W9-ADP-321
DOMI MINA
NVS TIO
ILLV MEA

THE OXFORD ENGLISH DICTIONARY

SECOND EDITION

THE OXFORD ENGLISH DICTIONARY

First Edited by

JAMES A. H. MURRAY, HENRY BRADLEY, W. A. CRAIGIE
and C. T. ONIONS

COMBINED WITH

A SUPPLEMENT TO THE OXFORD ENGLISH DICTIONARY

Edited by

R. W. BURCHFIELD

AND RESET WITH CORRECTIONS, REVISIONS
AND ADDITIONAL VOCABULARY

THE OXFORD ENGLISH DICTIONARY

SECOND EDITION

Prepared by
J. A. SIMPSON *and* E. S. C. WEINER

VOLUME XI
Ow–Poisant

CLARENDON PRESS · OXFORD

Oxford University Press, Great Clarendon Street, Oxford OX2 6DP
Oxford New York
Athens Auckland Bangkok Bogotá Buenos Aires Calcutta
Cape Town Chennai Dar es Salaam Delhi Florence Hong Kong Istanbul
Karachi Kuala Lumpur Madrid Melbourne Mexico City Mumbai
Nairobi Paris São Paulo Singapore Taipei Tokyo Toronto Warsaw
and associated companies in
Berlin Ibadan

First published 1989
Reprinted 1991 (with corrections), 1998

British Library Cataloguing in Publication Data
Oxford English dictionary.—2nd ed.
1. English language—Dictionaries
I. Simpson, J. A. (John Andrew), 1953–
II. Weiner, Edmund S. C., 1950–
423
ISBN 0-19-861223-0 (vol. XI)
ISBN 0-19-861186-2 (set)

Library of Congress Cataloging-in-Publication Data
The Oxford English dictionary.—2nd ed.
prepared by J. A. Simpson and E. S. C. Weiner
Bibliography: p.
ISBN 0-19-861223-0 (vol. XI)
ISBN 0-19-861186-2 (set)
1. English language—Dictionaries. I. Simpson, J. A.
II. Weiner, E. S. C. III. Oxford University Press.
PE1625.087 1989
423—dc19 88-5330

Data capture by ICC, Fort Washington, Pa.
Text-processing by Oxford University Press
Typesetting by Pindar Graphics Origination, Scarborough, N. Yorks.
Manufactured in the United States of America by
World Color Book Services, Taunton, Mass.

KEY TO THE PRONUNCIATION

THE pronunciations given are those in use in the educated speech of southern England (the so-called 'Received Standard'), and the keywords given are to be understood as pronounced in such speech.

I. *Consonants*

b, d, f, k, l, m, n, p, t, v, z *have their usual English values*

g as in *go* (gəʊ)
h ... *ho!* (həʊ)
r ... *run* (rʌn), *terrier* ('tɛrɪə(r))
(r) ... *her* (hɜː(r))
s ... *see* (siː), *success* (sək'sɛs)
w ... *wear* (wɛə(r))
hw ... *when* (hwɛn)
j ... *yes* (jɛs)

θ as in *thin* (θɪn), ba*th* (bɑːθ)
ð ... *then* (ðɛn), ba*the* (beɪð)
ʃ ... *shop* (ʃɒp), di*sh* (dɪʃ)
tʃ ... *chop* (tʃɒp), di*tch* (dɪtʃ)
ʒ ... vi*sion* ('vɪʒən), dé*j*euner (deʒøne)
dʒ ... *judge* (dʒʌdʒ)
ŋ ... si*nging* ('sɪŋɪŋ), thi*n*k (θiŋk)
ŋg ... fi*n*ger ('fɪŋgə(r))

(FOREIGN AND NON-SOUTHERN)

ʎ as in It. serra*gli*o (ser'raʎo)
ɲ ... Fr. co*gn*ac (kɔɲak)
x ... Ger. a*ch* (ax), Sc. lo*ch* (lɒx), Sp. fri*j*oles (fri'xoles)
ç ... Ger. i*ch* (ɪç), Sc. ni*ch*t (nɪçt)
ɣ ... North Ger. sa*g*en ('zaːɣən)
c ... Afrikaans baardmanne*tj*ie ('baːrtmanəci)
ɥ ... Fr. c*u*isine (kɥizin)

Symbols in parentheses are used to denote elements that may be omitted either by individual speakers or in particular phonetic contexts: e.g. *bottle* ('bɒt(ə)l), *Mercian* ('mɜːʃ(ɪ)ən), *suit* (s(j)uːt), *impromptu* (ɪm'prɒm(p)tjuː), *father* ('fɑːðə(r)).

II. *Vowels and Diphthongs*

SHORT

ɪ as in p*i*t (pɪt), -n*e*ss, (-nɪs)
ɛ ... p*e*t (pɛt), Fr. *sept* (sɛt)
æ ... p*a*t (pæt)
ʌ ... p*u*tt (pʌt)
ɒ ... p*o*t (pɒt)
ʊ ... p*u*t (pʊt)
ə ... *a*nother (ə'nʌðə(r))
(ə) ... beat*e*n ('biːt(ə)n)
i ... Fr. s*i* (si)
e ... Fr. b*é*b*é* (bebe)
a ... Fr. m*a*ri (mari)
ɑ ... Fr. b*â*timent (bɑtimɑ̃)
ɔ ... Fr. h*o*mme (ɔm)
o ... Fr. *eau* (o)
ø ... Fr. p*eu* (pø)
œ ... Fr. b*oeu*f (bœf) c*oeu*r (kœr)
u ... Fr. d*ou*ce (dus)
ʏ ... Ger. M*ü*ller ('mʏlər)
y ... Fr. d*u* (dy)

LONG

iː as in b*ea*n (biːn)
ɑː ... b*ar*n (bɑːn)
ɔː ... b*or*n (bɔːn)
uː ... b*oo*n (buːn)
ɜː ... b*ur*n (bɜːn)
eː ... Ger. Schn*ee* (ʃneː)
ɛː ... Ger. F*ä*hre ('fɛːrə)
aː ... Ger. T*a*g (taːk)
oː ... Ger. S*oh*n (zoːn)
øː ... Ger. G*oe*the ('gøːtə)
yː ... Ger. gr*ü*n (gryːn)

NASAL

ɛ̃, æ̃ as in Fr. f*in* (fɛ̃, fæ̃)
ɑ̃ ... Fr. fr*an*c (frɑ̃)
ɔ̃ ... Fr. b*on* (bɔ̃)
œ̃ ... Fr. *un* (œ̃)

DIPHTHONGS, etc.

eɪ as in b*ay* (beɪ)
aɪ ... b*uy* (baɪ)
ɔɪ ... b*oy* (bɔɪ)
əʊ ... n*o* (nəʊ)
aʊ ... n*ow* (naʊ)
ɪə ... p*eer* (pɪə(r))
ɛə ... p*air* (pɛə(r))
ʊə ... t*our* (tʊə(r))
ɔə ... b*oar* (bɔə(r))

aɪə as in f*ier*y ('faɪərɪ)
aʊə ... s*our* (saʊə(r))

The incidence of main stress is shown by a superior stress mark (') preceding the stressed syllable, and a secondary stress by an inferior stress mark (ˌ), e.g. *pronunciation* (prəˌnʌnsɪ'eɪʃ(ə)n).

For further explanation of the transcription used, see *General Explanations*, Volume I.

LIST OF ABBREVIATIONS, SIGNS, ETC.

Some abbreviations listed here in italics are also in certain cases printed in roman type, and vice versa.

a. (in Etym.)	adoption of, adopted from
a (as *a* 1850)	*ante*, 'before', 'not later than'
a.	adjective
abbrev.	abbreviation (of)
abl.	ablative
absol.	absolute, -ly
Abstr.	(in titles) *Abstract, -s*
acc.	accusative
Acct.	(in titles) *Account*
A.D.	*Anno Domini*
ad. (in Etym.)	adaptation of
Add.	Addenda
adj.	adjective
Adv.	(in titles) *Advance, -d, -s*
adv.	adverb
advb.	adverbial, -ly
Advt.	advertisement
Aeronaut.	(as label) in Aeronautics; (in titles) *Aeronautic, -al, -s*
AF., AFr.	Anglo-French
Afr.	Africa, -n
Agric.	(as label) in Agriculture; (in titles) *Agriculture, -al*
Alb.	Albanian
Amer.	American
Amer. Ind.	American Indian
Anat.	(as label) in Anatomy; (in titles) *Anatomy, -ical*
Anc.	(in titles) *Ancient*
Anglo-Ind.	Anglo-Indian
Anglo-Ir.	Anglo-Irish
Ann.	Annals
Anthrop., Anthropol.	(as label) in Anthropology; (in titles) *Anthropology, -ical*
Antiq.	(as label) in Antiquities; (in titles) *Antiquity*
aphet.	aphetic, aphetized
app.	apparently
Appl.	(in titles) *Applied*
Applic.	(in titles) *Application, -s*
appos.	appositive, -ly
Arab.	Arabic
Aram.	Aramaic
Arch.	in Architecture
arch.	archaic
Archæol.	in Archæology
Archit.	(as label) in Architecture; (in titles) *Architecture, -al*
Arm.	Armenian
assoc.	association
Astr.	in Astronomy
Astrol.	in Astrology
Astron.	(in titles) *Astronomy, -ical*
Astronaut.	(in titles) *Astronautic, -s*
attrib.	attributive, -ly
Austral.	Australian
Autobiogr.	(in titles) *Autobiography, -ical*
A.V.	Authorized Version
B.C.	Before Christ
B.C.	(in titles) British Columbia
bef.	before
Bibliogr.	(as label) in Bibliography; (in titles) *Bibliography, -ical*
Biochem.	(as label) in Biochemistry; (in titles) *Biochemistry, -ical*
Biol.	(as label) in Biology; (in titles) *Biology, -ical*
Bk.	*Book*
Bot.	(as label) in Botany; (in titles) *Botany, -ical*
Bp.	Bishop
Brit.	(in titles) *Britain, British*
Bulg.	Bulgarian
Bull.	(in titles) *Bulletin*
c (as *c* 1700)	*circa*, 'about'
c. (as 19th c.)	century
Cal.	(in titles) *Calendar*
Cambr.	(in titles) *Cambridge*
Canad.	Canadian
Cat.	Catalan
catachr.	catachrestically
Catal.	(in titles) *Catalogue*
Celt.	Celtic
Cent.	(in titles) *Century, Central*
Cent. Dict.	*Century Dictionary*
Cf., cf.	*confer*, 'compare'
Ch.	Church
Chem.	(as label) in Chemistry; (in titles) *Chemistry, -ical*
Chr.	(in titles) *Christian*
Chron.	(in titles) *Chronicle*
Chronol.	(in titles) *Chronology, -ical*
Cinemat., Cinematogr.	in Cinematography
Clin.	(in titles) *Clinical*
cl. L.	classical Latin
cogn. w.	cognate with
Col.	(in titles) *Colonel, Colony*
Coll.	(in titles) *Collection*
collect.	collective, -ly
colloq.	colloquial, -ly
comb.	combined, -ing
Comb.	Combinations
Comm.	in Commercial usage
Communic.	in Communications
comp.	compound, composition
Compan.	(in titles) *Companion*
compar.	comparative
compl.	complement
Compl.	(in titles) *Complete*
Conc.	(in titles) *Concise*
Conch.	in Conchology
concr.	concrete, -ly
Conf.	(in titles) *Conference*
Congr.	(in titles) *Congress*
conj.	conjunction
cons.	consonant
const.	construction, construed with
contr.	contrast (with)
Contrib.	(in titles) *Contribution*
Corr.	(in titles) *Correspondence*
corresp.	corresponding (to)
Cotgr.	R. Cotgrave, *Dictionarie of the French and English Tongues*
cpd.	compound
Crit.	(in titles) *Criticism, Critical*
Cryst.	in Crystallography
Cycl.	(in titles) *Cyclopædia, -ic*
Cytol.	(in titles) *Cytology, -ical*
Da.	Danish
D.A.	*Dictionary of Americanisms*
D.A.E.	*Dictionary of American English*
dat.	dative
D.C.	District of Columbia
Deb.	(in titles) *Debate, -s*
def.	definite, -ition
dem.	demonstrative
deriv.	derivative, -ation
derog.	derogatory
Descr.	(in titles) *Description, -tive*
Devel.	(in titles) *Development, -al*
Diagn.	(in titles) *Diagnosis, Diagnostic*
dial.	dialect, -al
Dict.	Dictionary; *spec.*, the *Oxford English Dictionary*
dim.	diminutive
Dis.	(in titles) *Disease*
Diss.	(in titles) *Dissertation*
D.O.S.T.	*Dictionary of the Older Scottish Tongue*
Du.	Dutch
E.	East
Eccl.	(as label) in Ecclesiastical usage; (in titles) *Ecclesiastical*
Ecol.	in Ecology
Econ.	(as label) in Economics; (in titles) *Economy, -ics*
ed.	edition
E.D.D.	*English Dialect Dictionary*
Edin.	(in titles) *Edinburgh*
Educ.	(as label) in Education; (in titles) *Education, -al*
EE.	Early English
e.g.	*exempli gratia*, 'for example'
Electr.	(as label) in Electricity; (in titles) *Electricity, -ical*
Electron.	(in titles) *Electronic, -s*
Elem.	(in titles) *Element, -ary*
ellipt.	elliptical, -ly
Embryol.	in Embryology
e.midl.	east midland (dialect)
Encycl.	(in titles) *Encyclopædia, -ic*
Eng.	England, English
Engin.	in Engineering
Ent.	in Entomology
Entomol.	(in titles) *Entomology, -logical*
erron.	erroneous, -ly
esp.	especially
Ess.	(in titles) *Essay, -s*
et al.	*et alii*, 'and others'
etc.	et cetera
Ethnol.	in Ethnology
etym.	etymology
euphem.	euphemistically
Exam.	(in titles) *Examination*
exc.	except
Exerc.	(in titles) *Exercise, -s*
Exper.	(in titles) *Experiment, -al*
Explor.	(in titles) *Exploration, -s*
f.	feminine
f. (in Etym.)	formed on
f. (in subordinate entries)	form of
F.	French
fem. (*rarely* f.)	feminine
fig.	figurative, -ly
Finn.	Finnish
fl.	*floruit*, 'flourished'
Found.	(in titles) *Foundation, -s*
Fr.	French
freq.	frequent, -ly
Fris.	Frisian
Fund.	(in titles) *Fundamental, -s*
Funk or *Funk's Stand. Dict.*	*Funk and Wagnalls Standard Dictionary*
G.	German
Gael.	Gaelic
Gaz.	(in titles) *Gazette*
gen.	genitive
gen.	general, -ly
Geogr.	(as label) in Geography; (in titles) *Geography, -ical*

Geol.	(as label) in Geology; (in titles) *Geology, -ical*
Geom.	in Geometry
Geomorphol.	in Geomorphology
Ger.	German
Gloss.	Glossary
Gmc.	Germanic
Godef.	F. Godefroy, *Dictionnaire de l'ancienne langue française*
Goth.	Gothic
Govt.	(in titles) *Government*
Gr.	Greek
Gram.	(as label) in Grammar; (in titles) *Grammar, -tical*
Gt.	Great
Heb.	Hebrew
Her.	in Heraldry
Herb.	among herbalists
Hind.	Hindustani
Hist.	(as label) in History; (in titles) *History, -ical*
hist.	historical
Histol.	(in titles) *Histology, -ical*
Hort.	in Horticulture
Househ.	(in titles) *Household*
Housek.	(in titles) *Housekeeping*
Ibid.	*Ibidem*, 'in the same book or passage'
Icel.	Icelandic
Ichthyol.	in Ichthyology
id.	*idem*, 'the same'
i.e.	*id est*, 'that is'
IE.	Indo-European
Illustr.	(in titles) *Illustration, -ted*
imit.	imitative
Immunol.	in Immunology
imp.	imperative
impers.	impersonal
impf.	imperfect
ind.	indicative
indef.	indefinite
Industr.	(in titles) *Industry, -ial*
inf.	infinitive
infl.	influenced
Inorg.	(in titles) *Inorganic*
Ins.	(in titles) *Insurance*
Inst.	(in titles) *Institute, -tion*
int.	interjection
intr.	intransitive
Introd.	(in titles) *Introduction*
Ir.	Irish
irreg.	irregular, -ly
It.	Italian
J., (J.)	(quoted from) Johnson's *Dictionary*
(Jam.)	Jamieson, *Scottish Dict.*
Jap.	Japanese
joc.	jocular, -ly
Jrnl.	(in titles) *Journal*
Jun.	(in titles) *Junior*
Knowl.	(in titles) *Knowledge*
l.	line
L.	Latin
lang.	language
Lect.	(in titles) *Lecture, -s*
Less.	(in titles) *Lesson, -s*
Let., Lett.	letter, letters
LG.	Low German
lit.	literal, -ly
Lit.	Literary
Lith.	Lithuanian
LXX	Septuagint
m.	masculine
Mag.	(in titles) *Magazine*
Magn.	(in titles) *Magnetic, -ism*
Mal.	Malay, Malayan
Man.	(in titles) *Manual*
Managem.	(in titles) *Management*
Manch.	(in titles) *Manchester*
Manuf.	in Manufacture, -ing
Mar.	(in titles) *Marine*
masc. (*rarely* m.)	masculine
Math.	(as label) in Mathematics; (in titles) *Mathematics, -al*
MDu.	Middle Dutch
ME.	Middle English
Mech.	(as label) in Mechanics; (in titles) *Mechanics, -al*
Med.	(as label) in Medicine; (in titles) *Medicine, -ical*
med.L.	medieval Latin
Mem.	(in titles) *Memoir, -s*
Metaph.	in Metaphysics
Meteorol.	(as label) in Meteorology; (in titles) *Meteorology, -ical*
MHG.	Middle High German
midl.	midland (dialect)
Mil.	in military usage
Min.	(as label) in Mineralogy; (in titles) *Ministry*
Mineral.	(in titles) *Mineralogy, -ical*
MLG.	Middle Low German
Misc.	(in titles) *Miscellany, -eous*
mod.	modern
mod.L	modern Latin
(Morris),	(quoted from) E. E. Morris's *Austral English*
Mus.	(as label) in Music; (in titles) *Music, -al; Museum*
Myst.	(in titles) *Mystery*
Mythol.	in Mythology
N.	North
n.	neuter
N. Amer.	North America, -n
N. & Q.	*Notes and Queries*
Narr.	(in titles) *Narrative*
Nat.	(in titles) *Natural*
Nat. Hist.	in Natural History
Naut.	in nautical language
N.E.	North East
N.E.D.	*New English Dictionary*, original title of the *Oxford English Dictionary* (first edition)
Neurol.	in Neurology
neut. (*rarely* n.)	neuter
NF., NFr.	Northern French
No.	Number
nom.	nominative
north.	northern (dialect)
Norw.	Norwegian
n.q.	no quotations
N.T.	New Testament
Nucl.	Nuclear
Numism.	in Numismatics
N.W.	North West
N.Z.	New Zealand
obj.	object
obl.	oblique
Obs., obs.	obsolete
Obstetr.	(in titles) *Obstetrics*
occas.	occasionally
OE.	Old English (= Anglo-Saxon)
OF., OFr.	Old French
OFris.	Old Frisian
OHG.	Old High German
OIr.	Old Irish
ON.	Old Norse
ONF.	Old Northern French
Ophthalm.	in Ophthalmology
opp.	opposed (to), the opposite (of)
Opt.	in Optics
Org.	(in titles) *Organic*
orig.	origin, -al, -ally
Ornith.	(as label) in Ornithology; (in titles) *Ornithology, -ical*
OS.	Old Saxon
OSl.	Old (Church) Slavonic
O.T.	Old Testament
Outl.	(in titles) *Outline*
Oxf.	(in titles) *Oxford*
p.	page
Palæogr.	in Palæography
Palæont.	(as label) in Palæontology; (in titles) *Palæontology, -ical*
pa. pple.	passive participle, past participle
(Partridge),	(quoted from) E. Partridge's *Dictionary of Slang and Unconventional English*
pass.	passive, -ly
pa.t.	past tense
Path.	(as label) in Pathology; (in titles) *Pathology, -ical*
perh.	perhaps
Pers.	Persian
pers.	person, -al
Petrogr.	in Petrography
Petrol.	(as label) in Petrology; (in titles) *Petrology, -ical*
(Pettman),	(quoted from) C. Pettman's *Africanderisms*
pf.	perfect
Pg.	Portuguese
Pharm.	in Pharmacology
Philol.	(as label) in Philology; (in titles) *Philology, -ical*
Philos.	(as label) in Philosophy; (in titles) *Philosophy, -ic*
phonet.	phonetic, -ally
Photogr.	(as label) in Photography; (in titles) *Photography, -ical*
phr.	phrase
Phys.	physical; (*rarely*) in Physiology
Physiol.	(as label) in Physiology; (in titles) *Physiology, -ical*
Pict.	(in titles) *Picture, Pictorial*
pl., plur.	plural
poet.	poetic, -al
Pol.	Polish
Pol.	(as label) in Politics; (in titles) *Politics, -al*
Pol. Econ.	in Political Economy
Polit.	(in titles) *Politics, -al*
pop.	popular, -ly
Porc.	(in titles) *Porcelain*
poss.	possessive
Pott.	(in titles) *Pottery*
ppl. a., pple. adj.	participial adjective
pple.	participle
Pr.	Provençal
pr.	present
Pract.	(in titles) *Practice, -al*
prec.	preceding (word or article)
pred.	predicative
pref.	prefix
pref., Pref.	preface
prep.	preposition
pres.	present
Princ.	(in titles) *Principle, -s*
priv.	privative
prob.	probably
Probl.	(in titles) *Problem*
Proc.	(in titles) *Proceedings*
pron.	pronoun
pronunc.	pronunciation
prop.	properly
Pros.	in Prosody
Prov.	Provençal
pr. pple.	present participle
Psych.	in Psychology
Psychol.	(as label) in Psychology; (in titles) *Psychology, -ical*
Publ.	(in titles) *Publications*
Q.	(in titles) *Quarterly*
quot(s).	quotation(s)
q.v.	*quod vide*, 'which see'
R.	(in titles) *Royal*
Radiol.	in Radiology
R.C.Ch.	Roman Catholic Church
Rec.	(in titles) *Record*
redupl.	reduplicating
Ref.	(in titles) *Reference*
refash.	refashioned, -ing
refl.	reflexive
Reg.	(in titles) *Register*

reg.	regular
rel.	related to
Reminisc.	(in titles) *Reminiscence, -s*
Rep.	(in titles) *Report, -s*
repr.	representative, representing
Res.	(in titles) *Research*
Rev.	(in titles) *Review*
rev.	revised
Rhet.	in Rhetoric
Rom.	Roman, -ce, -ic
Rum.	Rumanian
Russ.	Russian
S.	South
S.Afr.	South Africa, -n
sb.	substantive
sc.	*scilicet*, 'understand' or 'supply'
Sc., Scot.	Scottish
Scand.	(in titles) *Scandinavia, -n*
Sch.	(in titles) *School*
Sc. Nat. Dict.	*Scottish National Dictionary*
Scotl.	(in titles) *Scotland*
Sel.	(in titles) *Selection, -s*
Ser.	Series
sing.	singular
Sk.	(in titles) *Sketch*
Skr.	Sanskrit
Slav.	Slavonic
S.N.D.	*Scottish National Dictionary*
Soc.	(in titles) *Society*
Sociol.	(as label) in Sociology; (in titles) *Sociology, -ical*
Sp.	Spanish
Sp.	(in titles) *Speech, -es*
sp.	spelling
spec.	specifically
Spec.	(in titles) *Specimen*
St.	Saint
Stand.	(in titles) *Standard*
Stanf.	(quoted from) *Stanford Dictionary of Anglicised Words & Phrases*
str.	strong
Struct.	(in titles) *Structure, -al*
Stud.	(in titles) *Studies*
subj.	subject
subord. cl.	subordinate clause
subseq.	subsequent, -ly
subst.	substantively
suff.	suffix
superl.	superlative
Suppl.	Supplement
Surg.	(as label) in Surgery; (in titles) *Surgery, Surgical*
s.v.	*sub voce*, 'under the word'
Sw.	Swedish
s.w.	south-western (dialect)
Syd. Soc. Lex.	Sydenham Society, *Lexicon of Medicine & Allied Sciences*
syll.	syllable
Syr.	Syrian
Syst.	(in titles) *System, -atic*
Taxon.	(in titles) *Taxonomy, -ical*
techn.	technical, -ly
Technol.	(in titles) *Technology, -ical*
Telegr.	in Telegraphy
Teleph.	in Telephony
(Th.),	(quoted from) Thornton's *American Glossary*
Theatr.	in the Theatre, theatrical
Theol.	(as label) in Theology; (in titles) *Theology, -ical*
Theoret.	(in titles) *Theoretical*
Tokh.	Tokharian
tr., transl.	translated, translation
Trans.	(in titles) *Transactions*
trans.	transitive
transf.	transferred sense
Trav.	(in titles) *Travel(s)*
Treas.	(in titles) *Treasury*
Treat.	(in titles) *Treatise*
Treatm.	(in titles) *Treatment*
Trig.	in Trigonometry
Trop.	(in titles) *Tropical*
Turk.	Turkish
Typog., Typogr.	in Typography
ult.	ultimately
Univ.	(in titles) *University*
unkn.	unknown
U.S.	United States
U.S.S.R.	Union of Soviet Socialist Republics
usu.	usually
v., vb.	verb
var(r)., vars.	variant(s) of
vbl. sb.	verbal substantive
Vertebr.	(in titles) *Vertebrate, -s*
Vet.	(as label) in Veterinary Science; (in titles) *Veterinary*
Vet. Sci.	in Veterinary Science
viz.	*videlicet*, 'namely'
Voy.	(in titles) *Voyage, -s*
v.str.	strong verb
vulg.	vulgar
v.w.	weak verb
W.	Welsh; West
wd.	word
Webster	*Webster's (New International) Dictionary*
Westm.	(in titles) *Westminster*
WGmc.	West Germanic
Wks.	(in titles) *Works*
w.midl.	west midland (dialect)
WS.	West Saxon
(Y.),	(quoted from) Yule & Burnell's *Hobson-Jobson*
Yrs.	(in titles) *Years*
Zoogeogr.	in Zoogeography
Zool.	(as label) in Zoology; (in titles) *Zoology, -ical*

Signs and Other Conventions

Before a word or sense

† = obsolete
‖ = not naturalized, alien
¶ = catachrestic and erroneous uses

In the listing of Forms

1 = before 1100
2 = 12th c. (1100 to 1200)
3 = 13th c. (1200 to 1300), etc.
5–7 = 15th to 17th century
20 = 20th century

In the etymologies

* indicates a word or form not actually found, but of which the existence is inferred
:— = normal development of

The printing of a word in SMALL CAPITALS indicates that further information will be found under the word so referred to.

. . indicates an omitted part of a quotation.

- (in a quotation) indicates a hyphen doubtfully present in the original; (in other text) indicates a hyphen inserted only for the sake of a line-break.

PROPRIETARY NAMES

THIS Dictionary includes some words which are or are asserted to be proprietary names or trade marks. Their inclusion does not imply that they have acquired for legal purposes a non-proprietary or general significance nor any other judgement concerning their legal status. In cases where the editorial staff have established in the records of the Patent Offices of the United Kingdom and of the United States that a word is registered as a proprietary name or trade mark this is indicated, but no judgement concerning the legal status of such words is made or implied thereby.

ow, ou, *int.*[1] *ME.* and *mod.Sc.* Also 4 **ouȝ, owe, owh.** [The mod.Sc. interjection historically written *ow, ou,* is (uː); from the ambiguity of the spelling *ou, ow* in ME., it is not certain whether this is the same word.] An exclamation expressing surprise, or some allied emotion. ***ou ay*** (mod.Sc.) O yes (in concessive sense).

α. **13..** *Guy Warw.* (A.) st. lxxxii, 'Owe', seyd þe king, 'artow Inglis kniȝt, þan schuld y þurch skil and riȝt Hate þe euer more'. *a* **1330** *Otuel* 475 'Ouȝ', quaþ roulond, 'blame me nouȝt'. *c* **1380** WYCLIF *Sel. Wks.* III. 404 Owe, wheþer we shal se Anticrist so myghty! *Ibid.* 405 Ow, wheþer God, þat is treuþe ordained Cristen men to be marred! **1393** LANGL. *P. Pl.* C. XIII. 19 'Owh! how!' quaþ ich þo, and myn hefd waggede.

β. **1768** ROSS *Helenore* 74 He..says come ben, ow Bydby is that ye? **1814** SCOTT *Wav.* xxxix, 'Ow, ay, sir! a bra' night', replied the lieutenant. **1818** —— *Br. Lamm.* xxiv, 'Reasonable charges!' said the sexton: 'ou, there's grund-mail—and bell-siller..and the kist—and my day's wark—and my bit fee—' [etc.]. **1865** G. MACDONALD *A. Forbes* 20 Ow, bairn, are ye there yet?

ow (aʊ), *int.*[2] [A natural exclamation: cf. O *int.*, OH *int.* and varr., OW, OU *int.*[1], and OUCH *int.*[1]] An exclamation expressing sudden pain.

1919 G. B. SHAW *Great Catherine* iii. 146 (*Claire twists herself loose; turns on him; and cuffs him furiously*) Yow—ow! Have mercy, Little Mother. *Ibid.* iv. 155 Ow! Youve nearly pulled my teeth out. **1926** —— *Translations & Tomfooleries* 239 *Reginald.* Oh! Oh! Oh! The crocodiles! Stop! Ow! Oh! **1969** D. E. WESTLAKE *Up your Banners* (1970) xviii. 121 She threw another hammerlock on me. 'Ow,' I said. **1976** R. B. PARKER *Promised Land* (1977) xi. 60, I..hugged her. 'Ow,' she said. I eased up a little on the hug.

ow, obs. form of OWE, YOU.

owai, oway, owayward, obs. ff. AWAY, -WARD.

owar, var. OWHERE *Obs.*, anywhere.

owar, obs. Sc. f. WOOER.

oware, obs. f. HOUR.

owch(e, obs. form of OUCH *sb.*

owcht, obs. or dial. form of AUGHT, OUGHT.

owd, obs. and dial. form of OLD.

owdacious (aʊˈdeɪʃəs), *a. colloq.* (orig. *U.S.*) [? A 'portmanteau' blending of AUDACIOUS *a.* and OUTRAGEOUS *a.*] Impertinent, mischievous, bold. Hence **owˈdaciously** *adv.*, outrageously.

1846 in Bartlett *Dict. Amer.* (1848) 243 He had a daughter Molly, that was the most enticin', heart-distressin' creature that ever made a feller get owdacious. **1847** in *Ibid.* 243, I was never so owdaciously put out with the abominable abolitionists before. **1857** C. M. YONGE *Dynevor Terr.* I. vi. 81, I wonder you aren't ashamed of yourselves, and the family in such trouble! Downright owdacious! **1947** W. DE LA MARE *Coll. Stories for Children* 98 Some crabbed old woman said they were owdacious, or imperent, or mischeevious.

‖**owdell** (ˈaʊd(ə)l). [Welsh *awdl* a rime or assonance (pl. *odlau*); also in sense given below (pl. *awdlau*).] A poem consisting of compositions in all the 24 strict metres.

1612 DRAYTON *Poly-olb.* IV. 59 Some Makers..Rehearce their high conceits in Cowiths: other some In Owdells theirs expresse; as matter haps to come. *Ibid.* 67 *Note*, Owdells are couplets of variety in both time and quantity.

owdir, obs. form of OUTHER, either.

owe (əʊ), *v.* Forms: see below. [Comm. Teut.: OE. *áȝan*, pres. *ic áh*, pa. *ic áhte* = OFris. (*âga*), *âch* (*hâch*), *âchte*, OS. *égan* (*êh*), *êhta*, OHG. *eigan*, ON. *eiga*, *á*, *átta*, Goth. *aigan*, *aih*, *aihta*: one of the original Teutonic preterite-present verbs (see CAN, DARE, DOW, MAY). The OTeut. *aig-*, *aih-*, answers to a pre-Teut. *aik-*, ablaut-grade of *ik-*, the original stem of the present: cf. Skr. *iç* to possess, own. This vb. now survives only in Eng. and the Scandinavian langs. (Sw. *äga*, *ega*, Da. *eie* to own, have). In Eng. it has undergone much change both of form and sense. The original preteritive inflexion of the present tense (*áh*, *áht*, *áhst*, *áh*, *áȝon*) began in late OE. and early ME. to be supplanted by the ordinary pres. tense forms (e.g. 3rd sing., *áhð*, *aweþ*, *oweþ*, *awes*, *owes*, pl. *áȝað*, *aȝeþ*, *oȝeþ*, *oweth*, etc.); and in mod.Eng. the tense is entirely thus levelled, *owe*, *owest*, *owes*, *-eth*, *owe*. The OE. pa. t. *áhte*, ME. *âhte*, *ôhte*, survives as *ought*; but before 1200 this began to be used (in the subjunctive) with an indefinite and hence present signification, in a special sense, and thus gradually came to be in use a distinct verb from *owe* (for which see OUGHT *v.*); its function as pa. t. of *owe* being supplied in 15th c. by *owed*. The orig. pa. pple. in all the Teut. langs. became an adj., of which the mod.Eng. form is OWN *a.*; but as a pa. pple. OE. *áȝen* was still used in 16–17th c. as *owen*, *oune*. A later pa. pple. *aucht*, *ought*, conformed to the orig. pa. t., is found from the 14th c.: see OUGHT *v.* 7. The current pa. pple. is *owed*; so that the whole verb has now the ordinary weak conjugation *owe*, *owed*, *owed*. The change of signification from *habēre* to *dēbēre* can be best traced in the scheme of senses below; but the primitive sense 'have, possess' is not yet extinct in the dialects, which use *awe* or *owe* = *own*, and have not entirely lost the connexion of *owe* and *ought*.

OUGHT, being now in Standard English practically a distinct word, has been fully treated in its alphabetical place, and is not dealt with here; but, for the historical development, the two articles OWE, OUGHT, should be read together.]

A. Inflexional Forms.

1. *Infinitive.* α. 1 **áȝan,** 2–3 **aȝen,** (3 **aȝhenn, aȝæn, aȝe**), 3 **awen,** 3, *north.* 4–5 **agh(e,** 3–6 *north.* **awe,** 6– **aw.** β. 3 **oȝe(n,** 3–4 **owen,** 3– **owe,** (6 **ough,** 7 **ow**).

α. *c* **888** Aȝan [see B. 1]. *c* **1200** ORMIN 8173 Off þe bettste pall þatt aniȝ mann maȝȝ aȝhenn. *c* **1205** LAY. 11781 Þu scalt ..þas riche aȝen [*c* 1275 oȝe]. *Ibid.* 32085 No most þu nauere mære Ængle-lond aȝe. *c* **1300** Awe [see B. 1 b]. *c* **1400** Agh [see B. 1 c]. **1535** STEWART *Chron. Scot.* II. 470 For na dett that he can aw.

β. *c* **1275** LAY. 4149 Ne mai neuere mansipe leng oȝe [*c* 1205 aȝen]. *Ibid.* 18574 Ȝef he nolde þis owe. *c* **1320** *Cast. Love* 132 How miȝte he him more loue schowen þen his oune liknesse habben and owen? **1483** CAXTON *Gold. Leg.* 34/2 To haue cure and owe to wake. **1580** LYLY *Euphues* (Arb.) 415 Who should owe the calfe. **1649** LOVELACE *Poems* 143 What your whiter chaster brest doth ow.

2. *Pres. Indic.* **a.** *1st sing.* α. 1 **áh, áȝ,** 2–3 **ah,** (2 **auh, ach,** 3 **æh**), 3–4 **agh,** (**aghe**), 3–6 **aw,** 4 **au(e,** 4–6 **awe.** β. 3–4 **oȝ, oh,** 3 **ohȝ, ouh, ou,** 3–5 **ogh,** (4 **oghe**), 4–5 **owȝe,** 4–7 **ow,** 4– **owe,** (5 **howe**).

α. *a* **1000** *Byrhtnoth* 175 (Gr.) Nu ic ah mæste þearfe. *c* **1200** ORMIN 11815 Þatt I me sellf all ah itt wald. **13..** *Cursor M.* 13825 (Cott.) Wit-stand his biding agh [*a* 1425 *Tr.* ow] i noght. **13..** *Ibid.* 5145 (Fairf.) Bi þe faythe I aghe [*G.* aw, *Tr.* owe] to ȝou. *c* **1400** *Ywaine & Gaw.* 720, I aw the honor and servyse.

β. **1297** R. GLOUC. (Rolls) 6369 Bi þe treuþe ich ou to þe. *a* **1310** in Wright *Lyric P.* xxv. 70 The more oh ich to lovie the. *a* **1425** *Cursor M.* 10248 (Tr.) Þat I no chirche owȝe com inne. **1426** LYDG. *De Guil. Pilgr.* 22677 So I howe. *c* **1430** *Syr Gener.* (Roxb.) 7422, I wil worship as I ow. **1530** PALSGR. 650/1, I owe dette. *a* **1652** BROME *Queenes Exch.* v. Wks. 1873 III. 548, I ow thee a just reward.

b. *2nd sing.* α. 1 **áhst, áht, áȝt,** 2–3 **aȝes(t, aust,** 3 **ahes(t;** 3–4 **ahe,** 4 **agh, aghe, au,** 4–5 (6– *Sc.*) **aw, awe.** β. 3– **owest,** (4–5 **owist,** 5 **-yst,** 7– **ow'st**); 4 **ogh,** 5 **ow, owe.**

α. *a* **900** CYNEWULF *Elene* 726 Đu ðe ahst doma ȝeweald. *c* **950** Aht [see B. 2]. *c* **1175** *Lamb. Hom.* 15 Heore uuel..þu aȝest to hetiene. *c* **1200** *Vices & Virtues* 41 Đu aust te folȝin ðane..onfald Iob. *a* **1225** *Juliana* 48 Ne ahestu nan habben. *c* **1230** *Hali Meid.* 39 Þat þu ahes to don. *a* **1300** *Cursor M.* 23181 (Cott.) Þou agh [*Ed.* ahe, *Gött.* au] to min. **1375** BARBOUR *Bruce* IX. 733 As þou aw. *c* **1460** *Towneley Myst.* iii. 171 To luf me welle thou awe.

β. *a* **1225** *Ancr. R.* 126 Þe dette þet to owest me. **13..** *Cursor M.* 26965 (Cott.) Ne..þi-self ogh sai bot soth o þe. *a* **1425** *Ibid.* 4589 (Tr.) Þerfore owe [*earlier MSS.* au, aghe] þou bi riȝt. **1483** *Vulgaria abs Terentio* 16 b, Do as thow owyst to do. **1502** *Ord. Crysten Men* (W. de W. 1506) I. iii. 33 Yᵘ owest to meruayll and fere. **1651** HOBBES *Leviath.* II. xx. 106 Thou that owest me obedience.

c. *3rd sing.* (1) *Original:* α. 1 **áh, áȝ,** 2–3 **ah,** (2 **auh, ach,** 3 **æh**), 3–4 **agh, -e,** 3–6 **aw,** 4 **au, aue,** 4–5 **awe,** (5 **augh**). β. 3–4 **oh, oȝ,** 3 **ohȝ, ouh, ou,** 3–5 **ogh,** 4–5 **owȝe, ow, owe.** (2) *New formation:* γ. 2 **ahð, aweþ,** (3 **haht**), 4 **aws,** 5 **awiþ,** (**awthe**). δ. 3–4 **oȝþ, oȝeþ,** (**oȝet**), 3–5 **oweþ,** (3 **howeð**), 4– **oweth,** (4–5 **-iþ, -yþ,** 5 **-ith(e, howyth**); 6– **owes,** (6–7 **ows**).

α. *a* **1000** *Andreas* 518 (Gr.) Ah him lifes ȝeweald. *c* **1000** *Ags. Gosp.* Matt. xxiv. 47 Eall þæt he ah. *c* **1160** *Hatton G.* ibid., Eall þæt he aȝ. *c* **1175** *Lamb. Hom.* 139 Man ach to wurþen þis halie dei. *Ibid.*, Sunnedei ah efri..Mon...to chirche cume. *c* **1200** *Vices & Virtues* 35 Đat god ðat he aw te donne. *Ibid.* 45 Đe hlauerd..ðe ðat scip auh. *c* **1200** *Trin. Coll. Hom.* 17 Ne noman ne agh werne. *c* **1205** LAY. 13479 Þes king æh [*c* 1275 haht] al þis lond. **13..** *Cursor M.* 267 (Gött.) Coursur of þe werld men au [*Cott.* aght] it call. *Ibid.* 4380 He aue to thinck apon þe ending. **1432–50** tr. *Higden* (Rolls) IV. 461 A man awe not to departe. **1513** DOUGLAS *Æneis* IX. xii. 51 He that aw this swerd.

β. *c* **1200** *Moral Ode* 2 (Trin. MS.) Mi wit oh to be more. *c* **1200** *Trin. Coll. Hom.* 155 Al chirche folc ohȝ to ben gadered in chirche. *Ibid.* 189 Þat ilke wei ogh al mankin to holden. *c* **1220** *Bestiary* 370 Ne oȝ ur non oðer to sunen. *a* **1225** *Ancr. R.* 64 Þet he ouh to siggen. *c* **1308** *Pol. Songs* (Camd.) 204 The wreche was hard that ow the godе. *c* **1325** *Know Thyself* 46 in *E.E.P.* 131 Þenke on þi god as þe wel owe. *c* **1400** *Destr. Troy* 5357 As ogh myn astate. *a* **1425** *Cursor M.* 9686 (Tr.) Hit owȝe tried to be. ? **1490** CAXTON *Rule St. Benet* (E.E.T.S.) 139 He owe to fall downe prosstrate.

γ. *c* **1160** *Hatton Gosp.* Luke xi. 21 Þa þing þe he ahð [*Ags. Gosp.* ah]. **13..** *Cursor M.* 9636 (Gött.) Dede he aws to thole for-þi. *c* **1400** *Apol. Loll.* 30 Awiþ he not to bless[e] þe peple? **1486** *Bk. St. Albans* A ij b, As she awthe to be.

δ. *c* **1205** LAY. 3465 Þe man þat lutel oȝeþ. *c* **1250** *Gen. & Ex.* 324 Quat oȝet nu ðat for-bode o-wold? **1303** R. BRUNNE *Handl. Synne* 954 Pray..to oure lady þat owyþ þys day. **1340** *Ayenb.* 9 Þe wyl of him þet hit oȝþ. **13..** *Cursor M.* 6161 (Gött.) Þis owes [*Tr.* oweþ] euer to be in mind. **1382** WYCLIF *Eccl.* xi. 8 He owith to han mynde of the derke tyme. *a* **1450** *Cov. Myst.* (1841) 97 To whom the mayd howyth to be maryed. **1530–1** *Act 22 Hen. VIII*, c. 12 Lyke as a trewe man oweth to do. **1563–87** FOXE *A. & M.* (1684) I. 534 No bishop ows to let a true priest. *c* **1600** SHAKS. *Sonn.* lxxix, What he owes thee. **1651** HOBBES *Leviath.* II. xxx. 181 The debt that every man oweth.

d. *plural.* α. 1 **áȝon, -un,** (**áȝað**), 2–3 **aȝen, aȝe, aweð,** 3 **ahen, aȝeð, -æð, aweð;** 4 **agh(e, ah,** (**h)ach,** 4–5 **aue, awe,** 4–6 **au, aw,** 5 **augh.** β. 2–3 **oȝen, oȝeð,** 3 **ohen,** 3–5 **owen,** (5 **-in, -yn, -ne**), **oweþ, -eth, ouwe,** 4 **oen, howen, oghe, ouh,** 4–7 **ow,** 4– **owe,** (5 **howe,** 8 **ough**).

α. *c* **1000** *Ags. Gosp.* Matt. v. 4 (5) Hi eorðan aȝun. *c* **1200** *Vices & Virtues* 35 Swo aweð to donne alle. *c* **1200** *Trin. Coll. Hom.* 41 Swo we aȝeð to don. *Ibid.* 57 We aȝen to cumen. *a* **1240** *Sawles Warde* in *Lamb. Hom.* 245 Hu we ahen wearliche to biwiten us seoluen. **13..** *Cursor M.* 23824 (Edin.) We agh it noght to hald in were. *Ibid.* 11618 (Cott.) Þe lauerd agh [*G.* aue, *Tr.* owe, *L.* ow] yee worthli to lufe. *a* **1340** HAMPOLE *Psalter* ii. 4 Wele aghe we to brek. **1389** in *Eng. Gilds* (1870) 39 Þe ligeaunce þat þei awe. *c* **1500** *Lancelot* 3447 Yhe aw to be commendit. **1552** ABP. HAMILTON *Catech.* (1884) 8 The trew service..quhilk we aw to him. **1588** A. KING tr. *Canisius' Catech.* 57 Sa we au faith ..to the kirk.

β. *a* **1175** *Cott. Hom.* 235 Ure king we oȝeð wurhðmint. *c* **1200** *Trin. Coll. Hom.* 57 Alse we oȝen to don. *a* **1225** *Ancr. R.* 68 Uor þi owen þe gode..to habben witnesse. *c* **1275** LAY. 25110 Al þat we beie oweþ [*c* 1205 aȝæð]. *Ibid.* 25319 Þat we oweþ [*c* 1205 aȝen] cleane. *c* **1330** R. BRUNNE *Chron.* (1810) 313 Þe whilk ȝe salle & ouh to maynten. *c* **1380** WYCLIF *Sel. Wks.* III. 197 Þei owen to use þis doynge. **1380** *Lay Folks Catech.* (Lamb. MS.) 978 We owe to loue oure euyn-cristyn. **1444** *Rolls of Parlt.* V. 124/2 Profites that cometh, or oweth to come. **1463** MARG. PASTON in *P. Lett.* II. 142 Do as ye owe to do. **1473** *Rolls of Parlt.* VI. 86/1 The which VI marcs, the seid Priour..and his successours.. owyn to pay. **1647** COWLEY *Mistress, Sleep* ii, All my too much Moysture ow. **1711–1868** Owe [see B. 4].

3. *Past Indic.* (1) *Original*: **áhte, ôhte,** etc.: see OUGHT *v.* (2) *New formation*: 5 **awede,** 5– **owed,** (5 **-id, -yd,** 7 **ow'd**); *2nd sing.* **owedst,** (7 **ow'd'st**).

a **1425** *Cursor M.* 14045 (Trin.) Wheþer owed to loue him bettur þo. **1572** R. H. tr. *Lauaterus' Ghostes* (1596) 147 This man that owed the apparel. **1604** SHAKS. *Oth.* III. iii. 333 That sweete sleepe Which thou owd'st yesterday. **1627** MAY *Lucan* v. (1631) 18 The man that ow'd, and kept This boate. **1801** STRUTT *Sports & Past.* Introd. §3. 3 He owed his knowledge of letters to accident.

4. *Pa. pple.* α. 1 **áȝen,** 5–9 **owen,** (5 **owyn,** 6 **oune**). β. **aht, aught, ought,** etc.: see OUGHT *v.* γ. 4– **owed,** (6 **oughed,** 7 **owd, ow'd**).

α. **1460–4** Owyn [see B. 3]. **1570** LEVINS *Manip.* 220/12 Oune, *debitus*. **1642** *View Print. Bk. int. Observat.* 9 The King the supreame head..unto whom a body politique.. been bounden and owen next to God. *Ibid.*, Bounden and owen to beare..obedience. **1803** W. TAYLOR in Robberds *Mem.* I. 458, I have owen him a letter still longer.

γ. *c* **1374** CHAUCER *Boeth.* IV. pr. v. 102 (Camb. MS.) Tormentz of laweful peynes ben rather owed to felonos citezeins. *a* **1643** W. CARTWRIGHT *Ordinary* III. iii, All broken sleeps, are ow'd Only to you. **1715–20** POPE *Iliad* IX. 827 Strength consists in spirit and in blood, And those are owed to generous wine and food.

5. The negative *ne* blended formerly with this vb., making the OE. forms *náh*, *náȝon*, *náhte*, ME. *naȝen*, *nowen*, *nouh*, *nowest*, etc.

a **1225** *Ancr. R.* 256 Heo..nouh non uorte nimen Godes flesch & his blod. *Ibid.* 380 Ȝe nowen nout unnen. *a* **1240** *Lofsong* in *Cott. Hom.* 215 Þu nowest none mon nowiht.

B. Signification.

I. To have; to possess; to own.

†**1. a.** *trans.* To have; to have belonging to one, to possess; to be the owner of, to own; = OWN *v.* 2. *Obs.* (since *c* 1680) exc. *dial.*

For illustration of the original pa. t. see OUGHT *v.* 1.

c **888** K. ÆLFRED *Boeth.* xiv. §2 Þa micles beþurfon þe micel aȝan willaþ. *c* **1000** *Ags. Gosp.* Matt. xiii. 44 Se man.. gæð and sylþ eall þæt he ah, and ȝebiȝþ þone æcer. *c* **1175** *Lamb. Hom.* 103 Þe mon ne ah his modes iwald. **1297** R. GLOUC. (Rolls) 8890 Ne let me nomon owe, Bote he abbe an tuo-name. *c* **1386** CHAUCER *Pard. T.* 33 The goode man that the beestes oweth. *c* **1460** FORTESCUE *Abs. & Lim. Mon.* xi. (1885) 136 The eyres off thaim þat some tyme owed it. **1526** *Pilgr. Perf.* (1531) 117 He that of very ryght owed yᵉ cappe. *c* **1611** CHAPMAN *Iliad* XXIII. 325 The horse The Gods bred, and Adrastus ow'd. **1628** T. SPENCER *Logick* 117 The Oxe.. knowes who owes him, and feedes him. **1664** PEPYS *Diary* (1879) III. 7 Fine storehouses,..but of no great profit to him that oweth them. *a* **1825** FORBY *Voc. E. Anglia* s.v., Mr. Brown owes that farm.

†**b.** To get or take possession of; = OWN *v.* 1; HAVE *v.* 14. *Obs.*

c **1205** LAY. 28423 Þe feond hine aȝe! *c* **1300** *Havelok* 1292 Als I sat upon that lowe, I bigan Denemark for to awe.

†**c.** To acknowledge as belonging to oneself; = OWN *v.* 3 a. *Obs.*

c **1400** *Destr. Troy* 8956 The ost for to honour & agh hym as lord. **1613** WITHER *Abuses Stript* I. viii, Their fore-fathers ..would not know them, (If they were living) or for shame not owe them. **1622** MISSELDEN *Free Trade* 30 Him that wrote a little treatise..which it seemes for modesty he refuseth to owe.

II. To have to pay.

This branch and the next were expressed in OE., as in the other Teutonic langs., by the vb. *sceal*, pa. t. *sceolde*, inf. *sculan* (Goth. *skal*, *skulda*, *skulan*), mod.Eng. SHALL, SHOULD. The first traces of the mod. use appear in the Lindisf. Gloss, which renders L. *dēbēre* (where the Rushw., like the later Ags. Gosp., uses *sculan*) by the phrase *áȝan tó ȝeldanne* 'to have to pay'. Examples are wanting during the following two centuries to show the stages by which this was shortened to the simple *áȝan*, which is found by 1175 in full use, both in the sense 'to owe (money)', and 'to have it as a duty', 'to be under obligation (*to do* something)', both taking the place of OE. *sculan*. (See also OUGHT *v.* 2, 5.) The result was that *shall* gradually ceased to have the sense 'owe', retained that of obligation with a weaker force, and became mainly an auxiliary of the future tense; while *áȝan*, *aȝen*, *oȝen, owen, owe*, in taking *dēbēre* as its main sense, has in Standard Eng. lost that of *habēre*, or handed it over to the cognate OWN, which shares it with *have* and such Romanic synonyms as *possess*.

2. a. To be under obligation to pay or repay (money or the like); to be indebted in, or to the amount of; to be under obligation to render (obedience, honour, allegiance, etc.). Const. with simple dat. or *to*. (The chief current sense.)

For illustration of the pa. t. in earlier form see OUGHT *v.* 2.

[*c***950** *Lindisf. Gosp.* Matt. xviii. 28 ȝeld þæt ðu aht to ȝeldanne [*Vulg.* debes, *Rushw.* and *Ags. G.* scealt, *Hatt.* scelt]. —— Luke xvi. 5 Huu micel aht ðu to ȝeldanne hlaferde minum? [*Vulg.* debes domino meo, *Ags. G.* scealt þu minum hlaforde]. *Ibid.* 7 Huu feolo aht ðu to? [*Vulg.* debes, *Ags. G.* scealt þu].] *a* **1175** *Cott. Hom.* 235 Ure king we oȝeð uurþmint [*text* wrhmint], hur sceappend al þat we bieð. *c* **1200** ORMIN 16529, & ȝiff þu litell dost forr Godd, Godd ah þe litell mede. **1258** *Proclam. Hen. III*, l. 4 We hoaten alle vre treowe in þe treowþe þæt heo vs oȝen. **1382** WYCLIF *Luke* xvi. 5 He seide to the firste, Hou moche owist thou to my lord? **1484** CAXTON *Fables of Alfonce* vii, He is wyse that payeth that that he oweth of ryght. *a* **1533** LD. BERNERS *Gold. Bk. M. Aurel.* (1546) H viij b, The people owe obedyence to the prynce. **1588** A. KING tr. *Canisius' Catech.* 38 In it chyldrene ar taucht quhat thay aw vnto thair parents. **1735** SHERIDAN *Let. to Swift* 16 July, Swift's Lett. 1768 IV. 102, I cleared off the rent which I owed him. **1801** in A. H. Craufurd *Gen. Craufurd & Light Div.* (1891) 10 You owe it to yourself to prepare against this. **1860** TYNDALL *Glac.* I. iii. 29, I paid him what I owed him. **1871** FREEMAN *Norm. Conq.* IV. xviii. 140 On behalf of the land to which they owed a temporary allegiance.

b. *absol.* (or with indirect obj. only): To be indebted, be in debt.

1460, 1483 [see OUGHT *v.* 2 b]. **1607** HEYWOOD *Wom. Kild w. Kindn.* Wks. 1874 II. 143, I haue..nothing left, I owe euen for the clothes vpon my backe. **1865** MRS. CARLYLE *Lett.* III. 285, I owed for my summer bonnet and cloak. **1894** *Outing* (U.S.) XXIV. 256/1 She says she owes me for the preservation of her life on the island. **1970** 'E. QUEEN' *Last Woman* II. 135 'She'll come', Newly said grimly. 'After that yarn of hers, she owes me.' **1972** D. ANTHONY *Blood on Harvest Moon* i. 17 'Another job.'.. 'I couldn't turn this one down,' I said. 'I owe the lady.'

c. *Sports.* To be under an obligation to give one's opponent in a match (a number of strokes or points) as a handicap.

1904 J. P. PARET *Lawn Tennis* 345 *Owe-fifteen* (*thirty or forty*), a term used in handicap play to indicate that one player must make one (fifteen), two (thirty), or three (forty) points in each game before he begins to score. **1908** *Daily Chron.* 24 Aug. 9/3 Mr. F. Scarf..owing one stroke, beat Mr. R. C. Oppenheimer,..(handicap 15), by 7 holes up and 5 to play.

3. *transf.* **a.** To have or cherish towards another (a feeling, regarded as something which is yet to be paid or rendered in action); to bear (good or ill will). *Obs.* exc. in ***to owe a grudge***. **b.** To have or bear *to* some one or something (a relation, as dependence, etc., which has to be acknowledged); to 'own'. *rare.* (For earlier pa. t. see OUGHT 3, 3 b.)

a. *c* **1385** [see OUGHT 3]. **1460–4** *Paston Lett.* II. 81, I.. have owyn to your person ryght herty love. **1461** *Ibid.* 62 They wold owe yow ryth good wyll, so that ye wold owe hem good wyll. *a* **1533** LD. BERNERS *Huon* lxx. 240 Ye do me greate wronge to owe me youre yll wyll. *a* **1548** HALL *Chron., Hen. VIII* 70 To whom the Cardinall did not owe the best favor. **1613** PURCHAS *Pilgrimage* (1614) 209 They.. will wait two or three houres for some to whom they owe some speciall grudge, to bestow their curse vpon him. **1726** SWIFT *Gulliver* II. i, Being afraid the boy might owe me a spite. *a* **1904** *Mod.* The act of one who owes us a grudge.
b. 1644 [H. PARKER] *Jus Pop.* 59 Monarchy and Aristocracy are derivative forms and owe a dependance on Democracy. **1855** MOTLEY *Dutch Rep.* I. iii. (1866) 107 There was nothing in his character or purposes which owed affinity with any mood of this jocund and energetic people.

4. *fig.* **a.** To have to ascribe or attribute (something) to, or acknowledge as derived from (some person or thing); to have, as received from or caused by some one or something; to be indebted or beholden for. Const. *to* (or simple dative). Cf. DUE *a.* 9. (For the earlier pa. t. see OUGHT *v.* 4.)

1591 SYLVESTER *Du Bartas* I. iii. 115 But, th' Earth not only th' Oceans debter is For these large Seas; but owes him Tanäis [etc.]. **1605** SHAKS. *Lear* III. iv. 108 Thou ow'st the Worme no Silke; the Beast, no Hide. **1702** POPE *Jan. & May* 71 Abusive Nabal ow'd his forfeit life To the wise conduct of a prudent wife. **1711** ADDISON *Spect.* No. 60 ¶3 It was to this Age that we owe the Production of Anagrams. **1816** J. WILSON *City of Plague* III. i. 325, I owe my life to thee. **1838** J. L. STEPHENS *Trav. Greece* 13/1 Corinth owed her commercial greatness to the profits of her merchants in transporting merchandise across [the isthmus]. **1868** LOCKYER *Elem. Astron.* vi. (1879) 228 We owe the discovery of the prismatic spectrum to Sir Isaac Newton.

†**b.** Without direct object: To be indebted or beholden (*to* a person or thing *for* something). *Obs.*

1611 BEAUM. & FL. *King & no King* I. i, I think, we owe thy fear for our victory. **1638** JUNIUS *Paint. Ancients* 46 Accurate Artificers..owe more unto Doctrine than unto Nature. **1653** MARVELL *Corr.* Wks. 1872–5 II. 4 In this both he and I ow infinitely to your Lordship. **1686** tr. *Chardin's Trav. Persia* 93 Others assert, That they owe for their knowledge of Christianity to one Cyril.

III. To have it as a duty or obligation.

†**5. a.** To have as a duty; to be under obligation (*to do* something). (Followed by inf. with or without *to*.) *Obs.* (For the pa. t. see OUGHT *v.* 5 a.)

(*a*) with *to* and infin. = OUGHT *v.* 5 b (*a*).

c **1175** *Lamb. Hom.* 21 Swilcne lauerd we aȝen to dreden. *Ibid.* 81 Her me ah to understonden for whi hit seið [h]alf quic. *c* **1200** *Trin. Coll. Hom.* 57 Alse we oȝen to don. **1303** R. BRUNNE *Handl. Synne* 836 Þe seruyng man..Oweþ to come when he haþ leysere. **1386** *Rolls of Parlt.* III. 226/1 As we ben and owe to ben. **1432–50** tr. *Higden* (Rolls) II. 293 Thei awe to be namede raþer Agarenes. *c* **1500** *Melusine* 108 Therfore it oweth not to be refused ne gaynsayd. **1534** MORE *Treat. on Passion* Wks. 1314/1 You owe also one to weshe an others fete. **1537** *Let.* in *Cranmer's Misc. Writ.* (Parker Soc.) II. 352 As obedient..as a true Christian oweth to be.

(*b*) with simple infin. = OUGHT *v.* 5 b (*b*).

c **1200** *Trin. Coll. Hom.* 53 Nu aȝe we alle..nime forbisne. **13..** *Cursor M.* 5104 (Cott.) All your bidding agh be til vs als comanding. *c* **1470** HARDING *Chron.* CCIX. v, As prysoners owe home agayn repeire. *a* **1500** *Chaucer's Dreme* 1405 Forgotten was no thing That owe be done. **1524** HEN. VIII *Let. to Pace* in Strype *Eccl. Mem.* (1724) I. II. App. xiii. 28 They shuld & owe, not oonely forbere to geve ayde.

†**b.** In weakened sense: = Shall. *Obs. rare.*

c **1250** *Gen. & Ex.* 1944 Quat-so his dremes owen a-wold.

†**6.** quasi-*impers.* (usually with inf. clause as subject): (It) behoves, is the duty of, befits, is due (to); e.g. ***him owe*** (or ***oweth***) = it behoves him, he ought; ***as him owe*** = as befits him, as is due to him. *Obs.* (For the pa. t. see OUGHT *v.* 6.)

c **1220** *Bestiary* 350 Anoðer kinde. Ðat us oȝ alle to ben minde. *c* **1375** *Cursor M.* 18791 (Fairf.) Wele vs agh to loue him. **1382** WYCLIF *Exod.* xxi. 13 Y shal ordeyne to thee a place whidyr hym awe to flee. *c* **1440** *York Myst.* xxiii. 49 Full glad and blithe awe vs to be. *c* **1450** *Mirour Saluacioun* 4486 Hym awe serue and luf godde with his hert alle & some. **1470–1500** [see OUGHT *v.* 6 a, b].

†**7.** pa. pple. *owen* = under obligation, obliged, bound. *Obs.*

1541–2 *Act 33 Hen. VIII* in Bolton *Stat. Irel.* (1621) 211 To give money in almes, in as large a maner and forme as they are bownden or owen to doe. **1642** [see A. 4 a].

†**owe** *a.*, shortened ME. form of OWN *a.*

owe, obs. form of HOW *adv.*, YOU *pron.*

†'**owedness.** *Obs. nonce-wd.* [f. *owed* pa. pple. of OWE *v.* + -NESS.] The quality or fact of being possessed or owned.

1585–7 T. ROGERS *39 Art.* (1607) 354 Among the Familists (saith H. N.) none claimeth anything proper to himself for to possess the same to any owedness or privateness.

owelty ('əʊəltɪ). *Law.* Also 6–8 **ovelty**, 8 **ovealty**. [a. AF. *owelté*, earlier *oeltet* (Oxf. Psalter):—L. *æquālitāt-em*, f. *æquāl-is* (OF. *ewal, owel, oel*, etc.) equal.] Equality.

(The AF. adj. *owel* 'equal' (BRITTON I. 251, II. 79, etc.), does not appear to have come into Eng. use.)

1579 RASTELL *Expos. Termes Lawe, Oweltie*, is when there is Lord, mesne, and tenant, and the tenant holdeth of the mesne by the same seruices, that the mesne holdeth ouer of yᵉ lord aboue him. **1596** BACON *Max. Com. Law* iii. (1636) 14 There shall be ten shillings onely reserved upon the gift entaile as for ovelty. **1727–41** CHAMBERS *Cycl.*, *Owelty* or ovelty of services,..an equality of services; as when the tenant paravail owes as much to the mesn, as the mesn does to the lord paramount. **1818** CRUISE *Digest* (ed. 2) II. 524 Called a rent for owelty or equality of partition.

Owen ('əʊən). The name of E. E. *Owen* (1915–49), Australian inventor, used *attrib.* or alone to designate a sub-machine-gun invented by him.

1958 D. P. MELLOR *Role of Sci. & Industry* xv. 329 The Owen gun was an Automatic firearm of the usual recoiling breech bolt type, with a fire control member cooperating directly with the trigger. **1961** D. DEXTER *New Guinea Offensives* ii. 51 All sections testing the Owen preferred it to the Tommy-gun. **1965** *Austral. Encycl.* VII. 34/1 In the field of military inventions, one of the best-known is the Owen sub-machine gun, patented in 1941 by its inventor, E. E. Owen. **1967** 'E. LINDALL' *Time too Soon* iii. 32 An Owen gun slung across his body. **1970** M. KELLY *Spinifex* viii. 132 The Owen gun best and only friend.

†**owen**, *pa. pple. Obs.* obliged: see OWE *v.* B. 7.

owen, obs. f. OVEN; obs. inf., etc. of OWE *v.*

owen, owene, obs. forms of OWN *a.*

Owenian (əʊ'iːnɪən), *a.* [f. surname *Owen* + -IAN.] Of or pertaining to Robert Owen (1771–1858), a social reformer who advocated the reorganization of society on a system of communistic co-operation, which he endeavoured to carry into practice in various industrial communities. So **Owenism** ('əʊɪnɪz(ə)m), the theory or system of Owen; '**Owenist**, an adherent of Owenism; also *attrib.*; **Owenite** ('əʊɪnaɪt), a follower of Owen; also *attrib.*; '**Owenize** *v. trans.*, to bring under the influence of the system of Owen; to convert to Owenism.

1829 SOUTHEY *Sir Thomas More* I. vi. 144 But wherefore do you think that the Owenite scheme is likely to be carried into effect only by sectarian agency? **1830** *Mechanic's Press* (Utica, N.Y.) 10 June 254/2 What a precious compound of almost all that is unprincipled, is here presented :—Agrarianism, Owenism. **1831** E. G. WAKEFIELD *Householders in Danger from Populace* 9/2 The desperadoes ..may be divided into two classes, which I shall designate as *Huntites* and *Owenites*. *Ibid.* 10/1 The Owenites..are bent on the overthrow of all existing laws. **1833** J. S. MILL in *Tait's Edin. Mag.* III. 352 This doctrine..might easily have misled a less expanded mind..into the vagaries of Spenceanism and Owenism. **1833** *Edin. Rev.* LVI. 484 It is folly to expect that the whole nature of the problem is to be changed by the perfectibility of Owenised man. **1836** 'BRONTERRE' tr. *Buonarroti's Hist. Babeuf's Conspiracy* II. 363 My readers of the Owenite or co-operative school will be forcibly reminded..of the many doubts..addressed to Robert Owen, touching the posssibility of reducing his system to practice. **1843** MILL *Logic* II. vi. ii. 485 If the Owenite stops here, he is in a position from which nothing can expel him. **1848** MRS. GASKELL *M. Barton* xxxvii, You mean he was an Owenite; all for equality and community of goods. **1870** *Athenæum* 5 Feb. 187 That Owenism and Fourierism failed to accomplish their ends in the Old World the socialists allow. *Ibid.*, Glancing at the list of the Owenist associations, we see that the Forrestville community (Indiana)..died in its second year..and that New Harmony ..came to an end in its third year. **1880** T. FROST *Forty Yrs'. Recoll.* 14, I..knew nothing of the Owenian ethics and social economy. **1919** M. BEER *Hist. Brit. Socialism* I. II. ii. 131 George Mudie, an Owenite and journalist. **1950** G. B. SHAW *Farfetched Fables* Pref. 81, I am not stigmatizing all Owenites, Marxists, and Darwinists as immoral. **1956** W. H. G. ARMYTAGE in D. L. Linton *Sheffield* 205 This was an Owenite centre (Robert Owen had first visited the town on 30 December 1833), where a considerable amount of adult education was undertaken. **1975** V. CUNNINGHAM *Everywhere spoken Against* vii. 186 William Taunton..was a physical-force Chartist, an Owenite Socialist, manager of Coventry's first Co-operative Store.

ower ('əʊə(r)). [f. OWE *v.* + -ER¹.]

†**1.** A possessor, an owner. *Obs.*

c **1440** *Promp. Parv.* 375/1 (Harl. MS. 221) Owere of a schyp, or schyp-lord. **1447** *Rolls of Parlt.* V. 139/2 The owers of the seide Catell may never come to have replevyn of them. **1637** BP. HALL *Serm. at Excester* 24 Aug., Wks. (1662) III. [IV.] 95 He..will purchase with money that which the great ower of heaven gave him freely.

2. One who owes, a debtor. *rare.*

a **1637** B. JONSON *Underwoods* xxxiv. 1 They are not, sir, worst owers that do pay Debts when they can.

ower, obs. f. EWER², OAR, OVER, YOUR.

owerance, owrance ('əʊərəns, 'aʊrəns). *Sc.* and *north. dial.* [f. *ower, owre*, north. dial. form of OVER + -ANCE.] The position of being over; superiority, ascendancy, mastery, control.

1552 ABP. HAMILTON *Catech.* (1884) 154 To slay syn and dede quhilk had ouerance apon us. **1818** HOGG *Brownie Bodsbeck* I. iii. 39 Or it get the owrance o' auld Wat Laidlaw, od it sal get strength o' arm for aince. **1819** RENNIE *St. Patrick* II. 266 (Jam.) [He] hasna as muckle owrance o' himsel' as win up on the feet o' him. **1855** ROBINSON *Whitby Gloss.* s.v., 'She fairly haes t' owerance ower him', she completely rules him. *Mod. Sc.* She's his wife, but she hasna the owrance o' a penny! [Also in Northumbld., Cumbld., Ulster.]

†**owes, owse**, obs. forms of OOZE¹.

1575 in Ellis *Orig. Lett.* Ser. II. III. 30 The owse of Ashen barke dronke, is an extreme purgacion.. All the..connyng of a Tanner concistethe in the skillfull making of his owes.

o wey, owfe, obs. forms of AWAY, WOOF.

†**owgel**, var. of OUGLE *a.*, *Obs.* ugly, horrible.

?*c* **1400** LYDG. *Æsop's Fab.* i. 32 The owgel [*v.r.* vgly] blaknes of the derk nyght.

owȝe, obs. f. OWE.

owght, owȝt, obs. ff. OUGHT, OUT.

owgly, obs. f. UGLY *a.*

†**owhere**, *adv. Obs.* Forms: α. 1 **áhwǽr, áhwér, áhwár**, 1–3 **awer**, 4 **awher, aware**, 5 (?) **awre**. β. 3 *Orm.* **owwhar, owwhær, (eower)**, 3–4 **owhar, ouwhar**, 4 **owhore, ouwhere, ouwar, owar**, 4–5 **owher, -e, (ouwher, oughwhere, our**, 5 **ouȝwher(e, owȝwhere)**. [f. OE. *á* ever, O *adv.* + *hwǽr* WHERE: cf. *anywhere, aywhere, everywhere, somewhere*.] Anywhere.

α. *c* **888** K. ÆLFRED *Boeth.* vii. §3 Habbe ic þe awer benumen þinra gifena? *c* **1000** ÆLFRIC *Jos.* i. 18 Se man þe wiþcwiþ þinum bebodum ahwar, beo he deaþes scildiȝ. *c* **1000** *Ags. Ps.* (Th.) lxi. 6 Ne mæȝ ic hine ahwær befleon. *c* **1000** *Laws Edw. & Guth.* c. 11 Ahwar on lande. *a* **1300** *Leg. Rood* 30 Þat hit tre was fairest þo þat hi myȝte awer [*c* 1350 owhere] ise. **13..** *Cursor M.* 1837 (Gött.) Þe heiest montayn þat was aware [*T.* owhore, *C.* our-quare, *F.* awre-quare]. **1390** GOWER *Conf.* II. 349 For if mi fot wolde awher go.
β. *c* **1200** ORMIN 6509 To witenn ȝiff þeȝȝ haffdenn Crist Owwhar onn eorþe fundenn. *Ibid.* 6921 ȝiff þeȝȝ himm owhar wisstenn. *c* **1205** LAY. 8231 And ȝif ich hine mai eower [*c* 1275 owha] ifon. *a* **1225** *Ancr. R.* 60 Ham..þet ouðer oðer hondlie, oðer ouhwar ivele oðer. *c* **1320** *Cast. Love* 1278 Owher that he ȝode, Folk him sewed, bothe evyll and goode. *c* **1325** *Lai le Freine* 15 When kinges might our y-here Of ani meruailes that ther were. *c* **1350** *Will. Palerne* 2251 What man vpon molde miȝt ouwar finde tvo breme wite beres. *c* **1380** WYCLIF *Serm.* Sel. Wks. I. 262 If a man have al bileve þat Goddis lawe techiþ ouwher [*v.r.* owȝwhere]. *c* **1400** *Rule St. Benet* (E.E.T.S.) 90/1540 In bakkows, brewhows, or ourels [= owher els]. *c* **1449** PECOCK *Repr.* 211 It is not founde ouȝwhere in Holi Scripture. **1483** CAXTON *Gold. Leg.* 395/2 The beste grasse and herbys that is owhere.

†**owhither**, *adv. Obs.* Forms: 3 **ohwider, ouhwuder**, 4 **o whydre**. [f. ME. *ô* = OE. *á* ever + *hwider* WHITHER: cf. OWHERE, and OE.

ǣghwider everywhither.] To any place, anywhither.

a **1225** *Ancr. R.* 172 ȝif he ouhwuder wende ut. *a* **1240** *Sawles Warde* in *Cott. Hom.* 247 Hwon þat he slepe oðer ohwider [fare] from hame. **1382** WYCLIF *2 Kings* v. 25 Thi seruaunt ȝeede not o whydre [1388 to ony place].

owing (ˈəʊɪŋ), *vbl. sb.* [f. OWE *v.* + -ING[1].] The action of the verb OWE (sense 2); that which one owes; obligation to pay, indebtedness; debt.

1552 HULOET, Owynge, or the act of owynge, *debitio.* **1628** GAULE *Pract. The.* (1629) 109 Cæsar inuades the Fortunes of his Subiects, either to vphold his Honours, or absolue his Owings. **1839** FR. A. KEMBLE *Rec. Later Life* I. 235 Being in the mind to pay my owings, I proceed to do so.

owing (ˈəʊɪŋ), *ppl. a.* [f. as prec. + -ING[2]. Almost always used predicatively, or after its noun.]

1. That owes (see OWE *v.* 2, etc.); that is under obligation, bound (*to do* something); indebted, bounden, beholden (*to* a person *for* something). Now *rare* or *Obs.*

1362 LANGL. *P. Pl.* A. x. 69 Þenne is holy chirche a-signet [*v.rr.* owynge, awynge] to helpen hem and sauen. **1678** PEPYS *Corr.* 292, I am greatly owing to your Lordship for your last favour. **1691** T. H[ALE] *Acc. New Invent.* 13 One Instance..of what this Company is owing for, to the..Thoughtfulness of its Accusers.

2. Said of the thing: That is yet to be paid or rendered; owed, due. Const. *to* or simple dat. (The usual current sense.)

The origin of this use is obscure, there being no corresponding sense of the vb.; it might possibly be reflexive, 'owing itself', hence 'being owed'.

1411 in *E.E. Wills* 19 Of whiche somme ys owynge to me, to be payd, an.C. Mark by þe handes of my lady louell. **1435** *Rolls of Parlt.* IV. 493/1 Certeyn dette, which they clayme to be owyng hem by..ye Kyng. **1570** *Wills & Inv. N.C.* (Surtees 1835) 344 Dettis awand me. **1596** DANETT tr. *Comines* (1614) 179 At the yeeres ende there is not one penny owing them. **1782** MISS BURNEY *Cecilia* IX. v, She discharged all that was owing for the children.

3. *fig.* **owing to**: **a.** *pred.* That owes its existence to; attributable to; derived or arising from, caused by, consequent on, 'due to' (see DUE *a.* 9).

1655 STANLEY *Hist. Philos.* I. (1701) 43/1 Wise Cleobulus's Death, the Lyndian Shoar, To which his Birth was owing, doth deplore. **1695** WOODWARD *Nat. Hist. Earth* i. (1723) 17 These are the very Exuviæ of Animals, and all owing to the Sea. **1706** HEARNE *Collect.* (O.H.S.) I. 173 As to the Notes..they are in a great Measure owing to Mr. Potter. **1812** SIR H. DAVY *Chem. Philos.* 2 The effect is owing to the presence of light. **1858** BUCKLE *Civiliz.* (1873) II. viii. 582 It is to a knowledge of the laws and relations of things that European civilization is owing.

b. Hence, as prepositional phr.: In consequence of, on account of, because of. (Cf. *according to*.)

1814 SCOTT *Wav.* x, Owing to his natural disposition to study..he had been bred with a view to the bar. **1815** —— *Guy M.* xl, Owing to these circumstances, Brown remained several days in Allonby without any answers whatever. **1839** STONEHOUSE *Axholme* 163 Where the lands are divided into a great many selions, and, owing to the number of owners, are continually passing from one person to another. **1865** LIGHTFOOT *Comm. Gal.* (1874) 151 This rendering obtained currency..owing to the untoward circumstances of the times.

owir, obs. north. dial. var. OVER.

owirhaill, Sc. variant of OVERHALE *v. Obs.*

†**owirloft**, obs. Sc. form of ORLOP[1].

1564 *Reg. Privy Council Scot.* I. 281 The sey wattir to haif interes into thame, to the owirloft.

owk, obs. Sc. variant of *ouk*, *wouke*, WEEK.

owl (aʊl), *sb.* Forms: α. 1–3 *úle*, 4–6 *oule*, 5–7 *owle*, (5 *owele*, 5–6 *owll(e*, 7 *oole*), 6– *owl*. β. 5–6 *howle*, 5 *howylle*, 6 *houle*. [Com. Teut.: OE. *úle* wk. fem., = OLG. **ûla* (MDu., MLG., LG. *ûle*, Du. *uil*):—**ûlôn*, from **ûwlôn*: cf. OHG. *ûwila* (MHG. *iuwel*, *iule*, Ger. *eule*, mod.Fl. *uwele*), ON. *ugla*. These point back to OTeut. **uwwalâ*, **uwwilâ*, dim. of an echoic **uwwâ*, derived from the voice of the bird. Cf. OHG. *hûwo*, OLG. *hûo*, MHG. *hûwe*, also mod.G. *uhu*, names of the owl of similar echoic origin; also L. *ulula* owl, *ululāre* to howl, and HOWL, HOWLET.]

1. a. A nocturnal bird of prey, well known by its doleful 'hoot', having a large head, small face, raptorial beak, and large eyes directed forwards, beset by a disk of radiating feathers; feeding on mice, small birds, and the like, which it can approach noiselessly by reason of its soft plumage. The name has app. been applied in English from the beginning to all the native species, esp. the two or three common ones: see b.

c **725** *Corpus Gloss.* (O.E.T.) 1382 *Noctua, ulula*, ule. *Ibid.* 2150 *Ulula*, ulae. *c* **1000** ÆLFRIC *Lev.* xi. 16 Ne ete ȝe nan þing hafocynnes ne earncynnes: Ne ulan. *a* **1250** *Owl & Night.* 4 Iherde ich holde grete tale Ane ule and one nightegale. *c* **1385** CHAUCER *L.G.W.* 2249 *Philomene*, The oule [*v.r.* owle]..That prophete is of wo & of myschaunce. *c* **1440** *Promp. Parv.* 374/2 Owle, or howle, byrde, *bubo.* **1535** COVERDALE *Ps.* ci. 6 Like a Pellicane in the wildernes, and like an Oule in a broken wall. **1590** SHAKS. *Mids. N.* II. ii. 6 The clamorous Owle that nightly hoots. **1663** BOYLE *Usef. Exp. Nat. Philos.* I. iv. 66 As the eyes of owls are to the splendor of the day. **1714** GAY *Sheph. Week* vi. 53 For Owles, as Swains observe, detest the Light. **1826** DISRAELI *Viv. Grey* v. xv, The screech of the waking owl. **1887** RUSKIN *Praeterita* II. 363 Whatever wise people may say of them, I at least myself have found the owl's cry always prophetic of mischief to me.

b. The common British species are the ***barn owl*** (white, silver, yellow, church, hissing, hobby, screech owl); the ***tawny owl*** (brown, grey, beech, ferny, hoot, hooting, ivy, wood owl); the ***long-eared*** or ***horned owl*** (long-tufted, mottled-tufted owl).

Less common are the ***short-eared owl*** (fern, hawk, october, red, short-horn, woodcock owl), the ***eagle owl*** (stock owl of Orkney), ***little owl*** (bare-toed, little night owl), ***snowy*** or ***great white owl***.

1390 GOWER *Conf.* II. 265 Sche caste in..A part ek of the horned Oule. **1500–20** DUNBAR *Poems* xxxiii. 74 The myttane, and Sanct Martynis fowle, Wend he had bene the hornit howle. **1611** COTGR., *Lucheran*, a scrich-owle. **1623** WODROEPHE *Marrow Fr. Tongue* 399/2 With Stockes, Wood, Wolues, and Scrick-Ooles. **1674** RAY *Collect. Words, Eng. Birds* 83 The common gray or Ivy-Owl. **1678** —— *Willughby's Ornith.* 101 Our Church Owl and brown Owl..delight in lower and plain countrys. **1770** G. WHITE *Selborne* xxix. 81 *To Pennant*, I have known a dove-house infested by a pair of white owls, which made great havock among the young pigeons. **1830** TENNYSON *Song Owl* 7 Alone and warming his five wits, The white owl in the belfry sits. **1882** J. HARDY in *Proc. Berw. Nat. Club* IX. 428 The horned, white, and brown owls have here an undisturbed refuge. **1882** A. HEPBURN *Ibid.* 504 The Long-Eared, Tawny, and Barn Owls, were permanently resident.

c. *Ornith.* Any bird of the sub-order *Striges*.

These comprise the families *Aluconinæ* (*Strigidæ* of Sharpe) and *Striginæ* or *Strigidæ* (*Bubonidæ* of Sharpe), typified respectively by the Screech or Barn Owl (*Aluco flammeus* Fleming, *Strix* Linn.), and the Tawny or Brown Owl (*S. stridula* Linn.); and including, among 19 genera, those typified by the Hawk Owl (*Surnia*), Snowy Owl (*Nyctea*) which are diurnal in habit, the Horned or Eared Owls (*Asio*), Eagle Owl (*Bubo*), Cue Owl (*Scops*), Little Owl (*Carine noctua*), and American Burrowing Owl (*Speotyto cunicularia*). The known species are about 200.

1706 PHILLIPS s.v., In Virginia there is a sort of Owl as big as a Goose, that kills the Poultry in the Night. **1802** BINGLEY *Anim. Biog.* (1813) II. 62 The Great Horned or Eagle Owl ..which is common in many parts of Greece, was even considered as a favourite bird of Minerva. **1859** TENNENT *Ceylon* II. VII. vii. 257 Across the grey sky the owl flits in pursuit of the night moths. **1869** tr. *Pouchet's Universe* (ed. 11) 219 This species abounds in the Mississippi regions, where it shelters itself in subterranean abodes several yards in depth..It is called the burrowing-owl (*Strix cunicularia*). **1884–5** *Stand. Nat. Hist.* (1888) IV. 345 The great gray owl, *Syrnium cinereum*, an extremely rare winter visitor to the northern United States. **1894** NEWTON *Dict. Birds* 675 Among Owls are found birds which vary in length from 5 inches—as *Glaucidium cobanense*,..much smaller than a Skylark—to more than 2 feet..[A] characteristic of nearly all Owls is the reversible property of their outer toes. **1896** *Daily News* 6 June 8/1 In Valdivia, Dr. Plate observed the remarkable earth owl, which digs long shafts in the steppes, and is distinguished for its terrible scream.

d. In various proverbial sayings.

(*to carry* or ***send owls to Athens***, after Gr. γλαῦκ' Ἀθήναζε ἄγειν (Aristoph. *Birds* 301), to 'carry coals to Newcastle', to take a commodity where it already abounds; the owl being the emblem of Pallas Athene, the patron goddess of Athens, and represented on Athenian coins, etc.)

1390 GOWER *Conf.* I. 299 Bot Oule on Stock and Stock on Oule; The more that a man defoule, Men witen wel which hath the werse. **1590** SWINBURNE *Testaments* Pref., I may be thought to powre water into the Sea, to carrie owles to Athens, and to trouble the reader with a matter altogether needlesse and superfluous. **1602** SHAKS. *Ham.* IV. v. 41 They say the Owle was a Bakers daughter. *a* **1611** BEAUM. & FL. *Four Plays in one*, Induct., Could not you be content To be an owl in such an ivy-bush? **1622** MALYNES *Anc. Law-Merch.* 426 There is a Custome that no Officer may arrest after Sun set; such therefore as goe abroad but at those times, are said to Fly with the Owle, by a common Prouerbe. **1738–1869** [see IVY-BUSH]. **1764** H. WALPOLE *Let. to Earl of Hertford* 15 Feb., The noise, which made me as drunk as an owl. **1787** GROSE *Prov. Gloss.* s.v., *To take owl*, to be offended, to take amiss. **1840** MARRYAT *Poor Jack* xxxvi, The..men will be as drunk as owls.

2. *transf.* and *fig.* **a.** Applied to a person in allusion to nocturnal habits, to literal or figurative repugnance to light, to appearance of gravity and wisdom (often with implication of underlying stupidity), etc. Hence = wiseacre, solemn dullard.

1413 *Pilgr. Sowle* (Caxton) I. xxvii. (1859) 31 Peple, whiche the wretchyd horrible owle of helle had drawen out of theyr nest. **1508** KENNEDIE *Flyting w. Dunbar* 36 Fantastik fule,..Ignorant elf, aip, owll irregular. **1579** FULKE *Heskins's Parl.* 15 The Owles and Battes of our time, either can not, or will not see it. **1598** SYLVESTER *Du Bartas* II. i. II. *Imposture* 377 In heav'nly things..more blinde then Moals, In earthly, Owls. **1606** SHAKS. *Tr. & Cr.* II. i. 99, I bad thee vile Owle, goe learne me the tenure of the Proclamation. **1694** ECHARD *Plautus* 172 But without flattery, I was a great Owl for not falling in love before now. **1847** L. HUNT *Men, Women, & B.* II. ii. 32 It vexes one to see so fine a poet make such an owl of himself.

b. ***Brown Owl***, the name given to the adult leader of a Brownie Guides pack; ***Tawny Owl***, a Brown Owl's assistant.

1918 R. S. S. BADEN-POWELL *Girl Guiding* I. ii. 17 The Brown Owl (that is, the leader of the Pack) takes her place by the toadstool. *Ibid.* 21 Each Pack is under the charge of a grown-up leader—the Brown Owl. **1921** in —— *Brownies* (ed. 2) 60 A Brownie Pack consists of not less than two Sixes ..under a Brownie Guider, who is called the Brown Owl, and her assistant the Tawny Owl. **1932** [see PACK *sb.*[1] 3 d]. **1950** *Oxf. Jun. Encycl.* IX. 254/1 Brownies are divided into 'Packs' of 18–24 children, under the leadership of two adult leaders, known to the Brownies as 'Brown Owl' and 'Tawny Owl'. **1968** M. FINCH *Eye with Mascara* xiv. 149 She sounded like Brown Owl chivvying her Brownies. **1973** *Brownie* 10 Jan. 7/1 Our Pack has a membership of 20 keen Brownies... Our meetings are held at Brown Owl's house. .. Tawny Owl is a Sister at Hetune and walks all the way to our meetings. **1977** *Guider* July 331/2 She was a Guider in this Company, a Brown Owl of the 1st Teignmouth Pack, a Sea Ranger Skipper and a District Commissioner.

3. a. A name for the Lump Fish, more fully ***sea owl***. **b.** A variety of Ray, the ***owl-ray***.

1601 HOLLAND *Pliny* II. 428 The Lompe, Paddle or sea-Owle. **1862** COUCH *Brit. Fishes* I. 115 Sandy Ray, Owl, *Raia circularis*. *Ibid.* II. 183 Sea Owl, the Lumpfish. **1863** KINGSLEY *Water Bab.* iv, Where the great owl-rays leap and flap, like giant bats, upon the tide.

4. A fancy variety of the domestic pigeon distinguished by its owl-like head and prominent ruff; also called ***owl-pigeon***.

1725 BRADLEY *Fam. Dict.* s.v. *Pigeon*, There are..many sorts of pigeons, such as..Petits, Owls, Spots, Trumpeters, Shakers, &c. **1765** *Treat. Dom. Pigeons* 125 The owl is..a small Pigeon, very little larger than a jacobine. **1899** *Q. Rev.* Oct. 415 He crossed a white fantail cock with the offspring of an owl and an archangel.

5. A local name (in South Eng.) of certain moths.

1853 W. D. COOPER *Sussex Gloss.* **1883** *Hampsh. Gloss.*, *Owl*..(1) The tiger-moth...(2) Any small white moth.

†**6.** Name of some game. *Obs.*

1653 URQUHART *Rabelais* I. xxii. 95 There he played..At the billiards, At bob and hit, At the owle [Fr. *au hybou*]. **1660** HOWELL *Lexicon* xxviii, To play at the Owl, *alla civetta*; *a la chouëtte*.

7. *attrib.* and *Comb.*, as ***owl barn***, ***belfry***, ***-cote***, ***-down***, ***flight***, ***-hoot***, ***-light***, ***-time***; ***owl-eye***, ***-hole***, ***-shooter***, ***-sight***; ***owl's head***, ***wing***, etc.; instrumental, as ***owl-frequented***, ***-haunted*** adjs.; parasynthetic and similative, as ***owl-dark***, ***-downy***, ***-dusk***, ***-dusked***, ***-eyed***, ***-faced***, ***-headed***, ***-sighted***, ***-soft***, ***-winged***, ***-wise*** adjs.; also ***owl-like***; ***owl-wise*** adv.; † **owl-blasted** *a.*, bewitched; **owl bus** *N. Amer.*, a bus running during the night; **owl car** *N. Amer.*, a tramcar running during the night; **owl-catchers**, gloves of stout leather; **owl jug**, a porcelain jug shaped like an owl; **owl-train** (*U.S.*), a train running during the night; **owl trolley** = *owl car*.

1603 HARSNET *Pop. Impost.* xxi. 137 No doubt but mother Nobs is the witch, the young girle is *owleblasted and possessed. **1947** *Sun* (Baltimore) 24 June 10/2 Operators of all other all-night busses and trolleys have been directed to connect with the *owl bus, just as they did with the..owl trolley. **1975** *Washington Post* 26 Dec. A 22/3 Chances are the owl bus riders will..simply fade away.., just another segment of the population abandoned by the Metro system. **1889** FARMER *Americanisms* 405/2 **Owl-Car*, a tram-car plying late into the night. **1904** *N.Y. Even. Post* 7 May 1 The driver of an 'owl car' that rattled eastward on Spring street. **1911** *Daily Colonist* (Victoria, B.C.) 21 Apr. 12/7 An 'owl car' service has been inaugurated by the B.C.E.R. Company at Vancouver. **1947** *Sun* (Baltimore) 24 June 10/2 The No. 17 owl or all-night car has been supplanted by a No. 28 bus. **1879** JEFFERIES *Amateur Poacher*, A pair of '*owl-catchers', gloves of stout white leather. **1863** 'G. HAMILTON' *Gala-Days* 107 For the substantial stone city.. turns out to be a miserable little dirty, hutty, smutty, stagnant *owl-cote. **1920** E. SITWELL *Wooden Pegasus* 41 In *owl-dark garments goes the Rain. **1924** —— *Sleeping Beauty* ii. 18 Smoothing the dusky dawn's *owl-down. *a* **1849** POE *Enigma, Petrarch. stuff* Poems (1859) 79 *Owl-downy nonsense. **1928** E. SITWELL *Five Poems* 18 That sang sweet country songs in owl-dusked leaves:..but time drifts *owl-dusk o'er the brightest eyes. **1868** BROWNING *Ring & Bk.* VI. 1786 With a wink of the *owl-eyes of you. **1640** SIR E. DERING *Carmelite* (1641) 16 Others of your bent who are ..*owle-eyed in Sunshine. **1843** CARLYLE *Past & Pr.* II. xvii, Valiant Wisdom..escorted by owl-eyed Pedantry. **1925** F. SCOTT FITZGERALD *Great Gatsby* iii. 45 A..man, with enormous owl-eyed spectacles. **1542** UDALL *Erasm. Apoph.* 309 b, To begette suche foule babies & *oule faced doudes. *a* **1529** SKELTON *Dk. Albany* 312 He ran away by nyght In the *owle flyght Lyke a cowarde knyght. *a* **1839** PRAED *Poems* (1865) II. 38 Things hid In *owl-frequented pyramid. *c* **1795** YOUNG in *Ann. Agric.* XXIII. 376 Wool on the cheeks and throat (but not to the degree they term *owl-headed) [sheep]. **1960** AUDEN *Homage to Clio* 55 Steatopygous, sow-dugged and owl-headed. **1968** *Listener* 11 July 59/2 A Chou Dynasty bronze bell with tiger-handle and an owl-headed drinking vessel. **1898** *Board of Agric. Leaflet* No. 51 In many old barns..there are *owl-holes just under the eaves, formed with ledges specially made for ingress and egress. **1938** W. DE LA MARE *Memory* 11 Came *owl-hoot From the thicket. **1925** B. RACKHAM tr. *E. Hannover's Pott. & Porc.* I. 554 The origin of the faïence owls..is fully discussed..by Walter Stengel..in the *Jahrbuch für Kunstwissenschaft* for 1924, p. 26. He gives good reason for regarding these *owl-jugs,..as being of Nuremberg origin. **1936** [see DOUBLE EAGLE 2]. **1960** R. G. HAGGAR *Conc. Encycl. Cont. Pott. & Porc.* 339/1 Faience owl jugs were made at Nuremberg in Germany... Specimens dating between 1540 and 1560 are recorded by Rackham. **1934** *Owl light [see *moth-light* s.v. MOTH *sb.*[1] 3]. **1936** DYLAN THOMAS *Twenty-Five Poems* 42 Altarwise by owl-light in the halfway-house The gentleman lay graveward with his furies. *a* **1618** SYLVESTER *Maiden's Blush* 1063 *Owl-like in a Cloud involv'd. **1844** H. ROGERS *Ess.* I. ii. 84 The owl-like gravity of thousands of common readers. **1530** PALSGR. 250/1 *Oules heed, *hure*. [*Littré*: *hure*, tête hérissée et en désordre.] **1596** FITZ-GEFFRAY *Sir F. Drake* (1881) 31 *Oule-sighted eies, that dazled are with light, But see acutelie in the darksome night. **1924** E. SITWELL *Sleeping Beauty* xvi. 59 An *owl-soft shadow falling over folly. **1953** W. DE LA MARE *O Lovely England* 32 Owl-soft his wings. **1871** BROWNING *Pr. Hohenst.* 188 An outspread providential hand Above the *owl's-wing aigrette. **1972** R. ADAMS *Watership Down* xxiii. 159 By *owl-time Bigwig and his helpers had scratched out a kind of lobby inside the entrance to one of the runs leading down from the wood. **1856** *N. Y. Herald* 8 Jan. 1/2 The '*Owl Train', due at Jersey City at five o'clock yesterday morning, did not arrive until afternoon. **1876** S. & A. WARNER *Gold of Chickaree* 248 Must take the morning train. It's not quite an 'owl train' —but comes along, I believe, by eight o'clock. **1882** MCCABE *New York* 190 (Farmer) The Third avenue line runs its trains all night... These are the owl-trains. **1910** *N. Y. Even. Post* 22 Dec. 3 The engine of the 'owl train'—for by this term the one leaving New York after midnight is called.. went off the track. **1947** *Los Angeles Times* 18 Jan. 1/1 (*heading*) 7 killed and 86 hurt in wreck of owl train. **1947** *Owl trolley [see *owl bus* above]. *a* **1822** SHELLEY *Def. Poetry* Pr. Wks. 1888 II. 32 Those eternal regions where the *owl-winged faculty of calculation dare not soar. **1906** KIPLING in *Tribune* 16 Jan. 4/3 Jimmy.. rolled his congested eye-balls, *owl-wise. **1912** W. DEEPING *Sincerity* xxxviii. 276 His round, lard-coloured, mildly owl-wise face. **1939** JOYCE *Finnegans Wake* I. 78 The eternals were owlwise on their side every time.

b. esp. in names of animals, as **owl-butterfly**, a large South American butterfly (*Caligo eurylochus*) with large ocelli, likened to owls' eyes, on the posterior wings; **owl-faced bat**, the bat *Chilonycteris Macleayii*, a native of Cuba and Jamaica; **owl-faced monkey** = *owl-monkey*; **owl-fly**, (*a*) an angler's name for *Sialia lutaria*; (*b*) = *owl midge*; **owl-gazelle**, Sœmmering's Gazelle, the native name of which is *aoul*; **owl-gnat**, a gnat of the tribe *Noctuiformes*, family *Psychodidæ*; **owl midge** = *moth-fly* (MOTH *sb.* 3); **owl-monkey**, a South American monkey of the genus *Nyctipithecus*; **owl-moth**, a very large Brazilian moth (*Erebus strix*) resembling an owl in its colouring and in the appearance of its hind wings; **owl-parrot** = KAKAPO; **owl-pigeon**: see 4; **owl-ray**: see 3; **owl-swallow**, a bird of the family *Podargidæ*, akin to the night-jars.

1884 *Stand. Nat. Hist.* (1888) II. 489 *C. eurylochus* or the '*owl-butterfly'.. being common throughout South America. **1863** BATES *Nat. Amazon* II. 102 The nocturnal, *owl-faced monkey (*Nyctipithecus trivirgatus*). **1676** COTTON *Angler* II. 335 Late at night is taken the *Owl-fly. **1799** G. SMITH *Laboratory* II. 298 The yellow-miller, or owl fly. **1932** RILEY & JOHANNSEN *Med. Entomol.* xiv. 195 The *Psychodidae*, popularly known as moth flies, owl flies, sand flies, or papataci, are minute dark-coloured insects whose body and wings are densely covered with hairs. **1951** COLYER & HAMMOND *Flies Brit. Isles* 84 The *Owl Midges or Hairy Moth-flies are easily recognisable; they may often be seen on windows, where they either run actively with a curious, jerky gait or remain perfectly still. **1962** GORDON & LAVOIPIERRE *Entomol. for Students of Med.* xx. 131 Flies belonging to the other three subfamilies [of Psychodidae].. are known as moth flies or owl midges. **1862** T. W. HARRIS *Insects injur. Veget.* (ed. 3) v. 338 The *owl-moth (*Erebus Strix*) has wings which, though not so broad, expand eleven inches. **1880–1** *Libr. Univ. Knowl.* (U.S.) XI. 141 *Owl-parrot.. in New Zealand, the kakapo or night-parrot. **1890** W. P. BALL *Effects of Use & Disuse* 69 The rudimentary keel of the sternum in the owl-parrot of New Zealand. **1869–73** *Cassell's Bk. Birds* II. 136 The *Owl Swallows (*Podargi*).

c. Also **owl's crown**, a composite plant *Filago germanica*; (? erroneously) Wood Cudweed (*Gnaphalium sylvaticum*).

1787 W. MARSHALL *Norfolk* Gloss., Owlscrown, ..*gnaphalium sylvaticum*, wood cudweed. **1880** BRITTEN & HOLLAND *Plant-n.*, Owl's Crown, *Filago germanica*.

owl, *v.*[1] [f. OWL *sb.*] *intr.* To behave, hoot, look, or go about like an owl; to pry about, prowl, esp. in the dark. Now chiefly *dial.*

1542 UDALL *Erasm. Apoph.* 248 By reason of an oule, breakyng his slepe.. with hir oughlyng. **1656** HOBBES *Six Lessons* Wks. 1845 VII. 278 Is it not therefore.. well owled of you, to teach the contrary? **1778** WOLCOTT (P. Pindar) *Ep. to Reviewers* xxviii, Mousing for faults or, if you'll have it, owling. **1893** *Wilts. Gloss.*, *Owl about*, to moon about out of doors in the dark.

†**owl**, *v.*[2] *Obs.* [app. a back-formation from OWLER, OWLING.] *trans.* To smuggle (wool or sheep) out of England; to carry on the trade of an owler.

1738 *Obs. British Wool* Title-p., A Scheme for preventing our Wool from being Owled Abroad for the future, if put in Practice.

owlate, owld, obs. ff. OWLET, OLD, WOULD.

'owldom. *nonce-wd.* The domain of owls.

1850 CARLYLE *Latter-d. Pamph.* iii. (1872) 120 Owldom shall continue a flourishing empire.

†**owldron**, var. OLERON *Obs.*, a coarse fabric.

1550–1600 *Customs Duties* (B. M. Addit. MS. 25097), Owldrons, the bolte, containing xxx yards—xiijs. iiij*d.*

†**owlebie.** *Obs.* [cf. -BY *suffix* 2.]

1653 E. G. in *Bulwer's Anthropomet.* Pref. verses **ij, Men were swine and turn'd to Owlebies.

owler, dial. form of ALDER, the tree.

†**'owler.** *Obs.* exc. *Hist.* [Goes with OWLING: app. f. OWL *sb.*: see -ER[1] I.

To prevent the exportation of wool it was made illegal by Act 14 Chas. II, c. 18 §8 to transport it in the night-time; and it is probable that it was in reference to the fact that the smugglers of wool carried on their work, like owls, under cover of night, that the terms *owler* and *owling* arose: cf. quot. *a* 1700. Some have considered the words to be formed on the north. dial. form of *wool* ('*ool*), but from the district with which they were specially associated (Kent and Sussex) this is very improbable.]

One engaged in the illegal exportation or 'owling' of wool or sheep from England; also, a vessel so employed, an owling-boat.

1696 LUTTRELL *Brief Rel.* (1857) IV. 26 A messenger has seized the Owler, who carried over the duke of Barwick to France. *a* **1700** B. E. *Dict. Cant. Crew*, *Owlers*, those who privately in the Night carry Wool to the Sea-Coasts, near Rumney-Marsh in Kent, and some Creeks in Sussex, &c. and Ship it off for France against Law. **1701** T. BROWN *Advice* in *Collect. Poems* 106 To Gibbets and Gallow's your Owlers advance, That, that's the sure way to Mortifie France. **1778** *Eng. Gazetteer* (ed. 2) s.v. *Rumney Marsh*, This marsh is the place from whence the owlers have for so many ages exported our wool to France. **1892** *Blackw. Mag.* July 33 Ailesbury crossed the Channel in an 'owler' or smuggling vessel.

owlery ('aʊlərɪ). [f. OWL *sb.* + -ERY.]

1. A place where owls are kept; an abode or haunt of owls.

1817 *Sporting Mag.* I. 9 The Owlery at Arundel Castle. **1850** CARLYLE *Latter-d. Pamph.* iii. (1872) 93 England.. sunk now to a dim owlery. **1866** *Morn. Star* 31 Dec., Others made a dart at the owlery, and saved some of its occupants [from the fire].

2. The quality or characteristic of an owl; owlishness. (Cf. *tomfoolery*.)

1831 CARLYLE *Sart. Res.* III. iii, Perhaps too of all the owleries that ever possessed him [man], the most owlish.. is that of your actually-existing Motive-Millwrights. **1865** —— *Fredk. Gt.* XVI. i. (1872) VI. 133 The multiplied forms of stupidity, cupidity and human owlery.

owlet ('aʊlɪt). Also 6 **oulette, owlate.** [dim. of OWL: see -ET[1]; prob. altered from the earlier HOWLET.] An owl; a young owl or little owl.

1542 UDALL *Erasm. Apoph.* 248 He tooke veraye eiuill reste in the nightes, by reason of an oule... A launceknight .. tooke the peines to catche this oulette. **1567** MAPLET *Gr. Forest* 94 b, There is a certaine Shrickowle or Owlet which when she crieth, she shricketh. **1589** PUTTENHAM *Eng. Poesie* III. xix. (Arb.) 242 As egles eyes to owlates sight. **1798** WORDSW. *Idiot Boy* lviii, The owlets through the long blue night Are shouting to each other still. **1832** W. IRVING *Alhambra* II. 88 He loved his children too even as an owl loves its owlets.

b. *attrib.* and *Comb.*, as ***owlet-haunted*** adj., ***owlet wing***; **owlet light** = OWL-LIGHT; **owlet-moth**, an American name for any moth of the genus *Noctua* or family *Noctuidæ*.

1821 SHELLEY *Epipsych.* 221 Whose flight Is as a dead leaf's in the owlet light. **1831** CARLYLE in Froude *Life* (1882) II. 207 Ignorance eclipses all things with its owlet wings. **1862** T. W. HARRIS *Insects injur. Veget.* (ed. 3) v. 435 The injury done to vegetation by the caterpillars of the Noctuas, or owlet-moths. **1880** NIMMO *Hist. Stirlingsh.* I. vi. 99 Its owlet-haunted walls.

'Owl-glass. Forms: 6–7 **Ho(w)leglas,** 6 **Howliglasse,** 7 **Owli-, Owlyglasse, Owl glass.** See also HOLLIGLASS. [f. OWL *sb.* + GLASS *sb.* 8.] The English rendering of mediæval *Eulenspiegel*, the name of a German jester of mediæval times, the hero of an old German jest-book translated into English *c* 1560; a prototype of roguish fools; hence, A jester, buffoon.

c **1560** (*title*) A merye Ieste of a Man that was called Howleglas; and of many meruaylous Thinges and Iestes that he dyd in his Lyfe, in Eastlande and in many other Places. *Ibid.* Contents, How Holeglas was made a paryshe clarke. **1589** NASHE *Anat. Absurd.* 18 These.. beeing in their priuate Chambers the expresse imitation of Howli-glasse. **1601** B. JONSON *Poetaster* III. i, What, do you laugh, Howleglas!.. you perstemptuous varlet. **1630** J. TAYLOR (Water P.) *Coriats Commend.* Wks. II. 91/2 Then shall the fame which thou hast won on foot,.. Ride on my best Inuention like an asse To the amazement of each Owliglasse. **1890** K. R. H. MACKENZIE (*title*) The Marvellous Adventures of Master Tyll Owlglass.

'owl-head. a. *local* (See quot.) **b.** *local U.S.* 'The black-bellied plover, *Squatarola helvetica*' (*Cent. Dict.*).

1854 WOODWARD *Mollusca* II. 222 Internal casts of [the fossil bivalve] *Producta gigantea* are called 'owl-heads' by quarrymen in the North of England.

†**'owling**, *vbl. sb. Obs.* exc. *Hist.* [Goes with OWLER: app. f. OWL *sb.*: see -ING I c.] The practice of smuggling wool (and sheep) out of England; the trade of an owler. Also *attrib.*, as *owling boat, trade.*

1699 LUTTRELL *Brief Rel.* (1857) IV. 548 The owling trade is in a manner suppresst by the diligence of the officers appointed for that purpose. *c* **1728** EARL OF AILESBURY *Mem.* (1890) 316 That owling boat coming in generally twice a week with commodities. **1738** *Obs. British Wool* 6 By the Owling of Wool into Foreign Countries, we enable their own Manufacturers to make much better and finer Stuffs. **1769** BLACKSTONE *Comm.* IV. xii. 154 Owling, so called from it's being usually carried on in the night, which is the offence of transporting wool or sheep out of this kingdom, to the detriment of it's staple manufacture. **1887** LECKY *Eng. in 18th C.* VI. xxiii. 236.

owlish ('aʊlɪʃ), *a.* [f. OWL *sb.* + -ISH[1].] Owl-like; resembling an owl, or that of an owl.

1611 COTGR., *Cahuaille*, a companie of Owles; an Owlish companie. *Rab*[*elais*]. **1613** PURCHAS *Pilgrimage* 2 Whose owlish eyes are dazled with the brightnesse of this light. *a* **1764** LLOYD *Poet* Poet. Wks. 1774 II. 20 But eminence offends at once The owlish eye of critic dunce. **1880** MARG. LONSDALE *Sister Dora* viii, Her owlish habits of wandering at unearthly hours in all weathers. **1895** ZANGWILL *Master* III. ii. 300 The little man with his most owlish air of wisdom.

Hence **'owlishly** *adv.*, in an owlish manner; **'owlishness**, the quality of being owlish.

1888 *Boston* (Mass.) *Transcript* 7 July 5/5 It is very interesting to see him appearing for once in the guise of the newspaper correspondent, whose ordinary owlishness he so effectively ridicules. **1901** C. G. HARPER *Gt. North Road* II. 40 Old gabled houses that.. seem to nod owlishly to neighbours just as decrepit across the cobble-stoned path.

'owlism. *nonce-wd.* [f. OWL *sb.* + -ISM.] An owlish characteristic or practice.

1843 CARLYLE *Past & Pr.* II. xvii, Lawyers too were poets, were heroes.. Their Owlisms, Vulturisms.. will disappear by and by, their Heroisms only remaining.

owlk(e, obs. Sc. form of WEEK.

owl-light. Also 9 **owl's light.** [f. OWL *sb.* + LIGHT *sb.*] The dim and uncertain light in which owls go abroad; twilight, dusk; also (in early use) the cloud of night, the dark.

1599 NASHE *Lenten Stuffe* (1871) 67 Which drove Leander, when he durst not deal above-board.. to swim to her, nor that in the day, but by owl-light. **1630** J. TAYLOR (Water P.) *Merry Wherry-Ferry-Voy.* Wks. II. 8/2 When sodainly 'twixt Owle-light and the darke, We pluck'd the Boat beyond high-water mark. **1675** COTTON *Scoffer Scoft* 83 He has that won't endure the Sun, But is by Owl-light to be done. **1776** MRS. DELANY *Life & Corr.* Ser. II. II. 213, I must finish to-morrow, for I have written thus far by owllight. **1826** J. R. BEST *4 Yrs. France* 332 He.. arrived at Beaucaire in time to lead his ladies about both by owls-light and lamp-light. **1877** SIR P. WALLIS in Brighton *Mem.* (1892) 199 As I am now writing by owl's light, I must call a halt.

fig. **1761** WARBURTON *Charge to Clergy Diocese Gloucester* Wks. 1787 V. 592 The Antiquarian, who delights to solace himself in the benighted days of Monkish Owl-light.

†**owl-spiegle**, *sb. Obs. rare.* [After Ger. *Eulenspiegel*.] = OWL-GLASS. Hence **owlspiegle** *v.* (*nonce-wd.*), to make into an owl-spiegle.

1637 B. JONSON *Sad Sheph.* II. i, Thou shouldst have given her a madge-owl, and then Thou'dst made a present o' thy self, owl-spiegle! **1830** SCOTT *Doom Devorgoil* III. i, My nether parts Are goblinized and Owlspiegled.

'owly, *a.* [f. OWL *sb.* + -Y, or (in *oulelie*) -LY[1].]

a. = OWLISH.

a **1586** SIDNEY *Arcadia* v. (1598) 445 Our owly eyes, which dimm'd with passions be, And scarce discerne the dawne of comming day. **1647** *Strange Newes from Campania* 54 Whilst Treason and Rebellion start aside, And in each hole their Owly faces hide. **1654** GAYTON *Pleas. Notes* III. ii. 72 Her face was flat, and very much like an Owles, if not more Oulelie [*printed* Oulebie]. **1864** O. W. NORTON *Army Lett.* (1903) 203 Last night I was out all night in the rain.. and I feel owly to-day. **1873** C. G. LELAND *Egyptian Sketch-bk.* 33 Up started a little, dark, old, owly, goblin, night-ghoul of a creature. **1978** R. HOLLES *Spawn* vii. 61 The round, slightly owly features of the woman in nursing uniform.

b. *Comb.*, as **owly-eyed** *a.*, having eyes like an owl's, in respect of seeing badly in daylight. Also (*U.S. dial.*), intoxicated.

a **1586** SIDNEY *Arcadia* III. (1622) 303 Their wicked mindes blind to the light of vertue, and owly eyed in the night of wickednesse. *c* **1630** DRUMM. OF HAWTH. *Hymn on Fairest Fair*, Shadows of shadows, atoms of Thy might, Still owly-ey'd when staring on Thy light. **1900** *Dial. Notes* II. 47 *Owly-eyed*, intoxicated... Wise.

†**owlyst**, *a. Obs.* [app. of Scandinavian origin; cf. Norw. *ulyst*, mod.Icel. *úlyst*, *ólyst* want of desire or appetite, *úlystug* unwilling, uneager, f. *ú-* or *ó-* = un- + *lyst* desire, liking.] Listless, sluggish, slothful, inert. Hence †**owlysthede.**

c **1440** *Promp. Parv.* 374/2 Owlyst, *desidiosus, segnis. Ibid.*, Owlyst man, or womann.., *deses. Ibid.*, Owlysthede, *desidia, segnicies.*

owman, obs. form of WOMAN.

†**'owmawt**, *v. Obs. rare.* [cf. ON. *úmáttr* 'unmight', faintness, *úmætta* to swoon. The sb. may formerly have been in Eng., whence the vb.] *intr.* To swoon, to faint.

c **1440** *Promp. Parv.* 374/2 Owmawtyn, or swownyn.., *sincopiso.* O(w)mawtynge (or swownynge), *sincopis.*

owmbre, obs. form of UMBER.

owmlys, owmpere, owmpre, owmple, obs. ff. UMBLES, UMPIRE, UMPLE.

own (əʊn), *a.* Forms: α. 1 **áȝen (-an), æ̅ȝen;** 2–3 **aȝen, æȝen,** 3 **ahen, aȝwen (aȝein, haȝen, ahȝen, aȝhen,** *Orm.* **-enn;** *inflected* **aȝne, ahne);** 3–5 **awen,** (4 **auuen, ane, hawne,** 4–5 **aghen, aughen, awenn(e, aune),** 4– *north. Eng.* and *Sc.* **awn,** (4–6 **auin,** 4–7 **auen, aun,** 5 **avne, auwen, awyn, -e,** 5–7 **awne,** 5–8 **awin,** 6 **awine);** 8– *Sc.* **ain.** β. 2–4 **oȝen,** (3 **hoȝen),** 3–6 (7) **owen,** (3 **howen, owin,** 3–4 **owun,** 3–6 **oune,** 4 **ouen, owhen, oghne, on,** 5 **owyn(e,** 6 **howyn),** 4–7 **owne,** (5 **oughne, oun, oon, honne,** 6–7 **one),** 7– **own.** γ. 3 **aȝe,** (**æȝe, æhȝe, ahȝe),** 3–5 **awe.** δ. 2–4 **oȝe,** 3–6 **owe,** (3 **howe).** ε. 5 **nawen, nowun, noun,** 5–7 **nowne,** 6–8 (*dial.*) **nown,** 8–9 *dial.* **nawn, nain.** [OE. *æ̅ȝen*, *áȝen* =

OFris. êgen, eigen, ein, ain, OS. êgan (MLG. êgen, MDu. êghin, eighen, Du. eigen), OHG. eigan (MHG., Ger. eigen), ON. eiginn (Sw., Da. egen); adj. use of ágen (ǽgen), Goth. aigan:—OTeut., *aigano-, *aigino-, pa. pple. of aigan to possess, OE. ágan, OWE v. The primary sense was thus 'possessed, owned': cf. Goth. aigin sb. 'property'. The Early ME. âȝen, besides yielding the north. awen, awn, midl. and south. owen, own, was shortened a 1200 (chiefly in the south) to âȝe, ôȝe (parallel to the southern pa. pples. in which -n was dropped), giving later awe, owe, which last survived to the 16th c. Inflected forms both of the full and apocopate types, repr. OE. ágnes, ágenre, ágnum, ágenne, were used in early ME., and owne as definite form still in Chaucer; owne as a traditional spelling came down to early 17th c. The erroneous division of min own as my nown led also to his nown, her nown, still occasional in dialect use, esp. in north. form nain, etc.]

That is possessed or owned by the person or thing indicated by the preceding sb. or pron.; of or belonging to oneself, or itself; proper, peculiar, particular, individual.

1. a. Used after a possessive case of adj., to emphasize the possessive meaning. (The usual construction.)

In his, her, its, their own, the pronoun is usually (but not always) reflexive.

α. a 900 tr. Bæda's Hist. III. xii. [xiv.] (1890) 192 His aȝen sunu Alhfrið & Æðelwald his broðor sunu, se ær him riice hæfde. a 1000 Cædmon's Satan 10 Godes aȝen bearn. c 1000 Ags. Gosp. Matt. xxv. 15 Aihwilce be his aȝene mæȝene. c 1175 Lamb. Hom. 109 Þurh his ahȝene ehte. a 1200 Moral Ode 161 We sculen alre monne lif iknauwen . . alse ure ahen. c 1200 Vices & Virtues 9 Godes aȝwene name. c 1200 Ormin 6899 He wollde ȝifenn all Hiss aȝhenn sune hiss riche. c 1205 Lay. 66 For his awene [c1275 owene] saule. Ibid. 253 His ahne [c1275 owene] sune seoþen hine sceat to deaþe. Ibid. 18133 þin æȝen. a 1250 Owl & Night. 1284 Thu fallest mid thine ahene Iwenge. 13.. Cursor M. 462 (Cott.) Al sal be at myn auen [G. aun, F. awen, T. owne] weild. Ibid. 1116 Þat murþered sua [h]is ane [G. aun, F. awen] ymage. Ibid. 1214 Þat caym his aghen [G. aun] broþer slogh. Ibid. 12371 Efter his aun [G. auuen [pr. aunen] , F. awen, T. owne] ymage. Ibid. 17288 + 413 Als it was his aughen wille. c 1375 Sc. Leg. Saints xxxvi. (Baptista) 336 His hawne bruthir. a 1400 Sir Perc. 320 To wete his awenne [wille]. c 1400 Destr. Troy 9847 The laike is your avne. c 1440 York Myst. xxx. 226 He wende þis worlde had bene haly his awne. c 1450 Pol. Rel. & L. Poems (1866) 105, I am þe warke of þin aghen hende. 1462 Finchale Priory (Surtees) 95 With his auwen stuff and upon his auwen costez. 1486 Bk. St. Albans D ij b, Looke if the hawke can espie it by hir awyn corage. 1526 Tindale 1 Cor. xi. 21 His awne Supper. 1609 Skene Reg. Maj. II. 172 The trespassour convict, and condemned to the death, at his awin hand. c 1620 A. Hume Brit. Tongue (1865) 11 If Roben Hud wer nou leving, he wer not able to buu his aun bou, or to bou his aun boau. a 1657 J. Balfour Ann. Scot. (1824–5) II. 17 Thesse are the Lord Chancelers auen words to his Maiestie. 1816 Scott Old Mort. v, If ye be of our ain folk, gangna up the pass the night.

β. a 1175 Cott. Hom. 235 Maȝie wiman forȝeten his oȝe cild, þat hi ne milsi hire barn of hire oȝen innoð? c 1200 Trin. Coll. Hom. 173 Here owen sinnes. Ibid. 189 Mid his oȝene deaðe. a 1240 Ureisun in Cott. Hom. 197 Ich am . . ðin owune hine. a 1300 Sarmun liv. in E.E.P. (1862) 7 A man sal know is owin frend. 1303 R. Brunne Handl. Synne 872 Þe satyrday may here ouně be. c 1315 Shoreham 52 Tafonge þer-inne godes oȝen flesch. 1362 Langl. P. Pl. A. x. 75 Þe wit is his oune. c 1380 Wyclif Sel. Wks. III. 328 Bi here owene dom. c 1386 Chaucer Pars. T. ¶ 131 Who so hateth his owene [v. rr. owen, oughne] soul. 1405 Rolls of Parlt. III. 605/2 As hyt were don and accorded be our self in our owne propre persone. c 1425 Seven Sag. (P.) 2144 And love hyre as hys ouen lyfe. 1559 Mirr. Mag., Jack Cade v, The shame our owne, when so we shame her. 1603 H. Petowe in Farr S.P. Jas. I (1848) 108 Seal'd by Truthe's one hand. 1618 Bolton Florus IV. iv. 296 At that time hee did nobly with his own hand. 1637 Decree of Star Chamb. § 8 Thereon Print and set his and their owne name or names. 1764 Goldsm. Trav. 30 And find no spot of all the world my own. 1841 Thackeray Gt. Hoggarty Diamond (1849) viii. 91, I would not have taken the lord mayor's own daughter in place of Mary with a plum for her fortune. 1885 Law Times LXXX. 10/1 The ripe thoughts of such a writer have a value all their own. 1895 Bookman Oct. 23/1 To the reader who loves history for its own sake. 1896 M. Field Attila IV. 104, I saw him dead With my own eyes. 1931 M. Allingham Police at Funeral xiv. 200, I wonder if you would tell me in your own words how you came to have such a wound? 1962 L. Deighton Ipcress File 7 'Just tell me the whole story in your own words, old chap...' I was wondering whose words he thought I might have used.

γ. c 1205 Lay. 308 Þe fader heo bi-eode; to his aȝre unneode. Ibid. 4565 He þoðte heo to habben; to his awere bihoue. Ibid. 22099 Piram, þu ært min aȝe preost. c 1330 Arth. & Merl. 2672 Ac to the quen be nought biknawe That that child be thine awe. c 1440 York Myst. x. 240 To se myn nawe dere childe.

δ. c 1175 Oȝe [see β]. a 1250 Prov. Ælfred 85 in O.E. Misc. 106 Eeuruyches monnes dom to his owere [v.r. oȝe] dure churreþ. c 1250 Kent. Serm. ibid. 30 Ase godes oghe mudh hit seid. c 1275 Lay. 8238 And in to Kent wende; to his owe castle. a 1300 K. Horn 669, I schal me make þinowe. 1340 Ayenb. 17 Prede is þe dyeules oȝe doȝter. a 1450 Cov. Myst. (1841) 28 O tre I kept for my owe. 1586 Whetstone Eng. Mirror 69 He was . . come thither for . . his owe and the name of the Genowaines honour.

ε. c 1420 Sir Amadace (Camden) lviii, Is he comun, . . my nowun true fere? 1444 in Paston Lett. I. 50 The matier that is cause of your noun comyng hedir. 1512 Will Tho. Jenyns (Somerset Ho.), Scribile wt my nowne hande. a 1652 Brome New Acad. I. i, His nowne natural brother. 1721 Amherst Terræ Fil. No. 8 (1754) 38 Twenty chose rather to be fondled up, and Call'd mother's nown boys. 1828 Scott F.M. Perth xxxiii, If her nainsell be hammer-man hersell, her nainsell may make her nain harness.

b. Expressing tenderness or affection; also rarely in superl. = very own.

c 1386 Chaucer Friar's T. 269 Heere may ye se, myn owene deere brother. c 1430 Lydg. Min. Poems (Percy) 110 My nawen hony swett. c 1530 Redforde Play Wit & Sc. (1848) 38, I wylbe bolde wyth my nowne darlyng! Cum now, a bas, my nowne proper sparlyng! 1598 Shaks. Merry W. II. i. 15 By me, thine owne true Knight. 1691 Shadwell Scowrers I. i, Some wise lecture from nown daddy. 1855 Tennyson Maud I. xviii. 74 My own heart's heart and ownest own, farewell. 1907 G. B. Shaw Major Barbara I. 253 Lomax: How is my ownest today? Ibid. 272 My ownest, there is no danger. 1922 Joyce Ulysses 352 Then mayhap he would embrace her gently . . and love her, his ownest girlie, for herself alone. 1939 G. B. Shaw Geneva III. 53 My ownest and bestest, you are a Dame of the British Empire.

c. Phr. ***to be one's own man*** (or ***woman***): to be master of oneself; to be independent; to have the full control or use of one's faculties. Phr. ***to do one's own thing***: see THING sb.[1]

c 1374 Chaucer Troylus II. 750, I am myn owene woman wel at ese. 1390 Gower Conf. II. 349 If I be noght myn oghne man And dar noght usen that I can. 1598 B. Jonson Ev. Man in Hum. IV. vi, A tall man is never his own man till he be angry. 1610 Shaks. Temp. v. i. 213 Prospero [found] his Dukedome In a poore Isle: and all of vs, our selues, When no man was his owne. 1664 Cotton Scarron. IV, For though full light, when her own woman, Yet, in this heavy Dump, was no Man Could raise her up. 1685 Lovell Gen. Hist. Relig. 135 They are wholly their own Men, having no spiritual Exercise in Common for the service of their Neighbour. 1773 Goldsm. Stoops to Conq. v, So, Constance Neville may marry whom she pleases, and Tony Lumpkin is his own man again. 1966 J. Potts Footsteps on Stairs (1967) i. 14 This final encounter with Vic was a necessary part of the ritual of release. With it behind her, . . she was once more her own woman. 1969 Guardian 17 Feb. 2/7 He freely admitted that he had learned something from all the early masters... But . . he was determined to be his own man. 1972 P. Dickinson Lizard in Cup xi. 164 His own personal desire . . to be his own man, to act and conquer outside Caesar's provinces. 1974 Times 2 Nov. 4/8 Mr Brown insists he is not a liberal... In truth, Mr Brown is his own man. 1975 D. Bagley Snow Tiger xvi. 138 There'll be no strings. I'm my own woman, I am.

d. own in the predicate sometimes has the force of self in the subject, as in 'I am my own master' = 'I myself (and no other) am my master'; where 'my own master' is not opposed to 'some one else's master', but 'I' to 'some one else'.

1551 in Tytler Edw. VI (1839) II. 44 If they would keep their own counsel, he, for his part, would never confess any thing to die for it. a 1631 Donne Poems (1650) 57 Not that I shall be mine owne officer. 1692 Prior Ode Imit. Hor. III. ii. 146 Virtue is her own reward. 1767 T. Mawe (title) Every Man his own Gardener. 1800 Windham Sp. Parl. 18 Apr., Gentlemen, who in the game-season, . . become their own butchers and poulterers. 1848 tr. Hoffmeister's Trav. Ceylon & India, Cherishing it into a small fire, we boiled our own chocolate, the cook being ill. 1974 G. Butler Coffin for Canary ii. 47 If we were every man his own Hitchcock, we wouldn't need to go and see the films.

2. a. Without possessive preceding. Now rare, and usually with an or in pl., esp. in reference to relationship (e.g. ***an own brother***, as distinguished from a half-brother or brother-in-law, or one who is only figuratively a brother; ***own cousins***, first cousins). †***oune hyne***: see HOGHENHINE.

a 1000 Hymns vii. 66 (Gr.) Þu ȝeæðelodest þe ealle ȝesceafta, and . . sealdest ælcre ȝecynde aȝene wisan. a 1000 Boeth. Metr. xx. 14 Þu þe unstilla aȝna ȝesceafta To þinum willan wislice astyrest. c 1000 Ælfric Hom. I. 112 God . . forȝeaf him aȝenne cyre. a 1175 Cott. Hom. 221 God . . let ham habba aȝenne cire. 1292 Britton I. xiii. § 1 La premere nuyt . . cum uncouth, le autre nuyt geste, et la terce nuyt oune hyne. 1340 Ayenb. 109 Zuo þet he ne heþ ne oȝene wyt ne oȝene wyl. c 1375 Cursor M. 18708 (F.) Fra þen walde ihesus wiþ opin dede Conferme his trauþ til awin sede. 1546 J. Heywood Prov. (1867) 53 Alwaie owne is owne, at the recknyngis eend. 1632 Womens Rights 196 The owne pen of so great a lawyer. 1671 Autobiog. C'tess Warwick (Percy Soc.) 2 My lady Claytone, . . grew to make so much of me as if she had been an own mother to me. 1690 S. Sewall Diary 21 Nov. (1878) I. 335 Mr. Laurence, Capt. Davis's Son-in-Law, is buried this day; so that Five own Sisters are now Widows. 1737 Whiston Josephus, Hist. VI. iii. § 4 This horrid action of eating an own child. 1862 Merivale Rom. Emp. (1865) III. xxvii. 248 Octavia was own sister to Octavius. 1875 Whitney Life Lang. ii. 14 He does not see why each should not have an own name. 1895 Oliver tr. Kerner's Nat. Hist. Plants II. 406 We may now proceed to discuss . . the prepotency of foreign pollen over own pollen . . ; 'own' pollen . . is applied to such as has originated in one of the anthers of the same flower.

†b. ***the own*** was used, 14th to 17th c., in the sense of 'its own' (instead of his own, its own).

1340 Hampole Pr. Consc. 3133 Als it may be with þe awen body. 1526 Pilgr. Perf. (W. de W. 1531) 268 b, The soule . . hath suche aboundaunce of ioye, whan it seeth the owne saluacion. 1578 Ps. lxxvii. in Scot. Poems 16th C. II. 110 As water that fast rinnes ouer a lin, Dois nat returne againe to the awin place. 1601 Holland Pliny II. 71 As for Orach there is a wild kind of it, growing of the owne accord. 1643 Trapp Comm. Gen. i. 4 If ye would pronounce it according to the own letters.

c. ***own goal***: a goal (see GOAL sb. 3) scored against one's own side. Also fig. (see quots.).

1947 Sporting Mirror 7 Nov. 10/3 Huddersfield were extremely unlucky to go under by an own-goal score to Charlton. 1952 Times 27 Dec. 8/1 Yesterday the Albion, with the help of two 'own goals', won a great game. 1962 Punch 11 Apr. 569/4 Mal holds the record for equalising own-goals. 1976 Guardian 11 Aug. 10/8 Two youngsters of Provisional IRA blown up by premature explosion of own bomb while crossing peace line . . . described as own goals by smiling Army press officers. 1976 Norwich Mercury 10 Dec. 8/6 With no one taking control J. Purling eventually left M. Warman stranded with a back header that lopped just under the crossbar for an own-goal. 1977 Observer (Colour Suppl.) 2 Jan. 12/2 The two men who had blown themselves up—'own goals' in the army's gruesome parlance. 1978 Guardian 30 Nov. 1/6 The Parliamentary scene was set last week for one of those gentlemanly arrangements which allows the opposition to have its say without actually scuppering the Government. Unfortunately, the Government scored an own goal.

3. absol. (mostly with preceding possessive): That which is (one's) own; property, possessions; (one's) own goods, kinsfolk, friends, or whatever is implied by the context. Somewhat arch. (exc. in some phrases).

(Sometimes erroneously classed as a sb.; it is really the adj., invariable in plural.)

c 950 Lindisf. Gosp. John i. 11 In aȝan cuom. a 1035 Cnut's Secular Laws c. 24 (Schmid) Aȝife man þam aȝen-friȝean his aȝen. 12.. Moral Ode (Egerton MS.) 263 And of his owen nolde ȝiuen. a 1300 Cursor M. 8168 Sir, wel-cum to þin aun. Ibid. 14342, I haf tan flexs emang mine aun, And þof i am noght wit þam knaun. 13.. Seuyn Sag. (W.) 1610 To do bi me as bi thin awe. 1340 Ayenb. 21 Huanne he deþ to moche despense, oþer of his oȝen: oþer of oþre manne. 1467–8 Rolls of Parlt. V. 572/1 Y purpose to lyve uppon my nowne, and not to charge my Subgettes. c 1520 King & Barker 115 in Hazl. E.P.P. I. 9 Tho the barker had hes howyn, theyrof he was fayne. 1534 Tindale John i. 11 He cam amonge his awne and his awne receaved him not. 1611 Shaks. Wint. T. v. iii. 123 Tell me (mine owne) Where hast thou bin preseru'd? 1839 Yeowell Anc. Brit. Ch. ix. (1847) 92 He gave freely of his own. 1854 Thackeray Newcomes I. xxiv. 233 Her teeth [were] as regular and bright as Lady Kew's own. 1869 Tennyson Holy Grail 47 The cup . . from which our Lord Drank at the last sad supper with his own.

b. ***of (one's) own*** (also †***of the own***): that is one's own; belonging to oneself. (Cf. OF 44.)

13.. Coer de L. 4475 Ilke lord his baner gan upliffte, Off kynde armys off hys owen. 1490 Caxton Eneydos xxiii. 86 With alle his habilimentes and other thinges, his of owne. 1568 Grafton Chron. I. 84 The Scots . . had no money of their awne. 1610 Holland Camden's Brit. (1637) 138 Euery Kingdome . . had a speciall name of the owne by it selfe. 1743 Bulkeley & Cummins Voy. S.-Seas 102 Two Swords of the Captain's own. 1800 Helena Wells West Indian I. 302 A cousin of her own. a 1904 Mod. A great friend of my own.

c. Special phrases. ***to hold*** (†***maintain***) ***one's own***: to maintain one's position or standing against opposition or rivalry; not to suffer defeat or derogation. †***to tell one his own***: to tell him the plain truth about himself; to give him the reproof he deserves (obs.). ***on one's own***: on one's own account, responsibility, resources, etc.; by oneself. ***to call*** (a thing) ***one's own***: cf. CALL v. 17 d. ***to come into one's own***: to get possession of one's rightful property; to be properly esteemed. ***to get one's own back***: see GET v. 62 b (quots. 1910–22).

c 1350 Will. Pal. 3642 His men miȝt nouȝt meyntene her owne. 1526 Pilgr. Perf. (W. de W. 1531) 98 Be neuer ouercome in ony mater, but holde thyne owne. 1601 Holland Pliny I. 482 There is not a better Reed growing for to make shafts, . . it will hold the owne and stand in the weather. 1613–1857 To call a thing one's own [s.v. CALL v. 17 d]. 1679 Hist. Jetzer 17 He gave them a round rattle, and spared none of his course Eloquence to tell them their own. 1721 Amherst Terræ Fil. No. 1 (1754) 2 The famous saturnalian feasts . . when every scullion and skipkennel had liberty to tell his master his own, as the British mobility emphatically stile it. 1846 Young Naut. Dict. 151 A vessel is said to 'hold her own' when she makes no progress, but yet does not lose ground. 1895 Westm. Gaz. 4 Dec. 3/3 One can greet the play 'on its own', to borrow a popular phrase. 1900 Law Notes Dec. 355/2 The Times . . appear to have inserted the notice on their own. 1902 J. Milne Epistles of Atkins iv. 63 His one thought how to 'get his own back'. 1912 T. Dreiser Financier vii. 71 The ready-made shoe— machine-made to a certain extent—was just coming into its own. 1917 A. G. Empey Over Top 302 On your own, another famous or infamous phrase which means Tommy is allowed to do as he pleases. An officer generally puts Tommy 'on his own' when he gets Tommy into a dangerous position and sees no way to extricate him. 1925 D. H. Lawrence Phoenix II (1968) 482 At night, when the silence of the moon, and the stars, and the spaces between the stars, is the silence of me too, then I am come into my own by night. 1929 —— Ibid. 580 For what does goodness mean? It means, in the end, being like everybody else, and not having a soul to call your own. 1930 A. Huxley Let. 18 Oct. (1969) 343 I've really had very little time to call my own. 1931 Week-End Rev. 24 Oct. 515/1 It looks as if the music of Jean Sibelius were at last coming into its own this winter. 1936 Discovery July 222 Electrical instruments will not come into their own until a large repertory of music has been composed specially for them. 1946 R. Allen Home Made Banners x. 115 But in these last moments each of them was on his own. 1969 Listener 24 July 109/1 At this point, alas, the Art Nouveau comes into its own. 1976 National Observer (U.S.) 18 Dec. 1/1 'Nixon spurred interest in this type of prosecution, but since he left we're more or less on our own,' says a lawyer who works part time on obscenity matters.

4. Comb. **a.** with nouns, as **own brand**, a class of goods marked with the name of the retailer instead of the manufacturer; also attrib.; **own category** Psychol., a type of attitude test in which the subject is asked to select suitable categories into which to grade controversial statements and thereby reveals his own emotional involvement; also *attrib.*; **'own-form** *attrib.* (see quot.); **own-label** *attrib.*, of merchandise marked with a label showing the name of the retailer instead of the manufacturer; occas. (without hyphen) in non-*attrib.* position; **'own-'will**, self-will; **own-root**, growing from its own root; **b.** with *pa. pples.*, forming *adjs.*, as **'own-born**, born one's own, indigenous; **own-grown**, grown by oneself; **own-invented**, invented by oneself; **own-looking**, looking or seeming one's own, resembling oneself; **own-named**, having one's own name, named after oneself; **own-rooted** *a.* = *own-root*.

1849 ROCK *Ch. of Fathers* I. i. 13 Every..hamlet had its *own-born patron saint. **1970** *Times* 5 Feb. (Pedigree Dogs Suppl.) p. iii/6 A range of 23, some of which were '*own brands'. **1970** *Times* 16 Feb. (Food in Britain Suppl.) p. ix (*heading*) Own brands are money-savers. *Ibid.*, The principles of own-brand groceries date back to the turn of the century when stores such as Lipton and Home & Colonial did much of their own packaging. [**1953** SHERIF & HOVLAND in *Jrnl. Abnormal Psychol.* XLVIII. 135/2 Ultimately it may provide a means of utilizing the individual's own categorization of statements as a behavioral index of his stand on an issue.] **1961** —— & —— *Social Judgment* v. 118 (*heading*) Judgment of items with individual choice of categories—'*own' categories. *Ibid.* 126 If future investigations bear out the promise of our results, it may prove feasible to order the stands of individuals on a controversial social issue through their placement of relevant items within their 'own' categories. **1970** *Jrnl. Gen. Psychol.* LXXXII. 147 The basic task for the Ss was that frequently used in cognitive complexity research, the free-sorting or own-categories technique. **1972** *Jrnl. Social Psychol.* LXXXVIII. 84 In the present study, the Q-sort variant known as the own-categories technique was used to investigate some effects of redundancy and congruence on judgement scales. **1973** N. LEMON *Attitudes & their Measurement* vii. 199 The development of the own categories procedure as a method of measuring involvement. **1877** DARWIN *Forms of Fl.* i. 24 The fertilisation..of either form with its *own-form pollen [may be called] an illegitimate union. **1591** SYLVESTER *Du Bartas* I. iii. 1148 He is warm wrapped in his *owne-grow'n Wooll. **1642** J. EATON *Honey-c. Free Justif.* 242 His *owne-invented signe of washing by water of Baptisme. **1961** *Economist* 11 Mar. 983/2 In the grocery and provisions trade, the larger multiples were almost all engaged in some food manufacture between the wars, supplemented by agreements for '*own-label' products from other manufacturers. **1969** *Times* 13 Mar. 23/3 Tesco and Woolworths have withdrawn supplies of 'Tuf' shoes and launched 'own label' brands. **1972** *Sunday Times* 31 Dec. 63/3 Lyons is particularly a supplier of supermarket own-label items and catering foods. **1975** *Times* 16 May 8/3 'Own label'..is the trade term for shops that sell groceries made by well-known companies but with the name of the shop, not of the maker, prominent on the packet. **1977** *Daily Tel.* 14 Jan. 1/6 Sainsbury's said most of its London shops were without supplies of its own-label bread, which it was still selling at 17p, but had normal supplies of proprietary loaves selling at 19p. **1647** H. MORE *Song of Soul* I. I. xlii, Th' *own-litter-loving Ape, the Worm, and Snail. *a* **1814** *Love, Honor & Interest* III. iii. in *New Brit. Theatre* III. 283 Your *own looking child—The very mind and picture of yourself. **1612** DRAYTON *Poly-olb.* ii, By this her *own-named town the wand'ring Froom had past. **1881** *Gard. Chron.* XVI. 851 When Roses are properly budded and properly planted they strike out from the point of union, and become *own-root Roses. **1915** M. E. KING *Gothic Ruin & Reconstruction* 12 Let the renascent art blunder at first, as it must if it be *own-rooted and not parasitic. **1625** BP. MOUNTAGU *App. Caesar* 68 Thus hee fell to transgresse through his wicked *owne-will. **1893** J. PULSFORD *Loyalty to Christ* II. 297 For the crucifying and dying out of every vestige of own-will.

own (əʊn), *v.* Forms: *α.* 1 **áȝnian, áhnian,** 3 **ahnien,** (*Orm.*) **ahnenn,** (*pa. t.* **ahnede, æȝenede**). *β.* 3 **ohni,** (*pa. t.* **ohnede, hoþȝenede, hoþnode** (þ for p = w), 4 *ger.* **oȝninge**), 7 **owne,** 6– **own.** [OE. *áȝnian*, f. *áȝen* OWN *a.*: so OHG. *eiginen* (MHG. *eigenen*, Ger. *eignen*), MDu. *eechenen*, ON. *eigna* (Sw. *egna*, Da. *egne*).

Used in OE. and early ME. in senses 1 and 2; but after this scarcely found till the 17th c. The derivatives *owner* and *owning* are however found in the interim in sense 2. It seems as if the verb itself went out of use before 1300, but was restored from the derivative *owner*, when *owe* in its original sense of 'possess' was becoming obsolescent. Senses 3–6 are all of the later date.]

†**1.** *trans.* To make (a thing) one's own, appropriate, take possession of; to seize, win, gain; to adopt as one's own. *Obs.*

c **888** K. ÆLFRED *Boeth.* xiv. §1 Hu miht þu þon þe aȝnian heora god? *c* **950** *Lindisf. Gosp.* Matt. v. 4 Eadȝe biðon ða milde forðon ða aȝneȝað eorðo. *c* **1200** ORMIN 5649 þiss seollþe all heoffness ærdess land þe winnenn shall & ahnenn. *c* **1205** LAY. 4091 Al Logres þat lond He æȝenede [*c* 1275 hoþnode] to his æȝere hond. *Ibid.* 11864 He anan sone Ahnede [*c* 1275 ohnede] him al Rome. *c* **1275** *Ibid.* 2483 Gwendoleine hafde þe ouere hond And hoþȝenede hire al þis lond.

2. a. To have or hold as one's own, have belonging to one, be the proprietor of, possess.

a **1000** *Riddles* lxxxviii. 10 Ðone gleawstol broðor min aȝnode. *c* **1205** LAY. 1932 Nu wes al þis lond iahned a Brutus hond. **1340** [see OWNER].

1607 SHAKS. *Cor.* I. viii. 3 Not Affricke ownes a Serpent I abhorre More then thy Fame and Enuy. **1662** PEPYS *Diary* 20 May, It is not so well done as when Roxalana was there, who, it is said, is now owned by my Lord of Oxford. **1781** COWPER *Retirement* 579 The estate his sires had owned in ancient years. **1858** SEARS *Athan.* II. ii. 185 Gardens owned by the wealthier residents of the city. **1890** *Spectator* 19 July 77/2 Their [U.S. millionaires'] practice of 'owning', that is, controlling, both the professional politicians and the press.

†**b.** To have as one's function or business. *Obs.*

1611 SHAKS. *Wint. T.* IV. iv. 143, I wish..that you might euer do Nothing but that: moue still, still so: And owne no other Function. **1712–14** POPE *Rape Lock* II. 89 Of these the chief the care of Nations own, And guard with Arms divine the British Throne.

c. Of hounds: to show recognition of (the scent of the quarry).

1781 P. BECKFORD *Thoughts on Hunting* xx. 255 Foxes will run the roads at..times, and hounds cannot always own the scent. **1838** T. SMITH *Extracts Diary of Huntsman* v. 126 *Owning a scent*, when hounds throw their tongues on the scent. **1893** W. C. A. BLEW *Radcliffe's Noble Sci. Fox-Hunting* ix. 161 A couple or two, or a single hound, may have come across and struck upon the scent of a fox which has shifted, unseen, across a ride. The scent in the stuff is too stale for them freely to own. **1954** J. I. LLOYD *Beagling* 142 Hounds *own* a scent when it is strong enough for them to *speak* to it. **1971** G. WHEELER *Year Round* 21 Now the kale comes really alive as hounds drive through it converging on Ladybird's corner. One after another they own her line.

3. a. To call (a thing or person) one's own; to acknowledge as one's own.

1610 SHAKS. *Temp.* v. i. 275 Two of these Fellowes, you Must know, and owne, this Thing of darkenesse, I Acknowledge mine. **1611** —— *Wint. T.* III. ii. 89 Thy Brat hath been cast out..No Father owning it. **1691** WOOD *Ath. Oxon.* II. 642 He hath also published little trivial things.. which he will not own. **1772** *Ann. Reg.* 249/1 At last, the bishops were called to appear before the privy-council. They were asked, 'If they owned their petition?'

b. To acknowledge or recognize as an acquaintance; to give recognition to. *Obs.* exc. *dial.*

1650 FULLER *Pisgah* II. ix. 192 Our eares and eyes quickly own those objects far off, with which formerly they have been familiarly acquainted. **1662** PEPYS *Diary* 27 Apr., I.. met my Lord Chamberlaine..who owned and spoke to me. **1773** JOHNSON *Let. to Mrs. Thrale* 21 Sept., I was owned at table by one who had seen me at a philosophical lecture. **1868** ATKINSON *Cleveland Gloss.*, *Awn*, to own or acknowledge, as a friend or acquaintance, that is, to visit.

†**c.** To claim for one's own; to lay claim to. *Obs.*

1655 STANLEY *Hist. Philos.* III. (1701) 123/2 Menedemus accuseth him of owning many Dialogues of Socrates. **1658–9** *Burton's Diary* (1828) III. 5, I move to choose your clerk. The person in place may be deserving,..but own your privilege in choosing. **1712** STEELE *Spect.* No. 555 ¶3, I might have owned these several Papers with the free Consent of these Gentlemen. **1815** *Chron.* in *Ann. Reg.* 51/2 Both bodies..were carried to the bone-house to be owned.

†**d.** To attribute (a thing) *to* some source. *rare.*

1740 tr. *De Mouhy's Fort. Country-Maid* (1741) I. 51, I found no Difficulty in owning to them the Occasion of this dangerous Illness.

4. To acknowledge as approved or accepted; to declare or manifest one's acceptance or approval of; to countenance, vindicate. Somewhat *arch.*

c **1610** SIR. J. MELVIL *Mem.* (1683) 55 The too much owning of Rixio, a known minion of the Pope, would give ground of suspicion. **1649** MILTON *Eikon.* 79 Piracy become a project own'd and authoriz'd against the Subject. **1758** S. HAYWARD *Serm.* Introd. 13 We might hope to find our labours more owned. **1853** CONYBEARE *Ess. Eccl. & Soc.* (1855) 92 A preacher is said in this [Recordite] phraseology to be 'owned' [*i.e.* of God] when he makes many converts. *c* **1860** SPURGEON in *Daily News* 24 Aug. (1898) 6/2 God has owned me to the most degraded and off-cast; let others serve their class; these are mine, and to them I must keep.

5. a. To acknowledge (something) in its relation to oneself; also, more generally, to acknowledge (a thing) to be what is claimed, or to be the fact; to confess to be valid, true, or actual; to admit.

(*a*) with *simple obj.*

1655 STANLEY *Hist. Philos.* I. (1701) 6/2 Which Aristotle hath borrowed from him, not owning the Author. **1662** STILLINGFL. *Orig. Sacr.* III. iv. §8 Writers and historians, which did not own the authority of the Scriptures. **1666** PEPYS *Diary* 27 Oct., How high the Catholiques are every-where and bold in the owning their religion. **1711** *Lond. Gaz.* No. 4795/4 Stoln or strayed,..a..Mare,..lately paced, but does not freely own it. **1749** FIELDING *Tom Jones* XV. xi, Her Age was about thirty, for she owned six and twenty. **1814** CARY *Dante, Paradise* VIII. 134 Nature..no distinction owns 'Twixt one or other household. **1876** J. PARKER *Paracl.* I. viii. 114 The world has never cared to own its need of the Son of man.

(*b*) with *obj.* and *compl.*

1665 BUNYAN *Holy Citie* 90 The Servants of Christ are here owned to be the foundations of this Wall. **1684** *Pennsylv. Archives* I. 87[To] yeilde obediens to the Lord Balltemore and owne him for theire Proprietor. **1709** *Tatler* No. 63 ¶5 There are few, very few, that will own themselves in a Mistake. **1758** S. HAYWARD *Serm.* iv. 114, I readily own myself at a loss. **1815** W. H. IRELAND *Scribbleomania* 256 To the labours of Lindley Murray the rising generation will own itself highly indebted. **1828** SCOTT *F.M. Perth* xix, Surprised at last into owning thyself a woman.

(*c*) with *obj. clause* (rarely *inf.*).

1665 PEPYS *Diary* 31 Oct., She would not owne that ever she did get any of it without book. **1718** LADY M. W. MONTAGU *Let. to C'tess of Mar* 28 Aug., I hope you will own I have made good use of my time. **1745** ELIZA HEYWOOD *Female Spect.* No. 14 (1748) III. 70 You will here-after own to be guilty of an injustice you will be ashamed of. **1760** C. JOHNSTON *Chrysal* (1777) III. 70 What the chief commanders..owned to have reserved for each of themselves. **1873** HELPS *Anim. & Mast.* v. (1875) 115, I own to you that I have a great fear of the damage that ridicule might do.

b. *intr.* To confess (*to* something).

1776 GARRICK in *G. Colman's Posth. Lett.* (1820) 324 Jewel only owns to a treaty, but no bargain yet struck. **1814** BYRON *Wks.* (1832) III. 39 He owns to having reprinted some sheets [etc.]. **1853** MISS YONGE *Heir Redclyffe* iv, He owns to disliking the Doctor. **1869** J. MARTINEAU *Ess.* II. 214 We own to a feeling of shame and grief, when we find [etc.].

c. *to own up*: to make a full admission or confession (esp. when challenged or pressed); to confess frankly. (*intr.* with or without *to*, or with *obj. clause.*) *colloq.*

1853 J. A. BENTON *California Pilgrim* 55 However, you 'own up', and confess. **1858** S. A. HAMMETT *Piney Woods Tavern* 28 I'm willin' to own up that I'm ginerally considered to rather have a gift that way myself. **1861** *Harper's Mag.* Mar. 463/2 The English have long since resigned even the name of competitors,..as far as fishing on the Grand Bank is concerned... They have quit the field, 'owned up beat'. **1880** TROLLOPE *Duke's Children* xxxv, If you own up in a genial sort of way the House will forgive anything. **1883** GILMOUR *Mongols* xxiii. 285 If his two companions in accusation would not own up, he would take the responsibility of the loss. **1889** M. E. WILKINS *Indep. Thinker* in *Far-away Melody* (1891) 146 Then I asked him, an' he owned up it was so. **1890** *Boston* (U.S.) *Jrnl.* 23 May 1/6 On being arrested he owned up to his crime. **1951** *People* 3 June 7/1 It will be difficult to find many regular backers who could truthfully own up to a good week at Epsom. **1966** *Listener* 10 Mar. 342/1 It is the usual thing to address the class sternly and demand that the culprit should 'own up'.

6. *spec.* †**a.** *trans.* To acknowledge as due (*to* a person). *Obs. rare.*

Perh. an error for *owe*: see OWE *v.* 2.

1560 DAUS tr. *Sleidane's Comm.* 43 He must take his othe to owne him his faith and obeidience. **1699** BENTLEY *Phal.* Pref. 6, I said enough to make any Person of common Justice and Ingenuity have own'd me thanks for preventing him from doing a very ill Action.

†**b.** To acknowledge as due to oneself, to hold as deserved or merited; to merit, deserve. *rare.*

a **1643** LD. FALKLAND, etc. *Infallibility* (1646) 108 Guilt enough to owne that severity.

c. To acknowledge as having supremacy, authority, or power over one; to profess, or yield, obedience or submission to (a superior, a power, etc.).

1695 BLACKMORE *Pr. Arth.* I. 55 The Prince of Darkness owns the Conquerour, And yields his Empire to a mightier Pow'r. *c* **1709** PRIOR *First Hymn Callimachus* 99 Man owns the power of kings; and kings of Jove. **1814** SHELLEY *Summer-evening Churchy.* ii, Silence and twilight..breathe their spells..Light, sound, and motion own the potent sway. **1870** ELLERTON *Hymn*, '*The day Thou gavest*' v, Till all Thy creatures own Thy sway. **1874** GREEN *Short Hist.* i. §3. 23 Wessex owned his overlordship as it had owned that of Oswald.

own, owne, obs. forms of ONE *numeral adj.*

†**'ownage.** *Obs. rare.* [f. OWN *v.* + -AGE.] The fact of owning, ownership.

1576 FLEMING *Panopl. Epist.* 148 All my commendations and titles of dignitie (if I haue, at least, any in owneage). *Ibid.* 198, I challenge that vnto me by right of ownage, which the Atheniens..made ouer with assurance to Codrus. **1633** T. ADAMS *Exp. 2 Peter* iii. 10 A general distinction of ownages was added by the law of nations.

ownce, ownche, obs. forms of OUNCE.

ownded, owndynge, owndy: see OUND-.

owndir, obs. form of UNDER.

owned (əʊnd), *ppl. a.* [f. OWN *v.* + -ED[1].]

1. Possessed, held as one's own property.

Often in comb., as ***American-, British-, Chinese-, foreign-owned; employer-, government-, privately-owned.***

1628 GAULE *Pract. The.* (1629) 407 Seated in his owned, and earned Throne. **1863** *All Yr. Round* 18 July 488/1 Owned horses take cold, throw out splints or curbs. **1899** *Daily News* 24 Nov. 3/2 Occupying an employer-owned cottage, with no other available house in case the tenant for any offence loses work and home.

2. Acknowledged.

1674 N. FAIRFAX *Bulk & Selv.* 178 A more owned truth than that which this is brought to strengthen. **1827** SOUTHEY *Lett.* (1856) IV. 49 Theirs is an owned language.

owner ('əʊnə(r)). Forms: *α.* 4 **oȝenere,** 5 **ownere,** (5 **ownour,** 5–6 **owener**), 5– **owner.** *β.* 5 **awener,** (**awenner**), 5–7 **awner,** (7 **awiner**). [f. OWN *v.* + -ER[1].] **a.** One who owns or holds something as his own; a proprietor; one who has the rightful claim or title to a thing (though he may not be in possession); *spec.* one who owns a race-horse. Also (*slang*), the captain of a warship, barge, or other boat; also of an aircraft. So **owne'ress**, the captain's wife.

1340 *Ayenb.* 37 Zuych is þe zenne..of ham of religion þet byeþ oȝeneres, uor hi behoteþ to libbe wy[þ]-oute oȝninge. **1387** TREVISA *Higden* (Rolls) VI. 345 þinges..beeþ now more i-wasted in glotenye and outrage of honures [*v. rr.* ouners, owneres, *L.* possessorum]. **1432** *Rolls of Parlt.* IV. 390 The seide Merchauntz..aweners of the seid Merchaundisez. *c* **1489** *Plumpton Corr.* 84 The awenners of the same cattell. **1491** *Act 7 Hen. VII* c. 2 §5 Suche persons as the same feoffoure or ownour shall depute and assigne. **1552** ABP. HAMILTON *Catech.* (1884) 24, I am thair only awner, Lord and maister. **1598** SHAKS. *Merry W.* v. v. 64 Worthy the Owner, and the Owner it. **1631** *Tyninghame Sess. Rec.* in Ritchie *Ch. St. Baldred* (1880) 226 The awiners of the seittis wer not willing heirto. **1782** MISS BURNEY *Cecilia* x. iv, She now lived upon an estate of which she no longer was the owner. **1844** WILLIAMS *Real Prop.* (1877) 17 No man is in law the absolute owner of lands. He can only hold an estate in them. **1863** *Chambers's Encycl.* V. 428/2 The income of a jockey..is often very large: £1000 has frequently been given by a grateful owner. **1898** A. E. T. Watson *Turf* v. 124 The winner of a selling race has..to be sold by auction; the owner receives no more than the entered selling price. **1903** Kipling *Traffics & Discoveries* (1904) 49 I'm goin' to deviate to the owner's comfortable cabin direct. **1914** 'Bartimeus' *Naval Occasions* iii. 21 That there launch precious near fouled the mark-buoy... Their owner sailing 'er too. **1916** G. Taylor *With Scott* 213 Scott was invariably known as The Owner, a naval term always applied to the captain of a warship. **1923** *Blackw. Mag.* Apr. 445/2 The Owner and Owneress have a very jolly little cabin. **1930** in C. Allen *Raj* (1977) ix. 123 Cricket. Owners, Trainers and Jockeys, Vs. Patrons, Stewards and Officials. **1943** C. H. Ward-Jackson *Piece of Cake* 45 *Owner*, the Commanding Officer, the captain of an aircraft. **1971** 'D. Halliday' *Dolly & Doctor Bird* xiii. 192 Johnson slept for an hour. I left the wheel to go into the owner's cabin to rouse him. **1977** D. Francis *Risk* ii. 14 Binny, Tapestry's trainer, didn't want me on the horse. 'Not in the Gold Cup,' he'd said..when the owner had proposed it.

b. *attrib.* and *Comb.* appositive, as ***owner-breeder***, ***-driver***, ***-manager***, ***-occupant***, ***-occupier***, ***-operator***; also ***owner-occupation***, ***-occupiership***; ***owner-driven***, ***-managed***, ***-occupied*** adjs.

1937 E. Rickman *On & off Racecourse* i. 4 The most successful *owner-breeders are in the game because they have a genuine love of the thoroughbred and of the sport. **1971** *Daily Tel.* 20 Oct. 17/4 Sir Humphrey, the fourth baronet, owner-breeder of Parthia, the 1959 Derby winner. **1919** *Honey Pot* I. iii. 4 (Advt.), For immediate delivery. Daimler 57-hp special..*owner driven. **1960** *Amer. Speech* XXXV. 240 In truckers' language a 'gypsy' is an owner-driven truck. **1918** A. Bennett *Pretty Lady* xxxi. 214 The interior of the cab,..was ornate with toy-curtains..to indicate to the world that he was an *owner-driver. **1924** *Morris Owner* Mar. 20/1 A sympathetic understanding of his car and of road-craft by an owner-driver..makes for more pleasurable motoring. **1963** *Times* 23 May 8/3 Last year there were 7,000 cabs in London, and 10,400 drivers, of whom 2,919 were owner-drivers. **1972** *Police Rev.* 17 Nov. 1484/1 In the case of haulage firms, and in particular the owner-driver..it pays to overload. **1891** *Ibid.* 10 Jan. 3/1 Where that which the Board of Agriculture call '*owner-farming' is common. **1972** *Accountant* 5 Oct. 411/3 Independent '*owner-managed' business as distinct from the large multi-national corporations. **1965** H. I. Ansoff *Corporate Strategy* iv. 62 During the high-growth phase of the electronics industry many new firms were started by *owner-managers. **1967** C. Margerison in Wills & Yearsley *Handbk. Managem. Technol.* 18 While they were never entirely a law unto themselves, the owner-managers of the nineteenth century were largely role-determining actors—they were able to control their factories and affairs very much in the manner that they wished. **1970** *Globe & Mail* (Toronto) 26 Sept. B2/3 Residual lending activities of CMHC in the *owner-occupant market appear to have increased. **1958** *Ann. Reg. 1957* 71 The slowing up of the property market, especially in the sale of houses for *owner-occupation. **1970** *Daily Tel.* 16 Mar. 11/1 The change-over to owner-occupation really began to show about 1920, when some 20 per cent. of the land was in the hands of those who farmed it. **1952** *Time* 9 June 66 (Advt.), Here in Philadelphia, the percentage of *owner-occupied homes is greater than in any other large city in America.. greater than the national average. **1960** *Times* 23 May 3/5 Northern Ireland is a country of small farms, mainly owner-occupied. **1961** E. A. Powdrill *Vocab. Land Planning* iii. 44 This recognition is evolved from a study of the age and condition of buildings, densities, incidence of owner-occupied properties, and rateable values. **1972** M. Jones *Life on Dole* xi. 84 The old houses are, in general, owner-occupied. **1935** *Planning* II. xliii. 2 There are for example the approaches of State ownership at the one extreme, and of sub-division among many thousands of small *owner-occupiers at the other extreme. **1958** *New Statesman* 4 Jan. 7/3 Here and there an enterprising tenant, owner-occupier or determined landlord has repaired and repainted and the contrast is startling. **1971** *Reader's Digest Family Guide to Law* 460/1 An owner-occupier..does not pay capital gains tax on the sale of his home. **1974** *Times* 8 Aug. 18/7 It is questionable whether any public interest is served by requiring owner-occupiers to let commercial and factory premises where they have ceased to use them for their own purposes. **1924** *Glasgow Herald* 28 Nov. 9 As to *owner-occupiership, the figures were..encouraging. **1957** E. Bott *Family & Social Network* 161 *Owner-operator of a small tobacco and sweet shop. **1971** M. Tak *Truck Talk* 114 *Owner-operator*, a trucker who both owns and drives his rig. **1976** *Woman's Day* (N.Y.) Nov. 50/2 'You can do damage if you don't replace a radiator cap..correctly,' warns Jim Gottfredsen, longtime owner-operator of Gup's West Side Service in Racine, Wisconsin. **1885** *Daily News* 14 Oct. 6/1 The *owner vote must be given at municipal elections.

ownerless ('əʊnəlɪs), *a.* [f. prec. + -less.] Having no owner, without an owner.

1806 W. Taylor in *Ann. Rev.* IV. 227 A maroon gypsey-like population of ownerless negroes. **1865** *Sat. Rev.* 24 June 757/2 Inconveniences arising from ownerless dogs. **1886** J. Payn *Heir of Ages* II. xxiii. 89 She will turn out to be heiress of long-forgotten and ownerless millions.

ownership ('əʊnəʃɪp). [f. as prec. + -ship.] The fact or state of being an owner; legal right of possession; property, proprietorship, dominion. Also *attrib.*

1583 Golding *Calvin on Deut.* xxxix. 235 One that hath but onely the laying out of them, and not the ownership of them. **1652** Needham tr. *Selden* (*title*) Of the Dominion, or Ownership of the Sea. **1832** Austin *Jurispr.* (1879) I. xiv. 382 Ownership or Property may be described accurately enough in the following manner: 'the right to use or deal with some given subject in a manner, or to an extent, which, though it is not unlimited, is indefinite'. **1863** Fawcett *Pol. Econ.* ii. vi. (1876) 191 There are many advantages associated with the ownership of land. **1880** *Daily News* 6 Nov. 5/6 If allowance for ownership votes were made, the majority of voters were with him. **1899** T. Veblen *Theory of Leisure Class* ii. 23 The practice of seizing women from the enemy as trophies, gave rise to a form of ownership-marriage. **1906** *Westm. Gaz.* 20 June 7/1 These were the 'ownership' voters, which were a scandal of the franchise. The speaker knows of a case where one man had sixty-seven ownership votes. *Ibid.*, As an instance of this plural voting by ownership, Wimbledon had 3,350 non-resident voters who owned property in the borough. **1910** *Ibid.* 10 Jan. 2/1 What..are the advantages which are claimed for the ownership system? **1944** W. Temple *Church looks Forward* xxii. 158 At an earlier date Ownership and Management were very closely connected. **1956** H. Gaitskell in Gould & Kolb *Dict. Social Sci.* (1964) 457/2 Nationalization..is generally understood to mean the taking over by the State of a complete industry so that it is owned by and managed and controlled for the Community, and public ownership.. strictly speaking means the ownership by the community of any property whether individual or not, whether embracing the whole of an industry or only part of it. **1975** *Chinese Econ. Stud.* VIII. iv. 6 The ownership pattern refers to who owns the means of production (including means of labor, such as machines, plants, land, and objects of labor, such as raw materials).

ownest, obs. erron. form of honest *a.*

owney-oh ('əʊnɪəʊ). *joc.* Also owneo, ownio, ownie-o, owny-oh. [f. a popular song (1907) *Antonio & his Ice-Cream Cart.*] Phr. ***on one's owney-oh***, on one's own; alone. (Cf. own *a.* 3 c.)

1922 Joyce *Ulysses* 96 He's as bad as old Antonio. He left me on my ownio. **1956** A. Wilson *Anglo-Saxon Att.* i. iv. 117 As I see it, when you haven't anything more to give a person, well, then you're on your ownio. **1963** 'A. Gilbert' *Ring for Noose* xi. 132 'On your owney-oh?' she said. **1967** J. Symons *Man who killed Himself* i. vi. 54 Soon I shall be able to go shopping without worrying, all on my owneo. **1969** F. Sargeson *Joy of Worm* iii. 75 For that matter how in Hades have I managed with the job? Solo. All on my ownie-o. **1976** 'W. Trevor' *Children of Dynmouth* xi. 200 She was crying and moaning in the wind, sir, up there on her owny-oh with nobody giving a blue damn about her.

†'**ownhede**. *Obs. rare.* [f. own *a.* + *-hede* -head.] Right of possession; ownership.

1483 *Cath. Angl.* 16/1 An Awnhede, *proprietas*.

ownhood ('əʊnhʊd). [f. own *a.* + -hood: rendering Behmen's *eigenheit.*] The condition of being, or considering oneself, one's will, etc. as one's own or at one's own disposal; also (in quot. 1856) selfhood.

1649 J. E[llistone] tr. *Behmen's Ep.* x. §4. 111 Whosoever will attain to Divine contemplation and feeling within himselfe; he must mortify the Antichrist in his soule, and depart from all ownehood of the will. [So *passim.*] **1691** E. Taylor *Behmen's Theos. Philos.* 369 What he possesseth as an ownhood. **1856** R. A. Vaughan *Mystics* viii. viii. (1860) II. 93 With Behmen,..redemption is our deliverance from the restless isolation of Self, or Ownhood, and our return to union with God. *Ibid.* 238 The proprium, or ownhood of every angel, spirit, or man, is only evil. **1893** J. Pulsford *Loyalty to Christ* II. 297 Only through the extinction of all ownhood, can you become channels of the Father's universal sympathies.

owning ('əʊnɪŋ), *vbl. sb.* [-ing¹.] The action of the verb own. (Now *rare* exc. as gerund.)

1. Possession, holding of property.

1340 [see owner]. **1580** Hollyband *Treas. Fr. Tong, Proprieté & appertenance*, proprietie or owning. **1607** Hieron *Wks.* I. 194 Although the heire..come to the owning and fingering of that which hee hath prepared. **1657** W. Dillingham in *Sir F. Vere's Comm.* Pref. A iv, A copy ..in the owning and possession of Major-General Skippon.

2. Acknowledgement, countenancing, etc.

c **1610** [see own *v.* 4]. **1654** Cromwell *Sp.* 12 Sept. in *Carlyle*, Some owning of your call. **1695** Locke *Reas. Chr.* (R.), The owning, and profession of one God. **1701** *Life Chas. I.* 71 Too great an owning of the Scots.

owning ('əʊnɪŋ), *ppl. a.* [-ing².] That owns property, plant, business interests, etc.

1904 *Electrical Investments* 7 Dec. 773/1 A set-off against any advantage the owning company may be said to secure in extra traffic by the connection. **1909** *Westm. Gaz.* 19 Jan. 2/1 Of the five owning companies three at least have other routes which are more profitable to them. **1923** M. Sadleir *Desolate Splendour* 80 Morvane and the literal appellation of its owning family.

ownness ('əʊnnɪs). [f. own *a.* + -ness.] The fact or quality of being one's own or peculiar to oneself.

1642 R. Harris *Serm. Luke* xviii. 6-8. 32 Gods adversaries are some way his owne; and that Ownenesse works Patience. **1838** Carlyle *Misc.* (1872) VI. 97 Napoleon..with his ownness of impulse and insight..with his originality. **1873** Mrs. Whitney *Other Girls* xviii. (1876) 254, I would have rooms for them here, that they should feel the own-ness of.

owns, ownsce, obs. forms of ounce *sb.*

ownself, erroneous writing of *own self*, after *himself*, *oneself*: see self.

1633 Gerard *Part. Descr. Somerset* (1900) 26 Hated of all, and hateful to their kinred and ownselves. **1646** Fuller *Wounded Consc.* (1841) 322 Every man is best judge of his ownself, if he be his ownself.

ownsome ('əʊnsəm). [f. after lonesome *a.*] Phr. ***on one's ownsome***, alone.

1939 M. Harrison *What are we waiting For?* 130 You tucked up for bye-byes all on your little ownsome. **1948** D. Ballantyne *Cunninghams* 248 We'll call at the cottage.. and dance on our ownsome. **1961** J. Maclaren-Ross *Doomsday Book* 103 I'm absolutely on my ownsome, old feller. **1967** R. Petrie *Foreign Bodies* xi. 163 Oh, snap out of it. You'll pull through on your ownsome. **1976** G. Seymour *Glory Boys* xii. 149 He's been left on his ownsome, and doesn't like it.

ownty-downty ('əʊntɪ'daʊntɪ), *a.* Also **ownty-donty, owny-towny.** [A rhyming jingle.] A familiar or nursery extension of own *a.*

1815 D. Humphreys *Yankey in Eng.* 19 My owny, towny, Lydy Lovett. **1871** L. M. Alcott *Little Men* v. 68 How nice it is to do it all my ownty donty self! **1882** O. W. Holmes *Let.* 18 Mar. in J. Brown *Lett.* (1912) 449 It is told, the story, without any affectation, but so lovingly that the blessed little creature becomes our own child, our 'ownty-downty', as New England nursery small talk has it.

owrance, variant form of owerance *Obs.*

owre, obs. f. hour, ore², our, ure, your.

owre, owre- (in comb.), obs. and northern form of over, over-.

†**owreke**, var. of awreak *v.*, to avenge. *Obs.*

c **1205** Lay. 4402 To o-wreken þe uppon Beline.

ows, obs. f. us.

owse, owsey, obs. ff. ooze, oozy *a.*

owsel(l, -ille, -le, -yl, obs. ff. ouzel.

†'**owsell.** *Obs. rare.* [Etymology and sense obscure.]

1609 J. Melton *Sixefold Politician* v. 73 Neither the touch of conscience, nor the sense..of any religion, euer drewe these into that damnable and vntwineable traine and owsell of perdition.

owsen, owssen, dial. ff. *oxen*, pl. of ox.

['**owser.** A misprint for *ouse*, ooze *sb.*¹ 2, perpetuated in various Dicts.

[**1688** R. Holme *Armoury* iii. 350/2 A Tanners Pooler, or Poler..is..to stir up the Ouse, or Bark and Water.] **1704** *Dict. Rust., Pooler*, or *Poler*; it is an Instrument used about Tanners Pits, wherewith they stir up the Ouser [*ed.* 1726 Owser], or Bark and Water. **1715** Kersey, *Owser*, the Bark and Water, in a Tanner's Pit. **1730–6** in Bailey (folio). **1775** Ash, *Owser*.., the mixture of bark and water in a tanpit. **1823** in Crabb *Technol. Dict.* II. etc.]

owt (aʊt). Repr. dial. pronunc. aught *sb.*² Esp. in phr. ***owt for nowt***, anything for nothing.

1847 E. Brontë *Wuthering Heights* II. xviii. 344 'All well at the Heights?' I inquired of the woman. 'Eea, f'r owt Ee knaw!' she answered. **1895** J. T. Clegg *Works* I. 238 There's olez tuthri cliverdicks to smile At owt they thinken rayther eaut-o'th'-road. **1913** D. H. Lawrence *Let.* 1 Feb. (1962) I. 183, I should think you've forgotten the Yorkshire proverb, 'An' if tha does owt for nowt, do it for thysen'. **1935** 'L. Luard' *Conquering Seas* 128 He's got tongue that would fair make one think owt to nowt. **1963** [see nowt]. **1977** E. W. Hildick *Loop* xviii. 123 Owt's possible, any bloody thing.

owt, owt-, owte- (in comb.): see out, out-.

owt(e, obs. forms of ought.

owtake, owtane: see out-take, -taken.

owtas, owter, owth, owtrage (owterage), owtray, owtred, etc.: see outas, outer, outh, outrage, outray, outred, etc.

owtherquedaunce, erron. f. outrecuidance.

owtour, owttour, obs. forms of out-over.

owtouth, obs. Sc. form of *outouth*, outwith.

owtsept, owtt, obs. variants of outcept, out.

owul, owur, owyn, obs. ff. awl, our, your, oven.

owyr, obs. f. hour, over.

owze, obs. form of ooze.

ox (ɒks). Forms: 1 oxa, 2–7 oxe, 4, 7– ox, (5 hox, 6 oxce), 7– (*north.* and *Sc.*) owce, owse. *Pl.* 1 oxan, (œxen, exen), 2– oxen, (3 ocsen, oxene, 4–6 -in, -yn, -yne, 5 -one, exin, exon, 6 oxeson), *north.* and *Sc.* 6 oussin, 7– owsen, owssen, ousen. *β.* 4–6 oxes, (4 -is, 5 -ys). [Com. Teut.: OE. *oxa* wk. masc. = OFris. *oxa*, OS. *ohso* (MLG., LG. *osse*, MDu. *osse*, Du. *os*), OHG. *ohso* (MHG. *ohse*, Ger. *ochse*), ON. *uxe*, *oxe* (Sw., Da. *oxe*), Goth. *auhsa*:—OTeut. **ohs-n-*:—pre-Teut. **uksén-* (found also in Welsh *ych*, pl. *ychyn*, Skr. *ukshán*).

Ox is the only word in general Eng. use which retains the orig. plural *-en*, OE. *-an*, of the weak declension. An older umlaut pl. *œxen*, *exen* occurs in O.Northumb., whence app. *exin*, *exon* in 15th c. A new pl. *oxes* occurs 14–16th c., but has not survived. The genitive sing. *oxes* for *oxan* appears in Lindisf. Gosp. With the northern *owse*, *owssen*, cf. Du. and Flem. *os*, *ossen*.]

1. The domestic bovine quadruped (sexually distinguished as *bull* and *cow*); in common use, applied to the male castrated and used for draught purposes, or reared to serve as food.

Often with a word prefixed indicating breed, use, etc., as *Devon, domestic, draught, Herefordshire ox.*

*c***825** *Vesp. Ps.* viii. 8 Scep and oxan..and netenu feldes. *c***950** *Lindisf. Gosp.* John ii. 14 Bebycgendo exen & scipo. *Ibid.* Luke Pref. lv, Miδ bisseno oxes. *Ibid.* lviii, Asales oδδe oxes. *a* **1000** *Riddles* xxiii. 13 (Gr.), Swa hine oxa na teah ne esna mæȝen ne fæt hengest. **1016–20** *Charter of Godwine* in Thorpe *Cod. Dipl.* IV. 10 þrittiȝ oxna and twentiȝ cuna, and tyn hors. *a* **1100** *O.E. Chron.* an. 1085 An oxe ne an cu ne an swin næs belyfon. *c* **1200** *Trin. Coll. Hom.* 195 Half hundre ȝiokes of ocsen. *c* **1290** *S. Eng. Leg.* I. 39/169 Finde ȝe mowen þere Oxene and Bolen. *a* **1300** *Cursor M.* 6745 (Cott.) Oxen [*v.r.* oxin] fiue for an he pai. *Ibid.* 11272 And þe child..Lai in crib tuix ox and ass. **1375** BARBOUR *Bruce* x. 388 [He] has left all his oxyne out. *c* **1400** *Destr. Troy* 568 Fro þo proude exin, þat with flamys of fyre han so furse hete. *c* **1420** *Pallad. on Husb.* I. 513 For vche yok of exon in thi plough. *a* **1440** *Sir Degrev.* 147 Husbondus..He lent hem oxone and wayne Of his owne store. *c* **1475** *Pict. Voc.* in Wr.-Wülcker 757/41 *Hic et hec bos*, a hox. **1483** *Cath. Angl.* 49/1 A Buse for a noxe, *bocetum. c* **1511** *1st Eng. Bk. Amer.* (Arb.) Introd. 28/2 Ther bynde they ther oxeson with Arabie gold about ther hornes, and erys. *c* **1520** ANDREW *Noble Lyfe* I. xiv. C j, A bull lyueth .xv. yere, and a oxce .xx. yere. **1596** DALRYMPLE tr. *Leslie's Hist. Scot.* I. 29 *margin*, Ky Oussin and wylde bullis. **1607** TOPSELL *Four-f. Beasts* (1658) 197 If the bloud be fallen into an Oxens legs, it must be let forth. *a* **1653** GOUGE *Comm. Heb.* II. vii. (1655) 131 An oxes eating of the corn. **1667** MILTON *P.L.* XI. 647 A herd of Beeves, faire Oxen and faire Kine. **1671** SALMON *Syn. Med.* III. lxxxi. 707 Mix with it a little Gall of Oxe. **1683** G. MERITON *Yorks. Dial.* 67 (E.D.S. No. 76) Ta see me Owse dead at me feet. **1725** BRADLEY *Fam. Dict.* s.v., A Bull-Calf gelt in Time becomes an Ox. **1792** BURNS *My Ain Kind Dearie O*, Owsen frae the field come down. **1825** BROCKETT *N.C. Gloss., Ousen, Owsen*, oxen. **1870** BRYANT *Iliad* I. IX. 289 Many a slow-paced ox with curving horns They slew.

β. **1388** WYCLIF *1 Kings* i. 25 He..offride oxis [1382 oxen] and fatte thingis. —— *Ecclus.* xxii. 2. **1390** GOWER *Conf.* II. 63 In stede of Oxes He let do yoken grete foxes. **1426** LYDG. *De Guil. Pilgr.* (E.E.T.S.) 451 Haue my pasture ther with Rude Oxys. **1542** BECON *Potation for Lent* F, He should restore and gyue hym fyue oxes for an oxe.

2. *Zool.* Any beast of the bovine family of ruminants, including the domestic European species, the 'wild oxen' preserved in certain parks in Britain, the buffalo, bison, gaur, yak, musk-ox, etc.

With distinctive prefixed word: ***American ox***, the American bison or buffalo; ***Cape ox***, *Bos caffer*; ***Galla ox***, the sanga of the Galla country; ***grunting ox***, the yak; ***Indian, Brahmin***, or ***dwarf ox***, the Zebu (*B. indicus*); ***musk ox***, a ruminant of arctic America, *Ovibos moschatus*.

c **1000** ÆLFRIC *Gloss.* in Wr.-Wülcker 118/39 *Bubalus*, wilde oxa. **1388** WYCLIF *Deut.* xiv. 5 An hert, a capret, a wielde oxe [*Vulg.* bubalum]. **1607** TOPSELL *Four-f. Beasts* (1658) 53 The name *Bos*, or an Oxe as we say in English, is the most vulgar and ordinary name for Bugils, Bulls, Cows, Buffes, and all great cloven-footed horned beasts. **1611** BIBLE *Deut.* xiv. 5 The Pygarg, and the wilde oxe [*Vulg.* orygem], and the chamois. **1744** A. DOBBS *Hudson's Bay* 41 The American Oxen, or Beeves, have a large Bunch upon their Backs. **1785** tr. *Buffon's Nat. Hist.* VI. 240 The Zebu, or Dwarf Ox. **1816** BRACKENRIDGE *Jrnl. Voy. Missouri* 175 The hump in a large ox, is about a foot in length. **1836** *Penny Cycl.* VI. 378/2 The small Hindoo ox with a hump on the chine, and the African Cape ox. **1847** CARPENTER *Zool.* §269 None..are so remarkable as the Zebu or Brahmin Ox. *Ibid.* §271 The Musk-Ox, which is an inhabitant of the coldest regions of North America. **1860** GOSSE *Rom. Nat. Hist.* 119 The gaur, the gayall, and other great wild oxen of India. *Ibid.* 203 In the forests of Lithuania there yet linger a few herds of another enormous ox..the European bison.

3. *transf.* An ancient coin bearing a representation of an ox; also *attrib.*, as *ox-coin, -unit.*

1607 TOPSELL *Four-f. Beasts* (1658) 53 The Cryer is every publick spectacle made proclamation, that he which deserved well, should be rewarded with an Oxe, (meaning a piece of mony having that impress upon it). **1892** I. TAYLOR in *Academy* 10 Sept. 220/2 These ox coins to which Pollux refers have been identified with certain silver coins with a bull's head struck in Euboea. *Ibid.*, We must therefore take the value of the ox in Delos at two silver drachmas. *Ibid.*, The theory of a universal ox-unit of 130 grains of gold is.. difficult to reconcile with such evidence as we possess.

4. *fig.* **a.** A fool; esp. in phr. ***to make an ox of*** (any one). ***dumb ox***: see DUMB *a.* 7 b.

1566 ADLINGTON *Apuleius* 90 He by and by (being made a very oxe) lighted a candle. **1598** SHAKS. *Merry W.* v. v. 126 *Fal.* I do begin to perceiue that I am made an Asse. *Ford.* I, and an Oxe too. **1606** —— *Tr. & Cr.* v. i. 65 Hee is both Asse and Oxe. **1640** H. MILL *Night Search* 126 At last he findes she made an Oxe of him. **1906** E. DYSON *Fact'ry, 'Ands* x. 126 You don't see 'em buckin' up, or playin' ther frivolous ox. **1922** JOYCE *Ulysses* 9 Don't you play the giddy ox with me! **1923** *Brewer's Dict. Phr. & Fable* (new ed.) 809/2 *To play the giddy ox*, to act the fool generally; to behave in an irresponsible or over-hilarious manner.

b. ***the black ox***, misfortune, adversity; old age: in proverb, ***the black ox has trod on*** (*his*, etc.) ***foot.***

1546 J. HEYWOOD *Prov.* (1867) 14 The black oxe had not trode on his nor hir foote. **1581** MULCASTER *Positions* xxxvi. (1887) 139 Till the blacke oxe tread vpon his toes, and neede make him trie what mettle he is made of. **1591** LYLY *Sappho* IV. ii, She was a pretie wench,..now crowes foote is on her eye, & the black oxe hath troad on her foote. *a* **1700** B. E. *Dict. Cant. Crew* s.v., *The black Ox has not trod upon his Foot*, of one that has not been Pinch'd with Want, or been Hard put to it. **1748** RICHARDSON *Clarissa* (1811) I. 344 The common phrase of wild oats, and black oxen, and such-like were qualifiers. **1850** L. HUNT *Autobiog.* I. iv. 171 The 'black ox' trod on the fairy foot of my light-hearted cousin Fan.

5. *attrib.* and *Comb.* (In some of these the pl. *oxen* also occurs.) **a.** Appositive, in sense 'male' (cf. BULL *sb.*[1] 9), as *ox-calf, -stirk*; attrib., of or pertaining to an ox or oxen, bovine, as ***ox-chain, -dung, -fair, -flesh, -gad, -gut, -hoof, -market, -skin, -team, -track, -train***; drawn or worked by an ox or oxen, as ***ox-convoy, -mill, -plough, -sawmill, -sled, -transport, -wagon, -wain***; for the use, equipment, housing, etc., of an ox or oxen, as ***ox-bell, -boose, -close, -common, -goad, -lays, -loom, -pasture, -prod, -rung, -shoe, -whip***; **b.** objective and obj. genitive, as ***ox-butchering, -driver, -driving, -hunting, -loosing, -roasting, -slayer, -whitening, -worship***; instrumental, as ***ox-drawn*** (also ***oxen-drawn***), ***-fed*** adjs.; similative and parasynthetic, as ***ox-size***; ***ox-broad, -faced, -horned, -jawed, -red, -shaped*** adjs.

1674 RAY *N.C. Words* 36 An **Ox-boose*: an Ox-stall, or Cow-stall. **1953** DYLAN THOMAS *Under Milk Wood* (1954) 28 P.C. Attila Rees, *ox-broad, barge-booted, stamping out of Handcuff House in a heavy beef-red huff. *a* **1849** H. COLERIDGE *Ess.* (1851) II. 23 The sheep and *ox-butchering, at which the Homeric heroes are so expert. **1398** TREVISA *Barth. De P.R.* XVIII. cx[i]. (MS. Bodl.) lf. 288/2 The *oxe calfe hatte Vitulus. **1523** FITZHERB. *Husb.* §67 It is tyme to gelde his oxen calues in the olde of the mone, whan they be .x. or .xx. dayes olde. *c* **1830** *Glouc. Farm Rep.* 17 in *Libr. Usef. Knowl., Husb.* III, Six ox-calves of the Hereford breed. **1785** G. WASHINGTON *Diaries* (1925) II. 441 [1] *Oxe Chain. **1817** J. K. PAULDING *Lett. from South* I. 128 Next came three men,..chained together with an ox-chain. **1842** [see *goose-yoke* s.v. GOOSE *sb.* 8]. **1866** *Rep. Indian Affairs* (U.S.) 292, I also repaired 20 wagons, 15 ox chains, 15 grain cradles. **1546** *Yks. Chantry Surv.* (Surtees) 91) 113 Parkes, parockes, and the *oxcloses. **1641** in J. Merrill *Hist. Amesbury, Mass.* (1880) 19 Three hundred acres of upland inclosed for an *ox common. *c* **1820** S. ROGERS *Italy, Como* 47 Wains *oxen-drawn. **1900** DOYLE *Boer War* i. 9 In their huge ox-drawn waggons..they had vehicles and homes and forts all in one. **1828** A. ROYALL *Black Bk.* II. 114 He was one of your right down flat footed *ox-drivers. **1843** *Yale Lit. Mag.* VIII. 332 'Gee Bright!' shouted the stentorian voice of an ox-driver. **1870** BRYANT *Iliad* I. VI. 188 Beating them with an ox-driver's goad. **1916** G. B. SHAW *Androcles & Lion* I. 23 *The ox driver.* The menagerie service is the Emperor's personal retinue. **1937** K. BLIXEN *Out of Africa* IV. 269 One strong young animal gave..his Native ox-drivers endless trouble. **1572** MASCALL *Plant. & Graff.* (1592) 43 Couer it with *Oxe dunge. **1483** *Cath. Angl.* 265/1 An *Oxfayre..*locus vbi boues venduntur.* **1803** *Edin. Rev.* II. 132 [Animals] which the *ox-fed rustic never molests. **1836** *Knickerbocker* VIII. 681 His father kept a long *ox-gad to whip him with. **1611** BIBLE *Judg.* iii. 31 Shamgar..which slew..sixe hundred men with an *oxe goad [1535 COVERDALE Oxes gadd]. **1843** *Knickerbocker* XXI. 125 The ladies requested the loan of Mr. Diddlemas's ox-goad to knock down chestnut burrs. **1848** E. BRYANT *California* iii. 32 The crack of the ox-goad, the 'whoa-haws', ..create a most Babel-like and exciting confusion. **1916** G. B. SHAW *Androcles & Lion* I. 23 A man with an ox goad comes running through the central arch. **1658** ROWLAND *Moufet's Theat. Ins.* 1023 They set in the utmost void places *Ox-hoofs, Hogs-hoofs, or old cast things that are hollow. **1850** MRS. BROWNING *Prom. Bound* Poems I. 166 Hearest thou what the *ox-horned maiden saith? **1761** *Ann. Reg.* II. 3 Their chief employment at first was *ox-hunting. **1602** BRETON *Wonders worth Hearing* (1879) 7/2 Thou olde mangy, fiery faced, bottle nosed, horse lipped, *Ox lawed rascall. **1701** in K. Steuart *By Allan Water* iii. (1901) 73 Item the caldron and *oxen-looms £2. **1837** WHEELWRIGHT tr. *Aristophanes* I. 275 Is it *ox-loosing time, or later? **1634** BRERETON *Trav.* (Chetham) 61, I saw a late erected *ox-market. **1826** T. FLINT *Recoll.* 211 Steam-mills arose in St. Louis, and *ox-mills on the principle of the..tread-mill. **1837** J. M. PECK *Gazetteer Illinois* (ed. 2) I. 33 Ox mills on the inclined plane and horse mills by draught, are common throughout..the state. **1483** *Cath. Angl.* 265/2 An *Oxe pasture, *bovarium.* **1815** SIR J. SINCLAIR *Syst. Husb. Scot.* I. 371 Old grass certainly feeds large cattle better. In Northumberland it is the ox pasture. **1523** FITZHERB. *Husb.* §6 In some places, an *oxe-ploughe is better than a horse-plough. **1765** A. DICKSON *Treat. Agric.* (ed. 2) 177 The beam..may be made shorter in a two-horse plough, or an ox-plough. **1879** E. ARNOLD *Lt. Asia* 10 His slate of *ox-red sandal-wood. **1817** COBBETT *Pol. Reg.* 8 Feb. 162 After all the *ox-roasting and temple-building in commemoration of that glorious triumph. **1817** in *Trans. Illinois State Hist. Soc. 1910* (1912) 150 An inclined Wheel *ox Saw Mill with two saws. **1875** KNIGHT *Dict. Mech.* s.v., An *ox-shoe consists of a flat piece of iron with five or six holes near its outer margin to receive as many flat-headed nails. **1872** BROWNING *Fifine* lxxvii, Swell out your frog the right *ox-size. **1809** A. HENRY *Trav.* 265 We were obliged to wrap ourselves..in *ox-skins, which the traders call buffalo-robes. **1483** *Cath. Angl.* 265/2 An *Oxe slaer, *bovicida.* **1842** in *Kansas State Hist. Soc. Coll.* (1918) XIV. 755, I made also an *oxsled. **1844** *Knickerbocker* XXIII. 445 Let us ride.. home on the ox-sled. **1863** H. S. RANDALL *Pract. Shepherd* (ed. 7) xix. 228 The old-fashioned, lively and merry scene of hauling out hay on an ox-sled. **1904** M. E. WALLER *Wood-Carver of 'Lympus* 82 Uncle Shim is driving the ox-sled down the Pent Road. **1882** FISKE in *Harper's Mag.* Dec. 122/1 There were the ox-cart for summer and the ox-sled for winter. **1550** *Knaresborough Wills* (Surtees) I. 59 One *oxe stirke of one yere olde. **1573** TUSSER *Husb.* xvii. (1878) 36 For *oxteeme and horseteeme, in plough for to go. **1776** in *Huntington* (N.Y.) *Town Rec.* (1889) III. 17 Carting Genll Tryons Baggage from Huntington to Jamaica with an Ox team. **1848** E. BRYANT *California* i. 14 Ox-teams seem to be esteemed as preferable. **1913** J. LONDON *Valley of Moon* 297 The chest of drawers..had crossed the Atlantic by sailing ship and the Plains by ox-team. **1974** M. FIDO *R. Kipling* 77/1 Hiring labourers and ox-teams. **1849** in E. Page *Wagons West* (1930) 120 We will now push off for good and any *ox train that gets ahead of us will have to travele. **1850** L. H. GARRARD *Wah-to-Yah* 72 Overtaking a United States ox-train, with which I traveled and stayed all night. **1869** *Bradshaw's Railway Manual* XXI. 433 Four years ago the only way of traversing these 1,721 miles between the Missouri and the Pacific was by mail coaches, or by mule or ox trains. **1887** E. CUSTER *Tenting on Plains* 357 There is no picture that represents the weariness and laggard progress of life like an ox-train. **1968** E. MCCOURT *Saskatchewan* x. 112 Some settlers arrived..by ox train and Red River cart. **1831** J. M. PECK *Guide for Emigrants* II. 135 From twelve to fifteen large *ox waggons are employed..in hauling it [*sc.* coal] to market. **1857** D. E. E. BRAMAN *Information Texas* iii. 56 The ox-wagons, the 'peculiar institution' of this country, are hauling away cotton. **1878** T. J. LUCAS *Camp Life & Sport S. Afr.* iii. 42 The Cape ox-waggon is quite an institution, and has been called, like the camel, the 'ship of the plains'. **1895** *Catholic Mag.* Aug. 200 It was put into an ox-waggon. **1946** E. O'NEILL *Iceman Cometh* (1947) I. 44, I vas so tough and strong I grab axle of ox wagon mit full load. **1960** [see BACKVELD]. **1971** *Sunday Express* (Johannesburg) 28 Mar. 11/1 Students to whom I spoke described the move as 'archaic and back to the ox-wagon'. **1820** H. MATTHEWS *Diary of Invalid* (ed. 2) 18 Abundance of *ox-wains. **1831** J. MACQUEEN in *Blackw. Mag.* Nov. 752/2 With a good rattan or Mauritius *ox whip. **1650** FULLER *Pisgah* IV. vii. 129 Others..conceive *Oxe-worship in Egypt of far greater antiquity.

6. a. Special comb.: **ox-antelope**, a bovine antelope; in the Revised Version (*Num.* xxiii. 22) a marginal reading for 'wild ox', rendering Heb. *r'êm* ('unicorn' in 1611), identified as *Bos primigenius*; **oxback**, in phr. *on oxback*, sitting or riding on an ox; **ox-ball**: see quot.; **ox-beef**, the flesh of the ox used as food; **ox-bile** = *ox-gall*; **ox-biter**, a bird: (*a*) = *ox-pecker*, q.v.; (*b*) *U.S.* the cow-bird, *Molobrus ater* or *M. pecoris*; **ox-bot**, the larva of the gad-fly, infesting the skin of cattle; **ox-bot fly**, the fly producing this larva; **ox-boy**, a boy who tends oxen; a cowboy; **ox-brake**: see quot.; **ox-chip**, a piece of dry ox-dung; **ox-coin** (see 3 above); †**oxen and kine** (also **kye**), a local name of some sea-fowl, as the ruff, *Machetes pugnax*, or the dunlin, *Tringa alpina*; **ox-feather** (*humorous*), the 'horn', as the symbol of cuckoldry: cf. *bull's feather* (BULL 11 b); **ox-feller** (*jocular*), a butcher; **ox-fence**, a strong fence to confine cattle; *spec.* one consisting of a hedge with a stout railing on one side, and (often) a ditch on the other; hence **ox-fenced** adj.; **ox-fish**, a S. American sea-fish; **ox-fly, ox gad-fly**, the gad-fly or bot-fly, *Œstrus bovis*; **ox-foot**, (*a*) the foot of an ox, esp. as used to make *ox-foot jelly*; (*b*) (see quot. 1730–6); **ox-frame**, a frame for holding oxen while they are being shod; also **ox-shoeing frame**; **ox-gall**, the gall of the ox, used for cleansing purposes, also in painting and pharmacy; so **ox-gall-stone**; **ox-god**, Apis, the sacred bull of the Egyptians; †**ox-grass** (*-girse*), pasturage for an ox; **ox-heart** *a.*, heart-shaped and of unusual size; applied esp. to a variety of cherry; also as *sb.*; †**ox-hunger**, the disease Bulimy or Dog-hunger; **oxland** = OXGANG; also, plough-land; **oxman**, a man who looks after oxen, a herdsman; **ox-money**, a tax levied on oxen; **ox-noble**, a variety of potato; **ox-pecker**, the genus *Buphaga* of African birds, feeding on the parasitic larvæ that infest the hide of cattle (Craig 1848); also called *beef-eater*; **ox-penny** = *ox-money*; †**ox-pith**, the marrow of the ox's bones; **ox-rail** = *ox-fence*; **ox-ray**, a fish, the large horned ray, *Cephaloptera giorna* (Cuvier); **ox-rein**: see quot.; **ox-runner**, a kind of runner for a sleigh; **ox-sole** (*Irish*), the whiff, a flat fish; **ox-spavin**: see quot.; **ox-stone**, a name for jade; **ox-vomit**, corruption of *nux vomica* (*dial.*); **ox-warble**, (*a*) the tumour or swelling in the back of an ox caused by the ox-fly; (*b*) the gad-fly producing this; **oxyard**, a measure of land (? = *oxland*); also, a yard where oxen are kept. See also OXBANE, -BOW, -CHEEK, -EYE, -GANG, -GATE, -HARROW, etc.

1857 LIVINGSTONE *Trav.* iv. 75 That I might be able to visit Sebituane on *ox-back. **1851** STERNBERG *Dial. Northampt.* (E.D.D.), **Ox-ball*, a round, hairy ball often found in the stomach of an ox. **1590** SHAKS. *Mids. N.* III. i. 197 *Bot.*.. Your name I beseech you sir? *Mus.* Mustard-seede... *Bot.*.. That same cowardly gyant-like *Oxe-beefe hath deuoured many a gentleman of your house. **1878** *Amer. Home Cook Bk.* 5 Ox-beef, when it is young, will have a fine open grain, and a good red colour. **1819** BRANDE *Man. Chem.* 440 *Ox-bile..this secretion [etc.]. **1826** HENRY *Elem. Chem.* II. 438 When submitted to heat, ox-bile.. deposits a portion of coagulated matter. **1885** J. CORYELL in *Harper's Mag.* Feb. 420/1 The red-beaked *ox-biters (*Buphaga erythrorhynca*), more popularly known as rhinoceros-birds. **1841** *Encycl. Brit.* (ed. 7) XXI. 627 The *Ox-bot, *Œstrus bovis*,..is a cuticular insect, the eggs being deposited externally in the skin of cattle. **1862** T. W. HARRIS *Insects injur. Vegetation* vii. (ed. 3) 624 The maggots..of the *Œstrus bovis*, or *ox bot-fly, live in large open boils..on the backs of cattle. **1573** TUSSER *Husb.* lxiii. (1878) 143 The *oxboy as ill is as hee, Or worser, if worse may be found. **1875** KNIGHT *Dict. Mech.*, **Ox-brake.* The ox-brake resembles that used for shoeing refractory horses. **1857** E. BANDEL *Frontier Life in Army* (1932) 178 No timber to be seen yet, and our wood is gone. We must get along on what few buffalo or *ox chips we can gather. **1857** W. CHANDLESS *Visit to Salt Lake* I. vii. 122 Some one pitched on an old camping-place studded with 'ox-chips'. **1602** CAREW *Cornwall* 35 Amongst the first sort, we reckon the..Sea-larkes, *Oxen and Kine, Scapies, Puffins, Pewets. **1623** WHITBOURNE *Newfoundland* 8 There are also Godwits, Curlewes, and a certaine kinde of fowle that are called Oxen and Kine. **1894** NEWTON *Dict. Birds* 680 The Dunlin.. in connexion therewith Mr. Harting.. reasonably refers Oxen-and-kine, by which name some apparently small wildfowl were of old times known in the west country. **1615** SWETNAM *Arraignm. Wom.* (1880) p. xxv, She will make thee weare an *Oxe feather in thy cap. **1856** R. A. VAUGHAN *Mystics* (1860) I. 281 He stands aloof.. when grave doctors shake hands with *ox-fellers. **1829** *Sporting Mag.* XXIII. 372 Many *ox-fences and two rasping brooks. **1875** 'STONEHENGE' *Brit. Sports* I. II. iii. §3. 160 Horses and men make light of ox-fences, brooks, or gates in the first frenzy of their charges. **1852** *Fraser's Mag.* XLV. 539 The *ox-fenced pastures of Leicestershire. *a* **1642** SIR W. MONSON *Naval Tracts* VI. (1704) 534/1 The *Ox-Fish,.. esteem'd above all Fishes;.. it eats.. like Beef. **1601** HOLLAND *Pliny* II. 391 The little grubs or worms whereof come the *oxe-flies. **1809** W. IRVING *Knickerb.* (1861) 225 Victory, in the likeness of a gigantic ox-fly, sat perched upon the cocked hat of the gallant Stuyvesant. **1730-36** BAILEY (folio), *Oxfeet (in Horses) is said of a horse when the horn of the hind-feet cleaves just in the middle of the fore-part of the hoof from the coronet to the shoe. **1887** I. R. *Lady's Ranche Life Montana* 29 My next venture was pancakes; and the crowning success, *ox-foot jelly. **1844** *Knickerbocker* XXIII. 155 A little slab-roofed smithy... An *ox-frame standing by the door, and at one side a shed. **1890** N. P. LANGFORD *Vigilante Days* I. xxvi. 384 We sat down upon the ox-shoeing frame, and talked over the whole matter. **1802** BINGLEY *Anim. Biog.* (1813) III. 304 The *ox gad-fly. **1799** G. SMITH *Laboratory* I. 98 Take *ox-gall.. and some water; mix together and with it rub your gold or silver. **1816** J. SMITH *Panorama Sc. & Art* II. 766 This ink will easily mark the transparent paper, if mixed with a little ox-gall. **1863-72** WATTS *Dict. Chem.* I. 588 *Ox gall-stones consist mainly of cholochrome, cholic acid, and choloidic acid, with small portions of cholesterin. **1610** HEALEY *St. Aug. Citie of God* 663 All adored this *Oxe-god. **1568** *Wills & Inv. N.C.* (Surtees 1835) 297, I giue vnto my seruant Willm Sparrow an *oxe girse [= grass] yerelye in the Millfielde. **1846** J. BAXTER *Libr. Pract. Agric.* (ed. 4) II. 335 *Ox-heart yellow [turnip]. **1870** LOWELL *Cathedral* Poet. Wks. (1879) 442 And pulled the pulpy ox-hearts. **1884** ROE *Nat. Ser. Story* ix, The moist sultriness.. finished the ox-heart cherries. **1623** BINGHAM *Xenophon* 79 One, who had experience, told him, that it was a plaine *Oxe-hunger, and that they would immediatly stand vp, if they had any thing to eat. **1387** TREVISA *Higden* (Rolls) II. 97 Danegeld.. þat was þre pans of eueriche bouata terræ, þat is, of eueriche *oxeland. **1603** OWEN *Pembrokeshire* (1892) 135, viij acres make an Oxelande.. viij oxelandes make a ploweland.. x plowlands make a knightes ffee. **1663** in S. L. Bailey *Hist. Sk. Andover, Mass.* (1880) 13 All those my two parcells of oxland or ploughing ground on the westerly side of ye Shawshin river. *c* **1830** *Glouc. Farm Rep.* 19 in *Libr. Usef. Knowl., Husb.* III, Three *ox-men to work the oxen. **1616** *Manch. Crt. Leet Rec.* (1885) II. 333 Paide to Mr. Houlte.. *oxe money for his masters provision of howsehould. **1822** HIBBERT *Descr. Shetl. Isles* 321 All landholders.. pay the ox and sheep money... The average of scat, wattle, and ox money, is said to be about 8*d.* sterling. **1799** A. YOUNG *Agric. Surv. Linc.* 145 Kidneys do not take from the soil so much as *ox-nobles. **1793** *Statist. Acc. Scot.* VII. 583 The parish also pays to Sir Thomas Dundas, the superior, for scatt, wattle, and *ox-penny. **1822** HIBBERT *Descr. Shetl. Isles* (1891) 68 (E.D.D.). **1604** MARSTON *Malcontent* II. ii, Distild *oxe-pith [cf. 1614 J. TAYLOR *Sculler* Ep. xxxii, Pith that grows i' the ox's chine]. **1844** ALB. SMITH *Adv. Mr. Ledbury* (1856) I. xx. 155 The embankment.. beyond the *ox-rails. **1860-5** COUCH *Brit. Fishes*, *Ox Ray, horned Ray. **1858** SIMMONDS *Trade Dict.*, *Ox-reims, narrow strips of prepared hide, about 9 feet long, extensively used in the Cape colony for halters for horses, for passing round the horns, close to the head, of draught oxen, to keep them together. **1835** C. F. HOFFMAN *Winter in West* I. 295 Our sleigh [was] a low clumsy pine box on a pair of *ox-runners. **1727-41** CHAMBERS *Cyclopædia* s.v. *Spavin*, *Ox-Spavin, which is a callous tumour, at the bottom of the ham, on the inside; hard as a bone, and very painful. **1877** F. G. LEE *Gloss. Liturg. Terms* 167 *Jade*, a mineral of a greenish colour; sometimes termed '*ox-stone'. **1772** T. SIMPSON *Vermin-Killer* 2 Mix up a little flour with honey, and a little *ox-vomit till it comes to a paste. **1887** *Daily News* 3 May 3/6 Miss Ormerod has issued another warning on the subject of *ox-warble, a pest that is doubly injurious, for the warble maggots.. by the holes they leave in the hides, lessen the value of the latter to the tanner. **1885** W. MORRIS in *Commonweal* I. 12/1 The straw from the *ox-yard is blowing about. **1897** *Mem. of Tennyson* I. i. 1 To Margaret his wife he devises one ox-yard of land. **1910** J. MASEFIELD *Ballads & Poems* 42 The red cock in the ox-yard crows.

b. In names of plants (in some of which *ox-*, like 'horse-' in similar use, denotes a coarse or large species, or means 'eaten by' or 'fit for oxen'): **ox-balm**, the N. American plant, *Collinsonia canadensis*; also called horse-balm (Miller *Plant-n.* 1884); **ox-berry**, (*a*) the Black Bryony or Lady's Seal, *Tamus communis*; (*b*) the fruit of the Wake-Robin, *Arum maculatum*; **ox-daisy** = *ox-eye daisy*; **ox-heal** or **-heel**, Bear's-foot or Fetid Hellebore, *Helleborus fœtidus*; **ox-hoof**: see quot.; **ox-mushroom**, a name for very large specimens of the common mushroom (*Cent. Dict.*).

1854 *Trans. Michigan Agric. Soc.* V. 130 The plants were very numerous, among which were *oxbalm.. and marsh grass. **1931** W. N. CLUTE *Common Names of Plants* 97 The ox-balm (*Collinsonia*) is merely a larger balm. **1859** CAPERN *Ball. & Songs* 168 Rich as the cornelian, with its ruby sheen, Is the *ox-berry wreath round the bramble seen. **1882** *W. Worc. Gloss.*, *Oxberry*, the berry of the *Arum maculatum*. The juice is used as a remedy for warts. **1819** *Pantologia*, *Ox daisy, in botany... *Chrysanthemum*. **1597** GERARDE *Herbal* II. ccclxi. 825 The fourth kinde of Blacke Hellebor, called.. in English *Oxeheele, or Setterwoort. **1776-96** WITHERING *Brit. Plants* (ed. 3) II. 511 Bears-foot, Setterwort, Oxheel, Stinking Hellebore. **1846** LINDLEY *Veg. Kingd.* 550 The leaves of Caulotretus.. and various Bauhinias are used in Brazil under the name of Unha de Boy, or *Oxhoof, as mucilaginous remedies.

ox-, a formative of chemical terms.

1. = OXY- from *oxygen*; as in OX- or OXYACETIC, -ACID; OXANTHRACENE, OXIODIC, etc.

2. A shortening of OXAL-, as in OXAMIC, OXALDEHYDE, OXAMIDE, OXANILIC.

3. Form of OXA- before a vowel.

oxa-. Also before vowels **ox-**. Combining element in systematic chemical names used to denote the presence of an oxygen atom (regarded as replacing a $-CH_2-$ group), as in *6-oxa-3-thiadecanenitrile*, *1H-2-oxapyrene*, *oxirane*, *oxolane*.

1928 *Jrnl. Amer. Chem. Soc.* L. 3075 In order to avoid confusion with the ordinary meanings of oxy-, thio-, azo-, etc., it is recommended that the forms *oxa-*, *thia-*, *aza-*, etc., be employed to indicate the presence of hetero atoms in a ring (the *a* being dropped before a vowel). **1971** *Nomencl. Org. Chem.* (I.U.P.A.C.) (ed. 3) B. 53 (*table*) Element Oxygen.. *Prefix* Oxa.

oxacillin (ɒksəˈsɪlɪn). *Pharm.* [f. *is*)*oxa*(*zole* (s.v. ISO- b) + PENI(CILLIN.] A semisynthetic penicillin, $C_{19}H_{18}N_3O_5NaS.H_2O$, that is used as an alternative to methicillin, having the same resistance to penicillinase and being in addition resistant to acid so that it can be taken orally; (5-methyl-3-phenyl-4-isoxazolyl)-penicillin sodium. Also called ***oxacillin sodium*** and ***sodium oxacillin*** (in the British and U.S. pharmacopœias respectively).

1962 *Proc. Mayo Clinic* XXXVII. 137, 5-Methyl-3-phenyl-4-isoxazolyl penicillin (Prostaphlin*). [*Note*] *Trade name of Bristol Laboratories, Inc... Since this paper was prepared for publication, 'oxacillin' has been adopted as the generic name of this drug. **1963** *New & Non-Official Drugs* 148 Sodium oxacillin is a semisynthetic penicillin salt for oral administration. **1967** *Martindale's Extra Pharmacopoeia* (ed. 25) 994/1 Oxacillin sodium is more resistant to destruction by the acid gastric secretion than benzylpenicillin or methicillin sodium. **1970** *Atlantic Monthly* Mar. 50 He was also given heavy doses of antibiotics, including a gram of chloramphenicol, a gram of oxacillin, [etc.].

oxahverite *Min.*: see OXHAVERITE.

oxal-, combining element in chemical terms, used in the sense 'derived from or related to oxalic acid', or 'containing the radical oxalyl'. **oxala'cetic acid**, a dicarboxylic acid, HOOC·CO·CH_2·COOH, which crystallizes as an enol form and is produced ***in vivo*** by transamination from aspartic acid and in the Krebs cycle by oxidation of malic acid; so **oxa'lacetate**, the anion, or an ester or salt, of oxalacetic acid. ‖**oxalæmia** (ɒksəˈliːmɪə) *Path.* [mod.L., f. Gr. αἷμα blood]: see quot. **o'xalamide** = OXAMIDE. **'oxalan** [-AN 2; cf. *alloxan*] = OXALURAMIDE. **oxa'lantin** [cf. *alloxantin*]: see quot. **oxa'lethyline**, a poisonous oily liquid of composition $C_6H_{10}N_2$; also, a general name for the series to which this belongs, as *chloroxalethyline* $C_6H_9ClN_2$. **oxal'hydric acid**, a former name for SACCHARIC *acid*; hence **oxal'hydrate**, a salt of this acid, a SACCHARATE. **'oxalite** *Min.* = HUMBOLDTINE. Also OXALURAMIDE, OXALYL, etc.

1891 *Jrnl. Chem. Soc.* LX. 1333 On mixing.. a benzene solution of carbon oxychloride with copper *oxalacetate.. the copper salt takes up an appreciable quantity of chlorine. **1969** Oxalacetate [see GLYOXYLATE]. **1896** *Jrnl. Chem. Soc.* LXX. I. 599 Nef's ethylic ethoxyfumarate.. when hydrolysed with hydrochloric acid, gives *oxalacetic acid. **1939** *Ann. Reg. 1938* 375 In the biological fixation of nitrogen by root nodule bacteria the formation of aspartic acid via the oxime of oxalacetic acid was confirmed. **1972** *Arch. Biochem. & Biophysics* CLIII. 226/1 Oxalacetic acid.. functions as a key substrate in metabolism as the keto form; however, the pure compound crystallizes as the *cis* enol of hydroxymaleic acid. **1892** *Syd. Soc. Lex.*, *Oxalæmia, the presence of oxalates in the blood; a doubtful condition. **1836-41** BRANDE *Chem.* (ed. 5) 1181 When oxalate of ammonia is distilled.. the liquid which passes over contains a flocculent substance,.. to which M. Dumas has given the name of *oxalamide. **1866-77** WATTS *Dict. Chem.* IV. 248 **Oxalan*, syn. with *Oxaluramide*. *Ibid.*, **Oxalantin*, $C_6H_4N_4O_5$.. is related to parabanic acid in the same manner as alloxantin.. to alloxan. **1881** *Ibid.* VIII. 1450 **Oxalethylines*. **1838** T. THOMSON *Chem. Org. Bodies* 75 The *oxalhydrate of lead which fell was collected on a filter and thoroughly washed with water. *Ibid.*, The *oxalhydric acid is a new and peculiar acid. **1866-77** WATTS *Dict. Chem.* IV. 277 **Oxalite*, native ferrous oxalate, also called *Humboldtine*.

oxalate (ˈɒksələt), *sb. Chem.* [a. F. *oxalate* (G. de Morveau and Lavoisier, 1787), f. OXAL- in *oxalique* OXALIC + -ATE[4].] A salt of oxalic acid.

1791 HAMILTON tr. *Berthollet's Dyeing* I. 243 The acidulous oxalate of pot-ash may also be employed for this purpose. *Ibid.* II. 371 Oxalats. **1807** MARCET in *Phil. Trans.* XCVII. 303 The lime was precipitated by oxalat of ammonia. **1869** ROSCOE *Elem. Chem.* (1874) xxxiv. 314 Oxalic acid is a dibasic salt, and forms two classes of salts, called Normal Oxalates, and Acid Oxalates.

attrib. **1889** *Anthony's Photogr. Bull.* II. 297 Time.. is required for the development of a good negative, both with the pyro and oxalate developer.

Hence **oxa'latic** *a.*, relating to oxalates.

1853 in DUNGLISON *Med. Lex.* **1892** *Syd. Soc. Lex.*, *Oxalatic diathesis*, the *oxalic Diathesis*. [See OXALIC c.]

oxalate (ˈɒksəleɪt), *v. Med.* [f. the sb.] *trans.* To add an oxalate to, esp. so as to prevent coagulation of blood.

1911 *Amer. Jrnl. Physiol.* XXIX. 204 The tissue extract was itself oxalated to remove any calcium that may have been present. **1934** *Brit. Med. Jrnl.* 7 July 10/2 Blood collected under paraffin was oxalated and centrifuged and the plasma examined spectroscopically. **1954** *Blood* IX. 610 The serum was decanted and 2·8 ml. were oxalated by adding 0·5 ml. of 0·1 M. potassium oxalate.

So **'oxalated** *ppl. a.*, containing added oxalate.

1893 *Jrnl. Path. & Bacteriol.* I. 443 (*heading*) Effect of graduated additions of calcium chloride to oxalated blood. **1946** *Nature* 16 Nov. 708/2 The prothrombin concentration in normal human oxalated plasma averaged approximately 2 mgm. per 100 ml. when expressed as protein nitrogen. **1964** W. G. SMITH *Allergy & Tissue Metabolism* vi. 69 Oxalated blood samples were collected both before and for several minutes after shock.

ox'aldehyde. *Chem.* [f. OX- 2 + ALDEHYDE: = *oxalic aldehyde*.] A synonym of GLYOXAL.

oxalic (ɒkˈsælɪk), *a. Chem.* [ad. F. *oxalique* (G. de Morveau and Lavoisier, 1787), f. L. OXALIS: see -IC.] Of, derived from, or characteristic of the *Oxalis* or Wood Sorrel: *spec.*

a. ***oxalic acid***: a highly poisonous and intensely sour acid ($C_2H_2O_4$ = $C_2O_2.2HO$), the first member of the dibasic series having the general formula $C_nH_{2n-2}O_4$.

It exists in the form of salts (potassium, sodium, or calcium oxalate) in Wood Sorrel and many other plants, and is also obtained chemically from sugar, starch, sawdust, and other organic substances; it crystallizes in transparent colourless crystals, readily soluble in water or alcohol.

oxalic series (of acids): the dibasic acids derived from the glycols, which differ from the *lactic* or *monobasic* series by having an additional atom of oxygen in place of two of hydrogen; they include Oxalic, Malonic, Succinic, Pyrotartaric, Adipic, Pimelic, Suberic, Azelaic, Sebacic, Brassylic, and Roccellic acids (Roscoe *Elem. Chem.* (1874) xxxiv).

1791 HAMILTON *Berthollet's Dyeing* I. I. II. i. 123 Nitric acid.. forms oxalic acid, with part of the hydrogen and charcoal. **1800** tr. *Lagrange's Chem.* II. 210 Oxalic acid.. is extracted from sugar by combining the oxygen of the nitric acid with one of its constituent principles. **1847** E. TURNER *Elem. Chem.* 711 Oxalic acid. Discovered by Scheele in 1776. It occurs as a mineral Humboldite combined with oxide of iron. **1873** [see OXALYL]. **1876** HARLEY *Mat. Med.* (ed. 6) 313 Oxalic Acid derives its name from the wood sorrel.. which, like all the genus, abounds in oxalic acid in combination with potash.

b. ***oxalic ether***, a name for neutral ethyl oxalate ($C_6H_{10}O_4$ = $C_2O_2.2C_2H_5.O_2$); also extended to the oxalates of the alcohol-radicals in general.

1838 T. THOMSON *Chem. Org. Bodies* 328 Oxalic ether was mixed with sulphuret of potassium. **1866-77** WATTS *Dict. Chem.* IV. 268 *Oxalic Ethers*... Only those of methyl, ethyl, amyl and allyl have.. been yet obtained.

c. ***oxalic diathesis*** (*Path.*), that condition of the system in which there is a tendency to formation of calcium oxalate in the urine; also called ***oxalatic diathesis***, ***oxalic acid diathesis***.

1843 SIR T. WATSON *Lect. Princ. & Pract. Physic* lxxvi. II. 548 There is yet another diathesis sufficiently common and important to claim your best attention. I mean the *oxalic*: in which there is a tendency to the formation, in the kidney, of the oxalate of lime, or mulberry calculus.

‖**Oxalis** (ˈɒksəlɪs). *Bot.* [L. *oxalis*, *oxalid-* (Pliny), a. Gr. ὀξαλίς (Diosc.), f. ὀξ-ύς sour, acid. In mod.F. *oxalide*.] A large genus of plants (type of N.O. *Oxalidaceæ*, otherwise reckoned as a tribe, *Oxalideæ*, of *Geraniaceæ*), mostly ornamental herbs, with delicate five-parted flowers of various colours, and leaves usually of three leaflets; the common British species is *O. Acetosella*, Wood Sorrel.

[**1601** HOLLAND *Pliny* XX. xxi, Touching the Docke.. there is a wild kind thereof, which some call Oxalis in Greeke, (*i.* wild Sorrell, or Soure-docke).] **1706** PHILLIPS, *Oxalis*, wild Sorrel or Wood-Sorrel, an Herb. **1797** WOLLASTON in *Phil. Trans.* LXXXVII. 399 The saccharine acid is known to be a natural product of a species of oxalis. **1856** RUSKIN *Mod. Paint.* IV. v. xx. §5 The exquisite oxalis is preeminently a mountaineer.

oxalo-, combining element = OXAL-, as **oxalo'acetate** = *oxalacetate* s.v. OXAL-; **oxaloa'cetic acid** = *oxalacetic acid* s.v. OXAL-; **ˌoxalo-'nitrate**, a salt of oxalic and nitric acid; **oxa'losis** *Path.* [-OSIS], a rare disorder of metabolism in which crystals and stones of calcium oxalate are deposited in the kidneys and elsewhere, often causing death during childhood as a result of renal failure; **oxalo'succinate**, the anion, or an ester or salt, of oxalosuccinic acid; **ˌoxalosuc'cinic acid**, a tricarboxylic acid, HOOC·CO·CH(COOH)·CH_2·COOH, which is an intermediate in the formation of α-ketoglutaric acid from isocitric acid in the Krebs cycle; **oxalovinic**

(ˌɒksələʊˈvaɪnɪk) **acid**: a synonym of *ethyloxalic acid*, the acid oxalate of ethyl ($C_4H_6O_4$ = $C_2H(C_2H_5)O_4$); hence **oxalovinate** (ɒksələʊ ˈvaɪnət), a salt of this acid, an ethyloxalate.

1943 SUMNER & SOMERS *Chem. & Methods of Enzymes* xviii. 324 Malate, *oxaloacetate, or succinate could replace fumarate in reaction (c). **1962** S. G. WALEY in A. Pirie *Lens Metabolism Rel. Cataract* 356 Another γ-keto acid that undergoes enzymatic decarboxylation is oxaloacetate. **1937** *Nature* 18 Sept. 503/2 α-Ketoacids other than pyruvic, for example..*oxaloacetic or phenylpyruvic acid, may equally serve as acceptors for the amino group of glutamic acid. **1940** [see *α-ketoglutarate* s.v. KETO- a]. **1968** PASSMORE & ROBSON *Compan. Med. Stud.* I. ix. 14/2 Acetyl-CoA reacts with oxaloacetic acid to produce citric acid. **1873** WATTS *Fownes' Chem.* (ed. 11) 427 A basic *oxalo-nitrate is obtained by adding ammonium oxalate to the oxynitrate. **1952** YING CHOU & DONOHUE in *Pediatrics* X. 660 (*heading*) *Oxalosis. Possible 'inborn error of metabolism' with nephrolithiasis and nephrocalcinosis due to calcium oxalate as the predominating features. **1973** N. M. R. BUIST et al. in Forfar & Arneil *Textbk. Pediatrics* xix. 1171/2 Treatment of oxalosis includes alkalinization of the urine, dietary restriction of calcium and a large fluid intake. **1911** *Chem. Abstr.* V. 3240 Tri-Et *oxalosuccinate..is best prepared by means of EtOK. **1962** S. G. WALEY in A. Pirie *Lens Metabolism Rel. Cataract* 355 In the citric acid cycle..two molecules of CO_2 are formed per turn of the cycle; one comes from oxalosuccinate, a β-keto acid. **1925** *Chem. Abstr.* XIX. 4423 (Index), *Oxalosuccinic acid, triethyl ester. **1948** *Jrnl. Biochem.* CLXXIV. 144 The instability of oxalosuccinic acid makes an accurate estimation of this constant rather difficult. **1966** F. A. ROBINSON *Vitamin Co-Factors of Enzyme Syst.* viii. 541 In this organism [sc. *E. coli*], biotin appears to function in the conversion of oxalosuccinic acid into α-ketoglutaric acid. **1838** T. THOMSON *Chem. Org. Bodies* 172 *Oxalo-vinic acid..was discovered by Mitscherlich... It decomposes carbonates of barytes and lime, forming soluble *oxalo-vinates capable of crystallizing. From oxalovinate of barytes it is easy to obtain pure oxalovinic acid.

oxaluramide (ɒksəˈl(j)ʊərəmaɪd). *Chem.* [See OXALURIC and AMIDE.] The amide of oxaluric acid ($C_3H_5N_3O_3$), obtained as a white crystalline powder by the action of ammonia and hydrocyanic acid on alloxan; also called *oxalan*.

1866–77 WATTS *Dict. Chem.* IV. 277.

‖**oxaluria** (ɒksəˈl(j)ʊərɪə). *Path.* [mod.L., f. OXAL- + -URIA.] The presence of an excess of calcium oxalate in the urine.

1844 G. BIRD *Urin. Deposits* vii. (heading), Chemical pathology of oxalate of lime (oxaluria). **1899** CAGNEY tr. *Jaksch's Clin. Diagn.* vii. (ed. 4) 358 It [i.e. oxalic acid in the urine] is subject to very great increase in certain morbid states, and the condition is then called oxaluria.

oxaluric (ɒksəˈl(j)ʊərɪk), *a. Chem.* [f. OXAL- + URIC.] In *oxaluric acid*: a monobasic acid ($C_3H_4N_2O_4$), which may be regarded as consisting of oxalic acid and urea *minus* water, obtained as a white crystalline powder of a very acid taste. Hence **oxaˈlurate**, a salt of oxaluric acid.

1836–41 BRANDE *Chem.* (ed. 5) 1381 Oxaluric acid is formed by the union of 2 atoms of water with parabanic acid. *Ibid.*, With excess of ammonia, oxalurate of lime yields a gelatinous precipitate. **1866** ODLING *Anim. Chem.* 135 These dumbbells may consist of oxalurate of calcium. **1892** *Syd. Soc. Lex.*, *Oxaluric acid*,..the analogue of alloxanic acid, being uric acid in which one atom of hydrogen is replaced by one atom of the radical of oxalic acid.

oxalyl (ˈɒksəlɪl). *Chem.* [f. OXAL- + -YL.] The hypothetical radical (C_2O_2) of oxalic acid.

1859 FOWNES *Man. Chem.* 398 One molecule of C_4H_4 (ethylene) and C_4O_4 (oxalyl). **1873** RALFE *Phys. Chem.* p. xxi, Oxalic acid, $C_2H_2O_4$, is a double molecule of water in which half the hydrogen is replaced by oxalyl.

oxamic (ɒkˈsæmɪk), *a. Chem.* [f. OX- 2 = OXAL- + AMIC.] In *oxamic acid*: a monobasic acid, $C_2H_3NO_3$ (= $NH_2.C_2O_2.OH$), produced by the dehydration of acid oxalate of ammonium, and in other ways; its salts are **oxamates**. *oxamic ether*: an ether in which one or other of the hydrogen-atoms of oxamic acid is replaced by an alcohol-radical; e.g. *ethylic oxamate* or **oxamethane**, $C_4H_7NO_3$ = $NH_2.C_2O_2.O.C_2H_5$; *ethyloxamic acid*, $C_4H_7NO_3$ = $NH.C_2H_5.C_2O_2.OH$.

1838 T. THOMSON *Chem. Org. Bodies* 592 Of Oxamethane, or Etheroxamide. **1857** MILLER *Elem. Chem.* III. 172 This body,..originally termed *oxamethane*,..is now admitted to be oxamic ether, or the ether of amidated oxalic acid. **1873** RALFE *Phys. Chem.* p. xxvi, Thus we have Oxamic Acid, Silver Oxamate, Methyl Oxamate.

oxamide (ˈɒksəmaɪd). *Chem.* [f. OX- 2 + AMIDE first formed as F. *oxamide* (J. Dumas 1830, in *Ann. de Chim. et de Physique* XLIV. 130).] The diamide $C_2O_2.N_2H_4$, representing two molecules of ammonia in which two atoms of hydrogen are replaced by oxalyl, C_2O_2; also called *oxalamide*. Extended generically to the amides which also contain alcohol-radicals, as *dimethyloxamide*, $C_2O_2.N_2H_2.(CH_3)_2$, etc.

1838 T. THOMSON *Chem. Org. Bodies* 590 Oxamide. This substance, the first of the series of amides, was discovered by Dumas, in the year 1830. **1866–77** WATTS *Dict. Chem.* IV. 284 Oxamides containing Alcohol radicals. **1869** ROSCOE *Elem. Chem.* xxxiv. (1871) 367 By heating neutral ammonium oxalate, a white powder called Oxamide is left.

oxammite (ˈɒksəmaɪt). *Min.* [Named 1870, from OX- 2 + AMM(ONIA + -ITE[1].] Native oxalate of ammonium, found in yellowish-white crystals or crystalline grains.

1870 *Amer. Jrnl. Sci.* L. 274 Oxalate of Ammonia, which Professor Shepard names Oxammite. **1892** *Dana's Min.* 994 Oxammite..[is] found with mascagnite, which it resembles.

oxanilic (ɒksəˈnɪlɪk), *a. Chem.* [f. OX- 2 = OXAL- + ANILIC.] In *oxanilic acid* (= phenyloxamic acid): a crystalline substance ($C_8H_7NO_3$) obtained by heating aniline with an excess of oxalic acid; its salts are **oxˈanilates**. So **oxaˈnilamide** (= monophenyloxamide), a snow-white flaky substance ($C_8H_8N_2O_2$) obtained in the decomposition of cyaniline by hydrochloric acid; **oxˈanilide** (= diphenyloxamide), a substance ($C_{14}H_{12}N_2O_2$), crystallizing in white scales, obtained by heating aniline oxalate, or in the decomposition of cyaniline by dilute hydrochloric or sulphuric acid; **oxˈaniline**, a base (C_6H_7NO) obtained by heating amido-salicylic acid, forming a white inodorous mass, which dissolves in hot water or alcohol, and separates on cooling in slightly coloured crystals.

1857 MILLER *Elem. Chem.* III. 241 Oxanilide. **1866–77** WATTS *Dict. Chem.* IV. 287 Oxanilamide..Oxanilic acid.. Oxanilide..Oxaniline.

ox-antelope: see OX 6.

oxanthracene (ɒkˈsænθrəsiːn). *Chem.* Also oxy-. [f. OX- 1 + ANTHRACENE.] A neutral substance, $C_{14}H_8O_2$, derived from anthracene.

1862 MILLER *Elem. Chem.* III. 670. **1866–77** WATTS *Dict. Chem.* IV. 352 [It] forms light reddish-yellow crystals of oxanthracene, fusible, volatile without decomposition, and subliming in long needles.

oxarde, obs. form of OXHERD.

oxazepam (ɒkˈseɪzɪpæm). *Pharm.* [f. OX- 1 + AZ(O- + -*ep*(*ine* (suffix designating an unsaturated seven-membered ring containing nitrogen) + AM(IDE.] A tricyclic, creamy-white powder, $C_{15}H_{11}ClN_2O_2$, which is a tranquillizer given to relieve anxiety states and to control the withdrawal symptoms of alcoholism.

1964 *Jrnl. Pharmaceutical Sci.* LIII. 1181/1 Oxazepam, 7-chloro-1,3-dihydro-3-hydroxy-5-phenyl-2*H*-1,4-benzodiazepine-2-one, has been characterized pharmacologically in our laboratories as an anticonvulsant and mild central depressant and is currently under clinical investigation as an antianxiety agent. **1966** *Jrnl. Amer. Med. Assoc.* 21 Nov. 952/1 Six days after oxazepam was stopped completely, her husband reported she had been up all night, was talking irrationally, and was having visual hallucinations. **1974** *Brit. Jrnl. Clin. Pract.* XXVIII. 65/1 Oxazepam, one of the benzodiazepine group, has an anxiolytic action with very little sedative potential.

oxazole (ˈɒksəzəʊl). *Chem.* [ad. G. *oxazol* (Hantzsch & Weber 1887, in *Ber. d. Deut. Chem. Ges.* XX. 3119): see OX- 1, AZO-, and -OLE.]

a. A weakly basic, heterocyclic compound, O·CH:N·CH:CH, which is a volatile liquid. **b.** Any of the derivatives of this compound obtained by substituting for hydrogen.

1888 *Jrnl. Chem. Soc.* LIV. 574 Oxazoles are obtained by the condensation of α-halogen-ketones with amides. **1892** [see IMIDAZOLE]. **1929** R. A. GORTNER *Outl. Biochem.* xiv. 350 Polypeptides may be considered to enolize..yielding substituted imidazoles or substituted oxazoles. **1966** *McGraw-Hill Encycl. Sci. & Technol.* IX. 461/1 Oxazole is miscible with water and organic solvents. **1968** A. ALBERT *Heterocyclic Chem.* (ed. 2) vi. 289 Oxazole alkaloids have been isolated from flowering plants in the Rutaceae and Gramineae, and oxazolidines (their reduced analogues) occur in cabbages.

oxazolidine (ɒksəˈzɒlɪdiːn). *Chem.* [f. prec. + -IDINE.] Any of the compounds obtained by substituting for hydrogen in the hypothetical parent compound $CH_2CH_2NHCH_2O$ (which is the fully hydrogenated form of oxazole), some of which are anticonvulsants and are used in treating petit mal.

1902 *Jrnl. Chem. Soc.* LXXXII. I. 56 (*heading*) Synthesis of oxazolidines by the action of aldehydes on hydramines. **1953** *Chem. Rev.* LIII. 315 The oxazolidines are liquids or solids of basic character; their stability to hydrolysis is generally low. **1961** A. GOTH *Med. Pharmacol.* xix. 229 In the clinical use of the oxazolidine derivatives, the following toxic effects have been reported: drowsiness and ataxia, photophobia, and a strange visual disturbance.

oxazolone (ɒkˈsæzələʊn). *Chem.* [f. as prec. + -ONE.] Any compound containing the nucleus obtained by hydrogenating one of the double bonds of oxazole and replacing a methylene group by a carbonyl group; = AZLACTONE.

1899 JAPP & FINDLAY in *Jrnl. Chem. Soc.* LXXV. I. 1027 It occurred to us that, by substituting an α-hydroxy-acid for the α-keto-alcohol in the foregoing reaction, it might be possible to prepare oxazolones (ketodi-hydro-oxazoles). **1947** *Sci. News* IV. 70 The synthesis of penicillin G starts with a benzyl oxazolone and with penicillinamine, and attempts to recombine them. **1968** A. ALBERT *Heterocyclic Chem.* (ed. 2) vi. 290 Of the oxazolones, the 5-isomer..and its derivatives are the best known. **1968** R. O. C. NORMAN *Princ. Org. Synthesis* xviii. 604 The oxazolones or azlactones, prepared by the dehydration of *N*-acyl-α-amino-acids, are employed in Erlenmeyer's synthesis of α-amino-acids. **1975** *Nature* 13 Nov. 149/2 We have examined..the production of antiparasite antibodies and parameters of T-cell function (the response to phytohaemagglutinin (PHA) and oxazolone).

ˈox-bane. [f. OX + BANE *sb.*[1]] A plant injurious to cattle; now, applied to the Poison-bulb of South Africa, *Buphane toxicaria*.

1611 COTGR., *Mort aux bœufs*, ox-bane; an hearbe whereof if an Ox eat, he dies forthwith of the Squinzie. **1706** PHILLIPS, *Ox-bane*, a sort of Herb.

ox-bird, oxbird. [f. OX + BIRD *sb.* 2.]

1. A name applied to various British small wild-fowl; esp. the Dunlin (*Tringa variabilis*); also, locally, to the Sanderling (*Calidris arenaria*), Ringed Plover (*Ægialitis hiaticula*), Common Sandpiper (*Tringoides hypoleucus*).

a **1547** in *Househ. Ord.* (1790) 223 Prices of Foule—Oxe-birds, the doz. **1591–4** LANCASTER *Voy. to E. Indies* (1810) II. 590 A certaine kind of foule called oxe birds, which are a gray kind of sea-foule, like a snite in colour but not in beake. **1699** J. JONES in *Misc. Cur.* (1708) III. 393 Plovers, Snipes, Ox-birds, Pipers,..and a hundred other sort of Fowl. **1802** G. MONTAGU *Ornith. Dict.* (1833) 144 Ox-bird, a name for the Stint. **1813** COL. HAWKER *Diary* (1893) I. 89 Killing..1 jack snipe and 5 ox-birds. **1863** J. R. WISE *New Forest* 312 Ringed Plover..known..in the neighbourhood of Christchurch and Lymington, as the 'oxbird'. **1883** —— in *Hampsh. Gloss.*, *Ox-bird*, the common sand-piper. **1884** WOOD in *Sunday Mag.* May 306/2 The Dunlin..on the Medway Creeks..is known as Ox-bird. **1885** SWAINSON *Prov. Names Birds* 195 Sanderling (*Calidris arenaria*), also called..Ox bird (Essex; Kent). **1886** R. C. LESLIE *Sea-painter's Log* i. 11 The tiny broad-arrow mark of the oxbird.

2. Applied to **a.** a species of Weaver-bird, *Textor alector*; **b.** the African ox-pecker or -biter (*Cent. Dict.*).

1883 *List Anim. Zool. Soc.* 246. **1896** *Ibid.* (ed. 9) 258 *Textor alector*, Ox-bird.

ox-blood (ˈɒksblʌd). [f. OX + BLOOD.] The blood of the ox; a colour resembling this; also used *attrib.* or as *adj.*, *spec.* of a colour of opals, of porcelain, and of leather.

1705 *Whole Art of Dying* II. 53 *Ox-blood Colour*. First Tinge the Stuffs Yellow,..and work them till they are sufficiently beautiful, then..put into the Kettle a Tub of stale Urine, and boil it again till they take the Dye. **1707** *Curios. Husb. & Gard.* 350 Feed them with Ox-Blood. **1897** *Sears, Roebuck Catal.* 194b/3 Men's Hard Cash Lace, best Russia Calf, latest Ox Blood (dark wine) color. **1936** *Burlington Mag.* Jan. 10/2 The splendid ox-blood and peach bloom reds of the Ch'ing dynasty. **1937** D. JONES *In Parenthesis* 118 You feel the pack of the Ox-blood Kid—it's as light as the Reg'mentals—there's a whole lot of them that work it. **1941** 'BRAHMS' & 'SIMON' *No Bed for Bacon* ii. 37 It was Elizabeth of England in ivory and ox blood. **1950** H. MCCLOY *Through Glass, Darkly* i. 5 A bowl of ox blood porcelain. **1950** C. FRY *Venus Observed* II. i. 34 Umber, bronze and brass, ox-blood, damson, Crimson, scalding scarlet. **1967** S. LLOYD *Lightning Ridge Bk.* 24 In the reds, miners describe colour as 'ox blood', 'pidgeon's blood', 'port wine red', and so on. **1968** *Listener* 27 June 825/1 One of the occupants.. was wearing 'ski pants and ox-blood-coloured shoes'. **1968** D. TORR *Treason Line* 69 He..walked over to the Chinese vases in the window. He put one vase with an ox-blood glaze..into the window on the left. **1971** J. S. GUNN *Opal Terminol.* 32 *Ox blood*,..name given to the deepest of the red-coloured opals. **1974** 'G. BLACK' *Golden Cockatrice* x. 163, I got another vase..imitation ox blood. **1975** T. STOPPARD *Travesties* I. 27, I think to match the carnation, oxblood shot-silk cravat.

ox-bow, oxbow (ˈɒksbəʊ). [f. OX + BOW *sb.*[1]]

1. The bow-shaped piece of wood which forms a collar for a yoked ox and has its upper ends fastened to the yoke; = BOW *sb.*[1] 5.

1368–9 *Durham Acc. Rolls* (Surtees) 575 In hercis et Oxbouys emptis..xixd. ob. **1530** PALSGR. 250/2 Oxebowe that gothe about his necke, *collier de beuf*. **1573** TUSSER *Husb.* xvii. (1878) 36 With ox bowes and oxyokes, and other things mo, For oxteeme and horseteeme, in plough for to go. **1669, 1721** [see BOW *sb.*[1] 5]. **1833** S. SMITH *Life & Writings J. Downing* 106 A farmer ort to stick to his ox bows and goard sticks. **1846** R. B. SAGE *Scenes Rocky Mts.* iii. 26 An extra quantity of ox bows, axle-trees..in case of accidents or breakage. **1876** *Whitby Gloss.*, *Owce-bow*, an ox-collar; the wooden one for the neck when the animal is yoked. **1881** *Rep. Indian Affairs* (U.S.) 398 Ox-bows, 2-inch..doz. 51.

2. *U.S.* **a.** A semicircular bend in a river; hence, the land included within this. Also *attrib.*, as *ox-bow bend*.

1797 J. A. GRAHAM *Pres. St. Vermont* 148 In this town [Newbury, Vt.] are those extensive intervales known by the name of the great Ox-Bow, which form the River assumes in its course at this place. **1845** BARBER & HOWE *Hist. Coll. N. York State* 201 Oxbow, on the Oxbow of the Oswegatchie river. **1858** O. W. HOLMES *Aut. Breakf.-t.* x, The Connecticut..wantons in huge luxurious oxbows about the fair Northampton meadows. **1875** TEMPLE & SHELDON *Hist. Northfield, Mass.* 12 The high plain here trends to the west, and turns the course of the Connecticut so that it makes an ox-bow bend.

b. More fully *ox-bow lake*. A curved lake left in a former meander of an adjacent river after the river has changed its course and cut through the narrow neck of the meander.

1898 W. M. DAVIS *Physical Geogr.* ix. 245 An abandoned meander is occupied by nearly stagnant water... In time it becomes an ox-bow lake. **1902** [see MORTLAKE 2]. **1937** [see CUT-OFF *sb.* 2]. **1944** A. HOLMES *Princ. Physical Geol.* x. 165 If a flood occurs when only a narrow neck of lands is left between adjoining loops, the momentum of the increased flow is likely to carry the stream across the neck... A deserted channel is left, forming an ox-bow lake which soon degenerates into a swamp. **1957** L. EISELEY *Immense Journey* 22 Fishes of this type who get themselves immured in oxygenless ponds or in cut-off oxbows buried in winter drifts. **1961** *Listener* 19 Oct. 614/1 In his lifetime the river flowed through his ox-bow. **1962** [see MORTLAKE 2].

3. *Comb.* (in sense 1) **ox-bow key**, a key for fastening the end of an ox-bow; **ox-bow stirrup**, a stirrup resembling an ox-bow in shape; also *ellipt.*

1882 *Rep. Indian Affairs* (U.S.) 480 Ox-bow keys, 2 inch. *a* **1918** J. BRATT *Trails of Yesterday* (1921) xiii. 52 In the morning I was set to work.. making ox-bow keys and fitting bows to yokes. **1907** S. E. WHITE *Arizona Nights* I. i. 5 Uncle Jim sat placidly on his white horse, his thin knees bent to the ox-bow stirrups, smoking. **1942** BERREY & VAN DEN BARK *Amer. Thes. Slang* §915/5 *Ox bows*,.. wide old-fashioned wooden stirrups.

ox-boy, -close, etc.: see OX 5, 6.

Oxbridge (ˈɒksbrɪdʒ). [Short for '*Ox*ford and Cam*bridge*'.] A name used to designate the universities of Oxford and of Cambridge; the characteristics common to both, esp. as distinct from other universities in the British Isles. Also *attrib.* Cf. CAMFORD.

1849 THACKERAY *Pendennis* I. xxix. 286 'Rough and ready, your chum seems,' the Major said. 'Somewhat different from your dandy friends at Oxbridge.' **1906** V. WOOLF in Q. Bell *Virginia Woolf* (1972) I. 205 You see a pink cheeked boy whose only talk is of cricket.. enter upon his first term at Oxbridge. **1907** G. W. E. RUSSELL *Seeing & Hearing* v. 35 We ran a neck-and-neck race at the University... In those days I little thought of settling down in Oxbridge. **1912** H. G. WELLS *Marriage* i. § 1. 5 A.. meretricious dressing-bag of imitation morocco, which had been one of her chief financial errors at Oxbridge. **1924** E. F. BENSON *David of King's* i. 5 Useless.. to delude the intelligent reader into believing that it was Queen's Parade at Oxbridge or Prince's Parade at Camford. **1955** T. H. PEAR *Eng. Social Differences* i. 20 He would often wish his sons to go to a public (boarding) school and to Oxbridge. **1958** *New Statesman* 30 Aug. 244/1 Whatever its merits or demerits, Oxbridge remains first choice for a majority of university applicants. **1960** AUDEN *Homage to Clio* 88 Oxbridge philosophers, to be cursory, Are products of a middle-class nursery. **1960** *Times* 14 Mar. 13/4 The University 'Rag'.. is now more closely identified with what the jargon calls 'Redbrick' rather than 'Oxbridge', with the world of Kingsley Amis rather than that of the young Compton Mackenzie. **1964** S. BRITTAN *Treasury under Tories* i. 21 One characteristic that Whitehall does have in common with other *élite* groups is its overwhelmingly Oxbridge character. **1967** *New Scientist* 6 Apr. 39/2 Father is very likely public school and 'Oxbridge'. Son is 'redbrick'. **1973** D. ROBINSON *Rotten with Honour* 9 We'll have—Hale... Twenty-six, Oxbridge, degree in languages. **1975** *Sunday Tel.* 4 May 30/2 *(heading)* Fine win by Oxbridge. The Universities beat Worcestershire by 66 runs at Fenners. **1976** *Globe & Mail* (Toronto) 1 July 35/8 And as if to make the thing complete the prayer was often offered by a clergyman who read the liturgy with an Oxbridge accent even though he was a product of southern Ontario.

Hence **Ox'bridgean, -ian** *a.* and *sb.*

1959 *Cambr. Rev.* 7 Feb. 315/1 They [*sc.* the Americans] are so polite, so ready to believe that the visiting Oxbridgean must find Yale or Harvard an anti-climax. **1959** *Guardian* 14 Dec. 6/4 'The mere fact,' you fretted, that such Oxbridgean institutions 'have refused the student loan money may make their actions suspect'. **1960** *Mind* LXIX. 419, I have wished I was reading one of those Oxbridgean philosophers who, had they taken the right turning early in life, would long ago have brought the filing and card-indexing systems of the British Civil Service up to a new peak of perfection. **1970** *Atlantic Monthly* May 132 As apt as an eighteenth-century Oxbridgean with the Latin tag. **1971** *New Scientist* 17 June 706 The ivy-covered, Oxbridgian atmosphere of Yale.

ox cart. [OX 5.] A cart drawn by an ox. Also *transf.*

1749 J. HEMPSTEAD *Diary* 6 July (1901) 526 No ox Carts in these parts & very few Horse Carts. **1877** M. M. GRANT *Sun-Maid* i, And then emerged.. an ox-cart. **1918** E. S. FARROW *Dict. Mil. Terms* 427 *Ox Cart.*—A slang name for a heavy French shell which moves with a moderate velocity. **1973** *Country Life* 29 Nov. 1802/3 Continuously exploring.. deeper into veldt and jungle, leading, on his Arab pony, a train of ox carts. **1975** *Times Lit. Suppl.* 5 Dec. 1462/1 Crane's noble and well-loved print 'The Triumph of Labour' with its procession of garlanded oxcarts and rejoicing workers.

'ox-cheek. The cheek of an ox, esp. as an article of food. Also *attrib.*

1592 GREENE *Upst. Courtier* (1871) 44 He useth him as courteously as a butchers cur would an ox-cheek when he is hungry. **1693** DRYDEN *Juvenal* iii. 461 With what Companion-Cobler have you fed, On old Ox-cheeks, or He-Goats tougher Head? **1709** *Brit. Apollo* II. No. 61. 2/2 Ox-cheek-Women, Costermongers. **1769** MRS. RAFFALD *Eng. Housekpr.* (1778) 5 To make an Ox Cheek Soup.

‖**oxea** (ˈɒksɪə). *Zool.* [mod.L., f. Gr. ὀξύ-ς sharp.] A needle-shaped sponge spicule, pointed at both ends. Hence **'oxeate** *a.*, having the form of an oxea.

1886 R. VON LENDENFELD in *Proc. Zool. Soc.* 585. **1887** SOLLAS in *Encycl. Brit.* XXII. 416/1 *(Sponges)* By far the commonest form is the oxea, a needle-shaped form pointed at both ends and produced by growth from a centre at the same rate in opposite directions along the same axis... By the suppression of one of the rays of an oxea, an acuate spicule or stylus results. *Ibid.* 416/2 The spicular rays often become cylindrical; usually pointed (*oxeate*) at the ends, they are also frequently rounded off (*strongylate*).

oxen, pl. of OX. Hence †**i-oxned** *pa. pple.* (ME.), furnished with oxen.

c **1205** LAY. 31812 þer cheorl draf his fulȝe I-oxned swiðe fære.

oxer (ˈɒksə(r)). *Fox-hunting slang.* [See -ER[1] 1.] An ox-fence.

1859 LAWRENCE *Sword & Gown* vi. 67 A rattling fall over an 'oxer'. **1861** WHYTE MELVILLE *Mkt. Harb.* 51 The fence .. was an 'oxer', about seven feet high, and impervious to a bird.

ox-eye, oxeye (ˈɒksaɪ). Also 5 **oxie, oxeghe**, 6 **oxei**, *Sc.* **oxee**, 6–8 **oxey**.

1. The eye of an ox; an eye like that of an ox, a large (human) eye.

1688 BOYLE *Final Causes Nat. Things, Vitiated Sight* 258 If she had not had that sort of eyes, which.. some call ox-eyes; for hers were swelled much beyond the size of human eyes. **1869** C. GIBBON *R. Gray* viii, His ox eyes were rolling more stolidly. **1892** M. WYNMAN *My Flirtations* i, A sallow, undersized Italian, with handsome ox-eyes.

2. A popular name of various birds: *esp.* the Great Titmouse (*Parus major*); also locally, the Blue Titmouse (*P. cæruleus*) or Blue Ox-eye, and Cole Titmouse (*P. Britannicus*) or Black Ox-eye.

1544 TURNER *Avium* G v b, *Primum parum, Angli uocant* the great titmouse or the great oxei. **1549** *Compl. Scot.* vi. 39 The oxee cryit tueit. **1655** MOUFET & BENNET *Health's Improv.* (1746) 188 Oxeys or great Titmice, feed, as ordinary Titmice do, upon Caterpillars, Blossoms of Trees, Bark-Worms and Flies. **1817** *Sporting Mag.* L. 142 A bird of the oxeye species has this year built its nest in the valve of a pump.

b. Also, locally applied to the Ox-bird or Dunlin, *Tringa variabilis*; the Tree-creeper (also *ox-eye creeper*), *Certhia familiaris*; the Chiff-chaff, *Phylloscopus rufus*; the Willow Warbler, *P. trochilus*; in N. America, to the Black-bellied Plover, *Squatarola helvetica*, and the American Dunlin, *Pelidna americana*.

1589 RIDER *Bibl. Schol.*, *Birdes* 1703 An Oxeye, or creeper, *Certhia.* **1649** *Perf. Descr. Virginia* (1837) 17 Ducks .. Widgeons.. Dottrells.. Oxeyes. **1668** WILKINS *Real Char.* II. v. §4. 147 Those other Birds.. a little bigger then a Wren called Ox-eye-creeper. **1806** COL. HAWKER *Diary* (1893) I. 4 A wild duck, ox-eyes, rails, fieldfares. **1885** SWAINSON *Prov. Names Birds* 193 Dunlin.. Ox bird or Ox eye (Essex; Kent). **1886** ELWORTHY *W. Somerset Word-bk.*, *Ox-eye*, only name for both the chiff-chaff and the willow warbler. **1896** P. A. BRUCE *Econ. Hist. Virginia* I. 115 There was.. the duck in all those varieties so well known to modern sportsmen, the canvas-back, the red head, the mallard, the widgeon, the dottrell, the oxeye.

3. Applied to various plants: **a.** A species of the genus *Buphthalmum* (N.O. *Compositæ*), of which the Central European species *B. grandiflorum* and *B. cordatum*, herbaceous perennials with bright yellow radiate flowers, are often cultivated in gardens. **b.** The British wild plants *Chrysanthemum segetum*, the Corn Marigold or Yellow Ox-eye, and *C. Leucanthemum*, the White Ox-eye, Ox-eye daisy, Dog-daisy, or Moon-daisy; sometimes also (app. by confusion) applied to species of *Anthemis* with yellow or white flowers resembling these. **c.** Applied by Lyte to *Adonis vernalis* (N.O. *Ranunculaceæ*). **d.** The American composite plant *Heliopsis lævis* with large yellow flowers. **e.** The West-Indian composite plants, Creeping Ox-eye or West Indian Marigold, *Wedelia carnosa*, and Sea-side Ox-eye, *Borrichia arborescens*. (*Treas. Bot.* 1866.)

a. *a* **1400–50** *Stockh. Med. MS.* 210 Oxeye: *oculus bouis.* *c* **1450** *Alphita* 24/21 *Butalmon* uel *butalmos*, oculus bouis idem, anglice oxie [*v.r.* oxeghe]. **1551** TURNER *Herbal* I. G v, Buphthalmus or oxey.. hath leues lyke fenel and a yellowe floure greater then Camomill, lyke vnto an ey, wherupon it hath the name. *c* **1588** SPENSER *Virg. Gnat* 678 Oxeye still greene, and bitter Patience. **1597** GERARDE *Herbal* II. ccxlv. 606 The plant which we haue called Buphthalmum, or Oxe eie. **1760** J. LEE *Introd. Bot.* App. 321 Ox-eye, *Buphthalmum.*

b. **1625** B. JONSON *Pan's Anniv.*, Bring corn-flag, tulips, and Adonis' flower, Fair oxeye, goldy-locks, and columbine. **1688** R. HOLME *Armoury* II. 69/1 A wild Field Marygold.. this is also termed an Oxe-Eye if Yellow, and a Wild Daisie if White. **1706** PHILLIPS, *Ox-eye*,.. also an Herb otherwise call'd Great Margaret, good for Wounds and the King's Evill. **1753** CHAMBERS *Cycl. Supp.* App., *Ox-eye-daisy*, a name sometimes given to the *Leucanthemum* of botanical writers. **1760** J. LEE *Introd. Bot.* App. 321 Ox-eye of old Authors, *Anthemis.* *a* **1795** AIKIN *Even. at Home* xvi, One of the great ox-eye daisies in the corn. **1846** SOWERBY *Brit. Bot.* (ed. 3), Great White Ox-eye. **1870** MISS BROUGHTON *Red as Rose* I. 204 Her lap full of decapitated oxeyes. **1892** *Syd. Soc. Lex.*, Ox-eye chamomile, *Anthemis tinctoria.*

c. **1578** LYTE *Dodoens* II. xxxii. 189 This herbe.. is called in Latine *Buphthalmum* and *Oculus bouis*... This is the right Oxe eye described by Dioscorides. **1741** *Compl. Fam.-Piece* II. iii. 380 Oriental Ox-eye with red and white Flowers.

4. Applied to a sparoid fish, *Box* or *Boöps vulgaris*; also to an elopoid fish. *Megalops cyprinoides.*

a **1642** SIR W. MONSON *Naval Tracts* VI. (1704) 534/1 The Ox-Eye, is like the Tunney, an excellent Fish; and looks like the Eye of an Ox [coast of Brazil].

5. Applied to several things likened to the eye of an ox, as **a.** A drinking cup in use at certain Oxford colleges; **b.** *Naut.* A small glass bull's eye (Smyth *Sailor's Word-bk.* 1867); **c.** 'A small concave mirror made, especially in Nuremberg, of glass' (*Cent. Dict.* 1890); **d.** An oval dormer window = ŒIL-DE-BŒUF (Knight *Dict. Mech.* 1875).

1703 in *Hearne's Collect.* (O.H.S.) II. 461 Abest Creedus, quia bibit Ox-Eyes cum Bedelli uxore. [See also Note to this.] *a* **1843** SOUTHEY *Comm.-pl. Bk.* IV. 425 Oxford, All Souls... Their silver cups at the college are called ox-eyes, and an ox-eye of wormwood was a favourite draught there. **18..** *Oxford during Last Cent.* 65 At Corpus Christi were drinking-cups and glasses, which, from their shape, were called ox-eyes.

6. *Naut.* = BULL'S EYE 10: see quots.

1598 PHILLIPS tr. *Linschoten* (Hakl. Soc.) II. 240 A certayne cloude, which in shew seemeth no bigger than a mans fist, and therefore by the Portingals it is called *Olho do Boy*, (or Oxe eye). **1705** C. PURSHALL *Mech. Macrocosm* 172 Those Dreadful Storms on the Coasts of Guinea, which the Seamen call the Ox Eye, from their Beginning; because at first it seems no bigger than an Ox's-Eye. **1867** SMYTH *Sailor's Word-bk.*, *Ox-eye*, a small cloud, or weather-gall, seen on the coast of Africa, which presages a severe storm.

7. *Comb.* **ox-eye arch**, a pointed or Gothic arch; **ox-eye bean** = *horse-eye bean*: see HORSE *sb.* 28 c (Simmonds *Dict. Trade* 1858); **ox-eye camomile, daisy** (see 3 b); **ox-eye tom-tit** (see 2 a).

1736 DRAKE *Eboracum* II. ii. 532 In the Anglo-Norman age, all their arches.. were nearer to the Roman taste, than the acuter oxey arch.

ox-eyed (ˈɒks,aɪd), *a.* [f. prec. + -ED[2].]

1. Having large full eyes like those of an ox.

1621 BURTON *Anat. Mel.* III. ii. II. ii. (1676) 290/1 Homer useth that Epithite of Ox-eyed, in describing Juno, because a round black eye is the best. **1792** GIBBON *Misc. Wks.* (1814) II. 476 Your friend is.. not quite so great a vixen as the ox-eyed Juno. **1856** R. A. VAUGHAN *Mystics* (1860) I. 3 Eyes of hazel,.. such for size and lustre as Homer gives to ox-eyed Juno. **1895** *Westm. Gaz.* 13 Aug. 7/1 How stolid he looks! How ox-eyed!.. How mildly ruminative!

2. Of the form of a pointed or Gothic arch.

1736 DRAKE *Eboracum* App. p. xxxiii, The acuter, oxeyed, arch coming then into fashion.

Oxfam, OXFAM (ˈɒksfæm). [Short for *Ox*ford Committee for *Fam*ine Relief.] An organization for the distribution of food, funds, etc., in disaster areas and to poor countries.

1963 D. MITCHELL in *Oxfam Ann. Rep. 1962/63*, At first the Oxford Committee for Famine Relief—Oxfam, as it is now known all over the world—was one of many similar groups with a temporary mission: the emergency relief of war suffering in Europe. **1968** *Listener* 8 Aug. 162/1 A grim, obsessed Oxfam worker, struggling to get a few scraps and leavings to millions of starving children. **1969** N. W. PIRIE *Food Resources* 15 Oxfam posters used to read 'Oxfam hates hungry babies' and went on to suggest ways of getting rid of the hunger. **1974** I. MURDOCH *Sacred & Profane Love Machine* 304 Her few inexpensive jewels had gone to Oxfam. **1975** J. BLACKBURN *Mister Brown's Bodies* i. 10 Those disgusting pictures of famine victims you see in the Oxfam shops.

ox-feather, ox-foot: see OX 6.

Oxford (ˈɒksfəd). The name of a University town in England [in OE. *Oxena-*, *Oxnaford* 'ford of oxen', ME. *Oxneford*, *Oxenford*].

1. **a.** Used attributively in numerous expressions: **Oxford accent**, a style of pronouncing English popularly supposed to be particularly characteristic of members of the University of Oxford and (esp. before 1939) to be marked by affected utterance; **Oxford bags** [BAG *sb.* 16], a style of trousers very wide at the ankles; so **Oxford-bagged** *a.*; **Oxford blue**, a dark shade of blue, adopted as the colour of the university; **Oxford Blues**: see BLUE *sb.* 7 a; **Oxford chrome**, yellow ochre, formerly dug at Shotover, near Oxford; **Oxford clay** (*Geol.*), a deposit of stiff blue clay underlying the 'coral rag' of the Middle Oolite in the midland counties of England, and esp. in Oxfordshire; earlier called *clunch clay* (CLUNCH *sb.* 6), *plastic clay* (PLASTIC *a.* 5 b); **Oxford cloth** (see quots.); **Oxford corners**, in *Printing*, ruled border lines enclosing the print of a book, etc., crossing and extending beyond each other somewhat at the corners; **Oxford(shire Down**, a sheep of the breed so called, produced by crossing Cotswold and Hampshire Down sheep and developed by Samuel Druce at Eynsham about 1830; **Oxford English**, English spoken with an Oxford accent; the speech popularly supposed to be characteristic of a member of the University of Oxford; **Oxford frame**, a picture-frame the

sides of which cross each other and project some distance at the corners; **Oxford grey** (see *Oxford mixture*); also, the colour of such cloth; **Oxford Group**: see GROUP *sb.* 3 d; **Oxford hollow**, in *Bookbinding*, a flattened paper tube inserted between the spine of the book and its cover, to strengthen the spine and allow the book to be opened flat more easily; **Oxford John**, a dish of sauced and stewed mutton with other ingredients; **Oxford man**, a man who has been educated at the University of Oxford; **Oxford marmalade**, a kind of coarse-cut marmalade originally manufactured in Oxford (registered as a trade-mark by Frank Cooper in 1908 and 1931); also *attrib.* and *fig.*; **Oxford mixture**, a kind of woollen cloth of a very dark grey colour; called also *Oxford grey*, *pepper-and-salt*, *thunder-and-lightning*; **Oxford Movement** (*Ch. Hist.*), the movement for the revival of Catholic doctrine and observance in the Church of England, which began at Oxford about 1833; **Oxford ochre** = *Oxford chrome* above; **Oxford oolite** (*Geol.*), the middle division of the Oolitic system: see OOLITE 2; **Oxford plant** = *Oxford weed*; **Oxford punch** [PUNCH *sb.*[3]] (see quots.); **Oxford ragwort**, an annual herb, *Senecio squalidus*, belonging to the family Compositæ and bearing heads of yellow flowers (a native of southern Italy now naturalized in Britain, after having escaped from the Oxford Botanic Garden); **Oxford sausage**, a kind of sausage; also *fig.*; **Oxford scholar** *slang*, a crown; five shillings; a dollar; **Oxford School** (*Ch. Hist.*), the school of thought represented by the Oxford Movement; the body of persons belonging to this; **Oxford shirt**, a shirt made from Oxford cloth; **Oxford shirting** = *Oxford cloth*; **Oxford shoe**, a style of shoe laced over the instep; **Oxford Tracts**, the 'Tracts for the Times' issued 1833–41 in advocacy of the principles of the Oxford Movement, whence the movement and school are also known as TRACTARIAN; **Oxford trousers** = *Oxford bags*; **Oxford unit** *Pharm.*, a unit of penicillin originally adopted at the Sir William Dunn School of Pathology in the University of Oxford, being the amount which when dissolved in 1 c.c. of water gave the same inhibition as a certain partly purified standard solution; cf. *penicillin unit*; **Oxford voice** = *Oxford accent*; **Oxford weed**, the ivy-leaved toadflax, *Cymbalaria muralis*.

1904 J. K. JEROME *Tommy & Co.* v. 174 Somerville's *Oxford accent is wasted here. **1924** GALSWORTHY *On Expression* 8 And dare we condemn cockney—a lingo whose waters, in Southern England, seem fast flooding in over the dykes of the so-called Oxford accent, and such other rural dialects as are left? **1934** *S.P.E. Tract* XXXIX. 616 It might be said perhaps that the 'Oxford Accent' conveys an impression of a precise and rather foppish elegance, and of deliberate artificiality. **1940** G. ARTHUR *Concerning Winston Spencer Churchill* 194 Lacking the 'Oxford accent' he spoke as a Briton to Britons. **1959** J. BRAINE *Vodi* vi. 93 Dick assumed an Oxford accent. 'It's *naht* old-fashioned, dear brethren, to think of Hell in the language of fire and brimstone.' **1974** P. DICKINSON *Poison Oracle* ii. 45 The Sultan's manner is very deceptive... His Oxford accent and his slang..are all a sort of parody of our civilisation. **1961** *Times* 18 May 16/6 Eton-cropped maidens sporting decorously with *Oxford-bagged partners. **1927** *Dancing Times* Jan. 573/2 *Oxford bags, plus fours, in fact, any old thing. **1933** P. BALFOUR *Society Racket* ii. 61 We wore high-necked jumpers and 'Oxford bags'. **1938** J. BETJEMAN *Oxf. Univ. Chest* i. 9 The pale-faced mechanics in Oxford bags and tweed coats, walk down the Cornmarket. **1948** H. ACTON *Mem. Aesthete* vi. 119 Instead of the wasp-waisted suits with pagoda shoulders and tight trousers affected by the dandies, I wore jackets with broad lapels and broad pleated trousers. The latter got broader and broader. Eventually they were imitated elsewhere and were generally referred to as 'Oxford bags'. **1971** *Daily Tel.* 2 Aug. 9/5 By night you're either..Dietrich in a velvet blazer and Oxford bags, or Carole Lombard in a halter-neck satin top..and a long satin kilt. **1973** *Country Life* 19 Apr. 1115/1 A single-breasted striped suit for the bridegroom, which has Oxford bags and patch pockets. **1866** MRS. H. WOOD *Elster's Folly* I. viii. 191 'Strike your colours, ladies, you that sport the crimson and purple!' called out a laughing voice from one of the skiffs. '*Oxford blue wins.' **1875** *All Year Round* 20 Feb. 444/2 The hues peculiar to the best period of Sèvres were gros-blue, a dark heavy Oxford blue. **1923** JOYCE *Let.* 26 Feb. (1966) III. 72 The smaller Oxford blue volume. **1959** M. GILBERT *Blood & Judgement* xvii. 176 He picked up a thin, Oxford-blue folder. **1973** R. LUDLUM *Matlock Paper* xi. 101 A half-unbuttoned, oxford-blue shirt. **1875** *Ure's Dict. Arts* (ed. 7) III. 465 **Oxford chrome*, an oxide of iron used in oil and water-colour painting. **1818** W. PHILLIPS *Selection of Facts Geol. Eng. & Wales* 66 In these..are included the three strata..namely, the Forest marble, the Cornbrash limestone, and the clunch clay (*Oxford Clay). **1837** *Encycl. Brit.* (ed. 7) XV. 203/2 The Coralline Formation..Lower group..Oxford clay. **1865** PAGE *Handbk. Geol.*, *Oxford clay*, the lower member of the Middle Oolite, so called from its being well developed in Oxfordshire. **1967** D. H. RAYNER *Stratigr. Brit. Isles* ix. 298 Around Peterborough, vast pits have been dug in the Oxford Clay for brick-making. **1964** *McCall's Sewing* iv. 58/2 **Oxford cloth*, plain-, basket- or twill-weave cotton, often used for shirting. It is fairly heavy cloth in which two yarns travel as one in the warp, and one filling yarn is equal in size to the two-warp yarns. **1968** J. IRONSIDE *Fashion Alphabet* 243 *Oxford cloth*, a heavy cotton cloth used for shirts and sometimes jackets or summer suits. **1969** *Sears Catal.* Spring/Summer 24 Rajah shirt with soil release. Oxford cloth of polyester and cotton. **1976** *National Observer* (U.S.) 17 Jan. 10/3 (Advt.), Our fine quality, breathable, pure cotton oxford cloth pyjamas are unbeatable for wear all year 'round. [**1849** *Jrnl. R. Agric. Soc.* X. 436 The Cotswold is a large breed of sheep, and is the stock from which the class called new Oxford is sprung.] **1859** *Ibid.* XX. 345 Amongst the 'other short-woolled sheep' exhibited, we have Hampshire Downs, *Oxfordshire Downs, [etc.]. *Ibid.*, The *Oxford Downs date from the year 1833..when a neat, well-made Cotswold ram was used with Hampshire ewes. **1912** R. LYDEKKER *Sheep* v. 106 The formation of the Oxford down was commenced about the year 1833. **1970** *Observer* (Colour Suppl.) 26 Apr. 36/1 All six Down breeds..are shortwools, Oxford Down..being heaviest... Bold-looking sheep with top-knot of wool above dark face. **1926** D. H. LAWRENCE *Plumed Serp.* ii. 31 An odd, detached, yet cocky little man, a true little Indian, speaking *Oxford English in a rapid, low, musical voice. **1932** *S.P.E. Tract* XXXVII. (*title*) 'Oxford' English. **1952** M. STEEN *Phoenix Rising* iv. 72 Americans come over and proceed to acquire what they think is Oxford English. **1969** 'H. PENTECOST' *Girl Watcher's Funeral* (1970) II. ii. 100 It was Oxford English with a slight accent which I took to be French. **1975** *ITV Evidence to Annan Committee* 15 In the spoken word the traditional currency was, till recently, Oxford English. **1874** MICKLETHWAITE *Mod. Par. Churches* 322 The barbarism, called an *Oxford frame. **1939** 'N. SHUTE' *What happened to Corbetts* iii. 88 He laid her on the ornate, gilded iron bed beneath a picture of the 'Stag at Bay' and a text in a wood Oxford frame that told them 'God is love'. **1973** J. THOMSON *Death Cap* xiii. 177 The pictures on the walls were..pre-Raphaelite prints in Oxford frames. **1836** W. F. TOLMIE *Diary* 28 Oct. in *Jrnls.* (1963) 322, 1 pr Extra S. fine dark *Oxford grey trousers. **1864** J. S. LE FANU *Uncle Silas* II. xii. 191 An old Oxford gray surtout that showed his lank length to advantage. **1903–4** Oxford grey [see DONEGAL]. **1964** S. BELLOW *Herzog* 237 A stylish oxford gray summer suit. **1973** R. HAYES *Hungarian Game* xxxix. 235 Urkowitz' face was turning a shade of fine Oxford gray. **1956** H. WILLIAMSON *Methods Bk. Design* xix. 308 Another method is to fix on the spine of the section a tube of paper, or *Oxford hollow, and to fix the cover to this. **1960** G. A. GLAISTER *Gloss. Bk.* 289/1 Oxford hollow: a flattened paper tube which is attached to the back of a book..so that when the book is opened the back opens up independently of the spine... The O[xford] U[niversity] P[ress], who have supplied this note, state 'presumably the word Oxford was used to describe this kind of binding because undoubtedly the old Oxford bindery was the first to use it, particularly for leather-bound Bibles. It is properly applied only to a leather-bound book and is a style which is now used by most leather binders.' **1965** L. S. DARLEY *Introd. Bookbinding* 30 Another way of lining the spine, after the mull has been glued in place, is by making a tubular hollow—sometimes called an Oxford hollow—a device which provides a lining for the spine, a hollow for the cover and an additional point of union between the book and its case. **1892** *Encycl. Pract. Cookery* II. 68/2 *Oxford John. **1952** F. WHITE *Good Eng. Food* II. iv. 136 *Oxford John.* Take a well hung leg of mutton [etc.]. **1590** NASHE *Pasquil's Apol.* I. Biij, You that are *Oxford men, enquire whether Walpoole were not a Puritane? **1890** GLADSTONE *Sp. at Oxford Union* 5 Feb., To call a man a characteristically Oxford man is, in my opinion, to give him the highest compliment that can be paid to any human being. **1907** *Yesterday's Shopping* (1969) 24 *Marmalade*..*Oxford (Frank Cooper's). **1942** C. MORLEY *Thorofare* lxx. 459 There was Cooper's bitter Oxford marmalade—the only Oxonian product to which Uncle Dan would grant supremacy. **1962** *Sunday Express* 25 Feb. 6/3 Wyatt's thick-cut Oxford marmalade voice. **1973** 'S. HARVESTER' *Corner of Playground* I. viii. 74 A new jar of Oxford lime marmalade. **1837** DICKENS *Pickw.* xli, His legs ..graced a pair of *Oxford-mixture trousers, made to show the full symmetry of those limbs. **1868** HOLME LEE *B. Godfrey* iii. 18 He wore a long Oxford mixture coat. **1841** J. RATHBORNE (*title*) Are the Puseyites sincere? A letter most respectfully addressed to a right reverend catholic lord bishop on The *Oxford Movement. **1864** J. H. NEWMAN *Apol.* iv. 107 But there was another reason still,..which severed Mr. Rose from the Oxford Movement. *a* **1890** R. F. LITTLEDALE in *Chambers's Encycl.* (1901) IV. 359/2 The factor variously known as the Oxford or Tractarian movement, or by its advocates as the 'Catholic Revival'. **1891** CHURCH *Oxford Movement* 1 What is called the Oxford or Tractarian movement began..in a vigorous effort for the immediate defence of the Church against serious dangers, arising from the violent and threatening temper of the days of the Reform Bill. **1854** *Oxford ochre [see OCHRE *sb.* 1]. **1875** *Ure's Dict. Arts* (ed. 7) III. 430 A section of the ochre-pits at Shotover Hill, near Oxford, where the Oxford ochre is obtained. **1838** *Penny Cycl.* XI. 138 Oolitic System..5 Portland oolite. 6. *Oxford oolite. 7. Bath oolite. **1856** HAWTHORNE *Jrnl.* 31 Aug. in *Passages from Eng. Note-Bks.* (1870) II. 150 We looked also at the outside of the wall [of New College], and Mr. Parker..showed us a weed growing ..hanging plentifully downward from a shallow root. It is called the *Oxford plant, being found only here, and not easily, if at all, introduced any-where else. **1845** E. ACTON *Mod. Cookery* xxvi. 637 *Oxford punch... Lemons.. oranges..calf's foot jelly..white wine..French brandy.. Jamaica rum [etc.]. **1877** E. S. DALLAS *Kettner's Bk. of Table* 322 Oxford punch.—The great characteristic of this punch is its having a quantity of calf's foot jelly dissolved in it. **1892** *Encycl. Pract. Cookery* II. 69/1 Oxford punch. **1884** W. MILLER *Dict. Eng. Names Plants* 249/2 *Senecio...squalidus.* *Oxford Rag-wort. **1886** G. C. DRUCE *Flora Oxfordshire* 158 Oxford Ragwort... Very plentiful in and around Oxford, where it was first noticed by Sir Joseph Banks. Dillenius sent seeds to Linnæus but whether he gathered them from the Oxford Garden or the wall of the town no memorandum exists. **1926** *Nat. Hist. Oxford District* 72 A few brave adventitious plants may be seen on the walls, including the ubiquitous Oxford Ragwort. **1948** PRIME & DEACOCK *Shorter Brit. Flora* 149 Oxford Ragwort..; waste places, greatly on the increase. (This plant is very common on bombed sites in London.) **1969** *Nature* 27 Sept. 1303/2 Oxford ragwort (*Senecio squalidus*) spread throughout the railway system after seeds had been dispersed from the Botanic Garden to Oxford station. **1973** GILMOUR & WALTERS *Wild Flowers* (ed. 5) xiii. 198 The Oxford ragwort ..has achieved..an astonishing recent spread. **1764** (*title*) The *Oxford sausage. **1877** E. S. DALLAS *Kettner's Bk. of Table* 100 The Oxford sausage is a crêpinette, can be made at home. **1926** *Daily Colonist* (Victoria, B.C.) 5 Jan. 6/2 (Advt.), Fresh Made Oxford Sausage, 3 lbs. for 32 c. **1937** PARTRIDGE *Dict. Slang* 596/1 **Oxford Scholar*, five shillings (piece or sum): New Zealanders' rhyming s. on *dollar*: C. 20. Also from ca. 1870, in the S.W. of England. **1938** F. D. SHARPE *Sharpe of Flying Squad* 332 *Oxford Scholar*, dollar. **1960, 1965** Oxford scholar [see sense 2]. **1967** Oxford scholar [see CASER[2]]. **1926–7** *Army & Navy Stores Catal.* 717/1 *Oxford shirts—With stiff cuffs, soft turnover cuff or small wristband to link and button—each 12/9. **1959** *Listener* 4 June 982/1 The cloth cap and the collarless Oxford shirt. **1971** *New Yorker* 9 Oct. 29/2 (Advt.), Our own make long staple cotton oxford shirt. [**1907** *Yesterday's Shopping* (1969) 742/2 Fancy cotton shirting... Oxford mat, best quality.] **1926–7** *Army & Navy Stores Catal.* 697/2 *Oxford shirting (soft finish) 29 in. wide..1/1 Per yd. **1940** *Chambers's Techn. Dict.* 606/1 *Oxford shirting*, a plain-weave cotton fabric, generally striped, used for shirting. **1948** G. L. FRASER *Textiles by Britain* 165 *Oxford shirting*, plain or fancy woven striped shirting cloth. [**1721** AMHERST *Terræ Fil.* No. 46 (1754) 247, I have met them with bob-wigs and new shoes, Oxford-cut.] **1847** *New Monthly Mag.* LXXX. II. 457 High-lows (now called *Oxford shoes). **1870** MISS BRIDGMAN *Ro. Lynne* I. xiii. 213 Patent-leather Oxford shoes. [**1902** *Westm. Gaz.* 27 Aug. 8/1 The shoes would be low-cut, black calf, laced oxfords.] **1839** HOOK in Liddon, etc. *Life Pusey* II. 467 Let it be erected by contributors to the *Oxford Tracts and their friends—or by any other title by which you would prefer to have yourselves called. **1870** ALLIBONE *Dict. Eng. Lit.* 1709/1 Dr. Pusey had given great offence to some, and equal satisfaction to others, by his connection with the Oxford Tracts movement. **1925** *Punch* 4 Mar. 244 (*caption*) Perils of the Dance. The terror of the *Oxford trousers. **1937** J. LAVER *Taste & Fashion* xvii. 241 The advent of Oxford trousers in the middle twenties. **1942** FLOREY & JENNINGS in *Brit. Jrnl. Exper. Path.* XXIII. 122 For those using the dilution method it may be stated that the '*Oxford unit' is that amount of penicillin which when dissolved in 50 ml. of meat extract broth just inhibits completely the growth of the test strain of *Staphylococcus aureus*. **1948** WRIGHT & MONTAG *Textbk. Pharmacol. & Therap.* (ed. 4) xxxiii. 548 For the treatment of mild to moderately severe infections daily dosages of 80,000 to 120,000 Oxford units are sufficient. **1952** W. T. SALTER *Textbk. Pharmacol.* xlix. 1084/1 The new international unit and the old Oxford unit are very close. **1920** A. HUXLEY *Limbo* 85 When the Military Representative spoke, he could hear again that wretched Nut's rendering of the Eton and *Oxford voice. **1924** E. M. FORSTER *Passage to India* xxiv. 221 'We object to the presence of so many European ladies and gentlemen upon the platform,' he said in an Oxford voice. **1931** *Atlantic Monthly* Feb. 149/1 The pronunciation of the common people left its impress indelibly on the so-called best people, with a few languid drawls, terminal *aws*, clipped *gs* and feeble *hs* thrown in.., which..acquired the name of the Oxford voice. **1834** W. BAXTER *Brit. Phænogamous Bot.* I. 23 This very pretty plant is a native of Italy, and is said to have been originally introduced into England by means of its seeds having been brought in some marble sculptures from that country to Oxford, where it has long established itself on the walls of the Colleges, gardens, &c. in such abundance as to have obtained the name of '*Oxford-weed.'. **1976** C. OMAN *Oxford Childhood* vii. 133 Mrs Pember was a qualified botanist and I was soon flattered by being sent up to the top of a crumbling wall..to get her specimens of Oxford Weed.

b. Used *attrib.* or as *adj.* to denote the characteristic manner, speech, behaviour, etc., of a present or former member of the University of Oxford; freq. = *Oxford accent*.

1877 H. JAMES *Let.* 28 Feb. in R. B. Perry *Tht. & Char. W. James* (1935) I. 375, I lunched the other day with Andrew Lang to meet J. Addington Symonds,—a mild, cultured man, with the Oxford perfume. **1897** G. B. SHAW *Our Theatres in Nineties* (1932) III. 108 Stage smart speech, which, like the got-up Oxford mince and drawl of a foolish curate, is the mark of a snob. **1909** P. GIBBS *Street of Adventure* iii. 37 'Because I tell you so,' said Luttrell, with a touch of his Oxford manner. **1913** A. LUNN *Harrovians* ii. 27 Mr. Lee had neither a double chin nor an Oxford manner. **1919** J. B. MORTON *Barber of Putney* ii. 24 Up and down one heard the Oxford drawl. **1922** JOYCE *Ulysses* 6 He thinks you're not a gentleman... Because he comes from Oxford. You know, Dedalus, you have the real Oxford manner. *Ibid.* 431 In youth's smart blue Oxford suit with white vestslips. **1926** A. S. L. FARQUHARSON in J. C. Wilson *Statement & Inference* I. p. xxv, 'The trouble is that one feels life is so short, *ars longa* but philosophy seems very much longer.' This is the scholar's last lesson, the clue perhaps to what is sometimes called Oxford irony. **1928** D. H. LAWRENCE *Woman who rode Away* 152 But, in a voice more expostulatingly Oxford than ever, he said [etc.]. *Ibid.* 153 Jimmy got up, with a bit of an Oxford wriggle, and held out his hand. **1934** *Spectator* 5 Jan. 18/2 Surely it is permissible to suggest..the Oxford Bleat by writing down the directions given me the other day as 'past a whaite house, between the water-tah and the pah station'. **1937** *N. & Q.* 12 June 428/1 What we term Oxford pronunciation, and wrongly so call it. **1938** F. D. SHARPE *Sharpe of Flying Squad* xvii. 189 A gentleman with an Oxford drawl..in darkest Hoxton. **1957** G. AVERY *Warden's Niece* viii. 153 A young man..clumsily trying to propel his punt from the stern instead of the conventional Oxford position in front. **1958** B. NICHOLS *Sweet & Twenties* v. 74 If the worst came to the worst I could 'rely on the Oxford manner'. **1960** W. B. GALLIE *New University* vi. 115 They were delighted by the fact that he so often appeared to be joking—for so they described Lindsay's elaborate Oxford irony.

2. *ellipt.* for Oxford English Dictionary, Oxford grey, marmalade, mixture, scholar, shirt, shoe, trousers, etc.

c **1890** in *Amer. Mail Order Fashions* (1961) 28/2 Women's tan Dongola Kid, square or pointed toe, fox heel Oxfords. French stay. **1890** *Illustr. London News* 24 May in L. de Vries *Victorian Advts.* (1968) 51/3 New Range of Coloured

Oxfords, Cambrics, and Calcuttas for Shirts and Pyjamas. **1902** FARMER & HENLEY *Slang* V. 119/1 *Oxford*, a crown piece. **1903** in S. Nowell-Smith *Edwardian England* (1964) facing p. 180 (Advt.), The 'Oxford'. Blacking leather or glacé kid. **1914** *Glasgow Herald* 7 Sept. 10/2 Glasgow firms manufacture..zephyrs, Oxfords, shirtings, and dress goods. **1926** *Daily Colonist* (Victoria, B.C.) 21 July 16/4 (Advt.), A 4-ply worsted wool in shades of pink... Oxford. **1929** G. MITCHELL *Mystery of Butcher's Shop* xi. 120 He fell down, and tore chunks out of his Oxfords on the brambles. **1932** *New Yorker* 11 June 45 Waterproof leather oxfords or ghillies..; suede oxfords at Brooks and Rogers Peet.. Golf oxfords at Spalding [etc.]. **1945** M. D. POTTER *Fiber to Fabric* viii. 155 *Oxford*, a plain weave of medium and heavy weights. **1950** W. STEVENS *Let.* 21 Nov. (1967) 699, I look it up either at the office, where we have a Webster, or have someone look it up for me in the State library, where there is an Oxford. **1957** V. NABOKOV *Pnin* i. 8 His conservative black oxfords had cost him about as much as all the rest of his clothing. **1958** [see *beetle-crushers* s.v. BEETLE *sb.*[2] 5]. **1960** 'A. BURGESS' *Doctor is Sick* 103 'We'll say a quid deposit, returnable on return of the hat, and a straight charge of an Oxford for the loan. Right?' 'Right.' The young man handed over his Oxford scholar. **1962** L. DEIGHTON *Ipcress File* i. 13 He rocked on his hand-lasted Oxfords. **1964** J. SYMONS *End of Solomon Grundy* I. ii. 29 The routine of breakfast..Cooper's Oxford, the electric percolator. **1965** *Australasian Post* 4 Mar. 46 From 'dollar' we have the rhyming slang 'Oxford scholar', which eventually became shortened to an 'Oxford'. **1970** *Catal. L. L. Bean* (Freeport, Maine) Fall 32 Heavy duty nylon oxford outside is waterproof. **1971** D. E. WESTLAKE *I gave at the Office* (1972) 139 Dressed in..new clothes—down to expensive black oxfords. **1972** 'I. DRUMMOND' *Frog in Moonflower* 10 The Master..spread a piece of toast with Cooper's Oxford. **1976** *New Yorker* 26 Jan. 52/3 It is like seeing a pair of oxfords suspended from an ornate chandelier. **1978** *Spectator* (New Canaan High School, Connecticut) 66 Then I..pulled out four shirts: a turtleneck, a Lacoste 'alligator' shirt, a flannel shirt, and a wrinkled, white button-down Oxford.

b. The University of Oxford; *collect.*, the members of the University; quasi-adj., belonging to or supporting the University. With specific adj., any of various school examinations conducted under the auspices of the University.

a **1697** AUBREY *Wiltshire: Topogr. Coll.* (1862) 17 At Oxford, (and I believe at Cambridge) the rod was frequently used by the Tutors and Deans. **1886** H. BAUMANN *Londinismen* 129/2 Are you Oxford or Cambridge? **1899** BEERBOHM *More* 155, I was a modest, good-humoured boy. It is Oxford that has made me insufferable. **1916** W. OWEN *Let.* Apr. (1967) 389, I hear you are applying yourself to some solid study for the J[unior] Oxford. **1930** *Times Lit. Suppl.* 25 Dec. 1103/1 There is encouraging evidence elsewhere that young Oxford is beginning to recognize that mere cleverness is poetically sterile. **1966** *Rep. Comm. Inquiry Univ. Oxford* I. 17 Members of Oxford.

Ox'fordian, *a.* [f. prec. + -IAN.] **1.** *Geol.* Of, pertaining to, or designating a division of the Upper Jurassic in Britain lying below the Kimeridgian and above the Callovian (in continental Europe restricted to the lower part of this division). Also *absol.*, the Oxfordian stage or period. [In this sense ad. F. *oxfordien* (J. Thurmann 1830, in *Mém. de la Soc. d'Hist. nat. de Strasbourg* I. 22).]

1849 *Q. Jrnl. Geol. Soc.* V. 179 The clear definition of an equivalent of the Oxfordian group..had not been defined in the Southern Alps until M. von Buch demonstrated to the Italian geologists..that their 'Ammonitico rosso' was of Oxfordian age. *Ibid.* 182 The overlying stage..is therefore a good representative of the Oxfordian of the Alps. **1885** ETHERIDGE *Stratigraph. Geol.* 441 The Middle Jurassic rocks comprise two complete and distinct groups—1. The Oxfordian; 2. The Corallian. 1. Oxfordian—divisible into two sections, *a* and *b*, the Kellaways Rock and the Oxford Clay. **1885, 1946** [see CALLOVIAN *a.*]. **1967** D. H. RAYNER *Stratigr. Brit. Isles* ix. 275 The base of the Upper Jurassic is sometimes taken at the base of the Oxfordian stage. **1975** A. HALLAM *Jurassic Environments* ii. 16 The problem of correlation becomes much more serious from Upper Oxfordian times onwards. *Ibid.*, The increased difficulty of correlating the Upper Oxfordian is a consequence of northwards retreat of the boreal cardioceratid faunas which had ranged widely into southern Europe during the Lower Oxfordian.

2. [f. the title of Edward de Vere, Earl of *Oxford* (1550–1604) + -IAN.] Used with reference to the theory that the Earl of Oxford wrote the plays attributed to Shakespeare. Also as *sb.*

1930 P. ALLEN *Case for Edward de Vere* 20 These poems of Chapman..are, in my judgment, enough..to prove the Oxfordian authorship of 'Shakespeare'. **1930** *Times Lit. Suppl.* 11 Sept. 712/2 Oxfordians seem to start from the basic assumption that the association of the work of Shakespeare with the Stratford player needs explanation. **1932** *Ibid.* 23 June 462/4 For the ordinary reader, and especially for the reader unfamiliar with the Oxfordian theory, Mr. Allen's book is not wholly satisfactory. **1958** *Listener* 17 July 100/3 Baconians, Oxfordians, Rutlandians, Derbyites. **1970** S. SCHOENBAUM *Shakespeare's Lives* VI. ix. 609 Freud read the Looney book. It converted him to the Oxfordian faith. *Ibid.* 610 The contempt felt by reputable scholars for the Oxfordians.

Oxfordish ('ɒksfədɪʃ), *sb.* and *a.* [f. OXFORD + -ISH[1].] **A.** *sb.* Oxford jargon or slang. **B.** *adj.* Of, pertaining to, or suggestive of the University of Oxford.

1863 C. READE *Hard Cash* I. 16 Ploughed is the new Oxfordish for plucked. **1921** R. MACAULAY *Dangerous Ages* iv. 74 A pleasant, Oxfordish room, with the brown paper and plain green curtains of..college days. **1931** W. HOLTBY *Poor Caroline* v. 196 'Ah, a very opportune arrival, sergeant,' he began in his formal Oxfordish voice. **1962** J. D. SALINGER *Franny & Zooey* 127, I can never bring myself to smile back at him when he's being charming and Oxfordish. He's on lend-*lease* or something from Oxford.

Oxfordism ('ɒksfədɪz(ə)m). [f. OXFORD + -ISM.]

1. An Oxford habit or trait; the characteristics, habits, or peculiarities of Oxford scholars.

1830 CARLYLE *Misc., Richter* (1857) IV. 138 *note*, Burschenism is not without its meaning more than Oxfordism or Cambridgeism. **1895** *Daily News* 9 Jan. 6/3 The word 'festive' is good English, but to work the word very hard was, at one time an 'Oxfordism'.

†**2.** *Ch. Hist.* The principles and practices of the Oxford Movement (see OXFORD). *Obs.*

1847 G. B. CHEEVER *Wand. Pilgr.* xxv. 165 It was heart cheering to hear a Bishop of the Church of England, in the midst of the prevalence of Oxfordism..take these simple themes. **1849** O. BROWNSON *Wks.* VII. 145 He might, perhaps, write a passable essay or article for a magazine in favour of Oxfordism.

So †'**Oxfordist** *Ch. Hist.*, an adherent of the Oxford Movement. *Obs.*

1836 ARNOLD in Stanley *Life & Corr.* (1844) II. viii. 67 This the Romanists and the Oxfordists say is a view required to modify and add to that of the Scripture.

'**Oxfordy**, *a.* [f. OXFORD + -Y[1].] Oxfordish, Oxonian.

1924 D. H. LAWRENCE in *Criterion* Oct. 27 It was his manner, his rather Oxfordy manner, more than anything else, that went beyond her. **1927** in *Lett. Gertrude Bell* I. i. 12 My sister..begged me to send Gertrude to stay with them for the winter..opining that frequenting foreign diplomatic Society might be a help for Gertrude 'to get rid of her Oxfordy manner'. *a* **1935** T. E. LAWRENCE *Mint* (1955) II. iii. 108 The rough end of the hut tries to copy the accent he displays when he reads our nominal roll. It's an Oxfordy drawl. **1959** *Encounter* Aug. 74/1 This deliciously fat Oxfordy volume.

ox-gall: see OX 6.

oxgang ('ɒksgæŋ). *Obs.* exc. *Hist.* *Chiefly* northern. Also 7–8 *dial.* **osken, -in**; **ox-going**. [f. OX + GANG *sb.*[1] 3. In OE. two words with *oxan* gen. sing. or *oxena* gen. pl.]

1. The eighth part of the CARUCATE or plough-land varying from 10 to 18 acres, or more widely, according to the system of tillage, etc.; a bovate.

The carucate being the extent of land ploughed by one plough, with its team of eight oxen, an eighth of this was considered as the share of each ox of the team. Holders of less than a carucate united with their neighbours in the use of a co-operative plough, to the team of which each furnished as many oxen as he held oxgangs: see quot. 1425. (In quot. *c* 1375 strangely used to render L. *jugerum* JUGER.)

963 in Birch *Cartul. Sax.* (1887) III. 346 On hillum twegra oxena gang, and on Lundby twegra oxena gang. **972–92** *Ibid.* 370 An hide buton anes oxan gang. *c* **1375** *Sc. Leg. Saints* xvii. (*Martha*) 49 Of ane oxgange hale þe space [orig. *per spatium jugeris*], þat twa hundreth fet in lynth has And twenty, and in bred alsa Sewyne schore of fute and na ma. *c* **1425** WYNTOUN *Cron.* I. 400 Yhwmen, pewere Karl, or Knawe That wes of mycht an ox til hawe, He gert that man hawe part in pluche;..Swa than begowth, and eftyr lang Of land wes mesure, ane ox-gang. **14..** *Nominale* in Wr.-Wülcker 737/19 *Hec bovaga*, a noxgang. [*c* **1475** *Pict. Voc.* ibid. 796/7 *Hec bovata*, a hoxgangyn lond.] **1532** *Test. Ebor.* (Surtees) VI. 33 An oxgang of land and meadow. **1541** (18 July) *Acta Dom. Concilia et Sessiones* (Register Ho. Edin.) XVI. lf. 51 b, Because ilk Oxengang [SKENE (1609) oxengate] is estemyt ȝierly to twentie shillings in all dewities. **1610** W. FOLKINGHAM *Art of Survey* II. vii. 59 The Oxe-gang, or Oxengate..called *Bouata terrae* containes after the originall repute 13 acres. **1639** in *N. Riding Rec.* IV. 121 According to an auncient rate of 18[d] an oxgange of lande. **1703** THORESBY *Let. to Ray* (E.D.D.), An oxgang contains 10 acres in some places; in others sixteen, eighteen, twenty-four; and fifty in some parts of Bradford parish. **1788** W. MARSHALL *Yorksh.* Gloss. (E.D.S.), *Oskin*, an ox-gang. **1891** ATKINSON *Moorland Par.* 431 In the year 1272 there were fifty-six oxgangs or bovates in villanage in the township of Danby.

2. As a measure of length: ? a furlong.

1569 STOCKER tr. *Diod. Sic.* II. viii. 52 The Riuer of Tygre ..commonly aboue foure oxgangs broade.

†'**oxgate.** Chiefly *Sc. Obs.* Also 6–7 **oxengate**. [f. OX + GATE *sb.*[2], GAIT *sb.*[1]] A measure of land; the same as the OXGANG (for which this name appears to have been substituted after 1550).

1585 *Decree of Scotch Exchequer* in E. W. Robertson *Hist. Ess.* (1872) 136 Thirteen acres extendis and sall extend to ane oxgait of land, and four oxgait extendis and sall extend to ane pund land of auld extent. **15..** *Harl. MS.* 4628 The Lords fand that 13 aikers sall be ane oxengate of land. **1609** SKENE [see OXGANG, 1541]. **1628** COKE *On Litt.* 5 An oxgange or oxgate of land is as much as an ox can till. **1672** *Sc. Acts Chas. II* (1820) VIII. 147/1 The threttie two oxingaite of land of old extent..with the tower fortalice maner place.. walkemilnes and cornemilnes of the samyn milnelands.

ox-going, dial. synonym of OXGANG: see E.D.D.

'**ox,harrow**, *sb.* A large and powerful harrow used on clay lands; originally drawn by oxen.

1523 FITZHERB. *Husb.* §15 It is vsed in many countreys, the husbandes to haue an oxe harowe, the whiche is made of sixe smal peces of timbre, called harowe bulles. **1764** *Museum Rusticum* III. xxi. 89 A pair of ox-harrows, or the heaviest of all, in many counties called drags. **1766** *Ibid.* VI. 373 Were I to have two ox-harrows,..I should be obliged to have a much stronger team than four stout horses. **1813** A. YOUNG *Agric. Essex* I. 147 Very large and powerful harrows for their strong land, which they call ox harrows.

Hence **ox-harrow** *v. trans.*, to harrow with an ox-harrow.

1778 [W. MARSHALL] *Minutes Agric.* 15 Aug. 1775 Ox-harrowed A. 2 [a certain field], and gathered it up into five-'bout lands.

†**ox'haverite.** *Min. Obs.* Also (more correctly) **oxahverite**. [Named 1827 from *Oxa-* or *Uxa-hver* in Reykjadal, Iceland.] A pale green variety of Apophyllite, found in small green crystals on silicified wood.

1827 BREWSTER in *Edin. Phil. Jrnl.* VII. 115 Oxhaverite. **1829** *Nat. Philos.* I. *Polaris. Light* ix. 36 (U.K.S.) Some years afterwards he discovered the remarkable mineral of oxhaverite. **1837** DANA *Min.* 276 Oxahverite. **1868** *Ibid.* 416 Oxhaverite. **1896** CHESTER *Dict. Names Min.*, Oxhaverite.. an obs. syn. of apophyllite.

ox-head ('ɒkshɛd). [f. OX + HEAD.]

1. The head of an ox, or a representation of one.

In quot. 1595 with allusion to HORNING *vbl. sb.* 3.

1595 SHAKS. *John* II. i. 292, I would set an Oxe-head to your Lyons hide. **1703** MAUNDRELL *Journ. Jerus.* (1721) 12 The Chests were carved on the outside with Ox-heads.

2. *transf.* A stupid person; a dolt, blockhead; also *attrib.* or quasi-*adj.* stupid.

a **1634** MARSTON (W. 1864) Dost make a mummer of me, ox-head? **1806** FESSENDEN *Democr.* I. 93 Could equal ox-head celebration In honor of the frantic nation.

3. *dial.* = HOGSHEAD.

1886 ELWORTHY *W. Somerset Word-bk.* s.v., Plase, sir, I be come arter th' empty oxhead.

'**oxherd.** [f. OX (in OE. in gen. sing. *oxan* or gen. pl. *oxena*) + HERD *sb.*[2]] A keeper of oxen; a cowherd.

c **1000** ÆLFRIC *Colloq.* in Wr.-Wülcker 90/9 *Bubulci*, oxan-hyrdas. *Ibid.* 91/12 *O Bubulce*, eala oxanhyrde. *a* **1100** *Ags. Voc.* ibid. 274/28 *Aubobulcus*, oxnahyrde. **1398** TREVISA *Barth. De P.R.* XVIII. xiv. (MS. Bodl.) lf. 255 b/2 An oxe heerde hette Bubulcus, and is iordeyned bi office to kepe oxen. *c* **1425** *Voc.* in Wr.-Wülcker 669/5 *Hic bubulcus*, oxarde. **1875** JOWETT *Plato* (ed. 2) I. 329 The art of the oxherd is the art of attending to oxen.

'**ox-hide**, '**oxhide.** The skin of an ox.

c **1470** HENRYSON *Mor. Fab.* x. (*Fox & Wolf*) xiii, The wolf will not forgif the ane ox hide. **1497** *Naval Acc. Hen. VII* (1896) 229 An Oxe hyde all Redie coryed & Tanned. **1640–1** *Kirkcudbr. War-Comm. Min. Bk.* (1855) 148 That the best ox hyde be sold for viij merks, and inferior sorts of oxen hydes for v libs., vij merks. **1887** BOWEN *Virg. Æneid* I. 367 They..Bought such measure of land as an oxhide measures.

attrib. **1848** BUCKLEY *Iliad* 67 He drew together the notch of the arrow and the ox-hide string.

¶ *erroneously.* 'A measure of land, as much as could be encircled by a hide cut into narrow strips' (Simmonds *Dict. Trade* 1858: so in mod. Dicts.).

(An error arising from confusion of HIDE *sb.*[1] with HIDE[2].)

ox-horn ('ɒkshɔːn). [f. OX + HORN.]

1. A horn of an ox. (Sometimes used as a drinking-vessel.)

[*c* **1000** ÆLFRIC *Saints' Lives* xxxi. 776 Com se deofol.. and hæfde ænne oxan horn on hande.] **1601** HOLLAND *Pliny* I. 402 In the deep sea they light on certain little trees branched and full of boughes, in colour of an Ox horne. **1626** BACON *Sylva* §549 Hartshorn is of a fat and clammy substance, and it may be, Ox-horn would do the like [yield mushrooms]. **1868** BLACKMORE *Lorna D.* xxii, He took the large ox-horn of our quarantine-apple cider.

2. A name of the Black Olive or Olive-bark (*Bucida Buceras*) of Jamaica, the wood of which is not liable to the attacks of insects.

1866 *Treas. Bot.* 831/1.

3. *ox-horn cockle*, a bivalve mollusc, the heart-cockle, *Isocardia cor.*

oxhouse ('ɒkshaʊs). Now *local.* A house for the sheltering or stabling of oxen: cf. *cow-house*.

14.. *Nom.* in Wr.-Wülcker 727/2 *Hoc bostare*, a nox-hows. **1523** FITZHERB. *Surv.* 35 b, Two barnes and an oxe house, a hey house and a stable. **1533** *Test. Ebor.* (Surtees) VI. 39 All the haie that is in the oxhouse lathe. **1577** B. GOOGE *Heresbach's Husb.* 12 An entrie..to the Oxhouses. **1876** *Whitby Gloss.*, *Owce-house*, the stable for the oxen.

†**oxi.** *Obs.* Abbreviation of OXYGON.

1703 MOXON *Mech. Exerc.* 269 Fig. 3. is described by the *Oxi* in this manner. *Ibid.* 279 The Streight Arch may be described (as its vulgarly said) from the *Oxi*, which being but part of a Word, is taken from the word *Oxigonium*, signifying a..Triangle, with three sharp Angles. **1725** W. HALFPENNY *Sound Building* 8 A Gothick Arch, or Oxi.

oxi, obs. ME. inf. of ASK *v.*

oxi-, earlier spelling of many words, chiefly chemical, now spelt OXY-.

oxic ('ɒksɪk), *a.* [f. OX(IDE *sb.*, OX(YGEN + -IC.]

1. *Soil Science.* Applied to a subsurface mineral soil horizon more than 30 cm. thick that is characterized by the virtual absence of any weatherable materials and the presence of hydrated oxides of iron and aluminium, highly insoluble minerals such as quartz, and clays of the type in which single sheets of silica tetrahedra alternate with single sheets of alumina octahedra. Cf. OXISOL.

1960 *Soil Classification: 7th Approximation* (U.S. Dept. Agric.) v. 53/1 The concept of the oxic horizon presented here is very tentative, as it has had little testing... The oxic horizon is one from which weathering has..removed or altered a large part of the silica that is combined with iron and aluminium, but not necessarily the quartz or 1:1 lattice clays. **1970** P. M. AHN *W. African Soils* (1974) vii. 221 The boundaries of the oxic horizon are usually gradual and diffuse, and the horizon shows no rock structure or very little. **1972** FOTH & TURK *Fund. Soil Sci.* (ed. 5) x. 262 All soils with oxic horizons belong to the Oxisol order. **1976** D. STEILA *Geogr. Soils* xi. 151 It is believed that the most extensive areal development of the oxic horizon may have taken place under paleo-climates of much higher rainfal.

2. [Back-formation from ANOXIC *a.*] Involving, characterized by, or related to the presence of oxygen.

1970 *Acta Radiologica: Therapy, Physics, Biol.* IX. 257 The investigations..were conducted with the aim of comparing the reactions of different cell lines to oxic and anoxic roentgen radiation. **1972** *Radiation Bot.* XII. 151 The damage produced by anoxic irradiation can be enhanced by O_2, after irradiation, to give oxic damage. **1975** *Nature* 26 June 740/2 We have measured in oxic and anoxic cells the yield of strand breakage on bacteriophage λ DNA-superinfecting lysogenic bacteria. **1975** *Ibid.* 4 Dec. 415/1 It is formed from phytol thermocatalytically in oxic conditions.

Hence **o'xicity**, oxic condition.

1978 *Nature* 16 Mar. 216/2 The available data suggest that the oxicity/anoxicity of the sediment and the water column affects the amount and nature of the organic matter incorporated into the sediment during deposition.

oxidability (ˌɒksɪdə'bɪlɪtɪ). Also **oxy-**. [f. next: see -ITY.] The quality of being oxidable; oxidizability.

1803 CHENEVIX in *Phil. Trans.* XCIII. 297 All those of easier oxidability than mercury. **1866** R. M. FERGUSON *Electr.* (1870) 122 The greater the disparity in oxidability.. the greater is its power.

oxidable ('ɒksɪdəb(ə)l), *a. Chem.* Now *rare.* Also **oxy-**. [a. F. *oxidable* (Lavoisier, 1789), now *oxydable*, f. *oxider* to OXIDATE: see -ABLE.] Capable of being oxidated; oxidizable.

1790 R. KERR tr. *Lavoisier's Elem. Chem.* II. 179 Table of compound oxydable and acidifiable bases. **1796** PEARSON in *Phil. Trans.* LXXXVI. 435 Perhaps also the tin was added to render the copper less readily oxidable. **1866** R. M. FERGUSON *Electr.* (1870) 122 Silver being less oxidable than copper.

oxidant ('ɒksɪdənt). [a. F. *oxidant* (1806 in Hatz.-Darm., now *oxydant*), ppl. adj. from *oxider* to OXIDATE.] An oxidating agent; a substance that readily gives off oxygen; = OXIDIZER 1.

1884 *Health Exhib. Catal.* 62/2 Antiseptics, disinfectants, oxidants, and air-purifiers. **1930** M. STEPHENSON *Bacterial Metabolism* iii. 49 The position of a system..is determined by the Eh when [the concentration of] oxidant equals [that of] reductant. **1950** *Engineering* 29 Dec. 575/3 Fuels can be burned..with fluorine when no oxygen is present at all—although a fluorine compound would still be known as the 'oxidant'. **1961** *New Scientist* 12 Oct. 110/1 Oxidants may include oxygen, air, chlorine,..and so on, and many combinations of fuels and oxidants are possible for fuel cell development. **1972** *Daily Tel.* 27 Nov. 3/2 Engineers pumped more than a million gallons of fuel and oxidant in the fuel tanks in a count-down rehearsal.

oxidase ('ɒksɪdeɪz, -s). *Biochem.* Also †OXYDASE. [ad. F. *oxydase* (G. Bertrand 1896, in *Compt. Rend.* CXXII. 1217), f. *oxyde* OXIDE *sb.*: see -ASE.] Orig., any enzyme which brings about oxidation (now called an OXIDOREDUCTASE); now used only of such enzymes that react with molecular oxygen, esp. those that catalyse the transfer of hydrogen from a substrate to oxygen so as to form water or hydrogen peroxide (cf. OXYGENASE).

1896 *Chem. News* 19 June 293/2 (*heading*) A new oxidase, or oxidising soluble ferment of vegetable origin. **1935** *Times Lit. Suppl.* 28 Feb. 127 Xanthine oxidase is unable to attack nucleosides. **1946** P. H. MITCHELL *Textbk. Biochem.* xii. 340 Cytochrome Oxidase.—This enzyme specifically catalyzes the oxidation of cytochromes by molecular oxygen. **1956** *Sci. News* XL. 43 When fresh or withered [tea] leaf is damaged it absorbs oxygen from the air with the aid of an enzyme, an oxidase, occurring in the leaf cells. **1964** *Rep. Internat. Union Biochem. Comm. on Enzymes* in Florkin & Stotz *Comprehensive Biochem.* XIII. vi. 33 All enzymes catalysing oxido-reductions will be named 'oxidoreductases' in the systematic nomenclature... [In the trivial nomenclature] the terms 'dehydrogenase' or 'reductase' will be used much as hitherto... 'Oxidase' will be used only for cases where O_2 acts as an acceptor, and 'oxygenase' only for those cases where the O_2 molecule is directly incorporated into the substrate. **1970** R. W. MCGILVERY *Biochem.* xvii. 407 Aromatic rings may be opened by oxidations utilizing a complete molecule of oxygen. Examples:..the oxidation of hydroxyanthranilate by hydroxyanthranilate oxidase.

oxidate ('ɒksɪdeɪt), *v. Chem.* Now *rare.* Also **oxy-**. [f. F. *oxid-er* (G. de Morveau and Lavoisier 1787; *oxyder* in *Dict. Acad.* 1835) + -ATE[3].]

1. *trans.* To cause to unite with oxygen; to convert into an oxide; = OXIDIZE 1.

1790 R. KERR tr. *Lavoisier's Elem. Chem.* II. §14. 221 Iron and zinc..decompose the water, and become oxydated at its expence. **1822** IMISON *Sc. & Art* I. 386 The oxygen unites with, and oxydates the wire. **1866–77** WATTS *Dict. Chem.* IV. 302 It [ozone] oxidates black sulphide of lead into white sulphate of lead. **1882** *Nature* XXVI. 252/2 Make the red lead to be hydrogenated much smaller in amount than that to be oxidated.

2. *intr.* To unite with oxygen; to become converted into an oxide; = OXIDIZE 2.

1807 DAVY in *Phil. Trans.* XCVIII. 44 The basis of potash ..oxidates in carbonic acid and decomposes it. **1825** J. NICHOLSON *Operat. Mechanic* 352 The roleaus of wire,.. being still red, would oxydate quite as much as if they had been heated in the midst of the flames without the least precaution. **1879** G. PRESCOTT *Sp. Telephone* 115 The harder metals which do not oxidate readily, being preferred.

Hence **'oxidated** *ppl. a.* (in quot. 1855 *humorously* for 'rusty'); **'oxidating** *vbl. sb.* and *ppl. a.*

1791 HAMILTON tr. *Berthollet's Dyeing* I. 27 *note*, The oxydated (calcined) part of the surface of the tin. **1793** BEDDOES *Calculus* 236 It is to this oxygene..that the effect produced by oxidated mercury is owing. **1800** *Med. Jrnl.* IV. 121 The oxydating wire, namely, from the zinc side, was the lowest in the tube. **1855** O. W. HOLMES *Poems* 198 Where conversation runs Through mouldy toasts to oxydated puns. *c* **1865** WYLDE in *Circ. Sc.* I. 396/2 The use of the oxidating flame may..be tried on metals.

oxidation (ɒksɪ'deɪʃən). *Chem.* Also **oxy-**. [a. F. *oxidation* (G. de Morveau and Lavoisier, 1787; *oxydation* in *Dict. Acad.* 1835), n. of action from *oxider*: see prec.] **1. a.** The action or process of oxidating; combination with oxygen; conversion into an oxide or oxygen-compound. Also, the removal of hydrogen from a compound.

1791 HAMILTON *Berthollet's Dyeing* I. I. I. i. 10 The regular succession of colours in iron, according to its degree of oxydation (calcination). **1816** J. SMITH *Panorama Sc. & Art* II. 301 Oxidation, or oxygenation, or oxidizement, the combination of any other body with oxygen. **1862** DANA *Man. Geol.* §52. 51 The processes of oxydation and deoxydation..give a degree of activity even to the world of rocks. **1866** [see DEHYDROGENATION]. **1871** ROSCOE *Elem. Chem.* 13 In this act of combination, which is termed oxidation, heat is always, and light is frequently given off. **1885** GOODALE *Physiol. Bot.* (1892) 355 The reception of oxygen, the oxidation of the oxidizable matter..etc...are collectively called respiration. **1900** *Jrnl. Chem. Soc.* LXXVIII. I. 301 (*heading*) Oxidation of the nature of dehydrogenation by means of ferricyanides. **1959** CRAM & HAMMOND *Org. Chem.* vi. 73 In organic chemistry, oxidation involves the removal of hydrogen and (or) the addition of oxygen or some other hetero atom to a compound.

attrib. **1839** URE *Dict. Arts* 1162 [He] scrapes its entire surface clean and free from oxidation-scale or fire-strain.

b. In extended use: the partial or complete removal of an electron from an atom or molecule; an increase in the proportion of electronegative constituents in a molecule or compound.

1892 MORLEY & MUIR *Watts' Dict. Chem.* III. 657 The term *oxidation* has been widened until at present it is applied to all chemical changes which result in an addition of a negative radicle, simple or compound, to elements or compounds, or a decrease in the relative quantity of the positive radicle of a compound, whether this is or is not accompanied by substitution of a negative radicle..e.g. the following change: $4Fe + 3O_2 = 2Fe_2O_3$. **1907** WHITNEY & BROWN tr. *Le Blanc's Text-bk. Electro-Chem.* vii. 256 There must be, in every galvanic cell, an oxidation at one electrode and a reduction at the other. **1928** H. L. HIND tr. *Schoen's Probl. Fermentation* xiv. 167 There is a change from divalent iron to iron at a higher degree of oxidation. **1968** PASSMORE & ROBSON *Compan. Med. Stud.* I. viii. 5/2 It is also characteristic of biological oxidations that they are often linked together to form a chain along which the electrons flow.

2. Special combs.: **oxidation number**, the charge (expressed in units of the negative of the electron charge) which is assigned to an atom on the assumption that the bonding in the substance or radical in which it exists is completely ionic; the average formal charge so assigned to atoms of a particular element in a compound or radical; **oxidation potential**, the electrode potential required to bring about a particular oxidation reaction at the electrode; **oxidation-reduction** = REDOX; freq. *attrib.*; **oxidation state**, oxidation number; the state of having a particular oxidation number.

1948 *Jrnl. Chem. Educ.* XXV. 278/2 The O_2 molecule..is made up of two neutral atoms..; the oxidation number of the O atom is consequently zero. **1964** CRAM & HAMMOND *Org. Chem.* (ed. 2) vi. 98 The system described is similar to the inorganic system if effective oxidation numbers, ranging from -4 (in CH_4) to $+4$ (CCl_4 or CO_2), are assigned to *individual carbon atoms* within organic molecules. **1968** J. MARCH *Adv. Org. Chem.* xix. 853 Carbon in propane has an oxidation number of $-2{\cdot}67$ and in butane of $-2{\cdot}5$, though organic chemists seldom think of these two compounds as being in different oxidation states. **1900** *Jrnl. Chem. Soc.* LXXVIII. II. 642 An attempt was made to measure a number of oxidation potentials. **1942** C. E. K. MEES *Theory Photogr. Process* viii. 308 When a silver salt solution is added to a reducing solution, there is an adjustment of the oxidation potentials of each to a common value intermediate between the two. **1966** C. R. TOTTLE *Sci. Engin. Materials* x. 225 The readiness to ionize by losing electrons in the presence of an ionizing solvent is called the oxidation potential. **1909** *Chem. Abstr.* III. 2648 It is therefore unnecessary to assume..that the e.m.f. in an oxidation-reduction cell is due to H_2 or O_2 at definite pressure in the electrode. **1951** *New Biol.* XI. 29 The over-all reaction in photosynthesis is of a type, extremely important in living organisms, known as an oxidation-reduction, in which one compound becomes oxidized at the expense of another which is reduced. **1974** *Sci. Amer.* Dec. 65/2 Chemical processes of this kind, in which electrons are transferred from one molecule to another, are called oxidation-reduction reactions. **1975** *Jrnl. Biol. Chem.* CCL. 3929 The oxidation-reduction equilibrium of the γ chains of human fetal hemoglobin. **1942** SNEED & MAYNARD *Gen. Inorg. Chem.* vi. 120 In many cases an element in its oxide or chloride is not reduced to the free state [by hydrogen] but to a lower oxidation state. **1973** J. G. DICK *Analytical Chem.* ii. 15 The hydrogen atom is assigned an oxidation state of + 1, except in hydrides where the oxidation state is generally − 1.

oxidative ('ɒksɪdeɪtɪv), *a.* [f. as OXIDATE *v.* + -IVE.] Involving, pertaining to, or characterized by oxidation.

1878 FOSTER *Phys.* II. ii. §5. 286 The blood itself removed from the body has practically no oxidative power at all over substances which are undoubtedly oxidized in the body. **1898** *Allbutt's Syst. Med.* V. 398 Carbonic anhydride is only one of the several products of the oxidative metabolism. **1923** *Q. Jrnl. Med.* XVI. 145 (*heading*) The rate of oxidative recovery from exercise in man. **1935** C. F. & G. T. CORI in Harrow & Sherwin *Textbk. Biochem.* xx. 567 This so-called 'oxidative quotient' was found to be between 3 and 6 for all tissues examined. **1962** DARDENNE & KIRSTEN in A. Pirie *Lens Metabolism Rel. Cataract* 419 Oxidative deaminations are of greater importance for the degradation of amino acids. **1972** *Daily Colonist* (Victoria, B.C.) 13 Feb. 27/5 It may be that the human need for Vitamin E is increasing due to the oxidative atmosphere man is creating around the world.

Hence **'oxidatively** *adv.*, by an oxidative process.

1964 *Oceanogr. & Marine Biol.* II. 152 The reineckate ion is removed with silver nitrate, and interfering substances (basic amino acids) are oxidatively deaminated by boiling with silver oxide. **1972** COTTON & WILKINSON *Adv. Inorg. Chem.* (ed. 3) xxiv. 773 Molecules that contain multiple bonds may be added oxidatively without cleavage to form new complexes which have 3-membered rings. **1976** *Lancet* 11 Dec. 1312/2 *Pseudomonas* metabolises carbohydrates oxidatively.

oxidator ('ɒksɪdeɪtə(r)). Also **oxy-**. [Agent-n. from OXIDATE *v.*: see -OR 2 c.] **a.** Something that oxidates; an oxidizing agent. **b.** An apparatus for directing a stream of oxygen into the flame of a lamp.

a **1864** GESNER *Coal, Petrol.* etc. (1865) 167 It is supposed that hot air is a better oxidator than cold. *c* **1865** LETHEBY in *Circ. Sc.* I. 110/1 Common Lamp, with Oxydator.

oxide ('ɒksaɪd, 'ɒksɪd), *sb. Chem.* Also **oxid** (chiefly *U.S.*), **oxyde, oxyd.** [a. F. *oxide* (1787), now *oxyde*, f. *oxy-gène* + *-ide*, after the ending of *acide*: cf. Sp. *oxido*, Pg. *oxydo*, It. *ossido*.

Cf. 1787, G. de Morveau & Lavoisier *Nomencl. Chimique* 56 'Nous avons formé le mot *oxide*, qui d'une part rappelle la substance avec laquelle le métal est uni, qui d'autre part annonce suffisamment que cette combinaison de l'oxigène ne doit pas être confondue avec la combinaison acide, quoiqu'elle s'en rapproche à plusieurs égards.' This antithesis of *acide* and *oxide* was no doubt the reason why some early writers in Eng. used *oxid* (like *acid*), a spelling now favoured by American use. *Oxyde* and *oxyd* represent a feeling for closer written conformity to *oxygen*.]

a. A compound of oxygen with another element, or with an organic radical.

1790 R. KERR tr. *Lavoisier's Elem. Chem.* II. 187 Red oxyd of mercury..the oxyds of silver. **1793** BEDDOES *Calculus* 236 The oxid of mercury, in passing through the human body, parts with its Oxygene. **1795** PEARSON in *Phil. Trans.* LXXXV. 331 Wootz, from the surface of which oxide, and any other extraneous matter, had been carefully rubbed off. **1799** *Med. Jrnl.* I. 61 Substances, such as the oxydes of mercury, zinc, &c. **1800** HENRY *Epit. Chem.* (1808) 67 Every substance, capable of union with oxygen, affords, by combustion, either an oxide or an acid. **1864–72** WATTS *Dict. Chem.* II. 508 Simple ethers..are the oxides of the alcohol-radicles. **1878** A. H. GREEN *Coal* ii. 65 The red colour of the rocks..is caused by every grain being coated by a thin skin of ferric oxide. **1879** DANA *Man. Geol.* (ed. 3) 50 The oxyd of the metal calcium is common quicklime. **1890** *Cent. Dict.*, *Oxid, oxide.*

b. *attrib.* and *Comb.*, as ***oxide-coated*** adj., ***oxide coating***.

1933 J. H. MORECROFT *Electron Tubes* ii. 23 In making the modern oxide-coated filament the coating is applied in the form of a white carbonate. *Ibid.*, The amount of CO_2 released from the oxide coating of an ordinary rectifier tube .., when the carbonate is being reduced to the oxide, is sufficient to fill the bulb to about 10 mm Hg pressure. **1964** F. ROSEBURY *Handbk. Electron Tube & Vacuum Techniques* (1965) 95 Experimental tubes often do not require their oxide-coated cathodes to have exceptionally long life. **1966** *McGraw-Hill Encycl. Sci. & Technol.* XIV. 246/2 Oxide coatings commonly have a work function of the order of 1·1 ev.

So †**'oxide** *v.* [ad. F. *oxider* ('métaux oxidés', *Nomencl. Chim.* 1787), now *oxyder*] = OXIDIZE.

1798 *Nicholson's Jrnl.* Jan. 458 The iron does not form ink with the gallic acid, but in proportion as it is oxided. **1806** *Med. Jrnl.* XV. 274 Some of the mercury is, by the action of the air,..oxyded.

†**oxi'digerence.** *Obs. rare.* [f. as if from **oxidigerent*, f. OXIDE + L. *gerens, gerent-em*, bearing, carrying.] Surface oxidization, rusting.

1831 STEPHENSON in J. Holland *Manuf. Metal* I. 153 On no malleable iron railway has oxidegerence or rusting taken place to any important extent.

oxi'dimetry. [f. OXIDE + -METRY.] Measurement or estimation of the amount of oxide formed.

1896 *Invention* 25 Jan. 50/1 It represents a special branch of oxidimetry.

oxidizable ('ɒksɪdaɪzəb(ə)l), *a. Chem.* Also **oxy-**. [f. OXIDIZE *v.* + -ABLE.] Capable of being oxidized; capable of combining with oxygen so as to form an oxide or oxygen-compound.

1802 CHENEVIX in *Phil. Trans.* XCII. 336 The easily oxidizable metals cannot be employed. **1869** PHIPSON tr. *Guillemin's The Sun* (1870) 44 The chlorides, bromides, and iodides of metals not easily oxydisable. **1885** [see OXIDATION 1].

Hence ˌ**oxidiza'bility**.

1876 tr. *Wagner's Gen. Pathol.* (ed. 6) 301 Those peculiarities by which it is distinguished from other fats, e.g. easier oxidizability. **1884** *Athenæum* 8 Mar. 314/3 Researches on the oxidizability of iron and steel.

oxidization (ˌɒksɪdaɪ'zeɪʃən). *Chem.* Also **oxy-**. [n. of action from OXIDIZE *v.*] The action of oxidizing or process of being oxidized; oxidation.

1817 J. BRADBURY *Trav. Amer.* 287 *note*, Iron ore.. in a continued state of oxydization. **1885** J. R. ALLEN in *Mag. Art* Aug. 456/2 Objects of bronze, being less liable to oxidization than iron, have been preserved.

oxidize ('ɒksɪdaɪz), *v. Chem.* Also **oxy-**. [f. OXIDE + -IZE.]

1. a. *trans.* To cause to combine with oxygen; to convert into an oxide or oxygen-compound. (In the case of a metal, often = to cover with a coating of oxide, to rust, make rusty.) More widely, to cause to undergo oxidation; to remove an electron from, completely or partly.

1802 [implied in OXIDIZABLE, OXIDIZEMENT]. **1806** HATCHETT in *Phil. Trans.* XCVI. 119 Coal is apparently nothing more than carbon oxidized to a certain degree. **1872** HUXLEY *Phys.* vi. 138 It is highly probable that the amyloids and fats are very frequently oxidised in the blood. **1875** H. C. WOOD *Therap.* (1879) 123 There.. must be a limit to the powers of the system to oxidize alcohol. **1894** PERKIN & KIPPING *Org. Chem.* I. vi. 95 Alcohol is readily oxidised by chromic acid, yielding acetaldehyde. **1913** MCPHERSON & HENDERSON *Course in Gen. Chem.* xxxiv. 471 Ferrous chloride is said to be oxidized to ferric chloride. **1942** SNEED & MAYNARD *Gen. Inorg. Chem.* xviii. 438 Chlorine oxidizes bromide ions and iodide ions to free bromine and iodine respectively. **1968** R. O. C. NORMAN *Princ. Org. Synthesis* iv. 143 The methyl group is oxidized when methane is converted by bromine into methyl bromide, because the electron-pair in the C–Br bond is less under the control of the carbon atom than the pair in the original C–H bond.

b. *humorously* for 'rust' in *fig.* sense.

1895 *Forum* (N.Y.) Jan. 602 The naïf enthusiasm of the elderly traveller whose own Greek is oxidized an inch thick.

2. *intr.* To enter into combination with oxygen; to take up oxygen; to become converted into an oxide. (Of a metal, often = to become coated with oxide; to rust, become rusty.)

1826 HENRY *Elem. Chem.* I. 166 A piece of zinc, immersed under water which is freely exposed to the atmosphere, oxidizes very slowly. **1864** *Daily Tel.* 17 Mar., There they [iron rails] lie, and oxidise tranquilly. **1871** ROSCOE *Elem. Chem.* 199 Allowing thin pieces of the metal to oxidize in dry air.

Hence '**oxidized** *ppl. a.*; **oxidizing** *vbl. sb.* and *ppl. a.*

oxidized silver, in silversmith's work, a name erroneously given to silver with a dark coating of silver sulphide.

1839 G. BIRD *Nat. Philos.* 203 The paper.. will be found stained of a deep purple hue from the oxydized gold. **1842** PARNELL *Chem. Anal.* (1845) 371 Heated with rather a strong oxidizing flame. **1855** J. R. LEIFCHILD *Cornwall* 233 A long series of processes, alternately of an oxidizing and a deoxidizing character. **1871** *Giant* 31 The new invention of oxydised silver. **1893** *Athenæum* 1 Apr. 412/1 This reddening.. is due to the oxidizing action of moist air.

†'**oxidizement.** *Chem. Obs.* Also **oxy-**. [f. prec. + -MENT.] = OXIDATION, OXIDIZATION.

1802 CHENEVIX in *Phil. Trans.* XCII. 333, I can attribute their difference of colour only to the different state of oxidizement of the iron. **1836** BRANDE *Chem.* (ed. 4) 330 The terms *oxidizement* and *oxidation* imply the combination of oxygen with bodies. **1849** NOAD *Electricity* (ed. 3) 154 Iron, coated with brass or copper, as less liable to oxidizement.

'**oxidizer.** Also **oxy-**. [f. as prec. + -ER[1].]

1. A substance that oxidizes, or gives off oxygen to, another; an oxidizing agent. *spec.* one used to support the combustion of fuel in a rocket engine or fuel cell.

1875 H. C. WOOD *Therap.* (1879) 575 Chromic acid is a very active oxidizer. **1883** *Hardwich's Photogr. Chem.* (ed. Taylor) 257 Experiments performed with various oxidizers. **1950** *Sci. News* XV. 78 Liquid fluorine could be used as an 'oxidiser' with suitable fuels, but great care is needed when handling this liquid. **1952**, etc. [see FUEL *sb.* 3 c]. **1973** *Daily Tel.* 3 Aug. 34/3 Like all rocket engines they use a fuel, monomethyl hydroazine, and an oxydiser, nitrogen tetroxide.

2. A workman employed in making 'oxidized silver': see OXIDIZED.

1884 *Birmingham Daily Post* 23 Feb. 3/4 Gilders.—Wanted an experienced Parcel Gilder and Oxydiser.

oxidoreductase (ˌɒxɪdəʊrɪ'dʌkteɪz, -s). *Biochem.* Also †**oxydo-**. [ad. F. *oxydo-réducase* (Battelli & Stern 1921, in *Arch. internat. de Physiol.* XVIII. 413), f. *oxyde* OXIDE *sb.* + *réduction* REDUCTION: see -ASE.] Any enzyme that catalyses oxidoreduction.

1922 [see HYDRATASE]. **1922** [see HYDROLASE]. **1928** *Physiol. Abstr.* XIII. 141 The oxydoreductase of yeast, unlike that from milk, acts on methyl glyoxal almost as strongly as on acetaldehyde. **1958** *Nature* 15 Feb. 452/2 Enzymes catalysing oxido-reductions would be named oxidoreductases in the systematic nomenclature, according to the scheme 'donor-acceptor reductase'. **1964** [see OXIDASE]. **1974** *Encycl. Brit. Macropædia* VI. 897/2 Oxidoreductases and transferases account for about 50 percent of the approximately 1,000 enzymes recognized thus far.

oxidoreduction (ˌɒksɪdəʊrɪ'dʌkʃən). *Biochem.* [f. OXID(ATION + -O + REDUCTION.] A process in which one substance is oxidized and electrons from it reduce another substance.

1934 *Jrnl. Faculty Sci. Hokkaido Univ.* II. (Ser. 3) 18 In animal and in plant cells, oxidoreduction occurs in parallel with the formation of peroxide. **1958** [see OXIDOREDUCTASE]. **1971** *Ital. Jrnl. Biochem.* XX. 129 Crystalline lactate dehydrogenase.. catalyzes the dismutation of glyoxylate to glycolate and oxalate producing the oxido-reduction system of NAD coenzymes illustrated in Figure 1.

So ˌ**oxidore'ductive** *a.*, involving oxidoreduction.

1951 WHITBY & HYNES *Med. Bacteriol.* (ed. 5) xx. 314 Others obtain energy from amino-acids, probably by paired oxido-reductive deaminations. **1971** J. Z. YOUNG *Introd. Study Man* xxvi. 376 Oxido-reductive reactions are linked with phosphorylation to produce ATP.

†**o'xidulated,** *ppl. a. Chem. Obs.* Also **oxy-**. [f. obs. F. *oxydulé*, f. *oxydule*, 'lowest degree of oxidation, protoxide', dim. of *oxyde*; after L. *acid-us, acidul-us*: cf. *acidulated, acidulous*.] Combined with a smaller proportion of oxygen than in another compound; as in *oxidulated iron*, a former name for the magnetic oxide of iron (Fe_3O_4) as distinguished from the peroxide (Fe_2O_3). So †'**oxidule (oxydul)** [a. obs. F. *oxydule*], an oxide containing a smaller or the smallest proportion of oxygen; †**o'xidulous** *a.* = *oxidulated*.

1806 *Edin. Rev.* IX. 71 Those portions of the ore which contain the least quantity of oxygen.. are consequently denominated *oxydulated. **1852** TH. ROSS *Humboldt's Trav.* II. xxiv. 512 Vallies, which contain magnetic sands (granulary oxidulated iron). **1818** HENRY *Elem. Chem.* (ed. 8) II. 55 [In the case] of only two oxides.. we might have applied the term *oxide* to the metal fully saturated with oxygen, and of **oxidule* to the compound at an inferior stage of oxidizement, as has been done by several of the French chemists. **1814** *Edin. Rev.* XXIII. 68 *Oxidulous iron ore forms a rock. **1869** PHILLIPS *Vesuv.* x. 282 Magnetite, oxydulous Iron, occurs in blocks in Somma.

oxie, obs. form of OX-EYE.

'**oxify,** *v. nonce-wd.* [f. OX + -(I)FY.] *trans.* To make an ox of, turn into an ox.

1804 SOUTHEY in Robberds *Mem. W. Taylor* I. 515 Instead of oxifying or assifying myself, and crying wonderful! at every action of my perfect prince.

oxigen, -gon, etc., obs. ff. OXYGEN, -GON, etc.

oxime ('ɒksaɪm), **oxim** ('ɒksɪm). *Chem.* [f. OX- 1 + *-ime*, shortened from IMIDE (the imides containing the radical :NH, the oximes :N(OH)). Introduced by the German chemists V. Meyer and Janny in 1882.] A chemical compound containing the divalent group :N(OH) joined to a carbon atom, esp. in the combination C_nH_{2n}: as ***acetoxime*** C_2H_4:N(OH), ***formoxime*** = CH_2:N(OH). Also called **oximide**.

1891 *Athenæum* 23 May 669/3 The large class of substances known as the oximes, which have been so much investigated of late, has just been enriched by the discovery of its simplest possible member, formoxime, CH_2:N.OH. **1893** *Ibid.* 13 May 608/3 [A paper was read on] 'Organic Oximides: a Research on their Pharmacology', by Dr. H. Pomfret.

oximel(l, obs. form of OXYMEL.

oximeter (ɒk'sɪmɪtə(r)). *Med.* [f. OXI- + -METER.] A device for measuring the proportion of hæmoglobin in the blood which is in the oxidized form.

1942 G. A. MILLIKAN in *Rev. Sci. Instruments* XIII. 434 (*heading*) The oximeter, an instrument for measuring continuously the oxygen saturation of arterial blood in man. **1951** *Anesthesiology* XII. 549 With the oximeter it is possible to show how the anesthetist in his manipulations may induce trends which often lead to severe anoxemia. **1966** *McGraw-Hill Encycl. Sci. & Technol.* IX. 469/2 A second type of oximeter is designed to measure the oxygen saturation of blood outside the body during or shortly after withdrawal of the blood from various sites in the vascular system. **1975** *Sci. Amer.* Feb. 69/1 (Advt.), With the ear oximeter, the physician can make the measurement simply by attaching an optoelectronic device to the patient's ear and reading percent oxygen saturation on the display.

Hence **oxi'metric** *a.*, employing an oximeter; **o'ximetry**, the use of an oximeter.

1944 G. A. MILLIKAN in O. Glasser *Med. Physics* I. 900/1 (*heading*) Oximetry: continuous measurement of blood oxygen. **1948** *Federation Proc.* VII. 104/2 (*heading*) Oximetric determination of cardiac output in man. **1955** *Canad. Jrnl. Psychol.* IX. 67 (*heading*) Studies on the physiology of awareness: An oximetrically monitored controlled stress test. **1966** *McGraw-Hill Encycl. Sci. & Technol.* IX. 469/2 The physical basis of oximetry stems from the difference in absorption by oxygenated and reduced hemoglobin of red light of wavelengths in the region of 640 mμ. **1971** *Biol. Abstr.* LII. 9988 (*heading*) Cerebral venous oxygen saturation during rapid changes in the arterial blood pressure: an oximetric study in dogs.

oxindole (ɒk'sɪndəʊl). *Chem.* Also **-ol.** [f. OX- 1 = OXY- + INDOLE.] A colourless crystalline substance (C_8H_7NO), becoming an oil when heated, consisting of indole combined with one equivalent of oxygen. Hence ***dioxindole***, containing two equivalents of oxygen ($C_8H_7NO_2$): see DI-[2] 2 c.

1872 WATTS *Dict. Chem.* VI. 733 *Indol*.. is produced.. by passing the vapour of oxindol over heated zinc-dust. *Ibid.* 736 The oxindol.. forms long colourless needles or feathery groups,.. and at higher temperatures distils.. as a colourless or reddish oil which immediately solidifies in the crystalline form... On exposure to the air, it is partly converted by oxidation into dioxindol. **1881** *Nature* XXIV. 229/1 A body called oxindol, from which isatin, and therefore indigo, can be obtained. **1892** MORLEY & MUIR *Watts' Dict. Chem.* III. 661 Oxindole.. dioxindole.

oxine ('ɒksiːn). *Chem.* [ad. G. *oxin* (Hahn & Vieweg 1927, in *Zeitschr. f. anal. Chem.* LXXI. 123), f. *oxychinolin*, hydroxyquinoline.] 8-Hydroxyquinoline, C_9H_7NO, a crystalline phenol which forms water-insoluble complexes with many metal ions and is used in analysis and as a deodorant and antibacterial agent.

1927 *Chem. Abstr.* XXI. 2444 Oxine itself is difficultly sol. in water.. but is more sol. in AcOH. **1947** [see HYDROXYQUINOLINE]. **1956** R. G. W. HOLLINGSHEAD *Oxine & Its Derivatives* IV. xxxiv. 1167 The growth of athlete's foot is prevented by the use of an absorbent powder, such as talc or starch, containing oxine and finely divided boric acid. **1973** T. MOHÁCSY tr. *Burger's Organic Reagents in Metal Analysis* ii. 97 Oxine complexes are usually intensely coloured in chloroform. This renders possible the spectrophotometric determination of many metal ions.

oxiodic: see OXY-IODIC.

Oxisol ('ɒksɪsɒl). *Soil Science.* [f. OXI(C *a.* + -SOL.] A type of stable, highly weathered mineral soil found in tropical regions (see quots. 1960, 1971). Cf. OXIC *a.* 1.

1960 *Soil Classification: 7th Approximation* (U.S. Dept. Agric.) xvi. 238/1 The Oxisols include the soils that, in recent years, have been called Latosols, and many, if not most, of those that have been called Ground-Water Laterite soils... All soils that have oxic horizons are included in the order. **1970** P. M. AHN *W. African Soils* (1974) vii. 221 The Oxisol order probably includes only the oldest and most highly weathered of West African soils. **1971** *Gloss. Soil Sci. Terms* (Soil Sci. Soc. Amer.) 26/1 *Oxisols*, mineral soils that have an oxic horizon within 2 m of the surface or plinthite as a continuous phase within 30 cm of the surface, and that do not have a spodic or argillic horizon above the oxic horizon. (An order in the USDA soil taxonomy.) **1972** [see OXIC *a.* 1]. **1976** D. STEILA *Geogr. Soils* xi. 150 There are two main regions of Oxisol concentration: in South America surrounding the alluvial soils of the Amazon and in equatorial Africa.

'**oxless,** *a.* [-LESS.] Without an ox or oxen.

1819 BYRON *Juan* II. cliv, But beef is rare within these oxless isles.

'**ox-like,** *a.* and *adv.* [-LIKE.] Like, or resembling that of an ox; after the manner of an ox.

1616 W. FORDE *Serm.* 37 To exempt yourselves from this supine and oxelike securitie. **1728** POPE *Dunc.* II. 164 His be yon Juno of majestic size, With cow-like udders, and with ox-like eyes. **1847** CARPENTER *Zool.* §268 Boviform or Ox-like Antelopes,.. species that present various degrees of relationship to the Antelopes and Oxen respectively.

'**oxlip.** Forms: 1 **oxanslyppe, -sloppe,** 6 **oxelip(pe, oxslip,** 7– **oxlip.** [OE. *oxanslyppe* wk. fem., f. *oxan* genit. sing. of *oxa*, OX + *slyppe* slimy or viscous dropping: see COWSLIP.] The name of a flowering herb: applied (at least from 16th c.) to a plant intermediate in appearance between the Cowslip (*Primula veris*) and Primrose (*P. vulgaris*), agreeing with the former in having a common scape bearing an umbel of many flowers, but in the colour and form of the individual flowers resembling the latter; now ascertained to be a natural hybrid between the cowslip and primrose; by some 17–18th c. writers extended to include the cultivated varieties of many colours commonly comprised under the name *Polyanthus*. **b.** By recent botanists appropriated to *Primula elatior* (Jacq.), a species having the appearance of a luxuriant pale-flowered cowslip, found in Europe from Gothland southward, and in Britain only in Essex and parts of the adjacent counties.

The latter, discovered at Bardsfield in Essex in 1842, by Mr. H. Doubleday, is sometimes distinguished as the Bardfield or True Oxlip; in Essex it is included, with the hybrid oxlip, under the name 'Cowslip', the cowslip of English literature being there called 'Paigle'.

c **1000** *Sax. Leechd.* II. 32 Wiþ slie, oxanslyppan niþewearde, & alor rinde wylle on buteran. *Ibid.* III. 30ȝenim ..ȝearwan & wudubindan leaf, & cuslyppan & oxsanslyppan. **1568** TURNER *Herbal* III. 80 Coweslippe is named in..Latin herba paralysis, and there are two kinds of them,..the one is called in the West contre of some a Cowislip, and the other an Oxislip, and they are both called in Cambridgeshyre Pagles. **1578** LYTE *Dodoens* I. lxxxiii. 122 *Verbasculum album*, Oxelippe [Figure]. *Ibid.* 123 The Oxelip..is very like to the Cowslippe, sauing that his leaues be greater and larger, and his floures be of a pale or faynt yellow colour, almost white and without savour. *Ibid.*, The petie Mulleyns are called..in English Cowslippes, Primeroses, & Oxelips. **1590** SHAKS. *Mids. N.* II. i. 250, I know a banke where the wilde time blowes, Where Oxslips and the nodding Violet growes. **1611** —— *Wint. T.* IV. iv. 125 Pale Prime-roses,..bold Oxlips, and The Crowne Imperiall: Lillies of all kinds. **1686** PLOT *Staffordsh.* 350 Having improved the seed of *Primula veris* or common wild primrose to that height, that it has produced the *Primula polyanthos* or Oxlip. **1688** R. HOLME *Armoury* II. 70/2 The Oxlip Cowslip is like those of the field, but of several red colours. **1776** WITHERING *Brit. Plants* (1796) II. 233 Mr. Curtis tells us, that by cultivation it [primrose] may be brought to throw up a long common fruit-stalk like the Oxlip; which countenances the idea of the latter being a variety of this. **1830** TENNYSON *Talking Oak* 107 As cowslip unto oxlip is, So seems she to the boy. **1884** MILLER *Plant-n.*, *Ox-lip*, also applied to *P*[*rimula*] *variabilis* and *P. vulgaris caulescens.*

b. **1842** *Gard. Chron.* 12 Mar., The German Oxlip, the true *P. elatior*,..which is not yet known to be a native of England. **1842** H. DOUBLEDAY in *Phytologist* I. 204, I send you some oxlips from Bardfield in Essex which..appear to me to be identical with the true *Primula elatior* of Linnæus and the German botanists... Pagels or cowslips also occur in the neighbourhood. **1844** *Ibid.* I. 975 The Bardfield Oxlip. **1897** *Pall Mall G.* 19 May 3/2 If you are a bit of a botanist you will notice that all through Zeeland the oxlip takes the place of cowslip and primrose, a form intermediate between both, stalked like a cowslip, but with larger flowers. **1902** *Speaker* 23 Aug. 555/2 In East Anglia the true Oxlip is found.

Oxo (ˈɒksəʊ). Also oxo. [f. OX + -O.] The proprietary name of an extract of beef, orig. a liquid, later in solid tablets, used as the basis of drinks and soups; also, the drink made from such tablets.

1899 *Trade Marks Jrnl.* 24 May 626 Oxo... Fluid beef. Liebig's Extract of Meat Company, Limited,..London,..and..Antwerp; manufacturers of Liebig Company's extract of meat, and manufacturers, shippers, and importers of South American produce. **1904** C. L. NEIL *Mod. Physical Culture* 15 Perhaps the handiest and best form in which to take this [*sc.* beef tea] is Oxo, made by Liebig's Extract of Meat Company. **1905** *Car* 24 May p. viii/1 A 4 oz. bottle of Oxo, and a few biscuits. **1907** *Yesterday's Shopping* (1969) 5/2 (*heading*) Liebig Co.'s Oxo Fluid Beef. **1914** D. O. BARNETT *Let.* 6 Nov. (1915) 4 Chocolate would be very welcome, also Oxo tablets. **1922** *Glasgow Herald* 13 Apr. 2 We shall carry..a thermos flask for Oxo. **1936** E. M. ANDERSON *Pract. Camp Cookery* 84 Brown sauce... 1 or 2 Oxo cubes. *Ibid.*, Use Oxo, relish, etc., if required, and season to taste. **1963** B. NILSON *Bk. Meat Cookery* 14/2 Pour over the Oxo stock. **1975** C. FREMLIN *Long Shadow* i. 10 Popping in with cups of tepid Oxo. **1976** A. HILL *Summer's End* i. 6 It smelled like a ton of flowers pressed into the space of an oxo-cube.

oxo(-) (ˈɒksəʊ), *prefix* and *a. Chem.* [f. OX(YGEN + -O.] **1.** As a word-forming element in the names of organic compounds used to denote the presence of a carbonyl group, as in *oxodecanoic acid*, 3-*oxovaleric acid*, OXOSTEROID.

1971 *Nomencl. Org. Chem.* (I.U.P.A.C.) (ed. 3) C. 176 In the presence of a group having priority over carbonyl for citation as principal group, or when all the carbonyl groups cannot be included in the ketone functional class name, the presence of carbonyl-oxygen atoms is indicated by the prefixes 'oxo-', 'dioxo-', *etc.*

2. With a hyphen, as quasi-*adj.* without a hyphen, or joined, as one word, to a sb. **a.** Applied to an oxygen atom linking two other atoms, and to compounds containing such a grouping. Now *rare*.

1921 *Jrnl. Chem. Soc.* CXIX. 1657 This is the value of the factor for the oxo-linking, –O–. **1922** *Ibid.* CXXI. 1811 In the oxo-compound the molecule is in one straight line. **1934** *Jrnl. Amer. Chem. Soc.* LVI. 795/1 Ol compounds readily change to oxo compounds upon heating their solutions. **1962** [see OL].

b. Applied to compounds, ions or groups containing one or more oxygen atoms bonded to another atom (*spec.* in *Org. Chem.* indicating the presence of a carbonyl group; cf. 1 above), as *oxo acid*, *anion*, *group*, *ion*.

1935 H. J. LUCAS *Org. Chem.* xxxix. 514 If the oxo group is on the end of a carbon chain, the compound is an aldehyde acid. **1958** *Jrnl. Physiol.* CXL. 154 The normal metabolism of the intestinal cells overshadows or compensates for any changes in the oxo acid concentrations in the blood. **1959** *Nomencl. Inorg. Chem.* (I.U.P.A.C.) v. 44 Most of the common acids are oxoacids, *i.e.*, they contain only oxygen atoms bound to the characteristic atom. **1965** PHILLIPS & WILLIAMS *Inorg. Chem.* I. xiv. 523 Oxyacids are sometimes called oxo-acids to stress the fact that they contain XO groups in their structures. **1969** H. T. EVANS tr. *Hägg's Gen. & Inorg. Chem.* xxi. 500 Charged oxide molecules, that is oxo ions, should also be considered as oxides. The particular descriptions of these..and the corresponding oxo acids, are given under the respective central-atom element. **1971** *Nomencl. Org. Chem.* (I.U.P.A.C.) (ed. 3) C. 120 Trivial names for oxo carboxylic acids..may be used for the acyclic component. **1972** COTTON & WILKINSON *Adv. Inorg. Chem.* (ed. 3) v. 170 The second main class of acid behavior is shown by compounds with X–OH groups; these are called oxo acids, and generally have a formula of the type H_nXO_m, for example H_3PO_4. *Ibid.* xxi. 639 Many of the most important ligands having oxygen donor atoms are oxo anions, such as NO_2^-, NO_3^-, SO_4^{2-} and ClO_4^-. *Ibid.* xiv. 408 Tetrahedral oxo ions such as PO_4^{3-}, ClO_4^-, MnO_4^-.

c. Also **OXO, Oxo.** Applied to the hydroformylation process or reaction.

1947 *Chem. & Industry* 1 Feb. 73/2 The OXO reaction is one of general applicability to compounds containing the ethylenic double bond. **1949** R. F. GOLDSTEIN *Petroleum Chem. Industry* x. 187 The Oxo reaction is exothermic, 35k. cal. being liberated per mol of olefin reacted. **1966** *McGraw-Hill Encycl. Sci. & Technol.* VI. 543/1 Cobalt catalysts are universally used for the Oxo reaction. **1969** [see *hydroformylation* s.v. HYDRO-]. **1971** *Nature* 20 Aug. 537/1 Roden..discovered the oxo or hydroformylation reaction which generates aldehydes and alcohols from olefins, carbon monoxide, and hydrogen in the presence of cobalt catalysts.

‖**o'xoleon, o'xoleum,** obs. latinized forms (after L. *oleum* oil) of Gr. ὀξέλαιον 'a sauce of vinegar and oil', f. ὀξύς sharp, sour + ἔλαιον olive oil.

1699 EVELYN *Acetaria* 94 The discreet choice and mixture of the *Oxoleon* (Oyl, Vinegar, Salt, &c.). **1725** BRADLEY *Fam. Dict.* s.v. *Lettuce*, With the usual Oxoleum of Vinegar, Pepper, and Oyl.

Oxonian (ɒkˈsəʊnɪən), *a.* and *sb.* [f. *Oxonia*, latinized form of *Oxenford, Oxford* + -AN.]

A. *adj.* Of or belonging to Oxford.

1644 SIR E. DERING *Prop. Sacr.* e, The Oxonian complements grow up close to this. **1716** *Pol. Ballads* (1860) II. 175 Th' Oxonian doctors farther went. **1810** *Edin. Rev.* XVI. 172 We call them [*according as, classified, classification*] Oxonian barbarisms; because we know no other title descriptive of them. **1851** MAYHEW *Lond. Labour* (1861) II. 43/1 I've been selling Oxonian button-overs ('Oxonian' shoes, which cover the instep, and are closed by being buttoned instead of being stringed through four or five holes).

B. *sb.* **a.** A native or inhabitant of Oxford; more usually, a member of the University of Oxford. Also, used of residents of Oxford who are not members of the University.

c **1540** *Pilgr. T.* 676 in *Thynne's Animadv.* (1865) App. i, Then he asked me and I were cantibrygion. I sayd no, I was an oxonian. **1701** FARQUHAR *Sir H. Wildair* II. i, I'm priveleged to be very impertinent, being an Oxonian. **1878** *N. Amer. Rev.* CXXVII. 512 Oxonians and Cantabs twitted the Scotch with knowing no Greek and little Latin. **1966** *Oxford Mail* 16 Mar. 8/3 We real Oxonians do still exist.

b. A kind of shoe: see quot. 1851 in A.

1848 THACKERAY *Van. Fair* lviii, Then the sleepless Boots went..gathering up..the Bluchers, Wellingtons, Oxonians, which stood outside. **1851** MAYHEW *Lond. Labour* (1861) II. 42/2, I had a pair of very good Oxonians that had been new welted.

So **O'xonianize** *v.*, to make Oxonian in character, imbue with the ideas of Oxford; **Oxo'nolatry** [see -LATRY], worship of or devotion to Oxford.

1885 *Athenæum* 26 Sept. 400/1 He was..as little Oxonianized at the core..as a true son of Oxford could well be. **1893** SWINBURNE *Stud. Prose & Poetry* (1894) 34 The effusive Oxonolatry of Mr. Arnold. **1932** A. QUILLER-COUCH in *Fifty Years* 46 What we, the lighter-hearted, did not renounce was the charm of the place, that 'Oxonolatry', if you will, which Swinburne had scoffed at.

o'xonic (ɒkˈsɒnɪk), *a. Chem.* [f. OX- 2 + *carb*)*onic.*] In *oxonic acid*, $C_4H_5N_3O_4$, a substance formed by the gradual oxidation of uric acid in an alkaline solution, and yielding on decomposition glyoxyl-urea and carbon dioxide. Its salts are **'oxonates.**

(The name had previously been applied by Schulze to the acid obtained by the action of nascent hydrogen on pure oxalic acid. Watts *Dict. Chem.* IV. 288.)

1881 WATTS *Dict. Chem.* VIII. 1458 *Oxonic acid*, $C_4H_5N_3O_4$. An acid discovered by Strecker, who obtained it by the action of atmospheric oxygen on uric acid in alkaline solution. It forms two series of salts.

oxonium (ɒkˈsəʊnɪəm). *Chem.* [f. OX- 1 + -ONIUM.] The hydroxonium ion, H_3O^+, or any derivative of this in which one or more of the hydrogen atoms are replaced by organic radicals. Usu. *attrib.*

1899 COLLIE & TICKLE in *Jrnl. Chem. Soc.* LXXV. 717 If oxygen can replace phosphorus, nitrogen, or sulphur in bases, then these oxygen compounds can be viewed as derivatives of the hypothetical base, oxonium hydroxide, OH_3OH. **1929** R. A. GORTNER *Outl. Biochem.* xxx. 621 The anthocyanin compounds readily add acids to form oxonium salts. **1959**, **1966** [see HYDRONIUM]. **1974** *Nature* 31 May 474/2 By dynamic reversal of the H_2O binding step before pseudorotation, the two oxygens in the pair of oxoniums could equilibrate with the H_2O oxygens of the medium.

oxosteroid (ɒksəʊˈstɪərɔɪd, -ˈstɛrɔɪd). *Biochem.* [f. OXO- 1 + STEROID.] = *ketosteroid* s.v. KETO- a.

1956 *Biochem. Jrnl.* LXII. 1P Urinary 17-oxosteroid conjugates consist of a mixture of glucuronides and sulphates. **1968** PASSMORE & ROBSON *Compan. Med. Stud.* I. xxxi. 13/1 (*caption*) 17-Oxosteroids are derived mainly from androgens and are excreted in urine principally as their 3-sulphate derivatives.

oxotremorine (ɒksəʊˈtrɛmərɪːn). *Pharm.* [f. OXO- + TREMORINE.] A crystalline compound, 1-(2-oxopyrrolidino)-4-pyrrolidino-2-butyne, $C_{12}H_{18}N_2O$, a metabolite of tremorine, which is capable of inducing the symptoms of Parkinsonism and is used in research into this disease.

1961 A. K. CHO et al. in *Biochem. & Biophys. Res. Communications* V. 276 For purposes of rough measurement, a unit was defined as the dose per Kg. which on intravenous injection in mice gave this threshold effect. It proved to be equal to approximately 15 μg. of 2-oxotremorine base. **1970** PASSMORE & ROBSON *Compan. Med. Stud.* II. v. 560/2 Another method [of inducing symptoms of Parkinsonism] involves the use of the drug tremorine..or its active metabolite oxotremorine which induce tremor, rigidity, akinesia, analgesia and signs of peripheral cholinergic stimulation in many animal species. **1972** BRIMBLECOMBE & PINDER *Tremors* iv. 96 Leslie & Maxwell (1964) first suggested that oxotremorine is a more desirable tool in screening compounds for anti-Parkinson activity than is tremorine.

ox-pecker, -ray, etc.: see OX 6.

oxprenolol (ɒksˈprɛnəlɒl). *Pharm.* [f. OX- 1 + *pren-* (f. ISOPRENALINE) + reduplicated -OL (after PROPRANOLOL).] The compound 1-(*o*-allyloxyphenoxy)-3-isopropylamino-2-propanol, $C_{15}H_{23}NO_3$, which is an adrenergic blocking agent used mainly (in the form of the white crystalline hydrochloride) in the treatment of cardiac arrhythmia, angina and hypertension.

1968 *Jrnl. Amer. Med. Assoc.* 29 July 292/1 The following nonproprietary names..have been adopted by the United States Adopted Names (USAN) Council... Oxprenolol hydrochloride. **1969** *Jrnl. Appl. Physiol.* XXVII. 366/1 Oxprenolol, a specific beta-receptor blocking agent, diminished effort tachycardia by 15·0% and emotional tachycardia by 34·2%. **1977** *Lancet* 5 Nov. 954/1 Players receiving oxprenolol feel calmer before performing and happier with their recital.

oxsi, obs. inf. of ASK *v.*

†**oxskin.** *Obs.* In 7 oxe skinne. App. a perversion of the dial. *oskin* OXGANG, facilitated by popular association of HIDE *sb.*[1] and [2].

1610 HOPTON *Bac. Geodæt.* I. ii. 21 Foure akers (saith he) make a yard of land, fiue yards of land contain a hide..in Yorkeshire and other countries they call a hide an Oxe skinne.

oxspring, oxpring, obs. forms of OFFSPRING.

ox-stall (ˈɒksstɔːl). Also 4–5 oxes-, 8 *Sc.* owsen-staw. A stall or stable for oxen.

c **1386** CHAUCER *Clerk's T.* 342 She was born and fed in rudenesse As in a cote, or in an Oxe [*v. rr.* oxes, oxsis, ox] Stalle. **1492** RYMAN *Poems* xxxii. 4 in *Archiv Stud. neu. Spr.* LXXXIX. 199 A childe they founde In an oxe stalle in raggis wounde. **1530** PALSGR. 250/2 Oxestale, *creche.* **1599** MARSTON *Sco. Villanie* II. v. 194 Liu'd he now, he should lack, Spight of his farming Oxe-stawles. *Ibid.* III. Proem. 210 To purge this Augean oxstall from foule sinne. **1776** *Herd's Sc. Songs* II. 146 She sought it in the owsen-staw.

'ox-tail. The tail of an ox; esp. as an article of food. Also *attrib.* in ***ox-tail soup***, etc.

c **1460** *Towneley Myst.* xii. 225, I haue here in my mayll sothen and rost, Euen of an ox tayll that wold not be lost. **1681** COLVIL *Whigs Supplic.* (1751) 17 Some had slings, some had flails Knit with eel and oxen tails. **1834** H. W. BRAND *Simpson's Cookery* v. 64 Ox-tail soup. Blanch two ox-tails, cut into pieces of a size suited to be served at table. **1837** MARRYAT *Dog-fiend* xxxviii, To make soup of..; he can't afford ox-tail. **1841** THACKERAY *Gt. Hoggarty Diamond* (1849) xi. 142 Three silver tureens of soup: viz. mock-turtle soup, ox-tail soup, and giblet soup. **1865** C. M. YONGE *Clever Woman* II. iv. 53 The whole party were in a little den at the pastrycook's; the boys consuming mutton pies, and the ladies ox-tail soup. **1868** M. JEWRY *Warne's Model Cookery* 172/2 (*heading*) Ox-Tail Soup. **1882** *Standard* 23 Aug. 5/2 It was the Royalist refugees who taught us to prepare soup of the ox tails, which until then were tossed to the dogs. **1939** JOYCE *Finnegans Wake* I. 133 Can rant as grave as oxtail soup and chat as gay as a porto flippant. **1970** SIMON & HOWE *Dict. Gastron.* 286/1 It is said the first ox-tail soup was made by a starving French nobleman during the Reign of Terror.

oxter (ˈɒkstə(r)), *sb. Sc., Irish,* and *north. dial.* Also 6, 9 ox(s)tar(e, 6–7 oxster, 7–8 ockster. [A modified or extended form from OE. *óxta, óhsta*, from same stem as OE. *óxn*:—**óhsna* = OHG. *uohsana* and *uochasa, ôchasa*, MHG. *uohse, uehse*; stem *ôks-, ôhs-*, whence also Du. *oksel* (OKSELLE):—OLG. **ôksla, ôhsla*; also, with weak grade *aks-, ahs-*, OHG. *ahsala*, Ger. *achsel*; so L. *axilla*, dim. of **axula*, and OIr. *oxal*; all in the same or an allied sense.] **a.** The armpit.

15.. *Sir A. Barton* in *Surtees Misc.* (1888) 73 He shoote hime in at the left oxtere, The arrowe quiett throughe harte. **1597** LOWE *Chirurg.* (1634) 81 There is a sort of it that appeareth under the oxter and jawes. **1637–50** ROW *Hist. Kirk* (1842) 145 Being sent for to the castell, [he] went up with his Bible under his ockster, affirming that they would plead for him. **1674** RAY *N.C. Words* 35 An Oxter: an Armpit, *Axilla.* *a* **1745** SWIFT *Direct. Servants, Footman*, This will keep it at least as warm as under your arm-pit or ockster, as the Scots call it. **1818** SCOTT *Br. Lamm.* xxiv, Let her leddyship get his head ance under her oxter. **1881** R. BUCHANAN *God & Man* III. 214 Johnstone..had the telescope under his oxter. **1901** G. B. SHAW *Admirable Bashville* II. 304 But many felt that Byron shewed bad taste In taking old Ned Skene upon his back, And, with Bob Mellish tucked beneath his oxter, Sprinting a hundred yards to show the crowd The perfect pink of his condition. **1914** JOYCE *Dubliners* 206 Many a good man went to the penny-a-week school with a sod of turf under his oxter. **1932** AUDEN *Orators* II. 70 The madman keeper crawls through brushwood, Axe under oxter. **1956** H. SUTHERLAND *Irish Journey* iii. 25 Each carrying a loaf under his 'oxster'. **1964** *Listener* 19 Mar. 494/3 Alan Whicker..stood..on that bubbling pitch lake of Trinidad..and let us hear a calypso from a man who'd fallen into it up to his oxters. **1977** D. BAGLEY *Enemy* ix. 63 Benson's carrying a gun in his oxter. **1978** *Jrnl. Lancs. Dial. Soc. Jan.* 15/1 [Durham] *Oxter*, armpit.

b. More loosely, The under side or inside of the upper arm.

1500-20 DUNBAR *Poems* xiii. 17 His fa sum by the oxstar leidis. **1715** RAMSAY *Christ's Kirk Gr.* II. xvii, Twa sturdy chiels, Be 's oxter and be 's coller, Held up..The liquid logic scholar. **17..** —— *Jenny Nettles* i, Bag and baggage on her back, And a baby in her oxter. **1852** A. ROBB *Poems & Songs* 115 Grip me in your oxter. **1893** STEVENSON *Catriona* xi. 125, I would be blythe to have you at my oxter.

c. *Comb.* **oxter-plate** (see quot. 1904).

1885 H. PAASCH *From Keel to Truck* 46 Plate,..oxter—Tôle de voûte contre l'étambot. Achselgrube-Platte. **1904** A. C. HOLMS *Pract. Shipbuilding* I. 526 The oxter plates are those which take the sternpost, immediately below, or partly on, the transom. **1927** G. F. LEECHMAN *Theory & Pract. Steering* 51 The rotary current applies considerable pressure upon the hull in the vicinity of the oxter plate. **1948** R. DE KERCHOVE *Internat. Maritime Dict.* 511/1 *Oxter plate*, a shell plate riveted to the stern frame in way of the rudderpost head.

Hence **'oxter** *v. trans.*, to support by the arm, walk arm in arm with; to take or carry under the arm; to fold the arm round.

1780 J. MAYNE *Siller Gun* II, Lads oxter lasses without fear, Or dance like wud. *c* **1793** BURNS *Meg o' the Mill*, The Priest he was oxter'd, the Clerk he was carried. **1894** *Northumbld. Minstrel's Budget* in *Northumbld. Gloss.* s.v., When this master of minstrelsy oxtered his blether.

ox-tongue, oxtongue ('ɒks,tʌŋ).

1. The tongue of an ox.

c **1420** *Liber Cocorum* (1862) 26 Take tho ox tonge and schalle hit wele, Sethe hit, broche hit in lard yche dele. **1601** HOLLAND *Pliny* II. 279 The leaves..resemble an ox tongue. **1894** *Westm. Gaz.* 26 Oct. 6/3 He amassed a considerable fortune by the ox-tongue trade.

2. Popular name of several plants: = LANGUE DE BŒUF 1. †**a.** *orig.* applied to various plants having rough leaves, more or less tongue-shaped; chiefly species of bugloss, borage, and alkanet. *Obs.*

c **1325** *Gloss. W. de Bibbesw.* in Wright *Voc.* 162 E bucle [*gloss* oxe-tunge] ausy, une herbe seyne. *a* **1400-50** *Stockh. Med. MS.* 196 Langdebef or oxtunge, *lingua bouis.* **1483** *Cath. Angl.* 265/2 Oxtonge, *buglossa, herba est.* **1578** LYTE *Dodoens* I. vi. 12 The auncient Fathers called it [Borage] in Greeke βούγλωσσον,..in English Oxe tongue. **1597** GERARDE *Herbal* II. xxxii. 235 Sharpe Haukeweede hath leaues like to those of Langue de beefe or Oxetoong. **1611** COTGR., *Langue de bœuf*,..Ox-tongue, rough or small Buglosse.

b. In modern Botany: A composite plant, *Helminthia* (*Picris* Linn.) *echioides*, growing on clayey soil; also called ***prickly ox-tongue***.

1760 J. LEE *Introd. Bot.* App. 321 Ox-tongue, *Picris.* **1858** *Penny Cycl.* 2nd Suppl. 301/1 There is but one species [of the genus] inhabiting Great Britain, *H[elminthia] echioides*, the Ox-Tongue... The branches, stem, leaves, and involucre are covered with strong prickles springing from white tubercles, and with 3 minute hooks at the apex. **1885** *Pall Mall G.* 28 Oct. 4/2 In the long, dry grass at the foot of the hedge stands out the yellow 'bristly oxtongue'—stem and leaves all frosted with white glands.

3. A name occasionally applied to obsolete weapons with broad blades: = LANGUE DE BŒUF 2.

1890 in *Cent. Dict.* **1894** in *Funk's Stand. Dict.*

ox-vomit, -wagon, -warble, etc.: see OX 5, 6.

oxy, *a.*[1] *rare* [-Y.] **a.** Of or belonging to an ox.

c **1611** CHAPMAN *Iliad* IV. 139 He took his arrow by the nock, and to his bended breast The oxy sinew close he drew.

b. Resembling an ox.

In quot. with pun on *Oxford.*

1922 JOYCE *Ulysses* 9 Tell that to the oxy chap downstairs and touch him for a guinea.

oxy ('ɒksɪ), *a.*[2] *Chem.* The prefix OXY- (in sense 2) used without a hyphen as a quasi-*adj.*

1910 *Encycl. Brit.* VI. 51/1 Oxyaldehydes and oxyketones (viz. compounds containing an oxy in addition to an aldehydic or ketonic group) undergo both condensation and oxidation when treated with phenylhydrazine. **1923** W. M. CUMMING et al. *Systematic Org. Chem.* v. 74 In the following section are discussed the more important of those condensations which give rise to oxy compounds—aldehydes, ketones, and quinones. **1962** COTTON & WILKINSON *Adv. Inorg. Chem.* v. 136 Many metal ions whose solutions are acidic may be regarded as oxy acids. **1975** *Inorg. Chem.* XIV. 1232/1 These chloroaluminate solvents are known to be effective chlorinating agents for a number of oxides and oxy anions.

oxy, obs. ME. inf. of ASK *v.*

oxy- (ɒksɪ), repr. Gr. ὀξυ-, combining form of ὀξύς sharp, keen, acute, pungent, acid; used in various words, chiefly scientific. The more important of these will be found in their alphabetical places; others follow here, in two groups.

1. Words of various kinds, in which *oxy-* stands for 'sharp', 'acute' (in *lit.* or *fig.* sense): as **oxyacanthous** (-ə'kænθəs) *a. Bot.* [Gr. ἄκανθα thorn], having sharp thorns (Mayne *Expos. Lex.* 1857). ‖**oxyæsthesia** (-ɪs'θiːsɪə) *Phys.* and *Path.* [mod.L., f. Gr. αἴσθησις feeling], abnormal acuteness of sensation, hyperæsthesia (Mayne). ‖**oxyaphia** (-'æfɪə) *Phys.* and *Path.* [mod.L., f. Gr. ἁφή touch], excessive acuteness of the sense of touch (Mayne). **oxy'aster** *Zool.* [Gr. ἀστήρ star], a sponge-spicule having acute rays radiating from one point. ‖**oxy'blepsia** *Phys.* [mod.L., a. Gr. ὀξυβλεψία, f. βλέπειν to look], acuteness of sight, sharp-sightedness (Mayne). **oxy'carpous** *a. Bot.* [Gr. καρπός fruit], having pointed fruit (Mayne). **oxycephalic** (sɪ'fælɪk) *a. Anthropol.* [Gr. κεφαλή head], having a skull of pointed or conical shape; so **oxy'cephaly**, the condition of being oxycephalic. **'oxyclad** *Zool.*, a branched form of sponge-spicule: see quot. **oxy'dactyl** *Zool.* [Gr. δάκτυλος finger or toe], *a.* belonging to the division *Oxydactyla* of Batrachians, characterized by slender toes; *sb.* an oxydactyl batrachian. †**oxy'dercical** *a. Obs.* [Gr. ὀξυδερκικός], sharpening the sight. **oxy'diact** *a.* and *sb. Zool.* [DI-[2]; Gr. ἀκτίς ray], (a sponge-spicule) having two acute rays. ‖**oxyecoia** (-iː'kɔɪə) *Phys.* and *Path.* [mod.L., a. Gr. ὀξυηκοΐα, f. ἀκούειν to hear], abnormal acuteness of hearing, acoustic hyperæsthesia (Mayne). †**oxygal** [ad. L. *oxygala*, Gr. ὀξύγαλα], sour milk. ‖**oxygeusia** (-'gjuːsɪə) *Phys.* and *Path.* (also anglicized **-geusy**) [mod.L., f. Gr. γεῦσις taste], excessive acuteness of the sense of taste (Mayne). **oxygnathous** (ɒk'sɪgnəθəs) *a. Zool.* [Gr. γνάθος jaw], having the jaws of the shell quite or almost smooth, as certain pulmonate molluscs. **oxy'hexact** *a.* and *sb. Zool.* [Gr. ἕξ six, ἀκτίς ray], (a sponge-spicule) having six acute rays; so **oxyhe'xaster**, a hexaster with acute rays (? = prec.). **oxyklinocephalic** (-,klaɪnəʊsɪ'fælɪk), *a. Anthropol.*, ? said of a skull combining the oxycephalic and klinocephalic forms. ‖**oxy'opia** *Phys.* (anglicized **oxyopy**) [mod.L., f. Gr. ὀπ- to see], abnormal acuteness of sight (Mayne). ‖**oxyosphresia** (-ɒs'friːsɪə) *Phys.* [mod.L., f. Gr. ὄσφρησις smell], excessive acuteness of the sense of smell (Dunglison 1842). **oxy'pentact** *a.*, *sb. Zool.* [Gr. πέντε five, ἀκτίς ray], (a sponge-spicule) having five acute rays. **oxy'petalous** *a. Bot.*, having pointed petals (Mayne). ‖**oxy'phonia** *Phys.*, *Path.* (also anglicized **ox'yphony**) [mod.L., a. Gr. ὀξυφωνία, f. φωνή voice], excessive acuteness or shrillness of voice (Dunglison 1842). **oxyphyllous** (-'fɪləs) *a. Bot.* [Gr. φύλλον leaf], having pointed leaves (Mayne). **'oxyr(r)hine, oxy'r(r)hinous** *adjs. Zool.* [Gr. ῥίς, ῥιν- snout], sharp-nosed, sharp-snouted. **oxystomatous** (-'stɒmətəs) *a. Zool.* [Gr. στόμα mouth], having the mouth-parts sharply projecting, as the division *Oxystomata* (Milne Edwards) of crabs; so **'oxystome** *a.* = prec.; *sb.* a crab of the division *Oxystomata*. **oxystrongyle** (-'strɒndʒɪl), **-strongylus** *Zool.* [STRONGYLE], a sponge-spicule like a strongyle but sharp at each end; hence **oxy'strongylous** *a.*, of the nature of an oxystrongyle. **oxy'tetract** *a.* and *sb. Zool.* [Gr. τετρα- four, ἀκτίς ray], (a sponge-spicule) having four acute rays. **oxytylote** (ɒk'sɪtɪləʊt) *Zool.* [Gr. τύλος knob], a simple sponge-spicule sharp at one end and blunt at the other; hence **oxytylotate** (-'tɪləʊteɪt) *a.*, having the character of an oxytylote.

1886 R. VON LENDENFELD *Sponges* in *Proc. Zool. Soc.* 561 **Oxyaster.* With long, slender, pointed rays. **1878** BARTLEY tr. *Topinard's Anthrop.* v. 176 *Oxycephalic, elevated skull. **1890** H. ELLIS *Criminal* iii. 50 There is a generally recognised tendency to the pointed (oxycephalic) or sugar-loaf form of head. **1895** *Forum* (N.Y.) Sept. 36 Among these anomalies were..'*oxicephaly'. **1888** SOLLAS in *Challenger Rep.* XXV. p. lv, **Oxyclad* (κλάδος, a young branch). The esactine is oxeate, the ecactine terminates in two or more secondary actines or 'cladi'. **1657** TOMLINSON *Renou's Disp.* 195 Make an *oxydercical collyrie of such medicaments as cure caligation. **1886** LENDENFELD (as above) 562 **Oxydiact.* Four rays rudimentary, only two rays lying in one straight line remain. [**1706** PHILLIPS, **Oxygala*, Sower Milk.] **1745** tr. *Columella's Husb.* XII. viii, Make oxygal, or sour milk, after this manner. **1886** LENDENFELD (as above) 562 **Oxyhexact.* With six pointed rays, the ends of which form the corners of a double square pyramid. The rays represent the crystalline axes. **1886** LENDENFELD (as above) 562 *Hexaster.* A star with six, generally equal rays:—a. **Oxyhexaster.* Rays pointed. b. *Discohexaster.* Rays terminated by disks. **1878** BARTLEY tr. *Topinard's Anthrop.* v. 177 A certain deformed skull found in Silesia is *oxyklinocephalic. **1846** SMART, **Oxyo'py*, preternaturally acute vision. **1886** LENDENFELD (as above) 562 **Oxypentact.* One ray rudimentary, representing the axes of a simple square pyramid. **1846** SMART, **Ox'yphony*, acuteness of voice. **1890** *Cent. Dict.*, *Oxyrhine. **1892** *Syd. Soc. Lex.*, **Oxyrrhinous.* **1857** MAYNE *Expos. Lex.*, *Oxystomatus*, ..*oxystomatous. **1852** DANA *Crust.* I. 62 The triangular mouth of the *Oxystomes. **1888** SOLLAS (as above), **Oxystrongyle.*—The esactine is oxeate and the ecactine strongylate... **Oxytylote*... The esactine is oxeate, and the ecactine tylote. **1886** LENDENFELD (as above) 562 **Oxytetract.* Two rays rudimentary, representing the edges of a square pyramid.

2. Chemical words, in which *oxy-* is taken as the combining form of OXYGEN (cf. HYDRO- d); denoting either simply the presence of oxygen, as in OXYACID, OXYSALT, †*oxybase*, or the addition of oxygen to the substance denoted by the simple word, and thus practically = *oxygenated* or *oxidized*. For special uses, see OXYCHLORIDE, OXYSULPHATE, and other main words. A looser use is seen in **oxy-acetylene, oxy-alcohol** (or **oxy-spirit**), **oxy-coal-gas, oxy-house-gas, oxy-ether, oxy-fuel, oxy-gas, oxy-propane**, terms applied *attrib.* (after OXYHYDROGEN, OXYCALCIUM) to the flame produced by mixing acetylene, the vapour of a spirit lamp, ordinary house-gas, or sulphuric ether, etc. with oxygen; so ***oxy-alcohol blowpipe, lamp***, etc.; **oxy-helium**, a mixture of oxygen and helium, used as a breathing mixture in deep-sea diving; **oxy-paraffin** *a.*, applied to a paraffin lamp with arrangement for complete oxygenation of the flame.

But the most frequent use of *oxy-* is as a prefix to names of organic substances, to denote a derivative or related compound in which an atom of hydrogen is displaced by one of hydroxyl (HO); in which sense the more accurate *hydroxy-* is now often preferred: see OXYACID 2.

In earlier use often spelt *oxi-*; before a vowel sometimes reduced to *ox-*: see OX- 1.

The more important of the *oxy-* compounds are treated as main words; the *oxy-* or rather *hydroxy-* organic compounds are unlimited in number, including e.g. *oxy-* or *hydroxyacetal* ($CH_2(OH)CH(OC_2H_5)_2$); ***-aldehyde*** ($CH_2(OH)CHO$); ***-anthracene*** (= anthraquinone); ***-benzene*** or ***-benzol*** (= phenol, C_6H_5OH); ***-benzyl***; ***-camphor*** ($C_{10}H_{16}O_2$); ***-cannabin*** ($C_{20}H_{20}N_2O_7$); ***-caproamine*** (= leucine); ***-choline*** (= betaine); ***-cinchonine*** ($C_{19}H_{22}N_2O_2$); ***-cymene*** (= carvacrol, $C_{10}H_{13}OH$); ***-dimorphine*** ($C_{34}H_{36}N_2O_6$); ***-guanine***; ***-glycolyl-urea*** (= allanturic acid); ***-lanthopine***; ***-methyl***; ***-methylene*** (= formic aldehyde); ***-morphine*** ($C_7H_{19}NO_4$); ***-naphthylamine*** (or ***-naphthylidine***, $C_{10}H_9NO$), ***-narcotine*** ($C_{22}H_{23}NO_8$); ***-neurine*** (= betaine); ***-phenol*** (= pyrocatechin); ***-phenyl*** (C_6H_4OH); ***-quinine***; ***-quinoline*** (= carbostyril); ***-strychnine*** ($C_{21}H_{28}N_2O_6$); ***-sulphobenzide***; ***-thymoquinone*** ($C_{10}H_{12}O_3$); ***-toluene*** (= cresol, C_7H_8O); ***-toluyl***, etc.

Also in the names of oxy- or hydroxy-acids, as ***oxy-acetic*** (= GLYCOLLIC); ***-amygdalic***; ***-benzoic*** ($C_7H_6O_3$); ***-butyric*** ($C_4H_8O_3$); ***-caproic*** (= leucic); ***-chelidonic*** (= meconic); ***-cholic***; ***-cuminamic*** ($NH_2.C_{10}H_{10}O.OH$); ***-cuminic*** ($C_{10}H_{12}O_3$); ***-gummic*** ($C_4H_{10}O_{11}$); ***-hippuric*** ($C_9H_9NO_4$); ***-isouvitic*** ($C_9H_8O_6$); ***-lizaric*** acid (= purpurin); ***-mandelic*** (= phenylglycollic); ***-mesitylenic*** ($C_9H_{10}O_3$); ***-naphthoic*** ($C_{10}H_6(OH)CO_2H$); ***-phenic*** acid (= pyrocatechin); ***-picric*** (= styphnic, $C_6H_3N_3O_8$); ***-propionic*** (= lactic); ***-salicylic*** (= gentisinic, $C_6H_3(OH)_2COOH$); ***-tannic***; ***-terephthalic*** ($C_8H_{12}O_3$); ***-tolic*** ($C_7H_6O_3$); ***-toluamic***; ***-toluic*** (= cresotic, $C_6H_3(CH_3)(OH)CO_2H$); ***-trimesic***; ***-uric***, etc.

1864-72 WATTS *Dict. Chem.* II. 909 *Glycollic acid.* $C_2H_4O_3$..**Oxacetic acid.* **1873** —— *Fownes' Chem.* (ed. 11) 681 Nitrous acid converts glycocine into glycollic or oxyacetic acid. **1909** *Westm. Gaz.* 19 Jan. 4/2 A special weldless steel tubing brazed together by an *oxy-acetylene process. **1939** L. TIBBENHAM *Welding Cast Iron* iii. 29 The temperature of an air-acetylene flame is about three-quarters that of oxy-acetylene. **1959** *Listener* 8 Oct. 583/3 Before the days of oxy-acetylene. **1961** C. WILLOCK *Death in Covert* iii. 56 A desk which had been designed by a modern sculptor whose chosen tool was the oxy-acetylene welder's torch. **1975** R. C. JAIN tr. *Castro & de Cadenet's Welding Metall.* iii. 20 The oxy-acetylene process is being largely replaced by the electric-arc methods since it has a number of disadvantages in the welding of stainless steels. **1892** *Syd. Soc. Lex.* s.v., *Oxyalcohol blowpipe..invented by Marcet, in which the flame of a spirit lamp is urged by a blowpipe transmitting oxygen. **1899** CAGNEY tr. *Jaksch's Clin. Diagn.* vii. (ed. 4) 351 The aromatic oxy-acids which have been proved to exist in the urine are paroxy-phenyl acetic acid,..*oxyamygdalic acid. **1866-77** WATTS *Dict. Chem.* IV. 352 *Oxanthracene. $C_{14}H_8O_2$..When anthracene is boiled for some days with nitric acid, a resin is formed which becomes granular on cooling, and..forms light reddish-yellow crystals of oxanthracene. **1892** MORLEY & MUIR *Watts' Dict.* III. 670 Di-oxy-anthracene $C_{14}H_8(OH)_2$, Chrysazol. **1865** MANSFIELD *Salts* 45 An *Oxybase bears to the general idea of a salt and to Oxygen a relation just the converse of that which a Hydrostyle bears to that idea and to Hydrogen. The term Oxybase includes the Alkalies, commonly so called. **1866** ODLING *Anim. Chem.* 121 Ampelic or *oxi-benzoic acid. **1873** WATTS *Fownes' Chem.* 616 Quartene or butene glycol is converted by slow oxidation with nitric acid into *oxybutyric acid. **1897** *Allbutt's Syst. Med.* IV. 310 In diabetes..acetone and oxybutyric acid, are usually present with the sugar. **1882** *Nature* XXVII. 118/2 By the action of boiling 60 per cent. nitric acid, cellulose is converted into an amorphous substance $C_{18}H_{26}O_{16}$, oxy-cellulose. **1878** KINGZETT *Anim. Chem.* 99 By oxidation of a milder character..a white amorphous acid, termed *oxy-cholic, is produced. **1889** LOCKYER in *Harper's Mag.* Mar. 582/1 By means of the *oxy-coal-gas flame, we can determine the spectrum of any vapor given off. **1877** WATTS *Fownes' Chem.* (ed. 12) II. 490 *Carvacrol *Oxycymene*, or *Cymenol*, is..a thick oil. **1969** *New Scientist* 8 May 284/2 The *oxy-fuel burner was then lit and the charge melted with the burner operating under reducing conditions. **1951** E. G. WEST *Welding Non-Ferrous Metals* iii. 48 The *oxy-gas cutting of ferrous metals, except stainless steels, depends on the rapid oxidation of the iron by the oxygen stream. **1974** *Nature* 4 Jan. 53/2 In this operation, in which oxy-gas torches have been used at the work face, temperatures are in the region of 3,000–3,500° C. **1873** RALFE *Phys. Chem.* 93 By oxidation with potassium permanganate, guanin is converted into urea, oxalic acid, and *oxy-guanin. **1966** A. B. CAMERON in P. Hepple *Petroleum Supply & Demand* 38 The use of *oxyhelium equipment now enables them [*sc.* divers] to remain as deep as 525 ft for periods up to 30 minutes. **1969** *Physics Bull.* Feb. 51/2 There is a problem of speech communication between divers breathing oxy-helium and the men on the surface. **1976** *Offshore Engineer* Apr. 23/1 Comex physiologists first described the High Pressure Nervous Syndrome (HPNS) during oxy-helium dives as long ago as 1968. **1879** *Cassell's Techn. Educ.* IV. 407/2 If the oxy-spirit, *oxy-house-gas, or oxy-hydrogen jets, or the magnesium lamps . . are to be used. **1866–77** WATTS *Dict. Chem.* IV. 313 **Oxymethyl-carbonic acid*, a name applied by Kolbe . . to glycollic acid. **1875** *Ibid.* VII. 886 **Oxyneurine*. This base . . is identical with betaine from beet-juice. **1870** *Eng. Mech.* 21 Jan. 453/2 *Oxy-paraffin oil lamps. **1857** W. A. MILLER *Elem. Chem.* III. 572 *Oxyphenic Acid or Pyrocatechin ($C_{12}H_6O_4$) the formula of Oxyphenic differs from that of phenic acid by two equivalents of oxygen. **1963** A. C. DAVIES *Sci. & Pract. Welding* (ed. 5) vi. 371 Iron and steel can be cut by the oxy-hydrogen, *oxy-propane, oxy-coal gas and oxy-acetylene cutting blow-pipes with ease, speed and a cleanness of cut. **1970** *Daily Tel.* 24 Sept. 2/2 On the morning of the explosion two workmen were using oxy-propane cutting tools. **1873** WATTS *Fownes' Chem.* 683 Nitrous acid converts alanine into lactic or *oxypropionic acid. **1879** *Oxy-spirit [see *oxy-house-gas*]. **1866–77** WATTS *Dict. Chem.* IV. 321 **Oxytolic acid*, $C_7H_6O_3$. An acid, isomeric with salicylic and oxybenzoic acids. . . It is produced by the oxidation of toluene. **1873** —— *Fownes' Chem.* 704 Amylene glycol yields oxybutyric instead of *oxyvaleric acid.

oxyacanthin (ˌɒksɪə'kænθɪn). *Chem.* [f. botanical L. *Oxyacantha*, specific name of the Hawthorn, a. Gr. *ὀξυάκανθα* lit. 'sharp-thorn', a shrub, prob. *Cratægus Pyracantha* (Persoon): see -IN[1].] A name given to a bitter neutral substance obtained by Leroy from the Hawthorn.

1866 WATTS *Dict. Chem.* IV. 288.

Also **oxyacanthine** (ˌɒksɪə'kænθaɪn) *Chem.* [see -INE[5]], an alkaloid obtained from the root of the Barberry, *Berberis vulgaris*.

1866–77 WATTS *Dict. Chem.* IV. 288 *Oxyacanthine.* $C_{32}H_{46}N_2O_{11}$? *Vineline*. . . An alkaloid existing, together with berberine, in the root of *Berberis vulgaris*. *Ibid.* 289 Oxyacanthine, when pure, is a white powder ordinarily with a yellowish tinge. . . It has a bitter taste.

oxyacanthous, etc.: see OXY- 1.

oxyacid, oxy-acid (ɒksɪ'æsɪd). *Chem.* Also **oxi-**, **ox-acid**. [f. OXY- 2 + ACID.]

1. An acid containing oxygen (e.g. carbonic acid, CH_2O_3) as distinguished from a *hydracid* formed by the union of hydrogen with a halogen (e.g. hydrochloric acid, HCl).

1836–41 BRANDE *Chem.* (ed. 5) 1032 It is obvious . . that there are no salts, properly so termed, in which the oxy-acids are combined with silica, but that silicium forms haloid compounds. **1849** NOAD *Electricity* (ed. 3) 224 The hypothesis of Davy developing the general analogy of all salts, whether derived from oxyacids or hydracids. **1882** ROSCOE *Elem. Chem.* vi. 56 All acids contain hydrogen, combined either with an element, or with a group of elements, which almost always contain oxygen, and in this case the substances are termed oxy-acids.

b. *attrib.* or *adj.* Of or belonging to an oxyacid.

1854 J. SCOFFERN in *Orr's Circ. Sc., Chem.* 352 The attempt to assimilate oxyacid salts with the type of hydracid salts.

2. *Organic Chem.* In plural, a name given to several series of acids derived from those of the fatty or the aromatic series, by the substitution of one or more hydroxyl for one or more hydrogen atoms; hence called more exactly *hydroxy-acids*.

The diatomic monobasic acids derived from the fatty acids ($C_nH_{2n}O_2$) have the formula $C_nH_{2n}O_3$, and constitute the *fatty oxy-*, *(hydr)oxy-fatty*, or *lactic* series. The diatomic monobasic acids derived from the aromatic group or benzene derivatives ($C_nH_{2n-8}O_2$) have the formula $C_nH_{2n-8}O_3$, and constitute the *aromatic oxy-acids* or *(hydr)oxy-aromatic* series.

1877 WATTS *Fownes' Chem.* (ed. 12) II. 317 These acids are called *lactic acids*, after the most important member of the series, and *oxy-fatty acids*, because they may be derived from the acids $C_nH_{2n}O_2$ by the substitution of OH for H; thus: $CH_3.CO_2H$ Acetic acid; $CH_2OH - CO_2H$ Oxyacetic acid. *Ibid.* 534 These aromatic oxy-acids, like the corresponding acids of the fatty series (the lactic acids), exhibit alcoholic as well as acid characters. **1885** REMSEN *Introd. Organ. Chem.* 155 The first class which presents itself is that of the alcohol acids or acid alcohols; that is, substances which combine within themselves the properties of both alcohols and acids. They are commonly called oxy-acids or hydroxy-acids.

oxy-alcohol: see OXY- 2.

† **oxya'mmonia.** *Chem.* Obs. synonym of *Hydroxylamine*. (*Syd. Soc. Lex.*, 1892.)

oxyanion (ˌɒksɪ'ænaɪən). *Chem.* Also **oxy-anion** (with hyphen). [f. OXY- 2 + ANION.] An anion containing one or more atoms of another element each linked to one or more oxygen atoms.

1940 *Jrnl. Chem. Soc.* 131 (*heading*) The interchange of heavy oxygen between water and inorganic oxy-anions. **1952** *Chem. Rev.* L. 456 Since oxyanions have a large amount of resonance stabilization, it is necessary to overcome this stability in order that a chemical reaction take place. **1972** W. R. KNEEN et al. *Chemistry* xvii. 427 The phosphorus acids and oxyanions all contain approximately tetrahedral four-co-ordinate phosphorus.

oxy-arc ('ɒksɪɑːk). Also **oxyarc**. [f. OXY- 2 + ARC.] An arc struck in an atmosphere of oxygen between a work-piece and a hollow electrode through which the oxygen is supplied. Usu. *attrib.*

1956 A. C. DAVIES *Sci. & Pract. Welding* (ed. 4) vi. 349 (*heading*) Oxyarc cutting process. **1962** J. BELL *Crime in our Time* I. 15 They . . attempted to burn the safe open with oxy-arc equipment. **1974** *Petroleum Rev.* XXVIII. 676/1 Oxy-arc, at present widely used, may be replaced by the technique of arc-plasma. **1976** *Offshore Platforms & Pipelining* 155/3 This entails . . cutting the pipe with an oxy-arc tool.

oxyard: see OX 6.

oxy-aro'matic, *a. Chem.*, in *oxy-aromatic acid* = aromatic oxyacid: see OXYACID.

1887 A. M. BROWN *Anim. Alkaloids* 23 This is . . washed repeatedly with ether to get rid of the oxy-aromatic acids.

‖**oxybaphon** (ɒk'sɪbəfən). *Greek Antiq.* Pl. **-bapha**. [a. Gr. *ὀξύβαφον* vinegar-saucer, f. *ὀξυ-* acid, vinegar + *βαφ-*, stem of *βάπτειν* to dip, *βαφή* dipping, etc.] With classical archæologists: A bell-shaped wine-cup or vase.

1850 LEITCH tr. *C.O. Müller's Anc. Art* §358 (ed. 2) 440 An oxybaphon from Armentum at Naples. **1857** BIRCH *Anc. Pottery* (1858) II. 161 Deep bell shaped craters, called oxybapha, having on them mystic and Dionysiac subjects.

'**oxy-bird.** *dial.* = OX-BIRD.

1887 *Kentish Gloss.* (E.D.S.), *Oxbird*, the common dunlin. . . Called Oxybird in Sheppy. **1887** F. COWPER *Caedwalla* (1888) 87 The tide was nearly low, and a flock of oxy birds were settled on the mud-banks.

oxyblepsia, etc.: see OXY-.

oxy'bromide. *Chem.* [f. OXY- 2 + BROMIDE.] A bromine compound analogous to the oxychlorides; as ***phosphorus oxybromide***, $POBr_3$, produced by the decomposition of the pentabromide (PBr_5) in moist air.

1866–77 WATTS *Dict. Chem.* IV. 510 Oxybromide of phosphorus . . $POBr_3$. **1873** —— *Fownes' Chem.* (ed. 11) 227 Two bromides of phosphorus, an oxybromide and a sulphobromide, are known, corresponding in composition and properties with the chlorine compounds.

oxy-calcium (ɒksɪ'kælsɪəm). *Chem.* [f. OXY- 2 + CALCIUM.] In ***oxy-calcium light*** = LIMELIGHT *sb.* 1.

c **1865** J. WYLDE in *Circ. Sc.* I. 61/2 The oxy-calcium light is a very simple and useful contrivance. **1879** *Cassell's Techn. Educ.* IV. 232/2 The sources of light have been improved on by the adoption of the oxy-calcium, oxy-hydrogen . . and electric light.

† **oxy'carbonate.** *Chem. Obs.* A compound of a carbonate and an oxide; a hydrate carbonate.

1819 BRANDE *Man. Chem.* 306 These are probably the carbonate and the oxycarbonate. **1876** HARLEY *Mat. Med.* (ed. 6) 29 The caustic alkalies, 'lime and magnesia', are converted into carbonates or oxycarbonates from absorption of carbonic anhydride.

† **oxy'carburetted,** *a. Chem. Obs.* In ***oxycarburetted hydrogen***: see quots.

1807 T. THOMSON *Chem.* (ed. 3) II. 132 The first species is composed of carbon and hydrogen; the second, of carbon, hydrogen, and oxygen. . . He [Berthollet] calls the first carbureted hydrogen; the second, oxycarbureted hydrogen. **1812** SIR H. DAVY *Chem. Philos.* 310 What have been called different oxicarburetted hydrogene gasses are merely mixtures of olefiant gas, carburetted hydrogene, carbonic oxide, and hydrogene gasses. **1892** *Syd. Soc. Lex.*, *Oxycarburetted hydrogen gas*, an old term for *Carbonic oxide*.

† **oxy'cedar.** *Obs.* [ad. L. *oxycedros* (Pliny), a. Gr. *ὀξύκεδρος* (Theophr.), 'the red juniper with pointed leaves' (Liddell and Scott).] A species of Juniper (*Juniperus Oxycedrus*).

1646 SIR T. BROWNE *Pseud. Ep.* 335 Bellonius affirmeth that Charcoals made out of the wood of Oxycedar are white.

oxycellulose (ɒksɪ'sɛljuːləʊs). [f. OXY- 2 + CELLULOSE *sb.*] Any of various substances obtained by the oxidation of cellulose, some of which are used as gauze or lint in cases of hæmorrhage.

1893 CROSS & BEVAN in *Jrnl. Chem. Soc.* XLIII. 22 A portion of the mass [of cellulose] . . yields but slowly to the action of the nitric acid, in consequence, we find, of its conversion into an oxidised derivative, to which we have provisionally given the name *oxycellulose*. **1938** *Ann. Rev. Biochem.* VII. 58 When oxycelluloses are boiled with dilute alkalis, the fluidity is virtually unaffected and there is only a slight decrease in tensile strength. **1954** KIRK & OTHMER *Encycl. Chem. Technol.* XIII. 551 Oxycellulose, when properly prepared, is a hemostatic material and is gradually absorbed by bodily fluids when it is used to pack wounds. **1963** [see OVERBLEACHED *ppl. a.*].

oxycephalic, etc.: see OXY-.

'**oxychlor-**, '**oxychloro-**. *Chem.* Containing oxygen and chlorine, as ***oxychlor-ether***, a liquid, $CH_2Cl.CH(OH)(OC_2H_5)$, obtained by the action of water at high temperature on bichlor ether.

So † **oxy'chlorate** *of potash*, old name of Potassium chlorate, $KClO_3$. † **oxy'chloric** *acid*, old name of Perchloric acid, $HClO_4$. **oxy'chloride**, a combination of oxygen and chlorine with another element, as ***phosphorus oxychloride***, $POCl_3$; also, a compound of a metallic chloride with the oxide of the same metal. Also called **oxy'chloruret**. †***acetic oxychloride*** = chloracetic acid.

1818 SIR H. DAVY in Brande *Chem.* (1841) 99, I mentioned to you . . Count Stadion's Oxychloric acid. *Ibid.*, I have used detonating powder . . made with the oxychlorate of Potassa, to use Stadion's name. **1856** W. A. MILLER *Elem. Chem.* II. 717 In the bodies termed oxychlorides, oxyiodides, and oxycyanides . . one equivalent of the chloride, of the iodide, or of the cyanide of the metal is united with one or more equivalents of the oxide of the same metal. Turner's yellow . . is an oxychloride of lead (PbCl, 7 Pb.O). **1857** *Ibid.* III. 313 Oxychlorides of the Monobasic Acids.—The acids of the lower members of the series HO, $C_nH_{n-1}O_3$, can readily be made to furnish volatile compounds in which one equivalent of oxygen, as contained in the anhydrous acid, has its place supplied by chlorine. With acetic acid (HO, $C_4H_3O_2$) an acetic oxychloride may be obtained consisting of $C_4H_3O_2Cl$. **1866–77** WATTS *Dict. Chem.* IV. 596 Oxychloride of phosphorus is a colourless fuming liquid having a specific gravity of 1·7 and boiling at 110°. **1880** FRISWELL in *Soc. Arts* 447 The scarlet obtained by dyeing cochineal in the presence of oxichloride of tin.

oxychlorocruorin (ˌɒksɪklɔərəʊ'kruːərɪn). *Biochem.* [f. OXY- 2 + *chlorocruorin* s.v. CHLORO-[1].] The oxygenated form of chlorocruorin.

1870 *Jrnl. Anat. & Physiol.* IV. 129 (*caption*) Green blood of *Sabella ventilabrum*, shewing the two bands of Oxy-chlorocruorin. **1924** *Proc. Cambr. Philos. Soc.: Biol. Sci.* I. 217 The absorption bands of oxychlorocruorin and reduced chlorocruorin resemble those of oxy- and reduced haemoglobin shifted towards the red end of the spectrum. **1950** *Sci. News* XV. 89 Oxyhaemoglobin and oxychlorocruorin have each their characteristic absorption spectrum and the blood of *Serpula* shows both.

oxychromatin (ɒksɪ'krəʊmətɪn). *Biol.* [a. G. *oxychromatin* (M. Heidenhain 1894, in *Arch. f. mikrosk. Anat.* XLIII. 543), f. Gr. *ὀξυ-* sharp, acid: see CHROMATIN.] A supported component of chromatin characterized by a greater affinity for acid dyes and a smaller content of nucleic acid than chromosomal chromatin.

1895 *Jrnl. R. Microsc. Soc.* 159 'Oxychromatin' and 'cyanophilous granulation' are independent structural parts of the chromatin framework. **1924** E. G. CONKLIN in E. V. Cowdry *Gen. Cytol.* ix. 550 The oxychromatin which escapes into the cell body at mitoses is often more abundant than that which goes to form the chromosomes. **1948** W. ANDREW tr. *E.D.P. de Robertis's Gen. Cytol.* vii. 140 With ultracentrifugation the nucleus is deformed and the nuclear structures are stratified in the following layers . .: (1) nucleolus, (2) basichromatin, (3) oxychromatin, (4) karyolymph.

† **oxy'chromic**, *a. Chem.* Old synonym of *perchromic*.

oxy-coal-gas: see OXY- 2.

† '**oxycrate.** *Obs.* Also 6–8 **oxicrate**, 7 **oxicrat**, 7–8 **oxycrat**. [ad. Gr. *ὀξύκρᾱτ-ον*, f. *ὀξυ-* acid + *-κρᾱτος* (in comp.) mixed.] A mixture of vinegar and water.

1597 A. M. tr. *Guillemeau's Fr. Chirurg.* 27/2 Cause the patient to washe his mouth with a little Oxycrate. **1601** HOLLAND *Pliny* II. 422 If a man be poisoned with taking venomous mushroms, he shall find means to auoid the danger thereof by drinking nitre in oxycrat or vineger & water mingled together. **1747** WESLEY *Prim. Physic* (1762) 68 Cover the body with Cloths dipt in Oxycrate.

‖**oxy'croceum.** *Obs.* [mod.L., f. Gr. *ὀξυ-* sour, vinegar + L. *croceus* of or pertaining to saffron (*crocus*).] (See quot. 1696.)

1646 SIR T. BROWNE *Pseud. Ep.* 78 The same attraction wee finde not onely in simple bodies, but such as are much compounded, as the Oxicroceum plaster. **1696** PHILLIPS (ed. 5), *Oxycroceum*, a Plaister made of Saffron, Vinegar, and other Ingredients.

oxy'cyanide. *Chem.* [f. OXY- 2 + CYANIDE *sb.*] A combination of oxygen and cyanogen with another element, or of the oxide and cyanide of a metal, as ***oxycyanide of mercury***, $Hg''Cy_2.Hg''O$.

1854 J. SCOFFERN in *Orr's Circ. Sc., Chem.* 500 Oxycyanide of mercury is formed. **1864–72** WATTS *Dict. Chem.* II. 255 Warm aqueous cyanide of mercury dissolves a large quantity of mercuric oxide, forming an alkaline solution, which deposits small needles of oxycyanide of mercury.

oxyd(e, oxydate, etc., var. ff. OXIDE, etc.

'*Obs.* in general usage, though still preferred by some.' (N.E.D.)

oxydase ('ɒksɪdeɪs). *Chem.* [mod. f. *oxyd*, OXIDE + *-ase* (ad. Gr. *-ασις*) in names of ferments, as *diastase*.] A former variant spelling of OXIDASE.

1896 *Jrnl. Chem. Soc.* LXX. II. 571 The author gives the generic term *oxydase* to laicase, tyrosinase, and other oxidising ferments of vegetable origin. **1900** *Nature* 8 Feb. 339/1 The oxygen-carrying power of certain enzymes known at the present time as 'oxydases'. **1929** R. P. WALTON tr. *Waldschmidt-Leitz's Enzyme Actions* vii. 231 In these cases, special oxydases.. appear to be present.

oxydercical, -diact, etc.: see OXY- 1.

oxydoreductase, obs. var. OXIDOREDUCTASE.

oxy-ether: see OXY- 2.

oxy-fatty acid: see OXYACID 2.

oxy'fluoride. *Chem.* [f. OXY- 2 + FLUORIDE.] A fluorine compound analogous to an oxychloride. Formerly also called **oxyflu'oruret.**

1868–77 WATTS *Dict. Chem.* V. 813 The Difluoride [of tin] or Stannous fluoride, SnF_2.. when heated in the air,.. takes up oxygen, and forms stannic oxyfluoride, $Sn^{iv}OF_2$ or $SnO_2{\cdot}SnF_4$. **1880** CLEMINSHAW *Wurtz' Atom. The.* 146 Marignac.. regards as isomorphous the double fluorides of titanium, the double oxyfluorides of niobium and of tungsten.

oxygal, etc.: see OXY- 1.

oxygen ('ɒksɪdʒən). *Chem.* Also 8– oxi-, -gene. [a. F. *oxygène*, intended to mean 'acidifying (principle)', *principe acidifiant* (Lavoisier): see OXY- and -GEN 1; oxygen being at first held to be the essential principle in the formation of acids.

Lavoisier's original term, proposed in 1777, was *principe oxygine*, changed 1785–6 to *principe oxygène*; thence in 1786 *oxygène* as sb., spelt in *Nomenclature* of 1787 *oxigène*; admitted in *Dict. Acad.* 1835 as *oxygène*.]

1. a. One of the non-metallic elements, a colourless invisible gas, without taste or smell. Symbol O: atomic weight 16. Also *fig.*

It is the most abundant of all the elements, existing, in the free state (mixed with nitrogen), in atmospheric air, and, in combination, in water and most minerals and organic substances. It combines with nearly all other elements (forming *oxides*), the process of combination being in some cases so energetic as to produce sensible light and heat (*combustion*), in others very gradual, as in the rusting or *oxidation* of metals. It is essential, in the free state, to the life of all animals and plants, and is absorbed into the organism in *respiration*: hence it was formerly called *vital air*. Priestley, who isolated it in 1774, holding it to be common air deprived of PHLOGISTON (q.v.), called it *dephlogisticated air*.

[**1789** J. K[EIR] *1st Pt. Dict. Chem.* Pref. 18 Lavoisier.. having endeavoured to show that vegetable and other matters.. consist of air, charcoal, and inflammable gas, or, in his language, oxygene, carbone, and hydrogene.] **1790** R. KERR tr. *Lavoisier's Elem. Chem.* II. iv. 185 Oxygen forms almost a third of the mass of our atmosphere. [**1791** BEDDOES in *Phil. Trans.* LXXXI. 176 Cast iron.. contains a portion of the basis of vital air, the oxygène of M. Lavoisier.] **1791** HAMILTON *Berthollet's Dyeing* I. I. I. i. 3 Mercury, combined with a small quantity of oxygen is black. **1794** *Europ. Mag.* XXVI. 5 Dephlogisticated Air, or (as they are now pleased to call it) *Oxygene*. **1799** *Med. Jrnl.* I. 373 Opponents particularly object, that the base of vital air does not deserve the title of oxygen, as many combinations of it are far from being acids. **1811** DAVY in *Nicholson's Jrnl.* XXIX. 112 Combinations of Oximuriatic Gas and Oxigen. **1845** W. GREGORY *Outlines Chem.* 45 Oxygen was discovered by Priestley in 1774; and in the following year by the Swedish chemist Scheele without any knowledge of Priestley's discovery. **1872** HUXLEY *Phys.* i. 17 It is oxygen which is the great sweeper of the economy.

fig. **1849** LYTTON *Caxtons* I. II. i. 45 Having thus exhausted all the oxygen of learning in that little receiver [*sc.* a preparatory school], my parents looked out for a wider range for my inspirations. **1932** *Sunday Times* 15 May 6 That cheerful noise which is the oxygen of 'society'.

b. An atom of oxygen.

1950 F. H. HATCH et al. *Petrol. Igneous Rocks* (ed. 10) I. ii. 68 The essential hydroxyl groups are included in the planes containing the 'free' oxygens in the tetrahedra. **1966** *Mineral. Mag.* XXXV. 1071 These compounds contain oxygens associated with three nearly equidistant protons forming H_3O^+ ions. **1974** *Nature* 4 Jan. 15/1 The main chain carbonyl oxygens were not resolved from the rest of the main chain, so that the orientation of the peptide bonds could not be determined directly.

2. A manufacturer's name for bleaching-powder, i.e. so-called 'chloride of lime'. (Simmonds 1858.)

3. *attrib.* and *Comb.* **a.** *attrib.* or *adj.* (see etymology above), in †**oxygene air** (*obs.*), **oxygen gas,** names for oxygen in the free or gaseous state.

1790 R. KERR tr. *Lavoisier's Elem. Chem.* I. v. 54 The oxygen gas, or pure vital air. **1794** G. ADAMS *Nat. & Exp. Philos.* I. xi. 449 Vital, Dephlogisticated, or oxygene air. **1794** PEARSON in *Phil. Trans.* LXXXIV. 388 White lac burned in oxygen gaz without.. any smoke, and with a beautifully bright flame. **1843** J. A. SMITH *Product. Farming* (ed. 2) 19 Oxygen, in union with latent heat, forms Oxygen gas. **1896** *Daily News* 31 Oct. 5/3 The oxygen treatment is the application of oxygen gas to wounds and ulcers.

b. The sb. in attrib. use or in combination; as in *oxygen acid* (= OXYACID 1), *-carrier, inhalation, lack, saturation, supply, tension, treatment*; *oxygen-breeding, -carrying, -dependent, -free, -poor* adjs. **oxygen bottle,** a cylinder of compressed or liquid oxygen; **oxygen debt** (see quot. 1923); **oxygen lance** (see LANCE *sb.*[1] 8); **oxygen mask,** a mask fitting over the nose and mouth through which oxygen or oxygen-enriched air may be supplied for breathing; **oxygen tent,** a tent-like enclosure for placing over a patient in order to provide him with an oxygen-enriched atmosphere.

1878 ABNEY *Photogr.* (1881) 64 Any other oxygen absorbing medium. **1842** PARNELL *Chem. Anal.* (1845) 89 The combinations of oxide of gold with oxygen acids are almost unknown. **1932** *Illustrierte Technische Wörterbücher* XVII. 234/1 *Sauerstoffbombe* (f.)—oxygen bottle—bombe (f) à oxygène—bombola (f) d'ossigeno. **1941** *Flight* 16 Jan. 48/1 The rigger changes the oxygen bottles and fits the starting motor to the aircraft. **1974** HAWKEY & BINGHAM *Wild Card* xix. 156 The other [trolley], an anesthesia machine, carried three yoked oxygen bottles. **1888** *Jrnl. R. Microsc. Soc.* 596 Schunck.. regards chlorophyll as a respiratory pigment, but probably a carbonic acid-carrier, not an oxygen-carrier. **1897** *Allbutt's Syst. Med.* IV. 643 [The blood-corpuscles] cannot perform such an active part as oxygen-carriers. **1972** *Cytobiologie* V. 52 This was the first application of the perfusion medium with a fluorocarbon as oxygen carrier. **1916** A. P. MATHEWS *Physiol. Chem.* xi. 496 There may be in addition a union with the hemoglobin, which will retard its oxygen-carrying capacity. **1968** *Times* 13 Nov. 16/1 The beads may be minute clumps of haemoglobin, the oxygen-carrying protein. **1923** HILL & LUPTON in *Q. Jrnl. Med.* XVI. 142 The 'oxygen debt' is defined as the total amount of oxygen used, after cessation of exercise, in recovery therefrom. **1947** T. K. CURETON et al. *Physical Fitness Appraisal* xiv. 437 The lactic acid [in the blood] increases very rapidly, with an estimated increment of 7 grams for each liter of oxygen debt. **1969** J. H. GREEN *Basic Clin. Physiol.* xi. 66/1 It is possible to run a short distance (100 yards) without breathing... After the exercise has been completed the subject breathes deeply and rapidly for the next few minutes in order to take in oxygen to 'repay' the oxygen debt. **1956** *Nature* 17 Mar. 531/1 Oxygen-dependent reactions. **1972** *Jrnl. Exper. Marine Biol. & Ecol.* IX. 217 The respiratory rate of the oxygen-dependent prosobranch, *Buccinum undatum* L., increases with decreasing salinity. **1933** *Mining & Metallurgy* XIV. 340/1 Oxygen-free high-conductivity copper.. that is now being commercially offered for the first time represents a notable achievement in electro-metallurgy. **1972** *Radiation Res.* XLIX. 507 The oxygen-carrying capacity of *Busycon* and *Limulus* hemocyanins is eliminated following irradiation of the protein with cobalt-60 γ-rays in neutral, oxygen-free media. **1897** *Daily News* 12 July 5/3 The work of the Oxygen Home, opened by Princess Louise last May, appears to be progressing very satisfactorily. **1898** *Allbutt's Syst. Med.* V. 46 For this [shortness of breath] there is a remedy in oxygen inhalations. **1925** *Physiol. Rev.* V. 554 Carbon dioxide and oxygen lack produced marked increases in respiration with very little change in the reaction of the blood. **1963** R. P. DALES *Annelids* iv. 93 Among oligochaetes the abilities of *Tubifex* to withstand oxygen-lack are well known. **1874** tr. *Lommel's Light* 5 Termed the oxygen lamp or burner. **1920** *Abstr. Papers in Sci. Trans. & Periodicals* July 177 A description is given of the oxygen mask used by the French military aviators. **1930** E. RICE *Voy. to Purilia* i. 16 The air grew rarer... We were obliged to don the oxygen masks.. so carefully and laboriously constructed for us. **1964** L. S. BRUNNER et al. *Text-bk. Medical-Surgical Nursing* xii. 189/1 Those individuals whose need for supplemental oxygen is greatest.. are the very ones who are most prone to resist the application of an oxygen mask. **1975** *Times* 4 Sept. 1/8, I saw an air hostess run into the first-class compartment with an oxygen mask. **1951** M. ABERCROMBIE et al. *Dict. Biol.* 128 *Lung*... Present in early fishes before origin of Amphibia, probably as an accessory breathing organ adapted to oxygen-poor fresh waters in which earliest vertebrates probably lived. **1969** *Listener* 6 Feb. 163/1 Mars has an atmosphere which is appreciable, even though it is too thin and too oxygen-poor to support any Earth creatures. **1942** *Electronic Engin.* XIV. 724 The ratio of their output currents will remain constant for any given degree of oxygen saturation. **1969** CROFTON & DOUGLAS *Respiratory Dis.* i. 33/1 The oxygen saturation is relatively uninfluenced until the partial pressure of oxygen in alveolar gas falls to relatively low levels. **1916** A. P. MATHEWS *Physiol. Chem.* xi. 481 The arterial blood had an oxygen tension varying in different experiments from 91·6–104·4 per cent of the tension in the alveolar air. **1953** J. HUNT *Ascent of Everest* 273 The respiratory centre in the brain.. responds normally not to the oxygen tension of the blood.. but to the direct effect of carbon dioxide tension of the arterial blood. **1965** B. E. FREEMAN tr. *Vandel's Biospeleol.* xviii. 318 The oxygen tension of subterranean waters is variable. [**1921** *Jrnl. Physiol.* LV. p. xx (*heading*) A simple oxygen bed tent and its use to [*sic*] a case of œdema and chronic ulcer of the leg.] **1925** *Sci. Amer.* Sept. 181/2 (*caption*) A portable oxygen tent for pneumonia patients. **1974** C. HILL *Scorpion* 55 Michael was lying under an oxygen tent.. the top of his head covered in bandages.

oxygenant (ɒk'sɪdʒɪnənt). ? *Obs.* [a. F. *oxygénant*, pr. pple. of *oxygéner* to OXYGENATE.] A substance that oxygenates another; an oxidizing agent.

1802 *Edin. Rev.* I. 242 Oxygen, and particularly the gaseous oxygenants, evidently produce two effects, of the same tendency. **1803** BEDDOES *Hygëia* XI. 52 Air destroys contagion by acting as an oxygenant. **1866** ODLING *Anim. Chem.* 149 As an oxidising agent, there are many more energetic oxygenants than the [nitric] peroxide.

oxygenase ('ɒksɪdʒəneɪz, -s). *Biochem.* [a. G. *oxygenase* (Chodat & Bach 1903, in *Ber. d. Deut. Chem. Ges.* XXXVI. 607): see OXYGEN and -ASE.] Any enzyme which catalyses the incorporation of molecular oxygen into a substrate; orig. used in the narrowest sense of OXIDASE.

1903 *Jrnl. Chem. Soc.* LXXXIV. I. 378 Most oxydases contain principles of both types, and it is proposed to retain the term peroxydase for those substances.. which are not themselves oxidisers, but impart activity to, and thus destroy, peroxides, whilst the new term, 'oxygenase', is proposed for those substances.. which are capable of producing hydrogen peroxide, but leave it in an inactive condition. **1920** M. W. ONSLOW in *Biochem. Jrnl.* XIV. 536 The function of this additional enzyme is to catalyse the oxidation of the catechol substance with the formation of a peroxide... It is proposed to call this second enzyme an oxygenase, a term originally used by Chodat and Bach for the portion of an oxidase which can be replaced by hydrogen peroxide. **1964** [see OXIDASE]. **1971** M. F. MALLETTE et al. *Introd. Biochem.* viii. 282 Both oxygenases and hydroxylases use O_2 to alter substrates... Both classes of enzymes reduce O_2 but do it by incorporating oxygen atoms into organic substrates. On the other hand, oxidases reduce O_2.. and do not incorporate it into organic compounds.

†**o'xygenate,** *a. Obs.* In 8 oxi-. [f. F. *oxygéné* pa. pple.: see -ATE[2] 2.] = OXYGENATED.

1797 *Monthly Mag.* III. 351 Moistened with muriatic oxigenate acid.

oxygenate ('ɒksɪdʒəneɪt, ɒk'sɪdʒɪneɪt), *v.* Also 8 oxi-. [f. F. *oxygén-er* (G. de Morveau and Lavoisier, 1787), f. *oxygène*: see -ATE[3].] *trans.* To supply, treat, or mix with oxygen; to cause oxygen to combine with (a substance); to oxidate, oxidize; *esp.* to charge (the blood) with oxygen by respiration.

1790 KERR tr. *Berthollet's Bleaching* iii. 36 By decomposing common salt in the same process which is performed for oxygenating its acid. **1793** BEDDOES *Sea Scurvy* 53 Whether we oxygenate the blood by the lungs or the stomach. **1794** G. ADAMS *Nat. & Exp. Philos.* I. xi. 462 To oxygenate a substance, or make it combine with vital air. **1875** W. HOUGHTON *Sk. Brit. Insects* 58 To draw fresh currents of water to oxygenate the blood.

Hence **oxygenating** *vbl. sb.* and *ppl. a.*

1794 J. HUTTON *Philos. Light*, etc. 149 To explain all appearances in those burning and oxigenating bodies. *Ibid.* 385 Vegetables secrete and emit that very oxigenating substance, when growing in the sun. **1890** *Pall Mall G.* 4 Aug. 1/3 A much needed oxygenating of the life-blood of the nation.

oxygenated (see prec.), *ppl. a.* [f. prec. + -ED[1].] Mixed or combined with oxygen.

† *oxygenated muriatic acid*: = OXYMURIATIC *acid* (i.e. chlorine).

1790 R. KERR (*title*) Essay on the New Method of Bleaching, by means of Oxygenated Muriatic Acid, from the French of Berthollet. **1812** DAVY *Chem. Philos.* Introd. 46 A theoretical nomenclature is liable to continued alteration; oxygenated muriatic acid is as improper a name as dephlogisticated marine acid. **1871** ROSCOE *Elem. Chem.* 48 Hydrogen Dioxide has received the name of oxygenated water, as it easily decomposes into oxygen and water.

oxygenation (ɒksɪdʒə'neɪʃən). [a. F. *oxygénation*, noun of action from *oxygéner* to OXYGENATE.] The action of oxygenating or condition of being oxygenated; mixture with oxygen; combination with oxygen, oxidation.

1790 R. KERR tr. *Lavoisier's Elem. Chem.* II. iv. 186 Sometimes oxygenation takes place with great rapidity. **1794** G. ADAMS *Nat. & Exp. Philos.* I. 461. **1796** HATCHETT in *Phil. Trans.* 336 It [Molybdæna] appears to me to suffer four degrees of oxygenation. The first is the black oxyde; the second is the blue oxyde; the third is the green oxyde, which I am inclined to call molybdous acid, according to the distinction made by the new nomenclature; the last and fourth degree is the yellow acid, or that which is supersaturated with oxygen. **1865** LIVINGSTONE *Zambesi* xxii. 454 Not only is the most perfect oxygenation of the blood secured.

ox'ygenator. [Agent-n. from OXYGENATE *v.*]

a. A substance that oxygenates another; = OXIDATOR a.

1864 in WEBSTER.

b. (See quot.)

1875 KNIGHT *Dict. Mech.*, *Oxygenator*, a contrivance for throwing a stream of oxygen into the flame of a lamp.

c. *Med.* An apparatus for oxygenating the blood.

1928 *Jrnl. Physiol.* LXVI. 443 Drinker, Drinker and Lund used a modification of Hooker's oxygenator in bone marrow perfusion experiments. **1961** [see HOLE *sb.* 7 e]. **1968** *Sci. Jrnl.* Nov. 63/2 Attempts to replace the living heart and lungs by a mechanical pump and an artificial oxygenator were unsatisfactory.

†**oxyge'neity.** *Obs. rare*[−1]. [irreg. f. OXYGEN + -E)ITY: cf. *homogeneity*, etc.] = OXYGENITY.

1801 W. TAYLOR in *Monthly Mag.* XI. 645 The most probable [theory] is that which hints at the oxygeneity of light.

oxygenic (ɒksɪ'dʒɛnɪk), *a. rare.* [f. OXYGEN + -IC.] Of the nature of, or consisting of, oxygen.

1850 CLOUGH *Let. to T. Arnold* 3 Jan., Poems, etc. 1869 I. 167 Consider.. the long preparation of this strange marriage of coal and oxygenic air. **1885** *Sat. Rev.* 12 Dec. 781/2 You'll breathe an air ignored By oxygenic gases.

oxygeniferous (ɒksɪdʒə'nɪfərəs), *a. rare.* [f. as prec. + -FEROUS.] Bearing or conveying oxygen.

1838 *Blackw. Mag.* XLIII. 653 Fit for the entry of a great host of oxygeniferous particles.

oxy'genity. *nonce-wd.* [f. OXYGEN + -ITY.] The quality of being oxygen, or oxygenous.

1894 *Contemp. Rev.* Aug. 294 They..lose their 'oxygenity' and 'hydrogenity'.

ˈoxygeˌnizable, *a.* [f. next + -ABLE.] Capable of being oxygenized or oxygenated.

1802 CHENEVIX in *Phil. Trans.* XCII. 166 Besides its acid properties, this substance has others, common to oxygenizable bodies.

oxygenize (ˈɒksɪdʒənaɪz, ɒkˈsɪdʒɪnaɪz), *v.* [f. OXYGEN + -IZE: cf. *carbonize.*] *trans.* = OXYGENATE *v.* Chiefly in *pa. pple.* (or *ppl. a.*) **oxygenized** = OXYGENATED.

1802 CHENEVIX in *Phil. Trans.* XCII. 126 That the proportion of oxygen..was greater in the salt than in uncombined oxygenized muriatic acid. **1822–34** *Good's Study Med.* (ed. 4) II. 465 Unless the supply furnished by the food to the blood-vessels be sufficiently oxygenized by ventilation. **1895** *Pop. Sci. Monthly* Aug. 473 The food..is then passed through the oxygenizing process in the lungs.

Hence †**oxygenizement** = OXYGENATION, OXIDATION; **oxygenizer** = OXYGENATOR.

1802 CHENEVIX in *Phil. Trans.* XCII. 165 Of the oxygenizement of fluoric and boracic acids, we have no proof. **1816** J. SMITH *Panorama Sc. & Art* II. 419 The next degree of oxygenizement is expressed by the termination *ic*, thus we say sulphuric acid. **1882** OGILVIE, *Oxygenizer*.

oxygenless (ˈɒksɪdʒənlɛs), *a.* [f. OXYGEN + -LESS.] Not containing oxygen.

1935 E. R. BURROUGHS *Pirates of Venus* 46 Even though she [*sc.* the planet Venus] be oxygenless. **1963** I. FLEMING *On H.M. Secret Service* ix. 98 James Bond followed her, holding his breath against the searing impact of the Arctic, oxygenless air. **1972** *Sci. Amer.* Apr. 58/2 We still have the 'fossils' of this life-style in the universal process of anaerobic (oxygenless) fermentation.

oxygenous (ɒkˈsɪdʒɪnəs), *a.* [f. OXYGEN, or F. *oxygène* + -OUS.] †**a.** Producing acids, acidifying: ***oxygenous gas***, oxygen; ***oxygenous principle***, Kirwan's rendering (1787) of Lavoisier's *principe oxygine* (1777–84). *Obs.* **b.** Of the nature of, consisting of, or containing oxygen.

1787 KIRWAN *Essay on Phlogiston* ii. 22 The vitriolic acid, according to them [Lavoisier, etc.] consists of sulphur as its base, and pure air, in a concrete state, as its *acidifying* or *oxygenous* principle. *Ibid.* (*passim*), The oxygenous principle. **1788** PRIESTLEY in *Phil. Trans.* 157 The term *phlogiston*..may still be given to that *principle* or thing, which, when added to water, makes it to be inflammable air; as the term *oxygenous principle* may be given to that thing which, when it is incorporated with water, makes dephlogisticated air. **1794** SULLIVAN *View Nat.* I. 233 On account of this property..the denomination of oxigenous gas has been given to vital air. **1822** IMISON *Sc. & Art* II. 47 The reason of this is, that the oxygenous part of the air has united to the metal. **1875** MAINE *Village Communities* (1876) 213 The exclusive food of the natives of India is of an oxygenous rather than a carbonaceous character.

oxygon (ˈɒksɪgən), *a.* and *sb. Geom.* Now *rare* or *Obs.* Also 6–7 oxi-. [f. L. *oxygōni-us*, a. Gr. ὀξυγώνιος acute-angled, f. ὀξύ-ς sharp + γωνία angle: perh. through F. *oxygone* (1611 in Cotgr.).] **a.** *adj.* Having acute angles, acute-angled. **b.** *sb.* An acute-angled triangle: in early use also in L. form **oxygonium (-us)**.

1570 BILLINGSLEY *Euclid* I. def. xxix. 5 An oxigonium or an acuteangled triangle, is a triangle which hath all his three angles acute. **1598** SYLVESTER *Du Bartas* II. ii. IV. *Columnes* 199 Moreover, as the Building's Ambligon May more receive then Mansion's Oxigon. **1685** R. WILLIAMS *Euclid* 10 Oxygone, or Acutangle triangle is that whose angles are all acute. **1688** J. S. *Fortification* 3 [These figures] are called Oxygoniums. **1838** SIR W. HAMILTON *Logic* xxv. (1866) II. 24 *note*, Oxygon, i.e. triangle which has its three angles acute.

Hence **oxygonal** (ɒkˈsɪgənəl), †**oxyˈgonial**, **oˈxygonous** *adjs.*, having three acute angles.

1706 PHILLIPS, *Oxygonial*, belonging to an Oxygon, Acute-Angular. **1727–41** CHAMBERS *Cycl.* s.v. *Triangle*, If all the angles be acute..the triangle is said to be acutangular, or oxygonous. **1842** FRANCIS *Dict. Arts*, *Oxygonal*, acute angled.

ˈoxyhæmoˈcyanin, the oxidized blue form of HÆMOCYANIN, q.v. (*Syd. Soc. Lex.* 1892).

oxyhæmoglobin, -hemoglobin (ˌɒksɪhiːməʊˈgləʊbɪn). *Chem.* [OXY- 2.] 'The form in which hæmoglobin exists in arterial and capillary blood where it is loosely combined with oxygen' (*Syd. Soc. Lex.*).

1873 RALFE *Phys. Chem.* 178 Oxygen on entering the body chemically combines with hæmoglobin, forming oxy-hæmoglobin, which gives the scarlet colour to arterial blood. **1875** H. C. WOOD *Therap.* (1879) 184 The spectroscope shows plainly that the haemoglobin exists in the blood either in its pure state, or else as oxyhæmoglobin.

oxyˈhydrate. *Chem.* A hydrated oxide or hydrate of a metal, as ***oxyhydrate of iron***. So **oxyˈhydric** *a.*, consisting of oxygen and hydrogen combined; as ***oxyhydric acid***, a descriptive term for water (H_2O). †**oxy-hydrocarbon** *a.*, consisting of oxygen combined with a hydrocarbon.

1876 tr. *Wagner's Gen. Pathol.* (ed. 6) 88 If the water contains iron in solution, this is readily precipitated as an oxyhydrate. **1891** *Lancet* 23 May 1165/2 Carbonic acid unites with oxyhydrate to form carbonate of lead, which is soluble in excess of the gas.

1852 MORFIT *Tanning & Currying* (1853) 158 In modern chemistry water is known as oxy-hydric acid, or protoxide of hydrogen. **1866** ODLING *Anim. Chem.* 55 The building up of the primary oxihydrocarbon molecules.

oxyhydrogen (ɒksɪˈhaɪdrədʒɪn), *a.* [f. OXY- 2 + HYDROGEN.] Consisting of, or involving the use of, a mixture of oxygen and hydrogen.

oxyhydrogen blowpipe: a compound blowpipe in which two streams, of oxygen and hydrogen, meet as they issue; used to produce an extremely hot flame by the burning of the hydrogen in the oxygen. ***oxyhydrogen light***: the bright white light obtained by directing such a flame upon lime; the lime-light. So ***oxyhydrogen flame, jet, lamp***, etc. ***oxyhydrogen microscope***, etc.: one in which the object is illuminated by an oxyhydrogen light.

1827 E. TURNER *Elem. Chem.* 160 An apparatus of this kind, now known by the name of the oxy-hydrogen blow-pipe, was contrived by Mr. Newman. **1834** MEDWIN *Angler in Wales* II. 5 The microscope..notwithstanding all its oxyhydrogen improvements. *c* **1865** LETHEBY in *Circ. Sc.* I. 134/2 The Oxy-hydrogen Light..was first introduced to public notice by Lieutenant Drummond. **1871** tr. *Schellen's Spectr. Anal.* 16 *note*, The light of magnesia heated in the oxyhydrogen flame.

†**ˈoxyˌiode.** *Chem. Obs.* [f. OXY- 2 + IODE.] Obsolete name for an IODATE.

1815 HENRY *Elem. Chem.* II. 32 The metallic bases called by Sir H. Davy, *oxyiodes*, and by Gay Lussac,..*iodates*.

So †**oxyiˈodic** *a.* = IODIC. **oxyˈiodide**, an iodine compound analogous to an oxychloride. †**oxyˈiodine**, Davy's name for *iodic anhydride*, I_2O_5.

1815 SIR H. DAVY in *Phil. Trans.* I. 213, I venture to propose a name..that of *oxyiodic acid. **1815** HENRY *Elem. Chem.* (ed. 7) II. 32 For the watery solution of oxyiodine Sir H. Davy has proposed the name of *oxyiodic acid*, and is disposed to regard it as a triple compound of iodine, hydrogen, and oxygen; or an oxyiode of hydrogen. **1868–77** WATTS *Dict. Chem.* V. 815 Insoluble *Oxyiodides of variable composition. **1815** DAVY in *Phil. Trans.* I. 213, I venture to propose a name..**oxyiodine* for the new solid compound.

oxylith (ˈɒksɪlɪθ), Also **-lithe.** [ad. F. *oxylithe*, f. *oxy-* OXY- 2 + *-lithe* -LITH.] A commercial name for calcium peroxide, CaO_2, as used in breathing apparatus as a convenient source of oxygen (evolved by reaction with carbon dioxide).

1902 *Chem. News* 16 May 240/2 The recent invention of 'oxylith', due to M. Jaubert, will help to make the use of nascent oxygen still more wide in its applications. **1924** *Chambers's Jrnl.* Oct. 701/2 The helmet of this appliance.. is supplied with a substance called 'oxylithe', which gives off pure oxygen when breathed upon. **1948** R. H. DAVIS *Breathing in Irrespirable Atmospheres* vi. 206 Where 'Oxylithe' was employed as the main source of oxygen in the earlier designs, it took a couple of minutes to evolve oxygen in sufficient quantity to allow work to begin.

oxyluciferin (ɒksɪl(j)uːˈsɪfərɪn). *Biochem.* [f. OXY- 2 + LUCIFERIN.] The oxidised form of (a) luciferin produced by the action of luciferase. (Cf. the note s.v. LUCIFERIN.)

1919 E. N. HARVEY in *Jrnl. Gen. Physiol.* I. 135, I suggest also that luciferin when oxidized be designated oxyluciferin. **1953** J. RAMSBOTTOM *Mushrooms & Toadstools* xiv. 163 Luciferin is oxidised by luciferase in one part of a cell producing oxyluciferin which in another part is reduced again to luciferin. **1964** *Oceanogr. & Marine Biol.* II. 351 Chromatography yields three isolated substances, two of which are active in luminescence and have been designated oxyluciferin A and oxyluciferin B.

oxymel (ˈɒksɪmɛl). Also 4–7 **oxi-, -mell.** [a. L. *oxymel* (also *oxymeli*), a. Gr. ὀξύμελι, f. ὀξύ-ς sour + μέλι honey.] A medicinal drink or syrup compounded of vinegar and honey, sometimes with other ingredients.

oxymel of squills, oxymel made with 'vinegar of squills'.

[*c* **1000** *Sax. Leechd.* II. 212 Eac sceal mon oxumellis sellan þæt biþ of ecede & of hunige ȝeworht drenc suþerne.] **1398** TREVISA *Barth. De P.R.* XIX. lx. [xlvi.] (MS. Bodl.) lf. 304 b/2 Oximel is iȝeue wiþ hote water to defiynge and naisschinge of hard matere and to open pores. *c* **1400** *Lanfranc's Cirurg.* 189 Tempere hem wiþ oximel. *c* **1460** *Play Sacram.* 584 A drynke made full well wyth scamoly and wt oxymell [*MS.* oxennell]. **1533** ELYOT *Cast. Helthe* (1541) 36 Oximell is, where to one part of vyneger is put double so moche of honye, foure tymes as moche of water. **1684** EARL ROSCOM. *Ess. Transl. Verse* 130 And all, goes down like Oxymel of Squils. **1831** J. DAVIES *Manual Mat. Med.* 39 Oxymels are other species of syrups made from honey and vinegar.

oxymeter (ɒkˈsɪmɪtə(r)). *rare*⁻⁰. [ad. mod.L. *oxymetrum*: see OXY- 2 and -METER.] = EUDIOMETER. So **oxyˈmetric** *a.*, measured in regard to the amount of oxygen.

1857 MAYNE *Expos. Lex.*, *Oxymetrum*, a measurer of oxygen: an oximeter; another name for the instrument called a eudiometer. **1876** tr. *Schützenberger's Ferment.* 111 We may previously determine the oxymetric value of the hyposulphite, the volume of oxygen which is required to saturate the unit of volume of the solution.

‖**oxymoron** (ɒksɪˈmɔːrɒn). *Rhet.* [a. Gr. ὀξύμωρον, sb. use of neuter of ὀξύμωρος pointedly foolish, f. ὀξυ- sharp + μωρός dull, stupid, foolish.] A rhetorical figure by which contradictory or incongruous terms are conjoined so as to give point to the statement or expression; an expression, in its superficial or literal meaning self-contradictory or absurd, but involving a point. (Now often loosely or erroneously used as if merely = a contradiction in terms, an incongruous conjunction.)

[**1640** BP. REYNOLDS *Passions* xvii. 186 It was a bold but true ὀξύμωρον of Seneca. *Mortibus vivimus.*] **1657** J. SMITH *Myst. Rhet.* 121 Oxymoron, ὀξύμωρον, *Acutifatuum aut stulte acutum*, subtilly foolish. *a* **1677** BARROW *Serm.* (1826) VI. 132 Some elegant figures..lofty hyperboles, paranomasies, oxymorons..lie very near upon the confines of jocularity. **1792** W. ROBERTS *Looker-On* No. 30 (1794) I. 427 These contradictory gentlemen..were thus pressed together in a forced kind of union, like the figure oxymoron. **1890** *Q. Rev.* CLX. 289 Voltaire..we might call, by an oxymoron which has plenty of truth in it, an 'Epicurean pessimist'.

oxymoronic (ˌɒksɪmɔəˈrɒnɪk), *a.* [f. OXYMORON + -IC.] Suggestive of oxymoron; incongruous, self-contradictory. So **oxymoˈronically** *adv.*

1901 BEERBOHM *Around Theatres* (1924) I. 270 A little bore, whose oxymoronically belated-premature death we hail..as a merciful release. **1970** G. GREER *Female Eunuch* 164 It would be oxymoronic to claim to be gently, reliably or sensibly in love. **1972** P. GREEN *Shadow of Parthenon* 35 'Imperial democracy', that oxymoronic contradiction in terms. **1975** *Times Lit. Suppl.* 17 Oct. 1226/5 Professor Hardy's point..is signalled by the oxymoronic 'dubious consolations' of her title.

†**oxymuriate** (ɒksɪˈmjʊərɪət). *Chem. Obs.* [f. next: see -ATE[1] 1 c.] A salt of 'oxymuriatic acid': applied formerly to compounds now called either chlorates or chlorides, as ***oxymuriate of mercury, of tin***, = mercuric and stannic chloride, ***oxymuriate of potash*** = potassium chlorate.

1797 PEARSON in *Phil. Trans.* LXXXVII. 149 To this residue was added half its bulk of oxygen gaz, obtained from oxymuriate of potash. **1816** ACCUM *Chem. Tests* (1818) 124 Add..a quantity of oxy-muriate of mercury. **1830** M. DONOVAN *Dom. Econ.* I. 261 A small quantity of chloride of lime, or, as it was formerly called, oxymuriate of lime.

So †**oxyˈmuriated** *a. Obs.*, as in ***oxymuriated acid*** = OXYMURIATIC acid, ***oxymuriated quicksilver*** = OXYMURIATE of mercury.

1796 KIRWAN *Elem. Min.* (ed. 2) II. 215 An effervescence ..arising from the production of Oxymuriated Acid. **1822–34** *Good's Study Med.* (ed. 4) IV. 503 Dissolving a drachm of oxymuriated quicksilver in half a pint of water.

†**oxymuriatic** (ˌɒksɪmjʊərɪˈætɪk), *a. Chem. Obs.* [f. OXY- 2 + MURIATIC.] ***oxymuriatic acid*** (also ***oxymuriatic gas***): a former name of chlorine, as a supposed compound of oxygen and 'muriatic' (hydrochloric) acid. ***oxymuriatic matches***: matches tipped with chlorate of potash.

1796 KIRWAN *Elem. Min.* (ed. 2) II. 328 Oxymuriatic Acid and Aqua Regia scarcely affect it. *Ibid.* 462 He observed it to yield oxymuriatic Gas. **1807** T. THOMSON *Chem.* (ed. 3) II. 225 Oxymuriatic acid was discovered by Scheele in 1774. .. He gave it the name of dephlogisticated muriatic acid, from the supposition that it is muriatic acid deprived of phlogiston. The French chemists, after its composition had been ascertained, called it oxygenated muriatic acid; which unwieldy appellation Kirwan has happily contracted into oxymuriatic. **1835** SIR J. ROSS *Narr. 2nd Voy.* xxi. 317 Procuring a light by means of the oxymuriatic matches which he had seen us use.

oxymyoglobin (ˌɒksɪmaɪəˈgləʊbɪn). *Biochem.* [f. OXY- 2 + MYOGLOBIN.] The oxygenated form of myoglobin.

1935 *Physiol. Abstr.* XIX. 578 The dissociation curve of oxymyoglobin is a hyperbola. **1953** FRUTON & SIMMONDS *Gen. Biochem.* vi. 167 At a given oxygen pressure oxymyoglobin is less dissociated than oxyhemoglobin, i.e. myoglobin has a higher affinity for oxygen. **1974** M. D. RANKEN in Birch & Parker *Vitamin C* ix. 122 At the surface of fresh meat, in contact with oxygen, the colour is the bright red of oxymyoglobin.

oxyˈnitrate. *Chem.* [f. OXY- 2 + NITRATE.] A compound of the oxide and nitrate of a metal.

1809 GREGOR in *Phil. Trans.* XCIX. 199 The colourless liquid *oxynitrat* of lead. **1819** CHILDREN *Chem. Anal.* 440 Oxynitrate (qu. Nitrate?) of silver, and nitrate of mercury, dropped in excess into a dilute solution of any hyposulphite, give a precipitate of their respective metals in the state of sulphurets. **1873** WATTS *Fownes' Chem.* (ed. 11) 426 The normal [platinammonium] nitrate $N_2H_6Pt(NO_3)_4$, is obtained by dissolving the oxynitrate $[N_2H_6Pt(NO_3)_2O]$ in nitric acid.

†**oxyˈnitric**, *a. Chem.* In ***oxynitric acid, oxynitric gas***, obs. names of nitrogen peroxide.

1805 W. NISBET *Dict. Chem.* 369 Oxy-nitric gas. **1815** HENRY *Elem. Chem.* (ed. 7) I. 361 It will appear that the oxygen in nitrous gas is very nearly both in weight and volume a multiple of that in nitrous oxide by 2; in nitrous acid by 3; in nitric acid by 4; and in oxynitric acid by 6.

oxyntic (ɒkˈsɪntɪk), *a. Physiol.* [f. Gr. type *ὀξυντ-ος, verbal adj. from ὀξύ-νειν to sharpen, make acid, f. ὀξύ-ς sharp: see -IC.] Rendering acid, acidifying: applied to certain glands of the stomach, or to cells in them, supposed to produce the hydrochloric acid of the gastric juice.

1884 A. GAMGEE in *Encycl. Brit.* XVII. 674/1 The glands which possess these acid-forming cells have of late been termed (Langley) oxyntic glands. **1892** *Syd. Soc. Lex.*, Oxyntic cells.

ox yoke. [OX 5.] A yoke used for draught oxen. Also *transf.*

1573 [see OX-BOW 1]. **1688** R. HOLME *Armoury* III. 244/1 In the Cart-House..Oxeyokes, Horse Collars. **1785** G. WASHINGTON *Diary* 16 Nov. (1925) II. 441 A good Oxe Cart —2 Oxe yokes. **1809** *Austin Papers* (1924) I. 164 One Plough, one Harrow..and two Ox yokes. **1847** in H. Howe *Hist. Coll. Ohio* 188 Journeys..of 20 or 50 miles, for the sole purpose of having the staple of an ox-yoke mended. **1879** B. F. TAYLOR *Summer-Savory* xvii. 138 Awkward H's like a pair of leaning bar-posts with one bar, and B's like ox-yokes. **1938** M. K. RAWLINGS *Yearling* iv. 41 Penny..went to the sink-hole with a wooden ox-yoke supporting two wooden buckets over his thin shoulders.

oxyphil ('ɒksɪfɪl), *a. Biol.* Also **-phile.** [f. Gr. ὀξυ- sharp, acid + -φιλος loving, -PHIL(E.] 'Acid-loving': applied to certain white blood-corpuscles or other cells having an affinity for acid dyes.

1893 *Brit. Med. Jrnl.* 25 Feb. 400/1 The complete histological differentiation of a leucocyte depends upon staining it in such a manner that all the oxyphile and basophile elements are brought out in relief. **1896** *Allbutt's Syst. Med.* I. 79 Their [i.e. Kanthack and Hardy's] coarsely granular oxyphile cells are the eosinophile cells of most writers. *Ibid.* 80 Feeble oxyphile reaction. *Ibid.* 117 Other cells containing oxyphil granules. **1925** H. J. CONN et al. *Biol. Stains* vii. 79 Yellowish eosin..is used in various technics for staining the oxyphile granules of cells. **1970** *Jrnl. Path.* CII. 193 One of the adenomata in this series is composed of oxyphil cells and transitional oxyphil cells when viewed by light microscopy. **1976** *Clinical Endocrinol.* V. Suppl. 377 The one oxyphil adenoma tested by Schorr *et al.* (1972) showed no response.

oxyphilic (ɒksɪ'fɪlɪk), *a. Biol.* [f. prec. + -IC.] Readily stained by acid dyes; oxyphil.

1901 C. E. SIMON *Text-bk. Physiol. Chem.* xiii. 303 The granules which are found in certain forms of leucocytes are apparently of an albuminous nature. According to their affinity for acid, basic, or neutral dyes, they are termed oxyphilic, basophilic, and neutrophilic, respectively. **1973** *Cancer* XXXI. 253/1 The endoplasmic reticulum is poorly developed in oxyphilic cells, which means that protein-synthesis must be scanty.

oxyphilous (ɒksɪ'fɪləs), *a. Biol.* [f. as prec. + -OUS.] = prec.

1893 *Brit. Med. Jrnl.* 25 Feb. 400/2 All the granules found in normal circulating leucocytes are oxyphilous. **1968** *Zeitschr. f. Mikrosk.-Anat. Forsch.* LXXIX. 551 Oxyphilous Welsh cells of the parathyroid glands have glandular functions.

†**oxy'phosphate.** *Chem.* An obs. name for a metallic phosphate containing a larger proportion of oxygen, as ***oxyphosphate of iron*** = ferric phosphate.

1815 HENRY *Elem. Chem.* (ed. 7) II. 116 The phosphate of iron is almost insoluble in water. The oxy-phosphate of iron is, also, an insoluble salt.

oxyproline (ɒksɪ'prəʊliːn). *Biochem.* [ad. G. *oxyprolin* (H. Leuchs 1905, in *Ber. d. Deut. Chem. Ges.* XXXVIII. 1937): see OXY- 2 and PROLINE.] = *hydroxyproline* s.v. HYDROXY-.

1928 *Physiol. Abstr.* XII. 599 Tetrasulphocyandiamminchromic acid..may be used to give crystalline precipitates with proline and oxyproline. **1931** *Chem. Rev.* IX. 264 Hammarsten..has synthesized γ-oxyproline. **1935** A. K. ANDERSON *Essent. Physiol. Chem.* xvi. 177 The pyrrol rings are present in the amino acids proline and oxyproline. **1972** *Biol. Abstr.* LIV. 4493/2 As silicosis progressed the quartz and oxyproline content in the lungs increased.

oxyrhynch ('ɒksɪrɪŋk). [f. OXY- 1 + Gr. ῥύγχ-ος snout, beak.]

1. Any crab of the group *Oxyrhyncha*, characterized by a triangular cephalothorax with projecting rostrum; the group includes the spider-crabs.

1839 *Penny Cycl.* XIV. 297/2 The first joint of the external antennæ..being cylindrical..in nearly all the Oxyrhynchs. **1840** *Ibid.* XVII. 109 The Oxyrhynchs are all essentially marine.

2. A fish; = next, 1.

‖**oxyrhynchus** (ɒksɪ'rɪŋkəs). *Zool.* [ad. Gr. ὀξύρρυγχος sharp-snouted, epithet of a fish.]

1. A fish (*Mormyrus oxyrhynchus*) found in the Nile, esteemed sacred by the ancient Egyptians.

1706 PHILLIPS, *Oxyrinchus*, the Spit-nose, a sort of River-fish. **1851** *Museum Nat. Hist.* II. 152 The oxyrhinchus is very commonly represented in the paintings of Thebes, Beni-Hassan and Memphis. **1865** J. H. INGRAHAM *Pillar of Fire* (1872) 223 The oxyrhincus, the eel, the lepidotus, and some other kinds of fish are sacred; and at Thebes they are embalmed by the priests.

2. *Ornith.* A genus of American tyrant flycatchers, characterized by a long straight sharp-pointed bill.

1868 *Eng. Cycl.* s.v. *Picidae*, Neither does the intervention of the Wryneck with its wormlike tongue, or of Oxyrhyncus with its acute bill, do more than indicate the broken links of the chain.

†**oxyrrhodin, -ine** (ɒk'sɪrəʊdɪn). *Obs.* Also in L. form **oxyrrhodinum.** [ad. mod.L. *oxyrrhodinum*, ad. Gr. ὀξυρρόδινον (ἔλαιον), 'rose-oil mixed with vinegar' (Liddell and Scott).] A preparation of vinegar and oil of roses, formerly used medicinally. Also †**oxyrrhod,** ‖**oxyrrhodon.**

1639 J. W. tr. *Guibert's Char. Physic.* I. 31 Oyle of Roses, ..Rose water, and a spoonfull of vineger, mixe them well together, and your oxirrhod is done. **17..** FLOYER *Humours* (J.), The spirits, opiates, and cool things, readily compose oxyrrhodines. **1727-41** CHAMBERS *Cycl.*, *Oxyrrhodon*, or *Oxyrrhodinum*. **1754-64** SMELLIE *Midwif.* I. Introd. 19 A cloth dipped in oxyrrhodon must be laid on her abdomen.

‖**oxysaccharum** (ɒksɪ'sækərəm). Also 6 **oxi-.** [Late L., a. late Gr. ὀξυσάκχαρον, f. ὀξυ- sharp, acid + σάκχαρον sugar.] A medicine compounded of vinegar and sugar.

c **1550** LLOYD *Treas. Health* (1585) X viij, Let the matter be preparid with oxisaccharum in thre partes therof. **1727-41** in CHAMBERS *Cycl.*

oxy-salt ('ɒksɪsɔːlt). *Chem.* Also **oxi-.** [f. OXY- 2 + SALT.] A salt containing oxygen; a salt of an oxyacid.

1836-41 BRANDE *Chem.* (ed. 5) 593 The oxidizement of a metal is an essential preliminary to the formation of its oxy-salts, or, in other words, to its combinations with oxy-acids. **1841** SCHÖNBEIN in *Rep. Brit. Assoc.* 210 Mixed with chemically pure..sulphuric acid, with phosphoric acid, nitric acid, potash, and a series of oxi-salts. **1882** VINES *Sachs's Bot.* 698 Oxygen is introduced into the plant in the form of water, carbon dioxide, and oxy-salts.

†**oxy'sulphate.** *Chem.* An obs. name for a metallic sulphate containing a larger proportion of oxygen, as ***oxysulphate of iron*** = ferric sulphate.

1802 *Med. Jrnl.* VIII. 550 It has been proposed to distinguish them [iron sulphates] by terming that salt which contains the metal more highly oxydated, an oxysulphat. **1815** HENRY *Elem. Chem.* (ed. 7) II. 109 This salt has been called, but not with strict propriety, *oxy-sulphate*. Its legitimate name would be *sulphate of peroxide of iron*; but, as this is inconvenient from its length, it may be called the *red sulphate of iron*.

So **oxy'sulphide**, a compound of an element or positive compound radical with oxygen and sulphur; generally restricted to compounds of the oxide and sulphide of a metal. †**oxy'sulphion** *Obs.* 'Daniell's term for the acid compound of an oxy-salt containing sulphur which is set free at the positive pole of a galvanic battery, but which cannot exist in a free condition' (*Syd. Soc. Lex.*); = the group SO_4, now called SULPHION. †**oxy'sulphuret** *Obs.* = oxysulphide.

1854 J. SCOFFERN in *Orr's Circ. Sc., Chem.* 408 A mixture of insoluble *oxysulphide of lime and carbonate of soda. **1845** TODD & BOWMAN *Phys. Anat.* I. 6 A compound..called by Prof. Daniell *oxysulphion. **1849** NOAD *Electricity* (ed. 3) 225 Oxysulphion of hydrogen. **1854** J. SCOFFERN in *Orr's Circ. Sc., Chem.* 472 Oxide and sulphuret of antimony combine in many proportions, forming many *oxysulphurets.

oxytetracycline (ˌɒksɪtetrə'saɪkliːn). *Pharm.* [f. OXY- 2 + TETRACYCLINE.] The 5-hydroxy derivative, $C_{22}H_{24}N_2O_9$, of tetracycline (usu. administered in the form of its yellow hydrochloride), which is an antimicrobial substance produced by cultures of the bacterium *Streptomyces rimosus* and has actions and uses similar to those of other tetracyclines.

1953 *Jrnl. Amer. Med. Assoc.* 3 Jan. 46/1 Both compounds possess a common four-ringed skeleton, for which the generic term tetracycline has been proposed. They differ only in that aureomycin has a chlorine atom at ring one while terramycin has a hydroxyl group at ring three. The chemically descriptive generic names chlorotetracycline and oxytetracycline, respectively, have therefore been proposed for the two compounds. **1958** *Times* 29 Sept. 2/7 The promise of antibiotics as a means of controlling certain plant diseases has been brought a step nearer fulfilment by a recent Order which permits the use of streptomycin and oxytetracycline. **1966** *Economist* 9 Apr. 169/1 This February, Pfizer's patent monopoly on the drug, oxytetracycline, expired. **1969** CROFTON & DOUGLAS *Respiratory Dis.* xviii. 321/1 Sometimes oxytetracycline or chlortetracycline is better tolerated [than tetracycline]. **1974** R. M. KIRK et al. *Surgery* ii. 24 Oxytetracycline is given to prevent secondary infection.

oxytocic (ɒksɪ'tɒsɪk), *a.* and *sb. Med.* [f. Gr. ὀξυτόκιον = oxytocic *sb.*, f. ὀξυ-, OXY- 1 + τόκος childbirth.] **a.** *adj.* Serving to accelerate parturition. **b.** *sb.* A medicine having this property.

1853 DUNGLISON *Med. Lex.*, *Oxytocic*, ..a medicine which promotes delivery. **1873** R. BARNES *Dis. Women* xviii. 187 Indian hemp..is credited..with oxytocic properties. *Ibid.*, The powers of galvanism as an oxytocic, and even in originating uterine contraction. **1875** H. C. WOOD *Therap.* (1879) 69 The oxytocic action of quinia was believed in many years ago by numbers of our Southern practitioners.

oxytocin (ɒksɪ'təʊsɪn). *Med.* [f. OXYTOC(IC *a.* and *sb.* + -IN[1].] A hormone present in the neurohypophysis of mammals which stimulates uterine contractions and the ejection of milk from a lactating breast and is made synthetically for use in inducing labour and controlling bleeding after delivery.

1928 *Jrnl. Amer. Chem. Soc.* Feb. 575 α-Hypophamine is being supplied under the trade name of Oxytocin..and β-Hypophamine under the trade name Vasopressin... They were first supplied for clinical use in August, 1927. **1928** *Official Gaz.* (U.S. Patent Office) 11 Sept. 258/1 Parke, Davis & Company, Detroit, Mich... *Oxytocin* for preparation for stimulating contractions of uterine and other unstriped muscular fibers. Claims use since Sept. 15, 1927. **1930** *Druggists Circular* Oct. 60/2 In 1928 Oliver Kamm succeeded in separating the two principles of the posterior lobe of the pituitary body. One of them, which acts upon the uterus, Kamm named oxytocin. **1937** *Dispensatory U.S.A.* (ed. 22) 854/1 The oxytocic principle has been called pitocin, oxytocin, [etc.]. **1965** LEE & KNOWLES *Animal Hormones* ii. 29 The second hormone, oxytocin, appears to exert its action only in mammals, but it may play some part in oviposition in the other vertebrates. **1969** *Daily Tel.* 19 Dec. 11/8 Oxytocin is used regularly to start or speed up a labour that is lagging. **1974** *Nature* 20 Dec. 630/1 Neurones in the hypothalamus synthesise the hormones vasopressin and oxytocin. **1977** 'E. CRISPIN' *Glimpses of Moon* xii. 256 It read like an instruction from an obstetrician to a lady who.. has been given oxytocin to hurry matters up.

Hence **oxy'tocinase** [-ASE], an enzyme that inactivates oxytocin.

1949 *Chem. Abstr.* XLIII. 2330 *(heading)* Effect of cysteine and glutathione on the oxytocinase activity of blood plasma. **1974** PASSMORE & ROBSON *Compan. Med. Stud.* III. II. xl. 1/2 A serum oxytocinase which rapidly inactivates oxytocin appears in increasing amounts during pregnancy.

oxytone ('ɒksɪtəʊn), *a.* and *sb. Gram.*, chiefly *Gr. Gram.* Also **oxyton.** [ad. Gr. ὀξύτον-ος having the acute accent, f. ὀξυ- sharp, acute + τόνος pitch, tone, accent.] **a.** *adj.* Having an acute accent on the last syllable. **b.** *sb.* A word so accented.

1764 W. PRIMATT *Accentus redivivi* 109 Aristarchus..has pronounced it [ἀγυιαν] as an oxytone. **1869** J. HADLEY *Ess.* (1873) 111 On the last syllable of an oxytone word, when.. its higher pitch changes to a lower, the lower pitch is represented in..the same way as in the latter part of the circumflex accent. **1881** WESTCOTT & HORT *Grk. N.T.* II. App. 6/2 They are not independent or strictly final oxytones, being treated as fragments of a clause.

Hence **'oxytone, 'oxytonize** *vbs. trans.*, to make oxytone; to pronounce or write with the accent on the last syllable.

1887 *Science* 29 Apr. 412/2 There is also a tendency to oxytonize many words,..although the accent shifts, as in other Indian languages.

oxytonic (ɒksɪ'tɒnɪk), *a.* Also **oxy'tonical.** [f. OXYTONE *a.* and *sb.* + -IC.] Characterized by an oxytone; designating a language in which the majority of words are oxytones.

1890 *Century Dict.*, Oxytonical. **1954** PEI & GAYNOR *Dict. Linguistics* 156 *Oxytonic language*, a language in which the majority of the words bear the main accent on the last syllable. **1963** *Amer. Speech* XXXVIII. 217 Armenian, like French, is oxytonic; with rare exceptions, the stress in a word falls on the last syllable. **1972** HARTMANN & STORK *Dict. Lang. & Linguistics* 160/2 *Oxytonic language*, a language in which most words have fixed..stress on the final syllable.

oxytrichine (ɒk'sɪtrɪkaɪn), *a.* and *sb. Zool.* [f. mod.L. *Oxytrichina* neut. pl., f. *Oxytricha*, the typical genus, f. Gr. ὀξυ- sharp + θρίξ, τριχ- hair (cf. Gr. ὀξύτριχος adj.): see -INE[1].] **a.** *adj.* Belonging to the family *Oxytrichina* or *Oxytrichidæ* of infusorians. **b.** *sb.* An infusorian of this family. Also **oxy'trichinous** *a.* = a (Mayne 1857).

oxytrope ('ɒksɪtrəʊp). [ad. mod.L. *Oxytropis*, f. Gr. ὀξυ- sharp + τρόπις keel; from the pointed keel of the corolla.] A plant of the genus *Oxytropis* (N.O. *Leguminosæ*), closely allied to *Astragalus*, the species of which are chiefly alpine; they have pinnate leaves, and flowers of various colours in spikes or racemes; several are cultivated as ornamental rock-work plants.

1865 BENTHAM *Brit. Flora* 215 The point of the keel is short and straight as in the yellow oxytrope. **1883** G. ALLEN in *Longm. Mag.* Feb. 418 In the same exposed Clova range ..the closely-related yellow oxytrope still grows in diminishing numbers; while its ally the Ural oxytrope holds its own manfully over all the dry hills of the Highlands.

‖**Oxyuris** (ɒksɪ'(j)ʊərɪs). *Zool.* Pl. **oxy'urides** (-ɪdiːz). [mod.L. (Rudolphi, 1809), f. Gr. ὀξυ- sharp + οὐρά tail.] A genus of small thread-worms of the family *Ascaridæ*, inhabiting the rectum of various animals; *O. vermicularis* is frequent in that of man, especially of children.

1864 *Reader* IV. 669/3 The minute oxyurides, so frequent a source of weakness and irritability in children. **1868** *Eng. Cycl.* s.v. *Entozoa*, Oxyuris is characterised by being subulate posteriorly, having the mouth orbicular.

Hence **oxy'uric** *a.* [-IC], pertaining to or produced by an *Oxyuris*, as 'oxyuric irritation' (*Cent. Dict.*); **oxy'uricide** (-saɪd) [-CIDE 1], 'a medicine which destroys *Oxyurides*' (*Syd. Soc. Lex.*), an anthelmintic; **oxy'urifuge** [-FUGE] = prec.

1864 T. S. COBBOLD *Entozoa* xiii. 372 There is one Indian drug which appears to be very valuable, because it..is..a true Oxyuricide. **1881** —— in *Jrnl. Linn. Soc.* (1883) XVI. 187 The practical efficiency of the drug [milk of Papaw] as an oxyurifuge has been attested by Dr. Peckolt.

oxyurous (ɒksɪ'(j)ʊərəs), *a. rare*⁻⁰. [f. mod.L. *oxyūr-us* (cf. prec.) + -OUS.] Having a pointed tail.

1857 MAYNE *Expos. Lex.*, *Oxyurus*..having a tail ending in a point.., or the body attenuated and subulated to the posterior extremity: oxyurous.

oy, oe (ɔɪ, 'oɪ), *sb. Sc.* Forms: 5 o, 5- oy, oye, 8- oe. [a. Gael. *ogha*, also written *odha*, pronounced ('oːa) = Ir. *úa* grandson, OIr. *au* descendant. *O* and *oe* appear to be etymologically the original forms in Lowland Sc.; in many parts of Scotland the diphthong *oy* is pronounced (oe).] A grandchild.

c **1470** HENRY *Wallace* I. 30 The secund O he was of gud Wallace. **1508** KENNEDIE *Flyting w. Dunbar* 308 Belzebubbis oyis, and curst Corspatrikis clan. **1564-5** *Reg. Privy Council Scot.* I. 326 Jane Campbell, oy and ane of the airis of umquhile Finla Campbell. **1640-1** *Kirkcudbr. War-Comm. Min. Bk.* (1855) 131 James Lindsay of Auchenskeoch; Andro Lindsay, his sone;..Charles Lindsay, his oy. **1718** RAMSAY *Christ's Kirk Gr.* III. v, Auld Bessie..Came wi' her ain oe Nanny. **1728** —— *General Mistake* 193 Counting kin, and making endless faird, If that their granny's uncle's oye 's a laird. **1818** SCOTT *Hrt. Midl.* iv, There was my daughter's wean, little Eppie Daidle—my oe, ye ken. **1868** G. MACDONALD *R. Falconer* v, What's the auld leddy gaein' to du wi' that lang-leggit oye o' hers?

†**b.** A nephew; a niece. *Obs.*

1596 DALRYMPLE tr. *Leslie's Hist. Scot.* IX. 150 The 3oung prince his oye with him was in als gret affectione, as he of his awne body had bene gottne. *Ibid.* x. 282 The Erle of Lennox brocht with him his wyfe, Lady Margaret King Henrie his oy. **1673** *Wedderburn's Vocab.* 11 (Jam.) *Nepos*, a nephew or oye.

oy, *v.* Repr. variant pronunciation of HOY *v.*

1816 W. TAYLOR in *Monthly Mag.* XLI. 527 There let them burr and oy, while tow'd aside.

oy, oi (ɔɪ), *int.* [Yiddish.] An exclamation used by Yiddish-speakers to express dismay, grief, etc. Occas. in wider use. Also *oy vay, vey* [a. G. *Weh* woe] (see quot. 1968).

1892 I. ZANGWILL *Childr. Ghetto* I. xii. 270 The dispute thickened; the synagogue hummed with 'Ei's' and 'Oi's' not in concord. **1924** *Dialect Notes* V. 274 Exclamations in American English... Oy: ——, —— yoy. **1928** H. CRANE *Let.* 22 Feb. (1965) 317 Oy-oy-oy! I have just had my ninth snifter of Scotch. **1932** L. GOLDING *Magnolia Street* III. viii. 570 'And if you hadn't..oi! oi!' said Ada. 'It would have been awful!' **1934** WODEHOUSE *Right Ho, Jeeves* xi. 141 A story about a Scotchman, an Irishman, and a Jew... I said 'Hoots, mon,' 'Begorrah,' and 'Oy, oy.' **1939** MRS. P. CAMPBELL *Let.* 28 June in *B. Shaw & Mrs. Campbell* (1952) 332 A Jewish Mother... The Mothers dialogue consisting of: 'Oi; Oi; tch: tch.' **1959** B. KOPS *Hamlet of Stepney Green* I. 12 Children, *oy vay*, don't talk to me about children. **1963** V. NABOKOV *Gift* iii. 181 His trick of garbling Russian, in imitation of a farcical Jewish accent as when he said..'Oy, vat a mudnik!' **1968** L. ROSTEN *Joys of Yiddish* 14 Two *A*[lteren] *K*[ockern] had sat in silence on their favorite park bench for hours, lost in thought. Finally, one gave a long and languid '*Oy!*' The other replied, 'You're telling *me?*' *Ibid.* 273 *Oy* is often used as lead-off for '*oy vay!*' which means, literally, 'Oh, pain', but is used as an all-purpose ejaculation to express anything from trivial delight to abysmal woe. **1975** *New Yorker* 3 Mar. 34/3 The family gathered round for Passover. Oy, nephew! What's the world coming to. **1976** K. THACKERAY *Crownbird* v. 91 'Oy vey, but he's recovered well,' Stein thought.

‖**oyama** (o'jama). [Jap.] = ONNAGATA.

1963 *Guardian* 21 Jan. 9/3 The extraordinary verisimilitude achieved by the 'oyama' or actors playing female rôles. **1965** *This is Japan 1966* 51/2 He was considered to be the last of the great *oyama*, male performers of female roles on the Shimpa stage.

oyapock, a Brazilian opossum: see YAPOCK.

oyas, obs. f. OYEZ.

oyce, var. OYSE.

oych(e, obs. forms of OUCH, clasp.

oye, app. alteration of *oyes*, OYEZ *int.* and *sb.*

(Perh. meant as a sing. of *oyes*; possibly for OF. imper. sing. *oi* 'hear (thou)', or for *oyez* with *z* mute as in mod.F.)

a **1450** *Cov. Myst.* (Shaks. Soc.) 94 Oy! al maner men takyth to me tent. **1480** CAXTON tr. *Higden* (Rolls) VIII. 530 Thenne this Iac Strawe lete make an oye in the felde that all his peple sholde come nere and here his crye and wyll.

oyer ('ɔɪə(r)). *Law.* Forms: [3 oyer, 4 oier, oir], 4- oyer; also 5-7 oier, (5 oyeer, 6 oir, 6-7 oyre). [a. AFr. *oyer* (Britton I. i. §3) = OF. *oir, oyr:—odir, audir:*—L. *audīre* to hear, mod.F. *ouir*; an infinitive used subst.]

1. Short for *oyer and terminer*; a criminal trial under the writ so called (see OYER AND TERMINER).

1432-50 tr. *Higden, Harl. Contin.* (Rolls) VIII. 486 That paste, y schalle speke with oon of theym after an oyer. *a* **1568** ASCHAM *Scholem.* II. (Arb.) 137 Seing so worthie a Iustice of an Oyre hath the present oursight of that whole chace. **1651** N. BACON *Disc. Govt. Eng.* II. lxvi. 227 Upon security to appear before the Justices in Oyer. **1858** M. PATTISON *Ess.* (1889) II. 2 Some mighty issue has been trying in the great historical Oyer of the Reformation against the See of Rome. **1864** *Standard* 31 Oct., The great oyer of railway assassination came to a close on Saturday, and resulted in a verdict of guilty.

2. In *Common Law*, The hearing of some document read in court; esp. of an instrument in writing, pleaded by one party, when the other party 'craved oyer' of it. Abolished 1852.

1602 FULBECKE *2nd Pt. Parall.* 33 The defendant demaunded oier of the Testament. **1607** COWELL *Interpr.*, *Oyer de Record* (*Audire recordum*). **1672** *Ibid.* s.v., When an Action is brought upon an Obligation, the Defendant may pray Oyer of the Bond; or if Executors sue any one, the Party sued may demand Oyer of the Testament. **1670** *Tryal of Penn & Mead* 12 If you deny me Oyer of that Law. **1768** BLACKSTONE *Comm.* III. xx. 299 He may crave oyer of the writ, or of the bond, or other specialty upon which the action is brought; that is to hear it read to him. **1852** *Act 15 & 16 Vict.* c. 76 §55 If Profert shall be made it shall not entitle the opposite Party to crave Oyer of or set out upon Oyer such Deed or Document.

oyer, obs. spelling of *oþer*, OTHER.

oyer and terminer ('ɔɪər ənd 'tɜːmɪnə(r)). *Law.* [The Anglo-Fr. phr. *oyer et terminer* 'to hear and determine' partly anglicized: cf. OYER.]

a. In Anglo-Fr. used in proper verbal construction, and also, in *commission d'oir et de terminer*, as a sb. phrase = 'hearing and determining' (cf. -ER⁴). **b.** In English chiefly in the latter construction, as in **commission of oyer and terminer** (*† of oyer and determiner, of oyer determiner*, = AFr. *de terminer*), a commission formerly directed to the King's Judges, Serjeants, and other persons of note, empowering them to hear and determine indictments on specified offences, such as treasons, felonies, etc., special commissions being granted on occasions of extraordinary disturbance such as insurrections: also called ***writ of oyer and terminer***. Now, the most comprehensive of the commissions granted to judges on circuit, directing them to hold courts for the trial of offences. Hence in such phrases as ***commissioners*** or ***justices of*** (or *†in*) ***o. & t.***, ***writ, court of o. & t.***; and †**c.** elliptically, for 'commission or court of oyer and terminer'.

a. [**1278** *Rolls of Parlt.* I. 3/2 Furent assignes Justices, de enquere, oyer, e terminer selum la leye e la custume. **1292** BRITTON I. i. §1 Pur ceo qe nous ne suffisums mie en nostre propre persone a oyer et terminer totes les quereles del poeple. *Ibid.* §3 Estre ceo volums nous, qe Iustices errauntz soint assignetz de mesmes les chapitres oyer et terminer en chescun counté et en chescune fraunchise de vii aunz en vii. aunz. **1314-15** *Rolls of Parlt.* I. 290/1 Il forge trespas vers luy..et purchace Commissions d'oir & de terminer as gentz favorables a li.]

b. **1414** *Rolls of Parlt.* IV. 58/1 A Commission of Oyer and termyner, after the fourme of a Statut mad. **1433** *Ibid.* 458/1 Upon which Riot aforsaid, was graunted..writtes of Oyer and Termyner. **1455** *Ibid.* V. 332/2 Tyll your Commission of Oier and Determyner be direct to endifferent Commissioners. **1587** FLEMING *Contn. Holinshed* III. 1389/1 In the place where the court commonlie called the Kings bench is vsuallie kept by vertue of hir maiesties commission of oier and terminer. **1633** T. STAFFORD *Pac. Hib.* I. i. (1810) 16 The Lo. President and Councell shall have Commission, power, and authoritie..of Oyer, Determiner, and Goale deliverie. **1644** [H. PARKER] *Jus Pop.* 5 When discords arose..they might have been qualified and repressed by a friendly association, and either one or both might have had the oyer and terminer thereof. **1681** *Trial S. Colledge* 1 The Judges and Commissioners of Oyer and Terminer and Gaol-Delivery, met at the Court-House in the City of Oxford. **1693** C. MATHER *Wonders Invis. World* (1862) 6 Considering the Place that I hold in the Court of Oyer and Terminer. **1769** BLACKSTONE *Comm.* IV. xix. 269 The courts of oyer and terminer and general gaol delivery. **1846** McCULLOCH *Acc. Brit. Empire* (1854) II. 177 The commissions which confer the criminal jurisdiction are three in number: 1, a commission of peace; 2, a commission of oyer and terminer; and, 3, a commission of general gaol delivery.

c. **1469** J. PASTON in *P. Lett.* II. 357 When hys jugys sat on the oyeer determyner in Norwyche, he beyng ther. **1480** CAXTON tr. *Higden* (Rolls) VIII. 578 Anone after cam doune one Oyer determyne, for to doo iustyce on alle them that soo rebellyd in the cyte. **1494** FABYAN *Chron.* VII. 630 The mayre..by vertu of yᵉ sayd comyssyon, callyd an oyer determyner, and a day was kept at Guyldhall. **1577** FLEETWOOD in Ellis *Orig. Lett.* Ser. II. III. 55 Upon Saturday last in the after noone we had an Oier and Determiner in the Guyld Hall, the which we use to hold in the vacation tyme to kepe the people in obedience.

d. In some of the States of the American Union: A court of higher criminal jurisdiction.

1888 BRYCE *Amer. Commw.* II. xxxvii. 24 The governor is directed to appoint judges, commissioners of oyer and terminer.

oyez, oyes (əʊ'jɛs), *int.* (*sb.*, *v.*). Forms: 5- Oyes, O yes, (5 Oyas, 6 Oies, O is, O ys, ooyess); 6-7 *Sc.* hoyes; 7- Oyez, (7 oiez, O yez, oh yes, O ace, 7-9 oyess). [OF. *oiez, oyez*, hear ye! imperative pl. of *oir* to hear:—L. *audiātis*, pres. subj.; orig. pronounced *o'yets*, but subseq. reduced to *o'yes*, and so identified in sound with the two words *O yes!* and hence often so written.]

A. *imperative verb*, and *interjection.* 'Hear, hear ye'; a call by the public crier or by a court officer (generally thrice uttered), to command silence and attention when a proclamation, etc., is about to be made.

[*c* **1286** *Stat. Excestre* in *Stat. Realm* I. 211/1 Ceo oyez vus A. e B... Re jeo dirrai verite.] *c* **1440** *York Myst.* xxx. 369 *Pil.* Cry, Oyas! *Be.* Oyas! *Ibid.* xxxi. 319 Do crie we all on hym at onys. O3es! O3es! O3es! *Ibid.* 360 O yes! if any wight with þis wriche any werse wate Werkis. **1567** *Triall Treas.* (1850) 21 O yes, O yes, I will make a proclamation. **1584** LYLY *Campaspe* III. ii, O ys, O ys, O ys, all manner of men, women, and children. **1654** E. JOHNSON *Wond.-wrkg. Provid.* i. 2 Oh yes! oh yes! oh yes! All you the people of Christ that are here Oppressed. **1682** N. O. *Boileau's Lutrin* IV. 212 With Stentors Voice he make loud Proclamation O yez! I' th' Chapter House, A rare Collation Stands ready dress't. **1822** T. MITCHELL *Aristoph.* II. 257 Oyes! oyes! in virtue of my office—Waits any member of the court without? **1842** BARHAM *Ingol. Leg.*, *Misadv. Margate* xvi, But when the Crier cried, 'O Yes!' the people cried, 'O No!'

B. as *sb.* A call or exclamation of 'Oyez!' Plural †*oyesses*, also †*oyes*.

Quot. 1635 has *O's ace*, an eccentric plural of *O ace* (pronounced in the north *O yas* or *O yess*).

1494 FABYAN *Chron.* VII. 615 The sayde tayllours..wold nat cease for speche of the mayre nor oyes made by the mayres sergiaunt of armes. *a* **1548** HALL *Chron.*, *Hen. VIII* 4 And there with all, commaunded his Heraulde to make an Oyes. **1589** R. HARVEY *Pl. Perc.* (1590) 13 Crier, make an o yes, for Martin to come into the Court. **1598** SHAKS. *Merry W.* V. v. 45 *Qui.* Crier Hob-goblyn, make the Fairy Oyes. *Pist.* Elues, list your names: Silence you aiery toyes. **1600** W. WATSON *Decacordon* (1602) 131 Going with oyesses vp and downe the streets. **1619** DALTON *Countr. Just.* xxii. (1630) 61 He may cause three oyes for silence to be made. **1635** BRATHWAIT *Arcad. Pr.* II. 196 Having first commanded Cletor the pretorian cryer with three O's ace to command silence. **1752** J. LOUTHIAN *Form of Process* (ed. 2) 88 After the crying of three several Oyesses. **1873** H. SPENCER *Stud. Sociol.* v. 110 The oyez shouted in a law court to secure attention.

b. Erroneously confused with OUTAS (in Latin form *huesium*).

1597 SKENE *De Verb. Sign.*, *Huesium, hoyesium*..ane hoyes, or crie vsed in proclamations. **1609** —— *Reg. Maj.* 4 Quhen ane man is slane,..or is found dead in any place; in this case, the finder sall raise the hoyes, as said is.

†**C.** as *vb. trans.* To proclaim as by cries of 'Oyez!' *Obs. rare.*

1599 NASHE *Lenten Stuffe* 3 When the high flight of his lines in common brute was ooyessed.

oygnement, oyke, obs. ff. OINTMENT, OAK.

-oyl, ending of the names of acid radicals, formed on the names of the corresponding carboxylic acids ending in *-ic* or *-oic*; e.g. FUMAROYL, HEXANOYL.

1971 *Nomencl. Org. Chem.* (I.U.P.A.C.) (ed. 2) C. 185 The name of a univalent or bivalent acyl radical formed by removal of hydroxyl from all the carboxyl groups is derived from the name of the corresponding acid by changing the ending '-oic' to '-oyl'.

oylet, -ett, etc., obs. forms of OILLET.

oynct, oyne, obs. ff. OINT *v.* to anoint, OVEN.

oyneon, -ion, -yon, etc., obs. forms of ONION.

oyns, obs. form of OUNCE *sb.*¹, a weight.

oynt, oyntuose, -ture: see OINT, etc.

o ys, obs. form of OYEZ.

oys, oyse, oyss, obs. ME. and Sc. ff. USE *sb.*, *v.*

oyschere, oyser, -ier, obs. ff. USHER, OSIER.

oyse, oyst(e, obs. ff. OOZE, HOST *sb.*

oyster ('ɔɪstə(r)), *sb.* Forms: 4-5 oystre, -ere, 4-6 oistre, (4 hoister, -re), 5 oystur, -yr, (hoystyr, -er), 6-8 oister, 4- oyster; also 4-5 ostre, 5 ostur, -yr, oestre, 6 oster. [ME. a. OF. *oistre, uistre, huistre*, mod.F. *huître* = Pr., Sp., Pg. *ostra*, obs. It. *ostrea*, ad.L. *ostrea* fem., beside *ostreum* neut., a. Gr. ὄστρεον oyster.]

1. a. A well-known edible bivalve mollusc of the family *Ostreidæ*; *esp.* the common European species, *Ostrea edulis*, and the North American species, *O. virginica* of the Atlantic, and *O. lurida*, the Californian oyster, of the Pacific coast.

green oyster, an oyster which has fed on confervæ in tanks. ***hard oyster***, the native northern oyster of U.S., distinguished from the ***soft oyster*** found from the Chesapeake Bay southward. ***mangrove oyster***, an oyster growing on the submerged trunks or roots of mangroves, as in Florida. ***rock*** or ***sea oyster***, an oyster growing on rocks or natural beds, as opposed to those which are artificially cultivated.

1357-8 *Durham Acc. Rolls* (Surtees) 124 In Oystres empt. vjs. *a* **1377** *Abingdon Acc.* (Camden) 38 In ostreys ixs. *c* **1386** CHAUCER *Sompn. T.* 392 Many a Muscle and many an oystre [*v. rr.* oystere, oyster] Whan othere men hath ben ful wel at eyse Hath been oure foode. *c* **1420** *Liber Cocorum* (1862) 17 For to make potage of oysturs. **1483** *Cath. Angl.* 262/1 An Ostyr,..*ostreum, quidam piscis.* **1555** EDEN *Decades* 95 The fisshe it selfe is more pleasaunte in eatynge then are owre oysters. **1674** T. FLATMAN *Belly God* 57 Your Wall fleet Oysters no man will prefer Before the juicy Grass-green Colchester. **1756** Mangrove oyster [see *oyster-crab* under 7 d]. **1806** WOLCOTT (P. Pindar) *Tristia* Wks. 1812 V. 244 Who first an oyster eat, was a bold dog. **1817** J. EVANS *Excurs. Windsor*, etc. 451 The green oyster, eaten at Paris, is brought from Dieppe. **1838** *Encycl. Brit.* (ed. 7) XVI. 688/2 It abounds with small rock-oysters. **1883** MOLONEY *W. Afr. Fisheries* 43 (Fish. Exhib. Publ.) Women go in for the collection of mangrove-oysters. **1883** E. P. RAMSAY *Food Fishes N.S. Wales* 37 (ibid.) Recent experiments tend to prove that the Rock-Oyster of our shores.. which is left dry by every tide, is only a variety of the Drift-Oyster.

b. *fig.*

(In allusion to the fable of the monkey who, as judge, kept the oyster and gave a shell to each of the disputants.)

1839 THACKERAY *Major Gahagan* ii, The oyster remained with the British Government.

c. Phrases and proverbial expressions.

† ***to drink to one's oysters***, to fare accordingly. † ***a stopping*** or ***choking oyster***, a retort which puts a person to silence. ***as like as an apple to an oyster*** (and similar phrases), i.e. totally different. ***the world is my oyster***: the world offers opportunities for profit, etc.; also in extended uses.

1472 J. PASTON in *P. Lett.* III. 41 For and I had not delt ryght corteysly up on Holy Rood Day I had drownk to myn oystyrs. *a* **1529** SKELTON *Bowge of Courte* 477, I haue a stoppynge oyster in my poke. **1532** MORE *Confut. Tindale* Wks. 724/1 Hys similitude of grammer likened vnto fayth, is no more lyke then an apple to an oyster. **1542** UDALL *Erasm. Apoph.* (1877) 61 To a feloe laiyng to his rebuke, that he was ouer deintie of his mouthe and diete, he did with this reason giue a stopping oistre. **1546** J. HEYWOOD *Prov.* (1867) 36 His wife.. deuiseth to cast in my teeth, Checks and chokyng oysters. **1598** SHAKS. *Merry W.* II. ii. 2 Why then the world's mine Oyster, which I, with sword will open. **1648** JENKYN *Blind Guide* 71 Why do you bring him in speaking of apples, when you speake of oysters? **1930** J. A. WILLIAMSON *Short Hist. Brit. Expansion* (ed. 2) II. VI. ii. 183 *Laissez-faire*, with its cosmopolitan view of the world as the trader's oyster. *a* **1938** T. WOLFE *You can't go Home Again* (1940) III. xxix. 469 Drake was self-contained: the world his oyster, seas his pastures, mighty distances his wings. **1942** A. BRYANT *Yrs. of Endurance* xi. 230 He [*sc.* Napoleon] was not going to waste his incomparable genius to make the world—his oyster—safe for Barras and the plutocrats of the Luxembourg. **1949** A. MILLER *Death of Salesman* I. 39 The world is an oyster, but you don't crack it open on a mattress. **1975** *New Yorker* 26 May 66/3 A few weeks after the conference, he told American farmers that the world food market could 'be our oyster'. **1977** 'J. GASH' *Judas Pair* vi. 67 The world was my oyster. My uneasy mood had vanished.

d. A reserved or uncommunicative person.

1925 M. WILTSHIRE *Thursday's Child* xi. 221, I wouldn't mind betting Jane's worrying herself sick over it; and he—goodness knows what he's doing or feeling. I never saw such an oyster. **1930** J. B. PRIESTLEY *Angel Pavement* vi. 305, I never knew anybody so close, you old oyster you!

e. A type of unmoored submarine mine detonated magnetically or acoustically as a vessel passes over it. Also *attrib.*

1947 CROWTHER & WHIDDINGTON *Science at War* iv. 177 The mine mechanism [*i.e.* of German pressure mines] consisted of a rubber air bag with an aluminium diaphragm. With a change of pressure air escapes from the bag, the diaphragm is moved, and after a time closes an electrical detonating circuit. A change of about 1/1,000th in the total pressure, equivalent to that of about ½ inch of water, exerted for about six seconds, was needed to operate the mechanism. This device, called an 'oyster', is shown in Plate XLV. **1950** A. P. HERBERT *Independent Member* lii. 308 The enemy.. had new terrors by then—the 'oyster' or pressure mine. **1955** J. F. TURNER *Service most Silent* xi. 155 For the first four years of the War both the Germans and ourselves were developing the top secret mine of the War—the oyster. *Ibid.*, The Luftwaffe produced 'acoustic oysters' and the Navy 'magnetic oysters'. **1965** K. LANGMAID *Approaches are Mined!* xiv. 240 The first 'Oyster' minefields were laid by German light craft on the night of the 6th/7th of June [1944].

2. a. Commonly applied also to other bivalve molluscs resembling the oyster, as the PEARL-OYSTER, *Meleagrina margaritifera*, of the family *Aviculidæ*; also with qualifications, as **thorny oyster** of the genus *Spondylus*, **boat-oyster**, a fossil of the genus *Gryphæa*, **saddle-oyster**, etc.: see quots.

1398 TREVISA *Barth. De P.R.* XI. vi. (1495), By nyghte.. oystres open theymselfe ayenst dewe... And that dewe.. bredyth a full precious gemma, a stone that hyghte Margarita. **1600** SHAKS. *A.Y.L.* v. iv. 63 Rich honestie dwels.. in a poore house, as your Pearle in your foule oyster. **1755** YOUNG *Centaur* v. Wks. 1757 IV. 226 If we should find a small pearl in one oyster of a million, it would hardly make us fishers for life. **1828** G. YOUNG *Geol. Surv. Yorksh. Coast* 241 *Gryphœa*. Boat-oyster, or Miller's thumb. **1840** *Penny Cycl.* XVII. 363–4 *Placuna Placenta*, vulgarly known as the Chinese Window Oyster,.. and *Placuna Sella*, known to collectors as the Saddle-Oyster (from Tranquebar, etc.). **1869** WOOD *Comm. Shells* 85 We come now to the remarkable Saddle Oyster (*Anomia ephippium*).. recognized by its flat lower valve, in which is a large and nearly oval hole, just below the hinge. **1883** E. P. RAMSAY *Food Fishes N.S. Wales* 36 (Fish. Exhib. Publ.) The 'Hammer-head Oyster' (*Malleus albus*, Lam.), &c., are found on our coasts.

† **b.** ***long oyster.*** (See quot.) *Obs.*

1674 RAY *Collect. Words, Sea Fishes* 105 Long Oyster, Sea-gar, Red Crab: *Locusta marina*. The name long Oyster is no doubt a Corruption of Locusta. [Rather of Sp., Pg., Pr. *langosta*, OF. *langoste*:—L. *locusta*.]

3. The morsel of dark meat in the front hollow of the side bone of a fowl.

1883 H. P. SPOFFORD in *Harper's Mag.* Aug. 456/1 He rolled under his tongue the sweet morsel of the oyster out of a side bone. **1890** MISS BRADDON *One Life* II. 103 That particular morsel out of a fowl's back which epicures have christened the oyster.

4. ***vegetable oyster***: the salsify (also called *oyster-plant*: see 7 d).

1884 MILLER *Plant-n., Tragopogon porrifolius*, Jerusalem Star, Salsify, Vegetable Oyster.

5. A greyish-white colour resembling that of an oyster. Cf. 7 c.

1922 *Daily Mail* 11 Dec. 14 (Advt.), Silk hose... In black, white,.. peacock, flame, oyster. **1960** *Housewife* Apr. 97 Cotton sailcloth... In a choice of three good colours—oyster, light royal blue, or black. **1978** H. MACINNES *Prelude to Terror* ii. 18 A.. study in greys, from silver carpeting to pale oyster walls.

6. One of the cross-sections of wood in an oyster veneer.

1924 G. O. WHEELER *Old Eng. Furnit.* (ed. 3) iii. 22 These 'oysters' are often in kidney-shape and the welding of a mosaic was no easy task. **1974** *Country Life* 26 Sept. (Suppl.) 60 William III oyster olivewood chest. The top with concentric rings of oysters of decreasing size.

7. *attrib.* and *Comb.* **a.** simple attrib., as ***oyster family, kind, -shoal, spat***; connected with the taking, breeding, keeping, selling, or eating of oysters, as ***oyster-bar, -barrel, cry, -culture*** (hence ***-culturist***), ***-dish, -dredge, -fishery, -fork, -ground, house, -industry, -keg, -merchant, -monger, navy, -net, pirate, saloon, season, -shop, -smack, -stall, stand, supper, -tavern, voice***; made of oysters, as ***oyster cocktail, cracker, -patty, -pie, -sauce, soup, stew, stuffing***, etc.

1878 R. L. STEVENSON in *London* 8 June 441/1 They were driven by a sharp fall of sleet into an *Oyster Bar. **1925** E. SITWELL *Troy Park* 74 That child is the small wicked ghost Of Metropoles and oyster bars. **1972** E. HARGREAVES *Fair Green Weed* i. 12 I've been eating something called escovitched fish in an oyster bar. **1682** T. FLATMAN *Heraclitus Ridens* No. 74 (1713) II. 201 As much a Mock t' Esquire, 'midst all his Ruff, As empty *Oister-Barrel to a Muff. **1895** *Funk's Stand. Dict.*, *Oyster cocktail. **1905** *Granville Centennial Cook Bk.* 121 Oyster Cocktail. *c* **1938** [see COCKTAIL 4]. **1957** M. MCCARTHY *Memories Catholic Girlhood* viii. 203 Olympia oyster cocktail and devilled Dungeness crabs. **1975** M. ORR *Rich Girl, Poor Girl* (1977) xii. 147 The meal.. began with an oyster cocktail and progressed to a cold Senegalese soup. **1873** *Kansas Mag.* III. 273/2 Our commissary department was poorly supplied ..four small *oyster crackers. **1924** *Amer. Mercury* Apr. 430/1 The custom that some Baptist churches have fallen into of oyster crackers and cubes of bakers' bread in the Lord's supper is to my mind unscriptural. **1975** BYFIELD & TEDESCHI *Solemn High Murder* (1976) iii. 53 Baxter tore open a cellophane envelope of oyster crackers. **1714** GAY *Trivia* I. 28 When.. damsels first renew their *oyster cries. **1874** *Chambers' Encycl.* VII. 178/2 In such situations ..*oyster-culture can be most.. profitably carried on. **1882** *Daily Tel.* 18 Aug. 4/8 *Oysterculturists are becoming alarmed lest the superior oysters known as natives should be contaminated by the near presence of the inferior sort. **1865** GEO. ELIOT *Let.* 8 Jan. (1956) IV. 174, I am so much pleased with.. the pretty *oyster-dish. **1796** MORSE *Amer. Geog.* II. 126 About 10000 people are employed in the *oyster-fishery along the coasts of England. **1834** H. J. NOTT *Novellettes* I. 94 He can escape from the empty pageant to the substantial and homely comforts of a beefsteak or *oyster house. **1949** *Fishing Gaz.* Oct. 96/2 Hampton oyster houses are George T. Elliot, M. F. Quinn, and J. S. Daly and Son. **1774** GOLDSM. *Nat. Hist.* (1776) VII. 41 Of Bivalved Shell-Fish, or Shells of the *Oyster Kind. **1726** B. FRANKLIN *Jrnl. Voy. Philadelphia* in *Mem. Life & Writings* (1818) I. App. p. iii, The *oyster-merchants fetch them.. from other places. **1869** *Rep. Comm. Agric. 1868* (U.S. Dept. Agric.) 340 An oyster merchant of Rochelle, doing business with the growers of the adjacent islands of Oleron and Ré, will say £250,000 per annum. **1720** STRYPE *Stow's Surv. Lond.* (1754) I. I. v. 26/2 One Rufe de Reines, *Oystermonger, took a Custom of all Men and Women that washed their Clothes.. there. **1932** *Sun* (Baltimore) 19 Sept. 6/5 (*heading*) Sour note on a recent addition to the *oyster navy. **1962** *Daily Progress* (Charlottesville, Va.) 21 Mar. 3 (*heading*) 'Oyster navy' gets radar. **1726** LEONI *Alberti's Archit.* II. 122/2 You may take up the Mud from the bottom by means of an *Oyster-Net. **1807** M. E. RUNDELL *New Syst. Dom. Cookery* 133 (*caption*) *Oyster patties. **1843** *Ainsworth's Mag.* IV. 97 An eulogy of the excellence of Lord Marmiton's oyster patties. **1932** AUDEN in *Rev. Eng. Stud.* (1978) Aug. 285 Over oyster patties, I'll explain it all. **1953** K. TENNANT *Joyful Condemned* vi. 51 Mrs. Mike was carrying a plate of oyster patties. **1599** B. JONSON *Cynthia's Rev.* II. i, O, Hercules, 'tis your only dish; above all your potatoes or *oyster-pies in the world. **1851** A. O. HALL *Manhattaner* 59 Some of them [*sc.* mosquitoes] are dainty, and associate only with fat people whose nightmares are based upon turtle steaks and oyster pies. **1976** R. CONDON *Whisper of Axe* I. xxiii. 146 They ate oyster pie and crab cakes. **1903** J. LONDON *Let.* 9 Mar. (1966) 147 When the *oyster pirates.. arrived, they forced the two watchmen off into the water. **1930** J. DOS PASSOS *42nd Parallel* II. 133 Oyster pirates used to shanghai young fellers. **1833** *Knickerbocker* I. 117 To be seen about taverns and *oyster saloons. **1905** J. C. LINCOLN *Partners of Tide* vi. 105 The pair entered a little battered restaurant with the sign 'Atwood's Oyster Saloon' over the door. **1727** 'E. DORRINGTON' *Hermit* I. 27 The boil'd Meat and *Oyster-Sauce. **1798** JANE AUSTEN *Let.* 24 Oct. (1932) I. 9 We.. had some beef-steaks and a boiled fowl, but no oyster sauce. **1816** 'QUIZ' *Grand Master* VII. 24 To partake Of oyster-sauce and a beef-steak. **1861** MRS. BEETON *Bk. Househ. Managem.* p. xxiv. (Index), *Oyster.. season. **1866** 'F. KIRKLAND' *Pictorial Bk. Anecdotes* 181/2 [He] traded up and down the James and York rivers, especially during the oyster season. **1977** *Harpers & Queen* Nov. 276/3 When the British oyster season is over, the clam trade continues. **1827** J. L. WILLIAMS *View W. Florida* 16 The entrance to this bay is obstructed by sand bars and *oyster shoals. **1823** in *Spirit of Public Jrnls.* (1825) 8 Charged with assaulting David Tullock, *Esq.* at an *oyster-shop in Brydges-street. **1841** DICKENS *Old C. Shop* xxxix. 12 Kit, walking into an oyster-shop as bold as if he lived there. **1913** MRS. P. CAMPBELL *Let.* 25 Mar. in *B. Shaw & Mrs. Campbell* (1952) 102 Many a rendez-vous at Cheesmans oyster shop. **1802** E. WYNNE *Diary* 22 Oct. (1940) III. iv. 69 Several other sailors' bodies have been thrown on shore, it was an *oyster smack that was lost. **1976** *Times* 27 Aug. 17/1 A string of oyster smacks.. will be competing in the Thames Oyster Smack Race. **1741** E. SMITH *Compl. Housewife* (ed. 10) 62 (*heading*) *Oyster soop. **1861** MRS. BEETON *Bk. Househ. Managem.* 103 Oyster soup. **1935** M. MORPHY *Recipes of all Nations* 599 *Oyster soup*.. is one of the favourite soups in America. **1836** DICKENS *Pickw.* (1837) xxii. 227 Here's a *oyster-stall to every half-dozen houses. **1922** E. SITWELL *Façade* 15 Oyster-stall notes. **1830** *Boston Even. Transcript* 29 Sept. 2/4 The *oyster stands in New Orleans have been leased for .. the same price as last year. **1851** A. O. HALL *Manhattaner* 7 Oyster stands, where dirty mouths and flickering tallow candles grinned ghostly satisfaction. **1977** *Times* 14 May 13/4 For £4,000 to £6,000 each.. you may be able to buy two Sèvres oyster-stands. **1846** D. CORCORAN *Pickings* 128 Mrs. Smith was never known to have an *oyster stew of an evening that she did not divide it with Mrs. Jones. **1973** P. A. WHITNEY *Snowfire* xiii. 254 He.. brought me back a bowl of hot oyster stew and crackers. **1935** M. MORPHY *Recipes of All Nations* 611 *Oyster stuffings for poultry are frequently found in old English cookery books. **1971** M. G. EBERHART *Two Little Rich Girls* (1972) ix. 105 The dinner.. with its oyster stuffing for the turkey and its huge mince pie. **1741** B. LYNDE *Diary* 17 Apr. (1880) 107 *Oyster supper with all the Court. **1856** H. B. STOWE *Dred* II. 221 He drinks and frolics, and has his oyster-suppers. **1949** *Missouri Hist. Rev.* Apr. 215 He is uneasy at oyster-suppers at the 'Opera House'. **1612** R. DABORNE *Chr. turn'd Turke* 350 Affrighting of whole streetes With your full *Oyster voyce.

b. objective and obj. gen., as ***oyster-cultivator, -dredger, -eating, -fishing, -grower, -lover, -opener, -planting, -rearing, -seller, shucker, -trawler***; ***oyster-breeding*** adj.; also instrumental, as ***oyster-covered*** adj.

1697 DRYDEN *Virg. Georg.* I. 297 Thro' Helle's stormy Streights, and *Oyster-breeding Sea. **1882** W. D. HAY *Brighter Britain!* I. iii. 72 *Oyster-covered rocks. **1905** *Westm. Gaz.* 10 Aug. 1/3 Oyster-covered iron beams and girders. **1508, 1723** *Oyster-dredger [see DREDGER[1]]. **1853** FORBES & HANLEY *Hist. Brit. Mollusca* II. 320 Irish oyster-dredgers have a notion that the more the banks are dredged, the more the oysters breed. **1933** *Sun* (Baltimore) 7 Aug. 14/2 An old-fashioned Southern Maryland '*oyster eatin''. **1977** *Times* 22 Jan. 12/3 The return to oyster-eating. **1827** W. CLARKE *Every Night Bk.* 62 If the visitor make an ally of the waiter or *oyster-opener, he may often have people pointed out to him there, who are rather worth seeing. **1900** W. STEVENS *Let.* 21 Oct. (1967) 47 Fishmen, and grizzly oyster-openers. **1969** E. H. PINTO *Treen* 140 A simple but effective oyster opener, in Colchester Museum, is a wooden block, hollowed out to take a large oyster; [etc.]. **1891** W. K. BROOKS *Oyster* 127 In some of the Northern States *oyster-planting has been in existence for many years. **1483** *Cath. Angl.* 262/2 An *Ostre seller, *ostrearius*. **1898** GOULD *Pocket Med. Dict.* (ed. 2) 234 **Oyster-shuckers' keratitis*, a form due to corneal traumatism from pieces of embedded oyster-shell. **1969** L. HELLMAN *Unfinished Woman* vi. 61 The oyster shucker.. would open oysters for my father. **1973** *Daily Colonist* (Victoria, B.C.) 1 July 9/2 Rumor has it that the professional oyster shucker eventually becomes immune to the poison and simply counts his scars.

c. similative, as ***oyster eye, kiss, -lip; oyster-coloured, -grey, -white*** adjs.; oyster-coloured, as ***oyster brocade, satin***, etc.

1667 MARVELL *Instr. Painter Dutch Wars* 61 Paint her with Oyster-Lip. **1805** *Naval Chron.* XV. 35, I remained in an oyster state, between asleep and awake. **1893** *Daily News* 10 May 6/4 Lady F.'s dress was made of oyster brocade trimmed with old point. **1894** *Ibid.* 11 May 6/5 The train was in brocade of an oyster-grey ground shot with mother-o'-pearl. **1901** *Westm. Gaz.* 5 Sept. 6/3 Miss V. C. wore an oyster-satin skirt with swathed bodice. **1901** *Sketch* 11 Sept. 303 Her wedding-dress of oyster-white satin. **1904** *Daily Chron.* 5 May 8/4 Women are wearing bronze shoes with their golden-brown costumes,.. oyster-coloured suede with a costume of that shade. **1920** S. LEWIS *Main St.* xi. 141 An oyster-coloured blouse. **1922** JOYCE *Ulysses* 114 Oyster eyes. **1931** J. CANNAN *High Table* xi. 168 The mother of the bride wore a handsome dress of oyster satin. **1938** S. BECKETT *Murphy* 117 Oyster kisses passed between them. **1951** [see GIBSON[2]]. **1952** P. ATKEY *Juniper Rock* i. 5 A short, pink man in oyster silk pyjamas. **1958** L. DURRELL *Balthazar* i. 13 Pearl ground with shadowed oyster and violet reflections. **1960** *Harper's Bazaar* Apr. 84 A short narrow dress of delustred oyster satin. **1969** [see *Irish crochet* s.v. IRISH *a.* 2 c]. **1974** N. MARSH *Black as he's Painted* i. 20 The glossy walls were an agreeable oyster-white. **1975** G. MOFFAT *Miss Pink* iii. 48 Bridget wearing oyster lace over silk. **1976** *Southern Even. Echo* (Southampton) 11 Nov. 9/1 The bride wore an oyster-coloured empire-line dress.

d. Special combinations: **oyster-bank**, a bank of oysters, an oyster-bed: see BANK *sb.*[1] 5; † **oyster-barrel muff**, a muff having the form of an oyster-barrel; **oyster-bed**, (*a*) a layer of oysters covering a tract of the bottom of the sea, a place where oysters breed or are bred: see BED *sb.* 14 b; (*b*) a layer or stratum containing fossil oysters; **oyster-bird** = OYSTER-CATCHER; **oyster-biscuit** (see quot.); † **oyster-board**, a long narrow board or table of the kind used for displaying oysters for sale; applied contemptuously to the communion-tables introduced by the early Reformers and the Puritans; **oyster-boat**, a boat (in *U.S.* also a floating house built on a raft) used in the oyster-fishery or oyster cultivation; hence *oyster-boatman*; † **oyster-bread** (see quot.); **oyster-brood**, the spat of oysters in its second year; † **oyster-callet** = *oyster-wench*; **oyster-cellar**, a shop, orig. in a basement, where oysters are sold; **oyster-crab**, a small crab living as a commensal with an oyster, esp. *Pinnotheres ostreum*; **oyster-farm**, a tract of sea-bottom where oysters are bred artificially; hence **oyster-farmer, oyster-farming**; **Oyster Feast**, a traditional feast held at Colchester to mark the beginning of the oyster-fishing season; **oyster-field** = *oyster-bed*; **oyster-fish**, † (*a*) an oyster;

(*b*) the toad-fish (*Opsanus tau*); (*c*) the tautog (*Tautoga onitis*); (*d*) (see quot. 1903); **oyster fitting** (see quot. 1940); **oyster-green**, a name of the seaweed *Ulva lactuca*, also *U. latissima* (***broad-leaved** o.*); **oyster-knife**, a strong knife adapted for opening oysters; †**oyster-lay** = *oyster-bed* (*a*) (cf. LAYING *vbl. sb.* 2 c); **oyster-like** *a.*, resembling an oyster, esp. in sticking inside one's 'shell'; **oyster-man**, a man engaged in taking, breeding, or selling oysters; **oyster-meter**, an officer appointed by the Court of the Fishmongers' Company to supervise the oyster industry; **oyster-mushroom**, an esculent fungus, *Agaricus ostreatus*; **oyster-park**, an oyster-bed or oyster-farm; **oyster-piece**, a piece of oyster veneer; **oyster-plant**, (*a*) the sea-lungwort (*Mertensia maritima*), so called from the oyster-like flavour of its leaves; (*b*) the salsify (*Tragopogon porrifolius*); ***Spanish oyster-plant***, *Scolymus hispanicus*, the edible roots of which are used like salsify; **oyster-plover** = OYSTER-CATCHER; **oyster-rake**, a rake with a long handle and tines from six to twelve inches in length, usually well curved, used for gathering oysters in deep water; **oyster-scale**, the scale-insect *Mytilaspis pomorum*; †**oyster-scalp**, a scallop or bivalve mollusc of the oyster-family, or its shell; **oyster-scow** *U.S.*, a scow engaged in oyster-fishing; **oyster-seed**, oyster spat; also, young oysters suitable for transplantation to artificial beds; †**oyster-table**, a table inlaid with mother-of-pearl; **oyster-tongs**, an instrument used for gathering oysters in shallow water, consisting of a jointed pair of hinged rakes with inward-bending teeth and long handles; **oyster-tree**, the mangrove; **oyster-veneer**, a whorled veneer obtained esp. from small boughs of trees; cf. OYSTERING *vbl. sb.* b; also ***oyster-veneered*** adj., ***oyster-veneering***; **oyster walnut** (see quot. 1944); freq. *attrib.*; †**oyster-wench, -wife, -woman**, a girl or woman who sells oysters.

1612 *Proc. Virginia* 102 in *Capt. Smith's Wks.* (Arb.) 168 Hee..forced them to the *oyster banks. **1831** *Encycl. Brit.* (ed. 7) IV. 284 The oyster banks produce the finest pearls in the world. **1703** DE FOE *Reform. Manners* Misc. 101 Knights of the Famous *Oyster-Barrel Muff. **1591** PERCIVALL *Sp. Dict.*, *Ostiario*, an *oister bed. **1833** LYELL *Princ. Geol.* III. 354 The strata of sand which immediately repose on the oyster-bed are quite destitute of organic remains. **1898** *Daily News* 13 May 5/2 The ration..consists of..16 oz. of hard bread (called *oyster biscuits in the States). **1554** in *Latimer's Serm. & Rem.* (Parker Soc.) II. 275 *Weston.* 'In the same place he proveth a propitiatory sacrifice, and that upon an altar, and no *oyster-board'. **1849** MACAULAY *Hist. Eng.* i. (1871) I. 40 Tables which the Papists irreverently termed oyster boards. **1419** *Liber Albus* (Rolls) I. 343 Item, de *oystrebot, quantum dabit. **1538** BALE *Thre Lawes* 1344 He was sellynge of a Cod In an oyster bote a lyttle beyonde Quene hythe. **1813** J. K. PAULDING *Lay of Scottish Fiddle* i. 18 The sailors..urg'd in dreams the gallant chase Of oyster-boats far up the bay. **1891** *Scribner's Mag.* X. 472, I will try to describe how the deck of an oyster-boat must be trimmed for its work. **1859** G. A. SALA *Twice round Clock* 251 Listen to the slang of *oyster-boatmen and bargees. **1601** HOLLAND *Pliny* I. 556 *Oister-bread, so called for that it was good with oisters. **1827** *Act 7 & 8 Geo. IV*, c. 29 §36 If any Person shall steal any Oysters or *Oyster Brood from any Oyster Bed. **1621** BRATHWAIT *Nat. Embassie*, etc. (1877) 302 *Oister-callet, slie Vpholster. **1830** J. F. WATSON *Ann. Philadelphia* 220 *Oyster Cellars..did not at first include gentlemen among their visiters. **1842** DICKENS *Amer. Notes* I. vi. 208 Lamps, marking the whereabouts of oyster-cellars. **1889** R. BRYDALL *Art in Scot.* vi. 96 The then popular Oyster-cellars in Edinburgh. **1756** P. BROWNE *Jamaica* (1779) 420 The *Oyster-Crab. This little species is generally found with the Mangrove oysters, in their shells. **1844** J. E. DEKAY *Zool. N.Y.* VI. 12 The *P[innotheres] depressum* of Say, is..the male, or we suppose the young, of the Common Oyster Crab. **1884** J. A. RYDER in G. B. Goode *Fisheries U.S.: Nat. Hist. Aquatic Animals* I. x. 744 Some Oysters were dredged up by the crew which contained some Oyster-crabs. **1902** H. L. WILSON *Spenders* 131 Now the oysters will be due—fine fat Buzzard's Bays —and oyster crabs. **1938** L. BEMELMANS *Life Class* I. iii. 49 All maîtres d'hôtel..are especially fond of little fried things ..whitebait, oyster crabs, fried scallops. **1960** C. M. YONGE *Oysters* vii. 118 An essentially parasitic crab which has been the cause of considerable damage..., especially in Delaware Bay, is the small Oyster Crab. **1940** *Sun* (Baltimore) 18 Oct. 3 Chesapeake oysters, which are now raised on '*oyster farms'. **1975** *Times* 24 Apr. 3/4 Their oyster farm is claimed to be the only one of its kind in Europe. **1946** *Nature* 26 Oct. 587/1 Many of the newly settled spat perish in the first weeks of sedentary life, and in spite of all the care of the *oyster-farmers. **1953** *Sun* (Baltimore) 5 Feb. 19/5 If private leasing of such beds were allowed, they could produce enough seed to supply oyster 'farmers' their all-important seed oysters. **1977** *Harpers & Queen* Nov. 275/4 Fertilised eggs, which oyster farmers call..white, grey or black sick, depending on how ripe it is. **1943** *Sun* (Baltimore) 5 Feb. 10/1 A system of '*oyster farming' combining a free fishery with close State management. **1962** D. NICHOLS *Echinoderms* iii. 35 In the early days of oyster-farming the fishermen would drag a dredge across the beds to collect the starfish. **1974** *Country Life* 21 Nov. 1561/3 A high mercurial content in the water ..prevents oyster farming. **1888** E. L. CUTTS *Colchester* xviii. 171 The annual feast on the election of the mayor is called the *Oyster Feast...people take it for granted that the feast derives its name from the bivalve for which the town is famous; but this origin of the name may be questioned. 'Oyster feasts' are common at the beginning of a new official reign in many places. **1924** F. MUIRHEAD *England* (ed. 2) 575 The opening of the oyster fishing is celebrated by an 'Oyster Feast' on Oct. 20th. **1934** A. E. HOUSMAN *Let.* 15 Sept. (1971) 360 The chief ambition of my life has long been to be invited to the Colchester Oyster Feast. **1972** R. COBB *Reactions to French Revolution* 4 He had once dressed up as a Roman Emperor for the carnival at the time of the Oyster Feast. **1888** *Amer. Anthropologist* I. No. 4. 297 The *oysterfield..would supply a bounteous repast. **1611** FLORIO, *Ostreca*, any *oyster-fish. **1855** S. F. BAIRD in *Rep. Bd. Regents Smithsonian Inst.* IX. 340 The toad-fish, or, as it is called at Beesley's point, the oyster-fish, on account of its frequenting the oyster beds, is one of the fisherman's pests. **1878** *Proc. U.S. Nat. Mus.* I. 374 *Tautoga omitis* [sic].—Oyster-fish. Rather common. **1884** G. B. GOODE *Nat. Hist. Aquatic Anim.* I. III. 251 The toad-fish, *Batrachus tau*, called also on the coast of New Jersey and in some parts of the Southern States 'Oyster-fish', is one of the most repulsive looking fishes upon our coast. **1903** T. H. BEAN *Fishes N.Y.* 598 This [*sc. Tautoga onitis*] is better known in New York as the blackfish; farther south it is styled ..Moll, Will George and oyster fish. *Ibid.* 656 *Gobiosoma bosci*... Naked Goby; Mud Creeper; Oysterfish. **1940** *Sun* (Baltimore) 30 Apr. 6/3 The oyster fish, sometimes called 'devil fish' by local fishermen, has a big head and mouth with which it crushes oysters for food. **1962** K. F. LAGLER et al. *Ichthyology* xi. 361 In the oyster toad-fish (*Opsanus tau*).. blood sugar levels are raised upon intramuscular injection of corticosteroid compounds. **1892** J. W. URQUHART *Electric Ship-Lighting* vii. 227 The *oyster fitting, without the guard, is much used for cabins. **1940** *Chambers's Techn. Dict.* 606/2 *Oyster-fitting*, a bulkhead fitting designed to emit light on both sides of the bulkhead or other partition upon which it is mounted. **1597** GERARDE *Herbal* III. clix. 1377 Lungwoort..groweth vpon rockes..especially among Oisters..; this Mosse they call *Oister greene. **1866** *Treas. Bot.* 833/1 *Oyster-green*, a name commonly given to *Ulva Lactuca* from its bright-green tint, and its being frequently attached to the common oyster. **1694** MOTTEUX *Rabelais* IV. xxx. (1737) 124 Like an *Oyster-knife. *a* **1841** W. P. HAWES *Sporting Scenes* (1842) II. 120 Oyster-knives and blood become well acquainted. **1907** *Yesterday's Shopping* (1969) 120/3 Place a stiff knife similar to an oyster knife between the rubber ring and flat metal top, and..it will easily come off. **1973** *Daily Colonist* (Victoria, B.C.) 1 July 9/1 An oyster knife..is obviously patterned on the rapier. **1703** *Lond. Gaz.* No. 3897/4 The *Oyster-Lays in the Hundred of Rochford, in the County of Essex. **1784** R. BAGE *Barham Downs* I. 229 How I acquired any *oyster-like disposition.. I know no more than a coach-horse. **1937** *Daily Herald* 16 Feb. 19/6, I have never known Mr. Rinder so definitely oyster-like as when I tackled him yesterday on the line he proposed to take in the broadcast. **1975** *Country Life* 13 Sept. 1320/4 Its [*sc.* salsify's] stale fish flavour, described as oyster-like. *a* **1976** A. CHRISTIE *Autobiogr.* (1977) x. ii. 488 There was something oyster-like about Rosalind. **1552** HULOET, *Oyster man,..*ostrearius*. **1753** in E. Singleton *Social N.Y. under Georges* (1902) 350, I am informed that an oysterman..may clear eight or ten shillings a day. **1853** O. S. FOWLER *Home for All* (rev. ed.) 23 Those persons who would economize, have only to order those very shells which the oyster-man has to pay to have carted from his cellar. **1891** W. K. BROOKS *Oyster* 141 No particular set of oyster-men are to blame. **1955** *Times* 31 Aug. 5/1 But the oystermen of Cornwall eat the succulent grade four oyster with greater relish than its bigger brother. **1974** 'A. GARVE' *File on Lester* xxxix. 143, I talked first with some oystermen along the front here. **1780** *Chron.* in *Ann. Reg.* 201/1 Tried and learnedly argued between the *oyster-meters of London and the proprietors of oyster-beds in the county of Essex. **1875** COOKE *Fungi* iv. 86 The *oyster mushroom..included in almost every list and book on edible fungi. **1862** ANSTED *Channel Isl.* IV. xxii. (ed. 2) 509 About 250 men and women are employed in the *oyster parks in sorting, loading, and unloading oysters. **1925** *Oyster piece [see OYSTERING *vbl. sb.* b]. **1960** *Times* 9 Dec. 18/7 The beautiful 'oyster-piece' veneers and marquetry. **1973** *Daily Tel.* (Colour Suppl.) 16 Mar. 47/2 Laburnum wood which has a dark heart and a yellow sapring when cut across the grain produces highly decorative 'oyster pieces'. **1821** W. COBBETT *Amer. Gardener* iv. 257 Salsafy, called by some *oyster plant, is good in soups, or to eat like the parsnip. **1841** *Cultivator* VIII. 114 Oyster Plant, or Salsify..after boiling soft, make gravy of flour, butter, etc. and add to them, and really they are rich substitutes for oysters. **1858** HOGG *Veg. Kingd.* 542 *Mertensia maritima* is a native of the sandy sea-coasts of Scotland and the north of England, where it is called *Oyster Plant*. **1885** E. P. ROE *Nature's Serial Story* xxvi. 186 Will your nose become *retroussé* if I ask you to aid me in planting parsnips, oyster-plant, carrots and..onions? **1938** R. GATHORNE-HARDY *Wild Flowers in Brit.* vi. 40 Another beautiful blue flower to be found on the coasts of Scotland and northern England is the uncommon Oyster Plant, *Mertensia maritima*,..which spreads its fat leaves and drooping blue flowers over the sea-shingle. **1960** *Oxf. Bk. Wild Flowers* 170/1 Sea Lungwort or Oyster Plant (*Mertensia maritima*)..is a rare plant of stony sea-shores in the north. **1972** Y. LOVELOCK *Vegetable Bk.* 201 The roots [of salsify] also are eaten.. and are said to taste like asparagus; others suppose them to taste like oysters, from which belief it gains its name vegetable oyster and oyster plant. **1976** *Billings* (Montana) *Gaz.* 1 July 2-A/4 Ten percent vegetables and fruits: Beets, carrots, onion, oyster plant (salsify) rutabagas. **1705** *Providence Rec.* (1894) VI. 247 *Oyster Rake 3 hammer and a hand Bill. **1900** *Field* 7 July 45/2 The prevalence of *oyster scale on the gooseberries. **1552** HULOET, *Oyster scalph, *ostrifer*. **1824** *Nantucket Inquirer* 26 Jan. (Th.), He wore a hat of the new *oyster-scow cut. **1856** *Dollar Times* (Cincinnati, Ohio) 11 Dec. 2/5 Our river boats are palaces of paint and gilding, but a leak from the bowsprit of an oyster-scow will sink one in fifteen minutes. **1610** *Althorp MS.* in Simpkinson *Washingtons* (1860) App. p. ii, The Parlor. Impr. ij tables —a cup-bard..a round *oyster table. **1716** *Providence Rec.* (1894) VI. 161 To Iron Teeth for *Oyster Tongs and Carpenters Adds 00-05-00. **1835** J. J. AUDUBON *Ornith. Biogr.* III. 608 My host carried with him..a pair of oyster-tongs. **1949** R. J. SIM *Pages from Past Rural N.J.* 74 In oyster tongs the pin is thirty-two inches or more above the heads. **1909** G. O. WHEELER *Old English Furnit.* (ed. 2) iii. 115 Sections of small walnut branches were built in veneers, ..resembling..oyster-shells, and..this particular work has come to be classed as 'oyster veneer'. **1974** *Country Life* 30 May 1538/1 The use of walnut oyster-veneers in England is common. **1914** EBERLEIN & MCCLURE *Pract. Bk. Period Furnit.* 86 When the cabinets were '*oyster' veneered, inlaid with marqueterie or lacquered. **1976** *Country Life* 27 May (Suppl.) 48d/1 (Advt.), A rare 17th century oyster-veneered walnut side table. **1916** E. W. GREGORY *Furnit. Collector* vi. 91 The well-known '*oyster' veneering is also typical of the style. **1944** C. DREPPERD *Primer of Amer. Antiques* 241/2 **Oyster Walnut*, the burl in walnut having oyster shapes and forms in it and obvious when cut on the bias. A fine veneer pattern. **1972** *Country Life* 8 June (Suppl.) 51 A small William & Mary 'oyster walnut' chest of drawers. **1593** SHAKS. *Rich. II*, I. iv. 31 Off goes his bonnet to an *Oyster-wench. **1825** BROCKETT *N.C. Gloss.* s.v., *Ee-shee-ke-le-kaul-er-Oysteers*, the famous cry of the elder oyster-wenches in Newcastle. **1562** J. HEYWOOD *Prov. & Epigr.* (1867) 113 On whom gape thine Oysters so wide, *oysterwife? **1597** GERARDE *Herbal* III. clix. 1377 The poore *Oisterwomen which carrie Oisters to sell vp and down. **1663** BUTLER *Hud.* I. ii. 540 The Oyster-Women lock'd their Fish up, And trudg'd away to cry No Bishop.

Hence **'oyster** *v.*, (*a*) *intr.*, to fish for or gather oysters; (*b*) *trans.*, to feed on oysters; with *up*; (*c*) *intr.*, to shut *up*; be silent (*slang*); cf. CLAM *v.*[4] 2; so **'oysterer**, one who gathers or sells oysters; a boat employed in the oyster-fishery; See OYSTERING *vbl. sb.* Also (all more or less *nonce-words*) **'oysterage**, an oyster-bed; **'oysterdom**, the domain or realm of oysters; **'oyster-ˌfull** *a.*, replete with oysters; **'oysterhood**, the condition of an oyster, habitual seclusion or reserve; **oy'sterian** *a.*, of or pertaining to oysters; **'oysterish** *a.*, of the nature of or resembling an oyster (hence **'oysterishness**); **'oysterize** *v.*, to make an oyster of, treat as an oyster; **'oysterless** *a.*, having no oysters, devoid of oysters; **'oysterling**, a young or small oyster.

18.. E. INGERSOLL (Cent.), Many more are *oystering now than before the war. **1861** T. WINTHROP *Cecil Dreeme* 156 Boys, I've got a sick man to oyster up. **1896** *Voice* (N.Y.) 13 Feb. 3/3 Being near the Gulf some would oyster and fish. **1973** R. PARKES *Guardians* xii. 225 Once they got him down the station he oystered up proper. Not another word. **1866** *Morn. Star* 4 Jan., The Saltash *oysterage will ..be found a valuable acquisition by the company. **1865** J. G. BERTRAM *Harvest Sea* xi. (1873) 242 The Ile de Re..in the Bay of Biscay..may now be designated the capital of French *oysterdom. *a* **1618** SYLVESTER *Tobacco Battered* 267 Iakes-farmers, Fidlers, Ostlers, *Oysterers. **1828** BANIM *Anglo-Irish* II. 188 Be it in..merchantman, collier, oysterer, skiff, or open-boat. **1855** SINGLETON *Virgil* I. 83 Pontus and *oyster-full Abydos' straits Are tempted. **1854** LOWELL *Cambr. 30 Yrs. Ago* Pr. Wks. 1890 I. 90 He came out of his *oysterhood at last. **1838** *New Monthly Mag.* LIII. 545 We are now approaching the paradise of the *oysterian Adam and Eve..the locality of the first fossil occurrence of the *ostrea leviuscula*. **1834** BECKFORD *Italy* I. iii. 31 A certain *oysterishness of eye and flabbiness of complexion. **1793** SOUTHEY *Let.* in *Life* I. 196 Poor Southey will either be cooked for a Cherokee, or *oysterised by a tiger. **1865** *Sat. Rev.* 2 Dec. 710/2 The awful vision of an *oysterless generation [may] be prevented from becoming a fact. **1867** *Times* 15 Oct. 5/6 Not one of the young *oysterlings of the previous summer's spat was known to have been killed by the cold weather or frost.

'oyster-ˌcatcher. [Cf. Fris. *oestervisscher*, Ger. *austermann*, *austernfischer*, and Linnæus' L. name *ostralegus*, mod.F. *huîtrier*.] A maritime wading bird of the family *Hæmatopodidæ* with black-and-white or black plumage, and bill and feet of a brilliant red.

The common European species is *Hæmatopus ostralegus* Linn., the earlier Eng. name of which is Sea Pie; the N. American species is *H. palliatus*. As an English name 'oyster-catcher' appears first in connexion with the latter; it was used generically by Pennant *Genera of Birds* (1773) p. xxxi.

1731 M. CATESBY *Nat. Hist. Carolina* (1754) I. 85 *Hæmatopus*... The Oyster Catcher. **1732** MORTIMER in *Phil. Trans.* XXXVII. 448 *Hæmatopus*... The Oyster-Catcher, so called, because it feeds upon Oysters, which it finds gaping when left dry on the Banks at low Water. **1846** STOKES *Discov. Australia* II. vii. 254 Our game-bag was thinly lined with small curlews, oyster-catchers, and sanderlings.

oystered ('ɔɪstəd), *a.* [f. OYSTER *sb.* + -ED[2].]

1. Of a veneer: bearing an oyster-shaped or whorled pattern.

1914 EBERLEIN & MCCLURE *Pract. Bk. Period Furnit.* ii. 57 The middle or end of the Carolean epoch when the whorled or 'oystered' veneer made from the transverse slices of small boughs came into vogue.

2. Eaten with oysters. *Nonce-use.*

1932 DYLAN THOMAS *Let.* (1966) 4 Oh, woe..unto Mumbles and the oystered beer.

oystering, *vbl. sb.* [f. OYSTER + -ING[1].] **1.** The practice of gathering or selling oysters.

1662 *Virginia Stat.* (1823) II. 140 The poore Indians whome the seating of the English hath forced from their wonted conveniences of oystering. **1860** *My Experiences in Australia* 66 In summer..oystering..used to be a favourite amusement with the young folks of Sydney.

2. Oyster veneer or work done with this.

1914 EBERLEIN & MCCLURE *Pract. Bk. Period Furnit.* iii. 90 Marqueterie, oystering and lacquer were freely used in their decorations. **1925** PENDEREL-BRODHURST & LAYTON *Gloss. Eng. Furnit.* 117 The slices are referred to as Oyster-pieces, and the arrangement as Oystering.

†**'oysterloit.** Also -loyte, -loite. An old name of bistort, *Polygonum Bistorta*.

[Perh. an error in Lyte for **oysterloyce*: cf. '*Oosterlucye*, Aristolochia, *herba*, Ger. *osterlucey*' (Kilian). According to Turner *Names of Herbes* (1881) 83 'Bistorta is called..in the South countrey *Astrologia*': see the various forms of this word under ARISTOLOCHIA and ASTROLOGE.]

1578 LYTE *Dodoens* I. xiv. 23 The small Bistorte..is called in some places of England Oysterloyte. **1611** COTGR., *Couleuvrée*, Snakeweed, Oysterloit.

'oysterous, *a.* [f. OYSTER *sb.* + -OUS.] Of the nature of, or full of, oysters.

1836 T. HOOK *G. Gurney* III. 239 The conversation..of those oysterous, boisterous convivialists. **1882** H. C. MERIVALE *Faucit of Ball.* II. II. iv. 192 A little pair of oysterous eyes of no particular colour.

'oyster-shell. a. A shell of an oyster. Also *fig.*

c **1450** *Pol. Poems* (Rolls) II. 239 Falsehed and sche byn bothe of oon substaunce, Alle be they not worth an oyster-schelle. **1553** EDEN *Treat. Newe Ind.* (Arb.) 16 Theyr fete are round..of the bignes of great oystershelles. **1607** TOPSELL *Four-f. Beasts* (1658) 104 Harts marrow,..mingled with the powder of oyster shels,..cureth kibes and chilblanes. **1875** BUCKLAND *Log-bk.* 124 The black markings or Wampum-spots in the American oyster-shell were..cut out, made into beads, and used as money or ornaments by the Indians. **1876** TROLLOPE *Prime Minister* IV. vi. 87 When Aristides has been much too just the oyster-shells become numerous.

b. *attrib.* **oyster-shell bark-louse** *N. Amer.* = *oyster-shell scale* (*a*); **oyster-shell scale** *N. Amer.*, (*a*) a scale insect, *Lepidosaphes ulmi*, which attacks many trees and shrubs; (*b*) the disease produced by this insect, characterized by small curved scales on the plant's bark; **oyster-shell stains** (*Photogr.*), stains on the plate in the collodion process; **oyster-shell veneer, veneering** = *oyster veneer, veneering* s.v. OYSTER 7 d.

1757 WHYTT in *Phil. Trans.* L. 387 He put the first in oystershell lime-water. **1835** *Court Mag.* VI. 188/1 Careering it in Bath, in his oyster-shell phaeton. **1868** LEA *Photogr.* 247 *Marbled Stains.*—'Oyster-shell' stains of reduced silver, with a gray metallic surface and in curious curved and arabesque patterns occasionally make their appearance. **1868** *Rep. Comm. Agric. 1867* (U.S. Dept. Agric.) 73 The oyster shell bark louse or scale insect..is said to be exterminated by washing the tree with a mixture of two parts of soft soap, eight parts of water, and lime enough to give it the consistence of whitewash. **1877** *Rep. Vermont Board Agric.* IV. 150 Dr. Worcester has also shown me a branch covered with oyster shell bark-louse. *Ibid.*, The insect is shorter and stouter than that of the oyster shell scale. **1924** LAWRENCE & SKINNER *Boy in Bush* ii. 21 He was glad to reach the oyster-shell path running up Wellington Street. **1924** C. C. DEAM *Shrubs of Indiana* 233 Some individuals of several species are attacked and even killed both in cultivation and in the wild state by the oyster-shell scale. **1929** G. G. & F. GOULD *Period Furnit. Handbk.* xiv. 147 Veneer:..oyster-shell—in walnut, irregularly shaped oval pieces, cross sections cut from small boughs, the wood graining suggesting oyster-shells, popular in the late Charles II period. **1955** R. FASTNEDGE *Eng. Furnit. Styles* 286 This oystershell veneering, used for cabinet doors and drawer fronts, was introduced from Holland in the late seventeenth century. **1971** A. CHRISTIE *Nemesis* viii. 86 A William and Mary oyster-shell bureau. **1972** SWAN & PAPP *Common Insects N. Amer.* 163 Oystershell Scale: *lepidosaphes ulmi*... The armor is light to dark brown, shaped like a tiny oyster shell.

'oystery, *a.* [f. OYSTER *sb.* + -Y.] Characterized by or abounding in oysters; having the quality of an oyster.

1844 DICKENS *Lett.* III. 59, I..opened the dispatch with a moist and oystery twinkle in my eye. **1871** R. ELLIS *Catullus* Fragm. ii, A sea-shore Hellespontian, eminent most of oystery sea-shores.

oystre, oystry, obs. Sc. forms of HOSTRY.

oystreche, -ege, -ige, -yche, obs. ff. OSTRICH.

oyther, obs. form of OTHER.

oz. [a. It. *ōz* or *ōž*, 15th c. abbreviation of *onza*, *onze*.] An abbreviation used for 'ounce', 'ounces', esp. after a number, as in 3 lb. 8 oz.

(For Italian MS. forms of the abbreviation, see Cappelli *Dizionario di Abbreviature*, Milano, 1899. In MS. the *z* had the lengthened form, its tail being usually carried in a circle under, round, and over the *o*, so as to form the line of contraction over the word. Cf. the analogous (13–15th c.) ways of writing lb. for *libra, libre* pound, pounds.)

a **1548** HALL *Chron., Hen. VIII* 257 b, A C. liii. ounces in golden plate, and .iiii. M. iii. oz in gylte plate. **1891** *Penny Postage Jubilee* 173 A letter of ½ oz. to Hong-Kong is..2½*d.*

‖**ozæna, ozena** (əʊ'ziːnə). [L. *ozæna* (Pliny), a. Gr. ὄζαινα a fetid polypus in the nose, f. ὄζειν to smell. Cf. F. *ozène* (1603 in Hatz-Darm.).]

1. *Path.* A fetid muco-purulent discharge from the nose, due to ulcerative disease of the mucous membrane, frequently with necrosis of the bone.

1656 BLOUNT *Glossogr.*, *Ozena*..a disease or sore in the nose, causing a stinking savour. **1661** LOVELL *Hist. Anim. & Min.* 347. **1741** MONRO *Anat.* (ed. 3) 113 An *Ozæna* is..ill to cure. **1822–34** *Good's Study Med.* (ed. 4) III. 204 The first variety..is often found as a sequel in ozænas.

†**2.** Old name for the Cuttle-fish. *Obs.* [= Gr. ὄζαινα a strong-smelling sea polypus.]

1591 SYLVESTER *Du Bartas* I. v. 238 The subtle Smell-strong-Many-foot [*margin* The Ozena], that fain A dainty feast of Oyster-flesh would gain. **1706** PHILLIPS, *Ozæna*, a sort of the Fish Pourcoutrel or Many-feet, so call'd from the rank Smell of its Head.

Hence **o'zænic** *a.*, pertaining to ozæna.

1857 in MAYNE *Expos. Lex.*

Ozalid ('əʊzəlɪd). [Formed by reversing DIAZO- and inserting *l*.] A proprietary name used esp. in connection with a diazotype copying process in which the light-sensitive coating of the paper contains the coupling compound as well as the diazonium salt, so that the image may be made visible by exposure to gaseous ammonia. Hence, a photocopy produced by this process.

1924 *Trade Marks Jrnl.* 16 July 1608 Ozalid... Paper.., stationery, and bookbinding. Kalle & Co., Aktien Gesellschaft.., Biebrich-on-Rhine, Germany; manufacturers and merchants. **1928** *Official Gaz.* (U.S. Patent Office) 13 Nov. 292/2 Kalle & Co. Aktiengesellschaft, Wiesbaden-Biebrich, Germany. Filed Jan. 30, 1928. *Ozalid* for light-sensitive copying and photographic papers. Claims use since Mar. 19, 1923. **1929** *Encycl. Brit.* XVII. 803/1 G. Kögel has patented..the use of diazoanhydrides..for paper that may be used for the same purpose; this process is known as 'Ozalid'. **1939** *Thorpe's Dict. Appl. Chem.* (ed. 4) III. 589/2 Ozalide [*sic*] papers, which have largely displaced blueprint paper, are based on the principle that a light-sensitive diazoanhydride may be mixed with a phenol or aromatic amine without coupling until the mixture is rendered slightly alkaline. **1941** *Official Gaz.* (U.S. Patent Office) 23 Dec. 767/2 General Aniline & Film Corporation, New York, N.Y. Filed Oct. 22, 1941. *Ozalid.* For light-sensitive diazotype paper, cloths, films, etc., for machines for developing the photoprints thus produced and parts of such machines. Claims use for light-sensitive diazo type materials since Mar. 19, 1923; and for printing and developing machines since May 1, 1936. **1944** *Trade Marks Jrnl.* 12 Apr. 167/2 Ozalid... Photographic and photocopying apparatus, instruments, and utensils. Ozalid Company Limited,..London,..manufacturers and merchants. **1967** V. STRAUSS *Printing Industry* v. 267/2 Diazo papers..are also known as Ozalids and whiteprints. **1970** E. A. D. HUTCHINGS *Survey of Printing Processes* vii. 114 Development of the intermediates is carried out in an Ozalid ammonia vapour dyeline machine. **1975** J. BUTCHER *Copy-editing* v. 61 The final proof is a photographic proof (usually an Ozalid).

ozanna, obs. variant of HOSANNA.

Ozark ('əʊzɑːk). Also **Osark.** [ad. F. *aux Arcs* at the Quapaw, ult. ad. Illinois *akansea* Quapaw Indian.] The Quapaw, a North American Indian people, or perhaps a local group of this tribe.

1816 H. KER *Trav. Western Interior U.S.* 40 We were visited by a few of the Osark tribe of Indians, who came to us in canoes.... They are called by the name of a river they inhabit, on the west side of the Mississippi. **1821** T. NUTTALL *Jrnl. Trav. Arkansa* vi. 81 The aborigines of this territory, now commonly called Arkansas or Quapaws and Osarks, do not..number more than about 200 warriors. **1910** F. W. HODGE *Handbk. Amer. Indians* II. 180/2 *Ozark*, a term at one time applied to a local band of Quapaw, from their residence in the Ozark mountain region of Missouri and Arkansas.

ozarkite (əʊ'zɑːkaɪt). *Min.* [Named 1846 from *Ozark* + -ITE[1].] A white amorphous variety of Thomsonite, from the Ozark Mountains, Arkansas.

1846 C. U. SHEPHARD in *Amer. Jrnl. Sc.* Ser. II. II. 251.

oze, obs. form of OOZE.

ozen-, ozin-, oznabrig, var. OSNABURG *Obs.*

ozey, var. OSEY *Obs.*, a sweet wine.

oziar, ozier: see OSIER.

ozie, obs. f. OOZY.

†**ozimus, ozymus.** *Obs.* App. some error for OSMUND[1], iron imported from Sweden.

1550 EDW. VI *Jrnl.* in *Lit. Rem.* (Roxb.) 261 If he [King of Suethen] brought ozymus and stele, and cooper, etc., he shuld haue our commodites and pai custom as an Englishman. **1657–61** HEYLIN *Hist. Ref.* (1849) I. 232 (D.) If he sent ozimus, steel, copper, &c. **1761** HUME *Hist. Eng.* II. xxxv. 277.

ozocerite, ozokerit(e (əʊ'zɒsəraɪt, əʊ'zəʊkərɪt, -aɪt; əʊzəʊ'sɪəraɪt, -'kɪəraɪt). *Min.* [a. Ger. *ozokerit* (Glocker, 1833), arbitrarily f. Gr. ὄζ-ειν to smell (ὄζω I smell) + κηρός bees-wax + -ITE[1].] A wax-like fossil resin, of brownish-yellow colour and aromatic odour; a mixture of natural hydrocarbons, occurring in some bituminous coal-measure shales and sandstones. Also called *native paraffin, mineral tallow*, or *mineral wax*.

Originally found by Meyer in Moldavia; subsequently in Galicia and other countries. Used to make candles, and for insulating electrical conductors, etc.

1837 DANA *Min.* 441 *Ozokerite*, a variety of black bitumen lately discovered by Meyer. **1846** WORCESTER, *Ozocerite*, a mineral resembling resinous wax in consistence and translucency. **1884** *Blackw. Mag.* Sept. 341/2 The ozokerite or earth wax of Galicia is found in great abundance.

attrib. **1871** SCOFFERN in *Belgravia Mag.* Feb. 450 An entirely new source of candle-making material has been developed, from the exploration of the ozokerit mines bordering the Caspian Sea. **1885** W. L. CARPENTER *Soap, Candles* etc. 328 Ozokerit Candles.

Hence **o'zocerited, o'zokerited** *ppl. a.*, covered or treated with ozocerite, as ***ozocerited core***. (U.S.)

ozo'nation. = OZONIZATION.

1854 J. SCOFFERN in *Orr's Circ. Sc., Chem.* 286 Ozonation of the..oxygen..takes place. **1948** KIRK & OTHMER *Encycl. Chem. Technol.* II. 426 A triozonide is formed with difficulty by ozonation of benzene. **1972** *Adv. Chem.* CXII. 1 A competition exists during ozonation of olefins between ozonolysis and epoxide formation.

ozone ('əʊzəʊn). *Chem.* [a. F. *ozone* (1840), f. Gr. ὄζ-ειν to smell + -ONE.] **a.** An allotropic or altered condition of oxygen, existing in a state of condensation (having three atoms to the molecule, O_3), with a peculiarly pungent and refreshing odour.

It is produced in the electrolysis of water, and by the silent discharge of electricity or the passage of electric sparks through the air (whence it is sometimes perceived after a thunderstorm); it is more active than ordinary oxygen, is a powerful oxidizing agent, liberates iodine from potassium iodide, and, when heated, breaks up into ordinary oxygen, expanding by half its volume.

1840 SCHÖNBEIN in *Rep. Brit. Assoc.* (1841) 214, I shall..consider the odoriferous principle as an elementary body and call it 'Ozone', on account of its strong smell. *Ibid.* 217, I do not, therefore, hesitate to ascribe the familiar electrical odour to ozone. **1871** M. COLLINS *Mrq. & Merch.* II. vii. 195 Exhilarated by the fresh ozone of the mountains. **1880** CLEMINSHAW *Wurtz' Atom. The.* 119 Ozone is, as we all know, condensed oxygen.

b. *fig.*

1865 *Cornh. Mag.* Apr. 450 The aristocratic ozone being absent from the atmosphere, there was a flatness about the dancing of all those who considered themselves above the plebeian ranks of the tradespeople. **1896** *Godey's Mag.* Apr. 357/1 In the artistic ozone of that zealous body of workers her ambition received its first definite impulse.

c. *attrib.* and *Comb.*, as ***ozone apparatus, carrier, generator, machine, season***; ***ozone-bearing, -infusing*** adjs.; **ozone-box, -cage,** a box containing ozone test papers, used to indicate the presence and relative amount of ozone in the air; **ozone-hydrogen,** Osann's term for hydrogen evolved by electrolysis from sulphurated water, said to have more active properties than ordinary hydrogen; **ozone-sonde,** a radiosonde for transmitting information on the ozone content of the atmosphere; also without hyphen as one word or two; **ozone (test) paper** (see quot.); **ozone scale,** a scale of tints with which to compare ozone papers after exposure; **ozone-water,** a solution of ozone in water.

1890 *Daily News* 25 Jan. 5/7 The want..of *ozone-bearing south-westerly winds. **1861** *N. Syd. Soc. Year Bk. Med.* 124 A new *Ozone-box and Test-slips. **1872** C. B. FOX *Ozone* 20 A modification of Beane's *Ozone generator. **1866–77** WATTS *Dict. Chem.* IV. 323 **Ozone-hydrogen.* **1864** KEMP in *Times* 12 Oct., The discoloration of *ozone paper..did not at any time during the month reach the maximum observed here. **1960** *Monograph Internat. Geodetic & Geophysical Union* No. 3, 20 During the IGY many successful balloon soundings with the *ozone-sonde were obtained. **1964** *Bull. Atomic Sci.* Jan. 29 In the past two years there has been an increased emphasis on several aspects of antarctic meteorology...albedo programs, meteorological studies aboard the Eltanin, and the inclusion of vertical coverage through..ozonesondes, and gammasondes. **1969** MCINTOSH & THOM *Essent. Meteorol.* vii. 111 One form of ozone sonde..is that devised by A. W. Brewer. Air is bubbled through a small electrolytic cell filled with neutral potassium iodide solution. **1874** *Chambers's Encycl.* VII. 180/2 The effect..produced by the air on ..*ozone-test papers—papers steeped in iodide of potassium..which are rendered brown (or blue) by the liberation of iodine—is..due to ozone. **1866–77** WATTS *Dict. Chem.* IV. 323 **Ozone-water*, an aqueous solution of ozone, which, according to Meissner.., exhibits in certain cases an action opposed to that of peroxide of hydrogen.

'ozoned, *a.* [-ED[2].] Supplied with ozone.

1902 *Scotsman* 3 Sept. 6/8 The finely ozoned air in the Highlands has a gloriously recuperating power.

'ozoneless, *a.* [-LESS.] Having no ozone.

1887 *All Year Round* 29 Jan. 36 It allows of really beneficial exercise when it carries its rider out of an ozoneless region. **1893** F. ADAMS *New Egypt* 17 That ozoneless lake, immemorially stagnant in its depths, which we call the Mediterranean Sea.

ozoner ('əʊzəʊnə(r)). *U.S. slang.* [f. OZONE + -ER[1].] A drive-in cinema. Also ***ozoner cinema***.

1948 *Time* 26 Apr. 96/2 This week, New York City will get its first 'ozoner': a 600-car..affair on Staten Island. **1949** *Sat. Rev. Lit.* (U.S.) 11 June 4/1 There are now between 1,000 and 2,000 drive-ins in the U.S... Hollywood calls them 'ozoners'. **1962** *Punch* 24 Jan. 167/1 Virtually every picture window of the motel rooms face[s] out on the ozoner cinema.

ozonic (əʊ'zɒnɪk), *a.* [f. OZONE + -IC.] Of, of the nature of, or containing ozone.

ozonic ether, a solution of hydrogen peroxide in water with ether.

1840 SCHÖNBEIN in *Rep. Brit. Assoc.* (1841) 218 The electrolysis of our ozonic compound. **1872** C. B. FOX *Ozone* 28 The action of Dr. Richardson's Ozonic Ether on the Iodide of Potassium tests is due to the Peroxide of Hydrogen which has been mixed with it. **1878** FOSTER *Phys.* II. ii.

(1879) 320 The oxygen in combination with hæmoglobin was in an active, or ozonic condition.

'ozonide. [-IDE.] **1.** (See quot. 1872.)

1867 *N. Syd. Soc. Retros. Med.* 464 Ozonides, such as permanganate of potash and the persalts of iron, turn the resin blue. **1872** C. B. Fox *Ozone* 11 Schönbein called those bodies containing Oxygen in a negatively active condition Ozonides.

2. a. [ad. G. *ozonid* (C. Harries 1904, in *Ber. d. Deut. Chem. Ges.* XXXVII. 840).] Any of the compounds containing the ring C–O–O–C–O, which are formed by the addition of ozone to olefinic double bonds and are explosive oils or amorphous solids.

1904 *Jrnl. Chem. Soc.* LXXXVI. I. 361 The ozonides are mostly highly explosive. **1929** R. A. GORTNER *Outl. Biochem.* xxxi. 640 On treatment of the oleic acid ozonide with water, it decomposes into hydrogen peroxide, pelargonic acid, and azelaic acid semi-aldehyde. **1959** E. L. MASCALL *Pi in the High* 28 Though many facts that art. provides *Re* substances called Ozonides. **1968** R. O. C. NORMAN *Princ. Org. Synthesis* xviii. 505 Lithium aluminium hydride reduces ozonides to alcohols.

b. The ion O_3^-, or a salt of this ion.

1949 *Chem. Abstr.* XLIII. 4170 The compd. can be formulated K^+, O_3^-, and termed K ozonide. **1962** P. J. & B. DURRANT *Introd. Adv. Inorg. Chem.* xxi. 799 The ozonide ion, $(O-O-O)^-$, is present in potassium ozonide, KO_3. **1966** *McGraw-Hill Encycl. Sci. & Technol.* XII. 409/2 Sodium also forms an ozonide, NaO_3, when ozone is passed into a solution of sodium in liquid ammonia.

ozoniferous (əʊzəʊ'nɪfərəs), *a.* [f. OZONE + -(I)FEROUS.] Bearing or generating ozone.

1858 T. GRAHAM *Elem. Chem.* II. 640 Passing the ozoniferous oxygen..through a tube containing pumice-stone soaked in sulphuric acid, to dry it. **1881** *Sci. Amer.* XLIV. 265 Plants supposed to produce or evolve ozone, and hence called ozoniferous plants.

ozonify (əʊ'zəʊnɪfaɪ), *v.* [f. OZONE + -(I)FY.] *trans.* To convert into ozone; to ozonize.

1866–77 WATTS *Dict. Chem.* IV. 301 By means of platinum wires,..electric discharges are passed through the oxygen, whereby it becomes ozonified. **1896** *Pop. Sci. Monthly* 573.

Hence **ozonifi'cation**.

1864 in WEBSTER.

ozonization (ˌəʊzəʊnaɪ'zeɪʃən). [n. of action f. next: see -ATION.] **a.** Conversion into ozone; charging with ozone.

1866–77 WATTS *Dict. Chem.* IV. 300 Processes..attended with ozonisation of the air. **1872** C. B. Fox *Ozone* 18 A powerful ozonisation of the Oxygen..is immediately produced.

b. Reaction with ozone, esp. in an ozonolysis process.

1906 *Jrnl. Chem. Soc.* XC. 227 The ozonisation of elaidic acid could only be carried out in chloroform solution. **1936** *Jrnl. Amer. Chem. Soc.* LVIII. 2272 The isolation of 1,2-diketones from the ozonization of disubstituted acetylenes. **1964** ROBERTS & CASERIO *Basic Princ. Org. Chem.* vii. 192 Ozonides..may explode violently and unpredictably. Ozonizations must therefore be carried out with due caution.

ozonize ('əʊzəʊnaɪz), *v.* [f. OZONE + -IZE.] **1.** *trans.* To convert (oxygen) into ozone.

1858 T. GRAHAM *Elem. Chem.* II. 641 Ozonised oxygen was freed from ozone and aqueous vapour by passing through sulphuric acid [etc.]. **1866–77** WATTS *Dict. Chem.* IV. 300 Dry oxygen..can be only partially ozonised by electric discharges. **1893** *Times* 19 July 2/6 A condenser charge is obtained by means of which the oxygen around the points is condensed or ozonized.

2. To charge or impregnate with ozone; to treat or act upon with ozone; to cause to react with ozone.

1850 T. GRAHAM *Elem. Chem.* I. 304 In ozonized air, paper impregnated with a solution of iodide of potassium immediately becomes brown from the liberation of iodine. **1881** *Nature* XXIII. 363 The slip had been ozonized by exposure..to the air. **1906** *Jrnl. Chem. Soc.* XC. 227 A solution of sodium oleate was ozonised and then evaporated under reduced pressure. **1930** *Jrnl. Amer. Chem. Soc.* LII. 2550 Methyl neopentyl ketone..and trimethylacetaldehyde were produced in the ratio of approximately 3·7 to 1 when di-isobutylene was ozonized and the ozonide hydrolyzed. **1968** *Adv. Chem. Ser.* LXXVII. lxii. 35 To determine what mechanistic pathways might be operating to account for the different cis-trans ratios, we have ozonized the olefin stereoisomers in the presence of the respective, necessary aldehydes. **1971** *Nature* 26 Nov. 213/1 The source [*sc.* mercury] was ozonized and mechanically spread on the Pt backing plate.

Hence **'ozonized, 'ozonizing** *ppl. adjs.*

1850 Ozonized [see 2 above]. **1873** RALFE *Phys. Chem.* 165 This blue colour may be developed by guaiacum and ozonizing substances. **1878** FOSTER *Phys.* II. ii. §3 278 A mixture of ozonized turpentine and tincture of guaiacum.

ozonizer ('əʊzəʊnaɪzə(r)). [f. prec. + -ER[1].] An apparatus for producing ozone.

1875 WATTS *Dict. Chem.* VII. 887 Houzeau has constructed an apparatus called an 'ozoniser', by which ozone is produced in considerable quantity. **1893** *Times* 18 July 2/6 Other forms of ozonizers are also employed.

o'zonograph. [f. OZONE + -O[1] + -GRAPH.] A registering or self-acting ozonoscope.

1890 in *Cent. Dict.*

ozo'nographer. [f. as prec. + -GRAPHER.] One who observes and records the amount of atmospheric ozone.

1890 in *Cent. Dict.*

ozonolysis (əʊzə'nɒlɪsɪs). *Chem.* [f. OZON(E + -O + -LYSIS.] The cleavage of double or triple carbon—carbon bonds by reaction with ozone.

1931 *Jrnl. Amer. Chem. Soc.* LIII. 358 In order to obtain the ketone indicated from hydrocarbon number 1 it is necessary to assume that the pinacolone rearrangement suggested by Butlerow has taken place during ozonolysis. **1936** *Jrnl. Org. Chem.* I. 145 The ozonolysis of triple bonds has been studied with..six acetylene representatives. **1951** I. L. FINAR *Org. Chem.* I. iv. 57 Ozonolysis..is probably the best method for determining the position of a double bond in any olefinic compound. **1971** I. G. GASS et al. *Understanding Earth* ix. 133 The ozonolysis products of the kerogens are aromatic in the Onverwacht.

Hence **ozono'lytic** *a.*, involving ozonolysis.

1956 *Jrnl. Polymer Sci.* XXII. 213 A simple ozonolytic method has been developed which enables the natural rubber trunk chains of rubber-polymethyl methacrylate and rubber-polystyrene interpolymers to be degraded into low molecular weight fragments. **1972** *Angewandte Chemie* (Internat. Ed.) XI. 1089/2 (*heading*) Ozonolytic degradation of a catenane.

ozonometer (əʊzəʊ'nɒmɪtə(r)). [f. OZONE: see -METER.] An instrument or device for ascertaining the amount of ozone in the air.

It consists of a graduated scale of tints with which ozone test papers, after exposure for a fixed time, are compared.

1864 *Times* 13 Oct., Schœnbein's ozonometer is graduated from zero to 10 deg. **1868** *Eng. Cycl.* s.v., An ozonometer by which a strip of ozone-paper 24 inches in length is exposed successively for an hour to the action of the atmosphere.

So **ˌozono'metric** *a.*, pertaining to the measurement of ozone; **ozo'nometry**, the measurement of the amount or proportion of ozone in the air.

1857 SIR T. WATSON *Lect. Princ. & Pract. Physic* (ed. 4) (L.), He got several physicians at Basle to compare their lists of catarrhal patients with his table of atmosphero-ozonometric observations. **1864** WEBSTER, *Ozonometry.* **1867** BRANDE & COX *Dict. Sci.*, etc., *Ozonometry.* This term has been applied to the means of detecting the presence and proportion of ozone in the atmosphere.

ozonoscope (əʊ'zəʊnəskəʊp). [f. OZONE + Gr. -σκοπος viewing: see -SCOPE.] An instrument for showing the presence or amount of ozone in the air.

1872 C. B. Fox *Ozone* 41 Discussions..as to whether or not Schönbein's ozonoscope solely registers Ozone. *Ibid.* 43 This test appeared to him, then, to be useless both as an ozonometer and an ozonoscope.

So **ozonoscopic** (əʊzəʊnəʊ'skɒpɪk) *a.*, serving to indicate the presence or amount of ozone.

1872 C. B. Fox *Ozone* 17 If positive and negative electricity be allowed to impinge on ozonoscopic paper.. there is no difference in the effects of the two kinds of electricity.

ozonosphere (əʊ'zəʊnəʊsfɪə(r)). *Meteorol.* [f. OZON(E + -O + SPHERE *sb.*] The region of the atmosphere where there is a significant concentration of ozone, at an altitude of 10 to 50 km. (6–30 miles); esp. the part between about 20 and 25 km (12–15 miles) where the concentration is greatest.

1933 *Jrnl. Inst. Electr. Engin.* LXXIII. 578/2 The upper part of the stratosphere is conveniently dealt with under a different name, even though there is no definite boundary between the stratosphere and the ozonosphere. **1951** *Jrnl. Brit. Interplanetary Soc.* X. 22 The composition up to the ozonosphere is then fairly well established. Above this both oxygen and nitrogen still form the major part of the atmosphere. **1963** *New Scientist* 1 Aug. 232/2 Apart from the effect that this might have in..giving us acute sunburn, there is another potentially important outcome of contaminating the ozonosphere. **1965** K. E. SPELLS in J. A. Gillies *Textbk. Aviation Physiol.* iii. 49 The region from about 12 to 22 miles altitude is sometimes called the ozonosphere.

ozonous ('əʊzəʊnəs), *a.* [f. OZONE + -OUS.] Of the nature of or containing ozone.

1890 in WEBSTER.

†**'ozyat.** *Obs.* An illiterate spelling of ORGEAT.

1769 MRS. RAFFALD *Eng. Housekpr.* 312 To make Ozyat. Blanch a Pound of Sweet Almonds, and the same of Bitter, beat them very fine [etc.]. **1778** *Ibid.* (ed. 2), To make Ozyat a second way. *Ibid.*, Send it up in ozyat glasses..quite cold.

P

P. the sixteenth letter of the alphabet in English and other modern languages, was the fifteenth in the ancient Roman alphabet, corresponding in position and value to the Greek *Pi*, *Π*, Π, earlier Γ, Ր, originally written from right to left ᒣ, and identical with the Phenician and general Semitic *Pe*, forms of which were ᒣ, ᒣ. During its whole known history the letter has represented the same consonantal sound, viz. the labial *tenuis*, or lip unvoiced stop, to which the corresponding sonant or voiced stop is B, and the nasal, M. In English, the simple *p* has always this sound; but it is sometimes silent, as initially in the combinations *pn-*, *ps-*, *pt-* (representing Greek *πν-*, *ψ-*, *πτ-*), and medially between *m* and another consonant, as in *Hampstead*, *Hampton*, *Sampson*, *Thompson*, *Dempster*, *Tompkins*, where it is not etymological, but has the function of indicating for the preceding *m* the short and semi-sonant value which *m* naturally has before pronounced *p*: cf. *Simpson*, *crimson* (ˈsɪmsən, ˈkrɪmz(ə)n), with *wimple*, *wimble*. In words from Latin, such as *exempt*, *tempt*, *peremptory*, *assumpsit*, *consumptive*, *redemption*, and some others, as *Humpty-Dumpty*, where the *p* is (so far as English is concerned) etymological or consciously derivational, there is generally in careful utterance an intention to pronounce it, resulting in an incomplete *p*, which we indicate thus (tɛm(p)t), (riːˈdɛm(p)ʃən); but, in rapid or careless utterance, the *p* disappears, just as in *Ham(p)ton*, *Thom(p)son*.

The digraph PH, *ph*, is used, in continuation of Latin usage, to transliterate the Greek letter *Φ*, *φ*, the phonetic value of which is now identical with that of F. The words beginning with PH have thus the same relation to the P words proper that those in CH have to the C words; that is, they constitute an alien group, which, only for alphabetical convenience, occupy a place in the midst of the P words proper, between PE-, and PI-.

Original P in Germanic or Teutonic represents an Indo-European B. But, *initially*, B was of rare occurrence in Indo-European, and it is not certain that any of the words in which it so occurred were retained in Teutonic, where initial P was consequently very rare. Of the OE. words in P, a few were apparently Common West Germanic, a very few, Common Teutonic; of many of the remainder the origin is quite obscure, but the majority were manifestly adoptions within the historical period from other languages, chiefly from Latin. Notwithstanding these extraneous additions, P remained the smallest initial letter (the exotic K, Q, not being counted) in the Old English or Anglo-Saxon vocabulary, occupying less than half the space of I, and little more than two-thirds of that of Y. Its relation to the other mutes, C (= K) and T, and to its own sonant B, is seen by the pages which these occupy in Toller's edition of Bosworth's Anglo-Saxon Dictionary, which are C 50, T 64, B 78, P 8½ pages. P might be expected to comprise a correspondingly small part of the modern English vocabulary; on the contrary, it is actually the third largest initial, being surpassed only by S and C, with which it forms a triad of gigantic letters, which include nearly a third of all the words in the dictionary. This result is mainly owing to the vast accessions from Greek, Latin, and the modern Romanic languages (chiefly, of course, from French), and especially to the enormous number of words formed with the Latin prefixes *per-*, *post-*, *pre-*, *pro-*, and the Greek *para-*, *peri-*, *pro-*, along with the PH group already referred to. But, besides these, P has received great additions, not only in later times from Oriental, African, American, and other remote languages, but, during the Middle English and Modern periods alike, of a multitude of common, familiar, or lower-class words from sources which cannot be traced, often apparently from fresh word-formation. P thus presents probably a greater number of unsolved etymological problems than any other letter.

I. 1. The letter (piː). Plural P*s*, P's, p's (piːz).

attrib. as ***p-language***, a language which preserves original *p*, or substitutes it for other sounds, as Greek which has *πεντέ* against L. *quinque*, or Welsh which has *pedwar* against OIr. *cether*, from **qetwer*, L. *quatuor*. Used *spec.* to designate one of the two main groups of languages which developed from Common Celtic, so called because its distinctive phonological features include the development of IE. **q*ᵘ to *p*, as ***P-Celtic***, ***-division***, ***-group***, etc.; ***P-Celt***, a speaker of P-Celtic.

c **1000** [see B]. **1530** PALSGR. 33 The sounding of this consonant *P*. *P* in all thynges followeth the generall rules.. without any manner exception. *Ibid.* 21 Excepte *ps* whiche they sounde but *s*. sayeng for *psálme*, *psaltére*, *salme*, *saltere*. **15..** HEYWOOD (*title*) The playe called the foure P. A new and very mery enterlude of A Palmer. A Pardoner. A Poticary. A Pedler. **1573–80** BARET *Alv.* s.v., This letter p seemeth both by his name and forme to be of kind to b, and as it were a b turned vpside downe. **1601** SHAKS. *Twel. N.* II. v. 97 By my life this is my Ladies hand.. thus makes shee her great *P's*. **1612** DEKKER *If it be not good* Wks. 1873 III. 329 Three Pees haue peppered me, The Punck, the Pot, and Pipe of smoake. **1863** A. M. BELL *Princ. Speech* 161 With reference to the letter *P*, we observe, that it is not made by the conjunction of the lips, but by their separation; and this of course implies previous contact. **1891** J. RHYS in *Trans. Philol. Soc. 1891–4* 104 (*title*) The Celts and the other Aryans of the *P* and *Q* groups. *Ibid.* 111 We are entitled to conclude that the Q Celts arrived in the west before the P Celts, as they are found occupying the furthest parts of the Celtic area... The conclusion is scarcely to be avoided that the later comers, the P Celts, came as invaders and conquerors. **1892** *Blackw. Mag.* Mar. 409 The inability of Syrian lips to pronounce the letter P. **1892** JOHNSTON *Place Names Scotl.* 224 Windisch and Stokes' Classification of Celtic languages... The *p* group, Welsh, Pictish, Cornish, &c. **1900** *Contemp. Rev.* Feb. 272 Greek may be called a *p*-language, Germanic a *q*-language. **1913** J. M. JONES *Welsh Gram.* 1 Keltic: (*a*) the Q division, consisting of dialects in Gaul and Spain, and the Goidelic group, comprising Irish, Scotch Gaelic and Manx; (*b*) the P division, consisting of Gaulish, and the British group, comprising Welsh, Cornish and Breton. **1949** *Antiquity* XXIII. 23 By birth-place and blood, Kieran was closely associated with the P-Celtic tribe of Corcu-Loigde. *Ibid.* 27 The Ulaid (the Ulstermen of the Saga), were once P-Celts, in O'Rahilly's view. **1953** [see BRITTONIC *a.* and *sb.*]. **1972** W. B. LOCKWOOD *Panorama Indo-Europ. Lang.* 74 The term Goidelic is chiefly used to denote Irish as distinct from British or, more technically speaking, to denote Q-Celtic as opposed to P-Celtic. **1977** *Word 1972* XXVIII. 133 One may wish to see Pictish interpreted as somewhat less different from Cumbric and the rest of insular p-Celtic than Jackson would argue.

2. Used, like the other letters, to indicate serial order, as in the 'signatures' of the sheets of a book, the Batteries of the Horse Artillery, etc.

3. P and Q. a. ***to be P and Q*** (***Pee and Kew***).

According to Bound *Provincialisms* as quoted in Eng. Dial. Dict., this was used in 1876 in Shropsh. and Herefordsh. in the sense 'to be of prime quality'.

1612 ROWLANDS *Knave of Harts* (Hunterian Cl.) 20 Bring in a quart of Maligo, right true: And looke, you Rogue, that it be Pee and Kew.

b. ***to mind one's P's and Q's*** (***peas and cues***), to be careful or particular as to one's words or behaviour. So ***to be on*** (***in***) ***one's P's and Q's***.

1779 MRS. H. COWLEY *Who's the Dupe?* I. i, You must mind your *P's* and *Q's* with him, I can tell you. ? **1800** W. B. RHODES *Bomb. Fur.* iv. 30 My sword I well can use So mind your P's and Q's. *a* **1825** FORBY *Voc. E. Anglia* 266 'Mind your p's and q's', q.d. 'be nicely observant of your language and behaviour'. **1866** G. MACDONALD *Ann. Q. Neighb.* x. (1878) 181 Well, I thought it wasn't a time to mind ones peas and cues exactly. **1893** W. S. GILBERT *Utopia* I, He minds his P's and Q's,—And keeps himself respectable.

a **1814** *Apollo's Choice* II. ii. in *Mod. Brit. Drama* IV. 208, I must be on my P's and Q's here, or I shall get my neck into a halter. **1888** C. BLATHERWICK *Uncle Pierce* i, He was rather on his p's and q's. **1893** W. A. SHEE *My Contemp.* vi. 149 In a well-dressed crowd you are in your p's and q's.

c. ***one's P's and Q's***, put for 'one's letters'.

1820 COMBE *Consol.* I. 30 And I full five-and-twenty year Have always been school-master here; And almost all you know and see, Have learn'd their *Ps* and *Qs* from me.

[*Note.* As to the origin of these nothing has been ascertained. An obvious suggestion is that b. (for which the evidence does not go far back) refers to the difficulty which a child beginning to read has in distinguishing the tailed letters p and q; others have conjectured some cryptic reference to the words *peculiar*, or *particular*. There is no necessary connexion between b. and a., which belongs to an earlier date. In a still earlier passage from Dekker 1602, 'Now thou art in thy *pee* and *cue*', *pee* means the coat so called (see PEE *sb.*), and *cue* app. either *queue*, or CUE *sb.*² sense 3 or 4; but there may have been a punning allusion to the expressions here considered, if they were then current.]

4. ***P.Z. exercise*** (*R.N.*), an exercise at sea.

1905 *Trans. Inst. Naval Archit.* XLVII. II. 305 The P.Z. exercises have been so conducted as to be deceiving. **1916** 'TAFFRAIL' *Pincher Martin* viii. 140 Gunnery, gunnery, *toujours* gunnery—unless it was torpedo-running, steam tactics, or P.Z. Exercises—was carried on through-out the year. **1962** GRANVILLE *Dict. Sailors' Slang* 85/2 *PZ*, tactical exercise in the Fleet at sea in peacetime when the Code flags *PZ* were run up at the start of the exercise.

II. Abbreviations. **a. P.**, various proper names, as Peter, Paul, etc.; **P.**, **p.**, past, post; **P** (*chess*) = pawn; **P** (*Chem.*) = Phosphorus; **P** (*Mechanics*) = pressure; **P.**, 'prompter side' in a theatre; cf. *P.S.* below; **p.**, page; **p-** (*Chem.*), para-; **p**, parental generation (see quot. 1902); **p.** (in a ship's log) = passing showers; **p**, **p.**, pence, penny, in decimal currency (see NEW *a.* 4); ***p*** (*Music*) = *piano*, softly; *Π* (i.e. Greek *pi*) (*Math.*) continued product; *π* (*Math.*) = *pi*, the ratio of the circumference to the diameter of a circle, the incommensurable quantity 3·14159265...; **Pa**, pascal; **Pa.** (*U.S.*), Pennsylvania; **p.a.**, per annum (PER *prep.* I. 2); **P.A.**, personal assistant; **P.A.** [see quot. 1972], a canvas climbing boot with a rubber sole strengthened with a steel plate; **P.A.**, political agent; **P.A.**, Post Adjutant; **P.A.**, power amplifier; **P.A.**, press agent, Press Association, programme assistant; **P.A.**, **PA**, **p.a.**, public address; **PAL**, phase alternation line (name of a colour television system); **P. and O.**, **P. & O.**, Peninsular and Oriental Steam Navigation Co.; **PAR**, precision approach radar; **P.A.S.**, **PAS**, *para*-aminosalicylic acid; **PAYE**, **P.A.Y.E.**, pay as you earn; **PAYV**, pay-as-you-view; **Pb** (*Chem.*), *plumbum*, lead; **P.B.I.**, Poor Bloody Infantry(man), so *P.B.* used with other sbs.; **P.B.S.** (*U.S.*), Public Broadcasting Service; **p.c.**, per cent; **PC**, personal computer; **P.C.**, Police Constable; **p.c.**, **P.C.**, postcard; **P.C.**, Privy Councillor; **PC**, propositional calculus (see PROPOSITIONAL *a.* b); also *attrib.*; **PCB**, **pcb**, printed circuit board; (see also sense II. d below); **PCM**, **pcm**, pulse code modulation; **PCP**, phencyclidine; **p.c.u.**, passenger car unit; **P.D.**, **p.d.**, potential difference; **P.D.**, preventive detention (also, detainee); **Pd** (*Chem.*), Palladium; **PDI**, powered descent initiation (of a spacecraft); **P.D.Q.**, **p.d.q.**, pretty damn quick; **P.E.**, physical education; **P.E.**, **p.e.**, plastic explosive; **P.E.N.**, **PEN**, Poets, Playwrights, Editors, Essayists, and Novelists; **PEP** (*Radio*), peak envelope power; **PEP** (also with pronunc. pɛp), personal equity plan, an investment scheme intended to extend share-ownership in the U.K., whereby investors may acquire shares (up to a given value) in U.K. companies without paying tax on dividends or capital gains; **P.E.P.**, **PEP**, Political and Economic Planning; ***p/e ratio***, price-earnings ratio; **PERT** (orig. *U.S.*), program(me) evaluation (and) review technique (orig., program(me) evaluation research task); (= *network analysis* b, esp. as used to deal with events of uncertain duration); **P.E.S.C.**, Public Expenditure Survey Committee; **p.f.** (*Mus.*), pianoforte, [It. *piano forte*] soft then loud, [It. *più forte*] more loudly; **p.f.a.**, **P.F.A.**, pulverized fuel ash; **PFC**, **p.f.c.** (*U.S.*), Private 1st Class, poor foolish (forlorn, etc.) civilian; **PG**, parental guidance (orig. *N. Amer.*, a cinema film classification); **P.G.**, **p.g.**, paying guest; hence **p.g.** *v. intr.*, to reside as a paying guest; **PGR**, **P.G.R.** [ad. G. *p.g.R.* (O. Veraguth 1907, in *Monatsschr. f. Psychiatrie und Neurol.* XXI. 387)], psychogalvanic reflex, response; **Ph.D.** [L. *Philosophiæ Doctor*], Doctor of Philosophy, Doctorate of Philosophy; **P.I.** (*U.S. slang*), pimp; **PI**, **p.i.**, private investigator; **PIB**, Prices and Incomes Board; **PIDE** [Pg. *Polícia Internacional e de Defesa do Estado*], International Police for the Defence of the State; **PIN**, with pronunc. (pɪn), personal identification number (esp. one allocated by a bank, etc., to a customer for use with a cash card); **p-j**, **P.J.**, pyjama; **PK.**, **Pk.**, psychokinesis, psychokinetic (see quot. 1943); **P.K.I.** [Indonesian *Partai Komunis Indonésia*], Indonesian Communist Party; **PKU** (*Med.*), phenylketonuria; **P.L.A.**, People's Liberation Army; **P.L.A.**, Port of London Authority; **P.L.C.**, **p.l.c.**, public limited company; **P.L.M.** [Fr. *Paris-Lyon-Mediterranée*], Paris-Lyons-Mediterranean (Railway); **P.L.O.**, **PLO**,

Palestine Liberation Organization; **PL/I, PL/1** (*Computing*), 'Programming Language One', a versatile and powerful high-level language designed to replace both Fortran and Cobol in their respective fields; **PLP, P.L.P.,** Parliamentary Labour Party; **PLR,** Public Lending Right (s.v. PUBLIC *a.* 5 f); **PLSS,** personal life support system; **P.M.,** particular (*or* peculiar, *or* proper) metre; **P.M., p.m.,** *post meridiem*, afternoon; **p.m., P.M.,** *post mortem*; **P.M.,** Prime Minister; **P.M.A.** (*Dentistry*) (see quot. 1969); **P.M.G.,** Postmaster General; **P.M.S.,** pregnant mare's serum, or a gonadotrophic extract of it; **PNdb, PNdB,** perceived noise decibel(s) (see quot. 1959); **P.N.E.U.,** Parents' National Educational Union; **P.O.,** postal order; **P.O.,** post office; **P.O.A.,** Probation of Offenders Act; **P.O.D.,** pay on delivery; **P.O.D.** (*U.S.*), Post Office Department; **P. of W.,** Prince of Wales; **POL,** petrol, oil, and lubricants; **P.O.O.,** Post Office Order; **POP,** Post Office Preferred; **P.O.P., POP,** printing-out paper; **POPOP** [f. the repeated initials of PHENYL and OXAZOLE, the molecule consisting of five such rings joined in this order], 1,4-di[2-(5-phenyloxazolyl)] benzene, a substance used in solution as a scintillator; **POS,** point of sale; **POUM, P.O.U.M.** [Sp. *Partido Obrero de Unificación Marxista*], Workers' Party of Marxist Unity; **P.O.W.,** Prince of Wales; **P.O.W., POW,** prisoner of war; **P.P.,** parish priest; **p.p.,** *per procurationem*, by proxy; *pp* or *ppp* (*Music*) = *pianissimo*, very softly; **P-P, PP,** pellagra-preventive or -preventing (formerly a designation of the vitamin now called niacin); **ppb, p.p.b.,** parts per billion; **P.P.C.** (written on cards, etc.), *pour prendre congé*, to take leave; hence **P.P.C.** *v. intr.*; **PPC, P.P.C.,** progressive patient care; **P.P.D., PPD,** purified protein derivative (of tuberculin); **P.P.E., PPE,** Politics, Philosophy, and Economics (a course of study at Oxford University); **p.p.i.,** policy sufficient proof of interest; **P.P.I., p.p.i.,** plan position indicator; **PPK,** *Polizei Pistole Kriminal* [G., police criminal pistol], a type of handgun; **PPLO,** pleuropneumonia-like organism(s); **ppm,** parts per million; **P.P.S.,** Parliamentary Private Secretary; **PPU,** Peace Pledge Union; **P.Q., PQ,** parliamentary question; **P.R.,** photographic reconnaissance; **P.R.,** Pre-Raphaelite; **P.R.,** prize ring; **P.R.,** proportional representation; **P.R.,** public relations; **P.R., PR,** Puerto Rico, Puerto Rican; **P.R.A.,** President of the Royal Academy of Art; **P.R.B.,** Pre-Raphaelite Brother(-hood); **P.R.O.,** Public Record Office; **P.R.O.,** public relations officer; **PROM,** programmable read-only memory (cf. ROM s.v. R II. 2 a); **PROP,** Preservation of the Rights of Prisoners; **P.R.S.,** Performing Rights Society; **P.R.S.,** President of the Royal Society; **P.S.,** 'prompter side' in a theatre; **P.S.A.,** Pleasant Sunday Afternoon; **PSBR,** public sector borrowing requirement; **p.s.c.,** passed staff college; **p.s.i.(a.), psi,** pounds per square inch (absolute); **P.S.V., p.s.v.,** public service vehicle; **P.T.,** physical training; **P.T., PT,** purchase tax; **Pt.** (*Chem.*), Platinum; **pt.,** part, pint; **P.T.A.,** Parent-Teacher Association; **PT boat** (*U.S.*), patrol torpedo boat; **PTC,** phenylthiocarbamide; **P.T.I.,** physical training instructor; **P.T.O., p.t.o.,** = please turn over; **p.t.o., PTO,** power take-off; **Pty.** (*Austral. commercial*), proprietary; **P.U.O.,** pyrexia of unknown origin; **P.U.S., PUS,** Permanent Under-Secretary; **pw, p.w.,** per week; **P.W.D.,** Public Works Department; **PWR,** pressurized-water reactor; **PX** (*U.S. mil.*), Post Exchange; **p-y-o, PYO** = *pick your own* s.v. PICK *v.* 5 c. Also PABA, pH, P-N-P, P.S., P-TYPE.

1900 PERKIN & KIPPING *Organic Chem.* 316 The most usual course in the case of the di-derivatives is to employ the terms ortho-, meta-, and para-, or simply *o*, *m*, and **p*,.. para-nitrophenol or *p*- nitrophenol. **1740** J. GRASSINEAU *Mus. Dict.* 173 **P*, in the Italian music, frequently signifies *piano*, which is what we called soft. **1888** KIPLING *Masque of Plenty* in *Departmental Ditties* (1890) 48 (*adagio dim.*) Fillèd with praise... (*p*) Ay, paint our swarthy billions The richest of vermilions. **1957** H. SHANET *Learn to read Music* IV. 123 Between *f* and *p*, there are *mezzo forte*.., and *mezzo piano* (medium soft). **1977** G. WARFIELD *How to write Music Manuscript* 133 Place a 'p' under the first note and a 'pp' under the last in these two examples. **1902** W. BATESON et al. *Rep. Evolution Comm. R. Soc.* I. 160 We suggest as a convenient designation for the parental generation the letter *P. In crossing, the P generation are the pure forms... Starting from any subject-individual, P_2 is the grand-parental, P_3 the great-grandparental generation, and so on. **1918** BABCOCK & CLAUSEN *Genetics Rel. Agric.* x. 180 (*caption*) Re-appearance of parental values in the F_2 offspring. P_1 Leaf Factor. **1952** SRB & OWEN *General Genetics* ix. 164 Verify this by diagramming a sequence of crosses through F_2 where the P generation is the reciprocal of the one shown in the text. **1975** V. GRANT *Genetics of Flowering Plants* i. 9 The experimental results can be summarized as follows: P round yellow × wrinkled green. **1934** WEBSTER, **p.*,.. penny. **1968** *Times* 17 Apr. 6/1 The 10p. and 5p. coins could appear in small change almost at once. **1973** *Guardian* 18 Dec. 13/3 We couldn't get away with a half p in tax evasion—but they do. **1976** 'W. TREVOR' *Children of Dynmouth* iv. 95 Yesterday had officially been the last day for entries, but he'd seen no reason to turn away the man's fifty p. **1901** G. B. SHAW *Let.* 7 Nov. in *B. Shaw & Mrs. Campbell* (1952) 14 Titheradge's determination to die parrallel [*sic*] to the float with his heels O.P. and his head *P.. rather spoils the picture. **1933** P. GODFREY *Back-Stage* i. 18 The amber circuits in No. 1 batten, floats, and P. and O.P. perches. **1964** H. S. HVISTENDAHL *Engin. Units* iii. 29 In the French decree of May 3rd, 1961, the name pascal (*Pa), is adopted for the N/m². **1975** *Nature* 2 Oct. 371/2 The density of vitreous silica is affected irreversibly by the application of pressures of more than 2 × 10⁹ Pa. *a* **1912** W. T. ROGERS *Dict. Abbrev.* (1913) 145/2 **p.a.*, *Per annum* (For the year). **1931** *Times* 16 Mar. 22/4 (Advt.), Present rental value £300–£350 p.a. **1955** *Times* 7 July 1/5 Salary, £1,200–£1,600 p.a., plus free furnished quarters, fuel, light, water. **1942** PARTRIDGE *Dict. Abbrev.* 73/1 **P.A.*.. Personal Assistant. **1943** N. BALCHIN *Small Back Room* i. 14 D'you think Higgins goes in for women? We might hire him a suitable P.A. **1969** D. CLARK *Nobody's Perfect* ii. 61 Couldn't his P.A. have rung you when you got home? **1975** M. SINCLAIR *Long Time Sleeping* iii. 38 Gilbert Winter's office and the adjacent one of his long-suffering PA. **1963** *P.A. [see KLETTERSCHUH]. **1972** D. HASTON *In High Places* ii. 35 Neil and I [were] ahead leaving the other two arguing about who should wear the one pair of P.A.'s. (These are special boots for hard rock-climbing, with stiff, smooth rubber soles and canvas uppers. The initials are those of their inventor, Pierre Allain, a famous French climber before the Second World War.) **1913** E. M. FORSTER *Let.* 1 Jan. in *Hill of Devi* (1953) 25 The Political Agent from Neemuch.. brought a party... The *P.A... planted himself on the State for the night. **1937** F. STARK *Baghdad Sketches* 187 [They] send messages to the P.A. **1940** *Chambers's Techn. Dict.* 608/1 **P.A.*, power amplifier. **1971** *Melody Maker* 4 Sept. 20 The giant PA's distort their guitars out of all recognition. **1936** *Amer. Speech* XI. 220 In terms of the theater, the **P.A.* is the Press Agent. **1958** *Spectator* 11 July 53/2 The press box was empty except for PA and *The Times*. **1915** M. MACDONAGH *Diary* 6 Oct. in *London during Gt. War* (1935) II. iii. 80 My friend Howe, of the '*P.A.'. **1942** PARTRIDGE *Dict. Abbrev.* 73/1 *P.A.*.. Publishers' Association. But also Press Association. **1972** D. MCLACHLAN *No Case for Crown* iii. 45 I'll deal with the P.A.; their news editor used to work under me. **1968** *Listener* 4 Apr. 442/3 Four of these programme assistants form the nucleus of Radio Sheffield's staff... My immediate task is to look at the material.. left for me the previous night by one of the other *PA's. **1936** *Amer. Speech* XI. 220 In radio, a **P.A.* system is a public address system. **1953** POHL & KORNBLUTH *Space Merchants* (1955) ii. 23 The PA system announced that my flight was ready. **1963** *Times Lit. Suppl.* 1 Mar. 156/1 Marlowe anticipated Whitman's barbaric yawp by setting up a national PA system of blank verse. **1964** S. BELLOW *Herzog* (1965) 35 Over the p.a. system the management begged the spectators not to throw pennies. **1963** J. R. DAVIES *Understanding Television* xiii. 485 Mention must be made of the recently introduced *PAL system, developed by Telefunken... The PAL system has been investigated by the European Broadcasting Union... PAL is based on the N.T.S.C. system. **1968** *Listener* 21 Nov. 687/2 It's not quite true.. that PAL and SECAM are 'irreconcilable' now that at least one inventor is trying to market a cheap conversion kit. **1975** *New Scientist* 31 July 274/1 Commercial TV resolution in the US is 525 lines, against Europe's PAL standard of 625 lines. **1863** DICKENS *Uncomm. Trav.* in *All Year Round* 6 June 350/2 The well-known regularity of the *P. and O. Steamers. **1880** *Standard* 15 May 5/3 The trim mates of P. and O. liners. **1892** MRS. CLIFFORD *Aunt Anne* I. iii. 59 She fancied him on board a P. and O. **1951** *Gloss. Aeronaut. Terms* (*B.S.I.*) III. 21 *Final controller*, a radar controller employed in the transmission of *PAR talk-down instructions to the pilot of an aircraft on the final approach to the runway, and in passing monitoring information to the pilot when using a landing aid other than PAR. **1966** *McGraw-Hill Encycl. Sci. & Technol.* X. 578/2 In common practice, the ground PAR operators call instructions to the pilot. **1946** *Lancet* 5 Jan. 15/2 Treatment with *p*-aminosalicylic acid (*P.A.S.) was given in three periods with concomitant falls in temperature. **1959** J. BRAINE *Vodi* vi. 85 They'd tried strep. and P.A.S. **1971** *Brit. Jrnl. Dis. Chest* Jan. p. vi (Advt.), A choice of flavoured drinks... the acceptable way of taking PAS and Isoniazid. **1944** *Times* 4 Apr. 2/2 (*heading*) *PAYE begins. **1956** 'C. BLACKSTOCK' *Dewey Death* iv. 89 Miss Holmes.. [was] doggedly working out the P.A.Y.E. for the thirty members of I.L.D.A. staff. **1972** *Accountant* 21 Sept. 343/1 Scare stories.. about the implications of the proposed letter suffixes to employees' PAYE code numbers, have been officially denounced. **1958** *Spectator* 27 June 829/2 The need is to make the idea of *PAYV much more familiar than it is. There have been many references to it from time to time in the press in the last few years, but for some reason the idea has never caught on. **1916** *B.E.F. Times* 1 Dec. f. 4/1 So here's to the lads of the *P.B.I. Who live in a ditch that never is dry. *a* **1918** J. T. B. MCCUDDEN *Five Yrs. in R. Flying Corps* (1919) 134 The famous Ypres salient.. was by no means regarded with friendly feelings by the Infantry —or P.B.I. as they generally call themselves. **1946** *Jrnl. R. United Service Inst.* XCI. 52 He is the 'P.B.I.' of the service on whom the final success of the scheme depends. **1949** F. SWINNERTON *Doctor's Wife comes to Stay* 149 He's only the P.B. Author. **1952** *Sunday Times* 14 Dec. 7/3 Procedural remedies are being sought, mostly by back-benchers—the 'P.B.I.' of Parliament. **1968** W. WINWARD *Conscripts* xii. 154 The p.b.i. gets the chopper, but never the officer. **1972** *Guardian* 1 Feb. 12/2 In the trenches the PBI.. await the order to go over the top. **1976** *Times Lit. Suppl.* 30 Jan. 106/1 The Crossman interpretation of the position of the MP whom he sees as the PBI of the mass party. **1970** *N.Y. Times* 26 Feb. 95/4 Mr. Gunn is responsible for.. managing the country's 190-station public television network. *P.B.S. has been in existence for three months. **1972** *Newsweek* 4 Sept. 89 PBS abandoned floor reporting and trained its cameras only on speakers at the rostrum. **1978** *Broadcast* 16 Jan. 2/3 PBS takes 'Love for Lydia'... It will be screened on ..the [US] Public Broadcasting System. **1986** *N.Y. Times* 12 May C15/1 WPBT has earned respect and envy in the national PBS community by managing to drop on-the-air subscription campaigns—telethons that are called 'begathons' behind the scenes by station managers. **1874** 'MARK TWAIN' *Lett. to Publishers* (1967) 80 Bliss had contracted to pay me 10 *p.c. on my next book... He paid 7½ p.c. on Roughing It and 5 p.c. on Innocents Abroad. **1931** *N. & Q.* 26 Dec. 465/2 A 10 p.c. solution of oxalic acid will be useful if ink-stains be present. **1978** *Proc. Internat. Symposium Mini & Micro Computers 1977* 264/2 The *PC stores complex patterns of investment information and synthesizes them into investment decisions. **1982** *Computerworld* 27 Dec. 40/1 Then the next year the PC (Personal Computer) came out and you saw that for $3,000 you could do the same thing you had paid all that money for. **1986** *Your Business* Mar. 45/1 The functioning of word processors or PCs is only a minute part of the transformation that can be achieved. **1889** E. C. DOWSON *Let.* 21 Feb. (1967) 39, I enclose a *P.C. wh. I had just written—it is no longer necessary—but you may as well post it. **1951** R. MACAULAY *Lett. to Friend* (1961) 194, I had.. a nice picture p.c. from Father Pedersen from Rome. **1881** E. W. HAMILTON *Diary* 22 Nov. (1972) I. 185, I told Mr. G. he ought to make May a *P.C. **1973** *Whitaker's Almanack 1974* 84 The Duke of Buccleuch and Queensberry, P.C., K.T., G.C.V.O., aged 78. **1960** P. H. NIDDITCH *Elem. Logic Sci. & Math.* 29 In a *PC of the usual, axiomatic type the only definitions are those of connectives. **1965** HUGHES & LONDEY *Elem. Formal Logic* xv. 101 In 1910, in the first volume of *Principia Mathematica*, Whitehead and Russell presented an axiomatization of PC. *Ibid.* xxix. 211 Their validity can be determined by PC methods alone. **1973** J. J. ZEMAN *Modal Logic* xi. 181 One might ask if there is a modal system bearing an analogous relationship to the classical PC. *Ibid.* xii. 191 The definition of complete modalization was extended to include certain PC theorems. **1977** *Engin. Materials & Design* Aug. 9/2 Thought to be the most powerful calculator/watch combination on the market, hybrid construction is used to mount the chips on a small *pcb which also carries a miniature 5 by 4 matrix keyboard. **1977** *Gramophone* Nov. 960/3 It is not usual to mount heavy components on PCBs. **1947** *Bell Syst. Techn. Jrnl.* XXVI. 395 This paper describes an experiment in transmitting speech by *PCM, or pulse code modulation. **1966** *Punch* 10 Aug. 224 PCM will enable each existing pair of telephone cables to carry twelve times as many conversations as before. **1972** [see MODULATION 7]. **1977** *Broadcast* 7 Nov. 10/1 Sound radio signals.. are distributed in pcm multiplex form along analogue television links. **1973** *PCP [see PHENCYCLIDINE]. **1977** *Time* 18 July 35/3 Disturbing increases in the use of a dangerous new street drug called PCP. **1960** J. DRAKE in E. Davies *Roads* iv. 85 The term 'passenger car unit' or *p.c.u. is used in capacity measurements to make allowance for mixed traffic—all motor vehicles count as one unit, except heavy goods vehicles, buses, and coaches which count three. On a road having moderately high volumes of heavy traffic it is found that the p.c.u. count is 50% more than that for motor vehicles. **1966** *New Scientist* 29 Sept. 711/3 The unit of traffic he used was the 'passenger-car unit' (pcu) which is employed by the Ministry of Transport. A bus is rated at 3 pcu, for example. **1887** W. E. AYRTON *Pract. Electr.* vii. 371 An influence machine can produce a *P.D. between its terminals of some hundreds of thousands of volts. **1935** J. N. FRIEND *Text-bk. Physical Chem.* II. vii. 297 Experimental measurement of the P.D. between two liquids presents many difficulties. **1963** A. F. ABBOTT *Ordinary Level Physics* xxxvii. 487 The terminal p.d. is always less than the e.m.f., and the difference.. represents the p.d. required to send the current through the internal resistance of the cell. **1956** 'C. RAVEN' *Underworld Nights* 30 The last I heard of him he was done for pinching a shaving brush from Woolworth's and sentenced to eight years *P.D. under the new act. **1959** *New Statesman* 24 Jan. 102/2 My seven hosts were all preventive detainees (PDs) serving terms of five to 14 years imprisonment, and with three or more convictions. **1973** J. WOOD *North Beat* vi. 81 The thought of preventive detention appalled him. There was no remission with P.D. **1969** *New Scientist* 17 July 115/1 The critical operation is then a 'three-phase powered descent initiation' or *PDI, the braking manoeuvre which begins at this low point and reduces the vehicle's velocity to zero at a height of around 7000 feet. *c* **1875** B. WOOLF *Mighty Dollar* in B. H. Clark *Favorite Amer. Plays 19th Cent.* (1943) 489 That's right, you'd better step *P.D.Q., pretty damn quick. **1890** *Ladies' Home Jrnl.* July 12/4 The P.D.Q. Camera. **1891** KIPLING *Life's Handicap* 189 He went as his instructions advised *p.d.q.*—which means 'with speed'. **1926** [see MAKE *v.*¹ 65 c]. **1961** B. E. WALLACE *Death packs Suitcase* v. 55 I'd come back here P.D.Q., because here I'd know my way around. **1974** 'A. HAIG' *Peruvian Printout* 33 Whoever is messing about with our computers, I want him found p.d.q. **1956** J. EDMUNDSON *P.E. Teachers' Handbk.* vi. 30 Quite effective *P.E. lessons can be taken in a classroom even with.. very limited space. **1973** J. BURROWS *Like an Evening Gone* iii. 40 Sporting equipment of a modest kind,.. a vaulting horse and a set of P.E. mats. **1976** 'W. TREVOR' *Children of Dynmouth* v. 115 Stringer, the headmaster, was rubbish; the P.E. man went after the girls. **1949** F. S. CHAPMAN *Jungle is Neutral* ii. 19 We piled the dicky high with Tommy-guns, cases of *P.E. (plastic high explosive), grenades, and an assortment of demolition and incendiary devices. **1971** P. O'DONNELL *Impossible Virgin* xiii. 261 He had some fuse and plastic explosive, but.. using p.e. to set off a bullet would produce the wrong sort of noise. **1923** *Times* 2 May 11/3 Mr. John Galsworthy presided last night over a company of playwrights, poets, essayists, and novelists at an international dinner given by the *P.E.N. Club. **1924** G. S. GORDON *Let.* 20 Sept. (1943) 176 A private dinner in the evening with the Stockholm Pen Club (P—poets; E—editors; N—novelists). **1931** T. E. LAWRENCE *Let.* 13 Apr. (1938) 718 The P.E.N. suggestion is rather astonishing. **1966** 'H. MACDIARMID' *Company I've Kept* xiii. 270 Saurat rendered great service to the International P.E.N., as one of its Vice-Presidents. **1969** L. HELLMAN *Unfinished Woman* xiii. 195 A reception for the president of PEN, an Englishman. **1956** *Proc. IRE* XLIV. 1710/1 For a 0·5 watt SSB signal (1 w *PEP) there is 0·095 watt in the AM component. **1971** *Gloss. Electro-technical, Power Terms* (*B.S.I.*) III. vii. 23 *Peak envelope power*; *P.E.P.* of a radio transmitter. The power supplied to the aerial transmission line or specified artificial load by a transmitter during one radio frequency cycle at the highest crest of the modulation envelope, taken under conditions of normal operation. **1976** Perkowski & Stral *Joy of CB* vii. 70 As in AM transmissions, the peak envelope power (PEP) is still limited to 12 watts, but since the carrier is reduced or suppressed, additional power can be put into the sideband. **1986** *Daily Tel.* 19 Mar. 1/6 *PEPs are more flexible than pension arrangements. **1986** *Estates Gaz.* 9 Aug. 555/1 PEPs—Personal Equity Plans—are Mr Lawson's subtle persuaders which will, he hopes, turn us into a nation of shareholders. **1987** *Daily Tel.* 4 July 16 PEP managers were at pains.. to point out that the scheme is intended for long-term investment in United Kingdom shares. **1933** *Planning* VI. 15 They began more than two years ago to study.. the possibilities of renewing friction in.. industry, agriculture, finance, the social services... The *PEP budget.. is raised entirely from among those interested in the work. **1941** J. S. Huxley *Uniqueness of Man* xi. 233 It [*sc.* group work] is far more necessary in social science, where various bodies, such as P.E.P., are studying how to perfect it as a research method. **1970** I. Sieff *Mem.* ix. 164, I would not want to try and write a history of PEP here if I could but I would like to say something about it. **1965** *Acronyms & Initialisms Dict.* (Gale Research Co.) 558 *P/E, Price/Earnings Ratio (Relation between price of a company's stock and its annual net income). **1969** *Times* 30 Apr. 30/5 It leaves the historical p/e ratio on the ordinary shares.. looking vulnerable for a newspaper company at 20.8. **1959** *Amer. Statistician* Apr. 10/1 This Program Evaluation and Review Technique (code-named *PERT) is applied as a decision-making tool designed to save time in achieving end-objectives. **1960** *IRE Trans. Engin. Managem.* VII. 103/2 PERT (Program Evaluation and Review Technique) utilizes the network concept of R and D projects, and analyzes the 'time to completion' variable. **1962** [see *network analysis* s.v. network 5]. **1964** A. Battersby *Network Analysis* ix. 134 Pollack has published a detailed description of how PERT was brought in to control the construction of the $47,000,000 Zero Gradient Synchrotron at the Argonne National Laboratory. **1969** J. Argenti *Managem. Techniques* 72 The technique known as PERT.. is used when the duration of an activity is not accurately known. **1974** *Encycl. Brit. Macropædia* XIII. 600/1 Critical path method (cpm) is an optimizing procedure applicable only to certainty-type formulations of such problems. Project evaluation and review technique (pert) is applicable to risk- as well as certainty-type formulations but does not always yield optimal solutions. *a* **1974** R. Crossman *Diaries* (1976) II. 126 Then we moved on to housing where we had a very strange situation because, after agreeing to the cuts *PESC demanded, the Minister of Housing made an extraordinary Ministerial announcement virtually saying that the target of 500,000 houses a year had been abandoned. **1976** H. Wilson *Governance of Brit.* iii. 61 This meeting or 'PESC' was concerned not with detailed allocations of expenditure, as finally announced in February 1976, but with basic priorities. **1876** Stainer & Barrett *Dict. Mus. Terms* 348/2 **P.f.*, abb. of (1) Pianoforte. (2) *Piano, forte*, soft then loud. (3) *Più forte*, louder. **1938** *Oxf. Compan. Mus.* 712 *Pianoforte*,.. often abbreviated pf. **1958** *Archit. Rev.* CXXIII. 326 The ground-floor walls are of cavity construction with an inner skin of insulating *p.f.a. blocks and yellow bricks outside. **1970** *Sci. Jrnl.* Aug. 78/2 Marketing officers of the CEGB are today developing PFA sales for a wide range of civil engineering and building activities. **1941** *Amer. Speech* XVI. 167/2 *PFC, Private 1st Class. **1947** *Ibid.* XXII. 112 References to rates and ranks are numerous. One variously caricatures *P.F.C.* ('private first class') as 'poor foolish civilian'... A *double P.F.C.*, however, is a corporal, since he has two chevrons on his sleeve. **1948** J. T. Appleby *Suffolk Summer* iii. 13 The third, an embittered P.F.C., did odd jobs of typing and message carrying. **1955** *Daily Progress* (Charlottesville, Va.) 24 Aug. 18/1 Pfc's with PhD's teach generals and others the fundamentals of atomic weapons. **1963** T. Pynchon *V.* i. 13, 'I would like to sing you a little song.' 'To celebrate your becoming a PFC' said Ploy... 'Pore Forlorn Civilian, We're goin to miss you so.' **1977** 'E. McBain' *Long Time no See* xii. 198 'A man named James Harris, served with the Army.'.. 'Rank?' 'Pfc.' **1972** *New Acronyms & Initialisms* (Gale Research Co.) 81/2 **PG*, parental guidance suggested (some material may not be suitable for pre-teenagers) (movie rating). **1974** *Daily Colonist* (Victoria, B.C.) 6 Oct. 27/5, 61 per cent rated the film PG (Parental Guidance) or G (General Audience). **1976** *New Yorker* 12 Jan. 70/2 Why would anybody want a PG-rated Peckinpah film? **1977** *Time* 11 Apr. 38/3 Modest, well crafted, less bloody and less bloody-minded than most TV shows, it is a PG film that any P ought to be happy to G the kids through. **1923** U. L. Silberrad *Lett. J. Armiter* ii. 49 They have made the suggestion that I should *p.g. with them for the autumn and winter. **1925** F. Stark *Let.* 1 July (1974) I. 93, I am afraid I shall not be well enough to look after p.g.'s after all. **1933** M. Allingham *Sweet Danger* v. 62 We've got one P.G. already... She's been with us three years. **1959** D. Wallace *Richard & Lucy* v. 87 Terribly expensive rail fare, and they'd probably expect us to p.g. when we got there. **1972** *Times Lit. Suppl.* 28 Apr. 500/4 A decayed-gentlewoman's nice home for p gs. **1977** N. Slater *Crossfire* i. 22 I'm going to descend on you... I'd like to PG—handsome rental available. **1938** R. S. Woodworth *Exper. Psychol.* xiii. 277 The name 'psycho-galvanic reflex' was introduced by Veraguth.., who made a comprehensive study of the Féré effect... In the present chapter we will call it *PGR. **1949** *Brit. Jrnl. Psychol.* XL. 86 When the individuals' P.G.R. scores are obtained for a given attitude they must be expressed for each person relative to his own general P.G.R. reactivity. **1954** Woodworth & Schlosberg *Exper. Psychol.* (rev. ed.) vi. 137/2 The rapid changes in conductance have been studied extensively and suffer from too many names. The oldest is *psychogalvanic reflex* (PGR), but many dislike the implications that it is psychic or a reflex. **1962** *New Scientist* 22 Mar. 672 PGR (psychogalvanic response) records were taken for the same purpose. **1869** *Atlantic Monthly* Jan. 89/2 His cousin, the *Ph.D. from Göttingen, cannot help despising a people who do not grow loud and red over Aryans and Turanians. **1903** W. James *Mem. & Stud.* (1911) 331 A Ph.D. in philosophy would prove little.. as to one's ability to teach literature. *Ibid.*, He was of ultra Ph.D. quality. **1906** [see *D.Phil.* s.v. D III. 3] . **1936** *Discovery* May 156 Julius Grant, Ph.D., M.Sc., F.I.C. **1966** J. Betjeman *High & Low* 40 Doubtless some pedant for his Ph.D. Has ascertained the facts. **1973** G. Mitchell *Murder of Busy Lizzie* xv. 174 Why should any-body want to strangle a harmless little Ph.D. like Mr. Lovelaine? **1931** G. Irwin *Amer. Tramp & Underworld Slang* 144 **P.I.*, a pimp or pander, merely a euphemism by contraction. **1970** C. Major *Dict. Afro-Amer. Slang* 90 *P.I.*, pimp. **1960** *Acronyms Dict.* (Gale Research Co.) 165 *PI.. Private Investigator. **1970** G. F. Newman *Sir, You Bastard* vi. 170 The PI had his licence revoked. **1973** *Publishers Weekly* 13 Aug. 48/3 This is the third p.i. mystery featuring Shock and his partner. **1966** *Economist* 16 July 227/1 The Government should use the *PIB only when it is ready to back the board's recommendations to the hilt. *a* **1974** R. Crossman *Diaries* (1975) I. 421 We can't afford to let the policy fail and yet quite soon we are going to face the 18-per-cent increase of army pay which the P.I.B. will almost certainly award. **1959** *Listener* 9 July 45/1 The widespread activities of the state security police, known as *PIDE. **1970** *Ann. Reg. 1969* 276 On 19 November the [Portuguese] Government dissolved the PIDE and placed a similar organization under the direct control of the Ministry of the Interior. **1974** *Daily Tel.* 21 Aug. 4/7 The Portuguese Legion.. was outlawed together with the PIDE/DGS. **1981** *Sunday Times* 25 Jan. 15/3 Cards with *PIN numbers written on them have been stolen... It would be pointless to try a Lloyds' card without its PIN. **1982** *Daily Tel.* 30 Oct. 19/4 It will be his or her responsibility to ensure that the PIN is kept secret, but what of prying eyes at the checkout? **1986** *Financial Times Survey* 12 Mar. p. vi/2 Access and Barclaycard and Standard Chartered Visa card holders who have taken up the option of a PIN.. can draw cash from the ATMs of the supporting banks. **1964** S. Bellow *Herzog* 257 Put on those *p-j's now. **1967** R. De Sola *Abbrev. Dict.* (rev. ed.) 208/1 *Pj's*, peejays (pajamas). **1970** *New Yorker* 4 Oct. 122/3 (Advt.), Cotton sleep culotte rated perfect for P.J. parties. **1943** L. E. & J. B. Rhine in *Jrnl. Parapsychol.* VII. 20 This is the first of a long series of research reports describing experiments on what is called the 'psychokinetic' or '*PK' effect. The PK effect is colloquially called 'mind over matter', and means the direct influencing of a physical system by the action of a subject's effort, without any known intermediate energy or instrumentation. *Ibid.* 21 Up to the present, nothing has been published on the topic of the PK effect. **1949** *Mind* LVIII. 391 In PK the mind is supposed to cause changes in physical objects outside its own body, not by means of the nervous system and the muscular apparatus, but directly, by mere thought or 'will'. **1973** *Times* 4 Dec. 17/7 There is nothing new in PK (psychokinesis) and telepathy. **1976** *Times Lit. Suppl.* 13 Feb. 172/4 Demonstrating PK in chickens, and even in fertile eggs, which appear capable of influencing mentally an electronic randomizer controlling the switching mechanism of a lamp. **1939** J. S. Furnivall *Netherlands India* viii. 250 Semaoen, the leader of the revolutionary section, formed a Communist party (*P.K.I.). **1944** B. H. M. Vlekke *Nusantara* xv. 341 On May 23, 1920, the Social Democrat Club of Semarang decided to take the name Communist Party of the Indies, in Malayan, *Perserikatan Kommunist di India* (P.K.I.). **1973** J. M. van der Kroef in R. F. Staar *Yearbk. Internat. Communist Affairs* 469 The oldest such party in Asia, the Communist Party of Indonesia (Partai Komunis Indonesia; PKI) formally came into existence on 23 May 1920 as an out-growth of the 'Indies Social Democratic Association' founded six years previously by Dutch Marxists. **1964** *Observer* 19 July 8/6 The younger had been afflicted by the same dread disease—*PKU (phenylketonuria)—which had produced retardation in her sister. **1976** *Lancet* 6 Nov. 1031/1 We have looked for differences in the mono-oxidation of phenylalanine between plasma (or serum) from normal persons and patients with p.k.u. Identification of different enzymatic activities within these two groups would be one of the first steps in the development of a test for diagnosing variants of p.k.u. **1962** E. Snow *Other Side of River* (1963) xxxix. 290 Chinese don't use the old word *ping*, or 'soldier', any more; the *P.L.A. has only *chan-shih*, or 'fighters'. **1967** *Ann. Reg. 1966* 372 The Military Affairs Commission of the Central Committee appointed Mao's wife.. 'adviser on cultural work to the People's Liberation Army' (PLA). **1972** *Observer* 19 Nov. 8 The PLA is none the less a revolutionary army with traditions rooted in a guerrilla past. **1977** *Times* 12 Oct. (China Suppl.) p. iii/4 The People's Liberation Army, the PLA, is making little secret of its desire to modernize equipment under the leadership of Chairman Hua. **1925** *P.L.A. Monthly* Nov. 16/1 The warehouses of the *P.L.A. become the Mecca of the woolbuyers of the world. *Ibid.* 22/1 Final tests preparatory to the opening of the P.L.A. automatic telephone system were carried out. **1936** *Discovery* Aug. 232/1 As for using it [*sc.* the Thames] for transport, that is left to P.L.A. tugs, brick-barges, and an occasional pleasure steamer. **1969** S. Hyland *Top Bloody Secret* i. 27 The PLA man in charge of the landing stage. **1973** *Daily Tel.* 20 Dec. 15 Although the proposed new form of incorporation for small companies is temporarily shelved, a new designation for listed companies is introduced. Out goes 'Ltd' and in comes '*PLC' or 'Public Limited Company'. **1980** *Companies Act* c. 22 § 78(3) The alternative of 'public limited company' is the abbreviation 'p.l.c.'. **1980** *Daily Mail* 8 Oct. 26/3 Following the implementation of.. the 1980 Companies Act.. we will be faced with names which resemble the lyrics of a Goodies song: ICI plc; RHM plc; [etc.]. **1983** *Conc. Dict. Law* 290/1 The memorandum of association must state that it is a public company, that its name ends with the words 'public limited company' (*or* p.l.c.), and that its authorized capital is at least the authorized minimum (£50,000). **1986** *City Limits* 16 Oct. 95 Law plc has always been a generous employer. **1898** W. J. Locke *Idols* xvi. 230 The great *P.L.M. train carried Hugh swiftly northwards. **1919** R. Fry *Let.* 6 Oct. (1972) II. 458 The P.L.M. is really worse than the S.E.R... It's almost impossible to travel by it. **1948** W. Fortescue *Beauty for Ashes* xxxiii. 251 For the whole of my Paris visit.. he was indefatigable in his attentions, finding a free Entr'aide car.. to take me to my various destinations, and battling with the P.L.M. to get me a reserved seat and, if possible, a wagon-lit to take me to the South. **1972** R. Cobb *Reactions to French Revolution* iii. 87 The P.L.M... bypassed the river valley, to take in Montbard and Dijon. **1965** *Times* 23 Mar. 9/2 Ahmad Shukairy, leader of the Palestine Liberation Organization (*P.L.O.) has extended his search for help to China. **1974** *Guardian* 23 Jan. 2/4 According to the official Egyptian news agency, Yasser Arafat, the PLO chairman, addressed a message disowning the PLO statement. **1974** *Jewish Chron.* 20 Dec. 11/1 The Palestinians, through the PLO, must show magnanimity and statesmanship. **1976** *Time* 27 Dec. 14/1 Although badly battered from its losing role in the Lebanese civil war, the P.L.O. remains an important force. **1965** *PL/I : Language Specifications* (IBM Form C28-6571-0) *title-page*, This manual is a description of the full facilities of *PL/I to be implemented under Operating System/360. **1966** E. A. Weiss *PL/1 Converter* p. iii, Many of the limitations.. of FORTRAN have been eliminated in PL/I. **1970** A. Cameron et al. *Computers & Old Eng. Concordances* 27, I myself will be very surprised if the next generation of machines will not accept Fortran programming and probably Cobol, Algol, and pl i programming. **1972** *Computers & Humanities* VII. 12 Work in language computation is frequently done in pl/i. **1955** R. T. McKenzie *Brit. Pol. Parties* vii. 385 As a prelude to a discussion of the contemporary structure of the *PLP it is necessary to recall that the party in Parliament from its earliest years was plagued by two problems. **1963** Butler & Freeman *Brit. Pol. Facts 1900–60* ii. 94 During the war-time coalition the P.L.P. elected an Administrative Committee of twelve, with Peers' representation, all of whom were non-ministers. **1974** *Times* 22 Mar. 1/8 (*heading*) Mr. Mikardo elected PLP head. **1976** H. Wilson *Governance of Britain* viii. 160 A Labour prime minister has to operate in a number of intersecting party political circles. The first is PLP meetings. **1969** *Guardian Weekly* 27 Mar. 16/3 The present plan for a public lending right, or *PLR, has been drawn up by the Arts Council. **1984** *Listener* 26 Jan. 10/1 PLR, or the Public Lending Right Scheme, has just displayed its capacities as a support. **1968** *McGraw-Hill Yearbk. Sci. & Technol.* 359/1 A portable life support system (*PLSS) back pack will provide breathing oxygen, suit pressurization, carbon dioxide removal, liquid cooling and oxygen temperature control, biomedical monitoring package, suit pressure and high oxygen flow sensors, and communications. **1970** N. Armstrong et al. *First on Moon* iii. 63 Complete with the PLSS, the Armstrong and Aldrin suits weighed one hundred eighty-three pounds. **1764** A. Williams *Universal Psalmodist* (ed. 2) 87 Hallifax. Hymn 50th.. *P.M. *Ibid.* 91 Dalston. Psalm 122^{d} D^{r} W. P.M. **1798** [see metre *sb.*^{1} 1 b]. *a* **1912** W. T. Rogers *Dict. Abbrev.* (1913) 152/2 *P.M.* (mus.), peculiar metre (of hymns). **1666** Hook in *Phil. Trans.* 242 March 28th 3$^{h.}$ *p.m. *c* **1830** in M. Johnson *Amer. Advertising, 1800–1900* (1960), Worcester, Ms. and New York Mail Stage Line.. leaves Worcester, Wednesday and Saturday mornings at 3, and arrives in Norwich at 4 same p.m. *Ibid.*, The Fanny.. arrives in Norwich next morning; and in Worcester, by stage, in the p.m. **1845** *Punch* VIII. 54/2 The lights along the Hampstead Road still persist in turning day into night, and burning for several hours after p.m. *c* **1850** *Rudim. Navig.* (Weale) 14 With the astronomical day it is always P.M. **1965** *New Statesman* 23 Apr. 661/3 While I am abroad.. entries must reach the office Monday p.m. **1974** F. Nolan *Oshawa Project* xx. 119 Staff meeting this pm at 1500 hours. **1911** Webster, **P.M.* or *p.m.*.. post mortem, or post mortem examination. **1922** *Lancet* 12 Aug. 358/1 It seems possible that death resulted from a dislocation of the neck. Were the vertebræ examined p.m.? **1928** D. L. Sayers *Unpleasantness at Bellona Club* xvi. 187 The advisability of a P.M. in all cases of sudden death. **1938** S. Beckett *Murphy* xii. 259 They carried him into the p.m. room. **1973** R. Hill *Ruling Passion* I. ii. 15 We haven't had the PM yet, but the doctor was very certain it happened last evening. **1907** W. S. Churchill *Let.* 27 Mar. in R. S. Churchill *Winston Churchill* (1969) II. Compan. I. 653 Could not you or the *PM send him a 'private & personal' urging him not to fail us. **1915** Lloyd George *Family Lett.* (1973) 178 It was found impossible.. for the P.M. to hold Exchequer during the time I am occupied in organising Munitions. **1972** M. Sinclair *Norslag* ii. 15 The P.M. wants you round at the Cabinet Office. **1948** Schour & Massler in *Jrnl. Dental Res.* XXVII. 733 A quantitative method of assessing the prevalence of gingivitis in large groups of persons is proposed. Each gingival unit consisting of a papillary portion (P), a marginal portion (M), and an attached portion (A) is examined and counted separately. This method is tentatively termed the *P-M-A-Index (P-papillary gingivitis; M-marginal gingivitis; A-attached gingivitis). **1962** Blake & Trott *Periodontology* iii. 27 The difficulty of assessment of gingivitis has been partly overcome by the use of the P.M.A. index. **1969** *Gloss. Terms Dentistry* (*B.S.I.*) 67 *P.M.A. index* (papillary, marginal and attached index), an epidemiological index for scoring the extent of gingival inflammation. **1890** Webster, **P.M.G.*, Postmaster-general. **1908** G. B. Shaw *Coll. Lett.* (1972) II. 803 Your letter.. did not overtake me until I arrived here (Bayreuth), too late for a rejoinder to the P.M.G. **1927** [see franking machine]. **1968** *Listener* 29 Aug. 285/2 Vague recent statements by the PMG, Mr. Stonehouse. *a* **1974** R. Crossman *Diaries* (1976) II. 71 When Ted Short replaced Tony Benn as P.M.G. the Post Office was delighted. **1942** J. Hammond et al. in *Jrnl. Agric. Sci.* XXXII. 308 To avoid the constant use of cumbersome phrases, gonadotrophic extracts of the urine of pregnant women (chorionic gonadotrophin) are referred to through-out the text as 'u.p.', and extracts of the serum of pregnant mares as '*p.m.s.' **1957** *Times* 2 Dec. (Agric. Suppl.) p. vi/2 In experiments with Romney Marsh, Cheviot and Southdown sheep, P.M.S. injections have increased the number of lambs born of each ewe mated. **1970** W. H. Parker *Health & Dis. in Farm Animals* vii. 84 The method that appears most likely to succeed is a combination of progesterone and P.M.S. **1959** K. D. Kryter in *Jrnl. Acoustical Soc. Amer.* XXXI. 1425/1 The translation from perceived noisiness in noys to perceived noise level in *PNdb is expressed by the equation $PNdb = (1.2T \log_{10} N)/0.03$, where N is the number of noys. By definition, the perceived noise level of sound 'X' (in PNdb) is the sound pressure level in db *re* 0·0002 μbar of the 910– 1090 cps band of random noise that is judged by an average listener to be acceptable (or, inversely, as unacceptable) as sound 'X', under specified conditions of listening and testing. **1966** *Science* 18 Mar. 1346/3 As a practical matter, the loudness level, in phons, and the perceived noise level, in PNdb's, of a sound are usually calculated from acoustical measures of the sound rather than found by subjective judgement tests. **1971** *New Scientist* 18 Mar. 604/1 In calculating the NNI for any given point, a number of standard flight paths are assumed and the PNdB level for each type of aircraft moving along each possible flight path is then calculated, together with the number of aircraft movements. *a* **1912** W. T. Rogers *Dict. Abbrev.* (1913) 153/1 **P.N.E.U...*, Parents' National Educational Union. **1931** *Times Educ. Suppl.* 14 Mar. 98/1 P.N.E.U. methods... The paper on English Teaching..is of especial interest to the Parents' National Educational Union. **1972** R. Asher *Talking Sense* viii. 103, I was looking at the material my daughter of thirteen is studying at the P.N.E.U. school she attends. **1861** Geo. Eliot *Let.* 17 May (1954) III. 415 You are at liberty to imagine a kiss from me, or else to accept a note for it payable at sight. They don't give *P.O.'s for such payment here. **1891** A. Beardsley *Let.* 25 Dec. (1971) 31, I shall be glad of a few more copies of the November *Bee*, so enclosed PO for 1/-. **1824** E. Weeton *Jrnl.* May (1969) II. 280, I wished to see the General Post Office... I was close by the *P.O., and could not tell which was it. **1973** *Guardian* 18 Apr. 12/3 Is not the ratio of inland to EEC-bound mail such that the PO (which is no longer G) would more than cover its costs. **1944** J. H. Bagot *Punitive Detention* i. 13 In the years 1936 to 1939 a marked tendency is disclosed for the proportions discharged *P.O.A. and fined to decrease and for the proportion placed on probation to increase. **1945** *N. & Q.* 10 Mar. 106/1 'Dismissed P.O.A.' simply means that a case is dismissed under the Probation of Offenders Act, 1907... Such dismissals are of such daily occurrence in the courts that P.O.A. are initials as commonly understood as are R.A.F. or Y.M.C.A. in their respective spheres. **1859** *P.O.D. [see c.o.d.]. **1890** Webster, *P.O.D.*, Post-Office Department; pay on delivery. **1870** A. J. Munby *Diary* 13 July in D. Hudson *Munby* (1972) 288 Today the Thames Embankment was opened, *not* by the Queen, but by the *P. of W. and his sister Louise. **1974** *Listener* 3 Jan. 17/2 Lord Berners..invited a smart lady to luncheon to meet 'the P of W'. She arrived agog, expecting to meet the Prince of Wales and found it was the Provost of Worcester. **1944** *Times* 7 June 6/1 The operational planning for invasion had to be interpreted at an early stage in terms of *P.O.L. requirements. **1955** *Bull. Atomic Sci.* Feb. 56/3 As it was, POL (gasoline and liquid fuels) *were* excluded from Pusan and unloaded by offshore floating lines. **1977** *R.A.F. News* 22 June–5 July 11/3 Training is centred on the ground attack role, with simulated attack profiles (SAPs) being flown against..POL objectives (Petrol, Oil, Lubricants). **1856** J. A. Symonds *Let.* 28 June (1967) I. 75 Thank Papa very much for the *P.[ost] O[ffice] O.[rder] which I got cashed without difficulty. **1886** W. S. Churchill *Let.* 13 July in R. S. Churchill *Winston Churchill* (1967) I. Compan. I. iv. 123, I received the P.O.O. which you sent me and am very thankful for it. **1966** Gurnett & Kyte *Cassell's Dict. Abbrev.* 169/2 *P.O.O.*, Post Office Order. **1968** *Which?* 11 Jan. 2/2 The Post Office have told us that they are introducing a new system of envelope sizing, called Post Office Preferred (*POP). Packets which are not the size the Post Office prefers will not qualify for the cheapest postal rates. **1971** D. Potter *Brit. Eliz. Stamps* ix. 95 As part of the standardisation programme, the Post Office issued pop (Post Office Preferred) sizes during the course of 1968. **1895** W. K. Burton *Man. Photogr.* viii. 126 Paper for the [gelatino-chloride] process..is sold under various names... Examples are 'Solio-artistotype', 'Artisto-platino' and '*P.O.P.' **1925** P. R. Salmon *All about Photogr.* xx. 94 There is practically no difference between the cost of a finished print on P.O.P. and one on self-toning paper. **1972** A. Tyrrell *Basics of Reprogr.* vi. 105 POP should perhaps be remembered as more nearly a reprographic than a photographic process. **1955** *Science* 9 Dec. 1139/3 A solution of 0·4-percent PPO and 0·01-percent 1,4-di(5-phenyl-2-oxazolyl)benzene (*POPOP) has been used, which gives..a pulse height of 121 percent. **1975** *McGraw-Hill Yearbk. Sci. & Technol.* 261/2 The scintillator dye POPOP, heated in an oven to a vapor pressure of about 10 torrs..., when pumped with 400 kW of ultraviolet light from a nitrogen laser, has produced 30 kW of tunable laser output. **1972** *Newsweek* 16 Oct. 94/1 Throughout the trade..some 44,000 point-of-sale (*POS) terminals already are in service. **1984** *Times* 25 Oct. 37/8 The retailer does not and will not pay for the bankers' side of POS. **1937** F. Borkenau *Spanish Cockpit* ii. 82 The depth of the antagonism between Esquerra and PSUC on the one hand and CNT and *POUM on the other becomes intelligible. **1940** N. Mitford *Pigeon Pie* iii. 48 'It's Hitler and Stalin now, don't forget the wedding bells.' Mary had gone P.O.U.M., so she grudgingly conceded this point. **1916** F. M. Ford *Let.* 23 Aug. (1965) 69 The *P.O.W.—who was quite unrecongizable, was perfectly businesslike. **1966** Gurnett & Kyte *Cassell's Dict. Abbrev.* 170/1 *P.O.W...* Prince of Wales. **1919** W. H. Downing *Digger Dial.* 39 *P.O.W., prisoner of war. **1941** *War Illustr.* 31 Jan. 101/1 P.O.W. camps in Germany and Poland are shown in this map. **1953** *News Chron.* 2 June 2/3 In Pusan..Pyun Yung Tai repeated his threat that foreign troops arriving to supervise P.o.W.s after a ceasefire would have to 'fight their way into Korea'. **1957** J. Braine *Room at Top* xiii. 128 What do you think a POW gets to eat? **1973** *Black Panther* 21 July 6/3 Former POW Sergeant Robert P. Chenoweth, 25, of Portland. **1882** R. Bithell *Counting-House Dict.* 235 **P.P. Endorsements*. Endorsements by procuration—that is, *per-procuration*... The following is the usual form of a per-pro endorsement. 'Pay to the Order of Blanc & Co. 'Per Pro Shipley & Sons. 'Thos. Brown.' **1882** [see per *prep.* I. 7]. **1922** F. von Hügel *Let.* 29 Nov. (1927) 364 Yours very sincerely F. v. Hügel (pp. S.B.). **1967** E. Lemarchand *Death of Old Girl* i. 12 All the other letters can wait... Sign the ones we've done p.p. **1724** *Short Explic. Foreign Words in Mus. Bks.* 53 The letter P is often used as an Abbreviation of the Word *piano*: and *PP as an Abbreviation of the Words *piu piano*: and PPP as an Abbreviation of the Word *pianissimo*. **1966** *Listener* 2 June 815/2 Helga Pilarczyk.. often ignored the composer's repeated demands for *pp* or sometimes *ppp* singing. **1925** Goldberger & Tanner in *Public Health Rep.* (U.S. Public Health Service) XL. 77 It would seem as if the heretofore unrecognized pellagra-preventive factor, to which we shall hereafter refer as factor *P-P, were capable of preventing the disease with little if any cooperation from the protein factor of the diet. **1926** —— in *Ibid.* XLI. 307 If the so-called growth-promoting water-soluble vitamin of the yeast is distinct from the anti-neuritic and from the P-P factor, then [etc.]. **1935** *Biochem. Jrnl.* XXIX. 2830 (*heading*) The vitamin B_2 complex. Differentiation of the antiblacktongue and the 'P.-P.' factors from lactoflavin and vitamin B_6. **1942** Bicknell & Prescott *Vitamins in Med.* v. 259 Nicotinic acid was at first hailed as the PP or pellagra preventing factor, but it is now known that pellagra is a multiple deficiency disease and that lack of nicotinic acid is only one of the factors in its causation. **1967** H. A. Guthrie *Introd. Nutrition* xii. 240/2 Niacin, another water-soluble vitamin identified with the B complex, has been known as nicotinic acid and as the pellagra preventative (P–P) factor. **1956** J. Cholak in P. L. Magill et al. *Air Pollution Handbk.* xi. 10 The normal fluoride content of the atmosphere is extremely low (2 to 8 *ppb). **1970** *Nature* 25 July 403/1 Locally manufactured peanut butter was highly contaminated [with aflatoxin] in almost every case, with a mean approaching 500 p.p.b. **1975** *Ibid.* 23 Oct. 632/3 Figures in terms of p.p.b. (parts per 10^9) are as commonplace nowadays as p.p.m. once were and for some compounds analysts can measure as little as 1 part in 10^{12}. **1809–12** Mar. Edgeworth *Absentee* xvi, I shall make my *finale*, and shall thus leave a verbal *P.P.C. **1833** Marryat *P. Simple* lxv, The..count announced his departure by a P.P.C. **1838** H. C. Robinson *Diary* 30 Oct. (1967) 190, I called with a p.p.c. card on Samuel Rogers. **1863** Mrs. Gaskell *Dark Night's Work* vii. 108, I don't see any reason he had to come calling and P.P.C.-ing. **1883** Kipling *Let.* 14 Aug. in C. E. Carrington *Rudyard Kipling* (1955) iv. 53, I distributed my P.P.C. cards. **1909** J. R. Ware *Passing Eng.* 191/1 *To P.P.C.* (*Soc.*, 1880 on), to quarrel and cut. **1966** Gurnett & Kyte *Cassell's Dict. Abbrev.* 170/1 *p.p.c.*, pour prendre congé, to take leave. **1960** *Brit. Med. Jrnl.* 10 Sept. 783/2 You cannot travel far in the United States hospital world nowadays before hearing the phrase 'progressive patient care' (*P.P.C.)... P.P.C. is defined as 'the organization of facilities, services, and staff around the medical and nursing needs of the patient'. **1964** G. L. Cohen *What's Wrong with Hospitals?* vi. 128 The very consultants who attack P.P.C. for disrupting continuity of care champion the same idea in maternity units. **1934** *Amer. Rev. Tuberculosis* XXX. 766 Under current arrangements the Committee endorses the use of a special designation, namely 'Tuberculin, *P.P.D. (Purified Protein Derivative)', by these two manufacturing houses. **1951** *Proc. R. Soc. Med.* XLIV. 1046 Even the best P.P.D. preparations on the market, of about 90% tuberculo-protein content, still contain appreciable quantities of polysaccharide and nucleic acid which are not known to be concerned in the intradermal tuberculin reaction at all. **1963** Lincoln & Sewell *Tuberculosis in Children* iii. 41 The Heaf test requires a special apparatus that makes 6 skin punctures 1 mm deep through a layer of concentrated PPD containing 100,000 TU per ml. **1955** *20th Cent.* June 584 Every university may have its department of economics or philosophy or sociology, but only Oxford—with or without sociology—has *PPE. **1964** E. Waugh *Little Learning* viii. 173 A new, disreputable school named Modern Greats (now dubbed P.P.E.) was for 'publicists and politicians'. **1972** *Times Lit. Suppl.* 3 Nov. 1310/2 Edward Heath and Harold Wilson read PPE. **1895** Kennedy in *Law Times Rep.* LXXII. 861/1 All these 'disbursements' policies were *p.p.i. or 'honour' policies—policies, that is to say, wherein it was stipulated that the policy should be deemed sufficient proof of interest. **1945** *Electronic Engin.* XVII. 683/1 With the Battle of Britain by night must be associated..the use of G.C.I., or Ground Control Interception, which Dr. Denis Taylor developed, using the *P.P.I. (Plan Position Indicator) for the first of its many applications. **1959** *New Scientist* 23 July 97/2 In the ppi system the position of the echoes with respect to the ship is built up in plan or map form on the face of a cathode ray tube. **1966** *McGraw-Hill Encycl. Sci. & Technol.* I. 163/2 PPI presentations also change with altitude and direction of approach, making identification more difficult. **1946** W. H. B. Smith *Walther Pistols* 26 The *P.P.K. means *Polizeipistole Kriminal*, indicating that the arm is intended for detectives and other police not in uniform who need a smaller weapon which can be readily concealed about the person. **1948** —— *Small Arms of World* (ed. 4) 424 Characteristics of PPK Model: Length 5.8". Barrel 3.25". Weight 19 oz. Capacity 7. **1973** J. M. White *Garden Game* 173 The Jensen..had been thoroughly searched, but the PPK had been clipped back under the dash. **1975** J. McClure *Snake* iii. 36 Zondi..checked his PPK automatic. **1976** G. Seymour *Glory Boys* x. 121 For close protection work he favoured the PPK (Polizei Pistolen Kriminal) Walther... The PPK was a small weapon, manufactured..by..the Karl Walther factory at Ulm. **1947** *Proc. Soc. Exper. Biol. & Med.* LXIV. 165/2 The most reliable method for the identification of the *P.P.L.O. is the use of stained agar preparations. *Ibid.*, The P.P.L.O. are resistant to sulfonamides and to penicillin. **1965** *Listener* 11 Mar. 372/1 Unlike viruses, PPLO can grow in the absence of living host cells. **1972** *Science* 5 May 504/1 The mycoplasmas (originally called pleuropneumonia-like organisms or PPLO) have been studied both by people who want to grow them for study because of their pathogenicity and small size and by people who want to get rid of them because they are common tissue culture contaminants. **1913** *Bull. Univ. Illinois: Water Survey Series* No. 10, 42 (*table*) Dissolved oxygen, *p.p.m. **1948** *New Biol.* V. 64 At 1–5 ppm it can be used..as a means of inducing tomatoes to set without pollination. **1964** *Punch* 25 Nov. 806/2 A peregrine found dead on Lundy Island contained 78 ppm of total chlorinated hydrocarbon in its liver. **1936** H. Nicolson *Let.* 12 June (1966) 265 Then his *P.P.S. took him by the arm and he left the House for ever. **1959** *Times* 23 Oct. 14/6 Mr. Barber had served as a whip before he became P.P.S. to the Prime Minister in February, 1958. **1973** O. Lancaster *Littlehampton Bequest* 94 At the last Government reshuffle he was appointed P.P.S. to the Minister of Exploitation. **1976** H. Wilson *Governance of Britain* ii. 30 Apart from this, my experience of consultation is that, in ninety per cent of the cases, the senior minister concerned recommended his own P.P.S. for promotion in his own or another department—advice I did not always follow. **1937** A. Huxley *Let.* 30 Mar. (1969) 416, I have talked to the secretary of the *PPU and he agrees that it will be best to go ahead with the 6d. edition in paper. **1973** *Freedom* 1 Sept. 4/1 Convinced pacifists of the PPU type. **1948** *R.A.F. Rev.* Feb. 3 (*heading*) The path of the '*P.Q.' **1962** *Observer* 6 May 21/5 The parliamentary question—the 'P.Q.' **1975** M. Sinclair *Long Time Sleeping* ix. 117 'Everything stops for a PQ,' he said... 'Is there a Parliamentary Question down?' Pringle asked. **1976** H. Wilson *Governance of Britain* vii. 132 Prime ministers approach the bi-weekly ordeal by questions in different frames of mind, but of two things I am sure: no prime minister looks forward to 'PQs' with anything but apprehension; every prime minister works long into the night on his answers. **1943** *Aeroplane Spotter* 3 Dec. 278 (*caption*) The De Havilland *P.R. Mosquito. **1946** *R.A.F. Jrnl.* May 153 We are indebted for the photographs and specialized articles with which the P.R. people supplied us. **1958** *Times Lit. Suppl.* 24 Jan. 48/5 Another part of the secret was to have P.R. grouped together. **1851** *Art Jrnl.* July 186/2 A school..that..will continue to exist unless Mr. Ruskin and his friends the *P.-R.s upset it. **1874** L. Troubridge *Life amongst Troubridges* (1966) ix. 75 Amy's present rage..is to make her room pre-Raphaelite, with a border of P.R. bulrushes all round it. **1829** P. Egan *Boxiana* 2nd Ser. II. 8 A boxer of considerable notoriety in the London *P.R. **1863** 'Ouida' *Held in Bondage* I. iii. 64 Heroes of the Turf and the P.R. **1966** Gurnett & Kyte *Cassell's Dict. Abbrev.* 170/2 *P.R.*, Prize Ring. **1885** H. Sidgwick in A. & E. M. Sidgwick *Henry Sidgwick* (1906) 400 The application of the principle of *P.R. to University Constituencies. **1909** (*heading*) P.R. Pamphlet No. 1 (Revised March 1909). **1924** [see labour *sb.* 2 c]. **1935** H. Finer (*title*) The case against PR. **1974** *Times* 2 Mar. 14/4 If PR is to come in Britain the crucial issue is whether it is to be the single-member or multi-member kind. **1942** Partridge *Dict. Abbrev.* 77/1 **P.R...* Public Relations. (The publicity department of certain Services and Ministries.) **1944** A. Jacob *Traveller's War* 200 The remains of the P.R. unit set off down the desert road. **1963** H. Kubly *Whistling Zone* (1964) ii. xv. 177 Your students are giving you an excellent PR. **1977** *Time* 31 Jan. 48/3 The p.r. man behind this is the star. **1909** *Cent. Dict.* Suppl., **P.R.*, an abbreviation..(*b*) of *Porto Rico*. **1966** *Publ. Amer. Dial. Soc.* 1964 xlii. 41 Terms used exclusively for Puerto Rican include..*P.R.* **1972** D. E. Westlake *Cops & Robbers* (1973) 9 There were no customers in there; just the Puerto Rican clerk... The PR was neutral as gray paint. **1895** G. B. Shaw *Our Theatres in Nineties* (1932) I. 32 If the friend of Sir Joshua Reynolds had been Sir David Garrick, and if every successive *P.R.A. had had for his officially recognized peer the leading actor of his day. **1975** *Country Life* 18 Dec. 1736/2 Sir Gerald Kelly..the first of the televised art popularisers as PRA. **1849** D. G. Rossetti *Let.* 1 Oct. (1965) I. 73 Love to our family, the *P.R.B., and all. **1850** W. M. Rossetti *P.R.B. Jrnl.* in *Preraphaelite Diaries & Lett.* (1900) 283 Collins has not established a claim to the P.R.B.-hood..the connexion would not be likely to promote the intimate friendly relations necessary between all P.R.B.'s. **1852** J. Brown *Let.* (1912) 128 The other morning I saw a scene which, were I a P.R.B. and a genius, I would make immortal. **1973** *Country Life* 8 Feb. 330/1 Rossetti is strangely well suited to one aspect of today's tastes... His aims went sensationally beyond those of his fellow members of the PRB. **1892** F. W. Maitland *Let.* 6 Sept. (1965) 105, I ought to be at *P.R.O. next week. **1931** *N. & Q.* 5 Dec. 408/2, I cannot find the Returns of officers' services for these regiments at the P.R.O. **1958** *New Statesman* 6 Sept. 330/2 Farewell, adieu, BM and PRO, My time is up, reluctantly I go. **1941** H. Nicolson *Diary* 8 July (1967) 177, I drive down to White's Club with Duff [Cooper] and beg him to treat the *P.R.O.s this afternoon with all gentleness. They are a touchy lot. **1966** 'H. MacDiarmid' *Company I've Kept* i. 22 Philip Jordan, Attlee's P.R.O., was with us. **1970** J. Tunstall *Westminster Lobby Correspondents* v. 56 The Prime Minister's scarcity value to the Lobby men allows him (a) to speak to the Lobby mainly through a P.R.O. and personally only on irregular occasions; (b) the P.R.O. still attracts a substantial daily attendance even when he says little. **1973** *Jrnl. Electrochem. Soc.* CXX. 1001 (*heading*) Reliability of NiCr 'fusible link' used in *PROM's. **1977** *Sci. Amer.* Sept. 139/1 Information stored in ROM's and PROM's is nonvolatile. **1972** *Guardian* 1 Sept. 1/6 Prisoners were..vowing to stay up [on the roof] until the Home Office recognised the prisoners' union, *PROP. *Ibid.* 1/8 PROP—'Preservation of the Rights of Prisoners'. **1973** D. Curtis *Dartmoor to Cambridge* xiii. 121 We decided to organise the British movement by forming a prisoners' union. That was the first step in the conception of PROP, the Preservation of the Rights of Prisoners, a movement that was destined to shake the British prison system to its core four years later. **1976** *Daily Mail* (Hull) 16 Dec. 11/4 PROP, the prisoners' rights organisation, is to hold its own public inquiry into the riot at Hull Jail. **1976** A. Miller *Inside Outside* xi. 176 Where PROP went wrong..was in inviting men to break the prison rules. **1927** *Melody Maker* Aug. 755/2, I am assuming..that the hall is not already licensed by the *P.R.S. **1968** *Listener* 8 Aug. 177/3 A lot of the more superior publishers..weren't members of the PRS. **1682** *Grew's Anat. Plants* (Order Roy. Soc.), Chr. Wren *P.R.S. **1790** *P.S. [see *O.P.* s.v. O 6 d]. **1838** R. B. Peake *Quarter to Nine* i, in B. Webster *Acting National Drama* II. 5 Apartment; Frolick's lodgings; closet door. Enter Mrs. Jervis, P.S. **1942** Partridge *Dict. Abbrev.* 78/2 *p.s.*, prompt side (of a theatre). Also *P.S.* **1899** *Daily News* 27 Nov. 8/3 The *P.S.A.—or, to give it the full title, the Pleasant Sunday Afternoon—movement has now become pretty well known. **1976** *Economist* 16 Oct. 105/2 The £11½ billion public sector borrowing requirement (*PSBR). **1986** *Daily Tel.* 19 Mar. 10/4 This year's PSBR looks like turning out at a little under £7 billion. **1896** *Oxfordshire Light Infantry Chron.* 1895 26 Lt.-Colonels... (1) Johnstone, J., **p.s.c.* 16 Mar. 92. **1920** *Punch* 24 Mar. 225/1 Upon my first arriving on his Staff he had said to me, 'Oh, by the way, P.S.C., of course?'..'You have Passed Staff College, of course?' he said a little less affably. **1972** *Times* 7 Sept. 16/2 Without the magic letters 'psc' (passed staff college) after their names their chances of being promoted above major are, at best, doubtful. **1944** E. W. F. Feller *Air Compressors* xiv. 438 Figure 410 shows the piping arrangement for the 250 *psi method. **1959** *Motor* 2 Sept. 75/2 This is with 5·90–13 Goodyear tubed tyres, inflated to 26 p.s.i. back and front. **1968** M. Woodhouse *Rock Baby* xviii. 183 She fitted a little pressure gauge to the drill-guide... The needle on the gauge flicked across at once, to nine p.s.i. **1975** *Offshore Engineer* Sept. 44/1 Phillips has a contract with the British Gas Corporation (BGC) to meet the required amount per day at a specified pressure which is 1,000psi. **1951** *psia [see *isentropically* adv. s.v. iso-]. **1975** *Petroleum Rev.* XXIX. 91/1 The stabilised crude, with a vapour pressure of 5–7 psia, will be piped to the Greatham site. **1932** *Motor Transport* 28 Mar. 351/3 A bus driver who was refused a *p.s.v. driving licence ..has appealed with success to a bench of magistrates. **1944** L. D. Kitchin *Road Transport Law* 9/2 Every p.s.v., except those first registered on or before January 1, 1932, must be capable of turning in a circle not exceeding 60ft. **1972** *Police Rev.* 1 Dec. 1577/1 A licensed p.s.v. is not being used as a p.s.v. when it is not carrying passengers. **1922** T. E. LAWRENCE *Let.* 1 Sept. (1938) 364 If I can get able to sleep, and to eat the food, and to go through the *P.T. I'll be all right. **1938** *Times* 14 Feb. 10/4 A Half-Day Course in P.T. **1965** W. LAMB *Posture & Gesture* viii. 107 If a woman she may be respected for her vigour but is too likely to be drained of feminine attractiveness—'P.T. hag' is the profession's own term. **1973** M. AMIS *Rachel Papers* 137 The Darwin-born PT instructress, on the other hand, her glossy shoulder-muscles rippling in the ninety-degree heat, threw her bulk round the court in frank virility. **1958** *People* 4 May 2/1 (Advt.), Victor £498 plus £250 7s. *PT. **1963** *Which?* Mar. 71/1 [Price] excluding 10 per cent P.T. **1966** *Punch* 27 July 132/2 The Government's determination not to flinch, if necessary, from a ten per cent PT increase on musical instruments? **1925** *Kansas City* (Missouri) *Star* 4 Feb. 11/1 (*heading*) *P.-T.-A. plans celebration. **1962** L. DEIGHTON *Ipcress File* xviii. 106 The old stuff about re-treads, P.T.A. meetings, and where to go for a good divorce. **1973** J. BURROWS *Like an Evening Gone* iv. 47 We're doing a P.T.A. play at the school. **1976** *Publ. Amer. Dial. Soc.* 1973 LX. 12 Mother of Informant 8. Active in church affairs and P.T.A. **1942** *PT boat [see EXPENDABLE *a.*]. **1961** W. VAUGHAN-THOMAS *Anzio* v. 67 On 28 January Clark himself, after being nearly killed on the deck of his PT boat, arrived at Anzio. **1974** *Lebende Sprachen* XIX. 38/1 US *PT boat*—BE/US *motor torpedo boat*, BEa. *E-boat*. Schnellboot. **1932** BLAKESLEE & FOX in *Jrnl. Heredity* XXIII. 97/1 The long name, phenyl-thio-carbamide, we are shortening to the nickname **P.T.C.*, an abbreviation which we shall use throughout this paper. *Ibid.* 98/1 To those who find P.T.C. strongly bitter, it seems incredible that any one could call it tasteless. **1965** *Punch* 10 Nov. 688/1 Tallness, or colour-blindness, or the ability to taste the substance known as PTC (phenylthiocarbamide) are inherited. **1976** PTC [see *phenylthiocarbamide* s.v. PHENYL 2 b]. **1909** *Army & Navy Gaz.* 1 May 430/3 Foil v. Foil (*P.T.I.'s only). **1916** 'TAFFRAIL' *Pincher Martin* iii. 45 The next turn was by the P.T.I. (Physical Training Instructor). **1964** J. HALE *Grudge Fight* vi. 92 Buck Jones the P.T.I. **1968** M. WOODHOUSE *Rock Baby* xxi. 202 He was wearing a sweatshirt and blue drill trousers, like a grossly overweight P.T.I. **1977** *R.A.F. News* 11–24 May 2/4 There will also be a trampoline display by PTIs of the RAF. **1859** GEO. ELIOT *Let.* 24 Feb. (1954) III. 24 Yours ever truly George Eliot. *P.T.O. I have reopened my letter to ask you [etc.]. **1902** H. G. WELLS *Let.* 14 Feb. in *A. Bennett & H. G. Wells* (1960) 76 P.T.O. **1966** GURNETT & KYTE *Cassell's Dict. Abbrev.* 172/2 *P.T.O.*, Please Turn Over. **1951** A. B. LEES *Farming Machinery* xv. 144 If *p.t.o.-driven trailers of compact design could be made available to hill farmers at an economic price they might well prove to be a major factor in increasing food production from marginal land. **1967** *Jane's Surface Skimmer Systems 1967–68* 64/2 Air can be supplied from a PTO-driven blower mounted on the tractor unit. **1973** *Country Life* 28 June 1904/2 The Bearcat combined roughage and grain grinder... Available as a pto driven static or trailed machine..[it] incorporates a pre-breaker with bevel edge. **1904** *Age* (Melbourne) 20 May 1 (Advt.), Ball and Welch *Pty. Ltd. **1938** *Act* (Victoria) *3 Geo. VI* no. 4602, sect. xxvi, §5 The word 'proprietary' or the abbreviation thereof 'Pty.' shall form part of the name of a proprietary company. **1969** *Northern Territory News* (Darwin) 11 July 4/3 (Advt.), N.T. Real Estate Pty. Ltd. **1934** V. M. YEATES *Winged Victory* III. ix. 365 'I wish you'd tell me what *PUO means.' 'What do you want to know that for?' But the M.O. overcame his professional love of mystery, and added: 'It stands for Pyrexia of Unknown Origin.' **1964** M. HYNES *Med. Bacteriol.* (ed. 8) xii. 192 A clinical diagnosis of typhoid is rarely possible in the early stages, and the patient will be investigated as a case of 'P.U.O.' or pyrexia of unknown origin. **1976** *Proc. R. Soc. Med.* LXIX. 557/1, I..told him what a lot of interesting medical cases had come to the hospital under that useful army diagnosis of 'PUO'—pyrexia of unknown origin. **1933** C. MACKENZIE *Water on Brain* viii. 112 'The *P.U.S.?' 'The Permanent Under-Secretary,' Hunter-Hunt explained. **1974** P. GORE-BOOTH *With Great Truth & Respect* 324 What governed the whole of my life in this final period was the circumstance that, apart from the Secretary of State, the PUS was the only person in the Office whose obligation it was to have some knowledge of everything. **1939** *London Weekly Advertiser* 7 June 6/5, 35/- *P.W. Incl. **1968** *Punch* 19 June 871/1 Let's be terribly sympathetic to the BOAC pilots, skilled, resourceful and too well-mannered actually to call their £30 pw pay rise offer 'insulting', the vogue word for this sort of thing. **1975** *Irish Times* 9 May 22/3 (Advt.), Rent inclusive of heating. £10 p.w. **1976** *Burnham-on-Sea Gaz.* 20 Apr. 7/7 (Advt.), I have sacked my advertising man. I have been paying him £1.15 pw and what do I get. **1909** *Cent. Dict.* Suppl., **P.W.D.*, an abbreviation of *Public Works Department*. **1922** G. BELL *Let.* 17 July (1927) II. xxii. 645 Mr. Cooke, Major Wilson and I accepted the invitation of Sabih Bey, Minister of P.W.D., to bathe from his house in Muadhdham. **1958** G. DURRELL *Encounters with Animals* IV. 168 There was the little cockney P.W.D. man who..offered to drive me a hundred-odd miles, over atrocious African roads. **1971** *Illustr. Weekly India* 11 Apr. 45/3 Those of a structural nature which the P.W.D. were able and willing to solve. **1975** O. SELA *Bengali Inheritance* ix. 76 The flat was..originally built for European PWD engineers. **1954** *Mech. Engin.* July 585/1 The Westinghouse Electric Corporation, as of July 1953, was assigned responsibility for the development and design of a pressurized light-water reactor (*PWR). **1976** *New Scientist* 5 Aug. 290/2 PWRs are now better proven with a greater reliability than two years ago, and there are several large units now working in the US and West Germany. **1929** *Papers Mich. Acad. Sci., Arts & Lett.* X. 317/1 **PX*, post exchange. **1936** *Amer. Speech* XI. 62 The army took avidly to the name canteen—so avidly that after..the stores were officially re-named 'Post Exchanges', the name persisted... Even the modernistic abbreviation 'PX' does not seem to displace it. **1959** C. MACINNES *Absolute Beginners* 102 My ivy-league outfit a GI got for me last year from his PX. **1971** M. MCCARTHY *Birds of America* 184 If I give him a divorce, they'll take away my PX card and my QC privileges. **1975** *Publishers Weekly* 13 Jan. 59/1 Two American truck drivers get lost in Vietnam and take shelter in an abandoned supply depot that is still stocked with PX goodies like stereos, TVs and canned food. **1977** *Econ. Res. Ser.* XXII. 17 Some American farmers rely very heavily on *p-y-o and 100% p-y-o farms have been planned. **1983** *Washington Post* 1 June E13/1 It's strawberry season, and you can pick the fruits of the Schwartzes' labors at their Double-B Farms—one of more than 100 PYO farms in the Washington area. **1984** *Times* 27 July 26/4 P-y-o strawberries this week are about 35p a lb.

b. *Teleph.* P = 'private' in **PABX**, private automatic branch exchange; **PAX**, private automatic exchange; **PBX**, private branch exchange; **PMBX**, private manual branch exchange.

1923 *P.O. Electr. Engineers' Jrnl.* XV. 309 On P.A.B.X.'s a jack is provided on the manual board for every line. **1976** *Computing Europe* 2 Sept. 5/2 Lines can be intercepted within buildings (particularly at PABXs or distribution boards) and even at Post Office telephone exchanges. **1923** *P.O. Electr. Engineers' Jrnl.* XV. 315 These plants are in some cases working as single P.A.X.'s. **1974** *Ibid.* Oct. 19 (Advt.), Pye Business Communications' capability in PAX and PABX telephone systems can improve the efficiency of your existing installation or provide you with a completely new system. **1976** *Eastern Even. News* (Norwich) 9 Dec. 16/2 (Advt.), Norwich Airport has a vacancy for a temporary Clerk/Telephonist (part-time) involving manual operation of a small PABX switchboard, some simple accounts and typing. **1917** G. D. SHEPARDSON *Telephone Apparatus* xv. 253 The current through the talking subscriber's circuit experiences a considerable fall of potential due to the resistance in the trunk line between the control exchange battery and the P.B.X. board. **1940** R. CHANDLER *Farewell, my Lovely* xxxii. 240 A uniformed man dozed behind a pint-sized PBX set into the end of a scarred wooden counter. **1958** 'P. BRYANT' *Two Hours to Doom* 19 He lifted the phone to the PBX. **1976** *National Observer* (U.S.) 10 Apr. 9/2 The FCC program, which takes effect Aug. 1 for the PBX, key, main, and coin telephones. **1932** HERBERT & PROCTER *Telephony* (ed. 2) I. xiv. 614 Lines terminating on a P.M.B.X. are connected to consecutive jacks. *Ibid.* 619 The P.M.B.X. operator withdraws the plug from the exchange line jack. **1975** *Post Office Electr. Engineers' Jrnl.* LXVIII. 61/2 The PMBX No. 4 was originally designed to meet the requirements of single-position installations of up to 160 extensions.

c. p = PICO-, as in pF, picofarad(s).

1940 *Chambers's Techn. Dict.* 631/2 *pF.*, *pf.*, abbrev. for *pico-farad*. **1958** *Engineering* 21 Feb. 228/2 The sensitivity of the Tektor Major is better than 1·0 pF under all conditions.

d. P = 'poly-' in **PCB**, polychlorinated biphenyl; **PTFE**, polytetrafluoroethylene; **PVA**, (*a*) polyvinyl acetate; (*b*) polyvinyl alcohol; **PVC**, polyvinyl chloride; **PVP**, polyvinyl-pyrrolidone. (All these often occur with full stops, and some are occas. given in lower case letters.)

1966 *New Scientist* 15 Dec. 612/3 In Sweden, PCB is known to be used in electrical insulations, hydraulic oils, high-temperature and high-pressure lubricating oils, paints, lacquers and varnishes, and as pigments in various plastics. **1971** *Observer* 12 Dec. 4/3 Levels of PCBs..are roughly 10 to 100 times higher in plankton from the open ocean than from coastal waters. **1974** J. BURTON *Pollution* v. 33 Thousands of seabirds died in the Irish Sea in 1969, and it is believed that PCB was responsible. **1977** *Jrnl. R. Soc. Arts* CXXV. 240/1 Our wildlife has..been affected by the accumulation of the persistent organochlorine pesticides and by PCBs. **1949** *Electronic Engin.* XXI. 220/1 Two new types of seals will shortly be available, one of which is made from an entirely new material, polytetrafluorethylene (P.T.F.E.). **1962** *Which?* Aug. 255/1 There are two kinds of non-stick frying pans—those with a silicone finish and those with a plastic called polytetrafluoroethylene, or PTFE. **1973** *Materials & Technol.* VI. viii. 545 Trade names of PTFE plastics include: Teflon (USA); Fluon (UK); and Hostaflon TF (Germany). **1943** SIMONDS & ELLIS *Handbk. Plastics* viii. 393 (*table*) Polyvinyl alcohol 'PVA' Resin. *Ibid.* 1007 (*Gloss.*) Trade name/PVA Type/Polyvinyl alcohol Typical applications/Tubing, rubber substitute (see Resistoflex). **1960** *Farmer & Stockbreeder* 22 Mar. (Suppl.) 10/2 Again, modern materials come to the rescue, and this time it is the relatively new PVA (Polyvinyl acetate) emulsion. This is a synthetic resin which, when used in emulsion form and added to sand, cement, and certain aggregates, will give a jointless, waterproof floor. **1966** A. W. LEWIS *Gloss. Woodworking Terms* 38 *Polyvinyl acetate* (*pva*), emulsion glue of a white creamy consistency. It is used cold and does not require a hardener. **1969** L. S. MOUNTS in W. R. R. Park *Plastics Film Technol.* v. 140 Three water soluble plastic films are currently produced from polyvinyl alcohol (PVA), methyl cellulose and polyethylene oxide. **1977** *36 Home Handyman Projects* (Austral. Home Jrnl.) 74/2 Cut thin strips of very thin felt and apply a PVA glue to one side of the felt. **1941** *Electronic Engin.* XIV. 541/2 Polyvinyl chloride and copolymers. Examples—Welvic, B.X.P.'s, 'P.V.C.', Chlorovene. **1957** *Economist* 12 Oct. 161/1 Similar plastic-coated steels, all using pvc, have been offered in the United States for some time. **1971** *New Scientist* 10 June 630 The PVC-coated fabrics that have previously been the main synthetic material used in women's footwear. **1972** *Country Life* 16 Mar. 612/1 Playing around with a few old bricks.. and a cowl made of wire and pvc sacks. **1975** W. G. ROBERTS *Quest for Oil* (rev. ed.) vii. 77 Plastics, particular examples being Polythene, polystyrene, PVC and a number of synthetic resins. **1951** *Lancet* 19 May 1096/1 A Saline solution incorporating a P.V.P. compound was prepared and used in Germany with some success as a plasma substitute during the 1939–45 war. **1959** *Jrnl. Inst. Brewing* LXV. 73/2 Beer can be chill-proofed, with-out risk of pasteurization haze, by adding PVP during storage in the cellar. **1966** J. A. BRYDSON *Plastics Materials* xiv. 286 In the field of cosmetics p.v.p. is used because of its unique property of forming loose addition compounds with skin and hair. Hair lacquers may be formulated based on 4–6% p.v.p. in ethyl alcohol. **1974** M. C. GERALD *Pharmacol.* ix. 164 The plasma substitutes, dextran and polyvinylpyrrolidone, PVP.

III. 1. *P trap*, a trap consisting of a U bend the upper part of whose outlet arm is bent horizontal or nearly so.

1885 P. J. DAVIES *Stand. Pract. Plumbing* I. 103 Fig. 205 is the ordinary half ∽-trap, wrongly called Ⴖ-trap. **1890** W. R. MAGUIRE *Domestic San. Drainage* vi. 206 No. 1 is the **S**-trap; No. 2, half **S**-trap; No. 3, **P**-trap. **1976** R. DAY *All about Plumbing* 64/1 In a ground floor w.c. it is usual to fit an S trap,..but in an upstairs floor w.c., a P trap is usually installed.

2. *p* or *P* (*Physics* and *Chem.*) = principal: orig. used to designate one of the four main series of lines in atomic spectra, but now more frequently applied to electronic orbitals, states, etc., possessing one unit of angular momentum.

1890 J. R. RYDBERG in *Phil. Mag.* XXIX. 335 A few examples will suffice to show the arrangement and the use of this system. K (D_1, 4) denotes the fourth line of the first diffuse series of the spectrum of potassium.. Rb (P_{12}, 2) the second doublet of the principal group of Rb [etc.]. **1910** [see F III. 1 j]. **1922**, **1955** [see D III. 3 b]. **1964** J. W. LINNETT *Electronic Struct. Molecules* ii. 29 In the oxygen atom two 2*p* orbitals are half-filled..and so..bonds can be formed to two hydrogen atoms.

3. [initial letter of *primary*.] Used, chiefly in *P wave*, to denote an earthquake wave of alternate compression and rarefaction (the faster of the two main kinds of wave transmitted through the earth).

1908 C. G. KNOTT *Physics Earthquake Phenomena* xi. 199 Although Rebeur Paschwitz had suggested the possibility, Oldham, of the Geological Survey of India, was the first clearly to establish the existence in the complete record of two distinct phases in the Preliminary Tremors. These will be distinguished as *P* and *S*. *Ibid.* xii. 225 (*heading*) Chordal and arcual speeds of P and S phases of preliminary tremors in earth-radius per minute. **1936** V. B. MACELWANE in Macelwane & Sohon *Introd. Theoret. Seismol.* I. ix. 248 When it became clear that the *P*-waves were of the condensation-rarefaction type and the *S*-waves of the shear type, and individual earthquakes had been observed at a sufficient number of stations, attempts were made to draw up time—distance curves for the arrival times and to correlate these with the time of occurrence of the earthquake. **1966** *McGraw-Hill Encycl. Sci. & Technol.* XII. 152/1 The seismic body waves (*P*, *S*, and composite types like *PS*) have predominant periods in the range 1–15 sec, with *P* and *S*, respectively, at the short-period and long-period end of this range. **1971** I. G. GASS et al. *Understanding Earth* iii. 54/1 The core-mantle boundary is marked by an abrupt reduction in the velocity of compressional or *P* earthquake waves.

4. On the analogy of PH, used to denote the negative of the common logarithm of a concentration or activity expressed in moles per litre; similarly *pK*, the negative of the common logarithm of a dissociation constant; *pF* (see quot. 1971).

1924 N. H. FURMAN in H. S. Taylor *Treat. Physical Chem.* II. xiii. 828 By graphic interpolation, plotting—log *k* against pOH, we find pOH to be 5·1. **1929** H. T. S. BRITTON *Hydrogen Ions* iii. 43 The hydrogen-ion concentration has a *p*H value of $\frac{1}{2}pK_w$ at neutrality. **1935** R. K. SCHOFIELD in *Trans. 3rd Internat. Congr. Soil Sci.* II. 39 It has proved convenient to use a new scale, which I have called the pF scale, to express what has, in the previous pages, been called 'suction'... The symbol 'p' expresses its logarithmic character, while the symbol 'F' is intended to remind us that by defining pF as the logarithm of the height in centimetres of the water column needed to give the suction in question, we are really using the logarithm of a free energy difference measured on a gravity scale. **1946** LUTZ & CHANDLER *Forest Soils* ix. 292 Designation of the energy relations of soil water in terms of *pF* is analogous to specification of reaction in terms of *p*H. **1965** R. G. KAZMANN *Mod. Hydrol.* v. 141 The energy gradient of the soil (*pF*) works against the force of gravity. **1968** PASSMORE & ROBSON *Compan. Med. Stud.* I. vi. 5/2 In a solution containing a mixture of buffers the conjugate acid base ratio is determined at any pH by its p*K*. **1971** *Gloss. Soil Sci. Terms* (Soil Sci. Soc. Amer.) 12/2 *pF* (obsolete), the logarithm of the soil moisture tension expressed in centimeters height of a column of water. **1972** *Wastewater Engin.* (Metcalf & Eddy, Inc.) vii. 255 With pOH, which is defined as the negative logarithm of the hydroxyl-ion concentration, it can be seen..that, for water at 25°C, pH + pOH = 14. **1973** F. G. SHINSKEY *pH & pIon Control in Process & Waste Streams* i. 4 Increasing activity is indicated by a decreasing pIon.

5. *P-marker* (Linguistics) = *phrase-marker* (PHRASE *sb.* 7).

1955 N. CHOMSKY *Theory of Linguistic Struct.* (microfilm, Mass. Inst. Technol.) x. 735 We define 'K is the P-marker of *Z*' as: K is the set of strings which appear as a line of one of the members of E, where E is an equivalence class of S_1-derivations of *Z*. **1963** CHOMSKY & MILLER in R. D. Luce et al. *Handbk. Math. Psychol.* II. 301 A grammatical transformation, then, is a mapping of *P*-markers into *P*-markers. **1964** E. BACH *Introd. Transformational Gram.* iii. 39 A representation of immediate constituent structure for a string, such as is given by a labeled bracketing or labeled tree, is called a *phrase marker* (P marker). **1967** D. G. HAYS *Introd. Computational Linguistics* xiii. 210 The parser would..submit, to a higher level source-language processor or to a translator, base P-markers—constituency diagrams with all transformations undone. **1976** *Language* LII. 110 A successful asymmetrical derivation rule must operate on a P-marker and not on an individual lexical entry.

6. [repr. *proton*.] *p-process* (Astr.): a process believed to occur in stars by which heavy proton-rich nuclei are formed from other nuclei, esp. in circumstances of high proton flux such as may obtain in supernovae.

1956 F. HOYLE et al. in *Science* 5 Oct. 613/3 At such temperatures (*p*, *γ*) reactions occur in a time of the order of

10 seconds, even on the heaviest nuclei (*p*-process). **1957** *Rev. Mod. Physics* XXIX. 617/2 It is probable that the maximum number of protons which can be added to C^{12} through the duration of the *p* process is only two. **1977** J. NARLIKAR *Struct. Universe* ii. 50 Apart from these two processes there is a rarer process which produces proton-rich isotopes by exposing the r-process and s-process material to a fast flux of protons or of high-energy photons. This is known as the p-process.

p, variant of PEE *Obs.*, short coat, pea-jacket.

pa[1] (pɑː). A childish short form of 'papa'. Hence **pa** *v. trans. nonce-wd.*, to address as 'pa'.

1811 L. M. HAWKINS *C'tess & Gertrude* (1812) II. 219 The elder sat down [to the piano-forte] and..answered 'Yes, Pa',' to every thing that Pa' said. **1823** E. MOOR *Suffolk Words*, *Pa*, an abbreviation of pa-pa. Pretty general perhaps. It is sometimes rather comic to hear a great chuckle-headed lout—*paa*-ing his father—or *maa*-ing his mother. **1829** *Censor* 225 These exhibitions, affording wonderous delight to affectionate *Pas* and *Mas*. **1880** MISS BRADDON *Barbara* vi, With the exception of that decayed female, I have never seen a mortal in pa's offices.

‖**pa**[2] (pɑː), *sb.* Also **pah**. [Maori *pà*, f. *pà* vb. to block up. The form *hippah* arose from taking the prefixed definite article *he* as part of the word.] A native fort or fortified camp in New Zealand.

1769 COOK *Jrnl. 1st Voy.* (1893) 157 They have strong-holds—or Hippas, as they call them—which they retire to in time of danger. **1777** G. FORSTER *Voy. round World* I. 194 A hippah, or strong hold of the natives. **1842** W. R. WADE *Journ. in N. Zeal.* 27 (Morris) A native pa or enclosed village. **1845** *Ann. Reg.* 350 Our troops..attempting to carry the pah or fortified camp of Heké. **1858** *App. Jrnls. House Reps. N.Z.* E. IV. 4 They seem..at present inveterate in their adherence to their Native habits, and to their residence in Pas. **1859** A. S. THOMPSON *Story N. Zeal.* 132 (Morris) The construction of the war pas. **1863** T. MOSER *Mahoe Leaves* 14 A pah is strictly a *fortified village*, but..a collection of huts forming a native settlement is generally called a pah now-a-days. **1880** J. C. CRAWFORD *Recoll. Trav. N.Z. & Austral.* 28 A large pa (village) was visible at Pitone. **1884** BRACKEN *Lays of Maori* 25 Come, oh come, unto our Pah. **1900** H. LAWSON *Over Sliprails* 82 Things, according to pa gossip, had gone wrong with her from the date of the tragedy. *Ibid.* 88 A poor pa outcast who had negro blood in her veins. **1905** J. M. THOMSON *Bush Boys N.Z.* iii. 45 In every Maori 'pah' or village, there is one specially large 'whare', or house. **1911** W. H. KOEBEL *In Maoriland Bush* xii. 170 The old Maori did not appear to have lost caste among the brethren of his own race who still dwelt in their quaintly carved Pahs. **1920** *Outlook* (N.Z.) 29 Nov. 18/3 Her parish is roadless, deep ravines and steep hills separate pa from pa. **1938** R. FINLAYSON *Brown Man's Burden* 52 The old pa where many of the chieftain's ancestors and relatives were laid to rest on the topmost parapet. **1958** S. ASHTON-WARNER *Spinster* 72 When she got to the pa they cried in the Meeting House. **1959** G. SLATTER *Gun in my Hand* 99 Unpainted whares at the pa with cardboard at the windows and new cars parked on the lawn. **1963** D. ADSETT *Magpie Sings* 109 Perhaps they would go and live in the pa and get big and fat like lots of other Maori women.

paa, var. ME. PO, peacock.

paage, obs. var. PEAGE, toll paid by passengers.

paal(e, obs. forms of PALE *a.*

paalstab, -staff, -stave, var. of PALSTAVE.

paame, obs. form of PALM, name of a game.

paan: see PAGNE cloth, PANE.

paan, var. PAN *sb.*[5]

‖**pa'anga** (pɑːˈɑːŋgə). [Native.] The monetary unit of Tonga.

1966 *Times* 21 May 8 Tonga has decided against calling its new decimal currency unit the dollar because the native word, 'tola', also means a pig's snout, the soft end of a coconut, or, in vulgar language, a mouth. The new unit, to be introduced next year, will be called 'pa'anga', which has only two alternative meanings—a coin-shaped seed and, not surprisingly, money. **1973** *Whitaker's Almanac 1974* 986/2 Pa'anga (T$) of 100 *Seniti*.

paarche, paarform, paark, paart, obs. ff. PARCH, PERFORM, PARK, PART.

paarlmoer, var. PERLEMOEN.

paas, paast, obs. ff. PACE, PASCH, PASTE.

paauw, var. POU(W).

pab, Sc. dial. var. of POB[1], refuse of flax.

PABA (ˌpiːeɪbiːˈeɪ, ˈpɑːbɑː). *Pharm.* Also **Paba, paba**. [f. the initial letters of the formative elements of the chemical name.] = *para-aminobenzoic acid*.

1944 *Jrnl. Exper. Med.* LXXIX. 337 (*heading*) Comparison of PABA production by staphylococci (method of Lewis) with the concentration of sodium sulfathiazole required to inhibit *in vitro* growth of the cultures. **1945** *Proc. Soc. Exper. Biol. & Med.* LVIII. 262/1 In addition to its activity against typhus rickettsiae, preliminary experiments have shown that paba also inhibits growth of the rickettsiae of Rocky Mountain spotted fever. **1951** A. GROLLMAN *Pharmacol. & Therapeutics* xxvii. 606 The use of Paba has also been advocated in various 'collagen' diseases. **1963** *Times* 2 May 14/1 (Advt.), Para-aminobenzoic acid..has long been known simply as PABA which, even when pronounced 'pahbah' is clinically and aurally acceptable. **1966** *McGraw-Hill Encycl. Sci. & Technol.* XIII. 244/2 The mode of action of sulfonamides is considered to be an antimetabolite activity, dependent upon the inhibition of enzyme systems involving the essential PABA.

pabble (ˈpæb(ə)l), *v. Sc.* [Echoic.] *intr.* To make a sound like that of boiling liquid.

1832 J. WILSON in *Blackw. Mag.* XXXI. 879 The hissing, and the fizzing, and the pabbling of the great pan in which the basted trouts are writhing. **1834** —— *Ibid.* XXXV. 789 We hear them pabbling in the pan.

pablum (ˈpæbləm). Also **Pablum**. The proprietary name of a children's breakfast cereal. Also *fig.*

1932 *Official Gaz.* (U.S. Patent Office) 19 July 596/2 Mead Johnson & Company, Evansville, Indiana. Pablum. For specially prepared cereal food consisting of a mixture of wheat meal, to which have been added wheat embryo, dried yeast, powdered dehydrated alfalfa leaf and powdered beef bone prepared for human use. Claims use since June 4, 1932. **1941** *Trade Marks Jrnl.* 5 Feb. 47/2 Pablum... A food for infants and invalids. Mead Johnson & Company,.. Evansville, State of Indiana, United States of America; manufacturers. **1953** POHL & KORNBLUTH *Space Merchants* i. 9 Over the breakfast juices and the children's pablum.. they spoke persuasively to each other about how wise and brave they had been to apply for passage in the Venus rocket. **1956** P. FRANK *Forbidden Area* i. 40 He would want her to quit her job, and eventually..there would be children. She would find..her research downgraded to equations involving boiled water, evaporated milk, Karo syrup, and pablum. **1964** A. TYLER *If Morning ever Comes* xi. 160 *Joanne* never picks up. I had to scrape pablum off the damn *toaster* this morning. **1970** *Listener* 22 Oct. 538 In one week Spiro Agnew ascribed moral decay to the universities, Dr Spock, and the Presidential Commission on Campus Unrest, which, he said, had produced a report which 'was sure to be taken as more pablum for the permissivists'. **1971** W. HILLEN *Blackwater River* ii. 9 After a start on pablum and eggs and milk..he developed into a strong dog. **1976** *Amer. N. & Q.* XIV. 147/2 Its [*sc.* Oscar Wilde's *The Happy Prince*] obvious allegory and its appeal to a patronizing benevolence are palatable as pablum, but hardly to be trusted to sustain Eliot's confused, but intellectual Fisher King.

‖**pabouch** (pəˈbuːʃ). Also 7 **paboutch**. [See BABOUCHE, PAPOOSH.] A heelless Oriental slipper.

1687 A. LOVELL tr. *Thevenot's Trav.* I. 30 The heel..is shod with a piece of Iron made purposely half-round, and these Shoes they call Paboutches. **1813** MOORE *Post-bag* ii. 64 All sorts of dulimans and pouches, With sashes, turbans, and pabouches. **1824** SCOTT *St. Ronan's* xxx, I always drink my coffee as soon as my feet are in my pabouches; it's the way all over the East.

Pabst (pæbst). *U.S.* The name of a lager beer.

Registered in the U.S. as a proprietary name.

[**1906** *Official Gaz.* (U.S. Patent Office) 26 June 2969/2 Beer. Pabst Brewing Company, Milwaukee,..Used ten years..the name 'PABST' on the upper part of the band.] **1920** *Ibid.* 15 June 579/2 Pabst Brewing Company, Milwaukee.. Pabst..Beer and Malt Extracts. *Claims use* since June, 1889. **1963** R. WELLEK in N. Frye *Romanticism Reconsidered* 112 'It is impossible to think seriously with words such as Classicism, Romanticism, Humanism, or Realism.'.. But of course these terms are not labels: they have a range of meaning very different from Pabst Blue Ribbon or Liebfrauenmilch. **1974** *Black World* Mar. 59/1 He opened the refrigerator. In its confines were two cans of Pabst. **1976** *Time* 27 Sept. 47/2 The room is a cacophony of the ping-pong-dingdingding of the pinball machine, the pop-fizz of another round of Pabst, [etc.]. **1977** *Time* 7 Feb. 60/1 Belting down tumblers of Jim Beam and Pabst, they compared horror stories.

†ˈ**pabular**, *a. Obs. rare*$^{-0}$. [ad. L. *pābulār-is*, f. *pābulum* fodder: see -AR[1].] = next.

1656 BLOUNT *Glossogr.*, *Pabular, Pabulous*,..pertaining to fodder, Provender, forrage. [So in PHILLIPS, BAILEY, etc.]

pabulary (ˈpæbjʊlərɪ), *a.* [ad. L. *pābulāri-us* having to do with fodder: see prec. and -ARY.] Of or pertaining to pabulum, fodder, or aliment.

1835 J. S. FORSYTH (*title*) A Dictionary of Diet, being a Practical Treatise on all Pabulary and Nutritive Substances. **1839** G. RAYMOND in *New Monthly Mag.* LVII. 409 His gleanings had done..credit to his pabulary diligence.

pabulation (pæbjuːˈleɪʃən). *rare*$^{-0}$. [ad. L. *pābulātiōn-em*, n. of action from *pābulārī* to eat fodder, seek for food, forage.] (See quots.)

1623 COCKERAM, *Pabulation*, grasing, feeding. [So in BAILEY.] **1755** JOHNSON, *Pabulation*, the act of feeding or procuring provender. **1846** WORCESTER, *Pabulation*, act of feeding, fodder. **1864** in WEBSTER.

†ˈ**pabulatory**, *a. Obs. rare*$^{-0}$. [ad. L. *pābulātōri-us*, f. *pābulātōr-em* fodderer, forager: see -ORY.] Of or pertaining to pabulation.

1656 BLOUNT *Glossogr.*, *Pabulatory*, the same [with *Pabular, pabulous*.]. [So in BAILEY.]

pabulous (ˈpæbjʊləs), *a. rare.* [f. late L. *pābulōs-us* abounding in *pābulum* fodder: see -OUS.] Abounding in or affording pabulum or food.

1646 SIR T. BROWNE *Pseud. Ep.* III. xxi. 160 Wee doubt the common conceit, which affirmeth that aire is the pabulous supply of fire. **1755** JOHNSON, *Pabulous*.., affording aliment.

‖**pabulum** (ˈpæbjʊləm). [L. *pābulum* food, nourishment, fodder, f. stem *pā-* of *pā-sc-ĕre* (*pā-vi*) to feed.] Anything taken in by an animal or plant to maintain life and growth; food, aliment, nutriment. More usually said of the 'food' of plants, or of animal organs or organisms; rarely in reference to higher animals.

1733 TULL *Horse-Hoeing Husb.* i. 7 Roots must search out and fetch themselves all the *Pabulum* of a Plant. **1813** SIR H. DAVY *Agric. Chem.* i. (1814) 18 No one principle affords the *pabulum* of vegetable life. **1826** KIRBY & SP. *Entomol.* xliv. IV. 216 Affording a pabulum to these animals. **1845** TODD & BOWMAN *Phys. Anat.* I. 43 The blood is the immediate pabulum of the tissues. **1860** MAURY *Phys. Geog. Sea* x. §493 The rivers bring down and pour into the sea continually the pabulum which those organisms require.

b. That which supports or 'feeds' fire.

1678 CUDWORTH *Intell. Syst.* I. i. 46 Fire..needs a *Pabulum* to prey upon, doth not continue alwaies one and the same Numerical Substance. **1744** BERKELEY *Siris* §197 Oil, air, or any other thing that vulgarly passeth for a pabulum or food of that element [fire]. **1860** FARRAR *Orig. Lang.* v. 105 A necessary pabulum of combustion.

c. *fig.* That which nourishes and sustains the mind or soul; food for thought.

1765 STERNE *Tr. Shandy* VII. xxxi, Such a story affords more *pabulum* to the brain, than all the Frusts, and Crusts, and Rusts of antiquity. **1819** CRABBE *T. of Hall* x. 393 An age ..when tales of love Form the sweet pabulum our hearts approve. **1888** M. ROBERTSON *Lombard St. Myst.* iii, To furnish..more pabulum for reflection and rumination.

pac (pæk). *N. Amer.* Also **pack**. [Of Lenape (Delaware) Indian origin.]

a. A moccasin having a sole turned up and sewed on the upper; also applied to a heavy felt half-boot, worn by lumberers in winter. (See quots. *a* 1877 and 1961; cf. SHOEPACK.) **b.** With initial apostrophe, *ellipt.* for SHOEPACK.

a **1877** KNIGHT *Dict. Mech.* II. 1590/1 *Pac; Pack*, a moccasin having a sole turned up and sewed to the upper. Though now made of leather of various kinds, the *pac*, as used by the Indians of the Six Nations, for instance, was made of hide boiled in tallow and wax; or of *tawed* hide subsequently stuffed with tallow or wax. **1893** *Scribner's Mag.* June 715 Loggers' Footgear [Figures of] India-rubber brogan. Old-fashioned boot-pack. Modern rubber-soled boot-pack. Buck-skin and leather moccasin. **1922** *Outing* May 68/1 Footwear, pac boots 16 inches; rubber boots. **1931** 'GREY OWL' *Men of Last Frontier* 181 And here is where my hard-soled 'packs came in. **1944** *Sears, Roebuck Catal.* 345 Leather top work Pac... Not rationed... If you wear size 6½ or 7 shoe, order size 6 pac. **1961** WEBSTER 1616/1 *Pac* also *pack*,..2. a laced heelless sheepskin or felt shoe worn inside a boot or overshoe in cold weather. **1973** B. WRIGHT *Four Seasons North* 12 The trails are slippery in our rubber-soled pacs.

paca (ˈpækə). *Zool.* [a. Pg. and Sp. *paca*, a. Tupi *paca*, the native name (in Guarani, *paig*).

Gabriel Soares in his *Noticias do Brazil* 1587 spells it (in Pg.) *pagua*, Claude d'Abbeville *Mission en Maragnan* (1614) 251, has (in Fr.) *pac*.]

A genus (*Cœlogenys*) of large dasyproctid rodents, nocturnal in habit, native to Central and South America; the common species (*Cœlogenys paca*) is called also the *spotted cavy* and *water hare*.

[**1648** MARCGRAVE *Hist. Nat. Brasil.* II. 224 Paca Brasiliensibus, cuniculi etiam est species.] **1657** S. CLARKE *Geog. Descript.* 179 Their Pacas are like Pigs, their flesh is pleasant. **1796** STEDMAN *Surinam* II. xxii. 152 The Paca, or Spotted Cavey, called in Surinam the Aquatic Hare. **1871** *Routledge's Ev. Boy's Ann.* Sept. 517 When pacas and otters are in question, an Indian will do anything to kill them.

pacable (ˈpeɪkəb(ə)l), *a.* [ad. L. *pācābil-is*, f. *pācāre* to appease, pacify, f. *pāx*, *pāc-em* peace.] Capable of being pacified or appeased; placable.

a **1834** COLERIDGE *Church & State* (1839) 166 Reasonable men are easily satisfied: would they were as numerous as they are pacable! **1860** THACKERAY *Round. Papers* vi. *Screens in Din. Rooms*, That last Roundabout Paper..was written in a pacable and not unchristian frame of mind.

pacadile, bad form of PICCADILL.

†ˈ**pacal**, *a. Obs. rare.* [ad. L. *pācāl-is* peaceful.]

1656 BLOUNT *Glossogr.*, *Pacal*.., that brings or signifies peace, peaceable. **1730–6** in BAILEY (folio).

pacan, pacane, obs. forms of PECAN.

†ˈ**pacate**, *a. Obs.* [ad. L. *pācāt-us*, pa. pple. of *pāc-āre* to make peaceful, quiet, pacify.] Pacified, brought into a state of peace and calm, tranquil.

1644 J. GOODWIN *Innoc. Triumph.* (1645) 40 How pacate, flourishing, and free from disturbance this State hath been. *a* **1652** J. SMITH *Sel. Disc.* VII. i. (1821) 309 A pacate, humble, and self-denying mind. **1681** H. MORE *Exp. Dan.* vii, A man of a pacate mind and quick understanding.

Hence †ˈ**pacately** *adv.*, quietly; †ˈ**pacateness**, the state of being 'pacate' or peaceful.

a **1652** J. SMITH *Sel. Disc.* vi. 220 A gentle vocal air, such a one as breathed in the day-time more pacately. **1666** BP. REYNOLDS *Serm. in Westm. Abb.* 7 Nov. 13 This pacateness and serenity of Soul. **1681** H. MORE *Exp. Dan.* i. 10 There was not that pacateness nor tranquillity in the Medo-Persian Empire that there was in the Babylonian.

†**pa'cated**, *ppl. a. Obs.* [f. as prec. + -ED.]

1727 BAILEY vol. II, *Pacated*,..appeased, made peaceable. Hence in ASH and mod. Dicts.

pacation (pəˈkeɪʃən). [ad. L. *pācātiōn-em*, n. of action from *pāc-āre*: see PACATE *a.*] The action of pacifying or tranquillizing; the condition of being peaceful and tranquil; pacification.

1658 PHILLIPS, *Pacation*, a stilling or appeasing. **1730–6** BAILEY (folio). **1820** COLERIDGE in *Lit. Rem.* (1839) IV. 152 It was this that..prevented the pacation of Ireland.

† **'pacative**, *a. Obs. rare.* [f. L. *pācāt-*, ppl. stem of *pāc-āre*: see -ATIVE.] Stilling, sedative.

1684 tr. *Bonet's Merc. Compit.* XIX. 752 The pacative vertue of Vitriol [seems extended] to the effervescent bile.

‖ **pacay** (pa'kai, pə'keɪ). Also **paccay**. [a. Peruv. *pacay*, in Sp. *pacaya*.] A Peruvian leguminous tree (*Inga Feuillei*) of sub-order *Mimoseæ*, cultivated for its large white pods, which are esteemed as an article of food. Also applied to a tree of the genus *Prosopis*.

[**1748** *Earthquake of Peru* iii. 210 The..Pacayas..are there very plentiful.] **1866** *Treas. Bot.*, *Inga Feuillei*, a native of Peru, is cultivated in the gardens about Lima, where the inhabitants call it Pacay. **1880** C. R. MARKHAM *Peruv. Bark* xvi. 167 The paccay (*Mimosa Inga*), with its cottony fruit, was drooping over the bubbling waves.

paccage, paccan, obs. ff. PACKAGE *sb.*, PECAN.

pacche, obs. form of PATCH, PASH *v.*

Pacchionian (pækɪ'əʊnɪən), *a. Anat.* [f. the name of the Italian anatomist Pacchioni (1665–1726) + -AN.] Of or described by Pacchioni.

Pacchionian body, corpuscle, gland, granulation, one of the granular enlargements or outgrowths of the arachnoid membrane of the brain in the neighbourhood of the longitudinal sinus; ***P. depression, fossa, line***, a depression on the inner surface of the skull for the reception of the Pacchionian bodies.

1811 HOOPER *Med. Dict.*, *Pacchionian glands*. **1839–47** TODD *Cycl. Anat.* III. 644/1 The Pacchionian bodies are found principally along the edge of the great hemispheres of the brain. **1845** TODD & BOWMAN *Phys. Anat.* I. 255 The Pacchionian glands or bodies are whitish granules, composed of an albuminous material. **1893** *Syd. Soc. Lex.* s.v., They increase in size as the years advance, passing through holes in the dura mater and projecting into the sinus or lying in the Pacchionian fossæ of the skull bones.

paccioli, variant of PATCHOULI, the perfume.

pace (peɪs), *sb.*[1] Forms: 3–5 **pas**, 4–5 **paas**, **pass(e**, 4–7 **pase**, 5 **pasce**, 5–6 *Sc.* **pais(s**, 6 *Sc.* **paice**, 4– **pace**. [ME. a. OF. *pas*:—L. *passum* (nom. *passus*) a step, pace, lit. a stretch (of the leg), f. *pass-*, ppl. stem of *pandĕre* to stretch, extend.]

I. A step, and derived senses.

1. a. A single separate movement made by the leg in walking, running, or dancing; a step.

13.. *Coer de L.* 536, I bad hym ryde forth hys wey,.. Ageyn he com be another pas. *a* **1375** *Lay Folks Mass Bk.* App. iv. 105 Eueri fote þat þou gas þyn Angel poyntep hit vch a pas. *c* **1400** MAUNDEV. (1839) xvi. 174 Summe..at euery thrydde pas þat þei gon..þei knelen. **1489** CAXTON *Faytes of A.* I. xvi. 47 [They] shal marche paas by paas. **1593** SHAKS. *Lucr.* 1391 Pale cowards, marching on with trembling paces. **1634** [see PACE *v.* 1 d]. **1667** MILTON *P.L.* x. 589 Behind her Death Close following pace for pace. **1832** TENNYSON *Lady of Shalott* III. v, She made three paces thro' the room.

† **b.** *fig.* A 'step' in any process or proceeding.

[**1450–1530** *Myrr. our Ladye* 227 Her fete she suffered neuer to moue one pase, but yf she dyscussed fyrste what profyte shulde come therof.] *a* **1628** PRESTON *New Covt.* (1634) 210 We are not to be judged by a few actions, and a few paces, but by the constant tenor of our life. *a* **1698** TEMPLE (J.), The first pace necessary for his majesty to make, is to fall into confidence with Spain.

2. The space traversed by one step; hence as a vague measure of distance.

1382 WYCLIF *2 Sam.* vi. 13 And whanne thei hadden stied ouer, that baren the arke of the Lord, sexe paas, thei offreden an oxe and a wether. **1485** CAXTON *Chas. Gt.* 69 Olyuer.. came a foure paas nyghe vnto Fyerabras. **1587** FLEMING *Contn. Holinshed* III. 1332/1 On his left hand somewhat more than halfe a pase beneath him. **1667** MILTON *P.L.* VI. 193 Ten paces huge He back recoild. **1703** MAUNDRELL *Journ. Jerus.* (1732) 106 Five hundred and seventy of my paces in length. **1879** *Cassell's Technic. Educ.* IV. 92/2 In many cases the pace of the surveyor is used for determining distances.

3. A definite but varying measure of length or distance; sometimes reckoned as the distance from where one foot is set down to where the other is set down (about 2½ feet), as the ***military pace***; sometimes as that between successive stationary positions of the same foot (about 5 feet), as the ***geometrical pace***.

13.. *K. Alis.* 7804 An c. pas is hygh the wal. **1398** TREVISA *Barth. De P.R.* XIX. cxxix. (1495) 937 The pace conteyneth fyue fete and the perche enleuen pace and ten fete. *c* **1400** MAUNDEV. (Roxb.) xi. 46 A c. pascez þeine..es þe charnell of þe hospitale. **1555** EDEN *Decades* 323 To measure the earth by furlonges, paces and feete. **1692** *Capt. Smith's Seaman's Gram.* II. xxvi. 135 (At one deg. of Mounture) she conveyed her Shot 1125 Feet, or 225 Paces. **1756–7** tr. *Keysler's Trav.* (1760) II. 282 An open walk of an hundred and eight paces in length leads to the fountain. **1841** LEVER *C. O'Malley* vi. (The Man for Galway), To kiss your wife, Or take your life At ten or fifteen paces. **1842** BRANDE *Dict. Sci.* etc. s.v., The ancient Roman pace..was five Roman feet,..hence the pace was about 58·1 English inches, and the Roman mile, the '*mille passus*', equal to 1614 yards.

II. The action of stepping, and derived senses.

4. a. The action, or (usually) manner, of stepping, in walking or running; gait, step, walk, way of walking or progression. (See also 7.)

1297 R. GLOUC. (Rolls) 5635 For some meschaunce of þe king he made so glad pas. *c* **1386** CHAUCER *Miller's T.* 555 And Absolon gooth forth a sory pas. **1422** tr. *Secreta Secret.*, *Priv. Priv.* 235 Whoso hath the Paas large and slow, he is wyse and wel spedynge. **1513** DOUGLAS *Æneis* II. xi. 76 Litle Iulus.. With wnmeit paiss his fader fast followand. *c* **1586** C'TESS PEMBROKE *Ps.* L. vii, But loe, thou see'st I march another pace. **1697** DRYDEN *Virg. Georg.* III. 708 Late to lag behind, with truant pace. **1769** SIR W. JONES *Palace Fortune* Poems (1777) 20 Now came an aged sire with trembling pace. **1840** DICKENS *Old C. Shop* i, The little creature accommodating her pace to mine. **1851** LONGF. *Gold. Leg.* III. *Nativity* II. i, I steal with quiet pace, My pitcher at the well to fill.

† **b.** Course, way (in walking or running). *Obs.*

13.. *Cursor M.* 19076 (Edinb.) To þe tempil he sped his pas. **1390** GOWER *Conf.* III. 6 Wherof mi limes ben so dull, I mai unethes gon the pass [*rime* was]. *c* **1460** *Towneley Myst.* xxviii. 364 To Ierusalem take we the pace. **1608** TOPSELL *Serpents* (1658) 770 It is a small creature to see to, keeping on the pace very fearfully. **1657** HOWELL *Londinop.* 87 We will direct our pace downward now. **1727** GAY *Fables* I. xvii, In vain the dog pursu'd his pace.

† **c.** *transf.* and *fig.* Movement, motion; manner of going on. (Cf. 7 b.)

c **1386** CHAUCER *Man of Law's T.* 208 O fieble Moone vnhappy been thy paas [*v.r.* pas]. **1603** T. WILSON in Ellis *Orig. Lett.* Ser. II. III. 201 Our English affayres goe on with a smooth pace and a smilinge countenance. *c* **1611** CHAPMAN *Iliad* I. 394 The Pow'r whose pace doth move The round earth, heav'n's great Queen, and Pallas.

† **5.** A walking pace, walking (as distinguished from running, etc.). *Obs.*

a **1300** *Cursor M.* 15392 (Cott.) Fra þan he ran him ilk fote, ne yode he noght þe pas, til he com him til þat in. *Ibid.* 15872 (Cott.) His hend þai band and ledd him forth A-trott and noght þe pas [so *Gött.*; *Fairf.* & *Trin.* a pas]. *c* **1386** CHAUCER *Can. Yeom. Prol.* & *T.* 22 His hat heeng at his bak doun by a laas ffor he hadde riden moore than trot or paas. **1390** GOWER *Conf.* III. 41 Withinne his chambre..He goth now doun nou up fulofte, Walkende a pass.

6. a. Any one of the various gaits or manners of stepping of a horse, mule, etc., esp. when trained. Also *fig.*, esp. in such phr. as ***to put through his paces***, referring to the various accomplishments or actions of which a person or thing is capable.

1589 R. HARVEY *Pl. Perc.* (1590) 5 A horse may ouer reach in a true pace. **1600** SHAKS. *A.Y.L.* III. ii. 327 Time trauels in diuers paces, with diuers persons: Ile tell you who Time ambles withall, who Time trots withal, who Time gallops withal, and who he stands stil withall. **1667** *Lond. Gaz.* No. 200/4 A dark brown Gelding..having all his paces. **1713** *Ibid.* No. 5127/12 Stoln or stray'd.., a brown bay Gelding, ..his Pace, Trot and Gallop. **1727–41** CHAMBERS *Cycl.* s.v., The natural paces of a horse are three, *viz.* the walk, trot, and gallop: to which may be added an amble; because some horses have it naturally. **1766** GOLDSM. *Vic. W.* xiv, I had.. put my horse through all his paces,..at last a chapman approached. **1856** EMERSON *Eng. Traits*, *Voy. Eng.*, The captain affirmed that the ship would show us in time all her paces. **1871** B. TAYLOR *Faust* (1875) II. I. vii. 81, I see she means to put him through his paces.

b. A particular gait of the horse (or other quadruped); usually identified with *amble*, but now sometimes used as equivalent to *rack* (cf. PACE *v.* 3).

1663 BUTLER *Hud.* I. ii. 46 They rode, but Authors having not Determin'd whether Pace or Trot... We leave it, and go on. **1727–41** CHAMBERS *Cycl.*, *Pace* is more particularly understood of that easy low motion wherein the horse raises the two feet of the same side at a time; called also *amble*. **1840** BLAINE *Encycl. Rur. Sports* §1036 The walk may be irregular, though laterally conducted, as we see in the walk of the pace, which, if expedited, produces the amble. **18..** STRICKLAND FREEMAN *ibid.*, The poise being altered by the will of the horse, the off fore [leg] seemed to begin, and not to be succeeded by the off hind-foot being set down at the same time after it, as in the walk of the pace. **1885** *Field* 17 Oct., Col. Dodge's definition of a rack is that it is half-way between a pace and a trot.

III. Rate of movement, etc.

7. a. Rate of stepping; rate of progression (of a person or animal); speed in walking or running. Usually with qualifying adj. (Cf. also 4.)

c **1290** *S. Eng. Leg.* I. 393/15 þis best orn with gret pas. *c* **1330** R. BRUNNE *Chron. Wace* (Rolls) 3515 Ne go swyþer þan softe paas. *c* **1489** CAXTON *Sonnes of Aymon* xiv. 315 He sette hymselfe for to goo the waye so gret pase that no horse cowde not have waloped so fast. *a* **1533** LD. BERNERS *Huon* lv. 185 The horse wold nother trot nor galop but go styll his owne pase. **1642** FULLER *Holy & Prof. St.* III. xxi. 211 Their ordinary pace is a race. **1693** DRYDEN *Juvenal* x. (1697) 246 The Beggar Sings,..and never mends his pace. **1743** J. DAVIDSON *Æneid* VII. 185 Set forward with quick pace. **1863** GEO. ELIOT *Romola* xx, He quickened his pace, and took up new threads of talk.

b. *transf.* and *fig.* Rate of movement in general, or of action figured as movement; speed, velocity. *spec.*, in *Cricket*, the speed of a bowler's delivery; the velocity of a ball bowled; also *ellipt.*, = pace-bowling.

c **1430** LYDG. *Min. Poems* (Percy Soc.) 216 Fro silver wellys..Comethe cristal water rennyng a gret pas. **1599** SHAKS. *Much Ado* III. iv. 93 What pace is this that thy tongue keepes. *Mar.* Not a false gallop. **1659** *Burton's Diary* (1828) IV. 357 If they go the pace of their ancestors, I would tell them plainly they would not sit long. **1788** FRANKLIN *Autobiog.* Wks. 1840 I. 223 While we stood there the ship mended her pace. **1800** T. BOXALL *Rules & Instr. Cricket* 15, I think it very proper not to bowl always the same pace. *Ibid.* 34 The striker must judge for himself what pace the bowler is bowling. **1816** W. LAMBERT *Instr. & Rules Cricket* 18 Never bowl faster than you can do..well, varying your pace as you may judge proper. **1835** URE *Philos. Manuf.* 29 Had British industry not been aided by Watt's invention, it must have gone on with a retarding pace, in consequence of the increasing cost of motive power. **1900** P. F. WARNER *Cricket in Many Climes* 90 In Cobb and Kelly the New York team had two capital bowlers. The former is right-hand, and varies his pace well. **1955** [see *back-lift* s.v. BACK- B]. **1976** *0–10 Cricket Scene* (Austral.) 7/1 Many [innings] have been an amazing barrage of brutal driving, hooking and cutting against both pace and spin.

c. ***pace of the table*** (Billiards), ***of the wicket, ground*** (Cricket): the degree of elasticity of the cushions, or of the ground, as affecting the velocity of motion of the ball. (Cf. FAST *a.* 9.)

1873 BENNETT & CAVENDISH *Billiards* 77 The pace of the table makes a material difference in the strength with which this stroke should be played. **1888** R. H. LYTTELTON in Steel & Lyttelton *Cricket* ii. 52 In back play, unless the ball is very short, the pace of the ground may beat a man. **1897** *Daily News* 1 Nov. 7/2 He took four hours and fifty minutes to get his runs, and said that the extreme pace of the wicket bothered him. **1903** A. C. MACLAREN in H. G. Hutchinson *Cricket* ix. 252 Too much importance ought never to be attached to the opening game, owing to those who have not previously visited Australia being wholly unaccustomed.. to the fast pace of the wicket. **1955** *Times* 9 May 15/1 He spun it, too, and one can imagine how dangerous he might be on wickets with any pace in them.

8. Phrases. **a.** ***to keep (hold) pace***: to maintain the same speed of movement; to advance at an equal rate; to keep up *with*. (*lit.* and *fig.*)

1590 SHAKS. *Mids. N.* III. ii. 445 My legs can keepe no pace with my desires. **1601** HOLLAND *Pliny* I. 350 Lions and Camels only..keep pace in their march, foot by foot, that is to say, they never set their left foot before their right, nor ouer-reach with it. **1647** WARD *Simp. Cobler* 61 Who have held pace..with you in our evill wayes. **1762** GOLDSM. *Cit. W.* xv, His luxuries kept pace with the affluence of his fortune. **1776** ADAM SMITH *W.N.* II. iv. (1869) I. 359 The interest of money, keeping pace always with the profits of stock. **1782** MISS BURNEY *Cecilia* v. xii, [He] walked so fast that they could hardly keep pace with him. **1876** GRANT *Burgh Sch. Scotl.* II. xiii. 355 Boys..found incapable of keeping pace with the rest of their fellows. **1893** *Nat. Observer* 30 Sept. 505/1 Watts would have made a better race with La Flèche if he had pushed to the front, since she can hold a hot pace.

b. ***to go the pace***: to go along at great speed; *fig.* to proceed with reckless vigour of action; to indulge in dissipation; to 'go it'. ***to set the pace***: to fix or regulate the speed.

1829 *Sporting Mag.* XXIV. 47 The hounds went the pace over the heath towards Lymington. **1854** in *Brasenose Ale* 126 Each man will say you made them go the pace. **1866** MRS. HENRY WOOD *St. Martin's Eve* xxi, He went the pace ..as other young men do. **1890** *Licensed Victuallers' Gaz.* 5 Dec. 363/1 Fresh from Oxford, Arthur had been going the pace. **1892** [see BLIND *a.* (and *adv.*) 1 i]. **1905** A. BENNETT *Tales of Five Towns* I. 109 Well, you *have* been going the pace! We always knew you were a hot un, but really—. **1928** BARRIE *Peter Pan* I, in *Plays* 19 Nana must go about all her duties in a most ordinary manner..; naturalness must be her passion; indeed, it should be the aim of every one in the play, for which she is now setting the pace. **1928** E. WINGFIELD-STRATFORD *Hist. Brit. Civilization* II. iii. 1090 Britain was ceasing to set the pace to her neighbours; she was beginning to show signs of flagging in the race. **1958** *Engineering* 4 Apr. 424/2 Do things before anyone else not wait to see what someone else does—set the pace and keep them hopping.

IV. Special senses.

9. A step of a stair or the like; a part of a floor raised by a step; a stage, platform. Cf. FOOT-PACE 2, HALPACE.

a **1300** *Cursor M.* 9948 (Cott.) A tron of iuor graid.. Climband vp wit seuen pass [*v.rr.* pas, pace]. **1535** *Hampton Court Accts.*, 104 fote of hardston rought pase, for the steppes in the Quere. **1845** PARKER *Gloss. Archit.* (ed. 4) I. 267 *Pace*, a broad step, or slightly raised space about a tomb, etc.; a portion of a floor slightly raised above the general level.

† **10.** A passage, narrow way; esp. **a.** a pass between mountains, rocks, bogs, woods, etc.; **b.** a narrow channel at sea, a strait. *Obs.*

a **1300** *Cursor M.* 23735 We agh be bun at bide to pass þe pase þat es sa herd. **1377** LANGL. *P. Pl.* B. XIV. 300 ȝe, þorw þe pas of altoun Pouerte myȝte passe with-oute peril of robbynge. **1470–85** MALORY *Arthur* VII. ix, Thou shalt not passe a paas here that is called the paas perillous. *a* **1578** LINDESAY (Pitscottie) *Chron. Scot.* (S.T.S.) I. 368 [He] pullit wpe saillis and came stoutlie throw the pace of Calies. **1590** SPENSER *F.Q.* III. i. 19 She forward went, As lay her iourney, through that perlous Pace. *a* **1604** HANMER *Chron. Irel.* (1633) 1 Making paces thorow woods and thickets. **1612** *Stat. Irel.* (1765) I. 444 The high-ways and cashes and paces and passages throughout the woods of this kingdom. **1617** MORYSON *Itin.* II. 81 He caused..the woods to be cut downe on both sides of the Pace.

† **11. a.** In a church: A passage between the seats. **b.** ***middle pace***: the nave; ***of one pace***, of a nave only. *Obs.*

1499 *Will of J. Robert* (Somerset Ho.), To be buried in the myddell pace before the high crosse. **1507** *Will of Cornell* (ibid.), In the pace ayenst saint Kateryn Chapell dore. **1518** *Will of Hopkynson* (ibid.), The middill pase of the church. **1772** MUILMAN *Hist. Essex* VI. 164 The church consists of a middle pace and two aysles, but the chancel hath only a north aysle, all leaded. **1828** J. HUNTER *South Yorkshire* I. 84 The church is of one pace, with a tower at the west end. *Ibid.* 89.

† **12.** A passage (in a narrative or other writing); a section, division, chapter, canto, etc. *Obs.*

a **1300** *Cursor M.* 18583 Nu haf yee herd be tald þe pas, Hu þat he harud hell and ras. *c* **1400** *Destr. Troy* 663 The lady

..Past to hir priue chamber: & here a pas endis. **14..** *ABC Poem on Passion* 44 in *Pol., Rel. & L.P.* 245 Lystyn a lytyl pas. **1621** T. WILLIAMSON tr. *Goulart's Wise Vieillard* 24 Philosophers haue vsed to diuide old age as it were into certaine spaces, paces, or progresses.

†**13.** A 'company' or herd of asses. *Obs.*

1486 *Bk. St. Albans* F vj b, A Pase of Assis. **1688** R. HOLME *Armoury* II. 132/1 A company of..Asses [is] a Pace.

14. *attrib.* and *Comb.*, as *pace-goer*; **pace-aisle, pace-board** (cf. senses 9, 11); **pace-bowling** (hence *pace bowler*), **pace-change, pace-man** (cf. senses 7b, c); **pace-stick**, a stick used to measure (military) paces. See also PACE-MAKER, PACE-SETTER.

1877 LEE *Gloss. Liturg. Terms*, *Pace-aisle, the ambulatory round the back of a high altar. *Pace-board, a platform of wood before an altar. **1951** *People* 3 June 8/6 Good news to-day about Alec Bedser and Trevor Bailey, the two *pace bowlers likely to be chosen to open England's attack in the First Test. **1976** *Scotsman* 24 Dec. 15/7 But whatever flaws the Australian batting may suggest, their pace bowlers, Dennis Lillee and Jeff Thomson, seem the likeliest match-winners. **1958** *Listener* 16 Oct. 604/1 England had no powerful reserves of *pace-bowling strength to call on. **1951** R. ROBINSON in A. Ross *Cricketer's Compan.* **1960** III. 396 Not satisfied with..a wide range of *pace-changes, he rings in a leg-break or a round-armer now and again. **1870** MEADE *New Zealand* 328 A pair of legs which looked like *pace-goers by land or water. **1974** *Times* 25 Nov. 10/2 Prasanna, coming in at No. 10, edged, slashed and drove the West Indies *pacemen to distraction. **1976** *0-10 Cricket Scene* (Austral.) 11/1 The deadpan wickets in England were enough to cause a speedster to retire, but Lillee's speed genius and dedication earned him 21 wickets—more than any paceman on either side. **1833** *Regul. Instr. Cavalry* I. 16 The *pace stick must be used to measure..his step. **1876** ALBEMARLE *50 Yrs. Life* II. 219 Drill-sergeants followed them everywhere, to prove by the pace-stick whether they had accomplished the regulation number of inches at each stride.

pace (peːs), *sb.*[2] *Sc.* and *north. dial.* Also 4 **pas**, 5 (9) **paas**, 5–6 **pase**, *Sc.* **payce, paiss.** [In 15th c. *paas* from earlier *pask*; cf. northern *as*, *ass*, from *ask*, ASH *sb.*[2], etc. In Washington Irving perh. from Du. *paasch*, pronounced *paas*.] Easter, Easter-tide; = PASCH. **pace eggs**, *dial.* **paste-eggs** (LG. *paaschey*, F. *œufs de pâques*) Easter eggs; hence *pace-egger*, *-egging*: see Eng. Dial. Dict.

1385 in *3rd Rep. Hist. MSS. Comm.* 410/2 Deferryt tyl his lauchfull day next eftir pas. *c* **1425** WYNTOUN *Chron.* VIII. i. 3 The sextene day efftyr Pase. *c* **1440** *York Myst.* xxvii. 4 Here will I holde..The feeste of Paas. **1500–20** DUNBAR *Poems* xxxvi. 19 And nevir is glaid at ȝule nor Paiss. **1530** PALSGR. 805 At Pace, *a Pasques*. **1568** *Durham Depos.* (Surtees) 87 He wold stand up upon paysunday. *c* **1570** *Ibid.* 239 Upon Pase monday was a twelmonth last past. **1579** G. GILPIN tr. *Rabbotem's Bee-Hive Rom. Ch.* ii. (1580) 15 Holy ashes, holy paceegges, & flames, palmes and palme boughes. **1611** COTGR. s.v. *Pasque, Oeufs de Pasques*, Paste-egges. **1809** W. IRVING *Knickerb.* VII. ii, There was a great cracking of eggs at Paas or Easter. **1872** HARDWICK *Trad. Lanc.* 73 [They] sallied forth during Easterweek 'a pace-egging' as it was termed. **1876** *Prayer Bk. Interleaved* 117 The custom of asking for Pace..eggs.

†**b.** Extended, like med.L. *pascha* (see Du Cange) to other great church festivals, e.g. Christmas. (Cf. OF. *pasque de Noël*, Sp. *pascua de Natividad* or simply *Pascua*.) *Obs.*

c **1450** *St. Cuthbert* (Surtees) 3393 Done solempnite of pace.

pace (peɪs), *v.* Also 6–7 **pase.** [f. PACE *sb.*[1]]

1. a. *intr.* To move with paces or steps; to walk with a slow, steady, or regular pace: to step along.

1513 DOUGLAS *Æneis* XII. Prol. 161 The payntit povne, pasand with plomys gym, Kest vp his taill. **1570** LEVINS *Manip.* 7/3 To Pace, *gradi*. **1587** GREENE *Euphues his Censure* Wks. (Grosart) VI. 164 Hector pazing hand in hand with Achilles, Troilus with Vlisses. **1611** SHAKS. *Wint. T.* IV. iii. 120, I will euen take my leaue of you, & pace softly towards my Kinsmans. **1769** GRAY *Install. Ode* 35 Pacing forth With solemn steps and slow. **1814** CARY *Dante, Inf.* XXIV. 11 There paces to and fro, wailing his lot, As a discomfited and helpless man.

b. *transf.* and *fig.* To proceed or advance in speech or action.

1611 SHAKS. *Wint. T.* IV. i. 23, I..with speed so pace To speake of Perdita. **1639** W. SCLATER *Worthy Commun.* 49 Let not the moone pace over the Zodaicke oftner..then we performe, if possible, our course this way.

c. Also *to pace it*. (See IT 9.)

1597 BP. HALL *Sat.* I. vi. 8 The nimble dactyls striving to out-go, The drawling spondees pacing it below. **1652** PEYTON *Catastr. Ho. Stuarts* (1731) 23 Charles instead of pacing it, ran violently to destroy his subjects.

d. *trans.* with cognate or adverbial object.

1598 SHAKS. *Merch. V.* II. vi. 12 Where is the horse that doth vntread againe His tedious measures with the vnbated fire, That he did pace them first? **1634** *Documents agst. Prynne* (Camden) 20 Soe many paces as a man paceth in daunceinge soe manye steppes hee is forward to hell. **1849** MACAULAY *Hist. Eng.* ix. II. 438 Sentinels paced the rounds day and night.

e. With *away*: To spend (time) in pacing.

1820 KEATS *Hyperion* I. 194 He paced away the pleasant hours of ease.

2. *trans.* To traverse with paces or steps; to walk with measured pace along (a path) or about (a place); hence, To measure by pacing. Also *fig.*

1571 DIGGES *Pantom.* II. xi. Nj b, You maye..measure euery side, and line..as exactely as with corde, or pole, ye should paynfully pase it ouer. **1693** in *Hearne's Collect.* (O.H.S.) III. 342, I paced it, and found it to bee 70 of my Paces in Length. **1791** MRS. RADCLIFFE *Rom. Forest* v, Louis was pacing the room in apparent agitation. **1801** SOUTHEY *Thalaba* v. *note*, It..is, as far as I could judge by my pacing it, a large quarter of a league. **1878** *Masque Poets* 195 She rose and paced the room like one distracted. **1921** W. DE LA MARE *Veil* 24 She paced in pride The uncharted paths men trace in ocean's foam. **1955** *Sci. News Let.* 26 Mar. 201/1 The red maple is one of the first trees to wear its now flower-patterned spring frock. Experts use it as a milestick for pacing spring weather northward because it is one of the few trees that grows from Florida to Quebec.

3. a. *intr.* Of a horse, etc.: To move with the gait called a pace (see PACE *sb.*[1] 6 b): (*a*) to amble; (*b*) in recent use (chiefly *U.S.*), to rack (RACK *v.*[4]).

1614 B. JONSON *Barth. Fair* II. Wks. (Rtldg.) 317/2 I'll..have thy pasterns well roll'd, and thou shalt pace again by to-morrow. *c* **1620** Z. BOYD *Zion's Flowers* (1855) 137 Men for a space pace in prosperity, But at the last trot hard in misery. **1673** *Lond. Gaz.* No. 819/4 Stolen..one Bay Mare ..paces naturally. **1677** *Ibid.* No. 1222/4 A Sorrel Chesnut Gelding..walks well, paces little, but trotteth high. **1709** *Ibid.* No. 4543/4 Stray'd or stoln..a Sorrel Gelding..does not pace. **1833** HT. MARTINEAU *Manch. Strike* 42 The procession..overtook Mr. W.,..pacing to business on his gray pony. **1895** *Funk's Stand. Dict.*, *Pace*, to move, as a horse, at the pace, by lifting the feet on the same side synchronously. **1903** *Daily Mail* 11 Mar., A horse trots when his off fore and near hind legs strike the ground simultaneously, and he paces when the legs of a side move in unison, like those of two riders on a tandem cycle.

b. *trans.* (With cognate or adverbial object.)

1607 MARKHAM *Caval.* (1617) 148 In this ring you shall exercise your horse..making him pace it, and doe his changes first uppon foote pace onely; when he can pace them perfitely, then you shall make him trott. *Ibid.* 152 You may begin with the two distinct or several rings, which after he have pac'd, trotted and galloped, then..stop.

4. *trans.* To train (a horse) to pace; to exercise in pacing. Also *fig.*

1603 SHAKS. *Meas. for M.* IV. iii. 137. **1606** —— *Ant. & Cl.* II. ii. 64 The third oth' world is yours, which with a Snaffle, You may pace easie, but not such a wife. **1607** MARKHAM *Caval.* II. (1617) 82 You must then leaue exercising him in any lesson..and onely pace or trott him fairely forth right. **1724** *Lond. Gaz.* No. 6258/3 A bay Mare,..lately paced.

5. a. To set the pace for (a rider, boat's crew, etc.) in racing or training for a race. Also *transf.* and *fig.*

1886 *N.Y. Herald* in *Cyclist* 3 Nov. 82/1 Crocker was paced by Woodside, Rowe and Hender on bicycles. **1893** *Westm. Gaz.* 22 Mar. 5/3 Oxford had the advantage of the assistance of a Thames Rowing Club eight to pace them. **1961** A. BERKMAN *Singers' Gloss. Show Business* 65 *Pacing an act*, making a line-up plan of the songs used in an act, so that the interest and enthusiasm of the audience builds up to the end. **1962** *Listener* 31 May 947/1, I had been pacing him in meetings all over the country—that is, talking, to keep the crowd..until Cook should arrive. **1967** *Technology Week* 23 Jan. 64/1 The past history of the design and construction of the vehicles and their propulsion systems..has been paced by the major developments in the materials fields. **1968** *Globe & Mail* (Toronto) 15 Jan. 18/9 The Hawks outscored the Gens 4–1 in the third period to take the victory. Dennis Giannini paced the winners with two goals. **1968** P. OLIVER *Screening Blues* ii. 82 'Lining out' in which a lead singer paces a line and the congregation follows with the same line or a refrain response with a linear reply. **1969** *Times* 13 Dec. (Sat. Rev.) p. iv/4 He knows to a nicety just how to pace a book. **1973** *Internat. Herald Tribune* 15 June 15/4 In the American League, Jim Spencer drove in two runs, one with his third homer of the season, in the seventh, to pace Texas to a 4–2 triumph. **1977** *Sci. Amer.* June 138/3 It is the development of the remarkable military reconnaissance programs that has indirectly paced civilian technology in the postwar years.

b. *Med.* To make (the heart) beat at an appropriate rate by stimulating it with pulses of electricity.

1963 *Brit. Heart Jrnl.* XXV. 299 When the heart was paced by ventricular stimulation, mean left atrial pressure was higher..than when the atrium was paced at the same rate. **1973** SEGEL & SAMET in P. Samet *Cardiac Pacing* iv. 82 The coronary sinus provides another area from which the heart can be paced.

¶**6.** A corruption of or blunder for PARSE. *Obs.* (Showing that *pace* was pronounced as *pass*.)

1594 LYLY *Moth. Bomb.* I. iii, I am no Latinist Cand. you must conster it. *Can.* So I will and pace it too: thou shalt be acquainted with case, gender, and number.

pace ('peɪsiː, 'pɑːkeɪ), *prep.* [L., abl. sing. of *pax* PEACE as used e.g. in phr. *pāce tuā* by your leave.] By the leave of (a person).

Used chiefly as a courteous or ironical apology for a contradiction or difference of opinion.

1863 *Fraser's Mag.* Nov. 662/1 Mendelssohn was an artist passionately devoted to his art, who (*pâce* Dr. Trench) regarded art as *virtù*. **1883** *Standard* 1 Sept. 2/2 *Pace* the late Sir George Cornewall Lewis, Mr. Scofield is right. **1911** *Chambers's Jrnl.* Nov. 720/1 The colour [of fruit]..is a tacit invitation (*pace* the gardener) to the feast. **1931** R. L. MÉGROZ *Joseph Conrad's Mind & Method* vii. 170 Stevenson ..was regarded by the English critics who, (*pace* Mr. Olage) so dislike fine writing on fine subjects, as a master of prose in fiction. **1955** *Times* 7 July 9/6 Nor, *pace* Mr. Smith, was I for one moment defending immorality in the journalist. **1973** A. H. SOMMERSTEIN *Sound Pattern Anc. Greek* iv. 116 Indeed, pace Chomsky and Halle, we would probably want it to be impossible for mid glides to exist at all. **1974** 'M. UNDERWOOD' *Pinch of Snuff* iii. 23 It was something he greatly prized—*pace* Whitby-Stansford. **1976** *Conservation News* Nov./Dec. 4/2, I find (a) incredible (*pace* Herman Kahn).

b. In Latin phr. *pace tanti viri*: by the leave or favour of so great a man.

1771 SMOLLETT *Humph. Cl.* II. 101 Dr. Shaw..says, he has seen flakes of sulphur floating in the well.—*Pace tanti viri*; I, for my part, have never observed any thing like sulphur, either in or about the well. **1855** *Sat. Rev.* 8 Dec. 100/2 But who seeks for them in Harry Brougham's speeches, or even—*pace tanti viri* be it spoken—in Henry Lord Brougham's *Historical Sketches*? **1865** MILL *Exam. Hamilton's Philos.* xxvii. 544 Admiration, *pace tantorum virorum*, is a different thing from wonder.

pace, an early (14–15th c.) spelling of PASS *v.*

pacebil, obs. form of PEACEABLE *a.*

paced (peɪst), *a.* [f. PACE *sb.* and *v.* + -ED.]

1. Having a (specified) pace, gait, or rate of walking or going: chiefly in parasynthetic comb.

1583 GREENE *Mamillia* II. Wks. (Rtldg.) 316/1 Dames now-a-days..Pac'd in print, brave lofty looks, not us'd with the vestals. **1594** J. DICKENSON *Arisbas* (1878) 78 An high-pac'd Muse, treading a lofty march. *c* **1611** CHAPMAN *Iliad* XIII. 24 His brazen-footed steeds, All golden-maned, and paced with wings. **16..** DRYDEN (J.), Revenge is sure, though sometimes slowly pac'd. **1899** *Academy* 15 July 60/2 The best of life comes to the even-paced.

2. Traversed or measured by pacing. Also *fig.*

1869 LD. LYTTON *Orval* 169 The primly-paced saloons of Art and Science. **1882** FLOYER *Unexpl. Baluchistan* 177 Hills, each with a paced base of from half a mile to a mile. **1953** *Brit. Jrnl. Psychol.* Nov. 295 The task..was simply to touch the contact corresponding to the one lamp which was alight. In one condition (the 'paced' one) the lamp went out. *Ibid.* 296 Group II, which was paced, showed a fall-off. **1958** *Oxf. Univ. Gaz.* 27 Jan. 523/2 This year has seen the conclusion of a programme of work on 'Conditions influencing the rate of learning in paced and unpaced tasks'.

3. *Racing.* Having the pace set by a pace-maker.

1899 *Daily News* 8 Apr. 8/6 The National Cyclists' Union ..forbade all riders holding its licences..to attempt a paced ride of any description on the road.

pace-gard, -guard, var. PASSE-GARDE.

pace-maker. [PACE *sb.*[1]]

1. a. A rider (boat's crew, etc.) who makes or sets the pace for another in racing or training for a race. Also, one of the leading runners in a race. Also *transf.*

1884 *Pall Mall G.* 29 Mar. 2/2 The same scratch-crew acted as pace-maker for both the university eights. **1891** *Ibid.* 6 Aug. 1/3 To establish a record for a mile without pace-makers, in order that comparisons may be drawn between the times of an unassisted rider and one paced. **1900** *Field* 4 Aug. 186/1 Up to this he had been one of the pacemakers, but even now he was not to be left behind. *Ibid.* 8 Sept. 384/1 The value of the pacemaker as a mere leader who set a racing pace..was lost sight of when his utility as a wind-shield became recognized. **1942** *Sun* (Baltimore) 29 Apr. 19/1 El Toreador scored by three parts of a length over Seaway, pacemaker for most of the mile and 70-yard route of the seventh event. **1951** R. & N. MCWHIRTER *Get to your Marks!* iii. 66 Latching on to an over-awed local pace-maker in a 3-man field, Whitfield swept through. **1957** J. PETERS et al. *Mod. Middle- & Long-Distance Running* xii. 55 He.. missed a great opportunity of using Hansenne as a pace-maker. **1961** *Times* 11 Apr. 14/5 An athlete training with an automatic pacemaker. **1978** G. A. SHEEHAN *Running & Being* xii. 174 A pacemaker..had zeroed in on the perfect pace.

b. One who sets the rate of working for others or the standards to be achieved by others; a 'trend-setter'. Also *transf.*, of things.

1906 U. SINCLAIR *Jungle* xi. 130 They would get new pace-makers and pay them more. **1967** *Daily Tel.* 17 May 17/7 Public schools may well continue to act as pace-makers and trend-setters for this country's education as a whole. **1970** *Ibid.* 14 Feb. 9/8 Both Rameau and Gluck were pacemakers in their day, progressive composers who consciously set out to change the musical landscape of the society in which they lived. **1976** *Star* (Sheffield) 30 Nov. 14/4 Chris Guthrie's hopes of a return to face the Second Division's pacemakers Chelsea at Bramall Lane on Friday night soared today. **1977** *Times* 22 Dec. 12/5 Pacemakers to watch in 1978 are..good Victorian dining furniture, early Continental oak and walnut, and tallboys.

2. An apparatus fixed to a bicycle to indicate when the rider is going at the required pace.

1896 *Godey's Mag.* Apr. 377/1 On the same lines is a pace-maker that can be set at any desired rate... While this rate is maintained, it rings a bell.

3. *Physiol.* **a.** That part of an animal's heart which determines the rate at which it contracts and where the contractions begin (in man and other mammals normally the sino-atrial node).

1910 *Heart* II. 39 The normal auricular complex is most closely simulated by beats excited from the neighbourhood of Keith and Flack's node. The pace-maker of the heart is therefore situated in the neighbourhood of the superior cavo-auricular junction. **1927** HALDANE & HUXLEY *Animal Biol.* vii. 146 In a mammal the beat starts at the entrance of the great veins to the right auricle in a special piece of tissue known as the 'pace-maker' which does not contract but stimulates the neighbouring muscle. **1951** *Ann. Surg.* CXXXIV. 8/2 Pratt..stated that the pacemaker is governed, at least in part, by the chemical content of venous blood returning to the right auricle. **1961** *Lancet* 9 Sept. 574/1 After a 550-volt shock complete auriculo-ventricular dissociation with a nodal or high bundle pacemaker at a rate of 30 per minute evolved spontaneously. **1968** PASSMORE & ROBSON *Compan. Med. Stud.* I. xxviii. 10/2 If the rate of discharge of the SA node is depressed, the portion of the heart with the next highest spontaneous discharge rate becomes the pacemaker, usually the AV [*sc.* atrioventricular] node.

b. A structure which controls the rate of rhythmic activity of an organ other than the heart.
1949 KOESTLER *Insight & Outlook* xx. 138 A certain region near the sinus end of the heart controls the rate of beat, and similar 'pacemakers' function in the stomach, the ureters, and so forth. **1963** R. P. DALES *Annelids* vi. 132 If there are two pacemakers maintaining two muscular activities it may well be asked if one can dominate the other. **1966** S. OCHS in E. E. Selkurt *Physiol.* (ed. 2) vi. 147 A pacemaker for rhythmicity of the EEG wave was located in the thalamus. **1974** MCLENNAN & SANDBERG *Synopsis Obstetr.* (ed. 9) x. 145 Any group of excited myometrial cells anywhere in the uterus may serve in the pacemaker role and initiate electrical propagation throughout the myometrium.

c. A man-made device which supplies electrical signals to the heart, stimulating it to beat at an appropriate rate.
1951 *Ann. Surg.* CXXXIV. 9/1 Our attention has been directed to the study of the problem of cardiac arrest to determine if the use of an electrical artificial pacemaker in resuscitation would be of value. **1963** *Daily Tel.* 16 Apr. 17/1 A transistorised pacemaker little bigger than a match box and weighing only a few ounces has been devised for implanting in the abdominal wall. **1967** *New Scientist* 9 Feb. 331/1 Battery-powered pacemakers normally need their batteries replacing after no more than 2–3 years, needing a surgical operation each time. **1974** *Times* 4 Mar. 6/6 He is to undergo an operation for the installation of a pacemaker to help him overcome a heart condition which has affected him on several recent occasions.

'pace-,making. [PACE *sb.*[1]] **1.** The act or practice of making or setting the pace for competitors in a race.
1896 ADE *Artie* xi. 94 Ain't I tellin' you that we done the pacemakin'? **1900** *Field* 8 Sept. 384/1 Pacemaking has long since exceeded the original function it was designed to fulfil as a preventive of waiting tactics in ordinary bicycle races. **1911** *Encycl. Brit.* XXIII. 854/1 An element unknown to sprinting enters into middle- and long-distance runs, namely that of pace-making. **1968** B. TULLOH *On Running* ix. 114 You can often help each other along by sharing the pacemaking.
2. *Med.* = PACING *vbl. sb.* 3.
1963 *Amer. Jrnl. Cardiol.* XI. 594 (*heading*) Hemodynamic sequelae of idioventricular pacemaking in complete heart block. **1973** SCHERLAG & LAZZARA in P. Samet *Cardiac Pacing* xiii. 309 (*heading*) Pacemakers and pacemaking in the AV junction.

pacement, obs. form of PASSEMENT.

pacer ('peɪsə(r)). [Agent-n. from PACE *v.*]
1. *gen.* One who paces; one who walks with measured step; one who traverses or measures (a path, distance, etc.) by pacing.
1835 L. HUNT *Capt. Sword* ii, Pacer of highway and piercer of ford. **1886** DOWDEN *Shelley* II. 500 The pacers on the terrace descried a strange sail rounding the point.
2. A horse that paces, or whose ordinary gait is a pace: see PACE *sb.*[1] 6 b, *v.* 3.
a **1661** FULLER *Worthies, Huntington.* (1662) 51 It is given to thorough-paced-Naggs, that amble naturally, to trip much whilest artificial pacers goe surest on foot. **1708** J. CHAMBERLAYNE *St. Gt. Brit.* I. I. iv. (1737) 32 Your New England Pads are esteemed as the swiftest Pacers. **1740** BAYNARD *Health* (ed. 6) 31 Be your horse a pacer, or a trotter. **1809** W. IRVING *Knickerb.* v. vi, He entered New-Amsterdam as a conqueror, mounted on a Naraganset pacer. **1817** *Sporting Mag.* L. 25 The parson of the parish.. mounts the old pacer. **1829** *Sporting Mag.* XXIII. 266 The Narraganset pacer is extinct. **1884** E. EGGLESTON in *Century Mag.* Jan. 445/1 The awkward but 'prodigiously' rapid natural amble of the American pacer. **1900** *Field* June, A pacer.. canters with his hind legs, and trots with his fore legs.
b. One who trains a horse to pace; a trainer.
1656 EARL MONM. tr. *Boccalini's Advts. fr. Parnass.* I. xli. (1674) 54 Coults might not put Tramels upon their Pacers.
3. *Racing.* = PACE-MAKER I.
1893 *Pall Mall G.* 10 July 10/2 In the contest of Saturday the riders were permitted to have pacemakers; but the innovation was not entirely successful, the competitors several times overrunning the pacer.
4. *colloq.* Anything that goes at a great pace.
1890 *Cent. Dict.* **1901** FARMER *Slang.*

'pace-,setter. [PACE *sb.*[1]] One who sets the pace, trend, or fashion. (Chiefly *fig.*)
1895 *Westm. Gaz.* 25 Nov. 2/2 With Mr. Redmond as pace-setter, there will, we may be sure, be a lively competition between him, Mr. Dillon, and Mr. Healy. **1946** *Sun* (Baltimore) 2 Aug. 14/1 Perlina, the early pacesetter, was second about two lengths in front of.. White Ford. **1958** *Listener* 23 Oct. 653/3 The new middle-class society and the new pace-setters within it. **1961** *Times* 8 May 16/4 Music is limited to punctuation, .. or the role of pace-setter for words and action. **1969** *Times* 22 Oct. (Ghana Suppl.) p. i/2 Ghana was the pacesetter for modern Africa when it became the first sub-Saharan black country to move from colonial status to independence. **1970** *Globe & Mail* (Toronto) 25 Sept. 31/7 Keith Alexander of Calgary continued to be the Canadian pacesetter, firing a 71 yesterday for a two-round total of 143. **1973** A. E. WILKERSON *Rights of Children* 307 The White House Conferences on Children have served since 1909 as pacesetters in child welfare. **1975** *N.Y. Times* 16 Oct. 43/7 'For all the city's problems, New York has been and will continue to be the pace-setter for a high quality of urban life in this country,' the developer said in an interview.

'pace-,setting, *a.* [PACE *sb.*[1]] That sets the pace, trend, or fashion. (Chiefly *fig.*)
1965 *Economist* 13 Feb. 645/2 A moratorium on other settlements while a clearly 'pace-setting' wage claim for the year is under review. **1967** *Jane's Surface Skimmer Systems* *1967–68* 1/1 If the pacesetting operations by British Rail and Hover-Lloyd alone cannot silence the sceptics, they can be invited to look to the Mediterranean. **1976** M. BIRMINGHAM *Heat of Sun* iii. 24 The educational initiative which the state had taken over in founding the pace-setting Achimota school.

pacey ('peɪsɪ) *a.* Also **pacy.** [f. PACE *sb.*[1] + -Y[1].] Having pace or speed; fast. (*lit.* and *fig.*)
1906 J. J. MUNRO *Let. to F. J. Furnivall* (MS.) 25 Aug., In the practice of the day before yesterday, Cantab was perceptibly the pacier boat. **1927** *Observer* 29 May 28/4 These hitters, when once they get a real start, play havoc with pacey bowling. **1967** *Listener* 25 May 688/2 The production.. is.. pacey and vivid. **1968** *Daily Mirror* 27 Aug. 7/2 This is considered very pacey, which is the new word for trendy. Nobody, but nobody, says trendy any more. **1969** C. BOOKER *Neophiliacs* ii. 48 The whole world.. had been reduced to the same grainy, pacy, ever more 'realistic' dream. **1969** *Pony* July 512/1 *Show Jumping Summer* is a 'pacey' book, in which events follow each other in quick succession. **1977** *Daily Tel.* 13 Jan. 17 (Advt.), The Celeste's low slung, pacey appearance isn't just for show. The 2 litre model has a top speed of 105 mph. **1977** *Times Lit. Suppl.* 11 Feb. 145/4 (Advt.), Pacy, turbulent story with an excellent and authentically researched diamond mining setting.

pacha, pachalik, var. ff. PASHA, PASHALIC.

pachche, pache, obs. ff. PATCH.

pache, obs. var. PASCH, Easter.

pachemia = *pachyhæmia* s.v. PACHY-.

pachent, obs. form of PAGEANT.

pachinko (pə'tʃɪŋkəʊ). Also **pachinco.** [Jap. *pachin* onomatopœic word repr. the sound of something triggered off + *ko* dim. suffix.] A variety of pin-ball popular in Japan. Also *attrib.*
1953 *Encounter* Nov. 7/2 In Tokyo there are 5,000 registered *pachinko* halls. **1954** J. L. MORSE *Unicorn Bk. 1953* 262/1 An interesting development in Japan was the popular craze for *pachinko*, a kind of poor-man's pinball game. **1964** *Listener* 8 Oct. 540/2 Pachinko is played with handfuls of ball-bearings. You drop them, one by one, into the machine, flick them round, and if they land in a winning cup, the machine coughs back fifteen ball-bearings which are bought in the first place, twenty-five at a time, for fifty yen (one shilling). If you amass enough of them, they can be exchanged for prizes. **1971** *Guardian* 11 June 11/6 Pachinco machines, dozens of them side by side in rows.. are all identical. A trigger shoots off a ball which may find its way into a slot and produce a jackpot of balls. **1973** A. BROINOWSKI *Take One Ambassador* v. 55 This [joint] next door's *pachinko*.. reminds me of some of the leagues clubs at home. *Ibid.* 56 They'll [*sc.* the Japanese].. spend their time in a useless game like this *pachinko*.

pachisi: see PARCHEESI.

pachnolite ('pæknəʊlaɪt). *Min.* [Named 1863, f. Gr. πάχνη hoar-frost + -LITE.] Hydrous fluoride of aluminium, calcium, and sodium, occurring on cryolite in small white crystals.
1866 *Amer. Jrnl. Sci.* XLI. 199 Knop has named the new species Pachnolite. **1868** DANA *Min.* (ed. 5) 129 Found with pachnolite on the cryolite of Greenland.

pachometer (pə'kɒmɪtə(r)). *Physics.* = Pachymeter: see PACHY-.
1857 MAYNE *Expos. Lex.*, An instrument invented by Benoît for measuring the thickness of the glass of mirrors: a pachometer. **1875** in KNIGHT *Dict. Mech.*

‖**pachuco** (pə'tʃʊkəʊ). [a. Mexican Sp. *pachuco* flashily dressed, vulgar.] A juvenile deliquent of Mexican-American descent, esp. in the Los Angeles area; in extended use, a derogatory term for any Mexican-American. Also *attrib.*
1943 C. HIMES in *Crisis* July 200/1 *Pachuo* is a Mexican expression which originally meant 'bandit' but has degenerated by usage into a description of a juvenile delinquent... In Mexican districts in the county of Los Angeles, small bands of pachuos have organized into gangs to fight each other. **1944** *Time* 10 July 26/2 Pachuco... Mexican for zootsuiter. **1946** C. HIMES *Black on Black* (1973) 256 Some pachuco kids were ganged about the juke box, talking in Mex. **1947** *Common Ground* Summer 79/1 The Pachuco dialect is a mélange composed of *Caló*, Hispanicized English, Anglicized Spanish, and words of pure invention. **1950** G. C. BARKER (*title*) Pachuco: An American-Spanish argot and its social function in Tucson, Arizona. *Ibid.* (1958) I. 13 In many cities of the American Southwest there are today Mexican-American boys who are known.. as pachucos. These boys.. may be distinguished by certain peculiar characteristics of dress, behavior, and language. **1954** J. STEINBECK *Sweet Thursday* 11 In Los Angeles.. he led a gang of pachucos. **1966** T. PYNCHON *Crying of Lot 49* i. 11 Hostile Pachuco dialect, full of chingas and maricones. **1972** J. WAMBAUGH *Blue Knight* (1973) v. 70 '*Órale, panzón*,' he said, like a pachuco, which he put on for me. He spoke beautiful Spanish.. but the barrios of El Paso Texas died hard. **1976** *Word 1971* XXVII. 294 Pachuco, also known as *tirilí*, *tirilongo*, is used not only by felons, delinquents,.. and others outside respectable society, but also by younger males throughout the Southwest as a street variety and for its slangy effect.

pachy- ('pækɪ, pə'kɪ), before a vowel also **pach-**, combining form of Gr. παχύ-ς 'thick, large, massive', used in the formation of zoological, botanical, and pathological terms: ‖**pachy'æmia** = *pachyhæmia*. ‖**pachyblepharosis** (-blɛfə'rəʊsɪs) *Path.* [Gr. βλέφαρον eyelid], chronic inflammatory thickening of the eyelid (Mayne *Expos. Lex.* 1857). **pachycardian** (-'kɑːdɪən) *a. Zool.* [Gr. καρδία heart], of or belonging to the *Pachycardia*, or main body of the vertebrates having a thick muscular heart; *sb.*, a vertebrate of this group. **pachycarpous** (-'kɑːpəs) *a. Bot.* [Gr. καρπός fruit], having large thick fruit (Mayne 1857). **pachycephalic** (-sɪ'fælɪk) *a.* [Gr. κεφαλ-ή head], having a very thick skull, exhibiting pachycephaly. **pachycephaline** (-'sɛfəlaɪn) *a. Ornith.*, of or pertaining to the *Pachycephalinæ*, the thick-heads or thick-headed shrikes. **pachycephalous** (-'sɛfələs) *a.* = *pachycephalic*; spec., of or pertaining to the *Pachycephala*, a division of parasitic Crustacea or fish-lice. **pachycephaly** (-'sɛfəlɪ), thickness of the skull. **pachycholic** (-'kɒlɪk) *a. Path.* [Gr. χολή bile], relating to *pachycholia* or morbid thickness of the bile (Mayne 1857). **pachydactyl, -yle** (-'dæktɪl) *a. Zool.* [Gr. δάκτυλος finger], having thick fleshy digits; *sb.*, an animal with thick toes (Webster 1864). **pachy'dactylous** *a.* [-OUS], = prec. *a.* ‖**pachy'dermia** *Path.* [Gr. δέρμα skin], thickening of the skin; hence **pachy'dermial** *a.* **pachy'emy** = *pachyhæmia*; so *pachyemic*, *pachyemous*, adjs. (Mayne 1857). **pachy'glossal** *a. Zool.* [Gr. γλῶσσα tongue], of or pertaining to the *Pachyglossæ*, lizards with short or thick fleshy tongues, or the *Pachyglossi*, a tribe of Parrots; so **pachy'glossate**. **pachy'glossous** *a.*, thick-tongued (Mayne 1857). **pachygnathous** (pə'kɪgnəθəs) *a.* [Gr. γνάθ-ος jaw], thick-jawed (*Cent. Dict.*). ‖**pachy'hæmia** [Gr. αἷμα blood], thickness of the blood; so **pachy'hæmic** *a.*, relating to pachyhæmia. **pachy'hæmous** *a.*, having thick blood (*Syd. Soc. Lex.* 1893). ‖**pachyhy'menia, pachy'menia** *Path.* [Gr. ὑμήν membrane], thickening of the skin; hence **pachy'menic, -hy'menic** *a.*, thick-skinned (Mayne 1857). ‖**pachy'losis** (also **pachu-**): see quot. **pachymeningitis** (-mɛnɪn'dʒaɪtɪs) *Path.* [MENINGITIS], inflammation of the dura mater of the central nervous system, cerebral or spinal. ‖**pachy'meninx** (-'miːnɪŋks) [Gr. μῆνιγξ membrane], the dura mater (*Syd. Soc. Lex.* 1893). **pachymeter** (pə'kɪmɪtə(r)) [-METER] (also **pacho-**), an instrument for measuring the thickness of glass, metal plates, paper, etc. **pachyodont** ('pækɪəʊdɒnt) *a.* [Gr. ὀδούς, ὀδόντ- tooth], having massive teeth. **pachy'opterous** = *pachypterous*. **pachyote** ('pækɪəʊt) *a.* [Gr. οὖς, ὠτ- ear], having thick leathery ears; *sb.*, a thick-eared bat, of genus *Pachyotus*; so **pachy'otous** *a.* (*Syd. Soc. Lex.* 1893). **pachyphyllous** (-'fɪləs) *a. Bot.* [Gr. φύλλον leaf], having thick leaves (Mayne). **pachypod** ('pækɪpɒd), **pachypodous** (pə'kɪpəʊdəs) *adjs.* [Gr. πούς, ποδ- foot], having a large thick foot. **pachypterous** (pə'kɪptərəs) *a.* [Gr. πτερόν wing, feather], having thick wings or fins, as an insect, a bat, or a fish. **pachyrhynchous** (-'rɪŋkəs) *a.* [Gr. παχύρρυγχος, f. ῥύγχος snout], having a large thick bill. **pachysaurian** (-'sɔːrɪən), a thick-skinned saurian. **pachystichous** (pə'kɪstɪkəs), *a. Bot.* [Gr. στίχ-ος row, line], thick-sided, applied only to cells (*Treas. Bot.* 1866). **pachytrichous** (-'ɪtrɪkəs), *a.* [Gr. θρίξ, τριχ- hair], having thick hair (Mayne 1857).
1878 BARTLEY tr. *Topinard's Anthrop.* v. 177 *Pachycephalic, skull with thick hypertrophied parietes. **1858** HITCHCOCK *Ichnol. Mass.* 81 We should infer a larger number of *pachydactylous than leptodactylous animals to have made the tracks. **1897** *Allbutt's Syst. Med.* IV. 832 Chronic inflammation of the mucous membrane of the larynx.. may exist with the *pachydermial affection. **1893** *Syd. Soc. Lex.*, *Pachulosis,.. Sir Erasmus Wilson's term for a skin disease in which there is hypertrophy of the epidermis. **1866** A. FLINT *Princ. Med.* (1880) 693 Acute *pachymeningitis is always suppurative, and is chiefly of surgical interest. **1899** *Allbutt's Syst. Med.* VI. 854 A certain degree of compression of the cord is caused by pachymeningitis. **1884** KNIGHT *Dict. Mech.* Suppl., *Pachymeter, a Viennese instrument which determines the thickness of paper to the 1-1000th of an inch. **1842** BRANDE *Dict. Sci.* etc., *Pachyotes,.. the name of a family of bats,.. including those which have thick external ears. **1864** WEBSTER, *Pachyote.* **1857** MAYNE *Expos. Lex.*, *Pachypodus*, .. applied by Gray to an Order [of molluscs] corresponding to the *Conchifera Crassipedes* of Lamarck: *pachypodous. **1881** FREWER tr. *Holub's 7 Yrs. S. Africa* I. 140 In the abdomen of this *pachysaurian there is found a collection of lobulated fatty matter.

pachycaul ('pækɪkɔːl), *sb.* (*a.*) *Bot.* [f. PACHY- + Gr. καυλ-ός stem, stalk.] A tree having a thick primary stem and few or no branches; also *attrib.* or as *adj.* Hence **pachy'caulous** *a.*;

'**pachycauly**, development of this type. Cf. LEPTOCAUL *sb.* and *a.*

1949 E. J. H. CORNER in *Ann. Bot.* XIII. 392 The pachycaulous Cycad. *Ibid.* 393 The old clumsy pachycaul with massive and slow-growing branches. **1954** *Phytomorphology* IV. 264/1 In general, six effects accompany the transition from pachycauly to leptocauly. **1964** E. J. H. CORNER *Life of Plants* ix. 154 'Pachycaul' (with thick primary stem) denotes massive construction as of the rosette tree or cabbage tree. *Ibid.* 155 The pachycaul plants establish themselves by robust growth. **1967** E. A. MENNINGER *Fantastic Trees* 16 (*heading*) The pachycaulous trunks. *Ibid.*, One conspicuous example of this pachycaulous curiosity today in the forests of the Ivory Coast and Nigeria is the aky tree, also called the forest papaw. Despite its enormous size.. this tree's trunk is soft, porous, and spongelike, and it is generally unbranched. It is a living relic of an ancient age. **1973** A. J. WILLIS *Introd. Plant Ecol.* v. 55 A tendency to a pachycaul habit is seen in the ash, with its pinnate leaves and thick stubby twigs. **1974** *Kew Bull.* XXIX. 535 The pachycaul Giant Lobelias are some of the most spectacular plants of the tropical African highlands. *Ibid.* 549 In herbaceous species [of giant lobelia] ..the development is similar to that of the forest pachycauls. **1974** *New Phytologist* LXXIII. 971, I propose a general hypothesis on the evolutionary trends involving pachycauly in *Senecio*. **1976** *Phil. Trans. R. Soc.* B. CCLXXIII. 359 The purpose of this account [of climbing species of *Ficus*] is to provide new evidence for the general theory of angiosperm evolution from pachycaul to leptocaul vegetation.

pachyderm ('pækɪdɜːm), *sb.* and *a.* [a. F. *pachyderme* sb. (Cuvier 1797), ad. Gr. παχύδερμ-ος thick-skinned, f. παχύ-ς thick + δέρμα skin. In a general sense, *pachuderme* adj. occurs casually in Fr. *c* 1600 (Hatz.-Darm.).]

A. *sb. Zool.* A thick-skinned quadruped; spec. one of the *Pachydermata* of Cuvier.

1838 *Penny Cycl.* XII. 415/2 That the quadruped under consideration [Hyrax] is a true Pachyderm. **1853** KANE *Grinnell Exp.* xx. (1856) 160 That marine pachyderm, the tusky walrus. **1880** HAUGHTON *Phys. Geog.* ii. 53 England was inhabited by herbivorous pachyderms.. previous to the elevation of the east and west chain.

b. *fig.* Cf. PACHYDERMATOUS 2.

1867 GARFIELD in *Century Mag.* (1884) Jan. 417/2 Like all politicians he seems to have become a pachyderm. **1894** W. T. STEAD in *Review of Rev.* (Amer. ed.) Apr. 428 To shrink from the rude shocks and jars which tough pachyderms bear with unruffled composure.

B. *adj. Zool.* = PACHYDERMATOUS *a.*

1868 *Nat. Encycl.* I. 821 *Anthracotherium*, a fossil genus of pachyderm mammals.

Hence **pachy'dermal**, **pachy'dermic**, *adjs. Zool.*

1847 ANSTED *Anc. World* ix. 197 The gigantic living pachydermal mammals, such as the elephant, rhinoceros, and hippopotamus. **1838** *Penny Cycl.* XII. 416/2 The general balance of resemblance.. is strongly in favour of the Pachydermic relationship of the animal. **1840** *Ibid.* XVII. 151/2 These and other Pachydermic forms.

‖**Pachydermata** (pækɪ'dɜːmətə), *sb. pl. Zool.* [mod.L., f. Gr. παχύ-ς thick + δέρμα, δέρματ- skin.] An order of Mammalia in Cuvier's system of classification, consisting of the hoofed or ungulate quadrupeds which do not chew the cud, as the elephant, rhinoceros, hippopotamus, hyrax, horse.

Disused by more recent zoologists; its constituents being distributed into various orders.

1823 BUCKLAND *Reliq. Diluv.* 37 It is foreign to the habits of the hyæna to prey on the larger pachydermata. **1847** YOUATT *Horse* v. 107 The horse does not ruminate, and therefore belongs to the order pachydermata.

pachy'dermatocele. *Path.* [f. as prec. + Gr. κήλη tumour.] A tumour arising from hypertrophy of the corium and subcutaneous areolar tissue.

1854 V. MOTT in *Med.-Chirurg. Trans.* Ser. II. XIX. 155 (*title*) On a peculiar form of tumour of the skin, denominated 'Pachydermatocele'. **1900** *Lancet* 2 June 1593/2.

pachy'dermatoid, *a.* [See -OID.] Akin to the *Pachydermata*.

1882 in OGILVIE.

pachydermatous (pækɪ'dɜːmətəs), *a.* [f. PACHYDERMATA + -OUS.]

1. Of or belonging to the *Pachydermata*.

1823 BUCKLAND *Reliq. Diluv.* 18 Teeth of the larger pachydermatous animals are not abundant. **1874** WOOD *Nat. Hist.* 245 The last on the list of the pachydermatous animals is the well-known Hippopotamus, or River Horse.

2. *fig.* Thick-skinned; not sensitive to rebuff, ridicule, or abuse; not easily affected by outside influences.

1854 LOWELL *Keats* Prose Wks. 1890 I. 229 A man cannot have a sensuous nature and be pachydermatous at the same time. *a* **1876** M. COLLINS *Th. in Garden* (1880) II. 299, I doubt whether the poet might not find better employment than lashing pachydermatous fools.

Hence **pachy'dermatously** *adv.*, **pachy'derm-atousness**.

1854 WOOD *Anim. Life* (1855) 367 [An animal] of whose pachydermatousness, if we may coin such a word, there is no doubt. This is the Giraffe, whose hide is more than an inch in thickness. **1865** MORLEY *Mod. Characteristics* 35 The conditions of social and intellectual pachydermatousness are in themselves equally wonderful. **1900** *Westm. Gaz.* 1 Oct. 11/3 By being able pachydermatously to withstand the protests to which we have referred.

pachydermia, -dermial: see PACHY-.

pachy'dermoid, *a.* = PACHYDERMATOID.

1856 KANE *Arct. Expl.* II. i. 16 The frost-tempered junks of this pachydermoid amphibian [walrus]. **1877** LE CONTE *Elem. Geol.* III. (1879) 547 The Diprotodon..a pachydermoid Kangaroo as big as a rhinoceros.

pachydermous (pækɪ'dɜːməs), *a. rare.* [f. as PACHYDERM + -OUS.] Thick-skinned, pachydermatous. **b.** *Bot.* Thick-coated.

1836 *Encycl. Brit.* (ed. 7) XIV. 146/2 The removal of the genus Equus.. would enable us to simplify our definition of the pachydermous tribes.

pachyglossal to **pachymeter**: see PACHY-.

pachyntic (pæ'kɪntɪk), *a. Med.* [ad. Gr. παχυντικ-ός of thickening quality, f. παχύν-ειν to thicken.] **a.** Having the power of thickening the bodily fluids. **b.** Fleshy, fat.

1704 J. HARRIS *Lex. Techn.* I, *Pachuntick* Medicines. **1890** BILLINGS *Nat. Med. Dict.* **1893** *Syd. Soc. Lex.*

pachyodont to **pachytrichous**: see PACHY-.

pachysandra (,pækɪ'sændrə). [mod.L. (A. Michaux *Flora Boreali-Americana* (1803) II. 177), f. Gr. παχύς thick + ἀνήρ, ἀνδρό-ς male, in reference to the thick stamens of the male flowers.] A small evergreen subshrub of the genus so called, belonging to the family Buxaceæ, native to eastern North America or eastern Asia, and bearing white or pinkish-white flowers.

1813 W. T. AITON *Hortus Kewensis* (ed. 2) V. 260 Trailing Pachysandra. Nat[ive] of North America. Intro[duced] 1800, by Messrs. Fraser. **1818** *Curtis's Bot. Mag.* XLV. 1964 Trailing Pachysandra... Pachysandra was first described in Michaux's Flora of North-America, and received its name from the remarkable thickness of its stamens. It has very little beauty to recommend it to the flower-garden; but the curious Botanist will regard it with some interest. **1914** W. J. BEAN *Trees & Shrubs Hardy in Brit. Isles* II. 118 The Pachysandras thrive in any moist soil, and do not mind shade; they make neat tufts, but are of only moderate decorative value. **1941** R. S. WALKER *Lookout* 52 Pachysandra, or mountain spurge, blooms in March and April in the rich soil in Lookout Mountain woods. **1961** *Amat. Gardening* 18 Nov. 1/1 The pachysandra is..one of those borderline plants that are half shrub half herbaceous perennial. **1975** *New Yorker* 23 June 38/3 Both laughing, he supervised John's spitting out the lettuce and paper and tobacco into the pachysandra.

pachytene ('pækɪtiːn). *Cytology.* [ad. F. *pachytène* (H. von Winiwarter 1900, in *Arch. de Biol.* XVII. I. 63): see PACHY- and -TENE.] The third stage of the first meiotic prophase, following zygotene, during which the paired chromosomes shorten and thicken, the two chromatids of each separate, and exchange of segments between chromatids may occur.

[**1900** *Jrnl. R. Microsc. Soc.* 654 As the chromatic thread spreads itself again through the nuclear space, this duality disappears, and the thread is single, thick, and moniliform (pachytænic stage).] **1912** *Jrnl. Exper. Zool.* XIII. 378 All the threads still stain deeply and are very much thicker than in the leptotene-stage; hence these nuclei may be called the pachytene-nuclei. **1932** *Proc. 6th Internat. Congr. Genetics* I. 257 It is assumed that every chiasma represents a crossover which has occurred between two of the four chromatids at pachytene. **1965** BELL & COOMBE tr. *Strasburger's Textbk. Bot.* 34 In pachytene the pairing of homologous chromosomes is completed. **1974** *Cytogenetics & Cell Genetics* XIII. 330 Breakdown of spermatogenesis at the pachytene stage of meiotic prophase was observed in most germ cells.

pachytic (pæ'kɪtɪk), *a. Med.* [f. Gr. παχύτ-ης thickness + -IC.] = PACHYODONT.

1857 MAYNE *Expos. Lex.*, *Pachyticus*,.. of or belonging to *Pachytes*: pachytic. **1890** J. S. BILLINGS *Nat. Med. Dict.* II. 276 Pachytic..1 Thick, obese, 2 Pachyntic.

paci, obs. inf. of PASS *v.*

paciable, -ibil, obs. forms of PEACEABLE.

pacience, -ent, etc., obs. ff. PATIENCE, -ENT.

pacifarin (pæ'sɪfərɪn). *Med.* [f. L. *pācif(ic)ār-e* to make peace + -IN[1].] Any biologically produced substance which, when introduced into an organism, protects it from the harmful effects of an infection without killing the pathogen.

1963 H. A. SCHNEIDER in *Proc. Amer. Philos. Soc.* CVII. 445/2 As a new and third category of ecological ectocrines, which already embraces vitamins and antibiotics, we add as the first example of its class the substance I have described above, and name the class 'pacifarins' from the Latin verb 'pacificare', to make peace, to pacify. (I wish to thank my colleague, Dr. Ludwig Edelstein, for guiding me in this choice.) The particular pacifarin, the salmonellosis pacifarin, is, we believe, addressed only to the typhoid diseases, and for other diseases there are, we postulate, other pacifarins waiting to be identified. **1967** *Daily Tel.* 10 May 14/6 The basis of the discovery is that a microscopic amount of pacifarin extracted from wheat and dried egg-white will protect mice against infection by salmonella. **1975** *Infection & Immunity* XI. 69/2 Certain bacterial products other than enterobactin are also now known to possess pacifarin activity.

†**pa'ciferous**, *a. Obs.* [f. L. *pācifer* peace-bringing + -OUS.] Peace-bringing. Hence †**pa'ciferousness**.

1656 BLOUNT *Glossogr.*, *Paciferous*. **1727** BAILEY vol. II, *Paciferousness*,.. peace bringing quality.

pacifiable ('pæsɪfaɪəb(ə)l), *a.* [f. PACIFY + -ABLE.] Capable of being pacified or appeased.

1618 T. ADAMS *Fool & his Sport* Wks. 1861 I. 251 The conscience.. is not pacifiable whiles sin is within to vex it.

pacific (pə'sɪfɪk), *a.* and *sb.* [ad. L. *pācific-us* peace-making, peaceful, f. *pāx*, *pāc-em* peace; see -FIC: perh. through F. *pacifique*, *-ficque* (15th c. in Godef. *Compl.*).]

A. *adj.* **1.** Making, or tending to the making of, peace; leading to peace or reconciliation; conciliatory, appeasing.

a **1548** HALL *Chron.*, *Edw. IV* 248 b, Sore lamentyng.. that I did not performe and finally consumate, suche pollitique diuises..in my long life and paciffique prosperitie. **1581** MULCASTER *Positions* xxxix. (1887) 214 He appointed the pacificque, and friendly Embassages. **1667** MILTON *P.L.* XI. 860 An Olive leafe he brings, pacific signe. **1786** W. THOMSON *Watson's Philip III* (1839) 275 The marquis of Spinola..had strenuously supported the pacific counsels of Prince Albert at the court of Madrid. **1855** MILMAN *Lat. Chr.* III. vii. (1864) II. 135 The pacific influence which Gregory obtained in this momentous crisis.

2. a. Of peaceful disposition or character, not belligerent, peaceable.

1641 J. JACKSON *True Evang. T.* III. 189 See whether is more pacifique and charitable, and by consequent whether is the more Euangelicall. **1751** JOHNSON *Rambler* No. 185 ¶ 10 This pacifick and harmless temper. **1774** J. ADAMS in *Fam. Lett.* (1876) 40, I saw the tears gush into the eyes of the old grave pacific Quakers. **1879** DIXON *Windsor* II. xii. 132 In the end he brought them to a more pacific view.

b. = PEACEFUL *a.* 4.

1906 *Chambers's Jrnl.* Jan. 61/2 It is by their mastery of the policy of 'pacific penetration' that the Chinese make themselves such formidable neighbours.

3. a. Characterized by peace or calm, peaceful, at peace; calm, tranquil, quiet.

1633 T. JAMES *Voy.* lv, Pacificke and open Seas. **1865** CARLYLE *Fredk. Gt.* XVIII. xii. (1872) VIII. 26 The road has hitherto been mainly pacific.

b. ***Pacific Ocean***, ***Sea***, the 'Great Ocean' stretching between America on the east and Asia on the west; so called by Magellan, because found to be relatively free from violent storms.

[**1555** EDEN *Decades* 220 The sayde sea cauled *Pacificum* that is peaceable.] **1660** F. BROOKE tr. *Le Blanc's Trav.* 332 The great pacifick gulph, which may be said one of the calmest Seas of the world. **1777** ROBERTSON *Hist. Amer.* v. Wks. 1826, VI. 19 They enjoyed an uninterrupted course of fair weather, with such favourable winds, that Magellan bestow'd on that ocean the name of Pacific.

4. phr. ***pacific blockade*** (see quots.). ***pacific iron***, 'an iron band round a lower yard-arm into which the boom-iron screws' (*Cent. Dict.* 1890). †***pacific letters*** (also ***letters pacifical*** = L. *literæ pacificæ*, Gr. ἐπιστολαὶ εἰρηνικαί), orig. letters of commendation to the church in another city or country recommending the bearer as one in peace and communion with the Church; later, esp. letters recommending the bearer to the alms of the faithful.

1709 J. JOHNSON *Clergym. Vade M.* II. 85 Let no foreigner be received without pacifick letters. *Note. Pacifick Letters* were those given to any whether bishop, clergyman, or layman on any occasion he had to travel to another city. **1725** tr. *Dupin's Eccl. Hist. 17th C.* I. v. II. 69 By Letters pacifick, we understand, those which the Bishops gave to the Poor who were unjustly oppress'd or had need of Relief. **1880** *Encycl. Brit.* XIII. 194/1 The right of 'pacific blockade', *i.e.*, the blockade of ports belonging to a nation with which we profess not to be at war, has been asserted in a few doubtful instances. **1889** A. C. BOYD *Wheaton's Elem. Internat. Law* (rev. ed.) IV. i. 404 The above-mentioned proceedings against Greece and Brazil furnish instances of what is called 'pacific blockade'; the blockading power blockading the coast, or a certain portion of the coast, of the blockaded power, but declaring, at the same time, that a state of peace is maintained. **1895** T. A. WALKER *Man. Public Internat. Law* II. iv. 96 Pacific blockade consists in the cutting off by one state of communication with the ports or a particular portion of coast of another, otherwise than in the case of declared war, with the object of preventing commercial relations by sea. **1935** T. A. TARACOUZIO *Soviet Union & Internat. Law* x. 299 Another form of redress to which nations sometimes resort, and which is yet not considered war, is pacific blockade.

B. *sb.*

†**1. a.** *pl.* Peace-offerings [rendering L. *pācifica*.] **b.** An offer or overture of peace, an Eirenicon. *Obs.*

1609 BIBLE (Douay) *Ezek.* xlv. 15 One ramme of a flocke of two hundred..for holocaust, and for pacifiques. **1687** *Let. from Country* 10 If..she persists obstinately to refuse this national Paciffick; the Dissenters, I hope, will consider their honest Interest.

2. a. The Pacific Ocean.

a **1821** KEATS *Sonn.*, *On first looking into Chapman's Homer* 12 Like stout Cortez, when with eagle eyes He stared at the Pacific. **1855** MAURY *Phys. Geog. Sea* §54 The Atlantic is the most stormy sea in the world, the Pacific the most tranquil. **1894** *Westm. Gaz.* 4 Dec. 8/1 Because Keats made a mistake, is the real discoverer to be defrauded to all time? The Pacific was discovered September 26, 1513, by Vasco Nuñez de Balboa.

b. *attrib.* 'of the Pacific Ocean', as *Pacific coast, coaster, Northwest, seaboard, slope, state, style.* Comb., as *Pacificwards.* **Pacific slope,** (*a*) (see quot. 1902[1]); hence *Pacific sloper*; (*b*) an escape across the Pacific Ocean to avoid arrest (chiefly *Austral.* and *N.Z. slang*); **Pacific time,** time as reckoned on the 120th meridian west of Greenwich.

1855 MAURY *Phys. Geog. Sea* §276 The great chain [of mountains] that skirts the Pacific coast. **1872** R. G. MCCLELLAN *Golden State* xxxi. 523 The Pacific coast.. contains an area equal to one-half of the whole territory of the Republic of America. **1948** *Denison* (Texas) *Herald* 2 July 12/2 The most valuable fish is the Pacific Coast salmon. **1970** J. H. PATERSON *N. Amer.* (ed. 4) xix. 287/1 Like other Pacific coast cities, it has a small steel output, based on scrap. **1883** *Harper's Mag.* Nov. 943/1 [The completion of the Union Central route has not] given the 'boost' to California that the 'Pacific coasters' so fondly dreamed of. **1855** MAURY *Phys. Geog. Sea* §283 On the Pacific [Aleutian] islands there is an uninterrupted rain-fall during the entire winter. **1889** *Wealth & Resources of Oregon & Washington* (Union Pacific Railway Co.) 3 The resources and industries of the Pacific Northwest are so varied.. as to not only suggest but enforce its consideration in sections. **1938** G. CASH *I like Brit. Columbia* 100 The Provincial Library at the Parliament Buildings is quite one of the most interesting in the Pacific Northwest. **1977** *Time* 12 Dec. 61/3 They take the armchair beachcomber on a scenic tour.. past the cypresses of Monterey and the great coastal forests of the Pacific Northwest to the fog-shrouded Aleutians. **1838** *Knickerbocker* June 556 Where the prairie stretches away.. shall sweep the long, hissing train of cars, crowded with passengers for the Pacific seaboard. **1845** J. C. FRÉMONT *Rep. Exploring Expedition* 274 [We were] now about to turn the back upon the Pacific slope of our continent. **1855** MAURY *Phys. Geog. Sea* §355 The dry season on the Pacific slopes. **1901** HALL & OSBORNE *Sunshine & Surf* 38 There is such a thing known in Australia, America, and Canada as 'the Pacific slope', which, being interpreted, means a hurried departure, down to these regions [*sc.* Tahiti] of gentlemen who find these countries too hot to hold them. **1902** WEBSTER, *Pacific slope,* that part of North America.. lying west of the continental divide. **1902** W. S. WALKER *Zealandia's Guerdon* 292 Perhaps he [*sc.* the missing man] accomplished the 'Pacific Slope'. *Ibid.* 326 He [*sc.* the detective] has packed so many 'confidence men' off to penitentiary that the others have done the 'Pacific Slope' in various directions, chiefly towards Australia. **1915** H. B. NIVER *Elem. Geogr.* 167/1 By means of irrigation, the Pacific Slope has become one of the greatest fruit-growing sections of the world. **1938** R. GILKISON *Early Days in Dunedin* xiii. 133 In the 'seventies and 'eighties many fraudulent debtors, embezzlers and rich thieves escaped from New Zealand before arrest, by doing what came to be known as the 'Pacific Slope'. **1945** BAKER *Austral. Lang.* xiv. 243 *Eucalyptian, the Pacific slope,..* and *tiersman,* are not so important to our language that we could not do without them. Yet we would tend to class these as standard. **1954** E. GUNTHER in Freeman & Martin *Pacific Northwest* (ed. 2) 16 Salmon runs occur in all streams in the Pacific slope. **1876** *Benton Democrat* (Corvallis, Oregon) 18 Aug. 2/3 (*heading*) Pacific slopers. **1883** *Harper's Mag.* Mar. 648/1 'Well,' said the Pacific sloper, 'if it's a private funeral, what do they call it a reception for?' **1820** W. TUDOR *Lett. on Eastern States* 57 When the future Pacific states come to be represented in congress. **1949** *Los Angeles Times* 6 Nov. 1/8 The overall increase for Pacific States is 5,251,000 or 53·9%. **1976** *National Observer* (U.S.) 2 Oct. 1/2, 16 South Atlantic and South Central states got back $11.5 billion more than they paid in taxes. Thirteen Pacific and Mountain states came out $10.6 billion ahead. **1959** *Wall St. Jrnl.* 13 July 1/4 Increasing numbers of home builders.. are experimenting with the new style, often called.. 'Pacific style'. **1883** *N.Y. Herald* 18 Nov. 12/3 In the United States the standards will be known as the 'Eastern', 'Central', 'Mountain' and 'Pacific' times. **1958** 'CASTLE' & 'HAILEY' *Flight into Danger* ii. 36 'How soon do you expect to land?' 'About five a.m., Pacific Time.' **1976** *National Observer* (U.S.) 7 Aug. 16/1 Broadcast times apply to Eastern and Pacific time zones. **1897** *Daily News* 30 Dec. 6/5 Russia's progress Pacificwards.

c. Used to designate a type of steam locomotive with a 4-6-2 wheel arrangement designed to pull express passenger and freight trains; also *absol.*

1903 *Amer. Engineer & Railroad Jrnl.* Oct. 351 (*caption*) Pacific-4-6-2 Type Passenger Locomotive—Chicago, Rock Island and Pacific Railway. **1905** *Railroad Gaz.* 9 June 620/1 (*heading*) Pacific locomotive with superheater for the Erie Railroad. **1908** *Westm. Gaz.* 31 Dec. 3/1 The most interesting locomotive novelty of the year was the Great Western Company's 'Pacific' type of express engine. **1910** *Ibid.* 25 Jan. 2/1 French railways.. built their first 'Pacific' not long before ours, and this season most of the 'Riviera' expresses will be horsed by these vast machines. **1938** L. M. BEEBE *High Iron* iii. 97 The most important U.S.R.A. designs, for present purposes, fall into four wheel arrangements: the 4-6-2 or Pacific, the 4-8-2 or Mountain, the 2-8-2 or Mikado, and the 2-10-2 or Santa Fe types. **1972** B. C. BLANTON *400,000 Miles by Rail* iii. 37/1 The last major rail trip I took with my parents was in November, 1910. Our route was over the Katy's rails to St. Louis. The *Katy Flyer* was now headed by a Pacific locomotive. *Ibid.,* The *Royal Blue* was advertised as a solid-vestibuled train... It was headed by a Pacific and carried a Pullman parlor-observation car with open platform. **1978** *Observer* 26 Mar. 2/5 'Swanage'.. was built in 1950 and died in 1964. It is a 4-6-2 Pacific type.

Hence **pa'cificness** (Bailey vol. II, 1727).

†**pa'cificable,** *a. Obs.* [f. L. *pācificā-re* to pacify + -BLE.] = PACIFIABLE.

1621 BP. HALL *Heaven upon Earth* §4 The conscience is not pacificable, while sinne is within to vex it.

pacifical (pəˈsɪfɪkəl), *a.* [f. L. *pācific-us* (see PACIFIC) + -AL[1].] Of pacific or peaceful nature; peaceable. *letters pacifical*: see PACIFIC *a.* 4.

c **1485** *Digby Myst.* (1882) III. 1593 Bed hyr axke of his good be weyys pacyfycal. **1609** *Ev. Woman in Hum.* I. i. in Bullen *O. Pl.* IV, Sir, be pacificall, the fellowe was possest with some critique frenzie. **1876** G. MEREDITH *Beauch. Career* I. xiii. 197 He had to think of what was due to his pacifical disposition. **1883** *Canons of Antioch* vii. in Fulton *Index Canonum* 237 No stranger shall be received without letters pacifical.

pa'cifically, *adv.* [f. prec. + -LY[2].] In a pacific manner; peacefully, peaceably.

1793 *Residence in France* (1797) I. 231 A few dragoons have arranged the business very pacifically. **1865** CARLYLE *Fredk. Gt.* IV. x. (1872) II. 33 Friedrich Wilhelm's first step, of course, was to remonstrate pacifically.

pacificate (pəˈsɪfɪkeɪt). *v.* [f. L. *pācificāt-*, ppl. stem of *pācificāre* to make peace, to pacify.]

†**1.** *intr.* To make peace (*with*). *Obs. rare.*

1646 *Unhappy Game at Scotch & Eng.* 22 What is this other then to pacificate with him without their joynt advice and consent?

2. *trans.* To give peace to, to pacify.

1827 SOUTHEY *Hist. Penins. War* II. 388 He would now pacificate Roncal and the vallies of Aragon. **1865** CARLYLE *Fredk. Gt.* XIV. v. (1872) V. 222 There is one ready method of pacificating Germany. **1884** SIR C. WARREN *Memorandum on Bechuanaland* 29 Oct., The object.. is to remove the filibusters from Bechuanaland, to pacificate the territory.

Hence **pa'cificated** *ppl. a.*

1885 *Manch. Exam.* 14 Feb. 5/1 To make it [Khartoum] the capital of a pacificated or subjugated Soudan.

pacification (ˌpæsɪfɪˈkeɪʃən). [a. F. *pacification* (15th c. in Hatz.-Darm.), ad. L. *pācificātiōnem*, n. of action from *pācificāre* to pacify.] **a.** The action or fact of pacifying or appeasing; the condition of being pacified; appeasement, conciliation. spec. *U.S.*, a process or operation (usu. a military operation) designed to secure the peaceful cooperation of a population or an area where one's enemies are thought to be active.

Edict of Pacification, an ordinance or decree enacted by a prince or state to put an end to strife or discontent; esp. in *French hist.*, one of the royal edicts in the 16th century granting concessions to the Protestants; e.g. those issued in 1563, 1570, and the Edict of Nantes in 1598.

1490 CAXTON *Eneydos* xxi. 77 That the swete wyndes shalle putte hemselfe vp in pacifycacion of the see. *a* **1548** HALL *Chron., Hen. VI* 158 To begyn a shorte pacificacion in so long a broyle. **1573** E. VARAMUND *Rep. Outrages France* in *Harl. Misc.* (Malh.) I, The King.. gave his faith, that he would for ever most sacredly and faithfully observe his edict of pacification. **1615** BP. HALL *Contempl., O.T.* IX. vii, His pacification of friends [was] better than his execution of enemies. **1726** PENHALLOW *Ind. Wars* (1859) 66 They went into the Fort.. professing their desire for a pacification. **1881** SHORTHOUSE *J. Inglesant* I. xiv. 204 [This] had much helped towards the pacification of his mind. **1946** 'G. ORWELL' in *Horizon* XIII. 76 Defenceless villages are bombarded from the air, the inhabitants driven out into the countryside, the cattle machine-gunned, the huts set on fire with incendiary bullets: this is called *pacification.* **1966** *N.Y. Rev. Bks.* 3 Mar. 4/3 It would be wrong to predict a priori that President Johnson's new 'counter-insurgency' and 'pacification' programs, based on plans for economic and social development in the Southern villages, will fail as totally as did the quite similar plans sponsored by the French and later by the Diem regime. **1967** *New Yorker* 14 Oct. 55 For God's sake, Hinton! You mean all this time I've been talking about pacification you thought I meant *peace?* **1969** A. G. FRANK *Latin Amer.* xxv. 401 The latest effort, for instance, is to have the Latin American military occupation forces improve their reputation in the countryside by undertaking Latin American versions of the imperialist 'pacification' program in Vietnam. **1969** *Listener* 12 June 814/2 US civilians are busy with pacification programmes to make the peasants more hostile to communism and more loyal to Saigon. **1974** *Black Panther* 16 Mar. 2/3 This prison we're in is a military camp and it has the most propagandist and pacification program in all the camps in America. **1974** *Encycl. Brit. Macropædia* XIII. 847/1 The formula that peace is the aim of war.. has time and again been expressed in the paradoxical concept of pacification, which means exactly those violent actions through which an expanded area of peace shall be won and maintained.

b. A treaty of peace.

1560 DAUS tr. *Sleidane's Comm.* 458 b, In the meane season the pacification of Passawe to remayne in full strength. **1655** G. LANE in *Nicholas Papers* (Camden) III. 225 They haue made noe provision for their reception in the pacification. **1874** GREEN *Short Hist.* viii. §5. 516 The pacification at Berwick was a mere suspension of arms. **1874** STUBBS *Const. Hist.* I. xii. 522 The pacification was arranged on the 15th of May.

pacificator (pəˈsɪfɪkeɪtə(r)). [a. L. *pācificātor*, agent-n. from *pācificāre* to pacify. Cf. F. *pacificateur* (*c* 1500 in Godef. *Compl.*).] One who pacifies or brings to a state of peace; a peace-maker.

1539 CROMWELL in Merriman *Life & Lett.* (1902) II. 203 His highnes remitteth the conclusyon of thair affaires with any Ambassadours or pacificatours there. **1622** BACON *Hen. VII* 50 He had in consideration the point of honour, in bearing the blessed person of a pacificator. **1750** H. WALPOLE *Lett. H. Mann* (1834) II. 359 As he is a good pacificator.. we may want his assistance at home before the end of the winter. **1847** LEWES *Hist. Philos.* (1867) I. 25 Greece.. drawn into the contest as pacificator and arbiter. **1907** G. B. SHAW *Let.* 10 June (1972) II. 692, I.. have just created a scandal among the German pacificators by informing the leading Viennese newspaper that I consider disarmament.. absurd. **1968** *Daily Tel.* (Colour Suppl.) 13 Dec. 43/4 Drink, in other words, is becoming the opium of the people: the great pacificator.

pacificatory (pəˈsɪfɪkətərɪ), *a.* [ad. L. *pācificātōri-us*, f. *pācificātor*: see prec. and -ORY.] Tending to make peace.

pacificatory letters = *letters pacifical.*

1583 FOXE *A. & M.* 2154/2 Whervpon a certeine agreement pacificatory was concluded betwene them. **1659** HAMMOND *On Ps.* cxx. 7 Paraphr. 627 My words be never so friendly and pacificatory. *a* **1677** BARROW *Unity of Ch.* ix. Wks. 1831 VII. 497 All churches did maintain intercourse and commerce with each other by.. pacificatory, commendatory, synodical epistles. **1893** *Times* 27 Dec. 3/2 It will maintain in its political tendencies a pacificatory policy.

Hence **pa'cificatoriness** (Bailey vol. II, 1727).

pacificism (pæˈsɪfɪsɪz(ə)m). [f. PACIFIC *a.* + -ISM.] **a.** Rejection of war and violence as a matter of principle; = PACIFISM. **b.** Advocacy of a peaceful policy; rejection of war in a particular instance.

As an ideological term PACIFISM (infuenced by Fr. *pacifisme*) is now the preferred form.

1910 W. JAMES *Mem. & Stud.* (1911) xi. 283 Pacificism makes no converts from the military party. **1912** *Q. Rev.* July 203 With the old Pacificism, the Pacificism of the Quakers, of Tolstoi, and of all those who hold that war must not be tolerated.. the world has long been familiar. **1916** G. G. COULTON (*title*) The main illusions of pacificism. **1920** *Q. Rev.* Oct. 396 The revolution [in Japan, 1868].. was a reaction against these centuries of pacificism. **1936** F. M. FORD *Let.* 20 Aug. (1965) 254, I am just on the verge of litigation with the Oxford University Press over modifications they have arbitrarily made in my pacificisms quasi-communism and other outrages that they have committed. **1957** A. J. P. TAYLOR *Trouble Makers* ii. 51 By 'pacificism' I mean the advocacy of a peaceful policy; by 'pacifism' (a word invented only in the twentieth century) the doctrine of non-resistance. **1978** J. MEYERS *Katherine Mansfield* x. 131 Weekends [with Lady Ottoline Morrell].. were characterized by high spirits and high-mindedness, pacificism, poetry and all that was ultra-modern in the arts.

pacificist (pæˈsɪfɪsɪst). [f. as prec. + -IST.]

a. One who rejects war and violence as a matter of principle; = PACIFIST *sb.* **b.** One who advocates a peaceful policy as the first and best resort (see prec., sense b). Also *attrib.* or as *adj.*

In sense a PACIFIST (influenced by Fr. *pacifiste*) is now the preferred form.

1907 *Westm. Gaz.* 2 Apr. 2/2 We have.. a picture of Germany going to war in order 'to demonstrate the futility of the dreams of the Pacificists'. **1908** *Ibid.* 4 June 5/1 It is not sufficient to simply call him 'Pacificist' to prevent him denouncing these follies anew. **1910** W. JAMES *Mem. & Stud.* (1911) xi. 275 In my remarks, pacificist though I am, I will refuse to speak of the bestial side of the war-*régime*.. and consider only the higher aspects of militaristic sentiment. **1910** [see *milk-blooded* s.v. MILK *sb.* 10]. **1912** *Q. Rev.* July 204 To make war impossible, the older Pacificists appealed to the heart and soul of man; the new Pacificists make their appeal to his pocket. *Ibid.* 217 In places he draws the usual Pacificist conclusion. **1919** J. BUCHAN *Mr. Standfast* i. 21 It was bad enough for anyone to have to pose as a pacificist, but for me, as strong as a bull and as sunburnt as a gipsy and not looking my forty years, it was a black disgrace. *Ibid.* 35 You were bidden.. turn yourself from a successful general into a pacificist South African engineer. **1923** *Blackw. Mag.* June 822/2 These people are instinctive pacificists. **1923** R. MACAULAY *Told by Idiot* III. iv. 192 Stanley was in these days a stop-the-war, pacificist Little Englander, anti-militarist, anti-Chamberlain, anti-Concentration Camp. **1965** D. A. MARTIN *Pacifism* v. 73 The dissenting opposition to war discussed here is *pacificist* not pacifist. The dissenters did not hold that war was always wrong but that it should be avoided wherever humanly possible. **1966** *New Statesman* 3 June 815/2 We are all ..'Pacificists'—that is, we believe that war should be avoided wherever humanly possible.

paci'ficity. *rare.* [f. PACIFIC + -ITY.] The quality of being pacific, pacific character.

1800 W. TAYLOR in Robberds *Mem.* (1843) I. 356 We are ..trusting with the old confidence in Mr. Pitt's pacificity.

pacifico (pæˈsɪfɪkəʊ). [Sp.] A person of pacific or peaceful character, *spec.* a native of Cuba or the Philippines who submitted without active opposition to Spanish occupation.

1897 R. H. DAVIS *Cuba in War Time* 41 His [*sc.* General Weyler's] object.. was to prevent the pacificos from giving help to the insurgents. **1898** *Harper's Weekly* 19 Feb. 174/2 The pacificos who are in the fields supply the food for the army [*sc.* the insurgents in Cuba, February, 1898] and are under military supervision. **1905** A. G. ROBINSON *Cuba & Intervention* iii. 35 These became known as the *Pacificos.* **1916** G. B. SHAW in *To-day* 13 May 38/2 One who accidentally tackled Mr Ponsonby, and, miscalculating the mettle of the true British Pacifico, had his head heartily punched for his pains.

†**pa'cificous,** *a. Obs.* [See -OUS.] = PACIFIC.

1608 J. KING *Serm.* 24 Mar. 20 Salomon the pacificus, king of Salem, prince of peace. **1611** COTGR., *Pacifique*,.. pacificous. *a* **1670** HACKET *Abp. Williams* I. (1692) 79 Such as were transported with Warmth to be a fighting, prevail'd in Number, before the Pacificous.

pacifier (ˈpæsɪfaɪə(r)). [f. PACIFY + -ER[1].]

1. One who or that which pacifies or appeases.

1533 MORE *Apol.* xiii. 94 Yf this pacyfyer of this dyuysyon wyl say that this is nothing lyke the present mater. **1748** RICHARDSON *Clarissa* (1811) III. xxxii. 191 It looks as if he withheld them for occasional pacifiers. **1846** TRENCH *Mirac.* v. (1862) 169 The pacifier of the tumults and the discords in the outward world. **1956** H. GOLD *Man who was not with It* (1965) ii. 12 Telling *as if*, secure in morphine or other pacifiers,..we found in the show that forgotten moral thickness for which so many of us were sick. **1969** *Daily Tel.* 10 Nov. 2 By 1990 most of us..will be taking synthetic mood modifiers, pacifiers and general comforters.

2. A baby's dummy. *U.S.*

1904 F. CRISSEY *Tattlings Retired Politician* 367, I put away my teething ring and baby 'pacifier' several years ago. **1949** M. MEAD *Male & Female* xiii. 271 The very modern pediatrician may recommend a pacifier—the same old pacifier that still lingers on the back-street, in the little.. drug stores. **1960** *Encounter* Mar. 19/2 Minnie Foote's baby got held up to see and dropped his pacifier in the box. **1963** M. MCCARTHY *Group* xiv. 321 Norine removed the pacifier from the baby's mouth. **1976** *Billings* (Montana) *Gaz.* 4 July 5-A/3 The government has closed the books on a case that started with the choking death of a five-month-old boy and ended with the recall of more than 100,000 baby pacifiers.

pacifism ('pæsɪfɪz(ə)m). [ad. F. *pacifisme* (see quot. 1902): see -ISM, PACIFICISM.] The policy or doctrine of rejecting war and every form of violent action as means of solving disputes, esp. in international affairs; the belief in and advocacy of peaceful methods as feasible and desirable alternatives to war.

1902 *Proc. 10th Universal Peace Congr.* 74 M. Emile Arnaud... Speaking at length, in French,..said:... The negative programme of Pacifism is anti-War-ism. **1906** *Times* 30 July 5/4 It can bring its naval policy into harmony with its foreign policy and give pledges to 'pacifism'. **1915** *National Rev.* Mar. 54 The greatest war in history is now being fought in the cause of Pacifism. **1917** *Atlantic Monthly* June 745/2 To such people pacifism is a religion, an interpretation of Christianity. **1919** G. B. SHAW *Heartbreak House* p. xviii, There was only one virtue, pugnacity: only one vice, pacifism. That is an essential condition of war. **1929** CHESTERTON *Thing* 111 Nothing that I say here has any connection with what is commonly called pacifism. I think that our friends and brethren fell ten years ago in a just war. **1935** *Fellowship* Mar. 3/1 Pacifism does not renounce the struggle, but carries it on with the more effective weapons of non-violence. **1936** A. HUXLEY in G. K. Hibbert *New Pacifism* ii. 39 Humanism was once a favourable environment for pacifism. It has now become wholly inimical. **1937** P. S. MUMFORD *Introd. Pacifism* i. 10 Pacifism is not simply a negative policy of refusing to fight. It is a constructive policy of showing that there are more powerful and better ways of opposing your enemies. **1941** A. HUXLEY *Let.* 17 Nov. (1969) 470 In war time, it would seem, psychological conditions are such that the application of pacifism to politics is for all practical purposes impossible. **1945** G. C. FIELD *Pacifism & Conscientious Objection* 4 Pacifism..is not one single, simple creed, but a number of creeds. **1955** *Bull. Atomic Sci.* Sept. 265 If armaments are not acceptable to the pacifist, does this mean that he will submit to the aggressor and meekly resign himself to what he considers evil? The answer is emphatically no. This is to confuse pacifism with appeasement. The pacifist is definitely not a passivist. **1957** A. J. P. TAYLOR *Trouble Makers* ii. 51 Even Bright, who was sometimes nearer to pacifism, did not plead 'that this country should remain without adequate and scientific means of defence'. **1964** GOULD & KOLB *Dict. Social Sci.* 481/2 Pacifism has never yet been adopted as official policy by any state. **1976** *Pacifist* Jan. 10/1 It is an integral part of pacifism not only to expect one's own freedom but also to allow everybody else *their* freedom. **1976** *Christian Cent.* 15 Sept. 753/2 Most American evangelicals have been less than enthusiastic about pacifism.

pacifist ('pæsɪfɪst), *sb.* and *a.* [ad. F. *pacifiste*: see -IST, PACIFICIST.] **A.** *sb.* A proponent or advocate of pacifism; one who believes in resort to peaceful alternatives to war as means of settling disputes. Also in Comb., as *pacifist-minded* adj.

1906 *Times* 30 July 5/4 The French 'Pacifists' will appeal to England's example in order to induce France also to cut down her naval programme. **1907** *Academy* 2 Mar. 204/2 In 1890 he [*sc.* Carducci] wrote on 'War' an ode that passionately condemned the Pacifists. **1917** *Atlantic Monthly* June 748/1 My friend is a pacifist because he dreads the tantalizing consequences upon himself of resisting aggression by violent physical methods. **1929** CHESTERTON *Thing* 133 One does not need to be a pacifist to think that gunpowder need hardly go on being useful on quite such a grand scale. **1930** W. S. CHURCHILL *My Early Life* xxvi. 346, I have always been against the Pacifists during the quarrel, and against the Jingoes at its close. **1930** *Sun* (Baltimore) 30 Dec. 7/3 Most people like to have their soldiers represented as brave... But not these German pacifists and defeatists. **1936** A. HUXLEY *Let.* 2 Mar. (1969) 401 What the pacifist suggests is the eminently reasonable course of using intelligent generosity to begin with—rather than waiting to use it till the evil act has been committed. **1937** P. S. MUMFORD *Introd. Pacifism* ii. 15 The Pacifist believes: 1. That war, *i.e.* mass murder, as a political policy is morally wrong, and consequently will never produce good results... 2. That security for nations, ideals or personal freedom can be obtained only by non-violent resistance, [etc.]. **1948** 'J. TEY' *Franchise Affair* xix. 225 The murderous rage that fills the pacifist-minded when their indignation is roused. **1961** E. S. TURNER *Phoney War* xiii. 179 There was an arrogance among certain militant pacifists which..prevented them from respecting the views of those who thought freedom worth fighting for. **1969** *Listener* 10 Apr. 505/3 Perhaps the oddest aspect of dispatches from Vietnam is that pacifist-minded conscripts are so readily made available to say they don't think words like honour and patriotism make any sense out there. **1970** R. SAMPSON *Anarchist Basis of Pacifism* 1 My usage of the term 'pacifist' includes only those who live by the principle that they will not intentionally take human life, cost what it may. **1974** A. PRICE *Other Paths to Glory* i. 18 'What did your father do in the last war?'..'He worked on a farm... He was a conscientious objector—a pacifist.'

B. *adj.* Of or pertainig to pacifism; characterized by rejection of war and belief in peaceful alternatives. Also **paci'fistic** *a.*, suggestive of or inclined to pacifism; **paci'fistically** *adv.*

1908 *Times Lit. Suppl.* 10 Dec. 453/3 He made a speech remarkable for its string of pacifist commonplaces. **1909** *Westm. Gaz.* 1 Sept. 9/1 Prussia was led to 1806-7 by pacifist and humanitarian ideas. **1918** A. HUXLEY *Let.* 3 Mar. (1969) 146 The one blow at the eleventh hour was the Vice Provost's refusal to allow De La Warr's article on Labour and the War to be printed, as being too revolutionary and pacifist. **1920** W. J. LOCKE *House of Baltazar* xxi. 256 It contained the names of representatives of all the disgruntled and pacifist factions in England. **1927** H. D. LASSWELL *Propaganda Technique in World War* iii. 62 H. G. Wells may be taken as an example of the pacifistically inclined Liberal ..whose support of the War came at the cost of inner struggle. **1930** *Sun* (Baltimore) 31 Dec. 6/2 What Mr. Bouton characterizes as a peculiarly German Socialist, defeatist and pacifist attitude of 'a class apart' is far from that. **1936** A. HUXLEY *What are you going to do about It?* 4 It has seemed best to state the pacifist case in terms of a series of answers to common antipacifist objections. *Ibid.* 17 War ..can only be prevented from breaking out if at least one government of an important sovereign state chooses to act pacifistically towards its neighbours. **1945** *Fellowship* Aug. 152/1 A fearful responsibility rests upon us who believe in the pacifist way. **1956** A. H. COMPTON *Atomic Quest* i. 37 The public attitude..had been strongly pacifistic. **1961** E. S. TURNER *Phoney War* xix. 278 Vendors of Fascist, Communist or pacifist literature were liable to be arrested. **1973** D. AARON *Unwritten War* III. vii. 108 Both [*sc.* William and Henry James] felt the need..to display a pacifistic heroism. **1976** *Pacifist* Jan. 5/2 It doesn't seem to me to be a pacifist way of overcoming things we dislike just to use our position of power (as parents or as government) to impose our will upon the people over whom we happen to have some influence.

pacify ('pæsɪfaɪ), *v.* [a. F. *pacifi-er* (15th c. in Littré, OF. *pacefier* 1250 in Godef.), ad. L. *pācificāre*, f. *pācific-us* PACIFIC: see -FY.]

1. *trans.* To allay the anger, excitement or agitation of (a person); to calm, quiet; to appease.

(In first quot. *pacificie* is app. an error for *pacifie*.)

c **1460** G. ASHBY *Dicta Philos.* 841 To pacificie [orig. *pacificare*] your enemye, be studious, Thaugh of youre strengh & power ye be seure. **1484** CAXTON *Fables of Alfonce* viii, Thenne was the kynge wel appeased and pacyfyed. **1547** BOORDE *Introd. Knowl.* xxiv. (1870) 181, I haue money in my pooke To pacyfye the Pope, the Turke, and the Iue. **1601** SHAKS. *Twel. N.* III. iv. 309 He will not now be pacified. **1717** LADY M. W. MONTAGU *Let. to C'tess Mar* 16 Jan., Pray say something to pacify her. **1861** GEO. ELIOT *Silas M.* iii, You drain me of money till I have got nothing to pacify her with.

absol. **1548** UDALL *Erasm. Par. Luke* xv. 328 Eueri vain & void pleasure of the world, which dooeth but for a shorte space pacifie.

b. To calm or appease (passion, etc.).

1528 ROY *Rede me* (Arb.) 85 Howe be it ye do pacify The rigoure of god almighty. **1628** WITHER *Brit. Rememb.* III. 1575 Thy selfe apply Gods just incensed wrath to pacifie. **1758** JOHNSON *Idler* No. 2 ¶4 How skilfully I can pacify resentment. **1875** JOWETT *Plato* (ed. 2) I. 161 If they have wronged him and he is angry, he pacifies his anger and is reconciled.

2. To bring or reduce to a state of peace; to calm, quiet: **a.** strife, contention, rebellion, etc.

1494 FABYAN *Chron.* VI. clix. 149 The which was lyke to haue turnyd the pope to great trowble, if he by polytyke & wyse meanes had not shortly pacyfyed the mater. **1563** *Homilies* II. *Wilful Rebell.* I. (1859) 560 All domesticall rebellions being suppressed and pacified. **1759** HUME *Hist. Eng.* (1812) IV. xxix. 40 [The Emperor] in ten days arrived in Spain, where he soon pacified the tumults which had arisen in his absence.

absol. **1829** S. TURNER *Mod. Hist. Eng.* III. II. v. 171 The diet that was intended to pacify, broke up in July, leaving everything as unsettled and as discordant as before.

†**b.** parties at strife: to reconcile. *Obs.*

c **1500** *Melusine* xxxvi. 245 He dyscomfyted the Duc in batayll, and made hym to be pacyfyed with the kynge of Anssay. **1571** CAMPION *Hist. Irel.* II. i. (1633) 57 Certaine Bishops resciant there..pacified the Townesmen to their King. **1800** *Asiat. Ann. Reg., Misc. Tracts* 107/1 Having made choice of Abubekre, who had greatly exerted himself in pacifying the two parties.

c. a country or district: to reduce to peaceful submission, to establish peace and tranquillity in.

a **1548** HALL *Chron., Hen. VIII* 19 All the pillage almoste was restored, and the countrey pacified. **1565** *Reg. Privy Council Scot.* I. 394 To send fourtie..men of weir to the West Bordour for helping to pacifie the cuntre. **1651** HOBBES *Leviath.* I. x. 46 Counts..were left to govern and defend places conquered, and pacified. **1899** *Westm. Gaz.* 18 Apr. 7/1 It would take 100,000 men to pacify the islands.

d. *fig.* and *transf.* To calm, appease.

1526 *Pilgr. Perf.* (W. de W. 1531) 149 b, It shall pacifye the senses, quenche euyll thoughtes. **1582** T. WATSON *Centurie of Loue* c, Poems (Arb.) 137 But somewhat more to pacyfie my minde. **1738** JOHNSON *London* 197 Swift o'er the land the dismal rumour flies, And publick mournings pacify the skies. **1846** TRENCH *Mirac.* iv. (1862) 147 First blaming their want of faith, and then pacifying the storm.

3. *intr.* To become peaceful, calm down.

1509 HAWES *Past. Pleas.* xxxviii. (Percy Soc.) 198 My dolorous herte began to pacyfy. **1880** BARING-GOULD *Mehalah* vii. (1884) 94 She is a Pacific Ocean when not vexed with storms. She will pacify presently.

Hence '**pacified** *ppl. a.*, '**pacifying** *vbl. sb.* and *ppl. a.*, '**pacifyingly** *adv.*

1537 in W. H. Turner *Select. Rec. Oxford* 146 For the pacifying and determination of which variance. **1552** HULOET, Pacified, *delinitus*. *Ibid.*, Pacifyinge, or whyche doth pacifye, *pacificatorius*. *a* **1652** J. SMITH *Sel. Disc.* x. 511 A pacifying and quieting of all those riots and tumults. *a* **1704** T. BROWN *Pleasant Ep.* Wks. 1730 I. 111 Write a few pacifying strains. *a* **1708** BEVERIDGE *Thes. Theol.* II. 371 Is it not a blessed thing..to have a pacified conscience? **1843** D. JERROLD *Punch's Lett.* xviii. Wks. 1864 III. 486 The wine.. speaks pacifyingly, soothingly.

pacing ('peɪsɪŋ), *vbl. sb.* [f. PACE *v.* + -ING[1].]

1. The action of the verb PACE, q.v.

1706 *Lond. Gaz.* No. 4285/8 Stolen or strayed..a roan Mare..all her Ways, except Pacing. **1785** G. FORSTER tr. *Sparrman's Voy. Cape G.H.* (1786) II. 293 The beast [a rhinoceros]..kept on an even and steady course, which, in fact, was a kind of pacing. **1824** GALT *Rothelan* II. IV. iv. 126 He now and then turned, or paused in his pacing, to look over the battlement. **1876** T. HARDY *Ethelberta* (1890) 394 The..horse's pacing made scarcely more noise than a rabbit would have done in limping along.

attrib. **1681** W. ROBERTSON *Phraseol. Gen.* (1693) 970 A pacing saddle; *Ephippium tolutarium*. **1896** *Daily News* 28 Oct. 7/6 The suggested new rule and its sub-sections on the pacing question were favourably received.

2. *Cycle-Racing* and *Athletics*. The act of (tactical) pace-making, and hence of artificially increasing the speed of a competitor by allowing him to proceed in the slip-stream of a (usu. motorized) vehicle; also, the act of distributing effort carefully over a race to ensure optimum performance, esp. by utilizing the wind resistance offered by other competitors. Also *attrib.*

1895 G. L. HILLIER *Cycling* (ed. 5) 342 Appended are the Rules for 'Herne Hill Pacing', which, if strictly enforced, insure fair pacing all round... No pacer is to remain on the path, unless actually pacing. **1897** *Encycl. Sport* I. 62/1 (Athletics) *Pacing*, going in front so as to quicken the speed at which the race is being run, or at which some particular competitor is running. *Ibid.* 287/2 As a natural consequence the trade appeared upon the scene, the friendly character of the assemblies gradually disappeared, things became more business-like, pacing was supplied, tandems and often larger multicycles swooped down in shoals upon the highways. **1902** *Encycl. Brit.* XXVII. 327/2 The introduction of pacing by multicycles and motors next took from cycle racing what interest was left. **1935** *Encycl. Sports* 206/2 Surprising records have been created by pacing, since motorcycles and cars became available for this purpose, with wind-shields attached to the rear to protect the cyclist from wind resistance. These wind-shields also act as a sucker and help to draw him along. **1955** R. BANNISTER *First Four Minutes* x. 123 This was the first of many occasions when Chris Chataway helped me with the pacing in the early stages. **1974** *Encycl. Brit. Macropædia* XVIII. 544/2 Pacing styles have changed over the years, and this is particularly evident in mile running.. The early style was to start fast, relax somewhat during the middle two laps, then finish as rapidly as possible. **1974** *Sunday Mirror* 21 July 38/1 Schaer ..indulged in some unfair 'pacing', tucking himself in behind..Doyle and refusing official requests to move away.

3. *Med.* Artificial stimulation of the heart so as to make it beat at an appropriate rate. Cf. PACE *v.* 5 b.

1962 *Lancet* 29 Dec. 1369/2 We report here our experience of artificial pacing in nineteen patients, with special emphasis on the management of Stokes-Adams attacks in hospital, and the emergency control of rhythm by the electrode catheter. **1969** J. P. P. STOCK *Diagnosis & Treatment of Cardiac Arrhythmias* x. 144 Paired pacing has been employed in severe heart failure to increase the force of contraction of the heart. **1975** J. FLEMING in F. J. Fawcett *Cardiol.* I. 24 Electrical pacing of the heart on a short or long term basis is now firmly established as a valuable measure.

pacing, *ppl. a.* [f. as prec. + -ING[2].] That paces (see PACE *v.*); *spec.* of a horse (see PACE *v.* 3).

1652 EARL MONM. tr. *Bentivoglio's Hist. Relat.* 152 When the Coach-horses were tired; he and his wife got upon the pacing geldings. **1828** SCOTT *F.M. Perth* viii, First appeared Simon Glover on a pacing palfrey.

Pacinian (pə'sɪnɪən), *a.* [f. name of the Italian anatomist Pacini (1812–1883) + -AN.] Of or described by Pacini.

Pacinian body, corpuscle, one of numerous oval seed-like bodies attached to nerve endings, esp. of the cutaneous nerves of the hand and foot.

1876 DUHRING *Dis. Skin* 27 Pacinian corpuscles..are quite large, well-defined, oval or olive-shaped bodies. **1899** *Allbutt's Syst. Med.* VI. 252 It may be that the Pacinian corpuscles..are susceptible to painful impressions.

pack (pæk), *sb.*[1] Forms: 3-7 packe, 4-5 pakke, (4 palke), 4-6 pak, (5-6 pake), 4- pack. [ME. *packe, pakke* (early 13th c.) corresponds to early MFlem. *pac* (12th c.), MDu. (*a* 1300), MLG., Du., LG. *pak*; (late) MHG. and Ger. *pack*; also Icel. *pakki* (1337), Sw. *packa*, Da., Norw. *pakke*; obs. F. *pacque* (*c* 1510 in Godef.), AngloL. (15–16th c.) *paccus*; mod. It. *pacco*; mod. Ir. *pac*.

App. immediately from Flemish, Dutch, or Low German in 12th c. The earliest instance of the word yet recorded is of 1199 at Ghent, in Warnkönig-Gheldolf *Hist. de Gand* 236 'Omne pac, quod in curru fertur, sive parvum, sive magnum, si fuerit funiculatum, debet quatuor denarios'. *Pac* occurs also at Utrecht in 1244 (Höhlbaum *Hans. Urkundenbuch* I. 109). The verb (PACK *v.*[1]) appears at an early date in connexion with the wool trade, and it is known that the trade in English wool was chiefly with the Low Countries. The Fr. examples of *pacque* and *pacqhuus* packhouse (at Ghent and Lille) are prob. from Flemish. Ulterior history and origin unknown. The conjecture (in Diez, Körting, etc.), that *pac* is Romanic, seems ill-founded; the 'late L.' *paccus* being merely Anglo-Latin, i.e. the latinized form of Eng. *pack*; the word is quite late in It. Irish *paca*, *pac* is from Eng. (Senses 8–12 below, esp. 10–12 are rather from PACK *v.*)]

1. a. A bundle of things enclosed in a wrapping or tied together compactly, esp. to be carried by a man or beast; a package, parcel, esp. one of considerable size or weight; a bale; *spec.* a bundle of goods carried by a pedlar.

a **1225** *Ancr. R.* 166 Noble men & gentile ne bereð nout packes. **1313–14** *Durham Acc. Rolls* (Surtees) 512 In vj cordis pro Pakkis empt. 5*s.* **1377** LANGL. *P. Pl.* B. XIII. 201 Me were leuer, by owre lorde and I lyue shulde, Haue pacience perfitlich þan half þi pakke of bokes! *Ibid.* XIV. 212 Þere þe pore preseth bifor þe riche with a pakke at his rugge. **1472–5** *Rolls of Parlt.* VI. 155/2 To doo unpakke there tho Pakkes and Fardels. **1579** SPENSER *Sheph. Cal.* May 240 A pedler..Bearing a trusse of tryfles at hys backe, As bells, and babes, and glasses in hys packe. **1643** *Declar. Lords & Comm., Reb. Ireland* 49 Having taken out of her [a ship] eleven packs of Cloth. **1784** COWPER *Task* I. 465 A pedlar's pack, that bows the bearer down. **1803** WELLINGTON in Gurw. *Desp.* II. 20 Letter..from the Military Board, upon the subject of packs for bullocks. **1844** *Regul. & Ord. Army* 157 The Pack is to be invariably on when fitting the Accoutrements. **1884** H. SPENCER in *Contemp. Rev.* Feb. 161 There is a Pedlar's Act..giving the Police power to search pedlars' packs.

†**b.** Bundle of money, stock of cash; cash-box.

c **1394** *P. Pl. Crede* 399 Þer is no peny in my pakke [*MS.* palke] to payen for my mete. **1578** *Reg. Privy Council Scot.* Ser. I. III. 39 Having wairit thair haill pak thair-upoun.

c. *fig.* (Usually with conscious reference to the literal sense.)

1568 T. HOWELL *Arb. Amitie* (1879) 73 Bicause thou cleane deliuered art, of great and heauie pack. **1581** J. BELL *Haddon's Answ. Osor.* 128 There is no..skill in the learned that is not in Osorius packe. **1633** G. HERBERT *Temple, Ch. Porch* xxiv, Man is a shop of rules, a well-truss'd pack Whose every parcell under-writes a law. **1798** SOUTHEY *To Marg. Hill* 17 Like Christian on his pilgrimage, I bear So heavy a pack of business. **1897** *Outing* XXX. 374/1 Men.. shoulder their packs of general cussedness, and..hit the trail. **1962** J. BRAINE *Life at Top* vi. 101 Suddenly the pack was on my shoulders again; there was no quietness in the room.

d. *Photogr.* A set of two or three plates or films sensitive to different colours which are superimposed and exposed simultaneously. Cf. BI-PACK, TRI-PACK.

1907 *Brit. Jrnl. Photogr.* 19 July 547/2 By interspersing.. filters with films in sets for tri-chromatic negatives..the respective exposures can be made in rapid sequence without removing the pack from the camera. **1929** *Penrose Ann.* XXXI. 41 To assert that the colour analysis of the pack is equal to that of orthodox trichromatic work would be incorrect.

e. A knapsack, rucksack, usually with a wooden frame. Chiefly *Forces'* and *N.Z.*

1916 'BOYD CABLE' *Action Front* 49 The neutral ground.. was a sea of mud..littered with..packs which had been cut from or slipped from the shoulders of the wounded. **1925** FRASER & GIBBONS *Soldier & Sailor Words* 218 *Pack*, the infantry knapsack. **1958** *Tararua* XII. 27 Food and gear have to be carried. Everyone in New Zealand..puts it in a *pack*. **1968** *N.Z. Listener* 15 Mar. 6/1 You women can't go carrying all that stuff. Here, Joyce, give us your pack, Joyce! **1969** *Ibid.* 21 Feb. 4/1 Hobnail boots and canvas pack..just the gear for pushing through scrub and supplejack. **1971** *Ibid.* 22 Feb. 51/2 Pack carrying is still the same old personal battle between man and gravity. **1973** *Parade Sunday Bull.* (Philadelphia) 7 Oct. 31/2 Packs: Most versatile pack is a tubular metal pack frame, contoured to the body with a waist strap that transfers the weight to the legs and hip muscles.

f. A packet or package, esp. of cigarettes.

More usual in the U.S. than in the U.K.

1924 *Saucy Stories* May 54/1 Miss de Rose..reached for a pack of Strikes. **1936** *Discovery* Nov. 345/2 Ten nuts are the equivalent of one pack of Golden Bat cigarettes. **1937** J. A. LEE *Civilian into Soldier* v. 219 He emptied his pack of issue cigarettes. **1951** *N.Y. Times* 14 June 22/6 It comes in a little pack. **1958** *Listener* 19 June 1015/1 Six packs of American cigarettes. **1959** *Housewife* June 80 The fine white Table Salt in the gaily coloured packs! **1959** N. MAILER *Advts. for Myself* (1961) 218 Stoned with lush, with pot,..Milltown, coffee, and two packs a day, I was working live, and overalert, and tiring into what felt like death. **1963** *B.S.I. News* Apr. 20/1 The 'shelf-appeal' pack designed to catch the eye of the ordinary shopper. **1974** 'J. LE CARRÉ' *Tinker, Tailor* xxiii. 201 Gerstmann was a chain-smoker: Camels. I sent out for several packs of them—*packs* is the American word?

g. The container into which a parachute is packed.

1926 *Sci. Amer.* Aug. 100/1 (*caption*) This photograph.. shows the pilot parachute just emerging from the pack. **1930** C. J. V. MURPHY *Parachute* 43 The jumper, with the pack strapped on his back, dived from the wing of a plane. **1940** *Aeroplane* 13 Sept. 298/2 A small pilot chute..pulls the main parachute out of its pack. **1969** D. DWIGGINS *Bailout* vi. 88, I would have to jump, but first squeeze from my turret and reach my parachute pack from its rack in the fuselage. **1976** A. WHITE *Long Silence* vii. 59 The snap when the fixed line broke open the pack, and the jerk when the pack pulled out the chute.

2. As a measure, definite or indefinite, of various commodities: see quots.

1488–9 *Act 4 Hen. VII*, c. 22 The gold packed..weyeth not above vij unces, and sold for iij li. sterling the pack. **1545** BRINKLOW *Compl.* ii. (1874) 12 Whan he sold his clothys for a reasonable price the pack. **1706** PHILLIPS, *Pack of Wooll*, a Horse-load, consisting of seventeen Stone and two Pounds, or 240 Pound weight. **1744** A. DOBBS *Acct. Countries adjoining Hudson's Bay* 39 He had four Packs of Beaver of 40 each. **1774** S. HEARNE *Jrnl.* 11 Oct. (1934) 122 By the Masters account..65 or 70 Packs or Caggs, called by them Pieces, are put on board each canoe. **1778** *Eng. Gazetteer* (ed. 2) s.v. *Norwich*, The weavers here..use many thousand packs of yarn spun in other counties. **1805** FORSYTH *Beauties Scotl.* II. 127 Of wool... A pack is 12 stones; that is, 24 lib. of white, and 25½ lib. of..*laid* wool to the stone. **1812** SIR G. PREVOST in *Examiner* 5 Oct. 630/1, 700 packs of furs. *c* **1840** D. THOMPSON *Narr. Explorations W. Amer. 1784–1812* (1916) iv. 417, I traded three packs of Furrs (a pack is 90 lbs). **1847–78** HALLIWELL, *Pack*..a measure of coals, containing about three Winchester bushels. **1858** SIMMONDS *Dict. Trade Products* s.v., A pack of flour or Indian-corn meal, flax, etc. weighs 280 lbs.; of wool 240 lbs. net: formerly, in many parts of the country it was 252 lbs. **1890** *Cent. Dict., Pack*... A package of gold-leaf containing 20 'books' of 25 leaves each. **1961** PHILLIPS & SMURR *Fur Trade* II. 330 [He] fined him thirty packs of beaver, which was just the quantity he had.

3. a. A company or set of persons; generally implying low character, or association for some evil purpose, but often merely expressing contempt or depreciation, and formerly sometimes without such implication; a 'gang', 'lot'.

13.. *Cursor M.* 2212 (Gött.) Fra est he brohut ane euyl pack [*Cott.* felauscap]..Sexti werkemen þai wer. *c* **1385** CHAUCER *L.G.W.* 299 Yit they were hethene al the pak. *c* **1450** *St. Cuthbert* (Surtees) 3752 Þou hase destruyed vs, al þe pak. **1548** UDALL, etc. *Erasm. Par. Mark* vii. 50 The Scribes, Phariseis, yea, and almoste all the whole packe of the Iewes. **1578** BANISTER *Hist. Man* VIII. 111 The whole packe of the principall Anathomistes haue..affirmed fiue payre of sinewes to the loynes. **1652** SIR E. NICHOLAS in *N. Papers* (Camden) 316 Mr. Whitelocke is as mischievous to the K. and all his friends in England as any among the pack of rebels. **1698** FRYER *Acc. E. India & P.* 97 A Pack of Thieves that had infested the Roads a long time. **1768** GOLDSM. *Good-n. Man* I. i, A pack of drunken servants. **1820** SCOTT *Monast.* x, An the whole pack of ye were slain, there were more lost at Flodden. **1885** DUNCKLEY in *Manch. Exam.* 23 Mar. 6/1 The House..resembles in many respects a pack of schoolboys.

b. A large collection, or set (of things, esp. abstract); a 'heap', 'lot'. (Usually depreciative.)

1591 SHAKS. *Two Gent.* III. i. 20 Rather..Then (by concealing it) heap on your head A pack of sorrowes. **1633** G. HERBERT *Temple, Miserie* ix, No not to purchase the whole pack of starres: There let them shine. **1638** *Penit. Conf.* vii. (1657) 123 That ridiculous pack of heresies amassed by the Council of Constance. **1693** *Humours Town* 86 An endless pack of Knaveries. **1763** JEFFERSON *Corr.* Wks. 1859 I. 185 Would you rather that I should write you a pack of lies? **1862** MRS. CARLYLE *Lett.* III. 140 What a pack of complaints! **1880** GEN. SIR E. B. HAMLEY in Shand *Life* (1895) II. xvi. 17 Pack of nonsense.

c. *Rugby Football.* The forwards of a team, who form one half of the scrummage; also, the scrummage itself.

1887 M. SHEARMAN *Athletics & Football* II. iii. 305 The chief business of the half-back then became to snap up the ball..as soon as it came away from the pack. **1900** A. E. T. WATSON *Young Sportsman* 253 Form a compact scrummage with the heads down. Long and straggling packs are easily broken through. **1909** *Westm. Gaz.* 11 Dec. 20/2 Cambridge have an exceptionally fine pack, to whom they must look almost entirely for victory, their halves and three-quarters being but moderate. **1927** H. S. WALPOLE *Jeremy at Crale* xvi. 278 Mellon's probably the best three-quarter playing on any school side this season. But that needn't worry us. We've got a better pack than theirs. **1955** *Times* 1 Aug. 3/3 The British forwards..were beaten time and again by the Rhodesian pack. **1960** E. S. & W. J. HIGHAM *High-Speed Rugby* III. xii. 147 Only those who have played in the pack know what will-power it sometimes requires to stand up from a scrum in the last ten minutes and force the weary legs to run. **1972** G. SLATTER *Football is Fifteen* i. 16 Tom Morrison, manager of the All Blacks, said only the forwards would know what the loss of Simpson meant to the pack. **1976** *Eastern Even. News* (Norwich) 29 Nov. 13/7 Pressure from Beccles led to a five-metre scrum where they pushed the Union pack back over the line to give Shannon a try.

d. The organizational unit of the Brownie and Wolf Cub movements.

1918 [see BROWNIE[1] 2]. **1932** U. M. WILLIAMS *For Brownies* 111 Brown Owl is guarding the rest of the pack. **1945** 'GILCRAFT' *How to run a Pack* 5 The man or woman who in a weak moment has consented to run a Wolf Cub Pack. **1965** *Wolf Cub Jubilee Bk.* 31 Some Cub Packs in Canada have a real wolf's head on the top of their totem pole. **1973** *Guardian* 1 Apr. 11/3 Brown Owl said she'd understand if I wasn't quite happy in the pack.

e. In the war of 1939–45, a number of German submarines operating together.

1943 *Times* 13 Dec. 2/1 The story is told below of the defeat of a pack of U-boats in the North Atlantic. **1944** *Daily Tel.* 11 July 3 Captain Walker and his crew smashed U-boat packs lying across the Arctic and North Atlantic convoy routes. **1956** R. BRADDON *Nancy Wake* ix. 96 The Bay of Biscay was to be the main target area for U-Boat packs. **1961** S. E. ELLACOTT *Ships under Sea* x. 100 A common practice among U-boat packs was to lie in line at one- or two-mile intervals across a shipping lane. **1978** *Jrnl. R. Soc. Arts* CXXVI. 252/2 The German submarine packs..were threatening to starve us into submission.

†**4.** Applied to a person of low or worthless character; almost always with *naughty*. *Obs.*

1526 *Pilgr. Perf.* (W. de W. 1531) 37 b, Al though they be wretched lyuers & noughty packes amonge. **1540** HYRDE tr. *Vives' Instr. Chr. Wom.* I. vii. (1557) 18 Calle hir a naughtie packe: withe that one woorde thou haste taken all from hir, and haste lefte hir bare and foule. **1638** ROWLEY *Shoomaker a gentleman* IV. G iv b, Hence you Whore-master knave,.. Thou naughty packe. **1725** BAILEY *Erasm. Colloq.* (1878) I. 76 What does this idle Pack want? **1738** SWIFT *Pol. Conversat.* 106, I never heard she was a naughty Pack. [**1855** KINGSLEY *Westw. Ho!* xvii, Drake sent them all off again for a lot of naughty packs.]

5. a. A number of animals kept or naturally congregating together; applied *spec.* to a company of hounds kept for hunting, and to those of certain beasts (esp. wolves), and of birds (e.g. grouse) which naturally associate for purposes of attack or defence.

1648 *Hunting of Fox* 26 All joyn (like so many dogs in a pack) in pursuing these Foxes. **1688** R. HOLME *Armoury* II. 311/1 A Pack of Grous, or Heath-cocks. **1735** SOMERVILLE *Chase* II. 100 So from the Kennel rush the joyous Pack. **1774** GOLDSM. *Retal.* 107 He cast off his friends, as a hunts-man his pack, For he knew when he pleased he could whistle them back. **1795** SOUTHEY *Joan of Arc* Wks. 1837 I. 179 When from the mountains round reverberates The hungry wolves' deep yell;..The famish'd pack come round. **1862** JOHNS *Brit. Birds* 357 Coveys of Ptarmigan unite and form large packs.

b. 'The shepherd's portion in a "hirsel", or flock of sheep, grazed on the farm as his pay for looking after the whole herd' (Heslop *Northumbld. Wds.* 1894); also one of these, a ***pack-sheep***.

[By some viewed as a distinct word and connected with PACT, for which however no evidence has been found.]

1825 JAMIESON, *Packs*, the sheep, of whatever gender, that a shepherd is allowed to feed along with his master's flock, this being in lieu of wages. **1831** *Sutherland Farm Rep.* 77 in *Libr. Usef. Knowl., Husb.* III, Employing eleven married shepherds and eight young men, this gives the number of twelve hundred and fifty shepherds' sheep or packs mingled among the master's flocks. **1886** C. SCOTT *Sheep-Farming* 148 If the shepherd is allowed a 'pack', then of course the 'pack sheep' have marks totally different from the flock. **1888** *Scott. Leader* 23 Mar. 4 The 'pack' consisted of 50 sheep.

6. A complete set of playing-cards, varying in number according to the game and the country (see CARD *sb.*[2] 1).

c **1597** HARINGTON *On Play* in *Nugæ Ant.* (1804) I. 212 To skorne that gayne that is got with a packe of cards and dyce. **1653** H. COGAN tr. *Pinto's Trav.* xxxviii. 151 With three of the worst cards in the pack. **1684** *Lond. Gaz.* No. 1925/4 The very best Cards shall be sold in London by the last Retailer, at four Pence the Pack. **1711** ADDISON *Spect.* No. 93 ¶8 Shuffling and dividing a Pack of Cards. **1801** STRUTT *Sports & Past.* IV. ii. 291 The pack or set of cards, in the old plays, is continually called a pair of cards. **1816** SINGER *Hist. Cards* 38 The Spanish Pack consists, like the German, of forty-eight cards only, the tens in the former, and the aces in the latter, being omitted. **1878** H. H. GIBBS *Ombre* 7 A pack of forty Cards having no eights, nines, or tens, among them.

7. A large area of floating ice in pieces of considerable size, driven or 'packed' together into a nearly continuous and coherent mass (as found in polar seas).

1791 *Trans. Soc. Arts* IX. 164 Close to a pack of ice. **1820** SCORESBY in *Ann. Reg.* II. 1324/2 A pack is a body of drift-ice of such magnitude, that its extent is not discernible. **1824** PARRY *North West Passage* i. 4 We came to the edge of the 'pack' in the course of the forenoon. **18..** in Borthwick *Br. Amer. Rdr.* (1860) 264 If the field [of ice] is broken into a number of pieces none of which are more than forty or fifty yards across, the whole is called a *pack*.

8. *Coal-mining.* A mass of rough stones, etc., built up into a wall or pillar to support the roof.

1867 W. W. SMYTH *Coal & Coal-mining* 142 Such stone, and what breaks from the roof, is often built up in packs, or masses of dry rubble walling; and the roads which pass through the gob have thus to be protected by a pack wall of some feet thick on either side. **1881** RAYMOND *Mining Gloss., Pack*, a wall or pillar built of gob to support the roof.

9. A pyramidal pile of fish set to dry.

18.. PERLEY (Cent.), After a fortnight's drying, the fish should be put into a pack or steeple, for the purpose of sweating.

10. An act or the action of packing (in various senses: see PACK *v.*[1]).

a **1612** HARINGTON *Epigr.* (1633) II. xcix, And thus what with the stop, and with the pack, Poore Marcus, and his rest goes still to wrack. *a* **1700** B. E. *Dict. Cant. Crew, Pack*,.. Pack of Juries, Packing of Cards. **1745** H. PELHAM in W. Thompson *R.N. Advoc.* (1757) 11 Let William Thompson be continued as lately, in overlooking the Pack [of meat in casks], and Pickling. **1760–72** H. BROOKE *Fool of Qual.* (1809) IV. 125 All was hurry, pack, and dispatch.

11. a. *Hydropathy.* The swathing of the body in a wet sheet, blanket, etc. (PACK *v.*[1] 6 b); the state of being so packed; the sheet, etc., in which a patient is thus packed. Also ***dry-pack***: see quot.

1849 MRS. CARLYLE *Lett.* I. 47 The bath-woman should have stayed with me during the first 'pack'. **1859** J. SMEDLEY *Practical Hydrop.* 43 Wet packs may be repeated several times in the space of twelve hours. *Ibid.* 45 The dry pack is to produce a greater degree of perspiration, and is useful in chronic rheumatism [etc.]. *Ibid.* (1870) 87 It is not safe to leave a patient in pack without an attendant near. **1899** *Allbutt's Syst. Med.* VIII. 160 Wet sheets, packs, sitz-baths, and douches are of great value.

b. *Surg.* A soft pad usu. composed of several layers of gauze sewn together, used esp. for wedging organs of the body during an operation.

1916 PARKER & BRECKINRIDGE *Surg. & Gynæcol. Nursing* xx. 263 At the Mayo clinic three sizes of packs are used, (1) 4 × 8 inches, (2) 5 inches by 3 yards, (3) 3 inches by 2 feet. The latter are used for packing about the gall-bladder. **1944** W. W. BABCOCK *Princ. & Pract. Surg.* xviii. 285 Salt packs consist of gauze soaked in 10 per cent hypertonic solution in which 5- or 10-grain tablets of sodium chloride are embedded. **1955** *Times* 15 July 11/4 The plaintiffs' cause of action was that during an operation on Mrs. Urry for the delivery of a child by lower Caesarian section, a swab or pack was left in her body. **1955** M. G. Lynch in Ochsner & DeBakey *Christopher's Minor Surg.* (ed. 7) xxi. 500/1 Gelfoam packs will often control this bleeding. **1970** H. Haxton *Surg. Techniques* vii. 45 Most bleeding can be controlled by the pressure of a pack or a finger on the right spot.

c. *Dentistry.* A substance applied in a plastic state to the gums around and between the teeth, subsequently hardening, to serve as a dressing after disease or surgery of periodontal tissue.

1923 A. W. Ward in *Jrnl. Amer. Dental Assoc.* X. 478/2 In order to avoid infection, pain, sensitiveness of the roots.. I have devised a quick setting pack. This pack is mixed like cement and flowed between the teeth and all over the exposed surface. The tissues regenerate under the pack, which is allowed to remain four to six days after the operation. **1953** I. Glickman *Clin. Periodontology* xliv. 743 The mixed pack is separated into small masses. *Ibid.* 746 If a portion of the pack fractures off within three days after it was placed, the entire pack should be replaced. **1974** D. L. Allen et al. *Periodontics for Dental Hygienist* (ed. 2) x. 206 The placement of a periodontal dressing or pack following surgery is extremely important.

d. = *face-pack* s.v. face *sb.* 27.

1934 M. Verni *Mod. Beauty Culture* i. v. 29/1 In many schools of beauty, the pupils are taught to sponge the face with hot water before applying the pack. **1944** R. G. Harry *Mod. Cosmeticology* (ed. 2) v. 55 The tightening effect is produced by the drying of the pack, and is enhanced by the presence of albumin and/or certain gums. **1964** Wells & Lubowe *Cosmetics & Skin* ii. vii. 202 The significant mechanism operative in the use of face packs is the drying of the pack on the skin surface. **1972** *Vogue* Jan. 15/2 To transform a dry skin.. use this simple pack.

12. The quantity (of fish, fruit, etc.) packed in tins or cans in a particular season or year.

1889 *Pall Mall G.* 20 Sept. 6/3 The value of this year's pack, exclusive of salted fish and fresh salmon shipped, will be..2,640,000 dols. **1896** *Living Topics Cycl.* (N.Y.) II. 189 During the year the canned fruit pack amounted to 1,280,000 cases. **1901** *Scotsman* 26 Mar. 5/1 Canadian fisheries..the 'pack', or quantity canned amounted to 16,403 tons.

13. Short for *pack-horse*, *pack-beast*.

1866 N. Chevalier *Reminisc. Journey across South Island* (typescript) 7 The pack [was] a strong heavy old chap, the third pretty good. The fourth a flea bitten Arab mare. **1887** Mrs. Daly *Digging & Squatting* 154, I had two horses, one which I used as a 'pack', and the other I rode.

14. Slang phr. *to send to the pack* (see quot. 1916); also *to go to the pack*, to lose a (high) position, to 'go to pieces', to deteriorate. Chiefly *Austral.* and *N.Z.*

1916 C. J. Dennis *Songs Sentimental Bloke* 94 I've sent the leery bloke that bore me name Clean to the pack wivout one pearly tear. *Ibid.* 127 *To send to the pack*, to relegate to obscurity. **1919** W. H. Downing *Digger Dial.* 26 *Go to the pack*, deteriorate. **1934** T. Wood *Cobbers* xvi. 200 The country was going to the pack. **1939** Joyce *Finnegans Wake* 269 If she can't follow suit Renée goes to the pack. **1946** K. Tennant *Lost Haven* (1947) xvi. 250 Everything'ull go to the pack unless they're let go home again. **1952** D. Niland in *Coast to Coast 1951–52* 196, I can't let him go to the pack like that. **1958** G. Casey *Snowball* 118 You wait till he gets a bit older. Them abos always go t' the pack. **1963** D. Crick *Martin Place* 196 Things are goin' to the pack. If they get any shorter of work, they'll close down.

15. *attrib.* and *Comb.* **a.** *attrib.* Constituting or serving for a pack or bundle, as ***pack-bag***, ***-basket***, ***-box***, ***-load***, ***-paper***; loaded with or used for carrying a pack, as ***pack-animal***, ***-ass***, ***-beast***, ***-bullock***, ***-cow***, ***-dog***, ***-donkey***, ***-mule***, ***-ox***, ***-pony***. **b.** objective and instrumental, as ***pack-bearer***, ***-bearing*** adj., ***-carriage***, ***-driver***, ***-laden*** adj. **c.** Special Combs.: **pack and prime way** [cf. prime *a.*], local name for a way by which packs may be carried on horseback, etc., a bridle-way; so ***pack and prime bridge***, ***road***; **pack-cinch** (*U.S.*), a wide 'cinch' or girth, with a hook at one end and a ring at the other, used with a pack-saddle; **pack-clouds** (*poet.*), densely massed clouds; **pack-draper**, an itinerant draper carrying his goods in a pack; **pack-drill**, a military punishment (see quot. 1890); also in phr. ***no names, no pack-drill***: see name *sb.* 1 h; **pack-duck** [duck *sb.*[3]] (see quot.); **pack-fork** (see quot.); **pack-frame**, a frame, usu. of metal, into which a knapsack or other pack is fitted for easier transport; **pack-ice**, ice forming a pack (sense 7); **pack-leader**, the leader of a group of animals; †**pack-line**, packthread; **pack-moth**, a species of clothes-moth (*Anacampsis sarcitella*); †**pack-paunch**, ? a paunch like a pack, a big belly or big-bellied person; **pack-peddler**, one who travels round from village to village with a pack of small items for sale; **pack-rat**, the North American bushytailed woodrat, *Neotoma cinerea*; also *attrib.* and *fig.*; hence as *v. trans.*, to collect an assortment of objects, as a pack-rat does; **pack-road**, a road along which pack-animals are driven; **pack-sack**, the container into which goods comprising a pack are put, a rucksack; also *attrib.* in phr. ***pack-sack citizen*** (*Canad.*), a vagrant; **pack-sheet**, (*a*) a sheet for packing goods in; (*b*) *Med.*, a wet sheet for packing or wrapping a patient in; **packshot**, in television advertising, a close-up picture of the advertised product in its wrappings; **pack-strap(s**, the strap or straps which secure a load round the forehead or shoulders of a person or to the back of a pack animal; **pack tactics**, the practice of German submarines of operating in groups; **pack-track**, **-trail**, a path or route suitable for a pack-train; **pack-train**, a train of pack-beasts with their packs; **pack-twine**, twine used for tying up a pack, packthread; **pack-wall** (*Coal-mining*): see sense 8; **pack-ware**, 'ware' or goods carried in a pack (in quot. *fig.*); **pack-way** = *pack-road*; **pack-wool**, wool done up in packs. Also pack-horse, -house, etc.

1628 Coke *On Litt.* 56 A foot way and horse way.. vulgarly is called a *pack and prime way. **1798** in *Yorks. N. & Q.* I. 189 A carriage bridge would be more convenient to the public, than repairing the present pack and prime bridge. **1888** *Sheffield Gloss.*, *Pack-and-prime road*, a packhorse road across the moors. **1847** *Santa Fé* (New Mexico) *Republican* 16 Oct. 2/2 They left their wagons and took *pack animals, and ten days' provisions. **1884** J. Colborne *Hicks Pasha* 44 The pack animals we sent on as before. **1643** Prynne *Sov. Power Parl.* i. (ed. 2) 4 *Packe-asses with Bels about their neckes. **1656** Earl Monm. tr. *Boccalini's Advts. fr. Parnass.* i. xxix. (1674) 33, I should be baser than a *Pack-bearer, if I did not arrogate to my self the whole power. **1605** Daniel *Philotas* i. i. Poems (1717) 322 Still they preach to us *Pack-bearing Patience, that base Property..of th' all-enduring Ass. **1877** Besant & Rice *Son of Vulc.* I. 24 Myles..was sitting on an inverted box, his own *pack-box, in front of the fire. **1845** Stocqueler *Handbk. Brit. India* (1854) 38 *Pack-bullocks, camels, pack-horses. **1707** J. Chamberlayne *St. Gt. Brit.* i. i. iv. 45 No where greater plenty of horses..for Plough and *Pack-Carriage. **1871** G. M. Hopkins *Note-bks. & Papers* (1937) 141 If you look well at big *pack-clouds. **1880** Miss Bird *Japan* II. 268 *Pack-cows with velvet frontlets embroidered in gold. **1844** *New Orleans Picayune* 18 Mar. 38/1 The only assistant they took with them was an Indian-trained *pack dog. **1913** I. Cowie *Company of Adventurers* 323 Pack-ponies were also used; also pack dogs, the latter bearing frequently burdens mountains high in comparison with their size. **1933** B. Willoughby *Alaskans All* 18 We four stood clinging to the collars of our pack dogs, wondering what marvels lay beyond. **1976** T. Walker *Spatsizi* xii. 132 Travelling slowly with their pack dogs, they walked 150 miles through the mountains. **1889** *Pall Mall G.* 10 July 7/2 He had..five well-trained horses, sixteen *pack donkeys. **1880** Jefferies *Hodge & M.* II. 168 The *pack-drapers come round visiting every cottage. **1845** W. H. Maxwell *Hints to Soldier* I. 13 A full guard house, dozens at *pack-drill. **1890** R. Kipling *Soldiers Three* (1891) 76 Mulvaney was doing pack-drill—was compelled that is to say, to walk up and down in full marching order, with rifle, bayonet, ammunition, knapsack, and over-coat. **1846** Worcester, **Pack-Duck*, a coarse sort of linen for pack-cloths, etc. **1648–60** Hexham *Dutch Dict.*, *Een Refe*, a *Pack-forke which Travellers use to carry their packs upon. **1955** E. Hillary *High Adventure* vii. 118 Her [*sc.* the Sherpani's] method of carrying it [*sc.* her load] was with a headband, and as I had no *pack frame with me I had to follow suit. **1963** *Guardian* 9 Aug. 7/4 To get to Dyrfjoll was a whole day's march from the nearest road and the pair used a sledge pack-frame on the way in. **1973** [see above sense 1 e]. **1976** G. Moffat *Over Sea to Death* x. 119 The paraphernalia of [mountain] rescue: rucksacks, pack frames, radio sets. **1485** *Naval Acc. Hen. VII* (1896) 38 Shanke hokes..iij, *Pakke hokes..iiij, Leche hokes..iiij. **1850** R. A. Goodsir *Arctic Voy. Baffin's Bay* 108 As long as there was a chance of procuring whales in Prince Regent's Inlet, he might have perserved..great as the risk would have been in pushing through the heavy *pack-ice we had fallen in with. **1876** Davis *Polaris Exp.* iii. 71 At 5 a.m. of the 26th, close pack-ice was again encountered. **1930** *Times Educ. Suppl.* 25 Jan. p. iv/1 From the air it was also observed that the great region of heavy pack-ice..gives place to waters comparatively little encumbered. **1965** *Kingston* (Ontario) *Whig-Standard* 3 Apr. 4/5 About 300,000 of these seals are killed on the pack ice every spring. **1975** *Nature* 18 Dec. 594/1 In the foraminifera-poor beds which we believe represent periods free, at least seasonally, of packice. **1901** *Daily News* 4 Mar. 7/4 They saw the patient but wily mule *pack-laden with the sleeping bags and other impedimenta of the travellers. **1440** *Eton Accts.* in *Athen.* (1887) 69/1 [Purchase of string] voc. paklynes [for measuring foundations of the college]. **1902** J. H. M. Abbott *Tommy Cornstalk* 35 In work where there is a probability of being under fire..the *pack-leader might be left behind. **1975** W. H. Nesbitt in M. W. Fox *Wild Canids* xxvii. 394 The female pack leader [of a group of feral dogs] often 'scouted' ahead before moving the pack. **1858** Simmonds *Dict. Trade*, **Pack-load*, the average load an animal can carry on its back. .. The pack load for a man is about 60 lbs., for a pony 125 lbs., for a bullock 210 lbs., and for an elephant 1000 lbs. **1862** T. W. Harris *Insects injur. Veget.* (ed. 3) v. 493 The *pack-moth (*Anacampsis sarcitella*), which is very destructive to wool and fabrics made of this material. **1835** A. Underwood in *Southwestern Hist. Q.* (1928–9) XXXII. 139 In company with Messrs. Money, Gay..and William Pruit attended by a Mexican with a *pack mule we took our departure. **1839** Z. Leonard *Adventures* (1904) 61 We now scattered over a considerable range of country for the purpose of hunting, leaving ten or twelve men only to bring on the pack-mules. **1895** *Outing* (U.S.) XXVII. 246/2 The Indians, with their pack mules laden with kegs and canteens of water, were sent back over the trail. **1909** W. R. Harris *Catholic Church in Utah* 128 We..entered a small mountain forest of pine trees in which we lost one of our pack mules. **1934** F. Stark *Valleys of Assassins* ii. 74, I..crouched with my back to the gale on the pack-mule. **1785** G. Forster tr. *Sparrman's Voy. Cape G.H.* (1786) I. 238 These oxen are by the colonists called *pack-oxen. **1585** J. Higins *Junius' Nomenclator* 6 *Packe paper, or cap paper, such paper as Mercers and other occupiers vse to wrappe their ware in. **1582** Stanyhurst *Æneis* iv. (Arb.) 101 A foule fog *pack paunch. **1868** *Harper's Mag.* Aug. 348/2 Ten years ago a *pack peddler went through the town. **1880** *Ibid.* Nov. 892/1 There was a pack peddler with smuggled shawls and laces at the door. **1944** G. Wilson *Passing Institutions* 70 We ..married, and died in a small area, learning of the big outside world only through books and an occasional pack peddler or clock tinker who came in. **1870** De B. R. Keim *Sheridan's Troopers on Borders* 201 [Indians] drive the herds and *pack-ponies, or else on foot lead them. **1923** J. H. Cook *50 Yrs. Old Frontier* 98 We used pack ponies on the return trip. **1885** Roosevelt *Hunting Trips* 13 These rats were christened *pack rats, on account of their curious and inveterate habit of dragging off to their holes every object they can possibly move. **1936** D. McCowan *Animals Canad. Rockies* xxii. 196 From the fact that it habitually transports sundry articles from one place to another the animal [*sc.* the wood rat], in the West, is commonly called Pack rat. **1955** Priestley & Hawkes *Journey down Rainbow* iii. 47 A mass of bat and pack-rat droppings. **1963** *Spectator* 21 June 803/2 Obsessed with some impulse, like a packrat fear of throwing anything away. **1966** H. Marriott *Cariboo Cowboy* iii. 40, I had other visitors every so often in the shape of sharp-faced, long-tailed rats which were known as pack rats. **1970** R. Lowell *Notebk.* 22 The horrifying mortmain of Ephemera: keys, drift, sea-urchin shells, Packratted off with joy. **1970** *Publishers' Weekly* 8 June 154 A pack rat is somebody who wants to have his own information material, his own personal library or files, even if this means indulging in a little petty thieving. **1973** *Ann. N.Y. Acad. Sci.* CCXI. 308 The sporadic pack-rat collecting we all do every day by habit amidst the print, graffiti, and speech that encompass our peculiar lives. **1973** 'D. Shannon' *No Holiday for Crime* (1974) vi. 94 When I came to, they were busy as packrats carting stuff out. **1881** Green *Making of Eng.* ii. 64 A wild region of tumbled hills, traversed but by a few *pack-roads. **1851** W. Kelly *Excursion to California* I. ix. 159 We, the packers, were now busily employed making *pack-sacks of a uniform size. **1920** *Rod & Gun in Canada* Nov. 715/1 A good old-time packsack. **1966** *Globe & Mail* (Toronto) 18 Jan. B5/7 [He] was a pack-sack citizen and appeared on Skid Row streets..with..caulk boots which would be later hocked for the last bottle. **1970** 'E. Lathen' *Pick up Sticks* (1971) viii. 70 The packsacks under Thatcher's chair contrasted strongly to the matched sets of luggage piled everywhere. **1858** Simmonds *Dict. Trade*, **Pack-sheet*, a baling material, a large cover for goods in a wagon. **1960** O. Skilbeck *ABC of Film & TV* 94 **Pack Shot*, the egregious scene with which most T.V. 'Commercials' conclude: a C.U. of the Sponsor's wrapped product. **1966** G. N. Leech *Eng. in Advertising* v. 42 In seven-second commercials there is little time to show anything except a title card or a 'pack shot' establishing a visual image of the product. **1969** *Focal Encycl. Film & Television Techniques* 128/1 Television advertising, for instance, makes much use of cinemacrography in the so-called 'pack shots' but these are normally filmed at a scale of less than 1:1. **1897** J. W. Tyrrell *Across Sub-Arctics of Canada* 12 Western half-breeds, trained in the use of the *pack-straps as well as the paddle. *Ibid.* 70 We both took a turn at the pack-straps. **1902** S. E. White *Blazed Trail* 113 The solitary man with the packstraps across his fore-head and shoulders had never seen so many [wood creatures]. **1949** P. Newton *High Country Days* iv. 38 The swags..lashed together [on a pack-horse] with the long packstraps. **1956** M. Duggan *Immanuel's Land* 53 He walked along..with the packstraps cutting into his shoulders. **1956** H. S. M. Kemp *Northern Trader* 25 Our canoemen tied their packstraps around a hundred-pound piece, piled another hundred-pound piece atop it, squatted down cross-legged while they adjusted the headband, heaved themselves up and jogged off. **1960** B. Crump *Good Keen Man* 109 The only reason my pack-straps didn't go the same way was that I noticed Harry eyeing them. **1942** *Sun* (Baltimore) 21 Feb. 2/8 The Nazi in command of the U-boat fleet, had promised to use '*pack tactics' on the Eastern Atlantic and save the largest submarines and best crews for attacks off American shores, to cripple Allied tanker strength. **1944** *Hansard Commons* 7 Mar. 1897 It might have seemed as if perhaps after all, the U-boats with their pack tactics might defeat the convoy system. **1870** *App. Jrnls. House Reps. N.Z.* D. xl. 6 It will be desirable to connect them [*sc.* No Name diggings] by a metalled *pack-track with Marsden to the Greenstone. **1930** L. G. D. Acland *Early Canterbury Runs* (ser. 1) ix. 219 It [*sc.* a hut] is miles by pack-track from the nearest neighbour. **1843** in *Utah Hist. Q.* (1929) II. 116 There is little grass in the mountains and the *pack trail bad. **1911** *Daily Colonist* (Victoria, B.C.) 29 Apr. 17/6 The completion of a pack trail into the valley of the Naas. **1965** *Beaver* Autumn 54/1 Along the pack trail we met trappers coming out of the bush. **1849** K. Webster *Diary* 19 June in *Gold Seekers of '49* (1917) iii. 50 It is said at Fort Kearney that the wagons passed here already this season, en route for California, number 5,400, and also three *pack trains. **1862** R. C. Mayne *Four Yrs. Brit. Columbia & Vancouver I.* 148 From thence pack-trains could make Alexandria..in 14 or 15 days. **1872** Raymond *Statist. Mines & Mining* 257 Several Mexican pack-trains and wagons were engaged transporting ore. **1922** *Beaver* Nov. 64/1 The daily progress of a pack train is a single drive of ten to fifteen miles. **1965** *Beautiful Brit. Columbia* Summer 9/1 He..operated a pack train for the Hudson's Bay Company. **1852** W. Wickenden *Hunchback's Chest* Pref. 7 A roll..appeared tied round with a piece of coarse *pack-twine. **1583** Foxe *A. & M.* 1527/2 Desirous to vtter such Popishe pelfe and *packeware as he brought with him. **1754** T. Gardner *Hist. Dunwich* 39 A *Pack Way, now destroyed, went to Westleton-Walks. **1690** *Lond. Gaz.* No. 2558/4 Three Bags of Cotton-yarn.., four of *Packwoll.

†**pack**, *sb.*[2] *Obs.* [Goes with pack *v.*[2] of which it may be the n. of action.

In quot. 1605, either *pack* or *pact* may be a misprint.]

A private or clandestine arrangement, pact, or compact; a secret or underhand design agreed upon by two or more persons; a plot, conspiracy, intrigue.

1571 Campion *Hist. Irel.* ii. i. (1633) 65 Reymond.. lingered not for Letters Pattents, but stept over presently, and made his packe. **1579–80** North *Plutarch* (1595) 455 It was found straight that this was a grosse packe betwixt Saturninus and Marius. **1600** O. E. *Repl. to Libel* ii. v. 99 Vpon pretence of some pack against the Romish state. *Ibid.* iii. v. 29 This conference was nothing but a packe with the popes Nuncio for the aduancing of the popes credite. **1605** Daniel *Qveenes Arcadia* i. ii. (1623) 333 *A.* Was't not a pack agreed twixt thee and me? *C.* A pact to make thee tell thy secrecy. **1649** G. DANIEL *Trinarch., Rich. II* cclix, Glocester, wth the Cheife of his Complices, Indited are of Treason; for the Packe Was broken.

pack, *a. Sc.* [Origin obscure; perh. related to PACK *sb.*² or *v.*²] On terms of close intercourse; confederate or leagued together, intimate; 'thick'. Also as *adv.* Intimately.

1786 BURNS *Twa Dogs* 38 Nae doubt but they were fain o' ither, An' unco pack an' thick thegither. *a* **1824** *Gypsie Laddie* xii. in Child *Ballads* VII. (1890) 69/1 Sir, I saw this day a fairy queen Fu pack wi a gypsie laddie. **1863** JANET HAMILTON *Poems & Ess.* 37 John an' me hae lang been pack. **1893** STEVENSON *Catriona* 343 Him and me were never onyways pack; we used to girn at ither like a pair of pipers.

pack (pæk), *v.*¹ Forms: see PACK *sb.*; also *Pa. t.* and *pple.* **packed** (pækt); *pple.* in 6–7 pact. [f. PACK *sb.*: see Anglo-Fr. *packer* (1423), *enpaker* (1294), Anglo-L. *pakkare* (*c* 1341), *impaccare* (1280). Cf. MDu., MLG., Du., LG. *pakken*, late MHG., Ger. *packen*; late Icel. *pakka*, Norw. *pakka*, Sw. *packa*, Da. *pakke*; F. *pacquier* (1530 in Palsgr.), *pacquer* (1600 in Godef.).

Early examples in Anglo-Fr. and Anglo-L.:

1280 *Memoranda Roll* (L.T.R.) 7 & 8 Edw. I. m. 13 (P.R.O.) Inueniet..sarpellarios..ad predictam lanam impaccandam. **1294** *Acc. Exch., K.R.* Bundle 126 No. 7 (2) m. 4 E le apariller de ceste leine e les sarpellers a mesme la leine enpaker nous vnt couste cest an..iij.li. ij.s. vj.d. **1341** *Durham Acc. Rolls* (Surtees) 542 Pro lana pakkanda. **1409–10** *Rolls of Parlt.* III. 626/1 Certeyns Merchantz..en mesmes les packes sotelment enpackent layn fyne, et et argent. **1423** *Act 2 Hen. VI*, c. 11 Le Barelle de Harank danguilles [sil ne contiegnent] xxx. galons pleinement pakkez. *16th c. transl.* Nor barrell of Herring nor of Eeles vnles they contayn 30 gallons fully packed.]

I. 1. a. *trans.* To make into a pack, package, bale, or compact bundle; to put together compactly as a bundle, or in a box, bag, or other receptacle, esp. for convenience of transport or for storing.

13.. *E.E. Allit. P.* B. 1282 Now hatz Nabuzardan nomen alle þyse noble þynges, And pyled þat precious place and pakked þose godes. **1444** *Rolls of Parlt.* V. 104/2 There is grete plenty of Wolle Yerne, dailly pakkede and shippede. **1494** *Act 11 Hen. VII*, c. 23 The same Herring should be well, truly, and justly layed and packed. **1580** in *Rec. Convent. Roy. Burghs* (1870) I. 100 He sall pak..no grilses with salmound, bot sax grilses in ane barrell at the maist. **1598** HAKLUYT *Voy.* I. 210 So many folders to fold their clothes, and so many packers to pack their packs. **1693** DRYDEN *Juvenal* iii. 18 My Friend, just ready to depart, Was packing all his Goods in one poor Cart. **1776** ADAM SMITH *W.N.* IV. viii. (1869) II. 233 It cannot be packed in any box [etc.]..or any other package, but only in packs of leather or pack-cloth. **1863** GEO. ELIOT *Romola* xxxvi, The contents of the library were all packed and carried away.

absol. **1865** TROLLOPE *Belton Est.* xx. 234 He threw a heap of clothes into a large portmanteau, and set himself to work packing.

b. In *Commerce.* To prepare and put up in suitable receptacles, so as to preserve fresh or sound for use, or in a form suitable for the market.

An extension of the use in sense 1, as applied to herring, salmon, etc., now used to include the whole process of pickling or otherwise preparing, and tinning or canning, or otherwise putting up, meat, fish, eggs, fruit, and other commodities, so as to preserve them for future or distant sale and consumption. Hence PACK *sb.*¹ 12, PACKER¹ 2 b, uses of PACKING *vbl. sb.*¹ and *ppl. a.*, etc.

[**1494**, **1580**: see sense 1.] **1725** DE FOE *Voy. round World* (1840) 7 The beef being also well pickled or double packed (that we might have a sufficient reserve for the length of our voyage. **1831** *Reg. Deb. Congress U.S.* 8 Feb. 133 It is believed that, in Cincinnati alone, there were slaughtered and packed this year one hundred thousand hogs. **1852** *Trans. Mich. Agric. Soc.* III. 230 Mullet..are sometimes used as pan-fish, and are packed to a limited extent.

2. a. With *up*: To put *up* in a pack or packs.

1530 PALSGR. 651/1, I wyll packe up my stuffe... *Je pacqueray mes besoignes.* **1671** R. MONTAGU in *Buccleuch MSS.* (Hist. MSS. Comm.) I. 498 Thomas Bond has made an end of packing up all the pictures. **1753** FOOTE *Eng. in Paris* II. Wks. 1799 I. 52 So pack up a few things, and we'll off in a post-chaise directly. **1809** MALKIN *Gil Blas* II. vii. ¶27, I should be a great fool to pack up my alls when the prize was falling into my hands. **1860** TYNDALL *Glaciers* I. xvi. 107 We..packed up our provisions and instruments.

†**b.** *fig.* To put up with; to 'pocket'.

1624 T. SCOTT *Votivæ Angliæ* D iij b, Too generous sencible and delicate or digest to packe upp the least affront or injurie whatsoeuer.

c. *absol.* To pack clothes and other necessaries for a journey. Also with *up*, and used in passive of a person: to have finished packing.

1684 BUNYAN *Pilgr.* II. 5 They packt up and are also gone after him. *c* **1714** LADY M. W. MONTAGU *Let. to Mrs. Hewet* xcviii. 160 One who has nothing at present in her head but packing up. **1906** 'O. HENRY' in *N.Y. World Mag.* 1 July 8/1, I am packed and was to have left for the North Woods this morning. **1907** G. B. SHAW *John Bull's Other Island* I. 28 *Doyle*: Hodson. *Hodson*..: Did you call, sir? *Doyle*: Pack for me too. I'm going to Ireland with Mr. Broadbent. **1912** R. BROOKE *Old Vicarage Grantchester* (1916) 10 God! I will pack, and take a train, And get me to England once again! **1958** J. CANNAN *And be a Villain* iv. 83 I'm packed, but I must..tell them I'm leaving. **1962** J. BRAINE *Life at Top* xxii. 248, I turned away without speaking and went upstairs to pack. **1969** G. LYALL *Venus with Pistol* xxxv. 234 We're all packed up. I don't know if I've got all your things in the right bags. **1974** J. JOHNSTON *How Many Miles to Babylon?* 66, I have to catch the Dublin train. I..should go and pack.

d. *to pack up* (or *in*) (*intr.*), to stop working; to give up an enterprise; to surrender; to die; to cease to function; to collapse.

1925 FRASER & GIBBONS *Soldier & Sailor Words* 219 *Pack-up.., To*, to stop (as opposed to 'carry on'). To give up. To finish. To die. **1926** E. F. SPANNER *Naviators* i. 8 It was about five in the afternoon when Sir Joseph decided to pack up for the day. **1928** C. F. S. GAMBLE *Story N. Sea Air Station* xii. 201 To make matters worse another engine packed up, and this increased the stern list of the ship. **1940** 'GUN BUSTER' *Return via Dunkirk* II. xii. 174 The Belgians have packed up... They've laid down their arms. **1948** C. DAY LEWIS *Otterbury Incident* iv. 45 There seemed nothing to stop Toppy unless his voice packed up; so Ted and I left him. **1953** W. BURROUGHS *Junkie* (1972) vii. 70 He said, 'We've got to pack in. We can't last with this crowd.' **1956** 'J. WYNDHAM' *Seeds of Time* 87 The laterals aren't firing... I mean they *won't* fire. They've packed up. **1959** 'M. INNES' *Hare sitting Up* I. i. 17 The most surprising people will pack up under strain. **1962** *Economist* 3 Nov. 440/2 The Algerians seem to think that Mr Khemisti..broke off the talks as a gesture of solidarity with Cuba. But American reports suggest that it was the State Department itself that decided to pack in. **1967** J. L. ANDERSON *Vinland Voyage* 90 None of us had much confidence in it [*sc.* our ancient engine] and it packed up a few days later. **1973** A. BROINOWSKI *Take One Ambassador* i. 14 I'm Mrs Bert Norrice..Mr Norrice passed on last year..Bert's heart packed up. **1977** G. FISHER *Villain of Piece* iv. 40 Where is the nearest telephone?..It's packed in.

e. *to pack up* or *in* (*trans.*), to stop (doing something), to give up, finish with; freq. in phr. *to pack it up* (or *in*), to stop working, abandon an attempt, etc.; also as imp., be quiet, 'cut it out', behave yourself. *slang* and *colloq.*

1942 BERREY & VAN DEN BARK *Amer. Thes. Slang* §205/4 *Stop talking*; '*shut up*',..pack it up. **1943** HUNT & PRINGLE *Service Slang* 50 *Pack it up* or *in*, stop talking or fooling; cut it out. **1945** J. B. PRIESTLEY *Three Men in New Suits* iv. 104 'Pack it up,' she warned him. **1949** 'G. ORWELL' *Nineteen Eighty-Four* I. viii. 86 'Oh, pack it in!' said the third man. **1951** A. BARON *Rosie Hogarth* 210 Pack it up, Joyce. I'm telling you. **1951** 'N. SHUTE' *Round Bend* 10 It looked as if the public were getting a bit tired of it. Sir Alan packed it up. **1953** W. BURROUGHS *Junkie* (1972) xii. 121 Every month or so she hires a new lover, gives him shirts and suits and wrist watches, and then packs him in when she has enough. **1959** 'O. MILLS' *Stairway to Murder* viii. 92, I packed up my job last week... I just told you... I packed in my job last week. **1963** N. HILLIARD *Piece of Land* 43 They saw nothing... About eight o'clock they decided to pack it in..headed back for town. **1971** B. W. ALDISS *Soldier Erect* 47 'Why don't you pack in ordering us about, Wally?' I asked. **1972** J. WILSON *Hide & Seek* viii. 137 Rob Millar didn't finish work until gone eleven, and then decided he'd have to pack it in. **1974** K. CLARK *Another Part of Wood* ii. 56 He had long ago 'packed it in', and spent his life sitting by the window dozing, with a volume of Pepys' Diary upside down on his knee. **1976** *News of World* 14 Mar. 11/2 He has been ordered to pack in his job and return for the final four weeks of term. **1977** *Daily Mirror* 18 Mar. 24 Hey! You! That's my missus—pack it in!

3. a. To put together closely or compactly; to form into a compact mass or body; to crowd together.

1563 GOLDING *Cæsar* 122 He was fayne to packe vp his souldiers in lesse roume closer together. **1577** WHETSTONE *Gascoigne* B iij b, God graunt his woords, within your harts be pact. **1784** COWPER *Task* I. 80 Two citizens who take the air, Close pack'd, and smiling, in a chaise and one. **1864** TENNYSON *En. Ard.* 178 Almost as neat and close as Nature packs Her blossom or her seedling. **1887** *Spectator* 15 Oct. 1373 Audiences so packed as to be dangerous.

b. *Naut. to pack on all sail*: to put on or hoist all possible sail for the sake of speed; to crowd sail. Also *absol.* in same sense.

1562 J. SHUTE *Cambini's Turkish Wars* 34 b, The Captaine commaunded to packe on all the sayles. *c* **1594** CAPT. WYATT *R. Dudley's Voy. W. Ind.* (Hakl. Soc.) 9 Wee might..perceave a ship pack on all the saile they weare able to make after us. **1706** E. WARD *Wooden World Diss.* (1708) 11 He flies at her with all the Sail he can pack. **1805** NELSON in Nicolas *Disp.* VI. 479, I shall..be ready to pack after them, if they are gone to the Bay. **1850** SCORESBY *Cheever's Whalem. Adv.* xii. (1859) 168 They packed on all sail. **1884** H. COLLINGWOOD *Under Meteor Flag* 32 Turn the hands up, and pack on her..discretion is the better part of valour with us just now.

†**c.** *Gardening.* To graft in a particular way: see quot. *Obs.*

1615 W. LAWSON *Country Housew. Gard.* (1626) 30 Packing on, is, when you cut aslope, a twig of the same bigness with your graft, either in or besides the knot,..and make your graft agree jump with the cyon, and gash your graft and your cyon in the middest of the wound length-way, a straw breadth deep, and thrust the one into the other..then tye them close.

d. To press (anything loose) into a compact or solid mass.

1850 R. G. CUMMING *Five Yrs. Hunter's Life S. Afr.* II. 141 The ground all round was packed flat with their spoor. **1890** L. C. D'OYLE *Notches* 80, I packed down the snow, and climbed out on to the roof. **1893** *Outing* (U.S.) XXII. 134/1 The rain..had but little effect on the heavy dust;..it would probably take a week's constant rain to pack the road hard again.

e. *Mining.* In the process of washing ore: To cause the denser material or ore to subside to the bottom by striking (the tub or keeve) with mallets or hammers.

1875 *Ure's Dict. Arts* II. 153 The tub is then packed by striking its outside with heavy wooden mallets... The packing hastens the subsidence of the denser portions. *Ibid.* 154 This tub is packed by machinery... The hammers..are mounted upon iron bars..and violently driven upon the side of the kieve by means of springs.

f. *Theatr.* Phr. *to pack them in*: to attract a capacity audience. Also *transf.*

1943 *N.Y. Times* 9 May II. 5/4 Harry James and his band have been helping to pack them in at the Paramount. **1970** *Guardian* 31 July 9/3 Bolton's Octagon Theatre..is packing them in for Old Tyme Musical Hall. **1972** *Ibid.* 1 Dec. 11/1 She's still at it at 49; still packing 'em in, and getting the odd rave review. **1977** *New Statesman* 17 June 809/2 His rejigged Radio 4 *Today* programme is now packing the listeners in.

g. *Computers.* To compress (stored data) in a way that permits subsequent recovery; *spec.* to represent (two or more items of data) in a single word. Also *absol.*

1954 *Computers & Automation* Dec. 18/1 *Pack*, to combine several different brief fields of information into one machine word. **1959** M. H. WRUBEL *Primer of Programming* viii. 189 If the data consist of only a few significant digits, two or more numbers can be 'packed' into a single 10-digit word. They will be transferred from the card to the machine as a 10-digit word, which must subsequently be 'unpacked' by an appropriate program. **1961** L. W. HEIN *Introd. Electronic Data Processing* ix. 165 One of the bad situations is that of the 31-word record in a 60-word fixed record-length computer... A decision to pack means some rather complex programming. **1964** *IBM Systems Jrnl.* III. 125 Decimal digits, packed two to a byte, appear in fields of variable length (from 1 to 16 bytes). **1972** *Computer Jrnl.* XV. 199/1 A stream..might be formed by one stream function which unpacks words into bytes, followed by another one which packs them all up again. **1973** [see PACKED *ppl. a.*¹ 1 c].

4. To form into a 'pack', in special senses of the sb. **a.** To form (hounds) into a pack; **b.** To place (cards) together in a pack; **c.** To drive (ice) into a pack: usually passive.

1649 G. DANIEL *Trinarch., Hen. IV* cclxviii, Soe may Hounds well-pack't Pursue the Prey. **1681** W. ROBERTSON *Phraseol. Gen.* (1693) 971 To pack the cards; *componere chartas.* **1824** PARRY *North West Passage* i. 9 A very inconsiderable quantity of loose ice is sufficient to shelter a ship from the sea, provided it be closely packed. *c* **1887** MISS W. JONES *Games Patience* ii. 9 As the aces turn out, you place them below these heaps, packing on them at every opportunity. *Ibid.* xix. 44 You are not bound to pack on the side packets.

5. *intr.* for *refl.* **a.** To collect into a body; to come together or assemble closely; to crowd together. *esp.* To collect into or form a pack: said of animals, as wolves, grouse, etc., also of ice in the polar seas: see PACK *sb.* 5, 7. Also of a group of runners in a long-distance race.

1828 *Craven Gloss.* (ed. 2), *Pack*, to collect together. **1844** in *Rep. U.S. Comm. Patents 1846* (1847) 34 It [*sc.* cotton] does not pack and becomes hard. **1845** *Zoologist* III. 1170 The young follow their parents in a 'covey' till..autumn, when several coveys 'pack', i.e. become gregarious. **1855** KINGSLEY *Westw. Ho!* xvi, Sailors packed close in those days. **1858** GEIKIE *Hist. Boulder* ii. 10 The ice is then said to pack. **1884** *Pall Mall G.* 12 Aug. 4/1 In the Hebrides the grouse..will decline to pack. **1887** A. W. TOURGÉE *Button's Inn* 200 It [*sc.* the storm] filled the road with a slippery mealy mass, which did not cling or pack. **1890–3** E. M. TABER *Stowe Notes, Lett. & Verses* (1913) 8 The snow packs so readily that I can walk without much difficulty. **1908** *Westm. Gaz.* 27 July 9/3 The failure of the British representatives..was undoubtedly due to their failure to 'pack' well.

b. In passive sense: To admit of being packed in a bundle, or pressed into a compact mass.

1846 GREENER *Sc. Gunnery* 83 When the small balls did not pack perfectly tight. **1867** *Jrnl. R. Agric. Soc.* Ser. II. III. II. 591 It all takes to pieces, packs up easily. **1939–40** *Army & Navy Stores Catal.* 656/1 Foulard Silk [dressing gown]..of very light weight to pack small. **1946** *Mod. Lang. Notes* LXI. 444 This dress washes and irons and packs easily. **1974** *Janet Frazer Catal.* Spring & Summer 455/2 Pneumatic 'Igloo' tent... Packs away compactly.

c. Of the forwards in Rugby football: to form or take their places in the scrummage. Also const. *in* and *down.*

1874 *Rugby Union Football Ann. 1874–5* 15 A good forward will..pack in again at the back of the scrummage. **1887** M. SHEARMAN *Athletics & Football* II. iii. 313 There is many a good scrimmager who packs quickly. **1900** A. E. T. WATSON *Young Sportsman* 252 Be the first to form the scrummage and pack quickly. **1927** WAKEFIELD & MARSHALL *Rugger* II. iii. 162 If..his opponents have the right of putting the ball in, he ought to pack opposite their loose-head to be ready to check their scrum-half. **1949** *Rugby League Football* ('Know the Game' Series) 31 The front row forward who packs nearest to the referee has what is known as the 'loose head'. **1968** HUDSON & DYER *Your Bk. of Rugger* v. 49 'Number 8'..packs down in between the second row, with his back parallel to the ground and his feet spread evenly apart. **1970** G. SLATTER *On the Ball* vi. 139 The scrum packs down on our 25-yard line and Haigh takes the ball.

6. a. *trans.* To cover, surround, or protect with something pressed tightly around.

1796 C. MARSHALL *Garden.* viii. (1813) 102 Trees properly packed (i.e. the roots well covered) may live out of ground ten days or a fortnight in autumn. **1882** BUCKLAND *Notes & Jottings* 282 They [beavers] seem to have packed, repaired, and continually attended to the tender places which the stream might make in their engineering. **1890** *Daily News* 26 Dec. 7/1 Navvies are 'packing' the line as it crosses the deep valleys which they have..filled up with the chalk and gravel from the cuttings. **1896** *Allbutt's Syst. Med.* I. 428 If the surgeon be not at hand, the dressing should be 'packed', that is pads of absorbent wool bandaged over the points where the discharge appears.

b. *Med.* In hydropathic treatment: To envelop (the body or a part of it) in a wet sheet or cloth, with or without a dry outer covering.

1849 MRS. CARLYLE *Lett.* I. 46 The Doctor proposed to 'pack' me. **1859** SMEDLEY *Pract. Hydropathy* 43 It is important, in packing,..that the patient be tightly packed in the sheet and blanket. **1896** *Allbutt's Syst. Med.* I. 345 The diaphoretic methods by packing with woollen blankets or wet sheets are often found to be useful.

c. *Surg.* To fill, wedge, or cover with a pack. Also *absol.* ***to pack off***, to wedge (an internal organ) with packs so as to keep it away from a region of interest.

1889 CAIRD & CATHCART *Surg. Handbk.* vii. 53 The cavity of the nostril may be packed with a long strip of lint. **1897** STIMSON & ROGERS *Man. Operative Surg.* (ed. 3) I. 28 Much of the hemorrhage can be stopped..by packing with sponges or pads of gauze. **1906** H. M. DAVIES *Man. Minor Surgery & Bandaging* (ed. 13) ii. 36 Large pieces of gauze.. are very convenient for packing off the intestines..from the rest of the abdomen. **1924** R. HOWARD *Surg. Emergencies* iv. 74 The site of the obstruction should be isolated..by.. packing the surrounding intestine off with abdominal pads. **1940** R. MAINGOT *Abdominal Operations* I. I. ii. 46 The little sinus that remains may be lightly curetted out and packed with gauze which has been soaked in..penicillin. **1955** M. G. LYNCH in Ochsner & DeBakey *Christopher's Minor Surg.* (ed. 7) xxi. 499/2 If the hemorrhage is severe..the nose should be packed. **1972** NEALON & GROSSI in P. F. Nora *Operative Surg.* i. 7/2 The wound is packed open with gauze over a simple layer of nonadherent material.

7. a. To fill (a receptacle or space) *with* something packed in (*e.g.* a bag, box, trunk, etc., with clothes or goods of any kind compactly arranged; a crevice or interstice with something fitting tightly, as in making a vessel air-tight, water-tight, etc.); to cram, stuff. Also with *up*.

1581 J. BELL *Haddon's Answ. Osor.* 41 b, You packe up your trunckes, and returne to your former course of exhortation. **1583** *Leg. Bp. St. Androis* Pref. 124 Packand thair penche lyk Epicurians. **1825** J. NICHOLSON *Operat. Mechanic* 297 The head being often packed up with elastic substances, such as pasteboard, or even cork. **1884** G. ALLEN *Philistia* II. 75 Ernest had packed his portmanteau. **1910** C. E. MULFORD *Hopalong Cassidy* xxxviii. 242 Hall carefully packed his pipe and puffed quickly.

b. *transf.* and *fig.* To fill (any space) as full as it will hold; to cram, crowd (*with* people or with something immaterial). Usually in passive; also predicated of that which occupies the space. Also const. *out*.

1857–8 SEARS *Athan.* xi. 96 [A passage] crowded and packed with meaning. **1886** S. G. W. BENJAMIN in *Harper's Mag.* LXXII. 463/1 They opened a lane through the crowd that packed the great portal. **1932** C. C. MARTINDALE *What are Saints?* 58, I had to go straight from Westminster Cathedral..to a church in Chiswick,..packed out with people observing his [*sc.* St. Edward the Confessor's] feast-day. **1944** G. TEXIDOR in D. M. Davin *N.Z. Short Stories* (1953) 301 The domain in front of the hotel was packed out with cars and lorries. **1973** *Times* 7 June 15/5 The Rolling Stones couldn't play the Ken Colyer Club one night and The Dimensions appeared instead... It was packed out. **1977** D. CLARK *Gimmel Flask* vi. 101 This place is packed out for lunch.

c. ***to pack them***, to hold back diarrhœa caused by nervousness; hence to be terrified. Also with explicit alternative objs. *Austral. slang.*

1951 E. LAMBERT *Twenty Thousand Thieves* 132 He's packing them badly. He's quite useless. **1952** T. A. G. HUNGERFORD *Ridge & River* iii. 46, I suppose the poor cow *would* pack 'em a bit. He's on'y a kid, by the look of him. **1959** 'D. FORREST' *Last Blue Sea* 69 You know something, thought Ron Fisher, you're no good. You're packing them. **1961** R. BRADDON *Naked Island* 44 'Who's panicking?' 'You are, son. Fair packing 'em, y'are.' **1971** D. IRELAND *Unknown Industrial Prisoner* 132 They were packing the shits when he went off his head in the control room last time.

8. To load (a beast) with a pack.

1596 SHAKS. *1 Hen. IV*, II. i. 3 Charles waine is ouer the new Chimney, and yet our horse not packt. **1837** W. IRVING *Capt. Bonneville* III. 243 It was I that packed the horses, and led them on the journey. **1894** H. NISBET *Bush Girl's Rom.* 121 The bushrangers..packed a couple of spare horses with what he was likely to require.

9. a. To carry or convey in a pack or packs. Hence, to carry in any manner; to wear habitually; to possess. Also *absol.*

1805 W. CLARK *Jrnl.* 15 Dec. in Lewis & Clark *Orig. Jrnls. Lewis & Clark Expedition* (1905) III. xxi. 280 Proced up the 1st. right hand fork 4 miles & pack the meat from the woods to the canoes. **1816** U. BROWN *Jrnl.* in *Maryland Hist. Mag.* (1916) XI. 360, I let him know that I..meant to hire a horse of him to pack our provisions. **1845** J. C. FRÉMONT *Rep. Exploring Expedition* 73 It would have been a work of great time and labor to pack our baggage across the ridge. **1850** CULBERTSON in *5th Smithson. Rep.* (1851) 91 Joe killed an antelope... We packed the hams and shoulders to camp. **1863** S. BUTLER *First Year in Canterbury Settlement* v. 61 The back country..is inaccessible by dray, so that all stores ..have to be packed in and packed out on horseback. **1874** E. EGGLESTON *Circuit Rider* vii. 71 My shoes hurts my feet, an' I have to pack one of 'em in my hand most of the time. **1877** RAYMOND *Statist. Mines & Mining* 19 The ore.. having been packed a distance of ten miles on mules. **1886** *Fortn. Rev.* Jan. 52 The [gold] 'dust'..filled the buckskin pouches..to such plethoric dimensions as to require the assistance of a sumpter horse to 'pack' it down from the mines. **1890** N. P. LANGFORD *Vigilante Days* II. xviii. 282 No man that ever packed a star in this city can arrest me. **1902** A. H. LEWIS *Wolfville Days* v. 61 He finds this person ain't packin' no gun. **1903** *Dialect Notes* II. 323, I never did pack a watch. **1913** [see HEFT *v.*[1] 1]. **1927** *Amer. Speech* II. 361 He packed the child home. **1930** L. G. D. ACLAND *Early Canterbury Runs* (ser. 1) viii. 200 George Harper..used to pack the wool out on bullocks, three sacks on each. **1940** R. CHANDLER *Farewell, my Lovely* iii. 22 Don't you pack no rod? **1952** *Picture Post* 6 Dec. 37/2 A revival of flogging was in loud demand, and there was the barmaid who insisted she wouldn't feel safe until every policeman packed a gun. **1970** C. WILSON *Campbell of Yukon* ii. 9 Here the cargoes &c have to be 'packed' on the men's shoulders from water to water. **1973** *Washington Post* 5 Jan. B3/6 Actress Ali McGraw 'packs all the glamor of a worn-out sneaker'.

b. To travel with one's goods or merchandise in packs.

1842 M. CRAWFORD *Jrnl.* (1897) 14 Some of the company preparing to pack from here. **1857** W. CHANDLESS *Visit to Salt Lake* II. vii. 264 Waggoning through the settlements.. and thence 'packing' to California.. **1903** S. E. WHITE *Forest* ii. 15 Do not carry a coat..you will never wear it while packing. **1911** J. F. WILSON *Land Claimers* i. 1 It isn't much fun packing along that trail.

c. To be capable of delivering (a blow) with force; esp. in phr. ***to pack a punch***; also *fig. colloq.*

1921 H. C. WITWER in *Collier's* 19 Feb. 22/3 He packed a wicked right and had stopped a lot of good men before Kid Roberts cut him short with a one-round knockout. **1922** E. O'NEILL *Hairy Ape* (1923) i. 7 He packa da wallop, I tella you!.. No fightin', maties. **1934** M. H. WESEEN *Dict. Amer. Slang* 239 *Pack a terrific punch*, to hit hard, or to have the ability to do so. *a* **1938** T. WOLFE *Lett.* (1956) 45, I think my play 'The House' will 'pack a punch'. **1957** *Listener* 20 June 1008/1 An artist who packs such a violent literary punch might be expected to make use of a savage, expressionist line. **1958** WODEHOUSE *Cocktail Time* xvi. 137, I take it that she busted you one... These nannies pack a wicked punch. **1971** *Sunday Express* (Johannesburg) 28 Mar. 22/3 Like Kies, he packs a powerful punch, but he does not wade in like Jan. **1973** W. M. DUNCAN *Big Timer* xxi. 137 That Carver packed a wallop, didn't he? I should have plugged him sooner.

II. 10. *refl.* and *intr.* To take oneself off with one's belongings, be off; to go away, depart, esp. when summarily dismissed. **†a.** *refl.*

[So in Du. *zich weg pakken*; Plantijn, 1573, has *hem wech packen, packt v van hier, packt v t' huys*.]

1508 KENNEDIE *Flyting w. Dunbar* 442 For fault of puissance, pelour, thou mon pak the. **1601** CHESTER *Love's Mart.* lxxxiv. (1878) 21 Enuie go packe thee to some forreine soyle. *a* **1634** CHAPMAN *Alphonsus* Plays 1873 III. 255 Pack thee out of my sight. **1865** CARLYLE *Fredk. Gt.* XI. iv. (1872) IV. 63 Voltaire..lost no time in packing himself [cf. Germ. *sich packen*].

b. *intr.* Also ***to be*** (also ***go***) ***packing***. ***to send packing***, to send away, dismiss summarily (= sense 11).

1526 SKELTON *Magnyf.* 1797 As for all other let them trusse & packe. **1567** *Trial Treas.* in Hazl. *Dodsley* III. 294 Will ye be packing, you ill-favoured lout? **1594** NASHE *Unfort. Trav.* 9, I would..send him packing. **1612** CHAPMAN *Widdowes T.* Plays 1873 III. 35 For your owne sake, I advise you to pack hence. **1681** W. ROBERTSON *Phraseol. Gen.* (1693) 514 Let us be packing, We'll dwell no longer here; *migremus hinc*. **1766** GOLDSM. *Vic. W.* xxi, Out I say, pack out this moment. **1842** TENNYSON *Vision of Sin* IV. xii, Let the canting liar pack! **1842** BROWNING *Pied Piper* 32 Sure as fate, we'll send you packing. **1893** STEVENSON *Catriona* ii. 13, I had scarce breath enough to send my porter packing. **1926** T. E. LAWRENCE *Seven Pillars* lxxxviii. 468 As both example and guilt were blatant, the others went packing into the far room while their chiefs forthwith executed sentence.

c. Const. *off*. Also, to die.

1766 SEWEL & BUYS *Compl. Dict. Eng. & Dutch* I. 549/3 To pack off, (to die) *Stërven*. **1914** W. OWEN *Let.* 15 June (1967) 260 The alternative would be to come home immediately..and at once to pack off to some other part of the world. **1933** T. E. LAWRENCE *Let.* 10 Aug. (1938) 774, I would like myself and those I care for to pack off all together.

11. *trans.* To send or drive away, order off, send about his business, dismiss summarily, get rid of. Now usually with *off*.

1589 RIDER *Bibl. Schol.* 1047 To packe, or driue forwarde. **1602** WARNER *Alb. Eng.* x. lv. (1612) 243 Lord William Graie..Did with an armie hence pack thence our dangerous neighbour Guise. **1643** LIGHTFOOT *Glean. Ex.* (1648) 24 He was packed away. **1662–3** PEPYS *Diary* 19 Jan., My Lord did presently pack his lady into the Country. **1737** BRACKEN *Farriery Impr.* (1757) II. 79 They are pretty sure of packing him off to one or other that does not understand them. *c* **1817** HOGG *Tales & Sk.* V. 187 As soon as day-light appeared, I was packed about my business. **1894** NORRIS in *Cornh. Mag.* Mar. 227 He packed her off to bed at once.

12. ***to pack a jury, cards***: see next.

pack, *v.*[2] [Origin obscure: cf. PACK *sb.*[2]

The sense, both in vb. and sb., suggests some connexion with PACT *sb.* (also COMPACT *sb.*[1] c); the implication here being however always bad. As to the form, though final *-ct* is commonly reduced in Sc. and in some mod.Eng. dial. to *c* or *k* (e.g. *ack, fack, correck, direck*, etc.), we have no evidence of such change in Standard Eng. of 16–17th c.; yet a confusion between *pact* and *pack't, pack'd*, is conceivable. On the other hand, no connexion is apparent between sense 1 and any sense treated under PACK *v.*[1]; hence this has been provisionally ranked as a separate word. But the later senses, esp. 4 and 5, appear to arise from a blending of this with PACK *v.*[1], with which they are now in feeling associated. So with PACK *sb.*[2]]

†I. †1. *intr.* To enter into a private arrangement, to agree in a secret or underhand design; to plot, conspire, scheme, intrigue. *Obs.*

a **1529** [see PACKING *vbl. sb.*[2]]. **1582** STANYHURST *Æneis* IV. (Arb.) 97 With two Gods packing one womman sellye to coosen. **1588** SHAKS. *Tit. A.* IV. ii. 155 Goe packe with him, and giue the mother gold, And tell them both the circumstance of all. **1602** CAREW *Cornwall* 14 b, [This want of profit] they impute it partly to the Easterne buyers packing, partly to the owners not venting, and venturing the same.

†2. To bring or let (a person) into a plot, to engage as a confederate or conspirator; in *pass.* to be an accomplice or confederate in a plot. *Obs.*

1590 SHAKS. *Com. Err.* V. i. 219 That Goldsmith there, were he not pack'd with her, Could witnesse it. **1599** —— *Much Ado* V. i. 308 Margaret..I beleeue was packt in all this wrong, Hired to it by your brother. *c* **1600** DAY *Begg. Bednall Gr.* I. ii. (1881) 18 Do you but send away Sir Walter Playnsey, Let me alone to pack the Cardinal.

†3. a. *trans.* To contrive or plan (something) in an underhand way; to plot. *Obs.*

1613 [see PACKING *vbl. sb.*[2]]. **1614** SYLVESTER *Bethulia's Rescue* IV. 209 Their Marriage then was neither stoln, nor packt, Nor posted. **1655** FULLER *Ch. Hist.* II. ii. §10 She had purposely before-hand packed and plotted the same [his death]. **1694** F. BRAGGE *Disc. Parables* xii. 417 Had it been a pack'd business, they would have been careful not to have differed in a tittle.

b. *intr.* or *abs.*

1590 NASHE *Pasquin's Apol.* (Gros. I. 225), My Reformer doth nothing but play the Iugler: he packs under-boord, and shewes not how farre forth the Archb. hath affirmed it.

II. 4. To select or make up (a jury or a deliberating or voting body) in such a way as to secure a partial decision, or further some private or party ends. Also, to secure (a particular decision or result) by selecting or arranging the body of voters, etc.

1587 HARRISON *England* II. ii. (1877) I. 53 Grieued, that she had..wrested out such a uerdict against him, and therein packed vp a quest at hir owne choise. **1643** [see PACKED[2]]. **1665** J. WEBB *Stone-Heng* (1725) 159 What by impannelling of ignorant Jurors, what through packing and suborning Them. **1681** DRYDEN *Abs. & Achit.* 607 He packt a Jury of dissenting Jews. *a* **1715** BURNET *Own Time* IV. (1724) I. 626 All people saw the way for packing a Parliament now laid open. **1849** MACAULAY *Hist. Eng.* vi. II. 98 He had packed the courts of Westminster Hall in order to obtain a decision in favour of his dispensing power. *Ibid.* viii. 317 Having determined to pack a parliament, James set himself energetically and methodically to the work. **1925** A. TOYNBEE *Survey Internat. Affairs 1920–23* 80 In order to prevent any possiblity of 'packing' the vote, the date of residence was not fixed..as the day when the Treaty came into force, but as the day when it was signed. **1932** *Ann. Reg. 1931* II. 275 China... Together with others from the Canton faction they issued a manifesto declaring that the elections to the Convention would be a fiasco, that the Convention would be 'packed' by Chiang, and that its whole purpose was to seat him more firmly in the dictatorship. **1955** *Times* 26 May 8/3 The Minister had tried to cloak the Bill with respectability but this had to be seen against his earlier statements about 'packing' the courts and the Senate. **1965** *Mod. Law Rev.* XXVIII. 517 He was not above packing the House in order to curb such activities. **1973** *Black Panther* 14 Apr. 12/2 The Supreme Court is being systematically packed despite the defeat of Carswell and Haynesworth. **1976** *Daily Tel.* 24 Apr. 2/6 Vauxhall Labour party is to meet..to investigate allegations that the general management committee is being improperly 'packed' with members to ensure the selection of a merchant banker to succeed the present MP.

5. To arrange or shuffle (playing cards), so as to cheat or secure a fraudulent advantage. Hence *fig.*, ***to pack cards with*** (***any one***), to make a cheating arrangement with. (Cf. sense 1.) *Obs.* or *arch.*

1599 MINSHEU *Sp. Dict.*, *Barajar*, to packe cards, to shuffle cards. **1606** SHAKS. *Ant. & Cl.* IV. xiv. 19 Shee, Eros has Packt Cards with Cæsars, and false plaid my Glory Vnto an Enemies triumph. **1615** BACON *Sp. about Undertakers* Wks. 1879 I. 498/1 Some shall be thought practisers that would pluck the cards, and others shall be thought papists that would shuffle the cards... The king were better call for a new pair of cards, than play upon these if they be packed. **1667** DENHAM *Direct. Paint.* IV. ix. 11 in *Third Collect. Poems* 19/2 How to pack Knaves 'mongst Kings and Queens. **1753** *Scots Mag.* Oct. 492/1, I learned to pack cards and to cog a dye. **1890** MCCARTHY *French Revol.* II. 76 The poor King tried..to pack cards with fortune. **1927** *Amer. Speech* II. 352/2 They packed the deal on the other players.

packability (pækə'bɪlɪtɪ). [f. PACKABLE *a.*: see -BILITY.] The capacity to be packed; *spec.* of clothes and fabrics, the ability to be packed easily into, and to travel without damage in, a suitcase.

1958 *Vogue* May 108 A traveller's dream of packability, a pleated dress..that emerged uncreased after days in a suitcase. **1963** *New Yorker* 29 June 44/1 (Advt.), All the lightness, comfort, and packability that Arnel is famous for. **1967** *Daily Tel.* 24 Oct. 19 Dress and coat ensembles of great packability. **1977** *Shooting Times & Country Mag.* 13–19 Jan. 33/1 One of the main advantages of pistols—'packability'—is lost.

packable ('pækəb(ə)l), *a.* (and *sb.*) [f. PACK *v.*[1] + -ABLE.] Capable of being packed. Also *ellipt.* as *sb.*

1880 *Blackw. Mag.* Mar. 368 Guns packable on the backs of mules. **1932** *Times Lit. Suppl.* 21 Jan. 40/4 So easily packable, pocketable, readable a copy of the book. **1962** *Sunday Express* 30 Dec. 16/5 Opaque and eminently packable pyjamas. **1972** *New Yorker* 29 July 16/1 (*caption*) A packable that goes to town dressed up ndown! **1976** *Sci. Amer.* Feb. 123/3 In any Euclidean space an infinite set of boxes packable by a given brick has a finite subset of packable boxes that can be used for packing all the others.

package ('pækɪdʒ), *sb.* Also 7 paccage. [f. PACK *v.*[1] + -AGE.]

1. The packing of goods, etc.; the mode in which goods are packed; †*spec.* the privilege formerly held by the City of London of packing cloth and other goods exported by aliens or denizens (*obs.*).

1540 in *Proc. Privy Council* (1837) VII. 48 Certain leade.. was stayed at London by the packer for lack of payment of package money. **1611** COTGR., *Amballage*, package. **1640** *2nd Charter Chas. I to London* (cf. Luffman *Charters* (1793)), Officium Sarcinacionis sive Paccacionis, Anglice *Paccage*, omnium Pannorum [etc.]. [Confirmation of Charter 18 Edw. IV (1478) which reads: Officia sive occupaciones paccacionis omnimodorum Pannorum, etc.] **1691** *House of Lords MSS.* (1892) 299 The offices and duties of Bailliage, Paccage, Scavage, Portage. **1748** *Anson's Voy.* II. vii. 209 The whole was a very extraordinary piece of false package; and.. there was concealed amongst the cotton, in every jar, a considerable quantity of double doubloons and dollars. **1800** COLQUHOUN *Comm. Thames* xi. 332 The privileges of the Package of Cloths and certain other outward-bound Goods of Foreign Merchants, Denizens, or Aliens.. are confirmed to the City by Charter of.. 16 Charles I. **1849–52** TODD *Cycl. Anat.* IV. 1127/2 Artificial arrangement.. contributing to facilitate their package.

2. †**a.** The whole or mass of things packed together; a cargo. *Obs.*

1669 STURMY *Mariner's Mag.*, *Penalties & Forf.* 7 If any.. Person taking Charge of the Ship, shall permit any sort of the Package therein to be opened. **1802** PALEY *Nat. Theol.* xi. ii. §7. 209 The spleen may be merely a stuffing, a soft cushion to fill up a vacancy or hollow, which unless occupied, would leave the package loose and unsteady.

b. *fig.* (See quots.) *slang.*

1933 *Sun* (Baltimore) 17 Aug. 8/6 The 'package', as the kidnapped victim is called, is rushed across the State line and delivered to the 'keepers'. **1935** A. J. POLLOCK *Underworld Speaks* 85/1 *Package*, the kidnaped victim. **1945** L. SHELLY *Jive Talk Dict.* 15/2 *Package*, a girl. **1960** WENTWORTH & FLEXNER *Dict. Amer. Slang* 371/1 *Package*, an attractive, usu. small and neat, girl or young woman. **1963** *Listener* 4 Apr. 585/1 A 'package' was criminal jargon for a dead body with three or more bullets placed in a most efficient manner at the base of the skull.

3. (The chief current sense.) **a.** A bundle of things packed up, whether in a box or other receptacle, or merely compactly tied up; esp. such a bundle of small or moderate size, as an item of luggage; a packet, parcel.

1722 DE FOE *Col. Jack* (1840) 328 Cases, packages, and bales of European goods. **1810** CRABBE *Borough* i. 76 Package, and parcel, hogs-head, chest, and case. **1837** W. IRVING *Capt. Bonneville* II. 24 Their innumerable horses,.. some burthened with packages, others following in droves. **1897** GEN. H. PORTER in *Century Mag.* Jan. 351 At noon a package of despatches.. reached head quarters.

b. *transf.* and *fig.* orig. *U.S.* A combination or collection of interdependent or related abstract entities. (Cf. PARCEL *sb.* 7 b.) Hence *attrib.*, esp. (*a*) of negotiations, as ***package deal***, a transaction or proposal agreed to as a whole, the less favourable items as well as the more favourable; so ***package offer, proposal***, etc.; (*b*) of holidays, tours, etc., one in which all arrangements are the responsibility of agents, (*c*) of a series of acts in a vaudeville show, on television, etc. (For a considerable body of further evidence see *Amer. Speech* May 1958, 73 ff.)

Dict. Americanisms has an 1846 quot. for *package ticket* in the sense 'one entitling the holder to a specified number of journeys'.

1931 *Social Sci. Abstr.* 15838 Insurance in a 'package'... The exact size of the 'package' offered to any employee depends upon age, sex, and length of service. **1948** *Investor's Reader* 26 May 9 Often units of preferred and common shares are tied together in one big economy package which offers two for the price of one. **1951** W. F. BUCKLEY *God & Man at Yale* 40 This report is primarily a highly controversial package of political and economic ideas. **1952** *N.Y. Herald Tribune* 9 Apr. 26/7 On this basis the [steel] industry is confronted not with a package [*sc.* the wage recommendations of the Wage Stabilization Board] costing 29.8 cents an hour, but one that will cost 59.6 cents. **1953** in *Amer. Speech* (1958) XXXIII. Suppl. 74 Eventually the agency offers a package—a violinist, a pianist, a singer, a quartet and perhaps a small string orchestra. **1958** *Economist* 8 Mar. 849/1 The [U.S.] Administration is thinking of proposing a simplified 'package' [for summit talks]. **1959** *Observer* 26 Apr. 6/2 The package would link the future of Berlin with a settlement of the German problem and European security. **1962** M. McLUHAN *Gutenberg Galaxy* 128 (*heading*) The *camera obscura* anticipated Hollywood in turning the spectacle of the external world into a consumer commodity or package. **1965** *Melody Maker* 25 Sept. 20 Few fans will turn out every week for expensive concerts. Yet, in the past, some towns have had two or even three big packages in their area in one week. **1966** *Listener* 3 Mar. 300/2 It was the orthodox deflationary package that was to be expected in an off-year for the British balance of payments. **1967** M. McLUHAN *Medium is Massage* 22 The mass audience.. is.. merely given packages of passive entertainment. **1968** *Globe & Mail* (Toronto) 3 Feb. B3/3 Although the Canadian union gained the greatest economic package in its 30-year history from the company the day before, hundreds of workers were reluctant to return to work. **1969** L. G. ARTHUR in A. E. Wilkerson *Rights of Children* (1973) 132 The great advancement of the juvenile courts is that they can be imaginative and flexible: that they can design a package of dispositions to fit the needs of a particular child. **1969** *Listener* 2 Jan. 31/2 You can arrange as part of your package to hire a car. **1970** *Daily Tel.* 3 Mar. 2/1 The Hillman Minx de Luxe model will also cease to be available, but a 'comfort' package of carpets and central console will be available for the Minx. **1972** *Guardian* 25 Mar. 1/1 Northern Ireland's Parliament at Stormont is to be prorogued for a year under the peace package of Ulster announced in the Commons yesterday. **1972** *Times* 16 Aug. 1/4 National bargaining on the unions' package claim... The whole package amounted to 40 per cent... Union officials at local level will now be able to pursue those parts of the package that have not been met. **1975** J. DE BRES tr. *Mandel's Late Capitalism* xi. 358 The underdeveloped country sends its entire export package to the imperialist country. **1977** *Time* 17 Jan. 17/1 The Carter package offers something to just about everybody. **1977** 'A. STUART' *Snap Judgement* 192 The tired tanned look of tourists at the end of a two-week package.

attrib. (*a*) **1951** *N.Y. Herald Tribune* 14 Dec., President Truman in effect wrapped up the whole subject of creeping corruption in his administration.. into one package policy which he laid before the nation. **1952** *Ibid.* 4 Mar. 1/8 (*headline*) State to offer city 'Package' Aid Plan. *Ibid.*, The Dewey [State] administration was reported ready tonight to offer New York City a 'package' solution for the city budget crisis. **1952** *N.Y. Times* 9 Mar. 15/1 The plan for West German sovereignty was tied up in a 'package deal' with the plan for West Germany's military and financial contribution to Western defense. **1952** *N.Y. Herald Tribune* 19 May 14/3 The ensuing battle for diplomatic advantage.. seemed pretty well played out by the end of April, when the United Nations Command made up its 'package' offer of settlement. **1955** *Times* 13 May 8/4 An attempt at some sort of 'package deal', whereby a disarmament settlement is made dependent on the solution of other world problems. **1963** *Ann. Reg. 1962* 247 The Chancellor.. criticized the American suggestion for a 'package deal' with Moscow. **1964** M. McLUHAN *Understanding Media* (1967) II. xxxi. 334 He tends instead to accept the full image as a package deal. **1967** *Listener* 20 July 74/2 In the peculiarly modern field of mass productive factory design, the so-called package-dealer holds sway, with his offer of a complete design-and-build service. **1972** *New Building* Oct. 11/3 Fully conscious of the wastefulness of normal tendering methods, Simonbuild consider their package deal system the only sensible and economic approach for the needs of today. **1972** WODEHOUSE *Pearls, Girls & Monty Bodkin* iii. 41 This step-daughter who had come to him as part of the package deal when he and Grayce were joined in holy wedlock. **1973** I. M. SINCLAIR *Vienna Convention on Law of Treaties* v. 141 But the 'package' proposal did not envisage any stage of compulsory arbitration or judicial settlement, except in relation to the *jus cogens* articles. **1976** *Economist* 16 Oct. 73/3 It now says that what Mr Smith accepted in his September 24th broadcast was not—as he says he was told it was—a package deal that had been firmly agreed upon with Mr Kissinger by Britain and the African presidents; it was merely a set of 'proposals'.

(*b*) **1952** *N.Y. Herald Tribune* 14 Apr. 6 (Advt.), Unique, new, all-expense fishing 'package' trips. **1952** *N.Y. World-Telegram & Sun* 29 Apr. 25/1 Eastern Air Lines has mapped out an ambitious schedule of package vacations. **1958** *New Statesman* 11 Oct. 502/2 The great increase in British visitors, however, has been in the less expensive areas, and this is reflected in the range of 'package' tours offered by the travel agencies. **1960** *News Chron.* 11 Apr. 9/4 Pony trekking.. is probably the most popular of all the package-holidays. **1964** M. McLUHAN *Understanding Media* (1967) II. xx. 212 They can have.. Berlin or Venice in a package tour. **1967** *Spectator* 1 Dec. 699/3 Cut-price package trips [are] practically keeping the international airlines going during the slack season. **1971** *Daily Tel.* 9 Jan. 18/3 Moscow.. is one place where the package tourist scores heavily over the independent tourist. **1973** J. SYMONS *Plot against Roger Rider* II. 45 Are they going to be stranded in a foreign city?.. Reassured, the package tourists sink into their seats. **1976** A. GREY *Bulgarian Exclusive* xiv. 99 A large Russian package tour group. **1976** *Field* 18 Nov. 980/2 We read of the pilgrimages to Eton.. and the crowds who flocked there—'those package tourists of medieval times'. **1977** *Irish Times* 8 June 4/1 Mr. Adrian Hopkins, of Bray Travel, which organises package holidays in the Seychelles, said yesterday that they could have full refunds if they decided not to travel.

(*c*) **1946** *Sun* (Baltimore) 18 Feb. 11/5 The boys in blue finally have come up with touring package shows of their very own. **1952** *N.Y. Jrnl.-American* 23 May 13/1 Judy Garland and Sid Luft are investing close to $100,000 in producing their own package shows to tour the country. **1956** B. HOLIDAY *Lady sings Blues* (1973) xx. 165 When theatre dates began to slack off, Mr. Levy decided to get together a whole package show, with me as the star and fronting the band. **1958** *Amer. Speech* XXXIII. (Suppl.) 73 A package show on radio or television may involve a number of varied performances given once a week throughout the year, with a core of main performers and with others who are brought on for one or more performances, but not for all. **1959** *Tatler* 1 Apr. 34/1 Stan Getz, star of last year's 'Jazz At The Philharmonic' package show in Britain.

c. Any related group of objects that is viewed or organized as a unit.

1947 CROWTHER & WHIDDINGTON *Science at War* Pl. ix (*caption*) A late model; it is a 'package', with magnetron and magnet complete with rectangular wave guide out of which power pours. **1952** *New Yorker* 12 Apr. 45 (Advt.), The big, beautiful, package that comprises the restaurants of Rockefeller Center. **1958** *Observer* 12 Oct. 1/3 The objectives of this lavish experiment were.. to test the interaction of the three stages.. and.. to achieve a trajectory that could be controlled enough to put the final package within some 50,000 miles of the moon. **1962** F. I. ORDWAY et al. *Basic Astronautics* iv. 128 The cosmic ray package contains two proton monitors.. and devices to detect electrons. **1962** S. CARPENTER in *Into Orbit* 56 Another item which is thrown off, just before re-entry, is the package of three retro-rockets which ride strapped to the heatshield during most of the mission. **1965** *IEEE Trans. Reliability* XIV. 114 (*heading*) Impact testing of plug-in circuit packages for high reliability. **1968** *Times* 10 Dec. 6/7 The orbiting observatory carries two experimental packages, both intended to make observations in the ultraviolet region of the spectrum. **1970** *Sci. Amer.* Feb. 26/1 If.. one wanted to design a central processor with 1,000 logic elements, one could begin by selecting 200 integrated-circuit packages, each containing an average of five gates of the kind desired. **1972** *Computers & Humanities* VII. 82 A collection of canned programs maintained as a unit is a library. If they are closely related in content, e.g., all statistical, then the library is a package. **1976** *Offshore Platforms & Pipelining* 23/2 The pump package of Noble's Rig 27 varies slightly from the specification guide. **1976** *Physics Bull.* May 202/3 A Japanese company has recently developed a multicolour three-dimensional image video package, using 35 mm film for the storage of the holograms, which is aimed at the advertising, educational, medical and recreational markets. **1977** *Modern Boating* (Austral.) Jan. 81/2 Every boat-trailer-motor package which goes out of their doors is fully equipped with the recommended number of fire extinguishers as well as all other recommended safety gear as part of the package.

d. Misc. *attrib.* uses of sense 3 a. (All *N. Amer.*)

1821 *Deb. Congress U.S.* (1855) 16th Congress 2 Sess. App. 1526 Package sales.. by the assortments of merchandise they combine, excite most interest. **1888** M. DELAND *John Ward* i. 2 They were at the mercy of Phibbs, the package man, who brought their wares on his slow, creaking cart.. from Mercer. **1971** H. A. SMITH *View from Chivo* xiii. 127 Jim Davey closed the package store two hours early and shut off all beer sales. **1976** *Amer. Speech 1974* XLIX. 115 *Package bar*, establishment that sells packaged goods (wine, beer, and hard liquor) as well as serves liquor by the drink.

4. †**a.** Means, material, or requisites for packing.

1751 R. PALTOCK *P. Wilkins* (1884) II. xviii. 202 My greatest concern was, having broke up so many of my chests, to find package for the things.

5. A case, casing, box, or other receptacle in which goods are packed.

original package, the package or case in which goods are sent out from the place of manufacture.

1801 W. TAYLOR in *Monthly Mag.* XII. 580 The method of prizing, or squeezing.. the article into its package, so as to reduce its bulk for stowage. *a* **1827** *Pet. to Ho. Comm.* in Bischoff *Woollen Manuf.* II. 60 Your petitioners, there-fore, humbly pray your Honourable House to.. place the holders of wool, duty paid.. upon the same footing as importers and holders of silk in original packages. **1890** *Daily News* 28 June 6/2 Judge Foster [of Kansas] recently decided that liquor could only be sold in 'original packages', which is construed as meaning one or more bottles of beer or whisky. The merchants.. are not allowed to sell beer or whisky by the glass.

Hence **'packaging**, the action of making up into a package; also *attrib.* and *fig.*

1875 KNIGHT *Dict. Mech.*, *Packaging-machine*, a machine for bundling yarns or goods into compact shape for transportation; a bundling-press. **1934** *Planning* II. xxxvi. 10 They must submit samples, manufacturing formula, chemical analysis.., description of process of manufacture and packaging. **1950** *Sunday Times* 7 May 8/4 It is apparent.. that in the last 12 months packaging has improved considerably. **1954** *Economist* 20 Feb. 568/1 Some of the subsidiaries do 'quite a substantial amount of trade' in packaging materials. **1957** L. F. R. WILLAIMS *State of Israel* 96 Much attention is being paid to grading, packaging and marketing. **1962** *Rep. Comm. Broadcasting 1960* 34 in *Parl. Papers 1961–2* (Cmnd. 1753) IX. 259 A trivial presentation may consist.. in an excessive interest in smart 'packaging' at the expense of the contents of the package. **1962** M. McLUHAN *Gutenbrg Galaxy* 268 Language and the arts would.. become mere packaging devices. **1976** R. BARNARD *Little Local Murder* ix. 105 Slovenly shoppers who could be deceived by the most patently bogus special offer, the most obviously inflated packaging device. **1977** W. MARSHALL *Thin Air* ii. 24 I've seen the food packaging people... Apparently the packaging is done in the evenings.

package, *v.* [f. the sb.] *trans.* To wrap up, make into a package. Also *fig.* and *absol.*

1928 M. H. WESEEN *Crowell's Dict. Eng. Gram.* 445 *Package*, commercial cant as a verb. **1947** M. McCARTHY *On Contrary* (1961) 11 An image of happiness as packaged by the manufacturer. **1954** N. TOMALIN in *Granta* 6 Nov. 21/1 Two licensed pigeon-feed sellers who.. earn ten pounds a day, have factories in Ealing packaging the peas, and are worried acutely by their income tax. **1959** *Listener* 30 July 186/3 There is no lack of playwrights who carry on the old trade of packaging sentimental hokum into a tough shell. **1967** *Boston Sunday Herald* 26 Mar. VI. 7/6 Something for everybody is the way Air France describes its 1967 Jet Away Holidays tour program, recently packaged and distributed to travel agents. **1970** *Natural Hist.* Feb. 18/3 Philadelphia is now packaging its trash, putting it into empty coal cars and then shipping the material back to the strip mines as land fill. **1972** *New Yorker* 2 Dec. 162/2 The black films are packaged, financed, and sold by whites. **1976** N. POSTMAN *Crazy Talk* 70 Billy Graham has packaged his 'message' in a way not unlike that in which Scope packages its 'message'. **1976** *NBR Marketplace* (Wellington) III. 5/1 It brings in its products from factories overseas (US, UK, Australia, and even Brazil) and packages here.

packageable ('pækɪdʒəb(ə)l), *a.* [f. PACKAGE *v.* + -ABLE.] Capable of being packaged, in the various senses of the verb.

1961 *Aeroplane* CI. 578/2 From the present generation of packageable propellents (e.g. nitric acid and a mixed amine fuel), a practical realizable specific impulse of about 245 sec. can be obtained. **1977** *Church Times* 6 May 7/1 Fundamentalism, like Maoist Marxism, is positive and highly packageable.

packaged ('pækɪdʒd), *ppl. a.* [f. PACKAGE *v.* + -ED[1].] Wrapped up, made into a package; pre-packed.

1933 R. SIMMAT *Princ. & Pract. Marketing* viii. 67 The various types of packaged product may be divided into two classifications—the liquid and the solid. **1934** S. B. WHIPPLE *Noble Experiment* 173 The exorbitant prices for packaged spirits and wines. **1945** P. CHEYNEY *I'll say she Does!* ii. 41 This Confucius certainly knew his packaged goods. **1952** [see KNOCK-DOWN *a.* 3]. **1958** *Times* 4 Aug. 9/2 The pile of débris that results from unpacking a pound of packaged biscuits has to be seen to be believed. **1964** M. McLUHAN *Understanding Media* (1967) II. xx. 207 The age of the consumer of processed and packaged goods. **1969** *Jane's Freight Containers 1968–69* 184 Packaged Timber Berth.

b. *fig.*

1946 R. BLESH *Shining Trumpets* (1949) xiv. 325 The mediocre, but financially profitable slick packaged musical trash. **1947** *Richmond* (Virginia) *Times-Dispatch* 11 May 1-D/4 Scheduled for this Summer are some 14 weekly 'packaged' tours. **1951** *N.Y. Herald-Tribune* 24 Apr. 23/6 Fifteen 'packaged' lessons have been prepared. **1953** R. CHANDLER *Long Good-Bye* iv. 22 The goddam women will start..making up with the packaged charm. **1954** *Sun* (Baltimore) 16 Oct. 12/6 Many insurance companies offer homeowners a 'packaged' policy..at a saving over the cost of a multiplicity of policies each to cover a limited field. **1958** *Observer* 7 Dec. 15/6 Some of the units would be 'packaged' kitchens, bathrooms or bedrooms—that is to say, units with built-in furniture and fittings. **1959** *Economist* 7 Feb. 511/2 A packaged holiday, usually consisting of two weeks or ten days..for an all-in charge that includes air ticket and hotel bill. **1959** *Listener* 23 Apr. 700/1 A foreign policy that is a packaged deal. **1961** L. MACNEICE in *New Statesman* 30 June 1054/3 The weather is packaged and the spacemen In endless orbit. **1967** A. COWAN in Wills & Yearsley *Handbk. Managem. Technol.* 160 It is not possible to write a prescription which can be applied as a finite system to a business. This is a disappointment to those who hope that a neat, packaged solution can be found. **1970** *Daily Tel.* 10 Nov. 17/5 Even ghost-hunters have been offered a packaged tour of the haunted houses of England. **1975** *Times* 18 June 5/2 The packaged tourists pay homage and more solid currency to Anne Hathaway's cottage.

packager ('pækɪdʒə(r)). [f. PACKAGE *v.* + -ER[1].] One who packages, in the various senses of the verb.

1959 *Wall St. Jrnl.* (Eastern ed.) 14 Jan. 1/1 They're rough-and-tough 'action-adventure' shows, and all have been produced by independent packagers—TV program producers who assemble the ingredients of story, director and cast, and then put them together to make a show. **1969** *Listener* 17 Apr. 538/1 'These two are the outstanding producers and packagers of guilt in our time,' whines Alexander Portnoy of his parents. **1976** *New Yorker* 19 Apr. 31/2 Morty Mann, the packager of 'Back-Chat', who claims to have lost 'a small fortune' in the enterprise, says that the program failed because the Prince just couldn't 'relate'. **1977** W. MARSHALL *Thin Air* ii. 22 We'll go and see your food packager.

†**packald.** *Obs.* Also 5 **pakald.** [f. PACK *sb.*[1] The nature of the suffix is not clear: Jamieson suggests a corruption of *-et* in *packet*, and compares *fagald* for FAGGOT. But the first quot. is earlier than any we have of *packet*.] A pack, bundle; a burden, load; a packet.

c **1440** *York Myst.* xviii. 160 Þis pakald bere me bus, Of all I plege and pleyne me. **1516** *Inv. R. Wardrobe* (1815) 25 Item ane pakkald of lettrez with ane obligatioun with vi soverties for Alexander Boid for the landis of Kilmarnok. **1637** RUTHERFORD *Let. to Laird of Cally* Lett. (1671) 257 O how loath we are to forgoe our packalds and burdens.

packall, variant of PEGALL, Indian basket.

packaway ('pækəweɪ), *a.* [f. PACK *v.*[1] + AWAY *adv.*] Capable of being folded into a small space when not in use.

1957 *Archit. Rev.* CXXII. 355/3 Other garage doors will be shown... A new packaway door..which was exhibited in prototype at the last exhibition..has been modified and improved since. **1973** *Times* 4 May 15/1 Up in London's Seven Sisters Road, they are marketing the best value in child-to-adult, packaway bicycles I have seen. **1974** *Times* 5 Mar. 9/1 (*caption*) Those amorphous, ectoplasmic packaway jobs [*sc.* mackintoshes] the earnest tourists wear.

'**pack-cloth.** [f. PACK *sb.*[1] + CLOTH; cf. Du. *pack-kleed* (Kilian 1599).] A stout coarse kind of cloth used for packing; a piece of this.

14.. *Metr. Voc.* in Wr.-Wülcker 629/17 *Bumbicinium*, kotyn or pakclothe. **1565-73** COOPER *Thesaurus, Coactilia*, skinnes wherin clothes were packed in carriage: packe clothes. **1698** *Lond. Gaz.* No. 3368/4 Pack'd up in a Bundle of Packcloth. **1776** [see PACK *v.*[1] 1]. **1827** *Perils & Captivity* (Constable's Misc.) 230, I had no sort of clothing, but a piece of packcloth about my middle.

packed (pækt), *ppl. a.*[1] Also **packt.** [f. PACK *v.*[1] + -ED[1].]

1. a. Put or pressed together closely in a bundle or mass, crowded in, etc.; put into a package or packet: see PACK *v.*[1] 1-3. Of meals, packaged for transporting and eating on a picnic or in an informal manner.

1777 G. FORSTER *Voy. round World* I. 102 We sailed through a great quantity of packed or broken ice. **1851** HT. MARTINEAU *Hist. Peace* (1877) III. IV. xiv. 146 A closely packed assembly of business-like men. **1876** GEO. ELIOT *Dan. Der.* III. xxiii, The packed-up shows of a departing fair. **1897** R. KIPLING *Captains Courageous* 160 The packed mass ran from the cabin partition to the sliding door. **1958** B. PYM *Glass of Blessings* xvi. 186 Sitting on mackintoshes, eating packed lunches..tramping home again through the rain—one can see how he would yearn after Portugal. **1959** 'M. INNES' *Hare sitting Up* III. i. 167 He'll be back in no time. With a nice packed lunch. **1965** E. SALTER *Once upon a Tombstone* II. xvii. 152 How about a trip up the glacier? We could take a packed lunch and make a day of it. **1968** *Guardian* 30 Mar. 10/5 You can..be met at Benbecula by a hired car with a packed meal in it. **1973** G. MITCHELL *Murder of Busy Lizzie* iv. 49 We're going to explore the island. Do you think, Father, that we could ask for a packed lunch? **1976** *Times Lit. Suppl.* 5 Nov. 1398/4 What an outing that would have been; you would have needed a packed lunch.

b. *Med.* Applied to blood cells separated as much as possible from plasma (usu. by centrifugation); esp. in ***packed-cell volume***, the proportion of a sample of blood, by volume, occupied by cells after they have been allowed to settle; cf. *hæmatocrit* s.v. HÆMATO-, HEMATO-.

1933 *Amer. Jrnl. Med. Sci.* CLXXXV. 59 Several students of the blood have again become interested in the determination of the volume of packed red cells by means of various types of hematocrit. **1943** *Lancet* 6 Nov. 576/2 The mean corpuscular hæmoglobin concentration, which is the ratio of the hæmoglobin content of the blood (grammes per 100 c.cm.) to the volume of the packed red cells (hæmatocrit). **1955** *Ibid.* 17 Dec. 1274/2 *Investigations.*—Blood-count: hæmoglobin 4·7 g. per 100 ml.; packed-cell volume 14%; mean corpuscular hæmoglobin concentration 33%; [etc.]. **1961** *Ibid.* 26 Aug. 490/1 A thirteen-year-old boy required a 250 ml. packed-cell transfusion every four to five weeks. **1967** S. TAYLOR et al. *Short Textbk. Surg.* i. 11 Packed-cell transfusions are viscid and slow to flow. **1974** *Jrnl. Appl. Physiol.* XXXVII. 976/1 These data were obtained under very carefully controlled conditions (e.g., careful measurement of packed cell volume and resistivity..). **1976** *Nature* 1-8 Jan. 47/2, 0.25 ml of packed cells were added to 2 ml of a medium.

c. *Computers.* Of, pertaining to, or being a decimal number stored with successive digits represented by successive half-bytes and the sign by the rightmost half-byte.

1964 *IBM Jrnl. Res. & Devel.* VIII. 95 (*in figure*) Packed decimal number. **1966** R. SILVERSTONE in A. Opler *Programming the IBM System/360* xi. 126 All internal decimal arithmetic operation[s] must be performed in packed format. *Ibid.*, Since packed numbers require half as much space as zoned decimal numbers, they should be used in storing or writing intermediate files which are not to be directly printed. **1973** MURRILL & SMITH *Introd. Computer Sci.* vi. 219 To obtain the packed representation from the zoned (or unpacked) representation, we need only to (a) remove all zone fields and (b) transpose the sign and digit fields in the rightmost byte... Systems such as the IBM 360 have hardware instructions to 'pack' and 'unpack' decimal numbers.

2. Filled with something packed in; as full as it will hold; stuffed, crammed, crowded: see PACK *v.* 7.

1883 *Scotsman* 30 July 4/5 Packed trains were despatched every few minutes. **1886** R. KIPLING *Departm. Ditties*, etc. (1899) 69 How shall the women's message reach unto her Above the tumult of the packed bazar?

packed (pækt), *ppl. a.*[2] [f. PACK *v.*[2] + -ED.] Selected or manipulated to serve party ends, as a deliberative assembly, a jury: see PACK *v.*[2] 4.

1643 PRYNNE *Sov. Power Parl.* I. 12 It was by this packed over-awed Parliament, and Act, annulled, revoked, and holden as none. **1648** 'MERCURIUS PRAGMATICUS' *Plea for King* 5 By the subscription of a packt grand Jury. **1693** J. EDWARDS *Author. O. & N. Test.* 80 The pack'd Council of Trent. **1736** NEAL *Hist. Purit.* III. 530 This..met with some opposition even in that pack'd assembly. **1844** TUPPER *Heart* xi. 119 Loaded dice, packed cards. **1867** BRIGHT *Sp. Reform* 8 Aug., It was not a packed meeting.

packer[1] ('pækə(r)). Also 5 **pakker, -our.** [f. PACK *v.*[1] + -ER[1]; = Du. *pakker* (Kilian *packer*).]

1. One who packs; one who puts up something in a bundle or receptacle; with qualifying adj., one (well or ill) skilled in packing.

1598 [see PACK *v.*[1] 1]. **1722** DE FOE *Col. Jack* (1840) 328 They were..repacked by..packers of their own. **1882** MISS BRADDON *Mt. Royal* III. i. 2 Some valets are bad packers.

2. *spec.* †**a.** An officer charged with the packing or supervision of the packing of exported goods liable to custom, etc.: cf. *packing-officer* in PACKING *vbl. sb.*[1] 3 and PACKAGE *sb.* 1. *Obs.* (The earliest sense: in 14th c. Anglo-L. *paccator.*)

1353 *Rolls of Parlt.* II. 251/1 Certein noumbre des Portours, Packers, Gwynders, Overours, & autres Laborers des Leines. **1450** *Ibid.* V. 200/1 Surveyours of the serche, Packers or eny other Officers. **1488-9** *Act 4 Hen. VII*, c. 11 No manner of persone beyng sworn to be a wolle pakker. **1535** *Act 27 Hen. VIII*, c. 14 §2 Euery porte..where no tellers nor packers at this present time be.

b. One whose business or trade it is to pack goods for transportation; one who prepares and packs provisions, as meat, fish, fruit, etc. for future or distant markets.

1692 LUTTRELL *Brief Rel.* (1857) II. 449 Severall bundles of cloaths..seized at a packers in Coleman street. **1817** W. SELWYN *Law Nisi Prius* (ed. 4) II. 1175 Goods had been sent by orders from the vendee to a packer; the packer was considered as a middle man between the vendor and vendee. **1885** *Manch. Exam.* 7 Jan. 5/2 The closing of these markets caused a serious loss to the American breeders and packers.

c. One who packs people in seats.

1898 C. RALEIGH in *Daily News* 7 Nov. 2/3 The gentleman called the packer, whose business was to cry, 'Move up, please; sit closer, please'.

3. a. Now *N. Amer.* and *Austral.* (*N.Z.*). One who transports goods by means of pack-beasts. Also in extended use.

1694 MOTTEUX *Rabelais* (1737) V. 216 Burthen-Bearers, Packers. **1788** M. CUTLER in *Life*, etc. (1881) I. 402 Here we met a Packer with ten pack-horses. **1859** *Brit. Colonist* (Victoria, B.C.) 6 June 2/3 The arrival of over one hundred pack mules from the Chilliwak country, where they have been wintering, and offers by the packers to take freight to Lytton City for eighteen cents, has failed to revive trade. **1874** A. BATHGATE *Colonial Experiences* x. 135 The rear [of string of pack-horses was] brought up by the packer on horseback, his broad-brimmed wide-a-wake hat pulled well over his weather-beaten face. **1881** *Cheq. Career* 76 A packer offered me higher wages to drive pack-horses down the south coast. **1952** H. INNES *Campbell's Kingdom* 22, I was wakened with the news that the packer was in from Come Lucky and would be leaving after lunch. I was taken out and introduced to a great ox of a man who was loading groceries into an ex-army truck. **1958** G. TERRY *Hist. & Legends of Chilcotin* 7 Tom Hutchinson was a packer and worked with a pack train of 300 mules between Yale and Barkerville. **1968** R. M. PATTERSON *Finlay's River* 101 When they travelled with horses they had, in him, a competent packer.

b. *Austral.* and *Canad.* A pack-horse, pack-mule, etc. Also, a pack-dog.

1875 WOOD & LAPHAM *Waiting for Mail* 59 A horse, some old packer he looked like. **1890** *Melbourne Argus* 7 June 4/1 Starting back..from one of the Flemington hotels with his saddle horses and packers. **1908** A. C. LAUT *Conquest Gt. Northwest* II. 270 Getting two or three of the wise old bell-mares, that are in every string of packers, at the end of a long rope, the canoemen shot across the whirl of mid-stream and got footing on the opposite shore. **1944** J. MARTIN *Canad. Wilderness Trapping* 13 In spring and fall when it is impossible to haul your supplies, dogs come in handy as packers.

c. One who transports goods in a pack on his back; also, in more recent use, one who carries a rucksack containing all the necessities of travelling. Chiefly *Canad.*

1873 G. M. GRANT *Ocean to Ocean* 356 We could see that continuous labour for one or two years in solitary wilderness ..as surveyor, transit-man..or even packer, is a totally different thing from taking a trip across the continent. **1892** E. S. BROOKES *Frontier Life* xiii. 117, I have often watched the packers, who would carry a load of seventy-five pounds on their backs, through a rough survey line for six or seven weeks. **1921** A. HEMING *Drama of Forests* 320 Upon the first his companion placed two more packs; then, stooping beneath the weight of 240 pounds, the packers at a jog-trot set off uphill and down, over rugged rocks and fallen timber. **1968** R. M. PATTERSON *Finlay's River* 29 He was a short, stocky man—the ideal build for a packer—and it was nothing for him to pack a two hundred-pound load over a long portage. **1974** *Weekend Mag.* (Montreal) 9 Mar. 20/3 It is something peculiar to the Spanish that they look on every packer as a hippie-freak—and they don't like hippie freaks.

4. A machine or contrivance used for packing.

1890 *Cent. Dict., Packer*... 7. The variously constructed mechanism by which the grain cut by a reaping-machine is packed or compressed on the binding-table and held till embraced and bound by the twine. **1894** *Labour Commission Gloss., Packers*[2], laths used for packing calicoes in bales. **1902** *Census Bull.* (U.S.) No. 216. 28 June 61/1 Types succeed each other in the packer with 3-em space between the words, until a continuous line is formed.

5. A device inserted into an annular space in an oil well (such as that between the casing and the tubing) in order to block the flow of oil and gas. orig *U.S.*

1885 *Encycl. Brit.* XVIII. 718/1 An indiarubber packer is then attached in such a manner that within it the pipe that is above it slides in that which is below it, and the rubber is forced against the sides of the drill-hole. **1904** *Dialect Notes* II. 386 When a well has sufficient gas to flow its product through a two-inch pipe, but will not make its production through the casing, a packer is placed at or near the top of the sand to compel the gas or oil to relieve itself only through the tubing. **1922** D. T. DAY *Handbk. Petroleum Industry* I. 291 The fundamental principle of all types of packers embodies the vertical compression and lateral expansion of a resilient substance..between casing or tubing and the wall of the hole, between two strings of casing, or between tubing and casing. **1960** C. GATLIN *Petroleum Engin.* xiii. 256/1 The ratio of hole diameter to unexpanded packer diameter is kept as low as possible, and commonly ranges from 1·1 to 1·2. **1973** J. W. JENNER in Hobson & Pohl *Mod. Petroleum Technol.* (ed. 4) iv. 141 In some areas where the wells are not easily accessible..a packer is run on the tubing and set just above the pay zone. Completion fluid of high enough density to kill the well is contained in the annulus above the packer and production is via the tubing. **1977** *Sunday Times* 24 Apr. 17/4 The plug is called a packer, and it blocks off the bottom of the outer casing.

Hence **packership**, the office of a packer: see 2 a.

1495 *Letter Bk. City of London* I. lf. 317 b, Thoffices of Pakkership and Gawgership of the said Citee.

packer[2]. [f. PACK *v.*[2] + -ER[1].] One who 'packs' cards, juries, etc.; †a confederate in a fraudulent design, a conspirator, plotter.

1586 NEWTON tr. *Daneau's Diceplay* vi, As many foysting coseners and deceiptfull packers in playing..use to do. **1599** MINSHEU *Sp. Dict., Barajador*, a packer of cards, a shufler of cards. **1771** T. HULL *Sir W. Harrington* (1797) II. 165 A packer is one who is in league with a parcel of smart young fellows that are rather destitute of fortune, and for that reason are pushing for everything which can make it. **1807** E. S. BARRETT *Rising Sun* I. 95 Associating with Coggers of dice, packers of Cards. **1905** W. O'BRIEN *Recoll.* 295 Mr. Peter O'Brien..afterwards earned the titles of Lord O'Brien of Kilfenora and..'Pether the Packer'.

packery ('pækərɪ). *rare.* [See -ERY; = Du. *pakkerij.*] **a.** A place where goods are packed; a packing establishment. **b.** A collection of packs or packages.

1880 *Libr. Univ. Knowl.* (N.Y.) X. 447 Broom factories, pork packeries, soap-works. **1891** MISS DOWIE *Girl in Karp.* xii. 158 On his back his marvellous baggage was strapped... A pair of boots and his coat were tied with pieces of cotton-string to the whole packery.

packet ('pækɪt), *sb.* Also 6-9 **pacquet,** 7 **paquette,** 8-9 **paquet.** [Dim. of PACK *sb.*[1] Cf. F. *pacquet* (1530 in Palsgr.), *paquet* (1539 in R. Estienne), It. *pacchetto* (Florio 1611), Sp. *paquete.*

The Fr. and Eng. forms appear together in Palsgrave 1530; Hatz.-Darm. say the Fr. was from the Eng., and as *paquet* is masc., it could hardly be the dim. of obs. F. *pacque* fem., which would have been *pa(c)quette.* Possibly the Eng. was orig. an AngloFr. dim. of *pack.* The It. and Sp. forms are late, and app. from Fr.]

1. a. A small pack, package, or parcel: in earliest use applied to a parcel of letters or dispatches, and esp. to the State parcel or 'mail' of dispatches to and from foreign countries.

1530 PALSGR. 250/2 Pacquet of letters, *pacquet de lettres*. **1533** BRIAN TUKE *Let. to Cromwell* 17 Aug., I wrote unto my Lorde of Northumberlande, to write on the bak of his pacquettes the houre and day of the depeche. *a* **1548** SIR E. HOWARD in Ellis *Orig. Lett.* Ser. III. I. 151, I send you in this paquet a lettre to my wife. **1599** J. FRAUNCIS (Chester Post) in *Cecil Papers* (Hist. MSS. Comm.) IX. 377, I cannot hear of any passage..out of Ireland, saving the post bark which brought over two packets. **1604** E. G[RIMSTONE] *D'Acosta's Hist. Indies* VI. x. 452 How the Kings of Mexico and Peru had intelligence..seeing they had no vse of any letters, nor to write pacquets. **1653** in *Hatton Corr.* (Camden) 8 Your great packuitt is come to my hand. **1693** *Massachus. P.O. Act*, A pacquett shall be accounted 3 letters at the least. **1716** LADY M. W. MONTAGU *Let. to C'tess Mar* 21 Nov., I foresee I shall swell my letter to the size of a pacquet. **1762** *Gentl. Mag.* 53 His Excellency was making up a pacquet, which was to be sent to Berlin by his running footman. **1803** in *M. Cutler's Life*, etc. (1888) II. 304 We..present you a paquet of plants. **1849** MACAULAY *Hist. Eng.* iii. I. 393 The difficulty and expense of conveying large packets from place to place. **1871** T. T. COOPER *Pioneer Commerce* ix. 250, I..produced a packet of photographs of friends. **1875** *Ure's Dict. Arts* II. 728 Thus the packet [of leaf gold] becomes sufficiently compact to bear beating with a hammer of 15 or 16 pounds weight.

b. *fig.* A small collection, set, or lot (*of* things or persons): cf. PACK *sb.*[1] 3.

Sometimes (with obvious reference to a packet of letters or news), a false report, a falsehood, a 'packet of lies': cf. GALLEY-PACKET. ***to sell one a packet*** (colloq.): to tell him a falsehood, take him in, 'sell' him.

1589 NASHE *Pref. Greene's Menaphon* (Arb.) 6 The Italionate pen, that of a packet of pilfries, affoordeth the presse a pamphlet or two. **1613** PURCHAS *Pilgrimage* (1614) 93 The Heathenish and Popish, and..other packets of miracles. **1766** in J. H. Jesse *Geo. Selwyn & Contemp.* (1843) II. 72, I thank you, my dear George, for including me in your *pacquet* of friends. **1796** GROSE *Class. Dict.*, *Packet*, a false report. **1828** SCOTT *F.M. Perth* xix, Dorothy had..possessed herself of a slight packet of the rumours which were flying abroad. **1886** T. HARDY *Mayor Casterbridge* xliii, It never crossed my mind that the man was selling me a packet.

c. As title of a periodical publication containing news, etc.

1678–9 (*title*) The Weekly Pacquet of Advice from Rome. **1683** T. HOY *Agathocles* 6 The loathsome Cries Of daily Letters, Pacquetts, Mercurys. **1735** *H. Scougal's Life of God*, etc. Pref., The..Society for promoting Christian Knowledge..judged it worthy a place in their Annual Packet to their corresponding members. **1851** (*title*) The Monthly Packet of Evening Readings.

d. *transf.* Applied to natural formations.

1658 EVELYN *Fr. Gard.* (1675) 104 Caterpillars are easily gathered off during all the winter, taking away the packets which cleave about the branches. **1822–34** *Good's Study Med.* (ed. 4) I. 513 The texture of the heart is fleshy,..consisting of packets of fibres, more or less oblique.

e. A small pile or set of cards. *rare.*

1887 MISS W. JONES *Games Patience* ii. 9 The object..is..to build up packets from the ace to the king.

f. *slang* (chiefly *Mil.*). A bullet or other missile; hence, trouble, misfortune; *to stop* (or *cop*, etc.) *a packet*, to be killed or wounded; to get into trouble; to be reprimanded.

1917 P. MACGILL *Brown Brethren* xx. 284 Wot's she doin' standin' out in the street like that?.. She'll stop a packet if she's not careful. **1925** FRASER & GIBBONS *Soldier & Sailor Words* 219 *Packet*, a bullet wound, *e.g.* it would be said of a wounded man:—He 'stopped a packet' or 'bought a packet' —*i.e.*, got hit by a bullet. Also, any trouble or unexpected bad luck. **1933** D. L. SAYERS *Murder must Advertise* vii. 120 I'm really fearfully sorry you copped that packet that was meant for me. **1946** J. IRVING *Royal Navalese* 130 *Packet*, trouble, in some form or another. 'So-and-so caught his packet on the Russian convoys'... 'Smithie caught a packet from "The Bloke".' **1948** PARTRIDGE *Dict. Forces' Slang* 135 Blimey, old Bill didn't half cop a packet from the C.O. **1958** B. HAMILTON *Too Much of Water* xi. 236, I was a bit vague as to when Swete got his packet. **1960** 'H. CARMICHAEL' *Seeds of Hate* viii. 70 Frank Mitchell copped a packet on the river bank. **1978** A. PRICE *'44 Vintage* iii. 39 We've been disbanded... The same thing's happening to the 2nd Northants, they've caught a packet too.

g. A large sum of money. *slang.*

1922 M. ARLEN *Piracy* III. viii. 214 Tarlyan and Cypress had both won a packet at *chemin de fer*. **1928** WODEHOUSE in *Strand Mag.* Aug. 114/1 'Get in on the short end,' said Aurelia earnestly, 'and you'll make a packet.' **1930** W. S. MAUGHAM *Bread-Winner* II. 76 It cost me a packet. **1955** 'E. C. R. LORAC' *Ask Policeman* vii. 101 Lived in style for years and must have spent a packet. **1959** J. FLEMING *Miss Bones* xv. 171 I've cleaned up a nice little packet..but Walpurgis still owes me quite a bit. **1966** J. BETJEMAN *High & Low* 74, I bet your racket brings you in a pretty packet. **1972** P. D. JAMES *Unsuitable Job* iii. 80 That awful cross of roses... Poor old nanny, it must have cost her a packet.

h. *Physics.* A localized disturbance of a field or medium that retains its identity as it travels; usu. = *wave packet* (WAVE *sb.* 10).

1928 *Proc. R. Soc.* A. CXVII. 278 We may imagine that by means of Heisenberg's γ-ray microscope we have detected an electron near a hydrogen nucleus in the form of a packet like (5·4) with x_0, etc., so adjusted that on the older quantum theory the particle would describe the nth circular quantum orbit. **1934** *Discovery* May 125/1 Photons (quanta or packets of electro-magnetic energy) are in general more efficient in bringing about atomic changes than particles of corresponding energy. **1956** A. A. TOWNSEND *Struct. Turbulent Shear Flow* v. 102 If this is true, a packet of turbulent fluid that has been moved across the flow by large eddy motion will have a turbulent intensity determined by its rate of energy gain over a considerable part of its previous existence as turbulent fluid. **1970** *Nature* 29 Aug. 937/2 As long as the incoming packet is spatially sharp enough, the reflected packet will manifestly carry information about the scattering mass.

2. Short for PACKET-BOAT.

1709 STEEL *Tatler* No. 107 ¶1 You may easily reach Harwich in a Day, so as to be there when the Packet goes off. **1800** WELLESLEY in Owen *Desp.* 667 Monthly packets should be established to sail regularly both from Europe and India. **1852** J. R. PLANCHÉ *Invisible Prince* ii. 14 Fierce whiskered gents,..Smoked bad cigars, on board the penny packets. **1874** W. E. HALL *Rights & Duties Neutrals* 72 Vessels of the type of the packets plying between Dover and Calais. *a* **1936** KIPLING *Something of Myself* (1937) ii. 26 Turkey..turned up, usually a day or two late, by the Irish packet, aloof, inscrutable.

3. *attrib.* and *Comb.* Carrying a packet or packets, as ***packet-bark***, ***-ship***, ***-steamer***, ***-vessel*** (= PACKET-BOAT); ***packet-carrier***, ***-horse***; put up or sold in packets, as ***packet cigarettes***, ***goods***, ***mix***, ***soup***, ***tea***, ***tobacco***; **packet-day** (see quot.); † **packet-mail**, a 'mail' or bag containing letters or papers, a mail-bag (*obs.*); **packet-note**, a size of note-paper, 9 by 11 inches the sheet; **packet rat**, a derogatory name for a seaman, *spec.* one who specialized in the short voyage across the Atlantic; **packet-switching** *vbl. sb.*, a mode of data transmission in which a message is broken into a number of parts or 'packets' which are sent independently, over whatever route is optimum for each packet, and re-assembled at the destination; so **packet-switched** *ppl. a.*

1806 BOWLES *Banwell Hill* I. 320 The gay *packet-bark, to Erin bound. **1606** DEKKER *Newes fr. Hell* Wks. (Grosart) II. 122 The *Packet-caryer (that all this while wayted on the other side), cride A boate, a boat. **1909** *Westm. Gaz.* 5 June 11/1 The demand for *packet cigarettes..has given rise to the manufacture..of special brands. **1858** SIMMONDS *Dict. Trade*, **Packet-day*, the mail-day; the day for posting letters, or for the departure of a ship. **1958** *Observer* 9 Feb. 5/3 *Packet goods... Loose goods. **1977** 'J. FRASER' *Hearts Ease* ix. 103 Shelves of tinned and packet goods. **1689** *Lond. Gaz.* No. 2485/4 Three Persons on Horseback set upon the Chester Mail..taking the *Pacquet-Horse and Pacquet into an adjacent Wood. **1663** GERBIER *Counsel* 8 Postillions hasten with the *Packet-Maile to the Post Office. **1664** BUTLER *Hud.* II. i. 61 About her neck a Packet-Male, Fraught with Advice, some fresh, some stale. **1968** D. E. ALLEN *Brit. Tastes* i. 35 Housewives in the South are fonder of all the speeded-up ways of cooking... *Packet mixes are used with less compunction. **1894** STEVENSON & OSBOURNE *Ebb-Tide* II. ix. 172, I fought my way, third mate, round the Cape Horn with a push of *packet-rats that would have turned the devil out of hell and shut the door on him. **1906** *Daily Chron.* 11 Aug. 4/6 It is almost as far a cry from the days of the Liverpool 'packet rat' as it is from the craft of to-day to the 'coffin ships' of Plimsoll memory. **1920** *Punch* 7 Apr. 266/1 An' the blessed lights o' Liverpool a-winkin' through the rain To welcome us poor packet-rats come back to port again. **1935** J. MASEFIELD *Victorious Troy* 68 'Who in hell said "Time, too?"' Cobb asked... 'Which of your damned packet-rats said "Time, too", then?' **1967** A. L. LLOYD *Folk Song in England* iv. 296 The packet-rats sailing under the house-flags of the Black Ball, Red Star, Dramatic and Swallowtail lines. **1782** R. MORRIS *Let.* 7 Oct. in J. Jay *Corr. & Public Papers* (1891) II. 349 Joshua Barney..[is] now commanding the *Packet Ship *General Washington*. **1837** A. LANGTON *Jrnl.* in *Gentlewoman Upper Canada* (1950) 9, I should strongly recommend avoiding a crowded packet-ship..or perhaps a packet-ship at all. **1842** DICKENS in *Harper's Mag.* (1884) Jan. 217/1, I made arrangements for returning home in the George Washington packet-ship. **1962** *Which?* Jan. 20/1 For convenience in shopping, the *packet soups (the least heavy and bulky) are obviously better than the tinned soups. **1974** A. ROSS *Bradford Business* 125 We stoked up hurriedly on packet soup and woody pork chops. **1865** T. P. KETTELL *Hist. Great Rebellion* xx. 246 These two vessels had been *packet-steamers, running to New York. **1883** E. EGGLESTON *Hoosier School-Boy* 115 The little packet-steamer was landing at the wharf. **1972** *Proc. Inst. Electr. Engineers* CXIX. 1677 (*heading*) Proposed organisation for *packet-switched data-communication network. **1980** *Financial Rev.* (Sydney) 22 Apr. 3/3 A cheap alternative, the use of OTC's Midas packet-switched network where tariffs are based on volume of information rather than time, is being investigated. **1985** P. LAURIE *Databases* i. 30 The major telephone services have 'Packet Switched Networks' which transmit data at rates of around 50000 bits per second nationally and internationally. **1972** *Times* 17 May (Suppl.) p. iii/8 The technique..is known as 'store and forward' or *packet-switching... Only when the message has been completely and accurately received is it forwarded to the next centre. **1976** *Times* 8 June 10/8 In Data transmission, the new 'packet switching' technique which has evolved from message-switching (as opposed to circuit-switching) systems is being applied in a number of networks. **1986** *Times* 4 Mar. 22 New videotex targets to hack and new radio and packet-switching services to use. *c* **1870** in A. Davis *Package & Print* (1967) Pl. 192 (Advt.), Niblett's farm house bread stores... Agent for the celebrated *packet tea. **1907** *Yesterday's Shopping* (1969) 1 Packet Teas packed on the estates in China and India. **1931** *N. & Q.* 14 Nov. 353/2 One of the earliest distributors of packet tea was the one-time old-fashioned firm of Horniman. **1976** *Times* 28 July 1/6 Packet tea and large, sliced loaves are among the eight foods for which manufacturers have voluntarily restricted prices. **1894** *Westm. Gaz.* 14 Feb. 2/1 Twenty years ago there were scarcely a dozen *packet tobaccos; now they are innumerable.

'packet, *v.* [f. PACKET *sb.*: cf. F. *paqueter* (Cotgr. 1611).]

1. *trans.* To make up into, or wrap up in, a packet.

1621 *Summary of Du Bartas* To Rdr. *iv b, So many wonders as I behold enstated and packeted vp in a paucity of Verses. *a* **1745** SWIFT *Lett.* (R.), My resolution is to send you all your letters well sealed and packeted. **1755** H. WALPOLE *Lett.* (1846) III. 157 When Mr. Müntz has done, you will be so good as to pacquet him up, and send him to Straw-berry. **1853** MISS E. S. SHEPPARD *Ch. Auchester* i, There was unction in the packeted, ticketed drugs.

†**2.** *trans.* To dispatch by packet-boat. *Obs.*

1638 FORD *Fancies* I. i, The young lord of Telamon, her husband, Was packeted to France, to study courtship.

†**b.** *intr.* To ply with a packet-boat. *Obs.*

1806 WEBSTER *Dict.*, *Packet*, to ply with a packet. **1813** *Boston Daily Advertiser* 9 Mar. 3/4 The subscribers respectfully inform the publick that they continue the packeting business between Providence and New York.

packetarian (pækɪˈtɛərɪən). *U.S.* [f. PACKET *sb.* 2 + -ARIAN.] One of the crew of a packet-boat.

1882 *Harper's Mag.* July 281/1 The typical 'Jack' of the pre-propeller age—the 'packetarian', and the able seaman of the clipper-ship fleet—has..utterly vanished. **1887** S. SAMUELS *From Forecastle to Cabin* 265 The 'packetarians' came last, and they invariably found themselves reduced to the same toggery in which they boarded the ship. **1930** R. CLEMENTS *Grey Seas* 110 No 'packetarians' these days, Mr. Findlay.

packet-boat. [f. PACKET *sb.* + BOAT *sb.* Hence, F. *paquebot*, in 1634 *paquebouc* (Cleiriac *Termes de Marine* 35), in *Dict. Acad.* 1718 *paquet-bot.*]

A boat or vessel plying at regular intervals between two ports for the conveyance of mails, also of goods and passengers; a mail-boat. (Often shortened to *packet*: see PACKET *sb.* 2.)

Orig. the boat maintained for carrying 'the packet' of State letters and dispatches. Cf. 1598–9 (in *Rept. Secret Committee on Post Office*, 1844, 37) 'Postes towardes Ireland ..Hollyheade, allowance as well for serving the packett by lande as for entertaining a bark to carie over and to returne the packet, at x li. the moneth'. An early official name for this was POST-BARK (in *State Papers* as late as 1651), also POST-BOAT, q.v. In 1628 (*S.P. Dom. Chas. I*, CXXIV. 118 b, P.R.O.) 'Hollyhead for keepinge a Boate..to Transport the Packetts to Ireland. *Margin*, this to bee performed by the pacquets postmaster'; this 'Boate to Transport the Packetts' was prob. already familiarly known as the 'packet-boat', since this term was so well-known as to be borrowed in French before 1634. (In 1637 the 'Speedy Post' to carry the packet to and from the Continent was known as the 'Postmaster's Frigate' (Cal. S.P. *passim*).

1641 EVELYN *Diary* 11 Oct., I marched three English miles towards the packet-boate. **1649–50** *Commons' Journal* 21 Mar., The Charge of the Packet Boats for Ireland. **1657** *Acts & Ordin. Parl.* c. 30 §8 (Scobell) 513 Rules..for the Settlement of Convenient Posts, and Stages..and the providing and keeping of a sufficient number of Horses, and Pacquet-Boats. **1668** *Lond. Gaz.* No. 267/4 The passage is re-establist between Harwich and Helvoet-sluyce, with able and sufficient Pacquet-boats of 60 Tuns. **1693** G. COLLINS *Gt. Brit. Coasting Pilot* I. 14/1 Holyhead-Road... The Pacquet Boats for Ireland use this place. **1718** LADY M. W. MONTAGU *Let. to Abbé Conti* 31 Oct., I arrived this morning at Dover, after being tossed a whole night in the packet-boat. **1774** PENNANT *Tour Scot. in 1772*, 295 A pacquet-boat,..sails every fortnight. **1879** BLACK *Macleod of D.* xxx, The big open packet-boat that crosses the Frith of Lorn.

†**packeteer** (pækɪˈtɪə(r)). *Obs.* except *Hist.* [f. PACKET *sb.* + -EER.] **1.** *Canad.* A carrier (often an Indian) of letters and documents, esp. in the fur trade.

1784 J. THOMAS in *Publ. Hudson's Bay Rec. Soc.* (1954) XVII. 27 Tradesmen at their separate employs, Hunters, Trappers, fishermen, and pacqueteers. **1943** *Beaver* Mar. 30/1 Mail packets were operated on a time-table, just as are mail flights by aeroplanes today. 'Packeteers' were never armed.

2. = PACKETARIAN.

1922 *Short Stories* Feb. (early issue) 141/2 *Au revoir*, Joe Pichegru, you sun-smoked son of a packeteer!

packeter (ˈpækɪtə(r)). *Canad.* [f. PACKET *sb.* + -ER[1].] = PACKETEER 1.

1893 J. HORDEN *Forty-Two Yrs. amongst Indians & Eskimo* xv. 147 The packeters returning from Abbitibbe with the letters..to Moose. *Ibid.* xvii. 169 The 'packeters' were espied crossing the river, in snow-shoes. **1961** J. W. ANDERSON *Fur Trader's Story* iii. 24 Others again would drive dog teams..while others would be 'packeters', hauling the mail..in winter.

pack-flat (equal stress), *a.* [f. PACK *v.*[1] + FLAT *a.*, *adv.*] Capable of being made into a flat package.

1951 *Good Housek. Home Encycl.* 107/2 Glass-top coffee table with pack-flat base. **1969** E. H. PINTO *Treen* 375 The 18th-century, 'pack-flat', mahogany wig stand..is exactly like modern travelling millinery stands. **1974** *Sunday Tel.* 6 Oct. 20/1 (Advt.), Sportsmans snug will keep you warm & dry in the worst weather! Full size 54″ × 30″ × 20″. Pack flat 30″ × 6″ × 2″.

packfong, erroneous form for PAKTONG, Chinese nickel-silver.

pack-full, *a.* [f. PACK *v.*[1]] As full as can be packed.

1858 MRS. CARLYLE 16 Jan. in *New Lett. & Mem.* (1903) II. 172 Her head has been pack-full of nonsense.

'pack-,horse. [f. PACK *sb.*[1] + HORSE *sb.*] A horse used for carrying packs or bundles of goods.

c **1475** *Pict. Voc.* in Wr.-Wülcker 757/38 *Hic saginarius*, a pakhors [*printed* palhors]. **1552** HULOET, Packehorse or mule, *clitellarius*. **1630** *R. Johnson's Kingd. & Commw.* 481 Two hundred Horsemen in Moscovie, require three hundred Packe-horses. **1745** *De Foe's Eng. Tradesman* xxvi. (1841) I. 260 Carriage by packhorses and by wagons. **1859** THACKERAY *Virgin.* i, Strings of pack-horses that had not yet left the road.

b. *fig.* A drudge.

1594 SHAKS. *Rich. III*, I. iii. 122, I was a packe-horse in his great affaires. **1693** WOOD *Life* 27 Nov. (O.H.S.) III. 436 He has been a packhorse in the practical and old galenical way of physick. **1768** GOLDSM. *Good-n. Man* II. i, I'll be pack-horse to none of them.

c. *attrib.* and *Comb.*

1593 NASHE *Christs T.* 65 b, Violent are most of our packe-horse Pulpit-men. *a* **1703** POMFRET *Fortunate Compl.* 44 He ..pack-horse like, jogs on beneath his load. **1791** W. BARTRAM *Carolina* 384 The heat and the burning flies..such ..as to excite compassion even in the hearts of pack-horsemen. **1872** JENKINSON *Guide Eng. Lakes* (1879) 53 The old packhorse track from Kendal to Whitehaven.

packhouse ('pækhaʊs). [f. PACK *sb.*[1] + HOUSE *sb.*; = Du. *pakhuis* (Kilian *packhuys*), Ger. *packhaus*; obs. F. *pacqhuus*.] A building in which packs or bundles of goods are stored; a warehouse.

1601 J. WHEELER *Treat. Comm.* 16 [They] did let out the best of their houses to..strangers for chambers, and pack-houses. **1773** *Ann. Reg.* 65 Several hundred persons..at Dundee..carried off 400 sacks of wheat and barley, from the packhouse. **1893** *Daily News* 4 May 5/4 The..company's packhouses are just now overstocked with Russian cotton.

packie ('pækɪ). *N.Z. colloq.* [f. PACK *sb.*[1] + -IE.] = PACKMAN 2 b.

1945 J. D. PASCOE in *N.Z. Geographer* I. 20 Next on the list is the 'packie'—half-cook, half-handyman, always good with horses or mules—who takes blankets and provisions into 'camp'. **1947** P. NEWTON *Wayleggo* (1949) 14 The process is repeated, the 'packie' moving on again. **1963** *Weekly News* (Auckland) 8 May 39/1 The packie happened to come in that morning for more bread. **1972** P. NEWTON *Sheep Thief* iv. 31 An old packie by the name of Paddy Roper lost two of his team there.

packing ('pækɪŋ), *vbl. sb.*[1] [f. PACK *v.*[1] + -ING[1].]

I. The action of PACK *v.*[1]

1. a. The putting (of things) together compactly, as for transport, preservation, or sale; the filling (of a receptacle) with things so put in.

1389 *Act 13 Rich. II*, c. 9. §1 Null merchant nautre homme achate ses leynes par celles paroles *Goodpakkyng* ne par autres paroles semblables. **1391** *Earl Derby's Exped.* (Camden) 35 Pro pakkyng dictorum pannorum. **1494** *Act 11 Hen. VII*, c. 23 Neither the Tale-fish nor small Fish should be laid double in packing. **1506** *Burgh Rec. Edin.* (Rec. Soc.) I. 109 Throw pakking and peling of merchand gude in Leith to be had furth of our realme. **1760–72** H. BROOKE *Fool of Qual.* (1809) IV. 101 The night was employed in hastening and packing. **1802** MAR. EDGEWORTH *Irish Bulls* iv. 161 Little Dominick heaved many a sigh when he saw the packings up of all his school-fellows. **1841–71** T. R. JONES *Anim. Kingd.* (ed. 4) 755 A circumstance which much facilitates the packing of the abdominal viscera. **1897** *Longmans' Geog. Ser.* II. *The World* 333 Meat-curing and packing is a very important industry at Chicago and Cincinnati. [Cf. PACK *v.*[1] 1 b.]

b. The assembling of gregarious beasts or birds: see PACK *v.*[1] 5.

1879 JEFFERIES *Wild Life in S.C.* 303 The packing of birds is very interesting.

c. *Med.* Wrapping in a wet sheet.

1861 GEO. ELIOT *Let.* 10 Dec. (1954) III. 472 As I hope the Florentine hydropathist may not be a quack as Dr. Gully at Malvern certainly is, I shall be disappointed if there is no good effect to be traced to judicious 'packing' and sitz baths. **1874** BLACKIE *Self-Cult.* 51 The wet sheet packing, one of the most bruited of the hydropathic appliances.

d. The transporting of goods on pack animals.

1843 *Amer. Pioneer* II. 162 Merchandise..was principally carried on pack horses until after 1788. Packing continued to be an important business in Kentucky until 1795. *Ibid.* 215 The grain would not bear packing across the mountains; a horse could not carry more than four bushels of it. **1897** *Boston Daily Globe* (evening ed.) 4 Aug. 5/2 Prices for packing across the pass have risen. **1948** *Hungry Horse News* (Columbia Falls, Montana) 24 Sept. 8/1 Roy owns a valuable string of pack horses and does considerable packing for the forest service.

e. An extra charge added to the cost of delivered goods to cover the cost of packing them.

1901 *Pitman's Business Terms, Phr. & Abbrev.* 155 *Packing*... The *charge* made for packing. **1974** *Parker's Wholesale Catal.* (J. Parker Dutch Bulbs..Co.) Autumn 13/2 All our prices are inclusive of duty and packing.

f. The spatial arrangement of the constituent atoms of a crystalline structure relative to one another.

1917 [see HEXAGONAL *a.* 3]. **1945** C. W. BUNN *Chem. Crystallogr.* vii. 276 The mode of packing of atoms, ions, or molecules in crystals may be regarded as controlled by two principles—the principle of close packing.., and, where ions are concerned, the tendency for an electrically charged unit to surround itself with units of opposite charge. **1966** C. R. TOTTLE *Sci. Engin. Materials* iii. 54 The closeness of packing of atoms in a crystal lattice affects thermal and mechanical properties. **1973** H. D. MEGAW *Crystal Struct.* ii. 54 Packing of ions as rigid spheres determines the coordination number (the number of anions surrounding a cation).

II. 2. *concr.* **a.** Any material used to fill up a space or interstice closely or tightly; filling, stuffing.

Applied, *e.g.*, to a piece of some substance inserted in a joint, around a piston, etc., so as to render it air-tight or water-tight; a contrivance (such as a bag of flax-seed, which swells when wetted) for stopping the opening between the tube and the side of the boring in an oil-well; small stones embedded in mortar, for filling up the inside of a wall; in *Printing*, a cloth, board, or the like, placed between the impression-cylinder and the paper, for equalizing the impression.

1824 R. STUART *Hist. Steam Engine* 160 The ends of the wheels are made to move round steam-tight by packings or stuffings. **1837** *Civil Eng. & Arch. Jrnl.* I. 12/1 They..form a perfectly secure water-joint, without any assistance of packing, lead, or other material. **1842–76** GWILT *Archit. Gloss.*, *Packing*, small stones imbedded in mortar, used to fill up the interstices between the larger stones in rubble work. **1858** SIMMONDS *Dict. Trade*, *Packing*, a quantity of wood or coals piled up to support roofs in a mine or for other purposes; the stuffing round a cylinder, etc. **1890** W. J. GORDON *Foundry* 221 (*Rotary Press*) It was customary to work entirely with soft packing—that is to say, with a thick blanket or cloth between the impression cylinder and the paper.

b. *slang.* Food, particularly if of inferior quality.

1891 J. BENT *Criminal Life* 272 *Packing*,..food. **1925** FRASER & GIBBONS *Soldier & Sailor Words* 219 *Packing*, rations. Food in general. **1973** 'P. MALLOCH' *Kickback* iv. 27 'When you've had the kind of packing I've had for three years, this is a treat.' He..began to eat.

III. 3. *attrib.* and *Comb.* **a.** Used for, in, or in connexion with the packing of goods, as ***packing-awl, -cloth, -crate, -crib, -house, -knot, -paper, -plant, -room, -shed, -stick, -wood, -yard.*** **b.** Pertaining to or used in the packing of a piston, a joint, etc., as ***packing-block, -bolt, -expander, -gland, -leather, -nut, -ring.*** **c.** **packing-board**: see quot.; **packing box**, (*a*) a box for packing goods in; also *attrib.* = *packing case*; (*b*) a stuffing-box around the piston-rod of a steam-engine; **packing case**, a case or frame-work in which articles are packed or securely enclosed, for conveyance to a distance; also *attrib.* used disparagingly of a type of modern architecture alleged to resemble packing-cases in its regularity and monotony; **packing density** *Computers*, the density of stored information in terms of bits per unit of storage medium; **packing fraction** *Nuclear Physics*, 10,000 times $(M-A)/A$(or $(M-A)/M$), where M is the atomic weight of a nucleus and A is its mass number; cf. *mass defect* s.v. MASS *sb.*[2] 10 d; **packing needle** = PACK-NEEDLE; **packing-officer** (see quot.); †**packing-penny**, a penny given at dismissal; ***to give a packing-penny to***, to 'send packing', to dismiss; **packing-press**, a strong press, usually hydraulic, used to compress goods into small bulk for convenience of carriage; **packing-sheet**, (*a*) a sheet for packing goods in; (*b*) *Med.* a wet sheet in which a patient is enveloped in hydropathic treatment; **packing station**, *spec.* an official depot where eggs are graded and packed; also (with hyphen) *attrib.*; †**packing whites**, name for a kind of woollen cloth.

1875 KNIGHT *Dict. Mech.*, **Packing-awl*, one for thrusting a twine through a packing cloth or the meshes of a hamper. *Ibid.*, **Packing-bolt* (*Steam-engine*), a bolt which secures the gland of a stuffing-box. **1774** in *Mass. Hist. Soc. Coll.* (1914) LXXI. 214 To a *packing Box £0. 9. 4. **1800** JANE AUSTEN *Let.* 25 Oct. (1952) 77 The charge of 3*s* 6*d* for the Packing box. **1909** *Daily Chron.* 8 July 8/3 (*heading*) No 'packing box' houses. They are not turned out by the score or the hundred all to one pattern like packing cases. **1881** *Archit. Publ. Soc. Dict.*, **Packing-board*, the term applied to the boards used with poling boards over the intended soffit of an arch in tunneling, to the top of the heading wherever the earth shows symptoms of falling in. **1842** SELBY *Brit. Forest Trees* 212 The wood is soft and spongy, and only fit for *packing-boxes. **1791** in Picton *L'pool Munic. Rec.* (1886) II. 268 The frames, *packing cases and carriage. **1893** SELOUS *Trav. S.E. Africa* 26 A large open packing-case, in which had been stowed the trading goods. **1935** *Fortnightly* Apr. 410 So we are given the packing-case building—rectangular boxes with holes punched for doors and windows. **1961** *Times* 11 Apr. 4/2 Sir Jacob Epstein apparently intended a certain reproach to the 'packing-case' type of modern architecture in the bronze group, 'Pan'. **1890** *Cent. Dict.* s.v. *Lenticel*, The outer (not corky) cells of a lenticel are termed **packing* or *complementary cells*. **1859** W. S. COLEMAN *Woodlands* (1866) 44 For making *packing-crates. **1958** *Wescon Convention Record of IRE* IV. 49/1 The first limitation in *packing density is the number of pulses per inch that can be recorded on each track, which is limited by the basic resolution of the head and tape combination. **1967** MCLACHLAN & MOLSOM *Data Processing* xi. 171 The speed of reading and writing..will depend upon the physical speed of the tape past the read/write head, and the packing density of the information written. **1927** F. W. ASTON in *Proc. R. Soc.* A. CXV. 501 The mean gain or loss of mass per proton when the nuclear packing is changed from that of oxygen to that of the atom in question..will be called the '*packing fraction' of the atom and expressed in parts per 10,000. **1938** R. W. LAWSON tr. *Hevesy & Paneth's Man. Radioactivity* (ed. 2) xix. 179 The idea of the 'packing fraction' has been introduced, by which we understand the difference between the mass of the atom and the integral part of its mass-number, divided by the mass-number. **1949** FRIEDLANDER & KENNEDY *Introd. Radiochem.* ii. 38 The mass defect Δ is the difference between the atomic mass M and the mass number A: $\Delta = M-A$... The packing fraction f is the mass defect divided by the mass number: $f = \Delta/A$. (Sometimes f is defined as Δ/M; the difference is negligible.) **1955** A. E. S. GREEN *Nuclear Physics* ii. 55 Packing fractions are positive (0·6 to 0 mMU) for the stable nuclei from 1 to 20, negative (0 to − 0·8 to 0 mMu for nuclei from 20 to 170, and positive again (0 to 0·6 mMU) for the very heavy nuclei. **1968** G. M. MOSSOP *Advanced Level Atomic Physics* ix. 150 The packing fraction is the mass defect per nucleon. **1884** KNIGHT *Dict. Mech.* Supp., **Packing Gland*, an annular piece, the cover of a stuffing box, which is screwed or otherwise forced into the stuffing box to expand the packing against the piston. **1834** C. F. HOFFMAN *Winter in West* (1835) II. xxxii. 136 One of the *packing-houses, built of brick, and three stories high, is more than a hundred feet long, and proportionably wide. **1901** *Chambers's Jrnl.* Mar. 208/1 Two of the largest packing houses had in their cold-storage chambers no fewer than two hundred and sixteen million eggs. **1968** *Globe & Mail* (Toronto) 5 Feb. 5/4 He was leading the campaign to organize packinghouse workers. **1977** *Time* 22 Aug. 43/1 By 14 he had quit school and started work as a janitor and a packing-house laborer. **1871** *Routledge's Ev. Boy's Ann.* May 300 *Packing knots are used for binding timber together. **1662** in Pitcairn *Crim. Trials* III. 607 A sharp thing lyk a *paking neidle. **1880** L. HIGGIN *Handbk. Embroidery* iv. 34 It should now be braced with twine by means of a packing needle. **1937** A. M. MIALL *Making Home Furnishings* x. 161 Thread your long curved packing needle with string, and with a few large stitches through the hessian secure the tops of the springs to it. **1858** SIMMONDS *Dict. Trade*, **Packing-officer*, an excise-officer who superintends or watches the packing of paper, and other exciseable articles. **1861** D. G. ROSSETTI *Let.* Jan. (1965) II. 392, I shall have it printed on common brown *packing-paper. **1939** *Army & Navy Stores Catal.* 305/2 Packing paper and cloth for export parcels. **1598** B. JONSON *Case Altered* III. iii, Will you give A *packing penny to virginity? **1825** BROCKETT *N.C. Gloss.*, *Packing-penny-day*, the last day of the fair; when all the cheap bargains are to be had. **1921** *Daily Colonist* (Victoria, B.C.) 17 Mar. 2/5 Representatives of ten national *packing plant unions today pledged their support to the Amalgamated Order of Meat Cutters. *Ibid.* 9 Oct. 31/5 Fire, which apparently originated in a smokehouse last night, destroyed the packing plant of the H. F. Lewis Company. **1825** J. NICHOLSON *Operat. Mechanic* 292 A very ingenious and useful *packing-press has been invented by Mr. John Peek. **1854** *Harper's Mag.* Mar. 456/1 The '*packing-room' is the loft of the gin-house. **1900** H. LAWSON *On Track* 94 One day I went downstairs to the packing-room and saw a lot of phosphorus in jars of water. **1960** J. BETJEMAN *Summoned by Bells* ii. 12 Bang through the packing-room! **1901** *Chambers's Jrnl.* Feb. 99/1 An expert to accompany the fruit from the orchard, through the *packing-shed, on to the port of shipment. **1946** K. TENNANT *Lost Haven* (1947) vii. 100 Jack Starbrace had fallen over backwards into the packing shed. **1545** *Rates of Customs* c j, Olde shetes called *packinge shetes the dossen. **1869** CLARIDGE *Cold Water Cure* 81 Had this gentleman been subjected to the Packing-sheet followed by Tepid-bathing. **1930** E. BROWN *Brit. Poultry Husbandry* 347 *Packing stations. **1938** L. PEARCE-GERVIS *Compl. Poultry Keeper & Farmer* v. 150 Each grade has its own particular colour..and contains the registered number of the packing station. **1960** *Farmer & Stockbreeder* 1 Mar. 55/3 Many of us..are not at all happy about current packing-station prices. **1875** KNIGHT *Dict. Mech.*, **Packing-stick*, a *woolding* stick; one used in straining a twine around a rolled fleece of wool in tying. **1483** *Act 1 Rich. III*, c. 8 §4 Eny Clothes called *Pakkyng whites. **1816–30** BENTHAM *Offic. Apt. Maximized, Extract Const. Code* (1830) 64 *note*, Should peradventure any *packing-worthy occasion happen to take place. **1883** A. J. ADDERLEY *Fisheries Bahamas* 6 (Fish. Exhib. Publ.) The sponges are taken to the *packing-yard, where they are sorted, clipped, soaked in tubs of lime-water, and spread out to dry in the sun.

'packing, *vbl. sb.*[2] [f. PACK *v.*[2]]

†**a.** Private or underhand arrangement; fraudulent dealing or contriving, plotting: see PACK *v.*[2]

a **1529** SKELTON *Death Earl Northumbld.* 71 Ther was fals packing, or els I am begylde. **1587** HARRISON *England* II. iii. (1877) I. 77 Such packing..is vsed at elections, that..he that hath most friends,..is alwaies surest to speed. **1603** DEKKER *Batchelors Banquet* Wks. (Grosart) I. 208 Then fals hee into a frantick vaine of Iealousie: watching his wiues close packing. **1613** PURCHAS *Pilgrimage* (1614) 225 The forging and packing of miracles. *c* **1656** BRAMHALL *Replic.* ii. 103 If there be no miscarriage, no packing of Votes, no fraud used..like that in the Councel of Ariminum for..rejecting *homo-ousios*.

b. Corrupt constitution or manipulation of a deliberative body, etc.: see PACK *v.*[2] 4.

1653 [F. PHILLIPS] *Consid. Crt. Chancery* 20 Suborning or packing or laying of Juries. **1821** BENTHAM (*title*) The Elements of the Art of Packing as applied to Special Juries, particularly in cases of Libel Law. **1855** MACAULAY *Hist. Eng.* xv. III. 512 About the packing of the juries no evidence could be obtained. **1884** *Pall Mall G.* 23 July 1/1 The packing of Parliaments hardly secured to the Stuarts a perpetual lease of power.

'packing, *ppl. a.* [f. PACK *v.* + -ING[2].] **1.** That packs or is engaged in packing: see the verbs.

1636 DAVENANT *Wits* v. i, The nimble packing hand. **1890** *Boston* (Mass.) *Jrnl.* 25 Sept. 2/3 One large packing-firm [in S. California] will this year lose $50,000 on prunes alone.

2. As the second element in adj. combs.: habitually carrying, esp. of a weapon, as ***pistol-packing***, etc. (See PACK *v.*[1] 9 a.)

1936 E. AMBLER *Dark Frontier* xi. 174 How do you suppose we're going to stop a mob of eight dagger-packing Greeks? **1943**, etc. [see *pistol-packing* ppl. adj. s.v. PISTOL *sb.* 2]. **1959** *Times Lit. Suppl.* 13 Nov. 664/4 He is forced into carrying a Luger-packing German entomologist on a hunt for a rare and mysterious beetle.

†**'packishness.** *Obs. nonce-word.* The condition or quality of being a pack.

1672 EACHARD *Hobbs's State Nat.* 22 If any one trangam be taken out or missing, the pack then presently loses its packishness, and cannot any longer be said to be a pack.

packman ('pækmən). [f. PACK *sb.*[1] + MAN *sb.*]

1. A man who travels about carrying goods in a pack for sale; a pedlar.

a **1625** SIR J. SEMPLE (*title*) A Pick-tooth for the Pope: or the Pack-mans Pater-Noster, set down in a Dialogue betwixt a Pack-man and a Priest. *Ibid.* 1 The Priest said, Pack-man, thou must haunt the Closter, To learn the Ave, and the Pater noster. **1753** *Stewart's Trial* 89 James.. immediately dispatched Alexander Stewart packman. *c* **1817** HOGG *Tales & Sk.* V. 166 Auld Ingleby, the Liverpool pack-man. **1869** BLACKMORE *Lorna D.* ii, I hoped that he would catch the packmen.

2. a. *N. Amer.* One who transports goods by means of pack-animals or in a pack on his own back.

1828 in *Kansas Hist. Q.* (1936) Aug. 251, I & the two pack-men returned to the creek with six horses and all the baggage. **1847** *Ex. Doc. 31st U.S. Congress 1 Sess. House* (1849) No. 5. III. 627 Two of Judge Burt's packmen arrived today for provisions to take to the parties south. **1908** W. R. NURSEY *Story Isaac Brock* vi. 45 Brock would watch these packmen as, thus handicapped with a load weighing from two to five hundred pounds, they set out across the rough portage.

b. *N.Z.* A sheep-station handyman whose principal duties are conveying goods by pack-animal from camp to camp and cooking; hence also **packman-cook**.

1933 L. G. D. ACLAND in *Press* (Christchurch, N.Z.) 11 Nov. 15/7 *Packer, packman*, one who loads the packhorses and leads or drives them from camp to camp. He also cooks for the musterers. **1961** B. CRUMP *Hang on a Minute* 76 The packman-cook [on the sheep-station] was a muttering-to-himself old man called Joe. **1963** *Weekly News* (Auckland) 31 July 37/1 Packman-cook can be a tough job in some places. **1972** P. NEWTON *Sheep Thief* vii. 51 'Come and get it or I'll chuck it out.' The packman's rude yell rang through the hut and all hands stirred.

Hence **'packmanship**, the office of a packman.

1831 *Blackw. Mag.* XXX. 251 Denying the truth of his picture of packmanship.

packmantie, obs. Sc. var. POCKMANTEAU, etc., portmanteau.

pack-moth: see PACK *sb.*[1]

'pack-,needle. Forms: see PACK and NEEDLE. [f. PACK *sb.*[1] + NEEDLE; cf. Ger. *packnadel*, Du. *paknaald* (Kilian *packnaelde*).] A large strong needle used for sewing up packages in stout cloth.

1327 *Wardrobe Acc. 20 Edw. II* 26/10 Unus penner cum paknedlis. **1341** [see PACKTHREAD]. **1362** LANGL. *P. Pl.* A. v. 126, I..Brochede hem with a pak-neelde [*v.rr.* pacneld, pakke nedle]. **1545** *Rates Customs* c ij b, Packenedels the thousand iiis. iiiid. **1634** T. JOHNSON *Parey's Chirurg.* x. xxiv. (1678) 255 A long thick Triangular needle of a good length like to a large Pack-needle. **1736** AMYAND in *Phil. Trans.* XXXIX. 337 Thrusting close to the Bone a Pack-Needle armed with a strong Packthread. **1866** ROGERS *Agric. & Prices* I. xxi. 551 Sacks were made in the house, and pack-needles and thread were bought for the purpose.

packsaddle ('pæk,sæd(ə)l), *sb.* [f. PACK *sb.*[1] + SADDLE *sb.*; cf. Du. *pakzadel* (Kilian *packsadel*), Ger. *packsattel*.]

1. A saddle adapted for supporting a pack or packs to be carried by a pack-beast.

1388 WYCLIF *2 Macc.* iii. 27 In a pakke sadil *ether* hors litir. **1530** PALSGR. 250/2 Packesadyll, *batz, bas.* **1598** B. JONSON *Ev. Man in Hum.* I. iv, Born for the manger, pannier, or pack-saddle. **1641** MILTON *Ch. Govt.* II. (1851) 149 Ye may take off their packsaddles, their days work is don. **1772** NUGENT tr. *Hist. Fr. Gerund.* I. 348 He will as much apply to scholastic studies as it now rains pack-saddles. **1859** MARCY *Prairie Trav.* iv. 98 The Mexicans use a leathern pack-saddle without a tree.

2. Short for *pack-saddle roof*: see 3.

1848 B. WEBB *Continental Eccles.* 130 A point commands eight spires at once: two being pack-saddles.

3. *attrib.* and *Comb.*, as **'packsaddle-,maker**; **packsaddle roof** (see quot.); so ***packsaddle tower***.

1599 MINSHEU *Sp. Dict.*, A Packe-saddle maker, ..*albardero.* **1720** *Lond. Gaz.* No. 5904/4 William Milward, Pack-saddle-maker. **1845** PARKER *Gloss. Archit.* (ed. 4) I. 381 A very common..termination [of the church towers in Normandy] is a pack-saddle roof with gables on two sides. **1848** RICKMAN *Archit.* App. 43 The tower on two sides has high gables, and is roofed from these with a common house ridge roof. This sort of roof is called a pack-saddle roof.

packsaddle, *v.* [f. the sb.] *trans.* To convey on a packsaddle.

1912 *Red Mag.* Mar. 508/1 They had a burro on another ledge of the estate, which packsaddled things in from where the stage dropped them.

packstaff ('pækstɑːf, -stæf) [f. PACK *sb.*[1] + STAFF.] A staff on which a pedlar supports his pack when standing to rest himself. In proverbial phrase †***as plain as a packstaff*** (obs.; now *pikestaff*).

1542 BECON *David's Harp* Early Wks. (Parker Soc.) 276 He is as plain as a pack-staff. **1597** BP. HALL *Sat.* III. Prol. 4 Not, riddle like, obscuring their intent; But, packe-staffe plaine, uttring what thing they ment. **1691** DRYDEN *Amphitryon* III. i, O Lord, what absurdities! as plain as any packstaff. **1760-72** H. BROOKE *Fool of Qual.* (1792) I. iv. 153 Poundings of packstaves. **1881** DUFFIELD *Don Quix.* I. 310 The benedictions of the pack-staves.

†**b.** *attrib.* (expressing contempt). *Obs.*

1598 MARSTON *Sco. Villanie* I. i. B vij, O packstaffe rimes. *Ibid.* II. v. E v, A packstaffe Epethite, and scorned name.

packthread ('pækθrɛd). Forms: see PACK and THREAD. [f. as prec. + THREAD *sb.*] Stout thread or twine such as is used for sewing or tying up packs or bundles.

1341 *Durham Acc. Rolls* (Surtees) 542 In Paknedel et Paktrede emp. pro lana pakkanda, viijd. **1392-3** *Earl Derby's Exped.* (Camden) 158 Pro pacthred pro dictis ligandis. **1442** in Willis & Clark *Cambridge* (1886) I. 387, xvj Skaynys of grete packethrede for the masons for mesours. **1592** SHAKS. *Rom. & Jul.* v. i. 47 A beggerly account of emptie boxes,.. Remnants of packthred. **1604** T. M. *Black Bk.* in *Middleton's Wks.* (Bullen) VIII. 22 Apparelled in villanous packthread. **1712** ADDISON *Spect.* No. 407 ¶5 There was a Counsellor who never pleaded without a Piece of Packthread in his Hand. **1865** CARLYLE *Fredk. Gt.* XII. xi. (1872) IV. 239 His big Austrian Heritages..elaborately tied by diplomatic packthread and Pragmatic Sanction.

attrib. and *Comb.* **1720** *Lond. Gaz.* No. 5868/9 Shift.. ruffled with a Packthread striped Muslin with looped Mechlin Edging. **1723** *Ibid.* No. 6175/6 William Burdock .., Packthread-Spinner. **1863** FR. A. KEMBLE *Resid. in Georgia* 27 A pack-thread bell-rope.

packtong, var. PAKTONG, Chinese nickel-silver.

packwax: see PAXWAX.

‖**paco** ('pɑːkəʊ). Also **pacos**. [Sp. *paco*, a. Quichua *paco*, the native name in Peru.

Cf. Domingo de S. Tomas *Lex. Leng. Peru*, 1560, *Oveja*, llama, ó paco, ó guaca, ó guanaco, ó vicuña.]

1. = ALPACA.

1604 [see ALPACA 1, GUANACO]. **1613** PURCHAS *Pilgrimage* (1614) 873 The Sierras yeeld..Pacos, a kinde of sheepe-asses, profitable for fleece and burthen. **1752** SIR J. HILL *Hist. Anim.* 575 The Camelus, without any gibbosity. The Pacos..It is a native of Peru, and is sometimes employed, as the Glama, in carrying burthens. **1774** GOLDSM. *Nat. Hist.* II. 415 The natural colour of the paco is that of a dried rose leaf. **1834** *Nat. Philos.* III. *Phys. Geog.* 55/2 The paco, which in its domestic state is called bicunia or vigonia.

2. *Min.* An earthy brown oxide of iron, containing minute particles of silver. (From its colour).

1839 URE *Dict. Arts* 915 *Paco*, or *Pacos*, is the Peruvian name of an earthy-looking ore, which consists of brown oxide of iron. **1854** J. D. WHITNEY *Metallic Wealth U.S.* iii. 169 The principal ores [at Cerro de Pasco] are the *pacos* so called, analogous to the *colorados* of the Mexican miners: they are ferruginous earths, mingled with argentiferous ores.

pacock, north. form of *pocock*, PEACOCK.

†**'Pacolet.** *Obs.* Name of a dwarf in the old romance of Valentine and Orson, said to have made a magical horse of wood by which he could instantly convey himself to any desired place. Hence allusively, esp. in ***Pacolet's horse*** (F. *le cheval de Pacolet*), and *Pacolet* for a swift steed.

1581 SIDNEY *Apol. Poetrie* (Arb.) 64, I may speake..of Peru, and in speech, digresse from that, to the description of Calicut: but in action, I cannot represent it without Pacolets horse. *a* **1613** OVERBURY *Characters* (N.), The itch of bestriding the presse, or getting up on this wodden Pacolet. **1694** ECHARD *Plautus* 53 If I had got Pacolet's Horse, I cou'dn't ha' came sooner. **1728** RAMSAY *Monk & Miller's Wife* 230 I'll gar my Pacolet appear.

pacquet, obs. form of PACKET.

pact (pækt), *sb.* [a. OF. *pact* (14th c.), later *pacte* (in OF. also *pat, pac, pag*, pl. *pas*), ad. L. *pactum* agreement, covenant, neuter sb. f. *pactus*, pa. pple. of *pac-isc-ĕre* to agree, covenant.] An agreement between persons or parties, a compact.

nude, bare, or ***naked pact***, an agreement without consideration, which cannot therefore be legally enforced.

1429 *Rolls of Parlt.* IV. 361/1 No Merchaunt..shall.. bynde any of ye Kynges Lieges, be pact, covenant nor bond. **1485** CAXTON *Chas. Gt.* 216 He was contente to make a pacte and couenaunte wyth Charles. **1542** HENRY VIII *Declar. Scots* B ij b, That is due vnto vs by right, pactes, and leages. **1671** MILTON *P.R.* IV. 191 As offer them to me..on such abhorred pact, That I fall down and worship thee as God. **1790** BURKE *Fr. Rev.* Wks. 1808 V. 57 The engagement and pact of society, which generally goes by the name of the constitution. **1846** BROWNING *Lett.* (1899) I. 462/4 His pact with the evil one obliged him to drink no milk.

pact (pækt), *v. rare* [f. prec. Cf. obs. F. *pacter* (16th c. in Godef.).] **a.** *trans.* To stipulate; to agree to, conclude (something) with a person; to enter into a pact with (a person). **b.** *intr.* To enter into a pact, bargain (*for* a thing). Hence †**'pacted** *ppl. a.*

1535 CROMWELL in Merriman *Life & Lett.* (1902) II. 45 To pay the saide money..uppon suche conuenauntes as they shal pacte condiscende and conclude. **1567** TURBERV. *Ovid's Epist.* 63 Thy pacted spouse I am. **1646** GAULE *Cases Consc.* 35 The pacted witch is one only operative..by vertue of a superstitious compact or contract made with the Divell. **1654** VILVAIN *Theol. Treat.* ii. 41 A Covenant of Grace.. freely pacted with Man a sinner. **1940** *Economist* 6 Jan. 10/2 To-day Germany has pacted with Communism, Italy is neutral, the West fights Germany.

pact, obs. f. *packed*, from PACK *v.*

‖**pacta sunt servanda** ('pækta sʊnt sɜːˈvænda), *phr.* [L., lit. 'agreements must be kept': cf. Cicero *De Officiis* III. xcii pacta et promissa semperne servanda sint; *Digesta Iustiniani* II. xiv ideo servandum erit pactum conventum.] The principle, esp. in international law, that agreements are binding and inviolable.

1855 R. PHILLIMORE *Commentaries upon Internat. Law* II. v. vi. 56 *Pacta sunt servanda* is the pervading maxim of International, as it was of Roman jurisprudence. **1925** E. SATOW in *Cambr. Hist. Jrnl.* I. 295 (*heading*) *Pacta sunt servanda* or International Guarantee. **1939** E. H. CARR *Twenty Years' Crisis* xi. 232 War writers..have attempted to treat the rule *pacta sunt servanda* not merely as a fundamental rule of international law, but as the corner-stone of international society. **1945** J. L. KUNZ in *Amer. Jrnl. Internat. Law* XXXIX. 197 *Pacta sunt servanda* means the institution, by general international law, of a special procedure—the treaty procedure—for the creation of international norms... Valid treaty norms must be kept, but they can, by appropriate procedures, be revised. *Pacta sunt servanda* means the inviolability, not the unchangeability, of treaties. **1958** *Reports of Judgments* (Internat. Court of Justice) 121 The maxim *pacta sunt servanda* is of special significance in considering this contention of the Government of Sweden. **1962** *Times* 27 June 8/6 The ordinary rule was that contracts were to be enforced—*pacta sunt servanda.* **1973** I. M. SINCLAIR *Vienna Convention on Law of Treaties* iii. 53 Article 26 of the Convention reproduces, in lapidary language, the basic principle *pacta sunt servanda*, designated by the Commission as 'the fundamental principle of the law of treaties'.

pacthred, obs. form of PACKTHREAD.

paction ('pækʃən), *sb.* Now chiefly *Sc.* Also 5-6 **paccyon**, 5 **pactyon**, 6 **-tione**, 6-7 **-tioun**. [a. OF. *paction, paccion* (14th c. in Godef.), ad. L. *pactiōnem*, n. of action from *paciscĕre* to agree, covenant.] **a.** The action of making a bargain or pact; a bargain, agreement, compact, contract.

1471 CAXTON *Recuyell* (ed. Sommer) 8 The paccion and promys that he maad to his broder Tytan. **1484** —— *Fables of Æsop* II. xi, The convenaunces and pactyons made by drede and force oughte not to be holden. **1566** *Reg. Privy Council Scot.* I. 489 Ony setting, promeis, taking, pactioun, or conditioun. **1657** W. MORICE *Coena quasi Κοινή* v. 51 He entred into paction with man. **1754** ERSKINE *Princ. Sc. Law* (1809) 82 The provisions that the wife is entitled to, either by law or by paction. **1856** BOUVIER *Law Dict.* (ed. 6) II. 277 *Pactions.* International Law. When contracts between nations are to be performed by a single act, and their execution is at an end at once, they are not called treaties, but agreements, conventions or pactions. **1865** MAFFEI *Brigand Life* II. App. 311 Such pactions with the assassins as the Bourbonist kings were not ashamed to enter into. **1883** *Wharton's Law Lexicon* (ed. 7) 586/1 *Paction*, a bargain or covenant. **1964** *Mod. Law Rev.* XXVII. 314 In *Learmonth v. Sinclair's Trustees*..Moncrieff L.J.-C. said:..Now custom, whether general or local, when it is effectual operates not by implied paction or contract but by law.

b. Those leagued together, a confederation.

1877 BLACK *Green Past.* xx, And fight the whole paction of your enemies in Englebury.

'paction, *v. Sc.* [a. F. *pactioner, -onner* (14th c.), f. *paction*: see prec.] **a.** *trans.* To covenant or agree to (something); **b.** *intr.* To make a paction.

1640 R. BAILLIE *Canterb. Self-convict.* Postscr. 8 The King of Scotland is obliged at his coronation to paction under his great oath the preservation of the established Religion. **1725** MACFARLANE *Genealog. Collect.* (1900) II. 87 John Bisset..pactioned with Brisius Bishop of Murray anent the Transportation of Ecclesia St. Mauritij to Balbray. *a* **1839** GALT *Demon Destiny* III. 27 When they had paction'd to proceed together.

pactional ('pækʃənəl), *a.* Chiefly *Sc.* [f. PACTION *sb.* + -AL[1].] Of, pertaining to, or of the nature of a pact or covenant.

1624 F. WHITE *Repl. Fisher* 405 A relatiue, Pactionall, and Sacramentall Vnion. *a* **1659** BP. BROWNRIG *Serm.* (1674) II. ii. 22 The Promises..are..not simply free, but pactional and fœderal. **1726** E. ERSKINE *Serm.* Wks. 1871 I. 126 In a way of pactional debt. **1893** *Law Rep., Weekly Notes* 130/2 The contract..was pactional, and not testamentary.

Hence **'pactionally** *adv.*, by pact or agreement.

1884 LD. WATSON in *Law Rep.* 9 App. Cases 341 An estate ..which was being pactionally secured to the issue of the marriage into which she was entering.

†**pac'titious**, *a. Obs. rare*$^{-0}$. [f. L. *pactīci-us*, f. *pact-us* pa. pple.: see PACT *sb.* and -ITIOUS.] Characterized by being agreed upon or stipulated.

1656 in BLOUNT *Glossogr.* **1658** in PHILLIPS. **1755** JOHNSON, *Pactitious*, settled by covenant.

†**'pactive**, *a. Obs. rare*$^{-1}$. [ad. L. type **pactīv-us*, f. ppl. stem *pact-*: see PACT *sb.*] Pactional, settled by covenant.

1633 T. ADAMS *Exp. 2 Peter* i. 8 Heaven is..often called a reward; not factive, but pactive; of covenant, not of merit.

pactolian (pæk'təʊlɪən), *a.* [f. L. *Pactōlus*, Gr. *Πακτωλός* + -IAN.] Of, belonging or relating to, the river Pactolus in Lydia, famed in ancient times for its golden sands; golden.

1606 SYLVESTER *Du Bartas* II. iv. II. *Magnificence* 275 With either hand..shee pours Pactolian surges and Argolian showrs. *a* **1618** —— *Christian's Conflict* 98 The sacred hunger of Pactolian Dust, Gold, Gold bewitches mee. **1796** *Modern Gulliver's Trav.* 170 Each page invites to the pactolian coast. *a* **1845** HOOD *Black Job* ii, Flimsy schemes, For rolling in Pactolian streams.

pac'torial, *a. Sc. Law. rare.* [f. as next + -AL[1]: see -ORIAL.] = next.

1884 *Law Rep.* 9 App. Cases 332 The deed..contains no pactorial contract to do anything except for the marriage.

†**'pactory**, *a. Obs. rare.* [ad. L. type **pactōrius*, f. *pact-*: see PACT *sb.* and -ORY.] Of the nature of or pertaining to a pact or covenant.

1633 T. ADAMS *Exp. 2 Peter* ii. 10 Thine is a service.. Pactory; undertaking such a work for such wages.

pacu (pæ'ku:, 'pæku:). *Zool.* Also **pacou, paco, paku.** [a. Tupi *pacú.*] A large, vegetarian, freshwater fish, *Colossoma nigripinnis*, belonging to the family Characidæ and native to the northern parts of South America.

1825 WATERTON *Wand. S. Amer.* (1882) 35 The Pacou the richest and most delicious fish in Guiana. **1827** GRIFFITH tr. *Cuvier* X. 424 The Pacu. **1869** R. F. BURTON *Highl. Brazil* II. xvi. 240 The Pacú..The Carp-like body averages 2 to 3 palms in length. **1938** A. H. VERRILL *Strange Fish & their Stories* 218/1 Pacu. **1959** P. CAPON *Amongst those Missing* 181 Not too bad, I guess. A paku, and two of those fish sort of like bream. **1962** D. W. TUCKER tr. *Sterba's Freshwater Fishes of World* 112 (*caption*) The Pacu is a rarely-imported species from northern South America. **1974** H. MACINNES *Climb to Lost World* vi. 86 In the river there was plenty of Pakuweed, so called by the Indians because the Paku fish is supposed to feed on it. **1977** D. J. COFFEY *Encycl. Aquarium Fish* 89/1 *Colossoma nigripinnis*. Pacu. 71 cm. (28 in.) This fish comes from the Amazon... Body colour is silver. The dorsal and anal fins are red in colour.

pacy, var. PACEY *a.*

pad (pæd), *sb.*[1] *Obs.* exc. *dial.* Forms: 2, 5 **pade**, 3 **pode**, 5–7 **padd(e**, 6 **pod**; 5– **pad**. [Late OE. *pade* or ? *pad*, akin to ON. *padda* wk. fem. (Sw. *padda*, Dan. *padde*) = OFris. and MDu. *padde*, Du. *pad*, *padde*, MLG. *padde*, *pedde*, LG. *pad*, mod.Fris. dial. *padde*, *podde*, *podd*, *pod*, all in sense 'toad'. Cf. LG. or Du. *schildpad* tortoise, Ger. *schildpatt* tortoise-shell. Hence the diminutive PADDOCK, frog. Relations outside Teutonic unknown.]

1. †A toad (*obs.*); but in mod. dialects, the same as PADDOCK, a frog.

1154 *O.E. Chron.* an. 1137 Hi dyden heo in quarterne þar nadres & snakes & pades wæron inne & drapen heo swa. *c* **1250** *Gen. & Ex.* 2977 Polheuedes, & froskes, & podes spile Bond harde egipte folc in sile. *c* **1420** *Anturs of Arth.* 115 On þe chef of þe cholle A pade [*MS. Thornton* tade, *MS. Ingilby* padok] pikes one þe polle. *c* **1425** WYNTOUN *Cron.* I. xv. 1346 As ask or eddyre, tade or pade. *a* **1450** *Cov. Myst.* xvii. (Shaks. Soc.) 164, I xal prune that paddok and prevyn hym as a pad. *c* **1470** HENRYSON *Mor. Fab.* XIII. (*Frog & Mouse*) xiv, The fals ingyne of this foull carpand pad [*rime* bad]. **1570** LEVINS *Manip.* 7/33 A Padde, tode, *bufo*. *a* **1585** MONTGOMERIE *Flyting* 431 That this worme..some wonders may wirk; And, through the poyson of this pod, our pratiques prevaile. **1876** *Whitby Gloss.*, *Pads*,..frogs. **1876** *Mid. Yorks. Gloss.*, *Pad*,..a frog.

fig. **1593** HARVEY *New Let.* Wks. (Grosart) I. 291 The abiectest vermin, the Vilest padd, that creepeth on the earth.

2. A star-fish.

1613 *Howard of Naworth Househ. Bks.* (Surtees) 28 Mr. Sennoye's man bringing sea pads [*note*, the star-fish] and wilkes. **1661** LOVELL *Hist. Anim. & Min.* 283 Seepadde. *Stella marina*. **1834** SIR H. TAYLOR *Artevelde* II. v. iii, Seahedgehog, madrepore, sea-ruff, or pad.

†**3.** ***a pad in the straw***, a lurking or hidden danger.

1530 PALSGR. 595/1 Though they make never so fayre a face, yet there is a padde in the strawe. **1575** CHURCHYARD *Chippes* (1817) 136 Syr William Drury, (smelling out a pad in the straw). **1579** GOSSON *Sch. Abuse* (Arb.) 63, I haue.. poynted to the strawe where the padd lurkes, that euery man at a glimse might descry the beaste. **1590** NASHE *Pasquil's Apol.* I. C ij b. **1650** FULLER *Pisgah* III. II. viii. §3 *Latet anguis in herbâ*, there is a pad in the straw, and invisible mischief lurking therein. **1652** PEYTON *Catastr. Ho. Stuarts* (1731) 22 Altho' there lay a Pad in the straw.

4. *Comb.* †**pad-pipe** = *paddock-pipe*; †**pad-stool** = *paddock-stool*: see PADDOCK *sb.*[1] 3.

c **1450** *Alphita* (Anecd. Oxon.) 24/1 *Boletus*,..angl. tadestol [*v.r.* paddestol]. *Ibid.* 37/5 *Cauda Pulli* crescit in aquis. angl. padpipe. **1570** LEVINS *Manip.* 161/16 A Padstoole, *tuber*. **1607** TOPSELL *Four-f. Beasts* (1658) 384 A kind of Mushrom, or Padstoole.

pad (pæd), *sb.*[2] Also 7 **padde**, (*Sc.* 8 **pead**, 9 **paid**). [A word orig. of vagabonds' cant, introduced like other words of the class in 16th c.: cf. CRANK *sb.*[3]; a. Du. or LG. *pad* = OHG. *pfad*, cognate with Eng. PATH, q.v.]

1. a. A path, track; the road, the way. Orig. *slang*, now also *dial*.

1567 HARMAN *Caveat* 84 The hygh pad, the hygh waye. **1611** MIDDLETON & DEKKER *Roaring Girle* Wks. 1873 III. 216, I am..a maunderer vpon the pad. **1625** B. JONSON *Staple of N.* II. v, A Rogue, A very Canter, I Sir, one that maunds Vpon the Pad. **1666** BUNYAN *Grace Ab.* 12, I must say to the puddles that were in the horse pads, Be dry. **1768** ROSS *Helenore* 21 For her gueed luck a wie bit aff the pead [*ed.* 1812 paid], Grew there a tree wi' branches thick an' bred. **1790** W. MARSHALL *Midl. Counties* Gloss. (E.D.S.), *Pad*,..path. **1870** E. PEACOCK *Ralf Skirl.* II. 109 Slip ower Owse an' go by trods an' pads. **1898** J. A. BARRY *S. Brown's Bunyip*, etc. 21 Striking a well-beaten pad, he followed it.

fig. **1647** H. MORE *Song of Soul* I. II. cxxxii, The equall pad Of justice now, alas! is seldome trad.

b. *Austral. spec.* A track made by bullocks, cattle, camels, etc. Cf. *cattle-pad* s.v. CATTLE 9.

1911 C. E. W. BEAN *'Dreadnought' of Darling* xxiii. 207 The white track was the pad made by the feet of many camels. **1934** A. RUSSELL *Tramp-Royal in Wild Australia* ii. 20 The pad was winding and rocky and scarcely discernible. One sometimes wondered if it really was a pad, so little did it look like one. **1941** I. L. IDRIESS *Great Boomerang* ix. 67 You'll see the pad leanin' back to the horse paddock. **1954** B. MILES *Stars my Blanket* xix. 138 In places we were able to follow a wandering bullock-pad. **1966** 'J. HACKSTON' *Father clears Out* 19 We almost wore a series of pads through the bush trailing it. **1968** K. WEATHERLY *Roo Shooter* 37 They strode down the cattle pad at a fast walk.

2. a. Phr. ***on the pad***, on the road, on the tramp; ***to stand pad***, to beg by the way; ***gentleman, knight, squire of the pad***, a highwayman. **b.** Robbery on the highway. *slang*.

1664 ETHEREDGE *Comical Revenge* I. iii, I have laid the dangerous Pad now quite aside. **1699** R. L'ESTRANGE *Erasm. Colloq.* 43 A troop of lusty Rogues upon the Pad. **1700** T. BROWN *Amusem. Ser. & Com.* 105 Some-times they are Squires of the Pad, and..borrow a little Money upon the King's High-Way. **1706–7** FARQUHAR *Beaux' Strat.* II. ii, D'ye know of any other Gentlemen o' the Pad on this Road? **1851** MAYHEW *Lond. Labour* I. 246 He subsists now by 'sitting pad' about the suburban pavements. *Ibid.* 416 Her husband was on the pad in the country, as London was too hot to hold him. *Ibid.* III. 24 Beggars..who 'stand pad with a fakement' [remain stationary, holding a written placard].

†**3.** A highway robber; a highwayman. Cf. FOOTPAD. *Obs.*

1673 R. HEAD *Canting Acad.* 88 The *High-Pad*, or Knight of the Road. **1695** CONGREVE *Love for L.* I. iv. 16 Two suspicious Fellows like lawful Pads, that would knock a Man down with Pocket Tipstaves. *a* **1700** B. E. *Dict. Cant. Crew*, *High Pad*, a High-way Robber well Mounted and Armed. *Ibid.*, *Water-Pad*, one that Robbs Ships in the Thames. **1716** C'TESS COWPER *Diary* (1864) 100 Mr. Mickelwaite was set upon by nine Footpads... His Servants and he fired at them again, and the Pads did the same. **1823** BYRON *Juan* XI. xi, Four pads, In ambush laid, who had perceived him loiter Behind his carriage. **1834** H. AINSWORTH *Rookwood* III. v, High Pads and Low Pads.

4. A road-horse, an easy-paced horse, a pad-nag.

1617 MORYSON *Itin.* II. 47 He delighted in study, in gardens,..in riding on a pad to take the aire. **1690** in *12th Rep. Hist. MSS. Comm.* App. VII. 272, 60 sumpter horses, 6 war-horses, and 16 padds. **1703** SIR J. CLERK *Mem.* (1895) 46, I was mounted on a fine gray pad belonging to the Duke of Queensberry. **1708** [see PACER 2]. **1788** GIBBON *Decl. & F.* lviii. (1869) III. 434 He quietly rode a pad or palfrey of a more easy pace. **1832** TENNYSON *Lady Shalott* II. iii, An abbot on an ambling pad. **1858** R. S. SURTEES *Ask Mamma* xiv. 46 The very neatest lady's pad I ever set eyes on!

5. *attrib.* and *Comb.*, as (sense 1) ***pad-horse***, ***-mare***, ***-ram*** (humorous after *pad-horse*), †***-thief***; (sense 4) ***-boy***, ***-groom***; also ***pad-clinking***, ***pad-like*** adjs.

1633 B. JONSON *Tale Tub* IV. iii, Oh for a pad-horse, pack-horse, or a post-horse, To bear me on his neck, his back, or his croup. **1690** SHADWELL *Am. Bigot* II, De Pad-thief of the road. **1708** *Lond. Gaz.* No. 4478/8 Stoln or Stray'd.., a Padlike Mare light coloured in the Face. **1714** ADDISON *Spect.* No. 623 ¶5 Finding it an easy Pad-Ram..she purchased it of the Steward. **1725** T. THOMAS in *Portland Papers* VI. (Hist. MSS. Comm.) 81 A little pad mare. **1826** *Sporting Mag.* XVII. 378 These, with the squire's pad-groom..made a respectable appearance. **1865** H. KINGSLEY *Hillyars & Burtons* xix, My bonny, pad-clinking [*note* Alluding to the clinking of their spurs]..bucks, Good day. **1870** BLAINE *Encycl. Rur. Sports* §1074 The pad groom is employed in the hack stable and to follow his master.

pad (pæd), *sb.*[3] Also 6–7 **padde**, 7–8 **padd.** [Known from middle of 16th c.; origin obscure.

It is not certain that all the senses here placed have a common origin: 8 and 9 esp. seem to have little connexion with branch I. The only senses appearing to have relationship outside Eng. are 6 and 7, with which cf. 16th c. Flem. (now obs.) '*pad, patte* (vetus) palma pedis, planta pedis' (Kilian) i.e. sole of the foot, and LG. *pad* 'sole of the foot' *Bremisches Wbch.* 1767; but the history of the continental word is also unknown, it did not mean 'cushion', and it could not possibly be the starting-point of the Eng. senses.]

I. † **1. a.** A bundle of straw or the like to lie on.

1554 BP. HOOPER in *Fox's A. & M.* (1631) III. XI. 150/1 Hauing nothing appointed to me for my bed, but a little pad of straw, and a rotten couering. **1598** DRAYTON *Heroic. Ep.*, *Elenor Cobham to Dk. Humphry* Poems (1605) 52 b, Glad heere to kennell in a pad of straw. **1641** BROME *Jovial Crew* III. Wks. 1873 III. 394, I left 'em..sitting on their Pads of straw, helping to dress each others heads. **1719** DE FOE *Crusoe* II. iii, They lay..upon Goat-skins, laid thick upon such Couches and Pads, as they made for themselves.

b. A bed; hence, a lodging, a place to sleep; one's residence. Also, a room frequented by narcotic (esp. marijuana) users. (*slang*, orig. *U.S.*).

1718 C. HITCHING *Regulator* 19 The names of the Flash Words now in vogue amongst Thieves... The Padd, *alias* Bed [etc.]. **1846** *Swell's Night Guide* 67 The only question she asks is, 'vot pad do you vont?' **1914** JACKSON & HELLYER *Vocab. Criminal Slang* 64 Pad.., a bed; a place to sleep. **1938** *New Yorker* 12 Mar. 36/3 Pads where semi-conscious smokers are robbed of their money are creeper joints. **1956** 'E. MCBAIN' *Cop Hater* (1958) ix. 79 'If Ordiz is a junkie, what's he doing on Whore Street?' 'He's blind in some broad's pad.' **1959** [see *beatnik* s.v. BEAT GENERATION]. **1959** N. MAILER *Advts. for Myself* (1961) 346, I went with my wife and my friend..to a cold-water pad, south of the village. **1961** *Spectator* 25 Aug. 266 In this half world of cats, pads and hipsters there is a residual morality. **1965** 'MALCOLM X' *Autobiogr.* 57 Cats' pads, where with the lights and the juke down mellow, everybody blew gage and juiced back and jumped. **1967** *Boston Sunday Herald* 26 Mar. IV. 1/3 'Four out of five times when we go into a pad where we have been told there is pot, we find it', says the detective. **1967** N. LUCAS *C.I.D.* x. 134 A 'pad' is a bed—in a flat, a house, a bed-sitter or even in a shack. **1973** 'D. SHANNON' *No Holiday for Crime* (1974) vi. 89 She's got a pad over on Nadeau Street. **1974** K. MILLETT *Flying* I. 26 The usual university ghetto pad, an old house gone hip. **1977** *Time* 17 Jan. 8/3 They later searched the apartments of several employees, as well as Starckmann's swank pad in Neuilly.

c. A padded cell: cf. PADDED *ppl. a.*[2]

1938 S. BECKETT *Murphy* 167 The padded cells, known to the wittier as the 'quiet rooms', 'rubber rooms' or, in a notable clip 'pads'. **1964** G. L. COHEN *What's Wrong with Hospitals?* vii. 147 The side-rooms are in fact 'pads' remaining from the pre-tranquillizer regime. **1965** *New Statesman* 23 July 119/2 Quondam padded cells, now pink and chintzy, are given to old reliables who could leave hospital if they had anywhere to go. 'Yes, we do keep two 'pads' for isolation purposes,' barked the burly N.C.O.

2. a. A soft stuffed saddle without a tree, such as are used by country women or by equestrian performers, and by children in learning to ride; that placed on an elephant.

1570 LEVINS *Manip.* 7/32 A Padde, saddle, *penulatum*. **1600** DYMMOK *Ireland* (1843) 7 The horsemen..ryde upon paddes, or pillows without styrups. **1603** OWEN *Pembrokeshire* (1892) 280. **1633** T. STAFFORD *Pac. Hib.* III. xiii. (1810) 624 A choise Irish horse with a rich pad, and furniture. **1639** SHIRLEY *Ball* V. i, The pads, or easy saddles, Which our physicians ride upon. **1792** WOLCOTT (P. Pindar) *Odes of Condol.* Wks. 1792 III. 197 'Tis better riding on a pad, Than on a horse's back that's bare. **1813** MARIA GRAHAM *Jrnl. India* 75 On his [the elephant's] back an enormous pad is placed..upon this is placed the *howda*. **1875** S. SIDNEY *Bk. of Horse* 303 The best saddle for commencing is a pad, without a tree. **1879** F. POLLOK *Sport Brit. Burmah* I. 199, I was on a pad, as I found that I could shoot far better off it than out of a howdah.

b. That part of double harness to which the girths are attached, used in place of the gig-saddle; sometimes, also, a cart-saddle.

1811 *Sporting Mag.* XXXVII. 304 Arms and crests..will be introduced on the winkers, pads, nose-bands and breast-plates. **1875** S. SIDNEY *Bk. of Horse* 489 The pad or saddle of a four wheeled carriage has no weight to sustain beyond the shafts. **1894** ARMATAGE *Horse* vi. 88.

3. a. Something soft, of the nature of a cushion, serving esp. to protect from or diminish jarring, friction, or pressure, to fill up hollows and to fill out or expand the outlines of the body, to raise a pattern in embroidery, etc.

a **1700** B. E. *Dict. Cant. Crew*, *Padds*, worn by the Women to save their Sides from being Cut or Mark'd with the Strings of their Petty-coats. **1799** tr. *H. Meister's Lett. Eng.* 224 Some ladies make use of artificial means to procure this kind of deformity of shape. This gives rise to pads and padded ladies, of which you have lately [1791] read so many aukward pleasantries. **1850** J. F. SOUTH *Househ. Surg.* 151 Surgeons have a brass tourniquet with a bandage and a pad, the action of the pad being to press specially upon the artery. **1873** BESANT & RICE *Little Girl* II. iii. 70 Her wealth of hair wanted no artificial pads to set it up and throw it off, as it lay, ..upon her head. **1884** *Health Exhib. Catal.* 83/2 Patent Woollen Pads for laying under stair-carpets, landings, &c.

b. A cushion or stuffing placed beneath a saddle or gig-tree, or any part of a horse's furniture or harness, to prevent galling, or under the foot to keep the sole moist; a cap of leather stuffed to protect a horse's knee.

1843 YOUATT *Horse* xxi. 428 In the better kind of stables a felt pad is frequently used... It keeps the foot cool and moist, and is very useful, when the sole has a tendency to become flat. **1894** ARMATAGE *Horse* 259, 263.

c. In Cricket and other sports: A guard or protection for parts of the body, as the leg or shins.

1851 LILLYWHITE *Guide Cricketers* 14 Pads..to guard the legs..must also be obtained. **1866** *Routledge's Ev. Boy's Ann.* 357 Pads and gloves are at the present day necessaries. **1878** M. & F. COLLINS *Vill. Comedy* II. vi. 73 A cricket club ..won eternal fame because the players insisted on wearing their pads on the wrong leg. **1882** *Daily Tel.* 17 May, Watson was bowled off his pads.

d. = PADDING *vbl. sb.*[2] 2.

1860 THACKERAY *Four Georges* iv. (1876) 101 That outside, I am certain, is pad and tailor's work.

e. A strip of rubber (etc.) material fitted in the road which when depressed by traffic operates road signals. Cf. *detector-pad*.

1933 H. WATSON *Street Traffic Flow* ix. 165 Electric contact pads or strips, called 'detectors' laid in the carriageway, and actuated by vehicles. **1935** *Times* 3 Dec. 11/4 The installation of pedestrian control signals, to be operated by traffic pads. *Ibid.*, The Hendon Council, however, did not consider that the provision of pad-operated pedestrian signals would serve the desired purpose on such a road. **1960** H. MANZONI in E. Davies *Roads* vii. 176 The signals are actuated by vehicles passing over a detector pad consisting of two hollow rubber treads.

f. = *launching pad* s.v. LAUNCHING *vbl. sb.* b.

1949 *Gloss. Guided Missile Terms* (GM 51/8) (Res. & Devel. Board, U.S. Dept. Defense) 75 *Pad*, a permanent or semipermanent base constructed to support a missile-launching device. **1953** *Air Univ. Q. Rev.* Fall 32 (*caption*) To withstand the pressures and intense heat of the exhaust blast during take-off, the 100-foot-square pad must be two-and-one-half feet thick. **1958** *Times* 1 Mar. 6/3 The missile had been on its pad for days before firing. **1964** MRS. L. B. JOHNSON *White House Diary* 24 Mar. (1970) 101 Saturn I will be used to send an unmanned Apollo spacecraft into orbit—in fact, one is on the pad..now for launching later this spring. **1971** *Sci. Amer.* Sept. 229/3 In 1961..the Russians had just 14 big liquid-fuel SS-6's on open pads. **1973** *Times* 17 Oct. 1/4 Our Egyptian rockets..are now on their pads ready to be launched by the single order to press a button.

g. A take-off or landing point for a helicopter.

1960 *Washington Post* 1 Dec. D13/1 The mushrooming uses to which the 100-by-100 foot concrete helicopter 'pad' at the Pentagon is being put today. **1972** L. HANCOCK *There's a Seal in my Sleeping Bag* ix. 238 We were walking along the boardwalk past the helicopter pad. **1974** *BP Shield Internat.* Oct. 18/2 With a slight bump and shudder, we landed on the helicopter pad. **1976** 'L. BLACK' *Healthy Way to Die* ii. 17 The circling helicopter was descending towards the pad. **1977** *Time* 31 Jan. 15/1 On the drive from a helicopter pad to his office, his swift-moving convoy was guarded by three select commando battalions.

h. = *cow-pad* (cow *sb.*[1] 8).

1971 *New Scientist* 1 July 36/2 The dung is also the incubation medium of many helminth parasites of stock, the eggs of which are passed in the pads. **1973** *Nature* 30 Nov. 271/1 Such dung pads soon dry into a hard cake. **1974** *Sci. Amer.* Apr. 101/2 On the average 12 dung pads are dropped by a single adult bovine every day. **1976** *Australasian Express* 3 Sept. 2/1 Dung pads are being eaten at a rapid rate in the northern half of Australia.

4. A number of sheets of blotting-, writing-, or drawing-paper fastened together at the edge so as to form a firm block, from which the sheets may be removed one by one as used; called also ***blotting-***, ***drawing-***, or ***writing-pad***.

1865 DICKENS *Mut. Fr.* I. viii, A pen, and a box of wafers, ..and a writing-pad. **1876** PREECE & SIVEWRIGHT *Telegraphy* 282 On the service of the Post Office Department... Every [telegraph] circuit is supplied with pads of these forms, and in order that the clerk who is about to receive a message may know what particular form to use, every message is indicated by a prefix, which is the first signal always sent. **1880** BESANT & RICE *Seamy Side* xx. 168 The massive pad of blotting-paper..reminded the boy of his uncle. **1888** M. ROBERTSON *Lombard St. Myst.* xv, This ..sheet..had been torn off a blotting pad.

II. 5. Any cushion-like part of the animal body. ***optic pad***: see OPTIC A. 2.

1878 BELL tr. *Gegenbaur's Comp. Anat.* 117 The septa of the gastrovascular system..terminate as elongated bands or pads. **1881** MIVART *Cat* 36 The adjacent surfaces of the bodies of the vertebra are nearly flat, and are connected together by the intervention of a fibrous pad. **1883** *H. Gray's Anat.* (ed. 10) 492 Posteriorly, the corpus callosum forms a thick rounded fold, called the splenium or pad. **1897** *Allbutt's Syst. Med.* II. 690 In the mouth, the vesicles.. occur most frequently on the inside of the lips, the pad of the upper jaw, and the tongue. **1898** P. MANSON *Trop. Diseases* i. 21 Prick the congested finger pad with a clean needle... Then gently with finger and thumb squeeze the finger pad.

6. The fleshy elastic cushion forming the sole of the foot, or part of it, in various quadrupeds, as feline and canine beasts, the camel, etc. Also, a fibrous cushion at the bottom of the tarsus in a bird's foot; also, one of the tarsal cushions of an insect, a pulvillus.

1836–9 TODD *Cycl. Anat.* II. 61/2 The elastic pad placed beneath the foot of the dromedary. **1871** STAVELEY *Brit. Insects* ii. 38 Feet of insects..of two claws with one, two, or three soft pads; but the pads are often wanting. **1874** Heel-pad [see HEEL *sb.*[1] 27 c]. **1881** MIVART *Cat* 14 The skin of the fleshy pads beneath the paws. **1895** NEWTON *Dict. Birds* 866 They are soon buried in the fibrous interarticular pad, and in the majority of birds ultimately vanish.

7. The foot or paw of a fox, hare, otter, wolf, or other beast of the chase; also the footprint of such.

1790 NAIRNE *Tales* (1824) 99 (E.D.D.) His pads alternate play. **1859** JEPHSON *Brittany* vi. 79 Nailed against a barn-door, I observed the 'pads' (*pattes*) or feet of a wolf. **1865** R. S. SURTEES *Romford's Hounds* 76 Off went the brush, head, and pads... 'Brush is bespoke'... He then distributed the pads. **1878** JEFFERIES *Gamekeeper at H.* 27 Country housewives still use the hare's 'pad' for several domestic purposes. **1891** MRS. J. GORDON *Eunice Anscombe* 170 A smart little felt hat ornamented at one side with a silver-mounted otter-pad. **1901** *Wide World Mag.* VI. 447/2 Not a trace of cart-rut, hoof-mark, or camel-pad could I discern.

III. 8. *Mech.* The socket of a brace, in which the end of the bit is inserted; a tool-handle into which tools of different gauges, etc., can be fitted, as in a pad-saw.

1688 R. HOLME *Armoury* III. 368/1 (Joiner's tool) *Pad*, is the square piece of Wood in which the Bit is fixed. **1703** MOXON *Mech. Exerc.* 94 You ought to be provided with Bitts of several sizes, fitted into so many Padds. **1812–16** J. SMITH *Panorama Sc. & Art* I. 115 In the end of one of these limbs, which is called the pad, the piece of steel by which the boring is performed, is inserted. **1875** *Carpentry & Join.* 22 It also goes by the name of the pad saw, on account of the handle in which it is inserted. This handle, or pad, after being turned, is bored quite through and is fitted with a long brass ferrule. **1881** YOUNG *Every Man his own Mechanic* §319 The pads or patent tool-handles with tools contained within, and varying in number from 12 to 20, are very useful.

9. *Watch-* and *Clock-making.* A pallet.

1704 W. DERHAM in *Phil. Trans.* XXV. 1789 It is necessary..that the Power..do at all times exert the very same force upon the Pads or Pallets. **1884** F. J. BRITTEN *Watch & Clockm.* 183 [The] Pad..[is] the pallet of the Anchor recoil escapement for clocks.

10. A package of yarn of a definite amount or weight. *local.*

1746 *Exmoor Scolding* (E.D.S.) 113 Tha tedst net carry whome thy Pad. **1828** *Craven Gloss.* (ed. 2), *Pad*, a small pack or bundle. **1886** ELWORTHY *W. Somerset Word-bk.*, *Pad*..(By sellers of woollen yarn). The square-shaped package of yarn in which it is generally made up for sale, consisting of twelve bundles or hanks, and each bundle consisting of a great many skeins varying..according to the fineness of the yarn—a skein being always a fixed number of yards, and the pad a fixed weight. *Ibid.*, (By spinners.) A bundle of yarn consisting of twenty-four small hanks, each consisting of four skeins, each skein measuring 360 yards; consequently a pad of yarn always represented the same number of yards, whatever its size or weight.

11. *Shipbuilding.* (See quot.)

1867 SMYTH *Sailor's Word-bk.*, *Pad*, or *Pad-piece*, in ship-building, a piece of timber placed on the top of a beam at its middle part, in order to make up the round of the deck.

12. (More fully ***lily-pad***.) A broad floating leaf (of the water-lily). *U.S.*

1858 O. W. HOLMES *Aut. Breakf.-t.* (1883) 33 Pickerel lying under the lily-pads. **1891** *Anthony's Photogr. Bull.* IV. 46 The Indian canoe..stealing along sedgy lake shores, and through the lily pads of the long ponds. **1895** *Month* Aug. 499 There are no lily pads about.

13. A trade term for a thick double-faced ribbon, used as a watch-guard, and in masonic decorations; also for an extra-thick ribbon used for stiffening the waists of women's dresses, etc.

14. A padding machine. Freq. *attrib.*

1935 *Textile World* LXXXV. 1860/2 Formation of the patches is a danger signal, however, and—as is true of all danger signals in the pad dyehouse—should be taken heed of at once if serious trouble is to be avoided. **1951** *Jrnl. Soc. Dyers & Colourists* LXVII. 508/1 In dyeing practice, the nearest approach to printing technique was the so-called pigment-padding process, where the vat dye was applied on the pad as a suspension of unreduced dye. **1955** *Ibid.* LXXI. 896/1 Difficulties may arise from this increase [in width], e.g. from wrinkles passing the pad nip. *Ibid.* 900/1 Does the preferential uptake of water by the dry cloth entering the pad box cause a slight change in the concentration of direct dye and give a length of cloth off shade at the beginning of a run? **1961** COCKETT & HILTON *Dyeing of Cellulosic Fibres* xi. 358 The essential parts of a pad are a nip of two or more rollers, a trough, and means of applying pressure to the nip. **1966** *Encycl. Polymer Sci. & Technol.* V. 238 The machine consists of two or three squeeze rolls mounted over a shallow trough, or 'pad box', provided with guide rolls for the cloth.

15. *Electr.* A resistance network inserted into a transmission line to attenuate all frequencies equally by a known amount.

1931 *Electronics* Feb. 508/1 The term 'pad' as commonly employed in connection with audio frequency circuits, refers to an attenuation device used to reduce the power at a point in a circuit by some desired value... Regarded as an electric circuit, a pad consists of a one-section artificial line whose elements are pure resistances. **1951** W. J. CREAMER *Communication Networks & Lines* v. 46 Non-symmetrical pads may be employed for the purpose of matching impedances, but there will be a minimum loss below which it is not possible to go without getting into the difficulty of a negative resistance element. **1959** K. HENNEY *Radio Engin. Handbk.* (ed. 5) xxi. 22 The minimum attenuation setting of a ladder pad normally corresponds to its insertion loss, which amounts to approximately 2·5 db. **1967** D. H. HAMSHER *Communication Syst. Engin. Handbk.* vi. 31 Two-wire trunk circuits may contain a switchable 2-db pad.

16. *U.S. slang.* (See quots.)

1970 *Daily Tel.* 27 Apr. 3 New York police have their own secret slang to deal with illegal business... A 'pad' is an establishment that provides police with regular pay-offs. **1971** *N.Y. Times* 19 Oct. 47 The gamblers of the city paid off the policemen on a regular monthly basis after they had been placed on what is called 'the pad'. **1971** *Guardian* 28 Oct. 13/6 [He] was thrilled with becoming a plainclothesman because..'he was now on the pad'. The pad is the regular sum paid to officers for ignoring illegal activities. **1971** *Times* 1 Nov. 23 When a cop was transferred to a new post, the pad from his old station kept up for another two months. **1973** M. TRUMAN *Harry S. Truman* iii. 72 In Kansas City there was a tradition of carrying one or two thousand city employees 'on the pad' without requiring them to show up for work.

IV. 17. *attrib.* and *Comb.*, as (sense 3) ***pad-back***, ***electrode***, ***-foot***; ***pad-like*** adj.; (2 b) ***pad-housings***, ***-screw***, ***-terret***; (7) ***pad-mark***, ***-scent***; (8) ***pad-hole***; **pad-bracket** (see quot.); **pad-cloth**, a housing-cloth extending over the horse's loins; **pad-crimp press**, a press on which damped leather is pressed into shape between convex and concave surfaces; **pad-elephant**, an elephant having on its back a pad only (not a howdah), on which to carry burdens, baggage, game killed in hunting, and the like; **pad eye** *Engin.* (see quot. 1909); **pad-hook**, a hook on the harness-pad (see sense 2 b) of a horse, for holding up the bearing-rein; **pad mangle**, a padding machine; **pad money** *U.S. slang* (see quots.); **pad-piece**: see sense 11; **pad-plate**, a metal plate on which a harness-pad is made; **pad-play** (*Cricket*), the use of the leg-pads to protect the wickets; hence **pad-player**; **pad room** *U.S.*, in a theatre, a waiting-room for performers; **pad-saddle**, a treeless padded saddle; **pad-saw**: see sense 8 ; **pad-side** , a strip of leather attached to the harness-pad and to the girth; **pad-steam**, used *attrib.* and *absol.* to denote a process in which fabric is first padded and then steamed; **pad stitch** (see quot. 1968); also (with hyphen) as *vb.*; so **pad stitching**; **padstone** (see quots.); **pad-top**, an ornamental leather piece finishing off a harness-pad at the top; **pad-tree**, a frame of wood or metal giving shape and rigidity to a harness-pad.

1897 *Daily News* 9 Nov. 6/5 White and gilt Louis XVI standard chairs, seats and *pad backs in blue striped brocaded silk. **1884** KNIGHT *Dict. Mech.* Suppl., **Pad bracket*, a stable-wall bracket having a shape adapted to receive the saddle which rests thereon. **1870** BLAINE *Encycl. Rur. Sports* (ed. 3) §1087 The full set [of clothing for race-horses] comprises..breast-cloth, *pad-cloth, and fillet-cloth, with rollers to secure them. **1896** *Allbutt's Syst. Med.* I. 369 An accessory wire [may be] led from the foot-plate to a *pad electrode placed under the thigh. **1833** *Edin. Rev.* LVII. 367 With twenty *pad-elephants to beat the covert. **1864** TREVELYAN *Compet. Wallah* (1866) 151 We found the pad elephants, forty-four in number; which, with the howdah-wallahs, gave us a line of four dozen. **1909** *Cent. Dict.* Suppl., **Pad-eye*, in ship-building, a flat rectangular piece of metal with an eye or ring projecting edgewise from its surface, the whole forming one solid piece. It is attached to the surface on which it is placed by screws or rivets through the flat part. **1972** L. M. HARRIS *Introd. Deepwater Floating Drilling Operations* vi. 76 The principal use of buoys in floating-drilling operations is to mark anchors... The unit should have strong padeyes on top and bottom for attaching handling lines and pendants. **1976** *Offshore Platforms & Pipelining* 239/3 For added strength, cables are run from each corner of the frame to the existing pad eyes on the mass anchor. **1905** F. S. ROBINSON *Eng. Furnit.* xii. 181 The legs of these tables are somewhat too straight to be classed as cabriole, and have *pad feet. **1955** R. FASTNEDGE *Eng. Furnit. Styles* 286 *Pad foot*, resembling the club foot but set on a disk. **1974** *Country Life* 7 Mar. (Suppl.) 40 A fine quality George II red walnut Armchair in original condition having cabriole legs and pad feet. **1688** R. HOLME *Armoury* III. 368/1 *Bush* or **Pad Hole*, a four square hole in which the Bit is placed, so as it cannot turn. **1901** *Scribner's Mag.* Apr. 413/2 To stand there and see those mincing cobs go by, their *pad-housings all a-glitter. **1849** *Sk. Nat. Hist., Mammalia* IV. 216 (*Manis*) The hind-feet have five short, thick, blunt claws, edging a *pad-like sole covered with coarse granular skin. **1880** GÜNTHER *Fishes* 330 The lateral teeth are large, pad-like. **1955** *Jrnl. Soc. Dyers & Colourists* LXXI. 777/2 On leaving the *pad-mangle, the goods should pass directly into a Mather & Platt ager. **1966** R. C. CHEETHAM *Dyeing Fibre Blends* i. 59 Piece-dyeing is usually carried out on a pad-mangle, with the least possible duration in the wet state. **1900** *Blackw. Mag.* Mar. 393/2 Here again is the *pad-mark of a tiger. **1926** T. E. LAWRENCE *Seven Pillars* lxvi. 344 We..marched south..seeing tracks of gazelle..with, in one spot, stale padmarks of leopard. **1973** *Times* 14 Aug. 14/5 Only pad marks of mink were found. **1904** 'No. 1500' *Life in Sing Sing* 256/2 *Pad money, money for lodgings. **1927** *Dial. Notes* V. 457 *Pad money*..., money for a night's lodging or for admission into an opium den. **1920** E. R. WILSON in P. F. Warner *Cricket* 94 [They] used to bowl round the wicket in order to get batsmen l.b.w. with their off break, which, if bowled over the wicket, permitted '*pad play'. **1956** N. CARDUS *Close of Play* 15 Hobbs and Sutcliffe twice frustrated an Australian attack on 'sticky' pitches—on one of the most vicious of all, at Melbourne, largely by pad-play. **1960** J. FINGLETON *Four Chukkas to Australia* 39 His reliance on so much pad-play had ruined his stroke-play. **1888** *Pall Mall G.* 12 Apr. 5/2 Have you any intention of dealing with '*pad-players'? **1927** K. NICHOLSON *Barker* 149 **Pad room*, waiting room for performers. **1931** *Amer. Mercury* Nov. 353/2 *Pad room*, a dressing tent. **1622** SIR R. BOYLE in *Lismore Papers* (1886) II. 60, I receaved from Thomas Taylor..a fair *padd saddle and ffurneture. **1877** W. MATTHEWS *Ethnogr. Hidatsa* 19 They..make neat pad-saddles of tanned elk-skin, stuffed with antelope-hair. **1875** 'STONEHENGE' *Brit. Sports* I. II. v. §8. 182 Some can pick out a cold '*pad scent'. **1945** *Textile World* Jan. 84 (*heading*) *Pad-steam dyeing reaches volume production. **1961** COCKETT & HILTON *Dyeing of Cellulosic Fibres* xi. 361 The several forms of pad-steam..give greater production because of their continuous character. **1966** *Encycl. Polymer Sci. & Technol.* V. 240 The Du Pont pad-steam process employs steam under controlled conditions to bring about dye fixation. **1924** W. D. F. VINCENT et al. *Cutters' Pract. Guide Cutting & Making Body Coats* 30/3 Whether or not you *pad-stitch the collar, or stitch together by machine, give it firmness as well as shape. **1964** *McCall's Sewing* ix. 126/2 *Pad stitch*, this stitch is very similar to diagonal basting stitch. **1968** J. IRONSIDE *Fashion Alphabet* 84 *Pad-stitch*, 1. In Tailoring: A diagonal basting stitch used to hold interlining or canvas to fabric. 2. In Embroidery: Filling stitches over which fancy stitches are worked; used to give bulk. **1964** *McCall's Sewing* xiv. 254/1 End pad-stitching at seam line. **1963** *Gloss. Gen. Building Terms* (*B.S.I.*) 19 **Padstone*, a block of stone or concrete built into a wall to distribute the pressure from a concentrated load. **1964** J. S. SCOTT *Dict. Building* 222 *Padstone*, a stone or concrete pad in a wall. **1894** ARMATAGE *Horse* vi. 89 The leaders of a..four-in-hand..their reins are passed.. through the upper half of the *pad terret.

pad, *sb.*[4] [A variant of PED, perhaps affected in form by prec.] An open pannier, usually of osiers; a measure of fish, fruit, etc., varying in quantity according to the commodity, a 'basket'.

1579 E. K. *Gloss. Spenser's Sheph. Cal.* Nov. 16 A haske is a wicker pad, wherein they vse to cary fish. **1787** W. MARSHALL *Norfolk* Gloss. (E.D.S.), *Pads*,..panniers. **1851** MAYHEW *Lond. Labour* I. 57 He may buy a pad of soles for 2*s.* 6*d.*, and clear 5*s.* on them. **1858** SIMMONDS *Dict. Trade*, *Pad*,..a fish measure, which varies in number—60 mackerel go to a pad. **1887** *Daily News* 1 Dec. 2/8 Apples, 4*s.* to 9*s.* per pad. **1891** *Times* 3 Oct. 13/3 Crabs, 20*s.* to 25*s.* per pad.

pad, *sb.*[5] (*adv.*) [Partly echoic, partly associated with PAD *v.*[1]] The dull firm non-resonant sound of steps, or of a staff, upon the ground; also the repeated step or footfall producing this sound. In earliest example used advb. ***pad, pad***, = with repetition of this sound or action.

1594 NASHE *Unfort. Trav.* Wks. (Grosart) V. 150 As in an earth-quake the ground should open, and a blind man come feeling pad pad ouer the open Gulph with his staffe. **1879** BROWNING *Ivàn Ivànovitch* 125 'Tis the regular pad of the wolves in pursuit of the life in the sledge! **1890** KIPLING *Plain Tales fr. Hills* 123 There came from the compound the soft 'pad-pad' of camels. **1901** *Pilot* 19 Jan. 76/1 The..soft pad of naked feet passing along the dusty road.

†**pad**, *sb.*^{6} *Obs.* Shortened form of PADLOCK.
[In Rogers *Agric. & Prices* II. 519/1, 3, 520/4, of 1294, 1307, cited as *Pad*: in 520/4 of 1392 '2 pads & chains for horses'. But the original words are in no case given.]
1573 TUSSER *Husb.* (1878) 38 Soles, fetters, and shackles, with horselock and pad.

pad (pæd), *v.*^{1} [Related to PAD *sb.*^{2}: cf. LG. and E.Fris. *padden* = OHG. *pfadôn*, OE. *pæððan*, to tread, go along (a path). Also LG. (Bremisch. Wbch.) *padjan* to run with short steps: said of children; *pedden* to step, step often. But in some senses associated with the sound, like PAD *sb.*^{5}]

I. 1. a. *trans.* To tread, walk, or tramp along (a path, road, etc.) on foot.
1553 BRADFORD *Lett.* Wks. (Parker Soc.) II. 46 Other your brothers and sisters pad the same path. **1727** SOMERVILLE *Fables* XIV. ii, Two Toasts with all their Trinkets gone, Padding the Streets for Half-a-Crown. **1882** *Glasgow News* 17 May 4 Many an honest man..is forced to..'pad the road' in search of work.

b. *intr.* To travel on foot, to walk; to tramp or trudge along, esp. as a vagrant or person seeking work. Also, *to pad it.*
1610 ROWLANDS *Martin Mark-all* E iv b, Two Maunders ..wooing in their natiue language. O Ben mort wilt thou pad with me. **1796** MRS. M. ROBINSON *Angelina* II. 158 You can't be any great things, padding it at this time of the morning. **1824** SCOTT *St. Ronan's* vi, [He] might have been made to pad on well enough. **1837** MRS. SHERWOOD *Henry Milner* III. ii, Footsteps were heard padding along. **1883** W. C. SMITH *North Country Folk* 108 We padded, barefoot, to the school.

c. *to pad the hoof*, to go on foot, tramp: cf. HOOF *sb.* 4. *slang.*
1824 W. IRVING *T. Trav.* I. 225 Stout fellows to pad the hoof over them. **1860** THACKERAY *Lovel the Wid.* i, Bearded individuals, padding the muddy hoof in the neighbouring Regent Street. **1894** S. J. WEYMAN *Man in Black* 21 'If I knew, I should not be padding the hoof', said he. **1904** [see BOOT *sb.*^{3} 1 c]. **1916** J. B. COOPER *Coo-oo-ee* x. 130 A dog with you breaks the lonesomeness of the bush, I know. We've padded the hoof together. **1966** 'J. HACKSTON' *Father clears Out* 108 When the people..missed the coach, and had to pad the hoof into the town.., they'd take the short cut. **1970** *N.Z. Listener* 21 Dec. 8/4 We pondered on the day years ago when we were padding the hoof ourselves.

2. *intr.* (with reference to the manner of walking).
†**a.** Of a horse: To pace. **b.** Of other quadrupeds: To walk or run with steady dull-sounding steps. Also of a person, and reduplicated *pad-pad.*
[In this sense partly echoic with reference to the sound.]
a. 1724 *Lond. Gaz.* No. 6239/4 Stolen.., a..Mare,.. it Trots and Pads. **1737** BRACKEN *Farriery Impr.* (1757) II. 41 This Sort..are soonest taught to pace or pad well.
b. 1871 G. MACDONALD *Love's Ordeal* xxiii, A hound, Padding with gentle paws upon the road. **1898** G. W. STEEVENS *With Kitchener to Khartum* 72 When my camel padded into their camp by moonlight. **1899** C. J. C. HYNE *Further Adventures Capt. Kettle* v. 84 Naked feet pad-padded quickly up over the dust and grass. **1926** A. BENNETT *Lord Raingo* I. ii. 7 A nice thing, that with five servants in the place, and him a millionaire, he should be reduced to padding about in his socks! **1966** 'J. HACKSTON' *Father clears Out* 84 Father was changing as we padded along. **1975** M. BRADBURY *History Man* vii. 126 Felicity pads at Howard's side down the long bright passage.

3. a. *trans.* To tread or beat down by frequent walking; to form (a path) by treading. *dial.*
1764 *Museum Rusticum* III. xxi. 88 Whether the earth be in such a state of cohesion as to be padded under the horses feet. **1814** *Sporting Mag.* XLIII. 242 The cottagers'.. gardens..have been padded like sheep-folds. **1855** BROWNING *Childe Roland* xxii, Whose savage trample thus could pad the dank Soil to a plash. **1888** *Sheffield Gloss.*, Snow is said to be well padded when a path has been trodden thereon.

†**b.** *fig.* (?) To render callous, as if by treading.
(But the sense is doubtful; cf. PADDED *ppl. a.*^{1})
1607 *Schol. Disc. agst. Antichr.* I. iv. 194 As for them whom this heresie has so paded and benummed, that they thinke they are well enough.

II. †**4.** *intr.* To rob on the highway; to be a footpad. *Obs.*
1638 FORD *Lady's Trial* v. i, One Can..cant, and pick a pocket, Pad for a cloak, or hat, and, in the dark, Pistol a straggler for a quarter-ducat. **1680** *Vind. Conforming Clergy* (ed. 2) 38 What should they do then? but..go a padding upon the High-way. **1730-6** BAILEY (folio), *To Pad*,.. also to rob on the road on foot.

pad, *v.*^{2} [f. PAD *sb.*^{3} in various senses. Recent; not in J., Todd 1818, nor Webster 1828.]

I. 1. a. *trans.* To stuff, fill out, or otherwise furnish (anything) with a pad or padding; to stuff (something) in or about, so as to serve as a pad.
1827 LYTTON *Pelham* xliv, But, sir, we must be padded; we are much too thin; all the gentlemen in the Life Guards are padded, sir. **1846** LANDOR *Imag. Conv.* Wks. II. 105 What falsehoods will not men put on, if they can only pad them with a little piety! **1856** KANE *Arct. Expl.* I. xxviii. 373 Dry grass was padded round their feet. **1866** ROGERS *Agric. & Prices* I. xxi. 532 The saddle-tree must have been padded in the house. **1885** H. O. FORBES *Nat. Wand. E. Archip.* 158 Lichens and mosses padded every stone.

b. *absol.* or *intr.*; also for *refl.*
1821 BYRON *Juan* v. cxl, Eastern stays are little made to pad, So that a poniard pierces if 't is stuck hard. **1873** BESANT & RICE *Little Girl* II. v. 80 Fellows said he padded.

2. *trans.* **a.** To fill *out* or expand (a sentence, story, etc.) by the insertion of unnecessary or useless words or matter: see PADDING *vbl. sb.*^{2} 2 b.
1831 MACAULAY *Ess., Boswell's Johnson* (1887) 195 His [Johnson's] constant practice of padding out a sentence with useless epithets, till it became as stiff as the bust of an exquisite. **1870** *Eng. Mech.* 4 Mar. 600/3 The rest of the almanac is..not padded with matter from the pages of other journals. **1891** *Spectator* 12 Dec. 855 Conversations and descriptions with which the rather thin story is padded out.

b. To extend or increase (an official list, expense account, claim for payment, etc.) with unauthorized or fraudulent items.
1913 *Maclean's Mag.* Mar. 104 (*heading*) Padding the expense account. *Ibid.* 105/2 To pad this account by magnifying the cost of hotel accommodation, meals and railway fare, was most distasteful to him. **1921** *Daily Colonist* (Victoria, B.C.) 23 Oct. 1/2 John W. Duncan, charged with padding a cheque.., was found not guilty. **1928** *Observer* 15 Apr. 12 They claim that the list of members..was heavily 'padded' by the inclusion of persons without their knowledge and consent. **1967** *Boston Sunday Herald* 26 Mar. IV. 3/1 Beating the system can be done by padding bills, adding a dollar here, two dollars there, for medical items, clothing and so forth. **1968** *Economist* 14 Dec. 27/2 A report by a Granada television team in Britain showed that the [voting] lists were padded. **1976** 'M. ALBRAND' *Taste of Terror* xi. 67 Forster never paid but preferred to be sent a bill in spite of the fact that he knew it was padded.

3. To impregnate *with* a liquid or paste by squeezing between rollers, the substance applied being either on one of the rollers or in a bath preceding them.
1839 URE *Dict. Arts* 227 The goods are to be padded in a solution of the sulphate or muriate of manganese. **1897** C. T. DAVIS *Manuf. Leather* (ed. 2) 324 They first pad the leather with a solution of alizarine rendered slightly alkaline with ammonia. **1927** C. E. MULLIN *Acetate Silk* (1928) xxx. 375 In applying the developed colors on cotton, the fiber is usually first padded in the naphthol bath and then the color developed in a second bath. **1933** *Chem. Abstr.* XXVII. 2045 Fabrics having a cellulose acetate pile are printed or padded with a soln. of regenerated cellulose in caustic alkali to obtain a local or over-all deposition of cellulose. **1972** D. HILDEBRAND in K. Venkataraman *Chem. Synthetic Dyes* VI. iii. 431 The fabric which has been padded with dyestuff and anti-crease agent is stored in the presence of mineral acid as catalyst for 1-3 hours.

4. To glue the edges of (leaves of paper) together so as to form a pad.
18.. *Writer* III. 82 (Cent.) A half-pint of the cement will pad a vast quantity of sheets.

II. 5. *East Indies.* To place or pack (big game, etc.) on the pad of an elephant.
1878 J. INGLIS *Sport & W.* xx. 276 While game is being padded the whole line waits. **1879** F. POLLOK *Sport Brit. Burmah* I. 189, I..killed the deer. We padded it, and continued our way. *Ibid.* II. 143 Whilst we were padding this tiger, one of my elephants..walked off.

III. 6. To track by the pad or footmarks.
1861 G. F. BERKELEY *Eng. Sportsman* v. 70 Burnet, who.. was well up to any sort of woodcraft, padded a 'skunk' and a racoon.

IV. 7. To perforate with small holes, as in making the 'rose' of a nozzle.
1889 *Engineer* 11 Jan. 39 In order to prevent a false reading of the water gauge, it was 'padded', that is to say, the end of the tube in the top of the upcast shaft was perforated with numerous small holes.

pada ('pɑːdə). Also **padam.** [Skr., = foot.]
a. An Indian lyrical poem set to music. Also *attrib.*
1880 F. S. GROWSE *Mathurā* (ed. 2) 212 He is said to have written a Hindi poem called the Dasratna, together with a few short *Sâkhis* and *Padas* in the same language. **1898** B. A. PINGLE *Indian Mus.* (ed. 2) ii. 64 The Dhrupada is a later form of the original Padas or Bhajanas (prayer or praise). **1914** [see BHAJAN]. **1957** O. GOSVAMI *Story Indian Mus.* xx. 212 The *Padam* is sung in the same way as the *Kriti.* **1967** SINGHA & MASSEY *Indian Dances* ii. 43 Padas are love lyrics which cover every conceivable aspect of love from the mystic and divine to the earthly and profane. **1968** *Jrnl. Mus. Acad. Madras* XXXIX. 102 Annamacharya says that the songs of one ignorant of the proper style and pattern of *pada*-composition..would be worthless. **1972** P. HOLROYDE *Indian Mus.* 275 Padams demand a very dramatized technique of mime gesture and facial expression. **1974** B. C. DEVA *Indian Mus.* v. 76 The songs of Bhadrachala Ramadas ..are referred to as pada-s.

b. A group of words forming a section of Sanskrit verse; a mode of reciting this.
1887 M. MONIER-WILLIAMS *Brāhmanism & Hindūism* (ed. 3) xv. 409 These Vedic texts may be recited according to any one or more of the five different Pâthas, or modes of recitation, called Samhitā, Pada, Krama, Jaṭā, and Ghana. **1916** A. A. MACDONELL *Vedic Gram. for Students* 449 A hemistich of two or more Pādas is treated as a unit. **1917** —— *Vedic Reader for Students* p. xiii, The earliest expedient of this kind was the formation of the Pada or 'word' text, in which all the words of the Saṃhitā text are separated and given in their original form as unaffected by the rules of Sandhi. **1965** *Language* XLI. 11 Three instances are accounted for by the pāda *devân devayaté yaja.* **1971** *Language* XLVII. 59 The first three pādas are hyposyllabic as transmitted.

padanda, var. PEDANDA.

‖**padang** ('padaŋ). [Malay.] An open grassy space; a field, esp. a playing-field; also, scrub vegetation.
1915 *Blackw. Mag.* Dec. 793 Two others were caught near the Europe Hotel, sitting on the 'padang' by the sea. **1927** R. J. H. SIDNEY *In Brit. Malaya To-Day* 45 We are standing on my large verandah overlooking the school *padang.* **1933** L. AINSWORTH *Confessions Planter in Malaya* 74 They had been given leave to gather on our Padang (a large field in the centre of all our coolie lines). *Ibid.* 182 The clubhouse is set in very pleasant surroundings, with a large padang, or playing-field, attached. **1952** P. W. RICHARDS *Trop. Rain Forest* ix. 211 The vegetation was the so-called padang, a kind of heath-like scrub or poor forest. **1964** K. G. TREGONNING *Hist. Mod. Malaya* x. 226 E. W. Birch..was one of those whose delight it was to see a *padang*, a shady playing field, laid out in every kampong of the State. **1972** *Malay Mail* (Kuala Lumpur) 25 May 4/5 The pasar malam ..will be held at Dato Kramat padang from Wednesday. **1977** *Borneo Bull.* 7 May 4-A/2 Red Cross Day will be celebrated here tomorrow (Sunday) with a parade on the town padang followed by a ceremony in the Youth Centre.

[**padar.** Admitted by Johnson with the passage here cited, and thence in later dicts., but evidently an error of some kind.
The form suggests PODDER, beans and pease, but the sense appears to be that of POLLARD, the coarse part of flour, q.v.
a **1639** WOTTON *Life Dk. Buckhm.* in *Reliq.* (1651) 103 In the bolting and sifting of near fourteen years..all that came out could not be expected to be pure, and white and fine Meal, but must needs have withall among it a certain mixture of Padar and Bran.]

padasha, padasoy, obs. var. PADISHAH, PADUASOY.

padauk, var. PADOUK.

pad-bracket, -cloth, etc.: see PAD *sb.*^{3}

padd(e, obs. ff. PAD.

'**padded,** *ppl. a.*^{1} [f. PAD *v.*^{1}] Trodden, beaten firm and hard by treading; *fig.* (?) hardened or rendered callous as by treading.
1583 BABINGTON *Commandm.* iv. (1637) 36 They..who with benummed soules, parched, padded, senslesse, and every way most hardned hearts..lie and sleepe on the one side idle. **1821** CLARE *Vill. Minstr.* II. 199 Only a hedge-row track, or padded balk.

'**padded,** *ppl. a.*^{2} [f. PAD *sb.*^{3}, *v.*^{2}] Furnished or filled out with pads or padding; expanded by the insertion of needless or extraneous matter; impregnated throughout with a dye or the like by padding (see PAD *v.*^{2} 3). ***padded cell***, a room in a lunatic asylum or prison, having the walls padded, to prevent the person confined in it from injuring himself against them; also *fig.* and *transf.*; also (with hyphen) *attrib.*; ***padded room*** (see quot. 1976); ***padded shoulders***, the shoulders of a suit, etc., padded to give the appearance of breadth; also *fig.*; ***padded soap.***
1799 [see PAD. *sb.*^{3} 3]. **1823** LOCKHART *Reg. Dalton* II. vi. (1842) 155 A padded foot-stool sustained in advance his gouty left leg. **1839** URE *Dict. Arts* 655 This mode of drying the padded calicoes. **1846** TENNYSON *New Timon*, What! it's you, The padded man, that wears the stays. **1862** SALA *Seven Sons* III. i. 5 Who is so sane but he may need..the padded room some day? **1880** MISS BRADDON *Barbara* vii, In the padded corner of a Pullman car. **1891** S. P. SADTLER *Handbk. Industr. Org. Chem.* ii. 61 Soaps made in this way retain all the glycerine..and belong to the class known as 'filled' or 'padded' soaps. **1935** H. G. WELLS *Things to Come* 14 The fact that in the future various light apparatus such as a portable radio, electric torch, notebook, will have to be carried on the person and that this will probably necessitate a widening of those broadly padded shoulders which are already necessary in the costume of contemporary men because of their wallets and fountain pens. *a* **1936** KIPLING *Something of Myself* (1937) vii. 176 A 'comfortable nursery' proved to be a dark padded cell at the end of a discreet passage! **1959** N. N. HOLLAND *First Mod. Comedies* 39 'Dapperwit' implies a comparison of clothes and wit, as though Dapperwit's pretensions to wit were a kind of padded shoulders to cover his actually feeble intelligence. **1961** COCKETT & HILTON *Dyeing of Cellulosic Fibres* xi. 361 Where vat dyes are concerned, development of the padded goods with alkaline reducing agent may be carried out discontinuously on jigs. **1962** A. NISBETT *Technique Sound Studio* ii. 48 Of the various possible sound-deadening systems, it is best to try to avoid those which give a padded-cell effect. **1963** WODEHOUSE *Stiff Upper Lip, Jeeves* xxii. 167 Stiffy, who is pure padded cell from the foundations up, was planning to marry the Rev. H. P. Pinker. **1972** D. HILDEBRAND in K. Venkataraman *Chem. Synthetic Dyes* VI. iii. 424 If the substantivity of the dye is insufficient, the dye will migrate when the padded goods are dried under inhomogeneous drying conditions. **1973** *Jewish Chron.* 19 Jan. 14/5 To give readers some idea of what passes for dialogue in the padded cell of the drama department, here is the kind of exchange in which Mr Mackie specialises. **1976** *Amer. Speech* 1973 XLVIII. 207 An uncontrollable patient may be sent to the *quiet room* or *QR*, formerly called the *padded room.* **1977** *Time* 3 Jan. 56/3 You will recall that the last we saw of Inspector Clouseau he had succeeded in.. driving his immediate superior, Chief Inspector Dreyfus, completely, totally, padded-cell mad.

paddee, paddell, padde lock, obs. ff. PEDEE, footman, footboy, PADDLE, PADLOCK.

padder ('pædə(r)), *sb.*^{1} [f. PAD *sb.*^{2} or *v.*^{1} + -ER^1.] A footpad, highwayman, robber.
1610 ROWLANDS *Martin Mark-all* 50 Such as robbe on horse-backe were called high lawyers, and those who robbed on foote, he called Padders. **1678** DRYDEN *Limberham* Epil., Lord, with what rampant gadders Our counters will be thronged, and roads with padders! **1719** YOUNG *Busiris* IV. i, But sweep his minions, cut a padder's throat. **1889** DOYLE

Micah Clarke 237 We are not a gang of padders and michers, but a crew of honest seamen.
fig. **1667** DRYDEN *Sir Martin Mar-all* IV. i, If she had stirred out of doors, there were Whipsters abroad, i' faith, padders of maidenheads. **1708** *Brit. Apollo* No. 86. 3/2 Three Padders in Wit, Who must steal all they get.

ˈpadder, *sb.*[2] **1.** One who pads (see PAD *v.*[2] 1 b).
1827 LYTTON *Pelham* xi, Sir H. M. was close by her, carefully packed up in his coat and waistcoat. Certainly, that man is the best padder in Europe.
2. A padding machine.
1927 C. E. MULLIN *Acetate Silk* (1928) xxviii. 361 It is usually best to dye the acetate silk first and then cross-dye the cotton either in the padder or jig. **1955** *Jrnl. Soc. Dyers & Colourists* LXXI. 894/2 In order to get as good impregnation as possible before the fabric reaches the nip of the padder, this small volume is combined with a comparatively long path through the padder trough. **1971** E. I. VALKO in H. Mark et al. *Chem. Aftertreatment of Textiles* iii. 105 Impregnation of fabric is frequently carried out by first immersing the fabric and then pulling it between the rolls of a padder.
3. *Electronics.* Also **padder capacitor, condenser.** A usu. adjustable capacitor connected in series in a tuned circuit in order to improve the tracking with another tuned circuit at low frequencies when the tuning of the two circuits is ganged (as in a superheterodyne). Cf. TRIMMER.
1936 J. H. REYNER *Testing Radio Sets* (ed. 3) xiii. 190 (*in figure*) Padder. **1939** H. J. HICKS *Princ. & Pract. Radio Servicing* ii. 21 C10, C11, C12 and C13 are the trimmer and padder condensers employed in the oscillator circuit to make it track with the r.f. tuning condenser. **1950** A. MARCUS *Radio Servicing* xi. 453 In addition to the series padder, a small trimmer capacitor is usually connected in parallel with the main tuning capacitor. **1971** A. MARGOLIS *Mod. Radio Repair Techniques* vi. 82 To maintain the tracking difference, a smaller oscillator coil and padder capacitor is added to the circuit.

†**ˈpadder,** *v. Sc. Obs.* [Freq. of PAD *v.*[1]: see -ER[5].] *trans.* To tread, trample down.
1789 DAVIDSON *Seasons* 87 Less valid, some, Though not less dext'rous, on the padder'd green..shoot forth the penny-stane. **1824** MACTAGGART *Gallovid. Encycl.* s.v., A road through the snow is *padderd*, when it has been often trod.

paddeˈreen, -ine. *Irish.* Also 9 padhereen. [a. Ir. *paidrín* rosary, dim. of *paidir* Lord's prayer, paternoster, ad. L. *pater*.] A bead of the rosary. In quot. 1689 app. *fig.* a bullet.
1689 *Apol. Fail. Geo. Walker's Acct. Siege of Derry* 26 While the Hand of the Church is preparing Mandates, with a Present of Leaden Padderines to be sent Post by the French and Irish to Saint Patrick in Purgatory. **1849** S. LOVER *Rory O'More* 107 Padhereens is the name the Irish give to their beads, upon which they count the number of Paters (or Pathers) they repeat, and hence the name.

ˈpadding, *vbl. sb.*[1] [f. PAD *v.*[1] + -ING[1].] The action of PAD *v.*[1]; robbery on the highway, etc.
1674 *Jackson's Recantation* Title-p., That Wicked and Fatal Profession of Padding on the Road. **1820** L. HUNT *Indicator* No. 13 (1822) I. 102 'He [Claude du Val] took' says his biographer 'the generous way of padding'.
b. *Comb.*, as **padding-crib, -ken** (*slang*).
1851 MAYHEW *Lond. Labour* I. 243/2 Others resort to the regular 'padding-kens', or houses of call for vagabonds.

ˈpadding, *vbl. sb.*[2] [f. PAD *v.*[2] + -ING[1].]
1. The action of PAD *v.*[2], in its various senses.
1839 URE *Dict. Arts* 222 In padding, where the whole surface of the calico is imbued with mordant, the drying apartment..should..afford a ready outlet to the.. exhalations. **1874** HELPS *Soc. Press.* vii. (1875) 82 All padding is an abomination to me. **1890** D. S. MARGOLIOUTH *Place of Ecclus.* 8 Padding is not disapproved by the Orientals as it is by us. **1954** *Jrnl. Soc. Dyers & Colourists* LXX. 383/2 The polymer emulsion..is then suitably diluted for application to the fabric, and applied by padding and drying. **1964** 'E. LATHEN' *Accounting for Murder* (1965) x. 94 It would take more than a little juggling of expense accounts to explain the situation... Somebody must have gone into a panic about some minor padding. **1973** *Times* 31 July 1/8 Several delegations have submitted a variety of inflated expense statements ranging from high living to outright padding of the bills.
attrib. **1839** URE *Dict. Arts* 915 *Padding machine*, in calico-printing, is the apparatus for imbuing a piece of cotton cloth uniformly with any mordant. **1875** *Ure's Dict. Arts* (ed. 7) I. 641 A section of the padding flue used in mordanting. **1912** J. HÜBNER *Bleaching & Dyeing Veg. Fibrous Materials* XVI. 371 The padding machine may be used for..impregnating with the aniline solution in the dyeing of Aniline Black. **1935** *Chem. Abstr.* XXIX. 4179 Dyeing in concentrated dye bath... The mech. and operating details of padding mangles of various manuf. are described. **1963** A. J. HALL *Textile Sci.* iv. 193 The textile material..is impregnated evenly with the dye liquor with the aid of a so-called padding mangle. **1973** *Materials & Technol.* VI. vii. 461 The most popular type of padding machine has two or three rollers giving one or two immersions in the padding solution.
2. *concr.* **a.** That of which a pad is made; material, such as cotton, felt, hair, used in stuffing or padding anything.
1828 *Lights & Shades* II. 66 They put a padding in to make them sit on one side. **1844** G. DODD *Textile Manuf.* iv. 138 The fabric produced is only used for drugget, padding, and other inferior purposes. **1874** BURNAND *My Time* iii. 28 Chairs, without leather or padding of any sort. **1875** WHYTE MELVILLE *Riding Recoll.* vi. (1879) 101 Formerly every saddle used to be made with padding about half an inch deep.
fig. **1867** TROLLOPE *Chron. Barset* I. xxxv. 302 There is something imposing about such a man till you're used to it, and can see through it. Of course it's all padding.
b. Extraneous or unnecessary matter introduced into a literary article, book, speech, etc., to fill up space and bring it up to a certain size; whatever has the effect of merely increasing the size without enhancing the value of writing; in magazines, the articles of secondary interest (which would do equally well in any number), as distinguished from those of immediate importance and the continuous stories which 'run' in the publication.
In Painting, 'figures or accessories not regarded as essential to a picture' (Funk).
[**1861** *Illustr. Lond. News* 26 Jan. 80/1 'Padding' signifies the lumping together of the contents of a monthly magazine, classing apart the serial stories.] **1869** M. COLLINS *Ivory Gate* II. xvii. 235 To write..two or three articles of magazine 'padding' a month. **1877** R. H. HUTTON in *Fortn. Rev.* Oct. 482 It was he [Walter Bagehot] who invented the phrase 'padding', to denote the secondary kind of article.. with which a judicious editor will fill up perhaps three-quarters of his review. **1896** C. PLUMMER *Bede* I. p. xlvi, He amplifies the narrative with rhetorical matter which can only be called padding.
3. *Electronics.* The use of a padder; ***padding capacitor*** or ***condenser*** = PADDER *sb.*[2] 3.
1935 A. T. WITTS *Superheterodyne Receiver* iv. 37 Condenser C_3, the padding condenser, has a capacity that is large in comparison with the tuning condenser C_2, with the result that at the lower settings of the latter the padding condenser has very little effect. **1936** J. H. REYNER *Testing Radio Sets* (ed. 3) xiii. 190 The alternative method, that of padding and trimming, is usually adopted. *Ibid.* 191 We.. have three variables, namely, the oscillator inductance, the parallel trimming condenser, and the series padding condenser, and three frequencies which are to be 'spot on'. **1946** C. A. QUARRINGTON *Mod. Pract. Radio & Television* I. xviii. 140 The [condenser] vanes are shaped to give the necessary effect when working on the highest frequency band incorporated in the receiver, and the lower frequency band or bands are corrected by means of padding. *Ibid.* 141 The series condenser..is called the padding condenser and is usually..of the pre-set type..; the small parallel capacity ..is called the trimming condenser, and is invariably of the pre-set type. **1962** J. H. & P. J. REYNER *Radio Communication* ix. 371 The padding and trimming capacitances must..be altered for each wave range and are usually..changed over by the switching which alters the coils.
4. padding stitch = *pad stitch.*
1913 M. E. WILKINSON *Embroidery Stitches* 123 *Padding stitch*, close Satin stitch worked over a raised or padded grounding. **1955** E. A. MANSFIELD *Clothing Construction* xv. 323/2 To shorten the fold-line so that the collar will lie close to the neck,..put in two rows of small padding stitches along the fold line.

ˈpadding, *ppl. a.* [f. PAD *v.*[1] + -ING[2].]
†**1.** That practises highway robbery. In quot. *fig.*
1672 EACHARD *Hobbs's State Nat.* 73 That Humane Nature in general is a shirking, rooking, pilfering, padding Nature.
2. That pads or paces on; that walks or runs with steady dull-sounding footfall.
1684 BUNYAN *Pilgr.* II. 105 Mercy..saw, as she thought, something most like a Lyon, and it came a great padding pace after. **1888** A. RIVES *Quick or Dead* vi. (1889) 80 She.. began to move up and down the room with the long, padding gait peculiar to her. **1891** ATKINSON *Last of Giant Killers* 158 The dread Goat..tramping round and round the Castle with padding, dull-sounding steps.

†**ˈpaddist.** *Sc. Obs.* [f. PAD *v.*[1] 4 + -IST.] A padder, a professional highwayman.
1671 ANNAND *Myst. Pietatis* 85 A paddist, or Highwayman, attempting to spoil a preacher, ordering him to stand.

paddisway, obs. f. PADUASOY, kind of silk.

paddle (ˈpæd(ə)l), *sb.*[1] Also 5 padell. [Origin obscure; see also PADLE, PATTLE.
The implement in sense 1 was sometimes in 17–18th c. also called SPADDLE, which has been taken by some as the original form, and viewed as a dim. of *spade*. But *spaddle* is not known nearly so early as *paddle*, and may be altered from it, or the words may be unconnected.]
I. 1. A small spade-like implement with a long handle, used for clearing a ploughshare of earth or clods, digging up thistles, etc.
1407 in Rogers *Agric. & Prices* III. 545/3 Padell for plough /3. **1560** BIBLE (Genev.) *Deut.* xxiii. 13 Thou shalt haue a paddle among thy weapons [1611 upon thy weapon], and when thou woldest sit downe without, thou shalt dig therewith. **1679** C. NESSE *Antid. agst. Popery* Ded. 9 To turn it as easily as the ploughman doth his water-course with his paddle. **1733** TULL *Horse-Hoeing Husb.* xxiii. 380 Him that follows the Drill, whose chief Business is, with a Paddle to keep all the Shares and Tines from being clogged up by the Dirt sticking to them. **1850** *Jrnl. R. Agric. Soc.* XI. I. 141 Thistles removed by women with paddles. **1900** *Daily News* 17 Sept. 7/2 By paddle I mean a small, sharp, spade-like instrument, with a handle long enough to serve the purpose of a walking-stick.
II. A spade-shaped oar, or something having a like function.
2. A sort of short oar used without a rowlock, having a broad blade which is dipped more or less vertically into the water, and pulled and pushed backward so as to propel a canoe forward: orginally applied to those used by Indians, South Sea Islanders, etc. The name is applied more generally to any form of oar used without a rowlock.
double paddle, one having a blade at each end.
1624 CAPT. SMITH *Virginia* II. 32 Instead of Oares, they vse Paddles and stickes. **1712** E. COOKE *Voy. S. Sea* 336 Short Paddles, made like an Oar at each End. **1726** SHELVOCKE *Voy. round World* (1757) 281 On these the rower sits looking forward, with a double paddle. **1837** W. IRVING *Capt. Bonneville* II. 276 An Indian..plying the paddle, soon shot across the river. **1860** WHITTIER *Truce Piscataqua* 11 Let the Indian's paddle play On the unbridged Piscataqua!
3. †**a.** One of a series of paddle-like arms or spokes, radiating from a revolving axle, drum, or wheel in a ship or boat, so as to enter and push on the water in succession (*obs.*); hence, **b.** One of the boards or floats which perform the same function more effectively in the 'paddle-wheel' of a steamer; a paddle-board; also, **c.** A float of an undershot mill-wheel. **d.** Short for PADDLE-WHEEL. **e.** Short for *paddle-boat* or *-steamer*: see 11.
1685 PETTY in Fitzmaurice *Life* (1895) iv. 122 On each end of the Axis..a wheele of about 7 foot diameter, with 12 Stemms issuing out of each wheele and a Paddle or Oar at the end of each Stem of 3 feet square. **1685** [see PADDLE-WHEEL]. **1698** T. SAVERY *Navigation Impr.* 111 This engine is the least lyable to be injured by a shot..: for tho' it break some of the paddles, you suffer no inconvenience. **1758** EMERSON *Mechanics* (ed. 2) Gloss. 278 *Paddles*,..The laddle boards on the edge of a waterwheel. **1784** S. T. WOOD *Patent Specif.* No. 1447. 16 A wheel and axis is made to revolve, which in its revolution carry with it vanes, leavers or paddles, that are fixed to the extremity of the axis. **1786** J. FITCH in *Columbian Mag.* (Philad.) I. Dec., Each evolution of the axis moves twelve oars or paddles five and a half feet; they work [like] the strokes of a paddle of a canoe. **1809** FULTON *U.S. Patent Specif.* 11 Feb., I give the preference to a water wheel or wheels with propelling boards... Previous to adopting wheels I made experiments upon paddles. **1811** H. JAMES *Patent Specif.* No. 3426 The oars, paddles, or propelling boards,..revolving or turning in the direction of the lengthways of the boat or vessel. **1816** R. BUCHANAN *Propelling Vessels* 24 The paddle-wheels..are 9 feet dia. and 2 feet 11 ins. wide. This boat has 10 paddles. **1819** LAMBERT in J. Nicholson *Operat. Mechanic* (1825) 72 The great advantage..is not only the superior hold and pressure which the water takes on the paddles or floats of such wheels, but the very little back-water which they create. **1833** *Encycl. Brit.* (ed. 7) X. 549 Soon after this [1787], Mr. Miller built a boat with two keels, between which he introduced a propelling paddle; and Mr. William Symington of Falkirk applied the steam-engine to it. **1840** DICKENS *Old C. Shop* v, A great steam-ship, beating the water..with her heavy paddles. **1890** 'R. BOLDREWOOD' *Col. Reformer* (1891) 154 A stately ocean steamer, with throbbing screw or mighty paddle. **1897** *Daily News* 23 Sept. 5/3 The first steamers to cross the Atlantic were paddles. There were even paddles in the Royal Navy.
4. *Zool.* A limb serving the purpose of a fin or flipper; as that of a turtle, whale, ichthyosaurus, or plesiosaurus; the foot of a duck; the wing of a penguin; one of the ctenophores or ciliated locomotive organs of the *Ctenophora*; one of the natatory feet of crustacea.
1835 KIRBY *Hab. & Inst. Anim.* II. xvii. 143 Paddles, by which term the natatory apparatus of the Chelonian reptiles, and of the marine Saurians..are distinguished. **1850** H. MILLER *Footpr. Creat.* iii. (1874) 33 The sweeping paddles of the Ichthyosaurian genus. **1860** HARTWIG *Sea & Wond.* vi. 73 The pectoral fins or paddles are no more than 6 feet long. **1871** —— *Subterr. W.* ii. 14 Arms..resembling the paddle of the turtle. **1894** NEWTON *Dict. Birds* 705 In the water they [the wings of the penguin] are most efficient paddles. **1894** G. EGERTON *Keynotes* 33 The twelve weeks' ducklings..with..such dainty paddles.
5. An artificial disk or plate attached to the foot to increase its hold of the water in swimming, etc.
1823 J. BADCOCK *Dom. Amusem.* 208 The paddles, which are fastened to the soles of the feet or boots,..are made of block-tin four or five inches wide below.
III. Applied to various things shaped or used more or less like a paddle (senses 1 and 2).
6. a. A sliding panel or sluice in a weir or lock-gate which can be raised or lowered to regulate the quantity of water allowed to flow through; **b.** a panel regulating the amount of grain running out of a hopper.
1795 J. PHILLIPS *Hist. Inland Navig.* 361 The water in the lock is drawn off..by means of the paddles in the gates. **1815** *Pocklington Canal Act* 45 Any paddle, valve, or clough in any of the lock gates. **1837** WHITTOCK, etc. *Bk. Trades* (1842) 202 The lower gates are loosened, and the 'paddles' of the upper gates are gradually raised which allows the water to rush into the chamber of the lock.
b. 1825 J. NICHOLSON *Operat. Mechanic* 158 A paddle, regulating the quantity of corn to be delivered to the mill, and by raising or lowering which, a larger or smaller proportion of grain may be furnished.
7. A paddle-shaped instrument or tool, used in various trades: e.g. **a.** in *Glass-making*, for stirring and mixing the materials; **b.** in *Brickmaking* and similar industries, for tempering clay; **c.** in *Puddling*, for stirring the molten ore; **d.** in *Leather-making* (see quot. 1885).
1662 MERRETT *Neri's Art of Glass* App., A Padle to stir and move the Ashes and Sand in the Calcar. **1753** in CHAMBERS *Cycl. Suppl.* **1825** J. NICHOLSON *Operat. Mechanic* 460 The clay..is then cut into small pieces with a paddle, not much unlike a spade. **1868** JOYNSON *Metals* 73 The metal has now to be kept constantly stirred by the

puddler with an iron tool called a paddle. **1884** W. H. GREENWOOD *Steel & Iron* xiv. 280 The tools used by the puddler are..a long straight chiselled-edged bar called a 'paddle' [etc.].

1885 C. T. DAVIS *Manuf. Leather* xviii. 356 The motion of the wheels causes the stock to move up in front, pass under the wheels, and down on the concave bottom to the back of the vat, and thus by means of the paddles, and the constant changing position of the stock a thorough and gentle agitation is maintained.

8. An instrument with a flat blade or surface, used **a.** for beating clothes while they are being washed in running water; **b.** for administering corporal punishment to slaves, etc.; hence, a blow inflicted with this instrument.

1828 *Cherokee Phœnix* 10 Apr. (Bartlett s.v. *Cobb*), Such negro..shall receive fifteen cobbs or paddles for every such offence. **1856** OLMSTED *Slave States* 281 The paddle is a large, thin ferule of wood, in which many small holes are bored; when a blow is struck, these holes, from the rush and partial exhaustion of air in them, act like diminutive cups, and the continued application of the instrument.. produce[s] precisely such a result as that attributed to the strap. **1970** *Wall St. Jrnl.* 16 June 1 The 'board of education', a paddle applied smartly to the backside, may be making a comeback in the classroom. **1977** *New Yorker* 30 May 27/1 One of the boys..was said to have been struck more than twenty times with a paddle.

c. A short-handled bat with a broad, flat blade, used in various ball games.

[**1925**: implied in *paddle tennis*]. **1935** MASON & MITCHELL *Active Games & Contests* xxi. 388 Paddle Ball... This is an excellent game played with a paddle-tennis ball and paddle. **1949** P. B. BARRINGER *Natural Bent* xviii. 127 To play two-hole cat, four boys, two bases, a ball, and two bats were needed. These bats were sometimes called paddles. **1974** E. TIDYMAN *Dummy* vi. 80 He..accepted a challenge to play table tennis..offering the doctor instruction on the proper way to hold his paddle. **1975** *Oxf. Compan. Sports & Games* 745/1 Bigger and heavier paddles are used, and the ball may be played into court off the walls. **1976** *Webster's Sports Dict.* 299/2 The table tennis paddle is slightly smaller than the paddleball paddle.

d. *Computing.* A paddle-shaped device used to control the movement of an image on a VDU or television screen.

1980 *Kilobaud Microcomputing* Dec. 87/1 Like most TV games, this one has a pair of paddle controllers. **1985** *Personal Computer World* Feb. 124/4 Personal Peripherals.. has acquired TG products, makers of joysticks, paddles and related products.

9. The long paddle-shaped snout of the paddle-fish: see 12.

1890 in *Cent. Dict.*

10. *Astronautics.* A paddle-shaped array of solar cells projecting from a spacecraft.

1959 *Listener* 13 Aug. 247/1 The four 'paddles' recharge the satellite's batteries by converting sunlight into electricity. **1966** *Electronics* 17 Oct. 36 The two solar paddles each extend 19 feet from the Agena and together provide 15 kilowatts. **1972** *Nature* 17 Mar. 90/1 The solar paddles and antenna were also reported to be working satisfactorily.

IV. 11. *attrib.* and *Comb.*, as (sense 2) ***paddle-blade, -dip, -man, -stroke***; also ***paddle-like, -shaped*** adjs.; (sense 3) ***paddle arm, -crank, -guard***; 'having, or propelled by, paddles', as ***paddle-boat, punt, -sloop, steamer, tug***; (sense 4) ***paddle-foot***; (sense 7) ***paddle tool***.

1839 R. S. ROBINSON *Naut. Steam Eng.* 87 The ends of the *paddle arms pass through the centres. **1891** *Month* LXXIII. 28 Leaving space enough between the *paddle-blades to admit his head. **1874** J. W. LONG *Amer. Wild-Fowl Shooting* 79 Now the building of a *paddle-boat is not so simple an under-taking as many of my readers may suppose. **1891** *Scribner's Mag.* X. 13 She was a paddle-boat, built of wood, and was 207 feet long. **1938** M. K. RAWLINGS *Yearling* xx. 261 The remaining bears were scrambling across the swamp like paddle boats, churning the water behind them. **1875** KNIGHT *Dict. Mech.* 1594/2 The arrangement of the *paddle-cranks is intended to equally divide the weight of the controlling frame between the paddle-wheel and the paddle-wheel guard. **1899** E. J. CHAPMAN *Drama Two Lives, Canadian Summer-nt.* 68 With noiseless *paddle-dip we glide. **1954** J. R. R. TOLKIEN *Fellowship of Ring* II. ix. 399 It wasn't a log, for it had *paddle-feet. **1847** CARPENTER *Zool.* §458 The Penguin,.. aided by its *paddle-like wings,..swims and dives with great facility. **1861** J. R. GREENE *Man. Anim. Kingd., Cœlent.* 165 A row of strong cilia is attached in such a manner as to form a paddle-like plate, or comb. **1863** A. ROBB *Heathen World & Duty of Ch.* I. 19 We hear the song of the *paddlemen. **1909** *Yachting Monthly* Dec. 93/2 The '*paddle punt' is about 14 ft. long, strongly built on the Deal model. **1918** N. DUNCAN *Battles Royal* IV. ii. 242 Old Elihu Maul, with a hook and line, had fished the Boiling Pot in civil weather from a paddle-punt. **1970** E. J. MARCH *Inshore Craft Gt. Brit.* II. ii. 82 The second class [*sc.* punts]..cost £12. Generally known as 'paddle punts', they were used for inshore fishing. **1898** *Westm. Gaz.* 20 June 10/2 The *paddle-shaped limbs are 'fringed'. **1889** *Academy* 27 July 52/3 He was in command of the *paddle-sloop Argus. **1886** *Outing* VIII. 26/1 The Ripple, [a] *paddle steamer of the river steamer type. **1895** *Model Steam Engine* 80 The paddles in the paddle-steamers act as outriggers. **1923** *Man. Seamanship* (Admiralty) II. viii. 152 For long tows at sea the screw tug is the most efficient, as owing to the propellers being totally submerged they are not affected by the sea to the same extent as paddle tugs. **1930** J. MASEFIELD *Wanderer of Liverpool* 15 The Paddle-tug Wrestler arrived at an hour ere flood. **1955** *Times* 6 June 6/6 Experience has shown that paddle tugs are more efficient than screw-driven tugs for work in confined basins because of their great manoeuvrability and power. **1868** JOYNSON *Metals* 58 The iron..at a certain stage is collected at the ends of the '*paddle' tools into balls or lumps.

12. Special Combs.: **paddle ball**, a game played with a light ball and wooden bat in a four-walled hand-ball court; **paddle-beam** (*Shipbuilding*), one of two large beams lying athwart a ship, between which the paddle-wheels revolve; **paddle board**, (*a*) one of the floats or boards fitted on the circumference of a paddle-wheel (= 3 b); (*b*) a wooden board for supporting a person in water, esp. when surfing; **paddle-box**, the casing which encloses the upper part of a steamer's paddle-wheel; also *transf.*; hence **paddle-box boat**, a boat forming, when inverted and stowed, the upper section of a paddle-box; **paddle-crab**, a swimming crab, esp. the edible crab of N. America, *Callinectes hastatus*; **paddle-end**, in decoration, an oval enlargement of a line or band, like the end of a paddle; **paddle foot** *U.S. slang*, (*a*) an infantryman; (*b*) a member of an airforce ground crew; (see also sense 11 above); **paddle-hole**, a sluice hole in a lock-gate to admit or discharge water (cf. sense 6); †**paddle-plane** *Aeronaut.* = *cyclogiro, -gyro* s.v. CYCLO- 1; **paddle-row**, the ctenophore of a ctenophoran (cf. sense 4); **paddle-shaft**, the revolving shaft which carries the paddle-wheels of a steamer; **paddle tennis**, a type of tennis played in a small court with a sponge-rubber ball and wooden or plastic bat; **paddle-tumbler**, in leather-making, a tank in which skins are thoroughly washed by being kept in motion in water by means of a paddle-wheel; **paddle-vat** = *paddle-tumbler*; **paddlewheeler**, a paddle steamer; **paddle-wood**, the light elastic wood of a S. American tree, *Aspidosperma excelsum*, from which the Indians make canoe-paddles. Also PADDLE-FISH, -WHEEL.

1935 *Paddle ball [see sense 8c above]. **1962** *Times* 14 Nov. 3/6 Games of..paddle-ball (Rugby fives with table tennis bats). **1973** *Daily Colonist* (Victoria, B.C.) 20 May 2/2 Our daughter..gets blisters on her soles after a hard game of tennis or paddle ball. **1975** *Listener* 9 Oct. 484/1 A *cinquantaine sportive* concern to keep fit through paddle ball at the Downtown Club. **1864** WEBSTER, **Paddle-beam*. **1869** SIR E. J. REED *Shipbuild.* xv. 278 Paddle-boxes are usually built upon a framing, of which the paddlebeams form the athwartship, and the spring-beams the longitudinal boundaries. **1790** RUMSEY *Patent Specif.* No. 1738 The floats or *paddle-boards..may hang on hinges. **1830** KATER & LARDNER *Mech.* xiv. 179 In the paddle-wheel..the power is the resistance which the water offers to the motion of the paddle-boards. **1967** J. SEVERSON *Great Surfing* Gloss., *Paddleboard*, a square-sided, hollow surfcraft usually constructed of plywood. **1968** *Surfer Mag.* Jan. 56/1 He surfed a hollow paddle board that he made at home. **1974** 'R. B. DOMINIC' *Epitaph for Lobbyist* xvi. 139 He was going to find time for healthful exercise—paddle-board, or a few turns in the pool. **1833** *Chambers's Edin. Jrnl.* 1 June 140/2 The captain now takes his station on the *paddle-box. **1837** *Civil Eng. & Arch. Jrnl.* I. 13/1 Her extreme breadth athwart the paddle-boxes 46 feet. **1879** BLACK *Macleod of D.* xxxix. 351 When we get on to the paddle-box..he will not know what to do to welcome you! **1908** G. B. SHAW *Let.* 31 Dec. (1972) II. 823 Charlotte wrecked it [*sc.* the car] the first day. The professional kept her in countenance by knocking off the paddle-box against the gate. *a***1936** KIPLING *Something of Myself* (1937) iv. 102, I saw..a woman crouching on the paddle-box of a crowded boat. **1976** P. LOVESEY *Swing, swing Together* xxxvii. 175 A coat of white paint on the paddle-box, lifeboats and funnel. **1859** F. A. GRIFFITHS *Artil. Man.* (1862) 133 *Paddle-box boats answer extremely well. *c***1860** H. STUART *Seaman's Catech.* 9 Paddle-box boats stow on the top of the paddle boxes. **1946** *Amer. Speech* XXI. 34/2 **Paddlefeet*.., Infantrymen. **1948** MENCKEN *Amer. Lang.* Suppl. II. 727 The airmen..use many derisory terms in speaking of themselves..*e.g.*,.. *paddlefoot*..for a member of the ground crew. **1950** *Life* 2 Jan. 98/2 Murray was a paddlefoot in Europe. **1957** *New Yorker* 23 Nov. 67/3 A paddlefoot mess officer in North Africa. **1960** WENTWORTH & FLEXNER *Dict. Amer. Slang* 372/1 *Paddlefoot*.., an infantry soldier. **1933** *Flight* 2 Feb. 107/2 Our Berlin correspondent indicates that the Rohrbach '*paddle plane' has the circumferential speed of the paddles approximately equal to the top speed. **1950** *Gloss. Aeronaut. Terms* (*B.S.I.*) 1. 30 *Cyclogyro* (paddle-plane). **1815** DICKENSON *Patent Specif.* No. 3932 A small pinnion upon the *paddle-shaft. **1837** *Civil Eng. & Arch. Jrnl.* I. 55/1 Each paddle-shaft, after being turned, weighs 6½ tons. **1895** *Model Steam Engine* 72 Motion is imparted to the paddles by connecting the top of the piston-rods directly with the cranks on the paddle-shaft. **1925** *Playground* Mar. 710/1 He secured permission from Park Commissioner Francis B. Gallatin to mark several *paddle tennis courts in Washington Square Park. **1944** F. G. MENKE *Encycl. Sports* (rev. ed.) 490 Frank P. Beal..originated Paddle Tennis in 1924 to provide children with a game that would teach them the rudiments of tennis. **1972** *N.Y. Times* 3 Nov. 22/4 (Advt.), A new recreational facility featuring tennis, paddletennis..and a barbeque and picnic area with charming pavilion has been completed. **1883** HALDANE *Workshop Receipts* Ser. II. 373/1 The skins are now a second time washed in the '*paddle-tumbler', first in cold and then in tepid water. **1903** L. A. FLEMMING *Pract. Tanning* 23 Sheepskins are also very satisfactorily tanned with one-bath chrome liquors in *paddle-vats. **1924** H. A. TRIPP *Shoalwater & Fairway* vii. 128 That Belle steamer was a mine-sweeper in the War, and jolly useful they found the old excursion *paddle-wheelers. **1970** S. TRUEMAN *Intimate Hist. New Brunswick* vi. 83 He built the *Reindeer*, a paddlewheeler that easily outraced bigger and fancier river boats. **1976** *National Observer* (U.S.) 13 Mar. 8/1 (Advt.), Return to heartland America aboard the legendary paddlewheeler Delta Queen, or the luxurious new Mississippi Queen. **1866** *Treas. Bot.* 103/2 *Aspidosperma excelsum*, called by the colonists *Paddle-wood, is remarkable for its singularly fluted trunk, composed of solid projecting radii, which the Indians use as ready-made planks.

'paddle, *sb.*[2] *Sc.* Also 6 **paddill, padill**, 8–9 **padle, paidle.** [Origin unknown: Jamieson compares *haf-podde* 'sea-toad', a name mentioned by Schoneveld.] The common Lump-fish, *Cyclopterus lumpus*; also called ***paddle-cock***, COCK-PADDLE.

1591 *Aberdeen Recds.* in Cadenhead *New Bk. of Bon Acc.* (1866) 64 Partins and paddillis, with other sort of schell fish. **1601** HOLLAND *Pliny* II. 428 The Lompe, Paddle or sea-Owle. **1805** G. BARRY *Orkney Isl.* III. i. 295 The Lump Fish (*cyclopterus lumpus*..), here denominated the *Paddle*, frequents the harbours and sand-banks. **1810** NEILL *List Fishes* 23 (Jam.) The male (called by our fishermen *Cock-paddle*), is for the table, at the season, much preferable to the female, (the *Hush*, *Hen-paddle*, and in Fife the *Bagaty*). **1838** *Proc. Berw. Nat. Club* I. 174 The Paidle spawns towards the end of March. **1882** OGILVIE, *Paddle-cock*, a name given in the north of Scotland to the lump-fish.

paddle, *sb.*[3] *Sc.* [? dim. of PAD *sb.*[4]]

1. A little leather bag.

*a***1568** *Wowing of Jok & Jynny* vii. (Bannatyne MS.), Ane auld pannell of ane laid sadill, Ane pepper polk maid of a padill. **1887** *Suppl. to Jamieson, Padell, Paidle, Peddle*, lit. a little pad or pack: a small leathern bag, pouch, or wallet used by packmen;..also, the leathern pouch worn by country housewives.

2. Usu. in form **paidle.** (See quots.) Also *attrib.*

1879 *Cases Court of Session, Scotl.* (ser. 4) VI. 1324 Nets ..often have also a barrel-shaped trap or paidle attached to them. **1882** *Ibid.* IX. 186 The respondents..earn part of their living by fishing on the shores of the Solway by means of small stake-nets, locally called 'paidle-nets'. **1895** *Daily News* 5 July 5/3 The nets are set at low-water point,..and have pockets or 'paidles' in the corners, into which the fish, mostly flounders, are carried with the ebbing tide..of the Solway.

'paddle, *sb.*[4] [f. PADDLE *v.*[1]] †**1.** Fuss, ado. *rare.*

1642 ROGERS *Naaman* 865 That paddle and adoe which you have made to soder and play the Hypocrite.

2. (Also *Sc.* **paiddle, paidle.**) An act of paddling in mud or shallow water.

1866 W. GREGOR *Dial. Banffshire* 121 The twa bairns keepit a paidle..in the lint-cobble, catchin' wattir-horse. **1880** LONGMUIR & DONALDSON *Jamieson's Etym. Dict. Scottish Lang.* (rev. ed.) III. 430/1 We..had a gran' paidle in the saut watter. **1896** A. M. BISSET *Poets Linlithgowshire* 188 But woe to the imp that..damm'd up the burn for a paidle or wade. **1942** 'N. SHUTE' *Pied Piper* v. 106 Wouldn't you like to take your shoes off and have a paddle, then? **1976** *Morecambe Guardian* 7 Dec. 25/7 They decided to go for a swim and walked into the sea first for a paddle.

'paddle, *sb.*[5] [f. PADDLE *v.*[2]] The act of paddling, or of rowing lightly. ***at the paddle***, at the rate one moves when paddling; with easy rowing. *Comb.* **paddle-over** [after WALK-OVER], an easy victory in a boat race.

1861 HUGHES *Tom Brown at Oxf.* ii. (1889) 11 An old hand just going out for a gentle paddle. **1882** DE WINDT *Equator* 97 We arrived..at the mouth of the Sarawak river,..after a hard paddle. **1897** *Daily News* 13 Mar. 6/5 The practice consisted of a paddle down to the Hurlingham and back..to the Leander Hard..stopping short of Hammersmith, and coming back at the paddle to Putney. **1906** *Westm. Gaz.* 4 July 5/1 Little more than a paddle-over for the Cambridge men.

paddle ('pæd(ə)l), *v.*[1] Also 6 **paddyll**, 7 **padle**, 8–9 *Sc.* **paidle**, 9– *dial.* (in sense 4) **poddle** ('pɒd(ə)l). [Origin obscure: the form is dim. and frequentative.

The radical appears to be the same as in PAD *v.*[2], though only sense 4 seems directly derived from that. Cf. LG. *paddeln* to tramp about (Danneil), from *padjen, pedden* to tread. The special association of the word with mire or water in sense 1 is not explained.]

I. 1. *intr.* To walk or move the feet about in mud or shallow water; to wade about in play or for pleasure; to dabble with the feet, or the feet and hands, in shallow water.

1530 PALSGR. 651/1, I paddyll in the myre, as duckes do or yonge chyldren, *Je pestille*. I pray the, se howe yonder lytell boye padleth in the myre,..*pestille en la boue*. **1611** COTGR., *Patouiller*, to slabber; to padle, or dable in with the feet; to stirre vp and downe, and trouble, or make foule, by stirring. **1637** G. DANIEL *Genius of Isle* 164 Whole Shoales of Carren Crowes,..Paddle in the warme blood of people slaine. **1655** FULLER *Ch. Hist.* II. iii. §7 Could those infernal Fiends.. take any Pleasure, by padling here in Puddles. **1706** PHILLIPS, *To Paddle*, to move the Water with Hands or Feet, to dabble. **1781** COWPER *Retirem.* 499 Ducks paddle in the pond before the door. **1788** BURNS *Auld Lang Syne* iii, We twa hae paidl't i' the burn, From mornin sun till dine. **1816** SCOTT *Antiq.* xi, Paddling in a pool among the rocks. **1840** R. H. DANA *Bef. Mast* xiv. 33 The second mate..has to roll up his trousers and paddle about the decks barefooted. **1848** THACKERAY *Trav. Lond.* Wks. 1886 XXIV. 350 Look at the shabby children paddling through the slush. **1880** W. S. GILBERT *Pirates* I, Suppose we take off our shoes and stockings and paddle.

fig. **1621** QUARLES *Esther* viii, That take delight To bathe, and paddle in the blood of those Whom jealousies..oppose. **1635** —— *Embl.* I. *Invoc.* (1718) 2 Wherein Thy childrens leprous fingers, scurf'd with sin, Have paddled. **1703** COLLIER *Ess. Mor. Subj.* II. 78 An odd sort of bog for fancy to paddle in. **1870** SWINBURNE *Ess. & Stud.* (1875) 239 Boys and girls who paddled in rhyme or dabbled in sentiment.

2. a. *intr.* To play or dabble idly or fondly (*in*, *on*, *with*, or *about* something) with the fingers; to toy.

1602 SHAKS. *Ham.* III. iv. 185 And let him [the King] for a paire of reechie kisses, Or padling in your necke with his damn'd Fingers, Make you to rauell all this matter out. **1604** —— *Oth.* II. i. 259 Didst thou not see her paddle with the palme of his hand? **1746** *Exmoor Courtship* 374 (E.D.S.) He takes hold of her and paddles in her Neck and Bosom. **1824** GALT *Rothelan* I. vii, Adonijah..paddled, as it were unconsciously, with his fingers on the gems. **1837** THACKERAY *Ravenswing* v, He..let her keep paddling on with his hand.

†**b.** *trans.* To finger idly, playfully, or fondly.

1611 SHAKS. *Wint. T.* I. ii. 115 To be padling Palmes, and pinching Fingers, As now they are, and making practis'd Smiles As in a Looking-Glasse. **1622** in Arber *Story of Pilgr. Fathers* 414 There was also a heap of sand..newly done. We might see how they had paddled it with their hands.

†**3. a.** *trans.* To trifle away, waste, squander. **b.** *intr.* To trifle; to deal in a petty trifling way. (Cf. PEDDLE, PIDDLE.) *Obs.*

1616 J. DEACON *Tobacco Tortured* 62 Tell me in good sadnesse, whether it be not a superfluous waste, for any man of great place, to paddle forth yearely one hundred pounds at the least, for an hundred gallons of filthy fumes? *a* **1620** J. DYKE *Sel. Serm.* (1640) 160 Hee may be padling with these playsters and poulteyses that men in the world seeke ease by. **1642** ROGERS *Naaman* 176 Eating and drinking, padling in the world or about carnall objects. **1840** GEN. P. THOMPSON *Exerc.* (1842) V. 86 In the small way, they keep a perpetual paddling with the poor man's drink.

II. 4. a. *intr.* To walk with short, unsteady, or uncertain steps, like those of a child; to toddle.

1792 BURNS *The Deuk's Dang o'er my Daddie* i, He paidles out, and he paidles in, An' he paidles late and early, O. **1805** ANDR. SCOTT *Poems* (1808) 164 Aff the spat she wadna stir, But prance an' paidle. *c* **1817** HOGG *Tales & Sk.* III. 286 Old Sandy paddled away from the stable towards the house. **1836** T. HOOK *G. Gurney* III. 176, I hear the sound of feet pattering and paddling over the floor. **1860** THACKERAY *Four Georges* iii. (1876) 66 A hundred little children are paddling up and down the steps to St. James's Park. **1908** H. G. WELLS *War in Air* iii. 72 Then he got up, paddled about, rearranged the ballast bags on the floor,..and turned over the maps on the locker. **1970** F. DURBRIDGE *P. Temple & Harkdale Robbery* v. 51 Tam Coley paddled cheerfully out [of the room] with a nod to Paul.

1827 J. CLARE *Shepherd's Calendar* 69 The ruddy child, nursed in the lap of care,..Beside its mother poddles o'er the land. **1842** C. RIDLEY *Let.* 5 Mar. in *Cecilia* (1958) vii. 89, I..spend a great deal of time in poddling about the garden. **1869** R. D. BLACKMORE *Lorna Doone* I. x. 109 Now I am uncommonly fond of ducks..and it is a fine sight to behold them walk, poddling one after other. **1976** SCOLLINS & TITFORD *Ey up, mi Duck!* II. 59 *Poddlin'*, walking; implies a comical gait. Usually describes a small child, or a little old man, etc. As in: 'Eh wer *poddlin*' along wi'aht a care int wold!'

b. *trans.* (in *dial.* use). (*a*) To trample down by treading over; to mark with wet or muddy feet. (*b*) To lead or support a child learning to walk.

1805 STAGG *Misc. Poems* 144 (E.D.D.) Sauntrin' pace the paddled green. **1824** MACTAGGART *Gallovid. Encycl.* 371 These circular spots then shorn of grass are termed paddled rounalls. **1828** *Craven Gloss.* (ed. 2), *Paddle*, to support or lead a child by the hand in its first attempt to walk. **1877** *Holderness Gloss.*, *Paddle*, to trample over, tread down. **1889** *N.W. Linc. Gloss.* (ed. 2) s.v., Them bairns hes been paddlin yon clean floor fra end to end.

5. *Comb.* **paddle-pond**, a pond in which children may paddle.

1930 *Time & Tide* 14 Feb. 195/2 He saw that these spaces were..empty, and he resolved that some..of them should be filled; hence the goal-posts and paddle-ponds.

Hence **'paddling** *vbl. sb.*[1] (in *Comb.*, ***paddling pool***) and *ppl. a.*[1]

1642 ROGERS *Naaman* 367 How shall I speake to this wofull place for the padling out of her season of ease? **1679** JAS. POLLEY *Will*, Pay all my small padling debts. **1714** GAY *Sheph. Week* v. 155 While padling ducks the standing lake desire. **1828** *Craven Gloss.* (ed. 2), *Paddling-strings*, strings fixed to the frock of a young child to assist it in walking. **1840** [see sense 3]. **1884** *Athenæum* 22 Nov. 652/1 This undignified paddling recalls the fairy days of childhood, when paddling itself was a venturesome feat. **1895** CROCKETT *Men of Moss-Hags* I. 358 A paidling bairn of seven years. **1932** T. SHARP *Town & Countryside* x. 204 These playgrounds should be equipped with swings,..and a sand-pit and perhaps a paddling pool. **1958** *Listener* 6 Nov. 727/1 Children's paddling pools. **1972** *Guardian* 1 Aug. 15/6 Emma went to the crèche-playgroup where there were swings, slides, books, a paddling-pool, a Wendy-house.

paddle, *v.*[2] [f. PADDLE *sb.*[1]]

I. 1. a. *intr.* To move on the water by means of paddles, as in a canoe. Also said of the canoe.

1677 I. HUBBARD *Narrative* 129 He accidentally met with a Canooe..turned adrift, by which means he padled by some shift or other so farr out of the harbour. **1719** DE FOE *Crusoe* I. xiii, I saw them..row (or paddle, as we call it) all away. **1751** J. BARTRAM *Observ. Trav. Pennsylv.*, etc. 17 We borrowed a canoe, and paddled up the West branch. **1784** *Cook's Voy.* I. iv. 141 We had not long anchored, when two canoes paddled towards us. **1853** W. IRVING in *Life & Lett.* (1864) I. iii. 60 Paddling with them in Indian canoes on the limpid waters of the St. Lawrence.

b. *transf.* To row with oars lightly or gently; technically applied to the rowing of a racing crew when not exerting their full power.

1697 DAMPIER *Voy.* I. 247 Because they would not be heard, they hal'd in their Oars, and paddled as softly as if they [etc.]. **1737** M. GREEN *Spleen* 369 He paddling by the scuffling crowd, Sees unconcern'd life's wager row'd. **1842** *Bell's Life* 31 July 1/5 (Eton *v.* Westminster), The competitors paddled to their stations. **1861** HUGHES *Tom Brown at Oxf.* xi. (1889) 97 Being summoned to the boat, they took to the water again, and paddled steadily up home. **1866** *Oxf. Undergr. Jrnl.* 18 Apr. 38 Paddled to Barnes Railway Bridge, and rowed hard from there back to Hammersmith.

c. Of a paddle-steamer, etc.: To move by means of paddle-wheels.

1844 W. H. MAXWELL *Sports & Adv. Scotl.* xxxv. (1855) 279 The 'Sovereign' was paddling out of the harbour. **1847** TENNYSON *Princ.* Prol. 71 Round the lake A little clock-work steamer paddling plied And shook the lilies.

d. Of birds or other animals: To move in the water with paddle-like limbs. Hence ***paddling-crab*** = ***paddle-crab***: see PADDLE *sb.*[1] 12.

2. a. *trans.* To propel (a canoe, boat, etc.) by means of a paddle or paddles; also, to transport (a person) in a canoe.

1784 BELKNAP *Tour to White Mts.* (1876) 20 Our horses swam after a canoe, in which..an old woman paddled us over. **1863** FR. A. KEMBLE *Resid. in Georgia* 54, I met many of them paddling themselves in their slight canoes. **1875** T. W. HIGGINSON *Hist. U.S.* iii. 17 The canoes were very light, and could be paddled with ease.

b. Phr. ***to paddle one's own canoe***, to make one's way by one's own exertions.

1828 J. HALL *Lett from West* 261 It seems that they were not so well skilled in navigation as the *Lady of the Lake*, who 'paddled her own canoe' very dexterously. **1834** W. G. SIMMS *Guy Rivers* II. 225 He guessed therefore, best haul off, and each..'must paddle his own canoe'. **1844** MARRYAT *Settlers in Canada* viii, I think that it much better that as we all go along together, that every man paddle his own canoe. **1854** SARAH T. BOLTON *Song 'Paddle Your Own Canoe'* i, Where'er your lot may be, Paddle your own canoe. **1887** *Harper's Mag.* Mar. 547/1 They couldn't see how he was to paddle his canoe all alone by himself. **1924** [see BUNCH *v.*[2] 1 c]. **1924** M. KENNEDY *Constant Nymph* xvii. 232 Why can't she leave the fellow to paddle his own canoe? **1949** *Time* 4 July 25/2 They seem more interested in paddling their own canoes than shaping a strong third force that would be the best weapon against the communism they all hate.

II. 3. *trans.* To beat (a person) with a paddle or the like; to 'spank', 'smack'. *U.S.*

1856 OLMSTED *Slave States* 189, I thought it was.. sulkiness, so I paddled him, and made him go to work. **1896** STEVENSON *Weir of Hermiston* iv. 108 She had known him in the cradle and paddled him when he misbehaved. **1919** L. F. CODY *Memories Buffalo Bill* 31, I had started from the porch to paddle every one of them [*sc.* the children]. **1976** 'D. HALLIDAY' *Dolly & Nanny Bird* iv. 48 The first thing a Maggie Bee nurse does in any British household is to ask the mother if she minds if the offspring get paddled from time to time.

4. To use a paddle, in various special senses of the sb.: (*a*) to stir or mix (molten ore) with a paddle; (*b*) to wash or dye (leather) by means of a paddle; (*c*) to stir (the lye in soap-making) with a paddle.

1873 E. SPON *Workshop Receipts* (ser. 1) 382/2 The paddling should be continued until a ring drawn with the spatula may be recognized. **1874** J. A. PHILLIPS *Elem. Metallurgy* 544 The pot-skimmings..are now thrown into the furnace and well paddled with the charge. **1909** H. G. BENNETT *Manuf. Leather* 171 When a quick and even colouring is desired..the goods may be paddled in the first liquors.

5. To use (something) like a paddle.

1929 W. DEEPING *Roper's Row* xxxii. 363 He spread his table napkin, and finding the soup too hot, paddled his spoon in it.

Hence **paddling** *vbl. sb.*[2] and *ppl. a.*[2]

1719 DE FOE *Crusoe* I. x, I was..fatigu'd with Rowing, or Paddling, as it is called. **1855** KINGSLEY *Westw. Ho* xxix, Lazy paddlings through the still lagoons. **1856** OLMSTED *Slave States* 189, I sent them word to give him a good paddling, and handcuff him, and send him back to the railroad. **1874** J. A. PHILLIPS *Elem. Metallurgy* 542 The alternate raking and paddling of the charge is continued at regular intervals. **1875** 'STONEHENGE' *Brit. Sports* II. VIII. ii. §1. 648 Paddling is the portal to excellence in rowing of all kinds. **1888** L. A. SMITH *Music of Waters* 325 The following is a specimen of the paddling-songs, which really form the principal water-music of the Tonga Islands. **1894** *Outing* (U.S.) XXIV. 422/1 A small fleet of paddling canoes and row-boats. **1953** P. PROVENCHER *I live in Woods* i. 6 The crews commenced a lively paddling song on quitting the shore.

paddle-beam, -boat, -box, -crab, etc.: see PADDLE *sb.*[1]

paddle-cock: see PADDLE *sb.*[2]

paddled ('pæd(ə)ld), *a.* [f. PADDLE *sb.*[1] + -ED[2].] Furnished with paddles.

1870 J. ORTON *Andes & Amazons* vii. (1876) 114 Monstrous Saurians, footed, paddled, and winged.

'paddle-fish. [f. PADDLE *sb.*[1] + FISH *sb.*[1]]

A large freshwater fish of the family Polyodontidæ, which includes the two genera *Polyodon* and *Psephurus*, characterized by a projection resembling a paddle attached to the upper part of its head.

[**1686** tr. *Relation Invasion Florida* xxiv. 121 We caught another sort of fish also, called *Pexe-palla*, the *Palat-fish*; the head of it is covered with a kind of an elbow-hood, the upper point whereof is shaped like a Palet or Lingel.] **1807** JANSON *Stranger in America* 191 The paddle-fish..is four feet and four inches in length. The snout resembles in shape the paddle used by Indians in crossing rivers. **1892** J. A. THOMSON *Outl. Zool.* 430 (*Ganoidei*) The paddle-fish or spoon-bill of the Mississippi. **1908** *Century Mag.* July 457/1 In Louisiana it [sc. *Polyodon spatula*] is known as billfish, billdom, and paddlefish. **1948** *Sat. Rev. Lit.* (U.S.) 15 May 26/2 They were assailed by questions about the Paddlefish, the Brindled Stonecat, or the Tessellated Darter. **1962** K. F. LAGLER et al. *Ichthyol.* iv. 110 Examples of partly scaled fishes include the paddlefish (*Polyodon*)..that inhabits streams in Central North America and has also a near-relative, the fresh-water swordbill, *Psephurus*, in China. **1976** *Billings* (Montana) *Gaz.* 16 June 1-C/1 The paddlefish is a living fossil like the Coelacanth..and is found only in two places on earth, the Mississippi River and its tributaries and the Yangtze drainage in China.

2. = *oar-fish* (s.v. OAR *sb.* 6).

1953 *Sun* (Baltimore) 18 Sept. 11/5 One of the world's rarities, an oarfish, or paddle fish, believed to be the origin of sailors' tales of sea serpents, has been caught off Sydney Heads.

paddler[1] ('pædlə(r)). [f. PADDLE *v.*[1] + -ER[1].]

1. One who or that which paddles or dabbles in mire or shallow water. (In quot. 1882, a wild duck.)

1611 COTGR., *Patouillard*, a padler, dabler, slabberer; one that tramples with his feet in plashes of durtie water. *a* **1625** BEAUM. & FL. *Wit at Sev. Weapons* I. i, Well, he may make a padler i' th' world, From hand to mouth, but never a brave swimmer. **1822** *Blackw. Mag.* XI. 163 Those paddlers in sewers, with their mud-ammunition. **1882** SIR R. P. GALLWEY *Fowler in Irel.* 33, I have..seen a string of young paddlers tumble off a bank into the river.

2. *pl.* A child's waterproof knickers or overall.

1928 *Weekly Dispatch* 27 May 15/7 All-black bathing suits. Besides suits, there are the much needed rubber paddlers, caps, and shoes.

'paddler[2]. [f. PADDLE *v.*[2] + -ER[1].]

1. One who paddles a canoe or the like.

1799 *Naval Chron.* III. 63 The paddlers are directed by a man who stands up. **1861** DU CHAILLU *Equat. Afr.* xiv. 218, I had twelve stout paddlers in my canoe.

2. †**a.** = PADDLE *sb.*[1] 2 (*obs.*); **b.** A paddle-steamer (*colloq.*).

1682 WHELER *Journ. Greece* I. 38 They..Row with two Padlers, or little Oars. **1890** *Star* 2 Apr. 1/7 In command of H.M.S. Bulldog, a paddler.

'paddle-,staff. [f. PADDLE *sb.*[1] + STAFF *sb.*]

1. = PADDLE *sb.*[1] 1.

1609 C. BUTLER *Fem. Mon.* (1634) 126 You may make a shift with any ordinary Spade or Paddle-staff. **1622** in *Naworth Househ. Bks.* (Surtees) 195 For lying yron on a paddle staffe for the warriner. **1668** *Dict. Rust.*, *Paddle-staff*, a long Staff with an Iron Bit at the end, like a small Spade, much used by Mole-catchers. **1806** J. GRAHAME *Birds of Scot.* 3 Listening, leans Upon his paddle-staff.

2. *Brewing.* A wooden spade-shaped implement used in mashing. (Cf. PADDLE *sb.*[1] 7.)

1703 *Art & Myst. Vintners* 41 Beat them together with a Paddle-staff for half an hour. *Ibid.* 48 Put this mixture into the Wine, and mix them with a Paddle-staff.

'paddle-,wheel. [See PADDLE *sb.*[1] 3.]

1. A wheel used for propelling a boat or ship: as originally tried, consisting of or having a series of paddles or paddle-like spokes inserted in an axle, drum, or wheel, whence the name; but, eventually, having floats or paddle-boards fitted more or less radially round the circumference, so as to press backward like a succession of paddles against the water. These wheels rotate on a horizontal axis, so that only the lower paddle-boards are under water; they are generally arranged in pairs one on each side of the vessel; in river-steamers, sometimes single and placed in the stern.

Petty called his suggested wheel with actual paddles a 'paddle-wheel', but the term was app. avoided by the inventors and theorists of the 18th c., who wrote simply of 'the wheel', 'water-wheel', 'rowing-wheel', 'revolving oars', etc. And at the eventual employment of the wheel with float-boards instead of paddles, the name 'paddle-wheel' was at first felt to be inappropriate, but it gradually came in after 1815.

1685 PETTY in Fitzmaurice *Life* (1895) iv. 122 To make this Axis and the Paddle wheels turn round, so as the Paddles may take hold of the water in the nature of Oars one after another successively. *Ibid.* 123 The men betwixt decks heaving one way, the men on the upper deck must heave the other way, to give the Axis and Paddle wheels motion. **1805** O. EVANS *Yng. Steam Eng. Guide* p. viii, To propel a boat against the stream the paddlewheel may be attached to the shaft of the flywheel. [**1808** *Specif. Trevithick & Dickinson's Patent* No. 3148 A rowing wheel..furnished with floats or pallets, but which we call our propelling boards.] **1815** *Specif. of Dickinson's Patent* No. 3932 A more efficient method of applying the power or strength of men to turn paddle wheels fixed on the sides..of ships, boats. **1824** R. STUART *Hist. Steam Engine* 83 Mr. Jonathan Hulls..is entitled to the honourable notice of having proposed [1736] the application of paddle-wheels moved by a Steam Engine, to propel ships, instead of wind and sails. **1840** *Encycl. Brit.* (ed. 7) XX. 687/1 In this boat he [Jonathan Hulls] had two paddle-wheels suspended in a frame projecting from its stern. **1841** T. OXLEY in *Mech. Mag.* XXXV. 72 Sir Joseph [Banks] and I both called them oars, or revolving oars; I believe the word 'paddle-wheel' was not known at that time [1808]. **1868** A. K. H. BOYD *Less. Mid. Age* 329 The frith.. is to-day unruffled by a single paddle-wheel. **1897** *Daily News* 23 Sept. 5/3 The old paddle-wheel is already, for regular and rapid service, doomed.

attrib. **1857** G. MUSGRAVE *Pilgr. Dauphiné* II. i. 22 The Saone is..the most favourable to paddle-wheel locomotion. **1863** P. BARRY *Dockyard Econ.* 275 The celebrated *Vladimir*, so well known during the Crimean war, a paddle-wheel boat, and remarkably swift. **1875** KNIGHT *Dict. Mech.*

1592/2 On the axis of each paddle is an arm from which a rod proceeds to an eccentric on the paddle-wheel shaft.

2. A wheel fitted with paddles (PADDLE *sb.*[1] 7) used to keep skins in constant motion in water, in the manufacture of leather, and in similar processes.

1883 HALDANE *Workshop Receipts* Ser. II. 373/1 The skins .. are .. finally brought into a tank of water, not too cold, and kept in constant motion with a paddle-wheel.

3. A device shaped like the wheel of a paddle-boat, used in a game of chance.

1926 ADE *Let.* 26 Oct. (1973) 114 We had games as follows: one roulette, one hazard, .. one wheel of fortune for cash, one paddle wheel for fancy baskets, dolls, boxes of candy etc. **1935** *Sun* (Baltimore) 22 July 7/4 Operation of paddle wheels, bingo devices and other alleged games of chance would no longer be tolerated. **1939** *Ibid.* 24 Apr. 18/1 Prince George's county .. secured passage of a measure that would legalize not only pinball games, but bingo, paddle wheels and other similar devices. **1961** J. SCARNE *Compl. Guide Gambling* xix. 459 *Paddle wheel or raffle wheel,* a carnival wheel each of whose numbered sections contain one, two, or three numbers. Most such wheels have a counter laydown raffle chart on which bets are placed.

4. *attrib.* † **paddle-wheel aeroplane** or **aircraft** = *cyclogiro, -gyro* s.v. CYCLO-.

1935 *Technical Rep. Aeronaut. Res. Committee 1933–34* I. 8 We have also considered a number of proposals for the construction of .. paddlewheel aeroplanes. **1939** *Jrnl. R. Aeronaut. Soc.* XLIII. 756 Unusual aircraft such as flapping wing aircraft, paddle wheel aircraft, tail-first aeroplanes.

paddle-wood: see PADDLE *sb.*[1] 12.

paddo, paddow, also **padda, paddie,** northern forms of PADDOCK, frog, toad; so **paddo-pipe.**

c **1375** *Sc. Leg. Saints* ii. (*Paulus*) 770 A fowle padow at þe laste he keste, þat wes laythe to se. *a* **1568** *Lyndesay's Play* 976 (Bannatyne MS.) Quhat and the paddois [= *Satyre* 1381 padoks] nipt my tais? **1706** PHILLIPS, *Paddow-pipe,* a sort of Herb. **1776** WITHERING *Brit. Plants* (1796) II. 5 *Hippuris*... Common Mares-tail. Paddowpipe. **1870** R. CHAMBERS *Pop. Rhymes Scot.* 88 A Paddo then came loup-loup-louping out o' the well.

paddock ('pædək), *sb.*[1] (Also *Sc.* 9 poddock, 8–9 puddock.) [f. PAD *sb.*[1] + dimin. suffix -OCK.]

1. A frog. (Now *Sc.* and *north. dial.*)

c **1350** in *Rel. Ant.* I. 8 *Rana,* a paddoke. **1388** WYCLIF *Exod.* viii. 2, 3, Y schal smyte alle thi termys with paddoks [1382 frogges]; and the flood schal buyle out paddokis [1382 froggis]. **1530** PALSGR. 502/2 My bely crowleth, I wene there be some padockes in it, .. *des grenouilles dedans.* **1608** TOPSELL *Serpents* (1658) 725 There be three kindes of Frogs .. the first is the little green Frog: the second is this Padock, having a crook back .. and the third is the Toad. **1697** DRYDEN *Virg. Georg.* III. 812 The Water-Snake, whom Fish and Paddocks fed. **1724** RAMSAY *Health* 65 Bak'd puddock's legs. **1825** BROCKETT *N.C. Gloss., Paddick,* or *Paddock,* a frog... Never a toad. **1854** H. MILLER *Sch. & Schm.* xii. 126/1 Are we eels or puddocks, that we are sent to live in a loch?

† **b.** A toad. *Obs.* (exc. as literary archaism.)

13.. *K. Alis.* 6126 Evetis, and snakes, and paddokes brode, .. Al vermyn they eteth. *c* **1375** *Sc. Leg. Saints* ii. (*Paulus*) 750 þan þai .. a padok gert hym drink in hy. *c* **1440** *Promp. Parv.* 376/2 Paddok, toode, *bufo.* **1530** PALSGR. 250/2 Paddocke, *crapavlt.* **1579** SPENSER *Sheph. Cal.* Dec. 70 The grieslie Todestoole .. And loathed Paddocks lording on the same. **1656** BLOUNT *Glossogr., Paddock,* .. a Toad. **1870** MORRIS *Earthly Par.* II. III. 240 O'er his head the bat Hung, and the paddock on the hearth-stone sat.

c. *transf.* Applied in obloquy to a person.

In quot. 1605 a familiar spirit in the shape of a toad?

a **1450** *Cov. Myst.* xvii. (1841) 164, I xal prune that paddok [= frog], and prevyn hym as a pad [= toad]. **1563** WINƷET *Wks.* (1890) II. 31 Certane padokis, filthy verming, .. of the quhilk sort are the Pelagianis. **1605** SHAKS. *Macb.* I. i. 9 Padock calls anon: faire is foule, and foule is faire. **1893** STEVENSON *Catriona* xv. 174 But there was grandfather's siller tester in the puddock's heart of him.

2. A kind of rude sledge used for carrying large stones. *Sc.*

1824 MACTAGGART *Gallovid. Encycl., Paddock,* .. a machine shaped like a frog, for carrying large stones. **1825–80** in JAMIESON. **1887** BULLOCH *Pynours* vi, The slip, sled, or paddock came into use. It was a sort of strong wooden cradle.

3. *attrib.* and *Comb.* (chiefly *dial.*), as *paddock-brood, -face*; **paddock-cheese** = *paddock-stool*; **paddock-hair,** the soft down or hair on unfledged birds and on new-born babies; **paddock-pipe,** a species of *Equisetum* (Horse-tail), esp. *E. limosum*; also Mare's Tail, *Hippuris vulgaris*; **paddock-ride, -rod, -rud, -spew,** frogs' or toads' spawn; **paddock-spindle,** *Orchis mascula* (Britten & Holl.); **paddock-stone** = TOAD-STONE; **paddock-stool** = TOADSTOOL *sb.*

a **1627** MIDDLETON *Witch* I. ii, Here's a spawn or two Of the same *paddock-brood. **14..** *Harl. MS.* 1002, lf. 144 b/2 *Hic boletus,* a *padokchese. **1724** RAMSAY *Vision* xxi, Batavius, with his *paddock-face. **1827** TAYLOR *Poems* 67 (E.D.D.), I foun' sax bare wee things Wi' *paddock hair upon their wings. **1830** GALT *Lawrie T.* I. vi. (1849) 17 For nearly thirteen years I had sat on my hunkers in the paddock hair, under the wing of a kind parent. **1673** *Wedderburn's Vocab.* 18 (Jam.) *Aequisetum,* a *paddock-pipe. **1778** LIGHTFOOT *Flora Scotica* (1792) 648 Marsh Horse-tail, .. Paddock-pipe. **1720** RAMSAY *Rise & Fall of Stocks* 114 A shot starn .. found neist day on hillock side, Na better seems nor *paddock ride. [Cf. JELLY *sb.*[1] 2 b; *fallen star* s.v. FALLEN *ppl. a.*] **1508** KENNEDIE *Flyting w. Dunbar* 342 And thou come, Fule! in Marche or Februere, Thair till a pule, and drank the *paddok rod [*v.rr.* rude, roid]. **1488** *Inv. R. Wardrobe* (1815) 10 Item a ring with a *paddokstane, with a charnale. **1700** E. LHWYD in Rowlands *Mona Antiqua* (1723) 338 Besides the Snake-stones .. the Highlanders have their Snail-Stones, Paddoc-Stones .. etc. to all which they attribute their several Virtues. *c* **1450** *Alphita* (Anecd. Oxon.) 70/7 *Fungus* agaricus crescit in arboribus .. *paddoc-stol. **1483** *Cath. Angl.* 265/2 A Paddokstole, *boletus, fungus .. asparagus.* **1787** BURNS *Verses written at Selkirk* iv, Now gawkies, tawpies, gowks, and fools, .. May sprout like simmer puddock-stools. **1824** MACTAGGART *Gallovid. Encycl.* s.v. *Hillfowk,* As rotten as a yellow puddock stool.

Hence **'paddocky** *a.,* abounding in frogs.

1828 J. WILSON in *Blackw. Mag.* XXIV. 284 Over all the water-cressy and puddocky ditches.

paddock ('pædək), *sb.*[2] Also 7 puddock. [app. a phonetic alteration of PARROCK: cf. *poddish* for *porridge,* etc.]

1. a. A small field or enclosure; usually a plot of pasture-land adjoining or near a house or stable.

[**1547** in Hunter *Biggar & Ho. Fleming* xxiv. (1862) 312 Item in the Boghall, that draws in plough and paddock xiij oxin.] **1622** MABBE tr. *Aleman's Guzman d' Alf.* I. 82 A fierce Bull, which .. they had let out of the Paddok. **1669** WORLIDGE *Syst. Agric.* (1681) 330 A Puddock, or Purrock; a small Inclosure. **1759** WESLEY *Wks.* (1872) II. 471 A rude multitude quickly ran together, to a paddock adjoining to the town. **1872** YOUATT *Horse* iv. (ed. 4) 86 Let him [the hunter] therefore have his paddock as well as his loose box. **1885** MISS BRADDON *Wyllard's Weird* I. ii. 69 There was only the extent of a wide paddock and a lawn between the hall-door and that grand old gateway.

b. *spec.* Such an enclosure forming part of a stud farm.

1856 H. H. DIXON *Post & Paddock* iii. 59 For downright breeding .. Rawcliffe Paddocks quite bear the palm. *Ibid.* 62 The strength of the pasturage, and the beautiful combination of hill and dale make these paddocks a perfect paradise for blood-mares and foals. **1894** ARMATAGE *Horse* viii. 115 The colt may be mounted in the paddock.

c. In Australia and New Zealand, any field or piece of land enclosed by fencing, irrespective of size or land use.

1822 J. DIXON *Narr. Voy. New South Wales* 58, I saw a few paddocks of clover and English grasses, in as good condition as I have seen the same fields in England. **1832** BISCHOFF *Van Diemen's Land* vi. 148 There is one paddock of 100 acres, fenced on four sides. **1847** A. HARRIS *Settlers & Convicts* xiv. 279 In ten months' time from their occupying the farm, there was one of the sides of a paddock fence put up. **1869** TOWNEND *Remin. Australia* 180 The church .. stood by itself in the middle of a paddock. **1873** TROLLOPE *Austral. & N.Z.* II. xxiii. 368 Vast paddocks containing perhaps 20,000 acres each. **1881** *Gentl. Mag.* Jan. 67 The bullock paddock .. contained 6000 acres, and was securely fenced in with the usual post and rails. **1891** *'Coo-ee', Tales Austral. Life* 121 The fields, or paddocks, as they call them here [in Australia], were pretty. **1900** F. CAMPBELL *Three Moons* 314 Mrs. Tredwin cantering across the ten-mile paddock. **1911** C. E. W. BEAN *'Dreadnought' of Darling* i. 7 The Western Division is inhabited—indeed it is all fenced into paddocks. **1916** J. B. COOPER *Coo-oo-ee* ix. 115 Sandy was in his pumpkin paddock ('pumpkins were the things to feed pigs on'). **1924** H. T. GIBSON *That Gibbie Galoot* xv. 56 By the way, you Colonials call a field a paddock, or more often a paddeck. **1930** L. G. D. ACLAND *Early Canterbury Runs* (ser. 1) i. 7 In the early sixties .. expense and the scarcity of water prevented much sub-division into paddocks on most of the plains stations. **1937** 'W. HATFIELD' *I find Australia* iv. 59 The 'horse-paddock' near the homestead was eight miles by eight, and that wasn't a big 'paddock'. **1957** *N.Z. Listener* 22 Nov. 4/3 'Creek' and 'paddock' are New Zealandisms, because they mean something quite different in the English of England. It is of some significance that Katherine Mansfield uses both words only in their New Zealand sense. **1962** J. FRAME *Edge of Alphabet* xv. 81 With the gate into the field (they call it paddock) shut. **1963** B. PEARSON *Coal Flat* xvii. 310 In the lush paddocks on the river flat, a few prosperous farmers ran sheep. **1968** K. WEATHERLY *Roo Shooter* 7 In the forty-five-thousand-acre paddock at the bottom of the rocky hill country the rains have scoured great washouts in the slopes. **1977** *National Times* (Austral.) 17 Jan. 16/4 (Advt.), Lot 7: Homestead Block: 166.05 ha (410 acres) Freehold, gently undulating country running down to river, subdivided into 9 paddocks.

d. *fig.*

1841–4 EMERSON *Ess., Nature* Wks. (Bohn) I. 226 Estates of romance, compared with which their actual possessions are shanties and paddocks. **1875** DOWDEN *Shaks.* 22 Keble was born and bred in the Anglican paddock. **1880** G. MEREDITH *Tragic Com.* (1881) 21 A country where literature is confined to its little paddock, without influence on the larger field .. of the social world.

2. *spec.* **a.** (See quots.)

1678 PHILLIPS, *Paddock,* .. a walk or division in a Park. **1706** *Ibid., Paddock* or *Paddock-course,* a place in a Park pal'd in very narrow on both sides, for Hounds or Gray-hounds to run Matches. **1783** AINSWORTH *Lat. Dict.* (Morell) I, A paddock in a park, *septum, circus venatorius.*

b. *Horse-racing.* A turf enclosure near the race-course, where the horses and jockeys are assembled in preparation for the race.

1862 *All Yr. Round* Mar. 29 Three and thirty thorough-bred colts have dipped down from the paddock to the post. **1881** *Daily News* 2 June 5 The genuine public .. drove thoughtlessly past the paddock .. and disposed itself either in the cords near the winning-post or on the slope of the hill.

3. *Mining.* (*Colonial.*) **a.** An open excavation in a superficial deposit. **b.** A store-place for ore, etc.

1862 *Otago: Goldfields & Resources* 34 Sod walls .. are largely used in making dams and 'paddocks'. **1869** R. B. SMYTH *Gloss. Mining Terms, Paddock,* an excavation made for procuring washdirt in shallow ground. A place built near the mouth of a shaft where quartz or washdirt is stored. **1874** A. BATHGATE *Colonial Experiences* viii. 93 This process is carried on for months, the tail-race being prolonged into the space from which the ground has been washed away, until a larger hole or 'paddock' is taken out, with precipitous sides, varying in height from a couple of feet to two hundred or more. **1876** W. J. J. SPRY *Cruise Challenger* vi. (ed. 7) 85 Next the lime tufa was bored into, and now large 'paddocks' are sunk to a depth of over 20 feet in the decomposed igneous rock. **1895** *Otago Witness* 21 Nov. 22/5 (Morris) A paddock was opened at the top of the beach, but rock-bottom was found.

4. *attrib.,* as *paddock-course, -critic, fence, -gate, sheet.* **paddock-grazing,** in dairy farming, a method of pasture management developed by the French farmer, André Voisin, in which several fields are used in rotation; hence, as a back-formation, **paddock-graze** *v. trans.*

1704 F. FULLER *Med. Gymn.* (1711) 234 Horses run without Riders upon 'em something after the manner of a Paddock-Course. **1707** J. CHAMBERLAYNE *St. Gt. Brit.* III. vii. 313 The Nobility and Gentry have their .. Paddock Courses, Horse-Rases [etc.]. **1897** *Daily News* 21 June 10/6 His brilliant form .. made a great impression upon the paddock critics. **1864** R. HENNING *Let.* 4 Mar. (1966) 156 The 'Station Creek' .. came down a roaring river .. and swept down with it the whole of the paddock fence which crossed its bed, though it was built in that part of entire trunks of trees. **1800** MRS. HERVEY *Mourtray Fam.* I. 109 They were within a hundred yards of the paddock gate. **1908** E. J. BANFIELD *Confessions of Beachcomber* II. iii. 326 The tribe cut off the iron bracing from the paddock gates. **1911** C. E. W. BEAN *'Dreadnought' of Darling* i. 11 The coach had stopped at a paddock gate. **1969** 'J. ASHFORD' *Prisoner at Bar* v. 37 A herd of Frisians were paddock-grazing the nearest fields. **1960** *Farmer & Stockbreeder* 16 Feb. 77/3 It was no use introducing strip- or paddock-grazing unless this was accompanied by a marked increase in stocking. **1962** K. N. RUSSELL *Fishwick's Dairy Farming* (ed. 3) II. 228 This .. is the gospel according to Voisin, whose system of rotational paddock grazing Mr. Pearson has recently adopted. **1970** C. S. BARNARD et al. *Milk Production* xv. 240 Paddock grazing is an alternative to strip grazing which obviates the daily task of moving electric fences. Semi-permanent fences are erected to create paddocks of a size and number that enable fresh grazing to be offered every 1–7 days. **1970** R. JEFFRIES *Dead Man's Bluff* ix. 85 The bloke who invented paddock grazing knew a thing or two. **1971** *Power Farming* Mar. 40/2 Paddock grazing is the modern way to really efficient grassland management. It enables grass to be accurately rationed ensuring that each cow has the correct intake of highly nutritious herbage, resulting in increased milk yield per acre and improved milk quality. **1975** *Country Life* 26 June 1702/3 Modern paddock-grazing owes much to the work of ICI .. pioneers of the one-day, 21-paddock, two-sward system. **1963** E. H. EDWARDS *Saddlery* xxi. 160 The everyday exercise sheets .. are the same shape as a paddock sheet, but usually a few inches larger. **1977** *Horse & Hound* 10 June 28/1 (Advt.), Coloured Rollers, For day rugs or paddock sheets.

'paddock, *v.* [f. PADDOCK *sb.*[2]]

1. *trans.* **a.** To enclose or fence in (a sheep-run, etc.) (*Australia*). **b.** To shut up or enclose in or as in a paddock.

1873 TROLLOPE *Australia* I. xx. 302 When a run is 'paddocked' shepherds are not required;—but boundary-riders are employed. *Ibid.* II. xii. 214 The sheep are all 'paddocked',—that is, kept in by fences,—so that shepherding is unnecessary. **1873** [see PADDOCKED *ppl. a.*]. **1884** T. WALDEN in *Harper's Mag.* LXIX. 433 Droves of oxen, sheep, and swine were paddocked close by. **1930** L. G. D. ACLAND *Early Canterbury Runs* (ser. 1) v. 111 He paddocked the sheep one night at the Rangitata Bridge. *Ibid.,* Meaning to have breakfast at the hotel where his sheep were paddocked. **1941** BAKER *N.Z. Slang* v. 40 *To paddock land,* to put up fences; *to paddock stock,* to put stock into a paddock.

2. *Mining.* (*Colonial.*) To store (ore, etc.) in a paddock (see PADDOCK *sb.*[2] 3 b). Also, to excavate washdirt in shallow ground (see PADDOCK *sb.*[2] 3 a); occas. const. *out.*

1860 *National Mag.* VIII. 307/1 Those who have seen Chinamen at work 'paddocking' in the worn-out alluvial gold-diggings of Australia, can speak for their steady, untiring industry. **1863** V. PYKE in *App. Jrnls. House Reps. N.Z.* D. VI. 18 Many .. who held river claims worked very successfully by wing dams, consisting of bags of sand laid into the stream, so as to cut off a portion of its bed, which, being drained by pumping, was paddocked out and passed through the cradle. **1899** *N. Queensland Herald* 8 Feb. 31 They have gathered and stacked surface stone till they have paddocked sufficient for a crushing in the mill yard.

Hence **'paddocked** *ppl. a.,* **'paddocking** *vbl. sb.*

1873 RANKEN *Dom. Australia* v. (1874) 91 This will completely loosen the little dirt found in paddocked sheep. **1881** A. C. GRANT *Bush-Life Queensland* II. 175 Gathering up the paddocked horses, he caught and saddled his own and his master's. **1900** E. A. HILL (of N.S. Wales) in *Birm. Weekly Post* 25 Aug. 5/4 Paddocking was not universal, as is now the case.

† **'padduck.** *Obs.* In 6 paduck, padduke. Some kind of cloth. (Cf. *pack duck,* s.v. DUCK *sb.*[3])

1545 *Rates of Customs* c j b, Padduke the c. elles xxs. **1583** *Ibid.* D v b, Paduck the c. elles xxiiijs.

paddy ('pædɪ), *sb.*[1] Forms: (α. 6 batte, 7 batty.) β. 7 paddie, 8–9 paddi, 8 pady, (patty), 9 paddee, 9– padi, 7– paddy. [a. Malay *pādī* rice in the straw, in Javanese and other Malay langs. *pārī*. The identity of this with Canarese *batta, bhatta* rice in the husk, whence the *batte, batty* of early authors, is uncertain.]

1. a. Rice in the straw, or (in commerce) in the husk. Also, the rice plant. Now freq. written *padi.*

[**1598** W. PHILLIPS *Linschoten* 70 Rice, of a lesse price and slighter then the other Ryce, and is called Batte.] **1623** *St. Papers, Col.* 146 The people addict themselves wholly to the planting of paddie for their maintenance. [**1698** FRYER *Acc. E. India & P.* 67 The Ground between this and the great Breach..bears good Batty.] *Ibid.* 244 Furlongs loaded with Rice or Paddy, being courser than the Indian. **1782** *Ann. Reg.* 65 Collecting paddy and beating the rice from the straw. **1818** JAS. MILL *Brit. India* II. v. v. 490 His only remaining resource was in the paddy in the fields. **1879** *Cassell's Techn. Educ.* I. 18/2 Rice which comes to us in the husk is called by its Indian name 'paddy'. **1893** F. A. SWETTENHAM *About Perak* 41 The country for miles round Parit Buntar has been converted from jungle into fields of sugarcane and padi. **1894** [see NASI]. **1900** C. O. BLAGDEN in W. W. Skeat *Malay Magic* iii. 58 In the inland villages it is regarded as a great crime to use the sickle (*sabit*) for cutting the *padi.* **1931** *Economist* 19 Dec. 1168/2 Thousands of acres of paddy are being planted in isolated plots that were merely abandoned swamps. **1943** *Sun* (Baltimore) 10 June 12/2 Unmilled or rough rice, growing or cut, is known as 'paddy'. **1966** S. M. SADEEK *Windswept & Other Stories* (1969) 2 The strong winds whistled their..tunes.. through the whispering sugarcanes and the sheets and sheets of shimmering padi—green, or golden—under the tropic sun. **1969** J. M. GULLICK *Malaysia* ii. 47 'Padi' is the term for unhusked rice and is used to denote the rice plant. **1971** R. RUSSELL tr. *Ahmad's Shore & Wave* i. 9 All around is flat country..and dotted about the plains are muddy bluish pools which from the air look like big pieces of blue glass set in the fields of green waving paddy. **1972** M. SHEPPARD *Taman Indera* 163 The grey water bottles are left to dry for two or three days and are then fired in a shallow trench, using coconut fibre, coconut shells and padi husks.

b. = *paddy-field.*

1948 *Amer. Speech* XXIII. 229/2 *Paddy,* a rice field. **1972** *Sci. Amer.* May 23/1 The entire immediate area had been a rice paddy, but during the years when no cultivation had occurred, the rice had been replaced by a very tall reed. **1974** *Encycl. Brit. Micropædia* VII. 668/3 *Paddy,* a wet field used for growing rice. **1974** *Indonesian Observer* 26 July 1/3 The President was informed that the irrigation project whose construction work was begun 1936 but stopped until 1971 will be capable of irrigating 50,330 hectares of paddies. **1974** *Nat. Geographic* Aug. 252 A tree-lined road cut through harvested grainfields and paddies resting under a crystal-blue sky.

2. Short for PADDY-BIRD; *ellipt.* its feathers.

1777 G. FORSTER *Voy. round World* II. 568 Rice-birds, commonly called paddies. **1891** *Times* 24 Oct. 13/2 Feathers... Short selected are dearer, white and gray paddy firm.

3. *attrib.* and *Comb.*, as ***paddy-boat, clearing, -crop, -field, flat, -grinding, -ground, -pounder, tax***, etc.; **paddy-insect**, a Chinese species of silkworm from Hainan.

1698 FRYER *Acc. E. India & P.* 162 Two hundred Paddy-Boats with their Convoys. **1762** WOOD in *Phil. Trans.* LII. 417 You descend into the paddy, or rice fields. **1871** *Athenæum* 27 May 650 Mr. Cooper..was upset into a newly-flooded paddy-field by the great man's outriders. **1880** C. R. MARKHAM *Peruv. Bark* vi. 354 They call these low swampy valleys on each side of a stream paddy flats, whether they are actually cultivated or not. **1892** *Daily News* 15 Mar. 3/1 The Secretary of State has informed the Governor of Ceylon that..the time has arrived for abolishing the paddy tax. **1937** *Discovery* Jan. 7/2 Spacious padi fields. **1971** *Illustr. Weekly India* 25 Apr. 42/1 The large tracts of golden paddy fields blended with the molten gold of Niger flowers. **1977** *Borneo Bull.* 7 May 1/5 Four people..were electrocuted in a padi field at Kampong Keriam, near Tutong, last month when an overhead power cable collapsed on to the field.

paddy ('pædɪ), *sb.*² [Irish pet-form of *Padraig* or *Patrick*.]

1. (With capital initial.) Nickname for an Irishman; also used as a form of address, often felt to be derog.

1780 A. YOUNG *Tour Irel.* I. 116 Paddies were swimming their horses in the sea to cure the mange. **1826** DISRAELI *Viv. Grey* IV. iv, Paddy was tripped up. **1899** *Westm. Gaz.* 18 Mar. 8/1 We were surprised to see that our entire staff of office-boys had suddenly turned Paddies, wearing the green with a most becoming *bonhomie*. **1907** G. B. SHAW *John Bull's Other Island* III. 75 *Hodson*... Dont you be taken in by my ole man, Paddy. *Matthew*... Paddy yourself! How dar you call me Paddy? **1916** 'TAFFRAIL' *Pincher Martin* ii. 29 'Stop yer bloomin' noise, Paddy!'.. And Pincher suffered no further inconvenience at the hands of Peter Flannagan.

b. Phr. ***to come the paddy over***, to bamboozle, humbug. *slang.*

1821 *Blackw. Mag.* 608 Fairly came the paddy over him.

c. (With capital initial.) The proprietary name of an Irish whiskey; a drink of this. Also (sometimes with lower-case initial) Irish whiskey generally.

1925 *Trade Marks Jrnl.* 23 Dec. 2827 Paddy... Whisky. Cork Distilleries Company, Limited,..Cork, Ireland; distillers. **1971** J. AIKEN *Nightly Deadshade* vii. 77 Milly is drinking port..and O'Grady, double Paddys. **1974** D. SEAMAN *Bomb that could Lip-Read* vii. 51 Will you gentlemen join me in a drink now?.. Three Paddies, then, is it? **1975** *New Yorker* 25 Aug. 40/3 Did she put Irish whiskey in your glass, that Paddy junk? We asked for Scotch. **1976** N. FREELING *Lake Isle* xx. 140 The drop of paddy's fearfully dear here. I've no opinion of the stuff the supermarket calls Scotch.

2. A bricklayer's or builder's labourer.

1856 EMERSON *Eng. Traits* (1902) 165 The men were common masons, with paddies to help. **1877** *N.W. Linc. Gloss.* s.v., A bricklayer's paddy..brings him bricks and mortar.

3. An unlicensed almanac, called more fully ***Paddy's Watch*** and ***paddywhack almanac*** (see PADDYWHACK 1 b).

1876 *Mid-Yorks. Gloss.*, *Paddywatch*,..or *Paddy*,..an almanac. **1886** *N. & Q.* 7th Ser. I. 478/1, I have often heard [*a* 1834]..'Have you an almanac?' and the answer has been, 'We have a Paddy'.

4. A passion, a temper; = PADDYWACK 2. *colloq.*

1894 HENTY *Dorothy's Double* I. 132 They goes out looking red in the face, and in a regular paddy. **1929** J. OWEN *Shepherd & Child* i. 14 Tristina went—and that without pulling the door behind her 'in a paddy', as she would have done if the order had come from Miss Trellis. **1933** [see IRISH *sb.* 5]. **1959** 'O. MILLS' *Stairway to Murder* v. 56 It was my awful temper. I used to get into the biggest paddies when I was a kiddie. **1959** I. & P. OPIE *Lore & Lang. Schoolch.* x. 178 They taunt the person:..'Don't get in a paddy.' **1975** J. COWLEY *Mandrake Root* (1976) xvi. 280 You're a pigheaded Stilwell... Got a real paddy when you let go.

5. 'A well-boring drill having cutters that expand on pressure; *paddy-drill*' (Funk).

6. A name in North Carolina of the ruddy duck, *Erismatura rubida*; = PADDYWACK 4. Also ***paddywhack***.

7. In Black English, a white person; also *attrib.* or as *adj.*

1946 C. HIMES *Black on Black* (1973) 256 'Hey, don't spit in the sink where you wash the glasses,' some paddy down the bar said. **1962** [see BOOT *sb.*³ 1 e]. **1966** *Sat. Rev.* (U.S.) 15 Oct. 74/2 Man, how I hate Paddies (white people)! **1967** *Trans-Action* Apr. 6/1 This field worker..had run with 'Paddy' (white), 'Chicano' (Mexican), and 'Blood' (Negro) sets since the age of twelve. **1970** R. D. ABRAHAMS *Positively Black* i. 8 The black became beautiful and the white became nothing but a honky and a paddy. **1972** J. WAMBAUGH *Blue Knight* (1973) xiv. 240, I spotted a paddy hustler taking a guy up the back stairs. *Ibid.* 241 Paddy hustling was always a Negro flimflam and that's where the name came from, but lately I've seen white hustlers using this scam on other paddies. **1973** D. BARNES *See the Woman* (1974) 68 'What are you?' Grear said to West. 'This paddy's interpreter?' *Ibid.* 70 Biggest paddy whore in Normandie Avenue. **1976** —— *Yesterday is Dead* (1977) II. 199 Hollister..found he was the only white face in the place... 'You know..I'm the only paddy in here.'

8. *Railway* and *Colliery slang.* (See quots.)

1965 H. SHEPPARD *Dict. Railway Slang* 8 *Paddy*, colliery train from mine to railhead. **1971** D. J. SMITH *Discovering Railwayana* x. 58 *Paddy*, train conveying coal from the pithead to distant sidings. **1977** *Guardian Weekly* 4 Dec. 19/4 Once out of the cage, there was a quarter of a mile to walk over pit railway sleepers, dodging heavy equipment, to the 'paddy' whose proper name is 'the endless rope haulage manrider'.

9. In *Combs.* of **Paddy** or **Paddy's**: **Paddy Doyle** *Services' slang*, confinement in the cells, esp. in phr. ***to do***, or ***doing, Paddy Doyle***; **Paddy's hurricane** *Naval slang*, a flat calm; **Paddy's lantern** *colloq.*, the moon; **Paddy('s) lucerne** *Austral.*, a local name for the tropical evergreen shrub, *Sida rhombifolia*, of the family Malvaceæ, a pest in parts of Australia, although cultivated elsewhere for the fibre it yields; **paddy mail** = sense 8 above; **paddy wagon** *slang* (orig. *U.S.*), a police van; occas., a police car; **Paddy Wester** *slang*, an inefficient or inexperienced seaman; (see also quots.).

1919 Paddy Doyle [see C.B. s.v. C III. 3]. **1932** E. WEEKLEY *Words & Names* xii. 174 Doing '*Paddy Doyle*' as a euphemism for doing 'time' in the cells. **1948** PARTRIDGE *Dict. Forces' Slang* 136 *Paddy Doyle*, a lower-deck term for 'detention cell'—singular or collective. *a* **1865** SMYTH *Sailor's Work-bk.* (1867) 514 *Paddy's hurricane*, not wind enough to float the pennant. **1891** H. PATTERSON *Illustr. Naut. Dict.* 132 *Paddy's hurricane*, when there is little or no wind, so that the pennant hangs down alongside the mast. **1897** 'F. B. WILLIAMS' *On Many Seas* 43 We came on deck to find a 'Paddy's Hurricane'—a calm. **1903** A. SONNICHSEN *Deep Sea Vagabonds* vii. 114 The winds here never blew at all, or, after the manner of Paddy's hurricane, up and down. **1958** J. G. R. BISSET *Sail Ho!* v. 48 A dead calm was known as 'Paddy's hurricane'. **1933** P. A. EADDY *Hull Down* v. 104 Work round the deck and up aloft is a hundred times easier when 'Paddy's Lantern' is hung out. **1937** PARTRIDGE *Dict. Slang* 600/2 *Paddy's lantern*, the moon: nautical... Prob. after parish-lantern. **1898** MORRIS *Austral Eng.* 195/2 Hemp, Queensland,..name given to the common tropical weed *Sida rhombifolia*... Called also Paddy Lucerne. **1926** 'J. DOONE' *Timely Tips for New Australians* (Gloss.), Paddy's lucerne.—A prevalent type of weed. **1965** *Austral. Encycl.* VIII. 127/2 Paddy's lucerne is so tough and difficult to eradicate that it is reckoned one of the most formidable weed-pests in warmer parts of the Commonwealth. **1945** *Penguin New Writing* XXIII. 85 Colliers were drawn toward it from all the surrounding parts. His mate, Ron Loss, came in by the paddy-mail. **1976** *Star* (Sheffield) 29 Nov. 1/2 A man died today when ten miners were thrown from a paddy mail which crashed at a pit on the outskirts of Barnsley... The paddy mail—a train for carrying miners underground —struck a wooden roof support which had become dislodged, and was derailed. **1930** *Chicago Tribune* 26 Mar. 3/6 He was informed by the pink faced lockup keeper that all Chicago's 'paddy waggons' are motor driven. **1932** J. T. FARRELL *Young Lonigan* vi. 259 First thing you know they'll have you in a jam, and you'll be riding in the paddy wagon. **1946** C. HIMES *Black on Black* (1973) 260 The police..held all four of us there waiting for the ambulance and the paddy wagon. **1964** M. BANTON *Policeman in Community* iii. 51, 2 Patrolmen in a wagon ('Paddy-wagon' or 'Black Maria'). **1967** *N.Z. Listener* 20 Jan. 3/4 A policeman is my guide, and a paddy-wagon my carriage, for a late evening trip around the town's night-spots. **1972** H. C. RAE *Shooting Gallery* iv. 258 The Paddy-wagon, customarily on duty at the cul-de-sac beyond the junction. **1973** *Sunday Mail* (Brisbane) 18 Mar. 25/6 A Police paddy wagon..cruised by. **1974** *Times* 21 Sept. 14/2 Police, dogs, ambulances..a gigantic paddy-wagon. **1927** F. H. SHAW *Knocking Around* xiii. 125 He was not an actual Paddy-Wester, but he had sailed shipmates with many of them. **1929** F. C. BOWEN *Sea Slang* 100 *Paddy Wester*, a fake seaman with a dead man's discharge, after a notorious boarding-house keeper in Liverpool who shipped thousands of green men as A.B.'s for a consideration. **1937** PARTRIDGE *Dict. Slang* 600/1 *Paddy Wester*; occ. *paddywester*. A bogus seaman carrying a dead man's discharge-papers; a very incompetent or dissolute seaman. **1938** W. E. DEXTER *Rope-Yarns* 125 They had a pack of fake seamen sailing on dead men's discharges—a crew of 'Paddy Westers'.

Hence **'Paddyism**, an Irish peculiarity, Irishism.

1801 SOUTHEY *Lett.* (1856) I. 167, I have discovered two tricks of pure Paddyism. **1890** CLARK RUSSELL *Ocean Trag.* I. iv. 87, I could see, by hearing her (to use a Paddyism), the pout of her lip.

paddy ('pædɪ), *a.* [f. PAD *sb.*³ + -Y¹.] Having pads; cushion-like; soft, mild; also, 'comfortable', placidly self-satisfied.

Not in common use. The contextual sense is not entirely clear in some of the examples.

1865 C. M. YONGE *Clever Woman* II. iii. 38 A pair of plump, paddy-looking old friends. **1873** —— *Pillars of House* II. xix. 156 The paddy good-natured face in bed. **1958** L. M. BOSTON *Chimneys of Green Knowe* 132 He was woken by Orlando's whiskery face poking him in the ear, and a paddy foot on his eyelid. **1962** N. MARSH *Hand in Glove* ii. 53 The impressive things about Sergeant Raikes were his size and his mildness... He said: 'Good afternoon, miss,' in a loud but paddy voice.

[**paddy**, *a.*², an error for *baddy* in Motley, followed by recent dicts. Explained as: Low in character or manners; mean; contemptible; poor.

[**1585-6** T. DIGGES *Let. to Walsingham* 2/12 Jan. (P.R.O.) Such baddy persons as commonly, in voluntary procurements, men are glad to accept.] Quoted in **1864** MOTLEY *Netherl.* I. vii. 393 as 'paddy'. Hence in **1864** WEBSTER, and some later Dicts.]

'paddy-bird. [f. PADDY *sb.*¹ + BIRD *sb.*]

1. The Java sparrow, *Padda* (or *Munia*) *oryzivora.*

1727 A. HAMILTON *New Acc. E. Ind.* I. xiv. 161 The Paddy-bird is also good in their Season.

2. Anglo-Indian name for species of white egret, which frequent the paddy-fields.

1858 R. HUNTER in Mitchell *Mem. R. Nesbit* 406 Egrets or white herons, by Anglo-Indians with little taste termed paddy-birds. **1884** MISS C. F. G. CUMMING in *Macm. Mag.* Feb. 303/1 Multitudes of spirit-like white cranes, or paddy-birds, paddle about.

3. A species of Sheathbill, *Chionis minor.*

1894 NEWTON *Dict. Birds* 832 *note*, The cognate species of Kerguelen Land is named by the sealers 'Sore-eyed Pigeon', ..as well as 'Paddy-bird'—the last perhaps from its white plumage resembling that of some of the smaller Egrets.

paddymelon ('pædɪˌmɛlən). Also **paddymalla; pad-, paddi(e)-, pade-, pady-, -melon, -mellun.** [A corruption of an aboriginal name, the first element of which has been conjectured to be the same as in *pata-gorang* (in Sydney dialect) 'kangaroo': see Morris *Austral. Eng.* 336/2.] A small brush kangaroo.

1827 P. CUNNINGHAM *N.S. Wales* (1828) I. 289 The *wallabee* and *paddymalla*..inhabit the brushes and broken hilly country. **1830** R. DAWSON *Pres. St. Australia* 212 (Morris) Had hunted down a paddymelon (a very small species of kangaroo). **1897** *Outing* (U.S.) XXX. 138/1 Get a pady-melon, hare, or any coursing game. **1898** *Westm. Gaz.* 23 Feb. 8/1 Kangaroos, Wallabies, Kangaroo rats, Wombats, Bandicoots, Pademelons.

attrib. **1851** J. HENDERSON *Excurs. N.S. Wales* II. 129 (Morris) These are hunted in the brushes and killed with paddy-mellun sticks. **1885** MRS. C. PRAED *Head Station* 313 The plains..riddled with paddymelon holes.

paddy'whack, -wack. *colloq.* [f. PADDY *sb.*²]

1. a. An Irishman.

1811 *Lex. Balatr.* s.v. *Whack*, A paddywhack; a stout brawney Irishman. **1846** *Song* in *Slang Dict.* (1873), I'm Paddy Whack from Ballyhack, Not long ago turn'd soldier.

b. ***paddywhack almanac*** = PADDY *sb.*² 3.

1886 *N. & Q.* 7th Ser. I. 388, 477.

2. A rage, passion, temper.

1899 R. KIPLING *Stalky* 25 He's a libellous old rip, an' he'll be in a ravin' paddy-wack.

3. *dial.* A severe thrashing (*Eng. Dial. Dict.*). Also in occas. use in *Austral.* and *N.Z.*

1898 B. KIRKBY *Lakeland Words* 111 Ah gev yon beggar paddy-whack fer his sauce, an' he'll nut fergit it in a hurry. **1923** G. WATSON *Roxburghshire Word-bk.* 227 *Paddy-whack* .., a stroke or blow; a whack or whacking. **1924** *Truth* (Sydney) 27 Apr. 6 *Paddywhack*, a beating. **1965** F. SARGESON *Mem. Peon* iv. 75 'Of course Michael is not going to be unsociable,' she announced. 'I'll have to give him a paddy-whack if he is.'

4. The ruddy duck: = PADDY *sb.*² 6. (*U.S.*)

pade, obs. form of PAD *sb.*¹, toad, frog.

padelion. Var. PEDELION, the plant Lady's Mantle.

padell, obs. form of PADDLE *sb.*¹

‖**padella** (pəˈdɛlə). [It. *padella* flat pan, frying-pan, etc.:—L. *patella* flat pan or dish: see PATELLA.] A shallow metal or earthenware dish in which oil or fatty matter is burnt by means of a thick wick; used esp. in Italy for illuminations; also *attrib.*

[**1858** SIMMONDS *Dict. Trade, Padella* (Italian), a small frying-pan; a kind of oven.] **1882** *Society* 11 Nov. 6/2 The ivy-covered nooks..were lighted with padella lamps.

pademelon, variant of PADDYMELON.

padenda, var. PEDANDA.

paderero, obs. var. PEDRERO, piece of ordnance.

padesoy, obs. form of PADUASOY.

ˈ**pad-foot.** *dial.* [f. PAD *v.*[1] (*sb.*[1]) + FOOT *sb.*]

1. A dialectal equivalent of FOOTPAD.

1847 TOM TREDDLEHOYLE *Bairnsla Ann.* 41 (E.D.D.) Sitha, Bobby's catch't a padfooit. **1892** J. S. FLETCHER *When Chas. was King* (1896) 209 Here I am, winged in this way by some vile padfoot.

2. One of the dialect names of the goblin called the BARGHEST. (Chiefly in Yorkshire.)

1736 DRAKE *Eboracum* I. ii. 58 The Padfoot of Pontfrete, and the Barguest of York. **1828** *Craven Gloss.* (ed. 2), *Padfoot*, A Ghost. **1865** BARING-GOULD *Werewolves* viii. 106 The Church-dog, bar-ghast, pad-foit, wash-hound, or by whatever name the animal supposed to haunt a churchyard is designated. **1883** *Almondbury & Huddersfield Gloss.*, *Padfoot*,..described as being something like a large sheep, or dog; sometimes to have rattled a chain, and been accustomed to accompany persons on their night walks, much as a dog might; keeping by their side, and making a soft noise with its feet—pad, pad, pad—whence its name. It had large eyes as big as 'tea-plates'.

padge (pædʒ). *dial.* Also **pudge.** [Cf. PUDGE[1].] The barn owl, *Tyto alba*, which has white plumage flecked with brown or grey. Also *attrib.*

1848 A. B. EVANS *Leicestershire Words* 65 Padge-owl, the common owl. **1881** *Ibid.* (new ed.) 208 Padge..the common barn-owl. **1885** C. SWAINSON *Provincial Names & Folklore Brit. Birds* 126 Familiar names [of the barn owl]... Padge, Pudge, or Pudge owl (Leicestershire). **1937** AUDEN in Auden & MacNeice *Lett. from Iceland* viii. 103, I'll never grant a more than passing beauty To pudge or pilewort, petty-chap or pooty.

padgeant, -gion, obs. ff. PAGEANT.

pad-groom, -horse, etc.: see PAD *sb.*[2] 5.

pad-hook: see PAD *sb.*[3] 17.

padi, var. PADDY *sb.*[1]

padill, obs. f. PADDLE *sb.*[3]

‖**padishah, padshah** (ˈpɑːdɪʃɑː, ˈpɑːdʃɑː). Forms: 6 padenshawe, 7 padasha, (potshaugh, -shaw), pad(i)schach, 7, 9 padischah, 8 padeshah, -shau, 9 padichaw, padisha, 8– padishah, padshah. [a. Pers. *pādshāh*, in poetry *pādĕ-*, *pādīshah* (in Turkish *pādishāh*):—Pahlavi *pātaχšā* or *pātaχšāh*:—OPers. **pātiχšāyaθiya*, f. *pati* = Skr. *pati* master, lord, ruler + *šāh* king, SHAH. (P. Horn *Grundr. Neupers. Etymol.* 1893.)] A Persian title, taken as equivalent to 'Great King' or 'Emperor'; applied in Persia to the Shah, in Europe usually to the Sultan of Turkey, in India (where often pronounced *bādshāh*) to the Great Mogul, and (before 1948) by natives to the sovereign of Great Britain as Emperor of India; also extended by Orientals to other European monarchs.

1612 *E.I.C. Letters* (ed. Danvers) I. 175 He acknowledges no Padenshawe or King in Christendom but the Portugals King. **1613** PURCHAS *Pilgrimage* (1614) 543 This Selim Padasha rebelled against his father Ekher. **1614** SELDEN *Titles Hon.* 103 The Grand Signior rather hath in later times vsed the title of Padischah Musulmin i. Great King of the Musulmans..and they call the German Emperor Urum Padischah, the French King Frank Padischah. **1634** SIR T. HERBERT *Trav.* 97 At the end sate the Potshaugh or great King [the Shah of Persia]. **1665** *Ibid.* (1677) 211 Here we met the Pot-shaw again. **1662** J. DAVIES tr. *Olearius' Voy. Ambass.* 341 They [Persians] call their Kings *Schach*, *Padschach*, and *Padischach*. **1757** *Phil. Trans.* L. 180 The word Padishah, or rather Padeshah,..in the old Persic tongue, denoting King. **1800** *Hull Advertiser* 30 Aug. 4/2 Recognized by several Hindoos..to be 'Padshaw', i.e. the King. **1823** BYRON *Juan* VI. xxxix, Whom, if they were at home in sweet Circassia, They would prefer to Padisha or Pacha. **1896** *Peterson's Mag.* Jan. 47/1 The Padishah [Sultan] is supposed to speak no language but Turkish or Arabic.

‖**padkos** (ˈpatkɔs). *S. Afr.* Also **padkost**, erron. **pat-koss.** [Afrikaans, f. *pad* road + *kos* (Du. *kost*) food.] Food for the journey; provisions.

1848 R. GRAY *Jrnl.* 16 Dec. (1849) 95 Having got careless as to our 'pat-cop' [*sic*] as we approached home, we fared but badly, and finished our meal by a draught of not the clearest water in the world. **1850** —— *Jrnl.* 6 Nov. (1851) 173, I was not allowed to depart without a good supply of pat-koss, and other comforts provided by the kindness of the parishioners. **1878** *Cape Monthly Mag.* Nov. 273 A dish of 'sesaties' and a couple of loaves..often formed part of the 'padkos'. **1895** in *Funk's Stand. Dict.*, Padkost. **1950** *Cape Times* 19 Sept. 14/1 With apples, biscuits and fish and chips as padkos, Mr. C. J. Kirstein..arrived..from Cape Town..in 12 hours, 45 minutes. **1957** —— 3 Apr. 9 (*heading*) 'Padkos' Passengers. *Ibid.*, One thing the South African Railways have always had to contend with is South Africa's habit of taking along 'padkos' on a journey. **1971** *Sunday Mail Mag.* (Brisbane) 24 Oct. 11/2 No Afrikaner ventures forth on a journey of more than a few miles without his padkos ('food for the road'), and our new friends were seemingly equipped for a fortnight's safari.

padle, paidle (ˈpeɪd(ə)l), *sb. Sc.* Also 6 paiddill, 7 pedle. [app. Sc. form of PADDLE *sb.*[1]: cf. Sc. pronunciation of *daddle*, *saddle* (ˈded(ə)l, ˈsed(ə)l).] A field or garden hoe; a scraper of this shape.

a **1568** *Anon.* in *Bannatyne MS.* 325/33 Ane pluche, ane paiddill, and ane palme corss. **1644** *Register Univ. Edinb.* 49 (MS.) Duties of the Bursars. To make clean the stairs from dirt and dust with a pedle and a Besome. *a* **1800** *Old Scottish Song* (Jam.), The gardener wi' his paidle. **1812** FORBES *Poems* 144 (E.D.D.) Spades an' padles an' a'. **1819** THOMSON *Poems* 109 (E.D.D.) A coal-rake an' a paidle.

Hence **padle, paidle** *v. Sc. trans.*, to hoe; to loosen (the ground), scrape or 'harl' with a hoe.

1825 JAMIESON, *To Paidle, v.a.*, to hoe. **1884** SIR A. GRANT *Story Univ. Edin.* I. 141 The bursars..were also to 'paidell' the stairs and entrances to the schools [cf. 1644 above]. *Mod. Sc.* All the cottagers were employed paidling turnips.

padle, obs. form of PADDLE.

padlock (ˈpædlɒk), *sb.* Formerly often as two words, **pad lock**, or hyphened, **pad-lock.** [f. *pad*, of uncertain meaning + LOCK *sb.*[2]

An obvious suggestion is that the first element is PAD *sb.*[4], basket, pannier, hamper. But there is no early evidence that a *pad-lock* was orig. used to fasten a pannier. Also, if *pad* in Rogers' *Agric. & Prices*, cited under PAD *sb.*[4], occurs in the orig. documents, these are much earlier than any instance yet found of *pad*, *ped*, 'basket', which is besides of rare and local occurrence.]

A detachable or portable lock, designed to hang on the object fastened, having a pivoted or sliding bow or shackle, which can be opened to pass through a staple or ring, and then locked so as to engage a hasp, the links of a chain, etc.

dead padlock, a simple padlock having no spring.

[**1453** in Rogers *Agric. & Prices* III. 554/4 Padlock /3.] **1478–9** in Swayne *Sarum Churchw. Acc.* 366 A Padlokke to the Church, 1½d. **1508** in Kerry *St. Lawrence's, Reading* (1883) 24 Payed for a padlok to the font, iijd. **1562** J. HEYWOOD *Prov. & Epigr.* (1867) 170 Beware it breede not a pad-locke on thy heele. **1569** *Nottingham Rec.* IV. 134 A pad locke for the Coppy yatte. **1649** C. WALKER *Hist. Independ.* II. 56 The Zealots of the Commons were very angry at the Lords, and threatned to clap a Pad lock on the Dore of their House. **1663** GERBIER *Counsel* 96 Hung at the one end in an iron ring, at the other end in a like ring, both united with a strong Padlock. **1686** tr. *Chardin's Trav. Persia* 159 In a Portmantle lockt with a Padlock. **1703** MOXON *Mech. Exerc.* 22 Trunk-Locks, Pad-Locks, etc. **1874** MICKLETHWAITE *Mod. Par. Churches* 219 These may be fastened with staples and padlocks.

fig. **1658** GURNALL *Chr. in Arm.* Verse 14. III. v. (1669) 84/1 The light of a holy conversation hangs as it were a padlock on profane lips. **1742** POPE *Dunc.* IV. 162 We hang one jingling padlock on the mind. **1822** BYRON *Werner* IV. i, That Word will, I think, put a firm padlock on His further inquisition. **18..** LOWELL *Capture Fugit. Slaves*, Put golden padlocks on Truth's lips.

padlock (ˈpædlɒk), *v.* [f. prec. sb.] *trans.* To fasten with or secure by means of a padlock.

1645 MILTON *Colast.* Wks. (1851) 353 Let not..such an unmercifull..yoke bee padlockt upon the neck of any Christian. **1722** DE FOE *Plague* (Rtldg.) 71 The Officers had Orders to Padlock up the Doors. **1828** SCOTT *F.M. Perth* vii, My mouth shall never be padlocked by any noble of them all. **1884** *Law Rep.* 13 *Q. Bench Div.* 455 The dock company ..padlocked the doors.

Hence **padlocked** (ˈpædlɒkt) *ppl. a.*

1760–72 H. BROOKE *Fool of Qual.* (1809) III. 70 A little padlocked chest. **1856** EMERSON *Eng. Traits, Wealth* Wks. (Bohn) II. 73 High stone fences and padlocked garden gates.

padmelon: see PADDYMELON.

pad-nag (ˈpædˈnæg), *sb.* [f. PAD *sb.*[2] + NAG.] An ambling nag; an easy-going pad-horse.

1654 WHITELOCKE *Jrnl. Swed. Emb.* (1772) II. 220 A sober ..well-paced english padde nagge. **1684** DR. W. POPE *Old Man's Wish* ii. (Roxb. Ball. VI. 507), With a spacious plain, without hedge or stile, And an easy pad-nagg to ride out a mile. **1770** FOOTE *Lame Lover* I. Wks. 1799 II. 60 To buy a pad-nag for a lady. *a* **1845** BARHAM *Ingol. Leg.* Ser. III. *House-warming*, As horse-litter, coach, and pad-nag, with its pillion..Defiled from the Strand. **1849** MACAULAY *Hist. Eng.* vii. II. 172 To procure an easy pad nag for his wife.

Hence ˌ**pad-ˈnag** *v. intr.*, to ride a pad-nag, ride at an easy pace, amble; also ˌ**padˈnagging** *ppl. a.*

1748 RICHARDSON *Clarissa* (1811) III. xl. 235 Will it not.. give him pretence and excuse oftener than ever to pad-nag it hither? **1836** COL. HAWKER *Diary* (1893) II. 107 The green sub. of some padnagging regiment had walked off with my portmanteau instead of his own.

padock(e, padok, obs. ff. PADDOCK *sb.*[1]

‖**padou** (padu). [F. *padou* (in same sense), formerly *Padoue*, i.e. Padua in Italy.] (See quot.)

1858 SIMMONDS *Dict. Trade, Padou*, a sort of silk ferret or ribbon. Hence in mod. Dicts.

‖**padouk** (pæˈdaʊk). Also **padauk, padowk, peduk.** [Burmese native name.] A large deciduous or evergreen tree of the genus *Pterocarpus*, belonging to the family Leguminosæ, esp. *P. soyauxii* of West Africa, *P. dalbergioides* of the Andaman Islands, and *P. macrocarpus* of Burma and Thailand; also, the reddish hardwood produced by these trees. Also *attrib.*

1839 H. MALCOM *Trav. South-Eastern Asia* I. II. 189 The Pa-douk, or Mahogany.., is plenty in the upper provinces. .. It grows very large, and is mostly of the branched or knotty kind. **1858** in SIMMONDS *Dict. Trade.* **1858** C. T. WINTER *Six Months Brit. Burmah* xv. 115 The pa-douk..a highly ornamental ever-green tree with bright yellow papilionaceous flowers, which are very fragrant, exudes a gum. **1892** *Blackw. Mag.* Sept. 384 Thick among the huge 'padouks' the gray-stemmed 'gurjuns' gleam. **1893** *Westm. Gaz.* 20 Apr. 3/3 Peduk is darker in colour than the other woods generally used. **1895** *Daily News* 3 June 5/6 There is at least one thing which Cedric the Saxon never heard of —the Indian padouk wood of the fittings. **1900–1** PRAIN *Ann. Report Bot. Gard. Calcutta*, The true or Burma Padouk is the timber of *Pterocarpus macrocarpus*, a species that occurs only in Burma. 'Andaman Padouk' or 'Redwood' is the timber of *P. dalbergioides*..found only, in a wild state, in the Andamans. **1908** W. R. FISHER *Schlich's Man. Forestry* (ed. 2) V. 590 Many foreign woods are used for piano-cases—mahogany, American walnut and maple, padauk, stain wood, etc., ebony for keys, and Florida-cedar for the hammers. **1928** *Observer* 25 Mar. 13/2 Counter-tops at the Bank of England are made of Andaman padouk. **1930** *Times Lit. Suppl.* 5 June 483/3 He would be a tiro indeed who could mistake the fierce red and lively grain of padouk, or the dull heavy texture of sabicu for mahogany. **1956** *Handbk. Hardwoods* (Forest Prod. Res. Lab.) 182 Padouk wood is variable in texture. **1967** G. SIMS *Last Best Friend* vii. 61 The weight of the Padouk door might have been the first sign to the perceptive caller that this was a rather special house. **1973** *Times* 1 Feb. 19/3 In the furniture section padouk wood display cabinets..were selling in the £200–£500 range.

Padovan (ˈpædəvən), *sb.* and *a.* [f. It. *Padova* (see PADUAN *a.* and *sb.*) + -AN.] **A.** *sb.* = PADUAN *sb.* 1. **B.** *adj.* = PADUAN *a.*

1973 M. WEST *Salamander* i. 42 That girl in the Ferrari, she's a Venetian, a Veronese, a Padovan. **1978** *Sci. Amer.* June 26/1 Eighteen years a professor in Padua, he had published only two books, one an instruction manual.., the other a witty polemic against a Padovan student who had sought to rip off that very instruction book!

pad-piece, -plate, -play: see PAD- *sb.*[3] 14.

padpipe: see PAD *sb.*[1] 4.

‖**padre** (ˈpɑːdreɪ). [It., Sp., Pg. *padre*:—L. *patre-m*, acc. of *pater* father.] 'Father': a title applied in Italy, Spain, Portugal, and Spanish America, to the regular clergy; in India (from Portuguese), to a minister or priest of any Christian Church; and by natives (in speaking to Europeans) of native priests; hence, applied by English soldiers and sailors to a chaplain.

1584 in *Hakluyt's Voy.* (1810) II. 381 We found there 2 Padres, the one an Englishman, the other a Flemming. **1698** FRYER *Acc. E. India & P.* 8 A Chappel..the Rural Seat of one of their Black Padres. **1751** *Affect. Narr. of Wager* 7 A blind Subjection to the Padres, and a contemptuous Abhorrence of Heretics. *c* **1813** MRS. SHERWOOD *Ayah & Lady* iv. 25 Now there was in the place where I lay ill a Christian *padre*. *Ibid.* Glossary, *Padre*, a Christian minister. **1865** LIVINGSTONE *Zambesi* ii. 47 The Goanese padre of Tette..appointed a procession. **1898** *Daily News* 7 Apr. 6/2 The 'fighting padre' is by no means an unknown figure in British wars.

attrib. **18..** SIR T. LAWRENCE *Label* (in Kew Museum), Very fine quality Tea called Padre Oolong, prepared by the Chinese for their Priests. *Ibid.*, Padra Tea. [**1858** SIMMONDS *Dict. Trade Prod.* 271 *Padra*, a black tea.]

padrigon: see PERDRIGON, a variety of plum.

Padroadist (pɑːdrəʊˈɑːdɪst). [f. Pg. *padroado* patronage + -IST.] A Roman Catholic who favours or suports the *padroado* or ecclesiastical patronage claimed by the King of Portugal in India.

1890 *Tablet* 10 May 739 Padroadists and Propagandists are regarded as two distinct sects. [**1896** *Ibid.* 15 Feb. 258 At present the 'Padroado' is a veritable incubus on the Catholic Church in India.]

‖**padrone** (paˈdrone). [It.: cf. med.L. *patro*, *-ōnem* for cl. L. *patrōnus* PATRON.] An Italian term meaning, primarily, Patron, master; applied to †**a.** the Prime Minister of the Papal Curia (*Cardinal Patron*); **b.** the master of a trading-vessel in the Mediterranean; **c.** an Italian labour-contractor, an employer of street musicians, begging children, etc.; **d.** the proprietor of an inn in Italy.

1670 G. H. *Hist. Cardinals* I. III. 79 The Cardinal Nephew, whom they called *Padrone*. *Ibid.* II. III. 178 He exercis'd the office of Padrone. **1678** DRYDEN *Limberham* V. i, I shall never make you amends for this kindness, my dear Padron. *c* **1751** GRAY *Let. to Walpole* Nov., Wks. 1814 I. 546 As to my Eton Ode, Mr. Dodsley [the publisher] is *padrone*. **1804** W. IRVING in *Life & Lett.* (1864) I. v. 86 Our padrone immediately displayed the Genoese flag, and hailed the vessel. **1836** MARRYAT *Midsh. Easy* xix, The crew consisted of the padrone, two men, and a boy. **1860** *Once a Week* 14 July 72/1 They had not earned money enough in the day to secure them a favourable reception from the *padrone* at night.

Hence †'**padronancy**, †'**padronage**, †'**padronship**, the office of (Cardinal) Padrone, or First Minister in the Papal Court; '**padronism**, the system of bringing Italian children into a foreign country to perform street music or beg for the profit of the *padrone* or taskmaster.

1670 G. H. *Hist. Cardinal* II. II. 154 He will fall out of the hands of the Papacy, as he fell out of the *Padronage*. *Ibid.* III. 175 The declaration of a Cardinal Padrone.. in the beginning of his Padronship. *Ibid.* 178 He shew'd himself diligent enough in his office of Padronancy. *Ibid.* 206 They apply themselves immediately to the Pope, till they shall see the Cardinal a little more setled in his Padronancy. **1880** *Daily News* 15 Apr. 5/2 The King of the padroni.. was arrested under the United States law against 'padronism' passed in 1874.. which makes the bringing of such [Italian] children into the States a felony.

pad-saddle, -saw, -tree, etc.: see PAD *sb.*[3]

padshah, another form of PADISHAH.

†**pad-staff.** *Obs.* = PADDLE-STAFF.

a **1661** FULLER *Worthies* (1840) III. 203 With his pad-staff he did dig a square hole about it, and so departed.

padstool: see PAD *sb.*[1] 4.

Paduan ('pædju:ən), *a.* and *sb.* [f. *Padua* name of a city of northern Italy, in It. *Padova*, L. *Patavium* + -AN. Cf. PATAVINITY.]

A. *adj.* Of or pertaining to Padua.

1801 D. STEWART *Life & Writ. W. Robertson* 152 An admixture of Paduan idioms.

B. *sb.* **1.** A native or inhabitant of Padua.

1842 BRANDE *Dict. Sci.* etc. 867/1 The talents which these Paduans possessed to engrave dies.

2. One of the coins or medallions, in bronze and silver, forged in the 16th c. in imitation of ancient pieces, by two Paduan artists, Cavino and Bassiano.

1769 *Misc.* in *Ann. Reg.* 196/2 In a separate case are contained the Paduans and other counterfeit medals. [*Note.* A Paduan.. is a modern medal struck with all the marks and characters of antiquity.] **1842** BRANDE *Dict. Sci.* etc.

3. A kind of dance; the PAVAN.

1880 *Grove's Dict. Mus.* II. 627/2 Padua gave its name to the ancient dance Paduan, or Pavan.

4. A make of violin-strings.

1884 H. R. HAWEIS *Musical Mem.* iii. 94 Paduans are strong [violin-strings], but frequently false.

Hence '**Paduanism**, the dialectical characteristics of Patavium or Padua, of which Livy was a native, Patavinity; the use of patois.

1594 R. ASHLEY tr. *Loys le Roy* 24 b, Pollio obiected Paduanisme vnto Liuie.

paduasoy ('pædju:əsɔɪ). Forms: α. 7–8 poudesoy, (7 poodesoy, 8 pudisway). β. 7– paduasoy; 8 paduasuay, (paddi-, pattissway), pada-, padesoy, 9 padusoy. [*Poudesoy* (*poodesoy, pudisway*) is F. *pou-de-soie* (1667 Littré), *pout de soye, poul de soie* (1389–94 in Godef. *Compl.*), of unascertained origin; in recent F. spelt *pout-de-soie* and POULT-DE-SOIE, the latter also in 19th c. English. The forms in *-sway, -suay* represent the 17–18th c. F. pronunciation of *soie* as *soè, souè, souê*; the rimes show this still in 1730 when the spelling was *paduasoy*. *Paduasoy* is, in appearance, a combination of *Padua*, Eng. name of the Italian city + F. *soie* silk. (Padua has long had manufactures of silk and other textiles, and a kind of narrow silk ribbon is thence named in F. *padou*, in 1642 *padoüe*: Oudinot). But *Padua soy* could not well be of Eng. formation, since *soy, soye, soie*, was never in Eng. use. Nor could it originate in French, where 'Padua silk' would be *soie de Padoue*, not *Padoue soie*. The probability then is that *paduasoy* was an Eng. corruption of *pou-de-soie* or *poudesoy*, app. by association with *Padua say*, a kind of SAY or serge, actually from Padua, which had been known in England since 1633 or earlier:

1633 *Naworth Househ. Bks.* (Surtees) 300 For five yeardes of Padua saye for a peticote for my Ladie, xxjs. viijd. **1676** *Lond Gaz.* No. 1093/4 Stolen... A Padua Say Peticoat and Wastecoat. Cf. **1710** *Ibid.* No. 4706/4 Paduay Serges, and other Stuffs.]

A strong corded or gros-grain silk fabric, much worn in the 18th c. by both sexes, of which POULT-DE-SOIE is the modern representative. Also *attrib.*, and *ellipt.* a garment of this material.

α. **1663** S. FORTREY *Eng. Interest & Impr.* 22 In silk stuffs, taffeties, poudesoyes, armoysins, clothes of gold and silver .. silk ribbands, and other such like silk stuffs as are made at Tours. **1689** *Lond Gaz.* No. 2425/4 Also 3 Pieces of Checquer'd Silk,.. all Silk like a Poodesoy. **1694** CHAMBERLAYNE *Pres. St. Eng.* I. vii. 65 We yearly imported from France.. Silks, Sattins, Taffeta's, Stuffs, Armoysins, Poudesoy's [so all edd. to 1710; then 1716–1748 Paduasoys]. **1704** *Lond Gaz.* No. 3992/3 Also East-India Goods.., consisting of.. Pudisways. **1728–9** in *Mrs. Delany's Life & Corr.* I. 193 Princess Royal had white poudesoy, embroidered with gold, and a few colours intermixed. **1733–4** *Ibid.* 428 A pink plain poudesoy. [*Obs.* by 1750, but re-introduced from Fr. *c* 1850 in the form POULT-DE-SOIE q.v.]

β. **1672** *Acct. Earl of Shaftesbury's Wardrobe* (Stanf.), A black velvet coat, paduasoy suit laced. **1704** *Lond. Gaz.* No. 3984/4 An Olive-colour'd Gown and Petticoat strip'd, lin'd with a muddy-colour'd Pattissway. **1727** FIELDING *Love in Sev. Masques* I. ii, Two girls in paduasuay coats and breeches. **1727** GAY *Begg Op.* II. iv, A Piece of black Padesoy. **1730** JENYNS *Art of Dancing* I. 66 Let him his active limbs display In camblet thin, or glossy paduasoy. **1730** SWIFT *Robin & Harry* 47 Clad in a coat of paduasoy, A flaxen wig, and waistcoat gay. **1741** RICHARDSON *Pamela* (1824) I. 223 A fine laced silk waistcoat, of blue paduasoy. *a* **1845** HOOD *Bianca's Dream* iv, In vain the richest padusoy he bought. **1869** MRS. OLIPHANT *George II* (1879) II. 237 The pale primrose-coloured paduasoy.

padyan, padʒean, etc., obs. Sc. ff. PAGEANT.

padymelon, variant of PADDYMELON.

pæan ('pi:ən), *sb.* Also 6–7 pean. [a. L. *pæan*, a. Gr. παιάν a hymn or chant, properly (see below) one addressed to Apollo invoked under the name *Pæan* (Παιάν, Attic Παιών, Epic Παιήων), originally the Homeric name of the physician of the gods. The invocation being by the phrase Ἰὼ Παιάν, *Io Pæan* (see Io[1]), the song or hymn came itself to be called the *pæan*.]

1. In reference to *Greek Antiq.*: A hymn or chant of thanksgiving for deliverance originally addressed to Apollo or Artemis; esp. a song of triumph after victory addressed to Apollo, also a war-song in advancing to battle addressed to Ares; hence any solemn song or chant. The full phrase *Io pæan* occurs poetically as a sb. in same sense.

1592 LYLY *Midas* V. iii, Io paeans let us sing, To physicke's and to poesie's king. **1603** HOLLAND *Plutarch's Mor.* 1251 The Poets that composed the songs of victorie, named Pæanes. *c* **1611** CHAPMAN *Iliad* I. 457 That day was .. spent in pæans to the Sun. **1770** LANGHORNE *Plutarch* (1879) I. 60/2 The King.. himself began the pæan, which was the signal to advance. **1873** SYMONDS *Grk. Poets* v. 118 The Paean, sung to Phoebus.. was the proper accompaniment of the battle and the feast. **1878** GLADSTONE *Prim. Homer* xiii. 151 The triumphal hymn of praise, or *paian*, is commemorated in the *Iliad*, as already established in use.

2. In modern use: A song of praise or thanksgiving; a shout or song of triumph, joy, or exultation.

[**1544** E. GOSYNHYLL (*title*) The Prayse of all Women, called Mulierum Pean.] **1599** MARSTON *Sco. Villanie* III. viii. 210 Tut, rather Peans sing Hermaphrodite. **1604** DRAYTON *Owl* 1133 The warbling Mavis mirthfull Peans sung. **1646** BUCK *Rich. III*, III. 78 Who would have sung Peans to his glory. **1709** POPE *Ess. Crit.* 186 Hear, in all tongues consenting Pæans ring! **1842** TENNYSON *Two Voices* 127, I sung the joyful Pæan clear.. Waiting to strive a happy strife. **1869** LD. LYTTON *Orval* 198 The paean of the people's Liberty!

attrib. **1839** MRS. HEMANS *Tombs of Platea* ix, Where the pæan strains were sung.

Hence '**pæan** *v. trans.*, to sing in or as a pæan. So '**pæanism** [Gr. παιανισμ-ός], the chanting of the pæan; '**pæanize** *v. intr.* [Gr. παιανίζ-ειν], to chant or sing the pæan.

1820 T. MITCHELL *Aristoph.* I. 186 Notes of vict'ry *pæan'd high! **1669** GALE *Crt. Gentiles* I. II. iv. 40 For the Victories.. Io Pæan was sung to Apollo; at least hence *Pæanismes.. had their rise. **1702** C. MATHER *Magn. Chr.* VII. vi. (1852) 579 The Grecian ελελευ Ιου Ιου used in their Pæanisms. *a* **1827** W. MITFORD cited in *Cent. Dict.*, Pæanism. **1628** HOBBES *Thucyd.* (1822) 123 The Peloponneseans.. were *paeanizing as if they had already the victory.

pæan, variant of PÆON.

pædagogic, pædant, etc.: see PEDA-.

pædarchy: see PÆDO-.

pædeia (paɪ'daɪə). Also **paideia.** [a. Gr. παιδεία child-rearing, education.] In ancient Greek society: education or upbringing; more gen., a society's culture; the sum of physical and intellectual achievement to which the human body and mind can aspire. Also *transf.*

[**1875** F. HUEFFER tr. *Guhl & Koner's Life of Greeks & Romans* 196 The education proper of the boy (παιδεία) became a more public one, while the girl was brought up by the mother at home.] **1939** G. HIGHET tr. *Jaeger's Paideia* I. II. iii. 283 The age of Sophocles saw the beginnings of an intellectual movement... This was the movement mentioned in our introductory chapter: it was *paideia*, education, or rather culture, in the narrower sense. The word paideia, which at its first appearance meant 'childrearing', and which in the fourth century, the Hellenistic, and the Imperial Roman ages constantly extended its connotation, was now for the first time connected with the highest areté possible to man: it was used to denote the sum-total of all ideal perfections of mind and body. **1962** *Listener* 30 Aug. 323/2 The Lycurgan training for public service enriched Greek 'paedeia'. **1967** *Ibid.* 17 Aug. 201/3 Marx is.. built into my intellectual experience, what the Greeks would have called my *paideia*. **1977** G. W. H. LAMPE *God as Spirit* ii. 49 Wisdom is a holy spirit of *paideia*, which, in opposition to materialistic (Epicurean) culture, is the disciplined observance of the Law.

pæderasty, ped- ('pi:d-, 'pɛdəræstɪ). [ad. mod.L. *pæderastia*, a. Gr. παιδεραστία, f. παιδεραστής, f. παῖς, παιδ- boy + ἐραστής lover. In Fr. *pédérastie*.] Unnatural connexion with a boy; sodomy.

1613 PURCHAS *Pilgrimage* (1614) 293 He telleth of their Pæderastie, that they buy Boyes at an hundred or two hundred duckats, and mew them vp for their filthie lust. **1752** HUME *Ess. & Treat.* (1777) II. 382 Solon's law forbid pæderasty to slaves. **1788** GIBBON *Decl. & F.* (1846) IV. 233 The same penalties were inflicted on the passive and active guilt of paederasty. **1869** RAWLINSON *Anc. Hist.* 529 Hence the laws against infanticide, against adultery, against pæderasty.

So '**pæderast** [Gr. παιδεραστής], †**pæde'rastist**, a sodomite; **pæde'rastic** *a.* [Gr. παιδεραστικός], pertaining to or practising sodomy; hence **pæde'rastically** *adv.*

1730–6 BAILEY (folio), *Pederast.., a Sodomite, a buggerer. **1738** WARBURTON *Div. Legat.* I. 171 As the detestable Pæderasts of after Ages scandalized the godlike Socrates. **1925** R. FRY *Let.* 7 Sept. (1972) II. 581 We had a long talk on the tyranny of the Paederasts and Sapphists. **1935** E. E. CUMMINGS *Let.* 2 Jan. (1969) 131 Scientists are of course pederasts, as we neither know nor care; & unnaturally enough this natural history museum is a temple or cathedral of the scientific spirit. **1963** A. HERON *Towards Quaker View of Sex* 69 Socially the paederast is the most isolated of homosexuals. **1969** *Listener* 14 Aug. 205/3 A divorced woman on the throne of the House of Windsor would be a pretty big feather in the cap of that bunch of rootless intellectuals, alien Jews and international pederasts who call themselves the Labour Party. **1971** P. QUENNELL *Marcel Proust* 11 The sense of his own separateness, as a paederast who loved women,.. and a sick man.. intensified his gift of observation. [**1593** G. HARVEY *New Letter* Wks. (Grosart) I. 290 That penned.. another [Apology] of Pederastice, a kinde of harlatry, not to be recited.] **1704** SWIFT *T. Tub* Pref., There is first the *pæderastic school with French and Italian masters. **1864** tr. *Gaspar's Hand-bk. Forensic Med.* III. 333 *note*, Dohrn.. has observed this appearance in his old pæderastic hospitallers. *Ibid.* 332 A boy alleged to have been abused *pæderastically. **1684** T. GODDARD *Plato's Demon* 29 The little respect which he had for that Sex, and great love for the other, which made him so great a *Pæderastist.

pædeutics (pi:'dju:tɪks); rarely sing. **pædeutic.** Also **paid-.** [f. Gr. παιδευτικός of or for teaching, ἡ παιδευτική (sc. τέχνη) education: see -ICS.] The science or art of education.

1864 WEBSTER, *Paideutics*. **1885** *Life of Sir R. Christison* I. 28 Was it an error or not in the pædeutics of those times? **1885** *Sat. Rev.* 3 Oct. 459/1 We could wish such ugly barbarisms or neologisms as.. 'paideutics' and the like had been eschewed. **1899** *Blackw. Mag.* Aug. 253 The one substantial contribution.. made to the paideutic of the game.

pædiatric (pi:dɪ'ætrɪk), *a. Med.* Also **pediatric.** [see PÆDO-, PEDO-, and IATRIC *a.*] Of, pertaining to, or dealing with pædiatrics or the diseases of children.

1880 A. JACOBI in *Trans. Amer. Med. Assoc.* XXXI. 709 (*heading*) Address on the claims of paediatric medicine. **1894** *Lancet* 3 Nov. 1065 Professor Johann Bokai, the well-known pædiatric physician. **1927** W. P. LUCAS *Mod. Pract. Pediatrics* iii. 20 From the moment a child is conceived it is a pediatric problem. **1963** *Times* 16 May 13/3 For all these reasons it is not surprising that opinion among paediatricians and paediatric nurses is divided. **1965** *Math. in Biol. & Med.* (Med. Res. Council) v. 228 In a well known text book of paediatric surgery there is a photograph of nine children with tracheo-oesophageal fistula, successfully treated. **1973** D. MORLEY *Paediatric Priorities in Developing World* i. 1 Doctors with the relevant paediatric training can organize a service which will prevent more than one-half of the deaths in infancy and early childhood without awaiting any great change in environment.

Hence **pædi'atrically** *adv.*

1949 M. MEAD *Male & Female* ix. 192 If her suckling of the child [is] replaced by a formula pediatrically prescribed —then also we may find very serious disturbances in maternal attitudes.

pædiatrician (pi:dɪə'trɪʃən). *Med.* Also **ped-.** [f. prec. + -ICIAN.] A specialist or expert in pædiatrics.

1903 *Med. Rec.* (N.Y.) LXIII. 513/2 Dr. L. Emmett Holt said he thought all pediatricians would agree that most of the cases which had given trouble in diagnosis were those in which there was a prolonged fever. **1932** *Lancet* 12 Nov. 1072/1 (*heading*) Congress of German pædiatricians in Vienna. **1959** *Times Lit. Suppl.* 13 Mar. 148/1 The authors, a pediatrician and a psychiatrist, show a broad understanding of the sociological scope of adolescents' difficulties. **1971** C. G. PARSONS in S. M. Bates *Pract. Paediatric Nursing* p. ix, Paediatricians have always depended on nurses to help children to settle into hospital.. and to take the mother's place when she has to be separated from her baby. **1976** *Daily Tel.* 1 Mar. 2/1 Women who become pregnant despite being fitted with intra-uterine contraceptive devices.. may risk giving birth to seriously malformed babies, a consultant paediatrician has warned.

pædiatrics (pi:dɪ'ætrɪks), *sb. pl.* (const. as *sing.*). *Med.* Also **ped-.** [f. as prec.: see -IC 2.] The branch of medical science dealing with the study of childhood and the diseases of children.

1884 (*periodical title*) Archives of pediatrics. **1924** *Glasgow Herald* 10 June 6 The new foundation is the Sampson-Gemmell Chair of Medical Pædiatrics at the Royal Hospital for Sick Children. **1946** *Nature* 24 Aug. 277/2 Geriatrics must also come to occupy a part not less important in medicine than pediatrics to-day. **1956** LD. AMULREE in A. Pryce-Jones *New Outl. Mod. Knowl.* 213 Infant and child welfare services are available in most civilized countries, and pediatrics and the care of children is becoming more and more a preventive service. **1975** *Physics Bull.* Oct. 458/1 (*caption*) In the field of paediatrics the x ray examination of infants and young children is a diagnostic procedure that is on the increase.

pædiatrist (piːˈdaɪətrɪst, piːdɪˈætrɪst). *Med.* Also **ped-**. [f. as prec. + -IST.] = PÆDIATRICIAN. Also *attrib.* or as *adj.*

1897 *Trans. Amer. Pediatric Soc.* IX. 44, I wish to speak more especially to the general practitioner and pediatrist. **1928** O. WILKINSON *Strabismus* x. 143 The advice and insistent counsel of the family physician and the pediatrist. **1977** *Chicago Tribune* 2 Oct. XII. 12/2 (Advt.), 1 deluxe optometric or pediatrist suite.

pædo-, pedo- (ˈpiːdəʊ), occas. **paido-** (ˈpaɪdəʊ), before a vowel **pæd-, ped-**, combining form of Gr. παῖς, παιδ- boy, child, and element in several words, scientific and technical, of which the more important will be found in their alphabetical places.

pædarchy (ˈpiːdɑːkɪ) [Gr. -αρχια, ἀρχή rule], rule or government by a child or children. **pæˈdocracy, paid-** [see -CRACY], government by children. **pæˈdology, paid-** [see -LOGY], the study of the nature of children; so **pædoˈlogical**, pertaining to pædology; **pæˈdologist**, **pædoloˈgistical** *a.*, **pædoloˈgistically** *adv.* (see quot.). **pæˈdometer**, an instrument for measuring the weight and length of a child; hence **pædometric** *a.* **pædonosology** (-nəʊˈsɒlədʒɪ) [Gr. νόσος disease: see -LOGY], the study of the diseases of children. **pædonymic** (piːdəʊˈnɪmɪk) [after *patronymic*], a name given to a person from that of his or her child; so **pæˈdonymy**, the giving of such a name.

1830 *Hist. Eur.* in *Ann. Reg.* 245/2 The government was called the *paedarchy (or the regime of children). **1647** J. NOYES *Temple Measured* 34 Some are.. unseasonable, ignorant, youthful. This is a *Pedocracy as well as a Democracy. **1900** *Speaker* 5 May 131/2 Miss Vernon of the *Paidological Bureau. **1894** *Educ. News* (U.S.) 14 Apr. 233 A **paidologist* is one who studies boys. **Paidologistical* pertains to *paidology, and **paidologistically* is the adverb that refers to the acts of a paidologist while he is treating of paidology paidologistically. **1853** DUNGLISON *Med. Lex.*, **Pædometer*, baromacrometer. **1889** *Jrnl. Educ.* 1 Feb. 75/2 The terrors of a cast-iron Code and Inspectors with their *paedometric apparatus. **1857** MAYNE *Expos. Lex.*, *Pædonosologia*, term for a description or consideration of the diseases of children: *pedonosology. **1883** W. LEAF in *Jrnl. Philol.* No. 24. 286 Prof. Geddes quotes as a similar '*Pædonymic' the expression 'Althaea Meleagris'. *Ibid.* 287 Whether or no the custom of *Paedonymy has left any other trace.. must be left to anthropologists to decide.

pædobaptism (piːdəʊˈbæptɪz(ə)m). Also **pedo-**. [f. PÆDO- + BAPTISM; cf. mod.L. *pædobaptismus* (16th c.), F. *pédobaptisme* (17th c.).] The baptism of children; infant baptism.

1640 BP. HALL *Episc.* I. §10 Where is there expresse charge for the Lord's day? Where for pædobaptism? **1651** CARTWRIGHT *Cert. Relig.* II. 38 The administration of Pedobaptisme. **1755** JOHNSON, *Pedobaptism*. **1872** *Westm. Rev.* July 81 Persons who denied that pædobaptism is to be found in the New Testament.. were allowed to rot.. in gaols.

pædobaptist (piːdəʊˈbæptɪst). Also **pedo-**. [f. PÆDO- + BAPTIST, after prec.] One who practises, adheres to, or advocates infant baptism.

1651 BAXTER *Inf. Bapt.* 173 He might have called us Anti-pædobaptists, as being against Infant-Baptism. **1755** JOHNSON, *Pedobaptist*, one that holds or practises infant baptism. **1772** in Urwick *Nonconf. Worcester* (1897) 215 Ye Paedo-baptist Congregation is of late years much reduced. **1891** F. W. NEWMAN *Card. Newman* 62 The only part which I took was, to support Union with Pædo-Baptists, not to divide.

pædogamy (piːˈdɒgəmɪ). *Biol.* Also (chiefly *U.S.*) **pedogamy**. [ad. G. *pädogamie, paedogamie* (M. Lühe 1902, in *Schriften d. Physikal.-ökonom. Gesellsch. Konigsberg, Sitzung biol. Sektion* XLIII. 5), f. PÆDO- + -GAMY.] In certain protozoans, reproduction by the fusion of gametes derived from the same parent cell (see also quot. 1953).

1910 G. N. CALKINS *Protozool.* iv. 146 (*heading*) Fertilization by endogamy (pedogamy, Prowazek). **1953** R. P. HALL *Protozool.* ii. 80 Pedogamy appears to be an unusual type of syngamy in which the two gametes are not more than one or two cell-generations removed from a single gametocyte. **1965** POLJANSKIJ & CHEJSIN *Dogiel's Gen. Protozool.* (ed. 2) vii. 322 In certain cases sister individuals, originating from a single nucleus of one and the same mother cell, act as gametes. Phenomena of this type are known as paedogamy.

Hence **pæˈdogamous** *a.*, of or pertaining to this type of reproduction.

1926 G. N. CALKINS *Biol. Protozoa* xi. 510 Fertilizations have been described as exogamous, endogamous, autogamous, or pædogamous. **1940** L. H. HYMAN *Invertebrates* I. iii. 161 The fertilization [of Myxosporidia] is seen to be a paedogamous autogamy.

pædogenesis (piːdəʊˈdʒɛnɪsɪs). *Biol.* Also (chiefly *U.S.*) **pedo-**. [mod.L., coined in Ger. (K. von Baer 1866, in *Bull. Acad. Imp. Sci. St.-Pétersbourg* IX. 96), f. PÆDO- + GENESIS.] Reproduction by larval or immature forms of animals, esp. certain insects; cf. NEOTENY b. Hence **pædogeˈnetic** *a.*, pertaining to or characterized by pædogenesis.

1871 W. S. DALLAS tr. O. von Grimm in *Ann. & Mag. Nat. Hist.* VIII. 32, I had before me an insect [*sc.* a species of *Chironomus*] which is subject to what Von Baer calls pædogenesis. *Ibid.* 36 Different animals may be subject to pædogenesis at different stages of development. **1888** ROLLESTON & JACKSON *Anim. Life* 507 Pædogenesis or the production of ova by the immature animal is rare, and in Insecta always parthenogenetic. **1889** *Athenæum* 13 Apr. 471/1 A parthenogenetic and *pædogenetic generation occurs in the life-cycle [of the blood-worm]. **1891** F. V. THEOBALD *Acct. Brit. Flies* 42 The ovaries [of flies of the family Cecidomyidæ] become fully developed and bud off eggs; [*Note*] = Pædogenesis (i.e., the production of ova by the immature animal, and is in the insecta always parthenogenetic). **1895** D. SHARP in *Cambr. Nat. Hist.* V. iv. 142 A very rare kind of parthenogenesis, called paedogenesis, has been found to exist in two or three species of Diptera. **1920** H. REINHEIMER *Symbiosis* II. viii. 158 The 'wages' of a prolonged transgression against the law of Symbiosis is thus indeed death—in the shape of diathesis, dissolution, and of a kind of Paedogenesis—precocious sexuality. **1951** COLYER & HAMMOND *Flies Brit. Isles* iii. 71 Parthenogenetic reproduction by immature stages is known as paedogenesis. *Ibid.* iv. 83 Those [*Miastor* larvae] which are paedogenetic have no 'breast-bones', while those which will pupate and produce normal flies possess this organ. **1964** R. M. & J. W. FOX *Introd. Compar. Entomol.* vii. 243 Neoteny (pedogenesis) involves the precocious maturity of the ovary so that young are produced by a mother who has not reached the imaginal instar.

pædomancy, erron. form of PEDOMANCY.

pædomorphic (piːdəʊˈmɔːfɪk), *a.* Also **ped-**. [f. PÆDO- + MORPHIC *a.*] **1.** *Biol.* Exhibiting pædomorphism or pædomorphosis.

1891 *Proc. Acad. Nat. Sci. Philadelphia* 209 It might be expected that pedomorphic varieties closely resemble each other when the same disposition is exhibited in closely allied species. **1922** *Jrnl. Linn. Soc.* (*Zool.*) XXXV. 97 Crinoids are as 'pædomorphic' as any Perennibranchiate Amphibian. **1957** L. EISELEY *Immense Journey* 119 The pedomorphic features of man—his almost hairless body, his helpless childhood, his surprisingly developed brain. **1959** J. D. CLARK *Prehist. S. Afr.* iv. 90 The Boskop type exhibits a continuation of certain pedomorphic (infantile) characteristics into the adult state, as does the Bushman. **1965** B. E. FREEMAN tr. *Vandel's Biospeleol.* xi. 165 This feature may be considered in addition to that of small size, as a paedomorphic character. **1970** G. GREER *Female Eunuch* 31 This.. is an observation which is frequently made about the whole female body, that it is infantilized or pedomorphic.

2. (After *anthropomorphic*.) Having (or attributing to other objects) the form or characteristics of a child.

1903 H. G. WELLS in *Fortn. Rev.* Jan. 184 He will look out on the world with anthropomorphic (or rather with pædomorphic) eyes. **1907** H. ELLIS in *19th Cent.* May 767 The Child.. imagines a colossal magician, of anthropomorphic (if not paidomorphic) nature.

pædomorphism (piːdəʊˈmɔːfɪz(ə)m). *Biol.* Also **ped-**. [f. PÆDO- + -MORPHISM.] The retention of juvenile characteristics in certain adult mammals.

1891 *Proc. Acad. Nat. Sci. Philadelphia* 208 Dr. Harrison Allen spoke of the disposition occasionally exhibited in adult mammals, for the proportions of different parts of the body to remain as they were in the immature individuals... Dr. Allen proposed for this peculiarity the term pedomorphism. **1931** *Amer. Jrnl. Physical Anthropol.* XVI. 203 (*title*) Pedomorphism in the pre-Bushman skull. **1970** G. GREER *Female Eunuch* 333 The pedomorphism of women has always been remarked upon. **1973** B. J. WILLIAMS *Evolution & Human Origins* vii. 98/1 Paedomorphism is said to occur when certain developmental processes are retarded in such a way that important features of the larval or infantile form are maintained into sexual maturity.

pædomorphosis (piːdəʊˈmɔːfəsɪs, -mɔːˈfəʊsɪs). *Biol.* [f. PÆDO- + MORPHOSIS.] Phylogenetic change indicated by the retention of juvenile characteristics in the adult form.

1922 W. GARSTANG in *Jrnl. Linnean Soc.* (*Zool.*) XXXV. 100 In other articles I propose to deal with the origin and significance of larval forms, and to draw attention to some further examples of the influence of larval characters upon adult organisation, to which I apply the term 'Pædomorphosis'. **1932** J. S. HUXLEY *Probl. Relative Growth* vii. 240 (*caption*) Diagram to illustrate positive and negative mutations in rate-factors, leading to recapitulation and paedomorphosis, respectively. **1965** B. E. FREEMAN tr. *Vandel's Biospeleol.* ix. 134 Partial neoteny, a phenomenon to which Garstang's term paedomorphosis may be more exactly applied. **1970** *Times Lit. Suppl.* 4 June 619/4 The most serious lacuna in the book is the absence of any mention of the part which the well-known principle of retardation of development, or paedomorphosis, has played in the evolution of man. **1971** [see NEOTENY]. **1974** G. L. STEBBINS *Flowering Plants* xi. 249/2 The evolutionary mechanism by which this [*sc.* the evolution of herbs and subshrubs into shrubs or trees] could happen involves the principle of paedomorphosis.

pædonom (ˈpiːdəʊnɒm). *Gr. Antiq.* [ad. Gr. παιδονόμος.] A magistrate who superintended the education of youths.

a **1871** GROTE *Eth. Fragm.* vi. (1876) 224 Under the superintendence of the Pædonom.

pædophile (ˈpiːdəʊfaɪl), *sb.* and *a.* Also **pedo-**. [ad. Gr. παιδόφιλ-ος loving children (cf. -PHIL, -PHILE).] **A.** *sb.* A person with pædophilia. **B.** *adj.* = PÆDOPHILIAC, -PHILIC *adjs.*

1951 *Group Psychotherapy* IV. 166 (*heading*) Psychodramatic treatment of a pedophile. **1954** *Jrnl. Projective Techniques* XVIII. 352/1 This sexualized view of a late middle-aged female, by a 26-year-old subject, reflects the strikingly immature confusion of sexual and maternal figures found in the pedophile group. **1975** *Sunday People* 1 June 2/6 Many paedophiles who read the article will have heard of P.A.L. for the first time and will be anxious that the organisation survives to continue this service. **1976** *Publishers Weekly* 23 Aug. 75/2 Hilary is nine... She's at the mercy of the old man she calls the Devil, actually a pathetic pedophile. **1977** *Sunday Times* 30 Jan. 41/2 The paedophile authors he discusses include the diarist Kilvert, Lewis Carroll.. and J. M. Barrie.

pædophilia (piːdɒˈfɪlɪə). Also **pedo-**, † **paido-**. [f. PÆDO-, PEDO- + -PHILIA, or f. as prec. + -IA[1].] An abnormal, esp. sexual, love of young children.

1906 H. ELLIS *Stud. Psychol. Sex* V. i. 11 Paidophilia or the love of children.. may be included under this head [*sc.* abnormality]. **1926** *Med. Jrnl. & Rec.* CXXIV. 161/1 One must keep clearly in mind in dealing with pedophilia the distinction between that mediating homosexuality, and the much more pure perversion which is our subject. **1952** E. A. GUTHEIL tr. *Stekel's Patterns of Psychosexual Infantilism* i. 62 Some eager lady friends of the mistress of the house who expand their friendship to include the younger male generation, may be suspected of pedophilia. **1962** *Listener* 20 Sept. 438/1 The film certainly is not.. a study in paedophilia, of a middle-aged professor's grotesque passion for a twelve-year-old girl. **1963** A. HERON *Towards Quaker View of Sex* 69 Paedophilia is not always homosexual. **1973** *Times Lit. Suppl.* 8 June 647/2 He was driven to a pedophilia in which he played the role of both parents to the children of his fancy.

Hence **pædoˈphiliac, -ˈphilic** *adjs.*, pertaining to or characterized by pædophilia; also as *sb.*, a pædophilic person.

1927 *Psychoanal. Review* XIV. 191 It is only in rare cases that one encounters an individual who has pedophilic predilections and at the same time is suffering from venereal disease. *Ibid.*, Krafft-Ebing.. in his attempt at psychological explanation falls back on 'a morbid disposition only' on the part of the pedophalic [*sic*] as the motivating factor. **1951** *Group Psychotherapy* IV. 170 He then insisted he had never had the slightest amount of pedophiliac desire, and that his crime was a total mystery to him. **1954** *Jrnl. Projective Techniques* XVIII. 348/1 The rapists probably do differ from the pedophiles, however, on the variable of aggression, the majority of the pedophilic acts having been of a passive and seductive nature. **1960** *Spectator* 8 July 69 The.. survey.. shows the paedophiliac to be a type altogether distinct from the adult-seeking homosexual. **1963** A. HERON *Towards Quaker View of Sex* 69 A variety of early experiences and inadequacies of upbringing.. make the paedophilic especially sympathetic towards.. the state of childhood and immaturity. **1974** J. BANCROFT *Deviant Sexual Behaviour* vi. 157 Paedophiliac offenders frequently have personalities in which self-deception and deception of others is marked. **1976** *Publishers Weekly* 26 Apr. 52/1 He contacted fellow pedophiliacs and through them was able to sample many kinds of young girls.

pædotribe (ˈpiːdəʊtraɪb). *Gr. Antiq.* Also **pedo-**. [ad. Gr. παιδοτρίβης.] One who taught wrestling and other exercises; a gymnastic master.

1594 R. ASHLEY tr. *Loys le Roy* 29b, Gymnasts, pedotribes, athletes. **1656** BLOUNT *Glossogr.*, *Pedotribe.* *a* **1822** SHELLEY *Ess. & Lett.* (1852) I. 256 Herodicus being pædotribe.. united the gymnastic with the medical art.

pædotrophy (piːˈdɒtrəfɪ). [ad. Gr. παιδοτροφία.] The rearing of children. So **pædotrophic** (piːdəʊˈtrɒfɪk) *a.*, relating to the rearing of children; **pæˈdotrophist**, one skilled in rearing children.

1857 MAYNE *Expos. Lex.*, *Pædotrophia*, old term.. pedotrophy. **1890** J. S. BILLINGS *Nat. Med. Dict.* II. 271 Pædotrophy.. The hygiene of the rearing of children. **1889** J. SULLY in *Harper's Mag.* June 102/2 Pædotrophic Partnership, the term by which the new Socialism designated a particular and relatively permanent variety of sexual attachment. *Ibid.* 108/2 They could.. pronounce the plaintiff a properly qualified pædotrophist.

Paelignian (pɛˈlɪgnɪən, paɪ-), *sb.* and *a.* Also **Pelignian**. [f. L. *P(a)eligni* + -AN.] **A.** *sb.* **a.** A member of an Oscan-Umbrian people centred on Corfinium in southern Italy. **b.** The language of this people. **B.** *adj.* Of or pertaining to this people or their language.

1600, etc. [see MARRUCINIAN *sb.* and *a.*]. **1853** C. MERIVALE *Fall of Roman Republic* iii. 77 The Samnites and Pelignians reclaimed 4,000 of their own countrymen who had thus established themselves in the Latin town of Fregellæ. **1862** W. P. DICKSON tr. *Mommsen's Hist. Rome* II. xi. 332 When.. the Samnites and Pælignians applied to the senate for a reduction of their contingents, their request was based on the ground that during recent years 4000 Samnite and Pælignian families had migrated to the Latin colony of Fregellæ. **1909** W. E. HEITLAND *Roman Republic* II. xliii. 434 For the revolted Allies some centre was necessary as the headquarters of the confederate government. This was found at Corfinium in the Paelignian country on the eastern side of the Apennine. **1933, 1939** [see MARSIAN *sb.* and *a.*]. **1939** R. SYME *Roman Revolution* xiv. 193 The fierce Marsians and Paelignians had long and bitter memories. **1967** E. T. SALMON *Samnium & Samnites* iv. 177 Ovid.. had his own Paelignian homeland in mind.

paella (pɑːˈɛlə, paɪˈɛlə). [Cat. *paella*, f. OFr. *paele* (mod. *poêle*), f. L. *patella* pan, dish.] A Spanish dish of rice with chicken, seafood, vegetables, etc., cooked and served in a large shallow pan. Also *fig.*

1892 *Encycl. Pract. Cookery* II. 84/2 *Paela*, a favourite Spanish dish containing the usual oil and garlic. **1926** B. REYNOLDS *Cocktail Continentale* 66 You lunch at Antiqua Casa Botin. Crab soup. Paella a la Valencian, a mixture of chicken, fish, meat, rice, vegetables, snails and clams. **1939** R. CAMPBELL *Flowering Rifle* II. 52 Dead Charlies climbing on each other's backs To make a huge paella of the plains. **1955** J. THOMAS *No Banners* viii. 69 An appetizing *paella* and a goblet of *vino tinto* for each man. **1960** 'W. HAGGARD' *Closed Circuit* x. 121 The food was excellent: he could give her the *paella* which he knew she loved, and now she was eating it with relish.. her mouth still full of rice and chicken. **1965** *Punch* 24 Feb. 289/1 The locals mostly speak with a macaroni Italian accent, the Dons with some kind of *paella* Spanish. **1970** 'D. HALLIDAY' *Dolly & Cookie Bird* vii. 99 Paella with all the right things in it, squids and octopuses and chicken and lobster-tails and paprika and sherry and peas and onion and pimento and pork, all done with saffron rice. **1972** *Village Voice* (N.Y.) 1 June 24/3 The underworld provided the paella for the detective stories, including the celebrated 'Pinktoes'. **1976** *National Observer* (U.S.) 23 Oct. 19/3 The restaurant serves up an imaginative assortment of house specialities, many European inspired including.. the Spanish Paella Valenciana.

paen, -ene, var. PAYEN *Obs.*, pagan.

paene, obs. f. PANE *sb.*

pænitence, obs. f. PENITENCE.

‖**pænula** (ˈpiːnjʊlə). [L.] In *Roman Antiq.* A sleeveless cloak having an opening for the head only, and covering the whole body. Hence, An ecclesiastical garment of the same kind, an early form of the chasuble.

[**1270-1** *Pipe Roll* 55 Hen. III. m. I *d*, Pro.. xxxiii penulis de Lindeseye Ermyne & Coruelyne.]

1753 CHAMBERS *Cycl. Supp.*, *Pænula*, among the Romans, a thick garment fit for a defence against cold and rain. **1868** MARRIOTT *Vest. Chr.* p. lxii, We have abundant evidence in Roman literature of the uses to which the *Pænula* served, and of its gradual exaltation from a garb of slaves or of peasants to one which even emperors might wear in travelling, and which was expressly prescribed in the fifth century of our era as the dress of senators.

pæon (ˈpiːən). Also 7-8 **pæan**. [a. L. *pæon*, ad. Gr. παιών: see PÆAN.] A metrical foot of four syllables, one long and three short, named, according to the position of the long syllable, a first, second, third, or fourth pæon.

1603 HOLLAND *Plutarch* Explan. Words, *Pæon* or *Pæeon*, the name of Apollo, and of a metricall foot in verse, of which Pæans are composed. **1699** BENTLEY *Phal.* 459 The Poet was constrain'd of mere necessity to use a Pæon instead of a Dactyl. **1727-41** CHAMBERS *Cycl.*, *Paean* or *Paeon*.. so called, as commonly supposed, because appropriated to the hymn *Pæan*; though Quintilian derives the name from its inventor *Pæon*, a physician. **1867** R. C. JEBB *Sophocles' Electra* (1870) 125/2 The antistrophic verse has a paeon.. in the first place.

pæonic (piːˈɒnɪk), *a.* (*sb.*) [ad. L. *pæōnic-us*, ad. Gr. παιωνικός of or belonging to a pæon.] Of or pertaining to a pæon or pæons; composed of pæons; having the pedal ratio (2:3) of the pæon. **b.** as *sb.* A pæonic verse or foot.

1830 J. SEAGER tr. *Hermann's Metres* II. xl. 104 The ancient Greeks themselves appear not to have completely distinguished between Cretic and pæonic numbers... Pæonics catalectic on two syllables, and having an iambic anacrusis, are rarely met with. **1879** J. W. WHITE tr. *Schmidt's Rhythmic Class. Lang.* §21. 66 Paeonics and bacchii. *Ibid.* §22. 69 Paeonic sentences are rare in Aeschylus.

pæonin (ˈpiːəʊnɪn). *Chem.* [f. L. *pæonia*, PEONY (in reference to colour) + -IN.] = CORALLIN

1866 in WATTS *Dict. Chem.* IV. 324. **1878** tr. *Ziemssen's Cycl. Med.* XVII. 520 The same holds good as regards corallin or pæonin, a red colour composed of rosolic acid.

pæony, var. PEONY.

‖**paepae** (ˈpaɪpaɪ). Also 9 **pi-pi**. Pl. **paepae**. [Native name.] **a.** An elevated stone platform on which Polynesian houses were often built. **b.** A paved area in front of some Polynesian buildings. **c.** A type of raft.

1846 H. MELVILLE *Typee* xxiv. 219 Like all the other edifices of any note, it was raised upon a small pi-pi of stones. **1919** *Century Mag.* Aug. 446/1, I sat.. on the palm-shaded *paepae* of my cabin above the blue lagoon. **1923** R. LINTON *Material Culture of Marquesas Islands* 272 Many of the *paepae* on hill slopes were simple terraces with a trench at the rear to carry off water. *Ibid.* 273 The perfect *paepae* contains stones of three sorts. **1927** P. H. BUCK *Material Culture of Cook Islands* i. 39 In the well-preserved house site.. the cobbled *paepae* terrace was a foot lower than the house terrace. **1930** —— *Samoan Material Culture* 56 When a high *paepae* platform was made, most of the posts did not reach the ground level. **1958** T. HEYERDAHL *Aku-Aku* x. 334, I was the man who had travelled to Raroia with my friends on a *pae-pae*. **1968** N. A. ROWE in T. Heyerdahl *Sea Routes to Polynesia* 205, I had wondered for many years what this could mean but I see now.. that it was a reference to a raft or *pae-pae*. *Pae-pae* can also mean stone platform: hence the confusion. **1974** T. HEYERDAHL *Fatu-Hira* ii. 88 Here we stumbled upon human vestiges.. mostly over-grown terrace walls and stone platforms, *pae-pae*, where native huts had once stood. *Ibid.* iv. 155 Some *paepae* had been declared *tabu* by ancient medicine men and often contained burials and old artifacts.

paeyn, var. PAYEN *Obs.*, pagan.

paff (pæf), *int.* Also **paf**. [Imit.] An expression of contempt. Also used to represent the sound of a blow.

1851 LONGFELLOW *Golden Legend* v. 242 These beggars.. Lamed and maimed, and fed upon chaff, Chaunting their wonderful piff and paff. **1897** *Pall Mall Gaz.* 28 Sept. 2/3 The combatants used their fists only... Paf! paf! one for you, and paf! paf! for your opponent. **1910** [see CRASH *v.* 6 a]. **1922** JOYCE *Ulysses* 40 What offence laid fire to their brains? Paff!

paffle, var. POFFLE *Sc.*, a small holding.

‖**pagador.** *Obs.* [Sp. *pagador*:—med.L. *pācātōr-em* payer.] A pay-master.

1591 *Garrard's Art Warre* 338 The Treasurers and Pagadores Colateraly. **1596** SPENSER *State Irel.* Wks. (Globe) 657/2 This is the manner of the Spanyardes captaynes, whoe.. scorneth the name as base to be counted his souldiours pagador. **1604** DIGGES *4 Parad.* II. 46 The Captaines are become.. the Pagadores or Pay-Masters of their Bandes.

pagan (ˈpeɪgən), *sb.* and *a.* Forms: 4 **paygane**, 5 **pagayne**, 5-6 **pagane**, 5- **pagan**. [ad. L. *pāgān-us*, orig. 'villager, rustic; civilian, non-militant', opposed to *mīlēs* 'soldier, one of the army', in Christian L. (Tertullian, Augustine) 'heathen' as opposed to Christian or Jewish. The Christians called themselves *mīlitēs* 'enrolled soldiers' of Christ, members of his militant church, and applied to non-Christians the term applied by soldiers to all who were 'not enrolled in the army'. Cf. Tertullian *De Corona Militis* xi, 'Apud hunc [Christum] tam miles est paganus fidelis quam paganus est miles infidelis'. See also GIBBON xxi. *note*.

Cf. PAYEN.

The explanation of L. *pāgānus* in the sense 'non-Christian, heathen', as arising out of that of 'villager, rustic', (supposedly indicating the fact that the ancient idolatry lingered on in the rural villages and hamlets after Christianity had been generally accepted in the towns and cities of the Roman Empire: see Trench *Study of Words* 102, and cf. Orosius I Præf. 'Ex locorum agrestium compitis et pagis pagani vocantur') has been shown to be chronologically and historically untenable, for this use of the word goes back to Tertullian *c* 202, when paganism was still the public and dominant religion, and even appears, according to Lanciani, in an epitaph of the 2nd cent.]

A. *sb.* **1.** One of a nation or community which does not hold the true religion, or does not worship the true God; a heathen. (†In earlier use practically = non-Christian, and so including Muslims and, sometimes, Jews.)

c **1375** *Sc. Leg. Saints* viii. (*Philepus*) 6 Payganis, þat war dwelland þare. **1432-50** tr. *Higden* (Rolls) II. 281 The goddes, that paganes do worshippe, were men some tyme. **1456** SIR G. HAYE *Law Arms* (S.T.S.) 8 The hard hertis, and untrewe treuth of the pagans. **1593** SHAKS. *Rich. II*, IV. i. 95 Streaming the Ensigne of the Christian Crosse, Against black Pagans, Turkes, and Saracens. **1596** —— *Merch. V.* II. iii. 11 Adue,.. most beautifull Pagan, most sweete Iew. **1727** DE FOE *Syst. Magic* I. iii. (1840) 69 The emperor Julian.. was perverted from Christianity, and confirmed a pagan, by Maximus a Magician. **1805** SOUTHEY *Metr. T.*, *Yng. Dragon* I. i, Pithyrian was a Pagan, An easy-hearted man, And Pagan sure he thought to end As Pagan he began. **1846** WRIGHT *Ess. Mid. Ages* I. iii. 99 The later Saxons, after the crusade, used the word 'Saracen' in the sense of 'pagan', and.. applied it to the pagans of the north.

2. *fig.* or *allusively*. A person of heathenish character or habits, or one who holds a position analogous to that of a heathen in relation to Christian society.

1841 EMERSON *Lect.*, *Man Reformer* Wks. (Bohn) II. 247 Love would put a new face on this weary old world in which we dwell as pagans and enemies too long. **1877** BLACK *Green Past.* xv. (1878) 122 'But what are his politics?' said the Lady Sylvia to this political pagan. **1879** —— *Macleod of D.* xv, That bloodless old Pagan, her father.

†**b.** *spec.* A paramour, prostitute. *Obs.*

1597 SHAKS. *2 Hen. IV.* II. ii. 168 What Pagan may that be? **1632** MASSINGER *City Madam* II. i, In all these places I have had my several pagans billeted For my own tooth.

3. *Comb.*, as **pagan-like** adj.

1608 H. CLAPHAM *Errour Left Hand* 34 The formes of them be Pagan-like. **1668** H. MORE *Div. Dial.* IV. xxxv. (1713) 387 A wicked Apostacy into Pagan-like Superstitions.

B. *adj.* **1. a.** Not belonging to a nation or community that acknowledges the true God; worshipping idols; heathen.

c **1586** C'TESS PEMBROKE *Ps.* XLIV. i, Thy hand the Pagan foe Rooting hence,.. Leaveless made that braunch to growe. **1634** SIR T. HERBERT *Trav.* 200 The women here [Sumatra] (not differing from all other parts of the Pagan World) are much vnchast. **1765** BLACKSTONE *Comm.* I. 93 The antient and christian inhabitants.. retired to those natural intrenchments, for protection from their pagan visitants. **1865** M. ARNOLD *Ess. Crit.* vi. 201 The ideal, cheerful, sensuous, pagan life. **1894** J. T. FOWLER *Adamnan* Introd. 39 The first Christian architecture was.. a continuation of the pagan work.

b. Nature-worshipping, pantheistic.

1908 E. F. BENSON *Climber* vi. 107 She had read the account of the projected fair to them all two days before; it was a sort of pagan harvest festival, full of folk-lore, and was tremendously picturesque. **1953** L. WILKINSON *Seven Friends* 115 In all three brothers humour is rich and deep, as is love of Nature: but Llewelyn, more than John, much more than Theodore, found joy—a Pagan joy—in all his sensibilities and responses. **1973** R. WILLIAMS *Country & City* xxii. 270 The spiritual feeling for the land and for labour, the 'pagan' emphasis which is always latent in the imagery of the earth. **1987** *Church Times* 6 Nov. 12/4 Water—pond, river, or well—has a deep pagan appeal.

2. *fig.* Of heathen character, heathenish.

1550 W. LYNNE *Carion's Cron.* 279 To the pagane Papistes, arrogant Anabaptistes, licenciouse lybertines. **1606** CHAPMAN *Monsieur D'Olive* Plays 1873 I. 215 Said t'was a pagan plant, a prophane weede And a most sinful smoke [i.e. tobacco]. *a* **1704** T. BROWN *Sat. Marriage* Wks. 1730 I. 58 This pagan confinement.. Suits no order, nor age, nor degree.

†**paga'nalian**, *a. Obs. rare*$^{-0}$. [f. L. *Pāgānālia* neut. pl. (see below) + -AN.] Belonging to the *Paganalia* or annual festival celebrated in each *pagus* or rural district of ancient Italy. So †**'paganals** *sb. pl.* (anglicization of *Paganalia.*)

1656 BLOUNT *Glossogr.*, *Paganalian*,.. of or belonging to Wakes or Plough-mens Feasts, Country Holy daies, and the like. **1658** PHILLIPS (s.v. *Paganical*), Paganals *i.* Wakes, Country-Holidayes, Ploughmens Feasts.

pagandom (ˈpeɪgəndəm). [f. PAGAN + -DOM.] The realm or domain of pagans; the pagan world (as opp. to *Christendom*); heathendom.

1853 *Fraser's Mag.* XLVII. 295 It regarded Pagandom as its common foe. **1868** J. A. WYLIE *Road to Rome* xvii. 213 The one supreme deity of Pagandom. **1886** A. T. PIERSON *Crisis Missions* 194 Joining the centres of Christendom and Pagandom.

†**pa'ganic**, *a. Obs.* [ad. L. *pāgānic-us*, f. *pāgān-us* PAGAN: see -IC.] Of, belonging to, or characteristic of pagans; pagan.

1676 MARVELL *Gen. Councils* Wks. 1875 IV. 145 Churches, that with paganick rites they dedicated to Saint Mary. **1685** H. MORE *Paralip. Prophet.* xxxii. 293 It is indeed a Paganick Oracle. **1773** J. ROSS *Fratricide* III. 11 (MS.) All The black paganic Worship of the East.

†**pa'ganical**, *a. Obs.* [See -ICAL.] = prec.

1573 L. LLOYD *Marrow of Hist.* (1653) 149 Paganical rites of fond foolish observations. **1678** CUDWORTH *Intell. Syst.* I. iii. 138 [They] are not so much to be accompted atheists, as spurious, paganical, and idolatrous theists.

Hence †**pa'ganically** *adv.*

1664 H. MORE *Antid. Idolatry* ix. 96 Whereby it is deprehended to be still more coursly and Paganically Idolatrous. **1678** CUDWORTH *Intell. Syst.* I. iv. 279 The one and only God (saith Clemens) is worshipped by the Greeks Paganically, by the Jews Judaically, but by Us newly and Spiritually.

paganish (ˈpeɪgənɪʃ), *a.* [f. PAGAN + -ISH[1].]

†**1.** Of or belonging to pagans; pagan. *Obs.*

1583 HAYES *Narr. Gilbert's Voy.* in *Hakluyt's Voy.* (1809-12) III. 192 Those Paganish regions. **1599** *Broughton's Lett.* xii. 40 That sence which in Paganish writers is.. vsuall. *a* **1641** BP. MOUNTAGU *Acts & Mon.* (1642) 204 Paganish and Idololatricall rites. **1718** BP. HUTCHINSON *Witchcraft* 167 Paganish and Popish Superstitions.

2. Resembling or befitting a pagan; of pagan character or quality; heathenish.

1613 BP. HALL *Serm. Rev.* xxi. 3, 4 Wks. 1837 V. 70 Not to hope for it, is paganish and brutish. **1676** R. DIXON *Two Testaments* 208 To use Rites is comely,.. but to multiply them.. is Jewish and Paganish. **1795** W. MASON *Ch. Mus.* 238 He would not suffer verse to be.. sung as verse.. because it was gay and paganish. **1871** BLACK *Daughter Heth* (1876) 24 Variations, which he regarded as impudent and paganish.

Hence **'paganishly** *adv.*

1825 SCOTT *Betrothed* xiii, Mahound (so paganishly was the horse named) answered by plunging.

paganism (ˈpeɪgənɪz(ə)m). [ad. eccles. L. *pāgānism-us* (Augustine), f. *pāgān-us* PAGAN: see -ISM. Cf. F. *paganisme* (1611 in Cotgr.).]

1. The religious belief and practices of pagans; the condition of being a pagan; heathenism.

1433 LYDG. *St. Edmund* II. 417 That goddis creatoure.. Sholde in helle eternal peyne endure Thoruh mysbeleue for paganysme rage. **1561** T. NORTON *Calvin's Inst.* IV. xix. (1634) 729 They goe about a wittie thing, to make one Religion of Christianitie, Jewishnesse, and Paganisme, as it were of patches sowed together. **1602** WARNER *Alb. Eng.* IX. li. (1612) 230 Peruse all Lawes, euen Paganizme. **1781** GIBBON *Decl. & F.* xxi. (1846) II. 248 The divisions of Christianity suspended the ruin of Paganism. **1833** J. H. NEWMAN *Arians* I. iii. (1876) 80 The Book of Genesis contains a record of the dispensation of Natural Religion, or Paganism, as well as of the Patriarchal.

†**b.** The pagan world; pagandom, heathendom.

1640 tr. *Verdere's Rom. of Rom.* I. xxvii. 123 The revenge of those outrages, which from time to time all Paganisme had received from the Emperours of Greece. *c* **1650** *Don Bellianis* 18 The great destruction made of his people by you, and in all Paganisme.

2. *fig.* or *allusively*. Pagan character or quality; the moral condition of pagans.

1874 FERGUSSON in *Contemp. Rev.* Oct. 765 Views opposed to the Paganism of St. Paul's or to the attempt to mediævalize it. **1876** J. PARKER *Paracl.* II. xix. 356 The paganism of his logic should not be taken for more than it is worth.

b. A pagan or heathenish feature. *rare.*

1883 *Athenæum* 15 Dec. 783/1 Their crowning features are mere paganisms, quite out of keeping with the designs they deface.

paga'nistic, *a.* [f. PAGAN *sb.* and *a.* + -ISTIC.] = PAGANISH *a.* 2.

1933 DYLAN THOMAS *Let.* (1966) 71 But the more paganistic..one becomes, the less one feels the desire to write. **1938** *Sun* (Baltimore) 14 Nov. 2/5 He will ignore the madman Hitler and his cripple-minded Goebbels with their paganistic philosophy. **1948** L. SPITZER *Linguistics & Lit. Hist.* v. 194 A comparison of Claudel's Christian ode with the paganistic ode of Ronsard.

paganity (pə'gænɪtɪ). Now *rare* or *Obs.* [ad. late L. *pāgānitās* (Cod. Theod. 438), f. *pāgān-us* PAGAN: cf. *Christianity*. Cf. OF. *paieneté*.] The condition or quality of being pagan; paganism.

1548 UDALL, etc. *Erasm. Par. Mark* Pref. 5 Rome, which coulde not forget her old paganitie. **1678** CUDWORTH *Intell. Syst.* I. iv. 561 There is something of imperfection.. something of paganity likewise necessarily consequent thereupon. **1837** CARLYLE *Let. to Sterling* 25 Dec., What Christianity is to us and what Paganity is, and all manner of other anities. **1866** J. B. ROSE *Ecl. & Georg. Virg.* 142 Britain in primitive paganity is not 'almost divided from the world'.

paganize ('peɪgənaɪz), *v.* [a. F. *paganise-r* (1551 in Hatz.-Darm.) or med.L. *pāgānizāre*: see PAGAN and -IZE.]

1. *trans.* To make pagan; to give a pagan character or form to.

1615 BRATHWAIT *Strappado* (1878) 151 A Christian Paganis'd with name of Punke. **1678** CUDWORTH *Intell. Syst.* I. iv. §36. 628 Christianity.. was thereby itself Paganized and Idolatrized. **1812–29** COLERIDGE in *Lit. Rem.* (1838) III. 126 Even as early as the third century the Church had begun to Paganize Christianity.

2. *intr.* To become pagan; to act as a pagan; to assume a pagan character. Also *to paganize it.*

1640 CHILMEAD tr. *Ferrand's Love Melancholy* 176 They paganize it to their own damnation. **1641** MILTON *Animadv.* (1851) 206 This was that which made the old Christians Paganize. **1875** MRS. CHARLES in *Sunday Mag.* May 512 When Christendom begins to speak of her golden age as in the past, she paganises.

Hence **'paganized** *ppl. a.*, **'paganizing** *vbl. sb.* and *ppl. a.*; also **,pagani'zation**, the action of paganizing or fact or being paganized; **'paganizer**, one who paganizes.

1863 DRAPER *Intell. Devel. Europe* x. (1865) 228 The *paganization of religion was in no small degree assisted by the influence of the females of the Court of Constantinople. **1898** F. I. ANTROBUS tr. *Pastor's Hist. Popes* V. 9 Whether.. the paganisation of all the relations of life [was] so universal as has been maintained. **1732** WATERLAND *Chr. Vind. Charge* 74 *Paganized Christianity. **1873** MORLEY *Rousseau* I. 194 The paganized catholicism of the renaissance. **1727–41** CHAMBERS *Cycl.*, *Ethnophrones*,.. q.d. *paganizers, or persons, whose thoughts, or sentiments were still heathen or gentile. **1652** GAULE *Magastrom.* 110 To take heed of.. Judaizing, *Paganizing, of idolatry, atheism, superstition. **1855** MILMAN *Lat. Chr.* III. ii. (1864) I. 328 Christianity made some steps toward the old religion by the splendour of its ceremonial, and the incipient paganising, not of its creed, but of its popular belief. **1631** R. H. *Arraignm. Whole Creature* xi. §1. 96 Called abusively by Pagans and Heathens, and *Paganizing Christians, the Goods of Fortune. **1826** G. S. FABER *Diffic. Romanism* (1853) 347 The Bible knows nothing of those paganising distinctions between *relative worship* and *positive worship*.

paganly ('peɪgənlɪ), *adv.* [f. PAGAN *a.* + -LY[2].] In a pagan manner or degree; like a pagan.

1659 H. MORE *Immort. Soul* I. xiv. (1662) 53 This..I am not so paganly superstitious as to believe one syllable of. **1835** in Southey *Comm.-pl. Bk.* IV. 581 The Irish Papists are paganly superstitious.

pa,gano'christian, *a.* and *sb.* [f. *pagano-*, comb. form of L. *pāgānus* PAGAN + CHRISTIAN.] **A.** *adj.* Christian in a pagan way, or with an admixture of paganism. **B.** *sb.* A Christian corrupted by paganism. So **pagano-'christianism; pagano-'christianize** *v.*

1667 J. CORBET *Disc. Relig. Eng.* 17 That new kind of Paganism, or Pagano-Christianism. **1668** H. MORE *Div. Dial.* IV. xxi. (1713) 341 The Pagano-christian Tyranny of the Pope. **1680** —— *Apocal. Apoc.* ii. 23 These People.. shall at the end..get the Nations under them, that is, the Paganochristians. **1681** —— *Exp. Dan.* ii. 38 The Empire.. was beginning to Pagano-Christianize and grow Idolatrous again. **1685** —— *Paralip. Prophet.* xxvi. 229 The Pagano-christianizing Caesars or Emperours.

paganry ('peɪgənrɪ). [f. PAGAN *sb.* + -RY; cf. *popery*.] Pagan condition or practice; heathenry.

1583 STUBBES *Anat. Abus.* I. (1879) 144 It is all one, as if they had said, bawdrie, hethenrie, paganrie. **1866** J. B. ROSE tr. *Ovid's Fasti* Notes 259 The memory of this paganry did not disappear when all traces of lake and solar rites had passed away.

†**'pagany.** *Obs.* [Refashioning of PAYENY, after *pagan*. Cf. *Tuscany*.] = PAGANDOM.

a **1533** LD. BERNERS *Huon* lviii. 197 He slew Sorbryn, the moost valyant knyght in all pagany. **1594** CAREW *Tasso* (1881) 11 Where midst vnnumbred troopes of Paganie..few of his Countrey are.

page (peɪdʒ), *sb.*[1] Also 5 payge, 6 *Sc.* pege. [a. OF. *page* = It. *paggio*, med.L. *pagius* (*c* 1300, Du Cange): cf. Sp. *page*, Pg. *pagem* in same sense.

The origin of the Romanic word is unsettled. Diez conjectured for It. *paggio* derivation from Gr. παιδίον boy, which is very doubtful; Littré suggests that med.L. *pagius* is from *pāgus* the country, a country district, comparing Pr. *pages* villain, rustic:—L. *pāgensis*, and cites the statement of Fauchet (1601), that down to the time of Charles VI and VII, 1380–1461, *page* in Fr. seems to have been applied solely to *de viles personnes*.]

I. † **1.** A boy, youth, lad. *Obs.*

a **1300** *Cursor M.* 7499 Quat bot to lese þi lijf, leue page. *Ibid.* 10295 War pages nan for hirdes sett, Bot stalworth men þair bestes gett. **1375** BARBOUR *Bruce* I. 289 He had A Sone, A litill Knave, þat wes þan bot a litill page. *c* **1386** CHAUCER *Reeve's T.* 52 A child þat was of half yeer age In Cradel it lay and was a propre page. *c* **1440** *York Myst.* xviii. 101 þat yonge page [the infant Jesus] liffe þou mon for-gange, But yf þou fast flee fro his foo. **1582** STANYHURST *Æneis* II. (Arb.) 46 My father vnwelthy mee sent, then a prittye page, hither.

†**2.** A male person of the 'lower orders', or of low condition or manners: a term of contempt and sometimes of opprobrium; cf. KNAVE 2, 3. *Obs.*

13.. *K. Alis.* 6461 So wex yalow is heore visages, In the world no buth so foule pages! *c* **1386** CHAUCER *Frankl. Prol.* 20 He hath leuere talken with a page Than to comune with any gentil wight There he myghte lerne gentillesse aright. *c* **1430** *Hymns Virg.* 62 He [Satan] wolde haue peerid with god of blis; Now is he in helle moost looþeli page. *c* **1440** *York Myst.* xxix. 381 Sirs, we muste presente þis page [Jesus] to ser Pilate. **1508** DUNBAR *Tua Mariit Wemen* 313 That page was neuer of sic price for to presome anys Wnto my persone to be peir. *a* **1529** SKELTON *Dk. Albany* 416 A prince to play the page It is a rechelesse rage, And a lunatyke ouerage.

3. A boy or lad employed as a servant or attendant; hence, a male servant of the lowest grade in his line of service, corresponding to an apprentice in trade; one whose part it is to assist and learn from an upper or more experienced servant or officer. **a.** Formerly in the most wide and general use; also with special qualifications, as ***page of the kitchen, scullery*** (= scullion), ***stable*** (= stable-boy), etc. *Obs.* in general use; but **b.** Still applied in East Anglia to a shepherd's attendant, whether boy, lad, or man. (Cf. modern uses of *boy*, as in *cabin-boy, cow-boy, post-boy, stable-boy*, etc.)

a **1327** *Pol. Songs* (Camden) 237 Palefreiours ant pages. **13..** *Guy Warw.* (A.) st. 283 Wiþ him he hadde þer a page þat serued him in þat hermitage. **14..** *Metr. Voc.* in Wr.-Wülcker 623/2 A payge of the keschyn. *c* **1440** *Promp. Parv.* 377/1 Page of a stabylle, *equarius*. **14..** *Customs of Malton* in *Surtees Misc.* (1888) 61 þai schall haffe in þe sayd mylnes two mylners and j page. **1470–85** Kechyn page [see KITCHEN *sb.* 5 a]. **1530** PALSGR. 250/2 Page a servaunt, *page*. ? *a* **1550** *Freiris of Berwik* 447 in *Dunbar's Poems* (1893) 300, I haif ane pege..will..bring to me sic thing as I will haif. **1707** CHAMBERLAYNE *St. Gt. Brit.* 539 (The Queens Officers and Servants) Scullery..Yeoman..Joint Grooms..Page.. Servant..Child.

b. 1819 RAINBIRD *Agric.* (1849) 297 (Eng. Dial. Dict.). *a* **1825** FORBY *Voc. E. Anglia*, *Page*, the lad attending on a shepherd. **1847–78** HALLIWELL, *Page*, the common and almost only name of a shepherd's servant, whether boy or man... Extensively used through Suffolk, and probably further.

4. a. *Chivalry.* A boy or lad in training for knighthood, and attached to the personal service of a knight, whom he followed on foot, being not yet advanced to the rank of squire. Cf. *foot-page* (FOOT *sb.*), FOOTMAN 3. Now only *Hist.* Hence †**b.** A foot-soldier. †**c.** A camp-servant. *Obs.*

13.. *K. Alis.* 6022 Fyve hundrod thousand Knyghtis to armes, so Y fynde, Withowte pages and skuyeris. *c* **1440** *Generydes* 5460 With hir went ij squyers and noo mo, Save ij pages to kepe ther horses also. [**1847** JAMES *J. Marston Hall* vii, If we place you as page to any one else, it must solely be with a view to your military promotion hereafter. **1858** TRENCH *Synon. N.T.* viii. (1876) 30 Like that of the squire or page of the Middle Ages.]

b, c. *c* **1330** R. BRUNNE *Chron.* (1810) 163 A hundreth knyghtes mo..& four hundreth to bote, squieres of gode aray, & fiue hundreth o fote, to whilk I salle pay..Knyght, squier & pages, þe termes of two ȝere. *c* **1440** *Promp. Parv.* 337/1 Page, *pageta, pedissequus, pedes*. **1480** CAXTON *Chron. Eng.* VII. (1520) 120/1 Whyle this doynge lasted the englysshe pages toke the pylfre of the Scottes. **1563** GOLDING *Cæsar* (1565) 60 Learning by the flyght of oure horsemen and pages [*calonum*] in what case the matter stood. **1632** SHERWOOD, A souldiers page, *goujat*.

5. a. A youth employed as the personal attendant of a person of rank. (In earlier times often himself of gentle birth, and placed in this position in order to be trained in the usages of good society.)

c **1460** J. RUSSELL *Bk. Nurture* 1123 Yeff he be a..page.. receve hym as a..grome goodly in fere. **1585** T. WASHINGTON tr. *Nicholay's Voy.* II. xviii. 51 A place for yong children, which are pages. **1592** SHAKS. *Rom. & Jul.* III. i. 97. **1606** CHAPMAN *Monsieur D'Olive* Plays 1873 I. 197 Pages and Parasits [live] by making legges. **1727–41** CHAMBERS *Cycl.*, *Page*, a youth of state, retained in the family of a prince or great personage..to attend in visits of ceremony, do messages, bear up trains, robes, etc. and..to have a genteel education, and learn his exercises. **1756** tr. *Keysler's Trav.* (1760) I. 455 A lady of considerable rank, who..is allowed a page, or *ragazzo*, and he must not exceed fourteen years of age. **1808** SCOTT *Marm.* I. xv, Where hast thou left that page of thine, That used to serve thy cup of wine? **1855** MACAULAY *Hist. Eng.* xxii. IV. 789 Many coaches and six, attended by harbingers, footmen, and pages.

b. Hence, a title of various officers of a royal or princely household, usually with some distinctive addition, as ***page of honour, page of the back-stairs, of the chamber, of the presence***, etc.

c **1386** CHAUCER *Knt.'s T.* 569 A yeer or two he was in this seruyse Page of the chambre of Emelye the brighte. **1450** *Rolls of Parlt.* V. 193/1 Bryan Wager, page of oure Robes. **1509–10** *Act 1 Hen. VIII*, c. 14 Yomen Gromes and pagys of the Kynges Chambre. *a* **1562** G. CAVENDISH *Wolsey* (1893) 81, xii goodly yong gentilmen, called pages of honour. **1664** (*title*) Comedies and Tragedies. Written by Thomas Killigrew, Page of Honour to King Charles the First. **1698** LUTTRELL *Brief Rel.* (1857) IV. 416 A son of Mr. Secretary Vernon is made page of the presence to the duke of Glocester. **1707** CHAMBERLAYNE *St. Gt. Brit.* 544 (The Queen's Officers and Servants)..Pages of the Back-Stairs [6]..Their Salary 80*l.* per Annum each. Pages of the Presence-Chamber [4]..Their Salary 25*l.* per Annum each. Grooms of the Great-Chamber [10]..Their Salary 40*l.* *Ibid.* 551 (The Master of the Horse, and his Officers).. Equerry of the Crown Stable..256*l.* Pages of Honour [4].. 156*l.* each. Gentleman of the Horse..256*l.* **1899** *Pall Mall Mag.* Apr. 514 Loudon..was made a page of the backstairs to Queen Mary. **1900** *Whitacker's Alm.* 87 (Her Majesty's Household)..Pages of the Back Stairs [4]. State Pages [2]. Page of the Chambers... Pages of the Presence [5]. Pages, Men [3]. *Ibid.* 88 Master of the Horse..; Crown Equerry..; Pages of Honour [4].

c. Hence, in mod. usage, often applied to a boy or lad (usually in 'buttons' or livery) employed in a private house, a club, hotel, large shop, etc., to attend to the door, go on errands, and the like; a foot-boy; in U.S. to an attendant upon a legislative body. **d.** Also applied to little boys fancifully dressed at a wedding ceremony to bear the bride's train.

1781 COWPER *Truth* 146 She yet allows herself that boy behind;..His predecessor's coat advanced to wear, Which future pages yet are doomed to share. **1829** LYTTON *Devereux* II. i, There..a page, in purple and silver, sat upon the table, swinging his legs to and fro. **1833** T. HOOK *Parson's Daughter* (1847) 222 A small white-faced boy who was called 'page' to Aunt Eleanor,..superseding what commonly-minded persons were accustomed to consider footboys. **1840** *Boston Even. Transcript* 18 Feb. 2/1 A page took them to the Clerk—the Clerk handed them to the Speaker. **1878** B. HARTE *Man on Beach* 104 Obtaining political influence through caucuses, I became at last page in the Senate. **1897** W. W. JACOBS *Skipper's Wooing* xi. 127 And Henry'll be a little page in white satin knickers holding up the bride's train. **1949** *Time* 27 June 61/1 The Capitol Page School..is attended by the House's 49 page boys, the Senate's 21, the Supreme Court's four, and a few more Capitol-employed boys. **1955** *Times* 8 July 10/4 She was attended by two pages, James Mostyn and Viscount Quenington, two child bridesmaids, Harriet and Sarah Duckworth, and five older bridesmaids. **1973** 'M. YORKE' *Grave Matters* III. i. 54 Maybe he'll bring the girl to see us. .. Then you can start planning Andrew's page's outfit.

II. Transferred uses.

6. A clip or other contrivance, for holding up a woman's skirt in walking.

1864 SALA *Quite Alone* xxvii. 185 The artful arrangement of hooks and strings, known as 'ladies' pages'.

7. *Entom.* Collector's name for a black and green South American hawk-moth of the family *Uraniidæ*.

1886 in *Cassell's Encycl. Dict.* **1901** *Westm. Gaz.* 30 Nov. 4/2 During the last two years swarms of a singularly handsome butterfly, with dark green wings and white tails, have been noticed in Trinidad,..it is now known that they are the 'green pages' of the Venezuelan forests.

8. *Brick-making.* (See quot.)

1875 KNIGHT *Dict. Mech.*, *Page*, the track carrying the pallets, which support the newly molded bricks, and on which they are slipped to the off-bearing boy..at the end. [Fr. *page* was formerly applied to the brickmaker's boy who carried the newly moulded bricks on the pallets.]

9. *Comb.*, as ***page-work***; ***page-like*** adj.; **page-boy,** (*a*) = sense 5; (*b*) used *attrib.* and *absol.* to designate a woman's hair-style in which the hair is worn in a long bob with the ends turned under and hanging on the shoulders; (*c*) = PAGER *sb.*[3]

1623 MASSINGER *Dk. Milan* III. i, All the dangers That, page-like, wait on the success of war. **1874** A. J. MUNBY *Diary* 29 June in D. Hudson *Munby* (1972) 368 'Goodbye, William!' she said to the page boy who opened the hall door for us. **1888** LIGHTHALL *Yng. Seigneur* 53 'So, then, do your own page-work', said Haviland. **1902** *Spectator* 8 Feb. 201/1 Loitering in the division lobbies as if they were untrustworthy page-boys on a round of morning errands. **1903** *Daily Chron.* 10 Mar. 7/2 There are large numbers of page-boys employed in West-end clubs and hotels. **1939** R. CHANDLER *Big Sleep* i. 13 Her hair was a fine tawny wave cut much shorter than the current fashion of pageboy tresses curled in at the bottom. **1951** 'A. GARVE' *Murder in Moscow* i. 27 She still wore her fair hair in a fringe with a page-boy bob. **1961** L. P. HARTLEY *Two for River* 53 'Mr. Lenthall, please, Mr. Lenthall, please,' intoned a page-boy in a high-pitched nasal sing-song. **1971** *Guardian* 27 July 9/2 Hair is in long page-boy bobs with hair slides. **1973** *Times* 17 Jan. 4/5 The Post Office yesterday launched its radio 'pageboy', a tiny 'bleeper' which can be set off by a telephone call. **1975** H. MCCUTCHEON *Instrument of Vengeance* vi. 94 Her hair was..cut in pageboy style. **1976** G. MCDONALD *Confess, Fletch* (1977) xxvii. 125 Her hair was a perfect black, shining pageboy.

page (peɪdʒ), *sb.*[2] [a. F. *page* fem. (12th c. in Hatz.-Darm.) a page:—L. *pāgina* a leaf of a book, a written page, f. stem *pag-* of *pangĕre* to fasten, fix in, fix together.]

1. a. One side of a leaf of a book, manuscript, letter, etc. Also, a complete leaf of a book, etc. ***full page***, a page containing its full complement of printed lines, or containing an engraving or illustration which occupies the entire page; also *attrib.*: cf. FULL *a.* 12. ***page for page***, corresponding in the paging; also *attrib.*

1589 NASHE *Pref. Greene's Menaphon* (Arb.) 9 Seneca let bloud line by line and page by page, at length must needes die to our stage. **1601** HOLLAND *Pliny* XIII. xii. 393 If one leafe of this large Paper were plucked off, the more pages tooke harme thereby, & were lost. **1656** BLOUNT *Glossogr.* s.v., Some confound *folio* and *page*; when as a folio or leaf properly comprehends two pages. **1728** SWIFT *Poetical Works* (1967) 346 Tim set the Volume on a Table, Read over here and there a Fable, And found, as he the pages twirl'd, The Monkey, who had seen the World. **1786** BURNS *Poems, chiefly in Scottish Dial.* 71 Now moths deform in shapeless tatters Their unknown pages. **1791** MRS. RADCLIFFE *Rom. Forest* ix, Intending only to look cursorily over the few first pages. **1819** BYRON *Don Juan* I. xcv. 50 By the wind Even as the page is rustled while we look, So by the poesy of his own mind Over the mystic leaf his soul was shook. **1860** TYNDALL *Glac.* II. i. 224 The phenomena referred to in the foregoing pages. **1889** H. O. SOMMER *Malory's Arthur* Pref. 8 Caxton is reprinted page for page, line for line, word for word. **1895** CONRAD *Almayer's Folly* 254 Books open with torn pages bestrewed the floor. **1896** in *Moxon's Mech. Exerc., Printing* p. xviii, A line-for-line and page-for-page reprint of the original text. **1919** G. B. SHAW *Great Catherine* 115 A play that will leave the reader as ignorant of Russian history as he may be now before he has turned the page. **1925** F. SCOTT FITZGERALD *Great Gatsby* iii. 55 Knew when to stop, too—didn't cut the pages. **1950** W. STEVENS *Auroras of Autumn* 99 On the pedestal, an ambitious page dog-eared. **1969** I. MURDOCH *Bruno's Dream* 27 He..folded the page into a paper dart. **1974** 'J. LE CARRÉ' *Tinker, Tailor* I. xiii. 113 The pages had been excised with a razor blade.

b. *Printing.* The type set up, or made up from slips or galleys, for printing a page.

1727–41 CHAMBERS *Cycl.* s.v. *Printing*, The page, then, composed and ranged in the galley, he ties it up therein with a cord or packthread, and sets it by. **1824** J. JOHNSON *Typogr.* II. 193 A few observations on the method of tying up a page. **1891** W. MORRIS in Mackail *Life* (1899) II. 254, I will set up a trial-page of the G[olden] L[egend].

c. *Type-founding.* One of the parcels into which new type is made up by the founders, to be sent out: usually 8 inches by 4.

1882 J. SOUTHWARD *Pract. Printing* (1884) 15 Type is sent from the founders in parcels... The parcel is called a page. **1903** H. HART *Let. to Editor*, Moxon calls these type-founders' pages 'cartridges'.

d. That which is (actually or notionally) written, printed, etc., on a page. Cf. sense 2 a.

1805 W. BLAKE *Let.* 19 Jan. (1966) 857 The first page of the Poem was beautifully executed. *c* **1862** E. DICKINSON *Poems* (1955) I. 376 Tell him the page I didn't write. **1903** G. B. SHAW *Revolutionist's Handbk.* viii, in *Man & Superman* 210 Whilst these pages are being written an English judge has sentenced a forger to twenty years penal servitude. **1951** L. HUGHES *Montage of Dream Deferred* 39 Up to my room, sit down, and write this page. **1966** *McGraw-Hill Encycl. Sci. & Technol.* V. 177/1 Rail-roads employ high-speed facsimile (several pages per minute) for the transmission of waybills. **1975** *Times* 24 Sept. 2/8 Using the Keypad, the user would call up the Viewdata service and select the 'pages' of information to be displayed on the television screen. **1978** *Broadcast* 6 Mar. 10/2 Viewdata's standard page of 24 lines of text requires 480 lines of actual picture information.

e. *Computers.* A division of the main store of a computer consisting of a certain number of 'words' (commonly a few thousand); also, a corresponding amount of data or part of a program.

1948 *Ann. Computation Lab. Harvard Univ.* XVI. 46 A 'page' number marks a section of 'blocks' in much the same fashion as the page of a book would contain several lines of data, while the block number identifies the line of data. **1962** *IRE Trans. Electronic Computers* XI. 226/2 The main core store is..partitioned into blocks..which for identification purposes are called pages. **1970** O. DOPPING *Computers & Data Processing* ix. 124 In systems with extensive core swapping it is advantageous to have the program subdivided into 'pages' of a prescribed size, e.g. 1,000 words, and consider primary storage to be sub-divided into blocks, where each block has room for exactly one page.

2. *fig.* **a.** Any page, or the pages collectively, of a writing; hence, rhetorically, Writing, book, record. **b.** An episode such as would fill a page in a written history; a single phase of the 'book of nature', or of the 'book of life' (see BOOK *sb.* 4).

1619 DRAYTON *Past.* Ecl. v. viii, On the world's idols I do hate to smile, Nor shall their names e'er in my page appear. **1750** GRAY *Elegy* xiii, Her ample page Rich with the spoils of time. **1752** —— *Bentley* v, That..inspiration..That burns in Shakespeare's or in Milton's page. **1822** SOUTHEY *Ode King's Visit Scot.* xi, A deeper tragedy..hath never fill'd The historic page. **1851** TRENCH *Poems* 54 Nor merely in the fair page nature shows, But in the living page of human life To look and learn. **1885** *Daily Tel.* 24 July, A bright page in her military history.

3. *attrib.* and *Comb.*, *as **page-head**, **-heading**, **-picture**, **-size**, **-turning**; **page-long** adj.*; **page charge**, a fee of so much per page requested from an organization when a learned journal publishes a paper by one of its members; **page-cord, -gauge** (see quots. 1858, 1875); **page-galley**, (*a*) a galley containing enough type to print a page; (*b*) a galley proof on which the type has been divided into pages and numbered; **page-paper**, a piece of stiff paper on which a page of type is placed before being fastened up with others in a forme; **page printer**, a printer (sense 2) whose output is in the form of printed or typed pages; so **page-printing** *ppl. a.* and *vbl. sb.*; **page-proof**, a pull taken from type made up into paged form; **page reference**, a reference to a specific page or group of pages in a book or periodical; **page three girl**, a scantily-clad or nude model whose picture appears as a 'pin-up' in the popular press, *spec.* as part of a regular feature on page three of the *Sun* [*Page Three* is a proprietary name registered by News Group Newspapers, publishers of the *Sun*]; also in extended use; **page-turner**, (*a*) a mechanical device for turning the pages of a book (so **page-turning** *ppl. a.*); (*b*) *fig.*, a very enjoyable or readable book; (*c*) one who turns the pages of a musician's score, usu. during a performance.

1966 *Jrnl. Amer. Chem. Soc.* 5 Feb. 8A/2 A page charge is assessed to cover in part the cost of publication. Payment is expected but is not a condition for publication. **1968** J. M. ZIMAN *Public Knowl.* vi. 117, I am informed that the decision of the referees on the paper is quite independent of whether this 'page charge' is honoured. **1969** *Physics Bull.* Jan. 23/1 Page charges were first introduced by the AIP in 1930 for *The Physical Review*..; for *The Physical Review*, for example, they currently amount to $60 a page. The charges, which are not mandatory, are paid by authors' institutions and are honoured by the majority of institutions... These are used to offset those items of expenditure classified as 'input' production costs; subscription prices are kept relatively low and are applied towards 'output' production costs. **1970** *Nature* 29 Aug. 892/1 The actual pressure behind page charges is the desire of each editor to keep the selling price of his journal within the means of the individual subscriber. **1858** SIMMONDS *Dict. Trade*, *Pagecord*, thin twine used by printers to tie together the pages or columns [of type] previous to printing. **1875** KNIGHT *Dict. Mech.*, *Page-gage*, a standard of length for the pages of a given piece of work. **1927** R. B. MCKERROW *Introd. Bibliogr.* I. vi. 63 The page 'galley'... The compositors of the Elizabethan period normally finished a page of work at a time. **1964** F. BOWERS *Bibliogr. & Textual Crit.* III. i. 65 An example of the routine practice of the trade would be the transfer of lines of type from the stick directly into the Elizabethan page galley instead of the long or slip galley of later times. **1971** *Library* XXVI. 297 The earliest hint of a 'long' galley, as opposed to a 'square' or page galley, seems to appear in an 'oral testimony'..which claims that the news galley of 1770 contained at least 132 lines of matter in long primer between eighteen and twenty ems wide. This suggests a galley with dimensions of about 20 in. × 4 in. **1918** E. POUND *Let.* 4 June (1971) 136 You have got all the points I noted in the page-galleys, so I was right in not cabling about them. [**1975** J. BUTCHER *Copy-Editing* xii. 213 The printer may be asked to provide page-on-galley proofs. **1976** *Gloss. Documentation Terms* (*B.S.I.*) 46 *Page-on-galley proof*, a single-stage alternative to galley proof and page proof.] **1930** *Times Lit. Suppl.* 30 Oct. 886/2 The page-long questions and answers of the *cause célèbre*. **1961** *Times* 31 Aug. 11/1 These convoluted evocations, often in page-long parentheses. **1824** J. JOHNSON *Typogr.* II. 193 The compositor..takes a page paper into the palm of his hand, and puts it against the bottom of the page. **1901** *Daily Chron.* 15 July 3/2 The most continuous feature in this book is the series of attractive page-pictures. **1899** *Electrical Engineer* (N.Y.) 2 Mar. 249/2 There is..no simple page printer having such speed and such perfect control over page and line as is here secured. **1948** *Ann. Computation Lab. Harvard Univ.* XVI. 69 The output devices of the machine are page printers and tape punches. **1967** BURKHARD & CLARE in D. H. Hamsher *Communication Syst. Engin. Handbk.* ii. 30 Until recent years page printers were developed almost exclusively for teletype-writer use and were almost entirely mechanical. With a trend toward higher speeds and toward data applications many of the mechanisms are being replaced by electronic circuits. **1895** *Jrnl. U.S. Artillery* Oct. 593 (*heading*) Experimental use of the Essick page printing telegraph for transmitting information in sea-coast artillery firing 1895. **1959** J. W. FREEBODY *Telegr.* ii. 55/2 This machine, known as a teleprinter, printed the messages on a paper tape. In 1931, a page printing machine was introduced. **1881** W. WHITMAN 24 Aug. in *Daybooks & Notebooks* (1978) I. 256 The first batch of page-proofs of the new volume, to-day. **1901** T. L. DE VINNE *Pract. Typogr.: Correct Composition* xvi. 301 Page proofs seriously add to the expense of the work when the author makes much alteration. **1934, 1951** [see GALLEY *sb.* 5 b]. **1951** W. STEVENS *Let.* 30 July (1967) 724 On receipt of page proofs [I] will give them prompt attention. **1975** J. BUTCHER *Copy-Editing* v. 59 It is usually cheaper to proceed straight to page proof. **1925** *Manual of Style* (Univ. Chicago Press) (ed. 8) 195 Unfilled page references must be queried. **1953** R. L. COLLISON *Indexes & Indexing* I. 68 Page references should be carefully stated. **1971** *Nature* 30 Apr. 602/1 The index has suffered greatly from the speed of production, being incomplete both in subject matter and the page references given. **1975** J. BUTCHER *Copy-Editing* x. 184 Form of text reference. The author's name, date of publication and page reference (if one is needed) are given in parentheses. **1929** H. CRANE *Let.* 30 Aug. (1965) 344, I think we ought to change our plan regarding page size and use. **1946** *Nature* 24 Aug. 267/1 The members of the Institute hope that British periodicals which adopted reduced page-sizes as a war-time measure will as soon as possible revert to full size. **1975** *Sun* 12 June 3 (*caption*) Lovely Jackie Brocklehurst makes her bow today as a super Sun Page Three girl. **1977** *Sounds* 9 July 22/1 As far as homegrown pop papers are concerned Danny Fields' name is a long way from being a 'household word' (examples: corn-flakes, Vim, Tommy Cooper, Page Three Girl, Johnny Rotten etc. etc.). **1979** *Brit. Jrnl. Photogr.* 10 Aug. 766/2 If we saw such associations in an image *together* with a page 3 girl we would suspect a satirical intention. **1986** *Times* 6 May 3/1 Prostitution and 'page three' girls were the subjects chosen by a senior circuit judge. **1969** *Daily Tel.* 11 Aug. 18/3 The page-turner, made of plywood, plastic toy gears and commonplace lamp batteries, operates with the user's suck or blow a miniature electrical device. **1974** *Publishers Weekly* 27 May 5/1 (Advt.), What happens next makes *Eagle in the Sky* a moving, exciting, and ultimately joyous page-turner. **1976** *Gramophone* Mar. 1482/1 As host of the first runthrough by the composer..of the *Elegie*, and page-turner at the English premieres of the two string sonatas, I may be forgiven for having a nostalgia for this music. **1976** *Washington Post* 19 Apr. C5/1 The last time I saw her she was up on that stage without an orchestra; just herself, the piano player, and the page turner. **1976** *Publishers Weekly* 19 Apr. 81/2 Like the other crime novels from the British author, this is a real page turner. **1969** *Daily Tel.* 11 Aug. 18/2 I've been using this pageturning gear without trouble for 18 months.

page (peɪdʒ), *v.*[1] [f. PAGE *sb.*[1]] **a.** *trans.* To wait on, attend, or follow, like a page. **b.** *to page it*, to act as a page.

1596 H. CHETTLE in Nashe *Saffron Walden* Wks. (Grosart) III. 195 Ile square and set it out in Pages, that shall page and lackey his infamie after him. **1607** SHAKS. Timon IV. iii. 224 Will these moyst Trees..page thy heeles And skip when thou point'st out? **1638** FORD *Fancies* v. ii, Nitido has paged it trimly too. **1819** KEATS *Otho* I. i. 79 Go, page his dusty heels upon a march.

c. To send for, search for, or communicate with (a person) by means of a page; to have the name of (a person) called out by a page. Also in extended use (of various electrical or electronic devices). orig. *U.S.* So **'paging** *ppl. a.* and *vbl. sb.*[2]

1904 L. BELL *At Home with Jardines* 65 The name of Jardine was paged through the corridors and billiard-room and café. **1904** *Sun* (N.Y.) 21 Aug. 5 A bell boy is called. 'Here, page Mr. Smith, Room 186', the clerk will say. The process of 'paging' Mr. Smith consists of calling out his name in the dining and other public rooms of the hotel. **1916** H. L. WILSON *Somewhere in Red Gap* ix. 368 A..mining promoter from Arizona..has himself paged by the boys about twenty times a day so folks will know how important he is. **1923** *Daily Mail* 31 July 6/5 The telephone operator ..turned to me. 'Stay around awhile,' she instructed. 'I'll "page" you when I'm through.' **1936** H. F. OLSEN in *RCA Rev.* I. 1. 58 (*heading*) General announce and paging systems. *Ibid.* 59 For certain types of general announce, paging, and sound distributing installations,..the intensity level required is relatively low. **1938** WODEHOUSE *Code of Woosters* xiii. 283 Jeeves, go and page Mr. Spode. Tell him I want him to come and put a bit of stuffing into my alibi. **1959** A. SEXTON in *Hudson Rev.* Spring 80 Out in the hall The intercom pages you. **1960** *IRE Trans. Vehicular Communications* Dec. 48 (*heading*) Personal radio paging in the VHF band. **1970** *Railway Mag.* Oct. 579/1 Post Office staff at Waterloo have been issued with two-way speech radio paging equipment supplied by Modern Telephones Limited to enable a central control point to speedily contact personnel handling letter bags on the platforms and concourse. **1971** *Daily Tel.* (Colour Suppl.) 22 Oct. 9/2 It works on the principle of the short-range radio paging systems used in factories and large-office complexes. **1973** *Times* 21 May (Telecommunications Suppl.) p. v/2 In connexion with pocket paging systems, dialling a code on the telephone will signal the appropriate paging receiver. The person paged will then dial a reply code on his nearest telephone. **1976** *New Yorker* 26 Jan. 54/2 We'd better have him paged. **1977** *Time* 2 May 49/1 A portable paging device about the size of a cigarette pack, the beeper is a mini-radio receiver that puts the person carrying it on instant call from office, home or anywhere else.

page (peɪdʒ), *v.*[2] [f. PAGE *sb.*[2]]

1. *trans.* To put consecutive numbers upon the pages of (a book, manuscript, etc.); to paginate.

1628 PRYNNE *Cens. Cozens* 53 The first part of his Booke ..is not paged. **1817** *Cobbet's Weekly Pol. Pamphlet* 22 Mar. 353 The former part..is paged in such a way as to fit with the paging of Number Fifteen. **1878** EBSWORTH in *Brathwait's Strappado* Pref. 17 Even when consecutively paged, his volumes are often composed of several distinct works.

2. a. *Printing.* To make up (composed type) into pages.

1890 in *Cent. Dict.*

b. *Type-founding.* To pack up (new type) in pieces for sending out.

1903 H. HART *Let. to Editor*, When type has been cast, it is set up; then dressed; then paged; i.e. packed up in convenient pieces. The founder will, if requested, page his type otherwise than to the standard width.

3. *intr.* To look *through* the pages of a book.

1943 *Amer. Speech* XVIII. 138 The following notes, taken as I paged through the book at random. **1966** E. PALMER *Plains of Camdeboo* xviii. 291 Paging through the books is an experience for every Palmer of every generation, for a single entry can recall a drama..forgotten for many years. **1970** *Physics Bull.* Sept. 401/1 The selection of a metal..for use in the body is not a simple matter which can be accomplished by paging through a hand-book.

pageant ('pædʒənt, 'peɪ-), *sb.* Forms: *α.* 4–6 **pagyn**, (6 **pagen**, **-eon**, **padgin**, **-ion**, **paidgion**, *Sc.* **padʒ(e)ane**, **-yan**) 6–7 **pagin**. *β.* 5 **pagend(e**, (**padzhand**, **pachand**, **paiande**, **pageunt**, **pajant**, **padgeant**, **-iant**, **pacent**, **pachent**), 5–6 **pagent**, 6 **pageaunt**, (**-ia(u)nt**, **-ient**, **-y(a)nt**, **pageyond**, **paia(u)nt**, **-auntt**, *Sc.* **padʒand**), 6–7 **pageante**, (7 **paygend**, **pagiente**), 5– **pageant**. [Late ME. *pagyn*, *padgin*, etc., in contemporary Anglo-Latin, *pagina*; subseq. with accrescent *-t* or *-d*, as in *ancient*, etc.: see -ANT[3]. Origin and history obscure: see Note below.]

1. a. A scene acted on the stage; *spec.* one scene or act of a mediæval mystery play. *Obs.* exc. *Hist.*

c **1380** WYCLIF *Wks.* (1880) 206 He þat kan best pleie a pagyn [*v.r.* pagent] of þe devyl..schal haue most þank of pore & riche. **14..** *Cov. Myst.* Prol. (passim) Pagent. **1427–8** *Coventry Leet Bk.* lf. 45 b, The smythes of Coventre ..shewen..how thei were discharged of the cotelers pachand be a lete in the tyme of Iohn Gote then meire. **1457** *Ibid.* 173 b, She [Q. Margaret] sygh then alle the pagentes pleyde save domesday, which myght not be pleyde for lak of day. **1467** in *Eng. Gilds* (1870) 372 That v. pageunts be hadd amonge the craftes. **1468** J. PASTON jr. in *Lett.* II. 317 Many pagentys wer pleyed in hyr wey in Bryggys to hyr welcomyng. **1500–20** DUNBAR *Poems* xxvi. 109 Than cryd Mahoun for a Heleand padȝane [*v.r.* padȝeane]. **1523** SKELTON *Garl. Laurel* 1383 Of paiauntis that were played in Ioyous Garde. **1530** PALSGR. 250/2 Pagiant in a playe, *mistere.* **1548** UDALL, etc. *Erasm. Par. Mark* 21 a, I haue rehersed vnto thee..the persons of this scene or pageaunte. *a* **1603** T. CARTWRIGHT *Confut. Rhem. N.T.* (1618) 477 As they haue multiplyed the number of their Stages, so thus they multiply their pagins and parts. **1641** MILTON *Animadv.* (1851) 213 His former transition was in the faire about the Jugglers, now he is at the Pageants among the Whifflers. **1801** STRUTT *Sports & Past.* III. ii. 137 The prologue..contains the argument of the several pageants, or acts, that constitute the piece. **1828** SCOTT *F.M. Perth* xx, The morris-dancers..again played their pageant.

b. *fig.* The part acted or played by any one in an affair, or in the drama of life; performance; esp. in ***to play one's pageant***, to act one's part. *Obs.* or *arch.*

c **1380** WYCLIF *Serm.* Sel. Wks. I. 129 þes pagyn playen þei þat hiden þe treuþe of Goddis lawe. **1470–85** MALORY *Arthur* x. lxxix, How now, said Launcelot vnto Arthur, yonder rydeth a knyght that playeth his pagents. **1478** SIR J. PASTON in *P. Lett.* III. 235 As ffor the pagent..the Erle off Oxenforde hathe pleyid atte Hammys..he lyepe the wallys, and wente to the dyke, and in to the dyke to the chynne. *a* **1529** SKELTON *Death Edw. IV* 85, I haue played my pageyond, now am I past. **1548** UDALL, etc. *Erasm. Par. Matt.* vi. 44 Ye must not playe your pageant in the sight of menne. **1574** STUDELEY (*title*) The Pageant of Popes, contayninge the lyues of all the Bishops of Rome..to the Yeare of Grace 1555..written in Latin by Maister Bale [etc.]. **1878** BROWNING *Poets Croisic* lxiii, We must play the pageant out.

†**c.** A part acted to deceive or impose upon any one; a trick. ***to play one a pageant***, to play him a trick, to impose upon or deceive him. *Obs.*

c **1380** WYCLIF *Wks.* (1880) 99 In þis manere þei pleien þe pagyn of scottis; for as scottis token þe skochen of armes of seynt george & here-bi traieden englischemen, so þes anticristis prelatis taken name & staat of cristis apostlis. **1530** PALSGR. 658/2 He had thought to playe me a pagent, *il me cuyda donner le bout.* **1582** STANYHURST *Æneis* I. (Arb.) 22 This spightful pageaunt of his owne syb Iuno remembring [*Nec latuere doli fratrem Iunonis et iræ*]. **1607** R. C[AREW] tr. *Estienne's World of Wonders* 88 This pageant was plaid by a Hollander.

†**d.** A scene represented on tapestry, or the like.

1557 *More's Wks.* ¶ij b, Mayster Thomas More in his youth deuysed in hys fathers house in London, a goodly hangyng of fyne paynted clothe, with nyne pageauntes, and verses ouer euery of those pageauntes: which verses.. declared what the ymages in those pageauntes represented.

2. a. A stage or platform on which scenes were acted or tableaux represented; *esp.* in early use, the movable structure or 'carriage', consisting of stage and stage machinery (MACHINE *sb.* 6), used in the open air performances of the mystery plays. *Obs.* exc. *Hist.*

[**1392–3** *Cartulary of St. Mary's, Coventry* lf. 85 b (in Sharp *Diss. Cov. Myst.* 66), Domum pro le pagent pannariorum Coventre.] **1450** *Coventry Smith's Acct.* (*Ibid.* 20) Spend to bryng the pagent in-to gosford-stret *vd.* **1453** *Ibid.* 15 þe kepers of the craft shall let bring forth þe pajant & find clothys that gon abowte þe pajant, and find russhes þerto. **1483** *Cath. Angl.* 266/1 A Paiande, *lusorium.* **1500** in *York Myst.* Introd. 35 The cartwryghts [are] to make iiij new wheles to the pagiaunt. **1535** *Covent. Weavers' Accts.*, Paid to the wryght for mendyng the pagent iijs. ijd. *a* **1595** ARCHD. ROGERS in Sharp *Diss.* 17 The maner of these playes weare, euery company had his pagaint, or parte, which pageants weare a high scafolde with 2 rowmes, a higher and a lower, vpon 4 wheeles. **1691** tr. *Emilianne's Frauds Romish Monks* (ed. 3) 344 Judith was one of the most beautiful young Women of Italy, and..round about her (upon the same Frame or Pageant) they had placed..Musicians. **1698** FRYER *Acc. E. India & P.* 44 On a Pageant over-against the Pagod they had a Set of Dancers handled like Puppits, to the amusing of the Mobile. **1739** CIBBER *Apol.* (1756) II. 155 Pageants, that is, stages erected in the open street, were part of the entertainment. **1825** T. SHARP *Diss. Pageants Coventry* 20 It is evident that the 'scaffolds' were placed upon wheels, and moved with the Pageant, to which it probably was attached. **1954** *Oxf. Jun. Encycl.* XII. 261/1 Each guild was usually responsible for one play, which was performed on a special two-decker waggon called a *Pageant.* **1960** BECKSON & GANZ *Reader's Guide to Lit. Terms* (1961) 153 The pageant was built on wheels. **1974** S. J. KAHRL *Trad. Medieval Eng. Drama* ii. 36 What distinguishes the pageants referred to in this procession from the stages otherwise described is that the structures for the Jesse tree, for St John and St Edward, the four Cardinal Virtues, and the censing angels..are all built around permanent architectural features.

†**b.** A piece of stage machinery; also a mechanical contrivance or machine generally. *Obs.*

1519 HORMAN *Vulg.* 238 Of all the crafty and subtyle paiantis and pecis of warke made by mannys wyt, to go or moue by them selfe, the clocke is one of the beste. **1611** FLORIO, *Pegma*, a frame or pageant, to rise, mooue, or goe it selfe with vices. *a* **1719** ADDISON (J.), The poets contrived the following pageant or machine for the pope's entertainment; a huge floating mountain, that was split in the top in imitation of Parnassus. **1861** WRIGHT *Ess. Archæol.* II. xxi. 173 *Pageant*—a word..subsequently in general use to denote stage machinery of all kinds.

3. A tableau, representation, allegorical device, or the like, erected on a fixed stage or carried on a moving car, as a public show; any kind of show, device, or temporary structure, exhibited as a feature of a public triumph or celebration. ***dumb pageant*** = dumb show. *Obs.* exc. *Hist.*

(This sense, in which 'scene' and 'stage' are combined, may have been the intermediate link between 1 and 2.)

[**1432** *Let.* in *Munim. Gildh.* (Rolls) III. App. 459 Parabatur machina, satis pulchra, in cujus medio stabat gigas miræ magnitudinis..ex utroque latere ipsius gigantis in eadem pagina erigebantur duo animalia vocata 'antelops'.] **1511** GUYLFORDE *Pilgr.* (Camden) 8 Bytwene euery of the pagentis went lytill children..gloryously and rychely dressyd. **1533** *Coronation Q. Anne* in Arb. *Garner* II. 47 A rightly costly pageant of Apollo with the Nine Muses among the mountains. *Ibid.*, A sumptuous and costly pageant in manner of a castle wherein was fashioned a heavenly roof and under it upon a green was a root or stock, whereout sprang a multitude of white and red roses [etc.]. **1560** DAUS tr. *Sleidane's Comm.* 330 At Millan..were set up ..triumphant arkes, pageons, and images, with honourable posies written. **1611** COTGR., *Pegmate*, a stage, or frame whereon Pageants be set, or carried. **1642** ROGERS *Naaman* 55 To stand as a dumb pageant, without salutation. **1706** PHILLIPS, *Pageant*, a triumphal Chariot or Arch, or other pompous Device usually carry'd about in Publick Shews. *a* **1745** in *Swift's Lett.* (1768) IV. 27 You would have put me to an additional expence, by having a raree-shew (or pageant) as of old, on the lord-mayor's day. Mr. Pope and I were thinking to have a large machine carried through the city, with a printing-press, author, publishers, hawkers, devils, &c. and a satirical poem printed and thrown from the press to the mob. **1875** A. W. WARD *Eng. Dram. Lit.* (1899) I. 145 Those pageants, in the generally accepted later and narrower use of the term, which consisted of moving shows devoid of either action or dialogue, or at least only employing the aid of these incidentally, by way of supplementing and explaining the living figures or groups of figures brought before the eyes of the spectators.

4. *fig.* **a.** Something which is a mere empty or specious show without substance or reality.

1608 CHAPMAN *Byron's Conspir.* Plays 1873 II. 239 Without which love and trust; honor is shame; A very Pageant, and a propertie. **1635** QUARLES *Embl.* I. ix. (1718) 37 Think ye the Pageants of your hopes are able To stand secure on earth, when earth itself's unstable? **1781** GIBBON *Decl. & F.* (1869) II. xxxviii. 396 It was a name, a shadow, an empty pageant. **1818** JAS. MILL *Brit. India* II. v. ii. 354 The sovereign, divested of all but the name of king, sinks into an empty pageant.

b. ? A specious tribute or token.

1750 JOHNSON *Let. to Printer Gen. Advert.* 3 Apr. in Boswell *Life*, Many, who would, perhaps, have contributed to starve him when alive, have heaped expensive pageants upon his grave.

5. a. A brilliant or stately spectacle arranged for effect; *esp.* a procession or parade with elaborate spectacular display; a showy parade.

1805 SOUTHEY *Madoc in W.* xv, Embroider'd surcoats and emblazon'd shields,..Made a rare pageant, as with sound of trump, Tambour and cittern, proudly they went on. **1820** W. IRVING *Sketch Bk.* I. 299 Few pageants can be more stately and frigid than an English funeral in town. **1852** TENNYSON *Ode Dk. Wellington* iii, Lead out the pageant sad and slow,..Let the long long procession go. **1855** PRESCOTT *Philip II*, I. I. ii. 17 The glittering pageant entered the gates of the capital. **1868** FREEMAN *Norm. Conq.* II. vii. 6 The consecration of a King was then not a mere pageant.

b. A spectacular representation (usually in the form of a procession) of scenes or events belonging to the past history of a place.

1883 D. COOK *On Stage* I. x. 219 In the pantomime season, or whenever any great pageant or spectacle is to be produced, these plots are of prodigious extent. **1905** *To-day* 7 June 180/2 The inhabitants are preparing a pageant. **1908** *Westm. Gaz.* 1 Oct. 2/3 On the sixth of these [days]..there will be presented a historical pageant. **1939** W. WARD *Theatre for Children* xiii. 248 Many play-grounds end their season with a festival or pageant in which every group has some part. **1970** BURTON & LANE *New Directions* iii. 78 A great many pageants have been so gruesome—Merrie Englande with rain—the form has earned itself a bad reputation. **1977** K. O'HARA *Ghost of T. Penry* xvii. 173 It was that charity pageant the old mistress put on up Kelletts one year. She needed a robe for an archbishop..when they were acting a crowning.

6. a. *attrib.* passing into *adj.* Of or acting in a pageant; stage-, puppet-; specious.

1659 *Parl. Speech Other Ho.* 4 To these we are to stand bare, whilst their pageant stage Lordships daign to give us a conference upon their Breeches. **1701** *Lond. Gaz.* No. 3758/3 We will..Assist Your Majesty against the French King, his Pageant Prince of Wales, and all others. **1736** HERVEY *Mem.* I. 73 France and England the pageant mediators in a quarrel..which was made up without their privity. *c* **1800** H. K. WHITE *Poet. Wks.* (1837) 36 The pageant insects of a glittering hour. **1868** J. H. BLUNT *Ref. Ch. Eng.* I. 55 Campeggio was made to feel that he was a mere pageant-legate.

b. *Comb.*, as ***pageant cart, drama, -master, -play, -plot, stage, -tableau, vehicle, wagon, -wheel; pageant-like, -loving*** adjs.; **pageant-car**, the car which carried, or served as, a stage for acting in the open air; †**pageant-house**, the house in which the stage and properties for the play were kept; †**pageant-idol**, an idol which is a mere 'vain show'; †**pageant-money, -pence, -silver**, money contributed for the mystery-play; **pageant-thing**, a thing that is a mere 'vain show', an idol.

1893 G. S. TYACK in Andrews *Bygone Warwick.* 66 The stages of the *pageant-cars. **1974** S. J. KAHRL *Trad. Medieval Eng. Drama* ii. 39 Such structures occupy space, as they do in pictures of continental *pageant carts. **1975** P. HAPPÉ *Eng. Mystery Plays* 27 The civic records of York and Chester show that the plays were performed on pageant carts. **1953** *Travel* Apr. 36/2 This spectacular *pageant-drama is a civic non-profit enterprise of the twin cities of Hemet and San Jacinto in Riverside County, California. **1974** *Encycl. Brit. Macropædia* XIII. 862/1 The pageant dramas of the West have tended to be largely open-air performances given in front of mass audiences. **1420** in *York Plays* Introd. 36 Le *pagent-howse pelliparorium. **1531** *Order of Leet* in Sharp *Cov. Myst.* (1825) 43 A pagiaunt, with the pagiaunt house & playing geire. **1626** in *York Myst.* Introd. 36 Of the skinners for the pageante howse farme yerely due, xij*d.* **1696** TATE & BRADY *Ps.* xcvii. 7 All who of *Pageant-Idols boast. **1933** R. TUVE *Seasons & Months* i. 41 A *pageant-like processional march of familiar figures. **1973** M. AMIS *Rachel Papers* 215 I've included a break-down of one of your more pageant-like essays. **1899** *Academy* 12 Aug. 157/1 He provided 'Trionfi' for the delight of a *pageant-loving folk. **1479** in *York Myst.* Introd. 41 To chuse searchers and *pageant master. **1937** AUDEN *Spain* 11 Tomorrow the hour of the pageant-master and the musician. **1963** *Times* 17 Apr. 13/3 Miss Gwen Lally, O.B.E., pageant master, play producer, and lecturer, died on Sunday. **1977** *Daily Tel.* 23 June 18 Pageantmaster to Hammersmith & Fulham Silver Jubilee Committee. **1525** in Sharp *Weaver's Pageant* 20 Rec. of the masters for the *pagynt-money xvjs. iiij*d.* **1551–2** in Sharp *Diss. Cov. Myst.* 22 Reseyved of the craft for *pagent pencys iiis. 4*d.* **1607** MIDDLETON *Your Five Gallants* II. i, Some *pageant-plot, or some device for the tilt-yard. **1492** in *York Myst.* Introd. 23 *note*, *Paiaunt silver. **1974** S. J. KAHRL *Trad. Medieval Eng. Drama* ii. 34 The most usual event which called for the erection of *pageant stages in the street was a royal entry. **1696** TATE & BRADY *Ps.* cxv. 6 The *Pageant-thing has Ears and Nose, But neither hears nor smells. **1825** T. SHARP *Diss. Pageants Coventry* 18 The different Companies Accounts.. refer to the *Pageant vehicles. **1932** T. W. STEVENS *Theatre* vii. 61 The *pageant wagon, interesting in itself, was a sterile device. **1958** A. C. CAWLEY *Wakefield Pageants* p. xxvi, A pageant-wagon with the superstructure of a ship, would have provided a strong scenic attraction for the *Processus Noe.* **1974** S. J. KAHRL *Trad. Medieval Eng. Drama* ii. 37 Nor, when we come to visualize the early pageant wagons as opposed to the fixed pageant stages, are we helped by the nature of the surviving evidence. **1584** in Sharp *Cov. Myst.* (1825) 38 Payde for sope for the *pagent wheles iiij*d.*

[*Note.* The word in the preceding senses is known only in English, and in the Anglo-Latin *pāgina.* The two main early senses were 'scene displayed on a stage', and 'stage on which a scene is exhibited or acted'. The relative order of these is not certain; but, so far as instances have been found, the sense 'scene' appears first. The Anglo-L. *pāgina* is in form identical with the known ancient L. *pāgina* leaf (of a book), PAGE *sb.*[2]; and it is noteworthy that from *pāgina* French had, beside the popularly descended *page*, a literary form *pagine, pagene*, 'page of a book', which also came into Eng. in the forms PAGINE, *pagyn(e, pagen*, and even (in 15th c.) *pagent*, forms which are identical with some of those of *pageant.* There is thus no difficulty so far as concerns *form* in identifying *pāgina* 'pageant' with *pāgina, pagine, pagyn, pagent*, 'leaf' or 'page'. And it is easy to conceive how the sense 'page' or 'leaf' of a MS. play, might have passed into that of 'scene' or 'act'; but direct evidence connecting the two has not been found. On the other hand, some, who take 'stage' as the earlier sense, have suggested for *pāgina* a possible passage of sense from 'tablet or slab (for inscription)' to 'board', and so to 'stage'; or have seen in the 14–15th c. Anglo-Latin *pāgina* a more or less independent formation from the stem *pag-* of L. *pangĕre* to fix, cognate with L. *compāges, compāgo, compāgina* 'fixing together', 'joining', *compāginata* 'fixed together' (whence perh. 'framework'); or have thought it a representative, in some way, of L. *pēgma*, Gr. πῆγμα 'a framework fastened or joined together', spec. 'a movable stage or scaffold used in theatres'. This last exactly gives the sense of *pāgina*, 'pageant'; and not only has Du Cange examples of med.L. *pēgma* as 'a wooden machine on which statues are placed', but Cotgrave has F. *pegmate* 'a stage or frame whereon Pageants be set or carried'. Thus it is indisputable that 'pageant' in the sense 'stage' would exactly render L. *pēgma*, and it is further true that the stem *pag-* of *pāgina* is cognate with πηγ- of πῆγμα; but of any actual historical relation between the forms of these words, or any passage of *pēgma* into *pāgina* in med.L., there is no trace. It had been supposed that an earlier Anglo-L. example of *pāgina*, in a sense like 'boarding', existed in the final paragraph of the 12th or 13th c. treatise of Alexander Neckham *De Utensilibus*, printed (very inaccurately) in T. Wright's *Vol. of Vocabularies* 1857, pp. 96–119, from MS. Cott. Titus D. 20, lf. 48 b, where Wright has 'ut lingnum hujus pagine forti aderat tegminibus'; but the actual reading of the MS. is 'ut lingnum *hic com*pagine forti ad[h]ereat tegminibus'; so that the supposed *pāgina* 'boarding' has no existence.]

pageant ('pædʒənt, 'peɪ-), *v.* [f. prec.]

†**1.** *trans.* To imitate as in a pageant or play; to mimic. *Obs. rare.*

1606 SHAKS. *Tr. & Cr.* I. iii. 151 With ridiculous and aukward action, (Which Slanderer, he imitation call's) He Pageants vs.

2. To carry *about* as a show or in a procession.

1641 MILTON *Reform.* I. (1851) 4 Even that Feast of love and heavenly-admitted fellowship..became the subject of horror, and glouting adoration, pageanted about, like a dreadfull Idol. **1660** —— *Free Commw.* Wks. (1851) 429 To pageant himself up and down in Progress among the perpetual bowings and cringings of an abject People.

3. To honour with a pageant.

1891 *Murray's Mag.* Oct. 599 She who once pageanted with sumptuous pomp victorious Doges returning trophy-laden.

Hence **pageanting** *vbl. sb.*, display of pageantry.
1873 MASSON *Drumm. of Hawth.* iv. 54 One may guess the amount of pageanting, banqueting, and speechifying.

'pageanted, *a.* [f. PAGEANT *sb.* + -ED².]
†**a.** Adorned with 'pageants' or scenes (in tapestry or the like: see PAGEANT *sb.* 1 d). *Obs.* **b.** Attended with pageantry and pomp.
1539 in *Archæol. Jrnl.* (1852) VII. 279, IV alter clothes II pagented alter clothes. *Ibid.*, Pagented he[n]gyngs. **1902** W. TOYNBEE in *Westm. Gaz.* 15 Feb. 2/3 Well might his worth the final fee Of pageanted sepulture reap.

pagean'teer. *rare.* In 7 -gen-. [f. PAGEANT *sb.*: see -EER¹.] †**a.** A player in a pageant or mystery-play: in quot. *fig. Obs.*
1624 GEE *New Shreds* 16 Me thinkes these lewd pagenteeres should be questioned..in some Ecclesiasticall Court for Prophanation of heaven and holy things.
b. One who takes part in a pageant (sense 5 b).
1910 *Daily Chron.* 11 Apr. 1/7 The pageanteers must be enjoying themselves all the time. **1927** *Daily Express* 15 July 2/4 The pageanteers—3,000 of them—assembled on the green and sang 'Land of Hope and Glory'.

pageantic (pə'dʒæntɪk), *a. rare.* [f. PAGEANT *sb.* + -IC: cf. *gigantic.*] Of the nature of or belonging to a pageant or pageants.
1825 T. SHARP *Diss. on Cov. Myst.* 25 Illustration of the form and construction of Pageantic structures.

pageantry ('pædʒəntrɪ, 'peɪ-). [See -RY.]
1. Pageants collectively; the public acting of scenes or display of tableaux. *Obs.* or *rare.*
1608 SHAKS. *Per.* v. ii. 6 What pageantry, what feats, what shows, What minstrelsy, and pretty din, The regent made.. To greet the king. *a* **1656** USSHER *Ann.* vi. (1658) 437, 80 women gloriously decked..were carried in litters, having legs of gold, and 500 more in others, whose legs were of silver; These things were most remarkable in the Pageantry. **1714** J. WYETT *Ellwood's Autobiogr.* Suppl. (1765) 391 The Pageantry of which Day's Work, as acted there by himself he hath since published with his Name to it. **1908** *Daily Chron.* 21 July 4/6 The pageantry brings the classes together.
2. Splendid display, gorgeous spectacular show; pomp. Also in *pl.*, and *fig.*
1651 JER. TAYLOR *Serm. for Year* II. viii. 99 To prove that we are extreamly proud in the midst of all this pageantry. **1673** [R. LEIGH] *Transp. Reh.* 10 Not less ignoble then Cardinal Campejus his Pageantry. **1727** GAY *Fables* I. xi. 6 A peacock with the poultry fed, All view'd him with an envious eye, And mocked his gaudy pageantry. **1795** SOUTHEY *Joan of Arc* Wks. 1837 I. 186 Blazon'd shields and gay accoutrements, The pageantry of war. **1856** FROUDE *Hist. Eng.* (1858) I. v. 389 Experience..had probably subdued their inclination for splendid pageantry. **1909** E. POUND *Personae* 53 Slow-moving pageantry of hours.
3. Mere acting or show, empty or specious display, show without substance. Also with *pl.*
1687 BURNET *Contn. Reply to Varillas* 114 After a weeks Pageantry of her Queenship, she was kept there till her Head was cut off. **1715** BENTLEY *Boyle Lect.* Serm. x. 364 The standing Ceremony and continued Pageantry of Transubstantiation. *a* **1854** H. REED *Lect. Eng. Hist.* v. (1855) 153 Chivalry had not yet declined to mere formal pomp and pageantry.

paged (peɪdʒd), *a.* [f. PAGE *sb.*² or *v.*² + -ED.]
a. Having the pages numbered. **b.** Having pages of a specified kind or number, as ***yellow-paged.***
1868 GEO. ELIOT *Let.* 29 Apr. (1956) IV. 433 As I shall not see these paged sheets again, will you charitably assure me that the alterations are safely made? **1869** D. G. ROSSETTI *Let.* 21 Aug. (1965) II. 715 Replace it at the end of the first section of sonnets—not as paged. **1889** *Athenæum* 21 Dec. 853/3 Left by Mr. Bradshaw in a paged revise of 1877. **1930** A. E. HOUSMAN *Let.* 29 June (1971) 297 In the paged proofs ..I find that the printers have inserted..a comma.
c. *Computers.* Divided into pages (PAGE *sb.*² 1 e).
1966 *IEEE Trans. Electronic Computers* XV. 857/1 The relationship between hardware and software in a paged and segmented system environment greatly affects system performance. **1973** *Nature* 6 Apr. 361/2 Among the features that made it [*sc.* Atlas] one of the most advanced machines in the world at the time were a number of facilities that have since become standard such as its permanent master programme and paged store.

pagedom ('peɪdʒdəm). [f. PAGE *sb.*¹ + -DOM.] The office or function of a page. Also *attrib.*
1852 MISS YONGE *Cameos* II. vi. 68 The ladies could instruct him in no graces of pagedom. **1856** *Chamb. Jrnl.* VI. 61 Hyder's cow-boy belongings..became useful in his pagedom novitiate.

'pageful. [-FUL.] As much as fills a page.
1879 *Q. Rev.* Apr. 415 Virtuous indignation by the pageful.

'pagehood. [-HOOD.] The state or condition of being a page. **b.** The personality of a page.
1820 SCOTT *Abbot* xix, She bears herself like the very model of pagehood. **1828** —— *F.M. Perth* xxiv, It is not so, an it please your pagehood. **1890** E. J. LYSAGHT *Gold of Ophir* III. x. 172 He wore the buttons of pagehood.

pagen, pagent, obs. ff. PAGEANT; var. PAGINE.

pager ('peɪdʒə(r)), *sb.*¹ [f. PAGE *v.*² + -ER¹.] One who pages (papers, blank books, etc.).
1901 *Daily Chron.* 9 Sept. 9/4 (Advt.) Pager and Perforator wanted.

pager ('peɪdʒə(r)), *sb.*² [f. PAGE *sb.*² + -ER¹.] Following a numeral (usu. with hypen): a book, newspaper or the like having the number of pages indicated by the numeral.
1966 'H. B. TAYLOR' *Triumvirate* i. 9 He'd gone all out on school supply ads..and turned out a thirty-two pager. **1973** *Times* 5 Sept. 18/7 The Fabian pamphlet, a 50-pager which should be out in a fortnight. **1977** *Times* 12 Sept. 12/6 Pamphlets on..how to get the most out of your phone service. This last is a 14-pager containing 59 pieces of information.

pager ('peɪdʒə(r)), *sb.*³ [f. PAGE *v.*¹ + -ER¹.] A radio device that emits a sound when activated by a telephone call, used to contact a person carrying it.
1968 *Guardian* 10 Apr. 7/3 There are already..in this country devices called radio pagers. You carry in your pocket the pager, which is linked by radio connection to your telephone. When the telephone rings, the pager blips, and you can answer the call by speaking into the pager. As things stand the pager is illegal. **1973** *Sci. Amer.* Aug. 57 The receiving pager..has a range of 50 miles. It emits a tone when the person carrying it is wanted on the telephone. **1977** *Times* 2 May 49/1 Customers can either rent the pocket pagers..or buy them outright.

†**'pagery.** *Obs.* [f. PAGE *sb.*¹ + -RY.] The office or position of a page, service as a page.
1586 *Cyuile & Vncyuile Life* (1868) 25 [In France] young gentilmen bee brought vp as Pages in Court: so soone as their Pagery is past, they become souldiers in some Band or Garrison. **1630** B. JONSON *New Inn* I. i, These are the arts, Or seven liberal deadly sciences Of pagery. **1641** EARL MONM. tr. *Biondi's Civil Warres* II. 86 A Dutchman, who being come out of pagery, and not having whereon to ride, followed him on foot.

pageship ('peɪdʒʃɪp). [f. PAGE *sb.*¹ + -SHIP.] The office of a page. Also *humorously*, as a title.
1835 LYTTON *Rienzi* VII. vi, May I wait on thy pageship to-morrow? **1844** TUPPER *Crock of G.* xxiii. 187 The house-keeper had power to push her nephew on to pageship, footmanship—to the final post of butler. **1891–2** LOUNSBURY *Stud. Chaucer* I. i. 31 It was probably to fit the period of this assumed pageship that the year 1340 was fixed upon as the date of Chaucer's birth.

Paget ('pædʒɪt). *Path.* The name of Sir James Paget (1814–99), English surgeon, used in the possessive to designate: **a.** A disease (also called *osteitis deformans*) that affects chiefly the elderly and is often symptomless, being characterized by the localized alteration of tissue in one or more bones (most often in the spine, skull, or pelvis), which become thickened and may undergo fracture or bending.
1877 *Guy's Hosp. Rep.* XXII. 337 (*heading*) Osteoporosis or Paget's osteitis deformans. **1889** *Index-Catal. Library Surg.-General's Office, U.S. Army* X. 353/2 (*heading*) Paget's disease of the bones. *See* osteitis deformans. **1939** *Times* 18 May 4/6 Dr. Alexander Wilson said that Mr. Desnos had Paget's disease—the bones of his skull were brittle and at least 50 per cent. softer than a normal skull. **1963** *Lancet* 5 Jan. 34/2 In Paget's disease stones are formed as a result of increased excretion of calcium due to increased turnover of bone. **1966** WRIGHT & SYMMERS *Systemic Path.* II. 1390/2 Paget's disease is a precancerous condition. **1974** PASSMORE & ROBSON *Compan. Med. Stud.* III. xxvi. 17/2 Paget's disease is rarely a painful disorder in the absence of complications such as fracture, tumour or arthritis.
b. A reddish eczematous condition of the skin associated with cancer of the underlying tissue and usually occurring in the female nipple; freq. called ***Paget's disease of the nipple***; so ***Paget*** (†or ***Paget's***) ***cell***, a large cell with clear cytoplasm and hyperchromatic nuclei found in the epidermis of the affected area.
1880 *Brit. Med. Jrnl.* 24 Jan. 128/1 As attention was first called to it by Sir James Paget, he [*sc.* J. E. Erichsen] would suggest for it the name 'Paget's disease' of the nipple. **1910** *Jrnl. Cutaneous Dis.* XXVIII. 383 The epidermis.. contained many of the large round, so-called Paget cells. **1917** *Lancet* 7 Apr. 519/2 The degenerate deeper layers of the epidermis..contain the large clear cells known as Paget's cells. **1923** *Brit. Jrnl. Surg.* XI. 317 Carcinoma in the breast, with which Paget's disease of the nipple is usually associated, is a primary carcinoma of the breast epithelium. **1954** *Jrnl. Obstetr. & Gynæcol.* LXI. 758 (*heading*) Histochemical characterization of the specific cells in Paget's disease of the vulva. **1966** WRIGHT & SYMMERS *Systemic Path.* I. xxviii. 995/2 Paget's disease of the breast.. accounts for between 2 and 3 per cent of all mammary carcinomas. *Ibid.* 996/2 Patients with Paget's disease are still very likely to be treated for supposed dermatitis of the nipple. **1974** PASSMORE & ROBSON *Compan. Med. Stud.* III. xxx. 9/2 Some believe that the Paget cells represent intra-epidermal spread of this [*sc.* cancer].

pageunt, pageyond, obs. forms of PAGEANT.

†**'paggle,** *v. Obs.* [Deriv. uncertain.] *intr.* To bulge, swell out as a bag, hang loosely.
c **1590** GREENE *Fr. Bacon* x. 63 Forty kine..With strouting dugs that paggle to the ground.

paggle, pagil, obs. var. PAIGLE, cowslip.

pagh, obs. variant of PAH *int.*

paghant, pagia(u)nt, etc., obs. ff. PAGEANT.

†**'pagical,** *a. Obs.* [f. PAGE *sb.*¹ + -ICAL: cf. *magical.*] Of or relating to the pages of a book.
1606 *Sir G. Goosecappe* II. i. in Bullen *O. Pl.* III. 37, I yfaith will, and put their great pagicall index to them, too.

pagin, obs. form of PAGEANT, PAGINE.

‖**pagina** ('pædʒɪnə). *Bot.* [L. *pāgina* leaf, page.] A flat surface, as of a leaf.
1842 BRANDE *Dict. Sci.*, etc., *Pagina*,..the surface of a leaf. **1866** *Treas. Bot.*, *Pagina*, the surface of anything.

paginal ('pædʒɪnəl), *a.* [ad. late L. *pāgināl-is*, f. *pāgina* a page: see -AL¹.] Of or pertaining to a page or pages; consisting of or referring to pages; page for page.
1646 SIR T. BROWNE *Pseud. Ep.* v. vi. 244 He shut or closed the booke, which is an expression proper unto the paginall books of our times. **1811** *Puttenham's Eng. Poesie* in Haslewood *Eng. Poets* I. Introd. 15 The present edition is a verbal and paginal reprint. **1888** *Archæol. Rev.* Mar. 62 All quotations will be given in full with paginal references.

paginary ('pædʒɪnərɪ), *a.* [f. L. *pāgina* page + -ARY.] = prec.
1823 T. G. WAINEWRIGHT *Ess. & Crit.* (1880) 312 The paginary amount of your lucubrations. **1824** DIBDIN *Libr. Comp.* 247 The paginary numerals recommencing at ch. xii. **1864** T. WESTWOOD *Chron. 'Compl. Angler'* 26 Hawkins' second edition..was but a paginary reprint of the first.

paginate ('pædʒɪneɪt), *v.* [f. L. *pāgina* page + -ATE³, as if ad. L. type *pāgināre*, which occurs in med.L. in other senses. Cf. mod.F. *paginer* (*Dict. Acad.* 1835).] *trans.* To mark or number the pages of (a book); to page.
1884 *N. & Q.* 6th Ser. IX. 428/1 It is entitled *The Vievv of France*, and forms a small quarto, not paginated. **1890** *Athenæum* 21 June 802/2 In printing the book, a number of copies were wrongly paginated.

pagination (pædʒɪ'neɪʃən). [n. of action from prec.: so in Fr. (*Dict. Acad.* 1835).] The action of paging or of marking the numbers of the pages; an instance of this; the sequence of figures with which the pages are numbered.
1841 D'ISRAELI *Amen. Lit.* (1859) II. 181 They at first totally omitted the *Troilus and Cressida*, which is inserted without pagination, and with little discrimination in the writings of Shakespeare. **1867** DEUTSCH *Rem.* (1874) 41 Twelve folio volumes, the pagination of which is kept uniform in almost all editions. **1882–3** SCHAFF *Encycl. Relig. Knowl.* I. 289/1 The Apocrypha was to be placed at the end of the New Testament, with a distinct title and pagination.

†**'pagine.** *Obs.* Also 4–6 pagyn(e, 4 pagen (5 pagent). [ad. L. *pāgina* PAGE *sb.*², directly or through OF. *pagene*, *pagine* (12th c. in Godef.), a learned adaptation of the L. word, of which the inherited form was *page.*] A page or leaf; *transf.* pages collectively, book, writing.
a **1225** *Ancr. R.* 286 þe holie pagine [*pagina sancta*]. *a* **1300** *Cursor M.* 21295 (Cott.) þe stile o matheu, water it was, And win þe letter o lucas, And marc pagine [*Trin.* pagyn] it was milk, And john honi, suet als suilk. **1382** WYCLIF *Jer.* xxxvi. 23 Whan Judi hadde rad thre litle pagens [**1388** pagyns, *Vulg.* pagellas], or foure, he kutte it with a scraping knyf. *c* **1475** *Partenay* Prol. 79 The philosopher..Which declarid in hys first pagent, hys methephisike off noble corage. **1552** UDALL tr. *Geminus' Anat.* I ij/2 We comprehended all the fygures of the heade in foure pagines.

paging ('peɪdʒɪŋ), *vbl. sb.*¹ [f. PAGE *v.*² + -ING¹.]
1. The action of PAGE *v.*²; the consecutive numbering of the pages of a book; pagination.
paging machine, a machine for printing or stamping the consecutive numbers of the pages of an account-book, etc.
1775 ASH Suppl., *Paging*, the act of marking the pages. **1824** J. JOHNSON *Typogr.* I. 263 Throughout the volume the paging is very irregular. **1858** SIMMONDS *Dict. Trade*, *Paging-machine.* **1884** H. SPENCER in *Athenæum* 5 Apr. 446/3 The pagings of these extracts refer to the first edition. *Mod. Advt.*, Improved paging and perforating machines, hand and treadle.
2. *Computers.* Division (of storage) into pages (PAGE *sb.*² 1 e); the transfer of pages between the central store and an auxiliary store.
1966 *IEEE. Trans. Electronic Computers* XV. 855/1 The computer addressing techniques known as paging and segmentation will be familiar. **1970** O. DOPPING *Computers & Data Processing* ix. 124 Paging systems and hardware relocation..are comparatively new inventions. **1972** *IEEE Trans. Computers* XXI. 1053/1 Under demand paging, a single program's execution and its resulting page swapping can be overlapped.

paging, *vbl. sb.*²: see PAGE *v.*¹ c.

pagle, variant of PAIGLE, a cowslip.

†**'pagled,** *ppl. a. Obs.* [Cf. PAGGLE *v.*] Made or become pregnant; big with young: cf. BAGGED.
1599 NASHE *Lenten Stuffe* 46 Hero, for that she was pagled and timpanized. **1615** H. CROOKE *Body of Man* 314 Other creatures when they are pagled as we say, do neuer or very seldome admit the Male.

‖**pagne** (paɲ). Also 8 pane, 8–9 paan. [a. F. *pagne*, ad. Sp. *paño* = Pg., It. *panno*:—L. *pannum* cloth. In the form *paan*, a. Du. *paan*, ad. Pg. or Sp.] A cloth; the piece of cloth forming originally the single article of clothing variously worn by natives of hot countries; *spec.* a loin-cloth, or a short petticoat, worn by primitive peoples, or retained by the westernized as part of their costume.

1698 FROGER *Voy.* 14 The Marabous, cloath'd with a kind of Surplice made of white Pagnes or Cotton-stuff, sacrifice to Mahomet. **1705** BOSMAN *Guinea* 350 A Multitude of Cloaths or Panes, heaped one over another. *Ibid.* xxi. 440 The Wives of the great Lords wear Calico Paans.. beautifully Chequered with several Colours. These Paans or Cloaths are not very long. **1759** tr. *Adanson's Voy. Senegal* in Pinkerton *Voy.* (1814) XVI. 608 For their clothing they make use of two *paans*, one of which goes round their waist ..and supplies the place of an under-petticoat. **1789** tr. *Sonnerat's Voy.* I. II. 14 A simple piece of linen, called Pagne, is the whole dress of the women. **1863** BURTON *W. Africa* I. 154 A..negro, dressed in..scanty pagne or loin-cloth with red streamers [etc.]. **1902** *Westm. Gaz.* 4 Apr. 3/2 The loose tunic, over which is worn the quaintly shaped pagne, which..is draped tightly round the figure, and only just permits the free movements of the wearer.

pagod ('pægəd). *arch.* Also 6–8 **pagode**, 7 **pagothe**. [ad. Pg. *pa'gode* (1516 in Yule): cf. F. *pa'gode* (1609 in Hatz.-Darm.): see next. The stressing *'pagod* occurs in Butler's *Hudibras*; Pope has *pa'god* as well as *'pagod*.]

1. An idol temple: = next, 1.

1582 N. LICHEFIELD tr. *Castanheda's Conq. E. Ind.* I. xiv. 34 All the Kings doe dye in one Pagode, which is the house of praiers to their Idolls. **1588** PARKE tr. *Mendoza's Hist. China* 402 Like a monasterie, the which the naturall people doo call Pagode. **1630** LORD *Display Sects E. Ind.* (Y.), That he should erect pagods for God's worship. **1653** H. COGAN tr. *Pinto's Trav.* 114 A number of Temples, which they call Pagods. **1735** POPE *Donne Sat.* IV. 239 The mosque of Mahound, or some queer Pagod. **1829** TENNYSON *Timbuctoo*, Her pagods hung with music of sweet bells.

2. An image of a deity, an idol (esp. in India, China, etc.). (Often associated with *god*.)

1582 N. LICHEFIELD tr. *Castanheda's Conq. E. Ind.* lxviii. 140 And it is possible that..the Pagodes will not aide nor helpe me as they haue done before time. **1634** SIR T. HERBERT *Trav.* 38, I have seene some of their Pagothes or Idols, in wood, resembling a man. **1664** BUTLER *Hud.* II. II. 534 Their Classick-Model prov'd a Maggot, Their Direct'ry an Indian Pagod. **1755** J. SHEBBEARE *Lydia* (1769) I. 322 His lordship admired the lions and pagods, and all the chimney ornaments. **1892** J. PAYN *Mod. D. Whittington* I. 33 He looked more like some pagod than a man at all.

b. *fig.* A person superstitiously or extravagantly reverenced, or otherwise likened to a heathen deity; an 'idol'.

1719 D'URFEY *Pills* II. 315 Like the mad Pagod of the North, the Swede. **1738** POPE *Epil. Sat.* I. 157 See thronging Millions to the Pagod run, And offer Country, Parent, Wife, or Son! **1814** BYRON *Diary* 8 Apr., [I] find my poor little pagod, Napoleon, pushed off his pedestal. **1861** *Temple Bar Mag.* I. 254 The most hideous pagod of cruelty, vice, and depravity, that ever lived.

3. A gold (or silver) coin: = next, 3.

1598 W. PHILLIPS *Linschoten* I. xxxv. 69/1 They are Indian and Heathenish money, with the picture of a Diuell vpon them, and therefore are called *Pagodes*. **1667** H. OLDENBURG in *Phil. Trans.* II. 430 Esteemed at 20 old Pagodes in India, each Pagode being about 10 shillings English. **1698** FRYER *Acc. E. India & P.* 34 The Coin current here [Gulconda] is a Pagod, 8s. **1704** *Collect. Voy.* (Churchill) III. 822/2 A Pagode was formerly no more than 84 Stivers but is since raised to 120. *a* **1845** HOOD *To Lady on Dep. India.* x, Go to the land of pagod and rupee.

4. = *pagoda sleeve*: see PAGODA 5.

1890 in *Cent. Dict.* (*Pagode*).

5. *attrib.* and *Comb.*

1719 J. T. PHILIPPS tr. *Thirty-four Confer.* 82 The Absurdities of the Pagod-worship. *Ibid.* 193 If they knew the Pagod-Gods they had in their Temples. **1814** BYRON *Ode to Nap.* iii, Those Pagod things of sabre-sway. **1859** SALA *Gas-light & D.* ii. 29 Busily stitching..sedent, and not squatting Pagod-like, all of a row.

pagoda (pə'gəʊdə). Also 7 **pagotha**, **pogodo**, 8 **pagodoe**. [ad. Pg. *pagode*, pl. *pagodes* (1516 in Yule), It. *pagode*, pl. *-i*; app. a corruption of a name found by the Portuguese in India. (Yule has no example of the form *pagoda* in 16th c. Pg. or It.; the *-a* appears to have been an Eng. representation of final *-e*.)

The native form imitated by the Pg. *pagode* is disputed: whatever it was, the Pg. appears to have been a very imperfect echo of it. Many take it to have been Pers. *but-kadah* idol-temple, f. *but* idol + *kadah* habitation; some suggest Skr. *bhagavat* holy, divine, or some current modification of that word: see Yule & Burnell s.v.]

1. a. A temple or sacred building (in India, China, and adjacent countries); *esp.* a sacred tower, usually of pyramidal form, built over the relics of Buddha or a saint, or in any place as a work of devotion.

1634 SIR T. HERBERT *Trav.* 190 The place where the great Pagotha stands. **1638** W. BRUTON in *Hakluyt's Voy.* (1812) V. 49 At a great Pogodo or Pagod, which is a famous and sumptuous Temple. **1681** R. KNOX *Hist. Ceylon* 72 The Pagoda's or Temples of their Gods are so many that I cannot number them. **1779** BURKE *Corr.* (1844) II. 270, I could not justify to myself to give to the synagogue, the mosque, or the pagoda, the language which your pulpits so liberally bestow upon a great part of the Christian world. **1803** WELLINGTON in Owen *Desp.* (1877) 369 Harcourt dispatched a letter to the principal Bramins of the pagoda of Juggernaut. **1899** F. T. BULLEN *Log Seawaif* 289 The lofty shining summit of the great pagoda dominated everything else.

b. *fig.* = Temple.

1762 CHURCHILL *Prophecy of Famine* 69 In Love's Pagoda shall they ever doze.

c. A small ornamental building or structure in imitation of an Oriental pagoda.

1796 MORSE *Amer. Geogr.* II. 492 Their towers, the models of which are now so common in Europe under the name of *pagodas*. **1816** T. L. PEACOCK *Headlong Hall* iv, Pagodas and Chinese bridges..shall rise upon its ruins. **1860** *All Year Round* No. 52. 34 Purchased..at one of the little glass advertising pagodas..on the Boulevards.

†**2.** An idol or image; = prec. 2. *Obs. rare.*

1634 SIR T. HERBERT *Trav.* 235 Pagothaes, Idols or vgly representations of the Deuill, adored by the Indians. **1665** *Ibid.* 375 Many deformed Pagothas are here worshipped.

3. A gold (less commonly a silver) coin formerly current in Southern India, of the value of about seven shillings.

1681 R. KNOX *Hist. Ceylon* IV. ii. 126 A Gold Ring, a Pagoda, and some two or three Dollars and a few old Cloths. **1727** A. HAMILTON *New Acc. E. Ind.* I. xxix. 365 They also coin Gold into Pagodoes of several Denominations and Value. **1774** *Ann. Reg.* 115 Each pagoda being worth about eight shillings on the par, with a rupee valued at two shillings and three pence. **1831** TRELAWNY *Adv. Younger Son* I. xxi. 170 He shook my hand, threw a bag of pagodas on the table. **1862** BEVERIDGE *Hist. India* I. II. vii. 344 Held of the King of Golconda at a quit-rent of 1200 pagodas, or about £430.

4. Short for *pagoda sleeve*: see 5.

1900 *Daily Mail* 21 Apr. 7/4 The freshest fancy in sleeves is called the pagoda.

5. *attrib.* and *Comb.*, as ***pagoda-like*** *adj.*, ***-shaped*** adj., ***-structure***; **pagoda-flower**, the flower of the PAGODA-TREE, q.v.; **pagoda sleeve**, a funnel-shaped outer sleeve turned back so as to expose the lining and inner sleeve, fashionable in the 18th and early 19th century; **pagoda-stone**, (*a*) = PAGODITE; (*b*) see quot.

1837 *Lett. fr. Madras* (1843) 62 The flowers have no perfume, except the *pagoda-flowers, and those are sickly. **1860** O. W. HOLMES *Elsie V.* xiii, Their boughs disposed in the most graceful *pagoda-like series of close terraces. **1874** LISLE CARR *Jud. Gwynne* I. vii. 174 A fanciful pagoda-like cage. **1897** *Outing* (U.S.) XXIX. 586/2 Crowned with tall, *pagoda-shaped spires. **1872** *Queen* 3 Feb. 71/2 *Pagoda sleeves..embroidered all over. *Ibid.* 1 June 391/3 Pagoda sleeves with rich lace ruffles beneath. **1873** *Young Englishwoman* Apr. 183/1 The casaque..has a large pagoda sleeve. **1889** *Daily News* 12 Nov. 3/1 It has 'pagoda', or 'bell' sleeves, now reappearing after a long interval. John Leech's pretty women in *Punch* wore bell sleeves. **1900** *Westm. Gaz.* 28 Sept. 3/2 The wide pagoda sleeves are not, in my opinion, nearly so pretty as the narrow little open sleeve with close-fitting sleevelets. **1952** C. W. CUNNINGTON *Eng. Women's Clothing* ii. 33 A 'pagoda sleeve' (long and narrow, opening some five or six inches above the wrist with small white undersleeves). **1868** KINGSMILL *Geol. China* in *Q. Jrnl. Geol. Soc.* XXV. 126 At least one species of Orthoceratite.. They are much prized by the Chinese under the name of '*pagoda stones', and sold at fancy prices. **1845** G. MURRAY *Islaford* 26 The light *pagoda-structure of the larch.

pa'goda-tree.

1. Name given to several trees found or cultivated in India, China, etc.: **a.** *Sophora japonica*, an ornamental leguminous tree with white or cream-coloured flowers, cultivated in China and Japan; **b.** *Plumeria acutifolia*, a native of the West Indies, cultivated in India, with fragrant flowers; **c.** *Ficus indica*, the Banyan-tree of India.

1876 *Treas. Bot.* (new ed.) 836/1. **1884** MILLER *Plant-n.*

2. *fig.* A mythical tree humorously feigned to produce pagodas (sense 3). ***to shake the pagoda-tree***: to make a fortune rapidly in India.

1836 T. HOOK *G. Gurney* I. 45 The amusing pursuit of 'shaking the pagoda-tree' once so popular in our Oriental possessions. **1869** *Echo* 6 Feb., The fruits of the pagoda tree are no longer to be had for the mere shaking. **1886** MRS. LYNN LINTON *Paston Carew* III. ii, The service of John Company, under whose flag, as we know, the pagoda-tree was worth shaking.

pagodite ('pægədaɪt). *Min.* [a. F. *pagodite* (C. A. G. Napione 1798), f. *pagode* PAGOD + -ITE[1].] A soft mineral carved by the Chinese into figures of pagodas, images, etc.; also called *agalmatolite*.

1837 DANA *Min.* 254 Agalmatolite..Pagodite. **1842** BRANDE *Dict. Sci.*, etc., *Pagodite*, a species of steatite or serpentine, which the Chinese carve into figures.

†**pa'gody.** *Obs.* [ad. It. *pagodi*, pl. of *pagode*, in transl. of *Viaggio di Cesare de' Federici*.] = PAGODA 1, 2, 3.

1588 T. HICKOCK tr. *C. Frederick's Voy.* 8, 42. Pagodies for euery Horse which Pagody may be of starling money 6 shillings 8 pence: they be peeces of gold of that valew. *Ibid.* 10 (11) The *Pagodies* which are Idoll houses..made with lime and fine marble. *Ibid.* 33 b, Their Idoles, which they call *Pagody*, whereof there is great abundance.

pagri: see PUGGREE.

pagurian (pə'gjʊərɪən), *a.* and *sb. Zool.* [f. L. *pagūrus*, a. Gr. πάγουρος a kind of crab, in mod. Zoology the name of the typical genus of the family *Paguridæ* or Hermit-crabs: see -IAN.]

a. *adj.* Belonging to the genus *Pagurus* or family *Paguridæ* of decapod crustaceans. **b.** *sb.* A crustacean of this genus or family, a hermit crab. So **pa'gurid**; **pa'gurine**, **pa'guroid** *adjs.* and *sbs.*

1840 *Penny Cycl.* XVII. 130/1 *Pagurians*, a tribe..of the Anomourous family of crustaceans. **1876** *Beneden's Anim. Parasites* ii. 25 Naturalists have given the name of *Cenobitae* to some pagurians inhabiting the seas of warmer latitudes. **1893** STEBBING *Crustacea* xi. 162 Many of the Pagurids are very beautifully coloured. **1899** L. A. BORRADAILE in *Proc. Zool. Soc.* 937 On the Hatching-stage of the Pagurine Land-crabs. *Ibid.*, The land-pagurines might also have lost the whole or a part of their larval life. **1852** DANA *Crust.* I. 53 Three distinct grades of degradation,..i.e., the Dromioid, the Lithodioid, and the Paguroid.

-pagus, *suffix*, f. Gr. πάγος that which is fixed (f. πηγνύναι to fasten), used to form the names of different kinds of Siamese twins according to their site of attachment; as *thoracopagus* s.v. THORACO-.

pagyant, pagyn, obs. ff. PAGEANT, PAGINE.

pah (pəh, pɑː), *int.* (*a.*) Also 7 **pagh**. A natural exclamation of disgust.

1592 KYD *Sp. Trag.* III. xiv, Pah: keepe your way. **1604** SHAKS. *Ham.* V. i. 221 (Qo.) Doost thou thinke Alexander lookt a this fashion i'th earth?.. And smelt so, pah. **1605** —— *Lear* IV. vi. 132 Fye, fie, fie; pah, pah: Giue me an Ounce of Ciuet; good Apothecary sweeten my immagination. **1676** *Doctrine of Devils* 55 Pagh, this is but a poor trick. **1828** SCOTT *F.M. Perth* xii, Pah! I scorn a tale-bearer. **1880** MRS. FORRESTER *Roy & V.* I. 38 It was a horrid ..thought, it made one's flesh creep. Pah!

b. *attrib.* or as *adj.* (in childish lang.) Nasty; hence, Improper, unbecoming.

a **1654** SELDEN *Table-t.* (Arb.) 118 Like a Child that will continually be shewing its fine new Coat, till at length it all bedawbs it with its Pah-hands. **1835** *Court Mag.* VI. 239/1 But to pass o'er the rail was considered pah, pah.

pah, var. of PA[2].

‖**paha** ('pɑːhə). Pl. **paha**. [Malay.] In Malaysia, a unit of weight used esp. for gold and equal to $\frac{1}{4}$ tahil, equivalent to $\frac{1}{3}$ oz. (9·4 grammes-weight).

1839 T. J. NEWBOLD *Pol. & Statistical Acct. Straits of Malacca* II. xiv. 236 A fine of ten tahils and one paha is to be exacted. **1947** R. O. WINSTEDT *Malays* 42 If the ordinary person pay five *paha* of gold in consideration of his low birth, then the marriage can take place.

Pahari (pə'hɑːriː), *sb.* and *a.* Also **paharia**, **Pahaṛiya**. [Hind. *pahāṛī* (language) of the mountains, f. *pahāṛ* mountain.] **A.** *sb.* **a.** An Indo-Iranian language group to which belong the languages spoken in the lower ranges of the Himalayas from Nepal to Chamba. **b.** (Also **pahareen**.) A native or inhabitant of this region. **B.** *adj.* Of or pertaining to this region, its inhabitants, or the languages spoken by them.

The name was originally applied to one of the languages or dialects which formed the group (so quots. 1857, 1886).

1811, etc. [see MALER *sb.* and *a.*]. **1857** *Jrnl. Asiatic Soc. Bengal* XXVI. 317 The languages included in..these two papers are..Dahi or Darhi..Dénwár..Pahi or Pahari, [etc.]. **1876** [see KASHMIR 1]. **1884** [see MALTO *sb.*]. **1886** KIPLING *Plain Tales from Hills* (1888) 1 The Kotgarh Chaplain christened her Elizabeth, and 'Lispeth' is the Hill or *pahari* way of pronouncing it. **1887** R. N. CUST *Linguistic & Oriental Ess.* (ser. 2) iii. 73 It is..more convenient..to treat Hindi as the unit, and then allow full room to its magnificient dialects, such as..Bagri, Pahári, [etc.]. **1901** KIPLING *Kim* iv. 93 'Huh! It is only a *pahari*' (a hillman), said Kim over his shoulder. 'Since when have the hill-asses owned all Hindustan?' *Ibid.* 107 A *pahareen*—a hillwoman of Dalhousie, my mother. **1905** *Daily Chron.* 9 Sept. 3/1 This particular district has been inhabited, since the British occupation, by two distinct races, the Santals and Paharias. .. The Paharias are a mountain race. **1908** T. G. BAILEY *Lang. N. Himalayas* III. p. i, Of these all, except Lāhuḷī, belong to what is at present called the Western Pahāṛī language of the Northern Group of the Sanskritic Aryan Family. **1916** G. A. GRIERSON *Linguistic Survey India* IX. IV. 1 The Pahāṛī languages fall into three main groups. *Ibid.* 2 The mass of the Aryan-speaking population of the Himalayan tract in which Pahāṛī is spoken belongs, in the West, to the Kanēt and, in the East, to the Khas caste. **1923** A. TURNBULL *Nepali Gram. & Vocab.* (ed. 3) 1 They also frequently refer to the language as 'Pahāṛī', or 'Pahāṛiyā', though, strictly speaking, it is only one of the many forms of Pahāṛī. **1943** R. GODDEN *Rungli-Rungliot* 37 Monbad speaks Hindustani and Paharia. **1950** *Encycl. Brit.* XVIII. 773/2 The hill dialects, known as Pahari, are akin to the language spoken in Rajputana. **1971** *Hindustan Times* (New Delhi) 7 Apr. 7/3 Mr Khandalavala's books include Pahari Miniature Painting, an exhaustive survey of painting in the Punjab hills. **1974** *Encycl. Brit. Micropædia* VII. 676/3 *Pahari painting*, miniature painting and book illustration that developed in the independent states of the Himalayan foothills in India. **1974** *Listener* 31 Jan. 136/3 The shops are run by Sikhs: the Paharis, the hill people, are not really interested.

‖**pahit** ('pɑːhɪt). [Malay, = bitter.] In full ***gin pahit***. Gin and bitters.

1914 G. FRANKAU *Tid'apa* (1915) ii. 11 He had shouted for *pahit* and for *stinger* till the hot, strong bane of them swept In flame to each brain-cell's tinder. **1923** W. S. MAUGHAM in *Nash's & Pall Mall Mag.* Apr. 32/1 The Irishman ordered a dry martini for her and a gin pahit for himself. **1932** —— *Book-Bag* 21 Shall you be ready for a gin pahit in ten minutes? **1961** CONYN & MARTEN *Bali Ballet Murder* iii. 41 *Gin pahit* as an aperitif. **1963** J. KIRKUP *Tropic Temper* 213 Patrons are requested to reserve their tables for dinner before ordering their pahits. **1965** O. A. MENDELSOHN *Dict. Drink* 251 *Pahit*, Malay Club term for long gin drink. **1968** *Punch* 12 June 852/2 There was the euphoria of foreseeing ourselves in Maugham fiction—white-tuxedoed dinner-parties, the fans turning on the ceiling, gin *pahits* on the veranda, humid adultery behind the jalousies.

‖**Pahlavi** (ˈpɑːləviː), *a.* and *sb.* Also **Pehlavi, Pehlevee, Pehleví** (ˈpɛːləviː), **Pehlví.** [Persian *Pahlaví*, Parthian, f. *Pahlav*:—*Parthava*, Parthia.] The name given by the followers of Zoroaster to the character in which are written the ancient translations of their sacred books and some other works of the same age; now used generally to designate a kind of written language, or rather a mode of writing the language, used in Persia under the Sásánian kings; loosely, Old Persian. Also **Pehlevian.**

'The hot strife which raged till recently as to whether Pahlaví is Semitic or Persian has been closed by the discovery that it is merely a way of writing Persian, in which the Persian words are partly represented—to the eye not to the ear—by their Semitic equivalents'. Thus 'for *bread* they wrote LHMA, i.e. the Aramaic *laḥmá*, but they pronounced *nán*, which is the common Persian word for bread. Similarly BSRA, the Aramaic *besrá* flesh, was pronounced as the Persian *gósht*'. The alphabet actually used was derived from the Old Aramaic. Prof. Nöldeke in *Encycl. Brit.*

1773 W. JONES tr. *Astarabadi's Hist. Nader Shah* App. 159 Barzuien learned the Indian tongue, and, having..procured a copy of the book, translated it into the Pehlevian dialect: about an hundred and forty years after, his work was turned from Pehlevi into Arabick. **1777** J. RICHARDSON *Dict. Persian, Arabic, & Eng.* p. iv/2 The idiom of Farsistan (Persia Proper)..had an extensive range over the most civilized of the lower districts: whilst the Pehlavi prevailed chiefly around the Mazenderan or Caspian Sea. **1789** [see ZEND 1]. **1815** M. ELPHINSTONE *Acct. Kingdom of Caubul* II. iv. 191 Some of these Zend and Pehlevee words are, however, common to the Shanscrit. **1831** *Encycl. Brit.* (ed. 7) III. 691/1 About the era of Mahomet..the learned had a language of their own, which had the name of the Pahlavi. **1840** *Penny Cycl.* XVII. 479/2 A history of Persia in the Pehlvi dialect. **1855** LEPSIUS *Stand. Alph.* (1863) 120 It approaches most nearly to the Pehlevi writing. **1859** FITZGERALD tr. *Omar* vi, In divine High piping Pehlevi..the Nightingale cries to the Rose. **1885** TH. NÖLDEKE in *Encycl. Brit.* XVIII. 134/2 At first sight the Pahlaví books present the strangest spectacle of mixture of speech. *Ibid.* 136/1 Very little profane literature still exists in Pahlaví; the romance of Ardashír has been mentioned above. *Ibid.*, A Pahlavi grammar is of course an impossibility. **1950** R. G. KENT *Old Persian* 6/2 Middle Iranian includes the Iranian dialects as they appear from about 300 B.C. to about 900 A.D. They are in general called Pahlavi. *Ibid.* 7/1 Arsacid Pahlavi was the official language of the Arsacid dynasty of Parthia, which ruled from 250 B.C. to 226 A.D... The Sasanian or South-west Pahlavi was the official language of the Sasanian dynasty, which ruled from 226 A.D. until..652. **1968** K. JAHN *Rypka's Hist. Iranian Lit.* 34 There is a great wealth of Middle Persian book-literature, usually known as Pahlavi literature. The language is also called book-Pahlavi. **1972** W. B. LOCKWOOD *Panorama Indo-European Lang.* 235 Middle Persian or Pahlavi, as the language of this literature is also called.

‖**pahoehoe** (pəˈhəʊiːhəʊiː). *Geol.* Also †**pahoihoi.** [Hawaiian.] A form of solidified lava that is undulating or billowy in form and has a shiny appearance. Cf. AA².

1859 [see AA²]. **1864** R. ANDERSON *Hawaiian Islands* 142 The broken lava is piled ten or fifteen feet above the smooth, hard *pahoihoi*. **1869** *Q. Jrnl. Geol. Soc.* XXV. 434 From this a stream of the smooth satin-like lava called 'pahoehoe' in Hawaii flowed for a few hours. **1972** *Islander* (Victoria, B.C.) 24 Sept. 4/2 One is pahoehoe—a taffy-like lava that has hardened into folds and creases that give it a smooth, ropy look, like frosting that has spilled over the top of a cake. **1975** *Nature* 29 May 387/1 The eruptions of this period include two..which produced pahoehoe instead of the more normal aa flows of Etna.

pai, obs. f. PAY.

pai: see PIE (Indian copper coin).

paian, var. PAYEN *Obs.*, pagan.

paice, obs. Sc. form of PACE.

paiche (pɑːˈiʃeɪ). [Amer. Sp.] = ARAPAIMA, PIRARUCÚ.

1961 E. S. HERALD *Living Fishes of World* 99/1 The largest species in the family [*sc.* Osteoglossidæ] is the fabulous *Arapaima gigas*, called paiche in Peru, pirarucú in Brazil, and arapaima in British Guiana. **1962** N. MAXWELL *Witch-Doctor's Apprentice* xx. 251 At each stop, the block of salt fish grew higher. It was all *paiche*, a giant fish often attaining a weight of more than two hundred pounds, which is found only in the Amazon River system. **1976** 'A. HALL' *Kobra Manifesto* xiii. 174 We were eating *paiche* with *farinha*.

paid (peɪd), *ppl. a.* [Pa. pple. of PAY *v.*¹]

†**1. a.** *pred.* Pleased, satisfied, content. *Obs.*

c **1230** *Hali Meid.* 27 Eiðer is alles weis paied of oðer. *c* **1330** R. BRUNNE *Chron.* (1810) 70 William was not paied, þat falle mad him ofright. *c* **1400** *Rowland & O.* 640 Damesell, arte thou payed of me? *c* **1400** MAUNDEV. (Roxb.) xii. 52 Here es my son þat I luffe, of wham I am wele payd. **1480** CAXTON *Chron. Eng.* ccxliv. (1482) 295 Sore agreued and right euyll payed toward the frensshmen. **1483** *Cath. Angl.* 266/1 Payde, *pacatus, contentus.* **1825–80** JAMIESON s.v. *Paid*, 'I'm weel paid wi' the bargain'... 'I'm verra ill paid for ye', I am very sorry for you; Aberd.

†**b.** Intoxicated, drunk. *Obs. slang.*

1638 SHIRLEY *Royal Master* II. i. D iij b, *Jaca.* Heele be drunke presently... [*Bombo drinks on*]..*Piet.* Hees paid, the King will come this way... *Bom.* Dee heare no body say he saw me, I wonnot Be seene yet. (*He reeles in.*)

2. Remunerated or recompensed with money; in receipt of pay: see PAY *v.*¹ 2, 4.

1862 *All Year Round* 18 Oct. 133 The machinery of paid officials. **1866** DORA GREENWELL *Ess.* (1867) 60 The exchange of paid for voluntary labour. **1961** WEBSTER s.v., A good job and a paid vacation. **1967** *Listener* 30 Nov. 694/2 The shortening of hours of work, improvements in housing standards, paid holidays, the prohibition of child labour,.. should all, on the face of it, have helped to intensify family cohesiveness. **1978** *Ibid.* 19 Jan. 78/3 After the Second World War, paid holidays became common.

3. Given, as money, in discharge of an obligation; discharged, as a debt; for which the money has been given, as a bill, a cheque: see PAY *v.*¹ 5.

1866 CRUMP *Banking* iv. 96 The law..seems to be that a paid cheque is the absolute property of the customer. **1892** ZANGWILL *Bow Myst.* 134, I..found a paid cheque made out for £25 in the name of Miss Dymond.

4. a. With prep. or adv., as ***paid-for, paid-off, paid-up***: see various senses of PAY *v.*¹

paid for, esp., an instruction given to a dog that has 'earned' a reward. ***paid-up capital***: that part of the subscribed capital of an undertaking which has been actually paid.

1817 BROUGHAM in *Parl. Deb.* 776 The legal, professional, hired, and paid for dicta of two officers. **1848** MILL *Pol. Econ.* II. v. ix. 463 A known and large amount of paid-up capital. **1854** J. C. MAITLAND *Cat & Dog* 8 To please Lily, I learned to sit patiently watching the most tempting buttered crust on the ground under my nose, when she said 'Trust, Captain!' never dreaming of touching it till she gave the word of command, 'Now it is paid for;' when I ate it in a genteel and deliberate manner. **1874** TROLLOPE *Lady Anna* xxxvii. 290 They are paying twenty per cent. on the paid-up capital. **1874** 'MARK TWAIN' *Gilded Age* xlviii. 435 What the insurance companies call the 'endowment', or the 'paid-up' plan, by which a policy is secured after a certain time without further payment. **1883** *Pall Mall G.* 7 Sept. 2/2 The annual repairs..would amount to at least £10,000, and the paids-out above mentioned to about £25,000. **1883** *Daily News* 10 Sept. 2/5 The consignor, when he has not been paid for his goods, instructs the carrier to collect for him the price thereof, and this is called the 'paid on'. **1886** R. KIPLING *Departm. Ditties* (1899) 27 Steer clear of Ink Save when you write receipts for paid-up bills in't. **1894** H. NISBET *Bush Girl's Rom.* xi. 100 They were mostly the paid-off shearers and extra stockmen whom he had met. **1913** [see EXTENDED *ppl. a.* 2 c]. **1922** 'R. CROMPTON' *Just—William* xii. 238 They taught him to sit up and almost taught him 'Trust' and 'Paid For'. **1934** 'R. HULL' *Murder of my Aunt* ii. 107 It seemed eternity to me, and I suppose to So-so too, waiting, for the glad sound of 'Paid for'. **1970** J. FLEMING *Young Man, I think you're Dying* ix. 127 The manner of dogs put on *Trust* for a biscuit, watching the biscuit until the words: *Paid for!*

b. In phr. ***paid-up member***, a member of a club, society, etc., who has paid a subscription.

1959 H. HOBSON *Mission House Murder* xxvi. 176 A fully paid-up member of Medina, Soho's equivalent of the old Mafia. **1960** *News Chron.* 1 July 6/7 Prince Philip always ..[visits] the club when he attends Cowes Week—he's a fully paid-up member. **1970** 'H. CARMICHAEL' *Remote Control* ii. 24 He was a paid-up member of the Kennel Club. **1976** *Conservation News* Nov./Dec. 12 That issue contained the application for non-voting tickets for paid-up members not attending as delegates.

paideutics: see PÆDEUTICS.

paidgion, obs. f. PAGEANT.

paidle, var. PADLE, hoe; Sc. f. PADDLE *v.*

paidle, var. PADDLE *sb.*³

paido-: see PÆDO-, PEDO-.

paie, obs. f. PAY.

paien(e, var. PAYEN, *Obs.*, pagan.

paier, obs. form of PAIR *sb.*, PAYER.

paigeite (ˈpeɪdʒaɪt). *Min.* [f. the name of Sidney *Paige* (1880–1968), U.S. geologist + -ITE¹.] A borate of iron and magnesium, $(Fe^{II},Mg)_2Fe^{III}BO_5$ with more ferrous iron than magnesium, which is found as black orthorhombic crystals.

1908 KNOPF & SCHALLER in *Amer. Jrnl. Sci.* CLXXV. 324 The other mineral, for which we propose the name *paigeite*, in honor of Mr. Sidney Paige of the Geological Survey, was found at two localities, at Brooks Mountain [Alaska] in loose blocks, and at Ear Mountain, 40 miles to the northeast, *in situ.* **1954** [see HULSITE]. **1961** *Doklady Earth Sci.* CXXXIV. 1004 (*heading*) On the discovery of warwickite and paigeite in Precambrian dolomitic marbles of North Korea.

paigle, pagle (ˈpeɪg(ə)l). *dial.* Also 6 **pagyll, paggle,** 8–9 **pagil,** (9 *dial.* **paagle, paugle, peagle, pegle, peggle, peggall**: see E.D.D.) [In 16th c. *pagyll, pagle, paggle*, of uncertain origin; but cf. PAGGLE *v.*

See many conjectures in *N. & Q.* 7th s. VII, VIII, 1883.]

A local name for the cowslip, *Primula veris*; sometimes including the Oxlip; also applied locally to some other flowers, as the buttercup.

1530 PALSGR. 250/2 Pagyll a cowsloppe. **1548** TURNER *Names Herbes* (1881) 79 There are iij Verbascula... The fyrste is called in barbarus latin Arthritica, and in englishe a Primerose. The seconde is..Paralysis, and in englishe a Cowslip, or a Cowslap, or a Pagle. **1568** —— *Herbal* III. 80 A Cowislip, and..an Oxislip..are both call [sic] in Cambridgeshyre Pagles. **1573** TUSSER *Husb.* xlii. (1878) 95 Strowing herbes of all sortes..5. Cousleps and paggles. *Ibid.* xliii. 96, 25. Paggles, greene and yelow. **1597** GERARDE *Herbal* II. cclx. §7. 637 Called for the most part Oxelips and Paigles. **1629** PARKINSON *Paradisi* xxv. 247 In some countries they call them Paigles, or Palsieworts, or Petty Mulleins, which are called Cowslips in others. **1691** RAY *S. & E.C. Words* (E.D.S.), *Paigle*..is of use in Essex, Middlesex, Suffolk, for a cowslip: *cowslip* with us signifying what is elsewhere called an *oxslip*. **1760** J. LEE *Introd. Bot.* App. 321 Pagils or Paigles, *Primula*. **1866** *Treas. Bot.*, Paigle, Pagle, or Peagle, *Primula veris*.

‖**pai-hua** (paɪhwɑː). Also **bai hua, báihuà.** [Chinese *báihuà*, f. *bái* white, clear, plain + *huà* language, speech.] The standard written form of modern Chinese, based on the northern dialects, esp. that of Peking; the vernacular literary style (opp. WENYEN). Also *attrib.* Cf. PUTONGHUA.

1923 B. KARLGREN *Sound & Symbol in Chinese* iii. 37 Some modern newspapers have tried to introduce *pai hua* 'white language', i.e. vulgar style, colloquial, at least in one or two columns, but with no great success. **1932** O. M. GREEN in *Asiatic Rev.* XXVIII. 114 The Literary Revoltuion of 1917 to 1919..secured the adoption of the Pai Hua, the most widely spoken language in China, for all literary purposes. Not only newspapers and magazines but many standard works are now printed in the Pai Hua. **1936** N. WALES in E. Snow *Living China* 336 The healthy parvenu *pai-hua*, 'plain speech', literature of the people in the spoken language, ashamed of itself and despised and outcast by the *wen-yen literati*. **1937** E. SNOW *Red Star over China* i. 44 These Shensi hill people have a dialect of their own..but they understand *pai-hua*, or mandarin Chinese. **1950** J. DE FRANCIS *Nationalism & Lang. Reform in China* i. 7 The *paihua* or colloquial style was, roughly speaking, speech reduced to writing in the ideographic script. **1968** P. KRATOCHVÍL *Chinese Lang. Today* v. 163 Perhaps the most influential factor..was the out-burst of writing in the new style which followed the rejection of *wényán*. This style called *the new báihuà*, or only *báihuà* (usually translated as 'vernacular'; the etymology of the Chinese term which means something like 'plain language' is not quite certain), grew partly out of the tradition of popular old *báihuà* writing mainly represented by the great medieval novels.

paijama: see PYJAMA.

paik (peɪk), *sb. Sc.* and *north. dial.* [Goes with PAIK *v.*: origin unknown.] A firm stiff blow, esp. on the body; ***one's paiks***, the thrashing due to one, or that one comes in for.

1508 DUNBAR *Flyting* 70 How that thow, poysonit pelor, gat thy paikis [*rime* aix]. **1571** *Satir. Poems Reform.* xxv. 112 Cum þai heir, þir tuo yeir, They sall not misse þair paikis. **1768** ROSS *Helenore* 42 While monie a paik unto his beef they led, Till wi' the thumps he blue an' blae was made. **1819** W. TENNANT *Papistry Storm'd* (1827) 48 Ilk clapper gaif ilk bell sic paiks. **1822** BYRON *To Scott* 4 May, He got his paiks—having acted like an assassin. **1895** CROCKETT *Men of Moss Hags* 282 We always got our paiks for what little we had.

paik (peɪk), *v. Sc.* and *north. dial.* [See prec.] *trans.* To hit with something hard or solid, as the knuckles, a stick, a stone; to beat, pummel, thrash. Hence **ˈpaiking, ˈpaikment**, a thrashing; **ˈpaiker**, a beater; ***causey-paiker***, a street-walker.

a **1555** LYNDESAY *Tragedy* 378 Nor..Off Rome rakaris, nor of rude Ruffianis, Off calsay Paikaris, nor of Publycanis. *c* **1639** R. BAILLIE *Lett.* (1775) I. 74 That day Mr. Armour was well paiked. **1807** STAGG *Misc. Poems* (Cumberld.) 94 Weant heame—was paick'd agean by th' weyfe. **1822** SCOTT *Nigel* xxxvii, If she comes to dunts, I have twa hands to paik her with.

paik, obs. Sc. form of PAWK, trick.

pai kau (paɪ kaʊ). Also **pai kow, pie-gow.** [Cantonese, f. *p'ai* tablet + *kau* nine.] A Chinese gambling game played with dominoes.

1906 [see CHUCK-A-LUCK]. **1969** R. C. BELL *Board & Table Games* II. vi. 102 Pai Kow is played with a full set of Chinese dominoes. **1972** *Guardian* 29 May 16/2 Mr Liu..wants..to attract his countrymen away from Mah Jong and Pai Kau—a sort of dominoes played like poker. **1978** *Daily Tel.* 13 July 1/7 The legalising of exotic games such as fan tan and pai kau in casinos.

pail (peɪl), *sb.* Forms: 4–7 **payle,** 5 **paille,** (**payelle**), 6–7 **paile,** 7–8 **pale,** 6– **pail.** [Of uncertain origin: cf. OE. *pæᵹel* 'gill, wine-measure' (Sweet), and OF. *paelle, payelle, paielle* frying-pan, brazier, warming-pan, bath, liquid measure, saltpan:—L. *patella* small pan or dish, plate, dim. of *patina* broad shallow dish, pan; see Note below.]

1. A vessel, usually of cylindrical or truncated obconical shape, made of wooden staves hooped with iron, or of sheet-metal, etc., and provided with a bail or hooped handle; used for carrying milk, water, etc. (The sense in quots. *c* 1000 and 1423 is doubtful. In the latter the word appears to be OF. *payelle*, frying-pan, brazier, or flat-dish.)

[*c* **1000** ÆLFRIC *Gloss.* in Wr.-Wülcker 124/2 *Gillo*, pæᵹel [*mispr.* wægel]. **1392–3** *Earl Derby's Exped.* (Camden) 174 Pro ij payles ligneis, ijs. [**1423** in *Rolls of Parlt.* IV. 241 Item, XXXI Pottez du Bras..Item, XIX Pailles de Bras,..Item, XXVII Pailles de Bras rumpuz..Item, XII Pailles ovec longe handels, pris le pece VIIId.] *c* **1425** *Voc.* in Wr.-Wülcker 666/16 *Hec multra*, payle. *c* **1440** *Promp. Parv.* 377/2 Payle, or mylke stoppe, *multrale,..vel multra.* **1530** PALSGR. 250/2 Payle a vessell, *seau*. **1577** B. GOOGE *Heresbach's Husb.* 66 The Gardners in the end of Sommer, do take the rootes and set them in pannes, pottes, or payles. *a* **1636** FITZ-GEFFRAY *Bless. Birthd.* (1881) 153 Had they not come their empty pailes to fill At wisdomes well, they had beene empty still. **1697** DRYDEN *Virg. Past.* II. 28 New Milk that..overflows the Pails. **1703** MOXON *Mech. Exerc.* 259 Dip every Brick you lay, all over in a Pale of Water. **1798** SOUTHEY *Well of St. Keyne* v, There came a man from the house hard by At the Well to fill his pail. **1882** Ross in *Sunday Mag.* Feb. 96 A sea In which we children dip our tiny pails.

b. A pail full (of water, etc.); a pailful.

1600 HAKLUYT *Voy.* III. 418 Skins of those seales, contayning ech of them aboue a great paile of water. **1703** MOXON *Mech. Exerc.* 259 They may throw Pales of Water on the Wall after the Bricks are lay'd. **1886** HALL CAINE *Son of Hagar* I. v, Crossing the garden with a pail of water just raised from the well.

c. In phrases relating to the milk-pail.

1617 MORYSON *Itin.* III. 286 They pay..two stiuers weekely for each Cow for the Paile. **1758** R. BROWN *Compl. Farmer* (1759) 19 The best sort of cows for the pail. **1886** ELWORTHY *W. Somerset Word-bk.* s.v., A cow is said to be 'a come'd in to pail' when her calf is gone, and all her milk becomes available for the dairy. **1888** T. HARDY *Wessex Tales* I. 57 The cows were 'in full pail'.

†**2.** A shallow pan, such as is used for obtaining salt by the evaporation of brine; a salt-pan. *Obs.* (So OF. *paielle.*)

1481 CAXTON *Myrr.* II. xxi. 112 Nygh vnto metz the cyte is a water that renneth there, the whiche is soden in grete payelles of copper, and it becometh salt fayr and good.

3. *attrib.* and *Comb.*, as *pail-bottom, -brush, -handle, -lathe, -machine, -maker, -nail, -stake.*

1723 *Lond. Gaz.* No. 6224/6 Thomas Gibbons, Pailmaker. **1789** W. MARSHALL *Glouc.* Gloss. (E.D.S.), *Pailstake*..a bough, furnished with many branchlets, is fixed with its but-end in the ground, in the dairy-yard. The branchlets being lopped, of a due length, each stump becomes a peg to hang a pail upon. **1858** SIMMONDS *Dict. Trade, Pail-brush*, a hand brush to clean the corners of vessels. **1884** KNIGHT *Dict. Mech.* Suppl. 653/1 The workman..in an instant moves another chisel to form the groove for receiving the chine of the pail-bottom and chamfers the upper edge.

Hence **pail** *v.* (*nonce-wd.*), to pour out in pailfuls.

1807 W. TAYLOR in *Ann. Rev.* V. 559 The well-head of all the clear water which the Lockes and Hartleys have pailed abroad.

[*Note.* The OE. form *pægel* suits the mod. Eng. *pail* (cf. *hail, sail, tail*, etc.), but does not explain the final *-e* always present from 14th to 17th c., which is better accounted for by the OF. word. Neither source is quite satisfactory as to the sense: the OF. word being applied in all cases to a *shallow* dish; while OE. *pægel* appears to have been a small measure: cf. LG. *pegel*, Da. *pægel, pæl*, half a pint. The Dutch *pegel* is difficult to bring into line. Kilian 1599 has *peghel* 'capacity or measure of a vessel'; Hexham 1678 has 'the concavity or the capacity of a vessel or of a pot'. But mod.Du. *pegel, peil* has the sense 'gauge, scale, mark', which was also the sense in MDu., going back, according to Franck, to an ODu. **pagil* 'little peg or pin', esp. one 'used as a mark', to be compared with Eng. *peg* and Du. dial. *pegel* icicle; an original sense remote from that of Eng. *pail* or even OE. *pægel.*]

pail, *v.*[2] *dial.* [Origin unknown: see also PALE *v.*[4]] *trans.* To beat, thrash. Hence **pailed** *ppl. a.*, beaten; **pailing** *vbl. sb.*, **pailing-hammer**.

c **1746** J. COLLIER (Tim Bobbin) *View Lanc. Dial.* Wks. (1862) 53 He begun o possing, on peyling him. **1835** in Cornwallis *New World* (1859) I. 377 One shingle hammer, one pailing hammer. **1872** HARTLEY *Yorks. Ditties* Ser. I. 81 He's fit to pail his heead agean th' jaumstooan.

pail, paile, obs. forms of PALE, PALL, PEEL.

[**pailer**, mispr. for *pailet*, PALLET, in Holland *Pliny*, ed. 1634, XIX. i, included by Davies 1881, whence inserted in later dicts.]

pailet, obs. form of PALLET *sb.*[2], small bed.

pailful ('peɪlfʊl). [f. PAIL *sb.* + -FUL.] As much as a pail holds.

1591 LYLY *Endym.* IV. ii, He is resolved to weepe some three or four palefuls. **1607** MARKHAM *Caval.* v. (1617) 38 You shall take a Peale-full of colde water. **1707–12** MORTIMER *Husb.* (1721) II. 284 Bestow a Pale-full of Water on every Tree. **1853** MACAULAY in *Life & Lett.* (1880) II. 373 The rain was falling by pailfuls.

paill, obs. Sc. f. PALE *sb.*[1] and *a.*, PALL.

paillard, etc., var. PALLIARD, etc.

paillasse, palliasse (pæl'jæs, 'pælɪæs). Forms: 6 *Sc.* paillyeis, (pavilyeas, pales); 8– paillasse, palliasse, -ass. [a. F. *paillasse* (15th c. in Hatz.-D.), f. *paille* straw:—L. *palea* chaff, straw.

App. adopted in Sc. in 16th c.; then in Eng. in 18th c., first in Fr. spelling, and subseq. as *palliass(e).*]

A sack or mattress of stout material filled with straw and serving as an under-bed; a straw mattress; now, usually, an under-mattress stuffed with straw or similar material.

α. **1506** *Acc. Ld. High Treas. Scot.* III. 267 Item, for lxx elne Bertane clath to be four pair pales schetis. **1562** in *Maitl. Club Misc.* (1833) 31 Debursit..for paillyeisis to the Gaird. **1566** in Hay Fleming *Mary Q. of Scots* (1897) 499 Auchtein elnis of camves to be the pavilyeas and the cuvering of the pavilyeas.

β. **1759** tr. *Adanson's Voy. Senegal* in Pinkerton *Voy.* (1814) XVI. 608 Over this they throw a mat, which serves them for a *paillasse* or straw bed. **1842** LOUISA S. COSTELLO *Pilgr. to Auvergne* I. 95 A paillasse and two mattresses on the floor. **1868** *Regul. & Ord. Army* ¶929 The paillasse is to be rolled up in a Circular form. **1883** *War Office Advt.* in *Pall Mall G.* 15 Sept. 15/2 Tenders for the Supply of Forage and Straw for Paillasses, for Military Services.

γ. **1798** *Army Med. Board* in W. Blair *Soldier's Friend* 84 Where matts cannot be made, some fresh straw should be placed under each palliass. **1809** WELLINGTON in Gurw. *Desp.* V. 291 To provide the palliasses for the hospital. **1834** L. RITCHIE *Wand. by Seine* 81 They found no one but a man lying on a palliass. **1888** *Standard* 21 May 3/3 The Prisoner was found in bed..with the watch and chain under the palliasse.

paille, paille maille, obs. ff. PAIL, PALL-MALL.

paillet(t, obs. f. PALLET *sb.*[2], small bed.

paillette (pæ'ljɛt). Also -et. [a. F. *paillette* (pajɛt), dim. of *paille* straw, chaff, scale of grass.]

1. A piece of coloured foil or bright metal, used in enamel painting.

1878 F. W. RUDLER in *Encycl. Brit.* VIII. 184/2 The lights were picked out in gold, while the brilliant effect of gems was obtained by the use of *paillettes*, or coloured foils. **1894** *Times* 7 Apr. 9/5 A triptych, of Limoges enamel..in brilliant colours, with paillets of foil, date about 1490.

2. A small piece of gold or silver foil, mother-of-pearl, or some glittering material, used to ornament a woman's dress; a spangle.

1890 in *Cent. Dict.* **1897** *Westm. Gaz.* 9 Nov. 7/3 The dress is..embroidered in a design of Wisteria, carried out in paillettes of burnished silver. **1898** *Daily Chron.* 24 Sept. 8/2 Bodice..of lace, with the design traced with paillettes.

Hence **pai'lletted** *a.*, spangled.

1902 *Westm. Gaz.* 1 May 4/2 It is made of cream-embroidered mousseline, pailletted with mother-o'-pearl.

paillȝeoun, -ȝeon, -ȝon, -ȝoun, etc., obs. Sc. ff. PAVILION.

†**pai'llole.** *Obs.* [a. OF. *paillole* (13th c. in Littré), in med.L. *paleola*, dim. of *palea* scale of chaff.] A thin scale or grain of metal, as of gold.

1481 CAXTON *Myrr.* II. viii. 85 Ffro this parte toward thende of egypte cometh to vs the paillole whiche is of fyn golde.

‖**paillon** (pajõ, 'pæljən). [Fr., deriv. of *paille* scale of chaff.] A scale or small bit of bright metal foil used in enamelling and decorative art.

1890 in *Cent. Dict.*

paillyeis, obs. Sc. f. PAILLASSE.

pail-mail, paiment, paimistris, obs. ff. PALL-MALL, PAYMENT, PAYMISTRESS.

‖**pailou** (ˌpaɪ'ləʊ). [Chinese, f. *p'ai* tablet + *lou* tower.] An elaborate Chinese commemorative or ornamental gateway.

1836 J. F. DAVIS *Chinese* II. xviii. 321 The emperor occasionally orders a *pae-low* to be erected at the public expense. **1887** *Chinese Times* 1 Oct. 785/2 The homes of the dead, with their *p'ailou* and carved images of lions, sheep, &c. **1923** *Blackw. Mag.* Jan. 101/2 In front of one of them [*sc.* temples] stands a white stone *pailou*, which shines in the sunlight like a flamboyant Stonehenge trilith. **1947** *Archit. Rev.* CII. 13 The p'ailou is a commemorative gateway, set up either to mark a famous place or to serve as a monument to the dead and having three or five openings with double or triple lintels and tiled roofs. **1948** R. ALLEY *Gung Ho* 28 Under the great pailou framing the main street. **1958** W. WILLETTS *Chinese Arts* II. viii. 736 This class of monumental stone arch or gateway... Commemorative or triumphal in function... *P'ai-lou* are almost always built of stone, in close imitation of a wooden prototype and with carpentry technique. They have one, three, or five openings. **1977** *N.Y. Rev. Bks.* 26 May 21/2 The destruction of Peking started in the 1950s, when all the pailous that spanned the main thoroughfares of the old city were eliminated.

pailyeoun, -ȝeon, -ȝon, -ȝoun, etc., obs. Sc. ff. PAVILION.

pain (peɪn), *sb.*[1] Forms: 3–6 peyne, 3–7 peine, 4–7 paine, payne, payn, 4– pain, (4–6 *Sc.* pane, 5–6 pein, peyn, pene, *Sc.* pan, 6 peane, pœne). [ME. a. OF. *peine* (11th c. in Littré) = Pr., Sp., It. *pena*:—L. *pœna* penalty, punishment. Cf. also PINE, an earlier form of the same word from L.]

1. a. Suffering or loss inflicted for a crime or offence; punishment; penalty; a fine. *Obs.* exc. in phr. *pains and penalties*, and as in b.

1297 R. GLOUC. (Rolls) 7742 Þer to he nom gret peine of hom. *a* **1300** *Cursor M.* 6691 If he liue a dai or tuin, þe lauerd sal vnderli na pain. **1387** TREVISA *Higden* (Rolls) II. 231 Crist þat payed a payne [*pœnam solvit*] for vs alle. **1433** in *10th Rep. Hist. MSS. Comm.* App. v. 295 He shal pay the same payne as afor is saide. **1482** *Paston Lett.* III. 297 Wryttes of subpena..made upon gret peynys were delyvered to the seid William. **1577** tr. *Bullinger's Decades* (1592) 45 Condemnation vnto death set as a peine upon our heades, because of the transgression. **1689** *Col. Rec. Pennsylv.* I. 309 Which Ordinances..shall be observed inviolably..under paynes therein to be expressed. **1770** *Junius Lett.* xxxvii. 189 *note*, The courtiers talked of..a bill of pains and penalties. **1859** MILL *Liberty* i. 23 Compulsion, either in the direct form or in that of pains and penalties.

b. *esp.* in phr. *on, upon, under* (†*up*, †*of*, †*in*) *pain of*: followed by the penalty or punishment incurred in case of not fulfilling the command or condition stated, as *on pain of death*; also, formerly, that which one is liable to pay or forfeit, as *on pain of a hundred pounds, on pain of life*, or the crime with which one is liable to be charged, as *on pain of felony*. Formerly sometimes with ellipsis of *on*, etc. (*pain of* = 'on pain of').

c **1380** WYCLIF in Todd *Three Treat.* 133 Crist bad preche; & þei bidden leue in payne of prisonyng. *c* **1386** CHAUCER *Knt.'s T.* 849 Namoore vp on peyne of lesynge of youre heed. *Ibid.* 1685 No man ther fore vp peyne of los of lyf No maner shot..In to the lystes sende. **1389** in *Eng. Gilds* (1870) 4 Of peyne of a pond wax to þe bretherhede. *c* **1430** LYDG. *Min. Poems* (Percy Soc.) 151 Ther dar noon officeer Peyne of his lyff do noon extorcioun. *c* **1449** PECOCK *Repr.* (Rolls) I. 99 Vndir great payne of horrible death suffring. **1461** *Paston Lett.* II. 58 A writte chargyng hym in peyne of c *li* to brynge me in to the Kynges Benche. **1472** *Presentm. Juries* in *Surtees Misc.* (1888) 24 Opane of vjs. viijd. p[t] to be forfyt. **1529** RASTELL *Pastyme, Hist. Pap.* (1811) 55 That none shulde ley no violent hande upon a clerke, payne of cursynge. **1599** B. JONSON *Cynthia's Rev.* v. ii, Doe it, on pœne of the dor. **1650** HOWELL *Giraffi's Rev. Naples* I. 98 That every one upon paine of life shold return to their houses. **1652** *Ibid.* II. 19 That every one should open his Shop under pain of Rebellion. **1699** BENTLEY *Phal.* 439 He order'd every man upon the pain of death to bring in all the money he had. **1752** J. LOUTHIAN *Form of Process* (ed. 2) 92 To pass upon the Assize of C.D. each under the Pain of One hundred Merks. **1829** SOUTHEY in *For. Rev. & Cont. Misc.* III. 30 They shall be commanded, on pain of perpetual bondage, to depart out of the said kingdoms. **1884** *Times* (weekly ed.) 17 Oct. 14/1 A proclamation ordering the tribes to join him under pain of death.

†**c.** *pain fort and dure*: see PEINE.

†**d.** in *pl.* Judicial torture. *Obs. rare.*

1533 CROMWELL in Merriman *Life & Lett.* (1902) I. 361 They..wolde confesse sum grete matier if they might be examyned as they ought to be that is to sey by paynes.

2. a. A primary condition of sensation or consciousness, the opposite of *pleasure*; the sensation which one feels when hurt (in body or mind); suffering, distress. With *a* and *pl.*, a single feeling of this nature. In early use *esp.* suffering inflicted as punishment. (Cf. sense 1.)

a **1300** *Cursor M.* 20618 O paine þow sal noght thol a dele. **1390** GOWER *Conf.* III. 345 Of every lust thende is a peine. **1413** *Pilgr. Sowle* (Caxton) v. i. (1859) 69 Now ben ended the peynes and tormentes. **1481** CAXTON *Reynard* (Arb.) 32 Reynert the foxe..saide to Isegrym, shorte my payne. **1598** CHAPMAN *Blind Beggar Alexandria* Plays 1873 I. 29 But every pleasure hath a payne they say. **1601** SIR W. CORNWALLIS *Ess.*, [His] furthest wish being but to bee out of his paine. **1756** BURKE *Subl. & B.* I. ii, Pain and pleasure are simple ideas incapable of definition. **1883** A. BARRATT *Phys. Metempiric* 152 The simple reaction, which physically is expressed as the Law of Self-conservation, psychically as the Principle of following Pleasure and avoiding Pain. **1892** WESTCOTT *Gospel of Life* 162 The most universal fact in life is pain.

†**b.** *spec.* The punishment or sufferings of hell (or of purgatory). *Obs.*

1340–70 *Alex. & Dind.* 747 Ȝe schulle be punched and put in paine for euere. *c* **1400** *Rowland & O.* 1440 His saule wente vn-to payne. **1544** BALE *Chron. Sir J. Oldcastell* in *Harl. Misc.* (Malh.) I. 261 Euery man..is a pilgrym, eyther towardes blesse or els towardes payne. **1568** GRAFTON *Chron.* II. 345 Whosoeuer dyed in that time, and gaue his goodes to further that voyage, he was cleane absolued from paine and from sinne. **1598** BARCKLEY *Felic. Man* (1631) 183 Ar now cast downe into paines lowest abysse.

c. *to put out of* (one's) *pain*, etc.: to put to death, dispatch (a wounded or suffering person or animal).

1572 FORREST *Theophilus* 1233 in *Anglia* VII, God tooke him owte of this carcerall payne. **1596** SPENSER *F.Q.* v. xii. 23 He lightly reft his head to ease him of his paine. **1639** SHIRLEY *Maid's Rev.* v. iii, I would I were hanged, to be out of my pain! **1783** AINSWORTH *Lat. Dict.* (Morell) IV. s.v. *Lysimachus*, Lysimachus..at his request gave him a cup of poison to put him out of his pain. **1808** MARCHIONESS OF STAFFORD 15 Sept. in *C. K. Sharpe's Corr.* (1888) I. 346 A C[ss]. of Suth[d]...was half drowned..and after coming on shore, put out of pain by Andrew Davy, a fugitive.

3. a. In specifically physical sense: Bodily suffering; a distressing sensation as of soreness (usually in a particular part of the body).

1377 LANGL. *P. Pl.* B. XVII. 187 For peyne of the paume powere hem [the fingers] failleth To clucche or to clawe. **1486** *Bk. St. Albans* C vij b, Hawkys that haue payne in theyr croupes. **1590** SPENSER *F.Q.* I. xi. 37 Loud he yelled for exceeding paine. **1697** DRYDEN *Virg. Georg.* III. 64 Envy her self at last..The Pains of famisht Tantalus shall feel. **1722** R. WODROW *Suff. Ch. Scot.* (1837) II. II. xiii. §5. 458/1 At the ninth [stroke in the torture of the boot] Mr. Mitchel fainted through the extremity of pain. **1841–71** T. R. JONES *Anim. Kingd.* (ed. 4) 438 In Man, the power of feeling pain indubitably is placed exclusively in the brain; and if communication be cut off between this organ and any part of the body, pain is no longer felt, whatever mutilations may be inflicted. **1849** MACAULAY *Hist. Eng.* IV. I. 433 The king was in great pain, and complained that he felt as if a fire was burning within him.

b. *spec.* (now always *pl.*) The sufferings or throes of childbirth; labour.

a **1300** *Cursor M.* 3488 (Cott.) In trauelling..Ful herd it was þair moder pain [*Trin.* Muchel was þe modir peyn]. **1388** WYCLIF *John* XVI. 21 But whanne sche hath borun a sone, now sche thenkith not on the peyne, for ioye, for a man is borun in to the world. **1539** BIBLE (Great) *1 Sam.* IV. 19 She bowed her selfe, and traueled, for her paynes cam vpon her. **1547** BOORDE *Brev. Health* ccxlii, Wel she may be named a woman, for as much as she doth bere chyldren with wo and peyne. *c* **1611** CHAPMAN *Iliad* IV. 509 Feeling suddenly the pains of child-birth. *a* **1704** T. BROWN *1st Sat. Persius* Wks. 1730 I. 53 Here some pert sot, with six months pain, brings forth A strange, mishapen, and ridiculous birth. **1797** SOUTHEY *Eng. Eclogues, Hannah* 19 She bore unhusbanded a mother's pains. **1889** J. M. Duncan *Clin. Lect. on Dis. Women* xi. (ed. 4) 68 Brought about..by the contractions of the uterus in 'pains'.

†**c.** *pl.* A disease of the feet in horses. *Obs.*

c **1440** *Promp. Parv.* 390/2 Peynys, yvyl yn horsys fete. **1598** Florio, *Reste*, a disease in a horse which we call the paines. **1610** Markham *Masterp.* II. lxxviii. 350 The paines is a certaine vlcerous scabbe growing in the pastornes of a horse, betwixt the fetlocke and the heele.

d. ***pain in the neck*** (colloq.) (also simply *pain*), an annoying or tiresome person or thing; also, in same sense (but *vulg.*), ***pain in the arse***. Also, ***to give*** (someone) ***a pain*** (***in the neck*** or ***arse***), to be annoying or tiresome (to someone).

1908 R. E. Knowles *Web of Time* xiv. 144 'There's naethin' like the guid auld oatmeal.' 'You Scotch folks give me a pain,' broke in David. **1912** *Maclean's Mag.* Nov. 68/1 Bill, you give me a pain. **1924** Wodehouse *Leave it to Psmith* ix. 188 He got there first, damn him! Wouldn't that give you a pain in the neck! **1933** E. B. White *Let.* Mar. (1976) 112 All through the campaign I thought Mr. R. was something of a pain. **1934** [see ass *sb.*[2] 1 a]. **1937** [see dinkum *a.*]. **1941** W. A. Percy *Lanterns on Levee* 77, I was a sickly youngster ..a frail problem child, a pain in the neck. **1951** 'A. Garve' *Murder in Moscow* x. 102 What do we really know of Mullett, except that he was a pain in the neck to every-body? **1958** *Spectator* 7 Feb. 175/3 The Liu was almost as big a pain in the neck as the previous night's Preziosilla. **1967** W. Soyinka *Kongi's Harvest* 14 Your uncle is a pain in the neck. **1970** *Times* 7 Jan. 7/7 Anthony Quinn..plays a wise, noble, feckless, life-loving Greek dispenser of advice, lay preacher and general pain in the neck. **1972** D. Ramsay *Little Murder Music* 8 Hey, Jack, how does his royal pain in the ass intend to take the *Scherzo*? **1972** *Times* 13 Sept. 7/5 He represents about 1 per cent of the blokes... He is a pain. **1973** 'E. McBain' *Hail to Chief* i. 6 Homicide cops..were pains in the ass to detectives actually..trying to solve murder cases. **1975** *New Yorker* 21 Apr. 103/3 She is a pain, and, unconsciously, the source of many of the troubles that follow. *Ibid.* 17 Nov. 125/1 Fiction, in whatever form, about real people is more often than not a pain, and sometimes downright pernicious. **1976** A. White *Long Silence* xiv. 123 Lieutenant Otto Andersen..was a consistent pain in the arse to Colonel Birkenkamp, constantly reporting his men for slovenly dress. **1977** *Rolling Stone* 7 Apr. 12/2 It was an increasing pain in the ass to do the same material each night.

4. a. In specifically psychical sense: Mental suffering, trouble, grief, sorrow.

1375 Barbour *Bruce* II. 517 [Thai] wald partenerys off thar paynys be. *c* **1386** Chaucer *Knt.'s T.* 957 Syn I knowe of loues peyne. *c* **1430** *Syr Tryam.* 607 Hyt dothe the kyng mekylle payne When he thenkyth how sir Roger was slayne. *c* **1560** A. Scott *Poems* (S.T.S.) xxviii. 1 To luve vnluvit it is ane pane. **1656** Cowley *Misc., Gold*, A Mighty pain to Love it is, And 'tis a pain that pain to miss, But of all pains the greatest pain It is to love, but love in vain. **1754** Richardson *Grandison* IV. 51, I remember with pain the pain I gave to your generous heart. *c* **1850** *Arab. Nts.* (Rtldg.) 85 Their absence would cause me much pain.

†**b.** *spec.* Distress caused by fear of possible evil, anxiety; anxious desire or apprehension. *Obs.*

1668 R. Mountagu in *Buccleuch MSS.* (Hist. MSS. Comm.) I. 420, I am in a great deal of pain to know how my horses have performed the journey. **1758** *Ann. Reg.* 113/2 The public was in great pain for the Admirals..left..in sight of six large French ships of war. **1789** G. White *Selborne* (1875) 318 The foster mother [a cat] became jealous of her charge [young squirrels], and in pain for their safety.

†**5.** Trouble as taken for the accomplishment of something (= *pains*, sense 6); also, in early use, trouble in accomplishing something, difficulty. (F. *peine*.) Phrases. ***to do one's pain; to take pain; to lose one's pain***. *Obs.* in *sing.*: see 6.

a **1300** *Cursor M.* 14480 Fra þat time forth þai did þair pain þat he and lazar war bath slain. *c* **1330** R. Brunne *Chron. Wace* (Rolls) 12174 Þo þat ascaped, hit was wyþ payn. **1375** Barbour *Bruce* VIII. 350 Quhen he saw he tynt his pane, He turnit his bridill, and to ga. *c* **1410** Hoccleve *Mother of God* 108 Now do your bysy peyne To wasshe away our cloudeful offense. **1476** *Paston Lett.* III. 165, I have moche payne to gete so moche mony. **1481** Caxton *Myrr.* III. i. 131 Whiche may moche prouffyte to them that wyll doo payne to knowe them. **1509** Hawes *Past. Pleas.* vi. (1845) 25 Who wyll take payne to folowe the trace. **1513** Douglas *Æneis* I. Prol. 109 And ȝit, forsuith, I set my besy pane, As that I suld, to mak it braid and plane. **1533** Bonner in *St. Papers Hen. VIII*, VII. 410 After that, with moost great peane and difficultie, I was arryved at Rie. **1603** Owen *Pembrokeshire* viii. (1892) 62 The husbandman that spareth paine spareth thrifte. **1633** P. Fletcher *Purple Isl.* x. xl, A thousand Knights woo'd her with busie pain. **1702** *Eng. Theophrast.* 305 A man would not employ the least pain in the acquisition of sciences, if [etc.]. **1768** *Woman of Honor* I. 23 Taking some pain to excuse the girl's carelessness.

6. a. *pl.* Trouble taken in accomplishing or attempting something; labour, toil, exertions, or efforts, accompanied with care and attention, to secure a good or satisfactory result. Most freq. in phr. ***to take pains, to be at*** (***the***) ***pains***.

1528 Tindale *Wks.* (Parker Soc.) I. 260 To make them think that they must take pains, and do some holy deeds. **1538** Starkey *England* I. ii. 55 Apply themselfys to theyr laburys and paynys for the susteynyng of the hole body. **1589** Nashe *Pref. Greene's Menaphon* (Arb.) 8 They haue nought but..their paines for their sweate, and..their labour for their trauaile. **1608** Chapman *Byron's Conspir.* Plays 1873 II. 229 What idle paines have you bestowd to see A poore old woman? **1708** Swift *Sacramental Test* Wks. 1755 II. I. 121 The university was at the pains of publishing a Latin paper to justify themselves. **1774** Goldsm. *Nat. Hist.* (1776) II. 176 A person born deaf, may, by time, and sufficient pains, be taught..to speak, and, by the motions of the lips, to understand what is said to him. **1808** Scott *Marm.* I. xiii, Yet much he praised the pains he took, And well those pains did pay. **1865** Dickens *Mut. Fr.* Postscr. 292, I foresaw..that a class of readers..would suppose that I was at great pains to conceal exactly what I was at great pains to suggest. **1887** Ruskin *Præterita* I. xii. 426 He.. spared no pains on his daughter's education.

b. In this sense the pl. *pains* has been freq. construed as a *sing.* (Cf. *means, news.*)

1533 Cranmer *Let. to Boner* in *Misc. Writ.* (Parker Soc.) II. 269 Ye will be contented to take this pains. **1542** Udall *Erasm. Apoph.* 51 *margin*, The peines of teachyng is woorthie great wages. **1671** tr. *Erasm. Colloq.* 230 Recompensing one pains with another. **1766** Fordyce *Serm. Yng. Wom.* (1767) II. viii. 25 Why be at all this pains? **1884** Sir J. C. Mathew in *Law Rep. 13 Q. Bench Div.* 488 He..took every pains to arrive at a proper conclusion.

c. ***for*** (one's) ***pains***: in return or recompense for one's labour or trouble; now usually sarcastic or ironical, implying that the labour is misspent or futile, or that the return for it is the contrary of what was desired.

1538 Bale *Brefe Comedy* in *Harl. Misc.* (Malh.) I. 208 For your peynes ye haue appoynted by the emproure your stypende wages. **1598** Shaks. *Merry W.* III. iv. 103 Giue my sweet Nan this Ring: there's for thy paines. **1599** Chapman *Humorous Day's Mirth* C iv, Now she stops..and rates him for his paines. **1650** *Overseers' Acc., Holy Cross, Canterb.*, Paid Goodwife Bayly for paines o. o. 8. **1713** Addison *Guard.* No. 112. ¶2 When I talk of practising to fly, silly people think me an owl for my pains. **1778** Miss Burney *Evelina* (1791) I. xxi. 99 If you hadn't come, you might have staid..and been a beggar for your pains. **1801** Mar. Edgeworth *Castle Rackrent* Wks. 1832 I. 77, I had my journey for my pains. **1889** Corbett *Monk* xi. 154 The old general, in a fit of exasperation, publicly gave him a sound thrashing for his pains.

7. *attrib.* and *Comb.* **a.** attrib., as ***pain-sensation, -sense, -sensibility***; **b.** instrumental, as ***pain-afflicted, -bought, -chastened, -dimmed, -distorted, -drawn, -racked, -shot, -stricken, -worn, -wrung*** adjs.; **c.** objective, as ***pain-assuaging, -bearing, -dispelling, -giving, -inflicting, -killing, -producing, -relieving*** adjs.; ***pains-hating*** adj. [after painstaking: see 6]; **d. pain-free** *a.*, free from pain; **pain-killer**, one who or that which does away with pain; *spec.* name of a medicine for alleviating pain; †**pain-piss** *Obs.*, painful urination, strangury; **pain point** *Physiol.* = *pain spot*; **pain-proof** *a.*, having immunity from pain.; **pain spot** *Physiol.*, a small spot on the surface of the skin that is sensitive to pain; **pain-threshold**, the upper limit of tolerance to pain. See also painstaking, etc., painsworthy.

1645 Quarles *Sol. Recant.* ii. 35 And like a *pain-afflicted stripling, play With some new Toy, to while thy grief away. **1597** A. M. tr. *Guillemeau's Fr. Chirurg.* 49 b/1 *Payne-assuaging clisteryes, made of freshe milcke. **1870** Bryant *Iliad* I. v. 153 Pæan with his *pain-dispelling balms Healed him. **1889** Doyle *Micah Clarke* 149 The line of white *pain-drawn faces. **1628** Gaule *Pract. The.* (1629) 176 Men neyther shrinke, nor shrike..when they perceiue their Bodies pierce-free, or *paine-free. **1889** 'Mark Twain' *Connecticut Yankee* xviii. 215 The executioner..was a good, pains-taking and *pain-giving official. **1890** W. James *Princ. Psychol.* II. xxi. 306 Locke expressly makes the *pleasure-* or *pain*-giving quality to be the ultimate human criterion of anything's reality. **1934** R. Bodley *Japanese Omelette* iv. 30 The geta..supposed to fit the sole of a Japanese foot..are, to my mind, the most paingiving form of footwear ever devised. **1864** Pusey *Lect. Daniel* ix. 562 Indolent, conceited, soft, *pains-hating. **1803** J. Kenny *Society* 52 And Sickness..Awhile forgets her *pain-inflicting task. **1853** *La Crosse* (Wisconsin) *Democrat* 7 June 2/4 Ayer's Cherry Pectoral, Perry Davis' *Pain Killer. **1855** I. C. Pray *Mem. J. G. Bennett* 200 The many pain-killers invented have diminished largely the amount of human suffering. **1863** W. B. Cheadle *Jrnl. Trip across Canada* (1931) 102 Milton rubs his face with pain-killer. **1886** *N. Zealand Herald* 28 May 5/1 His wife gave him some hot water and milk with a little pain-killer... Subsequently he died. **1898** *Daily News* 1 Mar. 6/3 The late Sir James Y. Simpson, the inventor of chloroform, and great painkiller of his day. **1932** J. Steinbeck *Pastures of Heaven* x. 236 Pat could hear the sizzle of mentholatum and painkiller gushing from containers and boiling into the fire. **1959** [see *benzocaine* s.v. benzo-]. **1973** 'R. MacLeod' *Burial in Portugal* iii. 68 Finding the painkiller tablets, he swallowed a couple. **1977** A. Morice *Murder in Mimicry* I. iv. 33 In those days you had to get by with ordinary painkillers which were about as effective as a slug of brandy to a man having his leg amputated. **1964** J. J. Walsh *Understanding Paraplegia* iv. 24 In many cases, the so-called 'harmless' *pain-killing drugs are not sufficiently strong to stop the pain. **1974** 'J. Graham' *Bloody Passage* ix. 125 The pain-killing injection had helped. **1614** Markham *Cheap Husb.* I. xxix. (1668) 55 Of the pain in the Kidneys, *pain-piss, or the Stone. **1897** tr. *T. Ribot's Psychol. of Emotions* 27 Goldscheider..admits *pain-points (points sensible to pain), but not a specific organ for pain nor special nerves to transmit it. **1954** S. Rothman *Physiol. & Biochem. Skin* v. 136/2 There is no doubt that itching is produced with great ease when the stimulus is weak and repetitive and when several pain points are stimulated simultaneously. **1903** 'Mark Twain' in *North Amer. Rev.* Jan. 3 No C[hristian] S[cience] family would consider itself..*pain-proof without an Annex. **1908** *Practitioner* Dec. 850 The experiment was absolute proof of the *pain-relieving quality of congestion. **1935** *Discovery* Aug. 226/2 One very fortunate property which such a generator appears to possess is its pain-relieving virtue. **1966** *Lancet* 31 Dec. 1436/1 Digitalis, quinidine,..and pain-relieving drugs were given when indicated to both groups. **1897** *Trans. Amer. Pediatric Soc.* IX. 68 Touch, temperature, and *pain sense are normally developed. **1911** Beerbohm *Zuleika D.* iv. 44 He was gazing at the girl with *pain-shot eyes. **1888** W. Stirling tr. *Landois's Text-bk. Human Physiol.* (ed. 3) xiv. 831 The *pain-spots can be isolated by means of a needle, or electrically. **1927** Haldane & Huxley *Animal Biol.* v. 126 Stimulation of a single pain-spot will only cause movement after a long time or never. **1973** C. P. Swanson *Nat. Hist. Man* viii. 237/2 (*caption*) Pain spots on normal hands of two individuals. **1857** Geo. Eliot *Sc. Cler. Life, Janet's Repent.* xviii, The sight of the *pain-stricken face. **1902** *Pain-threshold [see misery 8]. **1969** 'I. Drummond' *Man with Tiny Head* xvi. 182 Sandro guessed that his pain-threshold would be high and that he would give nothing away. **1834** *Tait's Mag.* I. 134/2 Above the little *pain-worn thing The sailor's widow wept. **1838** Eliza Cook *Truth* iii, When the oozing *pain-wrung moisture drips.

pain, *sb.*[2] Forms: 4–6 payn, 5 payne, peyn, (8 pain). [a. F. *pain*:—L. *pānem* bread.]

†**1.** Bread. (Frequent in *Piers Ploughman*.) *Obs.*

1362 Langl. *P. Pl.* A. VIII. 106 Þe prophete his payn eet in penaunce and wepyng. **1377** *Ibid.* B. xiv. 76 Þorw plente of payn, & of pure sleuthe. **1393** *Ibid.* C. x. 92 Ther is payn and peny-ale as for a pytaunce y-take. *c* **1460** J. Russell *Bk. Nurture* 339 Þan take youre loof of light payne..and with the egge of þe knyfe nyghe your hand ye kett.

2. *Cookery.* Applied, usually with qualifying word, to various fancy dishes, mostly containing bread; as ***pain fondu*** [= dissolved], ***pain perdu*** [= lost], ***pain ragon, pain reguson***; **pain puff**, a kind of puff or small pie with soft crust.

c **1390** *Form of Cury* No. 59 in *Antiq. Culin.* (1791) 13 Payn fondew. Take brede, and frye it in grece, other in oyle... Grynde it with raisons [etc.]. *Ibid.* No. 67. 14 Payn ragonn. *c* **1430** *Two Cookery-bks.* 42 Payn pur-dew. *c* **1450** *Ibid.* 68 This is the purviaunce made for Kinge Richard..the xxiii day of September [1387]... The thirde course... Payne puff. *Ibid.* 112 *Peynreguson.* Nym resons and do out ye stones, and bray it in a morter with pepir and gingiuer, and salt and wastel bred [etc.]. **14..** *Noble Bk. Cookry* (Napier 1882) 46 To mak payn pardieu tak payn-mayne or freshe bred and paire away the cruste [etc.]. **1513** *Bk. Keruynge* in *Babees Bk.* 271 For standarde, venyson roste,..pecocke with his tayle,..plouer, rabettes, grete byrdes, larkes, doucettes, paynpuffe. **1615** Markham *Eng. Housew.* ii. 46 To make the best Panperdy, take a dozen egges [etc.]. **1706** Phillips s.v., In Cookery, *Pains* signifie certain Messes proper for Side-dishes, so call'd as being made of Bread, stuff'd with several sorts of Farces and Ragoos. **1723** [see cream *sb.*[2] 7 b]. **1941** W. A. Percy *Lanterns on Levee* 11 Oh, the poor little boys who never put a lump of butter into steaming butter-bread (spoon-bread is the same thing) or lolled their tongues over pain-perdu. **1961** T. Henrot *Belgium* 189 *Pain-perdu*—rusk softened in warm, sweetened milk then browned in butter. **1972** *Guardian* 28 Jan. 9/5 Pain Perdu or Gilded Crusts..are very popular with children.

pain (peɪn), *v.* Forms: see pain *sb.*[1] [a. OF. *pener*, 3rd sing. pr. *peine* (10th c. in Littré) = Pr., Sp. *penar*, It. *penare*, med.L. *pœnāre*, f. L. *pœna*, F. *peine*, pain *sb.*[1] Cf. also pine *v.*, OE. *pīnian*.]

I. †**1. a.** *trans.* To inflict a penalty or punishment upon; to punish; to torture by way of punishment; to fine. *Obs.*

c **1350** *Will. Palerne* 2898 And putte hem in hire prisoun to peyne hem at hire wille. **1495** *Trevisa's Barth. De P.R.* xiv. x. E iij b/2 Many deme that the hylle Ethna is a place of payne and some soules ben paynyd therin. *a* **1533** Ld. Berners *Gold. Bk. M. Aurel.* (1546) Nn v, Thou haste iusticied the Iustyce, and none dare peyne the. **1601** Holland *Pliny* I. 499 That whosoeuer..cut downe any trees growing in another mans ground, should be peined in the court for a trespasse don.

†**b.** To enjoin under penalty. *Obs.*

1607 *Henley-in-Arden Rolls* (1890), Wee paine all the Alehowse keepers, that they and euery of them make holsome & good drinke bothe ale & Beare. **1620** J. Wilkinson *Of Courts Baron* 148 If there was any thing pained at the last court to be done, and as yet is not done, you must enquire who hath made defalt therein.

II. 2. To inflict pain upon, cause to suffer; to hurt, distress. **a.** *gen.* or mentally: To inflict suffering upon, to afflict, give pain to; to grieve, to hurt the feelings of. Also *absol.* to cause suffering.

13.. *Cursor M.* 23261 (Gött.) Bot a point es þaim paines [*v.rr.* pines, pinis] mar, þan ellis all þair oþer fare. *c* **1450** tr. *De Imitatione* III. xxxv. 105, I peynyng þe wiþ sorwes spare þe not. *c* **1586** C'tess Pembroke *Ps.* lxix. x, Whome thou painest, more they paine. **1611** Bible *Joel* ii. 6 Before their face the people shall be much pained. **1780** A. Young *Tour Irel.* (Nat. Libr. Ed.) 85 There is not a single view but what pains one in the want of wood. **1807** Crabbe *Par. Reg.* Wks. II. 155 Transports that pain'd and joys that agonized. **1838** Lytton *Alice* II. ii, These gifts Caroline could not refuse, without paining her young friend.

b. To inflict bodily suffering upon, to torment; to cause bodily pain to, to hurt. (In quot. 1377, To put to physical inconvenience, incommode.)

1377 Langl. *P. Pl.* B. xii. 247 Riȝt as þe pennes of þe pecok peyneth hym in his fliȝte. *c* **1386** Chaucer *Monk's T.* 614 Many a mannes guttes dide he peyne. **1426** Lydg. *De Guil. Pilgr.* 11958 A body vp on a cross dystreyned, And, as me thouhtë, gretly peyned. **1530** Palsgr. 651/2 It payneth me very sore to speke, I am so horse. **1590** Spenser *F.Q.* I. ii. 33 Cold and heat me paines. *c* **1624** Chapman *Batrachom.* 11 So I lay Sleepless, and pain'd with headache. **1828** Scott *F.M. Perth* xxx, But your arm, my lord,..Does it not pain you? *a* **1864** Hawthorne *Amer. Note-Bks.* (1879) I. 152 Pained with the toothache.

†**3.** *intr.* To suffer pain or distress; to suffer. (*arch.* in quot. 1885.)

c **1315** Shoreham 38 And seue ȝer thou scholdest, man, O dedlyche senne peyny. **1393** Langl. *P. Pl.* C. xxii. 324 Þe croys..þat crist..for mankynde on peynede. *c* **1440** *Promp. Parv.* 390/2 Peynyn, or pynyn yn wo or sekenesse. *a* **1536** *Calisto & Melib.* in Hazl. *Dodsley* I. 81 Where is the patient that so is paining? **1591** DANIEL in *Sidney's Astr. & Stella* etc. Sonn. xi, So shalt thou cease to plague, and I to pain. **1885** W. PATER *Marius* II. 213 Christ, paining in him, set forth a copy to the rest.

III. 4. a. *refl.* To take pains or trouble; to exert oneself or put forth efforts with care and attention; to endeavour, strive. *Obs.* or *arch.*

a **1300** *Cursor M.* 19027 Petir painid him ful gierne in cristis lai þat folc to lerne. **1377** LANGL. *P. Pl.* B. VII. 42 Pledours sholde peynen hem To plede for swiche and helpe. **1481** CAXTON *Godeffroy* xxx. 64 The other that cam aftir peyned them moche for to goo more wysely. **1596** SPENSER *F.Q.* IV. vi. 40 She her paynd with womanish art To hide her wound. **1614** RALEIGH *Hist. World* IV. iii. §9 Eumenes pained himselfe to carrie succour to his left wing. **1700** DRYDEN *Cock & Fox* 669 While he pain'd himself to raise his note. **1870** LOWELL *Study Wind.* 217 Men still pain themselves to write Latin verses.

†**b.** *intr.* for *refl.* = prec. *Obs.*

c **1440** *Partonope* 2190 They peyned freshly to fyght bothe. **1484** CAXTON *Fables of Alfonce* vi, In vayne thou hast payned and laboured. *a* **1529** SKELTON *'Now synge we'* 68 Stand fast in faythe,..And payne to lyue in honeste.

c. *pass.* To be put to trouble or exertion; to be obliged to put forth effort. ? *Obs.*

1785 CRABBE *Newspaper* 310 We..Are pain'd to keep our sickly works alive.

†**5.** *trans.* To take pains about, endeavour. *Obs.*

a **1300** *Cursor M.* 28166 (Cott.) Quen I sagh my neghbur wele fare,..I paind oft at him vn-spede, bath in will and word and dede.

pain, variant of PAYEN *Obs.*, pagan.

†'**painable**, *a. Obs. rare.* [f. PAIN *sb.* or *v.* + -ABLE: cf. *comfortable.* Cf. *penible.*] Painful.

1649 EVELYN *Liberty & Servitude* iii, The manacles of Astyages were not therefore the lesse weighty, and paynable, for being composed of gold or silver.

painch(e, painct, obs. ff. PAUNCH, PAINT *v.*

†'**pain-de'maine.** *Obs.* Forms: 4 **paindemeine,** 4–5 **payn(e)demayn(e;** 5 **payn(e)mayne, -main, paynman, payman,** 6 **payne mayne.** [AF. *pain demeine, demaine*, med.L. *panis dominicus* 'lord's bread'. Also called simply DEMEINE.] White bread, of the finest quality; a loaf or cake of this bread.

[*c* **1330** *Durham Acc. Rolls* 17 In pane dominico et melle 5*d.* **1378** *Munim. Gildh. Lond.* (Rolls) III. 424 Etiam cum uno payndemayn.] *c* **1386** CHAUCER *Sir Thopas* 14 Whit was his face as Payndemayn Hise lippes rede as rose. *c* **1420** *Liber Cocorum* (1862) 40 Take floure of payndemayn. *a* **1440** *Sir Degrev.* 1393 Paynedemaynes [*Camb. MS.* paynemayn] prevaly Scho fett fra the pantry. *c* **1440** *Douce MS.* 55 lf. 9 Then cast feyre pecys of paynemayns or elles of tendre brede. *c* **1475** *Pict. Voc.* in Wr.-Wülcker 788/32 *Hic panis*, brede... *Hec placencia*, a payman. **1530** PALSGR. 250/2 Payne mayne, *payn de bouche.*

Comb. a **1377** *Househ. Edw. III* in *Househ. Ord.* (1790) 19 William Brynklowe Yoman Paymenbaker.

pained (peɪnd, 'peɪnɪd), *ppl. a.* [f. PAIN *v.* + -ED[1].] Affected with pain (physical or mental); hurt, distressed, grieved, etc.: see the verb; expressing or indicating pain.

1340–70 *Alex. & Dind.* 268 To oure painede peple inpossible hit semeþ. **1545** RAYNOLD *Byrth Mankynde* II. vi. (1634) 122 Which may be applyed to the pained places. **1608** SHAKS. *Per.* IV. vi. 173 The pained'st fiend Of hell. *a* **1661** FULLER *Worthies* (1840) III. 92 Others repairing thither.. the poor for alms; the pained for ease. **1873** BLACK *Pr. Thule* xviii. 299 There was a pained look about the lips.

painedly ('peɪndlɪ, 'peɪnɪdlɪ), *adv.* [f. PAINED *ppl. a.* + -LY[2].] In a pained manner.

1921 D. H. LAWRENCE *England, my England* (1922) 270 Mr. Enderby looked up painedly. **1926** FOWLER *Mod. Eng. Usage* 418/2 *Painedly.* A bad form.

painem, -en, obs. forms of PAYNIM.

painful ('peɪnfʊl), *a.* Forms: see PAIN *sb.*[1] [f. PAIN *sb.*[1] + -FUL.]

1. Full of, characterized by, or causing pain or suffering; hurting, afflictive, distressing, grievous; annoying, vexatious. **a.** In general, or mentally.

c **1340** HAMPOLE *Prose Tr.* 33 A gastely syghte of it how foule how vggly and how paynfull þat it [sin] es. *c* **1410** LOVE *Bonavent. Mirr.* xl. 87 (Gibbs MS.) þe paynfull passyoun of Ihc. **1548–9** (Mar.) *Bk. Com. Prayer, Visit. Sick*, After this painfull lyfe ended. **1658** *Whole Duty of Man* vii. §1 How pleasant a virtue this is, may appear by the contrariety it hath to several great and painful vices. **1794** MRS. RADCLIFFE *Myst. Udolpho* i, An uncertainty which would have been more painful to an idle mind. **1829** LANDOR *Imag. Conv., Maid of Orleans & Agnes Sorel* Wks. 1853 II. 39/1 Salutary pangs may be painfuller than mortal ones.

b. Physically.

1544 PHAER *Regim. Lyfe* (1560) Hj b, Nephretica is painfuller afore meat. **1612** CHAPMAN *Widowes T.* Plays 1873 III. 73 Alas shee's faint, and speech is painefull to her. **1703** ROWE *Ulyss.* I. i. 228 Midnight Surfeits, Wine And painful undigested Morning Fumes. **1860** TYNDALL *Glac.* I. xxv. 178 A sky the brightness of which is painful to the eyes.

c. Of a person: Inflicting pain or punishment; tormenting. *rare.*

c **1450** *Cursor M.* 18223 (Laud) Satan that paynefull [*Cott., Gött.*, pinful; *Trin.* pyneful] prynce he lawght And vnder myght of helle by-tawght. **1870** G. MEREDITH *France* vi. in *Odes Fr. Hist.* (1898) 60 The painful Gods might weep, If ever rain of tears came out of heaven.

2. Suffering or affected with (physical) pain. (Usually of a part of the body which has been wounded or hurt.)

1590 SPENSER *F.Q.* III. ii. 11 The loving mother, that nine monethes did beare In the deare closett of her painefull syde Her tender babe. **1612** BP. HALL *Contempl., O.T.* IV. iv, They see themselves lothsome with Lice, painful and deformed with Scabs. **1794** MRS. RADCLIFFE *Myst. Udolpho* iv, His wound was painful. **1877** L. MORRIS *Epic Hades* I. 7 He wore a crown Upon his painful brow.

3. Causing or involving trouble or labour; troublesome, difficult, irksome, toilsome, laborious. Now *rare* or merged in 1.

c **1375** *Sc. Leg Saints* xxvii. (*Machor*) 1342 It sall be done ..How paynefull or how hard it be. **1535** J. MASON in Ellis *Orig. Lett.* Ser. II. II. 55 Itt [Toledo] is the paynefullist towne that ever mann duellyd in. Itt is through so up hyll and downe hyll. **1604** E. G[RIMSTONE] *D'Acosta's Hist. Indies* III. x. 152 These eighteene leagues of land..is more painefull and chargeable then 2300 by sea. **1665–6** *Phil. Trans.* I. 90 The way of winding off the silk..which is the painfullest and nicest of all the rest. **1676** DRYDEN *Aurengz.* I. i, By quick and painful Marches hither came. **1858** FROUDE *Hist. Eng.* III. xiii. 97 Sums of money would be frequently offered them in lieu of a painful hospitality.

4. Characterized by painstaking; performed with labour, care, and attention; diligent, assiduous, laborious, careful. *Obs.* or *arch.*

c **1380** WYCLIF *Wks.* (1880) 124 To holde sich pore lif and meke and peyneful in resonable abstynence. *c* **1400** MAUNDEV. (1839) xvii. 184 He lost much peynfulle labour. **1565** T. STAPLETON tr. *Bede's Hist. Ch. Eng.* 79 In consideration of their vertuous sermons and painefull preaching. **1638** in *10th Rep. Hist. MSS. Comm.* App. v. 486 The long, paynfull and profitable service donne unto us by James Lynch. **1775** E. ALLEN in Sparks *Corr. Amer. Rev.* (1853) I. 464 This is the situation..according to my most painful discoveries. **1834–43** SOUTHEY *Doctor* vi. (1848) 18/2 The painful chronicle of honest John Stowe. **1894** *Nation* (N.Y.) 21 June 470/3 The little book..will reward a not too painful reading.

5. Of persons: Characterized by taking pains; working with labour and care; painstaking, laborious, assiduous, careful, diligent. *Obs.* or *arch.*

1549 LATIMER *3rd Serm. bef. Edw. VI* (Arb.) 91 We haue some as painfull magistrates, as euer was in Englande. **1612** CAPT. SMITH *Map Virginia* 22 The women be verie painefull and the men often idle. **1702** C. MATHER *Magn. Chr.* I. v. (1852) 76 The more learned, godly, painful ministers of the land. **1802** MRS. RADCLIFFE *Gaston de Blondeville* Posth. Wks. 1826 I. 46 The patience of a painful antiquary. **1877** PEILE *Philol.* i. §14. 16 The laws of etymology, which painful students have discovered.

painfully ('peɪnfʊlɪ), *adv.* [f. prec. + -LY[2].] In a painful manner.

1. In a way that causes or is accompanied by pain or suffering; distressingly; with pain.

1568 GRAFTON *Chron.* II. 857 Men were so sore handled, and so painfully pangued, that [etc.]. **1657** R. LIGON *Barbadoes* (1673) 10 Being painfully and pipeing hot, arriv'd at this exalted mansion. **1795** SOUTHEY *Soldier's Wife* 2 Weary way-wanderer, languid and sick at heart, Travelling painfully over the rugged road. **1872** BLACK *Adv. Phaeton* xxii. 312 Ambleside..looked painfully modern now.

2. In a way that gives trouble; with difficulty. *Obs.* or *arch.*

1533 ELYOT *Cast. Helthe* (1539) 85 Yf it were easily expulsed, or peynfully. **1573–80** BARET *Alv.* P 29 Painefully, hardly, *laboriosè.* **1835** J. H. NEWMAN *Par. Serm.* (1837) I. iii. 32 A depth of meaning..hardly and painfully to be understood. **1842** ALISON *Hist. Europe* (1849–50) X. lxv. §55. 51 Macdonald was thus painfully maintaining his ground in upper Catalonia.

3. With great pains, painstakingly, laboriously, with care and effort. *Obs.* or *arch.*

1555 BRADFORD *Let.* in Coverdale *Lett. Martyrs* (1564) 270 Lyuyng therein not so purely, louynglye, and painfully as I shoulde haue done. **1631** WEEVER *Anc. Fun. Mon.* 316 Painefully and expensfully studious of the common good. **1709** HEARNE *Collect.* (O.H.S.) II. 200 He..painfully collected the works of Geffrey Chawcer. **1855** MILMAN *Lat. Chr.* II. iv. (1864) I. 270 That no private man could hope to arrive at a sounder understanding..than had been painfully attained by so many holy bishops.

4. *fig.* Excessively, to an alarming degree.

1900 [see EFFORTFUL *a.*]. **1909** A. LANCASTRE SALDANHA *Recoll.* xi. 151 Sir Robert Peel was painfully shy with strangers. **1941** N. COWARD *Australia Visited* i. 2 An R.A.F. plane which seemed to me almost painfully small. **1961** *Flying* (N.Y.) Feb. 33/1 At this point it should be painfully obvious that cities, being 'soft', and the people within them are ideally suited to destruction by nuclear weapons.

painfulness ('peɪnfʊlnɪs). [f. as prec. + -NESS.] The quality of being painful.

1. The quality of being fraught or attended with pain; distressingness. Also in passive aspect: The condition of suffering pain; distress, affliction.

c **1485** *Digby Myst.* III. 608 O lord! wo xall put me from þis peynfulnesse? **1526** TINDALE *1 John* iv. 18 For fear hath paynfulnes. **1662** SOUTH *Serm.* I. 27 No Custom can make the Painfulness of a Debauch easy. **1777** J. RICHARDSON *Dissert. East. Nations* 2 To soften the extreme painfulness of incessant labour. **1884** PAE *Eustace* 79 Forget the painfulness of our situation, and think of its romance.

2. The quality of causing trouble or labour; difficulty, troublesomeness, irksomeness. *Obs.* or *arch.*

1526 *Pilgr. Perf.* (W. de W. 1531) 230 For the vncertainty of the same, and also for the paynfulnes and tedyousnes therof. **1631** R. BYFIELD *Doctr. Sabb.* 32 Ordinary labour with festivall services to God can neither easily concurre, because painfulnesse and joy are opposite, nor decently.

3. The quality of taking pains; laboriousness, careful industry, painstaking. *Obs.* or *arch.*

1531 ELYOT *Gov.* III. x, In theim which be either gouernours or capitaynes..Paynfulnesse, named in latyne *Tollerantia*, is wonderfull commendable. **1597** HOOKER *Eccl. Pol.* v. lxxvii. §13 To testifie loue by painefulnesse in Gods seruice. **1658** A. FOX *Wurtz' Surg.* I. ii. 3 A Skill in Surgery is obtained with great painfulness.

painim(e, obs. form of PAYNIM.

paining ('peɪnɪŋ), *vbl. sb.* [f. PAIN *v.* + -ING[1].] The action of the verb PAIN.

1. The action of causing or condition of feeling pain; pain, suffering. Now *rare.*

c **1440** *Pol. Rel. & L. Poems* 151/15, I askyd hym how he had paynyng, he said, '*Quia amore langueo*'. **1596** SPENSER *F.Q.* IV. ii. 41 To wype his wounds, and ease their bitter payning. **1760–72** H. BROOKE *Fool of Qual.* (1809) IV. 107 It was too much of joy, it was pleasure to paining. **1812** J. J. HENRY *Camp. agst. Quebec* 111 These subsequent annual painings uniformly attacked me.

†**2.** The taking of pains. *Obs.*

1633 P. FLETCHER *Elisa* I. xliii, There doth it blessed sit, and..Laughs at our busie care and idle paining.

'**paining,** *ppl. a.* [f. as prec. + -ING[2].] That pains; causing pain or suffering.

1698 M. LISTER in *Phil. Trans.* XX. 246 A paining Grief towards the bottom of their Bellies, which did grind and torment them. **1891** *Eastern Daily Press* 24 July 4/6 Beyond a slight paining sprain and some cuts about the mare, no harm was done.

pa-in-law. *colloq.* = FATHER-IN-LAW.

1886 H. BAUMANN *Londinismen* 130/1 *Pa-in-law*,..father-in-law. **1949** E. COXHEAD *Wind in West* xii. 289, I couldn't throw away the chance of poking my fingers into pa-in-law's pie. **1952** M. ALLINGHAM *Tiger in Smoke* xiv. 213 Are you worrying about..my future pa-in-law?

painless ('peɪnlɪs), *a.* [f. PAIN *sb.*[1] + -LESS.]

†**1.** Free from pain; not suffering pain. *rare.*

1570 LEVINS *Manip.* 91/10 Paynlesse, *indolens.* **1675** HOBBES *Odyssey* (1677) 158 That he should be brought home thus..Asleep, and painless.

2. Causing no pain; not accompanied with pain.

1591 SYLVESTER *Du Bartas* I. i. 590 With pain-lesse paine they tread A sacred path that to the Heav'ns doth lead. *a* **1700** DRYDEN (J.), Is there no smooth descent? no painless way Of kindly mixing with our native clay? **1795** SOUTHEY *Vis. Maid Orleans* II. 234 Then did they not regard his mocks Which then came painless. **1887** F. DARWIN *Life Darwin* III. 202 Dr. Wilder advocated the use of the word 'Callisection' for painless operations on animals.

Hence '**painlessly** *adv.*, without pain; '**painlessness**, freedom from pain.

1634 BP. HALL *Contempl., N.T.* IV. vii. *Bloody Issue healed*, Could the Physitians have given her, if not health, yet relaxation and painelessnesse, her meanes had not been misbestowed. **1861** BUMSTEAD *Ven. Dis.* (1879) 672 These swellings are usually developed..painlessly. **1864** MRS. CARLYLE *Lett.* III. 209 Shall I ever more have a day of ease, of painlessness? **1880** MISS BRADDON *Barbara* xlv, His disease was one in which death does not come painlessly.

†'**painliness.** *Obs. rare.* [f. **painly* adj. (f. PAIN *sb.*[1] + -LY[1]) + -NESS.] The condition of being in pain; distressful state.

1435 MISYN *Fire of Love* II. v. 78 Paynlynes..me down castis & prykkis to go to þe of qwhome onely I trow solas & remedy I sal see.

†'**painous,** *a. Obs. rare.* In 5 **peynous.** [a. OF. *penus, -os*, later *peineus* = It., Sp. *penoso*:—late L. *pœnōs-us* (Pseudo-Aug.) painful, f. *pœna*: see PAIN *sb.*[1]] Painful; severe.

c **1400** *Beryn* 2609 Peynous ordinaunce Is stallid for hir falshede. *Ibid.* 3766 She hath many a day led a peynous lyff.

painstaker ('peɪnzˌteɪkə(r)). Now *rare* or *Obs.* [f. *pains* (PAIN *sb.*[1] 6) + TAKER.] One who takes pains; a painstaking person.

1618 CHAPMAN *Hesiod* 188 *note*, Fit for mental painstakers, students [etc.]. **1666** PEPYS *Diary* 24 June, He was no great pains-taker in person. **1711** ADDISON *Spect.* No. 61 ¶5 There are actually such Pains-takers among our British Wits.

painstaking ('peɪnzˌteɪkɪŋ), *sb.* [f. *pains*, pl. of PAIN *sb.*[1] (sense 6) + *taking*, gerund of TAKE *v.*] The taking of pains; the bestowal of careful and attentive labour in order to the accomplishment of something; assiduous effort.

1556 OLDE *Antichrist* 85 This is their paynes taking and trauaile. **1623** LISLE *Ælfric on O. & N. Test.* 5 Their posterity haue liued in sorrow and paines-taking euer since. **1737** WHISTON *Josephus, Hist.* I. xviii. §2 (1777), They did not shew any want of pains-taking. **1888** BURGON *Lives 12 Gd. Men* II. v. 44 That mastery of the art of preaching which results from laborious painstaking.

painstaking ('peɪnzˌteɪkɪŋ), *a.* [f. as prec. + *taking*, pr. pple. of TAKE *v.*] That takes pains; bestowing attentive effort for the accomplishment of some result; careful and industrious; assiduous.

1696 TRYON *Misc.* i. 23 The Richer sort..[are] much more Distempered than the Ordinary pains-taking People.

1712 COOKE *Voy. S. Sea* 399 The Natives are..industrious, and Pains taking. **1882** SERJT. BALLANTINE *Exper.* xi. 116 The case was tried..before..a most painstaking judge.

b. Of actions, productions, etc.: Marked or characterized by attentive care.

1866 GEO. ELIOT *F. Holt* xxiv, The satisfaction of receiving Mr. Sherlock's painstaking production in print. **1895** J. W. BUDD in *Law Times* XCIX. 544/2 The..painstaking manner in which they superintend..this department.

Hence **'pains,takingly** *adv.*, with careful and attentive effort, assiduously.

a **1861** CLOUGH *Poems*, etc. (1869) I. 318 Setting himself laboriously and painstakingly to work. **1891** *Sat. Rev.* 19 Dec. 705/2 This little book has been painstakingly prepared.

'painstakingness. [f. PAINSTAKING *a.* + -NESS.] The fact or habit of taking pains; assiduous effort.

1927 *Sunday Express* 19 June 19/3 The sportingness of owners, the painstakingness of trainers, and the brilliance of jockeys. **1936** *Times Lit. Suppl.* 2 May 366/3 His dicta are analysed by the author with the same painstakingness.

painsworthy ('peɪnz,wɜːðɪ), *a. rare.* Also 7 **pain-worthy.** [f. *pains*, PAIN *sb.*[1] 6 + WORTHY.] Worthy of trouble; worth taking pains about.

1650 FULLER *Pisgah* III. ii. §1 It will be pain-worthy to enquire [etc.]. **1861** MAX MÜLLER *Sc. Lang.* Ser. I. vi. (ed. 4) 222 There is no painsworthy difficulty nor dispute about declension, &c., of nouns.

paint (peɪnt), *sb.* [f. PAINT *v.*]

1. The act or fact of painting or colouring.

1602 MARSTON *Antonio's Rev.* III. ii, Her cheekes not yet slurd over with the paint Of borrowed crimsone. *Mod.* Give it a paint, and it will look all right.

2. That with which anything is painted.

a. A substance consisting of a solid colouring matter dissolved in a liquid vehicle, as water or oil, used to impart a colour by being spread over a surface; also applied to the solid colouring matter alone, or to a cake of it, as in *a box of paints*; a pigment.

1712 ADDISON *Spect.* No. 416 ¶2 Expresses were sent to the Emperor of Mexico in Paint. **1735** BERKELEY *Querist* §118 A modern fashionable house,..daubed over with oil and paint. **1816** J. SMITH *Panorama Sc. & Art* II. 829 When two coats of this paint have been laid on, it may be polished. **1833** J. HOLLAND *Manuf. Metal* II. 250 Paint is commonly ground by means of a stone muller. **1881** BESANT & RICE *Chapl. of Fleet* I. 90 The timber had once been painted, but the paint had fallen off.

b. Colouring matter laid on the face or body for adornment; rouge, etc.

c **1660** DRYDEN *To Sir R. Howard* 76 His colours laid so thick on every place, As only showed the paint, but hid the face. **1718** LADY M. W. MONTAGU *Let. Lady Rich* 10 Oct., I have seen..beauties..monstrously unnatural in their paint! **1817** BYRON *Beppo* lxvi, One has false curls, another too much paint. **1865** PARKMAN *Huguenots* iii. (1875) 31 [The Indians] were in full paint in honor of the occasion.

c. *Med.* An external medicament which is put on like paint with a brush.

1899 *Allbutt's Syst. Med.* VIII. 582 Both tar and pyrogallol work better as paints and varnishes than the chrysarobin. *Ibid.* VIII. 727 Trichloracetic acid may be substituted [for tincture of iron] as a paint. *Mod.* Iodine paint is a good application in some cases.

d. (See quot.)

1875 KNIGHT *Dict. Mech.*, *Paint*,..stuff mixed with caoutchouc..intended to harden it, [e.g.] Sulphate of zinc, whiting, plaster-of-paris, lampblack, pitch.

e. Phr. *as smart* (*pretty*, etc.) *as paint*: superlatively smart, pretty, etc.

1850 F. E. SMEDLEY *Frank Fairlegh* xli. 340 Why, Oaklands, man, you are looking as fresh as paint; getting sound again, wind and limb, eh? **1883** R. L. STEVENSON *Treas. Isl.* viii. 65 You're a lad, you are, but you're as smart as paint. I see that when you first came in. **1905** *Tatler* 22 Feb. 306/3 Half the English [Rugby] side were played out twenty minutes before the end while the Irish-men were still as fresh as paint. **1918** A. QUILLER-COUCH *Foe-Farrell* 176 He stared..across at the grouped rustic buildings, all as pretty as paint. **1930** H. A. BRYDEN *Enchantments of Field* 187 After all, your hounds may be as handsome as paint, but if they fail you in nose, cry and hunting-power they are worse than useless. **1963** N. MARSH *Dead Water* (1964) iii. 58 Miss Emily arrived at noon on Monday. She had stayed overnight in Dorset and was as fresh as paint. **1975** J. I. M. STEWART *Young Pattullo* ii. 40 Not always wholly agreeable, perhaps, but as clever as paint.

3. *fig.* Colour, colouring; adornment, esp. such as is put on or assumed merely for appearance; outward show, fair pretence.

1647 COWLEY *Mistress, Written in Juice of Lemon* v, A sudden paint adorns the trees. **1650** HUBBERT *Pill Formality* 43 Even then shall thy paint appear and be dis-covered. **1681** W. PENN in *Hist. Soc. Pennsylv.* (1826) I. II. 204, I have forborne paint and allurement, and writt truth. **1728** YOUNG *Love Fame* v. 522 Virtue's the paint that can make wrinkles shine.

†**4.** A painting, a picture. *Obs. rare.*

c **1710** CELIA FIENNES *Diary* (1888) 299 On the Left side is a summer house wth paints of the seasons of y[e] yeare.

5. *Indian paint*: a name for two N. American plants, whose roots yield colouring matters formerly used by the Indians; *yellow Indian paint*, yellow puccoon, or yellowroot (*Hydrastis canadensis*), and *red Indian paint*, red puccoon, or bloodroot (*Sanguinaria canadensis*).

1893 in *Syd. Soc. Lex.*

6. = PINTO *sb.* Also as *adj.* (Chiefly *U.S.*)

1848 BARTLETT *Dict. Amer.* 243 In some of the Southern States, a horse or other animal which is spotted is called a *paint*. **1869** *Overland Monthly* III. 126 A black-and-white-paint horse, fifteen hands high. **1909** 'O. HENRY' *Roads of Destiny* vi. 96 Sam Kildrake's old paint hoss that killed hisself over-drinkin' on a hot day. **1948** *Sun* (Baltimore) 18 June 15/4 The Appaloosa somewhat resembles the paints, pintos and calicos, so popular with the plains Indians. **1955** W. FOSTER-HARRIS *Look of Old West* viii. 226 An animal violently splotched with different colors was called a paint. **1975** J. HANSEN *Trouble Maker* i. 2 She led out a little paint mare. *Ibid.* xii. 125 The sorrel followed the paint. **1976** *Billings* (Montana) *Gaz.* 2 July 11-C/6 (Advt.), 8 yr old paint gelding. Child broke. Possible show horse.

7. *attrib.* and *Comb.*, as *paint-cistern*, *-cloth*, *-drum*, *-job*, *-mark*, *-oil*, *-rag*, *-shop*, *-stoving*, *-water*, *-work*; *paint-grinder*, *-mixer*, *-remover*, *-stripper*, *-thinner*; *paint-beplastered*, *-dappled*, *-daubed*, *-speckled* *-removing*, *-stained*, *-worn* adjs.; **paint box**, a box of solid paints or pigments, usually water-colours; **paint-bridge** (*Theatr.*), a platform, capable of being raised or lowered, on which a scene-painter stands; **paint-brush**, (*a*) a brush for painting with; (*b*) = *Indian paint-brush* (INDIAN A. 4 b); **paint-burner**, an apparatus for burning or softening paint by a flame directed upon it, so that it can be removed (Knight *Dict. Mech.* 1875); **paint card**, a card showing a graduated range of paint colours; also *fig.*; **paint frame** (*Theatr.*), a movable iron framework for moving scenes from the stage to the paint-bridge; **paint-mill**, a machine for grinding paints or pigments; **paint-pot**, a pot in which oil-colour is contained, while being laid on; **paint-roller**, a roller covered in an absorbent material which holds paint to be applied to a surface; also *attrib.*; **paint-room**, (*a*) a room where paints are stored; (*b*) a room in a theatre where the scene-painter works; **paint-root**, the Carolina redroot (*Lachnanthes tinctoria*); **paint spray**, a device for spraying paint on to a surface; hence *paint-spray* vb. trans., *paint-sprayed* ppl. adj.; **paint-stone**, a stone used as a source of paint; **paint-strake**, *Naut.* 'the uppermost strake of plank immediately below the plank-sheer' (*Cent. Dict.*).

a **1843** SOUTHEY *Comm.-pl. Bk.* IV. 272 Thy *paint-beplaster'd forehead, broad and bare. **1725** *New-England Courant* 8-15 Feb. 1/2, I would oblige every Sign-Painter to serve seven Years at College, before he presum'd to handle Pencil or *Paint-Box. **1820** SHELLEY *Posthumous Poems* (1824) 62 Near that a dusty paint box, some old hooks. **1858** SIMMONDS *Dict. Trade*, *Paint-box*, a child's box containing cakes of water-colours. **1879** BLACK *Macleod of D.* xl, A poor creature—a woman-man—a thing of affectation, with his paint-box, and his velvet coat, and his furniture. **1827** J. WOODMAN *Patent Specif.* No. 5476. 2 My *paint brush is of bristles. **1842** J. COLE *Patent Specif.* No. 9228. 4 The paint brush, after it is formed is soaked. **1882** YOUNG *Ev. Man his own Mech.* §1576 The hair of this brush is longer than that of the ordinary paint brush. **1898** *Atlantic Monthly* LXXXII. 497/2 The exquisite vernal iris and the scarlet painted cup, otherwise known as the Indian's paint-brush and prairie fire, splendid for color. **1915** ARMSTRONG & THORNBER *Field Bk. Western Wild Flowers* 472 *Paint Brush. *Castilleja miniata*. Red. Summer. Northwest. This is a very handsome kind, from one to four feet tall. **1968** MRS. L. B. JOHNSON *White House Diary* 9 Apr. (1970) 656 Great splashes of wildflowers began to appear along the road and in the pastures..pale pink buttercups, wild verbena, coral paint brush, Indian blanket. **1931** D. RUNYON *Guys & Dolls* (1932) xiii. 266 A nervous man..with a blood pressure away up in the *paint cards must live quietly. **1961** Paint card [see *grey scale* s.v. GREY *a.* 8]. **1815** BURNEY *Falconer's Marine Dict.*, *Paint-Cisterns, in ships of war, are cisterns made of wood, and lined with lead, to contain the different kinds of paint. **1886** *All the Year Round* 28 Aug. 79 Snuffboxes, too, were found among the perfumes, *paintcloths, and washes. **1904** *Windsor Mag.* Jan. 234/1 He handed me a *paint-dappled copper stencil-plate, two feet square. **1945** W. DE LA MARE *Burning-Glass* 54 A *paint-daubed woman bound for lonely bed..Stood watching him. **1920** *Blackw. Mag.* Apr. 499 The *paint-drums..had been jolted bodily from their lashings. **1901** C. MORRIS *Life on Stage* v. 31 Run upstairs to the *paint-frame (three flights up) and ask the painter to put a little ad-libitum in this bottle for me. **1954** *Archit. Rev.* CXVI. 114 A similar movement may still be seen driving the paint-frame at the Leicester Theatre Royal. **1961** *New Statesman* 20 Jan. 81/1 Backstage, Mr Moro plans..a full-scale paint frame. **1970** *New Yorker* 14 Nov. 59/1 The danger is always that the result will be a *paint job, very superficial. **1971** *New Scientist* 22 Apr. 224/3 An imaginative and informed paintjob can achieve things which no camera or CRT could ever do. **1978** G. VIDAL *Kalki* xi. 251 The White House (which needs a paint job). **1894** *Outing* (U.S.) XXIV. 118/2 The tramper may leave the highway with impunity.., following the little signs and *paint-marks on the trees. **1825** J. NICHOLSON *Operat. Mechanic* 454 Curriers' shavings, which are used for cleaning *paint-mills. **1885** HOWELLS *Silas Lapham* (1891) I. 17 I've got a whole *paint-mine out on the farm. **1884** KNIGHT *Dict. Mech.* Suppl., *Paint Mixer*, a can with shaft and paddles, resembling an upright churn. Used to mix paint with the necessary oil, turpentine, [etc.]. **1727** in *Maryland Hist. Mag.* (1923) XVIII. 227 Glass, *Paint oile, Druggs and Stationary ware. **1840** R. H. DANA *Bef. Mast* viii. 18 We sat, with our brushes and *paint-pots by us. **1938** N. MARSH *Artists in Crime* i. 4 The painter..found..a handkerchief that had been used as a *paint-rag. **1975** N. FREELING *What are Bugles blowing For?* 73 The woman..was wiping dust off her hands with a paint-rag. **1885** *List of Subscribers, Classified* (United Telephone Co.) (ed. 6) 133 Manufacturers..*Paint Remover. **1890** *Cent. Dict.*, *Paint-remover*, a caustic alkaline paste used to take off old paint in order to prepare the surface for repainting. **1960** *Practical Wireless* XXXVI. 306/1 The enamel can then be softened..by immersing them in a paint remover for perhaps a quarter of an hour. **1962** L. DEIGHTON *Ipcress File* xx. 131 She offered me one of those menthol cigarettes that taste like paint remover. **1973** F. TAUBES *Painter's Dict.* 175 Paint remover is sold under various trade names, and each brand is of similar formulation. The fluid is used to remove old paint layers and oil-varnish films. **1951** N. & S. MAGER *Amer. Househ. Encycl.* 623 *Paint rollers. **1954** *Good Housek. Home Encycl.* 208/1 *Paint Rollers*: Covered in lamb's wool on special felt..these rollers are simple to use. **1958** *Times* 7 July 6/5 The latest paint roller improvement is a foolproof model which holds and automatically feeds the right amount of paint on to the surface. **1959** *Listener* 23 Apr. 739/1, I have been trying out the self-feeding paint rollers that have recently come on the market. **1971** *Handyman Which?* Nov. 25/2 There are lots of paint rollers and their prices vary..from 28p to about £2. *c* **1860** H. STUART *Seaman's Catech.* 62 The paint and paint oil is stowed in the *paint-room. **1866** DARWIN *Orig. Spec.* i. (ed. 4) 12 The pigs ate the *paint-root (*Lachnanthes*), which coloured their bones pink. **1866** *Oregon State Jrnl.* 23 June 3/4 Enquire of W. W. Winter, at *paint shop under picture gallery. **1899** *Sat. Even. Post* 10 June 795 Eight hundred tons of white lead are ground in the paint shop every twelve months. **1949** J. H. OUSBEY *Cellulose Spraying* xv. 61 The bodies, on which the doors have already been hung, come to the paintshop by overhead conveyor and are in bare metal. **1973** *Times* 18 May 26/5 By eliminating the solvents and attendant fumes, Fiat said the danger to the lungs of paintshop employees is sharply reduced. **1922** JOYCE *Ulysses* 442 Their *paint-speckled hats wag. **1962** *Punch* 11 July 57/1 Twenty thousand men downing *paint-sprays at Dagenham. **1967** M. CHANDLER *Ceramics in Mod. World* iii. 99 Almost all products of this kind..are glazed by spraying, in much the same way as car bodies are paint-sprayed. **1971** *Money Which?* Mar. 69/1 Small tools, such as hand drills, paint sprays, and so on, are strictly speaking capital. **1973** *Scotsman* 13 Feb. 8/6 Dundee's modern shopping precinct has now been further decorated with paint-sprayed gang slogans. **1797** A. BARNARD *Let.* 29 Nov. in *S. Afr. a Century Ago* (1901) 121 The '*paint stone' is found in this neighbourhood [*sc.* Paarl] in quantities—namely, an impalpable powder which, mixed with oil, serves the country people with colour to paint their waggons, houses, etc. **1896** *13th Ann. Rep. U.S. Bureau Amer. Ethnol.* *1891-92* 115 The articles known as paint-stones scarcely come under the head of implements... Most of them were used merely to furnish paint. **1951** *Engineering* 26 Jan. 100/2 An infra-red *paint-stoving plant..is being used for stoving No. 20 gauge aluminium panels for omnibus bodies. **1962** W. D. HISLOP in H. W. Chatfield *Sci. Surface Coatings* xviii. 531 All paint stoving ovens can be a hazard as the solvent vapour/air mixture is a potential fire risk. **1971** *Morning Star* 13 Apr. 4/5 While this may only be washing-up liquid, ..it could well be something far more dangerous, like bleach or *paint-stripper. **1973** J. ROSSITER *Manipulators* iv. 37 Paint-stripper fluid poured lavishly over the enamel..had boiled large blisters. **1959** *Sears, Roebuck Catal.* Spring/Summer 1397/6 *Paint Thinner. **1960** *Practical Wireless* XXXVI. 313/1 The following will be required:..paint, paint thinners and an artist's small brush. **1977** F. PARRISH *Fire in Barley* ix. 96 Two five-gallon drums... One was called paint-thinner, one creosote. **1866** S. B. JAMES *Duty & Doctrine* (1871) 83 Snow-white is far more forcible than mere *paint-white, or ceiling-white. **1888** M. B. HUISH in *Art Jrnl.* LI. 177/1 No expensive *paintwork, in feeble imitation of the wood it covers. **1933** L. A. G. STRONG *Sea Wall* i. 3 The mailboat..glided gracefully in, her white paintwork stained a rich orange. **1966** G. N. LEECH *Eng. in Advertising* v. 40 Handy Andy shifts grime from paintwork like this. **1973** *Handyman Which?* Aug. 104/1 Curtains..rubbing against a wall could, over a period of time, make marks on the paintwork. **1859** SALA *Gas-light & D.* vii. 85 That comfortable *paint-worn manginess about the handle.

paint (peɪnt), *v.*[1] Forms: 3-6 **peint(e, peynt(e,** 4-7 **paynt(e,** (5-6 **pant(t, poynt,** 5-6, 9 *dial.* **pent(e,** 6 **painct, paynct, peignt,** *Sc.* **pynt,** 6-7 **peinct),** 4- **paint,** (6 **painte).** *Pa. pple.* 3 **i-, y-peint,** 3-4 **y-, i-peynt,** 4 **peynt, paynt, paint;** 4-5 **y-, i-paynted; peinted, peynted, -id,** 5-6 **paynted, -yd, -yt,** 4- **painted.** [ME. ad. OF. *peind-re* (3rd sing. pres. *peint*, pa. pple. *peint*) = Pr. *pegner*, It. *pignere, pingere*:—L. *pingĕre* (3rd sing. *pingit*, pa. pple. *pinct-us*) to paint. The early ME. pa. pple. *peint, ypeint*, was a direct adoption of F. *peint*, and may have been the earliest part of the vb. adopted; cf. ATTAINT. Otherwise the natural form of the word in Eng. would be *pain* as in *complain, distrain*, etc.

But the earliest evidence for the vb. yet found is *peintunge*, PAINTING *vbl. sb.*, in *Ancren R.* *a* 1225.]

I. 1. a. *trans.* To make (a picture or representation) on a surface in colours; to represent (an object) to the eye on a surface by means of lines and colour; to depict, portray, delineate, by using colours.

to paint (an object) *black, white, red*, etc.: to depict or portray as of that colour.

c **1290** *Beket* 2127 in *S. Eng. Leg.* I. 167 For ȝwane men peyntiez an Anletnesse [*Harl. MS.* an halewe]: ȝe ne seoth it nouȝt bi-leued þat þere nis depeint [*v.r.* ypeint] a Roundel: al-a-boute þe heued. **1297** R. GLOUC. (Rolls) 3613 Þeron ypeint was..þe ymage of vre leuedy. **13..** *Coer de L.* 5728 In his blasoun, verrayment, Was y-paynted a serpent. *c* **1375** *Sc. Leg. Saints* xi. (*Symon & Judas*) 69 He send til hyme þane a paynteore, þat rycht sle wes in portratore, to paynt his fygur propirly. **1387** TREVISA *Higden* (Rolls) I. 13 Gregorius..seiþ, 'I haue peynt a wel faire man, and am my self a foule peyntour'. *c* **1400** MAUNDEV. (Roxb.) vii. 24 Þai wald paynt þe aungell black and þe fende qwhite. **1456** SIR G. HAYE *Law Arms* (S.T.S.) 41 This story is payntit in mony placis. **1517** TORKINGTON *Pilgr.* (1884) 3 He shewyd the pepyll a pictur poyntyd on a clothe, of the passion of our lorde. **1653** H. COGAN tr. *Pinto's Trav.* lxi. 257 A little child [who]..appeared in the same fashion as we are accustomed to paint Angells. **1805** SOUTHEY *Pious Painter* I. i, But chiefly his praise And delight was in painting the Devil. **1875** HAMERTON *Round my House* ii. (1876) 31 Picturesque old houses,..which an artist would be glad to paint. *Mod.* His portrait is to be painted for the Reform Club.

b. To adorn (a wall, tapestry, window, etc.) *with* a painting or paintings. (Mostly in *passive.*)

c **1386** CHAUCER *Knt.'s T.* 1112 Al peynted [*v.r.* peinted] was the wal in lengthe & brede..Ffirst on the wal was peynted a forest. **1387** TREVISA *Higden* (Rolls) II. 313 His schippe þat was i-peynt wiþ a dragoun. **1511** GUYLFORDE *Pilgr.* (Camden) 37 All the body of the churche..payntid with storyes from the begynnynge of the worlde. **1784** COOK *3rd Voy.* II. iii. 267 A kind of additional prow painted with the figure of some animal. **1813** MAR. EDGEWORTH *Patron.* (1833) I. vi. 105 To paint a new window for the gallery.

†**c.** Said of writing (as a kind of painting). *Obs.*

1561 *Reg. Privy Council Scot.* I. 174 Quhilkis markis nor descriptioun..is on na wyise specifiit, discrevit, nor payntit in nor upoun the said libell as aucht to haue bene. **1638** BAKER tr. *Balzac's Lett.* (vol. II) 142 These are not words that one reades, and are painted upon paper, they are felt.

d. *transf.* Said of the effect of coloured light.

1831 BREWSTER *Optics* ii. 6 The green light from G..and the blue light from B will fall upon the paper..thus painting upon the paper an inverted image of the object. **1851** RUSKIN *Stones Ven.* (1873) II. v. 150 Like the Iris painted upon the cloud.

e. *intr.* or *absol.* To practise the art of painting; to make pictures.

c **1386** CHAUCER *Knt.'s T.* 1229 Wel koude he peynten lifly that it wroghte. **1530** PALSGR. 651/2 He can paynte and portrer as wel as any man in al this countray. **1669** STURMY *Mariner's Mag.* VII. xxxiv. 50 To grind Gold to Write and Paint. **1821** CRAIG *Lect. Drawing* viii. 417 To paint also implies to draw.

f. *intr.* (for *neuter-passive*). To form a (good, bad) subject for painting.

1860 READE *Cloister & H.* xliii. (1896) 123 War was always detrimental... But in old times..it painted well, sang divinely, furnished Iliads.

2. *fig.* **a.** To depict or display vividly as by painting.

1561 T. HOBY tr. *Castiglione's Courtyer* III. (1577) Q iv, [He] meeteth her in the teeth, with such heauy passion paincted in his eyes. **1780** BENTHAM *Princ. Legisl.* xiv. §1 If even each atom of your pain could be painted on my mind. **1814** CARY *Dante, Par.* IV. 11 Desire Was painted in my looks. **1875** JOWETT *Plato* (ed. 2) IV. 85 The bad have pleasures painted in their fancy as well as the good.

b. To depict or describe in words; to set forth as in a picture; to present vividly to the mind's eye, call up a picture of.

1406 HOCCLEVE *Misrule* 247 Thogh fauel peynte hir tale in prose or ryme. **1560** DAUS tr. *Sleidane's Comm.* 119 b, Oh unsatiable woulves: howe ryghte..have the Prophetes and Apostles..paynted and set you forth in your colours. **1605** *1st Pt. Ieronimo* (1901) III. iii, Reueng, giue my toong freedom to paint her part. **1766** FORDYCE *Serm. Yng. Wom.* (1767) I. i. 13 What words can paint the guilt of such a conduct? **1783** CRABBE *Village* I. 53, I paint the Cot As Truth will paint it, and as Bards will not. **1865** GOSSE *Land & Sea* (1874) 308, I try to paint, in poor and feeble words, a few of the features and objects.

3. a. To colour with a wash or coating of paint; to cover the surface of (a wall, door, etc.) with paint; to colour, stain; hence, to adorn with colours.

a **1250** *Owl & Night.* 76 Þine eȝen beoþ colblake and brode Riht swo hi weren ipeint mid wode. *a* **1300** *Cursor M.* 9912 Þis castell..es painted..O thre colurs o sundri heu. *Ibid.* 9924 Þe thrid [colur]..þat þe kirnels ar paint [*v.rr.* paynt, peynt] wit-all. *c* **1400** MAUNDEV. (Roxb.) xxx. 137 Many faire halles and chaumbres, paynted with gold and azure. **1610** HOLLAND *Camden's Brit.* II. 30 Their ancient maner and custome of peincting their bodies. **1617** MORYSON *Itin.* (1903) 83 Commonly paynting the mayne and taile..of their horses with light coulers, as Carnation and the like. **1704** J. PITTS *Acc. Mahometans* viii. (1738) 163 The Women..paint their Hands and Feet with a certain Plant call'd Hennah. **1875** HAMERTON *Round my House* ii. (1876) 35 Wainscoted with old oak that had been painted grey. *Mod.* Are you going to paint or varnish the wood-work?

b. *transf.* To colour by any means.

1377 LANGL. *P. Pl.* B. XIX. 6 Pieres þe plowman was paynted al blody, And come in with a crosse. *c* **1385** CHAUCER *L.G.W.* 875 *Tisbe*, How with hise blod hire selue gan sche pente. *c* **1586** C'TESS PEMBROKE *Ps.* LXXI. x, Ages snow my head hath painted. *a* **1698** SOUTH *Serm.* III. xi. 420 If God so cloaths the Fields, so paints the Flowers. **1814** *Sporting Mag.* XLIII. 70 His eyes were much swollen and painted. **1851** TRENCH *Poems* 155 Where the sunbeam.. wound..to paint With interspace of light and colour faint That tesselated floor. **1876** GEO. ELIOT *Dan. Der.* lviii, Seeing the young faces 'painted with fear'.

c. *fig.* To adorn or variegate with or as with colours; to deck, beautify, decorate, ornament.

1377 LANGL. *P. Pl.* B. XV. 176 He can purtreye wel þe pater-noster and peynte it with aues. **14..** *Sir Beues* 1132 (MS. M.) All the wyndowes and all the wallis With cristall was peynted. **1509** HAWES *Past. Pleas.* xxvi. (1845) 114 A ryall playne, With Flora painted in many a sundry vayne. **1533** GAU *Richt Vay* 16 Thay that payntis thair body with precious clais. **1667** MILTON *P.L.* V. 187 Till the Sun paint your fleecie skirts with Gold. **1750** SHENSTONE *Rural Elegance* 60 Or humble harebell paints the plain. **1866** B. TAYLOR *Pine Forest Monterey*, Spring, that paints These savage shores.

4. a. To put colour on (the face in order to beautify it artificially); to rouge; also *refl.*

1382 WYCLIF *2 Kings* ix. 30 Forsothe Iezabel..peyntyde hyre eeȝen with strumpettis oynment, and sche anournede hyre heued. *c* **1400** *Destr. Troy* 434 Wemen haue wille in þere wilde youthe to fret hom with fyn perle, & þaire face paint. **1599** CHAPMAN *Hum. Day's Mirth* Plays 1873 I. 77 She is very faire, I thinke that she be painted. **1678** HEXHAM *Du. Dict.*, To Paint ones face as Gentle-women do, *Blancketten.* **1712–14** POPE *Rape Lock* V. 27 Since painted or not painted, all shall fade, And she who scorns a man, must die a maid. **1852** THACKERAY *Esmond* II. vii, 'She's not so —so red as she's painted', says Miss Beatrix.

b. *intr.* for *refl.*

13.. *Cursor M.* 28014 (Cott.) Yee leuedis..studis hu your hare to heu, hu to dub and hu to paynt. *c* **1532** DU WES *Introd. Fr.* in *Palsgr.* 945 To paynt as women do, *farder.* **1602** SHAKS. *Ham.* V. i. 213 Let her paint an inch thicke, to this fauour she must come. **1712** ARBUTHNOT *John Bull* III. i, She scorned to patch and paint. **1862** W. COLLINS *No Name* IV. iii. II. 187 'Shall I paint?' she asked herself..'the rouge is still left in my box'.

†**c.** *intr.* (*fig.*) To change colour; to blush. *to paint white*, etc.: to turn pale. *Obs.*

c **1613** MIDDLETON *No Wit like Woman's* II. i, Look to the widow, she paints white.—Some *aqua cœlestis* for my lady! **1616** B. JONSON *Devil an Ass* II. vi, You make me paint Sr. *Wit.* The' are fair colours, Lady, and naturall! **1623** MIDDLETON *More Dissemblers Besides Women* I. i, I'll kiss thee into colour: Canst thou paint pale so quickly?

5. *fig.* (*trans.*) To give a false colouring or complexion to; to colour highly, esp. with a view to deception. Now *rare* or *Obs.*

c **1386** CHAUCER *Pars. T.* ¶948 Thow shalt nat eek peynte thy confession by faire subtile wordes to couere the moore thy synne. *a* **1400–50** *Alexander* 4427 He can practise & paynt & polisch his wordis. **1551** T. WILSON *Logike* (1580) 2 b, Rhetorike at large paintes well the cause, And make that seeme right gaie. **1601** SIR W. CORNWALLIS *Ess.*, So are most of the actions of the last ages; but painted with counterfeite colours. **1778** SIR J. REYNOLDS *Disc.* viii. (1876) 443 The writers..where taste has begun to decline, paint and adorn every object they touch.

†**6. a.** *intr.* To talk speciously; to feign; to fawn; **b.** *trans.* To flatter or deceive with specious words.

c **1430** *How Wise Man Tauȝt Sonne* 105 in *Babees Bk.* 51 Y wole neiþir glose ne peynt, But y waarne þee on þe oþir side. **1513** BRADSHAW *St. Werburge* I. 52 Other to flater, and paynt the company. **1530** PALSGR. 655/2, I peynt, I glose or speke fayre, *je adule.* **1588** SHAKS. *L.L.L.* IV. i. 16 Nay, neuer paint me now, Where faire is not, praise cannot mend the brow. **1632** LITHGOW *Trav.* x. 488 You leye, you paint, you faine.

7. *trans.* To apply with a brush, as an external medicament; to treat (any part) in this way: see PAINT *sb.* 2 c.

1861 HEADLAND *Med. Handbk.* 233 The vinegar of cantharides..is painted over the part with a camel hair brush. **1899** *Allbutt's Syst. Med.* VIII. 524 Liquor potassæ, diluted with an equal part of water, should be painted on. *Mod.* The part affected should be painted with iodine.

8. *intr.* (*slang.*) To drink.

1853 WHYTE MELVILLE *Digby Grand* ii. I. 70 Each hotel we passed..called forth the same observation, 'I guess I shall go in and paint'. **1857** KINGSLEY *Two Y. Ago* xxiv, Pegasus doth thirst for Hippocrene, And fain would paint —imbibe the vulgar call—Or hot or cold, or long or short.

9. a. *trans.* To cause to be displayed or represented on the screen of a cathode-ray tube.

1946 *Jrnl. Inst. Electr. Engin.* XCIII. IIIA. 147/2 When an echo or the background has been painted it rapidly fades away according to a law determined by the properties of the screen. **1949** *Jrnl. R. Aeronaut. Soc.* LIII. 436/1 It will be seen that the area of towering cumulo-nimbus clouds..are clearly painted on the PPI picture. **1960** J. D. HAIGH *Radiolocation Techniques* xii. 192 A photographic display of this kind has the advantage that the whole display is of uniform brightness as compared with a normal p.p.i. in which, at any one moment, only that portion of the picture actually being painted by the rotating time-base is at maximum brightness. **1960** *Proc. Inst. Electr. Engin.* CVII. B. Suppl. 19. 54/2 The display console has a double-deflection system consisting of the main deflection circuits ..which position a spot on the tube face, and a second deflection coil..which paints a small raster about this position. **1977** *Sci. Amer.* Jan. 60/2 One kind of stimulus we find useful consists of a moving pattern of small, bright dots 'painted' on the screen of a cathode-ray tube with the aid of a computer.

b. *intr.* To show up on the screen of a cathode-ray tube. Also with *up.*

1946 *Jrnl. Inst. Electr. Engin.* XCIII. IIIA. 145/2 To obtain a satisfactory picture it is necessary to arrange that a fixed target 'paints' at approximately the same point on the screen for consecutive rotations of the aerial system. **1949** *Jrnl. R. Aeronaut. Soc.* LIII. 436/2 It was hoped to fly into some of the cloud forms, but the pilot decided that the risk of flying into any area which 'painted up' on the PPI tube was too great.

II. 10. *Phrases. **to paint** (any one) **black***: to represent as evil or wicked; so ***not so black as he is painted.*** ***to paint the town red*** (slang, orig. U.S.): to cause an excitement or commotion, to go on a boisterous or riotous spree. ***to paint by number(s***: to paint in a picture supplied marked out into sections which are numbered according to the colour to be used; hence ***paint-by-number(s, painting-by-number*** attrib. phrs.

1596, etc. [see DEVIL *sb.* 22 c]. *a* **1686** SOUTH *Serm.* II. ix. 356 Do but paint an Angel black, and that is enough to make him pass for a Devil. **1894** SIR E. SULLIVAN *Woman* 112 These husbands are..not always so black as they are painted. **1884** *Boston* (Mass.) *Jrnl.* 20 Nov. 2/4 Whenever there was any excitement or anybody got particularly loud, they always said somebody was 'painting the town red'. **1897** *Chicago Advance* 15 July 74/3 The boys painted the town [New York City] red with firecrackers [on Independence Day]. **1900** CAPT. M. H. HAYES *Among Horses in Russia* i. 36, I have found them..in no way inclined to paint town and country red on the slightest provocation. **1970** *Women's Household* July 6/3, I..paint by number and plan to try painting soon. **1971** 'P. KAVANAGH' *Triumph of Evil* (1972) vi. 50 He even bought this terrible oil painting... It looked as though it had been painted by numbers. **1976** *Billings* (Montana) *Gaz.* 26 June 14-B/6 But paint-by-number artists have nothing on 11 men at Our Savior's Lutheran Church. Led by Merle Brunsvold, the men put together an electronic pipe organ kit. **1976** *Sunday Post* (Glasgow) 26 Dec. 9/2 Our other products, like playing cards, jigsaws, painting-by-number kits, &c. **1977** J. HODGINS *Invention of World* iii. 42 She..spent the afternoon doing a paint-by-numbers picture, in the living room.

III. With *advbs.* †**11. paint forth** = *paint out* 12 a.

1558 KNOX *First Blast* (Arb.) 12 Nature I say, doth paynt them furthe to be weake, fraile..and foolishe. **1615** CHAPMAN *Odyss.* XIX. 684 My information well shall paint you forth. **1649** in *Nicholas Papers* (Camden) 148 Itt is of very great concernment towards the painting forth of the Presbitery.

12. paint out. a. †To express or display by painting; to execute in colours (*obs.*); *fig.* to depict as in a painting or vivid description.

1556 in *Robinson's transl. More's Utop.* (Arb.) 164 Drawen and painted oute with master Mores pensille. **1581** J. BELL *Haddon's Answ. Osor.* 461 b, Emongest many pictures of our Lady..the very same which Luke did painte out for his owne use, and reserved with great reverence. **1633** ABP. WILLIAMS in *Laud's Wks.* (1857) VI. 336 [They] have with their deceitful colours..painted me out as ugly unto your grace as they have done your grace formidable unto me. **1728** MORGAN *Algiers* I. vi. 177 That notable Amazon..is painted out as a very Masculine Lady. **1809** MALKIN *Gil Blas* IV. vi. ¶12 Some good-natured friend in the dark has painted you out for a reprobate.

†**b.** To copy in colours. *Obs.*

1670–98 LASSELS *Voy. Italy* II. 33 Tho. Earl of Arundel got leave to have it painted out. *Ibid.* 52.

c. To blot out or efface by covering with paint.

1862 WILKIE COLLINS *No Name* IV. vii, I am going to give the lie direct to that she-devil Lecount, by painting out your moles. **1901** *Daily Chron.* 11 July 9/7 The Star..has carried those of the Starfish, with the last four letters painted out, but so faintly that the painted-out letters could be read.

d. *Naut.* = sense 3.

1902 B. LUBBOCK *Round the Horn* viii. 302 The great day for cleaning and painting out the half-deck has come... The steward also painted out his berth to-day. **1924** 'P. BLUNDELL' *Confessions of Seaman* ii. 28 When was it painted out last, I should like to know? **1963** S. HAYDEN *Wanderer* (1964) i. 8 You've painted her out—you've even changed her name?

†**paint**, *v.*² *Obs. Naut.* [app. back-formation from PAINTER².] *trans.* To make fast (an anchor) on a ship with a 'painter'.

1485 *Naval Acc. Hen. VII* (1896) 68 Hokes to paynte thankers with.

†**paint**, *ppl. a. Obs.* In ME. peint, peynt. [a. F. *peint*: see PAINT *v.*¹] Painted.

[**1340** *Ayenb.* 26 Berieles ypeynt and y-gelt.] *c* **1394** *P. Pl. Crede* 193 Y-paued wiþ peynt til. **1399** LANGL. *Rich. Redeles* III. 196 No proude peniles, with his peynte sleve.

paintable ('peɪntəb(ə)l), *a.* [f. PAINT *v.*¹ + -ABLE.] Capable of being painted; suitable for a painting.

1833 *Blackw. Mag.* XXXIII. 957 If he would call the picturesque whatever is not beautiful nor sublime, yet paintable, (pardon the horrid word,) well. **1833** *New Monthly Mag.* XXXVIII. 162 This great poet is often more paintable than his brethren. **1862** W. W. STORY *Roba di R.* (1863) I. ii. 10 The new and clean is not so paintable..as the tarnished and soiled. **1900** HERKOMER *title* (Romanes Lecture) England Lovable and Paintable.

Hence '**paintableness.**

1894 *Athenæum* 23 June 810/1 A good example of that aspect of nature for the discovery of which and of its paintableness the world is greatly indebted to Mr. Whistler.

†'**pain-,taking.** *Obs.* [f. PAIN *sb.*¹ + *taking*, gerund of TAKE *v.*]

1. Receiving or suffering of punishment.

1382 WYCLIF *Ecclus.* v. 17 [14] Vp on a theef is confusioun, and peyne taking [**1388** penaunce, Vulg. *pœnitentia*].

2. = PAINSTAKING *sb.*; sometimes including the notion of enduring pain.

1528 TINDALE *Obed. Chr. Man* 108 b, They thinke also that God..reioyseth and hath delectation in oure payne takynge. **1556** OLDE *Antichrist* 92 b, Silvester the seconde, who..was promoted to be pope by the devilles diligent payne taking. **1567** MAPLET *Gr. Forest* 80 The other by his paine taking, sleepe quietly and take their rest.

painted ('peɪntɪd), *ppl. a.* [f. PAINT *v.*¹ + -ED¹.]

1. Depicted in colours, represented in a picture; executed in colours as a picture, likeness, or design.

a **1300** *Cursor M.* 23215 Painted fire..þat apon a wagh war wroght. **1552** HULOET, Paynted ymages in silinges and tables, *anaglypha.* **1601** SIR W. CORNWALLIS *Ess.* xlvii, What is [this] but to feed the auditory with dishes by the Painter, not the Cooke?—when examined..it proues a painted shoulder of mutton. **1798** COLERIDGE *Anc. Mar.* II. viii, As idle as a painted Ship Upon a painted Ocean.

2. a. Coated or brushed over with colour or paint; ornamented with designs or pictures executed in colour; having the face artificially coloured.

c **1420** LYDG. *Assembly of Gods* 1341 Resydyuacion gooth Toward Macrocosme, with a peyntyd fase. **1526** TINDALE *Acts* xxiii. 3 God shall smyte the thou payntyd wall. **1604** E.

G[RIMSTONE] *D'Acosta's Hist. Indies* v. ix. 354 It carried vpon the head, a pointed myter of painted paper. **1769** GRAY *Install. Ode* 8 Let painted Flatt'ry hide her serpent-train in flowers. **1784** COOK *3rd Voy.* I. Introd. 8 When Great-Britain was first visited by the Phœnicians, the inhabitants were painted Savages. **1851** RUSKIN *Stones Ven.* (1873) II. iv. 110 The traditions annealed in the purple burning of the painted window.

b. *fig.* Coloured so as to look what it is not; unreal, artificial; feigned, disguised, pretended.

1377 LANGL. *P. Pl.* B. xx. 114 With pryue speche and peynted wordes. *c* **1380** WYCLIF *Wks.* (1880) 271 Prelatis of þe world & peyntid foolis of religion. **1426** LYDG. *De Guil. Pilgr.* 10947 Ffor al thy peynted wordys swete, My staff in soth I wyl nat lete. **1621** ELSING *Debates Ho. Lords* (Camden) 46 Sir Ed. Villiers his paynted friend, and Mompesson an obdurate enemy. **1728** SHERIDAN *Persius* v. (1739) 67 Nor are you to be deceived by painted Expressions. **1852** ROBERTSON *Serm.* Ser. I. xix. (1866) 326 The life of men was a painted life.

3. *fig.* Adorned with bright or varied colouring, highly coloured, variegated.

c **1470** HENRYSON *Mor. Fables* v. (*Parl. Beasts*) xv, The peyntit pantheir, and the vnicorne. **1526** *Pilgr. Perf.* (W. de W. 1531) 63 The pecockes paynted fethers. **1714** L. EUSDEN *Speech of Pluto* in *Poet. Misc.* 140 And painted Meads smile with unbidden Flow'rs. **1844** LD. BROUGHAM *A. Lunel* III. vi. 189 The cattle, and painted birds, stretched their weary limbs..and soothed their hearts.

4. In specific collocations: often used to form the specific name of an animal or plant of conspicuous colouring, as *painted duck, goose, honey-eater, mallow, ray*, etc.; **painted bat**, an East Indian bat (*Kerivoula picta*) with brilliant orange colouring; **painted beauty**, a large North American butterfly, *Vanessa virginiana*, with black and white markings on its brownish-yellow wings; **painted bunting**, name for two birds: (*a*) the Nonpareil, *Cyanospiza ciris*; (*b*) = *painted longspur*; **Painted Chamber** (in contemporary AF. *chaumbre peynte*), a chamber in the old Palace of Westminster, in which in early times Parliament often assembled (first recorded in 1339) and in which the Sovereign sometimes met the two houses: its walls were painted with a series of battle scenes (see Stubbs *Const. Hist.* (1875) xx. §748; Brayley and Britton *Westminster* 401); **painted clam**, an edible porcelainlike bivalve (*Callista gigantea*) of the southern United States; †**painted cloth**: see CLOTH 5; **painted cup**, †a name for (*a*) the plant *Bartsia viscosa*; (*b*) any species of the N. American genus *Castilleia*, having bracts more brilliant and showy than the flowers; **painted finch**, 'one of several species of *Passerina* or *Cyanospiza*, the nonpareil, the indigo-bird, or the lazuli-finch: so called from their brilliant and varied colors'; **painted grass**, the striped variety of *Phalaris arundinacea*, Lady's laces; **painted ground**: see quot.; **painted hyena** = HYENA-DOG (*Lycaon pictus*); **painted lady**, (*a*) a species of butterfly (*Vanessa* or *Pyrameis cardui*) of orange-red colour, spotted with black and white; (*b*) a party-coloured variety of Pink or *Dianthus*; (*c*) also *painted lady pea*, a variegated species of *Lathyrus*, esp. of the Sweet Pea; (*d*) a name used in South Africa for several local species of gladiolus, distinguished by marks of a different colour on some of their petals; **painted longspur**, a North American bird, *Centrophanes pictus* (Coues *Key N. Amer. Birds* (1884) 358); **painted mischief** (*slang*), playing cards; **painted quail**, a name applied to several birds allied to the quail, esp. to those of the genus *Excalfactoria*; **painted snipe**: see quot. 1896; **painted terrapin, tortoise, turtle**, a small American freshwater turtle of the genus *Chrysemys*, distinguished by red and yellow rings on its greenish-brown shell; **painted top-shell**, a littoral gastropod mollusc, *Calliostoma zizyphinum* (formerly *Trochus* or *Gibbula magus*), which has a vividly coloured conical shell.

1899 *Lippincott's Monthly Mag.* Oct. 631 The *Painted Beauty and the Cosmopolitan resemble each other strongly. **1972** SWAN & PAPP *Common Insects N. Amer.* 237 Painted Beauty: *Vanessa virginiensis*... Also called American painted lady and Virginia lady. **1893** NEWTON *Dict. Birds* 459 The..gaudy *Painted Bunting or Nonpareil. [**1339** *Rolls of Parlt.* I. 106/1 En la Chaumbre de Peynte. **1350-1** *Ibid.* 225/1 En la Chaumbre Blaunche pres de la Chaumbre Peynte.] *c* **1543** in Parker *Dom. Archit.* III. 79 The parlement chambre & *paynted chambre. **1654** (*title*) Speeches of His Highnesse the Lord Protector to the Parliament in the Painted Chamber. **1875** STUBBS *Const. Hist.* III. xviii. 129 He [Hen. VI] had been brought into the painted chamber to preside at the opening of parliament. **1488** in *Ripon Ch. Acts* (Surtees) 286, j *pantid cloth cum pictura S. Antonii. **1528** *Test. Ebor.* (Surtees) V. 253 A paynted clothe wth Christe and ij thefes upon it, iiij*d.* **1542-1654** [see CLOTH *sb.* 5]. **1787** WITHERING *Brit. Plants* (ed. 2) II. 632 Bartsia, *Painted-cup. **1866** *Treas. Bot.*, *Painted cup*, an American name for *Castilleja*. **1730** MORTIMER in *Phil. Trans.* XXXVI. 431 *Fringilla tricolor*, the *painted Finch..; its Head and Neck are blue; its Back green, and the Belly red. **1597** GERARDE *Herbal* I. xix. §2. 25 Usually of our English women..called Ladies Laces, or *Painted grasse. **1884** MILLER *Plant-n.*, Painted Grass. **1881** *Standard* 3 Oct. 2/1 Designs which remind the ancient spectator of that portion of the old Fleet Prison once known as 'the *painted ground', because of the vivid illustrations that distinguished it. **1868** WOOD *Homes without H.* xii. 220 Called the *Painted Honey-Eater on account of the variety of its colouring. Its scientific name is *Entomophila picta*. **1753** CHAMBERS *Cycl. Supp.*, **Painted lady*, a term for a particular sort of carnations, the flowers of which have all their petals red or purple on the out side, and white underneath. **1760** J. LEE *Introd. Bot.* App. 321 Painted Lady Pease, *Lathyrus*. **1823** CRABB *Technol. Dict.*, *Painted lady*, the name of a beautifully variegated pea, the *Lathyrus odoratus* of Linnæus. **1829** *Glover's Hist. Derby* I. 174 *Papilio Pictus*, Painted Lady Butterfly. **1890** *Daily News* 14 Oct. 5/1 The butterflies of autumn, admiral and painted lady, sail from bush to bush. **1906** B. STONEMAN *Plants S. Afr.* xix. 198 Gladiolus... Painted Ladies and 'Kalkoentjes' belong here. Eighty-one species of this large genus are found in South Africa. **1927** [see AANDBLOM]. **1972** *Stand. Encycl. S. Afr.* V. 201/2 The Cape species [of gladiolus] are known as pypies, afrikaners, painted ladies, bells. *Ibid.* 202/1 The painted ladies (e.g. *G. carneus*) have white or pink trumpet-shaped flowers with markings on the lower perianth lobes. **1825** *Greenhouse Comp.* II. 25 *Malva miniata*, *painted Mallow, a shrub introduced from South America in 1798. **1879** *Daily News* 8 Mar. (Farmer), There are plenty of ways of gambling..without recourse to the '*painted mischief'. **1895** LYDEKKER *Roy. Nat. Hist.* IV. 416 The common *painted quail (*Excalfactoria chinensis*) inhabits the Indo-Chinese countries, especially the lower hills. **1836** YARRELL *Brit. Fishes* II. 433 The Small-eyed Ray, or *Painted Ray. *Raia microcellata*. **1811** *Sporting Mag.* 63 Called the *painted snipe. **1896** NEWTON *Dict. Birds* 886 The so-called Painted Snipes, forming the genus *Rostratula*, or *Rhynchæa*... Three species are now admitted, natives respectively of South America, Africa and southern Asia and Australia. **1839** STORER & PEABODY *Rep. Fishes, Reptiles & Birds Mass.* 208 *Chrysemys picta*... The *painted Tortoise. **1842** J. E. DEKAY *Zool. N. Y.* III. 12 The Painted Tortoise..is unquestionably the handsomest of our fresh-water species. **1876** D. S. JORDAN *Man. Vertebrates Northern U.S.* 163 C[*hrysemys*] *picta* (Herm.) Ag. Painted Turtle. Mud Turtle... One of the most common turtles. **1904** W. T. HORNADAY *Amer. Nat. Hist.* xxxvii. 327/1 The Painted Terrapin, hitherto called at random the Painted 'Turtle' and Pond-'Tortoise', is perhaps the most widely distributed species..in the United States. **1949** *Life* 11 Apr. 81 A painted turtle cranes its neck in the spring sun. **1973** M. CROWELL *Greener Pastures* 200 We..pick up a painted turtle intent on crossing the road. **1865** J. G. WOOD *Common Shells of Sea-shore* xi. 100 The *Painted Top-shell..is rather boldly ridged. *Ibid.* 101 The name of Painted Top is given to it on account of the magnificent hues of the animal. **1901** E. STEP *Shell Life* xi. 205 The Painted Top-shell..is a very distinct species, the shape of the three largest of the 8 whorls giving the solid shell a decidedly turreted appearance. **1972** S. P. DANCE *Shells* 18 (*caption*) The Painted Top Shell is a gaily coloured species and has long tentacles.

painter[1] ('peɪntə(r)). Forms: 4-5 **peyntour, peynteur, payntoure, -eore**, 4-6 **payntur**, 5 **paintour, payntor, peyntoure, poyntowre, panter**, 5-6 **payntour, peynter**, 5-7 **paynter**, (6 **peyntar, penter, peincter**), 5- **painter**. [ME. a. AF. *peintour* = OF. *peintour, -tor* (regimen-case of *peintre* = Pr. *pintor*, Sp., Pg. *pintor*, It. *pintore*):—Com. Romanic *pinctōr-em*, for L. *pictōr-em*, agent-n. from *pingĕre* to PAINT. In 15-16th c., the ending was conformed to the *-er* of native agent-nouns.] One who paints.

1. a. An artist who represents or depicts objects on a surface in colours; one who paints pictures.

1340 HAMPOLE *Pr. Consc.* 2308 Ne swa sleygh payntur never nan was,..þat couthe..paynt a poynt aftir þair liknes. *c* **1375** Paynteore [see PAINT *v.*[1] 1]. **1382** WYCLIF *Esther* i. 6 The whiche thing the peynteur with wonder diuersete made fair. *c* **1440** *Promp. Parv.* 407/1 Poyntowre, or peyntoure, *pictor*. **1538** in *Vicary's Anat.* (1888) App. xii. 238 Payde to Hans Holbyn, one of the Kingis paynters. **1561** T. HOBY tr. *Castiglione's Courtyer* I. Kb, A most excellent peincter. **1634** W. TIRWHYT tr. *Balzac's Lett.* 223, I avoid the sight of all Paynters..lest they shew me the patterne of my pale visage. **1759** JOHNSON *Rasselas* xxix, A painter must copy pictures. **1870** RUSKIN *Lect. Art* v. 121 The greatest of English painters..our own gentle Reynolds.

b. *fig.* One who describes something in a pictorial or graphic style; a pictorial describer.

1570 DEE *Math. Pref.* 37 To describe..how, vsuall howers, may be (by the Sunnes shadow) truely determined: will be found no sleight Painters worke. **1774** GOLDSM. *Retal.* 63 A flattering painter, who made it his care To draw men as they ought to be, not as they are. *a* **1877** BAGEHOT *Lit. Stud.* (1879) 205 The great works of the real painters of essential human nature.

2. a. A workman who coats or colours the surface of things (as woodwork, ironwork, etc.) with paint.

c **1400** *Destr. Troy* 1591 Of all þe craftes..Parnters, painters, pynners also; Bochers, bladsmythis, baxters amonge. **1483** *Act 1 Rich. III*, c. 12 §1 Artificers of the said Realm..Spurriers, Goldbeaters, Painters, Sadlers. *c* **1515** *Cocke Lorell's B.* 9 Fyners, plommers, and penters. **1711** *Act 10 Anne* c. 18 §57 All..Printers Painters or Stainers of any such Paper. **1862** *All Yr. Round* 18 Oct. 133 Orphans of parents—bricklayers, painters, carpenters—'who had never been upon the parish'. **1891** E. PEACOCK *N. Brendon* I. 26 We are compelled to call both the President of the Royal Academy and the man who paints our carts and hot-bed frames by the common name of painter.

b. With *of*, or in objective comb.: One who paints (i.e. either 'depicts', or 'adorns with colour') what is indicated by the context. Also *fig.*

1844 LD. BROUGHAM *A. Lunel* III. iv. 125 She has some pretensions as a painter of still life. **1853** WHITTIER *Garden* 1 O Painter of the fruits and flowers, We own Thy wise design. *Mod.* He was a famous painter of lions.

†**3.** (See quot.) *Obs.*

1688 R. HOLME *Armoury* III. 152/1 Colours, of which there is only seven used in Glass-painting..Black, called Painter by them.

4. *attrib.* and *Comb.*, chiefly appositive, as *painter-engraver, -etcher, -graver, -husband, -minister, -muse, -poet, -saint*; *painter-engraving, -etching*; **painter-like** *a.*, (*a*) resembling or characteristic of a painter; (*b*) picturesque, artistic; **painter's brush**, (*a*) (see quot. 1685); (*b*) = *Indian paint-brush* (INDIAN A. 4 b); **painter's colic**, a form of colic to which painters who work with poisonous preparations of lead are liable, lead-colic; †**painter's gold**, orpiment; **painter's** (or **painters'**) **mussel**, the freshwater mussel, *Unio pictorum*; †**painter's oil**, linseed oil.

1879 F. S. HADEN *About Etching* I. 18 We shall have to show that the adoption of the tool, (except in the case of the *painter-engraver, who..was an original artist,) implies the practice of a secondary art. **1937** *Burlington Mag.* Feb. 77/1 Elevation to the level of painter-engravers such as Hausbuchmeister and Martin Schongauer. **1890** F. S. HADEN *Art of Painter-Etcher* 4 This great-master engraving, this original engraving, this *painter-engraving. **1880** *Times* 23 Dec. 7/5 Society of *Painter Etchers.—.. The society.. has been formed to 'promote original etching and the interest of painters practising that branch of art'. **1920** E. H. HUBBARD *Etchings* 128 The work of 'painter-etchers' (men who execute original subjects direct on the plate). **1975** *Whitaker's Almanack 1976* 1104/2 Painter-Etchers and Engravers, Royal Society of.., 26 Conduit Street, W.1. **1890** F. S. HADEN *Art of Painter-Etcher* 5 The singular restriction of the Fine Arts to three—Oil painting, Sculpture, and Architecture, to the exclusion of Water Colour painting and *Painter-Etching. **1879** —— *About Etching* II. 47 *Leyden, Lucas Van*..A Flemish *painter-graver of great reputation. **1738** J. F. FRITSCH tr. *De Lairesse's Art of Painting* I. VI. xv. 331 But since Beauty is attracting, and Deformity offensive, this certainly is true *Painter-like, which supposes the best and most agreeable Objects. **1821** CRAIG *Lect. Drawing* ii. 138 The form will scarcely ever be forgotten..that has ever been looked on with a painter-like feeling. **1845** R. FORD *Hand-bk. for Travellers Spain* II. 595/2 *Villafranca del Vierzo* is truly Swiss-like,..with painter-like bridges. **1958** *Economist* 8 Nov. (Suppl.) 9/2 His painter-like method of composition 'over the whole surface at once'. **1693** WATTS *On Death Aged Relative* v, The *painter-muse with glancing eye Observ'd a manly spirit nigh. **1909** *Daily Chron.* 17 Mar. 3/3 Mr. Graham is what may be termed a *painter-poet. **1941** BLUNDEN *Thomas Hardy* 262 The painter-poet insists on being very much in the middle of things time and again in Hardy's verse. **1899** *Month* Jan. 38 The *painter-saint of Fiesole. **1685** G. MERITON *Nomencl. Cler.* 356 A *Painter's Brush or Pencill, *Penicillum*. **1869** S. BOWLES *Our New West* v. 104 The painter's brush, as familiarly called here, is a new flower to me. **1899** S. HALE *Let.* 22 Apr. (1919) 345 Mariposa lilies, painter's brush, poppies, and dozens of others. **1910** MRS. H. WARD *Canadian Born* x. 206 Anderson had brought her to a wild garden of incredible beauty... Painter's brush, harebell, speedwell, golden-brown gaillardias. **1822-34** *Good's Study Med.* I. 173 Two cases of violent *painter's colic. **1899** *Allbutt's Syst. Med.* VIII. 7 'Occupation neuroses' such as painter's colic or mercurial tremor. **1872** RUSKIN *Eagle's N.* §199 When the English gentleman becomes an art-patron, he employs his *painter-servant only to paint himself and his house. **1591** PERCIVALL *Sp. Dict.*, *Oropel*, leather gilt, *painters gold [**1599** *Minsheu adds*: Orpin or base gold for painters]. **1611** COTGR., *Oripeau*, base gold, leafe gold, false gold, Orpine, Painters gold. [**1862** J. G. JEFFREYS *Brit. Conchol.* I. 34 *U*[*nio*] *pictorum*... Painters'. **1865** L. REEVE *Conchologia Iconica* XXV. s.v. Unio, species 123 The painters' Unio. Shell elongately oblong,..fulvous-olive.] **1896** L. E. ADAMS *Collector's Man. Brit. Land & Freshwater Shells* (ed. 2) 148 The '*Painters' Mussel' is found in similar localities to *U*[*nio*] *tumidus*. **1901** E. STEP *Shell Life* 111 The Painter's Mussel.., so called because the valves were formerly used to hold artists' colours. **1952** J. CLEGG *Freshwater Life* xvi. 268 The Painter's Mussel..has a long, thin shell, about two to three inches in length. **1974** M. SAUL *Shells* 87 The more solid valves of the Painter's Mussel..were used by artists throughout Europe to hold their colours. **1545** *Rates of Customs* c ij, *Paynters oyle the barrel. **1583** *Ibid.* D vj, Painters or Linsed Oyle.

painter[2] ('peɪntə(r)). *Naut.* Also 5-9 **paynter**, 7-9 **penter**. [Derivation uncertain. Connexion with PAINTER *sb.*[2], net, snare, F. *pantière*, has been conjectured; but no corroborative evidence has been found. Cf. PAINT *v.*[2]

Cf. also OF. *pentoir, pendoir* anything for hanging things on, of which Godef. has one 15th c. instance glossed as 'cordage de forte resistance'.]

1. The rope or chain with which the shank and flukes of the anchor, when carried at the cathead, are confined to the ship's side. Now always SHANK-PAINTER, q.v.

1487 *Naval Acc. Hen. VII* (1896) 44 Paynters for the ankres..iiij. [**1495** *Ibid.* 258 Bowpayntours for destrelles feble j Shankpayntors for destrelles worne & feble ij.] **1661** J. TATHAM *London's Tryumphs* in Heath *Grocer's Comp.* (1869) 478 Stand ready by the Anchor Let go your open Penter, and hold fast your Stopper. [**1769** FALCONER *Dict. Marine* (1789), *Shank-Painter*, a short rope and chain which hangs the shank and flukes of an anchor up to the ship's side, as the *stopper* fastens the ring and stock to the cat-head.]

2. A rope attached to the bow of a boat, for making it fast to a ship, a stake, etc.

1711 W. SUTHERLAND *Shipbuild. Assist.* 154 For the Long-boat... Painter, ½ the Boat Rope and ⅛ of the Le(ngth). **1757** ROBERTSON in *Phil. Trans.* L. 34 The skiff was..let down; but the painter not being fast, the rope run an end, and the skiff went adrift. **1790** WOLCOTT (P. Pindar) *Adv. to Fut. Laureat* Wks. 1812 II. 338 Just like the Victory or Fame That by its painter drags the Gig or Yawl. **1806** *Naval Chron.* XV. 462 This..allowed time to cut the boat's penter. **1831** TRELAWNEY *Adv. Younger Son* (1890) 311, I..slipped the painter which held the boat. **1861** HUGHES *Tom Brown at Oxf.* ii. (1889) 15 [He] jumped out with the painter of his skiff in his hand. **1876** BESANT & RICE *Gold. Butterfly* xv. 130 Painters in London boats are sometimes longish ropes, for convenience of mooring.

b. *to cut* (or *slip*) *the painter* (*fig.*): to send a person or thing 'adrift' or away; to clear off; to sever a connexion, effect a separation.

a **1700** B. E. *Dict. Cant. Crew* s.v., *I'll Cut your Painter for ye*, I'll prevent ye doing me any Mischief. **1785** GROSE *Dict. Vulg. Tongue* s.v., *I'll cut your painter for you*, I'll send you off. **1867** SMYTH *Sailor's Word-bk.* s.v., 'Cut your painter', make off. **1888** T. W. REID *Life W. E. Forster* II. 99 The sooner we 'cut the painter' and let the Greater Britain drift from us the better it would be for Englishmen. **1891** E. KINGLAKE *Australian at H.* 4 On the contrary, the idea of 'cutting the painter' is not popular.

painter[3]. [Variant of PANTHER, prob. from 16th c. Eng. *panter* or F. *panthère* (pronounced *pantère*).] Name in some parts of N. America for the American panther or cougar (*Felis concolor*).

1803 J. DAVIS *Trav. U.S.A.* 382 My master..said that I ought to live among *painters* and wolves, and sold me to a *Georgia* man for two hundred dollars. **1823** J. F. COOPER *Pioneers* xxviii, It might frighten an older woman to see a she painter so near her, with a dead cub by its side. **1834** D. CROCKETT *Narr. Life* i. 5 This alarmed me, and I screamed out like a young painter. **1901** ROOSEVELT in *Scribner's Mag.* Oct., The cougar... In the Eastern States it is usually called panther or painter; in the Western States, mountain lion, or, toward the South, Mexican lion. The Spanish-speaking people usually call it simply lion. **1940** ARNOLD & HALE *Hot Irons* 9 You learn, accidentally, that a 'painter' is really a panther. **1972** *Amer. Speech 1968* XLIII. 218 Mountain cuisine consisted almost entirely of meat: rattlesnake, ..*painter* (panther), and rabbit.

'painterly, *a.* (*adv.*) [f. PAINTER[1] + -LY[1], [2].]

a. Like, or pertaining to, a painter; characteristic of a painter, artistic; *spec.* of a style of painting, characterized by qualities of colour, stroke, and texture rather than of contour or line. Also *transf.* **b.** *adv.* In a way proper to a painter, artistically. *rare.*

a **1586** SIDNEY *Arcadia* I. (1590) 55 It was a very white and red vertue, which you could pick out of a painterly glosse of a visage. **1822** T. G. WAINEWRIGHT *Ess. & Crit.* (1880) 248 A painterly arranged exclamation of this kind. *Ibid.* 261 How well made up—how painterly! **1932** *Times Lit. Suppl.* 16 June 441/1 A linear style and a 'painterly' (a translation of the German word *malerisch*, which can also mean picturesque). **1942** *Burlington Mag.* Jan. 24/2 A technique which foreshadows the painterly methods of Watteau. **1950** *Eng. Stud.* XXXI. 166 One should not forget the exciting Kiplingesque rhythm..or the painterly qualities of the dramatic, colourful poem of Cummerbund, the monster of India. **1952** H. READ in P. & L. MURRAY tr. *H. Wölfflin's Classic Art* p. vi, One word, however, calls for comment—the word 'painterly', which has been invented to convey the meaning of the German word *malerisch*... It stands for that depreciation and gradual obliteration of line (outline and tangible surface) and for the merging of these in a 'shifting semblance' of things—it is an attempt to represent the vague and impalpable essence of things. **1958** *Observer* 23 Mar. 16/5 Short lyrics of precision and beauty, painterly poems, touchingly infused with the poet's passion for what is beautiful. **1958** *Times* 24 July 5/2 His recent attempts to exchange a linear for a more painterly manner. **1962** *Punch* 1 Aug. 177/3 Alberta Wheeler, ex-night club dancer and painterly genius. **1963** *Guardian* 11 Mar. 7/2 He is becoming more painterly, his colour more subtle, and his surface dense with matter. **1969** H. E. BATES *Vanished World* xi. 147 It was not only the painterly quality of Crane's prose that attracted me. **1969** R. MAYER *Dict. Art Terms & Techniques* 276/1 *Painterly*, having the quality of expertly brushed workmanship... A term applied to the dominance of tonal masses over line as a means of defining form in painting, sculpture, and architecture. **1973** F. TAUBES *Painter's Dict.* 176 Botticelli is a linear painter, whilst Rembrandt's work would be considered painterly. **1973** *Times Lit. Suppl.* 3 Aug. 900/3 The painterly aspect of each drawing is never forgotten: apart from shading with chalk or wash, in order to enliven a line or contour, pastels are employed and often coloured paper used. **1974** A. DILLARD *Pilgrim at Tinker Creek* xv. 268 A photograph of earth from space, the planet so startlingly painterly and hung. **1978** P. PORTER *Cost of Seriousness* 2 Masts for Woodbridge Crowd three degrees of the horizon, edging A painterly Dutch sky.

Hence **'painterliness**, painterly quality.

1955 P. HERON *Changing Forms of Art* xiii. 202 Hilton's *conscious intention* has been to eliminate all charm, all painterliness, even that evidence of mastery of the material which is itself a seductive element in painting. **1958** S. SPENDER *Engaged in Writing* iii. 43 Marteau's very appearance transformed the atmosphere from the weighted inwardness of Bonvolio-directed programme music, to cracking outdoor painterliness. **1977** *Times Lit. Suppl.* 24 June 761/5 Manet's painterly procedures—as well as his acknowledged painterliness.

'paintership. *nonce-wd.* [f. as prec. + -SHIP.] The function or position of a painter.

1553 M. WOOD tr. *Gardiner's True Obedience* G viij, Let him striue also to continue stil in his chief paintourship, least another passe him in conning, & so haue the name of the cheif painter from him.

Painter-Stainer = PAINTER[1] 1 and 2.

The name by which the members of the City of London Livery Company of Painters (which included *painters* in senses 1 and 2), are designated in their charter, in which connexion it has continued in use to the present day. The restriction of meaning stated in quot. 1706, and repeated in later Dicts., does not seem to be in accordance with facts.

1504 *Deed* in J. G. Crace *Comp. Painter-Stainers* (1880), John Browne paynter-steyner. **1581** *Charter Painters Comp. Lond.*, Liberi Homines et Cives Civitatis London Artis sive Misterii pictorium vocati Anglice Paynters-Steyners. **1582** *Grant of Byelaws*, The..fellowship of the arte of paynters, alias paynters stayners of the City of London. **1604** *Act 1 Jas. I*, c. 20 No manner of person..shall..make any manner of worke or workes, or lay any manner of Colour or Colours, Painting or Paintings whatsoeuer, in the sayd Art or Mystery of Painters Stainers aforesaid..vnlesse [etc.]. **1706** PHILLIPS (ed. Kersey), *Painter-Stainer*, one that makes draughts of, and paints all sorts of Coats of Arms, with other Devices, belonging to the Art of Heraldry. **1709** STRYPE *Ann. Ref.* (1824) I. xiii. 268 Forced to become an apprentice for ten years to William Gardiner, painter stainer of London. **1880** J. G. CRACE [Master] (*title*) Some Account of the Worshipful Company of Painter-Stainers. *Ibid.* ad fin., This Company may fairly appeal to all good citizens to join in the wish expressed in their time-honoured toast 'May the Painter-Stainers' Company flourish root and branch for ever'.

paint-house, obs. variant of PENTHOUSE.

paint-in ('peɪntɪn). [f. PAINT *v.*[1] + -IN[3].] A gathering for the purpose of painting; *spec.* an organized attempt to improve and draw attention to shabby or neglected buildings by cleaning and redecorating them.

1966 *Maclean's Mag.* 14 May 3 What is a Paint-In? Well, it's a protest, like a sit-in, except that people paint and other people gather round. **1969** *Time* 20 June 64 Jane Shay.. organized a one-day paint-in by a group of Washington high school art students. **1969** *Parade* (N.Y.) 14 Dec. 12/2 A gigantic clean-up and paint-in began. **1974** *State* (Columbia, S. Carolina) 26 Apr. B-1/3 (*caption*) Gibson Hopper tries his hand at a paint-in during opening day of Fiesta '74.

paintiness ('peɪntɪnɪs). [f. PAINTY *a.* + -NESS.] The quality of being painty.

1884 *Bazaar* 22 Dec. 663/3 Faults of feeble colouring and splashy paintiness. **1885** BULLOCH *G. Jamesone* v. 55 With how little paintiness they shine forth from their frames.

painting ('peɪntɪŋ), *vbl. sb.* [f. PAINT *v.* + -ING[1].] The action of the verb PAINT, or that which is painted.

1. The result or product of applying paint or colour; colouring; pictorial decoration.

a **1225** *Ancr. R.* 392 Ine schelde beoð þreo þinges, þet treo, and þet leðer, & þe peintunge. **1495** *Trevisa's Barth. De P.R.* XVI. xcix. 587 Glasse is amonge stones as a fole amonge men for it takyth al manere of colour and payntyng. **1607** SHAKS. *Timon* I. i. 155 A peece of Painting, which I do beseech Your Lordship to accept. **1760–1** in Willis & Clark *Cambridge* (1886) II. 496 Repairing the painting of the room. **1817** J. EVANS *Excurs. Windsor* etc. 22 A rich piece of painting in enamel. *a* **1859** MACAULAY *Hist. Eng.* xxiii. V. 112 Gazers who admired the painting and gilding of his Excellency's carriages.

2. *concr.* A representation of an object or scene on a surface by means of colours; a picture.

c **1388** in *Wyclif's Sel. Wks.* III. 462 Alle men worschipynge..þoo ymagis or any payntyngus, synnen ande done ydolatry. **1483** *Cath. Angl.* 266/2 A Payntynge, *pictura, emble[m]a.* **1588** SHAKS. *L.L.L.* III. i. 21 With..your hands in your pocket, like a man after an old painting. **1639** N. N. tr. *Du Bosq's Compl. Woman* I. 10 To refresh the eyes with their paintings. **1809** W. BLAKE *Descr. Catal.* 62 The distinction made between a Painting and a Drawing. **1859** GULLICK & TIMBS *Painting* 275 Perhaps the most remarkable painting of the eighteenth century in France.

3. a. The representing of objects or figures by means of colours laid on a surface; the art of so depicting objects.

c **1440** *Promp. Parv.* 390/2 Peyntynge, or portrature ..*pictura.* **1638** JUNIUS *Paint. Ancients* 12 The facultie of Painters..knoweth no end in painting. **1770** SIR J. REYNOLDS *Wks.* (1855) 329 There are excellencies in the art of painting beyond what is commonly called the imitation of Nature. **1841–4** EMERSON *Ess.*, *Art* Wks. (Bohn) I. 148 Painting and sculpture are gymnastics of the eye.

b. *fig.* The depicting in words, representation in vivid language.

1615 CHAPMAN *Odyss.* XIX. 288 Thus many tales Ulysses told his wife, At most but painting, yet most like the life. **1695** DRYDEN *Troilus & Cressida* Pref. b iij, The painting of it is so lively, and the words so moving. *a* **1877** BAGEHOT *Lit. Stud.* (1879) 207 Few things in literary painting are more wonderful.

4. The action of colouring or of adorning with paint; the colouring of the face with paint; an instance of this. Also *fig.*

1497 *Nav. Acc. Hen. VII* (1896) 237 Workyng abought the payntyng of the seid ship. **1579** W. WILKINSON *Confut. Fam. Loue* 48 These his vayne payntynges of his margent, shall hereafter make his cause more odious. **1650** FULLER *Pisgah* IV. vi. 116 Painting was practised by Harlots, adulterated complexions well agreeing with adulterous conditions. **1715** SOUTH *Serm.* IV. i. 46 Like the Plaistering of Marble, or the Painting of Gold. **1880** OUIDA *Moths* iii. 17 It is all cant to be against painting.

†**5.** *concr.* Pigment, paint. *Obs.*

1591 PERCIVALL *Sp. Dict.*, *Mudas*, painting for womens faces, *Fucus.* **1594** GREENE & LODGE *Looking-Glass* Wks. (Grosart) XIV. 27 The costly paintings fetcht fro curious Tyre, Haue mended in my face what nature mist. **1608** TOPSELL *Serpents* (1658) 695 Adulterated with meal, chalk, white-earth, or painting. **1650** BULWER *Anthropomet.* 158 Thou defacest the features of God, if thou cover thy Face with painting.

6. *attrib.* and *Comb.*, as ***painting apron***, ***-cleaner***, ***-machine***, ***-room***, etc.; †**painting-cloth** = PAINTED cloth.

1668 R. HEAD *Eng. Rogue* II. 112 Old painting Cloath.. Dives in the flames..the Prodigal on Horse-back. **1769** C. LEADBETTER *Mech. Dialling* xxvii. 148 Painting Brushes of Several Sizes. **1804** *Europ. Mag.* May 329/1 The back offices and painting-room abutted upon Langford's..auction-room. **1837** MRS. SHERWOOD *H. Milner* I. xiii. 57 Bits of broken plates, which Henry used as pallets and painting-stones. **1852** THACKERAY *Esmond* i, As one has seen unskilful painting-cleaners do. **1876** LOWELL *Among my Bks.* Ser. II. 311 He would come to the painting-room and sit silent for hours. **1902** *Chambers's Jrnl.* Feb. 125/2 The spray painting-machine is brought into operation where large unbroken surfaces have to be covered. **1966** 'H. MACDIARMID' *Company I've Kept* ii. 59 A painting-machine like Jean Tinguely's to produce unexpected designs.

'painting, *ppl. a.* [f. as prec. + -ING[2].] That paints: see the verb.

1628 EARLE *Microcosm.*, *Player* (Arb.) 42 He is like our painting Gentle-women, seldome in his owne face, seldomer in his cloathes. **1752** FOOTE *Taste* II. Wks. 1799 I. 23 That gentleman..that we see'd at the painting man's.

Hence **'paintingness** (*rare*), pictorial quality.

1801 W. TAYLOR in Robberds *Mem.* I. 374 One cannot enough praise the expression and paintingness of the style.

paintless ('peɪntlɪs), *a.* [f. PAINT *v.* and *sb.* + -LESS.]

†**1.** Incapable of being painted or depicted.

1729 SAVAGE *Wanderer* II. 246 By woe, the soul to daring actions swells; By woe, in paintless patience it excels.

2. Destitute or devoid of paint.

1859 HELPS *Friends in C.* Ser. II. (ed. 2) I. 11 Sordid,.. paintless, blackened houses. **1868** DILKE *Greater Brit.* I. I. xi. 122 We met them with peaceful paintless cheeks.

†**'paintment.** *Obs. rare.* [f. PAINT *v.* + -MENT.] Painting, adornment with colours.

1597 BEARD *Theatre God's Judgem.* (1612) 67 Along the verdant fields all richly di'de With Natures paintments, and with Floraes pride. **1622** ROWLANDS *Good Newes & Bad N.* 15 Where..natures paintments, red, and yellow, blew, With colours plenty round about him grew.

paintress ('peɪntrɪs). [ad. F. *peintresse*, in 15–16th c. also *paintresse* (Godef.), fem. of *peintre* painter.] A female painter; a woman who paints.

†**1.** A woman who paints or rouges her face. *Obs.*

1633 T. ADAMS *Exp. 2 Peter* iii. 1 As the cunning paintress deals with her face.

2. A woman who paints pictures; a female artist.

1741 *Corr. betw. C'tess Hartford & C'tess Pomfret* (1805) III. 225 We went to see the paintress Rosalba, who is now old. **1836** *Blackw. Mag.* XXXIX. 353 Nature..adorning and touching up, like a paintress, her choice works. **1884** H. S. WILSON *Stud. Hist.* 160 She was a paintress of repute.

b. With *of*, or a genitive, or sb. attrib.

1790 H. WALPOLE *Let. to Miss Berrys* 10 Oct. (1846) VI. 370, I long to hear that its dear paintress is well. **1826** KIRBY & SP. *Entomol.* (1828) III. xxix. 72 This admirable paintress of natural objects. **1880** C. KEENE *Let.* in *Life* (1892) x. 314 A friend..a rattling fine animal paintress.

3. A woman employed in painting pottery-ware.

1825 J. NICHOLSON *Operat. Mechanic* 474 As both males and females are employed in this branch, the men are called *painters*, the women *paintresses*: but in blue-painting, where no men are employed, the women are called *blue-painters.* **1893** E. L. WAKEMAN in *Columbus* (Ohio) *Disp.* 4 May, One [daughter] may be a 'paintress', coloring the cheaper wares.

†**'paintrix.** *Obs. rare.* [See -TRIX.] = prec 2.

1547 in *Vicary's Anat.* (1888) App. ii. 117 Item to Misteris levyn Terling, Paintrix, x li. **1762** H. WALPOLE *Vertue's Anecd. Paint.* v. Wks. 1798 III. 90.

†**'paintry.** *Obs.* Also 6 -tre. [ad. obs. F. *peintrie* (15th c. in Godef.): see -RY.] The action or product of painting; also *fig.*

1511 *Acc. Ld. High Treas. Scot.* IV. 296 For certane colouris [etc.] boght be him for the paintre of the Kingis gret schip. **1533** GAU *Richt Vay* 16 Ymagis or payntre. **1573** G. HARVEY *Letter-bk.* (Camden) 103 No bombast or paintry to helpe deformity. **1653** MANTON *Exp. James* i. 11 When.. you walk in a garden or field..think thus with yourselves: Here is a goodly show and paintry.

†**painture.** *Obs.* Forms: 3–8 **pein-**, 4–5 **peyn-**, 5 **paynture**, **-toure**, 5–8 **painture.** [ME. a. OF. *peinture, painture* (11th c. in Godef.) = Pr., Sp., It. *pintura* (beside Pr. *pictura*, It. *pittura*):—late L. **pinctūra* for *pictūra* painting, f. *pingĕre, pict-, pinct-* to paint: see -URE. *Painture* is thus ult. a doublet of PICTURE.]

1. The action or art of painting, or depicting objects in colours; style of painting. Also *fig.*

c **1386** CHAUCER *Doctor's T.* 33 With swich peynture She peynted hath this noble creature. **1398** TREVISA *Barth. De P.R.* XIX. xxxvii. (1495) 879 The Egypciens fonde fyrst paynture. **1593** G. HARVEY *Pierce's Super.* Wks. (Grosart) II. 118 The next peece, not of his Rhetorique, or Poetry, but of his Painture. **1668** DRYDEN *Ess. Dram. Poesy* 59 Shall that excuse the ill Painture or designment of them? *a* **1718** PENN *Tracts* Wks. 1726 I. 482 The primitive Christians abhorred Painture. [**1846** LANDOR *Wks.* (1876) IV. 226 We have suffered to drop away from us the beautiful and commodious word..painture.]

2. That which is painted; painting, pictorial work; a painting, picture.

a 1225 *Ancr. R.* 242 Al nis bute ase a scheadewe—al nis bute ase a peinture. 1382 WYCLIF *1 Chron.* vi. 29 He made in hem cherubyn, and palmes, and dyuerse peynturis. *c* 1400 MAUNDEV. (Roxb.) viii. 29 To fordo þe paynture and þe ymages þat ware purtraid on þe walles. 1496 *Dives & Paup.* I. iii. 34/2 The lewde man sholde use his bookes, that is ymagery and paynture. *a* 1533 LD. BERNERS *Gold. Bk. M. Aurel.* (1546) Y ij b, The whiche paintures were sayed to bee of the handy warke of the expert Appelles. 1668 DRYDEN *Ess. Dram. Poesy* 69 The shadowings of Painture.. being to cause the rounding of it.

3. A substance used in painting; a paint, pigment.

1387 TREVISA *Higden* (Rolls) I. 387 þey wolde..make.. dyuers figures..and peynte hym wiþ ynke oþer wiþ oþir peynture and colour. *c* 1449 PECOCK *Repr.* II. ix. 193 Graued and ourned with gold and othere gay peinturis. 1620 THOMAS *Lat. Dict.*, *Atramentum*... Inke, blacke painture.

painty (ˈpeɪntɪ), *a.* [f. PAINT *sb.* + -Y.]

1. Of, belonging to, or abounding in paint.

1873 W. MORRIS in Mackail *Life* (1899) I. 292 The big room is bare and painty. 1891 C. JAMES *Rom. Rigmarole* 181 Do you mind this painty smell?

2. Of a picture: Overcharged with paint; having the paint too obtrusive.

1870 *Athenæum* 21 May 680 Being rather opaque, not to say painty, in some of its less important parts. 1884 *Ch. Times* 410/1 A telling landscape, too painty, but the composition is good.

pain-worthy: see PAINSWORTHY.

painy, painym: see PAYENY, PAYNIM.

† **paiocke.** [Known only in the passage cited. It has been variously viewed by editors as a misprint for *pacocke*, *pecocke*, or other obs. form of PEACOCK, or as some dialect form of that word, or as being the older spelling (with *i* for *j*) of *pajock*, for an alleged northern Sc. *pea-jock* = peacock. Various other conjectures have been offered.

The spelling *peacock* or *peacocke* is found in the First Folio in the 5 other places where the word occurs, and there seems no reason why Hamlet should here use a stray dialect word. The context suggests that Hamlet was going to say 'A very, very Ass', but checked himself at the last word and substituted this.]

1602 SHAKS. *Ham.* III. ii. 295 *Ham.* For thou dost know: Oh Damon deere, This Realme dismantled was of Ioue himselfe, And now reignes heere, A verie verie Paiocke. *Hora.* You might haue Rim'd. [Pope reads: For thou dost know, O Damon dear, This realm dismantled was Of Jove himself; and now reigns here A very very—peacock.] [Hence 1899 *Blackw. Mag.* Feb. 354/1 We think of Beau Brummell rather as a 'very, very pajock' than a man of bones and sinews.]

paip, pape (peːp). *Sc.* Also pep (Jam.). [var. of PIP.] The stone of a cherry, sloe, plum, or other stone fruit; an orange pip, etc. ***the paips***, a game played by schoolboys with cherry-stones.

1721 KELLY *Sc. Prov.* 2 A Head full of Hair, a Kirkle full of Hips, and a Briest full of Papes, are three sure Marks of a Daw. 1808–25 JAMIESON, *Paip*, a cherry-stone... Three of these stones are placed together, and another above them. These are called a castle. The player takes aim with a cherry-stone, and when he overturns this castle, he claims the spoil. [But in some districts the missile is a large flat metal button, a bit of slate, or a marble.] 1821 *Blackw. Mag.* IX. 401 *note*, *Papes* are cherry-stones, which are collected with care by the boys, and furnish them with numberless sources of amusement. 1885 SIR R. CHRISTISON *Autobiog.* I. ii. 33 Cherry trees in my young days were robbed as much for the papes as for the cherries.

paip, paiply, Sc. ff. POPE, POPELY.

pair (pɛə(r)), *sb.*[1] Forms: 3–5 peire, peyre, 4–7 paire, payre, (4–5 (9) pare), 4–6 payr, 5 peyr, (peyer, payir, 5–6 par, payer, 6 paier, parre, pere), 4– pair. [ME. a. F. *paire*:—L. *paria*, pl. neut. of *pār*, *pāri-* equal, taken as sing. fem. Cf. L. *pār* sing. neut. (more than 50 examples in *Durham Acc. Rolls*, Surtees), It. †*par*, *paio*, Sp., Pg. *par*, OF. *par*, *pair*; also Ger., Du. *paar* (OHG., MHG. *pār*), Da., Sw., Icel. *pār*; the form *par*, *pare*, was in use also in ME.; *pair*, *payr*, without final *-e*, is occasional in 14–15th c.

Pair is now followed by *of*, as in 'a pair of gloves'; but *of* was formerly omitted, as 'a pair gloves': cf. Ger. *ein paar handschuhe*. After a numeral *pair* was formerly used in the sing. form; 'three pair (of) shoes' = Ger. *drei paar schuhe*; this is still retained colloquially, and in certain connexions; but the tendency is now to say 'three pairs'.]

I. Two associated together; a set of two.

1. a. Two separate things of a kind that are associated or coupled in use, usually corresponding to each other as right and left (less frequently as upper and under). Such are things worn on or adapted to the right and left limbs or sides of the body, as 'a pair of gloves, leggings, shoes, stockings, spurs, stirrups, fetters, sculls', etc.; also (*colloq.* and somewhat *humorously*) the two bodily members themselves, as 'a pair of eyes, ears, lips, jaws, arms, hands, heels, legs, wings', etc.; also, other things used side by side, as 'a pair of folding doors, curtains', etc.

[1278 in *Durham Acc. Rolls* (Surtees) 487 In 2 paribus arsuns.] *c* 1290 *Beket* 20 in *S. Eng. Leg.* I. 107 Ake euere he hadde ane peire feteres faste him up-on. 1375 BARBOUR *Bruce* XIII. 463 Seven hundreth paris of spuris rede War tane of knychtis that war dede. 1377 LANGL. *P. Pl.* B. v. 256 And haue ymade many a knyȝte bothe mercere & drapere, þat payed neuere for his prentishode nouȝte a peire gloues. *c* 1386 CHAUCER *Wife's Prol.* 597 He hadde a paire Of legges and of feet so clene & faire. 1398 TREVISA *Barth. De P.R.* v. xx. (Bodl. MS.) lf. 10 b/2 Somme [teeth] bene pares twey ouer and tweyne neþir. 1478 W. PASTON jr. in *P. Lett.* III. 237 Ij. schyrtes, and a peyer of sclyppers. 1579 *Nottingham Rec.* IV. 184 A pere of shows for the neytar boye. 1647 WARD *Simp. Cobler* 75 Truth [doth] best, when it is spoken out, through a paire of open lips. 1678 BUTLER *Hud.* III. i. 791 Our Noblest Senses act by Pairs, Two Eyes to see, to hear two Ears. 1712 BUDGELL *Spect.* No. 425 ¶1 Thro' a Pair of Iron Gates. 1865 DICKENS *Mut. Fr.* I. i, The girl rowed, pulling a pair of sculls very easily.

b. Hence various colloquial or familiar locutions:

pair of hands, a man; ***to take*** or ***show a clean*** or ***fair pair of heels***: see CLEAN *a.* 3 g, FAIR *a.* 8 d; ***pair of lawn sleeves***, a bishop; ***pair of oars***: see OAR *sb.* 3 a; ***another*** or ***a different pair of shoes*** or ***boots***, a different matter; ***pair of wheels***, a two-wheeled vehicle.

1598 FLORIO s.v. *Trasti della barca*, As we saie the cushions in a paire of oares. 1623 COCKERAM I. s.v. *Fenchmonth*, Which fee, for a paire of Wheeles is foure pence, and for Paniers two pence. 1630 *R. Johnson's Kingd. & Commw.* 592 Her enemies brought ten hundred thousand paire of hands to pull downe the wals of Ierusalem. 1844 MACAULAY *Ess.*, *Earl of Chatham* (1887) 817 At every levee, appeared eighteen or twenty pair of lawn sleeves. 1849 T. ARNOLD *Let.* 28 Aug. in *N.Z. Lett.* (1966) 135 Nothing is easier than to make a beautiful scheme of education on paper, but to make it work is 'quite another pair of shoes', as they say in New Zealand. 1859 THACKERAY *Virginians* II. xvi. 130 If Mr. George had been in the army, that..would have been another pair of boots. 1865 DICKENS *Mut. Fr.* I. xv, 'That, sir', replied Mr. Wegg,..'is quite another pair of shoes'. 1931 G. B. SHAW *Widowers' Houses* III. 58 in *Works*, Dooty's another pair o' shoes. 1936 W. H. S. SMITH *Let.* 9 Aug. in *Young Man's Country* (1977) ii. 22 I've now had a good opportunity to get to know Hill... We haven't got many tastes in common, but I like him. Doha is a very different pair of shoes.

2. a. In the names of single articles of clothing, instruments, or tools, composed of two corresponding parts, which are not used separately, and consequently are named only in the plural: e.g. 'a pair of breeches, trousers, or stays; a pair of scissors, tongs, bellows, compasses, spectacles, balances, stocks'.

1297 R. GLOUC. (Rolls) 8013 Amorewe uor to werie a peire of hosen [*v.r.* a peyre hose] of say. 1390 GOWER *Conf.* II. 318 Out he clippeth also faste Hire tunge with a peire scheres. *c* 1425 *Eng. Voc.* in Wr.-Wülcker 657/16 *Hic cucigna*, A[e] pare belows. 1530 PALSGR. 182 Suche instrumentes or toles as we in our tong use to name by payres..a payre of bellows, a payre of stockes, a payre of spectacles. 1563 SHUTE *Archit.* D j b, Take a paire of compasses and set the one poincte of the compasses..vpon ye line vnder the Abacus. 1671 LADY M. BERTIE in *12th Rep. Hist. MSS. Comm.* App. v. 23 She was so ill with wearing a paire of perfumed bodyes that she was forced to goe to bed. 1784 COOK *3rd Voy.* II. vii. 351 Our new visitor had on a pair of green cloth breeches. 1870 DICKENS *E. Drood* ii, Two pairs of nut-crackers.

b. *Cricket.* = *a pair of spectacles* s.v. SPECTACLE *sb.*[1] 7 c.

1862 *Bell's Life in London* 29 June 7/5 Obtained that unenviable score, 'a pair'. 1960 *Times* 22 June 5/3 Willett and Gibson each completed a perfunctory 'pair'. 1974 *Daily Tel.* 12 June 34/1 Engineer, looking to save his pair, would have been run out first ball if Amiss's throw..had hit the stumps. 1977 *Sunday Times* 27 Feb. 29/7, I wouldn't swop that 'pair' for anything. It taught me much of life and cricket.

3. Two persons or animals of opposite sexes.

a. A man and woman united by love or marriage; an engaged or married couple. ***happy pair***: see HAPPY *a.* 3.

1377 LANGL. *P. Pl.* B. IX. 164 Many a peire sithen the pestilence, Han plight hem togideres. 1590 SPENSER *F.Q.* III. x. 16 A wanton payre Of lovers loosely knit. 1590 SHAKS. *Mids. N.* IV. i. 96 There shall the paires of faithfull Louers be Wedded, with Theseus, all in iollity. 1667 MILTON *P.L.* IV. 534 Live while ye may, Yet happie pair. 1727–46 THOMSON *Summer* 1172 Young Celadon And his Amelia were a matchless pair. 1807 CRABBE *Par. Reg.* II. 105 Next at our altar stood a luckless pair. 1869 A. B. EDWARDS *Debenham's Vow* lxiii, The newly-married pair were installed in a compartment by themselves.

b. Two partners in a dance.

1770 GOLDSM. *Des. Vill.* 25 The dancing pair that simply sought renown By holding out to tire each other down. 1781 COWPER *Hope* 13–14 As in a dance the pair that take the lead Turn downward, and the lowest pair succeed. 1844 DICKENS *Christmas Carol* ii, Three or four and twenty pair of partners;..people who would dance.

c. A mated couple of animals.

13.. *E.E. Allit. P.* B. 335 Of vche horwed, in ark halde bot a payre. ?*a* 1366 CHAUCER *Rom. Rose* 107 The smale foules .. They peyned hem, ful many a peyre, To synge on bowes blosmed feyre. 1567 MAPLET *Gr. Forest* 6 b, There is a paire of them, Male and Female. 1795 COWPER *Pairing Time* 44 All pair'd, and each pair built a nest. 1838 *Encycl. Brit.* (ed. 7) XVI. 733/1 They [eagles] not only pair, but continue in pairs all the year round; and the same pair procreates year after year.

4. a. A set of two; two individuals (persons, animals, or things) of the same kind taken together; esp. when associated in function, purpose, or position; a couple, brace, span. Sometimes said of two objects of different kind when intimately associated and viewed as a group. ***to be a pair***: of persons, to be two of a kind, to be as bad as one another (*colloq.*)

a 1300 *Floriz & Bl.* 566 Swiche him serueþ a day so faire Amoreȝe moste anoþer peire. 1418 *E.E. Wills* (1882) 32, ij peire of my best shetes. *c* 1430 LYDG. *Min. Poems* (Percy Soc.) 236 [He] Took out of helle soulys many a peyre. *c* 1430 —— *Reas. & Sens.* 218. *c* 1470 HENRY *Wallace* VII. 225 Vpon the bawk thai hangit mony par. 1486 *Bk. St. Albans* F vj, A Couple or a payer of botillis. 1575 LANEHAM *Let.* (1871) 8 A payree of great whyte syluer lyuery Pots for wyne. 1638–9 in Swayne *Sarum Churchw. Acc.* (1896) 210 Paire of Sawyers for 29 dayes. *a* 1703 BURKITT *On N.T.* Mark vi. 13 The Jesuits send forth their emissaries by pairs. 1776 WITHERING *Brit. Plants* (1796) III. 639 [*Vicia lutea*] Flowers sometimes in pairs. 1800 WORDSW. *Pet Lamb* 14, I watched them with delight, they [maiden and lamb] were a lovely pair. 1840 THACKERAY in *Fraser's Mag.* Jan. 107/2 'I' faith, I believe you're a pair,' said Mr. Wood. 'Pray, sir, keep your tongue to yourself..' cried Mrs. Catherine, with proper spirit. 1856 WHYTE MELVILLE *Kate Cov.* xii, The pair [horse and rider] looked what the gentlemen call 'all over like going'. 1873 PROCTOR *Elem. Astron.* xiii. 121 The stars of the pair are seen to circle round each other. The very fact that they so circle shows not only that they form a real pair, but that they attract each other. 1914 G. B. SHAW *Fanny's First Play* I. 178 Dora: We both get a bit giddy when we're lighthearted. Him and me is a pair, I'm afraid. 1931 M. ALLINGHAM *Police at Funeral* v. 69 She was a damned bad-tempered old harpy! And so was Andrew—they were a pair. 1967 J. ROSENBERG *Double Darkness* I. i. 46 It's only her own respectability she thinks of. Like you. You're a pair. 1976 'D. FLETCHER' *Don't whistle 'Macbeth'* 86 It's a creepy feeling... Aren't we a pair? Come on. Let's go back and cheer ourselves up.

b. Short for ***pair of horses***, two horses harnessed and running together.

1727 FIELDING *Love in Sev. Masques* v. xiii, Six Flanders mares the former drives, The latter but a pair. 1782 COWPER *Gilpin* 12 All in a chaise and pair. 1863 *Chambers's Bk. Days* I. 554/2 Who would dare to call two horses anything but a pair when they are harnessed to a carriage, though they may be two in any other situation? 1866 MRS. RIDDELL *Race for Wealth* xxiii, Let..Mrs. Robinson drive out with a pair.

c. In Parliamentary language, two voters on opposite sides who mutually agree to abstain from voting in order to be absent from a division without affecting the relative position of parties. Also, such an agreement between opposite sides.

1819 C. ARBUTHNOT *Let.* 14 Mar (1941) 16 It is expected of them all to be there during the whole course of every evening, & that the coming down merely to get a pair will not do. 1845 DISRAELI *Sybil* IV. i, 'We want a brace of pairs', said Lord Milford. 'Will you two fellows pair?' 1889 *Daily News* 5 Apr. 4/7 The actual majority, however, would have been the same in any case—a pair is a pair; one for, one against. 1894 *Ibid.* 11 May 5/2 Sir John Gorst..was originally paired with Mr. Robertson,..the pair being 'off', Sir John Gorst was available for pairing with the Home Secretary. A still later arrangement shifted the pair to another member of the Opposition, leaving Sir John Gorst free to vote. 1965 *New Statesman* 19 Mar. 426/2 One minister..was flatly refused a pair by his Tory opposite number. 1976 *Southern Even. Echo* (Southampton) 18 Nov. 3/4 Sir Harold had to cancel a flight to Geneva at the last minute because, he claimed, the Tories changed their minds about providing him with a pair in the Commons division.

d. Short for 'pair of oars': see OAR *sb.* 3 a, b.

1885 *Whitaker's Alm.* 400/1 The two old Oxonians, Lowndes and D. E. Brown, were undoubtedly the best pair. 1890 *Ibid.* 590/2 Looker and Clark of the Thames won the Senior Pairs.

e. In other connexions: e.g.

pair of cards, two of the same value (see also 6); ***pair of colours***, two flags belonging to a regiment, one the royal, the other the regimental flag; hence, the position or commission of an ensign; cf. COLOUR 7 c; ***pair of dice***, a set of two; ***pair of indentures***, ***knives***, etc.: see these words.

c 1386 CHAUCER *Pard. T.* 295 The kyng..Sente him a paire of dees of gold in scorn. 1680 COTTON *Compl. Gamester* in Singer *Hist. Cards* (1816) 348 A pair is a pair of any two, as two kings, two queens, &c. 1745 SWIFT *Direct. Servants, Footman*, From wearing a livery, you may soon probably carry a pair of colours. 1747–1871 [see COLOUR *sb.* 7 c]. 1870 HARDY & WARE *Mod. Hoyle* 80 (Cribbage) If the adversary were then to play another five, he would..score two for the pair.

f. *Mech.* Two mechanical elements that together constitute a kinematic pair (see KINEMATIC *a.* b).

1876 A. B. W. KENNEDY tr. *Reuleaux's Kinematics of Machinery* i. 43 The kinematic elements of a machine are not employed singly, but always in pairs; or in other words,.. the machine cannot so well be said to consist of elements as of pairs of elements. *Ibid.*, If a kinematic pair of elements be given, a definite motion can be obtained by means of them if one of the two be held fast or fixed in position. *Ibid.* xiii. 549 If we put a normal or normally crossed pair in place of one of the parallel pairs we obtain a chain which is constrained, and which contains five cylinder pairs. 1905 SMITH & MARX *Machine Design* i. 13 The helical surfaces by which a nut and screw engage with each other are called a twisting pair. 1969 G. D. REDFORD et al. *Mech. Technol.* ii. 24 Two links which interact directly with, and mutually constrain, each other form a kinematic pair. *Ibid.*, Shafts in plain bearings, pin-jointed links, slide bars and slide blocks, screw and nut assemblies are all forms of lower pairs. 1975 MABIE & OCVIRK *Mechanisms & Dynamics of Machinery* (ed. 3) i. 9 A pair that permits only relative rotation is a revolute or turning pair, and one that allows only sliding is a sliding pair.

g. In basket-making (see quots. 1910 and 1912).

1897 A. FIRTH *Cane Basket Work* vi. 42 Take No. 3 [spoke]..bringing it down beside No. 1 and behind No. 4.., making one 'pair' of ends turned down. The canes forming these 'pairs' must each in turn be kept side by side..and held perfectly flat under the thumb till the next 'pair' is down. **1904** O. T. MASON *Indian Basketry* I. iii. 94 *Two-rod foundation.*—One rod in this style lies on top of the other; the stitches pass over two rods in progress and under the upper one of the pair below, so that each stitch incloses three stems in a vertical series... The alternate rod, or the upper rod, in each pair will be inclosed in two series of stitches. **1910** *Encycl. Brit.* III. 482/2 The 'pair', two rods worked alternately one over the other, used for filling up bottoms and covers of round and oval baskets. **1912** T. OKEY *Introd. Basket-Making* 153 *Pair*, two rods of willow or cane worked alternately over and under each other—the reverse of a fitch. **1953** [see FITCH *sb.*[3]].

h. Ellipt. for 'a pair of breasts'.

1922 JOYCE *Ulysses* 231 Hell's delights! She has a fine pair. **1973** M. AMIS *Rachel Papers* 174 'Who was that tart you had round here before?' 'Gloria?' 'Yeah. Tell you what, she's got a right pair on her.'

5. Sometimes a mere synonym for *two*, and formerly used loosely for a few, two or three. Now mostly superseded in this use by *a couple*.

1599 MASSINGER, etc. *Old Law* II. ii, What is't to bide A little hardness for a pair of years, or so? **1611** SPEED *Hist. Gt. Brit.* IX. xii. (1623) 704 Fewer by a pair of thousands. **1629** SHIRLEY *Wedding* I, I may be compeld within A pair of minutes to turn ashes. **1630** B. JONSON *New Inn* II. ii, To entertain you for a pair of hours. **1837** LANDOR *Pentameron, 5th Day's Interview* Wks. 1853 II. 348/2 Your mention of eggs..has induced me to fancy I could eat a pair of them.

II. A set, not limited to two.

6. a. A set of separate things or parts forming a collective whole; e.g. a set (of gallows, harness, numbles, etc.); a suit (of armour); a string (of beads); a pack (of cards); a complex musical instrument, as 'a pair of organs, clavichords, virginals, bagpipes'; a chest (of drawers). ***a pair of arrows***, a set of three arrows (*Cent. Dict.* 1890). All *Obs.*, or only *dial.* (But see b, c.)

13.. *Cursor M.* 7896 (Cott.) þe king a pair o letters [*v.rr.* a letter, lettres] writte Did, and gaf him-self to ber. **1340** *Ayenb.* 258 þet on wyfman ssel habbe uor hare body ine one yere zuo uele payre of robes. **1377–1697** Peyre bedes, pare of bedes, etc. [see BEAD *sb.* 2]. *c* **1386** CHAUCER *Knt.'s T.* 1263 And somme woln haue a paire plates large. **1426** *Paston Lett.* I. 12 Certeyns maffaisours..the seyd John Grys..by the space of a myle to a payre galwes ledden. **1493** in Chappell *Pop. Mus.* (1879) I. 49 Delivered to a merchaunt for a pair of Organnes 30£. **1513** DOUGLAS *Æneis* VII. iv. 74 Apoune the postis also mony ane payr Off harnes hang. **1530** PALSGR. 182 *Vnes cartes*, a payre of cardes to playe with. **1558** *Will of Hinton* (Somerset Ho.), A paier of virginalls. **1632** LITHGOW *Trav.* VI. 285 Fourty paire of Chaplets. **1656** EARL MONM. tr. *Boccalini's Advts. fr. Parnass.* I. ii. (1674) 3 A pair of Cards, which the Serjeants..found in his pocket. **1706** E. WARD *Wooden World Diss.* (1708) 62 He's as proud of these, as a High-lander is of a Pair of Bag-pipes. **1825** JAMIESON s.v., 'A pair o' Carritches', a catechism; 'a pair o' Proverbs', a copy of the Proverbs, used as a school-book; 'a pair o' pullisees', a complete tackle of pullies, etc. **1852** THACKERAY *Esmond* III. vii, We had a pair of beautiful old organs in Castlewood Church. **1853** CARLETON *Traits & Stories* (1860) I. 263 A thin, sallow little man, with a pair of beads, as long as himself. **1880** J. H. SHORTHOUSE *John Inglesant* xx. 267 You remind me of some of the rich oratories I have seen ..; where everything is beautiful and costly, but where a classic statue of Apollo stands by the side of a crucifix, a Venus with Our Lady, a Cupid near St. Michael, and a pair of beads hanging on Mercury's Caduceus. **1894** *Northumbld. Gloss.* s.v. *Pair*, 'A pair (= chest) of drawers.' 'A pair of cards'... 'A pair o' pipes'... All these terms are in common general use. **1930** *Amer. Speech* V. 427 A necklace is sometimes called a *pair o' beads* in the Ozarks. **1962** A. JOBSON *Window in Suffolk* vi. 102 She would refer to a necklace as a pair of beads. **1976** *Publ. Amer. Dial. Soc. 1973* LX. 16 One informant called it [*sc.* a string of beads] *a pair of beads*.

b. ***pair of stairs***: a flight of stairs. Often used as equivalent to *floor* or *storey*, as ***two pair of stairs***, or shortly, ***two pair***, the second floor or storey. Also *attrib.*, as in ***a one*** (or ***two***) ***pair*** (***of stairs***) ***lodging***, ***room***, ***window***, etc.

1530 PALSGR. 182 *Vngz degrez*, a payre of stayres. **1628** EARLE *Microcosm.*, *Tauerne* (Arb.) 33 A Tauerne Is a degree, or (if you will) a paire of stayres aboue an Alehouse. **1662** J. STRYPE in *Lett. Lit. Men* (Camden) 178 One [Chamber], which is a very handsome one, and one pair of stairs high. **1710** *Lond. Gaz.* No. 4668/4 Numb. 5. in Brick Court in the Middle Temple Lane, two pair of Stairs, on the Right-hand. **1749** FIELDING *Tom Jones* XIV. vi, That Nightingale should procure him either the Ground Floor, or the two Pair of Stairs. **1761** MRS. F. SHERIDAN *Sidney Bidulph* III. 127 Working for my bread in a two pair of stairs room. **1836** DICKENS *Let. c* 24 Aug. (1965) I. 170 His notion of the Bedroom is rather more derived,..from his own fourth pair back. **1844** —— *Mart. Chuz.* ii, Mr. Pecksniff..turned him loose in a spacious room on the two-pair front. **1853** CLOUGH in *Longfellow's Life* (1891) II. 257, I stay in there, up two pair,..from eleven to five daily. **1922** JOYCE *Ulysses* 316 And who was he, tell us? A nobody, two pair back and passages, at seven shillings a week.

c. ***pair of steps***: a flight of steps; also, a portable set of steps used in a library, etc.

1755 in Picton *L'pool Munic. Rec.* (1886) II. 155 A breast wall and pair of steps from the shore or road up to the Ladies' Walk. **1761** COLMAN *Genius* No. 2. in *Prose Sev. Occas.* (1787) I. 25, I could as easily have scaled the monument, as have come at the tip of her chin without the help of a pair of steps. **1884** W. ALDIS WRIGHT *Bible Word-bk.* (ed. 2) s.v., We still speak of a 'pair' of steps or stairs.

7. (Also written *pare.*) A company of miners working together (Cornwall, America); a team of mules carrying tin.

1846 J. TRENOODLE *Spec. Dial.* 26 (E.D.D.) Ef Franky's peere wornt drunk. **1855** J. R. LEIFCHILD *Cornwall* 146 Though the takers or one pitch vary from two to twelve in number... This partnership is termed a pair of men, whatever the number may really be. **1871** *Trans. Amer. Inst. Mining Eng.* I. 202 One 'pair' (two or more men working in common) may be losing money. **1882** *W. Cornw. Gloss.*, *Pair of moyles* (mules), usually about thirty, for carrying tin. **1883** *Standard* 28 Sept. 3/6 (Cornwall) A 'pare' of ten men were working at a night shift underground.

8. In roulette (with pronunc. pɛr), an even number, or a number marked 'pair'.

1850, etc. [see NOIR 2 a]. **1902** [see IMPAIR *sb.*[2]]. **1953**, **1969** [see MANQUE]. **1973** [see IMPAIR *sb.*[2]].

III. 9. *attrib.* and *Comb.*: **pair-bond**, the relationship formed during the courtship and mating of a pair of animals or two people; so **pair-bonding** *vbl. sb.*, the formation of such a relationship or the patterns of behaviour that help to establish it; **pair case** (see quot.); **pair-feed** *v. trans.*, to feed two groups of (experimental animals) with a diet identical except for the item whose effects are being tested on one group; so **pair-fed** *ppl. a.*; **pair-formation**, the pairing of animals, esp. birds, in preparation for breeding; **pair-light**, a window of two lights (LIGHT *sb.* 10); **pair-mate** *v. trans.*, to test the sexual compatibility of (experimental animals) by allowing mating within and between each of two groups; also, to control the mating of (experimental animals) so that each male mates with only one female, or vice versa; so **pair-mating** *vbl. sb.*; **pair production** *Nuclear Physics*, the conversion of a gamma-ray photon into an electron and a positron.**pair-skating**, skating performed by pairs; **pair-toed** *a. Ornith.*, having the toes in pairs, two before and two behind.

[**1939** G. K. NOBLE in *Auk* LVI. 265 If pairs of birds or fishes are to form a bond between themselves they must develop behavior different from the feeding or locomotion of non-breeding members of the group.] **1940** D. LACK in *Condor* XLII. 282 In some species of birds, the sexes..form a very temporary *pair-bond. **1954** *Behaviour* VI. 279 The intruder male [*sc.* a zebra finch] succeeded in breaking the old pair-bond, won the female over, built her a new nest, and began a fresh cycle with her. **1963** *Listener* 31 Jan. 204/1 The two [*sc.* gannets] perform an elaborate mutual display which is concerned with strengthening the pair bond. *Ibid.* 204/2 The length and intensity of this display is greatest when the pair bond is weakest, that is, when the couple are newly mated. **1969** *Times* 11 Apr. 12/6 The..tree sparrow, a species in which the pair bond is usually strong. **1970** J. KEAR in J. H. Crook *Social Behaviour in Birds & Mammals* 358 The pair bond and its stability is obviously of great consequence to parental behaviour. **1974** *Country Life* 7 Mar. 491/1 In few mammals is the pair bond so strong;..a [beaver] couple may remain paired for up to 18 years. **1977** D. MORRIS *Manwatching* 88 A sign of old friendships or pair-bonds is that two people can sit together in a peaceful silence without feeling the need to keep up a stream of cheerful chatter. **1965** *New Scientist* 17 June 768/1 *Pair-bonding..is the ornithologist's in-phrase for procreative conjunction between sexually ardent cocks and hens. **1967** D. MORRIS *Naked Ape* ii. 62 The pair-bonding mechanism in our species [*sc. Homo sapiens*], although very powerful, is far from perfect. **1978** *Listener* 12 Jan. 35/2 The interplanetary visitor..would quickly conceptualise pair-bonding in what we call marriage. **1884** F. J. BRITTEN *Watch & Clockm.* 183 [The] *Pair Case [was] the old style of casing watches with an inner watch case containing the movement and an outer case quite detached from the inner. **1972** *Science* 19 May 795/1 Rat litter-mates were *pair-fed nutritionally adequate liquid diets. *Ibid.*, The animals fed alcohol had 72 percent more hydroxyproline in hepatic protein than did pair-fed controls. **1974** *Nature* 4 Jan. 48/2 Hamsters were made vitamin A deficient by maintenance on a vitamin A deficient diet starting at day 10–14 after birth; controls were pair-fed with the same diet supplemented with vitamin A... Tracheas were removed from the vitamin A deficient and pair-fed control hamsters. **1940** D. LACK in *Condor* XLII. 269 There is probably more ignorance concerning *pair-formation than there is of any other aspect of bird behavior. **1950** *Brit. Birds* XLIII. 392 Pair-formation [of marsh-tits] takes place at all times of the year. **1967** A. MANNING *Introd. Animal Behaviour* v. 105 In some birds the female becomes dominant after pair formation. **1970** J. KEAR in J. H. Crook *Social Behaviour in Birds & Mammals* 358 Pair-formation itself is influenced by plumage changes, display and maturity. **1971** J. Z. YOUNG *Introd. Study Man* xxxiv. 484 Apparently in baboons and even chimpanzees and gorillas there is no long-lasting pair formation. **1868** G. M. HOPKINS *Jrnls. & Papers* (1959) 183 It [*sc.* a tower] is pierced with *pair-lights first, higher with a triplet. **1944** *Genetics* XXIX. 526 One hundred and six Azusa wild males [*sc.* fruit-flies] were *pair-mated to standard grade 20 Wooster bobbed females. *Ibid.* 529 Two genes were tested by each pair-mating. **1968** R. RIEGER et al. *Gloss. Genetics & Cytogenetics* 327 *Pair mating*, a procedure used to determine the degree of sexual isolation between two groups (A and B) of individuals. Separate tests of mating success are made for the four possible mating combinations. **1934** *Physical Rev.* XLV. 137/1 For energies above twenty million volts the predicted *pair production is even greater than that computed by Oppenheimer and Plesset. **1958** W. K. MANSFIELD *Elem. Nucl. Physics* v. 43 The three methods of interaction of γ-rays with matter are Compton scattering, photo-electric absorption and pair production. **1973** L. J. TASSIE *Physics Elem. Particles* ii. 9 Electron-positron pair production has a threshold of 1·022 MeV. Pair production cannot occur in free space, because the conversion of a photon into a pair cannot conserve both total energy and momentum... Some other particle must be present. **1902** *Daily Chron.* 14 Feb. 4/7 To this event succeeded the *pair-skating competition. **1868** *Proc. Zool. Soc.* 316 A few Cuckoos represent the *Pair-toed Coccygomorphæ.

†**pair**, *sb.*[2] *Obs. rare*[−1]. [f. PAIR *v.*[2]; but the text is doubtful.] Impairment, abatement.

c **1375** *Cursor M.* 7382 (Fairf.) Iesse welcomed him ful faire Samuel him talde wiþ outen payre.

pair (pɛə(r)), *v.*[1] [f. PAIR *sb.*[1]]

1. a. *trans.* To make a pair by matching (two persons or things or one with another); to place together as adapted or suited to each other; to provide with a 'fellow' so as to make a pair.

1613 SIR E. SACKVILLE in *Guardian* No. 133 My lord.. had not paired the sword I sent him to Paris; bringing one of the same length, but twice as broad. **1695** WOODWARD *Nat. Hist. Earth* I. (1723) 26, I can pair, with Sea-Shells, several of these Fossil ones. **1849** BRYANT *Innoc. Child*, Innocent child and snow-white flower! Well are ye pair'd in your opening hour. **1855** MACAULAY *Hist. Eng.* xii. III. 231 The French ambassador and the French general were well paired.

†**b.** To be a match for; to match, equal. *Obs.*

1603 DRAYTON *Odes* xvi. 8 That Shee which I adore, Which scarce Goodnesse selfe can payre.

2. *intr.* To 'go' *with*, so as to match.

1611 SHAKS. *Wint. T.* v. i. 116 Had our Prince..seene this houre, he had payr'd Well with this Lord; there was not full a moneth Between their births. **1756** HOME *Douglas* II. i. 24 He might have..pair'd with him in features and in shape. **1879** E. GARRETT *House by Works* I. 52 There was no other figure which could pair with Barbara's.

3. a. *trans.* To arrange (two persons or things) in a pair or couple; to associate or bring together as mates or antagonists; ***to pair off*** (a number of persons or things), to put two by two or in pairs.

1607 BEAUM. & FL. *Woman-Hater* IV. ii, Virtue and grace are always paired together. **1706** E. WARD *Wooden World Diss.* (1708) 24 Thus these two [Captain and Lieutenant] are generally pair'd like marry'd Couples. **1711** STEELE *Spect.* No. 113 ¶4, I made new Liveries, new-pair'd my Coach-Horses. **1881** TYLOR *Anthropol.* ix. 223 Each warrior is paired with an opponent.

b. To arrange in couples of opposite sexes, as for dancing, dinner, etc.; *esp.* to unite in love or marriage; to mate (animals). Also *absol.*

1673 DRYDEN *2nd Pt. Conq. Granada* III. iii, Ye gods, why are not hearts first paired above? **1702** POPE *Sappho* 44 Turtles and doves of diff'ring hues unite, And glossy jett is pair'd with shining white. **1828** SCOTT *F.M. Perth* xxix, It is only whilst the timid stag is paired with the doe, that he is desperate and dangerous. **1841** E. C. GREY *Little Wife* II. vii. 61 If you go on pairing and matching in this manner.. you will be the terror of the whole of the male species. **1895** MARIE CORELLI *Sorrows Satan* xi, The Earl proceeded to 'pair' us all. 'Prince, you will take Miss Fitzroy,—Mr. Tempest, my daughter falls to your escort'.

c. In the British Parliament and other legislative bodies: to bring (an opponent) into an agreement to abstain from voting on a given question or for a certain time.

1956 ABRAHAM & HAWTREY *Parl. Dict.* 127 If a member wishes to be absent from the House, he may arrange with a member of the opposite party, who also wishes to be absent, that neither shall attend the House, or at least vote in a division, for an agreed time. They are then said to be 'paired'. **1968** W. SAFIRE *New Lang. Politics* 315/2 When supporters of John F. Kennedy explained that their candidate was seriously ill at the time of the McCarthy censure, liberal Democrats refused to accept the excuse because, they argued, 'the Senator could have been paired against McCarthy'. **1973** *Courier & Advertiser* (Dundee) 21 Feb. 11/3 Mr Teddy Taylor (Cathcart), who did not vote, as he was 'paired' with Mr Ronald King Murray (Leith), said, 'It is a victory for the people.' **1974** *Times* 18 Mar. 2/8 The Conservatives have said that they will only pair sick MPs with sick MPs, and there are no invalids on the Tory side.

4. a. *intr.* To come together in couples; to form a couple; to become companions or associates; esp. in the British Parliament and other legislative bodies, to make an agreement with an opponent that both shall abstain from voting on a given question or for a certain time (see PAIR *sb.* 4 c); also ***to pair off***.

a **1711** KEN *Sion* Poet. Wks. 1721 IV. 393 And tho' no Marriages are there, We yet may, like the Cherubs, pair. **1772** *Debates & Proc. Brit. House of Commons 1768–1770* 240 At dinner time many made no scruple, though the cause was not determined, of *pairing off*, as it is called; some pair'd off for every question in the election, others for a day, or a few hours only. **1810** G. ROSE *Diaries* (1860) II. 464 Several members had paired. **1811** T. CREEVEY *Let.* 21 Jan. in *Creevey Papers* (1963) iv. 76, I am not to vote to-night... Villiers won't release me from contract of pairing off. **1817** *Parl. Deb.* 744 Sir B. Hobhouse paired off in favour of the motion with General Thornton. **1852** MACAULAY in Trevelyan *Life* (1876) II. 352, I went down to the House and paired. **1866** *Harper's Mag.* May 805/2 This vote was given under peculiar circumstances. Mr. Morrill, of Maine, had sometime previously 'paired off' with Mr. Wright of New Jersey, [etc.].. **1885** *Times* (weekly ed.) 6 Mar. 14/2 Sir E. Watkin neither voted nor paired on Friday night. **1964** MRS. L. B. JOHNSON *White House Diary* 8 Apr. (1970) 102 Those committed as being safe for the bill..those who were absent and might 'pair' if you got to them and could find them an opposite number. **1965** *New Statesman* 19 Mar. 426/2 It is further alleged that one Conservative, at least, saw fit to pair with two Labour members.

b. To unite *with* one of the opposite sex; to become mates in love or marriage; to couple or mate.

1611 SHAKS. *Wint. T.* IV. iv. 154 Your hand (my Perdita:) so Turtles paire That neuer meane to part. **1775** SHERIDAN *Rivals* II. i, There never can be but one man in the world, whom a truly modest and delicate woman ought to pair with in a country-dance. **1793** COWPER *A Tale* 15 A chaffinch and his mate.. They paired, and would have built a nest. **1828** SCOTT *F.M. Perth* ii, Hawks, far less eagles, pair not with the humble linnet. **1877** A. B. EDWARDS *Up Nile* xxii. 680 The pigeons are pairing; the time of the singing of birds is come.

c. ***to pair off***, to go off or apart in pairs; also ***to pair off with*** (colloq.), to marry.

1803 G. COLMAN *John Bull* I. 9 Come, Mrs. Brulgruddery, let you and I pair off, my lambkin. **1827** LYTTON *Pelham* xxi, This couple soon paired off, and was immediately succeeded by another. **1860** EMERSON *Cond. Life, Consid.* Wks. (Bohn) II. 415 Suppose the three hundred heroes at Thermopylæ had paired off with three hundred Persians. **1865** MISS BRADDON *Sir Jasper* xxxv, [If they] would only make a match of it, I should be free to pair-off with the lively widow. **1881** MRS. A. B. CHURCH *Cecily's Debt* III. i, The other guests.. paired off amongst themselves.

d. In basket-making: to work two rods alternately one over the other.

1901 A. FIRTH *Cane Basket Work* (ser. 2) iv. 45 Pair round once to divide into twos, still keeping the central side spokes undivided. *Ibid.*, Now turn the basket upside down and pair round once, taking two lots of double spokes together each time, and keeping the row of pairing even with the edge of the weaving.

e. ***to pair up***, to form couples, esp. (of birds) to form pairs in preparation for mating; also, to match.

1908 A. W. MYERS *Compl. Lawn Tennis Player* 134 The prevalent custom.. is for the members to 'pair up' irrespective of style and temperament. **1920** E. O'NEILL *Beyond Horizon* II. 37 Don't you think them two'd pair up well? **1937** *Brit. Birds* XXX. 267 As soon as a couple of birds have paired up, they proceed to exclude other Grebes from a certain area. **1951** L. MACNEICE tr. *Goethe's Faust* 170 One's bosom finds this paper light to nurse, It pairs up snugly with a billet doux. **1965** D. LACK *Life of Robin* (ed. 4) v. 66 The blackbird apparently pairs up in late autumn.

Hence **'pairing** *ppl. a.*

1828 *Encycl. Brit.* (ed. 7) XVI. 733/1 Pairing birds.. flock together in February, in order to choose their mates.

pair, *v.*[2] *Obs.* or *dial.* Forms: 4–5 **peire, (pere,** 5 **peiere, pey(e)r),** 4–6 **peyre, payre,** 4–7 **paire,** 3–7 (*dial.* -9) **pair,** (*dial.* and *Sc.* 4–9 **pare,** 5–6 **par,** 6 **payr, peare).** [Aphetic f. *apeyre, apayre,* APPAIR, q.v.]

†**1.** *trans.* = APPAIR 1, IMPAIR 1; to make worse; to lessen. *Obs.*

a **1300** *Cursor M.* 8407 He that better can mend þen pere [*v.r.* paire, payre, peire]. **1362** LANGL. *P. Pl.* A. III. 123 Vr Fader Adam heo falde wiþ Feire biheste; Apoysende Popes and peyreþ holy chirche. **1387** TREVISA *Higden* (Rolls) VI. 399 He bulde newe citees and amended citees þat were i-peyred. **1503** HAWES *Examp. Virt.* v. 26 For that wyll payre and yll thy name. **1546** J. HEYWOOD *Prov. & Epigr.* (1867) 73, I will.. mend this house, and payre an other. **1573** TYRIE *Refut.* To Rdr. in *Cath. Tractates* (S.T.S.) 10 Nother eikand nor pearand ane word. **1625** BACON *Ess., Innov.* (Arb.) 527 Euer it mends Some, and paires Other.

2. *intr.* = APPAIR 2, IMPAIR 2; to become or grow worse, to deteriorate, to fall off. Now *dial.*

c **1320** *Cast. Love* 228 God whrowght never that thyng But hit peyred thowrgh his wonnyng. *c* **1330** R. BRUNNE *Chron.* (1810) 296 Now alle þe cuntre peires, vnneþis ouht þei left. *c* **1380** WYCLIF *Sel. Wks.* III. 438 þis is cause whi þe world peyreþ. *c* **1400** *Laud Troy Bk.* 11206 It was dight wel & fair That he myght neuere rote ne pair. *c* **1470** HENRY *Wallace* I. 14 Bot God abuff has maid thar mycht to par. **1491** CAXTON *Vitas Patr.* (W. de W. 1495) I. vii. 10 b/1 The whiche vestymentes neuer payred in desert. **1530** PALSGR. 655/2, I peyre, I waxe worse. **1597** BP. HALL *Sat.* VI. i. 84 Somewhat it was that made his paunch so peare, His girdle fell ten ynches in a yeare. **1650** T. FROYSELL *Serm.* (1652) 41 So doe his gifts begin to flag and paire in him. **1828** *Craven Gloss.* (ed. 2), *Pare,* to give a less quantity of milk. 'T'cow pares feafully'. **1870** R. CHAMBERS *Pop. Rhymes Scot.* 364 Februar, an ye be fair The hoggs 'll mend, and naething pair.

pair, obs. form of PARE *v.*

paired (pɛːəd), *ppl. a.* [f. PAIR *v.*[1] + -ED[1].]

a. Associated together in pairs or twos; coupled.

1611 COTGR., *Apparié,* paired, coupled, matched. **1711** STEELE *Spect.* No. 254 ¶3 A very loving Couple most happily paired in the Yoke of Wedlock. **1728** POPE *Dunc.* I. 66 Figures ill pair'd, and Similes unlike. **1880** A. WILSON in *Gentl. Mag.* CCXLVI. 44 The lancelet.. has no paired fins or limbs.

b. Special collocations, as **paired associates,** stimulus material presented in pairs to test the strength of associations set up between them at a subsequent presentation of one of the pair; also (freq. in form ***paired-associate***) *attrib.*; hence ***paired association***; **paired comparison,** a method of testing the discriminations made between different examples of the same type of stimulus by presenting them for comparison in pairs; also *attrib.*

1937 *Jrnl. Exper. Psychol.* XX. 60 (*heading*) The influence of the relative order of presentation of original and interpolated paired associates. **1949** B. J. UNDERWOOD *Exper. Psychol.* ix. 287 The number of pairs in a paired-associate list has varied, but from 8 to 15 have commonly been employed. **1971** *Jrnl. Gen. Psychol.* LXXXV. 212 Some are variants of such tasks as those for memory span.. and paired-associates learning. **1963** D. T. CAMPBELL in S. Koch *Psychol.* VI. 120 The preexperimental learning of the pro-Communists might be epitomized as a paired association of 'Communist—good'. **1901** E. B. TITCHENER *Exper. Psychol.* I. I. vii. 154 Smells have enough variety, but are extremely and insistently associative. However, it would be well worth while to apply the method of paired comparisons to them. **1937** G. W. ALLPORT *Personality* (1938) i. 5 The method of paired-comparison recommends itself as an objective and qualitative technique for studying judgements of the affective value of colors. **1951** S. S. STEVENS *Handbk. Exper. Psychol.* i. 28/1 Certain criteria of internal consistency, as in the method of paired comparisons. **1970** *Jrnl. Gen. Psychol.* LXXXII. 19 With the use of a paired-comparisons procedure, each group consisting of five animals was exposed to all three pairs.

†**'pairer.** *Obs. rare*[−1]. [f. PAIR *v.*[2] + -ER[1]: cf. APPAIRER.] One who impairs.

c **1400** *Wyclif's Bible, Jas.* Prol. (MS. Fairfax 2) Enuyouse men.. which seyn þat y am a peirer [*v.r.* apeirer] of holi scriptures.

pair-horse ('pɛəhɔːs), *a.* [Condensed from *pair of horse(s* used attrib.: cf. *two-horse, four-horse, four-wheel,* etc.] For a pair of horses. Hence **pair-horsed** *a.*

1842 *Ainsworth's Mag.* II. 429 The 'Bath pair-horse Invalid' now drew up.. for the elderly gentleman. **1854** C. D. YONGE tr. *Athenæus* III. 935 Bringing with him Glycera, the daughter of Thalamis in a pair-horse chariot. **1875** KNIGHT *Dict. Mech., Pair-horse Harness,* the general name given to double harness in England. **1900** *Daily News* 27 Sept. 9/1 His attempt to beat the one mile pair-horse English record of 2 minutes 35 1–5 seconds. **1902** [see DIFFERENTIAL *a.* 4 b]. **1905** *Daily Chron.* 22 May 6/3 The costly motor-cars of the humble workmen and the pair-horsed carriages of the lordly labourers. **1910** A. BENNETT *Clayhanger* I. iii. 19 A couple of pair-horsed trams. **1914** CONRAD *Chance* I. vii. 193 Just then the racket was distracting, a pair-horse trolley lightly loaded with loose rods of iron passing slowly very near us.

pairial, obs. form of PAIR-ROYAL.

'pairing, *vbl. sb.*[1] [f. PAIR *v.*[1] + -ING[1].]

a. The action of PAIR *v.*[1] in various senses. (For quots. 1915, 1969 cf. PAIR *sb.*[1] 4 f.) Also with *off* and *up.*

1611 COTGR., *Apparitation,* a matching, or pairing. **1792** J. PEARSON *Political Dict.* 40 Pairing-off. Two Sneaking Scoundrels, not worth a piece of dog's meat to either party. **1838** *Encycl. Brit.* (ed. 7) XVI. 733/1 The instinct of pairing is bestowed on every species of animals to which it is necessary for rearing their young, and on no other species. **1851** HT. MARTINEAU *Hist. Peace* v. v. (1877) III. 259 The custom of pairing in the Commons. **1897** A. FIRTH *Cane Basket Work* ii. 18 To begin by pairing, place each weaver singly behind two consecutive spokes. *Ibid.* vii. 60 This last inch may be all 'pairing'.. if preferred, but if woven in the ordinary way, a row or two of pairing must form the edge. **1900** *Daily News* 12 June 8/4 The pairings in the thirteenth round of the [Chess] tournament.. are as follows [etc.]. **1901** M. WHITE *How to make Baskets* i. 6 Pairing may be used either with an odd or even number of spokes. **1908** *Westm. Gaz.* 19 Nov. 14/3 The question of pairing-up arose, and the other [tennis] players naturally awaited the Prince's choice. **1909** E. STRASBURGER in A. C. Seward *Darwin & Mod. Sci.* vi. 109 Attention was drawn to the fact that during the reducing division of nuclei which contain chromosomes of unequal size, gemini are constantly produced by the pairing of chromosomes of the same size. This led to the conclusion that the pairing chromosomes are homologous, and that one comes from the father, the other from the mother. **1915** R. F. MCKAY *Theory of Machines* viii. 89 Line contact is undesirable.. in lower pairing. **1926** J. S. HUXLEY *Ess. Pop. Sci.* 175 In herons and egrets.. it is not the male who seeks out territory long before pairing-up, but pairing-up occurs on the communal feeding-grounds. **1939** *Auk* LVI. 265 No bond in the strict sense of the word, that is a pairing off, is formed. **1953** N. TINBERGEN *Herring Gull's World* xii. 105 Settling upon a territory will not occur until after pairing-up. **1955** A. W. BOOTHER *Basketry for Beginners* 13 Reverse pairing, used in conjunction with pairing, makes an attractive decoration for a basket... Reverse pairing is also used on cane bottoms and lids of baskets. **1958** B. HAMILTON *Too Much of Water* ix. 204 It was, indeed, a day of pairings-off. Annie Maxwell and Fred Upcher seemed to have settled for one another's company. **1964** H. HODGES *Artifacts* x. 146 Pairing was done with two rods woven simultaneously so that they crossed between the stakes to produce an effect similar to twined weave. **1965** D. LACK *Life of Robin* (ed. 4) v. 65 Tradition assigns St. Valentine's Day for the pairing up of wild birds. **1969** G. D. REDFORD et al. *Mech. Technol.* ii. 24 In higher pairing, contact is usually along a line or at a point, and the motion is that of, or equivalent to, rolling. **1970** AMBROSE & EASTY *Cell Biol.* x. 326 The result of this process, which is known as synapsis or zygotene pairing, is that there is now a haploid number of chromosome pairs, which are called bivalents. **1971** *Sci. Amer.* Sept. 89/3 Light absorbed by a molecule kicks one of the electrons associated with the molecule into an excited energy state, thereby making the electron available for pairing with an electron from a neighbouring atom or molecule in an electron-pair bond.

b. *attrib.* and *Comb.*, as **pairing-call,** a call used by birds during the mating season; **pairing-desk,** a desk in the House of Commons at which members arrange pairs; **pairing-season, -time,** the season at which birds pair; the age at which the sexes begin to pair off; also *transf.*

1911 J. A. THOMSON *Biol. Seasons* II. 149 The long-drawn-out, modulated pairing-call of many of the waders.. is on the border-line. **1899** *Daily News* 24 Apr. 7/3 Seeing him approach the pairing desk, I asked, 'Do you want to go away, Sir John?' **1860** O. W. HOLMES *Elsie V.* xii, Does the bird know why its feathers grow more brilliant.. in the pairing season? **1742** W. ELLIS *Mod. Husbandman* July xvi. 85 Every Pheasant.. that can be proved to be in the Mannor at Pairing-time. **1795** COWPER (*title*) Pairing time anticipated. **1850** *Punch* 10 Aug. 62/2 Parliamentary Almanack.—Latter end of July, 'pairing' time begins. **1867** O. W. HOLMES in *Atlantic Almanac 1868* 2/2 On the 14th of February the windows fill with pictures for the most part odious, and meant for some nondescript class of males and females, their allusions having reference to Saint Valentine's day, the legendary pairing-time of the birds.

†**pairing,** *vbl. sb.*[2] *Obs.* [f. PAIR *v.*[2] + -ING[1].] Injury, damage, impairment.

1382 WYCLIF *Matt.* xvi. 26 What profitiþ it to a man, ȝif he wynne al þe world, trewly he suffre peyrynge of his soule? *?a* **1500** *Chester Pl.* (E.E.T.S.) 251 He should.. suffer her not to come him nere, for payring of his fame. *c* **1617** EARL OF SOMERSET *Let. to K. Jas.* in *Cabala* (1654) 3 That which is so little, as that it will suffer no pairing, or diminution.

pairmain, obs. f. PEARMAIN, kind of apple.

'pairment[1]. Now only *dial.* [Aphetic f. *appairment,* APPAIRMENT: cf. PAIR *v.*[2]] = APPAIRMENT, IMPAIRMENT; injury, deterioration.

c **1330** R. BRUNNE *Chron. Wace* (Rolls) 2395 After þe peirement [*v.r.* after apeyrment] of his liuere. **1382** WYCLIF *2 Cor.* vii. 9 That in no thing ȝe suffre peirement of vs. *c* **1440** *Jacob's Well* 205 ȝif þe thyng be werse, when þou restoryst it,.. þe muste restore þe peyrement. **1874** R. E. LEADER in *Sheffield Gloss.* (1888), A gardener will say his plants will take no pairment under such and such conditions.

†**'pairment**[2]. *Obs.* In 4 **peyr-,** 4–5 **payrement.** [app. a. AF. ****pairement,*** f. *pairer* to couple.] ? Coupling, consortship; in phr. ***to hold (a woman) in pairment.***

c **1330** R. BRUNNE *Chron.* (1810) 58 Engle his wife he [Harald] drofe away, & held in peyrment Egyue, þat was an abbes, out of hir hous had Maugre hire wille [LANGTOFT Et l'abesse Eggyve de sa mesun robbayt, La tynt cum sa femme]. *c* **1400** *Laud Troy Bk.* 5969 His Aunte was rauysched with Thelamon; He held here longe In payrement And gat sir Ayax verament.

pair-oar ('pɛərɔə(r)). [Condensed from *pair of oars*: cf. PAIR-HORSE.] A boat rowed by a pair of oars: see OAR *sb.* 3. Also *attrib.* Hence **pair-oared** *a.*

1854 (*title*) Our Cruise in the Undine; the journal of an English pair-oar expedition through France. **1870** M. COLLINS *Vivian* II. xvi. 277, I declare there is a punt, and a pair-oar too. **1899** *Rowing Almanack* 209 It is the usual practice on the river for a pair-oar to give way to a four-oar. **1901** *Chambers's Jrnl.* Feb. 129/2 It comes by way of the river, a rotten, old, pair-oared skiff. **1938** C. S. FORESTER *Ship of Line* i. 7 Hornblower took his seat in a pair oared wherry.

pair-royal (pɛə'rɔɪəl). Also 6 **pa'rriall,** 7 **pa'royal(l, pe'rryall, pa'rreiall,** 8 **pai'royal, pai'rial, pa'rial,** 9 **'prial.**

A set of three of the same kind. **a.** In cribbage and other card games: Three cards of the same denomination, as three fives, queens, etc.; ***double pair-royal,*** four such cards.

1608 DAY *Hum. out of Br.* I. C ij, Shew perryall and take't. **1680** COTTON *Compl. Gamester* in Singer *Hist. Cards* (1816) 348 A pair-royal is of three, as three kings, three queens, &c. **1749** MRS. DELANY in *Life & Corr.* (1861) II. 519 We had in playing a 15, a pairoyal, a double peroyal, a second peroyal, and an end game, which was 27. **1801** STRUTT *Sports & Past.* IV. i. 267 The game is counted.. by fifteens, sequences, pairs, and pairials. **1870** HARDY & WARE *Mod. Hoyle* 78 In play [at cribbage] you cannot make a double pair-royal with any cards higher than sevens, as they would then exceed thirty-one, the limit of the hand.

b. A throw of three dice all turning up the same number of points, as three twos, three sixes, etc.

1656 [see RAFFLE *sb.*[1] 1]. **1880** HARDY *Ret. Native* III. vii. 225 The raffle began, and the dice went round. When it came to Christian's turn, he took the box with a trembling hand, shook it.. and threw a pair-royal. Three of the others had thrown common low pairs, and all the rest mere points.

c. *transf.* A set of three persons or things; three of a kind.

1592 NASHE *Strange Newes* C iij b, He coupled them both ..and.. thrust in the third brother, who made a perfect parriall of pamphleters. **1633** FORD *Broken H.* v. ii, On a pair-royal do I wait in death: My sovereign.. on my mistress ..and on Ithocles. **1635** QUARLES *Embl.* v. (1777) 282 That great pair-royal Of adamantine sisters. **1650** FULLER *Pisgah* IV. i. 26 The Moabites.. concluded.. that that paroyall of armies had smitten one another. **1803** W. TAYLOR in *Ann. Rev.* I. 352 The end.. might also be attained by vesting it in a prial of kings. **1840** DE QUINCEY in *Blackw. Mag.* XLVIII. 516/2 The year 333 before Christ. Here we have another '*prial*', a prial of threes, for the *locus* of Alexander.

d. *attrib.*, as ***pair-royal headed*** adj., three-headed.

1651 CLEVELAND *On Sir T. Martin* 19 Pair-royal headed Cerberus his Cozen: Hercules labours were a Bakers dozen.

pairt, pairtlie, Sc. ff. PART, PARTLY, PERTLY.

pairwise ('pɛəwaɪz), *adv.* and *a.* [f. PAIR *sb.*[1] + -WISE.] In or by pairs; with regard to pairing; forming a pair.

1831 CARLYLE *Ess., Nibelungenlied* (1872) III. 122 Such as continued refractory he tied together by the beards, and hung pair-wise over poles. **1876** [see KINEMATIC *a.* b]. **1956** *Nature* 21 Jan. 127/2 In the tetramer, pair-wise engagement of all the CONH groups is again geometrically possible. **1960** H. M. HOENIGSWALD *Language Change* xiii. 144 Pair-wise reconstructions from three related languages may probe the question of degrees of relationship within the language family. **1965** *Math. in Biol. & Med.* (Med. Res.

Council) III. 126 An observer or observers willing to assign a ranking order to the pair-wise resemblances among the objects. **1969** *Word 1967* XXIII. 302 The characters can be anything at all as long as they are pairwise distinguishable. **1971** POWELL & HIGMAN *Finite Simple Groups* viii. 260 K_1, .., K_c are pairwise disjoint, non-empty subsets of *G*. **1972** *Computers & Humanities* VI. 184 Used in roll-call analysis to count pair-wise voting agreement on isolated roll-call votes. **1975** *Language* LI. 378 Even if we allow pairwise (non-linear) extrinsic ordering, the problem is not solved.

‖**pais** [= OF. *pais*, F. *pays* country], in the phrase ***trial per pais***: see COUNTRY 7.

1664 *Spelman's Gloss.* s.v., *Trial per pais.* **1706** in PHILLIPS. **1766** BLACKSTONE *Comm.* II. xix. 294 Common assurances..By matter *in pais*, or deed; which is an assurance transacted between two or more private persons *in pais*, in the country. **1768** *Ibid.* III. xxiii. 349 The nature and method of the trial by jury; called also the trial per pais, or by the country.

pais, obs. f. PACE, PEACE.

pais, var. PEISE.

paisa (ˈpaɪsə). Pl. paise, -a, paisas. [a. Hindi *paisā*: see PICE.] **a.** = PICE. **b.** A coin and decimalized unit of currency, equal in value to one-hundredth of a rupee, in India (since 1957: see NAYA PAISA), Pakistan (since 1966), and Nepal, and to one hundredth of a taka in Bangladesh.

1884 [see DAM *sb.*[5]]. **1924** *Regions Beyond* XLV. 44 Flowers are scattered upon the waters, coins are dropped into the depths, perhaps only a paisa (farthing), but the giver is poor and needy. **1956**, etc. [see NAYA PAISA.] **1959** [see ANNA]. **1963** *Times* 8 May 21/4 Last year the Pakistan Government made a reduction of 40 per cent—from 25 paise to 15 paise per lb.—in export duty. **1969** *Sunday Tel.* 12 Jan. 7/3 Hashish candy..is available for 50 Nepalese paise. This is about 3d. **1969** *Enact* (Delhi) Dec. 7/3 Oh! You are a munim all over, always counting paisas. **1971** *Femina* (Bombay) 16 Apr. 55/1 Your family won't even know you've been counting every paise [*sic*]. **1975** *Bangladesh Observer* (Dacca) 26 July 2/4 (Advt.), Cement... Taka 7.50 (seven and paisa fifty) only per ton. **1978** L. HEREN *Growing up on The Times* v. 166 The more affluent Indians..gave beggars paise, or fractions of farthings.

paisage, obs. f. PAYSAGE, landscape.

paisan: see PAYSAN.

paisand, var. PEISANT.

‖**paisano** (paiˈsano). [Sp., = peasant, rustic: see PEASANT.]

1. In Spanish-speaking areas: a fellow-countryman; a peasant. Also *attrib.*

1844 G. W. KENDALL *Narr. Santa Fé Expedition* II. 230 [He] invariably called me his paisano, or country man. **1890** C. F. LUMMIS *Land of Poco Tiempo* iv. 88 Every one was out, but they were no longer the friendly *paisanos* we had known. **1935** J. STEINBECK *Tortilla Flat* 11 What is a paisano?.. His ancestors have lived in California for a hundred or two years. **1940** E. FERGUSSON *Our Southwest* xiv. 247 The Spanish clustered in towns. They fought Indians only when they had to, to assure safety and security. Security was what the *paisano* wanted. **1969** A. MARIN *Rise with Wind* x. 118 Carrasco was one of the few *paisanos*..who wore civilian clothes. **1971** *Publishers' Weekly* 18 Oct. 25/2 There are many cookbooks exploring the gourmet or *paisano* delights of foreign countries and places. **1977** H. FAST *Immigrants* 6 No use, paisano. Come back next week, the week after.

2. In Mexico and south-west of U.S.: A name of the chaparral-cock or road-runner, *Geococcyx californianus*.

1885 *Harper's Mag.* Feb. 423/2 The paisano..deserves.. kindness from man. **1893** K. SANBORN *S. California* 55.

paisant, -aunt, obs. forms of PEASANT.

paise, var. PEASE, to appease; PEISE.

paishcush, var. PESHCUSH.

paishe: see PASHE.

paishwa, obs. f. PESHWA.

paisible, -yble, obs. var. PEACEABLE.

Paisley (ˈpeɪzlɪ). The name of a town in Renfrewshire, Scotland, used *attrib.* or *absol.* to designate a garment or material made there or having the curvilinear design characteristic of cloth made there, or the pattern itself.

1834 Paisley shawl [see SHAWL *sb.* 2a]. *c* **1860** [see NORWICH]. **1866** R. S. CHARNOCK *Verba Nominalia* 215 *Paisley*, a shawl made at Paisley, co. Renfrew (Scotland); celebrated also for its manufactures of silk and other shawls, muslin, cotton thread, and ornamental fancy goods. **1898** *Daily News* 5 Mar. 6/4 If black stuffs were chosen, it was only that they might be trimmed with paisleys. **1900** *Ibid.* 28 Apr. 6/6 Paisley velvet is a favourite facing for collars and revers. **1911** *Daily Colonist* (Victoria, B.C.) 23 Apr. 7/1 (Advt.), Paisley silks. **1950** D. GASCOYNE *Vagrant* 15 Spread with a soft paisley-patterned cloth. **1951** E. PAUL *Springtime in Paris* vi. 125 One of the coffee-coloured men in a flashy paisley robe and wearing gold-bowed pince-nez. **1954** F. SARGESON in C. K. Stead *N.Z. Short Stories* (1966) 5 He hoped to better himself at the fine Paisley work. **1959** H. HOBSON *Mission House Murder* ii. 11 My Paisley silk bow-tie. **1964** *McCall's Sewing* iv. 58/2 *Paisley*, any cotton, wool, or rayon which is printed with the traditional scroll design which originated in Paisley, Scotland. **1966** R. THOMAS *Spy in Vodka* (1967) vii. 60 He wore a dark-blue flannel sports shirt, a blue and yellow Paisley ascot, a pair of grey flannels that must have cost sixty bucks, and black loafers. **1967** [see NORWICH]. **1975** G. LYALL *Judas Country* xxii. 163 He had his old brownish Paisley-pattern silk scarf folded as a choker. **1976** *Evening Advertiser* (Swindon) 31 Dec. (Advt.), Fur coats, capes and foxes. Victorian nighties, petticoats and camisoles, silk and Paisley shawls, beaded and sequined garments... Buyer calling regularly in the area. **1977** J. FLEMING *Every Inch a Lady* xiii. 63 A Paisley-patterned scarf in blue and red silk. **1977** J. WAMBAUGH *Black Marble* (1978) viii. 105 The long-legged asthmatic.. was trying to look dog show respectable in a three-button herringbone coat, gray woolen slacks and a paisley tie.

Paisleyite (ˈpeɪzlɪaɪt), *a.* and *sb.* [f. the name of Ian *Paisley* (b. 1926), Ulster Presbyterian minister and politician + -ITE[1].]

A. *adj.* Of or pertaining to Ian Paisley or his followers. **B.** *sb.* A supporter of Ian Paisley and his advocacy of Protestant interests in Northern Ireland and the independence of Northern Ireland from the Republic of Ireland. So ˈ**Paisleyism**, the religious and political principles of Paisleyites.

1966 *Guardian* 18 July 4/5 Paisleyism might have been expected to cause alarm and fierce anger in the [Irish] Republic. *Ibid.* 25 July 1/2 A Government order restricting a Paisleyite march. **1966** *New Statesman* 30 Sept. 468/3 The Cormac Square riots, when the Paisleyites marched on the General Assembly of the Irish Presbyterian Church. **1968** *Listener* 19 Dec. 823/2 Through the day, groups of Paisleyites infiltrated into the cordoned-off city. **1969** *Daily Tel.* 26 Feb. 16 Mr. Roy Bradford..increased his majority in his Belfast constituency..despite the intervention of a Paisleyite candidate. **1970** *Guardian* 18 Apr. 11/5 The likelihood is that the Paisleyite opposition will increase its numbers in Stormont. **1976** J. CARROLL *Madonna Red* (1977) iii. 98 He knew the bitter energy that faith could release against Paisleyites and Jews. **1978** D. MURPHY *Place Apart* vii. 148 However people may disagree in their analyses of Paisley the man, everybody recognises the danger of Paisleyism the cult.

paiss(e, obs. Sc. ff. PACE, PASS, PEISE.

paissaunte, obs. f. PEASANT.

paiste, paisterer, paistrie: see PASTE, PASTERER, PASTRY.

pait, obs. var. PATE, a badger; obs. Sc. f. *paid*: see PAY *v.*

†ˈ**paitclaith.** *Sc. Obs.* Also pet-, pait-. A corruption of *paitlet, -lat*, Sc. forms of PATLET, an article of clothing; associated with *claith*, CLOTH.

15.. *Aberdeen Reg.* XXIV. (Jam.), Gwnes, collaris, Pet-claythis, curschis, & slewis [sleeves]. *Ibid.* XXV. (Jam.), Four paitclaythis. **1568** in Hay Fleming *Mary Q. of Scots* (1897) 511 Item ane broun goun. Item ane saiting pait-cleyth.

paith, obs. Sc. form of PATH.

†ˈ**paithment.** *Sc. Obs.* [app. a blending of *pavement* and *paith*, PATH.] = PAVEMENT. (In quot. *c* 1470 the earth's surface, the ground.)

c **1375** *Sc. Leg. Saints* xviii. (*Egipciane*) 719 Done I fel one þe payhtment. *c* **1470** HENRY *Wallace* VIII. 936 Quhen the paithment was cled in tendyr greyn. **1538** *Aberdeen Reg.* XVII. (Jam.), The paithtment of the kirk.

paitlat, -let, Sc. var. PATLET, a partlet.

paitrel, variant of PEITREL, POITREL.

paitrick, paive, obs. Sc. ff. PARTRIDGE, PAVE.

Paiute (ˈpaɪuːt), *sb.* and *a.* Also 9 **Pah-Utah, Pah-Utche, Pah-Ute, Pa-Utah, Pie-Utaw**; 9- **Piute.** [ad. Sp. *Payuta*, or ad. native name (perhaps *payiutsi* fish people), influenced by *Utah* and *Ute*.] **A.** *sb.* **a.** A Shoshonean Indian people inhabiting parts of Utah, northern Arizona, and southeastern Nevada (more fully *Southern Paiute*); also, a culturally similar Shoshonean people of western Nevada and adjacent parts of California, Oregon, and Idaho (*Northern Paiute*); a member of either of these peoples.

The Southern Paiute and Northern Paiute are not subdivisions of a single people; their languages are distinct, and their territories are not contiguous.

1827 D. T. POTTS in D. M. Frost *Notes on Gen. Ashley* (1960) 63 This river [*sc.* the Sevier] is inhabited by a numerous tribe of miserable Indians... They call themselves Pie-Utaws, and I suppose are derived from the same stock [as the Utaws]. **1827** J. SMITH in H. D. Carew *Hist. Pasadena* (1930) I. 136 Passing down this river some distance, I fell in with a nation of Indians who call themselves Pah Utches. **1860** MAYNE REID *Odd People* 329 In the western & southern division of the Great Basin, the Digger exists under the name of *Paiute*, or more properly, Pah-Utah—so-called from his supposed relationship with the tribe of the Utahs. **1881** *Encycl. Brit.* XII. 825/2 In California and the south-western States, occupied by the morally debased and physically degraded Pah-Utes. **1910** F. W. HODGE *Handbk. Amer. Indians* II. 186/2 Paiute... In common usage it has been applied at one time or another to most of the Shoshonean tribes of W. Utah, N. Arizona, S. Idaho, [etc.] **1937** R. H. LOWIE *Hist. Ethnol. Theory* vi. 55 Had he begun his studies among the Eskimo or Paiute, his general views might have been different. **1947** B. HAILE *Prayer Stick Cutting* 43 Neckbands..should be of otter or beaver skin obtained from the..Paiutes. **1952** J. R. SWANTON *Indian Tribes N. Amer.* 375 With the Bannock, the Northern Paiute constituted one dialectic group of the Shoshonean Branch of the Uto-Aztecan stock. *Ibid.* 381 The Southern Paiute belonged to the Ute-Chemehuevi group of the Shoshonean branch of the Uto-Aztecan stock. **1959** E. TUNIS *Indians* 107/2 The southern Paiute, the Bannock, and the Gosiute were typical 'tribes', though they were not actually organized as tribes. **1973** A. H. WHITEFORD *N. Amer. Indian Arts* 39 One-rod coiling was done by the Pomo and Paiute. **1974** A. MACLEAN *Breakheart Pass* i. 12 They say the Paiutes kill every white man on sight. **1977** H. LANDAR in T. A. Sebeok *Native Lang. Americas* II. III. 327 The term Snake, applied to the Northern Paiute of Oregon, is used of other Shoshonean groups as well.

b. Either of the languages of the Paiute, technically distinguished as ***Southern Paiute*** and ***Northern Paiute***.

1915 *Everybody's Mag.* Oct. 461/2, I talked Piute to him all afternoon and he didn't understand a word of it. **1921** E. SAPIR *Language* 67 Paiute, for instance, may compound noun with noun. **1933** L. BLOOMFIELD *Language* iv. 72 The Shoshonean family (in southern California and eastward, including Ute, Paiute, Shoshone, Comanche, and Hopi). **1949** E. A. NIDA *Morphol.* (ed. 2) iv. 103 Alternating unvoicing and reduction as in Southern Paiute. **1975** *Language* LI. 124 Consider an alternating stress rule, such as that of Southern Paiute, which stresses every alternate vowel from left to right across a word. **1977** H. LANDAR in T. A. Sebeok *Native Lang. Americas* II. III. 327 Northern Paiute... 2,000 [speakers] in Nevada, California, Oregon and Idaho.

B. *adj.* Of or pertaining to the Paiute or their languages.

1845 J. C. FRÉMONT *Rep. Exploring Expedition* 260 They rarely carried home horses, on account of the difficulty..of guarding them..from the Pa-utah Indians. **1869** 'MARK TWAIN' *Innoc. Abr.* xx. 205 Tahoe means grasshoppers. It means grasshopper soup. It is Indian,.. They say it is Pi-ute —possibly it is Digger. **1938** W. DYK *Left Handed's Son of Old Man Hat* 11 A Paiute girl came to our place. **1949** *Natural Hist.* June 268/1 Major Powell..named it Tapeats Creek after a Paiute Indian in his employ. **1955** W. GADDIS *Recognitions* II. ii. 388 The Piute Indians followed the sun to that hole where it crawled in at the end of the earth. **1975** *Language* LI. 797 The Southern Paiute suffix *-'tɨ* is restricted to true passives.

‖**paiwari** (paɪˈwɒrɪ). Forms: 8 piworree, 9 -ie; piwaree, -i; -warry, -i, -ie; paiwari. [Carib of Guyana.] An intoxicating beverage prepared from cassava, used by the Indians of Guyana. Cf. CASSIRI. Also *attrib.*, as ***paiwari-drinking***, ***-feast***, ***-trough***.

[**1660** F. BROOKE tr. *Le Blanc's Trav.* 401 They have a drink of the root Cavain, which the Carmels call Piroa.] **1769** E. BANCROFT *Guiana* 278 The piworree is made from the bread of Cassava or Manioc. **1866** *Treas. Bot.* s.v. *Manihot*, Another of the products of Cassava is an intoxicating beverage called Piwarrie... It is made by the women, who chew Cassava cakes and throw the masticated material into a wooden bowl, where it is allowed to ferment for some days, and [is] then boiled. **1868** W. H. BRETT *Indian Tribes of Guiana* I. ix. 155 After a few lashes, they drank paiwari together, and returned to the main body of the dancers. **1880** BRETT *Leg. & Myths Guiana* 102 A large canoe is brought on shore And with paiwari running o'er. **1883** E. F. IM THURN *Among Indians of Guiana* xv. 319 All the festivals among all the tribes being occasions for much drinking of paiwari—the national beverage—they may all be called Paiwari Feasts. **1934** E. WAUGH *Handful of Dust* vi. 337 'They have been making *piwari*... You should try some.'.. Tony gulped the dark liquid, trying not to taste it. But it was not unpleasant, hard and muddy on the palate like most of the beverages he had been offered in Brazil, but with a flavour of honey and brown bread. **1938** *Amer. Anthropologist* XL. 228 Another method of manufacturing alcoholic beverages in South America was to ferment the starchy juice of the pressed or chewed cassava (*Jatropha manihot*)... It was called paiwari or paiva in British Guiana, ..cachiri among the Roucouyenne, and cauim or pajuarú among the aborigines of Brazil. **1958** H. G. DE LISSER *Arawak Girl* v. 50 Francisco had been drinking much piwari. **1964** V. G. C. NORWOOD *Jungle Life in Guiana* v. 108 Quantities of the three principal native beers or liquors brewed by forest Indians throughout Guiana: cashiri, yamanchi and paiwarrie.

paize, variant of PEISE.

pajala (ˈpɑːdʒələ). [Malay.] A type of boat used around the Macassar Strait (see quot. 1950).

1937 G. E. P. COLLINS *Makassar Sailing* 12 When the first stage is completed the ship is a pajala, a low undecked boat of island design. **1950** *Jrnl. Malayan Branch R. Asiatic Soc.* XXIII. 113 The Pajala is a beamy, undecked coasting boat which is normally fitted with a tripod mast setting a single, large rectangular sail. **1964** K. G. TREGONNING *Hist. Mod. Malaya* 59 There had been Bugis traders in Malayan waters for centuries. In the sixteenth century Malacca knew well their *pájalas*, their large prahus with distinctive tripod mast and a deep oblong sail.

pajamahs, -mas: see PYJAMAS.

Pajarete, var. PAXARETE.

‖**pajero** (paˈxero). [Sp. *pajero* lit. dealer in straw, f. *paja* straw.] The Pampas Cat of S. America (*Felis pajeros*).

Pajitanian, var. PATJITANIAN *a.*

pajock, a modernized spelling of PAIOCKE, q.v.

Pak (pæk), colloq. abbrev. of *Pakistan*, PAKISTANI *sb.* and *a.*

[**1935** C. RAHMAT ALI (*title*) Pakistan, the fatherland of the Pak nation.] **1954** G. S. RAO *Indian Words in Eng.* 134/1 *Pak*, contraction of Pakistan. **1965** P. ROBINSON *Pakistani Agent* v. 74 It was obvious the Paks were up to some new game. **1967** *Guardian* 24 Aug. 6/6 The official Pakistan news service reported yesterday that 'indecent miscreants' are smuggling Pak grain into India. **1969** *Indian Express* (Bombay) 28 July 11/3 (*heading*) Pak separatist parties merge. **1971** M. KELLY *25th Hour* iii. 214, I don't see all this secrecy and drama. Smuggling us out like a load of Paks. **1971** *Sun* (Ceylon) 17 Sept. 6/4 (*heading*) Pak refugees hit by floods. **1974** *New Society* 13 June 627/3 The chauvinists' scenario runs on about filthy foreigners and Pak shopkeepers (they *do* stay open later). **1975** *Bangladesh Times* (Dacca) 27 July 6/1 (*heading*) Pak flood death toll rises to 49. **1977** *Private Eye* 13 May 7/3 The foreign mission which serves booze in limitless quantities is the Russian Embassy in Islamabad, 200 miles away and many alcoholics are now signing up to join the Pak-Soviet Friendship Societies.

pak, pake, pakke, obs. ff. PACK.

pakald: see PACKALD.

pakapoo, pakapu (ˈpækəpuː, pækəˈpuː). Also **pak-a-peu, puka pu**, etc. [Chinese]. A Chinese gambling game resembling lottery with sheets of paper so marked as to be indecipherable except to an initiate. Phr. ***like a pakapoo ticket***, untidy, disordered (*Austral.*).

1911 L. STONE *Jonah* ix. 92 He had come down early to mark a pak-ah-pu ticket at the Chinaman's in Hay Street. **1913** *Chambers's Jrnl.* Feb. 155/1 All kinds of games of chance—'two up', 'pak-a-pu' (the latter a form of lottery imported by the Chinese). **1923** *Daily Mail* 12 Feb. 7 Five Chinese pleaded guilty at Liverpool Assizes to charges of running a gaming house... For the defence it was argued that Pak-a-Peu (or Puck-a-pu) was a game of skill. **1927** *Daily Express* 21 Sept. 7/2 A Japanese ship's captain.. appealed against a conviction..for employing two other Japanese to sell chances in an unlawful lottery known as 'Puka pu'. 'It is a favourite game with the Japanese and Chinese and others living in Limehouse,' explained Mr. Horace Fenton. **1932** H. SIMPSON *Boomerang* x. 275 Brought in evidence two flimsy pieces of printed paper, one a pakapu bet, the other a five-pound-note. **1936** 'R. HYDE' *Passport to Hell* i. 10 Chinese grocery-shops, masonic clubs, and pakapoo saloons. **1951** E. LAMBERT *Twenty Thousand Thieves* (1952) ix. 89 Henry opened Dooley's pay-book, the pages of which showed liberal sprinklings of the red ink with which fines and convictions were entered. 'What a pay-book!' he sighed. Dooley grinned. 'Like a pak-a-poo ticket,' he agreed. **1959** BAKER *Drum* 133 *Marked like a pakapoo ticket*, confusedly or incomprehensibly marked. **1960** *N.Z. Listener* 22 July 9/2 Some of the last of the old Chinese dwellings of the opium-smoking and pakapoo-playing generation are being pulled down in Haining Street in Wellington. **1961** PARTRIDGE *Dict. Slang* Suppl. 1212/1 *Look like a pakapu ticket*, to be completely indecipherable: Australian (esp. Sydney) coll.: since ca. 1940. 'Pakapu is a Chinese gambling game, not unlike housie. A pakapu ticket, when filled, is covered with strange markings'. **1964** A. WYKES *Gambling* 330 The only illegal gambling games in New South Wales are *fan-tan*, another Chinese game called *pak-a-p*, and *two-up*.

pakaru, var. PUCKEROO.

pak-choi (pakˈtʃɔɪ). [Cantonese, lit. 'white vegetable'; cf. PE-TSAI.] A Chinese species of cabbage, *Brassica chinensis*. Also *attrib.*

1847 R. FORTUNE *Three Years' Wanderings N. Provinces China* xvi. 306 The celebrated 'Pak-tsae', or white cabbage of Shastung and Peking, is a very different plant. **1894** *Bull. Cornell Univ. Agric. Exper. Station* LXVII. 183 The Pak-Choi, commonly called Chinese cabbage and frequently confounded with the Pe-Tsai..is a vegetable which never forms a head. **1900** L. H. BAILEY *Cycl. Amer. Hort.* I. 178/1 Pak-Choi Cabbage... This plant is grown by the American Chinese, and is occasionally seen in other gardens. **1931** H. C. THOMPSON *Vegetable Crops* (ed. 2) xix. 291 The Pak-choi varieties resemble swiss chard in habit of growth. The leaves are long, dark green and oblong or oval. This type does not form a solid head. **1969** *Oxf. Bk. Food Plants* 154/1 Pak-Choi (*Brassica chinensis*)..is more closely related to rape and swede than to the European cabbages... The plant does not form a heart and in appearance it resembles chard or spinach beet... Pak-choi does best when sown in July or August, to produce an autumn crop. **1972** Y. LOVELOCK *Vegetable Bk.* 72 The other [Chinese cabbage], Baak-choy (B[rassica] chinensis), is also called Chinese mustard, and is noted for its lack of smell when cooking.

pakeha (ˈpɑːkehɑː). Also 9 **packeah**. The Maori word used in New Zealand for a white man.

1817 J. L. NICHOLAS *Narr. Voyage to N.Z.* I. v. 139 Many of them had never before..beheld an European, and to see *packaka kiki* (the white man eat,) was a novelty. [**1820** *Gram. & Vocab. Lang. N.Z.* (Ch. Miss. Soc.) 187 (Morris) *Pakeha*, an European; a white man.] **1832** A. EARLE *9 Months' Resid. N.Z.* 146 The white taboo'd day, when the packeahs (or white men) put on clean clothes and leave off work. **1838** J. S. POLACK *New Zealand* II. iii. 102 He [*sc.* the chief] said I was a pákeha maori or native white man. **1845** E. J. WAKEFIELD *Adv. N.Z.* I. 73 We do not want the missionaries from the Bay of Islands, they are pakeha maori, or whites who have become natives. **1854** GOLDER *Pigeons Parlt.* III. 44 Aiding some vile pakehas In deeds subversive of the laws. **1859** [see *beach-comber*]. **1933** *Bulletin* (Sydney) 13 Sept. 8/4 The first pakehas were not at all ethical— rough whalers and adventurers. **1938** [see HALF-PIE *a.*]. **1938** R. FINLAYSON *Brown Man's Burden* 1 Rua came from Taupo to the coastal district to work on the farm of a Pakeha. **1959** G. SLATTER *Gun in my Hand* xxii. 224 The Maori must smile at the pakeha going all Maori when he's overseas. People on the ship to England wearing tikis and saying good kai this morning. **1960** *Guardian* 23 Sept. 13/1 Race relations in New Zealand..had been based on the absolute equality of Maori and Pakeha (European). **1963** *Evening Post* (Wellington, N.Z.) 25 July, Co-existence between Maoris and Pakehas had seriously affected Maori culture. **1978** *Islands* (N.Z.) Aug. 20 The pakehas' faces floated like white disks in a sea of brown.

pakhal (pəˈkɑːl). [Hind.: see PUCKAULY.] A vessel for carrying or keeping water, *spec.* a water-skin of leather.

1885 G. C. WHITWORTH *Anglo-Indian Dict.* s.v. *bhisti*, A double bag called a pakhál, which is carried by a buffalo or bullock. **1892** W. WICKHAM *Milit. Transport India* xv. 147 The leather packháls or water bags should..be dubbed before use. **1920** *Blackw. Mag.* Oct. 464/1 A couple of mules laden with metal pakhals of water. **1925** [see CHAGAL].

‖**pakhawaj** (ˈpakawadʒ). [Hind.] A doubleheaded drum used in Indian music, esp. that of the northern part of the country.

1867 E. M. TAYLOR in *Proc. R. Irish Acad.* IX. 116 Perhaps the *pukhwaj* is employed more than the other [*sc.* the tabla] by Hindu professionals. **1921** H. A. POPLEY *Mus. India* vii. 121 The *Pakhawāj* is a drum slightly larger than the mṛidaṅga but similar in shape, which is used in the north of India. **1957** *New Oxf. Hist. Mus.* I. iv. 222 Prominent in our days are the *pakhawaj* and the *tabla*. The former..has a clay body of irregular cylindrical shape, tapering slightly towards the left hand, with a large surface of parchment. **1969** R. SHANKAR *My Music, My Life* i. 41/1 The *pakhawaj*, a one-piece drum made of clay with two faces or heads, tuned to different pitches. **1977** B. C. DEVA *Mus. Instruments* 39 The *pakhavaj* is the king of drums in Hindustani music, though now it is more a constitutional monarch, respected from a distance.

Pakhto: see PASHTO *sb.* and *a.*

Pakhtun (pəkˈtuːn), *sb.* and *a.* Also **Pakhtoon, Pakhtun**, etc., and in form **Pashtun, Pushtun.** [Pashto.] **A.** *sb.* A member of a Pashto-speaking tribal people, also called PATHAN, inhabiting parts of south-east Afghanistan and north-west Pakistan; this people collectively. **B.** *adj.* Of or pertaining to this people.

1815 M. ELPHINSTONE *Acct. Kingdom of Caubul* II. i. 151 Their own name for their nation is Pooshtoon; in the plural, Pooshtauneh. The Berdooraunees pronounce this word Pookhtauneh. **1867** H. W. BELLEW *Dict. Pukkhto* p. vii, To have given place to all the words of those languages used in an unchanged form by Pukkhtūn authors, would have added unnecessarily to the bulk of the work. **1880** —— *Races of Afghanistan* vi. 56 The term Pathán is not a native word at all. It is the Hindustani form of the native word Pukhtána, which is the plural of Pukhtún, or Pakhtún..as it is pronounced by the Afrídí. And Pukhtún is the proper patronymic of the people inhabiting the country called Pukhtún-khwá, and speaking the language called Pukhtú or Pukhto. **1885** G. C. WHITWORTH *Anglo-Indian Dict.* 245/2 *Pathán* (Hindustáni, from the Pashto *pakhtána*, the plural of *pakhtun*, the name of a people inhabiting the country called by Herodotus Pactiya.) **1906** A. HAMILTON *Afghanistan* x. 263 After the Afghans the dominant people are the Pukhtun or Pathans, represented by a variety of tribes. **1908** *Encycl. Relig. & Ethics* I. 158/2 The Afghans themselves prefer the designation Pushtūn or Pukhtūn, older form Pashtūn, Pakhtūn (whence their Indian name Pathān). **1940** P. SYKES *Hist. Afghanistan* I. i. 13 The Afghan nomads organized on a tribal system, whose true national name is Pashtun or Pakhtun, generally termed 'Pathan' by Europeans, belong to the Turko-Iranian type. **1955** *Times* 11 May 9/6 Even before 1947 the Pathans (or Pakhtoons, as they are called in their own tongue) had been claiming the right to independence. **1956** *Ann. Reg. 1955* 116 The Afghan Prime Minister..stated that the proposed merger of West Pakistan would never be accepted or recognized either by the 'Pakhtun nation' or by his Government. **1963** *Times* 13 May 9/5 One consequence expected from Sardar Muhammad Daud Khan's resignation was an improvement of relations between Afghanistan and its neighbour Pakistan... Afghanistan is so publicly committed to the cause of the Pakhtuns, however, that no sudden relinquishment can be expected. **1971** *Illustr. Weekly India* 18 Apr. 21/2 West Pakistan in order to consolidate the Baluchis and the Pakhtoons in its north-west, may be forced into a diversionary adventure in Kashmir. **1973** *Times* 27 July 16/5 An attempt was made to raise the Pakhtun flag on the banks of the Indus. **1974** *Encycl. Brit. Micropædia* VII. 783/1 The Pashtuns believe themselves to have originated in Afghanistan and to be descended from a common ancestor.

Paki (ˈpækɪ). *slang.* Also **Pakki, Pakky.** [Abbrev. of PAKISTANI *sb.* and *a.*] A Pakistani, *spec.* an immigrant from Pakistan. Also *attrib.* and in *comb.*, as ***Paki-bashing***, wanton physical assault on or other violence directed against Pakistani immigrants (hence ***Paki-bash, Paki-basher***).

1964 *Guardian* 15 Apr. 8/4 Some big Paki over the water's got her set up for right trouble. **1969** B. KNOX *Tallyman* v. 94 Ali's a Paki—an' you know how it goes. Paki's pretty well look all the same to me. **1970** *Observer* 5 Apr. 3/2 The name of the game is Pakky Bashing... Any Asian careless enough to be walking the streets at night is a fool. **1970** *Daily Progress* (Charlottesville, Va.) 15 Apr. 7-c/2 They attack Asian immigrants, and term this 'paki-bashing'. **1972** J. BROWN *Chancer* iii. 47 Sergeant Burton and me, we broke in the Paki lodging house. **1973** C. MULLARD *Black Brit.* II. iv. 40 'Hunting the Barney'..a practice that has much in common with present-day 'Paki-bashing'. **1973** M. AMIS *Rachel Papers* 142 Joe, a young and ambitious cook, was fed up to the teeth with cooking steak and chips for the odd Pakki. **1975** J. SYMONS *Three Pipe Problem* v. 36 He wanted to send the nig nogs and the Pakis back where they belong, in the jungle. **1976** *Times* 20 Jan. 12/7 Argument over the precise number of Paki-bashers who can dance on the arms of a swastika. **1977** F. BRANSTON *Up & Coming Man* xii. 126 He let the half [of a house] he owned to a load of Pakis to use as a temple. **1977** *Daily Tel.* 17 Jan. 3/1 'Paki-busting' is suddenly a topical phrase in Canada. **1977** *Time* 12 Dec. 19/3 Bands of front backers, swinging fists and banner staves, have sallied into peaceful demonstrations by Indians and Pakistanis in what are cruelly called 'Paki bashes'.

pakihi (ˈpɑːkihi). Also **pakahi, paki.** [Maori.] An area of open, swampy, land, esp. characteristic of north-western parts of the South Island of New Zealand; also, the type of waterlogged soil associated with such land. Also *attrib.*

1861 J. VON HAAST *Rep. Topogr. & Geol. Explor. Nelson Province* iv. 131, I shall now enumerate the different pakis, or open tracts of land, and give a short description of them. **1871** C. L. MONEY *Knocking about in N.Z.* v. 63 We suddenly came out of the bush on to an open pakihi some miles in length. **1896** *N.Z. Alpine Jrnl.* II. 148 The only patch of rata bush on the flat, the rest being partly open 'pakihi' and partly covered with low scrub and timber. **1919** L. J. WILD *Soils & Manures in N.Z.* v. 53 Pakihi Soils of Westland..occur over considerable tracts of sour, swampy, but easily drained terrace lands. **1930** J. DEVANNY *Bushman Burke* 14 The supplies..had been packed by horse along a track cut out of the bush, and further, up towards the Ridge, the pakahi. **1947** P. NEWTON *Wayleggo* (1949) x. 110 Little pakihis ran up into the bush every here and there. **1959** A. MCLINTOCK *Descr. Atlas N.Z.* p. xiv, The souls in the scrub-covered terraces are gley podzols (pakihi). **1959** G. SLATTER *Gun in my Hand* 76 Green swamp-water, a tangle of black-berry or pakahi beside the twisting railway line. **1970** *N.Z. Listener* 7 Dec. 6/3 The 33 million acres of sour and barren 'pakihi' soil [on the West Coast of N.Z.]. *Ibid.* 6/5 So what about all that pakihi? It is red-brown, depressing land whose drainage is blocked by an impervious iron pan. **1972** P. NEWTON *Sheep Thief* ix. 72 He set off up the creek in search of the horses. He found them grazing in a little pakihi. **1973** *Massey Ferguson Rev.* (N.Z.) Mar.-Apr. 3/1 Two farmers a few miles away from Bald Hill have successfully transformed 170 acres of pakihi by using much the same over-sowing methods as the department.

pakisbrede, variant of PAXBRED.

Pakistani (pɑːkɪˈstɑːnɪ, pæk-), *sb.* and *a.* [f. the name *Pakistan* + -I.] **A.** *sb.* A native or inhabitant of Pakistan, an independent state formed in 1947 as a homeland for the Muslims of India from parts of Punjab, Sind, Baluchistan and North-West Province (East Pakistan, formerly East Bengal, achieved independence as Bangladesh in 1971). **B.** *adj.* Of or pertaining to Pakistan, its natives, or its inhabitants.

1941 L. S. AMERY *Let.* 25 Jan. in J. Glendevon *Viceroy at Bay* (1971) xvi. 198 Jinnah and his Pakistanis. **1948** *Sunday Times* 2 May 4/5 No Pakistani I have met is yet ready to admit that the achievement was not worth the sacrifice. **1950** *Times* 6 Mar. 5/7 The Pakistani Government soon set about filling the gap, taking care to ensure that the tribal areas and their peoples benefit from the development of West Pakistan as a whole. **1951** W. I. JENNINGS *Commonwealth in Asia* viii. 117 No Indian—or for that matter Pakistani or Ceylonese—politician wishes to sit at the same table as a representative of the Union of South Africa. **1957** *Times* 19 Dec. 15/2 The agreement signed by the World Bank and Pakistani officials yesterday completes the initial financing of the newly formed Pakistan Industrial Credit and Investment Corporation. **1965** *New Statesman* 30 Apr. 670/1 In neighbouring Sparkbrook, where faded vermilion posters..stare down upon shabbily dressed Pakistanis. **1967** *Listener* 17 Aug. 211/3 Radio comics with their unending imitations of Pakistani bus conductors must find other targets. **1971** *Peace News* 28 Oct. 5/2 We understood that the Pakistani army was burning the villages in the area, in retaliation for the previous day's attack. **1973** M. AMIS *Rachel Papers* 186 When I surfaced, dragged along in a tide of fat-legged girls and torpid Pakistanis,..there..was Rachel. **1976** 'W. TREVOR' *Children of Dynmouth* iii. 77 He'd seen the Dynmouth Hards beating up the Pakistani from the steam laundry in a bus-shelter.

Pakki, Pakky, varr. PAKI.

pakora (pəˈkɔːrə). Also **pakhora.** [a. Hind. *pakoṛā* a dish of vegetables in grain-flour.] A savoury Indian dish consisting of diced or chopped vegetables coated in batter and deep fried.

1954 J. MASTERS *Bhowani Junction* xxiii. 192 Our guests will be here in half an hour, and I have forgotten to make pakhoras. **1962** R. P. JHABVALA *Get Ready for Battle* iii. 135 She took a bite from a cheese pakora. **1963** *Guardian* 1 May 6/5 She can make fresh pakoras..dainty morsels of cauliflower, green pepper, onion, or slivers of potato, coated in highly seasoned batter and deep-fried in oil. **1971** *Femina* (Bombay) 30 Apr. 63/1 Even then they get only cold pakoras or oil potato chips. **1972** R. P. JHABVALA *New Dominion* II. 138 The tea..was very nice. They had pakoras and samusas and all sorts of other things. **1978** *Times of India* 18 Mar. 13/6 Delicious smells from the neighbouring *halvai's* shop. He is frying *samosas, pakoras, jalebis* and other mouth-watering delicacies.

‖**pak pai** (pak paɪ). [Cantonese, lit. 'white licence'.] In Hong Kong, a car used illegally as a taxi.

1972 *South China Morning Post* (Hong Kong) 4 Dec. 10/6 *Pak Pai*, a car which plies for hire, illegally. **1977** *Ibid.* 13 Apr. 11/7 Triad gangs are involved in the operation of extortion rackets with mini-buses, pak pais and goods vehicles illegally used for passengers in rural areas. **1977** 'J. LE CARRÉ' *Hon. Schoolboy* xix. 464 Collecting gambling debts from the *pak-pai* drivers.

‖**paktong** (ˈpæktɒŋ). Also **paak-, packtong.** [Cantonese dial. form of Chinese *peh t'ung*, f.

peh white + *t'ung* copper. (*Pakfong* is a mere scribal or typographical error, which has passed from Ure's *Dict. Arts* into various other works.] Chinese nickel-silver; an alloy of copper, zinc, and nickel, resembling silver.

1775 *Ann. Reg.* II. 34/2 A specimen of the ore paaktong, or white copper. **1839** URE *Dict. Arts, Packfong.* **1856** W. A. MILLER *Elem. Chem.* II. 864 Owing to the remarkable whitening power which nickel exerts on brass, it is now much used in the manufacture of packfong. **1883** S. W. WILLIAMS *Middle Kingdom* II. 19 The pehtung, argentan, or white copper of the Chinese is an alloy of copper, zinc, nickel and iron;..these proportions are nearly the same as German silver.

paku, var. PACU.

pal (pæl), *sb.*[1] *colloq.* (orig. *slang* or *low colloq.*) Also 7–9 **pall**, 9 **pell**. [a. Eng. Gipsy *pal* brother, mate (Smart & Crofton) = Turkish Gipsy *pral*, *plal*, Transylv. Gipsy *pçral* brother.] A comrade, mate, partner, associate, 'chum'; an accomplice in crime or dishonesty.

1681–2 *Hereford Dioc. Reg. Depos.* 29 Jan. 51 Wheare have you been all this day, pall?.. Why, pall, what would you have mee to doe? **178..** PARKER *Life's Painter* 136 *Pal*, a comrade, when highwaymen rob in pairs, they say such a one was his or my pal. **1807** BYRON *Let.* 30 June in *Works* (1898) I. 130 'Better late than never, Pal,' is a saying.. applicable on the present occasion. **1812** J. H. VAUX *Flash Dict.*, *Pall*, a partner; companion; associate; or accomplice. **1827** *Blackw. Mag.* XXII. 693 Suppose me,..my pells all around me, fighting that day's battle o'er again. **1841** S. BAMFORD *Passages in Life of Radical* (ed. 2) I. xxiv. 151 The thieves and their 'pals', as he termed the repulsive females. **1886** *Lantern* (New Orleans) 27 Oct. 2/3 Reynold Bowers and his pal, Jack Lacoste. **1890** KIPLING in *Pioneer Mail* 28 May 698/2, I was great pals with a man called Hicksey. **1894** ASTLEY *50 Years Life* I. 331 He was a great pal of mine. **1924** F. M. FORD *Some do Not* I. ii. 50 Eunice Vanderdecken is a bitterly misjudged woman. She's a real good pal. **1936** M. DE LA ROCHE *Whiteoak Harvest* v. 79, I have talked to her.. as I couldn't to anyone else... Well, she's been a complete pal—if you know what I mean. **1963** *Listener* 14 Feb. 279/1 The local battalion, the Bradford Pals, was butchered at the Somme. **1972** J. PORTER *Meddler & her Murder* x. 128 Be a pal and shove the marge across.

Hence **'pallish**, **'pally** (also in the extended form **pally-wally**) *adjs.*, on terms of fellowship; 'chummy'; **'palliness**; **'palship**, the relation of being pals, comradeship. (All slangy.)

1892 M. WILLIAMS *Round London* (1893) 127, I was at Eton with [him]..and, as boys say, we were very 'pallish'. **1895** *Westm. Gaz.* 27 June 3/2 A pleasant scene between 'Miss Brown' and a school-girl from Demerara, who tries to become 'pally' with her. **1896** *Blackw. Mag.* Mar. 300 There is no 'palship' between a thief and his 'fence'. **1915** H. L. WILSON *Ruggles of Red Gap* (1917) i. 9 The Honourable George..had..been almost quite too pally with him. **1916** [see NEVER *adv.* 9]. **1922** J. CANNAN *Misty Valley* 282 If you cared for me it was not pally to let me go on doing things I didn't know were wrong. **1923** [see *hell-brew* s.v. HELL *sb.* 11 a]. **1929** H. A. VACHELL *Virgin* i. 12 She had never been 'pally' with girls. **1936** W. R. TITTERTON *G. K. Chesterton* I. v. 60 [He] was on pally terms even with small shop-keepers, farmers and country squires. **1936** P. M. CLARK *Autobiogr. Old Drifter* xiv. 200 The wonderful pal-ship of dogs is to me an everlasting delight. **1951** R. HOGGART *Auden* ii. 38 Auden often wobbles..from the pally to the patronising. **1954** F. BROWN in *Astounding Sci. Fiction* Sept. 16/2, I *like* quarrelling. If you're going to go namby-pamby and pally-wally on me, I'll go find someone else. **1966** *Listener* 23 June 897/2 The whole feuding quartet had been invited..to join the presidential plane and put on a show of unanimity and palship. **1972** R. D. ABRAHAMS in T. Kochman *Rappin' & Stylin' Out* 236 The protected and licensed confines of palship groupings. **1974** *Publishers Weekly* 11 Feb. 56/2 His long, intimate palship with Marlon 'Bud' Brando. **1974** S. GULLIVER *Vulcan Bulletins* 47 Why would Anscudden go along with stealing Javits' shipment? I thought they were supposed to be pally. **1976** *Scottish Rev.* Spring 9 She joined a Whist club and got very pally with another auld maid like herself.

†**pal**, *sb.*[2] *Obs. rare.* [ad. L. *pāla* spade, blade, shoulder-blade.] A blade.

1541 R. COPLAND *Guydon's Quest. Chirurg.* F iv b, The bone spatulare..is lyke a pal, for it is large and thynne fro the backe parte with an apparence holden by yͤ myddes.

pal, *v.* [f. PAL *sb.*[1]] *intr.* To become or be a 'pal' of another; to keep company, associate (*with*). Often with *in, on, up*, and *around with, up with*.

1879 *Autobiog. of Thief* in *Macm. Mag.* XL. 500, I palled in with some older hands at the game. **1889** MRS. L. B. WALFORD *Stiff-necked Gen.* (new ed.) 95, I think you and I 'pal up' very well. **1899** E. PHILLPOTTS *Human Boy* 84 Bray bossed Corkey and palled with him. **1915** R. LARDNER in *McClure's Mag.* Aug. 21/3, I and Lefty and Mike used to pal round together. **1926** G. HUNTING *Vicarion* vi. 103 And I shan't have time to compromise *you* when I can pal around with Charlemagne, or Valentino, or Rameses Second, or Kublai Khan! **1943** I. WOLFERT *Tucker's People* viii. 167 All those poor people..were just like the people he palled around with. **1958** B. HAMILTON *Too Much of Water* xi. 249, I got tight one night with a chap I'd palled up with. **1975** *High Times* Dec. 24/1 Lenny picked up part of his *schtick* from the characters that he palled around with in New York. **1976** *New Society* 20 May 409/1 Y'know, who to pal up with. **1977** *Time* 28 Mar. 37/1 It has been reported that he occasionally palled around with gangsters on golf courses or in gambling casinos.

pal, obs. f. PALE, PALL.

pala ('pɑːlə). *Ent.* Pl. **palæ**. [a. L. *pāla* spade.] (See quot. 1906.) Hence **'palar** *a.*, of or pertaining to a pala.

1892 E. SAUNDERS *Hemiptera Heteroptera Brit. Islands* 336 *C*[*orixa*] *Fallenii*... The palæ of the male are truncate at the base. **1906** J. B. SMITH *Explanation Terms Entomol.* 95 Pala: the shovel-shaped tarsal joints in many aquatic *Heteroptera*. **1957** RICHARDS & DAVIES *Imms's Gen. Textbk. Entomol.* (ed. 9) III. 428 The pala is not a stridulatory organ, nor has it been shown conclusively that the peculiar strigil of these insects [*sc.* Corixidæ] is concerned with sound production. **1959** SOUTHWOOD & LESTON *Land & Water Bugs Brit. Isles* 387 Palar pegs numerous, extending in a row along most of the pala. *Ibid.* 388 Male palae more or less rounded on the top edge.

pala: see PALAY.

pala: see PALLAH.

‖**palabra** (pə'lɑːbrə). [Sp., = word: cf. PALAVER.] A word; speech, talk, palaver.

Chiefly in *pl. pocas palabras* (Spanish) few words: a phrase frequent *c* 1600, and variously corrupted.

1594 KYD *Sp. Trag.* III. xiv. 118 What new deuice haue they deuised, tro? *Pocas Palabras*, milde as the Lambe. **1596** SHAKS. *Tam. Shr.* Induct. i. 5 Therefore *Paucas pallabris*, let the world slide: *Sessa*. **1611** MIDDLETON & DEKKER *Roaring Girl* D.'s Wks. 1873 III. 221 *Pacus palabros*, I will coniure for you, farewell. **1821** SCOTT *Kenilw.* xi, An ye mend not your manners, and mind your business, leaving off such idle palabras. **1837** CARLYLE *Fr. Rev.* III. v. vi, To conquer or die is no theatrical palabra, in these circumstances, but a practical truth and necessity.

palace ('pæləs), *sb.*[1] Forms: 3–6 **paleys, -eis, -ais**, 4–5 **paleise, -eyse, -eice, -eyce, -as, -ys**, 4–6 **palays, -ayce, -es, -is**, 5 **palass(e, -aies, -yce, -ijs, payleysse, -ays**, 5–6 **palaise, -ice, -ois, -oys**, 6 **paliss, -ise, -ece, pal(l)aice, pallas(e, -ays, -es, -ys**, 6–8 **pallace**, 5– **palace**. *Pl.* **palaces**: in 4 **paleis, -eys**, 5 **-ice, -is, -yce, -ys, -es**; 6 **palacies**. [ME. a. OF. *palais, paleis*, F. *palais* = Pr. *palai, -ait*, Sp., Pg. *palacio*, It. *palazzo*:—L. *palātium*, orig. proper name of one of the seven hills of Rome (also called *Mons Palatinus*, the PALATINE Mount), hence, the house of Augustus there situated, and later the assemblage of buildings which composed the palace of the Cæsars, and finally covered the whole hill; whence transf. to other imperial and royal residences.

From the Fr. also Du. *paleis*, Ger. *palast*, LG. *palas*, Da. *palads*, Sw. *palats*; but the word appears originally to have entered the Teut. langs. in the form *palantium* or *palantia* (cf. Gr. παλλάντιον), whence OE. *palęnt* m., *palęnte*, *palęndse* wk. fem., OFris. *palense*, OS. *palencea*, *palinza*, OHG. *pfalanza*, *-inza*, MHG. *phalenze*, *pfalze*, *pfalz* fem.: cf. PALSGRAVE.]

1. a. The official residence of an emperor, king, pope, or other sovereign ruler.

c **1290** *S. Eng. Leg.* I. 39/194 A-midde þe paleys þis holi bodi huy bureden with grete pruyte. *a* **1300** *K. Horn* 1256 Horn him ȝede with his To þe kinges palais [*v.r.* paleyse]. **1362** LANGL. *P. Pl.* A. II. 18 In þe pope paleys heo is as priue as my-seluen. **1393** *Ibid.* C. XI. 16 Boþe princes paleis [*B* paleyses] and poure menne Cotes. *c* **1430** *Syr Tryam.* 488 The hounde, as the story says, Ranne to the kyngys palays. **1475** *Nottingham Rec.* II. 389 Yeuen vnder our Priue Seal, at our Palois of Westminster. **1500–20** DUNBAR *Poems* lix. 4 Hes magellit my making, throw his maliss, And present it into ȝowr paliss. **1529** RASTELL *Pastyme* (1811) 13 He was in his pales slayn by treason. **1549** *Compl. Scot.* 42 Lyik as plutois paleis hed been birnand. **1555** EDEN *Decades* 259 The dukes pallaice. **1589** *Hay any Work* (1844) 69 Going to the old pallas at Westminster. **1703** MAUNDRELL *Journ. Jerus.* (1732) 101 When David spied her from the Terrace of his Pallace. **1743** BULKELEY & CUMMINS *Voy. S. Seas* 110 That the worst Jail in England is a Palace to our present Situation. **1851** RUSKIN *Stones Ven.* (1874) II. vii. 233 The Ducal Palace stands comparatively alone.

b. The official residence of an archbishop or bishop within his cathedral city, e.g. Fulham Palace; in common parlance extended to any episcopal residence, e.g. 'Lambeth Palace', 'Cuddesdon Palace': see quots. 1886–96. (This use does not seem to obtain out of England.)

c **1290** *Beket* 1865 in *S. Eng. Leg.* I. 160 Seint thomas ne hadde i-beo at is paleis nouȝt longe. *c* **1380** WYCLIF in Todd *Three Treat.* 151 More þei shal be sett by..whenne þei comen to her paleices. *c* **1450** *Merlin* 105 The archebisshop drough hem alle to his paleis. **1547** BOORDE *Brev. Health, Extrav.* 4 b, All that Cardynalles palacis, be so sumptuously maynteyned. **1556** *Chron. Gr. Friars* (Camden) 27 The fest holden in the byshoppe of Londones palles. **1642–3** in Rushw. *Hist. Coll.* (1721) V. 109 To the Bishop of Lincoln's House,..commonly called the Bishop's Palace. **1781** COWPER *Truth* 122 Not all the plenty of a Bishop's board, His palace, and his lacqueys, and 'My Lord!' **1845** J. F. MURRAY *Tour of Thames* 36 The manor-house, or palace, of Fulham has been, from a very early period the principal summer residence of the Bishops of London. **1886** *Daily News* 28 Dec. 7/1 The style of 'palace' belongs strictly to a bishop's residence within his cathedral city only. Lambeth Palace was known correctly as Lambeth House within the past 90 years; and letters of Bonner are extant dated severally from his palace at Fulham and house at Lambeth. **1896** *Spectator* 22 Aug 235 Even the most ordinary of villa residences is a palace when lived in by a Bishop;..the Bishop will make anything short of furnished lodgings a palace.

c. In extended applications, chiefly due to translation or adaptation of foreign usage.

In some versions of the Bible, loosely used for Gr. αὐλή, L. *atrium*, hall, court; sometimes applied to a ducal mansion, e.g. *Blenheim Palace, Dalkeith Palace*; like It. *palazzo*, applied to the large mansions of noble families in Italian cities, as the *Farnese Palace*; in *palace of justice* applied, like F. *palais de justice*, to the supreme law-court; etc.

1526 TINDALE *John* xviii. 15 [He] went in with Iesus into the pallys [**1539**, **1611** palace] of the hye preste [αὐλήν, *atrium*, WYCLIF the halle of the bischop, *Geneva* hall, *Rhem.*, *R.V.* court]. **1596** DALRYMPLE tr. *Leslie's Hist. Scot.* I. 47 Vpon the Riuer of Douern ar castelis, Touris, palices, and gentil menis places nocht few. **1808** PIKE *Sources Mississ.* III. (1810) 212 The public square is in the centre of the town; on the north side of which is situated the palace (as they term it) or government house. **1818** *Burt's Lett. N. Scot.* I. Notes 6 People commonly denominate the house of a duke, as they do an episcopal residence, a palace. **1823** ROGERS *Italy* xviii. 4 Stop at a Palace near the Reggio-gate, Dwelt in of old by one of the Orsini.

†**d.** *U.S.* In allusive use: see quot. *Obs.*

1809 J. QUINCY in *Life* 174 The result was astonishing to Campbell and the leaders of the Palace troops [supporters of Jefferson's Administration]. *Ibid.* 185 Dawson, a man of the palace.

e. By metonymy, the monarch or monarchy.

1962 A. SAMPSON *Anat. Brit.* I. iii. 49 For much of this, it is unfair to blame the palace. Many of the pretensions spring from deeper causes than the monarchy. **1973** *Times* 14 Apr. (Nepal Suppl.) p. i/5 The primacy of the palace in the decision-making process was the principal feature of the constitution that King Mahendra introduced in 1962. **1974** *Listener* 14 Mar. 327/3, I thought the election was going to be a very close thing..actually, the Conservatives have more votes than the Labour Party. But I think the choice made by the Palace was inevitable. **1974** *Times* 6 May 14/7 The Palace..believed it did not *have* to accede to Mr Wilson's request.

2. In various figurative uses: e.g. ***the palace of heaven, a fairy palace***, etc.

a **1300** *Cursor M.* 412 He wroght þe angels all of heuen And sette þam in haly palais [*v.r.* pales]. **1362** LANGL. *P. Pl.* A. XI. 302 Percen wiþ a pater noster þe paleis of heuene. *c* **1400** *Rom. Rose* 5002 Peyne & Distresse, Syknesse & Ire,.. Ben of hir [Eldes] paleys senatours. **1526** *Pilgr. Perf.* (W. de W. 1531) 233 May..ouerthrowe yͤ spirituall hous or palays that he hath entended..to rere vp. **1597** HOOKER *Eccl. Pol.* v. lxv. §7 Which conceipt being entered into that palace of mans fancie. *c* **1614** SIR W. MURE *Dido & Æneas* I. 501 Some waxen pallaces with paine do reir. **1778** MISS BURNEY *Evelina* (1791) I. xii. 33 Made me almost think I was in some inchanted castle or fairy palace. **1898** WATTS-DUNTON *Aylwin* (1900) 65/1 The face of a wanderer from the cloud-palaces of the sylphs.

3. A dwelling-place of palatial splendour; a stately mansion.

1387 TREVISA *Higden* (Rolls) I. 213 þere were meny paleys [**1432–50** tr. *Higden* palice] real and noble i-bulde in Rome in worschippe of emperours and of oþere noble men also. *c* **1400** MAUNDEV. (Roxb.) xv. 66 þai schall hafe faire palaycez and grete and faire housez. *c* **1450** HOLLAND *Howlat* 668 Past till a palace of pryce plesand allane. **1589** GREENE *Menaphon* (Arb.) 30, I will imagine a small cotage to [be] a spacious pallaice. **1740** DYCHE & PARDON s.v. *Woodstock*, The Churchills..for whom is built a most magnificent palace. **1856** EMERSON *Eng. Traits, Wealth* Wks. (Bohn) II. 73 A hundred thousand palaces adorn the island.

4. *transf.* A building, usually spacious and of attractive appearance, intended as a place of amusement, entertainment, or refreshment: cf. GIN-, COFFEE-*palace*, etc. Also, ***palace of varieties***, a variety theatre.

Crystal Palace, the name of the building of the Great Exhibition of 1851, when removed and erected on Sydenham Hill, near London, as a permanent place of entertainment; it was destroyed by fire in 1936.

1834 *Oxf. Univ. Mag.* I. 327 The gin palaces, (as they have been not inaptly called). **1851** (*title*) Palace of Glass and the Gatherings of the People. **1851** (*title*) Crystal Palace and its Great Exhibition, as it was. **1855** *London as it is to-day* 121 The new Crystal Palace..is..a permanent addition to the means of amusement and instruction possessed by England and the world. **1875** *Chamb. Jrnl.* No. 133. 66 The gin palaces are filled with men, women, children, noise, smoke, and gas. **1890** *Pall Mall G.* 4 Sept. 6/2 'The Dockers' Palace' is the name of an institution..in connection with the parochial work of St. Matthew's, Stepney. **1894** STEAD *If Christ came to Chicago* 358 The coffee parlours and cocoa palaces of many English towns. **1899** BEERBOHM *More* 125 Oh, for the wasted glories of the old Oxford! Oh, for one hour in the Hoxton Palace of Varieties! **1902** O. WISTER *Virginian* xiii. 148, I came upon him one morning in Colonel Cyrus Jones's eating palace. **1933** P. GODFREY *Back-Stage* xiv. 179 Sir Oswald Stoll, by transforming the music-hall into the palace of varieties, achieved the same sort of result that Sir Joseph Lyons reached by converting tea-shops into Corner Houses. **1966** *Economist* 10 Dec. 1144/2 The plush restaurants..have been supplanted by the palaces *à go-go*. **1973** A. MACVICAR *Painted Doll Affair* ii. 32 A toilet palace dominates the head of Inveraray pier. **1976** J. M. BROWNJOHN tr. *Kirst's Time for Payment* 28 There was a big medium-priced restaurant, a porn palace, a hair stylist.

†**5.** The astrological 'house' of a planet: see HOUSE *sb.*[1] 8. *Obs.*

c **1374** CHAUCER *Compl. Mars* 53 Mars shal entre as fast as he may glyde In-to hir next paleys to abyde.

6. *attrib.* and *Comb.*: **a.** attrib. 'of or belonging to, or of the style of, a palace', as ***palace-castle, -chamber, -church, -door, -garden, -guard, -hall, -life, -politics, -prison, -yard***, etc. **b.** Instrumental, locative, objective, similative, etc., as ***palace-bordered, -covered, -like, -taught, -walking*** adjs. **c.** Special Combs.: **palace-car**, a railway-carriage fitted up in luxurious style; so ***palace tramcar***; **palace coup** = *palace revolution*; **palace-crown**, a counter used by officers of the Palais Royal in France; **palace**

guard, (*a*) one who guards a palace; (*b*) one who helps to protect a monarch, president, etc.; **palace-hotel**, a hotel of palatial splendour; **palace revolution** [cf. G. *palastrevolution*], the overthrowal of a sovereign, etc., without civil war, usu. by other members of the ruling group; also *fig.*; **palace style** *Archæol.*, a type of pottery associated with the Minoan palaces, or an imitation of this type.

1893 'MARK TWAIN' in *Century Mag.* Dec. 234/1 Along the *palace-bordered canals of Venice. **1900** J. K. JEROME *Three Men on Bummel* viii. 174 Through Prague's dirty, palace-bordered alleys must have pressed often in hot haste blind Ziska and open-minded Wallenstein. **1868** *Dispatch & Vanguard* (San Francisco) 28 Mar. 1/1, I enjoyed the equivocal luxury of traveling in a '*palace' or 'sleeping car'. **1884** *Pall Mall G.* 9 Dec. 11/1 When you sleep in a palace car you are liable to be jerked up on end by the sudden slowing up of the train. **1967** C. O. SKINNER *Madame Sarah* viii. 163 They travelled via .. three Pullmans .. and her own private car, known as a 'Palace Car'. **1899** J. H. METCALFE *Earldom of Wiltes* 11 A *palace-castle similar to Sheriff-Hutton. *c* **1374** CHAUCER *Former Age* 41 Yit were no *paleis chaumbres, ne non halles. **1738** WESLEY *Ps. & Hymns* CIV. iii, God .. forms His Palace-Chamber in the Skies. **1846** LOUISA S. COSTELLO *Tour Venice* 290 That gorgeous *palace-church, which it took ages to erect. **1970** *Guardian* 13 Jan. 1/2 Some kind of *palace coup occurred in Biafra on Friday... The Biafran doves 'invited' their leader to step down. **1970** *Daily Tel.* 16 Feb. 16 This adds another possibility to those of a bid by Reed or a rival—a palace coup which would allow new management to be called in to put through an internal re-organisation. **1865** J. H. INGRAHAM *Pillar of Fire* (1872) 153 This *palace-covered island. **1653** URQUHART *Rabelais* II. xxi. 148 A great purse full of *Palace-crowns [Fr. *d'escutz du Palais*] called counters. *c* **1374** CHAUCER *Troylus* II. 508 (459) In with þe *paleys gardyn by a welle. **1887** G. MEREDITH *Ballads & P.* 46 The *palace-guard Had passed the measured rounds. **1948** J. A. FARLEY *Jim Farley's Story* xxii. 232 Nathan Straus brought me word that the White House 'palace guard' realized the anti-Catholic campaign against me had failed. **1973** *Times* 11 May 1/1 This seemed his [*sc.* President Nixon's] most direct admission to date that he had allowed himself to be kept too isolated for too long by his departed 'palace guard'. **1833** TENNYSON *Poems* 70 And richly feast within thy *palacehall. **1847** MARY HOWITT *Ballads* 316 There were *palace-homes around her. **1870** J. D. SHERWOOD *Comic Hist. U.S.* 422 By the side of *palace hotels, now gleaming along golden bays. **1884** *Century Mag.* Mar. 643/1 It [*sc.* Washington, D.C.] has no elevated rail-roads, no palace hotels, no mammoth elevators. **1900** *Westm. Gaz.* 30 Aug. 8/1 The huge palace-hotels appear to have suffered most. **1934** G. B. SHAW *Too True to be Good* 11 Come to our palace hotels. **1969** *Sat. Rev.* (U.S.) 4 Jan. 64/2 Whether the world of the Superjet will allow the survival of the palace hotels is a question facing grand tours and grand tourists. **1865** GLADSTONE *Farew. Addr. Edin. Univ.* 24 That system exhibits a kind of royal or *palace-life of man. **1801** H. SKRINE *Rivers Gt. Brit.* 46 Buxton where Hygæa has created her *palace-like temple. **1608** SYLVESTER *Du Bartas* II. iv. IV. *Decay* 197 These *Palace-mice, this busie-idle sort Of fawning Minions, full of sooths and smiles. **1896** *Dublin Rev.* July 15 Eliakim is to succeed him as the king's *palace-prefect. **1904** *N.E.D.* s.v. *Palace* sb.[1] 6a., *Palace revolution. **1907** J. LONDON *Iron Heel* xiv. 188 They will be like the guards of the palace in old Rome, and there will be palace revolutions whereby the labour castes will seize the reins of power. **1932** M. EASTMAN tr. *Trotsky's Hist. Russ. Revolution* I. 83 (*heading*) The Idea of a Palace Revolution. **1935** H. A. L. FISHER *Hist. Europe* I. xii. 143 The [Byzantine] state was shaken by palace revolutions and civil war. **1949** *Mind* LVIII. 500 The ensuing changes must be classed with the 'palace revolutions' of other histories, since they scarcely affected the structure of the state. **1958** *Times* 1 Mar. 7/6 The palace revolution in ski racing technique. **1972** H. KEMELMAN *Monday the Rabbi took Off* xix. 123 The Persian King feared a palace revolution by Haman and plotted with Esther to bring about his ruin. **1902** A. J. EVANS in *Ann. Brit. Sch. Athens* 1900–1901 51 (*heading*) Mycenaean painted pottery of the '*Palace Style'. *Ibid.*, The view that this in fact represents the indigenous 'Palace Style' of Knossos in its highest development is confirmed by the evident parallelism which its motives present to the decorative wall paintings of the building. **1913** R. A. S. MACALISTER *Philistines* i. 18 In Palestine and elsewhere occasional scraps of the 'palace' styles come to light. **1939** J. D. S. PENDLEBURY *Archæol. Crete* iv. 180 L.M. II, in fact, was, like M.M. II, a true Palace style, though even more restricted in being confined to Knossos alone. **1974** *Encycl. Brit. Macropædia* XIX. 275/2 Between 1450 and 1375 BC, Mycenaean taste reduced the spontaneity of the early Marine style to a rigid formality, thereby creating the monumental Palace style. **1834** *Tait's Mag.* I. 232/2 The *palace-taught, and college-fed, Brings scandal on the meek unhonoured head. **1819** SHELLEY *Cenci* II. ii. 68 That *palace-walking devil Gold. **1725** POPE *Odyss.* XVIII. 123 He reels, he fails, Till propped, reclining on the *palace-walls.

† **palace**, *sb.*[2] *Obs.* Also 5–6 **palas, -ys, -ays.** [a. F. *palais* (13th c. in Hatz.-Darm.), ad. L. *palātium*, confounded with *palātum* (Darmesteter).] The palate or roof of the mouth: see PALATE.

1483 *Cath. Angl.* 266/2 A Palace (*v.r.* Palas) of a mouthe, *frumen, palacium.* **1506** *Kalender of Sheph.* K viij, The palys or rofe bone. **1541** R. COPLAND *Guydon's Quest. Chirurg.* F ij, What is the palays?.. It is the hyghest place or rofe of the mouth. **1547** BOORDE *Brev. Health* xxvi. 16 Ulceration in the palace or the roughe of the mouth.

ˈ**palace**, *sb.*[3] *s.w. dial.* Also **pallace.** [Of uncertain history; usually identified in spelling with PALACE *sb*[1], but perh. orig. a special use of PALIS *sb.*, in sense 'enclosed place', 'yard'.] (See quots.)

1506 *Will of R. Holland* (Som. Ho.), My place or howse that I dwell in and a litell howse or paleys adiownyng [Exeter]. **1703** *Lease Corporation Totnes* (in *N. & Q.* 1st Ser. (1850) I. 202/1), All that cellar and the chambers over the same, and the little pallace and landing-place adjoining to the river Dart. **1719** *Ibid.* (ibid. 233/2) All that great cellar lately rebuilt, and the plott of ground or pallace thereto belonging lately converted into a cellar. **1777** *Horæ Subsecivæ* 317 (E.D.D.) At Dartmouth in Devon there are some of these storehouses cut out of the rock still retaining their old name of palaces. **1871** QUILLER-COUCH *Hist. Polperro* 32. **1880** *E. Cornwall Gloss.*, *Palace*, a cellar for the bulking and storing of pilchards. This cellar is usually a square building with a pent-house roof, enclosing an open area or court. **1883** W. BLAKE in Walsh *Irish Fisheries* 27 (Fish. Exhib. Publ.), Even now in certain parts of the county of Cork there were remains of what were called fish palaces, where the Dutch used to cure the fish. **1890** QUILLER-COUCH *Three Ships* iv. (1892) 66 The towns-folk live on their first storeys, using the lower floors as fish cellars, or 'pallaces'.

ˈ**palace**, *v. rare.* [f. PALACE *sb.*[1]] *trans.* To place or lodge in a palace.

1873 BROWNING *Red Cott. Nt.-cap* 1588 Behold her palaced straight In splendor, clothed in diamonds. **1875** —— *Aristoph. Apol.* 5543 Elektra, palaced once, a visitant To thy poor rustic dwelling, now I come.

palace, erron. var. PALIS *Obs.*

Palace Court, ˈ**palace-**ˈ**court.** [= Court of the or a palace.]

1. Name of a court formerly held at the Marshalsea and having jurisdiction in personal actions arising within twelve miles of the palace of Whitehall, the city of London excepted: see quots.

1685 *Termes de la Ley* 525 *Palace-Court*, is a Court of Record, .. held at Southwark, and is a Court of Common Law. **1766** ENTICK *London* IV. 385. **1768** BLACKSTONE *Comm.* III. 76 King Charles I in the sixth year of his reign by his letters patent erected a new court of record, called the *curia palatii* or palace court, to be held before the steward of the household and knight marshal, and the steward of the court, or his deputy. **1773** *W. Salkeld's Rep. K.B.* 439 This must have been to the Palace Court, where neither plaintiff nor defendant must be of the king's house-hold; but, in a suit in the Marshalsea, both must be of the king's household. [**1849** *Act 12 & 13 Vict.* c. 101 §14 From and after the thirty-first day of December 1849 all the power, authority, and jurisdiction of the said Court of the Marshalsea, and of the said Court of the Palace of the Queen at Westminster .. shall cease and determine.] **1891** C. R. SCARGILL-BIRD *Guide to P.R.O.* Introd. 26.

2. The court-yard of a palace.

1801 SOUTHEY *Thalaba* VIII. xxxv, Open fly the iron doors, The doors of the palace-court. **1855** KINGSLEY *Heroes*, *Theseus* II. 211 His palace-court is full of their bones.

palaced (ˈpæləst), *a.* [f. PALACE *sb.*[1] and *v.* + -ED.] Having a palace or palaces; living in a palace.

1817 W. TAYLOR in *Monthly Mag.* XLIII. 46 Dearer than places of palac'd pride. *a* **1851** MOIR *Dark Waggon* iv, Till Lythgo shows, in mirrored gold, Its palaced loch so fair. **1886** *American* XIII. 21 The palaced rich and the homeless and houseless poor.

palace gate. The gate of a palace.

c **1374** CHAUCER *Compl. Mars* 82 Phebus, that was comen hastely Within the paleys yates ful sturdely. **14..** *Sir Beues* 306 (MS. M), He ranne hym forth at the ȝate, Till he come to the paleyse gate. **1523** SKELTON *Garl. Laurel* 468 Of elephantis tethe were the palace gatis. **1725** POPE *Odyss.* I. 140 On hides of beeves, before the palace-gate, .. the suitors sat. **1841** DOWNTON *Hymn, 'For Thy Mercy and Thy Grace'*, So within Thy palace-gate We shall praise, on golden strings, Thee, the only Potentate.

palaceous (pəˈleɪʃəs), *a. Bot.* [f. mod.L. *pālāce-us* (f. L. *pāla* shovel) + -OUS.] Of a leaf: Having a spade-like form, owing to the edge being decurrent on the support.

1835 LINDLEY *Introd. Bot.* (1848) II. 379 *Palaceous*, when the footstalk adheres to the margin.

ˈ**palaceward, -wards**, *adv.* [See -WARD.] Toward the palace. (Orig. †*to, unto the pallacewarde.*)

c **1374** CHAUCER *Troylus* II. 1252 (1203) (Campsall MS.) As was his wey to wende To paylaysward. **1587** TURBERV. *Trag. T.* (1837) 227 That made into the Pallacewarde, As fast as shee mought flie. **1894** SALA *London up to Date* I. 9, I .. advise you not to travel palacewards in a tramcar.

palach, variant of PELLOCK, a porpoise.

‖**palacio** (paˈlaθjo, pəˈlæsɪəʊ). [Sp., palace.] A palace, or a country seat, or an official building (in Spain or the Spanish-speaking territories in the Americas); also, the name of a specific building, as the former residence of the Spanish and Mexican governors in Santa Fe, New Mexico, or the former hunting-lodge of the Spanish kings in the Coto Doñana, Sevilla.

1844 J. GREGG *Commerce Prairies* I. 203 These bricks are called *adobes*, and every edifice, from the church to the *palacio*, is constructed of the same stuff. **1885** *Weekly New Mexican Rev.* 18 June 4/1 There he erected a palacio. **1893** CHAPMAN & BUCK *Wild Spain* xxxii. 350 The head of our cavalcade sighted the welcome light displayed from the turrets of the ancient shooting lodge of Doñana. Though now in a state of partial ruin, the old Palacio still shows of former grandeur, and has been .. a favourite sporting retreat for more than one Spanish king. **1963** *Times* 27 Feb. 11/6 It was frequently visited for hunting parties by the Kings of Spain for whom was created the palacio or hunting-lodge which is still the only substantial habitation many miles from the nearest road. **1968** R. F. ADAMS *Western Words* (rev. ed.) 218/2 *Palacio*, what the early freighters called the Palace of Governors in Santa Fe. **1969** A. MARIN *Rise with Wind* xiv. 170 A four-story white-stucco *palacio*. **1975** N. LUARD *Robespierre Serial* xiii. 113 The *palacio* had been .. used by the Spanish Kings who'd come to the Coto to shoot. **1977** P. SOMERVILLE-LARGE *Eagles near Carcase* vii. 132, I worked at the *palacio* before I was married.

†**paˈlacious**, *a. Obs.* Also **pall-.** [f. L. *palāti-um* PALACE *sb.*[1] + -OUS.] = PALATIAL.

1628 DEKKER *Brittannia's Honor* Wks. 1873 IV. 99 Faire, Spacious, and Pallacious Houses. **1662** GRAUNT *Bills of Mortality* vii. 41 The turning of great Palacious Houses into small Tenements.

palacye, obs. form of PALSY.

paladin (ˈpælədɪn). Also 6 **palladine, -yne,** 7 **paladine.** [a. F. *paladin* (16th c., Hatz.-Darm.), ad. It. *paladino* = Sp. *paladin, palatino*:—L. *palātīn-us* of or belonging to the palace, palatine; introduced after the equivalent OF. *palaisin, -asin, -azin* (see PALASIN) had become obsolete. Mod.F. has also, in another application, a third form of the same word, *palatin*: see PALATINE.] In modern forms of the Charlemagne romances, One of the Twelve Peers or famous warriors of Charlemagne's court, of whom the Count Palatine was the foremost; hence sometimes *transf.* a Knight of the Round Table; also *fig.* a knightly hero, renowned champion, knight errant.

1592 DANIEL *Delia* xlvi, Let others sing of Knights and Palladines. **1598** BARNFIELD *Poems* (Arb.) 85 Angellica the faire, (For whom the Palladine of Fraunce fell mad). ? *c* **1600** *Distracted Emp.* I. i, Of brave Orlando the great palladyne. *a* **1649** DRUMM. OF HAWTH. *Hist. Jas. V*, Wks. (1711) 165 They appeared upon the day armed from head to foot, like ancient paladines. **1658** PHILLIPS s.v. *Palatinate*, Certain knights of this Island, in ancient times called Knights of the round Table, were called Paladines. **1788** GIBBON *Decl. & F.* lii. V. 411 The true Peers and Paladins of French chivalry. **1832** tr. *Sismondi's Ital. Rep.* xiii. 283 Resolved on treading in the footsteps of Charlemagne and his paladins. **1879** B. TAYLOR *Stud. Germ. Lit.* 65 The 'Chanson de Roland' is no longer read, except by scholars, but the famous paladin still lives.

attrib. **1866** KINGSLEY *Herew.* xiv, The spirit of her old Paladin ancestor.

paladine, obs. form of PALATINE.

palæ-, form of PALÆO-, PALEO-, used before a vowel.

palæanˈthropic, *a.* Also **palæoanthropic** and with the prefix written **pale-.** [f. PALÆO-, PALEO- + ANTHROPIC *a.*] Of, pertaining to, or designating extinct prehistoric forms of man.

Quot. 1916 may represent an independent coinage.

1890 *Cent. Dict.* V, Paleo-anthropic. **1916** G. E. SMITH in *Amer. Museum Jrnl.* XVI. 325/2 If we refer to the epoch of the modern type of man as the Neoanthropic age, .. the Mousterian period and all of man's record that went before it can then be included in a Palæanthropic age. **1935** HUXLEY & HADDON *We Europeans* ii. 52 Modern types (Neanthropic) of man appear in Europe as the last ice-sheet began to retreat and the earlier types (Palæanthropic) seem to have disappeared. **1954** *Sci. Amer.* Sept. 52/3 Paleoanthropic man is clearly a tool user, a worker in stone and bone. **1962** C. S. COON *Origin of Races* viii. 334 How many grades .. shall we recognize in fossil and living men? .. A compromise nomenclature is Protoanthropic, Paleanthropic, and Neanthropic. **1973** B. J. WILLIAMS *Evolution & Human Origins* xi. 175/2 The paleanthropic line has included the finds of: Neandertal, Heidelberg, Peking, Java, Solo, Broken Hill (Rhodesia).

Palæarctic (pæliːˈɑːktɪk, peɪ-), *a.* Also **Palearctic** and with lower-case initial. [f. PALÆ- + ARCTIC.] Belonging to the northern region of the 'Old World' or eastern hemisphere; applied to the zoo-geographical region including Europe, North Africa, and Asia north of the Himālayas. Also *absol.*

1858 P. L. SCLATER in *Jrnl. Linn. Soc.* (*Zool.*) II. 135, I think we may consider Africa, north of the Atlas, Europe and Northern Asia, to form one primary division of the earth's surface, for which the name Palæarctic or Northern Palæogean Region would be best applicable. **1880** A. R. WALLACE *Isl. Life* iii. 39 Our first zoological region, which has been termed the 'Palæarctic' by Mr. Sclater. **1882** *American* V. 188 The 'Palæarctic' or Eur-Asiatic division. **1951** *Antiquity* XXV. 69 If Odysseus began as a bear, as Rhys Carpenter asks us to believe, it is well to know how palæarctic that makes him. **1957** P. J. DARLINGTON *Zoogeogr.* vii. 438 The Palearctic is north-temperate with an arctic fringe. **1974** *Environmental Conservation* I. 7/2 Huge numbers of palaearctic birds overwinter in the savanna zones south of the Sahara.

Palæasiatic, var. PALÆO-ASIATIC *sb.* and *a.*

palæchinoid, pale- (pæliːˈkaɪnɔɪd), *a.* and *sb.* *Zool.* [f. mod.L. *Palæchinoidea*, f. *Palæchinus* (for *Palææchinus*), name of the typical genus, f. Gr. παλαιός (see PALÆO-) + ἐχῖνος sea-urchin, ECHINUS.] **a.** *adj.* Belonging to the extinct division (*Palæchinoidea*) of Sea-urchins (*Echinoidea*), whose fossil remains are found in palæozoic rocks. **b.** *sb.* A sea-urchin of this division.

1889 NICHOLSON & LYDEKKER *Palæont.* I. 373 In all the Palechinoids there is a large peristomial aperture.

palæencephalon (ˌpæ-, ˌpeɪliːɛn'sɛfələn). *Anat.* Also (chiefly *U.S.*) **paleencephalon.** [a. G. *palaeencephalon* (L. Edinger *Vorlesungen über den Bau der nervösen Zentralorgane des Menschen und der Tiere* (ed. 7, 1908) II. xvi. 241): see PALÆO-, PALEO- b and ENCEPHALON.] The phylogenetically older portion of the brain, as contrasted with the neencephalon.

1917 *Jrnl. Compar. Neurol.* XXVIII. 216 It is becoming increasingly evident that the key to this difficult question is to be sought in the subcortical centers of the primitive types, that is, in the 'old brain' (palaeencephalon of Edinger, segmental apparatus of Adolf Meyer). **1972** [see NEENCEPHALON].

palæethnology, etc.: see PALÆO-, PALEO-.

Palæic (pə'liːɪk), *a. Geol.* [mod. f. Gr. πάλαι-ος ancient + -IC; after Norw. *palæisk* (Reusch 1900).] Applied to the old land surface as it existed at the close of the Tertiary Period, before the formation of valleys of erosion and other recent surface changes.

1902 H. W. MONCKTON in *Geol. Mag.* Dec. IV. IX. 410 Dr. Reusch..classes this moorland as belonging to what he names the Palæic surface of Norway. *Ibid.*, In Norway, where the rocks are hard, we have the Palæic hills and valley, with its river still flowing through it, the whole, no doubt, much modified by ice-action.

palæo-, paleo- (ˌpæliːəʊ, ˌpeɪliːəʊ), before a vowel usually **palæ-, pale-,** combining form of Gr. παλαιός ancient, used in various scientific words (often opposed to NEO-); for the more important of these see their alphabetical places.

The spelling with *æ* is preferred in Great Britain; but *pale-* (used by Webster, 1828) is common in America. When the main stress is on a later syllable of the word, the secondary stress is etymologically *paˌlæo-*, e.g. *paˌlæo-'lithic*; but the influence of *ˌpalæ'ography*, *ˌpalæ'ology*, etc., has made *ˌpalæo-* common also in *ˌpalæo'lithic*, etc.: cf. ORNITHO-.

palæeth'nology, palæo-, that branch of ethnology which treats of the most primitive races of men; so **palæ(o)ethno'logical** *a.*, pertaining to palæethnology; **palæ(o)eth'nologist**, one versed in palæethnology; **palæichthyan** (-'ɪkθɪən) *Zool.*, *a.* belonging to the *Palæichthyes* [mod.L., f. Gr. ἰχθύς fish], a division of fishes comprising the elasmobranchs and ganoids; *sb.* a member of this division; so **palæichthyic** (-'ɪkθɪk) *a.*; **palæ(o)ichthyology** (-ɪkθɪ'ɒlədʒɪ), that branch of ichthyology or of palæontology which treats of extinct or fossil fishes; so **palæ(o)ichthyo'logic, -al** *a.*, pertaining to palæichthyology; **palæ(o)ichthy'ologist**, one versed in palæichthyology; **palæoba'thymetry** *Geol.*, the bathymetric features of an area as they were at some period in the past; so **ˌpalæobathy'metric** *a.*; **palæobi'ology**, the biology of fossil plants and animals; hence **ˌpalæobio'logic, -ical** *adjs.*, **palæobi'ologist**; **palæoceanography**, etc., varr. *palæo-oceanography*, etc., below; **palæo'chemistry**, (the study of) the chemical features of something as they were in the geological past; hence **palæo'chemical** *a.*; **palæo'cosmic** *a.* [Gr. κόσμος world], of or pertaining to the first age of humanity upon the earth: see quot.; **palæo'crinoid** *Zool.*, *sb.* a crinoid of the division *Palæocrinoidea*, comprising the earlier extinct crinoids; *a.* belonging to or characteristic of this division of crinoids; **'palæocurrent** *Geol.*, a current, usu. of water, which existed at some period in the past, as inferred from the features of sedimentary rocks; **ˌpalæoen'vironment**, an environment at a period in the past; hence **ˌpalæoenviron'mental** *a.*; **'palæo-equator** *Geol.*, the equator as it was at some period in the past; hence **ˌpalæo-equa'torial** *a.*; **'palæofield** *Geol.*, (the strength of) the earth's magnetic field at a period in the geological past; **pa'læoˌgene** (-dʒiːn) *a. Geol.* [Gr. -γενης: see -GEN], a name proposed for a division of the Tertiary strata including the Eocene and Oligocene; **palæoge'netic** [GENETIC] *a.*, characterized by the existence in the early embryo of a germ which normally disappears, but in certain cases undergoes development; as in *palæogenetic atavism*; **palæo'geography** *Geol.*, (the study of) geographical features at periods in the geological past; hence **palæoge'ographer**; **ˌpalæogeo'graphic, -ical** *adjs.*; **ˌpalæogeo'graphically** *adv.*; **palæoge'ology**, (the study or reconstruction of) the geological features of an area in past ages; hence **ˌpalæogeo'logic, -ical** *adjs.*, **palæoge'ologist**; **ˌpalæogeomag'netic** *a. Geol.*, of or pertaining to the magnetic field of the earth in the geological past; **ˌpalæogeo'physics** *sb. pl.*, the study of the physical characteristics of the earth in past ages; hence **ˌpalæogeo'physical** *a.*; **palæo'geotherm** *Geol.* [*geotherm* f. GEO- + *-therm*, after ISOTHERM, etc.], a pattern of temperature variation which existed in the earth's crust at some time in the past; so **ˌpalæogeo'thermal** *a.*; **pa'læoˌglyph** (-glɪf) [after *hieroglyph*], an ancient graven character or inscription; **'palæoˌgravity** *Geol.*, the strength of the earth's gravity at some time in the past; **palæoherpe'tology** [HERPETOLOGY], the part of palæontology which deals with the extinct reptiles of earlier geological periods; so **palæoherpe'tologist**, one versed in palæoherpetology; **palæohy'drography** *Geol.*, (the study of) hydrographic features at periods in the geological past; **'palæoinˌtensity** *Geol.*, the intensity of a palæomagnetic field; **palæo'latitude** *Geol.*, the latitude of a place at some period in the past; hence **ˌpalæolati'tudinal** *a.*; **palæ'olatry** [-LATRY], worship of, or excessive reverence for, what is ancient; **palæolim'nology**, (the study of) the conditions and processes occurring in lakes in the geological past; hence **ˌpalæolimno'logical** *a.*, **palæolim'nologist**; **ˌpalæolitho'logic** *a. Geol.*, applied to a map showing the lithological features of an area at some period in the past; **palæo'longitude** *Geol.*, the longitude of a place at some period in the past; **palæomachic** (-'mækɪk) *a. nonce-wd.* [Gr. μάχη battle], of or pertaining to ancient warfare; **palæome'ridian** *Geol.*, the meridian of a place at some period in the past; **palæome'tallic** *a. nonce-wd.* [after PALÆOLITHIC], of or pertaining to the early part of the period characterized by a knowledge of metals, antecedent to the use of iron; of or pertaining to the Bronze Period; **ˌpalæometeo'rology**, the study of atmospheric conditions at periods in the geological past; so **ˌpalæometeoro'logical** *a.*, **-meteo'rologist**; **palæone'mertean, palæone'mertine** *Zool.*, *a.* belonging to the division *Palæonemertea* or *Palæonemertini*, comprising those nemertean worms which have the lowest or most primitive organization; *sb.* a member of this division; **palæoniscid** (-əʊ'nɪsɪd) *Zool.*, *a.* belonging to the family *Palæoniscidæ* of extinct lepidosteid fishes, typified by the genus *Palæoniscus* [mod.L., f. Gr. ὀνίσκος a sea-fish of the cod kind]; *sb.* a fish of this family; see also PALÆONISCOID *sb.* and *a.*; **ˌpalæo-ocea'nography** (also **palæoceanography**), (the study of) the conditions and processes occurring in oceans in the geological past; hence **ˌpalæ(o-)ocea'nographer**; **ˌpalæ(o-)oceano'graphic, -ical** *adjs.*; **palæope'dology** *Geol.*, (the study of) the features of soils in the geological past; hence **ˌpalæopedo'logical** *a.*, **palæope'dologist**; **palæophilist** (-'ɒfɪlɪst) *nonce-wd.* [Gr. -φιλος loving], a lover of antiquities, an antiquarian; **ˌpalæophysi'ography** *Geol.*, (the study of) the physical and topographical features of the earth's surface in the geological past; hence **ˌpalæophysi'ographer**; **ˌpalæophysio'graphic, -'graphical** *adjs.*; **palæophysi'ology**, the physiology of early races of mankind; **'palæoplain** *Geomorphol.*, a peneplain which existed at some period in the past and became overlain by other strata, being now buried or re-exposed; **'palæopole** *Geol.*, a magnetic pole of the earth at a period in the past; **palæo'psychic** *a. rare*, pertaining to the assumed (prehistoric) origins of behaviour patterns; so (also *rare*) **ˌpalæopsy'chology, -ist**; **'palæoradius** *Geol.*, the radius of the earth or another planet at some time in the past; **palæ'ornithine** *a. Zool.*, belonging to or having the characters of the *Palæornithinæ*, a group of parrots typified by the genus *Palæornis* [mod.L., f. Gr. ὄρνις bird: a bird of this kind having been known to the ancient Greeks and Romans]; **palæorni'thology**, that branch of palæontology or ornithology which treats of extinct or fossil birds; hence **palæornitho'logical** *a.*, pertaining to palæornithology; **palæosa'linity** *Geol.*, the salinity of the environment in which a sedimentary deposit was laid down; **pa'læosaur**, a fossil saurian reptile of the genus *Palæosaurus*; **palæoselachian** (-sɪ'leɪkɪən) *a.*, belonging to the division *Palæoselachii* of the *Selachoidei* [Gr. σέλαχος shark] or shark tribe of fishes; **'palæoslope** *Geol.*, the former or original slope of a region, or its direction; **'palæosol** [-SOL], a soil horizon which was formed as a soil in the geological past; hence **palæo'solic** *a.*; **palæ'osophy** [Gr. σοφία wisdom], ancient learning; **'palæospecies** *Palæont.*, a species including a group of fossils from different geological formations that make up a chronological series; **'palæostructure** *Geol.*, the geological structure of an area at some period in the past; hence **palæo'structural** *a.*; **palæotechnic** (-'tɛknɪk) *a.* [Gr. τέχνη art], pertaining to primitive art; *spec.* (see quot. 1960); **palæotec'tonic** *Geol.*, of or pertaining to tectonic features or events of previous stages in the earth's history; **'palæotemperature**, the average climatic temperature at a particular place and time in the past; **palæother'mometry**, the investigation of the temperature of climates and oceans in past ages; **palæoto'pography** *Geol.*, the topography of ancient landscapes, esp. as represented today by features that are buried or newly exhumed (cf. PALÆOGEOMORPHOLOGY); hence **ˌpalæotopo'graphic, -'graphical** *adjs.*, **ˌpalæotopo'graphically** *adv.*; **palæovol'canic** *a. Geol.*, applied to volcanic rocks of a period older than the Tertiary; **'palæowind** *Geol.*, a prevailing wind that existed at some period in the past; freq. *attrib.*; **ˌpalæoˌzooge'ography**, the study of the distribution of fossil animal remains; hence **ˌpalæoˌzoogeo'graphic** *a.*

1881 GÜNTHER in *Encycl. Brit.* XII. 676/1 Remnants of the *Palæichthyic fauna exist in the sturgeons and lampreys. **1880** *Nature* XXI. 428 The *palæichthyological treasures of [Scotland] began to attract attention. **1890** *Cent. Dict.*, **Paleichthyologist.* **1897** *Proc. Zool. Soc.* 317 Sending his specimen again across the Atlantic for re-examination by British palæichthyologists. **1881** *Nature* XXIII. 580 Sir P. Egerton, whose name will be ever associated with that of Agassiz in *palæichthyology. **1945** *Bull. Amer. Assoc. Petroleum Geologists* XXIX. 428 Maps of fossil distribution, with evaluation of the habitat of the organisms, add evidence. Thus from the lithology and fauna, it is possible to construct *paleobathymetric maps. **1964** H. W. MENARD *Marine Geol. Pacific* vi. 138/1 Since most of the islands existed at about the same time.., a consistent paleobathymetric map can be drawn. **1959** *Jrnl. Paleont.* XXXIII. 944/2 Critical comparative study is also called for of the characteristics of sedimentary rocks in areas where there is possibility of reconstructing a reasonably objective *paleobathymetry, as in the..Ventura Basin of California or other areas where the endemic fossils indicate a wide range of depth. **1971** *Nature* 2 Apr. 319/1 The magnitude of the cretaceous-Tertiary hiatus in the deep sea is therefore a function of palaeobathymetry with deeper water sections exhibiting a greater unconformity. **1948** *Bull. Geol. Soc. Amer.* LIX. 1337 (*heading*) *Paleobiologic implications of the measurement of paleotemperatures. **1961** WEBSTER, *Paleobiological. **1963** D. W. & E. E. HUMPHRIES tr. *Termier's Erosion & Sedimentation* ix. 192 Two palaeobiological aspects of this subject should be noted. **1974** *Nature* 15 Feb. 496/1 He [*sc.* D. M. S. Watson] joined Abel as one of the pioneers of palaeobiological thought. **1900** *Biol. Lect. Marine Biol. Lab. Woods Holl 1899* ix. 132 The method thus elaborated has been and is now in constant use by a number of *paleobiologists. **1975** *Nature* 1 May 16/1 Because they have become excited by new biological concepts and wish to apply them to fossils, a number of young researchers would now prefer to call themselves palaeobiologists. **1893** S. S. BUCKMAN in *Q. Jrnl. Geol. Soc.* XLIX. 482 The term 'hemera' will therefore enable us to record our facts correctly; and its chief use will be in what I may call '*palæo-biology'. **1943** *Mind* LII. 127 One can hardly think of a scientific fact better and more impressively documented than the phylogenetic hierarchy, established as it is by the threefold evidence of embryology, comparative anatomy, and paleobiology. **1948** *Jrnl. Paleont.* XXII. 265/1 Paleobiology is..mainly biological in objectives, but many of its techniques are unknown to biology. **1973** P. TASCH (*title*) Paleobiology of the invertebrates: data retrieval from the fossil record. **1854** *Edin. New Philos. Jrnl.* LVI. 9 The palæophysics are hardly studied, and even less the *palæochemistry. **1904** *Trans. Canad. Inst.* VII. 535 (*heading*) The palæochemistry of the ocean in relation to animal and vegetable protoplasm. **1926** *Physiol. Rev.* VI. 316 (*heading*) The paleochemistry of the body fluids and tissues. *Ibid.* 331 The high concentration of the salts, 2·852 per cent, in the serum of the lobster would appear to indicate that it is of neochemical rather than of paleochemical origin. **1942** *Proc. R. Irish Acad.* XLVIII. B. 119 An enquiry into oceanic palæochemistry and its bearing on the electrolytes of blood and cells. **1875** DAWSON *Nat. & Bible* v. 155, I have suggested the terms *Palæocosmic and Neocosmic, and I would hold as of the first age such men as can be proved to have lived in time of greatest elevation of the European land in the Post-glacial period, and of the second those who came in as their successors in the Modern period. **1877** —— *Orig. World* xiii. 285. **1884** *Leisure Hour* Mar. 148/2 The second continental period was that of palæocosmic, or 'palæolithic' man. **1872** NICHOLSON *Palæont.* 126 As a rule, also, the *Palæocrinoids have a calyx. **1885** *Athenæum* 11 Apr. 475/3 The particular recent crinoid..which shows the most marked affinities with the palæocrinoids is not a stalked form, but one of the Comatulidæ, *Thaumatocrinus*. *Ibid.*, It has an anal cone covered with plates—all palæocrinoid characters. **1955** *Bull. Geol. Soc. Amer.* LXVI. 1606 (*heading*) *Paleocurrents of Lake Superior Precambrian quartzites. **1971** *Nature* 28 May 245/2 A W.N.W. to N. palaeocurrent component predominates in the channel sandstones with pedogenic modification..occurring on most proximal floodplain deposits. **1957** R. J. BRAIDWOOD in *Publ. National Research Council* (U.S.) No. 565. 16/2 This field or axis of interrelated disciplines (perhaps 'Pleistocene ecology' or '*paleo-environment' or 'Quaternary geography'—I shall not attempt to name it!) would definitely include Man as an element in, and a factor acting upon, the environmental scene. **1970** *Nature* 29 Aug. 944/2 The palaeoenvironment of the Neolithic occupation site. **1975** *Ibid.* 20 Mar. 187/2 Reconstructions of palaeoenvironments often rely heavily on fossils, and thus engender circular arguments about the habitats occupied by different elements in the fauna. **1961** *Micropaleontology* VII. 366/1 Preliminary results of analyses of these data, in terms of biotic diversity, show interesting parallels with independent evidence concerning *paleoenvironmental changes and floral evolution. **1974** *Nature* 29 Mar. p. iv/3 (Advt.), An accompanying text describes each feature and discusses its ..preservation and occurrence in sedimentary rocks, and significance for paleoenvironmental reconstructions. **1976** *Ibid.* 20 May 223/1 These palaeoenvironmental similarities may be sufficient to explain the near identity of the two assemblages of micro-fossils. **1960** *Quaternary Res.* (Tokyo) May 212 (*heading*) The *palaeoequator and its relation to the recent distributional area of *Coriaria*. **1962** *Nature* 3 Nov. 427/2 The estimates of palæolatitudes are generally low, ranging from 59° S.–44° N., with 76 per cent of the values lying within 20° of the palæoequator. **1973** *Sci. Amer.* Nov. 111/1 An eastward extrapolation of paleo-equator positions determined from deep-sea drilling, together with a westward extrapolation of crustal age.., enables us to estimate the location and age of a series of points where the East Pacific Ridge and earlier 'paleo-equators' once intersected. **1966** *Nature* 15 Oct. 247 (*heading*) Summary of estimates of *palaeoequatorial [magnetic] intensity from igneous rocks in the temperature range 670° C to 500° C. **1882** OGILVIE, *Palæoethnological..*Palæoethnologist. **1883** *American* VI. 253 The views of the distinguished English palae-ethnologist. **1868** *Archæologia* XLII. 103 Of great importance to the students of Italian *palæo-ethnology and archæology. **1968** *New Scientist* 4 Apr. 16/1 Since the newly acquired moment is proportional to the known field, and the natural moment of the virgin rock is proportional to the ancient field, a simple equation allows the '*palaeofield' to be calculated. **1975** *Nature* 27 Feb. 685/2 The obvious ways of obtaining a palaeofield from a rock containing thermo-remanent magnetisation require that the rock be heated above its Curie point. **1882** GEIKIE *Text-bk. Geol.* VI. IV. 836 Some writers, recognizing a broad distinction between older and younger Tertiary deposits, have proposed a classification into two main groups: 1st Eocene Older Tertiary or *Palaeogene. **1892** *Athenæum* 25 June 829/2 Researches on the British paleogene Bryozoa, of which he recognized 30 species. **1886** J. B. SUTTON in *Proc. Zool. Soc.* 551 My object is to show that all examples of atavism belong to the *Palæogenetic group and that Neogenetic Atavism has no existence. **1911** *Bull. Geol. Soc. Amer.* XXII. 262 These results are of the greatest value to the *paleo-geographer. **1972** *Science* 12 May 665/2 A scholar who, as a paleogeographer, is not narrowly specialized in archeology or geology. **1906** *Bull. Geol. Soc. Amer.* XVII. 248 (*heading*) *Paleogeographic charts. **1971** *Nature* 16 July 180/2 The evidence..was taken from two series of palaeogeographic maps showing the distribution of land and sea since the early Cambrian. **1882** E. HULL *Contrib. Physical Hist. Brit. Isles* I. iii. 19 In endeavouring to prepare a series of maps representing the *palæo-geographical features of some region,..the requisite number of such maps and their proper order of succession..necessarily corresponds to those of the successive geological formations. *Ibid.* II. i. 55 (*heading*) Palæo-geographical and geological maps of the British Isles. **1956** L. J. WILLS *Concealed Coalfields* 6 The palaeogeographical treatment is capable of throwing new light on the problem of where the workable coals may originally have been deposited. **1965** B. E. FREEMAN tr. *Vandel's Biospeleol.* xvi. 274 A map of the distribution of the cavernicolous sphaeromids can easily be superimposed on the paleogeographical reconstruction of the Miocene epoch. **1934** *Bull. Amer. Assoc. Petroleum Geologists* XVIII. 784 (*heading*) Future research in *paleogeographically favorable zones. **1969** BENNISON & WRIGHT *Geol. Hist. Brit. Isles* xi. 265 Permian outcrops in Ireland, though not extensive, are palaeogeographically important. **1881** R. ETHERIDGE in *Q. Jrnl. Geol. Soc.* XXXVII. 228 Could we strip off all the Secondary and Tertiary rocks, and reveal or expose the extension of the older or Palæozoic series towards Germany on the east, and France on the south, then the vexed question of the old physical geology and geography (*palæogeography) of Britain and the relation and correlation of our area with that of Europe would be revealed. **1946** *Nature* 20 July 89/2 Grabau's widely ranging interests in stratigraphy, palæogeography, palæontology and sedimentation..were synthesized into a whole in his 'Principles of Stratigraphy' (1913). **1969** BENNISON & WRIGHT *Geol. Hist. Brit. Isles* i. 3 Changes in the distribution of land and sea, of the physiography of the land, and of climate have taken place and their study is called palaeogeography. **1971** I. G. GASS et al. *Understanding Earth* xx. 292/1 The direction of these currents can be established by studying the sedimentary structures the rocks contain; and this may assist in the determination of the palaeogeography of the times when sedimentation occurred. **1933** *Bull. Amer. Assoc. Petroleum Geologists* XVII. 1113 (*caption*) *Paleogeologic map of United States at beginning of Lower Cretaceous or Comanche time, representing areal geology of surface upon which Cretaceous sediments were deposited. **1966** *McGraw-Hill Encycl. Sci. & Technol.* IX. 519/1 Paleogeologic maps, showing the pattern of rocks on the surface at a past time, aid in the interpretation of landforms. **1882** *Sci. Trans. R. Dublin Soc.* I. 257 (*heading*) *Palæo-geological and geographical maps of the British Islands and the adjoining parts of the continent of Europe. **1940** *Geogr. Jrnl.* XCV. 208 The island re-emerged during the Tertiary from an ancient, drowned landmass named Palaeonotis, postulated by palaeogeologists..as having extended from Asia as far as New Caledonia. **1933** *Bull. Amer. Assoc. Petroleum Geologists* XVII. 1129 Northeastern Texas..is an excellent example of the application of *paleogeology to the problem of the accumulation of oil and gas. **1959** P. C. BADGLEY *Struct. Methods Exploration Geologist* v. 128 Figure 138 indicates the paleogeology immediately below the pre-Cretaceous erosion surface. **1960** A. I. LEVORSEN *Paleogeologic Maps* i. 2 Paleogeology ignores all subsequent sedimentation, volcanism, and deformation, and requires that the geologist consider the geology as it was when it was being formed. **1962** *Jrnl. Geophysical Res.* LXVII. 3461/2 Since different parts of formations became magnetized at different times, secular variation of the *paleogeomagnetic field must have produced a certain amount of scatter of the directions of magnetization. **1977** *Sci. Amer.* Dec. 42/1 The maps are computer-generated by rotation around the varying north paleogeomagnetic poles, the amount of rotation controlled by sea-floor magnetic measurements. **1965** *Phil. Trans. R. Soc.* A. CCLVIII. 1 Because no other *palaeogeophysical record is comparable in scope, palaeomagnetic surveys in the different continents have led to important conclusions about the Earth's evolution. **1970** *Nature* 18 July 227/1 Palaeogeophysical studies to determine whether present day processes were equally valid in past geological time. **1959** *Geophysical Abstr.* No. 175. 374 '*Paleogeophysics' includes all methods which can lead to an understanding of former physical conditions and processes in the earth during its evolution; it is a part of paleogeography. **1970** S. K. RUNCORN *Palaeogeophysics* iii. 17 The newest branch of palaeogeophysics is the record presumed to have been found in fossils of the biological rhythms of marine fauna. In the oceans it seems *a priori* reasonable to suppose that these biological clocks set themselves by the exactly periodic variations in their physical environment, which seem only to be the solar day, the synodical month and the tropical year. **1975** *Nature* 3 Apr. 406/2 The *palaeogeotherms which existed in the upper mantle immediately before incorporation and transport of the xenoliths by kimberlite eruptions have been derived from data from large numbers of individual xenoliths. **1970** R. G. J. STRENS in S. K. Runcorn *Palaeogeophysics* xl. 383 Apart from their usefulness in studying palaeogravity and *palaeogeothermal gradients, such geothermometers and geobarometers would be of inestimable value to petrologists. **1978** *Nature* 18 May 221/1 Much debate has centred upon whether some palaeogeothermal gradients are perturbed or not. **1861** F. HALL in *Jrnl. Asiatic Soc. Bengal* XXX. 7 Any the slightest conversancy with Sanskrit *paleoglyphs is incompatible with a decision so indulgent. **1970** R. G. J. STRENS in S. K. Runcorn *Palaeogeophysics* xl. 383 Prospects for measuring *palaeogravity with an accuracy sufficient to detect major variations (> 10%) over the last 3000 m. yr appear good. **1978** *Nature* 12 Jan. 153/2 Hypotheses involving substantial changes in Earth radius over geological time can be tested by measuring palaeogravity at, or near, the Earth's surface. **1898** *Natural Science* Dec. 435 [In opposition to] certain guesses of an eminent *palæoherpetologist. **1853** *Edin. New Philos. Jrnl.* LV. 298 (*heading*) On the *palæohydrography and orography of the Earth's surface. **1933** W. J. ARKELL *Jurassic Syst. Gt. Brit.* xviii. 557 To do justice to the palæogeography of the Jurassic period..we should have to proceed systematically from the points of view of .. palaeohydrography, palaeoceanography, palaeobiogeography, palaeoclimatology,..and many others. **1971** *Geol. Fӧrening. Stockholm Fӧrhandl.* XCIII. 59 (*heading*) Foraminifera and the paleohydrography of the Arabian Sea. **1965** *Jrnl. Geomagnetism & Geoelectr.* XVII. 417 (*heading*) Preliminary results of investigations made to study the use of Indian pottery to determine the *paleointensity of the geomagnetic field for United States 600–1400 A.D. **1974** *Nature* 17 May 227/2 If the Moon were uniformly magnetised, it would need to have had a dipole moment of about 10^{23} gauss cm^3 to give an ancient surface field of 2,000 gamma (γ) which is typical of several palaeointensity studies, although a much higher value has been reported. **1959** *Geophysical Jrnl.* II. 307 Thus the shape of the areas of confidence so calculated depends on the *palaeo-latitude. **1971** I. G. GASS et al. *Understanding Earth* xiii. 174/2 The study of wind systems associated with arid deposits of different ages gives evidence of palaeo-latitudes and so has a bearing on continental drift. **1964** *Prof. Papers U.S. Geol. Survey* No. 501-C. 109/1 (*heading*) *Paleolatitudinal distribution of ancient phosphorite. **1971** *Nature* 1 Jan. 17/1 The geometrical reconstruction presented here..was obtained using a palaeomagnetic computer program which plotted continental outlines in their palaeolatitudinal position relative to a pole determined palaeomagnetically. **1887** *Athenæum* 15 Oct. 498/2 A rare example of conscientious and loving typography, and what for want of a better word we must call *palæolatry. **1877** *Fraser's Mag.* XV. 541 Even to those who look upon war as ..now on its last legs, the reflections on military history will be an interesting study of those *palæomachic days. **1961** *Mem. Coll. Sci. Kyoto Univ.* B. XXVIII. 68 A *paleolimnological study of deep core-samples will indicate not only the developmental history of Lake Biwa-ko but the whole Pleistocene climatic history of the East Asiatic continent. **1973** *Nature* 16 Mar. 184/1 This aspect of the palaeolimnological work is being pursued in greater detail by magnetic, chemical and botanical investigations of the most recent sediments in Lough Neagh. **1960** *Amer. Jrnl. Sci.* CCLVIII. A. 1 (*heading*) Wilmot Hyde Bradley. Geologist, geomorphologist, *paleolimnologist, paleontologist, administrator. **1970** *Ann. Acad. Sci. Fennicae* A. 3. CV. 25 The two species *Bosmina coregoni* Baird and *B. longirostris* O. F. Müller..are of particular interest to limnologists and palaeolimnologists. **1942** *Amer. Jrnl. Sci.* CCXL. 237 One particularly significant contribution of *paleolimnology to glacial geology may be the derivation of an absolute chronology on the basis of quantitative counts of micro-fossils. **1948** *Bull. Geol. Soc. Amer.* LIX. 641, I have selected three distinctive features of the Green River formation to interpret in terms of the paleolimnology of the Eocene Green River lakes. These are the carbonate sediments and carbonate minerals, the oil shales, and the varved sediments. **1973** *Jrnl. Phycol.* IX. 395/2 The algal senescence system may prove valuable in lacustrine paleolimnology as a simple but experimentally accessible analogy to the processes of chlorophyll degradation in the water column. **1945** *Bull. Amer. Assoc. Petroleum Geologists* XXIX. 427 *Paleolithologic maps have lines, isoliths, connecting points of similar lithology and separating rocks of differing nature. **1966** *McGraw-Hill Encycl. Sci. & Technol.* IX. 519/1 Paleolithologic maps showing bottom sediment patterns suggest whether rocks were laid in depths of strong wave action or in quieter water of deeps or broad shoals. **1964** K. M. CREER in A. E. M. Nairn *Probl. Palaeoclimatol.* 274 Because of the assumed axial symmetry of the field, palaeomagnetic data cannot yield information about *palaeolongitude. **1961** *Nature* 17 June 1097/2 Localities along the same *palæo-meridian. **1965** *Phil. Trans. R. Soc.* A. CCLVIII. 27 A palaeomagnetic survey of a suite of rocks representing at least 10^4y thus provides information from which may be determined: (1) the palaeomagnetic latitude..of the sites, and (2) the palaeomeridian direction. **1890** HUXLEY in *19th Cent.* Nov. 770 The copper and early bronze stage—the '*palæo-metallic' stage, as it might be called. **1901** *Q. Jrnl. Geol. Soc.* LVII. 405 (*heading*) A *palaeometeorological explanation of some geological problems. **1962** REX & GOLDBERG in M. N. Hill *Sea* I. v. 295 Deep-sea deposits provide excellent source areas for paleometeorological investigations provided eolian materials can be recognised. **1964** K. W. BUTZER *Environment & Archeol.* xxii. 334 A great deal of more satisfactory paleoclimatic information must be available before this major barrier to paleometeorological study is removed. **1901** *Q. Jrnl. Geol. Soc.* LVII. 468 The *palæometeorologist must work with the best material he can obtain, content with the enunciation of general principles, and with the solution of some of the more simple problems. **1854** *Edin. New Philos. Jrnl.* LVI. 9 We have got very few notions on *palæometeorology and palæotemperature or thermics. **1901** *Q. Jrnl. Geol. Soc.* LVII. 469 Among the services which palæometeorology may hereafter render to the geologist..may be that of assisting him to determine the chronological relations of geological zones in different regions where no direct evidence..may be attainable. **1954** *Sci. News* XXXIII. 65 Paleoclimatology, the study of the climates of the past, is considerably more advanced than paleometeorology, the study of past weather. **1888** ROLLESTON & JACKSON *Anim. Life* 636 In the *Palæonemertean genera *Carinella* and *Cephalothrix*. *Ibid.* 638 Short longitudinal grooves present also in the Palæonemertean *Polia*. **1883** H. DRUMMOND in *Life* viii. (1899) 204 This is probably also a *palaeoniscid scale. **1890** *Athenæum* 12 Apr. 473/2 A specimen of a mesozoic palæoniscid fish from New South Wales. **1900** *Nature* 20 Sept. 507/1 *Cheirolepis* is a fully evolved palæoniscid, as shown by its oblique suspensorium. **1957** *Mem. Geol. Soc. Amer.* LXVII. II. xxiv. 684 The development of the method of paleotemperature research..using the O^{16}:O^{18} ratio in carbonates and other solid salts of oxyacids has provided the most powerful single tool yet invented in the equipment of the *paleo-oceanographer. **1945** *Paleo-oceanographic [see PALÆOCLIMATOLOGIC *a.*]. **1968** *Science* 29 Mar. 1461/1 The distribution of planktonic tests in fossil marine sediments are being used increasingly for paleo-oceanographic reconstructions. **1971** *Nature* 13 Aug. 469/1 Oxygen isotope and palaeontological determination of planktonic foraminifers allow us to make several generalizations on the palaeoceanographic history of the Arctic Ocean back to Mid Pliocene. **1971** *Ibid.* 30 Apr. 563/1 In the interesting *palaeoceanographical model proposed by Bandy, a thermal maximum is indicated in marine conditions during the same 9–8 m.y. periods. **1933** *Palæoceanography [see *palæohydrography* above]. **1957** *Mem. Geol. Soc. Amer.* LXVII. II. xxiv. 684 (*heading*) Future of the study of paleo-oceanography. **1972** *Nature* 17 Mar. 117/1 The gross geometric relationships of pelagic facies on a ridge system must be interpreted in the light of the spreading process itself before meaningful conclusions can be drawn about palaeoclimatology and palaeo-oceanography. **1927** B. B. POLYNOV *Contrib. Russ. Scientists to Paleopedology* 1 It is yet scarcely possible to speak of *paleopedology, as of a scientific theory that has assumed a wholly definite shape. *Ibid.* 14 As one of the most interesting recent Ukrainian papers on pedology may be especially mentioned the paleopedological map of Ukraina, drawn by Makhov. **1943** *Amer. Jrnl. Sci.* CCXLI. 197 A great deal more must be learned about the soil formation before paleopedologists will understand the true significance of the soil bones. *Ibid.* 199 Because of the nature of the pedogenic fossils it cannot be expected that paleopedology ever will be able to deal with much more than the general types of the ancient soil formation and the changes in the geographical pattern of the zones and regions in which these types prevailed during the different geological periods. *Ibid.* 200 The true paleopedological formations are rather rare. **1971** G. ROESCHMANN in D. H. Yaalon *Paleopedology* 319 In future, paleopedologists and geologists will only obtain satisfactory results..if they work as a team. **1973** *N.Z. Jrnl. Geol. & Geophysics* XVI. 723 Such paleopedological evidence may be employed to confirm and extend the chronology of the later part of the New Zealand Quaternary. *Ibid.* 735 This identification of these ancient episodes of erosion depends on the identification of tephra formations and paleosols and is a logical application of paleopedology to environmental reconstruction. **1822** *Blackw. Mag.* XI. 694 The gusto with which our zealous *Palæophilist listens to the rattling sound of certain ancient leaves of the rare volumes. **1898** J. E. MARR *Princ. Stratigr. Geol.* x. 121 The *palæo-physiographer..attempts to restore the physical conditions of greater thicknesses of deposit. **1950** *Bull. Illinois State Geol. Survey* No. 73. iii. 23 (*caption*) *Paleophysiographic diagram of the bedrock topography of Illinois. **1954** W. D. THORNBURY *Princ. Geomorphol.* ii. 31 (*caption*) A paleophysiographic diagram showing the major features of the preglacial topography of Illinois. **1898** J. E. MARR *Princ. Stratigr. Geol.* x. 122 The utmost that the maker of *palæophysiographical maps can expect to indicate, when dealing with considerable thicknesses of strata, is an approximation to the mean position of the shore-lines of the period when these strata were deposited. **1882** E. HULL *Contrib. Physical Hist. Brit. Isles* p. v, I had intended giving the title of '*Palæo-Physiography of the British Islands' to this volume; but certain friends in whose judgment I have the most implicit confidence assured me that no one would have the slightest conception from such a title of the contents of my book. **1915** C. SCHUCHERT *Text-bk. Geol.* II. xx. 450 There is..another record that has so far been almost refused recognition in our time-tables. This is the time evaluation of topographic form at any given stage of development (the physiography of the present, the paleophysiography of the past). **1880** tr. *Geiger's Hist. Developm. Hum. Race* 48 These questions..fall within the province of physiology, or if I am permitted to coin the term of *palæophysiology. **1900** R. T. HILL in *Topogr. Atlas U.S. Geol. Survey* Folio 3. 5/3 Destructional plains are sometimes evolved from constructional plains; the latter, after elevation in long erosion, are reduced in old age to the former. On the other hand, constructional plains are usually established upon areas which were once destructional plains. Ancient buried destructional plains thus veneered by constructional formations might be appropriately termed *paleoplains.

1966 *Bull. Amer. Assoc. Petroleum Geologists* L. 2302/2 Farther west along the flank of the Canadian shield..a vast paleoplain..was covered by Lower Cretaceous (locally Upper Jurassic) sediments which include a high percentage of sandstone which could serve as reservoir. **1962** *Geofisica Pura e Appl.* LIII. 52 (*heading*) Rock magnetism and the earth's *palaeopoles. **1971** I. G. Gass et al. *Understanding Earth* xv. 212 The evidence favouring drift including geomagnetic data (palaeopole investigations). **1904** G. S. Hall *Adolescence* II. xii. 194 The problem, whether there is any *paleopsychic race element, is as inevitable as it is unanswerable. **1916** *N.Y. Med. Jrnl.* CIV. 1077/1 We wish to maintain the idea that there may be other types of fossils to be studied than those derived from plants and animals, namely thought fossils, and that to paleobotany and to paleozoology we may add a science of paleopsychology. The happiest ground of the *paleopsychologist is..in history, in literature, in..possibly diseases. **1960** *Geofisica Pura e Applicata* XLV. 116 The *palaeo-radius corresponding to the time *t*. **1978** *Nature* 26 Jan. 316/1 Observations of the surface of Mercury and Mars by spacecraft enable constraints to be placed on the palaeo-radius of these extraterrestrial bodies. **1960** *Oil & Gas Jrnl.* 1 Feb. 154/1 A method for determining *paleo-salinities..would also be of considerable practical value in the search for various types of mineral deposits and petroleum. **1972** *Marine Geol.* XII. 335 (*heading*) Pollen and *paleosalinity analyses from a Holocene tidal marsh sequence. *Ibid.* 337 A method for determining paleosalinity was proposed by Nelson (1967) which utilized the relative proportions of iron and calcium phosphate in argillaceous sediments. **1871** H. Marshall *For very Life* II. vi. xi. 258 Ideas..are laid away in books, just as we find *palaeosaurs in the rocks. **1957** *Bull. Geol. Soc. Amer.* LXVIII. 469/1 Mapping of cross-bedding and other primary current structures has proved useful in reconstruction of regional *paleoslopes. **1965** *Bull. Amer. Assoc. Petroleum Geologists* XLIX. 341/1 Regional variation in stratigraphic position of the base of the landslide facies establishes the fact that the foot of the paleoslope migrated north-northwestwardly through time. **1975** Read & Watson *Introd. Geol.* II. i. iv. 82 Remarkably constant palaeocurrent directions determined from current-bedding throughout the Athabasca formation indicate a palaeoslope towards the west or north-west. **1950** Hunt & Sokoloff in *Prof. Papers U.S. Geol. Survey* No. 221. 109/1 An ancient soil, hereafter referred to as *paleosol, has been dated..as pre-Wisconsin in the Lake Bonneville and Denver basins. **1954** W. D. Thornbury *Princ. Geomorphol.* iv. 82 Paleosols may be found on buried landscapes, on exhumed portions of ancient landscapes, or upon features of the present topography which are relicts of previous geomorphic cycles. **1968** R. W. Fairbridge *Encycl. Geomorphol.* 554/2 A lateritic crust is essentially a paleosol, and reflects a polycyclic regime, usually as a result of repeated alternation of hot, humid conditions developing laterite, with dry, evaporating conditions favoring crust development. **1975** *Nature* 20 Mar. 189/1 Palaeoenvironmental indicators in the sediments include polygonal desiccation cracks, calcretes and other palaeosols. **1956** *Soil Sci.* LXXXII. 441 Erosive stripping of the protective mantle of sediment in many places, however, resulted in the resurrection of the *paleosolic profile *in toto*, so that now the paleosol occurs within the continuum of soils on the modern surface. **1965** R. V. Ruhe in Wright & Frey *Quaternary of U.S.* 759/2 These kinds of soil occur adjacent to each other and grade from one to another on the paleosolic surfaces of the older glacial tills. **1798** W. Taylor in *Monthly Mag.* VI. 452 They [the Eddaic poems] will afford a favourite text for commentary to all the antiquaries who shall in future busy themselves with arctic *paleosophy. **1806** —— in *Ann. Rev.* IV. 559 The whole range of the original writers on northern paleosophy. **1954** A. J. Cain *Animal Species* vii. 107 When good series are available, forms that seem to be good species at any one time may become indefinable since they are successive stages in a single evolutionary line... It is convenient to refer to such forms as *palaeospecies. **1956** P. C. Sylvester-Bradley *Species Concept in Palaeont.* 2 A third concept is the result of projecting the biospecies into a third dimension, that of time. It is the concept..others have called the 'palaeospecies'. **1964** *Nature* 1 Aug. 451/1 A species in palæontology..is a fundamentally different kind of unit and has been called a chromospecies or palæospecies. **1974** *Ibid.* 1 Nov. 85/2 Physical anthropologists have expanded the concept of variability in palaeospecies making it possible to lump greater ranges of morphological variation within a single species. **1966** *Bull. Amer. Assoc. Petroleum Geologists* L. 2323/1 To demonstrate a logical method of *paleostructural mapping by use of carefully selected isopachous intervals. **1972** *Internat. Geol. Rev.* XIV. 1320/1 In any platform region, paleostructural reconstructions should be preceded by a comprehensive study of the conditions of occurrence and distinctive lithologic features of the rocks. **1937** *Jrnl. Geol.* XLV. 51 A *paleo-structure map of southeastern Missouri at the end of Lamotte time. **1970** *Israel Jrnl. Earth-Sci.* XIX. 141 Systematic study of the thickness of Senonian strata yields conflicting data regarding palaeostructure. **1904** P. Geddes *City Devel.* xxv. 175/1 Must we not, therefore, call this earlier and crude mechanical civilisation which still predominates among us the '*Palæotechnic' stage, and recognise that the formerly less prominent industrial peoples..are passing more quickly than we into the 'Neotechnic' stage? **1915** —— *Cities in Evolution* iv. 63 We may distinguish the earlier and ruder elements of the Industrial Age as Paleotechnic, the newer and still often incipient elements disengaging themselves from these as Neotechnic. **1934** Paleotechnic [see eotechnic *a.*]. **1946** *Theology* XLIX. 94 The report.. praises the past but its vision for the future is lighted less by a doctrine of the creation than by paleotechnic ideology. **1960** C. Winick *Dict. Anthropol.* 399/1 *Paleotechnic*, in the development of the techniques of western civilization, referring to the period in which mineral resources became prominent and coal power and iron were widely used. It flourished around 1750. The factory system, finance capital, and competition developed. **1973** *New Society* 7 June 543/2 Its automated ticket system..makes London's machines seem paleotechnic by comparison. **1947** *Jrnl. Geol.* LV. 311 (*caption*) *Paleotectonic maps of the Cordilleran region in late Paleozoic time. Cross-ruled area is the volcanic archipelago and orogenic belt. Horizontally ruled areas were uplifted and eroded during the period designated. **1957** *Bull. Geol. Soc. Amer.* LXVIII. 151/2 These studies have revealed a paleotectonic framework composed of a geosynclinal basis in central Idaho and a relatively more stable cratonic shelf in southwestern Montana. **1975** *Nature* 10 July 117/1 The positions of Triassic seaways along the southern continental margin of the Tethys 'geosyncline' are defined by the effects of at least two main palaeotectonic events. **1854** *Palæotemperature [see *palæometeorology* above]. **1948** *Science* 5 Nov. 492/1 This particular application of the chemical differences in the processes of isotopes occurred to me a year and a half ago, and since that time my colleagues and I have been trying to solve the several difficult problems encountered in making such measurements of paleotemperatures. **1969** *Nature* 4 Oct. 66/2 Recent palaeotemperature measurements obtained from Caribbean cores..suggest that the coldest part of the Weichselian was around 17000 years BP. **1957** *Chem. Abstr.* LI. 12773 (*heading*) Determination of climatic conditions of some regions of the U.S.S.R. in the Upper Cretaceous period by the method of isotopic *paleothermometry. **1971** *Nature* 13 Aug. 466/2 Reconstruction of the climatic and hydrologic history of ocean basins has been based on either oxygen isotope palaeo-thermometry or studies of foraminiferal assemblages preserved in deep sea sediments. **1943** *Jrnl. Sedimentary Petrology* XIII. 111/1 Most *paleotopographic maps pass under the name of structural maps but there is a distinct difference. **1960** M. S. Bishop *Subsurface Mapping* ix. 135 Oftentimes the gentle slopes of paleotopographic surfaces are indicative of much steeper dips on the underlying beds, especially if a major unconformity is being mapped. **1960** *Canad. Mining & Metallurg. Bull.* LIII. 535/2 The oil has accumulated beneath the unconformity and the accompanying 'caprock' wherever the subcrop trend of a reservoir bed crosses a *paleotopographical ridge. **1966** *Bull. Amer. Assoc. Petroleum Geologists* L. 2296/1 These quantitative concepts are very useful in interpreting an area *paleotopographically; *i.e.*, they keep the number of tributaries, lengths of streams, and channel slopes within specific limits according to geomorphological principles. **1943** *Jrnl. Sedimentary Petrology* XIII. 108 The search for new deposits of petroleum is aided by the use of special paleogeographic maps... Other types of maps that may be used show salinity, thickness of sands, paleogeology and *paleotopography. **1970** *Jrnl. Geol. Soc. Australia* XVII. 39 The palaeotopography of an east-west valley on the eastern flank of the Great Divide is reconstructed from a consideration of early Tertiary and Palaeozoic rocks. **1957** *Bull. Geol. Soc. Amer.* LXVIII. 1870 (*heading*) *Paleo-wind directions in late Paleozoic and early Mesozoic time on the Colorado Plateau as determined by cross-strata. **1964** *Sedimentology* III. 52 The directional features of the dunes suggest that the paleowind pattern was similar to the present-day pattern around Bermuda. **1975** *Nature* 3 Jan. 19/1 We recommend experimental and analytical study of these currents taking into account continental dispersion and palaeowinds. **1967** *Palaeogeogr., Palaeoclimatol., Palaeoecol.* III. 201 *Palaeozoogeographic data are thought to be especially useful in establishing a timetable for continental drift. **1972** *Nature* 7 Apr. 297/3 Succeeding chapters..examine..the palaeozoogeographic patterns in the fossil record. **1967** *Palaeogeogr., Palaeoclimatol., Palaeoecol.* III. 210 Many ammonite species were able to disperse widely. While this renders them excellent for purposes of correlation it reduces their importance for *palaeozoogeography. **1975** *Nature* 17 Apr. 556/3 Palaeozoogeography can only make sense as the evolution of organisms in space and time.

b. In anatomical terms designating parts of the brain which are considered to be of relatively ancient development phylogenetically, as palæencephalon, palæocerebellum, palæocortex, palæopallium, palæostriatum, palæothalamus. Cf. neo- 1 e.

palæoanthropic: var. palæanthropic.

ˌpalæoanthroˈpology. Also (chiefly *U.S.*) **paleo-**. [ad. F. *paléoanthropologie* (P. Topinard *Élém. d'Anthrop. Gén.* (1885) vii. 177): see anthropology.] The branch of anthropology concerned with the study of fossil hominids.

1916 *Bull. Amer. Mus. Nat. Hist.* XXXV. 347 Then follows..the conclusion to which all M. Boule's own researches in palæonthropology [*sic*] and palæontology have evidently led him. **1935** *Times Lit. Suppl.* 14 Feb. 84/2 Dr. Leakey also..clearly sums up his results and shows their bearings on general palaeoanthropology and pre-history. **1957** *Antiquity* XXXI. 43 Rapid advances..are being made in palaeoanthropology at present. **1965** B. G. Campbell *Nomenclature of Hominidae* 3 New taxa are very rarely presented in palaeoanthropology according to the rules of the more recent zoological congresses. **1974** *Nature* 6 Sept. 10/2 Investigations of the development of locomotion within the hominid lineage provides one of the more active and fascinating areas of palaeoanthropology today. **1978** *Ibid.* 2 Mar. 10/3 Wherever physical anthropology is taught in British universities, palaeoanthropology is recognised as an important component of the courses.

Hence **ˌpalæoanthropoˈlogical** *a.*; **ˌpalæoanthroˈpologist**, an expert or specialist in palæoanthropology.

1934 Webster, Paleoanthropological,.. paleoanthropologist. **1935** *Times Lit. Suppl.* 14 Feb. 84/3 The problem of the prehistorical, especially the palaeoanthropological, relations between East Africa and the rest of the continent. **1947** *Sci. News* V. 44 The palæanthropologists [*sic*] went on with their researches..in the hope of one day discovering the hypothetical 'Tertiary man'. **1969** *Times* 17 Jan. 13/6 Dr. Louis Leakey..has for the past 40 years been exploiting the rich palaeoanthropological deposits in the Olduvai Gorge. **1975** *Nature* 10 Apr. 478/3 Although the article admirably reflects recent work in East Africa, it does scant justice to the palaeoanthropological researches in the Transvaal over the past decade. **1978** *Ibid.* 22 June 589/3 In almost all circumstances it now seems important that palaeoanthropologists try to work with a set of alternative hypotheses rather than simply with one favourite interpretation.

ˌPalæo-Asiˈatic, *sb.* and *a.* Also **Palæoasiatic, Palæasiatic**, and with the prefix spelt **Paleo-**. [f. palæo-, paleo- + Asiatic *a.* and *sb.*] = Palæo-Siberian *sb.* and *a.*

1909 A. C. Haddon *Races of Man* 48 The..western, and northern Ural-Altaians form one division, which includes such peoples as the Ugrians (in part), Palæasiatics, some of the Tungus, and the true Mongols. **1925** L. H. D. Buxton *Peoples of Asia* vii. 191 Some early type may, as one of the components of the highly complex physical form of the Koreans, include as a basis the aboriginal Palæasiatic type. **1929** —— *China* iii. 58 There is a clear division also between the Mongols and the Palaeasiatics, that is the old yellow-skinned tribes of north-eastern Asia, and other tribes on the north. **1932** [see Chukchee, chukchi *sb.* and *a.*]. **1948** D. Diringer *Alphabet* i. ix. 157 The Chukcha..are a.. Palæoasiatic, Mongoloid people. **1953** W. K. Matthews *Struct. & Devel. Russian* i. iv. 76 A variety of languages (e.g. Caucasian, Uralian, and Palaeoasiatic). **1962** W. P. Lehmann *Hist. Linguistics* ii. 44 Far to the east in Siberia the Palaeo-Asiatic or Hyberborean languages are spoken. **1976** *Language* LII. 482 The so-called Palaeo-Asiatic family..is ..more a geographical convenience than a genetic grouping.

palæobathymetry, etc.: see palæo-, paleo-.

ˌpalæobioˈchemistry. Also (chiefly *U.S.*) **paleo-**. [f. palæo-, paleo- + biochemistry.] The biochemistry of fossils and of organisms of the geological past, esp. as a means of investigating phylogeny; the investigation of the evolutionary development of biochemical processes.

1954 *Carnegie Inst. Yearbk.* 1953–4 97 (*heading*) Paleobiochemistry. **1966** *Science* 6 May 762/2 The Fig Tree organisms are comparable in size, shape, complexity of structure, and isolated habit to many modern bacillar bacteria. Although they may have had a nonphoto-synthetic metabolism, there is insufficient information available about their paleobiochemistry to realistically evaluate such a suggestion. **1967** *Compar. Biochem. & Physiol.* XX. 553 (*heading*) Paleobiochemistry of molluscan shell proteins. **1969** *Collier's Encycl. Year Bk.* 406 In one of the first applications of paleobiochemistry it has been found that hydrocarbon compounds in rock 3 billion years old may be composed of fossilized chlorophyll. **1969** G. Eglinton in Eglinton & Murphy *Org. Geochem.* ii. 21 Two main approaches can be taken to the biochemistry of organisms in past times. The first is to examine fossil specimens in the hope that some of the information is still there in the form of protein structure, secondary metabolites, etc... The second is to examine the biochemistry of present-day living organisms and make phylogenetic comparisons. From these one can attempt to infer evolutionary sequences in the development of biochemical processes..; this approach is known variously as paleobiochemistry, evolutionary biochemistry and chemical paleogenetics. **1969** M. Florkin in *Ibid.* xx. 498 Structurally preserved biopolymers kept *in situ* in their anatomical location in fossils..should constitute the most reliable material for studies in paleobiochemistry.

So **ˌpalæobioˈchemical** *a.*

Quot. 1937 is an isolated example, unrelated to the later use of *palæobiochemistry*.

1937 *Bull. Amer. Assoc. Petroleum Geologists* XXI. 770 Theories which appear to be in part applicable to such an accumulation are (1) the existence of paleo-biochemical conditions associated with the shallow-water near-shore deposits which controlled the abundance of petroleum-forming organisms. [Etc.] **1972** *Science* 31 Mar. 1461 (*heading*) Amino acid composition of planktonic foraminifera: a paleobiochemical approach to evolution. **1973** *Nature* 20 July 182/2 The recognition that keratin can survive tens of millions of years..could lead to further discoveries, enabling more palaeobiochemical analyses to be undertaken.

ˌpalæobiogeˈography. Also (chiefly *U.S.*) **paleo-**. [f. palæo-, paleo- + biogeography.] The study of the distribution of fossil plants or animals.

1934 in Webster. **1953** *Ecology* XXXIV. 811 (*heading*) A synthesis of paleobiogeography. **1961** P. E. Cloud in M. Sears *Oceanogr.* ii. 151 The patterns created in the struggle for perpetuity are the essence of descriptive biogeography and paleobiogeography. **1972** *Sci. Amer.* Mar. 12/2 He has written on such subjects as fossil carnivores, dating of early man,..evolutionary theory and paleobiogeography.

Hence **ˌpalæobiogeˈographer**, an expert or specialist in palæobiogeography; **ˌpalæoˌbiogeoˈgraphic, -ical** *adjs.*

1953 *Ecology* XXXIV. 812/2 Then come the paleobiogeographic maps. **1958** *Bull. Geol. Soc. Amer.* LXIX. 107/1 The amount of detail that can be shown on a paleogeographic or paleobiogeographic map depends on the length of the time interval which it attempts to represent. **1961** P. E. Cloud in M. Sears *Oceanogr.* ii. 159 For the paleobiogeographer, it is essential not to confuse temperature subdivisions with geodetic terms. *Ibid.* 162 An important paleobiogeographical exception to the direction of size increase is provided in the case of the shelled invertebrates. **1970** *Spec. Papers Geol. Soc. Amer.* No. 124. 23 During the late Paleozoic, unequal distribution and dispersal of biotas created changing paleobiogeographic provinces. **1978** *Nature* 9 Mar. 159/1 Palaeobiogeographic evidence is thus compatible with seafloor spreading and palaeomagnetic data.

palæobiology, etc.: see palæo-, paleo-.

palæobotany (ˌpælɪːəʊˈbɒtənɪ, ˌpeɪ-). Also (chiefly *U.S.*) **paleo-**. [f. palæo-, paleo- + botany.] The botany of extinct or fossil plants. (Correlative to palæozoology.) Hence **palæoboˈtanic, -ical** *adjs.*, belonging to palæobotany; **ˌpalæoboˈtanically** *adv.*, in terms of or as regards palæobotany; **palæo'botanist**, one versed in palæobotany.

1872 NICHOLSON *Palæont.* 473 The subject of Palæobotany or Palæophytology. **1879** *Ibid.* (ed. 2) II. 457 Professor Williamson, one of the ablest of living palæobotanists. **1895** *Pop. Sci. Monthly* Feb. 479 The preparation and study of..paleobotanic material. **1896** *Naturalist* Jan. 27 In that year he published the first palæobotanical paper. **1896** J. P. SMITH in *Proc. Amer. Philos. Soc.* Nov. 227 The paleobotany of the Coal Measures of Arkansas. **1934** *Bull. Amer. Assoc. Petroleum Geologists* XVIII. 1010 The Jackfork-Stanley is paleobotanically older than the Coal-bearing shale. **1968** R. W. FAIRBRIDGE *Encycl. Geomorphol.* 534/2 The last of the paleobotanically established Holocene stages is..also the historical period.

palæoceanography, etc.: see *palæo-oceanography* s.v. PALÆO-, PALEO-.

Palæocene ('pæliːəʊ-, 'peɪliːəʊsiːn), *a. Geol.* Also (chiefly *U.S.*) **Paleo-**. [ad. F. *paléocène* (W. Ph. Schimper *Traité de Paléont. végétale* (1874) III. 680), f. *paléo-* PALÆO-, PALEO + Gr. καινός new, recent (cf. EOCENE, OLIGOCENE, etc.).] Of, pertaining to, or designating the lowest series of the Tertiary system, lying below the Eocene and comprising the Montian and perhaps the Danian stages; (formerly often not recognized as a distinct series but incorporated in the Eocene). Also *absol.*

1877 *Proc. Geol. Soc.* XXXIII. 83 An attempt has been made to establish a zone intermediate between the European Cretaceous and Eocene, under the title of Palæocene. **1877** *Q. Jrnl. Geol. Soc.* XXXIII. Proc. 83 The Palæocene and other zones of European Eocene plant-bearing strata. **1899** *Nature* 26 Jan. 308/1 The Palæocene Volga Sea must have been a large sea extending northwards up the present lower Volga, and westwards as far as the meridian of Penza. **1921** A. W. GRABAU *Textbk. Geol.* II. xlv. 782 The Palæocene is not always recognized by American geologists, who class it as Lower or Basal Eocene. **1949** R. C. MOORE *Introd. Hist. Geol.* xvii. 399 In Europe and in North America, the Tertiary System is recognized as containing main divisions that in upward order are named Paleocene, Eocene, Oligocene, Miocene, and Pliocene. **1957** DUNBAR & RODGERS *Princ. Stratigr.* xvii. 298/1 The Paleocene is commonly not separated from the Eocene in Great Britain and France. **1965** KAY & COLBERT *Stratigr. & Life Hist.* xxiv. 617 There was an evolutionary explosion of mammals ..with the advent of the Paleocene Epoch. **1969** [see MONTIAN *a.*].

,palæocere'bellum. *Anat.* Also (chiefly *U.S.*) **paleo-**. [mod.L., f. PALÆO-, PALEO- b + CEREBELLUM.] A phylogenetically older portion of the cerebellum, comprising mainly the anterior lobe, pyramid, and uvula.

1925, 1954 [see NEOCEREBELLUM]. **1974** *Encycl. Brit. Macropædia* XII. 990/2 The anterior lobe of the cerebellum represents the paleocerebellum, an area that regulates equilibrium and muscle tone; it constitutes the main mass of the cerebellum in fish, reptiles, and birds.

So **,palæocere'bellar** *a.*, of or pertaining to the palæocerebellum.

1936 C. U. A. KAPPERS et al. *Compar. Anat. Nervous Syst. Vertebr.* I. vii. 777 The above mentioned group of authors has separated the cerebellum into a neocerebellar portion and a paleocerebellar portion. **1958** L. HAUSMAN *Clin. Neuroanat.* xxii. 203 (*heading*) Syndrome of paleocerebellar atrophy.

palæochemistry, etc.: see PALÆO-, PALEO-.

'palæoclimate. Also (chiefly *U.S.*) **paleo-**. [f. PALÆO-, PALEO- + CLIMATE *sb.*] The climate at a period in the geological past.

1924 *Geol. Mag.* LXI. 512 Conclusions regarding palæoclimates. **1954** *Jrnl. Geol.* LXII. 229/1 The organism-induced differentiation in recording varying fractions of the environmental temperature ranges and the fact that these types of skeletal-temperature records are at present our sole sources of data for paleotemperature investigations introduce uncertainty in evaluation of amplitudes in paleoclimates. **1963** *Times* 7 Jan. 9/7 The geological evidence of palaeoclimates. **1974** *Encycl. Brit. Macropædia* XIII. 908/2 Many ingested seeds, hair, feathers, and small animal bones within the coprolites may provide a reliable estimate of the paleoclimate of the time.

So **,palæocli'matic** *a.*, of or pertaining to a palæoclimate.

1893 C. A. WHITE in *Rep. U.S. Nat. Museum 1892* 301 This subject relates to what may be designated as paleoclimatic conditions, that is, to formerly existing conditions, which in certain parts of the earth were more or less materially different from those which now exist in the same parts. **1946** F. E. ZEUNER *Dating Past* vi. 163 The number of Palaeolithic sites which can be dated on local palaeoclimatic evidence is as yet very small. **1977** A. HALLAM *Planet Earth* 171 The occurrence of ancient calcareous rocks can be used as a paleoclimatic indicator.

,palæoclima'tology. Also (chiefly *U.S.*) **paleo-**. [f. prec. + -OLOGY.] The study or investigation of palæoclimates.

1920 G. W. BERRY in *Ann. Rep. Board of Regents Smithsonian Inst. 1918* 298 In the interpretation of the far distant past paleobotany and..paleozoology contribute fundamental data to geology..; not only as comprising the subject matter of the biology of the past,..but in the elucidation of the climate and other physical conditions of past times, subjects which may be embraced under the terms of Paleoclimatology and Paleoecology. **1946** F. E. ZEUNER *Dating Past* v. 145 Combining the geological evidence with the astronomical time-scale by means of the radiation curves, an absolute chronology is obtained which can be regarded as sufficiently reliable for the purposes both of palaeoclimatology and prehistoric archeology. **1974** *Encycl. Brit. Micropædia* VII. 690/2 Most research in paleoclimatology centres on explaining (1) the warmth of the Northern Hemisphere land masses during at least 90 per cent of the last 570,000,000 years, (2) the semiperiodic occurrence of widespread glaciation.., and (3) the irregular advances and retreats of the ice sheets during the glacial periods.

Hence **,palæoclimato'logic, -'logical** *adjs.*, **,palæoclimato'logically** *adv.*; **,palæoclima'tologist**, one who investigates palæoclimates.

1924 J. G. A. SKERL tr. *Wegener's Orig. Continents & Oceans* vi. 105 Information about deposits of rock-salt, which are so important for palæoclimatological purposes. **1927** *Geogr. Jrnl.* LXX. 167 For the palæoclimatologist.. Wegener's theory is a tempting haven of refuge from his perplexities. **1945** *Bull. Amer. Assoc. Petroleum Geologists* XXIX. 428 (*heading*) Paleoclimatologic and paleo-oceanographic maps. **1957** *Antiquity* XXXI. 78 The field research necessary for a meaningful paleoclimatological, paleobotanical, and paleozoological history of post-glacial south-western Asia is only beginning. **1963** *Amer. Jrnl. Sci.* CCLXI. 282 The hope that paleoclimatologic evidence may support or refute certain of the major rival hypotheses of global paleogeography. **1966** J. A. MABBUTT in G. H. Dury *Ess. Geomorphol.* 83 The zone offers a worthwhile challenge to the climatic geomorphologist,..partly because of its situation in the palaeoclimatologically little-known Southern Hemisphere. **1968** *Economist* 3 Feb. 42/3 He.. leaves one wondering once again whether the ups and downs of ancient history will ever be adequately understood until the palaeoclimatologists have done a proper job on the Mediterranean basin. **1972** *Nature* 17 Mar. 116/1 In either case, significant palaeo-climatological or palaeo-oceanographic variations might be detectable by analysis of the facies geometry.

palæo'cortex. *Anat.* Also (chiefly *U.S.*) **paleo-**. [mod.L., f. PALÆO-, PALEO- b + CORTEX.] A phylogenetically older portion of the cerebral cortex, which is coextensive with the palæopallium.

1909, 1947 [see NEOCORTEX]. **1964** J. Z. YOUNG *Model of Brain* xix. 306 In the vertebrate brain there are also such tiers of circuits provided, by the hypothalamus, thalamus, palaeocortex and neocortex.

Hence **palæo'cortical** *a.*, of or pertaining to the palæocortex.

1909 *Arch. Neurol. & Psychiatry* IV. 162 The palæocortical arrangement..is not nearly as typical as in the ventral grey substance. **1964** J. Z. YOUNG *Model of Brain* vi. 110 The palaeocortical centres and basal parts of the forebrain are also concerned largely with 'motivation' as well as being involved in learning.

palæocosmic, palæocrinoid: see PALÆO-, PALEO-.

palæocrystallic (-krɪ'stælɪk), *a.*, more etymological form of next.

1893 SIR R. BALL in *Fortn. Rev.* Aug. 182 That palæo-crystallic ocean which Arctic travellers have described. **1895** *Times* 23 Nov. 4/6 The hero and the villain are left alone.. with very little food, in the palæocrystallic ice.

palæocrystic, (,pæliːəʊ'krɪstɪk, ,peɪ-), *a.* Also (chiefly *U.S.*) **paleo-**. [f. PALÆO-, PALEO- + Gr. κρύστ(αλλος ice, κρυστ(αίν-εσθαι to freeze + -IC. The name was given by Capt. Nares during the Arctic expedition of 1875–6.] Consisting of ancient ice; applied to those parts of the polar seas which are believed to have remained frozen from remote ages.

1876 PETERMANN in *Academy* 16 Dec. 585/3 From Smith Sound to Behring Strait, the region of the Palaeocrystic Sea, our knowledge is entirely due to British enterprise and perseverance. —— in *Athenæum* 16 Dec. 804/1 Baffin Bay.. can receive but little of the palaeocrystic ice. **1878** A. H. MARKHAM *Gt. Frozen Sea* xvi. 200 After some discussion, Captain Nares decided upon calling the frozen sea, on the southern border of which we were wintering, the 'Palæocrystic Sea', the name being derived from the two Greek words παλαιός ancient, and κρύσταλλος ice.

palæocurrent: see PALÆO-, PALEO-.

,palæoe'cology. Also (chiefly *U.S.*) **paleo-**. [f. PALÆO-, PALEO- + ECOLOGY.] The ecology of fossil plants and animals.

1898 C. MACMILLAN in *Minnesota Bot. Stud.* I. 950 Paleoecology might be defined as the science of adaptations of fossil organisms. **1916** F. E. CLEMENTS *Plant Succession* xii. 193 Paleo-ecology develops its most fascinating aspect when it reaches the Human period. **1942** *Bull. Amer. Assoc. Petroleum Geologists* XXVI. 1697 Paleoecology, both organic and sedimentary, is a fertile field for geologic research. **1969** *Beaver* Summer 36/2 Too little is known about too few of the insects in Canadian amber to draw conclusions about their palaeo-ecology. **1976** *Nature* 29 Jan. 350/3 Palaeoecology is primarily concerned with the reconstruction of past ecosystems from palaeontological and lithological evidence.

Hence **,palæoeco'logic, -ical** *adjs.*, **,palæoeco'logically** *adv.*; **palæoe'cologist**, an expert or specialist in palæoecology.

1934 WEBSTER, Paleoecologist. **1940** *Bull. Amer. Assoc. Petroleum Geologists* XXIV. 1196 (*heading*) Inferred and possible paleoecological effects of the water medium. **1940** *Jrnl. Paleont.* XIV. 320/2 In a problem of this kind the paleoecologist is greatly handicapped by the fact that every criterion available is susceptible of a variety of interpretations. **1954** *Jrnl. Geol.* LXII. 234/2 Paleoecological factors, such as wide fluctuations in salinity and insolation-induced temperatures, are insufficient for such mean growth temperatures. **1959** *Jrnl. Palæont.* XXXIII. 936/1 More in need of emphasis paleoecologically, the change from water to sediment or between sediment layers may be almost as profound as that from air to water. **1961** WEBSTER, Paleoecologic. **1963** POTTER & PETTIJOHN *Paleocurrents & Basin Anal.* i. 2 Knowledge of current direction is also useful in paleoecologic studies. **1975** *Nature* 6 Feb. 400/1 Palaeoecological studies suggest that the species [sc. *Armeria maritima*] was widespread in distribution during the cold and disturbed conditions at the close of the last glaciation. **1977** A. HALLAM *Planet Earth* 218 Because they are far more abundant, the invertebrate fossil faunas of the sea are of more importance to stratigraphers and paleoecologists than are the vertebrates.

palæoenvironment to **-field**: see PALÆO-, PALEO.

palæogæan, -gean (,pæliːəʊ'dʒiːən, ,peɪ-), *a.* [f. PALÆO-, PALEO- + Gr. γαῖα, γῆ the earth.]

1. Belonging to *Palæogæa*, i.e. the 'Old World' or eastern hemisphere considered as a zoogeographical region.

1857 P. L. SCLATER in *Jrnl. Proc. Linn. Soc.* (Zool.) II. 130.

2. (See quot.)

1865 PAGE *Handbk. Geol. Terms*, *Palæogean*, belonging to the former conditions of the earth's surface as revealed by geology, as distinct from the existing terraqueous aspects as described by geography.

palæogene, to **-geomagnetic**: see PALÆO-, PALEO-.

,palæogeomorphic (-dʒiːəʊ'mɔːfɪk), *a.* Chiefly *U.S.*, in the form **paleo-**. [f. PALÆO-, PALEO- + GEOMORPHIC *a.*] Of, pertaining to, or formed by buried relief features; palæogeomorphological.

1945 M. KAY in *Bull. Amer. Assoc. Petroleum Geologists* XXIX. 427 (*heading*) Paleogeomorphic maps. **1960** *Prof. Papers U.S. Geol. Survey* No. 400-B. 186/1 Because of the subtle nature of the topography of this disconformable surface a regional paleogeomorphic pattern has not been generally recognized or described. **1966** *Bull. Amer. Assoc. Petroleum Geologists* L. 2279/1 Kay (1945, p. 427), discussing 'paleogeomorphic maps', did not really do justice to Thornbury's later definition of paleogeomorphology, because he omitted all mention of the use of subsurface data in constructing such maps; his main concern was the separation of seas from lands. **1972** *Ibid.* LVI. 538/2 Paleogeomorphic traps are formed where ancient subaqueous or land surfaces and the relief features on them ..are buried by younger strata of a different lithology.

,palæogeomor'phology. Also (chiefly *U.S.*) **paleo-**. [f. PALÆO-, PALEO- + GEOMORPHOLOGY.] The geomorphology of ancient landscapes, esp. as represented today by features that are buried or newly exhumed.

1954 W. D. THORNBURY *Princ. Geomorphol.* ii. 31 It might seem that the recognition of ancient erosion surfaces and the study of ancient topographies does not belong in the field of geomorphology, but the approach of the geomorphologist may be the most logical one. This aspect of geomorphology may well be called paleogeomorphology. **1966** R. MARTIN in *Bull. Amer. Assoc. Petroleum Geologists* L. 2278/1 Enlarging on Thornbury's concept, the writer groups under the term *paleogeomorphology* the study of all geomorphic phenomena which are recognizable in the subsurface and in outcrops of previously buried formations. **1968** R. W. FAIRBRIDGE *Encycl. Geomorphol.* 805/1 Paleogeomorphology is of practical importance insofar as many accumulations of oil, gas, certain ores and fresh water are related to buried relief features. **1972** *Geo Abstr.* A. 727 The palaeogeomorphology of the region is dominated by glacial features upon which karst features are now being superimposed.

Hence **,palæogeomorpho'logical, -'logic** *adjs.*; **,palæogeomor'phologist**, one who studies palæogeomorphology.

1960 *Canad. Mining & Metallurg. Bull.* LIII. 529/2 Buried relief features are of importance to the petroleum geologist whenever they lead to the trapping of hydrocarbons, either directly or indirectly. In areas where such features abound,..paleogeomorphological features rank in importance with sedimentation and structure as hydrocarbon trapping agents. **1963** *Oil & Gas Jrnl.* 21 Oct. 140/1 It is convenient for the paleogeomorphologist to know that water travelling at a certain speed can move particles of specific sizes and density. **1966** *Bull. Amer. Assoc. Petroleum Geologists* L. 2279/1 An important difference between stratigraphic and paleogeomorphologic traps is the pronounced three-dimensional aspect of the latter. *Ibid.* 2297/1 Although these [observations] have received practically no attention from 'modern' geomorphologists, they are of considerable importance to the paleogeomorphologist in the exploration for oil and gas. **1975** *Nature* 24 July 279/2 This work has resulted in the elucidation of the geographic extent, stratigraphic succession, facies change, palaeoenvironments and palaeogeomorphological setting of the basin.

palæogeophysical to **-glyph**: see PALÆO-, PALEO-.

palæography, (pælɪ'ɒgrəfɪ, peɪlɪ:-). Also (chiefly *U.S.*) **paleo-**. [ad. mod.L. *palæographia* (Montfaucon, title *Palæographia Græca* 1708), f. PALÆO-, PALEO- + Gr. -γραφία -GRAPHY. Cf. F. *paléographie* (1708).]

1. Ancient writing, or an ancient style or method of writing.

1822 *Q. Rev.* XXVI. 195 Dr. Young..whose acuteness and learning seem calculated to subdue the difficulties of Palæography. **1857** BIRCH *Anc. Pottery* (1858) I. 197 Judging from the palæography of the inscriptions, they may have been in use from the age of Augustus to that of..

Severus. **1900** G. C. BRODRICK *Mem. & Impressions* 255 Freeman..thought it a waste of time for an historian to grub in palæography.

2. The study of ancient writing and inscriptions; the science or art of deciphering and determining the date of ancient writings or systems of writing.

1818 in TODD. **1840** *Penny Cycl.* XVII. 149/1 The study of antient documents, called by modern antiquaries 'Palæography'. **1859** GULLICK & TIMBS *Paint.* 100 The art of deciphering ancient writings, or palæography. **1885** SIR E. M. THOMPSON in *Encycl. Brit.* XVIII. 143 Palæography is the study of ancient handwriting from surviving examples.

So **palæograph** ('pæli:əgrɑ:f, -æ-, 'peɪ-) [see -GRAPH], (*a*) an ancient writing; (*b*) = next [= F. *paléographe*]; **palæ'ographer**, one who studies or is skilled in palæography; **palæo'graphic, -ical** *adjs.*, of or pertaining to palæography, or ancient writing (hence **palæo'graphically** *adv.*, in relation to palæography); **palæ'ographist** = *palæographer*.

1864 WEBSTER, *Paleograph, an ancient manuscript. **1894** A. LANG in *Contemp. Rev.* Aug. 169 The great French palæograph and historian. **1850** C. T. NEWTON *Ess. in Archæol.* 12 The researches of the *Palæographer of classical antiquity embrace a far wider field than those of the mediæval Palæographer. **1881** HARTSHORNE *Glance 20th C.* 21 A Greek Codex..believed by palæographers to belong to the third century. **1846** WORCESTER, **Paleographic.* **1858** J. PRINSEP (*title*) Essays on Indian Antiquities, Historic, Numismatic, and Palæographic. **1842** BRANDE *Dict. Sci.* s.v. *Palæography*, The most valuable compilation of *palæographical knowledge is to be found in the *Traité de Diplomatique* of the Benedictines of St. Maur, 6 vols. 4to. 1748. **1846** ELLIS *Elgin Marb.* II. 135 One of the most celebrated palæographical monuments in existence. **1869** DEUTSCH in *Academy* 11 Dec. 83/2 Both these Phoenician characters, though to be distinguished *palaeographically only by the length and the bend of the tail, have a very distinct existence. **1882** *Athenæum* 29 July 139/2 The reading..is..palæographically impossible. **1846** WORCESTER, **Paleographist*, one versed in paleography. *T. Rood.* **1880** *Antiquary* May 227/1 MSS...declared by Roman palæographists to be unpublished compositions of St. Thomas Aquinas.

palæohydrography: see PALÆO-, PALEO-.

Palæo-'Indian, *sb.* and *a.* Also **PalæoIndian, Palæoindian, palæo-Indian,** and with prefix spelt **Paleo-**. [f. PALÆO-, PALEO- + INDIAN *a.* and *sb.*]

A. *sb.* **a.** The culture of the earliest Indian inhabitants of the Americas. **b.** One of these people. **B.** *adj.* Of or pertaining to Palæo-Indians or their culture.

1940 F. H. H. ROBERTS in *Smithsonian Misc. Coll.* C. 51 (*heading*) Developments in the problem of the North American Paleo-Indian. *Ibid.* 77 The morphological significance of the skeletons is considered..in conjunction with the other human remains attributed to the Paleo-Indian inhabitants. *Ibid.* 109 The work of recent years..demonstrates that there actually was a Paleo-Indian. **1941** *Bull. Geol. Soc. Amer.* LII. 2001 Evidences of the Paleo-Indian of the late Pleistocene or Early Recent times are present in Alaska. **1943** *Acta Americana* I. II. 194 The causes of this rapid and widespread disappearance [of Pleistocene forms of animals] are not known. It has been suggested that the Paleo-Indians may have been a contributing factor. **1959** J. J. HONIGMANN *World of Man* xliii. 791 In Union County, New Mexico, a site containing remains of 32 bison, 19 projectile points, and other artifacts indicates a mass kill by Paleoindians. *Ibid.*, The Paleoindian period yields none of the elaborate portable and mural art characteristic of the Upper Paleolithic in Europe. **1968** R. W. FAIRBRIDGE *Encycl. Geomorphol.* 454/2 The lake [*sc.* Lake Agassiz] influenced the movements of early man (paleo-Indian cultures), and artifacts typical of the period 5000–9000 B.C. are found around its margins. **1972** *Science* 16 June 1211/2 Although the literature on North American PaleoIndians is quite extensive, most of this information has been derived from the analysis of kill sites, and only limited data on Paleo-Indian campsites have been available.

palæointensity to **-limnology**: see PALÆO-, PALEO-.

palæolithic, (ˌpæli:əʊ'lɪθɪk, ˌpeɪli:-), *a.* (*sb.*) *Archæol.* Also (chiefly *U.S.*) **paleo-**. [f. PALÆO-, PALEO- + Gr. λίθ-ος stone + -IC.] Characterized by the use of primitive stone implements; applied to the earlier part of the prehistoric 'stone age'; also to things belonging to this period. Opp. to *neolithic*.

1865 LUBBOCK *Preh. Times* 2 Firstly, that of the Drift, when men shared the possession of Europe with the Mammoth, the Cave bear..and other extinct animals. This we may call the 'Palaeolithic' period. **1873** GEIKIE *Gt. Ice Age* Pref. 10 He considers that a glacial period had intervened since the disappearance of paleolithic man.

B. *sb.* A palæolithic implement.

1888 *Amer. Antiquarian* Mar. 123 Information as to the discovery of rude relics resembling paleolithics. *Ibid.* 124 (*heading*) Paleolithics and neolithics.

So **'palæolith**, a primitive stone implement; **palæo'lithical** *a.* = PALÆOLITHIC; **palæo'lithoid** *a.* [see -OID], resembling, or having the character of, what is palæolithic.

1879 WEBSTER *Suppl.*, *Paleolith*, a relic of the paleolithic era. **1887** *Boban Collect. Antiq.* II. 8 (Cent.) Paleolithical. **1895** *Folk-Lore* Mar. 76 From underground palæolith to exquisitely-shaped barbed arrow-head. **1896** SIR A. MITCHELL in *Proc. Soc. Antiq. Scotl.* Ser. III. VI. 357 Other things show that [this] palæolithoid weapon is found in the hands of a palæolithoid man.

palæology (pæli:'ɒlədʒɪ, peɪli:-). *rare*$^{-0}$. [f. PALÆO-, PALEO- + Gr. -λογία, -LOGY: cf. παλαιολογεῖν to discuss antiquities.] The science or study of antiquities. So **palæologian** (-'ləʊdʒɪən) *nonce-wd.*, an antiquarian; one who rests on the authority of antiquity; **palæo'logical** *a.*, relating to palæology; **palæ'ologist**, one versed in palæology.

1824 DIBDIN *Libr. Comp.* 248 Those of the latter are palæological or glossorial. **1828–32** WEBSTER, *Paleologist* [citing GOOD]. *Paleology*, a discourse or treatise on antiquities, or the knowledge of ancient things. **1880** BURTON *Reign Q. Anne* II. xiii. 329 His profound palæological erudition. **1894** MISS COBBE *Life* II. 39, I classify both parties..as Palæologians.

palæolongitude, -machic, etc.: see PALÆO-, PALEO-.

palæo'magnetism. *Geol.* Also (chiefly *U.S.*) **paleo-**. [f. PALÆO-, PALEO- + MAGNETISM.] (The study and interpretation of) the natural magnetism of rocks, which they are believed to have acquired at the time of their formation and is used as evidence for the past relationship of the rocks to each other and to the earth's magnetic field.

1854 *Edin. New Philos. Jrnl.* LVI. 9 The palæomagnetism ..will also give rise to most interesting discoveries, and even to magnetical maps in the various geological periods. **1953** T. NAGATA *Rock-Magnetism* vi. 213 Other people might be concerned with rock-magnetism as the medium or the fossil of the geomagnetic field in the past geologic times, namely, as the tool for palaeomagnetism, since the knowledge of the secular variation of geomagnetic field throughout the whole life of the earth is one of the basic subjects in the modern geophysics. **1955** *Nature* 10 Sept. 505/1 (*heading*) Palæomagnetism of sediments from the Colorado Plateau. **1962** *Listener* 17 May 849/1 This new subject of palaeomagnetism enables us to track the movement of the magnetic poles relative to the continents. **1970** *Nature* 6 June 934/1 The motion of these plates with respect to the Earth's spin axis can be determined using the methods of palaeomagnetism. **1971** I. G. GASS et al. *Understanding Earth* xv. 222/2 One may use palaeomagnetism as a tool for verifying continental drift.

Hence **ˌpalæomag'netic** *a.*, of or pertaining to palæomagnetism; **ˌpalæomag'netically** *adv.*, by means of or as regards palæomagnetism; **palæo'magnetist**, one who studies palæomagnetism.

1953 T. NAGATA *Rock-Magnetism* vi. 218 It seems that the Königsberger's [*sic*] conclusion quoted above is still substantially right at present and very useful as the criterion of available rock-magnetism for the palaeo-magnetic purposes. **1957** *Adv. Physics* VI. 166 Drab deltaic sediments of a cool environment are palaeomagnetically unsuitable. **1960** *Bull. Geol. Soc. Amer.* LXXI. 763/2 The paleomagnetist would like to know if it is at all possible for a nonaxial dipole field to exist for a long period of time. **1969** BENNISON & WRIGHT *Geol. Hist. Brit. Isles* iii. 51 As well as the marked angular unconformity, there is a difference in the palaeomagnetic pole position of about 50° which may indicate that this part of the Lower Torridonian is much older than the upper groups. **1970** *New Scientist* 17 Dec. 491/1 A stern criticism which palaeomagnetists have always had to face..is over the long-term stability of the magnetic minerals within their rock samples. **1973** *Nature* 23 Feb. 497/2 It is not difficult to distinguish palaeomagnetically between polar wandering and continental drift if one or the other acts alone. **1977** A. HALLAM *Planet Earth* 143 Paleomagnetic studies have been vital in establishing the theory of plate tectonics.

palæomeridian to **-meteorology**: see PALÆO-, PALEO-.

palæoniscoid, *sb.* and *a.* [f. mod.L. name of suborder Palæoniscoidei, f. generic name *Palæoniscus* (L. Agassiz *Recherches sur les Poissons fossiles* (1833) II. v. 41), f. PALÆO- + Gr. ὀνίσκος a sea-fish resembling cod + -OID.]

A. *sb.* A fossil fish belonging to the suborder Palæoniscoidei, a group that includes elongate fishes with heterocercal tails and diamond-shaped scales. **B.** *adj.* Of or pertaining to a fish of this kind.

1895 B. DEAN *Fishes Living & Fossil* vii. 166 (*caption*) Palaeozoic Palaeoniscoid. **1900** *Nature* 20 Sept. 507/2 Both the head and shoulder-girdle are of palæoniscoid type. **1928** *Palaeobiologica* I. 87 (*heading*) *Polypterus*, a palaeoniscoid? **1963** P. H. GREENWOOD *Norman's Hist. Fishes* (ed. 2) iv. 56 A modified palaeoniscoid scale occurs in the superorder Holostei, another group which is best known from extinct forms. **1968** A. S. ROMER *Procession of Life* viii. 161 A typical palaeoniscoid was a small, well-streamlined little fish, with thick shiny scales, long jaws with a powerful gape, and..a tail in which the fleshy, scale-covered tip of the body extends upward and backward to the tip of the fin. *Ibid.*, Today there survive only two small groups of palaeoniscoid descendants. **1974** D. & M. WEBSTER *Compar. Vertebr. Morphol.* viii. 162 True ganoid scales occurred in the palaeoniscoid fishes.

palæontography, (ˌpæli:ɒn'tɒgrəfɪ, ˌpeɪli:-). Also (chiefly *U.S.*) **paleo-**. [f. PALÆO-, PALEO- + Gr. ὄντα, pl. of ὤν being + -γραφία, -GRAPHY.] The description of fossil remains of extinct animals and plants; descriptive palæontology. So **palæon'tographer**, a person engaged in the description of fossil animals and plants; **ˌpalæonto'graphical** *a.*, relating to or engaged in palæontography.

1847 *Palæontographical Society, Laws*, 1. That the Society formed be called the Palæontographical Society, and that it shall have for its objects the illustration and description of British fossil organic remains. **1857** MAYNE *Expos. Lex.*, Paleontography. **1861** WILSON & GEIKIE *Mem. E. Forbes* xii. 412 The origin of the Palæontographical Society. **1924** P. GEDDES in P. Boardman *Worlds of Patrick Geddes* (1978) x. 357 The study of comparative religion too often readily gives an impression..[of] but the latest form of palaeontography and palaeography. **1973** *Nature* 1 June 308/2 The discussions liberally impinge on the cognate sciences of evolutionary palaeontography, biogeochemistry and statistics. *Ibid.* 308/3 It [*sc.* Schopf's *Models in Paleobiology*] should..infuse panic in the hearts of those palaeontographers who have got stuck in a rut.

palæontology, (ˌpæli:ɒn'tɒlədʒɪ, ˌpeɪli:-). Also (chiefly *U.S.*) **paleo-**. [f. PALÆO-, PALEO- + Gr. ὄντα, pl. of ὤν being + -λογία, -LOGY.] The study of extinct organized beings; that department of geology or of biology which treats of fossil animals and plants; often confined to that of extinct animals (palæozoology).

1838 LYELL *Elem. Geol.* II. xiii. 281 *note*, Palæontology is the science which treats of fossil remains, both animal and vegetable. **1851** RICHARDSON *Geol.* viii. (1855) 207 Palæontology may be defined to be the science of fossil animals. **1857** H. MILLER *Test. Rocks* 1 Palæontology.. deals, as its subject, with all the plants and animals of all the geologic periods.

So **palæonto'logic, -ical** *adjs.*, pertaining to palæontology; relating to extinct organisms; hence **palæonto'logically** *adv.*, in relation to palæontology; **palæon'tologist**, one versed in palæontology.

1854 R. G. LATHAM *Native Races Russian Emp.* 199 We get at it by that *palaeontologic line of reasoning which characterizes geology and archaeology. **1846** WORCESTER, **Paleontological*, relating to paleontology. *Conrad.* **1859** DARWIN *Orig. Spec.* ix. 287 That our palæontological collections are very imperfect is admitted by every one. **1854** R. G. LATHAM *Native Races Russian Emp.* 14 Upon the principles of ethnological criticism; or, changing the expression, *palaeontologically. **1876** PAGE *Adv. Text-bk. Geol.* xviii. 350 Palaeontologically. **1846** WORCESTER, **Paleontologist*, one versed in paleontology. **1871** TYNDALL *Fragm. Sc.* (1879) II. ix. 172 The riddle of the rocks has been read by the geologist and palaeontologist.

palæo-oceanography, etc.: see PALÆO-, PALEO-.

palæo'pallium. *Anat.* Also (chiefly *U.S.*) **paleo-**, and with hyphen. [mod.L., f. PALÆO-, PALEO- b + PALLIUM 3 d.] A phylogenetically older portion of the pallium of the brain, which comprises mainly the pyriform lobe (the hippocampal formation or archipallium is sometimes included).

1909 C. V. A. KAPPERS in *Arch. Neurol. & Psychiatry* IV. 161 This nervous substance, in order to distinguish it from the subventricular grey substance, should be called palæo-pallium. **1933** [see ARCHIPALLIUM]. **1948** A. BRODAL *Neurol. Anat.* x. 324 (*caption*) In amphibians..a dorsal area is found between the hippocampal area (archi-pallium) and the piriform area (palæo-pallium). **1962** E. C. CROSBY et al. *Correl. Anat. Nerv. Syst.* vii. 411/1 'Paleopallium' is a term applied to the pyriform cortex; that is, to portions at least of the hippocampal gyrus. **1972** T. W. JENKINS *Functional Mammalian Neuroanat.* ii. 35/1 Based on the phylogenetic age, the olfactory cortex at the base of the brain, which is the older cortex is referred to as the archipallium (archicortex), or paleo-pallium (paleocortex).

Hence **palæo'pallial** *a.*, of or pertaining to the palæopallium.

1936 C. U. A. KAPPERS et al. *Compar. Anat. Nerv. Syst. Vertebr.* II. ix. 1482 In mammals the discharge paths between the archipallial, paleopallial, and archistriatal regions and the diencephalic centers are essentially those which have been described for lower forms. **1962** E. C. CROSBY et al. *Correl. Anat. Nerv. Syst.* vii. 411 The non-olfactory functions of paleopallial and archipallial areas may become dominant in higher mammals.

ˌpalæopa'thology. Also (chiefly *U.S.*) **paleo-**. [f. PALÆO-, PALEO- + PATHOLOGY.] (The study of) the pathological conditions found in ancient human and animal remains.

1893 R. W. SHUFELDT in *Pop. Sci. Monthly* XLII. 679 Palæopathology..is a term here proposed under which may be described all diseased or pathological conditions found fossilized in the remains of extinct or fossil animals. **1923** R. L. MOODIE *Antiquity of Disease* iv. 66 Virchow, Mayer, Esper, Schmerling, and the other founders of paleopathology did their initial observations on the diseased bones of cave bears of Europe. **1952** *Bull. Hist. Med.* XXVI. 538 (*heading*) Evidence on the paleopathology of yaws. **1967** *Science* 11 Aug. 638/3 Since not only skeletal material but disease itself is the subject matter of paleopathology, many disciplines find a meeting ground in these studies. **1975** *Palestine Exploration Q.* CVII. 89 Excavated the cemeteries of four medieval leper hospitals in Denmark... Palaeopathology was, in this instance, able to contribute to clinical medicine.

Hence **ˌpalæopatho'logic, -'logical** *adjs.*; **ˌpalæopa'thologist**, one who investigates or studies palæopathology.

1917 *Johns Hopkins Hosp. Bull.* XXVIII. 261/1 Another American investigator, Dr. Aleš Hrdlička, has developed intensively the palæopathological side in his numerous explorations and studies of the aborigines on this continent. *Ibid.*, A very remarkable exhibition of palæopathologic specimens in San Diego. **1939** *Brit. Jrnl. Tuberculosis* XXXIII. 148 Egypt has provided the anatomist and the anthropologist, no less than the archæologist and the palæopathologist, with unrivalled opportunities and an unprecedented wealth of material for the prosecution of their respective researches. **1966** O. Temkin in S. Jarcho *Human Palaeopath.* 34 Material from Ancient Egypt looms very large in the discussions of palaeopathologists. **1966** W. G. J. Putschar in *Ibid.* 60 In palaeopathological material we have only the mineralized portion of the affected bone available. **1967** *Amer. Jrnl. Roentgenology* XCIX. 712 The Mochica-Chinú civilizations developed in the coastal deserts of northern Perú and the dry desiccating sands of these areas have preserved large quantities of their skeletal remains in a remarkably good state for paleopathologic study. **1975** *Palestine Exploration Q.* CVII. 88 To rule out the possibility that they were the disease now known as leprosy..; an opinion supported by the paleopathological evidence given below.

palæopedological to **palæophilist**: see PALÆO-, PALEO-.

‖**Palæophis** (pəˈliːəʊfɪs). *Palæont.* [f. PALÆ(O-, PALEO- + Gr. ὄφις serpent.] A genus of extinct Ophidians containing the oldest known fossil serpents.

1863 Lyell *Antiq. Man* xx. 402 The age of the Iguanodon was long anterior to that of the Eocene palæophis and living boa.

palæophysiology: see PALÆO-, PALEO-.

palæophytic (-ˈfɪtɪk), *a. rare*–⁰. [f. PALÆO-, PALEO- + Gr. φυτόν plant + -IC.] Of or relating to extinct plants.

1890 *Cent. Dict.*, Paleophytic.

palæophytology, (-faɪˈtɒlədʒɪ). Also paleo-. [f. as prec. + -LOGY.] The science of extinct or fossil plants; = PALÆOBOTANY. So **palæophyto'logical** *a.* = PALÆOBOTANICAL; **palæophy'tologist** = PALÆOBOTANIST.

1857 Mayne *Expos. Lex.*, Paleophytology. **1876** Page *Adv. Text-bk. Geol.* i. 29 To subdivide Palaeontology into two branches—palaeozoology..and paleophytology. *Ibid.* ix. 176 Under one or other of these divisions palaeophytologists have attempted to arrange their fossil flora. **1885** *Trans. Geol. Soc.* 6 From palæophytological reasons.

palæornithine to **-selachian**: see PALÆO-, PALEO-.

Palæo-Si'berian, *sb.* and *a.* Also **palæo-Siberian, Palæosiberian**, and with the prefix spelt **Paleo-**. [f. PALÆO-, PALEO- + SIBERIAN *a.* and *sb.*] **A.** *sb.* **a.** A member of any of several peoples of northern and eastern Siberia who are held to represent the earliest inhabitants of Siberia and whose languages do not belong to any of the major families. **b.** The Palæo-Siberian group of languages.

1914 M. A. Czaplicka *Aboriginal Siberia* ii. 15 If we are to provide a name for these unclassified tribes of the extreme north and east of Asia,..we would propose the name 'Palaeo-Siberians'... It implies a comparison and a contrast with the other tribes—Finnic, Mongolic, Turkic, Samoyedic, and Tungusic—who are comparatively recent comers to Siberia. **1965** *Language* XLI. 122 Soviet research in the rather exotic field of Paleosiberian. **1970** *Atlantic Monthly* Feb. 111 The Paleosiberians and a small Mongol enclave in Afghanistan..use these two methods of taking Soma. **1975** *Language* LI. 482 He suggests that the correspondence of certain Proto-Uralic items to those of other language families (e.g., Indo-European, Indo-Iranian, Turkic, Paleo-Siberian, and Eskimo) is due to an ancient areal affinity, not to linguistic relationship.

B. *adj.* Of, pertaining to, or designating Palæo-Siberians.

1923 R. B. Dixon *Racial Hist. Man* III. v. 334 The conclusion cannot be escaped that a relationship of some sort exists between these Palæo-Siberian peoples of Asia and the Indian tribes of the northwest coast of America. **1948** D. Diringer *Alphabet* 156 The aboriginal or Palaeo-Siberian group..are mainly nomad reindeer breeders and hunters. **1961** L. F. Brosnahan *Sounds of Language* viii. 177 The area of the simple stress accent is much larger: it extends.. from the west and south of Europe and includes..the.. Mongolian, Tungus and Paleosiberian languages of eastern Asia. **1964** tr. *Levin & Potapov's Peoples of Siberia* 56 The characteristics..show an ancient paleo-Siberian race, features of which are observed in other Siberian tribes.

palæoslope to **-species**: see PALÆO-, PALEO-.

,palæostri'atum (-straɪˈeɪtəm). *Anat.* Also (chiefly *U.S.*) paleo-. [mod.L. (coined in Ger. by C. U. A. Kappers 1908, in *Anat. Anzeiger* XXXIII. 322), f. PALÆO-, PALEO- b + STRIATUM.] The phylogenetically older portion of the corpus striatum, consisting essentially of the globus pallidus. Hence **,palæostri'atal** *a.*

1913 *Brain* XXXVI. 159 In analogy with the archi-striatal commissure which connects the nuclei amygdalæ, and a possible commissure between the palæostriata in Meynert's commissure, such a connexion of the phylogenetically most recent parts of the striatum would not be improbable. **1921** Tilney & Riley *Form & Functions Cent. Nervous Syst.* xliv. 805 In its process of evolution from the lower vertebrates to mammals, the primordial portion of the striate body corresponds to the globus pallidus. This structure may, therefore, be tentatively distinguished as the paleostriatum. *Ibid.* xlv. 819 This is known as the syndrome of the globus pallidus, juvenile paralysis agitans or the paleo-striatal syndrome of Ramsay Hunt. **1929** [see NEOSTRIATUM]. **1936** C. U. A. Kappers et al. *Compar. Anat. Nervous Syst. Vertebr.* II. ix. 1369 The paleostriatal and neostriatal areas of birds and their reptilean equivalents are basal in origin. **1972** [see NEOSTRIATUM].

palæostructural: see PALÆO-, PALEO-.

palæ'otalith. [app. for **palæotatolith*, f. Gr. παλαιότατο-ς oldest + λίθος stone.] (See quot.)

1897 T. McKenny Hughes in *Archæol. Inst. Jrnl.* Dec. 364 The supposed occurrence of a more ancient group of implements, for which the name Palæotaliths has been proposed. *Ibid.* 375 The term palæotalith seems.. unnecessary at present, as there is nothing to which it can be applied.

palæo'thalamus. *Anat.* Also (chiefly *U.S.*) paleo-. [mod.L., f. PALÆO-, PALEO- b + THALAMUS.] The phylogenetically older portion of the thalamus, usu. taken to include its anterior and medial parts.

1920 S. W. Ranson *Anat. Nervous Syst.* 391/1 (Index), Palæothalamus. See *Thalamus, old.* **1921** Tilney & Riley *Form & Functions Cent. Nervous Syst.* xxxi. 560 The primitive pars thalamica is known as the paleothalamus. **1958** L. Hausman *Clin. Neuroanat.* xxvii. 242 Phylogenetically, the hypothalamus, the epithalamus and part of the medial division of the dorsal thalamus constitute the old thalamus or paleothalamus. **1973** [see NEOTHALAMUS].

palæothere (ˈpæliːəʊθɪə(r), ˈpeɪliː-). Also (chiefly *U.S.*) **paleo-**. Often in L. form **palæo'therium.** [f. PALÆO-, PALEO- + Gr. θηρίον beast.] A perissodactyl mammal of the extinct genus *Palæotherium*, comprising several species of tapir-like form, varying from the size of a horse to that of a hog; their fossil remains are found in Eocene and Miocene strata. (In the Eng. form extended to other members of the extinct family *Palæotheriidæ*.)

1815 W. Phillips *Outl. Min. & Geol.* (1818) 89 In the gypsum, Cuvier discovered the bones of 5 varieties of an extinct animal, which he calls *palæotherium*..varying in size from a sheep to a horse. **1833** Lyell *Princ. Geol.* III. 317 On these lands we may suppose the Paleothere, Anoplothere, and Moschus of Binstead to have lived. **1854** *Fraser's Mag.* XLIX. 141 Cuvier predicted, from the fragment of a jaw-bone, the yet undiscovered Palæothere. **1880** Dawkins *Early Man* 143 The anoplotheres and palæotheres, the deinotheres and the mastodons..were either dragged in by the carnivores, or swept in by the flow of water.

Hence **palæo'therian** *a.*, of or pertaining to the palæothere; characterized by the palæotheres; **palæo'theriodont** [Gr. ὀδούς, ὀδόντ- tooth] *a.*, having teeth like those of the palæothere; *sb.*, an animal having such teeth; **palæo'therioid, -'theroid** *adjs.*, akin to the palæothere.

1834 Sir C. Bell *Hand* 120 The lower layer of this 'tertiary formation' is sometimes called the product of the Palæotherian period. **1868** Owen *Anat. Vertebr.* III. 341 The tooth assumes more of the palæotherian pattern. **1887** Cope *Orig. of Fittest* vii. 253 *Equus*..has been probably derived from Palæotheriodont ancestors. *Ibid.* 248 Palæotheriodonts.

palæothermometry to **-topography**: see PALÆO-, PALEO-.

palæotropical (ˌpæliːəʊˈtrɒpɪkəl, ˌpeɪliː-), *a.* Also (chiefly *U.S.*) **paleo-**. [f. PALÆO-, PALEO- + TROPICAL.] Belonging to the tropical parts of the 'Old World' or eastern hemisphere, considered as a zoogeographical region.

1857 P. L. Sclater in *Jrnl. Proc. Linn. Soc.* (Zool.) II. 138 Æthiopian or Western Palæotropical Region. *Ibid.* 140 Indian or Middle Palæotropical Region.

palæotype (ˈpæliːəʊtaɪp). [f. PALÆO-, PALEO- + TYPE.] A system of writing devised by A. J. Ellis, in which the 'old types' (i.e. existing Roman letters and other characters), in their various forms and combinations, are used to form a universal phonetic alphabet. Also *attrib.* or as *adj.* Hence **palæotypic** (-ˈtɪpɪk) *a.*

1867 A. J. Ellis *E.E. Pronunc.* I. 1 In order to be convenient to the Printer and Writer, the old types, παλαιοὶ τύποι..should be used, and no accented letters, few turned, and still fewer mutilated letters should be employed. The system of writing here proposed to fulfil these conditions will, in consequence of the last, be termed Palæotype. *Ibid.* 13 In order to fix the value of the palæotypic letters, they are on p. 15 compared with those of Mr. Melville Bell's *Visible Speech.* **1875** *Ibid.* IV. p. xii, The original list of Palæotypic symbols..has had to be supplemented and improved. **1887** —— in *Encycl. Brit.* XXII. 389/2 There are many more palaeotype letters and signs, here omitted for brevity, but found necessary for phonetical discussions.

palæotypography (-taɪˈpɒgrəfɪ). [f. PALÆO-, PALEO- + TYPOGRAPHY.] Ancient typography, early printing. So **palæoty'pographist**, one versed in early printing.

1872 W. Skeen *Early Typogr.* 80 One of the latest authorities, Mr. Blades, the able palæotypographist. **1881** *Athenæum* 16 Apr. 522 When the palæotypography of our own and foreign presses receives full and technical analysis.

Palæozoic (ˌpæliːəʊˈzəʊɪk, ˌpeɪliː-), *a. Geol.* Also **paleo-**. [f. PALÆO-, PALEO- + Gr. ζωή life, ζω-ός living + -IC.]

1. Characterized by, containing, or pertaining to ancient forms of life. As introduced by Sedgwick, in 1838, it was applied to the Cambrian and Silurian strata; as extended by Phillips, 1841, it comprises all the fossiliferous strata up to the Permian, the higher strata being MESOZOIC and CAINOZOIC.

1838 Sedgwick in *Q. Jrnl. Geol. Soc.* II. 685 Class II or Palæozoic Series. This includes all the groups of formations between Class I [Primary stratified rocks called by Sedgwick Protozoic] and the Old Red Sandstone, and subdivided as follows: 1 Lower Cambrian; 2 Upper Cambrian; 3 Silurian System. **1840** Phillips in *Penny Cycl.* XVI. 489/2 We include in the term 'Palæozoic', all the generally argillaceous and arenaceous strata between the mica schist and the old red-sandstone. *Ibid.* XVII. 154/1 The term Palæozoic may be retained, though it should be found that the application of it ought to be extended so as to include the carboniferous rocks or even the magnesian limestone. This indeed is not unlikely. **1841** Phillips *Palæozoic Fossils Devon* 160, I have suggested the..proposed titles; Cainozoic Strata.. Mesozoic Strata..Palæozoic Strata: Upper = Magnesian Limestone formation, Carboniferous System; Middle = (Eifel and South Devon); Lower = Transition Strata; Primary Strata. **1856** Darwin in *Life & Lett.* (1887) II. 80 Not a fragment of secondary or palæozoic rock has been found. **1880** Haughton *Phys. Geog.* iii. 78 During the Upper Palæozoic age, extensive land surfaces were in existence.

2. *fig.* and *transf.* Belonging to the most ancient, or to the lowest, stage.

1851 D. Wilson *Preh. Ann.* (1863) I. i. 36 How far back man is to be looked for in the palaeozoic chronicles of former life. **1864** Lowell *Fireside Trav.* 117 Uncle Z. was a good specimen of that palæozoic class, extinct.., or surviving, like the Dodo, in the Botany Bays of Society. **1869** Farrar *Fam. Speech* iv. (1873) 115 A large number of them belong to the lowest, palæozoic strata of humanity. **1889** Jacobs *Aesop* 54 [In] the Jātakas, we..come upon a really Palæozoic stratum of the Bidpai Fables.

B. *sb. ellipt.* (*pl.*) Palæozoic rocks or strata.

1865 Phillips in *Intell. Observ.* No. 40. 283 Below the Palæozoics.

palæozoology (-zəʊˈɒlədʒɪ, -zuː-). Also (chiefly *U.S.*) paleo-. [f. PALÆO-, PALEO- + ZOOLOGY.] That department of zoology, or of palæontology, which treats of extinct or fossil animals. (Correlative to PALÆOPHYTOLOGY.)

1857 in Mayne *Expos. Lex.* **1861** R. E. Grant *Tab. View Prim. Div. Anim. Kingd.* 8 The history of existing animals belongs to Cainozoology, and that of extinct forms to Palæozoology. **1862** Burton *Bk. Hunter* (1863) 2 Get the passive student once into palæozoology and he takes your other hard names..for granted. **1889** H. A. Nicholson in Nicholson & Lydekker *Man. Palæont.* (ed. 3) I. i. 3 Palæozoology and Palæobotany are inseparably connected with Neozoology and Neobotany. **1935** Twenhofel & Shrock *Invertebr. Paleontol.* i. 1 Paleontology..may be divided into paleobotany, treating of fossil plants, and paleozoology, treating of fossil animals. **1953** E. S. Barghoorn in H. Shapley *Climatic Change* xx. 238 Ecologic interpretation..will always require confirming evidence from the physical geology and paleozoölogy. **1978** D. Bloodworth *Crosstalk* iv. 38 A common interest in paleozoology.

Hence **,palæozoo'logical** *a.*, belonging to palæozoology; **,palæozo'ologist**, a student of extinct or fossil animals.

1866 *Phil. Trans. R. Soc.* CLVI. 672 A complete Monograph of the structure and life-history of that organism [sc. *Pentacrinus*] would be one of the most valuable contributions which Palæo-zoological science could receive. **1894** *Nat. Science* Sept. 175 A distinct revival of palæozoological interest in the Geological Society. **1909** Webster, Paleozoölogist. **1947** *Jrnl. Paleontol.* XXI. 574/1 This seems to be the favored path of some paleontologists (or should I call them paleo-zoologists?). **1957** *Antiquity* XXXI. 78 The field research necessary for a meaningful paleoclimatological, paleobotanical, and paleozoological history of post-glacial south-western Asia is only beginning. **1972** D. Bloodworth *Any Number can Play* x. 81 Max.. was a paleo-zoologist..doing some work on prehistoric monkeys.

‖**palæstra, palestra** (pəˈliːstrə, pəˈlɛstrə). *Gr. Antiq.* Also 5–6 **pal(l)estre, palastre, palester, palustre.** [a. L. *palæstra*, a. Gr. παλαίστρα, f. παλαί-ειν to wrestle; in form *palestre*, a. F. *palestre* (12th c. in Littré).] A place devoted to the public teaching and practice of wrestling and other athletic exercises; a wrestling-school, gymnasium: **a.** In Grecian antiquity.

1412–20 Lydg. *Chron. Troy* II. xi, In Martys honour they were dedicate And in palastre on wakes on the nyght. **1580** Lyly *Euphues* (Arb.) 447 To wrestle in the games of *Olympia*, or to fight at Barriers in *Palestra.* **1684** Bowles tr. *Theocritus* in *Dryden's Misc.* I. 243 To morrow I'll to the Palæstra go, And tell him he's unkind to use me so. **1776** R. Chandler *Trav. Greece* xxiii. 112 Socrates passing from the Academy to the Lyceum..discovers..an inclosure..which was a palæstra or place for exercises lately built. **1839** Thirlwall *Greece* lvi. VII. 143 Among his monuments were an arsenal,..a gymnasium, a palæstra, a stadium.

b. In transferred use; often put for the practice of wrestling or athletics; also *fig.*

14.. Lydg. *Balade Commend. our Lady* 69 Laureat crowne..To hem that putte hem in palestre for thy sake. **14..** *Circumsision* in *Tundale's Vis.* (1843) 96 Myghty champyons With won pallestre thorow hor hee renown. **1585** T. Washington tr. *Nicholay's Voy.* III. x. 86 The

Palester of the Athletes, which is..the wrestling. **1781** COWPER *Conversation* 842 Learned at the bar, in the palæstra bold. **1840** GEN. P. THOMPSON *Exerc.* (1842) V. 52 When the conduct of criminal justice is but a palæstra or course of exercise, to be turned on occasion against perhaps the most deserving members of the community.

pa'læstral, pa'lestral (see prec.), *a.* [f. prec. + -AL[1] (prob. through OF. or med.L.).] Of or pertaining to the palæstra, or to wrestling or athletics; athletic.

c **1374** CHAUCER *Troylus* v. 304 The feste and pleyes palestral At my vigile. **1513** DOUGLAS *Æneis* I. Pref. 174 The lusty gammys, and plais palustrale. *Ibid.* III. iv. 136 Our fallowschip exerce palestrale play. **1827** HONE *Every-day Bk.* II. 1009 In the 'Cornish hug', Mr. Polwhele perceived the Greek palæstral attitudes finely revived.

¶ App. misused for 'palatial'.

1500-20 DUNBAR *Poems* lxxxv. 73 Imperiall wall, place palestrall, Of peirless pulcritud.

So **pa'læstrian, -'estrian,** (*a*) *sb.*, one who practised wrestling in the palæstra; (*b*) *adj.* = PALÆSTRAL.

1599 R. LINCHE *Anc. Fiction* Q iv, The wrastlers, called also Palestrians. **1828** WEBSTER, *Palestrian, Palestric.*

palæstric, -estric (pə'li:strɪk, -'ɛstrɪk), *a.* [ad. L. *palæstric-us*, a. Gr. παλαιστρικός, f. παλαίστρα.] = prec.

1774 J. BRYANT *Mythol.* II. 46 They were so skilled in the Palæstric art. **1823** DE QUINCEY *Lett. Language* Wks. 1860 XIV. 125 An activity too palestric and purely human.

So †**pa'læstrical** *a. Obs.* (in same sense).

1579 TWYNE *Phisicke agst. Fort.* I. xc. 112 We entreated of Palestrical exercises. **1658** PHILLIPS, *Palestrical*, or *Palæstrical*, belonging to wrestling.

palætiology (pəli:tɪ'ɒlədʒɪ). *rare.* Also palaitio-. [(for **palæ-ætiology*), f. Gr. παλαιός ancient + ÆTIOLOGY; after *palæontology*.] Used by Whewell for the application of existing principles of cause and effect to the explanation of past phenomena.

1837 WHEWELL *Hist. Induct. Sc.* XVIII. III. 481 The sciences which treat of causes have sometimes been termed *ætiological*..; a portion of that science on which we are about to enter, geology, has..been termed *palæontology*, since it treats of beings which formerly existed. Hence, combining these two notions, the term *palætiology* appears to be not inappropriate, to describe those speculations which thus refer to actual past events, but attempt to explain them by laws of causation.

So **pa,lætio'logical** *a.*, of, belonging to, or using the methods of palætiology; **pa,læti'ologist**, one who investigates or treats of a subject in a palætiological way.

1837 WHEWELL *Hist. Induct. Sc.* XVIII. III. 486 Palætiological sciences..undertake to refer changes to their causes. *Ibid.* 487 The tendencies [etc.]..which direct man to architecture and sculpture, to civil government, to rational and grammatical speech..must be in a great degree known to the palætiologist of art, of society, and of language, respectively. **1840** —— *Philos. Induct. Sc.* (1847) II. 464. **1859** MAX MÜLLER *Sc. Lang.* Ser. I. ii. (1864) 29 Dr. Whewell classes the science of language as one of the palaitiological sciences.

‖**palafitte** ('pæləfɪt, ‖palafit). *Archæol.* [F. *palafitte*, ad. It. *palafitta* a fence of piles, f. *palo* stake, pile + *fitto* fixed, driven in: (Florio, 1611, has *palafitta* = *palificata* 'a foundation of piles ..in water-works': see PALIFICATION).] A hut of prehistoric age built on piles over the water of a lake; a lake-dwelling (in Switzerland or N. Italy).

1882 in I. Donnelly *Atlantis* 243 We must look, then, beyond both the Etruscans and Phœnicians in attempting to identify the commerce of the Bronze Age of our palafittes. **1893** *Amer. Cath. Q. Rev.* Oct. 727 About forty years ago special attention was directed by Dr. Keller to the Palafittes or Lake-Dwellings of Switzerland. **1899** BARING-GOULD *Bk. of West* II. 87 In the lake is a cranogue, or subaqueous cairn, on which was formerly a palafite dwelling.

palagonite (pə'lægəʊnaɪt). *Min.* [ad. Ger. *Palagonit* (Waltershausen, 1846), f. *Palagonia* in Sicily, one of its localities.] A volcanic rock of vitreous structure, allied to basalt. ***Palagonite-tuff***, a 'tuff' or porous rock composed of fragments of basaltic lava and palagonite.

1863 BARING-GOULD *Iceland* 208 The hill is composed of Palagonite tuff. **1879** RUTLEY *Stud. Rocks* xiii. 272 Under the microscope palagonite appears as a perfectly amorphous substance. **1896** CHESTER *Names of Min.*, *Palagonite*..a basaltic tufa, formerly considered a mineral species.

Hence **palagonitic** (-'ɪtɪk) *a.*, pertaining to or of the nature of palagonite.

1886 *Encycl. Brit.* XXI. 189/2 Lavas and scoriæ of anorthitic character, palagonitic tuffs, and basaltic ashes.

Palaic (pə'leɪɪk), *sb.* and *a.* [f. *Pala*, appar. a district of Asia Minor + -IC.] **A.** *sb.* The name of an Anatolian language, known from the Hittite archives. **B.** *adj.* Of or pertaining to this language.

1928 C. DAWSON *Age of Gods* xiii. 302 The Hittite archives also refer to three other tongues, Luvian, Palaic, and Harrian or Churrite. **1951** STURTEVANT & HAHN *Compar. Gram. Hittite Lang.* (ed. 2) I. i. 5 In the ritual of the deity Ziparwas certain passages are to be spoken *Pa-la-um-ni-li* 'in Palaic'. **1966** BIRNBAUM & PUHVEL *Anc. Indo-Europ. Dial.* 237 Watkins has..built a very ingenious hypothesis.. on the brittle back of the Palaic hapax *malitanna*. *Ibid.* 243 Among verb stems, Luwian, Hieroglyphic, and Lycian *-s(s)-* contrasts with the Hittite and Palaic 'iterative' *-sk-*. **1972** W. B. LOCKWOOD *Panorama Indo-European Lang.* 263 Palaic was spoken in an area to the north of Hattusa, say in the province later known as Paphlagonia. It occurs solely in interpolations in the Hittite text in connection with the cult of the god Ziparwa. **1973** *Trans. Philol. Soc. 1971* 159 The Palaic particle, unlike the Lycian one, is connective and adversative. **1974** *Encycl. Brit. Macropædia* I. 834/1 An interrogative or relative pronoun *kui-* (compare Latin *quis*) is common to Hittite, Palaic, and Cuneiform Luwian.

palais, obs. f. PALACE; var. PALIS *Obs.*

palaisade, -ado, obs. ff. PALISADE, -ADO.

palais de danse ('pæleɪ də dɑ̃:s). [Fr.] A public hall for dancing. Also *attrib.*, *fig.*, and *ellipt.* as **palais.**

1919 *Honey Pot* I. 14 The new Palais de Danse, which is to be opened on September 1st, is situated in Brook Green Road, two minutes walk from Hammersmith. **1926** *Punch* 13 Oct. 416/3 The young man you choose [as a dancing partner] out of a pen at sixpence a time at the Palais de Danse. **1928** *Melody Maker* Nov. 1193/3 Its rhythm had all the faults and few of the good points of the heavy 'Palais' style. **1940** HARRISON & MADGE *War begins at Home* 225 The manager of a large suburban palais. **1946** J. AGATE *Contemporary Theatre 1944-5* 73 Yes, but have they [*sc.* Delibes, Offenbach, and Johann Strauss] the lush, treacly, palais-de-danse Orientalism dear to the British heart? **1958** *New Statesman* 25 Jan. 102/3 The good old-fashioned pit and palais musicians. **1964** W. G. RAFFÉ *Dict. Dance* 368/2 The Palais is an accepted town centre, replacing the mediaeval marriage-market, or the Victorian Assembly Rooms, as a place where eligible young people can meet matrimonial partners. **1966** *Listener* 19 May 711/2 A Tashkent spinning and weaving mill..had its own..palace of culture (depreciated term—shades of the Palais de Danse!) with singing, dancing, and dramatic activities. **1972** P. BLACK *Biggest Aspidistra* I. iii. 30 He [*sc.* Jack Payne] broke up his..group to take a job as pianist with a band at the Birmingham Palais (the huge public-hall fashion of dancing was spreading outward from London). **1975** R. BUTLER *Where all Girls are Sweeter* iv. 36 While others studied at night we headed for the nearest Palais de Danse. **1976** *Times* 7 Aug. 2/5 Mrs Stonehouse, who has been married for 27 years, met her husband at the Hammersmith Palais when he was in the RAF. **1978** *Radio Times* 28 Jan. 69/4 Britain is renowned for its dance-skaters and has the strongest tradition of *palais de danse* in the world.

‖**Palais de Justice** (palɛ də ʒystis). [Fr., lit. 'palace of justice'.] In France (occas. elsewhere): a law court.

1792 T. BLAIKIE *Diary Scotch Gardener* (1931) 235, I told him..that I was here with a gang of theeves who had robbed my house..and the others and I [were] taken to the Palais de Justice. **1885** H. JAMES *Little Tour in France* xii. 92 His [*sc.* Jacques Cœur's] house..to-day is used as a Palais de Justice. **1962** N. FREELING *Love in Amsterdam* III. 133 At the Palais de Justice they made..an impressive entrance. **1974** —— *Dressing of Diamond* 187 Like all public buildings in France, the Palais de Justice is ruled entirely by the concierge. **1978** W. GARNER *Möbius Trip* iii. 65 They drove back to the Palais de Justice, crossed the chill courtyard.

palais glide ('pæleɪ glaɪd). [f. PALAIS (DE DANSE) + GLIDE *sb.* 1 c.] A type of ballroom dance in which large groups dance together.

1938 A. MOORE *Ballroom Dancing* (ed. 2) VII. 251 The Palais Glide can hardly be termed a dance; it is reminiscent of the Gallop which has been a feature of Hunt Balls for many years... It can be danced to any Foxtrot tune..and it is played at a tempo of about 30 bars a minute. **1939** *Britannica Bk. of Year* 196/2 Another instance of the desire to add more festiveness to British ballrooms has been the occasional introduction, at all kinds of dances, of the old 'Palais Glide'... This is even more of a romp than the 'Lambeth Walk'. **1969** *Listener* 8 May 640/1 The tune stayed alive in dance-halls where, during the 1930s, it could be used for the 'Palais Glide'. **1970** *Guardian* 24 Dec. 9/3 The girls..engaged in a perpetual Palais Glide, regardless of rhythm. **1974** R. INGHAM *Yoris* xvii. 54 Do you remember the Palais Glide?..Lovely dance.

‖**Palais Royal** (palɛ rwajal). The name of a Parisian theatre used *attrib.* to designate a type of indelicate farce said to be typical of this theatre.

1877 *Illustr. Sporting & Dramatic News* 21 Apr. 109/1 In my remarks about *Pink Dominos*..I alluded to the inevitable comparison that must be made between that piece and the other Palais Royal adaptations. *Ibid.* 20 Oct. 109/2, I consider the libretti of three-fourths of the French opéras-bouffes which have been translated..into English, practically and palpably cynical, and they are indecent withal. I may say the same of some Palais Royal pieces, mightily popular amongst us. **1951** N. MITFORD *Blessing* II. v. 195 What a curious thing—intrigues and misunderstandings, just like a Palais Royal farce. **1967** *Oxf. Compan. Theatre* (ed. 3) 715/1 In England the term 'Palais-Royal farce' was applied to the broad suggestiveness of such productions as the *The Pink Dominos* (1877) and *The Girl from Maxim's* (1902).

palamede: see PELAMYD.

palamedean (pæləˈmi:dɪən), *a. Ornith.* [f. mod.L. *Palamēdea*, fancifully f. Gr. Παλαμήδης, one of the Grecian heroes at the siege of Troy.] Of or belonging to the genus *Palamedea* or family *Palamedeidæ* of birds, the type of which is the kamichi or horned screamer, *Palamedea cornuta*.

†'**palamie.** *Obs.* [a. F. *palamie* (Liebault, 16th c.), 'the bloudie rifts; a disease, or impostumation in the roofe of a horses mouth' (Cotgr.).] An abscess in the palate of a horse.

1600 SURFLET *Country Farme* I. xxviii. 193 *margin*, The palamie or bloudie chops in the palate.

palamino, var. PALOMINO.

Palamite ('pæləmaɪt), *sb.* and *a. Eccl. Hist.* [f. the name of St. Gregory *Palamas*, an intellectual leader of the Hesychasts + -ITE[1].]

A. *sb.* = HESYCHAST. **B.** *adj.* Of or pertaining to the Palamites or their doctrines; = HESYCHASTIC *a.* 2.

1859 *Encycl. Brit.* XVII. 177/1 At the councils which were severally held in 1341 and 1351 he [*sc.* Gregorius Palamas] pled the cause of his party, and so identified him-self with the tenets he advocated that his fellow-sectarians were thenceforth called *Palamites*. **1877** MCCLINTOCK & STRONG *Cycl. Bibl. Lit.* VII. 547/2 The peculiar leading tenets of the Palamites were the existence of the mystical light discovered by the more eminent monks and recluses in their long exercises of abstract contemplation and prayer, and the uncreated nature of the light of Mount Tabor seen at the transfiguration of Christ. *Ibid.* 548/1 These alleged heresies were, however, mostly..the inferences deduced by Nicephorus Gregoras and other opponents from the Palamite dogma of uncreated light, and not the acknowledged tenets of the Palamite party. **1900** 'ODYSSEUS' *Turkey in Europe* vi. 252 The quarrel between the Palamites and Barlaamites, after distracting the Eastern Church, was at last settled by a Synod in a sense favourable to the former. **1949** E. L. MASCALL *Existence & Analogy* vi. 151 For the Thomist, supernatural grace means a communication of God himself to the creature... For the Palamite, it means a communication of the uncreated energy of God though not of his uncommunicable essence. **1957** *Oxf. Dict. Chr. Ch.* 633/2 In the second half of the 14th cent. Hesychasm was accepted throughout the Greek Church, its adherents being also generally known as 'Palamites'. **1961** *Times* 24 Nov. 14/4 Moghila did not admit the Palamite doctrine of energies. **1971** *Catholic Dict. Theol.* III. 15/1 This controversy, also known as the Palamite controversy.., was concerned not so much with the spiritual doctrine of the Hesychasts as with its ultimate theological and metaphysical justification.

‖**palampore** ('pæləm,pɔə(r)). Also 7-9 **palempore**, 9 **-pour.** [Derivation uncertain.

Yule and Burnell suggest a corruption of hybrid (Hind. and Pers.) *palangpōsh* bed-cover; which occurs as *palangapuze* in an Indo-Portug. Dict. of 1727. But Mr. Pringle (*Madras Selections* ser. IV. 71) suggests derivation from Pālanpur in Guzerat, 'which seems to have been an emporium for the manufactures of North India'. Perhaps these words have been confused.]

'A kind of chintz bed-cover, sometimes of beautiful patterns, formerly made at various places in India' (Yule and Burnell).

1698 FRYER *Acc. E. India & P.* 34 Staple Commodities are Calicuts white and painted, Palempores, Carpets, Tea. **1786** tr. *Beckford's Vathek* (1868) 51 These were only the dangling palampores and variegated tatters of his gay retinue. **1813** BYRON *Giaour* 666 A stain on every bush that bore A fragment of his palampore. **1837** *Civil Eng. & Arch. Jrnl.* I. 78/1 The chintz and palampore of India long continued to be the prototypes of European printed calicoes. **1880** BIRDWOOD *Ind. Art* II. 98 The celebrated *palampores*, or 'bed-covers', of Masulipatam..which in point of art decoration are simply incomparable.

†**palander** ('pæləndə(r)). *Obs.* exc. *Hist.* Also 6 **palandre**, 7 **palendar**; *pl.* 6 **palandrie**, 7 **palandarie.** [app. ad. It. *palandra, palandaria* (Florio), 'a kind of flat bottomed Barges or Ships vsed in time of war to transport Horses', etc., Sp. *palandre*, 16th c. F. *palandrie*, med.L. (14th c.) *palandaria* (Jal). Origin unascertained.]

1. A flat-bottomed transport vessel used esp. (by the Turks) for transporting horses.

1572 in Hakluyt *Voy.* II. I. 122 *margin*, Palandrie be great flat vessels made like Feriboats to transport horse. **1603** KNOLLES *Hist. Turks* 671 Solyman had by night sent over certaine troupes of light horsemen, in great palendars. **1658** EARL MONM. tr. *Paruta's Wars Cyprus* 44 About fifty Palandarie, which are made like small Gallies,..much covered, containing about a hundred Horse a peece. **1788** GIBBON *Decl. & F.* lx, The chargers..were embarked in the flat palanders. **1855** MILMAN *Lat. Chr.* IX. vii, They [the Venetians] would furnish palanders and flat vessels to transport 4500 horses.

2. A fire-ship; and in 17th c. a bomb-ketch.

1562 J. SHUTE *Cambini's Turk. Wars* 34 b, They tawed the palandre after them at yͤ sterme of some of their galleys. **1693** *Lond. Gaz.* No. 2861/1 They [the French]..could not ..bring on their Palanders, or Fireships, to make any attempt upon the Spanish Ships. *Ibid.* No. 2878/2, 4 Ketches or Palanders carrying Mortar Pieces.

‖**palang** (pa'laŋ). *Borneo* and *Philippines.* [Native name.] (See quot. 1974.)

1959 T. HARRISON *World Within* I. 59 The rapid spread of the *palang*, a cross-piece driven through the male penis, has shown that behind the easy acceptance of many upland women there is a readiness to react in a more elaborate and erotic manner. **1964** *Jrnl. Malaysian Branch R. Asiatic Soc.* XXXVII. 163, I have here chosen the term *palang* as the most widespread of the indigenous Bornean terms (cf. *utang*, etc.) and also the one known over parts of the outside world. *Ibid.* 164 It is safest to take the people nowadays called Kayans and some of the Kenyahs closely associated with them as the main west Borneo *palang* users in proto-historical times. **1974** S. E. MORISON *European Discovery of America: Southern Voyages* xvii. 422 The gentle Limasawans, says Pigafetta, went about nearly naked...

Here, and at Cebu, he describes a sexual practice known as *palang*. 'The males, large and small, have their penis pierced from one side to the other near the head, with a gold or tin bolt as large as a goose quill. In each end of the bolt some have what resembles a star, with points; others are like the head of a cast nail... In the middle of the bolt is a hole, through which they urinate'. *Ibid.* 435 Although certain writers..have either omitted this story or called it one of Pigafetta's tall tales, *palang* did exist. It persists to this day in Borneo and parts of the Philippines.

‖**pa'lank, -ka.** [a. F. *palanque*, It. *palanca* 'a defence made of great poles or stakes'; so Pol. *palanka*, Rom. *palanca*, Turkish *palanqah*.
The med.L. forms *palanga*, *phalanga* (Du Cange, Körting) appear to be from Gr. φάλαγξ, φάλαγγα trunk, log, pole. The *pal-* forms may be influenced by L. *pālus* stake.]
A kind of fortified camp: see quot. 1853.
1691 Luttrell *Brief Rel.* (1857) II. 302 [They] hop'd.. to make themselves masters of the suburb and palank on the other side the river. **1853** Stocqueler *Mil. Encycl.*, *Palankas*, a species of permanent intrenched camp, attached to Turkish frontier fortresses, in which the ramparts are reveted with large beams,..so as to form a strong palisade.

‖**palankeen, palanquin** (pælən'kiːn), *sb.* Forms: α. 6 palanchin, pal(l)anchine, pallankin, 7 palankine, -quine, pallenkine, pallanquin, (pollankan, palamkin, -keen, palakin, pallaquin), 7–8 pallankeen, palenkeen, 8 pallenkeen, 7– palankin, palanquin, 8– palankeen. Also β. 7 palanke, -ka, 7–8 palankee, 8 palanque. See also palkee. [orig. a. Pg. *palanquim* (1515 in Correa *Lendas da India*), whence also It. *palanchino*, Sp. and F. *palanquin* (1611 in Hatz.-Darm.), repr. an E. Ind. vernacular word **pālankī*: cf. Malay and Javanese *palangki* 'litter or sedan' (Crawford), Hindī † *pālakī*, *pālkī* 'palankeen', f. Skr. *paryaṅka*, *palyaṅka* couch, bed, Pālī *pallaṅko* 'couch, bed, litter, or palankin' (Childers), Hindī and Marāthī *palang* bedstead, couch. The final nasal appears to have been a Portuguese addition as in *mandarin*, and is often absent from the forms given by early travellers, as also from palkee.
There is a curious resemblance between this and the Sp. *palanca*:—L. *phalanga*, pole to carry a burden, cowl-staff, whence *palanquino*, 'a bearer, one of two who carry a burden between them on a pole', which some earlier writers held to be the source of the E. Indian word. Yule & Burnell suggest that the Portuguese may have associated the two.]
A covered litter or conveyance, usually for one person, used in India and other Eastern countries, consisting of a large box with wooden shutters like Venetian blinds, carried by four or six (rarely two) men by means of poles projecting before and behind.
α. **1588** T. Hickock tr. *C. Frederick's Voy.* 10 (11) Making readye to depart, with two Palanchines or little Litters, which are very commodious for the waye. **1598** W. Phillips *Linschoten* I. xv. 27/1 Great and thicke reeds, which are vsed in India to make the Pallankins, wherein they carry the women. **1612** R. Coverte *Voy.* 37 He is brought vpon an Elephant..and sometimes in a Pollankan, carried by foure slaues. **1613** Purchas *Pilgrimage* v. ix. 416 Set it in a Palamkin, which was borne by the chiefe men of the Towne. **1653** H. Cogan tr. *Pinto's Trav.* lvi. (1663) 218 They caused themselves to be born in Pallaquins or Arm-chairs, upon the shoulders of other Priests their inferiors. **1662** J. Davies *Mandelslo's Trav.* 82 Some-times carried in Palanquines, which are a kind of Litters or Sedans, carried by two men upon their shoulders with a bar. **1678** Phillips (ed. 4), *Palakin* (from the Spanish Palanquino a Porter). **1704** *Collect. Voy.* (Churchill) III. 690/1 Then the Empress's *Palankin* or Litter. **1785** in *European Mag.* (1786) IX. 177 They handed us each to a fly pallenkeen. **1885** Bible (R.V.) *Song Sol.* iii. 9 King Solomon made himself a palanquin. **1885** A. Dobson *Sign of Lyre* 177 Behold the hero of the scene, In bungalow and palankeen.
β. **1625** Terry in Purchas *Pilgrims* II. ix. vi. §3. 1475 Carried vpon mens shoulders..in a slight thing they call a Palankee. *Ibid.* §4. 1481 His [Great Mogol's] Wiues and Women of all sorts..are carryed in Palankas, or vpon Elephants. **1738** [G. Smith] *Curious Relat.* II. 504 He is carried on a stately Palanque. **1747** *Gentl. Mag.* 341 The enemy..lost..2 chests of arms, their provisions, palankees.
b. *attrib.* and *Comb.*, as *palankeen-bearer*, *-boy*, *-phaeton*, *-pole*, etc.
1698 Fryer *Acc. E. India & P.* 34 Ambling after these a great pace, the Palenkeen-Boys support them. *c* **1813** Mrs. Sherwood *Ayah & Lady* xii. 73 One of the palanquin-bearers came into the verandah. **1837** *Lett. fr. Madras* (1843) 89, I have had all the palanquin-boys, who are the best housemaids here, hard at work. *Ibid.* 163 He..put his shoulder under the palanquin-pole, and set off with his song again. **1877** Black *Green Past.* xlvi. (1878) 368 The roof of our palanquin-phaeton was of blue cloth.
Hence **palan'keen, -'quin** *v. intr.*, to travel in a palankeen: also *to palankeen it*.
1832 *Examiner* 340/1 They..are content to hookah and palanquin it. **1840** E. Napier *Scenes & Sp. in For. Lands* II. vi. 210 About one months marching, or rather palankeening, brought me to Madras. *a* **1845** Hood *To Lady on Dep. India* vi, Go to the land of slaves and palankeening.

†**palanthropic** (pælæn'θrɒpɪk), *a. Obs. rare.* [Irreg. f. palæo-, paleo- + anthropic *a.*] = palæanthropic *a.*
1894 [see neanthropic *a.*].

palantine, -yne, obs. forms of palatine.

Palantype ('pæləntaɪp). [f. the name *Palan(que* (see quot. 1940) + type *sb.*[1]] The proprietary name of a machine for typing in shorthand; also, the system of shorthand used. Hence '**palantypist**.
1940 *Trade Marks Jrnl.* 14 Aug. 782/1 Palantype.. . Typewriters and parts thereof, typewriter inks, typewriter ribbons, typewriting paper, and stands for typewriters (not being furniture). Clementine Camille Marie Palanque,.. London,..manufacturer. **1959** *Times* 9 Apr. 3/1 Palantype operator..required by Uganda Government. **1959** *Economist* 23 May 745/2 The institute's courses range from the training of district officers to that of clerks, typists and palantypists. **1964** *Financial Times* 25 Feb. 6/7 The small nucleus of reporting palantypists, the ladies who translate scientific jargon into shorthand hieroglyphs on a small, silent, rubber keyboard—later to convert it back. **1970** *Nature* 12 Sept. 1090/2 Several major hurdles still have to be overcome to transpose the twenty-nine symbols of palantype, the British form of mechanical shorthand, into proper English.

palar ('peɪlə(r)), *a. rare.* [ad. L. *pālāris*, f. *pāl-us* stake: see -ar.] Of the nature of, or resembling, a pale or stake.
1708 J. Chamberlayne *St. Gt. Brit.* II. III. x. (1737) 427 On the Foot of the Palar Part of the Cross. **1857** Mayne *Expos. Lex.*, *Palaris*,..palar.

‖**palari** (pə'lɑːrɪ). [Malay.] A type of boat (see quot. 1948)
1936 *Times Lit. Suppl.* 7 Nov. 899/3 He wanted a chance of seeing a *palari* working to windward in bad conditions. **1937** G. E. P. Collins *Makassar Sailing* 12 During the second stage, which turns a pajala into a palari, the sides are raised and a deck and high stern added. **1948** R. de Kerchove *Internal. Maritime Dict.* 516/1 *Palari*, an East Indian trading boat from southern Celebes and eastern Madura... It is rigged with one or two masts. 2. In Macassar the term 'palari' refers to a fast-sailing pleasure craft with two masts and an elaborately carved stern. **1950** *Jrnl. Malayan Branch R. Asiatic Soc.* XXIII. 112 The Palari is now characterised by the possession of a double-ended hull with a heavy, tripartite bowsprit and a high, overhanging stern. **1964** K. G. Tregonning *Hist. Mod. Malaya* 59 The Bugis copied their craft from the Portuguese, and the *pajala* was adapted into the famous *palari*, which..is..like a miniature seventeenth century fore and aft rigged galleon.

palarie (pə'lɑːrɪ), *v. Tramps'* and *Circus slang.* Also palari. [ad. It. *parlare.*] *trans.* and *intr.* To talk, to speak. Cf. parlyaree.
1846 *Swell's Night Guide* 77 The chanting cadger stalls the chummy's daughter off to a single padded lumber; ranks her of five bob and a bender;..palaries sweat patter, and nobbs on for more blunt. **1893** P. H. Emerson *Signor Lippo* xx. 91 She looked for all the world like a gippo, and she knew all the cant, and used to palarie thick to the slaveys. **1933** E. Seago *Circus Company* iii. 29 A subject not meant for a 'gajo's' ears, to be checked immediately... 'Nante palari before the josher cul.'

‖**palas, pulas** (pə'lɑːs). Also pa-, pulash. [Hindī *palāç*, *palās*, Skr. *palāça*.] The dhak-tree of India (*Butea frondosa* and *B. superba*). *palas kino*, the kino yielded by this tree, Bengal kino.
1799 Colebrooke in *Life* (1873) 407 *note*, *Butea frondosa*, named Palás, or Dhac. **1841** Elphinstone *Hist. Ind.* I. III. xi. 343 Spaces of several days' journey across covered with the palás or dák tree, which in spring loses all its leaves and is entirely covered with large red and orange flowers, which make the whole of the hills seem in a blaze. **1866** *Treas. Bot.* 183 The Dhak or Pulas of India. **1883** *Cassell's Fam. Mag.* Oct. 685/1 The Palash tree..is considered the most suitable tree for the production of lac.

palas, obs. form of palace *sb.*[1] and [2].

†**pala'sin,** *a. Obs. rare.* In 5 -syn. [a. OF. *palasin*, *palaisin*, f. *palais* palace *sb.*[1]: cf. paladin.] Belonging to the palace or court.
c **1400** *Rom. Rose* 6862 Thise Abbessis and eke bygyns These gret ladyes Palasyns [F. *dames palasines*].

palastre, obs. f. palæstra.

palasy, -sie, obs. ff. palsy.

palat, obs. f. palate, pallet.

palatable ('pælətəb(ə)l), *a.* [f. palate *sb.* and *v.* + -able.]
1. Agreeable to the palate; pleasant to the taste; having a good flavour: savoury.
1669 W. Simpson *Hydrol. Chym.* 165 Spirit..of harts-horn..is not very palatable, which makes some disgust it. **1748** *Anson's Voy.* II viii. 220 An almost constant supply of fresh and palatable food. **1840** Dickens *Old C. Shop* iv, Ask the ladies to stop to supper, and have a couple of lobsters and something light and palatable.
2. *fig.* Pleasing or agreeable to the mind or feelings; acceptable; that is or may be 'relished'.
1683 Kennett tr. *Erasm. on Folly* 53 Truth..is seldom palatable to the ears of kings. **1782** Miss Burney *Cecilia* IX. i, This counsel [was] by no means palatable. **1831** Carlyle *Sart. Res.* III. vii, Such Fighting-titles will cease to be palatable.
Hence **palata'bility**; '**palatableness**; '**palatably** *adv.*
1886 *Voice* (N.Y.) 16 Dec. (Advt.), Its medicinal value and *palatability were not impaired. *c* **1720** W. Gibson *Farrier's Dispens.* II. iii. (1734) 112 These are seldom or never used otherwise than in Substance,..for *Palatableness. **1770** *New Dispens.* 336/1 Greater regard being here had to palatableness than medicinal efficacy. **1677** Plot *Oxfordsh.* 37 Other waters..that are *palatably salt. **1741** Middleton *Cicero* I. vi. 426 A way of dressing mushrooms..palatably.

palatal ('pælətəl), *a.* and *sb.* [a. F. *palatal* (1752 *Dict. Trévoux*), f. L. *palāt-um* palate + -al[1].]
A. *adj.* **1. a.** *Anat.*, *Zool.*, etc. Pertaining to the palate: = palatine *a.*[2] 1.
1828–32 Webster, *Palatal*, pertaining to the palate. **1834** R. Mudie *Brit. Birds* (1841) II. 19 Bill..having the palatal knob very large. **1874** Lyell *Elem. Geol.* xxi. 358 A terrestrial reptile having numerous palatal teeth. **1888** Rolleston & Jackson *Anim. Life* 360 [In Mammalia] The præmaxillary, maxillary and palatine bones possess palatal plates which constitute the hard palate.
b. *Conchol.* (See quot.)
1854 Woodward *Mollusca* II. 165 *Pupa Uva*:..Shell.. aperture rounded, often toothed. (Dr. Pfeiffer terms those teeth 'parietal' which are situated on the body-whirl; those on the outer lip, 'palatal'.)
2. *Phonetics.* **a.** Of a consonant or vowel sound: Produced by placing the tongue against the palate, esp. the hard palate. The palatal consonants are formed further forward in the mouth than the velar or gutturals, and are represented by (c, ɟ, ç, and j).
In the Devanāgarī or Sanskrit alphabet the palatal consonants are those of the second row *c*, *ch*, *j*, *jh*, *ñ*, with the semivowel *y* and sibilant *ç*; the name is also often given to the sounds into which these have passed in modern Indian languages. *palatal vowels* are our (i, ɪ, e, ɛ, æ), more commonly called *front vowels*.
1728 Chambers *Cycl.* s.v. T., The *T* is one of the five Consonants which the Abbot de Dangeau calls *Palatal*. **1828–32** Webster, *Palatal*,.. uttered by the aid of the palate. **1844** Key *Alphabet*, etc. 25 In the Sanskrit alphabet, the series of guttural, palatal, lingual, dental, and labial consonants, have an *n* belonging to each class. **1875** Whitney *Life &c. Lang.* iv. 46 A sibilant with following palatal mute. **1876** Douse *Grimm's L.* §60. 146 The palatal semi-vowel (*y*).
b. Of a sound change: occurring in the environment of a palatal consonant or vowel.
1888 H. Sweet *Hist. Eng. Sounds* 124 This *c*-smoothing is by the Germans called 'palatal-umlaut'. **1894** —— *Anglo-Saxon Reader* (ed. 7) p. xiv, Why then continue..to call the change of *weorc* into *werc* 'palatal mutation', when the change is not a mutation, and is caused not by front, but invariably by back consonants? **1908** J. & E. M. Wright *Old Eng. Gram.* iv. 28 Umlaut is of two kinds: Palatal and Guttural. Palatal umlaut, generally called *i*-umlaut, is the modification (palatalization) of an accented vowel through the influence of an *ī* or *j* which originally stood in the following syllable. **1914** H. C. Wyld *Short Hist. Eng.*, v. 75 'Palatal Mutation'. This term was suggested by Bülbring to denote primarily the loss in Anglian of the second element of the diphthong *ea* (which thus appears merely as *e*) before the consonant-groups *ht*, *hs*, *hp*, when followed by a front vowel, or when final. **1939** *Trans. Philol. Soc.* 126 By the assumption that 'Breaking', 'Palatal Diphthongization', and 'Back-Mutation' were developments which can be dated within limits, a system of 'sound-changes' has been built up, which in some cases may be purely fictitious, in others only part of a long-drawn-out process. **1959** A. Campbell *Old Eng. Gram.* v. 70 *Sċīp* sheep, presumably from **sċēp* with palatal diphthongization of nW-S *sċēp*. **1975** Lass & Anderson *Old Eng. Phonol.* iv. 123 'Palatal diphthongization' of *ē̆*. As we show..there is no very good evidence for such a process in OE.
B. *sb.*
1. *Anat.* Short for *palatal bone*: = palatine *sb.*[2] 1.
1886 in *Cassell's Encycl. Dict.* **1890** *Cent. Dict.* s.v., In their simplest form the palatals are mere rods or plates extending horizontally from the pterygoids to the maxilliaries.
2. *Phonetics.* A palatal sound; usually, a palatal consonant. (See A. 2.)
1828–32 Webster, *Palatal*, a letter pronounced by the aid of the palate. **1844** Key *Alphabet*, etc. 23 The other letters ..according to their organs: 1st, the guttural and palatals,.. 2ndly, dentals,..3rdly, labials. **1862** Marsh *Eng. Lang.* 492 The combination *gh* was originally a guttural or perhaps a palatal.
Hence '**palatalism, pala'tality**, palatal quality or character; '**palatally** *adv.*, towards the palate; by means of the palate.
1864 F. Hall in *Lauder's Tractate* Notes (1869) 32 A device for preserving the palatality of its *g*. **1876** Douse *Grimm's L.* §64. 171 Different destinies of the combinations *kya* and *kwa*, according as the palatalism and gutturalism represented by *y* and *w*, attack the consonant or the vowel. **1934** *Dental Items of Interest* LVI. 206 Any extension of the preparation under the gingiva..palatally is to be avoided as being unnecessary. **1940** J. Osborne *Dental Mech.* xiv. 156 The use of black rubber palatally and lingually will give a better appearance to the finished denture. **1963** C. R. Cowell et al. *Inlays, Crowns, & Bridges* iv. 39 The withdrawal path must be inclined palatally. **1970** *Archivum Linguisticum* I. 7 When the following syllable contained an *i* the medial vowel could be palatally coloured.

palatalize ('pælətəlaɪz), *v. Phonetics.* [f. palatal + -ize.] *trans.* To render palatal; to modify into a palatal sound; esp., to change the gutturals k, g, etc., into (c, ɟ), etc., by advancing the point of contact between tongue and palate. Also *intr.*, to become palatal, to undergo palatalization. Hence '**palatalized** *ppl. a.*
1867 A. J. Ellis *E. E. Pronunc.* I. iii. §4. 204 The older French seem to have generally palatalized the Latin *c* before *a* as (*kamp*) from *campus*, whence afterwards (champ, shañ). **1886** *Athenæum* 25 Dec. 867/1 In Russian..a vowel like the final *ĭ* palatalizes the preceding consonant. *Ibid.*, Traces of these palatalized consonants are seen in 'singe' from *sangjan*.

1887 COOK *Sievers' O.E. Gram.* 110. *a* **1904** *Mod.* In OE. phonology, the palatalized *c* and *g* are often distinguished as *ċ, ġ*; by Bülbring as *ĉ, ĝ*. **1943** E. A. NIDA *Handbk. Descriptive Linguistics* II. v. 83 This may be the result of an original *e* which did palatalize but later this *e* changed to *a* and the palatalization remained. **1964** *Language* XL. 28 Cunter does not palatalize before unstressed /a/.., and.. Trun does not palatalize before any allophone of /a/. **1973** J. M. ANDERSON *Struct. Aspects Lang. Change* 154 The frontal allophone of /g/ appears to have palatalized first.

Hence **palatali'zation**.

1863 LEPSIUS *Stand. Alph.* 159 The palatalisation of *r* has ..in several..Sclavonic languages, passed into a slight assibilation. **1867** ELLIS *E.E. Pronunc.* I. iii. 206 The palatalisation of a consonant.

palate ('pælət), *sb.* (*a.*) Forms: 4–7 **palat, palet,** 5 **palett,** 6–7 **pallate,** 7 **pallat, pallet,** 5– **palate.** [ad. L. *palātum* palate. See also the obs. PALACE *sb.*² a. F. *palais*.]

1. The roof of the mouth (in man and vertebrates generally); the structures, partly bony and partly fleshy (see b), which separate the cavity of the mouth from that of the nose.

1382 WYCLIF *Lam.* iv. 4 Cleuede to the tonge of the soukende to his palet in thrist [*ad palatum eius in siti*]. **1450–1530** *Myrr. our Ladye* 249 The anguysshe of harte dryed so the tongue & palate of the vyrgyn. **1597** A. M. tr. *Guillemeau's Fr. Chirurg.* 24 b/2 The pallate or Vvula of the mouth. **1668** WILKINS *Real Char.* III. xii. 367 (*Ng*) is framed by an appulse of the Root of the Tongue towards the inner part of the Palat. *a* **1756** MRS. HAYWOOD *New Present* (1771) 167 To fricasey Ox Palates. *c* **1817** HOGG *Tales & Sk.* V. 112 My tongue and palate became dry and speechless. **1844** KEY *Alphabet*, etc. 25 *M, n, ng*..sounds depending partly upon the nose, and partly upon the lips, teeth, and palate, respectively.

b. ***bony*** or ***hard palate***: the anterior and chief part of the palate, consisting of bone covered with thick mucous membrane. ***soft palate***: the posterior part of the palate, a pendulous fold of musculo-membranous tissue separating the mouth-cavity from the pharynx, and terminating below in the uvula; also called ***veil of the palate***. ***cleft palate***: see CLEFT *ppl. a.* b.

1774 GOLDSM. *Nat. Hist.* (1776) VI. 161 In the bony palate of fish..all powers of distinguishing are utterly taken away. **1811** HOOPER *Med. Dict.*, *Palatum molle*, the soft palate. This lies behind the bony palate. **1890** SWEET *Prim. Phonetics* 8 The roof of the mouth consists of two parts, the 'soft' and the 'hard' palate.

†**c.** ***falling down of the palate, the palate down***, etc.: 'a term for a relaxed uvula' (*Syd. Soc. Lex.*).

1618 FLETCHER *Loyal Subj.* III. ii, Your Pallat's downe Sir. **1664** PEPYS *Diary* 23 Sept., My cold and pain in my head increasing, and the palate of my mouth falling, I was in great pain. **1684** A. LITTLETON *Lat. Dict.*, *Columella*, the swelling of the uvula, or falling down of the palate of the mouth. **1687–8** G. MIEGE *Gt. Fr. Dict.* s.v. *Luette*, The palate of the mouth down, *la luette abattue*.

2. Popularly considered as the seat of taste; hence *transf.* the sense of taste.

1526 *Pilgr. Perf.* (W. de W. 1531) 87 b, Breed to a sore mouth is sharpe & harde, whiche to a hole palate is swete & pleasaunt. **1596** SHAKS. *Merch. V.* IV. i. 96 Let their pallats Be season'd with such Viands. **1642** FULLER *Holy & Prof. St.* III. xiii. 184 As soon may the same meat please all palats. **1712** ADDISON *Spect.* No. 409 ¶2 Every different Flavour that affects the Palate. **1823** J. BADCOCK *Dom. Amusem.* 16 Meats that require salt,..according to the palate of the consumers. **1885** BIBLE (R.V.) *Job* xii. 11 Even as the palate tasteth its meat.

b. *fig.* Mental taste or liking.

1435 MISYN *Fire of Love* 90 þa haue..þe palate of þe hart filyd with feuyr of wykkyd lufe, qwarfor þai may not fele swetnes of heuenly Ioy. **1606** SHAKS. *Tr. & Cr.* I. iii. 338 Heere the Troyans taste our deer'st repute With their fin'st Pallate. **1644** MILTON *Areop.* (Arb.) 39 Any subject that was not to their palat, they..condemn'd. **1742** YOUNG *Nt. Th.* IX. 2067 Thou, to whose Palate Glory is so sweet. **1876** GEO. ELIOT *Dan. Der.* VI. xlvi, I heard a little too much preaching, ..and lost my palate for it.

3. *Bot.* A convex projection of the lower lip closing the throat of the corolla of a personate flower, as the snapdragon.

This curious use goes back to early botanists, e.g. Tournefort, Dillenius, Linnæus. It may have arisen from taking *palātum* in the wider sense of Germ. *gaumen*, Sw. *gom*, OHG. *goumo*, 'interior of the mouth, palate, throat, jaws'.

[**1732** DILLENIUS *Hort. Eltham.* 200 Labium..inferius tripartitum cuius palatum grandiuscula productio.. occupat.] **1760** J. LEE *Introd. Bot.* III. xxii. (1765) 228 *Palatum*, the Palate, is a Gibbosity or bunching out in the Faux of the Corolla. **1880** GRAY *Struct. Bot.* 248 A bilabiate corolla is..Personate, or masked, when the throat is closed, more or less, by a projection of the lower lip called the Palate.

4. *Entom.* The epipharynx of an insect, a fleshy lobe beneath the labrum.

1867 J. HOGG *Microsc.* I. iii. 220 Entomological specimens such as..tongues, palates, corneae, etc. show best in balsam.

5. *attrib.* and *Comb.*, as ***palate-bone, -myograph, -plate, -pleaser, -pleasure; palate-biting, -pleasing***, etc., adjs.; †**palate-man**, a man given to the pleasures of the palate, an epicure (so ***palate people***.)

1812 W. TENNANT *Anster F.* II. viii, Some bring..From Flushing's port, the *palate-biting gin. **1727–41** MONRO *Anat.* (ed. 3) 138 Each *palate-bone may..be divided into four Parts. **1876** *Clin. Soc. Trans.* IX. 124 The horizontal plate of the palate-bone. **1899** *Allbutt's Syst. Med.* VIII. 207 The commonness of *palate-defect..appears to be largely due to its correlation with some degree of brain-deficiency. *a* **1661** FULLER *Worthies, Bucks.* I. (1662) 128 Whether these tame be as good as wild-pheasants, I leave to *Pallate men to decide. **1890** J. S. BILLINGS *Nat. Med. Dict.* II. 277 **Palate-myograph*, an instrument for recording graphically the motions of the soft palate in speaking. *a* **1661** FULLER *Worthies, Cornwall* (1662) 194 Our *Palate-people are much pleased therewith [garlic]. **1782** MONRO *Anat.* 102 The *palate-plate is cribriform about the middle. **1620** VENNER *Via Recta* iii. 52, I will here aduertise all *pallat-pleasers, that they shall sooner surfet..with pork, then with any other flesh. **1611** COTGR., *Suave*,..sweet,..*palate-pleasing, delicious. **1657** G. STARKEY *Helmont's Vind.* To Rdr., Ridiculous (barely palat-pleasing) toyes. **1638** T. WHITAKER *Blood of Grape* 48, I speake not phantastically, or from any *palate-pleasure. **1800** LAMB *Lett.* (1886) I. 286 The..*palate-soothing flesh of geese.

†**B.** *adj.* Pleasant to the palate or taste; palatable. *Obs. rare.*

1617 HIERON *Wks.* (1619–20) II. 210 The most perfit and palate wine (they say) doth make the quickest vinegar.

palate ('pælət), *v. rare.* [f. prec. sb.]

1. *trans.* To perceive or try with the palate, to taste; to gratify the palate with, to enjoy the taste of, relish. Also *fig.*

1606 SHAKS. *Tr. & Cr.* IV. i. 59 You..that defend her, Not pallating the taste of her dishonour. **1739** R. BULL tr. *Dedekindus' Grobianus* 32 What fairest seems and best, when palated, offends th' unwary Guest. **1760** C. JOHNSTON *Chrysal* (1822) II. 299 'This wine?' answered my master, palating it two or three times. **1844** TUPPER *Twins* xxix. 213 The proud, unsullied family of Stuart, could not palate it at all. **1860** RUSKIN *Mod. Paint.* V. IX. v. §5. 247 Nothing was to be fed upon as bread, but only palated as a dainty.

†**2.** To make palatable, to season. *Obs.*

1610 W. FOLKINGHAM *Art of Survey* Ep. Ded. 2 Labouring, with invulgar Ingredients, to palate an ill seasoned Seruice. **1845** [see BLANC 2].

palate, obs. or erron. form of PALLET.

'palated, *a. rare.* [f. PALATE *sb.* + -ED².] Having a 'palate' or taste (of a specified kind).

1804 COLLINS *Scripscrap* vi, If kindly palated, with Taste unprejudic'd.

palateless ('pælətlɪs), *a.* [f. as prec. + -LESS.] Without a palate: *fig.* void of delicacy of taste.

a **1831** A. THOMSON in Butler *Bible Wk.* (1883) I. 122 Cries came out from palateless mouths..wildly imploring. **1860** RUSKIN *Mod. Paint.* V. IX. viii. §6 He delivers his.. articles..to his ravenous customers; palateless; gluttonous.

palatial (pə'leɪʃəl), *a.*¹ [f. L. *palāti-um* PALACE + -AL¹.] Of the nature or character of a palace; pertaining to or befitting a palace; splendid, magnificent (as a building).

1754 A. DRUMMOND *Trav.* xiii. 271 A very magnificent structure..built in the palatial stile of those days. **1858** HAWTHORNE *Fr. & It. Note-bks.* I. 12 Palatial edifices, which are better for a stranger to look at, than for his own people to pay for. **1884** *Graphic* 9 Aug. 134/1 Some of the most palatial hotels.

Hence **palati'ality** (-ʃɪ'ælɪtɪ); **pa'latially** *adv.*

1894 *Harper's Weekly Mag.* 7 Apr. 317 In point of 'palatiality' the newly..reconstructed house..leads the list. **1893** F. F. MOORE *Gray Eye or So* III. 130 Not palatially,.. but still pleasantly.

†**palatial**, *a.*², *sb.*, obs. irreg. form for PALATAL.

1775 ASH Suppl., *Palatial*. **1792** SIR W. JONES *Orig. & Fam. of Nations* Wks. 1799 I. 139 Dentals being changed for dentals, and palatials for palatials. **1828–32** WEBSTER, *Palatial*, pertaining to the palate; as, the palatial retraction of the tongue. *Barrow*.

pa'latian, *a. rare.* [f. L. *palāti-um* + -AN.] Of or belonging to a palace; = PALATIAL.

1845 DISRAELI *Sybil* II. i, The..easy chairs..imparted even to this palatian chamber a lively and habitable air.

†**pa'latiate**, *a. Obs. rare.* Also **-at**. [f. L. *palāti-um* + -ATE² 2.] = PALATIAL *a.*¹ Hence †**pa'latiately** *adv.*

1632 LITHGOW *Trav.* VII. 307 The great Palatiat Mansion, where the..Vicegerent hath his residence. *Ibid.* VIII. 366 Palatiat Tauernes, the worst whereof, may lodge a Monarchicke trayne. *Ibid.* IV. 139 Externall decorements of fabricks palatiatly extended.

palatic (pə'lætɪk), *a.* (*sb.*) *rare.* [f. L. *palātum* PALATE + -IC.] Of or belonging to the palate; palatal. **b.** *sb.* = PALATAL B. 2.

1669 HOLDER *Elem. Speech* 38 The 3 Labial B.P.M. are Parallel to the 3 Gingival T.D.N, and to the 3 Palatick K.G.Ng. **1828** *Blackw. Mag.* XXIII. 590 [It] nullifies the palatic susceptibility. **1889** J. M. ROBERTSON *Ess. towards Crit. Method* 69 Palatic taste is a matter of native bias.

So †**pa'latical** *a. Obs.*; †**pala'tician** (pælə'tɪʃən) *nonce-wd.* [after *politician*], one skilled in matters of the palate.

1656 BLOUNT *Glossogr.*, *Palatical*, pertaining to, or that pleaseth the palate. **1821** *Edin. Rev.* XXXV. 61 A profound palatician, and mistress of the art of..combining flavours.

palatiform (pə'lætɪfɔːm), *a. Entom.* [f. L. *palāt-um* + -FORM.] Applied to the tongue of an insect when closely united with the inner surface of the labium.

1826 in KIRBY & SP. *Entomol.* IV. 312. **1857** in MAYNE.

palatinal (pə'lætɪnəl), *a.* [f. L. *palātīn-us* PALATINE *a.*¹ + -AL¹.] Belonging to a palatinate.

1793 *State Papers* in *Ann. Reg.* 222/2 A continued correspondence between the military commanders, the palatinal confederations,..and the general confederation.

palatinate (pə'lætɪnət, 'pælətɪneɪt), *sb.* Also 7 **-at**. [f. PALATINE *sb.*¹ + -ATE¹; in F. *palatinat* (1611 in Cotgr.).]

1. The territory or district under the rule or jurisdiction of a palatine or count-palatine.

1658 PHILLIPS, *Palatinate*, the Country or chief Seat of a Count Palatine or Paladine. **1669** *Lond. Gaz.* No. 420/1 The Deputies of the Palatinates of Eraslavie, Podolie and Volime have put in a claim for a reimbursement of their Noblesse. **1684** *Scanderbeg Rediv.* II. 20 The Realm [of Poland] being divided into Thirty four Palatinates or Governments. **1768** *Ann Reg.* 13/2 The Russian army..formed a line in the palatinate of Cracovia. **1864** BURTON *Scot Abr.* I. v. 260 Over Europe there were inexhaustible varieties of palatinates, margravates, regalities, and the like, enjoying their own separate privileges.

b. In England or Ireland: A county palatine or palatine earldom: see COUNTY¹ 7, PALATINE *a.*¹ 2 b. Also applied to American colonies the Proprietors of which had palatine rights.

Such were Carolina, Maryland (1634–92, 1715–76), Maine: see PALATINE *a.*¹ 2 b, *sb.*¹ 2 d.

1614 SELDEN *Titles Hon.* 247 These two [Chester and Lancaster]..may be called Lay Palatinats with vs; for also of great autoritie are the other two of Durham and Ely, but both Bishopriques. **1656** BLOUNT *Glossogr.*, *Palatinate*, or County Palatine, is a principal County or Shire, having as it were the same authority, as the Palace or Kings Royal Court hath. **1669** J. LOCKE *Const. Carolina* ix. in *33 Dep. Kpr. Rep.* 259 To every county there shall be three as yᵉ hereditary nobility of this pallatinate [Carolina]. **1827** HALLAM *Const. Hist.* (1876) III. xviii. 351 In all these palatinates [in Ireland]..the king's process had its course only within the lands belonging to the church. **1874** STUBBS *Const. Hist.* I. ix. §98. 271 Two of these palatinates, the earldom of Chester and the bishopric of Durham, retained much of their character to our own days. **1882** L. STEPHEN *Swift* i. 2 Godwin Swift was made Attorney-General in the palatinate of Tipperary by the Duke of Ormond.

c. ***the Palatinate, Rhine P.***, a state of the old German Empire, under the rule of the Pfalzgraf or Count Palatine of the Rhine, one of the seven original electors of the Empire.

It originally included the district immediately dependent upon Aachen, the original imperial capital, but afterwards comprised two districts called the Upper and Lower Palatinate, which were later absorbed in Bavaria and other adjacent states. Now part of Rhineland-Palatinate.

c **1580** BACON *State Europe* Wks. 1879 I. 367/1 During the life of the last elector, Ludovic dwelt at Amberg in the higher Palatinate. **1619** LUSHINGTON *Repetit. Serm.* in *Phenix* (1708) II. 477 The Catholick is for the Spanish Match, and the Protestant for restoring the Palatinate. **1637** *Documents agst. Prynne* (Camden) 74 It is said that some messinger shall be forthwith sent to the Emperour to demaund the Palatinates and the Electorate, and to give his Imperiall Majestie notice of this confederacy. **1791** MACKINTOSH *Vind. Gallicæ* Wks. 1846 III. 12 Who..issues with calm and cruel apathy his orders to butcher the Protestants of Languedoc, or to lay in ashes the villages of the Palatinate. **1876** BANCROFT *Hist. U.S.* II. xxviii. 205 Germans, fugitives from the devastated Palatinate.

2. An inhabitant or native of the German Palatinate; cf. PALATINE *sb.*¹ 5.

1709 *Lond Gaz.* No. 4561/3 Proposals..for the Encouragement of the Palatinates Transportation into the Province of Carolina. **1890** *Critic* (U.S.) 1 Feb. 51/2 Washington..encouraged the importation of the Palatinates who fled from Germany to find peace and comfort in the American colonies.

3. *attrib.* or *adj.* Of or belonging to a palatinate.

1672 PETTY *Pol. Anat.* vi. Tracts (1769) 326 There is also a palatinate court in Tipperary. **1781** S. PETERS *Hist. Connecticut* 75 He..procured from the incaution of Charles II. as ample a charter as was ever given to a palatinate state. **1874** STUBBS *Const. Hist.* I. ix. §98. 271 *note*, The palatinate jurisdiction of Durham was transferred to the crown in 1836. **1900** *Q. Rev.* Apr. 425 A chief reason for his acceptance of the Palatinate See.

Hence **pa'latinate** *v. trans.* (*nonce-wd.*), to make into a palatinate or county palatine.

a **1661** FULLER *Worthies, Chesh.* I. (1662) 171 Lancashire ..relateth to Cheshire as the copy to the original, being Palatinated but by King Edward the third, referring the Duke of Lancaster to have his regal jurisdiction.

palatine ('pælətaɪn, -ɪn), *a.*¹ and *sb.*¹ Also 5 **palatyn(e,** 6 **pallatyne,** (7 **-een**), 7–8 **pallatine, palatin;** 7 **paladine;** 5 **palen-, palyntyne,** 6 **pallentine,** 6–7 **palentine, palantine, -yne.** [a. F. *palatin, -ine* (15th c. in Hatz.-Darm.), ad. L. *palātīn-us* of or belonging to the *palātium* or PALACE, as sb. 'an officer of the palace, a chamberlain'.]

A. *adj.* **1.** Of or belonging to the imperial palace of the Cæsars; of or belonging to the palace or court of the German emperors; of or belonging to a palace; of the character of or befitting a palace; palatial.

1598 STOW *Surv.* 37 The Citie of London..hath in the East a very great & most strong Palatine Tower. **1604** R. CAWDREY *Table Alph.*, *Palatine*, belonging to a Princes Court, or pallace. *a* **1735** HEARNE tr. *Petrus Blesensis* in Agnes Strickland *Queens Eng.* (1842) I. 317 Your king.. gave himself up to palatine idleness. **1819** KEATS *Lamia* 211 In Pluto's gardens palatine. **1859** PARKER *Dom. Archit.* III.

II. vii. 372 The pure palatine nature of these is shewn in an excellent treatise abstracted by Pennant.

2. Possessing royal privileges; having a jurisdiction (within the territory) such as elsewhere belongs to the sovereign alone.

a. In ***Count, Earl (Lord) Palatine***: see COUNT *sb.*² 2 (also COUNTY *sb.*²).

Count Palatine was sometimes used in 17th c. as = (English) ***Earl Palatine***; but occurs in Eng. Hist. chiefly as the title of the *Pfalzgraf*, PALSGRAVE, or Count Palatine of the Rhine, and esp. of Frederick who married Elizabeth daughter of James I, ancestress of the Royal House of Great Britain, also called, as an elector of the German Empire, ***Elector Palatine***, and sometimes ***Prince Palatine***.

a **1548** HALL *Chron., Hen. VIII* 237 b, Came to London Duke Frederyke of Bauyre Countye Palantyne or Palsgraue of the Ryne. *c* **1580** BACON *State Europe* Wks. 1879 I. 367/1 The elector palatine Ludovic, a Lutheran; his chief abode is at Heidelberg. **1596** SPENSER *State Irel.* Wks. (Globe) 621/2 A Palsgrave..that is, an Earle Palentine. **1612** SELDEN *Illustr. Drayton's Poly-olb.* xi. 181 William the Conqueror, first created one Hugh Wolfe a Norman, Count Palatine of Chester. **1612** *Harl. MS.* 5176, lf. 212 [Ceremonial of the Marriage] On St. John day, the 27 of Decembre Frederick Count Palatin and Elector was affianced and contracted in the Banquetting House at White-hall, in the presence of the King sitting in state. **1640** YORKE *Union Hon.* 106 Randolph, surnamed Blundevile..the sixth Earle Palatine of Chester. **1658** PHILLIPS s.v. *Palatinate*, One of the Electors of the Roman Empire called the Palsgrave, or Prince Palatine of the Rhene. **1684** *Scanderbeg Rediv.* iii. 31 The Daughter of the Princess Pallatine. **1786** W. THOMSON *Watson's Philip III* (1839) 331 Frederick elector palatine, a prince young, high-spirited, and in power not inferior to any of the Protestants. **1818** BYRON *Mazeppa* viii, An angry man, ye may opine, Was he, the proud Count Palatine. **1900** LAPSLEY *County Pal. Durham* 2 To-day the queen-empress is also countess palatine of Durham. *Ibid.* 218 *n.* 3 It was said by justice Newton that the lord palatine, in producing a vouchee was acting as the servant of the king's court (*Yearbk.* 19 Hen. VI Hil. 52).

b. In ***County Palatine, Palatine County***: see COUNTY¹ 7; rarely used in sense of the (German) PALATINATE. ***Palatine earldom***, the territory or dominion of an earl palatine = County Palatine.

1436 *Rolls of Parlt.* IV. 497/2 The Justices of our saide Soveraigne Lorde of his Countee Palentyne. **1461** *Ibid.* V. 478/2 That the Counte of Lancastr' be a Counte Palatyne. **1620** BACON *Draught of Proclam.* Wks. 1879 II. 118/2 Neither can we think it safe for us..that the county Palatine carrying with itself an electorate..should now become at the disposing of that house [of Austria]. **1639** *Charter of Maine* in Baxter *Sir F. Gorges* (1890) II. 127 Together with.. as large and ample..Prerogatives Royalties Liberties..within the said province..as the Bishop of Durham within the Bishoprick or County Palatine of Durham. **1874** STUBBS *Const. Hist.* I. xi. §124. 363 *note*, The first creation of a palatine earldom under that name is that of Lancaster in 1351.

c. Of or belonging to a count or earl palatine, or to a county palatine, or palatinate.

1638–9 *Laws Maryland* in *Archives of M.* (1883) I. 48 The Lord Proprietarie shall he allowed all..the like prerogatives and Royall Rights as are usually or of right due or belonging to a Court Pallatine. **1824** GALT *Rothelan* I. II. x. 229 The rich palatine city of Durham. **1827** HALLAM *Const. Hist.* (1876) I. i. 7 In a few counties there still remained a palatine jurisdiction, exclusive of the king's courts. **1874** STUBBS *Const. Hist.* I. xi. §124. 364 He [Roger Montgomery] also may have possessed palatine rights.

3. Of or belonging to the German Palatinate.

1644 in Neal *Hist. Purit.* (1736) III. 222 His Grace has forgot his refusing to licence the Palatine Confession of Faith. **1695** *Lond. Gaz.* No. 3139/3 The Palatin Troops are returned from the Upper Rhine. **1755** CARTE *Hist. Eng.* IV. 1 The Palatine alliance flattered James with the expectation of acquiring a mighty interest in Germany. **1768** *Chron.* in *Ann. Reg.* 64/1 The elector..instituted a new order of knighthood, entitled the order of the Palatine-lion.

b. Of or pertaining to the palatines: see PALATINE¹ B. 5.

1710 GOV. R. HUNTER in *N.Y. Col. Docs.* (1855) V. 165 We want still three of the Palatin Ships and those arrived are in a deplorable sickly condition.

B. *sb.* [elliptical uses of the adj. (which began already in L.).]

I. 1. As proper name: short for Palatine Hill, *Mons Palatinus*, at Rome. (See PALACE *sb.*¹)

1656 BLOUNT *Glossogr.*, *Palatine*,..may also be taken for the Hill Palatinus in Rome. **1841** W. SPALDING *Italy & It. Isl.* I. 229 Of the Circus Maximus we can still trace the shape, in the hollow between the Palatine and Aventine.

II. Repr. L. *palātinus* officer of the palace, and senses thence historically arising.

2. An officer of the imperial palace; orig. the chamberlain, the mayor or major of the palace; a chief minister of the empire.

1598 BARCKLEY *Felic. Man* (1631) 313 Constantine the Great..caused this proclamation to be made: If there be any ..that assureth himself he can truly..prove anything against any of my Judges, Earles, Friends or Palatines,..let him come safely, and informe me. **1614** SELDEN *Titles Hon.* 27 Publique Notaries are to bee made only by the Emperor, his Palatines, or such like. **1679** EVERARD *Prot. Princes Europe* 28 The Election of a Palatine or Major of the Palace, who was the Consul and Head of the People.

b. Hence, by development of the authority delegated to such officers of the palace: A lord having sovereign power over a province or dependency of an empire or realm; a great feudatory; a vassal exercising royal privileges in his province.

Applied esp. in the Middle Ages to the rulers of Hungary, the great lords of Poland and Lithuania, Counts Palatine of Germany, Burgundy, etc.

1591 HORSEY *Trav.* (Hakl. Soc.) 260 To..stir up the kinge of Polland and greatest pallentines and princes of power in Littuania. **1603** KNOLLES *Hist. Turks* (1638) 73 Many other great Princes..namely,..Henry Palatine of Rhine,..with some others. **1630** *R. Johnson's Kingd. & Commw.* 402 Saros Patak, where the Palatine or Earle-marcher of that part of Hungaria, subject to Bethlen Gabor, usually keepes his residence. **1652** J. WRIGHT tr. *Camus' Nat. Paradox* I. 3 Certain great Officers, named Castellains and Palatines, who are little Sovereign Lords, or Petty Kings, every one in his own Territorie. **1681** NEVILE *Plato Rediv.* 157 Poland is both Governed and Possessed by some very great Persons or Potentates, called Palatines. **1693** *Mem. Cnt. Teckely* I. 12 Francis Wesselini was then Palatine of the Kingdom [of Hungary]. **1710** WHITWORTH *Acc. Russia* (1758) 32 Descended from their Waywodes, or Palatines. **1830** MRS. OPIE 7 Dec. in *Mem.* (1854) xviii. 271 The costume of a Polish Palatine, who soon after entered. **1855** MILMAN *Lat. Chr.* IX. ii. IV. 38/212 There were besides..Otho the palatine of Burgundy..the palgraves of Thuringia, Wittlesbach, and numberless other counts and nobles.

c. In England and Ireland: An earl palatine; the lord of a county palatine.

1612 DAVIES *Why Ireland*, etc. (1787) 107 These absolute Palatines made Barons and Knights,..made their own judges,..so as the King's writ did not run in those counties. **1647** N. BACON *Disc. Govt. Eng.* I. lxxi. (1739) 189 Divers men had Prisons to their own use; some as Palatines, others of Lords of Franchise, and others by power and usurpation. **1867** FREEMAN *Norm. Conq.* I. v. 322 The spiritual Palatine of Durham and the temporal Palatine of Chester stood alone in the possession of their extraordinary franchises.

†**d.** In some of the American Colonies, the title of the Lord Proprietor or senior Proprietor of the province. (Esp. in Carolina: see PALATINATE 1 b.) *Obs.* exc. *Hist.*

1669 J. LOCKE *Const. Carolina* ii. in *33 Dep. Kpr. Rep.* 258 The eldest of the lords proprietors shall be palatin, and upon yᵉ decease of yᵉ palatin yᵉ eldest of the seven surviving proprietors shall always succeed him. *Ibid.* xxvii. 261 Yᵉ Palatin's Court, consisting of yᵉ Palatine and yᵉ other seaven proprietors. **1707** J. ARCHDALE *New Descr. Carolina* 12. **1808** D. RAMSAY *Hist. S. Carolina* I. ii. 31.

3. *pl.* In reference to the later Roman Empire: The troops of the palace; the prætorians.

c **1630** DRUMM. OF HAWTH. *Poems* Wks. (1711) 26/2 With joyful cries The all triumphing palatines of skies Salute thy rising. **1781** GIBBON *Decl. & F.* xvii. (1846) II. 36 From the reign of Constantine a popular and even legal distinction was admitted between the Palatines and the Borderers: the troops of the court, as they were improperly styled, and the troops of the frontier. **1788** *Ibid.* xli. IV. 21 Belisarius was instructed..to compute the military force of palatines or borderers that might be sufficient for the defence of Africa.

†**4.** The territory ruled by a palatine; a county palatine or palatinate. *Obs.*

1586 J. HOOKER *Hist. Irel.* in *Holinshed* II. 142/1 He.. vsed his authoritie to decide matters in and throughout the palantine of Kerrie. **1600** DYMMOK *Ireland* (1843) 18 This cuntry [Kerry] was a Pallatyne to the Erle of Desmond, the lyberties and royalties whereof..caused him to grow insolent aboue measure.

5. An inhabitant or native of a palatinate.

In quot. 1610, applied to inhabitants of Chester; in those from 1709 onwards, to the refugees from the Rhine Palatinate, in Great Britain and Ireland and the Colonies.

1610 *Chester's Tri.* Ded. 3 We (poore Palatines) from our best hearts..object to thy eye, The fruit of rich Loues industrie. **1708** *Lond. Gaz.* No. 4438/2, 10000 Palatines are order'd to march towards the Moselle. **1709** in Picton *L'pool Munic. Rec.* (1886) II. 23 Thirty persons of the poor Pallatines. *Ibid.*, The Pallatines lately receiv'd into this burrough. **1773** *Hist. Brit. Dom. N. Amer.* II. i. 70 The British Colonies have received many emigrant Palatines and Saltzburghers from Germany. **1855** MACAULAY *Hist. Eng.* xx. IV. 485 It was idle, they said, to talk about the poor Huguenots or the poor Palatines.

III. 6. [a. F. *palatine*: so called (1676) from the Princess Palatine, wife of the Duke of Orleans: see Littré.] A fur tippet worn by women. Also ***palatine tippet***.

1686 *Lond. Gaz.* No. 2132/4 Lost.., a black laced Palatin with Diamond Tags upon black Ribon. *a* **1687** COTTON *Scarron., Æn.* II. (1692) 63 (D.) With top-knots fine to make 'em pretty, With tippet pallateen and settee. **1745** *Gentl. Mag.* 54 An ordinance has been published at Copenhagen.. prohibiting the wear of all ribbons, palatines, womens handkerchiefs, &c...imported from abroad. **1835** *Court Mag.* VI. p. vi/1 A sable palatine tippet..should be worn with this dress for the promenade. **1880** MRS. L. B. WALFORD *Troublesome Daughters* II. xvi. 72 Had not Mademoiselle.. permitted Bertha to accompany her and Fräulein Lebrunn to purchase their new muffs and palatines?

palatine (ˈpælətaɪn, -ɪn), *a.*² and *sb.*² [a. F. *palatin, -ine* (Cotgr. 1611), f. L. *palāt-um* PALATE.]

A. *adj.* **1.** *Anat.*, etc. Of or belonging to the palate; situated in or upon the palate.

1656 [see 2]. **1720** HALE in *Phil. Trans.* XXXI. 7 These Glands..receive different Names, according to the Part they belong to; as Labial, Buccal, Palatine. **1828** STARK *Elem. Nat. Hist.* I. 354 *Anguis*,..no palatine teeth. **1881** MIVART *Cat* 73 The maxilla sends inwards a large horizontal process called the palatine plate.

b. Produced by malformation of the palate.

1822–34 *Good's Study Med.* (ed. 4) I. 429 The obscure palatine voice..can only be assisted by filling up the fissure in the palate with a silver plate.

†**2.** *Phonetics.* = PALATAL A. 2. *Obs.*

1656 BLOUNT *Glossogr.*, *Palatine*, of or belonging to the Palate. Hence, Palatine letters are such as are pronounced by the help of the Palate, as G.T.R. etc. **1711** J. GREENWOOD *Eng. Gram.* 286 Guttural, Palatine and Labial sounds. **1773** MONBODDO *Language* (1774) I. III. xiv. 675 In Greek, γ, κ, ξ, χ..are all palatine consonants.

B. *sb.* **1.** *Anat.* (*pl.*) Short for ***palatine bones***: The two bones, right and left, which form the hard palate.

1854 OWEN *Skel. & Teeth* in *Circ. Sc., Organ. Nat.* I. 178 The pleurapophyses..are called 'palatines'. **1878** BELL *Gegenbaur's Comp. Anat.* 461 In front of the pterygoid lie the palatines.

†**2.** *Phonetics.* = PALATAL B. 2. *Obs.*

1696 *Wallis's Acc. Pass. Life* in *Hearne's R. Brunne* (1725) App. i. to Pref. 166 Some letters were Labials, some Dentals, some Palatines, and some Gutturals. **1776** J. RICHARDSON *Arabic Gram.* 8. **1822–34** *Good's Study Med.* (ed. 4) I. 434 The consonants..gutturals, compounds, palatines, dentals, and labials.

ˈpalatineship. *rare.* [f. PALATINE *sb.*¹ + -SHIP.] The office of a palatine or count palatine.

1671 F. PHILLIPS *Reg. Necess.* 424 Our Nation was not without its Local Count Palatines..as those of Chester, Lancaster, Pembroke, and the Palatineships belonging to the Bishopricks of Durham and Ely.

†**ˈpalatiˌness.** *Obs.* [f. as prec. + -ESS.] A female palatine; the wife of a (count) palatine.

1559 AYLMER *Harborowe* F ij, Conrad Palatin, left behinde him one only doughter Agnes, which was Palatinesse. **1652** J. WRIGHT tr. *Camus' Nat. Paradox* XI. 288 The two Palatinesses strove..which should render best Offices to the Prisoner.

paˈlatinoid. [f. as PALATINE *a.*² (from L. *palātum* palate) + -OID.] A proprietary name for a particular form in which medicines are made up in a cachet of soluble jujube, so as to render them tasteless and easily assimilated.

1890 *Lancet* 1 Nov. 38 (Advt.) The new tasteless form of administering Nauseous Drugs. Palatinoids convey to the stomach Powders in their Natural free state.

ˈpalatist. *rare.* [f. PALATE *sb.* + -IST.] A person who studies his palate; an epicure.

1620 VENNER *Via Recta* iv. 75, I will plainly deliuer my opinion, whatsoeuer the sensuall Palatist shall deeme.

palatitis (pæləˈtaɪtɪs). [f. L. *palātum* palate + -ITIS.] Inflammation of the mucous membrane of the palate; a form of stomatitis (*Syd. Soc. Lex.*).

palative (ˈpælətɪv), *a. rare.* [f. PALATE *sb.* + -IVE.] Appealing to the palate or taste.

1682 SIR T. BROWNE *Chr. Mor.* II. §1 Glut not thy sense with palative Delights. **1880** *Academy* 21 Aug. 143/2 The dirge..for female voices, is very pleasing..; but the interest is not maintained to the very end. The last few bars are popular rather than palative.

palato- (pəˌleɪtəʊ, ˌpælətəʊ), comb. form of L. *palātum* PALATE, in scientific words, chiefly anatomical.

palato-alveolar *a.* (*Phonetics*) (see quots. 1932 and 1962). **palato-ˈdental** (*Phonetics*) *a.*, pertaining to palate and teeth; applied to consonants produced by placing the tongue against the palate immediately behind the teeth; *sb.*, a consonant so produced. **palato-ˈglossal** *a.*, belonging to or connecting the palate and the tongue; *sb.*, the palatoglossal muscle or *palatoglossus*. **palatognathous** (-ˈɒgnəθəs) *a.* [Gr. γνάθος jaw], affected with cleft palate. **palato-ˈmaxillary** *a.* [L. *maxilla* jaw], belonging to or connecting the palate and the (upper or lower) jaw or jaw-bone. **palato-ˈnasal** *a.*, belonging to or connecting the palate and the nose. **palato-pharyngeal** (-fəˈrɪndʒiːəl) *a.*, belonging to or connecting the palate and the pharynx; *sb.*, the palato-pharyngeal muscle or *palatopharyngeus*. **ˈpalatoˌplasty** *Surg.* [Gr. πλάσσειν to mould], plastic surgery of the palate. **palato-pterygoid** (-ˈtɛrɪgɔɪd) *a.*, belonging to the palatine and pterygoid bones; *sb.*, a bone composed of these united. **palato-ˈpterygo-ˈquadrate** *a.*, pertaining to the palatine, pterygoid, and quadrate bones; *sb.*, a cartilaginous structure representing these in certain fishes. **palato-quadrate** (-ˈkwɒdrət) *a.*, pertaining to or combining the palatine and quadrate bones; also *sb.* (*sc.* bone, cartilage). **palatorrhaphy** (pæləˈtɒrəfɪ) *Surg.* [Gr. ῥαφή suture]: see quot. **palato-velar** (*Phonetics*) *a.*, articulated with the tongue in contact with the palate and velum simultaneously or successively; also either palatal or velar.

1932 D. JONES *Outl. Eng. Phonetics* (ed. 3) ix. 45 *Palato-alveolar, articulated by the blade of the tongue against the teeth-ridge with raising of the main body of the tongue towards the palate. **1962** B. M. H. STRANG *Mod. Eng. Struct.* iii. 30 *Palato-alveolar* (tongue tip to palatal edge of alveolar ridge). **1964** R. H. ROBINS *Gen. Linguistics* iii. 101 Palato-alveolar fricatives. **1973** J. C. WELLS *Jamaican Pronunc. in London* i. 10 An unexpectedly large number of confusions between post-alveolar and palato-alveolar affricates turned up. **1844** KEY *Alphabet*, etc. 55 D..is the medial letter of the order of dentals, or *palato-dentals. *Ibid.* 99 T is the thin letter of the dental or palato-dental series.

1893 *Syd. Soc. Lex.*, **P[alatoglossal] fold*, the anterior pillar of the fauces. **1782** MONRO *Anat.* 92 Each of the two **palato-maxillary* [sutures] is at the back part of the side of each nostril. **1880** GUNTHER *Fishes* 76 The palato-maxillary apparatus. **1878** BELL *Gegenbaur's Comp. Anat.* 448 A firm framework for the *palato-pharyngeal cavity. **1893** *Syd. Soc. Lex.*, *P[alato-pharyngeal] fold*, the posterior pillar of the fauces. **1890** BILLINGS *Nat. Med. Dict.* II. 278 *Palatoplasty. **1854** OWEN *Skel. & Teeth* in *Circ. Sc.*, *Organ. Nat.* I. 235 The *palato-pterygoid process. **1888** ROLLESTON & JACKSON *Anim. Life* 396 The palato-pterygoid of *Urodela* appears as a continuous membrane-bone subsequently divided. *Ibid.* 413 In the latter [*Holocephali* among *Pisces*] the *palato-pterygo-quadrate cartilage is continuous with the cranium... The palato-pterygo-quadrate is continuous with the cranium in *Dipnoi*. **1870** ROLLESTON *Anim. Life* 38 The *palato-quadrate cartilages. **1871** HUXLEY *Anat. Vert.* 135 [In osseous fishes] the palato-quadrate arch is represented by several bones, of which the most constant are the palatine in front and the quadrate behind and below. **1857** MAYNE *Expos. Lex.*, **Palatoraphy*, term for the operation of uniting by suture the cleft palate. **1893** *Syd. Soc. Lex.*, *Palatorrhaphy*, the suturing of a cleft palate. **1895** P. GILES *Short Man. Compar. Philol.* II. viii. 113 Osthoff argues that there were originally three series of guttural consonants [in Indo-Germanic], making the velars which are not followed by *u̯* the third intermediate or '*palato-velar' series. **1902** E. W. SCRIPTURE *Elem. Exper. Phonetics* xxix. 443, 3d Series (middle and back of tongue) ..k^2, g^2 palato-velar. **1935** W. F. TWADDELL *On defining Phoneme* v. 48 The 'p-phoneme' is therefore the sum of *all* those phonological differentiae which correspond to a bilabial articulation as opposed to alveolar or palato-velar, [etc.]. **1964** R. A. HALL *Introd. Linguistics* I. xvi. 96 In the case of French, we can, on the grounds of complementary distribution, bring bilabial and labio-dental together under 'labial' position; palatal and velar together under 'palato-velar'; and fricative and sibilant together under 'spirant' manner.

palatogram (ˈpælətəʊgræm). *Phonetics.* [f. PALATO- + -GRAM.] A diagram produced by palatography.

1902 E. W. SCRIPTURE *Elem. Exper. Phonetics* xxi. 296 The diagram recording the contact of the tongue with the palate is called a 'palatogram'. *Ibid.* 298 The points at which the tongue touches the palate..in forming sounds can be registered by a mixture of meal and mucilage or by carmine water color or Chinese ink spread over the previously dried tongue. The sound is spoken naturally; the mouth is at once opened and the marks on the palate are observed... The results obtained are called 'palatograms'. **1917** *Nature* 4 Oct. 96/2 Palatograms will be found to corroborate observations of tongue-positions made by other methods. **1932** D. JONES *Outl. Eng. Phonetics* (ed. 3) xxi. 171 Fig. 97 is a palatogram of the sound *s*, as pronounced by me. **1948** J. R. FIRTH in *Bull. Sch. Orient. & Afr. Stud.* XII. IV. 859 Palatograms are not much use for any velar articulation, but throw light on many articulations forward of the soft palate. **1957** [see *linguistic analysis*].

palatography (pæləˈtɒgrəfɪ). *Phonetics.* [f. PALATO- + -GRAPHY.] A technique of recording the position of the tongue during articulation from its contact with the hard palate. Hence **palatoˈgraphic** *a.*

1902 E. W. SCRIPTURE *Elem. Exper. Phonetics* xxi. 296 (*heading*) Tongue Contacts; Methods of Palatography; American, Irish and Hungarian Records. **1908** H. SWEET *Sounds of English* 108 There are other methods whose results are obtained only indirectly, such as the palatographic, by which 'palatograms' are made. **1917** *Nature* 4 Oct. 96/1 Palatography..consists in using a special kind of artificial palate, in order to find out what parts of the roof of the mouth are touched by the tongue in the production of different speech sounds. **1935** *Amer. Speech* X. 230/1 Extensive palatographic and kymographic study. **1940** *Ibid.* XV. 102/1 Palatography cannot be used extensively in the correction of foreign brogue and speech defects. **1948** J. R. FIRTH in *Bull. Sch. Orient. & Afr. Stud.* XII. IV. 863 The possibility of a large proportion of palatographic abstractions in any given language. **1957** D. ABERCROMBIE in *Zeitschr. für Phonetik* X. 21, I use the expression '*direct* palatography' to mean the investigation of articulatory movements by means of marks made directly on the roof of the mouth as distinct from the more usual technique which employs an artificial palate. **1960** P. STREVENS in *Lang. & Speech* III. 34 Palatographic studies.. show that there are often large variations of the shape of the orifice.., within the speech of a single individual as well as between different speakers. **1970** *Times Lit. Suppl.* 23 July 817/1 The motion of the tongue in speech can be studied by 'dynamic palatography'. **1976** *Language* LII. 508 No mention is made of palatography as an observational technique.

‖**palatschinken** (pæləˈtʃɪŋkən), *pl.* [Austrian Ger. dial., f. Hungarian *palacsinta*, f. Rom. *plăcintă*, f. L. *placenta* a cake.] An Austrian dish of stuffed pancakes.

1929 K. BAEDEKER *Austria* p. xxvii, Farinaceous dishes. *Strudel*,..*Palatschinken*, pancakes [etc.]. **1941** 'R. WEST' *Black Lamb* (1942) I. 144 For the sweet course we were given two apiece of palatschinken, those pancakes stuffed with jam which one eats all over Central Europe. The Balkans inherited the recipe from the Byzantines, who ate them under the name of palacountas. **1952** I. RHODE *Viennese Cookery Bk.* v. 67 The pancakes in this chapter.. are strictly Viennese—thin *Palatschinken* and the thick *Schmarren*... Although the name *Palatschinken* is a corruption of the Hungarian *Palacsinta*, these pancakes are more French in origin. **1963** R. CARRIER *Great Dishes of World* xv. 270 Just before serving, dust *palatschinken* with icing sugar. **1971** LYON & BENTON *Eggs, Milk & Cheese* 171 *Palatschinken with Chicken.* This is an Austrian form of pancake which can be used with different kinds of flavouring and stuffing.

palaulays: see PALLALL.

Palaung (pəˈlaʊŋ), *sb.* and *a.* Also 9 **Paloung**, **Poloung**. [Native name.] **A.** *sb.* **a.** A people of the Shan States of Burma; a member of any of the various tribes constituting this people. **b.** The Mon-Khmer language of this people. **B.** *adj.* Of or pertaining to this people or their language. Hence **Paˈlaungic** *a.*

1860 F. MASON *Burmah* iii. 69 The Paloungs..are a Shan tribe found north and east of Bamoo. **1885** A. R. COLQUHOUN *Amongst Shans* v. 72 The Paloungs, or Poloungs, are darker and smaller than the Shans. *Ibid.* 75 The slopes of the hills to the west of Thai-nee are cultivated by the Paloungs. **1923** H. T. WHITE *Burma* xiii. 136 Palaungs, timid, peaceable folk, to the number of 144,000, are found principally in the Northern Shan States. *Ibid.* 140 The Austro-Asiatic family is represented by Môn-Hkmer [*sic*] languages, of which the most noticeable are Talaing.. and Palaung. **1934** 'G. ORWELL' *Burmese Days* xi. 165 The Palaungs..admire long necks in women. **1942** J. L. CHRISTIAN *Mod. Burma* ii. 15 The Wa and Palaung tribal groups of the Shan hills belong to the Mon Khmer family. **1948** A. KROEBER *Anthropol.* (rev. ed.) x. 424 Asia is particularly rich in tribal societies with 'internally marginal' cultures. Examples are:..Palaung, [etc.]. **1957** *Encycl. Brit.* XVII. 114/2 The Palaung is darker than the Shan in complexion. **1971** N. BIXLER *Burma* vi. 133 The Palaung, who live less than 3,000 feet above sea level and cannot grow opium, have within this century begun to specialize quite successfully in raising tea. **1974** *Encycl. Brit. Micropædia* VII. 688/2 *Palaungic languages*, branch of the Austroasiatic language family, including..Palaung, [etc.]. **1978** *Language* LIV. 206 The Mon-Khmer languages Palaung, Riang-Lang, and Praok.

palaver (pəˈlɑːvə(r)). *sb.* Also 8 **palaaver**, **palaber**, 9 *dial.* **fa-**; also **palava**. [ad. Pg. *palavra* word, speech, talk = Sp. *palabra* (in OP. *paravoa*, OSp. *paraula*, Diez), It. *parola*, F. *parole*:—L. *parabola* parable, in early med.L. 'story, tale, word'. *Palavra* appears to have been used by Portuguese traders on the coast of Africa for a talk or colloquy with the natives (quot. 1735), to have been there picked up by English sailors (quot. 1771), and to have passed from nautical slang into colloquial use: cf. *fetish*.

Hotten's Slang Dict. has *nantee palaver* = 'cease talking', app. corr. of Pg. *não tem palabra* = 'have or hold no speech'.]

1. A talk, parley, conference, discussion: chiefly applied to conferences, with much talk, between African or other tribespeople, and traders or travellers. Also *fig.*

1735 J. ATKINS *Voy. Guinea* 103 He found it as the Fetish-Man had said, and a Palaaver being called, Peter recovered two Ounces of Gold Damage. **1771** GOLDSM. *Prol. to Cradock's Zobeide* 28 (*Spoken in the character of a sailor*) No doubt they're all barbarians..I'll try to make palaver with them though. **1824** SCOTT *St. Ronan's* vi, Next morning a solemn palaver (as the natives of Madagascar call their national convention) was held. **1835** MARRYAT *Jac. Faithf.* xxix, Now take the other sofa, and let us have a long palaver, as the Indians say. **1878** *N. Amer. Rev.* CXXVI. 345 Like the word palaver, which Portuguese discoverers lent to the dusky natives of Western Africa. **1897** MARY KINGSLEY *W. Africa* 252 'How long does a palaver usually take to talk round here?' I ask. 'The last one I talked', says Pagan, 'took three weeks'. **1951** DYLAN THOMAS in *World Rev.* Oct. 66 In his house on stilts high among beaks And palavers of birds.

2. a. Applied contemptuously to (what is considered) unnecessary, profuse, or idle talk; 'jaw'.

1748 SMOLLETT *Rod. Rand.* (1812) I. 265 Damme, said the outlaw, none of your palaver. **1764** FOOTE *Mayor of G.* I. Wks. 1799 I. 173 Let's have none of your palaver here. *c* **1817** HOGG *Tales & Sk.* V. 272 It was probably as well that I did not make too great a palaver. **1839** CARLYLE *Chartism* ix. 170 One's right..to send one's 'twenty-thousandth part of a master of tongue-fence to National Palaver'. **1885** R. GARNETT *De Quincey's Confess.* Introd. 16 [De Quincey's] besetting sin is palaver—not however imbecile garrulity, but ..the..expatiation of the princess whose lips dropped diamonds.

b. Talk intended to cajole, flatter, or wheedle.

1744 A. HAMILTON *Itinerarium* (1948) 160 The pedlar.. sold some dear bargains to Mrs. Williams, and while he smoothed her up with palaber, the Bostoner amused her with religious cant. **1809** MALKIN *Gil. Blas* IX. ii. (Rtldg.) ¶5 What is the meaning of all this palaver? **1837** HOWITT *Rur. Life* III. i. (1862) 195 The peculiar style of palaver..the unique flattery..with which the gipsy accosts you. **1887** *S. Chesh. Gloss.*, *Falahver*, unctuous politeness, exaggerated civility expressed in words. 'Hey'd sich a lot o' falahver with him'.

†**c.** In West Africa: a dispute or contest. *Obs.*

c **1740** F. MOORE *Trav. Inland Afr.* (ed. 2) 221 They..call a Dispute *a Palaver*. **1744** W. SMITH *New Voy. to Guinea* 32 The English..once had a Settlement upon Charles Island, but having a Pallaver with the Natives they..waded over from the Main; by which Surprize they got Possession, and beat the English off that Island. **1789** *Rep. Lords Comm. Council: Evidence* I. 5 in *Parl. Papers 1731–1800* (Brit. Libr.) LXXXIV, If any Dispute or *Palavers* arose between Two or more Persons, they called a Council of the head Men, where the Persons were tried.

d. Business, concern. *slang* and *African colloq.*

1899 C. J. C. HYNE *Further Adventures Capt. Kettle* 21 It's not your palaver..or mine. **1953** *Eng. Stud.* XXXIV. 286 [West Africa] That's your palaver.

e. Jargon. ? *U.S.* (*rare*).

1909 'MARK TWAIN' *Is Shakes. Dead?* vii. 74, I have been a quartz miner..and know all the palaver of that business.

f. In Africa: trouble.

1953 P. CHRISTOPHERSEN in *Eng. Stud.* XXXIV. 286 *Palaver*..is now part of Standard English in the sense of 'talk' or 'parley'. But in West Africa this meaning is obsolete. In Pidgin and very largely in Coast English the word has come to mean 'business' or 'trouble' (e.g...'That has caused a lot of palaver' and 'He had some tummy palaver last week'). **1954** [see *D.O.* s.v. D III. 3]. **1970** *Drum* (E. Afr. ed.) Feb. 39/2, I am a boy of 21 and I am still unemployed. I want a girl friend, someone to pet me. But I feel I should get a job before getting involved with woman palava.

3. *attrib.* and *Comb.*, as ***palaver-court***, ***-house***, ***-man***, ***-room***.

1735 J. ATKINS *Voy. Guinea* 53 So much as he can prove ..at the Palaaver-Court, to have been defrauded of. *Ibid.* 63 Every Town hereabouts had a Palaaver-Room. *Ibid.* 74 The Palaaver-Man [demands] 10*s.* **1803** T. WINTERBOTTOM *Sierra Leone* I. v. 85 The Africans..hold their meetings in the búrree, or palaver house. **1861** DU CHAILLU *Equat. Afr.* vi. 50 The chief's house and the palaver-house are larger than the others.

palaver (pəˈlɑːvə(r)), *v.* Also 8 *dial.* **fa-**. [f. prec. (There is no corresponding vb. in Pg. or Sp.).]

1. a. *intr.* To talk profusely or unnecessarily; to 'jaw', 'jabber'; to talk plausibly or flatteringly. (In quot. 1877, to hold a colloquy, to parley.)

1733, **1764** [see PALAVERING below]. **1778** MISS BURNEY *Evelina* xvi, And palaver in French gibberish? **1791–3** in *Spirit Pub. Jrnls.* (1799) I. 372, I heard Mr. Thelwall palaver one day. **1840** BARHAM *Ingol. Leg.*, *Spectre Tappington* (1882) 342 [I] had no time to stop palavering with him any way. **1877** A. B. EDWARDS *Up Nile* x. 285 The worthy man, having spent all day in Assouan, visiting, palavering, bargaining, was now going home.

b. *trans.* with what is spoken as obj.

1853 C. BRONTË *Villette* xiii, Telling her nursery tales and palavering the little language for her benefit.

c. To talk *out of* or *into* something; to talk (any one) *over*, by palaver.

1767 *Woman of Fashion* II. 170, I won't be palaver'd out of my Prerogative. **1782** ELIZ. BLOWER *Geo. Bateman* II. 115 They easily palavers themselves into ladies favours. **1798** WOLCOTT (P. Pindar) *Tales of Hoy* Wks. 1812 IV. 418 No palavering me over with 'my dear friend'.

2. To treat with palaver; to flatter, wheedle.

1785 GROSE *Dict. V.T.*, *Pallaver*, to flatter. **1815** W. H. IRELAND *Scribbleomania* 149 To write silly odes, and palaver the great. **1863** READE *Hard Cash* I. vii. 214 Dodd never spoke to his officers like a ruffian, nor yet palavered them.

3. *intr.* const. *to*: to ask (someone) for something, to beg from. *slang.* ? *Obs.*

1858 A. MAYHEW *Paved with Gold* III. i. 255, I thought he was a 'queer gill' (suspicious) at first, and smoked us, from what he palavered to Phil when he gave him his 'deux-wins' (twopence). **1859** HOTTEN *Dict. Slang* 71 'Palaver to the nibs for a shant of bivvy,' ask the master for a quart of beer.

Hence **paˈlavering** *vbl. sb.* and *ppl. a.*

1733 *Revolution Politicks* II. 53 Here's Bo-Peep.—Pious falavering.—A Protestant Mask under two Faces. **1764** FOOTE *Mayor of G.* II. Wks. 1799 I. 179 Have a..caution that [he]..does not cajole you; he is a damn'd palavering fellow. **1778** MISS BURNEY *Evelina* xx, A truce with all this palavering. **1882** MISS BRADDON *Mt. Royal* II. v. 91, I could ..sue to her as a palavering Irish beggar sues for alms.

palaverer (pəˈlɑːvərə(r)). [f. prec. vb. + -ER[1].] One who palavers. So (*nonce-wds.*) **paˈlaverist**, one given to palaver; **paˈlaverment**, verbiage.

1788 J. MAY *Jrnl. & Lett.* (1873) 31 They are Irish palaverers, and the truth is not in them. **1816** CHALMERS *Let.* in *Life* (1851) II. iii. 66 Floundering its uncertain way through amongst the palaverments of law. **1822** J. WILSON *Blackw. Mag.* XI. 485 He is contented to be a critic—that is, a palaverer. *a* **1873** LIVINGSTONE in Blaikie *Life* xiii. (1880) 268 See to what a length I have run. I have become palaverist.

‖**palay** (pəˈleɪ). Also **pala**. [Tamil *palay*.] Name of two East Indian shrubs or trees with milky juice; **a.** *Cryptostegia grandiflora* (N.O. *Asclepiadaceæ*), which yields a flax-like fibre and a kind of caoutchouc; **b.** *Wrightia tinctoria* (N.O. *Apocynaceæ*), which yields an inferior kind of indigo (*pala indigo*).

1866 *Treas. Bot.* 836 *Palay*, an Indian name for *Cryptostegia grandiflora*. *Ibid.* 1237 An inferior kind of indigo, prepared from the leaves of *W[rightia] tinctoria* in some parts of Southern India, is called Pala Indigo, from Pala or Palay, the Tamil name for this and some allied milky trees. The wood of the Palay is beautifully white, close-grained, and ivory-like, and is commonly used..for making toys.

palayl, erron. f. POLAYL, poultry.

palays, obs. f. PALACE, var. PALIS *Obs.*

palazado, obs. f. PALISADO.

palazzo (paˈlattso). [It.: see PALACE *sb.*[1]]

1. Pl. palazzi. A palatial mansion; a large and imposing building.

a **1666** EVELYN *Diary* an. 1644 (1955) II. 228 The Palazzo Barberini..I take to be as..princely an object, as any moderne building in Europ. **1758** M. W. MONTAGU *Let.* May (1967) III. 149 He brags..that you found the Palazzo very clean. **1892** W. JAMES *Let.* 28 Dec. (1920) I. 335 You seem to me something ideal, off there in your inaccessible Cambridge palazzo. **1924** M. ARLEN *Green Hat* v. 143 In drawing-rooms, up and down terraces of palazzos, in clubs and cabarets. **1930** E. POUND *XXX Cantos* xvii. 77 On past the palazzi. **1958** *Oxf. Mag.* 13 Mar. 357/2 What activities it [*sc.* the Institute of Statistics] wishes to pursue in the great *palazzo* which it now demands. **1962** A. SAMPSON *Anat. Brit.* v. 66 The taxis and government Humbers draw up outside the palazzi of Pall Mall, and bowlers and umbrellas disappear through the great stone doorways, acknowledged by reverent porters. **1968** 'E. LATHEN' *Stitch in Time* I. 1

The..Sloan Guaranty Trust, an opulent palazzo of glass, marble and brass that had replaced the stately and venerable edifice on Pearl Street. **1978** W. M. Spackman *Armful of Warm Girl* 12 But now anyhow in her 73rd Street palazzo her phone rang.

2. Usu. as pl. **palazzos.** Loose, wide-legged trousers worn by women.

1972 *New Yorker* 9 Sept. 8/1 (Advt.), Our haltered palazzos come in champagne beige... The no-waistband, back-zip palazzos. **1973** *Harper's Bazaar* Apr. 5 (Advt.), Lollipops loll on a plunging palazzo... Shirring and sashing halt the halter above billowing pyjamas. **1973** *Telegraph* (Brisbane) 6 Sept. 18/2 Female employees..now are being permitted to wear the pants—in the form of trim pants suits, or, we guess, baggies—or palazzos, if they please.

3. *attrib.* and *Comb.*, as (sense 2) ***palazzo outfit, pants, pyjamas, shape, suit, trouser***; **palazzo sleeve,** a wide, flowing sleeve.

1973 *Today's Health* Oct. 36/1 Linda stopped at the dry cleaners to pick up the flowered silk pallazzo [*sic*] outfit she planned to wear to the theater on Saturday. **1972** *New Yorker* 7 Oct. 18/1 (Advt.), Velvety fleece palazzo pants. **1973** *Woman's Day* Sept. 168/1 (Advt.), Choose from smashing palazzo pants and clothes with the bare look. **1966** *Listener* 3 Feb. 171/2 The mannequins start with a natural advantage over most other mortals. Who but they could wear palazzo pyjamas..made entirely of ostrich feathers. **1968** *N.Y. Times* 30 Apr. 52 All these varieties continued into the nineteen-sixties, when they were joined by such other forms as palazzo pajamas (wide enough to sweep around a palace in), culottes, pants dresses and pants suits. **1976** *Times* 1 Sept. (Fashion Suppl.) p. viii/5 Emilio Pucci..introduced..the famous palazzo pyjamas. **1973** *New Yorker* 17 Mar. 56 (Advt.), We like the palazzo shape as a slashback culotte. **1972** *Ibid.* 26 Aug. 55 (Advt.), Our fluid navy wool knit with permanent pleated polyester chiffon palazzo sleeves. **1974** *Country Life* 3–10 Jan. 55/1 Drip-dry dresses and palazzo suits. **1972** *N.Y. Times* 3 Nov. 11/4 (Advt.), The palazzo-trouser.

palde, obs. f. PALLED.

paldron, var. PAULDRON.

pale (peɪl), *sb.*[1] Also 5 pal, payll, 6 paile, payl, *Sc.* paill, 6–7 palle, pail, 7 payle. [a. F. *pal* (15th c. in Littré), ad. L. *pālus* stake: = It., Sp. *palo*, Pg. *pao.*]

1. a. *orig.* A stake; a pointed piece of wood intended to be driven into the ground, esp. as used with others to form a fence; now, usually, One of the upright bars or strips of wood nailed vertically to a horizontal rail or rails to form a paling (cf. *pale-board*, 1483, in 8).

[**1347** *Rolls of Parlt.* II. 169/1 Estopez & transversez par goors, molins, piles, & pales par chescun Seignur contre sa terre demeigne.] **1382** Wyclif *Zech.* x. 4 Of hym corner, and of him a litil pale [Vulg. *paxillus*], of hym bowe of batel. *c* **1400** *Destr. Troy* 5610 Pals haue þai pight, with pittis and caves. *c* **1440** *Promp. Parv.* 378/2 Pale, for vynys, *paxillus.* **1530** Palsgr. 251/1 Pale or a stake, *piev.* **1555** Eden *Decades* 177 Inclosynge it with stakes or pales as his owne. **1675** Hobbes *Odyssey* (1677) 165 With a quickset-hedge enclosed round, And pales of heart of oak the hedge without Set close together, and stuck deep i' th' ground. **1760–72** H. Brooke *Fool of Qual.* (1809) I. Pref. 11 They stand like pales about a park. **1807** Crabbe *Par. Reg.* III. 314 In that small house, with those green pales before. **1881** Young *Every Man his own Mechanic* §181. 62 Pales, cleft pales, or pale boards may be used to complete the fencing.

†b. The stake (*palus*) at which Roman soldiers practised fighting (Veg. *Mil.* I. xi, II. xxiii.). *Obs.*

1622 Bp. Hall *Heaven upon Earth* vi. 18 As therefore good soldiers exercise themselves long at the pale: and there use those activities, which afterwards they shall practise upon a true adversary.

2. a. A fence made of stakes driven into the ground, or of upright bars or strips nailed to horizontal rails supported by posts; a paling, palisade. *Obs.* or *arch.*

c **1330** R. Brunne *Chron. Wace* (Rolls) 5831 An ouerthwert dik..& per-on a pale wel y-poynt. **1382** Wyclif *Luke* xix. 43 Thin enemyes schulen enuyroune thee with pale [**1388** with a pale]. **1491** *Act 7 Hen. VII*, c. 14 The Abbas and Convent of Berking were bounde to repaire..the pale of the parke of Haveryng. **1523** Fitzherb. *Husb.* §40 To haue a shepefolde made with a good hedge or a pale. **1607** Topsell *Four-f. Beasts* (1658) 213 Richmen..inclosed a piece of land by pail, mudwall, or bush, storing the same with divers wilde beasts. **1792** A. Young *Trav. France* 535 Herds of deer not confined by any wall or pale. **1810** Miss Mitford in L'Estrange *Life* (1870) I. iv. 94 We have received a summons from the under-sheriff..given over the pale to William this morning.

b. *transf.* and *fig.* A fence or enclosing barrier or line of any material. *Obs.* or *arch.*

1564 *Will of H. Lacye* (Morrison & Crimes 2, Somerset Ho.), My standing Mazer of silver gilte, with a pale of silver aboute the foote. **1615** Chapman *Odyss.* I. 110 What words fly, Bold daughter, from thy pale of ivory [i.e. teeth]? **1663** Charleton *Chor. Gigant.* 41 The exterior Muniment or pale of great stones. **1869** Tennyson *Holy Grail* 21 Never have I known the world without, Nor ever stray'd beyond the pale.

c. *fig.* A limit, boundary; a restriction; a defence, safeguard. Sometimes with direct reference to the literal sense, as in ***to break*** or ***leap the pale***, to go beyond bounds, indulge in extravagance or licence. *Obs.* exc. as in 5.

c **1400** *Destr. Troy* 13874 The buerne..Past ouer the pale and the pale ythes. *c* **1460** *Play Sacram.* 207 Myt we yt gete onys wᵗin our pales I trowe we shuld sone affter putt yt in a preve. **1585** T. Washington tr. *Nicholay's Voy.* IV. xx. 134 b, The Cordicque [mountaines] out of which the [Riuer] Tiger groweth and extendeth vnto the pales of Tospie the Taur. **1612** T. Taylor *Comm. Titus* ii. 12 This is the pale, and preseruatiue of pietie. **1671** F. Phillips *Reg. Necess.* 515 Nothing within the pale or verge of Reason, or the fancy or imagination of any. **1751** Johnson *Rambler* No. 163 ¶14 When the pale of ceremony is broken.

3. An area enclosed by a fence; an enclosed place; an enclosure.

c **1400** *Destr. Troy* 8970 He..No more in the mater mellit hym as then, But past furth to his pale. **1464** *Rolls of Parlt.* V. 543/2 Closure of certain parcell of the pale of oure Park. **1587** Churchyard *Worth. Wales* (1876) 77 Make Wales the Parke, and plaine Shropshiere the pale, If pale be not a speciall peece of Parke. **1698** Fryer *Acc. E. India & P.* 180 They cut a whole Tree down..shoulder'd it..brought it into the Pale of their Pagods. **1719** De Foe *Crusoe* I. iv, I brought all my goods into this pale. **1871** B. Taylor *Faust* (1875) II. II. iii. 154 One starts there first within a narrow pale.

4. a. A district or territory within determined bounds, or subject to a particular jurisdiction, e.g. †***English pale***, the confines or dominion of England, the pale of English law; *spec.* b. the ***English Pale*** in France, the territory of Calais (now only *Hist.*); c. the ***English Pale*** (also simply ***the Pale***) in Ireland, that part of Ireland (varying in extent at different times) over which English jurisdiction was established. †d. the ***English Pale*** in Scotland in 1545–9 (*obs.*). e. From 1791 to 1917, specified provinces and districts within which Russian Jews were required to reside. (The Russ. expression corresponding to 'pale of settlement' is *chertá osédlosti* (lit. 'boundary of settlement').)

1560 Daus tr. *Sleidane's Comm.* 396 b, The Frenche king went out of his owne pale. **1600** Holland *Livy* VII. xii. 257 The Tarquinians overran all the marches of the Roman pale. **1615** Heywood *Foure Prentises* Wks. 1874 II. 199 To breake into my Soueraignes royall pale. **1670** Blount *Law Dict.* s.v. *Palingman*, A Merchant Denizen; one born within the English Pale. **1683** *Brit. Spec.* 112 The Britains had also (even within the Roman Pale) for a time kings of their own.

b. **1494** Fabyan *Chron.* VII. 539 A lytle beyonde Guynys, wᵗin yᵉ Englysshe pale, was another lyke pauylyon pyght for Kyng Rycharde. **1547** Boorde *Introd. Knowl.* i. (1870) 120 The Cornyshe tongue [is spoken] in Cornewall,..and Frenche in the Englysshe pale. **1577–87** Holinshed *Chron.* III. 892/1 A great number of men of warre laie at Bullongne, ..which diuerse times attempted..to spoile the English pale. **1622** Bacon *Hen. VII* 75 Upon pretence of the safety of the English pale about Calais. **1893** *Archæologia* LIII. 289 The Pale extended from Gravelines to near Wissant, and reached inland about six to nine miles.

c. *c* **1547** Boorde *Introd. Knowl.* iii. (1870) 132 Irland..is deuyded in ii. partes, one is the Engly[sh] pale, & the other, the wyld Irysh. **1586** J. Hooker *Hist. Irel.* in *Holinshed* II. 95/1 The lord deputie..marched with the English armie, and the power of the pale to Mainoth. **1643** *Declar. Comm. Reb. Irel.* 10 Lord Gormanston and other Lords and Gentlemen of the Pale, all now in Rebellion. **1724** Swift *Drapier's Lett.* Wks. 1755 V. II. 52 A various scene of war and peace between the English pale and the Irish natives. **1892** Olden *Ch. Irel.* 277 The Pale was not a definite territory, it merely meant the district in which the king's writ ran, and in which the Irish Parliament actually exercised authority.

d. **1549** Jas. Henrison *Mem. to Somerset* xviii. in *St. Papers Edw. VI*, V. lf. 53 (P.R.O.) Lands lying within the English Pale of Scotland on this syde the strayte water of muscellburughe.

e. **1890** A. Reader *Russia & Jews* viii. 78 The Jews,..as soon as the contract was completed..had to return within the 'pale' of settlement. **1892** I. Zangwill *Children of Ghetto* III. 329 The whole history of her strange, unhappy race flashed through her mind... She was overwhelmed by the thought of its sons in every corner of the earth proclaiming to the sombre twilight sky the belief for which its generations had lived and died—the Jews of Russia sobbing it forth in their pale of enclosure. **1897** [see GOLEM]. **1927** *New Statesman* 6 Nov. 104/1 Bolshevism, whilst destroying the livelihood of the Jewish masses in the so-called 'Pale'—small traders and artisans—has disorganised Russia's economic system. **1969** *Observer* 23 Feb. 23/2 With the Revolution in 1917, the Jews were released from the Pale and allowed to move in great numbers into Russia proper. **1976** *Times* 8 Apr. 11/3 Generally it has been held that Jews had arrived in what was known as the Pale of Settlement, between Russia and Poland, because they were driven there, under expulsion first from England and France, then from Germany. **1977** Y. Menuhin *Unfinished Journey* i. 4 The Mnuchins..had settled in Gomel, a smallish city..at the very center of the Pale.

5. *fig.* esp. in ***within*** (or ***outside***) ***the pale of***, in which the senses 'limits', 'bounds' (see 2 c) and 'area' or 'region' (see 4) become indistinguishable.

1483 Caxton *Gold. Leg.* 414/1 The abbote..and xxi monkes..went for to dwelle in deserte for to kepe more straytelye the professyon of theyr pale. **1611** Shaks. *Wint. T.* IV. iii. 4 The red blood raigns in ye winters pale. **1649** Jer. Taylor *Gt. Exemp.* II. xii. 53 The Diocese of Palestine, which was afterwards enlarged to the pale of the Catholicke Church. **1654** Bramhall *Just Vindic.* i. (1661) 2 For we acknowledge that there is no salvation to be expected ordinarily without the pale of the Church. **1788** Jefferson *Autobiog. & Writ.* (1859) II. 418 The exercise of foreign jurisdiction, within the pale of their own laws. **1822** Hazlitt *Table-t.* II. xii. 270 She is out of the pale of all theories, and annihilates all rules. **1867** Freeman *Norm. Conq.* (1876) I. ii. 31 The conversion..brought England..not only within the pale of the Christian Church, but within the pale of the general political society of Europe.

6. a. *Her.* An ordinary consisting of a vertical strip or band in the middle of the shield, usually occupying one third of its breadth. Formerly also applied in pl. to a number of vertical stripes or divisions on the shield: see PALLET *sb.*[4], PALY *a.* ***in pale***: said of a charge or row of charges in the position of a pale; formerly also more generally = in the direction of a pale, palewise, vertically. (***party***) ***per pale***: said of the shield when divided by a vertical line through the middle.

1486 *Bk. St. Albans, Her.* D viij b, Iff the palys of bothe the colowris ben not equall thoos armys be not palyt. *Ibid.*, He berith gowlys and ij palis of golde. **1572** Bossewell *Armorie* II. 90 The fielde is of the Pearle, two Spurres in pale, Rubye. *Ibid.* 123 He beareth Vert and Sable, parted per pale vndade, two Towers embatiled Dargent. **1614** Day *Dyall* vi. 108 Ther 's party per pale, part of yron, and part of clay. **1677** Plot *Oxfordsh.* To Rdr. b ij b, If Gules, lineated perpendicularly, or in pale. **1709** Hearne *Collect.* 6 Nov. (Oxf. Hist. Soc.) II. 303 The Third window hath Nevill's Arms in Pale with those of the Sea of York. **1715** Ashmole *Antiq. Berks.* (1723) I. 145 On a Chief *Bar Nebule* A Pale charg'd with a Pelican. **1810** Scott *Lady of L.* IV. viii, I..marked the sable pale of Mar. **1867** Boutell *Eng. Her.* (1875) 34 A shield..may be divided into any number of quarterings by lines drawn per pale and per fesse, cutting each other.

†b. A vertical stripe on cloth, etc. *Obs.*

c **1384** Chaucer *H. Fame* III. 750 But what art thow that seyest this tale, That werest on thy hose a pale?

†7. *Bot.* a. The 'ray' or outer set of florets in composite flowers. b. Each of the parts or leaves of the 'impalement'; a calyx-leaf or sepal, or (in composites) a bract of the involucre: = IMPALER.

a. **1578** Lyte *Dodoens* I. xi. 19 Floures yellow in the middest, and compassed aboute as it were with a little pale of small white leaues. **1683** Ray *Corr.* (1848) 131 Whether ..naturally a full or double flower, or only consisting of a pale or border of leaves?

b. **1676** Grew *Anat. Flowers* i. §4 In the Empalement.. the Pales or Pannicles of every Under-Order, serve to stop up the Gaps made by the Recess of the Upper.

8. *attrib.* and *Comb.*, as ***pale-board*** (see sense 1), ***-cleaver*** (who makes cleft pales), ***-fence, -gate, -row***; ***pale-enclosed*** adj. See also PALEMAN, PALEWISE.

1483–4 *Durham Acc. Rolls* 98, 12 plaustrat. de lez payll-bordes. **1577** B. Googe *Heresbach's Husb.* (1586) 106 The Mastholme..maie also be made in Wainscot, and Paile boorde. **1578** *Faversham Par. Reg.* (MS.), Wyll'm Smythe, a palle cleuer. **1645** Quarles *Sol. Recant.* II. 51 Take pleasure in thy pale-enclosed Grounds. **1667** Duchess of Newcastle *Life of Dk. of N.* (1886) II. 136 Only the pale-row was valued at £2000. **1834** J. Kemper in *Wisconsin State Hist. Soc. Coll.* (1898) XIV. 423 In walking over the meadow..passed an indian burial place, 2 poles with white flags flying a pale fence partly surrounding the place. **1836** W. Dunlap *Mem. Water Drinker* (1837) I. 12 It was..a ricketty wooden pale-gate drawn back by a chain and bullet. **1845** M. M. Noah *Gleanings* 77 His house is..surrounded with a white pale fence. **1850** H. C. Watson *Camp-Fires of Revolution* 28 Their ranks looked like a broken pale-fence. **1889** Stockton in *Cent. Mag.* Dec. 300/2 A high pale fence surrounded the house yard.

pale, *sb.*[2] Now *rare* or *Obs.* [f. PALE *a.*] Paleness, pallor.

a **1547** Surrey *Æneid* IV. 666 The pale her face gan staine. **1592** Shaks. *Ven. & Ad.* 589 A suddain pale,..Vsurpes her cheeke, she trembles at his tale. **1635** A. Stafford *Fem. Glory* (1860) 116 You..on whose cheeks Solitude, Prayers, Fasts, and Austerity have left an amiable pale. **1797** Mrs. A. M. Bennett *Beggar Girl* (1813) III. 205 The deadly pale of her countenance increasing. **1832** Bowles *St. John in Patmos* I. 236 The sun is of an ashy pale. **1887** M. E. Wilkins *Humble Romance* 110 'It ain't so much the pale,' said Mrs. Potter, 'but thar's..a kind of a look around..the mouth that I've seen a good many times.'

pale, *sb.*[3] ? *dial.* [ad. L. *pāla* spade, oven-pale or -peel: see also PEEL.] a. A baker's shovel, a PEEL. b. A cheese-scoop (Simmonds *Dict. Trade* 1858).

1728 [sense b. is implied in PALE *v.*[4]]. **1816** Muir *Minstrelsy* 46 (E.D.D.) I'se gie a cheese..the very wale, To try it ye may bring a pale. **1857** *Gentl. Mag.* Aug. 181 The 'Pale' is the name given to the long wooden shovel on which the bread is placed in order to be pushed into the oven.

pale, *sb.*[4] *Bot.* [ad. L. *palea* chaff.] = PALEA.

1866 *Treas. Bot.* 836/2 *Paleæ*, or *Pales*.., membranous scales resembling chaff. The inner scales of the flower in grasses are pales. **1891** Oliver *Elem. Bot.* 45 Wheat... Each flower is enclosed between a flowering-glume and a pale.

[**pale,** in *cross-pale*, error for SPALE, SPALL.]

pale (peɪl), *a.* Also 4 pal, 4–6 paal(e, 5 palle, payll, 5–6 *Sc.* paill, 6 *Sc.* pail(e. [ME. a. OF. *palle, pale* (mod. F. *pâle*):—L. *pallid-um* pale, f. *pallēre* to be pale.]

1. a. Of persons, their complexions, etc.: Of a whitish or ashen appearance; not ruddy or fresh of complexion; pallid; wan (either naturally, or temporarily as a result of fear or other emotion).

a **1300** *Cursor M.* 24004 Ful pale [*v.r.* pal] wex al mi hide. *c* **1350** *Will. Palerne* 881 He cast al his colour and bi-com pale. *c* **1385** Chaucer *L.G.W.* 866 *Thisbe*, And pale as box sche was. *c* **1470** Henry *Wallace* x. 565 Behaldand his paill face, He kyssyt him. **1470–85** Malory *Arthur* x. xxxiv, He starte abak and waxed paale. **1545** Joye *Exp. Dan.* v. 69 Then was yᵉ kynges face paal and his cogitacions so ferefully troubled him that [etc.]. **1602** Shaks. *Ham.* III. i. 85 The Natiue hew of Resolution Is sicklied o're, with the pale cast of Thought. **1709** Steele *Tatler* No. 23 ¶2 The Man grew pale as Ashes. **1828** Scott *F.M. Perth* xiv, The Fair Maid of Perth's complexion changed from red to pale, and from pale to red. **1870** MORRIS *Earthly Par.* I. I. 436 Then pale as privet, took she heart to drink.

b. *generally.* Of a shade of colour approaching white; lacking intensity or depth of colour; faintly coloured.

1382 WYCLIF *Rev.* vi. 8 And loo! a paal hors; and the name Deeth to him that sat on him. *c* **1400** *Sege Jerus.* 743 Suþ putteþ þe prince ouer his pale wedes A brynye, browded þicke. *c* **1400** *Destr. Troy* 2004 Euer in point for to perysshe in the pale stremys. **1560** DAUS tr. *Sleidane's Comm.* 360 b, Thre sunnes,..one while of a pale colour, an other while as red as bloud. **1630** MILTON *May Morning* 4 The yellow Cowslip, and the pale Primrose. **1699** LISTER *Journ. to Paris* 108 The first Writing was turned so pale, that they took no pains to rub it out. **1784** COWPER *Task* III. 573 The ruddier orange, and the paler lime. **1868** J. E. A. BROWN *Lights thro' Lattice* 27 The pale Grey duskiness of olive foliage.

c. Qualifying adjs. (or sbs.) of colour. (Usually hyphened in attrib. construction.)

1588 SHAKS. *L.L.L.* I. ii. 107 Blushing cheekes by faults are bred, And feares by pale white showne. **1717** PRIOR *Alma* II. 332 Her scarf pale pink, her head-knot cherry. **1783** LIGHTFOOT in *Phil. Trans.* LXXV. 12 The eggs..of a pale-blush colour. **1798** SOUTHEY *Sonnets* xi, And timidly did its light leaves disclose, As doubtful of the spring, their palest green. **1811** W. R. SPENCER *Poems* 54 Like thee, whose pale-rose lips they press. **1876** GEO. ELIOT *Dan. Der.* xxxv, The pale-golden straw.

d. Used to distinguish things of lighter colour than others of the same kind: esp. of certain liquors, and flowers or plants. *spec.* as *pale ale* (also *ellipt.*); *pale sherry*, a general term for light-coloured, dry sherries.

1708 *Diss. on Drunkenness* 6 Numbers of Pale Ales, nam'd after the..Brewers that prepare them. **1833** C. REDDING *Hist. Mod. Wines* vi. 189 Pale sherry is made from the same grape as the brown, to the wine from which is added a couple of bottles of very pure brandy to each butt. **1838** T. THOMSON *Chem. Org. Bodies* 801 Three different kinds of cinchona bark..the pale, the yellow, and the red. **1846** R. FORD *Gatherings from Spain* xiv. 161 Pure genuine sherry.. will stand the importer from 100 to 130 guineas in his cellar. .. The reader will now appreciate the bargains of those 'pale' and 'golden sherries' advertised in the English newspapers at 36*s.* the dozen, bottles included. **1849** Pale ale [see *brown sherry* s.v. BROWN *a.* 7]. **1853** *Q. Jrnl. Chem. Soc.* V. 173 *(heading)* Alleged adulteration of pale ales by strychnine. **1861** MISS PRATT *Flower. Pl.* VI. 162 Oak Fern ..is sometimes called Pale Mountain Polypody. **1891** in C. Ray *Compleat Imbiber* (1967) IX. 122 Pale Sherry..Per. Doz. 20/-. **1965** A. SICHEL *Penguin Bk. Wines* III. 231 Intermediate types of sherry are described as brown, light golden, pale, etc., and are for the most part excellent wines, blended to the taste and needs of importers. **1976** 'J. FRASER' *Who steals my Name?* ix. 104 Don't guzzle down that Clos de Vougoet as if it was Watney's Pale. That's worth six pounds a bottle. **1977** *Berry Bros. & Rudd Catal.* Apr. 6 South African Sherry...pale extra dry—per bottle £1·70.

e. Pale Brindled Beauty, a geometrid moth, *Apocheima pilosaria*, usually having light-coloured wings flecked with darker markings.

[**1803** A. H. HAWORTH *Lepidoptera Britannica* 274 *(heading)* The pale Brindle. **1824** G. SAMOUELLE *Entomologist's Useful Compendium* 363 The pale brindle. Trunks of trees.] **1860** H. N. HUMPHREYS *Genera Brit. Moths* 81 *(caption)* The Female of the Pale Brindled Beauty. **1908** R. SOUTH *Moths Brit. Isles* (ser. 2) 295 Pale Brindled Beauty... The fore wings of this species are greyish,.. sprinkled with darker grey or brownish. **1955** E. B. FORD *Moths* xiii. 191 A black form of the Pale Brindled Beauty has become well established in some of the industrial areas of the north and round London. **1964** *Sunday Times* (Colour Suppl.) 2 Feb. 33 *(caption)* The male Pale Brindled Beauty moth may have these typical markings, but others have black wings. **1966** *Punch* 30 Mar. 463/1 Some ancient apple trees,..generous hosts, in season, to the Capsid Bug and.. the Pale Brindled Beauty.

2. Of something luminous or illuminated: Wanting in brightness or brilliancy; of faint lustre; dim.

c **1374** CHAUCER *Boeth.* II. met. iii. 26 (Camb. MS.) Wan the sonne is rysyn the day sterre wexeth paale and leseth hir lyht. **14..** *Circumsision* in *Tundale's Vis.* (1843) 85 That lyght was pale and nothyng clere. **1549** *Compl. Scot.* 38 Also fayr dyana, the lantern of the nycht, be cam dym ande pail. **1596** SHAKS. *Merch. V.* V. i. 125 This night methinkes is but the daylight sicke, It lookes a little paler, 'tis a day, Such as the day is, when the Sun is hid. **1736** GRAY *Statius* i. 54 The Sun's pale sister, drawn by magic strain. **1867** HAYNE *Bk. Sonnet* II. 230 Rugged December..Marshals his pale Days to the mournful dirge.

3. *fig.* (with various implications): Dim, faint, feeble; lacking intensity, vigour, or robustness; fearful, timorous, etc.

c **1530** L. COX *Rhet.* (1899) 53 Poetes haue..made many lyes of the pale kyngdome of Pluto. **1599** SHAKS. *Hen. V*, II. Prol. 14 The French..shake in their feare, and with pale Pollicy Seeke to diuert the English purposes. **1820** SHELLEY *Ode Liberty* xvi, That the pale name of Priest might shrink and dwindle Into the hell from which it first was hurled. **1891** G. MEREDITH in *Academy* (1898) 8 Oct. 14/2 My health is of a pale sort at present.

4. a. *Comb.*, chiefly parasynthetic, as ***pale-blurred, -breasted, -cheeked, -coloured, -complexioned, -eyed, -hued, -leaved, -lipped, -mouthed, -snowed, -spotted, -starred, -tinted, -visaged***; sometimes *fig.* with implication of fear, feebleness, etc., as ***pale-blooded, -hearted, -livered, -souled, -spirited***. Also advb., as †***pale-dead*** (or ? two words), ***pale-gleaming, -glimmering***. (See also PALE-FACE, -FACED.)

1579–80 NORTH *Plutarch* 739 These pale visaged and carion leane people, I feare them most, meaning Brutus and Cassius. **1599** SHAKS. *Hen. V*, IV. ii. 48 The gumme downe roping from their pale-dead eyes, And in their pale dull mouthes the Iymold Bitt Lyes foule with chaw'd-grasse. **1605** —— *Macb.* IV. i. 85 That I may tell pale-hearted Feare, it lies. **1624** MASSINGER *Parl. Love* IV. ii, Whose cruelty.. Would with more horror strike the pale-cheeked stars. **1629** MILTON *On Nativity* xix, The pale-ey'd Priest from the prophetic cell. **1688** *Lond. Gaz.* No. 2407/4 A..Man of a middle size,..and pale Complexion'd. **1746** *Brit. Mag.* 7 Yon overgrown pale-liver'd Rascal. **1789** PILKINGTON *View St. Derbysh.* I. 417 *Ranunculus hirsutus*, pale-leaved Crowfoot. **1820** KEATS *Ode to Psyche* in *Lamia & other Poems* 119 No shrine, no grove, no oracle, no heat Of pale-mouth'd prophet dreaming. **1876** GEO. ELIOT *Dan. Der.* II. xxv. 142 Deronda, who considered Grandcourt a pale-blooded mortal. **1913** D. H. LAWRENCE *Love Poems* 8 Pale-breasted throstles and a blackbird. **1918** D. H. LAWRENCE *New Poems* 32 Pale-blurred, with two round black drops.. my own reflection! *a* **1918** W. OWEN *Coll. Poems* (1963) 103 And when the land lay pale for them, pale-snowed. **1920** BLUNDEN *Waggoner* 33 But, alas, she falls in a swoon, Pale-lipped like a withering moon. **1921** W. DE LA MARE *Veil* 6 But with set, wild, unearthly eyes Pale-gleaming, fixed as if in fear, She couched in the water. **1954** J. R. R. TOLKIEN *Two Towers* III. iii. 52 Mist lay there, pale-glimmering in the last rays of the sickle moon. **1929** BLUNDEN *Near & Far* 46 While unamazed I view the siege of pale-starred horror raised By dawn.

b. Special Comb.: **pale crêpe** (or **crepe**) **(rubber)**, crêpe rubber of a pale yellowish colour, made by treating the latex with a chemical such as sodium bisulphite to prevent its turning brown.

1913 *India-Rubber Jrnl.* XLVI. 222/1 The preparation of pale crepe..is confined to the plantation rubber industry. *Ibid.*, In the preparation of pale crepe rubber the latex is coagulated in volumes varying from a few gallons to 500 or 600 gallons. **1937** [see CRÊPE 2]. **1938** C. F. FLINT *Chem. & Technol. Rubber Latex* iv. 126 Pale crêpe rubber may disappear from the market owing to the increasing use of latex for purposes for which pale crêpe was formerly used. **1970** *Encycl. Polymer Sci. & Technol.* XII. 187 Pale crepe is a long-established special rubber used for high-grade shoe soling and for applications needing a very light-colored, pure rubber.

pale (peɪl). *v.*[1] Now *rare.* Also 5–7 **payle**, 6 *Sc.* **peill**. [a. OF. *pale-r*, f. *pal* PALE *sb.*[1]: cf. L. *pālāre*, f. *pālus* stake.]

1. *trans.* To enclose with pales or a fence; to furnish with a fence; to encircle, surround, fence *in.*

c **1330** R. BRUNNE *Chron. Wace* (Rolls) 1055 þe kyng dide ȝyt pale hit efte. **1469** *Paston Lett.* II. 337 They..shulde payle certeine of the Parke of Weverston. *a* **1548** HALL *Chron., Hen. V* 65 b, The Frenchmen diched, trenched and paled their lodgynges. **1610** HEALEY *St. Aug. Citie of God* 179 Curtius the Consull payled it [the lake] about. **1667** DUCHESS OF NEWCASTLE *Life Dk. of N.* (1886) II. 137 He hath stocked and paled a little park belonging to it. **1706** LONDON & WISE *Retir'd Gardner* 24 A Trelliss, or Pole-Hedge, to pale up our Trees. **1778** *Eng. Gazetteer* (ed. 2) s.v. *Malwood-Castle*, K. Charles II. ordered it to be paled in. **1831** *Eastern Ross Farm Rep.* 89 in *Lib. Usef. Kn., Husb.* III, A hedge was planted,..paled on that side to protect the hedge until it should be able to protect itself.

b. *transf.* and *fig.* To encircle, encompass, hem in; to enclose as a paling or fence. Const. *in, up.*

1563–87 FOXE *A. & M.* (1596) 7/2 Yet it becommeth euerie man..there to keepe him, wherein his owne precinct dooth pale him. *c* **1596** *Declar. Fun. Lady K. Berkely* in *Gentl. Mag.* (1819) LXXXIX. I. 24 In the first aisle stood the foresaid 70 poor women, paling the passage on either side. **1599** SHAKS. *Hen. V*, V. Prol. 10 Behold the English beach Pales in the flood; With Men, Wiues, and Boyes. **1650** O. SEDGWICK *Christ the Life* Ep. Ded., He still desired that Justice might be as a River, and never coveted to pale it in as a pond for his private use. **1766** GOLDSM. *Vic. W.* xxvii, All our possessions are paled up with new edicts every day.

c. With *out*: To shut out or exclude by a fence.

1597 J. KING *On Jonas* (1618) 106 All the ground of the earth besides was paled out.

†**2.** To fix or stretch by means of stakes, to stake. *Sc. Obs.*

1584 *Reg. mag. Sig.* 28 Aug. (Rec. Ser.) 225/2 To haill, schutt, peill and draw nettis.

†**3.** To stripe, to mark or adorn with vertical stripes. *Obs.* (Almost always in pa. pple.: see PALED *ppl. a.*[1] 1, PALING *vbl. sb.*[1] 1.)

4. (See quot.) [Origin uncertain.]

1703 NEVE *City & C. Purchaser* 194 The Method of Paleing (as they call it,) or Soddering on of Imbost Figures on Leaden Work. *Ibid.*, Suppose a..Head in Bass-relief, were to be Pal'd on a Pump cistern for an Ornament..the Plate where it is to be pal'd on must be scrap'd very clean. **1734** *Builder's Dict.* II. B 7 b. **1881** *Archit. Publ. Soc. Dict.* s.v. *Paleing.*

pale (peɪl), *v.*[2] [ad. OF. *palir* (12th c.), F. *pâlir* to grow pale, make pale, f. *pâle* adj. pale; cf. L. *pall-ēre* to be pale, *pallesc-ēre* to become pale. See also PALL *v.*[1]]

1. a. *intr.* To grow pale or dim; to lose colour or brilliancy; to become pale in comparison. Also *fig.*

13.. *E. E. Allit. P.* A. 1003 þe calsydoyne þenne withouten wemme, In þe þryd table con purly pale. *c* **1430** *Syr Gener.* (Roxb.) 1559 Her colour gan to pale in hast. **1509** HAWES *Past. Pleas.* xix. (Percy Soc.) 92 Her gaye whyte coloure began for to pale. **1637** G. DANIEL *Genius of Isle* 140 The Red Rose pal'd, the White was soil'd in red. **1822** BOWLES *Grave of Last Saxon* I. 72 The morning stars Began to pale. **1860** J. W. WARTER *Sea-Board & Down* II. 458 All other beauty pales before the Beauty of Holiness. **1871** R. ELLIS *Catullus* lxviii. 138 Must I pale for a stray frailty?

b. In phr. *to pale into insignificance*: to lose importance (freq. in comparison with a greater achievement).

1909 *Daily Graphic* 26 July 10/1 He..made a flight of twenty-five miles across country; but that, of course, pales into insignificance by the side of the Channel flight. **1966** *Listener* 27 Oct. 602/1 This..will..be a standard biography upon a scale which will make..the rest pale into insignificance.

2. *trans.* To make pale, cause to become pale; to dim.

c **1374** CHAUCER *Boeth.* II. met. iii. 26 (Br. M. MS.) þe sterre ydimmyd paleþ hir white cheres by þe flamus of þe sonne. **1602** SHAKS. *Ham.* I. v. 90 The Glow-worme showes the Matine to be neere, And gins to pale his vneffectuall Fire. **1709** PRIOR *Solomon* III. 26 To..Pale it with Rage, or redden it with Shame. **1883** S. C. HALL *Retrospect* II. 287, I can..see his sunburnt face not yet paled by a month..in London.

†**pale**, *v.*[3] *Obs. rare.* [Derived ult. from L. *palliāre* or F. *pallier* (16th c. in Oresme).] = PALLIATE *v.* 3.

c **1400** *Lanfranc's Cirurg.* 91 It is an vnperfiȝt cure, but þou maist pale it [L. *palliare*], & do it awey þe stinche with hony waischinge. *Ibid.* 96 Sese fro þe verreye cure and turne ageyne to þe forseyde cure of þe oygnement of tuetye, whiche þat palyth þe cancre.

pale, *v.*[4] *dial.* [f. PALE *sb.*[3]] *trans.* To cut or scoop (cheese) with a cheese-scoop.

1728 RAMSAY *Fables* xi. 19 The cheese he pales, He prives, its good; ca's for the scales.

pale, *v.*[5] Now *dial.* [Origin uncertain. Darlington *S. Cheshire Folk-sp.* has *pale*, a barley-spike or awn: but cf. PAIL *v.*[2]] *trans.* To beat (barley) so as to detach the awns. Hence **paling** *vbl. sb.*; **paling-irons**, an implement with which barley is 'paled'.

1688 R. HOLME *Armoury* III. 74/1 Paling of Barley, is the beating of it, to get the beards from it. **1847–78** HALLIWELL, *Pale*, to beat barley. *Chesh.* **1887** DARLINGTON *South Cheshire Folk-sp.*, *Pale* v. to remove the awns of barley with 'paling-irons'.

pale, obs. form of PAIL *sb.*, PALL.

‖**palea** (ˈpeɪliːə). Pl. **-eæ** (-iːiː). [L. *palea* chaff.]

1. *Bot.* A chaff-like bract or scale; *esp.* the inner bracts enclosing the stamens and pistil in the flower of grasses (opposed to the *glumes* or outer bracts); also, those at the bases of the individual florets in many *Compositæ*; the scales on the stems of certain ferns.

1753 [see PALEACEOUS]. **1760** J. LEE *Introd. Bot.* I. viii. (1765) 16 *Palea*, a Chaff, is a thin Substance, springing from the Receptacle to part the Florets. **1830** LINDLEY *Nat. Syst. Bot.* 198 (*Compositæ*) *Bracteæ*..when present, stationed at the base of the florets, and called *paleæ of the receptacle. Ibid.* 292 The paleæ of Grasses approach the nature of a calyx. **1847** W. E. STEELE *Field Bot.* 179 Outer palea awned from the base or centre.

2. *Ornith.* A pendulous caruncle on the throat of a bird; a wattle or dewlap.

1890 in *Cent. Dict.*

paleaceous (peɪlɪˈeɪʃəs), *a. Bot.* [f. L. *palea* (see prec.) + -ACEOUS.] Furnished or covered with paleæ or chaff-like scales; of the nature or consistence of chaff; chaffy.

1753 CHAMBERS *Cycl. Supp.* s.v. *Receptaculum*, Its surface is sometimes naked, and sometimes paleaceous..all over beset with narrow pointed paleæ. **1816** *Encycl. Perth.* V. 639/2 The receptacle is paleaceous. **1825** *Greenhouse Comp.* I. 99 *Elichrysum*..Yellow paleaceous flowers of long duration. **1872** OLIVER *Elem. Bot.* II. 196.

Palearctic, var. PALÆARCTIC *a.*

paleate (ˈpeɪliːət), *a. Bot.* [ad. L. *paleātus*, f. *palea* chaff: see -ATE[2] 2.] Furnished with paleæ or chaffy scales; chaffy.

1880 GRAY *Struct. Bot.* v. (ed. 6) 147 When they [the bracts] are present, it [the receptacle] is paleate or chaffy.

So †ˈ**paleated** *a. Obs. rare*$^{-0}$.

1661 BLOUNT *Glossogr.* (ed. 2), *Paleated*.., made or mingled with chaff, full of chaff or straw.

palece, obs. form of PALACE.

paled (peɪld, *poet.* ˈpeɪlɪd), *ppl. a.*[1] [f. PALE *v.*[1] or *sb.*[1] + -ED.]

†**1.** Furnished or marked with (vertical) stripes; striped; in *Her.* = PALY. *Obs.*

1395 *E. E. Wills* (1882) 5 A bed paled blak and whit, with the tapites of sute. ? *a* **1400** *Morte Arth.* 1375 A preker.. That beres alle of pourpour, palyde with sylver. *c* **1530** LD. BERNERS *Arth. Lyt. Bryt.* (1814) 452 All in cotes of scarlet paled with grene. **1572** BOSSEWELL *Armorie* II. 30 b, Such Armes be called Armes pailed, for they bee made after the manner of payles. **1596** SPENSER *F.Q.* VI. ii. 6 Buskins he wore..Pinckt upon gold, and paled part per part.

2. Enclosed or furnished with pales; fenced.

1531 *Nottingham Rec.* III. 371 The paled garden in the Narro Mersshe. **1602** *2nd Pt. Return fr. Parnass.* II. i. 581 Musty mewes, where we haue spent Our youthfull dayes in paled langushment. **1795** *Fate of Sedley* II. 20 A little paled garden fronting the cottage. **1821** CLARE *Vill. Minstr.* I. 51 The paled road..The only path that freedom's rights maintain'd.

†**b.** *Bot.* Having 'pales' (PALE *sb.*[1] 7). *Obs.*

1704 *Dict. Rust.*, *Paled-Flowers*, ..those..that have Leaves set about a Head or Thrum, as in Marigolds. **1782** *Chambers' Cycl.* (ed. Rees), *Paled flowers.*

3. Constructed with pales or vertical bars.

1816 *Sporting Mag.* XLVIII. 27 The poachers.. advanced down the ride towards the paled gate.

paled (as prec.), *ppl. a.*^{2} *rare.* [f. PALE *v.*^{2} + -ED^{1}.] Rendered pale. Hence **'paledness.**

1593 T. WATSON *Teares Fancie* xix, Eies in their teares my paled face disclosed. **1594** R. CAREW *Tasso* (1881) 55 Seely children, and vnarmed old, And womens rout of feare ypaled hew. **1648** J. BEAUMONT *Psyche* VII. lxxi, Her doubtful Look, Where Paledness and Blushes mutually Their timorous and graceful station took.

paled, obs. form of *palled*: see PALL *v.*

pale-face ('peɪlfeɪs). **1.** A person who has a pale face; a name for a white man attributed to the North American Indians.

1822 in *G. A. McCall's Lett. fr. Frontiers* (1868) 72 [At a masquerade ball, a man dressed as] an Indian chief..thus accosted him,—'Ah, Paleface! what brings you here?' **1831** *Ibid.* 226. **1826** F. COOPER *Mohicans* iv, 'The pale faces make themselves dogs to their women', muttered the Indian, in his native language. **1851** MAYNE REID *Scalp Hunters* xxxviii. 292 They know it to be the war-trumpet of the pale faces! **1895** S. R. HOLE *Tour in Amer.* 237 Julius Berge was the first pale-face born here [Whitewater] some fifty-four years ago.

2. In American Blacks' use, a contemptuous term for a white man.

1945 MENCKEN *Amer. Lang.* Suppl. I. 637 The Negroes use various other sportive terms for whites, *e.g., pale-face, chalk* and *milk.* **1964** *N.Y. Times Mag.* 23 Aug. 62/2 *Whitey*, the latest word of contempt for a white person, superseding *ofay* and..*paleface.* **1971** *Publ. Amer. Dial. Soc. 1969* LI. 33 To Negroes, a white convict is a..*paddy, pale face.* **1971** E. E. LANDY *Underground Dict.* 145 *Pale face*, (B) white person.

pale-faced ('peɪlfeɪst), *a.* Having a pale face; pale in complexion, or (*fig.*) in aspect.

1592 SHAKS. *Ven. & Ad.* 569 Affection faints not like a pale-faced coward. **1635** QUARLES *Embl.* II. ii. 15 The pale-faced lady of the black-ey'd night. **1758** GOLDSM. *Mem. Protestant* (1895) I. 192 He was humped-back'd, pale-faced [etc.]. **1841** CATLIN *N. Amer. Ind.* (1844) II. lviii. 229 The Indian's inferiority to their pale-faced neighbours. **1893** *Scribner's Mag.* June 743/1 The vast wealth of pale-faced lotos and shrinking water-lilies.

palefrai, -fray, -frey, etc., obs. ff. PALFREY.

palefrenier: see PALFRENIER.

paleiform ('peɪliːɪfɔːm), *a. Nat. Hist.* [f. L. *palea* (see PALEA) + -(I)FORM.] Having the form or appearance of chaff; chaffy. (Mayne, 1857.)

paleis, obs. form of PALACE; var. PALIS *Obs.*

Palekh ('pɑːlɛk). The name of a town in Ivanovo province in northwest U.S.S.R. used *attrib.* to designate the iconography for which the town was renowned in the 18th century, and also a type of miniature painting on such articles as boxes and trays which was developed there during the 19th century.

[**1916** R. NEWMARCH *Russian Arts* iii. 65 Palekh 'the heart-centre of Russian popular ikonography'.] **1960** *Guardian* 1 Dec. 10/6 A Russian and Bulgarian shop opens in London tomorrow... There should be a rush on..examples of palekh iconography. **1963** M. CHAMOT *Russ. Painting & Sculpture* i. 7 The famous Palekh work, as it is called from the village where it is produced, is executed with incredible delicacy and carries on to this day something of the inventiveness and charm of early Russian Painting. **1964** *Punch* 16 Dec. p. xii, Gifts at the Russian Shop..include.. Palekh painted boxes. **1976** *Times* 19 Mar. 16/6 A sale of Russian and Greek icons totalled £35,609... A private buyer paid £1,400 for an early nineteenth-century Palekh school calendar.

palely ('peɪllɪ), *adv.* Also 6 paly. [f. PALE *a.* + -LY^{2}.] In a pale manner; with a pale look or appearance; dimly, wanly.

a **1548** HALL *Chron., Edw. IV* 237 Ihon Cheulet..there stode so sadly and so paly, without any worde speakyng, that [etc.]. *a* **1718** PENN *Sandy Found. Shaken* Wks. 1726 I. 250 T. V. came very palely down the Stairs. **1817** MOORE *Lalla R., Fire-worshippers* 358 The morn..o'er the Green Sea palely shines. **1880** L. WALLACE *Ben-Hur* IV. x. 225 If he looked up, it was to see the sky palely blue.

pale maille: see PALL-MALL.

†**'paleman.** *Obs.* [f. PALE *sb.*^{1} + MAN *sb.*]

1. = PALER.

1503 *Acc. Ld. High Treas. Scot.* II. 372 Item..to the pale men of the park of Strivelin..in drinksilver, xiiij s.

2. A man of the English Pale in Ireland.

1851 KELLY tr. *Cambrensis Eversus* III. 158 *note*, A feeling for other Irishmen not unlike what the old palemen had against the mere Irish.

palempore, -pour: see PALAMPORE.

palen ('peɪlən), *v. rare*$^{-1}$. [f. PALE *a.* + -EN^{5}.] *trans.* To make pale, cause to turn pale.

1790 W. TAYLOR tr. *Goethe's Iph. in Tauris* (R.), So turn'd the sun His palen'd visage from the damned deed.

palendar: see PALANDER.

paleness ('peɪlnɪs). [f. PALE *a.* + -NESS.] The condition or quality of being pale; pallor.

a **1340** HAMPOLE *Psalter* lxvii[i]. 14 þe hyndire of hire bak in palnes of gold [L. *pallore auri*]. *c* **1440** *Promp. Parv.* 378/2 Palenesse, of colowre, *pallor.* **1578** LYTE *Dodoens* II. xcii. 273 [It] taketh away the colour, and bringeth such a paalnesse, as is in dead bodies. **1661** LOVELL *Hist. Anim. & Min.* Introd., Melancholick diseases, palenesse, and smallnesse of pulse. **1797** MRS. RADCIFFE *Italian* i. (1826) 8 Her countenance changed to an ashy paleness. **1835** URE *Phil. Manuf.* 395 Natural paleness, and that paleness proceeding from bad health, are readily distinguished by the town practitioner.

Comb. **1654** WHITLOCK *Zootomia* 429 Their Palenesse-breeding Labours wo'n't yeild Sack.

palenkeen, obs. form of PALANKEEN.

‖**palenque** (pa'lenke). *Jamaica.* [Sp., = enclosure.] (See quots.)

1707 SLOANE *Jamaica* I. p. xvii, A Palenque is here a place for bringing up poultry. **1873** GARDNER *Jamaica* 80 The little farms called palenques.

palentine, obs. form of PALATINE.

paleo-: see PALÆO-.

†**'paleous**, *a. Obs. rare.* [f. L. *palea* chaff + -OUS.] Of the nature of chaff; chaffy.

1646 SIR T. BROWNE *Pseud. Ep.* II. iv. (1686) 60 This attraction have we tried in straws and paleous bodies.

palepuntz: see PUNCH *sb.*, the beverage.

†**'paler.** *Obs.* [f. PALE *v.*^{1} + -ER^{1}.] One who puts up a paling or fence; an officer of a park charged with keeping the fences in repair.

1464 *Mann. & Househ. Exp.* (Roxb.) 275 My mastyr payd to the paler for wagys, vj. *s.* viij. *d.* **1647** HAWARD *Crown Revenue* 51 Paler of the Park. **1670** *St. Papers, Dom.* 14 The offices of Keeper of the Middle Park and Bushy Park, and of paler thereof. **1800** D. LYSONS *Env. London, Suppl.* 74 With the custody of the parks, has been held two other offices, called paler of the parks, and mower of the brakes.

Palermitan (pə'lɜːmɪtən), *sb.* and *a.* [ad. It. *palermitano.*] **A.** *sb.* A native or inhabitant of the Sicilian town or province of Palermo. **B.** *adj.* Of, pertaining to, or characteristic of Palermo.

1673 J. RAY *Observations Journey Low-Countries* 279 There is a great emulation and enmity between the Palermitans and Messanese, which involves the whole Island. **1826** M. KELLY *Reminisc.* I. 80 The Palermitans are all fond of music. **1835** N. P. WILLIS *Pencillings by Way* I. xxi. 257 The oddity of the Palermitan style of building struck me forcibly. **1847** J. H. NEWMAN *Let.* 25 Aug. (1962) XII. 109 There was a Palermitan father at dinner... He has warmly invited us to Palermo. **1908** *Westm. Gaz.* 6 July 4/2 The editor..is a Palermitan, and his family is the Sicilian branch of the Roman Colonnas. **1936** G. F.-H. & J. BERKELEY *Italy in Making* II. xxii. 339 Even in Sicily, La Masa and his Palermitans would rise against Ferdinand with shouts of 'Viva Pio Nono!' **1961** *Times* 14 Jan. 9/2 Palermo's cathedral church..is in its own way more typically 'palermitan' than them all. **1968** D. M. SMITH *Medieval Sicily* x. 110 St. Cristina's fair during which Palermitans had had the valuable privilege of not paying customs or excise duty. **1978** *Harpers & Queen* Sept. 42/4 We had.. spaghetti con sarda, a Palermitan dish, with sardines, fennel and raisins.

†**Pa'lermo.** *Obs.* A wine from Palermo in Sicily.

1584 LYLY *Campaspe* I. ii. 89 O for a Bowle of fatt Canary, Rich Palermo, sparkling Sherry. **1632** MASSINGER *Maid of Honour* III. i, Till I set my foot In Sicily again, and drink Palermo.

paleron, obs. form of PAULDRON.

pales, obs. f. PALACE; var. PALIS *Obs.*

†**'palesate**, *v. Obs. rare*$^{-1}$. [f. late med.L. *palezāre* (Du Cange), ad. It. *palesare* 'to reveal, bewray, publish' (Florio), f. *palese* public, in open view:—L. type **palensis*, f. *palam* adv. openly, publicly. Cf. OF. *palaiser, paliser* and *palesement* sb., and see -ATE^{3}.] *trans.* To manifest, reveal.

1613 SHERLEY *Trav. Persia* 35 The counsell of the Turke had not palesated itselfe openly.

palesman ('peɪlzmən). *rare.* [f. *pale's* (PALE *sb.*^{1}, sense 4) + MAN; cf. *dalesman.*] = PALEMAN 2.

1894 P. J. MCCALL *Irish Nóinins, Green Woods of Slew* 27 The Palesmen he vanquished; they parleyed with you.

paless, palesser, var. PALIS, PALISER *Obs.*

†**palester.** *Obs.* [f. PALE *v.*^{1} + -STER, or var. of *palesser*, PALISER.] = PALER, PALISER.

1574 in J. J. Cartwright *Hist. Yorks.* (1872) 74 Fees to the keeper and palester.

Palestine ('pæləstaɪn). The name of a territory on the eastern shore of the Mediterranean (see next) used *attrib.* to designate a cream soup made from Jerusalem artichokes.

1834 J. ROMILLY *Diary* 13 Apr. (1967) 55 He told us that he had given Palestine Soup yesterday: he asked the B. of London the origin of the name..he told him it was because it was made of Jerusalem Artichokes. **1861** MRS. BEETON *Bk. Househ. Managem.* 912 (*heading*) Dinner for 6 persons. .. First course. Palestine soup. **1907** *Yesterday's Shopping* (1969) 41/1 Soups..Palestine—0/8½. **1929** A. E. HOUSMAN *Let.* 14 Sept. (1971) 284, I was however agreeably surprised by a Palestine soup which had not the faintest trace of artichoke. **1970** SIMON & HOWE *Dict. Gastron.* 287/1 *Palestine soup*, the term for a soup made of Jerusalem artichokes.

Palestinian (ˌpælə'stɪnɪən), *a.* and *sb.* [f. *Palestine* (see below) + -IAN.]

The name *Palestine* is derived from Gr. *Παλαιστίνη* (used in early Christian writing), L. *Palaestina* (the name of the Roman province), and designates that territory on the eastern Mediterranean coast which in biblical times comprised the kingdoms of Israel and Judah. There have been many changes in the frontiers in the course of history. It was revived as an official political title for the land west of the Jordan mandated to Britain in 1920. Palestine ceased to exist as a political entity in 1948 when the state of Israel was established, but the name continues to be used to describe a geographical entity, particularly in the context of Arab aims for the resettlement of people who left the area when the state of Israel was established.

A. *adj.* Of, pertaining to, or connected with Palestine.

1875 *Encycl. Brit.* II. 181/1 The books bearing this name are not contained in the Jewish or Palestinian Canon. **1902** D. G. HOGARTH *Nearer East* 163 The Palestinian highlands. **1920** *Glasgow Herald* 13 July 6 Mr. Balfour said that for long he had been a convinced Zionist but..he never foresaw.. that the great work of Palestinian reconstruction would happen so soon. **1934** [see GÖTTERDÄMMERUNG]. **1936** A. W. CLAPHAM *Romanesque Archit.* v. 113 Certain churches in southern Italy..show evidence of being the product of the Palestinian school. **1936** *Discovery* Aug. 250/1 Palestinian objects of the Bronze Age. **1949** *Radio Times* 15 July 27/2 Musa Alami, a prominent Palestinian Arab. **1962** *New Jewish Encycl.* 476/1 The initial compilation of the Palestinian Talmud is ascribed to Rabbi Johanen ben Nappaha (third century). **1972** *Guardian* 4 Sept. 3/7 Black September operations do generate a local Palestinian activism. **1973** *Jewish Chron.* 2 Feb. 22/4 Eventually the teachings of the Palestinian Amoraim were gathered together to form the Palestinian Talmud. **1976** *Daily Tel.* 30 June 4/8 He accused the Syrians of collaborating with the Right-wing Christians to suppress the Palestinian commando movement. **1977** M. MAZZAWI in *Times* 13 June 14/1 This promise, coupled with 30 years' occupation of the country by Britain, and compounded by a decision of the United Nations in 1947, has resulted in the Palestinian people (who now number three million) being either in refugee camps, in exile, or under alien military rule.

B. *sb.* A native or inhabitant of Palestine in biblical or later times.

1905 *Daily Chron.* 31 July 5/3 Territorialists..flooded the hall with leaflets declaring that 200 Russian Palestinians were illegally present. **1909** *Ibid.* 9 Sept. 3/6 Those who are for a mass return to the country of their origin..are termed 'Palestinians'. **1920** *Glasgow Herald* 12 July 12 The higher ranks of the Civil Service..would consist mainly of British officials until an increasing number of Palestinians were fully qualified... Other ranks would be open to Palestinians, irrespective of creed. **1968** *Guardian* 12 May 9/3 The other card the Israelis reckon to play is the Palestinians' actual experience of Israeli occupation. **1973** *Ibid.* 21 Apr. 12/1 The Arabs..[must] put the rights of the Palestinians (to the exclusion of Israel) before anything else. **1974** *Times* 30 Oct. 15/3 King Husain..is not himself a Palestinian and indeed has a vested interest in preventing the assertion of a distinct Palestinian identity. **1977** *Listener* 19 May 642/1, I do not necessarily equate the Palestinians with the PLO: can you rationally and logically expect me to go along with the covenant that says that the liberation of Palestine means to purge the Zionist presence from Palestine. **1977** M. MAZZAWI in *Times* 13 June 14/2 The Palestinians who left their homes were driven out by danger and threats. **1979** *Time* 13 Aug. 13/2 The Administration's first goal then, would be to bring Palestinians, perhaps even some P.L.O. officials, into the talks between the Israelis and the Egyptians on the future of the West Bank and Gaza.

palestra, etc.: see PALÆSTRA, etc.

Palestrinian (pælə'strɪnɪən), *a.* [f. the name *Palestrin(a* (see below) + -IAN.] Of, pertaining to, or in the style of the Italian composer Giovanni Pierluigi da Palestrina (*c* 1525–94).

1954 *Grove's Dict. Mus.* (ed. 5) VI. 512/1 Equally important, in any examination of the Palestrinian style, is it to bear in mind the fact that the order of publication of such of his works as appeared in the composer's lifetime offers no reliable evidence as to date of composition. **1958** *Listener* 2 Oct. 540/1 There always was a Palestrinian tradition.

palesy, -ie, etc., obs. forms of PALSY.

palet ('peɪlɪt). *Bot.* [f. PALE *sb.*^{4} + -ET^{1}: cf. F. *paillette*, dim. of *paille* straw.] = PALEA 1.

1880 GRAY *Struct. Bot.* v. (ed. 6) 142 *Palets*, ..also called Chaff, are diminutive or chaff-like bracts or bractlets on the axis (or receptacle) and among the flowers of a dense inflorescence, such as a head of Compositæ..; and the name is also given to an inner series of the Glumes of Grasses.

palet, obs. form of PALATE, PALLET.

paleth'nology, shortened form of *palæethnology*: see PALÆO-, PALEO-.

a **1898** BRINTON in Haddon *Study of Man* 493.

‖**paletot** ('pælətəʊ, 'pæltəʊ). [mod.F. *paletot* (palto, in verse palǝto), formerly *palletot* (1403 in Godef. *Compl.*), *palletocq* (1455), *palto* (1505), *paletoc* (16th c.), *palletoc* (Cotgr. 1611); cf. *paltof* (1483 in Godef.); also Sp. *paletoque*, Breton *paltôk*: of uncertain derivation: see PALTOCK.] A loose outer garment, coat, or cloak, for men or women.

1840 LOUISA S. COSTELLO *Summer amongst Bocages* II. 206 A man of about five-and-twenty, attired in a kind of furred palletot. **1844** ALB. SMITH *Adv. Mr. Ledbury* vi.

(1886) 20 Some wore dark blouses; others paletôts—a species of light shooting-jacket. **1864** MRS. H. WOOD *Trev. Hold* I. xi. 182 She wore a puce silk paletot, as they are called, made coat fashion, and a brown hat. **1892** J. KENT *Racing Life Ld. G. Cavendish Bentinck* i. 7 Wearing a light-coloured zephyr paletot above his scarlet [hunting-] coat.

paletoted ('pælətəʊd), *a. nonce-wd.* [f. PALETOT + -ED².] Provided with, or wearing, a paletot.
1947 V. NABOKOV *Bend Sinister* 34 A mild bore who used to take out his two polite paletoted dachsunds at nightfall.

palett, -ette, obs. forms of PALLET.

palette ('pælɪt). Forms: 7–9 **pallet,** (7–8 **pallat**), 8– **palette,** 9 (sense 2) **pallette.** [a. F. *palette* (of which the painter's palette is one of many senses), dim. of *pale* shovel, blade of oar:—L. *pāla* spade, shovel, baker's peel, shoulder-blade; cf. It. *pala* spade, shovel, peel, blade, plate, etc.; dim. *paletta* flat spoon, trowel, battledore, apothecary's spatula. (The Ital. word for painter's palette is *tavolozza,* dim. of *tavola.*)]

1. a. A flat thin tablet of wood or porcelain, used by an artist to lay and mix his colours on.
Its ordinary form is more or less oval, with a hole for the left thumb.
1622 PEACHAM *Compl. Gent.* xiii. (1634) 130 Having all your colours ready ground, with your pallet on the thumbe of your left hand..lay your colours upon your pallet thus. **1658** PHILLIPS, A *Pallat* [ed. **1706** *-et*], ..a thin piece of wood which a Painter makes use of to place his colours upon. **1727** GAY *Fables* I. xviii. 34 All things were set; the hour was come, His pallet ready o'er his thumb. *a* **1783** H. BROOKE *Temple of Hymen* Poems (1810) 406/1 On his left hand a palette lay, With many a teint of colours gay. **1859** GULLICK & TIMBS *Paint.* 199 Artists differ greatly in the number of tints they arrange on the palette.
fig. **1824** GALT *Rothelan* I. II. v. 188 The colours on our pallet consist of the universal elements and properties of the heart. **1868** J. E. A. BROWN *Lights through Lattice* 28 And now the Spring..From her bright palette brought the emerald of the young corn, and of the indigo.

b. *transf.* The set or selection of colours used by a particular artist or for a particular picture.
1882 HAMERTON *Graphic Arts* xxi. 238 It is impossible to give Turner's palettes, which probably varied very much at different times. **1890** *Spectator* 17 May 694/2 He has..a palette of his own that gives pleasure to a great many artists.

c. Of sounds (*spec.* in music): variety or range of tonal or instrumental colour (see COLOUR *sb.* 15).
1959 [see DEBUSSYAN *a.* and *sb.*]. **1965** *Listener* 28 Oct. 680/2 If you want to be reminded of his mastery of the orchestra and the richness of his [*sc.* Ravel's] instrumental palette, listen again to *Daphnis et Chloé*, and the *Rapsodie espagnole.* **1975** *Broadcast* 3 Nov. 14/3 Relaxed circumambient dialogue... You may find Pinter's subdued palette somewhat baffling. **1977** *Listener* 7 Apr. 452/1 The shock of moving from one tonal palette to another.

2. a. A name given to a small rounded plate formerly used in armour to protect the armpit.
1834 PLANCHÉ *Brit. Costume* 186 Two circular plates called pallettes, are sometimes fastened to them in front so as to protect the armpit. **1853** —— *Mon. Cockayne Fam.* in *Archæol. Jrnl.* 379 A pair of plates to protect the arm-pits called pallettes, introduced in the reign of Henry V. **1860** FAIRHOLT *Costume in Eng.* (ed. 2) Gloss., *Palettes.*

b. The breast-plate by means of which pressure is applied to the hand-drill: see BREAST-PLATE 3 b.
1875 in Knight *Dict. Mech.*

†**3.** An instrument of wood shaped like a spatula or palette-knife, formerly used for massage. *Obs.*
1857 in DUNGLISON. **1887** D. MAGUIRE *Art of Massage* (ed. 4) 20 The palette, which is also called ferule, tapette, battoir,..is an instrument..ending at one extremity in a handle, and the other in a disc.

4. *Zool.* A disc-like structure in certain animals. **a.** *Conch.* An accessory valve in some molluscs. **b.** *Entom.* A flat expansion upon the legs of some insects.
1834 MCMURTRIE *Cuvier's Anim. Kingd.* 269 (Teredo) The base..is furnished on each side with a stony and moveable kind of operculum or palette. **1863** BATES *Nat. Amazon* viii. (1864) 229 The female of the handsome golden-and-black *Euglossa Surinamensis* has this palette of very large size.

5. A parrot of the genus *Prioniturus* (racket-tailed parakeets): from the appearance of the tail, which with its two long spatulate central feathers suggests a painter's palette and brushes.
1890 in *Cent. Dict.*

6. In certain card games, a device used by the banker to facilitate the movement of cards and money.
1949 J. SCARNE *On Cards* (1955) xxi. 205 The croupier, squatting in the concavity of the kidney table, needs an ebony-finish palette to slide the cash and cards around. **1966** 'W. HAGGARD' *Power House* xi. 114 The croupier had one hand on the shoe, the other playing with the *palette.* **1968** D. TORR *Treason Line* 105 Vittoria's mother had invited him..for his dexterity in wielding the *palette.* As *chef de partie* in the high chair he could run a game of baccarat *banque* or chemin-de-fer as slickly as any professional.

7. *attrib.* and *Comb.*
1896 *Cosmopolitan* XX. 407/2 Art..holds forth her willing palette-laden hand to Youth. **1900** *Westm. Gaz.* 28 July 8/2 We have received a new Palette Album.., giving a series of views in colours of scenery in the English Lake District.

palette-knife. a. A thin flexible blade of steel fitted with a handle, of various forms, used for mixing colours on a palette, for distributing printing-ink on a surface, for spreading oil-paint on canvas, and similar purposes. Also *attrib.*
1759 COLEBROOKE in *Phil. Trans.* LI. 46 When the ground was near dry, I smoothed it with a pallat-knife. **1785** J. REYNOLDS *Discourse to Students of R. Acad.* 28 Rembrandt, in order to take the advantage of accident, appears often to have used the palate-knife [*sic*] to lay his colours on the canvass. **1811** *Self Instructor* 518 Take your pallet knife.. scrape your colour together. **1859** GULLICK & TIMBS *Paint.* 199 The Palette-knife, or Spatula, has a pliable blade. **1931** L. RICHMOND *Technique Oil Painting* xi. 86 With palette knife painting..the charm lies to a certain extent in accidental qualities. **1938** D. SHARP *Student's Bk. Oil Painting* vii. 45 A different style of work is palette-knife painting, and this method certainly gives a very fascinating texture to a picture. **1958** *Times* 11 Mar. 3/4 Aix-en-Provence has a 'Self-portrait' with heavy impasto ascribed to Rembrandt (which arrived there in 1863 a year or two before Cézanne painted his palette-knife studies of 'Uncle Dominique'). **1967** W. GAUNT *Compan. Painting* 93 Some equivalent of work with the spatula may be found in the practice of palette-knife painting. **1970** *Oxf. Compan. Art* 562/1 Some modern artists, working with palette knife or fingers or squeezing paint from the tube, have treated oil paint almost as if it were a substance for modelling.

b. A similar instrument used as a culinary tool.
1889 A. B. MARSHALL *Cookery Bk.* iii. 41 Royal Icing... Put on to the cake with a clean palette knife. **1906** MRS. BEETON *Bk. Househ. Managem.* xlvii. 1431 Scrape down the sides with a palette-knife, and with the point of the knife mix in all the material scraped down. **1951** E. DAVID *French Country Cooking* 20 A first-class pliable palette knife,..a selection of wooden spoons. **1975** *Habitat Catal.* 64 Kitchen equipment... Palette knife. Wood handle, steel blade.

Hence **palette-knifing,** the use of a palette-knife.
1891 R. KIPLING *Light that Failed* v, I know what palette-knifing means.

†**palew,** *a.* (*sb.*) *Obs.* Also **pallew.** [app. a derivative of PALE *a.*; but the nature of the formation is obscure. The later authors appear simply to follow Recorde.] Light or pale yellow.
1547 RECORDE *Judic. Ur.* viii. 31 Palew and lyght safferne ..are the best coloures. *Ibid.* 32. *Ibid.* 66 b, After it followyth pallew, which is a kynde of light yellow, sum thing lyghter in colour then Crowne golde. **1607** WALKINGTON *Opt. Glass* 108 The first is *vitellina bilis* of the colour of an egge yolke generated of palew choler. **1625** HART *Anat. Ur.* II. iii. 62 This colour is called..*Subrufus, subaureus,* or *subcroceus*: in English, palew, or light saffron.

† '**paleway,** *adv. Her. Obs.* = next.
1705 *Lond. Gaz.* No. 4163/3 All engraved with 3 Escallop Shells Pale-way.

paleways ('peɪlweɪz), *adv. Her.* ? *Obs.* [f. PALE *sb.*¹ + -WAYS.] = next. (In quot. 1610 = PALY.)
1610 GUILLIM *Heraldry* v. ii. (1611) 243 To these will I adde..an Italian Coat of rare use viz. palewaies of six argent and gules on a chiefe as the field is many cressants. **1691** WOOD *Ath. Oxon., Fasti* I. 646 And hath behind it, paleways [*ed.* 1721 palewise], an Abbats Crosier. **1769** *New Peerage* I. 270 Two demi garters paleways, argent.

palewise ('peɪlwaɪz), *adv. Her.* [f. PALE *sb.*¹ + -WISE.] In the direction of a pale; vertically (either in the middle of the shield = *in pale,* or in any part of the shield).
1721 [see PALEWAYS, quot. 1691]. **1864** BOUTELL *Her. Hist. & Pop.* viii. 36 Paly Bendy..is produced by lines drawn palewise, crossed by others drawn bendwise. **1867** —— *Eng. Heraldry* (1875) 142 *Pale-wise,* or In Pale..that is, set vertically, or arranged vertically one above another.

paley, variant of PALY *a.*¹

paleyce, -eys, obs. ff. PALACE; var. PALIS *Obs.*

palfrenier (pælfrə'nɪə(r)). *arch.* Forms: 5 palfreynyer, -frenyer, 9 palefrenier, -freneer, palfrenier. [a. F. *palefrenier* (1350 in Godef. *Compl.*), also *pare-, palfrenier* = It. *palafreniere,* Sp. *palafrenero,* Pg. *palafreneiro,* med.L. *pala-, palefrenarius, -frenerius, -fridiarius,* orig. *paraverēdārius* (*Lex Baiwar., Capitulare de Villis,* Du Cange), f. *paraverēdus*: see next and -IER 2.] A man having charge of horses; a groom.
c **1489** CAXTON *Sonnes of Aymon* x. 257 Mawgys sayd to yᵉ palfreynyer that kepte bayerde 'frende, goo & set the sadell vpon bayerde'..'syr', sayd yᵉ palfrenyer, 'I may not doo it'. **1820** SCOTT *Monast.* xxxv, A legion of godless lackeys, and palfreniers, and horse-boys. **1840** THACKERAY *Paris Sk.-bk.* (1872) 74 He calls his palefrenier a groom. **1863** SALA *Capt. Dangerous* II. iv. 147 Palefreneers littered him down with straw, as though he had been a Horse.

palfrey ('pɔːlfrɪ, 'pæl-). Forms: 2–4 palefrai, 3 -frei, -fray, 3–4 -frey, 4 palfre, 4–6 -frei, 4–7 -fray, 4– palfrey, (5 palfroy(e, 5–7 -freie, -freye, -fraie, -fraye, 6 paulfrey, pawlfre, 7 palfery, palefroy, palphrie, -frie, -fry, 8 -phry). [ME. a. OF. *palefrei,* in 11th c. *palefreid* (later *palefroy, -froi*:—late L. *palafrēd-us,* by dissimilation from *parafrēdus, -vrēdus* (in *Capit. Charlemagne*):—late L. *paraverēdus* (6th c.), f. Gr. παρά beside, extra + *verēdus* light horse, post-horse. Cognate Romanic forms are Pr. *palafre, -frei,* Sp. †*palafré, palafren,* Pg. *palafrem,* It. *palafreno*; in med.L. also *parefredus, -fridus, palafridus, palefredus, -fridus, palfredus, pala-, palefrenus*: see Du Cange. The forms in *-frenus, -freno, -fren* (whence *palfrenier*), show popular association with L. *frēnum,* It. *freno* bridle, rein.
Parafrēdus also passed into German: OLG. *parafrid, parevrit*; MLG. *pêrid,* LG. *perd,* MDu. *paert,* Du. *paard*; OHG. *pfarifrid, pferfrit*; MHG. *pferit*; Ger. *pferd*; the ordinary word for 'horse'.]

A saddle-horse for ordinary riding as distinguished from a war-horse; *esp.* a small saddle-horse for ladies. (Now *Hist.,* or in romantic or poetic lang.)
c **1175** *Lamb. Hom.* 5 He mihte ridan..on riche stede and palefrai. *c* **1200** *Trin. Coll. Hom.* 89 Noðer stede ne palefrei, ne fair mule. *c* **1330** R. BRUNNE *Chron. Wace* (Rolls) 11184 Many fair palfray & stede. *c* **1386** CHAUCER *Prol.* 207 His palfrey was as broun as is a berye. *c* **1450** *Merlin* xvi. 260 Thei lefte theire palfreyes and lepe upon stedes covered in maile. **1470–85** MALORY *Arthur* II. vi, A damoysel that came ryde ful fast..on a fayr palfroy. *a* **1547** HEN. VIII in Ellis *Orig. Lett.* Ser. I. II. 32 Some faire white, or white gray palfreies, or geldings. **1556** WITHALS *Dict.* (1568) 16 a/1 A pawlfre, *cantherius candidus.* **1614** CHAPMAN *Maske Inns of Crt.* 2 Dwarfe Palfries, with yellow foot-cloathes. **1719** D'URFEY *Pills* (1872) IV. 10 A Palphry proud, prick'd up with Pride, Went prancing on the way. **1803** SOUTHEY *Queen Orraca* IV. vii, Upon her palfrey she is set, And forward then they go. **1813** SCOTT *Trierm.* II. xiv, A maiden on a palfrey white. **1856** R. A. VAUGHAN *Mystics* (1860) I. 9 The fair damosels of the olden time on their palfreys. **1859** TENNYSON *Geraint & Enid* 126 [He] shook his drowsy squire awake and cried, 'My charger and her palfrey'.

b. *attrib.* and *Comb.,* as ***palfrey-man, -mare, -money, -page.***
1297 *Placita coram Rege* m. 39 (1897) 263 Ricardus le Palfreyman. **1360–1** *Durham Acc. Rolls* (Surtees) 562 Perot palfraypage Prioris. *a* **1500** *Mankind* (Brandl 1896) 240 And ȝe were þe kynges palfrey mare. **1502** *Will Ep. Cicest.* (Somerset Ho.), Soluendum post decessum meas domino Regi debitas pro le palfray money. **1530** PALSGR. 251/1 Palfrayman, *palefronier.*

Hence, '**palfreyed** *a.* [-ED²], provided with or riding on a palfrey.
1713 TICKELL *On Prospect of Peace* Poems (1790) 159 The bard, that tells Of palfrey'd dames, bold knights, and magic spells.

†**palfreyour.** *Obs.* Forms: [3 **palfreur, palefreyur**], 4 **palefreiour,** 7 **palfreour, palfrer.** [a. AF. *palefreyur, -our,* f. *palefrei* PALFREY + -OUR.] = PALFRENIER.
[**1297** *Placita coram Rege* (1897) 72 Ricardum le Palfreur'. **1300** *Pat. Roll* 28 *Edw. I,* m. 15d. in *Calendar* 550 Adam le Palefreyur, Henry le Palefreyur.] *a* **1327** *Pol. Songs* (Camden) 237 Palefreiours ant pages, Ant boyes with boste. **1601** F. TATE *Househ. Ord. Edw. II* §87 (1876) 52 Al palfreours & somters of the kinges house. *Ibid.* §90. 55 For the palfrers & coursers j herberger named.

palgrave: see PALSGRAVE.

Pali ('pɑːlɪ), *sb.* and *a.* Also **Pāli, Páli,** [Short for *pāli-bhāsā,* i.e. language of the canonical texts (as opposed to 'commentary'), f. *pāli* line, canon + *bhāsā* language.]

1. a. The language used in the canonical books of the Buddhists, composed in North India. This 'Middle High Indian' was the literary form of the language spoken in Kosala, the country now called the Uttar Pradesh (Oudh, etc.), which was the *lingua franca* of North India from the 6th or 5th to the 2nd century B.C. Also often used to include **b.** The language of the chronicles, commentaries, and other literary works of later Buddhists, which bears the same relation to the language of the canonical texts as mediæval bears to classical Latin; and **c.** The kindred language used in the early Indian inscriptions.
[**1693** A.P. tr. *De la Loubère's Siam* 9 The terms of Religion and Justice, the names of Offices, and all the Ornaments of the [Siamese] Vulgar Tongue are borrow'd from the Balie.] **1800** SYMES *Embassy to Ava* 338 That the Pali, the sacred language of the priests of Boodh, is nearly allied to the Shanscrit of the Bramins. **1833** TANDY tr. *Sangermano's Burmese Emp.* 141 The grammar of the Pali language or Magatà. *Ibid.,* All these books are written in the Pali tongue. **1837** G. TURNOUR *Mahāwanso* Introd. 22 Buddhists are impressed with the conviction that their sacred and classical language, the Mágadhi or Páli, is of greater antiquity than the Sanscrit. **1871** ALABASTER *Wheel of Law* 246 Others believe that Pali..was the vernacular language of Magadha, the Holy Land of Buddhism. **1877** RHYS DAVIDS *Buddhism* 237 A list of the Pali commentaries now extant. **1903** —— *Buddhist India* 152 Pali is a literary language based on the dialect of Kosala.

2. ***Pali plague***: see quots.
1869 E. A. PARKES *Pract. Hygiene* (ed. 3) 484 The Pali plague differs from the Egyptian plague, in having a marked lung disease. **1875** tr. *von Ziemssen's Cycl. Med.* I. 482 He thinks that he can recognise the black death of the fourteenth century in the so-called Indian Plague or Pali Plague, a disease which prevailed from 1815 to 1821 in the East Indian provinces of Kutch and Guzerat.

3. *Comb.,* as ***Pali-Prakrit, -Pyu.***

1948 D. Diringer *Alphabet* vi. 388 Pali-Prakrit Sinhalese. This language.. may be dated from the third century B.C. to about the fourth century A.D. *Ibid.* vii. 410 A mixed Pali-Pyu inscription.

pali, plural of PALUS[2].

paliard, palice, obs. ff. PALLIARD, PALACE, PALIS.

palichthyologic, etc., irregular form of *palæichthyologic*, etc.: see PALÆO-, PALEO-.
1848 *Q. Jrnl. Geol. Soc.* IV. 302.

palie, variant of PAULIE *a. Sc.*

†**palifi'cation.** *Obs.* (*Erron.* palli-.) [ad. med.L. *pālificātiōn-em*, It. *palificazione* (Florio), f. L. *pālificāre* to make a foundation of piles, f. *pāl-us* pile, stake, pale + *-ficāre* to make.] The action of driving piles or stakes into the ground in order to render it more firm for building operations.
1624 Wotton *Archit.* I. 26, I haue sayd nothing of Pallification, or Pyling of the Ground-plot.. when we build vpon a moist or marshy soile. Hence **1656** in Blount, **1658** in Phillips, **1823** in Nicholson *Pract. Builder.*

paliform ('peɪlɪfɔːm), *a. Zool.* [f. L. *pālus* stake, etc. + -(I)FORM.] Resembling, or having the form of, a palus.
1890 in *Cent. Dict.* **1900** *Proc. Zool. Soc.* June 126 A ring, often incomplete, of large septal teeth rises up.. or else one large paliform tooth.

palify, palijs, obs. f. PALLIFY, PALACE.

paligorskite, obs. var. PALYGORSKITE.

‖**palikar** ('pælɪkɑː(r)). Also pallecar. [ad. mod.Gr. παλικάρι, παλληκάρι lad, f. Gr. πάλλαξ, -ηξ youth; in F. *palikare.*] A member of the band of a Greek or Albanian military chief, esp. during the war of Independence.
1812 Byron *Ch. Har.* II. lxxi, Each Palikar his sabre from him cast. **1826** *Blackw. Mag.* XX. 719 The remnant of the Suliot palikars.. were reduced to capitulate. **1853** Felton *Fam. Lett.* xxxv. (1865) 277 Two very handsome, genteel, and civil pallecars, who were very attentive to us. **1854** *Blackw. Mag.* LXXVI. 417 The third prominent feature in the social condition of the Greek population is the existence of a military caste called Palikars.
Hence **'palikarism**, the palikar system or institution.
1854 *Blackw. Mag.* LXXVI. 418 Otho [was] re-established in absolute power by the assistance of palikarism and municipal corruption.

palilalia (pælɪ'leɪlɪə). *Path.* [mod.L., ad. F. *palilalie* (A. Soques 1908, in *Rev. Neurol.* XVI. 340), f. Gr. πάλι-ν again + λαλιά talk, speech.] A speech disorder characterized by repetition of words, phrases, or sentences.
1908 *Index Medicus* VI. 157/1 (Index), Palilalia. **1927** *Jrnl. Neurol. & Psychopath.* VIII. 26 The palilalia (as with stammering) disappears during pre-formed speech automatisms, as for instance, when the patient reads aloud, sings or recites. **1934** *Jrnl. Amer. Med. Assoc.* 1 Dec. 1711/2 Those familiar with such symptoms as automatic writing, palilalia, perseveration and verbigeration are inclined to wonder whether or not the literary abnormalities in which she [*sc.* Gertrude Stein] indulges represent correlated distortions of the intellect. **1955** J. M. Nielsen in A. B. Baker *Clin. Neurol.* I. iv. 376 Palilalia is a repetitive disturbance encountered in parkinsonism and in encephalitis (as representatives of organic causes), and in schizophrenia. **1961** W. R. Brain *Speech Disorders* vii. 107, I have once met with palilalia as a temporary phenomenon in a patient who suffered from compression of the medulla.

palilogy, palillogy (pə'lɪlədʒɪ). *Rhet.* Also in Gr. and L. forms. [ad. L. *palilogia, -illogia*, Gr. παλιλλογία, f. πάλιν over again + -λογία speaking.] The repetition of a word or phrase, esp. in immediate succession, for the sake of emphasis.
1657 J. Smith *Myst. Rhet.* 160 This figure and *Palalogia*, which signifies Repetition of the same word, are alike. **1678** Phillips (ed. 4), *Palilogia.* **1731** Bailey (ed. 5), *Palilogy.*
So †**palilo'getic** *a.* [f. Gr. παλιλλογεῖν], characterized by palilogy. *Obs.*
1652 Urquhart *Jewel* Wks. (1834) 292, I could have introduced.. exargastick, and palilogetick elucidations.

‖**palimbacchius** (ˌpælɪmbæ'kaɪəs). *Pros.* [L., a. Gr. παλιμβάκχειος, f. πάλιν back, backwards + βακχεῖος BACCHIUS.] A metrical foot consisting of two long and one short syllable; a reversed bacchius: = ANTIBACCHIUS. Also **palim'bacchic.**
1586 W. Webbe *Eng. Poetrie* (Arb.) 69 Palimbachius, of two long and one short, as --∪ *accorded.* **1749** *Numbers in Poet. Comp.* 19 Palimbacchic --∪ Spondee -- and half Pyrrhic ∪. **1773** Kenrick *Rhet. Gram. Eng. Lang.* in *Dict.* 22 When I hear an English prosodist thus talk of his Iambics, his Trochees.. and his Palimbacchics.

palimony ('pælɪmənɪ). *slang* (chiefly *U.S.*). [Blend of PAL *sb.*[1] and ALIMONY.] Compensation claimed esp. by the deserted party after the separation of a couple living together out of wedlock.
1979 *Telegraph* (Brisbane) 10 Jan. 16/2 If.. Michelle Triola Marvin.. wins her claims for what Americans call 'palimony', the outcome could set off a wave of similar claims across the United States by women whose live-in boyfriends walked out on them. **1979** *Sunday Star* (Toronto) 8 July A9/4 Sherry Steiger.. has lost her bid for palimony and a substantial part of her husband's holdings. **1980** *Time* 28 Jan. 90/2 Palimony, the term for sharing money after an unmarried couple have split, survives the Lee Marvin case. **1981** *Times* 11 Dec. 9/5 Miss Barnett.. has alleged in a separate civil action seeking 'palimony' (financial support) that she and Mrs King became lesbian lovers in 1972. **1984** M. Amis *Money* 154 Palimony sounds like bad news for the boys. **1986** *Illinois Bar Jrnl.* Feb. 286 Despite the Illinois Supreme Court's rejection of 'palimony', an unmarried cohabitant—regardless of age or gender—may be able to recover a portion of assets acquired during the period of cohabitation under the approach proposed in this article.

palimpsest ('pælɪmpsɛst), *sb.* and *a.* Also 7–8 in L. or Gr. form. [ad. L. *palimpsēstus* sb., a. Gr. παλίμψηστος scraped again, παλίμψηστον a parchment whence writing has been erased, f. πάλιν again + ψηστός, from ψάω, ψῆν to rub smooth.]
A. *sb.* †**1.** Paper, parchment, or other writing-material prepared for writing on and wiping out again, like a slate. *Obs.* [So It. *palimsesto* (Florio).]
1661 Lovell *Hist. Anim. & Min.* 7 The chalked skinne for a palimpsestus, serving in stead of a table book. **1662** Evelyn *Chalcogr.* (1769) 52 In writing, the use of the palimpsestus.. and the like. **1706** Phillips, *Palimpseston*,.. a sort of Paper or Parchment, that was generally us'd for making the first draught of things, which might be wip'd out, and new wrote in the same Place.
2. A parchment or other writing-material written upon twice, the original writing having been erased or rubbed out to make place for the second; a manuscript in which a later writing is written over an effaced earlier writing.
1825 *Gentl. Mag.* XCV. I. 348 Monsignore Angelo Mayo .. celebrated for his discoveries in the 'Palimpsestes'. **1838** Arnold *Hist. Rome* I. 256 *note*, The Institutes of Gaius.. was first discovered.. in a palimpsest, or rewritten manuscript of.. works of S. Jerome, in the Chapter Library at Verona. **1875** Scrivener *Text N. Test.* 18 To decipher a double palimpsest calls for the masterhood of a Tischendorf.
fig. **1845** De Quincey *Suspiria* Wks. 1890 XIII. 346 What else than a natural and mighty palimpsest is the human brain? **1856** Mrs. Browning *Aur. Leigh* I. 826 Let who says 'The soul's a clean white paper' rather say A palimpsest.. defiled. **1879** Lewes *Study Psychol.* viii. 153 History unrolls the palimpsest of mental evolution. **1918** D. H. Lawrence *New Poems* 33 Darkness comes out of the earth.. Wanes the old palimpsest. **1929** *Oxford Poetry* 17 The world is all a palimpsest That hails the spurious pugilist. **1949** 'G. Orwell' *Nineteen Eighty-Four* I. iv. 42 All history was a palimpsest, scraped clean and re-inscribed exactly as often as was necessary. **1962** R. Page *Educ. Gardener* x. 294 In Italy every town and house.. is a palimpsest of two or three thousand years of building and decay. **1977** *Times* 3 Sept. 9/1 Alan Watts will be principally remembered as the architect of that peculiar theological palimpsest which served as an ideology for the hippie generation: that odd blend of rural fundamentalism and eastern mysticism.
3. A monumental brass slab turned and re-engraved on the reverse side.
1876 *Encycl. Brit.* IV. 219/2 A large number of brasses in England are palimpsests, the back of an ancient brass having been engraved for the more recent memorial. **1877** L. Jewitt *Half-hrs. among Eng. Antiq.* 132 They were frequently laid down to other persons, or re-engraved on the other side, and hence called palimpsests.
B. *adj.* **1.** (Applied to a manuscript) Written over again; of which the original writing has been erased and superseded by a later: see A. 2.
1852 H. Rogers *Ecl. Faith* (1853) 237 A friend who used to mourn over the thought of palimpsest manuscripts. **1875** Poste *Gaius* Pref. (ed. 2) 5 The codex is doubly palimpsest, i.e. there are three inscriptions on the parchment. **1898** R. Harris in *Expositor* Dec. 402 It is useless to apply reagents in search of palimpsest writing where the vellum has only been used once.
fig. **1873** W. Cory in *Lett. & Jrnls.* (1897) 308 The pretty song, rising one will never know how, from a palimpsest memory.
2. Of a monumental brass: see A. 3.
1843 *Archæologia* XXX. 124 Palimpsest brasses are also found at Berkhampstead. **1877** J. C. Cox *Ch. of Derbysh.* III. 241 This monument is a remarkable.. example of the palimpsest or re-used brass.
3. *Petrogr.* Of a rock: partially preserving the texture it had prior to metamorphism. Also in *Geol.*, exhibiting features produced at two or more distinct periods.
1912 R. W. Clark tr. *Weinschenk's Petrogr. Methods* x. 198 In the normal case the newly developed substance is confined strictly to the border of the original crystal, but the texture of the altered rock may be recognized excellently, palimsest [*sic*] structure. **1926** G. W. Tyrrell *Princ. Petrol.* xvi. 271 (*caption*) A palimpsest structure. Garnetiferous biotite-hornfels... Shows alternations of psammitic and pelitic sediments preserved, although the rock is thoroughly hornfelsed with the production of muscovite and biotite. **1951** Turner & Verhoogen *Ign. & Metamorphic Petrol.* xx. 503 It frequently happens.. that fabric relicts (palimpsest structures), like mineral relicts, survive metamorphism and provide valuable indications of the parentage of the metamorphic rock. **1962** A. D. Howard in *Bull. Amer. Assoc. Petroleum Geologists* XLVI. 2255/1 A particularly interesting part of the anomaly is the drainage pattern, an unusual superposition of modern and ancient patterns that is convenient to refer to as palimpsest. In palimpsest drainage, the modern pattern is anomalous with respect to the older; it clearly indicates different topographic and possibly structural conditions at the time of development. **1972** D. J. P. Swift et al. *Shelf Sediment Transport* xxiii. 499 The floor of the central and southern Atlantic shelf is a palimpsest or multiple imprint surface.
Hence **'palimpsest** *v. trans.*, to make into a palimpsest, to write anew on (parchment, etc.) after erasure of the original writing; **palimp'sestic** *a.*, that is, or that makes, a palimpsest.
1823 *New Monthly Mag.* VIII. 13 Discoveries.. of Palimpsestic parchments had not yet furnished fresh matter for research. **1836** F. Mahony *Rel. Father Prout, Songs Horace* I. (1859) 376 Thy MSS. have come down to us unmutilated by the pumicestone of palimpsestic monk. **1900** *Expositor* June 420 We may wonder less at this Sinaitic .. codex having been palimpsested.

palinal ('pælɪnəl), *a. Physiol.* [irreg. f. Gr. πάλιν backward + -AL[1].] Characterized by or involving backward motion, esp. of the lower jaw in mastication.
1888 Cope in *Amer. Nat.* Jan. 7 *note*, The propalinal mastication is to be distinguished into the proal, from behind forwards,.. and the palinal, from before backwards. **1896** —— *Primary Factors Evolution* vi. 321 Ryder is of the opinion that the mastication of the Proboscidia is palinal.

palindrome ('pælɪndrəʊm), *sb.* and *a.* [ad. Gr. παλίνδρομ-ος running back again: so in mod.F. (Littré).]
A. *sb.* **1.** A word, verse, or sentence that reads the same when the letters composing it are taken in the reverse order.
c **1629** B. Jonson *Underwoods, Execr. upon Vulcan* (1640) B j b, Had I.. weav'd fifty tomes Of Logogriphes, or curious Pallindromes. **1706** Phillips, *Palindrome*.. as *Lewd did I live, and evil I did dwel.* **1821** *New Monthly Mag.* II. 170 The Palindromes, or Canorine, or recurrent verses, as they were called.
2. *transf.* **a.** *Mus.* A piece of music of which the second half is the first half in retrograde motion.
1947 E. Blom *Everyman's Dict. Mus.* 430/1 *Palindrome*, a word or poem reading the same backwards as forwards. In m[usic] a piece constructed in the same way, more or less loosely, as e.g. the prelude and postlude in Hindemith's *Ludus tonalis.* **1961** *Listener* 21 Sept. 445/3 The palindrome is another symmetrical form that she has used several times, most notably and extendedly in the recent *Symphonies* where the strict symmetry of the reversed 'reprise' is relieved only by changes of scoring, [etc.]. **1963** *Ibid.* 28 Mar. 570/3 Huber.. is obsessed with musical palindromes. **1979** *Gramophone* Aug. 327/2 Hers is a gorgeous performance, and its orchestral match may be summarized by the moment when Berg moves into a palindrome.
b. *Biol.* A palindromic sequence of nucleotides.
1974 Wilson & Thomas in *Jrnl. Molecular Biol.* LXXXIV. 115 We call these regions in double-chain DNA palindromes, because, given the antiparallel arrangement of the polynucleotide chains, these sequences read the same both backwards and forwards. **1977** *Nature* 3 Nov. 10/2 If these inverted repeats are adjacent (forming a palindrome) renaturation produces a double-stranded hairpin.
B. *adj.* That reads the same backwards as forwards.
1638 Peacham *Truth of our Times* 123, I caused this to be written over the porch of their free-schoole doore, *Subi dura a rudibus*: It is Palindrome. **1821** *New Monthly Mag.* II. 171 In English but one Palindrome line is known.
Hence **'palindromist**, a writer or inventor of palindromes.
a **1876** M. Collins *Th. in Garden* (1880) I. 226 A dear friend of mine, poet and palindromist and archæologist.

palin'dromic, *a.* [f. PALINDROME *sb.* + -IC.]
1. a. Of the nature of a palindrome.
1862 H. B. Wheatley *Anagrams* 11 A singularly appropriate Greek palindromic inscription.. occurs upon very many fonts in England.
b. More widely (esp. in *Math.* and *Mus.*), having a structure or composition that reads the same in both directions.
1957 W. J. Reichmann *Fascination of Numbers* ix. 90 The most simple form of palindromic numbers is the one containing a number of identical digits. **1961** *Listener* 23 Nov. 889/1 Schönberg makes his ternary-form prelude in effect a prelude-and-fugue, the middle section being fugal, with a powerfully melodic subject of palindromic construction, and a counter-subject that is also palindromic. **1963** *Ibid.* 17 Jan. 140/3 This act is the only formal success, having clear-cut musical ideas worked out logically in a neat palindromic structure. **1964** A. H. Beiler *Recreations in Theory of Numbers* xx. 228 There are an infinite number of palindromic primes. Here are a few: 101, 131, 151, 181, 313. **1972** *Times* 1 Aug. 15/2 The sole point of this letter is the date [*sc.* 27.7.72] at its foot. Apart from the three rather less pleasing palindromes arising on the 27th of the 8th 9th and 11th months of this year, today's is the last palindromic date until 18.1.81. **1974** *Nature* 9 Aug. 467/2 The central assumption of my theory is that the nucleotide sequences at the ends of eukaryote linear DNA molecules are palindromic. **1975** W. Safire *Before the Fall* 181 Prince Norodim Sihanouk, had been deposed by Lon Nol, his palindromic Prime Minister.
2. *Med.* Characterized by frequent, irregular recurrences of short-lived rheumatic attacks.
1941 Hench & Rosenberg in *Proc. Staff Meetings Mayo Clinic* XVI. 814 When an etiologic term cannot be applied, a distinctive descriptive term should be used. Such a designation we found in the term 'palindromic

rheumatism', suggested to us by Profs. A. D. Fraser and A. L. Hench, respectively, of the departments of Ancient languages and of English literature of the University of Virginia. **1959** *Ann. Rheumatic Dis.* XVIII. 331/2 When the histories of patients with definite rheumatoid arthritis were reviewed, a palindromic or episodic type of onset was found in 10 to 15 per cent. *Ibid.*, Finger contractures had been a common feature during the palindromic phase. **1972** *Lancet* 5 Aug. 269/2 Palindromic rheumatism is a condition in which an acute arthritis develops over a few hours, lasts for a day or two, and disappears the way it came.

Hence **palin'dromical** *a.* = prec.; **palin'dromically** *adv.*, in a way that reads the same backwards as forwards.
1864 WEBSTER, *Palindromical.*

paling ('peɪlɪŋ), *vbl. sb.*[1] [f. PALE *v.*[1] + -ING[1].]
†**1.** Decoration with 'pales' or vertical stripes.
c **1386** CHAUCER *Pars. T.* ¶ 343 The cost of embrowdynge, ..barrynge, owndynge, palynge.

2. The action of constructing a fence, or of enclosing a place, with pales; fencing.
1469 *Paston Lett.* II. 337 They that ben possessioners.. shulde payle certeine of the Parke of Weverston; and by cause this is nat performyd..thoo that ben possessioners shall..be amersid. And it is agreed that Sir William Yelverton, Sir Thomas Hoo..wolle pay the amercyment, and to delyver the said Duchesse possession of the said service and palyng. **1543** *Act 35 Hen. VIII*, c. 17 §6 For.. pailing, railing, or enclosing of Parkes [etc.]. **1667** DUCHESS OF NEWCASTLE *Life Dk. of N.* (1886) II. 153 The..paling, stubbing, hedging, &c., of his grounds and parks. **1703** T. N. *City & C. Purchaser* 212 Much us'd in Essex..; but in few other Countreys, except for Paleing.

3. *concr.* **a.** Wood prepared for or made into pales; pales collectively; fencing.
1788 *Trans. Soc. Arts* VI. 22 The firs answer for..paling for fences. *c* **1830** CARLYLE *Four Fables* iv, Thou art felled and sawed into paling. **1881** YOUNG *Every Man his own Mechanic* §181. 62 When park paling of cleft pales is made.

b. A fence made of pales. (with *a* and *pl.*)
1558 *Nottingham Rec.* IV. 120 The palyng for the seyd pynfold. **1766** BLACKSTONE *Comm.* II. iii. 38 It is not every field..which a gentleman pleases to surround with a wall or paling..that is thereby constituted a legal park. **1814** SCOTT *Wav.* lx, Waverley groped his way the best he could along a small paling. **1866** ROGERS *Agric. & Prices* I. xviii. 425 Split oaken planks to be used for strong palings.

c. Each of the pales of which a fence is made; usually in *pl.* = a set of pales, a fence.
1834 H. AINSWORTH *Rookwood* III. i, A rough..lane which skirted..the moss-grown palings..of the park. **1861** MRS. H. WOOD *East Lynne* (1888) 195 He plunged..over some palings into a field.

4. *attrib.*, as *paling board, fence.*
1805 R. W. DICKSON *Pract. Agric.* I. 110 Plate xxx, Two different sorts of paling fences. **1812** J. SMYTH *Pract. of Customs* (1821) 282 A paling Board is the outside or sappy part of a tree, sawed off from the four sides, in order to make the remaining part square. **1843** *Amer. Pioneer* II. 308 A strong body occupied the yard of Ebenezer Zane..using the paling fence as a cover. **1873** 'MARK TWAIN' & WARNER *Gilded Age* v. 60 Hawkins put up the first 'paling' fence that had ever adorned the village. **1894** R. BRIDGES *Feast of Bacchus* I. 179 The hedge and paling bounds. **1901** MERWIN & WEBSTER *Calumet 'K'* v. 68 They were standing..near the paling fence which bounded the C. and S.C. right of way. **1925** W. J. BRYAN *Mem.* 17 Our yard was enclosed in the old-fashioned paling fence with a baseboard about a foot high.

paling, *vbl. sb.*[2] [f. PALE *v.*[2] + -ING[1].] The action of becoming or turning pale.
c **1410** LYDG. *Life Our Lady* (MS. Ashm. 39 lf. 47), For in here face alwey was the blode, With oute palynge or eny drawynge doune. **1887** G. MEREDITH *Ballads & P.* 158 Like the paling of the dawn-star.

paling, *ppl. a.*[1] [f. PALE *v.*[1] + -ING[2].] Enclosing, surrounding.
c **1630** *Trag. Rich. II* (1870) 34 That dost allowe thy paleing flatterers To guild them selues with others misseryes.

paling, *ppl. a.*[2] [f. PALE *v.*[2] + -ING[2].] Becoming or turning pale.
1623 MIDDLETON *More Dissemblers Besides Women* I. iv, Your nice paling physicking gentlefolks. **1832** J. BREE *St. Herbert's Isle* 41 The sun looks downward with a paling light. **1899** *19th Cent.* Nov. 817 By the dual light of paling moon and rising sun.

‖**palingenesia** (ˌpælɪndʒɪ'niːsɪə). [med.L. (969 in Du Cange), a. Gr. παλιγγενεσία birth over again, regeneration, f. πάλιν again + γένεσις birth, origination.] = PALINGENESY.
1621 BURTON *Anat. Mel.* I. i. II. ix, The Pythagoreans hold metempsychosis and palingenesia that soules go from one body to another. **1707** *Curios. in Husb. & Gard.* 336 The Palingenesia or Resurrection of Plants from their Ashes. **1829** SOUTHEY *Sir T. More* II. 245 We might then hope for a palingenesia, a restoration of national sanity and strength. **1870** FARRAR *Witn. Hist.* v. (1871) 172 This is why it became the Palingenesia of a dead and miserable world.

Hence **palinge'nesian** *a.*, relating to palingenesia.
1816 J. LAWRENCE in *Monthly Mag.* XLII. 296 Gaffarel.. meditated a palingenesian experiment upon human bodies.

palingenesis (pælɪn'dʒɛnɪsɪs). [f. Gr. πάλιν again + γένεσις birth, origination: a modern compound not on Greek analogy: see prec.]
1. = PALINGENESY.
1818 HOBHOUSE *Italy* (1859) II. 351 A poem which he [Monti] published..and called the 'Palingenesis'. **1871** H. MACMILLAN *True Vine* iv. (1872) 169 The palingenesis of creation is accomplished, not by the rooting-up of evil, but by the sowing of good.

2. *Biol.* †**a.** The supposed production of animals from putrescent animal matter. *Obs.*
1866 in BRANDE & COX *Dict. Sci.* etc.

b. Haeckel's term for the form of ontogenesis in which ancestral characters are exactly reproduced, without modification; true hereditary genesis or evolution; the 'breeding true' of an organism (opp. to *kenogenesis*).
1879 tr. *Haeckel's Evol. Man* I. 11 This distinction between Palingenesis or inherited evolution, and Kenogenesis or vitiated evolution, has not..yet been sufficiently appreciated by naturalists.

c. *Entom.* = METAMORPHOSIS.
1886 in *Cassell's Encycl. Dict.*

3. *Petrol.* [ad. Sw. *palingenes* (J. J. Sederholm 1907, in *Bull. Comm. Géol. Finlande* XXIII. 89).] The formation of a new magma by the remelting of existing rocks.
1907 J. J. SEDERHOLM in *Bull. Comm. Géol. Finlande* XXIII. 102 The granitic magma, once solidified and, in part, decomposed, undergoes again, when brought into the deeper parts of the earth, a resurrection, or, as the author expresses it, palingenesis. **1965** A. HOLMES *Princ. Physical Geol.* (ed. 2) xxx. 1131 The following list of the radiometric ages of some of the uplifted basement rocks shows how successfully they escaped the widespread palingenesis..that rejuvenated similar old rocks during the Nevadan orogenies farther west. **1974** L. N. KOGARKO in H. Sørensen *Alkaline Rocks* vi. 480/1 The significant reductions of the melting temperatures of rocks caused by the volatile components is probably of great importance for palingenesis.

Hence **palin'genesist**, one who holds some doctrine of palingenesy.
1860 *All Year Round* No. 43. 389 Monsieur Doyère, the most ardent palingenesist of the age,..pretends that these animals are able to support..absolute desiccation, without losing the faculty of resurrection. **1869** tr. *Pouchet's Universe* (1871) 35 Our modern palingenesists.

palingenesy (pælɪn'dʒɛnɪsɪ). Also 7 -ie. [a. F. *palingénésie*, ad. med.L. *palingenesia*: see above.] Regeneration, birth over again; revival, re-animation, resuscitation. (*lit.* and *fig.*)
1643 SMALLWOOD *On Death Cartwright* in *C.'s Poems* (1651) **iij, Buried Ashes may as eas'ly see Theirs, as we this glad Palingenesie. **1660** tr. *Amyraldus' Treat. conc. Relig.* II. vii. 258 There must also be another burning of the world, and another Palingenesie or renovation of things. **1718** J. FOX *Wanderer* 57 While the World seems to rejoice in a perfect Palingenesy. **1801** W. TAYLOR in *Monthly Mag.* XI. 19 The..doctrines of an imminent palingenesy, and of the speedy coming of Antichrist. **1858** TRENCH *On Author. Vers.* (1859) 52 Nothing would so effectually hinder this rejuvenescence, this palingenesy of words, as the putting a ban upon them directly they pass out of vulgar use.

palingenetic (-dʒɪ'nɛtɪk), *a.* [f. PALINGENESIS: see GENETIC.] Of or belonging to, or of the nature of palingenesis (senses 2 b, 3). Hence **palinge'netically** *adv.*
1877 LANKESTER in *Q. Jrnl. Microsc. Sci.* XVII. 411 What he [Haeckel] terms 'heterochrony in the palingenetic phenomena of ontogeny'. **1879** tr. *Haeckel's Evol. Man* I. i. 10 It is..most important to distinguish clearly and exactly between the original, palingenetic processes of evolution, and the later kenogenetic processes of the same. **1942** M. P. BILLINGS *Structural Geol.* xv. 296 Palingenetic granites were actually molten and, in the simplest case, they have the same chemical composition as the rocks from which they were derived. **1974** BORODIN & PAVLENKO in H. Sørensen *Alkaline Rocks* vi. 523/1 In the Mongol-Tuva province palingenetic and metasomatic formations of alkaline rocks are widespread.

pa'lingenist. *nonce-wd.* = PALINGENESIST.
1839 *Fraser's Mag.* XIX. 50 We are Palingenists, and desire..to reanimate the dead.

†**'palingman.** *Obs.* [a. Du. *palingman*, f. *paling* eel + *man*.] A man who deals in eels.
1482 *Rolls of Parlt.* VI. 221/2 Aswell Merchauntes, as other sellers of Elys called Palyngmen. **1482** *Act 22 Edw. IV*, c. 2 Ascun tiel marchant ne palingeman. **1495** *Act 11 Hen. VII*, c. 23 Noe such Marchaunte nor paling man shuld sell nor put to sale any Elys by barell, &c. [*Variously misunderstood*: **1670** BLOUNT *Law Dict.*, *Paling-man*, seems to be a Merchant Denizen; one born within the English Pale. Similarly **1706** in KERSEY; **1721–** BAILEY; **1823** CRABB, etc. **1864** WEBSTER, *Paling man*, one born within that part of Ireland called the *English Pale*: so in later Dicts.]

palinode ('pælɪnəʊd), *sb.* Also 7 palinod. [ad. L. *palinōdia*: see PALINODY; or a. obs. F. *palinod* (16th c. in Littré).] *orig.* An ode or song in which the author retracts something said in a former poem; hence *gen.* a recantation; *spec.* in *Sc. Law* (see quot. 1861).
1599 B. JONSON *Cynthia's Rev.* v. iii, You, two and two, singing a Palinode, March to your several homes. **1600** (*title*) The Palinod [*ed.* 1604 or recantation] of Iohn Colvill, wherein he doth penitently recant his former proud offences. **1636** G. SANDYS *Par. Div. Poems, Job* (1648) 62, I ..there-fore in this weeping Palinod Abhorre my selfe, that have displeas'd my God. **1814** SCOTT *Wav.* xiv, That Balmawhapple [had given satisfaction] by such a palinode as rendered the use of the sword unnecessary. **1861** W. BELL *Dict. Law Scot.* s.v., In actions for damages on account of slander or defamation raised in the Commissary Court.., it was formerly the practice to conclude not only for damages, expenses, and a fine, but also for a judicial recantation or palinode by the defender. **1898** R. L. STEVENSON *St. Ives* xiii, I..abounded in palinodes and apologies.

Hence **'palinode** *v.* [cf. Gr. παλινῳδεῖν to recant], to recant, retract (*intr.* and *trans.*).
1886 TUPPER *My Life as Author* 364, I have seen fit more than once to 'palinode'. **1892** *Sat. Rev.* 2 Apr. 392/1 The first stanza..being most ingeniously palinoded by the second.

pali'nodial, *a.* *rare*$^{-1}$. [a. F. *palinodial* (Godef.), f. L. *palinōdia* PALINODY + -AL[1].] Of the nature of a recantation.
1813 JEFFERSON *Writ.* (1830) IV. 188 Their Prince issued a palinodial proclamation, suspending the orders on certain conditions.

palinodic (pælɪ'nɒdɪk), *a.* *Gr. Pros.* [ad. Gr. παλινῳδικ-ός, f. παλινῳδία: see PALINODY and -IC. In mod.F. *palinodique.*] Applied to verse in which two 'systems' of corresponding form, as a strophe and antistrophe, are separated by two others also of corresponding form but different from the former.
1883 JEBB *Œdipus Tyrannus* p. lxx, This is called the palinodic period: meaning that a group of rhythmical sentences recurs once, in the same order. **1885** *Athenæum* 3 Oct. 432/3 Alterations make vv. 875..to 882..into a complete palinodic period.

†**pali'nodical,** *a.* *Obs.* [f. as prec. + -AL[1].] Making or containing a 'palinode' or recantation.
1602 DEKKER *Satiromastix* Wks. 1873 I. 234 *Hor.* I could be pleas'd..to quaffe downe The poyson'd Inke, in which I dipt your name. *Tuc.* Saist thou so, my Palinodicall rimester?

'pali,nodist. *rare*$^{-0}$. [f. PALINODE + -IST.] The author of a palinode.
In mod. Dicts.

palinody ('pælɪnəʊdɪ). Now *rare* or *Obs.* Also 6–7 -odie; and in L. form **palinodia** (pælɪ'nəʊdɪə). [a. F. *palinodie*, ad. L. (It., Sp., Pg.) *palinōdia*, a. Gr. παλινῳδία singing over again, repetition, *esp.* recantation, f. πάλιν back again, over again, + ᾠδή song: 'a name first given to an ode by Stesichorus, in which he recants his attack upon Helen' (Liddell and Scott).]
1. = PALINODE.
1589 PUTTENHAM *Eng. Poesie* I. xxiv. (Arb.) 62 So did the Poet Stesichorus..in his Pallinodie vpon the disprayse of Helena, and recouered his eye sight. **1643** PRYNNE *Sov. Power Parl.* III. 143 (2) If I have over-shot my self..I shall promise them a thankfull acknowledgement, and ready palinody. **1691** WOOD *Ath. Oxon.* II. 359 He was..forced to make his Palinody in a Declamation in the public Hall. **1759** GOLDSM. *On Butler's Rem.* Misc. Wks. 1837 IV. 473 Then follows a palinody to the same gentleman. **1893** *Columbus* (Ohio) *Disp.* 5 Oct., The New York Sun says the President should recall Mr. Van Alen's appointment without regard to Republican ridicule of palinody.
β. **1590** BARROW in *Conferences* i. 13 Some of your chief Teachers haue preached palinodā concerning your ministerie. **1611** BIBLE *Transl. Pref.* 9 Saint Augustine was not afraid to exhort S. Hierome to a Palinodia or recantation. **1632** MARMION *Holland's Leaguer* v. iv, That he shall sing a Palinodium, And recant his ill courses. **1837–9** HALLAM *Hist. Lit.* (1847) I. iv. §46. 285 A limitation of his tyrannical doctrine, if not a palinodia.

†**2.** Singing over again, repetition. *Obs.*
1599 *Broughton's Let.* x. 35 Nothing..but a palinody, I meane not a recantation, but a repetition. **1609** [BP. W. BARLOW] *Answ. Nameless Cath.* 196 His old Palinodie of scorne and malediction.

palinspastic (pælɪn'spæstɪk), *a.* *Geol.* [f. Gr. πάλιν again + σπαστικ-ός drawing in (see SPASTIC *a.*).] Of a map or the like: representing layers of rock as returned to their supposed former positions. Hence **palin'spastically** *adv.*, by means of such maps; **palin'spastics** *sb. pl.*, the production of such maps.
1937 G. M. KAY in *Bull. Geol. Soc. Amer.* XLVIII. 291 The resulting map displays the several slices in their conceived relative positions... The name *palinspastic*..is proposed for base maps of this character. **1945** *Bull. Amer. Assoc. Petroleum Geologists* XXIX. 426 Palinspastics concern the placement of rocks in their relative original positions. *Ibid.* 435 Palinspastic maps..have been used to illustrate concepts of continental drift and of intracontinental movements in the development of mountain systems. **1969** J. F. DEWEY in M. Kay *N. Atlantic* xxiv. 331/2 No attempt was made in Figures 2 and 3 to reconstruct palinspastically the original shape of the paratectonic cover sequence, in terms of thickness or extent. **1971** *Nature* 2 Apr. 319/1 Fig. 2 is an upper Palaeocene palinspastic reconstruction of Fig. 1.

†**pa'lintocy.** *Obs.* [a. obs. F. *palintocie*, ad. Gr. παλιντοκία repayment of interest; in quot. 1693, taken in sense 'regeneration'; f. τόκος birth, offspring, interest of money.] (See quots.)
a **1693** *Urquhart's Rabelais* III. xviii. 147 In him is..begun again the Palintocy of the Megarians, and the Palingenesie of Democritus. [**1847** GROTE *Greece* II. ix. III. 60 Passing a formal *Palintokia* or decree, to require from the rich who had lent money upon interest the refunding of all past interest paid to them by their debtors.]

†**'palinure.** *Obs.* [f. the name of *Palinūrus*, the pilot of Æneas (Virg. *Æn.* iii. 202, v. 833, etc.).] A pilot; in quots. *fig.*
1631 R. H. *Arraignm. Whole Creature* i. 7 Wanting the Pilote and Palinure of reason and Religion, they runne

themselves vpon the rocks. 1640 FULLER *Joseph's Coat, David's Sin* xx. (1867) 209 The winding shelves do us detain, Till God, the Palinure, returns again. [1849 E. B. EASTWICK *Dry Leaves* 23 We were driven right across the stream..leaving our Palinurus and his comrade standing up to their middles in water.]

palinuroid (pælɪˈnjʊərɔɪd), *a. Zool.* [ad. mod.L. *Palinūroidea*, neut. pl., f. *Palinūrus*: see -OID.] Resembling or akin to the genus *Palinurus* (Spiny Lobster) of decapod crustaceans; belonging to the group *Palinuroidea* or family *Palinuridæ*, of which this genus is the type.

‖**palio** (ˈpælɪəʊ). Also 7, 8 pallio. [a. It. *palio*, ad. L. *pallium* a covering, cover.] A traditional horse-race held every July and August in the Italian city of Siena; a similar horse-race held in other Italian towns; the cloth or banner of velvet, silk, etc., given as the prize for this race.

1673 J. RAY *Observations Journey Low-Countries* 338 He entertains and diverts the Citizens of Florence..with sports and shows, especially races for prizes (Pallio's they call them). 1791 E. WYNNE *Diary* 4 Apr. (1935) I. iv. 60 The King of Naples arrived today [at Padua] and they prepare a Pallio for him. 1863 GEO. ELIOT *Romola* I. viii. 138 The Porta Santa Croce..where the richest of *Palii*, or velvet and brocade banners.., were..awaiting the winner or winner's owner. *Ibid.* xvi. 291 You are going towards the Piazza della Signoria... we shall perhaps see who has deserved the *palio* among these racers. 1873 S. & J. HORNER *Walks in Florence* I. xvii. 296 The Corso..was at one time celebrated for horse-races, in which the Florentine youth competed for a piece of cloth of gold, called the *Pallio*, and which gave its name to the diversion. 1881 K. BAEDEKER *Central Italy* (ed. 7) 21 On 2nd July and 15th August, horse-races, called *il Palio*, take place, presenting a very picturesque scene. 1902 E. G. GARDNER *Story of Siena* v. 131 The race is still called the Palio, from the rich stuff (now represented as a banner) given as prize. 1904 W. HEYWOOD *Palio & Ponte* I. i. 11 Besides the Palio of St John the Baptist, at Florence, another palio is referred to in the *Divina Commedia*. 1925 A. HUXLEY *Along Road* II. 100 The *Palio* itself—the painted banner which is given to the *contrada* whose horse wins the race. *Ibid.* 101 The Palio is probably the most dangerous flat-race in the world. 1930 E. POUND *XXX Cantos* xxiv. 109 Zohanne da Rimini Has won the palio at Milan with our horse. 1970 C. FRY *Yard of Sun* I. 6 You know it is the first practice-run for the Palio—And you know this parish has got the best horse It has ever had. 1972 *Times* 18 Sept. 19/1 Over the weekend the historic Tuscan town was enlivened with..the Palio horse race in Renaissance costumes. 1974 *Radio Times* 27 July–2 Aug. 33/2 Old traditions also continue [in Siena], like the famous annual horse-race, the *Palio*, held every summer on the city square.

palione, obs. Sc. form of PAVILION.

‖**paliotto** (paliˈɔtto). [It.] The frontal painting on an altar-piece. Also *attrib.*

1937 *Burlington Mag.* July 18/1 The *St. Peter* paliotto of about 1280–85. 1958 *Times Lit. Suppl.* 27 June 356/3 'Judas receiving Payment', the 'Baptism of Christ' from the thirteenth-century St John *paliotto* in the Siena Gallery, the head of Pietro Lorenzetti's St Catherine of Alexandria, [etc.]. 1961 M. LEVY *Studio Dict. Art Terms* 82 Paliotto painting.

†**palis**, *sb. Obs.* Forms: 4 palice, 4–5 palais, -ays, palis, -ys, 5 palaies, paleys, paless, palyce, 5–6 pales. [a. F. *palis*, OF. also *paleis*, and *palisse*, in med.L. *pālicium*, sb. neuter, from **pālicius* composed of stakes, f. *pālus* stake, PALE. Cf. also PALACE *sb.*[3]]

1. A fence of pales, a palisade, paling.

13.. *Gaw. & Gr. Knt.* 769 A park al aboute, With a pyked palays, pyned ful þik. *c*1374 CHAUCER *Boeth.* I. pr. iii. 7 (Camb. MS.) Warnestored and enclosyd in swich a palis. *Ibid.* II. met. iv. 31 Thow that art put in quiete and weleful by strengthe of thi palys [*robore uallı*] shalt leden a cler age. 14.. *Voc.* in Wr.-Wülcker 599/45 *Palicium, -cij, est quedam clausura facta ex palis*, a Palys. *c*1475 *Stans Puer ad Mensam* 200 in *Q. Eliz. Acad.* 63 Iff þou go with any man.. Be wall or by hege, by pales or by pale.

2. A place enclosed by a palisade or fence; an enclosure: see PALACE *sb.*[3]

(The first quot. is doubtful, and may belong to 1.)

*c*1420 *Anturs of Arth.* 148 (Douce MS.) Of palaies [*Thornton MS.* Of pales], of parkes, of pondes, of plowes. 1581 STYWARD *Mart. Discipl.* I. 59 He that shall enter in or goe foorth by any other gate, streete, or waie..into the citie, pales or lyst or fort where ye campe is lodged.

†ˈ**palis**, *v. Obs.* Forms: see prec. [f. prec. or a. OF. *palisser*, f. *palis*, *palisse*.] *trans.* To surround or enclose with a palisade; to fence in.

*c*1330 R. BRUNNE *Chron. Wace* (Rolls) 9940 He..palysed hit [a wood] aboute ful þykke. *c*1330 R. BRUNNE *Chron.* (1810) 110 Withouten palaised parke. *c*1440 *Stacyons Rome* in *Pol. Rel. & L. Poems* (1866) 122 *note*, That stoone is vndyr an Awter Palysyd with Iren and stele.

palis, obs. form of PALACE.

palisade (pælɪˈseɪd), *sb.* Also 6 pal(l)aisade, 7 palisad, pallasade, 7–9 pallisade. [a. F. *palissade* (15th c. in Hatz.-Darm), f. *palisser* to enclose with pales: see -ADE. Cf. PALISADO.]

1. a. A fence made of pales or stakes fixed in the ground, forming an enclosure or defence. Also applied to a fence made of iron railings.

1600 HOLLAND *Livy* XXVIII. v. 670 The avenues of the forest Thermopylæ..were stopped up by the Ætolians with a trench and pallaisade. 1697 DRYDEN *Æneid* XI. 718 Others aid To ram the stones, or raise the palisade. 1788 GIBBON *Decl. & F.* xl. (1846) III. 531 A ditch and palisade might be sufficient to resist the..cavalry. 1885 MISS BRADDON *Wyllard's Weird* I. 4 The wooden palisade had been removed in the progress of the work.

†**b.** *Gardening.* A light fence or trellis-work on which trees or shrubs are trained, an espalier; hence *transf.* a row of trees or shrubs so trained, or a row of trees or shrubs forming a close hedge.

1658 EVELYN *Fr. Gard.* (1675) 14 Concerning espaliers (which I will call *palisades*) I will shew you several formes of accommodating them. 1712 J. JAMES tr. *Le Blond's Gardening* 21 When the Trees are spread, and the Palisades grown up.

2. *Mil.* A strong pointed wooden stake, of which a number are fixed deeply in the ground in a close row, either vertical or inclined, as a defence.

1697 DRYDEN *Æneid* VII. 214 And Palisades about the Trenches plac'd. 1777 ROBERTSON *Hist. Amer.* I. II. 102 The ramparts were fortified with pallisades. 1828 J. M. SPEARMAN *Brit. Gunner* 317 Palisades are 9 feet long, and 6 or 7 inches square. When fixed, they are generally planted 3 feet in the ground and about 3 inches asunder. 1834 *Tait's Mag.* I. 188/2 They..began to dig a trench, and to heap up a mound, on which the palisades they brought with them were to be driven in. 1853 STOCQUELER *Mil. Encycl.*, *Palisades*, or *Palisadoes*, in fortification, stakes made of strong split wood, about nine feet long.

3. *fig.* Anything resembling or likened to a fence of stakes (or one of such stakes). **a.** *gen.*

1601 HOLLAND *Pliny* XVIII. vii. 558 Seed..contained.. within eares..defended (as it were) with a pallaisade of eales [AIL *sb.*[2]]. 1713 DERHAM *Phys.-Theol.* IV. ii. 109 Out of these Cartilages grow a Pallisade of stiff hairs. 1831 CARLYLE *Misc.* (1857) II. 325 To drive down more or less effectual palisades against that class of persons. 1865 B'NESS BUNSEN in Hare *Life* (1879) II. vii. 351 The gigantic palisade of mountains on each side. 1871 L. STEPHEN *Playgr. Eur.* (1894) v. 122 A vast palissade of blue ice-pinnacles.

†**b.** A wire supporting the hair, a part of the head-dress fashionable in the early part of the 17th century. *Obs.*

1690 EVELYN *Fop-Dict.*, *Palisade*, a Wire sustaining the Hair next to the Dutchess, or first Knot.

c. *pl.* Name for the lofty cliffs extending about 15 miles along the western bank of the Hudson above New York. Also applied to similar formations elsewhere.

1838 N. P. WILLIS *Amer. Scen.* I. 14 The Palisades—Hudson River... This singular precipice varies in height from fifty to two hundred feet, and presents a naked front of columnar strata, which gives it its descriptive name. 1861 N. A. WOODS *Pr. of Wales in Canada* etc. 405 The mighty river [Hudson] at first hemmed in by lofty cliffs, called the Palisades, which, striped with thin red and black strata, look like coloured palings erected by Nature to keep within bounds the stream. 1886 A. WINCHELL *Walks Geol. Field* 96 High cliffs of basaltic columns, like those exposed on the Hudson and Columbia rivers, are often called palisades.

d. *Biol.* A region of parallel elongated cells, often at right angles to the surface of the structure of which they form part; *esp.* the palisade parenchyma of a leaf. Freq. *attrib.* (see sense 4).

1914 M. DRUMMOND tr. *Haberlandt's Physiol. Plant Anat.* vi. 263 A remarkable modification, and one which is of great importance for the understanding of the palisade form, is the so-called arm-palisade-cell; in this case the palisade, instead of consisting of entire cells, is made up of groups of cell-branches or -arms. 1956 R. W. EVANS *Histol. Appearances of Tumours* vi. 79 In one of Chase's tumours the cells tended to form palisades. 1965 BELL & COOMBE tr. *Strasburger's Textbk. Bot.* 349 The outer leaves on the southern sunny side of a tree commonly possess a deeper palisade..than the 'shade leaves' of the northern side. 1971 *Nature* 19 Feb. 561/1 Here the so-called palisades of Vogt are found: fine radial lines about 1 mm long and four per mm of the corneal circumference. 1972 *Arch. Dermatol.* CVI. 865/3 The schwann cells which are closely aggregated often appear to be arranged in palisades.

4. *attrib.* and *Comb.*, as ***palisade-hedge***, ***-tree*** (see 1 b), ***-trench***; ***palisade-like*** adj.; **palisade-cell**, a cell of the *palisade-tissue*; **palisade-parenchyma**, the parenchymatous palisade-tissue of leaves; **palisade-tissue**, tissue consisting of elongated cells set closely side by side, as the parenchyma immediately below the epidermis of the upper surface in most leaves; **palisade-worm**, name for various parasitic nematode worms, esp. *Strongylus armatus*, infesting the horse, and *Eustrongylus gigas*, infesting various mammals.

1875 BENNETT & DYER tr. *Sachs' Bot.* 657 These changes are usually more complete in the '*pallisade-cells' on the upper side than in the parenchyma which lies deeper. 1664 EVELYN *Kal. Hort.*, *Feb.* Orchard 60 Trim up your *Palisade Hedges, and Espaliers. 1897 *Allbutt's Syst. Med.* II. 62 The rete mucosum between the cells of the *palisade and other layers. 1877 ROSENTHAL *Muscles & Nerves* 10 Cylindrical cells standing, *palisade-like, side by side. 1884 BOWER & SCOTT *De Bary's Phaner.* 407 Not inappropriately designated palisade-cells, or *palisade-parenchyma. 1875 BENNETT & DYER tr. *Sachs' Bot.* 465 The chlorophyll-tissue ..is developed on the upper side of the leaves..as the so-called *Pallisade-tissue. 1699 EVELYN *Kal. Hort.*, *Jan.* Orchard (ed. 9) 15 Keep your Wall and *Palisade-Trees from mounting too hastily. 1935 *Proc. Prehistoric Soc.* I. 124 In this barrow the posts (set in a *palisade-trench) were smaller. 1963 W. F. GRIMES in Foster & Alcock *Culture & Environment* v. 142 The entrance took the form of a passage between the ends of the bank which was defined by narrow trenches resembling palisade-trenches. 1888 ROLLESTON & JACKSON *Anim. Life* 685 *Strongylus armatus*, the *palisade Worm..is a common cause of aneurism,..in the Horse and Ass.

palisade (pælɪˈseɪd), *v.* Forms: see prec. [f. prec. sb.] *trans.* To furnish, surround, enclose, or fortify with a palisade or palisades; to fence in. Also *absol.*, and *fig.*

1632 LITHGOW *Trav.* VIII. 349 The Ditch..is mainly pallasaded with wooden stakes. 1719 LONDON & WISE *Compl. Gard.* I. 2 There is daily some new Thing to be done, as to Sow, Plant, Prune, Pallisade. 1796 H. HUNTER tr. *St.-Pierre's Stud. Nat.* (1799) I. 269 Jaws palisaded with teeth. 1850 *Fraser's Mag.* XLII. 10 The frowning cliffs that palisade the shore.

Hence **paliˈsaded** *ppl. a.*, (*a*) enclosed or fortified with a palisade; (*b*) *Med.*, consisting of, or arranged as in, a palisade (PALISADE *sb.* 3 d); **paliˈsading** *vbl. sb.*, (*a*) the action of furnishing or surrounding with a palisade; *concr.* a palisade, paling; (*b*) *Med.*, arrangement of cells in a palisade.

1719 LONDON & WISE *Compl. Gard.* 188 This Method of Pallisading has seldom or never been us'd in England. 1804 C. B. BROWN tr. *Volney's View Soil U.S.* 356 Five pallisaded forts..were the only stages in this journey. 1845 *Jrnl. Asiat. Soc. Bengal* XIV. 257 Running a light palisading between two precipices. 1890 'R. BOLDREWOOD' *Miner's Right* (1899) 75/1 A stout palisaded fence was at once run across the neck ..on the side facing the diggings. 1951 M. S. MCKEEHAN in *Jrnl. Exper. Zool.* CXVII. 39 During the period of nuclear orientation, the lens ectoderm rapidly changes from a cuboidal to a high columnar epithelium. This phenomenon may be called 'palisading'. 1956 R. W. EVANS *Histol. Appearances of Tumours* xvi. 300 When palisading is present it is usually a conspicuous microscopical feature. *Ibid.* xix. 403 This palisaded columnar epithelium lies in contact with the adjacent fibrous tissue. 1966 WRIGHT & SYMMERS *Systemic Path.* II. xxxviii. 1435/1 The zones of necrosis.. are surrounded by radially oriented ('palisaded') connective tissue cells. 1972 *Arch. Dermatol.* CVI. 865/1 The palisaded, encapsulated neuroma is a..benign cutaneous tumor. 1974 *Nature* 18 Jan. 145/1 This 'palisading' gives the lens anlage a regular appearance, but individual cells may deviate considerably from the columnar shape.

paliˈsado, *sb. Obs.* or *arch.* Also 6 palaisado, 6–8 palizado, 6–9 pallisado, 7 palisadoe, -zadoe, palysado, (pallaisada, -asado, pal(l)azado, pallozado), 7–8 pallisadoe, -zado, palissado. [ad. Sp. *palizada* palisade: see -ADO.]

1. = PALISADE *sb.* 1.

1589 IVE *Fortif.* 38 A palizado (placed at the outer edge of the parapet raysed vppon the sayd courtine or bulwarke) of sparres or such like. 1603 HOLLAND *Plutarch's Mor.* 438 They..plucked downe the pallaisada, mounted over the rampar, entred the campe. 1625 PURCHAS *Pilgrims* II. 1369 A deepe Ditch, and a Pallizado of young Firre-trees. 1725 DE FOE *Voy. round World* (1840) 65 They had..a covered pallisadoe round where they lodged their ammunition. 1780 COXE *Russ. Disc.* 212 The fortress..is a square enclosed with palisadoes. 1816 F. H. NAYLOR *Hist. Germany* II. xxiv. 426 They rushed into the trenches..and having torn up the palisadoes, made themselves masters of the imperial batteries.

†**b.** *Gardening.* = PALISADE *sb.* 1 b. *Obs.*

1604 E. G[RIMSTONE] *D'Acosta's Hist. Indies* v. xiii. 362 In the midst of which walke was a Pallisado, artificially made of very high trees, planted in order a fadome one from another. 1689–90 TEMPLE *Ess. Gardening* Wks. 1731 I. 181 The best Fruits not ripening without the Advantage of Walls or Palisadoes. 1725 BRADLEY *Fam. Dict.* s.v. *Garden*, The Space between the Bason and Pallisade should be fill'd with Pieces of Embroidery, or green Plots adorn'd with Yew, Boxes and Flower Pots.

2. = PALISADE *sb.* 2.

1623 BINGHAM *Xenophon* 113 They..strengthened all the Rampier with Palizadoes. 1635 BARRIFFE *Mil. Discip.* xcv. (1643) 306 To impale those parts..with sharp-pointed pallisadoes. 1659 PEARSON *Creed* (1839) 289 They..always take it for a straight standing stake, pale, or palisado. 1770 LANGHORNE *Plutarch* (1819) VI. 48 To repair the wall..he ordered each of the citizens to furnish a palisado. 1860 T. MARTIN *Horace* 216 A Roman soldier..A woman's slave, her arms doth bear, And palisadoes now.

3. *fig.* = PALISADE *sb.* 3 a.

1643 MILTON *Divorce* II. xvi. Wks. (1851) 103 No marvell anything, if letters must be turn'd into palisadoes to stake out all requisite sense from entring to their due enlargement. 1658 SIR T. BROWNE *Gard. Cyrus* iii. 47 The notable palisadoes about the flower of the milk-thistle. *a*1658 LOVELACE *Falcon* 78 When now he turns his last to wreak The palizadoes of his beak.

†**b.** = PALISADE *sb.* 3 b. *Obs.*

1607 *Lingua* IV. vi, Tires, Fannes, Palizadoes, Puffes, Ruffes.

c. = PALISADE *sb.* 3 c.

1840 *Penny Cycl.* XVI. 179/2 From Tappan to a distance of about 8 miles from the town of New York, the Palisadoes, as they are called, extend along the river.

4. *attrib.* and *Comb.*

1688 R. HOLME *Armoury* II. 86/2 Pallisado Hedg..made to uphold young Plants that they keep within pounds. 1720 STRYPE *Stow's Surv. London* III. 254 Freestone pavements and palisado pales before the houses.

paliˈsado, *v. Obs.* or *arch.* Forms: see prec. [f. prec. sb.] = PALISADE *v.*

1607 *Relat. Disc. River* in *Capt. Smith's Wks.* (Arb.) Introd. 53 Thursday we laboured, pallozadoing our fort. 1608 CAPT. SMITH *True Relation* Wks. (Arb.) 8 With all speede we pallisadoed our Fort. *c*1710 CELIA FIENNES *Diary* (1888) 71 In ye middle is a Bowling green palisado'd round.

1813 COLERIDGE *Lett., to D. Stuart* (1895) 615, I found Southey so..pallisadoed by preëngagements that I could not reach at him. **1823** BYRON *Juan* VIII. xlvi, The Greek or Turkish Cohorn's ignorance Had palisadoed in a way you'd wonder To see in forts of Netherlands or France.

Hence **pali'sadoed** *ppl. a.* = PALISADED; **pali'sadoing** *vbl. sb.* = PALISADING.

1611 COTGR., *Palissé*, palisadoed, staked, or paled about. **1624** CAPT. SMITH *Virginia* 60 They conducted us to their pallizadoed towne. **1740** PINEDA *Span. Dict., Empalizáda*, the Palizadoing that goes round any fortify'd Place. **1851** C. L. SMITH tr. *Tasso* III. xxxii, Thus the huge bull in palisadoed field Turns with his horn on the pursuing hounds.

palisander (pælɪ'sændə(r)). Also **palissander.** [a. F. *palissandre, palisandre*, prob. of Amer. Ind. origin.] The hard, dark, black-streaked wood of the Brazilian tree, *Dalbergia nigra*, of the family Leguminosæ; also known as Brazilian rosewood. Cf. ROSEWOOD 1. Also *attrib.*

1843 C. HOLTZAPFFEL *Turning & Mech. Manipulation* I. 104 The furniture rose-wood..was afterwards imported as Jacaranda, Palisander, and Palaxander-wood, by which names it is still called on the Continent. **1902** G. S. BOULGER *Wood* II. 270 Palisander-wood... A valuable wood, chiefly used in pianofortes. **1930** *Heal & Son Catal.* 14 The timbers that invite the craftsman's hand..Macassar Ebony, Amaranth and Palisander. **1936** *Burlington Mag.* Aug. 88/2 Furniture in mahogany, palissander, rose- or satinwood. **1941** *Archit. Rev.* LXXXIX. 16 (*caption*) The study, with palisander wood furniture. **1947** J. C. RICH *Materials & Methods Sculpture* x. 294 Brazilian rosewood, also known as Palisander and Jacaranda, is an extremely fine, rare, and expensive variety. **1957** *Times* 4 Nov. 13/1 There is plain Bangkok teak, and palisander wood from South America. **1966** *House & Garden* Dec. 57/1 The Clairtone [hi-fi]..is solid-state encased in rare Brazilian Palisander. **1971** *Country Life* 3 June 1361/1 The top is lined with gilt tooled leather in a surround of palisander wood. **1974** *Ibid.* 3 Oct. 939/1 (*caption*) An 18th-century secretaire bookcase in palissander wood attributed to William Vile. **1977** *Early Music* July 455 (Advt.), The Roessler 'Meister' range [of recorders] is available in rosewood, palisander, olivewood and box-wood.

palise, obs. form of PALACE; var. PALIS *Obs.*

†**paliser.** *Obs.* Also **palliser, palesser, -aser.** [f. PALIS *sb.* + -ER.] **a.** A maker of palings or fences. **b.** One who has charge of a park.

[**1368–9** *Durham Acc. Rolls* (Surtees) 575 Palicero de Mugleswyk et Joh'i Rogerson custodientibus duas portas parci ibidem.] **1442** in Willis & Clark *Cambridge* (1886) I. 387 Thomas Combe paliser..to make the pale of the closure of the college. **1536–7** *Durham Acc. Rolls* (Surtees) 703 Jacobo Foster, palaser de Beaurpark.

palish ('peɪlɪʃ), *a.* [f. PALE *a.* + -ISH[1].] Somewhat pale, rather pale.

1398 TREVISA *Barth. De P.R.* XIX. xi. (Bodl. MS.) lf. 295 b/1 Wateri colour & melky coloure..þat is whitissche oþer palische. **1564–78** BULLEYN *Dial. agst. Pest.* (1888) 45 When nature is so stronge to caste it forthe with a redde colour, palishe or yellowishe. **1627** HAKEWILL *Apol.* (1630) 428 Palish and wanne as a sicke man. **1753** GOLDSM. *Let.* Wks. 1881 IV. 475 Her face has a palish cast too much on the delicate order. **1898** WATTS-DUNTON *Aylwin* (1900) 49/1 A little feathery cloud of a palish gold.

†'**palish,** *v. Obs. rare*[−1]. [ad. F. *paliss-*, extended stem of *palir* to become or render pale.] *trans.* To make pale.

1483 CAXTON *G. de la Tour* L ij, The cold was..grete the whiche made her black and palysshed her colour.

‖**palissé** ('palise), *a. Her.* [F. pa. pple. of *palisser* to furnish with pales or with a palisade.] Said of a dividing line when broken into parallel vertical pointed projections like a palisade; as, ***party per fess palissé.*** **b.** Said of the field when divided into vertical piles (see PILE) of alternate tinctures: the same as *pily paly*.

1780 EDMONDSON *Compl. Body Her.* II. Gloss., *Palissé* is like a range of pallisadoes before a fortification, and so represented on a fesse rising up a considerable length, and pointed at the top, with the field appearing between them.

palissy ('pælɪsɪ). The name of the French master potter Bernard *Palissy* (*c* 1510–*c* 1590), used *attrib.* to designate pottery made by him, his successors, or his imitators.

1858 TROLLOPE *Three Clerks* I. vii. 137 He..was inclined to ridicule the growing taste of the day for torsos, Palissy ware, and Assyrian monsters. **1867** G. M. HOPKINS *Jrnls. & Papers* (1959) 155 Dish of Palissy ware with a pike. **1900** F. LITCHFIELD *Pott. & Porc.* vii. 255 The manufacture of the Palissy ware was continued until the time of Henri IV. **1902** S. WEYMAN *In Kings' Byways* I. 68 The table gleamed with ..Palissy ware and Cellini vases. **1969** S. SITWELL *Gothic Europe* xiv. 162 The rather horrible imitation Palissy pottery made in Portugal with fruit and vegetable and crustacean motifs.

†'**paliure.** *Obs.* [ad. L. *paliūrus*, a. Gr. παλίουρος (Theophrastus).] Name of a thorny shrub, prob. *Paliurus aculeatus* or Christ's-thorn.

1382 WYCLIF *Micah* vii. 4 He that is best in hem, is as a palyure [*gloss*, that is, a sharp bushe, or a thistil, or frijse; **1388** as a paluyre, *marg.* A paluyre is a tasil, ether a scharp buysch]. [**1785** MARTYN *Rousseau's Bot.* xvi, Paliurus or Christ's-Thorn... Being common in Palestine, it is supposed to be the thorn with which our Saviour was crowned.]

palizado, obs. form of PALISADO.

palk(e, erroneous form of *pakke*, PACK *sb.*[1]

‖**palkee, palki** ('pɑːlkiː). *East Ind.* Also 7 **pallakee, palleki(e.** [Hindī †*pālakī, pālkī* palankeen, litter.] = PALANKEEN.

1678 J. PHILLIPS tr. *Tavernier's Voy.* II. II. 175 The Princesses are carried in Palleki's. **1771** J. R. FORSTER *Toreen's Voy. Suratte* in tr. *Osbeck's Voy.* etc. II. 201 The greater nobility are carried in a *palekee*, which looks very like a hammock fastened to a crooked pole. **1828** *Asiatic Costumes* 67 (Stanf.) The doolies..are, like the palkee, borne only by two men. **1896** A. FORBES *Camps, Quarters &c.* 266 The ladies travelled in palanquins, or palkis, as they are more familiarly called.

b. *attrib.* and *Comb.*, as ***palkee-bearer***; **palkee dāk**: see DĀK; **palkee gharry (gharee)** [Hindī *pālki-gāṛī*, f. *gāṛī* carriage]: 'a carriage shaped somewhat like a palankin on wheels' (Yule).

1859 LANG *Wand. India* 121, I was stopped by a set of twelve palkee bearers. **1872** E. BRADDON *Life in India* iv. 121 The weak-springed..box upon wheels (called a *palkee gharee*) of India generally. **1878** *Life in the Mofussil* I. 38 (Y.) The Governor-General's carriage..may be jostled by the hired 'palki-gharry', with its two wretched ponies. **1882** MRS. CUPPLES *Mem. Mrs. Valentine* ii. 24 The journey at that time was performed by means of the palki-dâk.

pall (pɔːl), *sb.*[1] Forms: 1 **pæll**, 1, 4 **pell**, 3 **pel, peal**, 3–5 **pelle**, 3–7 **pal, palle**, 5 *Sc.* **paulle**, 5, 7 **pale**, 6 **paule, pawl(e**, *Sc.* **paill**, 3– **pall.** [OE. *pæll, pęll* 'costly cloak or robe, purple robe, purple', ad. L. *palli-um* pall, coverlet, curtain, cloak; a Greek cloak or mantle, the philosophers' cloak; in Tertullian, the garment worn by Christians instead of the Roman *toga*; later in various eccles. uses: see Du Cange. The historical order of the senses in Eng. is not that of the development of L. *pallium*.]

I. Cloth, a cloth.

1. Fine or rich cloth (as a material); esp. as used for the robes of persons of high rank; in OE. purple cloth, 'purple'. *Obs.*, exc. as poet. *arch.*

c **900** tr. *Bæda's Hist.* I. i. (1890) 26 Of þam bið ʒeweorht se weolocreada tælgh [*MS. B.* pæl]. *c* **1000** ÆLFRIC *Colloquy* in Wr.-Wülcker 96/19 Pællas and sidan (*purpurum et sericum*) deorwyrþe gymmas and gold. *c* **1200** ORMIN 8173 & all þatt wæde þatt tær wass Uppo þe bære fundenn, All wass itt off þe bettste pall þatt aniȝ mann maȝȝ aȝhenn. *a* **1225** *Leg. Kath.* 1461 I-schrud & i-prud ba wið pel & wið purpre. *c* **1330** *King of Tars* 364 In cloth of riche purpel palle. *c* **1400** *Laud Troy Bk.* 2836 And in the temple..Arne clothes fele of gold and palle. *c* **1430** *Hymns Virg.* 86 Where is bicome cesar, þat lorde was of al, Or þe riche man cloþid in purpur & in pal? *c* **1460** *How a Marchande* etc. 197 in Hazl. *E.P.P.* I. 205 Sche put on hur a garment of palle, And mett the marchand in the halle. **1579** SPENSER *Sheph. Cal.* July 173 They bene yclad in purple and pall. *a* **1700** *Little Musgrave* in Ritson *Eng. Songs* II. 215 The one of them was clad in green, The other was clad in pall. **1810** SCOTT *Lady of L.* IV. xii, If pall and vair no more I wear. **1814** —— *Ld. of Isles* IV. xxiii.

2. A rich cloth spread upon or over something; a coverlet, canopy, etc.· *Obs.* or *arch.* in *gen.* sense.

13.. *K. Alis.* 370 Hire bed was mad, forsothe, With pallis, and with riche clothis. *c* **1330** R. BRUNNE *Chron. Wace* (Rolls) 11235 And in hure chaumbre vpon a pal þey corouned hure wyþ a coronal. **1457** in *Somerset Med. Wills* (1901) 173 [A piece of cloth of gold called] le palle. **1500–20** DUNBAR *Poems* lxxvii. 13 To beir the paill of veluet cramase Abone hir heid. *a* **1529** SKELTON *Col. Cloute* 943 Hangynge aboute the walles Clothes of golde & palles. *a* **1578** LINDESAY (Pitscottie) *Chron. Scot.* I. 359 Ane paill of gould sett witht pratious stouns sett abone the kingis heid quhene he sat at meit. **1725** POPE *Odyss.* XIX. 364 With splendid palls the downy fleece adorn. **1794** MRS. RADCLIFFE *Myst. Udolpho* xlii, Over the whole bedding was thrown a counterpane, or pall, of black velvet. **1858** MORRIS *Judgm. of God* 170 He sat beneath a broad white pall.

3. *Eccl.* **a.** A cloth spread upon the altar, an altar-cloth; *esp.* a corporal. *arch.* **b.** A cloth or hanging for the front of an altar, a frontal. *arch.* **c.** A linen cloth with which the chalice is covered. (Cf. PALLA 2.)

c **1000** ÆLFRIC *Hom.* I. 508 And þær stod..arwurðe weofod, mid readum pælle ʒescrydd. *c* **1290** *S. Eng. Leg.* I. 302/92 Weouedes huy founden þreo, With rede palles huy weren i-heoled. **1432–50** tr. *Higden* (Rolls) V. 33 A myncheon scholde not towche the palles of the awter. **1480** CAXTON *Chron. Eng.* IV. (1520) 32 b/1 A woman sholde not touche the holy vessell of the auter, ne the palle. **1519** *Churchw. Acc. St. Giles Reading* 7 For coleryng ed mendyng of the pall. **1699** tr. *Dupin's Eccl. Hist. 11th C.* IX. 95 Why the Chalice is usually cover'd with a Vail or Pale before the Consecration? **1725** tr. *Dupin's Eccl. Hist. 17th C.* I. v. 63 The Linen with which they covered the blessed Eucharist, was called *Corporal*, the *Pall*, the *Shrowd*, *Co-opertorium* or *Syndon*. **1838** *Coronation Service* in Maskell *Mon. Rit.* (1847) III. 83 The Queen..makes her first Oblation; which is a Pall or Altar-Cloth of Gold. **1846** KEBLE *Lyra Innoc.* (1873) 172 The Altar's snow-white pall.

4. A cloth, usually of black, purple, or white velvet, spread over a coffin, hearse, or tomb.

c **1440** *Promp. Parv.* 378/1 Palle, or pelle, or other clothe leyd on a dede body,..*capulare*. **1463** *Burial Ord.* in *Antiq. Rep.* (1807) I. 315 The first herse coueryd with whit within the pale & parclose. *c* **1515** *Cocke Lorell's B.* 8 A ryche pal to ly on yᵉ corse late fro rome is come. **1538** *Croscombe Churchw. Acc.* (Som. Rec. Soc.) 43 Received of Edyth Honythorne for a knylle and the pall vj.ᵈ. *a* **1674** CLARENDON *Hist. Reb.* XI. §245 When the Coffin was put in, the black Velvet Pall that had covered it was thrown over it. **1712** ADDISON *Spect.* No. 517 ⁋2 The coffin was carried by six of his tenants, and the pall held up by six of the quorum. **1852** TENNYSON *Ode Wellington* 6 Mourning when their leaders fall, Warriors carry the warrior's pall.

II. A garment, a vestment.

5. A robe, cloak, mantle; in early times, esp. of rich stuff. *Obs.* or *arch.* in *gen.* sense.

c **1000** ÆLFRIC *Gram.* xliii. (Z.) 257 *Pallium*, pæl, *palliatus*, mid pælle ʒescryd. *c* **1205** LAY. 897 Ȝef us peal [*c* **1275** pal], ȝeue us hors, ȝeue us haihe scrud. *Ibid.* 24597 Ælc oniht hafde pal on And mid golde bigon. **1382** WYCLIF *Esther* viii. 15 Mardoch..schynede in kingis clothis..wrappid with a silken pal and purper. **1483** CAXTON *Gold. Leg.* 44/2 Anon she toke her palle or mantel & covered her. **1575** LANEHAM *Let.* (1871) 5 One of the ten Sibills..cumly clad in a pall of white sylk. **1590** SPENSER *F.Q.* II. ix. 37 In a long purple pall, whose skirt with gold Was fretted all about, she was arayd. **1652** NEEDHAM *Selden's Mare Cl.* 245 It is represented in the Figure of a woman, clothed with a Pall or linen frock. **1745** T. WARTON *Pleas. Melanch.* 214 Divine Melpomene.. Queen of the stately step, and flowing pall. **1824** BYRON *Juan* XVI. xl. *song*, He sweeps along in his dusky pall.

6. *spec.* **a.** *Eccl.* A woollen vestment worn by the Pope, and conferred by him on certain ecclesiastics, esp. metropolitans or archbishops (such conferment being a necessary preliminary to the special functions of their office); it is now a narrow band passing over the shoulders, with short lappets hanging down before and behind, and ornamented with crosses. (Now more usually called PALLIUM; formerly also PALLION.) Hence *transf.* The office or dignity of metropolitan or archbishop.

1480 CAXTON *Descr. Brit.* 25 Offa worshiped Adulph bisshop of lichfeld with the archebisshops palle. **1494** FABYAN *Chron.* VII. ccxxi. 243 This palle is an indument that euery archebysshop must haue, and is nat in full auctoritie of an archebysshop tyll he haue receyued his palle of the pope. **1538** LELAND *Itin.* IV. 102 After such tyme as the Pall of the Archb. of Lichfeild was taken from Lichfeild and restored againe to Canterbury. **1563** *Homilies* II. *Agst. Rebell.* (1859) 592 The Romish rag, which he calleth a pall, scarce worth twelve-pence. **1650** SIR R. STAPYLTON *Strada's Low C. Warres* III. 54 Besides his Pall, the Popes Chamberlain, brought him from Rome, a Cardinalls hat. **1726** AYLIFFE *Parergon* 92 After Consecration he shall have the Pall sent him. **1848** A. HERBERT in *Todd's Irish Nennius* Notes 5 The copier places York and Canterbury, the two palls or archiepiscopates of England, first and second.

b. A robe or mantle put upon the sovereign at coronation; now called the 'royal robe'.

1643 BAKER *Chron., Rich. II* 2 After this, he [the Archbishop] put upon him [Richard II] an upper Vesture called a Pall, saying, *Accipe Pallium*. **1847** MASKELL *Mon. Rit.* III. 115 This now called 'Royal Robe' is the ancient pallium; the 'open pall' as it is called in the orders of Charles II and James II.

7. *Her.* A bearing representing the front half of an archbishop's pall, consisting of three bands in the form of a capital **Y**, charged with crosses. (Also called ***cross-pall.***)

(party) per pall: said of the shield when divided into three parts, of different tinctures, by lines in the directions of those of a capital Y.

1562 LEIGH *Armorie* 182 The fielde is Azure, a Paule Sable. **1610** GUILLIM *Heraldry* IV. ii. 193. **1766** PORNY *Heraldry* (1777) Dict., *Pall*, a figure like a Greek *Y*, about the breadth of a Pallet: it is by some Heralds called a Cross-Pall. **1864** BOUTELL *Her. Hist. & Pop.* (ed. 3) xxi. 356 Surmounted by a pall of the last.

III. 8. *fig.* (Chiefly from 5, or now esp. 4.) Something that covers or conceals, a 'mantle', 'cloak'; in mod. use *esp.* something, such as a cloud, that extends over a thing or region and produces an effect of gloom.

c **1450** tr. *De Imitatione* III. lv. 130 There shal I yelde glory & worship for shame & repreef, a palle of preisyng for mornyng [cf. Isa. lxi. 3]. **1504** ATKYNSON tr. *De Imitatione* III. viii. 203 (heading) Howe grace is to be hyd vnder the palle of humlyte. **1526** *Pilgr. Perf.* (W. de W. 1531) 154 Vnder the pall of very mekenes & symplicite. **1742** YOUNG *Nt. Th.* IX. 2110 By this dark Pall thrown o'er the silent World! *c* **1817** HOGG *Tales & Sk.* V. 353 The sky was overspread with a pall of blackness. **1866** B. TAYLOR *Winter Solstice* Poems 301 Too cold to melt its pall of snow. **1882** F. HARRISON *Choice Bks.* (1886) 438 Overhead by day and by night a murky pall of smoke.

IV. 9. *attrib.* and *Comb.*, as ***pall-canopy, -cloth, -cloud***; ***pall-like*** adj.; **pall-bearer, -holder, -supporter**, one of those attending the coffin at a funeral, to hold up the corners and edges of the pall; †**pall-work**, work in 'pall' or rich cloth (*obs.*).

1707 HEARNE *Collect.* 29 Sept. (O.H.S.) II. 53 *Pall Bearers were Dr. Aldrich, Dr. Turner [etc.]. **1786** MISS E. CLAYTON in *Mrs. Delany's Corr.* Ser. II. III. 411 Lord and Lady Howard are gone to town this morning for poor Pˢˢ. Amelia's funeral. She is one of the pall-bearers. **1898** *Westm. Gaz.* 28 May 8/1 The pall-bearers had taken up their position. **1875** S. HADEN *Earth to Earth* 52 The old English hearse or *pall-canopy. **1541** *Yatton Churchw. Acc.* (Som. Rec. Soc.) 154 Payd for iij stavys to bere yᵉ *pawle cloth. *a* **1425** *Cursor M.* 5125 (Trin.) He dud on him *pal cloping And on his hond sett riche ring. **1886** CORBETT *Fall of Asgard* II. 28 To raise the storm that was to rive the *pall-cloud that hung over Asgard. **1814** M. CUTLER in *Life*, etc. (1888) II. 348 The other *pall-holders—Mr. Thurston, Dr. Worcester [etc.]. *c* **1420** *Anturs of Arth.* ii, Of purpure, and *palle werke, and perrè to pay. *a* **1440** *Sir Degrev.* 632 All of pall work fyn,..Anerlud with ermyn.

pall (pɔːl), *sb.*² *rare.* [f. PALL *v.*¹] A feeling of disgust arising from satiety or insipidity.

1711 SHAFTESB. *Charac.* II. II. §2 (1737) II. 149 The Palls or Nauseatings which continually intervene, are of the worst and most hateful kind of Sensation.

pall (pɔːl), *v.*¹ Also 6–7 **pawl, paul.** [app. aphetic from APPAL *v.*, to which the early senses are parallel. But the literal sense of 'become' or 'make pale' is of rare occurrence, being expressed by the cognate PALE *v.* from PALE *a.*]

I. Intransitive senses.

†**1.** To become pale or dim. *Obs.*

1412–20 LYDG. *Chron. Troy* III. xxv, The name of whom shall pallen in none age, But ever yliche without eclipsing shine.

†**2.** To become faint; to faint, fail (in strength, virtue, etc.). *Obs.*

1390 GOWER *Conf.* III. 13 That other biter as the galle, Which makth a mannes herte palle. **1540–54** CROKE *Ps.* (Percy Soc.) 22 Therefore at his hert woll pall. **1562** PHAER *Æneid* IX. Ee ij, Vnuicted strengthes begin to pal. **1602** SHAKS. *Ham.* V. ii. 9 When our deare plots do paule.

†**b.** To decay, waste away, rot. *Obs. rare.*

?*c* **1475** *Sqr. lowe Degre* 1030 Thus have ye kept your enemy here Pallyng more than seven yere.

†**3.** Of fermented or aerated liquors: To lose briskness or sharpness by exposure to the air; to become flat, vapid, stale, or insipid. **b.** Of blood: To become pale (?) by separation of clot and serum.

c **1430** LYDGATE [see PALLED *ppl. a.*¹ 2]. *c* **1440** *Promp. Parv.* 379/2 Pallyn, as ale & drynke,..*emorior.* **1513** *Bk. Keruynge* in *Babees Bk.* 267 Also yf your swete wyne pale, drawe it in to a romney vessell for lessynge [cf. *c* 1460 J. RUSSELL *Bk. Nurture* 116 ʒiff swete wyne be seeke or pallid put in a Rompney for lesynge]. **1530** PALSGR. 651/2, I palle, as drinke or bloode dothe, by longe standyng in a thynge, *je appallys.* This drinke wyll pall (*s'appallyra*) if it stande vncouered all nyght. **1596** NASHE *Saffron Walden* 115 A cup of dead beere, that had stood pawling by him in a pot three dayes. **1634** HABINGTON *Castara* (Arb.) 63 Sooner..then let pall So pure Canary. **1693** J. CLAYTON *Virginia* in *Misc. Curiosa* (1708) III. 287 When the Weather breaks the Blood palls, and like over-fermented Liquors is depauperated, or turns eager and sharp. **1703** *Art & Myst. Vintners* 11 Lest such Wines should Pall and die upon their hands.

4. *transf.* and *fig.* To become tasteless, vapid, or insipid to the appetite or interest.

a **1704** T. BROWN *Sat. on Marriage* Wks. 1730 I. 58 Oh, the virtue and grace of a shrill caterwauling. But it palls in your game. **1709** STEELE *Tatler* No. 2 ¶1 Beauty is a Thing which palls with Possession. **1748** JOHNSON *Vanity Hum. Wishes* 265 Now pall the tasteless meats. **1868** FARRAR *Seekers* II. ii. (1875) 200 Pleasure may pall or cease to be obtainable. **1882** PEBODY *Eng. Journalism* xviii. 137 His position lost all its charm the instant the work began to pall.

b. Const. *on, upon* (the sense, mind, or organ).

1713 ADDISON *Cato* I. iv, Beauty soon grows familiar.. and palls upon the sense. **1846** RUSKIN *Mod. Paint.* I. II. I. iv. §2 They would satiate us and pall upon our senses. **1879** DIXON *Windsor* II. xxiii. 236 The pastimes of the tilt-yard.. began to pall on him.

5. Of the person or organ: To lose relish or interest; to become satiated or cloyed *with.*

1765 STERNE *Tr. Shandy* VIII. xxxiv, If thy stomach palls with it, discontinue it from time to time. **1832** *Examiner* 673/2 The laity have done much wrong to the clergy in allowing it to..surfeit, and pall..with forbidden wealth.

II. Transitive senses.

†**6.** To make pale, to dim. *Obs.*

1533 ELYOT *Cast. Helthe* II. xxi. (1541) 35 The men and women have the colour of their vysage pallyd [*edd.* 1541–1612 palled]. **1593** Q. ELIZ. *Boeth.* I. met. v. 12 And Luciphar palled by Phebus vpriseth.

†**7.** To make faint or feeble; to enfeeble, weaken; to daunt, appal. *Obs.*

1390 GOWER *Conf.* II. 311 Unkindeschipe..The trouthe of mannes herte it palleth. **1423** JAS. I *Kingis Q.* xviii, The prolixitee Off doubilnesse that doith my wittis pall. **1494** FABYAN *Chron.* VI. clxx. (1533) 98 b/1 His knyghtes and soldyours were tyred & palled wyth ouer watche and laboure. **1556** J. HEYWOOD *Spider & F.* lxxiv. 62 Which.. did their harts so pall, That they cride for peace. **1607** DEKKER *Hist. Sir T. Wyatt* Wks. 1873 III. 119 Tis not the name of Traytor Pals me nor pluckes my weapon from my hand. **1686** F. SPENCE tr. *Varillas' Ho. Medicis* 302 A caprice which pawl'd fortune in such manner that she utterly turn'd tale.

†**b.** To render (breath) inoffensive. *Obs.*

1547 BOORDE *Brev. Health* xx. 14 A remedy to pall or make swete the breth.

†**8.** To render flat, stale, or insipid; to stale.

1625 MASSINGER *New Way* I. i, The remainder of a single can Left by a drunken porter, all night pall'd too. **1682** OTWAY *Venice Preserved* II. i, I cannot think Of tasting any thing a fool has pall'd. **1725** BRADLEY *Fam. Dict.* s.v. *Brewing*, Leaving your Vent-Peg always open palls it [March Beer].

fig. **1700** DRYDEN *Palamon & Arcite* III. 686 A miracle.. Their joy with unexpected sorrow pall'd. **1711** P. H. *View two last Parlts.* 145 The fortunate issue of that Expedition had pall'd the Enquiry. **1807** E. S. BARRETT *Rising Sun* I. 154 He palls enjoyment by excess.

9. To deprive of one's relish for something; to satiate, cloy (the appetite, senses, or sentient being).

1700 ADDISON *Epil. Brit. Enchanters*, And pall the sense with one continu'd show. **1725** N. ROBINSON *Th. Physick* 321 For fear of too much palling his Appetite. **1797** GODWIN *Enquirer* II. xii. 479 He must not pall his readers. **1829** *Examiner* 355/1 Can even the choicest viands fail to pall the stomach? **1856** BAGEHOT *Lit. Stud., Shelley* (1879) I. 113 Languor comes, fatigue palls, melancholy oppresses.

†**pall**, *v.*² *Obs. rare.* [Origin obscure: cf. PALE *v.*⁴]

1. *trans.* To beat, strike, knock (*down*).

a **1375** *Joseph Arim.* 499 Þei miȝte I-seo sone His polhache go and proude doun pallede. **1377** LANGL. *P. Pl.* B. XVI. 30 Þanne with þe firste pyle I palle hym down. *Ibid.* 51 Þanne *liberum arbitrium*..palleth adown þe pouke.

2. *intr.* or *absol.* To fight (one's way) *through.*

c **1400** *Destr. Troy* 10022 Þai met on the Mirmydons, macchit hom hard, Pallit thurgh the persans, put hom beside. *Ibid.* 11132 Þai..Put hom doun prestly, pallit hom þurgh, Slogh hom full sleghly for sleght þat þai couthe.

pall (pɔːl), *v.*³ [f. PALL *sb.*¹] *trans.* To cover with or as with a cloth; to drape with a pall.

c **1400** *Destr. Troy* 8385 The halle..was pight vp with pilers all of pure stones, Palit full prudly. **1605** SHAKS. *Macb.* I. v. 52 Come thick Night, And pall thee in the dunnest smoake of Hell. **1804** J. GRAHAME *Sabbath* 332 Why pall'd in state, and mitred with a wreath Of nightshade, dost thou sit portentiously? **1854** DE QUINCEY *Autobiog. Sk.* Wks. II. 226–7 Nature..so powerless and extinct as to seem palled in her shroud. **1869** TENNYSON *Holy Grail* 844, I saw the Holy Grail, All pall'd in crimson samite.

pall, obs. form of PAL; variant of PAWL.

‖**palla** ('pælə). [L., perh. related to *pallium.*]

1. *Rom. Antiq.* A loose outer garment or wrap worn out of doors by women (sometimes by men); an outer robe, mantle.

1706 in PHILLIPS. **1834** LYTTON *Pompeii* III. ix, The slave ..divested herself also of her long *palla.* **1866** J. B. ROSE tr. *Ovid's Met.* 72 Her palla to another she resigns. **1898** *Westm. Gaz.* 24 Jan. 4/3 Calpurnia..is robed in a brilliant green palla over a long yellow tunic.

2. *Eccl.* An altar-cloth; a chalice-cloth.

1706 PHILLIPS, *Palla*,..it is also often taken for an Altar-cloth. **1885** *Catholic Dict.*, *Palla*, a small cloth of linen used to cover the chalice and usually stiffened with cardboard, &c. The upper part may be covered with silk.

palla, variant of PALLAH, S. African antelope.

pallace, obs. form of PALACE *sbs.*¹ and ³.

pallad, obs. erron. form of PALLET *sb.*²

pallad- ('pæləd), *Chem.*, used as combining form of PALLADIUM, in names of certain compounds, as **'pallada,mine, pallada'mmonium, palla'ddiamine**: see quots.

1859 FOWNES *Man. Chem.* 329 Palladamine, $NPdH_3.O$, may be obtained from the chloride by oxide of silver... Müller also obtained another compound..to which he gives the name of palladdiamine; it contains N^2PdH^6. **1866–77** WATTS *Dict. Chem.* IV. 329 Hugo Müller regards..the yellow [compound] as chloride of palladammonium, $N_2H_6Pd''.Cl_2$. The yellow compound..yields the oxide of palladammonium, or palladamine, $N_2H_6Pd''O$.

Palladian (pæ'leɪdɪən), *a.*¹ [f. L. *palladi-us* of or belonging to Pallas + -AN.] Of or pertaining to Pallas, the goddess of wisdom; hence, pertaining to wisdom, knowledge, or study.

1562 LEIGH *Armorie* 29 b, Perseus the Palladian knight.. when he had slayne..Medusa, he consecrated yᵉ same [shield] to the mighty Goddes Pallas. **1644** MILTON *Areop.* (Arb.) 56 Unlesse he carry..all his midnight watchings, and expence of Palladian oyl, to the hasty view of an unleasur'd licencer. **1803** GODWIN *Life Chaucer* I. 470 (Jod.).

Pa'lladian, *a.*² *Arch.* [f. *Palladi-o* + -AN.] Of, belonging to, or according to the school of the Italian architect Andrea Palladio (1518–80), who imitated the ancient Roman architecture without regard to classical principles.

1731 POPE *Ep. Burlington* 37 Conscious they act a true Palladian part, And, if they starve, they starve by rules of art. **1792** GIBBON *Let.* in *Misc. Wks.* (1796) I. 696 To pass some hours in the palladian Chiswick. **1838** *Civil Eng. & Arch. Jrnl.* I. 94/1 The thrust..directed against that arch-heresy of all, the Palladian style. **1874** MICKLETHWAITE *Mod. Par. Churches* 250 Europe has never seen a worse style than the Palladian.

Hence **Pa'lladianism**, the Palladian school or style of architecture; **Pa'lladianize** *v.*, to make Palladian in style.

1838 *Civil Eng. & Arch. Jrnl.* I. 94/1 The sworn champion of Palladianism, and the bitter foe of all amateurs. **1851** RUSKIN *Stones Ven.* I. App. xv. 386 We shall get rid of Chinese pagodas, and Indian temples, and Renaissance Palladianisms, and Alhambra stucco and filigree, in one great rubbish heap. **1893** GILTSPUR *Church Street Stoke Newington* 27 The south front was Palladianised about the middle of the last century.

palladic (pæ'lædɪk), *a. Chem.* [f. PALLAD(IUM² + -IC 1 b.] Applied to compounds of palladium containing a smaller proportion of the metal than those called *palladious*; as ***palladic oxide*** or ***dioxide of palladium***, PdO_2.

1857 in MAYNE *Expos. Lex.* **1866–77** WATTS *Dict. Chem.* IV. 327 The tetrachloride or Palladic chloride, $Pd^{iv}Cl_4$. *Ibid.* 328 Palladic salts are very unstable, being easily reduced to palladious salts by heat, and by reducing agents.

†**palladie.** *Obs.* = PALLADIUM¹ 1.

1548 W. PATTEN *Exp. Scotl.* Pref. a iij, The well kepyng of the Palladie in Troy was euer the conseruacion..of the citie.

palladiferous (pælə'dɪfərəs), *a.* [See -FEROUS.] Containing or yielding palladium.

1866–77 WATTS *Dict. Chem.* IV. 325 The palladiferous gold of Brazil.

palladine, -yne, obs. forms of PALADIN.

palladio- (pæ'leɪdɪəʊ), *Chem.*, combining form of PALLADIUM², in names of certain compounds.

1841 BRANDE *Chem.* 1089 Palladio-bichloride of Potassium. *Ibid.*, Palladio-protochloride of potassium. *Ibid.* 1090 Prismatic crystals of palladio-cyanuret of potassium. **1866–77** WATTS *Dict. Chem.* IV. 330 Chloride of palladio-phenyl-ammonium.

palladious (pæ'leɪdɪəs), *a. Chem.* Also **palladous.** [f. PALLADI-UM² + -OUS.] Applied to compounds of palladium containing a larger proportion of the metal than those called *palladic*: as ***palladious oxide*** or ***protoxide of palladium***, PdO.

1842 PARNELL *Chem. Anal.* (1845) 95 A solution of palladious oxide. **1866–77** WATTS *Dict. Chem.* IV. 327 Palladious salts are for the most part brown or red; their taste is astringent, but not metallic.

palladium¹ (pæ'leɪdɪəm). Forms: 4–5, 7 **palladion**, 5 **palladioun, -dyon, -dian, -done, -din, paladion**, 6– **palladium.** [a. L. *palladium*, a. Gr. παλλάδιον, neuter of παλλάδιος of Pallas.]

1. *Gr.* and *Lat. Myth.* The image of the goddess Pallas, in the citadel of Troy, on which the safety of the city was supposed to depend, reputed to have been thence brought to Rome.

c **1374** CHAUCER *Troylus* I. 153 (97) But þough þat Grekes hem of Troye shetten,.. Thei hadde a relyk hight Palladion [*v.rr.* palladioun, paladion] That was hire tryst a bouen euerichon. **1390** GOWER *Conf.* II. 188 The Priest Thoas.. Hath soffred Anthenor to come And the Palladion to stele. *c* **1400** *Laud Troy Bk.* 17865 Palladin that thing called is Afftir Pallas..Fro hir It come also, I wene. **1585** T. WASHINGTON tr. *Nicholay's Voy.* II. xiii. 48 Diuers antiquities.., and amongst others the Palladium of antient Troy. **1601** HOLLAND *Pliny* I. 178 Metellus..lost his eies in a skare-fire, at what time hee would haue saued and got away the Palladium..out of the temple of Vesta. **1779** W. ALEXANDER *Hist. Women* (1782) I. vi. 213 Vestals..whose office was to preserve the sacred fire of the goddess in perpetual vigour, and guard the palladium. **1807** ROBINSON *Archæol. Græca* I. xv. 69 The Palladium, or statue of Minerva brought from Troy.

2. *transf.* and *fig.* Anything on which the safety of a nation, institution, privilege, etc. is believed to depend; a safeguard, protecting institution.

1600 HOLLAND *Livy* Pref. 6 These 35 bookes [of Livy].. preserued as another Palladium out of a generall skarefire. **1621** BURTON *Anat. Mel.* II. iii. VII. (1676) 223/2 My Palladium, my breast-plate, my buckler, with which I ward all injuries [etc.]. **1761** HUME *Hist. Eng.* I. xiii. 321 This stone..was carefully preserved at Scone as the true palladium of their monarchy. **1769** BLACKSTONE *Comm.* IV. xxvii. 343 The liberties of England cannot but subsist, so long as this palladium [trial by jury] remains sacred and inviolate. **1769–72** *Junius Lett.* Ded. 6 The liberty of the press is the palladium of all the civil, political, and religious rights of an Englishman. **1845** MCCULLOCH *Acc. Brit. Emp.* (1854) II. 91 The *Habeas Corpus* Act..denominated the palladium of an Englishman's liberty. **1888** M. BURROWS *Cinque Ports* iv. 62 The Charter of 6 Edward I (1278) is the palladium of the Cinque Port liberties.

pa'lladium². *Chem.* [a. mod.L., f. *Pallas*: cf. prec.

Named 1803 by its discoverer Wollaston, from the newly discovered asteroid *Pallas*: cf. CERIUM.]

A hard white metal of the platinum group, resembling silver, occurring in small quantities, chiefly in association with platinum, in S. America and elsewhere. Symbol Pd: atomic weight 126.

1803 *Phil. Trans.* 290 A metallic substance late sold in London as a new metal under the title of Palladium. **1805** WOLLASTON *ibid.* XCV. 316, I..subsequently obtained another metal, to which I gave the name Palladium, from the planet that had been discovered nearly at the same time by Dr. Olbers. **1884** F. J. BRITTEN *Watch & Clockm.* 180 The balance spring is usually of palladium.

attrib. **1866** WATTS *Dict. Chem.* IV. 329 Palladium-bases.

Hence **pa'lladiumize** *v. trans.*, to coat with palladium.

a **1851** *Mech. Mag.* in *Herrig's Archiv* VIII. 268 This process may be called palladiumizing with as much propriety as we say, zinking, or gilding. **1864** in WEBSTER.

pallah ('pælə), Also **palla, paala, pala, phalla, phaala.** [ad. Sechwana *p'hala*, Zulu *im-pala.*] An antelope (*Æpyceros melampus*) inhabiting parts of S. Africa; it is dark-reddish above, dull-yellowish on the sides, and white beneath; the male has horns about twenty inches long and spreading in a lyrate figure.

1806 SIR J. BARROW *Journ. Leetakoo* 407 This species of deer was called by the Booshuanas the Palla. **1812** PLUMPTRE tr. *Lichtenstein's Trav.* II. 324 That beautiful species of Antelope..which is called by the Beetjuans *Phalla.* **1822** BURCHELL *Trav.* II. xi. 300 One is called Paala by the Bichuanas. **1857** LIVINGSTONE *Trav.* iii. 56 The presence of the..pallah..is always a certain indication of water being within a distance of seven or eight miles. **1896** KIRBY *Haunts Wild Game* 546 Impala of the Swazis and Zulus, Pala of the Basuto.

pallaice, -as(e, obs. forms of PALACE.

pallaisada, -ade, obs. ff. PALISADO, -ADE.

pallall (pəˈlɑːl, -æ-). *Sc.* and *north. dial.* Also **pallalls, palall, pallaly, pallaldies palaulays, pally-ully.** [Derivation unknown.] A Scotch and Northern English name for the game of HOPSCOTCH; sometimes, the stone used in the game.
1808–18 JAMIESON, *Pallall, Pallalls,* a game of children, in which they hop on one foot through different triangular spaces chalked out, driving a bit of slate or broken crokery before them. **1828** MOIR *Mansie Wauch* i. 14 Some of her companions took her out to the back of the house to have a game at the pallall. **1847** J. WILSON *Chr. North* I. 3 Pall-lall..or any other of the games of the school play-ground. **1891** BARRIE *Little Minister* xxvii. 292 There were..girls playing at palaulays. **1896** MELDRUM *Grey Mantle* 251 Mony's the time I've played the palladies bare-fit wi' 'm on the plainstanes. **1898** R. BLAKEBOROUGH *Wit, etc. N. Riding Yorksh.* (E.D.D.), Divisions are chalked on the pavement, and the 'pally-ullies' are impelled within the lines by a hop on one leg and a side-shuffle with the same foot.

pallanchine, -kee(n, -kin, pallaquine, obs. ff. PALANKEEN.

pallart, obs. f. PALLIARD.

pallasade, -ado, -zado, obs. ff. PALISADE, -ADO.

pallasite (ˈpæləsaɪt). *Geol.* [f. the name of P.S. *Pallas,* who discovered such a meteorite in 1772, + -ITE[1].] Any of a class of stony-iron meteorites which consist largely of iron (usu. with a small proportion of nickel) and olivine. Hence **pallaˈsitic** *a.*
1868 *Geol. Mag.* V. 78 The arrangement of the meteorites in the museum of Berlin University, by M. G. Rose, is based on their mineral character, and forms two divisions—the metallic and the stony meteorites, the first containing meteoric iron and the Pallasite, the second the Chondrites, Howardites, [etc.]. **1920** *Mineral Mag.* XIX. 59 In most pallasites the iron is poor in nickel,..and the olivine is correspondingly poor in ferrous oxide. **1956** *Nature* 28 Jan. 156/1 From 60 to 1,600 km. the material of the mantle is identified as dunite and from 1,600 to 3,000 km. it is taken as of the same composition as pallasitic meteorites. **1962** [see MESOSIDERITE]. **1977** A. HALLAM *Planet Earth* 134/2 This led to the speculation that ancient peridots were extraterrestrial, extracted from the meteorites known as pallasites.

pallat, -ate, obs. forms of PALATE, PALLET.

pallatine, -yne, obs. forms of PALATINE.

pallavi (pəˈlɑːvɪ). Also **pallevi.** [Origin uncertain.] In the music of southern India, the first section of a song.
1891 C. R. DAY *Mus. & Mus. Instruments S. India* v. 60 Almost all [melodies] consist of a burden or refrain called Pallevi, a kind of answer to this refrain styled Anupallevi, and stanzas (called Charanam) of which there is usually an uneven number. These parts are in the several compositions arranged in different ways. **1914** A. H. F. STRANGWAYS *Mus. Hindostan* iii. 86 A *Pallavi* was then sung round. **1968** *Jrnl. Musical Acad. Madras* XXXIX. 26 A whole line of the Pallavi..had been absent from the piece as current. **1971** *Shankar's Weekly* (Delhi) 11 Apr. 23/1 The pallavi was set to Rupakam with a sub-initial take-off.

palle, obs. form of PALL, PALY *a.*[2]

palled (pɔːld), *ppl. a.*[1] [f. PALL *v.*[1] + -ED[1].]
†**1.** Enfeebled, weakened, impaired. *Obs.*
c **1386** CHAUCER *Manciple's Prol.* 55 So vnweedly was this sory palled goost. *c* **1386** —— *Shipman's T.* 102 (Corpus MS.) Eny old palled [*v.r.* appalled] wight. **1494** FABYAN *Chron.* VII. ccxlv. 288 Than began the trumpettys and tabours to blowe, whiche reuyued the palled hartys. **1601** HOLLAND *Pliny* XII. xii. 364 The colour is more pallat and weake [*colore languido*] inclining to white. **1605** *1st Pt. Ieronimo* II. iv, Which strooke amazement to their pauled speeche. **1606** SHAKS. *Ant. & Cl.* II. vii. 87 Ile neuer follow Thy paul'd Fortunes more. **1668** CULPEPPER & COLE *Barthol. Anat.* II. vi. 100 It receives the Liver blood..which ..is become pauled and sluggish, and has lost its heat.
2. Of fermented liquor, etc.: That has lost its briskness or freshness; flat, stale, vapid. *arch.*
c **1430** LYDG. *Min. Poems* (Percy Soc.) 168 Who forsakithe wyne and drynkithe ale pallid. **14..** *Song temp. Hen. VI* (Harl. MS.), Bryng us home no sydyr, nor no palde wyne. **1565–73** COOPER *Thesaurus, Mucidum vinum,* a palled wine or dead. **1629** MASSINGER *Picture* v. i, With a spoon-ful of palled wine poured in their water. **1711** E. WARD *Vulgus Brit.* v. 58 Or that the Turky..Should..Be pall'd, o'er-roasted, and unfit, For such a Fine-mouth'd Saint to eat. **1884** *Longm. Mag.* Feb. 384 Her high spirits were as flat as palled soda-water.
3. Deadened to pleasant tastes or impressions; satiated, cloyed, disgusted.
1691 DRYDEN *Amphitryon* III. i, Palled in desires, and surfeited of bliss. **1709** STEELE *Tatler* No. 54 ¶1 Pall'd Appetite is humorous, and must be gratify'd with Sauces rather than Food. **1795** SOUTHEY *Vis. Maid Orleans* II. 112 The epicure Here pampers his foul frame, till the pall'd sense Loathes at the banquet. **1859** KINGSLEY *Misc.* (1860) I. 222 The palled taste of an unhealthy age.

palled (pɔːld, *poet.* -ɪd), *ppl. a.*[2] [f. PALL *v.*[3] (or *sb.*[1]) + -ED.] Covered with or robed in a pall.
1839 BAILEY *Festus* xxiii. (1848) 289 Swathed in clouds As though in plumed and pallèd state. **1850** TENNYSON *In Mem.* lxx, Palled shapes In shadowy thoroughfares of thought.

†**ˈpallen,** *a. Obs.* [OE. *pællen, pellen,* f. *pæl,* PALL *sb.*[1] + -EN[4].] Made of 'pall' or rich cloth; in early use, 'of purple'.
c **1000** ÆLFRIC *Hom.* I. 64 Bicgað eow pællene cyrtlas. *c* **1000** —— *Hom.* in *Leg. Rood* (1871) 103 Se casere..dyde of his purpuran & his pellenan gyrlan. *c* **1205** LAY. 23762 A ræf swiðe deore..& ænne pallene curtel. *a* **1400–50** *Alexander* 1517 He plyes ouer þe payment pallen webbes. **14..** *Siege Jerus.* (E.E.T.S.) 322 Piȝten pauelouns doun of pallen webbes, With ropis of riche silk.

pallenkeen, -kine, pallentine, palles, obs. ff. PALANKEEN, PALATINE, PALACE.

pallescent (pəˈlɛsənt), *a. rare.* [ad. L. *pallēscent-em,* pr. pple. of *pallēscĕre* to become pale.] Growing or becoming pale. So **paˈllescence,** a blanching or paling.
1657 TOMLINSON *Renou's Disp.* 345 It beares Apples like the masculine, but lesser and luteously pallescent. **1817** T. L. PEACOCK *Nightmare Abbey* ix, The spirit of black melancholy began to set his seal on her pallescent countenance. **1822** —— *Maid Marian* ii, An awful thought, which caused a momentary pallescence in his rosy complexion.

pallesie, -ye, obs. forms of PALSY.

pallet, *sb.*[1] *Obs.* exc. *Sc.* Forms: 4–5 palet, -ete, pallette, 5–6 palett(e, 6 pallat(t, 6 (9 *Sc.*) pallet, (7 -ed). [a. OF. *palet,* dim. of *pal* stake.]
†**1.** A piece of armour for the head, a head-piece (usually of leather). *Obs.*
1374 *Inv.* in *Promp. Parv.* 379 *note,* Item, ij. ketelhattes, et ij. paletes, *prec'* vj.*s.* viij.*d.* **1399** LANGL. *Rich. Redeles* III. 325 A preuy pallette her pannes to kepe, To hille here lewde heed in stede of an houe. **1405** in *Promp. Parv.* 379 *note,* Doublettes, jakkes, basynettes, vysers, palettes, aventailles. **1411** *E. E. Wills* (1882) 19 An aburioun of stele with a pallette couerte with reede velwette. *c* **1440** *Promp. Parv.* 378/2 Palet, armowre for the heed, *pelliris, galerus.* *c* **1475** *Pict. Voc.* in Wr.-Wülcker 782/34 Nomina Armorum... *Hec tassis,* a palett...*galea.*
2. *transf.* The head, pate. Now only *Sc.*
c **1330** *Arth. & Merl.* 4016 On the helme he smot for soth, Thurch helme and palet to the toth. *a* **1352** MINOT *Poems* vii. 131 Inglis men sall..Knok þi palet or þou pas, And mak þe polled like a frere. **1500–20** DUNBAR *Poems* xxxiii. 51 As blaksmyth bruikit was his pallatt, For battering at the study. *a* **1529** SKELTON *Elynour Rummyng* 348, I shall breake your palettes, Wythout ye now cease! **1582** STANYHURST *Æneis* I. (Arb.) 21 Neptun..his pleasing pallet vp-heauing Hee noted Aeneas. **1596** NASHE *Saffron Walden* 50 Not a pinnes head or a moaths pallet. **1638** BRATHWAIT *Barnabees Jrnl.* I. C ij, Till I brake a Blacksmith's palled. **1826** G. BEATTIE *John o' Arnha'* in *Life* (1863) 248 The ither bore The gausty pallet, grim with gore.

pallet (ˈpælɪt), *sb.*[2] Forms: α. 4–5 paillet(t, 4–6 payllet, paylet, 4–7 pailet, 5 palyet, 6 *Sc.* pelat; β. 5–6 palet(t, 6 -ette, 6–7 pallate, (6–8 -ad, 7 palate), 7–8 pallat, 6– pallet. [ME. *paillet*: cf. dial. F. *paillet* heap or bundle of straw, deriv. of *paille* straw:—L. *palea* chaff; also AF. *paillette* straw, in Bestiary 475.]
1. A straw bed; a mattress; a small, poor, or mean bed or couch.
c **1374** CHAUCER *Troylus* III. 229 (180) On a pailet [*v.r.* paylet] al þat glade nyght By Troylus he lay. *c* **1440** *Promp. Parv.* 379/2 Palyet, lytylle bed, *lectica.* *c* **1450** *Bk. Curtasye* 435 Gromes palettis. **1505** *Acc. Ld. High Treas. Scot.* III. 150 Item, for stra to the Quenis pelat.. xijd. **1557** *Order of Hospitalls* G ij, Of Beddes, Bolsters, Mattresses,..Pallads. **1615** BP. HALL *Contempl., O.T.* XI. iv, This man, though great in Bethlehem, lays him down to rest upon a pallet. **1758** GOLDSM. *Mem. Protestant* (1895) I. 115, I perceived the Water had soaked through the Pallet. **1827** MOORE *Epicur.* xvi. (1839) 165 Content with a rude pallet of straw. **1883** FROUDE *Short Stud.* IV. I. xi. 128 The monks then sought their pallets.
fig. **1601** HOLLAND *Pliny* I. 527 All this preuaileth not in a leane and hungry ground, vnlesse fatter earth be laied as a pallet vnderneath. **1634** MILTON *Comus* 318 Ere..the low roosted lark From her thatch't pallat rowse.
b. *Comb.,* as ***pallet-bed, -chamber, -couch.***
1513 MORE *Rich. III* (1882) 82 King Richard..came out in to the pallet chamber, on which he found in bed sir James and sir Thomas Tyrels. **1618** SIR S. D'EWES *Autobiog.* (1845) I. 111, I assisted at her pallet-side, kneeling, weeping, and praying with others. **1707** CHAMBERLAYNE *St. Gt. Brit.* II. xiv. 175 The Gentlemen of the Bed-Chamber..whose Office..is to lie by the King on a Pallet-Bed all Night. **1814** SCOTT *Ld. of Isles* IV. xxiii, That pallet-couch, and naked wall.
†**2.** *Naut.* See quots. *Obs.* (It is not certain where this belongs; some place it under the next.)
1704 J. HARRIS *Lex. Techn.* I, *Pallet* is a Room within the Hold of a Ship, closely parted from it, in which by laying some Pigs of Lead, &c. a Ship may be sufficiently ballasted, without losing room in the Hold; which therefore will serve for Stowing the more Goods. **1867** SMYTH *Sailor's Word-bk., Pallet,* a ballast-locker formerly used, to give room in the hold for other stowage.

pallet (ˈpælɪt), *sb.*[3] Also 8 palet, pallat, (8–9 palate). [a. F. *palette,* dim. of *pale* spade, shovel, blade, etc., a word of many senses, some of which in English retain the form PALETTE, q.v.]
1. A wooden instrument consisting of a flat blade or plate, with a handle attached; *spec.* that used, in various forms, by potters and others for shaping their work.
1558 WARDE tr. *Alexis' Secr.* 114 Styrynge it well fyrste with a sticke, and than with a pallet broade at the ende. **1686** PLOT *Staffordsh.* 390 A rodd of Iron fastned to a pallet, that reaches out a little beyond the Anvil. **1725** BRADLEY *Fam. Dict.* s.v. *Ointment,* Beat it with a wooden Palet, and change the Water, so that it becomes as white as Milk. **1727–41** CHAMBERS *Cycl., Pallet,* among potters, crucible-makers, etc., is a wooden instrument..for forming, beating, and rounding their works. They have several kinds; the largest are oval with a handle;..others..in manner of large knives. **1837** J. T. SMITH tr. *Vicat's Mortars* 95 *note,* The pallet or board (called the 'hawk'), used by plasterers for mixing small quantities of stucco as they apply it.
2. An artist's tablet for paints; a PALETTE, q.v.
†**3. a.** A flat board, plate, or disk; e.g. the blade of an oar, the float of a paddle-wheel. *Obs.*
1721 *Phil. Trans.* XXXI. 244 There's no Improvement to be made, either with respect to the Proportion of the Oars, their Length, the Breadth of the Pallets. **1725** H. DE SAUMAREZ *ibid.* XXXIII. 412 At each End of the Lines, which constitute the Angle,..are two Pallets not much unlike the Figure of the Log. **1727** BRADLEY *Fam. Dict.* s.v. *Fox,* The Fox..will endeavour..to pull out the Food he smells in the Hole..and cause the Pallet to fall. **1808** *Specif. Trevithick & Dickinson's Patent* No. 3148 A rowing wheel.. furnished with floats or pallets, but which we call our propelling boards.
spec. **b.** *Brickmaking.* A board for carrying away a newly moulded brick: cf. PLANCHET. **c.** Each of the series of disks in a chain-pump.
1839 URE *Dict. Arts* 189 As the wheel revolves, the piston rods..will cause the pistons to force the new-moulded bricks, with their pallet or board under them, severally up the mould. **1875** KNIGHT *Dict. Mech., Pallet*...3. One of the series of disks or pistons in the chain-pump or chapelet... 7. (*Clay.*) *a.* A board on which a newly molded brick is carried away to the *hack. Ibid.* [see PAGE *sb.*[1] 8].
d. A portable tray or platform used, esp. in conjunction with a fork-lift truck, for moving or stacking heavy loads in convenient units. Also *attrib.*
1921 R. V. WRIGHT et al. *Material Handling Cycl.* 97 *Pallet,* a flat platform..used to pile material on. **1948** *P.O. Telecomm. Jrnl.* I. IV. 119/2 A pallet is a double-faced wooden or metal platform with a space between the top and bottom faces significantly large to permit the entry of the forks of a forklift truck. **1958** [see FORK *sb.* 16]. **1961** *Times* 10 June 11/6 Tomatoes..packed, 120 at a time, into 'pallets' or metal trays supplied by British Railways. **1963** *Times* 23 July 7/3 The soldiers will sit in what are called 'people pallets' which will be dropped from low-flying Lockheed C130 assault aircraft. The pallets, which hold 12, 24 or 48 men, will be carried on the open cargo ramp at the rear end of the aircraft. **1971** *Power Farming* Mar. 13/2 Five-ton high-lift pallet trailers were used to transport the carrots from the field to the packing station. **1974** *Guardian* 20 Mar. 5/4 Pack your goods onto a standard pallet up to 40″ × 48″. .. We lift the whole pallet and take it to any of..17 different European destinations. **1976** *Farnborough Internat. Exhib.* (Official Programme) 17 Hawker Siddeley Dynamics..has a £6m. contract to build experiment carrying pallets for Spacelab. **1978** S. BRILL *Teamsters* vii. 266 Pallets are the wooden trays under which any heavy cargo is loaded.
†**4.** *Gilding.* A flat brush for taking up gold-leaf.
1727–41 CHAMBERS *Cycl., Pallet,* in gilding, is an instrument made of a squirrel's tail; used to take up the gold leaves from the pillow, to apply and extend them on the matter to be gilt.
5. A projection on some part of a machine, which engages with the teeth of a wheel, and thus converts a reciprocating into a rotary motion, or *vice versâ*; *esp.* a projection upon the pendulum or the arbor of the balance-wheel of a clock or watch, engaging with the escapement-wheel. [So in Fr.]
1704 DERHAM in *Phil. Trans.* XXV. 1788 It is scarce possible to manage the Pallets so, as nicely to make the same Vibrations as were *in Vacuo.* **1730–6** BAILEY (folio), *Pallats,* two nuts that play in the fangs of the crown wheel of a watch. *a* **1774** GOLDSM. *Surv. Exp. Philos.* (1776) I. 149 The pendulum has two palates,..which at equal intervals rise and fall, and let the teeth of the wheels pass under them in equable succession. **1830** KATER & LARDNER *Mech.* xiv. 194 The pallets are connected with the pendulum so as to oscillate with it.
6. In an organ: Any one of the valves in the upper part of the wind-chest, each of which is connected with a key of the keyboard, and, on being opened by pressing down the key, admits the 'wind' or compressed air to a groove beneath the set of pipes corresponding to that key.
Also applied to other valves, as ***waste-pallet,*** a valve allowing escape of air from the storage-bellows when too full.
1840 *Penny Cycl.* XVI. 493/2, E is the spring which keeps the pallet in its place when not in use. **1852** SEIDEL *Organ* 48 Of various sorts of valves..those called palates are the most important ones. **1898** STAINER & BARRETT *Dict. Mus. Terms* 338 In order to prevent an undue rising of the bellows when more wind is supplied than used, a *waste-pallet* is placed in every bellows.
7. *Bookbinding.* A tool for impressing letters or figures on the back of a book, consisting of a metal block mounted on a handle and having the letters, etc. engraved upon it, or the required types fastened in it.
1875 *Ure's Dict. Arts* I. 425 The tools..whether single letters or figures, or 'pallets' (that is, the title of a book, &c., cut in a single metal block) are mounted on wooden handles, and applied before use to a gas burner, in order to obtain the requisite heat.
8. *Conch.* = PALETTE 4 a.

9. *attrib.* and *Comb.*, as *pallet-frame*, *-spring*, *-wheel*, *-wire*; **pallet-arbor**, an arbor on which a pallet (in a clock, etc.) is fixed; **pallet-board** = sense 3 b; **pallet-box**, in an organ, a box or chest forming part of the wind-chest, containing the pallets belonging to one keyboard; **pallet-eye**, in an organ, a loop of wire at one end of a pallet, to which is attached the wire by which it is pulled down; **pallet-leather**, in an organ, the soft leather with which the inner surface of a pallet is faced; **pallet-moulding**, in *Brick-making*, a process in which each brick as moulded is turned out on a pallet, and the mould sanded to prevent adhesion of the clay; **pallet-tail**, each of the rocking arms which bear the pallets in certain escapements.

1883 SIR E. BECKETT *Clocks & Watches* 185 In all clocks of this kind the *pallet-arbors are set in small cocks. **1875** *Ure's Dict. Arts* I. 529 (*Brick-making*) This operation is repeated each time that a *pallet-board comes under the hopper. **1898** STAINER & BARRETT *Dict. Mus. Terms* 339 Attached to a loop of wire called the **pallet-eye*, fastened to the moveable end of the pallet. **1825** J. NICHOLSON *Operat. Mechanic* 521 That part of the *pallet frame.. in which is set the stone for receiving the action or impulse of the small pin teeth, is formed into a rectangular shape. **1875** KNIGHT *Dict. Mech.* s.v., In *pallet-molding the molds are usually sanded; in slop-molding they are wetted. **1876** PREECE & SIVEWRIGHT *Telegraphy* 84 The wheel has fifteen teeth cut on its circumference; its play is regulated by two small pallets.. and two small steel *pallet-springs. **1884** F. J. BRITTEN *Watch & Clockm.* 226 The *pallet staff holes are found to wear very much if not jewelled. **1793** SIR G. SHUCKBURGH in *Phil. Trans.* LXXXIII. 88 The index that is carried round immediately by the pendulum, viz. on the same arbor with the *pallet wheel. **1852** SEIDEL *Organ* 51 Muller has tried to put all the *palate-wires, belonging to one manual, into one common hole.

pallet (ˈpælɪt), *sb.*[4] *Her.* Also 7 **palett.** [dim. of PALE *sb.*[1] 6.] An ordinary resembling the pale (PALE *sb.*[1] 6), but of half its breadth.

1572 BOSSEWELL *Armorie* 12 But it [the Pale] may be diminished, as from a Paile to a Pallet which is ye halfe of the Paile. **1661** MORGAN *Sph. Gentry* II. iii. 33 The pale, whose content is the third part of the whole field, and is divided again into the Pallet, which is half the pale, and the Endors which is half the Pallet. **1864** BOUTELL *Her. Hist. & Pop.* iii. 15 The arms of Raymond, Count of Provence—or, 4 pallets gules.

†**pallet**, *sb.*[5] *Obs.* [a. F. *palette*, OF. *paellete* (Gloss. de Salins, 13–14th c.), dim. of *paele* shallow pan:– L. *patella*.] A vessel of a definite measure used to receive the blood in blood-letting.

1627 HAKEWILL *Apol.* III. v. §5. 205 A.. Surgeon.. reports that he drew from a patient.. in foure dayes twenty seven pallets, euery pallet.. containing three ounces and more.

†**pallet**, *a. Obs. rare.* [a. OF. *palet* (13–14th c. in Godef.), dim. of *pâle* PALE *a.*; but in reference to wine, cf. *vin paillet* light or straw-coloured wine.] Of a light colour between red and white; pale red, flesh-coloured.

1565 COOPER *Thesaurus*, *Heluus color*, a pallet colour, or a fleash colour of white and redde. **1573–80** BARET *Alv.* C 792 Horseflesh colour, or pallet colour in wine. *c* **1600** BURELL *Pilgr.* in J. Watson *Coll. Scot. Poems* (1709) II. 11 Vpon thair brest.. The Rubie pallet and Th' opall, Together with the Amatist. **1611** COTGR., *Vin baillet*, a pallet, or pale Claret, wine. **1632** SHERWOOD, Pallet wine, *vin baillet, vin paillet*.

pallet, obs. form of PALETTE, PALATE.

pallet (ˈpælɪt), *v. rare.* [f. PALLET *sb.*[2]] *intr.* To lie *down* to sleep on or as on a pallet.

1921 G. C. SHEDD *Lady of Mystery House* xix. 263 He and I could pallet down on the porch.

palleting (ˈpælɪtɪŋ). *Naut.* [cf. PALLET *sb.*[2] 2.] 'A slight platform made above the bottom of the magazine, to keep the powder from moisture' (*Weale's Rudim. Nav.* 136). Also *attrib.*, as *palleting-beam*, *-hatches*.

1815 BURNEY *Falconer's Dict. Marine*, *Palletting Hatches* .. are small apertures, about 20 inches square, formed by the palletting-beams and carlings in the fore-magazine. *c* **1850** *Rudim. Navig.* (Weale) 95 *Palletting-Beams* are those beams under the flat of the magazine, bread-room, and powder-room, where there is a double palleting.

palletization (ˌpælɪtaɪˈzeɪʃən). [f. PALLETIZE *v.* + -ATION.] The action or process of palletizing or of becoming palletized. Also *attrib.*

1946 *Chem. Industries* Aug. 294 (*heading*) Palletization. **1957** *Economist* 19 Oct. 257 They will advise on palletisation, mechanical handling and other modern techniques. **1965** R. B. ORAM *Cargo Handling* v. 83 Whisky in cases and cartons, insulation material in bags and fire bricks; all this was cargo that lent itself to palletization. **1967** *Times Rev. Industry* Feb. 71/3 The introduction of more efficient cargo-handling techniques, i.e., palletisation, containerization, packaged timber, roll-on, roll-off, &c.

palletize (ˈpælɪtaɪz), *v.* [f. PALLET *sb.*[3] + -IZE.] *trans.* To place on a pallet; to transport on a pallet; to convert a loading system to the use of pallets. (See PALLET *sb.*[3] 3 d.) So **ˈpalletized** *ppl. a.*; **ˈpalletizing** *vbl. sb.*

1954 in WEBSTER Add. **1959** *Times Rev. Industry* Apr. 77/2 Wagons specially designed for palletized loading. **1960** *Farmer & Stockbreeder* 1 Mar. 71/3 Palletizing, widely used in industry, and for fruit and potatoes, has not, it is believed, been used in this. **1964** *Economist* 3 Oct. 61/2 Goods being palletised in advance. **1967** *Jane's Surface Skimmer Systems 1967–68* 21/2 Palletised loads can be 'floated' in on hover-pallets supplied with air from the main compressor. **1970** *Financial Times* 13 Apr. 9/7 A feature of the building is that the structural steel frame is designed as a space frame to perform the function of storing palletised goods. **1977** *R.A.F. News* 22 June–5 July 3 (Advt.), Removals—Home and overseas Storage—Palletised containers.

palletot, pallew: see PALETOT, PALEW.

pallial (ˈpælɪəl), *a.* [ad. mod.L. *palliāl-is*, f. PALLIUM: see -AL[1].] **a.** *Zool.* Of or pertaining to the pallium or mantle of a mollusc (or of a brachiopod).

pallial adductor, the anterior adductor muscle of a bivalve; ***pallial cavity, impression, line, lobe, sac***: see quots.; ***pallial sinus***, a sinus or recess in the pallial impression of certain molluscs, being the mark of their retractile siphons.

1836 TODD *Cycl. Anat.* I. 706/1 It is in this pallial sac that the animal establishes a current of water. **1851–6** WOODWARD *Mollusca* 26 The border of the 'mantle' is also muscular; and the place of its attachment is marked in the shell by a line called the 'pallial impression'. **1858** GEIKIE *Hist. Boulder* vi. 96 The inner surface of each valve is lined with a soft membranous substance, called the pallial lobe. **1872** NICHOLSON *Palæont.* 216 The 'pallial line' or 'pallial impression'. **1877** HUXLEY *Anat. Inv. Anim.* i. 59 In some Mollusks (e.g. Pteropoda), the delicate lining membrane of the pallial cavity serves as the respiratory organ. **1888** ROLLESTON & JACKSON *Anim. Life* 698 (Brachiopoda) A circumpallial sinus uniting the terminations of the pallial sinuses is figured by Joubin in *Discina*.

b. *Anat.* Of or pertaining to the pallium of the brain.

1901 [see NEOPALLIUM]. **1933** *Proc. Nat. Acad. Sci.* XIX. 7 Below the reptiles the entire pallial field is dominated by the olfactory system. **1965** L. B. AREY *Developmental Anat.* (ed. 7) 495 [The commissures] cross partly in the lamina and partly in the fused adjacent portions of the median pallial walls.

†**ˈpalliament.** *Obs.* [ad. med.L. *palliāment-um*, f. *palliāre* to cloak.] A robe, gown: in quots. the white gown of a candidate for the Roman consulship.

1588 SHAKS. *Tit. A.* I. i. 182 Titus Andronicus, the people of Rome.. Send thee by me.. This Palliament of white and spotlesse Hue, And name thee in Election for the Empire. **1593** PEELE *Honour of Garter* 92 A goodly king in robes most richly dight, The upper like a Roman palliament.

palliard (ˈpæljəd). *Obs.* or *arch.* Forms: 5 **payllard, -art,** 6 **palȝard, -ȝart, -yarte, pallart,** 6–7 **palyard(e, pallyard,** 6–9 **paillard,** 6– **palliard.** [a. F. *paillard*, in 13th c. *paillart*, f. *paille* straw: see -ARD.] A professional beggar or vagabond (who sleeps on the straw in barns and outhouses); *transf.* a low or dissolute knave; a lewd fellow, a lecher, a debauchee.

1484 CAXTON *Fables of Æsop* II. xviii, The foxe was but a theef and a payllart and a knaue of poure folke. *c* **1500** *Melusine* 294 Ye ought not to meue your self for suche a theef & palyard. **1525** LD. BERNERS *Froiss.* II. clxix. [clxv.] 492 He was but a false palyarte, and alwayes agaynste the Crowne of Fraunce. **1561** AWDELAY *Frat. Vacab.* 4 A Palliard is he that goeth in a patched cloke. **1567** HARMAN *Caveat* vii. 44 The worst and wickedst of all this beastly generation are scarse comparable to these prating Pallyardes. **1614** RALEIGH *Hist. World* II. (1634) 476 A most luxurious and effeminate Palliard he [Sardanapalus] was. *c* **1690** KIRKTON *Hist. Ch. Scotl.* ii. (1817) 84 Not only a debauched paillard but a cruel murtherer. **1834** H. AINSWORTH *Rookwood* III. v, Palliards,.. and Jarkmen. **1851** BORROW *Lavengro* III. 315 The male part of the upper class are.. a parcel of poor, shaking, nervous paillards.

b. *attrib.* or *adj.* Knavish; dissolute.

1484 CAXTON *Fables of Æsop* II. xvi, Ha a payllart Mule, why goost thow not faster? **1581** *N. Burne's Disput.* in *Cath. Tractates* (S.T.S.) 170 Vsurpit Bischopis, apostat preistis and palliard Ministeris. **1638** *Sat. on Gen. Assembly* in *Scott. Pasquils* (1868) 42 A palyard drunkard charlitan.

†**palliardise.** *Obs.* Also 6 **-ice,** 6–7 **-ize.** [a. F. *paillardise* (1539 in R. Estienne), f. prec. + -ISE[2].] Lewdness, fornication, lechery.

1591 LODGE *Diogenes* (Hunter. Cl.) 46 Nothing.. more weakeneth an Armye.. than luxuritie and palliardize. **1614** RALEIGH *Hist. World* I. vi. §5 Hee [Jupiter] gave himself over wholly to palliardize and adultery. **1646** BUCK *Rich. III* v. 136 Nor can they tax him with Palliardise, Luxury, Epicurism.

So †**ˈpalliardry,** †**ˈpalliardy** [= F. *paillardie* (Villon)], roguery, knavery; lechery, fornication.

1513 DOUGLAS *Æneis* IV. Prol. 178 ȝe that list of ȝour palȝardry neuir blyn. *c* **1560** A. SCOTT *Poems* xxxiv. 82 Thocht ȝung perwersit natouris To palȝardy applawddis. **1570** *Satir. Poems Reform.* xxii. 80 Thy subteltie and palȝardrie Our fredome bringis in thrall.

†**ˈpalliardize,** *v. Obs.* [f. PALLIARD + -IZE.]
1. *intr.* To fornicate.

1619 T. MILLES tr. *Mexia's, etc. Treas. Anc. & Mod. T.* II. 364/1 Charlemaigne, whose eldest daughter was found paillardising with.. Eginhard, his Secretary. **1650** ANNE BRADSTREET *Four Mon., Assyr., Sardan.* 3 Sardanapalas.. That palliardizing sot.

2. *trans.* To be a procurer of.

1644 PRYNNE & WALKER *Fiennes's Trial* 2 To.. let the Parliament see, they had not employed such a man as would palliardise Lies, and become a pander unto Falshood.

palliasse: see PAILLASSE.

palliate (ˈpælɪət), *ppl. a.* [ad. L. *palliātus* cloaked, f. *palli-um* cloak (-ATE[2] 2); afterwards pa. pple. of late L. *palliāre* to cloak, palliate.]

†**A.** as *pa. pple.* Cloaked, covered, concealed; mitigated. *Obs.*

a **1548** HALL *Chron., Hen. IV*, Introd. (1550) 4 b, They sente the reuerent father Thomas Arundell.. in habite pallyate and dissimuled, into the citee of Paris. **1605** BACON *Adv. Learn.* II. x. §5 The fault.. must be accommodate and palliate by dyets and medicines familiar. **1637–50** ROW *Hist. Kirk* (1842) 242 That was still the cloak under whilk was palliat all the wicked plotts aganis the Kirk of God.

B. as *adj.* †**1.** Wearing a cloak (in quot., a philosopher's cloak: see PALLIUM 1). *Obs.*

1610 HEALEY *St. Aug. Citie of God* XIII. xvi. (1620) 457 Lest the communication of this name with the vulgar, should debase the proud.. number of the Palliate.

†**2.** Cloaked; having its real nature concealed.

1612 R. FENTON *Usury* 128 That.. may in matter bee a palliat or cloaked vsurie. **1648** HAMMOND *Serm.* iv. Wks. 1684 IV. 494 God may.. give us a treacherous settlement, a palliate peace.

†**3.** Of a cure: Superficial or temporary. *Obs.*

a **1625** COPE in Gutch *Coll. Cur.* I. 131 All his industry and sales, did in your estate make but a palliate cure. **1679** PRANCE *Addit. Narr. Pop. Plot* 30 Cardinal Poole.. did not .. absolve their Consciences from Restitution, but only made a palliate Cure.

4. *Zool.* Having a PALLIUM (sense 3 b); tectibranchiate.

1890 in *Cent. Dict.*

palliate (ˈpælɪeɪt), *v.* [f. PALLIATE *ppl. a.*; cf. late L. *palliāre* (Apuleius, 2nd c.) to cloak, F. *pallier*, which may have aided the formation.]

†**1.** *trans.* To cover with or as with a cloak; to cloak, clothe, shelter; to invest. Also *fig. Obs.*

a **1548** HALL *Chron., Hen. VII* 32 Surmyse set foorth and palliated with the vesture.. of a professed veritee. **1613** R. CAWDREY *Table Alph.* (ed. 3), *Palliate*, cloake. **1630** T. WESTCOTE *Devon.* (1845) 60 Her sheep.. are palliated under the coverture of the high-grown hedges of enclosures. **1635** GELLIBRAND *Variation Magn. Needle* 3 The Ocean, which palliates the imperfect parts of the Earth. **1656** BOULTON *Medicina* Ded. A ij b, It is the accustomed manner of our modern Writers, alwaies to palliate themselves under the Protection of some worthy Patron.

†**2.** *fig.* To hide, conceal, disguise. *Obs.* or *arch.*

1598 BACON *Sacred Medit.* vii. (Arb.) 117 Hipocrites with their dissembling holinesse towardes God doe palliate and couer their iniuries towardes men. **1706** PHILLIPS, *To Palliate*, to disguise, daub, colour or cloak. **1795** GOUV. MORRIS in Sparks *Life & Writ.* (1832) III. 58 The bankruptcy of their India Company, long palliated, now stands confest. **1809–12** MAR. EDGEWORTH *Almeria* vii, Her name was printed among the list of subscribers, and there was no palliating the fact.

3. To alleviate the symptoms of a disease without curing it; to relieve superficially or temporarily; to mitigate the sufferings of; to ease.

In early use the notion was that of cloaking, disguising, patching up; this passed gradually into that of alleviating the symptoms: cf. 4.

1588 J. READ *Compend. Method* 60 They [bone-diseases] eyther bee neuer cured, or else onelie so palliated that they breake out againe. **1601** HOLLAND *Pliny* II. Explan. Words Art A v b, So sweet Pomanders doe palliat a stinking breath, occasioned by a corrupt stomack or diseased lungs, and such like. **1646** FULLER *Wounded Consc.* (1841) 351 Let mountebanks palliate, cures break out again, being never soundly but superficially healed. *a* **1714** ABP. SHARP *Serm.* (1738) V. ix. 284 He is but half a Physician; he hath palliated our sores and diseases, but he hath not removed them. **1876** ROGERS *Pol. Econ.* xxi. (ed. 3) 281 That which cannot be cured must be palliated.

4. To disguise or colour the real enormity of (an offence) by favourable representations or excuses; to represent (an evil) as less than it really is; to cause to appear less guilty or offensive by urging extenuating circumstances; to extenuate, excuse.

This has passed gradually from the sense of cloak (as in 2), disguise, colour, to that of extenuate, lessen the gravity of.

1634 W. TIRWHYT tr. *Balzac's Lett.* 317, I neede not seeke colours to palliate my actions or words. **1653** H. COGAN tr. *Pinto's Trav.* ix. 27 This advice causing him to see his fault .. he labored to have palliated it with certain excuses. **1777** ROBERTSON *Hist. Amer.* I. III. 215 They endeavoured to palliate what they could not justify. **1856** FROUDE *Hist. Eng.* (1858) II. vi. 83 The illegal imprisonment cannot be explained away, and cannot be palliated. **1878** LECKY *Eng. in 18th C.* I. i. 119 These considerations only slightly palliate his conduct.

b. To excuse (a person).

1862 M. B. EDWARDS *John & I* xxxi. (1876) 236 As well endeavour to show that black is white, as to prove that any temptations you may have had can in the smallest degree palliate you.

†**5.** To make less emphatic or pronounced; to moderate, mitigate, qualify or tone down (esp. one's action or statement). Also *absol.* or *intr.* To take up a more moderate position, to compromise. *Obs.*

1665 PEPYS *Diary* 31 Dec., The great evil of this year.. is the fall of my Lord of Sandwich, whose mistake about the prizes hath undone him.. though sent (for a little palliating it) Embassador into Spayne. **1672** MARVELL *Reh. Transp.* I. 223 Do you think the Christians would have palliated so far, and colluded with their Consciences? **1711** HEARNE *Collect.* (O.H.S.) III. 135 The Author.. is forc'd to palliate what he said about Mr. Harley's being an Accomplice by an Advertisement he has in his Paper last Night. **1748** RICHARDSON *Clarissa* (1749) II. xxxvi. 241 To obtain this time, you must palliate a little, and come into some seeming compromise. **1796** MORSE *Amer. Geog.* II. 489 This fanciful piece of beauty [small feet] was probably invented by the ancient Chinese, to palliate their jealousy.

†**b.** To appease, please, or indulge (one's taste).

1631 WEEVER *Anc. Fun. Mon.* 154, I haue inserted these parcels of the Psalter, that by this occasion my Reader might palliate his taste with an Essay of our Ancestors old English. *a* **1632** T. TAYLOR *God's Judgem.* II. vii. (1642) 110 Next all the Candies, Preserves, all the Junkets.. to palliate his taste.

†**c.** To moderate the hostility of. *Obs. rare.*

1678 BUNYAN *Pilgr.* Apol. 59 Yea, that I might them better palliate [*ed.* 1684 *altered to* moderate], I did too with them thus Expostulate.

palliated (ˈpælɪeɪtɪd), *ppl. a.* [f. prec. + -ED[1]; taking the place of the earlier PALLIATE *ppl. a.*]

1. Cloaked (*lit.* and *fig.*); †covered over, concealed; †superficially healed; mitigated, extenuated: see the vb.

1612 SELDEN *Illustr. Drayton's Poly-olb.* x, Merlin Ambrose.. slighted that pretended skill of those magicians, as palliated ignorance. **1643** PRYNNE *Sov. Power Parl.* App. 192 That they might act a certain palliated Fable. **1665** NEEDHAM *Med. Medicinæ* 400 The palliated Diseases return with more severity than before. **1840** BARHAM *Ingol. Leg.* Ser. I. *Passage Life H. Harris*, The half-avowed, and palliated confession of committed guilt. **1857** MAYNE *Expos. Lex.*, *Palliatus*.. covered with a cloak; veiled; mantled; applied to pains subdued or lulled by the use of opiates: palliated.

2. Having the archiepiscopal PALLIUM.

1892 *Tablet* 6 Aug. 204 This very Vicarial and Palliated See of Arles.

palliating (ˈpælɪeɪtɪŋ), *ppl. a.* [f. as prec. + -ING[2].] That palliates: in the senses of the vb.

1679 *Gentl. Calling* Pref. §5 Palliating Medicines. **1710** in Somers *Tracts* II. 261 The Majority of that House were.. satisfied with a palliating Answer, jumbled up by the Junto. **1758** JORTIN *Erasm.* I. 514 Luther.. discountenanced and rejected all such palliating schemes, and.. was determined never to yield an inch. **1845** MRS. S. C. HALL *Whiteboy* ii. 14, I wish I could show those who cry out against Irish outrage.. a few of the palliating circumstances.

palliation (pælɪˈeɪʃən). [a. F. *palliation* (13–14th c. in Littré), ad. med.L. *palliātiōn-em*, n. of action from *palliāre*: see PALLIATE.]

†**1.** The action of palliating; the cloaking or concealing (of an act, etc.); that which serves to conceal or hide; a cloak, covering. *Obs.*

1577 PATERICKE tr. *Gentillet* (1602) 228 They make her [justice] serve.. as a palliation or coverture, for all assassi[n]ments, murders, and vengeances. **1649** MILTON *Eikon.* xxvii. **1660** H. MORE *Myst. Godl.* To Rdr. 9 The generality of Christians make the external frame of Religion but a palliation for sin. **1794** SULLIVAN *View Nat.* V. 344 Candour would wish to throw a veil over the failings of an illustrious character; but deliberately perpetrated crimes have no claim to palliation.

2. The action of disguising or seeking to make less conspicuous, the enormity of (a crime, etc.) by excuses and apologies; extenuation; excuse; often in phrase ***in palliation of***.

1605 BACON *Adv. Learn.* II. xi. §3 Herein comes in crookedly and dangerously, a palliation of a great part of Ceremoniall Magicke. **1766** GOLDSM. *Vic. W.* xxx, This.. though not a perfect excuse, is such a palliation of his fault as induces me to forgive him. **1867** FREEMAN *Norm. Conq.* I. vi. 570 He could not.. invoke even the tyrant's plea of necessity in palliation of his evil deeds.

3. The alleviation of the symptoms and incidents of disease without curing it; hence *gen.* alleviation, mitigation, temporary relief.

1626 BACON *Sylva* §61 A wise physician will consider whether a disease be incurable;.. if he find it to be such, let him resort to palliation; and alleviate the symptom. **1651** BIGGS *New Disp.* ¶83 Palliations of diseases. **1783** JOHNSON *Let. to Dr. Mudge* in Boswell, Excision is doubtless necessary to the cure, and I know not any means of palliation. **1863** HOLLAND *Lett. Joneses* xxii. 314 You utterly refuse to admit that there is any palliation of your misery.

palliative (ˈpælɪətɪv), *a.* and *sb.* [a. F. *palliatif, -ive* (13–14th c. in Littré), f. L. type **palliātīv-us*: see PALLIATE and -IVE.]

A. *adj.* †**1.** Serving to cloak or conceal. *Obs.*

1611 COTGR., *Paliatif*, palliatiue; cloaking, hilling ouer, couering. **1656** BLOUNT *Glossogr.*, *Palliative*, that cloaketh, covereth or concealeth.

2. Serving to relieve (disease) superficially or temporarily, or to mitigate or alleviate (pain or other evil).

1543 TRAHERON *Vigo's Chirurg.* 43 b/2 We wyll speake of his cure aswel eradicatyue as palliatyue. **1651** BIGGS *New Disp.* ¶263 At the best a Fontanel is.. but a palliative cure. **1750** JOHNSON *Rambler* No. 32 ¶6 The cure for the greatest part of human miseries is not radical, but palliative. **1889** *Allbutt's Syst. Med.* VIII. 887 These drugs at best are no more than palliative.

3. Tending to extenuate or excuse.

1779 J. DUCHE *Disc.* (1790) I. iv. 62 The palliative arts they make use of to reconcile their duty with their passions. **1782** WARTON *Rowley Enq.* 85 He openly defends his new attempt, not in a palliative apology, but in a peremptory declaration. **1849** C. BRONTE *Shirley* x. 148 If her auditress ventured.. to put in a palliative word, she set it aside with a certain disdain.

B. *sb.* **1.** That which gives superficial or temporary relief; that which serves to alleviate or abate the violence of pain, disease, or other evil.

1724 SWIFT *Drapier's Lett.* Wks. 1755 V. II. 134 Those palliatives which weak, perfidious, or abject politicians are .. in all diseases, so ready to administer. **1803** *Med. Jrnl.* X. 549, I.. confined myself to palliatives, the principal of which was laudanum. **1846** H. ROGERS *Ess.* I. iv. 179 We are promised a cure of our malady, and we are treated with palliatives. **1877** OWEN *Wellesley's Desp.* Introd. 27 A timely palliative, if not a radical cure, for immediate and urgent evils.

2. An extenuating representation.

1748 RICHARDSON *Clarissa* (1811) II. xxix. 184 What shall we think of one, who seeks to find palliatives in words? *a* **1797** H. WALPOLE *Geo. II* (1847) III. xi. 309 [This was] a palliative of the latter's obliquity, if justice would allow of any violation. **18..** W. SCOTT (Webster 1864), He had been what is called, by manner of palliative, a very gay young man.

Hence **ˈpalliatively** *adv.*, in a palliative manner; in a way that serves to lighten or mitigate.

1714 MANDEVILLE *Fab. Bees* (1733) II. 345 The weakness of the language it self may be palliatively cured by strength of elocution. **1822–34** *Good's Study Med.* (ed. 4) III. 490 In such cases we should proceed gently and palliatively.

palliator (ˈpælɪeɪtə(r)). [agent-n. in L. form from PALLIATE.] One who palliates or alleges extenuating considerations; an extenuator.

1792 MAD. D'ARBLAY *Lett.* 20 Dec., The worst.. will not risk losing their only abettors and palliators in this kingdom. **1824** *Examiner* 435/1 He is.. a palliator of every powerful and profitable abuse. **1878** SPURGEON *Treas. Dav.* Ps. cvi. 30 Phinehas.. was no trimmer, or palliator of sin.

palliatory (ˈpælɪətərɪ), *a.* [f. as prec. + -ORY.] Characterized by palliation; having the function or effect of palliating.

1665 M. NEEDHAM *Med. Medicinæ* 401 There remains no more room for the like palliatory proceeding. **1845** BUNTING in B. Gregory *Side Lights Confl. Meth.* (1898) 414 Some explanations are very palliatory but not justificatory.

pallid (ˈpælɪd), *a.* Also 7 **palid.** [ad. L. *pallid-us*, f. root *pall-* in *pall-ēre* to be pale, *pall-or* paleness.] Lacking depth or intensity of colour, faint or feeble in colour, wan, pale. (Said chiefly of the human face as affected by death, sickness, or passion, hence *transf.* of these causes themselves.) Chiefly *poet.* before 1800, exc. in *Bot.*

1590 SPENSER *F.Q.* III. ii. 28 So soone as Night had with her pallid hew Defaste the beautie of the shyning skye. **1591** —— *Ruines Rome* xv, Ye pallid spirits, and ye ashie ghoasts. **1596** —— *F.Q.* v. xi. 45 Gainst which the pallid death findes no defence. *c* **1611** CHAPMAN *Iliad* VIII. 65 Pallid fear made boldest stomachs stoop. **1700** DRYDEN *Fables, Ceyx & Alcyone* 484 Then flick'ring to his palid Lips, she strove To print a Kiss. **1776** WITHERING *Brit. Plants* (1796) III. 409 Involucrum slender, pallid, cloven into segments. **1795** SOUTHEY *Joan of Arc* III. 315 A blush suffused Her pallid cheek. **1816** KIRBY & SP. *Entomol.* (1818) II. xix. 125 *note*, The dorsal segments are covered with very short pallid.. hairs. **1876** BRISTOWE *The. & Pract. Med.* (1878) 606 The symptoms due to loss of blood get developed.. the patient.. becomes excessively pallid.

b. *Comb.*, as *pallid-faced, -looking, -tomentose* adjs.; also in comb. with a word of colour, as *pallid-grey, -fuliginous, -ochraceous*, etc.

1887 W. PHILLIPS *Brit. Discomycetes* 61 Cup subsessile, contorted, pallid-fuliginous. *Ibid.* 185 Hymenium pale umber or pallid-grey. *Ibid.* 265 Scattered or gregarious, hemispherical, pallid-tomentose. **1897** P. WARUNG *Tales Old Regime* 248 Among the crowd which lined the height was a pallid-faced girl. **1897** *Outing* (U.S.) XXX. 437/1 With the mullet came the pallid-looking suckers.

Hence **ˈpallidly** *adv.*, **ˈpallidness.**

1656 *Artific. Handsom.* 43 [They] sometimes appear pallidly sad, as if they were going to their graves. **1838** POE *A. G. Pym* Wks. 1864 IV. 185 Gigantic and pallidly white birds. **1661** FELTHAM *Resolves* II. lxvi. (ed. 8) 328 Let no man then be discouraged with the pallidness of Piety. **1826** SCOTT *Woodst.* xvi, The stern repose of the eye, and death-like pallidness of the countenance.

ˌpallidi-, combining stem of L. *pallid-us* pale, used in some terms of Nat. Hist., as **pallidiˈflorous** *a.*, pale-flowered. **pallidiˈpalpate** *a.*, having pale palpi. **pallidiˈtarsate** *a.*, having pale tarsi. **pallidiˈventrate** *a.*, having a pale abdomen.

1857 in MAYNE *Expos. Lex.*

pallidity (pəˈlɪdɪtɪ). [f. L. *pallid-us* pale + -ITY.] Paleness of countenance, pallor.

1808 W. HERBERT *Ella Rosenberg* II. 185 Our looks indicated the pallidity and languor of sorrow. **1835** *New Monthly Mag.* XLIV. 469 He.. sinks into pallidity and paralysis.

pallie, variant of PAULIE *a. Sc.*

pallieȝoun, obs. Sc. form of PAVILION.

pallification: see PALIFICATION.

†**ˈpallify**, *v.*[1] *Obs.* [irreg. f. L. *palli-āre* or F. *palli-er* + -FY.] *trans.* = PALLIATE *v.* 3.

1544 PHAER *Regim. Lyfe* (1553) B v, Remedy to pallyfie the coppred face that is vncurable. **1576** BAKER *Jewell of Health* 59 b, It.. palifyeth or rather hydeth the forme of the Leprie. *Ibid.* 108 a, It pallyfieth any contagious sore or griefe.

†**ˈpallify**, *v.*[2] *Obs. rare*$^{-1}$. [f. L. *pallē-re* to be pale + -FY: cf. *horrify*.] *trans.* To make pale.

1576 NEWTON *Lemnie's Complex.* (1633) 148 So much had the horrour of death.. within few houres pallified his colour.

†**ˈpalliment.** *Naut. Obs. rare.* [ad. obs. F. *palemente*, also *palmante, palamente*, 1543 in Jal, = It. *palamento*, Sp. *palament*, the oars of a galley collectively, oarage, f. It. *pala* blade of an oar, etc. Cotgr. has '*pallamente*, part of the Orelop or vpper decke of a Galley'; so *palamento* in Florio.] The oarage of a galley (or ? as in Cotgr. and Fl.)

1585 T. WASHINGTON tr. *Nicholay's Voy.* II. x. 44 Hauing mended and newe couered a peece of our palliment.

palling (ˈpɔːlɪŋ), *vbl. sb.* [f. PALL *v.*[1] + -ING[1].] The action of PALL *v.*[1]; the losing of freshness, flavour, or interest, etc.: see the verb.

1703 *Art & Myst. Vintners* 5 The Palling or Flatting of Wines. **1833** DISRAELI *Cont. Flem.* III. xvii, I know not the palling of passion. **1873** SYMONDS *Grk. Poets* v. 129 To prevent the palling of so much luxury on sated senses.

ˈpalling, *ppl. a.*[1] [f. as prec. + -ING[2].] That palls upon the taste, etc.: see the verb.

1666 DRYDEN *Ann. Mirab.* ccix, Their palling taste the journey's length destroys. **1749** FIELDING *Tom Jones* VIII. xiv, The trifling amusements, the palling pleasures, the silly business of the world. **1858** HAWTHORNE *Fr. & It. Note-Bks.* II. 180 The fresh fruit flavor; rich, luscious, yet not palling.

Hence **ˈpallingly** *adv.*

1821 CAMPBELL in *New Monthly Mag.* II. 236 Their subjects remind us of fables rather pallingly familiar to our school-boy memories.

palling, *ppl. a.*[2] [f. PALL *v.*[3] + -ING[2].] That covers with, or as, a pall.

1832 R. CATTERMOLE *Beckett*, etc. 175 Terror, first, In frenzied haste withdraws the palling shroud.

pallio- (ˌpælɪəʊ), combining form of PALLIUM, used in zoological terms relating to the pallium or mantle of a mollusc, etc.; as **palliobranchiate** (-ˈbræŋkɪət) *a.*, belonging to the *Palliobranchiata* or *Brachiopoda*, the tubes of the mantle being supposed to be branchia or gills; **pallioˈcardiac** *a.*, pertaining to the mantle and the viscero-pericardial sac of a cephalopod; **palliopedal** (-ˈpɛdəl) *a.*, pertaining to the mantle and foot of a mollusc.

1851–6 WOODWARD *Mollusca* 281 The only argument for supposing the *Rudistes* to have been *palliobranchiate. **1883** E. R. LANKESTER in *Encycl. Brit.* XVI. 677/2 Certain membranes.. and a curious muscular band—the *pallio-cardiac band—traverse the sac. **1878** BELL *Gegenbaur's Comp. Anat.* 348 In Haliotis.. they [nerves] pass off from the common pedal ganglionic mass (the *pallio-pedal ganglia).

†**ˈpallion**[1]. *Obs.* Also 3 **palliun**, 3–6 **-oun**, 4 **-oune.** [a. OF. *pallion, -un* (12th c. in Godef.), ad. L. *pallium*: see PALLIUM.] = PALL *sb.*[1] (usually in sense 6 a), PALLIUM.

c **1290** *Becket* 306 in *S. Eng. Leg.* I. 115 Heo gonne sende sone Aftur is palliun [*Harl. MS.* 248 pallioun] to rome. *c* **1330** R. BRUNNE *Chron.* (1810) 148 Biside þam on þer schip com a bisshop doun, þe mast in hand gan kip, with croice & pallioun. *c* **1450** *St. Cuthbert* (Surtees) 7793 With his pallion his eyen he hidde. **1480** CAXTON *Chron. Eng.* xcvii. 78 Saynt gregory.. sent to seynt Austyn his pallion & made hym primat and Archebisshop of Englond. *a* **1510** DOUGLAS *King Hart* xli, Dame Danger hes of dolour to him drest Ane palliou n that na proudnes hes without.

pallion[2] (ˈpæljən). [Derivation obscure: cf. Sp. *pallon* (paˈʎon), a quantity of gold or silver from an assay, It. *pallone*, augm. of *palla* ball.] A small piece or pellet.

1727 *Philip Quarll* 170 In the Manner as they make Pallions on Board with old Cable Ends. **1799** G. SMITH *Laboratory* I. 101 Cut it into little bits, or pallions, lay the bits or pallions of solder upon it. **1884** BRITTEN *Watch & Clockm.* 243 Run small pallions of suitable solder evenly over it.

pallion, -oun, obs. Sc. forms of PAVILION.

pallisade: see PALISADE.

pallish: see PAL.

pallite (ˈpɑːlaɪt). *Min.* [a. F. *pallite* (Capdecomme & Pulou 1954, in *Compt. Rend.* CCXXXIX. 288), f. *Pall-o*, the name of its locality in Senegal + -ITE[1].] A white or greyish ferrian variety of millisite.

1954 *Mineral. Abstr.* XII. 440 Two types of Ca-Al phosphates are distinguished: (1) Pallite.. formed by the action of calcium phosphate on montmorillonite; (2) Crandallite.. formed by the leaching of (1). **1960** *Amer. Mineralogist* XLV. 257 Uranium is present in amounts up to 140 ppm U in pallite.

‖**pallium** ('pæliəm). Pl. pallia. [L. *pallium*: see PALL *sb.*[1]]

1. *Antiq.* The Latin name for the large rectangular cloak or mantle worn by men, chiefly among the Greeks; esp. by philosophers, and by ascetics and others in the early Christian Church. (= Gr. ἱμάτιον, HIMATION.)

1564 *Brief Exam.* ****** iiij, Paule..sent for his *Pallium.* **1596** SPENSER *State Irel.* Wks. (Globe) 630/2 The Greekes ..afterwardes..chaunged the forme therof into their cloakes, called Pallia, as some of the Irish also doe. **1766** SMOLLETT *Trav.* xxviii. II. 61 He is larger than the life, cloathed in a magnificent pallium. **1850** MRS. JAMESON *Sacr. & Leg. Art* 44 Except in the wings and short pallium they resemble the figures of Grecian kings.

2. *Eccl.* **a.** The woollen vestment conferred upon archbishops in the Latin Church: = PALL *sb.*[1] 6 a.

1670 LASSELS *Voy. Italy* I. 227 Whose Bishop hath the ensignes of an Archbishop, to wit, the vse of the Pallium, and the Crosse. **1807** COXE *Austria* I. ii. 23 In order to receive the confirmation of his office, and the pallium from the hands of the Pope. **1851** HUSSEY *Papal Power* III. 133 The first recorded instance of a grant of the pallium, the consecrated scarf, which was the badge and certificate of Metropolitan authority. **1874** GREEN *Short Hist.* vii. §2. 359 Whatever had been his part in the schism, Cranmer had received his Pallium from the Pope.

b. An altar-cloth: = PALL *sb.*[1] 3 a.

1865 KINGSLEY *Herew.* xxvi, The altar was bare; the golden pallium which covered it gone.

3. †**a.** *Anat.* (See quot.) *Obs.*

1793 HOLCROFT *Lavater's Physiog.* x. 60 Anatomists have not..bestowed any name on the curtain, or pallium, extending from the beginning of the nose to the red upper lip proper.

b. *Zool.* The integumental fold or MANTLE of a mollusc (or of a brachiopod).

1872 NICHOLSON *Palæont.* 201 The inner surface of the valves..is lined by expansions of the integument which secrete the shell,..called the 'lobes' of the 'pallium' or 'mantle'. **1880** BASTIAN *Brain* 85 These same contractions of the pallium are also subservient.

c. *Ornith.* The MANTLE of a bird, i.e. the back and folded wings taken together, when distinct in colouring, etc. (*rare.*)

d. *Anat.* The wall of the cerebral hemispheres (including, in mod. use, the rhinencephalon). Cf. ARCHI-, NEO-, and PALÆOPALLIUM.

1890 *Jrnl. Anat. & Physiol.* XXV. 106 When the surface of a cerebral hemisphere is carefully examined, it is seen to be capable of a natural division into two parts: a basal region, or Rhinencephalon, and a superior portion, or Pallium. **1901** *Ibid.* XXXV. 442 And His..freely admits that the rhinal fissure is the line of demarcation between the 'pallium' and the 'rhinencephalon'. **1934** L. B. AREY *Developmental Anat.* (ed. 3) xv. 414 The telencephalon consists of three regional parts. One is the corpus striatum. .. The second division is the rhinencephalon, or archipallium, while the remainder of the hemisphere makes up the neopallium. The last two portions comprise all of the externally visible hemispheres, and together may be called the pallium. **1948** A. BRODAL *Neurol. Anat.* 323 It is only in mammals that the dorsal cortex undergoes a marked development, and increases progressively in the phylogenetic ascent, to reach its peak of development in man, in whom it forms the bulk of the entire pallium. **1972** *Jrnl. Neurochem.* XIX. 2031 During the last third of the gestational period, the cerebral pallium of the rabbit develops from a primitive vesicle with a total weight of about 100 mg to a highly organised structure 10 times as large.

4. *Meteorol.* A sheet of cirro-stratus cloud uniformly covering the whole sky.

1883 SCOTT *Meteorol.* I. vii. 126 For the uniform sheets.. M. Poëy has proposed the name of *Pallium*, a cloak, but this term has not met with general acceptance. **1885** T. W. BACKHOUSE in *Nature* No. 799. 361 The nearest approach here to a pallium of these singular clouds was on the morning of December 12.

5. *attrib.*

1894 MOYES in *Dublin Rev.* Oct. 419 The Archiepiscopal or Pallium oath was naturally held to be a sufficiently binding tie between the entire bishops of the province and the Holy See. **1895** G. MEREDITH *Amaz. Marr.* x, They must be the very ancient pallium philosophers, ensconced in tubs.

pallizado, obs. form of PALISADO.

pall-mall (pɛl'mɛl, pæl'mæl). Also 6–7 pallemaille, 7 pallemaile, paille maille, -mail, palemaille, pelemele, pelmel, pal-mall, 7–9 pell mell. [a. obs. F. *pallemaille*, *palmaille*, *palmail* (16th c.), *paillemail*, *palemail*, *-maille* (17th c.), a. It. *pallamaglio* (Florio 1598–1611: see quot. in sense 1), lit. 'ball-mallet', f. *palla* 'any kind of ball, ballet, or boule', + *maglio* 'a mallet or a beetle'. It. *palla* is a variant of *balla* ball; *maglio*:—L. *malleus* hammer. Cf. also MALL.]

†**1.** A mallet for striking a ball; *spec.* that used in the game described in sense 2. *Obs.*

1568 *Cal. Scot. Papers* (1900) II. 558 [Mary was playing at Seton] richt oppinlie at the feildis with the palmaill and goif. **1605** ERONDEL *Fr. Garden for Eng. Ladies* N iij b, If one had Paillemails, it were good to play in this Alley, for it is of a reasonable good length, straight and euen. **1611** FLORIO, *Palamaglio*, a pale-maile, that is a stick with a mallet at one end of it to strike and cast a wooden ball with, much vsed ..in Italy. Also the game or play with it.

2. A game practised in Italy, France and Scotland, from the 16th c., and in England in the 17th c., in which a boxwood ball was driven through an iron ring suspended at some height above the ground in a long alley; the player who, starting from one end of the alley, could drive the ball through the ring with the fewest strokes or within a given number of them winning the game.

1598 DALLINGTON *Meth. Trav.* (1606) T iv b, Among all the exercises of France, I preferre none before the *Pallemaille*... I maruell wee haue not brought this sport also into England. **1599** JAS. I Βασιλ. Δωρον III. (1603) 121 The exercises I would have you to use are..playing at the caitche or tennise, archery, palle maille. **1634** PEACHAM *Compl. Gent.* xix. §3. 233 Their [the French] exercises are for the most part Tennise play, Pallemaile [etc.]. **1647** *Perfect Occurr.* 15–22 Oct. in *Thomasson Tracts* (Br. Mus.) XXIX. No. 42. 292 His Majesties [Chas. I] usuall Recreations are Hunting, Pelmel, and Tennes. **1650** SIR R. STAPYLTON *Strada's Low C. Warres* v. 113 Playing at Pall Mall. **1656** BLOUNT *Glossogr.* s.v. *Pale Maille*, This game was heretofore used at the Alley near St. Jameses, and vulgarly called Pel-Mel. **1661** PEPYS *Diary* 2 Apr., To St. James's Park, where I saw the Duke of York playing at Pelemele, the first time that ever I saw the sport. **1884** *Chambers's Jrnl.* 1 Nov. 695/1 A couple of the mallets and a ball used in the old game of pall-mall. **1890** A. LANG in *Golf* (Badm. Libr.) (1895) 11 The game of pell mell is probably older in Scotland than in England, and was borrowed from our 'auld ally' of France.

†**b.** Applied to the Persian *changān* or polo. *Obs.*

1684 PHILLIPS tr. *Tavernier's Trav.* IV. v. 154 Here [at Ispahan] the men play at Pall-mall on horseback, the Horseman being to strike the Ball running at full speed, between the two Goals.

†**3.** The alley in which the game was played.

1644 EVELYN *Diary* 27 Feb., [St. Germains] a very noble garden and parke, where is a pall-maill. *Ibid.* 1 May, At Blois..we walked up into yᵉ Pall Mall. **1663** PEPYS *Diary* 15 May, I walked in the Parke, discoursing with the keeper of the Pell Mell, who was sweeping of it; who told me of what the earth is mixed that do floor the Mall, and that over all there is cockle-shells powdered. **1671** *Phil. Trans.* VI. 2152 The Alleys are of the largeness of a Pal-mall. **1679–88** *Secr. Serv. Money Chas. & Jas.* (Camden) 133 To Lawrence Dupuy,..to be laid out and expended towards the repayring the Pall Mall in St. James's Parke.

b. The name of a street developed from one of these alleys in London, now the centre of London club life; also used as a synonym for the War Office which was situated in Pall Mall.

[**1650** *Ret. Commiss. Crown Lands* in *Archæol. Jrnl.* (1854) XI. 256 Elm trees standing in Pall Mall Walk, in a very decent and regular manner on both sides the walk, being in number 140.] **1656–7** in P. Cunningham *Handbk. Lond.* (new ed.) 372/2 Down the Haymarket and in the Pall Mall. **1660** PEPYS *Diary* 26 July, We went to Wood's at the Pell Mell (our old house for clubbing). **1661** T. RUGGE *Diurnall* Sept. (B. M. MS.), [The road] from Charing Cross to St. James', by St. James' Park wall and at the backside of Pall Mall, is now altered, by reason a new Pall Mall is made for the use of His Majesty in St. James' Park by the wall. **1691** WOOD *Ath. Oxon.* II. 573 He died in his house situated in the Pall Mall within the Liberty of the City of Westminster. **1714** GAY *Trivia* II. 258 O bear me to the path of fair Pall Mall; Safe are thy pavements, grateful is thy smell! **1854** WAY in *Archæol. Jrnl.* XI. 256. **1861** THACKERAY *Four Georges, Geo. III* 71 Pall Mall is the great social Exchange of London now..the mart of news, of politics, of scandal, of rumour. **1893** *Daily News* 17 Apr. 4/7 It would be a very strong thing for Whitehall or Pall Mall to overrule the joint discretion of the military and municipal authorities.

4. *Comb.*, as †**pall-mall-beetle** [BEETLE *sb.*[1]], the mallet used in the game.

1644 DIGBY *Nat. Bodies* ix. 73 We see a stroak with a rackett vpon a ball, or with a pailemaile beetle vpon a boule maketh it fly from it.

pall-mall, obs. form of PELL-MELL.

‖**pallone** (pal'lone). [It. *pallone* foot-ball, balloon, augm. of *palla* ball.] An Italian game, somewhat resembling tennis, played with a large ball struck with a cylindrical wooden guard, worn over the hand and wrist.

1873 'OUIDA' *Pascarèl* I. 33 Riding in the bullock waggons, and driving the ball at pallone. **1885** *New Bk. Sports* 90 Pallone, though a far simpler game [than tennis], is, to the layman, a pretty sight. **1886** SYMONDS *Renaiss. It., Cath. React.* (1898) VII. xi. 166 Her [Italy's] lyrist had to sing of pallone-matches instead of Panhellenic games.

pallor ('pælə(r)). [a. L. *pallor*, n. of state from root *pall-* in *pallēre*: see PALLID.] Paleness.

1656 *Artific. Handsom.* 42 There is some little change of the complexion from a greater degree of pallor, to a lesse. **1656** BLOUNT *Glossogr.*, *Pallor*, a pale colour, paleness, wanness. **1866** HUXLEY *Elem. Physiol.* ii. (1869) 59 It is quite possible to produce pallor and cold in the rabbit's ear. **1885** MISS BRADDON *Wyllard's Weird* I. i. 8 It was a pretty little face, even in the pallor of death.

b. *Comb.*, as ***pallor-dimmed*** adj.

1857 J. L. TUPPER in *Ruskin: Rossetti* (1899) 161 Pallor-dimmed frozen, nakedling!

Pallottine ('pælətaın), *a.* and *sb.* [f. the name of Vincent *Pallotti* (1795–1850), an Italian priest who founded in 1835 the Society of the Catholic Apostolate, a society of R.C. priests, lay brothers, sisters, and associates, known formerly as the Pious Society of Missions, and known popularly as the Pallottine Fathers.]

A. *adj.* Also **Pallottian, Pallotine**. Belonging or pertaining to the Society founded by Pallotti.

B. *sb.* A member of the Society.

1890 *Tablet* 19 July 98/2 The English Pallottine Fathers (Society of Missions) have bought the Palazzo Caccia in Rome, and intend converting it into a seminary. **1894** M. E. HERBERT *Life Vincent Pallotti* xiv. 153 The Pallottine Sisters have also large schools adjoining the church. **1896** [see CONSULTOR 1 b]. **1903** P. J. CHANDLERY *Pilgrim-Walks in Rome* xvi. 409 The church is served by the Pallotine Fathers. **1962** J. S. GAYNOR *Eng.-Speaking Pallottines* 5 They set about realising the Pallottian ideal in the world. **1962** *Times* 1 Sept. 8/3 Provincial of the Pallottine Fathers. **1971** *Shrewsbury Diocesan Year Bk.* 84 Pallottine Missionary Sisters, Pallotti Hall, Siddington, near Macclesfield. **1976** *Billings* (Montana) *Gaz.* 20 June 12-B/6 Church and state Saturday were ready to crack down on the Pallottine Fathers, an order of Roman Catholic priests dedicated to helping the poor abroad but accused of using millions in charitable funds for land ventures and loans to local politicians.

pallour, var. PALOUR, a shell-fish.

pallozado, obs. corrupt f. PALISADO.

pallsay, obs. f. PALSY.

pally ('pælı). Colloq. abbrev. and spelling of PALAIS DE DANSE.

1928 D. H. LAWRENCE *Lady Chatterley* xi. 189 The new girls in their silk stockings, the new collier lads lounging into the Pally or the Welfare. **1947** I. BROWN *Say Word* 72 Whether with hurdy-gurdy on the pavement or with boogie-woogie in the 'Pally', still they favour a word with rhyming syllables. **1948** *Amer. Speech* XXIII. 319/2 *Pally*, dance hall (in England abbreviation for Palais de Dance).

pally, *a.*, *slang*, companionable, 'chummy': see PAL.

pally, variant of PALY *a.*[2] *Her.*

pallyard, pallys, obs. ff. PALLIARD, PALACE.

palm (pɑːm), *sb.*[1] Also 4–7 **palme**, 9 *dial.* **paum**. [OE. *palm* str. m., *palma* wk. masc., and *palme* wk. fem. = OS. *palma* fem., OHG. *palma* fem., MHG. *palme* fem. and masc., ON. *pálmr* masc., all a. L. *palma*; ME. *palme* agreeing also with F. *palme* (12th c. in Littré), ad. L. *palma* (instead of the inherited OF. form *paume*). L. *palma* was a transf. sense of *palma* palm of the hand, expanded hand: see PALM *sb.*[2]]

1. a. Any tree or shrub of the Natural Order *Palmæ* or *Palmaceæ*, a large family of monocotyledons, widely distributed in warm climates, chiefly within the tropics, remarkable for their ornamental forms and various usefulness to man.

They have the stem usually upright and unbranched, a head or crown of very large pinnate or fan-shaped leaves, and fruit of various forms (nut, drupe, or berry). In different species, the fruit-pulp, seed, pith, head of young leaves, or young root is used as food (*e.g.* date-palm, coco-nut, sago-palm, cabbage-palm, palmyra-palm); oil is obtained from the fruit (oil-palm) or seed (coco-nut); wine (*toddy*) and sugar (*jaggery*) from the sap; fibre from the leaf-stalk (date-palm, kittul) or fruit-husk (coco-nut); the wood is used for building and other purposes; the leaves for thatching, and for making paper, hats, baskets, etc.; with various other uses. The palm of Scripture is the date-palm. The only European species of the order is *Chamærops humilis*, the Dwarf Fan Palm of Southern Europe.

c **825** *Vesp. Psalter* xci. 13 Se rehtwisa swe swe palma bloweð. *c* **950** in *Rit. Dunelm.* (Surtees) 65 Swælce pælm' [*L.* quasi palma]. *Ibid.* 95 Pælma' [*L.* palmarum]. *c* **950** *Lindisf. Gosp.* John xii. 13 ȝenomon tuicgo ðara palmana & foerdon toȝænes him. *c* **1000** ÆLFRIC *Hom.* II. 402 Se palm is siȝebeacen. *c* **1290** *S. Eng. Leg.* I. 379/113 A ȝeord of palm cam in is hond. *a* **1340** HAMPOLE *Psalter* xci[i]. 12 þe rightwis as palme sall floryss. **1382** WYCLIF *Lev.* xxiii. 40 And ȝe shulen take to ȝow.. the braunches of palmes. *c* **1420** *Pallad. on Husb.* VI. 91 The palme ek now men setteth forth to stonde. **1535** COVERDALE *Judg.* iv. 5 She dwelt vnder yᵉ palme of Debbora betwene Rama & Bethel. **1613** PURCHAS *Pilgrimage* (1614) 647 A pot of Wine of Palme, or Cocoa, which they draw forth of Trees. **1635–56** COWLEY *Davideis* I. *Note* 7 In the publique Games of Greece, Palm was made the sign and reward of Victory. **1727–46** THOMSON *Summer* 678 And from the palm to draw its freshening wine! **1870** YEATS *Nat. Hist. Comm.* 102 Of the many species of palms, the date and the cocoa-nut palm are the most distinctive.

b. Applied *fig.* to a person.

1500–20 DUNBAR *Poems* lxxxvi. 21 Princes [= princess] of peiss, and palme imperiall. **1607** SHAKS. *Timon* v. i. 13 You shall see him a Palme in Athens againe. **1860** WARTER *Seaboard & Down* II. 350 Hear what the palm and prince of Knighthood said.

c. With defining words, denoting various species of the order *Palmæ*, as **bamboo palm, broom palm, catechu palm, dragon's-blood palm, feather palm**, etc. (see quots.); also occasionally plants of other orders, as **club palm**, the genus *Cordyline* (N.O. *Liliaceæ*), also called *palm-lily* (see 7); **fern-palm**, a general name for the N.O. *Cycadeæ*, from their resemblance to both palms and ferns. See also CABBAGE-PALM, COCO-NUT, COHUNE, COQUITO, DATE, FAN, HEMP, ITA, IVORY, OIL, SAGO-*palm*, etc., etc.

1866 *Treas. Bot.* 960/1 *R*[*aphia*] *vinifera*, the Bamboo Palm... The Africans..make very pliable cloth and neat baskets of the undeveloped leaves. *Ibid.* 1147/2 *T*[*hrinax*] *argentea* is..a native of Panama, where it is called *Palma de escoba*, or Broom-palm, its leaves being there made into brooms. *Ibid.* 837/1 Catechu Palm, *Areca Catechu*. *Ibid.*

88/1 A sort of Catechu is furnished by boiling down the seeds of this palm. *Ibid.* 379/2 D[*æmonorops*] *Draco* (formerly *Calamus Draco*)..is called the Dragon's Blood Palm,..its fruits yielding a portion of the substance known ..as dragon's blood. **1884** MILLER *Plant-n.*, *Cordyline*, Club Palm, Palm-Lily. *Ibid.*, *Ptychosperma*, Australian Feather-palm. *Ibid.*, *Cycadeæ*, Fern-Palms. *Cycas revoluta*, Fern-Palm, or Sago-Palm, of Japan.

2. A 'branch' or leaf of the palm-tree, esp. as anciently carried or worn as a symbol of victory or triumph, and on festal occasions (as still in the Roman and Greek Churches), or in mediæval times by pilgrims (PALMER *sb.*[1] 1). (See also 4.)

c **1200** *Trin. Coll. Hom.* 89 Þet folc com toȝenes him mid blostmen and mid palmes. *a* **1300** *Cursor M.* 20161 Tak þis palme her in þi hand. **1382** WYCLIF *Rev.* xii. 9 Clothid, with whijte stoolis, and palmes in the hondis of hem. *c* **1420** LYDG. *Assembly of Gods* 1174 Hauyng in her hande the palme of vyctory. **14..** *Tundale's Vis.* 419 But a preste, þat a palmare was A palme in his hande he hadde. **1645** EVELYN *Diary* 17 Apr., The Pope's benediction of the *Gonfalone*, or Standard, and giving the hallowed palmes. **1700** DRYDEN *Palamon & Arcite* III. 396 And Mars..With palm and laurel shall adorn his knight. **1827** KEBLE *Chr. Y.*, *Holy Innocents* i, Their palms and garlands telling plain, That they are of the glorious martyr train.

3. *fig.* Put emblematically for Victory, triumph; supreme honour or excellence, prize; esp. in such phrases as ***to bear the palm***, ***yield the palm***, etc.

c **1386** CHAUCER *Sec. Nun's T.* 240 With the palm of martirdom Ye shullen come un-to his blisful feste. **1483** CAXTON *Gold. Leg.* 382 b/2 He callyd clemente fro the bottom of the see to the palme of vyctorye. **1601** B. JONSON *Poetaster* v. i, Well said! This carries palm with it! *Ibid.*, It still hath been a work of as much palm..as to invent or make. **1606** SHAKS. *Tr. & Cr.* III. i. 170 What he shall receiue of vs in duetie, Giues vs more palme in beautie then we haue. *c* **1611** CHAPMAN *Iliad* XXIII. 557 Actor's sons.. bore The palm at horse-race. **1697** DRYDEN *Virg. Georg.* III. 153 In Peace t' enjoy his former Palms and Pains. **1781** GIBBON *Decl. & F.* xvii. II. 33 As an orator, he disputed the palm of eloquence with Cicero himself. **1827–35** WILLIS *Parrhasius* 160 Were there no palm beyond a feverish fame. **1875** JOWETT *Plato* (ed. 2) I. 151 He cannot make a speech —in this he yields the palm to Protagoras.

4. A branch or sprig of any one of several trees and shrubs substituted in northern countries, esp. in the celebrations of Palm Sunday, for the true palm; also applied to the plants themselves.

Most commonly some species of willow (or its catkins), esp. the goat-willow, *Salix Caprea*; also, locally, hazel, yew, laurel, larch, spruce fir, and (in America) hemlock spruce.

1375 BARBOUR *Bruce* v. 312 The folk of the cuntre Assemblit at the kirk vald be,..thar palmys to bere. **14..** *Cott. MS. Claud. A. ii*, lf. 52 For encheson we have non olyfe þat beruth grene leves, we takon in stede of hit hew [yew] and palmes wyth, and beruth abowte on procession, and so þis day we callyn Palme Sonnenday. **1530** PALSGR. 251/2 Palme, the yelowe that groweth on wyllowes. **1562** BULLEYN *Def. agst. Sickness*, *Compounds* 40 Woolly knottes, growing upon sallowes, commonly called palmes. **1600** SHAKS. *A.Y.L.* III. ii. 187 Looke heere what I found on a Palme tree. **1669** WORLIDGE *Syst. Agric.* (1681) 330 *Palms*, the white excrescencies of Buds of Sallies or Withy coming before the leaf. **1779** *Gentl. Mag.* Dec. 580/1 [Yew-trees in East Kent are] to this day universally called palms. **1864** HOLME LEE *Silver Age* (1866) 475 The palms were budding downy and gray in the narrow copse. **1880** *Antrim & Down Gloss.*, *Palms*, small branches of the Spruce fir, also budded twigs of the willow. These are supplied on Palm Sunday to persons attending service in the Roman Catholic Churches. **1896** A. E. HOUSMAN *Shropsh. Lad* x, Afield for palms the girls repair, And sure enough the palms are there.

†**5.** A branch (of a tree); in quot. 1796, a 'branch' or leaf of the palm-tree (= sense 2). *Obs.*

1559 W. CUNNINGHAM *Cosmogr. Glasse* 201 Couered with leaues and palmes of trees. **1796** H. HUNTER tr. *St.-Pierre's Stud. Nat.* (1799) I. 530 The stellated and radiating forms of it's palms, likewise taken from the straight line, constitute a very agreeable opposition with the roundness of it's stem.

†**6.** Short for palm-wine, or palm-sack (see SACK).

1708 W. KING *Cookery* iv, Two bottles of smooth Palm or Anjou white shall give a welcome. **1725** WELSTED *Oikographie* 12 Nor Cyprus soft, the Lover's Balm, Is here; nor Vine sirnam'd the Palm.

7. *attrib.* and *Comb.* **a.** attrib., as ***palm awning***, ***bark***, ***bough***, ***-fibre***, ***-flower***, ***-frond***, ***-grove***, ***-nut***, ***-sap***, ***-stem***, ***-thatch***, ***-trunk***, ***-twig***, ***-wood***. **b.** objective, instrumental, similative, etc., as ***palm-bearing***, ***-bowered***, ***-crowned***, ***-flanked***, ***-fringed***, ***-graced***, ***-like***, ***-lined***, ***-o'erspread***, ***-rising***, ***-shaded***, ***-thatched*** adjs. **c.** Special Combs.: † **palm-bag**, the fibrous spathe of the flower-spike of a species of palm, *Manicaria saccifera*, of the Lower Amazon, which forms a bag or cap; also called *palm-net* and *palm-sack*; **palm-bark-tree**, an Australian shrub, *Melaleuca Wilsoni* (Miller *Plant-n.* 1884); **palm-bird**, a weaver-bird which nests in palm-trees; **palm-borer** = *palm-grub*; **palm bottom**, a hollow or valley in which palms grow; **palm-branch**, a leaf of the palm-tree with its stalk, used as a symbol of victory, as a decoration, etc. (see 2); **palm-butter**, palm-oil in the solid state; **palm-cabbage**, the terminal bud or head of young leaves in various species of palm, eaten as a vegetable (see CABBAGE-TREE); **palm-cat**, (*a*) a viverrine animal of the genus *Paradoxurus* or sub-family *Paradoxurinæ*, which frequents palm-trees; (*b*) the ocelot; **palm-civet** = *palm-cat* (*a*); **palm-colour**, used to render Gr. φοῖνιξ a dark-red colour (first used by the Phœnicians), taken as if from φοῖνιξ date-palm; **palm-crab**, the tree-crab (*Birgus latro*), which climbs palm-trees for the fruit; **palm-fern**, a name for the *Cycadeæ* (= *fern-palm*: see 1 c); **palm-grub**, the larva of a palm-weevil; **palm-heart** = *palm-cabbage* (cf. HEART *sb.* 18); **palm-honey**: see quot.; **palm-house**, a glass house for growing palms and other tropical plants; **palm-hut**, a small cabin made from palm-trees; **palm-kale**, a variety of cabbage with a stem 10 or 12 feet high and a crown of leaves like a palm; **palm-kernel**, the kernel of the drupaceous fruit of the Oil Palm (*Elæis guineensis*), which yields an oil (*palm-kernel oil*); **palm-lily**, name for the palm-like liliaceous plants of the genus *Cordyline* and allied genera (Miller 1884); **palm-marten** = *palm-cat* (*a*); †**palm-net** = *palm-bag*; **palm-room**, a room, usu. in a hotel, adorned by potted palms; **palm-soap**, a soap made from palm-oil; †**palm-sack** = *palm-bag*; **palm-squirrel**, a small, greyish-brown, tree squirrel with three white stripes along its back, belonging to the genus *Funambulus*, esp. *F. palmarum*, which is found in India; **palm-stand**, a stand for supporting a palm grown in a plant-pot; **palm-sugar**, the sugar procured from palm-sap, esp. that of *Caryota urens*: see JAGGERY; **palm-swift**, a small Jamaican swift (*Micropus phœnicobia*) which nests in palm-leaves; **palm toddy**: see quot.; **palm-viper**, a venomous serpent of South America (*Lachesis* or *Craspedocephalus bilineatus*); **palm-warbler**, a bird (*Dendrœca palmarum*) common in the eastern United States; **palm-wasp**, a kind of wasp (*Polybius palmarum*) which makes its nest in palm-trees; **palm-wax**, a waxy substance produced by various species of palm, esp. *Ceroxylon andicola*; **palm-weevil**, any one of various weevils whose larvæ bore into palm-trees; **palm-willow**, any species of willow the sprigs of which are used instead of palm-branches (see 4), esp. *Salix Caprea*; **palm-wine**, wine made from the sap of the palm-tree; **palm-withy** = *palm-willow*; **palm-worm**, (*a*) some large American centipede; (*b*) = *palm-grub*. See also PALM-CROSS, PALM-LEAF, PALM-OIL, etc.

1681 GREW *Musæum* II. 185 The Palm-Net or *Bag.. Originally, entire, like a taper'd Bag commonly call'd Hippocrates's Sleive..'Tis naturally sewed or woven together with admirable Art..Another Palm-Sack or Net, almost a yard long. **1865** TYLOR *Early Hist. Man.* viii. 210 They catch them in nets of *palm-bark. **1552** HULOET, *Palme bearynge, *palmifer*, *palmiger*. **1636** J. TRUSSELL in *Ann. Dubrensia* (1877) 7 Carnivalls, Palme and Rush-bearing, harmlesse Whitson-ales. **1866** J. B. ROSE tr. *Ovid's Met.* 297 Palm-bearing Araby. **1902** D. G. HOGARTH *Nearer East* 141 Stony slopes..only at very rare intervals relieved by *palm bottoms. **1828** SCOTT *F. Maid Perth* xxxiv, Bearing branches of yew in their hands, as the readiest substitute for *palm boughs. **1804** J. GRAHAME *Sabbath* (1808) 29 How sweet the tinkle of the *palm-bowered brook! **1535** COVERDALE *Neh.* viii. 15 Go vp vnto ye mount and fetch Olyue braunches, Pynebraunches, Myrtbraunches, *Palme-braunches. **1807** ROBINSON *Archæol. Græca* III. xx. 319 The token of victory was commonly a palm-branch. **1863** M. L. WHATELY *Ragged Life in Egypt* v. 31 Dusting furniture with a palm-branch. **1914** W. OWEN *Let.* 25 Feb. (1967) 235, I had huge success with my Costume: Nothing more elaborate than my Gown on my back a laurel wreath on my head, & a palm branch in the hand. **1928** D. H. LAWRENCE *Woman who rode Away* 16 Simply marvellous people! And the way they strewed palm-branches under her feet! **1977** H. KAPLAN *Damascus Cover* xii. 122 He was tied to the gate of the Al-Frange Synagogue. .. Then he was beaten with palm branches. **1878** H. M. STANLEY *Dark Cont.* II. xiii. 387 They brought me a mixture of india-rubber and *palm-butter. **1705** BOSMAN *Guinea* xvi. (1721) 271 At the top grows a Fruit,..called *Palm-Cabbage, because it hath a sort of Cabbagy Taste. **1827** *Perils & Captivity* (Constable's Misc.) 321 They were fain to subsist on a few seeds, wild fruit and the palm cabbage. **1966** E. J. H. CORNER *Nat. Hist. Palms* iv. 93 Not all palm-cabbages are edible. **1972** J. W. PURSEGLOVE *Tropical Crops: Monocotyledons* II. 443 The freshly cut terminal bud [of *Cocos nucifera*], known as palm cabbage, is considered a delicacy and may be eaten cooked or raw. **1849–52** TODD *Cycl. Anat.* IV. 911/1 These Indian *Viverridae*..have been called '*Palm-cats'. **1859** TENNENT *Ceylon* (1860) I. 144 The palm-cat..lurks by day among the fronds of the coco-nut palms, and by night makes destructive forays on the fowls. **1893–4** LYDEKKER *Royal Nat. Hist.* I. 458 The *palm-civets are purely nocturnal and thoroughly aboreal in their habits. **1774** J. BRYANT *Mythol.* I. 327 The horse was of a *Palm-colour, which is a bright red; we call such horses bays. **1881** SEMPER *Anim. Life* Introd. 5 Diagram of the lungs and circulation of *Birgus latro*, the *Palm Crab. **1895** CLODD *Primer Evol.* v. (1900) 54 The cycads or *palm-ferns, so called from their resemblance to palms, for which, with their crown of feathery leaves, they are often mistaken. **1801** SOUTHEY *Thalaba* III. xviii, As patiently the Old Man Entwines the strong *palm-fibres. **1928** H. CRANE *Let.* 31 Jan. (1965) 314 The great *palm-flanked arena of Angelus Temple. **1610** HEALEY *St. Aug. Citie of God* 570 Some thinke they [Bees] doe not ingender, but fetch their issue,..from the *Palme-flowre. **1859** KINGSLEY *Misc.* (1860) I. 86 *Palm-fringed islets. *a* **1904** *N.E.D.* s.v. *Palm* sb.[1] 7a, *Palm frond. **1938** M. K. RAWLINGS *Yearling* i. 5 The palm-frond mill-wheel must just brush the water's surface. **1972** 'M. RENAULT' *Persian Boy* xxvi. 349 He looked up at the waving palm-fronds, and played lazily with my hair. **1973** *Nat. Geographic* Feb. 211/1 On a plain before the fort of Rustaq, I sat on a palm-frond mat with a wiry old sheik. **1974** *Observer* (Colour Suppl.) 13 Oct. 20/3 (*caption*) Swinging from palm fronds like a teenage Tarzan, this Arab boy performs acrobatics for the benefit of admiring tourists at the oasis of Gafsa in Tunisia. **1839** BAILEY *Festus* xx. (1848) 248 The *palm-graced pilgrims of truth's holy land. **1801** SOUTHEY *Thalaba* I. ii, Nor *palm-grove, islanded amid the waste. **1856** STANLEY *Sinai & Pal.* ii. (1858) 145 From the palmgroves,..came the name of Phenicia or 'the Land of Palms'. [**1901** tr. C. G. O. Drude in L. H. Bailey *Cycl. Amer. Hort.* III. 1193/1 [From many species are cut out the soft terminal bud (heart), which is eaten as Palm salad.] **1938** M. K. RAWLINGS *Yearling* xx. 250 He sliced the *palm-hearts thinly. **1971** 'D. HALLIDAY' *Dolly & Doctor Bird* v. 67 We had palm hearts, a matter of flaccid white tubing, followed by prime rib steak. **1976** *Times* 1 June 6/3 We have found..tinned palm hearts and artichoke bottoms. **1866** *Treas. Bot.* 639/1 In Chili, a sweet syrup, called Miel de Palma, or *Palm-honey, is prepared by boiling the sap of [the Coquito Palm] to the consistency of treacle. **1871** KINGSLEY *At Last* xi, Let him transport his stream into the great *Palm-house at Kew. **1930** R. MACAULAY *Staying with Relations* ii. 20 The forest would recede a little, and small clearings and plantations make themselves apparent.., with groups of *palm huts dumped among them like bee-hives. **1936** *Discovery* Dec. 382/1 A riverside palm-hut. **1885** OGILVIE, **Palm-kale*, a variety of the cabbage extensively cultivated in the Channel Islands. **1863** R. F. BURTON *Abeokuta* I. 129 The *Palm-kernel oil,.. so fast becoming an important article of traffic, is of two kinds. **1899** MARY KINGSLEY *W. African Stud.* App. i. 444 Two tons of palm kernels should be counted to equal one ton of palm oil so far as regards fiscal arrangements. **1819** SHELLEY *Prometh. Unb.* III. iii. 163 Distinct with column, arch, and architrave, And *palm-like capital. **1884** MILLER *Plant-n.*, *Cordyline*, Club Palm, *Palm-Lily. **1902** D. G. HOGARTH *Nearer East* 74 The abundant waters of its own *palm-lined defiles. **1930** R. MACAULAY *Staying with Relations* xviii. 265 They rode into the bay, and saw before them the palm-lined harbour front of the Pacific's greatest pearl city. **1623** BINGHAM *Xenophon* 31 There was much Wheat, and Wine of Palme to be found, and Vineger boiled out of *Palme nuts. **1855** KINGSLEY *Westw. Ho!* xxiii, From the ashes of those palm-nuts you could make good salt. **1735** THOMSON *Liberty* II. 10 Beneath the rural Portal, *Palm-o'erspread, The Father-Senate met. **1598** TOFTE *Alba* (1880) 5 Whilst thou thy Noble House noblest indeede.. through thy *Palme-rising Fame. **1903** 'C. E. MERRIMAN' *Lett. from Son* 46, I met him in the *palm room last night. **1930** E. POUND *XXX Cantos* xxix. 137 'No not in the palm-room.' The lady says it is Too cold in the palm-room. **1931** F. L. ALLEN *Only Yesterday* i. 11 In the more dimly lighted palm-room there may be a juvenile petting-party or two going on. **1846** *Jewish Manual, or Pract. Information Jewish & Mod. Cookery* Toilette iv. 212 *Palm soap, Castille soap ..should always be preferred. **1966** J. S. COX *Illustr. Dict. Hairdressing* 108/1 *Palm-soap*, a soda soap of palm oil. (*Piesse*). **1831** *Proc. Zool. Soc.* I. 103 The *Palm Squirrel is very abundant in gardens in Dukhun. **1891** W. T. BLANFORD *Fauna Brit. India: Mammalia* II. 384 The cry of the palm-squirrel is a shrill chirp, resembling the note of a bird. **1908** *Westm. Gaz.* 15 June 5/3 The workers [*sc.* white ants] are preyed upon by true ants and many other insects; ..by rats, mice, and palm-squirrels. **1955** I. T. SANDERSON *Living Mammals of World* 115/2 Palm-Squirrels... It is virtually impossible for the non-specialist to identify or even define this tribe. **1926** M. LEINSTER *Dew on Leaf* v. 55 A large writing-desk and shelf of books,..and a blackwood *palm-stand, were some of the surrounding objects. **1855** KINGSLEY *Westw. Ho!* xxiii, The nymph had..darted between the *palm-stems to her canoe. **1866** *Treas. Bot.* 158/1 Palm toddy is intoxicating, and when distilled yields strong arrack..but its most important product is jaggery, or *palm-sugar. **1937** M. COVARRUBIAS *Island of Bali* (1972) vi. 125 The child is weaned after three birthdays.., when the mother puts a mixture of lime and palm-sugar to her nipples. **1971** *Nat. Geographic* Mar. 344 (*caption*) Train of oxcarts, laden with baskets of palm sugar, rumbles toward a landing on the Irrawaddy River. **1897** MARY KINGSLEY *W. Africa* 175 It had a certain amount of *palm-thatch roof. **1871** C. KINGSLEY *At Last* x, The two first settlers regretted the days when the house was a mere *palm-thatched hut. **1857** LIVINGSTONE *Trav.* xxi. 411 The men..spend most of their time in drinking the *palm-toddy. This toddy is the juice of the palm-oil tree..a sweet clear liquid, not at all intoxicating while fresh, but, when allowed to stand till the afternoon, causes inebriation. **1950** 'D. DIVINE' *King of Fassarai* vii. 48 Fishing, canoe-building..and palm toddy. **1974** *Nat. Geographic* Dec. 754 A feast of marinated raw fish ..was washed down with palm toddy. *c* **1200** *Trin. Coll. Hom.* 89 [Hi] beren on here honde blostme, sum *palm twig, and sum boh of oliue. **1896** *List Anim. Zool. Soc.* (ed. 9) 646 *Lachesis bilineatus* (Wied). Two-lined *Palm-Viper. *Hab.* South America. **1889** JEFFERIES *Field & Hedgerow* 202 The *palm-willow bears its yellow pollen. **1613** PURCHAS *Pilgrimage* (1614) 698 Their *Palme-wines, which they draw out of the toppe of a kinde of Palme. **1836** MACGILLIVRAY tr. *Humboldt's Trav.* xxii. 311 They found several inhabitants collecting palm-wine. **1957** M. BANTON *W. Afr. City* iii. 52 War-time prosperity multiplied the demand for palm-wine in Mende country. **1964** J. P. CLARK *Three Plays* 5 A big gourd of palm wine and three heads of kola-nut split before the dead of the land. **1969** J. M. GULLICK *Malaysia* i. 31 There may be a shop for the restricted sale of 'toddy' (palm wine). **1976** *Daily Times* (Lagos) 8 July 32/4 But Obadeya told the tribunal that he was in a palm-wine bar with Chidi that night. **1609** C. BUTLER *Fem. Mon.* (1634) 136 *Palm-withys, or other trees whereon they [bees] gather. **1798** SOTHEBY tr. *Wieland's Oberon* (1826) I. 179 Underneath the *palm-wood's shelt'ring height. **1865** J. H. INGRAHAM *Pillar of Fire* (1872) 207 This beautiful door was of palm-wood. **1706** PHILLIPS, **Palm-Worm*, an American Insect half a Foot long..remarkable for its infinite Number of Feet, and two Claws at Head and Tail, with which it wounds and poisons Men.

palm (pɑːm), *sb.*² Forms: α. 4–6 **paume, pawme, pame** (also 8–9 *dial.*), 5 **paame.** β. 5–6 **paulme,** 5–7 **palme,** 7– **palm.** [ME. *paume*, a. F. *paume*:—L. *palma* palm of the hand; subseq. assimilated, through *paulme* (also in OF.), to the L. The latter was cognate with Gr. παλάμη, Skr. *pāṇi* (from **palni*), OE. *folm*, OHG. *folma* str. fem., palm of the hand.]

I. 1. a. The part of the hand between the wrist and the fingers, esp. its inner surface on which the fingers close, and which is nearly flat when extended. (In early use sometimes = hand.)

α. **13..** *E.E. Allit. P.* B. 1533 Þer apered a paume, with poyntel in fyngres þat watz grysly and gret, and grymly he wrytes. **1377** LANGL. *P. Pl.* B. XVII. 175 Þe paume hath powere to put oute alle þe ioyntes. **1382** WYCLIF *Matt.* xxvi. 67 Other ȝouen strokis with the pawm of hondis in to his face. **1387** TREVISA *Higden* (Rolls) III. 311 A childe drynke of þe pame of his hond. *c* **1475** *Partenay* 4306 Plain pawme of hande the swerde made entre.

β. *c* **1400** MAUNDEV. (Roxb.) xxxii. 147 Þe visage and þe palmez of þe hend. **1484** CAXTON *Curiall* 4 She lawgheth.. and smyteth her paulmes to-gydre. **1535** COVERDALE *2 Kings* ix. 35 They founde nothinge of her, but the szkull and the fete, and the palmes of her handes. **1616** CHAPMAN *Homer's Hymn to Apollo* 305 But here the fair-hair'd Graces,.. Danc'd, and each other's palm to palm did cling. **1740** SOMERVILLE *Hobbinol* III. 183 She of the Gypsy Train.. artful to view The spreading Palm, and with vile Cant deceive The Love-sick Maid. **1813** SCOTT *Rokeby* VI. xii, He pressed his forehead with his palm. **1871** R. ELLIS *Catullus* lxiv. 261 Part with a slender palm taborines beat merrily jangling.

fig. **1825** LONGF. *Spir. Poetry* 5 The leaves above their sunny palms outspread.

b. In various figurative phrases, esp. referring to the receiving of money as a reward or bribe.

1601 SHAKS. *Jul. C.* IV. iii. 10 Let me tell you Cassius, you your selfe Are much condemn'd to haue an itching Palme. **1807** E. S. BARRETT *Rising Sun* III. iv. 42 You would imply that if we were greased in the palm, we should, like them, be ready to turn a courtier. **1855** MOTLEY *Dutch Rep.* (1861) II. 347 He should believe that their palms had been oiled. **1899** BARING-GOULD *Bk. of West* I. xi. 178 Large landed proprietors managed to get slices by a little greasing of palms.

c. The part of a glove that covers the palm.

Cf. quot. 1852 s.v. PALMED *a.* 3.

1891 CONAN DOYLE *Adv. Sherlock Holmes, Speckled Band*, I observe the second half of a return ticket in the palm of your left glove.

2. In *Zool.* and *Comp. Anat.* (and occasionally in wider use) extended to **a.** The corresponding part of the fore-foot of a quadruped. †**b.** The claw of a bird, etc. *Obs.* **c.** The sole of the foot. *rare.* **d.** *Entom.* The first joint of the fore-leg of an insect when specially developed. **e.** A prehensile structure on the tails of certain monkeys.

? *a* **1400** *Morte Arth.* 776 A blake bustous bere.. With yche a pawe as a poste, and paumes fulle huge. **1426** LYDG. *De Guil. Pilgr.* 17480 Myn handys off merveyllous fasoun, Lyk the pawmys off a gryffoun. **1460** *Stacyons Rome* 252 in *Pol. Rel. & L. Poems* (1866) 122 In heuen to dwelle for euur more, To þe palme wylle we goo. **1821** SHELLEY *Prometh. Unb.* IV. 123 Our feet now, every palm, Are sandalled with calm. —— *Adonais* xxiv, The invisible Palms of her [Urania's] tender feet. **1826** KIRBY & SP. *Entomol.* III. 370 *Palma* (the *Palm*). The first joint of the *Manus*, when longer and broader than the subsequent ones, or otherwise remarkable; answering to the *Planta* in the legs. **1843** BROWNING *Return of Druses* III, A fire curls within us From the foot's palm and fills up to the brain. **1861** MAYHEW *Lond. Labour* III. 150/1 They form a hollow in the palm of the foot, or the waist of the foot as some call it. **1863** BATES *Nat. Amazon* ii. (1864) 40 The South-American monkeys.. which have a fifth hand for climbing in their prehensile tails, adapted for this function by their strong muscular development, and the naked palms under their tips.

3. The flat expanded part of the horn in some deer, from which finger-like points project.

13.. *Gaw. & Gr. Knt.* 1155 Þe breme bukkez also, with hor brode paumez. **1590** SIR T. COCKAINE *Treat. Hunt.* D j, Diuers Buckes haue sundrie slots in their palmes. *c* **1611** CHAPMAN *Iliad* IV. 124 The forehead of the goat Held out a wondrous goodly palm that sixteen branches brought. **1630** J. TAYLOR (Water P.) *Navy Landships, Horsemanship* Wks. I. 93/1 A Buckes hornes are composed of Burre, Beame, Branch, Aduancer, Palme, and Spelter. **1770** G. WHITE *Selborne* xxviii. *To T. Pennant* 80 The horn of a male-moose, which had.. a broad palm with some snags on the edge. **1861** HULME tr. *Moquin-Tandon* II. III. 181 In the fourth year the horn terminates in an expansion termed the 'palm'.

4. A flat widened part at the end of an arm or arm-like projection. **a.** *gen.*

1526 *Pilgr. Perf.* (W. de W. 1531) 304 b, & than after they .. drewe the other arme to the palme of the crosse, & also smote in it another nayle. **1844** H. STEPHENS *Bk. of Farm* I. 414 The arm *c* is furnished.. with an oblique palm or ear upon which the fore-edge of the mould-board rests, and to which it is bolted. **1869** SIR E. J. REED *Shipbuild.* iv. 66 The palm here spoken of was shaped like the palm of a vice, and was run in underneath the iron flat of the lower saloon, and riveted to it.

b. *spec.* The blade of an oar.

1513 DOUGLAS *Æneis* x. iv. 122 Quhil that the famy stour of stremis le Vp weltis from the braid palmis of tre. **1867** *Contemp. Rev.* VI. 253 At length we marked our steersman smile, And broadened the oar-palm to rest awhile.

†**c.** Applied to the hand of a clock. *Obs. rare.*

1629 Z. BOYD *Last Battell* 519 The Palme turneth about, and with its finger pointeth at the houre.

d. The broad triangular part of an anchor, the inner surface of the fluke.

1706 PHILLIPS, *Palm of an Anchor*, the Flook or broad part which fastens into the Ground. **1772–84** COOK *Voy.* (1790) IV. 1264 They were.. obliged to.. drag the anchor after them, till they had room to heave it up, when they perceived that one of its palms was broken. **1867** J. MACGREGOR *Voy. Alone* (1868) 27 It needs a good scrubbing to get rid of it from each palm of the anchor.

5. An instrument used by sailmakers instead of a thimble: see quot. 1769–76.

1769–76 FALCONER *Dict. Mar., Palm, paumet*,.. is formed of a piece of leather or canvas, on the middle of which is fixed a round plate of iron, of an inch in diameter, whose surface is pierced with a number of small holes, to catch the head of the sail-needle. The leather is formed so as to encircle the hand, and button on the back thereof, while the iron remains in the palm. **1897** R. KIPLING *Captains Courageous* 108 Harvey spent his leisure hours.. learning to use a needle and palm.

II. †**6. a.** A game in which a ball was struck with the hand; = *palm-play* (see 9), F. *la paume, jeu de la paume.* **b.** The ball used in this game.

1440 J. SHIRLEY *Dethe K. James* (1837) 56 Whane he playd there at the pawme, the ballis oft ranne yn at that fowle hole. **1467** *Eng. Gilds* 372 Item, that no man pley at tenys or pame wᵗʸn the yeld halle. **1482** in *Paston Lett.* III. 303 At the Paame ther, ther pleasure for to take. **1530** PALSGR. 252/2 Paume to play at tennys with, *paulme*.

7. A measure of length, equivalent either to the breadth of the palm of the hand (= HAND *sb.* 20, HANDBREADTH), i.e. about three to four inches, or to the whole length of the hand from the wrist to the finger-tips, i.e. about seven to nine inches.

1485 CAXTON *Chas. Gt.* 221 He had the face a cubyte brode, the nose a palme longe. *c* **1500** *Melusine* xlix. 325 Geffray.. made his swerd to entre in his flesshe wel a palme deep. **1607** TOPSELL *Four-f. Beasts* (1658) 172 The tail is not above two hands or palms long. **1625** BACON *Ess., Empire* (Arb.) 303 During that Triumuirate of Kings,.. there was such a watch kept, that none of the Three, could win a Palme of Ground, but the other two, would straightwaies ballance it. **1771** *Ann. Reg.* 78 The corpse.. was.. placed on a.. scaffold, fifty-four palms high. **1801** A. RANKEN *Hist. France* I. I. v. 451 There was a circular window of five palms or three feet nine inches diameter. **1857** C. GRIBBLE in *Merc. Marine Mag.* (1858) V. 4 The Brazilian palm being reckoned at 8¾ inches, not 9 as generally supposed.

III. [f. PALM *v.*] **8.** The act of palming a card, etc.: see PALM *v.* 2.

1664 J. WILSON *Cheats* IV. i, Did not I.. teach you your top, your palm, and your slur?

IV. 9. *attrib.* and *Comb.*, as ***palm-breadth, -marking, -reader; palm-reading, -tickling*** adjs.; **palm-ball** *U.S. Baseball*, a pitch of the ball gripped with the thumb and palm; †**palm-barley** (see quot.); **palm-grease** (*humorous*), money given as a douceur or bribe (cf. 1 b); so **palm-greasing**, petty bribery, 'tipping'; †**palm-pear** (see quot.); **palm-play** [Fr. *jeu de la paume*], an old game resembling tennis, in which the ball was struck with the palm of the hand instead of a racket; so ***palm-playing***; **palm-print**, the impression left by the palm of the hand; **palm-veined** *a. Bot.*, palmately veined; **palm-wise** *adv.*, with open palm; **palm-worker**, a person who works with a palm (sense 5).

1948 *Richmond* (Virginia) *Times-Dispatch* 15 Mar. 17/4 The lanky Cincinnati Reds' sidewheeler has added a new pitch to his repertoire—a *palm ball. **1950** *Sun* (Baltimore) 28 Aug. 16/2 He carries his own little notebook and can tell you many of the pitches he has made, when he threw the slider, the palm ball and even the gopher ball. **1973** *Times* 15 Aug. 7/3 There are numerous ways of hurling a ball legally to increase its effectiveness, such as the.. screw-ball, the fork-ball and the palm-ball. **1976** *Webster's Sports Dict.* 300/2 *Palm ball*,.. an off-speed pitch that is gripped between the thumb and the palm instead of with the ends of the fingers and that is thrown so that the fingers do not impart rotation to the ball. **1706** PHILLIPS, *Palmare Hordeum* (in old Records), *Palm-Barley or Sprat-Barley;.. a sort of Grain that is fuller and broader than common Barley [cf. 1611 COTGR., *Orge paumé*, Beere Barlie, big Barlie, Barlie with the square eare]. **1597** A. M. tr. *Guillemeau's Fr. Chirurg.* 45/1 We must then from palme to *Palmebreadthe, a little more than half throughe cutt the same. **1897** 'OUIDA' *Massarenes* iii, She'll want a lot of *palmgrease. **1886** BARING-GOULD *Court Royal* I. iv. 56 The police.. were extortionate in their demand for *palm-greasing. **1883** *Longm. Mag.* Sept. 497 Belief in fortunate *palm-markings. **1655** MOUFET & BENNET *Health's Impr.* (1746) 310 Wardens or *Palm-Pears, so called, because one of them will fill the Palm of a Hand. *a* **1547** EARL OF SURREY in *Tottell's Misc.* (Arb.) 13 The *palme play, where, dispoyled for the game, With dazed eies oft we.. Haue mist the ball, and got sight of our dame. **1801** STRUTT *Sports & Past.* II. iii. 85 The game of hand-ball is called by the French, palm-play. **1870** ROSSETTI *Dante at Verona* xxviii, He comes upon The women at their *palm-playing. **1929** A. C. & C. EDINGTON *Studio Murder Myst.* xv. 202 In wearing gloves the criminal nearly always leaves a very legible *palm print. **1946** *Nature* 12 Oct. 526/1 A drawing of a hand emphasizing the features of finger- and palm-print patterns is reproduced from this article. **1954** F. CHERRILL *Cherrill of Yard* vii. 69 'Are palm-prints as infallible as finger-prints?' he asked. **1955** *Times* 10 May 4/2 It had now been established that no two human beings had the same palm prints. **1967** N. LUCAS *C.I.D.* v. 61 In 1930 .. for the first time, palm-print evidence was accepted in a criminal court. **1977** D. HARSENT *Dreams of Dead* 5 Her palm-print shrinks on the mirror as she turns away. **1867** CRAIG *Palmistry* 304 In Palmistry and in chiromancy, many collateral circumstances often go to read off an individual, as well as the mere *palm-reading. **1920** R. MACAULAY *Potterism* III. ii. 131 She is the most wonderful *palm reader and crystal gazer I have come across. **1809** MALKIN *Gil Blas* VIII. vii. (Rtldg.) ¶3 *Palm-tickling petitioners for the loaves and fishes. **1866** *Treas. Bot.* 838/2 *Palm-veined, having the principal veins radiating from a common point. *a* **1603** T. CARTWRIGHT *Confut. Rhem. N.T.* (1618) 514 The same hand.. being first stretched forth *palm-wise, is after gathered in fist-wise. **1889** *Critic* 27 July 65/1 *Palm workers.. are obliged to do their work standing up; sitting down they would not have enough force to pass the long needles through the stiff canvas.

palm (pɑːm), *v.* Also 7 **paume, pawme, paulm,** 7–8 **paum,** 7–8 (9 *dial.*) **pawm.** [f. PALM *sb.*²: in most senses, orig. slang or low colloquial. Cf. It. *palmare* to grip with the palm of the hand, also, to stroke or smooth with the palm; F. *paumer* to stroke with the flat hand.]

1. a. *trans.* To touch with the palm, or pass the palm across; to handle; to stroke with the hand; to take or grasp the hand of, shake hands with.

1685 CROWNE *Sir C. Nice* III. Dram. Wks. 1874 III. 294 *Sur.* Is there not salt enough in London for you? *Sir Co.* Ay, stuff pawm'd by butlers and waiters. *c* **1704** PRIOR *Epigr.*, Frank carves very ill, yet will palm all the meats. **1784** *New Spectator* No. 12. 1 And what with palming one fellow, kissing another and coaxing with thousands, has driven me almost hornmad. **1876** T. HARDY *Ethelberta* (1890) 268 He became gleeful,.. nervously palming his hip with his left hand, as if previous to plunging it into hot water for some prize. **1881** *Confess. frivolous Girl* 176. **1974** *Guardian* 23 Sept. 24/8 Farmer palmed over a header from the impressive Thompson. **1976** *Wymondham & Attleborough Express* 3 Dec. 27/2 From the kick off the ball was put to Chambers on the wing and his hard shot was palmed into the path of Bartrum who put Pollastra 1–0 up in 45 seconds.

b. *intr.*

1678 DRYDEN *Kind Keeper* IV. i, I think in my conscience, he is palming and topping in my belly. **1855** ROBINSON *Whitby Gloss.*, *To Palm* or *Pawm*, to climb, to ascend progressively by the use of the hands and feet, as a monkey 'palming' up a pole with its paws and legs.

2. a. *trans.* To conceal in the palm of the hand, as in cheating at cards or dice, or in juggling.

1673 [see PALMING *vbl. sb.*¹ 2]. **1680** COTTON *Compl. Gamester* xv. 96 He palms them as much as he can, nimbly passing the last Card. **1706** PHILLIPS, *To palm*, to juggle in one's Hand; to cog or cheat at Dice. *a* **1732** GAY *Fables* II. xii. 104 Is't I who cog or palm the dice? **1882** BESANT *All Sorts* III. 34 He began to 'palm' the egg in the most surprising manner. **1882** *Sat. Rev.* LIV. 629 You may show a dozen men how to 'palm' a card, yet not one of them will be able to do it.

b. ? To perform or play (a trick) by palming.

1717 PRIOR *Alma* II. 242 But Space and Matter we should blame; They palm'd the Trick that lost the Game.

†**3.** *intr.* To play a trick, to cheat; to impose *upon* a person. *Obs.*

1686 F. SPENCE tr. *Varillas' Ho. Medicis* 414 The Germans paulm'd upon Francis the First. **1707** J. STEVENS tr. *Quevedo's Com. Wks.* (1709) 204 The Dog paum'd upon us so slily. **1724** J. MACKY *Journ. thro. Eng.* I. iv. 68 At Play .. the Ladies think it no Crime to pawm handsomely.

4. a. *trans.* To impose (a thing) fraudulently (*on* or *upon* a person); to pass *off* by trickery or fraud. *spec.* in *U.S. Law* = PASS *v.* 64 c.

1679 CROWNE *Amb. Statesman* IV. 59 Thinking you cou'd pawme such stuffe on me. **1711** ADDISON *Spect.* No. 117 ¶4 She.. has made the Country ring with several imaginary Exploits which are palmed upon her. **1755** SMOLLETT *Quix.* (1803) IV. 160 My lord duke has palmed his lacquey upon us, in lieu of my lawful husband. **1822** LAMB *Elia* Ser. I. *Dist. Corresp.*, Have you not tried to palm off a yesterday's pun? *a* **1862** BUCKLE *Civiliz.* (1869) III. iv. 274 Pernicious notions palmed on the people. **1880** *Federal Reporter* (U.S.) I. 36 Nor is it necessary, in order to give a right to an injunction, that a specific trade-mark should be infringed, but it is sufficient that the court is satisfied that there was an intent on the part of the respondent to palm off his goods as the goods of the complainant. **1904** *Judicial & Statutory Definitions* VI. 5159/2 'To palm off' means to impose by fraud; to put off by inferior means. The language also imports that plaintiff must have been deceived and cheated by the representations, which he could not have been had he relied upon them. **1939** *Northeastern Reporter* XXI. 837/2 Defendants so conducted their business as to intentionally palm off on the public goods of the defendants as the goods of the plaintiff. **1956**, etc. [see PALMING *vbl. sb.*¹ 3]. **1973** *N.Y. Law Jrnl.* 17 Apr. 4/5 A claim that Borden attempted to 'palm off' its dried soup package as that of Lipton's.

b. with inverted construction: to put (a person) *off with* (something).

1830 tr. *Aristophanes, Acharnians* 21 The Chorus.. should stand by like fools, that I may palm them off with diminutive words. **1894** *Idler* Sept. 168 The public.. cannot always get the books it wants.. and is frequently palmed off with other books which it does not in the least care about. **1934** *Punch* 30 May 592/3, I lost seven holes running this morning absolutely and entirely because I had been palmed off with a little swine who sniffed whenever I was about to strike my ball. **1960** B. KOPS *Dream of Peter Mann* III. 66 We couldn't have our Superstore just yet and we were palmed off with promises.

5. To 'grease the palm' of, bribe, 'tip'.

1747 *Advent. Kidn. Orphan* 40 (F. Hall). **1812** J. H. VAUX *Flash Dict.* s.v., It is then said that the party who receives it [the bribe] is palmed, or that Mr. Palmer is concerned. **1812** *Spirit Pub. Jrnls.* XVI. 345 A candidate in full career.. Palming each greasy raggamuffin. **1890** *Pall Mall G.* 6 Feb. 3/3 The heads of this particular firm.. admit that they 'palmed' right and left. **1899** C. G. HARPER *Exeter Road* 135 Votes which would in other days have been acquired by palming the men and kissing all the babies.

palmaceous (pæl'meɪʃəs), *a. Bot.* [f. mod.L. *Palmāceæ* fem. pl. (f. L. *palma* PALM *sb.*[1]) + -OUS.] Of or belonging to the Natural Order *Palmaceæ*, *Palmæ*, or Palms.

1730 MARTYN in *Phil. Trans.* XXXVI. 385 The same Botanists have placed the *Musa* in the Palmaceous Class. **1857** in MAYNE *Expos. Lex.*

Palmach ('palmax). Also ‖Palmakh. [Heb. shortening of *pᵉluggōṯ maḥaṣ* striking force.] A commando force of the Jewish HAGANAH, active esp. during the war which preceded the formal establishment of the state of Israel in 1948, and incorporated in the Israeli national army in that year.

1945 *Times* 26 Sept. 5/7 The present strength of the *Haganah* itself is variously estimated at 50,000 to 75,000 men, with first-rate equipment,..and a motorized field force (*Palmakh*) capable of throwing in a task force of several thousand men at a few hours' notice at any threatened point of the country. **1949** KOESTLER *Promise & Fulfilment* III. i. 298 The military cadres of the extreme Left, *Palmach*, became the best and most ferocious shock troops. **1950** H. LEVIN *Jerusalem Embattled* 288 *Palmach* (Heb.), abbreviation for *Plugot Machatz*. Mobile detachment of the Jewish Defence Organization. **1955** S. D. GOITEIN *Jews & Arabs* viii. 224 The best boys of the *Palmach*, the 'Commandos' of the *Haganah*. **1960** H. AGAR *Saving Remnant* ix. 219 The Jews began the war with five thousand trained men: the *Palmach*, or shock companies of the Haganah. **1966** *New Statesman* 7 Oct. 506/2 He [*sc.* Ben Gurion] risked unpopularity in dissolving the Palmach, the crack commando troops who formed the potential core of a political and military elite. **1968** P. DURST *Badge of Infamy* iii. 27 There are a hundred of my old friends from the Palmach who would jump at the chance. **1971** *Guardian* 21 Oct. 7/5 The Palmach, the underground Jewish commando movement.

Palma Christi ('pælmə 'krɪstɪ). [The med.L. name (also, in sense 1, Fr., It., Sp., Pg.) for the two plants (= palm or hand of Christ); from the hand-like shape of the leaves (in 1), and of the tubers (in 2). See also PALMCHRIST.]

1. The Castor-oil plant, *Ricinus communis*.

1548 TURNER *Names of Herbs*, Ricinus is called..in english Palma Christi. **1578** LYTE *Dodoens* III. xxix. 355 The seede of Palma Christi is hoate and drie in the thirde degree. *a* **1687** WALLER *Battel Summer-Isl.* I. Wks. (1729) 86 The Palma-Christi and the fair papà,..In half the circle of the hasty year Project a shade, and lovely fruits do wear. **1736** BAILEY *Househ. Dict.* 59 He may take an ounce of the juice of the root of *Palma Christi*, with as much sugar, fasting. **1833** M. SCOTT *Tom Cringle* xviii, We applied an embrocation of the leaves of the *Palma Christi* or Castor oil nut.

†**2.** A name for species of *Orchis* having palmate tubers, as *O. maculata* and *O. latifolia*. *Obs.*

1578 LYTE *Dodoens* II. lix. 225 Of Royall Standergrasse or Palma Christi. [Three kinds described.] **1597** GERARDE *Herbal* I. ciii. 170 Roiall Satyrion or finger Orchis, is called of the Latines Palma Christi.

†**palma'coco.** *Obs.* The coco-palm, COCO 2.

1681 GREW *Musæum* II. 201.

palmar ('pælmə(r)), *a.* and *sb.* [ad. L. *palmāris*, f. *palma*: see PALM *sb.*[1] and [2], and -AR.]

A. *adj.* †**1.** (See quots.) *Obs. rare*⁻⁰.

1656 BLOUNT *Glossogr.*, *Palmar* (*palmaris*), pertaining to victory or to a hand breadth, or to the palm of the hand. **1658** PHILLIPS, *Palmar*, belonging to a Palm.

2. *Anat.* Pertaining to, situated in, or connected with the palm of the hand (or the corresponding part of the fore-foot of a quadruped).

palmar arch: name for the continuation of the radial artery (*deep p.a.*) and that of the ulnar artery (*superficial p.a.*) in the palm.

1831 R. KNOX *Cloquet's Anat.* 211 Palmar or Anterior Ligaments. **1840** G. ELLIS *Anat.* 408 The artery that forms the superficial palmar arch is the continuation of the ulnar. **1872** HUMPHRY *Myology* 37 The anterior or palmar part of the ulnar condyle. **1878** T. BRYANT *Pract. Surg.* I. 173 On the plantar surface of the foot or the palmar of the hand.

B. *sb.* **1.** *Anat.* A palmar muscle, nerve, or other structure.

1890 in *Cent. Dict.*

2. *Zool.* Name for certain joints in the 'arms' of a crinoid: see quot. 1888. (Also in Lat. form *palmāre*, pl. *-ia*.)

1877 HUXLEY *Anat. Inv. Anim.* ix. 584 These again bifurcate to give rise to the palmaria. **1879** CARPENTER in *Trans. Lin. Soc.* II. I. 24 Complete series of distichals and palmars. **1888** ROLLESTON & JACKSON *Anim. Life* 572 If the arms [of a Crinoid] branch twice the joints between the first and second places of division are known as *distichals*; if thrice, the joints between the second and third places of division are designated *palmars*.

palmarian (pæl'mɛərɪən), *a. rare.* [f. L. *palmāri-um* that which bears the palm, a masterpiece + -AN.] = PALMARY *a.*[1]

1815 T. KIDD in *Tracts & Misc. Crit. of Porson* Pref. 33 The chief merit of this palmarian emendation. **1825** *Blackw. Mag.* XVIII. 212 The palmarian charge of all,..the climax of his sins, negligences, and offences. **1889** *Athenæum* 16 Feb. 206/3 [Theobald's] palmarian emendation of the passage in 'Henry V.' describing the death of Falstaff should make his name dear to all lovers of poetry.

palmarosa (,pælmə'rəʊsə). [It.]. **1.** *palmarosa oil*, an essential oil distilled from the grass *Cymbopogon martinii* var. *motia* and used in soaps, perfumes, and cosmetics.

1897 *Jrnl. Chem. Soc.* LXXII. I. 81 Palmarosa oil... This oil, formerly known as Turkish geranium oil, is prepared in the province of Bombay by distilling with water the leaves of a grass. **1902** C. SALTER tr. *Koller's Cosmetics* iv. 64 Palmarosa oil dissolves in 3 parts of 70 per cent. alcohol. **1923** W. A. POUCHER *Perfumes & Cosmetics* I. 105 Palmarosa oil is a useful adjunct in preparing almost any perfume of rose type. **1940** H. TROTTER *Man. Indian Forest Utilization* xiii. 243 Rosha grass oil..is also known as palmarosa or geranium oil. **1945** E. SAGARIN *Sci. & Art of Perfumery* iii. 33 Geraniol..is present in oil of citronella, gingergrass, palmarosa, attar of rose, and a host of others. **1950** E. GUENTHER *Essent. Oils* IV. 5 In India..the bulk of commercial palmarosa oil originates. **1972** *Stand. Encycl. S. Afr.* V. 320/2 From others [*sc.* aromatic grasses]..essential oils like palmarosa oil and citronella oil are extracted.

2. In full, *palmarosa grass*. A tropical grass, *Cymbopogon martinii* var. *motia*, cultivated, esp. in India, for the sake of the essential oil it produces; also known as rosha grass.

1950 E. GUENTHER *Essent. Oils* IV. 9 Distillation of palmarosa grass in direct steam stills increased the yield of oil. *Ibid.* 13 All palmarosa plantings [in Java] were..in excellent condition. **1975** F. KENNETT *Hist. Perfume* ix. 183 Geraniol..can be obtained with greater facility and abundance from oils of citronella, geranium, or palmarossa [*sic*] grass.

†**palmary** ('pælmərɪ), *sb. Obs. rare.* [ad. L. *palmāri-um*, that which carries off the palm of victory, neuter sb. use of *palmāri-us* of or pertaining to a palm: see next.] A token of victory or supreme excellence, a prize: cf. PALM *sb.*[1] 3.

1657 THORNLEY tr. *Longus' Daphnis & Chloe* 163, I give thee this, the palmary of thyne [sc. beauty].

palmary ('pælmərɪ), *a.*[1] [ad. L. *palmāri-us* that bears off the palm of victory, f. *palma* palm: see -ARY.] That bears, or is worthy to bear, the palm (see PALM *sb.*[1] 3); holding the first or highest place; of supreme or first-rate importance; pre-eminent, principal, chief.

1657 W. MORICE *Coena quasi Κοινὴ* Diat. iii. 144 Three favourite and palmary Texts. **1703** QUICK *Dec. Wife's Sister* 23 But the Palmary Argument for these Marriages..is this, their great Expediency. **1879** FARRAR *St. Paul* (1883) 38 That palmary truth of the Pauline theology. **1888** I. BYWATER in *Class. Rev.* II. 278 He has given us a goodly number of emendations of the kind which in old days would have been called 'palmary'. [Cf. mod.L. *emendatio palmaria*.]

'**palmary**, *a.*[2] *rare.* [ad. L. *palmār-is*, f. *palma* palm: see -ARY[2]. Cf. F. *palmaire* (Paré 16th c.).] Pertaining to the palm of the hand; palmar.

1696 PHILLIPS (ed. 5), *Palmary Muscle*, the Muscle that contracts the Palm of the hand. **1897** *Chicago Advance* 21 Oct. 547/2 It began with ordinary palmary and pedal applause.

palmate ('pælmeɪt), *sb. Chem.* [f. PALM-IC + -ATE[4].] A salt of palmic acid.

1838 T. THOMSON *Chem. Org. Bodies* 432 Palmate of soda is obtained by mixing palmic acid with a solution of carbonate of soda. *Ibid.*, Palmate of ammonia may be obtained in the same way.

palmate ('pælmət), *a. Nat. Hist.* [ad. L. *palmāt-us*, f. *palma* palm (of the hand) + -ATE[2] 2.]

1. Of a form like that of an open palm or hand; applied to parts or members of a plant or animal which have narrow or spreading divisions like fingers, properly when these project or radiate from an expanded entire portion like the palm.

spec. **a.** *Bot.* Of leaves having lobes or divisions (strictly five in number) whose midribs all radiate from one point at the end of the leaf-stalk, the sinuses being either shallow or deep (see PALMATI-), or even extending to the base so that the leaf consists of separate leaflets (in this case more properly called *digitate*); also of tubers having divisions like fingers, as in some species of *Orchis*. **b.** *Zool.* Of the horns of deer when of broad flat form with lateral projecting points, as in the reindeer and moose. **c.** *Entom.* Of the antennæ and legs of certain insects: see quot. 1826.

1760 J. LEE *Introd. Bot.* III. v. (1765) 179 *Palmate*. **1785** MARTYN *Rousseau's Bot.* xxvii. (1794) 424 The leaves are palmate or handed. **1807** J. E. SMITH *Phys. Bot.* 109 Globular or palmate knobs or bulbs. **1826** KIRBY & SP. *Entomol.* IV. 321 *Palmate*. Very short antennæ which send forth externally a few long finger-shaped branches, giving them some resemblance of a hand. *Ibid.* 329 *Palmate*. When towards the apex the cubit is armed laterally with several divaricate spiniform teeth. **1855** KINGSLEY *Westw. Ho!* vi, The great palmate oarweeds which waved along the chasm. **1880** GRAY *Struct. Bot.* iii. §4 (ed. 6) 101 *Digitate* (fingered) was the old name, when the term *palmate* was restricted to a simple but palmately lobed leaf of this type. But since the time of De Candolle the two names have been used interchangeably.

2. Of the foot of a bird: Having the toes connected by an expanded membrane; webbed.

1826 GOOD *Bk. Nat.* (1834) II. 41 A palmate or web-foot, formed for swimming.

palmated ('pælmeɪtɪd), *a. Nat. Hist.* [-ED[1].]

1. = prec. 1.

1753 CHAMBERS *Cycl. Supp.* s.v. *Leaf*, Palmated Leaf, one in form of an open hand. **1794** S. WILLIAMS *Vermont* 82 His horns are palmated. **1851** MAYNE REID *Scalp Hunt.* xx. 139 Thatched with the palmated leaves of the yuca. **1881** B. DAWKINS in *Nature* 24 Nov. 85/2 Antlers palmated in front, instead of behind the beam.

2. = prec. 2; also applied to the foot of some quadrupeds, etc.

1768 PENNANT *Zool.* I. 129 The Osprey... The left [foot] is not at all palmated, as Linnæus..asserts it is. **1776** *Ibid.* I. 119 Seal..Five palmated toes on each foot. **1802** PALEY *Nat. Theol.* xv, The strong short legs of that animal [mole], the palmated feet armed with sharp nails. **1856** KANE *Arct. Expl.* I. xxiv. 320 A novel use of a palmated foot.

palmately ('pælmətlɪ), *adv.* [f. PALMATE *a.* + -LY[2].] In a palmate manner. (Chiefly *Bot.*)

1845 LINDLEY *Sch. Bot.* iv. (1858) 26c, Leaves divided palmately into many narrow lobes. **1870** HOOKER *Stud. Flora* 153 Sanicula... Leaves palmately cut. **1872** OLIVER *Elem. Bot.* II. 175 A..herb with palmately-lobed leaves.

palmati- (pæl'meɪtɪ, pæl'mætɪ), combining form of L. *palmātus* PALMATE, in botanical terms relating to leaves. **palmatifid** (-'mætɪfɪd) *a.* [L. *-fidus* split, divided], palmately cleft or divided at least half-way to the base. **palmatiform** (-'mætɪ-) *a.*, approaching a palmate form, or having the ribs palmately arranged. **pal,mati'lobate, pal'matilobed** (-meɪtɪ-) *a.*, palmately divided with rounded divisions or lobes. **pal,mati'parted, -'partite** (-,meɪtɪ-) *a.* [L. *partītus* divided: see PARTITE], palmately divided nearly to the base; so **pal'matisect, pal,mati'sected** (-meɪtɪ-) *a.* [L. *sectus* cut: see -SECT].

1840 WHEWELL *Phil. Induct. Sci.* I. 466 Leaves may be called pinnatifid, pinnatipartite, pinnatisect, pinnatilobate, palmatifid, palmatipartite. **1857** MAYNE *Expos. Lex.*, Palmatifid,..palmatiform,..palmatilobate,..palmatipartite,..palmatisected. **1870** BENTLEY *Man. Bot.* 155 When there are more than 5 lobes, the leaf is palmatifid or palmately-cleft. **1872** OLIVER *Elem. Bot.* I. vii. 76 If the segments be separated nearly to the petiole, the leaf is palmatipartite. **1882** VINES *Sachs' Bot.* 416 Lamina being usually pinnatifid, but sometimes palmatifid.

palmation (pæl'meɪʃən). [n. of action from PALM *v.*, and PALMATE *a.*: see -ATION.]

†**1.** The action of touching or feeling with the palm of the hand. *Obs.*

1688 R. HOLME *Armoury* II. 387/1 Palpation, or Palmation ..by which the object is discovered to be either rough or smooth, hairy or naked.

2. *Nat. Hist.* Palmate formation (as in the horns of a deer, the feet of a bird, etc.); *concr.* each of the divisions of a palmate structure.

1883 *Chambers' Encycl.* s.v. *Deer*, [Antlers] are renewed with increase of size, and of breadth of palmation. **1884-90** *Cassell's Nat. Hist.* III. 79 The gigantic Irish Deer, a species originally included with the Elk, on account of the palmation and outward inclination of its huge antlers. **1889** *Sci. Amer.* N.S. LXI. 296/1 The curious axis deer..its horns, when developed, will have no palmations. **1890** COUES *Ornith.* II. iii. 194 The palmation is usually complete, extending to the ends of the toes.

palmato- (pæl,meɪtəʊ), occasional advb. combining form of L. *palmātus* PALMATE (cf. PALMATI-). **pal,mato-'peltate** *a.*, peltate and palmately divided. **pal,mato-ra'mose** *a.*, palmately branched, having branches spreading like fingers.

1846 DANA *Zooph.* (1848) 545 Cespitose, slenderly palmato-ramose. **1876** HARLEY *Mat. Med.* (ed. 6) 441 Leaves large, palmato-peltate.

Palm Beach. The name of a coastal resort in Florida, U.S.A., used to designate a kind of light-weight fabric used for clothing. Also *attrib.*, as *Palm Beach cloth, suit*.

Palm Beach is a proprietary name in the U.S. in this sense.

1915 *Policeman's Monthly* Sept. 21/2 A lady and a daughter thinking to give the husband a pleasant surprise, bought him a fine new silk 'Palm Beach' suit. **1915** *Official Gaz.* (U.S. Patent Office) 26 Oct. 1221/1 Palm Beach... Woolen piece goods, mohair piece goods, and piece goods of combinations of cotton, wool, mohair, alpaca, camel-hair, silk, and artificial silk. **1916** *Daily Colonist* (Victoria, B.C.) 2 July 6/1 (Advt.), Palm Beach Suits in an exceptionally fine quality of mercerized Palm Beach cloth. **1922** H. L. FOSTER *Adventures Trop. Tramp* 1, I had just applied for a job as stoker, but a Palm Beach suit, a Panama hat, and a cane did not seem to be a convincing costume on the figure of an applicant for this position. **1928** —— *If you go to S. America* 17 In..tropical lands white linen or palm beach are desirable. **1928** *Daily Mail* 25 July 12/1 The ideal is a sports shirt with a low open neck, flannel trousers, and a jacket of the material used in Palm Beach suits. **1940** *Chambers's Techn. Dict.* 610/1 *Palm Beach*, a light fabric of plain weave made from cotton warp and lustre worsted weft, or entirely of cotton. **1959** J. THURBER *Years with Ross* vi. 99 Ingersoll had appeared..dressed in a Palm Beach suit. **1973** 'I. DRUMMOND' *Jaws of Watchdog* xi. 148 He was elegant in a white Palm Beach suit and a dark pink shirt.

palmchrist ('pɑːmkrɪst). Also 7 palmecrist. [Cf. mod.Ger. *Christpalme*; obs. F. *paulme de Christ, paulme Dieu* (Cotgr.).] Anglicized form of PALMA CHRISTI (sense 1).

1611 BIBLE *Jonah* iv. 6 God prepared a gourd [*marg.* palmecrist]. **1860** PUSEY *Min. Proph.* 286 We have each, his own palmchrist; and our palmchrist has its own worm.

palm court. Also with capital initials. [f. PALM *sb.*[1] + COURT *sb.*[1] 1.] A large room or patio, esp. of a hotel, named from the palm-trees used as decoration. Now usu. in *attrib.* use, esp. **palm-court music**, the kind of light music associated with the palm court (also *ellipt.*); **palm-court orchestra**, a small band which plays such music.

These associations are now regarded as old-fashioned.

1908 *Westm. Gaz.* 12 Mar. 10/2 The lounge or palm-court of to-day was merely a revival of the Greek hall. **1910** *Bradshaw's Railway Guide* Apr. 1151 Plymouth, Royal Hotel..Magnificent Palm Court. Orchestra plays daily. **1930** E. WAUGH *Vile Bodies* x. 197 The manager of the 'Imperial'..upheld the integrity of British hotel-keeping. Tea, he explained, was served daily in the Palm Court, with orchestra on Thursdays and Sundays, between the hours of four and six. **1945** S. HUGHES in C. Madge *Pilot Papers* 89 The 'light' music public thinks of the music it wants in terms..of palm-court orchestras. **1955** *Radio Times* 22 Apr. 13/2 David Galliver sings with the Palm Court Orchestra in Grand Hotel at 9.0 tonight. **1959** *Observer* 21 June 18/4 The sugary tones of the Palm Court orchestra are never far away. **1962** *Ibid.* 28 Oct. 23/7 A retreat into daydream-fantasy that eventually either nauseates or numbs, as palm-court music does. **1966** M. BREWER *Man against Fear* xvi. 171, I recognised a popular Palm Court number from *Traviata*. **1969** *Times* 30 Apr. (Brighton Suppl.) p. i/3 The bingo hall with a palm court bar and lounge. **1970** E. LEE *Music of People* vii. 138 Music which would now be called 'Palm Court' was still widely popular. **1973** J. RYDER *Trevayne* (1974) vi. 50 Trevayne had gone to a corner pay phone to call his wife at the Plaza..but..he was told she wasn't in the Palm Court. **1977** J. WAINWRIGHT *Do Nothin'* viii. 124 He sometimes plays pure 'Palm Court'..without that extra lilt which can make a band swing.

palm-cross. †**a.** A cross, usually a monumental cross in a churchyard, formerly decorated with palm-branches (or substitutes for them) on Palm Sunday. *Obs.* **b.** (See quot. 1855.)

1469–70 in Swayne *Sarum Church-w. Acc.* (1896) 13 Pro emend'e le Palmecros. **1525** in Glasscock *Rec. St. Michael's, Bp. Stortford* (1882) 39 Pd. for quarter of lyme to set up w[t]alle the palme crosse..xvjd. **15..** *Will* in *Ripon Ch. Acts* (Surtees) 334 Palme Crose within the kirkegarth. **a1568** [see PADLE]. **1855** ROBINSON *Whitby Gloss.*, *Palm Crosses*, ornamental combinations of small crosses made of the peeled willow palm, put together with pins and studded with the blossoms. These memorials of the season are then suspended from the top of the room.

palmed (pɑːmd), *a.* [f. PALM *sb.*[2] + -ED[2]; repr. L. *palmātus*.]

1. Having a 'palm' or flat expanded part with projecting points, as a deer's horn; palmate; carrying palmate horns. ? *Obs.*

1486 *Bk. St. Albans* E iv, Too brawnchis first pawmyd he most haue. **1575** TURBERV. *Venerie* 56 This heade should be called a palmed toppe. **1622** DRAYTON *Poly-olb.* xxiii. (1748) 355 The proud palmed deer Forsake the closer woods. **1697** *Phil. Trans.* XIX. 505 All of the Deer Kind, carrying the same sort of Palmed Horns.

2. PALMATE as a leaf.

1766 J. BARTRAM *Jrnl.* 17 Jan. 40 Here we cut down three tall palm or cabbage trees, and cut out the top bud, the white tender part of the rudiments of the great leaves, which will be 6 or 7 foot long, when full grown, and the palmed part 4 in diameter.

3. In parasynthetic comb.: Having a palm or palms (of a specified kind).

c1400 *Master of Game* (MS. Digby 182) iii, Of the bucke ..His heede is pamynge and longe pamed. **1611** COTGR. s.v. *Paumé*, A full-paulmed Stags head. **1613** CHAPMAN *Masque* Wks. 1873 III. 115 She..loves hounds and high pallmd harts. **1852** R. S. SURTEES *Sponge's Sp. Tour* (1893) 197 He carried the smart dogskin wash-leather palmed glove of his right hand in his left one. **1889** *Daily News* 18 July 7/1 The average palmed, square tipped man is the average man of sense.

palmed (pɑːmd), *ppl. a.* [f. PALM *v.*[2] + -ED[1].] Concealed in the palm of the hand.

1896 *Daily News* 3 June 8/3 Keeping the hand closed, until the opportunity occurs for getting rid of the palmed article.

palmellaceous (pælmɛˈleɪʃəs), *a. Bot.* [f. mod.L. *Palmellāce-æ* fem. pl. + -OUS.] Belonging to the *Palmellaceæ*, a doubtful order of fresh-water Algæ (typical genus *Palmella*), consisting of simple cells, of various colours, with thick jelly-like integument, and multiplying by cell-division; supposed by some to be transitional states of some undetermined higher plants. So **palˈmellin** [-IN[1]], a red colouring matter found in *Palmella cruenta*; **palˈmelloid** *a.* [-OID], resembling or apparently akin to the genus *Palmella*.

1877 *Q. Jrnl. Microsc. Sci.* XVII. 185 On a 'palmelloid' modification of Stigeoclonium. [**1878** MCNAB *Bot.* 54 The algae were formerly known as the green gonidia of the lichen thallus, and belong chiefly to the Palmelleaceae with chlorophyll.] **1881** *Philadelphia Rec.* No. 3455. 6 Substances which he had succeeded in extracting from fresh-water algae. They are palmelline, xanthophyll, chlorophyll and characine. **1890** COOKE *Freshw. Algæ* iv. 41 Considerable surfaces are covered with a palmelloid growth.

†**ˈpalmeous,** *a. Obs.* [f. L. *palme-us* of or made of palms + -OUS.] Of palms or palmwood.

1657 TOMLINSON *Renou's Disp.* 722 They make the palmeous Emplaister after the form prescribed, agitating it alwayes with a palmeous spatle. [*Ibid.*, Agitating it with a rudicle of the Palm, or some other astrictive Tree.]

palmer (ˈpɑːmə(r)), *sb.*[1] Forms: 3–6 **palmere**, 4 **paumer**, 4–6 **palmare**, 6 **paulmer**, **palmar**, 4– **palmer**. [a. AF. *palmer*, *paumer* = OF. *palmier*, *paumier* (= Sp. *palmero*, Pg. *palmeiro*, It. *palmiere*):—med.L. *palmārius*, f. *palma* palm.]

1. A pilgrim who had returned from the Holy Land, in sign of which he carried a palm-branch or palm-leaf; also, an itinerant monk who travelled from shrine to shrine, under a perpetual vow of poverty; often simply an equivalent of *pilgrim*.

a1300 *K. Horn* 1027 A palmere he þar mette. **c1330** R. BRUNNE *Chron. Wace* (Rolls) 15834 A schort staf he dide hym make, Als palmeres in handes take. **1362** LANGL. *P. Pl.* A. Prol. 46 Pilgrimes and Palmers Plihten hem to-gederes For to seche seint Ieme. **14..** *Tundale's Vis.* 418 He se non ..But a preste, þat a palmare was, A palme in his hande he hadde, And in a sclaven was he cladde. **1530** PALSGR. 252/2 Paulmer a poore man, *blistre*. **1592** SHAKS. *Rom. & Jul.* I. v. 102 For Saints haue hands, that Pilgrims hands do tuch, And palme to palme, is holy Palmers kisse. **1674** STAVELEY *Rom. Horseleach* 93 The Pilgrim had some home, or dwelling place, but the Palmer had none. The Pilgrim travelled to some certain designed place, or places, but the Palmer to all. The Pilgrim went at his own charges, but the Palmer profest wilful poverty, and went upon Alms. **1808** SCOTT *Marm.* I. xxiii, Here is a holy Palmer come, From Salem first, and last from Rome. **1856** STANLEY *Sinai & Pal.* ii. 144 Hence too [Phoenicia], at least in recent times, came the branches, which distinguished the pilgrims of Palestine, from those of Rome, Compostella, and Canterbury, by the name of '*Palmer*'.

transf. **1906** *Bungalow* Dec. 8/2 The exodus of these infatuated palmers is ever to the land of Shakespeare.

2. a. Name for a destructive hairy caterpillar. [Orig. applied to those of migratory or wandering habits, or that moved about in swarms: see PALMER-WORM.]

1538 ELYOT *Dict.*, *Campe*, a worme which..is callyd a palmer. *Ibid.*, *Centipeda*, a worme called a Palmer, whiche is heary, and hath many feete. **1578** LYTE *Dodoens* II. xxv. 177 Whose leaves be holy as though they had bene eaten with Locustes, Paulmers, or Snayles. **1613** PURCHAS *Pilgrimage* (1614) 803 Mingling likewise with these ashes, scorpions, spiders and palmers aliue. **1867** F. FRANCIS *Angling* xiv. (1880) 501 Palmers..are the..caterpillars of various moths.

b. *Angling.* An artificial fly, of various kinds, covered with bristling hairs like the caterpillar so called; a hackle.

1651 T. BARKER *Art of Angling* (1653) 5 There are several kinds of Palmers that are good for that time. **1787** BEST *Angling* (ed. 2) 93 Golden Palmer, or Hackle. **1884** *St. James's Gaz.* 21 June 6/1 In certain waters a big red or black palmer is the best and best recognized lure for perch.

c. A wood-louse.

1725 BRADLEY *Fam. Dict.* II, Its held to be a great secret to drink pounded Palmers found in cellars in some white wine. **1847–78** HALLIWELL, *Palmer*, a wood-louse.

3. *attrib.* and *Comb.*, as (in sense 1) ***palmer-like*** adj., ***-man***, ***-staff***, ***-weed***; (in sense 2) ***palmer bob*** (BOB *sb.*[1] 9), ***fly***; †**palmer-serpent**: see quot.; **palmer-trout**, a local name of the samlet.

1814 COL. HAWKER *Diary* (1893) I. 94 My flies..were the yellow dun at bottom and red *palmer bob. **1651–7** T. BARKER *Art of Angling* (1820) 33 We will begin to make the *Palmer flye. **1858** HAWTHORNE *Fr. & It. Note-bks.* II. 11 White head and *palmer-like beard. **1885** BURTON *Arab. Nts.* (1887) III. 276 The *palmer-man drank the bitter draught. **1608** TOPSELL *Serpents* (1658) 745 Unto this Porphyre I may add the *Palmer Serpent, which Strabo writeth doth kill with an unrecoverable poyson, and it is also of a Scarlet colour. **1623** WODROEPHE *Marrow Fr. Tongue* 460/2 The Pilgrimes of my Deseignes shall alwayes be furnished with the *Palmer Staffe of Courage. **1836** YARRELL *Brit. Fishes* I. p. xxxvii, *Palmer Trout. **1865** COUCH *Brit. Fishes* IV. 245 Samlet, or Parr... Branlin. Palmer Trout... *Salmo Salmulus*. **1845** G. MURRAY *Islaford* 33 He reached his home in *Palmer-weeds.

†**palmer,** *sb.*[2] *Obs.* Also 5 **pawmer**, **palmeir**, **-yer**, 6 **palmier**. [a. F. *palmier*, *paumier* palm-tree, date-tree (12th c.):—L. *palmāri-us*, f. *palma* palm. Cf. It. *palmero*, Sp. *palmera*, Pg. *palmeira*.] A palm-tree; a date-tree; the palmyra.

c1470 HENRY *Wallace* IX. 1923 His handis maid rycht lik till a pawmer [*v.r.* to ane Palmeir]. **1481** CAXTON *Myrr.* II. x. 88 In ynde groweth a tree moche grete and right fayr.. and is called palmyer and bereth dates. **1491** —— *Vitas Patr.* (W. de W. 1495) II. 261/2 The sayd Symeon..was clommen on a palmyer. **c1532** DU WES *Introd. Fr.* in *Palsgr.* 914 Palmier, *datiers*. **1599** HAKLUYT *Voy.* II. I. 252 Sugar which is made of the nutte called Gagara: the tree is called the palmer.

b. *attrib.* and *Comb.*: **palmer-nut**, ? coco-nut; **palmer-tree**, palm-tree (in quots. coco-nut palm).

14.. *Nominale* in Wr.-Wülcker 711/17 *Hic cucumur*, *vel -mis*, a palmernutte. **1599** HAKLUYT *Voy.* II. I. 218 There come euery yeere from Cochin..great shippes laden with great Nuts cured, and with Sugar made of the selfe same Nuts called Giagra: the tree whereon these Nuts doe grow is called the Palmer tree. *Ibid.* 264 Here are very many palmer or coco trees.

palmer, *sb.*[3] ? *Obs.* Forms: 4 **pamere**, 5 **paumere**, **pawmer(e**, **palmare**, 5–7 (?–9) **palmer**, 7 **paulmer**. [a. OF. *paumer* in same sense, f. *paume* palm of the hand: cf. PALMERY[1].] A flat piece of wood used for striking the palm of the hand as a punishment; a ferule.

1387 TREVISA *Higden* (Rolls) VIII. 221 Seynt Iohn þe Evangelist appered to hym in his slepe, and manassede hym to smyte wiþ a pamere [*v.rr.* pawmere, paumere, pawmer: **1432** palmer: L. *ferula*]. **1483** *Cath. Angl.* 267/1 A Palmare in þe scole, *ferula*,..*palmatorium*. **c1500** in Peacock *Stat. Cambridge* (1841) App. A. p. xxxvii, The Bedyll in Arte shall bring the Master of Gramer to the Vice-chauncelar, delyveryng hym a Palmer with a Rodde. **1561** DAUS tr. *Bullinger on Apoc.* (1573) 61 Children are kept in awe with the Palmer, least they forget them selues. **1611** COTGR., *Ferule*, a Ferula, or Paulmer vsed in Schooles for correction. **1658** PHILLIPS, *Palmer*, a certain instrument where-with school-boys are struck on the palms of their hands.

palmer (ˈpɑːmə(r)), *sb.*[4] [f. PALM *v.* 2 + -ER[1].] One who palms, or conceals in the hand (a card, die, or other object, in cheating, conjuring, etc.); one who practises sleight of hand.

1671 SHADWELL *Humourists* iii, I saw you,..by help of a dozen men, chastise one poor Topper or Palmer. **1706** PHILLIPS, *Palmer*,..one that deceitfully cozens or cogs at Cards or Dice, by keeping some of them in his Hand unseen. **1885** *Pall Mall G.* 19 Mar. 5/1 The clever conjurer..as a palmer and a passer..takes a high rank.

palmer, *v. Sc.* and *north. dial.* [f. PALMER *sb.*[1]] *intr.* To wander about like a palmer or vagrant; to go about idly from place to place.

1807 STAGG *Poems* 60 A palmer'd out as chance wad heft, An' till a neybors house a tuok. **1816** SCOTT *Antiq.* xxix, Ony auld palmering body that was coming down the edge of Kinblythemont. **1875** W. ALEXANDER *Ain Folk* (1882) 208 Up an' paumerin' aboot the toon o' the seelence o' the nicht.

Palmerin (ˈpælmərɪn). [From *Palmerin de Oliva*, the legendary illegitimate son of a Byzantine princess, whose name (f. Sp. *palmera* palm-tree) is said to have been derived from his exposure as an infant in a wicker basket among palms and olives on a mountain side. He was the original hero of the Palmerin romances which appeared in Spain in the 16th c.] Any one of the knightly heroes of the Palmerin romances; hence, allusively, any redoubtable champion of the age of chivalry.

1611 BEAUM. & FL. *Knt. Burn. Pestle* III. ii, And, by that virtue that brave Rosicler That damned brood of ugly giants slew, And Palmerin Frannarco overthrew. **1640** GLAPTHORNE *Hollander* III. Wks. 1874 I. 110 Ha, thy arme in sling, my Palmerin. **1823** SCOTT *Peveril* xv, To be an absolute Palmerin of England is not in my nature.

Palmerstonian (pɑːməˈstəʊnɪən), *a.* [f. the name of Henry John Temple, Viscount *Palmerston*, English statesman (1784–1865) + -IAN.] Of, pertaining to, or characteristic of Lord Palmerston, or the forceful, assertive diplomacy associated with him. Also as *sb.*, a supporter of Lord Palmerston. So **Palmerˈstonianism**; **ˈPalmerstonism**.

1854 *Punch* 17 June 246/2 We also wish he [*sc.* Lord Palmerston] would open a school in Downing Street wherein to furnish instruction in penmanship on the Palmerstonian system. **1858** *Illustr. News of World* 24 Apr. 187/1 Exposed to an attack from Palmerston and the Palmerstonians. *Ibid.* 5 June 283/2 Thunderbolts in the *Times* which made Mr. Disraeli, at Slough, virtuously protest against Palmerstonian corruption of the press. **1866** R. S. CHARNOCK *Verba Nominalia* 217 *Palmerstonism*,..old-soldierism; soft-soap. **1898** *Westm. Gaz.* 14 Dec. 8/1 The revived Palmerstonianism of Lord Rosebery. **1900** [see ELDONIAN *a.*]. **1927** *Observer* 20 Nov. 10/2 Because, in the hard old Palmerstonian phrase, we are not geese. **1928** *Ibid.* 11 Mar. 6/4 In private he was never chary of urging his chief to a more Palmerstonian line of policy. **1946** J. W. DAY *Harvest Adventure* xii. 195 One old man, with a Palmerstonian pippin face, in a full-skirted, snuff-coloured greatcoat with a velvet collar, talked of Culford as had done the beater half an hour before. **1954** A. J. P. TAYLOR *Struggle for Mastery in Europe 1848–1918* 414 Lansdowne did not need much encouragement to abandon the bankrupt Palmerstonian policy. **1966** *Economist* 12 Nov. 683/2 Palmerstonism was already hopelessly bankrupt. **1973** *Listener* 7 June 742/1 You will wonder why such a Palmerstonian view of television cuts any ice with the broadcasting authorities.

ˈpalmer-ˌworm. [f. PALMER *sb.*[1] 2 + WORM *sb.*: see quot. 1608.] Name for various hairy caterpillars destructive to vegetation; in North America, the larva of a tineid moth, *Ypsilophus pometellus*, destructive to apple-leaves.

In O.T. rendering Heb. *gāzām*, prob. a kind of locust.

1560 BIBLE (Geneva) *Joel* i. 4 That which is left of the palmer worme, hathe the grashopper eaten. **1608** TOPSELL *Serpents* (1658) 667 There is another sort of these Caterpillers, who have no certain place of abode, nor yet cannot tell where to finde their food, but like unto superstitious Pilgrims, do wander and stray hither and thither,..these have purchased a very apt name amongst us Englishmen, to be called Palmer-worms, by reason of their wandering and roguish life, (for they never stay in one place, but are ever wandering). **1660** BOYLE *New Exp. Phys. Mech.* Digress. 377 One of those hairy wormes that resemble caterpillars, and are wont to be call'd Palmer-wormes. **1668** *New Eng. Hist. & Gen. Reg.* (1880) XXXIV. 298 It pleased God to restrain the Palmer worm amongst vs in y[e] Bay and to spare our fruit trees. **a1817** T. DWIGHT *Trav. New Eng. etc.* (1821) II. 400 The palmer-worm, were it to appear annually, would, within a few years, empty New-England of its inhabitants. **1880** *Boy's own Bk.* 265 The palmer-worm, woolbed, or canker is found on herbs, plants, and trees.

†**palmery**[1]. *Obs.* In 3-4 paumerie, pameri. [As PALMER[3], with change of suffix.] = PALMER[3].

c **1290** *S. Eng. Leg.* I. 437/219 Seint Ioan þe Ewangelist to him cam..And a paumerie [*v.r. E. Eng. P.* (1862) 76/208 pameri] bar on is hond: gret and strong i-nouȝh; Seint Eadmund he nam bi þe hond: and is paumerie op drouȝh.

palmery[2] (ˈpɑːmərɪ). [f. PALM *sb.*[1] + -ERY; cf. *fernery*.] A collection of palm-trees; a place or house in which they are grown, a palm-house.

In recent Dicts.

palmester, -try, obs. ff. PALMISTER, -TRY.

palmeta, -to, obs. var. PALMETTO.

palmette (pælˈmɛt). [a. F. *palmette*, in sense 1 palmetto, palm-leaf ornament, dim. of *palme*; in 2 dim. of L. *palma*, F. *paume* palm of the hand.]

1. *Archæol.* An ornament (in sculpture or painting) with narrow divisions or digitations, somewhat resembling a palm-leaf. Also *transf.* and *attrib.*

1850 LEITCH tr. *C. O. Müller's Anc. Art* §320 (ed. 2) 373 A stele on a vase from Volci, on which the painter represents yellowish palmettes on a white ground. **1857** BIRCH *Anc. Pottery* (1858) I. 301 A peculiar floral ornament..the antefixal ornament, or palmette, appears at the handle. **1889** J. HIRST in *Archæol. Inst. Jrnl.* No. 181. 28 The artist having wished thus to fill in every vacant space at his disposal with a leaf, a palmette, or a flower. **1908** *Times Lit. Suppl.* 14 Aug. 260/2 From the tenth to the fourteenth century the palmette-motive disappears. **1931** A. ESDAILE *Student's Man. Bibliogr.* vi. 212 Two..London binders..produced about 1815 some really beautiful bindings decorated with classical palmette borders. **1931** A. U. DILLEY *Oriental Rugs & Carpets* iii. 61 A fourth group of superior rugs, distinguished by pattern of palmette and now called Ispahan. **1975** *Ashmolean Mus. Rep. Visitors 1973–4* 17 A fragment of an Attic black-figure amphora decorated with a lotus and palmette pattern, languettes, and part of a battle scene.

2. *Zool.* An appendage of the head in certain gastropod molluscs.

1843 *Penny Cycl.* XXV. 379/2 There is an internal prismatic appendage, which MM. Quoy and Gaimard call a *palmette*, because it is frequently digitated. *Ibid.* 380/1 The head is red-brown and striated, with a narrow green band at the base of the eyes and the palmettes.

palmetto (pælˈmɛtəʊ). Forms: 6-7 (9) **palmito**, 7 **palmita**, 7-8 **palmeto, -ta**, 8- **palmetto**. [Originally a. Sp. *palmito* dwarf fan-palm, dim. of *palma* palm; subseq. conformed to diminutives in *-etto* from Italian.] **a.** Name for several smaller species of palms, esp. the dwarf fan-palm, *Chamærops humilis*, of Southern Europe and North Africa, and the cabbage palmetto, *Sabal Palmetto*, of the South-eastern United States; also other species of *Chamærops*, *Sabal*, and *Thrinax*. By early writers used more vaguely.

1583 E. COTTON in Hakluyt *Voy.* (1589) 188 The Palmito with his fruite inclosed in him. **1601** R. JOHNSON *Kingd. & Commw.* (1603) 204 The inhabitants liue vpon rice, palmito, cattell and fish. **1613** PURCHAS *Pilgrimage* (1614) 649 The Palmita is without branches, the fruit growes on the top, which within is like Pomegranats, ful of grains, without of a golden colour. **1624** CAPT. SMITH *Virginia* v. 170 Plants of seuerall Kinds, as..Cedars, infinite store of Palmetoes. **1631** R. H. *Arraignm. Whole Creature* xii. §2. 120 Better than the African and Spanish rootes: the American Palmitos and Potatos. **1634** SIR T. HERBERT *Trav.* 209 The most beneficiall tree to Travellers is the Palmeto; it growes like the Date or Coco-tree. **1727-46** THOMSON *Summer* 675 And high palmettos lift their graceful shade. **1760** J. LEE *Introd. Bot.* App. 321 Palmetto, *Chamærops.* **1765** J. BARTRAM *Jrnl.* 31 Dec. in Stork *Acc. E. Florida* (1766) 18 We came now to plenty of the tree palmetto, which the inhabitants call cabbage-tree. **1808** PIKE *Sources Mississ.* III. App. 27 There is the palmetto, which grows to the height of 20 and 25 feet, with a trunk two feet in diameter. **1847** LONGF. *Ev.* II. ii. 97 They glided along,..behind a screen of palmettos. **1901** *Scribner's Mag.* XXIX. 447/2 The only vegetation is a clump of stunted palmettoes, marking the burial-place of some forgotten Moorish saint.

b. With qualifying words, as **blue palmetto**, *Chamærops Hystrix*, of Southern U.S.; **cabbage p.**, *Sabal Palmetto* (see above); **dwarf p.**, *Sabal Adansoni*, of South-eastern U.S.; **royal p.**, *Sabal umbraculifera* and *Thrinax parviflora*, of the West Indies; **saw p.**, *Chamærops serrulata*; **silk-top p.**, name in Florida for *Thrinax parviflora*; **silver-leaved** or **silver-top p.**, *Thrinax argentea*, of the West Indies, Panama, etc. Also **humble p.**, **small p.**, names for the palm-like genus *Carludovica* of *Pandanaceæ* or Screw-pines, of S. America and the W. Indies, esp. *C. insignis*.

1756 P. BROWNE *Jamaica* 190 Palmeto Royal, or Palmeto Thatch. This tree..covers whole fields in many parts of the island. *Ibid.* 330 The humble Palmeto with round foot-stalks. **1866** *Treas. Bot.* 838/2. **1884** MILLER *Plant-n.*

c. *attrib.* and *Comb.*, as ***palmetto country***, ***ground***, ***hat***, ***juice***, ***leaf***, ***palm***, ***swamp***, ***tree***, ***wine***; also in sense 'thatched with palmetto leaves', as ***palmetto cabin***, ***house***, ***hut***; ***palmetto-covered***, ***-thatched***, adjs.; **palmetto basket**, a basket made of palmetto leaves; **palmetto brush**, a hard brush made from the roots of the palmetto; **palmetto bush**, a young or dwarfed plant of one of the species of palmetto; **palmetto cabbage** = *cabbage palmetto* (see sense b); **palmetto flag**, the flag of the State of South Carolina, which bears a figure of a cabbage palmetto tree; so **Palmetto State**, a name for South Carolina; **palmetto thatch**, the leaves of several kinds of palmetto, esp. *Thrinax argentea*, used for making hats, baskets, etc.; also the tree itself.

1813 SCOTT *Trierm.* III. xxv, Their hands *palmetto baskets bare. **1913** *Country Life* Nov. 94/3 For the making of *palmetto brushes the problem is to remove the pith without destroying the fibres. **1784** T. HUTCHINS *Hist. Narr. Louisiana & W. Florida* 34 The whole is..covered with thick wood, *Palmetto bushes, &c. **1812** *Niles' Reg.* III. 237/1 Many more must have been slain, but were hid from our view by the thick and high Palmetto bushes. **1901** *Scribner's Mag.* Apr. 433/1 Narrow grooves have been worn in the hillsides, divided one from the other by..pyramids of earth and clay, crested with the stunted stems and roots of palmetto bushes. **1802** J. DRAYTON *View South-Carolina* 6 Their soil is of very sandy nature; producing..*palmetto cabbage, palmetto royal, silk grass. **1870** *Amer. Naturalist* III. 458 With a *palmetto cabin, plenty of oysters, game and fish, he lives a free and easy life. **1942** S. KENNEDY *Palmetto Country* 24 The *Palmetto country rests upon what is geologically known as the Floridian plateau. **1883** J. MACGREGOR in *Sunday Mag.* Nov. 686/2 We passed vast *palmito-covered and absolutely treeless plains. **1860** in *South Carolina Hist. Mag.* (1964) LXIV. 156 This evening the *Palmetto Flag was inaugurated. **1861** *Mitchell's Maritime Reg.* 403/2 The Peter Maxwell sailed off with the Palmetto flag flying at her main. **1744** F. MOORE *Voy. Georgia* 124 The Indians were prevailed upon to return to the *Palmetto ground. **1765** J. BARTRAM *Jrnl.* 24 Dec. (1766) 5 A perch or more of palmetto-ground. **1747** *N. Jersey Archives* XII. 364 The woman..Had on,..blue worsted stockings, *palmeta hat, scarlet red cloak [etc.]. **1877** E. S. WARD *Story of Avis* 410 She looked very young and girlish that day in her palmetto hat and white linen dress. **1889** G. W. CABLE in *Century Mag.* Feb. 516/2 Before the end of the month all the women in St. Martinville were wearing palmetto hats. **1974** 'B. MATHER' *White Dacoit* vi. 64 His hideous palmetto hat..flopped down over his face in a ragged veil. **1741** in *South Carolina Hist. Soc. Coll.* (1887) IV. 42 They came to some *Palmetto Houses, where they halted about ane hour. **1763** W. ROBERTS *Nat. Hist. Florida* 9 The town, consisting of about forty palmetto houses. **1739** W. STEPHENS *Jrnl.* 29 Dec. in *Colonial Rec. Georgia* (1906) IV. 480, I found them well covered from bad Weather, by a strong *Palmeta Hut. **1741** in *South Carolina Hist. Soc. Coll.* (1887) IV. 33 The first Palmetto Hut on the sea beach ..where the Spaniards had once a lookout. **1845** T. J. GREEN *Jrnl. Texian Expedition* 152 Several were left on the road exhausted for the want of water and here they commenced unfortunately, the use of the *palmetto juice as a substitute. **1662** GERBIER *Princ.* 3 Wilde Indians, who have no other Roofs but of *Palmito-Leaves. **1731** M. CATESBY *Nat. Hist. Carolina* I. 69 A man..builds a hut with Palmetto-Leaves, for the shelter of himself and family while they stay. **1763** tr. Du Mont in *Le Page du Pratz' Hist. Louisiana* I. 351 Making thus the form of a house of an oblong square..and cover..with cypress-bark, or palmetto-leaves. **1825** SCOTT *Talism.* viii, An umbrella of palmetto leaves. **1880** G. W. CABLE *Grandissimes* xiv. 89 On it [*sc.* the floor] were here and there in places white mats woven of bleached palmetto leaf. **1891** *Harper's Mag.* Dec. 47/1 Perhaps the colonel would not wave the palmetto leaf too vigorously. **1976** C. LARSON *Muir's Blood* xxx. 159 Ferns as wide as palmetto leaves drooped and swayed. **1837** *Globe* (Washington) 14 Jan. 3/3 After exchanging all kinds of civilities..which induced them to believe that the Judge was certain of the *Palmetto State. **1843** *Knickerbocker* XXI. 222 The merry days of good old Christmas are still observed in the Palmetto State. **1948** *Sat. Even. Post* 10 July 12/3 Although Palmetto State folks may have hesitated to brag the first year, they're safe now. **1974** *State* (Columbia, S. Carolina) 15 Feb. 1-A/3 Officials of the U.S. Justice Department firmly rejected a disputed reapportionment plan Thursday for the S.C. House of Representatives charging that it could deny equal voting rights to blacks in the Palmetto State. **1853** 'P. PAXTON' *Stray Yankee in Texas* 56 The '*marais*' or slough,..according to my friend Joe's account, changed into a 'branch'; then after running through a cypress brake or two, ultimately assumed the form of a *palmetto swamp. **1756** *Palmeto Thatch [see b]. **1866** *Treas. Bot.* 1147/1 T[*hrinax*] *argentea*, the Silver Thatch-palm, is usually said to yield the young unexpanded palm-leaves imported from the West Indies under the name of Palmetto Thatch, and extensively employed for making palm-chip hats, baskets, and other fancy articles. **1888** G. W. CABLE *Bonaventure* 86 On a bank of this bayou..[stood] the *palmetto-thatched fishing and hunting lodge. **1895** G. KING *New Orleans* 34 There is absolutely no seeing of Bienville's group of palmetto-thatched huts by the yellow currents of the Mississippi. **1908** *Daily Chron.* 1 Sept. 7/5 As they strolled together towards the palmetto-thatched, open-face camp fronting on Ruffle Lake. **1971** 'D. HALLIDAY' *Dolly & Doctor Bird* xiv. 202 Brady led me..up to the Begum's long palmetto-thatched bar. *c* **1565** J. SPARKE *J. Hawkins' Sec. Voy.* (Hakl. Soc.) 19 Mats..made with the rine of *Palmito trees. **1778** *Chron.* in *Ann. Reg.* 169 The device for the great seal of South-Carolina:—a palmetto tree supported by twelve spears. **1792** MAR. RIDDELL *Voy. Madeira* 100 The *palma camaerops*, or palmetto tree, rises to the height of fifty or sixty feet. **1865** 'G. HAMILTON' *Skirmishes* xiii. 172 If he is concocting..rebellion, can he not go on just as blithely under the Stars and Stripes as under the Palmetto tree? *c* **1565** J. SPARKE *J. Hawkins' Sec. Voy.* (Hakl. Soc.) 19 *Palmito wine..is gathered by a hole cutte in the toppe of a tree, and a gorde set for receauing thereof.

‖**palmetum** (pælˈmiːtəm). [mod. use of L. *palmētum* palm-grove.] (See quot.)

1854 HOOKER *Himal. Jrnls.* II. xxvii. 252 A large *Palmetum*, or collection of tall and graceful palms of various kinds.

palmful (ˈpɑːmfʊl), *sb.* [f. PALM *sb.*[2] + -FUL 2.] A quantity that fills the palm of the hand; as much as the palm will contain.

1812 W. TENNANT *Anster F.* I. iii. 6 Some little palmfuls of the blessed dew. **1823** LAMB *Elia, Old Benchers Inner Temple*, He took it not by pinches, but a palmful at once. *a* **1861** T. WINTHROP *John Brent* (1883) xxii. 194 They took their water by the throatful, not by the palmful. **1940** C. H. WARREN *Corn Country* 3 He pulled out a palmful of unprepared flour.

palmful (ˈpɑːmfʊl), *a. rare.* [f. PALM *sb.*[1] + -FUL 1.] Full of or abounding in palm-trees.

a **1618** SYLVESTER *Job Triumphant* 67 Neer wher Idume's dry and sandy soil Spreads palmful forests.

palm garnete, obs. corrupt f. POMEGRANATE.

palmi- (pælmɪ), combining form of L. *palma* palm of the hand, palm-tree, etc. (PALM *sb.*[1] and [2]), occurring in scientific (chiefly botanical) terms, as **palˈmicolous** *a.* [L. *-colus* inhabiting], growing upon or inhabiting palm-trees; **ˈpalmiform** *a.* = PALMATIFORM; **ˈpalmigrade** *a. Zool.* = PLANTIGRADE; **ˈpalmilobed** *a.*, palmately lobed; **palmiˈnervate**, **ˈpalminerve**, **ˈpalminerved** *a.*, palmately nerved or veined, as a leaf; **ˈpalmi-veined** *a.* = prec.; **palˈmivorous** *a.* [L. *-vorus* devouring], feeding on, or obtaining food from, palm-trees.

1857 MAYNE *Expos. Lex.*, *Palmicolous..*Palmiform. **1864** WEBSTER, *Palmigrade* [citing HITCHCOCK]. **1876** HARLEY *Mat. Med.* (ed. 6) 711 Leaves alternate, more or less *palmilobed. **1857** MAYNE *Expos. Lex.*, *Palminervate. **1880** GRAY *Struct. Bot.* iii. §4 (ed. 6) 93 Palmately, Digitately, or Radiately Veined (or *Palminerved) class, of which leaves of common Maples and the Vine are..examples. **1852** TH. ROSS *Humboldt's Trav.* II. xxii. 336 The assertion of Linnæus, that..man is essentially *palmivorous.

palmic (ˈpælmɪk), *a. Chem.* [ad. F. *palmique* (Boudet 1832), f. L. *palma* (in PALMA CHRISTI) + -IC.] Of or pertaining to castor oil: in ***palmic acid***, ($C_{18}H_{34}O_3$) obtained by saponifying palmin and decomposing with hydrochloric acid; it crystallizes in white silky needles; = *ricinelaïdic acid*.

1838 T. THOMSON *Chem. Org. Bodies* 431 Palmic acid when pure, fuses at 122° [Fahr.].

palmier, var. PALMER *sb.*[2] *Obs.*, palm-tree.

palmierite (pælˈmiːəraɪt). *Min.* [ad. F. *palmiérite* (A. Lacroix 1907, in *Compt. Rend.* CXLIV. 1400), f. the name of Luigi *Palmier-i* (1807–1896), Italian meteorologist: see -ITE[1].] A sulphate of potassium, sodium, and lead, $(K,Na)_2Pb(SO_4)_2$, found as colourless hexagonal crystals.

1907 *Mineral. Mag.* XIV. 406 Palmierite..found enclosed in aphthitalite amongst the products of the Vesuvian eruption of April, 1906. **1954** *Mineral. Abstr.* XII. 332 Palmierite..was prepared as pearly scales by fusing a mixture of $PbSO_4$ and K_2SO_4.

palmiet (ˈpalmɪt). [Afrikaans, a. Du., f. Sp. and Pg. *palmito*, dim. of *palma* palm.] A South African plant found in swamps and along river-banks, *Prionium serratum* (= *P. palmita*), of the family Juncaceæ, which has a woody stem, topped with a cluster of long, narrow, serrated leaves two or three feet long, and small, greenish-gold flowers borne in a large panicle.

1785 G. FORSTER tr. *Sparrman's Voy. Cape Good Hope* I. iii. 42 A little river or stream covered with *palmites*, a kind of *acorus* with a thick stem and broad leaves, which grow out from the top, as they do in the palm-tree, a circumstance from which the plant takes its name. **1800** A. BARNARD *Let.* 14 May in *S. Afr. a Century Ago* (1901) xvii. 286, I am living out of town.., removed from all party work, except working parties in our fields, rooting up of palmite roots, and planting of fir trees and potatoes. **1822** W. J. BURCHELL *Trav. S. Afr.* I. iv. 89 The boors believe this brownness [of the water] to be caused by the great quantity of Palmite (Palmiet), which every where grows in these streams. *Ibid.* 91 Most of the rivers which we passed in this excursion, are choked up with the plant called *Palmiet* by the colonists, and from which this one [*sc.* river] derives its name. **1868** J. CHAPMAN *Trav. S. Afr.* I. ix. 193 The flower and root of the bulrush as well as the tsetla root or palmiet..forms the main article of the diet of the Makobas. **1871** H. H. DUGMORE *Reminisc. Albany Settler* I. 17 The beaver gave way to the home-made palmiet or coffee straw, and the tiger-skin cap. **1944** V. POHL *Adventures Boer Family* xvi. 106 The only hats they possessed were those made by my mother and Sophia from straw, palmiet (a water plant) or mealie leaves. **1952** *Cape Times* 20 Sept. 3/2 The boat..was steered to a clump of palmiet. **1973** *Stand. Encycl. S. Afr.* VIII. 439/2 Palmiet... This waterside plant..has a fairly stout, erect or decumbent, woody stem covered with old leaf-bases.

palmiferous (pælˈmɪfərəs), *a.* [f. L. *palmifer* palm-bearing + -OUS: see PALM *sb.*[1] and -FEROUS.] **a.** Bearing or producing palm-trees. *rare*$^{-0}$. **b.** Bearing or carrying 'palms' or palm-branches.

1656 BLOUNT *Glossogr.*, *Palmiferous*,..bearing or yeelding Palm or Date Trees; also victorious. **1664** H. MORE *Myst. Iniq.* 376 Satan is bound, the Palmiferous Company triumphs, and the Heavenly Jerusalem is seen upon Earth.

1866 Neale *Sequences & Hymns* 57 Christ's own Martyrs, valiant cohort, White-robed and palmiferous throng.

palmification (ˌpælmɪfɪˈkeɪʃən). [f. L. *palma* palm, after *caprification*.] (See quot.).

1876 *Encycl. Brit.* IV. 72 The Babylonians suspended male clusters from wild dates over the females;..the process was called *palmification*.

palmin (ˈpælmɪn). *Chem.* [ad. F. *palmine* (Boudet 1832), f. L. *palma* (in Palma Christi) + -in.] A fatty substance obtained on treating castor-oil with nitric peroxide. Now called *ricinelaïdin*.

1838 T. Thomson *Chem. Org. Bodies* 431 Palmin is very soluble in alcohol and in ether.

palming (ˈpɑːmɪŋ), *vbl. sb.*[1] [-ing[1].] The action of palm *v.*

1. Touching or grasping with the palm of the hand. (In quot. 1686 with play on sense 2.)

1686 Dryden *Sp. Fryar* ii. iii, (*He strokes her Face*) ..*Gom.* Hold, hold, Father,..Palming is always held foul Play amongst Gamesters. **1734** Fielding *Univ. Gallant* iii. Wks. 1882 X. 75 There's no good ever comes of romping and palming: I never gave my hand to any man without a glove—except Sir Simon.

2. The action of concealing something in the palm of the hand, as in cheating at cards or dice, or in conjuring.

1673 R. Head *Canting Acad.* 17 Spent..in palming, napping, with how to fix a Die for any purpose. **1710** H. Bedford *Vind. Ch. Eng.* Pref. 54 The palming by Religious Juglers. **1803** *Sporting Mag.* XXI. 326 Palming, or handling the cards—so called from the cards being secured in the palm of the hand. **1899** *Daily News* 6 May 8/5 Such as are fond of palming and conjuring.

3. ***palming off*** (U.S. Law) = passing *vbl. sb.* 2 b. Also *attrib.*

1891 *Atlantic Reporter* XXI. 613/2 The language of the court imports an intentional deceit and palming off. **1925** *Federal Reporter* (1926) VII. 604/1 In the case at bar the means are as plainly unlawful as in the usual case of palming off. It is as unlawful to lie about the quality of one's wares as about their maker. **1942** *Ibid.* CXXIV. 706/1 Under Illinois law the 'palming off doctrine' is not treated as merely the designation of a typical class of cases of unfair competition, but as a rule of law itself. **1956** *Dior* v. *Milton* in *N.Y. Suppl.* 2nd Ser. CLV. 452 With the passage of those simple and halcyon days when the chief business malpractice was 'palming off', and with the development of more complex business relationships..many courts..have extended the doctrine of unfair competition beyond the cases of 'palming off'. **1965** A. Bogsch in *Ibid.* 329/2 The principle of 'passing off' or 'palming off'.

4. *attrib.*

1812 Byron *Waltz* xiii, Till some might marvel, with the modest Turk, If 'nothing follows all this palming work?' **1812** J. H. Vaux *Flash Dict.*, *Palming-racket*, secreting money in the palm of the hand.

ˈpalming, *vbl. sb.*[2] [f. palm *sb.*[1] 4 + -ing[1]; cf. *blackberrying*, etc.] Gathering 'palms'.

1825 Hone *Every-day Bk.* I. 396 It is still customary..to go a palming..on Palm Sunday morning;..gathering branches of the willow or sallow with their grey..buds.

ˈpalming, *ppl. a.*[1] [f. palm *v.* + -ing[2].] That palms; touching or grasping with the hand.

1775 Sheridan *Rivals* ii. i, But country-dances!..to run the gauntlet through a string of amorous palming puppies.

†**palming,** *ppl. a.*[2] *Obs.* [f. palm *sb.*[2] + -ing[2].] Of a deer's horn: Bearing palms.

c **1400** [see palmed *a.* 3].

palmiped, -pede (ˈpælmɪpɛd, -piːd), *a.* and *sb.* [ad. L. *palmipēs, palmiped-em*, f. *palma* palm *sb.*[2] + *pēs, ped-em* foot.]

A. *adj.* Of a bird: Having palmate feet (see palmate *a.* 2); web-footed.

1661 Lovell *Hist. Anim. & Min.* Introd., Birds which are..granivorous, as the..barnicle..palmipede daw. **1694** Ray in *Lett. Lit. Men* (Camden) 200, I fancied they were no palmiped Bird. **1850** *Fraser's Mag.* XLII. 28 She would lead her palmipede brood to the water.

B. *sb.* A web-footed bird.

In pl. often as L. *palmipedes* (-dīz).

1610 Guillim *Heraldry* iii. Table (1660) 95 Having their feet Whole and plain, and are called *Palmipedes*, as the Swan, Goose, Ducks. **1681** Grew *Musæum* 67 Of Palmipede's, or Webfooted Fowles. **1691** Ray *Creation* (1692) 150 Water-Fowl, which are Palmipeds, or whole-footed. **1774** Pennant *Tour in Scot. in 1772*, 312 The little Petrel—these are the last of the palmipeds. **1854** Owen *Skel. & Teeth* (1855) 62 In the palmipedes or web-footed order.

So †**palˈmipedous** *a. Obs.* = prec. A.

1646 Sir T. Browne *Pseud. Ep.* v. i. (1686) 191 The Pelican is palmipedous or fin-footed like Swans and Geese.

palmist (ˈpælmɪst, ˈpɑːmɪst). [f. palm *sb.*[2] + -ist; perh. back-formation f. palmistry.] = next.

1886 *Pall Mall G.* 16 July 4/1 There is a Sibyl's cave, where a hardened palmist will tell your fortune and your future. **1892** *Literary World* 20 May 485 The phrenologist and the palmist take infinite pains to dispel the prevailing ignorance.

palmister (ˈpælm-, ˈpɑːmɪstə(r)). Now *rare.* Also 5–7 **palmester**, 6 **-estrer**. [In 15–17th c. *palmester*, also *palmestrer*, app. f. *palmestry*, palmistry: cf. *sorcer-er, sorcer-y*, etc.] One who practises palmistry; one who professes to tell people's characters and fortunes by examining the palms of their hands; a chiromancer.

a **1500** P. Johnston *Thre Deid Pollis* 42 Quhat phisnamour, or perfyt palmester. **1561** T. Hoby tr. *Castiglione's Courtyer* iv. (1577) X iij b, Palmestrers by the visage know many times the conditions, and otherwhile the thoughts of men. **1565** Cooper *Thesaurus, Chiromantes*.., a Palmester. **1578** Banister *Hist. Man* iv. 63 These three Muscles make that fleshy part of the thombe, which Palmesters do terme the hill of Mars. **1594** Carew *Huarte's Exam. Wits* xii. (1596) 183 Imagination..inuiteth a man to be a witch, superstitious,..a palmister, a fortune-teller. *a* **1670** Hacket *Cent. Serm.* (1675) 424 No soothsayer, no Palmester, no judicial Astrologer is able to tell any man the event of his life. **1888** Bryce *Amer. Commw.* III. vi. cxiv. 639 *note*, Fortune-tellers, clairvoyants, palmisters, and seers.

palmistry (ˈpælm-, ˈpɑːmɪstrɪ). Forms: 5 **pawmestry**, 6–7 **palmestrie**, **palmistrie**, (6 **paulmistrie**, **palmastry**, **palmesy**, **pampestrie**, **-y**, 6–8 **palmestry**), 6– **palmistry**. [ME. f. *paume, palme*, palm (of the hand) + an element (orig. *-estrie, -estry*) of obscure origin, which has been gradually changed to *-istry*, so that the word now appears like a derivative of the 19th c. *palmist*.]

1. Divination by inspection of the palm of the hand; the art or practice of telling persons' characters and fortunes by examination of the lines and configurations of the palm; chiromancy.

c **1420** Lydg. *Assembly of Gods* 870 Adryomancy, Ornomancy, with Pyromancy, Fysenamy also, and Pawmestry. *a* **1425** *Gower's Conf.* III. 134 Gebuz and Alpetragus eke Of Planisperie [*v.r.* palmestrie]..The bokes made. **1530–1** *Act 22 Hen. VIII*, c. 12 Some of them feynynge them selfes to haue knowlage in physike, phisnamie, palmestrie or other craftie sciences. **1538** Elyot *Dict.*, *Chiromantia*, palmestry. **1546** Langley *Pol. Verg. De Invent.* i. xviii. 34 b, Chiromantie..called commonly Palmistry. **1562** *Lanc. Wills* i. (1857) 183 On litle boke of palmesy. **1567** Harman *Caveat* (Shaks. Soc.) 23 Egiptians ..practising paulmistrie to such as would know their fortunes. **1575** *Mirr. Mag., Bladud* 46 b, For fooles..And such as practise pampestry. **1613** Purchas *Pilgrimage* (1614) 310 They professe palmistry and fortune-telling. *a* **1658** Cleveland *Gen. Poems* (1677) 2 He tipples Palmestry, and dines On all her Fortune-telling Lines. *c* **1704** Prior *Henry & Emma* 133 A frantic gipsy..With the fond maids in palmistry he deals. **1832** De Quincey *Charlemagne* Wks. XIII. 160 *note*, It is in fact upon this infinite variety in the superficial lines of the human palm, that palmistry is grounded.

attrib. **1899** *Daily News* 21 July 5/1 There were raffles, a palmistry tent, and a café chantant. **1900** Pinero *Gay Ld. Quex* ii. 87 The palmistry profession is a flourishing one.

b. *fig.* (*nonce-uses.*)

1841 De Quincey *Rhetoric* Wks. 1860 XI. 407 The impossibility of finding any two leaves of a tree that should be mere duplicates of each other, in what we might call the palmistry of their natural marking. **1877** Stubbs *Lect. Med. & Mod. Hist.* (1886) 76 A science of historical palmistry.. that attempts to refer..every manuscript to its own country, district, age, school, and even individual writers.

2. Applied allusively to the use of the hands in applause (quot. 1698), or in pocket-picking (quot. 1711), or to bribery (quot. 1828: cf. palm *sb.*[2] 1 b, palm *v.* 5); also used erroneously as = sleight of hand (cf. palm *v.* 2).

1698 Farquhar *Love & Bottle* iv. ii, If you would tell a poet his fortune, you must gather it from the palmistry of the audience. **1711** Addison *Spect.* No. 130 ⁋3 He found his Pocket was picked: That being a Kind of Palmistry at which this Race of Vermin [Gipsies] are very dextrous. **1828** *Burton's Diary* III. 535 *note*, If he would only, by an allowed and well-understood palmistry, conciliate 'a king of heralds', that prime officer in the court of honour..would presently discover among 'old registers', arms..belonging to the applicant's remote 'ancestors'. **1859** Wraxall tr. *R. Houdin* iii. 26, I..devoted myself to the manipulation of cards and palmistry. *Ibid.* xii. 175, I had recourse to palmistry to influence his decision.

†**ˈpalmit.** *Obs. rare.* [ad. L. *palmes, palmit-em.*] A shoot or sprig of a vine.

1657 Thornley tr. *Longus' Daphnis & Chloe* 48 The vines protrude their palmits towards the ground. *Ibid.* 185 Bunches of Grapes hanging still upon their palmits.

palmita, obs. f. palmetto; see also pelamyd.

palmitate (ˈpælmɪteɪt). *Chem.* [f. palmit-ic + -ate[4].] A salt of palmitic acid.

1873 Ralfe *Phys. Chem.* 49 The Potassium Palmitate, Stearate and Oleate are then removed. **1880** J. W. Legg *Bile* 54 Some soaps, salts of the fatty acids, palmitate, stearate, and oleate of soda are found in the bile.

palmite (ˈpælmaɪt). [ad. Sp. and Pg. *palmito*, S. Afr. Du. *palmiet*: see palmetto.]

†**1.** Some kind of palmetto; in quot. 1595 ? the fibre of some variety of palm. *Obs.*

1555 Eden *Decades* 359 Theyr drynke is eyther water or the iuse that droppeth from the cut braunches of the barren date trees cauled Palmites. **1595** R. Hasleton in Arb. *Garner* VIII. 382 Tying them [sheepskins] together over my shoulders and under my arms with Palmite..a weed like to that whereof our hand-baskets are made [at Majorca].

2. A South African aquatic plant, *Prionium Palmita* (N.O. *Juncaceæ*), growing in the beds of rivers, and bearing a tuft or large serrated sword-shaped leaves, affording a strong fibre.

[**1824** Burchell *Trav.* I. 91 Most of the rivers which we passed, are choked up with the plant called *Palmiet* by the colonists.] **1834** Pringle *Afr. Sk.* 25 Girt by the palmite's leafy screen.

palmitic (pælˈmɪtɪk), *a. Chem.* [ad. F. *palmitique* (Frémy 1840), arbitrarily f. L. *palma* palm *sb.*[1] (or ? F. *palmite* pith of the palm-tree) + -ic.

The natural formations from *palma* would have been *palmic, palmin*, etc.; but these were preoccupied by derivatives of *Palma Christi* (castor oil).]

Of or obtained from palm-oil; in ***palmitic acid***: a fatty acid ($C_{16}H_{32}O_2$) contained in palm-oil and in vegetable and animal fats generally; a colourless substance, without taste or smell, lighter than water, solid at ordinary temperatures.

1857 Miller *Elem. Chem.* III. 394 Palmitic Acid..is obtained most readily from palm oil, the solid portion of which consists chiefly of the glycerin compound of palmitic acid. **1871** Roscoe *Elem. Chem.* 334 This palmitic acid bears the same relation to cetyl alcohol as acetic acid does to common or ethyl alcohol.

palmitin (ˈpælmɪtɪn). *Chem.* [a. F. *palmitine* (Frémy 1840), f. as prec. + *-ine*, -in[1].] A natural fat contained in palm-oil and many other animal and vegetable fats, obtained as a white solid, the tripalmitate of glyceryl, $C_3H_5(C_{16}H_{31}O_2)_3$. In *pl.* applied to the palmitates of glyceryl or glycerides of palmitic acid in general; the above being distinctively called *tripalmitin*.

1857 Miller *Elem. Chem.* III. 368 *Palmitin*..is contained abundantly in palm oil, from which it has received its name. **1866** Odling *Anim. Chem.* 42 Palmitin is an important constituent of palm oil or butter, and also exists in human and other soft fats to a considerable extent. **1866–77** Watts *Dict. Chem.* IV. 335 Palmitates of Glyceryl or Palmitins. *Monopalmitin,..Dipalmitin,..Tripalmitin.* **1877** —— *Fownes' Chem.* II. 299 By cautious pressure it [palm-oil] may be separated into fluid olein and solid palmitin.

palmito, obs. form of palmetto.

palmi-veined, palmivorous: see palmi-.

palm-leaf (ˈpɑːmliːf). **a.** A leaf of the palm-tree, used for thatching, or for making hats, baskets, etc., and esp., in the Southern U.S., as a fan.

1660 F. Brooke tr. *Le Blanc's Trav.* 58 All the houses.. are covered with palm-leaves. **1802** Southey *Thalaba* iii. xxiii, Knitting light palm-leaves for her brother's brow. **1871** Kingsley *At Last* x, A small sugar-press..under a roof of palm-leaf.

b. Short for *palm-leaf hat*.

1852 Mrs. Stowe *Uncle Tom's C.* viii, Sam soon appeared, palm-leaf in hand, at the parlour door. **1854** Mary Holmes *Tempest & Sunshine* 15 So mounting Prince again, he gave his old palm-leaf three flourishes round his head.

c. *attrib.* Made of a palm-leaf or palm-leaves. ***palm-leaf book, fan, hat, manuscript, roof***; **palm-leaf pattern**, a device resembling a palm-leaf used in the decoration of oriental carpets.

1937 M. Covarrubias *Island of Bali* (1972) i. 7 The second half of the manuscript [of the Tjatur Yoga] is extremely obscure, full of errors, and appears incomplete, perhaps owing to careless copying of an older palm-leaf book. **1860** J. G. Holland *Miss Gilbert's Career* viii. 132 Then Mrs. Ruggles helped herself to a palm-leaf fan. **1891** *Century Mag.* Mar. 734 Chad substituted a palm-leaf fan from the hall table. **1836** O. W. Holmes *September Gale* 156 The wind whisked off my palm-leaf hat. **1842** Dickens *Amer. Notes* (1850) 34/1, I saw them first at their work (basket-making, and the manufacture of palm-leaf hats). **1948** D. Diringer *Alphabet* vi. 360 Many palm-leaf manuscripts..are also written in this [Nagari] script. **1897** Mary Kingsley *W. Africa* 427 Above all is a roof of palm-leaf mats, in good old Coast style. **1931** A. U. Dilley *Oriental Rugs & Carpets* Pl. 28 (*caption*) Saraband Rug. Palm Leaf Pattern. **1930** R. Macaulay *Staying with Relations* ix. 119 They..went to find her, but found nothing except wrecked posts and a smashed palm leaf roof sprawling on the shaken earth.

palmless (ˈpɑːmlɪs), *a.* [f. palm *sb.*[1] + -less.] Destitute of palm-trees.

1894 B. Thomson *S. Sea Yarns* 185 The bitter winds and the sterile palmless shore.

palmlet (ˈpɑːmlɪt). *Entom.* [f. palm *sb.*[2] 2 d + -let.] = palmula.

1826 Kirby & Sp. *Entomol.* III. xxxiii. 370 *Palmula* (the *Palmlet*). A minute accessory joint between the claws, answering to the *Plantula* in the legs.

palm-oil. [In sense 1, f. palm *sb.*[1] + oil; in 2, f. palm *sb.*[2], with humorous allusion to sense 1.]

1. Oil produced by various species of palm-tree; *esp.* that obtained from the fruit-pulp of the Oil Palm (*Elæis guineensis*) of West Africa, which in cooler climates becomes of the consistence of butter and of an orange-red colour; it is used as food by the natives, and elsewhere for making soap and candles, lubricating machinery, etc.

1705 Bosman *Guinea* xvi. (1721) 267 The Palm-oil..is obtained by Contusion and Expression. **1712** tr. *Pomet's Hist. Drugs* I. 136 Palm Oil..is an unctuous Liquor, as thick as Butter. **1870** Yeats *Nat. Hist. Comm.* 204 Palm oil is used in England principally in the manufacture of yellow soap, but with the Africans it is an article of food.

attrib. **1863** R. F. BURTON *Wand. W. Africa* II. 145 'Palm-oil-chop' is the curry of Western Africa. **1896** SIR H. H. JOHNSTON in *Daily News* 9 Dec. 10/2 The sneered at 'palm-oil-ruffians' of the first half of this century, who did more than anyone else to unconsciously abolish the slave trade. **1897** MARY KINGSLEY *W. Africa* 208 The Negroes cook uniformly very well, and at moments are inspired in the direction of palm-oil chop and fish cooking.

2. *humorously*. That with which the palm is 'greased' or 'anointed'; money given as a douceur or bribe; a 'tip'.

a **1627** MIDDLETON *Game at Chess* III. i, Palm-oil will make a pursuivant relent. **1867** *Routledge's Ev. Boy's Ann.* June 368, I had plenty of money, and 'palm oil' goes as far in those latitudes as in our more civilized communities. **1896** E. A. KING *Ital. Highways* 190 Palm-oil will always produce temporary blindness in the officials.

palmoscopy (pæl'mɒskəpɪ). *Med.* [f. Gr. παλμός pulsation + -σκοπία -SCOPY.] (See quots.)

1857 MAYNE *Expos. Lex., Palmoscopia, Med.* Term for divination or prognostication from palpitation, as of the heart, arteries, bowels, or muscles: palmoscopy. **1890** J. S. BILLINGS *Nat. Med. Dict.* II. 280 *Palmoscopy*.. Observation of the beats of the heart or of the pulse.

palm sack: see SACK *sb.*[2]

Palm Sunday. The Sunday next before Easter, observed in commemoration of Christ's triumphal entry into Jerusalem; in the mediæval church, and still in the Roman, Greek, and other churches, by processions in which branches of palm or (in northern regions) other trees (see PALM *sb.*[1] 2, 4) are carried.

c **1000** *Ags. Gosp.* Luke xix. 29 *margin*, Ðys ȝebyrað feower wucon ær middan wyntra & on palm-sunnandæȝ. *c* **1290** *Beket* 1855 in *S. Eng. Leg.* I. 159 Ase ore louerd a-palme-sonenday. *c* **1300** *St. Brandan* 348 Aboute Palm-sonede hi bihulde about faste. **1375** BARBOUR *Bruce* xv. 100 [Thai] helde the sege full stalwardly Quhill palmesonday wes passit by. *c* **1449** PECOCK *Repr.* (Rolls) I. 202 In eeldir daies, whanne processioun was mad in the Palme-Sundai bifore masse. **1530** PALSGR. 251/2 Palmesonday, *pasques flevry, dimanche de blanches.* **1645** EVELYN *Diary* Mar., [At Rome] On Palm Sunday there was a greate procession after a papal masse. **1828** SCOTT *F. Maid Perth* xxi, On the 30th of March next to come, being Palm Sunday.

attrib. **1563** FOXE *A. & M.* 1712/2 Vpon Satterdaye being Palme Sonday Euen. **1627** DRAYTON *Miseries Q. Margaret* in *Batt. Agincourt* etc. 99 Fatall Towton that Palme-Sunday fight. **1874** in *Ripon Ch. Acts* (Surtees) 109 *note*, The battle of Towton, which was called Palm-Sunday Field.

So † **Palmsun even**, the eve of Palm Sunday (*obs.*); also **'Palmsun** *a.*, occurring on or about Palm Sunday (cf. *Whitsun*); **'Palmsun** *v. dial.* (see quot. 1779).

1571 *Satir. Poems Reform.* xxviii. 218 On Palmsoneuin this paper I compleit. *c* **1605** *Acc.-bk. W. Wray* in *Antiquary* XXXII. 213 The 21 day of Aprill, beinge palme sonn even. **1779** *Gentl. Mag.* XLIX. 580 With us in the North, the children go out into the fields.. a palmsoning or palmsning, as they call it, and gather the flowering buds of the sallow. **1813** *Sporting Mag.* XLII. 43 The Palmsun Horse Show, at Malton.

palm-tree ('pɑːmtriː). **a.** A tree of the order *Palmaceæ* or *Palmæ*: = PALM *sb.*[1] 1.

c **950** *Lindisf. Gosp.* John xv. 4 Suæ ðio palm-treo [L. *palmes*] ne mæȝe ȝebrenge uæstem from him seolfum buta ȝeuuniȝa in winȝearde. *c* **1000** ÆLFRIC *Exod.* xv. 27 Þær wæron twelf wyllas and hundseofontiȝ palmtreowa. *c* **1250** *Gen. & Ex.* 3305 An ten and sexti palme tren bi ðo welles men miȝte sen. *a* **1300** *Cursor M.* 11660 A palme tre sco sagh hir bi. **1543** TRAHERON *Vigo's Chirurg.* IV. 147 Some allowe, that the water be drawen out wyth the woode of a palmetre, or drye elder. **1634** JACKSON *Creed* VIII. xviii. §6 The palmtree.. was as true an embleme or hieroglyphick of righteousnesse or justice, as the sword is of authority, and power. **1842** LONGF. *Slave's Dream* ii, Beneath the palm trees on the plain Once more a King he strode.

b. Applied popularly to other trees: see PALM *sb.*[1] 4.

1653 WALTON *Angler* iii. 92 You see some Willows or Palm trees bud and blossome sooner then others do. **1736** PEGGE *Kenticisms, Palm-tree*, a yew-tree. **1887** *Kentish Gloss.* s.v., There is, in.. Woodnesborough, a public-house called 'The Palm-tree', which bears for its sign a clipped yew tree.

c. *attrib.* Also *Comb.*, as **palm-tree justice**, justice summarily administered, usu. with little regard for legal principle or precedent (with reference to the Islamic cadi (see CADI) administering justice under a palm-tree: see also quot. 1634 in sense a).

1781 SMEATHMAN in *Phil. Trans.* LXXI. 167 *note*, The caterpillar or maggot of the Palm-tree Snout-beetle, *Curculio Palmarum*, which is served up at all the luxurious tables of the West Indian epicures.. as the greatest dainty of the Western world. **1802** SOUTHEY *Thalaba* v. Notes, Wks. 1838 IV. 210 Houses made of palm-tree branches. [**1916** A. UNDERHILL in *Shakespeare's England* I. xiii. 383 In Shakespeare's time the Court of Chancery was almost as unfettered by precedent as the typical Cadi under the Palm Tree.] **1959** *Sunday Times* 24 May 5/4 What are the origins and associations of the phrase.. 'palm-tree justice', which has recently been used several times by Her Majesty's Judges in legal contexts? **1963** *Times* 7 May 9/2 It would be perhaps rather hard luck for Simpson's now to have to part with their North Road site at prices which no longer represented modern prices. It would be no more than palm-tree justice. **1968** *Economist* 3 Feb. 42/3 In this period the [Roman] emperors themselves considered the letters that came up to them and dictated their answers personally: palm-tree justice was still obtainable.

‖**palmula** ('pælmjʊlə). *Entom.* [mod.L., dim. of L. *palma* palm.] A process between the tarsal claws in certain insects.

1826 KIRBY & SP. *Entomol.* III. xxxv. 692 You will find between the claws [of Lamellicorns] a minute but conspicuous joint terminated by two bristles which seem to mimic the *ungula* and its claws; these parts are what are denominated the *palmula, plantula*, and *pseudonychia*. **1895** *Cambridge Nat. Hist.* V. 105 A lobe or process.. very varied in different Insects, called empodium, arolium, palmula, plantula, pseudonychium, or pulvillus.

Palmus Christi, variant of PALMA CHRISTI.

1530 PALSGR. 251/2 Palmus christi an herbe.

palmy ('pɑːmɪ), *sb. Sc.* Also **pammie, pawmie.** [Corresponds to F. *paumée* 'coup dans la main' (Littré); but OF. *paumée, palmée* = It. *palmata*, Pr., Sp., Pg. *palmada*, had the sense 'a slap with the palm'; cf. med.L. *palmata* (Du Cange), f. *palma* PALM *sb.*[2] Cf. PALMER *sb.*[3]] A stroke on the palm of the hand, given as a punishment.

1785 R. FORBES *Poems* (1812) 95 Nae school being in, Our pammies o'er, syne aff we'd rin. **1826** GALT *Lairds* iv, There was na a day I didna get a pawmy but ane, and on it I got twa. **1854** H. MILLER *Sch. & Schm.* (1858) 142 The same number of palmies, well laid on, were awarded to each. **1883** *Q. Rev.* Apr. 400 He got.. many a 'palmy' on his hand with a thick strap of leather.

palmy ('pɑːmɪ), *a.* [f. PALM *sb.*[1] + -Y.]

1. Containing or abounding in palms; of or pertaining to a palm or palms; palm-like. Chiefly *poet.*

1667 MILTON *P.L.* IV. 254 Or palmie hilloc, or the flourie lap Of som irriguous Valley. **1734** THOMSON *Liberty* II. 82 The neighbouring Land, whose palmy Shore The silver Jordan laves. **1764** GOLDSM. *Trav.* 70 The naked negro.. Boasts of his golden sands, and palmy wine. **1819** HEBER *Hymn 'From Greenland's icy Mountains'* i, From many an ancient river, From many a palmy plain. **1866** B. TAYLOR *Palm & Pine* Poems 267 Her lithe and palmy grace.

2. *fig.* Bearing or worthy to 'bear the palm', triumphant, flourishing; esp. in *palmy state* (a Shaksperian phrase), *palmy days*.

1602 SHAKS. *Ham.* I. i. 113 In the most high and palmy state of Rome. **1617** DRUMM. OF HAWTH. *Forth Feasting* Poems (1656) 152 And like Augustus palmy Raigne be deem'd. **1796** BURKE *Regic. Peace* i. Wks. VIII. 82 In the high and palmy state of the monarchy of France, it fell to the ground without a struggle. **1837** DICKENS *Let.* 31 Jan. (1965) I. 232, I hope you will meet with every happiness that you picture to yourself in these palmy days. **1848** TROLLOPE *Kellys & O'Kellys* I. iv. 80 Mrs. Lynch had died before the commencement of Sim's palmy days. They had seen no company in her time. *a* **1854** H. REED *Lect. Brit. Poets* (1857) ix. 301 The period was a palmy one for men, who held a pen of power. **1893** J. C. JEAFFRESON *Bk. of Recoll.* (1894) I. xiii. 218 Persons who belonged to the brotherhood in its palmy days.

Hence **'palmily** *adv.*; **'palminess.**

1886 G. B. SHAW *How to become Mus. Critic* (1960) 112 When old-fashioned people.. regret the palmy days of the drama, superstitious ones are apt to take the desirability of palminess for granted... The young London play-goer can hardly judge; for he has no experience of palminess. *Ibid.*, A palmily stall-less pit.

palmyra (pæl'maɪərə). Forms: 7 **palmero**, 8 **palmeira, palmira**, 9 **palmyra.** [Formerly *palmeira*, a. Pg. *palmeira* (It. *palmero*, Sp. *palmera*) palm-tree: cf. PALMER *sb.*[2] Fryer's *palmero* may have been from an It. source. The mod. spelling is app. erroneously conformed to that of the ancient *Palmyra*, Gr. Παλμύρα, a city of Syria.]

A species of palm (*Borassus flabelliformis*), with rounded fan-shaped leaves, and large roundish drupes each containing three seeds; commonly cultivated in India and Ceylon, and important for its variety of uses.

The wood is used as timber; the leaves for thatch, matting, hats, baskets, umbrellas, fans, paper, etc.; the sap yields wine (toddy) and sugar (jaggery); the outer pulp of the fruit is eaten roasted or made into jelly; the seedling plants are used as food, etc.

1698 FRYER *Acc. E. India & P.* 199 The Poorer [Buildings] are made of Boughs or Oleas of the Palmeroes, or Leafs of Teke. **1718** *Propag. Gosp. in East* III. 85 (Y.) Leaves of a Tree called Palmeira. **1778** R. ORME *Milit. Trans. Ind.* II. 90 The interval.. was planted with rows of palmira and coco-nut trees. **1828** *Asiat. Costumes* 45 (Stanf.) The punkha, or fan, represented in the plate, is the leaf of the palmyra. **1870** ANDERSON *Missions Amer. Bd.* I. vii. 138 Sixty trees, twenty-nine of which were fruitful palmyras capable of supporting a native family.

b. *attrib.* and *Comb.*

1854 SIMMONDS *Commerc. Prod. Veg. Kingd.* 376 Eating the bulb or root, which is the first shoot from the Palmyra nut. **1857** HENFREY *Bot.* 394 *Borassus flabelliformis* yields what is called Palmyra-wood. **1858** HOGG *Veg. Kingd.* 752 The Palmyra Palm.. is the most common palm of India. **1900** G. SMITH *Twelve Pioneer Missionaries* 196 The palmyra-climbers make use of a sort of movable girdle to help them in climbing the trees.

palmyre ('pælmaɪə(r)). *rare*$^{-0}$. [ad. mod.L. *Palmyra*.] A sea-worm of the genus *Palmyra* of marine polychætous annelida.

1890 in *Cent. Dict.*

Palmyrene ('pælmɪriːn, pæl'maɪriːn), *sb.* and *a.* Also **Palmy'renian.** [ad. L. *Palmyrēn-us*, f. Gr. Παλμύρα, L. *Palmyra* Palmyra.] **A.** *sb.* **a.** A native or inhabitant of the ancient city of Palmyra in Syria. **b.** The language and script in use at Palmyra. **B.** *adj.* Of or pertaining to Palmyra, its inhabitants, its language, or its script.

1609 HOLLAND tr. *Ammianus Marcellinus' Roman Hist.* 339 Praysing and extolling of her, as much as the Parthyans do Semiramis, Ægypt Cleopatra.. or the Palmyrenes Zenobia. **1609** JONSON *Masque of Queenes* sig. E2ᵛ The ninth, in time, but equall in fame, and (the cause of it) vertue, was the chast Zenobia, Queene of the Palmyrenes. **1695** E. HALLEY in *Phil. Trans. R. Soc.* XIX. 161 But the Palmyrenes being informed of the Design [of M. Antonius to plunder Palmyra], took care to prevent them, and so escaped Plunder. *Ibid.* 172, I have taken care to have the Stone purposely viewed, as also to get from thence the exact Figure of the Syrian or Palmyrene Characters thereon... By the help of these, compared with two others.., I hope we may be able, one day, to make out the Palmyrene Alphabet. **1753** R. WOOD *Ruins of Palmyra* 6 Odenathus, a Palmyrene, ..made so proper a use of this situation.. as to get the balance of power into his hands. *Ibid.* 25 The ancient inscriptions we found at Palmyra were all Greek, or Palmyrene, except one in Latin. **1776** GIBBON *Decl. & F.* I. xi. 309 The emperor [Aurelian], by his salutory edicts, recalled the fugitives, and granted a general pardon to all who.. had been engaged in the service of the Palmyrenian queen. *Ibid.* 310 They.. engaged the Palmyrenians in a laborious pursuit. **1875** [see NABATÆAN *sb.* and *a.*]. **1886** W. P. DICKSON tr. *Mommsen's Provinces Roman Empire* II. ix. 96 Even in votive inscriptions which Palmyrenes set up to their native gods in Rome, and in tombs of Palmyrene soldiers that died in Africa or Britain, the Palmyrene rendering is added. **1900** G. BELL *Let.* 20 May (1927) I. 108 As we drew near Palmyra, the hills were covered with the strangest buildings, great stone towers, four stories high, some more ruined and some less, standing together in groups or bordering the road. They are the famous Palmyrene tower tombs. **1932** D. & T. RICE tr. *Rostovtzeff's Caravan Cities* v. 149 The external aspect of Palmyrene culture strikes the eye with its complexity and peculiarity. **1948** D. DIRINGER *Alphabet* iv. 280 Cantineau considers the Syriac alphabet as related to the cursive Palmyrene, the former having been influenced by the latter thanks to the commercial activities of the Palmyrenians. **1957** *Encycl. Brit.* XVII. 162/2 The Palmyrene princes cherished the idea of an independent empire of their own. *Ibid.* 163/2 The technical terms of municipal government are mostly Greek, transliterated into Palmyrene. **1963** W. F. ALBRIGHT *Biblical Period from Abraham to Ezra* i. 9 Nearly all.. parallels come from Nabataean or Palmyrene, as well as later Syrian inscriptions. **1972** P. M. FRASER *Ptolemaic Alexandria* I. i. 12 It was their destruction in the reign of Aurelian, at the time of the Palmyrene invasion, which led to the abandonment of Brucheion. **1978** *Times Lit. Suppl.* 3 Mar. 249/2 There is an interesting section discussing the scattered but far from negligible artistic traces left by Palmyrenes resident *in partibus*.

palo blanco ('pæləʊ 'blænkəʊ). *U.S.* [Amer. Sp., = 'white tree'.] A small tree or shrub of the genus *Celtis*, esp. *C. reticulata*, the western hackberry, belonging to the family Ulmaceæ, native to south-western North America and distinguished by its light-coloured bark, downy leaves, and red berries (see also quot. 1947).

1838 S. MAVERICK *Let.* 30 Dec. in 'R. M. Green' *Samuel Maverick* (1953) v. 83 Griffin & Granville can cut posts or pickets, and haul them to the (palo-blanco) hackberry tree. **1901** J. C. VAN DYKE *Desert* 147 All the common growths like the sage, the mesquite, the palo fierro, and the palo blanco, are blossom bearers. **1926** D. H. LAWRENCE *Plumed Serp.* xix. 326 The car went on, the great lights glaring upon the hedges of cactus and mesquite and palo blanco trees. **1927** —— *Mornings in Mexico* 33 A valley bed, where is.. the *palo-blanco*.. with big white flowers like pure white, crumpled cambric. **1938** L. N. GOODDING *Notes Native & Exotic Plants* (U.S. Dept. Agric. Soil Conservation Service) 52 Palo Blanco or White Bark Hackberry.. furnishes shade along many of the dry washes. **1947** J. C. RICH *Materials & Methods Sculpture* x. 293 *Palo Blanco* means 'white wood' and the name is applied to many woods of different species. **1951** KEARNEY & PEEBLES *Arizona Flora* 220 *Celtis reticulata*... Netleaf hackberry, palo-blanco, sugar-berry. **1958** E. M. REISS *Garden of Chaparral* 140 Palo-blanco; Hackberry (*Celtis laevigata*). A thirty-foot tree with whitish bark which accounts for its local name. **1960** R. VINES *Trees, Shrubs & Woody Vines of Southwest* 203/2 A vernacular name [of *Celtis lindheimeri*] is Palo Blanco.

palo de hierro ('pæləʊ deɪ hɪ'eərəʊ). *U.S.* Also palo fier(r)o. [Amer. Sp., = 'iron tree'.] The Sonora or desert ironwood, *Olneya tesota*, of the family Leguminosæ, which bears racemes of white flowers; also used as a name for other trees producing particularly hard wood, or the wood itself.

1894 *Amer. Anthropologist* VII. 293 During the rest of the year the Indians devote themselves to.. the gathering of the fruit of the cactus, mesquite beans, and the bean of the *palo fiero*. **1912** K. LUMHOLTZ *New Trails in Mexico* 224 All the mules, donkeys, and horses gathered at once around a lone but very large palo fiero tree to eat its dark green juicy leaves. **1931** W. A. DAYTON *Important Western Browse Plants* 86 Tesota (*Olneya tesota*) is variously known as arbol (or palo) de hierro, and desert (Mexican, or Sonora) ironwood. **1949** *Desert Mag.* June 22/2 The great washes along the highway were crowded with palo verde trees and ironwood, or palo fierro. **1951** KEARNEY & PEEBLES *Arizona Flora* 442 *Olneya Tesota*... Known commonly in Arizona as ironwood, or palo-de-hierro. **1963** W. J. SCHALDACH *Path to Enchantment* vi. 74 A tree unique in several ways is the ironwood, or *palo-fierro*. True to its name, the ironwood tree possesses wood so tough that it dulls an ax.

palois, obs. form of PALACE.

‖**palolo** (pə'ləʊləʊ). [Native name in Samoa and Tonga.] A nereid worm (*Palolo viridis*), abundant in some parts of the Pacific, and esteemed as food by the natives, who catch it when it annually visits the shores to spawn.

1895 *Edin. Rev.* July 102 The palolo worm, greatly esteemed as an article of food by the Pacific islanders. **1903** *Daily Chron.* 31 Jan. 3/2 A very interesting account.. of the well-known annual fishery of the Palolo worm.

‖**palombino** (palom'bino). [It. *palombino* (L. *palumbīnus*) dove-coloured, f. *palomba*, *-bo* pigeon, dove.] A greyish-white Italian marble.

1861 SIR G. G. SCOTT *Westm. Abbey* (1863) 97 The palombino is a white stone, not unlike clunch, only much harder.

palomino (pæləʊ'mi:nəʊ). orig. *U.S.* Also **palamino.** [Amer. Sp., a. Sp. *palomino* f. L. *palumbīnus* of or resembling a dove.] A light brown or cream-coloured horse with pale mane and tail, believed to have been developed from Arab stock. Also *attrib.*

1914 *Sunset* May 995/1 A Palomino stallion with arching neck and muscle-ridged barrel led the dozen brown and mottled mares of his seraglio up a silent hillside. **1932** H. W. BENTLEY *Dict. Spanish Terms in Eng.* 176 Palomino.. A term commonly used in the Southwest and California to describe a horse of a silver yellow color. **1935** J. STEINBECK *Tortilla Flat* x. 180 You will ride a palomino horse. **1936** *New Yorker* 18 Apr. 12/3 He made a fine entrance on his palomino. **1949** *Esquire* Mar. 29/1 They'll reserve a golden palomino horse for you—all yours for the length of your stay. **1955** W. FOSTER-HARRIS *Look of Old West* viii. 239 Palominos are gold-colored horses, light tan or cream, with white manes—a color variant, not a breed. **1958** *Times* 18 Sept. 13/3 Her favourites are not only Arabs, but, also, Thoroughbreds, Percherons.. with, as runners-up, Hackneys, Hunters, Palominos. **1959** *Sunday Express* 19 Apr. 5/6 Her Palamino pony-breeding business in Warwickshire. **1967** [see *circus-trick*]. **1973** *Country Life* 8 Mar. 654/3 (*heading*) British Palomino Society annual show. **1976** *Billings* (Montana) *Gaz.* 2 July 11-C/6 (Advt.), 4 year old Palamino mare. Good kid & ranch horse. $300.

2. A pale golden-brown colour.

1951 H. MACINNES *Neither Five nor Three* I. ii. 27 Her blonde palomino-rinsed head turned towards Mrs. Hershey. **1960** *Times* 31 Oct. 1/3 Mink Coat.. and Palamino Stole. **1968** J. IRONSIDE *Fashion Alphabet* vii. 159 The mink breeders.., always searching for different colours... name each variety, the more generally known being:... Palomino ..: Honey-gold.

palone, polone (pə'ləʊn). *slang.* Also polony (pə'ləʊnɪ), pollone. [Etym. uncertain; conceivably a phonet. var. of BLOWEN.] A derogatory term for a young woman; also, an effeminate man.

1934 P. ALLINGHAM *Cheapjack* xvi. 202 I'd rather 'andle a man any day than a lot of these silly palones. *Ibid.* 203 Charlie was not a lady's man, and by 'palones' he meant girls. **1937** PARTRIDGE *Dict. Slang* 646/2 *Polone*,.. a girl or woman. **1938** H. W. WICKS *Prisoner Speaks* vi. 95 The jogars and griddlers.. had a language of their own, such as: omie, meaning man, pollone—woman, feelia—boy,.. and so on. **1938** G. GREENE *Brighton Rock* I. ii. 30 'What about that polony he was with?' 'She doesn't matter,' the Boy said. 'She's just a buer.' *Ibid.* II. ii. 88 'Napoleon the Third used to have this room,' Mr. Colleoni said, 'and Eugenie.' 'Who was she?' 'Oh,' Mr. Colleoni said vaguely, 'one of those foreign polonies.' **1947** *Penguin New Writing* XXIX. 99 The authentic flavour of life among the small-time spivs, of caffs and gaffs, grafter and palone. **1969** J. GARDNER *Complete State of Death* v. 66 There was another possibility. Hart could be a palone. Fanny Hart. No. **1979** R. RENDELL *Make Death love Me* iv. 37 'When the polone comes to lock up, Groombridge'll be due to split.'.. 'Call her a girl, can't you? You're not a poove.'

palooka (pə'lu:kə). *slang* (chiefly *U.S.*). Also paluka, palooker. [Orig. unknown.] An inferior or average prizefighter; any stupid or mediocre person; a lout. Also *attrib.*

1925 H. C. WITWER *Roughly Speaking* (1926) 287 Ben will make at palooka's pan over for you in any style you wish, Reverend Jephtha. **1927** D. HAMMETT in *Black Mask* Feb. 28/1 A paluka who leads with his right. **1932** WODEHOUSE *Hot Water* vi. 112 One of these palookas suddenly pulls out a young carving-knife and sticks me in the wish-bone with it. **1933** *Amer. Speech* Oct. 37/2 He still looks plenty good enough to take the English palooka. **1936** J. TULLEY *Bruiser* v. 48 Don't let these palookers around here laugh you outta seein' me go—all you'll ever get outta these stumble bums is the holes in the doughnuts. **1950** J. DEMPSEY *Championship Fighting* ii. 11 It was only natural that the tide of palooka experts should sweep into the amateur ranks. **1950** A. LOMAX *Mister Jelly Roll* (1952) 139 You won't kick me in the ass, because I can beat this palooka. **1977** *New Yorker* 8 Aug. 12/2 A romantic fable about a Philadelphia palooka who gains his manhood. **1978** *N.Y. Times* 27 Feb. c2/6 Leon Spinks.. does not rate highly with at least one former heavyweight title holder. 'He is a palooka,' says Ingemar Johansson.

†**palour.** *Obs.* Also 6–8 pallour. [ad. F. *palourde*:—late pop. L. *pelorida*, for cl. L. *pelōris*, *-idem*, a. Gr. πελωρίς, -ίδα giant-mussel.] A bivalve shell-fish; a kind of cockle or mussel.

1589 RIDER *Bibl. Schol.*, *Fishes* 1722 A pallour, a shell fish. **1601** HOLLAND *Pliny* II. 443 The Palours also doe mollifie and soften the bellie [*Et pelorides emolliunt aluum*]. **1611** COTGR., *Clonisse*, the little, sharpe, and muddie cockle, tearmed, a Palour. *Ibid.*, *Pallourde*, a little, narrow, and seldome-gaping Cockle, which we also call, a Palour. **1657** C. BECK *Univ. Charac.* I. v, Pallour fish. **1694** MOTTEUX *Rabelais* IV. lx. (1737) 246 Chevins, Pallours.

‖**palourde** (palurd). [Fr.] A marine bivalve mollusc belonging to the genus *Venerupis*; a Venus clam or carpet-shell. Cf. PULLET 2

[**1863** J. G. JEFFREYS *Brit. Conchology* II. 361 According to Collard de Cherres, the Breton designation is 'palourde'.] **1942** E. PAUL *Narrow St.* xxxiv. 303 Baby sea snails to be picked out with a pin; huge *palourdes* and giant snails; the tender coquilles St. Jacques. **1951** —— *Springtime in Paris* xi. 189 Sampling eagerly the oysters, clams, palourdes, cockles, mussels, snails, razor-fish or sea-urchins. **1960** E. DAVID *French Provincial Cooking* 141 We.. cannot obtain the various kinds of exquisite little clams, the *praires*, the *palourdes* and the *clovisses* which one gets in France. **1976** *Times* 2 Oct. 10/2 Palourdes on a buttery spinach puree.

palouser (pə'lu:zə(r)). *U.S. colloq.* [f. the *Palouse*, a region in the north-western U.S.] (See quots. 1918 and 1958.)

1903 *Outing* May 144/2 No, all were not British 'remittance men', Arizona 'palousers', and bank clerks on the trail. **1918** *Dialect Notes* V. 27 *Palouser*, n. 1. A greenhorn; a country fellow. From the fact that the Palouse is a farming country. 2. A lantern made by attaching a bale, horizontally, to an empty can and by inserting a candle through a hole in the side. 3. A gorgeous sunset. From the circumstance that the sunsets in the Palouse are very magnificent. **1958** W. F. MCCULLOCH *Woods Words* 131 *Palouser*, a lantern made by sticking a candle through a hole in a tin can.

palo verde ('pæləʊ 'vɛrdeɪ). *U.S.* [Amer. Sp., = 'green tree'.] A name used for several small trees or shrubs belonging to the genera *Cercidium* or *Parkinsonia* of the family Leguminosæ, native to south-western North America and distinguished by green bark and racemes of yellow flowers. Also *attrib.*

1854 J. R. BARTLETT *Pers. Narr. Explor. Texas* II. 188 The vegetation consisted of mezquit and palo verde. **1860** *Proc. Calif. Acad. Sci.* II. 129 In the eastern part of the *Papagoria*, the country is.. covered with a low growth of *mesquite* and *palo verde* brush. **1881** *Amer. Naturalist* XV. 982 The 'Palo[v]erde' of the Mexicans... grows to be some fifteen or twenty feet high. **1891** [see MESCAL 2]. **1913** *Rep. Brit. Assoc. Adv. Sci. 1912* 533 The valleys [in the Sonora Desert] contain in abundance trees—of which the most common are mesquito (*Prosopis velutina*) and paloverde (*Parkinsonia torreyana*)—shrubs and cacti. **1947** *Southern Sierran* May 4/2 The flaming red of the Ocotillo and the bright lemon yellow of the Palo Verde were outstanding. **1955** *Sci. Amer.* Apr. 72 (*caption*) Desert wash is traced by ironwood (*Olneya*) and paloverde (*Cercidium*) plants. **1969** T. H. EVERETT *Living Trees of World* 200/2 The Jerusalem thorn or palo verde.. is not an Old World native but is indigenous from Texas to Argentina. **1972** Y. LOVELOCK *Vegetable Bk.* I. 177 Another close American relative [of the Judas tree] is the palo verde.., whose Spanish name refers to the distinctive green bark. **1974** P. A. MUNZ *Flora S. California* 437 *Cercidium* Tulasne. Palo Verde. Shrubs or small trees with green bark and ± spinose twigs. *Ibid.* 465 *Parkinsonia* L. Palo Verde. Low trees with green branches and twigs.. *P. aculeata* L. Mexican Palo Verde.

palox, paloys, obs. ff. POLE-AXE, PALACE.

palp (pælp), *sb. Zool.* [a. F. *palpe*, ad. L. *palpus*.] A feeler: = PALPUS.

1842 BRANDE *Dict. Sci.* etc., s.v. *Palpators*, A family of Clavicorn beetles, including those which have very long maxillary feelers, or palps. **1870** ROLLESTON *Anim. Life* Introd. 109 (Class, Insecta) The mandible has never even a rudiment of a palp. **1880** HUXLEY *Crayfish* iv. 167.

palp (pælp), *v. rare.* [ad. L. *palpāre* to touch softly, pat, caress, coax, flatter; cf. F. *palper* (16th c. in Hatz.-Darm.) 'to handle gently.. also, to flatter, soothe' (Cotgr.), It. *palpare*.]

1. *trans.* To touch, feel; to handle gently, pat. Also *fig.* To speak fair to, flatter, cajole.

1534 *St. Papers Hen. VIII*, II. 218 That they may palpe and clayme, also handle as blynde men dothe in darknes. **1650** T. VAUGHAN *Anthroposophia* To Rdr., Aquinas palps him gently, Scotus makes him winch. **1657** THORNLEY tr. *Longus' Daphnis & Chloe* 187 He began to palpe him with soft words. **1793** GIBBON *Lett.* Misc. Wks. 1796 I. 291, I sent for Farquhar, who is allowed to be a very skilful surgeon. After viewing and palping, he.. desired to call in assistance. **1967** S. BECKETT *Stories & Texts for Nothing* III. 86 Palp your skull, seat of the understanding.

2. *intr.* Short for PALPITATE *v.* 1.

1903 'MARJORIBANKS' *Fluff-Hunters* 30 Georgie panted and palped, and the old man gurgled and gasped. *Ibid.* 149 'I am Phyllis Tremayn!' exclaimed the excited bit of fat, palping all over.

palp, obs. Sc. form of PAP, teat.

palpability (pælpə'bɪlɪtɪ). [f. next + -ITY. Cf. F. *palpabilité*.] The quality of being palpable; *concr.* a palpable person or thing.

1601 DEACON & WALKER *Spirits & Divels* 342 Concerning the non visibility and palpability of spirits. *c* **1714** POPE, etc. *Mem. Mart. Scriblerus* xiv, He it was that first found out the Palpability of Colours. **1841** L. HUNT *Seer* (1864) 77 In the shape of any Viola, or Julia, or other such flattering palpability. **1873** M. ARNOLD *Lit. & Dogma* (1876) 64 The word Eternal has less of particularity and palpability for the imagination.

palpable ('pælpəb(ə)l), *a.* (*adv.*) Also 6 -abil, -yble. [ad. late L. *palpābilis* (Orosius), f. *palpāre*: see PALP *v.* and -ABLE. Cf. F. *palpable* (14–15th c. in Hatz.-Darm.).]

A. *adj.* **1. a.** That can be touched, felt, or handled; apprehensible by the sense of touch; tangible, sensible.

palpable darkness (tenebræ tam densæ ut palpari queant, 'darkness which may be felt' Exod. x. 21), thick, gross, utter darkness (a strong figure of speech). In ***palpable hit***, the orig. physical sense often passes into sense 2.

c **1384** CHAUCER *H. Fame* II. 361 That he may shake hem be the biles, So palpable they shulden be. *c* **1450** *Mirour Saluacioun* 4355 Ferefulst derknesse palpable. **1558** BP. WATSON *Sev. Sacram.* vii. 39 The Sacrament, signifieth and representeth the same visible, mortall, and palpable bodye of Christe vpon the crosse. **1600** HOLLAND *Livy* x. xxxii. 375 There chanced to be a foggie mist, which continued a good part of the day, so thick and palpable, as men could not see before them. **1602** SHAKS. *Ham.* v. ii. 292 A hit, a very palpable hit. *a* **1633** AUSTIN *Medit.* (1635) 59 Such an Object as shall bee palpable now as well as Visible; flesh of our flesh. **1786** tr. *Beckford's Vathek* 42 For two whole hours, a palpable darkness prevailed. **1799** G. SMITH *Laboratory* I. 9 Nealed and beaten to a palpable powder. **1860** TYNDALL *Glac.* I. ii. 18 The stones were palpable enough, carried down by the cataract.

b. *Med.* Perceptible by palpation.

1897 *Allbutt's Syst. Med.* II. 769 The spleen was not palpable. *Ibid.* IV. 108 The edge of the liver being palpable. **1974** *Nature* 22 Mar. 344/2 At 72 and 96 h the lesions were smaller but still palpable.

2. *transf.* Readily perceived by some one of the other senses, as the sight, hearing, etc.; perceptible; plainly observable, noticeable, patent.

c **1430** LYDG. *Min. Poems* (Percy Soc.) 206 Merciful Leonard! gracious and benigne! Shew to thy seruauntis som palpable sygne. *c* **1450** LYDG. & BURGH *Secrees* 2568 Evident toknys and signes palpable, Of a fool nyce and varyable. **1659–60** PEPYS *Diary* 6 Jan., Dinner.. was very good; only the venison pasty was palpable beef, which was not handsome. **1664** POWER *Exp. Philos.* I. 82 [Eyes of spiders] which indeed are so palpable that they are clearly to be seen by any man that wants not his own. **1766** FORDYCE *Serm. Yng. Wom.* (1767) I. vi. 236 What is dancing.. but the harmony of motion rendered more palpable? **1819** BYRON *Juan* II. xcvii, For shore it was, and gradually grew Distinct, and high, and palpable to view. **1880** MISS BRADDON *Barbara* xxvi. 199 'Head's very hot', said the surgeon, a fact also painfully palpable to the patient.

3. *fig.* Easily perceived; open to recognition; plain, evident, apparent, obvious, manifest.

1545 JOYE *Exp. Dan.* iv. 61 b, In stormes and derkenes of errours more palpable then in the seruitute of egypt. **1576** FLEMING *Panopl. Epist.* 281 The ignoraunce of the world is grosse and palpable. **1597** HOOKER *Eccl. Pol.* v. lxv. §15 Opinions of palpable idolatrie. **1612** BRINSLEY *Lud. Lit.* xx. (1627) 227 Keeping all in palpable ignorance to be drawne to dumb Idols. **1791** COWPER *Odyss.* XIV. 440 Should'st thou invent Palpable falsehoods? **1864** BOWEN *Logic* ix. 295 A Circle so palpable as this would, indeed, be committed by no one. **1867** FREEMAN *Norm. Conq.* I. vi. 559 Rejecting palpable fables and contradictions.

†**B.** as *adv.* = PALPABLY. *Obs.*

1585 T. WASHINGTON tr. *Nicholay's Voy.* Ep. Ded., To exclude olde men.. [is] palpable erronious. **1607** *Schol. Disc. agst. Antichr.* I. ii. 83 Those who.. see them daily with our eyes,.. yea.. feele them palpable with our hands.

'**palpableness.** [f. prec. + -NESS.] The quality or fact of being palpable.

1608 D. T. *Ess. Pol. & Mor.* 8 b, Such is the palpablenesse of their irregular enormities. **1793** JEFFERSON *Writ.* (1830) IV. 481 The palpableness of these resolutions rendered it impossible the House could reject them. **1847** A. BENNIE *Disc.* iii. 39 Giving to the abstractions of feeling the palpableness of sense.

palpably ('pælpəblɪ), *adv.* [f. as prec. + -LY[2].] In a palpable manner; so as to be felt, plainly seen, observed, etc.; clearly, obviously, manifestly.

1584 R. SCOT *Discov. Witchcr.* v. viii. (1886) 85 Doo you not see how reallie and palpablie the divell tempted and plagued Job? **1699** BURNET *39 Art.* xxii. (1700) 246 Things .. too palpably False to be put upon us now. **1793** SMEATON *Edystone L.* §184 The sea salts.. render the wall visibly and palpably moist. **1875** GLADSTONE *Glean.* VI. 195 For Italy it is palpably matter of life or death.

†'**palpabrize,** *v. Obs.* [Arbitrary f. L. *palpāre*: see PALPATE *v.*] *trans.* To feel, touch, handle. (With quot. 1623 cf. PALP *v.*)

1593 NASHE *Christ's T.* (1613) 119 They cannot grosly palpabrize or feele God with their bodily fingers. **1623** COCKERAM, *Palpabrize*, to flatter.

palpacle ('pælpək(ə)l). *Zool.* [f. L. *palp-us* feeler, after *tentacle*.] A tentacle-like organ in the *Siphonophora*, belonging to a palpon.

1888 HAECKEL in *Challenger Rep.*, *Zool.* XXVIII. 18 Palpacles or Tasting Filaments. Under this designation I include only the long, extremely contractile, hollow, simple filaments, which occur in the majority of Physonectæ at the base of the palpons. **1898** SEDGWICK *Student's Text-bk. Zool.* I. 139 The palpacles are similar organs of the palpons, found in one order.

palpal ('pælpəl), *a. Zool.* [ad. mod.L. *palpālis*, f. *palpus*: see -AL[1]. Cf. F. *palpal*.] Of the nature of, pertaining to, or serving as a palp or feeler.

palpal organ: a modification of the termination of the pedipalp of a male spider, which serves as a genital organ.

1857 MAYNE *Expos. Lex.*, *Palpalis*, *palpatus*, *Entomol.*, applied to an insect having palpi,.. palpal: palpate. **1874** MOGGRIDGE *Ants* Suppl. 299 The terminal palpal claw has two teeth towards its base on the underside. **1893** SHIPLEY

& MACBRIDE *Zool.* 188 The spermatozoa are conveyed to the palpal organs of the pedipalpi of the male.

palpate (ˈpælpeɪt), *v.* [f. ppl. stem of L. *palpāre* to PALP.] *trans.* To examine by the sense of touch; to feel; *spec.* as a method of medical examination. Also *absol.* or *intr.*

1849–52 TODD *Cycl. Anat.* IV. 1151/1 The bird sifts and strains..the mud and water which it palpates in search of food. **1898** *Allbutt's Syst. Med.* V. 655 Its [the spleen's] rounded margin can be readily palpated. **1901** W. OSLER *Princ. & Pract. Med.* (ed. 4) 25 There may be early muscle rigidity and increased tension, and spasm on any attempt to palpate. **1963** D. G. W. CLYNE *Textbk. Gynaecol. & Obstetr.* xv. 374 The examiner..then gently palpates with the pulps of the fingers so as to distinguish between the soft, wedge-shaped breech and the hard, round ballottable head.

Hence **palˈpating** *ppl. a.*

1901 G. R. BUTLER *Diagnostics Internal Med.* xxxiii. 431 The re-enforcement of the palpating hand by the other preserves the perceptive delicacy which the former would otherwise lose. **1974** PASSMORE & ROBSON *Compan. Med. Stud.* III. II. xxxix. 15/1 If the palpating fingers on the appropriate side can reach below the occipital prominence ..the head is not engaged.

ˈpalpate, *a. rare.* [ad. mod.L. *palpāt-us.*] Furnished with palps.

1857 MAYNE *Expos. Lex.* [see PALPAL].

palpation (pælˈpeɪʃən). [ad. L. *palpātion-em* stroking, flattering, flattery, n. of action of *palpāre* to PALP; cf. F. *palpation* (15th c. in Godef.).] Touching, feeling by touch, handling; gentle handling; *spec.* medical examination by feeling.

1483 CAXTON *Gold. Leg.* 19/2 Forthly by palpacion of his very body. **1640** WATTS tr. *Bacon's Adv. Learn.* v. ii. 226 When a man essayes all kind of Experiments without sequence or method that is a meere palpation [L. *palpatio*]. **1656** BLOUNT *Glossogr.*, *Palpation*, flattery, cogging, fair speaking, soothing. **1688** [see PALMATION 1]. **1853** DUNGLISON *Med. Lex.*, *Palpation*, the sense of touch. It is also used for the mode of exploring disease by feeling..the diseased organ. **1879** G. MACDONALD *Sir Gibbie* I. xxii. 320 A hairy thing lay by his side, which..he examined by palpation, and found to be a dog.

attrib. **1898** *Allbutt's Syst. Med.* V. 898 The presence of emphysema tends to mask the percussion and palpation signs very considerably.

ˈpalpatory, *a. rare.* [f. L. *palpāt-*, ppl. stem of *palpāre* (PALP *v.*): see -ORY[2].] Of the nature of or tending to palpation.

1876 tr. *von Ziemssen's Cycl. Med.* V. 76 Palpatory percussion shows a distinct increase of resistance at all points.

‖**palpebra** (ˈpælpɪbrə). *Anat.* Pl. **-ae.** [L.] An eyelid.

1706 PHILLIPS, *Palpebræ*, the Eye-lids, or Coverings of the Eyes. **1727–41** CHAMBERS *Cycl.* s.v., In quadrupeds the lower *Palpebra* is moveable, and the smaller. **1875** WALTON *Dis. Eye* 137 Œdematous swelling of the palpebra.

palpebral (ˈpælpɪbrəl), *a.* [ad. L. *palpebrālis*, f. *palpebra* eyelid + -AL[1]. Cf. F. *palpébral* (1748 in Hatz.-Darm.).] Of or pertaining to the eyelids; esp. in designating parts connected with these, as ***palpebral arch, artery, muscle, nerve, vein***, etc.

1840 G. V. ELLIS *Anat.* 76 The lachrymal artery perforates the palpebral ligament of the upper eyelid,..and it divides into branches that supply the lids, and anastomose with the upper and lower palpebral arches. **1842** E. WILSON *Anat. Vade M.* (ed. 2) 281 The Palpebral arteries, are given off from the ophthalmic. **1859** O. W. HOLMES *Prof. Breakf.-t.* i. (1891) 14 What I should call a palpebral spasm, affecting the eyelid and muscles of one side. **1880** FLOWER in *Nature* XXII. 99/1 Eyes black, the palpebral openings elongated.

[¶ An erroneous definition in Dunglison, 'Relating to the eyebrows', is repeated in the American Dictionaries.]

ˈpalpebrate, *a. rare.* [ad. mod.L. *palpebrāt-us*, f. *palpebra*: see -ATE[2].] Furnished with eyelids.

1857 in MAYNE *Expos. Lex.* **1893** *Syd. Soc. Lex.*, *Palpebrate*, having eyelids.

†**ˈpalpebre.** *Obs. rare*[−1]. [a. obs. F. *palpebre* (15th c. in Godef.), ad. L. *palpebra*.] An eyelid.

1541 R. COPLAND *Guydon's Quest. Chirurg.* D iij, The palpebres or eye lyddes, the nosethyrlles, and eares.

ˈpalpebrous, *a. rare.* (See quots.)

1846 SMART, *Palpebrous*, having large brows. **1857** MAYNE *Expos. Lex.*, *Palpebrosus*, applied to the *Crocodilus palpebrosus*, because it has its eyebrows converted into a single osseous scutcheon..; palpebrous.

†**ˈpalped,** *ppl. a. Obs.* [f. PALP *v.* + -ED[1].] Felt; apprehended by the touch. Cf. PALPABLE 1.

1609 HEYWOOD *Brit. Troy* xv. xlii, Fearlesse he through the palped darknesse scowres. **1613** —— *Braz. Age* Wks. 1874 III. 206 And bring a palped darknesse ore the earth. *a* **1639** WEBSTER *Appius & Virg.* III. i, His smooth crest hath cast a palped film Over Rome's eyes.

palphrie, -phry, obs. forms of PALFREY.

palpi, pl. of PALPUS.

palpicil: see PALPOCIL.

palpicorn (ˈpælpɪkɔːn), *a.* and *sb.* [f. mod.L. *palpicornes*, pl. of *palpicornis*, f. *palp-us* feeler + *cornu* horn. Cf. F. *palpicorne* (Cuvier).]

A. *adj.* Having palpi like horns or antennæ; *spec.* of or pertaining to the *Palpicornes*, a tribe of pentamerous beetles having slender palpi usually longer than the antennæ.

1882 in OGILVIE. **1886** in *Cassell's Encycl. Dict. Mod.* The palpicorn beetles are now classed as *Philhydrida*.

B. *sb.* **1.** A beetle of the tribe *Palpicornes*.

[**1832** GRIFFITH *Cuvier's Anim. Kingd.* XIV. 424 The fifth family of the Pentamerous Coleoptera—Palpicornes.] **1882** OGILVIE, *Palpicorn.* **1886** in *Cassell's Encycl. Dict.*

2. A long labial palp. (*Cent. Dict.*)

ˈpalpifer. *Entom.* [f. L. *palpus* PALP *sb.* + *-fer* bearing, bearer.] An outer lobe of the maxilla, bearing the maxillary palp.

1841 NEWMAN *Hist. Insects* 162 The feeler-bearer or *palpifer*,..is usually placed above the stalk of the feeler-jaw. **1895** WATERHOUSE *Labium* etc. 8 We need not expect the division between the palpifer and stipes to be specially marked here.

palˈpiferous, *a.* [f. mod.L. *palpifer* (f. *palpus*) + -OUS: see -FEROUS; cf. F. *palpifère* (Littré).] Bearing palps, esp. maxillary palps.

1857 in MAYNE *Expos. Lex.*, and in mod. Dicts. **1890** *Century Dict.* s.v., Any insect which has palps is both palpiferous and palpigerous, but mouth-parts of insects are either palpiferous or palpigerous, according as they bear maxillary or labial palps.

palpiform (ˈpælpɪfɔːm), *a.* [f. L. *palpus* feeler + -FORM; cf. F. *palpiforme* (Littré).] Having the form of or resembling a palp, palpus, or feeler.

1819 G. SAMOUELLE *Entomol. Compend.* 305. **1826** KIRBY & SP. *Entomol.* III. xxxii. 341 A pair of biarticulate palpiform organs. **1852** DANA *Crust.* I. 609 The palpiform natatory appendage of the thoracic legs.

palpiger (ˈpælpɪdʒə(r)). *Entom.* [f. L. *palpus* + *-ger* carrying, carrier.] The part of the labium of an insect which bears the labial palpi.

1841 NEWMAN *Hist. Insects* 160 The labial feelers or *labiopalpi* originate one on each side of the *palpiger*. **1877** HUXLEY *Anat. Inv. Anim.* vii. 403 Between the mentum and the ligula, on each outer edge of the labium, a small piece, the palpiger, is articulated. **1895** WATERHOUSE *Labium* etc. 6 The part that bears the labial palpi...called the palpiger by Newman.

palpigerous (pælˈpɪdʒərəs), *a.* [f. as prec. + -OUS.] Having or bearing palpi or feelers.

1826 KIRBY & SP. *Entomol.* xlviii. IV. 451 *Eleutherata* (*Coleoptera L.*). Maxilla naked, free, palpigerous. **1870** ROLLESTON *Anim. Life* 75 A largely developed and palpigerous labium.

palping (ˈpælpɪŋ), *ppl. a. rare.* [f. PALP *v.* + -ING[2].] That palps or feels.

1929 R. BRIDGES *Testament of Beauty* iv. 128 It thrusteth out its finely adapted tentacles in their first palping movements to the encounter of life.

palpitant (ˈpælpɪtənt), *a.* [a. F. *palpitant* (1519 in Hatz.-Darm.), ad. L. *palpitānt-em*, pr. pple. of *palpitāre*: see next.] Palpitating.

1837 CARLYLE *Fr. Rev.* II. v. iv, The Grocer, palpitant, with drooping lip, sees his Sugar *taxé*. **1864** LOWELL *Fireside Trav.* 195 Cascades, delicately palpitant as a fall of northern lights. **1868** GEO. ELIOT *Sp. Gipsy* IV. 312 Palpitant with memories From streets and altars.

palpitate (ˈpælpɪteɪt), *v.* [f. L. *palpitāt-*, ppl. stem of *palpitāre* to move frequently and quickly, tremble, throb, freq. of *palpāre* PALP *v.* Cf. F. *palpiter* (16th c. in Godef. *Compl.*).]

1. *intr.* To pulsate or beat rapidly and strongly, as the result of exercise, strong emotion, or as a symptom of disease: said of the heart, and transf. of the body or its members; to throb.

1623 COCKERAM II, To Beate or leape like the heart, *Palpitate.* *a* **1715** BURNET *Own Time* III. (1724) I. 511 His heart..continued to palpitate some time after it was on the Hangman's knife. **1766** GOLDSM. *Vic. W.* (1876) 204 My heart palpitating with fears of detection. **1838** DICKENS *Nich. Nick.* ix, 'I do so palpitate', observed Miss Squeers.

fig. **1871** M. ARNOLD *Friendsh. Garl.* viii. 67 [Burlesquing the style of a popular newspaper] Researches concerning labour and capital, which are hardly, as our Paris correspondent says, palpitating with actuality. **1901** *Lady's Realm* X. 548/2 London may still palpitate with functions and festivities.

b. *gen.* To move with a vibrating or quivering motion; to tremble, quiver.

1849 NOAD *Electricity* 471 The limb [of the frog] traversed by the direct current palpitated for a certain time. **1863** LONGF. *Wayside Inn, Stud.* T. 87 Fountains palpitating in the heat. **1886** SHELDON tr. *Flaubert's Salammbô* 16 Her thin nostrils palpitated.

2. *trans.* To cause to pulsate rapidly or throb.

1790 MRS. A. M. JOHNSON *Monmouth* I. 163 What strange transporting sensations palpitated my heart. **1833** T. HOOK *Widow & Marquess* vii, These..palpitated a bosom pure and at rest from every fiercer passion.

palpitating (ˈpælpɪteɪtɪŋ), *ppl. a.* [f. prec. + -ING[2].] That palpitates; throbbing, quivering.

1791 COWPER *Iliad* XXII. 535 She rushed with palpitating heart And frantic air abroad. **1863** LD. LYTTON *Ring Amasis* I. I. II. i. 103 A pretty woman, bosomed in an airy cloud of palpitating gauze. **1882** ROSSETTI *Ball. & Sonn.* 201 Some shadowy palpitating grove that bears Rest for man's eyes and music for his ears.

Hence **ˈpalpiˌtatingly** *adv.*

1849 *Fraser's Mag.* XL. 518 Heart-palpitatingly entered he that well-remembered portal. **1891** G. MEREDITH *One of our Conq.* II. x. 259 It lifts her out of timidity into an adoration still palpitatingly fearful.

palpitation (pælpɪˈteɪʃən). [ad. L. *palpitātiōn-em*, n. of action f. *palpitāre* PALPITATE. Cf. F. *palpitation* (1545).] The action of palpitating.

1. The beating of the heart; esp. a violent and rapid pulsation resulting from exercise, strong emotion, etc.; throbbing; *spec.* such increased activity of the heart arising from disease of the organ itself or other parts of the body.

1604 JAS. I *Counterbl.* (Arb.) 102 If..a man would..lay a heauy pound stone on his breast, for staying and holding downe that wanton palpitation. **1656** RIDGLEY *Pract. Physic* 273 Palpitation of the Heart comes first from something troubling the Heart. **1834** J. FORBES *Laennec's Dis. Chest* (ed. 4) 553 The symptoms of this affection..are—a soft and weak pulse, and feeble and indistinct palpitations. **1872** HUXLEY *Phys.* ii. 53 Other emotions cause that extreme rapidity and violence of action which we call palpitation.

2. *gen.* A trembling or quivering motion; a tremble.

1677 GALE *Crt. Gentiles* III. 66 When any parts of their members suffered a palpitation or leaping they foretold something prosperous or sad to happen. **1778** MAD. D'ARBLAY *Diary* 26 Aug., Mrs. Thrale..felt herself in a little palpitation for me. **1827** LYTTON *Pelham* lxxxiii. (1853) 293 Dawson trembled like a leaf, and the palpitation of his limbs made his step audible and heavy. **1891** T. HARDY *Tess* (1900) 102/1 She heard a new strange sound among the leaves... Sometimes it was a palpitation, sometimes a flutter; sometimes it was a sort of gasp or gurgle.

ˈpalpless, *a.* [f. PALP *sb.* + -LESS.] Having no palpi, palps, or feelers.

1880 BASTIAN *Brain* 95 Two other nerves on each side are in relation with the palpless mandibles.

palpocil (ˈpælpəsɪl). *Zool.* Also **palpicil.** [f. L. *palpo-*, taken as comb. form of L. *palpus* PALP + *cilium* eyelash.] A fine hairlike palp or palpus; a tactile hair.

1881 E. R. LANKESTER in *Encycl. Brit.* XII. 549/2 Tactil hairs (palpocils), however, occur on the ectodermal cells. **1888** ROLLESTON & JACKSON *Anim. Life* 806 (Porifera) Nervous elements... There are two forms of them, the palpocil and synocil. The former is a delicate free process, springing from a mesoglæal cell with one or more basal outrunners.

palpon (ˈpælpən). *Zool.* [mod. f. L. *palp-us* feeler, after *siphon*.] An individual member of a siphonophoran colony developed as a feeler; a dactylozooid.

1888 HAECKEL in *Challenger Rep., Zool.* XXVIII. 16 Palpons or Tasters... These are always simple, thin-walled, very contractile sacs, in which the proximal portion communicates with the cavity of the stem, while the distal end is closed. **1898** SEDGWICK *Stud. Text-bk. Zool.* I. 138 The structures called palpons (hydrocysts, dactylozooids) are to be looked upon as mouthless manubria of medusoids.

‖**palpus** (ˈpælpəs). *Zool.* Pl. **palpi** (ˈpælpaɪ). [L. *palpus* a feeler, cognate with *palpāre*: see PALP *v.*] A jointed organ attached to the labia, maxillæ and mandibles of insects, arachnids, etc., and serving as an organ of sense; a feeler. Also, each of the two fleshy lobes at the sides of the mouth of bivalve molluscs.

1813 BINGLEY *Anim. Biog.* (ed. 4) I. 41 The mouth..has also, in most instances, four or six palpi, or feelers. **1835** KIRBY *Hab. & Inst. Anim.* II. xvi. 83 The *Palpi*, or feelers, which in some cases emerge from the side of the maxilla. **1852** DANA *Crust.* I. 41 The members of Crustacea consist normally of three parts or branches, a tigellus, a palpus, and a fouet. **1877** W. THOMSON *Voy. Challenger* I. iv. 258.

Comb. **1880** BASTIAN *Brain* 97 Nerves..from the two pairs of antennæ, and from the palpi-bearing mandibles.

palsa (ˈpælsə). *Geomorphol.* [ad. Sw. *palse*, *pals* (pl. *palsar*), introduced as a techn. term (*palse*) by Fries & Bergström 1910, in *Geol. Fören. i Stockholm Förhandl.* XXXII. 195, from Finnish and Lappish *palsa*. The pl. *palsen*, sometimes found in Eng., reflects Ger. usage.] A mound or ridge of peat covered with vegetation and containing a core of frozen peat or mineral soil in which are numerous ice lenses, occurring in subarctic regions (usu. in bogs).

1942 *Geogr. Rev.* XXXII. 420 Peat knobs in swamps and bogs and hillocks in tundra, commonly called *Palsen*, are described from northern Europe and Siberia in an extensive foreign literature. *Ibid.* 421 The solid cores of ice show that the mounds are not due solely to upward movement of fine material, as in the case of most *Palsen*. **1954** W. D. THORNBURY *Princ. Geomorphol.* iv. 89 On surfaces covered by a good growth of tundra vegetation low, rounded mounds composed of fine materials are often found. They are called earth hummocks or palsen. **1973** A. L. WASHBURN *Periglacial Processes* 152 The ice lenses generally distinguish palsas from pingos. **1973** *Nature* 9 Nov. 64/1 In Finland palsas are only found north of the coniferous forest limit.

Palsgrave (ˈpɔːlzgreɪv). *Hist.* Also 6–7 **paltsgrave,** 7 **pauls-, palse-;** *β.* 7–9 **palgrave.** [a. 16th c. Du. *paltsgrave* (Kilian), mod.Du.

paltsgraaf = Ger. *pfalzgraf*, MHG. *pfalzgrâve*, OHG. *pfalenzgrâvo*, f. *pfalenza* palace + *grâvo* count.

L. *palātium* PALACE appears to have been altered in Teutonic lands to **palantium*, whence app. OHG. *pfalanza*, *pfalenza*, MHG. *pfalenze* (*pfalze*, *pfalz*), OS. *palencea*, *palinza* (Heliand), OE. *palente*, *palendse* fem., *palent* masc.]

A Count Palatine: see COUNT *sb.*[2] 2, PALANTINE *a.*[1] 2 a.

a **1548** HALL *Chron.*, *Hen. VIII* 237 b, Came to London Duke Frederyke of Bauyre Countye Palantyne or Palsgraue of the Ryne. *Ibid.*, The Palsgraue was receyued & conducted to Wynsore by the Duke of Suffolke. **1599** SANDYS *Europæ Spec.* (1632) 172 Though the Princes and heads of the weaker side.., both Paltsgrave and Lantsgrave, have.. imposed silence in that poinct. **1612** SIR C. MOUNTAGU in *Buccleuch MSS.* (Hist. MSS. Comm.) I. 241 If my Lord of Exeter had gone with the King now to the Instalment of the Paulsgrave [i.e. as a Knight of the Garter]. **1641** FRENCH *Distill.* iv. (1651) 100 John Casmire Palse-grave of the Rhene..did alwayes drinke of it. **1656** BLOUNT *Glossogr.*, *Palts-grave*..the Title of the Prince Elector Palatine of the Rheine. **1700** DE FOE *Dang. Prot. Relig.* Misc. (1703) 250 He had not Courage enough to break with Spain in the just Quarrel of the Palsgrave, King of Bohemia. **1819** SCOTT *Leg. Montrose* ii, I have myself commanded the whole stift of Dunklespiel on the Lower Rhine, occupying the Palsgrave's palace.

β. **1612** W. PYE in Ellis *Orig. Lett.* Ser. III. IV. 170, I thought good to stay vntill I might advertyse you of the Palgraves arryvall. **1855** MILMAN *Lat. Chr.* IX. ii. IV. 38 Otho the palatine of Burgundy..the palgraves of Thuringia, Wittlesbach, and numberless other counts and nobles.

So **'Palsgravine** [Du. *paltsgravin* = Ger. *pfalzgräfin*], a countess palatine.

1835 in BOOTH *Dict. Eng. Lang.* **1846** in WORCESTER. **1894** *Westm. Gaz.* 26 Sept. 3/3 Her children [were distinguished] as 'Rhinegraves' and 'Rhinegravines,' instead of Palsgraves and Palsgravines respectively.

† **'palsical**, *a. Obs.* [f. PALSY + -ICAL.] Of or pertaining to the palsy; paralytic.

1716 M. DAVIES *Athen. Brit.* II. To Rdr. 9 Their Hands are lyable to strange Paralitical Changes and Palsical Motions. **1727** BAILEY vol. II, *Palsical*..having the Palsey.

Hence † **'palsicalness** (Bailey vol. II. 1727).

palsied ('pɔːlzɪd), *ppl. a.* [f. PALSY *sb.*[1] or *v.* + -ED.] Affected with palsy, paralysed; *fig.* deprived of muscular energy or power of action; rendered impotent; tottering, trembling.

1550 BALE *Eng. Votaries* II. 96 As that so many sycke, so many blynde, so many..palseyd, leprosed..were by them [the Apostles] as by him [Becket] deliuered. **1603** SHAKS. *Meas. for M.* III. i. 36 For all thy blessed youth Becomes as aged, and doth begge the almes Of palsied-Eld. **1756** SMART *Hymn Supreme Being* xi, He fix'd the palsied nerves of weak decay. **1814** SOUTHEY *Roderick* v. 50 He did not feel how Roderick's hand Shook like a palsied limb. **1868** FARRAR *Silence & V.* iii. (1875) 62 From the palsied hands of Greece, Rome rudely snatched the sceptre. **1889** STEVENSON *Edinburgh* 58 Old palsied houses.

palsify ('pɔːlzɪfaɪ), *v. rare.* [f. PALSY + -FY.] *trans.* To afflict with palsy, to paralyse; also *fig.*

1775 ASH, *Palsified*,..diseased with the palsy. **1851** G. OUTRAM *Legal Lyrics*, *Annuity* x, She's palsified—an' shakes her head sae fast about, ye scarce can see't. **1882** J. WALKER *Jaunt to Auld Reekie* 296 She'll palsify Industry's arms.

Hence **palsifi'cation**, paralysing action.

1866 R. CHAMBERS *Ess.* Ser. I. 138 Through the very palsification of despair.

palstave ('pɔːlsteɪv). *Archæol.* Also **-staff**, ‖**paalstave**, ‖**paalstab**. [ad. Da. *paalstav*:—Icel. *pálstaf-r*, f. *páll* hoe or spade + *staf-r* stave, staff.] A form of celt of bronze or other metal, shaped so as to fit into a split handle, instead of having a socket into which the handle fits.

1851 D. WILSON *Preh. Ann.* 255 Implements to which archæologists are now generally agreed in applying the old Scandinavian term Paalstab, or its recently adopted English synonyme, Palstave, originally..designating a weapon employed in battering the shields of the foe. **1877** LL. JEWITT *Half-hrs. among Eng. Antiq.* 51 In others the entire weapon is made thicker, with a groove (answering to flanged sides, so far as it goes) on either side, and a stop-ridge. These are generally denominated 'palstaves', from the old Scandinavian term *paalstaf*. **1894** *Notts & Derbysh. N. & Q.* Aug. 110 Sixteen socketed celts, four spear-heads,..a palstave with three ribs on the diaphragm above the stop-ridge, a ferrule, and other objects.

palster. *Obs.* or *arch.* [a. MDu. and Du. *palster* stick with iron spike, pilgrim's staff: cf. OE. *palstr*, *palester* spike:—? OTeut. **palstro-* 'stick with a thorn' (Franck); cf. MLG. *palte*, LG. *palt*, *palter*, *pult*, Sw. *palta* tatter, splinter.] A pilgrim's staff.

1481 CAXTON *Reynard* xix. (Arb.) 47, I desire of your grace that I may haue male and staff [*orig.* palster ende mael] blessyd, as belongeth to a pilgrym,..he shal goo on pylgrymage, and gyue to hym male and staf [mael ende staf] ..He hynge on the foxes necke a male couerd wyth the skynne of bruyn the bere, and a lytil palster [een cleyn palsterkijn] therby. *c* **1489** —— *Sonnes of Aymon* xxi. 466 To gyve me a newe sloppe and a large hode, a palster well yrende. [**1894** F. S. ELLIS *Reynard the Fox* 147 Then in his hand a sturdy palster He put.]

palsy ('pɔːlzɪ), *sb.*[1] (*a.*[1]) Forms: *α.* 3–6 **parlesie**, **-esi**, 3–5 **parlasy**, 4–5 **parlesy(e**, **perlesy**, 5 **parlsy**, **perlocy**. *β.* 3–4 **palasie**, 4 **-asye**, **-acye**, **-esy**, **pallesye**, 4–5 **palesye**, **-sie**, **palasy**, 5 **pallesie**, **palysy**. *γ.* 4–5 **palsye**, 4–8 **palsie**, **palsey**, (5 **pallsay**, 6 **pawsey**), 4– **palsy**. See also PARALYSIE. [ME. a. OF. *paralisie*, *-lysie* (12–13th c. in Hatz.-Darm.), ad. Romanic type **paralysia* (cf. It. *paralisia*, Pg. *paralysia*, Sp. *perlesia*), for L. *paralysis*, Gr. παράλυσις, acc. -λυσιν, whence also OF. *paralisin*, *palacin*, *palazine* (Littré), OE. *paralisin*; cf. PARALYSIS.]

A. *sb.* **1. a.** A disease of the nervous system, characterized by impairment or suspension of muscular action or sensation, esp. of voluntary motion, and, in some forms, by involuntary tremors of the limbs; paralysis.

α. *a* **1300** *Cursor M.* 19048 (Edin.) A man was criplid in parlesie [*Cott.*, *Gött.* parlesi, *Trin.* palesy, *Laud* palsy]. **1340** HAMPOLE *Pr. Consc.* 2996 Som for ire sal have als þe parlesy. *c* **1400** tr. *Secreta Secret.*, *Gov. Lordsh.* 76 Lightly he rynnys yn-to perlesy. **1483** *Cath. Angl.* 269/2 þe Parlesy (*A.* Parlsy), *paralysis*. *c* **1500** *Rowlis Cursing* 46 in Laing *Anc. Poet. Scot.*, Appostrum or the perlocy. *a* **1510** DOUGLAS *K. Hart* 455 Heidwerk, Hoist, and Parlasy. **1580** J. HAY in *Cath. Tractates* (S.T.S.) 69 Miracolouslie delyveret from ane Parlesie.

β. *c* **1290** *S. Eng. Leg.* I. 16/514 Four men of strongue palasie heore hele huy hadden. **1303** R. BRUNNE *Handl. Synne* 11922 A lymme þat ys dede or drye þurghe sykenes, or smete yn pallesye. **1362** LANGL. *P. Pl.* A. v. 61 As pale as a pelet, In a palesye [B. v. 78 palsye, palacye] he seemede. **1382** WYCLIF *Mark* ii. 10 He seith to the sike man in palasie ..ryse vp, take thi bed. *c* **1412** HOCCLEVE *De Reg. Princ.* 3735 A Romayn, smyten with þe pallesie.

γ. **13..** *Cursor M.* 11817 (Gött.) þe palsy [*Cott.* parlesi; *Trin.* palesy] has his a side. **1382** WYCLIF *Matt.* ix. 2 The man sike in palsie. **14..** *Nom.* in Wr.-Wülcker 708/32 *Hec paralisis*, pallsay. **1533** ELYOT *Cast. Helthe* (1539) 26 b, Rosemarye..helpeth agaynst palseys. **1552** HULOET, *Pawsye.* **1590** SPENSER *F.Q.* I. iv. 35 The shaking Palsey, and Saint Fraunces fire. **1673** RAY *Journ. Low C.* 70 To be drunk by those that have the Palsie. **1757** FRANKLIN *Lett.* Wks. 1840 V. 360, I never knew any advantage from electricity in palsies, that was permanent. **1813** MAR. EDGEWORTH *Patronage* (1833) I. x. 164 The paralytic incumbent..had just at this time another stroke of the palsy. **1843** SIR T. WATSON *Lect. Princ. Physic* xxxi. I. 528 That species of palsy which is called *hemiplegia*. **1860** THACKERAY *Round. Papers*, *Carp at Sans Souci*, Having to lie out at night she got a palsy which has incapacitated her from all further labour.

b. With defining words: **Bell's palsy**, paralysis of the facial nerve; **cerebral palsy**, any of various non-progressive forms of paralysis caused by damage to motor areas of the brain before or during birth, manifested in early childhood by weakness and imperfect control of the affected muscles; hence **cerebral-palsied** *a.*, affected with cerebral palsy; also *absol.*; **creeping p.**, gradually growing paralysis; **crossed p.**, paralysis affecting the upper limb of one side and the lower of the other; **crutch-p.**, paralysis of the arm caused by the pressure of a crutch; **diver's palsy**, paralysis of the heart caused by diving; **lead-p.**, **mercurial-p.**, that induced by lead or mercurial poisoning; **scrivener's p.** = *writer's cramp*, see WRITER; **shaking p.**, tremulous paralysis in the aged; **transverse p.** = *crossed palsy*. Also DEAD PALSY.

1858 COPLAND *Dict. Pract. Med.* III I. 15/1 When the upper limb of one side, and the lower of the opposite side is affected, the palsy is usually called *transverse* or *crossed palsy*. [**1888** *Lancet* 14 Apr. 709/1 There are two classes of birth palsies, the 'peripheral' and the 'cerebral'.] **1889** W. OSLER *Cerebral Palsies of Children* i. 2 The cases are usually arranged under the generic terms cerebral palsies—the German *Cerebrale Kinderlähmung*—or spastic palsies, while the specific designation indicates the distribution of the paralysis, whether unilateral, bilateral, or paraplegic. **1900** *Westm. Gaz.* 22 Nov. 8/1 A man engaged in sinking an artesian well at Merton Abbey has been killed by 'diver's palsy'—paralysis of the heart caused by the change from high air pressure at a depth of 105 ft. to normal pressure. **1940** *Jrnl. Amer. Med. Assoc.* 14 Dec. 2119/1 Treatment depends on..the particular kind of cerebral palsy: spastic, athetoid or ataxic. **1955** *Lancet* 15 Jan. 146/1 Cerebral palsies may occur in mentally normal and in mentally deficient subjects. **1961** *Ibid.* 19 Aug. 433/2 The Pædiatric Research Unit..is contributing to the study of..the special psychological problems of learning in cerebral-palsied children. **1973** *Times* 30 Oct. 2/7 Buildings and land housing St Margaret's School, Croydon, which provides specifically for the cerebral palsied, were leased rent-free to the school by two sisters. **1974** PASSMORE & ROBSON *Compan. Med. Stud.* III. II. xxxvi. 9/1 Many children with mild cerebral palsy require no medical treatment and, if they are of average intelligence, should be considered as normal children, though allowances may have to be made.

2. *fig.* **a.** Any influence which destroys, or seriously impairs, activity or sensibility; a condition of utter powerlessness; an irresistible tremor.

1433 LYDG. *S. Edmund* III. 90 Hand and penne quake for verray dreed..Of which palsy, but grace be my leche,..I not who shal me teche. **1602** MARSTON *Antonio's Rev.* IV. iv, I will live, Onely to numme some others cursed bloode With the dead palsie of like misery. **1652** HOWELL *Giraffi's Rev. Naples* II. 150 The next morning the City had a hot good morrow given her by the Castles, that put her in a palsie for a great while. **1791** PAINE *Rights of Man* (ed. 4) 35 Is the calmness of philosophy, or the palsy of insensibility, to be looked for? **1848** W. H. BARTLETT *Egypt to Pal.* ii. (1879) 28 So thoroughly does the region now lie under the palsy of Mohammedanism.

b. *gentleman's palsy*: used allusively in reference to the shaking of the dice-box. *nonce-use.*

1608 *Yorksh. Trag.* I. iv, To..draw thrice three thousand acres into the compass of a little round table, and with the gentleman's palsy in the hand shake out his posterity, thieves or beggars.

† **3.** A palsied person, a paralytic. *Obs.*

a **1300** *Cursor M.* 18543 (Cott.) To parlesi [*Trin.* palesie] and to mesele, And to þe wode, gifand þair hele. **1483** *Cath. Angl.* 269/2 þe Parlesy, (*A.* Parlsy)..*paraliticus qui habet.. infirmitatem*. **1526** R. WHYTFORD *Martiloge* (1893) 14 He heled yᵉ blynde & defe, lepres & palseys.

† **B.** *adj.* (always *attrib.*, and app. attrib. use of sb.: cf. C.) Affected with palsy, palsied. Also *fig. Obs.*

1563 HYLL *Art Garden.* II. xlvi. (1608) 116 This hearb eaten doth strengthen the palsie members. **1607** TOPSELL *Four-f. Beasts* (1658) 22 A palsie man will fall down if he taste of the perfume made of the hairs of an asse or mule. **1635** SWAN *Spec. M.* vii. §3 (1643) 350 With what a palsie pace [winter]..cometh. **1703** KELSEY *Serm.* 297 Aged Men, whose Palsy Heads and fainting Powers are [etc.].

C. *attrib.* and *Comb.* **a.** *attrib.* of or of the nature of palsy, as † ***palsy-evil***, † ***-pine***, ***-stroke***; used to cure palsy, as ***palsy drop***, ***pill***, ***water***; **b.** instrumental, as ***palsy-quaking***, ***-shaken***, ***-shaking***, ***-sick***, ***-stricken***, ***-struck*** adjs., ***palsy-strike*** vb. **c.** Also ***palsy-like*** adj.

13.. *Propr. Sanct.* (Vernon MS.) in Herrig *Archiv* LXXXI. 92/116 Mony he heled in þat tyme þat weren in þe palesy pyne. **1387–8** T. USK *Test. Love* III. vii. (Skeat) l. 40 Me thinketh the palse yuel hath acomered thy wittes. **1581** MULCASTER *Positions* xvi. (1887) 73 Some palsilike trembling from the legges. **1592** SYLVESTER *Tri. Faith* IV. xi, By Faith, Saint Peter likewise did restore A Palsie-sick. **1606** SHAKS. *Tr. & Cr.* I. iii. 174 With a palsie fumbling on his Gorget. **1648** HERRICK *Hesper.*, *To friend on untuneable Times*, Griefe..has..Wither'd my hand, and palsie-struck my tongue. **1710–11** SWIFT *Lett.* (1767) III. 91 Bid him tell you all about the bottle of palsey water by Smyth. **1744** MRS. DELANY *Autobiog. & Corr.* (1861) II. 293 Cannot you prevail with her to take palsy drops? **1820** KEATS *Eve St. Agnes* xlii, Angela the old Died palsy-twitch'd. *a* **1837** CAMPBELL *Dead Eagle* 68 A palsy-stroke of Nature shook Oran.

palsy ('pælzɪ), *sb.*[2] (*a.*[2]) *slang.* Also **palsie** and in extended forms **palsy-walsy**, **palsie-walsie**, **palsey-walsey**. [f. PAL *sb.*[1] + -SY.] **A.** *sb.* A friend, a 'pal'; a form of (ostensibly) friendly address.

1930 *Amer. Speech* Dec. 82 Call me Palsy. **1937** J. CURTIS *There ain't no Justice* xxvi. 287 What are you having, palsy-walsy? **1941** H. SMITH *Gang's All Here* 266 There was nothing to do but I must go along with them. I even went into SRO with them. Talk about palsy-walsies! **1945** P. CHEYNEY *I'll say she Does* i. 18 How come, palsie? **1945** E. WILSON *I am gazing into my 8-Ball* 118 Ratoff appealed to him. 'Look, palsy,' he said, 'whawt time I wawz in your house this morning?' **1962** *Coast to Coast 1961–62* 25 'Well, well, if it's not my old palsie-walsie Bert,' one of the detectives said. **1966** 'W. HAGGARD' *Power House* x. 111 There was nothing quite so expendable as dear old palsy-walsies who had by now outgrown their usefulness.

B. *adj.* Friendly, 'pally'. So **'palsy-,walsiness**.

1947 *Philadelphia Bull.* 17 Feb. 8/3 Army planes will drop on them pictures of General MacArthur and Hirohito in palsey-walsey attitudes, to convince them that hostilities have ceased. **1957** 'P. QUENTIN' *Suspicious Circ.* vii. 75 What if all that revolting *Daddy Long Legs* palsy-walsiness had been fake? **1959** 'J. R. MACDONALD' *Galton Case* (1960) xviii. 149 Him and Pete were palsy-walsy. **1962** BROWN & GILMAN in J. A. Fishman *Readings Sociol. of Lang.* (1968) 268 Very 'palsy' parents may invite their children to call them by first name. **1963** WODEHOUSE *Stiff Upper Lip, Jeeves* xiii. 101 What do you call it when a couple of nations start off by being all palsy walsy and then begin calling each other ticks and bounders? **1969** *Daily Tel.* (Colour Suppl.) 11 Apr. 41/4 The New York police and I are not too palsy right now. **1974** WODEHOUSE *Aunts aren't Gentlemen* vii. 56 Being a Communist, he was probably on palsy-walsy terms with half the big shots at the Kremlin. **1977** J. WAINWRIGHT *Pool of Tears* 218 He's one of those matey types... Very palsy-walsy.

'palsy, *v.* [f. PALSY *sb.*[1]]

1. *trans.* To affect with palsy, to paralyse. Chiefly *fig.* To render powerless or inert.

1615 CHAPMAN *Odyss.* XVIII. 558 Ask'd, if overcome With wine he were, or,..were palsied In his mind's instruments. **1795** SOUTHEY *Vis. Maid Orleans* I. 283 Two Gouls came on, of form more fearful-foul Than ever palsied in her wildest dream Hag-ridden Superstition. **1838** PRESCOTT *Ferd. & Is.* Introd. (1846) 9 These circumstances so far palsied the arm of the Christians. **1874** BLACKIE *Self-Cult.* 24 It lames and palsies his utterance.

2. *intr.* To shake or tremble as if palsied (*nonce-use*); to become palsied (*rare*): cf. PALSYING b.

1582 STANYHURST *Æneis* II. (Arb.) 63 With menacing becking thee branches palsye beforetyme [L. *tremefacta comam concusso vertice nutat*]. **1834**, **1849** [see PALSYING b].

palsying ('pɔːlzɪɪŋ), *ppl. a.* [f. prec. + -ING[2].] That palsies or paralyses; paralysing.

1803 MISS PORTER *Thaddeus* (1826) III. xii. 260 Thaddeus gazed at him with a palsying uncertainty in his heart. **1898** G. MEREDITH *Odes Fr. Hist.* 47 On fields where palsying Pythic laurels grow.

b. Becoming palsied or paralysed.

1834 WHITTIER *Mogg Megone* 171 Until the wizard's curses hung Suspended on his palsying tongue. **1849** C.

BRONTE *Shirley* x. 152 The heaviness of a broken spirit, and of pining and palsying faculties.

†**palsywort** (ˈpɔːlzɪwɜːt). *Obs.* [f. PALSY + WORT]. A former name of the cowslip.

1597 GERARDE *Herbal* II. cclx. §7. 637 They are commonly called.. in English pettie Mulleins, or Palsie woorts, of most Cowslips. [Cf. *Ibid.* 638 The Cowslips are commended against the.. slacknes of the sinewes, (which is the palsie).] 1629 PARKINSON *Paradisi* xxv. 247 In some countries they call them Paigles, or Palsieworts, or Petty Mulleins, which are called Cowslips in others.

†**palt**, *sb. Obs.* [f. PALT *v.*: by-form of PELT *sb.*²] A blow, a stroke: = PELT *sb.*²

1625 PURCHAS *Pilgrims* II. VI. vi. 887 Lifting vp the wooden weapon, he gaue him such a palt on the pate. 1630 *Tinker of Turvey* (1859) 17 Another gave me three palts on the head, my scull was cracked.

†**palt**, *v.*¹ *Obs.* [By-form of *pelt*, *pilt*, PULT *v.*] *trans.* To thrust, put forcibly.

a 1380 *Cristene-mon & Jew* 99 in *Min. P. Vernon MS.* 487 Men schal in prison þe palt [*rimes* malt, for-talt] And putte þe to pyne.

†**palt**, *v.*² *Obs.* Also 6 pault. [By-form of PELT *v.* The phonetic change is unexplained.]

1. *trans.* To drive with missiles.

1637 HEYWOOD *Dial.* iv. Wks. 1874 VI. 184 Yon hill, from whose high crest I with more ease with stones may palt them hence.

2. To strike with repeated blows of missiles; to assail with missiles.

1579 GOSSON *Apol. Sch. Abuse* (Arb.) 64 The dirty Champions that stoode a loofe, paulted the buckler bearers on the shinnes. 1653 H. COGAN tr. *Pinto's Trav.* iv. 8 The whole multitude to the very children, pursued and palted them with staves and stones. 1700 T. BROWN *Amusem. Ser. & Com.* 110 Their Father was palted with hundreds of them [eggs].. on the Pillory. 1740 DYCHE & PARDON, *Palting* or *Pelting*, the act of throwing stones, dirt, &c. at a person.

b. *fig.* To assail with obloquy or reproaches.

1697 COLLIER *Immor. Stage* iii. (1698) 111 Do the Antient Poets palt it in this Manner? 1701 —— *M. Aurel.* (1726) 28 When the Emperor was once dead, he palts his memory to some purpose.

3. *intr.* To deliver repeated blows; to discharge missiles.

1606 SYLVESTER *Du Bartas* II. iv. II. *Trophies* 263 Am I a Dog,.. To be with stones repell'd and palted at?

4. To go with effort; to trudge.

1560 *Nice Wanton* in Hazl. *Dodsley* II. 165 Now pretty sister, what sport shall we devise? Thus palting to school, I think us unwise.

palter (ˈpɔːltə(r)), *v.* Also 6–7 paulter. [Appears first in 16th c. The form is that of an iterative in *-er*, like *faulter*, *totter*, *waver*; but no suitable primitive *palt* is known, and no corresponding vb. is known in any other lang.]

I. †**1. a.** *intr.* and *trans.* To speak indistinctly or idly; to say or recite in an indistinct tone; to mumble, babble. *Obs.*

1538 BALE *Thre Lawes* 496, I neuer mysse but paulter, Our blessed ladyes psaulter. 1575 *Gammer Gurton's Needle* II. iii, One while his tongue it ran, and paltered of a cat. 1872 in C. Sumner *Wks.* VI. 34 Some weak-backed quietist, who, afraid to look this thing in the face, would palter weak commonplaces.

†**b.** *trans.* To jumble *up*; to patch *up* (a composition). *Obs. rare.*

1588 GREENE *Perimedes* To Rdrs., I keepe my old course, to palter vp some thing in Prose, vsing mine old poesie still, *Omne tulit punctum.*

II. †**2.** *trans.* To shift or alter (in position). *Obs.*

1577 HARRISON *England* II. ix. (1877) I. 209 Sith most of them [ecclesiastical feasts] are fixed, and palter not their place of standing.

3. a. *intr.* To shift, shuffle, equivocate, prevaricate, in statement or dealing; to deal crookedly or evasively; to play fast and loose, use trickery. Usually const. *with.*

1601 SHAKS. *Jul. C.* II. i. 126 What other Bond [neede we] Then secret Romanes, that haue spoke the word, And will not palter? 1605 —— *Macb.* v. viii. 20 Be these Iugling Fiends no more beleeu'd, That palter with vs in a double sence, That keepe the word of promise to our eare, And breake it to our hope. 1606 —— *Ant. & Cl.* III. xi. 63 Now I must.. dodge And palter in the shifts of lownes. 1648 MILTON *Tenure Kings* 2 After they have juggl'd and palter'd with the World. 1706 PHILLIPS, *Palter*, to play fast and loose, to deal unfairly. 1813 MAR. EDGEWORTH *Patron.* (1833) I. xviii. 302 Oh! Caroline, don't go back—don't palter with us—abide by your own words. 1823 SCOTT *Quentin D.* xxxii, If you palter or double in your answers, I will have thee hung alive in an iron chain. 1847 EMERSON *Poems, Sphinx* 52 He creepeth and peepeth, He palters and steals. 1884 LD. BLACKBURN in *Law Rep.* 9 *App. Cases* 201 If they palter with him in a double sense [*i.e.* by ambiguous expressions], it may be that they lie *like* truth; but I think they lie, and it is a fraud.

b. To shuffle or haggle in bargaining; to huckster, bargain, or parley in matters of duty or honour.

1611 COTGR., *Harceler*,.. to haggle, hucke, hedge, or paulter long in the buying of a commoditie. 1618 BOLTON *Florus* 93 But the Carthaginians paltring in the case, quoth Fabius,.. What meanes this delay? 1838 DICKENS *O. Twist* xlvii, Hatred of the girl who had dared to palter with strangers. 1852 TENNYSON *Ode Dk. Wellington* 180 Who never sold the truth to serve the hour, Nor palter'd with Eternal God for power. —— *Third of February* 24 What! have we fought for Freedom from our prime, At last to dodge and palter with a public crime? 1883 J. HAWTHORNE *Dust* I. 90 Only fools and cowards palter about morality.

c. To play fast and loose *with* (a matter or thing); to dilly-dally, to trifle *with.*

1814 MRS. J. WEST *Alicia de Lacy* IV. 252 If my courage palters with my duty. 1841 L. HUNT *Seer* (1864) 35 Time will not palter with the real state of the case. 1877 L. MORRIS *Epic Hades* II. 137 My good Lord Who loved too much, to palter with the past. 1880 C. R. MARKHAM *Peruv. Bark* 428 He urged that nothing should be allowed to come in the way of this great work, that it should not be paltered with.

†**d.** *trans.* To barter; to corrupt. *Obs.*

1641 MILTON *Ch. Govt.* II. iii. Wks. (1851) 173 Where bribery and corruption solicits, paltring the free and monilesse power of discipline with a carnall satisfaction by the purse.

†**4.** *trans.* To trifle away, squander. *Obs.*

1625 FLETCHER *Elder Brother* II. i, 'Tis not to be a justice of peace as you are, And palter out your time i' th' penal statutes. 1706 PHILLIPS, *To Palter*,.. also to squander away.

Hence †ˈ**paltered** *ppl. a. Obs.*, ?gained by paltering (sense 3 b).

a 1625 SIR J. SEMPLE *Picktooth for Pope* (1669) 13 Puft vp with pampering pride of paltred pelfs.

palterer (ˈpɔːltərə(r)). Also 6–7 paltrer. [f. prec. + -ER¹.] One who palters; an equivocator; a shuffler; one who plays fast and loose; a haggler, a huckster; a trifler (*with* serious matters).

1589 J. RIDER *Bibl. Schol.*, A Palterer, *sordidus*, vide dodger. 1598 FLORIO, *Miseróne*, a chuffe.. a pinch-penny, a paltrer, a penie-father. 1599 NASHE *Lenten Stuffe* 7 There be of you.. that will account me a paltrer for hanging out the signe of the redde herring in my titlepage and no such feast towards for ought you can see. 1642 ROGERS *Naaman* 564 Turn our eyes off from all slighters and paltrers with God. 1819 SHELLEY *Cenci* IV. i, Vile palterer with the sacred truth of God. 1860 MOTLEY *Netherl.* (1868) I. i. 20 The well-known voice, which had so often silenced the Flemish palterers and intriguers.

paltering (ˈpɔːltərɪŋ), *vbl. sb.* [f. PALTER *v.* + -ING¹.] The action of the verb PALTER: equivocation, shuffling, playing fast and loose, trifling (*with* serious matters).

1600 HOLLAND *Livy* XXXVIII. xiv. 991, I can no longer endure this paltering and mockerie. 1607 SHAKS. *Cor.* III. i. 58 The people are abus'd, set on: this paltring Becomes not Rome. 1642 ROGERS *Naaman* 848 She cannot endure any dalliance or paltring. 1829 SOUTHEY *All for Love* II. xxxii, But, mark me!.. on conditions, youth! No paltering here we know! 1884 MRS. C. PRAED *Zéro* vii, There must be no paltering with present duty.

†**b.** *concr.* A trifle, a worthless or paltry thing.

1611 FLORIO, *Ciabattarie*, triflings, paltrings [*ed.* 1598 paultrie] not worth an old shoe.

ˈ**paltering**, *ppl. a.* Also 6 paltring, 6–7 paultring. [f. PALTER *v.* + -ING²; but in sense 1 app. influenced by PALTRY *a.*]

†**1.** Trifling, worthless, despicable, paltry. *Obs.*

1553 M. WOOD tr. *Gardiner's True Obed.* To Rdr. A iij, An idle belied carnal Epicure, that for worldly honor and paltring pelfes sake, hath euer holden with the Hare, and run with the Hounde. 1556 OLDE *Antichrist* 181 b, For feare of losing of a litel paltring pelfe. 1588 GREENE *Pandosto* (1843) 2 The paultring poet Aphranius. 1602 NEWTON *Tryal of Man's own Selfe* 44 Hereunto is to be referred the paultring mawmetrie. *Ibid.* 116 Whether by any secret sleight,.. or any such like paltering instruments.

2. That palters: see the vb.

†ˈ**palterly**, *a. Obs.* or *dial.* [app. altered from PALTRY *a.*, as if f. PALTER *v.* + -LY¹.] Paltry, mean, shabby.

1666–7 PEPYS *Diary* 22 Feb., It is instead of a wedding-dinner for his daughter, whom I saw in palterly clothes, nothing new but a bracelet. 1825 BROCKETT *N.C. Gloss.*, *Palterley*, *Paltery*, paltry.

†ˈ**palterly**, *adv. Obs. rare*⁻¹. In 7 paul-. [irreg. f. PALTER *v.* + -LY².] In a paltering manner, shiftily, trickily.

1598 R. BERNARD tr. *Terence, Eunuch* I. ii. 120 Thou lewd woman,.. dealing thus paulterly with me.

paltery, -ye, obs. forms of PALTRY *sb.*

ˈ**palting**, *ppl. a. Obs.* exc. *dial.* Also 6 paulting. [By-form of PELTING *a.*: cf. PALT *v.*²] Pelting, petty, trifling, paltry.

1579 G. HARVEY *Letter-Bk.* (Camden) 63 As for this paultinge letter I most affectionately praye the, retourne it me back againe. 1580 —— *Lett.* Wks. (Grosart) I. 62 To send me.. some odde fresh paulting three-halfepennie Pamphlet for newes. 1895 *Leeds Merc.* Suppl. 7 Dec. (E.D.D.), Whativer he does it's allus a paltin' job he maks on't.

†ˈ**paltock.** *Obs.* Forms: 4–6 paltok, -e, (*pl.* 4 paltokes, 4–5 paltokkis, 5 paultockes, 5–6 paltockes), 6–7 paltocke, 7 paltock. [a. OF. *paltoc*, *paletoc*, *palletoc* (now *paletot*, final *t* always mute), in Breton *paltôk*, Sp. *paletoque.* By Diez considered a compound of *palle* cloak and *toque* hood, cap. The Du. *paltrok*, in Plantijn 1573 *paltrock*, *paltsrok*, is, according to Franck, a perversion of the Fr. word, assimilated by popular etymology to *rok* coat, and later to *palts* in *paltsgraaf*, etc., so as to be = 'palatine or palace coat'.]

A short coat, sleeved doublet, or 'jack', worn by men in 14th and 15th centuries.

1350–70 *Eulogium Historiarum* (1863) III. v. clxxxvi. 230 Habent etiam aliud indumentum sericum quod vulgo dicitur 'paltok'. 1356, 1378 in Riley *Mem. London* 283, 418 Paltoke, paltockes. *c* 1375 in *Rel. Antiq.* I. 41 Callis, rokettis, colers, lacis, jackes, paltokis [*printed* pattokis], with her longe crakowis. 1377 LANGL. *P. Pl.* B. XVIII. 25 In Piers paltok þe plowman þis priker shal ryde. *c* 1400 *Laud Troy Bk.* 13342 Thei schotte arwes & keste gauelokkis, Thei dyght foule her paltokkis. *c* 1460 *Medulla Gram.* (Promp. Parv. 380 *note*), *Acupicta, i. vestis actu texta*, a paltoke or a doublette. *a* 1529 SKELTON *Poems agst. Garnesche* Wks. 1843 I. 118 Ye cappyd Cayface copious, your paltoke on your pate. 1530 PALSGR. 251/2 Paltocke a garment, *halcret.* 1658 PHILLIPS, *Palletoque* or *Pallecoat*, a cassock or short cloak with sleeves, such as Pages wear.

b. *Comb.* **paltock-maker.**

1378 in Riley *Mem. London* (1868) 418 [John Tilneye] paltoke-maker.

†**Paltock's inn.** *Obs. rare.* [perh. from a proper name.] A mean or inhospitable place.

1579 GOSSON *Sch. Abuse* (Arb.) 52 Comming to Chenas, a blind village, in comparison of Athens a Paltockes Inne. 1582 STANYHURST *Æneis* III. (Arb.) 72 Swiftlye they determind too flee from a countrye so wycked, Paltocks Inne leauing, too wrinche thee nauye too southward.

†ˈ**paltrement.** *Obs. rare.* [?irreg. f. PALTER *v.* or PALTRY *a.* + -MENT.] Worthless stuff, rubbish.

1641 J. TRAPPE *Theol. Theol.* iii. 87 [The heart] a world of contemplative wickednesse, a very pesthouse of all sorts of paltrement. 1643 TRAPP *Comm. Gen.* xlviii. 19 Images and other like popish paltrement, pressing in upon us again.

paltriness (ˈpɔːltrɪnɪs). [f. PALTRY *a.* + -NESS.] The quality of being paltry; an instance of this.

1727 BAILEY vol. II, *Paltriness*,.. Pitifulness, sorriness. 1816 J. SCOTT *Vis. Paris* (ed. 5) 93 Dirty walls, a foul fire-place, and various other signs of paltriness. 1871 CARLYLE in *Mrs. C.'s Lett.* III. 298 Those new neighbours, and their noises and paltrinesses. 1874 BLACKIE *Self-Cult.* 79.

†**paltriˈpolitan.** *Obs.* Also paultri-, pautry-. An opprobrious perversion of *metropolitan*; associating it with *paltry*. Hence †**paltriˈpolitanship.**

1588 *Marprel. Epist.* (Arb.) 24 Against the vsurped state of your Paultripolitanship. *Ibid.* 25 Such buggs words being in these daies accounted no lesse then high treason against a Paltripolitan. 1589 *Marprel. Epit.* F iij. 1637 BASTWICK *Litany* I. 11, I will soe thunderthump Your Pautry Politans, as.. I will make them come tumbling downe like Phaeton.

paltry (ˈpɔːltrɪ), *sb.* Now only *dial.* Also 6 paultry, paltery(e, 6–7 paltrie; see also PELTRY. [*Paltry* sb. and adj. appear nearly together in third quarter of 16th c. The sb. seems to be a deriv. in -RY of a sb. *palt*, *pelt*, exemplified in the latter form in Harman, 1567, and in Sc. dial. (Banffsh.) 'a piece of strong coarse cloth, or of a thick dirty dress; anything waste or dirty, trash' (Jam.); in the former in mod. Eng. dial. (Northamptonsh.) *palt* refuse, rubbish; which is perhaps identical with Fris. *palt*, E.Fris. *palte*, *palt*, MLG. and LG. *palte*, *pulte* a rag, MDu. ('Sax., Fris., Sicamb.', in Kilian 1599) *palt* broken or torn piece, fragment, Da. *pialt* tatter, clout, rag, pl. *pialter*, Sw. *palta*, pl. *paltor* rags. See also the adj. and PELTRY.] Refuse, rubbish, trash; anything worthless.

1556 J. HULLIER in Foxe *A. & M.* (1583) 2004/2, I thank ye all, that ye haue deliuered and lightened me of all this paltry. 1566 *Pasquine in Traunce* To Rdr., [They] use al the fetches possibly how they may keepe all things vpright, and cloute vp with stable straw, and such paltry, the reuynes, breaches, and decayes, of this their Chaos. *Ibid.* 52 How the Popes paltrie must be estemed. 1577–87 HOLINSHED *Chron.* III. 1222/1 From thense to Donfrise, which they sacked and spoiled of such paltrie as the fugitiues had left. 1580 HOLLYBAND *Treas. Fr. Tong*, *Badinage*, paltrie or peltrie, or riffe raffe, or ceremonies. 1586 FERNE *Blaz. Gentrie* 99 In those dayes, we leawd and vnlearned people durst not passe by it in the Church yarde without bending of a knee, now these paltryes.. been taken away. 1589 BRUCE *Serm.* (1591) Y iv, Gif a mans heart be set vpon the geare of this warld, vpon the paltrie that is in it, greedines commandeth that man. 1602 WARNER *Alb. Eng.* IX. li. (1612) 232 Your Pardons, pilgrimages, and your halowed paltries vaine. *a* 1825 FORBY *Voc. E. Anglia*, *Paltry*, rubbish; refuse or trash of any sort.

paltry (ˈpɔːltrɪ), *a.* Also 6 paultery, pawltre, 6–7 paltrie, paultrie, 7–8 paultry. [Appears in 16th c. nearly with prec. sb., of which it may be an attrib. use, as in *trumpery* sb. and adj.; cf. also LG. *paltrig*, *pultrig* (Brem. Wbch.), E.Fris. *palterig*, *paltrig* ragged, torn, f. dial. Ger. *palter*, pl. *-ern* rag, MLG. *palter-*, *polter-* (in *palter-*, *polterlappen* rags), E.Fris. *palter*, *pulter* a rough broken or splintered piece (e.g. of wood or stone), derivatives of *palte*, *palt* sb., mentioned in prec.]

Rubbishy, trashy, worthless; petty, insignificant, trifling; contemptible, despicable; of worthless nature. **a.** Of things.

1570 B. GOOGE *Pop Kingd.* III. (1880) 30 For this such strange religion haue they framde, and paultrie gere. 1573 G. HARVEY *Letter-Bk.* (Camden) 131 It gav then sownde owte like a paultery belle. 1592 *Nottingham Rec.* IV. 238 For byldyng a sort of pawltre howses wyche hathe downe gret hurt to owar towne. 1678 R. L'ESTRANGE *Seneca's Mor.* (1702) 96 For every paultry Sum of Money, there must be

Bonds. **1692** BENTLEY *Boyle Lect.* i. 7 Such a contemptible paultry Hypothesis. **1751** SMOLLETT *Per. Pic.* (1779) III. lxxx. 69 A paultry chamber in the third story. **1784** COWPER *Task* v. 348 We love the man, the paultry pageant you. **1791** SIR J. MACKINTOSH *Vind. Gallicæ* Wks. 1846 III. 104 The most paltry and shallow arts of sophistry. **1867** FREEMAN *Norm. Conq.* I. v. 347 The paltry trick was successful. **1892** STEVENSON *Across the Plains* 222 Quite dead to all but the paltriest considerations.

b. Of persons.

c **1592** MARLOWE *Jew of Malta* II. Wks. (Rtldg.) 159/1 My daughter here, a paltry silly girl. **1598** SHAKS. *Merry W.* II. i. 163 Our Messenger to this paltrie Knight. **1602** *2nd Pt. Return fr. Parnass.* Prol. 11 Yon paultry Crittick Gentlemen. **1642** MILTON *Apol. Smect.* Introd., Wks. (1851) 262 The idlest and the paltriest Mime that ever mounted upon banke. **1704** SWIFT *T. Tub* Author's Apol., He is a paultry imitating pedant. **1773** GOLDSM. *Stoops to Conq.* I. i, A low, paltry set of fellows. **1828** SCOTT *F. M. Perth* xxix, I.. showed little of that paltry apprentice boy, whom you used to—use just as he deserved. **1874** BLACKIE *Self-Cult.* 57 With all this, if he is not good, he may be a paltry fellow.

paltsgrave, obs. form of PALSGRAVE.

paludal (pəˈl(j)uːdəl, ˈpæl(j)uːdəl), *a.* [f. L. *palūs, palūd-em* marsh + -AL[1].] Of or pertaining to a marsh or fen; *Med.* and *Path.* produced by or arising from a marsh; malarial; esp. *Bot.*, of a plant, growing in marshy ground. Also, as *sb.*, a plant requiring a marshy habitat.

1818-20 E. THOMPSON *Cullen's Nosol. Meth.* (ed. 3) 317 Order II. Pyrexiæ. Fevers... 19... Paludal. **1822-34** *Good's Study Med.* (ed. 4) I. 602 Dr. Young gives to intermittents and remittents the common name of paludal fever. **1847** H. C. WATSON *Cybele Britannica* I. 65 The proposed series of terms runs thus:—.. Paludal. Plants of marshy ground, the roots of which are in water or wet ground most part of the year, or constantly. **1856** TODD & BOWMAN *Phys. Anat.* II. 115 Persons exposed to the paludal poison. **1896-7** *Allbutt's Syst. Med.* I. 47 Every variety of land-surface from Mount Olympus to the paludal lakes of the plain. *Ibid.* II. 308 Lancisi pointed out its [intermittent fever's] connection with paludal miasmata. **1926** *Nat. Hist. Oxford District* 88 Many of these paludals.. can grow equally well on either soil. **1932** G. C. DRUCE *Comital Flora Brit. Isles* p. xxv, The Hydrophytes or Water-loving plants .. include first the Paludal or Marsh and Bog plants. **1974** *Kew Bull.* XXIX. 542 The paludal species [of giant lobelia] .. have little secondary wood.

paludament (pəˈl(j)uːdəmənt). [ad. L. *palūdāmentum* (also in Eng. use); cf. F. *paludament* (Cotgr. 1611).] A military cloak worn by Roman generals and chief officers; hence, a royal cloak; a herald's coat.

1614 T. WHITE *Martyrd. St. George* B iv b, A Rich Paludament is cast about The Martyres shoulders. **1656** BLOUNT *Glossogr.*, *Paludament*.. a Coat-armor or Horseman's coat, a Soldier's garment, an Herald's Coat of Arms. **1702** ADDISON *Dial. Medals* iii. Wks. (Bohn) I. 349 Our modern medals are full of *togas* and *tunicas, trabeas* and *paludamentums*. **1821** DE QUINCEY *Confess.* Wks. 1856 V. 263 Immediately came 'sweeping by', in gorgeous paludaments, Paullus or Marius. **1879** FARRAR *St. Paul* I. 485 The two statues of Augustus, one in the paludament of an Imperator.

Hence **paludaˈmental** *a.*, of the nature of a paludament. *rare.*

1652 URQUHART *Jewel* Wks. (1834) 239 Having apparelled himself with a paludamental vesture, after the antick fashion of the illustrious Romans.

†**paˈlude.** *Obs. rare.* [a. OF. *palude* (also *palud*), 14th c. in Godef., ad. L. *palūs, palūd-em*, marsh.] A marsh, fen.

1412-20 LYDG. *Chron. Troy* I. iii, The serpent Hydra he slough eke in pallude. *c* **1420** *Chaucer's Boeth.* iv. metr. vii. 115 (Camb. MS.) [*gloss*] In þe palude of lyrne. **1480** CAXTON *Ovid's Met.* xv. iv, That which was somtyme deep paludes & see is now sandy ground. **1585** T. WASHINGTON tr. *Nicholay's Voy.* IV. xxix. 150 The Palude lerne wher Hercules killed yͤ serpent Hidra.

paludi- (before a vowel **palud-** and improperly **paludi-**), a formative element from L. *palūs, palūd-em* marsh, in **paˈludic** *a.*, of or pertaining to marshes; **paˈludicole**, **paluˈdicoline**, **paluˈdicolous** *adjs.*, inhabiting marshes; **paluˈdiferous** *a.*, producing a marsh or marshes; also erron. **paˈludial**, **paˈludian**, †**paˈludiate**, **paˈludious** *adjs.* = *paludic*, PALUDAL, PALUDOUS.

1897 MARY KINGSLEY *W. Africa* 301 A personal acquaintance with fluvial and *paludial ground deposits. **1860** *All Year Round* No. 53. 66 The true specific against *paludian fever. **1632** LITHGOW *Trav.* x. 439 To choose his lodging.. far from *palludiat Ditches. *Ibid.* 493, I set face.. for Scotland, suiting my.. feete with the palludiat way. **1897** M. L. HUGHES *Medit. Fever* i. 2 This endemic fever of the Mediterranean.. [is] distinguished from other diseases, more particularly from enteric and *paludic fevers. **1857** MAYNE *Expos. Lex.*, *Paludicolous [*printed* -culous]. **1656** BLOUNT *Glossogr.*, **Paludiferous*.. that causeth a Fen or Marsh. **1594** T. BEDINGFIELD tr. *Machiavelli's Florentine Hist.* (1595) 27 The Cittie of Venice, seated in a place *paludious, and vnwholesome. **1659** GAUDEN *Tears Church* I. v. 60 The Lions in Mesopotamia.. are destroyed by gnats; their importunity being such in those paludious places.

‖**Paludina** (pæl(j)uːˈdaɪnə). *Zool.* [mod.L., f. L. *palūs, palūd-* + *-īnus, -īna*: see -INE[1].] A genus of fresh-water gastropod molluscs, also called *pond-snails*.

1833 LYELL *Princ. Geol.* III. 244 Where the same Planorbes, Paludinæ, and Limnei occur. **1902** CORNISH *Nat. Thames* 15 The paludinas being large, thick-striped shells.

paludine (ˈpæl(j)uːdɪn, -aɪn), *a.* [f. L. *palūs, palūd-* + -INE[1].] Of or pertaining to a marsh. So in same sense **paˈludinal**, **paˈludinous** *adjs.*

1858 BUCKLAND *Curios. Nat. Hist.* (1859) 14 To prevent the slumbers of the lords and ladies being broken by their paludine neighbours [frogs]. **1866** *Morn. Star* 10 July, A little below Guastalla you come upon the paludinous tracts of land along the river [Po].

paludism (ˈpæl(j)uːdɪz(ə)m). *Path.* [f. L. *palūs, palūd-em* marsh + -ISM.] 'The condition of ill health produced by exposure to marsh miasmata' (*Syd. Soc. Lex.*).

1890 J. S. BILLINGS *Nat. Med. Dict.* II. 280 *Paludism*, the morbid condition produced by exposure to marsh malaria. **1897** *Allbutt's Syst. Med.* II. 308 The term 'malaria' is preferable to paludism. *Ibid.* 722 In Europe paludism has gradually lessened.

paludose (ˌpæl(j)uːˈdəʊs), *a. rare*[−0]. [f. as next: see -OSE[1].] = next.

1866 *Treas. Bot.*, *Paludose*,.. growing in marshy places.

paludous (pəˈl(j)uːdəs), *a. rare.* [ad. L. *palūdōs-us* marshy: see -OUS.] Of or belonging to marshes, marshy; inhabiting marshes.

1803 *Med. Jrnl.* X. 462 Uncompounded with, either febrile, or paludous, or limose gas. **1857** in MAYNE *Expos. Lex.*

Paludrine (ˈpæl(j)uːdriːn). *Pharm.* Also **paludrine.** [f. L. *palūs, palūd-em* marsh + *-rine*, after ATABRINE, MEPACRINE.] A proprietary name for proguanil hydrochloride, used as an anti-malarial drug.

1944 *Trade Marks Jrnl.* 22 Mar. 127/2 Paludrine... Pharmaceutical substances for the treatment of malaria. Imperial Chemical (Pharmaceuticals) Limited,.. Slough, Buckinghamshire; manufacturers and merchants. **1945** *Times* 6 Nov. 6/4 The new drug, which is to be distributed in a form known as Paludrine marks a revolutionary departure in anti-malarial research. **1951** 'N. SHUTE' *Round Bend* 288 Connie had taken Paludrine regularly.. and his malaria had not recurred. **1966** D. FORBES *Heart of Malaya* vi. 65, I.. pour my tea and take a paludrine tablet with the first gulp. **1974** P. DICKINSON *Poison Oracle* iv. 111 The malaria season was not yet at its height, but he had been giving them both Paludrine. **1977** P. THEROUX *Consul's File* 45 They went off on one of their usual expeditions. No compass, no paludrine, no torch.

†**palumbine**, *a. Obs. rare*[−0]. [ad. L. *palumbīn-us*, f. *palumbēs, -is, -us* wood-pigeon.] Belonging to the wood-pigeon or ring-dove.

1656 in BLOUNT *Glossogr.* **1658** in PHILLIPS.

palus[1]. Also 5 **palusche, palusshe.** [a. OF. *palus*, *paluz* (12th c. in Godef.), ad. L. *palūs* marsh.]

†**1.** A marsh, a fen; an abyss. *Obs. rare.*

1471 CAXTON *Recuyell* (ed. Sommer) 390 In myddis of this palus was a grete lake or ponde. **1489** —— *Faytes of A.* I. xiv. 38 A place.. fer from eny palusche or mares grounde. **1490** —— *Eneydos* xi. 42 The depe palusshe infernalle.

2. With capital initial and pronunc. (palys): a wine produced in the Palus region of Bordeaux in France. Also *attrib.*

1833 C. REDDING *Hist. Mod. Wines* v. 144 Bassens and Mondferrand grow the second class of Palus wines. **1861** MRS. BEETON *Bk. Househ. Managem.* 888 The genuine wines of Bordeaux are of great variety.. and the principal vineyards are those of Medoc, Palus, Graves, and Blanche. **1953** E. HYAMS *Vineyards in England* 90 Such *palus* wines are good enough of their kind. **1968** *New Statesman* 29 Nov. 744/2 How many little Palus and/or Bourg wines reach the market as Médoc, or even as St Julien?

‖**palus**[2] (ˈpeɪləs). *Biol.* Pl. **pali.** [L. *pālus* stake.] In corals, one of the thin, upright, calcareous laminæ or plates, which extend up from the bottom of a corallite to the calix, and are connected by their outer edges with the septa. Hence the dim. ‖ˈ**palulus**, pl. **paluli.**

1872 NICHOLSON *Palæont.* 92 The chief remaining structures.. are what are called 'pali', 'dissepiments', and 'tabulæ'. **1877** HUXLEY *Anat. Inv. Anim.* iii. 163 Small separate pillars between the columella and the septa are termed paluli.

palus: see PALAS.

palustral (pəˈlʌstrəl), *a. rare.* [f. L. *palustr-is* pertaining to a marsh (f. *palus* marsh) + -AL[1].] Pertaining to or inhabiting marshes; paludal. So **paˈlustrian** *a.* (*sb.*); **paˈlustrine** *a.*

1607 TOPSELL *Four-f. Beasts* (1658) 162 The Palustrains or Marishie Elephants are hair-brained and inconstant. **1787** W. MARSHALL *Norfolk* I. 311 Palustrean productions. **1879** WEBSTER Suppl., *Palustral*, pertaining to a bog or marsh. **1882** OGILVIE (Annandale) Suppl., *Palustrine.* **1900** *Brit. Med. Jrnl.* No. 2041. 301 All the palustral mosquitos are not malarial.

palustral, -tre, obs. erron. ff. PALÆSTRAL, -TRA.

†ˈ**paly**, *sb. Obs.* Also 5 **paley, payly.** [a. OF. *paille* (12th c. in Littré):—L. *palea* chaff.] Bran.

c **1440** *Promp. Parv.* 49/2 Bren, or bryn, or paley, *cantabrum, furfur.* *Ibid.* 379/1 Paly of brynne, *cantabrum.* *Ibid.* 457/1 Syvedys, or brynne, or palyys, *furfur.*

paly (ˈpeɪlɪ), *a.*[1] Chiefly *poet.* Also 6-7 **palie**, 9 **paley.** [f. PALE *a.* + -Y.] Of a pale kind or aspect; pale, or somewhat pale.

c **1560** A. SCOTT *Poems* (S.T.S.) xiv. 3 Hornit Dyane, with hir paly glemis. **1584** LODGE *Hist. Forbonius & Prisc.* (Shaks. Soc.) 103 Bloud forsooke His palie face. **1593** SHAKS. *2 Hen. VI*, III. ii. 141. **1742** GRAY *Propertius* II. 20 Monthly waning hides her paly fires. **1778** LANGHORNE *Owen of Carron* XII. iii, Fear O'er all his paly visage glides. **18..** J. H. NEWMAN *Verses on Var. Occas.* (1868) 210 See, the golden dawn is glowing, While the paly shades are going. **1886** STEVENSON *Prince Otto* ii, You look paley.

paly (ˈpeɪlɪ), *a.*[2] *Her.* Also 6 **palle, palie.** [ad. F. *palé* (13th. c. in Littré), f. *pal* PALE *sb.*[1]] Said of the shield (or of a bearing) when divided palewise, *i.e.* by vertical lines, into an even number of equal stripes of alternate tinctures.

paly bendy, divided both palewise and bendwise, *i.e.* vertically and diagonally, with alternate tinctures. ***Paly pily***: see PILY.

1486 *Bk. St. Albans, Her.* B iv b, Whan a cootarmure is paly of dyuerse colouris to the poynt. **1525** LD. BERNERS *Froiss.* II. xxv. 70 His armes are palle golde and goules. **1610** GUILLIM *Heraldry* v. iv. (1611) 245 Pales and bends born one ouerthwart the other, for which cause the same is termed paly-bendy. **1769** *New Peerage* I. 118 Arms. Paly of six, *or* and *azure*; a canton, *ermine.* **1892** C. E. NORTON *Dante's Paradise* 109 *note*, His scutcheon was paly of four, argent and gules.

palyard(e, -ȝard, etc., obs. ff. PALLIARD, etc.

palyce, -lys, obs. ff. PALACE; var. PALIS *Obs.*

palyeon, -youn, -ȝeon, -ȝeown, -ȝon, obs. Sc. forms of PAVILION.

palyet, obs. form of PALLET *sb.*[2], small bed.

palygorskite (pælɪˈgɔːskaɪt). *Min.* Also †**paligorskite.** [ad. G. *paligorskit* (T. v. Ssaftschenkow 1862, in *Verh. d. k. Ges. für d. Ges. Mineral. zu St. Petersburg* 102), f. *Palўgorsk*, name of a locality by the Popovka river in the Ukrainian S.S.R.: see -ITE[1].] A silicate of magnesium and aluminium that occurs as soft, light-coloured, fibrous layers and has a structure based on silica tetrahedra arranged in double chains.

1868 J. D. DANA *Syst. Min.* (ed. 5) 406 (*heading*) Paligorskite. **1916** *Chem. Abstr.* X. 581 (*heading*) Studies in the magnesian silicates. The group of zillerite, zermattite and palygorskite. **1921** *Mineral. Abstr.* I. 237 Paligorskite ('mountain-cork') from Billowitz near Brünn [Moravia]. **1968** I. KOSTOV *Mineral.* II. v. 352 Sepiolite can be dense or spongy.. whereas palygorskite resembles leather or parchment... Both minerals are secondary products found in altered serpentinitic rocks in association with opal, dolomite, and other minerals. **1973** *Clay Minerals* X. 28 Under a binocular microscope, the palygorskite shows fine interwoven fibres similar to those of coarse-textured paper.

palynology (pælɪˈnɒlədʒɪ). [f. Gr. παλύνειν to sprinkle (cf. πάλη fine meal = L. *pollen*) + -OLOGY.] The study of the structure and dispersal of pollen grains and other spores, as indicators of plant geography, taxonomic characteristics of plants, fossils used in dating geological formations or archæological remains, or causative agents of allergic reactions. So **palynoˈlogical** *a.*, of or pertaining to this study; **palynoˈlogically** *adv.*; **palyˈnologist**, a student of palynology.

1944 HYDE & WILLIAMS *Let.* 15 July in *Pollen Analysis Circular* 28 Oct. 6 We would therefore suggest palynology ..: the study of pollen and other spores and their dispersal, and applications thereof. We venture to hope that the sequence of consonants p-l-n, (suggesting pollen, but with a difference) and the general euphony of the new word may commend it to our fellow workers in this field. **1944** H. A. HYDE in *Museums Jrnl.* XLIV. 146/1 In view of the admitted inadequacy of the expression pollen analysis it has recently been proposed to substitute for it the new word palynology (Gk. παλύνω (paluno), I scatter; πάλη (pale), meal): the study of pollens and other plant spores and their dispersal, and applications thereof. **1946** *Svensk Bot. Tidskr.* XL. 303 (*title*) Palynological aspects of the pioneer phase in the immigration of the Swedish flora. **1953** *Proc. 7th Pacific Sci. Congr.* V. 172 It is a matter of no small concern to palynologists and plant geographers that our [*sc.* New Zealand's] peat deposits are being greatly modified by draining and burning. **1956** H. GODWIN *Hist. Brit. Flora* iii. 48/1 They [*sc.* pollen-grains] confer much increased sensitiveness and power upon the palynological technique. **1958** *Antiquity* XXXII. 54 Palynology, or the science of pollen analysis, has developed during the past three decades into a major source of knowledge of the past. **1959** *Micropaleont.* V. 27/2 Several samples were investigated palynologically in order to confirm, if possible, the supposed Pleistocene age. **1962** *Courier-Mail* (Brisbane) 10 Sept. 15/9 (Advt.), A major oil company.. is setting up a regional stratigraphic laboratory in Perth, Western Australia. A palynologist is required to organise and run the palynological section of this laboratory. **1963** G. ERDTMAN in A. & D. LÖVE *N. Atlantic Biota* 367 (*title*) Palynology and Pleistocene ecology. **1972** *Courier-Mail* (Brisbane) 15 Apr. 9/7 (Advt.), B.O.C. of Australia Limited.. requires a Senior Palynology Technician to supervise its laboratory staff. **1973** *Microscopy* XXXII. 319 This same resistance to attack permits the palynologist to employ selective oxidation techniques to concentrate microfossils from peats and coals. **1973** *Nature* 16 Mar. 187/1 These [*sc.* Pleistocene sediments] were analysed palynologically, and indicated four or five alterations of pluvial and interpluvial conditions.

Ibid. 8 June 342/1 The date of the appearance of marine grasses is not traceable by palynology because they produce pollen without exine, and so are not fossilized. **1975** *Times* 27 May 14/6 The lake beds [of Hoxne] contain fossil pollen and constitute the palynological type site of the Hoxnian Interglacial.

Pam (pæm). [Corresponds in sense to Sc. *Pamphie*, also *Pawmie*, 'a vulgar name given at cards to the knave of clubs' (Jamieson), and to F. *pamphile* name of the card game, and of the knave of clubs in it (Littré); of which *Pamphie*, *Pawmie*, *Pam* appear to be abbreviations. F. *pamphile* is, according to Littré, ad. Gr. personal name Πάμφιλος 'beloved of all', in L. *Pamphilus*.]

1. The knave of clubs, esp. in the game of five-card loo, in which this card is the highest trump.

1685 Crowne *Sir Courtly Nice* III. 22 Thou art the only Court card women love to play with; the very Pam at Lantereloo, the knave that picks up all. **1707** J. Stevens tr. *Quevedo's Com. Wks.* (1709) 338 The Apothecary is like Pam at Loo, he is everything that is wanting. **1712–14** Pope *Rape Lock* III. 61 Ev'n mighty Pam, that Kings and Queens o'erthrew, And mow'd down armies in the fights of Lu. *a* **1845** Hood *Storm at Hastings* iv, A living Pam, omnipotent at loo! **1849** *Chambers' Inform.* II. 671/1.

fig. **1706** Estcourt *Fair Example* I. i, Let me tell ye, Madam, Scandal is the very Pam in Conversation.

2. Name of a card-game, akin to Nap, in which the knave of clubs was the highest trump card.

1691 *Weesils* ii. 11 She wanted Counters too to play at Pam. **1713** Addison *Guard.* No. 120 ⁋6 She..grows more fond of Pam than of her husband. **1898** *Longm. Mag.* Nov. 58 A sumptuous ball at the Pantheon, silver loo with a princess, 'Pam' with a duchess.

Hence † **pam-child**, *nonce-wd.*, 'knave-child', male child.

1760 H. Walpole *Lett., to G. Montagu* 14 Jan. (1846) IV. 16, I have sat up twice this week..with the Duchess of Grafton, at loo, who..has got a pam-child this morning.

pam- (pæm-), repr. Gr. παμ- the form of παν-, PAN-, all-, before a labial, as in **pambrittanick**, obs. form of PAN-BRITANNIC.

pamaquin ('pæməkwɪn). *Pharm.* Also **-ine**. [f. P(ENTYL + A(MINO- + M(ETHOXY- + -*a*- + QUIN(OLINE.] An orange-yellow crystalline salt, $C_{19}H_{29}N_3O.C_{23}H_{16}O_6$, which is a toxic compound formerly used in the treatment of malaria. Cf. PLASMOCHIN, PLASMOQUINE.

1941 *Brit. Pharmacopœia 1932* Add. IV. 24 Pamaquin is the 6-methoxy-8-[ω-diethylamino-α-methylbutyl]-aminoquinoline salt of 2:2′-dihydroxy-1:1′-dinaphthylmethane-3:3′-dicarboxylic acid. **1951** A. Grollman *Pharmacol. & Therapeutics* xxxiii. 483 Because of its toxicity and the availability of safer and better drugs, pamaquine is no longer of therapeutic importance. **1961** *New Scientist* 4 May 261/1 The anti-malarial drugs pamaquin and primaquine produce anaemia in certain susceptible persons. **1974** B. G. Maegraith in A. W. Woodruff *Med. in Tropics* ii. 65/1 The 8-aminoquinoline most widely given [for vivax malaria] is primaquine; pamaquine or quinocide are alternatives.

'**pamby**, shortening of NAMBY-PAMBY *a.*

1823 Byron *Let.* 25 Jan. in *Wks.* (1901) VI. 164, I will bet you a flask of Falernum that the most stilted parts of the political *Age of Bronze*, and the most pamby portions of the Toobonai Islands, will be the most agreeable to the enlightened public. **1947** I. Brown *Say Word* 89 Defeating the accusation that..Ambrose [Philips] composed nothing but 'pamby' stuff.

pame, obs. ME. form of PALM *sb.*[2]

‖**pamé** ('pɑːmeɪ), *a.* *Her. rare.* [F. *pâmé*, formerly *pasmé*, pa. pple. of *pâmer*, *pasmer* to swoon:—pop. L. *pasmāre* for *spasmāre*, lit. 'to have a spasm' (Hatz.-Darm.).] Said of a dolphin: Represented with gaping mouth.

1867 Boutell *Eng. Heraldry* (1875) 82 If their [Fishes'] bodies are bent, as the Dolphin is generally represented, they are 'embowed',..and if with open mouth, 'pamé'.

pament, obs. ME. form of PAVEMENT.

pamfilet, pamflet, etc., obs. ff. PAMPHLET.

† **pamp, pampe**, *v.* *Obs. rare.* [app. the primary vb. of which PAMPER is the frequentative. Cf. Ger. *pampen* (dial. and colloq.) to cram, Bavarian *pampfen*, *sich voll pampfen* to gorge oneself (Schmeller); also Sw. dial. *pampen* swollen up; Lith. *pampti* to swell. See below.] *trans.* To cram; to pamper.

? *a* **1400** [*On Christ's Temptation*] in Wright *Rel. Ant.* II. 41 He stirith him [= them] to pappe and pampe her fleische, desyrynge delicous metis and drynkis.

[*Note.* The existence of this vb. is not altogether certain. The MS. whence the first quot. comes cannot now be found, so that its date is uncertain, and the reading might be interpreted as an error for *pampre*, PAMPER. The existence of *pampe* is however supported by the verb *pomp* (POMP *v.*[2]), which appears to be the same word. Prof. Skeat suggests the existence of an ablaut series *pimp-*, *pamp-*, *pump-*, to swell.]

‖**pampa** ('pæmpə), usually *pl.* pampas ('pæmpəz, -əs). [a. Sp. *pampa* (pl. *pampas*), ad. Peruv. *bamba*, a steppe, a flat: cf. the place-names *Moyo-bamba*, *Chuqui-bamba*, etc.]

1. a. The name given to the vast treeless plains of South America south of the Amazon, esp. of the Argentina and the adjacent countries. (The similar plains north of the Amazon are known as *llanos*.)

1704 *Collect. Voy.* (Churchill) III. 46/1 There are also bred in the *Pampas*..many Hares. **1810** *Edin. Rev.* XVI. 241 The *pampas* of Buenos Ayres are plains of the same kind [as the llanos or savannahs], but still more extensive. **1837** *Penny Cycl.* XVIII. 210/1 In the direction due north the pampa narrows between the Parana and a ridge..called the Sierra de Cordova. **1852** Th. Ross *Humboldt's Trav.* II. xvii. 87 The Llanos and the Pampas..are really steppes. **1880** C. R. Markham *Peruv. Bark* 104 At length we came to a rocky ridge which bounded the vast pampa of Vilque.

b. Short for *pampa sheep*, reared on the pampas.

1892 W. H. Hudson *Nat. La Plata* 108 The pampa descends to us from the first sheep introduced into La Plata about three centuries ago.

2. *attrib.* and *Comb.*, as **Pampas Indian**; **pampas-cat**, a wild cat of the pampas (*Felis pajeros*), about three and a half feet long, having long yellow-grey fur marked with oblique brownish stripes; **pampas clay**, an ossiferous bluish clay, beds of which occur in many parts of the pampas; **pampas deer**, a small deer of South America, *Blastoceros bezoarticus*, the male of which has partly dichotomous antlers; **pampas flicker**, a black, white, and yellow woodpecker, *Colaptes campestris*, found in the eastern part of South America; **pampas fox**, one of several small mammals resembling a fox or a dog, esp. *Dusicyon gymnocercus*, or Azara's fox, found in eastern and southern parts of South America; **pampas rice**, a name given in the southern U.S. to a variety of the common Millet (*Sorghum vulgare*), with a drooping panicle; **pampas woodpecker** = *pampas flicker* above.

1883 *List Anim. Zool. Soc.* (ed. 8) 56 *Pampas Cat. **1887** Heilprin *Geog. & Geol. Distrib. Anim.* 383 Unspotted cats ranging from Paraguay to the northern boundary of Mexico, the Chilian colollo, the pampas-cat, and the lynx. **1886** *Cassell's Encycl. Dict.*, **Pampas-clay*. **1860** Mayne Reid *Odd People* 446 A man on foot can approach much nearer to any game, than if he were mounted upon a horse. This is true..also of the large *pampas deer. **1883** *List Anim. Zool. Soc.* (ed. 8) 174 *Cariacus campestris* F. Cuv., Pampas Deer. **1894** Lydekker *Roy. Nat. Hist.* II. 388 The pampas deer is the smaller of the two species, standing about 2½ feet at the shoulder. *Ibid.* 389. **1972** G. K. Whitehead *Deer of World* iv. 63 The Pampas deer is the most elegant of all the South American deer. **1912** Brabourne & Chubb *Birds S. Amer.* I. 168 *Colaptes...campestris...* *Pampas Flicker. Carpentero. **1926** *Bull. U.S. Nat. Mus.* No. 133. 223 In habit and general appearance the pampas flicker differs little from the familiar *Colaptes aureus* of the eastern United States. **1957** M. H. Mitchell *Obs. Birds S.E. Brazil* 120 Pampas Flickers, on first sight or hearing, immediately recall to the northerner *Colaptes aureus*. **1923** *Proc. Biol. Soc. Washington* XXXVI. 55 Specimens from the high savanna of Bogotá..indicate that the *pampa fox of this area is a depauperate pallid race of the lowland *Cerdocyon thous*. **1956** G. Durrell *Drunken Forest* v. 105 He was a small, delicately made, grey pampas fox, with slender legs and enormous brush and eager brown eyes. **1972** *Vogue* Jan. 12/2 South American fur rugs..viscacha, guanaco, grey and pampas foxes. **1975** H. J. Stains in M. W. Fox *Wild Canids* i. 13 The pampas fox is found in Paraguay and southeastern Brazil south through the pampas region of Argentina. **1826** Sir F. B. Head *Journ. Pampas* 9 The south part of the Pampas is inhabited by the *Pampas Indians, who have no fixed abode. **1870** *Proc. Zool. Soc.* 705 (*title*) Notes on the habits of the *pampas woodpecker.

pampano, var. POMPANO.

'**pampas-,grass.** [f. PAMPA] The popular name of a gigantic grass, *Cortaderia selloana*, having ample silky panicles of silvery hue borne on stalks rising to the height of twelve or fourteen feet; a native of South America, whence it was introduced into Europe in 1843 as an ornament of lawns and shrubberies.

1850–1 Paxton *Flower Garden* I. 175. **1851** Lindley & Paxton *Paxton's Flower Garden* I. 175 This noble plant, now called the Pampas Grass, in consequence of its inhabiting the vast plains of S. America so named, has been introduced within a few years through Mr. Moore, of the Glasnevin Botanic Garden. **1858** Hogg *Veg. Kingd.* 821 The beautiful Pampas grass..throwing out leaves six or eight feet long. **1897** O. Stapf in *Gard. Chron.* Ser. III. XXII. 396 The occurrence of C. argentea in the pampas is by no means so general as to justify the name 'Pampas-grass', and the less so as the Cortaderia is much more common in the Andes, ascending there to high altitudes. **1900** L. H. Bailey *Cycl. Amer. Hort.* II. 703/1 The popular name 'Pampas Grass' is now unchangeable, but the plant does not grow on the pampas or vast grassy plains of South America, but in the mountains. **1934** C. Lambert *Music Ho!* II. 76 A Picasso reproduction is not considered 'amusing' unless flanked by pampas grass. **1950** G. Brenan *Face of Spain* iii. 56 Red branched tamarisks and tufts of pampas grass. **1973** F. A. Boddy *Foliage Plants* vii. 126 The pampas grass..makes such a splendid specimen plant in a lawn, with or without its great feathery plumes in the autumn.

pampaylyon, obs. form of PAMPILION.

pampean, pampæan (pæm'piːən, 'pæmpiːən), *a.* [f. PAMPA on analogy of *Hyblæan*, *Scyllæan*, *European*.

The pronunciation '*pampean* is etymologically incorrect, since *pampa* could not give a L. *pampēus*; the L. adj. would be *pampān-us* giving *pampan*, the Gr. παμπαί-ος giving *pampæan*, which, like *Euro'pean*, might be written *pam'pean*.]

Of or pertaining to the pampas.

1839 Darwin *Jrnl. Researches Voy. 'Beagle'* vii. (1860) 130 In the Pampæan deposit at the Bajada. **1846** —— *Geol. Obs. S. Amer.* iv. 76 The Pampean formation is highly interesting from its vast extent, its disputed origin, and from the number of extinct gigantic mammifers embedded in it. *Ibid.* 77 For convenience sake, I will call..the reddish argillaceous earth, Pampean mud. **1887** *Amer. Naturalist* XXI. 460 In the presence of various extinct forms..it agrees with the Pampean fauna of South America. **1892** Hudson *Nat. La Plata* 4 The humid, grassy, pampean country extends..halfway from the Atlantic Ocean..to the Andes.

pampelmousse (also **pample-**, **-mouse**): see POMPELMOOSE.

pampelyon, obs. form of PAMPILION.

pamper ('pæmpə(r)), *v.* Also 6 **pampyr, -ir, -re.** [Occurs *a* 1380; *forpampred* is in Chaucer's *Boethius c* 1374. It corresponds in form and sense with W. Flem. *pamperen* (De Bo), and in stem with the words mentioned under PAMP *v.*, of which it is in form the frequentative.]

1. *trans.* To cram with food; to over-indulge with rich food; to feed luxuriously. ***pamper up***: to feed up. *Obs.* except as included in b.

a **1380** *Prov. of S. Bernard* (Vern. MS. 304/3. l. 73) And þat is þi flesch,..þat þou pamprest and servest so. *c* **1440** *Jacob's Well* 157 A man, þat hyȝt Theodorus, in glotonye, euermore pamperyd his bely in exces of mete & of drynk. **1530** Palsgr. 652/1, I pampyr, as a man dothe that bringeth up a horse or any other beest whan he fedeth hym to make hym spedely fatte. **1577** B. Googe *Heresbach's Husb.* III. (1586) 120 b, Horse coursers..do feed them with sodden Rie, or beanmeale sod, pampering them up, that they may be the fairer to the eie. **1614** Bp. Hall *Contempl.*, *O.T.* v. ii, But now God will pamper their famine; and gives them..bread of angels. **1775** Johnson *Let. to Mrs. Thrale* 26 July, After dinner I went to Snowhill; there I was pampered, and had an uneasy night. **1820** Syd. Smith *Wks.* (1867) I. 291 Taxes on the sauce which pampers man's appetite. **1870** Emerson *Soc. & Solit.*, *Farming* Wks. (Bohn) III. 61 As he nursed his..turkeys on bread and milk, so he will pamper his peaches and grapes on the viands they like best.

b. To over-indulge (a person) in his tastes and likings generally; to bring up daintily; to indulge with what gratifies or delights the senses.

1530 Palsgr. 651/2, I pamper, I bring up dayntely, as a mother that loveth inordynately dothe her chylde. **1551** Robinson *More's Utop.* I. (1895) 47 Beynge deyntely and tenderly pampered vp in ydilnes and pleasure. **1615** Brathwait *Strappado*, etc. (1878) 338 Vaine is the flower, soone fading, soone forgot, which you do pamper to your ouerthrow. **1687** tr. *Sallust* (1692) 29 They purchase Pictures, Statues, Sculptures..to pamper their Eyes. **1829** Lytton *Disowned* xx, Petted and pampered from my childhood, I grew up with a profound belief in my own excellences. **1870** Emerson *Soc. & Solit.*, *Civiliz.* Wks. (Bohn) III. 10 Where the banana grows, the animal system is indolent and pampered.

c. *fig.* To over-indulge or 'feed' (any mental appetite, feeling, or the like).

1576 Fleming *Panopl. Epist.* 180 Pampering their minds with this imagination. **1628** Prynne *Love-lockes* 37 Which pampers the Vaine, and Sinfull humours, Lusts, and dispositions of our carnall Hearts. **1741** Fielding *Conversation* Wks. 1784 IX. 381 To pamper his own vanity at the price of another's shame. **1892** Zangwill *Bow Mystery* 112 She had stifled yet pampered her grief by working hard at it [a portrait] since his death.

† **2.** *intr.* To indulge oneself with food, to feed luxuriously. *Obs.*

1573 [see PAMPERING *ppl. a.*]. **1620** Rowlands *Night Raven* 19 To be at horse expence for oates and hay, Which idle stands and pampers in the stable. **1635** Quarles *Embl.* v. vii. 270 To day, we pamper with a full repast Of lavish mirth; at night, we weepe as fast.

† **3.** *trans.* (See quot. and cf. sense 1, quot. 1577).

1611 Cotgr., *Mangonisme*, the craft of pampering, trimming, or setting out of saleable things. *Ibid.*, *Mangonner* to pamper, trimme, sleeke, or set out vnto the eye sale things.

Hence '**pamperdom** (*nonce-wd.*), pampered condition, state of luxury; '**pamperer**, one who or that which pampers; '**pamperize** *v.* (*nonce-wd.*), to pamper.

1847 in *J. Brown's Horæ Subs.* (1882) 410 When from such pamperdom exiled. **1775** Ash, *Pamperer*,..one that pampers. **1781** Cowper *Conversat.* 48 A plea..For making speech the pamperer of lust. *a* **1845** Syd. Smith (Worcester), Pamperize.

pampered ('pæmpəd), *ppl. a.* [f. PAMPER *v.* + -ED[1].] Over-fed (*obs.*); luxuriously fed; over-indulged, spoiled by luxury: see the verb.

a **1529** Skelton *Vppon Deedmans Hed* 25 For all oure pamperde paunchys, Ther may no fraunchys..Redeme vs from this. **1576** Gascoigne *Steele Gl.* 366 Their stables ful yfraught with pampred Iades. **1641** Milton *Ch. Govt.* I. Wks. (1851) 31 The knotty Africanisms, the pamper'd metafors; the intricat, and involv'd sentences of the Fathers. **1697** Dryden *Virg. Georg.* III. 323 The pamper'd Colt will discipline disdain. **1759** Johnson *Idler* No. 52 ⁋2 A pampered body will darken the mind. **1805** *Med. Jrnl.* XIV.

276 A pampered and consequently distempered imagination. **1890** W. A. WALLACE *Only a Sister* 69 The spoilt and pampered children of the present day.

Hence ˈ**pamperedness**, pampered condition.

a **1618** SYLVESTER *Mayden's Blush* 1002 The fruits.. Of wanton Pride, of wastefull Pamprednesse. **1748** RICHARDSON *Clarissa* (1811) II. xxxvii. 267 No crosses, no vexations, but what we gave ourselves from the pamperedness, as I may call it, of our own wills.

ˈ**pampering**, *vbl. sb.* [f. as prec. + -ING[1].] The action of the vb. PAMPER; luxurious feeding; over-indulgence.

1526 *Pilgr. Perf.* (W. de W. 1531) 137 Pamperyng or ouermoche cherysshyng of our bodyes. **1555** W. WATREMAN *Fardle Facions* II. viii. 183 Not in the.. pamperinges of the bealy. **1623–4** MIDDLETON & ROWLEY *Sp. Gipsy* IV. iii, Can .. taffeta girls look plump without pampering? **1844** LEVER *T. Burke* xxxi. (1857) 299 The animal fresh from long pampering, sprang forward madly.

ˈ**pampering**, *ppl. a.* [f. as prec. + -ING[2].] That pampers: see the verb.

1573 L. LLOYD *Marrow of Hist.* (1653) 100 A heap of vices wait on pampering Princes. **1699** POMFRET *Choice* 47 Pamp'ring food Creates diseases and inflames the blood. **1742** SHENSTONE *Schoolmistr.* 301 With pamp'ring look draw little eyes aside.

‖**pampero** (pamˈpero). [Sp. *pampero*, f. Peruv. *pampa* + suffix *-ero*:—L. *-arius*.] A piercing cold wind which blows from the Andes across the S. American pampas to the Atlantic.

1818 *Amer. St. Papers, For. Rel.* (1834) IV. 277 (Stanf.) The keen blasts called the pamperos sweep over the houseless and unsheltered plain. **1826** SIR F. B. HEAD *Journ. Pampas* 9 The pampero or south-west wind, which, generated by the cold air of the Andes, rushes over these vast plains.

attrib. **1892** W. H. HUDSON *Nat. La Plata* 132 Some-times flying like thistledowns before the great pampero wind.

pampestrie, obs. corrupt form of PALMISTRY.

pamphagous (ˈpæmfəgəs), *a. rare.* [f. Gr. παμφάγος all-devouring (f. παμ-, παν- all + -φαγος eating) + -OUS.] All-devouring, omnivorous.

1702 C. MATHER *Magn. Chr.* II. (1852) App. 194 He eat with such a pamphagous fury as to cram himself with.. eighteen biskets at one stolen meal. (In some modern Dicts.)

pampharmacon, variant of PANPHARMACON.

†ˈ**pamphelet.** *Obs. rare*⁻¹. [Origin obscure: perhaps a cant term formed from Gr. πάμφιλος beloved of all, with dim. ending. Sibbald *Gloss.* compared obs. Du. or Fl. *pampoelie* 'mulier crassa'.] A courtesan, a wench.

1500–20 DUNBAR *Poems* lv. 14 Dame Venus fyre sa hard tham sted, Thai brak vp durris, and raeff vp lockis, To get ane pamphelet on ane pled.

†ˈ**pamphil.** *Obs. rare.* [Cf. next.] A memorandum or note.

1571 SIR T. SMITH *Let. to Ld. Burleigh* 3 Mar. in Digges *Compl. Ambass.* (1655) 192 The next day.. Mr. de Foix came to us and brought us a draught of the whole League in French,.. we perused it with our Pamphils, as Mr. Hall termeth them, *schediæ* or *adversaria*..(some other tho will have them called pieces, as some Frenchmen do name them).

pamphlet (ˈpæmflɪt), *sb.* Forms: [4 *panfletus*], 4–7 **pamflet**, (6 **pamflete**, **-flett(e**, 5 **pamfilet**, **pampelet**, **paunflet**, **plaun-**); 6– **pamphlet**, (6 **pamphelet**, 7 **-lett(e)**, **pamphlete**, **-lette**, **pampfelette**. [Appears in 14th c. in Anglo-Latin (*panfletus*), English (*pamflet*, 15th c. *pamfilet*, *paunflet*); app. a generalized use of *Pamphilet* or *Panflet*, a familiar name of the 12th c. Latin amatory poem or comedy called *Pamphilus, seu de Amore* (in OF. *Pamphilet*, MDu. *Panflet*), a highly popular opuscule in the 13th c. Cf. the familiar appellations of other small works similarly formed with dim. *-et*, e.g. *Catonet* the Distichs of (pseudo-) Cato, *Esopet*, the Fables of Æsop, etc. (See note below.) Hence in 17–18th c. adopted in French and other langs.]

1. A small treatise occupying fewer pages or sheets than would make a book, composed and (*a*) written, or (*b*) (since *c* 1500) printed, and issued as a separate work; always (at least in later use) unbound, with or without paper covers.

In a general sense used irrespective of subject (applied e.g. in 1495, to a codicil to a will, of only about 170 words), and in 17th c. including issues of single plays, romances, poems, novelettes, newspapers, news-letters, and other periodicals; still sometimes applied to chap-books, and the like; but not now usually to anything of purely literary character, or of religious nature, even though issued 'in pamphlet form'.

(*a*) [**1344** R. DE BURY *Philobiblon* viii, Sed revera libros non libras maluimus, codicesque plus dileximus quam florenos, ac panfletos exiguos incrassatis prætulimus palefridis.] **1387–8** T. USK *Test. Love* III. ix. (Skeat) I. 54 Christe.. graunte of thy goodnes to euery maner reder, full vnderstanding in this leud pamflet to haue. *c* **1412** HOCCLEVE *De Reg. Princ.* 2060 þogh þat þis pamfilet Non ordre holdē, ne in him include. *c* **1430** LYDG. *Min. Poems* (Percy Soc.) 180 My purpose, Out of the Frenssh a tale to translate, Whiche in a paunflet I redde and saw but late. **1490** CAXTON *Eneydos* Prol. 3 Sittyng in my studye where as laye many dyuerse paunflettis and bookys. **1495** *Test. Ebor.* IV. 26 And this pampelet I will stand as parcell of my forsaid will.

(*b*) **1496** *Fysshynge with Angle* (1883) 37 That this present treatyse sholde not come to the hondys of eche ydle persone whyche wolde desire it, yf it were enpryntyd allone by itself & put in a lytyll plaunflet, therfore I haue compylyd it in a greter volume of dyuerse bokys. **1523** SKELTON *Garl. Laurel* 1191 And of Soueraynte a noble pamphelet. *a* **1548** HALL *Chron., Edw. V.* 2 As I my selfe that wrote this pamphlet [Chronicle of Edw. V] truly knewe. **1552** ASCHAM *Let. to Astely* Wks. (1761) 5 Syr Thomas More in that pamphlet of Richard the thyrd, doth in.. these pointes so content all men. **1559** *Mirr. Mag.* (1563) H viij, I have recounted thus much.. which if it should haue bene spoken in hys tragedye would rather haue made a volume than a Pamphlete. **1577** R. WILLES *Eden's Decades* Epist. 7 R. Eden.. translated.. some other prety pamflettes concernyng the Spanyardes and Portugalles voiages. **1582** STANYHURST *Æneis* (Arb.) Ded. 4 Askam,.. in his goulden pamphlet, intituled thee Schoolemayster. **1623** GOUGE *Serm. Extent God's Provid.* Ded., In regard of the smalnesse of it, it [this Sermon] is indeed but as a little Pamphlet. **1681** LUTTRELL *Brief Rel.* (1857) I. 119 The publisher of the Observator, Heraclitus Ridens, and the Loyall Protestant domestick Intelligence (three pamphlets that come out weekly). **1778** JOHNSON 25 Apr. in *Boswell*, A few sheets of poetry unbound are a pamphlet as much as a few sheets of prose.

2. More specifically, a treatise of the size and form above described on some subject or question of current or temporary interest, personal, social, political, ecclesiastical, or controversial, on which the writer desires to appeal to the public.

This is merely a consequential specialization, arising from the fact that works of this kind are those for which the pamphlet form is now mainly employed.

1592 G. HARVEY *3rd Lett.* in *Shaks. Allusion Bks.* I. (1874) 149 Were it not more for other,.. I would be the first, that should cancell this impertinent Pamflet. **1606** CHAPMAN *Gentleman Usher* Plays 1873 I. 294 Some words, pickt out of Proclamations Or great mens Speeches; or well-selling Pamphlets. **1641** MILTON *Ch. Govt.* i. Wks. (1851) 99 These wretched projectors of ours that bescrawl their Pamflets every day with new formes of government for our Church. **1683** CROWNE *City Politiques* IV. i, As paper in Holland passes for money, Pamphlets with us pass for religion and policy. **1714** SWIFT *Pres. St. Affairs* Wks. 1755 II. I. 203 Systems that.. are supplies for pamphlets in the present age, and may probably furnish materials for memoirs and histories in the next. **1791** MACKINTOSH *Vind. Gallicæ* Wks. 1846 III. 20 Pamphlet succeeded pamphlet, surpassing each other in boldness and elevation. **1792** BURKE *Corr.* (1844) III. 428 Grattan's incomparable speech.. ought to make a little separate pamphlet. **1824** J. JOHNSON *Typogr.* II. xiv. 490 When pamphlets and other works of temporary and urgent nature are required. **1841** D'ISRAELI *Amen. Lit.* (1867) 687 The age of Charles the First may be characterised as the age of pamphlets. **1874** GREEN *Short Hist.* vii. §5 The brief form of these novelettes soon led to the appearance of the 'pamphlet'; and a new world of readers was seen in the rapidity with which the stories or scurrilous libels which passed under this name were issued.

3. *attrib.* and *Comb.* **a.** *attrib.*

1646 SIR T. BROWNE *Pseud. Ep.* 34 We are to cast a wary eye on those diminutive, and pamphlet Treaties dayly published among us. **1715** M. DAVIES *Athen. Brit.* I. 4 Tracts.. often since publish'd separately, in Pamphlet-Forms, as well as mostly upon Pamphlet-Subjects. **1730** FIELDING *Author's Farce* III. i, The scribbler in a pamphlet war. **1899** *Daily News* 13 June 8/3 An Introductory Letter .. which occupies sixty-nine pages, and is in pamphlet form, and pamphlet spirit.

b. *Comb.*, as ***pamphlet-book***, ***-history***, ***-octavo***, ***-shop***, ***-stall***, ***-title***, ***-writer***, ***-writing***; ***pamphlet-sized*** adj.; ***pamphlet-wise*** adv.

1716 M. DAVIES *Athen. Brit.* II. 86 Spending about six Years more in composing such *Pamphlet-Books. **1715** *Ibid.* I. 5 The first Treatise.. publish'd.. at Milan, 1607, in a small *Pamphlet-Octavo. **1750** *Let. to A. Johnson* 3 Nor have I omitted to call at every skulking *Pamphlet-shop. **1778** MISS BURNEY *Evelina* (1791) II. xxv. 153 Mrs. Selwyn had business at a pamphlet-shop. **1716** M. DAVIES *Athen. Brit.* II. 1 Several *Pamphlet-siz'd Writings. *c* **1720** *Ibid.* VI. *Conclus. Diss. Physick* 32 He deals chiefly.. with the Librarians of Morefields, *Pamphlet-stawls of old Books, and poor Ushers and Head-Form-Boys. **1613** BEAUM. & FL. *Honest Man's Fort.* III. ii, Have copies of it posted on posts, Like *pamphlet-titles, that sue to be sold. **1716** M. DAVIES *Athen. Brit.* II. 30 Some of King Henry the 8th's, and Queen Anne Bolen's reciprocal Letters, were printed *Pamphlet-wise, about two or three Years ago. **1735** BOLINGBROKE *On Parties* Ded. 28 To follow the generous and equitable Advice of the *Pamphlet-writer. **1751** *Pope's Dunciad* II. 314 *note*, Not a Pension at Court, nor Preferment in the Church,.. was bestowed on any man distinguished for his Learning separately from Party merit, or *Pamphlet writing.

Hence (*nonce-wds.*) ˈ**pamphletage**, the aggregate of pamphlets, pamphlets collectively; **pampheˈtette**, a small pamphlet; ˈ**pamphletful**, as much as a pamphlet will contain; **pamˈphletic**, **-ical** *adjs.*, pertaining to or of the nature of a pamphlet; ˈ**pamphletism**, an expression or manner of speech characteristic of pamphlets; ˈ**pamphletize** *v.*, *intr.* to write a pamphlet or pamphlets; *trans.* to write a pamphlet upon; ˈ**pamphletless** *a.*, without a pamphlet.

1896 A. LANG in *Longm. Mag.* July 110 The *pamphletage of the subject must be vast. **1882** RUSSELL *Hesperothen* I. 64 In a small *pamphletette from Robinson's 'Epitome..', there is a very pleasant account of some of the treasures. **1876** *N. Amer. Rev.* CXXIII. 426 It included in ten words a *pamphletful of political insight. **1715** M. DAVIES *Athen. Brit.* I. Pref. 8 Expressing the *Pamphletick Character, and the Pseudonymous Inconsiderableness of those Libelling Insults. *Ibid.* 10 Of the same Pamphletick genuineness is St. Barnaby's Epistle. **1654** GAYTON *Pleas. Notes* III. viii. 122 Severall Editions of some small *Pamphleticall labors of his. **1716** M. DAVIES *Athen. Brit.* II. To Rdr. 4 Those Libel-Granado's and Dragooning *Pamphletisms. **1652** GAULE *Magastrom.* To Rdrs., Books of late.. crowded in amongst us (some in their *pampheletizing edition, some in their voluminous translation). **1828** *Blackw. Mag.* XXIV. 21 Our Irish preacher.. did not intend to preach, but merely to pamphletize. **1837** MARRYAT in *New Monthly Mag.* LI. 175 Martin.. has obtained a great celebrity in France... He is lithographed, pamphletized [etc.]. *a* **1845** SYD. SMITH *Sir G. C. Lewis in Hades*, For ever and ever bookless, essayless, *pamphletless, grammarless.

[*Note.* The amatory poem of Pamphilus appears as *Panflet* in the Middle Dutch *Floris & Blaunchefleur* of Diderik van Assenede (*c* 1250) I. 333, where it is said of the hero and heroine 'Ende men se oec te lesene sette In Juvenale ende in Panflette, Ende in Ovidio de Arte Amandi' (And they were set also to read In Juvenal and in Panflet, And in Ovid on the Art of Loving). In French, *Pamphilet* appears in the inventory of the Library of the Louvre (Chas. V, and Chas. VI) dispersed by John, Duke of Bedford (L. Delisle *Cabinet des Manuscrits* III. 160). As to its popularity, the students of the University of Paris were rebuked because they preferred this erotic production to more edifying reading. Pamphilus was also well known in England, and is twice quoted or referred to by Chaucer; also by Gower *Mirour* 14449 (where see Editor's note). To connect the work with our 'pamphlet', we have to suppose that here also, as in France and the Low Countries, it was familiarly termed *Pamphilet* or *Panflet*, and that this name was in course of time extended to other opuscula produced or circulated 'in pamphlet form', i.e. as small detached works. This transference of sense must have been complete before 1340, when the name was applied in *Philobiblon* to what were evidently serious treatises, and before Thomas Usk, Hoccleve, and Lydgate applied it to single works of their own.]

ˈ**pamphlet**, *v.* ? *Obs.* [f. prec. sb.] **a.** *intr.* To write a pamphlet or pamphlets. **b.** *trans.* To report or describe in a pamphlet. Chiefly in ˈ**pamphleting** *vbl. sb.* and *ppl. a.*

1592 G. HARVEY *Four Lett.* ii, Who like Elderton for Ballating: Greene for pamphletting: both, for goodfellowship, and bad conditions? **1592** NASHE *P. Penilesse* Ep. to Printer, To the Ghost of Robert Greene, telling him, what a coyle there is with pamphleting on him after his death. **1613** JACKSON *Creed* II. xix. §11. 370 A common place trodden almost bare by the English pamphleting Papist. **1716** M. DAVIES *Athen. Brit.* II. 42 This Discourse being Pamphleted about, to Court, City, and Country. *Ibid.* 217 He bravely underwent above fourteen several Tryals and Examinations,.. besides many other Conferences, which were not written or pamphleted.

pamphletary (ˈpæmflɪtərɪ), *a.* [f. PAMPHLET *sb.* + -ARY[1].] Pertaining or relating to pamphlets; of the nature of a pamphlet.

1600 NASHE *Summers Last Will* in Hazl. *Dodsley* VIII. 73 For baldness a bald ass, I have forgot, Patch'd up a pamphletary periwig. **1815** *Paris Chit-Chat* (1816) I. 205 The pamphletary fever, which has spread during a few months past. **1878** BAYNE *Purit. Rev.* Pref. 6 The Pamphletary catacombs of the British Museum.

pamphleteer (pæmflɪˈtɪə(r)), *sb.* Also 7 **-etteer**, **-etere**, **etier**, 7–8 **-ettier**. [f. PAMPHLET *sb.* + -EER[1].] A writer of pamphlets; the author of a pamphlet. (Often contemptuous.)

1642 *Vind. King* 13 Seditious Preachers and Pamphletteers. **1642** J. TAYLOR (Water P.) *Seasonable Lect.* title-p., Henry Walker,.. a late Pamphletere, and now a double diligent Preacher. **1648** HEYLIN *Relat. & Observ.* I. App. 12 Though you doe not speak plaine, your Pamphlettiers doe. **1771** *Junius Lett.* liv. 288 That miserable pamphleteer.. reduced his argument.. to something like.. a syllogism. **1847** TENNYSON *Princ.* Concl. 89 A patron of some thirty charities, A pamphleteer on guano and on grain. **1874** GREEN *Short Hist.* iii. §1. 117 The pungent pen of the pamphleteer played its part in rousing the spirit of the nation.

pampheˈteer, *v.* [f. prec. sb.] **a.** *intr.* To write and issue pamphlets. Also, to engage in propaganda involving the issue or distribution of pamphlets. Also *fig.* Chiefly in **pamphleˈteering** *vbl. sb.* and *ppl. a.*

1698 E. WARD *Trip to Jamaica* 3 The condition of an author is much like that of a strumpet... If the reason be requir'd Why we betake our selves to so scandalous a profession as whoring or pamphleteering, the same excusive answer will serve us both. **1715** M. DAVIES *Athen. Brit.* I. Pref. 2 The Jesuitical Subornation of a Foot-Soldier's Pamphleteering against a Protestant Vicar. **1763** THACHER in *J. Adams' Diary* 5 Feb., I pamphleteer for him again? No! I'll pamphleteer against him. **1815** *Edin. Rev.* XXV. 188 Vulgar slander.. eked out by pamphleteering declamation. **1883** BRODRICK in *19th Cent.* 920 The coarse pamphleteering literature of which Swift and Junius produced the choicest specimens. **1897** *Granta* 24 Apr. 264/2 The result.. will be a compromise, which will permanently injure that future of women's education, which has been endangered enough already by the impatient folly of those who try to do a century's work in a week of garrulity and pamphleteering. **1930** T. S. ELIOT tr. *St.-J. Perse's Anabasis* 39 Let me go alone with the airs of the night, among the pamphleteering Princes. **1938** E. WILSON *Triple Thinkers* 284 Long-range literature attempts to sum up wide areas and long periods of human experience... Short-range literature preaches and pamphleteers with the view to an immediate affect. **1943** *Sun* (Baltimore) 22 June 1/4 OWI officials acknowledged that they have 'pamphleteered' several times in the past. **1976** *Time* 27 Dec. 5/1 Since when is pamphleteering per se bad manners or bad art in theatre or film, with such historic examples as Ibsen, Shaw, Eisenstein and Odets?

b. *trans.* To influence or persuade by means of pamphlets. *rare.*

1944 G. B. Shaw *Everybody's Pol. What's What?* iii. 29 The peasants and peasant soldiers, neither of them Communists, but all more or less talked and pamphleteered and journalized into believing that the Bolsheviks were the boys to give them land and peace.

† **ˈpamphleter.** *Obs.* Also 7 **-etter.** [f. PAMPHLET + -ER[1].] A writer of a pamphlet, a PAMPHLETEER.

1581 Nowell & Day in *Confer.* I. (1584) E iv, Here saith one of the Pamphleters, silence was the answere. **1592** G. Harvey *Pierce's Super.* (1593) 181, I have seldom..tasted a more unsavory slaumpaump of wordes and sentences in any shittish Pamfleter. **1679** J. Smith *Narr. Pop. Plot* 17 Calling those Pamphletters to a further Account.

pamphobia, variant of PANOPHOBIA.

1890 in Billings *Nat. Med. Dict.* **1900** in Gould *Dict. Med. Biol.*

pamphract (ˈpæmfrækt), *a. rare.* [f. Gr. παμ-, PAM- + φρακτός fenced, protected.] Completely covered or protected, as with a coat of mail.

In recent Dicts.

† **pamˈphysic**, *a. Obs. nonce-wd.* [f. Gr. παμ- PAM- + φυσικός natural, f. φύσις nature.] Of or concerning all nature.

1610 B. Jonson *Alch.* II. v, Is..Spagirica, Or the pamphysick, or panarchick knowledge, A heathen language?

pamphysical (pæmˈfɪzɪkəl), *a. rare.* [f. as prec. + -AL[1].] Considering material nature as the source of all phenomena.

1885 J. Martineau *Types Eth. The.* I. Introd. 19 The extreme points between which philosophy has oscillated.. are the pantheistic and (if I may invent a phrase) the pamphysical poles of doctrine. *Ibid.* II. Introd. 3 It may be regarded as determined into existence either from God, or from Nature...if from Nature, we take the pamphysical [track], within sight of Comte.

So **pamphysicism** (pæmˈfɪzɪsɪz(ə)m), the pamphysical doctrine or theory.

1895 Fairbairn *Catholicism* viii. (1899) 360 Under the impulse given to pamphysicism by evolution, agnosticism became belligerent and constructive.

† **pampilion.** *Obs.* Also 5 **pampaylyone,** 6 **-pelyon, -ion, -pilioun, -ian, -pillion, -eoun, -pyllon, pawmpilyon.** [Origin unknown.

According to quot. 1619 (supported by 1503, 1532) the name of a fur-bearing animal. For sense 2, connexion has been suggested with Pampellone, a town of France near Alby, and Pampeluna in Spain: cf. OF. *pampelune* 'étoffe fabriquée à Pampelune' (Godef.).]

1. A kind of fur used in the 15th and 16th centuries for trimming.

1487 (in Fairholt (ed. Dillon) *Costume* Gloss. s.v.), Pampaylyones of bozy. **1502** *Priv. Purse Exp. Eliz. York* (1830) 33 A gowne of cloth of gold furred with pawmpilyon. **1503** *Ibid.* 189 Two skynnes of pampelyon for the cuffes of the same gowne. **1505** *Acc. Ld. High Treas. Scot.* III. 43 Item, for xj skinnis of pampilioun to fill furth the lynyng of the samyn [goun]. **1532** *Privy Purse Exp. Hen. VIII*, For xxv dousin skynns of fyne pawmpelion, lx li. **1619** Middleton *Love & Antiq.* Wks. (ed. Bullen) VII. 331 Those beasts bearing fur... The ounce,..ginnet, pampilion.

2. A coarse woollen fabric of rough surface.

1567 in Swayne *Sarum Church-w. Acc.* (1896) 113, ij yerdes of Jene fustyan and ij yerdes of pampyllon to cast y[e] [organ] pypes vppon, ijs. vjd. **1580** Hollyband *Treas. Fr. Tong, Vn habillement de Bureau, ou autre drap meslangé de petit pris, dont les serfs & menu peuple souloit estre accoustré,* a coate of chaungeable colours for seruauntes, slighte rugge, or pampilion. **1597–8** Bp. Hall *Sat.* IV. ii. 19 Lolioes sidecote is rough Pampilian Guilded with drops that downe the bosome ran.

pampinary (ˈpæmpɪnərɪ), *a. rare.* [ad. L. *pampinārius*, f. *pampinus* vine-shoot, vine-tendril.] Pertaining to vine-tendrils or vine-shoots.

c **1420** *Pallad. on Husb.* III. 114 The squorges hie & graffes from the folde,..& scions pampinari. *Ibid.* 320 The secunde yer to kitte of al yfere, That they or dede or pampinary, were.

b. *Biol.* 'Of or pertaining to a young shoot' (Gould *Dict. Med. Biol.* 1900).

† **pampiˈnation.** *Obs. rare.* [ad. L. *pampinātiōn-em*, n. of action f. *pampināre*, f. *pampinus*: see prec.] The pruning or trimming of vines.

1398 Trevisa *Barth. De P.R.* XVII. clxxvii[i]. (MS. Bodl.) lf. 234/2 Also vines..nedeþ pampynacion, þat is to menynge pullinge awey of superfluite of leues. *c* **1420** *Pallad. on Husb.* VI. 22 This mone is ek for pampinacioun Conuenient—void leves puld to be. **1656** in Blount *Glossogr.* **1745** tr. *Columella's Husb. & Bk. Trees* IV. vi, All superfluities may be plucked off them by frequent pampination.

So † **ˈpampinate**, † **ˈpampine** *vbs. Obs.* [L. *pampināre*], *trans.* to prune or trim (a vine).

c **1420** *Pallad. on Husb.* x. 198 A vyne whos fruyt humour wol putrifie, Pampyned is to be by euery side. **1745** tr. *Columella's Husb. & Bk. Trees* IV. xxviii, The time for pampinating or pulling off the superfluous twigs and leaves.

† **ˈpamping.** *Obs.* [? for *pampin(e*, ad. L. *pampin-us.*] A tendril or young shoot of a vine. In quot. *attrib.* or *appositive.*

1607 Heywood *Fair Maid Exch.* Prol., Meane while shore up our tender pamping twig That yet on humble ground doth lowely lie.

pampiniform (pæmˈpɪnɪfɔːm), *a. Anat.* [f. L. *pampin-us* + -(I)FORM, in mod.F. *pampiniforme.*] Curled like a vine-tendril; applied *esp.* to a convoluted plexus of veins proceeding from the testis or ovary (also called *spermatic* or *ovarian plexus*).

1668 Culpepper & Cole *Barthol. Anat.* I. xxi. 53 This Intertexture of Veins and Arteries..is by some called Corpus varicosum, pampiniform, Pyramidal. **1836–9** Todd *Cycl. Anat.* II. 704/1 The corresponding vein..forming the pampiniform plexus. **1899** *Allbutt's Syst. Med.* VI. 233 The veins in which retrograde embolism..has been found are the hepatic, the renal, the mesenteric, the pampiniform plexus.

† **pampiˈnose**, *a. Obs. rare*[−1]. [ad. L. *pampinōsus*, f. *pampinus* vine-shoot: see -OSE.] Profuse of twigs and leaves (said of untrimmed vines).

c **1420** *Pallad. on Husb.* Tab. 507 Vynys, pampynose and not fructuose, to remedie.

† **pamˈpinulate**, *v. Obs. nonce-wd.* [f. L. type **pampinulātus*, f. **pampinul-us*, dim. of *pampinus*: see PAMPINARY.] *trans.* To furnish or deck with minute curling or convoluted threads.

1592 R. D. *Hypnerotomachia* 99 Hir starrie forehead pampynulated with threds of gold.

pampir, obs. form of PAMPER.

‖ **pamplegia** (pæmˈpliːdʒɪə). *Path.* Also **pan-**, and in Eng. form **pamplegy**. [mod.L., f. PAM- + Gr. πληγή stroke.] General paralysis.

1842 Dunglison *Med. Lex.*, *Pamplegia* [also *Panplegia*], general paralysis. Palsy of the body. **1893** in *Syd. Soc. Lex.*

pamplemousse, etc., variants of POMPELMOOSE.

pampootie (pæmˈpuːtɪ). *local Irish.* Also **pampooter, pampootee.** [Said in Folk-Lore Journal (1884) II. 261, to have been introduced some two hundred or more years ago by an East Indian ship-captain who settled on the South Isle of Aran: possibly a popular corruption of some form of PAPOOSH, *papouche*, or Sp. *babucha*; cf. *papouches, pampooties.*]

A kind of slipper or sandal of undressed cow-skin sewn together and tied across the instep. Used in the Isles of Aran off the west coast of Ireland.

1881 *Harper's Mag.* 510 Sandals, called pampootees, made of untanned cowhide, universally worn by the inhabitants of the Arran islands. **1884** *Folk-Lore Jrnl.* II. 261 The Aranites and inhabitants of some of the other Galway islands wear pampooters. **1892** Emily Lawless *Grania* I. ii. 13 Twisting her small pampootie-clad feet round a rope.

‖ **pampre** (‖ pɑ̃pr, ˈpæmpə(r)). Chiefly *Arch.* [a. F. *pampre*:—L. *pampinus*: see PAMPINARY.] An ornament or decoration representing vine-leaves and grape-clusters.

1842–76 Gwilt *Archit.* (ed. 7) Gloss., *Pampre* (Fr.). **1886** Sheldon tr. *Flaubert's Salammbo* xv. 413 A tunic of violet, brocaded with golden pampre.

pamprodactylous (pæmprəʊˈdæktɪləs), *a. Ornith.* [f. Gr. παμ-, PAM- all + πρό before + δάκτυλ-ος finger or toe + -OUS.] Having all the toes pointing forwards, as the colies (*Pamprodactylæ* of Murie), and a few other birds.

1899 *Camb. Nat. Hist.* IX. 10 Certain Swifts, and to a less degree some Nightjars, have the whole number [of toes] permanently pointing to the front (pamprodactylous).

pampsychism (and derivs.): see PANPSYCHISM.

pampyllon, pampyr, obs. forms of PAMPILION, PAMPER.

pan (pæn), *sb.*[1] Forms: 1–7 panne, (1 pǫnne, 4–5 ponne), 4– pan, (5 pon, 6 pane). [OE. *panne*, *pǫnne* wk. fem. = OLG. *panna* (OFris., MLG., LG., MDu. *panne*, Du. *pan*), OHG. *phanna*, *pfanna* (MHG., Ger. *pfanne*); cf. Icel. *panna* (late 14th c.), Sw. *panna*, Da. *pande*, prob. from LG.; not found in Gothic. From its occurrence in OE. as well as in Continental WGer., and its having in OHG. *pf* for *p*, the word was evidently Com. WGer. in 4th or 5th c., but its ulterior history and origin are uncertain.

Some think it a (prehistoric) adaptation of L. *patina*, *patena*, in same sense (as **pat'na*, **padna*, *panna*), but there are obvious difficulties. A med. (Ger.) L. *panna* occurs in 12th c. (Du Cange), but this may be the German word, or the result of associating it with L. *patina*. The Ir. *panna* was from med.L. or Eng. The Lith. *pana* and Slavonic forms are admittedly from Ger.]

1. A vessel, of metal or earthenware, for domestic uses, usually broad and shallow, and often open. (Often in pl. in conjunction with *pots.*)

c **897** K. Ælfred *Gregory's Past. C.* xxi. 165 Mid ðisse pannan hierstinge wæs Paulus onbærned. *c* **1000** Ælfric *Voc.* in Wr.-Wülcker 123/6 *Patella*, panne. *a* **1100** *Gerefa* in *Anglia* IX. 264 Pannan, crocca, brandiren. **13..** *K. Alis.* 4939 Hy nymeth the fyssh, and eteth it thanne, Withouten fyre, withouten panne. *c* **1375** *Sc. Leg. Saints* xxxii. (*Justin*) 731 A gret pane gert brocht be sowne. *Ibid.* xlvi. (*Anastace*) 181 Pottis or pannis vald he hynt in armys & kise. *c* **1386** Chaucer *Reeve's T.* 24 With hire he yaf ful many a panne of bras. *c* **1420** *Pallad. on Husb.* I. 909 So hit be thicke and pourid in a ponne. *a* **1529** Skelton *Elynour Rummynge* 317 A good brasse pan. **1543** *Nottingham Rec.* III. 398, ij. sawcers, one pane, one candylstyke. **1552** Huloet, Panne for coales, *larcus.* Panne to bake in, *testus.* **1596** Dalrymple tr. *Leslie's Hist. Scot.* I. 94 To karie pottis, panis, and vthir kitchine veshels. **1646** B. Ryves *Mercur. Rust.* 164 They steale his Pots, Pannes and Kettles. **1718** Mrs. M. Eales *Receipts* 3 Lay a thin Strainer in a flat earthen Pan. *c* **1802** Mar. Edgeworth *Ennui* xv, Let him get home and to bed: I'll run and warm it with the pan myself. **1871** M. Legrand *Cambr. Freshm.* iii. 47 They sent a porter off for the hot-water pans—so often forgotten until applied for.

b. With defining words, indicating purpose, etc., e.g. *bed-pan, bread-pan, frying-pan, milk-pan, saucepan, stew-pan, warming-pan*: see these.

c. As part of any apparatus esp. a lavatory.

1611 Cotgr., *Bassin à selle percée*, the pan of a close stoole. *Ibid.*, *Le bassinet d'un reschaut*, the pan of a chafing dish. *a* **1693** *Urquhart's Rabelais* III. xxii. 183. **1842** Parnell *Chem. Anal.* (1845) 15 With the weights in the opposite pan of the balance. **1869** E. A. Parkes *Pract. Hygiene* (ed. 3) 4 More water must be used for thoroughly flushing the pan and soil-pipe. **1919** R. Fry *Let.* May (1972) II. 451 A real Victorian W.C. with a pull up plug... But..there's no sham Chinese landscape in the pan. **1961** Partridge *Dict. Slang.* Suppl. 1212/2 *Down the pan*... A Cockney equivalent of *down the drain*, ruined with no chances left. **1972** J. Wainwright *Requiem for Loser* iv. 75 A race from one shithouse to the next. A lifetime of sitting on the pan. **1974** *Listener* 14 Mar. 347/3 'It's just money down the pan,' said one pensioner.

d. 'Originally the pan or bowl for the oil-lights in a church: afterwards applied to the frame for candles' (Gloss.). *Sc.*

1554 *Burgh Rec. Edinb.* (Rec. Soc.) II. 345 Item, for xiiij faddome of corde to hing the pan in the meids of the kirk, iiijs. iiijd. **1556** *Ibid.* 247 The sowme of xxs. for x half pund wecht candill furnist be tham to the pane on the hie altar.

e. Phrases. ***(to leap, fall) out of the pan into the fire***, to escape from one evil only to fall into a greater one: cf. FRYING-PAN 1 b; ***to savour of the pan***, to betray its origin; ***to turn the cat in the pan***: see CAT *sb.* 12; ***on the pan*** (U.S.), under reprimand or adverse criticism (said of a person).

c **1380** Wyclif *Sel. Wks.* III. 332 Many men of lawe..bi here suteltes turnen þe cat in þe panne. **1554** Ridley in *Bradford's Writ.* (Parker Soc.) II. 160 A work of Æneas Sylvius,..In the which..there be many things that savoureth of the pan. **1596** Spenser *State Irel.* Wks. (Globe) 659/1 This..were but to leape out of the pann into the fire. **1645** Quarles *Sol. Recant.* ii. 60 Those Bellowes mount the blaze the higher, Thou leap'st but from the Pan into the fire. **1923** H. C. Witwer *Fighting Blood* v. 140 Even when the newspapers puts him on the pan..the safe-playing, money-grabbing middleweight king just laughs at us. **1937** C. Boothe *Women* I. i. 9 *Edith.* I'll bet you had me on the pan. *Sylvia.* I never say behind my friends' backs what I won't say to their faces. I said you ought to diet. **1939** A. Aylesworth in *Better English* May 13/1 Five college professors sitting around a table... A sixth professor who wasn't there because he had snagged a job at a better institution, was on the pan. MacSnuft leaned across at the rest of us and contributed: 'He's an ignoramus!' **1941** J. Smiley *Hash House Lingo* 41 *On the pan*, being reprimanded.

f. A metal drum in a West Indian steel band. Also, steel-band music and the way of life associated with it.

1955 *New Commonwealth* 28 Nov. (Suppl.) p. xix/1 To make a 'pan' the end of a metal oil drum is cut off and the bottom of the circular pan so formed is shaped into sections by beating and chiselling. **1958** J. P. Hickerton *Caribbean Kallaloo* i. 15 The steel bands have reached a high pitch of virtuosity... 'Beating the pan' is a West Indian passion, and we once discovered an old man sitting outside our back gate beating out a rhythm on our up-turned rubbish bin. **1960** *Times* 17 Sept. 7/7 In Trinidad a steelband is known as a 'pan-side' and the word 'pan' has two connotations. The first refers to the instrument, the second to a way of musical life. Pan, the instrument, is..a tuned gong, made from the top of a 44-gallon steel barrel. *Ibid.*, The intermarriage of musical cultures—the offspring of which is pan. Pan is the core of national culture and the first expression of a truly West-Indian art-form. **1973** *Trinidad Guardian* 1 Feb. 8/5 The question of having tuners specialise in particular pans.

2. In many technical uses, applied to pan-like vessels in which substances are exposed to heat, or to mechanical processes: e.g.

a. An open vessel used for boiling, evaporating, etc.; also in *Chem.* a closed vessel for evaporation, a vacuum-pan. See also SALT-PAN, SUGAR-PAN, etc. **b.** *Metallurgy.* A pan-shaped vessel, usually of cast-iron, in which ores are ground and amalgamated; also, a vessel in which ore is smelted. **c.** *Soap-making.* A broad shallow iron vessel, usually forming the bottom of a large frame into which the tallows or oils are poured to be treated with soda lyes, etc., and from which the spent lyes are drained off: see SOAP-PAN. **d.** *Tinplate Manuf.* The fourth in a series of five cast-iron rectangular pots used in tinning, having a grated bottom, in which the tinned plates are placed on edge to drain and cool. **e.** A circular sheet-iron dish in which gold is separated from gravel, crushed quartz, etc., by agitation and washing.

a. 1674–91 Ray *Coll. Words, Making Salt* (E.D.S.), They ..leave about a pottle or gallon of brine in the pan, lest the salt should burn, and stick to the sides of the pan. **1721** *Lond. Gaz.* No. 6006/4 A Moiety of Salt-works, containing 12 Pans. **1818** Marshall *Review* II. 91 (E.D.D.) The pans used in Cheshire for the evaporating of the salt brine, are now made of wrought iron. **1823** Ure *Dict. Chem.* 436/1 The evaporating pan, or still, is a hemispherical dish of cast-iron ..furnished with an air-tight flat lid. 1854 RONALDS & RICHARDSON *Chem. Technol.* (ed. 2) I. 280 Open pans..are heated by the waste heat of the pan-furnace. 1875 KNIGHT *Dict. Mech.* 1600/2 Overflow furnace-pans are used in concentrating sulphuric acid.

b. 1839 URE *Dict. Arts* 1133 (s.v. *Silver*) The crystallization refinery of Mr. Pattinson is an extremely simple smelting-house... Each pan has a discharge-pipe, proceeding laterally from one side of its bottom, by which the melted metal may be run out when a plug is withdrawn. 1881 RAYMOND *Gloss. Mining, Pan*,..a cylindrical vat of iron, stone, or wood, or these combined, in which ore is ground with mullers and amalgamated.

c. 1839 URE *Dict. Arts* 1142 The spent lyes, which are not at all alkaline, are run off by a spigot below, or pumped off above, by a pump set into the pan. *Ibid.* 1149 The apparatus employed for making these soaps is a copper pan heated by a water-bath; in the bottom of the pan there is a step, to receive the lower end of a vertical shaft, to which arms or paddles are attached, for producing constant agitation.

d. 1839 URE *Dict. Arts* 1253 A range of rectangular cast-iron pots is set over a fire-flue in an apartment called the *stow*... The first rectangle in the range is the tin-pot; the second is the wash-pot, with a partition in it; the third is the grease-pot; the fourth is the pan, grated at bottom; the fifth is the list-pot.

e. 1875 KNIGHT *Dict. Mech.* 994/1 (*Gold-mining*) The operator dips his pan..and then imparts to it a rotary and oscillatory motion [etc.]. 1879 *Encycl. Brit.* X. 745 The most characteristic [appliance] being the 'pan', a circular dish of sheet-iron with sloping sides about 13 or 14 inches in diameter.

3. The contents of a pan, a panful.

[1674–91 RAY *Coll. Words, Making Salt* (E.D.S.), Out of two pans of forty-eight gallons they expect seven pecks of salt.] 1762 GOLDSM. *Cit. W.* lxx, He..had found a pan of money under ground. 1800 VINCE *Hydrostat.* xi. (1806) 116 By means of a pan of coals, we brought the water to the same degree of heat. 1839 URE *Dict. Arts* 1142 Six or seven days are required to complete the formation of a pan of hard soap.

4. A more or less pan-shaped depression or concavity of any vessel, or part of any structure.

1764 *Museum Rusticum* III. lvii. 240 A spade made about four inches broad, and eighteen inches long in the bit, or pan. 1823 P. NICHOLSON *Pract. Build.* 406 At the end of the table, nearest to the copper, a box, called the Pan, is adapted. 1852 SEIDEL *Organ* 38 Where the pedal comes in contact with the beam, the latter has a deepening in the form of a half-circle (called the pan). 1869 *Eng. Mechanic* 24 Dec. 352/3 On the top [of a harmonium] is the 'pan' containing the reeds. 1869 BOUTELL *Arms and Arm.* vi. (1874) 89 This boss, a kind of deep, circular pan made of iron, was fixed to the front of the shield, where it had a considerable projection.

b. *spec.* In various obs. types of guns and pistols: That part of the lock which holds the priming. ***flash in the pan***: see FLASH *sb.*[2] ***to shut one's pan*** (slang), to hold one's tongue, keep silent.

1590 SIR J. SMYTH *Disc. Weapons* 21 b, Because the same doth..wett the powder in their pannes and touch holes. 1660 BOYLE *New Exp. Phys. Mech.* xiv. 101 Most of our attempts to fire the Gun-powder in the Pan of the Pistol succeeded not. 1662 GURNALL *Chr. in Arm.* verse 18. lvi. §2 (1669) 427/2 Like false fire in the pan of an uncharged gun, it gives a crack but hurts not. 1761 *Brit. Mag.* II. 110 The pistol flash'd in the pan, and a spark flew into the cask. 1809 MALKIN *Gil Blas* VII. x. ¶9, I was not remiss in composing a fine compliment..with which I meant to launch out on her part; but it was just so much flash in the pan. 1833 MARRYAT *P. Simple* xx, Shut your pan. 1864 A. LINCOLN in *Century Mag.* (1889) Sept. 704/1, I shall be very 'shut pan' about this matter. 1871 W. H. G. KINGSTON *On banks of Amazon* (1876) 368 If I had tinder I could get [a light] with the help of the pan of my gun.

c. A socket, as of the thigh bone (*obs.*), or for a hinge, etc.

1598 FLORIO, *Accettabolo*,..Also the hollownes or pan wherein the huckle bone turneth. 1605 WILLET *Hexapla in Gen.* 335 We may name it acetabulum, the panne of the hucklebone. 1875 KNIGHT *Dict. Mech.* 1601/1 *Pan*,..the socket or sole for a hinge.

5. A hollow or depression in the ground, esp. one in which water stands; *spec.* a basin, natural or artificial, in which salt is obtained by evaporation of sea-water; a SALT-PAN. So ***oyster pan***.

1573 *Reg. Privy Council Scot.* Ser. I. II. 286 It being menit be the awnaris and pan maisteris of certane pannis on the coist sydes. *Ibid.*, The awnaris and panmaisteris of the salt pannis. 1594 PLAT *Jewell-ho.* I. 32 Of all Channels, Pondes, Pooles, Riuers, and Ditches, and of all other pannes and bottomes whatsoeuer. 1706 *Phil. Trans.* XXV. 2265 The Sea-Water being in hot Countries grained in Pans called Salt-Marshes. 1790 *Trans. Soc. Arts* VIII. 88 Frequent pools of sea-water in the middle of the Saltings. These are not improperly called the Pans. 1836 BRAY *Tamar & Tavy* I. 57 (E.D.D.) Mis-tor, a height of whose..rocks there is found so large and perfect a rock-basin as to be called by the peasantry 'Mis-tor Pan'. 1852 WIGGINS *Embanking* 96 Fill up the nearest of such hollows or 'pans', as they are called, with the stuff out of the circular dyke. 1884 JEFFERIES *Red Deer* x. 199 Another kind of hollow in the hills is called a pan.

b. *spec.* in *South Africa*, A shallow depression containing water or mud, at least in the rainy season; a dried-up salt-marsh or pool-bed.

1850 R. G. CUMMING *Hunter's Life S. Afr.* (1902) 33/2 Heavy rains fill the pan or basin with water, and, the dry season succeeding, the water disappears, and large deposits of salt are found. These pans or salt-licks are met with in several parts of South Africa. 1889 RIDER HAGGARD *Allan's Wife*, etc. 321 A dry pan, or water-hole, which..was densely covered with reeds. 1900 *Daily News* 26 Apr. 5/6 The Boers, ..surrounding the pan, opened a murderous fire.

c. = *skid-pan*.

1966 T. WISDOM *High-Performance Driving* ii. 30 The first skid pan was introduced at Chiswick [in 1922]. On this 'pan' solid-tyred K and D buses were put through their paces. *Ibid.* 31 'Pans'—circular areas covered with a mixture of grease or oil and water—were by now out of date.

6. The skull, especially its upper part; = BRAIN-PAN, HARN-PAN. *Obs.* or *dial.*

c1330 R. BRUNNE *Chron. Wace* (Rolls) 10899 In þe forehed Arþur he smot, þorow þe flesche, vnto þe pan. 1362 LANGL. *P. Pl.* A. IV. 64 Pees putte forþ his hed and his ponne blodi. c1386 CHAUCER *Knt.'s T.* 307 Loue is a gretter lawe, by my pan, Than may be yeue of any erthely man. c1440 *Promp. Parv.* 381/1 Panne of an heed, *craneum*. 1548–77 VICARY *Anat.* iii. (1888) 27 They be numbred seuen bones in the pan or skul of the head. 1658 A. FOX *Wurtz' Surg.* II. vi. 62 All Wounds in the head are dangerous..especially.. when the pan or scull is broken. 1839 MOIR *Mansie Wauch* (ed. 2) xxiv. 306, I feared the fall had produced some crack in his pan, and that his seven senses had gone a wool-gathering.

†**b.** The patella or KNEE-PAN. *Obs.*

1657 RUMSEY *Org. Salutis* xi. (1659) 63 The said Pitch-plaister, applyed to cover the pans of both knees. 1753 A. MURPHY *Gray's Inn Jrnl.* No. 53 Manifest Danger of.. hurting the Pan of the Knee, or some such Disaster.

c. A face. (Perh. influenced by ***to shut one's pan*** s.v. sense 4 b. Cf. also DEAD-PAN *a.*, *sb.*, *adv.*, and *v.*) *slang* (orig. *U.S.*).

1923 [see HEEBIE-JEEBIE(S)]. 1931 E. LINKLATER *Juan in Amer.* III. viii. 262, I never want to see that pan of yours again! 1943 HUNT & PRINGLE *Service Slang* 50 *Pan*, slang for face. 1944 E. B. WHITE *Let.* 8 Oct. (1976) 260 He starts toward her bearing a bouquet of American Beauty roses, and falls on his pan before he gets there. 1972 *Jazz & Blues* Nov. 11/4 This must have been funny enough when it happened; relayed through the medium of Rich's sourly contemptuous pickled-walnut pan. 1977 *Rolling Stone* 13 Jan. 41/2 As Belushi filled out the registration card, the manager remarked with a deadly pan: 'Write down the name of the person you're staying with.'

†**7.** A steel cap. *Obs.*

1638 W. MOUNTAGU in *Buccleuch MSS.* (Hist. MSS. Comm.) I. 282 A pan for the head, back and breast piece, and gaunts.

8. A hard substratum of the soil, usually more or less impervious to moisture: see HARD-PAN.

[1630 *R. Johnson's Kingd. & Commw.* 372 The soile barren:..being onely a flat Rocke with a pan of earth a foot or two thicke.] 1784 BELKNAP in *B. Papers* (1877) II. 180 It [the water] descends to the hard stratum, commonly called the pan. 1786 YOUNG *Ann. Agric.* V. 133 What Norfolk farmers call the pan, or that subsidence of the marle or clay which always forms immediately under the path of the plough. 1805 R. W. DICKSON *Pract. Agric.* I. 413 Upon all light soils it is necessary to preserve, at six or eight inches below the surface, what farmers call a pan; that is, the staple, at that depth, should be kept unbroken. a1817 T. DWIGHT *Trav. New Eng.*, etc. (1821) I. 374 The stratum, lying immediately under the soil;..what is here called the hard pan, a very stiff loam, so closely combined, as wholly to prevent the water from passing through it. 1846 J. BAXTER *Libr. Pract. Agric.* (ed. 4) II. 303 The pan, or old plough-floor, of this field. 1875 *Lyell's Princ. Geol.* II. III. xliv. 508 At the bottom of peat mosses there is sometimes found a cake, or 'pan', as it is termed, of oxide of iron.

9. A small ice-floe.

1863 A. C. RAMSAY *Phys. Geog.* xxiv. (1878) 396 The pans rise over all the low-lying parts of the islands, grinding and polishing exposed shores. 1883 *Fish. Exhib. Catal.* (ed. 4) 175 Running across Channel over small pans of ice. 1892 W. PIKE *North. Canada* 240 Ice was running in large pans, and steering was difficult.

10. The broad posterior end of the lower jaw of a whale.

1887 *Fisheries of U.S.* Sect. v. II. 232 *note*, Canes made full length from the ivory of the 'pan' of the sperm whale, turned and polished, with a hand-piece of the same material.

11. Severe or dismissive criticism. orig. *U.S. colloq.*

1936 *Esquire* Sept. 160/3 A pan on a show is a damp blanket. 1958 *Spectator* 24 Oct. 543/1 'Is it a pan?' asked the reporter from *Time* hopefully... 'No, bigod, it's a smashin' crit.' 1960 P. TOMPKINS *To a Young Actress* 60 The notice in *Punch* appeared next to a long pan of *Back to Methuselah*. 1972 *N.Y. Times* 3 Nov. 24/5 This Hunanese restaurant... Appraisals..included the whole possible spectrum of opinion from rave to pan. 1977 *Zigzag* Apr. 34/1 Afterwards they wrote a pan and then had a huge article criticising the pan.

12. *attrib.* and *Comb.* **a.** gen., as ***pan hand***, ***process***, ***system***; ***pan-dish***, ***-furnace***, ***-house***, ***-lid***, ***-load***, ***-metal***, ***-sherd***, etc.; (sense 1 f) ***pan music***.

1854 RONALDS & RICHARDSON *Chem. Technol.* I. 280 The open pans..are heated by the waste heat of the *pan-furnace. 1818 MARSHALL *Review* II. 92 (E.D.D.) There is a separate *pan-house to each pan. 1902 BARNES GRUNDY *Thames Camp* 72 Jane polishes the *pan-lids and scours the kitchen tables. 1939 J. STEINBECK *Grapes of Wrath* xxii. 414 Ma had taken up a *panload of brown pone. 1963 *Which?* 6 Feb. 48/2 Each [dish-washing machine] had to deal..with three separate assortments of dishes, which we call *standard*, *capacity* and *pan* loads respectively. 1552 *Inv. Ch. Goods York*, etc. (Surtees) 65 One crosse of *pane mettall, one challes of pane mettell gilt. 1669 STURMY *Mariner's Mag.*, *Penalties & Forfeit.* 6 Bell-mettle, Pan-mettle, Gun-mettle, or Shroof-mettle. 1960 *Times* 17 Sept. 7/7 Pan music casts a spell of enchantment on the Trinidadian... The essential feature of pan music is that the melody is carried by one instrument at a time while the others play more or less 'free' variations on the theme. 1977 *Times* 14 May 12/4 'Pan' music, as the drums are called, originated in Trinidad. 1877 RAYMOND *Statist. Mines & Mining* 328 The Del Norte has yielded exceedingly rich *pan-prospects. 1851 MAYHEW *Lond. Labour* II. 284 The potsherds and *pansherds, as the rubbish-carters call them. 1880 JEFFERIES *Gt. Estate* 194 The hives..were all in a row, each protected by large 'pansherds' from heavy rain. 1882 *Rep. to Ho. Repr. Prec. Met. U.S.* 609 The introduction of the Comstock *pan system.

b. Special comb.: **pan-amalgamator**, an amalgamating pan: see 2 b; **pan-broiling** *vbl. sb.* (hence, as a back-formation, ***pan-broil*** vb.) (see quot. 1970); **pan-charge**, the contents of an amalgamating pan during the metallurgical pan process; **pan-closet**, a water-closet having a pan; **pan-cover**, the piece covering the priming pan in old fire-arms; **pan-head**, a form of rivet-head used in shipbuilding; **pan-ice**, loose ice in blocks which form on the shores of Labrador and break away; **pan-latrine** = *pan-closet*; †**pan-licker**, a parasite; **pan-maker**, one whose business it is to make pans; **pan-man**, (*a*) a man in charge of a pan in a manufacturing process; (*b*) one who plays the pan (sense 1 f) in a steelband; †**pan-master**, the owner of a salt-pan: see sense 5, quot. 1573; †**pan-meat**, cooked food; **pan-mill**, a miner's apparatus used in separating gold from the alloy of earth, with which it is found mingled (Farmer); **pan-mug** (*local*), a large earthenware vessel; **pan-pie** = PANDOWDY; **pan-pulp** (*Metallurgy*), the ground ores and other materials in the amalgamating-pan; **pan-rock**, the rock-fish, *Roccus lineatus*, when fit for frying; **pan-sand**, the sand-bottom of an oyster-park or oyster-bed; **pan-scale**, **-scratch**, the scale that forms on the bottom of a pan; **pan-scourer**, **-scrubber**, a scourer, often in the form of a wire pad, for cleaning pans; **pan-side** *West Indian* (see quot.).; **pan-washing**, the separating of gold from gravel, etc., by stirring it in water in a pan; **pan-wood** (see quot.). Also PANCAKE, PANTILE, etc.

1874 RAYMOND *Statist. Mines & Mining* 429 Dodge's *pan-amalgamator and settler. 1950 L. H. GROSS *Meats, Poultry & Game* 14 Rib steaks—Broil, or *pan-broil. 1970 SIMON & HOWE *Dict. Gastron.* 287/2 *Pan-broil.* An American cooking term meaning to cook meat in a hot pan with almost no fat, pouring off fat as it accumulates. 1896 F. M. FARMER *Boston Cooking-School Cook Bk.* ii. 22 When coal is not used, or a fire is not in condition for broiling, a plan for **pan broiling* has been adopted. This is done by placing food to be cooked in a hissing hot frying-pan, turning often as in broiling. 1882 *Rep. to Ho. Repr. Prec. Met. U.S.* 651 The *pan-charge is drawn into the settlers and thinned down. 1884 *Century Mag.* Dec. 262/2 The absolute inadmissibility of the almost universal *pan-closet. 1869 BOUTELL *Arms & Arm.* (1874) 246 This [flint of a flintlock] is made to strike against a movable steel *pan-cover. 1869 SIR E. REED *Shipbuild.* xvii. 328 The common form of rivet head employed for shipbuilding is that known as a *pan head. 1874 THEARLE *Naval Archit.* 127 The pan-head rivet..is slightly conical under the head, [to] fill the hole made by the punching tool. 1878 H. Y. HIND in *Can. Naturalist* N.S. VIII. 277 The gradual rise of the land.. brings the successively rising surfaces under the influence not only of *pan-ice, but of snow-drifts. 1898 *Westm. Gaz.* 2 Mar. 4/3 No heavy vessels..could have withstood the terrible pan ice, which was frequently twenty to thirty feet thick. 1897 HUGHES *Medit. Fever* ii. 58 An inspection.. disclosed a leaking *pan-latrine. 1641 *Bull from Rome* A iij, *Panlickers are those who are Flatterers of Kings, Princes. 1483 *Cath. Angl.* 267/2 A *Panne maker, *patinarius*. 1635–6 *Canterb. Marriage Licences* (MS.), Thomas Lashfeild of S. Mary Northgate,..panmaker. 1832 A. DAVIS in P. D. Curtin *Two Jamaicas* (1955) 234 One stocker-man, one *pan-man, three boiler-men... These were all slaves. 1879 *Spons' Encycl. Manuf.* I. 108 This communication..is closed..by a sliding damper..under the ready control of the pan-man. 1892 *Labour Commission Gloss.*, *Pan-men*, men in the chemical industry engaged in boiling down the liquor obtained from black ash. 1959 W. A. SIMMONDS *'Pan'—Story of Steelband* 15 In order to understand fully the story of the Pan, one must understand the Panmen, who drew their music from every source that is Trinidadian. 1960 *Times* 17 Sept. 7/7 Some people say that the 'pan-men' take themselves too seriously. 1974 *Trinidad Guardian* 2 Nov. 9/2 Pan men would be trained to become teaching assistants. c1000 *Ags. Voc.* in Wr.-Wülcker 281/7 *Uiuertitum*, *ponmete. c1050 *Ibid.* 409/9 *Ferculum*, ælces cynnes panmete. 1888 *Daily Inter-Ocean* (U.S.) 8 Mar., On their way to inspect the California *pan mill. 1688 R. HOLME *Armoury* II. 173/1 *Cream*, the top of Milk standing in a pot or *pan-mug. 1901 *N. & Q.* 9th Ser. VIII. 406/2 A thick glazed earthenware vessel..called a *pancheon* in the Midland counties,..a *pan-mug* in Cheshire, and a *kneading-pan* in most cookery books. 1882 *Rep. to Ho. Repr. Prec. Met. U.S.* 651 This is found entirely sufficient to heat the *pan-pulp. 1898 *Westm. Gaz.* 25 Nov. 2/1 Oyster culturists and connoisseurs would..find..giants from the '*pan sands'. 1959 'A. GILBERT' *Death takes Wife* ix. 112 'Packet of *pan-scourers,' she said. 1960 *Guardian* 19 Sept. 6/4 The very first electric pan scourer. 1971 C. BONINGTON *Annapurna South Face* App. B. 252 Pan-scourers..24. 1879 *Cassell's Techn. Educ.* IV. 338/1 The carbonate and sulphate of lime..gradually accumulates on the bottom of the pan... This *pan-scratch has therefore to be removed periodically. 1926–7 *Army & Navy Stores Catal.* 118/3 **Pan scrubber.* A Metal Sponge for cleaning pots, pans, etc. 1960 *John o' London's* 14 Apr. 440/2 The sound of a wire pan-scrubber chasing grease round a frying pan. 1960 Pan-side [see sense 1 f above]. 1874 RAYMOND *Statist. Mines & Mining* 21 [It] will yield, under *pan-washing..very often a notable quantity of gold. 1880 SUTHERLAND *Tales of Goldfields* 4 They got a lesson in pan-washing. 1805 FORSYTH *Beauties Scotl.* (1806) III. 511 The small coal used in [the salt-works] has,..from time immemorial, received the singular appellation of *panwood,..which has suggested..a suspicion that wood was formerly used as fuel in these works. **1808** Ball *Coal-Trade* 52 (E.D.D.) Great coals, chews, lime-coal, and pan-wood or dross.

Pan (pæn), *sb.*^{2} [a. Gr. *Πάν*.] The name of a Greek rural deity, represented as having the head, arms, and chest of a man, while his lower parts were those of a goat, of which he sometimes also bore the horns and ears.

The original seat of his worship was in Arcadia, and he was supposed to preside over shepherds and flocks, and to delight in rural music; he was also regarded as the author of sudden and groundless terror seizing upon beasts or men (panic); in later times, from association of his name with *τὸ πᾶν* the all, everything, the universe, he was considered as an impersonation of Nature, of which his attributes were taken as mysterious symbols.

c **1369** Chaucer *Dethe Blaunche* 512 Pan that men clepe the god of kynde. *c* **1420** Lydg. *Assembly of Gods* 324 The rewde god Pan, of sheperdys the gyde. **1579** E. K. *Gloss. Spenser's Sheph. Cal.* Apr. 50 Christ..is the verye Pan and God of Shepheardes. **1584** R. Scot *Discov. Witchcr.* vii. xv. (1886) 122 They have so fraied us with bull beggers, spirits, ..elves, hags, fairies, satyrs, pans, fauns. **1606** Sylvester *Du Bartas* ii. iv. ii. *Magnif.* 870 Heer, many a horned Satyre, many a Pan. **1678** Norris *Coll. Misc.* (1699) 55 The gentle God of the Arcadian plains, Pan that regards the sheep, Pan that regards the swains, Great Pan is dead. **1844** Mrs. Browning *The Dead Pan*, (Refrain) Pan, Pan is dead.

pan (pæn), *sb.*^{3} Also 5 panne. [= F. *panne*, med.L. *panna* (Du Cange); of uncertain origin.

The med.L. word is very frequent in the 13th c. Close Rolls, in the forms (as printed) *pauna* and *palna*, which are difficult to reconcile with *panna* and F. *panne*. An OF. *penne* (Godef.) raises further difficulty.]

In a timber-framed house, the beam which rests upon and is fixed to the posts, and which supports the rafters, etc. See also quots. 1611, 1813.

Hence app. the phrase *post and pan*, which however is now taken in a different sense: see next.

[**1225** *Rot. Litt. Claus.* II. (1884) 65/2 Habere faciat.. duos postes et duos paunas in bosco nostro. *Ibid.*, viii postes, viii trabes, viii palnas, et c cheuerones. *Ibid.* II. 104, c cheuerones, x postes, xii paunas. *Ibid.* 137, xx cheuerones, iiii trabes et iiii palnas. So *passim*.]

1420 *Searchers Verdicts* in *Surtees Misc.* (1888) 15 In hys tenement in Coppergate in York walles even uppe thurgh fra the grunde uppe to the panne. **1483** *Cath. Angl.* 267/2 A Panne of a howse, *panna*. **1501** *Searchers Verdicts* in *Surtees Misc.* (1888) 22 The sparrez & tymbre of ye said William, which is shot & hyngeth over ye ground of ye same Ric' ther by viijth ynchez & more anenst ye pan of his house. **1600** *Burgh Rec. Glasgow* (Rec. Soc.) I. 206 Sic as biggis with poist and pan and layes with blak morter. [**1611** Cotgr., *Panne de bois* (is particularly) the peece of timber that sustaines a gutter between the roofes of two fronts, or houses.] **1674–91** Ray *N.-C. Words* s.v. *Pan* v., It seems to come from pan in buildings, which in our stone houses is that piece of wood that lies upon the top of the stone wall, and must close with it, to which the bottom of the spars are fastned. **1813** Leslie *Agric. Surv. Nairn & Moray* Gloss., *Pan*,..the great timbers of a cottage laid across the couples parallel to the walls, to support the laths or kebbers laid above the pans and parallel to the couples.

pan, *sb.*^{4} Also pane. [a. F. *pan* pane, compartment, etc.: see pane *sb.*^{1}]

1. In a timber-framed or half-timbered house, a square or compartment of timber framework, filled in with bricks or plaster.

1842–76 Gwilt *Archit.* (ed. 7) Gloss., *Pan*, a square of framing in half-timbered houses, the uprights being filled in with work. It is called post and pan, or post and petrail work, in the north of England. **1855** Robinson *Whitby Gloss.* s.v. *Post and Pan*, The posts being the framing, and the pan the flat surface or plastering with which the framing is filled up. **1886** *Chesh. Gloss.*, *Pane*, a panel of doab or of bricks between the wooden framework of the old black-and-white buildings.

†**2.** The space between the flanked or salient and shoulder angles of a bastion, a face of a bastion.

1742 Bailey, Pan of a Bastion, see *Face of a Bastion*. **1823** in Crabb *Technol. Dict.*

‖**pan, pán** (pɑːn), *sb.*^{5} Also pawn, paun, paan. [a. Hind. *pān* betel-leaf:—Skr. *parṇa* feather, leaf.]

1. The leaf of the betel pepper, *Piper betle*, used to enclose slices of betel nut (*Areca catechu*) mixed with lime; hence, the masticatory formed by this mixture.

1616 Sir T. Roe in Purchas *Pilgrims* (1625) I. iv. xvi. 576 The King giuing mee..two pieces of his Pawne out of his dish. **1809** Ld. Valentia *Voy. & Trav.* I. 101 On our departure, paun and roses were presented. **1885** *Macm. Mag.* Nov. 78/2 All..chew pan as a sailor chews his quid. **1891** R. Kipling *City Dreadf. Nt.* 39 They grin and jabber and chew pan and spit. **1964** *New Statesman* 3 Apr. 517/3 Eating the green leaf called paan..and the nut of the betel palm..is common in India, in Malaya and in Ceylon... The best paan leaf comes from Banaras. **1967** Singha & Massey *Indian Dances* vi. 68 The betel or *paan* as it is called, is covered with silver leaf and sprinkled with rose water. **1971** *Illustr. Weekly India* 4 Apr. 51/2 The Mughal rulers were great connoisseurs of paan. **1974** *Times* 7 Dec. 10/8 Paans, those leaf-wrapped chews.

2. *attrib.* and *Comb.*, as *pan-box*, *-chewing*, *-garden*, *-juice*; **panwala**, **-wallah** [see wallah], a person who sells pans.

1922 E. M. Forster *Abinger Harvest* (1936) 314 Bidar.. has produced beautiful pan-boxes of a lead alloy inlaid with silver. **1939** R. Godden *Black Narcissus* v. 53 A peon..who carried the General's pan-box. **1892** *Chambers's Jrnl.* 14 May 320 After a long course of pawn-chewing, the utterance becomes thick and indistinct, and the teeth black. **1971** *Illustr. Weekly India* 4 Apr. 48/1 Paan chewing is an ancient Indian habit. **1923** *Blackw. Mag.* Dec. 769/1 In one of these pan-gardens, as they are called, a boar had taken up his quarters. **1901** Kipling *Kim* ii. 47 He spat red *pan*-juice on the floor. **1955** R. P. Jhabvala *To whom she Will* xxvi. 186 He stopped at a pānwala's and..asked for a pān with cardamons and aniseed. *Ibid.* 294 The stalls of pānwalas are found everywhere, and they sell not only pāns but also cigarettes, matches, mineral drinks, biscuits, hard-boiled eggs and anything else suitable for a quick cheap snack. **1969** *Hindusthan Stand.* (Calcutta) 5 Aug. 2/4 As one waits..for the panwallah to stuff a betel leaf with hot or sweet masallah ..and roll it into a shapely pan. **1975** O. Sela *Bengali Inheritance* xix. 166 That bloody pan-wallah..lied to you.

‖**pan** (ban), *sb.*^{6} [Chinese *bǎn* slab.] A Chinese percussion instrument (see quots.).

1872 *Catal. Special Exhib. Anc. Mus. Instr. S. Kensington Museum* viii. 39 Pan. A piece of wood, with a groove cut nearly through its substance, and bamboo sticks for percussion. Used principally by Chinese beggars. **1954** *Grove's Dict. Mus.* (ed. 5) II. 234/1 *P'ai-pan* (or *pan*), percussion clapper. A popular instrument consisting of two slabs of the red wood *huai*, attached by a silk cord, on which a third slab is struck to beat time. **1975** C. P. Mackerras *Chinese Theatre in Mod. Times* viii. 131 (*caption*) The *pan* (clapper) consists of three pieces of wood, two of them fastened together (patterned surface visible), the other behind.

pan, *sb.*^{7} *Cinemat.* [Abbrev. panorama or panoramic. *a.*] **1.** The action of panning a camera (see pan *v.*^{3}); a panoramic sequence.

1922 *Opportunities Motion Pict. Industry* 111 *Pan*.., moving the camera up and down or from side to side to follow the action from one place to another. **1931** J. H. Reyner *Cine-Photogr. for Amateurs* viii. 92 *Rapid pan*. An exception to this slow movement is the case of the rapid panoram which is sometimes necessary in order to keep a moving object within the field of vision. **1937** H. B. Abbott *Compl. 9·5-mm. Cinematographer* vi. 88 A satisfactory 'pan' can sometimes be effected by slowly turning the camera on its tripod screw. **1942** *Amer. Cinematographer* May 235/2 The layout-man..figures out all of the camera moves such as..pans (following a character along). **1960** C. Morris *Unloved* in D. Wilson *Television Playwright* 447 Camera panning, moves round a stone seat... As the car circles, the pan reveals a boy on the stone seat apparently sketching the front façade. **1962** *Listener* 5 Apr. 596/2 The opening shot of *Exodus* is a huge 200-degree pan across the landscape and coastline of Cyprus. **1970** *Daily Tel.* (Colour Suppl.) 3 July 23 A tripod's a bit of a bind to lug around but it does give a rock steadiness and a touch of professionalism, especially on pans and telephoto shots. **1977** *Spare Rib* June 42/2 A story unfolded in a series of 360° camera pans.

2. *attrib.* and *Comb.*, as *pan shot*, *-tilt*; **pan-and-tilt** *a.*, used with reference to a tripod or other unit that allows the camera to move in both horizontal and vertical planes; **pan head** (see quot.).

[**1937** H. B. Abbott *Compl. 9·5-mm. Cinematographer* v. 69 The metal top has both pan and tilt movements with locking device for each.] **1938** G. H. Sewell *Amateur Film-Making* iii. 34 The ideal tripod..should also incorporate a 'pan-and-tilt' head. **1962** M. Bardwell *Amateur Cinematogr.* ii. 32 A tripod must not only give firm support —it must also allow controlled horizontal and vertical movement. This is achieved by means of a 'pan-and-tilt' head, which also enables you to lock the camera in position at almost any angle. **1977** *Offshore Engineer* May 97/2 It occupies only a fraction of the space normally dedicated to a camera mounted on a pan and tilt unit. **1940** *Amer. Speech* XV. 359/2 *Pan head*, the mechanism at the top of a tripod which permits the camera to be moved in both horizontal and vertical planes. **1941** Steinbeck & Ricketts *Sea of Cortez* xxiii. 223 We made jerky little pan shots back and forth. **1956** L. Mallory *Ciné Camera Secrets* 20 Pan shots must be slow and even. **1975** *New Yorker* 26 May 113/3 An 'atmospheric' tape background such as accompanies pan shots over bleak, windswept headlands. **1970** *Ibid.* 3 Oct. 108/3 Two..spots..could be directed by means of pan-tilt.

‖**p'an** (pan), *sb.*^{8} *Archæol.* [Chinese *pán*.] A vessel or wash basin.

1958 W. Willetts *Chinese Art* I. iii. 154 It is not altogether certain that *p'an* date back as far as Shang-Yin times. **1973** *Genius of China* 57/2 Dish on a high foot *p'an*, of burnished black pottery. **1977** Kwangchih Chang *Archaeol. Anc. China* (ed. 3) vii. 368 Water utensils: p'an, i, chien, yii, p'en, cheng, chu, wan.

pan (pæn), *v.*^{1} [f. pan *sb.*^{1}]

1. *trans.* To wash (gold-bearing gravel, sand, etc.) in a pan, in order to separate the gold; to separate by washing in a pan. Const. *off*, *out*.

1839 *Amer. Railroad Jrnl.* VIII. 99 Old machines are invariably burnt up, and the ashes 'panned out' for the fine gold that has lodged in the joints of the wood. **1872** 'Mark Twain' *Roughing it* lxi, He never could altogether understand that eternal sinkin' of a shaft an' never pannin' out anything. **1879** Atcherley *Boërland* 143 This [gravel-wash] was panned off in the dish. **1879** *Encycl. Brit.* X. 745 The gold is finally recovered by careful washing or 'panning out' in a smaller pan. **1880** *Daily Tel.* 3 Dec., They 'panned' the surface dirt for gold.

b. *absol.* or *intr.* To search or try for gold with the pan.

1850 N. Kingsley *Diary* 27 May (1914) 123 About 200 Indians & squaws came down and began to pan all around us. **1872** 'Mark Twain' *Roughing it* lxi, We had panned up and down the hillsides till they looked plowed like a field. **1881** Raymond *Mining Gloss.*, *Panning*... Washing earth or crushed rock in a pan, by agitation with water. **1896** *Daily News* 9 May 6/4 All tests made by dolly and panning off gave me good results.

2. To separate (salt) by evaporation in a pan.

1877 Ouida *Puck* xxxv. 462 We might perhaps get our salt panned, and our cotton carded.

3. *transf.* and *fig.* (*U.S.* and *Colonial.*) To bring forth, yield (with *out*).

1884 *Melbourne Punch* 4 Sept. 91/2 The department on being searched only panned out a few copper coins. **1891** *Boston* (Mass.) *Jrnl.* Nov., Their queer bee tree will pan out a good day's work after all.

b. To get by any process, capture, catch. *colloq.*

1887 *Fisheries of U.S.* Sect. v. II. 477 The crew 'panned' about 10,000 seals.

4. *intr.* (usually with *out.*) To yield gold, as gravel, etc. when washed in a pan; hence *transf.* of the vein or mine, to yield precious metal.

1849 J. D. Dana *Mineral.* (ed. 2) 317 Gravel or soil..is said to *pan well* or *pan poorly* according to the result. **1866** 'Mark Twain' *Lett. from Hawaii* (1967) 85 In the mining camps of California..it is etiquette to say, 'Here's hoping your dirt'll pan out gay.' **1874** Aldrich *Prud. Palfrey* vii. (1884) 152 Though it did not yield so bounteously as the silver lode, it panned out handsomely. **1893** *Times* 24 May 5 The new find..proves the reef to be 6 ft. wide, and it pans well right through. **1898** *Daily News* 8 Aug. 2/1 Assuming that all the land located on these creeks would pan out as well as the few claims that were opened.

b. *fig.* To yield good results, show to advantage, succeed; also, to work out, to have a result (not necessarily something favourable).

1868 F. Whymper *Trav. Alaska* 282 'It panned out well' means that 'it gave good returns'. **1870** 'Mark Twain' *Lett. to Publishers* (1967) 31 January and November didn't pan out as well as December. **1884** *Brandon* (Manitoba) *Blade* 24 Jan. 4/3 If the domineering Attorney-General 'pans out' well during the coming session he will probably be the man. **1890** *Athenæum* 2 Aug. 166/3 How disappointingly the product of antiquarian digging will 'pan out'. **1892** *Pall Mall G.* 21 Nov. 2/3 Unfortunately this business did not 'pan out', to use the American phrase. **1923** Wodehouse *Adv. Sally* xiv. 177 He was hoping all along that this fight would pan out big and that he'd be able to pay you back what you had loaned him. **1925** A. Huxley *Let.* 16 Sept. (1969) 253 However, I shall see how things pan out when I get there. **1947** 'N. Shute' *Chequer Board* vii. 191, I think it may pan out all right. **1956** S. Bellow *Seize Day* (1957) i. 23 If I don't pan out as an actor I can still go back to school. **1967** *Electronics* 6 Mar. 316/2 Machines that automatically feed and place flatpacks on printed circuit boards haven't panned out, largely because girls with tweezers excel at gently handling the fragile IC packages. **1972** *Daily Tel.* 14 Dec. 5 But Dr Brett cautioned that what sounds exciting from the Moon does not always pan out in the laboratory. **1977** P. Dickinson *Walking Dead* i. v. 69 They decided to give it a year and see how it all panned out.

c. To speak freely or at length; to expatiate.

1871 J. Hay *Little Breeches*, I don't pan out on the prophets And free-will and that sort of thing. **1915** W. J. Locke *Jaffery* xxi. 291 I'm panning out about this, because it seems so deuced interesting. **1917** —— *Red Planet* xv. 182, I had..made up my mind to pan out to you like this. **1928** *Observer* 18 Mar. 9/3 Mr. Lewis..resists even the temptation to 'pan out' about that obviously born temptress.

5. *trans.* To cook or dress in a pan.

1871 Napheys *Prev. & Cure Dis.* i. ii. 64 Shellfish are preferable either raw, roasted, or panned. **1883** Annie Thomas *Mod. Housewife* 75 Panned Oysters.

6. *Agric.* and *dial. intr.* Of soil: To cake on the surface. Cf. pan *sb.*^{1} 8.

a **1825** Forby *Voc. E. Anglia*, *Pan*, to be hardened, as the surface of some soil is, by strong sunshine suddenly succeeding heavy rain.

7. *trans.* To criticize severely; to judge (a performance) to be unsuccessful or inadequate. orig. *U.S. colloq.*

1911 G. Ade in *Chicago Daily News* 16 Dec. 28/2 They would open up on Rufus and Pan him to a Whisper. **1914** *Sat. Even. Post* 7 Mar. 7/3 Kelly got nasty and begun to pan me for quitting and for the way I played. **1926** S. Lewis *Mantrap* xii. 150 I've never done one single thing to give her any excuse for panning me. **1927** *Vanity Fair* XXIX. 134/3 Will Shakespeare..was panned by the critics because he delved into the argot of his day to put it over. **1935** *Hot News* Apr. 14/3 Don't mistake me. I am not panning 'Hawk' as a player. **1938** G. Heyer *Blunt Instrument* iii. 52 'I have no dealings with actresses.' 'Well, then, stop panning them.' **1939** 'N. Blake' *Smiler with Knife* v. 78 The lurid headline, 'Famous Woman Explorer Pans Domesticity.' **1947** R. Chandler *Let.* 8 Mar. in *R. Chandler Speaking* (1966) 137 MacCarthy panned me, said the toughness was largely bluff. **1960** *Daily Mail* 27 Apr. 8/8 The idea that critics like panning shows is a myth. **1971** *Sunday Times* (Johannesburg) *News Mag.* 28 Mar. 6/1 Dirk de Villiers' latest South African film drama..is being panned by the critics. **1974** *Times* 2 Oct. 14/5 The play was roundly panned by many of our correspondents. **1977** *Time* 26 Dec. 36/2 Colleagues are quick to pan Simon in return: 'The Count Dracula of critics!'

pan (pæn), *v.*^{2} *Sc.* and *n. dial.* [Derivation unascertained.] *intr.* To fit, tally, correspond, agree.

1572 *Satir. Poems Reform.* xxxiv. 30 Say and promeis quhat thay can, Thair wordes and deidis will neuer pan. **1674–91** Ray *N.-C. Words*, *Pan*, to close, joyn together, agree. Prov. 'Weal and Women cannot pan, but Wo and Women can'. **1825** Brockett *N.C. Gloss.*, *Pan*, to match, to agree, to assimilate. **1877** *Holderness Gloss.* s.v., Jack an his wife didn't seem to pan togither at fost, but noo they get alang pratty weel. **1883** *Almondbury & Huddersf. Gloss.* s.v., Boards pan when they lie close together.

b. *trans.* To fit, join, or unite together.

1884 *Leeds Mercury Suppl.* 31 May (E.D.D.), Pan it down —press an article into its proper place. **1888** *Sheffield Gloss.* s.v., To pan boards together.

pan (pæn), *v.*^{3} *Cinemat.* [Abbrev. panorama or panoramic *a.*] **1.** *trans.* **a.** To follow or pass along (a person or object) with a camera.

1913 *Sat. Even. Post* 1 Nov. 64/3 We'll 'pan' you right down the middle of the picture to the raft. **1960** N. Kneale

Mrs. Wickens in Fall in D. Wilson *Television Playwright* 167 The Camera pans him away. He calls to the two Englishwomen.

b. To turn (a cine or television camera) in a horizontal plane, esp. in order to keep a moving object in view.

1930 *Electronics* Nov. 373/2 With the advent of sound, the operation of 'panning' the camera to afford a changing point of view became a more complicated process. **1956** *Railway Mag.* Nov. 779/1 Taking up a stance broadside to his target, he 'panned' his camera—that is, swung the camera round with the train—so that the engine remained in the same portion of the viewfinder throughout. **1973** P. L. CAVE *Speed Freaks* v. 43 Gerry panned the camera slowly over the remnants of the once-beautiful TR6. **1977** *Film & Television Technician* Feb. 4/2 The camera is supported by a counterweighted arm, and the arm is attached to a harness worn by the operator. The camera floats in space and the operator can pan, tilt, or crane it with one hand.

2. *intr.* Of a camera: to swing from one scene to another, or along objects or a place; to give a panoramic view in closing up to an object or a place.

1931 R. DYKES *Amateur Cinematographer's Handbk.* iii. 31 The tilting handle..is used to panoram down into valleys... It is also used to 'pan' up cathedral spires. **1932** A. BUCHANAN *Films* vi. 174 The camera 'pans' around the room, bringing to view the shabby furniture. **1936** *Words* Oct. 6/1 One of those inserts in which the camera seems to swing, or 'pan' dizzily from action going on in one place to what is going on in another. **1960** N. KNEALE *Quatermass & Pit* I. 11 The camera pans, to take in all that remains of a little working-class street. **1963** *Listener* 14 Feb. 300/3 The camera pans over photographs of tribesmen. **1971** *Daily Tel.* 21 Aug. 7/2 A camera panned dramatically in on a manorial notice. **1975** *New Yorker* 19 May 81/1 Then the camera moves to a worker with a cart, and pans with him to the end of the assembly line.

pan (pæn), *a.* Abbrev. of PANCHROMATIC *a.* Also *ellipt.* for *panchromatic film.*

1940 *Amer. Speech* XV. 357 'Going to use pan or N.C.?' 'Neither. Ortho.' **1940** 'C. I. JACOBSON' *Developing* 106 On no account must the dark green safelight provided for pan materials be used. **1954** C. WALLACE *Enjoy your Photogr.* iv. 44 Pan films photograph reds well. **1969** J. ELLIOT *Duel* I. iv. 82, I brought ten thousand feet of pan but only three of high speed for interiors.

pan, obs. form of PANE; obs. Sc. form of PAIN.

pan-, combining form and formative element, repr. Gr. παν- from πᾶν, neuter of πᾶς all, which was freely used in Greek, esp. with adjs. to which it stood in advb. relation in the sense 'all, wholly, entirely, altogether, by all, of all', as in πανάγαθος altogether good, πανάγιος all-holy, πανακής all-healing, πανάριστος best of all, παναρμόνιος suited to all musical modes, πάνδημος pertaining to all the people, public, πάνοπλος fully-armed, πανσέληνος of the full moon, πάνσοφος all-wise; so from national names, as πανελλήνιος of all the Greeks, πανιώνιος of all the Ionians; also in sbs., etc. derived from these adjs., and some other sbs., as πανδέκτης an all-receiver, πανηγεμών ruler of all, πανήγυρις a universal or general assembly, πανοπλία panoply.

Hence *pan-* occurs in English in words taken or derived from Greek, and in many others formed more or less on the same analogy either in English, med. or mod. Latin, or French. It is especially common with national names, after πανελλήνιος, πανιώνιος, etc., where it has become a living suffix, prefixed whenever needed. Before a labial παν- became παμ-, and before a guttural παγ- (=*paŋ*-), as πάμφιλος, παμφίλητος beloved of all, πάγκρεας the sweetbread, the pancreas; the former of these is retained in some English derivatives (see PAM-).

The following are examples of the uses of *pan-*; the more important words will be found in their places as Main words.

1. With national names, and words formed in imitation of them, with the sense 'Of, pertaining to, or comprising all (those indicated in the body of the word)'; with sbs. in *-ism* and *-ist*, generally expressing the notion of or aspiration for the political union of all those indicated, a sense which also tends to colour the adj. Of modern formations of this kind, PANSLAVISM and PANSLAVIST, with their related words, appear to have been the earliest. Among others are: **pan-ˌAnglo-'Saxon** *a.*, of or including all of 'Anglo-Saxon' race. **pan-anthropo'logical** *a.*, of all anthropologists. **pan-a'tomic** *a.*, consisting of all the atoms (*humorous*). **pan-'Buddhist** *a.*, of or embracing all Buddhists; so **pan-'Buddhism**. **pan-'Celtic** *a.*, of all Celts, or all the Celtic peoples; hence **pan-'Celticism**; (as a back-formation) **pan-Celt**, one who believes in the unity of all the Celtic peoples. **pan-'Christian** *a.*, universal Christian. **pan-denomi'national** *a.*, of or embracing all religious denominations. **pan-ecclesi'astical** *a.*, representing a whole church or ecclesiastical body. **pan-'Gothic** *a.*, common to or including all the Gothic or Teutonic races or languages, Germanic. **pan-'human** *a.*, of or pertaining to all human beings. **pan-I'onian, pan-I'onic** *adjs.*, of or comprising all Ionians. **pan-'Israelitish** *a.*, of or pertaining to all Israelites. **pan-'Latinist** *a.*, of or embracing all the Latin races. **pan-'Orthodox** *a.*, of, pertaining to, including, or representing all the Orthodox churches of the East; hence **pan-'Orthodoxy**, the principle of a union of all the Orthodox churches. **pan-'Protestant** *a.*, of or common to all Protestants. **pan-'Saxon** *a.* = *Pan-Anglo-Saxon.* **pan-Teu'tonic** *a.*, of or embracing all Teutonic peoples; hence **pan-'Teutonism**, the principle of a union of all Teutonic peoples. **pan-Tu'ranian** *a.*, embracing all the speakers of Ural-Altaic languages; hence **pan-Tu'ranianism, -Tu'ranism**, the principle of a union of all speakers of these languages.

1899 *Daily News* 8 May 8/4 The Admiral's '*Pan-Anglo-Saxon' ideas are popular on the other side. **1883** WRIGHT *Sci. Scepticism* 13 Were a *pananthropological congress..to vote that [etc.]. **1883** *Contemp. Rev.* Dec. 800 One great Evolutionist is inclined to..insinuate that the universe is the product of a *Pan-atomic Council. **1902** *Ibid.* Dec. 849 Something like a *Pan-Buddhist movement. *Ibid.* 851 *Pan-Buddhism and Eastern Russian policy are now inseparable factors on the political chessboard of Asia. **1904** *Westm. Gaz.* 3 Sept. 3/2 The *Pan-Celts also considered..the question of clothes, and it appears that Ireland is in need of a satisfactory and distinctive national costume. **1955** R. GRAVES *Crowning Privilege* 155, I was introduced to Welsh poetry nearly fifty years ago, when my father became an enthusiastic pan-Celt; and, this noun being new to Merioneth where we lived, he had a famous argument with Mr Postoffice-Griffiths as to whether it would count as one word in a telegram. **1891** YEATS *Let.* Nov. (1954) 181 He [*sc.* Ernest Rhys] has a kind of *Pan-Celtic enthusiasm. **1895** *Athenæum* 6 Apr. 434/1 The president of various Young Ireland and Panceltic societies. **1901** *Scotsman* 20 Sept. 3/7 [He] remarked that the Pan-Celtic Conference had laid the foundations of an abiding intellectual and moral union of the Celtic races. **1973** *Stornoway Gaz.* 24 Feb. 9/2 (*caption*) Discussing the programme for the Pan-Celtic Week, to be held in Killarney, Ireland, during May 12–20. **1868** VISCT. STRANGFORD *Select.* (1869) II. 291 An explanation..from the *Pan-Christian point of view. **1892** *Scott. Leader* 14 Mar. 7 The Carrubber's Close Mission, which is thoroughly *pan-denominational in its character. **1897** *Westm. Gaz.* 2 Nov. 9/1 Like Toynbee Hall, the new settlement is pan-denominational, welcoming all shades of opinion. **1888** *Pall Mall G.* 6 July 1/2 Two of these *pan-ecclesiastical assemblies are meeting this week in our midst. **1880** EARLE *Philol. Eng. Tongue* (ed. 3) §236 Specimens..which we derive from the old ancestral *pan-gothic stock. **1900** *Contemp. Rev.* Apr. 571 The *pan-human type spreads. **1830** J. DOUGLAS *Err. regard. Relig.* iii. 76 The *panionian Confederacy or the Amphictyonic Council. **1878** *Encycl. Brit.* VIII. 675/2 The purification of Delos..and the restoration of the *Pan-ionic festival there, in 426 B.C. **1881** *Ibid.* XIII. 204/2 Pan-Ionic. **1891** CHEYNE *Orig. Psalter* iv. 148 A fine monument of the *Pan-Israelitish sentiment of the Persian period. **1882** *Echo* 29 Aug. 1/5 She regards it as highly important that a '*Pan-Latinist' movement should be started, in order to oppose and neutralise the advancing aggression of 'Pan-Germanism' and 'Pan-Islamism'. **1888** *Pall Mall G.* 6 July 1/2 They are endeavouring to hold a *Pan-Orthodox Council in Kieff. **1900** 'ODYSSEUS' *Turkey in Europe* vi. 286 But *Panorthodoxy, if I may use the word, tends to regard Russia as the head, not only of the Slav races, but of all orthodox nations. **1902** *Q. Rev.* Apr. 604 The principles which inspire her rulers are those of Panorthodoxy and Panslavism. **1898** *Q. Rev.* Apr. 469 The old *pan-Protestant theories. **1901** A. BIRRELL in *N. Amer. Rev.* Feb. 260 A *Pan-Saxon Idea, to go down into the lists and strike the shields of the Pan-Slavonic Idea,..and of the Pan-Germanic Idea. **1884** *Manch. Guard.* 26 Sept. 5/2 An imaginary deep-laid scheme..a *Pan-Teutonic or Pan-Africander combination against the British power in South Africa. **1898** *Westm. Gaz.* 12 Nov. 5/1 The Organ of the Pan-Teutonic League. **1894** E. P. EVANS in *Pop. Sci. Monthly* XLIV. 306 Germany has long since outgrown the swaddling-clout of *Panteutonism. **1926** *Glasgow Herald* 3 Apr. 5/1 The *Pan-Turanian movement..began not more than 40 years ago. **1950** E. H. CARR *Bolshevik Rev.* I. xi. 338 The pan-Turanian aspirations of the 'young Bokhara' movement. **1926** *Glasgow Herald* 3 Apr. 5/1 The alphabet of the West will..give a new aspect to *Pan-Turanianism. **1932** *Times Lit. Suppl.* 21 July 525/2 A policy which..has been based in turn upon Panislamism, Ottomanism, Panturanianism. **1974** *Encycl. Brit. Macropædia* XIII. 789/2 Pan-Turanianism developed from a now much-disputed 19th-century theory of the common origin of Turkish, Mongol, Tungus, Finnish, Hungarian, and other languages; in certain very limited circles it looked forward to a great political federation of speakers of these languages. **1977** *Guardian Weekly* 25 Dec. 8/1 Panturanism (the dream of uniting the Turks in Asia with those of Turkey).

2. Other words: **pan'anthropism** [Gr. ἄνθρωπος man, after *pantheism*]: see quots. **pan-a'pospory**: see quot. **pan-ath'letic** *a.*, of or pertaining to the whole circle of athletic contests. **pan'atom**, an atom of a supposed primary substance of which all the elements are composed. **pan'blastic** *a. Biol.* [Gr. βλαστός sprout], originating from all the germinal layers (Billings *Nat. Med. Dict.* 1890). **pan'christic** *a.*, identifying Christ with the universe. **pan'clastic**, an explosive that shatters everything. **pan-con'ciliatory** *a.*, conciliatory to all. †**pan'crastical** *a.* ? for *panchrestical* [Gr. πάγχρηστος good for everything], good for all diseases, of the nature of a panacea. **pancyclo'pædic** *a.*, of or pertaining to the whole circle of science. **ˌpancyto'penia** (also *erron.* **-pœnia**) *Path.* [-PENIA], a condition in which the blood shows a relative deficiency of all three cellular components (erythrocytes, leucocytes, and platelets). †**pan-dæ'dalian** *a.* [Gr. πανδαίδαλος], of all curious workmanship. **pan-de'struction**, universal destruction. **pandi'abolism** [after *pantheism*] = *pan-Satanism.* **pan-dia'tonicism** (see quot. 1937); hence **pandia'tonic** *a.* **pandyna'mometer**: see quot. **pan-'egoism**, an extreme form of subjective idealism, restricting reality to the percipient ego; solipsism; hence **pan'egoist**, a solipsist. **ˌpanencepha'litis** *Path.* [prob. coined in Ger.: cf. G. *panenzephalitisch* adj., *panenzephalomyelitis* (H. Pette 1938, in *Münch. med. Wochenschr.* 29 July 1138/2), *panencephalitis* (Pette & Döring 1939, in *Deutsch. Zeitschr. f. Nervenheilkunde* CXLIX. 32)], a rare form of encephalitis in which both the grey matter and the white matter are affected and there is a gradual but progressive loss of mental and motor functions. **pa'nentheism** [Gr. ἐν in + θεός God]: see quot.; hence **pa'nentheist** *a.* and *sb.*, **panenthei'stic** *a.* **pan-'eulogism**, universal or indiscriminate praise. **pan-fri'volium** *nonce-wd.* [from *frivolous*, after *pandemonium*, etc.], a scene of all frivolity. **pan'germism**, a doctrine that attributes all disease to germs; so **pan'germic** *a.* †**pan-'glyphic** *a.*: see quot. **pan'grammatist**: see quot. **pan'graphic** *a.*, writing on all subjects or in all forms. **pangym'nasticon**, a device combining many gymnastic appliances (Funk 1895). **panhi'drosis, panid-**, perspiration over the whole body. **pan'hygrous** *a. rare* [Gr. πάνυγρος quite damp or wet], damp over the whole surface (*Syd. Soc. Lex.* 1893). **pan-hype'ræmia**, general hyperæmia or plethora of blood (*Ibid.*). **panˌhypopi'tuitarism** *Path.* (see quot. 1941). **panhyste'rectomy**, complete excision of the womb. **panichthy'ophagous** *a.*, eating fish of all kinds. **panidio'morphic** *a. Min.*, having all its components idiomorphic. **pan-materia'listic** *a.* [after *pantheistic*], holding the material universe to be all. **pan-me'lodicon, -me'lodion**: see quot. **pan-neu'ritis** *Path.*, general inflammation of the nerves; multiple neuritis (*Syd. Soc. Lex.* 1893). **'pannomy** *Philos.*, the 'law of reason as universal' (Funk 1895). **pano'istic** *a. Entom.* [Gr. ᾠόν egg], having an ovary producing eggs only without vitelligenous or other cells. †**pa'nolethry** [Gr. πανωλεθρία utter destruction], general destruction or slaughter. **pan'oral** *a. Dentistry*, of or pertaining to radiography of the whole mouth in one exposure. †**pan'organon**, a universal instrument. **pano'titis**, inflammation involving both the middle and internal ear (Billings *Nat. Med. Dict.* 1890). **'panpathy** [Gr. πάθος suffering], a feeling common to all. **panphe'nomenalism** *Philos.*, a theory that the universe is purely phenomenal. †**pan'plegia**: see PAMPLEGIA. **pan'pneumatism**: see quot. **'panpolism** [Gr. πόλις city, πόλισμα community], equality of civil rights. **pan-'popish** *a.*, pertaining to universal papal jurisdiction or power. **pan-'Satanism** [after *pantheism*], the belief or doctrine that Satan is the informing spirit of the universe. **pan'sciolism**, universal sciolism or smattering of knowledge. **panscle'rosis** *Path.*, complete induration of a part (*Syd. Soc. Lex.* 1893). †**panselene** [Gr. πανσέληνος full-mooned], the full moon (Phillips 1706, etc.). †**'pansperm**: see quot. **pan-'sphygmograph** = CARDIOGRAPH, or a combination of cardiograph and sphygmograph (Mayne 1857). **pan'sporoblast** *Zool.*, a structure formed by protozoans of the subclass Neosporidia, comprising several sporoblasts and two other cells. **panstereo'rama** [Gr. στερεός solid + ὅραμα sight, spectacle]: see quot. **pansy'stolic** *a. Med.*, (of a heart murmur) continuing throughout a systole. **pan'telegraph**, a form of telegraph invented by Casseli in 1856, for transmitting facsimile messages and portraits along a line connecting two isochronously vibrating pendulums, of which the first guides an iron point over the original portrait or message, setting up equivalent motions in the other. So **pante'legraphy**, 'facsimile telegraphy' (Funk 1895). **pan-'telephone**, a highly sensitive microphone capable of reproducing minute sound-vibrations at great distances; hence **pantele'phonic** *a.* **panthe'lematism** *Philos.* [Gr. θεληματ- will: see -ISM], the theory of Schopenhauer that the Ultimate and Absolute is Will. **'panthelism** [Gr. θέλ-ειν to will] = prec. **pantropic** (-'trəʊpɪk, -'trɒpɪk) *a. Med.* [-TROPIC], attacking or affecting many kinds of tissue indiscriminately. **pan-tropical** *a.*, of plants or animals, found in all regions of the tropics; also, including all tropical areas. **pan'zoism** *Biol.* [Gr. ζωή life], a name given to a synthesis of all the elements or factors of vitality. **pan'zoöty** [Gr. ζωότης animal nature], a zymotic disease affecting animals generally in a district or country; so **panzo'ötic** *a.* and *sb.*

1871 H. B. FORMAN *Living Poets* 367 If Mr. Swinburne's creed is describable in one word, that word must be made for the occasion—*pananthropism:..he sees the spirit of man (which be it borne in mind he calls 'God') everywhere animating and informing the universe. **1879** J. J. G. WILKINSON *Let.* 20 May in R. B. Perry *Tht. & Char. W. James* (1935) I. 27 Nothing is left to my apprehension but pananthropism, a composite form of pantheism. **1936** *Theology* XXXIII. 265 The poem is an impassioned plea for the truth not of Pantheism but of *Pananthropism. **1892** *Athenæum* 12 Nov. 667/3 A seedling..showing prothalli developed aposporously over general surface of frond (*pan-apospory). **1897** *Westm. Gaz.* 27 Jan. 2/1 That Cambridge Under-graduates..are not all marching through a cycle of *pan-athletic triumphs to double firsts. **1872** WATTS *Dict. Chem.* VI. 896 *Panatoms..the hypothesis that all the elements are formed of a single primary substance, pantogen, the atoms of which are regarded as material points, and as equal to one another. **1897** *Expositor* Dec. 416 Grotesque Egyptian Gnostic Gospels which..exhibit a *pan-Christic conception. **1892** *Times* 2 Apr. 7/2 A *panclastic more terrible in its effects than any hitherto known. **1901** M. J. F. MCCARTHY *Five Yrs. Irel.* xxvi. 383 That *panconciliatory gentleman. **1698** FRYER *Acc. E. India & P.* 377 Their Prescriptions are *Pancrastical, a Salve for every Sore, without respect had to difference of Temperament, or Constitution. **1852** DE QUINCEY *Sir W. Hamilton* Wks. 1863 XVI. 130 A *pancyclopædic acquaintance with every section of knowledge that could furnish keys for unlocking man's inner nature. **1944** W. DAMESHEK *Leukopenia & Agranulocytosis* ii. 44 The designation of pancytopenia may be applied to conditions in the blood in which there is a well-defined reduction in red cells, white cells and platelets. **1956** M. W. WINTROBE *Clin. Hematol.* (ed. 4) xi. 560 Pancytopenia is not a disease entity but rather a triad which is found under a number of different circumstances. **1974** *Nature* 17 May 263 Three patients, two males and a female, were studied: two suffered from aplastic anaemia and one from a pre-leukaemic state with pancytopoenia. **1618** LITHGOW *Pilgr. Farewell* E iv, To see thy gallant Youthes, so rich arrayde, In *Pandedalian Showes, did shine like Ore. **1884** RAE *Contemp. Socialism* 302 Bakunin, the Russian nihilist,..says that to attain '*Pandestruction' requires 'a series of assassinations and audacious, or even mad enterprises, horrifying the powerful and dazzling the people'. **1899** L. A. TOLLEMACHE in *Literature* 16 Sept. 281 [Some pessimists] will contend that ..her [Nature's] cult is in reality, not Pantheism but *Pandiabolism. **1937** N. SLONIMSKY *Mus. since 1900* (1938) p. xxii, *Pan-diatonicism sanctions the simultaneous use of any or all seven tones of the diatonic scale, with the bass determining the harmony. *Ibid.*, Gebrauchsmusik, proletarian music, and most forms of absolute music make use of pan-diatonic technique. **1963** *Times* 13 May 8/2 The immense profusion of counterpoint was under complete control, and the pandiatonic climaxes were shattering. **1970** *Composer & Conductor* Aug. 6/1, I myself [*sc.* N. Slonimsky] ventured into musical neologism with Pandiatonicism to describe a 20th-century technique in which all seven tones of the diatonic scale are used freely in dissonant combinations. **1876** *Catal. Sci. App. S. Kens.* 59 Flexion *Pandynamometer. An instrument designed to determine the work done by a steam engine, by means of the flexion of the beam. **1896** BENN in *Academy* 25 Jan. 70/1 *Pan-egoism (better known as solipsism—the extreme form of subjective idealism). **1898** *Q. Rev.* Jan. 65 Secondly, a philosophy of Immaterialism and Panegoism, in which, if consistent, we become subjective idealists and solipsists. **1890** *Eng. Illustr. Mag.* Nov. 130, I am the great *Panegoist, the would-be Conservator of Self, the inspired prophet of the Universal I. **1950** *Brain* LXXIII. 150 Perhaps the term '*Pan-encephalitis' already adopted by Pette (1942) for forms which attack both grey and white matter could be usefully employed here, i.e. 'Sub-acute sclerosing pan-encephalitis'. **1974** *Sci. Amer.* Feb. 35/1 In 1969..measles virus was isolated from brain cells of patients suffering from the brain inflammation called subacute sclerosing panencephalitis (SSPE). **1874** tr. *Ueberweg's Hist. Philos.* II. 230 Krause (1781–1832)..sought to improve upon the pantheism of the System of Identity by developing a doctrine of *Panentheism, or a philosophy founded on the notion that all things are in God. **1891** tr. *Amiel's Jrnl.* 194 The panentheism of Krause is ten times more religious than their dogmatic supernaturalism. **1940** *Theology* XL. 270 He [*sc.* Eckehart] oscillates between non-duality and modified duality, between pantheism and panentheism. **1959** I. EPSTEIN *Judaism* 244 Cordovero..safeguards the theistic position by defining his attitude in the formula: 'God is all reality, but not all reality *is* God'—an attitude which came to be known in modern philosophy as 'panentheism'. **1970** P. BERTOCCI *Person God Is* xi. 207, I shall..argue that a temporalistic form of personalistic theism (not pantheism, not panentheism) can reasonably illuminate what we actually do find in human experience and the world. **1959** W. N. PITTENGER *Word Incarnate* vii. 155 They [*sc.* 'Hartshorne and the other theistic 'process' philosophers'] ..offer us a **pan-entheist* view of the world which presents God and his creation, supremely God and man, in continued and intimate relationship. **1974** *Church Times* 22 Nov. 15/1 We regret that, in Canon David Edwards's review of Martin Thornton's *My God*, Fr. Thornton was described as a 'pantheist'. This was a misprint for 'panentheist'. **1918** M. D. PETRE *Modernism* viii. 177, I..began slowly to form an optimistic and panentheistic belief. **1959** W. N. PITTENGER *Word Incarnate* vii. 200 A panentheistic conception, in which God is seen as above and beyond the world yet ceaselessly active in it and intimately related to it. **1970** P. BERTOCCI *Person God Is* xi. 221 But persons have too much autonomy, and God has too much autonomy, in 'essence' and 'content', to fit into a part-whole model, either in the 'organic' sense or the panentheistic. *a* **1864** *National Rev.* (Webster), Her book has a trace of the cant of *paneulogism. **1834** *Tait's Mag.* I. 597/1 Within the walls of that exquisite *Panfrivolium—the ball-room at Willis's! **1887** A. M. BROWN *Anim. Alkal.* 160 *Pangermic doctrines bolstered up by hazy, vague, hypotheses. *Ibid.* 126 *Pangermism has been exhausting its energies in sensational demonstrations of bacterial surprises and bacillar blunderings. **1592** R. D. *Hypnerotomachia* 6 Fragments of strange histories, *Panglyphic and Hemy-gliphic. *Margin*, Panglyphic be wholy carved from the head to the foot in all members. **1739** J. HERRICK *Tryphiodorus* p. xxvii, There is yet another style of Writers which..may not improperly be called *Pangrammatists... It was not sufficient for them that their Poems consisted of the proper feet and measure, unless all the letters of the Alphabet were crowded into every single line of them. **1825** *New Monthly Mag.* XIV. 254 Rivalling the Pangrammatists and Lipogrammatists of old in quaint and laughter-stirring conceits. **1821** *Blackw. Mag.* VIII. 356 A sort of Hermes Trismegistus—in short, he may be reckoned omniscriptive or *pangraphic. **1857** MAYNE *Expos. Lex.*, *Panidrosis. **1893** *Syd. Soc. Lex.*, *Panhidrosis.* **1941** F. ALBRIGHT et al. in *Trans. Assoc. Amer. Physicians* LVI. 48 By '*panhypopituitarism' is meant a condition in which the anterior pituitary gland as a whole has impaired function. **1954** K. E. PASCHKIS et al. *Clin. Endocrinol.* xiii. 293 Tendency to hypoglycemia..is regularly present in panhypopituitarism. **1972** *Obstetrics & Gynecol.* XXXIX. 397/1 In a woman hypophysectomized at the time a craniopharyngioma was performed and who showed full panhypopituitarism, several regimens of human menopausal gonadotropin..failed to induce ovulation. **1977** *Lancet* 9 Apr. 779/2 The underlying pituitary tumour was not diagnosed until she presented with panhypopituitarism at the age of 76 (serum-prolactin 950 μg/l). **1890** BILLINGS *Nat. Med. Dict.*, **Panhysterectomy.* **1900** *Lancet* 18 Aug. 500/2 Panhysterectomy and vaginal extirpation were favoured in continental Europe. **1853** *Fraser's Mag.* XLVII. 265 A dry coarse fish, fit only for hungry boatmen and *panicthyophagous puss. **1888** W. S. BAYLEY in *Amer. Naturalist* Mar. 209 When..all of the constituents are idiomorphically developed, the rock is *panidiomorphic. **1877** *Fraser's Mag.* XV. 103 A most striking pourtray, in pantheistic or *panmaterialistic form, of the wondrous living guise of the Unknowable. **1838** *Encycl. Brit.* (ed. 7) XVI. 789/2 **Panmelodicon*, an instrument invented by Leppich at Vienna in 1810. By means of a conical barrel moved by a wheel, rods of metal, bent to a right angle, were made to sound when the finger-keys were pressed down. **1890** *Cent. Dict.*, *Panmelodion.* **1877** HUXLEY *Anat. Inv. Anim.* vii. 443 So far as is at present known, only the Orthoptera and the Pulicidae possess *panoistic ovaria. **1888** ROLLESTON & JACKSON *Anim. Life* Introd. 23 *note*, An ovary in which every ovarian cell becomes an egg, may be termed panoistic; one in which some only become eggs,.. meroistic. The terms are Brandt's, and were originally applied by him to Insectan ovaries. **1668** M. CASAUBON *Credulity* (1670) 58 Such persecutions, confusions, internecions, and *Panolethries, as they have suffered in most places. **1959** *Dental Practitioner* X. 270 (*heading*) *Pan-oral radiology. The most recent advance in dental radiography. **1967** L. M. ENNIS et al. *Dental Roentgenol.* (ed. 6) X. 287 (*caption*) Exposure mechanism and shieldings used..for the panoral technic. **1672** LEYBOURN (*title*) *Panorganon; or, a Universal Instrument performing all such conclusions as are usually wrought by Spheres, Sectors, Quadrants, Planispheres, etc., and to Solve Problems in Astronomy, Dialling, etc. **1900** P. CARUS *Hist. Devil* 462 There is..a mysterious longing, a yearning for the fulness of the whole, a *panpathy which finds a powerful utterance in the psalms of all the religions on earth. **1871** FRASER *Life Berkeley* x. 410 This philosophy of ultimately unintelligible *pan-phenomenalism. **1897** *Scotsman* 25 Mar. 7/5 This psychology..leaves no room for reality anywhere, and can only result in a panphenomenalism akin to that of Hume. **1901** *Baldwin's Dict. Philos.* II. 256/1 **Panpneumatism*, a term used by v. Hartmann (only) to designate a 'higher synthesis of Panlogism..and Panthelism ..according to which the absolute is both will and thought'. **1884** RAE *Contemp. Socialism* 190 Equality of right was the mark of the new period: Marlo calls it *panpolism. **1883** *Chr. Commw.* 6 Dec. 174/3 They have, while escaping from the *pan-popish bondage,..been led into metaphysical mazes of divinity. **1894** tr. *Harnack's Hist. Dogma* iv. 257 *note*, Some Gnostics advanced to *Pan-Satanism with regard to the Conception of the World. **1868** *Pall Mall G.* 2 Dec. 12 The attempt at pansophism, even in the arts, must end in *pansciolism. **1731** BAILEY, **Pansperm*, universal seed, also a mixture of all sorts of seeds. **1893** R. R. GURLEY in *Bull. U.S. Fish Comm.* *1891* 408 **Pansporoblast*, the transparent plasma-sphere formed by the condensation of a portion of the plasma around one of the numerous nuclei of the endoplasm of the myxosporidium; in distinction from the sporoblasts which result from the segmentation of the pansporoblast. **1932** BORRADAILE & POTTS *Invertebrata* ii. 93 In the syncytium,..there arise..bodies known as pansporoblasts, each composed of a couple of envelope cells with one or more cells known as sporoblasts. **1973** K. G. GRELL *Protozool.* 464 In most species [of *Myxosporidia*] the sporoblast forms several spores. It is then referred to as a pansporoblast. **1842** BRANDE *Dict. Sci.*, etc., **Panstereorama*,..in Rilievo, a model of a town or country in cork, wood, pasteboard, or other substances. **1889** in *Public Opinion* 27 Apr., In place of a picture he shows us a panstereorama. **1954** *Brit. Heart Jrnl.* XVI. 257 A *pan-systolicapical murmur was always associated with some degree of regurgitation at operation. **1966** *Lancet* 24 Dec. 1389/2 There was a harsh pansystolic murmur..radiating into the axilla. **1875** KNIGHT *Dict. Mech.* 1602/2 **Pantelegraph.* **1881** *Nature* XXIV. 225 Of telephone-specialists M. de Locht-Labye will show his *pan-telephone in action. **1887** *Sci. Amer.* 28 May 343/2 When the diaphragm was [affected] by damping either with the fingers or by placing the ear directly against its surface, the molecular or *pantelephonic vibration predominated, and all sounds were heard, including the first harmonic. **1877** SHIELDS *Final Philos.* 293 Hartmann, endeavoring to reconcile the panlogism of Hegel with the *panthelematism of Schopenhauer (or so called doctrine of universal will). **1896** W. CALDWELL *Schopenhauer's Syst.* i. 37 Though Schopenhauer's system has a strong materialistic colouring it is not materialism. It is rather animism or panpsychism (*panthelism, in point of fact). **1901** *Baldwin's Dict. Philos.* II. 257–8 *Panthelism*, the doctrine that will is the basis of the universe. **1917** *Encycl. Relig. & Ethics* IX. 612/1 The affirmation that the real is irrational (a blind will, panthelism [πᾶν + ἐθέλω]) in Schopenhauer's pessimism. **1937** *Jrnl. Path. & Bacteriol.* XLIV. 410 The neurotropic virus protects to a certain extent against the *pantropic strain. **1967** *Res. Vet. Sci.* VIII. 414 Antibodies will persist..for many years in the sera of cattle and sheep infected with pantropic virus. **1937** *Discovery* Sept. 263/1 Its [*sc.* the fern, *Ceratopteris thalictroides*'] distribution is *pan-tropical. **1946** *Nature* 20 July 86/1 The once-popular 'tiger nut' (swellings on the rhizomes of a pan-tropical water sedge). **1953** *New Biol.* XV. 35 The Scale Insect *Aspidotus destructor* is a pantropical species which is found wherever the coconut palm grows. **1967** *Palaeogeogr., Palaeoclimatol., Palaeoecol.* III. 203 There are no pan-tropical mammals, as there are pan-tropical plants. **1976** *Nature* 19 Feb. 528/2 A demonstrably Australian flora with many common pantropical plants missing. **1878** *N. Amer. Rev.* CXXVII. 53 The great world-powers, such as Evolution, Persistence of Force, Heredity, *Panzoism, and Physiological Units. **1890** BILLINGS *Nat. Med. Dict.*, **Panzoötic*, an epizoötic affecting many different kinds of animals. **1893** *Syd. Soc. Lex.*, *Panzoötic*, relating to *Panzoötia*. **1857** MAYNE *Expos. Lex.*, *Panzootia*,..term for a disease which affects the cattle and other animals of a country or district generally; similar to Pandemia as applied to human beings; *panzoöty.

†**panabase** ('pænəbeɪs). *Min. Obs.* [irreg. mod. f. Gr. πᾶν all + BASE *sb.*[1] Named (in French) by Beudant 1832.] A synonym of TETRAHEDRITE.

1847 in WEBSTER; and in later Dicts. **1896** A. H. CHESTER *Dict. Names Min.*, *Panabase*,..because of the number of bases which may replace one another in its composition.

†**panabasite** (pə'næbəsaɪt). *Min. Obs.* = prec.

1870 J. ORTON *Andes & Amazons* II. xxxiii. 443 Native silver with arsenuret of silver, panabasite pyrites and blende.

†**pana'cæon**, erron. form of PANACEA.

1684 tr. *Bonet's Merc. Compit.* XVI. 563, I think I have found a Panacæon for all Scorbutick pains.

panace ('pænəsiː). Also 6–7 **panaces**, 8 **panacee**. [Adapted or adopted forms of L. *panax* and *panaces*, synonyms of *panacēa* (see below), as name of a plant. *Panaces* retains the L. form; *panacee* was prob. from Fr.; Lyly's *panace*, if of two syllables, would represent L. *panax*.] A fabulous herb to which was ascribed the power of healing all diseases; 'All-heal'.

Variously identified, as by Pliny, with *Ligusticum*, Lovage, and Opopanax, and by the 16th c. herbalists with several other plants: cf. ALL-HEAL.

1513 DOUGLAS *Æneis* XII. vii. 91 The weill smelland herb hait panaces. **1580** LYLY *Euphues* (Arb.) 425 Where is that precious herbe Panace which cureth all diseases? **1611** BIBLE *Transl. Pref.* 3 Men talke of Panaces the herbe, that it was good for all diseases. **1697** DRYDEN *Æneid* XII. 617 Venus.. brews Th' extracted Liquor with Ambrosian Dews, And od'rous Panacee. **1740** C. PITT *Virg. Æneid* XII. 583 The queen..Tempers with scented panacee the whole. **1866** CONINGTON *Æneid* XII. 424 With juices of ambrosia blent And panace of fragrant scent.

panacea (pænə'siːə). Also 6 **-chæa, -chea**, 7 **-cæa**. [a. L. *panacēa*, a. Gr. πανάκεια universal remedy, f. πανακής 'all-healing'.]

1. A remedy, cure, or medicine reputed to heal all diseases; a catholicon or universal remedy.

1548 UDALL, etc. *Erasm. Par. Luke* Pref. 8 b, [That] which they call *panacea*, a medicine (as they affirme) effectual and of muche vertue, but knowen to no man. **1599** NASHE *Lenten Stuffe* Wks. (Grosart) V. 234 Physitions deafen our eares with the Honorificabilitudinitatibus of their heauenly Panachea. **1625** HART *Anat. Ur.* Pref. B, This Panacæa was a certaine medicine made of saffron, quick siluer, vermilion, antimonie, and certaine sea shels made vp in fashion of triangular lozenges. **1652** EVELYN *St. France* Misc. Writ. (1805) 89 Phlebotomie, which is their panacea for all diseases. **1759** WESLEY *Wks.* (1872) XIV. 243 There cannot be..an absolute panacea—a medicine that will cure every disease incident to the human body. **1867** MRS. H. WOOD *Orville College* (1876) 185 Coffee was his panacea for most ailments.

fig. **1616** *Rich Cabinet* 24 The godly Preacher..procures the generall panacea of patience, to ease all paines. **1755** P. WHITEHEAD *Ep. to Dr. Thompson* Poems (1790) 160 What sovereign med'cine can its course reclaim? What, but the poet's panacea—shame! **1803** JANE PORTER *Thaddeus* (1826) III. vii. 151 A panacea for worse ills. **1884** SIR C. S. C. BOWEN in *Law Rep.* 26 Ch. Div. 711 There is one panacea which heals every sore in litigation, and that is costs.

†**2.** Applied to a reputed herb of healing virtue, vaguely and variously identified; All-heal. *Obs.*

1590 SPENSER *F.Q.* III. v. 32 Whether yt divine Tobacco were, Or Panachæa, or Polygony, Shee fownd, and brought it to her patient deare. **1706** PHILLIPS, *Panacea*,..the Herb All-heal or Wound-wort. **1727–41** CHAMBERS *Cycl.*, *Panacea*,..All-heal, is also applied to several plants, by reason of the extraordinary virtues ascribed to them.

3. *panacea of mercury*: see quot.

1823 J. BADCOCK *Dom. Amusem.* 96 Add what is called, white panacea of mercury, (calomel washed in spirits of wine).

panacean (pænə'siːən), *a.* [f. prec. + -AN.] Of the nature of a panacea; all-healing.
1638–48 G. DANIEL *Eclog.* v. 102 Panacean Asphodil And fresh Nepenthe. **1782** WHITEHEAD *Odes* xlii, Still does reluctant Peace refuse To shed her Panacean dews. **1880** *Med. Temp. Jrnl.* July 145 Our slowness to believe the panacean qualities of alcohol.

panaceist (pænə'siːɪst). [f. as prec. + -IST.] One who believes in or applies a panacea.
1803 COLERIDGE *Lett., to Southey* (1895) 438 If the coach-man do not turn Panaceist, and cure all my ills by breaking my neck. **1849** LEWIS *Influence Authority* x. §6. 382 The panaceist..[has] one principle, which he introduces everywhere, and which he expects to prove a complete and immediate remedy for numerous political ills of the most discordant natures.

panache (pə'nɑːʃ, -æ-). Also 6 pannach, 6–7 pinnach, 7 penache, -ashe, 7–8 pannache, 7–9 pennache, 8 panashe, (-ack). [a. F. *panache*, ad. It. *pennacchio*, deriv. of *penna* feather.]
1. a. A tuft or plume of feathers, esp. when used as a head-dress or an ornament for a helmet; †hence extended to ornaments of similar appearance, as a tassel.
1553 in Hakluyt *Voy.* II. I. 113 A little pinnach of white Ostrich feathers. **1585** JAMES I *Ess. Poesie* (Arb.) 43 Like as ane hors, when he is barded haile, An fethered pannach set vpon his heid, Will make him seame more braue. **1601** HOLLAND *Pliny* I. 270 Their feathers so faire, that they serue for pennaches. **1651** EVELYN *Diary* 7 Sept., He had in his cap a pennach of heron. **1669** WYCHE *Short Rel. River Nile* (1798) 40 The tail is worn by children for a Penashe. **1719** D'URFEY *Pills* VI. 133 Like to a Panack it covers my Face. **1796** STEDMAN *Surinam* II. xvii. 31 This bird [the cockatoo] is crowned with a panashe or bunch of feathers. **1819** H. BUSK *Vestriad* I. 428 The tow'ring panache sweeps the chalky floor. *a* **1848** SIR S. MEYRICK in Cussans *Her.* vi. (1882) 94 The distinction between the Panache and Plume is, that the former was fixed on the top of a Helmet, while the latter was placed behind, in front, or on the side.
b. *Astron.* A plume-like solar protuberance.
1887 LOCKYER *Chem. of Sun* 441 At the poles there is an exquisite tracery curved in opposite directions, consisting of plumes or *panaches*.
c. *Comb.*, as ***panache-crest.***
1864 BOUTELL *Her. Hist. & Pop.* xvii. §2 (ed. 3) 267 The Garter-Plates..display panache-crests.
2. *fig.* Display, swagger, verve.
1898 THOMAS & GUILLEMARD tr. *Rostand's Cyrano de Bergerac* v. vi. 294 *Cyrano*... One thing is left, that, void of stain or smutch, I bear away despite you... *Roxane*... 'Tis?.. *Cyrano*... My *panache*. **1900** J. T. GREIN *Dramatic Crit.* (1902) III. 65 No one displayed that 'panache' which is the paramount demand of romantic comedy. **1903** G. B. SHAW *Man & Superman* p. xxxi, Shakespear..never conceived how any man who was not a fool could, like Bunyan's hero..with the panache of a millionaire, bequeath 'my sword to him that shall succeed me in my pilgrimage, and my courage and skill to him that can get it'. **1932** R. FRY *Characteristics French Art* III. 53 In real life the fun of soldiering, its bustle, its swagger, its panache, sometimes leads to being mutilated. **1949** F. MACLEAN *Eastern Approaches* III. vi. 370 His must have been, I think, an engaging character, a mixture of southern *panache*, rustic guile, and a childlike desire to please. **1960** D. WALKER *Where High Winds Blow* II. viii. 117 Mac wore his flying clothes, the half-laced boots and the old suède jacket; but with his clean blue shirt and a silk handkerchief knotted at his neck, he had a workaday panache. **1972** D. FRANCIS *Smokescreen* v. 58 A certain *panache* about him, but also some of the ruthless cynicism of experienced journalists. **1976** *New Yorker* 22 Mar. 128/3 When he did join the Maquis, late in March, 1944, Malraux exhibited his customary panache. **1978** *Listener* 12 Jan. 49/1 He plays the piano with panache, but cannot read music.

panached (pə'nɑːʃt, -æ-), *a.* Also 7 pen(n)ached [f. prec. + -ED²; cf. F. *panaché*.] Diversified with stripes of colour like a plume.
1664 EVELYN *Kal. Hort.* Apr. 65 Carefully protect from violent storms of Rain..your Pennach'd Tulips. **1665–76** REA *Flora* (ed. 2) 93 The flowers are white and red panached like a tulip. **1719** LONDON & WISE *Compl. Gard.* IX. 286 Purple, violet colour'd and panached or striped yellow, and violet Pansies.

†**'panacy.** *Obs. rare*$^{-1}$. = PANACEA.
a **1690** T. WATSON in Spurgeon *Treas. Dav.* Ps. cxix. 72 The Scripture is..the panacy, or universal medicine for the soul.

panada (pə'nɑːdə). Also 7 pannada; *β.* 6–9 panado. [a. Sp. (Pg., Pr.) *panada* = It. *panata*, F. *panade* PANADE², f. It. *pane*, L. *pāne-m* bread: see -ADE, also -ADO.] A dish made by boiling bread in water to a pulp, and flavouring it according to taste with sugar, currants, nutmegs, or other ingredients.
1625 F. HERING *Cert. Rules* C b, Burnet will doe well, or thinne pannada. **1625** MASSINGER *New Way* I. ii, She keeps her chamber, dines with a panada, Or water-gruel. **1732** ARBUTHNOT *Rules of Diet* I. 252 Mealy Substances and Panadas, or Bread boiled in Water. **1782** JONES *Let.* in Ld. Teignmouth *Life* (1804) 218 The nation..will be fed like a consumptive patient, with chicken-broth and panada. **1881** J. A. SYMONDS *Shelley* iv. 73 His favourite diet consisted of pulse or bread, which he ate dry with water, or made into panada.
fig. **1822** *Blackw. Mag.* XII. 12 [They] swallow, without flinching, all the theological panada with which she may think fit to cram them.
β. **1598** FLORIO, *Panada*, a kinde of meate called a Panado. **1617** MORYSON *Itin.* II. 46 Before these warres, he vsed to haue nourishing breckefasts, as panadoes, and broths. **1776** *Phil. Trans.* LXVI. 430 The regimen enjoined him..was gruel, panado, and sage-tea. **1835–40** J. M. WILSON *Tales of Borders* (1851) XIX. 252 A ruined constitution, which sack, and sago-pudding, and panado, could scarcely support.

†**panade¹.** *Obs. rare.* [app. related in its radical part to OF. *pann-*, *pan-*, *penart*, *penard* 'cutlass, a kind of large two-edged knife, poniard' (Godef.), med.L. *penardus* (Du Cange), but the suffix is different. Cf. also med.L. *pennatus* a kind of sword (Du Cange), It. *pennato* 'a kind of cutting-hooke that gardiners vse' (Florio); also (for the radical part) L. *bipennis* a two-edged axe.] A kind of large knife.
[**13..** *Annales Paulini* an. 1330 in *Chron. Edw. I & II* (Rolls) I. 350 Quando episcopus erat moriturus clamavit et præcepit 'Occide, occide'; et ad hoc tradidit suum panade, unde caput episcopi fuerat abscisum. **1883** STUBBS *ibid.* II. p. xcix, [Bishop Stapleton was] stripped and beheaded with a panade or butcher's knife, which one of the bystanders offered.] *c* **1386** CHAUCER *Reeve's T.* 9 And by his belt he baar a long panade [*mispr. by Thynne* pauade]. *Ibid.* 40 Wiþ panade and wiþ knyf or boydekyn.

panade² (pə'neɪd). [a. F. *panade*.] = PANADA.
1598 FLORIO, *Panadella, Panadina*, a little messe of Panad. **1603** HOLLAND *Plutarch's Mor.* 714 They give pappes and panades unto their little babes. **1655** J. PHILLIPS *Sat. agst. Hypocr.* (1674) 14 It was no Christmas-dish with Pruens made, Nor White-broath, nor Capon-broth, nor sweet ponade. **1892** W. B. SCOTT *Autobiog. Notes* I. 127 His [Leigh Hunt's] own food seemed to be panade.

panado, variant of PANADA. *Panado'd* in *Discolliminium* (1650) 46: see MARCH-PANADO *v.*

Panadol ('pænədɒl). *Pharm.* Also **panadol**. A proprietary name for paracetamol.
1955 *Trade Marks Jrnl.* 14 Dec. 1231/2 Panadol... All goods included in class 5 [*sc.* pharmaceutical, veterinary, and sanitary substances, etc.] for sale in the United Kingdom. Bayer Products Limited,..Kingston-on-Thames, Surrey; merchants and manufacturers. **1959** WILSON & SCHILD *Appl. Pharmacol.* (ed. 9) xvi. 326 The analgesic activity of N-acetyl p-aminophenol (paracetamol, panadol)..has been shown to be about as great as that of the parent compounds. **1967** M. CULPAN *In Deadly Vein* viii. 176 A low table—with..a couple of novels, and a bottle of Panadol tablets. **1971** D. LAMBERT in C. Bonington *Annapurna South Face* 293 The majority who attended had to be given some form of placebo, and panadol or aspirin were found best for this purpose. **1975** *Sunday Times* 16 Nov. 44/3, I was going crazy trying to find things: the Panadol for my husband's head.

‖**panæsthesia, -esthesia** (pænɪs'θiːsɪə, -iːsθ-). [a. Gr. *παναισθησία* full vigour of the senses, f. *παν-*, PAN- + *αἴσθησις* perception.] The total sum of the perceptions of an individual at a given moment.
1884 McDOWALL tr. A. Herzen in *Jrnl. Mental Sci.* Apr. 51 Each [element] awakens its own *quantum* of consciousness, which unites with that of the other elements simultaneously disintegrated, to form the *panæsthesia* of the individual. *Note.* I propose this name of *panæsthesia* to express 'the totality of what an individual feels at a given moment'.

panæsthetism (pæ'nɛs-, pæ'niːsθɪtɪz(ə)m). [f. Gr. *παν-*, PAN- + *αἰσθητ-ής* one that feels + -ISM.]
1. The theory that consciousness may inhere in matter generally.
1882 E. D. COPE in *Amer. Naturalist* June 468 Panæsthetism... The admission of the possibility of the existence of consciousness in other forms of matter than protoplasm, and in other planets than the earth.
2. = PANÆSTHESIA.
1900 GOULD *Dict. Med. Biol.*, *Panesthetism*, same as *Panesthesia*.

pan-'African, *a.* [PAN- 1.] All-African; of or pertaining to all persons of African birth or descent; of, pertaining to, or comprising all the peoples of Africa generally.
1900 *Daily News* 16 July 7/5 A pan-African Conference will be held at the Westminster Town Hall on July 23,..and will be attended and addressed by those of African descent from all parts of the British Empire, the United States of America, Abyssinia, Liberia, Hayti, &c. *Ibid.* 26 July 4/4 A permanent Pan-African Association was formed to protect the rights and aid the development of Africans and their descendants throughout the world. **1944** *Ann. Reg. 1943* 132 Sir Godfrey Huggins, Prime Minister of Southern Rhodesia,..foreshadowed a possible Pan-African Council to coordinate problems common to African countries. **1955** [see next]. **1960** *Times* 29 Sept. (Nigeria Suppl.) p. xii/2 Dr. Nkrumah's pan-African way of thinking. **1962** *Listener* 25 Jan. 157/1 The Ghana Government has also tried to promote pan-African schemes of unity. **1967** *Freedomways* VII. 174 It is only by planning along Pan-African lines ourselves can Africa hope to free herself. **1973** *Caribbean Contact* Feb. 16/2 Garvey's views in the 1920's already foreshadow the later Pan African movement. **1975** C. E. GRIFFITH *Afr. Dream* viii. 105 The pan-African advocate was disturbed by contemporary works which assigned Africans last place among the three major races of the world.
So **pan-Afri'cander** *a.* [PAN- 1], of or belonging to all Africanders, or of a government or state which should include all South Africans of Dutch descent or sympathies. Hence **pan-Afri'canderdom** (see -DOM).
1884 *Manch. Guard.* 26 Sept. 5/2 An imaginary deep-laid scheme..a Pan-Teutonic or Pan-Africander combination against the British power in South Africa. **1899** T. SCHREINER in *Daily News* 29 Nov. 6/6 Their dream of a Pan-Africander Republic. **1900** *Ibid.* 12 June 3/4 He never pretended to hide his ideal of Pan-Afrikanderdom under its own flag.

pan-Africanism (pæn'æfrɪkənɪz(ə)m). [f. PAN-AFRICAN *a.* + -ISM.] A movement which advocates the political union of all the indigenous inhabitants of Africa; the ideals of this movement. Hence **pan-'Africanist** *sb.*, an advocate or supporter of pan-Africanism, also as *adj.*, of or pertaining to pan-Africanism.
1955 B. TIMOTHY *Kwame Nkrumah* iii. 38 In October, 1945, the fifth International Conference of the Pan-African Congress was held in Manchester... The proceedings of the Conference were conducted under the joint chairmanship of ..Dr. P. Milliard, and Dr. W. E. B. Du Bois, who gave birth to Pan-Africanism. **1959** *Cape Times* 7 Apr. 1/7 African leaders from all parts of the Union decided to establish the Pan Africanist Congress. **1960** *Times* 22 Mar. 12/1 The Pan-Africanists' campaign against the pass laws exploded today on the banks of the Vaal river. **1963** *Listener* 17 Jan. 110/1 The fourth political ideal, Pan-Africanism, or continental federation. **1973** S. HENDERSON *Understanding New Black Poetry* 17 The changing world in which Black Americans of the post-World War II generation found themselves, a world in which articulate men and women rediscovered Africa and Pan-Africanism. **1973** *Black World* Mar. 53/2 An indiscriminate listing of pan-Africanist and Africanist resources. **1975** *Times Lit. Suppl.* 17 Oct. 1238/5 Like many pan-Africanists from the New World, there was often an element of utopianism in Delany's vision of Africa. **1976** *Survey* Summer–Autumn 289 Among black people outside there was often a strong link between Marxism and pan-Africanism. *Ibid.*, Black Americans and West Indians who were pan-Africanists were disproportionately left of centre in their political ideologies.

panage, obs. f. PANNAGE.

Panag(h)ia (pænaɪ'jiːə), *Gr. Ch.* Also 9 **Panhagia**. [a. Gr. *παναγία*, fem. of *πανάγιος* all-holy.] A title of the Virgin Mary in the Orthodox Eastern Church; the All-holy. Also, an image or representation of the Virgin Mary.
[**1686** B. RANDOLPH *Pres. St. Morea* 13 Many People came from the City of Zant to pay their devotions to the *Panaija* there.] **1775** R. CHANDLER *Trav. Greece* (1825) II. 59 The picture of the Panagia, or Virgin Mary, in Mosaic, on the cieling of the recess. **1866** FELTON *Anc. & Mod. Gr.* I. II. iii. 314 The Parthenon which had been converted into a church of the Panhagia, or Blessed Virgin. **1903** G. F. ABBOTT in *Daily Chron.* 16 June 3/1 A small table..placed under the lamp which burns in front of the icon of the Panhagia. **1910** *New Schaff-Herzog Encycl. Relig. Knowl.* VIII. 327/1 Panagia ('All Holy'), the usual (though not official) title of the virgin in the Greek Church. **1911** [see HODEGETRIA]. **1931** *Times Lit. Suppl.* 19 Mar. 231/2 Devotees who implore the Panagia of Kykko for rain or the Panagia of Tenos for health. **1958** L. DURRELL *Balthazar* vi. 135 'I ask you to sleep with him as I would ask the Panaghia to come down and bless him while he sleeps—like in the old ikons.' How ..Greek! **1961** D. ATTWATER *Christian Churches of East* I. 223 *Panagia*.., 'all-holy', used for the Mother of God as we say 'our Lady'. Also another name for the *enkolpion*.

panagirick, obs. f. PANEGYRIC.

panagraphic, etc., varr. PANOGRAPHIC, etc.

Panama (pænə'mɑː, 'pæn-). [The name of a city and state in Central America, and of the isthmus uniting North and South America.] *attrib.* Of or pertaining to Panama: spec. ***Panama disease***, a vascular wilt disease of banana trees, caused by the soil-borne fungus *Fusarium oxysporum* f. sp. *cubense*, and characterized by the yellowing and wilting of the leaves, first described from infected trees in Central America in 1910. ***Panama fever***: see quot. 1890. ***Panama hat***, a misnomer for a hat made from the undeveloped leaves of the stemless screw-pine (*Carludovica palmata*) of tropical South America; now often applied to hats made in imitation of this; also *absol.* *Panama* sb. ***Panama hat palm, plant***, the screw-pine, *Carludovica palmata*, which produces leaves used in the manufacture of Panama hats; = JIPIJAPA a. ***Panama red***, a local variety of marijuana grown in Panama.
1848 *Colburn's United Service Mag.* III. 67 One veteran in a panama and rosette deputed by the body, addressed me in Spanish. **1873** J. MILLER *Life amongst Modocs* 44 He could not push his panama any further back. **1885** LADY BRASSEY *The Trades* 177 It is sometimes called..the hat-palm, the young shoots making excellent sombreros or panamas. **1900** *Jrnl. Soc. of Arts* 17 Aug. 744 In buying a panama it is necessary to ascertain two things—that the straw is whole and that it is not stiffened. **1975** G. AVERY *Childhood's Pattern* ix. 216 School uniform was no badge of servitude... Nobody sat viciously on their Panamas.
1910 E. ESSED in *Ann. Bot.* XXIV. 488 The Panama Disease.—Preliminary Notice.—This fungoid disease on the *Musa sapientum* var. *Gros Michel* was, it seems, first detected in Central America. **1913** W. FAWCETT *Banana* xiii. 87 The true Panama disease also exists in Trinidad. **1934** A. HUXLEY *Beyond Mexique Bay* 16 That insidious Panama Disease..has ruined so many [banana] plantations throughout the Caribbean. **1949** *Caribbean Q.* I. III. 43 Bananas resistant to Panama disease..are being grown commercially. **1956** H. G. DE LISSER *Cup & Lip* x. 119, I instructed him to go to Napleton to see Sampson about the treatment of Panama Disease. **1969** *New Scientist* 16 Jan. 142/2 Panama disease of bananas is not controlled by eliminating the pathogen but by selecting resistant strains of banana. **1972** J. W. PURSEGLOVE *Tropical Crops*:

Monocotyledons II. 368 Panama disease, also known as banana wilt and vascular wilt,..is one of the world's most catastrophic plant diseases. **1850** J. L. TYSON *Diary of Physician in Calif.* 29 The so-called *Panama fever* rarely occurs, unless previous disease has wasted the powers. **1868** *Overland Monthly* Dec. 561/1 After hearing all about how she felt, his diagnosis was a mild case of fever—Panama fever. **1890** BILLINGS *Nat. Med. Dict.* II. 281 Panama fever. Sometimes malarial and sometimes yellow fever. **1940** F. RIESENBERG *Golden Gate* 109 Complaints charged that the frequent burials at sea resulted from improper care of those who had contracted 'Panama fever' or 'yellow fever'. **1833** MARRYAT *P. Simple* xxx, Men, with large panama straw hats on their heads. **1856** C. M. YONGE *Daisy Chain* II. xi. 455 Dr. Spencer was in the hall, with his bamboo, his great Panama hat, and grey loose coat. **1858** SIMMONDS *Dict. Trade, Panama-hats*, very fine plaited hats made from the fan-shaped leaves of *Carludovica palmata*, which are generally worn in the West Indies and American Continent, and fetch a high price. In Central America where they are made, the palm is called Jipijapa. **1900** *Jrnl. Soc. of Arts* 17 Aug. 744 Jipijapa or Panama hats. Ecuador is the real home of the hats wrongly designated under the name of 'panama'. .. Everywhere in Latin America the hat is known under the name of 'Jipijapa' in honour of the city where its manufacture was first started. **1916** 'TAFFRAIL' *Pincher Martin* iii. 34 Vernon Hatherley, the lieutenant-commander (T.), clad in an ancient Panamá hat and a suit of indescribable overalls. **1974** *Country Life* 4 Apr. 816/1 Simple panama hat with gros-grain ribbon. **1931** P. C. STANDLEY in *Publ. Field Mus. Nat. Hist. Bot. Ser.* X. 117 *Carludovica palmata*... Panama hat palm... Common in wet forest; ranging to Guatemala and southward to Peru. **1941** T. H. GOODSPEED *Plant Hunters in Andes* v. 146 Along such forest margins small species of bamboo, 'Panama hat' palms, tree ferns, the ginger, and other attractive plants disported themselves. **1954** R. W. SCHERY *Plants for Man* vii. 176/1 The Panama hat palm..grows wild in most of the American tropics. **1972** J. W. PURSEGLOVE *Tropical Crops: Monocotyledons* I. 94 Panama Hat Plant...occurs wild in the humid forests of Central America. **1967** *Boston Sunday Herald* 26 Mar. IV. 1/1 Traffic in marijuana—Acapulco Gold and the better quality Panama Red and Yakatanga Purple —out of Mexico has steadily increased in the last three years. **1972** *Last Whole Earth Catalog* (Portola Inst.) 62/3 Acapulco Gold, Panama Red, and other strains of grass are reputed to be particularly potent.

Panaman ('pænəmən), *sb.* and *a.* [f. PANAMA + -AN.] = PANAMANIAN *a.* and *sb.* Also **Pa'namic** *a.*

1901 W. H. DALL in *Proc. U.S. Nat. Museum* XXIII. 285 The northern limit of the Panamic fauna is Point Conception, California. **1904** *Sun* (N.Y.) 25 Feb. 2/6 The constitution settled the question of what the people of that republic are to be called by specifying that they are 'Panamans'. **1906** W. F. JOHNSON *Four Centuries of Panama Canal* (1907) xx. 360 The Panaman sense of justice is as highly cultivated, and the Panaman sensitiveness to and resentment of injustice are as keen as our own. **1913** E. PEIXOTTO *Pacific Shores from Panama* 26 Verandas.. overhang all the thoroughfares, and the indolent Panamans spend much of their time upon them or lounging about the ..cafés and hostelries. **1937** *Times Lit. Suppl.* 22 May 397/3 The friction between Yanqui indifference to diplomatic etiquette and Panaman pride are all candidly described here.

Panamanian (pænə'meɪnɪən), *a.* and *sb.* Also †**Panamenian.** [Irreg., f. PANAMA + *-n-* + -IAN.] **A.** *adj.* Of or pertaining to Panama. **B.** *sb.* A native or inhabitant of Panama.

This form with medial *-e-* (quots. 1869, 1892) is an adaptation of the Spanish term *Panameño.*

1855 R. TOMES *Panama in 1855* vii. 216, I had no means of judging of the intimate character of the Panamanian dames. **1869** PIM & SEEMANN *Dottings in Panama* xi. 184 The Panamenians displayed great heroism, but..the buccaneers could not be repulsed. **1889** W. NELSON *Five Yrs. Panama* 50 The native Panamanians being great stay-at-homes. **1892** J. BORNN in G. S. Minot *Hist. Panama* xv. 74 The Buccaneer..desired..precious metals and stones... But their search for these disclosed to them the fact that the Panamenian had provided against this emergency by placing these aboard a ship, with orders to sail away if the city should fall. **1906** M. A. CHATFIELD *Let.* 21 Jan. in *Light On Dark Places at Panama* (1908) 45 The best [hotel], the Central, charged $4.00 gold per day, $8.00 Panamanian. **1913** *Chambers's Jrnl.* July 503/2 Travelling without any Spanish and without binoculars puts one wholly at the mercy of the secretive Panamánian or the wily Indian. **1934** [see HONDURAN, HONDUREAN *a.* and *sb.*]. **1959** *Listener* 23 Apr. 718/1 A former Panamanian ambassador in London. **1964** *Daily Tel.* 11 Jan. 16/6 Panamanian claims to sovereignty over the Canal Zone. **1976** *Times* 5 Feb. 20/4 The Lloyd's report shows that 14 of last year's casualties were registered under the Panamanian flag. **1976** *Sci. Amer.* Sept. 140/2 Nicolás Ardito Barletti, a Panamanian, attempted to place a value on the social benefit from research.

pan-American (pænə'mɛrɪkən), *a.* [PAN- I.] Of or pertaining to all the states of North and South America or to all Americans.

1889 *Evening Post* (N.Y) 27 Sept. 4/3 European Opinion on the Pan-American Congress. **1901** *Daily News* 11 Apr. 5/1 The Buffalo Pan-American Exposition. **1901** *Westm. Gaz.* 23 Oct. 4/2 The Pan-American Congress was opened at four o'clock yesterday afternoon at Mexico. **1927** *New Republic* 21 Sept. 110/1 The existence of the Pan-American Union, and the calling of an occasional Pan-American Congress, should not deceive anyone as to the predominant position of the United States in this hemisphere. **1934** A. HUXLEY *Beyond Mexique Bay* 200 Pan-American Airways.. are responsible for the long-distance international services. **1966** *Times* 28 Feb. (Canada Suppl.) p. xiv/5 Canada's 1967 Pan-American Games.

Hence **pan-A'mericanism**, the idea or sentiment of a political alliance or union of all the states of North and South America; also, a movement towards better commercial and cultural relations among American nations.

1902 *Monthly Rev.* Oct. 66 The French-Canadian,.. should a change be forced upon him, would incline towards Pan-Americanism. **1915** W. WILSON *Public Papers* (1926) III. 409 This is Pan-Americanism. It has none of the spirit of empire in it. **1954** H. C. ALLEN *Gt. Brit. & United States* xiv. 526 His Pan-Americanism, which aimed at the economic and political consolidation of the Western hemisphere,..led him to leap into action on the Isthmian issue. **1966** *Oxf. Compan. Amer. Hist.* 611/2 Pan-Americanism, a new contribution to U.S. policy during the 1880's,..was formulated by Secretary of State Blaine.

pan-Anglican (pæn'æŋglɪkən), *a.* [PAN- I.] Of, pertaining to, or embracing the whole Anglican Church with its branches and related communities, esp. Colonial and American.

[**1679** *Lyndwood's Provinc., Const. Legat.* 3 *heading*, Concilium Pan-Anglicum Londini habitum..Anno Domini 1236.] **1867** [A 'Pan-Anglican Synod', consisting of 75 British, Colonial, and American Protestant bishops, met at Lambeth Palace from 24 Sept. to 10 Dec.]. **1868** W. S. GILBERT *Bab Ballads, Bishop of Rum-ti-foo*, To synod called Pan-Anglican. **1888** *Pall Mall G.* 6 July 1/2 The Pan-Anglican Episcopal Council, which is sitting at Lambeth.

pan-Anglo-Saxon, etc.: see PAN- I.

panans, obs. form of PENANCE.

pananthropism, -apospory: see PAN- 2.

panaquilon (pə'nækwɪlɒn). *Chem.* [f. *panax quinquefolium* (see PANAX) + -ON.] An amorphous sweet substance found in ginseng (*Panax Schinseng*) by Garrigues, in 1854.

1859 FOWNES *Man. Chem.* 355 Panaquilon, from Panax quinquefol..very much resembles glycyrrhizin, but is not precipitated from its solution by sulphuric acid. **1890** BILLINGS *Nat. Med. Dict.* II. 281 Panaquilon. $C_{12}H_{25}O_9$.

pan-Arabism (pæn'ærəbɪz(ə)m). [f. PAN- + ARAB *sb.* and *a.* + -ISM.] The ideal of political union of all the Arab states; a movement advocating such a union. Hence **pan-'Arab** *a.* and *sb.*, **pan-'Arabic** *a.*, **pan-'Arabist**.

1930 *Encycl. Social Sci.* III. 148/2 Pan-Arabism is scarcely more possible when Moslems speaking the Arabic language are ruled in such diverse ways as in French North Africa, Egypt, Syria, Iraq and the divisions of Arabia. **1939** *Asia* Aug. 450 (*heading*) Pan-Arab nationalism. **1958** *Spectator* 7 Feb. 159/1 In a sense pan-Arabism proved Farouk's downfall. *Ibid.* 1 Aug. 155/3 By joining the UAS the ruler [of Kuwait] would preserve his sheikdom and his subjects would have their pan-Arabic aspirations satisfied. **1959** *Times* 10 Mar. 11/2 This uncertainty at the top is bound to encourage others, who know more clearly what they want, to take over, whether they are pan-Arabists or Communists, idealists or self-seekers. **1962** *Listener* 1 Mar. 365/1 To young Arab Nationalists—to young Pan-Arabists everywhere—Egypt under President Nasser seemed destined to unite the Arab world. *Ibid.* 5 Apr. 597/1 The Ba'ath leaders are doctrinaire pan-Arabs of the frontier-smashing variety. **1963** M. KHADDURI *Mod. Libya* xi. 330 At the outset, those who advocated Pan-Arabism were limited to the articulate intelligentsia who had received their education in neighboring Arab countries. **1968** *Listener* 15 Aug. 195/2 The commandos themselves are pan-Arab in a new sense... The fedayin have no state. **1974** *Florida FL Reporter* XIII. 52/1 They admitted that each had also learnt (besides Classical Arabic) a pan-Arabic Standard dialect. **1975** N. LUARD *Robespierre Serial* iv. 16 Twice Saudi-Arabian delegate to Pan-Arab conferences. **1978** *Times* 10 Aug. 12/7 Messianic Pan-Arabism was rapidly declining, while the Arab national state triumphed.

†**pa'narchic**, *a. Obs. nonce-wd.* [f. Gr. πανάρχ-ος all-ruling + -IC.] All-ruling.

1610 B. JONSON *Alch.* II. v, Is Ars sacra,..Or the pamphysick, or panarchick knowledge, A heathen language?

panarchy ('pænɑkɪ). *rare.* [f. PAN- + Gr. ἀρχή, -αρχία rule, realm.] Universal realm.

1839 BAILEY *Festus* xix. (1848) 208 The starry panarchy of space. **1948** L. MACNEICE *Holes in Sky* 49 He is separate too, who had but now ascended Into the panarchy of created things Wearing his halo cocked.

†'**panaret.** *Obs. rare*$^{-1}$. [ad. Gr. πανάρετος all-virtuous.] An all-virtuous one.

1609 J. DAVIES *Holy Roode* (1878) 13/1 Wilt haue our Bodies which thou didst create? Then take them to thee thou true Panaret.

‖**pana'ricium, -itium.** *Obs.* Also 6 -is. [late L. *panaricium*, for *paronychium*.] A whitlow.

c **1400** *Lanfranc's Cirurg.* 223 Panaricium is an enpostym þat is in þe heed of a mannes fyngir about þe nail. **1597** A. M. tr. *Guillemeau's Fr. Chirurg.* 39/1 Ther commethe in the endes of the fingers, somtimes a certayn vlceratione callede *Panaris* or *Paronichia*. **1663** BOYLE *Usef. Exp. Nat. Philos.* II. v. xi. 229 A Counsellor's wife, who..was cured of a panaritium.

panarmony: see PANHARMONY.

‖**panarthritis** (pænɑː'θraɪtɪs). *Path.* [f. PAN- + ARTHRITIS.] Inflammation involving the whole structure of a joint.

1890 BILLINGS *Nat. Med. Dict.*, *Panarthritis.* **1897** *Allbutt's Syst. Med.* III. 79 The disease [rheumatoid arthritis] has been called a pan-arthritis, because it involves all the parts of a joint—cartilage, bone, and synovial membrane.

†'**panary**, *sb. Obs. rare*$^{-1}$. [ad. L. *pānārium* bread-basket, neuter of *pānārius*: see next and -ARY.] A storehouse for bread, a pantry.

1611 BIBLE *Transl. Pref.* 3 It [the Scripture] is a Panary of holesome foode, against fenowed traditions.

panary ('pænərɪ), *a.* [a. L. *pānāri-us*, f. *pān-is* bread: see -ARY.] Of or pertaining to bread; esp. in the phrase *panary fermentation.*

1818 COLEBROOKE *Import Colonial Corn* 128 That fermentation, which takes place in the making of leavened or raised bread,..named the panary fermentation. **1844** H. STEPHENS *Bk. Farm* I. 41 Trying the relative panary properties of different kinds of flour and meal. **1875** *Encycl. Brit.* III. 254 The so-called panary fermentation in bread-making is a true alcoholic fermention [*sic*]. **1942** *Proc. Food Group* V. 70/1 During the latter half of the last century the microbiological aspect of panary fermentation attracted considerable attention. **1971** A. R. DANIEL *Bakers' Dict.* (ed. 2) 139/2 *Panary fermentation*, the fermentation of bread dough.

panashe, obs. form of PANACHE.

†**pana'tel.** *Obs. rare*$^{-1}$. [ad. It. *panatella* or *panadella* 'a little messe of Panad' (Florio).] A light panada.

1603 LODGE *Treat. Plague* (Hunterian Cl.) 55 If sharpenesse be displeasant to his stomacke... Barly, creame, Almond milke, and panatels, are fit meates in this cause. [**1727-41** CHAMBERS *Cycl.*, *Panada, Panata*, or *Panatella*, a diet, consisting of bread boiled in water, to the consistence of a pulp; given to sick persons whose digestion is weak.]

panatela (pænə'tɛlə). Also **panatella, panetela.** [Amer. Sp., a long, thin biscuit, etc.] **a.** A long slender cigar tapering at the sealed end. Also *attrib.* **b.** A cigarette made of Central or South American marijuana.

1901 'H. MCHUGH' *Down Line* 32 A young chap..who had been out in the smoking room working faithfully on one of those pajama panatella cigars. **1904** W. STEVENS *Let.* May (1967) 74 My idea of life is a fine evening..+ a soft, full Panatela. **1906** L. J. VANCE *Terence O'Rourke* II. i. 190 Gravely he inspected the end of the commendable panetela, which he was enjoying by the grace of Chambret; and he puffed upon it furiously, twinkling upon his friend through a pillar of smoke. **1912** G. FRANKAU *One of Us* v. 41 Apart, unmoved, behind his Panatela, Old Hiram stood, of journalists surrounded. **1928** ADE *Let.* 27 May (1973) 130 For many years after I took up the writing game I smoked whatever was readily obtainable, with a preference for a mild Havana Cigar of the Panatella shape. **1943** R. CHANDLER *Lady in Lake* (1944) ii. 9 He reached himself a panatela..and lit it. **1946** MEZZROW & WOLFE *Really Blues* xii. 229 Some Spanish guys..rolled it [*sc.* marijuana] in a different sized paper, about half an inch longer than mine and much thinner, and they called their product a 'panatella'. **1956** B. HOLIDAY *Lady sings Blues* (1973) iv. 43 'Girl,' he said, 'come *here*. Jimmy's got the best panatella you ever smoked in your life.' **1969** R. R. LINGEMAN *Drugs from A to Z* 194 *Panatella*.., bigger, fatter, more potent marijuana cigarette made of Central or South American marijuana. **1970** E. MCGIRR *Death pays Wages* vii. 156 The Sergeant produced a small box of midget panatellas and a box of matches.

‖**Panathenæa** (pænæθiː'niːə). Also **-aia.** [a. Gr. παναθήναια adj. neut. pl. (sc. ἱερά solemnities), f. παν- all + Ἀθηναῖ-ος Athenian, f. Ἀθῆναι Athens, or Ἀθήνη Athene, Minerva, the patron goddess of Athens.] The national festival of Athens, held, in a lesser form every year, in a greater every fifth year, to celebrate the union of Attica under Theseus. It included a splendid procession to the shrine of the goddess Athene, with gymnastic games and musical competitions. Hence **Panathe'næan** *a.*, pertaining to or characteristic of this festival.

1603 HOLLAND *Plutarch* Explan. Words, *Panathenæa*, a solemnity held at Athens... Such games..as were then exhibited..they called Panathenaik. **1727** BAILEY vol. II, *Panathenaea.* **1775** R. WOOD *Ess. Homer* 240 Could Homer have heard his Poems sung or recited, even at the Panathenæan Festival. *a* **1822** SHELLEY *Ion* Pr. Wks. 1888 II. 114 You have now only to consider how you shall win the Panathenaea. **1853** HICKIE tr. *Aristoph.* (1872) II. 590, I was quite spent with laughing at the Panathenaia. **1882** SWINBURNE *Tristram of Lyonesse, Athens* 179 None so glorious garland crowned the feast Panathenæan.

Panathenaic (pænæθiː'neɪɪk), *a.* (*sb.*) [ad. Gr. παναθηναϊκ-ός, f. παναθήναια: see prec.] Of or pertaining to the Panathenæa.

Panathenaic frieze, a frieze, designed by Phidias, representing the procession at the festival, which surrounded the exterior of the cella at the Parthenon.

1603 [see prec.]. **1638** JUNIUS *Paint. Ancients* 152 The pageants of their Panathenaïke solemnitie. **1835** *Court Mag.* VI. 179/2 That unrivalled production of Greek art, the Panathenaic procession. **1869** RUSKIN *Q. of Air* §39 The earliest Panathenaic vase known—the 'Burgon' vase in the British Museum. **1880** POYNTER & HEAD *Classic & Ital. Paint.* Pref. 13 The beauty which receives its full expression in the Panathenaic frieze.

†**B.** *sb. pl.* The Panathenaic celebrations. *Obs.*

1678 CUDWORTH *Intell. Syst.* I. iv. 401 The Peplum or Veil of Minerva, which in the Panathenaicks is with great pomp and ceremony brought into the Acropolis.

pan-athletic, panatom: see PAN- 2.

Panatrope ('pænətrəʊp). Also panotrope and with small initial. [f. *pana-*, *pano-*, of unknown origin + Gr. τροπή turn, turning.] The proprietary name of a form of (electric) record-player capable of relatively loud reproduction.

1926 *Glasgow Herald* 5 Oct. 5 There was no graduation of musical vibrations that the 'Panatrope' could not reproduce. **1928** E. WAUGH *Decline & Fall* II. iii. 168 In a minute the panatrope was playing, David and Martin were dancing, and Peter was making cocktails. **1933** *Punch* 16 Aug. 181/1 Whatever you may lack in the way of plush seats and panotropes you wouldn't see that at an ordinary cinema. *c* **1940** DYLAN THOMAS & DAVENPORT *Death of King's Canary* (1976) vii. 125 A panatrope sounded over the crack of rifles, the smashing of crockery, the complaining of beasts. **1954** *Trade Marks Jrnl.* 15 Sept. 921/1 Panatrope... Gramophones, radio gramophones, apparatus and instruments for recording and reproducing sound, parts and fittings..for all the aforesaid goods; and gramophone needles and gramophone records. The Decca Record Company Limited,..London,..manufacturers. **1961** *Times* 28 Mar. 12/7 They must now man the ticket office, sell programmes, start the recalcitrant generator, warm up the panotrope. **1968** D. BRAITHWAITE *Fairground Archit.* 165 *Panatrope*, successor to the mechanical organ—gramophone turntables, amplifier and loudspeakers relaying noisy pop records. **1978** C. HUMPHREYS *Both Sides Circle* x. 114, I had a fight with the representative of the firm who had hired us the panatrope, or long-playing record machine.

Panavision ('pænəvɪʒən). [f. PAN(ORAMA + *a* + VISION *sb.*] A proprietary name for a type of anamorphic lens; *loosely*, wide-screen cinematography. Also *fig.*

1955 *Jrnl. Soc. Motion Pict. & Television Engin.* LXIV. 233/1 Anamorphic printer lenses used..are the Tushinsky and Panavision. **1963** *Punch* 3 July 30/1 Panavision and colour make the whole thing incongruously cheerful to look at. **1967** *Trade Marks Jrnl.* 24 May 669/2 Panavision... Cinematographic and photographic apparatus..; anamorphic lenses... Panavision Incorporated.., City of Los Angeles. **1973** W. DANCY in S. Henderson *Understanding New Black Poetry* 300 Frail we cringe before Dante's Italic vision Its cineramic focus and panavision scale Swells brain-mind.

‖**Panax** ('pænæks). [L. *panax*, ad. Gr. πανακής, -κες all-healing, πάνακες the plant yielding opopanax.] Panace, All-heal; now a Linnæan genus of plants (N.O. *Araliaceæ*), containing herbs, shrubs, and trees, of tropical and Northern Asia and America, some of them noted for real or supposed medicinal virtues, esp. the Ginseng (*P. Schinseng*) and American species (*P. quinquefolium*).

c **1617** MIDDLETON *Witch* III. iii. 29 Marmaritin and mandragora, thou wouldst say. Here's panax too. **1638** NABBES *Bride* IV. i, Panax Coloni Is known to every rustick; and Hipericon. **1819** *Pantologia* s.v., Ginseng was formerly supposed to be confined to the mountains of Chinese Tartary: it is now, however, fully ascertained that the American panax quinquefolia is precisely the same.

panblastic: see PAN- 2.

† '**pan-bone**. *Obs. rare*$^{-1}$. [f. PAN *sb.*[1] 6 + BONE] The bone of the skull.

1545 RAYNOLD *Byrth Mankynde* Y vj, Vnsensyble swettinge euaporatith, and yssuyth furth of the poores in the skyn that coueryth the panbone.

pan-Bri'tannic, *a.* Also 8 Pambritannick. [PAN- 1.] †**a.** Of or consisting of all the Britons or of all parts of Britain. *Obs.* **b.** Of or comprising all the British dominions.

1709 ELIZ. ELSTOB *Ags. Hom. on birthday St. Gregory* Pref. 17 And be it plain as to the Britains, even from their Behaviour at that most celebrated Pambritannick Council at Augustine's Ac. **1900** *Daily News* 24 Mar. 4/7 The momentous outburst of pan-Britannic patriotism. **1902** *Q. Rev.* July 329 A Pan-Britannic Customs Union, if practicable, would prove efficacious in cementing the union of the empire.

pan-Buddhism, -ist, etc.: see PAN- 1.

pancake ('pænkeɪk), *sb.* [f. PAN *sb.*[1] 1 + CAKE *sb.*]

1. A thin flat cake, made of batter fried in a pan. Often taken as the type of flatness; phr. *as flat as a pancake* (and varr.) (also used with reference to the *fig.* senses of FLAT *a.*)

c **1430** *Two Cookery-bks.* I. 46 Putte a litel of þe Whyte comade in þe panne, & late flete al a-brode as þou makyst a pancake. **1555** W. WATREMAN *Fardle Facions* I. v. 53 For their meate they vse, moche a kynde of pancake made of rye meale. **1611** MIDDLETON & DEKKER *Roaring Girl* II. i, A continual Simon and Jude's rain Beat all your feathers as flat down as pancakes! **1619** *Pasquil's Palin.* (1877) 152 And every man and maide doe take their turne, And tosse their Pancakes up for feare they burne. **1757** SMOLLETT *Reprisal* I. ii, I'll beat their skulls to a pancake. **1761** STERNE *Tr. Shandy* III. xxvii. 138 He has crush'd his nose..as flat as a pancake to his face. **1828** *Craven Gloss.* (ed. 2) s.v. *Pancake Tuesday*, In some farm houses the servants, according to seniority, fried and tossed the pancake. **1830** MARRYAT *King's Own* I. xvii. 261 Under which it had lain, jammed as flat as a pancake. **1860** LD. BLOOMFIELD in *Lady G. Bloomfield's Remin.* (1883) II. xiv. 97 The country is as flat as a pancake. **1909** *Dialect Notes* III. 411 *Flatter than a pancake*, very flat, of persons and things. **1921** GALSWORTHY *To Let* I. ix. 79 Fleur was not yet home... Here were her aunt, and her cousins the Cardigans, and this fellow Profond, and everything flat as a pancake for the want of her. **1922** JOYCE *Ulysses* 735 The last [stout] they sent from O'Rourkes was as flat as a pancake. **1936** 'G. ORWELL' *Keep Aspidistra Flying* i. 15 He was nearly thirty and had accomplished nothing; only his miserable book of poems that had fallen flatter than any pancake. **1959** *Daily Tel.* 14 Mar. 6 His statement to the House of Commons yesterday fell as flat as a pancake.

2. Applied to various objects thin and flat like a pancake, and in more extended applications, e.g.

a. An imitation of leather consisting of leather-scraps glued together and stamped into sheets by hydraulic pressure, used for in-soles (Knight *Dict. Mech.* 1875). **b.** An arrangement of six playing-cards, in which one card is laid down and another transversely across it; round these are then placed four others, held in their places by the overlapping ends of the first two, and by overlapping each other, so that all form one cohering whole. **c.** *Palæont.* (See quot. and cf. the existing CAKE-URCHIN.) **d.** *dial.* (*a*) The leaf of the Kidney-wort, *Cotyledon Umbilicus* (Devon); (*b*) The fruit of the Common Mallow, *Malva sylvestris* (N. Linc.). **e.** *Naut.* A single cake of *pancake-ice*: see 3. **f.** A type of flat hat. *U.S.* **g.** A vertical descent made by an aircraft in a level position (see quot. 1918[1]); the landing of an aircraft in an emergency with the undercarriage retracted (see *pancake landing*). **h.** An opaque facial treatment used as a base for make-up. *Freq. attrib.*, as *pancake make-up*. orig. *U.S.*

b. 1844 ALB. SMITH *Adv. Mr. Ledbury* I. ix, I'll bet you.. that I make the whole of this pack of cards into 'pancakes'.

c. 1843 HUMBLE *Dict. Geol. & Min.*, *Pancake*, the name given by Klein to the Echinodiscus laganum, a species of fossil echinus, belonging to the division catocysti.

d. 1886 BRITTEN & HOLLAND *Plant-n.*, Pancakes.

e. 18.. in Borthwick *Brit. Amer. Rdr.* (1860) 263 This sludge [of ice]..forms itself into small plates, which, being rounded by continual rubbing, are called by the sailors *pancakes*. **1867** SMYTH *Sailor's Word-bk.*, *Pancakes*, thin floating rounded spots of snow ice, in the Arctic seas, and reckoned the first indication of the approach of winter, in August.

f. 1875 E. S. NADAL *Impressions London Social Life* 143 The cap was peculiar, though about the year '56 we had something like it called the 'Pancake'. **1945** *Amer. Speech* XX. 233/1 She had on her duty dress and a French pancake. *Ibid.* 234/1 *French pancake*, flat hat. **1957** M. B. PICKEN *Fashion Dict.* 241/2 *Pancake beret*, broad flat beret. **1975** G. HOWELL *In Vogue* 188 (*caption*) Pancake and huge gloves in looped emerald green crochet. **1976** M. & G. GORDON *Ordeal* (1977) xiii. 92 She wore..a pancake Stetson that she could tilt over her face.

g. 1912 *Aero* Mar. 66/1 Pride cometh before a pancake. **1913** C. MELLOR *Airman* 25 Landings must be 'normal'—not of the 'pancake' order. **1914** HAMEL & TURNER *Flying* 66 He must be able to learn how to make a fairly safe 'pancake'. **1918** H. BARBER *Aeroplane Speaks* (ed. 6) 14 *Pancakes*, pilot's slang for stalling an aeroplane and dropping like a pancake. **1918** COWLEY & LEVY *Aeronautics* x. 225 Dangerous consequences due to a landing of a pancake type are usually guarded against by a strong under-carriage and by the insertion of shock absorbers. **1974** P. WRIGHT *Lang. Brit. Industry* 5 In the R.A.F. during the last war crash landings were *pancakes*.

h. 1937 *Official Gaz.* (U.S. Patent Office) 13 July 251/1 Max Factor & Co., Los Angeles, Calif... Pan-cake. The word 'cake' is disclaimed apart from the mark. For cosmetic in the nature of a solidified cream used for a make-up base. **1940** *Sears Catal.* Spring/Summer 99 (*caption*) Pan-Cake Makeup. **1946** *Trade Marks Jrnl.* 15 May 244/2 Pancake... Cosmetic preparations for toilet use and for use in theatrical, motion picture, television, and photographic make-up. Max Factor & Co..., Hollywood, United States of America; manufacturers. **1951** H. MACINNES *Neither Five nor Three* I. v. 66 Miss Guttman's face flushed with pleasure even under the pan-cake make-up. **1953** *New Yorker* 13 June 61/1 Like his Cabinet members, he used pancake makeup. **1955** W. GADDIS *Recognitions* III. ii. 737 It's too bad they didn't get some pancake on him before he went up. **1960** L. COOPER *Accomplices* II. ii. 84 A private life that you can put over your real one..like your pancake make-up. **1962** E. O'BRIEN *Lonely Girl* ii. 22, I put pancake on Baba's back to hide her spots. **1970** *Sunday Times* 3 May 28/6 Women take hours getting themselves done up to attract men, slapping on pancake, painting their eyes. **1975** J. CROSBY *Affair of Strangers* iii. 25 Chantal wore only light pancake, dimming but not obliterating the brown skin. **1975** *Daily Colonist* (Victoria, B.C.) 20 June 4/6 The candidate had ugly mannish hands and, under the heavy pancake make-up, the suspicion of beard stubble. **1978** *Chicago* June 14/3, I didn't used to wear pancake at all—it was a macho thing with me. But now I do.

3. *attrib.* and *Comb.*, as *pancake-making*; *pancake-like*, *-shaped* adjs.; *pancake fashion*, *-wise* advbs.; **pancake batter**, the mixture from which pancakes are made; **pancake coil** *Electr.*, any flat or very short inductance coil (see quots.); **Pancake Day, Tuesday**, Shrove Tuesday, from the custom of eating pancakes on that day; **pancake descent, landing** [cf. PANCAKE *v.* b], the landing of an aircraft in an emergency with the undercarriage retracted; **pancake-ice**, floating ice in thin flat pieces, forming in the polar seas at the approach of winter; **pancake-plant** *dial.*, the common mallow (*N. Linc.*); **pancake race**, a race held on Shrove Tuesday, in which the participants are required to toss pancakes as they run; **pancake roll** (see quot. 1967).

1739 E. SMITH *Compl. Housewife* (ed. 9) 114 Mix all well together a little thicker than *pancake batter. **1747** H. GLASSE *Art of Cookery* vii. 69 Make it up into a thick Batter with Flour, like a Pancake Batter. **1965** A. CHRISTIE *At Bertram's Hotel* xi. 103 She made herself three pancakes with the pancake batter. **1910** H. M. HOBART *Dict. Electr. Engin.* I. 108 **Pancake coil*, a flat former-wound coil used in the construction of the early smooth-core rotating armatures of alternators. The term is also sometimes applied to the flat separately insulated unit coil used in modern high-pressure transformers. **1921** *Physical Rev.* XVIII. 138 Coursey's curves do not cover the case of coils whose radial dimension exceeds the axial (pancake coils). **1940** *Chambers's Techn. Dict.* 611/1 *Pancake coil*, an inductance coil in which the windings are arranged spirally, in the form of a flat disc. **1960** COOKE & MARKUS *Electronics & Nucleonics Dict.* 322/2 *Pancake coil*, a coil having a diameter appreciably greater than its length. **1961** *Guardian* 18 Jan. 1/1 The transformer..will be made up of a series of 'pancake' coils of primary and secondary windings. *a* **1825** FORBY *Voc. E. Anglia*, **Pancake-day*, Shrove Tuesday. **1914** W. J. CLAXTON *Mastery of Air* xlviii. 249 It is considered faulty piloting to make a *pancake descent where there is ample landing space. **1863** ATKINSON *Stanton Grange* (1864) 164, I have seen them [hares] work their way —*pancake fashion, I should call it—under a wire fence. **1817** SCORESBY in *Ann. Reg.*, *Chron.* 556 Its exterior is always sludge, and its interior *pancake ice. **1886** A. W. GREELY *Arctic Service* I. vi. 56 No semblance of a pack was noted until about 5 p.m. It then consisted of small pieces of pancake ice, which would in no way interfere with the progress of any steaming vessel. **1928** *Pancake landing [see LEVEL *v.*[1] 6]. **1938** *Encycl. Brit. Bk. of Year* 57/2 Nothing better could be expected than a 'pancake' landing which would destroy the undercarriage without seriously injuring the crew. **1960** WENTWORTH & FLEXNER *Dict. Amer. Slang* 374/1 *Pancake landing*, Specif., in aviation, the act or instance of landing an airplane on its fusilage rather than on its wheels, done when the landing gear is damaged. **1887** W. RYE *Norfolk Broads* 75 A mound, a considerable one for this *pancake-like county. **1951** *Sun* (Baltimore) 17 Jan. 3/2 (*caption*) Mrs. Virginia Leete..takes a spill in the snow during a practice run..in preparation for the annual *pancake race scheduled for Shrove Tuesday. **1955** *Ibid.* 23 Feb. 2/3 Pancake races have featured Shrove Tuesday observances in Olney for some 510 years. **1967** D. BRICE *Folk-Carol of England* iii. 86 The well-known 'pancake race' that takes place in the Buckinghamshire village [of Olney] every Shrove Tuesday. **1972** *Guardian* 15 Jan. 14/5 Shrovetide brings pancake races like that at Olney in Buckinghamshire, with housewives tossing pancakes as they belt along. **1976** *Times* 3 Mar. 14/6 The annual women's pancake races in Lincoln's Inn Fields. **1967** *Observer* (Colour Suppl.) 30 Apr. 38/4 **Pancake roll*, a pancake with savoury meat and vegetable fillings, deep fried. **1968** R. V. BESTE *Repeat Instructions* xi. 121 They had a more adventurous meal than the..vegetable chop suey and pancake rolls he usually ordered. **1969** O. BLAKESTON *For crying out Shroud* vii. 59 Jim orders fried oysters and crispy pancake rolls. **1976** M. BUTTERWORTH *Remains to be Seen* iv. 68 The diligent Chinese..laboured over their crab foo yung and their crispy pancake rolls. **1902** *Daily Chron.* 19 Nov. 8/5 She wears a *pancake shaped silk hat on her head. **1825** BROCKETT *N.C. Gloss.*, **Pancake Tuesday*, Shrove Tuesday; on which it is a general custom in the North to have pancakes. **1599** PORTER *Angry Wom. Abingd.* (Percy Soc.) 50 [She] makes him sit at table *pancake wise, Flat, flat, God knowes.

Hence (*nonce-wds.*) '**pancakish** *a.*, somewhat like a pancake; '**pancakewards** *adv.*, towards a pancake.

1883 *Blackw. Mag.* July 62 A pancakeish omelette and wine were very acceptable. **1867** *Cornh. Mag.* Mar. 362 Her allowance would not admit of..a surreptitious egg, might her desire pancakewards be never so strong.

'**pancake**, *v.* [f. PANCAKE *sb.*] **a.** *trans.*, to squeeze flat like a pancake. Also *fig.* and in sense 2 h of the sb.

1879 G. MEREDITH *Egoist* II. 226 These conquerors of mountains pancaked on the rocks in desperate embraces. **1941** *Time* 6 Oct. 17/1 A..near-hurricane..that killed three people, leveled grain fields, pancaked buildings, blocked highways. *Ibid.* 20 Oct. 2/1 Starting the bill in the House, with a steam roller set to pancake all opposition. **1942** *Capital* (Topeka, Kansas) 15 Mar. (*caption*) Sure! He's pancaked 17 guys in a row! Hits like a train at a grade crossing. **1948** L. MACNEICE *Holes in Sky* 13 They tell me report at the first police station. But the station is pancaked —so what can I do? **1953** DYLAN THOMAS *Let.* 22 June (1966) 409 Sober, airsick, pancaked flat, I saw these intelligent old friends as a warren full of blockish stinkers. **1973** R. L. SIMON *Big Fix* vii. 50 His face was pancaked in layers, his hair laquered. **1974** *Listener* 23 May 678/2 Rows of pancaked Cadillacs and burnt-out Rolls-Royces. **1977** *S. Wales Echo* 18 Jan. 1/4 Police reported 21 confirmed deaths but said it was likely 60 to 70 more bodies remained in a pancaked carriage crushed to a quarter of its bulk by a giant slab of concrete weighing hundreds of tons.

b. *Aeronaut. intr.* Of an aircraft: to descend rapidly in a level position in stalled flight, *spec.* to land in this manner in an emergency with the undercarriage retracted (cf. *pancake landing*). Of the pilot: to cause an aircraft to pancake. Also *transf.* and *fig.* Hence '**pancaking** *vbl. sb.*

1911 *Aero* Aug. 136/2 In the meanwhile Conway Jenkins had..'pancaked' badly, and smashed it pretty conclusively. **1912** *Ibid.* Mar. 66/1 He..then shut off his engine, calmly waiting for the machine to return to the ground, which it did with a resultant bump, commonly known to the aviation world as pancaking (falling flatly). **1914** *Aeronaut. Jrnl.* Oct. 316 *Pancake, to*, to descend steeply, with the wings at a very large angle of incidence, like a parachute. **1914** H. M. BUIST *Aircraft in German War* 35 The craft pancaking, diving and banking are monoplanes. **1916** C. WINCHESTER *Flying Men* 68 So..the 'pancaking' of aircraft is not an advisable method of landing. **1920** *19th Cent.* Mar. 570 This pancaking device by which the National Socialists tried at the last moment to save the crash. **1928** C. F. S. GAMBLE *Story N. Sea Air Station* xv. 263, I took my chance and about 10 feet up 'pancaked'—a horrid crash. **1929** E. W. SPRINGS *Above Bright Blue Sky* 73, I came out of the spin at five hundred feet and pancaked in the reserve lines. **1936** F. CLUNE *Roaming round Darling* xxv. 271 All at once she [*sc.* a lorry] slithered like hell, and, knifing a corner, pancaked on to a mulga-tree. **1938** *Daily Progress* (Charlottesville, Va.) 30 July 1/8 He suggested the planes might be ordered to comb isolated mountain forests on the Pacific side of Luzon Island on the possibility the 'Clipper' pancaked into the trees. **1943** P. BRENNAN et al. *Spitfires over Malta* 91, I told my boys to pancake as soon as they had finished engaging. **1950** *Gloss. Aeronaut. Terms (B.S.I.)* I. 12 *Pancaking*, the alighting of an aircraft at an abnormally high rate of descent or low forward speed. **1952** M. TRIPP *Faith is Windsock* vi. 97 'Beany Able funnels; we are on three engines and must land.' 'Pancake, Able.' 'Able pancaking.' **1962** R. W. CLARK *Rise of Boffins* ii. 53 Another great time-saver was the use of a code for passing instructions to the fighters, and such R.A.F. terms as.. 'pancake' (for land), were invented during these experiments. **1977** *Listener* 28 Apr. 559/2 His plane.. pancaked into it. The Germans..came out..to take him and the plane.

'pancake-'bell. A bell formerly (still in some places) rung on Shrove Tuesday at or about 11 a.m., popularly associated with the frying of pancakes.

Generally held to have been originally the bell calling to confession. It was observed as the signal for the cessation of work, and beginning of the holiday.

1599 DEKKER *Shoemaker's Holiday* v. i, Upon every Shrove-Tuesday, at the sound of the pancake bell, my fine dapper Assyrian lads shall clap up their shop windows, and away. **1620** J. TAYLOR (Water-P.) *Jacke-a-Lent* Wks. (1630) 115/1 Shroue-Tuesday,..by that time the clocke strikes eleuen, which (by the helpe of a knauish Sexton) is commonly before nine, then there is a bell rung, cald The Pan-cake Bell, the sound whereof makes thousands of people distracted. **1640–1** in Swayne *Sarum Churchw. Acc.* (1896) 212 Making a frame for the Pancake bell. **1896** *Leeds Merc.* 29 Feb. Suppl. (E.D.D.), Richmond and Darlington have also their pancake bells, also Northallerton, at which place the same bell is used as for the curfew. The pancake bell called the people to be shriven before Lent.

†**pan'carpial,** *a. Obs. rare*$^{-1}$. [f. L. *pancarpi-us*, ad. Gr. πάγκαρπ-ος, f. παν- all + καρπός fruit.] Composed of all kinds of fruits.

1592 R. D. *Hypnerotomachia* 86b, [Nymphs] with Pan-carpiall garlands of all manner of Flowers, upon their heades.

†**'pancart.** *Obs.* [a. F. *pancarte*, ad. med.L. *pancarta, pancharta*: see PANCHART.]

a. = PANCHART. **b.** A placard bearing a public notification.

1577 HOLINSHED *Chron.* II. 530/2 Iohn Bouchet.. meruayleth of an olde Pancarte [*ed.* 1587 panchart] or Recorde, whyche he had seene, by the tenoure whereof, it appeareth, that this Otho entitled hymselfe Duke of Aquitayne. **1656** BLOUNT *Glossogr.* [from Cotgr.], *Pancart*, a paper containing the particular rates of Tolls or Customs due to the King, etc. Thus termed because commonly hung up in some publick place, either single, or with a frame. **1741** tr. *D'Argens' Chinese Lett.* xl. 310 The poorest of them when they die, leave Alms enough to pay for the spirtual Pancart.

pance, obs. form of PANSE, PANSY *sb.*, PAUNCH.

†**'pancelet.** *Obs. rare.* [? dim. of *pance*, PAUNCE, cuirass: see -LET.] A kind of horse-shoe.

1607 MARKHAM *Caval.* VI. x. 64 The Pancelet to help the weake heele. **1726** *Dict. Rust.* (ed. 3) s.v. *Horse Shooe*, Horse-shooe of ..several sorts. 1. That called the Planch-shoe or Pancelet.

pan-Celtic, etc.: see PAN- 1.

pancer(e, -cher, variants of PAUNCER *Obs.*

panch, -e, obs. variants of PAUNCH.

panchama ('pʌntʃʌmə). *India.* [Skr., = fifth.] A member of the fifth division of early Indian society, outside the four main divisions of Brahmin, Kshatrya, Vasiya and Sudra; a pariah, an outcaste. This caste was also called *Pancham Bandam.*

1800 F. BUCHANAN *Jrnl.* 30 Apr. in *Journey from Madras* (1807) I. i. 19 Their farms they chiefly cultivate by slaves of the inferiour casts, called Sūdra, and Panchum Bundum. The Panchum Bundum are by far the most hardy and laborious people of the country. **1874** *Madras Census Rep. 1871* I. xi. 168 We now come to that great division of the people, spoken of by themselves as the 'fifth caste', and described by Buchanan and other writers as the *Pancham Bandam.* **1909** E. THURSTON *Castes & Tribes of S. India* VI. 44 The Government ruled that there is no objection to the proposal that Paraiyas and kindred classes should be designated Panchama Bandham or Panchama in future, but it would be simpler to style them the fifth class. *Ibid.*, Panchama students under training as teachers get stipends at rates nearly double of those for ordinary Hindus. **1917** *Rangoon Gaz.* 10 Oct. 12/1 A mass meeting of Panchamas (depressed classes) was held in Madras. **1932** G. S. GHURYE *Caste & Race in India* i. 10 In the Tamil and Malayalam regions..sometimes the village is divided into three parts: that occupied by the dominant caste in the village or by the Brahmins, that allotted to the Sūdras, and the one reserved for the Panchamas or untouchables. **1968** N. W. ROSS *Hinduism, Buddhism, Zen* 29 Outside the four main caste divisions,..there has also existed from the earliest times a group familiarly known as the Untouchables. They were called Panchamas, literally 'the fifths'.

†**'panchart.** *Obs.* [ad. med.L. *pancharta* (*-carta*), f. Gr. παν- all + L. *charta* leaf, paper, in med.L. 'charter'.] A charter, orig. app. one of a general character, or that confirmed all special grants, but in later use applied to almost any written record.

1587 [see PANCART, quot. 1577]. **1621** MOLLE *Camerar. Liv. Libr.* v. xi. 361 The Constitutions of the Emperor Charles the fourth, gathered together in the Panchart, commonly called the Golden Bull. **1762** *Gentl. Mag.* 256 The consul's chaplain has shewed me a panchart of a great Rabbin... This good Rabbin says in his Panchart..that all men should regard each other as brothers.

‖**panchayat, punchayet** (pʌn'tʃɑːjət). *E. Ind.* Also **panchaet, -ait, -aeet.** [Hindī, f. *panch* five, Skr. *pañca* five.] A council of five (or now usually more) persons, assembled as a jury or court of arbitrators, or as a committee to decide on matters affecting a village, community, or body. Also *attrib.* Hence **panchayat samiti** [f. Hindi *samiti* committee].

1805 *Asiatic Ann. Reg.* Misc. 14/2 The panchaets are anxious for the examination of collateral facts. **1812** MAR. GRAHAM *Jrnl. Resid. Ind.* 41 The Parsees..are governed by their own *panchait*, or village council..[it] consists of thirteen of the principal merchants of the sect. **1826** HOCKLEY *Pandurang Hari* I. iii. 32 Assemble a *punchayet*, and give this cause patient attention, seeing that Hybatty has justice. **1844** H. H. WILSON *Brit. India* II. 515 The fullest possible employment of the..village courts, or Panchayats, in the adjudicature of civil suits. **1875** MAINE *Hist. Inst.* vii. 221 The normal number of a Jury or Board of Arbitrators is always five—the panchayet familiar to all who have the smallest knowledge of India. **1881** E. B. EASTWICK *Murray's Handbk. Bombay Presidency* (ed. 2) II. 141/1 In order to see the Towers of Silence, permission must be obtained from the Secretary to the Pársí Pancháyat. **1893** KIPLING *Many Inventions* 84 Create, further, councils other than the panchayats of headmen, village by village and district by district. **1945** 'P. WOODRUFF' *Call next Witness* 14 He was chairman of the village panchayat, the court which could try the smallest local offences. **1955** *Times* 29 Aug. 9/6 Mansingh tried to negotiate peace at a special meeting of the Panchayats, or village councils. **1963** *Times* 11 Mar. 11/7 The emphasis was corrected and laid on agricultural production—but no sooner than the establishment of *panchayat raj* had led villagers to express their needs more outspokenly, and their satisfaction had become the business of the village politicians. **1963** *Economist* 23 Nov. 752/1 His [the King of Nepal's] system of 'panchayat democracy', an elaborate four-tier edifice of indirect elections. **1965** E. LINTON *World in Grain of Sand* vi. 73 Were all members of the Panchayat present? No. Then send for them! Panchayats, literally meaning 'councils of five', have existed in villages since ancient times... Numbers need not necessarily be confined to five. **1969** *Listener* 2 Jan. 5/1 The panchayat system is little more popular than Pakistan's basic democracy. **1969** *National Herald* (New Delhi) 29 July 7/4 Mr. Thana Ram, pradhan of panchayat samiti, has criticised the demotion of education extension officers who have completed five years of service. **1971** *Hindustan Times Weekly* (New Delhi) 4 Apr. 8/2 The Agriculture Refinance Corporation will provide Rs 25 lakhs for disbursement as loans among the orange-growers of Halrapatan panchayat samiti in Halawar district. **1971** *Nat. Geographic* Nov. 662/1 Panchayat means 'five elders', a traditional informal council that runs the affairs of Nepalese villages. **1973** *Times* 14 Apr. (Nepal Suppl.) p. i/5 Limited popular representation is permitted through a pyramidal structure of partly elected and partly nominated *panchayats*, or councils, beginning at the village level. **1976** D. HIRO *Inside India Today* 50 What then emerged was a three-tiered system whereby the old district boards..were replaced by zilla parishads (i.e. district councils) with responsibility for co-ordinating development plans to be channelled through panchayat samitis (i.e. council committees) consisting of a number of popularly elected panchayats encompassing one or more villages—all interlinked through indirect elections. This system, popularly known as the panchayat raj, was first introduced in..1959.

panchen ('pæntʃən). *Tibet.* Also **Banchen, Pantchan,** etc. [Tibetan, abbrev. of *pandi-tachen-po* great learned one (cf. PUNDIT).] A Tibetan Buddhist title of respect, applied *esp.* to the lama of Tashi Lhunpo, who is held to be the reincarnation of Buddha Amitbha and is next in importance to the Dalai Lama, being styled the *Panchen Lama* or *Panchen Rinpoche* (rinpoche = precious, jewel). Cf. RINPOCHE.

1763 J. BELL *Trav. from St. Petersburg* I. 284 The Kontaysha is of the same profession with the Delay-Lama. .. I am informed there is a third Lama, called Bogdu-Pantzin, of still greater authority... He lives..near the frontiers of the Great Mogul. **1784** S. TURNER *Let.* 2 Mar. in *Acct. Embassy to Court of Teshoo Lama in Tibet* (1800) III. 373, I was..strongly dissuaded by the Regent Punjun Irtinnee. **1794** A. DALRYMPLE *Oriental Repertory* II. 273 This Pantchan-lama is the Second Person of Tibeth and of all the Lama-Hierarchy. *Ibid.* 274 The Pan-tchan..asked permission of his Majesty to proceed to the Capital of the Empire. **1800** S. TURNER *Acct. Embassy to Court of Teshoo Lama in Tibet* II. viii. 325 *Punjin Rimbochay*, Great Apostolic Master; the mitred professors of religion. **1834** C. GÜTZLAFF *Sk. Chinese Hist.* II. xvii. 64 One of the chiefs of Tibet, on hearing of the death of Banchen Lama at Peking, had gone to Nepaul with an immense treasure. **1851** H. T. PRINSEP *Tibet, Tartary & Mongolia* 108 The highest of existing regenerate Boodhs are the Delai Lama of Lassa; the Bandshan Remboochi, of Teeshoo Loomboo, the same who was visited by Captain Turner, in the time of Warren Hastings. **1876** C. R. MARKHAM *Narr. Bogle & Manning* p. cxi, The Pundit went..to Teshu Lumbo, to do homage to the Teshu Lama or Panchen Rimboché, a boy eleven years old. **1895** L. A. WADDELL *Buddhism of Tibet* x. 235 The Sa-kya Grand Lāmas had been called 'Pan-ch'en', or the 'Great doctor' from the twelfth century. **1925** *Glasgow Herald* 13 Apr. 9 The Panchan Lama is one of the two lama popes, the other being the Dalai Lama, or Ocean Priest, who resides at Lhassa. **1931** C. BELL *Relig. of Tibet* xii. 155 During the reign of the eighth Dalai Lama it is the Panchen Rim-po-che who looms largest in Tibetan history. **1935** *Discovery* Aug. 239/2 On the high altar itself the central position was occupied by an excellent photograph of the Panchen Lama. **1956** K. W. MORGAN *Path of Buddha* vi. 256 The present Panchen Lama is the ninth in succession and was selected jointly by the former National Government of China and the followers of the exiled Panchen Lama. **1962** *Listener* 12 July 71/1 People interested in Tibetan institutions will also pay attention to the few pages devoted to the Panchen Lama. **1964** J. P. MITTER *Betrayal of Tibet* 98 The Chinese Amban violated the Trade Regulations of 1908 by forbidding the Pan-chen Lama and his officials to communicate with the British Trade Agent at Gyantse. **1978** *Guardian* 25 Feb. 6/8 The Panchen Lama..remained behind in Tibet when the Dalai Lama and other religious leaders fled to India in 1959.

pancheon ('pænʃən). Also 7 **panshin, -shion,** 7–9 **-chion,** 9 **-chin, -shin, -shon.** [Origin obscure: app. derived in some way from PAN *sb.*[1]

Some would identify it with *pankin*, which is known much earlier; but there are no other instances of the dim. *-kin* becoming *-chin*. Influence of *puncheon* has been suggested.]

A large shallow earthenware bowl or vessel, wider at the top than at the bottom, used for setting milk to stand in to let the cream separate, and for other purposes: sometimes applied to a bread-pan.

1601 HOLLAND *Pliny* xv. vi. 433 Pans and panchions of earth. **1687** H. MORE *Contn. Remark. Stor.* (1689) 421 A great many Earthen Milk-pans or Panchins, as they call them. **1784** WESLEY *Wks.* (1872) XIII. 502 A shelf where several pancheons of milk stood. **1829** *Glover's Hist. Derby* I. 99 Pancheons, or shallow red glazed pans for setting of milk in dairies. **1897** GURDON *Mem.* 43 (E.D.D.) She was pouring the new milk into the great earthenware panchions that are brown without and cream colour within.

b. Humorously used for 'paunch'.

1804 ANNA SEWARD *Mem. Darwin* 142 Lakes of milk ran curdling into whey, within the ebon concave of their [cats'] pancheons.

†**'panchrest.** *Obs.* Anglicized form of next.

1727–41 CHAMBERS *Cycl.*, *Panchrest, Panchrestos*,..a panacea. **1753** —— *Cycl. Supp.*, *Panchrestarii*, among the Romans, those who prepared the pancrest, or universal remedy.

‖**panchreston** (pæn'kriːstən). *Obs.* Also 7 **-chrestum, -creston,** (8 *erron* **panchrestos, -us**); *pl.* **-chresta.** [a. Gr. πάγχρηστον adj. neut. 'good for everything', whence L. *panchrēstum medicāmentum* (Cicero and Pliny) sovereign medicine.] A universal medicine, a panacea. Also *fig.*

1632 WINTERTON *Drexelius' Consid. Eternity* To Rdr. 4 A pancreston profitable for all things. **1640** HARVEY *Synagogue, Bible* iii, The true Panchreston 'tis for every sore. **1654** WHITLOCK *Zootomia* 176 Empiricks..that with some Panchrestum, Catholike Medicines, undertake every thing. **1706** PHILLIPS, *Panchestra*, Medicines that are good against all or many Diseases. [So in KERSEY BAILEY, etc.] **1727–41** Panchrestos [see prec.].

pan-Christian, panchristic: see PAN- 1, 2.

panchromatic (pænkrə'mætɪk), *a.* [f. PAN- + CHROMATIC *a.*] **1.** *Photogr.* Sensitive (though not equally so) to light of all colours in the visible range. Also *ellipt.*, a panchromatic emulsion or plate.

1903, etc. [see ORTHOCHROMATIC *a.* 1]. **1906** *Chambers's Jrnl.* May 416/2 This layer..is re-covered with yet another layer of panchromatic, and sensitised. **1921** *Glasgow Herald* 6 Apr. 7 My dark-room lamp has three interchangeable safe-lights,..one a dark green for panchromatics. **1952** *Proc. R. Soc. Edin.* A. LXIII. 206 The usual type of orthochromatic emulsion is a little slow to this radiation, but a panchromatic emulsion might record some red. **1978** *SLR Camera* Aug. 82/1 Panchromatic film—the type almost exclusively used these days for normal photography—..is very much more sensitive to blue and blue-green, than the eye, but less sensitive to green, yellow and orange.

2. = POLYCHROMATIC *a.*

1971 J. MCCLURE *Steam Pig* iii. 39 The poser of the panchromatic panties. **1975** M. KENYON *Mr Big* xix. 180 Two boisterous black girls in patched panchromatic trousers.

Hence **pan'chromatize** *v. trans.*, to render panchromatic; **pan'chromatizing** *vbl. sb.*

1922 E. J. WALL *Pract. Color Photogr.* ii. 15 Many dyes have been suggested for panchromatizing. **1925** —— *Hist. Three-Color Photogr.* vii. 246 A. Miethe recommended the following mixture for panchromatizing plates. **1960** K. M. HORNSBY tr. *P. Glafkidès' Photogr. Chem.* II. xxxv. 729 To make them [*sc.* photographic emulsions] sensitive to the other colours, green, yellow, red and infra red—or to ortho- or panchromatize as we say—it is necessary to incorporate certain special dyes.

panchronic (pæn'krɒnɪk), *a. Linguistics.* [tr. F. *panchronique* (F. de Saussure *a* 1913, in *Cours de Linguistique générale* (1916) I. iii. 138), f. PAN- 2 + CHRONIC *a.*] Pertaining to or designating linguistic study applied to all languages at all stages of their development. Also **panchro'nistic** *a.* Hence **pan'chronically** *adv.*; **'panchrony.**

1931 *Amer. Jrnl. Philol.* LII. 79 Scientific grammar must be based on a combination of ideo(syn)chrony and panchrony. **1939** L. H. GRAY *Foundations of Lang.* 24 The components of such a panchronic grammar, which may technically be termed *general grammar*, will be few in number. **1949** *Archivum Linguisticum* I. II. 127 On the *panchronistic* plane, there is the usual argument of the complete diversity of words for the same idea in different languages. **1951** S. ULLMANN *Princ. Semantics* v. 261 He [*sc.* de Saussure] did admit the possibility of 'panchronistic laws' resembling the universal regularities of natural science, e.g. the ubiquitousness of sound-change. **1952** *Times Lit. Suppl.* 10 Oct. 659/3 A final chapter, devoted to panchronistic or general semantics, is merely a programmatic sketch. **1957** *Archivum Linguisticum* IX. II. 81 Finally, hyper- and hypocharacterization may be used panchronically. **1964** *Ibid.* XVI. I. 23 Clusters so shaped may panchronically tend to undergo just this development. **1966** M. Pei *Gloss. Ling. Terminol.* 192 *Panchronic grammar*, applicable to all languages and at all historical stages of their development. **1969** *Eng. Stud.* L. 417 General phonetics is by definition synchronic, or rather panchronic. *Ibid.* 422 Comparatism was supposed..to lead to diachrony, not to the establishment of common, general features of language, to panchrony. **1974** R. A. Hall *External Hist. Romance Lang.* 4 The panchronic approach treats those aspects of language for which the passage of time is not relevant. **1978** *Language* LIV. 238/2 In Chapter V, he treats 'Lingua, stile, dialetti'..from a primarily panchronic point of view.

‖**panchshila** (pɑːn'ʃiːlə). Also **panchsheel, panchsila**, and as two words. [Hindī and Skr., f. *panch* five, *shila* foundation.] The five principles of peaceful relations formulated between India and China (and, by extension, other communist countries).

The five principles, stated in the preamble of a treaty signed by India and China in April 1954, are: 1. Mutual respect for each other's territorial integrity and sovereignty. 2. Non-aggression. 3. Non-interference in each other's internal affairs. 4. Equality and mutual benefit. 5. Peaceful co-existence.

1955 *Times* 18 July 7/5 After analysing the popular enthusiasm in Russia over the Nehru visit, the newspaper [sc. *Times of India*] says, 'It would be foolish, even dangerous, to work oneself up into a frenzy of apocalyptic fervour and hail those who hailed our Prime Minister as comrades good and true demonstrating in their mammoth enthusiasm the resolve to march in step to the golden melody of Panchshila.' **1958** *Times* 4 July 9/3 India tried to act upon the principles of *panchsila*, and did not wish to interfere in other people's affairs. **1959** *Manch. Guardian* 15 Aug. 5/4 China has slapped India's face, and the Panchshilas (the 'five principles of co-existence') have popped. **1961** *Economist* 2 Dec. 939/2 India was drawing up the *Panch Shila*—the five principles of peaceful co-existence—with the Chinese. **1965** J. Nehru in A. Appadorai *Documents Political Thought* (1976) II. 739 Panchsheel has begun to acquire a specific meaning and significance in world affairs. **1967** L. J. Kavic *India's Quest for Security* iii. 59 On 1 August 1955, a joint communiqué issued in Kathmandu by representatives of the Nepalese and Chinese governments declared that an agreement had been reached which affirmed panch sheel as the basis of Sino-Nepalese relations. **1978** L. Heren *Growing up on The Times* v. 178 Despite the Indian name, the *panchsila* were of Chinese origin, and were written into the preamble of the Sino-Indian Tibetan Treaty on the instance of Peking.

‖**panchway, pansway** ('pæntʃweɪ, 'pænsweɪ). *E. Ind.* Also 8 **panguay, ponsway, paunchway.** [a. Hindī *pansoī*, Bengālī *panço̤ī*, *pançī* a boat.] 'A light kind of boat used on the rivers of Bengal, with a tilted roof of matting or thatch, a mast and four oars' (Yule).

1757 J. H. Grose *Voy. E. Ind.* 20 Their larger boats, called panguays, are raised some feet from the sides with reeds and branches of trees, well bound together with small-cord. **1766** *Ibid.* (ed. 2) Gloss., *Ponsways*, Guard-boats. **1793** W. Hodges *Trav. India* 39 The paunchways are nearly of the same general construction [as budgerows]. **1823** Heber *Narr. Journ. India* (1828) I. 4 A Panchway, or passage boat ..large and broad, shaped like a snuffer dish; a deck fore and aft, and the middle covered with a roof of palm branches.

†**panchymagogue** (pæn'kɪməgɒg). *Obs.* [Formerly *panchymagogon*, a. Gr. type *παγχυμάγωγον, f. παν- all + χύμα fluid, humour + ἀγωγός, -όν leading.] (See quot. 1657.)

1657 *Physical Dict.*, *Panchymagogon*, such purgers as are universal, purging all humors. **1671** Salmon *Syn. Med.* III. xlix. 560 There are many Panchymagogons extant. *Ibid.* li. 570 Electuary of Turbith..is a good Panchymagogue. **1676** Cooke *Mellificium Chirurg.* VII. I. iv. 814 Of Water-Purgers, Simple, Compound, and Panchymagogons. **1706** Phillips, *Panchymagoga* or *Panchymagogues*,..Medicines that disperse all Humours of the Body. **1893** *Syd. Soc. Lex.*, *Panchymagogue*, a medicine anciently believed to drive out all peccant humours.

panclastic, -conciliatory, etc.: see PAN- 2.

panclastite (pæn'klæstaɪt). [f. Gr. παν- all + κλαστός broken, -κλαστης breaker + -ITE[1] 4.] An explosive formed by mixing liquid nitrogen tetroxide with carbon disulphide, nitrotoluene, or other liquid combustible, in the proportion of three volumes of the former to two of the latter.

1883 *Eng. Mechanic* 9 Mar. 9 A Parisian has invented a new explosive which is more powerful than dynamite. Panclastite, as he calls it, consists of hypoazotic acid..mixed either with essence of petroleum or sulphuret of carbon. **1890** *Daily News* 31 May 5/7 An analysis..shows that the Nihilists were manufacturing 'panclastite'.

pancosmic (pæn'kɒzmɪk), *a.* [f. as next + -IC: cf. *cosmic*.] Pertaining or relating to the whole universe; of or pertaining to pancosmism.

1853 *Fraser's Mag.* XLVIII. 459 In the most melodious verse, illustrated by the most startling and pancosmic metaphors. **1891** *Daily News* 3 Apr. 5/2 Miss Naden's poetry began to bear the burden of Pancosmism... She rejoices in being 'One with the essence of the boundless world'... A microbe or a bluebottle fly is just as Pancosmic as anything else, on this showing.

pancosmism (pæn'kɒzmɪz(ə)m). *Philos.* [f. Gr. παν- all + κόσμος world, universe + -ISM, after *pantheism*.] The doctrine that the material universe or cosmos is all that exists.

1865 Grote *Plato* I. i. 18 The fundamental tenet of Xenophanes was partly religious, partly philosophical, Pantheism, or Pan-kosmism. **1876** Fairbairn *Stud. Philos. Relig. & Hist.* (1877) 392 Pantheism and Pankosmism are but the ideal and real sides of the same thought. **1901** R. M. Wenley in Baldwin *Dict. Philos. & Psychol.* I. 84/2 Pancosmism is, for orthodox theology, the sole atheism.

b. *nonce-use.* Ideal oneness with the whole world.

1891 [see PANCOSMIC].

Hence **pan'cosmist**, one who holds the doctrine of pancosmism.

1876 Fairbairn *Stud. Philos. Relig. & Hist.* (1877) 392 The pantheist is a metaphysician, the pankosmist a physicist.

pancratian (pæn'kreɪʃɪən), *a.* [f. L. PANCRATI-UM + -AN.] Of or belonging to the pancratium.

1810 F. Lee tr. *Pindar's Isthmian Odes* v. 474 To thee and to thy Pytheas were decreed The garlands of the stout Pancratian toil.

pancratiast (pæn'kreɪʃɪæst). [ad. L. *pancratiastēs*, a. Gr. παγκρατιαστής, agent-n. from παγκρατιάζειν to practise the παγκράτιον, PANCRATIUM. Cf. mod.F. *pancratiaste*.] A combatant or victor in the pancratium.

1603 Holland *Plutarch* Explan. Words, *Pancratiast*, one that is skilfull and professed in the said Pancration. **1610** Marcelline *Triumphs Jas. I* 1 To plaite Wreathes, Chaplets, and Coronets of honor for this worthy Pancratiaste. **1765** *Antiq.* in *Ann. Reg.* 181/1 An Olympian Pancratiast. **1880** Waldstein *Pythag. Rhegion* 15 This statue belongs to the heavier genus of athletes, the boxer or the pancratiast.

So **pancratiastic** (pænkreɪʃɪ'æstɪk), *a.* [ad. Gr. παγκρατιαστικ-ός], of, pertaining to, or characteristic of a pancratiast.

1749 G. West *Pindar's Nemean Odes* xi. Strophe ii, The Wrestler's Chaplet..Mix'd with the great Pancratiastick Crown. **1875** Jowett *Plato* (ed. 2) I. 194 They have at last carried out the pancratiastic art to the very end.

pancratic (pæn'krætɪk), *a.* [ad. L. type **pancratic-us* (in adv. *pancraticē*; Sp. *pancratico*, F. *pancratique*), irreg. f. παγκράτιον, or f. Gr. παγκρατής all-powerful + -IC.]

1. Of or pertaining to the pancratium; hence, fully disciplined or exercised in mind, having a universal mastery of accomplishments.

a **1660** Hammond *Serm. Jer.* xxxi. 18 Wks. 1683 IV. 488 Advanced and arrived already to a spiritual height, to a full pancratick habit, fit for combats and wrastlings. **1731** Bailey, *Pancratick*, all-powerful, almighty. **1820** *Ann. Reg.* II. 1296 The evolutions and manœuvres of the old Pancratic contests. **1848** Lowell *Biglow P.*, *Notices Indep. Press*, The advantages of a pancratic or pantechnic education.

2. Of an eye-piece: Capable of adjustment to many degrees of power.

1831 Brewster *Optics* xliii. 363 It..has more recently been brought out as a new invention,..under the name of the Pancratic Eye Tube. **1878** Lockyer *Stargazing* 113 This arrangement is called Dollond's Pancratic eyepiece. **1884** Knight *Dict. Mech.* Suppl. 654/1 Pankratic Microscope..has a sliding tube containing the eye-piece, by which its distance from the object glass may be changed, and various degrees of enlargement..obtained without change of glasses.

†**pan'cratical**, *a.* *Obs.* [-AL[1].] = prec. 1.

1581 Mulcaster *Positions* xvii. (1887) 76 Not to deale with the catching pancraticall kinde of wrastling. **1646** Sir T. Browne *Pseud. Ep.* VII. xviii. 381 Milo..was the most pancraticall man of Greece.

Hence †**pan'cratically** *adv.* *Obs.*

1727 Bailey vol. II, *Pancratically*,..almightily.

pancratist ('pænkrətɪst). [cf. It. *pancratista*, for L. *pancratiastēs*, with modification of suffix.] = PANCRATIAST.

1775 Ash, *Pancratist*,..one skilled in gymnastic exercises. **1873** Symonds *Grk. Poets* iii. (1877) 87 Boxers, pentathletes, wrestlers, pancratists. **1885** Jane E. Harrison *Stud. Grk. Art* iv. 191 A wrestler, a boxer, a pancratist.

‖**pancratium** (pæn'kreɪʃɪəm), **-ion** (-ɪən). [L. *pancratium*, a. Gr. παγκρατιον an exercise of all the forces, f. παν- all + κράτος bodily strength, mastery: cf. παγκρατής all-powerful. As a plant-name (see sense 2), in Dioscorides and Pliny.]

1. *Gr. Antiq.* An athletic contest, combining both wrestling and boxing.

1603 Holland *Plutarch's Mor.* 364 Feats of activity,..not onely in that generall exercise *Pancration*, wherein hand and foote both is put to the uttermost at once, but also at buffets. *Ibid.*, Another general *Pancratium*. **1749** G. West *Odes Pindar*, *Pancratium* (1753) II. 92 An Athlete must borrow many Things from each of those Sciences to render himself eminent in the Pancratium. **1837** Wheelwright tr. *Aristophanes* II. 215 How could one, Arm'd with a breastplate, fight in the pancratium? **1875** Jowett *Plato* (ed. 2) V. 402 The pancration shall have a counterpart in a combat of the light-armed.

fig. **1807** *Edin. Rev.* IX. 395 Epic poetry has been considered by critics as a sort of poetical *pancratium*.

2. *Bot.* A genus of bulbous plants of the N.O. *Amaryllidaceæ*, bearing an umbel of large white flowers terminating a solid scape.

1664 Evelyn *Kal. Hort.* Dec. in *Sylva*, etc. (1729) 227 Lychnis double white, Matricaria double flo. Olives, Pancration. **1767** J. Abercrombie *Every Man own Gard.* (1803) 47 Gladioluses, pancratiums, fritillaries, crown imperials. **1846** Mrs. Lee *African Wand.* xviii. (1854) 314 Above that exquisite white pancratium.

attrib. **1890** *Pall Mall G.* 12 July 5/2 A magnificent pancratium lily.

pancreas ('pæŋkriːæs, -əs). [a. mod.L., a. Gr. πάγκρεας (stem -κρεατ- sweetbread, f. παν- all + κρέας flesh. So F. *pancréas*, It., Sp. *pancreas*.] A lobulated racemose gland situated near the stomach, and discharging by one or more ducts into the duodenum a digestive secretion, the *pancreatic juice*; called in animals, when used as food, the *sweetbread*.

1578 Banister *Hist. Man* v. 68 This body is called Panchreas, that is, all carnous or fleshy, for that it is made and contexed of Glandulous flesh. **1681** tr. *Willis' Rem. Med. Wks.* Vocab., *Pancreas*, called in a hog the sweet bread. **1731** Arbuthnot *Aliments* i. (1735) 15 The Pancreas is a large salivary Gland separating about a Pound of an Humour like Spittle, in twelve Hours. **1831** R. Knox *Cloquet's Anat.* 784 The Pancreas..lying across the vertebral column, between the three curvatures of the duodenum, behind the stomach, and to the right of the spleen.

b. *transf.* (See quots.)

1841–71 T. R. Jones *Anim. Kingd.* (ed. 4) 475 To these secreting cæca [of Rotifera], Ehrenberg has chosen to give the name of pancreas; but..the first rudiments of a pancreas are only met with in animals far higher in the scale of animal existence. **1883** E. R. Lankester in *Encycl. Brit.* XVI. 676/2 Upon the bile-ducts in Dibranchiata are developed yellowish glandular diverticula, which are known as 'pancreas', though neither physiologically nor morphologically is there any ground for considering [them] ..equivalent to the glands so denominated in the Vertebrata.

pancreatectomy (ˌpæŋkriːə'tɛktəmɪ). *Surg.* [f. Gr. stem παγκρεατ- (PANCREAS) + -ECTOMY.] Excision of the pancreas.

1900 in Dorland *Med. Dict.* **1903** W. S. Bickham *Text-bk. Operative Surg.* v. 834 Anatomically, complete pancreatectomy is very difficult. **1968** *New Scientist* 27 June 701/2 Pancreas transplantation..might also be useful.. where pancreatectomy is needed because of malignancy. **1974** R. M. Kirk et al. *Surgery* vi. 112 Occasionally distal pancreatectomy, the removal of ductal stones, and drainage of the cut end of the pancreas into the jejunum, improves the patient. **1977** *Proc. R. Soc. Med.* LXX. 160/1 One man of 44 died of massive haemorrhage the day after a complicated procedure to relieve intestinal and biliary obstruction, following a pancreatectomy less than three weeks previously.

Hence ˌ**pancrea'tectomize** *v. trans.*, to excise the pancreas of; ˌ**pancrea'tectomized** *ppl. a.*

1912 *Amer. Jrnl. Physiol.* XXX. 341 The glycolytic action of muscle extracts of both normal and pancreatectomized animals has been tested. **1960** *Recent Progress Hormone Res.* XVI. 503 Rats were fasted and underfed for 8–10 days and then pancreatectomized. **1965** Lee & Knowles *Animal Hormones* vii. 111 If a dog is pancreatectomized and the circulation connected to one, two or three pancreases from normal dogs, the blood glucose is normal in the pancreatectomized animal, irrespective of the number of the pancreases utilized.

pancreatic (pæŋkriː'ætɪk), *a.* [ad. mod.L. *pancreatic-us*, f. Gr. παγκρεατ-: see PANCREAS and -IC. So mod.F. *pancréatique*, Sp., It. *pancreatico*.] Of or belonging to the pancreas.

pancreatic juice, the clear viscid fluid secreted by the pancreas, forming an important agent in digestion.

1665–6 *Phil. Trans.* 12 Mar. 178 Produced by the conflux of the said acid Pancreatick-juyce, and some Bilious matter. **1758** *Ibid.* L. 588 Two bodies or glands, one of which may be called hepatic, and the other pancreatic. **1827** Abernethy *Surg. Wks.* I. 31. **1872** Huxley *Phys.* vi. 153 Pancreatic juice is an alkaline fluid not unlike saliva in many respects.

†**pancre'atical**, *a.* *Obs.* [-AL[1].] = prec.

1670 W. Simpson *Hydrol. Ess.* 158 The subacid ferment of the pancreatical juyce.

pancre'atico-, combining form, as in **pancre'atico-duo'denal** *a.*, connecting or pertaining to both the pancreas and the duodenum; **pancreˌaticoduode'nectomy** = *pancreatoduodenectomy*.

1848 in Craig. **1897** *Allbutt's Syst. Med.* III. 724 Loss of blood due to ulceration of the pancreatico-duodenal arteries. **1941** *Ann. Surg.* CXIV. 612 Until 1935, pancreaticoduodenectomy for cancer involving the pancreas was not attempted. **1973** V. L. Stevenson *Biliary Tract Surg. & Cholangiogr.* xii. 124 Those undergoing pancreaticoduodenectomy generally afforded a longer survival than those undergoing palliation.

pancreatin ('pæŋkriːətɪn). *Chem.* [f. Gr. stem παγκρεατ- (PANCREAS) + -IN[1].] A proteid compound, one of the active principles of pancreatic juice; also, a preparation extracted from the pancreas and used to aid digestion.

1873 Ralfe *Phys. Chem.* 145 Pancreatin is obtained by rubbing down the pancreas of a freshly killed animal, in full digestion, with pounded glass,..from which the pancreatin may be precipitated by alcohol. Pancreatin is an albuminoid substance which rapidly decomposes. **1883** *Q. Rev.* July 21 The digestive ferments, as pepsin and pancreatin.

‖**pancreatitis** (pæŋkriːə'taɪtɪs). *Path.* [f. as prec. + -ITIS.] Inflammation of the pancreas.

1842 in Dunglison *Med. Lex.* **1866** A. Flint *Princ. Med.* (1880) 646. **1897** *Allbutt's Syst. Med.* II. 859 Chronic pancreatitis may be caused by alcoholism.

Hence **pancrea'titic** *a.*, pertaining to or affected with pancreatitis (*Cent. Dict.* 1890).

pancreatize (ˈpæŋkriːətaɪz), *v.* [f. as prec. + -IZE.] *trans.* To treat with pancreatin so as to make digestible. Hence **ˈpancreatized, ˈpancreatizing** *ppl. adjs.*; also **pancreatiˈzation.**
1890 *Century Dict., Pancreatize.* **1897** *Allbutt's Syst. Med.* III. 135 Reducing..the pancreatising agent. *Ibid.*, Pancreatised milk diluted with..water. *Ibid.* 140 The milk may be pancreatised for a time and diluted—the pancreatisation being gradually reduced. **1898** *Ibid.* V. 615 The process of peptonisation or pancreatisation of milk.

pancreato-, comb. form (= PANCREATICO-), as in **pancreˌatoduodeˈnectomy** (see quot. 1928); **ˌpancreaˈtography**, radiological examination of the pancreas.
1928 R. J. E. SCOTT *Gould's Med. Dict.* (ed. 2) 1044/2 *Pancreatoduodenectomy*, excision of the head of the pancreas with the surrounding loop of duodenum. **1937** *Surg., Gynecol. & Obstetr.* LXV. 681 (*heading*) Resection of head of pancreas and duodenum for carcinoma—pancreatoduodenectomy. **1977** *Proc. R. Soc. Med.* LXX. 153/1 Unfortunately, Whipple's operation or pancreatoduodenectomy for carcinoma of the head of the pancreas was seldom possible. **1971** RAINS & CAPPER *Bailey & Love's Short Pract. Surg.* (ed. 15) xlii. 877 (*heading*) Pancreatography. **1977** *Lancet* 9 July 68/1 A screening test which makes possible the detection of pancreatic disease at an early stage and gives an indication for invasive procedures such as endoscopic pancreatography and selective arteriography is urgently needed.

pancreatoid (ˈpæŋkriːətɔɪd), *a.* and *sb.* [f. as PANCREATIZE *v.* + -OID.] **a.** *adj.* Resembling the pancreas. **b.** *sb.* A tumour resembling the pancreas.
1842 DUNGLISON *Med. Lex., Pancreatoid*,..a tumour resembling the pancreas in structure. **1867** C. A. HARRIS *Dict. Med. Terminol., Pancreatoid*, resembling the pancreas.

pancreˈatomy. [For **pancreatotomy*, f. as prec. + Gr. -τομια, -TOMY, cutting.] Excision or extirpation of the pancreas.
1890 in *Cent. Dict.* **1893** in *Syd. Soc. Lex.*

pancreˈectomy. [See -ECTOMY.] = prec.
1890 in *Cent. Dict.* **1893** in *Syd. Soc. Lex.*

pancreozymin (pæŋkriːəʊˈzaɪmɪn). *Biochem.* [f. PANCRE(AS + -O + ZYMIN.] A hormone which stimulates the production of enzymes by the pancreas.
1943 HARPER & RAPER in *Jrnl. Physiol.* CII. 116 We have obtained preparations which increase the output of enzymes from the cat's pancreas without having any secretin activity. .. For the active substance producing this effect we suggest the name 'Pancreozymin'. **1956** *Nature* 7 Jan. 22/2 Cholinergic drugs and pancreozymin in the pancreas, and acetylcholine and adrenalin in the salivary glands, all stimulate the secretion of protein. **1965** LEE & KNOWLES *Animal Hormones* viii. 120 It may be that under normal conditions both secretin and pancreozymin are released together. **1974** R. M. KIRK et al. *Surgery* vi. 110 Pancreozymin..is liberated in response to the presence of protein and fat in the duodenum.

pancuronium (pænkjʊˈrəʊnɪəm). *Pharm.* [f. *pan-*, of uncertain etym. + CUR(ARE + -ONIUM.] A steroid whose bromide is used as a neuromuscular blocking agent.
1967 *Brit. Jrnl. Anæsthesia* XXXIX. 775/1 Pancuronium bromide (NA97), was first synthesized in 1964 by Hewett and Savage (1966, personal communication). **1976** *Billings* (Montana) *Gaz.* 17 June 1-D/6 Many of the breathing failures at the hospital were caused when unknown assailants injected patients with a potentially lethal muscle-paralyzing drug, pancuronium bromide. **1976** *Lancet* 18 Dec. 1334/1 One group of eight patients received general anæsthesia with thiopenthone, suxamethonium chloride, pancuronium bromide or gallamine, and enflurane ('Ethrane') with nitrous oxide plus oxygen.

pancy, obs. form of PANSY *sb.*

pancyclopædic: see PAN- 2.

pand (pænd). *Sc.* Also dial. pan', pawn. [Cf. OF. *pandre* = *pendre* to hang, *pend* pendant.] A narrow curtain or piece of drapery, hung horizontally (usually box-pleated) from the framework of a bed; a valance.
1561 *Inv. Royal Wardr.* (1815) 123 Item ane claith of stait of blak velvot..with thre pandis quhairof thair is ane without frenyeis. **1648** *Inv.* in *Spottiswoode Misc.* (1844) I. 370 Ane stand of courtingis, with two piece of pand. **1692** *Inv.* in *Scott. N. & Q.* (1900) Dec. 92/1 Ane highe wanscot bed with purpure hingins and pand furnished with silk frenzies. **1756** MRS. CALDERWOOD *Jrnl.* (1884) 72 Commonly a muslin or point ruffled pawn round it. **1818** SCOTT *Br. Lamm.* xxvi, Where's the..beds of state, twilts, pands and testors, napery and broidered wark?
Hence **ˈpanded** *a.*, having a pand or valance.
1578 *Inv. Roy. Wardr.* (1815) 210 Ane bed of claith of gold and silvir double pandit.

pand, obs. or dial. form of PAWN.

panda (ˈpændə). [Said to be one of the names in Nepal.]
1. A racoon-like animal (*Ælurus fulgens*) of the south-eastern Himalayas, about the size of a large cat, having reddish-brown fur and a long bushy ring-marked tail; the red bear-cat.
[**1824** F. CUVIER *Hist. des Mammifères* livrais. 50 Panda.] **1835** SWAINSON *Nat. Hist. Quadrupeds* 107 The panda..has been discovered only of late years, in the mountains of India. It has been termed the most beautiful of all known quadrupeds. **1861** J. G. WOOD *Nat. Hist.* I. 420 This beautiful creature is a native of Nepal, where it is known under the different names of Panda, Chitwa, and Wah. **1901** C. J. CORNISH *Living Anim.* 126 The bear Cat or Panda.
2. a. A large, black and white, bear-like mammal, *Ailuropoda melanoleuca*, native to limited, mountainous areas of forest in China, where the first scientific description of it was made by the French missionary, Armand David (1826–1900), in 1869; formerly known as the parti-coloured bear, until its zoological relationship to the red panda was established in 1901.
1901 E. R. LANKESTER in *Trans. Linn. Soc.* (*Zool.*) VIII. 165 *Æluropus* must be removed from association with the Bears..and is no longer to be spoken of as 'the Parti-coloured Bear', but as 'the Great Panda'. **1928** *Proc. Zool. Soc.* 975 The systematic position of the Giant Panda..is a question about which there has been much disagreement amongst zoologists. **1933** *Discovery* Mar. 91/1 In outward appearance there is considerable difference between these two animals, the giant panda..being very bear-like, while the little panda is about the size and somewhat the shape of a cat. **1939** *Daily Mail* 12 Apr. 8/4 This sickly sentimental panda plague has infected far more people than can ever hope to eye it in the flesh... Would-be fashionable young women are carrying panda mascots. **1940** N. MITFORD *Pigeon Pie* ix. 140 Ming, the panda, would soon eat no food until one of them was played to her. **1943** *Jrnl. Mammalogy* XXIV. 267 The New York Zoological Society has recently acquired a pair of giant pandas... The principal natural diet of the panda is bamboo. **1966** R. & D. MORRIS *Men & Pandas* vi. 105 There were panda postcards.., panda toys (almost obliterating the teddy bear for a brief period), panda novelties, panda strip-cartoons, panda brooches, and panda hats. **1973** *Times* 2 May 9/8 Children [in Peking] played a multitude of games including ' feed the panda', a variation on 'pin the tail on the donkey'. **1976** *Times Lit. Suppl.* 27 Feb. 231/5 It is rumoured that China has sited her nuclear testing grounds not far away from Panda country.
b. Used *attrib.* to designate a type of pedestrian crossing (see quot. 1962[1]). Also *absol.*
1962 *Daily Tel.* 7 Mar. 15/7 'Panda' pedestrian crossings are to be introduced..to supplement zebra crossings. Their warning lights will be operated by push-buttons and they will be given a 12-month trial. *Ibid.*, Differences in appearance between the 'Pandas' and the zebras are that the black-and-white carriageway markings at the 'Pandas' will be altered in shape from rectangles to blunted chevrons. **1962** *Times* 3 Apr. 12/6 Panda crossings, introduced yesterday, held up Croydon's evening traffic. **1963** *Times* 24 May 17/4 The amber lights system used on panda crossings was so complex and ambiguous that the ordinary driver could not understand it. **1965** A. CHRISTIE *At Bertram's Hotel* xi. 106 On the whole, the Canon was not what we would call accident prone... Whilst taking no care or thought, they could still survive even a Panda crossing.
c. A police patrol car, so named from the resemblance of a broad white stripe on the car to the markings of the giant panda. Also *attrib. colloq.*
1966 *Guardian* 13 Sept. 8/4 Special one-man patrol cars —painted blue with a broad white stripe and known as 'Pandas'. **1969** J. WAINWRIGHT *Take-Over Men* i. 13 What about your Panda Patrols? Your closed-circuit television? **1970** *Times* 17 Mar. 2 Five children, who..helped catch two thieves, are to be given a ride in a police panda car. **1971** *Daily Tel.* 10 May 2/2 It was felt that panda drivers should be warned that the vehicles were not meant to be pursuit cars. **1974** 'A. GILBERT' *Nice Little Killing* vi. 82 He got out his old second-hand car—the village bobby didn't rate a panda.

pan-dædalian, etc.: see PAN- 2.

pandæmonium: see PANDEMONIUM.

pandaite (ˈpændəaɪt). *Min.* Also **pandaïte**. [f. *Panda*, the name of the hill in Mbeya, Tanzania, where it was first found + -ITE[1].] A hydrated oxide of barium, strontium, niobium, and titanium, $(Ba,Sr)(Nb,Ti)_2(O,H_2O)_7$, belonging to the pyrochlore group and found as yellow or white octahedral crystals.
1959 E. JÄGER et al. in *Mineral. Mag.* XXXII. 24 Some authors prefer to include under pyrochlore all the members of the group. Others give distinct names to the various members of this group. We prefer the latter and therefore propose to give the mineral described above the name of *pandaite* (after Panda Hill). This name shall be used for those minerals of the pyrochlore group in which Ba predominates over other elements in the *A* positions. **1971** *Mineralium Deposita* VI. 154/2 This pandaïte shows large deficiencies in A ions and only 20–25% of the A positions are occupied. *Ibid.* 155/1 The mineral from Bingo [in the Congo] is a hydrated rare-earth variety of pandaïte. **1977** *Amer. Mineralogist* LXII. 407 *Pandaite*..is a synomym for *bariopyrochlore*. The name should be dropped.

‖**pandal** (ˈpændəl, pænˈdɑːl). *E. Ind.* Also 8 **bandel, pundull,** 9 **pan-, pendaul.** [a. Tamil *pendal* shed.] A shed, booth, or arbour, esp. for temporary use.
1717 J. T. PHILLIPS *Acc. Malabar* 19 Water-Bandels (which are little Sheds for the Conveniency of drinking Water). **1800** SIR T. MUNRO in G. R. Gleig *Life* (1830) I. 283, I would not enter his pundull, because he had not paid the labourers who made it. **1810** SOUTHEY *Curse of Kehama* IX. Notes *Wks.* 1838 VIII. 259 The Pandal is a kind of arbour or bower raised before the doors of young married women. **1815** *Sporting Mag.* XLVI. 20 A magnificent pendaul..to accommodate 10,000 people. **1815** MᶜKENZIE in *Asiat. Res.* XIII. 329 (Y.) Pandauls were erected opposite the two principal fords on the river. **1893** *Westm. Gaz.* 18 Nov. 4/3 The town was gaily decorated in honour of his visit, twenty pandals having been erected along the route to Government House. **1929** F. T. JESSE *Lacquer Lady* I. xii. 86 Her mother, the Kalawoon's wife, was running the pandal or festival pavilion for Thibaw. **1956** *Times* 13 Jan. 3/3 All the music is amplified, since the temporary *pandal*, which is the equivalent of an Eisteddfod 'tent', seats nearly 1,500 people. **1962** *Housewife* (Ceylon) Feb. 19 It was decided to hold the reception at the 39th lane sports club, where there was ample room for two large pandals to be erected. **1963** *Guardian* 11 Apr. 11/3 The Hindu wedding, celebrated under the flowered palm leaf pandal. **1971** *Weekend* (Ceylon) 8 Aug. 3/3 Permanent pandals will be built to decorate the entrances to sacred cities. **1977** *Oxford Mission Q. Paper* Jan.–Mar. 10 An enormous *pandal* had been erected which covered the whole area on the south side of the church, and the altar was placed on a mound in the middle of it.

pandall, *Her.*: see SPINDLE-CROSS.

‖**pandan**[1] (ˈpɑːndɑːn). *E. Ind.* [Urdū *pāndān*, f. Hindī *pān* PAN *sb.*[5] + Pers. *dān* vessel, holder.] A small box of Indian manufacture, generally of decorated metal, used for holding pán (PAN *sb.*[5]).
1886 *Catal. Colon. & Ind. Exhib.* 51 The articles shown include hookahs, *pandans* or betel-nut boxes.

pandan[2] (ˈpændən). Also **pandang.** [Malay.] = PANDANUS.
1777 G. FORSTER *Voy. round World* I. 270 The pandang or palm-nut tree had given its long prickly leaves to thatch the roofs of the buildings. **1783** W. MARSDEN *Hist. Sumatra* 87 Of the *pandan*, which is a shrub with very long prickly leaves, like those of the pine apple or aloe, there are many varieties. **1935** I. H. BURKILL *Dict. Econ. Products Malay Peninsula* II. 1646 The compound pine-apple-like fruit of a *Pandan* is composed of the fused fruits of the individual flowers. **1954** R. E. HOLTTUM *Plant Life Malaya* ii. 23 Pandans have much in common with palms. **1959** 'M. DERBY' *Tigress* iii. 125 A clump of *pandan*..edged the near end of the pool. **1972** M. SHEPPARD *Taman Indera* 158 Pandan leaves are used to make mats of finer quality, for sitting, praying or sleeping on.

pandanaceous (pændəˈneɪʃəs), *a.* [f. Bot. L. *Pandānāce-æ* + -OUS.] Pertaining to or connected with the Natural Order *Pandanaceæ* or screw-pines.
1889 NICHOLSON & LYDEKKER *Palæont.* II. 1541 Fruits.. which are regarded by their describer, Mr. Carruthers, as undoubtedly Pandanaceous.
So **panˈdanad**, a pandanaceous plant; **panˈdaneous** *a.*, pandanaceous.
1857 MAYNE *Expos. Lex.*, Pandaneous. **1892** *Daily News* 20 Apr. 5/5 The palms and pandanads which, with the Cycads, now form the most striking feature of the large Palm House at Kew.

‖**pandanus** (pænˈdeɪnəs). *Bot.* [mod.L. (G. E. Rumphius *Herbarium Amboinense* (1743) IV. 139/1), f. Malay *pandan.*] A tree or shrub of the genus so called, belonging to the family Pandanaceæ, native to Malaysia, tropical Africa, or Australia, and distinguished by forked trunks with thick aerial roots, long, narrow, prickly leaves arranged in spiral tufts, and large, sometimes edible fruits resembling a pineapple. Also *attrib.*
[**1777**: see PANDAN[2].] **1830** J. LINDLEY *Introd. Nat. Syst. Bot.* 285 The seeds of Pandanus are eatable. **1846** L. LEICHHARDT in J. D. Lang *Cooksland* 326 The fruit of the pandanus forms another apparently very-much-liked eatable of the natives. **1875** MISS BIRD *Sandwich Isl.* (1880) 86 She wore..a *lei* of the orange seeds of the pandanus. **1885** G. S. FORBES *Wild Life Canara* 216 Jackals and hyaenas occasionally lurked among the pandanus thickets on the shore. **1908** E. J. BANFIELD *Confessions of Beachcomber* I. i. 15 Groups of pandanus palms bearing massive orange-coloured fruits. **1915** *Chambers's Jrnl.* Nov. 698/1 A net..is woven from a strong fibre found in a species of pandanus-tree. **1936** I. L. IDRIESS *Cattle King* xxxvi. 314 Plenty of water there, rock-bound rivers, pandanus-palm creeks, grass, trees, lily-covered lagoons. **1946** —— *In Crocodile Land* i. 5 They chopped pandanus nuts for breakfast. **1964** R. PERRY *World of Tiger* xv. 231 The palms and pandanus wilderness in southern parts of the Island [*sc.* Java]. **1971** *World Archaeol.* III. 140 Unworked river pebbles, used for such purposes as breaking bones and crushing pigments or pandanus nuts. **1977** *Bulletin* (Sydney) 22 Jan. 65/1 The spindly eucalypts and pandanus palms in the Alligator River district were filled with the rasping shriek of millions of cicadas and crickets.
2. The fibre produced from pandanus leaves or the material woven from it. Also *attrib.*
1894 *Outing* (U.S.) XXIV. 354/2 On the pandanus-leaf mats. **1930** M. MEAD *Growing up in New Guinea* ix. 156 A pandanus rain mat is a clumsy thing to carry about. **1963** *House & Garden* Feb. 61/2 Storage unit..teak, with pandanus grasscloth doors. **1971** *Daily Tel.* 23 Dec. 3/7 The children [of Pitcairn Island] will have found their presents in pandanus-leaf baskets suspended by the front porch or above their beds. **1972** M. SHEPPARD *Taman Indera* 141 The floor is hard and smooth and there is usually a low platform at one end on which spectators can sit, cross-legged, on pandanus mats. **1974** *Nat. Geographic* Dec. 778/1 The scene was one from yesterday—the pandanus-thatched houses under the palms, the circle of grinning, tattooed men.

pandar, etc.: see PANDER, etc.

‖**pandaram** (pənˈdɑːrəm). *E. Ind.* [Tamil *paṇḍāram.*] A low-caste Hindu ascetic mendicant; also applied to the low-caste Hindu priests of S. India and Ceylon.

1711 in J. T. Wheeler *Madras* (1861) II. 163 The destruction of 50 or 60,000 pagodas worth of grain..and killing the Pandarrum. **1814** W. Brown *Hist. Propag. Chr.* (1823) I. 184 With the view of becoming a distinguished Pandaram, he placed himself under the tuition of one of the most celebrated priests. **1859** Tennent *Ceylon* I. iii. vii. 373 A little temple..in which consecrated serpents were tenderly reared by the Pandarams.

pandaric (pæn'dærɪk), *a. rare.* [f. *Pandar-us* (see pander *sb.*) + -ic.] Of, or similar to that of, Pandarus; of or pertaining to a pander.

1885 *Nation* (N.Y.) 26 Mar. 257/1 One might..infer..that..the servants and hangers-on of kings and princes are no longer capable, in modern days, of discharging pandaric offices for their masters.

pandation (pæn'deɪʃən). *Arch. rare.* [ad. L. *pandātiōn-em* (Vitruv.), n. of action from *pandāre* to bend, bow.] A bending, bowing, or warping.

1860 Weale *Dict. Terms, Pandation*, in architecture, a yielding or bending in the middle.

pandean, -dæan (pæn'diːən), *a.* and *sb.* [irreg. f. Pan *sb.*[2], on some mistaken analogy.]

A. *adj.* Of or pertaining to Pan. ***pandean pipe*** = pan-pipe. ***pandean harmonica***, a mouth-organ resembling the Pan's pipe.

1807 (*title*) The Complete Preceptor for Davies's new invented Syrrynx or patent Pandean Harmonica. **1820** W. Irving *Sketch Bk.* II. 106 Wandering musicians with pandean pipes and tambourine. **1834** Hood *Tylney Hall* (1840) 249 A pandean band in those days as fashionable..as Weipparts' or Colinet's at the present time. **1864** Pinkerton in *N. & Q.* 3rd Ser. VI. 430 Their band, represented by one man with pandean pipe and drum.

B. *sb.* A member of a pandean band.

a **1845** Hood *To Mrs. Fry* xiii, I like to hear your sweet Pandeans play. **1880** in Grove *Dict. Mus.* II. 644/1 At the commencement of the present century..itinerant parties of musicians, terming themselves Pandeans, went about the country, and gave performances.

pandect ('pændɛkt). [a. F. *pandecte*, ad. L. *pandecta* or *-tēs*, a. Gr. πανδέκτης an all-receiver; esp. in pl. L. *pandectæ*, Gr. πανδέκται, in sense 1.]

1. a. *pl.* (rarely *sing.*) A compendium in fifty books of Roman civil law made by order of the Emperor Justinian in the sixth century, systematizing opinions of eminent jurists, to which the Emperor gave the force of law.

1531 Elyot *Gov.* i. xiv, Called the Pandectes or Digestes. **1614** Selden *Titles Hon.* Pref. d iv, When Lothar took Amalfi, he there found an old Copie of the Pandects or Digests. **1758** Blackstone *Comm.* Introd. i. 17 A copy of Justinian's pandects being newly discovered at Amalfi, soon brought the civil law into vogue all over the west of Europe. **1765** *Ibid.* iii. 81 The present body of civil law..consists of, 1. The institutes... 2. The digests, or pandects, containing the opinions and writings of eminent lawyers, digested in a systematical method. **1878** Smith *Dict. Antiq.* 860/2 These two works, the Pandect and the Code.

b. *transf.* and *fig.* (Also *sing.*) A complete body of the laws of any country or of any system of law.

1553 Paynel (*title*) The Pandectes of the Evangylicall Lawe, comprisyng the Whole Historye of Christes Gospell. **1611** Bible *Transl. Pref.* 3 The Scripture is..a Pandect of profitable lawes, against rebellious spirits. **1692** Bentley *Boyle Lect.* ix. 316 The Code and Pandect of the Law of Nature. **1731** *Hist. Litteraria* II. 303 Proposals for printing by Subscription, a new Pandect of Roman Civil Law, as..now receiv'd and practis'd in most European Nations. **1900** *Expositor* Oct. 264 Some of the Moslem codes are called 'Pandects' i.e. 'all containing'.

2. (*sing.*) **a.** A treatise covering the whole of a subject; a complete treatise or digest.

1591 Sylvester *Du Bartas* i. i. 209 Therefore by Faith's pure rayes illumined, These sacred Pandects I desire to read. **1611** Donne *On Coryat's Crudities* 50 Thus thou, by means which th' Ancients never took, A Pandect mak'st and universal book. **1701** Swift *Contests Nobles & Comm.* Wks. 1755 II. i. 46 That..the commons would please to form a pandect of their own power and privileges. **1813** Mar. Edgeworth *Patron.* (1833) II. xxi. 26 On these points it is requisite to reform the pandects of criticism.

b. A manuscript volume containing all the books of the bible.

1887 F. J. A. Hort in *Academy* 26 Feb. 148/2 There cannot now be a shadow of doubt that the Codex Amiatinus is the 'Pandect' which Ceolfrid sent as a present to Gregory II. **1893** E. G. Browne *Lessons Early Eng. Church Hist.* 68 A pandect means a copy of the whole Bible. **1912** D. S. Boutflower *Life of Ceolfrid* 69 He [*sc.* Ceolfrid] caused three Pandects to be transcribed. **1969** *Jrnl. Brit. Archaeol. Assoc.* XXXII. 1 One of the three pandects, as they were then called (complete bibles in one volume) has survived miraculously intact. This is the Codex Amiatinus.

¶ Catachr. for pundit *sb.*

[Similarly in Fr.: cf. quot. 1791 in Yule s.v. *Pundit.*]

1794 J. Williams *Parental Didactics* in *Cabinet* etc. 18 Pandects and Bramins, Molhas and Cantabs.

Hence **pan'dectist**, one skilled in the Pandects.

1901 F. W. Maitland *Rede Lect.* 26 Georg Beyer, a pandectist at Wittenberg, set a precedent for lectures on German law in a German university.

Pandee, variant of Pandy *sb.*[2]

‖**pandemia** (pæn'diːmɪə). Also anglicized 'pandemy. [mod.L., f. Gr. πανδημία the whole people, πανδήμιος of or belonging to the whole people, public, general.] = pandemic *sb.*

1853 Dunglison *Med. Lex., Pandemy*, pandemic. **1857** Mayne *Expos. Lex., Pandemia*, pandemy. **1900** Gould *Dict. Med. Biol.* etc., *Pandemia*, an epidemic that attacks all persons. [Also] *Pandemy.*

pandemian (pæn'diːmɪən), *a.* [f. Gr. πανδήμι-ος of or pertaining to all the people + -an.] Vulgar, popular, human; = pandemic 2.

1818 T. L. Peacock *Rhododaphne* Wks. 1875 III. 158 Uranian Love..is the deity or genius of pure mental passion for the good and the beautiful; and Pandemian Love, of ordinary sexual attachment. *a* **1822** Shelley *Pr. Wks.* (1888) II. 64 Of necessity must there also be two Loves, the Uranian and Pandemian companions of these two goddesses.

pandemic (pæn'dɛmɪk), *a.* and *sb.* [f. Gr. πάνδημ-ος of or pertaining to all the people, public, vulgar, f. παν- all + δῆμος people, populace: in sense 2 repr. Gr. πάνδημος ἔρως common, vulgar, or sensual love, as opposed to οὐράνιος the heavenly or spiritual; so πάνδημος Ἀφροδίτη the earthly or human Venus, etc. Cf. Plato *Symp.* 180 E.]

A. *adj.* **1.** General, universal. *esp.* Of a disease: Prevalent over the whole of a country or continent, or over the whole world. Distinguished from *epidemic*, which may connote limitation to a smaller area.

1666 Harvey *Morb. Angl.* i. 2 Some [diseases] do more generally haunt a Country..whence such diseases are termed Endemick or Pandemick. **1799** Hooper *Med. Dict., Pandemic*, a synonim of Epidemic. **1873** Mrs. Whitney *Other Girls* xxviii, It is absolutely exceptional; it will never be pandemic. **1892** *Times* 2 Sept. 9/1 We are face to face with a pandemic outbreak of cholera similar to those which fell upon Europe in 1830, 1847, 1853, and 1866.

2. Of or pertaining to vulgar or sensual love.

a **1822** Shelley *Pr. Wks.* (1888) II. 67 That Pandemic lover who loves rather the body than the soul is worthless. **1883** *Pall Mall G.* 8 Sept. 5/1 It is the Pandemic not the Heavenly goddess whose praises he chants.

B. *sb.* A pandemic disease: see A. 1.

1853 Dunglison *Med. Lex., Pandemic*,..an epidemic which attacks the whole population. **1876** tr. *Wagner's Gen. Pathol.* (ed. 6) 141 An epidemic exists in one community only,..but in its greater extension, over a whole land, it is called a pandemic. **1899** *Allbutt's Syst. Med.* VI. 192 Nearly all of our knowledge of thrombosis in influenza dates from the pandemic of 1889–90.

pandemoniac (pændiː'məʊnɪæk), *a.* [f. as pandemoni-um, after *demoniac.*] **a.** Of all divinities. **b.** Of or pertaining to Pandemonium; infernal. **c.** as *sb.* A pandemoniac person; a denizen of Pandemonium. *rare.*

a. 1848 W. R. Williams *Lord's Prayer* (1854) 217 He..in whose Pandemoniac alembic all religions and all existences are found to coagulate into one Being.

b. 1849 E. E. Napier *Excurs. S. Africa* II. 239 To move with the restlessness of condemned spirits at some pandemoniac feast. **1890** Talmage *Fr. Manger to Throne* 45 That awful struggle against pandemoniac cohorts which rode up to trouble, baffle and destroy..the Son of God.

c. 1923 Galsworthy *Captures* 81 Success, power, wealth—those aims of profiteers and premiers, pedagogues and pandemoniacs.

pandemoniacal (ˌpændiːməʊ'naɪəkəl), *a.* [f. as prec. after *demoniacal.*] Characteristic of, or like that of, Pandemonium: esp. of din or noise.

1862 *Temple Bar Mag.* IV. 502 A more fearful and pandemoniacal din arises. **1875** Ruskin *Fors Clav.* lvii. 251 The Pandemoniacal voice of the Archangel-trumpet thus arouses men out of their sleep.

pandemonian (pændiː'məʊnɪən), *a.* and *sb.* [f. pandemoni-um + -an.] **a.** *adj.* = prec. **b.** *sb.* An inhabitant of Pandemonium.

1795 Bentham *Mem. & Corr.* Wks. 1843 X. 313 He is preparing some dishes for the entertainment of your countrymen, and my fellow-citizens, the Pandemonians. **1889** C. C. R. *Up for Season* 159 Shrieks and pandemonian revels, Hell let loose.

pandemonic (ˌpændiː'mɒnɪk), *a.* [f. as prec. + -ic, after *demonic.*] Of or pertaining to Pandemonium, or to all the demons.

1879 M. D. Conway *Demonol.* I. iii. viii, Every constituent feature..rolled together in one pandemonic expression.

pandemonium (ˌpændiː'məʊnɪəm). Also -dæmon-. [In form, mod.L. f. Gr. παν- all + δαίμων divinity, demon[1].]

1. (With capital initial.) The abode of all the demons; a place represented by Milton as the capital of Hell, containing the council-chamber of the Evil Spirits; in common use, = hell or the infernal regions.

1667 Milton *P.L.* i. 756 A solemn Councel forthwith to be held At Pandæmonium, the high Capital Of Satan and his Peers. *Ibid.* x. 424 About the walls Of Pandæmonium, Citie and proud seate Of Lucifer. **1713** Addison *Guardian* No. 103 ⁋4 He would have a large piece of machinery represent the Pan-dæmonium [of Milton]. **1743** Chesterf. in *Old England* No. 3 Misc. Wks. 1777 I. 116 'This..is certainly levelled at us', says a conscious sullen apostate patriot to his fallen brethren in the Pandæmonium. **1831** Carlyle *Sart. Res.* ii. iii, And, in this hag-ridden dream, mistake God's fair living world for a pallid, vacant Hades and extinct Pandemonium.

2. *transf.* A place regarded as resembling Pandemonium: **a.** A centre or head-quarters of vice or wickedness, a haunt of wickedness. **b.** A place or gathering of wild lawless violence, confusion, and uproar.

1779 Swinburne *Trav. Spain* xlii. 367 Every province..would in turn appear a Paradise, and a Pandaemonium. **1800** Colquhoun *Comm. Thames* iv. 190 The various ramifications of this Pandæmonium of Iniquity. **1813** *Examiner* 17 May 317/2 The Emperor Tiberius..wrote to the Senate from his pandæmonium at Capreæ. **1816** Byron *Dom. Pieces* ii. ii, To make a Pandemonium where she dwells, And reign the Hecate of domestic hells. **1827** Lytton *Pelham* xlix, We found ourselves in that dreary pandaemonium,..a Gin-shop. **1876** Black *Madcap V.* vi. 47 She would turn the place into a pandemonium in a week. **1897** F. T. Bullen *Cruise Cachalot* 155 Ribald songs, quarrelling, and blasphemy made a veritable pandemonium of the place.

c. Wild lawless confusion or uproar, a distracting fiendish 'row'.

1865 Parkman *Pioneers Fr.* i. iv. (1885) 55 When night came, it brought with it a pandemonium of dancing and whooping, drumming and feasting. **1897** *Daily News* 29 Nov. 4/5 On Saturday pandemonium again reigned in the Reichsrath.

3. = hell *sb.* 7.

1807–8 W. Irving *Salmag.* (1824) 386 Which like a tailor's Pandemonium, or a giblet pie, are receptacles for scientific fragments of all sorts and sizes.

pandemy: see pandemia.

pan-denominational, etc.: see pan- 1.

pander ('pændə(r)), *sb.* Also 6- pandar, 6–7 pandare, pandor. [Properly *pandar*, orig. *Pandare*, Eng. of AFr. form of L. *Pandarus*, Gr. Πάνδαρος, a proper name used by Boccaccio (in form *Pandaro*), and after him by Chaucer in *Troilus and Criseyde*, as that of the man fabled to have procured for Troilus the love and good graces of Chryseis, name and character being alike of mediæval invention: see Skeat *Chaucer* II. Introd. lxiii–iv. The later spelling *pander* is due, no doubt, to association with agent-sbs. and freq. vbs. in -er.]

1. (With capital initial.) As proper name.

c **1374** Chaucer *Troylus* i. 548 A frend of his þat called was Pandare [*rimes* care, fare]. *Ibid.* 582 This Pandare, þat neigh malt for sorwe and routhe. *Ibid.* 822 And how þat hym soth seyde Pandarus. **1606** Shaks. *Tr. & Cr.* iii. ii. 210 *Pandarus.* If euer you proue false one to another, since I haue taken such paines to bring you together, let all pittifull goers betweene be cal'd to the worlds end after my name: call them all Panders.

2. A go-between in clandestine amours; one who supplies another with the means of gratifying lust; a male bawd, pimp, or procurer.

1530 Lyndesay *Test. Papyngo* 390 Pandaris, pykthankis, custronis, and clatteraris. **1579–80** North *Plutarch* (1612) 93 He that was the Pandor to procure her. **1591** Spenser *M. Hubberd* 808 Ne, them to pleasure, would he sometimes scorne A pandares coate (so basely was he borne). **1598** Shaks. *Merry W.* v. v. 176 One Mr Broome,..to whom you should haue bin a Pander. **1632** Lithgow *Trav.* i. 2 Ruffian Pandors..are now clothed..and richly rewarded. **1791** Mrs. Radcliffe *Rom. Forest* xiv, He now saw himself the pander of a villain. **1840** Macaulay *Ess., Clive* (1851) II. 534 Squandering his wealth on pandars and flatterers. **1869** Lecky *Europ. Mor.* I. xi. 293 The Pander and the Courtesan are the leading characters of Plautus.

b. Less usually said of a woman: a panderess.

1585 Greene *Planetomachia* Wks. (Grosart) V. 77 Pasylla smiling at the diligent hast of the old Pandar [Clarista], commaunded she should be brought in. **1766** Fordyce *Serm. Yng. Wom.* (1767) I. vii. 304 Employed as a handmaid ..if not as a pandar. **1853** Kingsley *Hypatia* xix. 223 Sorceress she was, pander and slave-dealer.

c. *transf.* and *fig.* Said of a thing.

1582 Stanyhurst *Æneis*, etc. (Arb.) 139 Forgerye thee pandar; thee messadge mockrye. **1622** Hakewill *David's Vow* iii. 113 The Eye beeing as it were the Pandar or Broker. *a* **1704** T. Brown *Sat. on Quack* Wks. 1730 I. 63 Thou church yard pimp, and pander to the grave. **1791** Burke *App. Whigs* Wks. VI. 40 Make virtue a pander to vice.

3. One who ministers to the baser passions or evil designs of others.

1603 Knolles *Hist. Turks* (1621) 7 One of her Eunuches, whom she purposed to use as her pander for the circumventing of the Patriarch. **1682** Dryden *Medal* 256 The Pander of the People's Hearts. **1752** Johnson *Rambler* No. 195 ⁋12 In a place where there are no pandars to folly and extravagance. **1874** L. Stephen *Hours in Library* (1892) II. iii. 92 He crowns a torrent of abuse by declaring that Scott has encouraged the lowest panders of a venal press.

†**4.** ? = bully 3, 4. *Obs.*

1592 G. Harvey *Pierce's Super.* Wks. (Grosart) II. 111 He would neuer dare me, like a bold Pandare, with such stout challenges.

pander ('pændə(r)), *v.* Also -ar. [f. pander *sb.*]

1. *trans.* To act as a pander to; to minister to the gratification of (another's lust). Also *fig.*

1602 Shaks. *Ham.* iii. iv. 88 Since Frost it selfe, as actiuely doth burne, As Reason panders Will. **1666** E. M. *Converted Twins* ii. iii, Ah! that a Lady's love should be Thus pandar'd by a Gypsie. **1827** R. H. Dana *Buccaneer* xlii, Lust panders murder—murder panders lust!

2. *intr.* To play the pander; to subserve or minister to base passions, tendencies, or designs. Const. *to.*

1603 [see PANDERING]. **1641** MILTON *Ch. Govt.* II. (1851) 64 Excommunication servs for nothing with them, but to prog, and pandar for fees. **1812** SOUTHEY *Omniana* II. 23 These traitors..who lampooned the noblest passions of humanity in order to pandar for its lowest appetites. **1868** J. H. BLUNT *Ref. Ch. Eng.* I. 359 He pandered to the king's gross immoralities. **1879** BLACK *Macleod of D.* xvi, Pandering to the public taste for pretty things.

Hence **ˈpandering** *vbl. sb.* and *ppl. a.*; **ˈpanderer**, one who panders; = PANDER *sb.* 2.

1603 DEKKER *Wonderfull Yeare* Wks. (Grosart) I. 90 To be plaid heere By English-men, ruffians, and pandering slaues. **1839** *John Bull* 29 Apr., Pretenders, panderers, parasites, hypocrites. **1875** JOWETT *Plato* (ed. 2) V. 41 He should be the enemy of all pandering to the popular taste. **1884** RITA *Vivienne* IV. iv, Panderers to popular taste and popular error.

†**ˈpanderage.** *Obs. nonce-wd.* [f. PANDER *v.* + -AGE.] The practice or trade of pandering.

1612 CHAPMAN *Widowes T.* Plays 1873 III. 21 Thou shalt hold thy Tenement to thee and thine eares for euer, in free smockage, as of the manner of Panderage. **1675** J. SMITH *Chr. Relig. App.* (Webster 1828).

panderess (ˈpændərɪs). Now *rare.* Also 7- pandar-, 7 pandresse, 8 pandress, -ass. [f. PANDER *sb.* + -ESS.] A female pander, a bawd.

1606 WARNER *Alb. Eng.* XIV. lxxxix. 362 But all in vaine, so opposite to Loue did she perseuer, As that vnto his Pandresse Arte he was enforc't to leaue her. *a* **1652** BROME *Mad Couple* II. i, I have ingag'd my selfe for her to be your Pandaresse. **1721** D'URFEY *Operas*, etc. 274 This Pandrass, ..he charges to Timandra's Hand To give the Scroll. **1859** TRENCH *Sel. Gloss.* 20 *Bawd* once could have been applied to pandar and pandaress alike.

panderism (ˈpændərɪz(ə)m). Also pandar-. [f. PANDER *sb.* + -ISM.] The practice or trade of a pander; systematic pandering.

1601 *Downfall Earl Huntington* II. ii. in Hazl. *Dodsley* VIII. 136 Suffering their lines To flatter these times With pandarism base. **1604** T. M. *Black Bk.* in *Middleton's Wks.* (Bullen) VIII. 24 He should excel even Pandarus himself, and go nine mile beyond him in pandarism. **1726** SWIFT *Gulliver* III. viii, Perjury, oppression, subornation, fraud, pandarism. **1809** MALKIN *Gil Blas* IX. vii. (Rtldg.) ¶4 Lemos managed that intrigue by the panderism of Signor de Santillane. **1818** *Blackw. Mag.* III. 453 His paid panderism to the vilest passions of that mob.

†**ˈpanderize**, *v. Obs.* Also pandar-. [f. as prec. + -IZE.] *intr.* To act the pander. Hence †**ˈpanderizing** *vbl. sb.* and *ppl. a.*

1603 FLORIO *Montaigne* (1634) 489 Venus..who so cunningly enhanced the market of her ware, by the brokage or panderizing of the lawes. **1606** MARSTON *Fawne* III, Your father shall not say I pandarizde. **1616** R. C. *Times' Whistle* vi. 2890 Incarnate devill! pandarizing page!

ˈpanderly, *a. Obs.* or *arch.* [f. as prec. + -LY¹.] Of the nature of or befitting a pander.

1581 B. RICH *Farewell* Tivb, She would make her vnderstande..how ill she could awaie with suche pandarly practises. **1601** SHAKS. *Merry W.* IV. ii. 119 Oh you Panderly Rascals, there's a knot: a gin, a packe, a conspiracie against me. **1640** GENT *Knave in Gr.* To Rdr., Some [are] pimping, some panderly knaves. **1823** SCOTT *Quentin D.* xxvii, A panderly barber.

pandermite (pænˈdɜːmaɪt). *Min.* [Named 1877, from Panderma in Asia Minor: see -ITE¹.] A variety of Priceite.

1886 in *Cassell's Encycl. Dict.* **1896** in CHESTER *Dict. Names Min.*

†**ˈpanderous**, *a. Obs.* Also 6 -drous, 7 -darous. [f. PANDER *sb.* + -OUS.] Of the nature of or characterizing a pander. In quot. *c* 1575 as *sb.*

c **1575** *Balfour's Practicks* (1754) 378 He may be repellit fra passing upone ane assise, or being witness..that is ane pandrous (i.e. *leno*), or juglar (i.e. *joculator*). **1611** *2nd Maiden's Trag.* III. i. in Hazl. *Dodsley* X. 427, I set before thee, panderous lord, this steel. *a* **1627** MIDDLETON *Witch* III. ii, The same wary pandarous diligence Was then bestow'd on her. **1633** *Costlie Whore* IV. ii. in Bullen *O. Pl.* IV, I dare in single combat any knight, Any adventurer, any pandorus hinde.

ˈpandership. *rare.* [f. as prec. + -SHIP.] The function or trade of a pander.

1656 J. BENTHAM *Two Treat.* (1657) 51 Calvin..saith, That mixt dancing of men and women together, are nothing else then panderships and provocations to whoredome.

pan-destruction, -diabolism: see PAN- 2.

pandiagonal (ˌpændaɪˈægənəl), *a. Math.* [f. PAN- + DIAGONAL *a.*] Used to describe a magic square with the property that, if any number of columns be removed from one side of the diagram and added *en bloc* to the other, another magic square results.

1897 *Amer. Jrnl. Math.* XIX. 99 The square A is magic because each row, column, and diagonal has the same sum, 175; it is pandiagonal because not only the two main diagonals, but also the twelve broken diagonals..have each the same sum. **1919** *Monist* XXIX. 308 Magic squares of order ≡ 2 (mod. 4) made with consecutive numbers cannot be pandiagonal. **1939** H. S. M. COXETER *Ball's Math. Recreations & Ess.* (ed. 11) vii. 203 A magic pandiagonal square of the fourth order..was inscribed at Khojuraho, India, as long ago as the eleventh or twelfth century. **1976** *Sci. Amer.* Jan. 120/1 And it is pandiagonal (sometimes called Nasik or diabolic), which means that its broken diagonals add up to 65, the constant.

Hence **ˌpandiˈagonally** *adv.*

1911 W. W. R. BALL *Math. Recreations & Ess.* (ed. 5) vii. 157 If a pandiagonal square be cut into two pieces along a line between any two rows or any two columns, and the two pieces be interchanged, the new square so formed will be also pandiagonally magic.

panˈdiculated, *a. rare.* [f. L. *pandiculāt-us*, pa. pple. of *pandiculārī* to stretch oneself, f. *pandĕre* to stretch + dim. element.] 'Stretched out, opened, extended' (Ash, 1775).

pandiculation (pændɪkjuːˈleɪʃən). [n. of action from L. *pandiculārī*: see prec.] An instinctive movement, consisting in the extension of the legs, the raising and stretching of the arms, and the throwing back of the head and trunk, accompanied by yawning; it occurs before and after sleeping, also in certain nervous affections, as hysteria, and at the accession of a fit of ague. Sometimes loosely used for 'yawning'.

1611 COTGR., *Pendiculation*, a pendiculation; or, a stretching in th' approach of an Ague. **1649** BULWER *Pathomyot.* II. ix. 225 Pandiculation is a Deliberate Action of the other Muscles of the Body. **1668** *Phil. Trans.* III. 812 About Sneezing, the Hickocke, Yawning, Pandiculation, and their Causes. **1822–34** *Good's Study Med.* (ed. 4) III. 333 Pandiculation..is an instinctive exertion to recover a balance of power between the extensor and flexor muscles. **1822–56** DE QUINCEY *Confess.* (1862) 217 By mere dint of pandiculation, vulgarly called yawning.

pandionine (pænˈdaɪəʊnaɪn). *Ornith.* [f. Zool. L. *Pandion*, generic name of the OSPREY, L. *Pandīon*, Gr. *Πανδίων*, in Mythology the father of Procne and Philomela.] Of or belonging to the genus *Pandion* or osprey.

In recent Dicts.

pandit, variant of PUNDIT *sb.*

pandle (ˈpænd(ə)l). Also 8 pandell. [Origin unascertained; app. the source of Leach's generic name *Pandalus.*] A local name of the shrimp; applied by some writers to an allied crustacean, perhaps *Pandalus annulicornis*, Leach.

1786 *Gentl. Mag.* II. 853 A small fish is caught on the sands [at Hastings] which they call pandells; they are bigger than shrimps, smaller than prawns... Their claws are not like those of a lobster, but shut up like a knife with a short blade. **1835** KIRBY *Hab & Inst. Anim.* II. xv. 38 The smaller Crustaceans, as the shrimp, prawn, pandle. **1875** *Sussex Gloss.*, *Pandle*, a shrimp. Also used in Kent.

b. *Comb.*, as **pandle-whew**, a local name of the wigeon (Norfolk).

1885 SWAINSON *Prov. Names Brit. Birds* 154.

ˈpandoor, -dore. *Sc. dial.* [See quot. 1796; but proof of the alleged derivation is wanting.] A kind of large oyster, found near Prestonpans.

1796 *Statist. Acc. Scot.* XVII. 70 Oysters caught nearest to the town [Prestonpans] are the largest and fattest: hence the largest obtained the name of Pandoors, i.e. oysters caught at the doors of the pans. **1805** FORSYTH *Beauties Scotl.* I. 458. **1894** HALIBURTON *Furth in Field* 58 (E.D.D.) With a dish o' mussel-brose at Newhaven, or with a prievin' o' fat pandores a little further east the coast.

pandoor, pandor: see PANDOUR, PANDER.

Pandora¹ (pænˈdɔərə). Also 7 Pandore. [a. Gr. *Πανδώρα* lit. 'all-gifted', f. *παν-* all + *δῶρον* gift.] In Greek mythology, the name of the first mortal woman, on whom, when made by Vulcan and brought to Epimetheus, all the gods and goddesses bestowed gifts.

1633 J. FISHER *Fuimus Troes* I. iv. in Hazl. *Dodsley* XII. 461 To frame the like Pandore, The gods repine, and nature would grow poor. **1643** MILTON *Divorce* II. iii, The Academics and Stoics, who knew not what a consummat and most adorned Pandora was bestow'd upon Adam.

Hence **Pandora's box**: the gift of Jupiter to Pandora, a box enclosing the whole multitude of human ills, which flew forth when the box was foolishly opened by Epimetheus; according to a later version, the box contained all the blessings of the gods, which, on its opening, escaped and were lost, with the exception of hope, which was at the bottom of the box. Hence in fig. and allusive uses.

1579 GOSSON *Sch. Abuse* (Arb.) 44, I cannot lyken our affecton better than..to Pandoraes boxe, lift vppe the lidde, out flyes the Deuill; shut it vp fast, it cannot hurt vs. **1610** B. JONSON *Alch.* II. i. 92 Such was..Pandora's tub. **1672** SIR T. BROWNE *Lett. Friend* §14 And if Asia, Africa, and America should bring in their List [of diseases]. Pandoras Box would swell, and there must be a strange Pathology. **1679** J. GOODMAN *Penit. Pardoned* II. i. (1713) 264 There may be some hope left in the bottom of this Pandora's box of calamities. **1840** CARLYLE *Heroes* v. 268 The Eighteenth was a Sceptical Century; in which little word there is a whole Pandora's Box of miseries. **1886** MRS LYNN LINTON *Paston Carew* xlii, Pandora's box was opened for him, and all the pains and griefs his imagination had ever figured were abroad.

pandora² (pænˈdɔərə), **pandore** (pænˈdɔə(r)). Also 7–8 pandure, (8 pandola), 9 pandura, pandur. [a. It. *pandora* (also *pandura*), F. *pandore*, ad. L. *pandūra*, a. Gr. *πανδοῦρα*, a musical instrument the invention of which was attributed to Pan. (But the word was prob. of foreign origin.)]

A stringed musical instrument of the cither type, the same as the BANDORE.

The original Greek and Roman *pandura* is described as a kind of lute with three strings; such an instrument is still used in some eastern lands under the name *pandur*. But the original type has, at different times, and in different countries, undergone many changes in form, in the number and material of the strings, the use or non-use of a plectrum, etc. Equally numerous are the modifications of the name: cf. BANDORE, BANJO, MANDOLINE. The changes of thing and name have not always gone together: the Neapolitan *pandura*, for instance, retaining the ancient name, is 'a musical instrument larger than the mandoline, strung with eight metal wires, and played with a quill'.

α. **1597** MORLEY *Introd. Mus.* 166 Take an instrument, as a Lute, Orpharion, Pandora, or such like. **1762** SMOLLETT *L. Greaves* iii. (1793) I. 51 Their raw red fingers..being adorned with diamonds, were taught to thrum the pandola, and even to touch the keys of the harpsichord. **1825** FOSBROOKE *Encycl. Antiq.* I. 628 The Orpharion was like a guitar, but..was strung with wire... The Bandore, nearly similar, had a straight bridge; the Orpharion slanting. The Pandura was of the lute kind, the Mandura a lesser lute. **1838** *Encycl. Brit.* (ed. 7) XVI. 788/2 *Pandora*, a small kind of lute, with fewer strings than the ordinary lute,..believed to have originated in the Ukraine. **1880** A. J. HIPKINS in Grove *Dict. Mus.* II. 644 *Pandora* or *Pandore*. A Cither of larger dimensions than the Orpharion.

β. **1612** DRAYTON *Poly-olb.* iv. 63 Some that delight to touch the sterner wyerie chord, The cythron, the pandore, and the theorbo strike. **1706** PHILLIPS, *Pandore* or *Pandure*, a kind of Musical Instrument. **1880** *Grove's Dict. Mus.* II. 612 A larger orpharion was called Penorcon, and a still larger one Pandore. **1889** ABERCROMBIE *East. Caucasus* 171 Akim's eyes at once fell upon a pandur, or three-stringed lute.

pandour, pandoor (ˈpænduə(r)). Also pandur. [= F. *pandour*, Ger. *pandur*; all a. Serbo-croatian *pàndūr*, 'a constable, bailiff, beadle, summoner, or catchpole; a mounted policeman or guardian of the public peace; a watcher of fields and vineyards', having also in earlier times the duty of guarding the frontier districts from the inroads of the Turks. For ulterior etymology see Note below. The sense in which the word became known in Western Europe is involved in the history of Trenck's body of pandours.]

1. In *pl.* The name borne by a local force organized in 1741 by Baron Trenck on his own estates in Croatia to clear the country near the Turkish frontier of bands of robbers; subsequently enrolled as a regiment in the Austrian Army, where, under Trenck, their rapacity and brutality caused them to be dreaded over Germany, and made *Pandour* synonymous in Western Europe with 'brutal Croatian soldier'.

1747 (*title*) Memoirs of the Life of Francis Baron Trenck ..Colonel of a body of Pandours and Sclavonian Hussars. *Ibid.* 15, I set out with a retinue of twenty pandour-tenants of mine. *Ibid.* 16 My haram-bascha or captain of pandours. **1754** RICHARDSON *Grandison* (1781) II. iv. 51, I beheld six Pandours issue from that inner part of the wood. **1791** HAMPSON *Mem. J. Wesley* III. 124 His style might have better suited a colonel of pandours than a christian bishop. **1799** CAMPBELL *Pleas. Hope* I. 352 When leagued Oppression pour'd to Northern wars Her whisker'd pandoors and her fierce hussars. **1843** *Penny Cycl.* XXV. 185/2 On Maria Theresa's succession to the throne, Trenck offered his own and the services of his men, his regiment of Pandours, as he called them, to the young empress.

fig. **1768** FOOTE *Devil on 2 Sticks* II, The hussars and pandours of physic..rarely attack a patient together.

‖**2.** In local use, in Croatia, Servia, Hungary, etc.: A guard; an armed servant or retainer; a member of the local mounted constabulary.

1880 *Sat. Rev.* 7 Feb. 178/2 A small body of guards, called pandours, is, by immemorial usage, attached to the establishment [the monastery of St. John of Rylo]. **1886** W. J. TUCKER *E. Europe* 155 The 'pandurs' came to fetch him, and..dragged him before the commission. *Ibid.* 169 These Pandurs, your police, your mounted constabulary, or whatever you call them, are they of no use?

[*Note.* The word *'pandūr*, with all or some of the senses mentioned above, is found in nearly all the South-Slavonic (Servian) dialects, and in Magyar, also as *pan'dur* in Roumanian; it has entered Turkish as *pan'dul*. Earlier forms in Magyar and Serbo-croatian were *bàndūr*, *bàndor*; the former is still used in and near Ragusa. The word is not native either in Magyar or Slavonic, and the question of its origin and course of diffusion in these langs. is involved in considerable obscurity. But Slavonic scholars are now generally agreed in referring it through the earlier *bàndūr*, *bàndor*, to med.L. *banderius*, orig. 'a follower of a standard or banner' (see BANNER), or to some Italian or Venetian word akin to this. Among senses evidenced by Du Cange for *banderius* (and *bannerius*), are those of 'guard of cornfields and vineyards', also 'summoner, apparitor', which are both senses of *pàndūr*; It. *banditore* (Venetian *bandiore*) has also the sense of 'summoner'. The alleged derivation of the word from Pandur or Pandur Puszta, 'a village in Lower Hungary', given in Ersch & Grüber's Cyclopædia, and repeated in many English Dictionaries, is absolutely baseless.]

pandowdy (pæn'daʊdɪ). *U.S.* [Of obscure origin; perh. a compound of PAN *sb.*[1] Halliwell cites from Bp. Kennett's MS. *pandoulde* a custard (Somerset); but this is now unknown in Eng. dialects.] A kind of apple pudding, variously seasoned, but usually with molasses, and baked in a deep dish with or without a crust.

1846 WORCESTER, *Pandowdy*, food made of bread and apples baked together. **1852** HAWTHORNE *Blithedale Rom.* xxiv, Hollingsworth [would] fill my plate from the great dish of pandowdy. **1893** LELAND *Mem.* I. 74 Pan-dowdy—a kind of coarse and broken up apple-pie.

pandrass, -ess, obs. forms of PANDERESS.

pan-drop. *Sc.* [f. PAN *sb.*[1] + DROP *sb.* 10 e.] A hard, peppermint-flavoured sweet, shaped like a flattened sphere.

1877 *Encycl. Brit.* VI. 257/1 A core or centre of some kind is required, and this may consist either of a seed or fruit..; or it may be a small lozenge, as in the case of pan drops. **1904** 'H. FOULIS' *Erchie* v. 29, I thoucht it was pan-drops ye cam' oot for, or conversation-losengers. **1927** *Glasgow Herald* 7 Sept. 12/7 An' there's nae mae tears since ye've got him wi' the poke o' pan-draps in his han'. **1956** C. M. COSTIE *Benjie's Bodle* 106 Wir haean a duff, an' treacle.. an twa pan drops. **1964** *Scotsman* 14 Oct. 5 What was described in court as 'a classical line of traditional Scottish sweet—pan drops'. **1966** W. MERRILEES *Short Arm of Law* 184 These.. were not chocolates at all but hard peppermint sweets.. pan-drops as we called them in Scotland.

pandur, variant spelling of PANDOUR.

pandur, pandura, pandure: see PANDORA[2].

pandurate ('pændjʊərət), *a.* [f. L. *pandūra* PANDORA[2] + -ATE[2].] = next. Also † '**pandurated** *a.*

1775 ASH *Suppl.*, *Pandurated*, having a leaf in the form of the pandore. **1847** WEBSTER, *Pandurate.* **1881** *Gard. Chron.* XVI. 717 The lip is pandurate, undulate, emarginate at the top. **1882** *Garden* 29 July 104/1 The large pandurate labellum is pure white on its upper part.

panduriform (pæn'djʊərɪfɔːm), *a.* [f. L. *pandūra* PANDORA[2] + -FORM.] Fiddle-shaped: chiefly in *Bot.* and *Entom.*

1753 CHAMBERS *Cycl. Supp.* s.v. *Leaf*, *Panduriform Leaf*, one of the shape of a violin:.. larger at both ends than in the middle, where it is deeply cut, in a rounded manner. **1760** J. LEE *Introd. Bot.* III. v. (1765) 178 *Panduræform*, Pandure-shaped. **1826** KIRBY & SP. *Entom.* xxxv. III. 609 In ..*Acheta monstrosa* they [the tegmina] are rather panduriform. **1870** BENTLEY *Man. Bot.* (ed. 2) 155 When a lyrate leaf has but one deep recess on each side, it is termed *panduriform* or fiddle-shaped.

pandurina (ˌpændjuː'riːnə). [It., f. *pandura* (see PANDORA[2], PANDORE) + dim. suffix *-ina*.] A small musical instrument of the mandoline type.

1893 J. S. SHEDLOCK tr. *Riemann's Dict. Mus.* 53/1 *Bandola.* (Span.), Bandolon, Bandora, Bandura, an instrument of the lute family, with a smaller or larger number of steel or catgut strings, which were plucked with the finger like the Pandora, Pandura, Pandurina, [etc.]. **1910** F. W. GALPIN *Old Eng. Instruments of Mus.* iii. 40 At this period [*sc.* the sixteenth century] there was another small instrument called by Prætorius *Mandürichen* or *Pandurina*, which could be conveniently carried under the cloak. **1938** *Oxf. Compan. Mus.* 683/1 *Pandurina*, a very small instrument of the lute type, strung with wire—probably the ancestor of the mandoline. **1954** *Grove's Dict. Mus.* (ed. 5) V. 549/1 The pandurina returned to popularity, particularly about 1760–80, under the name Milanese mandoline. **1976** D. MUNROW *Instruments Middle Ages & Renaissance* 79/3 Praetorius.. also mentions a smaller size [of mandora], the *pandurina*, with four strings tuned to g, d', g', d''.

† **pan'durist.** *Obs. rare.* [f. as PANDURIFORM *a.* + -IST.]

1656 BLOUNT *Glossogr.*, *Pandurist*, he that plays on a musical instrument called a Rebech, or on a Violin.

pandy ('pændɪ), *sb.*[1] Chiefly *Sc.* [Supposed to be L. *pande* 'stretch out!', imper. of *pandĕre* to stretch or spread.] **a.** A stroke upon the extended palm with a leather strap or *tawse*, ferule, or rod, given as a punishment to schoolboys; = PALMY *sb.*

1805 A. SCOTT *Poems* 12 But if for little rompish laits, I hear that thou a pandy gets. **1865** G. MACDONALD *A. Forbes* 30 The punishment was mostly in the form of pandies—blows delivered with varying force, but generally with the full swing of the tag, as it was commonly called. **1876** GRANT *Burgh Sch. Scotl.* I. v. 204 Breaches of order and bad conduct.. at the Elgin academy [are punished] by 'pandies'. **1895** W. HUMPHREY in *Month* Oct. 230 The pandies took their name from *Pande manum*—'Stretch out your open hand'. [The usual Sc. explanation is from *pande palmam*! as the source at once of *pandy* and *palmy*.]

b. *attrib.* and *Comb.*, as *pandybat.*

1916 JOYCE *Portrait of Artist* (1969) i. 49 Fleming held out his hand. The pandybat came down on it with a loud smacking sound. **1922** —— *Ulysses* 547 Twice loudly a pandybat cracks.

Hence '**pandy** *v. trans.*, to strike on the palm of the hand with the tawse or ferule, as a punishment.

1863 KINGSLEY *Water-Bab.* v, And she.. pandied their hands with canes. **1875** A. R. HOPE *My Schoolboy Fr.* 11 When he was going to be pandied.

‖**Pandy** ('pændɪ), *sb.*[2] *E. Ind.* Also -ee. [According to Yule, from the surname *Paṇde*, the title of a *Jōt* or subdivisional branch of the Brahmins of the Upper Province, which was very common among the high-caste sepoys of the Bengal army. One of those bearing the surname was *Mangul Paṇde*, the first man to mutiny in the 34th Regiment.] A colloquial name for a revolted sepoy in the Indian Mutiny of 1857–9.

1857 H. GREATHED *Lett. Siege Delhi* (1858) 99 As long as I feel the entire confidence I do.. I cannot feel gloomy. I leave that feeling to the Pandees. **1864** TREVELYAN *Compet. Wallah* (1866) 247 He was separated from his squadron, and surrounded by a party of desperate Pandies. **1893** FORBES-MITCHELL *Remin. Gt. Mutiny* 164 We captured those guns that the Pandies were carrying off. **1897** LD. ROBERTS *41 Yrs. in India* I. vi. 62

Pandy ('pændɪ), *sb.*[3] *Med.* The name of Kalman *Pandy* (b. 1868), Hungarian neurologist, used *attrib.* or in the possessive to denote a reaction or test he devised for globulins in the spinal fluid, in which a sample is treated with a dilute aqueous solution of phenol.

1916 L. F. BARKER *Monographic Med.* II. 83 Pandy's test has not received the attention it deserves. **1933** W. R. BRAIN *Dis. Nervous Syst.* 113 Pandy's reaction is the most sensitive, and may yield a weakly positive result with normal fluids. **1963** *Lancet* 12 Jan. 108/1 Lumbar puncture on the ninth day of the illness yielded clear fluid..; the Pandy test was negative.

pan-dynamometer, etc.: see PAN- 2.

pane (peɪn), *sb.*[1] Forms: 4–5 **pan**, 6 **paene**, **paan**, **pein**, 6–7 **payn(e**, 6–8 **pain(e**, 4– **pane**. [a. F. *pan* (11th c. in Littré) = Pr. *pan*, Sp. *paño*, Pg. *panno*, It. *panno*:—L. *pannum*, acc. of *pannus* a cloth, a piece of cloth.]

I. A piece of cloth.

† **1. a.** A cloth; a piece of cloth; any distinct portion of a garment, a lap, a skirt. *Obs.*

a **1300** *Cursor M.* 4387 Sco drou his mantel wit þe pan,.. He drou, sco held, þe tassel brak. *c* **1320** *Sir Tristr.* 994 Tristrem gan it wiþ hald As prince proude in pan. **1387–8** T. USK *Test. Love* II. ii. (Skeat) l. 29 Among pannes mouled in a wiche [WHITCH], in presse among clothes laid. *c* **1450** *Merlin* 501 Thei kneled to sir Gawein, and folded the panes of her mantels. *c* **1475** *Rauf Coilȝear* 234 Gif thow dwellis with the Quene, proudest in pane. *c* **1475** *Partenay* 5654 Which so well was Anoynted indede, That no sleue ne pane had he hole of brede. **1573–80** BARET *Alv.* P 57 A Pane of cloth, *panniculus, segmen*, ῥάκιον.

† **b.** = COUNTERPANE[2]. *Obs.*

13.. *Gaw. & Gr. Knt.* 855 Þer beddyng watz noble, Of cortynes of clene sylk, wyth cler golde hemmez, & couertorez ful curious, with comlych panez. **1459** *Invent.* in *Paston Lett.* I. 484 Item, ij blankettys, j payre of schettys. Item, j rede pane furryd withe connyngs. **1495** *Acc. Ld. High Treas. Scot.* I. 226, iij ellis of scarlot to be a pane to the Kingis bed. **1516** *Ibid.* III. 50 For ij elne iij quartaris Inglis scarlet to be ane pane for the Kingis bede in the schip. **1578** *Invent.* in Hunter *Biggar & Ho. Fleming* xxvi, Ane pein of purpour weluot freinzeit wᵗ blak and reid silk.

† **2. a.** A piece, width, or strip of cloth, of which several were joined together side by side, so as to make one cloth, curtain, or garment. *Obs.*

The 'panes' might be narrow pieces or strips of alternate or different colours (e.g. red and blue) or different materials (e.g. velvet and cloth of gold), or pieces of the same colour with lace or other trimming inserted in the seams, or (in later use) strips of the same cloth distinguished by colour or separated by lines of trimming, etc.

1480 *Wardr. Acc. Edw. IV* (1830) 118, iiij costerings of wool paled rede and blue with rooses sonnes and crownes in every pane. **1517** in Kerry *St. Lawr. Reading* (1883) 106 An Awter Cloth of panes of Cloth of gold & velwett imbrowdred wᵗ archangells & floures. *a* **1548** HALL *Chron., Hen. VIII* 207 b, Another chamber was hanged with grene Veluet.. in the middle of euery pane or pece, was a fable of Ouid in Matamorphoseos embraudered. **1592** GREENE *Upst. Courtier* in *Harl. Misc.* (Malh.) II. 219 A very passing costly paire of veluet breeches, whose panes.. was drawne out with the best Spanish satine. **1611** CORYAT *Crudities* 43 The Switzers weare.. doublets and hose of panes, intermingled with red and yellow, and some with blew, trimmed with long puffes of yellow and blewe sarcenet rising up between the panes. **1613** CHAPMAN *Masque* Plays 1873 III. 92 But betwixt every pane of embroidery, went a row of white Estridge feathers. *a* **1639** T. CAREW *Cœl. Brit.* Wks. (1824) 150 The curtain was watchet and a pale yellow in paines. **1686** *Lond. Gaz.* No. 2170/4 One Green Satin Peticoat laced with Gold and Silver Lace, in Panes. **1694** MOTTEUX *Rabelais* IV. lii. (1737) 212 Breeches with Panes like the outside of a Tabor.

† **b.** *pl.* Strips made by cutting or slashing a garment longitudinally for ornamental purposes; e.g. to show the fine stuff with which it was lined, or of which an undergarment was composed. *Obs.*

1613 CHAPMAN *Masque* Plays 1873 III. 94 Wide sleeves cut in panes. *a* **1648** LD. HERBERT *Life* (1886) 166 Her gown was a green Turkey grogram, cut all into panes or slashes, from the shoulder and sleeves unto the foot. **1653** URQUHART *Rabelais* I. viii. (Rtldg.) 36 They [breeches] were, within the panes, puffed out with the lining.

II. A piece, portion, or side of anything.

† **3.** A section or length of a wall or fence. *Obs.*

e.g. the length between two angles, bastions, buttresses, posts, etc.

c **1380** *Sir Ferumb.* 5188 By þat were Sarazyns.. come inward.. At a pan þat was broken. **1489** CAXTON *Faytes of A.* II. xv. 119 Closed rounde about with seuen panes of strong walles. **1524** *Churchw. Acc. St. Giles, Reading* 21 For makyng of v panys of the church pale iiijd. **1525** LD. BERNERS *Froiss.* II. xxii. 53 Than the knyght shewed me a pane of the wall, and said, sir, se you yonder parte of the wall whiche is newer. **1530** PALSGR. 251/2 Pane of a wall, *pan de mur.* **1672** DRYDEN *Assignation* II. ii, There's the wall; behind yond pane of it we'll set up the ladder. [**1795** SOUTHEY *Joan* Notes Wks. 1837 I. 200 (tr. Froissart) The miners.. overthrew a great pane of the wall, which filled the moat where it had fallen.]

4. A side of a quadrangle, cloister, court, or town.

13.. *E.E. Allit. P.* A. 1033 Vch pane of þat place had þre ȝatez. **1447** *Will of Hen. VI* in Carter *King's Coll. Cha.* 13 A cloistre square the est pane conteyning in lengthe clxxv fete, and the west pane as muche. **1481** CAXTON *Godeffroy* clxxix. 264 Thyse thre castellys.. were alle square, the sydes that were toward the toun were double, in suche wyse that one of the panes that was without myght be aualed vpon the walles, and thenne it shold be lyke a brydge. **1560** ROLLAND *Crt. Venus* II. 490 Ane Closter weill ouir fret.. Quhairin was all thir ten Sibillais set In euerilk Pane set ay togidder thre. **1912** T. D. ATKINSON *Eng. & Welsh Cathedrals* 268 The north pane of the cloisters with its sunny aspect.

5. A flat side, face, or surface of any object having several sides: e.g. (*a*) the dressed side of a stone or log; (*b*) one of the divisions or sides of a nut or bolt-head; (*c*) one of the sides of the upper surface or table of a brilliant-cut diamond.

1434 *Indent. Fotheringhey* in Dugdale *Monast.* (1846) VI. 1414/2 [The steeple is to be square in the lower part, and after being carried as high as the body of the church] hit shall be chaungid, and turnyd in viij panes. *c* **1530** in Gutch *Coll. Cur.* II. 305 Oone odar Challes with a patten gilte the foote of vj panes and in oone of theyme a Crucifixe. **1875** LASLETT *Timber* 74 *note*, Pane is the hewn or sawn surface of the log. **1875** KNIGHT *Dict. Mech.* 1601/2 *Pane*.., the divisions or sides of a nut or bolt-head; as, a six-paned nut, *i.e.* a hexagonal nut.

III. A division of a window, and derived uses.

6. a. One of the lights of a mullioned window (*obs.*), or a subdivision of this; now, One of the compartments of a window, etc. consisting of one sheet or square of glass held in place by a frame of lead, wood, etc.; the piece of glass itself, or of horn, paper, or the like substituted for it.

1466 *Paston Lett.* II. 268 To the glaser for takyn owte of ii. panys of the wyndows of the schyrche. *a* **1490** BOTONER *Itin.* (1778) 93 Item quælibet fenestra.. continet 5 vel 6 pagettas, anglice panys. *c* **1535** in *Yorksh. Archæol. Jrnl.* (1886) IX. 322 One glasse wyndow wᵗ iij panes of vij ffoote longe and ij foote wyde euery pane. **1607** WALKINGTON *Opt. Glass* 139 The glazier should.. haue vsed him for quarrels and paines. **1662** GERBIER *Princ.* 17 Glass Windows of small Payns. **1663** —— *Counsel* 47 Suffer no Green paines of Glasse to be mixt with white. **1709** STEELE *Tatler* No. 77 ¶2 She had found several Panes of my Windows broken. **1799** G. SMITH *Laboratory* I. 179 Choose such panes of glass as are clear, even, and smooth. **1801** SOUTHEY *Thalaba* VI. xxiv, Silvering panes Of pearly shell. **1816** J. SMITH *Panorama Sc. & Art* II. 754 Take now a pane of glass, and place it upon the print. **1836** MACGILLIVRAY tr. *Humboldt's Trav.* v. 69 The windows being without glass, or even the paper panes which are often substituted. **1898** G. B. SHAW *Plays* II. 274 The ornamental cabinet.. its corner rounded off with curved panes of glass protecting shelves of.. pottery.

b. ***fulminating pane***, see FULMINATING *ppl. a.*; ***luminous*** or ***magic pane***, a sheet of glass on which pieces of tin-foil, arranged in some design, are made luminous by the discharge of an electric condenser through the foil.

1894 BOTTONE *Electr. Instr. Making* (ed. 6) 75 Fulminating Panes, or 'Franklin's plates' as they are also called, are easily made by coating both sides of a sheet of glass with tinfoil, to the extent of half of the entire surface, leaving the margins all round clear glass.

7. = PANEL *sb.*[1] 9.

1582 STANYHURST *Æneis* I. (Arb.) 34 Æneas theese picturs woonderus heeded, And eeche pane throghly with stedfast phisnomye marcked. **1593** NASHE *Christ's T.* 79 b, False counterfet panes in walls, to be opened and shut like a wicket. *a* **1625** FLETCHER *Elder Bro.* IV. iv, He had better have stood between two panes of Wainscot. **1706** PHILLIPS, *Pane*, a Square of Glass, Wainscot, etc. *c* **1850** *Rudim. Navig.* (Weale) 136 *Panel*, a square or pane of thin board.

8. a. A rectangular division of some surface; one of the compartments of a chequered pattern.

1555 EDEN *Decades* 198 Diuers shietes weaued of gossampyne cotton of sundry colours, wherof two are rychely fryngéd with golde and precious stones,.. and chekered lyke the panes of a cheste borde. **1724** J. MACKY *Journ. thro. Eng.* (N.), One wall.. took up the whole length of a street, built of pains of this stone about a foot square. **1875** KNIGHT *Dict. Mech.* 1601/2 *Pane*,.. one square of the pattern in a plaid or checker-work fabric.

b. Each of the blocks of burr-stone of which a mill-stone is constructed.

1839 URE *Dict. Arts* 829 The pieces of buhr-stones are.. cut into parallelopipeds, called panes, which are bound with iron hoops into large millstones. **1874** KNIGHT *Dict. Mech.* 400/2 The separate blocks which are hooped together to form a buhr-stone are known as panes.

9. A section or plot of ground more or less rectangular in shape; spec. in *Irrigation*, a division of ground bounded by a feeder and an outlet-drain.

[*c* **1480** HENRYSON *Test Cress.* 427 Quhair is thy garding.. with.. fresshe flouris, quhilk the quene Floray Had painted plesandly in every pane.] **1819** RAINBIRD *Agric.* (1849) 297

(E.D.D.) *Pane*,..a regular division of some sorts of husbandry work, as digging, sawing, etc. Some are saffron-panes, where saffron has been grown. **1848** W. Barnes *Poems* Gloss. (E.D.D.), *Pane*, a compartment of tedded grass between the raked divisions. **1866** *E. Anglian N. & Q.* II. 363 *Pane*,..used by cottagers for a garden bed, or any small piece of ground, having a defined boundary. **1879** Wrightson in *Cassell's Techn. Educ.* vii. 23 The water trickles down the sides of the ridges, finding its way into gutters—between the elevated 'panes' or 'stetches'.

10. A sheet or page of stamps.

1912 *Chambers's Jrnl.* Nov. 749/1 The print would have represented a 'pane' of one hundred and twenty stamps. **1916** F. J. Melville *Postage Stamps in Making* I. xvi. 173 Where the sheet is in panes, only the pane containing the defective print is discarded. **1971** D. Potter *Brit. Eliz. Stamps* viii. 83 From September 1967 until May 1968 only 6s booklets contained Machin Head stamps, with three panes of 4ds. *Ibid.* xv. 174 In those days British stamps were printed by typography, and the printers' rule placed round the edge of the panes relieved the edges of the plates from the pressure which always falls more heavily on those parts. Marginal arrows..indicate the points of division into counter book panes, less unwieldy than complete sheets.

†**pane**, *sb.*[2] *Obs.* [ME. a. OF. *panne, pane, penne, pene*, etc. (Cotgr. *panne* a skin, fell, or hide) = Pr. *pena, penna*, OSp. *peña, pena*, Sp. *pana*, in med.L. *panna, penna* fur, skin (Du Cange).

Referred by Diez to L. *penna* feather (the sense after MHG. *federe* downy fur or peltry); others take it as a fem. formation from L. *pannus*, but here the OF. form *penne, pene*, presents difficulty.]

1. Fur, esp. as used for a lining to a garment; a fell or skin (of ermine, sable, minever, or other fur).

a **1300** *Floriz & Bl.* 110 He lat bringe a cupe of seluere And eke a pane of meniuier. **13..** *Guy Warw.* (A.) 711 Þe panis al of fow & griis [*MS. Caius* riche panys of faire grys], Þe mantels weren of michel priis. *c* **1440** *Promp. Parv.* 381/1 Pane, of a furrure, *penula*,..(P. *panula*). **1494** in *Househ. Ord.* (1790) 120 Item, On New-yeare's day, the King ought to weare..his pane of arms; and if his pane bee 5 ermins deepe, a Duke's ought to bee but fower. *c* **1500** *Sc. Poem Heraldry* 177 in *Q. Eliz. Acad.*, etc. (1869) 100 Ȝhit sum haldis in armis ij certane thingis, Nothir metallis nor colouris to blasoune, Ermyne and werr, callit panis, bestly furring, And haldin so without other discripcioune. **1503** *Acc. Ld. High Treas. Scot.* II. 236 Payit to the Quenis Maister of Wardrob for ane payn of mynever to fill furth the lynyng of the samyn..xls. **1530** Palsgr. 251/2 Pane of a gray furre, *panne de gris*.

2. A package or bundle of furs containing a hundred skins: also called mantle.

(But this may belong to pane *sb.*[1])

[**1423** *Rolls of Parlt.* IV. 136, iii panes de Foynes, chescun contenant .c. Bestes, pris le pece xd.] **1612** *Bk. Customs & Valuat. Merch.* in *Halyburton's Ledger* 305 Budge..Powtes the fur contening four pans ix li. *Ibid.*, Calaba..seasoned the pane..x li, stag the pane..vi li.

pane (peɪn), *sb.*[3] [Cf. F. *panne*, in same sense, of uncertain origin.] The pointed or edged end of a hammer opposite to the face; = pein.

1881 *Metal World* No. 12. 181 What writer..has decided the proper orthography of the top part of a machinist's hammer? Some call it the 'pene', some write it 'pene', and some 'peane'. **1883** Crane *Smithy & Forge* 20 Some-times the handle is nearer to the pane or narrow end, the broad end being known as the face. **1902** Marshall *Metal Tools* vi. 65 An engineer's ball-pane hammer... The 'ball-pane' is the small round knob at the back of the hammer-head, and is chiefly used for riveting.

Hence **paned** *a.*, in comb., having a pane of a specified kind, as ***ball-paned, small-paned***.

1901 *J. Black's Carp. & Build., Home Handicr.* 30 Give every alternate tooth [of a saw] a sharp tap with a..small-paned hammer.

†**pane**, *v.*[1] *Obs.* [f. pane *sb.*[2]] *trans.* To border or line with fur. ***paned, i-paned***, furred.

c **1330** *Florice & Bl.* (1857) 131 And a mantel of scarlet Ipaned al wiȝ meniuer.

pane (peɪn), *v.*[2] [f. pane *sb.*[1]]

1. *trans.* To make up (a piece of cloth, a garment) of pieces or strips of different sorts or colours, joined side by side. Chiefly in *pa. pple.*

1504 *Will of Goodyer* (Somerset Ho.), iij curteynis paned bluwe & red of stamen. **1509** *Burgh Rec. Edinb.* (1869) I. 122 That thair baneris of baith the saidis craftis be paynitt with the imagis figuris and armis of the webstaris. **1552** *Inv. Ch. Goods Surrey* in *Surrey Archæol.* (1869) IV. 16 Item one aulter cloth of grene and yellow crewell pained. **1704** *Lond. Gaz.* No. 4033/4 Lost.., 3 Damask Window-Curtains, pain'd with Orange-colour Shagareen. **1774** *Ann. Reg.* 117/2 A rich mantle of purple, paned with white. **1861** H. Ainsworth *Constable of Tower* (1862) 17 He wore a doublet and hose of purple velvet, paned and cut.

2. To fit (a window) with panes.

1726 Leoni *Alberti's Archit.* II. 46/1 The Window must be grated, tho' not paned with scantling talc.

†**3.** To panel (a room). *Obs.*

1728 *Brice's Weekly Jrnl.* 28 June 4 The other [room] wainscotted and paned with fine Dutch Canvass.

pane, obs. f. pain, pan *sb.*[1], penny.

pan-ecclesiastical, -egoism, etc.: see pan-.

paned (peɪnd), *ppl. a.* [f. pane *v.*[2] (*sb.*[1]) + -ed.]

1. Made of strips of different coloured cloth joined together, or of cloth cut into strips, between which ribs or stripes of other material or colour are inserted.

1555 in *Wills Doctors' Comm.* (Camden) 43 Item, a paned blue hanging for the same use. **1583** in *North N. & Q.* I. 77 A payr of blew paynd hosse, drawin furthe wt Dewrance. **1607** Beaum. & Fl. *Woman-Hater* i. ii, All the swarming generation Of long stocks, short pain'd hose, and huge stuff'd doublets. *a* **1658** Ford, etc. *Witch Edmonton* iv. i, Oh! my ribs are made of a payn'd hose, and they break. **1822** Scott *Nigel* ii, His paned hose were of black velvet, lined with purple silk, which garniture appeared at the slashes. *a* **1825** Forby *Voc. E. Anglia* s.v. *Pane*, Paned curtains are made of long and narrow stripes of different patterns or colours sewed together. [**1827** W. Gifford *Ford* Introd. 177 Paned hose..were a kind of trunk breeches, formed of stripes of various coloured cloth, occasionally intermixed with slips of silk, or velvet, stitched together.]

2. Of a window or door: Having panes of glass. (Chiefly with qualification.)

1756 Mrs. Calderwood *Jrnl.* v. (1884) 127 The windows are all of the small pained kind. **1814** *Sporting Mag.* XLIV. 43 A fox..took a direction through a glass paned door. **1888** F. Hume *Mad. Midas* i. ii, A quaint little porch and two numerously paned windows on each side.

panee, paneel, var. pawnee, panele.

panegas, obs. form of *pence*, pl. of penny.

panegurie, obs. variant of panegyry.

†'**panegyre**. *Obs.* [ad. Gr. πανήγυρις panegyris: in sense 1 identified with *panegyric*.]

1. A eulogy: = panegyric *sb.* 1.

1603 B. Jonson (*title*) A panegyre on the happy entrance of James, our sovereign, to his first high session of Parliament. *a* **1618** Sylvester *Mayden's Blush* Ded. 4 Instead..of precious Gifts, of solemne Panegyres: Accept a Heart.

2. A general assembly: = panegyris 1.

1757 Stukeley in *Mem.* (Surtees) III. 358 Here was in British times the great panegyre of the Druids, the mid-summer meeting of all the country round. **1763** —— *Palæograph. Scara* 8 At public sacrifice, which they called Panegyres; a meeting of a side of a country, a province.

panegyric (pænɪ'dʒɪrɪk), *sb.* and *a.* Also 7 **panegyrike, -gyrique, -girick, pani-, panne-, pana-, -gyrick, -girike, -gerick(e, 7–9 panegyrick**. [a. F. *panégyrique* (1512 in Hatz.-Darm.), ad. L. *panēgyric-us* public eulogy, orig. adj., a. Gr. πανηγυρικός fit for a public assembly or festival, f. πανήγυρις panegyris.]

A. *sb.* **1.** A public speech or writing in praise of some person, thing, or achievement; a laudatory discourse, a formal or elaborate encomium or eulogy. Const. *on, upon*, formerly *of*.

1603 Daniel (*title*) A Panegyrike Congratulatorie delivered to the Kings most excellent Maiestie. **1620** in *Fortesc. Papers* (Camden) 132, I also composed a panagirick of the immortality of glorie. **1656** Blount *Glossogr.*, *Panegyrick*,..a licentious kinde of speaking or oration, in the praise and commendation of Kings, or other great persons, wherein some falsities are joyned with many flatteries. **1673** Marvell *Reh. Transp.* II. 45 The Mountebanks..decrying all others with a Panegyrick of their own Balsam. **1697** Potter *Antiq. Greece* iv. viii. (1715) 227 The Company..were some-times entertain'd with a Panegyrick upon the dead Person. *a* **1704** T. Brown *Pleas. Ep.* Wks. 1730 I. 109 Write a panegyric upon custard. **1791** Boswell *Johnson* i, I profess to write, not his panegyrick.. but his Life. **1836** *Johnsoniana* i. 71 Had I meant to make a panegyric on Mr. Johnson's excellencies. **1879** Froude *Cæsar* xxviii. 491 After Cato's death Cicero published a panegyric upon him.

2. Elaborate praise; eulogy; laudation.

1613 R. Cawdrey *Table Alph.* (ed. 3), *Panigirike*, praise. **1702** Evelyn in *Pepys' Diary* (1879) VI. 255 Not doubting but the rest which follows will be still matter of panegyric. **1762** Goldsm. *Cit. W.* I. Pref. 5 In this season of panegyric, when scarce an author passes unpraised either by his friends or himself. **1879** Farrar *St. Paul* I. 6 He stands infinitely above the need of indiscriminate panegyric.

†**3.** = panegyrist. *Obs.*

1600 W. Watson *Decacordon* (1602) 13 Father Stanney, a Iesuit Priest, called (of the Panigericks) the lanterne of England.

B. *adj.* †**1.** = panegyrical 1. *Obs.*

1603 Holland *Plutarch* Explan. Words, *Panegyricke*, Feasts, games, faires, marts, pompes, shewes, or any such solemnities, performed or exhibited, before the generall assembly of a whole nation.

2. = panegyrical 2.

a **1631** Donne *Litanie* xxiii. Poems (1654) 344 In Panegyrique Allelujaes. **1706** Maule *Hist. Picts* in *Misc. Scot.* I. 17 The panegyrick author after a sort doth show. **1737** Pope *Hor. Epist.* ii. i. 405 I'm not used to panegyrick strains. **1774** Mason *Elegies* i. Poems 46 Cautious I strike the panegyric string.

Hence †**pane'gyric** *v. intr.*, to utter or write a panegyric; *trans.*, to praise in an elaborate oration or eulogium.

1708 De Foe *Review Affairs France* IV. Pref., I am not going about to panegyric upon my own Work. **1732** *Gentl. Instr.* (ed. 10) 539 (D.), I had rather be..lampooned for a virtue than panegyrick'd for a vice.

pane'gyrical, *a.* [f. as prec. + -al[1].]

†**1.** Of the nature of a general assembly. *Obs.*

a **1617** Bayne *Diocesans Tryall* (1621) 4 Their ordinary meeting, as it is, Acts 2. 46, daily, could not be a Panegericall meeting. *a* **1679** T. Goodwin *Govt. Ch. Christ* iv. vi. Wks. 1865 XI. 231 In the primitive church the persons of the bishops..were chosen by all the people, and by panegyrical meetings.

2. Of the nature of a panegyric or eulogy; publicly or elaborately expressing praise or commendation; eulogistic, encomiastic, laudatory.

1592–3 G. Harvey *Pierce's Super.* Wks. (Grosart) II. 326 To addresse a plausible discourse, or to garnish a Panegyricall Oration in her prayse. **1596** Nashe *Saffron-Walden* Wks. (Grosart) III. 76 **1616** Bullokar *Eng. Expos.*, *Panegyricall*,..spoken flatteringly in praise of some great person. **1755** J. Shebbeare *Lydia* (1769) I. 405 A dead lord ..is always to receive honourable interment and a panegyrical epitaph. **1858** J. H. Newman *Hist. Sk.* (1876) II. ii. i. 222 The Duke of Wellington's despatches..tell us so much more about him than any panegyrical sketch.

Hence **pane'gyrically** *adv.*, in or by means of a panegyric; by way of elaborate eulogy.

1680 *Religion of Dutch* vi. 57 You must also Panegyrically celebrate the Cantons..for their refusal. **1814** W. Taylor in *Monthly Rev.* LXXIII. 360 Winkelmann..fell in love with its sculptured reliques of antient art, and undertook to describe them panegyrically.

pane'gyricize (-saɪz), *v. rare.* [f. panegyric *sb.* + -ize.] = panegyrize *v.* 1.

1787 Ann Hilditch *Rosa de Montmorien* II. xiv. 68 He suffered me to panegyricize him in a dedication of a piece.

‖**panegyris** (pə'niːdʒɪrɪs, -'ɛdʒɪrɪs). [a. Gr. πανήγυρις, f. παν- all + ἄγυρις = ἀγορά assembly.]

1. *Gr. Antiq.* A general assembly; *esp.* a festal assembly in honour of a god. In quots. 1647–79 in allusion to Heb. xii. 23.

1647 Trapp *Comm. Matt.* iii. 12 Amidst a panegyris of angels, and that glorious ampitheatre. **1679** J. Goodman *Penit. Pard.* iii. v. (1713) 367 There shall be the glorious *Panegyris*, the assembly and church of the first-born. **1775** Chandler *Trav. Asia Minor* xl. 143 A panegyris or general assembly was held there yearly. **1879** C. T. Newton *Art & Archæol.* viii. (1880) 330 The Olympic *panegyris*..was still a reality.

†**2.** = panegyric A. 1. *Obs.*

1646 Crashaw *Steps to Temple* 23 Their silence speaks aloud, and is Thy well pronounced panegyris.

panegyrism ('pæniːdʒɪrɪz(ə)m). *nonce-wd.* [f. panegyrize + -ism. Cf. Gr. πανηγύρισμα, -ισμός celebration of a public festival.] A panegyrizing; a composition of panegyrical character.

1894 T. Sinclair in *Athenæum* 17 Nov. 677/2 A work which has been called a panegyrism.

panegyrist ('pæniːdʒɪrɪst). [f. next: see -ist. Cf. Gr. πανηγυριστής one who celebrates a public festival.] One who writes or utters a panegyric; one who elaborately praises; an encomiast.

1605 Camden *Rem.* (1637) 3 Adde..these few lines out of a farre more ancient Panegyrist. **1782** Miss Burney *Cecilia* ix. iii, The panegyrist of human life! **1815** W. H. Ireland *Scribbleomania* 25 Panegyrists, Errant Knights! That whitewash one as grim'd as Nero, And make him shine abroad—an hero. **1876** Freeman *Norm. Conq.* V. xxiii. 156 The high-flown rhetoric of a panegyrist.

panegyrize ('pæniːdʒɪˌraɪz), *v.* [ad. Gr. πανηγυρίζ-ειν to celebrate πανήγυρις or a public festival; to deliver a panegyric: see -ize.]

1. *trans.* To pronounce or write a panegyric or elaborate eulogy upon; to speak or write in praise of: to eulogize.

1617 Collins *Def. Bp. Ely* ii. vi. 250 Among so many Saints, as he Panegyrizeth in these Orations. **1791** Mad. D'Arblay *Diary* 2 June, The friends of Government.. panegyrised him while they wanted his assistance. **1833–6** J. H. Newman *Hist. Sk.* (1876) I. ii. ii. 251 Meanly panegyrizing the government of an usurper.

2. *intr.* To compose or utter panegyrics.

a **1827** Mitford cited in Webster (1828).

Hence '**panegy,rized**, '**panegy,rizing** *ppl. adjs.*; also '**panegy,rizer**.

1823 *Valperga* II. 239 He was an earnest panegyrizer of republics and democracies. **1852** Davies & Vaughan *Plato's Republic* x. (1868) 341 More anxious to be the panegyrized than the panegyrist. **1855** Doran *Hanover Queens* I. xi. 436 In his panegyrising epitaph on the monarch.

panegyry (pə'niː-, pə'nɛdʒɪrɪ, 'pæniːdʒɪrɪ). Also 7 **pani-, panegery, panegury**. [f. Gr. πανήγυρις panegyris, with change of suffix.]

1. *Gr. Antiq.* = panegyris 1. Also more generally, A religious festival.

1641 Milton *Ch. Govt.* ii. Pref., That the call of wisdom and virtue may be heard everywhere;..not only in pulpits, but..at set and solemn paneguries in theatres. **1659** H. L'Estrange *Alliance Div. Off.* 136 These dayes [the Nativity, Epiphany, Easter, Ascension and Pentecost] were called..The Christian Panegyries, as a note of distinction from those of lesser account. **1839** *Fraser's Mag.* XX. 207 The..panegyries or great monthly festivals of the [Egyptian] gods. **1894** G. Rawlinson in *Lex Mosaica* 24 The institution of panegyries or 'solemn assemblies'.

†**2.** = panegyric A. 1 (*if not mispr. in quots.*)

1600 W. Watson *Decacordon* (1602) 72 Then would he [Erasmus]..sound foorth the Panigeries of their praises. **1636** Heywood in *Ann. Dubrensia* (1877) 69 Having these Panegeries now read over, To thy perpetuall fame.

paneity (pə'niːɪtɪ). [ad. med.L **pāneitās*, f. **pāne-us* of bread, f. *pān-is* bread.] The quality or condition of being bread, 'breadness'.

a **1687** S. Parker *Reasons Abrogat. Test* (1688) 22 They could not onely separate the Matter and Form, and Accidents of the Bread from one another, but the Paneity or Breadishness it self from them all. **1689** Prior *Ep. Shephard* 66 Romish bakers praise the deity They chipp'd, while yet in its paneity. **1782** Priestley *Corrupt. Chr.* II. vi. 42

Innocent..acknowledged that..there did remain a certain paneity and vineity.

panel (ˈpænəl), *sb.*[1] Forms: 3- panel; also 4-6 panell, -e, (5 -yll, -ȝell, -ele, pannule, penelle), 5-8 pannal, 6 -ale, 6-7 -all, 6-8 -ell, 6-9 -el, (7 -elle, -iell). [ME. a. OF. *panel* piece of cloth, saddle-cushion, piece (of anything), etc., mod.F. *panneau* = It. *pannello*, med.L. *pannellus*, dim. of *pannus* cloth: see PANE *sb.*[1] (several senses of which are found also under *panel*). OF. had also *panele* f., piece, etc., which in ME. would run together with *panel*.]

I. A piece of cloth, and connected uses.

1. A piece of cloth placed under the saddle to protect the horse's back from being galled (*obs.*); now, the pad or stuffed lining of a saddle employed for this purpose.

a **1300** *Cursor M.* 14982 Broght þai noþer on hir bak Na sadel ne panel. *c* **1400** *Ywaine & Gaw.* 473 Luke thou fil wele thi panele, And in thi sadel set the wele. **1483** *Cath. Angl.* 267/2 A Panelle of a sadelle, *panellus, subsellium.* **1497** *Naval Acc. Hen. VII* (1896) 117 Cartsadell without panell. **1607** MARKHAM *Caval.* VI. (1617) 56 The pannells of his Saddle shall be made of strong linnen cloath. **1724** DE FOE *Mem. Cavalier* (1840) 74, I cut a hole in the pannel of the saddle. **1835** *Encycl. Brit.* (ed. 7) XI. 621 Hunting saddles should have their pannels well beaten and brushed to prevent sore backs.

2. A kind of saddle: generally applied to a rough treeless pad; but formerly sometimes to an ass's wooden saddle.

[**1390–1** *Earl Derby's Exped.* (Camden) 46 Pro iij panellis nouis pro cursore domino, xxs. pr.] **1530** PALSGR. 251/2 Pannell to ryde on, *batz, panneau.* **1573** TUSSER *Husb.* (1878) 36 A panel and wantey, packsaddle and ped. **1591** PERCIVALL *Sp. Dict., Acitára de Silla*, the pannell or the saddle tree, *Stragulum ligneum.* **1597** BP. HALL *Sat.* IV. ii. 26 So rides he mounted on the market-day, Upon a straw-stufft pannel all the way. **1617** MORYSON *Itin.* I. 215 Our Asses had pannels in stead of saddles..and ropes laid crosse the pannels, and knotted at the ends in stead of stirrups. **1742** JARVIS *Quix.* I. IV. xliii. (1885) 243 Sancho Panza, stretched on his ass's pannel and buried in sleep. **1869** E. A. PARKES *Pract. Hygiene* (ed. 3) 419 Weight of Horse Appointments.. 5th Dragoon Guards 1 Pair pannels 5 lb. 4½ oz.

†**3.** In more general sense: A small piece of anything. *Obs.*

(Common in OF. but of doubtful existence in Eng.)

1628 COKE *On Litt.* II. ii. §234. 158 b, A Pane is a part, and a Pannel a little part.

II. A small piece or slip of parchment, and related legal uses.

4. A slip or roll of parchment, *esp.* the slip on which the sheriff entered the names of jurors and which he affixed to the writ.

[*c* **1307** *Writ to Sheriff of Somerset* Chancery File, New Ser. 1 *dorso*, Responsum istius breuis est in Panello huic annexo.] *c* **1440** *Promp. Parv.* 381/1 Panele, *pagella, panellus.* **1562** *Act 5 Eliz.* c. 22 §1 Vnlesse such person or persons so making any pelts, or buying such skinnes,.. conuert the same into semits, pannels, or other their owne necessary vses. **1628** COKE *On Litt.* II. ii. §234. 158 b, A Jury is said to be im-pannelled when the Sheriff hath entred their names into the Pannel, or little piece of Parchment, *in Pannello assisæ.* **1670** BLOUNT *Law Dict., Panel*, a Schedule or Page; as a Panel of Parchment, or a Counterpane of an Indenture: But it is used more particularly for a Schedule or Roll containing the names of such Jurors, as the Sheriff returns, to pass upon any Trial. **1752** J. LOUTHIAN *Form of Process Sc.* (ed. 2) 202 Which Panel must be in Parchment, intitled. *The County ss. Nomina Jur. ad Triand. inter Dominum Regem, et —— Prisonar. ad Barram. Ibid.*, The Panel must have Margin-room, to mark their Appearances and Challenges. **1768** BLACKSTONE *Comm.* III. 353 He returns the names of the jurors in a panel (a little pane, or oblong piece of parchment) annexed to the writ. **1875** STUBBS *Const. H.* III. xx. 408 Under the name of 'pannel' the sheriff's return had been endorsed on or sewed to the writ.

5. a. A list of jurors, the jury itself.

[**1292** BRITTON I. xxii. §10 Pur uns remuer hors des panels et autres mettre. **1314–15** *Rolls of Parlt.* I. 333/2 Ipsi panellum debitum de probis & legalibus hominibus retornarunt.] **1377** LANGL. *P. Pl.* B. III. 315 Ne put hem in panel To don hem pliȝte here treuthe. **1444** *Rolls of Parlt.* V. 127/1 The Coronours..have power to make the array of the enquest or panell for the triell of the same offencers. **1543–4** *Act 35 Hen. VIII*, c. 6 §6 Persons so..impanelled..shalbe added to the former panell. **1682** *Enq. Elect. Sheriffs* 24 The Pannel that brought in an Ignoramus upon the Bill against the Earl of Shaftsbury. **1730** FIELDING *Rape upon Rape* II. i, I think half of that pannel are bailiff's followers. **1827** HALLAM *Const. Hist.* (1876) II. xii. 458 The sheriffs..had taken care to return a panel in whom they could confide. **1862** BURTON *Bk. Hunter* (1863) 136 A panel means twelve perplexed agriculturists, who..are starved till they are of one mind.

b. *transf.* A list of persons, or (quot. 1575) of beasts. *spec.* a list or group of people called upon to advise, judge, take part in a discussion or contest, etc.

1575 LANEHAM *Let.* (1871) 16 A great sort of bandogs whear thear tyed in the vtter Coourt, and thyrteen bearz in the inner. Whoosoeuer made the pannell, thear wear inoow for a Queast, and one for challenge, and néed wear. **1716** M. DAVIES *Athen. Brit.* II. 242 If the following..Pannel be labell'd to the former Catalogue of that most August Assembly. **1888** *Standing Orders Ho. Comm.* (1897) §49. 13 The Committee of Selection shall nominate a Chairmen's Panel to consist of not less than Four nor more than Six Members..the Chairmen's Panel shall appoint from among themselves the Chairman of each Standing Committee. **1934** G. B. SHAW *Too True to be Good* 24 The formation of panels of tested persons eligible for the different grades in the governmental hierarchy. **1947** *Ann. Reg. 1946* 53 The method of forming panels for juvenile courts. **1952** W. J. H. SPROTT *Social Psychol.* vi. 103 Another device for assessing the attitudes of special groups of people is to use panels of respondents who are prepared to give their views on expert or general questions. **1958** *New Statesman* 1 Feb. 127/2 Perhaps..he believes the Brainstrusters really are equipped to pronounce themselves upon, virtually, anything... Radio and television have given a great impetus here. 'Do the panel think that there is an after life?' **1958** *Listener* 4 Dec. 916/1 A small panel of experts who were also good broadcasters. **1959** *Times* 28 Feb. 7/4 If one of those contests which require the competitor to list a number of items in order of popularity were to turn its attention to the months of the year, the panel of judges (each one an expert) would surely find February at the bottom of the poll. **1961** *Which?* Sept. 231/2 The assessments were made by a panel of people experienced in listening to tape recorders. **1962** *Listener* 1 Feb. 211/2 It was a panel of architects of many nationalities who sketched out the main design. **1966** *Ibid.* 4 Aug. 168/1, I thought the panel skirted the subject. Why the BBC did not have a child psychologist on it I cannot guess. **1967** C. L. WRENN *Word & Symbol* 11 The committee of scholars who translated the *New English Bible* New Testament..sought..to weld the whole into agreeable and dignified English with the aid of a 'literary panel'. **1973** *N.Y. Law Jrnl.* 31 Aug. 1/6 In reversing and remanding the case to the Southern District, the Second Circuit panel assigned it to Judge Constance Baker Motley. **1975** *Irish Times* 10 May 3/4 They named a panel of players from which the Ballybofey line-out will be chosen tomorrow. **1976** *Horse & Hound* 3 Dec. 54/3 He introduced a panel of experts for an open forum and considerable discussion ensued. **1977** *Sunday Express* 30 Jan. 31/5 It is customary for the touring side to see the full panel of Test umpires in action in the games outside the Tests.

c. The official list of doctors in a district who accepted patients under the National Health Insurance Act of 1913 (since superseded by the National Health Service Act of 1946). ***on the panel***, (*a*) of doctors, registered as accepting patients thus; (*b*) of patients, under the care of a 'panel doctor'; also in extended use.

1913 *Punch* 30 July 101/1 The proposed Laureate was a medical man and not on a panel. **1914** *Times* 12 Feb. 6/5 Of these [doctors] 1500 are already on the panel for the county. **1914** T. SMITH *Everybody's Guide Insurance Acts* (ed. 3) 124 Which practitioners are collectively to be known as 'the panel'. **1957** R. HOGGART *Uses of Literacy* i. 21 Almost every worker has been on the 'panel' at the local doctor's. **1964** G. L. COHEN *What's Wrong with Hospitals?* i. 22 Working people still talk about 'going on the Panel' when they're off sick, and don't see why they should use another term. **1974** *Daily Tel.* (Colour Suppl.) 29 Mar. 19/2 The average GP has 2,460 people on his panel. **1975** P. G. WINSLOW *Death of Angel* v. 117 It's the National Health... If only the government had left things alone, like they always was, with the Panel. **1976** 'J. BELL' *Trouble in Hunter Ward* i. 6 There were thousands of Health Service patients who put themselves upon their doctor's panel because they could no longer, after the war, afford to be private patients.

6. *Scots Law.* **a.** In the phrase ***on*** or ***upon the panel*** = upon (his, one's) trial. Also, in later use, ***in the panel***, etc.

The original sense of *panel* here is conjectural. It seems most probable that (on the analogy of sense 4) it meant a slip of parchment, containing the indictment, or the name or names of the persons indicted. *To be on the panel* would thus be *to be indicted*, and so on one's trial. It would also be easy to use the term elliptically for the name or names, and so, the person or persons, on the panel, as in b, where note that the word is collective. In later times, 'the panel' has been sometimes understood as a place, viz. 'the bar of the court' (so Jamieson), or the dock. Cf. the phrases *in the panel*, to put or bring *into the panel*, to enter *the panel*.

1557 *Books of Adjournal* (High Court of Justic.) 8 Apr., The personis upone the pannell askit instrumentis. **1560** ROLLAND *Crt. Venus* III. 128 Thay callit the criminall, With ane twme scheith set him on the Pannall. **1582** *Reg. Privy Council Scot.* Ser. I. III. 502 Few complenaris hes offerit thame to persew the personis enterit on pannell. **1660** DICKSON *Exp. Job* x. Writ. 1845 I. 5 God has put the man on the pannel, and is entered in a contest, and will condemn us. ? *a* **1700** in *Kirkton's Hist. Ch. Scot.* (1817) 384 Mr. James Mitchel was upon the pannell at the criminal court for shutting at the Archbishop of St Andrews. **1714** THOMSON in *Cloud of Witnesses* (1730) 134, I was brought and set in the Pannel, with the Murderers, and they read over my Indictment. **1752** J. LOUTHIAN *Form of Process* (ed. 2) 16 The Day of Compearance being come, the Prisoner is sent for, and enters the Pannal (from this the Prisoner is called Pannel).

b. The person or persons indicted, the accused. (The pl. form in quot. 1801 is a 'foreigner's' error.)

1555 *Bks. of Adjournal* 7 Dec., The pannell protestit for the panis contenit in the actis of parliament. **1562** *Ibid.* 13 May, Intrandi as secund pannale, the laird of Wester Ogill, etc. **1695** *Ibid.* 18 Nov., Ordains that for hereafter the pannalls advocats in all their wryten debates title the defenders by the name of pannall, as has bein always in use before the Justice Court, and not by the name of defender. **1708** J. CHAMBERLAYNE *St. Gt. Brit.* II. II. vi. (1737) 386, 15 ..are chosen to be the Assize upon the Pannal (or Prisoner at the Bar). **1795** *Scots Mag.* LVII. 479/1 He saw no marks of insanity about the pannel, who always behaved with great propriety. **1801** *Sporting Mag.* XVII. 30 Mr. Clark, Counsel for the pannels, made no objection. **1883** EDERSHEIM *Life Jesus* (ed. 6) II. 169 On the assumption of their being the judges, and He the panel.

III. A distinct piece or portion of some surface, etc., usually contained in a frame or border.

(This appears to be the underlying idea in this group, but the arrangement is tentative and provisional.)

†**7.** The general sense of 'compartment' or 'section' appears to be exemplified in the following:

c **1440** *Jacob's Well* 273 þis ground of equyte is ij. panellys. In þe to panel equyte acordyth resoun wyth wyll, and þe oþer panel equite acordyth wyll wyth resoun. Eyther of þise ij. panys is iiij. fote brode.

8. A section or compartment of a fence or railing; a hurdle. Cf. PANE *sb.*[1] 3.

1489 CAXTON *Faytes of A.* II. xxiv, In the said forest..to be made palebordes called penelles. *Ibid.* II. xxx, To make fyue penellys of palysses to be sette vp. **1530** PALSGR. 251/2 Panell of a wall, *pan de mur.* **1658** EVELYN *Fr. Gard.* (1675) 138 A reed-hedge handsomely bound in pannels. **1882** *Gard. Chron.* XVII. 809/2 Each panel is composed of three vertical parallel posts, two longitudinal rails..and two boards attached to the posts between the rails. **1890** 'R. BOLDREWOOD' *Col. Reformer* (1891) 226 A panel of fencing is not quite nine feet in length.

9. a. A distinct compartment of a wainscot, door, shutter, side of a carriage, etc., consisting usually of a thinner piece of board or other material, normally rectangular, set in the general framework.

1600 SHAKS. *A.Y.L.* III. iii. 89 This fellow wil but ioyne you together, as they ioyne Wainscot, then one of you wil proue a shrunke pannell, and like greene timber, warpe, warpe. **1688** R. HOLME *Armoury* III. 100/1 *Pannell*, little cleft Boards, about 2 foot high, and 16 or 20 inches broad, of these Wainscot is made. **1703** MOXON *Mech. Exerc.* 109 Bevil away the outer edges of the Pannels. **1784** COWPER *Task* I. 282 Rural carvers..with knives deface The pannels. **1825** COBBETT *Rur. Rides* 411 A stage-coach came up to the door, with 'Bath and London' upon its panels. *c* **1850** *Rudim. Navig.* (Weale) 136 *Panel*, a square or pane of thin board, framed in a thicker one called a stile... Such are the partitions by which the officers' cabins are formed. **1866** GEO. ELIOT *F. Holt* xxxviii, She had..seen herself..in the crystal panel that reflected a long drawing-room. **1874** KNIGHT *Dict. Mech.* 720/2 A panel wider than its height is a *lying-panel*... If its height be greater than its width, a *standing panel*.

b. In architecture and other constructive arts: A compartment of a surface either sunk below or raised above the general level, and set in a moulding or other border, as in a frame, sometimes of different colour or material.

1693 TIGON (*title*) A New Book of Drawings, containing Several Sortes of Iron Worke as Gates,..Staircases, Pannelles, etc. **1715** LEONI *Palladio's Archit.* (1742) II. 27 A large pannel occupying the whole Architrave and Frize to place the Inscription upon. **1842–76** GWILT *Archit.* (ed. 7) 960 The tower of St. Peter Mancroft, at Norwich, is a good specimen of flint building with stone panels. **1874** MICKLETHWAITE *Mod. Par. Churches* 214, I can see no reason why the panels should not be formed of some of the concretes which we are now able to procure.

c. *Bookbinding.* (*a*) A compartment of the external cover of a book enclosed in a border or frame. (*b*) Also, the space between the raised bands on the back of a book.

1875 *Ure's Dict. Arts* (ed. 7) I. 425 'Raised bands' are formed of strips of pasteboard or parchment at regular intervals across the back of the book, leaving a space termed 'panels' between them. **1880** ZAEHNSDORF *Bookbinding* 129 Panel mitred in gold, with title and small corners... Small tail panel with date. **1903** *Studio* Aug. 175 A solid leather outer binding with an inlaid..panel in the centre to contain coats-of-arms..amid a framework of gold tooling.

d. (*a*) A piece of stuff of different kind or colour, laid or inserted lengthwise in the skirt of a woman's dress; also, the portion of the original material enclosed between two such pieces. (*b*) A panel-shaped piece of embroidery or appliqué work for insertion in any drapery.

1889 *John Bull* 2 Mar. 149/3 The skirt, of grey silk, had broad panels of dark grey velvet, on which a design of feathers was embroidered in silver. **1899** W. G. P. TOWNSEND *Embroidery* iv. 43 Design for an appliqué panel, ..Worked in the Windermere linens, in blues and green. *Ibid.*, Design for..a long panel for the back of a settee. **1903** *Westm. Gaz.* 19 Feb. 4/2 On the skirt these [flatly stitched inverted box pleats] are set about five or six inches apart, except in the front, where a wider space is left to give a panel effect—a space amounting to about twelve inches.

e. *fig.* Something resembling a panel in shape and relation to the surrounding space.

1902 A. E. W. MASON *Four Feathers* xviii. 174 Through the open window the moon threw a broad panel of silver light upon the floor of the room.

f. A section of a tapestry or other ornamental work, usu. one surrounded by a decorative border. Also, a tapestry regarded as a whole.

1856 O. JONES *Gram. Ornament* xvi, The painter began to usurp the office of the scribe... We have the first stage.. where a geometrical arrangement is obtained with conventional ornament enclosing gold panels, on which are painted groups of flowers. **1911** *Encycl. Brit.* XXVI. 405/1 Other tapestries..are fantastic with schemes of abstract ornament into which are introduced as subsidiary details figure subjects set in panels and medallions. **1918** G. L. HUNTER *Decorative Textiles* xii. 243 Tapestry screen panels woven in New York. **1923** F. DE ZULUETA *Embroideries M. Stuart & E. Talbot* 10 This again is a green velvet curtain, measuring 7½ × 6 feet and mounting twenty-four needle-work panels. *Ibid.* 15 If the centre-piece is not enough, there is the octagonal panel immediately above it. **1946** H. LÉJARD *French Tapestry* 24 The tapestry panels intended for the decoration of the same room soon came to be composed on related themes. **1953** E. FISHER *Swedish Embroidery* 38 The stimulating colours of this unique hanging panel can be seen in the colour reproductions. **1964** D. DUBON *Tapestries S.H. Kress Coll. at Philad. Mus. of Art: Hist. Constantine* 20 The sarcophagus is framed by an oval wreath of ribbon within an oval panel, bound laurel leaves with a shell form at the top and bottom. *Ibid.* 21 The ornament surrounding the central panels on all of the over-doors is similar. **1965** P. Hentgès tr. *Biryukova's Hermitage, Leningrad: Gothic & Renaiss. Tapestries* Pl. 33 The left-hand panel shows the betrothal of Mary and Joseph. **1974** *Encycl. Brit. Macropædia* XVII. 1055/1 A tapestry set is a group of individual panels related by subject, style, and workmanship and intended to be hung together.

g. One of the shaped sections of a parachute.

1930 O. H. Kneen *Everyman's Bk. Flying* xii. 223 Two men straighten out the twelve 'panels' of silk. **1938** *Flight* 25 Aug. 168*c*/1 The canopy, which is 24ft. in diameter, is made up of 24 triangular gores cut from high-quality silk. Each gore is composed of four panels, the stitching of which forms a zig-zag pattern round the complete canopy. **1974** *Encycl. Brit. Micropædia* VII. 740/2 The canopy is given extraordinary strength by fabrication from up to 28 separate panels, or gores, each made up of smaller sections.

10. †**a.** A window-pane. *Obs.* **b.** A compartment in a stained glass window, containing a separate subject. Also *transf.*

1727–41 Chambers *Cycl.* s.v., Hence also Panels, or panes of glass, are compartments or pieces of glass of various forms, square, hexagonal, etc. **1873–5** Jas. Fowler in *Yks. Arch. Jrnl.* III. 199 The arrangement is a succession of panels, each containing a subject. **1891** J. T. Fowler *Ibid.* XI. 499 This panel certainly does not belong to the window. **1898** C. H. Turner in J. Hastings *Dict. Bible* I. 421/1 This picture is cut up, as it were, into six panels, each labelled with a general summary of progress. **1927** A. H. McNeile *Introd. New Testament* 79 He [*sc.* St. Luke] cuts the history into 'panels'.

11. *Coal-mining.* **a.** A piece of coal left uncut in a mine. **b.** A compartment or division of a mine separated from the rest by thick masses or ribs of coal.

1747 Hooson *Miner's Dict.*, *Pannell* , a small Piece of Wholes that is left uncut, either to support some Weight from falling, or else..left, because it is..not worth the cutting. *Ibid.* K iij, Huttrill [is] any hard Pannel in a Vein or Pipe..bound up and crossil'd by mixt Stuff, as Chirts, hard Tufts, Caukes, or Kevills. **1847** E. Cresy *Encycl. Civ. Eng.* I. 695 Panel work..is performed by dividing the entire mine into panels, separated by walls of coal from 40 to 50 yards in thickness. **1882** R. L. Galloway *Hist. Coal Mining* xv. 149 It occurred to Mr. Buddle [*c* 1810] that a great improvement ..might be effected by dividing a colliery, in the course of the first working, into districts, or panels, surrounded on all sides by barriers of solid coal.

12. *Gardening.* A compartment of some design in carpet-bedding.

1805 Repton *Landscape Gard.* 185 The pannel..may be removed in winter. **1892** *Gard. Chron.* 27 Aug. 243/3 These need frequent thinning out and clipping into shape, so as to confine each colour to its own panel or boundary-line, so as to properly define and preserve the character of the several designs.

13. A compartment or division of a pavement.

1893 *Daily News* 21 Sept. 5/3 A 'panel' of karri wood has been laid opposite the West Strand Post Office, where the wear and tear is exceedingly heavy.

IV. A thin board, etc., such as might form a panel in sense 9.

14. a. A thin wooden board used as a surface for oil painting; also, a painting on such a board.

1709 Prior *Protogenes & Apelles* 59 He [Apelles] gave the Pannel to the Maid. **1765** H. Walpole *Otranto* ii. (1798) 32, I am not in love with a coloured panel. **1821** Craig *Lect. Drawing* ii. 117 It was the custom of the first practitioners in this process, to cover the pannels of their pictures with grounds of thin plaster. **1859** Gullick & Timbs *Paint.* 217 For small cabinet pictures, panels of well-seasoned mahogany are prepared. **1875** Fortnum *Majolica* iii. 26 Were they even painted in oil on panel. **1956** Hedström & Taylor tr. *Bergström's Dutch Still-Life Painting* 58 We may now compare Bosschaert's panel with two early works by other artists... The farther edge of the table is considerably more than half way up the panel.

b. A large size of photograph, of a height much greater than its width. Chiefly *attrib.*

1888 *Lady* 25 Oct. 374/3 Some of the most delightful panel screens for photographs I ever set eyes on. *Ibid.*, The two-fold screens with..sufficient space for panel portraits. **1891** *Pall Mall G.* 14 May 6/1 The panel photo is..as much part of the ceremony of presentation as, in the courtly times of Sir Joshua Reynolds, a few sittings at his studio in Leicester-square were part of the business of a fashionable marriage.

c. A leaf or section of a folding screen or triptych, etc. Also *fig.*

1880 E. Glaister *Needlework* vi. 62 Panel screens..are excellent subjects for fine embroidery. **1896** F. Simmonds tr. *Ricci's Correggio* vii. 122 On the high altar of the oratory ..there was once a triptych, the central panel of which represented Christ. **1936** E. G. Troche *Painting in Netherlands* 26/2 Possibly half of a diptych, of which the panel with Our Lady is now lost. **1959** P. & L. Murray *Dict. Art & Artists* 324 Usually the central panel [of a triptych] is twice the width of the wings, so that they can be folded over it to protect it. **1967** N. Amphoux tr. *Troyat's Tolstoy* (1970) II. viii. 223 In painting the third panel of his triptych he had, as in *Boyhood*, combined the story of his friends, the Islenyevs, with his own. **1970** *Oxf. Compan. Art* 494/1 Panel painting was not developed fully until altars were furnished with painted retables.

15. A board used by a baker, tailor, etc.

1612 in *Naworth Househ. Bks.* (Surtees) 42 A pannell for the baker. **1658** J. Jones tr. *Ovid's Ibis* 120 Dominus Mechanick that leaps from the pannel to the pulpit.

16. A control panel or instrument panel.

1897 E. Wilson *Electr. Traction* x. 219 The panel system of switchboards, whereby the various switches, complete for a given purpose, can be mounted on a panel of slate or marble and placed in line with those already installed. **1923**, etc. [see *control panel* s.v. control *sb.* 5]. **1926** *Wireless World* 8 Dec. 760/3 A neat method of mounting a flash lamp bulb so that it may..illuminate the panel and tuning dials at night. **1929** V. W. Pagé *Ford Model 'A' Car* ix. 314 Remove the four screws which hold the instrument panel in place and pull panel back. **1933**, etc. [see *instrument panel* s.v. instrument *sb.* 6]. **1940** *Railway Signalling & Communications* xix. 353 Points within 350 yds. of the signal box are mechanically operated by levers and the signals by switches on the panel. **1941** G. E. Irvin *Aircraft Instruments* xvii. 438 Large transport planes carrying two pilots require a dual set of instruments. This necessitates a large panel. **1964** M. Allward *Inside Jet Airliner* v. 39 The main panels contain the indicators and controls for the hydraulic and electrical systems, engine and fuel functioning, anti-icing and air-conditioning. **1969** T. C. Millington *Hillman Imps* x. 117 It is just possible to contrive a panel to mount two 2 in. gauges immediately above the speedometer. **1977** D. Beaty *Excellency* i. 8 He..clambered gingerly inside the fuselage..ran his fingers round the dusty panel.

V. Unclassed senses.

17. (See quot.)

1853 Stocqueler *Milit. Encycl.*, *Pannels*, in artillery, are the carriages which carry mortars and their beds upon a march.

18. *Mining.* (See quot.)

1858 Simmonds *Dict. Trade*, *Panel*,..in mining, a heap of ore dressed and ready for sale. **1881** Raymond *Mining Gloss.*, *Panel.* 1. A heap of dressed ore.

19. (See quot.)

1894 *Northumbld. Gloss.*, *Panels*, the several strata composing a bed of stratified rock: chiefly used with reference to the bands of a limestone, as 'Blue limestone with strong panels'.

20. (See quot.) (A rendering of Fr. *panneau*, perh. never actually in Eng. use: cf. pane *sb.*[1] 5.)

1727–41 Chambers *Cycl.* s.v., Pannel in masonry, denotes one of the faces of a hewn stone.

VI. 21. *attrib.* and *Comb.*, as ***panel-cupboard***, ***-ledge***, ***-maker***, ***-opener***, ***-painting***, ***-picture***, ***-sleeve***; (sense 5 b) ***panel discussion***, ***member***; (sense 5 c) ***panel system***; (sense 14 a) ***panel painter***; ***panel-backed***, ***-bodied***, ***-lined*** adjs.; **panel analysis** *Sociol.*, analysis of attitude changes using the panel technique (see below); **panel-back** *a.*, applied to chairs with panelled backs (see quot. 1925); also *absol.* as *sb.*; **panel-beater**, one whose occupation is beating out the metal panels of motor vehicles; hence ***panel beating***; **panel board** (see quot. 1954); **panel-den** = *panel-house*; **panel doctor**, formerly, a doctor registered as accepting patients under the National Insurance Act of 1913; **panel fence** *U.S.*, a fence constructed in panels or sections (see panel *sb.*[1] 8); **panel fire** = *panel heater*; **panel-furring**, a furring to which the external panels of a railway-carriage are fastened; **panel-game**, (*a*) stealing in a panel-house (*Cent. Dict.* 1890); (*b*) a 'quiz' or similar game played before an audience by a small group of people; hence ***panel gamester***; **panel gauge** (see quot. 1966); **panel heater**, an electrically-heated panel mounted on a wall; hence ***panel-heated*** adj., ***panel heating***; **panel-house**, a brothel in which the walls have sliding panels for the purpose of robbery; **panel patient**, one who received medical treatment from a doctor under the Insurance Act of 1913; **panel pin**, a kind of thin nail, usu. having a tapered head, for securing panels; **panel-plane**, 'a long stocked plane having a handle or toat' (Knight *Dict. Mech.* 1875); **panel-planer**, (*a*) a machine for thinning the edges of panels so as to fit into the grooves in the stiles; (*b*) = *panel-raiser*; **panel practitioner** = *panel doctor*; **panel-raiser**, a machine for forming a raised panel on a board by working away the surrounding surface; **panel-robbery**, the business of a panel-thief; **panel saw**, a fine-toothed saw used for cutting out panels; **panel show** = *panel-game* (b); **panel stamp**, a stamp for decorating the panels in the cover of a book; hence ***panel-stamped*** adj.; **panel-strip**, a strip of wood or metal to cover the joint between a post and a panel or between two panels in a railway-carriage; **panel study** *Sociol.*, an investigation of attitude changes using a constant set of people and comparing each individual's opinions at different points in time; **panel technique** *Sociol.*, the technique used in panel studies; **panel-thief**, a thief in a panel-house; so **panel-thieving** *sb.*; **panel truck** *U.S.*, a small lorry or van with a closed body; **panel-truss**, a truss having timbers or bars arranged in rectangular divisions diagonally braced; **panel van** now *Austral.* = *panel truck*; **panel wall**, (*a*) a division between two panels in a coal mine; (*b*) a wall in a building that does not bear any structural weight; hence ***panel-walled*** adj.; **panel warming**, warming by means of panel heaters; **panel-wheel**, a wheel which cuts a groove with a flat bottom and sloping or bevelled sides. See also panel-work.

1968 *Internat. Encycl. Social Sci.* XI. 371/1 *Panel analysis gives rise to the study of an aspect of social change that tends to be neglected in studies of aggregate trends. **1969** J. J. Linz in Dogan & Rokkan *Quantitative Ecol. Anal. Social Sci.* v. 102 The possibility of using ecological units for a kind of panel analysis of aggregate data to explore problems of change over time. **1904** P. Macquoid *Hist. Eng. Furnit.* ix. 223 The late *panel-back chair..dated 1691. **1925** Penderel-Brodhurst & Layton *Gloss. Eng. Furnit.* 119 *Panel-back or wainscot chair*, a cumbrous high-seated oak chair with heavy legs, stretchers, and high wainscotted back, in use in Tudor and Jacobean times. **1975** *Oxf. Compan. Decorative Arts* 360/2 The panel-back chair (which was also panelled beneath the arms and seat) was to establish for two centuries the standard pattern of the chair with back of square or rectangular shape. *Ibid.* 361/1 Richly upholstered chairs..were found with more refined types of panel-backs. **1908** *Daily Chron.* 21 Feb. 10/7 (Advt.), *Panel beaters, used to hammering landaulette..panels in steel and aluminium. **1973** J. Wainwright *Devil you Don't* 14 The mechanics and panel-beaters working Sunday, double-time. **1978** *Cornish Guardian* 27 Apr. 6/1 (Advt.), Qualified mechanic and/or Panel Beater Sprayer required. **1968** *Gloss. Terms Mechanized & Hand Sheet Metal Work* (*B.S.I.*) 15 **Panel beating*, a method of roughly forming a hollow body, usually by hammer blows. **1972** K. Bonfiglioli *Don't point that Thing at Me* iii. 21 Moishe Spinoza Barzilai is, as a matter of fact, Basil Wayne & Co., the great coach-builders of whom even you, ignorant readers, must have heard, although not point one per cent of you will ever afford his lovely panel-beating, still less his princely upholstery. **1932** *Panel-board [see *corner-block* s.v. corner *sb.*[1] 16]. **1954** *Paper Terminol.* (Spalding & Hodge) 43 *Panel boards*, thick, tough, rigid boards made in various ways... Used in the manufacture of cars and in the building trade. **1972** *Gloss. Terms Timber* (*B.S.I.*) 27 *Panel-board*, fibre building board generally made from wood fibres. **1835** *Court Mag.* VI. 10/2 Mark the perfectly self-complacent air with which he sits in his quiet *pannel-bodied Tilbury. **1895** Clive Holland *Jap. Wife* (ed. 11) 63 She goes to a *panel cupboard, where we keep our..English biscuits. **1860** *Panel-den [see *panel-house*]. **1936** *Panel discussion [see creative *a.* 1 d]. **1956** W. H. Whyte *Organization Man* (1957) 55 It had started conventionally enough with a panel discussion in which I and two other men spoke. **1971** *Archivum Linguisticum* II. 20 A recent investigation of recorded panel discussions has shown that the average length of a unit of intonation used by the ten Present-English speakers involved was 5·3 (institutional) words. **1913** *Punch* 12 Feb. 127/2 To ask the Secretary of the Treasury if he could state the total population of the island of Canna, and who is the *panel doctor. **1932** Kipling *Limits & Renewals* 300 A private party of thirty-two gentlemen and ladies,..all near enough neighbours in Shoreditch to use the same panel-doctor, poured into that man's consulting-room. **1957** R. Hoggart *Uses of Literacy* iii. 63 Working-class people have had years of experience of waiting at labour-exchanges, at the panel doctor's and at hospitals. **1800** W. Tatham *Hist. & Pract. Ess. Tobacco* 10 The *worm* or **pannel* fence,..consists of malled rails. **1858** J. A. Warder *Hedges & Evergreens* 113 A half-acre lot, with a seven foot panel-fence on one side and a hedge on the other. **1949** W. Faulkner *Knight's Gambit* 154 They would ride past mile after mile of white-painted panel fence. **1951** *Southern Folklore Q.* June 130 'Farm Fences'..pictures a panel fence adapted to rocky fields. **1934** *Archit. Rev.* LXXV. 110/1 *Panel fires are less than five years old. **1844** G. Wilkes *Mysteries of Tombs* 54/1, I forgot to mention..that Malinda Hoag was convicted..in robbing a countryman of $54 by the *panel game. **1857** *Porter's Spirit of Times* 5 Dec. 213/3 Females are employed as decoy-ducks to induce the yokels from the rural districts into places of *un*questionable character, where they are sure to be plundered of their money by the panel-game. **1928** Panel game [see creep *sb.* 1 e]. **1953** *Evening News* 2 Jan. 5/3 The first edition of the new TV panel game 'Down You Go' was not an unqualified success. **1957** P. Wildeblood *Main Chance* 55 A singularly witless panel-game in which the contestants, in turn, thought of somebody whom they would like to be and their fellow-panellists had to guess the name. **1971** *Morning Star* 25 June 3/6 The new [radio] shows vary from current affairs, comedy, court dramas, Radio 4's answer to 'World in Action', and panel games. **1976** *Dumfries & Galloway Standard* 25 Dec. 9/3 The weather has continued to play havoc with the football programme and to reduce the 'Pools' to something of a 'panel game'. **1969** *Listener* 6 Sept. 308 Gilbert Harding..brought a compelling viewability to everything he did, whether as *panel-gamester..or television cook and general pundit. **1909** *Cent. Dict.* Suppl., *Panel-gage. **1966** A. W. Lewis *Gloss. Woodworking Terms* 34 *Panel gauge*, marking gauge with a long stem and extra-wide stock for gauging the widths of wide boards. **1936** *Archit. Rev.* LXXIX. 109/2 The library is *panel-heated, the criss-cross net-work of heating tubes being woven round the slots of the skylights. **1951** *Good Housek. Home Encycl.* 11/1 An electric fire..in the form of a *panel heater mounted on the wall. **1928** *Domestic Engin.* XLVIII. 101 (*heading*) The physical and physiological effects of *panel heating. **1848** 'N. Buntline' *Mysteries & Miseries N.Y.* iii. 44 This is a *panel-house and I have led a bad, bad life for many a year. **1860** Bartlett *Dict. Amer.* (ed. 3), *Panel-house*, or *Panel-den*, a house of prostitution and theft combined. **1948** [see lush *sb.*[2] 2]. **1967** *Parade* (Austral.) Oct. 61/3 After that Katie Marks and her gang decided to branch out into the panel-house racket —a brothel equipped with sliding panels which allowed thieves to rifle clients' clothing. **1901** *Academy* 5 Oct. 293/2 On the *panel-ledge stands an unframed sketch. **1591** Percivall *Sp. Dict.*, *Albardero*, a *pannell maker, *Clitellarius.* **1938** *Public Opinion Q.* Oct. 602 A small magazine..which is published expressly for *panel members. **1952** *Radio Times* 15 Aug. 37/2 What makes *What's My Line?* so popular? The personalities of the panel members, certainly. **1975** *Listener* 2 Jan. 21/3 What was spent on running the Arts Council? How many artists sat on your panels: who were they: who were the other panel-members? **1896** *Westm. Gaz.* 24 Oct. 4/1 [A] collection of burglar's tools, including a fine brace and centre-bit, and a 'patent *panel-opener', shaped much like the common or domestic tin-opener, but on a larger scale. **1911** *Encycl. Brit.* XXVI. 405/2 The earlier painters whether illuminators of MSS. or wall and *panel painters. **1937** *Burlington Mag.* Feb. 77/2 The group of Upper Rhenish panel-painters. **1954** M. Rickert *Painting in Brit.: Middle Ages* v. 120 The ability of Matthew Paris as a panel painter. **1890** W. J. GORDON *Foundry* 157 Trucks do not want upholstering or glazing or *panel-painting. **1913** *Outlook* 23 Aug. 247/1 Green tickets such as are used by ordinary *panel patients when temporarily from home. **1924** J. BUCHAN *Three Hostages* i. 12 He would pay three visits a day to a panel patient, which shows the kind of fellow he was. **1950** T. H. MARSHALL *Citizenship & Social Class* 57 The early health service added 'panel patient' to our vocabulary of social class. **1964** A. BRIGGS in S. Nowell-Smith *Edwardian England* ii. 91 Other persons earning less than £160 a year could insure themselves voluntarily and become 'panel patients'. **1977** *Lancet* 8 Oct. 776/1 He took on no panel patients. **1880** LITTLEDALE *Plain Reas.* vii. 16 We should disprove the genuineness of a *panel picture declared to be four hundred years old, if we showed it to be painted on mahogany. **1951** *Good Housek. Home Encycl.* 320/1 Secure the glass.. with a small sprig or *panel pin. **1957** *Practical Wireless* XXXIII. 542/1 Fix the panel to the base with panel pins or small screws. **1960** *Farmer & Stockbreeder* 8 Mar. (Suppl.) 5/2 Take piece P and pin it to the frame with deep-drive panel pins, making sure hole S lines up with the drawer space. **1873** J. RICHARDS *Wood-working Factories* 182 To these standard planes may be added a *panel, plough, and right and left rebate planes. **1914** *Aberdeen Univ. Rev.* Nov. 50 The *Panel practitioner being obliged to provide only what is termed ordinary medical treatment. **1922** *Encycl. Brit.* XXXI. 384/2 Medical men who act as panel practitioners continued to recommend their panel patients to the hospitals in increasing numbers. **1875** KNIGHT *Dict. Mech.* 1602/1 A double-head *panel-raiser, working upon two edges of the board at once. **1882** *Harper's Mag.* Feb. 400/1 Stories designed to teach our girls that theft, and arson, and *panel-robbery.. are the noblest exploits in which they can engage. **1754** *South Carolina Gaz.* 1 Jan. 2/2 Thomas Evance Has just imported.. tenent, *pannel and compass Saws. **1812–16** J. SMITH *Panorama Sc. & Art* I. 106 The pannel-saw.. is used for cutting very thin boards in any direction which may be required. **1825** J. NICHOLSON *Operat. Mechanic* 584 The panel-saw, either for cross-cutting, or cutting very thin boards longitudinally. **1964** W. L. GOODMAN *Hist. Woodworking Tools* 151 The Hand, Panel, and Ripping Saws, ranging from 10 in. to 30 in. **1954** G. MARX *Let.* 16 Aug. (1967) 93 The gibbering idiots on *panel shows, quiz shows, and other half hours of tripe. **1958** M. DICKENS *Man Overboard* vii. 99 That long-lipped ass from the panel show. **1884** *Daily News* 27 Oct. 2/1 The sleeves are of a different material from the other portions... The brocade of which these long *panel sleeves are.. made deserves description. **1893** *Portfolio* XXIV. 55 John Reynes ..often used a large *panel stamp, representing the instruments of the Passion treated as a coat-of-arms. **1961** T. LANDAU *Encycl. Librarianship* (ed. 2) 52/2 Many elaborate panel stamps and roll stamps appear in the 14th and 15th centuries. **1952** J. CARTER *ABC for Bk.-Collectors* 130 **Panel-stamped*, a term used by writers on book-binding to describe leather bindings of the 15th and 16th centuries decorated in blind with engraved blocks. **1958** M. ARGYLE *Relig. Behaviour* iii. 22 *Panel studies in which the same subjects are repeatedly studied while their attitudes are changing. **1963** T. & P. MORRIS *Pentonville* vii. 182 Panel studies by Fiedler and Bass.. indicate that inmate attitudes undergo a kind of cyclical change. **1964** M. ARGYLE *Psychol. & Social Probl.* xiii. 165 Panel studies during election campaigns have shown that there are some individuals who are more likely to change their voting intention than others. **1913** *Act 3 & 4 Geo. V* c. 37 §11 Medical treatment under the *panel system. **1926** *Encycl. Brit.* II. 861 At the time of its initiation the panel system met with great opposition from the medical profession. **1938** *Public Opinion Q.* Oct. 596 Instead of taking a new sample for each poll, repeated interviews with the same group of people have been tried. The experiences met with and the problems involved in such a *panel technique will be discussed here. **1949** R. K. MERTON *Social Theory* I. iii. 107 We may anticipate that the recent introduction of the panel technique—the repeated interviewing of the same group of informants—will in due course more sharply focus the attention of social psychologists upon the theory of attitude formation. **1844** G. WILKES *Mysteries of Tombs* 48/1 Oh, he's a *panel thief. **1860** BARTLETT *Dict. Amer.* (ed. 3), *Panel-thief*, a thief, who ..enters the room by a secret opening, and abstracts [the victim's] money, watch, etc. **1868** M. H. SMITH *Sunshine & Shad. N. York* 306 She was one of the most notorious panel-thieves in New York. **1947** *True* Nov. 69/1 The two lawyers had in addition the business of every free-lance safecracker, forger,.. and panel thief whose business was worth having. **1937** *Panel truck [see *bookmobile* s.v. BOOK *sb.* 19]. **1966** H. KEMELMAN *Saturday Rabbi went Hungry* v. 31 A light panel truck bearing the sign Jackson's Liquor Mart drove up. **1973** *Black World* Jan. 58/1 The panel truck followed. **1976** *CB Mag.* June 40/1 The Army Reserve Sergeant and afternoon soap opera buff suddenly switched on his headlights and churned onto the roadway in pursuit of a panel truck. *a* **1904** *N.E.D.*, *Panel-van. **1969** *Age* (Melbourne) 24 May 60/11 (Advt.), Falcon panel van, 1962 mod[el]. **1977** *Western Morning News* 1 Sept. 6/2 (Advt.), Volkswagen LT 31 Panel Van, white, petrol. **1839** URE *Dict. Arts* 976 Through the *panel walls roads and air-courses are driven. **1962** *Listener* 11 Jan. 64/1 They have shown how sensitively the new and economical materials like concrete frames and panel walls can be handled. **1957** J. KEROUAC *On Road* (1958) I. xi. 64 We had our headquarters in the main building, just a wooden contraption with *panel-walled offices. **1934** *Times* 19 Feb. 20/5 They have got the latest ideas in *panel warming, and the heat required in the type foundry is also supplied by gas. **1707–12** MORTIMER *Husb.* (1721) II. 202 Those Walls which are built *Pannel-wise, with square Pillars at equal distance,.. look much handsomer.

† **'panel**, *sb.*² *Obs.* [Origin obscure: treated by some as a sense of prec.] The fundament or lower part of the alimentary canal of a hawk.

c **1575** *Perf. Bk. Kepinge Sparhawkes* (1886) 7 Meates wᶜʰ endew sonest and maketh the hardest panell are best. *Ibid.* 26 Tokens of Wormes. Strayning sodaynly on the fyste,.. champpinge wᵗ her beake, offeringe her beake ofte to the panell, mutes smotty [etc.]. **1611** COTGR., *Brayeul*, the parts, or feathers, about a hawkes fundament, called by our Faulconers the brayle in a short-wingd, and the pannell in a long-wingd, hauke. **1678** PHILLIPS (ed. 4), *Pannel*, in Faulconry, is the Pipe next to the Fundament of the Hawk, there she digesteth her meat from her body.

panel ('pænəl), *v.* [f. PANEL *sb.*¹]

I. 1. *trans.* To empanel (a jury).

1451 *Paston Lett.* I. 208 The Shereff wille panell gentylmen to aquyte the Lorde, and jowroures to a quyte his men. **1530** PALSGR. 652/1, I panell a quest of men after the lawes of Englande. **1599** MASSINGER, etc. *Old Law* v. i, The jury's panell'd, and the verdict given Ere he appears.

II. 2. *Sc. Law.* To bring to trial; to indict.

1576 *Reg. Privy Council Scot.* Ser. I. II. 567 That the cuntre men arreistit.. may.. certanelie knaw at quhat day to be pannellit. **1660** DICKSON *Serm. Isa.* xli. 14–15 Writ. 1845 I. 138 Thou art a rotten hypocrite, thou hast never pannelled thyself before God's tribunal for sin. **1721** WODROW *Ch. Hist.* III. viii. (1830) IV. 124 Some country women were pannelled for being helpful to the wife of one of the persons alleged to have been concerned. **1814** SCOTT *Wav.* lxvi, He.. was soon to be panelled for his life.

III. †**3.** To furnish (a saddle) with a panel or pad. *Obs. rare.*

1508 *Acc. Ld. High Treas. Scot.* IV. 135 For grathing of foure sadilles, new pannalit.

4. To put a panel on (a beast, esp. a mule or ass); to saddle with a panel.

1530 PALSGR. 652/1 Panell my horse, I wyll ryde to market. **1742** JARVIS *Quix.* I. IV. xlvii. (1885) 257 They ordered him to saddle Rozinante and pannel the ass. **1881** DUFFIELD *Don Quix.* I. 144 Don Quixote.. ordered Sancho to saddle and pannel at once.

IV. 5. To fit or furnish (a room, wall, etc.) with panels; to adorn with panels.

1633 *Wilmslow Churchw. Acc.* in Earwaker *East Cheshire* (1877) I. 108 Paid for pannelling the church in the toppe. **17..** PENNANT (T.), A very handsome bridge, the battlements neatly pannelled with stone. **1823** P. NICHOLSON *Pract. Build.* 192 Where the principal stairs were constructed of wood, it was customary to panel the soffit. **1890** W. J. GORDON *Foundry* 73 We look into the saloon, which the cabinetmakers are panelling with satin-wood.

6. To fit or place as a panel in its frame.

1832 LYTTON *Eugene A.* I. v, A few old pictures were panelled in the open wainscot. **1858** —— *What will he do?* I. vi, Panelled in wood that had once been painted blue.

7. To ornament (a skirt or piece of drapery) with a panel or panels: see PANEL *sb.*¹ 9 d. Also *absol.*

1901 *Westm. Gaz.* 11 July 3/1 A lace flounce might border a skirt of net, or.. the lace might panel a skirt of net. **1908** *Westm. Gaz.* 14 Mar. 13/2 All the gauzy fabrics will panel well.

8. *Telegr.* To arrange (wires) in parallels.

1890 in *Cent. Dict.*

panel, dial. form of PARNEL.

†**panele.** *Obs.* Also 6–7 **panell, pannel**, 7–8 **penele**, 8 **paneel, panial.** [a. Sp. *panela*; cf. Ger. *panelle*.] Brown unpurified sugar from the Antilles.

1562 BULLEYN *Bk. Simples* 72 Although Suger can not bee simply made, from the panell, or sande whiche cometh from the Cane. **1592** in *Acts Privy Council* N.S. XXII. 465, 9 chests of sugar muscovathes.. 10 chests of sugar pannels. **1657** R. LIGON *Barbadoes* (1673) 91 They make Peneles, a kind of Sugar somewhat inferiour to the Muscavado. **1712** tr. *Pomet's Hist. Drugs* I. 56 A Sort of duskish, pale-grey Sugar called Paneels. **1740** *Hist. Jamaica* 229 Muscovadoes and Panial Sugar, 6*s.* per Hundred. **1774** *Ann. Reg.* 215/1 Molasses, syrups, paneles,.. from the British plantations.

paneless ('peɪnlɪs), *a.* [f. PANE *sb.*¹ + -LESS.] Of a window: Having no panes, lacking panes.

a **1763** SHENSTONE *Economy* III. 111 The shifts enormous that in vain he forms To patch his paneless window. **1886** W. J. TUCKER *E. Europe* 220 To keep out the cold by fastening our towels securely across the paneless window.

panellation (pænə'leɪʃən). [n. of action f. med. (Anglo-) L. *pannellāre*, f. *pannellus* PANEL *sb.*¹ 4, 5.] The empanelling of a jury.

a **1695** WOOD *Hist. Univ. Oxf.* (1796) II. 9 They in the said pannellation did put Rich. Wotton.. and other privileged persons, which were not wont anciently to be impannelled. **1848** in WHARTON *Law Lex.*

panelled, paneled ('pænəld), *ppl. a.* [f. PANEL *v.* + -ED.]

1. *Sc. Law.* Brought to the bar, put on trial.

1636 W. SCOT *Apol. Narr.* (1846) 153 Many were unknown to the pannelled.

2. Fitted or made with panels: divided into panels or decorative compartments.

1760–72 H. BROOKE *Fool of Qual.* (1809) IV. 123 A folding door of pannelled looking-glass. **1819** SHELLEY *Lett.* Pr. Wks. 1888 II. 285 Within this arch are two panelled alto relievos. **1902** BESANT *Five Yrs.' Tryst* 95 The dark panelled old room that they called Oliver Cromwell's Library.

panelling, paneling ('pænəlɪŋ). [f. PANEL *sb.* + -ING¹.]

1. Wood or other material made into panels, panels collectively, panel-work.

1824 SCOTT *Redgauntlet* ch. v, The very old wainscot which composed the floor and the panelling of the room. **1851** LAYARD *Pop. Acc. Discov. Nineveh* xiii. 343 This alabaster, cut into slabs, served as a kind of panelling to the walls of sun-dried bricks. **1875** W. S. HAYWARD *Love agst. World* 1 The oak paneling, of a sombre but rich brown.

2. *Mining.* (See PANEL *sb.*¹ 11.)

1900 *Daily News* 26 Nov. 2/1 Ground.. opened out and drained preparatory for panelling.

panellist ('pænəlɪst). Also (chiefly *U.S.*) **panelist.** [f. PANEL *sb.*¹ 5 b + -IST.] **a.** A panel doctor. **b.** A member of a discussion panel, committee, group of judges, etc., esp. one taking part in a radio or television progamme.

1937 G. FRANKAU *More of Us* 14 Alas! Came dawn when local panelist Pronounced Jack's Ladye Alice a cadaver. **1952** *N.Y. Times* 14 June 13 Bennett Cerf.. television panelist and anthologist, has compiled another book of humor. **1955** *Picture Post* 14 May 10/3 This programme concludes with a gay, exciting parlour variation on musical chairs, in which the panellists exchange faces. **1958** K. AMIS *I like it Here* iii. 36 Bowen.. had something of the air of a television panellist. **1958** *New Statesman* 19 Apr. 501/1 A member of the audience has a go first; the panellists comment on what he has said; and he has a final brief right of reply. **1959** *Encounter* Dec. 52/1 The panelists at the Socialist meeting. **1971** C. FICK *Danziger Transcript* (1973) 131, I picked up a few bucks being a panelist on one of those Sunday political shows on TV. **1974** H. L. FOSTER *Ribbin'* vii. 316 Panel presentations were followed by ten small group meetings with panelists, former addicts and parents of addicts leading discussions. **1976** *Nature* 15 Apr. 633/2 Indeed the effect at the lower concentration of bitterness investigated was so marked that four out of the five panellists could detect no bitterness at all after presaturation of their tongues with sucrose.

'panel-work.

1. Work in wood, stone, etc., consisting of or containing panels; *esp.* panelled woodwork.

1874 PARKER *Gothic Archit.* I. vi. 195 The windows frequently appear to be only openings in the panel-work. **1886** WILLIS & CLARK *Cambridge* II. 510 The spaces between the windows.. are decorated with panelwork.

2. The working of a mine by division into panels.

1847 E. CRESY *Encycl. Civ. Eng.* I. 695 Panel work was introduced, fifty years ago. [See PANEL *sb.*¹ 11.] **1882** GALLOWAY *Hist. Coal Mining* xv. 149 Panel-work.. was first introduced [at Wallsend] in the year 1810.

So **panel-working.**

1883 GRESLEY *Gloss. Coal-mining*, *Panel-working*, a system of working coal seams.. in the North of England.

‖**panem et circenses** ('pænɛm ɛt sɜː'kɛnziːz). [L.] = *bread and circuses* (BREAD *sb.* 2 g).

1787 P. H. MATY tr. *Riesbeck's Trav. Germany* I. xxvi. 303 Every thing here cries out *panem et circenses*, and the multitude seem to have no other wishes than to have their paunches well filled, and a theatrical entertainment by way of dessert. **1864** C. M. YONGE *Bk. Golden Deeds* 100 Their [*sc.* the Romans'] cry was that they wanted *panem ac Circenses*. **1903** G. B. SHAW *Man & Superman* p. xxiv, At this moment the Roman decadent phase of *panem et circenses* is being inaugurated under our eyes. **1928** D. H. LAWRENCE *Lady Chatterley* xiii. 219 The masses are unalterable... Panem et circenses! **1961** D. L. MUNBY *God & Rich Society* iii. 61 Leaders who.. win votes by offering *panem et circenses* to those they despise. **1966** *Listener* 29 Sept. 458/2 Sir Joseph Hutchinson is concerned with the provision of *panem*, but what of *circenses* for a *populus* with vast leisure time created by cybernation?

panemye: see PAYNIMY *Obs.*

panence, obs. f. PENANCE.

panentheism, pan-eulogism: see PAN- 2.

paner, -ere, obs. ff. PANNIER.

panes, obs. f. *pence*, pl. of PENNY.

panetela, var. PANATELA.

paneter, -tre, -trie, obs. ff. PANTER *sb.*¹, PANTRY.

Paneth ('pænɛθ). *Histology.* The name of Joseph *Paneth* (1857–90), Austrian physiologist, used *attrib.*, in the possessive, and with *of* to designate a secretory cell present at the base of the crypts of Lieberkühn in the small intestine, and also the eosinophilic granules characteristic of their cytoplasm.

1899 *Veterinarian* LXXII. 555 These granular cells of Paneth showed the same reaction, and I was forced to conclude that they were mucus-forming. *Ibid.* 560 The cytoplasm in some instances has been observed to contain granules—Paneth's granules. **1938** *Gray's Anat.* (ed. 27) 1329 The deeper cells, especially in the duodenal glands, contain granules which stain characteristically with phosphotungstic haematoxylin and are termed granules of Paneth. **1968** PASSMORE & ROBSON *Compan. Med. Stud.* I. xxx. 21/1 There are only about a dozen Paneth cells in each crypt, but because of the enormous number of crypts the total mass of Paneth cells is large. **1976** *Cell & Tissue Kinetics* IX. 72 The number and localization of Paneth cells was not affected by changes in crypt cell kinetics during recovery after irradiation.

‖**panettone** (panet'tone). Also **panetone.** Pl. **pane'ttoni.** [It.] A rich Italian bread made with eggs, fruit, and butter.

1922 D. H. LAWRENCE *Aaron's Rod* xvii. 251 He shoved a lump of cake—or rather panetone, good currant loaf—through the window, with a knife to cut it. **1938** JOYCE *Let.* 20 Apr. (1966) III. 420, I spent all Easter Day with Lucia, ..eating *panettoni di Milano* and fooling generally. **1967** *Economist* 28 Oct. 450/3 Motta's success is inevitably connected to 'panettone', a traditional Milanese Christmas cake. Owing to Motta's successful marketing of this one hand-made product, 'panettone' is now all over Italy, the recognised symbol of Christmas, perhaps even more so than the Christmas tree and the crib. **1969** R. & D. DE SOLA *Dict. Cooking* 167/1 *Panettone*: (Italian—a kind of cake bread).

Often orange flavoured and raisin filled. **1972** L. O'DONNELL *Phone Calls* iv. 48 She..pushed forward a plate on which there was a high glossy cake with only one slice cut out of it. 'Please, have some *panetone*. Is very good—.' **1978** *Nieman-Marcus Christmas Bk.* 91 From Italy, the traditional semi-sweet panettone..bread studded with candied fruits and nuts.

pan-Euroˈpean, *a.* [f. PAN- + EUROPEAN *a.*] Pertaining to, affecting, or extending over the whole of Europe. Hence **pan-Euroˈpeanism.**

1901 CONRAD & HUEFFER *Inheritors* viii. 117 There was an 'All Round the World Cable Company'.., and a 'Pan-European Railway, Exploration, and Civilization Company' that let in light in dark places. **1931** *Ann. Reg. 1930* 172 This same trend in Italian policy was also manifested in Italy's reply to M. Briand's 'Pan-European' proposal in the course of which the Fascist Government declared its disagreement with any scheme of this kind which excluded Turkey and Russia. **1942** L. B. NAMIER *Conflicts* 2 The two great nations of Central Europe..burdened with Pan-European past..remained in a condition of political disunion and dynastic subdivision. **1961** *Guardian* 9 June 8/6 The later Pan-Europeanism of this loneliest of poets [*sc.* Rilke]. **1966** *New Statesman* 14 Oct. 540/2 This journal repeatedly emphasised that the famous breeze of European competition, or the large accumulations of capital open to pan-European industries, were no substitute for a successful socialist economy. **1979** *Daily Tel.* 20 Jan. 16/6 The new flowers..have been put through their paces under the Fleuroselect scheme which is run by a pan-European organisation for testing them.., with a secretariat in The Hague.

panewes, -ȝes, obs. ff. *pennies*, pl. of PENNY.

panfan (ˈpænfæn). *Geomorphol.* [f. PAN- + FAN *sb.*[1]] = PEDIPLAIN.

1915 A. C. LAWSON in *Univ. California Publ. Geol.* IX. III. 33 The surface thus evolved is, in its ideal completion, wholly one of aggradation, a vast alluvial fan surface to which for convenience in discussion I propose to give the name *panfan*. **1931** *Jrnl. Geol.* XXXIX. 138 Pediments are essentially compound graded flood plains excavated by ephemeral streams. As their growth corrodes the mountain mass they eventually coalesce to form smooth graded domes to which Lawson applied the term 'panfan'..—a name that is etymologically unfortunate because these features are not concerned with alluvial fans at all. **1933** *Geol. Mag.* LXX. 345 The rock-floors of the desert, known as pediments and panfans. **1954** W. D. THORNBURY *Princ. Geomorphol.* xi. 291 Lawson (1915) proposed the term *panfan* to designate 'an end stage in the process of geomorphic development in an arid region in the same sense that the peneplain is an end stage of the general process of degradation in a humid climate'. He also recognized that both peneplains and panfans represent penultimate rather than ultimate stages of degradation. **1974** [see PEDIPLAIN].

ˈpanfish. *U.S.* [f. PAN *sb.*[1] + FISH *sb.*[1]]

1. A fish suitable for frying whole in a pan.

1833 J. F. WATSON *Hist. Tales Philad.* 49 Before the house flows a small but deep creek, abounding in pan-fish. **1838** J. F. COOPER *Home as Found* II. v. 71 The Egyptians use them as a pan-fish. **1852** *Trans. Mich. Agric. Soc.* III. 226 These little fish are sometimes used as pan-fish. **1888** G. B. GOODE *Amer. Fishes* 36 In season the White Perch is *the* pan-fish, excelled by none. **1894** *Outing* (U.S.) XXIII. 403/2 The cat-fish, also a good pan-fish. **1899** B. W. GREEN *Virginia Word-bk.* **1969** R. & D. DE SOLA *Dict. Cooking* 167/1 *Panfish*, any fish suitable for frying, usually hand-caught fish like sunfish or catfish. **1970** *Globe & Mail* (Toronto) 26 Sept. 40/5 In addition to the ancestral stock of Atlantic salmon, Lavalee Lake holds bass, pan fish.

2. A name for the king-crab (*Limulus*), from its supposed resemblance to a saucepan. (*Cent. Dict.*)

panfry (ˈpænfraɪ), *v.* Chiefly *N. Amer.* [f. PAN *sb.*[1] + FRY *v.*[1]] *trans.* and *intr.* To fry in a pan with shallow fat. Also *transf.* So **ˈpanfried** *ppl. a.*

1942 M. K. RAWLINGS *Cross Creek Cookery* Pan-Fried Young Quail or Dove. **1957** J. KEROUAC *On Road* (1958) x. 174 That pan-fried chow mein flavored air. **1973** *Sat. Rev. World* (U.S.) 18 Dec. 48/3 It [*sc.* the Kahala's Maile Room] imports filets of trevally from New Zealand..and panfries them with tomatoes. **1974** *Globe & Mail* (Toronto) 20 Mar. 35/1 Ling or freshwater cod can be cooked in a variety of ways—the simplest being to panfry. **1976** *Woman's Day* (N.Y.) Nov. 104 Panfried liver and onions. **1977** *N.Z. Jrnl. Agric.* Jan. 63/1 Grill or pan-fry the bacon.

panful (ˈpænfʊl). [f. PAN *sb.*[1] + -FUL.] The quantity that fills a pan.

1874 RAYMOND *Statist. Mines & Mining* 319, I preferred to calculate upon the result of 40 panfuls worked by rocker. **1887** I. R. *Lady's Ranche Life Montana* 167, I often used to take a panful of salt, and get the whole band round me. **1894** *Outing* (U.S.) XXIII. 356/2 A panful of water.

pang (pæŋ), *sb.*[1] Also 6–7 **pangue.** [*Pang*, sb. and vb., are known only after 1500, the vb. being exemplified first (which may be accidental). Origin uncertain.

It has been suggested that *pang* sb. was a phonetically-lightened variant of an earlier *prang* (cf. *speech*, OE. *spræc*, where however *three* consonants came together), and thus identical with a word occurring twice as *pronge a* 1450, and once as *prange c* 1530, app. in the same sense as *pang*: see below. These have naturally been viewed as fig. uses of PRONG *sb.*, a stabbing or piercing point; the difficulty is that this has not been found in the literal sense till much later (1567), and is not frequent before 1600.

1447 BOKENHAM *Seyntys* (Roxb.) 151 As thow the prongys of deth dede streyn Here hert root. *a***1450** *Cov. Myst.* (Shaks. Soc.) 287 These prongys myn herte asondyr thei do rende. *c***1530** *Crt. of Love* 1150 The prange of loue so straineth them to crie.]

1. A brief keen spasm of pain which appears suddenly to pierce or shoot through the body or any part of it; a shooting pain.

In 16th c. chiefly in 'pangs of death'; also 'of childbirth'.

1526 *Pilgr. Perf.* (W. de W. 1531) 242 b, In the pange & distresse of deth. **1530** PALSGR. 251/2 Panges of dethe, *les traictz de mort.* *a***1548** HALL *Chron., Edw. IV* 250 The pangues and fittes of his sickenes. *c***1586** C'TESS PEMBROKE *Ps.* XLVIII. ii, The wife, whose wofull care The panges of child bed findes. **1601** F. GODWIN *Bps. of Eng.* 338 This man being very olde, died in a pang. **1603** SHAKS. *Meas. for M.* III. i. 80 The poore Beetle that we treade vpon In corporall sufferance, finds a pang as great, As when a Giant dies. **1609** BIBLE (Douay) *2 Kings* xxii. 5 The pangues of death have compassed me. **1611** BIBLE *Isa.* xxvi. 17 Like as a woman with childe..is in paine, and cryeth out in her pangs. **1709** STEELE *Tatler* No. 27 ¶2 The Man in the Pangs of the Stone, Gout, or any acute Distemper. **1833** HT. MARTINEAU *Cinnamon & Pearls* vii. 118 The pang which shot through her yesterday. **1851** CARPENTER *Man. Phys.* (ed. 2) 288 The attempt to allay the pangs of hunger by filling the stomach with non-nutritious substances.

2. *fig.* A sudden sharp mental pain or feeling of intense mental anguish.

1570 DEE *Math. Pref.* 1, I am in no little pang of perplexitie. **1590** SPENSER *F.Q.* II. i. 48 The bitter pangs that doth your heart infest. **1601** SHAKS. *Twel. N.* II. iv. 94 Say that some Lady..Hath for your loue as great a pang of heart As you haue for Oliuia. **1687** DRYDEN *Hind & P.* III. 287 O sharp convulsive pangs of agonizing pride! **1749** SMOLLETT *Regicide* I. iii, Keen are the pangs Of hapless love. **1808** SCOTT *Marm.* III. xiii, High minds, of native pride or force, Most deeply feel thy pangs, Remorse! **1877** BLACK *Green Past.* xxxviii. (1878) 303 Cheerfully and without a pang sacrifice the dollars you have paid.

†**3.** A sudden access of keen feeling or emotion of any kind; a sudden transitory fit. *Obs.*

1542 UDALL *Erasm. Apoph.* 117 b, This pangue or guierie of love dooeth especially..invade & possesse suche persones. **1548** UDALL, etc. *Erasm. Par. Luke* iv. 54 There bee in vs certayne affeccionate pangues of nature, whiche we are not able to cast awaye from vs. **1565** JEWEL *Def. Apol.* Wks. (Parker Soc.) III. 392 O, what a merry pang was this, M. Harding! **1642** ROGERS *Naaman* 6 Only to amuse their minds, and stirre up pangs of affection. **1643** TRAPP *Comm. Gen.* xix. 32 [He] does that in a drunken pang. **1693** *Humours Town* 138 Among their Fits of Devotion they shall have such Amorous Pangs for Heav'n, that one wou'd think [etc.]. *a***1694** TILLOTSON *Serm.* (1743) VIII. 3417 Galen..when he had anatomized man's body, and carefully surveyed the frame of it..fell into a pang of devotion and wrote a hymn to his Creator.

pang (pæŋ), *sb.*[2] [Echoic.] Vocal imitation of a short, resonant sound, such as that produced by a drum, a horse's hoof, etc.; a sound of this character.

1925 E. SITWELL *Troy Park* 65 As the hoofèd sound of a drum marched on With a pang like darkness. **1955** E. POUND *Classic Anthol.* III. 188 Every man eager to pace the stallions, 'Pang, pang' and Rein bells chink. **1958** L. DURRELL *Mountolive* vii. 144 There were two excellent hard courts which rang all day to the pang of racquets. **1958** —— *Balthazar* vii. 155 The tattling flutes and the pang of drums.

pang (pæŋ), *a. Sc.* [cf. PANG *v.*[2]] Packed tight, stuffed, crammed. Also *pang-full*.

*c***1560** A. SCOTT *Poems* (S.T.S.) ii. 178 Thair avairis fyld vp all the feild, Thay wer so fow and pang With drafe. **1807** RUICKBIE *Wayside Cottager* 110 (E.D.D.) The bench is fill'd, the house is pang. **1895** CROCKETT *Men of Moss Hags* 367 A rude man, and pang full of oaths.

b. Tight, compactly framed.

1813 HOGG *Queen's Wake* (1871) 27 Sae pang was our pearily prow Quhan we cudna speil the brow of the wavis We needilit them through below.

pang (pæŋ), *v.*[1] Now *rare.* [See PANG *sb.*[1]] *trans.* To afflict with pangs; to pierce or penetrate with acute physical or mental pain. Also *absol.*

*c***1502** *Joseph Arim.* (E.E.T.S.) 47/323 His chylde in the pestylence was in Ieopardy, And sore panged. *a***1529** SKELTON *P. Sparowe* 44 What heuynesse dyd me pange. *a***1548** HALL *Chron., Hen. VII* 3 b, By the tormentyng..of which sicknes, men were so..peynfully pangèd. **1598** FLORIO, *Accorare*, to pang or pinch at the hart. **1613** SHAKS. *Hen. VIII*, II. iii. 15 'Tis a sufferance, panging As soule and bodies seuering. **1748** SMOLLETT *Rod. Rand.* (1817) II. lii. 177 The news of your misfortune panged me to the very intrails. **1838** *Fraser's Mag.* XVIII. 531 May the mortal stroke Be balanced well, and pang not.

†**b.** To move by any sudden feeling. *Obs.*

1613 PURCHAS *Pilgrimage* (1614) 526 Heere the kinde-hearted Iesuit is panged with a fit of Charitie to yoke the Lutherans with them.

Hence **ˈpanged** *ppl. a.*, **ˈpanging** *vbl. sb.*

1827 HOOD *Mids. Fairies* lxxviii, Like a pang'd nightingale, it made him pause. **1876** C. WELLS *Joseph & Brethren* I. vi, But he is dead, and I am left to mourn, And tire on pangèd recollection. **1863** LD. LYTTON *Ring Amasis* I. I. II. ii. 124 Never shall the panging of your spirits be at rest.

pang (pæŋ), *v.*[2] *Sc.* and *north. dial.* [Origin uncertain: perhaps onomatopœic.

Identity with Goth. *praggan*, i.e. *prangan* to press, with loss of *r*, has been suggested.]

trans. To pack tight, fill by pressure, stuff, cram.

1637 RUTHERFORD *Lett.* 14 July (1671) 9 Hell will be empty..and heaven panged full. **1718** RAMSAY *Christ's Kirk Gr.* III. iii, As fou 's the house could pang. **1785** BURNS *Holy Fair* xix, It pangs us fou o' Knowledge. **1814** SCOTT *Wav.* lxiv, The auld gudeman o' Corse-Cleugh has panged it wi' a kemple o' strae amaist. **1825** BROCKETT *N.C. Gloss.*, *Pang*, to fill, or stuff. **1899** *Speaker* 4 Feb. 157 Men whose minds are panged with the lore of old Scotland.

panga[1] (ˈpɑːŋgə). Also **ponga, pongo.** [a. Amer. Sp. *panga* a boat.] A flat-bottomed boat with rising stem and stern.

1927 G. BRADFORD *Gloss. Sea Terms* 124/2 *Panga*, a flat-bottomed rowboat of Central America. **1948** R. DE KERCHOVE *Internat. Maritime Dict.* 517/1 *Panga*, a dug-out canoe from Panama, double-ended with rising stem and stern. These craft are about 18 ft. long by 4 ft. 6 in. wide and are cut out of one cedar log. **1970** *National Fisherman* Jan. 18B/4 The chaser-skiffs, also called speed-boats or pongos, are lowered overboard. **1971** *Islander* (Victoria, B.C.) 4 July 15/3 The reds and greens and yellows of the double-ended pongas which the lobster and bonito fishermen took far out to sea. **1978** *Daily Colonist* (Victoria, B.C.) 7 May 17/2 We haul anchor as soon as the ship-to-shore shuttle, called a panga, brings aboard the last of our cruise-mates.

panga[2] (ˈpæŋgə). [Swahili.] A large knife used in Africa either as an implement or as a weapon. Also *attrib.*

1935 E. HEMINGWAY *Green Hills Afr.* (1936) IV. i. 216 Chopping our way through with the long brush knives that are called pangas. **1952** *Time* 3 Nov. 36 Once pooh-poohed as mere 'press exaggeration', the Mau Mau have already mutilated scores of whites and 'loyal' blacks, with their favorite weapon, the *panga*—a long, machete-like knife. *Ibid.* 10 Nov. 38/3 On the front of the governor's car waved his official flag: two crossed *pangas* (broad-bladed African knives used to chop bananas). The *pangas* seemed symbolic last week, for Kenya Colony, the brightest jewel in Britain's East African Empire, is bleeding badly in a *panga* war. **1953** *Ibid.* 12 Jan. 26/1 There was a noise at the door, a shout, and a gang of Mau Mau thugs, led by the ranch's male cook, burst into the living room, brandishing *panga* knives. **1953** *Newsweek* 6 Apr. 38/3 As the villagers ran from their blazing homes, waiting Mau Maus struck them down with *pangas* (long knives) and hatchets. **1954** D. H. RAWCLIFFE *Struggle for Kenya* ix. 86 The isolated loyalist groups in the reserves ..were still armed with little more than *pangas* and spears. **1955** O. MEEKER *Report on Afr.* xii. 199 But until I reached Kenya no-one said a word about the Mau Mau terrorists, secret society oaths, the long knives called *pangas*, or the other Kikuyu specialities. **1964** C. WILLOCK *Enormous Zoo* viii. 138 African butchers sharpened their pangas on stone. **1969** *Daily Tel.* 28 Oct. 16 An African Presbyterian Minister was killed by a panga gang for refusing to take Kikuyu tribal oaths. **1972** J. MCCLURE *Caterpillar Cop* iii. 34 'I hear the murder was sometime around six.'.. 'Usual bit of passion and panga.' **1976** *Maclean's Mag.* 6 Sept. 51/2 Zulu mobs rampaged through Soweto armed with pangas (cane cutters), axes, spears, and knives. **1976** *Survey* Summer-Autumn 303 Forest fighters had..often only the ordinary rural blade of East Africa, the *panga*. **1977** D. BEATY *Excellency* xii. 139 The soldiers had taken out panga knives and were cutting down thorn bush and scrub.

Pangæa (pænˈdʒiːə). *Geol.* [f. PAN- + Gr. γαῖα land, earth.

The name is freq. stated to have been coined by A. Wegener 1914, in *Die Entstehung der Kontinente und Ozeane*, but it has not been found in the 1st ed. of that book (actually published in 1915); *Pangäa* does occur in ed. 2 (1920), p. 120, but with no indication that Wegener is coining it.]

A vast continental area or supercontinent comprising all the continental crust of the earth which is postulated to have existed in late Palæozoic or Mesozoic times before breaking up into Gondwanaland and Laurasia.

1924 J. G. A. SKERL tr. *Wegener's Orig. Continents & Oceans* xiii. 192 Thus the Pangæa of the Carboniferous era had already an anterior margin (America), which became folded (Precordilleras)..; and a posterior margin (Asia), from which littoral ranges and fragments became detached, and remained fast in the sima of the Pacific as groups of islands. **1928** C. SCHUCHERT in *Theory Continental Drift* (Amer. Assoc. Petroleum Geol.) 106 The rifting of Pangaea and the floating away of Australasia, Antarctica, and the Americas are said to have begun east of Africa in Jurassic time and west of Euro-Africa in early Cretaceous time. **1958** *Continental Drift* (Tasmania Univ. Geol. Dept.) 177 Apart from the dissociation of Pangaea into independent Laurasia and Gondwana, the fundamental picture is much as Wegener saw it. **1971** I. G. GASS et al. *Understanding Earth* xv. 230/2 Before the Pangaea of Permo-Triassic time was formed, one must envisage a different mosaic of continental fragments reassembled in a different way. **1974** *Sci. Amer.* Apr. 81/1 Ancient ocean currents in the vicinity of Pangaea, the single 'supercontinent' that is believed to have existed near the beginning of the Triassic period some 225 million years ago, are indicated here. **1977** *Ibid.* Mar. 92/3 About 600 million or perhaps one billion years ago the ancestors of all the present continents were evidently combined into one immense supercontinent, named Pangaea, which may have come into existence as much as 2.7 billion years ago.

Pangan (ˈpæŋgən). [Malay, = 'forest country'.] = NEGRITO.

1839 T. J. NEWBOLD *Pol. & Statistical Acct. Straits of Malacca* II. v. 60 In the interior of Pakaa, an aboriginal race is said to exist, termed Pangan. **1929** A. CHAMBERS tr. *Schebesta's Among Forest Dwarfs Malaya* v. 162 From the Malays in Tadoh I first heard the word *Pangan*. This was the name they gave to the Orang-Utan tribes. **1947** R. O. WINSTEDT *Malays* 8 The oldest of Malaya's existing races anthropologically is the Negrito, termed Semang in Perak and Pangan in Kelantan. **1965** R. MCKIE *Company of Animals* i. 35 Pangans had been digging with fire-hardened sticks for tubers, and later we found one of the small camps of these jungle aborigines.

Pangasinan (pɑːŋgɑːsiːˈnɑːn). Pl. **Pangasinans, Pangasinanes.** [Native name.]

a. (A member of) a people inhabiting the central area of the Luzon district of the Republic of the Philippines. **b.** The Austronesian language of this people.

1840 [see ILOCANO]. **1885** [see IBANAG *sb.* and *a.*]. **1948** D. DIRINGER *Alphabet* vii. 432 The other important vernaculars spoken by the Filipinos are: (1) Pangasinan, [etc.]. **1954** PEI & GAYNOR *Dict. Linguistics* 158 *Pangasinan*, a language spoken in the Philippine Islands by almost 400,000 persons; a member of the Indonesian sub-family of the Malayo-Polynesian family of languages. **1964** E. BACH *Introd. Transformational Gram.* v. 89 Some languages that have been worked on from this point of view.. are English, .. Pangasinan. **1974** *Encycl. Brit. Micropædia* VII. 717/2 *Pangasinan*, eighth largest cultural-linguistic group in the Republic of the Philippines. They occupy the central area of the province of Pangasinan in Luzon.

pangene (pæn'dʒiːn). *Biol.* Also **pangen.** [f. Gr. παν- all + stem of γένος race, offspring, γεν- to beget: cf. next.] De Vries's name for a (supposed) primary constituent unit of a germ-cell.

1899 J. A. THOMSON *Sci. Life* xi. 146 The theory of 'Pangenes' advocated by De Vries in 1889.. incorporates the distinctively modern conception of germinal continuity. *Ibid.* 153 To these hypothetical units numerous names have been given—biophors, pangenes, idiosomes [etc.].

pangenesis (pæn'dʒɛnɪsɪs). *Biol.* [f. Gr. παν-, PAN- all + γένεσις birth: see -GENESIS.] The name given by Darwin to his hypothesis, advanced to explain the phenomena of heredity, that every separate unit or cell of an organism reproduces itself by contributing its share to the germ or bud of the future off-spring. See quot. 1868.

1868 DARWIN *Anim. & Pl.* II. 359, I venture to advance the hypothesis of *Pangenesis*, which implies that the whole organization, in the sense of every separate atom or unit, reproduces itself. Hence ovules and pollen-grains—the fertilized seed or egg, as well as buds—include or consist of a multitude of germs thrown off from each separate atom of the organism. **1869** F. GALTON *Hered. Genius* 363. **1870** TYNDALL *Sci. Use Imag.* in *Lect. & Ess.* (1903) 72/2 He [Mr. Darwin] has drawn heavily upon time in his development of species, and he has drawn adventurously upon matter in his theory of pangenesis. According to this theory, a germ, already microscopic, is a world of minor germs. **1877** HUXLEY *Anat. Inv. Anim.* i. 40. **1892** J. A. THOMSON *Outlines Zool.* 65 This hypothesis has been repeatedly modified, but, except in the general sense that the body may influence its reproductive cells, 'pangenesis' is discredited by most biologists.

b. ***intracellular pangenesis***: see quot.

1900 GOULD *Dict. Med. Biol.*, *Intracellular Pangenesis*, the origin of ultimate vital principles (pangenes, gemmules, biophors) within the cell.

pange'netic, *a.* [See prec. and -GENETIC.] Of or pertaining to pangenesis: see quot.

1875 *Contemp. Rev.* XXVII. 90 We cannot understand how colloid bodies, such as the Pangenetic gemmules must be, could pass freely through membranes. **1899** THOMSON *Sci. Life* xvi. 217 Maupertuis.. distinctly stated a pangenetic theory of heredity.

Hence **pange'netically** *adv.*

1890 C. L. MORGAN *Anim. Life & Intell.* (1891) 134 [It] is (pangenetically) due to the fact that it takes some time for the modified gemmules to accumulate.

pan'genic, *a.* = PANGENETIC.

1900 *Brit. Med. Jrnl.* No. 2046. 636 The one [point of view] was known as the 'pangenic theory' of Darwin.

pangeometry (pændʒiː'ɒmɪtrɪ). [f. PAN- all + GEOMETRY.] Geometry extended to space of more than three dimensions; universal geometry. So **pan'geometer; ˌpangeo'metrical** *a.*

1882 J. B. STALLO *Concepts Mod. Physics* 216 The peculiar tenets of pangeometry. *Ibid.* (1883) 214 The pangeometers erect a transcendental structure on empirical foundations. *Ibid.* 208 *note*, The connection of Gauss's metageometrical or (to use the expression of Lobatschewski) pangeometrical views with his investigations respecting the geometrical interpretation of imaginary quantities.

pangeran (pæŋgə'ræn). Also **pangarang.** [Malay.] A Malay prince or noble.

1817 T. S. RAFFLES *Hist. Java* I. ii. 79 His [*sc.* the sovereign's] family are called *Pang' érans.* **1821** J. LEYDEN tr. *Malay Annals* viii. 272 The pangeran of Surabaya.. came to Malaca. **1831** *Canton Miscellany* II. 79 The Princes or Pangarangs who were seated on chairs walked with us. **1900** CONRAD *Ld. Jim* xx. 219 He came into the Council-hall where all the rajahs, pangerans, and head-men were assembled, with the queen,.. reclining on a high couch under a canopy.

pan-German (pæn'dʒɜːmən), *a.* and *sb.* [f. PAN- 1 + GERMAN: cf. Ger. *Alldeutscher.*]

A. *adj.* Of or pertaining to all Germans, or to the union of all Germans in one political state.

1892 *Daily News* 27 Feb. 5/2 The present difficulty is not Prussian merely; it is Pan-German. The riots in Vienna are just as serious as those in Berlin. **1902** *Q. Rev.* July 155 The Pan-German ideal, as presented by the lyric poets of the Liberation. *Ibid.* 160 The Pan-German League.. was founded in 1894.

B. *sb.* An advocate of pan-Germanism.

1899 *Daily News* 26 Oct. 3/4 The Pan-Germans and Anti-Semites at Hamburg. **1901** *Scotsman* 28 Feb. 7/5 The radical Czechs, by making speeches in their own tongue, caused the Pan-Germans to raise a protest.

So **pan-Ger'manic** *a.*, pan-German; **pan-'Germanism,** the notion or principle of the comprehension of all German peoples in an extended Germany; **pan-'Germany,** a Germany including all German peoples.

1900 tr. *von Bülow* in *Westm. Gaz.* 13 Dec. 2/2 There are laurels of higher worth than those which the Pan-Germanic League has to bestow. **1882** *Times* 30 Mar. 5/4 The Clericals .. will no more tolerate Pan-germanism than the Poles Pan-slavism. **1882** *Echo* 29 Aug. 1/5 In order to oppose and neutralize the advancing aggression of 'Pan-Germanism'. **1902** *Q. Rev.* July 152 It is only quite recently that the term *Alldeutschtum* was coined.. or the foreign equivalent Pan-Germanism.. supplied. *Ibid.* 161 What the Pan-German League wants is.. a 'Greater Germany', or as the exponents of this idea would say, a 'Pan-Germany'.

pan-'Germanist. [f. PAN-GERMAN *a.* and *sb.* + -IST.] A supporter of pan-Germanism. Also *attrib.*

1909 *Daily Chron.* 25 June 4/6 A racing yacht devised, built, and.. manned in Germany—an object of idolatry.. to the Pan-Germanists. **1914** *Atlantic Monthly* Oct. 448/2 The schemes of the Pan-Germanists indeed reach to the creation of a vast confederation of states. **1939** *Tablet* 3 June 706/1 He defends himself as best he can against the Pan-Germanist propaganda of the turbulent German minority. **1957** ELLIOTT & SUMMERSKILL *Dict. Politics* 251 Pan-Germanists have advocated particularly the absorption into Germany of the German-speaking provinces of Austria. **1974** *Encycl. Brit. Micropædia* VII. 717/b Pan-Germanists continued to press for expansion; the most articulate and active force toward that end was Hitler and the Nazi Party.

Hence **pan-Germa'nistic** *a.*, of, pertaining to, or supporting pan-Germanism.

1915 *World's Work* (N.Y.) Aug. 456/1 To block the Pan-Germanistic plan.

pangermic, -germism: see PAN- 2.

[**pangetive** (in Lodge's *Poore Mans Talent*, Hunterian Cl., 69), error for PUNGITIVE.]

'pangful, *a. rare.* [f. PANG *sb.*[1] + -FUL.] Full of pangs, sorrowful.

1748 RICHARDSON *Clarissa* (1811) VII. 224 He bowed his head upon his pangful bosom. **1897** *Chicago Advance* 5 Aug. 178/3 [To live] far from home.. is as pangful to him as to an absent school-boy.

pang-full: see PANG *a.*

panghulu, var. PENGHULU.

pangless ('pæŋlɪs), *a.* [f. PANG *sb.*[1] + -LESS.] Without a pang.

1811 BYRON *To Thyrza* iv, Death for thee Prepared a light and pangless dart. **1879** E. ARNOLD *Lt. Asia* 4 So brought she forth her child Pangless.

Hence **'panglessly** *adv.*

1877 PATMORE *Unknown Eros* Proem, The furiously gibbering corse Shakes, panglessly convuls'd, and sightless stares.

'pang-like, *a.* [f. PANG *sb.*[1] + -LIKE.] Like or befitting a pang.

a **1586** SIDNEY *Arcadia* IV. (1629) 412 With pang-like grones and gastly turning of his eyes, immediately all his limmes stiffened, and his eyes fixed.

panglima (pəŋ'gliːmə). Also **penglima.** [Malay *pĕnglima.*] A Malay leader of secondary rank; a Malay chief.

1839 T. J. NEWBOLD *Pol. & Statistical Acct. Straits of Malacca* I. v. 237 For further security, two panglimas sat on each side. **1900** W. W. SKEAT *Malay Magic* 169 Two swords were produced and placed crosswise, and a couple of Panglimas selected for the dance. **1939** A. KEITH *Land below Wind* xv. 264 The Penglima, or native chief.. met our *perahus* with much ceremony.

Pangloss ('pænglɒs). Name of the philosopher and tutor in Voltaire's *Candide* (1759) who believes that 'all is for the best in the best of all possible worlds', used allusively for one who is optimistic regardless of the circumstances. Also *attrib.* Hence **'Panglossism,** an unrealistically optimistic attitude or saying; **Pan'glossic** *a.*, characteristic of Pangloss.

1844 DISRAELI *Coningsby* I. II. i. 153 The political Panglosses who.. were continually proving that this was the best of all possible governments. **1926** J. S. HUXLEY *Ess. Pop. Sci.* xii. 147 This conclusion, from its inception with some of the Stoics to its Panglossic latter end in certain evolutionists, he dismisses. **1928** A. HUXLEY in *Life & Letters* 1 Oct. 345 We are to interpret them, Pangloss fashion, in terms of preconceived philosophy. **1931** *Times Lit. Suppl.* 10 Dec. 994/4 We can best envisage him.. still the sworn disciple of Pangloss the optimist. **1959** *Encounter* Nov. 66/2 He includes.. some of his pet Panglossisms, such as that learning is happiness. **1964** *Economist* 11 July 128/2 This is cheerfulness raised to the level of Panglossism. **1973** *Listener* 5 Apr. 438/1 The [Egyptian] regime's official Dr. Pangloss, Culture Minister Dr Abdel Khader Hatem.

Pan'glossian, *a.* and *sb.* [f. prec. + -IAN.]

A. *adj.* Of, pertaining to, or characteristic of the philosophy of Pangloss. **B.** *sb.* One who shares this philosophy.

1831 DISRAELI *Young Duke* I. I. iii. 23 He was quite disembarrassed of that Panglossian philosophy, which had hitherto induced him to believe, that the Earl of Fitz-pompey was the best of all possible uncles. **1922** HARDY *Late Lyrics* Apol. p. xi, Hence should anything of this sort in the following adumbrations seem 'queer'—should any of them seem to good Panglossians to embody strange and disrespectful conceptions of this best of all possible worlds, I apologize; but cannot help it. **1936** G. B. SHAW *Simpleton* Pref. 3 If author and journalist are both placid Panglossians, convinced that their civilization is the best of all possible civilizations.. there is no trouble. **1937** A. HUXLEY *Ends & Means* vii. 68 In those who make the identification it induces a kind of busy, Panglossian fatalism. **1957** M. MCCARTHY *Memories Catholic Girlhood* p. xxiv, Some of my relations philosophize to this effect, in a somewhat Panglossian style. **1967** *Guardian* 17 May 1/3 This somewhat Panglossian interpretation of the significance of General de Gaulle's press conference. **1976** *Nature* 18 Mar. 196/2 The first, and most widely appreciated, is the old Panglossian fallacy that natural selection favours adaptations that are good for the species as a whole, rather than acting at the level of the individual.

Pangola, var. PONGOLA.

pangolin (pæŋ'gəʊlɪn). Also 9 **pen-.** [a. Malay *peng-gōling* roller, f. *peng-* denominative + *gōling* to roll, in reference to its power of rolling itself up. The Malays distinguish *peng-goling sisik* scaly pangolin, from *peng-goling rambut* hairy pangolin (Marsden).] An edentate mammal of the genus *Manis*, of tropical Asia and Africa, the greater part of whose body is covered with horny scales; a scaly ant-eater. The name originally belongs to *Manis Javanicus*, a native of Java, etc.; but has been extended to Indian and African species, of which there are several.

[**1734** SEBA *Thesaur. Rer. Natural.* I. 88 Javanensibus et aliis populis orientalibus *Panggoeling*, quae vox *Convolutorem* notat.] **1774** GOLDSM. *Nat. Hist.* (1862) I. VI. 468 The Pangolin, which has been usually called the *scaly lizard*,.. is about three or four feet long. **1822** SIR T. S. RAFFLES in *Trans. Linn. Soc.* XIII. 249 Pangolin Sisik or Tangiling.. of Sumatra. **1840** *Penny Cycl.* XVII. 188 The Pangolins are slow in motion, and live on worms and insects, especially termites and ants. **1893** SELOUS *Trav. S.E. Africa* 108 The curious ant-eaters (earth pigs and pangolins) are probably relics of an earlier fauna.

†**pangony, -ie.** *Obs.* [ad. L. *pangōni-us* (Pliny), a. Gr. παγγώνιος, i.e. all-angled.] Name of an unidentified precious stone mentioned by Pliny: in 18th c. employed by some as a class-name.

1658 PHILLIPS, *Pangonie*,.. a kinde of precious stone, so called from its multitudes of Angles. **1692** COLES, *Pangonie*, .. a precious stone with very many corners. **1753** CHAMBERS *Cycl. Suppl.*, *Pangonia*,.. The bodies of this genus are single-pointed, or imperfect crystals, composed of dodecangular or twelve-planed columns, terminated by twelve-planed pyramids, and the whole body, therefore, made up of twenty four planes. Of this genus there are only three known species: 1. A brownish-white one, with a long pyramid. This is found in Silesia and Bohemia;.. and is esteemed a very valuable crystal.

pan-Gothic to **pangymnasticon:** see PAN-.

pangram ('pængræm). [f. PAN- + -GRAM.] A sentence containing all the letters of the alphabet (see also quot. 1953). So **pangra'mmatic** *a.*

1933 M. E. OHAVER *Cryptogram Solving* 31 Pangrammatic, containing all the letters of the alphabet. **1953** W. R. TRASK tr. *Curtius's European Lit.* xv. 283 The 'pangrammatic' affection, which consists in having as many successive words as possible begin with the same letters. **1963** *Medium Ævum* XXXII. 149 'Pangrammatic' verses are far older than the thirteenth century. **1964** *Sci. Amer.* Sept. 222 The pangram, an ancient form of word play, is an attempt to get the maximum number of different letters into a sentence of minimum length. **1965** *Time* 17 Sept. 72 Also represented: Sotadic [palindromic] verses, pangrammatic rubaiyat and problems in alphametics (alphabet arithmetic).

†**'panguts.** *Obs.* [app. f. PAN- all + *guts.*]

1617 MINSHEU *Ductor*, *A Panguts*,.. an vnweldie Drossel nothing but guts. **1658** PHILLIPS, *A Panguts* (as it were all guts), a drossel, a gorbelly, an unwieldy fellow. **1704** COCKER, *Pangut*, or *Paunchgut*, a huge fat bellied fellow. **1775** ASH, *Panguts* (*s.* a low word), a fat hulky lazy fellow.

Panhagia, var. of PANAG(H)IA.

panhandle ('pænˌhænd(ə)l), *sb.* [f. PAN *sb.*[1] + HANDLE.]

1. The handle of a pan; hence in *U.S.* a denomination for a narrow prolongation of a State or Territory extending between two others, e.g. the Panhandle of West Virginia. Also applied to territories outside the U.S.A. Also *attrib.*

1856 *Porter's Spirit of Times* 8 Nov. 159/1 He was from old Virginny—from what, he said, they called the *Pan-handle.* **1861** *Vanity Fair* (N.Y.) 25 May 246/2 We will wrap the flag of our fathers around the 'Pan Handle' of Virginia, and upset the entire dish of Old Dominion Secession. **1877** E. E. HALE *G.T.T.* 30 So they.. whirled relentlessly across the Pan Handle by which domestic name that funny strip of West Virginia is known which shoots up like an inverted icicle between Pennsylvania and Ohio. **1888** *Missouri Republican* (U.S.) 24 Feb. (Farmer *Americanisms*), The Panhandle of Texas offers desirable homes to a million of people, at a nominal price. **1890** *Cent. Dict.* s.v., The Panhandle of Idaho; the Panhandle of West Virginia, projecting northward between Pennsylvania and Ohio. **1932** *Atlantic Monthly* Mar. 295/1 Your atlas will show that Idaho has a panhandle jutting up to the Canadian border. **1952** B. ULANOV *Hist. Jazz in Amer.* (1958) iv. 33 Jack Teagarden, a big burly Texan with an infectious Panhandle accent in his singing, has always been associated with the blues. **1960** *20th Cent.* Mar. 248 The 'panhandle' of North Wiltshire near Lechlade. **1967** *Economist* 14 Oct. 141/2 These targets are usually in the 'panhandle', as Americans call the thin southern part of North Vietnam. **1974** *Union* (S. Carolina) *Daily Times* 22 Apr. 1/3 Mt. Hermon straddles the Lebanese-Syrian border and is just north of the Israeli panhandle. **1977** *Time* 7 Mar. 52/1 In a grimy arc, from

Nebraska through the plains of Kansas and Colorado, on into the panhandles of Oklahoma and Texas, scenes right out of *The Grapes of Wrath* suddenly materialized in the swirl of dust billowing up to 12,000 feet.

2. The act of begging (cf. next).

1849 J. J. Hooper in *Spirit of Times* 14 Apr. 87/3 The elephant was the great point of attraction. 'I want his hide and frame for a corn crib,' said a fellow from the Pan-Handle Beat. **1849** *Harper's Weekly* 5 May 429/2 'Workin' the pan-handle.' 'Eh?' 'I mean, are you beggin'?' **1900** Ade *More Fables* 142 He usually found some one waiting on the Door-Step to give him the Sign of Distress and work the fraternal Pan-Handle on him. **1942** Berrey & Van den Bark *Amer. Thes. Slang* §486/2 *A solicitation*, .. panhandle.

Hence (sense 1) **'panhandled** *a.*

1976 T. Stoppard *Dirty Linen* 65 Enormous women in taffeta dresses stir the air with panhandled fans.

panhandle ('pænhænd(ə)l), *v. slang.* (orig. and chiefly *U.S.*). [Back-formation from next.] *trans.* and *intr.* To beg (from); to steal or purloin. Hence **'panhandling** *vbl. sb.* and *ppl. a.*

1903 *N.Y. Even. Post* 9 Dec. 1 The prisoners were members of a 'panhandling' corporation which operated extensively throughout the financial district. **1904** G. H. Lorimer *Old Gorgon Graham* 53 A lot of men.. who wouldn't think of asking for money, will panhandle both sides of a street for favors. **1907** 'O. Henry' *Strictly Business* (1910) xix. 242 He felt his sleeve grasped and held. Suspecting that he was about to be panhandled, he turned a cold and unprofitable face, and saw that his captor was—Dawe. **1931** 'D. Stiff' *Milk & Honey Route* viii. 84 Domestic panhandling, or hitting back doors, .. seems to be on the decline. **1932** L. C. Douglas *Forgive us our Trespasses* (1937) xiv. 276 It's never been in a suppliant attitude, panhandling the brethren and sisters for sixpences to pay the parson's coal-bill. **1951** E. Paul *Springtime in Paris* xi. 198 The street music .. was strictly for panhandling —stray accordion players, atrocious old fiddlers, and half-crazed women with cracked voices and maudlin lyrics. **1959** *Times Lit. Suppl.* 6 Nov. p. xxxv/5 A poor art scholar .. has his precious manuscript on Giotto destroyed by the panhandling Jewish refugee from Israel. **1973** 'A. Blaisdell' *Crime by Chance* (1974) ix. 173, I ain't had a bite to eat since yesterday. I was in that bar panhandlin'. **1976** *Yellowstone Explorer* July 1/3 The absence of bears along the park's roads is a major concern of visitors, especially those who were here just a few years ago and saw literally dozens of bears panhandling picnic items passing cars. **1977** *It* June 5/2 They tackled the dilemma facing anyone who has been pan-handled—'Why don't I take this poor bastard home with me,'—and they did it on a massive scale.

panhandler ('pæn,hændlə(r)). [f. panhandle *sb.* or panhandle *v.* + -er[1].] **1.** A beggar. *slang* (orig. *U.S.*).

1897 F. Moss *Amer. Metropolis* II. vii. 393 A party of petty thieves and 'pan-handlers' (able-bodied street beggars), went into the 'Morgue'. **1899** Ade *Doc. Horne* xxiii. 255 The freckled boy then announced that he had 'sized' the hustler for a 'panhandler' from the start. **1909** [see lone *a.* 3 c]. **1929** *Daily Tel.* 8 Jan. 11/6 Large profits from begging in the rich Fifth Avenue business districts have produced a 'king of the pan-handlers'. **1954** *Manch. Guardian Weekly* 30 Dec. 14/3 The delicatessen stores alone in this city [*sc.* New York] would make the Phoenicians feel like pan-handlers and the merchant princes of Venice like fugitives from a soup kitchen. **1962** H. Hood in R. Weaver *Canad. Short Stories* (1968) 2nd Ser. 202 In a minute they would speak to him. They always did, drunks and panhandlers. **1966** F. Shaw et al. *Lern Yerself Scouse, A pan'andler*, a scrounger of food. **1973** 'E. McBain' *Hail to Chief* vi. 113 Don't .. start screaming if a panhandler taps you on the shoulder. He may only want a quarter for a drink. **1975** *Globe & Mail* (Toronto) 5 July 2/1 Panhandlers .. urinate in doorways, sleep in the streets. **1978** G. Vidal *Kalki* vi. 136 First they would approach a well-dressed person of the sort who would normally run a mile to avoid a panhandler for god, any god.

2. (With capital initial.) A native or inhabitant of a Panhandle.

1936 *Sun* (Baltimore) 12 May 12/5 If the gentleman from Texas wants us to revise our lingo so that it meets the approval of the Panhandlers, the least he could do is offer a substitute for the word he wishes eliminated. **1940** E. Fergusson *Our Southwest* xviii. 335, I talked all this over with a native-born Panhandler. **1949** *10 Story Western* May 28/2 He remembered how it was down there in the Panhandle—how the Panhandlers hated these Rio Valley floaters as no Idaho man could.

panharmonic (,pænhɑː'mɒnɪk), *a.* [f. pan- all + harmonic: cf. next.] **a.** Adapted to all the 'harmonies' or musical modes. **b.** Universally harmonic, harmonizing with all.

1875 Jowett *Plato* (ed. 2) III. 274 We shall not want multiplicity of notes or a panharmonic scale. **1886** Farrar *Hist. Interpretation* iv. 236 St. Augustine .. demanded that all interpretation should be panharmonic.

So **panhar'monicon**, a mechanical musical instrument of the orchestrion type, invented by J. N. Maelzel in 1800.

1848 J. H. Newman *Loss & Gain* iii. x. 381 The whole congregation was as though one vast instrument or Panharmonicon, moving all together. **1879** *Grove's Dict. Mus.* II. 194 Maelzel .. devoted himself to constructing an automaton instrument of flutes, trumpets, drums, cymbals, triangle, and strings struck by hammers... His next machine was the Panharmonicon, .. with clarinets, violins and cellos added.

†**panharmony** (pæn'hɑːmənɪ). *Obs.* [f. pan- + harmony; after Gr. παναρμόνιος all-harmonious.] Universal or general harmony.

1651 Collier tr. *Comenius' Patterne Univ. Knowl.* 52 Pansophy by its owne desirable Panarmony, or generall agreement will be fit and convenient.

Panhellenic (pænhɛ'liːnɪk, -'ɛnɪk), *a.* [f. pan- 1 + Hellenic; after Gr. πανελλήνιος of or pertaining to all the Greeks, πανέλληνες all the Hellenes, the united Greeks.] Of, concerning, or representing all men of Greek race (including in ancient times the Greek colonies in Asia, Sicily, Italy, etc.; in modern times, the Greeks living in the Turkish dominions, in Crete, etc.).

1847 Grote *Greece* ii. xlvii, The schemes of Periclês were .. eminently Pan-Hellenic. **1853** *Ibid.* lxxii, Athens had never had the power of organizing any such generous Pan-hellenic combination.

Panhellenism (pæn'hɛlɪnɪz(ə)m). [f. pan- 1 + Hellenism, or Gr. πανέλληνες + -ism: see prec.] The idea or plan of a political union of all Greeks; the Panhellenic spirit and aims.

1860 ['Remembered in spoken use in Oxford' (Prof. Bywater).] **1874** Fiske *Outl. Cosmic Philos.* ii. xviii. II. 205 The struggle between the higher and the lower patriotism, —between the two feelings known to the Greeks as Pan-Hellenism and Autonomism. **1884** J. T. Bent in *Macm. Mag.* Oct. 429/2 A secret society which was the backbone of Panhellenism.

So **Pan'hellenist**, one who favours Panhellenism.

1882 in Ogilvie *Imper. Dict.* **1900** *Pilot* 2 Sept. 263/1 There is an aloofness that lies deeper down in his [the Cretan's] nature than any pan-Hellenist piety.

panhidrosis to **panhysterectomy**: see pan-.

Panhonlib (pænhɒn'lɪb). [f. *Pan*ama, *Hon*duras, *Lib*eria.] Designating a merchant ship of Panama, Honduras, and Liberia flying a 'flag of convenience'. Cf. flag *sb.*[4] 1 f, Panlibhonco.

1958 *Times* 1 Apr. 11/5 There has recently been an intensification of the campaign against registration of ships, particularly tankers, under what have come to be known as 'PanHonLib' flags. **1958** [see Panlibhonco]. **1962** S. G. Sturmey *Brit. Shipping & World Competition* 228 Few British owners have sought Panholib registration.

panial, variant of panele *Obs.*

panic ('pænɪk), *sb.*[1] Also 5–6 -yk(e, 6–7 -ik(e, -icke, 6–9 -ick; 6 pannycke, 9 -ick. [ad. L. *pānicum*, in It. *panico*, F. *panic.*] **a.** A grass or graminaceous plant: originally applied to *Panicum italicum* of Linnæus (*Setaria italica* of later botanists), otherwise called Italian Millet, largely cultivated in Southern Europe, etc.; also extended to other species of the genus *Panicum* and its subgenera, many of which are cultivated in different parts of the world as cereal grains.

Panicum is a very extensive genus; Steudel describes 850 species, grouped under eighteen sections, many of these being distinct genera with other authors. (*Treas. Bot.*).

c **1420** *Pallad. on Husb.* iv. 50 Panyk & mylde in hoot & drie is sowe As now. **1555** Eden *Decades* 260 Of Moscouia .. the fieldes beare .. also mylle and panyke whiche the Italians caule Melica. **1562** Turner *Herbal* ii. 76 b, Panic is of the kynde of pulses, and in lykenes lyke vnto millet. **1597** Gerarde *Herbal* i. lvi. 78 There be sundrie sorts of Panick. *Ibid.*, The Panick of India groweth vp like Millet. **1610** W. Folkingham *Art of Survey* i. vii. 14 Saffron, Mill, Millet, Panick, Amilcorne, Spelt-corn, Garences. **1732** Arbuthnot *Rules of Diet* i. 251 Panick, aperient, boil'd with Milk. **1814** Southey *Roderick* Wks. 1838 IX. 378 *note*, The Hermit took a loaf .. made of pannick and of rye. **1852** Badger *Nestorians* I. 214 Three kinds of millet or pannick .. make the bread-flour in general use.

b. *attrib.* and *Comb.*, as *panic-bread*, *-seed*; **panic-grass**, any grassy species of *Panicum*, as *P.* (*Echinochloa*) *Crus-galli*, a weed of cultivated and waste ground in England.

1591 Percivall *Sp. Dict.*, *Panojo*, pannycke seede, *Pannicula*. **1597** Gerard *Herball* i. 7 Pannicke grasse is garnished with chaffie and downie tufts. **1668** Wilkins *Real Char.* ii. iv. 73 Panic-Grass. **1797** W. Johnston tr. *Beckmann's Invent.* II. 248 *note*, The slender spiked cock's foot panic-grass, *panicum sanguinale*. **1814** Southey *Roderick* Wks. 1838 IX. 399 *note*, The king would eat only of the pannick bread, as he had been wont to do. **1835** Hooker *Brit. Flora* I. 43 *Panicum Crus-galli*, Loose Panick-grass. **1870** W. Robinson *Wild Garden* ii. 121 Twiggy Panic Grass .. is an elegant plant. **1901** C. T. Mohr *Plant Life Alabama* 355 Wiry Panic-Grass... Exposed places in light soil. **1929** Weaver & Clements *Plant Ecol.* vii. 134 (*caption*) Competition between tall panic grass and evening primrose. **1963** Gleason & Cronquist *Man. Vascular Plants Northeastern U.S.* 101 Panic grass. Spikelets lanceolate or hisiform to ovate.

panic ('pænɪk), *a.* and *sb.*[2] Forms: 7– panic; also 7 -ique, -ik, 7–8 -ick, pannick, -ic. [a. F. *panique* adj. (15th c. in Littré) = It. *panico* (Florio); ad. Gr. πανικός adj. of or for Pan, groundless (fear), whence πανικόν neut. sb. panic terror, a panic.

'Sounds heard by night on mountains and in vallies were attributed to Pan, and hence he was reputed to be the cause of any sudden and groundless fear' (Liddell and Scott). Stories more or less elaborated, accounting for the origin of the expression, are found in Plutarch's *Lives* (Langhorne's tr. (1879) II. 701/2), Polyænus' *Stratagems* (written *c* 160 a.d.; cf. Potter *Greece* iii. ix.), etc.]

A. *adj.* (Now often viewed as attrib. use of B.)

1. a. In *panic fear*, *terror*, etc.: Such as was attributed to the action of the god Pan: = B. 2.

1603 Holland *Plutarch's Mor.* 425 Sudden foolish frights, without any certeine cause, which they call *Panique Terrores*. *Ibid.* 1293 All sudden tumults and troubles of the multitude and common people, be called Panique affrights. **1647** Ward *Simp. Cobler* 11, I hope my feares are but panick. **1665** Sir T. Herbert *Trav.* (1677) 241 That great Army .. were put into that pannick fear that they were shamefully put to flight. **1700** Dryden *Fables, Cock & Fox* 731 Ran cow and calf and family of hogs, In panique horror of pursuing dogs. **1770** Langhorne *Plutarch* (1879) II. 701/2 A panic fear ran through the camp. **1850** Merivale *Rom. Emp.* (1865) II. xiv. 134 A sound of panic dread to the populations of Italy.

b. Of the nature of or resulting from a panic; exhibiting unreasoning, groundless, or excessive fear.

1741 in *Johnson's Debates Parl.* (1787) I. 386 The tumults of ambition in one place, and a panic stillness in another. **1824** Galt *Rothelan* II. iii. vii. 70 He cried, with a shrill and panic voice, for Shebak.

†**2.** Of noise, etc.: Such as was attributed to Pan.

a **1661** Holyday *Juvenal* 120 Which .. they thought might be prevented by making a loud and panick noise with brasen vessels.

†**3.** Universal, general. *Obs. nonce-use.*

a **1661** Fuller *Worthies* xxiv. (1662) 77 Seeing sometimes a Pannick silence herein.

4. (cap.) Of or pertaining to the god Pan: as, Bacchic and Panic figures.

1890 in *Cent. Dict.*

B. *sb.*[2] [= mod.F. *une panique.*]

†**1.** Contagious emotion such as was ascribed to the influence of Pan. *Obs.*

1627 tr. *Bacon's Life & Death* (1651) 15 Seeing Pan was their God, we may conceive, that all Things about them were Panicks [L. *Panica* adj.], and vaine, and subject to Fables. **1708** Shaftesb. *Charact.* (1711) I. i. ii. 15 We may .. call every Passion Pannick which is rais'd in a Multitude, and convey'd by Aspect, or as it were by Contact or Sympathy. *Ibid.* 16 There are many Pannicks in Mankind, besides merely that of Fear. And thus is Religion also Pannick.

2. a. (= *panic fear*, *terror*, etc.; see A. 1): A sudden and excessive feeling of alarm or fear, usually affecting a body of persons, originating in some real or supposed danger vaguely apprehended, and leading to extravagant or injudicious efforts to secure safety. (With and without *a* and *pl.*)

1708 Shaftesb. *Charact.* (1711) I. i. ii. 15 The Uncertainty of what they fear'd made their Fear get greater. .. And this was what in after-times men call'd a Pannick. **1709** Steele *Tatler* No. 18 ¶6 The Approach of a Peace strikes a Pannick thro' our Armies, tho' that of a Battle could never do it. **1818** Jas. Mill *Brit. India* II. iv. viii. 277 The General .. fulfilled the fondest wishes of Hyder, by taking the panic, and running away from the army. **1856** Kane *Arct. Expl.* II. xii. 123 Parental instinct was mastered by panic. **1867** Freeman *Norm. Conq.* I. v. 375 An unaccountable panic seized on all men. **1879** Froude *Cæsar* xxii. 382 Cæsar's soldiers were seized with panic.

b. *spec.* A condition of widespread apprehension in relation to financial and commercial matters, arising in a time of monetary difficulty or crisis, and leading to hasty and violent measures to secure immunity from possible loss, the tendency of which is to cause financial disaster.

1757 Harris *Coins* 31 No alteration can be made in the standard of money without .. producing .. distrusts and panics. **1826** C. Knight *Pop. Hist. Eng.* VIII. xi. 195 This pecuniary crisis [in 1825] .. universally obtained the name of 'The Panic'. **1826** T. Attwood 27 Feb. in *Life* viii. (1885) 104 Smith, Payn and Smith, and Barclays have had last week very sharp runs upon them. In many Country Towns also these pleasant 'panics' have prevailed. **1863** Fawcett *Pol. Econ.* iii. xi. (1876) 442 Commercial panics are caused by a reckless employment of credit.

c. *fig.* A noteworthy or amusing person, thing, or situation.

1936 R. Ackland *After October* i. 47 Oh, my dear, aren't you *swell!* All grown up and sophisticated. Doesn't she look a panic, Timmy? *Ibid.* 49 My dear, it was a panic! **1946** T. Williams *27 Wagons Cotton* iii. 27 *Flora*: Says—(She goes off into another spasm of laughter.) *Jake*: What ever he said must've been a panic!

3. *attrib.* and *Comb.* **a.** *attrib.* Of or pertaining to a panic or panics; resulting from panic.

1842 *Southern Q. Rev.* I. 88 The sudden and violent contraction of 1833 .. produced the scenes of what is usually termed the 'panic session'. **1854** T. H. Benton *30 Years' View* I. 369/2 On the second day of December, 1833, commenced the first session of the Twenty-third Congress, commonly called the Panic Session. **1884** Giffen in *Pall Mall G.* 19 Dec. 4/1 The appreciation .. was one not to be regarded with a panic feeling. **1894** *Daily News* 12 July 5/1 The Bill, .. as a pure panic measure, must stand or fall by the general estimate of the gravity of the circumstances which have given rise to it.

b. *Comb.* (often not distinctly separable from attrib. use), as *panic-cry*, *-cure*, *-dread*, *-flight*, *-master*; *panic-driven*, *-like*, *-pale*, *-stunned* adjs.; **panic bolt**, a special bolt for a door designed to unfasten readily in emergencies; **panic button**, a switch or button for operating various devices in emergencies (see quots.); also *fig.* in phr. *hit*, *press*, *the panic button*, to become over-excited, take emergency measures (the origin of the expression is discussed in *Amer. Speech* XXXI (1956) no. 3, 240); **panic buying**, the buying in large quantities of goods of which a shortage is threatened or suspected; hence (as a back-formation) **panic-buy** *v.*; **panic-monger**, one who endeavours to bring about or foster a panic, esp. on a political, social, or financial question; an alarmist: a term of opprobrium; hence **panic-mongering**; **panic party** (see quots. 1929, 1943); **panic stations**, a state of emergency (freq. *fig.*); **panic-stricken, -struck**, *a.*, stricken with panic; so **panic-strike** *v.*; **panic-striking**, causing, or likely to cause, a panic.

1930 *Aberdeen Press & Jrnl.* 1 May 7/3 When he took the cinema in July, 1928, he put *panic bolts on the wooden door.. where there were ordinary slip bolts before. **1940** *Chambers's Techn. Dict.* 611/2 *Panic bolt*, a special form of door-bolt which is released by pressure at the middle of the door; commonly used on exit-doors in public buildings. **1964** J. S. SCOTT *Dict. Building* 223 *Panic bolt*, a door bolt often used at the double exit doors of theatres. It is opened by pressure from inside on to a horizontal bar within the door at waist height. **1972** *Times* 28 Dec. 1/8 London fire brigade checked the new arrangements last night and said that 'panic bolts' on the inside complied with regulations. **1955** *Amer. Speech* XXX. 117 *Hit the *panic button*, panic, get excited. **1956** *Ibid.* XXXI. 240 Discussion with several pilots.. reveals at least four buttons or switches, each one of which may be referred to as the 'panic button'. **1958** *Ibid.* XXXIII. 183 *Panic button*, the release button on the one-point release harness worn by the smokejumper. When a jumper is hung up in a tree,.. he twists a metal knob (the 'panic button') on his harness fifteen degrees to the left and hits it. This releases the webbing straps of the harness, and the entire parachute and harness fall off. 'I hit the panic button and let down about sixty feet.' **1959** *Times* 9 Mar. 13/4 *Hit the panic button*, get over-excited. **1962** *Review & Herald* 25 Oct. 24/3 Dr. Franklin Clark Fry, president of the Lutheran Church in America, warned here that the time is coming for world Christian missions 'to press the panic button', because Christianity is dying out. **1970** *Washington Post* 30 Sept. D4/5, I haven't thrown the panic button yet and I'm not going to. **1970** D. FRANCIS *Rat Race* iv. 45 Someone in the control tower had pressed the panic button. Fire engines screamed up. **1970** *Motoring Which?* July 113/1 As a last resort, pressing the 'panic-button' would 'dump' the craft, but could cause damage on a hard surface. **1972** T. ARDIES *This Suitcase* viii. 71 The President reacted reasonably enough. He didn't push the panic button... He .. ordered a stand-by alert. **1973** *Listener* 15 Feb. 200/3 The panic-button was pressed: foreign-exchange markets slammed their doors. **1974** *Scottish Daily Express* 14 Oct. 1/6 But one grocery chain manager stressed last night there was no immediate need for customers to *panic buy as stocks were high and many stores' supplies were still unaffected by the strike. **1974** *Times* 15 Nov. 18/3, I had already panic-bought five gallons of petrol.. saving 42p on next week's prices. **1942** *Washington Post* 23 Nov. 11/6 An anti-hoarding regulation for householders.. to curb *panic-buying of foods. **1949** *Sun* (Baltimore) 2 Dec. 4/5 There is no question but that panic buying has contributed to the current price rise. **1972** *Guardian* 18 Aug. 13 Concern over the number of mortgages available in the future and fears that selling [houses] could become more difficult have created a flood of panic-selling (which makes a change from panic-buying). **1973** *Times* 7 Dec. 18/8 Panic buying of spirits in the High Street, caused largely by forecasts of the shortage. **1974** *Guardian* 19 Jan. 20/2 Panic-buying would in itself lead to 'artificial shortages'. **1873** BURTON *Hist. Scot.* VI. lxxii. 301 The old *panic-cry about a Scots invasion. **1806–7** J. BERESFORD *Miseries Hum. Life* (1826) II. xviii, When he has.. scattered your whole party in a *panic-flight. **1877** RAYMOND *Statist. Mines & Mining* 227 This produced a *panic-like consternation. **1793** H. WALPOLE *Lett., to Miss Berrys* 7 Oct. (1846) VI. 494 The *panic-master-general. **1849** COBDEN *Speeches* 8 Those wicked alarmists and *panic-mongers whom I will never forgive. **1894** LD. WOLSELEY *Life Marlborough* II. 14 Sunderland succeeded in pursuading James that Lewis XIV's warnings were those of the 'panic-monger'. **1886** *Times* 30 Mar. 12/1 This *panicmongering has had the effect of suggesting strikes and rioting. **1883** G. MEREDITH *Poems & Lyrics* 143 How bold when skies are blue; When black winds churn the deep, how *panic-pale. **1919** *Boy's Own Paper* XLI. IX. 456/2 The 'Farnborough'.. disembarked a '*panic party'.. to pretend that the officers and crew were abandoning their ship. **1929** *Papers Mich. Acad. Sci., Arts, & Lett.* X. 313 *Panic party*, a feigned demonstration of alarm or panic on board a decoy (mystery) ship in order to lure the commander of a submarine alongside. When a mystery ship was torpedoed, the panic party took to the boats, apparently abandoning the vessel, but always leaving on board another crew to man the guns and finish the submarine if it came near enough. **1929** F. C. BOWEN *Sea Slang* 100 *Panic Party*, the men whose job it was to leave a Decoy Ship (Q-boat) in disorder when a German submarine opened fire. **1932** 'N. SHUTE' *Lonely Road* vii. 144 They shelled the panic party in the boats. **1943** BAKER *Dict. Austral. Slang* (ed. 3) 57 *Panic party*, any rush move (Digger slang). **1961** in Partridge *Dict. Slang* Suppl. 1213/1 :**Panic stations, be at*, to be prepared for the worst. **1963** 'J. PRESCOT' *Case for Hearing* iii. 53 Someone has been into Greenwood's again.. and got away with another three hundred... The police seem to be at panic stations about it. **1972** A. DRAPER *Death Penalty* xviii. 113 Let's face it, Caleb, you'll be the first to run to panic stations. **1804** M. HAYS *Harry Clinton* xxxii. 199 A ladder was.. speedily brought, the *panic-stricken family assisted to descend, and charitably conducted to a neighbouring inn. **1814** SOUTHEY *Roderick* xxv, The Moors, confused and captainless, And panic-stricken, vainly seek to escape The inevitable fate. **1859** W. COLLINS *Q. of Hearts* (1875) 19 Owen and I looked at one another in panic-stricken silence. **1904** [see DIXIE^2 1 b]. **1977** M. T. BLOOM *13th Man* iii. 39 They both turned their faces to me and the car and they looked panic-stricken, stuck in place. **1798** LADY HUNTER in *Jrnl. Sir M. Hunter* (1894) 122 Our formidable appearance *panic-struck them, and they were moving off. **1898** HENDERSON *Stonewall Jackson* I. xi. 448 They need only a movement on the flank to panic-strike them. **1851** H. MELVILLE *Moby Dick* III. vii. 56 Pip loved life, and all life's peaceable securities; so that the *panic-striking business in which he had somehow unaccountably become entrapped, had most sadly blurred his brightness. **1934** R. CAMPBELL *Broken Record* ii. 46 A senseless, dutiful exposure of panic-striking and depressing facts is worse than any amount of mischievous lying. **1776** J. THACHER *Mil. Jrnl.* (1823) 70 [Washington] made every effort to rally them, but without success; they were so *panic struck that even the shadow of an enemy seemed to increase their precipitate flight. **1835** J. E. ALEXANDER *Sk. Portugal* vi. 139 The Miguelites at last became panic-struck. **1848** BUCKLEY *Iliad* 130 A panic-struck and turbulent council. **1791** COWPER *Iliad* XVI. 983 *Panic-stunn'd he stood.

Hence **ˈpanicful** *a.*, 'full of panic, fearful'.

1846 WORCESTER, *Panicful* (cites C. B. Brown).

ˈpanic, *v.* [f. PANIC *sb.*^{2}] **1.** *trans.* To affect with panic.

1827 HOOD *Hero & Leander* xlii, The crew.. Struck pale and panick'd by the billows' roar. **1917** 'CONTACT' *Airman's Outings* 184 Nothing seems to panic the Boche more than a sudden swoop by a low-flying aeroplane. **1919** H. L. WILSON *Ma Pettengill* iv. 127 He was sure going to annoy Ben from time to time, even if he didn't panic him much. **1932** KIPLING *Limits & Renewals* 169 Then I'd come round the corner and hailed him, and that panicked him. **1932** *New Yorker* 4 June 46/1 Gough.. had a violence and fervor on the platform which packed them and panicked them everywhere. **1957** *Economist* 30 Nov. 795/1 The markets are healthy and not likely to be panicked into headlong fall. **1966** A. SACHS *Jail Diary* xxi. 189 That will panic the Whites in South Africa even further. **1971** *Daily Tel.* 2 Nov. 2/5 A radio dramatisation of H. G. Wells's 'War of the Worlds'.. panicked thousands throughout America in 1938. **1974** 'M. INNES' *Appleby's Other Story* xi. 93 At least it panicked her. She came.. to tell me a pack of lies. **1975** *Daily Tel.* 1 May 13/6 When I received a tax demand asking for £600 by Tuesday it panics me completely. **1977** *Time* 23 May 24/3 The Defense Secretary is by no means panicked.

2. *intr.* To get into a panic, to lose one's head.

1910 KIPLING *Divers. Creatures* (1917) 310 Jules was, so to speak, panicking in a water-tight flat through his unfortunate lack of language. **1921** 'SAPPER' *Man in Ratcatcher* 30 For a few agonizing seconds.. she panicked; then.. she pulled herself together and tried to stop him. **1924** M. NEWMAN *Consummation* v. xxii. 240 They panicked one night, started rapid fire and killed two of their own men. **1930** J. CANNAN *No Walls of Jasper* 196 Martin helped Phyl to unpack. All at once she panicked, rummaging wildly among the paper in the tea-basket and saying, 'Good heavens, Martin! there's no sugar for his tea!' **1946** M. PEAKE *Titus Groan* 371 Swelter,.. thinking the thin man to have panicked, pursued him. **1958** N. MARSH *Singing in Shrouds* (1959) xi. 235 I'd had one or two drinks over the eight and I suppose that's why I panicked. **1971** *Radio Times* 4 Nov. 72/4 Their headmaster.. rather panicked at the word 'drug'. **1975** P. SOMERVILLE-LARGE *Couch of Earth* iii. 48, I thought you might have panicked and hared off.

Hence **ˈpanicked** *ppl. a.*, stricken with panic; also *fig.*

1916 G. FRANKAU *Guns* 15 His panicked watchers spy us, a droning threat in the void. **1920** E. SITWELL *Wooden Pegasus* 107 The light falls like a rain of panick'd leaves Through the gold heart of eves. **1978** R. LEWIS *Uncertain Sound* iii. 80 With a sense of panicked claustrophobia I felt I had to get out of the office.

panical (ˈpænɪkəl), *a. rare.* [f. as PANIC *a.* and *sb.*^{2} + -AL^1.]

1. = PANIC *a.* 1.

1605 CAMDEN *Rem., Poems* 7 Chaucer our English Homer in the description of the sodaine stirre and Panicall feare when Chanteclere the cocke was caried away by Reynold the Foxe. **1890** CLARK RUSSELL *Shipmate Louise* xx. 128 Was ever panical terror more incomparably suggested?

2. Of or pertaining to the god PAN: = PANIC *a.* 4.

1794 T. TAYLOR *Pausanias' Descr. Greece* III. 235 The Sun produces Angelical, Demoniacal, Heroical, Nymphical, Panical, and such-like powers.

panically (ˈpænɪkəlɪ), *adv.* [f. prec. + -LY^2.] With panic-like fear.

1882 STEVENSON *Merry Men* v. (1887) 55 Had the sea been a lake of living flames, he could not have shrunk more panically from its touch.

panicky (ˈpænɪkɪ), *a. colloq.* [f. PANIC *sb.*^{2} + -Y.] **a.** Of the nature of, or characterized by a tendency to, panic; subject to panic; unreasonably or excessively apprehensive; said esp. in reference to commercial and financial matters.

1869 *Echo* 12 Oct., Hence the delays, mystification, and consequent panicky results. **1882** *St. James's Gaz.* 13 Feb., Wheat fell on Saturday, and the wheat market is described as being 'panicky'. **1900** *Scotsman* 2 June 8/3 All of a sudden he made a panicky speech in the House of Lords which was held by the panicky newspapers to justify all that they had said.

b. quasi-*sb.* That which is panicky.

1924 GALSWORTHY *White Monkey* I. xii. 96 'That appears to savour of the panicky,' he said.

panicle^1 (ˈpænɪk(ə)l). *Bot.* Also 6–9 pannicle. [ad. L. *pānicula* (*-ucula*), dim. of *pānus* a swelling, an ear of millet.] A compound inflorescence, usually of the racemose type, in which some of the pedicels branch again or repeatedly, forming a loose and irregularly spreading cluster, as in oats and many grasses.

1597 GERARDE *Herbal* I. iii. 4 The bushie top, with his long feather-like pannicles do resemble the common Reede. **1792** MARIA RIDDELL *Voy. Madeira* 98 The blossoms are disposed in a pannicle, or diffused spike. **1832** *Veg. Subst. Food* 120 When millet is ripe, the panicles are cut off near to the top of the stalk. **1872** OLIVER *Elem. Bot.* I. i. 83 An inflorescence which branches irregularly, like that of Bramble, Horse Chestnut, and most Grasses, is called a panicle.

†**panicle^2**. *Obs.* = PANIC *sb.*^{1}

Johnson's example from Miller is erroneous; M.'s entry is *Panicum*, Panic (etc.).

1606 PEACHAM *Graphice* (1612) 135 September in his left hand a handful of Millet, Oates and Panicle. **1656** W. D. tr. *Comenius' Gate Lat. Unl.* §92. 31 Oats, Rice, Millet, Panicle, Beech-wheat.

panicle, obs. form of PANNICLE.

panicled (ˈpænɪk(ə)ld), *a.* [f. PANICLE^1 + -ED^2.] Arranged in form of a panicle; paniculate; furnished with or bearing a panicle or panicles.

1677 PLOT *Oxfordsh.* 84 Fair panicled corn or bent-grass. **1800** *Asiatic Ann. Reg., Misc. Tr.* 267/1 Flowers panicled about the ends of the branches. **1830** LINDLEY *Nat. Syst. Bot.* 292 Arranged in a spiked, racemed, or panicled manner.

paniconograph (pænaɪˈkɒnəʊgrɑːf, -æ-). Also paˈnicograph. [f. PAN- + ICONOGRAPH.] (See quot.)

1875 KNIGHT *Dict. Mech.* 1602/1 *Panicograph*, a mode of obtaining printing-plates direct from a subject or transfer by applying it to the face of a plate of zinc, and building up a printing surface in relief corresponding to the design transferred. **1890** *Cent. Dict.*, Paniconograph. **1902** WEBSTER *Suppl.*, *Paniconograph*,.. a photozincograph.

So **paˌniconoˈgraphic, -icoˈgraphic** *a.*, pertaining or related to paniconography; **panicoˈnography**, a name given to a process for obtaining printing-plates directly from a design or transfer, by producing the design in relief on a zinc plate; photozincography.

1854 *Chamb. Jrnl.* I. 69 There is a paneiconographic process—a long name, which seems to imply a power of copying or reproducing any or all kinds of engravings. **1890** *Cent. Dict.*, *Paniconographic*, *Paniconography*.

paniculate (pəˈnɪkjʊlət), *a.* [ad. mod.L. *pāniculāt-us*, f. *pānicula* PANICLE^1 + -ATE^2.] Arranged in a panicle; panicled.

1727 BAILEY vol. II. s.v., A Plant is said to be *floribus paniculatis*, i.e. with paniculate Flowers, when it bears a great Number of Flowers standing upon long Foot-Stalks, issuing on all Sides from the middle Stalk. **1760** J. LEE *Introd. Bot.* III. xxi. (1765) 217 *Paniculate*, with the Flowers in Panicles. **1846** DANA *Zooph.* (1848) 578 Incurvate, paniculate in a plane, subtripinnate. **1877–84** F. E. HULME *Wild Fl.* p. vi, The inflorescence paniculate.

Hence **paˈniculately** *adv.*

1870 HOOKER *Stud. Fl.* 306 Scapes.. paniculately branched.

paˈniculated, *a. rare.* [See -ED^2.] = prec.

1719 QUINCY *Med. Dict.* (1726) 349/2 Such are call'd Panniculated Plants. **1860** TYAS *Wild Fl.* 117 St. John's wort.—The inflorescence is.. branched in paniculated clusters.

paˈniculato-, comb. form of mod.L. *pāniculāt-us*, paniculately, paniculate and ——.

1846 DANA *Zooph.* 582 Sparingly ramose, above paniculato-corymbose. *Ibid.* 666 Paniculato-ramose, branches terete.

panicum (ˈpænɪkəm). [L. name of a type of millet, adopted by Linnæus (*Species Plantarum* (1753) I. 55) and earlier botanists as the name of a genus.] A grass belonging to the large genus so called, including the European millet, *Panicum miliaceum*, and several other important cereals or fodder grasses; = PANIC *sb.*^{1}

1844 J. D. HOOKER *Let.* 10 Feb. in L. Huxley *Life J. D. Hooker* (1918) I. viii. 169 Fancy two new Panicums; I cannot make them agree with any others. **1870** W. ROBINSON *Wild Garden* II. 121 Elegant Panicum... America. Annual... Banks, slopes, fringes of shrubberies. **1932** *Discovery* Jan. 24/2 A shade plant grows rankly and below is a mat of *Panicum* to the exclusion of everything else. **1966** C. A. W. GUGGISBERG *S.O.S. Rhino* iv. 92 *Panicum*, which grows to a fair height, is eaten more especially when short, and the rhino have a tendency to keep it down. **1968** F. W. GOULD *Grass Systematics* 214 Bulb Panicum is an important forage grass of the southwestern mountain ranges.

panidiomorphic, panidrosis, etc.: see PAN-.

panier, variant of PANNIER.

‖**panier de crabes** (ˈpanje də krab). [Fr., lit. basket of crabs.] An internal struggle, a 'rat race'.

1963 *Economist* 30 Mar. 1218/2 The visitor is.. not able to move around in this communist *panier de crabes*. **1979** *Dædalus* Summer 137 In what the French would term the *panier de crabes* of sixteenth century Toledan society.

panifiable, *a. rare*$^{-1}$. [a. F. *panifiable*, f. *panifier*.] Capable of being made into bread.

1849 *Lond. Jrnl.* 10 Mar. 8 An ingenious instrument, called.. the *aleurometer*, the purpose of which is to indicate the panifiable properties of wheat flour.

panification (pænɪfɪˈkeɪʃən). [a. F. *panification* (*p. des pommes de terre*, 1781 in Hatz.-Darm.), noun of action f. *panifier* to make into bread.] The making into bread; conversion into the substance of bread, esp. as a chemical process.

1779 *Projects* in *Ann. Reg.* 100/1 It is from this very simple operation that the whole fabrication of potatoe-bread depends; without it, no panification. **1818** COLEBROOKE *Import Colonial Corn* 129 Whether the panification of the meal of rye or barley..be complete. **1854** *Fraser's Mag.* L. 326 See the blessed idea of Christian communion.. degraded into a mere act of divine panification! **1886** JAGO *Chemistry of Wheat, Flour & Bread* 314 Summing up the changes produced in panification—they are alcoholic fermentation of the sugar, softening and partial peptonising of the albuminoids, and a limited diastasis of the starch by the albuminoids so changed.

†**'panifice.** *Obs. rare.* [ad. L. *pānificium* making of bread, anything baked, f. *pānis* bread. Cf. obs. F. *panifice* 'bread-making,..also bread' (Cotgr.).] (See quot. 1656.)

1656 BLOUNT *Glossogr.*, *Panifice*,..the craft of baking or making Bread; also Bread it self, or a Loaf of Bread. **1657** TOMLINSON *Renou's Disp.* 398 These animalls do not expose their panifice to the injuryes of the aire and Heavens. **1658** in PHILLIPS.

panigerick(e, -gery, etc., obs. ff. PANEGYRIC, etc.

panikelle, obs. form of PANNICLE.

panime, obs. form of PAYNIM.

Paninean (pæ'nɪnɪən), *a.* Also **Paninian.** [f. Skr. *Pāṇinīyā* in the same sense (also used), f. the name *Pāṇini*: see below.] Of or pertaining to the Sanskrit grammar of Pāṇini (6th or 5th c. B.C.); adhering to the rules formulated by Pāṇini.

1801 H. T. COLEBROOKE in *Asiatic Researches* VII. 204 A performance, such as the Páninïya grammar, must inevitably contain many errors... The studied brevity of the Páninïya Sútras renders them in the highest degree obscure. **1807** W. JONES *Wks.* IV. 107 Asked what he thought of the Páninïya, he answered very expressively, that 'it was a forest'. **1879** W. D. WHITNEY *Skr. Gram.* ii. 9 The Paninean scheme..classes *a* as guttural. **1900** A. A. MACDONELL *Hist. Skr. Lit.* ix. 268 But the most important information we have of pre-Pāninean grammar is that found in Yāska's work. **1915** S. K. BELVALKAR *Acct. Syst. Skr. Gram.* 43 For most of those writers who followed Kaiyyata there was very little original work in the Pāṇinīya school that was left to be done. **1929** L. BLOOMFIELD in *Language* V. 273 A brief survey of both the Pāṇinean and the later systems is given by Belvalkar. **1967** S. M. KATRE *Pāṇinian Stud.* I. p. viii, With the resurgent interest in linguistic studies..it is appropriate that Pāṇinian studies should form part of the Building Centenary and Silver Jubilee Series. **1977** *Language* LIII. 222 Given the above, it is not impossible that Kātyāyana and Patañjali might have suggested additions or modifications to Pāṇinian rules.

†**'panion.** *Obs.* Also 6 panyon. [Shortened from COMPANION.] = COMPANION, mate, fellow.

1553 T. WILSON *Rhet.* 50 Whether he be a gamester, an alehouse haunter, or a panion among ruffians. **1581** J. BELL *Haddon's Answ. Osor.* 496b, Loe here a very pleasaunt panion and Maister of his Arte. **1589** NASHE *Martins Months Minde* Wks. (Grosart) I. 165 These Panions, scorning all modestie, and reiecting al reason. **1592** GREENE *Def. Conny Catching* Wks. (Grosart) XI. 80 He was a kind of Scholastical panyon.

pan-Ionian, pan-Ionic: see PAN- 1.

†**'paniot.** *Obs. rare.* [a. OF. *paniot* (1282 in Godef.), f. *pan* cloth.] Covering; horse-cloth.

1310 *Acc. Exors T. Bp. of Exeter* (Camden) 6 De iijs. vjd. de iij pecis de panyot debili venditis.

panisc, panisk ('pænɪsk). *Mythol.* [ad. Gr. πανίσκ-ος, L. *Panisc-us*, dim. of Πάν, PAN *sb.*[2]] A little Pan; an inferior deity representing or attending on Pan. Hence **pa'nisca** as feminine of this.

1604 B. JONSON *Penates*, The Paniskes, and the Siluanes rude. **1850** LEITCH tr. *C. O. Müller's Anc. Art* (ed. 2) §361. 448 A panisca at the music of Apollo opens her mouth wide. *Ibid.* §387. 501 A good-natured panisc plucks a thorn from the foot of a satyr.

panisic (pæ'naɪsɪk), *a. nonce-wd.* [f. PAN- all + Gr. ἴσ-ος equal + -IC.] Relating to a social state in which all are equal; = PANTISOCRATIC.

1864 BLACKMORE *Clara Vaughan* lxii, Platonic no doubt, and panisic, but not altogether adapted to double entry. **1887** —— *Springhaven* (ed. 4) II. vii. 76 A meek salutation which proved his panisic ideas to be not properly wrought into his system as yet.

Panislam (pæn'ɪslæm, -ɪ'slɑːm). [f. PAN- 1 + ISLAM.] All Islam; (the conception of) a union of the Muslim world.

1883 *Contemp. Rev.* Jan. 57 Panislam must be crushed by a new crusade.

So **Panislamic, -Islamic** (-ɪs'læmɪk, -ɪs'lɑːmɪk), of or pertaining to all Islam, or to a union of all Muslims. **Pan'islamism,** the Panislamic aspiration.

1881 *Times* 22 Dec. 9 Some encouragement being given in Egypt to the Panislamic dreams of the present Sultan. **1883** *Contemp. Rev.* Jan. 62 The phantom of a Panislamic league. **1885** *Encycl. Brit.* XIX. 93/1 The most famous, after the Pan-Islamic pilgrimages, are the great Shiite sanctuaries. **1882** *Echo* 29 Aug. 1/5 In order to oppose the advancing aggression of..'Pan-Islamism'.

pa'nivorous, *a. rare*—[0]. [f. L. *pānis* bread: see -VOROUS.] Devouring or feeding upon bread.

1830 in MAUNDER *Treas. Knowl.* **1848** in CRAIG.

pani-wallah. *India.* [f. Hindi *pānī* water + WALLAH.] A water-carrier (see also quot. 1957).

1934 'G. ORWELL' *Burmese Days* xxv. 368 Ba Pe is pani-wallah in the same house at sixteen rupees a month. **1936** W. H. S. SMITH *Let.* 2 Aug. in *Young Man's Country* (1977) ii. 20 My nice young pani-wallah has had to return to Rajshahi. **1957** D. G. O. BAILLIE *Sea Affair* 244 *Pani-wallahs*..are not really watermen at all, but oilmen, or greasers. **1960** *Times* 16 Mar. (Canberra Suppl.) p. xiv/6 Greasers are called panniwallahs, where 'panni' means water (once a more popular lubricant than grease). **1971** *Blitz* (Bombay) 6 Mar. 9/2 Householders are cursing him loudly, calling him 'paniwala maharaj'.

Panjabi: see PUNJABI *sb.* and *a.*

panjandrum (pæn'dʒændrəm). In origin, a nonsense word (simulating compounds of PAN-, and burlesquing a title), occurring in the farrago of nonsense composed by S. Foote to test the memory of old Macklin, who had asserted that he could repeat anything after once hearing it.

1755 FOOTE in *Q. Rev.* (1854) XCV. 516 And there were present the Picninnies, and the Joblillies, and the Garyulies, and the Grand Panjandrum himself, with the little round button at top. **1825** MAR. EDGEWORTH *Harry & Lucy Concl.* II. 153. **1867** F. H. LUDLOW *Little Brother* 39 The little wide-awake, like the Panjandrum 'with the little round button at the top'.

Hence **a.** A mock title for an imaginary or mysterious personage of much power, or a personage of great pretensions; a self-constituted high mightiness or magnifico; a local magnate or official of grand airs; a pompous pretender.

[**1825** MAR. EDGEWORTH *Harry & Lucy Concl.* II. 46 He [the gardener] began to praise his carnations... One he called..' The envy of the world, or the great panjandrum'.] *a* **1880** FITZGERALD (Brewer), He was the Great Panjandrum of the place. **1880** BREWER *Reader's Hand-bk. Allusions, Panjandrum (The Grand)*, any village potentate or Brummagem magnate. **1887** *Pall Mall G.* 11 Oct. 1 Wanting to cut a fine figure in high life, as official panjandrums generally do want. **1892** F. HARRISON in *Pall Mall G.* 19 Sept. 4/3, I do not think the future of Ireland can be affected by the utterances of the Panjandrum of Biblical Science and Scotch Presbyterianism. **1896** A. MORRISON *Child of the Jago* 148 A sudden quacksalver, a Panjandrum of philanthropy, who undertook to abolish poverty and sin. **1900** *Pall Mall G.* 16 Feb. 3/2 So will the great British public, even though it may scarcely know what sort of a Panjandrum a Senior Wrangler is.

b. Official and ceremonial fuss or formality.

1883 NASMYTH *Autobiog.* xv. 281, I did not care for all this panjandrum of punctiliousness.

panji(e, varr. PUNJI.

panjrapol, var. PINJRAPOL.

pank (pæŋk), *v. dial. intr.* To pant.

1663 DRYDEN *Wild Gallant* v. iii, We met three or four hugeous ugly devils..that made my heart so panck ever since, as they say! **1746** *Exmoor Scolding* (E.D.S.) 48. **1864** YOUNG *Rabin Hill* 7 (E.D.D.) Jist hark how he do pank an' blow.

†**pank,** *sb. Obs.* Of uncertain origin and sense. (The date seems to oppose its being connected with prec. vb., as a collateral form of PANT *sb.*[2])

c **1430** LYDG. *Min. Poems* (Percy Soc.) 31 War the sicknesse that called is the pank,..A maladie called *male de flank*, A bocche that nedeth a good cirurgian.

pankin ('pænkɪn). Now *dial.* [f. PAN *sb.*[1] + -KIN: cf. PANNIKIN.] A small earthenware pan or jar; also, such a vessel without restriction of size, a pancheon.

1420 *E. E. Wills* (1882) 46 Also ij pankyns & a posnet of a potell. **1533** in Weaver *Wells Wills* (1890) 19 To Aves Philipps, my auntes doughter, a pankyn. **1647–8** *N. Riding Rec.* (1887) V. 9 Presented for stealing an earthen pankin (8d.). **1788** W. MARSHALL *Yorksh.* Gloss. (E.D.S.), *Pankin*, any small earthen jar. **1863** ATKINSON *Stanton Grange* (1864) 231 You get a big pankin,..a large earthenware jar.

Panlibhonco (pænlɪb'hɒnkəʊ). [f. *Pan*ama, *Lib*eria, *Hon*duras, *Co*sta Rica.] Designating or pertaining to a merchant ship of Panama, Liberia, Honduras, and Costa Rica flying a 'flag of convenience'. Cf. FLAG *sb.*[4] 1 f, PANHONLIB.

1958 *Hansard Lords* 20 Mar. 369 We have to be very careful lest any action taken by Her Majesty's Government may harm British shipping more than 'Panlibhonco' owners. **1958** *Times* 14 Nov. 13/3 This great and growing block of virtually stateless tonnage—the tonnage of what is commonly known as 'PanHonLib' or 'Panlibhonco'. *Ibid.* 15 Nov. 8/2 Many of the big Panlibhonco fleets pay rates well above the average. **1959** P. PADFIELD *Sea is Magic Carpet* vi. 97 We sunbathed and watched the tankers sweep by on either side—many of them magnificent, streamlined beasts of the PanLibHonCo variety.

pan-loaf [PAN *sb.*[1]] A loaf baked in a pan; chiefly *Sc.* Also used *fig.* of an affected or cultured accent, or of someone whose behaviour is regarded as pretentious, this usage originating in the fact that a pan-loaf, being more expensive, was a sign of affluence. Hence **pan-loafy** *a.*

1886 WILLOCK *Rosetty Ends* (1889) 10 (E.D.D.) He lat drive at Simpson's head wi' a pan-loaf. **1906** 'H. FOULIS' *Vital Spark* i. 5 Four men and a derrick, and a water-butt and a pan loaf in the fo'c'sle. **1907** J. KIRKLAND *Mod. Baker* I. 112 Tin or Pan Loaves... Scotch pan loaves..are generally baked four in a pan, and to ensure that they separate with a smooth face each loaf is greased on the ends before being placed in the tin. **1922** JOYCE *Ulysses* 143 They buy..four slices of panloaf at the north city dining rooms in Marlborough street. **1946** 'D. TWITTER' *Tales o' the Toonie* 48, I warned Sarah Amelia no' tae start speakin' pan-loafy fin I wiz wi' her. She thrapit doon my thrapple that if I spak braid Farfar fowk wud tak me for a Turk. **1947** H. W. PRYDE *First Bk. McFlannels* vi. 61 An' yer pan-loaf talk! 'Good-marning, Mrs. McTweed,' says you, 'fehn weather we've heving for this tehm of the year!' **1957** *Bulletin* (Glasgow) 25 Feb. 11/2 Pan loaves are coming back into favour again. **1959** M. PUGH *Chancer* 61 'The little kids used to shout, "Grey breeks, grey breeks, let's hear you speaking pan-loafy,"' she said... An all girls' school where they paid fees and wore grey uniforms and didn't talk in the local accent was splendidly ridiculous. **1964** *Weekly Scotsman* 16 June 8 Ah dinna like her, she's oafy pan loaf. **1973** BOYD & PARKES *Dark Number* v. 58 Him and his fancy clothes and his pan-loaf accent and his money! Why couldn't he stay on his own side of the tracks? **1974** *New Society* 28 Feb. 500/3 It was the authentic voice of the people of Glasgow.., and not the 'pan-loaf' (falsely polished) accents of the Scottish BBC. **1976** *Scotsman* 24 Dec. (Weekend Suppl.) 1/7 His pan-loaf accent would make you die. He's gettin' ready, y'see, to be a great sports commentator on the telly after he's made his mark in athletics.

panlogism ('pænləʊdʒɪz(ə)m). [ad. mod.L. *panlogismus*, f. Gr. παν- all + λόγος speech, word, reason: see -ISM.] A term formed by J. E. Erdmann (*Deutsche Speculation seit Kant* (1853) II. 853) on the analogy of *pantheismus*, to describe the philosophy of Hegel, as one which holds that only the rational is truly real. (Generally used with an implication of dissent from the position so characterized.) Hence **pan'logical, panlo'gistic** *a.*, pertaining to or of the nature of panlogism.

1871 LEWES *Hist. Philos.* (ed. 4) II. 619 By Erdmann, Hegel's system is happily characterized as Panlogism rather than Pantheism, since, instead of presenting the universe as the evolution of God, he presents it, and God also, as the evolution of the abstract idea. **1872** *Contemp. Rev.* XX. 538 The panlogical system of Hegel. **1893** *Athenæum* 12 Aug. 221/1 In the course of expounding his 'panlogistic' theory. **1901** DEWEY in Baldwin *Dict. Philos.* II. 255/2 *Panlogism*, a term applied to philosophic systems which make thought the absolute—usually to the system of Hegel.

pan-materialistic, -melodicon, etc.: see PAN- 2.

‖**panmixia** (pæn'mɪksɪə). *Biol.* Also **panmixis, panmixy.** [mod.L., = Ger. *panmixie* (Weismann), f. Gr. παν- all + μιξία, from μίξις mixing, mingling; lit. 'universal or general mingling' (*sc.* of ancestral qualities).]

1. Weismann's term for a supposed promiscuous reproduction of all manner of ancestral qualities or tendencies, consequent on the cessation of natural selection in relation to organs which have become useless or little used, and tending to the degeneration of these organs. Now used to mean random mating within a breeding population. Also *transf.*

1889 POULTON, etc. tr. *Weismann's Ess. Heredity* 90 This suspension of the preserving influence of natural selection may be termed *Panmixia*, for all individuals can reproduce themselves and thus stamp their characters upon the species, and not only those which are in all respects, or in respect to some single organ, the fittest,..the great variability of most domesticated animals essentially depends upon this principle. **1889** [see GALTON]. **1890** RAY LANKESTER in *Nature* 27 Mar. 487/2 The doctrine of panmixia is this. When there is no longer, owing to changed conditions of life, any use for an organ, it will cease to be the subject of natural selection. Consequently all possible variations..will have (so far as the now lapsed use of the organ is concerned) an equal chance. **1890** W. JAMES *Princ. Psychol.* II. xxviii. 687 The obsolescence of disused organs he [*sc.* Weismann] explains very satisfactorily..by his theory of panmixy. **1895** MIVART in *Harper's Mag.* Mar., A fortuitous mixture of ancestral tendencies..called panmixia. **1896** A. TILLE in T. Common tr. *Nietzsche's Case of Wagner* p. x, In a tribe the members of which..assist each other in every kind of danger natural selection must soon come to an end, a kind of panmixy must arise and lead to a rapid decline. **1909** W. M. URBAN *Valuation* xi. 341 Social pan-mixia, the breaking down of class barriers, makes impossible that fixity and contrast of ideals. **1943** *Genetics* XXVIII. 114 Mass selection..is all that can occur under panmixia. **1949** DARLINGTON & MATHER *Elem. Genetics* 408 Panmixis, unrestricted Random Mating. Properly excluded by any restriction, but sometimes used where random mating is assumed within the operation of a restriction, especially with dioecy in animals. **1955** *New Biol.* XVIII. 35 Panmixia or random mating..does not mean promiscuity. **1968** J. W. PURSEGLOVE *Tropical Crops: Dicotyledons* II. 360 Panmixia: by growing a number of c[ulti]v[ar]s together and hand-pollinating between them a highly variable population can be synthesized. **1971** L. N. MORRIS *Human Populations* (1972) ii. 34 Panmixis does not take place within the total [human] species.

2. In form **panmixis.** A population within which random mating takes place.

1968 J. W. PURSEGLOVE *Tropical Crops: Dicotyledons* II. 360 In Uganda a panmixis of 19 [*Gossypium*] *latifolium* c[ulti]v[ar]s from a number of countries was chosen.

Hence **pan'mictic** *a.*, characterized by panmixia.

1943 *Genetics* XXVIII. 117 The term random breeding or panmictic unit will be used for any local population of the same effective size as the parental group. **1971** *Nature* 12 Feb. 468/1 It is possible that in animal species..well able to migrate, no local population is sufficiently isolated to prevent the entire species or subspecies forming effectively one panmictic population. **1975** S. K. JAIN in Frankel & Hawkes *Crop Genetic Resources* ii. 18 All individuals within a colony might be one panmictic group.

pannach(e, -ashe, pannada, pannal(l, obs. ff. PANACHE, PANADA, PANEL *sb.*[1]

‖**pannade.** *Obs.* [obs. F. *pannade* (Cotgr.), OF. *pennade, penade* (15–16th c. in Godef.), whence F. *panader* to strut, caper, curvet. Given by Blount in an entry taken verbally from Cotgrave and repeated in most of the Dicts. to the present day. But app. never in Eng. use.]

[**1611** COTGR., *Pannades*, the curuettings, prauncings, or boundings of lustie horses.] **1656** BLOUNT *Glossogr.*, *Pannades* (Fr.), the curvettings, prauncings, or boundings of lusty Horses. **1658–1706** in PHILLIPS. **1721–** in BAILEY. **1755** in JOHNSON citing AINSWORTH. Hence in mod. Dicts.

‖**ˈpannag.** [Heb. *pannag.*] ‘Perhaps a kind of confection’ (R.V. margin).

1611 BIBLE *Ezek.* xxvii. 17 They traded in thy market wheate of Minnith, and Pannag, and honie, and oyle.

pannage (ˈpænɪdʒ). Also (4–5 **pownage**), 6 **pannadge**, 6–9 **panage**, (7 **pawnage**, 7–9 **paunage**). [a. OF. *pasnage*, 1272 in Godef. (also *paasn-, parn-, paan-*), *panage* (*paisn-, pain-*), *pennage* (Godef.), mod.F. *panage*, in med.L. *pasnāticum, pastināticum*:—late L. *pastiōnāticum* (921 in Du Cange), f. *pastiōn-em* feeding, pasturing, from *pascĕre, past-um* to feed.]

1. *Law.* **a.** The feeding of swine (or other beasts) in a forest or wood; pasturage for swine; **b.** The right or privilege of pasturing swine in a forest; **c.** The payment made to the owner of a woodland for this right; the profit thus accruing.

[**1217** *Charter of Forest* ix, Unusquisque liber homo agistet boscum suum in foresta..et habeat pannagium suum. **1292** BRITTON III. vii. §5 Et puis soit enquis de mel et de pannage et de pesson des glans des noyz et de autre manere des fructz. **1321–2** *Rolls of Parlt.* I. 388/2 Porcs a pesczer en temps de pestzon..santz doner pasnage. **1347–8** *Ibid.* II. 205/2 En lieu de Disme de Pannage.] **1450** *Ibid.* V. 184/1 All maner of Grauntes..of eny Herbage or Pannage, Fisshyng, Pasture or commyn of Pasture. **1461** *Ibid.* 476/1 A summe of money called custume pannage for Swyne. **1495** *Act 11 Hen. VII*, c. 33 §10 The office of kepyng of the Parke of Maylewyg..with the Herbage and Pownage of the same. **1523** FITZHERB. *Surv.* viii. (1539) 12 Also it is to be enquered of panage, and herbage. **1598** MANWOOD *Lawes Forest* xii. §1 (1615) 87/2 The profite of the Mast, which is called Pawnage:..Pawnage is rather the money that is receiued for the Agistment of the Mast, then the Mast, or the Agistment it selfe. **1610** W. FOLKINGHAM *Art of Survey* III. iv. 70 Immunities and Exemptions from Theolonie, Pontage,..Pannage, Passage. **1770** HASTED in *Phil. Trans.* LXI. 165 To afford pannage for so large a number as 1200 hogs. **1878** *Law Rep.* 7 Ch. Div. 562 The Plaintiff..claimed to have..a right of pannage or common of pannage for his swine commonable in the forest. **1880** J. WILLIAMS *Rights of Common* 21 Nuts, acorns, the mast of trees, the right to which is known by the name of pannage.

2. *concr.* Acorns, beech-mast, etc., on which swine feed.

c **1374** CHAUCER *Former Age* 7 They eten mast hawes and swych pownage. **1668** WILKINS *Real Char.* II. vi. 171 Mast, Acorn, Pannage. **1713** E. GIBSON *Codex* 706 Acorns..are the chief of those things, which the ancient Laws call Pannage. **1882** *Athenæum* 19 Aug. 232 Herds of wild ponies and droves of wilder pigs thriving on the pannage.

transf. **1647** WARD *Simple Cobl.* 28 What usefull supplies the pannage of England would afford other Countries.

pannam, -um (ˈpænəm). *Thieves' Cant.* Also 7–8 **panam**. [prob. corrupt form of L. *pānem*, acc. of *pānis* bread, as in the prayer *panem nostrum da nobis hodie.*] Bread.

1567 HARMAN *Caveat* 83 Here followyth their pelting speche... *Pannam*, bread. **1609** DEKKER *Lanthorn & Candlelight* ciij b, If we mawn'd Pannam, lap, or Ruff-peck. **1641** BROME *Jovial Crew* II. Wks. 1873 III. 388 Here's Pannum and Lap, and good Poplars of Yarrum, To fill up the Crib, and to comfort the Quarron. *a* **1700** B. E. *Dict. Cant. Crew*, *Panam*, Bread. **1880** MISS BRADDON *Just as I am* vi. 34 Bits o' mouldy pannam.

attrib. *c* **1742** in Hone *Every-day Bk.* II. 527 Tickets to be had, for three Megs a Carcass to scran their Pannum-Boxes.

panne (pan, pæn). [F. *panne* (15th c. in Littré), earlier *pene, penne, pane* (13th c.), *pienne* (14th c.) = Pr. *penna, pena*, OSp. *peña*, med.L. *panna* (1406 in Du Cange); origin uncertain; see PANE *sb.*[2]] A soft kind of cloth with a long nap, resembling velvet.

1794 A. YOUNG *Trav. France* (ed. 2) I. II. xix. 550 St. Omers. There is a manufacture of..a kind of stuff called *pannes*. **1875** KNIGHT *Dict. Mech.*, *Panne*,..worsted plush of French manufacture. **1898** *Daily News* 10 Dec. 6/3 Among the new materials is that called panne, a very silky make of cloth, almost resembling velvet in softness of surface. **1899** *Westm. Gaz.* 18 Sept. 4/1 We see her in a dress of grey panne. **1919** [see BUD *sb.*[1] 3 d]. **1923** [see MAROCAIN]. **1940** *Chambers's Techn. Dict.* 611/2 *Panne velvet*, a warp pile fabric with silk pile; used for dresses and furnishings. **1972** *New Yorker* 7 Oct. 24/1 (Advt.), Pants are perfect for evening when they're lush panne velvet. **1977** *Vogue* Dec. 124/3 *Big sister*..in chocolate brown panne velvet.

panne, obs. form of PAN *sb.*[1] and [3].

pannel, variant of PANEL, PANELE.

[**pannell**, *v.* Only found in the following passage: app. an error of some kind. Editors have conjectured *spanieled, pantl'red*, and *paged*.

1606 SHAKS. *Ant. & Cl.* IV. xii. 21 The hearts That pannelled me at heeles, to whom I gaue Their wishes.]

pannery (ˈpænərɪ). [f. PAN *sb.*[1] + -ERY.]

1. The making of salt in pans: see PAN *sb.*[1]

1762 tr. *Busching's Syst. Geog.* V. 470 The pannery here, or the right of salt-works, depends on chancery-writ.

2. *nonce-use.* Pans collectively.

1889 *Pall Mall G.* 30 Apr. 7/2, I asked the manager..what he thought of the new pottery and pannery; he said, ‘Not much’.

†**ˈpannicle.** *Obs.* Also 5 **panikelle, pannycele**, 5–7 **panicle**, 6 **pannycle, -ickle, -ikell, -icule**, 7 **-ikle**. [a. OF. *panicle, pannicle*, ad. L. *pannicul-us* small piece of cloth, rag, dim. of *pannus* cloth; in mod.F. *pannicule*.]

1. *Anat.* A membrane or membranous structure in an animal body, as the peritoneum, the membranes of the brain, and *esp.* the *panniculus carnosus* (*fleshy pannicle*), a layer of muscular fibres lying just beneath the skin, specially developed in some quadrupeds.

c **1440** *Lanfranc's Cirurg.* 27 After hem comeþ panniclis [*Add. MS.* pannyceles]—þat is to seie smal cloop, þat is maad of sutil þredis of senewis, veynes & arteries. *Ibid. marg.* panikelles. *Ibid.*, þe panicle of þe heed byndiþ seuene boones. **1545** RAYNOLD *Byrth Mankynde* I. (1634) 70 A pannicle springing and growing forth from the right seate of Peritoneum. **1562** BULLEYN *Bulwark, Dial. Soarnes* 40 The rimme or pannicle, whiche from out foorthe, covereth the scalpe. **1603** HOLLAND *Plutarch's Mor.* 1337 That all their braines should be contained within one and the same membrane or pannicle. **1621** CRASHAW *Fiscus Papalis* L iv, Also, there is the very skinne or pannikle that came out of the most holy body of the Virgin Mary, which her sonne Jesus Christ our Lord, in his birth, brought with him. **1656** BLOUNT *Glossogr.* s.v., The fleshy Pannicle. *c* **1720** W. GIBSON *Farrier's Guide* I. i. (1738) 5 Underneath the Skin is placed the fleshy Pannicle, which is Muscular. [**1871** DARWIN *Desc. Man* I. i. 19 The power which many animals, especially horses, possess of moving or twitching their skin ..is effected by the panniculus carnosus.]

¶ **b.** App. misused as = brain-pan, skull.

1590 SPENSER *F.Q.* III. v. 23 He..Smote him so rudely on the Pannikell, That to the chin he clefte his head in twaine.

2. *Bot.* A membranous covering in plants, as the scales investing a leaf-bud.

1671 GREW *Anat. Plants* I. iv. §17 Every Bud, besides its proper Leaves, is covered with divers Leafy Pannicles or Surfoyls. **1736** H. BROOKE *Univ. Beauty* III. 403 The flowers' forensic beauties now admire, The impalement, foliation, down, attire, Couch'd in the pannicle or mantling veil.

pannicle, variant of PANICLE.

†**paˈnnicular**, *a.* *Obs.* [f. L. *pannicul-us*, PANNICLE + -AR.] Of the nature of ‘pannicle’.

1548–77 VICARY *Anat.* ix. (1888) 81 The tayle gutte, whose substance is panniculer.

panniell, obs. form of PANEL.

pannier (ˈpænɪə(r)), *sb.*[1] Forms: 4–7 **panyer**, 4– **panier**, 6 **pannyer**, 6– **pannier**, (also 4 **panyar, payngnier**, 4–5 **paner, panyȝer**, 5 **panere, -yere, -ȝer(e, -ȝar, -yher**, *Sc.* **panȝell**, 6 **paniar**, 7 **panniar, -ard**, 7–8 **panyard, -erd**). [ME. *panier*, a. F. *panier* (in 15th c. rarely *pannier*) = Pr. *panier*, Cat. *paner*, It. *paniere*:—L. *pānāri-um* bread-basket, f. *pān-is* bread: see -ARIUM.]

1. a. A basket; *esp.* one of considerable size for carrying provisions, fish, or other commodities; in later use mostly restricted to those carried by a beast of burden (usually in pairs, one on each side, slung across the back), or on the shoulders of a man or woman.

c **1300** *Havelok* 760 Gode paniers dede he make..to beren fish inne. *c* **1358** *Durham Acc. Rolls* (Surtees) 562, j par. de Panyars empt. apud London. *c* **1384** CHAUCER *H. Fame* III. 849 Or maken of these [twigs] panyers. **1426** LYDG. *De Guil. Pilgr.* 21050 Vp-on hyr hed a gret paner. *c* **1440** *Gesta Rom.* I. xc. 414 (Add. MS.) All thofe I solde the þe fyshe, I solde the not the panyere. **1578** LYTE *Dodoens* IV. lii. 511 The frayle Rushe..they vse to make figge frayles and paniers therwithall. **1598** HAKLUYT *Voy.* I. 448 (R.) Baskets made like bakers panniers. **1600** *Ibid.* (1810) III. 389 Little Paniers made of Palme leaves. *a* **1656** USSHER *Ann.* vi. (1658) 272 Beasts of..carriage, some for pack-saddles, and some for panniards. **1727** GAY *Fables* I. xxxvii. 21 Betwixt her swagging panniers' load A farmer's wife to market rode. **1859** THACKERAY *Virgin.* xxii, A costermonger with his donkey and a pannier of cabbage. **1886** HALL CAINE *Son of Hagar* (1887) I. i. 21 Mounted on a pony that carried its owner on a saddle immediately below its neck, and a pair of panniers just above its tail.

b. The amount contained by a pannier.

1714 *Fr. Bk. Rates* 43 Glass in Metal per Cart-load, containing 4 Panniers. **1880** DISRAELI *Endym.* I. xi. 89 The gardener's wife..threw..a pannier of cones upon the logs.

c. A covered basket for holding surgical instruments and medicines for a military ambulance.

(By a curious blunder this was explained by the Secretary at War in the House of Commons on 25 July, 1854, as a horse litter or ambulance for the transport of the sick or wounded, and no one in the House knew any better. The error is repeated in Kinglake's *Crimea*.)

1854 SIDNEY HERBERT in *Hansard* CXXXV. 719 Almost the first thing upon which my eye glanced was forty pair of panniers, for the conveyance of the sick. [Cf. quot. 1895.] **1880** KINGLAKE *Crimea* VI. ii. 7 He was carried in the invalid's pannier. *Ibid.* vi. 144 The cart or pannier used in transferring him to some other kind of hospital. **1895** SIR E. WOOD *Crimea in 1854 & 1894*, 11, I suppose it would be difficult now to find any one in the House of Commons, who could mistake a medical pannier, i.e. a covered basket for holding surgical instruments and drugs, for an ambulance.

†**2.** *Arch.* = CORBEIL 2. *Obs.* [Littré has (*Panier* 14) ‘Ornement d'architecture plus étroit et plus haut que la corbeille, portant des fleurs et des fruits’. The Eng. works here cited erroneously confuse CORBEIL with CORBEL.]

1781–6 REES *Chambers' Cycl.*, *Pannier*, in *Architecture*. See CORBEL. [*Ibid.*, *Corbel*, in *Architecture*, the representation of a basket.] **1842–76** GWILT *Archit.* (ed. 7) Gloss., *Pannier*, the same as CORBEL. [So Webster 1864 and mod. Dicts., all confusing *corbeil* with *corbel*.]

3. (See quot.)

1875 KNIGHT *Dict. Mech.*, *Pannier*..(*Hydraulic Engineering*), a basket or gabion of wicker-work containing gravel or earth,..used in forming a basis for earthy material in the construction of dikes or banks.

4. A basket-carriage. *rare.*

1880 ‘OUIDA’ *Moths* xvii. 199 Vere, with her husband, drove in the panier, with four white ponies.

5. A frame of whalebone, wire, or other material, used to distend the skirt of a woman's dress at the hips. [F. *panier* (Littré).] *erron.* A bunched up part of a skirt forming a protuberance behind.

1869 *Punch* 31 July 33/2 The singular excrescences which are worn now on the back are spoken of as ‘paniers’. **1877** ‘OUIDA’ *Puck* xxxi. 390 Chignons and co-respondents, plunging and panniers, Americanism and cocotteism. **1902** *Daily Chron.* 11 Jan. 8/3 Paniers are among the very latest dress importations received in London. They..have been used on a gown of mahogany brown velvet in the form of a tunic, opened in front to show a petticoat, with sides sweeping into a train at the back.

6. *attrib.* and *Comb.*, as *pannier-bearer*, *-maker*, *-rush*, *-shaped* adj.; **pannier bag**, a bag or similar container (usu. one of a pair) placed above or to the side of the rear wheel of a bicycle or motor cycle; also *ellipt.*; †**pannier-hilt** = BASKET-HILT; **pannier pocket**, a large pocket attached to the side of a skirt or dress; **pannier tank**, a type of small steam locomotive which has a water tank on each side of the boiler. Also PANNIERMAN.

1939–40 *Army & Navy Stores Catal.* 783/3 Cycle accessories..pannier bags and carriers. **1959** I. JEFFERIES *Thirteen Days* (1961) i. 9, I was forced to pull off the road. .. I had a bottle of cold beer..in the pannier. *Ibid.* xi. 170, I was taking the letters out of the pannier bag when the phone rang. **1975** J. WOOD *North Kill* x. 139 The speaker kicked his bike into life... The others were storing their cleaning materials into side pannier bags. **1976** *Times* 27 Aug. 12/8 The world's most expensive bicycle... For nearly £600 you get neither mudguards nor pannier bags, and not even a rear reflector. **1451** *Acc.* in Sharp *Cov. Myst.* (1825) 206 Item, þe panȝerberrer..ijd. **1641** S. SMITH *Herring Buss Trade* 19 Fresh or Pannier Herring. **1633** B. JONSON *Tale Tub* II. i, Your dun, rusty, Pannier-hilt poniard. **1472** *Presentmts. of Juries* in *Surtees Misc.* (1888) 25 Oone panyermaker houses & harbers suspect persones in his hous. **1922** JOYCE *Ulysses* 501 Those pannier pockets of the skirt.. are devised to suggest bunchiness of the hip. **1973** *Times* 11 Dec. 13/3 Bill's new skirt with its slung pannier pockets is pretty. **1578** LYTE *Dodoens* IV. lii. 511 The frayle Rushe or panier Rushe. **1828** KIRBY & SP. *Entomol.* (ed. 2) III. xxx. 229 The larva..constructs a pannier-shaped cocoon of the parenchyma of leaves. **1949** C. J. ALLEN *Locomotive Pract. & Performance 20th Cent.* vi. 65 Shunting on all railways is entrusted in large measure to small 0-6-0 tanks (pannier tanks on the Western Region). **1950** H. C. WEBSTER *Railways for All* ix. 83 Frequently such locomotives carry the water in tanks fitted on top of the boiler and are therefore termed ‘saddle tanks’. Others carry the water in two tanks secured high up along the boiler sides, and these are known as ‘pannier tanks’. **1957** *Railway Mag.* Nov. 751/2 Today 0-6-0 pannier-tanks usually deal with the traffic. **1970** *Ibid.* Oct. 549 (*caption*) Wellington to Much Wenlock afternoon passenger train..headed by 0-6-0 pannier-tank No. 7754. **1973** *Country Life* 8 Mar. 593 A type peculiar to the GWR —the pannier tank..these modest 0-6-0 engines, which carried their water in ‘panniers’ at either side of the boiler.

pannier (ˈpænɪə(r)), *sb.*[2] [See below.] The name by which the robed waiters at table are known in the Inner Temple.

1823 CRABB *Technol. Dict.*, *Pannier* or *Pannier-man*, a name..now commonly applied to all the domestics who wait in the hall at the time of dinner. **1859** F. BRANDT *Frank M.* viii. 107 The most awkward of waiters (called according to custom pannyers; scilicet pannifers, or bread-bearers). **1861** *Illustr. Lond. News* 9 Nov. 481/1 The Inner Temple Hall waiters are called *panniers*, from the *pannarii* who attended the Knights Templars[!]. **1903** F. A. INDERWICK *Letter to Editor*, The term ‘pannier’ during the whole of my time, now extending over 45 years, has been used as meaning ‘waiter’, and applied to the attendants of the inn waiting at meals... I have not found the term used anywhere officially, but it has apparently long been employed by members of the inn. **1903** T. F. HOWELL *Let.*, As no new ‘panniers’ are now appointed, the name will drop out of use.

[*Note.* The name *pannier* is merely colloquial, and does not occur in the Records. It may have originated or been derived in some way from that of the PANNIERMAN, but it is not identical with that word, as erroneously assumed by Crabbe (followed by later dictionaries); still less is it, as sometimes stated, the source of that word. There is no evidence to connect it with L. *pānārius* (bread-seller) or *pannārius* (cloth-seller), as conjectured by some.]

ˈ**pannier**, *v. rare.* [f. PANNIER *sb.*[1]] *trans.* **a.** To furnish with a pannier or panniers. **b.** To place in, or as in, a pannier.

1596 NASHE *Saffron Walden* 146 He hath so pannyerd and drest it that it seemes a new thing. **1804** CHARLOTTE SMITH *Conversations*, etc. II. 190 Panier'd in shells, or bound with silver strings Of silken Pinna.

panniered (ˈpænɪəd), *a.* [f. PANIER *sb.*[1] + -ED[2].] Laden with a pannier or panniers.

1735 SOMERVILLE *Chase* III. 131 Drove like a pannier'd Ass, and scourg'd along. *c* **1820** S. ROGERS *Italy, Como* 47 Wains oxen-drawn and panniered mules are seen.

ˈ**pannierman.** [f. PANNIER *sb.*[1] + MAN.]

1. A man in charge of a pannier or panniers; *esp.* a hawker of fish, etc., who conveys his goods to market in panniers. ? *Obs.*

1583 *N. Riding Rec.* N.S.I. (1894) 251 Divers of the inhabytantes and other poore men panier-men. **1614** B. JONSON *Barth. Fair* II. Wks. (Rtldg.) 321/2 If the pannier-man's jack was ever better known by his loins of mutton, I'll be flayed. **1678** RAY *Prov.* (ed. 2) 78 Mock no panyer-men, your father was a fisher. **1736** F. DRAKE *Eboracum* I. vi. 219 Sea fish market is kept..for panniermen free of the city. **1900** [see *Eng. Dial. Dict.*].

2. The name of a paid officer in the Inns of Court, who brought provisions from market (with a horse and panniers), and (in later times at least) had various duties in connexion with the serving of the meals, etc.: see quots. (Now obsolete.)

1482-3 *Black Bks. Linc. Inn* lf. 54 Et de xvjs. solut. a le panereman. **1538** *Ibid.* (ed. 1897) 251 No horses shall be putt in the Conygarye, butt onlye one horse for the Panyar man. **1601** *Pension Bk. Gray's Inn* 156 The paniarman.. shall alsoe have iii *li.* allowed him for..his wantinge of pasture and provision..for his horse. **1616** *Bl. Bks. Linc. Inn* 185 It is further ordered that the flesh and fish shall not be caryed in one pannyer uncleanelye and uncovered, but that the Pannyerman shall have one pannyer for fish and another for flesh. **1624** *Pens. Bk. Gray's Inn* 263 It is ordered ..that the panierman shall have thirtie shillings a yeare.. more..towards the bringinge home of the meat from the market. **1630-1** *Calend. Inner Temple Recds.* (1898) II. 191 For a new horn for the panierman. **1650** *Wits Recreations* Epit. lxxviii. M iij, On T. H. the Pannierman of the Temple. **1661** BLOUNT *Glossogr.* (ed. 2), *Pannierman*, in the Inns of Court, is one whose Office is to blow the Horn for Dinner, and wait at the Barristers Table. **1842** *Bl. Bks. Linc. Inn* 214 That the Pannierman do see that this order be observed. **1846** *MS. Bks. Linc. Inn* 19 Nov. [Latest mention] The daughters of Edward Clark late Pannierman to this Society. [**1900** Abolished at Inner Temple.]

panniform, *a. Bot.* [f. L. *pannus* cloth + -FORM.] = PANNOSE *a.*

1894 J. M. CROMBIE *Monogr. Lichens Brit.* I. 238 The thalline reactions, in conjunction with the general aspect of the plant, show that it belongs to *P[armelia] revoluta*, produced no doubt by a panniform condition of this species. **1921** A. L. SMITH *Handbk. Brit. Lichens* 141 *Panniform*, *Pannose*, felted. **1957** SNELL & DICK *Gloss. Mycol.* 110/1 Panniform. Having a felted or matted appearance.

pannikell, obs. form of PANNICLE.

pannikin (ˈpænɪkɪn). Also pannican, panakin, panikin. [f. PAN *sb.*[1] + -KIN: cf. *mannikin.*] **a.** A small metal (usually tinned iron) drinking vessel; a cannikin; also, the contents of such a vessel.

'Exceedingly common in Australia' (*Austral Eng.*).

1823 E. MOOR *Suffolk Words*, *Pannikin*, a little vessel or pan for warming children's pap, etc. A diminutive of pan. **1830** R. DAWSON *Pres. St. Australia* 101 (Morris) Several tin pannicans. *Ibid.* 200 He went to the spring and brought me a pannican full. **1835** MARRYAT *Jac. Faithf.* xxi, Bringing out the bottle and tin pannikins, ready for the promised carouse. **1865** MASSON *Rec. Brit. Philos.* i. 19 If saucers and pannikins are all that we have, let us at least take an inventory of our saucers and pannikins. **1880** SUTHERLAND *Tales of Goldfields* 44 A small pannikin full of gold dust. **1908** E. J. BANFIELD *Confessions of Beachcomber* II. i. 280 One day a bucket of milk was brought to the camp at dinner-time and served out with pannikins. **1911** C. E. W. BEAN '*Dreadnought*' *of Darling* xxxii. 282 There was a case of pannikins that had come up as freight. **1924** *Truth* (Sydney) 27 Apr. 6 *Pannikin*, small drinking vessel, made out of tin, carried by the sundowner, and tied to his billy. **1936** I. L. IDRIESS *Cattle King* ii. 14 The boy stared, then snatching his pannikin pushed the reluctant foal away and commenced milking the mare. **1945** BAKER *Austral. Lang.* 169 *A friendly pannikin*, a drink with a companion.

b. The head; in slang phr. *off one's pannikin*, off one's head.

1895 C. CROWE *Austral. Slang Dict.* 56 *Off his pannikin*, silly. **1899** 'S. RUDD' in Murdoch & Drake-Brockman *Austral. Short Stories* (1951) 110, I seen 'im just now up in your paddick, an' he's clean off he's pannikin. **1916** C. J. DENNIS *Moods of Ginger Mick* 126 Per'aps I'm orf me pannikin wiv' sittin' in the sun. **1934** B. PENTON *Landtakers* (1935) IV. vii. 360 He's gone raving off his pannikin in Sydney.

c. = *pannikin-boss.*

c **1926** 'MIXER' *Transport Workers' Song Bk.* 7 My power is such to make or break—I'm a pannikin, get me?

d. *Comb.* **pannikin-boss** (see quot. 1898).

1898 MORRIS *Austral Eng.*, *Pannikin-boss*, or *Pannikin-overseer*,..applied colloquially to a man on a station, whose position is above that of the ordinary station-hand, but who ..is only a 'boss' or overseer in a small way. **1930** L. G. D. ACLAND *Early Canterbury Runs* (ser. 1) v. 105 At 'smoke-oh' he used to take a standing jump over a bale of wool and then Brucksaw, the 'pannikin boss' (head general hand), used to carry it out of the shed single-handed. **1936** A. RUSSELL *Gone Nomad* ix. 70 There in the Silver City a telegram awaited me. It contained the offer of a job, that of 'pannikin-boss' and book-keeper on a sheep run east of Broken Hill, on the Milparinka Track. **1959** D. HEWETT *Bobbin Up* viii. 97 All this unshakable distrust of the pannikin boss, the boss's man..the lowest of the low in a world where dog ate dog. **1966** G. W. TURNER *Eng. Lang. Austral. & N.Z.* vii. 146 The manager of a sheepstation was called a *pannikin boss*, a term I have heard used..for a foreman on building jobs in New Zealand. **1969** D. NILAND *Dead Men Running* iv. 98 Father Vaughan seemed to project himself as no more than the mouthpiece of a pannikin boss of a God who sounded like a brutal and violent pirate.

panning (ˈpænɪŋ), *vbl. sb.*[1] [f. PAN *v.*[1] + -ING[1].]

1. a. The action or process of washing auriferous sand, gravel, or crushed rock, by agitation in a pan, so as to obtain the particles of gold or other substance of greatest specific gravity. Also with *out.*

1839 *Amer. Railroad Jrnl.* VIII. 99 This operation is continued until all the sand is removed, and nothing but the gold left. It is called 'panning out'. **1870** TUCKER *Mute* 40 Others to these the precious dirt convey, Linger a moment till the panning's through. **1872** 'MARK TWAIN' *Roughing It* lxi. 443 'Panning out' refers to the washing process by which the grains of gold are separated from the dirt. **1901** *Munsey's Mag.* XXV. 662/1 Panning is the crudest and simplest method of getting out gold dust.

b. The proceeds of such washing; the gold (or other valuable substance) obtained.

1891 *Times* 15 Jan. 5/2 Samples from the surface of the various reefs..show rich pannings. **1893** *Westm. Gaz.* 6 Dec. 6/1 My pannings from these claims are splendid.

c. The action of denouncing or criticizing severely. (Cf. PAN *v.*[1] 7.)

1914 *Sat. Even. Post* 15 Aug. 9/1 Speed sure got a pannin' in the clubhouse... Everybody..roasted him, but it didn't do no good. **1946** *Jazz Writings* 21/2 All this sounds like a merciless panning, I'm afraid, and yet it is kindly meant. **1958** *Spectator* 16 May 624/2 The Council of Industrial Design's exhibition..has had a panning from the design critics. Speaking..as a consumer, I agree with the criticism. **1960** *News Chron.* 27 Feb. 4/8 It was about the only thing in the show which did not get a panning from the critics.

d. *attrib.*, as *panning test, trough.*

1850 N. KINGSLEY *Diary* 17 May (1914) 122 Stoped down to day and made a panning trough to pour quick-silver from the riffler into and fix the pump. **1951** *Oxf. Jun. Encycl.* VII. 21/1 One of the oldest methods of assay..is the miner's concentration or 'panning' test.

2. *Agric.* The action of PAN *v.*[1] 6: the hardening of a layer of soil.

1939 *Geogr. Jrnl.* XCIV. 468 A heavy black clay of undetermined depth without any evidence of panning, no iron concentrations and no characteristics of laterite. **1960** *Farmer & Stockbreeder* 26 Jan. 78/3, I am completely convinced that a panning effect is negligible compared with that of a plough. **1971** *Power Farming* Mar. 50/2 (Advt.), Even in sticky conditions the Soilmaster acts efficiently without 'bulldozing'—Positively no panning. Before buying a new cultivator get the facts on the Soil-master range.

ˈ**panning**, *vbl. sb.*[2] [f. PAN *v.*[3] + -ING[1].] The action of PAN *v.*[3] Also *attrib.*, esp. in *panning shot.*

1917 C. N. BENNETT *Guide to Kinematogr.* ii. 22 Sweeping round the camera from side to side is called panoraming or 'panning'. **1939** G. GREENE *Lawless Roads* vi. 147 If I had moved a camera all round..the little plaza in a panning shot. **1946** *Electronic Engin.* XVIII. 207 The trick of camera panning from one speaker to another. **1953** K. REISZ *Technique Film Editing* ii. 42 A scene..shot from a large number of set-ups, some of them with a panning or tracking camera. **1967** *Spectator* 6 Oct. 392/2 The producer..was not helped by his camera crews, who, if their panning shots were tremulous, zoomed in on things like homing missiles. **1969** *Amat. Photographer* 23 Apr. 51/4 When you are forced to work more or less broadside-on,..swing the camera as you expose in the same direction as the movement. This technique, known as 'panning', is much used by press photographers. **1977** *Radio Times* 28 May 17/1 A long panning shot across some velvet cushions.

pannon, -oun, obs. forms of PENNON.

Pa'nnonic, *a.* Of or pertaining to ancient Pannonia, corresponding to modern Hungary. Also **Pa'nnonian** *a.* and *sb.*

1597 GERARDE *Herbal* I. xxxv. §7. 50 Carolus Clusius.. hath set foorth in his pannonick Epitome. **1605** BACON *Adv. Learning* II. f. 70v We see a notable example in Tacitus of two Stage-plaiers, Percennius and Vibulenus, who by their facultie of playing, put the Pannonian armies into an extreame tumulte and combustion. **1652** ASHMOLE *Theat. Chem.* Prol. 3 When the World was troubled with Pannonick Invasions. **1656** BLOUNT *Glossogr.*, *Pannonian*..of or belonging to..Hungary. **1804** *Europ. Mag.* May 333/2 The sons of Britain..animated with even more than Panonian ardour. **1912** *Q. Rev.* Oct. 335 His happiest days were certainly spent away from Rome in German and Pannonian wars. **1975** R. BROWNING *Emperor Julian* i. 13 Decius, a Pannonian senator who found himself proclaimed emperor against his will in 249. **1976** *Classical Q.* XXVI. 302 It was established in Dalmatia in or soon after A.D. 9, in the wake of the Pannonian uprising.

pannose (pæˈnəʊs), *a. Bot.* [ad. L. *pannōs-us* ragged, rag-like, f. *pannus* cloth: see -OSE.] 'Having the texture of coarse cloth' (*Treas. Bot.* 1866). Hence **pa'nnosely** *adv.*

pannous (ˈpænəs), *a. Path.* [f. as prec. + -OUS.] 'Pertaining to or of the nature of pannus' (*Cent. Dict.* 1890).

pannum, variant of PANNAM.

‖**pannus** (ˈpænəs). *Path.* [? L. *pannus* cloth; in F. *panus* (by Littré referred to L. *pānus*, Gr. πῆνος web).]

1. A vascular condition of the cornea of the eye, with thickening and opacity.

[*c* **1400** *Lanfranc's Cirurg.* 189 Pannus is a superfluite þat fallip in a wommans face, & comeþ ofte in childberyng.] **1706** PHILLIPS, *Pannus*..a Disease of the Eye, when the Vessels that run to the corners swell with Blood, by reason of a stoppage or inflammation; so that a fleshy Web afterwards covers the whole Eye, or part of it. **1875** H. WALTON *Dis. Eye* 873 Such opacity with vascularity is called pannus.

2. *Path.* A layer of granulation tissue that forms by a thickening of the synovial membrane and tends to spread over and absorb adjacent cartilage in a joint affected by rheumatoid arthritis.

1904 *Boston Med. & Surg. Jrnl.* 17 Nov. With the swelling which results the membrane at times extends in or over the cartilage, forming a pannus, and wherever this persists for any length of time.., the cartilage under the pannus is more or less absorbed. **1929** R. PEMBERTON *Arthritis & Rheumatoid Conditions* iii. 53 The proliferation of the synovial membrane causes a layer of granulation tissue to extend in the form of a thin pannus more or less completely over the joint cartilage. **1973** *Nature* 14 Dec. 419/1 The pannus of the rheumatoid joint has the ability to produce an active collagenase and invade and degrade cartilage *in vitro.*

pannuscorium (ˌpænəsˈkɔərɪəm). [Illiterate comb. of L. *pannus* cloth, and *corium* hide, leather.] A trade-name for a kind of soft leather cloth, used for the uppers of boots and shoes.

1858 SIMMONDS *Dict. Trade*, *Pannuscorium*, a name given to a species of leather cloth, used for shoes and boots for those who have tender feet. *c* **1860** *Popular Song*, Here is a Necropolis, There is an Emporium, Your boots are Antegropolis, Your shoes are Panuscorium. **1860** *All Year Round* No. 46. 467 The pannus corium, which has abolished corns.

panny (ˈpænɪ), *a. rare.* [f. PAN *sb.*[1] + -Y.] Like or characteristic of a pan.

1872 ELLACOMBE *Ch. Bells Devon, Bells Ch.* i. 209 A panny, harsh, iron-like sound.

pannycele, -cle, obs. forms of PANNICLE.

pannyer, pannyter, obs. ff. PANNIER, PANTER.

panoche (pæˈnɒtʃiː). *U.S.* Also **panocha, penoche, penuche.** [Amer. Sp., 'brown sugar'.]

1. A type of coarse brown sugar.

1847 *Californian* 10 Apr. 3/2 The cargo consists of 180 bales..of Mexican Sugar; 30 Packages Panoche and one Bale of Zarapies. **1856** L. J. F. JAEGER *Jrnl.* 17 Aug. in *S. Calif. Hist. Soc. Publ.* (1928) XIV. 124 Had to leave 3 cargoes of flour and one fanega of beans & ½ cargo of panocha. **1881** H. T. WILLIAMS *Pacific Tourist* 300/2 The ordinary brown sugar (panoche) of the Mexicans is also obtained from this plant. **1887** *Outing* Apr. 10/2 It is ordinarily made of corn, roasted and crushed and slightly sweetened, the most common sweetening being *panoche*, a crude sugar. **1936** J. A. MCKENNA *Black Range Tales* 52 With ten pounds of jerky, a cone of *penoche* or pressed brown sugar, and a serape, or gray blanket, a Mexican is fitted for a trip of several hundred miles through the mountains.

2. A kind of sweet resembling fudge, made with brown sugar, butter, milk or cream, and nuts. Also *fig.*

1872 *Rep. Indian Affairs 1871* (U.S.) 359, I doubt the good policy of issuing bread, and at times candy (panoche), to the pupils. **1921** M. L. MATTHEWS *Foods & Cookery* 274 Panocha... Mix sugar, milk, and salt. Boil until it reaches the 'soft-ball' stage. **1930** *Sunset* Dec. 30/2 At lower left are seen fondant-dipped and penoche-dipped figs and prunes. **1949** *Arizona Q.* Autumn 255 He made the most luscious panocha and rich syrups, which he sold to the public. **1949** *Chicago Tribune* 28 Sept. II. 2/2 Our recipe for Butterscotch Cake, and Penoche Icing, is printed on the recipe folder. **1952** J. STEINBECK *East of Eden* xix. 226 Faye twisted around in her chair to reach a piece of brown panocha studded with walnuts. When she spoke it was around a mouth full of candy. **1966** *Cookies & Candies* (Better Homes & Gardens) 79/2 Penuche. Rich and creamy brown-sugar fudge. A favorite of grandmothers (granddads, too!) **1968** *Cook's & Diner's Dict.* (Funk & Wagnalls) 167/2 Pe-nu-che..A candy made with brown sugar..Also called panocha. **1971** *Islander* (Victoria, B.C.) 7 Feb. 14/1 There are recipes for all the classic home candies like fudge, butterscotch, penuche, etc. **1976** *Publishers Weekly* 29 Mar. 59/3 With its story of aggressive hatred.., murder attempts.., a later revealed illegitimate birth, and a love interest as well, it's a well-iced piece of penuche.

panographic (pænəʊˈgræfɪk), *a. Dentistry.* Also **panagraphic.** [f. PANO(RAMIC *a.* + RADIO)GRAPHIC *a.*] Of, pertaining to, or designating radiography of several teeth and the adjacent bones in a single exposure by means of a small X-ray source placed inside the mouth and a film outside it.

1952 *Jrnl. Dental Res.* XXXI. 165 In the evaluation of the panographic technique it is well to remember that it must be judged as an adjunct to conventional radiography and not as a substitute for it. **1963** *Dental Radiogr. & Photogr.* XXXVI. 81/2 (*caption*) Panagraphic equipment and technic for the maxilla and the mandible. **1967** *Amer. Jrnl. Roentgenology* CI. 989/2 (*caption*) Panographic study reveals a large expansile cystic lesion in the right mandible, proven to be a dental cyst.

Hence **'panograph**, (*a*) a panographic radiograph; (*b*) an X-ray machine for use in panography; **pa'nography**, panographic radiography.

1961 *Oral Surg., Oral Med., Oral Path.* XIV. 1178 (*heading*) Panagraphy. *Ibid.* 1179 The x-ray tube used in the Panagraph is the Swiss Panoramix tube. **1963** BLACKMAN & POYTON *Man. Dental & Oral Radiogr.* xvi. 160 (*caption*) Panagraph of lower jaw showing unerupted and supernumerary teeth. **1967** *Amer. Jrnl. Roentgenology* CI. 988/1 Panography is a radiographic technique recently described by Blackman for use predominantly in dentistry. **1969** WUEHRMANN & MANSON-HING *Dental Radiol.* (ed. 2) viii. 161 Panagraphy suggests a technic to study structures in a panoramic fashion. The Panagraph or Panoramix is an x-ray machine utilizing an intraoral source of radiation to expose film placed extra-orally. *Ibid.* 163 The main advantages of the Panagraph appear to be that it is relatively portable, is easy to operate, and may be used effectively for mass dental radiography.

panoistic, panolethry: see PAN- 2.

Panomphæan, -ean (pænɒm'fiːən), *a.* [f. Gr. πανομφαῖ-ος, f. παν- all + ὀμφή voice of a god, oracular response: an epithet of Zeus.] Of or pertaining to Zeus, as sender of all ominous voices. (Misused humorously in French by Rabelais, and misunderstood by Cockeram, etc.)

1623 COCKERAM, *Panomphean*, All hearing. **1656** BLOUNT *Glossogr.*, *Panomphean*..pertaining to Jupiter. **1694** MOTTEUX *Rabelais* v. xlvi, *Trinc* is a Panomphean Word, that is a Word understood, us'd and celebrated by all Nations and signifies Drink. **1856** MRS. BROWNING *Aur. Leigh* v. 114 We want no half-gods, Panomphaean Joves.

So **Panom'phaic, Pa'nomphic** *adjs.* (*nonce-wds.*)

1822 T. L. PEACOCK *Maid Marian* xvii. 266 That very Panomphic Pantagruelian saint, well known..as a female divinity, by the name of La Dive Bouteille. **1878** J. THOMSON *Plenip. Key* 7 Whose supreme oracle is the panomphaic Trincq.

‖**panophobia** (pænəʊ'fəʊbɪə). *Path.* Also 9 **panphobia**. [mod.L., f. Gr. Πάν, gen. Πανός PAN + -φοβία from φόβος fear.] A form of melancholia marked by causeless or excessive terror.

1799 HOOPER *Med. Dict.*, *Panophobia*, that kind of melancholy which is attended with groundless fears. **1870** MAUDSLEY *Body & Mind* 97 That form of melancholia.. which is sometimes described as panphobia. **1893** *Syd. Soc. Lex.*, *Panophobia*, sudden fear or panic, which was supposed to be inspired by Pan.

‖**panoph'thalmia** = next.

1890 in *Cent. Dict.* **1893** in *Syd. Soc. Lex.*

‖**panophthal'mitis.** *Path.* [PAN-.] Inflammation of the whole eyeball.

1842 in DUNGLISON *Med. Lex.* **1899** *Allbutt's Syst. Med.* VI. 789 Evidence of destructive changes and panophthalmitis.

panoplied ('pænəplɪd), *a.* [f. PANOPLY + -ED[2].] Clad in complete armour. Also *fig.*

1877 BLACKIE *Wise Men* 218 She with nice craft had moulded from the clay A panoplied Pallas. **1901** LD. MILNER *Sp.* 26 May, Panoplied hatred, insensate, ambitious, invincible ignorance.

panoply ('pænəplɪ), *sb.* [ad. Gr. πανοπλία a complete suit of armour, the full armour of the ὁπλίτης, f. παν- all + ὅπλα pl. arms. Cf. F. *panoplie* (occurring casually 1551, but adm. in *Dict. Acad.* 1835). The original Gr. and a latinized form *panoplia* occur in early use.

1607 SIR J. H. in *Harington's Nugæ Ant.* (ed. Park 1804) II. 213 As well episcopall as temporall panoplia, or furniture, beseeming both a gentleman, a deane, and a bishop. **1624** GEE *Foot out of Snare* 24 Let vs..arme our selues with the πανοπλία of God.]

1. A complete suit of armour, the 'whole armour' of a soldier (*a*) of ancient or (*b*) of mediæval times. (In (*b*) its brightness and splendour are chiefly connoted.)

(*a*) **1632** B. JONSON *Magn. Lady* III. iv, *Iron*... More.. Than all your fury, and the panoply—*Prac.* Which is at best, but a thin linen armour. **1667** MILTON *P.L.* VI. 760 Hee in Celestial Panoplie all armd. **1750** JOHNSON *Rambler* No. 78 ¶1 Encumbered and oppressed, as he will find himself, with the ancient panoply. **1838** THIRLWALL *Greece* II. 346 Their short spears and daggers were..ill fitted to make an impression on the Spartan panoply. **1881** JOWETT *Thucyd.* I. 243 Three hundred panoplies which were allotted to Demosthenes he brought home with him.

(*b*) **1813** SCOTT *Trierm.* II. xix, As all around the lists so wide In panoply the champions ride. **1839** LONGF. *Coplas de Manrique* xxxii, Scarf, and gorgeous panoply, And nodding plume. **1867** FREEMAN *Norm. Conq.* (1876) I. vi. 516 Armed with all the magnificence of the full panoply of the time.

2. In various fig. and transf. applications:

a. *fig.* Complete armour for spiritual or mental warfare.

Often with direct allusion to την πανοπλίαν τοῦ Θεοῦ 'the whole armour of God' in Eph. vi. 11, 13.

1576 FLEMING (*title*) A Panoplie of Epistles, Or, a looking Glasse for the vnlearned. **1650** S. CLARKE *Eccl. Hist.* (1654) I. 4 Patience is the Panoply or whole Armour of the man of God. **1658** GURNALL *Chr. in Arm.* (1669) 245/1 These words present us with another piece in the Christians panoply. **1784** COWPER *Task* II. 345 Armed himself in panoply complete Of heavenly temper. **1854** J. S. C. ABBOTT *Napoleon* (1855) II. xxv. 464 Napoleon was armed with the panoply of popular rights. **1884** TENNYSON *Becket* v. ii, Mail'd in the perfect panoply of faith.

b. *transf.* Any kind of complete defence, covering, or clothing. **c.** Any splendid enveloping or surrounding array, material or ideal.

1829 LYTTON *Devereux* IV. iii, What a panoply of smiles the duchess wears to night. **1832** LANDER *Adv. Niger* III. xvii. 57 Another charm..a panoply, for preserving all persons, while bathing, from the fangs of the crocodiles. **1850** MERIVALE *Rom. Emp.* (1865) I. viii. 322 Before him lay ..the mighty City..gleaming in the sun with its panoply of roofs. **1856** KANE *Arct. Expl.* II. i. 22 His many-coated panoply against King Death. **1867** LYDIA M. CHILD *Romance of Repub.* xxxv. 400 Mist..as it grew colder, had settled on the trees..covering every little twig with a panoply of ice. **1872** JENKINSON *Guide Eng. Lakes* (1879) 278 The two lakes, Buttermere and Crummock,..surrounded by a grand panoply of mountains. **1887** BOWEN *Æneid* III. 517 Both of the Bears, and Orion, in golden panoply dight.

3. A group of pieces of armour arranged as a kind of trophy or ornament.

1890 in *Cent. Dict.* **1896** *Daily News* 5 Mar. 7/5 Some Russian shields, serving as panoplies, were added to the French shields.

panoply ('pænəplɪ), *v.* [f. prec. sb.] **a.** *trans.* To arm completely, to furnish with a panoply.

1832 L. HUNT *Gentle Armour* II. 4 To-morrow sees me panoplied indeed. **1885** *Homilet. Rev.* Sept. 264 To panoply fearful souls with the armor of..heaven-inspired thoughts.

b. *fig.* To array with something brilliant.

1873 'MARK TWAIN' *Gilded Age* xxxii. 290 It would be.. judicious to send her forth well panoplied for her work.—So he had added new and still richer costumes to her wardrobe, and assisted their attractions with costly jewelry. **1880** —— *Tramp Abroad* xxviii. 284, I and my agent panoplied ourselves in walking costume. **1895** *Daily News* 14 Sept. 5/7 There was..a train of saloon carriages for the excursionists. It was panoplied with flags and garlanded with vine leaves. **1940** 'GUN BUSTER' *Return via Dunkirk* I. i. 11, I was panoplied for War.

panoptic (pæn'ɒptɪk), *a.* [f. Gr. πάνοπτος seen of all, fully visible, πανόπτ-ης all-seeing + -IC.]

1. All-seeing.

1826 *Blackw. Mag.* XX. 844 He..vainly conceits that the great forest of books will hide him from our panoptic view. **1856** J. MARTINEAU *Ess.* (1891) IV. 52 Any class of teachers free to assume this panoptic position.

2. In which all is seen: cf. PANOPTICON.

1845 R. W. HAMILTON *Pop. Educ.* ix. (ed. 2) 239 The school [in France] is the ward of one great panoptic prisonhouse, with the keepers before the door.

pan'optical, *a.* [f. as prec. + -AL[1].] Of or pertaining to a view of everything at once.

1879 SIR G. SCOTT *Lect. Archit.* II. 252 The internal effect does not, however, trust exclusively to this panoptical theory.

panopticon (pæn'ɒptɪkən). [f. Gr. παν- + ὀπτικόν neuter of ὀπτικός of or for sight: cf. πάνοπτος fully seen or visible.]

1. a. The name given by Bentham to a proposed form of prison of circular shape having cells built round and fully exposed towards a central 'well', whence the warders could at all times observe the prisoners. Also *attrib.* or as *adj.*

The Penitentiary, Millbank, London, was originally constructed according to Bentham's plan.

1791 BENTHAM (*title*) Panopticon; or, the Inspection-House. *Ibid.* I. Postscr. 86 In a Panopticon prison..there ought not any where be a single foot square, on which man or boy shall be able to plant himself..under any assurance of not being observed. **1813** *Edin. Rev.* XXII. 19 The Panopticon was to be open at all times to every magistrate; and at certain hours to the public generally. **1818** HAZLITT *Eng. Poets* v. (1870) 128 He..superintends, as in a panopticon, a select circle of rural malefactors. **1882** MRS. OLIPHANT *Lit. Hist. Eng.* III. 310 Bentham's Panopticon.

b. *fig.* and *transf.* A place where everything is visible; a show-room for novelties.

1850 *Deed of Settlement of Royal Panopticon of Science & Art* 1 Royal Panopticon of Science and Art. An institution for Scientific exhibitions and for promoting discoveries in arts manufactures. **1851** J. HAMILTON *Roy. Preacher* xix. (1854) 239 From this panopticon of all the possible, His holy wisdom chose the best. **1882** OGILVIE (Annandale), *Panopticon*..2. An exhibition room for novelties. *Art Journal.*

2. Name given to an optical instrument. (In quot. 1768, app. a kind of telescope.)

1768 FRANKLIN *Lett.* Wks. 1840 V. 420 Mr. Martin, when I called to see his panopticon, had not one ready. **1871** *Routledge's Ev. Boy's Ann.* Mar. Suppl. 1/1 Statham's 'Panopticon'..a powerful achromatic Telescope and Microscope combined.

pano'ram, *a.* and *sb.* [A commercial shortening of *panoramic*.] **a.** *adj.* = PANORAMIC. **b.** *sb.* = *panoramic camera.*

1893 *Photogr. Ann.* 291 The Panoram: a perfected panoramic camera. **1902** *Westm. Gaz.* 26 May 4/2 Holiday pictures..taken with a Panoram type of camera. *Ibid.* 16 June 4/2 He should make it a point to use a Panoram for his exposures. **1903** *Ibid.* 27 May 12/2 The North-Eastern Railway Company publish a series of what they call 'Panoram' post-cards.

pano'ram, *v.* [A shortening of PANORAMIC *a.*] *intr.* = PAN *v.*[3] Hence **pano'raming** *vbl. sb.*

1915 *Wells Fargo Messenger* Oct. 18/3 We are before the Erie cut, and as the camera 'panorams' around, we get a glimpse of our splendid Eleventh Avenue Stable in Jersey City. **1938** G. H. SEWELL *Amateur Film-Making* ix. 80 The revolution of a camera on its vertical axis, so that it covers the features of a landscape, is known as 'panoraming' or 'panning'. *Ibid.* 81 To panoram with a hand-held camera, set your feet firmly on the ground,..brace yourself up and turn from the hips.

panorama (pænɒ'rɑːmə, -'æmə). [f. Gr. παν- all + ὅρᾱμα view: a name invented by R. Barker *c* 1789.

(In his specification of patent 1787, he called his invention *La Nature à coup d'Œil.*)]

1. a. A picture of a landscape or other scene, either arranged on the inside of a cylindrical surface round the spectator as a centre (a *cyclorama*), or unrolled or unfolded and made to pass before him, so as to show the various parts in succession.

1796 *Repertory of Arts* IV. 165 Patent granted to Mr. Robert Barker [No. 1612 of 1787]. (*Footnote*) This invention has been since called the Panorama. **1801** *Encycl. Brit.* Suppl. II. 326/2 *Panorama*, a word..employed of late to denote a painting..which represents an entire view of any country, city, or other natural objects, as they appear to a person standing in any situation, and turning quite round. **1806-7** J. BERESFORD *Miseries Hum. Life* v. xvii, Prolonging your stay in London for the express purpose of going to the Panorama. **1807** T. YOUNG *Lectures* I. 455 In the panorama, which has lately been exhibited in many parts of Europe, the effects of natural scenery are very closely imitated. **18..** (*title*) Panorama of the Thames from London to Richmond, exhibiting every Object on both banks of the River. **1866** BRANDE & COX *Dict. Sci.* s.v., The first panorama exhibited in London was painted by Robert Barker in 1789; it represented a view of Edinburgh.

b. *transf.* and *fig.* A continuous passing scene; a mental vision in which a series of images passes before the mind's eye.

1813 M. EDGEWORTH *Let.* 16 May (1971) 56 Pray do not think because I name these fine people..that my poor little head is turned... Be assured that the whole panorama passes before me as a panorama. **1818** 'T. BROWN' *Brighton* I. p. xi, A novel should be a panorama of life; and we trust that our *views* will be found correct in the present one. **1836** MARRYAT *Japhet* lvii. 104/1 A deep reverie, during which the various circumstances and adventures of my life were passed in a rapid panorama before me. **1859** GEO. ELIOT *A. Bede* xliv, You perceive clearly what sort of picture Adam and Hetty made in the panorama of Arthur's thoughts on his journey homeward. **1876** BESANT & RICE *Gold. Butterfly* iv, She began to recall the endless moving panorama of the London streets.

2. a. An unbroken view of the whole surrounding region.

1805 M. WILMOT *Russ. Jrnls.* (1934) 151 Up at Cock Crow to drive to Sparrow Mount from which spot Moscow is seen as a Panorama, & a most exquisite view it is indeed. **1828** SCOTT *Chron. Canongate* Ser. II. Introd., The Calton had always the superiority of its unrivalled panorama. **1836** *Murray's Handbk. for Trav.* 321 The Panorama from the top of the Brocken is very fine. **1878** K. JOHNSTON *Africa* ii. 22 From the summit..there opens out one of the grandest panoramas which the eye of man could behold.

b. *fig.* A complete and comprehensive survey or presentation of a subject.

1801 (*title*) The Political Panorama. **1806** MRS. STERNDALE (*title*) The Panorama of Youth. **1812** J. SMITH (*title*) The Panorama of Science and Art. **1813** MARIA EDGEWORTH *Patron.* (1833) II. xxvii. 137 In his rapid panorama of foreign countries, he showed variety of knowledge. **1860** PUSEY *Min. Proph.* 425 Habakkuk, in one vast panorama,..exhibits the future in pictures of the past.

3. *attrib.* and *Comb.*; also ***panorama-wise***.

1809 W. IRVING *Knickerb.* III. vi, The panorama view of the battery was given merely to gratify the reader with a correct description of that celebrated place. **1822** *Blackw. Mag.* XII. 86 A thousand other scenes..come up.. panorama-wise before us. **1896** *Daily News* 19 Nov. 7/4 A prospecting party came across a vein of gold quartz in the famous panorama walk.

pano'ramal, *a. nonce-wd.* [f. prec. + -AL[1].] Passing everything under survey or review.

1808 E. S. BARRETT *Miss-led General* 120 Those satirical, critical, panoramal, cynical..drudges, the Reviewers.

panoramic (pænɒ'ræmɪk), *a.* [f. prec. + -IC.] Of, pertaining to, or of the nature of a panorama.

panoramic camera, a photographic camera devised to rotate automatically so as to take a complete or extended landscape.

1813 REES *Cycl.* s.v. *Panorama*, The cylindrical surface on which objects are to be painted is called the panoramic surface. **1815** J. CAMPBELL *Trav. S. Africa* 361 (Jod.), I.. expressed a wish, that my friends in London could be gratified with a panoramick view of it. **1838** ROBINS (*title*) Panoramic Representation of the Queen's Coronation Procession from the Palace to the Abbey. **1856** SIR B. BRODIE *Psychol. Inq.* I. ii. 35 An extensive panoramic view of the whole of the surrounding country. **1878** ABNEY *Photogr.* (1881) 214 In a panoramic camera the eye is supposed to travel round the view, the point of sight altering at each movement of the eye.

b. Commanding a view of the whole landscape.

1880 D. W. FRESHFIELD in *Academy* 11 Dec. 418 The panoramic peak of Monte Incudine.

So **pano'ramical** *a.*; **pano'ramically** *adv.*, after the manner of a panorama.

1840 *Fraser's Mag.* XXII. 671 Emblazoned panoramically upon the mind's perception. **1846** WORCESTER, *Panoramic, Panoramical.* **1889** *Athenæum* 28 Dec. 902/1 The subject.. treated panoramically, is exceptionally difficult.

panoramist (pænɒˈrɑːmɪst, -ˈæmɪst). [f. as prec. + -IST.] A painter of panoramas.

1881 *N. & Q.* 6th Ser. III. 247/2, I shall be glad to know if there is any record of the panoramist's religious history. **1888** *Pall Mall G.* 14 Mar. 5/2 The illusion produced by the art of the panoramist is so great that even with the aid of an opera glass it is almost impossible to determine at what exact point the solid objects end and the painted picture begins.

panorganon, -Orthodox, etc.: see PAN-.

‖**Panorpa** (pəˈnɔːpə). *Entom.* pl. -æ. [mod.L. (Linnæus 1748); derivation not stated.] A genus of neuropterous insects, the type of a family *Panorpidæ*, taken by some as an order *Panorpatæ*, the scorpion-flies. Hence **paˈnorpate,** †**paˈnorpatous** *adjs.*, of or pertaining to the scorpion-flies as an order; **paˈnorpian, paˈnorpine** *adjs.*, of or pertaining to the genus *Panorpa*; **paˈnorpid,** an insect of the family *Panorpidæ*; **paˈnorpoid** *a.*, resembling or related to the scorpion-flies.

1878 BELL *Gegenbaur's Comp. Anat.* 272 Some of Panorpa have an enlargement at the end of the fore-gut. **1857** MAYNE *Expos. Lex.*, Panorpatous. **1890** WEBSTER, *Panorpian, Panorpid.* **1890** *Cent. Dict.*, *Panorpine.* **1895** *Funk's Stand. Dict.*, *Panorpate, Panorpoid.*

panotype (ˈpænətaɪp). [f. *pano-*, irregularly for PAN- or PANTO- + TYPE.] A name for a photographic picture obtained by the collodion process.

1875 in KNIGHT *Dict. Mech.* 1602/2. [Also in later Dicts.]

panpardie, -perdy, obs. ff. *pain perdu*: see PAIN *sb.*[2] 2.

panpathy, -phenomenalism: see PAN- 2.

†**panˈpharmacal,** *a. Obs. rare.* [f. next + -AL[1].] Of or pertaining to a panpharmacon, panacean.

1657 TOMLINSON *Renou's Disp.* 289 The Indians use this medicament as panpharmacal in all diseases. **1657** *Physical Dict.*, *Panpharmacal*, an universal medicine.

panpharmacon, pam- (pænˈfɑːməkən, pæm-). *rare.* [f. PAN- all + Gr. φάρμακον drug; cf. Gr. παμφάρμακος adj. 'skilled in all drugs'.] A remedy against all diseases and poisons, a universal remedy, a panacea.

1661 BLOUNT *Glossogr.* (ed. 2), *Panpharmacon* (Gr.), a medicine for all diseases. **1694** SALMON *Bate's Dispens.* (1713) 575/2 It is used by some as Panpharmacon, but what Diseases it will absolutely cure I think is scarcely determin'd. **1700** T. BROWN *Amusem. Ser. & Com.* 95 The Outsides of their Pots were Gilded with the Titles of Preservatives, Cordials and Panpharmacons. **1731** BAILEY, *Pampharmacon.* [So **1775** ASH.] **1845** FORD *Handbk. Spain* I. 193 The divine Isaac Barrow resorted to this panpharmacon whenever he wished to collect his thoughts.

panphobia, variant of PANOPHOBIA.

pan-pie. *U.S.* [f. PAN *sb.*[1] + PIE *sb.*[2]] = PANDOWDY.

1723 J. NOTT *Cook's & Confectioner's Dict.* sig. Y8ᵛ This Paste is proper for Pan pies that are set on the Table without a Desert or Banquet of sweet Meats. **1862** 'G. HAMILTON' *Country Living* 70 No pan-pie with hot brown bread on Sunday morning. **1883** *Rep. Maine Board Agric. 1882* 403 You have all heard of the pan-dowdy, or pan-pie, the pride of our grandmothers.

pan-pipe (ˈpæn,paɪp). Also Pan's pipe, Pan's-pipe. [f. PAN *sb.*[2] + PIPE.] A primitive musical instrument made of a series of reeds graduated in length so as to form a scale, the upper and open ends being level, so as to permit the easy passage of the lips from one to another; its invention was ascribed by Greek legend to Pan; a syrinx, mouth-organ.

1820 T. MITCHELL *Aristoph* I. p. xxxv, Olympus is generally represented, as a young man.. taking lessons on the pan-pipe from Marsyas. **1825** HONE *Every-day Bk.* I. 1114 A man playing the Pan-pipes, or 'mouth organ'. **1846** GROTE *Greece* I. i. (1862) I. 52 Hermês surrenders to Apollo, the lyre, inventing for his own use the syrinx or panspipe. **1855** THACKERAY *Newcomes* xlvii, At the end of the lime-tree avenue is a broken-nosed damp Faun, with a marble panpipe. **1875** JOWETT *Plato* (ed. 2) III. 37 The harp may be permitted in the town, and the Pan's-pipe in the fields.

panplain (ˈpænpleɪn). *Physical Geogr.* Also **-plane.** [f. PAN- + PLAIN *sb.*[1]] A plain formed by the coalescence of previously separate flood-plains.

1933 C. H. CRICKMAY in *Geol. Mag.* LXX. 345 We would expect the growing floodplains to become confluent, making one broad universal plain shared by all the streams of the region. The surface will be flat, and will have a general slope like that which now characterizes the lower floodplains of great rivers. The only relief will be remnants of some of the interfluves which may persist as low monadnocks. This plain, formed of floodplains joined by their own growth, may be called a panplain. **1942** O. D. VON ENGELN *Geomorphol.* vi. 97 Eventually the level surfaces of adjacent stream floors, concurrently developed by such planation, become confluent and a panplane, a very level plain with a general downward inclination, is produced. **1960** B. W. SPARKS *Geomorphol.* xv. 340 There seems little doubt that river planation is an important agency of erosion,.. but whether these can extend indefinitely to form a panplain seems more doubtful. **1967** J. HAYS in Jennings & Mabbutt *Landform Stud. Austral. & New Guinea* ix. 200 Near Darwin, the panplains of north-flowing and west-flowing streams have coalesced.

panplanation (,pænplæˈneɪʃən). *Physical Geogr.* [f. PAN- + PLANATION, after PANPLAIN.] The formation of a panplain.

1933 C. H. CRICKMAY in *Geol. Mag.* LXX. 345 The essential difference between panplanation and peneplanation is that the former starts from the lower floodplains of rivers and grows laterally in all landward directions, whereas the latter is of universal occurrence. **1942** O. D. VON ENGELN *Geomorphol.* xvi. 356 It is now considered improbable that flood-plain accumulation and panplanation (Crickmay, C.H., 1933) combined.. could completely dispose of all relief in a peneplaned region. **1970** R. J. SMALL *Study of Landforms* v. 168 Many authorities have regarded lateral plantation by running water as a major factor in the formation of desert surfaces.., and a process akin to panplanation has been assumed by some to account for savanna plains.

panplegia to **panpsychism:** see PAN-.

panpot (ˈpænpɒt), *sb.* [f. *pan(oramic) pot(entiometer)*.] A kind of potentiometer used to vary the apparent position of a sound source by varying the strengths of the signals to individual speakers without changing the total signal strength.

1941 *Jrnl. Soc. Motion Pict. Engin.* XXXVII. 130 A special 3-circuit differential junction network, nicknamed 'The Panpot', is used to dub one original track onto one, any two, or all three of our Fantasound program tracks. **1964** H. B. HADDEN *Pract. Stereophony* iii. 39 To present a monophonic signal, as a point source at a given position.., a control known as a 'panoramic potentiometer' is employed... This control, known as a 'panpot' for short, is a two-gang fader with the two halves arranged back to back, so that as the gain of one half of the particular channel is increased, the other half is decreased. **1975** *Gramophone* Dec. 1122/1 The deck was plugged into a large discothèque type console with a quadrophonic pan-pot in the middle.

Hence **ˈpanpot** *v. trans.*, to process by means of a panpot; **ˈpanpotted** *ppl. a.*, **ˈpanpotting** *vbl. sb.*

1973 *Jrnl. Audio Engin. Soc.* XXI. 3/2 The recording may ..be made by 'pan-potting' sounds into the channels to stimulate [*read* simulate] pickup by directional microphones. **1976** *Gramophone* Jan. 1269/1 This 'pan-potting' method also enabled the balance to be adjusted after the recording session. *Ibid.* 1269/2 The medium is largely confined to pan-potted multi-track material.

,pan-Presbyˈterian, *a.* [PAN- 1.] Of or pertaining to all Presbyterians.

1877 *Proc. Free Ch. Scot.* 273 Representatives to the Pan-Presbyterian Council—The names of gentlemen.. proposed [to] represent the Assembly at the General Presbyterian Council in July next. **1888** *Pall Mall G.* 6 July 1/2 The Pan-Presbyterian Council meets once in four years.

panpsychism (pænˈsaɪkɪz(ə)m). *Philos.* Also **pampsychism.** [PAN-.] (See quot. 1901.) Hence **panˈpsychic** *a.*, pertaining to or based on panpsychism; **panˈpsychist,** one who believes in panpsychism; also *attrib.* or as *adj.*; **panpsyˈchistic** *a.*, connected with or characterized by panpsychism; **panpsyˈchistically** *adv.*

1879 G. H. LEWES *Mind as Function of Organism* ii. 34 We must therefore pronounce against the hypothesis of Panpsychism. **1881** W. JAMES in *Unitarian Rev.* Nov. 415 All modern thought converges toward idealistic or, as I should rather call them, pan-psychic, conclusions. **1901** *Baldwin's Dict. Philos.* II. 256/1 *Panpsychism*, the theory that all matter, or all nature, is itself psychical, or has a psychical aspect; that atoms and molecules, as well as plants and animals, have a rudimentary life of sensation, feeling, and impulse which bears the same relation to their movements.. that the psychical life of human beings does to their objective activities. **1903** C. A. STRONG *Why Mind has Body* p. vi, Hence I think panpsychists are justified in maintaining that with their principles they are able to explain the connection of mind and body. *Ibid.*, I have chosen my title with the object of putting this panpsychist pretension distinctly on record. **1904** J. MCCABE tr. *Haeckel's Wonders of Life* xv. 354 His [*sc.* Fechner's] system is.. panpsychistic and at the same time pantheistic. **1911** J. WARD *Realm of Ends* i. 20 To this principle pampsychism appeals. *Ibid.* 21 On this, the pampsychist view, Nature.. resolves into a plurality of conative individuals. *Ibid.* iii. 62 The pampsychist.. maintains.. that at all events there are no things wholly inert. **1924** B. EDGELL *Theories of Memory* 133 The present writer has failed to find any link between M. Bergson's pampsychism and his individualism. **1935** R. B. PERRY *Tht. & Char. W. James* II. 443 Whether this 'beyond', this thing-in-itself, shall be interpreted panpsychistically, is questioned and again left unsettled. **1937** A. H. MURRAY *Philos. of James Ward* v. 98 The pampsychistic solution, at which he arrives, dates back to Leibniz and earlier. **1940** *Mind* XLIX. 43 Berkeley probably saw that pampsychism, for him, spelled pantheism. *Ibid.* 45 With this new background the Berkeleian immaterialism took on a new aspect; it is no longer pampsychist. **1955** H. J. KOREN *Introd. Philos. Animate Nature* I. i. 35 The ancient hylozoists.. and modern panpsychists.. imply or state that all things are alive. **1959** *Chambers's Encycl.* XII. 718/2 Should pampsychism replace the older hylozoism, the truth being that the inner side of everything is its soul, the outer aspect observable by an outsider being its body? **1968** F. COPLESTON *Hist. Philos.* VIII. v. xvii. 393 Neither Strong nor Drake meant to imply that stones, for instance, are conscious. Their panpsychism was linked with the idea of emergent evolution. **1973** *Nature* 20 July 183/1 At one time he expressed panpsychic ideas, thinking there could be some consciousness even in a mug, but later was prepared to restrict it to animals with a nervous system. **1975** C. BURT *ESP & Psychol.* vi. 99 Theists and panpsychists.. have no qualms about ascribing minds to human beings.

†**ˈpan-,pudding.** *Obs.* or *dial.* A pudding cooked or baked in a pan; see quot. 1839.

1606 *Choice, Chance,* etc. (1881) 47 Quoth he, Panpudding is a good dish for a grosse stomack. **1630** J. TAYLOR (Water-P.) *Gt. Eater Kent* Wks. I. 146/1 The Pan-puddings of Shropshire, the White puddings of Somersetshire, the Hasty-puddings of Hamshire, and the Pudding-pyes of any shire, all is one to him. **1736** BYROM *Rem.* (Chetham Soc.) II. I. 17, I ate pan puddings, as they called them (fritters) heartily. **1839** STONEHOUSE *Axholme* 47 About forty or fifty years ago.. Saturday, pan pudding, i.e. a pudding made of flour, with small bits of bacon in it.

b. *attrib.* (in contemptuous use.)

1593 NASHE *Four Lett. Confut.* Wks. (Grosart) II. 277 Not ..to corrupt the aire, and imposthumate mens ears with their pan-pudding prose any more.

c. Phr. ***to stand to one's pan-pudding***, to stand to one's duty; to stand firm, hold one's ground.

1690 *Pagan Prince* xxv. 71 And so, noble Tritons, every one to his command; stand to your Panpudding. **1694** MOTTEUX *Rabelais* IV. lxiv. (1737) 264 How bravely did they stand to their Pan-puddings!

panpygoptosis (,pænpaɪgəʊpˈtəʊsɪs). *nonce-wd.* [A fanciful formation combining the elements PAN-, PYGO-, OPTO-, -OSIS.] = *duck's disease* s.v. DUCK *sb.*[1] 12. Hence **pan,pygopˈtotic** *a.*

1938 S. BECKETT *Murphy* v. 97 Duck's disease is a distressing pathological condition in which the thighs are suppressed and the buttocks spring directly from behind the knees, aptly described in Steiss's nosonomy as Panpygoptosis. *Ibid.* 104 Miss Dew's control, a panpygoptotic Manichee of the fourth century,.. had not.. been raised so wholly a spiritual body as yet to sit down with much more comfort than she had in the natural.

Pan-Roman, Panroman (,pænˈrəʊmən). [PAN- + ROMAN *sb.*[1] 3.] An artificial language invented for universal use by H. Molenaar; also known as UNIVERSAL.

1907 W. J. CLARK *Internat. Lang.* II. vi. 103 The last few years have produced quite a crop of artificial languages.. Idiom Neutral; Pan-Roman or Universal, by Dr. Molenaar; Latino sine flexione [etc.]. *Ibid.* 105 The victorious Esperantists.. poke fun at these new-fangled schemes. A parody in Esperanto verse.. narrates the fickleness of Pan-Roman and how it changed into Universal. **1922** *Nature* CIX. 494/1 A language of the Neo-Latin type, somewhat similar to Neutral Idiom, is the 'Panroman' (or 'Universal') of the German positivist and pacifist, Dr. H. Molenaar. **1927** E. S. PANKHURST *Delphos* vi. 81 Universal (1903), later called Panroman (1906), by Dr. H. Molenaar, is another neo-Latin language.

pans, obs. form of *pence*, pl. of PENNY.

‖**pansala** (ˈpʌnsələ). [Sinhala, f. *pan* leaf + *sala* dwelling, f. Skr. *parṇaśālā*, Pali *paṇṇasālā*.] A Buddhist temple or monastery; orig., a forest hut constructed from leaves.

1850 R. S. HARDY *Eastern Monachism* xiii. 129 The dwelling of the priest is called a pansala, from pan, leaves, and sala, a dwelling, or a place to which any one is accustomed to resort, from a root which signifies to go. **1913** L. WOOLF *Village in Jungle* i. 12 He had fallen ill.. and had stayed for a month or two in the priest's pansala. **1927** *Missionary Herald* Sept. 219/2 Mr. Weeraratua went to see him at his pansala and talked to him about Christ. **1956** R. PIERIS *Sinhalese Social Organization* II. ix. 73 There was, in almost every village, temple land, the property of which was vested in.. a local *vihāra* or *pansala*.

pan-Satanism to **-sclerosis:** see PAN-.

pansch, obs. form of PAUNCH.

panse (pans), *v. Sc.* and *dial.* Also 6 **pans, panss,** 6–8 **pance,** (9 **panch**). [a. OF. *panser*, *pancer*, to take thought for, take care of, treat (the sick), attend (to wounds, etc.), parallel form of *penser* to think: see PENSE.]

†**1.** *intr.* To think; to meditate. *Obs.*

a **1500** HENRYSON *Garment gude Ladies* 27 Hir patelet of gude pansing. **1500–20** DUNBAR *Poems* lviii. 24 Thay panss nocht off the parrochin pure. **1528** LYNDESAY *Dream* 397 To pans on his prudens. **1530** —— *Test. Papyngo* 444 My hart is peirst with panes for to pance. **1594** A. HUME *Hymns*, etc. (Bannatyne Club) 63 Studie not nor panse not meikle on the feeding of the flesh. **1637–50** ROW *Hist. Kirk* (Wodrow Soc.) 12 The faithfull servants of God.. pansed how this great work might be effectuat to God's glorie.

†**2.** *trans.* To think of, consider, heed. *Obs.*

1560 ROLLAND *Crt. Venus* III. 879 Perfitlie pance thir pointis last pregnant. *c* **1600** MONTGOMERIE *Cherrie & Slae* 1357 And pance not, nor skance not, The perril nor the pryce. **1629** SIR W. MURE *True Crucif.* 2825 If God bee for thee, panse no who oppose.

3. To attend to surgically or medically; to dress (a wound).

a **1584** MONTGOMERIE *Cherrie & Slae* 491 Gif ony pacient wald be pancit, Quhy suld he loup quhen he is lancit. **1676** W. ROW *Contn. Blair's Autobiog.* xii. (1848) 576 They had a singular care of him causing panse his wounds. **1752** J. LOUTHIAN *Form of Process* (ed. 2) 124 He was carried to a neighbouring House, where his Wounds were panced. **1890** LOWSON *Guidfellow* 281 (E.D.D.) Having pansed and dressed the wound. **1891** *Hartland Gloss.*, *Panch*,.. to prick and work a wound to extract matter or any foreign substance.

Hence **'pansing** *vbl. sb.*, (*a*) thinking; (*b*) the dressing of a wound; also **pansement** *rare.*

1500–20 DUNBAR *Poems* xxix. 13 Than pansing of penuritie Revis that fra my remembrance. **1579–80** *Burgh Rec. Edin.* (Rec. Soc.) IV. 152 The pansing, dressing, curing and handling of Robert Asbowane, quha wes laitlie hurt and woundit be James Dowglas. **1590** A. HUME *Hymns*, etc. (Bannatyne Club) 45 My pansing dois augment my paine. **1842** DUNGLISON, *Pansement*, dressing.

†**panse**, *sb. Obs. rare*⁻¹. [a. OF. *pense, panse*, thought.] A thought.

a **1500** *Colkelbie Sow* I. 456 (Bann. MS.) And all thair plat pure pansis.

panse, obs. variant of PAUNCE, a breast-plate.

panse, pansie, obs. forms of PANSY *sb.*

pan-'sexual, *a.* [f. PAN- 2 + SEXUAL *a.*] Of or pertaining to pan-sexualism; that is not limited in sexual choice; **pan-'sexualism**, the view that the sex instinct plays a part in all human thought and activity and is the chief or only source of energy. Hence **pan-'sexualist** *a.*, pertaining to the theory of pansexualism; **pan-sexu'ality**.

1917 C. R. PAYNE tr. *Pfister's Psycho-anal. Method* 60 Which .. has brought the reproach of 'pansexualism' against psychoanalysis. **1922** J. STRACHEY tr. *Freud's Group Psychol.* iv. 39 Psycho-analysis, then gives these love instincts the name of sexual instincts... The majority of 'educated' people have regarded this nomenclature as an insult, and have taken their revenge by retorting upon psycho-analysis with the reproach of 'pan-sexualism'. **1926** W. MCDOUGALL *Outl. Abnormal Psychol.* i. 20 It has led Freud .., as Janet has said, to construct 'an enormous system of medical philosophy', the theory of Pan-sexuality. *Ibid.* vi. 131 Freud, in accordance with his pansexualist tendency, expressed the opinion [etc.]. *Ibid.* xviii. 314 The dogma that the Œdipus complex is present in all men is the principal instrument of the pan-sexual theory. **1972** *Jrnl. Social Psychol.* LXXXVII. 51 In the beginning the human organism has the potential of pansexuality. **1974** *Observer* 7 Apr. 36/6 Eventually, no doubt, some biographer will tell us how far he [*sc.* H. de Montherlant] was homosexual, heterosexual or—as seems to be suggested by some discreet passages about bestiality and incest—pansexual. **1977** *Guardian Weekly* 7 Aug. 18/2 An exquisitely Victorian taste for extravagant, pansexual erotic fantasy.

pansheon, -shon, obs. or dial. ff. PANCHEON.

pansied ('pænzɪd), *a.* [f. PANSY *sb.* + -ED².] Adorned with or abounding in pansies.

1819 WIFFEN *Aonian Hours* (1820) 41 A pansied dell. **1835** TALFOURD *Ion* II. i, When pansied turf was air to winged feet.

pansified ('pænzɪfaɪd), *ppl. a.* [f. PANSY + -FY + -ED¹.] Excessively stylized or adorned; affected, effeminate.

1941 C. KING *Diary* 17 July in *With Malice toward None* (1970) 135 These birds from Portland Place... think anything said with feeling is rather vulgar, so usually give out a very pansified BBC message. **1944** 'G. ORWELL' *Crit. Ess.* (1951) 145 The rather pansified drawings of youths. **1959** W. D. PEREIRA *North Flight* iv. 56 You don't know this place. Like a pansified rabbit warren. Architect designed. **1973** *Listener* 20 Dec. 860/3 Hervey's relationship with .. the pansified international Algarotti. **1976** *Ibid.* 27 May 679/1 Being not only a Londoner, but a central Londoner, .. I can breakfast and dine in my pansified quarters in the heart of the soft South, having spent most of the intervening time in the gritty, bracing, humorous, individualistic North.

pansive, obs. Sc. form of PENSIVE *a.*

pan-Slav (pæn'slɑːv), *a.* [PAN- 1.] = next.

1903 *Mod. Newspaper*, In 1905 a Pan-Slav exhibition will be held at St. Petersburg, when representatives will be sent from all the Slavonic nations of eastern Europe.

Panslavic, -Slavic (-'slɑːvɪk), *a.* [PAN- 1.]

a. Of or pertaining to all the Slavic races. **b.** = PANSLAVISTIC a.

1860 MARSH *Eng. Lang.* i. 8 The Panslavic invasion, which will be the next source of danger to the civil and intellectual liberties of Christendom. **1880** *Daily Tel.* 2 Mar., A fresh outburst of Panslavic anger.

Panslavism (pæn'slɑːvɪz(ə)m). Also 9 -sclavism. [f. PAN- 1 + SLAV + -ISM: after Ger. *Pansclavismus*.] The movement or aspiration for the union of all Slavs or Slavonic peoples in one political organization.

[**1846** JOWETT in *Life & Lett.* (1897) I. v. 157 My balance of power would be .. France and England against Pansclavismus and despotism.] **1850** LONGF. in *Life* (1891) II. 188 He [Gurowski] is a Pole .. believing in Panslavism, or the union of all the Slavonic tribes under one head, and that head Russia. **1877** *Public Opinion* 7 July 1 The advance of Russia is as hateful to the hopes of Hellenic Christians as it can be welcome to the zealots of Panslavism. **1880** *Fraser's Mag.* May 616 Here Panslavism is distinctly repudiated; Philo-Slavism is defined... I have never met a Panslavist among the Southern Slavs.

So **Pan'slavist**, an adherent or promoter of Panslavism; also as *adj.* = next; **Pansla'vistic** *a.*, (*a*) of, pertaining to, or favouring Panslavism; (*b*) = PANSLAVIC a.

1850 LONGF. in *Life* (1891) II. 189 At tea we had Panslavistic Gurowski. **1877** D. M. WALLACE *Russia* xxvi. 419 But what of their Panslavistic Aspirations? **1883** *Athenæum* 29 Dec. 855/1 It saved him from those Panslavist tendencies. **1884** *Harper's Mag.* May 859/1 The .. aspirations of the Muscovite panslavists were not satisfied. **1903** *Contemp. Rev.* Jan. 65 The first Pan-Slavistic Congress took place in Prague in June, 1848.

Pansla'vonian, -Slav-, *a.* Also -sclavonian. [Pan- 1.] Of or pertaining to, or including all Slavonians; Panslavic, Panslavistic. So **Pansla'vonic, -Sl-, -scla'vonic** *a.*; **Pan'slavonism** = PANSLAVISM.

1854 R. G. LATHAM *Native Races Russian Emp.* 331 The fundamental fact on which Pan-slavonism rests, is the vast .. area over which the different dialects of the Slavonic language are spoken, combined with the small amount of difference they exhibit. **1864** WEBSTER, *Panslavonian*. **1877** *Public Opinion* 7 July 1 Under the supreme direction of Prince Tcherkasski .. and his colleagues of M. Akeakoff's Panslavonic bureau. **1877** D. M. WALLACE *Russia* xxxiv. 600 There was but one step to the conception of a Panslavonic empire.

pansophic (pæn'sɒfɪk), *a.* [f. as PANSOPHY + -IC] Of or pertaining to pansophy. Also **pan'sophical** *a.* Hence **pan'sophically** *adv.*, in a pansophic manner.

1651 COLLIER *Comenius' Patterne Univ. Knowl.* 93 We have three chiefe and essentiall properties of Pansophicall method. *Ibid.* 146 Every theame that's handled pansophically hath propositions making demonstrations. **1660** WORTHINGTON *Let. to Hartlib* in *Remains* (Chetham Soc.) I. 242 It were to be wished, indeed, that it were done into Latin .. for the humbling of many conceited enthusiasts and Pansophical pretenders. **1882** *Athenæum* 4 Mar. 279 His [Comenius's] great design of a Pansophic Institute, or College of the Sciences, was pressed upon the Long Parliament by Hartlib and others.

pansophism ('pænsəʊfɪz(ə)m). [f. Gr. πάνσοφος all-wise + -ISM.] The possession or profession of universal knowledge. So **'pansophist**, a claimant or pretender to universal knowledge.

1864 BLACKMORE *Clara Vaughan* xxxix, Choose .. between my services, and the maunderings of some pansophist. **1868** *Pall Mall G.* 2 Dec. 12 As a general rule .. the attempt at pansophism, even in the arts, must end in pansciolism.

pansophy ('pænsəʊfɪ). Also 7 -sophie, 7–8 ‖**pansophia**. [f. Gr. παν- all + σοφία wisdom; forming an abstr. sb. to Gr. πάνσοφος adj. 'all-wise'.]

1. Universal or cyclopædic knowledge; a scheme or cyclopædic work embracing the whole body of human knowledge.

In its Latin form used by J. A. Comenius (Komensky) of Moravia in 1639, in the title of a book, *Prodromus Pansophiæ*, giving a sort of prospectus of a universal cyclopædia.

1642 HARTLIB *Ref. Schooles* 90 The seven parts of the Temple of Christian Pansophie. **1651** COLLIER *Comenius' Patterne Univ. Knowl.* 16 Pansophy therefore by wholesome Counsel takes all things in generall into its consideration, that it may evidently and most clearly appeare, how lesser things are, and come to be, subordinate to the greater [etc.]. **1674** BOYLE *Excell. Theol.* I. i. 50 The Encyclopedia's and Pansophia's, that even men of an elevated genius have aimed at. **1882** *Athenæum* 4 Mar. 279/1 Comenius's scheme .. was to collect and maintain learned men from all nations, and to give them leisure for their special studies, and generally to foster 'Pansophy'. **1899** *Academy* 29 July 108/2 Komensky and Hartlib tried to found in England a 'Christian Academy of Pansophy'.

2. The claim or pretension to universal knowledge.

1792 BOOTHBY *On Burke's App. Whigs* 265 The French philophers .. affect .. a sort of pansophy, or universality of command over the opinions of men. **1886** *Standard* 30 Dec. 2/1 His pansophy teaches him that the affections are the cause of all the misery in the world.

pansperm: see PAN- 2.

†**pansper'matic**, *a. Obs.* [f. Gr. παν- all + σπερματ- seed + -IC, after *spermatic*.] That is the seed or seminal principle of all things.

1690 LEYBOURN *Curs. Math.* 445 b, To the end it [the Solar Ocean] might more effectually communicate its Panspermatick Virtue to all those Bodies, to which it is to afford Light and Influence.

pan'spermatism. [f. as prec. + -ISM.] = PANSPERMIA. Hence **pan'spermatist**, one who holds the doctrine of panspermatism.

1874 J. FISKE *Cosmic Philos.* I. II. viii. 420 The hypothesis, devised by Spallanzani, that the atmosphere is full of invisible germs which can penetrate through the smallest crevices. This hypothesis is currently known as 'panspermatism', or the 'theory of omnipresent germs', or .. the 'germ-theory'. **1874** *Contemp. Rev.* XXIV. 518 It rested more especially with the Panspermatists, who chose still to be opponents of 'spontaneous generation', to show this belief .. was erroneous. **1878** TYNDALL *Gragm. Sc.* II. xiii.

panspermia (pæn'spɜːmɪə). Also Anglicized pan'spermy. [mod.L. *panspermia*, ad. Gr. πανσπερμία the doctrine of Anaxagoras and Democritus that the elements were a mixture of all the seeds of things, f. πάνσπερμος: see PANSPERMIC.] The biogenetic theory that the atmosphere is full of minute germs which develop on finding a favourable environment. Also called PANSPERMATISM. In recent use applied to the idea that micro-organisms or chemical precursors of life are present in space and able to initiate life on reaching a suitable planet.

1842 DUNGLISON *Med. Lex.*, *Panspermia*. **1857** MAYNE *Expos. Lex.*, *Panspermia* .., panspermy. **1882** *Pop. Sci. Monthly* XX. 824 The weight of his opinion in favor of his own theory of panspermy. **1893** *Syd. Soc. Lex.*, *Panspermia*, the physiological system according to which there are germs disseminated through all space which develop when they encounter a suitable soil. **1908** H. BORNS tr. *Arrhenius' Worlds in Making* viii. 217 The so-called theory of panspermia really shows a way. According to this theory life-giving seeds are drifting about in space. They encounter the planets, and fill their surfaces with life as soon as the necessary conditions for the existence of organic beings are established. **1938** S. MORGULIS tr. *Oparin's Origin of Life* ii. 39 At the beginning of the twentieth century the idea of the transfer of genus from one celestial body to another was again revived in the form of the so-called theory of panspermia, originated by the great Swedish physical chemist S. Arrhenius. **1970** *Daily Tel.* 9 Jan. 19 The theory of 'panspermia', the idea that the seeds of life drift through the Galaxy until they find a planet on which to settle, was eagerly discussed on the .. final day of the moon-rock conference in Houston. **1971** I. G. GASS et al. *Understanding Earth* ix. 140/2 The hypothesis of 'panspermia' .. is an old one which has never found much favour. **1975** *Times Lit. Suppl.* 25 July 846/3 The possibility of panspermia—the idea, recently revived by Leslie Orgel and Nobel laureate Francis Crick, that life did not originate on earth at all, but arrived here from elsewhere in the universe.

panspermic (pæn'spɜːmɪk), *a.* [f. Gr. πάνσπερμος composed of, or containing all sorts of seeds (f. παν- all + σπέρμα seed) + -IC.] Of or pertaining to panspermia.

1857 MAYNE *Expos. Lex.*, *Panspermicus* .., of or belonging to Panspermia: panspermic.

So **panspermism** (pæn'spɜːmɪz(ə)m) = PANSPERMATISM; **pan'spermist** = PANSPERMATIST.

1869 tr. *Pouchet's Universe* (1871) 504 The name of panspermism has been given to this pretended universal dissemination of the reproductive bodies of animals and plants. **1870** NICHOLSON *Man. Zool.* 33 By the 'panspermists' or the opponents of spontaneous generation, it is alleged, that the production of Bacteria .. in organic infusions is due simply to the fact that the atmosphere and probably the fluid itself, is charged with innumerable germs. **1874** *Contemp. Rev.* XXIII. 710 The hypothesis of Panspermism .. supposes that these minutest living things have merely developed in the fluids owing to the accidental presence of invisible germs thrown off from pre-existing living organisms. **1881** TYNDALL *Floating Matter of Air* 208 Panspermism.

pansphygmograph, etc.: see PAN- 2.

pan's-pipe, pan's pipe: see PAN-PIPE.

panstick ('pænstɪk). Also Pan-Stik (proprietary name). [f. PAN(CAKE *sb.* 2 h + STICK *sb.*¹] A kind of matt cosmetic in the form of a stick.

1949 *Trade Marks Jrnl.* 10 Aug. 705/2 Pan-Stik... Non-medicated toilet preparations, cosmetic preparations and perfumes. Max Factor & Company .., Los Angeles, State of California, United States of America; manufacturers. **1962** *New Statesman* 18 May 708/2 We were crushed in the toilets. All round girls smeared on pan-stick. 'I can't go with him, he's too short.' 'All the grey glitter I put on me hair come off on his cheek and I hadn't the heart to tell him.' **1967** *Guardian* 1 Feb. 6/6 The kids I meet .. just don't wash enough. And they plaster their faces .. with layers of cover creams, and thick tinted foundations and then probably panstick make-up as well. **1973** J. BURROWS *Like an Evening Gone* i. 13 Talk .. as superficial as panstick.

pansy ('pænzɪ), *sb.* Forms: 5 **pensee**, 6 **pensy**, **pawnsy**, **paunsie**, 6–7 **pancy**, 6–8 **pansie**, 7– **pansy**. Also β. 6 **pances** (?*pl.*), **pawnce**, **paunse**, 6–7 **panse**, **paunce**. [Formerly *pensee*, *pensy*, a. F. *pensée*, *pencée* (*a* 1500 in Godef. *Compl.*), a fanciful application of *pensée* 'thought'. The β form *panse* is not given in Fr. dicts.; but OF. had *pense*, *panse*, beside *pensée*, *pansée*, in the sense 'thought'.

A reference to the popular or 'vulgar' standing of the name in France occurs in the French botanist Ruel or Ruellius *De natura stirpium* (1536) 595 'Violæ inodoræ genus esse putaverim quam vulgus gallicum *penseam* vocat'.]

1. a. The common name of *Viola tricolor*, esp. of the cultivated varieties; the wild plant is a common weed in cornfields, etc., with small flowers compounded of purple, yellow, and white; the cultivated form is a favourite garden plant, with very numerous varieties having large richly and variously coloured flowers. Also called HEARTSEASE, q.v., and dialectally and locally by various fanciful names, as *kiss-me-at-the-garden-gate*, *love-in-idleness*, *three-faces-under-a-hood*, etc.

a **1500** *Assembly of Ladies* 62 With margarettes growing in ordinaunce .. Ne-m'oublie-mies and sovenez also; The povre pensees were not disloged there. **1530** PALSGR. 251/2 Pancy floure, *menve pencee* [cf. 231/1 Hertesease, *menve pensee*]. *Ibid.* 253/1 Pensy floure, *pensee*. **1592** GREENE *Upst. Courtier* in *Harl. Misc.* (Malh.) II. 217 The checkerd paunsie, or party coloured harts ease. **1597** GERARDE *Herbal* II. ccxcix. § 1. 703 Harts ease is named .. Pansies, Liue in Idlenes. **1629** PARKINSON *Paradisi in Sole* lii. 283 In English Hartsease, and Pansies of the French name *Pensees*. Some giue it foolish names, as Loue in idlenesse, Cull me to you, and Three faces in a hood. **1637** MILTON *Lycidas* 144 The

Pansie freakt with jeat. **1697** DRYDEN *Virg. Past.* II. 66 Pancies to please the Sight, and Casia sweet to smell. **1771** LANGHORNE *Fables of Flora, Violet & Pansy* vii, On that fair bank a Pansy grew, That borrow'd from indulgent skies A velvet shade and purple hue. **1866** *Treas. Bot.* 1218 The endless varieties of Heartsease, or Pansy, are all derived from the cornfield weed *V[iola] tricolor*, and the allied species *V. altaica* from Tartary, and *V. grandiflora* from Switzerland.

β. **1548** TURNER *Names of Herbes* H v, Called in english two faces in a hoode or panses. **1579** SPENSER *Sheph. Cal.* Apr. 142 The pretie Pawnce And the Cheuisaunce, Shall match with the fayre flowre Delice. **1601** HOLLAND *Pliny* XXI. x. 92 The purple March Violet..after them the Panse. **1617** B. JONSON *Vision of Delight* 164 The shining Meads Doe boast the Paunce, the Lillie, and the Rose. *c* **1620** ROBINSON *Mary Magd.* I. 316.

b. A figure or representation of the flower of the pansy as an ornament. [So in 16th c. Fr.]

1553 *Richmond Wills* 76, I beqhweytt and gyff to my broder Constable my pawnsy of golde with the ruby in it.

c. *Comb.*, as ***pansy-culture***, ***-flower***, ***-grower***, ***-growing***, ***-tint***, ***-velvet***; ***pansy-coloured***, ***-dark***, ***-like***, ***-purple***, ***-violet***, ***-yellow*** adjs.

[Cf. F. *pensée* 'couleur d'un violet brun' (Littré).]

1891 *Daily News* 22 June 6/2 A yoke of pansy-coloured velvet. **1909** *Daily Chron.* 18 Mar. 10/3 Lady Kenmare in black and Georgiana Lady Dudley, tall and beautiful in pansy-coloured cloth, were Lady Mayo's assistants. **1897** *Westm. Gaz.* 26 Jan. 10/1 He turned his attention to pansy-culture. **1862** G. M. HOPKINS *Vision of Mermaids* (1929), Their pansy-dark or bronzen locks were strung With coral shells. *a* **1548** HALL *Chron., Hen. VIII* 81 The Frenche kyng & his bende..with garlondes of friers knottes of white satten, and in euery garlond liij. paunse flowers, whiche signified, thinke on Fraunces. **1865** R. BUCHANAN *Sutherland's Pansies* iv, But pansy-growing made his heart within Blow fresh. **1898** *Atlantic Monthly* Apr. 460/1 The velvety, pansy-like variety of the birdfoot violet. **1898** *Daily News* 11 May 4/4 A gown of pansy-purple velvet. **1901** *Westm. Gaz.* 13 July 2/1 A wild upheaval of pansy-purple volcano-shaped peaks. **1940** C. DAY LEWIS tr. *Virgil's Georgics* IV. 89 Eridanus, than which through fertile lands no river Rushes with more momentum to the pansy-purple sea.

2. The colour of a pansy; *spec.* a shade of blue or purple.

1914 JOYCE *Dubliners* 227 A red-faced young woman, dressed in pansy. **1926** *Eaton's News Weekly* 26 June 13/1 Bathing suit...in blue, cardinal, pansy, black. **1935** *Amer. Speech* X. 193/2 The following terms are applied to blue..: *slate, aster, indigo, pansy*, [etc.].

3. a. An effeminate man; a male homosexual.

1929 M. LIEF *Hangover* 210 'Say, what do you know about this?' he said. 'One of those pansies was trying to date me up!' **1937** M. ALLINGHAM *Dancers in Mourning* xiv. 192 You don't want to feel that every other user of the road privately feels that your club is nothing but a pack of pansies on bicycles. **1947** A. P. GASKELL in D. M. Davin *N.Z. Short Stories* (1953) 276 He struck a chesty attitude standing naked on the seat. 'Do I look like a pansy?' 'Not with that thing.' **1956** [see CAMP *a.* (and *sb.*[5])]. **1957** [see *boy friend, boy-friend* s.v. BOY *sb.*[1] 7]. **1960** J. BETJEMAN *Summoned by Bells* ix. 98 There Bignose plays the organ And the pansies all sing flat. **1967** G. JACKSON *Let.* 16 May in *Soledad Brother* (1971) 115 They make emotional pansies of the boys with that sanctimonious dogma. **1971** F. FORSYTH *Day of Jackal* xx. 335, I don't like you in that stuff. It makes you look like all those nasty pansies back in there. **1975** *Amer. N. & Q.* XIII. 146/2 Evidence that Sir Thopas is a 'pansy' or a 'queer', who would be ridiculed as a homosexual. **1976** BOTHAM & DONNELLY *Valentino* vii. 52 A group of degenerate art students, most of whom he considered pansies.

b. *Comb.*, as ***pansy-ass***, ***-boy***.

1934 *New Statesman* 15 Sept. 318/2 Reminiscences of the fate of Heines and Röhm were reflected in shouts about 'pansy-boys'. **1976** N. THORNBURG *Cutter & Bone* viii. 192 He learned all about the ingratitude and stupidity of the man's..pansy-ass sons.

ˈpansy, *a.* [f. PANSY *sb.* 3.] Effeminate; homosexual; affected. So **ˈpansyish** *a.*

1929 J. DEVANNY *Riven* xvii. 112 'Thanks. Don't bother.' The voice was warm... A rich telephone voice. To an artist a pansy voice; a purple pansy. **1934** M. HODGE *Wind & Rain* III. 83 She'll forget all about it, in the arms of Roger Cole! I think he's pansy, anyhow. **1942** E. PAUL *Narrow St.* xxxvi. 323 Pierre..started sending affectionate notes to certain homosexual French officers who were rabidly anti-Left... One by one, these pansy reactionaries began to disappear from their units. **1951** 'E. CRISPIN' *Long Divorce* viii. 84 I'd want her to be walking out with a decent lad, not a pansy little foreign gramophone-record. **1953** E. TAYLOR *Sleeping Beauty* ii. 27 Laurence leant awkwardly against the chimney-piece in a rather pansyish pose. **1971** *Daily Tel.* 21 Aug. 3/4 'Most of these new designs are too pansy, too effeminate,' said Leading Seaman Robert Nelson.

ˈpansy, *v.* [f. PANSY *sb.* 3] **a.** *trans.* To dress or adorn in an affected or effeminate manner. Freq. *refl.* and const. *up.* **b.** *intr.* To act or walk in an effeminate manner.

1946 'BRAHMS' & 'SIMON' *Trottie True* 154 Luke Lovelock had pansied himself into a feature of every fashionable production. Luke had such perfect taste. **1951** N. MARSH *Opening Night* i. 27 The theatre was shut dahn for a long while until they 'ad it all altered and pansied up. **1966** J. WAINWRIGHT *Crystallised Carbon Pig* xxxix. 172 Originally, his hair had been mousy brown. He'd tried to pansy himself up—and failed. **1972** M. KENYON *Shooting of Dan McGrew* i. 10 It's over a month old..and the last word from McGrew before he went pansying off.

pant (pænt), *sb.*[1] *northern.* [Origin unknown: sense 2 suggests Romanic *pantano* slough, bog; but the resemblance is prob. fortuitous.]

1. A public fountain, cistern, or well; usually a stone or iron erection with a spout, whence water is drawn, a conduit; also called **pant-well** (Jamieson 1825–80).

1586 in *Mem. St. Giles's, Durham* (Surtees) 13 Payd for the poore men's dycke that dwell att the pant. **1595** in R. Welford *Hist. Newcastle* III. 130 Every street hath his cistern or pant. **1857** JEFFREY *Roxburgh.* II. iii. 112 Water was brought from a well in Sudhope-Path to a pant erected for its reception at the Cross. *Ibid.* III. i. 12 A huge and unseemly pantwell, surmounted by a lamp stood in one corner. **1884** BESANT *Dorothy Forster* iii. (1887) 28 A triangular green, having the village pant at the end. **1887** *Newcastle Weekly Chron.* Suppl. 23 July 2/5 Besides the numerous public pants,..there were [*a* 1846], in the most populous districts [of Newcastle], 'farthing pants', [at which]..one farthing was charged for a 'skeel' full of water.

2. A pool into which water or moisture drains; a puddle.

1807 STAGG *Misc. Poems* 15 Lang stretch'd i' th' midden pant. **1808** R. ANDERSON *Cumbld. Ball., Codbeck Wedding* xii, He..stuck in a pant 'buin the middle. **1878** *Cumbld. Gloss., Pant*, a sump. [*Ibid., Sump*..a hole at the bottom of a pit to collect water in.] **1899** *Speaker* 23 Dec. 309/2 Where the water from the pant flows out of the farm-yard under a wall, the grass is soft and green.

pant (pænt), *sb.*[2] [f. PANT *v.*]

1. One of a series of short quick efforts of laboured breathing, from exertion or agitation; a gasp, a catching of the breath.

1500–20 DUNBAR *Poems* xiii. 53 Thair cumis ȝung monkis...And in the courte thair hait flesche dantis, Full faderlyk, with pechis and pantis. **1603** DRAYTON *Bar. Wars* (1619) v. lxiv, As yet his Breath found Passage to and fro, With many a short Pant, many a broken word. **1682** BUNYAN *Holy War* 248 Here were groans, there pants. **1834** W. GODWIN *Lives Necromancers* 221 The loud strokes of the hammer,..intermixed with the pants and groans of the workmen. **1845** E. WARBURTON *Crescent & Cross* xxiv. II. 212 Not a pant escaped from her [a mare's] deep chest.

2. A throb or heave of the breast in laboured breathing or palpitation of the heart.

1581 T. HOWELL *Devises* E ij b, The hardest harte by proofe, doth yeelde an inwarde pante When good desyres are deprest. **1606** SHAKS. *Ant. & Cl.* IV. viii. 16 Leape thou..Through proofe of Harnesse to my heart, and there Ride on the pants triumphing. **1800** in *Spirit Pub. Jrnls.* IV. 270 The bosom's pant, the rosy-winding arm. **1805** W. GODWIN *Fleetwood* I. vi. 139, I felt the quick pants of my bosom.

3. *transf.* The regular throb and gasping sound of a steam-engine, as the valves open and shut.

1840 RUSKIN *Let. College Friend* 4 July, Wks. 1903 I. 407 For you..have heaved the dark limbs of the colossal engine—its deep, fierce breath has risen in hot pants to heaven. **1853–8** HAWTHORNE *Eng. Note-Bks.* (1879) II. 53 Every pant of the engine.

pant (pænt), *sb.*[3] [sing. back-formation f. PANTS *sb. pl.*] **1.** = PANTS *sb. pl. U.S.*

1893 H. A. SHANDS *Some Peculiarities of Speech in Mississippi* 49 *Pant*.., an abbreviation of *pantaloons*, used by clerks in dry-goods stores. They say: 'I have a pant that I can sell you,' etc. Of course, *pants* is a well-known abbreviation, but I think *pant* is rather a new word. **1936** A. L. HENCH (*MS. note dated Feb.*), For six or seven years now, I have been hearing clothes dealers speak of a pair of pants as 'a fine pant'. The reasoning seems to be that if a pile of pairs of pants is *pants*, then one pair is a *pant*. **1962** *L.L. Bean Catal.* Spring 10 A practical and well made pant for general sportswear. **1976** *Billings* (Montana) *Gaz.* 16 June 3-A/4 (Advt.), You just can't beat the value of this 3-piece jacket/dress/pant ensemble at our irresistible price... The pull-on pant makes a good thing better.

2. *attrib.* and *Comb.*, as ***pant-leg***, ***look***; **pantcoat**, a women's coat designed for wearing with trousers; **pantdress**, a dress with a divided skirt; **pantskirt**, a divided skirt; **pant suit**, **pantsuit** = *trouser suit.*

1970 *N.Y. Post* 16 Dec. 6 Pantcoat, on duty for wintry weather and for city traffic. **1974** *New Yorker* 25 Feb. 62/1 (Advt.), A great pantcoat: this Weatherbee, with its easy swing and snappy fit. **1964** *Women's Wear Daily* 30 Nov. 44 Julie Isles..likes the pantdress that stops just above the knee. **1967** *Maclean's Mag.* Dec. 35 At far left a Persian pantdress in pure wool (with a matching mini-nightie, about $60). **1968** Pantdress [see *pantskirt* below]. **1956** H. GOLD *Man who was not with It* (1965) ix. 73 The pantleg was sticky where it was bruised. **1974** D. RICHARDS *Coming of Winter* i. 6 He moved uphill very quickly, his boots and pantlegs soaking from the water. **1976** *New Yorker* 5 Jan. 22/3 We glanced down the row and saw..the next straightening the pant leg over his right calf in a single motion, and so on. **1970** *Women's Wear Daily* 23 Nov. 31/2, I think another pant look will take over. **1964** *Times* 3 Aug. 11 The pants and pantskirt as shown by Marc Bohan at Dior are for the country and around the house. **1968** *N.Y. Times* 15 July 43 This time, it is a more coordinated trend—pant-skirts, pant-dresses, pant-suits, tops and pants and so on. **1977** *Evening Post* (Nottingham) 27 Jan. 9/5 Stride ahead in this all-season look of a classic shirt paired with a trim pant-skirt. **1966** *Sun* 15 June 3/1 'At least they didn't come in trouser suits.' Two girls did. One wore a pant suit in pink and green linen. **1968** *Telegraph* (Brisbane) 24 Oct. 31/6 Model Kelly shows off the latest pantsuit in white stretch towelling. **1970** *Harrods Christmas Catal.* 14/1 Pant suit hangers. **1975** *N.Y. Times* 8 Sept. 33/4 Another woman..sits by herself looking aloof, brushing hairs off her well-pressed rust pantsuit.

pant (pænt), *v.* Also 5 pont, 6–7 paunt. [Common from *c* 1440: earlier history not evidenced. App. related to (? shortened from) OF. *pantoisier*, *-eisier*, *-aiser*, *-uisier*, *-iser*, 'to pant, to have the breath short, to breathe with labour' (12th c. in Godef.); according to Gaston Paris (*Romania* VI. (1877) 628):—popular L. *phantasiāre* to be oppressed with nightmare, to gasp or pant with oppression, f. *phantasia* phantasy, nightmare.

Such a shortening of the Fr. vb. in Eng. is not very easy to account for: but *pantiser* may have been felt as a vb. with stem *pant-* and formative suffix *-iser* (cf. *advert, advertise*). In 16th c. F. there was also the vb. *pantoier, pantoyer*, while mod.F. has *panteler* to pant, in both of which *pant-* is app. taken as a stem and furnished with various formative suffixes.]

1. *intr.* To breathe hard or spasmodically, as when out of breath; to draw quick laboured breaths, as from exertion or agitation; to gasp for breath.

c **1440** *Promp. Parv.* 381/2 Pantyn, *anelo.* *c* **1440** HYLTON *Scala Perf.* (W. de W. 1494) II. xxxiv, They streyne hemself ..and panten soo strongly that they brast in to bodily feruours. *c* **1460** *Towneley Myst.* xvi. 238 War! I say, lett me pant, now thynk I to fyght ffor anger. **1470–85** MALORY *Arthur* VII. xvii, Thus they foughte..tyl att the laste they lacked wynde both, and then they stode waging and scateryng pontyng, blowynge and bledynge. **1576** FLEMING *Panopl. Epist.* 288 They blowe, and pant like discomfited souldiers. **1607** SHAKS. *Cor.* II. ii. 126 He neuer stood to ease his Brest with panting. **1615** MANWOOD *Lawes Forest* (ed. 2) 3 *marg.*, He that doth hunt a wilde beast, and doth make him paunt, shall pay 10. shillings. **1735** SOMERVILLE *Chase* III. 509 He pants, he sobs apall'd; Drops down his heavy Head to Earth. **1860** TYNDALL *Glac.* I. xvi. 112 He sometimes paused,..and panted like a chased deer. **1873** HALE *In His Name* vi. 49 The poor beast he rode came panting into the crowd.

b. *fig.* Said of the wind or waves.

1666 DRYDEN *Ann. Mirab.* xcviii, Weary waves, withdrawing from the fight, Lie lulled and panting on the silent shore. **1717** POPE *Eloisa* 159 The dying gales that pant upon the trees. **1782** COWPER *Expost.* 721 A cold blast sings Through the dry leaves, and pants upon the strings. **1819** SHELLEY *Ode to West Wind* iv, If I were..A wave to pant beneath thy power, and share The impulse of thy strength.

c. To go or run panting.

1713 YOUNG *Last Day* I. 207 Words all in vain pant after the distress. **1770** GOLDSM. *Des. Vill.* 94 As a hare..Pants to the place from whence at first he flew. **1871** BROWNING *Balaustion* 71 We could hear behind us plain the threats And curses of the pirate panting up In..passion of pursuit.

d. *transf.* To emit hot air, vapour, etc., in loud puffs, as a furnace or engine.

1743 DAVIDSON *Æneid* VIII. 250 The fire in the furnace pants. **1878** BROWNING *La Saisiaz* 98 Not a steam-boat pants from harbour.

2. To gasp (for air, water, etc.); hence *fig.* To long or wish with breathless eagerness; to gasp with desire; to yearn (*for*, *after*, or *to* with *inf.*).

1560 BIBLE (Genev.) *Ps.* xlii. 1 As the hart braieth for the riuers of water, so panteth my soule after thee o God. **1605** SHAKS. *Lear* V. iii. 243, I pant for life. **1611** BIBLE *Ps.* xlii. 1 As the Hart panteth after the water brookes, so panteth my soule after thee, O God. **1719** YOUNG *Revenge* V. ii. When all the bliss I pant for, is to gain In hell a refuge from severer pain. **1752** JOHNSON *Rambler* No. 193 ¶ 2 Every man pants for the highest eminence within his view. **1781** COWPER *Retirement* 476 He..Pants to be told of battles won or lost. **1822** BYRON *Werner* I. i, 'Tis to be amongst these sovereigns My husband pants! **1863** GEO. ELIOT *Romola* xxiv, He panted for the threatening voice again.

3. To throb or heave violently or rapidly; to palpitate, pulsate, beat: said of the heart, bosom, etc.; also of the blood.

c **1460** *Towneley Myst.* xxiii. 52, I shall fownde, if that I may,..To cause his hart pante. **1535** COVERDALE *Ps.* xxxvii[i]. 10 My hert paunteth, my strength hath fayled me. —— *Isa.* xxi. 4 Myne herte paunted. **1573–80** BARET *Alv.* P 71 To pant as the heart, or braine doth... My veines do beate, or pant. **1608** *Merry Devil Edmonton* in Hazl. *Dodsley* X. 228 His blood is good and clear, As the best drop that panteth in thy veins. **1781** COWPER *Expost.* 473 A breast that panted with alarms. **1819** SHELLEY *Cenci* II. ii. 140 Her very name, But spoken by a stranger, makes my heart Sicken and pant.

4. *transf.* Of an iron ship: To have its plating bulge in and out in the struggle with the waves.

1869 SIR E. J. REED *Shipbuild.* i. 12 Instances..of ships 'panting' in their fore compartments. **1890** W. J. GORDON *Foundry* 67 In the fore body and aft body there is much strutting and bracing, to prevent the new ship 'panting' in her struggles with the waves.

5. *trans.* **a.** To utter gaspingly; to gasp *out*, etc.

1605 SHAKS. *Lear* II. iv. 31 Came there a reeking Poste,..halfe breathlesse, painting [*Globe* panting] forth From Gonerill his Mistris, salutations. **1778** MISS BURNEY *Evelina* xlvi, 'No,—no,—no—' I panted out, 'I am no actress'. *c* **1830** S. FERGUSON *Forging of Anchor* ii, And thick and loud the swinking crowd at every stroke pant 'ho!' **1847** TENNYSON *Princess* v. 23 At length my Sire..Panted from weary sides 'King, you are free!'

†**b.** *poet.* To expel or drive *forth* or *out* by agitated gasping. *Obs.*

c **1624** CHAPMAN *Batrachom.* 110 His heart within him panted out repose, For th' insolent plight in which his state did stand. **1821** SHELLEY *Prometh. Unb.* III. iii. 125 My spirit Was panted forth in anguish whilst thy pain Made my heart mad.

pant, obs. form of PAINT.

pant- = Gr. παντ-, the shortened form in which παντο- 'all-' appears before a vowel: see PANTO-. The following words have *pant-* followed by an element with initial *a-*. **ˈpantagogue** *Med.* [Gr. ἀγωγός driving forth, leading], a medicine that expels all morbid matter. **pantaˈmorphic** *a.* [Gr. ἄμορφος formless, unshapen], generally deformed. **ˌpantanenceˈphalic** *a. Terat.* [Gr. ἀνεγκέφαλος without brain], congenitally destitute of brain (Gould *Dict. Med.* 1900). **panta'phobia** [Gr. ἀφοβία fearlessness], total absence of fear (*Syd. Soc. Lex.* 1893). **pan'tarchic** *a.*, of or pertaining to a pantarchy. **'pantarchy** [Gr. ἀρχή rule], a state in which the rule is vested in the whole people. †**pan'tarete**, erron. **-arite** [Gr. ἀρέτη virtue], all-virtuousness. **pan'tatrophy** *Path.* [Gr. ἀτροφία ATROPHY], general atrophy; so **pan'tatrophous** *a.* See also PANTHODIC, PANTISOCRACY.

[**1811** HOOPER *Med. Dict.*, *Pantagoga*, medicines which expel all morbid humours.] **1854–67** C. A. HARRIS *Dict. Med. Terminol.*, **Pantagogue*, that which expels all morbid humours. **1893** *Syd. Soc. Lex.*, *Pantagogue*, the same as *Panchymagogue*. **1857** MAYNE *Expos. Lex.*, *Pantamorphicus*, ..*pantamorphic. **1890** BILLINGS *Nat. Med. Dict.*, *Pantamorphic*, generally amorphous or deformed. **1883** L. F. WARD *Dynamic Sociol.* I. 466 The cosmopolitan, or *pantarchic stage. **1899** FISKE *Cent. of Sci.* viii. 217 Never did a philanthropic world-mender contemplate his grotesque phalanstery or *pantarchy with greater pleasure. **1624** HEYWOOD *Gunaik.* III. 123 Of whose omniscience, *pantarite, and goodnesse, all men heretofore haue spoke too little. **1857** MAYNE *Expos. Lex.*, *Pantatrophus*,..totally without nutrition or nourishment; *pantatrophous. **1893** *Syd. Soc. Lex.*, *Pantatrophous*, without nutrition. **1857** MAYNE *Expos. Lex.*, *Pantatrophia*,..term for complete innutrition, *pantatrophy. **1900** GOULD *Dict. Med.*, *Pantatrophy*.

panta-, erron. form of PANTO-, in PANTACOSM, PANTAGAMY, PANTATYPE; also *pantagraph*, *pantamorphic*, *pantascopic*: see PANTOGRAPH *sb.*, PANTO-.

pantable, -cle, -fle, obs. var. PANTOFLE.

'pantacosm. [Erroneous form for *pantocosm*, f. PANTO- + Gr. κόσμος world.] Another name of the instrument called COSMOLABE.

1864 in WEBSTER; and in later Dicts.

pantagamy (pæn'tægəmɪ). [An illiterate formation for *pantogamy*, f. Gr. παντο- PANTO- all + -γαμία, from γάμος marriage. (*Pantagamy* is etymologically, from Gr. ἀγαμία celibacy, 'universal or total celibacy'.)] A communistic system of complex marriage, in which all the men and women of a household or community are regarded as married to each other, as formerly practised among the Perfectionists at Oneida Creek in U.S.

1852 J. NICHOL *Amer. Lit.* i. 20 The American mind delights in..social and political experiments, as Shakerism, Mormonism, Pantagamy. **1867** DIXON *New Amer.* II. xxiv. *heading*, Pantagamy. [*Ibid.* 256 In the Bible Family living at Oneida Creek, the central domestic fact of the household is the complex marriage of its members to each other, and to all.] **1894** *Q. Rev.* Oct. 311 Has not Oneida Creek invented 'Complex Marriage' or Pantagamy?

pantagraph, etc., erron. f. PANTOGRAPH *sb.*, etc.

Pantagruelian (pæntəgru:'ɛlɪən), *a.* and *sb.* [f. *Pantagruel*, the name given to the last of the giants in Rabelais + -IAN.]

A. *adj.* Of, pertaining to, characteristic of, or appropriate to, Pantagruel, represented by Rabelais as a coarse and extravagant humorist, dealing satirically with serious subjects.

1694 MOTTEUX *Rabelais* v. 223 The Most Certain, True and Infallible Pantagruelian Prognostication. For the Year that's to come, and every and aye. **1839** *Fraser's Mag.* XX. 521 The liberality, ability, and Pantagruelian zeal of Theodore Martin of Edinburgh. **1883** F. W. POTTER tr. *Fr. Celebrities* II. 113 The Pantagrulian chef-d'œuvre, 'L'Ami Fritz'.

B. *sb.* = PANTAGRUELIST.

1899 W. E. HENLEY in *Nutt's Circular* Apr. 2 Rabelais.. had been dead a full century,..ere Sir Thomas Urquhart.. best of Pantagruelians and rarest of Scotsmen, produced (1653) his amazing rendering of Books I and II.

So **Pantagru'elic** [F. *pantagruélique*], **-'grueline** *adjs.* = prec. A.; **Pantagru'elically** *adv.*

c **1804** DOUCE in *Bibl. Cornub.* (1878) II. 869/1 An antiquarian hash..under the whimsical appellation of 'the Ancient Cathedral of Cornwall' pantagruelically surveyed by John Whitaker, B.D. **1838** *Fraser's Mag.* XVII. 111 Call you this writing Pantagruellically? **1857** LAWRENCE *Guy Livingst.* xxxi. 304 A German philosopher..(eating and drinking all the while Pantagruelically). **1882** TRAILL *Sterne* iv. 34 Pantagruelic burlesque. **1882** *Daily News* 2 Jan. 5/2 A Pantagrueline prognostication for 1882.

‖**Pantagru'elion.** [F. *pantagruélion.*] A humorous name given by Rabelais to hemp, as the source of the hangman's rope.

1857 KINGSLEY *Two Y. Ago* x, An immediate external application..of that famous herb Pantagruelion, cure for all public ills and private woes.

Pantagruelism (pæntə'gru:əlɪz(ə)m). [a. F. *pantagruélisme*, f. *Pantagruel*: see above and -ISM.]

1. The theory and practice ascribed to Pantagruel, one of the characters of Rabelais; extravagant and coarse humour with a satirical or serious purpose.

1835 SOUTHEY *Doctor* III. Interch. xiii. 340 Ignorant of humorology! more ignorant of psychology! and most ignorant of Pantagruelism. *a* **1849** H. COLERIDGE *Ess.* (1851) II. 234 An unsuccessful attempt at pantagruelism, with all the outrageousness and none of the richness of Rabelais. **1860** DONALDSON *Theatre of Greeks* (ed. 7) 77 By Pantagruelism we mean..an assumption of Bacchanalian buffoonery as a cloak to cover some serious purpose. **1865** WRIGHT *Hist. Caricat.* xix. 342 Pantagruelism, or, if you like, Rabelaism, did not, during the sixteenth century, make much progress beyond the limits of France.

¶**2.** 'The theory or practice of the medical profession: used in burlesque or ridicule'. (Webster.)

(App. an error from misunderstanding quot. 1835 above.) **1864** WEBSTER (citing Southey as authority). [So in OGILVIE; also in CASSELL, and later Dicts.]

Pantagruelist (pæntə'gru:əlɪst). [a. F. *pantagruéliste*: or f. as prec. + -IST.] An imitator, admirer, or student of Pantagruel, or of Rabelais.

1611 COTGR., *Pantagrueliste*, a Pantagruellist; a merrie Greek, faithfull drunkard, good fellow. (Hence in BLOUNT 1656, PHILLIPS 1658, BAILEY 1721.) **1834** SOUTHEY *Doctor* (ed. 2) I. 175 In humour however he was by nature a Pantagruelist. *Ibid.* 178. **1847** LOWELL *Lett.* I. 130 Had I mixed more with the world than I have, I should probably have become a Pantagruelist. **1886** SAINTSBURY *Ess. Eng. Lit.* (1891) 251 Peacock was a Pantagruelist to the heart's core.

Hence **Pantagrue'listic, -istical** *adjs.* = PANTAGRUELIAN *a.*

1838 *Fraser's Mag.* XVII. 317 In a work Pantagruelistical they would be..out of place. **1880** *Libr. Univ. Knowl.* (N.Y.) VII. 319 A very absurd and indecorous work of a pantagruelistic kind.

pantaleon (pæn'tæli:ən). Also -lon, -lone, -loon. [Named after Pantaleon Hebenstreit, a German, who invented the instrument in 1705.]

A musical instrument: a large dulcimer having one or two hundred strings, sounded by hammers or sticks held in the player's hands.

1757 A. LINDE tr. *Keysler's Trav. Germany* IV. lxxxvi. 125 M. Panthaleon Hebenstreit, never refuses to gratify strangers with a sight of the Panthaleon, a musical instrument called by his own name, who was the inventor of it. **1774** WRAXALL *Tour North. Europe* ii. (1775) 11 She plays on an instrument resembling our spinet, and which they call a pantaloon. **1838** *Encycl. Brit.* (ed. 7) XVI. 790/2 *Pantaleone*. **1880** A. J. HIPKINS in Grove *Dict. Mus.* II. 645 *Pantaleon* or *Pantalon*, a very large Dulcimer invented and played upon in the early part of the last century by Pantaleon Hebenstreit, whose name was transferred to the instrument by Louis XIV. The name was also given in Germany to horizontal pianofortes with the hammers striking downwards.

pantalettes, -lets (pæntə'lɛts), *sb. pl.* (*rare* in *sing.*) *Chiefly U.S.* Also (in *sing.*) **pantelette.** [Dim. formation after *pantaloon*: see -ETTE.]

a. Loose drawers or 'trousers' with a frill at the bottom of each leg, worn by young girls *c* 1825–53; *transf.* euphemistically to drawers, trousers (see BLOOMER), cycling 'knickerbockers', or the like, worn by women.

1834 *Knickerbocker* IV. 117 In the first place, in their blushing girlhood, they assume the pantalettes, or little pantaloons. **1838** *Southern Lit. Messenger* IV. 28/1 Two pretty sisters, in pantalettes, waited on table. **1847** PORTER *Big Bear* 104 (Farmer) If I hadn't a had on pantalets. **1857** READE *Course True Love* II. ii. 133 The company..were very severe on this [Bloomer] costume, and proceeded upwards from the pantalettes to the morals of the inventor. **1879** *Lond. Soc.* Christm. No. 51/2 You are only fit for a pinafore and pantalettes. **1881** in Mrs. Power O'Donoghue *Ladies on Horsebk.* v. 316 [Mexican horsewomen], clad in loose Turkish pantalettes tucked into the riding-boots of soft yellow leather. **1882** *Standard* 19 Sept. 5/2 Dr. Mary Walker lectured..in 'pantalettes'. **1887** J. ASHBY STERRY *Lazy Minstrel* 229, *Song of School-girls*, Come the dainty dimpled pets, With their tresses all in nets, And their peeping pantalettes Just in view. **1887** in *Girl's Own Paper* 8 Oct. 19/3. **1888** *N. & Q.* 7th Ser. VI. 390. **1897** *Daily News* 30 Aug. 5/7 There are very pretty possibilities with a short skirt and pantalette [for the bicycle]. **1922** JOYCE *Ulysses* 528 The scanty, daringly short skirt, riding up at the knee to show a peep of white pantelette, is a potent weapon. **1975** R. PLAYER *Let's talk of Graves* iii. 78 Little girls in pantalettes bowled their hoops.

b. *transf.* The frills used to adorn certain joints when brought to the table.

1883 *Harper's Mag.* July 246/1 The paper pantalets which adorn the broiled lamb chop.

Hence **panta'letted** *a.*, dressed in pantalettes.

1865 MRS. WHITNEY *Gayworthys* i, A child of seven, sashed, pantaletted and bronze-booted. **1880** *World* 31 Mar. 12 The short-frocked pantaletted contingent [of girls].

pantalon, -one, -oon, variants of PANTALEON.

pantaloon (pæntə'lu:n). Forms: 6 **pantaloone, -loun, -lowne,** 7 **panteloun, -lown,** 7–8 **pantalon, -lone,** 7– **-loon.** [a. F. *pantalon* (1550 in Hatz.-Darm.), ad. It. *pantalone* 'a kind of mask on the Italian stage, representing the Venetian' (Baretti), of whom *Pantalone* was a nickname, supposed to be derived from the name of *San Pantaleone* or *Pantalone*, formerly a favourite saint of the Venetians.]

1. a. The Venetian character in Italian comedy, represented as a lean and foolish old man, wearing spectacles, pantaloons (see 3), and slippers. **b.** Hence, in modern harlequinade or pantomime, a character represented as a foolish and vicious old man, the butt of the clown's jokes, and his abettor in his pranks and tricks.

c **1590** in Collier *Ann. Stage* (1831) III. 403 (Stage Direction) Enter the panteloun, and causeth the cheste or truncke to be broughte forth. **1592** NASHE *P. Penilesse* 27 Our representations..not consisting like theirs of a Pantaloun, a Whore, and a Zanie, but of Emperours, Kings and Princes. *a* **1610** HEALEY *Epictetus' Man.* (1636) 24 Hee is not ashamed..to dance Country dances, and Matachines, as a Zanie or Pantalon. **1632** HEYWOOD *2nd Pt. Know not me* Wks. 1874 I. 257 Now they peepe like Italian pantelowns Behind an arras. [**1704** ADDISON *Italy*, *Venice* (1766) 68 Pantalone [in Italian comedy] is generally an old cully.]

b. 1781 *Westm. Mag.* IX. 709 No Pantaloon with peaked beard to-night Shall screaming boys and trembling maidens fright. **1835** W. IRVING *Tour Prairies* xxix. 275 Their tail cocked up like the queue of Pantaloon in a pantomime. **1855** *Times* 3 Apr., Never did Clown and Pantaloon belabour each other more heartily. **1867** [see HARLEQUINADE].

†**2.** Hence applied in contempt to an enfeebled tottering old man; a dotard, an old fool. *Obs.* exc. as echo of Shaks.

1596 SHAKS. *Tam. Shr.* III. i. 37 My man Tranio, *regia*, bearing my port, *celsa senis* that we might beguile the old Pantalowne. **1600** —— *A.Y.L.* II. vii. 158 The leane and slipper'd Pantaloone, With spectacles on nose, and pouch on side, His youthfull hose well sau'd, a world too wide, For his shrunke shanke. **1862** T. A. TROLLOPE *Marietta* I. iii. 53 He became a withered and shrivelled pantaloon.

†**b.** A nickname (app.) for Scottish courtiers after the Restoration. *Obs.* [Perhaps from their dress: cf. 3.]

1660 *Cavalier's Complaint* in W. W. Wilkins *Pol. Ball.* (1860) I. 163 But truly there are swarms of those Who lately were our chiefest foe, Of pantaloons and muffs. *c* **1690** KIRKTON *Hist. Ch. Scot.* iii. (1817) 114 This parliament [1662] was called the Drinking Parliament. The commissioner [Middleton] had £50 English a-day allowed him, which he spent faithfully among his northern pantalons.

3. Applied at different periods to garments of different styles for the legs. (Chiefly in pl.)

†**a.** A kind of breeches or trousers in fashion for some time after the Restoration. *Obs.*

Said by Evelyn (in context of quot. 1661) to have been taken by the French from the costume of the stage-character of the period 'when the freak takes our Monsieurs to appear like so many Farces or Jack Puddings on the stage'.

1661 EVELYN *Tyranus* in *Mem.* (1871) 751, I would choose ..some fashion not so pinching as to need a Shooing-horn with the Dons, nor so exorbitant as the Pantaloons, which are a kind of Hermaphrodite and of neither Sex. [Cf. 'petticoat-breeches' in Fairholt *Costume* (ed. 1860) 254–5.] **1663** BUTLER *Hud.* I. iii. 924 And as the French we conquer'd once Now give us laws for pantaloons, The length of breeches. **1667** DRYDEN *Wild Gall.* III. i, I have not yet spoke with the gentleman in the black pantaloons [the Devil]. **1674** BLOUNT *Glossogr.* (ed. 4), *Pantalones*, a sort of Breeches now in fashion, and well known. **1686** tr. *Chardin's Trav. Persia* 87 They [Persians] wear little shirts, that fall down to their knees, and tuck into a streight Pantaloon. **1691** *Satyr agst. French* 6 They taught our Sparks to strut in Pantaloons. **1719** DE FOE *Crusoe* I. xi, The breeches were made of the skin of an old he-goat, whose hair hung down such a length..that, like pantaloons, it reached to the middle of my legs. *a* **1734** NORTH *Lives* (1826) I. 289 [referring to events of *c* 1680], I could not but wonder to see pantaloons and shoulder-knots crowding among the common clowns.

†**b.** Applied to other styles, either historically, or in reference to the dress of the stage character, which, according to quot. 1727–41, was at one time of the nature of 'tights'. *Obs.*

The quot. from Chambers is merely translated from the Fr. *Dictionnaire de Trévoux*, and does not prove English usage. In French the name became associated with the tight garments of the 15–16th c., familiar in the paintings of the Italian artists of the period; but this was nowhere a contemporary application. From this arose the use in c.

1696 PHILLIPS (ed. 5), *Pantaloon*, a sort of Garment formerly worn, consisting of Breeches and Stockings fastned together and both of the same Stuff. **1727–41** CHAMBERS *Cycl.* [from French], *Pantaloon* or *Pantalon*, the name of an ancient garment frequent among our forefathers, consisting of breeches and stockings all of a piece. The denomination comes from the Venetians, who first introduced this habit, and who are called Pantaloni... Also used for the habit or dress these buffoons [in the Italian comedy] usually wear; which is made precisely to the form of their body, and all of a piece from head to foot.

c. A tight-fitting kind of trousers fastened with ribbons or buttons below the calf, or, later, by straps passing under the boots, which were introduced late in the 18th c., and began to supersede knee-breeches. **d.** Hence extended to trousers generally (especially in U.S., where this use may have been independently taken directly from F. *pantalon, a* 1800).

1798 [implied in PANTALOONED]. **1804** C. B. BROWN tr. *Volney's View Soil U.S.* 360 He was dressed in the American style; in a blue suit, with round hat and pantaloons. **1806–7** J. BERESFORD *Miseries Hum. Life* (1826) x. lxxxix, Loudly bursting..the fastenings of your braces, and the strings of your pantaloons behind. **1825** *Retrospect. Rev.* XII. 25 *note*, In October 1812, an order was made by St. John's and Trinity College, that every young man who appeared in Hall or Chapel in pantaloons or trowsers, should be considered as absent. **1834** PLANCHÉ *Brit. Costume* 316 Pantaloons and Hessians boots were introduced about the same period [i.e. *c*1789]. **1855** WHITTIER *Barefoot Boy* 3 With thy turned-up pantaloons, And thy merry whistled tunes. **1857** CHAMBERS *Inform. People* I. 798/1 Pantaloons, which fitted close to the leg, remained in very common use by those persons who had adopted them till about the year 1814, when the wearing of trousers, already introduced into the army, became fashionable. **1858** GEN. P. THOMPSON *Audi Alt.* I. xlviii. 187 British officers, in all the priggery of sash and white pantaloon. **1865** DICKENS *Mut. Fr.* III. xi, Dressed in.. pepper and salt pantaloons. **1877** M. M. GRANT *Sun-Maid* viii, His loose shirt hung outside his pantaloons.

e. See quot. and cf. PANTALETTES.

1821 *Ladies' Museum* Feb. (Parisian news), Female children wear pantaloons of merino, with short petticoats of the same. **1881** in Mrs. Power O'Donoghue *Ladies on Horseback* v. 235 [For horsewomen] Pantaloons of chamois leather, buttoning close at the ankles.

4. *attrib.* and *Comb.*, as ***pantaloon-like*** adj.

1675 PHILLIPS *Theat. Poet*, Pref. **iij, Whether the Trunck-Hose Fancy of Queen Elizabeth's days or the Pantaloon Genius of ours be best. *a* **1822** SHELLEY *Devil* xvi. 4 Could make his pantaloon seams start. **1858** SIMMONDS *Dict. Trade, Pantaloon Stuff*, material for men's trousers. **1892** SIR J. C. BROWNE in *Pall Mall G.* 5 May 7/1, I should describe them as pantaloon-like girls, for many of them had a stooping gait and withered appearance, shrunk shanks, and spectacles on nose.

pantalooned (-ˈluːnd), *a.* [f. prec. + -ED².] Wearing pantaloons; having pantaloons on; trousered.

1798 CHARLOTTE SMITH *Yng. Philos.* I. 27 He..was pantalooned and waistcoated after the very newest fashion. **1801** in *Spirit Pub. Jrnls.* V. 233 No more the pantaloon'd, unpowder'd spark, Displays his figure in the dusty Park. **1857** READE *Course of True Love* II. iv. 160 These pantalooned females practise a reserve, compared with which the modesty of Europe is masculine impudence.

pantaˈloonery. [f. as prec. + -ERY.]

1. The performance of a pantaloon in the pantomime.

1821 LAMB *Elia* Ser. I. *My First Play*, The clownery and pantaloonery of these pantomimes have clean passed out of my head. **1855** *Times* 2 Apr., The difficulties of Clownery and Pantaloonery had yet to be surmounted.

fig. **1885** *Society* Nov. 11/1 At last that pantaloonery is 'over'.

2. 'Materials for pantaloons' (Webster 1864); trouserings.

pantaˈlooning, *vbl. sb. rare.* [f. PANTALOON + -ING¹; cf. *tailoring, colonelling.*] Playing the part of Pantaloon.

1861 MAYHEW *Lond. Labour* III. 121 He has given up clowning, and taken to pantalooning instead. **1862** *All Year Round* 13 Sept. 12 Pantalooning is bad for a man's spirits, bad for his manners, bad for his opinion of himself.

pantameter, -morph, etc.: see PANTOMETER, PANTO-.

†**pantap,** an abbreviation of *pantaple*, PANTOFLE.

1570 LEVINS *Manip.* 27/28 Pantap, *callopodium.*

pantaphel, -ap(p)le, obs. corrupt ff. PANTOFLE.

†**panˈtarbe.** *Obs.* [a. OF. *pantarbe* (Cotgr. 1611), ad. Gr. παντάρβη some kind of precious stone.] A precious stone fabled to act as a magnet to gold: the stone of the sun.

1587 T. UNDERDOWN *Heliodorus' Æthiop. Hist.* 54 The stoane is a Pantarbe, of secrete vertue. **1647** TRAPP *Comm. 1 Pet.* ii. 4 *And precious.* Far beyond that most orient and excellent stone *Pantarbe*, celebrated by Philostratus. **1694** MOTTEUX *Rabelais* v. xliii. 201 That Carbuncle alone would have darken'd the Pantharb of Joachas the Indian Magician. **1753** CHAMBERS *Cycl. Supp.*, *Pantarbe*,..an imaginary stone, the virtues of which were similar to those of the magnet; but exerted upon gold as those of the loadstone upon iron.

†**ˈpantarch.** *Obs. rare.* [a. F. *pantarche, -arque* (Rabelais), erron. form of *pancarte* PANCART.] A paper; a general chart.

1694 MOTTEUX *Rabelais, Pantag. Prognost.* To Rdr., I have tumbled over and over all the Pantarchs of the Heavens, calculated the Quadrates of the Moon.

†**ˈpantas, ˈpantais.** ? *Obs.* Also 6 panties, 7 -asse, -ise, 8 -ess. [a. F. *pantais, -ois*, from *pantoiser*, earlier *pantaisier, -teisier* to PANT.] A pulmonary disease of hawks; also applied to the 'yellows' in cattle.

1577 B. GOOGE *Heresbach's Husb.* (1586) 134 b, If he haue the Panties he will pant much, and shake in the Flanke. **1611** COTGR., *Pantois*, short wind, pursinesse;..in Hawkes we call it, the Pantais. **1614** MARKHAM *Cheap Husb.* II. xliv. (1668) 84 The Pantas is a very faint disease, and maketh a Beast to sweat, shake and pant much. **1688** R. HOLME *Armoury* II. 237/2 (Diseases in Hawks) The *Pantas*, or Asina: a Disease in the Breast, which causeth shortness of breath, or hinders the drawing of breath, called also the Pantise. **1741** *Compl. Fam.-Piece* III. 476 Of the Yellows in a Cow or Bullock, which some call the Pantess. **1847–78** HALLIWELL, *Pantas.*

pantascope, erron. f. PANTOSCOPE.

†**ˈpantatype.** *Obs.* [f. Gr. πάντα *pl.* 'all things' + TYPE; but the etymological form is PANTOTYPE.] The name given by Charles, Earl Stanhope, 1803, to a system of 'universal type-printing' projected by him.

1803 A. WILSON *Let. to Authors*, etc., Aug. (in *Collectanea* (O.H.S.) III. 377) Earl Stanhope has lately purchased the two important Secrets of Pantatype Printing and of Stereotype Printing, in order to give them to the Public. Pantatype Printing means universal type printing; being applicable to all subjects. **1896** H. HART *Stanhope & Oxford Press* (ibid. 411) What then was Pantatype? My own opinion is that..Ld. Stanhope thought he saw his way to a wide-spread adoption of what we now call 'process' work..Hard metal relief blocks [were to be used] in place of wood-cuts; intaglio engravings were to be copied and turned into relief blocks by the processes of Gengembre and others.

pantechnic (pænˈtɛknɪk), *a. rare.* [f. Gr. παν- all + τεχνικός belonging to the arts.] Of, pertaining to, or comprehending all the arts.

1848 LOWELL *Biglow Papers, Notices Indep. Press*, Then do I perceive..the advantages of a pancratic or pantechnic education.

pantechnicon (pænˈtɛknɪkən). [f. Gr. παν- all + τεχνικόν, neut. of τεχνικός: see prec.] A word, invented as the name of a bazaar of all kinds of artistic work, which has (through the fortune of the building) come to be applied to a large warehouse for storing furniture, and also to be colloquially used as short for *pantechnicon van*, a furniture-removing van.

1830 *Mech. Mag.* XV. 393 Pantechnicon [Heading of Article, describing the building, in Motcomb Street, Belgrave Square, which was originally intended for a bazaar, and was afterwards converted into a warehouse for storing furniture]. **1848** THACKERAY *Van. Fair* lxi, The rich furniture and effects,..rolled away in several enormous vans to the Pantechnicon, where they were to lie until Georgy's majority. **1865** DICKENS *Mut. Fr.* I. ii, He would have come home in matting from the Pantechnicon. **1876** JOS. IRVING *Ann. Our Time, Suppl.* (ed. 2) 155/2, 1874 [Feb.] 13. —The Pantechnicon, in Motcomb Street,..used as a repository for furniture and all kinds of goods, destroyed by fire, together with its valuable contents. **1891** *Pall Mall G.* 31 Aug. 2/3 The friends..who sent pantechnicons and heavy waggons doubtless meant well.

b. The attempt to reconcile the use with the etymology has given the following:

1842 BRANDE *Dict. Sci.* etc., *Pantechnicon*, signifies a place in which..every species of workmanship is collected and exposed for sale. The large building near Belgrave Square is an excellent specimen of this modern invention. **1845** FORD *Handbk. Spain* II. 731 The rest of the Peninsula considers them [the shops of Madrid] to be the magazine, the Pantechnicon of the universe.

c. *attrib.*, as ***pantechnicon-driver, -van.***

1892 *Daily Chron.* 28 Apr. 9/1 Situation wanted in household removals in pantechnicon vans. **1897** MARY KINGSLEY *W. Africa* vii. 142 When you are an unsophisticated cannibal Fan you don't require a pantechnicon van to stow away your one or two mushroom-shaped stools, knives, and cooking-pots, and a calabash or so. **1902** *Daily Chron.* 28 Apr. 11/3 Pantechnicon Driver required; smart.

pantee, see PANTIES *sb. pl.*

panteen, -ein, var. forms of PANTINE.

pantel, -ell(e, obs. forms of PANTLE.

pantelegraph, -telephone: see PAN- 2.

panˈtellerite. *Min.* [Named by Förstner from *Pantelleria*, an island between Sicily and Tunis.] A mineral found at Pantelleria, intermediate in composition between dacite and liparite, and more or less trachytic in character.

1890 in *Cent. Dict.*

panteloun, -own, obs. ff. PANTALOON.

[**pantener,** a freq. misreading of PAUTENER.]

panteon(e, obs. forms of PANTHEON.

†**ˈpanter¹.** *Obs.* (exc. *Hist.*) Forms: α. 3 paniter, 3–4 -eter, 4 -yter, -ytere; β. 4– panter, (4 painter, 5 pant(t)ere, -yr). [ME. *paneter*, etc., a. AF. *paneter* = F. *panetier* (12th c. in Hatz.-Darm.) = Pr. *paneter*, Sp. *panadero*, It. *panatiere*, in med.L. *pāna-, pānetārius, -terius*, baker (cf. OF. *paneter* to bake bread), f. L. *pān-em*, It. *pane*, Sp. *pan*, bread.] A word originally meaning 'baker', but in ME. usually applied to the officer of a household who supplied the bread and had charge of the pantry (an office now merged in that of butler); the controller of the bread in a large establishment.

α. **1297** R. GLOUC. (Rolls) 3868 He ȝef..þat lond of aungeo kaye is paneter [*v. rr.* panyter, panter]. *Ibid.* (Rolls) 9034, & is paniter & is chamberlein & is botiler al so. **1393** LANGL. *P. Pl.* C. XVII. 151 Pacience is hus paneter and payn to pouerte fyndeþ. *c* **1450–60** *Bp. Grosseteѕt's Househ. Stat.* in *Babees Bk.* 330 Command the panytere with youre brede, & the botelare with wyne and ale, come to-gedur afore ȝou at the tabulle. **1496** *Acc. Ld. High Treas. Scot.* I. 305 Item, to the cuke and the panetare in Methven..xiiijs.

β. **14..** *Metr. Voc.* in Wr.-Wülcker 624/8 *Arthocopus*, botelere, bakere *uel* panttere. *c* **1450** *Bk. Curtasye* 667 in *Babees Bk.* 322 Þenne comes þe pantere with loues thre. *c* **1460** J. RUSSELL *Bk. Nurture* ibid. 66 If thou be admitted in any offyce, as Butler or Panter,—in some places they are both one. *c* **1530** TINDALE *Jonas* Prol. C iv, Though all the bred be committed vn to the panter. **1580** HOLLYBAND *Treas. Fr. Tong*, *Vn Panetier*, a Panter. [**1851** TURNER *Dom. Archit.* I. iv. 137 The Pantry..was superintended by the panter or pannetier.]

ˈ**panter².** *Obs.* exc. *dial.* Also 4 paunter, 5 pantire, -yr, 5–6 -ere, (6 panther). [ME. a. OF. *panter* 'tendicula, lacum' (13th c. in Godef.); cf. F. *pantière* (Cotgr. '*panthiere*, a great swoope-net or drawing-net') = It. *pantiera* 'a kind of tramell or fowling net' (Florio), in med.L. *panthēra* (Du Cange) 'a species of net with which ducks are taken'; L. *panthēra* hunting-net, Gr. πανθήρα large net, f. πᾶν all + θήρ wild beast, θηρᾶν to hunt.] A fowling net, a fowler's snare; a net, snare, trap, noose. Also *fig.*

c **1325** *Poem Times Edw. II.* 457 in *Pol. Songs* (Camden) 344 Pride hath in his paunter kauht the heie and the lowe. *c* **1325** *Metr. Hom.* 69 Als a fouler Tas foules wyt gylder and panter. *c* **1380** WYCLIF *Sel. Wks.* III. 200 Ydilnesse is þe develis panter. *c* **1385** CHAUCER *L.G.W.* Prol. 119 The smale foulis..That from the panter..ben skapid. ? *a* **1420** LYDG. *Chorle & Byrde* 77 This birde was trapped, & caught with a pantere. *c* **1440** *Promp. Parv.* 381/2 Pantere, snare for byrdys, *laqueus, pedica.* **1483** [see PANTLE *sb.*]. **1509** BARCLAY *Shyp of Folys* (1874) II. 297 As fysshe or byrde to panter, net or snare. **1530** PALSGR. 251/2 Panther to catche byrdes with, *panneau.* **1652** ASHMOLE *Theat. Chem.* 215 The Byrd was trapped and cawt in a Panter. **1782** ELPHINSTON *Martial* III. xciii. 173 Thy panters, unpropt, are decay'd To nets of Arachne's control. **1900** *E.D. Dict.*, *Panter* (N.E. Lancash.), a snare for birds made of hair.

panter³ (ˈpæntə(r)). [f. PANT *v.* + -ER¹.]

1. One who or that which pants.

a **1729** CONGREVE *On Mrs. Arabella Hunt's Singing* ii, Which, warbling mystic sounds, Cements the bleeding panter's wounds. **1823** BYRON *Juan* VII. xxxix, All panters for newspaper praise. **1840** *New Monthly Mag.* LX. 492 Panters after posthumous reputation.

2. *slang.* The heart. (Partly a pun upon 'hart'.)

a **1700** B. E. *Dict. Cant. Crew*, *Panter*, a Hart. *c* **1725** *Old Song* in Farmer *Musa Pedestris* (1896) 44 Didst thou know ..but half of the smart Which has seized on my panter, since thou didst depart. **1785** GROSE *Dict. Vulg. T.*, *Panter*, a hart, that animal is, in the psalms, said to pant after the fresh water brooks. [*ed.* 1796 *adds*] Also the human heart, which frequently pants in time of danger.

†**3.** (See quot.) *Obs.*

1706 PHILLIPS, *Panter*, the Paunch or Belly; also a Sore or Gall on the Neck of Draught-Beasts.

panter, obs. form of PAINTER, PANTHER.

panterer (ˈpæntərə(r)). Now only *Hist.* Also 5–6 -trer. [Expanded form of PANTER¹, as if from *pantry* + -ER: cf. *adulterer, upholsterer*, etc.] = PANTER¹.

14.. *Nom.* in Wr.-Wülcker 684/20 *Hic panterius*, a pantrer. *c* **1420** *Chron. Vilod.* 506 His Panterere to[k] a lofe þo ywys. **1552** HULOET, Pantrer, *Panarius.* *a* **1641** BP. MOUNTAGU *Acts & Mon.* (1642) 427 They meet in the Refectory..where..the Panterer sets bread before them. **1859** PARKER *Dom. Archit.* III. iii. 80 The Cloth being laid, the panterer brought forth the bread. **1883** *Times* (weekly ed.) 6 Apr. 9 Dukes and earls and knights acted as stewards and butlers and panterers, and..haggled for their perquisites of scarlet cloth and wine and candles..like commoner people.

pan-Teutonic, -Teutonism: see PAN- 1.

Panthalassa (pænθəˈlæsə). *Geol.* Also **panthalassa.** [f. PAN- + Gr. θάλασσα sea.] A universal sea or single ocean, such as would have surrounded PANGÆA.

1893 E. SUESS in *Natural Sci.* II. 186 We might..rather be induced to infer that in Prepalæozoic times there may have existed a universal hydrosphere or panthalassa covering the whole of the planet. **1924** J. G. A. SKERL tr. *Wegener's Orig. Continents & Oceans* x. 149 It is..not improbable that in the most ancient 'pre-geological times' the film of sial..could then have been..only about 30 km. thick, and have been covered with a 'Panthalassa'..which probably left exposed only small proportions, or none at all, of the earth's surface. **1937** A. L. DU TOIT *Our Wandering Continents* x. 210 The Drift Hypothesis..has to view the great geosynclinal seaways of earlier geological history as branches, albeit important ones, of a universal ocean or 'Panthalassa', which was transformed into the present oceans through the horizontal drifting of the crustal blocks. **1970** R. S. DIETZ in Johnson & Smith *Megatectonics Continents & Oceans* iii. 36 (*caption*) Accretionary development of two supercontinents (Laurasia and Gondwana)..producing two super-continents of equal area, surrounded by the equatorial universal ocean of Panthalassa. *Ibid.* iii. 43 The Pacific Ocean may be regarded as the remnant of Panthalassa, with the Atlantic, Arctic, and Indian Oceans being mostly rift oceans.

panthan, pantharb, variants of PANTHEON, PANTARBE.

†**panˈthean,** *a. Obs.* = next.

1730–6 BAILEY (folio), *Panthean Statues*, statues that represented all or the most considerable of the heathen deities.

pantheic (pænˈθiːɪk), *a. rare.* [f. PANTHE-UM + -IC.] Of the nature of a pantheum: combining in one figure the symbols or attributes of many different gods.

1818 R. P. KNIGHT *Symbolic Lang.* (1876) 81 Diana..has ..titles and symbols expressive of almost every attribute, whether of creation, preservation, or destruction; as appears from the Pantheic figures of her. *Ibid.* 143 In engravings upon gems,..we often find the forms of the ram, goat, horse, cock, and various others, blended into one, so as to form Pantheic compositions, signifying the various attributes and modes of action of the Deity.

pantheism ('pænθiːɪz(ə)m). [mod. f. Gr. παν- all + θε-ός God + -ISM; app. after PANTHEIST.

Panthéiste and *panthéisme* were used in French in 1712 (E. Benoist *Mélanges* 252, 265) the former app. taken from Toland's English use (see next), the latter formed after it on the ordinary analogy of pairs in *-ist* and *-ism*. Toland does not appear to have used *pantheism*.]

1. The religious belief or philosophical theory that God and the universe are identical (implying a denial of the personality and transcendence of God); the doctrine that God is everything and everything is God.

1732 WATERLAND *Chr. Vind. Charge* 76 Pantheism..and Hobbism are scandalously bad, scarce differing from the broadest Atheism. *a* **1766** J. BROWN *Honour* 176 *note*, That species of atheism commonly called Pantheism. **1823** COLERIDGE *Table-t.* 30 Apr., Pantheism and idolatry naturally end in each other: for all extremes meet. **1848** R. I. WILBERFORCE *Doct. Incarnation* v. (1852) 121 Pantheism, the principle of which is to merge the personality of the moral Governor in the circle of His works.

2. The heathen worship of all the gods.

1837 SIR F. PALGRAVE *Merch. & Friar* i. (1844) 21 The greater portion of the Tartar tribes professed a singular species of Pantheism, respecting all creeds, attached to none. **1861** PEARSON *Early & Mid. Ages Eng.* (1867) I. 18 The spirit of Roman pantheism, which erected a temple to the divinities of all nations.

pantheist ('pænθiːɪst). [f. as prec. + -IST. First used by Toland 1705; thence F. *panthéiste*.] One who holds the doctrine of pantheism.

1705 (*title*) Socinianism truly Stated..; to which is prefixt Indifference in Disputes: Recommended by a Pantheist [J. Toland] to an Orthodox Friend. **1705** TOLAND *ibid.* 7 The Pantheists..of which number I profess myself to be one. **1721** BP. HARE *Script. Vind. fr. Misrepr. Bp. Bangor* Pref. 21 Thus prays this *Pantheist* (i.e. the impious author of the *Pantheisticon*) whose impudent Blasphemies loudly call for the Animadversions of the Civil Power. **1750** WARBURTON *Note Pope's Ess. Man.* I. 268 We are parts of him, his offspring, as the Greek poet, a pantheist quoted by the Apostle, observes: And the reason is, because a religious theist, and an impious pantheist, both profess to believe the omnipresence of God. **1778** APTHORPE *Preval. Chr.* 223 He is therefore a Spinozist or a philosophic pantheist. **1876** GLADSTONE in *Contemp. Rev.* June 24, I am by no means sure that Dante is not a Pantheist.

pantheistic (pænθiː'ɪstɪk), *a.* [f. as prec. + -IC: cf. Toland's title *Pantheisticon*.]

1. Of or pertaining to pantheists, or pantheism.

[**1718** J. TOLAND (*title*) Pantheisticon: sive Formula celebrandæ Sodalitatis Socraticæ.] **1732** WATERLAND *Chr. Vind. Charge* 44 The Pantheistick System..supposes God and Nature, or God and the whole Universe, to be one and the same Substance, one Universal Being; insomuch that Mens Souls are only Modifications of the divine Substance. **1856** SIR B. BRODIE *Psychol. Inq.* I. iv. 118 The pantheistic theory..has descended from the school of Pythagoras to these latter times.

†**2.** = PANTHEIC. *Obs.* (? an error.)

1842 BRANDE *Dict. Sci.* etc., *Pantheistic*,..a term applied to statues and figures.

So **panthe'istical** *a.* = sense 1; hence **panthe'istically** *adv.*

1840 THACKERAY *Paris Sk.-bk.* (1872) 176 In this work, the lady asserts her pantheistical doctrine. **1848** *Tait's Mag.* XV. 150 The Creator [is never] pantheistically identified with the works. **1870** DISRAELI *Lothair* xxx. 151 There is that human reason..which insists on being atheistical, or polytheistical, or pantheistical.

pantheize ('pænθiːaɪz), *v. rare.* [f. PANTHE(IST + -IZE 1.] To imbue with the characteristics and ideas of pantheism; to make compatible with pantheism.

1909 W. JAMES *Pluralistic Universe* iii. 118 Theologians have felt its irrationality acutely, and the 'fall', the predestination, and the election which the situation involves have given them more trouble than anything else in their attempt to pantheize Christianity.

panthelematism, -thelism: see PAN- 2.

pantheology (pænθiː'ɒlədʒɪ). [mod. f. Gr. παν-, PAN-, all + THEOLOGY.]

†**1.** The whole sum of theology or divinity. *Obs.*

1656 BLOUNT *Glossogr.*, *Pantheology*, the whole sum of Divinity. **1658** PHILLIPS, *Pantheologie*.

2. A synthetic theology comprehending all deities and all religions.

a **1693** *Urquhart's Rabelais* III. ii. 29 The true Spring and Source of the lively Idea of Pantheology. **1893** *Temple Bar Mag.* XCVII. 69 [His] intimacy with Greek pantheology was scarcely orthodox.

Hence **panthe'ologist**, one who studies or is versed in pantheology.

1727 BAILEY vol. II, *Pantheologist*, a Student or Writer of universal or a whole Body of Divinity. (So in later Dicts.)

pantheon (pæn'θiːən, 'pænθiːən). Also 4 **panteon(e**, 6 **panthan, -ean, (panthee)**. [a. L. *panthēon*, *-theon*, a. Gr. πάνθειον a temple consecrated to all the gods (f. παν- all + θεῖος of or sacred to a god, θεός a god). Cf. F. *panthéon*.

The ME., early mod. Eng., and recent pronunc. (e.g. in Cowley and Bailey's Dict.) is '*pantheon*; Johnson has *pan'theon*, which was the more prevalent in England *c* 1900.]

1. A temple or sacred building dedicated to all the gods, or where images or other memorials of all the deities of a nation are collected; *spec.* (with capital initial) that at Rome which was originally built by Agrippa *c* 25 B.C., and being on a circular plan has also been called the *Rotunda*; since A.D. 609 it has served as a Christian church, being known as Santa Maria Rotonda.

? **13..** *All Saints* 37 in Herrig's *Archiv* LXXIX. 435 That temple was callyd panteone..Panteone is to sey in greke: 'Of all godis & deuellus eke'. *c* **1350** *All Saints* 37 in Horstm. *Altengl. Leg.* (1881) 143 Panteon þai calde þe name; 'þe hows of goddes', þat menes þe same. **1549** COVERDALE etc. *Erasm. Par. Rev.* xvi. 25 The firste plage is fallen vpon all ydols and false goddes whiche they had set and packed together in one tempel of Pantheon, that is to saye all goddes. [**1585** T. WASHINGTON tr. *Nicholay's Voy.* II. xx. 57 The proportion of the Panthee of Rome.] **1586** SIR E. HOBY *Pol. Disc. Truth* xxx. 140 The Romanes allowed the seruice of all gods, hauing for that ende builded a Temple to all gods called Pantheon. **1588** SHAKS. *Tit. A.* I. i. 242 Lauinia will I make my Empresse..And in the Sacred Panthan her espouse. **1617** MORYSON *Itin.* I. 135 Marcus Agrippa..built this Church, and dedicated it to Jupiter..and to Ceres, and to all the gods, whereupon it was called *Pantheon*. **1727-** BAILEY, *Pan'theon*. **1740** DYER *Ruins of Rome* Poems (1761) 28 Yon venerable dome, Which virtuous Latium, with erroneous aim, Rais'd to her various deities, and nam'd Pantheon. **1860** HAWTHORNE *Marb. Faun* I. (1883) 516 The world has nothing else like the Pantheon.

b. *fig.* 'Temple' or 'shrine of all the gods'.

1596 NASHE *Saffron-Walden* Wks. (Grosart) III. 155 Of this John Thorius..I will speake.., his Church another Pantheon or *Templum omnium deorum*, the absolutest Oracle of all sound deuinitie. **1639** FULLER *Holy War* (1640) 4 Poland, the Pantheon of all religions. **1663** COWLEY *On bk. present. itself to Univ. Libr. Oxf.* 1 Hail, Learning's Pantheon! Hail the sacred Ark, Where all the World of Science does embarque! **1882** *Athenæum* 30 Dec. 878/1 Scherer..has room in his literary pantheon for every legitimate form of art. **1899** EARL ROSEBERY *Sp. Cromwell* 14 Nov., Everyone, I think..has, in their heart of hearts a Pantheon of their historical demigods..a shrine in which they consecrate the memories of the deaths of the noblest and bravest men.

c. *transf.* A building resembling or compared to the Pantheon at Rome; now, especially, a building serving to honour the illustrious dead of a nation, who are either buried there or have memorials erected to them in it.

The latter use had app. its origin in the church of St. Geneviève in Paris, which in some respects resembles the Pantheon at Rome, and which, both before the Revolution and since, has been used for this purpose, being so renamed at that period.

1713 *Ward's Simp. Cobler* 12 It were..requisite, that the City should repair Pauls..for an English Pantheon, and bestow it upon the Sectaries, freely to assemble in. **1727-41** CHAMBERS *Cycl.* s.v., The chapel of the Escurial, which is the burying place of the kings of Spain, is also a rotondo; and in imitation of that of Rome, is also called pantheon. **1801** [see PANTHEONIZE below]. **1838** *Encycl. Brit.* (ed. 7) XVII. 76/2 The Pantheon, or church of St. Geneviève, is perhaps the most magnificent of the modern edifices in Paris... The west portico bears some resemblance to the Pantheon at Rome. **1855** *London as it is to-day* 29 Westminster Abbey may not inaptly be called the pantheon of the glory of Britain. **1890** *Whitaker's Almanack* 346/2 The French Chamber..decided to transfer the remains of Carnot, Marceau, and Baudin to the Pantheon.

2. A habitation of all the gods; the assemblage of all the gods; the deities of a people collectively.

1550 BALE *Image Both Ch.* xvi. Sel. Wks. (Parker Soc.) 491 The blasphemous Pantheon of Rome once perishing, all other churches of the unfaithful must needs follow soon after in their course. **1806** T. MAURICE *Fall of Mogul* Introd. 15 To that superstitious race the universe is a vast pantheon, filled with intellectual beings of various classes and powers. **1853** MAURICE *Proph. & Kings* xxv. 435 However intricate the relations of the gods may seem to us in the Greek pantheon. **1862** BEVERIDGE *Hist. India* II. IV. ii. 22 The Hindoo pantheon now boasts of being able to muster 330,000,000 deities. **1878** MACLEAR *Celts* ii. (1879) 22 Highest in the Celtic Pantheon was the golden-handed sun.

b. A name for a treatise on all the gods.

1698 [A. TOOKE] (*title of transl.*) The Pantheon, Representing the Fabulous Histories of the Heathen Gods and Most Illustrious Heroes..Written by Fra. Pomey. **1790** (*title*) Bell's New Pantheon, or Historical Dictionary of Gods, Demi-Gods, Heroes, and Fabulous Personages of Antiquity. **1824** WATT *Bibliotheca Brit.* I. s.v. *Stephen Bateman*, Golden Book of Heathen Gods... This work has been considered as one of the first attempts towards a Pantheon, or descriptions of the Heathen Gods.

c. A collection of wax-work models of the gods.

1711 *Spect.* No. 46 Advt., Mr. Penkethman's Wonderful Invention call'd the Pantheon: or, the Temple of the Heathen Gods..The Figures..move their Heads [etc.].

3. Name of a large building in London ('having a dome like the Pantheon'—Walpole, *Let. to Mann* 26 Apr. 1771), opened as a place of public entertainment in 1772: hence allusively.

1772 *Chron.* in *Ann. Reg.* 69 Last night was opened..the much-talked-of receptacle of fashionable pleasure, The Pantheon, to a crouded company. **1774** FOOTE *Cozeners* I. Wks. 1799 II. 146 Expences in attending plays, operas, masquerades, and pantheons. **1782** WESLEY *Wks.* (1872) XI. 158 We are making swift advances toward it [lewdness], by playhouses, masquerades, and pantheons.

4. *attrib.* = Of all the gods or heroes.

1767 H. WALPOLE *Let. to Mann* 30 May, I shall make a solemn dedication of it in my pantheon Chapel.

Hence **pan'theonic** *a.*, of the nature of or resembling a pantheon; **pan,theoni'zation**, admission into the pantheon; **pan'theonize** *v. trans.*, to admit into the pantheon; to inter in the Pantheon.

1801 *Paris as it was* II. xlviii. 137 Marat..was..pantheonized, that is, interred in the Pantheon. **1804** *Europ. Mag.* XLV. 437/1 The insanity of the people in pantheonizing and dispantheonizing Marat and Mirabeau. **1865** J. H. INGRAHAM *Pillar of Fire* (1872) 223 All these sacred figures decorated this pantheonic portico. **1883** R. BROWN *Eridanus* 4 The formal pantheonization of divinities.

panther ('pænθə(r)). Forms: 3-6 **panter**, 4-6 **pantere**, (5 **panteere**), 5-6 **panthere**, (7 **-ar**), 5- **panther**. [ME. *pantere*, a. OF. *pantère* (Ph. de Thaun, 12th c.), mod.F. *panthère*, ad. L. *panthēra*, ad. Gr. πάνθηρ. (The solitary instance in OE. is merely an alien word from L or Gr.)

The subjective analysis of the name, as from Gr. παν- all + θήρ beast, gave rise to many fancies and fables: see Ph. de Thaun *Bestiaire* 224, etc.]

1. Another name for the Leopard (*Felis pardus*); popularly applied to large leopards.

As with other exotic animals, the name, handed down from the Latin writers, was known long before the animal; all the early references merely reflect the statements of ancient authors and their mediæval continuators. These statements were long believed to refer to a beast distinct from the leopard; a belief encouraged by there being two Latin names *panthēra* and *pardus*, as to the relation between which the ancient writers themselves were not clear, and by fabulous notions as to the generation of the leopard as a hybrid between the lion and the 'pard', and as to the sweet fragrance fabled to be exhaled by the panther. Down to modern times (cf. quot. 1813) the 'panther' was supposed to be at least a larger and more powerful kind of leopard, a distinction not scientifically tenable.

[*a* **1000** *Panther* 12 (Gr.) Is þæt deor Pandher bi noman haten, þæs þe niðða bearn wisfæste weras on ȝewritum cyððan bi þam anstapan.] *c* **1220** *Bestiary* 733 Panter is an wilde der, Is non fairere on werlde her. **1398** TREVISA *Barth. De P.R.* XVIII. lxxxii. (1495) 834 Lyons in Siria ben blacke wyth white speckis and ben lyke to Panteres. *c* **1430** LYDG. *Reas. & Sens.* 6438 In his sheelde, yif ye lyst here, Hath enprented a pantere. **1484** CAXTON *Fables of Æsop* IV. v, Fable of a panthere whiche felle in to a pytte. **1503** S. HAWES *Examp. Virt.* ix. 4 And by a swete smelle I knewe a pantere. **1545** JOYE *Exp. Dan.* vii. 98 The leoparde or spotted panthere..signifieth the kingdom of great Alexander. **1642** ROGERS *Naaman* Ep. Ded. 4 Which (as the Panthars breath..) hath made your name sweet. **1658** PHILLIPS, *Panther*, a kinde of spotted beast, the Leopard, or Libard being the Male, the Panther the Female. **1687** DRYDEN *Hind & P.* II. 228 The Panther's breath was ever famed for sweet. **1813** BINGLEY *Anim. Biog.* I. 261 In his general habits he [the Leopard] resembles the Panther, lying in ambush for prey. **1814** CARY *Dante's Inf.* I. 30 Lo! a panther, nimble, light, And cover'd with a speckled skin, appear'd. **1891** FLOWER & LYDEKKER *Mammals* xi. 515 The attempts to separate a larger and more robust variety, under the name of Panther, from a smaller and more graceful form, to which the name Leopard might properly be restricted, have failed.

fig. **1821** SHELLEY *Hellas* 316 Her slow dogs of war..see The panther, Freedom, fled to her old cover, Amid seas and mountains, and a mightier brood Crouch round.

2. Applied in America to the puma or cougar, *Felis concolor*, also called PAINTER³; and, sometimes, to the jaguar, *F. onca*.

1730 *N. Jersey Archives* XI. 202 On Monday..was killed..a monstrous large Panther. **1774** GOLDSM. *Nat. Hist.* I. 146 The jaguar or panther of America. **1808** PIKE *Sources Missis.* (1810) 66 Saw a very large animal, which, from its leaps, I supposed to have been a panther; but if so, it was twice as large as those on the lower Mississippi. **1822** *Niles' Register* XXII. 304/2 A panther, nine feet long, was lately found dead on the shore of lake Ontario. **1839** *Penny Cycl.* XIII. 434/2 The Jaguar, or American Panther,..is the form of the Leopard found in the New World. It is..the Panther or Great Panther of the furriers. **1843** MARRYAT *M. Violet* xliv. 369 *note*, The puma, or red panther, is also called 'American lion, cougar'. **1894** *Cent. Mag.* Apr. 849 The panther was long called a 'tyger' in the Carolinas, and a 'lyon' elsewhere.

3. *fig.* **a.** Applied to a fierce or savage man.

1868 *Sat. Rev.* 18 Jan. 75/2 Even authoresses seem to accept with perfect equanimity the idea that taming the male panther is out of the question.

b. *ellipt.* f. *Black Panther* s.v. BLACK *a.* 19; also used *attrib.* or as *adj.*

1968 *Guardian* 28 June 20/7 The Panthers wear a uniform consisting of Black Leather jacket and beret. **1968** *Listener* 5 Sept. 290/2 The hotel cops, baited in the beginning not only by rocks and bottles but by language of insane obscenity, and having waded into the advance guard of panthers, militants white and black, perambulating trouble-makers, then went berserk. **1970** G. JACKSON *Let.* 4 Apr. in *Soledad Brother* (1971) 220 The young Panther party member, our vanguard, must be embraced, protected, allowed to develop. **1972** J. MILLS *Report to Commissioner* 120 The Panthers are worse than the Shylocks. They won't let you alone. **1973** E. BULLINS *Theme is Blackness* 141 A Black Panther selling Panther newspapers. *Ibid.*, Say, brother..you Panthers sell papers just like the Muslims..don't cha? **1973** *Black Panther* 3 Mar. 8/1 Yet there are some people who say..that Panther rhetoric invites repression and destruction.

c. *ellipt.* for *panther juice* (sense 5 below).

1942 BERREY & VAN DEN BARK *Amer. Thes. Slang* §100/9 *Gin*,..panther. **1960** WENTWORTH & FLEXNER *Dict. Amer. Slang* 374/2 *Panther*,..inferior liquor, esp. gin. From 'panther sweat'.

†**4.** Name of a (? sweet-smelling) drug. *Obs.*

1656 *Acts & Ord. Parl.* c. 20 (Scobell) 464 Drugs called Panther, the pound, £2. **1662** in *Stat. Ireland* (1765) II. 403.

5. *attrib.* and *Comb.*, as *panther jump*, *-killing*, *-springer*, *-tooth*, *-tread*; *panther-like*, *-spotted* adjs.; **panther-cat**, the ocelot (Funk

1895): **panther-cowry**, a spotted cowry, *Cypræa pantherina* of the East Indies (*ibid.*); **panther juice, panther('s) piss, panther sweat**, strong liquor, usu. spirits, esp. of local or home manufacture; **panther-lily**, *U.S.*, the Californian lily, *Lilium pardalinum*; **panther-moth**, a collector's name for a European geometrid, *Cidaria unangulata* (*Cent. Dict.* 1890); **panther's bane**, a plant, also called Wolf's bane; **panther-toad**, a South African toad, *Bufo pantherinus* (*Cassell's Encycl. Dict.* 1886); **panther-wood**, a variety of the citron wood or sandarach tree, *Callistris quadrivalvis* (*Cent. Dict.* 1890).

1960 J. PHILIPS *Whisper Town* (1961) I. i. 4 Here's your *panther juice, Judge. **1774** GOLDSM. *Nat. Hist.* (1776) III. 254 An animal of the *panther kind. **1857** C. BRONTE *Professor* I. xii. 197 Envy and *panther-like deceit about her mouth. **1884** MILLER *Plant-n.* 78/1 *Panther Lily. **1900** *Field* 23 June 903/3 *L[ilium] superbum*..requires a vegetable soil like the Panther lily. **1941** BAKER *Dict. Austral. Slang* 52 *Panther's p—s*, liquor, esp. spirits. **1946** T. HEGGEN *Mister Roberts* 134 'That whiskey they make,' said Dowdy, 'is really panther-piss.' **1955** W. GADDIS *Recognitions* II. i. 308 Yeah? Well did you ever drink panther piss? the liquid fuel out of torpedoes? **1973** 'B. MATHER' *Snowline* v. 57 Locally distilled stuff of the genus known as panther piss. **1820** SHELLEY *Witch of Atlas* xxxviii, Amid The *panther-peopled forests. **1712** tr. *Pomet's Hist. Drugs* I. 39 Wolf or *Panther's bane..is a Root divided by Lumps or Clods. **1593** NASHE *Christ's T.* Wks. (Grosart) IV. 77 Some soules of this *Panther-spotted Ierusalem, may bee extraught to ioy with me. **1898** G. MEREDITH *Odes Fr. Hist.* 48 The smiter, *panther-springer, trapper sly. **1929** *Amer. Speech* IV. 386 Whiskey is sometimes called *donk* or *mule* because of its..'kick'... *Panther-sweat*..and *rat-track whiskey* are less easily classified. **1834** *Tait's Mag.* I. 341/2 With *panther-teeth their victim's heart They tear. **1899** *Westm. Gaz.* 9 Feb. 2/1 The cat..still keeps..the bold, free *panther-tread with which it paced of yore the temple courts of Thebes.

pantheress ('pænθərɪs). [f. prec. + -ESS.] A female panther.

1862 FROUDE in Sir J. Skelton *Shirley's Table-t.* 127 Mary Stuart..was something between Rachel and a pantheress. **1877** DIXON *Diana, Lady Lyle* II. VII. iv. 201 A pantheress is not armed with a more stealthy foot.

b. *fig.* Applied to a fierce or cruel but beautiful woman. Also *attrib.*

1868 *Sat. Rev.* 18 Jan. 75/1 A heroine of the beautiful pantheress order. **1890** 'R. BOLDREWOOD' *Miner's Right* (1899) 43/1 You are just as much carried away by this infernal scoundrel's regular features and soft voice, as that handsome pantheress that he's stolen somewhere.

pantherine ('pænθəraɪn, -rɪn), *a.* [ad. L. *panthērin-us*, f. *panthēra* PANTHER: see -INE[1].] Resembling a panther, spotted like a panther; of, belonging to, or characteristic of a panther.

1656 BLOUNT *Glossogr.*, *Pantherine*. **1753** CHAMBERS *Cycl. Supp.*, Pantherine tables, *pantherinæ mensæ*, among the Romans, tables made of citron wood..had this name from their being spotted after the manner of panthers. **1883** FENN *Eli's Children* (ed. 2) I. I. xix. 314 [She] curled herself gracefully..in a pantherine style in the corner of the carriage. **1890** —— *Double Knot* I. i. 73 Marie made a pantherine bound across the room.

'pantherish, *a.* [f. PANTHER + -ISH[1].] Somewhat like, or characteristic of, a panther.

1892 *Blackw. Mag.* CLI. 114/2 Graceful in a lithe, pantherish way. **1895** *Athenæum* 27 July 125/2 A..boneless puppet, at the mercy of any specimen of 'pantherish' grace (there are several panthers) who takes him in hand.

‖**pantheum** (pæn'θiːəm). Mostly in pl. **panthea**. [late L. *panthēum*, f. Gr. πάνθειος: see PANTHEON. In mod.F. *panthée*.] More fully ***signum pantheum***: A statue combining the figures, symbols, or attributes of several deities.

1706 PHILLIPS, *Panthea* or *Signa Panthea*. **1727–41** CHAMBERS *Cycl.*, *Panthea*, Πανθεια, among the ancients were single statues, composed of the figures, or symbols of several different divinities combined. **1730–6** in BAILEY (folio). **1775** ASH, *Pantheum*... A statue adorned with the figures or symbols of the gods. **1838** in *Encycl. Brit.* XVI. 790/2. **1882** FENNELL tr. *Michaelis' Anc. Marbles Gt. Brit.* 628 In the fashion of the *signa panthea* this youth unites in his own person the attributes of various gods..Poseidon..Apollo..Dionysos..Ares..Eros.

†**panth'netist.** *Obs. rare.* [f. Gr. παν- all + θνητός mortal + -IST.] (See quot.)

1660 INGELO *Bentiv. & Ur.* II. (1682) 208, I will premise a few things concerning the Temper and Design of the Panthnetists. [*margin*] Such as think the Soul and Body to perish in Death.

panthodic (pæn'θɒdɪk), *a. Physiol. rare.* [f. Gr. παντ(ο- PANTO- + Gr. ὁδός way.] Said of nervous action: Proceeding in all directions from a single point.

1850 MARSHALL HALL *Synops. Diast. Nerv. Syst.* i. §7 (1852) 13 (*heading*) Panthodic Law of Action of the Vis Nervosa. *Ibid.*, I use the term panthodic in a very emphatic sense; I believe that no spot of the diastaltic system can be excited without telling upon every other. **1853** in DUNGLISON *Med. Lex.* **1893** in *Syd. Soc. Lex.*

panti-, see PANTIES *sb. pl.*

pantible, corrupt form of PANTOFLE.

panties ('pæntiːz), *sb. pl.* Also occas. **pantees**. [dim. of PANTS *sb. pl.*]

1. a. Men's trousers or shorts. Usu. in derog. contexts.

1845 *Knickerbocker* XXVI. 433 If your panties weren't sheeted home at the bottom, you'd out-jump a monkey. **1848** W. E. BURTON *Waggeries* 19, I hadn't on nothin'..only a blue cotting shirt and sail-cloth pantys. *Ibid.* 95 I've a Colt's revolver in each pantey's pocket. **1910** KIPLING *Divers. Creatures* (1917) 310 The umpires, all in short panties, conferred. **1928** *Weekly Dispatch* 27 May 15/7 Panties for boys and skirts for girls..are being made *very* short. **1930** E. POUND *XXX Cantos* xviii. 82 And he was my gawd scared out of his panties.

b. Short-legged or legless knickers worn by women and girls.

1908 M. MORGAN *How to dress Doll* vi. 59 The undergarment is..easily made, for the little waist and panties are cut in one piece. **1932** *New Yorker* 11 June 40/1 There is a lace brassière top on a circular satin slip, and panties..are built in underneath. **1958** *Times* 25 Apr. 13/3 Brand new ex-Wren officers' silk/wool panties. **1969** M. PEI *Words in Sheep's Clothing* (1970) v. 34 'Panties'..short, abbreviated pants worn by women and children (men, as everyone knows, wear shorts, not panties). **1972** F. WARNER *Maquettes* 39 Bra and panties. **1976** J. CROSBY *Snake* (1977) xxxv. 216 She..picked up her panties, and slipped them on. After that the sweater, the skirt, stockings, and shoes.

c. Also *transf.* and *fig.*

1909 *Sat. Even. Post* 24 Apr. 15/3 New York..would be inhabited by cow-persons in décolleté leather panties. **1936** L. C. DOUGLAS *White Banners* ii. 42 There won't be any French chops with pink panties and a little bite of meat about the size of a peppermint lozenge. **1949** *Sat. Even. Post* 26 Mar. 35/2 Large bottles in woven straw panties stood on the checked table top.

2. *sing.*, as **pantie, panty**. = sense 1 b above. Also *attrib.* orig. *U.S.*

1932 *New Yorker* 11 June 28 (Advt.), If ever a garment could outwit that old ogre depression, it's the pantie in this picture... It is made of celanese. **1939** *Reader's Digest* May 107/2 There is nothing so mournful as a pantie manufacturer who cannot get space in the pantie section [of the garment-making area of New York City]. **1951** C. W. & P. CUNNINGTON *Hist. Underclothes* 246 For sports, pantie trunks and pantie briefs. **1960** *Harper's Bazaar* Apr. 56/1 Striped pantie; boned perforated foam bra. **1961** *New Yorker* 2 Dec. 48 Rogers places you there in the briefest baby doll and matching panty. **1970** *Focus* June 11/3 No apparent dye loss when washed, but pantie part shrank an inch all round.

3. *Comb.* of **pantee, panti, pantie, panty**. **a.** In names of women's undergarments combining the function of panties with that of some other undergarment, as ***panty-belt***, ***-blouse***, ***-brassière***, ***-girdle***, ***-hose***, ***-stockings***, ***-tights***.

1957 A. ADBURGHAM in *Punch* 27 Mar. 419/1 How pert the little pantie-belt, blue-spotted, with its blue-spotted suspenders to match. **1961** S. PRICE *Just for Record* iii. 26 The sort of birds I lie me down with..shimmy out of their pantie-belts. **1971** *Guardian* 24 Aug. 9/1 Pantie-blouses are ..the newest thing in all-in-one garments. **1925** *Ladies' Home Jrnl.* May 87/3 Panty-brassiere, $12. **1941** HERMER & MAY *Havana Mañana* 43 We recommend panty-girdles of mesh elastic and net or lace bras. **1946** [see LASTEX]. **1961** *She* Feb. 42 Au Fait's panty girdle..evenly supports tummy, behind, hips and thighs. **1961** *Housewife* Apr. 103/1 Wear a strong pantie-girdle—not a roll-on. **1968** J. IRONSIDE *Fashion Alphabet* 71 *Panti-girdle*, lightly elasticated briefs, exercising some control over bulges. **1972** E. T. RENBOURN *Materials & Clothing in Health & Dis.* xix. 387 The pantie-girdle syndrome has crept into the recent literature. Here, marked constriction of the circulation of the upper thigh.. leads to aching legs and..swelling ankles. **1972** J. WAMBAUGH *Blue Knight* (1973) vii. 98 A micro-mini that showed her red-flowered panty girdle when she sat down. **1963** *N.Y. Times* 22 Dec. 19 Our exclusive panti-hose... She'll enjoy the comfort and freedom of..panty tops and micromesh stockings, all in one. No garters, no seams. **1967** *Vogue* 15 Oct. 16 (Advt.), For 12/11 you can treat yourself to Panti-hose seam tights. **1970** *Focus* June 9/2 Invented ten years ago, tights (or pantie-hose) gained ground with the advent of the mini-skirt in 1968. **1970** *Toronto Daily Star* 24 Sept. 38/8 (Advt.), The first quality panty hose at a sensible price. **1972** G. V. HIGGINS *Friends E. Coyle* xviii. 108 She don't own no pants... Wears them panty hose. **1975** *Publishers Weekly* 1 Dec. 67/2 The type of wan, lightweight heroine who can't support her own pantyhose let alone a mystery novel. **1976** M. SPARK *Takeover* iv. 41 She pulled, through her dress, at the top of her panty-hose, setting herself to rights like a schoolgirl. **1966** P. O'DONNELL *Sabre-Tooth* vii. 104 The combined pantie-stockings she always wore. **1968** S. E. ELLACOTT *Everyday Things in Eng. 1914–1968* iv. 69 For some years previously [to 1966], during cold weather, women had worn 'tights' (pantee stockings), and these were now developed in sheer nylon for everyday wear with mini-skirts. **1968** *Vogue* 15 Apr. 92 Pantie-stockings,..3 gns. **1971** *Sunday Nation* (Nairobi) 11 Apr. 37/1 (Advt.), Stockings, Panty-stockings..Tights. **1971** *Guardian* 24 Aug. 9/1 Stocking tights and pantie stockings. **1970** *Guardian Weekly* 11 Apr. 14 'Sorry,' the man in overalls said. 'We're right out of them. What about a pair of panti-tights?' **1970** G. F. NEWMAN *Sir, You Bastard* viii. 207 Her lunch-break dash to Selfridges for pantie-tights, or whatever.

b. *spec.* **panty leg**, the leg part of a pair of panties; (with hyphen) *attrib.*, having such legs; **panty raid** *U.S.*, a prank involving the raiding of women's rooms for trophies of underwear; also *transf.* or *fig.*; **panty-waist** *U.S.*, (*a*) a sissy, a coward; used *attrib.*, effeminate, weak; (*b*) (*rare*) a garment, usu. for children, consisting of panties attached to a bodice.

1908 M. MORGAN *How to dress Doll* vi. 61 Face the arm-holes, neck and panty legs with a narrow facing. **1963** *New Yorker* 8 June 62 Favorite panty-leg bathing suit. **1966** *Time* 2 Dec. 53 Gold and silver pantyleg stockings..are selling so fast stores can't keep them in stock. **1952** *Stars & Stripes* (Pacific ed.) 21 May 2/3 A wild wave of panty raids swept a dozen college campuses Monday night... The [Univ. of] Colorado raid was staged by 1500 male students intent on seizing intimate trophies of lingerie. *Ibid.* 2/5 More than 1000 Northwestern university male students Monday went on a gleeful 'panty raid', stealing 'all the underwear in sight' and carrying a bewildered police sergeant on their shoulders. **1953** *Newsweek* 11 May 94/1 Traditionally, American undergraduates seem to regard the coming of spring as the rightful time to raise various kinds of hell. Be it goldfish eating, panty raids, or general disturbance of the town peace, boys will be boys, and, more recently, girls will be girls. **1957** TURNER & KILLIAN *Collective Behavior* 208 The fad may also exist as a *permission* to act contrary to the folk-ways and mores, as in the example of college 'panty raids'. **1968** *Listener* 3 Oct. 428/2 'I think we should organise a political panty raid.' There is little organised opposition to the radicals from other students, although one group did deplore 'holding members of the administration captive and burning irreplaceable files of professors who are unsympathetic.' **1936** *Amer. Speech* XI. 280/1 *Panty-waist*, a sissy. **1937** *Sun* (Baltimore) 28 Apr. 6 (Advt.), Now Mike don't be calling *me* a panty waist. **1939** C. MORLEY *Kitty Foyle* 15 Some of my pantywaists and nightgowns. **1942** *Short Guide Gt. Brit.* (U.S. War Dept.) 5 The English language didn't spread across the oceans and over the mountains and jungles and swamps of the world because these people were panty-waists. **1951** M. MCLUHAN *Mech. Bride* (1967) 125/1 No panty-waist humanitarianism here. **1952** N. SPAIN in C. Asquith *Second Ghost Bk.* 33, I should have said that I was pretty tough... I didn't do too badly in the War. I was in the Marines and they don't encourage panty waists in the Marines. **1971** 'A. BURGESS' *MF* x. 116 Some goddam British poet with one of these pantiwaist names, like Vere de Vere. **1971** H. A. SMITH *View from Chivo* i. 7 He is a pantywaist kind of fellow, very *dainty* about things. **1975** *Daily Colonist* (Victoria, B.C.) 30 July 5/3 When they [*sc.* the police] do lay hands on the culprits and get them to the courtroom they are let down by our pantywaist judges.

pantile ('pæntaɪl). Also 7–9 **pan tile, pan-tile**, 8 **pan-tyle**. [f. PAN *sb.*[1] + TILE *sb.* Cf. Du. *dakpan* (Kilian *dack-panne*), lit. roof-pan; Ger. *dachpfanne*, *pfannenziegel* pan-tile.]

1. a. A roofing tile transversely curved to an ogee shape, one curve being much larger than the other; when laid on the roof the greater part of their surface forms a concave channel for the descent of water, while one side forms a narrow convex ridge, which overlaps the edge of the adjoining tile.

The name has also been applied to tiles made with a single curve, which were laid edge to edge, on their convex sides, the junction of two edges being covered by another tile laid with its concave side downward; also, improperly, to flat overlapping roofing tiles.

1640 *Charter City London* Table of Rates, Tyles vocat' Pan Tyles or Flaunders Tyles the thousand, ijd. **1703** MOXON *Mech. Exerc.* 240 *Pan-Tiles*, being about thirteen Inches long, with a Nob or Button to hang on the Laths.. The best sort..are called Flemmish Pan-Tiles. **1738** [G. SMITH] *Curious Relations* II. v. 108 Those Leaves..serve instead of Pan-Tiles to cover their Dwellings. **1816** J. SMITH *Panorama Sc. & Art* I. 190 Common tiles for roofs are called pan tiles. **1880** BARING-GOULD *Mehalah* i, A small farm-house..roofed with red pan-tiles. **1881** YOUNG *Every Man his own Mechanic* §1206. 561 Plain tiles are perfectly flat, while pantiles are curved in form ~ something after the manner of the letter s.

b. in sing. collectively, or as a material.

1697 DAMPIER *Voy.* (1729) I. 387 The Houses are large, strongly built, and covered with Pan-tile. **1727** *Philip Quarll* 65 Their Houses are..Cover'd with Pantile.

c. †Erroneously applied to flat Dutch or Flemish paving tiles (*obs.*), and so to the Parade at Tunbridge Wells paved with these.

1774 FOOTE *Cozeners* II. Wks. 1799 II. 171 At Tunbridge ..they have the oddest pantile walk. **1784** H. WALPOLE *Brit. Traveller* 25 (Tunbr. Wells) [The shops] are ranged on one side of a walk called the Pantiles, from its pavement. **1805** MOORE *To Lady H.* 1 When..Tunbridge saw, upon her Pantiles, The merriest wight of all the kings That ever ruled these gay gallant isles. **1806** *Guide to Watering Pl.* 419 The former [Upper Walk] was once paved with pantiles, raised about four steps above the other. **1831** M. EDGEWORTH *Let.* 16 Apr. (1971) 525 Yesterday I went to Tunbridge Wells.., saw the Pantiles... The pantiles looked to me wondrous small and narrow and the roof over the row too low. **1907** *Daily Chron.* 29 Jan. 8/5 It is at the east end of the Pantiles that the original spring,..comes to the surface. **1936** *N. & Q.* 26 Dec. 461/2 The old Chapel of Ease..at entrance to the Pantiles, Tunbridge Wells..was built in 1684. *Ibid.*, When I was at school at Tunbridge Wells..I used to be taken to a church, close to the Pantiles. **1974** *Encycl. Brit. Micropædia* X. 179/1 The Pantiles Parade, with the original chalybeate spring..is preserved.

2. Humorously applied to hard sea biscuit, etc.

1873 *Slang Dict.* s.v., Pantile also means a flat cake with jam on it, given to boys at boarding-schools instead of pudding. **1891** *Labour Commission Gloss.*, *Pantiles*, term used to express the hardness of old sea biscuits ground into meal and then re-baked. **1901** FARMER *Slang*, *Pantile* (nautical) a biscuit.

3. a. *attrib.* and *Comb.*, as ***pantile-roof***, ***-works***; **pantile-lath**, an extra stout lath used for supporting pantiles on a roof.

1776 G. SEMPLE *Building in Water* 66 A nine Foot *Pantile-lath. **1873** E. SPON *Workshop Receipts* Ser. I. 127/1 Laths called by bricklayers double laths, and the larger ones pan-tile laths. **1837** HOWITT *Rur. Life* II. iv. (1862) 127 A long shed, stone walls and *pantile roof. **1703** *Proclam.* 10 Jan. in *Lond. Gaz.* No. 3879/4 The Brick and *Pantile Works near Tilbury Fort.

†**b.** Applied contemptuously in 18th c. to rural Dissenters' meeting-houses (sometimes, like ordinary cottages, roofed with pantiles), and to those who attended them: see quots. *Obs.*

1715 MRS. CENTLIVRE *Gotham Election* Wks. 1760 III. 163 Mr. Tickup's a good Churchman.. none of your occasional Cattle; none of your hellish pantile Crew. *Ibid.* 181 I'll have you hang'd for 't, I will, you Pantile Monster. **1785** GROSE *Dict. Vulg. T.*, *Pantile house* [ed. 1796 *Pantile Shop*], a Presbyterian, or other dissenting meeting house, frequently covered with pantiles.

Hence **'pantiled** *a.*, covered with pantiles; †**'pantiler**: see 3 b.

1778 *Love Feast* 12 Led by the Spirit to John's *pantil'd Roof. **1870** F. R. WILSON *Ch. Lindisfarne* 89 [It] rises over the thatched and pantiled roofs.. notably. **1951** [see *mansarded* adj. s.v. MANSARD]. **1963** *Guardian* 5 Mar. 7/2 A precipitous assembly of orange pantiled houses. **1978** M. BUTTERWORTH *X marks Spot* III. i. 121 They passed over a red pantiled roof of a farm-house. **1856** MAYHEW *World Lond.* 249 The officers.. used to designate the extraordinary religious convicts as '*pantilers'. **1889** DRYSDALE *Hist. Presbyter. Eng.* 443 Their frequenters were in some localities nick-named 'Pantilers', these pantiles forming a substantial yet economical roof.

'pan-,tiling. [f. PANTILE + -ING[1].] The covering of a roof with pantiles; pantiles collectively or in the mass.

1805 R. W. DICKSON *Pract. Agric.* I. 89 Pan-tiling, with small-sized deal lath, and sparkled within side. **1825** J. NICHOLSON *Operat. Mechanic* 550 A square of pan-tiling requires 180 tiles, laid at a ten-inch gauge. **1894** *Times* 23 Apr. 13/2 Wood and pantiling and boarded roofs taking the place of brick or stone and slate.

†**'pantine.** *Obs.* Also **pantein, -een, -in.** [In F. *pantin*, formerly *pantine* ('une jatte de Saxe, une pantine de Boucher', Diderot *Promenade du Sceptique*, 1747–9), which some French etymologists have referred to *Pantin* a village near Paris; but see quot. 1748.] A pasteboard figure of a human being, having the neck, body, and limbs jointed, so as to move when pulled by a thread or wire: a fashionable toy in the middle of the 18th c.

1748 *Lond. Mag.* 271 The ridiculous folly of Panteins [*note.* Paper or pastboard puppets, contriv'd to move in all postures, so call'd from mademoiselle Pantein, one of the marshal Saxe's [ob. 1750] ladies, who is said to be the inventer]. **1749** MRS. DELANY *Life & Corr.* (1861) II. 505 She has begun and almost finished.. a set of pantines. **1754** SHEBBEARE *Matrimony* (1766) II. 75 She resembled a Pantine, and wanted nothing but a Whalebone in her Head to give her a Twirl, and flirt her two long Arms into Motion. **1790** *Bystander* 174 Edwin is as much of an actor as a panteen is of a puppet. [**1881** BESANT & RICE *Chapl. of Fleet* II. v, Pantines, a ridiculous fashion of paper doll then in vogue as a toy for ladies with nothing to do.]

panting ('pæntɪŋ), *vbl. sb.* [f. PANT *v.* + -ING[1].]

a. The action of the verb PANT, in various senses.

c **1440** *Promp. Parv.* 381/2 Pantynge, *anelacio, vel anelatus.* **1580** SIDNEY *Ps.* XLII. i, My soul in panting plaieth, Thirsting on my God to looke. **1647** CLARENDON *Hist. Reb.* I. §35 The Prince's Journey into Spain, which.. had begot such a terrible panting in the hearts of all good English-men. **1715–20** POPE *Iliad* XVI. 134 His breath, in quick, short pantings, comes and goes. **1837** HAWTHORNE *Twice-told T.* (1851) I. xvi. 251 The horses.. heave their glistening sides in short quick pantings.

b. *spec.* In Shipbuilding: the movement of the plates of the ship's hull under stress, esp. occurring at the fore and aft ends of the ship. Also *attrib.*, often in names of structures designed to prevent such movement.

1885 H. PAASCH *From Keel to Truck* 24/1 Panting (of a ship). **1899** E. L. ATTWOOD *Text-bk. Theoret. Naval Archit.* 212 Panting beams and stringers to be fitted at the after end. **1904** A. C. HOLMS *Pract. Shipbuilding* I. ix. 105 At the stern, panting stresses are usually unimportant. **1922** C. M. SWAINSTON *Reed's Seamanship* (ed. 23) I. 187 The principal methods to resist panting are:—Closer spacing of frames, double frames, an extra tier of beams called *panting beams*, broadening of the stringers called *panting stringers*, [etc.]. **1927** G. BRADFORD *Gloss. Sea Terms* 124 *Panting strains*, those produced by.. the pressing in and out of a ship's plates due to the pressure of the waves. *Ibid.* 125 The *panting stringers* reinforce the plates against these stresses, along the sides, and *panting beams* and *frames* at the bow. **1961** F. H. BURGESS *Dict. Sailing* 156 *Panting*, the vibrations of the forward plates caused by the variable resistance of the water. *Ibid.*, *Panting beam*, a strengthened beam fitted forward to decrease vibration.

'panting, *ppl. a.* [f. as prec. + -ING[2].] That pants, in various senses: see PANT *v.*

1572 GASCOIGNE *Dan Bartholomew* Wks. (1587) 91, I feele my panting heart begins to rest. **1616** CHAPMAN *Musæus, Hero & L.* 368 She hugg'd her panting husband. **1718** PRIOR *Power* 172 Frequent for breath his panting bosom heaves. **1828** *Lights & Shades* II. 73 One poor panting girl. **1897** *Allbutt's Syst. Med.* III. 83 The respirations are short and panting.

Hence **'pantingly** *adv.*, in a panting manner; with short quick breaths.

1605 SHAKS. *Lear* IV. iii. 28 (Qo.) Once or twice she heau'd the name of father Pantingly foorth, as if it prest her heart. **1744** ARMSTRONG *Preserv. Health* III. 559 Thick and pantingly The breath was fetch'd. **1892** *Harper's Mag.* July 190/2, 'I came—on the first—train', answered Lois, pantingly.

pantiple, corrupt form of PANTOFLE.

pantisocracy (pæntɪ'sɒkrəsɪ, -aɪs-). [f. Gr. παντ-, PANTO- all + ἰσοκρατία ISOCRACY.] A form of social organization in which all are equal in rank and social position; a Utopian community in which all are equal and all rule.

1794 SOUTHEY *Let.* 20 Sept. in *Life* I. 221 We preached Pantisocracy and Asphete[r]ism everywhere. **1821** BYRON *Juan* III. xciii, All are not moralists like Southey, when He prated to the world of 'Pantisocrasy'. **1887** DOWDEN *Shelley* I. iv. 135 Southey and Coleridge.. had dreamed of pantisocracy on the banks of the Susquehanna.

pantisocrat (pæn'taɪsəkræt). [f. as prec. after *aristocrat, democrat.*] One who advocates or promotes pantisocracy.

1794 SOUTHEY *Let.* 20 Sept. in *Life* I. 221 It will then be time for you to take leave of the navy, and become acquainted with all our brethren, the pantisocrats. **1895** SAINTSBURY *Ess. Eng. Lit.* Ser. II. 10 It was impossible to start it without money, of which most of the Pantisocrats had none.

So **pantiso'cratic, pantiso'cratical** *adjs.*, pertaining to, involving, or upholding pantisocracy; **panti'socratist** = *pantisocrat.*

1794 COLERIDGE *Let.* 18 Sept. in *Life Southey* I. 219 C——, the most excellent, the most *Pantisocratic of aristocrats, has been laughing at me. **1794** SOUTHEY *Let.* 14 Oct. ibid. 222 This Pantisocratic scheme has given me new life. **1887** W. HUNT *Bristol* 186 Here the young poets elaborated their scheme of a pantisocratic settlement on the Sesquehanna. **1803** W. TAYLOR in Robberds *Mem.* I. 442 To found a Christian platonical *pantisocratical republic. **1880** DOWDEN *Southey* 39 With such a sum they might both qualify by marriage for membership in the pantisocratical community. **1835** MACAULAY *Ess.*, *Mackintosh's Hist. Rev.* (1843) II. 216 Rushing from one wild extreme to another, out-Paining Paine, out-Castlereaghing Castlereagh, *Pantisocratists, Ultra-Tories, heretics [etc.]. **1883** HALL CAINE *Cobw. Crit.* ii. 37 Coleridge, Southey and Lovell.. were all three passionate pantisocratists.

pantle ('pænt(ə)l), *sb.* Now *dial.* Forms: 5 **pantelle**, 6 **-el(l**, 9 **pantle.** [app. an altered form of PANTER[2].] A snare for birds, esp. snipe.

1483 *Cath. Angl.* 268/1 Pantelle strynge (*A.* A Pantyr), *pedica.* **1552** HULOET, Pantell, setter, or snare, *pedica.* **1856** J. DAVIES *Races* 237 (E.D.D.). **1882** *Lancash. Gloss.*, *Pantle*, a bird-snare made of hair. **1893** J. WATSON *Conf. Poacher* 39 We used to take them [snipe] in pantles made of twisted horsehair. **1897** MACPHERSON *Wild-fowling* 458 (E.D.D.) In South Furness men snare snipe by means of engines locally called pantles.

'pantle, *v. Obs.* exc. *dial.* [f. PANT *v.* with dim. or frequentative ending -LE.] *intr.* To pant.

[**1632** ROWLEY *Woman Never Vexed* II. in Hazl. *Dodsley* XII. 128 My heart! O my heart! if it does not go pantle, pantle, pantle.. I am no honest woman.] **1652** URQUHART *Jewel* Wks. (1834) 222 The Italian.. foamed at the mouth.. and fetched a pantling breath. **1678** COTTON *Scarron.* IV. 142 Although her woful heart did pantle. **1875** PORSON *Quaint Words* 15. **1890** *Glouc. Gloss.*, *Pantle*, to pant. [Also S. Worcestersh. (E.D.D.).]

pantler ('pæntlə(r)). Now only *Hist.* [app. an altered form of PANTER[1], PANTERER, ? after *butler.* (Not in French, nor app. in med.L.)] = PANTER[1].

c **1330** R. BRUNNE *Chron.* (1810) 33 The kyng tok þis pantelere, & strangled him right þore. *c* **1440** *Promp. Parv.* 381/2 Pantlere, *panitarius.* **1483** *Cath. Angl.* 268/1 A Pantelere, *vbi* A butlere. **1533** WRIOTHESLEY *Chron.* (1875) I. 21 The Earle of Arrondell butler, the Viscount Lisle pantler. **1597** SHAKS. *2 Hen. IV*, II. iv. 258 Hee would haue made a good Pantler, hee would haue chipp'd Bread well. **1679** BLOUNT *Anc. Tenures* 36 The Mannor.. to be held by the service of being Pantler to the Kings.. at their Coronations. **1706** *Lond. Gaz.* No. 4252/2 The Butler and the Pantler have taken his Name off the Tables in their Offices. **1842** BARHAM *Ingol. Leg.* Ser. II. *Lay St. Cuthbert*, Pantler and serving-man, henchman and page, Stand sniffing the duck-stuffing (onion and sage).

pantless ('pæntlɪs), *a.* [f. PANT *sb.*[3] + -LESS.] Wearing no pants.

1880 S. LAKEMAN *What I saw in Kaffir-Land* xi. 136 They [*sc.* Cape baboons] shot from branch to branch,.. like flying fish, or as pantless Zazel shoots from the cannon's mouth to her swinging rope. **1948** D. BALLANTYNE *Cunninghams* 260 Three pantless Maori kids met him. **1969** N. BEHN *Shadowboxer* (1970) ix. 79 He stared directly up the plump pantless female thighs. **1971** W. HANLEY *Blue Dreams* xxi. 331 Then, bra-ed but pantless, she moved toward Walter.

panto ('pæntəʊ). [Abbrev. PANTOMIME *sb.* (*a.*).] = PANTOMIME *sb.* (*a.*) 3; also *attrib.*

1852 E. L. BLANCHARD *Jrnl.* 15 Sept. in Scott & Howard *Life E. L. Blanchard* (1891) I. 98 At home till 5 p.m. fixing on titles for pantos... Arrange for panto with Smith for Drury. **1914** C. MACKENZIE *Sinister St.* II. IV. ii. 865 'You're on the stage, aren't you?' 'I usually get into panto,' she admitted. **1922** JOYCE *Ulysses* 533 Immoral panto boys in flesh tights. **1929** J. B. PRIESTLEY *Good Companions* II. i. 251 That's right. A lot of experience. C.P. work, halls, panto, low comedy in legit., know it all. **1937** G. FRANKAU *More of Us* xi. 121 Eke tho' of words bard still commands a brainful Which she can still make dance like panto elves. **1962** *Oxford Times* 1 June 23/4 Orsino and Viola.. the latter part, although difficult in its mixture of boyishness and charm, should not really be played as a principal boy in panto. **1968** *Listener* 26 Dec. 871/3 Nor has the standard of the witless, panto-type sketches been raised. **1969** *Ibid.* 28 May 663/1, I was glad that Hazel Hughes should play her.. like Kenneth Williams as painless panto dame. **1976** *Sunday Post* (Glasgow) 26 Dec. 3/3 She was transporting it from Calderpark Zoo to the Pavilion panto, where it was due to appear in the cartoon spot featuring TV personality Glen Michael. **1977** *R.A.F. News* 11–24 May 3/5 The organizers ran an 'ad lib' version of the panto 'Cinderella'.

panto- (pæntəʊ), before a vowel PANT-, repr. Gr. παντο- (παντ-, πανθ-), combining form of πᾶς, πᾶν (stem παντ-) all, already used in ancient Gr. (where often interchangeable with παν- PAN-) in forming adjs. and a few substantives used attrib., as πάνταρχος (Soph.) all-ruling, παντοδαπός of all kinds, παντοκράτωρ almighty, παντοκτίστης creator of all; in later Gr. it became much more frequent. The word παντόμῖμος was adopted in L. as *pantomimus* and thence came into French and English as *pantomime* before 1600. Otherwise, the formation of words in *panto-* began in the 17th c., and became more frequent in the 19th; but this has not become a living element forming compounds like the cognate PAN- 1 in *Pan-Anglican*, *Pan-American*, and the like. The chief derivatives of *panto-* appear in their alphabetical places; the following are of minor importance:

†**panto-chro'nometer**: see quot. †**panto-'devil**, *nonce-wd.*, a complete or entire devil. **,pantogan'glitis** *Path.*: see quots. **,panto-ge'lastic, -al** *adjs.* [Gr. γελαστικός risible], all-laughable. **pan'togenous** *a. Min.* [Gr. -γενης born, produced; in F. *pantogène*]: see quots. †**panto-i'atrical** *a.*, universally healing, all-healing. †**'pantomancer,** a diviner upon all kinds of things. **'pantomorph** (erron. **panta-**) [Gr. παντόμορφος], that which takes any or all shapes; so **panto'morphic** *a.* (**panta-**), assuming any or all forms. **pantope'lagian** *a.* [Gr. πέλαγος sea: cf. F. *pantopélagien* (Littré)], frequenting or inhabiting all seas. †**'pantophile** [F. *pantophile*], a lover of all. **panto'plethora** *Path.*, general plethora. **pan'topterous** *a. Zool.* [Gr. πτερὸν wing, fin], of or pertaining to the *Pantoptera*, a family of fishes having all fins but the ventral (Mayne *Expos. Lex.* 1857). **panto'therian** *a.* [Gr. θήρα, θηρίον beast], of or pertaining to the *Pantotheria*, an extinct order of American Jurassic mammals; *sb.* a member of this order. ‖**pantozo'otia** = *panzooty*: see PAN- 2 (Harris *Dict. Med. Terminol.* 1854–67).

1842 BRANDE *Dict. Sci.* etc., **Pantochronometer*, a term recently invented and applied to an instrument which is a combination of the compass, the sun-dial, and the universal time-dial, and performing the offices of all three. **1694** MOTTEUX *Rabelais* v. xiii, Oh you Devils, cry'd Friar Ihon, Proto-Devils, *Panto-Devils, you would wed a Monk, would you? **1857** MAYNE *Expos. Lex.*, **Pantoganglitis*,.. term for inflammation of the *ganglia*, central and peripherical; also for oriental cholera. **1893** *Syd. Soc. Lex.*, *Pantoganglitis*, a term for malignant cholera, introduced on the assumption that it was caused by inflammation of all the sympathetic ganglia. **1808** *Pantogelastical [see PANTOLOGICAL]. **1805–17** R. JAMESON *Char. Min.* (ed. 3) 220 *Pantogenous (pantogene), that is to say, which derives its form from all parts of the crystal, when every edge and angle suffers a decrement. Example, Pantogenous heavy-spar. **1857** MAYNE *Expos. Lex.*, *Pantogenus*, applied by Haüy to crystals in which each edge and each solid angle has undergone a decrease.. pantogenous. **1716** M. DAVIES *Athen. Brit.* III. *Diss. Physick* 14 Religiously inclin'd Doctors of the same *Panto-Iatrical Scriptures. **1652** GAULE *Magastrom.* 335 Of astromancers turning *pantomancers, or presaging not onely upon prodigies, but upon every slight occasion, by every vile and vaine means. **1841** SCUDAMORE *Nomencl.*, **Pantamorph*.., that which has all shapes. **1836** SMART, **Pantamorphic*, taking all shapes. **1890** *Cent. Dict.*, Pantomorph, Pantomorphic. **1857** MAYNE *Expos. Lex.*, *Pantopelagian. **1893** *Syd. Soc. Lex.*, *Pantopelagian*, frequenting all seas, or the whole sea; applied by Fleurien to such birds as the albatross and the stormy petrel. **1898** *Allbutt's Syst. Med.* V. 925 'The heart of a *pantophile', as Voltaire called that removed from Diderot's body. **1857** MAYNE *Expos. Lex.*, **Pantoplethora*,.. universal or general plethora, or fulness of the blood-vessels.

pantoble, pantocle: see PANTOFLE.

pantocain ('pæntəʊkeɪn). *Pharm.* Also **-caine.** [a. G. *pantocain*, f. Gr. παντο- PANTO- + *-cain*, after G. *cocain* COCAINE.] The hydrochloride salt, $C_{15}H_{24}N_2O_2 \cdot HCl$, of a diamino-ester which is used as a local anæsthetic; also called *amethocaine* or *tetracaine hydrochloride.*

1931 *Manuf. Chem.* II. 105/1 The new local anæsthetic of the I.G. Farbenindustrie, Pantocain,.. has been systematically evolved from the novocaine series and is the hydrochloride of *p*-butylaminobenzyldimethylamino-ethanol. **1937** *Brit. Med. Jrnl.* 20 Nov. 1036/2 Local infiltration with 0·5 per cent. pantocaine caused excessive oedema of the lids and face.. and intense itching. **1942** PARSONS & STALLARD *Dis. Eye* (ed. 10) xxi. 431 Particles of lime must be perseveringly picked out with forceps, after previous application of pantocain. **1970** *Brain Res.* XIX. 102 The neck afferents were eliminated by.. the blockage of afferent fibers by Pantocain injection into the intervertebral foramen.

Pantocrator (pæn'tɒkrətə(r)). Also **Pantokrator.** [ad. Gr. παντοκράτωρ almighty.] With reference to God or Christ: the Almighty, all-ruler; hence, an artistic representation of the figure of Christ, esp. as a characteristic form in Byzantine art.

1871 RUSKIN *Fors Clavigera Letter* 12 11 In the Apocalypse it is 'Lord, All governing'—Pantocrator—which we weakly translate 'Almighty'. **1911** O. M. DALTON *Byzantine Art & Archaeol.* xii. 672 In the Last Judgement, and as the Pantokrator, Christ is bearded, because in his function as Judge he is regarded as merely continuing his earthly mission. **1931** *Antiquity* V. 508 With the exception of the Pantocrator in the dome.. the Daphni mosaics belong to the pictorial, representational, Hellenic tradition. **1947** C. STEWART *Byzantine Legacy* v. 111 The condition of the Church of Christ Pantocrator is typical of many. **1950** A. HUXLEY *Themes & Variations* 174 Young Domenikos received a sound Greek education and studied painting... That indecently human personage—was that supposed to be the Pantocrator? **1962** *New Statesman* 25 May 768/3 It [*sc.* a cathedral tapestry] fails to achieve the commanding presence of a Byzantine pantocrator. **1963** D. T. RICE *Art of Byzantine Era* 88 In Basil's church the bust of Christ Pantocrator dominated the building from the dome. **1970** *Oxf. Compan. Art* 182/1 The Iconoclastic crisis.. culminated in the formation of a new religious iconography. .. It was then that the decorative scheme of the Byzantine church was fixed..: in the dome the Pantocrator (Christ the Ruler) surrounded by archangels. **1974** D. YARWOOD *Archit. Europe* iii. 110/2 The mosaics and frescoes.. of the dome.. illustrate the Christ Pantocrator in all His Glory.

Hence **panto'cratic** *a. rare.*

1949 AUDEN *Under Sirius* in *Horizon* Oct. 210 And out of the open sky The pantocratic riddle breaks;—'Who are you and why?'

pantod: see OD[2] b.

pantofle ('pæntəf(ə)l, pæn'tɒf(ə)l, -'tuːf(ə)l). Forms: 5 *Sc.* pantufle, (-uiffil), 6 -uffle, 6–7 -afle, -aphel, -of(f)el, -ophle, -ophel, 6– pantofle, -offle, 7–9 pantoufle, 9 -oofle. Also *β*. 6 pantocle, -acle; pantapple, 7 pantaple, 6–8 pantable, (6 pantiple, 7 -ible, -oble). [a. F. *pantoufle* (1489 in Hatz.-Darm.) = Cat. *plantofa*, Sp. *pantuflo*, Pg. *pantufo*, It. *pantofola*, *-ufola*; also Ger., Du. *pantoffel* (from It.), Flem. *pattoffel*. Ulterior origin unknown; see Diez and Littré. The English stress on the first syllable facilitated the corruptions *pantaple*, *pantocle*, *pantable*, assimilated to words in *-ple*, *-cle*, *-ble*. The stress on second syllable follows Fr. and Ger.]

A slipper; formerly applied very variously, app., at one time or another, to every sort of indoor slippers or loose shoes; esp. to the high-heeled cork-soled chopins; also to out-door overshoes or goloshes; and to all manner of Oriental and non-European slippers, sandals, and the like. (In Scottish use from 15th c.; in common Eng. use from *c* 1570 to *c* 1650–60; after that chiefly an alien or historical word.)

1494 *Acc. Ld. High Treas. Scot.* I. 224 Item, to Home the cordinare, for schone, brodykinnis and pantuiffillis tane fra him be Jame Dog. **1497** *Ibid.* 334 Item, for ane par of Franch pantuflis.. viij[s]. **1565** COOPER *Thesaurus*, *Baxeæ*,.. a kynde of slippers, or pantofles. **1577** B. GOOGE *Heresbach's Husb.* (1586) 101 Of his [beech's] barke, are made Pantoffels, and Slippers. **1579** GOSSON *Sch. Abuse* (Arb.) 30 The litle crackhalter that carrieth his maisters pantouffles. **1579–80** NORTH *Plutarch* (1895) IV. 22 A payer of pantophles. **1589** PUTTENHAM *Eng. Poesie* I. xv. (Arb.) 49 The actors.. did walke vpon those high corked shoes or pantofles, which now they call in Spaine and Italy *Shoppini*. **1607** R. C[AREW] tr. *Estienne's World of Wonders* 203 The Pope would not entertaine him, except he would.. kisse his pantoufle. *c* **1618** FLETCHER *Queen of Corinth* I. ii, [He] takes his oath Upon her Pantoffles. **1624** BURTON *Anat. Mel.* III. ii. I. i. (ed. 2) 356 She.. whipped him [Cupid] besides on the bare buttocks with her pantophle. **1636** MASSINGER *Bashf. Lover* v. i, Pray you, let me be your page; I can swear already, Upon your pantofle. **1679** OLDHAM *Sat. Jesuits* Wks. (1686) 44 Spurns to Hell For jearing Holy Toe, and Pantofle. *a* **1715** BURNET *Own Time* (1823) III. IV. 77 [The pope] would give me a private audience abed, to save me the ceremony of the pantoufle. **1767** STERNE *Tr. Shandy* IX. xxi, Nothing.. but trunk-hose and pantofles. **1820** SCOTT *Abbot* v, I have been too long the vassal of a pantoufle, and the slave of a silver whistle. *a* **1845** BARHAM *Ingol. Leg.*, *Ld. Thoulouse* vi, *Pantoufles* with bows Each as big as a rose. **1852** THACKERAY *Esmond* I. iii, Great gold clocks to her stockings, and white pantofles with red heels. **1887** ANNA FORBES *Insulinde* i. 9 Indian-looking pantoffles,.. with no upper heels, but very high wooden ones.

β. Corrupt forms. (*pantable* was exceedingly common from 1580 to *c* 1650.)

a **1568** ASCHAM *Scholem.* I. (Arb.) 84 As it is free.. to chose.. whether a man lust to weare Shoo or Pantocle. **1571** *Damon & Pithias* in Dodsley *O.P.* I. 215 Even here with a pantacle I wyll you disgrace. **1573–80** BARET *Alv.* P 72 A Pantapple, *vide* Shooe. *a* **1586** SIDNEY *Arcadia* I. (1629) 49 Chafing and swearing by the pantable of Pallace and such other oathes as his rusticall braverie could imagine. **1591** PERCIVALL *Sp. Dict.*, *Calçado de alcorques*, in pantoples, *Crepidatus*. **1596** *Lanc. Wills* III. 2 A payre of pantables and ij payre of slippers. **1602** MARSTON *Ant. & Mel.* II. Wks. 1856 I. 19 By my ladies pantable, I feare I shall live to heare [etc.]. **1676** D'URFEY *Mad. Fickle* v. iii, Out of my doors, by Jacobs Pantible—a Relique of Renown'd memory. **1688** R. HOLME *Armoury* II. 112/2 The Lady Slipper so called from the resemblance the fore-part of the flower hath to a Slipper, or Pantable. **1883** J. PAYNE *1001 Nights* VI. 291 Except he bring her.. another crown and girdle and pantable of gold.

b. Phrase. *to stand* (*be*, etc.) *upon* (*one's*) *pantofles*, i.e. on one's dignity; so *the high pantofle*, etc.

1573 G. HARVEY *Letter-bk.* (Camden) 14 He was now altogither set on his merri pinnes and walkd on his stateli pantocles. **1579** LYLY *Euphues* (Arb.) 47 For the most part they stand so on their pantuffles. **1591** R. TURNBULL *Exp. Epist. James* 171 b, To stand too much vpon our pantiples. **1591** GREENE *2nd Pt. Conny-catch.* Wks. (Grosart) X. 119 Then are they vpon their pantophles, because there is nothing found about them. **1594** CAREW *Huarte's Exam. Wits* xiii. (1596) 224 A Caualiero, who stood much on the pantophles of his gentilitie. **1665** BRATHWAIT *Comment Two Tales* 22 This sets the Carpenter upon his Pantofles. **1685** BUNYAN *Pharisee & Publ.* Wks. (1845) 140 Thou standest upon thy points and pantables, thou wilt not bate God on all of what thy righteousness is worth. *c* **1740** A. ALLEN *MS. Dict.* s.v. *Pantoble*, Pantofle, or Pantoufle, Slippers with high Soles. These, as well as high Heels, making People appear taller,.. gave birth to our Proverb, to stand upon ones Pantables, is to stand upon high Terms, carry his head Loftily. **1755** H. WALPOLE *Lett.* (1846) III. 156, I could not possibly to-day step out of my high historical pantoufles to tell it you.

†**c.** *Comb.* **pantofle-shoe** [F. *fer à pantoufle*, or *pantoufle*] = PANTON-*shoe* (for a horse). *Obs.*

1696 HOPE tr. *Solleysel's Parfait Mareschal* I. xl. 131, I have called this shoe the *Panton* or Pantable shoe to distinguish it from those of any other fashion or shape. **1717** *Dict. Rusticum* (ed. 2), *Pantons* or *Pantable-shoes*, a sort of Horse-shoes that serve for narrow and low Heels. **1722** W. GIBSON *Farrier's New Guide* xciv. (ed. 3) 256 The Cure is.. to shoe him with Lunets or Half-moon Shoes, or with those Pantofle Shoes describ'd by Solleysell.

pantogamy: see PANTAGAMY.

pantoganglitis, -genous, etc.: see PANTO-.

†**panto'glossical**, *a. Obs. rare*[−1]. [f. Gr. παντο- all + γλῶσσα tongue + -ICAL.] Of or belonging to all tongues.

1716 M. DAVIES *Athen. Brit.* II. 299 [It] may stand in full Defyance of ever being express'd, even with any Paraphrastical Periphrasis, or any Pantoglossical Mint of Words.

pantoglot ('pæntəʊglɒt), *a.* and *sb.* [f. Gr. παντο- all + γλῶσσα, γλῶττα tongue, after *polyglot*.]

a. *adj.* Knowing or speaking all languages. **b.** *sb.* One who speaks all languages. So **panto'glottism**.

1848 LOWELL *Biglow P.* Ser. I. ii. Poems 1890 II. 61 This would argue for the pantoglottism of these celestial intelligences. **1895** H. CALLAN *From Clyde to Jordan* ix. 101, I disapprove of a man being a polyglot, or worse, an approach to a pantoglot.

pantograph ('pæntəgrɑːf, -æ-), *sb.* Also *erron.* **panta-, panti-, penta-, pento-, pente-**. [mod. f. Gr. παντο- PANTO-, all + -γράφος writing, writer. So F. *pentographe* (Bion 1723), *pantographe* (1743 in *Hist. Acad. des Sci.*), the proximate source. Erroneously spelt by Bion and his translator Stone *pento-*, and by Chambers 1727 *penta-* (as if from Gr. πεντα- five); the latter still frequent in commercial and technical use.] **a.** An instrument for the mechanical copying of a plan, diagram, pattern, etc, on the same or an enlarged or reduced scale. In 17th c. called *parallelogram*.

It consists of four rods, perforated at uniform distances, and jointed together, two opposite joints being terminal and constant in position, the other two capable of being shifted according to the scale desired; one of the free ends carries a tracing-point, and one of the terminal joints a similar tracing-point; when one of these points is moved over the lines of the diagram, etc., the other traces the copy required.

[**1631** C. SCHEINER (*title*) Pantographice, seu Ars Delineandi res quaslibet per parallelogrammum lineare.. mobile. **1723** BION *Instr. de Math.* 89 L'instrument.. est nommé Pentographe; on le nomme aussi Singe.] **1723** E. STONE tr. *Bion's Math. Instr.* 86 Of the Pentograph, or Parallelogram. **1727–41** CHAMBERS *Cycl.*, *Pentagraph*, an instrument whereby designs, prints, etc. of any kind, may be copied in any proportion;.. otherwise called a parallelogram. [**1743** *Mach. approuv. par l' Acad. des Sci.* VII. 207 Pantographe, ou singe perfectionné, Par M. Langlois.] **1766** B. MARTIN *Surv. by Goniometer* 18 There remains therefore only the Pantagraph to be described. **1803** HAWKINS *Patent Specif.* No. 2735 Attaching.. pencils, etc. to a double pantograph. **1844** G. DODD *Textile Manuf.* vi. 200 An instrument called a pantograph has been introduced for producing an exquisite embroidery on plain silk goods after weaving. **1844** *Mech. Mag.* XL. 92 The Eidograph,.. invented about the year 1821.. is considered superior in many respects to the Pentograph. **1879** G. PRESCOTT *Sp. Telephone* 303 By using a form of pantograph, Prof. Mayer has obtained magnified tracings on smoked glass. **1897** [see PANTOGRAPHER 2].

attrib. **1875** KNIGHT *Dict. Mech.* s.v. *Pantograph*, The plate is then laid on the curved bed of the pantograph machine. **1895** *Oracle Encycl.* I. 585/2 Patterns are also etched on the rollers with nitric acid, by lines cut.. by means of Rigby's pentagraph machine. **1897** *Westm. Gaz.* 26 June 6/3 The pantograph power-shuttle machine.

b. A device of similar construction for mechanically reducing the cross-head motion of the indicator used for recording the pressure in a steam cylinder.

1893 WHITHAM *Constr. Steam Eng.* 154 A simple form of pantagraph, for use when the indicators are attached to the side of the cylinder. *Ibid.*, Pantagraph motions have been devised for overcoming these defects.

c. A jointed, self-adjusting framework on the top of an electric locomotive for conveying the current from overhead wires.

1907 F. H. DAVIES *Elect. Power & Traction* xxiii. 269 The.. collecting gear is that known as the pantograph, and the object.. is to permit of high speed running and reversal of direction without any corresponding adjustment of the gear. **1920** *Glasgow Herald* 23 Sept. 7 Electric locomotives can.. be fitted.. with pantograph collectors. **1930** *Engineering* 20 June 793/3 Only one pantograph was used at all speeds, so long as the current did not exceed 1800 amps. **1957** *Railway Mag.* Mar. 159/2 The pantograph is raised by pressing the push-button in the driving trailer. **1970** *Daily Mail* 8 Jan. 1/4 The pantograph.. appears to have jumped on top of the wire instead of running beneath it. **1977** *Modern Railways* Dec. 492/1 The primary reason for the central position was power collection problems at high speed in a two-power-car formation if each power car had its own pantograph.

d. Used of other mechanisms in the form of a movable diamond-shaped trellis or lazy tongs.

1942 *Archit. Rev.* XCII. 46 (*caption*) The early tube carriages of 1906, *seqq.*, had pantograph doors at both ends. **1975** *Observer* 9 Mar. 33/5 The driver's screen-wiper is a pantograph type and sweeps a commendably large area but the passenger's section of the screen has a big unswept corner.

Hence '**pantographing** *vbl. sb.*, the manipulation of a pantograph.

1897 *Sketch* 26 May 181/2 A front girl who must always have had experience in pantagraphing.

pantograph ('pæntəgrɑːf, -æ-), *v.* [f. the sb.] *trans.* To enlarge by means of a pantograph. Cf. PANTOGRAPHING *vbl. sb.*

1934 in WEBSTER. **1936** J. AGATE in *Sunday Times* 12 Apr. 5/1 Can a drop-earring be pantographed to chandelier-size without loss of exquisiteness?

pan'tographer. [f. PANTOGRAPH *sb.* + -ER[1].]

†**1.** = PANTOGRAPH *sb. Obs.*

1750 J. HAMMOND (*title*) Practical Surveyor, with Description of Sliding Rule, Universal Dial Pantographer [etc.]. **1774** S. DUNN (*title*) Theory and use of the Pantographer.

2. One who produces patterns, etc., by means of a pantograph.

1897 *Sketch* 26 May 181/2 The pantagrapher follows, or traces, with his pantagraph, the course of the stitches in the sketch of the pattern to be produced. **1897** *Advt. Brit. Embroidery Machine Co.*, The Jacquard producing the pattern and dispensing with the Pantagrapher.

pantographic (pæntəʊ'græfɪk), *a.* Also (in sense 1) erron. **penta-, panta-**.

1. [f. as prec. + -IC.] Pertaining to or of the nature of a pantograph. In quot. 1759 *fig.* Reproducing copies like the pantograph.

1759 STERNE *Tr. Shandy* I. xxiii, From the honourable devices which the Pentagraphic Brethren of the brush have shewn in taking copies. **1875** KNIGHT *Dict. Mech.* s.v., A system of connected pantographic levers. **1890** W. J. GORDON *Foundry* 175 The prettiest process of all is the pantagraphic one;.. The tiny fingers scratching so quietly and humanly the long cylinder of copper once seen will never be forgotten.

2. [f. PANTO- + Gr. γραφικός GRAPHIC.] ? Able to write in every language or character. *nonce-use.*

1801 W. TAYLOR in *Monthly Mag.* XII. 583 The author is polyglottic as the hydra, pantographic as Fry's letter-foundery.

panto'graphical, *a.* [See -ICAL.] = prec. 1.

1828 WEBSTER, *Pantographical*, pertaining to [or] performed by a pantograph. **1831** CARLYLE *Germ. Poetry* in *Misc. Ess.* (1872) III. 243 We have no original portrait here, but a pantagraphical reduced copy of some foreign sketches.

Hence **panto'graphically** *adv.*: (*a*) by means of or in the manner of a pantograph; (*b*) in the manner of a general description.

a. 1884 in STORMONTH. **1911** E. C. WORDEN *Nitrocellulose Industry* II. xiv. 697 These enamels may be closely imitated.. by taking a given pattern, enlarging it pantographically or otherwise, [etc.]. **1945** F. J. CAMM et al. *Newnes Plastics Manual* xii. 135 This machine [*sc.* the 'Keller' die-sinking machine] will produce all kinds of dies and jigs by a process of copying from a pattern pantographically.

b. 1890 in *Cent. Dict.*

pantography (pæn'tɒgrəfɪ). *rare.* [f. Gr. παντο- PANTO-, all + -GRAPHY.]

1. Complete description.

1828 WEBSTER, *Pantography*, general description; view of an entire thing. **1836** SMART, *Pantography*, description of *all*, view of an entire thing. (Also in later Dicts.)

2. The use of the pantograph. (So F. *pantographie* (Littré).)

1890 in *Cent. Dict.*

panto-iatrical: see PANTO-.

pantoic (pæn'təʊɪk), *a. Chem.* [f. as PANTOYL + -IC.] ***pantoic acid***, the unstable parent carboxylic acid $C_6H_{12}O_4$, of the pantoyl radicle.

1945 *Jrnl. Biol. Chem.* CLXI. 513 In connection with studies on the antagonistic action of pantoyltaurine on salicylate inhibition of *Escherichia coli* we have observed that pantoic acid, or, more properly, the pantoate ion, is more active than pantolactone. **1966** *McGraw-Hill Encycl. Sci. Technol.* XIV. 259/2 α-Ketoisovaleric acid.. is also a precursor of leucine and of the pantoic acid moiety of pantothenic acid.

Hence '**pantoate**, the anion, or a salt or ester, of pantoic acid.

1945 [see above]. **1968** *Compar. Biochem. & Physiol.* XXVII. 647 Pantothenate and pantoate inhibit the growth of *Trypanosoma lewisi in vitro.*

pantologic (pæntəʊ'lɒdʒɪk), *a.* Also *erron.* **panta-**. [f. as PANTOLOGY + -IC.] Of or pertaining to pantology; of universal knowledge.

1858 J. BROWN *Horæ Subs., Educ. through Senses* Ser. I. (1862) 316 We may say of our time in all seriousness, what Sydney Smith said..of the pantologic master of Trinity—Science is our forte; omniscience is our foible.

So **panto'logical** *a.*, dealing with pantology.

1808 (*title*) Fashionable Biography..with a Preface and Notes, Pantological and Pantogelastical. **1852** *Fraser's Mag.* XLV. 175 The development section of the new Pantological Museum. **1868** M. PATTISON *Academ. Org.* v. 266 Still less is the scientific habit generated by the pantological schemes now so much in favour.

pantology (pæn'tɒlədʒɪ). Also *erron.* **panta-**. [f. Gr. παντο- PANTO-, all + -λογια -LOGY.] A survey or systematic view of all branches of knowledge; universal knowledge; also, a compendium of universal information.

1819 *Pantologia* IX, *Pantologia, Pantology*, a work of universal instruction, or science: a cyclopædia or encyclopædia. **1822** *Blackw. Mag.* XII. 56 You, North, are undoubtedly a living pantology. **1841** B. PARK (*title*) Pantology, a Systematic Survey of Human Knowledge. **1852** *Fraser's Mag.* XLV. 175 The celebrated Hokus will lecture..on Pantology.

Hence **pan'tologist**, one who studies or is versed in universal knowledge. (Humorous or sarcastic.)

1840 *Fraser's Mag.* XXII. 148 *Multum legere non multa* is the student's motto—rather disregarded by the pantologists of the day. **1878** *Ibid.* XVII. 533 One more Pantologist—Professor of the Universal.

pantomancer, etc.: see PANTO-.

pantometer (pæn'tɒmɪtə(r)). Also *erron.* **pantameter.** [ad. F. *pantomètre* (1675 Bullet (title) *Usage du pantomètre*), f. Gr. παντο- PANTO-, all + μέτρον measure.] (See quots.)

1696 PHILLIPS (ed. 5), *Pantometer*, an Instrument in Geometry that serves to measure all sorts of Angles, Lengths and Heighths. **1823** CRABB, *Pantometre.* **1867** SMYTH *Sailor's Word-bk.*, *Pantometer*, an instrument for taking angles and elevations, and measuring distances.

b. Applied to other instruments.

(*a*) 'A graduated level' (Gwilt *Archit.* 1842–76). (*b*) An instrument for the mechanical production of portraits in profile (*Funk's Stand. Dict.* 1895).

pan'tometry. [f. Gr. παντο- PANTO-, all + Gr. -μετρία measurement.]

†**1.** Universal measurement: see quots. *Obs.*

[**1571** DIGGES (*title*) A Geometrical Practise, named Pantometria, diuided into three Bookes, Longimetra, Planimetra, and Stereometria.] **1656** BLOUNT *Glossogr.*, *Pantometrie*, a measuring of all kinde of quantities: It is the title and subject of a Mathematical Book, set forth by one Mr. Digs. **1692** COLES, *Pantometry*, a measuring of all things. **1797** J. DAWES (*title*) Pantometry; or an Attempt to systematize every Branch of Admeasurement.

2. The use of the pantometer. (*Cent. Dict.* 1890.)

Hence **panto'metric, panto'metrical** *adjs.*, of, pertaining to, or dealing with pantometry.

1828 in WEBSTER (both words).

pantomime ('pæntəmaɪm), *sb.* (*a.*) [ad. L. *pantomīmus* one who plays a part by dumb show, a ballet-dancer, ad. Gr. παντόμῖμος imitator of all, f. παντο- PANTO-, all + μῖμος mimic. So F. *pantomime* (1570 in Hatz.-Darm.); in Eng. the word was at first used in the L. form.]

1. A Roman actor, who performed in dumb show, representing by mimicry various characters and scenes; hence, generally, a mimic actor; one who represents his meaning by gestures and actions without words; a pantomimist. Now only *Hist.*

α. **1589** PUTTENHAM *Eng. Poesie* I. xi. (Arb.) 42 Betweene the actes when the players went to make ready for another, ..and the people waxt weary, then came in these maner of conterfaite vices, they were called *Pantomimi*, and all that had before bene sayd,..they gaue a crosse construction to it very ridiculously. **1626** BACON *Sylva* §240. **1630** B. JONSON *Love's Triumph* §1 With antic gesticulation and action, after the manner of the old pantomimi, they dance over a distracted comedy of love. *a* **1656** HALES *Gold. Rem.* I. (1673) 160 A Panto-mimus, a Poppet-player and Dancer in Rome.

β. **1615** BRATHWAIT *Strappado* 126 In time No question but hee'l prooue true Pantomime, To imitate all formes, shapes, habits, tyres Suiting the Court. **1621** SANDERSON *Serm. 1 Cor.* vii. 24 (1681) 202, I would our Pantomimes also and Stage-players would examine themselves and their Callings by this Rule. **1678** BUTLER *Hud.* III. ii. 1287 Pantomimes Who vary Action with the Times. **1709** STEELE *Tatler* No. 51 ⁋4 This Pantomime may be said to be a Species of himself: He has no Commerce with the rest of Mankind, but as they are the Objects of Imitation. **1781** GIBBON *Decl. & F.* xxxvi. (1869) II. 318 Buffoons and pantomimes are sometimes introduced, to divert, not to offend, the company. **1869** LECKY *Europ. Mor.* I. xi. 277 The immense increase of corrupt and corrupting professions, as actors, pantomimes, hired gladiators.

2. 'A kind of dramatic entertainment in which the performers express themselves by gestures to the accompaniment of music, and which may be called a prose ballet' (Husk in Grove *Dict. Mus.*).

a **1735** ARBUTHNOT (J.), He put off the representation of pantomimes till late hours, on market-days. *a* **1755** (in Johnson), Exulting folly hail'd the joyful day, And pantomime and song confirm'd her sway. **1760–72** H. BROOKE *Fool of Qual.* (1792) IV. 75 A great number of burlesque comedians entered the pales, in order to act one of their African drolls or pantomimes. *a* **1842** ARNOLD *Later Rom. Commw.* (1846) II. xi. 416 The exhibition of the pantomime was prohibited; an entertainment very different from that which is now known by the same name; and an outrage upon all decency. **1875** A. W. WARD *Eng. Dram. Lit.* I. i. 8 In the early days of the Empire..the pantomime, a species of ballet of action, established itself as a favourite class of amusement.

3. a. An English dramatic performance, originally consisting of action without speech, but in its further development consisting of a dramatized tale, the dénouement of which is a transformation scene followed by the broad comedy of clown and pantaloon and the dancing of harlequin and columbine. Now a feature of the Christmas holidays.

By the 20th century, the traditional form changed, with the loss of the pantaloon and harlequin features. The entertainment, primarily for children, is now based on the dramatization of a fairy tale or nursery story, and includes songs and topical jokes, buffoonery and slapstick, and standard characters such as a pantomime 'dame', played by a man, a leading boy, played by a woman, and a pantomime animal, e.g. horse, cat, goose, played by actors dressed in a comic costume, with some regional variations.

1739 CIBBER *Apol.* (1756) II. 50 It may not..be..improper to shew how our childish pantomimes came to take so gross a possession of the stage. **1749** FIELDING *Tom Jones* v. i, The inventor of that most exquisite entertainment, called the English pantomime. **1780** T. DAVIES *Garrick* (1781) I. x. 99 Rich [in 1717] created a species of dramatic composition unknown to this, and I believe, to any other country, which he called a pantomime: it consisted of two parts, one serious and the other comic. **1797** SOUTHEY *Joan of Arc* Pref., After the publication of this poem, a pantomime upon the same subject was brought forward at Covent-Garden Theatre. **1807** *Director* II. 331 Those very confined and partial transfigurations of our Harlequinades, termed Pantomimes. **1879** BLACK *Macleod of D.* xxxiv. 307 It is like a pantomime. You would expect to see a burst of limelight and Neptune appearing with a silver trident and crown. **1880** HUSK in Grove *Dict. Mus.* II. 646/2 In the early pantomime Harlequin was the principal character, and continued so until the genius of Grimaldi placed the Clown in the most prominent position. **1892** *Daily News* 24 Dec. 5/2 The pantomime has gradually interwoven itself into our recognised Christmas festivities, so as to become an essential part of them. **1896** *Pall Mall Mag.* Oct. 302/1 She was still playing principal boy in the pantomime—a gay, gallant Prince, in plumed cap and tights. **1901** R. J. BROADBENT *Hist. Pantomime* xxi. 225 Present-day Pantomime, with the immense sums spent annually on its gorgeous spectacular display and costly dresses..is a subject that is well known to us all... The best parts are, as a general rule, allotted to music-hall 'stars' whose names will draw the most money. **1911** *Times* 7 Nov. 9/4 Some of us would have passed through a childhood of tasteless pantomimes, lacking the most exciting of their three annual thrills, which were always the clown, the 'principal boy', and 'Jimmie' Glover. **1950** *Oxf. Jun. Encycl.* IX. 273/2 Pantomimes of to-day are on a spendidly lavish scale, with hundreds of performers. They all have their stock characters... They provide many of the catch phrases and popular songs of the season during their long runs.., often from Christmas till Lent. **1965** D. ARUNDELL *Story of Sadler's Wells* xii. 149 Phelps began his 1847–8 season on 23rd August..with of course a grand pantomime at Christmas (pantomime now meaning the extravaganza fairy-tale as we under-stand it today). **1978** *Times Lit. Suppl.* 24 Feb. 247/2 The town is agog over the annual pantomime which opens on Boxing Day.

b. *transf.* and *fig.*

1781 G. SELWYN *Let.* 27 Feb. in *15th Rep. R. Comm. Hist. Manuscripts* App. VI. 464 in *Parl. Papers 1897* (C. 8551) LI. 1, I believe there is no actor upon the stage of either theatre who, repeating what the author has wrote, does not, at the same time, recite his own private sentiments oftener, than our pantomimes in Parliament. **1837** DICKENS *Let.* 13 Feb. (1965) I. 236 Oliver and the Pantomime of Life are both finished, and with the Printer. **1941** *Penguin New Writing* III. 109 It's a proper pantomime. The old Tabbies'll have to mind their dignities if they steps out to-day. **1972** *Times* 7 Aug. (Jamaica Suppl.) p. v/4 The uniquely Jamaican 'pantomime'..has evolved into the musical comedy formula incorporating topical allusions..along with folklore characters.

4. Significant gesture without speech; dumb show.

1791 MRS. RADCLIFFE *Rom. Forest* v, Peter acted a perfect pantomime. **1814** SCOTT *Wav.* xxix, The entrance of Mrs. Cruickshanks..interrupted this pantomime of affectionate enthusiasm. **1871** L. STEPHEN *Playgr. Eur.* (1894) v. 118 As ..he could not speak a word of French..he was obliged to convey this sentiment into pantomime. **1873** OUIDA *Pascarèl* I. 42 Florio shrugged his shoulders with the most expressive pantomime in the world.

5. *attrib.* passing into *adj.* **a.** Of the nature of pantomime (sense 2); pantomimic. **b.** Of, belonging to, or characteristic of the pantomime (sense 3). Also *Comb.*

1746 in *Wesley's Wks.* (1872) II. 40 An Obnubilative, Pantomime Entertainment to be exhibited at Mr. Clark's. **1755** RICHARDSON *Corr.* (1804) VI. 265, I am sorry that the visits between you and Miss Talbot were so very pantomime. **1765** H. TIMBERLAKE *Mem.* 80 [The Cherokees] are..very dexterous at pantomime dances; several of which I have seen performed that were very diverting. **1777** G. FORSTER *Voy. round World* I. 412 In the intervals of the dance three men performed something of a pantomime drama. **1838** DICKENS *Nich. Nick.* xxiii, Mr. Folair made a funny face from his pantomime collection. **1861** THACKERAY *Four Georges* iv. (1862) 222 The king in the pantomime, with his pantomime wife, and pantomime courtiers,..whom he pokes with his pantomime sceptre. **1883** D. COOK *On Stage* I. x. 219 In the pantomime season, or whenever any great pageant or spectacle is to be produced, these plots are of prodigious extent. **1892** ANSTEY *Voces Pop.* Ser. II. 153 The Pit during Pantomime Time. **1901** R. J. BROADBENT *Hist. Pantomime* xix. 196 This clashing..cannot but..adversely affect the box-office receipts, unless, of course the Pantomime-goer makes a point of 'doing the round'. **1908** G. B. SHAW *Pen Portraits* (1932) 74 A pantomime animal with two men in it is a mistake when the two are not very carefully paired. **1919** —— *Great Catherine* 114 They..produced scene after scene of..tragic relief in the torture chamber with the monarch as pantomime demon committing real atrocities. **1922** JOYCE *Ulysses* 431 In pantomime dame's stringed mob-cap, crinoline and bustle, widow Twankey's blouse..and cameo brooch. **1935** T. S. ELIOT *Murder in Cath.* i. 41 All things are unreal, Unreal or disappointing; The Catherine wheel, the pantomime cat, The prizes given at the children's party. **1939** —— *Old Possum's Pract. Cats* 37 In the Pantomime season I never fell flat. **1946** M. DICKENS *Happy Prisoner* ix. 189 He had been afraid they were going to guy her up like a pantomime dame. **1967** *Listener* 19 Oct. 513/2 Everyone will want to see Alec Guinness do his pantomime-dame act in *Wise Child.* **1973** 'A. HALL' *Tango Briefing* viii. 99 Whether you die like a man or the back end of a pantomime horse you're going to stop breathing. **1976** M. GILBERT *Night of Twelfth* xvii. 156 Think of old Dip in a wig and falsies. He'd look like a pantomime dame.

'pantomime, *v.* [f. prec. sb.]

1. *intr.* To express oneself by dumb show. Also, to behave as though in a pantomime.

1768 [DONALDSON] *Sir B. Sapskull* I. xviii. 174 An unhappy girl..for want of friends to appear, or money to pantomime in her favour, is hurried to gaol. **1888** *Sat. Rev.* 24 Mar. 354 Where it is necessary for her to pantomime, the attitudes she assumes are in the best style of plastic art. **1958** *Spectator* 8 Aug. 187/2 The vanity of a Lloyd George or a Ramsay MacDonald, who preferred pantomiming round the world in a continual circus to staying put where they belonged.

2. *trans.* To express or represent by pantomime or dumb show.

1847 LEVER *Knt. of Gwynne* lviii, Pantomiming the action of drinking with his now empty glass. **1852** R. F. BURTON *Falconry Vall. Indus* v. 55 He then placed his forefinger on his lips, pantomiming that a little 'Bamboo-bakhshish' had ..stopped the unreasonable complainant's tongue. **1861** DUTTON COOK *P. Foster's D.* x, Septimus pantomimed deprecation of any such notions.

Hence **'pantomimed** *ppl. a.*

1950 A. RONELL in Manvell & Huntley *Technique Film Music* (1957) iii. 137 His pantomimed thoughts find voice through the inflection of instruments whose colours express Harpo's spirited style.

pantomimic (pæntəʊ'mɪmɪk), *a.* and *sb.* [ad. L. *pantomīmic-us*, f. *pantomīm-us*: see -IC.]

A. *adj.* **1.** Of the nature of pantomime or mimicry; expressed by dumb show.

a **1680** BUTLER *Rem.* (1759) I. 233 That counterfeits all pantomimic Tricks. **1788** *Warburton's Div. Legat.* VI. Notes, Wks. III. 555 Pantomimic gesture was amongst the Romans one way of exhibiting a Dramatic Story. **1879** GEO. ELIOT *Theo. Such* xv. 268, I do not forgive myself for this pantomimic falsehood.

2. Of or belonging to the pantomime.

1805 WORDSW. *Prelude* VII. 262 Music, and shifting pantomimic scenes, Diversified the allurement. **1840** *Penny Cycl.* XVII. 194/2 Noverre, in France, distinguished himself likewise in the composition of pantomimic 'ballets'. **1879** SALA in *Daily Tel.* 30 May, The jury were moved to irresistible laughter when they were told that the Brothers Dare, Mr. Marquez Gonza, and the pantomimic Martinetti had far better, instead of flying through the air, have 'devoted their attention to the Bar or the Church'.

b. Characteristic of or like a pantomime, in its quick or sudden transformations.

1895 J. MCCARTHY in *Forum* June 453 Mr. C.'s change of front and change of opinions were something pantomimic in their swiftness, and their completeness, and their surprise.

B. *sb.* = PANTOMIME *sb.* 1.

1617 MIDDLETON & ROWLEY *Fair Quarrel* IV. iv, I am acquainted with one of the pantomimics. **1689** T. PLUNKET *Char. Gd. Commander* 24 Fools and Pantomimmicks bear the Bell.

panto'mimical, *a.* Now *rare.* [See -ICAL.]

1. Of, belonging to, or of the nature of pantomime or dumb show.

1644 BULWER *Chiron.* 11 This was in that Pantomimicall Roscius, who could vary a thing more by gestures, then..Tully could by Phrase. **1649** —— *Pathomyot.* II. vi. 187 Such..seeme to have a Patent for excellent Pantomimicall utterance. **1780** T. DAVIES *Garrick* (1781) I. x. 98 He [Rich] applied himself to the study of pantomimical representation. **1787** *Generous Attachment* III. 25 Which..betrayed the rest of the company into the same pantomimical behaviour. **1824** SCOTT *St. Ronan's* xx, Action, even pantomimical action, was not expected.

2. = PANTOMIMIC *a.* 2.

1736 FIELDING *Pasquin* v. i. How came they to give the name of entertainments to their pantomimical farces? **1808** *Mem. Female Philos.* I. 106 That..for which she had the greatest predilection, was pantomimical dancing. **1813** T. BUSBY *Lucretius* I. III. *Comm.* p. xii, I might instance the constant effects of pantomimical music.

Hence **panto'mimically** *adv.*, in a pantomimic manner; by way of pantomime.

1839 LADY LYTTON *Cheveley* (ed. 2) III. iv. 99 Pushing over a banker's book..on which he began to write pantomimically. **1884** COLLINGWOOD *Under Meteor Flag* 27 Perched on the crosstrees, from which..position he reminded me pantomimically of the potent charm to be found in a comic song.

†**panto'mimicry.** *Obs. nonce-wd.* [f. PANTOMIMIC + -RY, after *mimicry*.] = PANTOMIME 4.

1728 NORTH *Mem. Music* (1846) 35, I desire to know to what end panto-mimikery was so much used.

'pantomimish, *a.* [PANTOMIME *sb.* (*a.*) + -ISH[1].] = PANTOMIMIC *a.* 2.

1923 *Glasgow Herald* 3 Feb. 6/6 A few veterans may recall how pantomimish Mr. Gladstone looked when..he borrowed the hat of a colleague.

pantomimist ('pæntəmaɪmɪst). [f. PANTOMIME + -IST.] One who acts in, or writes, a pantomime; a comic or burlesque actor; also = PANTOMIME 1.

1838 DICKENS *Nich. Nick.* xxiii, 'This is Mr. Lenville..', said the pantomimist. **1871** SMILES *Charac.* i. (1876) 9 Even the poor pantomimist of Drury Lane felt himself his superior. **1882** FARRAR *Early Chr.* 9 The actors who absorbed the greatest part of popular favor were pantomimists.

pantomography (pæntə'mɒgrəfɪ). *Med.* [f. PAN(ORAMIC *a.* + TOMOGRAPHY.] A form of tomography for obtaining radiographs of curved layers of an object, *spec.* the teeth and jaws, by rotation of the body and film during exposure; a further modification of the technique is ORTHOPANTOMOGRAPHY.

1952 Y. V. PAATERO in *Suomen Hammaslääkäriseuran Toimituksia* XLVIII. 7 Pantomography—a tomographic method for roentgenographing curved surfaces. **1954** —— in *Acta Radiologica* XLI. 321 A new method of tomographic roentgenography (which I subsequently named pantomography.) *Ibid.* 326 Since the roentgen beam in pantomography is relatively narrow, it is obvious that secondary radiation emanates from only a narrow portion of the object. **1956** K. C. CLARK *Positioning in Radiog.* (ed. 7) xxviii. 536/2 Pantomography..By this method of simultaneous movement of head and film in front of the slit diaphragm of the tube, a progressive panoramic view of the whole jaw is produced. **1969** G. J. VAN DER PLAATS *Med. X-Ray Technique* (ed 3) iv. 104 Pantomography is mainly applied in dental radiography.

Hence **pan'tomogram**, a radiograph obtained by pantomography; **pan'tomograph** (see quot. 1954[1]); **,pantomo'graphic, -'graphical** *adjs.*

1952 Y. V. PAATERO in *Suomen Hammaslääkäriseuran Toimituksia* XLVIII. 7 Divergence of rays in pantomographical roentgenography. *Ibid.*, Taking of lateral roentgenograms of jaw with the pantomographic method. **1954** —— in *Acta Radiologica* XLI. 321 *Pantomograph*, a device used with a normal roentgen apparatus, which produces pantomographic roentgenograms = pantomograms. *Ibid.*, Thus, pantomographic roentgenography must be distinguished from all previous tomographic methods which produce roentgenographic representations of level surfaces. *Ibid.* 326 The pantomograph used rotates around its axis once every 20 seconds.

pantomorph, -morphic: see PANTO-.

'panton. *Sc.* (Now *local.*) Also 5–6 **pantoun(e**, 9 *Shetland* **-in.** [Origin unknown. App. related in some way to *pantofle*.]

1. A slipper; = PANTOFLE.

1489 *Acc. Ld. High Treas. Scot.* I. 111 For xxx[ti] payre of schone and xxx[ti] paire of pantonis to my Lorde of Ross. **1500–20** DUNBAR *Poems* liii. 27 He trippet, quhill he tint his pantoun. **1585** JAS. I *Ess. Poesie* (Arb.) 55 The counsale quhilk Apelles gaue to the shoomaker..seing him find falt with the shankis of the Image of Venus, efter that he had found falt with the pantoun, *Ne sutor vltra crepidam.* **1615** *Rec. Sterling Council* in *Trans. Nat. Hist. & Arch. Soc. Sterling* (1902) 62 Buitts, schone, pantones and pickedaillis. **1692** *Sc. Presb. Eloq.* (1738) 142 That all the Kings in the World may..kiss his Soles, not the Popes Soles, &c., no nor his stinking Panton neither. [**1897** *Shetland News* 15 May (E.D.D.) What..is tempid dee ta come butt..'ithoot dee pantins?]

attrib. **1618** LITHGOW *Pilgr. Farewell* C iij b, The Papall Panton heele. **1641** *Sc. Acts Chas. I* (1817) V. 541 In name and behalff of..wrichtis, Couperis..panton heil makeris.

†**2.** *Comb.*: **panton-shoe** (*Farriery*), a horseshoe having the sponges thick inside sloping to a thin outer edge, as a remedy for narrow or contracted heels; also called PANTOFLE-*shoe*. *Obs.*

1696 HOPE tr. *Solleysel's Parfait Mareschal* I. xl. 130 For those horses which are hoof-bound..you must have Panton shoes. **1727** BAILEY vol. II, *Panton-Shoe*, a Shoe contrived for recovering narrow and Hoof-bound Heels in Horses. **1753** CHAMBERS *Cycl. Supp.*, *Panton-shoe*, in the manege.

pantonal (pæn'təʊnəl), *a.* [PAN- + TONAL *a.*] Used as a synonym for 'atonal', in twelve-tone music; including all tonalities; hence **pan'tonalism, panto'nality.**

1958 R. R. RETI *Tonality, Atonality, Pantonality* III. iii. 70 The question of how in the realm of pantonality the problem of consonance and dissonance is treated. *Ibid.*, 73 The first example tending towards the pantonal, the second towards the atonal concept. **1961** *Times* 6 Dec. 17/6 It is true enough that a crowd of Muscovites do not sing pantonal fugues. **1963** *Listener* 31 Jan. 220/3 In some sections I have expanded this pantonality into harmonic structures which vertically include up to twenty-three notes. **1966** *Ibid.* 19 May 736/1 Schoenberg disliked the word 'atonal', and preferred the expression 'pantonal', inclusive of all tonalities. **1970** W. APEL *Harvard Dict. Mus.* (ed. 2) 640/1 *Pantonality, pantonal*, the inclusion of all tonalities. The terms are sometimes used instead of atonality and atonal.

[**pantoner**, a freq. misreading of PAUTENER.]

pantopelagian, -phile, etc.: see PANTO-.

pantophagist (pæn'tɒfədʒɪst). [f. Gr. παντοφάγ-ος all-devouring + -IST.] A man or animal that devours things of all kinds; an omnivorous eater.

1822–34 *Good's Study Med.* (ed. 4) I. 116 Borelli gives us an instance of a pantophagist who swallowed a hundred louis-dor's at a meal. **1848** CRAIG, *Pantophagist*, an animal that eats all kinds of food.

So **panto'phagic** *a.* = next (Mayne *Expos. Lex.*).

pan'tophagous, *a.* [f. as prec. + -OUS.] All-devouring, eating all kinds of food, omnivorous.

1848 in CRAIG. **1893** in *Syd. Soc. Lex.*

So **pantophagy** (pæn'tɒfədʒɪ) [ad. Gr. παντοφαγία], the eating of all sorts of food.

1841 *Fraser's Mag.* XXIV. 26 The premier..gloriously crams With a power of pantophagy ultra-Herculean. **1857** MAYNE *Expos. Lex.*, *Pantophagia*, term for the capability of enjoying all eatables without distinction: pantophagy.

pantophobia (pæntəʊ'fəʊbɪə). Also **pan'tophoby.** [f. Gr. παντοφόβος all-fearing (f. παντο- all + φόβος fear) + -IA[1].] 'A form of monomania characterised by causeless or excessive terror. Also, a synonym of *Hydrophobia*' (*Syd. Soc. Lex.* 1893).

1842 DUNGLISON *Med. Lex.*, *Pantophobia*, Hydrophobia, Panophobia. **1857** MAYNE *Expos. Lex.*, *Pantophobia*, term for a species of melancholy, characterised by causeless fears: pantophoby.

So **panto'phobic, pan'tophobous** *adjs.*

1857 MAYNE *Expos. Lex.*, *Pantophobicus*, of or belonging to Pantophobia: pantophobic. **1893** *Syd. Soc. Lex.*, *Pantophobous*, afflicted with Pantophobia.

pantopod ('pæntəpɒd). *Zool.* [f. Gr. παντο- all + ποδ- stem of πούς foot.] One of the *Pantopoda*, a name for the *Pycnogonidæ* or Sea-spiders, when treated as a sub-order; a sea-spider.

1887 *Encycl. Brit.* XXII. 409/2 Arachnids, and especially Pantopods..are very common.

Pantopon ('pæntəʊpɒn). *Pharm.* Also **pantopon.** [f. PANT- + OP(IUM *sb.* + *-on*.] A proprietary name in the U.S. for a mixture of the hydrochlorides of the opium alkaloids. Cf. OMNOPON.

1909 *Chem. Abstr.* III. 944 Pantopon..contains according to Sahli..all the opium alkaloids. 1g. = 5g. opium. **1910** *Offical Gaz.* (U.S. Patent Office) 1 Feb. 183/1 F. Hoffmann-La Roche & Co., Basel, Switzerland. Filed Sept. 8, 1909. *Pantopon*... A pharmaceutical preparation containing all the alkaloids of opium in an easily-soluble state and in a form suitable for subcutaneous injections. **1940** H. A. MCGUIGAN *Appl. Pharmacol.* 524 It is claimed that pantopon causes less depression of the respiration, less nausea, and has a slower and more prolonged action [than morphine]. **1953** W. BURROUGHS *Junkie* (1972) xii. 121 Lupita sells her stuff in papers. It is supposed to be heroin. Actually, it is pantopon cut with milk sugar and some other crap. **1972** *Biol. Abstr.* LIV. 1738/2 The changes in histamine may have been affected by the narcotics—amobarbital and Pantopon.

pantopragmatic (,pæntəʊpræg'mætɪk), *a.* and *sb. humorous* and *satirical.* [f. PANTO- + PRAGMATIC.] **a.** *adj.* Universally meddling, occupied with everything. **b.** *sb.* A 'pantopragmatic' person; also, in *pl.*, a satirical name for the alleged 'science' of universal meddling.

1861 T. L. PEACOCK *Gryll Gr.* viii, Two or three..arch-quacks have taken to merry-andrewizing in a new arena, which they call the Science of Pantopragmatics. *Ibid.* xxxi, There is a meeting of the Pantopragmatic Society, under the presidency of Lord Facing-both-ways. *Ibid.*, I wonder the Pantopragmatics have not a department of cookery. **1875** *Contemp. Rev.* XXV. 735 One or two of his contemporaries, whom he could never forbear satirizing as leaders of the Pantopragmatic and kindred movements. **1891** *Sat. Rev.* 4 July 4/1 He was beginning one of those curious pantopragmatic tours of his.

pantoscope ('pæntəskəʊp). Also *erron.* **panta-.** [f. Gr. παντο-, PANTO- all + -SCOPE.]

1. A form of photographic lens having a very wide angle.

1875 tr. *Vogel's Chem. Light* xii. 124 Lenses have been made with a very large field of view. They are called pantoscopes. **1889** E. J. WALL *Dict. Photogr.* 105 In 1860 Harrison, of New York, introduced his globe lens..Busch improved upon this with the pantoscope.

fig. **1894** E. H. AITKEN *Naturalist on Prowl* 129 It grows more wonderful under the pantoscope of modern science.

2. A panoramic or pantoscopic camera.

1890 in *Cent. Dict.*

panto'scopic, *a.* Also *erron.* **panta-.** [f. as prec. + -IC.] Having a wide range of vision.

pantoscopic camera, a panoramic camera. ***pantoscopic spectacles***, those so constructed as to have different focal lengths in the upper and lower parts, the upper being for long distance vision, and the lower for short; bi-focal spectacles; also applied to spectacles so shaped that the wearer looks over them for longer, and through them for shorter distances.

1875 H. WALTON *Dis. Eye* 259 Spectacles made according to this principle have long been sold..under the name of pantoscopic. **1882** OGILVIE, *Pantascopic camera*, in *photog.* an instrument for taking panoramic views, including any angular extent up to 360°..by means of mechanism and clock-work. Very successful views of Swiss scenery have been taken by this instrument. **1893** *Photogr. Ann.* 292 Rotate the lens and film as..in the pantascopic camera.

pantosophy, rare synon. of PANSOPHY.

pantostomate (pæn'tɒstəmət), *a. Zool.* [f. Gr. παντο-, PANTO- all + στομα(τ-) mouth.] Having a body of which any part can be used for the absorption of food, as in *Amœba* and other protozoans; belonging to the class *Pantostomata* of Protozoa.

1895 in *Funk's Standard Dict.*

So **panto'stomatous** *a.* (in same sense); **'pantostome,** a member of the *Pantostomata.*

1880 W. SAVILLE KENT *Infusoria* I. 40 It needs only the withdrawal of the radiating pseudopodia, with the retention of the flagellum, to produce the Pantostomatous Flagellate genus *Oikomonas.* **1895** *Funk's Stand. Dict.*, Pantostome.

pantothenic (pæntəʊ'θɛnɪk), *a. Biochem.* [f. Gr. πάντοθεν from every side (f. παντο- PANTO-) + -IC.] ***pantothenic acid***: an oily, optically active carboxylic acid, $HOCH_2C(CH_3)_2CHOH \cdot CO \cdot NH(CH_2)_2COOH$, which is widely distributed in plant and animal tissues (mainly in combined form as coenzyme A), is essential for the growth of yeast and certain bacteria, and is a member of the vitamin B complex.

1933 R. J. WILLIAMS et al. in *Jrnl. Amer. Chem. Soc.* LV. 2925 We can safely regard the activity [in stimulating the growth of yeast] as due to a single acid. Since this acid appears to be of very widespread occurrence..we have tentatively called it 'pantothenic' acid. **1953** J. RAMSBOTTOM *Mushrooms & Toadstools* viii. 82 Some strains of *Saccharomyces cerevisiae* require inositol, biotin, aneurin, pantothenic acid and other factors. **1960** *Times* 2 July 2/6 Certain..vitamins [in royal jelly]..are almost entirely members of the B-complex, and include an unusually high proportion of pantothenic acid. **1974** PASSMORE & ROBSON *Compan. Med. Stud.* III. 1. xxiv. 30/1 Pantothenic acid deficiency has been considered, on the basis of therapeutic trials, to be the cause of the burning feet syndrome.

Hence **panto'thenate,** the anion, or an ester or salt, of pantothenic acid.

1941 *Chem. Abstr.* XXXV. 3606 $[\alpha]_D^{25}$ for the pantothenate ion is calcd. to be −26·8°. **1955** *Sci. News Let.* 1 Oct. 211/1 The cancer cells, Dr. Eagle finds, need these seven vitamins: choline, folic acid, nicotinamide, pantothenate, pyridoxal, riboflavin and thiamine. **1974** R. W. DOSKOTCH in W. O. Foye *Princ. Med. Chem.* xxv. 613/2 The commercial synthesis of calcium pantothenate starts with isobutyraldehyde and formaldehyde.

pantotherian: see PANTO-.

pantothermal (pæntəʊ'θɜːməl), *a.* [f. PANTO- + THERMAL *a.*] Able to stand a wide range of temperature.

1906 *Athenæum* 10 Feb. 175/1 A revision of all captures..appeared to show one species..as cosmopolitan and pantothermal.

†**pantotype** ('pæntətaɪp). *Obs.* [f. PANTO- + TYPE.] A universal type.

1644 BULWER *Chirol.* A ij, In Nature's Hieroglyphique grasp'd, the grand And expresse Pantotype of Speech, the Hand.

pantoum, a French spelling of PANTUN.

pantoyl ('pæntɔɪl, 'pæntəʊaɪl). *Biochem.* [f. PANTO(THENIC *a.* + -YL.] The optically active radical $HOCH_2C(CH_3)_2CH(OH)CO-$, present in pantothenic acid.

1942 BARNETT & ROBINSON in *Biochem. Jrnl.* XXXVI. 357 Dr. McIlwain..suggested a simplified nomenclature, following which we have adopted a system based on the name 'pantoyl' for the α:γ-dihydroxy-β:β-dimethyl-γ-butyryl radicle. **1971** *Analytical Biochem.* XLII. 8 Pantoyl lactone, the other product of hydrolysis of pantothenates, can be easily and directly evaluated by gas chromatography, providing a simpler method for the quantitation of Vitamin B_5.

Hence **pantoyl'taurine,** a sulphonic acid, $C_8H_{17}O_6NS$, which inhibits the action of pantothenic acid in microorganisms.

1942 *Biochem. Jrnl.* XXXVI. 366 The degree of inhibition by pantoyltaurine depends on the amount of pantothenic acid present in the medium. **1954** E. E. SNELL in Sebrell & Harris *Vitamins* II. ix. 680 Addition of pantoyltaurine increased the lag phase and decreased the rate of growth during the first half of the logarithmic phase of *Streptococcus hemolyticus.* **1968** *Compar. Biochem. & Physiol.* XXVII. 649 When pantoyltaurine, an analogue of pantothenic acid, was incorporated into the culture media, inhibition of growth [of *Trypanosoma lewisi*] was observed.

pantrer, obs. form of PANTERER.

pantry ('pæntrɪ), *sb.* Forms: α. 3–5 **panetrie**, 5 **panetre**; β. 5–6 **pantrye**, 5–7 **-trie**, 5– **pantry**, (4–6 **panterie**, 5 **pantre**, 6 **pan-**, **paintree**, 8 **pantrey**). [a. AF. *panetrie* = OF. *paneterie* bread-room, bread-closet (1392 in Godef.), in med.L. *pāna-*, *pānetāria*, *-teria*, It. *panetaria* bread-shop, stall, f. med.L. *pānetārius*, F. *panetier*: see PANTER[1].

In Eng. the sense has been from an early period gradually extended and transferred, until that of 'bread-room' is now practically lost sight of: cf. quots. 1706 and 1768.]

1. a. A room or apartment in a house, etc., in which bread and other provisions are kept; also (*butler's* or *housemaid's pantry*), one in which the plate, linen, etc. for the table are kept (see BUTLER *sb.* 3).

a **1300** *Marina* 82 in Horstm. *Altengl. Leg.* (1878) 172 þe abbot & þe couent bo.. maden him maister of panetrie. *c* **1330** R. BRUNNE *Chron.* (1810) 33 Whilom he serued in his panterie, & was outlawed for a felonie. **1438** *E.E. Wills* (1882) 110 To the officers of my said lords hall, pantrie, Seler, Boterie. *c* **1450** *Bk. Curtasye* 499 in *Babees Bk.* 315 þen to pantré he hyȝes be-lyue. **1541** *Act 33 Hen. VIII*, c. 12 §9 The sergeant of the pantrie.. shall.. giue bread to the partie, that shal haue his hande so striken of. **1572** *Inv. Skipton Castle* in Whitaker *Craven* (1805) 290 In the Kytchine, West Larder, Paintree. **1660** JER. TAYLOR *Worthy Commun.* i. §1. 28 In the cupboords or Pantries where bread or flesh is laid. **1706** PHILLIPS, *Pantry*, a Room or Closet where Bread and cold Meat is kept. **1768** GOLDSM. *Good-n. Man* II. i, Him that I caught stealing your plate in the pantry. **1822** SCOTT *Pirate* iv, The cookmaid.. indemnified him for his privations by giving him private entrée to the pantry. **1900** *Plan Ocean Passenger-steamship*, Pantry.. Saloon pantries.

fig. **1432-50** tr. *Higden* (Rolls) I. 77 Paradise.. is the pantre or place of alle pulcritude [*universæ pulcritudinis erat promptuarium*]. *Ibid.* 273 The cite callede Parisius.. the pantry of letters [*pincerna litterarum*]. **1662** GURNALL *Chr. in Arm.* III. xxix. (1669) 377/1 God.. carried the key of their Pantry for them.

b. Used in the names of tea rooms and cafés.

1948 J. BETJEMAN *Sel. Poems* 79 The shops.. on the Esplanade—The Circulating Library, the Stores, Jill's Pantry. **1958** J. CANNAN *And be a Villain* i. 16 Pam's Pantry started to serve tea at three-thirty. **1967** M. KENYON *Whole Hog* xvii. 169 They agreed on the Pancake Pantry.. Liz said the pancakes were good. **1971** S. PHILLIPS *Death in Sheep's Clothing* iv. 36 A teashop known as *Pam's Pantry*.. with fresh chintz curtains, flowers on each tiny oak table, and a lot of unidentifiable brass objects hanging from the beams.

2. *attrib.* and *Comb.*, as *pantry* †*coffin*, *-door*, *-knife*, *-linen*, *-window*, *work*; **pantry-boy**, an assistant in the commissariat department on board a passenger ship; **pantry-cock**, a faucet with upward-rising pipe, which curves semicircularly and discharges downward (Funk); **pantry-fly** (see quot.); **pantry-maid**, a maidservant who has duties in the pantry.

1897 *Daily News* 16 June 2/3 *Pantry boy.. on board the British ship Illovo, of London. **1611** in *Coryat's Crudities* Panegr. Verses l j b *note*, A *pantrie coffin made of paste. **1721** RAMSAY *Prospect of Plenty* 113 May she not open her ain *pantry-door. **1822-34** *Good's Study Med.* (ed. 4) I. 278 These deposit their eggs in game and other meats that have been long kept.. as *musca carnaria*, or flesh-fly;.. *m. citaria* or *pantry-fly. **1465** *Paston Lett.* III. 435 Item.. ij. *pantre knyves, a pyce of sylver. **1921** *Dict. Occup. Terms* (1927) §900 **Pantry maid*.. washes china and glass and cleans up in pantry. **1928** *Daily Tel.* 5 June 4/7 He had paid her 22s a week as a pantrymaid. **1892** E. REEVES *Homeward Bound* 127 Greater *pantry-window and other similar convenience. **1973** *Courier & Advertiser* (Dundee) 12 Jan. 1/3 (Advt.), Part-Time woman required for general cleaning and *pantry work in hotel.

Hence †**pantry** *v. Obs.*, to keep in a pantry.

1637 RUTHERFORD *Lett., to D. Dickson* 3 Mar. (1671) 189 Christ wil not pantry-up joyes.

'pantryman. A man in charge of or employed in the pantry (or in the commissariat department of a passenger ship); a butler or his help.

1563-7 BUCHANAN *Reform. St. Andros* Wks. (1892) 6 The Cuik, The Portar, The Stewart, The Pantriman. **1849** JAMES *Woodman* xxv, The pantry-men cleaned out the cups. **1891** *Daily News* 9 Nov. 7/2 Prisoner had been in the employ of the Savoy Hotel Company as pantryman, and after he had left in June a quantity of plate was missed.

pants (pænts), *sb. pl.* orig. *U.S.* [Abbreviation of PANTALOONS.]

1. a. *orig.* = Pantaloons; subsequently used for trousers, worn by either men or women. Chiefly *U.S.* **b.** *orig.* colloquial and 'shoppy' for 'drawers'; now used for underpants, panties, or shorts worn as an outer garment: cf. *hot pants* (HOT *a.* 12 c).

1840 E. A. POE *Peter Pendulum* in *Burton's Gentleman's Mag.* Feb. 88 Standing on one leg three hours, to show off new-touch strapped pants. **1846** O. W. HOLMES *Rhymed Lesson* 515 The thing named 'pants' in certain documents, A word not made for gentlemen, but 'gents'. **1853** E. BRADLEY *Verdant Green* (1857) 22 Seated with wash-leather.. like the eleventh hussars.. with their cherry-coloured pants. **1880** *Daily News* 8 Nov. 2/7 Pants and shirts sell rather freely, and jerseys are still in request. **1884** *Philad. Even. Tel.* XLI. No. 8. 2 His assailant tore the pocket from his pants. **1893** A. S. ECCLES *Sciatica* 37 Cutting off from a pair of merino pants the leg corresponding to the sound and unaffected limb. **1928** R. CAMPBELL *Wayzgoose* ii. 58 Through pants and vest the God explored. **1930** H. G. WELLS *Autocracy of Mr. Parham* II. i. 95 He grows more and more independent of the idea that his pants are him. **1940** O. NASH *Face is Familiar* 91 Sure, deck your lower limbs in pants. **1951** T. STERLING *House without Door* xiii. 152 She chose her blue underwear... She laid the pants and brassière on her bed. **1956** H. GOLD *Man who was not with It* (1965) i. 5 Grack.. plucked a tricksie in shorts as she wiggled by. He took the thin pants between his horny fingers. **1964, 1968** [see *pantskirt* s.v. PANT *sb.*³ 2]. **1971** *New Yorker* 11 Sept. 12/1 (Advt.), The back-zippered tunic is a great topper for skirts and pants. **1973** N. MOSS *What's the Difference?* p. ix, I heard an American student at Cambridge University telling some English friends how he climbed over a locked gate to get into his college and tore his pants, and one of them asked in confusion, 'But how could you tear your pants without tearing your trousers?' **1976** *National Observer* (U.S.) 20 Nov. 13/2 The men in flannel hillside shirts and work pants stood in the driveway outside the hillside house and talked about Vivien Kellems.

c. Slang phr. *to be caught with one's pants down*: in a state of embarrassing unpreparedness. orig. *U.S.*

1932 *Amer. Speech* VII. 330 To be caught with one's pants down, to be caught off guard. **1943** N. BALCHIN *Small Back Room* xiv. 164 We just let him carry on alone. Now, we're caught with our pants down, with nobody knowing anything about the damned thing. **1959** *Times Lit. Suppl.* 10 July 407/2 Here were the 'better elements' caught with their pants down, as Americans coarsely put it. **1963** P. MCCUTCHAN *Man from Moscow* iii. 36 There was.. four days to go before the arrival of the Foreign Ministers but the West was not going to be caught with its pants down. **1974** 'M. INNES' *Appleby's Other Story* xvi. 133 He overheard Maurice Tytherton, in a great fury, say something to his nephew about having caught him with his pants down. **1976** N. THORNBURG *Cutter & Bone* v. 129 His record.. did not amount to much more than indiscretion, an embarrassing talent for getting caught with his pants down.

d. Slang phr. *to bore* (or *scare, talk*, etc.) *the pants off* (someone): to bring about (the action of the verb) to a state of extremity.

1933 E. O'NEILL *Ah, Wilderness!* I. 38, I tell you you scared the pants off him. **1934** E. WAUGH *Handful of Dust* iii. 133 She bores my pants off, but she's a good trier. **1937** N. COWARD *Present Indicative* IV. 164 Even if I had known then how much time and ink he [*sc.* a critic] was going to waste in the future roasting the pants off me, I [etc.]. **1939** E. B. WHITE *Quo Vadimus?* II. 65 And if I *did* have a butler named Fish, wouldn't I kid the pants off him? **1940** O. NASH *Face is Familiar* 74 And that Mrs Comfitmonger while pounding her beat has dealt with personalities who would scare the pants off Lombroso. **1953** H. CLEVELY *Public Enemy* i. 2 'Did you win?' 'We took the pants right off them.' **1956** B. HOLIDAY *Lady sings Blues* (1973) i. 6 Once a girl hit me on the nose and it just about finished me. I took my gloves off and beat the pants off her. **1966** R. ELLISON in A. Chapman *New Black Voices* (1972) 402 Where does that idea come from?.. One place (which almost frightened the pants off me) was in *Commentary*. **1968** M. WOODHOUSE *Rock Baby* vi. 51 He.. told me there was an international athletics meeting at White City.. and that Denmark would undoubtedly thrash the pants off us. **1972** G. BROMLEY *In Absence of Body* ix. 119 Usually they take the pants off us, which is not surprising—they play regularly and it's our only game. **1975** 'W. HAGGARD' *Scorpion's Tale* ii. 23 There's some stupid story the island is haunted.. there's something which scares the pants off the local peasantry.

e. In other phrases: *to wear the pants*: to be the dominant member of a household; *to keep one's pants on*: to keep calm, not to panic or get angry; (*by*) *the seat of one's pants*: in the handling of an aeroplane, car, etc.: (by) human instinct or experience, as opposed to technical aid or scientific knowledge. Also in extended uses and with hyphens (*seat-of-the-pants*) as adj. phr.

1931 *Amer. Mercury* Nov. 331/1 He claimed that Peggy was bossy, that she wore the pants and gave orders to Pal. **1936** J. STEINBECK *In Dubious Battle* vi. 83 'I wish it would start,' Jim said... 'Keep your pants on,' said Mac. **1942** *Harper's Mag.* May 626/2 When you check your instruments you find it is doing a correct job of flying and that the seat of your pants and your eyes would have tricked you had you been allowed to do the 'co-ordinating'. **1947** *Richmond* (Virginia) *Times-Dispatch* 26 Dec. 2/3 Even expert flyers can't tell by the feeling in 'the seat of their pants' when a airplane is about to stall. **1957** L. P. HARTLEY *Hireling* x. 77 She's older than he is and she wears the pants. **1958** *Listener* 20 Nov. 835/3 That's no help to the man who's driving by the seat of his pants, as we used to say in the R.A.F. police. **1965** R. SHECKLEY *Game of X* (1966) xxi. 146 Flying *was* in fact extremely difficult, but.. I was just one of those seat-of-the-pants naturals who instinctively do everything right. **1971** *Sunday Nation* (Nairobi) 11 Apr. 29/1 The type of car which I have just put through one of my seat-of-the-pants road tests—the Alfa-Romeo 1300 GT Junior. **1972** *Times* 18 Sept. 20/4 There was a feeling among the workforce that the firm was being run 'by the seat of the pants'. **1973** E. BULLINS *Theme is Blackness* 68 [Mother] Now, put it some place where they'll be safe.. understand? Safe! [Daddy] Okay.. okay.. Matilda.. just keep your pants on, will ya? **1977** M. WALKER *National Front* i. 17 Mussolini had governed by the seat of his pants, guided in part by his early Socialism, in part by his.. bombastic nationalism and above all.. by his flair for presentation and publicity. **1978** R. JANSSON *News Caper* viii. 85 Thackray was not looking at the instruments... Perhaps that was what they meant by flying by the seat of the pants.

2. A colloquial abbreviation of PANTALETTES.

1851 *Washington Telegraph* (U.S.) in *Illustr. Lond. News* 19 July 86/1 Garments as graceful and becoming as are the 'frock and pants'. [Bloomer costume.]

3. *attrib.* and *Comb.*, as *pants pocket*; **pants dress**, a dress with a divided skirt; **pants rabbit** *U.S. slang* (chiefly *Mil.*), a body louse; **pants skirt** = *pantskirt* s.v. PANT *sb.*³ 2; **pants suit** = *pant suit, trouser suit.*

1964 *Women's Wear Daily* 30 Nov. 4 Catherine Deneuve ordered at Heim a pantsdress in multicolored striped chiffon. **1969** *Sears Catal.* Spring/Summer 32 Floral print especially smart in this pants dress because it's done in navy and white. **1931** E. O'NEILL *The Hunted* IV, in *Mourning becomes Electra* (1932) 170 He fumbles in his pants pocket. **1951** T. STERLING *House without Door* vi. 78 He walked down the stairs, struggling for change in his pants pocket. **1974** R. B. PARKER *Godwulf Manuscript* xii. 99, I took a jackknife out of my pants pocket. **1918** *Nat. Geogr. Mag.* June 499 They call the things 'pants rabbits' and 'seam squirrels'. **1928** W. H. UPSON *Me & Henry & Artillery* 11 Some of the wise crackers in the battery used to call them pants-rabbits, which is not real scientific, as they usually roam around your back and shoulders and seldom hit below the belt. **1937** J. STEINBECK *Of Mice & Men* ii. 36 What the hell kind of bed you giving us, anyways? We don't want no pants rabbits. **1964** *Glamour* July 77 A blouse that looks like challis edged in wool lace, with a wine-dark leather pants-skirt. **1969** *Sears Catal.* Spring/Summer 34 Plaid pants skirt. Twill. Front panel hides plaid culotte. **1964** *Glamour* Dec. 112, 1 and 2 [*sc.* jacket and pants] make a pants-suit that's very current and handsome. **1968** MRS. L. B. JOHNSON *White House Diary* 26 June (1970) 691, I changed into a beige pants suit. **1975** *New Yorker* 5 May 81/3 Elizabeth Franz.. looked fine in a becoming pants suit.

pantuffle, -ufle, obs. forms of PANTOFLE.

‖**pantun** (pæn'tuːn). Also **pantoum**. [Malay *pantun*; in Fr. misspelt *pantoum* for *pantoun* (Devic in Littré *Suppl.*).] A verse-form in Malay (see quot. 1883), also imitated in French and English. Also *attrib.*

1783 W. MARSDEN *Hist. Sumatra* 162 The essentials in the composition of the *pantoon*.. are the rythmus and the figure, particularly the latter, which they consider as the life and spirit of the poetry. **1821** J. LEYDEN tr. *Malay Annals* 83 They sing of it in Pantuns. *Ibid.* 259 There came a Pantun poet, who was famous for his skill in horsemanship. **1883** *Encycl. Brit.* XV. 326 The *pantuns* are improvised poems, generally of four lines, in which the first and third and the second and fourth rhyme. The meaning intended to be conveyed is expressed in the second couplet, whereas the first contains a simile or distant allusion to the second, or often has, beyond the rhyme, no connexion with the second at all. **1887** *Sat. Rev.* 3 Dec. 770 Among the verse-forms that are little used we must notice as new to us the droll and clever pantoum 'En Route'. **1897** *Daily News* 2 Aug. 4/6 Very few people know what a Pantoum is; it.. is a Malay form of verse patented by Mr. Austin Dobson. **1964** M. TAIB BIN OSMAN in Wang Gung-Wu *Malaysia* III. xv. 211 The *pantun* can be considered as folk-ditty; it is used on almost all occasions in Malay life. **1970** *New Yorker* 14 Nov. 58/1 She drafted three poems—another rondeau, a pantoum, and a cynghanedd. **1975** 'G. BLACK' *Big Wind* x. 183 She was singing a Malay *pantun*, a verse form tending to the obscene.

panty, see PANTIES *sb. pl.*

†**pantyr.** *Obs. rare.* [Shortened form of *pantré*, PANTRY, or a. OF. *panetière*.] = PANTRY.

c **1475** *Pict. Voc.* in Wr.-Wülcker 803/30 (Nomina domorum), *Hec panatria*, a pantyr.

pantyr, obs. form of PANTER[1] and [2].

‖**panung** ('pɑːnʊŋ). [Thai.] A Siamese garment, worn by men and women, consisting of a long piece of cloth draped round the lower part of the body.

1857 J. BOWRING *Kingdom & People of Siam* I. 132 Of the garments worn by the Siamese, the *panung*.. is worn round the waist and thighs. **1886** *Pall Mall Gaz.* 3 Aug. 4/1 Two men dressed in their ordinary garb—only a dark blue 'panung' about their loins (all Siamese wear the panung). **1928** *Daily Express* 13 Mar. 12/2 The Eton crop in Bangkok is as old as the 'panung'—that peculiar garment worn by men and women alike, which resembles a cross between a 'sarong' and a baby's napkin. **1958** *Listener* 18 Dec. 1039/3 Siamese girls.. wear their traditional *panung*, or slim skirt folded in front adapted from their own *pasin*.

panurgic (pæ'nɜːdʒɪk), *a. rare.* [ad. late Gr. πανουργικός knavish, f. πανοῦργος ready to do anything, knavish, f. παν- all + ἔργον work.] Able or ready to do anything.

1873 MORLEY *Rousseau* I. 291 Rousseau bade.. the panurgic one to attend to his own affairs. **1878** —— *Diderot* II. xvii. 279 No less panurgic and less encyclopædic a critic than Diderot himself could [etc.].

†'**panurgy.** *Obs. rare*⁻⁰. [ad. Gr. πανουργία knavery, f. πανοῦργ-ος: see prec.] (See quot.)

1656 BLOUNT *Glossogr.*, *Panurgy*,.. craftiness, subtilty, deceit; guile; a medling in all matters. (So in PHILLIPS, BAILEY, etc. Not in JOHNSON.)

panurine (pæ'njʊəraɪn), *a. Ornith.* [f. mod.L. *panūr-us* (f. Gr. πᾶν all (see PAN-) + οὐρά tail) + -INE[1].] Pertaining or allied to the genus *Panurus* or Bearded Titmouse. So **pa'nuroid** *a.*

1890 in *Cent. Dict.*

pany, panyme: see PAYENY, PAYNIM.

‖**panyar** (pə'njɑː(r)) *v. W. Africa.* [ad. Pg. *penhorar* to distrain, seize as a pledge or security (cf. *penhor* pawn):—L. *pignorāre*, *-erāre* to pledge, in med.L. to take in pledge, to plunder, invade an enemy's lands (Du Cange).] *trans.* To seize as a guarantee or security; hence, a euphemism for To seize as plunder, to raid, steal, esp. to kidnap (natives as slaves).

1735 J. ATKINS *Guinea* 53 Panyarring is a term for man-stealing along the whole coast; here it's used also, for stealing anything else. **1744** W. SMITH *Voy. Guinea* 99 To panyar is to kidnap, or steal men. **1853** CRUICKSHANK *18 Yrs. on Gold Coast* I. ii. 35 The words palaver and panyar.. are in very frequent use upon the Gold Coast... The latter is used to express the forcible seizure of a person or property, to obtain redress or restitution. *Ibid.* v. 98 He threw the guns over the batteries, and released a number of Cape Coast prisoners, who had been panyarred by the Dutch at Appam.

panyar, -yard, -yer(e, -yerd, -yȝer, -yell, obs. ff. PANNIER.

panyon, var. PANION, *Obs.*

panzer ('pænzə(r), ‖'pantsər). [G., 'mail, coat of mail'.] Used *attrib.*, of or pertaining to a German armoured unit; also in G. form *panzerdivision*. As *sb.*, a panzer unit or a member of such a unit. Also *transf.* and *fig.*

1940 *Economist* 20 Apr. 729/1 It is more than silly..to calculate the speed at which Germany's *panzerdivisionen* could traverse the Hungarian plain. **1940** *Topeka* (Kansas) *Daily Capital* 24 June 1 b Delegations deploying to stop Willkie's 'panzer' wire attacks. **1941** *Hutchinson's Pict. Hist. War* 19 Mar.-13 May 189 An Imperial division concentrated round Bengazi was left in the air when the German Panzer inrush swept aside the British armoured brigade. **1942** *R.A.F. Jrnl.* 3 Oct. 5 You were in danger of breaking your leg by falling over a complete panzer division of dachshunds moving from bar to shove ha'penny table on a broad front. **1943** E. J. PRATT *Coll. Poems* (1958) I. 82 And what specific can unmesh The tangle of civilian flesh From the traction of the panzers? **1945** KOESTLER *Yogi & Commissar* III. iv. 250 Geniuses are panzer-spearheads. **1949** —— *Promise & Fulfilment* II. iii. 234 Just after Glubb's panzers had begun the shelling of the Jewish quarter. **1962** *Listener* 28 June 1117/1 German Panzer troops arriving in Wales last week. *a* **1963** S. PLATH *Ariel* (1965) 55, I have always been scared of *you*, with your Luftwaffe..your Aryan eye, bright blue Panzer-man, panzer-man, O You. **1965** *New Statesman* 14 May 759/1 They tried to defend the Book of Genesis against Darwin's *panzers*. **1969** G. MACBETH *War Quartet* 74 Each panzer was a coiled spring, oiled For instant action. **1973** R. LEWIS *Blood Money* iii. 30 He served in North Africa during the Second World War in the Panzer Corps. **1975** *Times* 24 June 4/7 Three new brigades have been addd to the West German army... The number of tanks in a Panzer battalion is being reduced. **1976** A. WHITE *Long Silence* ix. 83 A lean panzer major walked from the other half track.

panzoism, panzoötic, -ty: see PAN- 2.

‖**pao-chia** (baodʒiɑː). Also **pao chia, paochia.** [Chinese *bǎojia*.] In China, a system by which households were organized for the purposes of administration. Also *attrib.*

1937 E. SNOW *Red Star over China* II. i. 50 The *pao-chia* system, an ancient method of controlling the peasantry..is now being widely imposed..by the Kuomintang in China and the Japanese in Manchukuo. *Pao-chia* literally means 'guaranteed armour'. **1959** C. K. YANG *Chinese Village in Early Communist Transition* vii. 103 To increase the effectiveness of governing such a large population..there had developed the system of collective responsibility, or *pao chia*, rooted far back in Chinese history, especially in the 'new policy' of the Sung prime minister Wang An-shih. **1965** J. CH'ÊN *Mao & Chinese Revolution* (1967) I. xi. 246 In the 'orderly' areas, they used the age-old system of collective responsibility known as the *pao-chia*—every 100 families were organized into a *chia* and every 1,000 families into a *pao* in which all members were made responsible for each other's actions. **1973** T. R. TREGEAR *Chinese* iii. 68 Law and order are maintained very largely through a modification of the old *pao chia* system by which every group of ten households was held responsible for the behaviour of its own members.

‖**paolo** ('paolo, 'paʊləʊ). [It. *Paolo*:—L. *Paulus* Paul: see quot. 1617.] An obsolete Italian silver coin, worth about fivepence sterling.

1617 MORYSON *Itin.* I. 99 Each man payed foure Poli, or Poali (a coine so called of Pope Paul). *Ibid.* 118 We..gaue a Clowne one Poalo for conducting vs. **1756-7** tr. *Keysler's Trav.* (1760) II. 141 Manuscript pasquinades..sold in the coffee-houses for half a paolo a sheet. **1805** M. G. LEWIS *Bravo of Venice* I. i. 3 No, not one paolo, by heavens! and I hunger almost to death! **1837** MARRYAT *Dog-fiend* xxxiii, Five hundred thousand paolis, amounting to about thirteen thousand pounds in sterling money.

‖**pao-tzu** (baodzɜː). Also **bao zi.** [Chinese *bāozi*.] A steamed roll with savoury or sweet fillings.

1956 B. Y. CHAO *How to cook & eat in Chinese* II. xx. 228 When *man-t'ou*, or Steamed Bread, is filled with stuffing, then it is *pao-tzŭ*. **1972** K. LO *Chinese Food* I. 61 The miniature *pao-tzu* (steamed buns with various fillings) are sometimes steamed first and finally fried until they are crisp, and served as crispy savouries. *Ibid.* III. 233 *Pao-tzu* are meant to be eaten on their own, like hot sandwiches. **1973** T. R. TREGEAR *Chinese* iv. 93 The staple diet is boiled millet or kaoliang, *pao tzu* (steamed bread), *tu fu* (bean curd) and vegetables. **1978** *Nagel's Encycl.-Guide: China* 376 The same variety of preparation is to be found in the different sorts of *bao zi*, or rolls stuffed with vegetables and meat (*cai rou bao zi*), or meat alone (*tian jin bao zi*).

pap (pæp), *sb.*[1] Forms: 3-7 **pappe**, 4-6 **papp**, 4-7 (chiefly *Sc.*) **pape**, (*Sc.* 5-6 **palp**, 6 **paup, pawp**), 4- **pap.** [ME. *pappe*, in northern and north-midl. writings, and app. from Scandinavian. Not recorded in ON. or MSw., but *pappe*, *papp* is widely diffused in Sw. dialects (Rietz); also ENorw. dial. *pappe*, North Fris. *pap*, *pape*, and dim. *papke* (Outzen) all in sense 'nipple, teat, breast giving suck'; cf. Lith. *pāpas* in same sense. Supposed, like the next, to have its origin in the sound made by an infant in opening and shutting the lips, as associated with the notion of food.]

1. A teat or nipple: **a.** of a woman's breast (now *arch.* or *northern*); **b.** a teat of a beast (chiefly *northern*); **c.** the corresponding part of a man, the mamilla (chiefly *literary*, somewhat *arch.*).

a. *c* **1200** ORMIN 6441 þatt fedd himm wiþþ þatt illke millc þatt comm off hire pappe. *a* **1225** *Ancr. R.* 330 Bi þeo tittes [*MS. T.* pappes] þet he sec þe milc þet hine uedde. *a* **1300** *Cursor M.* 16659 Blisced..þe papp þat neuer suken was. **1340** HAMPOLE *Pr. Consc.* 6767 Als a childe þat sittes in þe moder lappe And when it list, soukes hir pappe. **1398** TREVISA *Barth. De P.R.* v. xxxiv. (1495) i vj b/2 The pappes is a nedfull membre to fede and nourysshe the chylde. **1509** HAWES *Past. Pleas.* xxx. (Percy Soc.) 146 Her pappes round & therto right prety. **1513** DOUGLAS *Æneis* I. Prol. 474 The sweit liquare of thi palpis quhite. **1526** TINDALE *Luke* xi. 27 The pappes [so **1611**; WYCLIF teetis; *R.V.* breasts] which gave the sucke. **1552** LYNDESAY *Monarche* 4009 The barren paupis, than thay sall blys. **1600** J. PORY tr. *Leo's Africa* Introd. 33 These women..seare off their left paps, that they might not be an hinderance vnto them in their shooting. **1621** BURTON *Anat. Mel.* I. ii. I. iii. (1651) 56, I have seen those that..dryed up womens Paps, cured Gout, Palsie: by touch alone. **1669-70** DRYDEN *Tyrannic Love* v. i, Her paps then let the bearded tenters stake. **1701** RAY *Creation* (ed. 3) II. 236. [Now in ordinary use in Sc. and North Eng. to Lancash. and Lincolnsh.]

b. 1634 SIR T. HERBERT *Trav.* 212 The Mannatee or Cowfish..creepes vpon her paps. **1759** BROWN *Compl. Farmer* 49 She had as many teats or paps as pigs. **1774** GOLDSM. *Nat. Hist.* (1776) II. 299 The distinctions of quadrupedes, or animals with paps, as he [Buffon] calls them. *Mod.* (*north.* and *north midl.*) A cow's paps.

c. *c* **1440** *York Myst.* xl. 103 Inne with a spere-poynte atte þe pappe To the harte full thraly he throste hym. **1526** TINDALE *Rev.* i. 13 One lyke vnto the sonne of man..gyrd aboute the pappes [so **1611**; WYCLIF teetis; *R.V.* at the breasts] with a golden gyrdle. *c* **1611** CHAPMAN *Iliad* IV. 517 He strook him at his breast's right pap. **1712** ARBUTHNOT *John Bull* III. App. i, Whether the said Timothy Trim and Jack were the same person? which was proved..by a mole under the left pap. **1870** BRYANT *Iliad* II. xv. 103 Beneath the pap, it smote him as he came.

2. *transf.* Something resembling a pap in form. **a.** A small round tumour or swelling; a pimple. *pap of the hause* (Sc.: see HALSE *sb.*[2]): the uvula.

1552 HULOET, Pappe or pyle in the fundment of a man *Annates*. **1639** T. DE GREY *Compl. Horsem.* 217 This whay is also good to cure..barbs, pappes, and all fevers. **1774** GOLDSM. *Nat. Hist.* (1776) IV. 109 After the skin [of the porcupine] is taken off, there appear a kind of paps on those parts of the body from whence the large quills proceed. **1898** N. MUNRO *J. Splendid* xxix, Just a tickling at the pap o' the hass, he said in English.

b. *pl.* Formerly, a name for two (or more) conical hill summits, rising side by side; still retained in local nomenclature.

1632 LITHGOW *Trav.* III. 123 The length of Troy hath been..fifteene English miles; lying along the sea side betweene the three Papes of Ida. **1703** MARTIN *Western Isl.* 231 There are four Hills of a considerable heighth; the two highest are well known to Sea-faring Men, by the Name of the Paps of Jurah. **1745** P. THOMAS *Jrnl. Anson's Voy.* 104 There being two Mountains appearing like Paps..those they told us were the Paps over that Harbour. **1748** *Anson's Voy.* II. ix. 228 We observed two remarkable hummocks, such as are usually called paps. **1774** PENNANT *Voy. Hebrides* 217 The other paps are seen very distinctly; each inferior in height to this, but all of the same figure, perfectly mamillary. **1873** BLACK *Pr. Thule* xxv, The great 'Paps of Jura' were hidden in the mist.

3. *attrib.* and *Comb.*, as †**pap-bone** (app.) a name for each of the pair of ribs beneath the paps; †**pap-head**, the nipple; **pap-pox**, a name for cow-pox; **pap-shell**, a name for the limpet.

1581 MULCASTER *Positions* xiv. (1887) 65 This kind of laughing..oftimes therewith both the *papbones be loosed. **1530** PALSGR. 251/2 *Pappeheed, *bout de la mamelle*. **1610** MARKHAM *Masterp.* II. clix. 469 In the searing you shall see the ends of the veines start out like pape heads. **1889** *Lancet* 9 Mar. 503/2 A possible origin of the term Cow-pox or *Pap-pox. **1842** JOHNSTON in *Proc. Berw. Nat. Club* II. No. 10. 36 The Limpet..shell is often used to apply Fuller's earth, and similar remedies, to the sore nipples of nurses; hence probably the origin of '*Pap-shell', which Lister tells us is one of its English names. **1615** CROOKE *Body of Man* 157 The Mammarie or *Pap-veines and Arteries.

pap (pæp), *sb.*[2] Forms: 5 **papp**, 5-7 **pape**, 6 **pappe**, (*Sc.* **paup**), 5- **pap.** [Known from 15th c. Corresponds to MLG., LG. *pappe*, MG. *pappe*, *pap*, Ger. *pappe*, *papp*, Du. *pap* (1573 Plantijn). Cf. also OF. *papa* (13th c. in Godef.), Walloon *pape*, Sp., Pg. *papa*, It. *pappa* 'pap for children, any kind of pap or water-grewell', *pappare* 'to feede with pap' (Florio), also L. *pāpa* (*pappa*) 'the word with which infants call for food', *pappāre* (*papāre*) to eat pap; med.L. *pappa* pap. As the word appears to originate (like PAP *sb.*[1]) in the early utterance of infants, it may have been formed independently in various langs.]

1. a. Soft or semi-liquid food for infants or invalids, made of bread, meal, etc., moistened with water or milk. Also *fig.*; *spec.* in *U.S.*, a political appointment or grant; patronage, 'graft'.

c **1430** *Voc.* in Wr.-Wülcker 600/22 *Papatum*, pap. **1530** PALSGR. 251/2 Pappe meate for chyldre, *boville*. *a* **1548** HALL *Chron.*, *Hen. VI* 89 Will you haue an Englishe infant, whiche liueth with pappe to bee your Kyng and gouernor? **1597-8** BP. HALL *Sat.* IV. ii. 33 Or water-grewell, or those paups of meale That Maro makes his Simule and Cybeale. **1688** R. HOLME *Armoury* III. 84/1 Pap, of Nurses called papes, is Milk and Flour boiled together. **1781** COWPER *Conversation* 480 Give it the breast, or stop its mouth with pap! **1896** *Allbutt's Syst. Med.* I. 392 To begin with milky arrowroot..then to pass on to boiled pap of breadcrumb and milk.

fig. **1548** UDALL *Erasm. Par.* Pref. 14 Pappe for yonglinges in the feith. *a* **1631** DONNE *Lett.*, *to Sir T. Lucey* (1651) 13 Many doctrines..have place in the pap of Catechismes. **1825** *Delaware* (Ohio) *Patron* 10 Feb. 3/2 An irresistible desire..to serve the state, and to taste a little of the 'Treasury Pap', impelled us towards the capital. **1826** SCOTT *Jrnl.* 14 Sept., No man that ever wrote a line despised the pap of praise so heartily as I do. **1841** *Congress. Globe* 26th Congress 2 Sess. App. 300/2 The very new States are nursed from their chrysalis territorial condition into existence upon Federal pap from the Executive spoon. **1862** in J. B. Ranck *Albert Gallatin Brown* (1937) 217 Young, strong men..were feeding on government pap whilst wounded soldiers..were in a state of positive want. **1894** *Voice* (N.Y.) 6 Sept. 1/6 The Prohibition Party is the only party that is not controlled by public pap-seeking politicians. **1894** H. GARDENER *Unoff. Patriot* 223 A self-indulgent moralist, who feeds expensive pap to his personal conscience, but gives a stone to his starving neighbor! **1965** *Chicago Schools Jrnl.* Feb. 197/2 Most of the new clientele will have little taste for or interest in traditional literary values. This does not mean that we should give them over to pap. **1976** *Sounds* 11 Dec. 34/2 To describe this record as 'maudlin pap' must be extremely hurtful to Bernie Taupin. His lyrics are the result of his own poignant experience of a broken marriage. **1977** *Lebende Sprachen* XXII. 10/2 The spoils of office, the rewards for political activities..are called sweets, fat, spices, pap (baby food), plum, pie, persimmon, melon, pork, grease, and gravy. **1977** *Rolling Stone* 21 Apr. 84/3 Spector retreated into an increasingly contrived world of sound, lavishing his skill and money on cutting..such soft-core pap as the Righteous Brothers 'Unchained Melody'.

†**b.** *pap with a hatchet*: an obs. ironical phrase.

This expression, says Park (in editing *Harl. Misc.* 1808), 'seems to have been a cant phrase for doing a kind thing in an unkind manner; as it would be so to feed an infant'. But the sense appears rather to be 'the administration of punishment under the ironical style of a kindness or benefit'. It was the title of an anonymous pamphlet in the Marprelate controversy attributed to John Lyly by Gabriel Harvey (*Pierce's Supererogation* 69), who also frequently styles the author *Papp-hatchet*.

1589 ? LYLY (*title*) Pappe with an Hatchet. **1589** G. HARVEY *Pierce's Super.* (1593) 69 Would God, Lilly had always been Euphues, and neuer Papp-hatchet; that old acquaintance [i.e. Harvey himself] is neither lullabied with thy sweete Papp, nor scarre-crowed with thy sower hatchet. **1592** —— *Foure Lett.* ii. Wks. (Grosart) I. 164, I neither name Martin-mar-prelate: nor shame Papp wyth a hatchet. **1594** LYLY *Moth. Bomb.* I. iii. 104 They give us pap with a spoone before we can speake, and when we speake for that wee love, pap with a hatchet. **1615** A. NICCHOLES *Disc. Marr.* ix. 30 He that so old seekes for a nurse so yong, shall haue pappe with a Hatchet for his comfort. **1719** D'URFEY *Pills* IV. 329 A Custard was to him Pap with a Hatchet.

2. a. Anything of the consistence of the preceding; a soft semi-liquid substance; a mash, paste, pulp (such as is made by mixing a powdery substance with water or some other liquid).

1435 MISYN *Fire of Love* 90 Flee we þerfor bodily and warldly lufe..qwos flowre is anoytt with gall, & þe pape of neddyrs. **1608** TOPSELL *Serpents* (1658) 776 Of the pap of barley and the broth of lupines make a cataplasm. **1678** EVELYN *Diary* 24 July, They cull the rags..then stamp them in troughs to a papp with pestles or hammers like the powder-mills. **1691** RAY *Creation* I. (1692) 139 An oily Pap or Liniment. **1839** URE *Dict. Arts* 1010 The clay..is conveyed into a cylindrical vat, to be worked into a pap with water.

†**b.** The pulp of an apple, esp. when roasted.

1594 PLAT *Jewell-ho.* II. 45 [To] be giuen in powder, in the pappe of an apple. **1633** HART *Diet of Diseased* III. xv. 287, I hold it not amisse to take Pills in the pap of a rosted apple. *a* **1691** BOYLE *Med. Exp.* i. 1 Let the Patient take it at Bed-time in the Pap of an Apple. **1761** STERNE *Tr. Shandy* III. xvi, A child's head is naturally as soft as the pap of an apple.

3. *Comb.*, as *pap-bottle*, *-devourer*, *-food*, *-maker*, *-meat*, *-pan*, *-spoon*; *pap-feed* vb. **pap-warmer**, formerly, a contrivance for keeping food or drink warm, usu. incorporating a night-lamp. See also PAP-BOAT.

1857 HUGHES *Tom Brown* II. ii, Put him in with plenty of cotton-wool and a *pap-bottle. **1841** THACKERAY *St. Philip's Day at Paris* Wks. 1900 XIII. 552 The fools..who have gratified the young *pap-devourer with the present of a fine sword. **1809** COBBETT *Pol. Reg.* XV. 872 This measure has been..nursed and dandled, rocked, swathed, and *pap-fed by..whom? **1905** *Daily Chron.* 13 May 4/5 Too prolonged use of artificially digested and '*pap-foods' must be avoided. **1590** NASHE *Pasquil's Apol.* I. Bij b, I warrant you the cunning *Pap-maker knewe what he did. *c* **1440** *Promp. Parv.* 382/1 *Papmete for chylder, *papatum*. **1869** TENNYSON *Pelleas & Ettarre* 188 Keep him off, And pamper him with papmeat, if ye will. **1458** *Will of Guybon* (Somerset Ho.), *Pappepanne. **1533** in Weaver *Wells Wills* (1890) 155 My best panne, my best cawdren, a pape panne. **1792** WOLCOTT (P. Pindar) *Odes to Kien Long* II. xxiv, His sacred *Pap-spoon, and the Virgin's Dish. **1841** EMERSON *Lect.*, *Conservative* Wks. II. 274 His social frame is..a universe in slippers and flannels, with bib and pap-spoon. **1920** W. J. POUNTNEY *Old Bristol Potteries* x. 141 Another most interesting piece..is a caudle cup or pap warmer. **1961** L. G. G. RAMSEY *Connoisseur New Guide Antique Eng. Pott., Porc. & Glass* 66 Food warmers, catalogued as pap-warmers, performed the duties of night-light shelter as well as keeping liquids warm enough to drink during the night. **1969** E. H. PINTO *Treen* 122 The majority of wooden night-light holders are combined with pap warmers.

pap (pæp), *sb.*[3] Abbreviation of PAPA[1]. Also applied to an older man. Chiefly *U.S.*

1844 *Knickerbocker* XXIII. 15 They said, pap wasn't at home. **1854** M. J. HOLMES *Tempest & Sunshine* v. 69 Come here, and shake your old pap's paw. **1886** C. M. YONGE *Chantry House* I. xxi. 207 She never took liberties with him, nor called him Pap or any other ridiculous name. **1899** A. NICHOLAS *Idyl of Wabash* 53 His pap left him right smart of a lump. **1924** W. M. RAINE *Troubled Waters* ii. 24 There can't any of you..run me out the way you did Pap Thomson. **1955** D. W. MAURER in *Publ. Amer. Dial. Soc.* XXIV. 105 A *pappy* (or *pap*) is an elderly man.

Pap (pæp), *sb.*[4] Also pap. Abbrev. of PAPANICOLAOU (used only *attrib.*).

1963 GREISHEIMER & TROYER *Physiol. & Anat.* (ed. 8) xx. 789 The so-called 'Pap' test is so named after Papanicolaou, who with Stockard called attention to the importance of the changes in the vaginal epithelium first in lower animals in connection with estrous cycles. **1969** *Awake!* 8 Nov. 15/1 A study conducted at the University of Chicago 'reportedly shows a sixfold increase in positive Pap smears.. among women who have taken oral contraceptives'. **1973** *Sci. Amer.* July 22/3 Of the estimated 2·6 million women served last year by organized family-planning programs,.. eight in 10 had annual breast examinations and Pap tests. **1973** *Nation* (Barbados) 16 Dec. 10/4 I'd like to see all of the women who should be having pap smears coaxed into their doctor's offices. **1977** *Spare Rib* May 20/4 Pap smear and breast cancer tests could have been lost.

pap, *v.*[1] [f. PAP *sb.*[2] Cf. It. *pappāre* to eat pap.] **1.** *trans.* To feed with pap; to feed *up*.

a **1616** BEAUM. & FL. *Custom of Country* IV. iv, Oh, that his body were not flesh, and fading! But I'll so pap him up—Nothing too dear for him. **1820** *Examiner* No. 657. 721/1 It had been.. swaddled, and papped, and called beautiful like its father. **1878** E. JENKINS *Haverholme* 97 The babies.. were taken in, and papped, and provided with toys and soothing syrups.

†**2.** To treat with pap; to apply a pap or pulp to.

1658 A. FOX *Wurtz' Surg.* I. viii. 34 Which moisture.. turnes into a water, as we see it in such wounds which are thus papp'd up.

3. To make into pap.

1927 *Observer* 6 Feb. 14/4 This does not mean papping food for babes; it means speaking intelligibly to grown-ups.

pap, *v.*[2] [Echoic.] *intr.* To make a noise of which *pap* is an imitation.

1837 THACKERAY *Ravenswing* ii, Big square-toed shoes with which he went papping down the street.

pap, Sc. dial. form of POP *v.*

papa[1] (pə'pɑː). Also 8 pappa. [a. F. *papa*, in 1552 *pappa* (Hatz.-Darm.) = It. *pappa* 'the first word that children are taught to call their Father by, as ours say Dad, Daddie, or Bab' (Florio 1598, 1611), L. *pāpa* father, papa; cf. Gr. πάππας, later πάπας 'a child's word for father'. From F. also Ger. *papa*, introduced in 17th c. as *papà*, and at first only in courtly use, passing into common use late in 18th c. In Eng. in 17th and early 18th c. the form varied between *pa'pā* and *'pappa*; from the latter the American *'poppa*.]

1. A word employed as the equivalent of *father*: chiefly used in the vocative, or prec. by a possess. pronoun (as 'my papa'); also without any article in the manner of a proper name (e.g. 'I will ask Papa'); less usually with *a* or in *plural*.

At its first introduction from Fr., courtly and polite, and used even by adults; long considered 'genteel'; but more and more left to children, and in second half of 19th c. largely abandoned even by them.

1681 OTWAY *Soldiers Fort.* I. (1683) 7 Oh Papa, Papa! where have you been this two days, Papa? **1709** MRS. MANLEY *Secret Mem.* I. 57 The Maid.. in her usual fawning Language calls him dear Papa [*ed.* **1720** Pappa]. **1720–1** *Lett. fr. Mist's Jrnl.* (1722) II. 74 Not her Husband, but her Pappa. **1731** SWIFT *Strephon & Chloe*, The bashful nymph no more withstands, Because her dear papa commands. **1765** FOOTE *Commissary* II. Wks. 1799 II. 26 The right honourable Peer that is to be my pappa.. has flatly renounc'd the alliance. **1782** MISS BURNEY *Cecilia* VI. v, May be he thinks it would not be pretty to be very frisky, now he's a papa. **1812** H. & J. SMITH *Rej. Addr., Baby's Debut* i, Papa (he's my papa and Jack's) Bought me, last week, a doll of wax, And brother Jack a top. *Ibid.* v, And while papa said, 'Pooh, she may!' Mamma said, 'No, she shan't!' *a* **1845** HOOD *Stage-Struck Hero* vii, Genteelly taught by his mamma To say, not father, but papa. **1862** THACKERAY *Philip* xxi, Papa-in-law was well enough, or at least inoffensive. **1887** RUSKIN *Præterita* II. vi. 186 How papa and mamma took this new vagary, I have no recollection.

2. *transf.* **a.** A woman's lover or husband. *U.S. slang.*

1904 'No. 1500' *Life in Sing Sing* 261, I blew out and rung in with a couple of penny-weighters. A Tommy and his papa... I left them and went with two expert thieves who make it a practice to rob jewelers, a woman and her lover. **1926** L. HUGHES in *New Republic* 14 Apr. 223/2, I met a yellow papa, He took my last thin dime... I give it to him cause I loved him But I'll have more sense next time. **1942** —— *Shakespeare in Harlem* 107 That's one time, pretty papa, You'll sure stay in your place. You was a mighty lover and you Ruled me many years. **1960** WENTWORTH & FLEXNER *Dict. Amer. Slang* 375 *Papa*, a male lover.

b. Phr. *tell papa*, confide in the speaker.

1929 E. WALLACE *Red Aces* v. 48 'Tell papa,' he said. **1961** A. CHRISTIE *Pale Horse* xvi. 166 'Come now, tell Papa', said the odious Bradley.

3. *attrib.* or as *adj.*, paternal.

1900 'S. GRAND' *Babs* (1901) lxxv. 350 So long as he does not assume papa airs with me, I don't mind.

‖**papa**[2] ('pɑːpə). *Obs.* [In sense 1, a. med.L. *pāpa*, ultimately a. Gr. πάππας, πάπας father, later παπᾶς: see prec. In sense 2, a. med.L. *pāpa* as translating πάππας, παπᾶς.

The Gr. and L. words (meaning 'Father') were, like the latter, and mod. Romanic *padre*, addressed or applied to spiritual fathers; in the West at first to bishops generally (as in Prudentius and Gregory of Tours), but gradually confined to the Bishop of Rome (see POPE); in the East, in the form παπᾶς, applied more widely, so as to include the lower clergy. In this sense also sometimes rendered in Eng. by 'pope'.]

1. The pope (of Rome).

[**1555** in *Hakluyt's Voy.* (1810) II. 476 Prester John whom some call Papa Johannes.] **1559** in Strype *Ann. Ref.* (1824) I. II. App. viii. 424 In what age the name of *papa* had his original. **1563** WINȜET *Four Scoir Thre Quest.* To Rdr., Wks. 1888 I. 59 The successour of Petir, now commonlie callit Papa: albeit Papa be a terme efter the myndis of the aunciant Fatheris commoun to ony bischope, as efter in this buik is schawin. **1588** *Marprel. Epist.* (Arb.) 19 Here lies Iohn Bridges late Bishop, friend to the *Papa*. **1813** MOORE *Post-bag* iv. App. 298, I made thee Cardinal—thou mad'st me—ah? Thou mad'st the Papa of the World—Mamma! **1851** BORROW *Lavengro* xlix. (1893) 193 Their spiritual authority had at various times been considerably undermined by the emissaries of the Papa of Rome, as the Armenian called him. **1861** STANLEY *East. Ch.* iii. (1869) 98.

2. A parish priest or any member of the lower orders of the clergy in the Orthodox Eastern Church. Also in Gr. form *papas*.

1591 G. FLETCHER *Russe Commw.* (Hakluyt Soc.) 111 Their priestes (whom they call *papaes*) are made by the bishops. **1679** SIR P. RICAUT *Pres. St. of Gr. & Armen. Ch.* 92 From the Monasteries he receives a certain annual Income or Rent.. and from every *Papa*, or Priest, a Dollar yearly per Head. **1686** tr. *Chardin's Trav. Persia* 71 The Oriental Christians as well as the Turks, call Papa's all manner of Ecclesiastical Persons that Officiate in Holy Orders, whether Single or Married. **1687** A. LOVELL tr. *Thevenot's Trav.* I. 83 While the Papas says some Prayers, the Godfather and Godmother hold a Garland of Flowers. **1775** WRAXALL *Tour North. Europe* 237 The papas or priests are dressed in vestments which very much resemble the Romish. **1812** BYRON *Ch. Har.* II. *note*, He.. boxed the ears of the first 'papas' who refused to assist. **1897** *Daily News* 30 Mar. 6/1 Cyprian was now Papa, Papas or Pope of Carthage, and he at once began, like the Apostle Paul, to magnify his office.

papa[3] ('pɑːpɑː). [Maori.] A soft bluish clay or mudstone found in the North Island of New Zealand.

1873 J. H. H. ST. JOHN *Pakeha Rambles through Maori Lands* xi. 183 We descended a steep slide into.. a river with a bed of papa rock. **1892** E. S. BROOKES *Frontier Life* xvii. 150 The country [Taranaki].. is principally composed of papa rock. **1905** J. M. THOMSON *Bush Boys N.Z.* ix. 62 That Papa Rock is beastly stuff to slip... The Papa Rock, of which many of the cliffs in the bush country in New Zealand are formed, is really a very hard blue clay. **1909** G. H. SCHOLEFIELD *N.Z. in Evolution* i. 12 Papa country produces the readiest crops of grass. **1911** W. H. KOEBEL *In Maoriland Bush* xxiii. 239 The track.. has dented a passage upon the soft pa-pa rock. **1921** H. GUTHRIE-SMITH *Tutira* ii. 9 The materials of which the station is formed are marl or 'papa', sandstone, sandy marl, limestone, and conglomerate. **1949** F. SARGESON *I saw in my Dream* II. xiii. 128 Nearly all the soil had slipped away and left only great faces of papa. **1969** —— *Joy of Worm* iii. 105 The river had been willing.. to slide in casual ripples over slabs of papa, as though to look more closely at a tiny curve of beach.

papa, obs. form of PAWPAW.

‖**papabile** (pa'pabile), *a.* [It.; cf. PAPABLE *a.*] Of a prelate: worthy of becoming Pope; having good prospects of being elected Pope. Also in pl. form *papabili* and in L. form *papabilis*. Also as *sb.*, a prelate regarded as a possible Pope (during a conclave).

1934 G. SELDES *Vatican* v. 94 Certain cardinals always are *papabili*, or in line for the papacy. **1935** V. PIRIE *Triple Crown* 9 Not too many virtues were necessary for a candidate to be considered 'papabile', that is, acceptable to a reasonable amount of voters. **1938** *Times Lit. Suppl.* 1 Jan. 6/2 At the next Conclave he was *papabilis*. **1939** *Daily Tel.* 11 Feb. 12 Cardinal Hlond.. and Cardinal Copello.. are both considered papabile. **1958** *Times* 29 Oct. 11/3 A number of the younger Cardinals.. will still be *papabili* at the next election. **1958** *New Statesman* 1 Nov. 583/3 This week, there were scarcely half-a-dozen *papabili* and the only suitable 'neutral', Roncalli, was 76. **1963** *Times* 4 June 10/1 Cardinals Montini of Milan, Lecaro of Bologna, and Siri of Genoa remain, however, among the *papabile*. **1963** *Economist* 29 June 1342/1 He, alone among the *papabile* cardinals, made a point of nailing his.. colours to the mast. **1973** A. MANN *Tiara* viii. 71 His own integrity, combined with his consummate administrative ability, led many observers to consider him the most *papabile* of the European Cardinals. **1976** *Church Times* 9 July 14/3 The other Italian '*papabile*' figures are numerous. **1978** *Guardian Weekly* 10 Sept. 11/1 The cardinals, who had a wide range of ten papabili to choose from.

papable ('peɪpəb(ə)l), *a. rare.* [a. F. *papable* (16th c. in Hatz.-Darm.), after It. *papabile* 'able to be pope' (Florio), f. *papa* POPE: cf. med.L. *pāpābilitās* (Du Cange).] Capable of being elected pope; qualified for the office of pope.

1592 WOTTON *Let. to Ld. Zouch* in *Reliq.* (1685) 707 By the Death of the other two, the Conclave hath received little alteration; though Mondovio were papable, and a great Soggetto in the List of the Foresters. **1670** G. H. *Hist. Cardinals* III. II. 282 Cardinals, antient and Papable. **1900** *Speaker* 17 Feb. 538/2 The Cardinal, a man of worth and papable.. esteemed Crashaw.

papacy ('peɪpəsɪ). [ad. med.L. *pāpātia* (Florence of Worc. in Du Cange), f. *pāpa* POPE.

Pāpātia appears to have been altered from *pāpātus* papal office, after other abstract nouns in *-ia*, e.g. *abbātia* abbacy.]

1. The office or position of pope (of Rome); tenure of office of a pope.

[*a* **1118** FLORENCE OF WORC. an. 1044 Hic [Benedictus] cum Papatiam emisset.] **1390** GOWER *Conf.* I. 258 This innocent, which was deceived His Papacie anon hath weyved, Renounced and resigned eke. **1480** CAXTON *Chron. Eng.* ccliii. (1482) 327 Pope Felyx resygned the hole papacye to Nycholas. **1611** CORYAT *Crudities* 121 (*Mantua*) This Pius Secundus was that learned Pope which before he vntertooke the Papacy was called Æneas Syluius. **1759** HUME *Hist. Eng.* I. ii. 111 The hope of attaining the papacy. **1777** WATSON *Philip II* (1839) 23 He engaged that such a number of cardinals, partisans of France.. should be nominated at the next promotion, as would secure to Henry the absolute disposal of the papacy, in the event of the Pontiff's death.

2. a. The papal system, ecclesiastically or politically; esp. *Hist.* the papal government as one of the states of Europe.

1550 BALE *Eng. Votaries* II. Biij, The Papacy of Rome. **1553** BECON *Reliques of Rome* (1563) 135 b, In times paste before the papacye bare rule. **1615** G. SANDYS *Trav.* 2 The Venetians are Lords of this Sea: but not without contention with the Papacy. **1624** BEDELL *Lett.* x. 136 The Papacie falsely calling it selfe the Church of Rome is such. **1706** COTES tr. *Dupin's Eccl. Hist. 16th C.* II. IV. xix. 289 We cannot say the Institution of the Papacy comes from Jesus Christ, unless we say that of Episcopacy does so too. **1835** I. TAYLOR *Spir. Despot.* vi. 285 The preparations for the papacy—that is to say the church ascendancy of Italy and of Rome its centre, had already been carried very far [at end of 4th c.]. **1875** JOWETT *Plato* (ed. 2) III. 191 Another Roman Empire, existing by the side of the Papacy.

fig. *a* **1716** SOUTH *Serm.* V. xii. 531 There is a Papacy in every Sect, or Faction; they all design the very same Height, or Greatness, though the Pope alone hitherto has had the Wit and Fortune to compass it.

b. = PAPISM.

1914 *Trans. Shropshire Archæol. & Nat. Hist. Soc.* IV. 45 Mr. Jermor seems to have been himself suspected of a leaning towards papacy.

†**3.** Applied to the Caliphate: cf. POPEDOM.

1613 PURCHAS *Pilgrimage* (1614) 240 Kaim succeeded in the Papacie Anno Hegiræ 422.

papadam, papadum, varr. POPADAM.

†**papagan**, *sb.* and *a. Obs. nonce-wd.* A hostile formation: = Papist, Popish (with allusion to *pagan*).

1641 TRAPPE *Theol. Theol.* vii. 283 How much cause have wee to blesse God that wee were not borne Pagans or Papagans. **1647** TRAPP *Comm. 1 Cor.* vii. 9. **1679** C. NESSE *Antid. Popery* 12 As there is a pagan superstition.. so there is a papagan superstition. *Ibid.* 19.

papagay, obs. form of POPINJAY.

Papago ('pæpəgəʊ, 'pɑːpəgəʊ), *sb.* and *a.* [Sp., ad. native name.] **A.** *sb.* **a.** An Indian people of the south-western U.S. and northern Mexico; a member of this people. **b.** The Uto-Aztecan language of this people and (in some uses) of the closely related Pima Indians; also called Pima. **B.** *adj.* Of or pertaining to the Papago or their language.

1839 A. FORBES *California* 162 On the River Gila.. Papaga, 4000. **1864** *Harper's Mag.* Dec. 25/1 The Papago Indians also do good service by.. killing the hostile savages. **1875** *Encycl. Brit.* II. 538/2 The inhabitants of Arizona are mostly Indians... 4000 Papagoes, a wandering tribe in the south-eastern part of the territory, have no grounds allotted them. **1878** R. J. HINTON *Hand-bk. Arizona* 227 South and west of these lie the old Papago villages and wells. **1911** H. B. WRIGHT *Winning of Barbara Worth* 101 She pointed to a smoky, copper-colored Papago in a green headcloth and decorated shirt. **1912** K. LUMHOLTZ *New Trails in Mexico* 185 Hydrophobia is called in Papago *nótakik*. **1936** *Univ. Arizona Gen. Bull.* III. 118 These caterpillars feed on a spreading four-o'clock or on the Papago spinach on the desert. **1946** E. E. CUMMINGS *Let.* 31 Jan. (1969) 170, I sat opposite a Papago Indian. **1964** E. A. NIDA *Toward Sci. Transl.* viii. 162 Certain problems of translating magic incantations of the Papago Indians of Southern Arizona. **1968** P. M. POSTAL *Aspects Phonol. Theory* i. 10 The situation described here is based to a certain limited extent on that existing in Papago, a Uto-Aztecan language of the American Southwest. **1973** A. H. WHITEFORD *N. Amer. Indian Arts* 13 Modeling and paddling is a technique.. still used by the Papago and Yuma of Arizona. **1977** *Language* LIII. 459 L now recognizes.. that Papago *hɨjɨl* and *PaPay*.. probably do not belong in this cognate set.

papagoite (pə'pɑːgəʊaɪt). *Min.* [f. prec. + -ITE[1].] A basic silicate of calcium, copper, and aluminium, approximately $CaCuAlSi_2O_6(OH)_3$, which is found as blue monoclinic crystals.

1960 HUTTON & VLISIDIS in *Amer. Mineralogist* XLV. 600 The mineral described herein has been named papagoite after the Indian tribe that inhabited the area in which the active mining center of Ajo is situated. **1965** *Mineral. Abstr.* XVII. 359/2 Papagoite from the type deposit at the Ajo Mine, Arizona.., is monoclinic, with *a* 12·94, *b* 11·52, *c* 4·68Å, *β* 100°30′; space group *C 2/m*.

papaia, var. *papaya*: see PAWPAW.

papain (pə'peɪɪn). *Chem.* Also papayin. [f. *papay-a* (see PAWPAW) + -IN[1].] **a.** A proteolytic ferment obtained from the half-ripe fruit of the pawpaw (*Carica papaya*) which is used to assist the digestion of patients suffering from chronic dyspepsia and gastritis, as a meat tenderizer, and in clarifying beverages. **b.** The pure crystalline protease extracted from papaya latex.

1890 in *Cent. Dict.* **1893** *Syd. Soc. Lex.*, *Papáin*, a preparation from the juice of the papaw. A whitish, amorphous powder, containing a proteolytic ferment. **1898** *Allbutt's Syst. Med.* V. 33 The chemical objection which may be urged against..the vegetable ferments papayotin and papain. **1937** *Science* 22 Oct. 379/1 (*heading*) Crystalline papain. **1943** *Sumner & Somers Chem. & Methods of Enzymes* 158 The impure papain of commerce is a mixture of two distinct enzymes. **1963** *Daily Tel.* 14 June 17/6 British meat traders are concerned about the use of papain, an enzyme preparation, injected into animals before they are slaughtered, to produce artificially tenderised meat. **1969** T. C. THORSTENSEN *Pract. Leather Technol.* vi. 100 The enzyme papain introduced into this system exhibited very strong unhairing action. **1972** *Materials & Technol.* V. xix. 700 Papain is a relatively small enzyme, with a molecular weight of 21 000 and an isoelectric point of 8·75.

papal (ˈpeɪpəl), *a.* (*sb.*) [a. F. *papal* (1380 in Gower *Mirour*) or ad. eccl. L. *pāpālis* belonging to the Pope, f. *pāpa* POPE: see PAPA[2]. So Sp., Pg. *papal*, It. *papale*: see -AL[1].]

1. Of or pertaining to a pope, or to the pope, his dignity or office.

papal cross, one with three transoms; a triple cross. *papal crown*, or *tiara*: see quot. 1727.

1390 GOWER *Conf.* I. 257 The Pope..Of his Papal Autorite Hath mad..the decre. **1432-50** tr. *Higden* (Rolls) VI. 395 The clothynge papalle taken awey, and indued with seculer clothynge. **1512** *Act 4 Hen. VIII*, c. 19 *Preamble*, That our seid holy Fader shulde..be sequestered of & fro all Jurisdiccion and admynystracion Papal. *a* **1661** FULLER *Worthies, Herts.* (1840) II. 42 His own font-name was a papal one. **1687** T. BROWN *Saints in Uproar* Wks. 1730 I. 79 Having received the Papal benediction. **1727** CHAMBERS *Cycl.*, *Papal Crown*, is a deep cap, or mitre of cloth of gold, encompassed with three coronets or circles of gold, adorned with flowers..having a globe at top, finished with a cross. **1860** J. GARDNER *Faiths World* II. 601/2 Hildebrand accepted of the papal tiara under the title of Gregory VII.

b. That is a pope.

a **1802** BOWLES *Poems* I. 200 When it bade a Papal tyrant pause and tremble.

†**2.** Adhering to or supporting the pope; belonging to the Church of Rome; popish. *Obs.*

c **1592** MARLOWE *Massacre Paris* II. vi, To beat the papal monarch from our lands. *a* **1715** BURNET *Own Time* (1724) I. 265 Dr. Lloyd..thinks their time of hurting the Papal Christians is at an end. **1814** SOUTHEY *Ode War Amer.* ix, They who from papal darkness, and the thrall Of that worst bondage..Saved us in happy hour.

3. *Comb.*, as *papal-imperial* adj.

1874 STUBBS *Const. Hist.* I. i. 6 The permanency of the papal-imperial system.

†**B.** *sb.* = PAPIST. *Obs.*

1611 SPEED *Hist. Gt. Brit.* IX. xxiv. (1623) 1190 To salute this puppet King, and to welcome these papals.

†**ˈPapalin, -ine.** *Obs.* [a. F. *papalin* (17th c. in Hatz.-Darm.), relating to the pope, f. It. *papalino*, f. *papale*: see PAPAL and -INE[1].] A member of the papal party or papal church; an adherent of the pope; a papist.

1624 BEDELL *Lett.* i. 42 The wise State of Venice haue a little different notion of their Papalines, excluding..such of the Nobilitie as are obliged to the Pope by Ecclesiasticall promotions. **1626** C. POTTER tr. *Sarpi's Hist. Quarrels* 206 The Doctrine of the Romane Writers, or Papalins. **1669** BAXTER *Power Mag. & Ch. Past.* II. lxiv. (1671) 42 The Wars between the German Emperours and the Papalines. **1784** J. BROWN *Hist. Brit. Ch.* (1820) I. 6 Their uncommon holiness distinguished them from the Papalins.

‖**Papaˈlina.** *Obs. rare*[-1]. [It., fem. of *papalino*: see prec.] A female papist.

1671 in *Mem. Verney Fam.* (1899) IV. 203 By ye best and truest intellegence she did not dy a Papalina, but she made noe profession or confession eyther way.

papalism (ˈpeɪpəlɪz(ə)m). [f. PAPAL + -ISM.] The papal system.

1870 *Contemp. Rev.* XIV. 496 Bavaria..began to be disposed towards Papalism and Jesuitism. **1887** *Times* (weekly ed.) 7 Oct. 4/1 The modern advocate of the new Papalism.

ˈpapalist. [f. as prec. + -IST. Cf. obs. F. *papaliste*.] A member of the papal party, an adherent of the papal system. Also *attrib.*

1750 HODGES *Chr. Plan* (1755) Pref. 25 For my reader's satisfaction and reflection, and the Papalists conviction and confusion. **1826** G. S. FABER *Diffic. Romanism* (1853) 373 Unless I wholly mistake, the very hardiest of the Papalists pretend not to assert the Infallibility of Ecumenical Councils in regard to Facts. **1881** *Times* 12 Aug. 7/5 The stage to which the deliberate fury of Papalists and anti-Papalists..has carried the quarrel. **1903** *Eng. Hist. Rev.* XVIII. 482 What little significance lies in the expression depends on Llywelyn's clerk's serving up to the papalist primate the conventional phraseology of Roman documents. **1964** P. F. ANSON *Bishops at Large* ix. 325 The year 1920 saw the first of several Anglo-Catholic Congresses, and with them a rapid increase of baroque and rococo furnishings in Anglican Papalist churches.

Hence **papaˈlistic** *a.*, of the nature of a papalist; papistic.

1886 SYMONDS *Renaiss. It., Cath. React.* (1898) VII. x. 92 His papalistic enemies could get no grip upon him.

†**paˈpality.** *Obs.* [a. F. *papalité*, in med.L. *pāpālitās* (14th c. in Du Cange): see PAPAL and -ITY.]

1. The papal office, dignity, or authority; the popedom; the papal see.

1456 SIR G. HAYE *Law Arms* (S.T.S.) 111 [He] ourthrew wrangwisly the legis of the papalitee. **1480** CAXTON *Chron. Eng.* v. (1520) 54/1 It was in the 6 yere of Seynt Gregoryes papalyte. **1525** LD. BERNERS *Froiss.* II. clx. 440 Pope Clement was redy in his chambre of consystorie, syttyng in his chayre of papalyte. **1652** URQUHART *Jewel* Wks. (1834) 279 Joynt to the power wherewith he is invested by his Papality, he ruleth over those parts by the right of a temporal prince. **1661** BLOUNT *Glossogr.* (ed. 2), *Papality*,..the Popedom, the Dominion of the Pope, Popishness.

2. A papal doctrine. *rare.*

1826 W. S. LANDOR *Imag. Conv.* (ed. 2) I. viii. 163 He resisted the authority of the pope, and refuted the doctrine of transubstantiation, with several other papalities.

papalize (ˈpeɪpəlaɪz), *v.* [f. PAPAL + -IZE.]

1. *intr.* To become papal or popish in practice or sympathies; to romanize.

1624 GEE *Foot out of Snare* ii. 10 Concerning the.. behauiour of this Papalizing Church-man. **1783** COWPER *Let. to J. Newton* Wks. 1837 XV. 128 Approaching nearer to the church of Rome than ever any Methodist did, though papalizing is the crime with which he charges all of that denomination. **1886** SYMONDS *Renaiss. It., Cath. React.* (1898) VII. x. 86 Her nobles became.. more papalising in their private sympathies.

2. *trans.* To render papal; to imbue with papal or papist principles or doctrines.

1839 *Watchman* 4 Sept., Let him especially look at Ireland, intensely papalised as it is. **1856** E. G. K. BROWNE *Ann. Tractarian Movem.* (1861) 470 Mr. Golightly.. accused Dr. Wilberforce of Papalizing the See committed to his charge. **1898** G. W. E. RUSSELL *Coll. & Recoll.* iv. 55 He believed that he had been divinely appointed to papalize England.

Hence **ˈpapalized** *ppl. a.*, **ˈpapalizing** *vbl. sb.* and *ppl. a.*; also **papaliˈzation**, the action of papalizing, **ˈpapalizer**, one who papalizes.

1624, 1783 Papalizing [see sense 1]. **1842** G. S. FABER *Prov. Lett.* (1844) II. 100 In order to retain these faithful papalisers in our ecclesiastical garrison. **1843** —— *Sacr. Calend. Prophecy* (1844) I. p. xxv, In these evil days of Scepticism and Papalisation. **1879** BOULTBEE *Hist. Ch. Eng.* 60 The canon and the civil law of the papalised mediæval period. **1882** *Ch. Times* 3 Feb. 68 The thorough Papalizing of the Church under Cardinal Kemp.

ˈpapally, *adv.* [f. PAPAL + -LY[2].] In a papal manner; from a papal point of view; as a pope.

1627 H. BURTON *Baiting Pope's Bull* 68 It reigned then Imperially: it reigneth now Papally. **1888** *Daily News* 29 Oct. 6/3 Henry VIII..was..one of the most papally-minded men in England. **1901** F. W. MAITLAND *Rede Lect.* 25 Very rarely do we see elsewhere the academic teaching of any law that is not Roman: imperially or papally Roman.

papaloi (ˈpapalwa). [ad. Haitian Creole *papalwa*, f. *papa* father + *lwa* LOA[2].] A voodoo priest. Cf. MAMALOI.

1884 S. ST. JOHN *Hayti* v. 184 He again consulted the Papaloi or priest. *Ibid.* v. 194 The Haytians have corrupted the compounds Papa Roi and Maman Roi into Papaloi and Mamanloi. **1935** [see MAMALOI]. **1965** J. VON STERNBERG *Fun in Chinese Laundry* i. 16 My mind seems full of stealth, it has no goal, no conclusions, and no ambitions, as if a Haitian 'papa loi' had made me into a zombie. **1976** *Billings* (Montana) *Gaz.* 11 July 2-F/5 So he consulted the voodoo 'papaloi', who diagnosed the ailment as a minor spell which had been laid on him by an enemy.

†**ˈpapalty.** *Obs.* [a. OF. *papalté*, *papaulte* (*a* 1550 Calvin in Godef. *Compl.*), mod.F. *papauté*, f. *papal* after *royalté*, *royauté*.] = PAPALITY.

1577 *F. de Lisle's Legendarie* C viij b, Through whose aide he might conquere the Papaltye for him selfe. **1641** MILTON *Reform.* II. (1851) 42 To uphold the decrepit Papalty. **1859** J. C. HOBHOUSE *Italy* II. 239 The Papalty, like the Ottoman Empire in Europe, subsists by sufferance.

†**ˈpapane**, *a.* and *sb. Obs. rare.* [f. L. *pāpa* pope, after L. type **pāpānus*: see -AN, -ANE.] = PAPAL *a.* and *sb.*

1581 J. BELL *Haddon's Answ. Osor.* 20 Although the same doth not acknowledge your Papane principalitie. *Ibid.* 476 Peruse throughly this whole Papane.

Papanicolaou (ˌpæpənɪkəˈlɑːuː, pæpəˈnɪkəlaʊ). *Med.* The name of George Nicholas *Papanicolaou* (1883–1962), Greek-born U.S. anatomist, used *attrib.* and in the possessive with reference to a technique he devised for examining exfoliated or secreted cells, used chiefly as a means of detecting cancer, esp. of the vagina, cervix, and uterus.

1947 *Surg., Gynecol. & Obstetr.* LXXXV. 275 (*heading*) Modifications of the Papanicolaou technique. *Ibid.* 276/2 A number of flakes..were prepared with Papanicolaou's stain. **1956** *Nature* 18 Feb. 330/1 The cells were smeared on microscopical slides coated with egg-albumin or human serum and fixed in Papanicolaou's fixative. **1958** E. DAY in R. W. Raven *Cancer* III. xxii. 450 In taking cervical smears by the Papanicolaou method a cotton-tipped applicator is used. **1966** W. H. COLE in R. W. Cumley et al. *Recent Adv. Diagnosis of Cancer* 183 The Papanicolaou stain (1942) represents one of the greatest advances in diagnosis and treatment of cancer during the past several decades. **1972** GRAHAM & URBACH in J. H. Graham et al. *Dermal Path.* xxx. 675/1 During the past three decades the Papanicolaou technique, or various modifications of this method, has been applied to most organ tissues where secretions, exudates, or exfoliated cells can be obtained.

papaphobia (peɪpəˈfəʊbɪə). *rare*[-1]. [f. L. *pāpa* pope + Gr. -*φοβία* fear.] Distempered dread of the pope or of popery. Hence **ˈpapaˌphobist**, one who is affected with papaphobia. (*nonce-wd.*)

1798 BISSET *Life of Burke* I. 32 (Jod.) The puritanical papaphobia. **1818** COLERIDGE in *Lit. Rem.* (1838) III. 189 In the same spirit I excuse the opposite party, the Puritans and Papaphobists.

ˌpapa-preˈlatical, *a. nonce-wd.* Of or pertaining to papal prelates, or prelates who act papally. So **papa-ˌprelatist**, one who supports such prelates.

1692 *Scotch Presbyt. Eloq.* (1738) 76 She [Ch. of Eng.] is Papa-prelatical; nay, she is Archi-papa-prelatical. **1816** SCOTT *Old Mort.* vi, To mix in the ranks of malignants, papists, papa-prelatists, latitudinarians, and scoffers.

‖**paparazzo** (papaˈrattso). Pl. **paparazzi**. [It.] A free-lance photographer who pursues celebrities to take their pictures. Also *attrib.*

1968 *Daily Tel.* (Colour Suppl.) 29 Nov. 66/4 The anticipated horde of detested *paparazzi*—those scavenging Italian street photographers whose sole purpose appears to be to make every film celebrity's life a misery. **1972** W. GARNER *Ditto, Brother Rat!* xxii. 163 Pik..hoisted his camera and began zip-click-zipping at the delegation like a *paparazzo* who's suddenly found nothing between him and royalty in the nude. **1972** *N.Y. Times* 6 July 1 United States District Court Judge Irving Ben Cooper ruled yesterday that the activities of Ronald E. Galella, the self-styled 'paparazzo' photographer, had 'relentlessly invaded' the right to privacy of Mrs. Aristotle Onassis. **1974** V. GIELGUD *In Such a Night* vii. 64 The Roman *paparazzi*..are so frequently the terror of film-actors with thin skins. **1974** *Times Lit. Suppl.* 20 Dec. 1439/4 The London Clinic which she had entered a week before with the defiant exclamation to the vulturine *paparazzi* at the entrance, 'Don't think I'm coming here to die, I'm not.' **1977** *Maclean's Mag.* 21 Mar. 64/1 If Margaret was troubled by the publicity or the paparazzi that followed her during her New York stay, she certainly didn't show it.

paparchy (ˈpeɪpɑːkɪ). *rare.* [f. L. *pāpa* pope + Gr. -*αρχία* -*archy*, sovereignty.] Papal rule or sovereignty; government by a pope.

1839-40 I. TAYLOR *Anc. Chr.* (1842) II. viii. 400 Assumptions on which the Paparchy has been made to rest. **1895** *N. Amer. Rev.* Aug. 139 The paparchy is a law unto itself.

So **paˈparchical** *a.*, pertaining to papal rule.

1895 *N. Amer. Rev.* Aug. 132 The Pontiff reserves to himself the full powers conferred upon him by paparchical laws.

papas, a Greek priest: see PAPA[2] 2.

papaship (pəˈpɑːʃɪp). [f. PAPA[1] + -SHIP.] The position of being a 'papa', fatherhood; also (with possessive) as a mock title. (*humorous.*)

1816 BYRON *Let. to Moore* 5 Jan., My approaching papaship detained us. **1838** *Fraser's Mag.* XVII. 679 The boring intrusions of papa-ship. **1883** BLACK *Yolande* III. x. 191 You will convey the information to his Papa-ship.

†**ˈpapate.** *Obs. rare.* [a. OF. *papat* (15th c. in Godef.) or ad. med.L. *pāpātus* (Du Cange), f. *pāpa* pope: see -ATE[1].] The office of pope, the papacy.

1390 GOWER *Conf.* I. 254 A Cardinal was thilke tide, Which the papat longe hath desired. **1456** SIR G. HAYE *Law Arms* (S.T.S.) 216 [If] the subject had bene als evill to the haly papatis as the maister man was.

papaumu (papaˈuːmʊ). *N.Z.* Also **papauma**. [Maori.] A small evergreen tree or shrub, *Griselinia littoralis*, belonging to the family Cornaceæ, native to New Zealand, and distinguished by thick, ovate leaves with shiny upper surfaces; = *broad-leaf* s.v. BROAD *a.* D. 2.

1882 W. D. HAY *Brighter Britain!* II. vi. 199 The Karamu or Papaumu.., a family of pretty flowering shrubs. **1928** COCKAYNE & TURNER *Trees N.Z.* 57 Papaumu, Broadleaf. A small tree, 30–50 ft. high, or a shrub, with short irregular trunk. **1956** [see *broad-leaf*]. **1966** *Encycl. N.Z.* I. 252/1 Broadleaf, papauma (*Griselinia littoralis*)..is a common hardwood tree throughout the mixed and beech forests.

papaveraceous (pəpeɪvəˈreɪʃəs), *a. Bot.* [f. mod.L. *Papāverāce-æ* (f. L. *papāver* poppy) + -OUS.] Of or belonging to the N.O. *Papaveraceæ*, the poppy family.

1846 WORCESTER cites *Penny Cycl.* **1863** MARY HOWITT *F. Bremer's Greece* I. viii. 260 A little golden yellow flower of the papaveraceous family.

†**papaˈveric**, *a. Chem. Obs.* [f. as next + -IC.] In *papaveric acid*, a synonym of MECONIC acid.

1857 in MAYNE *Expos. Lex.* **1876** HARLEY *Mat. Med.* (ed. 6) 738.

papaverine (pəˈpeɪvəraɪn). *Chem.* [f. L. *papāver* poppy + -INE[5].] An alkaloid ($C_{20}H_{21}NO_4$) contained in opium, obtained in colourless needles.

1857 W. A. MILLER *Elem. Chem.* III. 282 Papaverine..is distinguished from the other opium bases by giving with concentrated sulphuric acid a deep blue colour. **1876** HARLEY *Mat. Med.* (ed. 6) 762 Opium contains about 1 per cent. of Papaverine.

papaverous (pəˈpeɪvərəs), *a.* [f. as prec. + -OUS.] Pertaining to, resembling, or allied to the poppy; papaveraceous; *fig.* soporific.

1646 SIR T. BROWNE *Pseud. Ep.* VII. vii. (1686) 288 Mandrakes afford a papaverous and unpleasant odor. **1845** *Blackw. Mag.* LVIII. 243 Papaverous volumes, with which only a superhuman endowment of vigilance could hope successfully to contend. **1874** BLACKIE *Self-Cult.* 5 A botanist..will class a water-lily with the papaverous or poppy family.

papaw: see PAWPAW.

papaya, freq. used as an alternative to PAWPAW 1.

papayaceous (pæpəˈjeɪʃəs), *a. Bot.* [f. mod.L. *Papāyāce-æ* (f. *Papāya*: see PAWPAW) + -OUS.] Belonging to the N.O. *Papayaceæ* (sometimes reckoned as a suborder of *Passifloraceæ*), of which the Pawpaw-tree, *Carica Papaya*, is the type. So **paˈpayad** (-AD 1 d), a papayaceous tree or shrub; **paˈpayal** *a.*, allied to the *Papayaceæ*; *sb.* a plant of the papayal alliance; **papayotin** (pəˈpeɪəʊtɪn) *Chem.*, a ferment, akin to *papaïn*, contained in the sap of the pawpaw-tree.

1846 LINDLEY *Veg. Kingd.* 320 The..Papayal alliance. *Ibid.*, [The plants] brought into closest contact with Papayals. *Ibid.* 321 *Papayaceæ*, Papayads. **1857** MAYNE *Expos. Lex.*, Papayaceous. **1866** *Treas. Bot.* 843 *Papayaceæ* (*Caricea, Papayads*), a natural order of calycifloral dicotyledons belonging to Lindley's papayal alliance of diclinous Exogens. **1885** *Lancet* 11 July 86/2 Papayotin (in diphtheritis) exercises a feeble solvent effect on the membrane when it is beginning to decompose. **1898** *Allbutt's Syst. Med.* V. 33 Papain..the more powerful product yielded by the fruit of *Carica Papaya* (papayotin being derived from the milky sap) has been recommended.

pap-boat. [f. PAP *sb.*[2] + BOAT *sb.* 2 a.]

1. A boat-shaped vessel for holding pap for feeding infants.

1782 MISS BURNEY *Cecilia* VI. viii, I have a vast inclination to get a pap-boat myself, and make him a present of it. **1854** THACKERAY *Rose & Ring* iii, [She] merely sent her compliments and a silver papboat for the baby.

2. A shell of the family *Turbinellidæ*, as *Turbinella rapha*, used on the Malabar coast to hold anointing oil.

1886 in *Cassell's Encycl. Dict.*

Pape (peɪp). *Sc.* and *Ulster*. Also pape. [f. POPE *sb.*[1] or as shortening of PAPIST.] An opprobrious term for a Roman Catholic.

1935 L. KERR *Woman of Glenshiels* iv. 56 Mary... wouldn't click with a 'pape' or a boy who whistled after them. **1939** JOYCE *Finnegans Wake* III. 440 Skim over *Through Hell with the Papes* (mostly boys) by the divine comic Denti Alligator. **1957** *Bulletin* (Glasgow) 11 Oct. 15/3 Lucas had been drinking. When charged he said, 'I set the house on fire to burn these Papes and Niggers.' **1968** J. BRAINE *Crying Game* v. 118 Adam's a good Catholic... It's smart to be a Pape now. *Ibid.* xii. 217 When I marry..it must be a Catholic... I mean, who else would I marry but a Pape? **1970** G. M. FRASER *General danced at Dawn* 48 Years later, when he led a famous league side out to play Celtic, this same corporal, having said his Hail-Mary and fingered his crucifix, instructed his team, 'Awright, fellas, let's get stuck intae these Papes.' **1972** *Listener* 7 Sept. 304/3 Gerry Fitt has been bawling about the number of Roman Catholics..who have been found shot dead... Gerry deduces that the dead papes have been killed by Protestant guns. **1974** *Socialist Worker* 2 Nov. 11/1 During my childhood it was constantly hammered home to me that I should be a good boy at school, that I shouldn't question what my elders told me, and that I should join the Orange Lodge because the 'Papes' are bastards.

pape, obs. form of PAP; Sc. form of POPE.

papegay, -jay, -joy, obs. forms of POPINJAY.

†**papelard.** *Obs.* Also 5 papularde, papelart. [a. F. *papelard* adj. and sb. (13th c. in Littré); in It. *pappalardo* glutton, greedy-gut, hypocrite (Baretti); med.L. *pape-, papalardus* (Du Cange); f. OF. *paper*, It. *pappare* to eat + *lard*, It. *lardo* bacon, fat; lit. a parasite, a sponge, a 'sucker'.]

A flattering parasite, a sycophant; a hypocrite. Also *attrib.* or as *adj.* Hypocritical (for greed or gain).

1340 *Ayenb.* 26 Þet me ne by yhyealde ypocrite ne papelard huer me dret more þe wordle þanne god. *c* **1400** *Rom. Rose* 7283 That papelard, that him yeldeth so, And wol to worldly ese go. *c* **1440** *Gesta Rom.* lxx. 401 (Add. MS.) He, this papularde preste, hathe herde oure Cownsaylle, and hathe delyuered here from syn. **1491** CAXTON *Vitas Patr.* I. li. (1495) 106 Lete us entree in: And slee this papelart.

So †**papelardry,** †**papelardy** (**papyllardie**), sycophancy, hypocrisy (for greed or gain).

c **1400** *Rom. Rose* 6796 Bifore the puple patre and prey, And wrye me in my foxerye Under a cope of papelardye. *c* **1400** tr. *Secreta Secret., Gov. Lordsh.* 136 In false Papelardry of word or of dede. **1426** LYDG. *De Guil. Pilgr.* 13921 Papyllardie Wych is a maner of ypocrysie.

papeling, obs. Sc. form of POPELING, a papist.

†**papelito** (pæpəˈliːtəʊ). *Obs.* [a. Sp. *papelito* slip of paper, bit of paper (cf. *papelillo* cigarette).] A cigarette.

1845 R. FORD *Hand-bk. for Travellers Spain* II. 784 So they jogged on, smoking their *papelitos*, to the Escorial. **1861** L. WRAXALL tr. *Aimard's Freebooters* xvi. 211 He rolled a husk cigarette..lit his papelito, and was soon surrounded by a dense cloud of bluish and fragrant smoke. **1867** 'OUIDA' *Under Two Flags* I. i. 15 Something to drink and something to smoke, were it only a glass of brown sherry and a little papelito.

†ˈ**papelote.** *Obs.* Also 5 paplote, paplette. [app. AF. *pape*, f. *pappe* PAP *sb.*[2] + *-lotte* dim. suff. Not in OF. (Godef. has *papelote, -lotte* small piece of paper).] Porridge.

1393 LANGL. *P. Pl.* C. x. 75 Boþe in mylk and in mele to make with papelotes. **14..** *Voc.* in Wr.-Wülcker 601/46 *Peraptum*, an^ce Papelotes. **1483** *Cath. Angl.* 268/2 Paplote (*A.* Paplette), *papatum*.

papengay, obs. form of POPINJAY.

paper (ˈpeɪpə(r)), *sb.* Also 4 papure, 4–6 papir, 5 papire, papyre, (paupire, 5–6 pauper), 5–7 papyr, 6 papre. [a. AF. *papir* = OF. *papier* (= Pr. *papier*, Cat. *paper*, Sp. *papel* 'paper', It. *papiro* papyrus), ad. L. *papȳrus* the papyrus or paper-reed of the Nile, also writing-material made of it, a. Gr. πάπυρος the papyrus-reed. From the writing-sheets made of the thin strips of papyrus the name was transferred to paper made of cotton, and thence to paper of linen and other fibres. These extensions took place before the word became English, so that here its application to *papyrus* is only a later retrospective use.]

I. The simple word. * Without *a* or *pl.* (exc. as denoting a particular kind).

1. a. A substance composed of fibres interlaced into a compact web, made (usually in the form of a thin flexible sheet, most commonly white) from various fibrous materials, as linen and cotton rags, straw, wood, certain grasses, etc., which are macerated into a pulp, dried, and pressed (and subjected to various other processes, as bleaching, colouring, sizing, etc., according to the intended use); it is used (in various forms and qualities) for writing, printing, or drawing on, for wrapping things in, for covering the interior of walls, and for other purposes.

1341–2 in *Ely Sacr. Rolls*, papyr. **1359–60** *Ibid.*, paper. **13..** *Gaw. & Gr. Knt.* 802 So mony pynakle payntet watz poudred ay quere,..þat pared out of papure purely hit semed. *c* **1374** CHAUCER *Troylus* v. 1597 Youre lettres ful þe papir al y-pleynted Conseyued hath myn hertes pite. *c* **1400** MAUNDEV. (1839) xxii. 239 He maketh no Money, but of Lether emprented, or of Papyre [*Roxb.* papire]. **1463** *Bury Wills* (Camden) 42 A book of papyr to wryte in expensis. *a* **1529** SKELTON *Poems agst. Garnesche* Wks. 1843 I. 131 A reme of papyr wyll nat holde [all]. **1548** *Privy Council Acts* (1890) II. 179 To the Clerkes of the Counsaile for paper, pens and ink. **1600** J. PORY tr. *Leo's Africa* 24 All their books..are written in parchment, for paper they haue none. **1712** *Act 10 Anne* c. 18. §44 Paper..printed painted or stained..to serve for Hangings. *a* **1716** SOUTH *Serm.* IV. x. 440 He sells his Soul with it, like brown Paper, into the Bargain. **1730** FIELDING *Author's Farce* II. v, A good handsome large volume,..printed on a good paper and letter. **1887** *Pall Mall G.* 21 Sept. 12/1 A growing tree is now often cut down, made into paper, and turned out as a newspaper in thirty-six hours.

b. Also applied to other substances used for writing upon, of similar consistence but differently made, as the PAPYRUS of the ancients; or to substances of similar texture, as that made by wasps for their nests (see *paper-wasp* in 12).

1398 TREVISA *Barth. De P.R.* XVII. cxxvi. (Bodl. MS.), Of þese russchis..þei makeþ & weueþ botes and seiles,..& also þei makeþ þerof papir to write in. **1613** PURCHAS *Pilgrimage* (1614) 506 Of the pith or heart of the tree, is made paper for bookes. **1615** G. SANDYS *Trav.* 102 The sedgie reeds,.. called formerly *Papyri*, of which they made paper; and whereof ours made of rags, assumeth that name. **1843** *Penny Cycl.* XXVII. 105/1 This [ligneous] fibre..is made into a paper, of which are constructed the combs [of a wasps' nest].

c. Applied familiarly to substances made from paper-pulp, used in the industrial arts, such as mill-board, papier mâché, slabs prepared for use in roofing, building, and other purposes.

c **1670** BOYLE *Uses Nat. Things* iv. Wks. 1772 III. 485 Though paper be one of the commonest bodies that we use, yet there are very few that imagine..that frames for pictures and divers fine pieces of embossed work, with other curious moveables, may..be made of it. **1778** *Tour thro' Gt. Brit., Birmingham*, Mr. Clay's manufactory for japanning, &c., making paper cases, stands, waiters, tea-boards, coach-pannels, &c., all of paper, finely varnished, and painted. **1897** BADEN-POWELL *Matabele Campaign* ii. 25 [Buluwayo] well filled with buildings, all single-storeyed, some brick, some tin, some 'paper' (i.e. wire-wove, ready-made in England, sent out in pieces), all with verandahs. *Ibid.* iii. 80 These 'paper' houses are common in Buluwayo—they are really wire-wove, with wooden frames, iron roofs, cardboard walls.

d. In various phrases and connexions, with allusion to writing or drawing; as ***to commit to paper***, to write down. ***to put pen to paper***, to commence writing, to write. ***on paper***: in writing, in print; said esp. of something described or represented in a preliminary sketch or plan, in contrast to the reality; hence = in theory, theoretically. ***paper-and-pencil*** (*attrib.*): executed in writing, carried out with paper and pencil.

1582 STANYHURST *Æneis*, etc. (Arb.) 139 But shal I looue the lady, so as Petrarck Laura regarded? In paper her dandling? her person neauer atayning? **1624** CAPT. SMITH *Virginia* IV. 161 All those..are rather things in words and paper then in effect. *c* **1654** DOR. OSBORNE *Lett.* (1903) 146 The fellow thought that putting 'pen to paper' was much better than plain 'writing'. **1771** SMOLLETT *Humph. Cl.* 10 June i, A man may be very entertaining and instructive upon paper..and exceedingly dull in common discourse. **1788** *Amer. Museum* III. 336/2 The form of their constitution, as it is on paper, admits not of coercion. But necessity introduced it in practice. **1795** WASHINGTON *Lett.* Writ. 1892 XIII. 64 All this looks very well on paper; but [etc.]. **1865** L. CARROLL *Alice's Adv. Wonderl.* vi. 122 Humpty Dumpty looked doubtful. 'I'd rather see that done on paper', he said. **1888** BURGON *Lives 12 Gd. Men* I. III. 296 The intention..of committing to paper some recollections of the holy man. **1948** [see CONNIPTION]. **1965** N. CHOMSKY *Aspects of Theory of Syntax* i. 10 Let us use the term 'acceptable' to refer to utterances that are..comprehensible without paper-and-pencil analysis. **1971** *Jrnl. Gen. Psychol.* Oct. 308 The five measures described here—three paper-and-pencil inventories and two visual tasks—all appear to be concerned with a central phenomenon, that of the individual's need to maintain an optimal level of stimulus input or variability. **1972** *Jrnl. Social Psychol.* LXXXVII. 156 Test anxiety scales are typically self-report, paper-and-pencil measures. **1973** *Jrnl. Genetic Psychol.* Sept. 35 The measure of approach was a paper and pencil measure. **1973** D. WESTHEIMER *Going Public* i. 19 For every point it goes up you've made yourselves a hundred twenty seven thou five hundred dollars. On paper. I must warn you that paper profits are often illusory. **1976** *Verbatim* Sept. 5/2 Six nifty paper-and-pencil games. **1977** *World of Cricket Monthly* June 82/3 On paper, Hampshire looked a short-odds bet for any of the one-day competitions.

2. Paper bearing writing; written documents collectively.

1386 CHAUCER *Cook's T.* 40 Vp on a day whan he his papir soghte, that [etc.]. **1393** LANGL. *P. Pl.* C. XIV. 38 The marchante mote nede be lette lengere þen þe messagere; For þe parcels of hus paper and oþer pryuey dettes Wol lette hym, as ich leyue.

1966 *Rep. Comm. Inquiry Univ. Oxf.* I. 241 Upon this depends the ability of the Vice-Chancellor to make himself felt, his capacity to think ahead and to give a lead without having continually to submerge himself in paper. *Ibid.* 253 Only thus can it [*sc.* the General Board] see over the top of the piles of paper and look at those general topics..which ought to be its principal concern. **1977** D. AITKIN *Second Chair* ii. 19 Watch out that you don't get smothered in paper. That foxy little friend of ours wants you to do all his hackwork while he..thinks great thoughts.

3. *Comm.* **a.** Negotiable documents, bills of exchange, etc. collectively. **b.** Paper money or currency as opposed to coin, bank-notes, etc.

a **1674** CLARENDON *Hist. Reb.* XVI. §241 The custom.. being to make their payments in Paper by Assignations. *c* **1722** LD. MAR *Legacy to Scotl.* (1896) 201 The paper could not exceed more than a certain quantity..in proportion to the specie in the nation. **1727–41** CHAMBERS *Cycl.* s.v., I have no money to give you, but only Paper; Paper indeed as good as ready money. **1728** SWIFT *Answ. Memor.* Wks. 1755 V. II. 173 Will foreigners take our bankers paper? **1775** R. MONTGOMERY in Sparks *Corr. Amer. Rev.* (1853) I. 491 It will be necessary to send hard money here..as paper will not yet go down. **1824** BYRON *Juan* XVI. xxii, But rarely seen, like gold compared with paper. **1850** THACKERAY *Pendennis* II. xxvi. 259 It was whispered among the tradesmen, bill-discounters, and others..that the Captain's 'paper' was henceforth of no value. **1883** *Manch. Exam.* 14 Dec. 4/1 For three months' bills the terms were..2⅝ per cent., but for January paper the rate was stiffer. *a* **1904** *Mod.* The bankers will not look at his paper. **1906** *Westm. Gaz.* 20 Oct. 12/2 Without..feeling—as he puts it—that he is 'a pawn with a breech-loader on an open-air chess-board, to be moved at the bidding of a despotic keeper who only takes paper'. **1925** [see HOT *a.* 7 e]. **1930** *Liberty* 5 July 23/2 Next day the news cracks about a twenty-grand payroll robbery at the factory in Sheffield. Bob comes in at night loaded with paper and gives me five hundred bucks of it. **1937** E. SNOW *Red Star over China* VI. iv. 234 Only Soviet paper was in use, except in the border counties, where White paper was also accepted. **1949** J. CARY *Fearful Joy* 255 Now they've got some loose paper they're going to make it float. **1969** *Times* 26 Mar. 28/8 A 'proper' level for three-month paper is thougth to be about 8⅝ per cent compared with a frequently quoted level of between 9$\frac{5}{16}$ and 8⅞ per cent. **1977** *Law Rep.* 5 July 620 The bank..also bought them, in the recognised international market in what was called 'medium-term paper'.

4. *slang.* **a.** Free passes of admission to a theatre or other entertainment; *transf.* persons admitted by free passes.

1785 *Apol. Life G. A. Bellamy* (ed. 2) II. xliii. 114 The piece [*sc. Romeo and Juliet* at Drury Lane and Covent Garden] was performed so many nights, that the public as well as the performers were tired and disgusted with it. We, [at Drury Lane] however, got the advantage of some nights. But this was not done without a great deal of paper, which was bestowed upon the occasion. **1820** C. MATHEWS *Let.* in A. Mathews *Mem. Charles Mathews* (1839) III. 165 He had spoken to the cash-taker of the rooms, who said, this is *all* the money (not much), and there's plenty of paper. **1825** P. EGAN *Life of Actor* iv. 144 '*Theatrical paper*' has been frequently known to *silence* many a harsh tongue; and also to change the looks of an angry creditor. **1873** *Routledge's Yng. Gentl. Mag.* Apr. 277/1 The house is filling well without the aid of paper or free tickets. **1885** *St. James's Gaz.* 30 Jan., Another point; I mean the distribution of 'paper', or free admissions. **1888** *Pall Mall G.* 19 May 4/2 How much paper there was in St. James's Hall yesterday we do not know, but the hall, in any case, must have been remuneratively full. **1927** *Vanity Fair* XXIX. 132/3 'Paper' is a pass. **1951** 'J. TEY' *Daughter of Time* ii. 21 Johnny Garson can tell you how much paper there is in the house what time he is sobbing his heart out.

b. *U.S.* Marked cards for sharpers.

1894 MASKELYNE *Sharps & Flats* 43 In America..one may still find 'saloons' which are stocked entirely with this kind of 'paper' as the cards are called. **1929** M. A. GILL *Underworld Slang* 9/2 *Paper*, marked playing cards. **1938** H. ASBURY *Sucker's Progress* 37 In the early days of Poker the marked cards used by sharpers were prepared beforehand by the gamblers themselves, and were known as 'paper'; or were marked during the process of the game with the finger nail or a needle point embedded in a ring.

c. *U.S.* A forged cheque or document.

1850 [see KITE-FLYING *vbl. sb.* 2]. **1925** *Flynn's* 7 Mar. 191/2 *Paper*,..forged notes or checks. **1930** *Liberty* 19 July 27/1, I turn out bills of sale by the dozen. I don't like to do it as it is not playing square with my dealers. They don't know they're getting worthless papers.

d. *U.S.* Posters or similar publicity material. Also individual singular: a poster or placard.

1878 *Harper's Mag.* Mar. 599/2 Struggling families who have 'one room to let', or..a modest paper in a window 'Borders wanted'. **1896** *N.Y. Dramatic News* 18 July 12/1 Car No. 6..was here July 7–8, posting very attractive paper, which reads 'coming soon'. **1903** W. C. THOMPSON *On Road with Circus* i. 23 The posters and lithographs sent out in advance are 'paper'. **1942** BERREY & VAN DEN BARK *Amer. Thes. Slang* §571/6 *Paper*, posters.

†**5.** ***herb paper, water paper***: suggested names for the papyrus plant. *Obs.*

1548 TURNER *Names of Herbes, Papyros*... It maye be called in englishe water paper, or herbe paper.

** Individual singular with *a*, and plural.

(The earliest sense here is 7, the *papers* which first attained to individual distinction being written documents. In 6 also, the specialized b. naturally took precedence of the general sense.)

6. a. A piece, sheet, or leaf of paper.

1628 EARLE *Microcosm.*, *A Childe*, His Soule is yet a white paper vnscribled with obseruations of the world. **1634** J. BATE *Myst. Nat. & Art* 30 Straine it through a browne paper rowled within a tunnel. **1718** MRS. EALES *Receipt* 5 Let 'em stand all Night in the Pan they are boil'd in, with a Paper laid close to 'em. **1833** J. H. NEWMAN *Arians* I. iii. (1876) 85 The mind is often compared to a tablet or paper. .. But, in truth, the mind can never resemble a blank paper. **1875** H. C. WOOD *Therap.* (1879) 19 Papers are medicated leaves or sheets of paper for external use.

b. A piece of paper serving as a wrapper or receptacle; often including the contents, a packet done up in paper, a small paper parcel; a paperful; a sheet or card of paper containing pins or needles stuck in it.

1511 GUYLFORDE *Pilgr.* (Camden) 39 The warden..toke a basyn full of folden papres with relyquis in eche of them. **1567** in Hay Fleming *Mary Q. of Scots* (1897) 508 Item xxiiij papir of prenis to the Quenis dule. **1662** J. DAVIES tr. *Mandelslo's Trav.* 227 A paper of Fruits and Conserves for the Desert. **1698** A. BRAND *Emb. Muscovy to China* 82 Two Papers of Thee. *a* **1776** R. JAMES *Dissert. on Fevers* (1778) 48, I gave him half a paper more of the Powder. **1836** DICKENS *Sk. Boz* I. 229 A little basket which..contains a small black bottle and a paper of sandwiches. **1844** —— *Mart. Chuz.* xix, Give me the paper of gloves. **1901** *Academy* 17 Aug. 138/1, 'I want a paper of pins'.

c. A curl-paper. (Usually in *pl.*)

a **1746** M. LEAPOR *Poems* (1748) I. 5 Let Isabel unload her aking Head Of twisted Papers, and of binding Lead. **1772** J. WOODFORDE *Diary* 21 Apr. (1924) I. 114 We..caught my Sister Jane at table with her hair up in papers. **1819** KEATS *Let.* 16 Apr. (1958) II. 92 Do you put your hair in papers of a night? **1838** DICKENS *Nickleby* (1839) vii. 60 The lady.. was dressed in a dimity night jacket with her hair in papers. **1876** MISS BRADDON *J. Haggard's Dau.* ix. 122 Take their hair out of papers.

d. *U.S.* A playing card. (Cf. sense 4 b).

1842 *Southern Lit. Messenger* VIII. 412/1, I found myself ..around a table in a corner, and the 'papers' in motion. **1862** O. W. NORTON *Army Lett.* (1903) 41 Those whose taste inclines them that way are playing with the 'spotted papers'. **1935** A. J. POLLOCK *Underworld Speaks* 86/1 *Papers*, playing cards.

7. a. A sheet, leaf, or piece of paper, bearing writing; a document written or printed on paper, as a note, bill, or other legal instrument; in *pl.* written notes, memoranda, letters, official documents, etc. With quot. *c* 1475 cf. F. *être sur les papiers de quelqu'un*, to be in his books, in his debt. †***papers of concern***: cf. F. *papiers de conséquence, papiers d'affaires.*

[**1364–5** *Rolls of Parlt.* II. 287/1 Surmettantz a eux qe sont Dettours, & ce voillent ils prover par lour papirs.] **1389** in *Eng. Gilds* (1870) 5 To kepe wel & trewely alle þe pointz of þis papir. *c* **1475** *Partenay* 4735 Now full merily demene you amonge, For of his paupires strike oute plain be ye! **1590** SPENSER *F.Q.* I. xii. 25 Which he disclosing read thus, as the paper spake. **1682** BUNYAN *Holy War* 203 His name is Pitiless; so he has writ himself in all papers of concern, wherein he has had to do. **1706** MRS. RAY in *Lett. Lit. Men* (Camden) 208 As to my husband's papers I have put them all..into Mr. Dale's hands. **1750** GRAY *Long Story* 66 Papers and books a huge Imbroglio! **1824** J. JOHNSON *Typogr.* II. xvi. 573 Papers printed by authority of either House of Parliament. **1861** C. KNIGHT *Pop. Hist. Eng.* VII. xxvi. 453 Mr. James Paull..moved for papers, upon which he proposed to ground grave charges against the late governor-general. **1872** YEATS *Growth Comm.* 99 From a state paper of the Doge Moncenigo we learn some particulars of the trade with Italy. **1902** BESANT *Five Yrs. Tryst* 29 'You've signed some paper or other, of course?' 'I've signed a dozen papers'. *Mod.* The honourable gentleman concluded his speech by moving for papers. The Prime Minister promised that papers should be laid on the table of the House.

†**b.** A note, fastened on the back of a criminal undergoing punishment, specifying his offence. *Obs.*

a **1529** SKELTON *Sp. Parrot* 472 So myche papers weryng for ryghte a smalle ex[c]esse. *a* **1548** HALL *Chron., Hen. VIII* 59 He so punyshed periurye with open punyshment & open papers werynge, that in his tyme it was lesse vsed. **1577** KNEWSTUB *Confut.* (1579) 82 b, Allegories, which are H.N. his best witnesses: be as those men who haue heretofore worne papers. **1588** SHAKS. *L.L.L.* IV. iii. 47 Why he comes in like a periure, wearing papers. **1593** —— *2 Hen. VI*, II. iv. 31 Led along, Mayl'd vp in shame, with Papers on my back, And follow'd with a Rabble. **1688** R. HOLME *Armoury* III. 310/1 To stand on the Pillory..with Papers of his Offence set on his Back.

†**c.** *pl.* = STATE-PAPERS, as in ***Office of His (Her) Majesty's Papers, Clerk, Keeper, Register of the Papers***; cf. also PAPER-OFFICE a. *Obs.*

Cf. 'Calendar of Documents relating to the History of the State Paper Office' in *30th Rep. Dep. Kpr.* App. pp. 212–293. The 'Office of Her Majesty's Papers and Records for Business of State and Council' was established in 1578. About 1800 the terms 'papers of state', 'paper-office' etc. became superseded by those of 'State papers', 'State paper office' etc.

1612 in *30th Rep. Dep. Kpr.* App. 225 The Othe of the Clerke of the Papers for matters of State. **1612** *Indorsement* ibid., A Register of the later Bookes and Papers of English business..delivered into the Office of the Papers at Whitehall, at the death of the Earle of Salisbury, late Lord Treasurer. **1629** SIR T. WILSON *Petition* ibid. 239 Clerk, Keeper and Register of Your Majesty's Papers and Records for business of State and Council. ? **1782** *Ibid.* 270 To preserve the Papers of State for the use of the public. **1799** *Ibid.* 287 The King's papers require an arrangement applicable to the dispatch of business.

d. *pl.* The collection of documents which establish the identity, standing, etc., of an envoy, traveller, or other person; the certificates which accompany an officer's application for permission to resign; hence ***to send in one's papers***, to resign; (***ship's papers***) the set of documents carried by a ship for the manifestation of her ownership, nationality, destination, etc.

1685–8 in *Black Bk. Admiralty* (1871) I. 29 To examine them well about their ladeing and likewise their papers and documents. **1794** in *Story's Pract. Prize Courts* (1854) 4 Every ship must be provided with complete and genuine papers. *Ibid.*, If there be false or colourable papers; if any papers be thrown overboard;..if proper ship's papers are not on board. **1796** PITT *Let.* 2 Nov., I accompanied your memorial with all your papers. **1855** MACAULAY *Hist. Eng.* xx. IV. 473 A fine ship named the Redbridge... Her papers had been made out for Alicant. **1872** *Routledge's Ev. Boy's Ann.* Apr. 302/1, I sent in my papers, packed up my traps, and here I am. **1890** W. E. NORRIS *Misadventure* xvi, He wished him..to send in his papers before his marriage. **1914** E. A. POWELL *Fighting in Flanders* ii. 45 One never stirred out of doors in Antwerp without one's papers, which had to be shown before one could gain admission to the post office ..or any other public buildings. **1960** O. MANNING *Great Fortune* II. 142 Recalled to his regiment. His papers came yesterday and off he had to go. **1960** *Victorian Studies* June 326 Those, like Captain Gadsby..in the end sent in their papers for the sake of their wife and family. **1963** R. D. SYMONS *Many Trails* xi. 110 The great steam-engine..was attended by a proper steam engineer, with 'papers'. **1966** *Listener* 24 Feb. 267/2 The Moscovite lives by the rules. 'Without "papers" a man is nothing,' my exasperated interpreter once asserted. **1970** *Globe & Mail* (Toronto) 28 Sept. 29/2 (Advt.), Applicant must possess thorough knowledge of hot water heating systems and preferably possess engineers papers. **1977** H. KAPLAN *Damascus Cover* xiv. 140 Some [Nazis]..proceeded to Rome and Geneva where clandestine processing stations..supplied them with the papers necessary for travel to the Middle East.

e. A set of questions in an examination, usually written or printed on one sheet; also, the written answers to such a set of questions.

1838 ARNOLD in Stanley *Life* (1844) II. 114 The recommendation of the Vice-Chancellor, that the Examinations should be conducted entirely through the medium of printed papers. *Ibid.*, We..know the value of printed papers, and we know also the advantages to be derived from a vivâ voce examination. **1852** BRISTED *5 Years in Eng. Univ.* I. 186 Our best classic had not time to floor the paper. **1859** FARRAR *Julian Home* xi. 131 The papers suited him excellently. **1861** M. BURROWS *Pass & Class* (1866) 21 The Pass papers occupy one day, the Class papers from four to five. *Mod.* I was busy correcting examination papers.

8. a. = NEWSPAPER, journal. *pl.* The publicity afforded by the newspapers; esp. in phr. ***to make the papers***: to gain publicity.

1642 PR. RUPERT *Declaration* 3 Those impudent unpunished papers cried daily in the streets. **1716** ADDISON *Freeholder* No. 19 ¶4 The *Examiner* was a Paper in the last Reign. **1727–41** CHAMBERS *Cycl.* s.v., We have daily Papers, weekly Papers, morning Papers, evening Papers..political Papers, literary Papers, Papers of entertainment, etc. **1810** LAMB *Let. to Manning* 2 Jan., Coleridge is bringing out a paper in Weekly Numbers, called the *Friend*. **1852** MRS. STOWE *Uncle Tom's C.* xix, She entered the room where St. Clare lay reading his paper. **1883** STEVENSON *Silverado Sq.* 14 The office of the local paper (for the place has a paper —they all have papers). **1963** 'A. GILBERT' *Ring for Noose* viii. 97 At all events he hadn't made the morning papers. **1967** WODEHOUSE *Company for Henry* iii. 47 One of these days that woman is going to get herself Into The Papers. **1972** *Village Voice* (N.Y.) 1 June 16/2 Through many lonely months McGovern had trouble making the papers.

b. = WALL-PAPER.

1764 in E. Singleton *Social N.Y. under Georges* (1902) 43 The Dining-Room is 14 × 19, hung with genteel Paper; the Entry or Passage from the Door, is hung with the same. **1830** M. EDGEWORTH *Let.* 17 Nov. (1971) 430 When I went down to the library..I was charmed even with the fuschia-trellis looking paper. **1873** C. M. YONGE *Pillars of House* II. xiv. 53 What our paper may have been in its earlier stages of existence I am not prepared to say; but since I can remember ..the wall presented every *nuance* of purplish salmon. **1945** *Catal. Exhib. Eng. & Hist. Wallpapers* (Central Inst. Art & Design) 6 The most beautiful of all..are the hand-painted Chinese papers. **1967** WODEHOUSE *Company for Henry* iv. 57 His spiritual home would have been some such establishment as Edgar Allen Poe's House of Usher, into which he would have fitted like the paper on the wall. **1975** 'A. HALL' *Mandarin Cypher* vii. 104 We had all the paper off the wall at the Hong Kong Cathay [Hotel].

9. A written or printed essay, dissertation, or article on some particular topic. Now *esp.* A communication read or sent to a learned society.

1669 W. HOLDER *Elem. Speech* 113 A Paper presented to the Royal Society. **1700** T. BROWN *Amusem. Ser. & Com.* 2, I know not what Success these Papers will find in the World. **1754** CHATHAM *Lett. Nephew* iii. 16 Spectators, especially Mr. Addison's papers, to be read very frequently. **1790** *Trans. Soc. Arts* IX. 210 A short paper on the Cinnamon tree. **1882** *Nature* XXV. 351/1 The second paper was..on the system of dredging introduced..on the rivers of France. **1887** *Pall Mall G.* 28 Oct. 3/2 This new theory, on which a paper was read at the late meeting of the British Association.

II. *attrib.* and *Comb.*

10. Simple *attrib.* in special senses, passing into *adj.* **a.** Of paper; made or consisting of paper.

(Also, made of paper of a particular form or kind, as in a ***large-paper*** copy of a book, a ***brown-paper*** parcel, an ***oiled-paper*** bag, etc. See LARGE, etc.)

(Often unnecessarily hyphened to following sb. The hyphen is needed only when the combination itself is used attrib.)

1594 T. NASH *Unfortunate Traveller* sig. H 4v As if it had beene a candle in a paper lanterne. **1596** NASHE *Saffron Walden* Wks. (Grosart) III. 173 These Boyes paper-dragons that they let fly with a pack-thrid in the fields. **1662** J. DAVIES tr. *Olearius' Voy. Ambass.* 236 Certain Cords whereat hung Paper-Lanthorns. **1670** W. CLARKE *Nat. Hist. Nitre* 60 The paper-Bills on the walls..remain'd like the Gold unburn'd. **1707** HEARNE *Collect.* 1 May (O.H.S.) II. 10 The Bp...desires a large-paper Livy. *Ibid.* 1 June 17 A royal paper copy of Mill's N.T. **1708** *Ibid.* 8 Apr. 101, 3 small-paper Livys. **1723** J. NOTT *Cook's & Confectioner's Dict.* sig. Cc 2v (*heading*) To dry Plums..when they are dry put them into Paper Bags full of small Holes, and hang them up. **1723** *Amer. Weekly Mercury* 7 Nov. 2/2 The natural Situation of these Counties and the Practice of our Neighbours, has laid us [of Penna.] under the necessity of coming into a Paper Currency. **1757** [BURKE] *Europ. Settlem. Amer.* II. 297 Money of credit, which they commonly call paper currency. **1780** COWPER *Table-T.* 385 The inestimable 'Estimate' of Brown Rose like a paper-kite, and charmed the town. *a* **1790** B. FRANKLIN *Autobiogr.* in *Writings* (1905) I. 306 The wealthy inhabitants..being against all paper currency. *Ibid.*, I wrote and printed an anonymous pamphlet..entitled 'The Nature and Necessity of a Paper Currency'. **1796** JANE AUSTEN *Let.* 9 Jan. (1952) 3 We have trimmed up and given away all the old paper hats of Mamma's manufacture. **1808** *Ibid.* 24 Oct. 225 We do not want amusement: bilbocatch,..spillikins, paper ships, riddles, conundrums, and cards..keep us well employed. **1828** P. CUNNINGHAM *N.S. Wales* (ed. 3) II. 102 Our colonial council has lately committed a great error in prohibiting..all paper issues below one pound. **1849** NOAD *Electricity* 167 A thick paper bag. **1864** *Harper's Mag.* Dec. 58/2 With an umbrella and a shawl, inclosing a box of paper collars. **1867** J. LAING *Theory of Business* vi. 77 With Austria, Russia, America, and other countries using paper currencies..the par is exceedingly uncertain. **1870** J. K. MEDBERY *Men & Mysteries Wall St.* 23 A broker cannot.. innocently fling a 'paper dart' at neighbour without being amerced ten dollars. **1871** KINGSLEY *At Last* v, Paper-nests, ..like those of our tree-wasps at home, hang from the trees. **1875** KNIGHT *Dict. Mech.*, *Paper Collar*, one made from paper in imitation of linen. **1897** MARY KINGSLEY *W. Africa* 477 Seedy young men with us object to carrying paper parcels for fear of being taken for tailors. **1899** 'MARK TWAIN' in *Forum* (N.Y.) Mar. 31 A billionaire in a paper-collar, a king in a breech-clout. **1905** *Daily Chron.* 15 May 8/5 There is a craze just now for 'paper hats'. It sounds crude, but the smartest and prettiest tricornes, mushrooms, and shady river hats are daintily woven from a soft paper. **1907** *Yesterday's Shopping* (1969) 352 c/1 *Paper d'oyleys*. Star pattern. **1913** C. MACKENZIE *Sinister St.* I. II. iv. 190 They threw paper darts and paper pellets with unerring aim. **1922** JOYCE *Ulysses* 423 A bandy child..with a papershuttlecock. **1934** A. HUXLEY *Beyond Mexique Bay* 6 He..decreed..that we should be given paper hats, balloons, and card-board trumpets. **1935** H. EDIB *Clown & his Daughter* xlii. 233 Women distributing sweets in coloured paper bags passed in and out of the audience. **1951** 'J. TEY' *Daughter of Time* i. 17 She was carrying various paper bags and a small tight bunch of anemones. **1951** R. W. JONES *Thomson's Dict. Banking* (ed. 10) 452/1 *Paper currency*, the paper instruments such as bank notes, cheques, bills, and other forms which take the place of money and act as a currency or circulating medium. **1955** A. MARSHALL *I can jump Puddles* (1956) xix. 136 'Skeeter couldn't fight his way out of a paper bag,' Joe asserted. **1958** Paper doily [see DOILY *sb.* or *a.*]. **1969** 'H. PENTECOST' *Girl Watcher's Funeral* (1970) II. i. 94 That first punch.. smashed through my guard like a paper doyley. **1972** M. WOODHOUSE *Mama Doll* xi. 145 Andy Dylan made paper darts. **1973** M. AMIS *Rachel Papers* 153 Not, for her, the wet Brillo-pad, nor the paper-bagful of kedgeree. **1973** J. LEASOR *Mandarin Gold* ii. 18 Paper lanterns were glittering above shop fronts and over stalls. **1974** *Sunday Times* (Colour Suppl.) 17 Feb. 55/3 Strange how people assume at once the personalities of their paper hats. That man, for instance, in a boiled shirt and three exiguous Red Indian feathers. **1974** M. G. EBERHART *Danger Money* xiii. 134 Shoes, stockings and paper tissues littered the room. **1975** *New Yorker* 3 Mar. 38/3 She never got over her spending a hundred and twenty-five dollars on paper lanterns for the engagement party. **1977** R. BARNARD *Death on High C's* ix. 87 She went through men like other women go through paper tissues.

b. *fig.* Like paper; slight, thin, flimsy, frail, feeble (as if made of paper).

1615 CROOKE *Body of Man* 60 The excellent proportion and structure..maketh this Paper-sconce high perill-proofe. *a* **1716** SOUTH *Serm.* IV. iv. 177 What Paper Walls such persons are apt to inclose themselves with. **1730** FIELDING *Rape upon Rape* I. viii, Pox of my paper skull! **1804** COLLINS *Scripscrap* 4 Go patter to paperscull saps, do ye see. **1854** *2nd Rep. Select Comm. Emigrant Ships* 61 in *Parl. Papers* XIII. 267 These advertisers..have a kind of arrangement with the owners of vessels; they are like recruiters, they collect emigrants; their ships are known in the trade by the name of 'paper' ships. **1891** *Labour Commission Gloss.*, *Paper Ship*, a ship built of inferior material and badly put together.

c. *fig.* Consisting of, pertaining to, or carried on by means of letters to journals, pamphlets, or books; literary. (Cf. 1 d.)

1592 NASHE *P. Penilesse* Wks. (Grosart) II. 16 So..was this Paper-monster, Pierce Penilesse, begotten. **1592** G. HARVEY *Foure Lett.* iv. Wks. (Grosart) I. 223 Meere Paper-bugs, and inckehorne-pads: or a greate deale worse. **1599** SHAKS. *Much Ado* II. iii. 249 Shall quips and sentences, and these paper bullets of the braine awe a man? **1636** PRYNNE *Unbish. Tim.* (1661) Ep. 22 Books of controversie, and paper-battels. **1641** MILTON *Animadv.* iv. Wks. (1847) 65/1 It will stand long enough against the battery of their paper pellets. **1672** CLARENDON *Ess.* Tracts (1727) 252 It thought it seasonable to discontinue those paper-skirmishes. **1727** W. STUKELEY in *Mem.* (Surtees) I. 199 My retreat secures me from malice and envy and all other kinds of paper-gall. **1761** *Ann. Reg.* 187 A very acrimonious paper war. **1809** 'D. KNICKERBOCKER' *Hist. N.Y.* I. IV. iv. 231 This all potent word, which served as his touchstone in politics, at once explains the whole system of proclamations, protests, empty threats, windmills, trumpeters, and paper war. **1826** M. KELLY *Reminisc.* II. 119 Most of the popular songs which he sang in Sacchini's operas were composed by himself, although the credit of them was given to Sacchini; but upon a severe quarrel between them, Rauzzini, in a paper war, actually avowed himself the author of them, and accused Sacchini of the greatest ingratitude. **1895** C. R. B. BARRETT *Surrey* 80 A life of perpetual paper warfare. **1963** D. OGILVY *Confessions Advertising Man* (1964) i. 15, I abhor people who wage paper-warfare. **1970** *Times* 13 Feb. 10/5 In the much larger Arab world, it is a paper war for many people.

d. Written on paper, in written form; *esp.* existing only 'on paper' (see 1 d) and not in reality; theoretical, hypothetical.

1638 CHILLINGW. *Relig. Prot.* I. Pref. to Auth. 'Charity Maint.' §18 The paper fortresses of an imaginary Infallibility. **1658–9** *Burton's Diary* (1828) IV. 37 If they have a mind to break in upon a paper law. **1793** SMEATON *Edystone L.* §122, I determined, from the paper materials that I had..at once to construct the models. **1802** M. CUTLER in *Life*, etc. (1888) II. 74 We see how insignificant the best constructed paper Constitution will prove when opposed to the interests and passions of men. **1803** *Deb. Congress U.S.* 23 Feb. (1851) 129 Paper blockades were substituted for actual ones, and the staple commodities of our country lay perishing in our storehouses. **1812** *Boston Gaz.* 20 July 1/5 The paper-blockades, which have justly occasioned so much irritation, are now abandoned. **1854** H. MILLER *Sch. & Schm.* iii. (1857) 50, I remained simply a fictitious or paper cock-fighter. **1872** *Wharton's Law Lex.* (ed. 5), *Paper blockade*, the state of a line of coast proclaimed to be under blockade in time of war, when the naval force on watch is not sufficient. **1882** OGILVIE, *Paper baron, paper lord*, one who holds a title which is not hereditary, or holds it by courtesy. **1893** *Times* 2 May 10/1 Paper profits were divided as if they were real. **1932** *Sun* (Baltimore) 15 Aug. 7/5 It was granted there might be a half-dozen 'paper' agreements at least..from the conference. **1941** J. S. HUXLEY *Uniqueness of Man* xiii. 270 Hedonism, like utilitarianism, is another of those paper schemes, beautifully logical, that just are not true. **1960** *Washington Post* 27 Nov. E3 At least 70 anti Castro groups have been formed in Miami, but many of them are paper organizations. **1965** A. NICOL *Truly Married Woman* 43 One more week towards the time when Olu Jones and his brethren would take over. He was not worried, however, Perhaps..because I have paper qualifications. **1970** *New York* 16 Nov. 54/3 Abbie is a simple bourgeois basket case, a paper Yippie, and over 30 anyway. **1973** *Time* 25 June 66/2 Lloyd also has a number of paper companies set up in Liechtenstein. **1977** E. AMBLER *Send No More Roses* xi. 266 A chain of twenty different corporations..all making paper profits. **1978** *Jrnl. R. Soc. Arts* CXXVI. 607/2 These targets are real, and not just paper objectives.

11. General Combs.

a. *attrib.* Of, pertaining or relating to, or used for, paper or papers; as ***paper-case***, ***-circulation***, ***-clamp***, ***-clip*** (so ***paper-clip*** vb.), ***-colour*** (= white), ***-excise***, ***-factory***, ***-fibre***, ***-file***, ***market***, ***-merchant***, ***-payment*** (sense 3), ***-press***, ***-pulp*** (see PULP), ***-punch***, ***-size***, ***-stuff***, ***-system*** (sense 3 in quots.), ***trade***, etc.

1679 OATES *Narr. Popish Plot* 48 Who..there drew out of a *Paper-Case a Paper. **1857** HUGHES *Tom Brown* I. viii, A leather paper-case. **1803** *Edin. Rev.* II. 114 The doctrine of unlimited *paper-circulation. **1875** KNIGHT *Dict. Mech.*, **Paper-clamp*,..for holding newspapers, sheet music, periodicals. *Ibid.*, **Paper-clip*, a clasp for holding papers together. **1904** CHESTERTON *Nap. Notting Hill* III. ii. 151 One of those queer little shops..which must be called toy-shops only because toys..predominate; for the remainder of goods seem to consist of almost everything else in the world—tobacco, exercise-books,..halfpenny paper clips. **1921** V. SACKVILLE-WEST *Orchard & Vineyard* 97, I watched..And thought how London clerks with paper-clips Had filed the bills of lading of those ships. **1962** A. NISBETT *Technique Sound Studio* ii. 40 Thin paper..individually paper-clipped to thick paper or card. **1963** A. ROSS *Australia 63* ii. 49 The two banks of the city paper-clipped together by harp-like steel bridges. **1969** P. HIGHSMITH *Tremor of Forgery* xi. 101 Ingham paper-clipped his notes and put them on a corner of his desk. **1973** *Time* 25 June 44/2 With roads, the North Vietnamese can bring in the stuff of life—the paper clips for a bureaucracy, the beginning of a postal system, school supplies, the works. **1974** H. L. FOSTER *Ribbin'* vi. 284 He entered, took a tray of paper clips from her desk and sat down on a chair directly in front of her. **1976** *New Yorker* 1 Mar. 64/2 The note was paper-clipped to a collection of President Nixon's Vietnamization speeches. **1978** N. FREELING *Night Lords* xv. 64 A thin pile of letter paper, neatly squared off and paper-clipped by her fair hand. **1888** STEVENSON *Black Arrow* 11 He will turn *paper-colour. **1860** BRIGHT *Sp.*, *Tax bills* 6 July (1876) 497 Persons who were interested in this question of the *paper-excise. **1862** H. MARRYAT *Year in Sweden* II. 400 Next year a *paper-factory will rise. **1871** KINGSLEY *At Last* xvi, The culture of bamboo for *paper-fibre. **1875** KNIGHT *Dict. Mech.*, **Paper-file*, a device to hold letters or other papers in a pack. **1871** KINGSLEY *At Last* xvi, To supply the United States' *paper market. **1600** J. PORY tr. *Leo's Africa* VIII. 307 Next followeth the streete of the *paper-merchants. **1822** COBBETT *Weekly Reg.* 11 May 353 The scheme for making *paper-payments perpetual. **1825** J. NICHOLSON *Operat. Mechanic* 291 The screws employed for *paper-presses are generally formed with such coarse threads, and so rapid a spiral, that the elasticity of the paper is sufficient to force it to run back. **1839** URE *Dict. Arts* 937 The two sheets of *paper pulp thus united are carried forward by the felt over a guide roller. **1900** *Dict. Nat. Biog.* LXI. 146/2 He started a paper-pulp manufactory at Chiswick. **1839** URE *Dict. Arts* 936 [A] sieve is employed to strain the *paper-stuff previously to its being used in the machine. **1803** *Edin. Rev.* II. 105 Dabblers in the *paper-system. **1823** in Cobbett *Rur. Rides* (1885) I. 398 We can have no war, as long as the paper-system lasts.

b. Objective and obj. gen., as ***paper-blessing***, ***-saving***, ***-selling***, ***-sparing***, ***-using*** adjs.; ***paper-colourer***, ***-dauber***, ***-glosser***, ***-holder***, ***-keeper***, ***-maker***, ***-making***, ***-marbler***, ***-reader***, ***-seller***, ***-sorter***, ***-spiller***, ***-splitting***, ***-tester***, ***-waster***. **c.** Instrumental and parasynthetic, as ***paper-bound*** (see also sense 12 below), ***-capped***, ***-clothed***, ***-collared***, ***-covered***, ***-insulated***, ***-mended***, ***-palisaded***, ***-panelled***, ***-patched***, ***-shuttered***, ***-soled***, ***-wrapped*** adjs. **d.** Similative, etc., as ***paper-hearted***, ***-like***, ***-thick***, ***-thin***, (freq. *fig.*), ***-white*** adjs., ***paper-whiteness***.

1597 DRAYTON *Mortimeriados* S ij b, What *paper-blessing Charrecters are you? **1882** W. WHITMAN *Daybks. & Notebks.* (1978) II. 287 *Paper-bound L of G with revisions prop. **1901** *Sketch* 24 July 26/2 The unsold paper-bound books in Germany are returned to the publisher, who re-binds them. **1928** A. HUXLEY *Let.* 12 Dec. (1969) 304 He'd be able to get rid of the paper bound copies at the same time. **1942** E. WAUGH *Put out More Flags* i. 32 The Vichy water and the paper bound-volume of Balzac on the table before her..spoke of what..she would have called her 'personality'. **1976** *National Observer* (U.S.) 2 Oct. 14/4, I disappeared into the bathroom..with a jar of bath salts and a paper-bound novel. **1598** E. GILPIN *Skial.* (1878) 5 So euery *paper-clothed post in Poules To thee (Deloney) mourningly doth speake. **1874** A. BATHGATE *Colonial Experiences* viii. 86 A section of the community known as the '*paper-collared swells', who are the government officials, medical men, bank employees *et hoc genus omne*. **1867** GEO. ELIOT *Let.* 21 Mar. (1956) IV. 354 People write..to tell me of one *paper-covered American copy of Felix Holt being brought to Europe. **1872** *Routledge's Ev. Boy's Ann.* Apr. 264/2 To jump through a paper-covered hoop. **1923** J. M. MURRY *Pencillings* 18 The paper-covered book, in fact, a rough and ready test of literary curiosity. **1952** *Amer. Speech* XXVII. 149 The paper-covered book in the United States is earning a place for itself much above that of the 'paper-back' and 'dime novel'. **1978** *Jrnl. R. Soc. Arts* CXXVI. 702/1 To have a catalogue of all the Institute's *dix-huitième* drawings in the small compass of a paper-covered 8vo volume including a coloured illustration of every one of them, is most valuable. **1682** T. FLATMAN *Heraclitus Ridens* No. 58 (1713) II. 110 We shall ne'er have done, if every whiffling *Paper-dauber must be regarded. **1882** OGILVIE, **Paper-glosser*, a hot-presser for glossing paper or cards; one who gives a smooth surface to paper. **1939** DYLAN THOMAS *Let.* Mar. (1966) 226 The English poets now are such a ..*paperhearted crowd you could blow them down with one bellow out of a done lung. **1900** *Jrnl. Inst. Electr. Engin.* Dec. (Advt., verso rear cover), Diatrine *paper-insulated.. cables. **1967** *IEEE Trans. Power Apparatus & Systems* LXXXVI. 34 (*heading*) Drying and impregnation of paper-insulated power cables. **1927** *Daily Tel.* 3 May 3 In the opinion of the Postmaster-General the *paperkeepers were amply remunerated at the present rates. **1970** *Ibid.* 12 Jan. 1/6 There would be a series of strikes by 10,000 messengers and paper-keepers in Whitehall. *Ibid.*, The effect of the strike..will be that documents will not be circulated to departments by the paper-keepers. **1663** GERBIER *Counsel* 93 *Paper-like walls. **1857** MRS. GATTY *Parables fr. Nat.* (1859) II. 33 Little pieces of his delicate paper-like bark. **1573–80** BARET *Alv.* P 77 A *paper maker, *chartarius*. **1832** BABBAGE *Econ. Manuf.* xxxi. (ed. 3) 320 If the author deals at once with the paper-maker. **1816** SINGER *Hist. Cards* 20 The art of *paper-making not being introduced into England before the reign of Henry VII. **1887** in Moloney *Forestry W. Afr.* 195 We think the West African Colonies specially adapted to the supply of paper-making basts. **1886** CASSELL, **Paper-marbler*, one who marbles or colours paper with veins in imitation of marble for book-binding, paper-hangings, etc. **1902** CONRAD *Typhoon* ii. 19 A mournful,..Chinaman, walking behind in *paper-soled silk shoes, and who also carried an umbrella. **1726** SWIFT *Adv. to Grub-Street Verse-Writers* iv, Lend these to *paper-sparing Pope. **1691** WOOD *Ath. Oxon.* II. 327 This grand scripturient *paper-spiller..Was strangly tost from post to pillar. **1875** KNIGHT *Dict. Mech.*, **Paper-splitting*, two pieces of muslin are firmly cemented on the sides of the paper and dried. By a pull on each piece the paper is split open. **1655** MRQ. WORCESTER *Cent. Inv.* xliv, A Key..which ..hath its Wards and Rose-pipe but *Paper-thick. **1929** E. BOWEN *Last September* vii. 85 The door went *paper-thin as they raised their voices. **1939** 'N. BLAKE' *Smiler with Knife* 99 His old, paper-thin voice. **1971** *Guardian* 17 Sept. 4/6, I do want to dedicate what is left of my life..to..this paper-thin thing of law and order. **1976** *Liverpool Echo* 24 Nov. 5/4 The Government's paper-thin majority. **1977** *Guardian Weekly* 28 Aug. 3/1 Even a paper thin majority in favour of the rule at Congress would ensure TGWU support. **1978** B. NORMAN *To nick Good Body* vii. 57 There was this thumping in their bedroom. Paper-thin the walls are in those houses. **1881** H. H. GIBBS *Double Stand.* 67 To supply..a *paper-using country with a required metal. **1682** *Modest Account* 13 For your Lordship to turn *Paper-waster. *c* **1385** CHAUCER *L.G.W.* 1198 *Dido*, Up on a thikke palfrey *paper whit. **1806** *Curtis's Bot. Mag.* XXIV. 947 (*heading*) Italian or *paper-white Narcissus. **1938** [see GRANDIFLORA *a.*]. **1957** L. DURRELL *Justine* 66 They [*sc.* Egyptian women] have become tuns of pleasure, rolling on paper-white blue-veined legs. **1973** J. BURROWS *Like an Evening Gone* xi. 128 [He] had turned paper-white when given the news. **1977** P. MOYES *To kill Coconut* v. 66 Paper-white legs proclaimed him a new arrival. **1874** R. TYRWHITT *Sketch. Club* 21 You have only the *paper-whiteness to stand for both. **1973** M. AMIS *Rachel Papers* 32 An old woman passed by surreptitiously dropping *paper-wrapped sugar-lumps on to the chair opposite.

12. Special Combs.: †**paper-bank**, a bank issuing notes; **paper birch** (see BIRCH *sb.* 1 b); **paper-blurrer**, a contemptuous name for an inferior writer; **paper-board**, (*a*) pasteboard = BOARD *sb.* 4; (*b*) *pl.* boards with a paper cover, used in book-binding; **paper boat**, (*a*) a model boat made from folded paper; (*b*) a lightly made vessel; **paperbound** *sb.* (see sense 11 c above) (chiefly *U.S.*) = PAPERBACK; **paper box**, (*a*) a box made of paper; (*b*) a box in which to keep papers; **paper-boy**, a boy employed to sell newspapers; **paper cable**, an electric cable insulated with paper; **paper cap**, (*a*) a cap made of usu. coloured paper and worn at festivals, parties, etc.; (*b*) a cap made of paper worn by carpenters and other workmen; **paper chain**, a chain made of usu. coloured paper as a decoration, esp. at Christmas; **paper-chase**, the game of hare and hounds (see HARE *sb.* 3 b) when paper is used for the 'scent'; hence ***paper-chaser***, ***-chasing*** adj.; also *transf.* and *fig.*; **paper-chewing** *slang* (*rare*), official correspondence; **paper chromatogram** *Chem.*, a chromatogram made on a paper support; **paper chromatography** *Chem.*, the separation of substances by chromatography on a paper support; hence ***paper chromatographic*** adj., ***paper-chromatographically*** adv.; †**paper-cigar**, a cigarette; **paper-cloth**, (*a*) a kind of cloth faced with paper; (*b*) a fabric made by Polynesians from the inner bark of the paper-mulberry and other trees; **paper-coal**, (*a*) a variety of coal or lignite of the Tertiary period, which splits into thin layers; (*b*) = DYSODYLE; **paper cover**, (*a*) see quot. 1960; (*b*) = PAPERBACK; **paper credit** (*Comm.*), 'credit given on the security of any written obligation purporting to represent property' (Wharton *Law Lex.* 1883); 'the term as commonly used includes book-debts, I.O.U.'s, and instruments of credit of all kinds' (Bithell *Counting-ho. Dict.* 1893); **paper cup**, a drinking cup made of thin cardboard; **paper-cutter**, (*a*) a paper-knife; (*b*) a machine for cutting the edges of paper; **paper day** (*Law*): see quot.; **paper doll**, (*a*) a doll-shaped figure cut or folded from a sheet of paper; (*b*) *U.S. slang*: (see quots. 1968–70, 1970); **paper dress**, an inexpensive disposable dress made of paper; **paper dust** *Printing* (see quot. 1964); **paper-faced** *a.*, (*a*) having a face like paper, i.e. thin or pale; (*b*) faced with paper; **paper-fastener**, a metallic contrivance for fastening separate leaves of paper together more conveniently than a pin; **paper-feed**, a device for inserting sheets of paper into a typewriter, printing machine, or the like; **paper-feeder**, a workman or contrivance supplying a printing machine with sheets of paper: cf. FEEDER 8 a and c; **paper flower**, (*a*) an imitation flower made from paper; (*b*) *U.S.*, a name used for several plants with flowers of a papery texture, esp. *Psilostrophe cooperi*, a small shrub of the family Compositæ, native to south-western desert areas of the United States and bearing panicles of yellow flowers; **paper-folder**, an instrument for folding paper, as a paper-knife, or the folding-stick used in bookbinding; **paper-folding**, the making of objects by folding paper, origami; **paper game**, a game played using pencil and paper; **paper-gauge**, **-gage** (*Printing*), = GAUGE *sb.* 12 a; **paper gold** = *special drawing rights* (SPECIAL *a.* 3 d); **paper guide**, an adjustable device on a typewriter for ensuring that the left edge of each sheet of paper is inserted at the same place; **paper handkerchief**, a disposable handkerchief made from soft tissue paper; **paper hankie, hanky** *colloq.*, = *paper handkerchief*; **paper-hornet**, a hornet that makes a papery nest (cf. *paper-wasp*); **paper-hunt** = *paper-chase*; **paper kiosk**, a kiosk at which newspapers are sold; **paper-machine**, a machine for making paper; **paper-making wasp** = *paper-wasp*; **paper man**, a man employed in some way about paper, as a paper-maker, a paper-hanger, etc.; one who sells or supplies papers; a musician, esp. a drummer, who plays from written music; **paper-marl**, a kind of marl occurring in thin layers; **paper-match** = *book match* (BOOK *sb.* 18); **paper minister** (*Sc. colloq.*), a minister who reads his sermons; † **paper-moth**, a moth of which the larva devours paper; *fig.* one who is constantly occupied with paper (cf. *bookworm*); **paper-mulberry**, a small tree (*Broussonetia papyrifera*) allied to the mulberry, from the bark of which paper is made in China and Japan; **paper-muslin**: see quot.; **paper napkin**, a disposable table-napkin made of paper; **paper nautilus** = ARGONAUT 2; **paper nylon**, a stiff paper-like form of nylon; † **paper paste** [= F. *carton pâte*], papier mâché; **paper pattern**, a pattern cut out of paper; *spec.* a dressmaking pattern printed on paper, now usu. on tissue paper with printed instructions; **paper pholas**, see PHOLAS; † **paper-plant**, papyrus; **paper plate**, (*a*) a disposable plate made of paper or cardboard; (*b*) a specially treated paper used as an offset printing plate in certain office duplicating machines; † **paper-plot**, the plot of a play, etc., drawn up on paper; **paper poplar**: see POPLAR; **paper priest**, ? = *paper minister*; **paper-reed**, the papyrus; **paper ribbon**, (*a*) = *paper tape* below; (*b*) = *paper streamer* below; **paper-round**, the job of regularly delivering newspapers; the particular route covered; **paper route** *U.S.*, = *paper-round* above; † **paper-royal**: see ROYAL; **paper-ruler**, an instrument used for, or person employed in, ruling straight lines on paper, a ruler; **paper run** *N.Z.*, = *paper-round* above; **paper-rush**, the papyrus; **paper sack**, (*a*) *U.S.* a paper bag; (*b*) a large sack-like container made of strong paper; **paper sailor**, the argonaut or paper nautilus; **paper sculpture**, the making of three-dimensional structures from one or more pieces of paper by folding, cutting, etc.; **paper shale** *Geol.*, shale which readily splits into very thin paper-like laminæ; **paper-shell**, anything with a very thin shell, as a soft-shelled crab; so **paper-shelled** *a.*, having a very thin shell; **paper shredder**, a machine that tears up esp. secret documents into small unreadable fragments; so ***paper-shredding*** adj.; **paper-spar**, a form of calcite occurring in very thin plates (also called *slate-spar*); † **paper-stealth**, literary piracy, plagiarism; **paper-stock**, raw material from which paper is made; **paper streamer**, a long narrow strip of coloured paper used as a decoration, etc.; † **paper-table**, a sheet or leaf of paper; **paper-taffeta**, a lightweight taffeta with a crisp papery finish; **paper tape**, tape made of paper; *esp.* such on which data is represented by means of holes punched in it; freq. *attrib.*; cf. TAPE *sb.*[1] 2 b, *perforated tape* (PERFORATED *ppl. a.* 1), *punched tape* (PUNCHED *ppl. a.* 2); **paper tiger** [tr. a Chinese expression first used by Chairman Mao], a person, country, etc., that appears outwardly powerful or important but is actually weak or ineffective; **paper towel**, a small disposable towel made of absorbent paper; **paper tower**, the part of a Monotype machine (MONOTYPE *sb.* 3) in which the perforated paper tape is held; **paper town** *N. Amer.*, (*a*) a town that is projected or promoted but not always actually founded; (*b*) a town or city supported by the paper-making industry; **paper-tree**, name for various trees and shrubs from which paper is made, as the Chinese *paper-mulberry*, *Daphne cannabina*, *Edgeworthia Gardneri*, and *Trophis aspera*, all of the East Indies; **paper ware**, (articles made of) papier-mâche; **paper-washing** (*Photogr.*), water in which silver prints have been washed, esp. before toning, which often contains a considerable proportion of silver; **paper-wasp**, a wasp that constructs its nest of a papery substance made from dry wood moistened into a paste; **paper-weight**, a small heavy flat-bottomed object, of stone, metal, glass, etc., often ornamental, intended to be laid upon loose papers to prevent their being removed or disarranged; **paper window**, a window in which paper is used instead of glass; hence **paper-windowed** *a.*; **paper-work**, (*a*) work in paper, a structure made of paper; (*b*) a writing, a literary work; (*c*) the written work of a student in a class or examination; (*d*) work done on paper, the filling-in of esp. official forms, the keeping of administrative records; **paper-works**, a set of buildings in which paper is made, a paper-factory, paper-mill; † **paper-worm** = BOOKWORM 2.

1796 MORSE *Amer. Geog.* II. 26 Two trading-companies, ..an Insurance company, and a *paper-bank. **1866** *Treas. Bot.* 141 The *Paper Birch, *B[etula] papyracea*, so called from the brilliant white colour of the bark of young trees, is an American species. **1581** SIDNEY *Apol. Poetrie* (Arb.) 61, I, that..am admitted into the company of the *Paper-blurers. **1652–62** HEYLIN *Cosmogr.* III. (1682) 182 Every foolish and idle paper-blurrer. **1852** K. H. DIGBY *Compitum* VI. 269 The conventional, exaggerated effusions of mere paper-blurrers. **1549** *Bk. Com. Prayer* (Colophon), Bounde ..in *Paper Boordes. **1888** C. T. JACOBI *Printers' Vocab.* 95 *Paper boards*, a term applied to cheap bindings in boards, but with paper instead of cloth sides. **1929** A. J. VAUGHAN *Mod. Bookbinding* IV. 216 *Paper or Cloth Boards*, a binding consisting of a case made from a paper or cloth cover. **1944** *Sun* (Baltimore) 9 Jan. 3/5 The Robert Gair Company plant, manufacturing paperboard for containers and boxes for war purposes, was shut down today because of a lack of wastepaper. **1959** R. HOSTETTLER et al. *Technical Terms Printing Industry* (ed. 3) 103/1 (Bound) in paper boards. **1959** A. MCLINTOCK *Descr. Atlas N.Z.* 59 The value of production of pulp, paper, and paperboard for 1956–7 was £12·4 million. **1961** J. CARTER *ABC for Bk.-Collectors* (ed. 3) 143 Notwithstanding that 'original boards'..are in fact covered with paper, the term *paper boards*, if used of any but quite modern books..suggests boards..covered with paper of a plain colour, usually not the original binding. **1965** B. J. KIRKPATRICK *Bibliogr. E. M. Forster* 47 Pale green paper boards; printed in black on upper cover. **1971** *New Scientist* 27 Apr. 259/2 Scrap paper..is used to make some forms of paperboard for packaging. ? **1846** MRS. GASKELL *Let.* (1966) 48 All the children were very kind to Florence, and made her paper boxes, and *boats. **1863** DICKENS in *All Year Round* 26 Sept. 108/1 My voyages (in paper boats) among savages often yield me matter for reflection at home. **1929** F. C. BOWEN *Sea Slang* 101 *Paper boat*, a lightly-built vessel of any sort, but particularly applied to paddle excursion steamers. **1931** R. CAMPBELL *Georgiad* III. 61 The anecdotes Of Alfred's cakes and Shelley's paper boats. **1961** F. H. BURGESS *Dict. Sailing* 156 *Paper boat*, any boat with very thin planking. **1964** M. CLIVE *Day of Reckoning* viii. 73 Parlour tricks, such as making cocked hats out of newspaper or paper boats from half-sheets of writing paper. **1978** *Listener* 12 Jan. 57/2 A parting gift from his cell-mate..a little paper boat..not more than two or three millimetres long. **1961** *Spectator* 26 May 765 (Advt.), Yale *Paperbounds. Yale University Press. **1970** *Scholarly Publishing* I. 419 Yale Fastbacks will be made available as paperbounds, at low cost, and they will often reflect the newest techniques of rapid book production. **1973** *Publishers Weekly* 7 May 10 (Advt.), Now *The Divine Vision* is a Quest paperbound. **1754** *Connoisseur* I. 189 The man of taste takes his Strasburgh veritable tabac from a right Paris *paper-box, and the pretty fellow uses a box of polished metal, that by often opening it he may have the opportunity of stealing a glance at his own sweet person reflected in the lid of it. **1757** in S. M. Hamilton *Lett. to Washington* (1899) II. 80 Paper Box of Tarsils..1. **1776** J. WEDGWOOD *Let.* 14 July (1965) 195 They have not much expectation in those articles (unless in very cheap paper Boxes) from any market where they have the French for their Rivals. **1861** D. G. ROSSETTI *Let.* 19 Jan. (1965) II. 389 Will you tell her we are very thankful for her paper-box, which is very useful? **1869** *Boyd's Business Directory N.Y. State* 460 H. Lettington, Manufacturer of Paper Boxes. **1913** J. LONDON *Valley of Moon* I. xi. 96 As if I didn't know..how long you worked in ..the paper-box factory. **1926–7** *Army & Navy Stores Catal.* 383/2 Paper boxes, japanned tin. **1876** BESANT & RICE *Gold. Butterfly* v. 38 The *paper-boy was beginning, with the milkman, his round. **1893** W. J. HOPKINS *Telephone Lines* xiv. 209 In the *paper cables made by John A. Roebling & Sons Company, two paper strips are laid on lengthwise, as loosely as possible, being held in place by thread wound about them. **1936** *Economist* 22 Feb. 437/1 The board intended to extend the business of the company into new lines, the main business being the manufacture of paper cables. **1973** R. W. SILLARS *Electr. Insulating Materials* v. 88 Drying of high voltage oil-filled paper cables ..is more critical than transformer drying, for the stress at working voltage is considerably higher and therefore discharge is more difficult to avoid. **1809** 'D. KNICKERBOCKER' *Hist. N.Y.* II. vi. viii. 162 Little urchins.. followed in droves after the drums, with *paper caps on their heads. **1835** DICKENS *Sk. Boz.* (1836) 1st Ser. II. 149 An unshaven, dirty, sottish-looking fellow, whose tarnished paper-cap..communicates an additionally repulsive expression to his very uninviting countenance. **1887** KIPLING *Plain Tales from Hills* (1888) 231 A big blue paper cap from a cracker. **1967** C. V. BARK *See Living Crocodiles* iii. 44 The guests wore paper caps and pulled crackers. **1974** L. LAMB *Man in Mist* vi. 37, I can well remember when carpenters and masons wore paper caps, as they still do in Italy and in Tenniel's *Alice*. **1943** N. BALCHIN *Small Back Room* iii. 31 It's a damned shame we haven't got a few *paper chains and a bit of misletoe for the old boy. **1971** M. MCCARTHY *Birds of America* 31 He..preferred the [Christmas] tree..with..the paper chains he cut and pasted. **1973** E. JONG *Half-Lives* 82, I tie you to the bed with paper chains. **1856** DICKENS *Scapegrace* in *Househ. Wds.* XIII. 28/2 What leapers of brooks, what runners in *paper chases! **1914** Paperchase [see *cycle-car*]. **1932** *Times Lit. Suppl.* 9 June 425/4 This is not the usual paper-chase of clues from crime to detection. **1977** *Arab Times* 14 Nov. 2/1 Now, in what local journalists call the great paper chase, three newspapers for blacks are competing at the newsstands. **1884** *Manch. Exam.* 6 Dec. 5/4 There are by-roads and field-paths enough..to satisfy the wants of the *paper chasers. **1884** C. DICKENS *Dict. Lond.* 28/1 There is plenty of cross-country sport promoted by the *paper-chasing clubs. **1934** 'G. ORWELL' *Burmese Days* ii. 30, I can't stick my bloody office..signing one chit after another. *Paper-chewing. *Ibid.* 38 All this paper-chewing and chit-passing. **1944** *Biochem. Jrnl.* XXXVIII. 231/2 The *paper chromatograms are by no means united to the separation of aminoacids. **1972** K. NARITA in M. Funatsu et al. *Proteins* II. 246 Radioactivity of acetylglycylserine was almost the same as that found in the material which stayed at the origin on the paper chromatogram. **1956** *Nature* 7 Jan. 22/1 He described preliminary studies on the successful *paper-chromatographic separation of intact tissue phospholipids. **1971** *Jrnl. Chromatogr.* LX. 381 Almost the entire present knowledge on the composition of human urinary sugar content in health and disease can be ascribed to paper chromatographic studies. **1966** *Bot. Mag.* (Tokyo) LXXIX. 507 Three amino acids are formed that can be identified *paper-chromatographically. **1948** *Science* 7 May 483/2 It appears that..*paper chromatography will be found to be an increasingly important research tool in analyzing for amino acids. **1971** C. T. KENNER *Analyt. Separations & Determinations* xv. 282 Two-dimensional paper chromatography is used to separate complex mixtures of amino acids produced by hydrolysis of protein. **1833** MARRYAT *P. Simple* xvii, A *paper segar. **1843** [see CIGARETTE 1 a]. **1852** DICKENS *Bleak H.* xliii, Walking about ..smoking little paper cigars. **1843** HUMBLE *Dict. Geol. & Min.*, **Paper coal*..composed..of a congeries of many kinds of leaves. **1896** CHESTER *Dict. Names Min.*, *Paper-coal*, an early name for dysodile, alluding to the paper-like leaves in which it occurs. **1856** GEO. ELIOT *Let.* 24 Dec. (1954) II. 282 George definitely votes for..boards. He thinks a *paper cover for a philosophical book a bad augury. **1903** *Daily Chron.* 10 July 3/4 Paper-cover issues of scientific and other serious books. **1913** T. E. LAWRENCE *Let.* 5 Apr. (1938) 152 If you have any cheap paper-covered copy..(paper-covers are customs free)..I would be exceedingly grateful. **1952** *Amer. Speech* XXVII. 149 It is not clear whether the *Matrix*..uses *limp-cover* in contradistinction to *hard-cover* or *paper-cover*. **1960** G. A. GLAISTER *Gloss. Bk.* 295/1 *Paper covers*, a style of binding much used for cheap reprints, and, especially on the Continent, for original works in which no boards are used, and the stiff paper cover which encloses the book is adhered to the back. *a* **1697** [? POLLEXFEN] *Disc. Trade* A v, *Paper Credit ever was, and will be, necessary for the carrying on of Trade. **1704** *Lond. Gaz.* No. 3991/3 They have set up a sort of Paper Credit at Strasburg, where they pay..in Bills. **1732** POPE *Ep. Bathurst* 39 Blest paper-credit! last and best supply! That lends Corruption lighter wings to fly! **1803** *Edin. Rev.* II. 102 Paper-credit is the visible sign of public credit, and identical with it. **1907** *Yesterday's Shopping* (1969) 352E/2 *Paper drinking cups, complete with holders. **1939** G. GREENE *Lawless Roads* xi. 272 The odious child takes all the paper cups from the water-tap by the lavatory. **1971** J. HENDERSON *Copperhead* (1972) xv. 191 A girl appeared with..the usual paper cups. **1978** R. HILL *Pinch of Snuff* xxiv. 239 She..poured tea from the flask into the paper cups. *a* **1828** D. WORDSWORTH *Jrnl.* (1941) II. 128, I purchased a ladle and a *paper-cutter..made by the peasants of these mountains. **1829** LYTTON *Disowned* xxxv, A pause ensued... Lord Borodaile played with a paper-cutter. **1901** *Harper's Mag.* CII. 797/1 There he was fitted out with everything he wanted, down to a silver paper-cutter. **1969** *New Yorker* 14 June 46/3 His overhead is hit with his whole arm—no mere flick of the wrist. The arm comes down like the moving part of a paper cutter. **1838** CHITTY *Archbold's Pract. Crt. Q.B.* (ed. 6) 101 In each of the courts there are certain days in each term called **Paper Days*, because the court, on those days, hear the causes which have been entered in the paper for argument before they enter upon motions. **1849** G. S. APPLETON *Mother Goose in Hieroglyphicks* (1963) (Advt., recto rear cover), Chandler's *paper dolls of the latest Paris fashions. No. 1 —Carrie, with her Dresses and Bonnets. **1903** H. KELLER *Story my Life* I. ii. 12 Two little children..were busy cutting out paper dolls. **1968–70** *Current Slang* (Univ. S. Dakota) III–IV. 81 *Make like a paper doll, and cut out*,..to leave. **1970** C. MAJOR *Dict. Afro-Amer. Slang* 89 *Paper doll*,..to play hookey from school; to leave. **1972** T. I. ELLIOTT in *Kawai's Origami* (ed. 4) p. iv, Playing with paper dolls is for girls, and the closest a guy approaches a paper doll is in the famous song where he buys 'a paper doll that other fellows will not steal'. **1976** *New Yorker* 15 Nov. 50/2 Maria undresses her paper doll and deliberately rips a feather off its hat. **1966** *Listener* 15 Dec. 893/1 This..is the year of the *paper dress that can be worn and then tossed in the waste basket. *Ibid.* 893/2 Paper-dress fabrics take colour well, and can be shortened with scissors. **1967** *Observer* 21 May 28/6 The best use so far of so-called 'paper' dresses—as instant summer bargains to be chucked away with no regrets. **1970** *New Society* 5 Mar. 385/2 It's a market that started developing in the fifties, boomed briefly in the mid-sixties with gimmicks like paper dresses, reassessed itself and looks set for a genuine boom in the mid-seventies. **1906** E. DYSON *Fact'ry 'Ands* iii. 27 Over these [*sc.* side-whiskers] the feathery *paper-dust collected till they looked like the wings of an adolescent gosling. **1964** *Gloss. Letterpress Rotary Printing Terms* (*B.S.I.*) 5 *Paper dust or fluff*, fibre (fluff) or loading (dust) which leaves the web as it passes through the printing press or slitters. **1971** *Engineering* Apr. 79 (Advt.), Clean air in every facet of industry... Paper dust. **1597** SHAKS. *2 Hen. IV*, v. iv. 12 Thou *Paper-fac'd Villaine.. Thou thin man. **1892** GREENER *Breech Loader* 174 The wadding used in the shot-gun is of three varieties..3rd, a hard felt paper-faced wad,..the 'pink edge' or Field wad. **1864** *U.S. Patent Specif.* No. 43,435 A new and useful Legal Cap-*Paper Fastener. **1867** *Patent Specif.* No. 2276 An eyelet and paper fastener combined. **1897** *Daily News* 9 Dec. 7/7 [He] secured the envelope..with a paper-fastener, which he ran through the envelope, doubling over the ends. **1920** H. ETHERIDGE *Dict. Typewriting* 177 The *paper feed of a typewriter consists of a paper roller (or platen) and two or more small feed rollers, which latter are kept in contact with the platen by means of springs, to allow of different thicknesses of paper being inserted. **1960** *Times* 24 Feb. 9/2 New fast paper-feed with integrated controls to reduce hand-movement. **1961** T. LANDAU *Encycl. Librarianship* (ed. 2) 120/2 The modern electric duplicator with its automatic paper-feed, counting mechanism and automatic stopping device, is a highly efficient and economical machine. **1967** KARCH & BUBER *Offset Processes* ix. 369 The delivery paper-feed control..controls the feed of paper from the delivery end. **1854** *Rep. Trans. Pennsylvania State Agric. Soc.* 176 The first premium on *paper flowers, is awarded to No. 177. **1892** *Jrnl. Amer. Folk-Lore* V. 99 *Xeranthemum*, *Helichrysum*, paper-flowers. **1915** ARMSTRONG & THORNBER *Field Bk. Western Wild Flowers* 542 Paper Flowers. *Psilostrophe Cooperi*. Yellow. Spring. Southwest. **1935** R. MACAULAY *Personal Pleasures* 256 Like those Japanese paper flowers which gently unfold and bloom in bowls of water..the mind puts out boughs and sprigs of blossom and ripe fruits, inebriating and enticing the charmed soul. **1972** *Islander* (Victoria, B.C.) 2 Apr. 2/3 Paper-flower and sun-drop raced up the hills. **1974** C. FREMLIN *By Horror Haunted* 94 Just look at all these mats, and doilies, and paper flowers! **1864** LOWELL *Fireside Trav.* 123 A useful old jackknife will buy more than the daintiest

..*paper-folder. **1875** Knight *Dict. Mech.*, *Paper-folder*, a bone knife used in folding paper, folding signatures for sewing, and feeding paper from the bank to the press. **1893** T. S. Row (*title*) Geometric exercises in *paper folding. **1905** *Westm. Gaz.* 30 Sept. 13/2 Paper folding has long been a favourite amusement in our Kindergartens. **1908** W. F. White *Scrap-bk. Elem. Math.* 144 (*heading*) Symmetry Illustrated by Paper Folding. **1968** [see origami]. **1972** T. I. Elliott tr. *Kawai's Origami* (ed. 4) p. i, Origami, paper-folding, can be enjoyed by children and adults alike. **1879** C. M. Yonge *Magnum Bonum* III. xxxv. 759 To listen to an exposition of the microphone, to share in a Shakespeare reading, or worse still, in a *paper game, was..such a bore. **1934** E. Waugh *Handful of Dust* i. 21 'No paper games?' 'Oh, no, nothing like that. A certain amount of bridge and back-gammon and low poker.' **1961** A. Wilson *Old Men at Zoo* iii. 125, I felt..that it would not be long before we were involved in paper games or even a sing-song round the piano. **1975** R. Player *Let's talk of Graves* iv. 108 We played games—paper games and Ludo. **1966** *Wall St. Jrnl.* 1 Dec. 5/2 World monetary reform negotiators removed some of the major stumbling blocks in their path to creating '*paper gold', although many more still remain. **1971** *Daily Tel.* 10 May 14 'Paper gold'..is a credit, listed in a computer in Washington, for each country which is a member of the International Monetary Fund. The members agree to use it to pay debts among themselves under certain rules, the only one of which need bother us is that no one except governments ever owns 'paper gold'. **1973** *Times* 15 Nov. 25/6 The nations of the world should start doing something to find a more catchy name for the Special Drawing Right, whose popular (well, fairly popular) nickname of 'paper gold' has recently been coming under attack in Britain. **1978** *Guardian Weekly* 19 Nov. 5/1 An agreement..to begin to phase out the world role of the United States dollar and its progressive replacement with so called 'paper gold', the basket of international currencies known as the IMF Special Drawing Rights. **1952** Leslie & Pepe *Methods of Teaching Typing Simplified* i. 9 *Paper guide should be set and paper inserted by the teacher. **1962** *Which?* Dec. 354 Only four of the machines..had a paper guide for helping to get the left edge of the paper at the same place each time. **1970** L. Gartside *Teaching Business Subjects* viii. 173 Adjustment of margin stops with special reference to the paper-guide. **1907** *Yesterday's Shopping* (1969) 510/1 Handkerchiefs, *Paper (Medicated)—These soft, silky papers are specially prepared for invalids, and are invaluable to sufferers from bronchial affections, catarrh, &c. **1939** R. Stout *Red Threads* (1941) viii. 109 A luxury brand of paper handkerchief, used for wiping creams from the skin. **1954** I. Murdoch *Under Net* iv. 62, I was choking and sneezing and using up a sackful of paper handkerchiefs. **1976** P. Ferris *Detective* i. 2 Rubbing the sweat off his bald head with a paper handkerchief. **1969** *Woman* 19 July 9/2 What man will pick up a dropped *paper hanky? **1970** A. Ross *Manchester Thing* 66 Purse, loose change, paper hankies, comb—that kind of stuff. **1974** N. Freeling *Dressing of Diamond* 171 Vera..gave him a paper hanky. Bernard..mopped at his face. **1886** *Pop. Sci. Mo.* XXVIII. 642 The positions of the *paper-hornets' nests..are variously asserted to be indicative of a 'hard' or 'open' winter, as they chance to be placed in the upper or lower branches of a tree. **1871** *Routledge's Ev. Boy's Ann.* Jan. 52 Hilton backed up Gordon at the *paper-hunt yesterday. **1935** E. Bowen *House in Paris* i. 11 A *paper kiosk opened to take its stock in. **1839** Ure *Dict. Arts* 937 The pulp being diluted to a consistency suitable for the *paper machine, is delivered into a vat. **1867** *Amer. Naturalist* I. 140 The odor that arises from the Tarantula killer when she uses her sting..resembles the odor of the *paper-making wasp (Vespa), only much stronger. **1619** Purchas *Microcosm.* lv. 522 The Printer.., Inke-man, *Paper-man, Corrector. **1753** H. Walpole *Lett.* (1846) II. 469, I have..paper-men to scold. **1936** *Metronome* Feb. 21/4 *Paper man*, drummer who plays only what's written. **1936** *Delineator* CXXIX. 10/3 We have heard that no music is used... No, indeed! *Papermen* are not welcome in this esoteric milieu. **1970** C. Major *Dict. Afro-Amer. Slang* 89 *Paper man*, musician..who plays according to written music. **1707–12** Mortimer *Husb.* (1721) I. 87 *Paper-Marle, which lies near Coals, and [is] like Leaves or Pieces of brown Paper, only 'tis something lighter for Colour. **1832** F. Trollope *Dom. Manners Amer.* II. xxvi. 74 Four ink-wipers, three *paper-matches, and a paste-board watch-case. **1844** Dickens *Mart. Chuz.* xlv. 519 Little Ruth ..had a particular interest in some delicate paper-matches on the chimney-piece: wondering who could have made them. **1854** H. Miller *Sch. & Schm.* v. (1857) 86 The skin-flint wife of a *paper minister. **1698** Farquhar *Love & Bottle* iii. i, Are my clothes so coarse, as if they were spun by those lazy spinsters the Muses?.. Do my hands look like *paper-moths? **1777** G. Forster *Voy. round World* I. 354 Cloth made of the bark of the *paper-mulberry, which we commonly called the cloth-tree. **1872** Oliver *Elem. Bot.* ii. 133 The Paper Mulberry..furnishes to the Polynesian Islanders the useful Tapa cloth, which is fabricated from its fibrous bark. **1864** Webster, **Paper-muslin*, glazed muslin, used for linings, and the like. **1895** *Montgomery Ward Catal.* 109/1 *Paper Napkins..for tourists, travelers, lawn parties, lunches, picnics. **1945** G. Brooks in S. Henderson *Understanding New Black Poetry* (1973) 175 Some paper napkins in a water glass. **1972** L. Lamb *Picture Frame* xiv. 122 He put in his order, saw it..served in paper napkins on plates. **1959** J. T. Story *Mix me a Person* iv. 42 The fossilised remains of juke boxes and female frolic skeletons in *paper-nylon slips. **1960** C. MacInnes *Mr. Love & Justice* 82 The man in Italian drape.., the woman with.. paper nylon petticoat and white stilettos. **1763** W. Lewis *Comm. Phil. Techn.* 367 This varnish, mixed with ivory-black,..is applied..on the dried *paper paste. **1702** Pepys *Let.* 13 Sept. (1926) II. 272 A strict measure cutt in paper of the originall writeing..and..a strict copy taken of the sayd writeing..one copy thereof and of the *paper-patterne, attested by the Doctor, to be delivered to him. **1833** in A. Adburgham *Shops & Shopping* (1964) iv. 40 A great variety of Morning, Dinner, Evening, Ball & Opera Dresses,.. which are made in models and full-size Paper Patterns. **1909** G. Stratton-Porter *Girl of Limberlost* iv. 54 Margaret Sinton was busy with the gingham and the intricate paper pattern. **1969** *Times* 30 Sept. 15/2 Sales of paper patterns —an invention claimed by an American, Mrs. Butterick more than 100 years ago but almost certainly extant in London earlier—are quoted at more than 22 million per year. **1974** M. Cecil *Heroines in Love* iv. 84 Paper patterns for home dressmaking. **1597** Gerarde *Herbal* i. xxvii. §4. 37 This kinde of reede, which I haue englished Paper reede, or *Paper plant, is the same..that paper was made of in Egypt. **1723** J. Nott *Cook's & Confectioner's Dict.* sig. B2ᵛ Almond Bisket..bake them on *Paper-Plates in a moderate Oven. **1948** R. R. Karch *Graphic Arts Procedures* viii. 242 Three kinds of plates are used on the Multilith Duplicators. On the paper plate provided for one-run jobs, you can type, write, letter, draw, paint, rule, or trace the image desired in special inks. The plate is then placed on the press without further preparation. **1966** 'D. Shannon' *With a Vengeance* (1968) iii. 48 [He] confiscated one of the hot cookies she'd just transferred to the paper plate. **1971** R. K. Smith *Ransom* (1972) iv. 167 Greer took the paper plate of hamburgers in one hand..and walked to the standup counter. **1975** *New Yorker* 16 June 25/2 Some girls went to wash their hands, and others..killed time by wearing paper plates on their heads. **1976** *Times* 1 Apr. 32/9 (Advt.), Multilith paper plates, large surplus stock, variety of sizes. **1628** Ford *Lover's Mel.* iii. iii, Enter Palador, Aretus, Corax (with a *paper-plot). **1716** M. Davies *Athen. Brit.* II. 56 His Book limited not his design, nor his Paper-Plot his undertakings. **1781** *Reading not Preaching* ii. 11 Let our *paper-priests and reading clergy apply this to themselves. **1597** *Paper Reede [see *paper-plant* above]. **1611** Bible *Isa.* xix. 7 The paper reeds by the brookes..shall wither. **1876** *Paper ribbon [see perforator 1]. **1888** *Encycl. Brit.* XXIII. 120/2 The paper ribbon R is moved forward by its centre row of holes. **1903** [see *paper tape* below]. **1922** [see *paper tower* below]. **1935** G. Greene *Basement Room* 102 He hadn't blown whistles or thrown paper ribbons. **1965** Paper ribbon [see monotype *sb.* 3]. **1948** C. Day Lewis *Otterbury Incident* iv. 47, I asked if he'd let me take on part of his *paper-round that evening. **1960** C. Dale *Spring of Love* i. 22 If I'm ever hard up for a job I'll come to you for a paper round... So if you ever need a paper boy, remember yours truly. **1971** C. Storr *Thursday* i. 15 The paper-round money had to provide Thursday with the things other children got without having to work. **1868** *Figaro* (San Francisco) 23 July 2/1 A *Paper Route—One of the best on the most substantial city daily. **1929** T. Wolfe *Look Homeward, Angel* (1930) xxvi. 349 He found a substitute for his paper route. **1973** *Publishers Weekly* 19 Nov. 60/3 Isabelle gets to use some of that energy taking over her brother's paper route. **1975** *New Yorker* 28 July 28 (*caption*) Thank goodness, Winant has got himself a paper route, so we have a little something coming in. **1948** D. Ballantyne *Cunninghams* i. viii. 48 Gilbert wanted..a bike for Christmas so's he could have a *paper run. **1727–41** Chambers *Cycl.* s.v. *Paper*, The description given by Pliny of the *Papyrus*, or *Paper-rush. **1884** Miller *Plant-n.*, Paper-reed, or Paper-rush, of the Nile, or of the Ancients. **1904** *Dialect Notes* II. 420 Put the apples in a *paper *sack.* **1940** W. Faulkner *Hamlet* iii. ii. 207 The note was in pencil, on a scrap torn from a paper sack, unsigned. *Ibid.* iv. i. 279 Eck had gone on into the store and emerged with a paper sack, from which he took a segment of cheese. **1944** *Chicago Daily News* 14 July 9/2 She carried a thermos jug of coffee and a couple of sandwiches in a paper sack to eat on the bus. **1955** *Times* 5 July (Reed Suppl.) p. iii/5 In little more than twenty-five years the development of the multi-wall paper sack, in which Medway Paper Sacks Limited has been largely instrumental, has established new standards of efficiency, convenience and cleanliness in the packaging of powdered and granular products. **1971** 'R. Macdonald' *Underground Man* xi. 74, I..had a double hamburger with a paper sack of French fried potatoes. **1974** S. Marcus *Minding Store* (1975) ix. 185 A little old lady in shabby clothes, carrying a paper sack instead of a hand-bag. **1843** Humble *Dict. Geol. & Min.*, Argonauta, the *Paper Sailor. **1901** *Daily Chron.* 14 Nov. 3/4 The Argonaut or Paper Sailer..so called from the delicate consistence of its shell. **1946** A. Sadler *Paper Sculpture* 17 *Paper Sculpture..is composed of sheets of finished paper, so rolled, bent, scored, cut and folded, that it makes a desired form. **1957** B. Angrave *Sculpture in Paper* 24 A legend has already grown up that modern paper sculpture was born in Poland, and is a development of the folk-art paper-cut tradition in that country. **1973** 'D. Halliday' *Dolly & Starry Bird* viii. 111 A fantasia of pure abstract design; a garden of convoluted plastic as fine as paper sculpture. **1978** *Cornish Guardian* 27 Apr. 33/5 Mrs. Phillips, president, welcomed Mrs. Spargo who gave a talk and demonstration of her paper sculpture. **1877** A. H. Green *Phys. Geol.* ii. 85 In some very finely laminated rocks as many as 30 or 40 layers may be counted in the thickness of an inch: such beds are..called Paper shales. **1931** *Prof. Papers U.S. Geol. Survey* No. 168, 7/2 'Paper shale' is the term applied to finely laminated claystones, siltstones, mudstones, and marlstones that show a pronounced tendency to part along the closely spaced bedding planes. **1969** Bennison & Wright *Geol. Hist. Brit. Isles* xiii. 292 An abundant fauna of ammonites and lamellibranchs is present, except in thin paper-shales. **1884** G. B. Goode *Fisheries U.S.: Nat. Hist. Aquatic Animals* 776 The terms 'Soft Crab', '*Paper-shell', and 'Buckler' denote the different stages of consistency of the shell. **1890** *Century Dict.* s.v., When the shell has hardened..the *paper-shell [crab] becomes a crackler. **1893** Kate Sanborn *Truthf. Wom. S. California* 132, 190 California paper-shell almond trees. **1912** *Outing* Oct. 377/1 The only difference between the so-called 'paper-shell' pecan and the fruit from wild trees is that the former has been grown on a budded or grafted tree. **1945** *New England Homestead* 27 Oct. 20/2 Paper-shell pecan in Shell 50¢ per pound. **1948** F. N. Howes *Nuts* 110 Among the many varieties [of almond] cultivated in France are those that range from the thinnest of shells or 'paper shells' to thick hard-shelled forms. **1969** R. & D. De Sola *Dict. Cooking* 167/2 Papershell: Soft-shell pecan. **1974** *Anderson* (S. Carolina) *Independent* 22 Apr. 5A/3 Georgia is the leader in the production of papershell pecans in this country. **1911** *Webster*, Paper-shelled, *a.* Having a very thin shell, as a *paper-shelled almond, or a crab whose shell is beginning to harden. **1946** *Nat. Geogr. Mag.* Apr. 526/2 Immediately after molting the animal [*sc.* a lobster] is soft-shelled. In a few days it is paper-shelled. **1948** F. N. Howes *Nuts* 110 It is usual to classify almonds according to the thickness of the shell—thin- or paper-shelled, soft-shelled and thick- or hard-shelled. **1962** L. Deighton *Ipcress File* xxx. 195 A small machine like a typewriter carriage. It was a *paper shredder. Jay fed the sheet in and pressed a button. It disappeared. **1973** 'D. Jordan' *Nile Green* xiii. 54 The House has an obsession with security so it provides paper shredders on every floor. **1958** S. Hyland *Who goes Hang?* xxxii. 137 John Wintour's bankruptcy..was now officially expunged..by..the *paper-shredding machines. **1968** A. Diment *Bang Bang Birds* i. ii. 14, I fed the telex strip into my paper-shredding device. **1647** H. More *Song of Soul* i. ii. xxxix, The words that he by *paper-stealth had got. **1875** Knight *Dict. Mech.*, **Paper-stock Bleacher*,..for expressing the bleaching material from paper-stock, without having recourse to the draining-vat... *Paper-stock Washer*, a machine for cleansing shredded rags preparatory to pulping. **1930** A. P. Herbert *Water Gipsies* xxv. 373 It was a Gala Night; and the waiters were distributing *paper streamers, balloons, dolls, squeakers and fans. **1935** C. Isherwood *Mr. Norris changes Trains* iii. 41 The ruffled plumes of a paper streamer.. stirring like seaweed in the draught from an electric fan. **1941** M. Treadgold *We couldn't leave Dinah* xvii. 266 A box of crackers and paper streamers left over from the famous Carnival. **1969** N. Freeling *Tsing-Boum* xvi. 117 Broken paper streamers knee deep. **1591** Sylvester *Du Bartas* i. v. 908 Blush not (my book)..To bear about upon thy *paper-Tables [F. *paints sur ton blanc papier*], Flies, Butterflies, Gnats, Bees, and all the rabbles Of other Insects. **1957** M. B. Picken *Fashion Dict.* 344/1 **Paper taffeta*, crisp lightweight taffeta with a somewhat papery feel. **1963** *Times* 27 Feb. 12/2 The bride, who was given away by her father, wore a gown of white paper taffeta, the bodice and trained-skirt trimmed with knife-pleated frilling. **1972** *Vogue* 15 Mar. 3/2 Plaid paper taffeta dress. **1890** *Electrician* 4 July 233/2 Each of these styles can be pressed against the *paper tape by the armature of a corresponding electromagnet. **1903** C. H. Sewall *Wireless Telegr.* iii. 133 There is a telegraphic apparatus known as the 'Wheatstone', in which a paper ribbon is first perforated and then sent through a machine, recording at the distant end with ink marks upon paper tape. **1924** P. J. Risdon *Wireless* xvi. 135 When the operator depresses the keys,..instead of typing letters and figures, it perforates the paper tape with holes corresponding to the dots and dashes of the Morse code. **1943** *Rep. Progress Appl. Chem.* XXVIII. 131 In the standard test for the adhesive power of gummed paper tape the sample is moistened under standard conditions. **1961** *Times* 3 Oct. (Computer Suppl.) p. vi/4 Each day the paper-tape readers feed into the computer more than nine million characters relating to long-distance calls. **1971** *Ann. Rep. Curators Bodl. Libr. 1969–70* 45 The correction of records.. suffered from rapid changes of the staff operating the paper-tape typewriters. **1975** J. B. Harley *O.S. Maps* i. 14 The names are then typed on a 'Monotype' keyboard which reproduces them on punched paper tape to operate the filmsetter. **1952** 'Han Suyin' *Many-Splendoured Thing* v. 313 America is only a *paper tiger... That's what the Peking government says. **1958** *Peking Rev.* 11 Nov. 7 In August 1946 Comrade Mao Tse Tung gave an interview to the American journalist Anna Louise Strong and expressed his famous view point that all reactionaries are paper tigers. **1963** *Economist* 12 Jan. 98/1 In the Chinese view, the 'rotten, decadent, paper-tiger nature' of imperialism cannot change. **1973** *Black Panther* 10 Nov. 14/3 Our minority may be powerful now, but in the end even that power will prove to be a paper tiger once the people unite. **1976** J. Snow *Cricket Rebel* 25 We [*sc.* Sussex] were something of paper tigers when it came to the championship games. **1943** D. Baker *Trio* i. 55 She jerked a *paper towel off the roller and did a careful job of drying. **1953** *Times* 31 Oct. 1/11 Many paper manufactures, including..paper towels and handkerchiefs. **1972** *Guardian* 17 May 9/5 Plain coloured paper towels cost 17p for a two-roll pack. **1975** *New Yorker* 8 Dec. 41/2 The stenographers and typists had to make do with paper towels that scratched when new and dissolved when damp. **1916** *Monotype System* (Lanston Monotype Machine Co.) Gloss. p. lxvi, *Paper Tower... The mechanism of both the Keyboard and Casting Machine..that carries the paper ribbon and advances it one marginal perforation for each character, or space, struck at the Keyboard or cast at the Casting Machine. *Ibid.* xi. 35 The operator has only to turn the small Valve Handle..at the left side of the bottom of the Paper Tower. **1922** *Casting Machine Adjustments* (Lanston Monotype Machine Co.) 17 The Paper Tower is the controlling mechanism of the Casting Machine. In it is placed the paper ribbon prepared at the Keyboard by the compositor, and the ribbon compels the Casting Machine to produce the characters required. *Ibid.*, The Paper Tower mechanism provides that the advance of the paper will be absolute. **1951** S. Jennett *Making of Bks.* iv. 68 Above the keybank [of the Monotype] is the paper-tower, in which is a roll of paper perforated along the edges like cine-film. **1819** E. Evans *Pedestrious Tour* 228 On this river too is General Simcoe's *paper town called London. **1943** T. Pratt *Barefoot Mailman* xi. 90 How do we know you are not a paper-town shark yourself? How do we know you have not come here to boom our city to false values? **1948** E. N. Dick *Dixie Frontier* 151 Many towns..never got beyond the stage of 'paper towns'. **1957** B. Hutchison *Canada: Tomorrow's Giant* 307 Logging camps, mills, paper towns, the new aluminium town of Kitimat..pour their products into Vancouver. **1959** *Tararua* XIII. 49 *Paper road* and *paper town*..describe those roads and towns which have been surveyed but whose actual existence has got no further than the maps. **1969** H. Horwood *Newfoundland* i. 4 Driving back through the star-studded night towards the paper town of Grand Falls. **1839** Ure *Dict. Arts* 940 Processes..in China to make paper with the inner bark of their *paper-tree ..or Chinese mulberry. **1884** Miller *Plant-n.*, Indian Paper-tree, *Daphne cannabina* and *Edgeworthia Gardneri. Ibid.*, Paper-tree, of Siam, *Trophis aspera.* **1925** G. Dickinson *Eng. Papier-Mâché* i. 3 In 1772 Henry Clay, japanner, of Birmingham, invented a material which had certain heat-resisting properties, that made it suitable for japanning or lacquering processes. The body of the material was made by pasting sheets of paper together, and the articles made from it were called '*paper ware'. **1969** *Canad. Antiques Collector* Jan. 8/1 The craze for making 'Paper-ware' spread from the 17th to the 19th century, when recipes for making and decorating bowls, vases and plates, were printed in such papers as the '*Gentleman's Magazine*'. **1858** Simmonds *Dict. Trade*, **Paper-weight*, a fancy ornament for keeping loose letters or papers on a table or desk from blowing about. **1893** Q. [Couch] *Delectable Duchy* 283 He spread the plan on the table, with a paper-weight on each corner. **1580** Hollyband *Treas. Fr. Tong*, *Vn Chassis*, a *paper window. **1683** Moxon *Mech. Exerc. Printing* 361 The Journey-men..make every Year new Paper Windows, whether the old will serve again or no. **1889** *Pall Mall G.* 26 Feb. 2/2 We were shown to a clean *paper-windowed room.

1587 HARRISON *England* II. xv. (1877) I. 268 Many goodlie houses..yet they are rather curious to the eie like *paper worke, than substantiall for continuance. 1599 *Broughton's Lett.* ix. 32 Euery later paperwork of yours is but a Tautology of the former. 1889 W. FRASER *Words on Wellington* 136, I have heard it said that a vivâ voce examination is not fair upon a young man; and that, what at Oxford we call 'paper work' should be used for military examinations. 1898 F. HARRISON in *19th Cent.* Nov. 802 Books are tested, precisely like an undergraduate's paper-work. 1900 *Daily News* 15 Dec. 6/1 The paper work is much above the average, though as yet only the well-educated part of the audience undertakes paper work. 1917 R. KIPLING *Let.* in C. E. Carrington *Rudyard Kipling* (1955) xvii. 445 Both sides groan together over the enormous amount of unnecessary paper-work. 1958 I. MURDOCH *Bell* viii. 120 Time was badly needed to catch up on the paper work of the previous week. 1961 [see *feed-house* s.v. FEED *sb.* 6]. 1969 J. ARGENTI *Managem. Techniques* v. 24 Too much paperwork. Symptoms: masses of complicated forms. 1971 S. HILL *Strange Meeting* ii. 123 They sat in their dug-out in the evening, reading or doing paperwork, listening to the gramophone. 1973 C. BONINGTON *Next Horizon* xxi. 290 Back to Base Camp, to start wading through the mass of paper-work which the end of the expedition..entailed. 1977 *New Yorker* 8 Aug. 68/3 (Advt.), We do the paperwork, you do the legwork. 1841 DOUGLAS in *Proc. Berw. Nat. Club* I. No. 9. 246 They reached Mill-Bank *paper-works. 1902 *Westm. Gaz.* 18 Mar. 2/1 The great paper works at Bermondsey, founded in 1803. 1691 WOOD *Ath. Oxon.* II. 316 Prynne..was one of the greatest *paper worms that ever crept into a closet or library.

paper ('peɪpə(r)), *v.* [f. prec. sb.]

1. *trans.* To write or set down on paper; to write about, describe in writing. Also *absol.* or *intr.* (quot. 1606). Now *rare.*

1594 CAREW *Tasso* (1881) 116 Foorthwith then ech ones name is papered. 1606 WARNER *Alb. Eng.* XIV. To Rdr. (1612) 337 Set is the soueraigne Sonne did shine when paperd laste our penne. 1655 *Nicholas Papers* (Camden) II. 341 How farther to deale with them I will not paper with my sence therein. 1865 F. T. BUCKLAND *Curios. Nat. Hist.* Ser. III. (1882) 31 A lady..asked him if he was Robinson Crusoe that Mr. Buckland had papered. 1886 STEVENSON *Kidnapped* 185 I'll have to paper your friend from the lowlands.

2. To enclose in, put *up* in, or cover with paper; to stick (pins, etc.) in a sheet or card of paper.

1599 [see PAPERED *ppl. a.* 1 a]. 1683 MOXON *Mech. Ex.*, *Print.* xxi. ⁋ 2 The Boy Papers up each sort in a Cartridge by it self. 1718 MRS. EALES *Receipt* 6 Put 'em in Pots or Glasses, paper 'em close. 1832 BABBAGE *Econ. Manuf.* xix. (ed. 3) 183 A woman gains about 1*s.* 6*d.* per day by papering [pins]. 1871 *3rd Rep. Dep. Kpr. Irel.* 33 The following, being unsuitable for the cartons, have been papered and indorsed.

3. a. To stick paper upon (a wall, etc.); to furnish or decorate (a room) with paper-hangings. (In quot. 1774 the thing stuck on is the subject of the vb.)

1774 *Westm. Mag.* II. 95 Bills plaister posts, songs paper ev'ry wall. 1775 ASH, *Paper*, to adorn with paper, to furnish with paper hangings. 1823 J. BADCOCK *Dom. Amusem.* 170 Walls..may be papered immediately. 1884 G. ALLEN *Philistia* I. 164 I've had my room papered again since you saw it last.

b. To line with paper.

1683 MOXON *Mech. Exerc.*, *Printing* xxii. ⁋ 1 Of Papering and Laying the Case. *Ibid.*, The other sides of the Box, he Papers so smooth and tight.

c. *Bookbinding.* To paste the end-papers and fly-leaves at the beginning and end of (a volume) before putting on the cover.

1875 *Ure's Dict. Arts* I. 423 The books..having been ..'folded, collated, placed and sewn', and afterwards 'papered'.

d. *to paper out*: to exclude by papering.

1855 MRS. H. A. ROPES *Six Months Kansas* (1856) 87 We must paper out the cold wind.

e. Fig. phr. *to paper over*: temporarily to conceal; esp. in phr. *to paper over the cracks* (see CRACK *sb.* 7 f).

1955 *Times* 16 Nov. 10/5 This document was treated by the western Ministers as no more than an attempt to paper over the complete divergence in policy. 1957 *Economist* 28 Dec. 1114/2 The party's usual split has been papered over. 1966 J. DEAKIN *Lobbyists* 79 Not even the impressive legislative accomplishments under Lyndon Johnson can paper over Congress's serious..frailties. 1969 *Sunday Sun* (Baltimore) 16 Mar. K 1/3 The two sides were still able to paper over their differences and agree to a compromise program. 1974 *Times* 6 Apr. 1/2 Mrs Meir has persuaded the party previously to paper over such differences.

4. a. To supply or furnish with paper.

1883 *N.Y. Even. Post* 13 May, The paper-manufactures are able to paper the country for a year in..less than a year. 1890 *Sat. Rev.* 10 May 583/1 Two stately volumes, very handsomely printed, papered, and otherwise got up.

b. *slang.* To fill (a theatre, etc.) by means of free passes: see PAPER *sb.* 4 a.

1859 E. FITZBALL *35 Yrs. Dram. Author's Life* II. 113 The second night comes, the unfailing 'Lady of Lyons'... House well papered, but badly *gilt*—calls similar. 1879 WEBSTER *Suppl.* s.v., The house is well papered tonight. 1885 *Punch* 31 Jan. 53/2 When on the first night of a new piece the house is badly 'papered', the effect is likely to be fatal. 1897 W. C. HAZLITT *Four Gen. Lit. Fam.* I. III. i. 229 The modern practice of papering the theatres was comparatively unknown. 1959 *Times* 3 Nov. 15/3 'Papering a house' is all very well when a company is playing to empty stalls, but is hardly a good idea when the house is full. 1973 *Courier-Mail* (Brisbane) 26 July 9/5 Surely the theatre could..at least have 'papered' the house with complementary guests for the opening if the box office was looking so poorly. 1978 A. MORICE *Murder by Proxy* xx. 155 We should be playing to an audience of approximately thirty-five, about two thirds of it papered.

5. To treat in any way with paper, *e.g.* to smooth with sand-paper.

1875 *Carpentry & Join.* 144 This will scrape down the surface of the wood until it is ready for 'papering', i.e. being further smoothed by glass or sand paper.

6. *intr.* and *trans.* To pass forged cheques; to defraud by issuing forged cheques. Also in extended use. *U.S. slang.*

1925 *Flynn's* 7 Mar. 191/2 *Paper*,..to pass worthless or forged checks. 1941 *Amer. Speech* XVI. 248/2 *To paper the burg*, to pass a quantity of forged checks. 1958 *Daily News* (N.Y.) 16 Apr. 60 Helped by phony..credentials and a blonde, a former stable boy..papered Queens and Long Island with $10,000 to $15,000 worth of bum checks. 1976 SCOTT & KOSKI *Walk-In* xi. 63, I want to know that this *is* Li we're dealing with and not some ringer they've papered on us.

7. *trans.* To preserve (insects) by storing them in triangular packets made of folded paper.

[1894 W. F. KIRBY *Hand-bk. Lepidoptera* I. p. lii, Collectors abroad generally put their captures into papers folded to resemble a triangular envelope. *Ibid.* p. lv, The cheapest way of buying Butterflies is to buy miscellaneous lots at an auction, especially lots in papers.] 1955 WAGSTAFFE & FIDLER *Preservation Nat. Hist. Specimens* I. 186 Specimens may often have to be stored for considerable periods before they can be set to form part of the permanent collection. The usual method of storing such specimens is to 'paper' them.

‖**paperasserie** (papərasəri). [Fr.] An accumulation of paper-work; administrative red tape.

1928 *Observer* 22 July 12 The Frenchman loves to make fun of 'paperasserie', the elaborate and meticulous bureaucracy, whose spirit he really admires in his heart. 1955 D. BARTON *Glorious Life* 123 Even though I make a great parade of enthusiasm and am far too conscientious about my work.., all this *paperasserie* is not my element. 1965 *New Statesman* 21 May 809/1 The complaints universally made against Indian administrators today—delay and file-passing—seem to be just the complaints that Curzon made against the British administrators of his time. His first battle was against paperasserie.

paperback ('peɪpəbæk). Also **paper-back**. [f. PAPER *sb.* + BACK *sb.*[1]] A book with a paper back or cover. Also *attrib.*, and as *v. trans.*, to publish in a paperback edition.

1899 R. KIPLING *Stalky* 35 There are a pile of paper-backs on that shelf. 1954 etc. [see HARDBACK 2]. 1957 *Times Lit. Suppl.* 12 July i/2 The revolution wrought in the world of books by the emergence of the paperback can best be measured by comparing a classical private library with a contemporary collection of books. *Ibid.* ii/3 In one way or another most English publishers have accepted, and come to terms with, the paperback revolution. 1960 *N.Y. Times Mag.* 5 June 2 Has Emily Post been paper-backed? 1962 A. HUXLEY *Let.* 11 Feb. (1969) 929 In this context see the list of 112 exercises in awareness..printed at the end of *Zen Flesh, Zen Bones* (now in paperback). 1963 *Sunday Times* (Colour Suppl.) 24 Nov. 23/2 They paperback their *World of Art* series at 18s. 1964 M. MCLUHAN *Understanding Media* (1967) II. xxxi. 347 The paperback, especially in its highbrow form, was tried in America in the 1920s and thirties and forties. It was not, however, until 1953 that it suddenly became acceptable. 1968 *Guardian* 27 Apr. 7/1 The worse the rubbish the wider the market: trash is paperbacked in many languages. 1971 *Country Life* 18 Feb. 381/2 His *Highland Year*..which is already in three editions and about to make paperback, is followed by *Highland Deer Forest.* 1971 *New Scientist* 19 Aug. 433/1 It looks as if most people are going to have to wait for the paperback. 1973 'M. INNES' *Appleby's Answer* xvii. 149 The paper-back rights.. would pay for far more than Miss Pringle's customary inexpensive holiday. 1974 *Times* 28 Feb. 15/8 Paperback rights bring £27,000 bid... Hardback rights in Britain are held by Alison Press. 1975 *Bookseller* 11 Oct. 2038/2 The book was called *Harris in Wonderland*, and Cape published it. It was adapted for radio, and paper-backed in Hungary, of all places. 1976 H. M. HARRISON in Aldiss & Harrison *Decade the 1950s* 12 With the coming of the paperback revolution..SF found new places to go.

So **'paper-backed** *a.* or *ppl. a.*, having a paper back, published in paper-back form; also (*fig.*), lacking in strength, feeble.

1888 KIPLING *Soldiers Three* (1889) 52 'Push, men!' sez Crook; 'Push ye paper-backed beggars!' he sez. 1903 *Work* 14 Mar. 89/3 (*heading*) Handy method of binding paper-backed books. 1909 *Chambers's Jrnl.* Sept. 610/2 The man then buys a paper-backed novel for fourpence-halfpenny. 1932 D. L. SAYERS *Have his Carcase* x. 116 One or two paper-backed books. 1957 *Times Lit. Suppl.* 12 July p. ii/3 American bookstalls and bookshops are nowadays crowded with solid, well made, often highbrow but still paperbacked volumes. 1968 *Guardian* 29 July 20/8 Paperbacked D. H. Lawrence floods the bookshops. 1974 C. FREMLIN *By Horror Haunted* 58 Years of..reading of lurid paper-backed stories under the desks at school had not provided him with this sort of solid..information.

'paper-bark. [f. PAPER *sb.* + BARK *sb.*[1]]

1. A name used for several Australian trees distinguished by flaky layers of pale bark, esp. *Melaleuca leucadendron*, the cajeput, and other members of the genus *Melaleuca*, belonging to the family Myrtaceæ. Also *attrib.*

1842 *Western Australia* 81 It [*sc.* the Melaleuca, or tea-tree] is sometimes known by the name of the paper-bark tree, from the multitudinous layers (some hundreds) of which the bark is composed. These layers are very thin, and are loosely attached to each other, peeling off like the bark of the English birch. 1846 STOKES *Discov. Austral.* I. v. 106 The face of the country was covered with specimens of the red and white gum, and paper bark tree. 1866 *Treas. Bot.* 197 *Callistemon*... The outer bark of some of the kinds.. peel off in layers, hence the trees are called Paper Bark trees. 1908 E. J. BANFIELD *Confessions of Beachcomber* I. iv. 216 Few of the forest trees are more picturesque than the paper-bark or tea-tree..of free and stately growth, the bark white. 1920 B. CRONIN *Timber Wolves* 88 From the paper-bark swamps came the reverberating boom of frogs. 1924 LAWRENCE & SKINNER *Boy in Bush* 100 It was salty paper-bark country. 1946 K. TENNANT *Lost Haven* (1947) 2 Wide, soggy moors..from which the great, white paper-barks tower. 1957 P. WHITE *Voss* 59 She walked in the garden, amongst the camellia bushes..and the scurfy native paperbarks. 1961 A. UPFIELD *Bony & White Savage* ix. 78 A ring of paperbark trees, all grey-white of trunk and branch... He was able to tear off a strip, to find it composed of layer above layer of paper-thin wafers... Under the outer one the wafers were flesh-coloured. 1969 *Northern Territory News* (Darwin) *Focus '69* 85/1, I took up my most pleasant sentry duties amongst the paperbark trees.

2. The durable bark of *Melaleuca leucadendron.*

1857 J. ASKEW *Voy. Austral. & N.Z.* 433 The dead bodies are burnt or buried, though some in North Australia place the corpse in the paper bark of the tea-tree, and deposit it in a hollow tree. 1908 E. J. BANFIELD *Confessions of Beachcomber* I. ii. 82 It became necessary..to keep the ridge covering of paper-bark in position. 1941 I. L. IDRIESS *Great Boomerang* iv. 28 It was she who found him paperbark and fashioned his first sandals.

3. paper-bark maple, *Acer griseum*, a maple native to central China, introduced into Europe in 1901, and characterized by flaky, light brown bark; **paper-bark tea-tree, ti-tree** = sense 1 above.

1927 A. REHDER *Man. Cultivated Trees N. Amer.* 577 Paperbark M[aple]. Tree to 8 m., with cinnamon-brown bark separating in thin papery flakes. 1938 *Amer. Nurseryman* 15 Oct. 3/3 The leaves of the paperbark maple ..are finely and thickly hairy underneath. 1969 T. H. EVERETT *Living Trees of World* 223/1 The paper-bark maple (*A[cer] griseum* of western China is remarkable for its beautiful rich cinnamon brown bark which peels in broad paper-thin strips. 1974 A. MITCHELL *Field Guide Trees Britain* 349 Paper-bark Maple... Now much planted in gardens. 1967 A. RULE *Forests Austral.* xiv. 154 An enterprising firm manufactures cork from the bark of the paperbark tea tree. 1944 *Living off Land* vii. 137 Open-grained Timbers... Paper-bark Ti-tree [etc.].

†**'paper-book.** *Obs.* [f. PAPER *sb.* + BOOK.]

1. A book of blank paper to write in.

1548 ELYOT *Dict.* s.v. *Codex*, *Cartaceus codex*, a paper booke. *a* 1568 ASCHAM *Scholem.* I. (Arb.) 26 After this, the childe must take a paper booke, and sitting..by him self, let him translate into Englishe his former lesson. 1642 HOWELL *For. Trav.* (Arb.) 23 In reading hee must couch in a faire Alphabetique paper-book the notablest occurences. 1747 CHESTERF. *Lett.* (1774) I. xc. 266 To take memorandums of such things in a paper book. 1751 EARL ORRERY *Remarks Swift* (1752) 129 On his birth-day..I sent him a paper-book, finely bound.

2. *Law.* A copy of the demurrer book which contains the pleadings on both sides in an action, when the issue is one of law, not of fact.

1768 BLACKSTONE *Comm.* III. xxi. 317 Copies thereof, called paper-books, are delivered to the judges to peruse. 1796 *Mod. Gulliver* 152 Pleas and paper books conclude this term. 1818 CRUISE *Digest* (ed. 2) II. 472 He had compared the case of Smith *v.* Parker in the report, with the paper-book, which was delivered to one of the Judges who then sat upon the bench. 1872 *Wharton's Law Lex.* (ed. 5), *Paper book*, the issues in law, etc., upon special pleadings, formerly made up by the clerk of the papers..an officer for that purpose, but now by the plaintiff's attorney or agent.

papered ('peɪpəd), *ppl. a.* [f. PAPER *v.* + -ED[1].]

1. a. Covered, lined, decorated, etc., with paper.

1599 T. M[OUFET] *Silkwormes* 56 Their papred boord whereon they take repast. 1785 PEACOCK in *Phil. Trans.* LXXV. 368 Slip the papered board..into the recess. 1810 CRABBE *Borough* xviii. 307 There mark the fractured door and paper'd pane. *a* 1828 D. WORDSWORTH *Jrnl.* (1941) II. 335 The little room so snug—the carpets—the papered walls. 1846 *Jewish Manual, or Pract. Information Jewish & Mod. Cookery* vi. 158 Bake in a papered tin. 1860 F. NIGHTINGALE *Notes on Nursing* ii. 16 Old papered walls of years' standing..are..ready sources of impurity to the air. 1869 E. A. PARKES *Pract. Hygiene* (ed. 3) 127 The ordinary plastered and papered walls. 1977 M. T. BLOOM *13th Man* ii. 13 The papered corridors had the palpable feel of transitoriness, of waiting to be called—up or out.

b. *slang.* Of a theatre, etc.: filled by means of free passes.

1936 *Amer. Speech* XI. 221 The house will be *papered*, which means that free passes to the show will be given away. 1959 *Oxf. Mag.* 12 Feb. 244/1 Last week the B.B.C. was able to fill the Festival Hall decently full (even allowing for 'papered' seats). 1974 *Plain Dealer* (Cleveland, Ohio) 27 Oct. 2-c/3 If there is a large crowd at ringside the suspicion will be a papered house, for the government doesn't want the world to see an empty stadium.

2. Of insects in a collection, stored in triangular packets made of folded paper.

1937 C. LONGFIELD *Dragonflies Brit. Isles* 27 Preserving the brilliant colours after death is extraordinarily difficult, and for that reason a 'pinned' or 'papered' collection of dragonflies is often very disappointing. 1955 WAGSTAFFE & FIDLER *Preservation Nat. Hist. Specimens* I. 187 (*caption*) Box for storing papered insects.

paperer ('peɪpərə(r)). [f. as prec. + -ER[1].]

a. One who papers (see the verb); *spec.* one who papers a room, a paper-hanger; one who fixes pins in paper, as the final process in their manufacture.

1837 J. ROMILLY *Diary* 25 May (1967) 119 Set the Painters & Paperers to work in the new house. **1844** MRS. CARLYLE *Lett.* I. 292 The painter, preparatory to the paperer,..has kept me expecting him till now. **1875** *Ure's Dict. Arts* III. 580 The pins are then taken to the paperers, who are each seated in front of a bench. **1928** A. HUXLEY *Let.* 8 Oct. (1969) 302 The house is in a state of chaos—painters and paperers still at work, furniture huddled here and there.

b. *slang.* One who issues or receives free passes to a theatre, etc.

1885 *Referee* 14 June 3/3 Results showed that the 'paperer' understood his business. **1895** *Punch* May 230/1, I took Lil, Dannel's youngest, last week to the play with some tickets I'd got. Well paperers mustn't be choosers.

ˈpaperful. [-FUL 2.] As much as fills a paper.

1722 DE FOE *Col. Jack* (1840) 45 There was a great deal in it [a bag of money], and among it a paper-full by itself.

ˈpaper-ˌhanger.

1. A person whose business it is to cover or decorate the walls of rooms, etc., with paper-hangings.

1796 M. EDGWORTH *Parent's Assistant* (ed. 2) 164 A new carpenter and paper-hanger..were appointed. **1809–12** MAR. EDGEWORTH *Vivian* xii, The vulgar present, full of upholsterers and paper-hangers,..pressed upon his attention with importunate claims. **1901** *J. Black's Carp. & Build., Home Handicr.* 42 It is more general to pass the paperhanger's brush down it first and follow this by applying a paperhanger's roller. **1969** *New Yorker* 12 Apr. 80/2 'We'll be as busy as one-armed paperhangers,' says Lind. **1975** *Ibid.* 21 Apr. 95/1 According to some twenty separate lists that were obtained from underwriters' manuals..occupations that various insurance companies consider to be grounds for rejection of applications for auto insurance, or acceptance only after careful study or on a restricted basis, included those of..paperhangers,..sports coaches and assistants, travelling salesmen,..and doctors.

2. *slang.* (orig. *U.S.*). One who passes forged or fraudulent cheques; a forger.

1914 JACKSON & HELLYER *Vocab. Criminal Slang* 101 Whoever thoughtlessly leaves his check book in accessible places incurs the jeopardy of..personal loss, seeing that 'paper hangers' are vigilant in the search for these. **1938** *Detective Fiction Weekly* 23 Apr. 73/1 Next to the con man is the 'paperhanger' or a 'writer of sad, short stories', these terms referring to a forger. **1941** J. G. BRANDON *Death in Quarry* xiii. 126 'Paper-hanger,' McCarthy echoed. 'That's a new one on me, William.' 'Passin' the snide, sir,' Withers informed him. 'Passing flash paper. Bank of Elegance stuff.' **1945** L. SHELLY *Jive Talk Dict.* 31 *Paper hanger*, one who deals in counterfeit money. **1976** *Times Lit. Suppl.* 16 Apr. 457/4 A legendary confidence man and 'paperhanger' (described as 'a criminal who specialises in hanging, or passing on stolen or counterfeit securities on brokerage houses, insurance companies, and individuals').

ˈpaper-ˌhanging.

1. *pl.* Paper, usually printed in ornamental designs, used for covering and adorning the walls of a room, etc. (so called as taking the place of the cloth hangings formerly used); wall-paper. Rarely in *sing.* A piece or length of wall-paper.

1693 *Lond. Gaz.* No. 2899/4 At the Warehouse for New-fashion'd Hangings,..are made and sold strong Paper-Hangings,..at Three-Pence..per Yard. **1759** SYMMER in *Phil. Trans.* LI. 365, I was surprised to find it..sticking against the paper-hangings of my room. **1867** SMILES *Huguenots Eng.* vi. (1880) 101 The art of printing paper-hangings was introduced by some artizans from Rouen.

2. a. The decorating of a room with wall-paper.

Mod. An expert in paper-hanging.

b. The affixing of bills, advertisements, etc., on a bill-board or hoarding.

1851 DICKENS in *Househ. Words* 22 Mar. 604/2 [I] Hired a large one [*sc.* hoarding]..let out places on it, and called it 'The External Paper-Hanging Station'. **1961** *Times* 21 June 13/6 A hundred years ago 'paper hanging' (a term for bill-posting inherited from the eighteenth century) was an irresponsible and pirate trade.

3. *slang.* (orig. *U.S.*). The passing of forged cheques; forging.

1927 *Dialect Notes* V. 458 *Paper hanging*,..passing forged cheques. **1930** *Detective Fiction Weekly* 30 Aug. 697/2 'Paperhanging', or passing fictitious checks..is not always a mere matter of offering a check to a merchant and trusting to luck that he will cash it. Many tradesmen make it a rule never to cash a check for a stranger, unless it be a pay check or a certified check; but a clever paper-hanger can get around this easily enough. **1932** *Evening Sun* (Baltimore) 9 Dec. 31/5 *Paper hanging*, forging. **1975** C. WESTON *Susannah Screaming* (1976) viii. 42 From paperhanging to murder—that's a pretty big jump. **1976** A. SCHROEDER *Shaking it Rough* 95 It all involved paper-hanging—fake credit cards, rubber checks, [etc.].

paperie, obs. Sc. form of POPERY.

paperiness (ˈpeɪpərɪnɪs). [f. PAPERY *a.* + -NESS.] Papery quality.

1890 *Athenæum* 26 Apr. 537/3 When he has rid his surfaces of a certain dryness and 'paperiness'.

papering (ˈpeɪpərɪŋ), *vbl. sb.* [-ING[1].]

1. a. The action of the verb PAPER; covering or decoration with paper. **b.** *concr.* Paper with which the walls of a room are covered, paper-hangings.

1825 *Greenhouse Comp.* I. 248 The most suitable colours ..for the temporary painting, chalking, or papering. **1841** THACKERAY *Gt. Hoggarty Diamond* (1849) x. 130 The painting, papering, and carpeting of my house. **1843** MRS. CARLYLE *Lett.* I. 203 Your modest allowance for painting and papering. **1855** MRS. GASKELL *North & South* I. viii. 97 It needed the pretty light papering of the rooms to reconcile them to Milton. **1883** *Harper's Mag.* Feb. 365/1 This room remains in its original state, with the exception of the papering. **1928** A. HUXLEY *Let.* 25 Oct. (1969) 302 The main work is done..all painting and papering. **1975** P. DICKINSON *Lively Dead* xxi. 125, I do want to get the papering done before my son comes back. He's an absolute devil with glue.

2. (See quot. 1966.)

1798 JANE AUSTEN *Let.* 1 Dec. (1952) 35 My long hair is always plaited up out of sight, and my short hair curls well enough to want no papering. **1815** R. FENTON *Mem. Old Wig* 9 Having undergone the varied ordeal of papering, pinching, crimping, baking, and torture a thousand ways, I was promoted to thatch the cranium of the notorious judge Jefferies. **1966** J. S. COX *Illustr. Dict. Hairdressing* 108/1 *Papering*, 18th cent. term for placing the paper papillotes around the wound hair preparatory to pinching it with hot pinching irons.

ˈpaper-knife. A knife of ivory, bone, wood, or other substance, used to cut paper along a fold, esp. to cut open the leaves of an uncut book.

1806–7 J. BERESFORD *Miseries Hum. Life* (1826) VIII. iii, Being reduced to make a paper-knife of your finger. **1848** THACKERAY *Lett.* 28 July, A paper-knife with a Mother of pearl blade. **1889** BESANT *Bell St. Paul's* II. 137 Standing thoughtfully at a table, playing with a paper-knife.

Hence **ˈpaper-knife** *v.*, to cut with a paper-knife.

1898 *Academy* 17 Sept. 267/2 A fresh batch of publications..has reached us. The first to be paper-knifed was *The Meaning of Education.*

ˈpaperless, *a.* [-LESS.] Of an automated business system, etc.: in which paper is not used as a medium for the storage, transmission, etc., of information; computerized. Freq. in phr. ***paperless office.***

1971 *New Scientist* 13 May 386 An experimental paperless service in San Francisco already provides computer transfer of funds from the accounts of industrial corporations to those of their employees. **1975** *Business Week* 30 June 48/1 Some believe that the paperless office is not that far off. Vincent E. Giuliano of Arthur D. Little, Inc., figures that the use of paper in business for records and correspondence should be declining by 1980, 'and by 1990, most record-handling will be electronic'. **1981** *Bookseller* 14 Nov. 1688/3 B Dalton Booksellers is now exchanging 'paperless orders and invoices' with more than 20 firms. **1986** *Sci. Amer.* June 31/1 The 'paperless office' remains a scheme of the future.

ˈpaper-ˌmill. A mill in which paper is made.

1498 *Privy Purse Exp. Hen. VII* 25 May (in Bentley *Excerpta* (1831) 117), For a rewarde yeven at the paper mylne, 16*s.* 8*d.* **1545** ELYOT, *Chartariæ officinæ*, paper mylles. **1593** SHAKS. *2 Hen. VI*, IV. vii. 41. *a* **1658** CLEVELAND *Pet. Poem* 64 Where Scholars Teeth are their own Paper-mills. **1707** J. STEVENS tr. *Quevedo's Com. Wks.* (1709) 227 As the Rag-women do for the Paper-Mills. **1825** J. NICHOLSON *Operat. Mechanic* 370 A very large and capital paper-mill, at Maidstone, in Kent, which is the principal seat of the paper trade in England. **1875** *Ure's Dict. Arts* III. 482 Paper-mills, moved by water-power, were in operation in Tuscany at the commencement of the 14th century.

Hence **ˈpaper-miller**, a man who works in a paper-mill.

1865 DICKENS *Mut. Fr.* IV. vi, No jealous paper-miller.

ˈpaper ˌmoney. [PAPER *sb.* 1, 3.] Negotiable documents used instead of money, esp. bank-notes, passing unquestioned from hand to hand; more strictly, a paper currency, which by the law of the country represents money and is a legal tender.

[Cf. *c* **1400** MAUNDEV. (Roxb.) xxv. 117 He [the Grete Caan] makez na monee but owþer of lether or of papire.] **1691** C. MATHER *Consid. Bills Credit* in A. M. Davis *Tracts* (1902) 13, I therefore cannot a little wonder at the great indiscretion of our Countrymen who Refuse to accept that, which they call Paper-Mony, as pay of equal value with the best Spanish Silver. *a* **1697** [? POLLEXFEN] *Disc. Trade* A. 5 We have improved Paper Credit, and turn'd it into Paper-Money, by giving Notes and Bills the privilege of a new Specie of Coin, and using them for making of most great payments. *Ibid.* A. 4 For promoting the sending of Silver Money abroad, and using Paper Money at home. **1735** BERKELEY *Querist* §219 Whether the abuse of banks and paper-money is a just objection against the use thereof? **1776** ADAM SMITH *W.N.* II. ii. (1869) I. 291 There are several different sorts of paper money; but the circulating notes of banks and bankers are the species which is best known. **1821** in Cobbett *Rur. Rides* (1885) I. 35 The desolating and damnable system of paper-money. **1880** BON. PRICE in *Fraser's Mag.* May 669 What is real paper money? The answer is, banknotes. They are written promises by a bank or Government to pay a certain quantity of coin to the bearer on demand.

attrib. **1740** W. DOUGLAS *Disc. Curr. Brit. Plant. Amer.* 19 We see..in our Paper Money Colonies, the Currencies have incredibly depreciated from Sterling. **1823** in Cobbett *Rur. Rides* (1885) I. 268 To put an end to the gains of the paper-money people. **1828** P. CUNNINGHAM *N.S. Wales* (ed. 3) II. 93 [Each] has charged about the same paper-money price for his articles.

papern (ˈpeɪpən), *a.* Now *dial.* [f. PAPER *sb.* + -EN[4].] Of paper.

1616 J. LANE *Cont. Sqr.'s T.* v. 442 With deedles wordes ..papern shott. *Ibid.* VII. 542 But kinge Cambuscan noold spend manie shott on papern-gunners barrells (waxinge hott).

[Now common in s.w. dial. Hampsh. to Cornw., e.g. 'papern shoes', 'a paperen bag': see Eng. Dial. Dict.]

†paper-office. *Obs.* An office or place where documents were kept: cf. PAPER *sb.* 7. **a.** The older name for the STATE PAPER *office*; spec. the place near Whitehall where the state papers used to be kept. **b.** A place attached to the King's (Queen's) Bench where legal documents were kept.

1637 WOTTON *Will*, Item I leave his said Majesty all the Papers..that perchance his Majesty will think fit to be preserved in his Paper-Office. **1670** EVELYN *Diary* 21 Oct., Mr. Jos. Williamson, Master of the Paper Office. **1704** J. HARRIS *Lex. Techn.* I. s.v., All..Letters of Intelligence, and many other Publick Papers communicated to the King's Council, or the two Secretaries of State, are afterwards transmitted to the Paper-Office, wherein they are all disposed in a place of good Security and Convenience within the King's Royal Palace. **1707** *Chamberlayne's St. Eng.* III. 692 The Custos Brevium, Nisi Prius, and the Paper Offices, are in the Queen's-Bench Office in the Temple. **1707** in Hearne *Collect.* 9 Aug. (O.H.S.) II. 32 The Keeper of y[e] Paper-Office at Whitehall. ? **1782** in *30th Rep. Dep. Kpr.* App. 270 Paper Office, Application for the old office adjoining to Whitehall Chapel.

ˈpaper-ˌstainer. [STAINER, f. STAIN *v.*]

1. One who stains or colours paper. Humorously used for an author, esp. an inferior author.

1596 NASHE *Saffron Walden* Wks. (Grosart) III. 42 Let anie man but finde mee meate and drinke..while I am playing the paper stainer. **1771** *Gentl. Mag.* XLI. 201 The whole tribe of Paper-stainers, from the sleek Divine, to the more active Devil at the Printing Office. **1887** *Pall Mall G.* 10 Sept. 3/1 The..author..lacks something of the true poet, but rises far above the mere purposeless paper-stainer.

2. A maker of paper-hangings.

1756 MOUNSEY in *Phil. Trans.* L. 19 Mr. Butler, a paper-stainer, trying to make some discoveries for the better fixing of colours. **1819** *P.O. Lond. Direct.* 353 Vincent & Co., Paper-stainers. **1902** *Westm. Gaz.* 3 Oct. 4/3 The wife of a paper-stainer.

papery (ˈpeɪpərɪ), *a.* [f. PAPER *sb.* + -Y.] Of the consistence of paper; resembling paper; thin or flimsy in texture. Also *fig.*

1627 MAY *Lucan* IV. (1631) 5 So the Ægyptians saile with woven boates Of papery rushes. **1648** HERRICK *Hesper.*, *Oberon's Feast*, The hornes of paperie butterflies. **1853** SEEMAN in *Pharmac. Jrnl.* XIII. 385 Texture from coriaceous to papery. **1900** *Daily News* 12 May 6/5 China silks..look meagre and papery except when they are of the best. **1924** R. FRY *Let.* 27 June (1972) II. 554 Ingres's *Stratonice* is a shock..it's so thin and papery. **1937** D. CANFIELD *Fables for Parents* (1938) 55 It was..more apparent that it was a papery idea out of a book.

[**papescent**, error for PAPPESCENT in J. and subseq. Dicts.]

papess (ˈpeɪpɪs). [ad. F. *papesse* (1567 in Hatz.-Darm.), It. *papessa* 'a shee-pope, a pope-Ione' (Florio), med.L. *papissa*, f. *pāpa*: see -ESS[1].]

A female pope; = POPESS.

Historically used of the alleged Pope Joan 853–55.

1620 BP. HALL *Hon. Mar. Clergy* II. ix. 196 Was the Historie of that their monstrous Papesse of our making? **1678** R. BARCLAY *Apol. Quakers* x. §10. 294 *note*, Onuphrius annotations upon this Papess (or Popess). **1866** BARING-GOULD *Cur. Myths Mid. Ages, Antichr. & Pope Joan* 170 She is commonly called the Papess Joan.

‖papeterie (papetri). [F., = paper-manufacture, paper-trade, stationery-case, f. *papetier* paper-maker, paper-merchant, in med.L. *papeterius* (1414 in Hatz.-Darm.) irreg. deriv. of *papier* paper.] A case or box, usually ornamental, for paper and other writing materials; a stationery-case.

1847 in WEBSTER. **1880** *Print. Trades Jrnl.* No. 31. 13 A combination of desk, papeterie, and dispatch-box.

†ˈpapey. *Obs.* Also **pappey.** [app. a deriv. of L. *pāpa* pope.] A fraternity of priests in Aldgate ward, London, or their residence.

1598 STOW *Surv.* 110 Then come you to the Pappey, a proper house, wherein sometime was kept a Fraternitie, or brotherhood of S. Charitie, and S. Iohn Euangelist, called the Papey, for poore impotent Priestes, (for in some language Priestes are called Papes) founded in the yeare 1430. **1790** PENNANT *London* (1813) 607.

papey, obs. form of PAWPAW.

†ˈpap-hawk. *Obs. rare*[−1]. [f. PAP *sb.*[1] + HAWK.] A child at the breast, a suckling.

c **1450** *Cov. Myst.* (Shaks. Soc.) 179 Popetys and pap-hawkes I [Herod] xal puttyn in peyne With my spere prevyn, pychyn, and to-pende.

Paphian (ˈpeɪfɪən), *a.* and *sb.* [f. L. *Paphi-us* adj. (f. *Paphos*) + -AN.] **A.** *adj.*

1. Of or belonging to Paphos, a city of Cyprus sacred to Aphrodite or Venus (the ***Paphian Goddess, Paphian Queen***).

c **1614** SIR W. MURE *Dido & Æneas* II. 753 The Paphyen Queen such brood did never beare. **1879** FARRAR *St. Paul* (1883) 403 The orgies of the Paphian goddess.

2. *transf.* Pertaining to love; *esp.* pertaining to, or devoted to, unlawful sexual indulgence; belonging to the class of prostitutes.

1656 BLOUNT *Glossogr.* s.v., Hence..Paphian fire or shot [is taken] for the fire or Arrows of Love. **1742** YOUNG *Night Thoughts* VIII. 994. **1812** BYRON *Ch. Har.* I. vii, Now

Paphian girls were known to sing and smile. **1879** E. WALFORD *Londoniana* I. 27 The Paphian sisterhood.

B. *sb.* **1.** An inhabitant or native of Paphos.

2. A devotee of the Paphian Venus; a prostitute.

1811 BYRON *Hints fr. Horace* 690 In turns she'll seem a Paphian or a prude. **1828** P. CUNNINGHAM *N.S. Wales* (ed. 3) II. 270 A miraculously converted Paphian.

Paphlagonian (pæflə'gəʊnɪən), *a.* and *sb.* [f. Gr. Παφλαγωνία, L. *Paphlagonia*, an ancient region in northern Asia Minor + -AN.]

A. *adj.* Of or pertaining to Paphlagonia or its inhabitants. **B.** *sb.* A native or inhabitant of Paphlagonia.

Also (spelt *Paflagonian*) with reference to the fictional people in Thackeray's *The Rose and the Ring*.

1596 T. NASHE *Have with you to Saffron-Walden* sig. O2^v, Procris and Cephalus, and a number of Pamphlagonian things more, that it would rust & yron spot paper, to have but one sillable of their names breathed over it. **1607** TOPSELL *Foure-f. Beasts* 291 Touching the Paphlagonians about the education of their horsses see more among the Venetians. *Ibid.* 562 The Paphlagonians, which before the Troyan warre were called *Eneti*, and afterwards *Veneti*. **1748** HUME *Philos. Ess. conc. Human Understanding* x. 189 The Impostor..was enabled to proceed, from his ignorant Paphlagonians, to the inlisting of Votaries, even among the Grecian Philosophers. **1855** THACKERAY *Rose & Ring* i. 4 Two nations which had been engaged in bloody and expensive wars, as the Paflagonians and the Crimeans had been. *Ibid.* ii. 5 The Paflagonian nobility did not care who was king. **1954** T. GUNN *Fighting Terms* 32 Here in a cave the Paphlagonian King Crouched. **1974** *Encycl. Brit. Micropædia* VII. 734/1 The Paphlagonians were one of the most ancient peoples of Anatolia.

pap-holy: see POPEHOLY.

paphood ('pæphʊd). *nonce-wd.* [f. PAP *sb.*^{2} + -HOOD.] Infancy.

1837 *Fraser's Mag.* XV. 576 Betrothed to thee as thy 'little wife' since the days of paphood.

papia, var. *papaya*: see PAWPAW.

‖**Papiamento** (papja'mento). Also **Papiamentu**. [Sp.] A Spanish-based creole language of Curaçao, Aruba, and Bonaire, in the Caribbean Sea.

1949 *Caribbean Q.* I. III. 36 The remnants of the African culture, are fast disappearing... There are no signs, however, that their language, the papiamento, which is still in use everywhere, will disappear. **1953** *Ibid.* III. I. 27 Dialects such as Papiamento..were unworthy of the grammarians' labour. **1956** *Publ. Amer. Dial. Soc.* XXVI. 11 The derivative of Spanish spoken in Curaçao (called Papiamentu or Papiamento), of French in Haïti (Creole), of English in Guiana (Ningro-Tongo), in the West Indies, and in South Carolina (Gullah) are some examples of languages which can either be regarded as dialects of the colonial languages or as new languages of their own. **1967** *Language* XLIII. 818 Papiamentu 'may well represent a fusion of two earlier pidgins or creoles'. **1972** J. L. DILLARD *Black English* i. 24 Some of them [*sc.* pidgin and creole languages] are vehicles of education and literature, like Papiamento, whose speakers have profited from an enlightened Dutch attitude toward languages. **1974** R. A. HALL *External Hist. Romance Lang.* vii. 157 In other languages, however, such as Papiamentu, the dominant lexical influence in later centuries has come from a non-Romance language, in this case Dutch. **1976** *San Francisco Examiner & Chron.* 13 June (Travel Suppl.) 8/3 Although Papiamento is spoken on radio and TV, and newspapers and books are printed in it, the official language on the island [*sc.* Aruba] is Dutch.

papiay, obs. form of POPINJAY.

†**pa'picolist**. *Obs. rare.* [f. L. *pāpa* pope + *-cola* worshipper + -IST.] A 'worshipper of the pope', a papist. So **pa'picolar** *a.*

1633 T. ADAMS *Exp. 2 Peter* i. 17 The word Trinity, say our papicolists, is not found in the Scriptures. **1644** *Speculum Impietatis* 19 The Romish Papicolists are in arms. *c* **1810** COLERIDGE in *Lit. Rem.* (1838) III. 364 As a German would have expressed himself,..'a-not-of-the-Roman-Catholic-Papicolar-polemics-unmerited, sneer'.

‖**papier** (papje). The French word for 'paper' used in various phrases, as **papier collé** (kɔle) ['gummed paper'], a collage made from paper; also *attrib.*; **papier déchiré** (deʃire), paper torn haphazardly for making collages; a collage made of such paper; **papier poudré** (pudre), a paper impregnated with face-powder. See also PAPIER MÂCHÉ

1907 *Yesterday's Shopping* (1969) 539/1 Papier Poudre. In 3 shades, white, rose and rachel... These exquisitely perfumed leaves are designed to supersede the use of 'puff and powder box'. **1919** R. FIRBANK *Valmouth* xi. 189 'A book is anathema to her.' 'Even a *papier poudré* one; for, when I gave her my little precious volume of *blanc de perle* in order to rub her nose, she started grating her teeth at me.' **1935** D. GASCOYNE *Short Survey Surrealism* v. 107 The *papiers collés* of Picasso and Braque (newspaper, wallpaper, cigarette packets). **1959** *Listener* 30 Apr. 766/3 It is a picture as utterly *original* as the first *papiers collés*. *Ibid.* 19 Nov. 868/1 Arp even welcomed the ravages wrought by time on his own works, and started to help nature along by doing the destruction for her, making *collages* of *papiers déchirés*, roughly and haphazardly torn. **1960** E. H. GOMBRICH *Art & Illusion* x. 356 His [*sc.* Picasso's] more playful creations, such as his *papiers déchirés*. **1960** D. HOLMAN-HUNT *My Grandmothers & I* iv. 121 Grandmother was scrubbing her nose with a sheet of Papier Poudre. **1962** *Listener* 15 Feb. 305/1 In using the technique of *papier collé* they were substituting fragments of reality itself for the earlier fragmented images of reality. *Ibid.*, Their *papier collé* pictures. **1963** *Times* 8 Feb. 14/3 The reliefs..and the sculpture..are built up of plywood layers treated in the manner of a *papier dechiré* collage. **1965** *New Statesman* 12 Nov. 758/2 The introduction of *trompe-l'œil* and *papier-collé*. **1973** *Country Life* 1 Mar. 556/3 Tiny booklets.. containing *papier poudre*, for 12p..very popular years ago for taking the shine off noses. It works.

‖**papier mâché** (papje maʃe, ˌpæpɪeɪ 'mæʃeɪ, mɑː-). Also with hyphen, and with simple *a* in *maché*, which is also found variously misspelt. [a. F. *papier* paper, *mâché* chewed, pa. pple. of *mâcher*:—L. *masticāre* to chew. (See below.)]

a. A substance consisting of paper-pulp or paper reduced to a pulp (often mixed with other substances), and shaped by moulding; used for boxes, jars, trays, various fancy articles, etc.; finer kinds consist of sheets of paper pasted together. Also *fig.*

1753 MRS. DELANY *Life & Corr.* (1861) III. 262 The ceiling ornamenting with *papier-machée*. **1758** [R. DOSSIE] *Handmaid to Arts* III. iv. §1. 407 Paper..is rarely made the subject of japanning till it is converted into *papier maché*. **1759** *Compl. Lett. Writer* (ed. 6) 229 A beautiful and exquisitely carved and gilt chariot of papier mashè. **1766** T. MARTYN *Connoisseur* No. 91 Some large and elegant Jars and Vases in *Papier macheè*. **1816** TINGRY *Varnisher's Guide* (ed. 2) xi, Colouring articles made of papier maché. **1818** 'T. BROWN' *Brighton* I. i. 13 He has a clay-cold heart, and a mere papier maché mind. **1879** G. PRESCOTT *Sp. Telephone* 305 Thin sheets of papier-maché. **1920** F. M. FORD *Let.* 24 July (1965) 115 The plaster Pillars of the State and the papier maché hearts of men. **1977** *Broadcast* 7 Feb. 7/2 It's unlikely that he would want to be party to a papier maché exercise.

b. *attrib.* (usually = made of papier mâché).

1753 MRS. DELANY *Life & Corr.* (1861) III. 260 A *papier-machée* ceiling. **1777** SIR A. I. ELTON in *Burke's Corr.* (1844) II. 137 A *papier-mâché* snuff-box. **1899** *Daily News* 26 June 8/4 The foundry room, wherein the papier-mâché moulds, or matrices, receive the boiling lead and turn out complete castings of pages of type.

[*Note.* Although composed of French words, the name *papier mâché* appears not to be of French origin; it is not recognized in the French Dictionaries of the Académie, Littré, or Hatz.-Darm. (except in the sense of 'chewed paper', *papier mouillé*, and figurative uses of this: see Littré). The term is not in the *Description des Arts et Métiers..par l' Academie des Sciences* of 1761; the *Journal de l' Agriculture, du Commerce*, etc., of Sept. 1778, cites it from an English source, translating from the *Handmaid to Arts* of 1758 (see above); so later French works. It seems to be meant as French for 'mashed paper'. Cf. the instructions for making this substance in Boyle's *Uses of Nat. Things* iv, 'First soak a convenient quantity of whitish paper..then *mash* it in hot water', etc.]

papilio (pə'pɪlɪəʊ). [a. L. *pāpilio* butterfly, adopted as a generic name by Linnæus in *Systema Naturæ* (ed. 10, 1758) I. 458.] A swallow-tail butterfly belonging to the large genus so called, frequently distinguished by tail-like projections on the hind pair of wings; formerly, any butterfly.

1789 *Loiterer* 26 Sept. 9 The Wings of Moths, and Papilios. **1835** J. DUNCAN *Brit. Butterflies* 92 The word *Papilio* was used by Linnaeus in the comprehensive sense which he was accustomed to attach to such terms, to designate generically all the diurnal lepidoptera. **1932** J. S. HUXLEY *Probl. Relative Growth* ii. 55 Many of these [*sc.* holometabolous insects] possess organs which increase in relative size with increase of absolute size of body..[like] the 'tail' on the hind wing of Papilios. **1936** *Discovery* July 213/2 Many large Papilios were flying about. **1965** R. MCKIE *Company of Animals* xiii. 178 Papilios and pierids and danaids, the Browns, the Blues, the Skippers, and many many more. **1972** L. E. CHADWICK tr. *Linsenmaier's Insects of World* 41/1 The males [of *Papilio dardanus*] occur throughout the range in the normal, long-tailed costume of the papilios.

papilionaceous (pəˌpɪlɪə'neɪʃəs), *a.* Also 7 papill-. [f. mod.L. *pāpiliōnāceus* (of insects), in F. *papilionacé* (Réaumur 1734); *pāpiliōnāceæ* (of plants), Ray 1682; f. L. *pāpiliōn-em* butterfly: see -ACEOUS.]

1. Of or pertaining to a butterfly or butterflies; of the nature of a butterfly; belonging to the butterfly tribe. Now *rare* or *Obs.*

1668 WILKINS *Real Char.* II. v. §2. 126 Papilionaceous Fly. **1713** DERHAM *Phys.-Theol.* IV. xiii. 235 A good though very brief Description of the Papilionaceous Fly. **1771** *Gentl. Mag.* XLI. 401 He takes pleasure to impale for days and weeks the papilionaceous race with corking pins. **1837** T. HOOK *Jack Brag* xviii, Psyche..the lovely lively lady with the papilionaceous wings.

b. *fig.* Having the character of which a butterfly is taken as a type: cf. BUTTERFLY *sb.* 2.

1832 CARLYLE *Misc., Boswell's Johnson* (1857) III. 91 A bright papilionaceous creature. **1875** MISS BRADDON *Hostages to Fortune* I. i. 37 The women he has admired hitherto belong to the papilionaceous tribe.

2. *Bot.* Applied, from its fancied resemblance to a butterfly, to that form of flower found in most leguminous plants, having an irregular corolla consisting of a large upper petal (the *vexillum* or standard), two lateral petals (the *alæ* or wings), and two narrow lower petals between these (forming the *carina* or keel). Also said of the plant.

1668 WILKINS *Real Char.* II. iv. §5. 96 Herbs.. Papillionaceous; the flower having some resemblance to a Butterfly, as the blooms of Pease or Beans, &c. **1693** *Phil. Trans.* XVII. 766 Many papilionaceous and winged Plants. **1797** HOLCROFT *Stolberg's Trav.* (ed. 2) III. lxxviii. 191, I saw the..tree of Judas, covered with its..red papilionaceous flower. **1876** DARWIN *Cross-fertil.* i. 5 Papilionaceous flowers..offer innumerable curious adaptations for Cross-fertilisation.

papilionine (pə'pɪlɪənaɪn), *a.* *Entom.* [ad. mod.L. *Papiliōnīn-æ* (fem. pl.), f. *papilio* butterfly, in mod. Zool. the name of the typical genus.] Belonging to the subfamily *Papilioninæ* or swallowtail butterflies.

†**pa'pilious**, *a.* *Obs. rare*$^{-1}$. [irreg. f. L. *papilio* butterfly + -OUS.] Allied to the butterfly.

1733 CHEYNE *Eng. Malady* I. x. §4 (1734) 98 Silk-worms, and the other Insects of the papilious Kind.

‖**papilla** (pə'pɪlə). Pl. **-æ**. [L., = nipple, dim. of PAPULA swelling, pimple.]

1. *Zool.* and *Anat.* **a.** The nipple of the breast; the mamilla. (*rare* in Eng. use.)

[**1398** TREVISA *Barth. De P.R.* v. xxxiv. (Bodl. MS.), þe tette þe heed of þe pappe hatte papilla in latyne.] **1693** tr. *Blancard's Phys. Dict.* (ed. 2), *Papilla*, a red Excrescency in the middle of the Breast. **1727-41** CHAMBERS *Cycl.* s.v., The lacteal tubes, coming from the several parts of the breasts, terminate in the *Papillæ*.

b. Any minute nipple-like protuberance, usually soft and fleshy, in a part or organ of the body:

e.g. those on the skin, specially abundant at the tips of the fingers and elsewhere, and constituting the apparatus for the sense of touch (***tactile papillæ***); those on the tongue (***circumvallate, conical, filiform, foliate,*** and ***fungiform papillæ***), most of which are connected with the sense of taste (***gustatory papillæ***); those at the tips of the Malpighian pyramids in the kidney (***renal papillæ***); those in the embryo which ultimately produce the teeth (***dental papillæ***); and those in various parts of insects and other invertebrates, *esp.* two malodorous organs which can be protruded from the abdomen in certain beetles. ***lachrymal papilla***: a slight protuberance on the edge of the eyelid, traversed by the lachrymal duct. ***optic papilla***: see OPTIC A. 2.

1713 DERHAM *Phys.-Theol.* IV. vi. 144 Mr. Cowper hath.. given us very elegant Cuts both of the skin, and the Papillae. **1748** HARTLEY *Observ. Man* I. i. 43 The nervous Papillae which are the immediate Organ in the Senses of Feeling, Taste, and Smell. **1844** CARPENTER *Princ. Hum. Phys.* §316 The *papillæ*,..are little elevations of the surface of the cutis, easily perceptible by the aid of a lens. **1853** *Ibid.* (ed. 4) §279 The Dentinal pulp..makes its appearance in the form of a papilla, budding-out from the free surface of a fold or groove of the mucous membrane of the mouth. **1881** MIVART *Cat* 23 Each hair grows from a single dermal papilla only, of which it is the greatly prolonged epidermal covering. **1888** ROLLESTON & JACKSON *Anim. Life* 551 [In *Holothurioidea*] The tube feet are either partially or completely retractile, and furnished with a terminal disc..or they are conical *papillæ* without discs.

c. *Path.* A small papule or pimple.

1797 M. BAILLIE *Morb. Anat.* (1807) 152 Papillæ and pustules, somewhat resembling the small-pox. **1892** *Syd. Soc. Lex.*, *Papilla*..Also, a diminutive of *Papula*.

2. *Bot.* A small fleshy projection upon any part of a plant.

1848 CRAIG, *Papillæ*..in Botany, the minute puncta upon the surface of a leaf; the vesicles on leaves of twigs [etc.]. **1870** HOOKER *Stud. Flora* 37 Pepperwort..*papillæ* scale-like when dry. **1885** GOODALE *Physiol. Bot.* (1892) 155 In the earliest stage of its development the leaf is a mere papilla consisting of nascent cortex..and nascent epidermis.

papillar ('pæpɪlə(r), pə'pɪlə(r)), *a.* [ad. mod.L. *papillār-is*: see next.] = next.

1830 R. KNOX *Béclard's Anat.* 143 Small papillar eminences, which are much more distinct upon the denuded dermis, than when seen through the epidermis. **1861** HULME tr. *Moquin-Tandon* II. VI. vi. 306 A case of papillar and vesicular inflammation.

papillary ('pæpɪlərɪ, pə'pɪlərɪ), *a.* [f. L. *papilla* (see above) + -ARY; cf. F. *papillaire* (1690 in Hatz.-Darm.).] Of the form or nature of a papilla; containing, furnished with, or consisting of papillæ; of, pertaining to, or affecting papillæ.

papillary body: the papillary layer of the skin. ***papillary muscles***: bundles of muscular fibre springing from the walls of the ventricles of the heart and attached to the *chordæ tendineæ*.

1667 *Phil. Trans.* II. 492 Concerning the Tongue, the same Author [Malpighi] has discovered in it many little Eminences, which he calls Papillary. **1713** DERHAM *Phys.-Theol.* IV. v. (1727) 140 *note*, The outward Cover of the Tongue..under which lie papillary Parts. **1886** FAGGE & PYE-SMITH *Princ. Med.* (ed. 2) II. 613 The papillary layer of the cutis. **1899** *Allbutt's Syst. Med.* VII. 847 Irregular contraction of the papillary muscles.

b. *Bot.* Of the nature of a PAPILLA (sense 2).

1874 LUBBOCK *Wild Flowers* iii. 54 The papillary edge of the summit of the pistil is the stigma.

papillate ('pæpɪleɪt, pə'pɪlət), *a.* [ad. mod.L. *papillāt-us*, f. *papilla*: see -ATE^2 2.]

1. Furnished or covered with papillæ.

1857 MAYNE *Expos. Lex.*, *Papillatus*..papillate. **1874** E. COUES *Birds N.W.* 629 Two short, obtuse cornua, which are thickly papillate. **1887** W. PHILLIPS *Brit. Discomycetes* 96 Hymenium same colour, papillate, granular.

2. Formed into a papilla, papillary.

1890 in *Cent. Dict.*

papillated (ˈpæpɪleɪtɪd), *a.* [f. as prec. + -ED¹.] = PAPILLATE *a.*

1828 STARK *Elem. Nat. Hist.* II. 69 Branchiæ projecting, in the form of scaly plates, papillated, or like cirri. **1834** MCMURTRIE *Cuvier's Anim. Kingd.* 141 The neck invested with a plumeless and papillated skin. **1897** *Allbutt's Syst. Med.* II. 1058 A papillated, or a simple mouth.

papiˈllectomy. *Surg* [f. PAPILLA + Gr. ἐκτομή excision.] The excision of papillæ.

1900 *Brit. Med. Jrnl.* 3 Feb. 248 Renal Papillectomy.

papilliferous (pæpɪˈlɪfərəs), *a.* [f. mod.L. *papillifer*, in F. *papillifère* (Littré), f. *papilla* + *-fer* bearing + -OUS.] Bearing papillæ.

1826 KIRBY & SP. *Entomol.* IV. 351 Cauda..5. Papilliferous (*Papillifera*). When at the last segment but one the tail exerts two soft fleshy organs, which secrete a milky fluid and yield a powerful scent. Ex. *Staphylinus*. **1866** *Treas. Bot.* 844/2 *Papillose, Papilliferous*, covered with minute soft tubercles or excrescences. **1900** *Brit. Med. Jrnl.* 20 Jan. 137 The perforation of papilliferous cysts.

papilliform (pəˈpɪlɪfɔːm), *a.* (*erron.* papillæform.) [f. mod.L. *papilliform-is*, f. as prec. + -FORM.] Of the form of a papilla; nipple-shaped.

1828 STARK *Elem. Nat. Hist.* II. 396 Anus at the posterior extremity, and a papilliform filament near it. **1861** HULME tr. *Moquin-Tandon* II. III. iv. 143 The Leech then draws a small papiliform piece of the skin into its mouth. **1878** BELL *Gegenbaur's Comp. Anat.* 139 A thicker cuticular layer is formed on papilliform processes.

‖**papillitis** (pæpɪˈlaɪtɪs). *Path.* [mod.L.: see -ITIS.] Inflammation of the optic papilla.

1892 *Syd. Soc. Lex.* s.v. *Papilla, congestion*, All cases of inflammation of the Optic disc are now usually designated *Papillitis*. **1899** *Allbutt's Syst. Med.* VII. 657 Attended with headache and a slight degree of papillitis.

papillœdema (pæpɪliːˈdiːmə). *Ophthalm.* Also (chiefly *U.S.*) **papilledema.** [f. PAPILL(A + ŒDEMA, as repr. G. *papillenödem* (A. Eloching 1895, in *A. von Græfe's Arch. für Opthhalm.* XLI. II. 276).] Non-inflammatory swelling of the optic disc due to increased intracranial pressure on the optic nerve, usu. as a result of a tumour or abscess of the brain.

1908 J. H. PARSONS *Path. of Eye* IV. xxvii. 1349, I suggest the use of the term 'papillœdema' to replace 'choked disc' (Stauungspapille). **1922** R. F. MOORE *Med. Ophthalm.* i. 23 In a few cases papillœ dema runs its course to complete subsidence in one eye, the other remaining normal throughout. **1950** BERENS & SIEGEL *Encycl. of Eye* 34 Papilledema is a common finding in increased pressure, although it is by no means an early sign. **1961** *Times* 11 May 9/1 The pathogenesis of papilloedema. **1972** *Pediatrics* XLIX. 248/1 Papilledema in a patient with cyanotic congenital heart disease is not necessarily a sign of brain abscess. **1977** *Proc. R. Soc. Med.* LXX. 235/2 Acute blockage of the shunt is usually obvious because of the clinical signs, the most valuable being bradycardia. Papillœdema is not to be relied upon.

‖**papilloma** (pæpɪˈləʊmə). *Path.* Pl. **-ata.** [f. PAPILLA + Gr. ending -ωμα, -*ōma* = formation; cf. CONDYLOMA.] A tumour of the skin or of a mucous membrane, consisting of an overgrown papilla or group of papillæ, usually covered with a layer of thickened epidermis or epithelium; *e.g.* a wart, corn, condyloma, etc.

1866 A. FLINT *Princ. Med.* (1880) 45 A papilloma is composed of papillae, often very large and irregular in shape. **1873** T. H. GREEN *Introd. Pathol.* (ed. 2) 151 The Papillomata are new formations resembling in structure ordinary papillæ, and like these they grow from cutaneous, mucous, or serous surfaces.

Comb. **1897** *Allbutt's Syst. Med.* II. 1122 Papilloma-like growths in cysts. *Ibid.* IV. 837 A papilloma-like mass.

Hence ‖**papillomaˈtosis**, the formation of a papilloma; **papiˈllomatous** *a.*, of, pertaining to, or of the nature of a papilloma.

1872 PEASLEE *Ovar. Tumors* 20 The benign papillomatous or dendritic form of tumor. **1897** *Allbutt's Syst. Med.* IV. 683 A small papillomatous growth. **1899** J. HUTCHINSON *Arch. Surg.* X. No. 38. 182 Family proclivity to cancer and to papillomatosis go together.

papillon (ˈpæpɪjɔ̃). [a. F. *papillon* butterfly.] A breed of toy dog related to the spaniel, having a white coat with a few darker patches, esp. on the head, and erect ears resembling the shape of a butterfly's wings. Also *attrib.*

1907 R. LEIGHTON *New Bk. Dog* XVII. lxi. 536/1 A very engaging little dog is the Papillon, or Squirrel Spaniel. *Ibid.* 536/2 The name Papillon is obviously given to the dog in reference to its ears, which stand out large and erect like the wings of a butterfly, heavily feathered. **1910** *Encycl. Brit.* VIII. 376/1 At the annual show of the Kennel Club in the autumn of 1905..additional breeds..[were] Chesapeake Bay dogs, Chihuahuas, Papillons and Roseneath terriers. **1924** *Glasgow Herald* 4 Apr. 8 A new toy dog has been brought from Belgium, the Papillon. It is very small, weighing when full grown 3 to 5 lb. **1927** M. B. COOPER in C. C. Sanderson *Pedigree Dogs* 341 The Papillon or Butterfly dog was first introduced into England in any number in 1923. **1929** R. GRAVES *Poems* 25 Those pugs and papillons and in-betweens. **1960** *Times* 11 Mar. 1/7 (Advt.), Adorable Papillon Puppies. **1971** F. HAMILTON *World Encyl. Dogs* 541 The Papillon has bred true to type for some 700 years or more, as can be verified in the art galleries and museums of the world. **1972** *N.Y. Times* 4 June 6/2 Deja.. has been best Papillon 125 of the 135 times he has been shown.

papillose (ˌpæpɪˈləʊs), *a.* [ad. mod.L. *papillōsus*, f. *papilla*: see -OSE¹.] Full of or beset with papillæ or nipple-like projections.

1752 HILL *Hist. Anim.* 425 The Anas, with a naked papillose face. The Muscovy Duck. **1753** CHAMBERS *Cycl. Supp.* s.v. *Leaf, Papillose Leaf*, one whose surface is covered with little roundish protuberances, or vesicles. **1835–6** TODD *Cycl. Anat.* I. 532/1 The tongue..becomes soft and papillose. **1877–84** F. E. HULME *Wild Fl.* p. xvi, Burdock.—Anthers exserted: filaments papillose.

Hence **papiˈllosity**, papillose condition.

1881 WEST in *Jrnl. Bot.* X. No. 220. 115 The papillosity of the upper part of the back of the nerve alone thoroughly distinguishes it.

papilloso-, used as combining adverbial form of mod.L. *papillōsus* PAPILLOSE, as in **papiˈlloso'asperate** *a.*, rough with closely set papillæ.

1846 DANA *Zooph.* (1848) 491 Surface of the coralla papillosoasperate.

papillote (ˈpæpɪləʊt, -ɒt). Also 8 **papillot, papilliot(e**, 8–9 **papillotte**, 9 **papilotte.** [a. F. *papillote* (Mme de Sevigne *a* 1696), app. a verbal sb. from **papilloter*, a supposed deriv. of *papillon* butterfly.]

1. A curl-paper. Also *fig.*

1748 H. WALPOLE *Let. to H. S. Conway* 6 Oct., I wish you could see him making squibs of his papillotes. **1778** *Refutation* 19 The wild Devonia still on fashion doats, And turns thy satire into papillotes. **1797** MRS. A. M. BENNETT *Beggar Girl* (1813) III. 169 A papilliot having dropped from madame's tête. **1831** BREWSTER *Nat. Magic* iii. (1833) 42 Her fingers were in active motion among the papillotes. **1848** THACKERAY *Van. Fair* xliii. 392 Glorvina, trembling with all the papillotes. **1860** QUEEN VICTORIA *Let.* 3 Nov. in R. Fulford *Dearest Child* (1964) 278 We drove over..to Clifden which unfortunately was en papillote. **1959** S. G. FLITMAN *Craft of Ladies' Hairdressing* viii. 74 For years the posticheur had used papilottes (small triangles of paper) to hold damp flat curls until they were dried.

attrib. **1845** STOCQUELER *Handbk. Brit. India* (1854) 80 A good supply of papillote paper. **1960** CUNNINGTON & BEARD *Dict. Eng. Costume* 156/1 *Papillotte comb*.., a decorative comb of tortoise-shell. **1966** J. S. COX *Illustr. Dict. Hairdressing* 108/2 *Papilotte tongs*, pinching irons.

2. A paper wrapper, usu. greased, in which certain types of meat and fish are cooked or served.

1818 T. MOORE *Fudge Fam. Paris* v. 38 One's hair and one's cutlets both *en papillotte*. **1868** M. JEWRY *Warne's Model Cookery* 296/2 Wrap them [*sc.* mutton cutlets] in buttered papers... The fat of the dressed meat is absorbed in the papillotes. **1959** R. POSTGATE *Good Food Guide 1959–1960* 109 Tamar salmon en papillotte, ham soufflé, or chicken à la crème, may appear on the menu. **1961** *Guardian* 10 Mar. 10/6 Trout can..be grilled..in paper-bags (*papillotes*)... first spread the inside of the *papillote* generously with maître d'hôtel batter.

papillous (pəˈpɪləs), *a.* Now *rare* or *Obs.* [ad. mod.L. *papillōsus*: see -OUS.] = PAPILLOSE.

1718 J. CHAMBERLAYNE *Relig. Philos.* (1730) I. xiv. §6 The Particles of the Olfactory Matter..must strike with some Force against the Papillous Tegument, to produce the Sense of Smelling. **1822–34** *Good's Study Med.* (ed. 4) IV. 486 Cuticle below the scabs..dotted with papillous apertures, oozing fresh matter.

papillule (pəˈpɪl(j)ʊl). [ad. mod.L. *papillula*, dim. of *papilla*.] A minute papilla; in *Entom.* applied to a small elevation or depression with a minute papilla in the centre. Hence **paˈpillulate** *a.*, beset with papillules.

1826 KIRBY & SP. *Entomol.* IV. 274 *Papillule* (*Papillula*), a tubercle or variole with an elevation in its centre. *Papillulate* (*Papillulata*), beset with many papillules. Ex. Elytra of *Dynastes Hercules* ♀.

†**ˈpapin.** *Obs.* In 5 papyn. [app. a. F. *papin*, now 'pap for children'. Cf. Sc. *Pappin* 'a sort of batter or paste, generally made of flour and water, used by weavers for dressing their linen warp, or their webs' (Jam.).] A dish composed of milk, flour, and yolks of eggs, sweetened with sugar.

c **1430** *Two Cookery-bks.* 9 Papyns.—Take fayre Mylke an Flowre, an drawe it þorw a straynoure, an set it ouer þe fyre, an let it boyle a-whyle [etc.].

papinga, -gay, -go, -jay, obs. ff. POPINJAY.

papin's digester: see DIGESTER 4.

†**papion, -oun.** *Obs.* [a. OF. *papion*, ad. med.L. *papio, -ōnem*, of unknown origin.] A carnivorous beast used in hunting; app. the cheetah or hunting leopard.

[*a* **1244** JAC. DE VITRIACO *Hist. Orient.* (Du Cange), Papiones quos appellant canes silvestres acriores quam lupi. *a* **1375** MAUNDEV. (French text) (Roxb.) v. 14 En Cipre lem chace ouesqe papions, qi semblent leopardz priuez, qi preignont trop bien les bestes sauvages.] *c* **1400** (English text) *ibid.*, In Cipre men huntes with papiouns [*MS. Cott. Tit.* papyouns; *v. rr.* papions, pampeons], þe whilk er lyke to leoperds. **1598** HAKLUYT *Voy.* I. 98 (tr. *Itin. fr. Will. de Rubruquis*, 1253) The Tartars..make themselues two gownes..of woolues skins, or Fox skins, or else of Papions [*orig.* de pellibus lupinis, vel vulpibus, vel papionibus].

papir, papire, obs. forms of PAPER.

papish (ˈpeɪpɪʃ), *sb.* and *a.* *Now dial.* [app. f. *pape*, dial. form of POPE (F. *pape*, L. *pāpa*).]

A. *adj.* Papistical, popish. (A hostile epithet.)

1546 GARDINER *Declar. Joye* 21 b, This they wyll aske me. Thow papysshe bysshop and folish lawer, doest thow deny predestination? [*Side note*] They vse the word papish, to stop euery mans mouth withall. **1566** in Peacock *Eng. Ch. Furniture* (1866) 137 The vestments, albs, amesses..that belong to the papishe priste. **1759** DILWORTH *Pope* 148 None but apish and papish brats will heed him. *c* **1817** HOGG *Tales & Sk.* III. 160 The rebel crew, and their papish prince. **1898** CROCKETT *Stand. Bearer* xiv. 118 He had been a Papish priest some-gate in his youth.

B. *sb.* = PAPIST. *dial.* or *illiterate.*

1604 in R. E. C. Waters *Parish Reg. Eng.* (1883) 68 Christian Steevens..was buried by women, for she was a papishe. **1668** DRYDEN *Sir M. Mar-all* IV. i, There are some Papishes, I'll warrant, that lie in wait for my daughter. **1792** MAD. D'ARBLAY *Let. to Mrs. Phillips* Sept., Upon the.. supposition that, being nothing but French papishes, they would never pay. **1802** COLERIDGE *Lett., to T. Wedgwood* (1895) 417 The climate and country are heavenly, the inhabitants Papishes. **1828** *Craven Gloss.* (ed. 2), *Papish*, a papist. **1894** LYTTLE *Betsy Gray* 16 (E.D.D.) Ye ca'd him a Papish an' a rebel.

ˈpapisher. *Obs.* or *dial.* [See -ER¹.] = prec. B.

1823 SCOTT *Peveril* xxi, This plot..that they are pursuing the Papishers about. **1836** J. H. NEWMAN *Lett.* (1891) II. 199 Dr. Wiseman (somewhat coolly) has sent me down two fresh Papishers last night.

papism (ˈpeɪpɪz(ə)m). [a. F. *papisme* (1578 in Hatz.-Darm.), f. as next + -ISM.] The papal system; popery; Roman Catholicism.

1550 BALE *Apol.* 83 If all thynges muste be persolued, that hathe bene promysed in papisme. **1553** BECON *Reliq. Rome* (1563) 138 So long as yᵉ Masse endureth, so long shall papisme continue. *a* **1614** P. LILIE *Two Serm.* (1619) 47 Papisme..is not a total defection, but an aberration, from Christ. **1716** M. DAVIES *Athen. Brit.* II. 381 Invocation of Saints, Church-Ornaments, Priest-Vestments, Altar-Garments, or such like Fundamental Articles of Papism. **1850** H. W. GREVILLE *Diary* (1883) 373 He [Bennet] enters into the whole case of Puseyism,..Papism, his own position.

papist (ˈpeɪpɪst). [a. F. *papiste* (1525 in Godef. *Compl.*), or ad. 16th c. L. *pāpista*, f. *pāpa* pope: see -IST.]

1. An adherent of the pope; esp. an advocate of papal supremacy; also, more generally, a member of the Roman Catholic Church; a Roman Catholic or Romanist. (Usually hostile or opprobrious.)

[**1521** FISHER *Serm. agst. Luther* Wks. (1876) 344 The popes holynes & his fauourers, whom he [Luther] calleth so often in derysyon papistas, papastros, & papanos, & papenses.] **1534** (*title*) A Litel Treatise ageynst the Mutterynge of some Papistis in Corners. **1657** J. SERGEANT *Schism Dispach't* 656 'Tis clear that al Roman-Catholikes, that is, all Communicants with the Church of Rome or Papists (as they call them) hold the substance of the Pope's Authority. **1699** TANNER 28 Apr. in *Pepys' Diary* (1879) VI. 186 The Papists and other enemies of the Ch. of England. **1781** GIBBON *Decl. & F.* xx. II. 152 *note*, In the beginning of the last century, the Papists of England were only a thirtieth, and the Protestants of France only a fifteenth part of the respective nations. **1891** *Times* 10 Oct. 5/3 In spite of the clamour of the extreme Papists, the Vatican recognized that it had still to look to the Italian Government for protection.

2. *attrib.* or *quasi-adj.* = PAPAL.

1819 LADY MORGAN *Autobiog.* (1859) 277 There, and in the bright hopes that opened to them of getting rid of papist government, it is that Bonaparte is a loss to Europe.

3. (With capital initial) An imitator or follower of the poet, Alexander Pope. Also *attrib.*

a **1849** H. COLERIDGE *Ess. & Marginalia* (1851) II. 118 Nor would so many really monotonous jinglers have passed for correct, orthodox Papists. **1902** F. HARRISON *John Ruskin* ii. 22 Many a prize poem has had worse couplets in the Papist vein than these on Etna.

Hence **ˈpapistlike** *a.*; **ˈpapistly** *adv.*

1579 FULKE *Refut. Rastel* 739 To reason from the authoritie of men negatiuely, is Papistlike. **1716** M. DAVIES *Athen. Brit.* III. *Diss. Drama* 29 He was suspected to be a Papist or Papistly affected.

paˈpistic, *a.* (*sb.*) [f. as PAPIST + -IC; cf. F. *papistique* (16th c. in Littré).]

1. = PAPISTICAL. (Usually hostile.)

1545 JOYE *Exp. Dan.* vii. 108 b, Lykewyse in the papistik chirche, what a multitude & variete is there of laudable in syghte ceremonis. **1624** *Brief Inform. Aff. Palatinate* 49 The Armie of the Papistique League..did extreamely rauage the low Palatinate. **1774** WARTON *Hist. Poetry* xliv. (1840) III. 130 Service-books for the old papistic worship. **1844** LINGARD *Anglo-Sax. Ch.* (1858) II. xiii. 259 *note*, I do not see why the papistic prelate Dunstan has not as good a claim to the honours of a reformer as either Alfred or Ælfric.

2. *absol.* or *sb.* = PAPIST 1.

1589 *Marprel. Epit.* (1843) 21 The papistics affirming all their traditions to be agreeable..to the word.

papistical (pəˈpɪstɪkəl), *a.* [f. as prec. + -AL¹.] Of, pertaining to, or of the nature of a papist or papists; adhering to the pope; of, pertaining, or adhering to the Church of Rome and its doctrines, ceremonies, and traditions; popish. Usually hostile or opprobrious. (In quot. 1568 = PAPAL.)

1537 CROMWELL in Merriman *Life & Lett.* 17 July (1902) II. 65 Soo his grace cannot a little mervayl to here of the papisticall facion that is mayntained in that town. **1568** GRAFTON *Chron.* II. 599 Aspiryng to ascend to the Papisticall Sea. **1654** WHITLOCK *Zootomia* 358 Our Protestant Jesuites..(as well as the Papisticall) care not for converting those Indians that have no Gold. **1767** S. PATERSON *Another Trav.* II. 66 A papistical or a calvinistic saint. **1873** M. COLLINS *Squire Silchester* II. ii. 17 The decorations had become unpopular. Somebody had called them Papistical.

pa'pistically, *adv.* [f. prec. + -LY².] In a papistical manner; popishly.

1572 ABP. PARKER *Corr.* (Parker Soc.) 403 Inquire of such unordered persons papistically set. **1655** BAXTER *Quaker Catech.* 30 These Quakers that Pharisaically and Papistically justifie themselves. **1848** J. H. NEWMAN *Loss & Gain* 207 What is called papistically inclined.

†**pa'pisticate**, *v. Obs. nonce-wd.* [f. PAPISTIC + -ATE³.] *trans.* To render papistic.

1746 W. HORSLEY *Fool* (1748) II. 67 Though he may not make them Traitors, yet he may Popefy, or Papisticate them.

papistry ('peɪpɪstrɪ). [f. PAPIST + -RY.] The doctrine or system of papists; popery; the Roman Catholic religion or faith. (A hostile term.)

15.. *Pore Helpe* in *Skelton's Wks.* (Dyce) I. p. cix, Sayinge it is but papistrie, Yea, fayned and hipocrisy. **1549** *Latimer's 2nd Serm. bef. Edw. VI*, To Rdr. (Arb.) 54 The abolishmente of all papestrie. **1549–62** STERNHOLD & H. *Ps.*, *Come Holy Spirit*, Keepe us from sects and errors all, and from all Papistrie. **1617** MORYSON *Itin.* I. 121 There was now small hope of reducing England to papistry. **1732** NEAL *Hist. Purit.* I. 596 Because Papistry was odious. **1856** WHITTIER *Mary Garvin* xxix, Beholding..The stranger cross his forehead with the sign of Papistrie.

†'**papize**, *v. Obs.* [f. L. *pāpa* POPE + -IZE.] *intr.* To act or play the pope; to act on the side of the pope or papal system; **b.** *trans.* To render papal or popish. Hence †**papized** *ppl. a.*, imbued with popery, conformed to the papal system; †**papizing** *vbl. sb.* and *ppl. a.*, playing the pope; following papal doctrines or practices.

1612 R. CARPENTER *Soules Sent.* 41 It is only an opinion of papizing Paganes. **1629** BRENT tr. *Jewell's Epist.* in *Sarpi's Council Trent*, etc. 854 When we see that nothing is decreed in the Councell, but at the Popes pleasure, why may wee not say that the oracles of the Councels doe Papize? **1639** FULLER *Holy War* III. xxix. (1840) 170 Protestants cut off the authority from all papized writers of that age. **1692** *Scotch Presbyt. Eloq.* (1738) 80 Papising Prelates. *a* **1843** SOUTHEY *Comm.-pl. Bk.* III. 519 He is accused of Papizing, because he wishes for conciliation.

paplette, paplote, variants of PAPELOTE *Obs.*

papodam, -dum, varr. POPADAM.

papolater (peɪ'pɒlətə(r)). [f. L. *pāpa* pope + *-later* (see -LATRY).] One who practises papolatry.

1913 A. FORTESCUE *Lesser Eastern Churches* i. 4 We are Creed-tamperers, Papolaters, gross disturbers of the peace by our shameless way of sending missionaries.

papolatry (peɪ'pɒlətrɪ). *nonce-wd.* [f. L. *pāpa* pope + -LATRY.] Worship of, or excessive reverence for, the pope. So **pa'polatrous** *a.*, characterized by 'papolatry'.

1894 *Contemp. Rev.* Aug. 302 Preachers of papolatry. *Ibid.* 303 The new papolatrous and dogmapoeic movement.

‖**papoose** (pə'pu:s). Also 7 **pappouse, papouse**, 8–9 **pappoose**. [An Algonquin word: in Narragansett *papoos*, Pequot *pouppous* (i.e. poopoos).] **a.** A North-American Indian young child.

1634 W. WOOD *New Eng. Prosp.* (1865) 108 This little Pappouse travells about with his bare footed mother to paddle in the Icie Clammbankes. **1677** I. MATHER *New Eng.* (1864) 197 They thought..to make the English believe those base Papooses were of royal Progeny. **1809** KENDALL *Trav.* I. xiii. 152 From *papoose*, a word by which, as it is said, some of the Indians mean a child. **1865** F. PARKMAN *Champlain* xii. (1875) 348 Naked pappooses screamed and ran. **1890** L. C. D'OYLE *Notches* 28 Strapped in that queer contrivance in which squaws carry their papooses.

b. papoose-root, a perennial plant, *Caulophyllum thalictrioides*, of the family Berberidaceæ, native to eastern North America, and bearing panicles of small yellowish flowers and blue berries; the thick, twisted root was formerly used medicinally.

1815 D. DRAKE *Nat. View Cincinnati* ii. 85 Poppoos root. **1843** J. TORREY *Flora N.Y.* I. 33 Blue Cohosh. Pappoose-root... The root of this plant is in some repute as a diuretic and bitter. **1866** *Treas. Bot.* 844/2 *Papoose-root*, the root of *Caulophyllum thalictroides*. **1943** R. PEATTIE *Great Smokies* 190 The old wives of the mountains today are not averse to ..giving their teething children a little papooseroot.

‖**papoosh, papouch(e** (pə'pu:ʃ). Also 7 **papucha**, 9 **papoush**: see also BABOUCHE, PABOUCH. [a. Pers. *pāpōsh* (Turkish *pābutch*) slipper, shoe, f. Pers. *pā* foot + *pōsh* covering.] A Turkish or Oriental slipper.

1682 WHELER *Journ. Greece* II. 187 They slip off their Papuchas, or Shoes, when they go in to do their Devotions. *Ibid.* v. 349 They never wear Papouches, or Slippers, like the Turks. **1835** WILLIS *Pencillings* II. liii. 115 A ragged and decrepit dervish, with his papooshes in his hand. **1847** THACKERAY *Eastern Adv. Fat Contrib.* Wks. 1900 XIII. 621 His pipes, narghilés, yataghans, and papooshes made him a personage of no small importance.

papovavirus (pə'pəʊvəvaɪərəs). *Microbiol.* Also **papova virus**. [See quot. 1962.] Any of a group of small animal viruses which includes those causing polyoma, papilloma, sarcoma, and warts, the members of which consist of double-stranded DNA in an icosahedral capsid with no envelope.

1962 J. L. MELNICK in *Science* 30 Mar. 1128 In the course of work in this laboratory with papilloma (wart) virus of man, polyoma virus of mice, and vacuolating virus of monkeys, I have been made conscious of the similarities in properties between each of them and papilloma virus of rabbits. This has led me to group these viruses together in the pa'po'va virus group, the name being derived from the first two letters of each virus name: *pa*pilloma, *po*lyoma, *va*cuolating, in the order in which the viruses became known. *Ibid.* 1129 The papova viruses contain DNA. **1969** S. T. LYLES *Biol. Microorganisms* xxvi. 536 Papovaviruses characteristically produce warts in human infections; the most common type is the *verruca vulgaris*, called the common wart. **1973** R. G. KRUEGER et al. *Introd. Microbiol.* xxi. 562/1 Members of the papova-virus group can produce tumours readily when injected into tissues of immunologically undeveloped neonatal animals and with difficulty when injected into older animals. **1977** *Proc. R. Soc. Med.* LXX. 393/2 Dulbecco (1976) has recently considered evidence suggesting that cellular mutations may be needed for the full expression of cell transformation by papova viruses.

†**pappe**, *sb. Obs.* [a. F. *pappe*, ad. L. *pappus*.] = PAPPUS.

1657 TOMLINSON *Renou's Disp.* 356 Flowers, which.. wither and turne into pappe or down.

†**pappe**, *v. Obs. rare*⁻¹. [? Connected with PAP *sb.*² and *v.*¹ Cf. It. *pappare* 'to feed with pap' (Florio).] *trans.* To feed, cram, pamper.

? *a* **1400** in Wright *Req. Ant.* II. 41 To pappe and pampe her fleische.

Pappenheimer ('pæpən'haɪmə(r)). *Med.* [The name of Alwin M. *Pappenheimer* (b. 1908), U.S. biochemist, who described such bodies in 1945 (*Q. Jrnl. Med.* XXXVIII. 75).] ***Pappenheimer('s) body***: a siderosome that stains with Romanowsky's or Wright's stain.

1947 MCFADZEAN & DAVIS in *Glasgow Med. Jrnl.* XXVIII. 238 Preparations of the peripheral blood of this case were sent to Dr. Pappenheimer, who..confirmed their apparent identity with those studied by him... We shall in this paper refer to these inclusion bodies as Pappenheimer's bodies. *Ibid.* 255 It would appear that the siderotic granules described by Grüneberg..and by Doniach *et al.*..are probably similar to the Pappenheimer bodies. **1966** J. W. LINMAN *Princ. Hematol.* iii. 63 Siderocytes are red cells that contain one or more hemosiderin granules; these inclusion bodies..are usually demonstrable only with special stains, such as Prussian blue. Occasionally they are associated with sufficient basophilic material to be evident with Romanowsky stains and are then referred to as Pappenheimer bodies. **1972** W. J. WILLIAMS et al. *Hematol.* viii. 80/2 Siderosomes staining with Wright's stain have been called Pappenheimer bodies.

pappescent (pæ'pɛsənt), *a. Bot.* Also *erron.* **papesc-**. [f. L. *papp-us*: see -ESCENT.] Producing a pappus, as composite plants.

1720 BLAIR in *Phil. Trans.* XXXI. 33 The *Esulæ* and *Tithymali* are Cathartick; tho' both these are Lactescent, yet they differ from those which are Pappescent also. **1731** ARBUTHNOT *Aliments* vi. (1735) 211 Cooling, lactescent, papescent Plants, as Cichory, Lettuce, Dandelion. **1732** —— *Rules of Diet* 346 Some lactescent papescent Plants as Endive.

pappet, obs. variant of POPPET, PUPPET.

pappiferous (pæ'pɪfərəs), *a. Bot. rare*⁻⁰. [f. L. *papp-us* + -FEROUS.] Bearing a pappus.

1890 in *Cent. Dict.* **1893** in *Syd. Soc. Lex.*

pappiform ('pæpɪfɔ:m), *a. Bot. rare*⁻⁰. [f. L. *papp-us* + -FORM.] Having the form of a pappus.

1866 *Treas. Bot.* 844/2.

papple, dial. var. POPPLE, cockle (weed).

papponymic (pæpəʊ'nɪmɪk). *nonce-wd.* [f. Gr. πάππ-ος grandfather, after *patronymic*.] (See quot.)

1875 M. A. LOWER *Eng. Surnames* (ed. 4) II. vii. 73 Those who assumed the latter [*Mac*] adopted the father's name or *Patronymic*, while those who took the former [O'], chose the designation of the grandfather, the *Papponymic*.

pappoose, pappouse, variants of PAPOOSE.

pappose (pæ'pəʊs), *a. Bot.* [ad. mod. Bot. L. *pappōsus* (in 17th c. botanists): see PAPPUS and -OSE.] Furnished with a pappus; of the nature of a pappus, downy.

1691 RAY *Creation* I. (1692) 99 That pappose Plumage growing upon the Tops of some of them [Seeds]. **1703** J. PETIVER in *Phil. Trans.* XXIII. 1422 Above a dozen pappose spikes. **1861** BENTLEY *Man. Bot.* 575 Calyx..superior, with a membranous or pappose limb.

pappous ('pæpəs), *a. Bot.* [See prec. and -OUS.] = prec.

1658 SIR T. BROWNE *Gard. Cyrus* iii. 155 The seeds of many pappous or downy flowers. **1785** MARTYN *Rousseau's Bot.* xxviii. (1794) 430 It consists of pappous or villous hairs. **1806** GALPINE *Brit. Bot.* 409 Salix..Seeds pappous.

‖**pappus** ('pæpəs). [mod.L., a. Gr. πάππος.]

1. *Bot.* The downy or feathery appendage on certain fruits, esp. on the achenes or 'seeds' of many *Compositæ*, as thistles, dandelions, etc.; hence extended to the reduced calyx of *Compositæ* generally, whether downy, bristly, scaly, toothed, or membranous.

1704 J. HARRIS *Lex. Techn.* I, *Pappus*, in Botany, is that soft light Down, which grows out of the Seeds of some Plants, such as Thistles, Dandelion, Hawkweed, etc. **1811** A. T. THOMSON *Lond. Disp.* (1818) 405 The capsule is crowned with a feathery pappus. **1866** *Treas. Bot.* 844/2 *Pappus*, the calyx of composites, in which that organ is reduced to a membrane, or scales, or hairs, or a mere rim.

Comb. **1847** W. E. STEELE *Field Bot.* 22 Cal. with a superior membranous or pappus-like limb. **1870** HOOKER *Stud. Flora* 212 Tragopogon..pappus-hairs in many series. *Ibid.* 188 Centaurea nigra..pappus-scales short unequal or O.

2. *Anat.* (See quots.)

1857 MAYNE *Expos. Lex.*, *Pappus*. *Anat.* Term for the first downy beard of the chin. **1893** *Syd. Soc. Lex.*, *Pappus*... Also, the downy hair of the skin and cheeks.

pappy ('pæpɪ), *sb.*¹ Also **pappie**. [dim. of PAPA.] A child's pet-name for 'father'.

1763 BICKERSTAFF *Love in Village* 66 Come, be a dear good-natured pappy. **1782** MISS BURNEY *Cecilia* VI. viii, O no, Pappy has a world of business to settle first. **1897** 'OUIDA' *Massarenes* xx, Now they were doing the same with poor pappy. **1909** JOYCE *Let.* 29 July (1966) II. 230 All are delighted with Georgie, specially Pappie. **1918** —— *Exiles* 20 Do you want to speak to my pappie? **1929** W. FAULKNER *Sartoris* III. iv. 206 Whut you hear, pappy? **1962** L. DEIGHTON *Ipcress File* xx. 130 My pappy used to say, 'Drink Scotch by itself, with rye mix a little water.' **1963** M. DUGGAN in C. K. Stead *N.Z. Short Stories* (1966) 109 Fanny never chattered much and less than ever in the presence of her pappy. **1978** D. BAGLEY *Flyaway* xxix. 280 He wanted to find his Pappy's airplane.

pappy, *sb.*² [dim. of PAP *sb.*²] A nursery equivalent of PAP *sb.*² (also *dial.* of PAP *sb.*¹).

1807 E. S. BARRETT *All Talents* 38 A giant sputt'ring pappy from the spoon.

pappy ('pæpɪ), *a.* [f. PAP *sb.*² + -Y.] Of the nature or consistence of pap; soft and wet.

1676 WISEMAN *Chirurg. Treat.* v. ix. 386, I saw it [his head] swell'd in severall places: some of the Swellings were big and pappy. **1762** MILLS *Syst. Pract. Husb.* I. 137 A sward of their roots laid over a very pappy mud. **1849** *Blackw. Mag.* LXVI. 103 A pappy potato, salted in the boiling. **1896** *Allbutt's Syst. Med.* I. 402 Bread crumbs and milk in fine pappy condition.

b. *fig.* Feeble in character, 'milk-and-watery'.

1809 W. BLAKE *Descr. Catal.* No. 9 There would soon be an end of proportion and strength, and it would be weak, and pappy,..and thick-headed, like his own works. **1893** G. ALLEN *Scallywag* I. 67 You..left me to talk half the day to that pappy, sappy, vappy big Englishman.

c. *Comb.*, as ***pappy-headed***.

1828 SOUTHEY *Ep. to A. Cunningham*, An honest fellow of the numskull race; And, pappier-headed still, a very goose.

papre, papry, obs. forms of PAPER, POPERY.

paprika ('pæprɪkə, pə'pri:kə). [Hungarian, f. Serbo-Croat *pàpar* pepper (see H. H. Bielfeldt 1965, in *Sitzungsber. d. deutsch. Akad. d. Wissensch. zu Berlin: Klasse für Sprachen, Literatur u. Kunst* I. 20).]

1. A condiment made from the dried, ground fruits of certain varieties of the sweet pepper, *Capsicum annuum*. Also *attrib.* and *fig.*

1896 J. T. LAW *Grocer's Manual* 521/1 Paprika, or Hungarian Red Pepper. **1897** *Sears, Roebuck Catal.* 9/3 Pure Ground Spices..Paprika—Hungarian (¼ lb boxes), sweet pepper. **1898** C. H. SENN *Culinary Encycl.* 70 *Paprika*, Hungarian red pepper. A kind of sweet capsicum of a brilliant scarlet colour. **1908** *Daily Chron.* 29 Apr. 9/6 Beat together, adding oil every two minutes; paprika to taste. **1918** A. QUILLER-COUCH *Foe-Farrell* 91 You rubbed a soupsong of garlic into them with three drops of paprika. **1930** *Time & Tide* 14 Feb. 206/2 The Master of the pig-stick had a face and a temper as scarlet as paprika. **1962** H. T. MOORE *Coll. Lett. D. H. Lawrence* I. p. x, He [*sc.* Lawrence] often sprinkled in the paprika of gossip. **1974** *Times* 14 Mar. 11/5 Prawn cocktail... Garnish with a sprinkling of paprika pepper. **1976** *Times* 3 Mar. 13/6 A touch of paprika in the finale was not allowed to lessen appreciation of contrapuntal cunning.

2. One of several European varieties of the sweet pepper, *Capsicum annuum*, bearing mildly flavoured fruits.

1925 J. A. HAMMERTON *Countries of World* V. 3586/1 Onions, garlic, paprika (Turkish pepper), beans and cabbage are common [in Serbia]. **1941** 'R. WEST' *Black Lamb* II. 55 Tomatoes and paprikas glowed their different reds. **1960** E. DAVID *French Provincial Cooking* 96 Red or green sweet peppers, also called capsicums. The pimientos of Spain, paprika peppers of Hungary and peperoni of Italy. **1969** *Oxf. Bk. Food Plants* 128/1 In general, the term 'paprika' is applied to European types [of sweet pepper] with large mild fruits; Spanish paprikas are called pimiento. **1978** *Times* 16 Mar. 25/4 The paprikas grow freely [under glass] as though Holland were a tropical country.

3. The orange-red colour of paprika. Also *attrib.*

1934 in WEBSTER. **1938** L. BEMELMANS *Life Class* II. vii. 191 The little rough-haired dachshund, almost paprika red. **1972** *Guardian* 11 Aug. 9/6 The colour combinations are.. lemon with navy/lemon plaid, and paprika with wine/yellow plaid. **1976** *National Observer* (U.S.) 22 May 19/3 (Advt.), Any body looks better in our ribknit turtle-neck... One size fits all men. Colors: Natural, Yellow, Paprika, Forest Green, Light Blue, Navy.

4. Used *attrib.* to designate various dishes flavoured with either the condiment or the vegetable.

1935 M. MORPHY *Recipes of All Nations* 337 Among the most famous of all Hungarian dishes are.. their paprikas.. being divided into pörkölt, the paprika dish without sour cream, and the other being paprika dishes containing sour cream. *Ibid.* 345 Pork chops with paprika sauce. *c* **1938** *Fortnum & Mason Price List* 26/2 Paprika Chicken—per tin 2/6. **1963** *Guardian* 25 Jan. 10/6 An excellent Viennese meal which included paprika chicken (strictly speaking a dish of Hungarian antecedents). **1966** *Harrods Food News* Sept. 2/1 Paprika Goulash—2 [Portions] 11/6. **1968** R. V. BESTE *Repeat Instructions* xiv. 145 He ordered Bulgarian salata, paprika chicken and a bottle of Riesling. **1969** R. & D. DE SOLA *Dict. Cooking* 168/1 *Paprika butter*, butter sauce colored and flavored with paprika. **1977** K. BENTON *Red Hen Conspiracy* ix. 53 The table was set with dishes.. ranging from the delicate flesh tones of Parma ham, the rusty scarlet of paprika sausage, [etc.].

paprikahuhn (pəˌpriːkəˈhuːn). Also (pl.) **-hühner**. [G., = paprika chicken.] An Austrian dish, perhaps of Hungarian origin, consisting of poached chicken in a rich cream sauce flavoured with paprika.

1905 K. BAEDEKER *Austria-Hungary* p. xvii, Some of the Austrian dishes have curious names;.. 'Gulyás', Hungarian baked meat, peppered; 'Paprikahuhn', fowl prepared in a similar way. **1906** [see GOULASH 1]. **1957** S. STRONG *Good Food from Vienna* 112 Chicken Paprika (Paprika Hühner)... This is a typical Viennese dish deriving from Hungary and should on no account be missed. **1965** R. PHILPOT *Viennese Cookery* 95 Paprikahuhn... Get a good spring chicken.. two ounces of butter, a medium-sized onion,.. very mild paprika,.. tomatoes,.. chicken stock, double cream. **1969** B. SIAS *Chicken Cookbook* 426 Paprika Huhn—Paprika Chicken—Austria's most famous chicken dish, even though Hungary has a claim on it. **1975** *Times* 9 Aug. 8/5 The *Paprikahuhn* proved as bland as baby food.

†**papse.** *Obs. rare*$^{-1}$. The name of some game or sport; or perh. *pl.* pranks.

c **1440** *York Myst.* xxix. 358 And sone schall ye see Howe we schall play papse for þe pages þrowe.

†**Papua** (ˈpæpuːə, -jʊə). *Obs.* Also **Papoo, Papu.** [ad. Malay *papuah, pĕpuah* frizzled.] = PAPUAN *sb.* 1.

1619 W. PHILLIP tr. *Schouten's Relation of Voiage from Straights of Magelan* 62 Wee thought those people to be Papoos, for all their haire was short, and they eate Betell and Chalke mingled with it. *Ibid.* 66 A kind of ill favoured people, all Papoos, their haire short, and curled, having rings in their noses and eares, and.. hogs teeth hanging about their neckes. **1684** LOCKE *Jrnl.* 20 Apr. in K. Dewhurst *John Locke* (1963) 242 Amongst the draughts he had of severall Esterne people in their natural colours and habits were the Kakerlacks and Papu's. *Ibid.*, The Papua was an olive coloured man with a taile. **1840** *Penny Cycl.* XVII. 219/2 Along the coast of the western half of the island are the Papuas, who have received that name from the Malays, in which language the word signifies 'frizzled hair'. **1845** *Encycl. Metrop.* XXV. 239/1 The Papúas of New Guinea.. seem to approach more nearly to the make and strength of the African. **1885** *Encycl. Brit.* XVIII. 231/1 New Guinea.. and other islands peopled by Papuas.

Papuan (ˈpæpjʊən), *sb.* and *a.* [f. *Papua* (see prec.), formerly a name for the island of New Guinea and later for a territory consisting of its south-eastern part (now incorporated in the state of Papua New Guinea, independent since 1975): see -AN.] **A.** *sb.* **1.** A native or inhabitant of Papua (or Papua New Guinea); also, a member of the racial type found there.

1814 J. MAVER tr. *J. Martinez De Zũniga's Hist. View Philippine Islands* I. p. xii, It is generally allowed that the language spoken by the Papuans, Samangs, and Negritos of the Philippines, and adjacent islands, is totally different from the Malayan. **1869** A. R. WALLACE *Malay Archipelago* II. xl. 445 In stature the Papuan decidedly surpasses the Malay. **1876** *Encycl. Brit.* V. 790/2 The rite of circumcision .. is still kept up.. among the Papuans. **1902** *Chambers's Jrnl.* May 287/2 [With] the Negro.. he throws in the Papuans and Malays, who have black or olive skins. **1913** J. G. FRAZER *Belief in Immortality* I. ix. 190 The Papuans, a tall, dark-skinned, frizzly-haired race, inhabit apparently the greater part of New Guinea, including the whole of the western and central portions of the island. **1954** M. K. WILSON tr. *Lorenz's Man meets Dog* p. ix, Even highly civilized peoples.. were accustomed to treat their prisoners no better than domestic animals... The Papuans eat them even to-day with excellent appetite. **1975** J. VAN DE WETERING *Outsider in Amsterdam* (1976) i. 12 Suddenly de Gier knew what this man had to be. Not a Negro but a Papuan.

2. The Papuan group of languages.

1925 H. MURRAY *Papua of Today* ii. 33 The Territory shows even a greater variety of languages. These languages are classified as Papuan and Melanesian. **1939** L. H. GRAY *Foundations of Lang.* 388 The Dravidian family seems to be isolated within India, all attempts to connect it either with Uralic, Altaic, Elamite, Subaraean, Burushaskī, Andamanese, Australian, or Papuan having proved unsuccessful. **1949** M. MEAD *Male & Female* 416 The Arapesh are a Papuan-speaking people. **1960** C. WINICK *Dict. Anthropol.* 401/1 *Papuan*, a New Guinea linguistic stock, non-Melanesian or non-Austronesian. **1978** *Language* LIV. 467 This vast area contains two well-established language families (Austronesian and Australian), as well as a bewildering congeries of seemingly diverse speech communities centering in New Guinea which until recent years were known only under the negative collective label 'Papuan' (= non-Austronesian, non-Australian).

B. *adj.* **1.** Of, pertaining to, or characteristic of Papua (or Papua New Guinea) or its inhabitants.

1869 A. R. WALLACE *Malay Archipelago* II. xl. 449 These people.. are tall and well-made, with Papuan features, and curly hair. **1875** *Encycl. Brit.* III. 739/1 The Papuan Subregion.. comprises, besides the large and imperfectly-known island whence its name is derived, three other provinces, which may be named the Timorese, the Celebesian, and the Moluccan. **1930** A. HUXLEY *Let.* 7 Jan. (1969) 326 The way every trace of beauty, originality, charm, nobility, existing in the various indigenous arts and crafts—from Papuan and Melanesian to Chinese and Indian —had been utterly stamped out. **1957** P. WORSLEY *Trumpet shall Sound* v. 98 Its leader.. declared that he was charged by God to convert his Papuan fellows. **1973** A. BEHREND *Samarai Affair* xii. 124 A small roundish lump now shrunken and indeterminate but once the head of a Papuan tribesman.

2. *spec.* Of or pertaining to a group of non-Austronesian languages spoken in Papua (or Papua New Guinea).

1885 *Encycl. Brit.* XVIII. 780/1 Still less known are the Papuan or Negrito languages, belonging to the black race with frizzled hair inhabiting most of New Guinea, and found also in the interior of some of the other islands having been driven from the coasts by superior intruders of the Malay race. **1908** T. G. TUCKER *Introd. Nat. Hist. Language* 145 The Papuan languages, in New Guinea and some smaller islands, breaking the geographical continuity of the Malayo-Polynesian family. **1912** J. H. P. MURRAY *Papua* v. 135 The languages of the islands at the east end of Papua are all classed as Melanesian, with the exception of Rossel Island, the language of which is considered to be Papuan. *Ibid.* v. 137 The language is.. unmusical in sound... It seems to be a Papuan language. **1925** —— *Papua of To-Day* ii. 33 The Papuan and Australian languages meet,.. in Torres Straits. **1933** L. BLOOMFIELD *Language* iv. 71 The other families of this part of the earth have been little studied; the Papuan family, on New Guinea and adjacent islands, and the Australian language. **1943** *Official Handbk. New Guinea* v. 343 The Papuan languages.. are said to differ as much among themselves as do the languages of the Indo-European group. **1957** *Oceania* XXVIII. 159 There is a distant genetic relationship between a group of Papuan (non-Austronesian) languages in the Vogelkop peninsula of Netherlands New Guinea and the equally non-Austronesian languages of North Halmahera. **1971** LAYCOCK & VOORHOEVE in *Current Trends in Linguistics* VIII. 509 It is rare for speakers of Papuan languages to have a name for themselves. **1975** *Encycl. Papua & New Guinea* II. 610/2 The Papuan languages are not a single family.

‖**papula** (ˈpæpjʊlə). Pl. **-æ.** [L., = pustule, pimple, in form a dim. of **papa*, app. from a root *pap-* to swell.]

1. *Path.* = PAPULE 1.

1706 PHILLIPS, *Papula*, a Swelling with many reddish Pimples that eat and spread. **1875** B. MEADOWS *Clin. Observ.* 22 The papulæ remain, a hair plainly seen in the centre of each. **1876** DUHRING *Dis. Skin* 41 Papulæ are circumscribed, solid elevations of the skin, varying in size from a pin-head to a split pea.

2. *Zool.* and *Bot.* = PAPULE 2.

1857 [see PAPULIFEROUS]. **1870** BENTLEY *Man. Bot.* (ed. 2) 58 Those with one secreting cell placed above the level of the epidermis are frequently termed papulæ or papillæ.

papular (ˈpæpjuːlə(r)), *a.* [f. prec. + -AR.] Pertaining to or of the nature of papules or pimples.

1818–20 E. THOMPSON tr. *Cullen's Nosol. Method.* (ed. 3) 321 These papular affections are peculiar to infants. **1879** *St. George's Hosp. Rep.* IX. 221 Administration interfered with by.. a papular eruption.

papularde, obs. form of PAPELARD.

papulate (ˈpæpjuːlət), *a.* [f. PAPULA + -ATE[2] 2.] = PAPULATED *a.*

1876 J. S. BRISTOWE *Treat. Theory & Pract. Med.* II. ii. 318 Not unfrequently these patches are papulate,.. gyrate, or marginate.

ˈ**papulated,** *a.* [f. L. *papula* + -ATE[2] 2 + -ED[1].] Covered with or marked by papules or pimples.

1822–34 *Good's Study Med.* (ed. 4) IV. 463 A harsh papulated or watery rind. **1874–88** W. WILLIAMS *Princ. & Pract. Vet. Med.* (ed. 5) 218 The disappearance of the papulated eruption.

papulation (pæpjuːˈleɪʃən). [n. of action f. L. *papulāre* to produce *papulæ* or pimples.] The formation of papules or pimples.

1877 ROBERTS *Handbk. Med.* (ed. 3) I. 161 Papulation is deferred till the 7th, 8th, 9th, or 10th day. **1899** *Allbutt's Syst. Med.* VIII. 607 The papulation.. is as frequently the consequence of the scratching as its cause.

papule (ˈpæpjʊl). [ad. L. *papula*; cf. F. *papule* (1555 in Hatz.-Darm.).]

1. *Path.* A small, solid, somewhat pointed swelling of the skin, usually inflammatory, without suppuration; a pimple.

[**1857** MAYNE has only *Papula*.] **1864** W. T. FOX *Skin Dis.* 30 Papules and vesicles may exist in abundance with very little erythema. **1893** *Syd. Soc. Lex.* s.v., The minute anatomy and pathology of papules are very various.

2. *Zool.* and *Bot.* = PAPILLA 1 b, 2.

1872 H. C. WOOD *Fresh-Water Algæ* (1874) 223 Nodules approximate, with their papules applanate.

papuˈliferous, *a.* [f. L. *papula* + -(I)FEROUS bearing.] Bearing papules; papilliferous.

1857 MAYNE *Expos. Lex.*, *Papuliferus*, *Bot.* Having or bearing papulæ, as the branches, leaves and calyces of the *Mesembryanthemum papuliferum*: papuliferous.

papulo- (ˈpæpjuːləʊ), used as combining form of PAPULA, PAPULE, in pathological terms, as ˌ**papulo-eryˈthema,** erythema accompanied by papules; hence ˌ**papulo-eryˈthematous** *a.*, characterized by papulo-erythema. ˌ**papulo-ˈpustular** *a.*, characterized by swellings resembling papules but containing pus. ˌ**papulo-ˈsquamous** *a.*, characterized by papules covered by scales. ˌ**papulo-ˈvesicle,** a swelling resembling a papule, but containing fluid; hence ˌ**papulo-veˈsicular** *a.*, characterized by papulo-vesicles.

1899 *Allbutt's Syst. Med.* VIII. 808 Gyrate patches of erythema or *papulo-erythema. *Ibid.* 697 Preceded by a *papulo-erythematous condition. *Ibid.* 869 A *papulo-pustular skin-affection. **1876** DUHRING *Dis. Skin* 247 Where the process runs into a *papulo-squamous stage. *Ibid.* 67 A great variety of stages of exudation.. giving rise to the papule, *papulo-vesicle, vesicle [etc.]. **1875** B. MEADOWS *Clin. Observ.* 47 An irritable and *papulo-vesicular patch on the back of each hand.

papulose (ˌpæpjuːˈləʊs), *a.* [ad. mod.L. *papulōs-us*: see PAPULA and -OSE.] Covered with papules or papillæ; papillose.

1776 J. LEE *Introd. Bot.* Explan. Terms 385 *Papulosum*, papulose, covered with vascular Punctures. **1830** LINDLEY *Nat. Syst. Bot.* 57 Stigmata.. papulose, or pencil-formed.

So **papuˈlosity.**

1656 BLOUNT *Glossogr.*, *Papulosity*, fulness of pimples or blisters. **1658** in PHILLIPS.

papulous (ˈpæpjuːləs), *a.* [f. as prec. + -OUS.] Covered with or characterized by papules, papulose; of the nature of a papule, papular.

1818–20 E. THOMPSON tr. *Cullen's Nosol. Method.* (ed. 3) 320 The varieties of papulous eruption are comprehended under three genera. **1899** *Allbutt's Syst. Med.* VIII. 606 Among the papulous diseases of the skin.

papure, obs. form of PAPER.

†ˈ**papwort.** *Obs.* [f. PAP *sb.*[2] (?) + WORT.] An old name of the herb Mercury.

a **1400–50** *Stockh. Med. MS.* 203 Mercurie or papwourtz or þe more smerewourt: *mercurialis*. **1597** GERARDE *Herbal* App., Papwort is Mercurie.

papy, obs. form of POPPY.

papyllardie, variant of PAPELARDY *Obs.*

†**papyr, papyre,** anglicized forms of PAPYRUS.

1601 HOLLAND *Pliny* XIII. xi. I. 392 The very bodie.. of the Papyr it selfe, serveth very well to twist and weave therwith little boats. **1662** STILLINGFL. *Orig. Sacr.* Ded. 1 Moses, when exposed in an Ark of Nilotick papyre. **1855** BAILEY *Spir. Leg.* in *Mystic*, etc. (ed. 2) 88 Nile born papyr.

papyr, -e, obs. forms of PAPER.

papyraceous (pæpɪˈreɪʃəs), *a.* *Nat. Hist.* [f. L. *papyr-us* (see PAPER) + -ACEOUS.] Of the consistence or thinness of paper; of the nature of paper; papery.

1752 SIR J. HILL *Hist. Anim.* 169 The violet-purple, papyraceous Solen... It's whole substance is not thicker than that of a sheet of tolerably thick paper. **1824** C. DUBOIS *Epit. Lamarck's Arrangem. Testacea* 142 Shell thin, fragile, and papyraceous. **1836–9** TODD *Cycl. Anat.* II. 156/2 The scapula is.. quite papyraceous in some places. **1882** HUXLEY in *Nature* 9 Mar. 437 This papyraceous substance has taken the place of the epidermis.

papyral (pəˈpaɪərəl), *a.* *nonce-wd.* [f. L. *papyr-us* + -AL[1].] Made or consisting of paper.

1848 LYTTON *Caxtons* VII. ii, Uncle Jack, whose pocket was never without a wet sheet of some kind,.. drew forth a steaming papyral monster.

papyrian (pəˈpɪrɪən), *a.* Also **-ean.** [f. L. *papȳrius* of papyrus + -AN.] Pertaining to or composed of papyrus.

1754 DODSLEY *Agric.* Poems (1810) 360/1 And from whence, A second birth, grows the papyrean leaf, A tablet firm, on which the painter-bard Delineates thought. **1836** I. TAYLOR *Phys. Theory Another Life* (1858) 77 An inscription, which heretofore had been committed to a leaf, or papyrian scroll.

papyriferous (pæpɪˈrɪfərəs), *a.* [f. L. *papyrifer* papyrus-bearing + -OUS: see -(I)FEROUS.]

a. Producing or yielding papyrus. **b.** Producing or yielding paper, or a substance resembling or serving as paper.

1656 BLOUNT *Glossogr.*, *Papyriferous*, that bears or brings forth Paper, or the Rush Papyrus. **1857** MAYNE *Expos. Lex.*, *Papyriferus*, *Bot.* Bearing paper... papyriferous. **1866** J. B. ROSE tr. *Ovid's Metam.* 463 To steer To Papyriferous seven-mouth Nile.

papyrin ('pæpɪrɪn). Also -ine. [mod.f.L *papȳrus* (see PAPER) + -IN¹.] The same as *parchment paper* or *vegetable parchment*: see PARCHMENT.

1860 *Edin. Philos. Jrnl.* N.S. XII. 324 Vegetable parchment.—Papyrine. **1863–72** WATTS *Dict. Chem.* I. 819 Unsized paper plunged..into [dilute] sulphuric acid..and then washed with weak ammonia..[is] converted..into a tough substance very much resembling animal parchment. .. The formation of this remarkable substance was first noticed in 1847, by Messrs. Poumarède and Figuier, who gave to it the name of *Papyrin*. **1864** WEBSTER, *Papyrine*.

papyrine (pə'paɪrɪn), *a.* [ad. L. *papȳrin-us* of papyrus: see -INE².]

a. Made of papyrus. **b.** Resembling paper (Mayne *Expos. Lex.* 1857).

1816 G. S. FABER *Orig. Pagan Idol.* I. 211 They made a papyrine vessel, which in form represented the head of the deity [Osiris]. **1819** —— *Dispensations* (1823) I. 372 The active missionaries..whom the great maritime people..is to send by sea with papyrine volumes.

papyritious (pæpɪ'rɪʃəs), *a. rare*⁻¹. [f. L. *papȳr-us* (see PAPER) + -ITIOUS¹: cf. L. *cinericius*.] = PAPYRACEOUS.

1840 WESTWOOD *Classif. Insects* II. 206 It is of a white, slender, and papyritious texture.

papyro-, combining form of Gr. πάπῡρος PAPYRUS (also in sense 'paper'): as in **papyrocracy** (pæpɪ'rɒkrəsɪ) *nonce wd.* [-CRACY], government by paper, i.e. by newspapers or literature; **papy'rographer**, a writer on papyrus; **papyro'logical** *a.*, pertaining to or dealing with papyrology; **papy'rologist**, a student of papyrology; **papyrology** (pæpɪ'rɒlədʒɪ) [-LOGY], the study of papyri; **papyrophobia** (pəpaɪərəʊ'fəʊbɪə) *nonce-wd.* [-PHOBIA], dread of paper; † **papy'ropolist** *Obs. rare*⁻⁰ [Gr. πωλεῖν to sell], a seller of paper; **pa'pyrotint**: see quot.; **papyroxylin** (pæpɪ'rɒksɪlɪn) [after *pyroxylin*] (see quot.).

1843 *Tait's Mag.* X. 238 A vow..against sparing one drop of blood which the tribunals had once devoted to the altars of the *Papyrocracy. **1906** J. H. MOULTON *Gram. N.T. Greek* I. 159 In the less educated papyrographers we find blunders of this kind. *c***1904** *Encycl. Dict.* Suppl., Papyrological. **1925** H. S. JONES in *Liddell & Scott's Greek-Eng. Lexicon* (1940) I. Pref. p. viii, Mr. H. Idris Bell..has supplied valuable notes on recent papyrological publications. **1939** A. TOYNBEE *Study of Hist.* VI. 74 The benefit of half a century of papyrological enterprise and ingenuity. **1922** *Glasgow Herald* 14 Apr. 5/2 A most helpful Guide prepared..by the well-known papyrologist Mr. H. I. Bell. **1968** *Sunday Times* 25 Aug. 3/5 He spent his winters as a young papyrologist excavating the rubbish-mounds of Græco-Roman cities in Egypt for the significant 'waste-paper' of a forgotten civilization. **1977** *Times* 28 Oct. 14/3 A famous lost play of antiquity has been discovered..among the Oxyrhyncus papyri,..by Professor Eric Turner, the great papyrologist. **1898** *Athenæum* 24 Dec. 887/1 In the department of *papyrology; if we may use such a word. **1900** *Ibid.* 3 Feb. 140/3 Papyrology is the Greek study which is devouring all the rest. **1790** BEATTIE *Moral Sci.* I. I. ii. §320 Of this *papyrophobia*..I was cured long ago. **1656** BLOUNT *Glossogr.*, **Papyropolist*..a Seller of Paper. **1897** WALL *Dict. Photogr.* (ed. 7) 435 *Papyrotype, Papyrography*, or **Papyrotint*, modifications of photo-lithography, in which paper is used as material on which the original transfer is made. **1894** BOTTONE *Electr. Instr. Making* (ed. 6) 26 Gun-paper, or *papyroxyline, is paper which has been immersed for a few seconds in a mixture of nitric and sulphuric acids, and then washed in an abundance of water. *Ibid.* 27 If papyroxyline is used, it should be made from stout millboard.

papyrograph (pə'paɪərəgrɑːf, -æ-), *sb.* [f. Gr. πάπῡρ-ος papyrus (see PAPER) + -γραφος -GRAPH.] Name of an apparatus patented (1874) by E. Zuccato for copying documents by chemical agents acting through a porous paper-stencil.

(In quot. 1878 erroneously put for *photo-papyrography*.)

[**1876** *Papier-Zeitung* 188 (*title*) Zuccato's Papyrograph.] **1877** *Echo* 22 Oct. 4/1 Besides the old-fashioned carbon paper..we have the papyrograph, the auto-polygraph, the autographic, and various other systems of so-called printing. **1878** ABNEY *Photogr.* (1881) 181 This method has been named by Sir H. James as the papyrograph. It must not be mistaken for another process, used for copying letters or circulars, and known by the same name. **1883** R. HALDANE *Workshop Receipts* Ser. II. 179/2 In the early days of papyrograph printing, a pad, saturated with persulphate of iron, was placed at the back of the stencil.

Hence **pa'pyrograph** *v. trans.*, to copy with a papyrograph; **papyro'graphic** *a.*, pertaining to or produced by a papyrograph or papyrography.

1848 H. E. STRICKLAND in *Jardine's Contrib. Ornith.* 20 If [a person] adopts the Papyrographic process, he has merely to draw on paper with lithographic chalk instead of a lead pencil, and to send his design..to an anastatic printer, who will speedily strike off the requisite number of impressions. **1874** *Specif. Zuccato's Patent* No. 1078, I shall..refer to the paper so prepared..as papyrographic paper. *a* **1890** W. R. WARE *Wood-working Tools* (Cent. Dict.), The first draft of these lessons was printed or papyrographed.

papyrography (pæpɪ'rɒgrəfɪ). [f. as prec. + -GRAPHY.] A term applied to a process of writing or drawing on paper and transferring the design to a zinc plate whence it is printed.

The name had already been given in French (*papyrographie*) to various transfer processes introduced in 1819, 1822, and 1840 respectively. More recently it has been loosely applied in English to Captn. Abney's papyrotype, etc.

1848 H. E. STRICKLAND in *Jardine's Contrib. Ornith.* 20, I found that drawings made on paper with this [lithographic chalk] could be readily transferred to zinc, and would supply an indefinite number of impressions... This new process, the original design being made on paper, I have distinguished by the name of Papyrography. **1849** P. H. DE LA MOTTE (*title*) Anastatic Printing and Papyrography. **1888** LIETZE *Heliographic Processes* 112 Capt. Abney's Papyrography [= Papyrotype].

b. The process of copying with a papyrograph.

In mod. Dicts.

papyrotype (pə'paɪərəʊtaɪp). [f. PAPYRO- + TYPE.] Name given to a modification of photolithography, devised by Captain Abney, in which the picture is first printed on a sensitized gelatin film supported on paper, and afterwards transferred to a lithographic stone or to zinc.

1874 ABNEY *Instr. Photogr.* 122 To make a transfer by Papyrotype. **1892** BROTHERS *Photogr.* 159 A process called Papyrotype was patented by Capt. Abney. [*Specif.* 615 of 1873.]

‖ **papyrus** (pə'paɪərəs). Pl. papyri (-'aɪəraɪ). Also 4–7 papirus. [L. *papȳrus*, a. Gr. πάπῡρος the paper-rush; also, the writing material prepared from it.]

1. An aquatic plant of the sedge family, the Paper Reed or Paper Rush (*Cyperus Papyrus* or *Papyrus antiquorum*), with a creeping rootstock which sends up stems from 8 to 10 feet high, bearing spikelets of flowers on long stalks in a large cluster at the top; formerly abundant in Egypt, and the source of the writing material used by the ancients (see 2); still found in Ethiopia, Syria, Sicily, etc.

1388 WYCLIF *Isa.* xviii. 2 The lond..that sendith messangeris bi the see, and in vessels of papirus on watris. **1398** TREVISA *Barth. De P.R.* XVII. cxxvi. (Bodl. MS.), Papirus is þe name of a rusche þᵗ is idruyed to tende fuyre & lanterns. **1548** TURNER *Names of Herbes* 60 Papyrus groweth not in Englande, it hath the facion of a greate Docke... It maye be called in englishe water paper; or herbe paper. **1615** SANDYS *Trav.* (1632) 102 The sedgie reeds which grow in the marishes of Ægypt, called formerly Papyri, of which they made paper. **1727–41** CHAMBERS *Cycl.* s.v. *Paper*, Besides Paper, they made sails, ropes, and other naval rigging; as also mats, blankets, clothes, and even ships, of the stalk of the Papyrus. **1827** MOORE *Epicur.* xvi. (1839) 173 Planks..bound rudely together with bands of papyrus. **1865** LIVINGSTONE *Zambesi* iii. 82 The shore..was covered with reeds and papyrus.

2. A substance prepared, in the form of thin sheets, from the stem of the papyrus plant, by laying thin slices or strips of it side by side, with another layer of similar strips crossing them, and usually a third layer again parallel to the first, the whole being then soaked in water, pressed together, and dried; used by the ancient Egyptians, Greeks, Romans, etc., as a material for writing on.

1727–41 CHAMBERS *Cycl.* s.v. *Paper*, Taking the MS. of St. Mark's Gospel at Venice to be written on Egyptian Papyrus. **1824** J. JOHNSON *Typogr.* II. xii. 430 Ancient manuscripts written on Papyrus, both in Greek and Latin. **1834** LYTTON *Pompeii* I. iii. 14 The few rolls of papyrus which the ancients deemed a notable collection of books. **1877** A. B. EDWARDS *Up Nile* xv. 397 These invaluable letters, written on papyrus in the hieratic character.

3. (With pl. *papyri*.) An ancient manuscript or document written on papyrus.

1824 J. JOHNSON *Typogr.* II. xii. 430 The first Papyrus was at length unrolled, and proved to be a Treatise of Music. **1863** LD. LYTTON *Ring Amasis* I. II. I. v. 267 This mummy was accompanied by a papyrus. **1875** SCRIVENER *Lect. Text N. Test.* 20 Those Biblical codices which most resemble the Herculanean papyri.

4. *attrib.* and *Comb.*

1837 SIR J. G. WILKINSON *Anc. Egypt.* viii. III. 62 Purposes to which the papyrus plant is said to have been applied. **1866** LIVINGSTONE *Last Jrnls.* (1873) I. ix. 234 Papyrus roots are hard to the bare feet. **1875** SCRIVENER *Lect. Text N. Test.* 16 The papyrus fragments rescued from the ruins of Herculaneum.

paquet, -ette, obs. forms of PACKET.

par (pɑː(r)), *sb.*¹ [a. L. *pār* equal, (as sb.) that which is equal, equality. Cf. It. *pare*, Sp., Pg. *par*, F. *pair* equal; It., Ger. *pari*, Pg. *paro*, par of exchange.]

1. a. Equality of value or standing; an equal footing, a level. Now chiefly in phr. *on* or *upon a par*.

1662 PETTY *Taxes* 26 A natural par between land and labour. **1672** —— *Pol. Anat.* (1691) 63 The most important [is] to make a Par and Equation between Lands and Labour, so as to express the Value of any thing by either alone. **1706** PHILLIPS s.v., *To be at Par*, i.e. to be equal. **1710** PALMER *Proverbs* 255 Thus matters were brought to a par, and victory stood hovering o're the illustrious combatants. **1726** SWIFT *Gulliver* I. iii, The rest of the great officers are much upon a par. **1741** MONRO *Anat.* (ed. 3) 16 The Renewal and Waste keeping pretty near *par* in adult middle Age. **1753** A. MURPHY *Gray's-Inn Jrnl.* No. 61 II. 53 It will..set the Ladies upon a Par with the Men. **1761–2** HUME *Hist. Eng.* (1806) III. App. iii. 629 Industry..increased as fast as gold and silver, and kept commodities nearly at a par with money. **1802** H. MARTIN *Helen of Glenross* II. 211 Lord Dorville is almost at par with you. **1832** I. TAYLOR *Saturday Even.* 481 All are to beseem themselves as if all were on a par. **1850** W. IRVING *Goldsmith* xv. 181 Elevated almost to a par with his idol. **1873** BURTON *Hist. Scot.* V. lxiii. 404 Something near to par with what Scotland had to render in return. **1876** MOZLEY *Univ. Serm.* v. 120 The rights of natural society are not to be put upon a par with the rude ideas of early ages.

†**b.** An equal numerical strength. †**c.** A match, something that is equal or a match *to* another. *Obs.*

1708 SWIFT *Sacr. Test* Wks. 1755 II. I. 130 So many of our [Irish] temporal peers live in England, that the bishops are generally pretty near a par of the [Irish] house. **1711** P. H. *View two last Parlts.* 234 The Tryal of this worthless Tool was made a Par to that of Arch-Bishop Laud's.

2. *Comm.* **a.** The recognized value of the currency of one country in terms of that of another; in full, *par of exchange*: see EXCHANGE *sb.* 4.

1622 MALYNES *Anc. Law-Merch.* 416 The diuersitie of the said Par of Exchanges of thirtie three shillings foure pence for the Low-countreys, and twentie foure shillings nine pence for Hamborough. **1691** LOCKE *Lower. Interest* Wks. 1727 II. 72 The *Par* is a certain Number of Pieces of the Coin of one Country, containing in them an equal Quantity of Silver to that in another Number of Pieces of the Coin of another Country. **1727–41** CHAMBERS *Cycl.* s.v., The Par differs from the course of exchange, in this, that the Par of exchange shews what other nations should allow in exchange; which is certain and fixed, by the intrinsic values of the several species to be exchanged: but the course shews what they will allow in exchange. **1832** MCCULLOCH *Commerc. Dict.* (1852) 579 The thousand circumstances which are daily and hourly affecting the state of debt and credit, prevent the ordinary course of exchange from being almost ever precisely at par. **1838** *Penny Cycl.* X. 108/2 Between two countries making use of the same metal a par may exist; but between two countries one of which makes use of gold and the other of silver an invariable par cannot exist. **1861, 1868** [see EXCHANGE *sb.* 4]. **1861** GOSCHEN *For. Exch.* (1864) 6 If the exchanges were at par—that is to say if the indebtedness of the two countries were equal. **1882** R. BITHELL *Counting-Ho. Dict.* (1893), *Mint Par of Exchange*, the weight of pure gold or silver in a coin of one country, as compared with that in a coin of another.

b. Equality between the market value of stocks, shares, bonds, etc., and the nominal or face value. Chiefly in the expressions *at par*, at the face value; *above par*, at a price above the face value, at a premium; *below par*, at a discount. *mint par*: see MINT *sb.*¹ 6.

1726 SWIFT *Gulliver* I. vi, The exchequer bills would not circulate under nine per cent. below par. **1744** TINDAL *Rapin's Hist. Eng.* III. Contin. 336/1 The credit of the Exchequer notes being thus secured, they daily rose nearer to par. **1755** H. WALPOLE *Let. to J. Chute* 20 Oct., Lottery tickets rise: subsidiary treaties under par—I don't say, no price. **1802** *Edin. Rev.* I. 104 A stock bearing one half per cent. would not find many purchasers at par. **1848** W. ARMSTRONG *Stocks* 5 The par value of any stock is that proportion of the capital stock which it represents [etc.]. **1892** BARN. SMITH & HUDSON *Arithm. for Schools* 304 When the price of £100 stock is £100 in money, the stock is said to be at par. **1952** *Economist* 27 Dec. 904 No par value shares were not endorsed by the Cohen Committee when it studied the company law nearly ten years ago, and Sir John Barlow's private Bill, which sought to make no par value shares permissible, went virtually unsupported by the City and by the Government. *Ibid.*, The n.p.v. share is distrusted on the Left,..simply because it tells the truth about an equity share in a way that the share with a nominal or unrealistic par value never could. **1960** NANASSY & SELDEN *Business Dict.* 142 *No par value*, refers to stock issued with no par value printed on the face. Each share represents a fractional part of the total value of the business. **1964** *Financial Times* 25 Feb. 5/2 The shares will have a par value of Kr. 100 each. **1973** D. WESTHEIMER *Going Public* i. 18 There's not a high degree of relationship between par value and what a share of stock will bring on the market.

c. *attrib. par value* = value at par. Also *no par*, having no face value.

1861 GOSCHEN *For. Exch.* 6 Thus those who have the bills to sell are able to obtain more than the actual par value for them. *Ibid.* 48 The limits within which the exchanges may vary..are on the one extreme, the par value, plus the cost of transmission of bullion; on the other extreme the par value, minus this identical sum.

3. a. An average or normal amount, quality, degree, or condition. *on a par*, on an average.

1778 [W. MARSHALL] *Minutes Agric.* 5 Nov. an. 1775, From five bushels of malt, I find, are brewed, on a par, forty-four gallons of strong, and eighty of small. **1796** W. MARSHALL *W. England* I. 12 Taking the par of years, we may fairly place West Devonshire ten days or a fortnight behind the Midland District. **1805** FORSYTH *Beauties Scot.* (1806) IV. 255 The nominal farms..contain on a par about..ninety acres within the head dike, and about 250 acres of moor or hill lands. **1812** SIR J. SINCLAIR *Syst. Husb. Scot.* I. 382 A very small sacrifice of this sort would bring good clover and rye grass to the par of old turf. **1863** FITZROY *Weather Bk.* 15 *note*, Its [the barometer's] average height being 29·95 inches at the mean sea level in England on the London parallel of latitude; which height may be called 'par' for that level.

attrib. Ibid. 323 The barometer had risen..but not to its normal or par height.

b. *above* or *below* (*under*) *par*, above or below the average, normal, or usual amount, degree, condition, or quality. So *up to par*.

1767 STERNE *Tr. Shandy* IX. xxiv, For the livre or two above par for your supper and bed. **1776** H. NEWDIGATE *Let.* in A. E. Newdigate-Newdegate *Cheverels* (1898) i. 11 As to my Spirits they are rather above than below par. **1778** [W. MARSHALL] *Minutes Agric.* 5 Nov. an. 1775, The last brewing..costs but 5*d.* a gallon, but it is below par. **1782** MISS BURNEY *Cecilia* II. i, Soon find out if they are above par. **1790** M. CUTLER in *Life*, etc. (1888) I. 461 Some of them [speeches in the House] far below par. *c* **1793-4** JANE AUSTEN *Lady Susan* (1925) 111 Sir James is certainly under par. **1809** MALKIN *Gil Blas* VII. iv. ¶6 A little below par with respect to your own works in general. **1826** ANNE ROYALL *Sketches* 270 The females appeared to be rather under par, as did some of the other sex. **1880** GEO. ELIOT *Let.* 1 Aug. (1956) VII. 308 These conditions found him a little below par from long protracted anxiety and excitement... But.. he has been getting strong again. **1886** BARING-GOULD *Court Royal* xlviii, I think he caught a chill, and being below par he succumbed. **1899** H. SPENCER in *Westm. Gaz.* 20 May 4/3 Thanks for your inquiry. I am about up to par, and not without hope of rising above it presently. **1934** G. B. SHAW *Too True to be Good* I. 31 There is nothing constitutionally wrong. A little below par: that is all. **1940** WODEHOUSE *Quick Service* x. 104 Mrs. Chavender's Pekinese..had woken up that morning a little below par, and Sally was driving her and it to the veterinary surgeon in Lewes. **1958** A. HUXLEY *Brave New World Revisited* (1959) viii. 99 Whenever anyone felt depressed or below par, he would swallow a tablet or two of a chemical compound called Soma.

4. *Golf.* The number of strokes which a first-class player should normally require for a hole or course, calculated from the length of the holes with two putts for each green, and in some cases taking account of difficulties and obstacles in the course. Also *fig.*, ***par for the course*** (see quot. 1961[1]).

1898 *Westm. Gaz.* 30 Mar. 9/2 Comparison between the par value of the different championship courses and the winning scores in the last championship meetings over them. **1900** *Ibid.* 9 Mar. 3/2 The professionals went round in the par of the green—74. **1924** J. BRAID *Golf Guide* 164 *Par Play*, perfect golf without flukes. Thus, if a green can be reached in two strokes, the hole is a Par four; two putts being allowed on each green. **1947** *Partisan Rev.* XIV. 363 Nancy had married and moved to San Francisco and had had three children immediately. 'Par for the course,' said Seymour to Jasper. **1957** *Encycl. Brit.* X. 507/1 Distance is the chief factor in determining the par for a hole. Following are the divisions: all distances up to 250 yd., par 3; 251 to 445, par 4; 446 to 600, par 5; more than 600, par 6. **1961** PARTRIDGE *Dict. Slang* Suppl. 1213/2 *Par for the course, that's (just) about*, that's pretty normal; that's what, after all, you can expect. Canadian c.p.: since ca. 1946. Ex golf. **1961** M. BEADLE *These Ruins are Inhabited* (1963) x. 137 While waiting..I caught a fragment of another subscriber's telephone conversation. This is also par for the course in making an Oxford phone call. **1973** A. MACVICAR *Painted Doll Affair* viii. 96 Let's see if you can still keep shooting all these pars and birdies. **1974** *Encycl. Brit. Macropædia* VIII. 250/2 Par is essentially a U.S. term that came into use in the early 1900s as a base for computing handicaps under the system devised by L. Calkins of Plainfield, New Jersey. **1975** A. BERGMAN *Hollywood & Le Vine* (1976) ix. 129 I'm not sure about his sex life... But that's par for the course out here, you don't even give it a second thought. **1976** *Scotsman* 15 Dec. 19/8 A perfect approach gave him another birdie at the thirteenth and with pars at the other inward holes he set a target which was not successfully challenged all day. **1977** *Times* 23 Mar. 16/8 *Mail* readers.. will, it is true, be getting their news a day later than you who take *The Times*, but that is about par for the course.

‖**par**, *sb.*[2] *Anat.* [L. *pār* equal (see prec.); also, a pair.] A pair, in L. names of the pairs of cranial nerves; chiefly in ***par vagum***, lit. 'wandering pair', the two pneumogastric nerves.

1704 J. HARRIS *Lex. Techn.* I, *Par Vagum*, a Pair of Nerves arising below the Auditory ones. **1727-41** CHAMBERS *Cycl.* s.v., *Par Vagum*, or the eighth Pair, is a very notable conjugation of nerves, of the medulla oblongata; thus called from their wide, vague distribution. **1893** *Syd. Soc. Lex.* s.v., *Par vagum nervorum*, the two pneumogastric nerves.

par (pɑː(r)), *sb.*[3] *dial.* [Related to PAR *v.*[1], ME. *parren* (13th c.), and thus possibly going back to a ME. **parre*, and even to an OE. **pearre*, radical form of *pearruc*, PARROCK, q.v.] An enclosure for beasts; also in comb., as ***par-yard***: see quots.

1819 RAINBIRD *Agric.* (1849) 297 (Eng. Dial. Dict.). *a* **1825** FORBY *Voc. E. Anglia*, *Par*, an inclosed place for domestic animals, for calves, perhaps, in particular. *Ibid*, *Par-yard*, the farm-yard, which is itself well separated and inclosed, and contains *pars* for the many and various animals which inhabit it. **1863** MORTON *Cycl. Agric.*, *Par* (Suff., Norf.), an enclosed place for domestic animals.

par (pɑː(r)), *sb.*[4] *colloq.* A printer's, reporter's, and journalistic abbreviation of *paragraph*.

1844 E. L. BLANCHARD *Diary* 27 Sept. in Scott & Howard *Life E. L. Blanchard* (1891) I. 36 Wrote some little pars for Alderton about 'screw Penholder'. **1854** GEO. ELIOT *Let.* 17 May (1954) II. 155, I intend to have the first sentence or par[agraph] in every § of the appendix in italics. **1879** BLACK *Macleod of D.* xviii. 155 Occasionally a reporter..will drop into the theatre on his way to the office, and 'do a par.', as they call it. **1891** E. NESBIT in *Longm. Mag.* Oct. 605 A picker-up of unconsidered pars, a reporter. **1891** *Publ. Opin.* 27 Mar. 404/1 Knowing something of the way these pars are worked in the Continental Press. **1928** D. L. SAYERS *Unpleasantness at Bellona Club* i. 9, I am ready to sacrifice my nearest and dearest in order to curry favour with the police and get a par. in the papers. **1969** *Daily Tel.* (Colour Suppl.) 31 Oct. 21/2 A story that the *Daily News* would splash might make only a couple of pars well back in the [*New York*] *Times*. **1973** K. GILES *File on Death* v. 119 There was a par. in the evening papers. **1976** *Listener* 2 Dec. 712/3 My business [as television reviewer] is not to bore the readers, to get 'em in the first par and bounce 'em with a last par they'll remember.

attrib. **1892** *Daily News* 2 Feb. 7/2 He had paid.. hundreds of pounds for par advertisements in the country papers.

par, parr, *v.*[1] Now *dial.* [ME. *parren*; app. related to PAR *sb.*[3] *dial.*, and possibly representing an unrecorded OE. **pearrian*: see PARROCK.] *trans.* To enclose, confine; to shut up in an enclosure; to fold, pen, etc.

c **1300** *Havelok* 2439 He bunden him ful swiþe faste,..þat he rorede als a bole, þat he wore parred in an hole, With dogges forto bite and beite. *c* **1380** WYCLIF *Serm.* Sel. Wks. I. 25 þin enemyes schulen..parre þee in Jerusalem, as sheep ben parrid in a foold. *c* **1400** *Ywaine & Gaw.* 3228 Yn al þis [? tyme] was sir Ywayn Ful straitly parred with mekil payn. *c* **1440** *York Myst.* xxxiii. 33 *Cayphas.* In pynyng payne bees he parred. **1863** W. BARNES *Dorset Dial.*, *Par*, to inclose, shut up.

par (pɑː(r)), *v.*[2] [f. PAR *sb.*[1]]

1. *trans.* To equate in value. *rare.*

1878 *Encycl. Brit.* VIII. 789/2 When two countries par their gold coins, the object is to arrive at a common term, for which value for value will be paid.

2. *Golf.* To complete (a hole or a course) with a score equal to par.

1961 WEBSTER s.v., [3]*Par*.., to make a golf score on (a hole) equal to par. **1974** *Spartanburg* (S. Carolina) *Herald* 19 Apr. B5/1 Heard, who parred the course Wednesday, said he was driving badly 'but I chipped and putted very well.' **1976** *Scotsman* 24 Dec. (Weekend Suppl.), We won every par five we parred. **1977** *Evening Post* (Nottingham) 24 Jan. 16/6 He parred the next nine holes before his second bogey of the day at the 18th.

‖**par** (par, pɑː(r)), *prep.* [F. *par*:—L. *per* 'through, by way of, by means of, by'.]

A French preposition meaning 'through, by': occurring in Fr. phrases, but never itself adopted as an English word.

1. Occurring in ME., in certain asseverations and adverbial expressions (where it was sometimes confused with OF. *pur*, F. *pour*:—L. *pro* 'for'). Many of these subseq. became obsolete, some continued into later use with change of *par* to *per*, others coalesced in popular use into words: see PERADVENTURE (*par aunter*), PARAMOUNT, PARAVAIL, PARAVAUNT, PARDIE, PERCASE, PERFAY.

†**a. par (per) amour**, by way of love, for love's sake: see PARAMOUR *adv.*

†**b. par (per, pur) charite (cheryte**, etc.), by or for Christian love, out of charity (chiefly in adjurations): see CHARITY 1. Also **par seinte charite** [OF. (13th c.) *pour sainte charité* (Littré)], for the sake of holy charity.

c **1250** *Hymn Virg.* 19 in *Trin. Coll. Hom.* 258 Bisech þin sune par cherite þat he me sschilde from helle pin. **1297** R. GLOUC. (Rolls) 6972, I nam noȝt wurþi to be þi sone ac par seinte charite..uor ȝif it me. *a* **1300** *Cursor M.* 20248 (Cott.) Quarfor i prai yuu, parcharite [so *G.*; *F.* for, *Tr.* pur charite] ..Yee sai it me and helis noght. *c* **1330** R. BRUNNE *Chron.* (1810) 97 Anselme..kried, pes per charite. *c* **1375** *Sc. Leg. Saints* xxx. (*Theodera*) 403, & askit hym parcheryte þat scho mycht þare resawit be. *c* **1430** *Freemasonry* (Halliw.) 794 Amen! amen! so mot hyt be! Say we so alle per charyte. *c* **1450** *Guy Warw.* (C.) 4551 Y bydde yow now pur charyte, That body ye delyuyr to mee.

†**c. par ma fay (fey)**, by my faith. Cf. PERFAY.

c **1300** [see FAY *sb.*[1] 6 b]. **13..** *Cursor M.* 636 (Gött) þai were noght schamed par ma fay. *c* **1435** *Torr. Portugal* 830 Ryght gladly, par ma fay!

†**d. par cœur (ceur)**, by heart, accurately: see PERQUER(E.

†**e. par chaunce**, by chance: see PERCHANCE.

†**f. par (per) compaigny(e**, by way of or in company, for company's sake: see COMPANY 1 b.

c **1386** CHAUCER *Miller's T.* 653 To sitten in the roof par compaignye. —— *Reeve's T.* 247 The wenche rowteth eek par compaignye. **1390** GOWER *Conf.* III. 218 And tawhte hem hou they sholde ascrie Alle in o vois per compaignie. **1413** *Pilgr. Sowle* IV. xx. (Caxton 1483) 67 Now lete vs steruen here per companye.

†**g. par-entrelignarie** [cf. OF. *entreligneure*, etc. (Godef.)], with interlineation.

1377 LANGL. *P. Pl.* B. XI. 298 A chartre is chalangeable byfor a chief iustice; If false latyne be in þe lettre þe lawe it inpugneth, Or peynted parenterlinarie [or] parceles ouer-skipped. [**1393** C. XIV. 119 Oþer peynted par-entrelignarie].

2. a. In mod.Eng., in advb. phrases from modern French, often hardly naturalized. Such are PARBLEU, q.v.; †***par complaisance***, by deference or indulgence; †***par derrière***, backward, on the back side, behind; ***par éminence***, by way of eminence, pre-eminently; ***par exemple***, for example, for instance; ***par force*** = PERFORCE *adv.*; ***par parenthèse***, by way of parenthesis.

1597 J. PAYNE *Royal Exch.* 21 So yt ys par derriere. **1791** A. S. DAMER *Let.* 18 Aug. in 'L. Melville' *Berry Papers* (1914) 63 They have seen her, and..admire her talents, and, *par parenthèse*, I do really believe that he means to marry her. **1819** H. BUSK *Dessert* 106 And I became a volunteer *par force*. **1847** in F. A. Kemble *Rec. Later Life* (1882) III. 264 There are a few expressions I should like to have stricken out of it, *par exemple*, I hate the word *stink*. **1847** C. BRONTË *Jane Eyre* I. xii. 204 This, *par parenthèse*, will be thought cool language. **1853** THACKERAY *Let.* in H. Ritchie *Lett. A. T. Ritchie* (1924) iv. 49 (This is par parenthèse). **1857** C. KINGSLEY *Two Yrs. Ago* I. p. ix, You shall see enough to-day..*Par exemple*—' And Claude pointed to the clean large fields. **1863** GEO. ELIOT *Let.* 4 Dec. (1956) IV. 118 Miss Hennell is staying there and writes me word that Miss Remond is a fellow guest lecturing (par parenthèse) on Slavery. **1867** H. JAMES *Let.* 22 Nov. in R. B. Perry *Tht. & Char. W. James* (1935) I. 251 Tonight, *par exemple*, I am going into town to see the French actors. **1878** SIR G. SCOTT *Lect. Mediæv. Archit.* I. 9 Pointed architecture..is not exclusively, but *par eminence*, Christian. **1878** H. JAMES *Europeans* I. iii. 111 'Ah, par exemple!' cried the young man. 'You deserve that I should never leave you.' **1889** E. DOWSON *Let.* 30 Jan. (1967) 30 Is he *the* Coquelin, par exemple or is he another? **1893** F. ADAMS *New Egypt* 25 A small European force, and one, *par parenthèse*, by no means extraordinary as to its military character. **1916** E. POUND in *Lett. J. Joyce* (1966) II. 375 And par exemple, the 'practical' Pinker was able to do less than I was.

b. par excellence [L. *per excellentiam*], by virtue of special excellence or manifest superiority; pre-eminently; by the highest claim or title to the designation; above all others that may be so called.

[**1598** TOFTE *Alba* I. (1880) 57 My bright Sunne, renowmd *per Excellence*, Through the illustrious splender of her gleames.] **1695** EARL OF PERTH *Lett.* (Camden) 61 The Santo (which is St. Antonio's church, called il Santo *par excellence*). **1777** in W. Roberts *Mem. Hannah More* (1834) I. 118 The whole house groaned at poor Baldwin, who is reckoned, *par excellence*, the dullest man in it. **1804** *Edin. Rev.* V. 85 Of the class of narratives usually denominated 'anecdotes' *par excellence*, M. Kotzebue has given several that deserve notice. **1873** C. ROBINSON *N.S. Wales* 80 The fashionable quarter par excellence is the east end of the city.

par-, *prefix*, repr. F. *par-*, L. *per-* (see PAR *prep.*), 'through, thoroughly', occurring in words from F., as PARBOIL, PARDON, PARTERRE, PARVENU; esp. common in ME. in words now obs., or in which *par-* has since been changed to PER- after Latin, as *parceve* PERCEIVE, *parfit* PERFECT, *parfourme* PERFORM, *partene* PERTAIN, etc.

par, var. PARR *sb.*, young salmon; obs. f. PAIR.

‖**para**[1] ('pɑːrə). Also 8 parrah, perau. [Turkish (Pers.) *pārah* piece, portion, morsel; the small coin so called. In F. *para.*] A small Turkish coin, the fortieth part of a piastre, in the 17th and 18th c. of silver, but later of copper, and sunk by successive depreciations.

('Its value is at present (1903) about one-twentieth of a penny. In other countries formerly Turkish the para has a greater value.' (*N.E.D.*))

1687 A. LOVELL tr. *Thevenot's Trav.* II. 62 The *Piastre Ryal* is worth eight *Chais*, and each *Chai* five *Paras*, and the *Para* four *Aspres*, which are all pieces of Silver. **1704** J. PITTS *Acc. Mohammetans* 68 Three or four *Parrahs*. **1776** R. CHANDLER *Trav. Greece* 123 The [Albanian] girls wear a red skull-cap plated with peraus or Turkish pennies of silver perforated, and ranged like the scales of a fish. **1808** A. PARSONS *Trav.* i. 3 Small fish..sell for a para, or three farthings English for a Turkish *oka*, which is forty-two English ounces. **1858** SIMMONDS *Dict. Trade* s.v., In Greece the para passes for about the third of a penny, and 100 make a drachma. **1880** J. NICHOL *Byron* x. 196 He discarded animal food, and lived..on toast, vegetables, and cheese, olives and light wine, at the rate of forty paras a day. **1886** *Cassell's Encycl. Dict.* s.v., The Para of Servia is the equivalent of the French centime. **1907** [see DINAR b]. **1935** H. EDIB *Clown & his Daughter* xvii. 90 'Rabia Abla, ten paras' worth of chewing-gum!' shouted a shrill voice from the street. **1960** O. MANNING *Great Fortune* I. 12 He took the coins from his pocket... They comprised a few *lire*, *filler* and *para*. **1971** *Daily Tel.* 18 Sept. 7/7 The first stamps issued in 1941 took the form of the Yugoslavian issues overprinted 'NEZAVISNA DRZAVA HRVATSKA' (Independent State, Croatia). Denominations ranged from 50 paras to 5·50 dinars. **1971** *Whitaker's Almanack 1972* 988 Dinar of 100 Old Dinars or 100 Paras.

‖**Pará**[2] (pə'rɑː). Also **Para** and in some collocations **para**. **a.** Name of a seaport (now usu. known as Belém) on the south estuary of the Amazon, in Brazil, and of the state in which it is situated. Used *attrib.* in the following:

Pará cress, a composite plant (*Spilanthes oleracea*), cultivated in tropical countries as a salad and pot-herb; **Pará grass**, (*a*) = PIASSABA; (*b*) a forage grass, *Panicum purpurascens*, native to Brazil but widely cultivated in tropical or sub-tropical regions; **Pará-nut** = Brazil-nut: see BRAZIL 4; **Pará rubber**, an india-rubber obtained from the coagulated milky juice of *Hevea brasiliensis* (N.O. *Euphorbiaceæ*), a tree growing on the banks of the Amazon.

1866 *Treas. Bot.* 1083 *Spilanthes*,..the leaves..have a singularly pungent taste, which is especially noticeable in the *Pará Cress, *S. oleracea*. **1882** *Garden* 30 Sept. 295/3. **1858** SIMMONDS *Dict. Trade*, **Para-grass*, a name for the fibres of the leaves of the *Attalea funifera*. **1858** HOGG *Veg. Kingd.* 759 *Attalea funifera* furnishes that fibre, resembling whalebone, which is now so much used in this country for making brushes and brooms,..their fibre..is called in commerce *Piassaba fibre*, *Monkey Grass*, or *Para Grass*. **1871** KINGSLEY *At Last* x, The creeping Para grass. **1916** L. H. BAILEY *Stand. Cycl. Hort.* V. 2453/1 Pará-Grass... Intro[duced] from Brazil. *P*[*anicum*] *numidianum*, Lam., is a closely related species of the E. Indies, sometimes confused with the true para-grass. **1929** J. W. BEWS *World's Grasses* vi. 230 'Para grass' (a perennial, with stout stolons, as much as 15 feet long..)..is cultivated for forage. **1958** J. CAREW *Black Midas* iv. 65 Here and there amidst lotus lilies, reeds or paragrass were alligator's eyes. **1968** E. LOVELACE *Schoolmaster* xiv. 221 Silence, and the many fingers of para grass at the roadside..gesturing skyward. **1973** TOTHILL & HACKER *Grasses S.E. Queensland* I. 17 Para grass..is an introduced pasture grass which is planted in wet places. **1848** CRAIG, **Para Nut*, the fruit of the tree, Bertholetia excelsa. **1866** *Treas. Bot.* 138 Brazil nuts form a considerable article of export from the port of Para (whence they are sometimes called Para nuts). **1884** *Encycl. Brit.* XVII. 761/1 Para-nut or Brazil-nut oil, yielded by the kernels of *Bertholletia excelsa*, is employed in South America as a food-oil and for soap-making. **1931** B. MIALL tr. *Guenther's Naturalist in Brazil* iv. 77 It [*sc.* the sapucaja] yields.. edible fruits.. whose nuts, known to the trade as Pará-nuts, appear on our Christmas dinner-tables as Brazil-nuts. **1857** T. HANCOCK *Personal Narr. Caoutchouc* 281 (Index), Para rubber. **1860** *Chem. News* 25 Aug. 125/1 The Para rubber, which is of a superior quality, is generally sent in the shape termed bottle rubber. **1898** *Daily News* 31 Aug. 5/1 The area producing Para rubber extends over 1,000 square miles. **1947** J. C. RICH *Materials & Methods of Sculpture* v. 98 Clarke states that the rubber cement can be made by dissolving ½ ounce of caoutchouc (para rubber) in 25 ounces of benzene. **1968** A. S. CRAIG *Dict. Rubber Technol.* (1969) 112 Para rubber was the best variety of all wild rubber but the advent of plantation rubber steadily reduced its importance until it is now of little significance in world rubber production.

b. Used *absol.* for *Pará rubber*.

1897 *Outing* (U.S.) XXX. 280/1 The crude rubber, which .. is the best up-river Para that the market affords. **1922** [see OVERVULCANIZE *v.*]. **1954** H. J. STERN *Rubber* i. 17 Apart from some domestic consumption the wild rubber of South America is now of small commercial importance, although the so-called 'fine hard Para' is still favoured in some quarters. **1963** A. S. CRAIG *Rubber Technol.* iii. 18 As late as 1920, the best quality of Para (pa-rá) rubber (known as 'Fine Hard Para') was the standard by which the newer plantation rubbers were judged.

para[3] ('pɑːrə). [Maori.] A New Zealand name for the large, evergreen fern, *Marattia salicina*, or its swollen rhizome, formerly used as food.

1855 J. D. HOOKER *Bot. Antarctic Voy.: Flora Novæ-Zelandiæ* II. 49 *Marattia salicina*... Northern and eastern parts of the Northern Island... Nat[ive] name, 'Para',..(Cultivated at Kew.). **1890** H. C. FIELD *Ferns of N.Z.* 153 *Marattia fraxinea*..'Para', 'Para reka', or 'Para tawhiti' of the Maoris. 'Horse-shoe fern' of Europeans. **1906** T. F. CHEESEMAN *Man. N.Z. Flora* 1026 Para; Parareka... The large starchy rhizome was formerly eaten by the Maoris, and hence the plant was occasionally cultivated near their villages. It is now fast becoming rare. **1921** [see *king fern* s.v. KING *sb.* 13 c]. **1946** *Jrnl. Polynesian Soc.* LV. 149 If there is no distinguishing suffix para is understood to mean the fern-tuber [of *Marattia fraxinea*].

para[4] ('pærə). Abbrev. of PARAGRAPH *sb.*

1859 J. BLACKWOOD *Let.* 18 Apr. in *Geo. Eliot Lett.* (1954) III. 52 We had better set a paragraph afloat... If you send a para(graph) to me here I will set it afloat among the Edinr. papers. **1885** R. KIPLING *Let.* 26 Sept. in C. E. Carrington *Rudyard Kipling* (1955) iv. 70 How am I to tackle your letter. .. Para. two from the butt end asks me if I know *The City of Dreadful Night*. **1938** 'G. ORWELL' in *New English Weekly* 9 June 169/1 Casual half-inch paras in every issue of the newspapers. **1951** WODEHOUSE *Old Reliable* x. 123 There is a morality clause in my contract.. Para Six. **1972** 'G. BLACK' *Bitter Tea* (1973) viii. 124 After this 'Dealer' para the news of your sunk ship could push them to a decision.

para[5] ('pærə), *a.* (*adv.*) [f. PARA-[1].] **1.** *Chem.* (Now usu. italicized.) Characterized by or relating to (substitution at) two opposite carbon atoms in a benzene ring; at a position opposite *to* some (specified) substituent in a benzene ring. Also as *adv.*

1876, etc. [see ORTHO *a.* (*adv.*) 1]. **1903** A. J. WALKER tr. *Holleman's Text-bk. Org. Chem.* II. 446 There remains no possibility, except the *para*-structure, for the third hydroxybenzoic acid melting at 210°. **1938** L. F. FIESER in H. Gilman *Org. Chem.* I. ii. 132 The para coupling of a free phenol is regarded as a 1,4-addition to the conjugated system of the nucleus, followed by loss of water. **1949** [see ORIENT *v.* 4a]. **1968** R. O. C. NORMAN *Princ. Org. Synthesis* xii. 402 The inductive effect is relayed through one more carbon atom than is the case for *ortho* or *para* substitution. **1972** R. A. JACKSON *Mechanism* ii. 12 Explanations based on the resonance effects of the methyl group do not.. explain the more pronounced effect of *meta* compared with *para* substitution.

2. *para* (or *Para*) *red*, any of various dyes that consist chiefly of the coupling product of diazotized paranitraniline and β-naphthol and are used in printing inks and paints.

1907 *Jrnl. Soc. Dyers & Colourists* XXIII. 20/2 Para red discharges on indigo have been produced for the last ten years. **1930** A. W. C. HARRISON *Manuf. Lakes & Precipitated Pigments* xii. 163 When Para red is present in old water paint on a wall surface, it is again best to remove the old material. **1967** [see FIRE-RED *sb.*].

3. See PARA-[1] 3.

para[6] ('pærə). *Obstetr.* [the ending of *nullipara, primipara, multipara*.] A woman who has had a specified number of confinements, as indicated by a preceding or following numeral.

1881 *Trans. Edin. Obstetr. Soc.* VI. 70 Of the 48 cases, 26 were primiparæ and 22 multiparæ, as follows: ii. paræ, 11; iii. paræ, 4; [etc.]. **1908** *Practitioner* Aug. 312 Fromme records the case of a vi-para, aged 34, who developed pyæmia after an abortion. **1923** *Jrnl. Obstetr. & Gynæcol.* XXX. 568 In one patient, a iii-para,.. the second stage of labour occupied 1¼ hours. **1950** *Amer. Jrnl. Obstetr. & Gynecol.* LIX. 737 The second maternal death occurred in a 40-year-old, para ii, gravida iv, whose diabetes was of two years' standing. **1966** *Fertility & Sterility* XVII. 336 A 24-year-old para 2 who had menstrual irregularity prior to insertion of the spiral. **1967** [see MULTIPARA]. **1977** *Lancet* 23 Apr. 910/1 A 36-week gestation 2·2 kg Black male infant was born to a 36-year-old gravida 7, para 5 mother by vaginal delivery.

para[7] ('pærə). Abbrev. of PARATROOPER.

In early quots. a. Fr. *para*, abbrev. *parachutiste*.

1958 *Spectator* 20 June 807/2 This has not greatly endeared him to the 'paras'. **1962** A. BUCHWALD *How Much is that in Dollars?* 15 My son assured me paras could never land in the Parc Monceau. **1966** M. CATTO *Bird on Wing* ii. 24 Louis.. had been a captain in the *paras*. He had learned certain things in Algeria. **1967** L. FORRESTER *Girl called Fathom* xii. 148 Commandant Daniel Jules Delavigne, late of the Paras—Indo-China, Algeria. **1972** *Listener* 9 Nov. 625 The First Battalion of the Parachute Regiment pulls out of Northern Ireland at the end of the month... Incidents like Bloody Sunday.. have earned the Paras a reputation for toughness. **1973** *Ibid.* 26 Apr. 534/1 A gun battle between the Paras and the Provos. **1977** J. CARTWRIGHT *Fighting Men* vii. 95 Right, paras get ready to jump.

para[8] ('pærə). Slang abbrev. of PARAPLEGIC *a.*

1961 PARTRIDGE *Dict. Slang* Suppl. 1213/2 *Para*. 2. A *para*plegic (a spinal-cord paralytic): Canadian doctors' and nurses': since ca. 1946. **1969** *Sun* (Melbourne) 18 Apr. 7/3 I'd like to say it's a disgrace that quadras (quadraplegics) and paras (paraplegics) have to wait so long before courts get around to clearing up the mess.

para-[1] (pærə), before a vowel or *h* usually **par-**, repr. Gr. παρα-, παρ-, combining form of παρά *prep.*, occurring in words already formed in Greek, their adaptations, and derivatives, and in modern words formed on the model of these, and, in certain uses, as a living element, in the formation of technical nomenclature.

As a preposition, Gr. παρά had the sense 'by the side of, beside', whence 'alongside of, by, past, beyond', etc. In composition it had the same senses, with such cognate adverbial ones as 'to one side, aside, amiss, faulty, irregular, disordered, improper, wrong'; also expressing subsidiary relation, alteration, perversion, simulation, etc. These senses also occur in English derivatives: see PARABAPTISM, PARABLE, PARADOX, PARASITE; PARALLEL; PARENTHESIS; PARHELION; PARISH; PAROCHIAL, PARODY, PAROXYSM, etc. Two groups of less usual technical words follow here.

1. Terms (substantival or adjectival) chiefly of Anatomy and Natural History, denoting or relating to an organ or part situated beside or near that denoted by the second element, or standing in some subsidiary relation to it; of Pathology, denoting diseases affecting such parts, or designating disordered conditions and functions (often Latin in form); and of miscellaneous other terms in the sense 'analogous or parallel to, but separate from or going beyond, that which is denoted by the root word'.

‖**para-anæst'hesia** *Path.*, anæsthesia of both sides of the body, esp. its lower half (Billings 1890). **para'bronchus** *Zool.*, any of the minutest ramifications of the bronchi in the lung of a bird. ‖**paracan'thosis** *Path.* [Gr. ἄκανθα prickle + -OSIS], morbid growth of the prickle-cell layer of the skin (*Syd. Soc. Lex.*). **'paracarp** *Bot.* [Gr. καρπός fruit], also in L. form ‖**para'carpium**, Link's term for an aborted ovary. **para'cellular** *a.*, passing or situated alongside and between cells. **para'cervical** *a.*, pertaining to or designating the region surrounding the cervix; hence **para'cervically** *adv.* **para'chromatin** *Biol.*, that portion of the nucleoplasm (differing from the rest in taking a faint stain) which forms the spindle in karyokinesis. **para'chromatism** *Path.*, 'faulty perception of colours' (*Syd. Soc. Lex.* 1893): colour-blindness. **para-church** (see quot. 1970). ‖**paracol'pitis** *Path.* [Gr. κόλπος womb], inflammation of the outside of the vagina. **para'condyloid** *a.*, applied to a process of the occipital bone adjacent to the condyle. **paracon'formity** *Geol.* = NON-SEQUENCE. ‖**paracope** (pə'rækəupiː) [Gr. παρακοπή], delirium of fever; hence **para'copic** *a.* (Billings 1890). **paraco'rolla** *Bot.*, an appendage to the corolla, as in *Narcissus* (Mayne *Expos. Lex.* 1857). ‖**para'cousia, para'cusis** [Gr. ἄκουσις hearing], disordered hearing. ‖**paracy'esis** *Path.* [Gr. κύησις conception], extra-uterine pregnancy. **'paracyst**, a subsidiary cyst, esp. in the reproductive organs of certain fungi. ‖**paracy'stitis** *Path.*, inflammation in the *paracystium* or connective tissue round the bladder. ‖**parade'nitis** *Path.* [Gr. ἀδήν gland], inflammation around a lymphatic gland. ‖**para'didymis** = *parepididymis*; hence **para'didymal** *a.* **para'fiscal** *a.*, ancillary to or containing elements not usually regarded as fiscal. ‖**parafla'gellum** (pl. **-a**), a small supplementary flagellum in an infusorian; hence **para'flagellate** *a.*, provided with a paraflagellum or paraflagella. **ˌparageo'syncline** *Geol.*, (*a*) a geosyncline situated at the edge of a continental kratogen (craton) (? *obs.*); (*b*) a geosyncline situated within an older kratogen (craton); [in sense (*b*) ad. G. *parageosynklinale* (H. Stille 1935, in *Sitzungsber. d. preuss. Akad. d. Wissensch.* (*Phys.-mat. Kl.*) 182)]; hence **ˌparageosyn'clinal** *a.* **para'germinal** *a.*, situated alongside of the germen in a seed. ‖**parageusia** (-'gjuːsɪə) [Gr. γεῦσις sense of taste], perversion of the sense of taste; also ‖**para'geusis**; hence **para'geusic** *a.* **para'glenal** [Gr. γλήνη socket of a joint] *a.*, epithet of the coracoid bone or cartilage in fishes; *sb.*, the coracoid bone or cartilage of a fish. **paragnath** ('pærəgnæθ), **paragnathus** (pə'rægnəθəs) *Zool.* (usu. in pl. **-gnaths,-gnatha**) [Gr. γνάθ-ος jaw], (*a*) one of the pair of lobes forming the lower lip in most Crustacea; (*b*) one of the pair of lobes forming the hypopharynx in certain insects; (*c*) one of several paired, tooth-like scales found inside the mouth of certain annelid worms. **'paragneiss** *Petrogr.* [a. G. *paragneiss* (H. Rosenbusch *Elem. d. Gesteinlehre* (1898) 467)], gneiss derived from sedimentary rocks. **para'gnosis** [GNOSIS], knowledge which is beyond that which can be accounted for by known methods; so **'paragnost**, a person possessing or allegedly possessing powers of clairvoyance or foreknowledge; **para'gnostic** *a.* **para'grammatism**, the confused or incomplete use of grammatical structures found in certain forms of speech disturbance; so **paragra'mmatic, -gra'mmatical** *adjs.* **para-hippo'campal** *Anat.* [HIPPOCAMPUS], a gyrus on the inferior surface of each cerebral hemisphere that posteriorly is continuous via the isthmus with the cingulate gyrus and anteriorly ends in the uncus. **para'hyal** *a.* (see quot.). ‖**parahyp'nosis**, abnormal sleep, as in hypnotized states or somnambulism. ‖**parakera'tosis** *Path.* [Gr. κερᾶτό-ω to become horny], skin disease characterized by abnormal development of the horny layer. **parakera'totic** *a. Path.*, affected by or symptomatic of parakeratosis. ‖**paraki'nesia** *Path.* [Gr. κίνησις motion], disordered motor function; also ‖**paraki'nesis**. ‖**para'lalia** *Path.* [Gr. λαλιά talking, speech], disordered or defective articulation. †**para'lampsis** *Path.* [Gr. παράλαμψις, f. λάμψις shining], a pearly-looking opacity of the cornea. ‖**parale'rema** *Path.* [Gr. παραλήρημα talking nonsense], slight delirium, 'wandering' in speech; also ‖**parale'resis**; so **para'lerous** *a.* [Gr. παράληρος talking nonsense], slightly delirious. ‖**para'lexia** *Path.* [Gr. λέξις speaking], a form of sensory aphasia in which one word is read for another; hence **para'lexic** *a.* ‖**paral'gesia** *Path.* [Gr. ἄλγησις sense of pain], (*a*) disordered sense of pain; (*b*) diminished sensibility to pain. ‖**pa'ralgia** *Path.* [Gr. ἄλγος pain] sensation akin to pain. **parali'turgical** *a.*, parallel or ancillary to the liturgy. †**para'menia** *Path.* [Gr. μῆν-ες menses], disordered or irregular menstruation (Good 1822–34). **para'menstruum** [MENSTRUUM], the period of eight days consisting of the first four days of each menstruation and the preceding four days; hence **para'menstrual** *a.* **para'metrial** *a.*, of or pertaining to the parametrium. ‖**parame'tritis** [Gr. μήτρα uterus, coined in Ger. by R. Virchow 1862, in *Arch. f. path. Anat. u. Physiol.* XXIII. 416: see quot. 1869], inflammation of the **parametrium** [back-formation from prec.], the connective tissue by the side of the uterus; hence **parame'tritic** *a.*, of, affected with, or pertaining to parametritis. **para'mitom(e**, the more fluid part of protoplasm, as distinguished from the denser and reticulated *mitome*. ‖**param'nesia** [ad. F. *paramnesie* (Lordat *Analyse de la Parole* (1843) 31, f. Gr. -μνησις memory], disordered or perverted memory, esp. of the meaning of words; now usu. = DÉJÀ VU a; hence **param'nesic** *a.* ‖**paramy'oclonus** *Path.* [Gr. μῦ-ς, μυο- muscle + κλόνος tumult], a form of convulsions in symmetrically placed muscles. **para'myotone** *Path.* [as prec. + Gr. τόνος stretching], a nervous disease, characterized by persistent tonic spasm. **para'nasal** *a. Anat.*, situated beside the nose: the epithet of certain sinuses. ‖**para'nema** (pl. **-mata**) *Bot.* [Gr. νῆμα thread] = PARAPHYSIS; hence **parane'matic** *a.*, pertaining to a paranema. **paranephric** (-'nɛfrɪk) *a.* [Gr. νεφρός kidney], occurring in the tissue beside the kidneys. ‖**parane'phritis**, inflammation of the *paranephros* or suprarenal capsule; hence **parane'phritic** *a.*, pertaining to or affected with paranephritis. **para'notum** *Ent.* (pl. **-nota**) [NOTUM], in certain insects, a lateral expansion of the dorsal part of a thoracic segment; so **para'notal** *a.* ‖**para'paresis** *Path.* [Gr. πάρεσις letting go, paralysis], partial paralysis of the lower limbs; hence **parapa'retic** *a.* **parapa'tagial** *a.*, pertaining to the *parapatāgium*, a fold of skin between the neck and shoulder in birds. ‖**para'pathia** *Path.* [Gr. πάθος suffering], moral insanity, pathomania. **para'petalous** *a. Bot.*, situated at each side of a petal, as stamens. ‖**para'phasia** *Path.* [cf. APHASIA], disordered speech characterized by the incorrect use of words; see also quot. 1972; hence **para'phasic** *a.* ‖**pa'raphia** *Path.* [Gr. ἁφή sense of touch], disordered tactile sense. ‖**para'phyllum** *Bot.* [Gr. φύλλον leaf], (*a*) a stipule; (*b*) in certain mosses, a small foliaceous organ between the leaves. **para'physical** *a.*, subsidiary or collateral to what is physical; of or pertaining to physical phenomena for which no adequate scientific explanation exists. **para'polar** *a.*, situated beside a pole, or beside the polar cells, as certain cells in *Dicyemidæ*. **parapo'litical** *a.* (see quot. 1965). †**pa'rapoplexy** *Path.*, an attack simulating apoplexy, false apoplexy. ‖**para'proctium** *Anat.* [Gr. πρωκτός anus], the connective tissue surrounding the rectum; hence ‖**paraproc'titis**, inflammation of this. **para'psychic** *a.*, of or pertaining to mental phenomena etc., for which no adequate scientific explanation exists; also **para'psychical** *a.* **para'rectal** *a.*, situated beside the rectum. **parare'ligious** *a.*, parallel to, or outside, the sphere of orthodox religion. ‖**pa'rarthria** *Path.* [Gr. ἄρθρον joint, ἀρθροῦν to articulate], defective or disordered articulation of speech. **parasa'gittal** *a. Anat.*, situated adjacent or parallel to the sagittal plane. ‖**parasalpin'gitis** *Path.* [Gr. σάλπιγξ trumpet, taken in sense 'Fallopian tube'], inflammation of the connective tissue around the Fallopian tube. **parase'cretion** *Path.*, abnormal or excessive secretion. **parasi'noidal** *a.*, situated beside a sinus, e.g. of the brain. **para'stemon** *Bot.* [Gr. στήμων thread, taken as 'stamen'], a stamen-like appendage, a staminodium. ‖**para'stremma** *Path.* [Gr. στρέμμα twisting], a convulsive spasm, distorting the face. †**parasy'napsis** *Cytology*, the side-by-side pairing of chromosomes at meiosis; hence **parasy'naptic** *a.*, **-sy'naptically** *adv.* †**para-syn'desis** *Cytology* [ad. G. *parasyndese* (V. Häcker 1907, in *Ergebnisse und Fortschritte der Zool.* I. 74), f. Gr. σύνδεσις binding together] = *parasynapsis* above; hence **parasyn'detically** *adv.* ‖**parasyno'vitis** *Path.*, inflammation of the connective tissue next to the synovial membrane of a joint. **parasyphi'litic** *a.*, indirectly related to or arising from syphilis. **para'tarsial** *a.*, pertaining to the *paratarsium* or lateral portion of the tarsus in birds. **paratec'tonic** *a. Geol.*, (*a*) accompanying deformation (? *obs.*); (*b*) [ad. G. *paratektonik* sb. (H. Stille in *Einführing in den Bau Amerikas* (1940) i. 9)], formed by, or of the nature of, a deformation which is chiefly epeirogenic and produces relatively simple, broad folds such as those in Germany north of the Alps (believed to be characteristic of parageosynclines); cf. *orthotectonic* adj. s.v. ORTHO- 1. **para'terminal** *a. Anat.*, epithet of a strip of cortex in the rhinencephalon that lies immediately in front of the lamina terminalis at the anterior end of the third ventricle and superiorly is continuous with the indusium griseum; chiefly in *paraterminal gyrus* (or †*body*). **para'thecium** *Bot.* [THECIUM], in cup fungi and lichens, the outer, dark-coloured layer of an apothecium; so **para'thecial** *a.* **parathyroid** (-'θaɪərɔɪd), [ad. mod.L. (*glandula*) *parathyreoidea* (coined in Sw. by I. Sandström 1880, in *Upsala Läkareförenings Förhandl.* XV. 466)] one of several bodies adjacent to the thyroid gland; freq. *attrib.* or as *adj.*, esp. in *parathyroid gland, hormone* (= PARATHORMONE); hence **parathy'roidal** *a.*, pertaining to a parathyroid. **para'tomial** *a.*, situated beside the *tomium* or cutting edge of a bird's bill; pertaining to the *paratomium* or lateral part of the upper jaw in birds. **pa'ratomous** *a.*, (*a*) See quot. 1857; (*b*) *Zool.*, of or pertaining to paratomy. **pa'ratomy** *Zool.* [ad. G. *paratomie* (F. von Wagner 1890, in *Zool. Jahrbücher. Abth. für Anat.* IV. 393): see -TOMY], in certain annelid worms, asexual reproduction in which new organs are developed before the division of the animal into two or more parts. **para'tracheal** *a. Bot.*, describing the structure of wood in which the position of the parenchyma depends on that of the vessels. †**para'tripsis** [Gr. τρῖψις rubbing] rubbing; hence **para'triptic** *a.*, pertaining to or effected by rubbing (Billings 1890). ‖**para'trophia**, **pa'ratrophy** *Path.* [Gr. τροφή food], disordered nutrition; hence **para'trophic** *a.* ‖**paraty'phlitis** *Path.* [Gr. τυφλός blind, taken in sense 'cæcum'], inflammation of the connective tissue next to the cæcum; perityphlitis. ‖**parau'chenium** *Ornith.* [Gr. αὐχήν neck], Illiger's term for the lateral region of the neck. ‖**paravagi'nitis** = *paracolpitis*. **paraven'tricular** *a. Anat.*, situated next to a ventricle: epithet of (*a*) a nucleus in the hypothalamus situated above the supra-optic nucleus, and (*b*) one of the mid-line nuclei of each thalamus. **para'vesical** *a.* [L. *vēsīca* bladder], situated beside the bladder. Also PARABASAL, PARACHORDAL, PARAGASTER, PAROTID, etc., q.v.

1893 A. NEWTON *Dict. Birds* II. 522 Secondary Bronchi.., besides opening into Air-sacs, send off a number of radially-arranged *parabronchia [*sic*], all of which extend to and end blindly near the surface of the Lungs. **1971** *Sci. Amer.* Dec. 75/1 The bird lung is perforated by the finest branches of the bronchial system, which are called parabronchi. **1900** G. EISEN in *Jrnl. Morphol.* XVII. 16, I designate as *paracellular bodies numerous non-cellular bodies situated between the regular cells of the testes. **1977** *Lancet* 15 Jan. 139/2 During intestinal secretion considerable ion movement occurs by a paracellular route via lateral intercellular spaces and the so-called tight junctions rather than through the cells. **1922** R. T. FRANK *Gynecol. & Obstetr. Path.* xii. 439 Three zones [of pelvic connective tissue spaces] are readily demonstrable—a para-vesical, *para-cervical and para-rectal one. **1945** *Amer. Jrnl. Obstetr. & Gynecol.* L. 527 (*heading*) Para-cervical anesthesia for the relief of labor pains. *Ibid.* 532 The injection of anesthetic solutions paracervically produces prompt relief from the pain caused by uterine contractions. **1977** *Lancet* 29 Jan. 260/1, I learnt my lesson whilst demonstrating to a colleague how simple is a termination of pregnancy using paracervical block as a local anæsthetic. **1970** *Guardian Weekly* 12 Dec. 14 Groups that don't attract or seek publicity, that meet in upper rooms... This is sometimes called the *para-church, the church of the future which is beginning to take shape. **1976** *Church Times* 17 Dec. 6/3 The author shows that the 'underground' churches that sprang up in the late 1960s have rightly given place to a new form—namely the 'para-church', or alternative church— which exists alongside the institutional churches. **1889** J. M. DUNCAN *Lect. Dis. Women* xxii. (ed. 4) 171 *Para-colpitis. **1957** DUNBAR & RODGERS *Princ. Stratigr.* VI. 119/2 We propose to restrict the term *disconformity* to the third type, in which two units of stratified rocks are parallel but the surface of unconformity is an old erosion surface of appreciable relief, and to introduce a new term **paraconformity* for the fourth type, in which the beds are parallel and the contact is a simple bedding plane. **1975** *Nature* 3 Jan. 15/1 Here we use the term unconformity to refer to a significant gap (demonstrated or inferred) in the stratigraphic record (disconformity or paraconformity). **1888** *Nature* 19 July 288/2 Paradoxal deafness..the *paracousia of Willis, in which the patient is deaf to words uttered in the silence of a room, but not in a noisy street. **1657** *Physical Dict.*, **Paracousis*, noise in the ears which comes from a præternatural motion of the air which is naturally contained in the ears. **1822–34** *Good's Study Med.* (ed. 4) IV. 123 *Paracyesis. Morbid pregnancy. **1876** tr. *Wagner's Gen. Pathol.* 243 Inflammation of..the loose adipose and connective tissue of the lower and lateral parts of the urinary bladder..known as..*paracystitis. **1968** *Economist* 30 Nov. 66/3 Either it would mean higher prices for French farmers ..or else some *parafiscal expedient to prevent this which would be a breach in the whole common price principle. **1974** B. PEARCE tr. *Amin's Accumulation on World Scale* I. ii. 257 It is not practicable to take a share of their profits away from these enterprises by fiscal or parafiscal measures. **1978** *Guardian Weekly* 26 Mar. 12/1 Sums collected as parafiscal levies..by employer associations. **1885** E. R. LANKESTER in *Encycl. Brit.* XIX. 856/1 With a single anterior large flagellum or some-times with two additional *paraflagella. **1956** L. V. DE SITTER *Struct. Geol.* xxiv. 346 The blocks or nuclei sometimes became partly nuclear (*para-geosynclinal) basins, and partly remained continuously above sea level. **1961** *Jrnl. Geol.* LXIX. 650/2 Northern Sakhalin..was characterized during the Tertiary by parageosynclinal conditions. **1923** C. SCHUCHERT in *Bull. Geol. Soc. Amer.* XXXIV. 199 These recording basins can not be grouped into any of the mentioned types of geosynclines, since some of them have oceanic depths, but all are actually a part of the Asiatic continent. They are marginal geosynclines or *parageosynclines (geosynclines beside a continent). **1936** tr. H. Stille in *Bull. Amer. Assoc. Petroleum Geologists* XX. 853 Less intense orogenies..may take place in areas prepared by having been 'special basins' (parageosynclines) in regions that had become consolidated earlier. **1941** *Ibid.* XXV. 1403 The influx of orthogeosynclinal clastics into the Artinskian parageosyncline (in the sense of Stille) is comparable with the invasion of Ouachita-derived geosynclinal sediments into the base of the Strawn in the Oklahoman geosyncline. **1968** R. W. FAIRBRIDGE *Encycl. Geomorphol.* 446/2 A ring of Paleozoic basins ('parageosynclines') surrounds both the Canadian and the Scandinavian shields. **1876** KLEIN in *Q. Jrnl. Microsc. Sci.* XVI. 116 That portion..which is..over-hanging the *paragerminal groove. **1899** *Allbutt's Syst. Med.* VIII. 327 *Parageusia is seen in nearly every form of insanity. **1822–34** *Good's Study Med.* (ed. 4) III. 204 *Parageusis. Morbid Taste. **1888** ROLLESTON & JACKSON *Forms Animal Life* (ed. 2) 170 The sides of the mouth [of the common crayfish] are overhung by the bases of the mandibles, and behind the latter are two small soft lobes united by the posterior margin of the mouth. These lobes are the *paragnatha, metastoma, or lower lip. **1921** *Psyche* XXVIII. 86, I would claim that the so-called 'superlinguæ' of insects most emphatically do represent the paragnaths of Crustacea. **1952** R. C. MOORE et al. *Invertebr. Fossils* xi. 454/2 (*caption*) Morphologic features of worms... Paragnaths. One or more pairs of minute denticulate distal plates. **1963** R. P. DALES *Annelids* ii. 43 Between this muscular part or 'pharynx' and the mouth [of nereids] is a membraneous buccal tube bearing small immovable teeth or paragnaths. **1902** A. HARKER *Petrol.* (ed. 3) xxii. 331 All these have the chemical composition of sedimentary rocks; Rosenbusch styles them '*paragneisses', in contra-distinction to 'orthogneisses', which have the composition of, and are believed to represent, igneous rocks. **1932** Paragneiss [see *orthogneiss* s.v. ORTHO- 1]. **1965** *Mem. Geol. Survey Dept. Malawi* No. 3 vii. 102 The dominant paragneisses in the hilly area around the Chaumbwi vent are quartzo-feldspathic granulites which occur as belts up to 1,100 yards wide. **1933** 'W. CARINGTON' *Death of Materialism* viii. 193, I shall..use the words '*paragnosis', 'paragnostic' and the like; the point being that all the phenomena I have in mind..show signs of the possession or acquisition of knowledge (gnosis) which is, *prima facie*, beyond (para) what can be ascribed to the operation of classical law. **1946** G. N. M. TYRRELL *Personality of Man* v. 53 *Paragnosis*, awareness of additional to normal knowledge. **1964** J. H. POLLACK *Croiset* (1965) i. 14 His mentor, Professor W. H. C. Tenhaeff, calls him a '*paragnost', a word which he coined in 1932. **1973** *Radio Times* 1 Nov. 67/4 More Things in Heaven and Earth... Gerard Croiset paragnost and healer. **1958** GOODGLASS & HUNT in Saporta & Bastian *Psycholinguistics* (1961) 449/1 Most authorities have distinguished between an 'agrammatic' form [of aphasia], marked by simplification and loss of grammatical detail, and a '*paragrammatic' form, marked by confused and incomplete, but not necessarily simplified constructions. **1962** FISH & STANTON tr. *Kleist's Sensory Aphasia* v. 71 'Then it is left had'..is paragrammatical. **1924** A. A. BRILL tr. *Bleuler's Textbk. Psychiatry* xiii. 397 At times grammar fails them [*sc.* schizophrenics] (*paragrammatism). Many words are used incorrectly. **1946** *Brit. Jrnl. Psychol.* XXXVII. 11 Paraphasia and paragrammatism are generally associated with the receptive ('temporal') syndromes. **1961** W. R. BRAIN *Speech Disorders* iv. 43 Sentence-deafness is characterized by a difficulty in understanding sentences and by 'paragrammatism' in expression, a term intended by Kleist to describe confusion in the use and order of words and grammatical forms. **1962** FISH & STANTON tr. *Kleist's Sensory Aphasia* v. 67 (*heading*) Sentence deafness and its abortive form with paragrammatism. **1958** *Gray's Anat.* (ed. 32) 1031 The *parahippocampal gyrus..commences at the isthmus, where it is directly continuous with the gyrus cinguli, and passes forwards bounded on its lateral side by the collateral and rhinal Sulci. **1969** TRUEX & CARPENTER *Human Neuroanat.* (ed. 6) xxi. 522/2 The lateral olfactory stria, the uncus, and the anterior part of the parahippocampal gyrus constitute the..pyriform lobe. **1972** M. L. BARR *Human Nervous Syst.* xiii. 213/1 The parahippocampal gyrus.. hooks sharply backward as the uncus. **1895** *Athenæum* 16 Mar. 348/3 Dr. Mivart..represented two lateral processes of the basihyal (for which he proposed the name *parahyal processes) as probably distinctive of the whole of the Psittaci. **1899** *Allbutt's Syst. Med.* VIII. 882 Bowen.. regards the disease as a *parakeratosis. **1943** *Arch. Dermatol. & Syphilol.* XLVII. 9 In an area above a large focal infiltration of the cutis the epidermis was thin and covered by a condensed *parakeratotic horny layer. **1973** *Internat. Jrnl. Dermatol.* XII. 153/1 This histologic picture consists of a parakeratotic column that stains lighter than the adjacent stratum corneum on hematoxylin and eosin stains. **1878** tr. *von Ziemssen's Cycl. Med.* XIV. 845 *Paralalia is that affection in which the patient..brings forth a different sound from the one he wishes to utter. **1878** tr. *von Ziemssen's Cycl. Med.* XIV. 790 In *paralexia incorrect words are uttered. **1950** *Jrnl. Speech & Hearing Disorders* XV. 291/1 Paralexia is defined as the substitution of any other word or words for the given symbol in reading. **1900** *Lancet* 15 Sept. 822/1 On being asked to read aloud from a newspaper..his reading was markedly *paralexic. **1885** LANDOIS & STIRLING *Text-bk. Hum. Physiol.* II. 1097 The term 'cutaneous *paralgia' is applied to..itching, creeping, formication. **1893** A. S. ECCLES *Sciatica* 60 Hyperæsthesia, paralgia, and anæsthesia are also greatly modified. **1977** *Times Lit. Suppl.* 25 Feb. 225/1 Much hagiographical material was transmitted through the liturgy. Eventually, miracle plays based on saints' lives made their appearance as a *para-liturgical halfway-house between ritual and drama. **1978** G. WAINWRIGHT in C. Jones et al. *Study of Liturgy* II. I. i. 38 Paraliturgical activities flourished: the Stations of the Cross, the rosary, the cult of the Sacred Heart. **1968** *Sunday Times* 29 Dec. 3 The *para-menstrual failure rate in 'O' level candidates was 17 per cent. for girls whose menstrual loss lasted up to four days. **1966** K. DALTON in *Proc. R. Soc. Med.* LIX. 1015/2 **Paramenstruum* is used in this study for the four days immediately before menstruation and the first four days of menstruation. **1970** *Times* 30 Sept. 14 Recent studies have shown that in women half of all medical and surgical admissions to hospital occur during the paramenstruum. **1976** *Drive* Sept.-Oct. 31/2 The paramenstruum (the four days before menstruation and the first four days of blood-loss). **1869** J. M. DUNCAN *Pract. Treat. Perimetritis & Parametritis* 4 It is..to Virchow that I am indebted for the suggestion of the chief terms I propose to use habitually. Taking example from the heart and other organs, he proposes to use *peri* to imply inflammation of serous membrane, and he uses *para* to imply inflammation of [adjacent] cellular or connective tissue... *Perimetritis*, then, will strictly imply inflammation of the uterine peritoneum. **Parametritis* will imply inflammation of the cellular tissue in connection with the uterus. **1903** *St. Louis Med. Rev.* XLVII. 449/2, I advised that the patient submit to examination under anesthesia, when the obstructing mass could be cleared away and the extent of the *parametrial involvement approximately determined. **1962** J. W. HUFFMAN *Gynecol. & Obstetr.* vi. 140/2 Cervical tears at labor may extend upward into the..parametrial tissues. **1889** J. M. DUNCAN *Lect. Dis. Women* xxx. (ed. 4) 244 The frequent occurrence of albuminuria in *parametritic cases.

1874 JONES & SIEV. *Pathol. Anat.* (ed. 2) 758 *Parametritis is..inflammation by the side of the uterus. **1889** J. M. DUNCAN *Lect. Dis. Women* xxviii. (ed. 4) 225 A very common name for parametritis is pelvic cellulitis. **1878** tr. *H. von Ziemssen's Cycl. Pract. Med.* VIII. 281 These abnormal conditions in the *parametrium are described by various authors under different names..: for example, phlegmon of the pelvis (Erichsen), parametritis phlegmonosa (Virchow), and purulent oedema (Pirogoff). **1908** *Practitioner* Aug. 312 Nine days later rigors commenced, and in the right parametrium there was a diffuse infiltration, though thrombosed veins were not palpable. **1967** G. M. WYBURN et al. *Conc. Anat.* i. 43 The general condensation of tissue around the base of the broad ligament and lower end of the cervix of the uterus is known as 'parametrium'. **1888** ROLLESTON & JACKSON *Anim. Life* p. xxi, Protoplasm..as a rule..is more or less vesicular, consisting of a denser substance (mitome) enclosing droplets of a more fluid character (enchylema, *paramitome). **1893** *Syd. Soc. Lex., Paramitom.* **1888** *Amer. Jrnl. Psychol.* I. 735 Several philosophers..have noticed that illusions of memory occur in dreams; and, judging from the writer's own experience, such phenomena are not uncommon. Several dreams illustrative of *paramnesia have come to my notice. **1941** *Mind* L. 323 However strong the feeling that this has all happened before, it may turn out that one is not remembering, but suffering from paramnesia, a feeling of *déjà vu*. **1961** J. HELLER *Catch-22* (1962) xx. 202 The subtle, recurring confusion between illusion and reality that was characteristic of paramnesia fascinated the chaplain. **1897** *Mind* VI. 285, I frequently read a new poem with a vague sense of familiarity, but such an experience never puts on a really *paramnesic character, as I quickly realise that it is explainable by the fact that the writer of the poem has fallen under the influence of Heine, or Tennyson, or Rosetti, as the case may be. **1963** *Lancet* 19 Jan. 164/2, I emerged from my paramnesic reverie to see the two attendants pursuing me across the hall. **1899** *Allbutt's Syst. Med.* VII. 896 All cases of *paramyoclonus cannot be hysterical. **1892** GOWERS *Man. Dis. Nerv. Syst.* I. 540 Ataxic *paramyotone. **1909** J. P. SCHAEFFER in *Univ. Pennsylvania Med. Bull.* XXII. 235/1 While making a study of the sinus maxillaris..my attention was called to some anatomical conditions which to my mind are of great importance in arriving at the etiology, diagnosis, and proper treatment of some affections of this *paranasal chamber. **1954** L. B. AREY *Developmental Anat.* (ed. 6) xxvi. 528 Lodged within the adjoining bones, and in communication with the nasal cavity, are several irregular chambers known collectively as the paranasal sinuses. **1973** J. DAVIES in Paparella & Shumrick *Otolaryngology* I. iii. 166/2 The paranasal air sinuses comprise the maxillary, the ethmoidal, the frontal, and the sphenoidal sinuses. **1866** *Treas. Bot.* 845/2 **Paranemata*, the paraphyses of algals and other cryptogams. **1897** *Allbutt's Syst. Med.* IV. 454 *Paranephric cysts. **1857** MAYNE *Expos. Lex.*, *Paranephritis..*Paranephritic. **1916** G. C. CRAMPTON in *Jrnl. N.Y. Entomol. Soc.* XXIV. 8, I would refer to these lateral folds as the '*paranota', regardless of whether they are entirely tergal in origin, or entirely pleural, or a combination of both. The theories dealing with this origin of the wings may therefore be referred to as the *paranotal theories. **1935** R. E. SNODGRASS *Princ. Insect Morphol.* viii. 158 A third stage was inaugurated with the transformation of the paranotal lobes of the mesothorax and the metathorax into movable organs of true flight. **1964** R. M. & J. W. FOX *Introd. Compar. Entomol.* iv. 112 Although no insect, living or fossil, is known to have paranota that can be clearly interpreted as precursory to wings, paranota are present in certain living insects. **1973** *Nature* 16 Nov. 127/1 He [*sc.* G. C. Crampton] pronounced judgment unequivocally in favour of the paranotal theory. **1880** GRAY *Struct. Bot.* vi. §2 (ed. 6) 178 *note*, **Parapetalous*, those stamens which stand at each side of a petal, yet not necessarily before a sepal. **1866** A. FLINT *Princ. Med.* (1880) 657 A difficulty of speech may consist in an inability to use the proper words to express the mental ideas... This difficulty is sometimes distinguished as *paraphasia. **1946** Paraphasia [see *paragrammatism* above]. **1959** SCHUELL & JENKINS in H. Schuell *Aphasia* (1974) xi. 212 Jargon and paraphasia were present. **1972** *Sci. Amer.* Apr. 78/2 Verbal paraphasia is the substitution of one word or phrase for another... Literal or phonemic paraphasia is the substitution of incorrect sounds in otherwise correct words. **1899** *Allbutt's Syst. Med.* VII. 428 A possible cause of *paraphasic speech. **1863** BERKELEY *Brit. Mosses* Gloss. 312 **Paraphylla*, variously shaped foliaceous or filamentous bodies produced near the leaves, but not at definite points like stipules. **1866** *Treas. Bot.* 845/2 **Paraphyllia*, stipules. **1826** *Blackw. Mag.* XX. 853 Physical or *paraphysical; logical or paralogical; nay, even metaphysical or parametaphysical; nothing comes amiss to a German romancer. **1933** O. LODGE in T. Besterman tr. *Driesch's Psychical Res.* p. ix, For the experimental establishment of reality the paraphysical stand first, although they are admittedly on a lower plane and have less important consequences than the psychical variety. **1934** *Mind* XLIII. 255 The 'theories' of psychical research in their application to 'paraphysical' and 'parapsychical' phenomena. **1961** *Ann. Reg. 1960* 420 A lady had bought an instrument which was claimed by its maker to be capable of diagnosis and treatment on a para-physical plane. **1877** HUXLEY *Anat. Inv. Anim.* xi. 653 Cells of the adjacent part of the body (*parapolar cells). **1965** D. EASTON *Framework Polit. Anal.* iv. 52, I shall refer to the internal political groups and organizations as **parapolitical systems* and retain the concept 'political system' for political life in the most inclusive unit being analyzed, namely, in a society. **1968** F. G. BAILEY in M. J. Swartz *Local-Level Politics* (1969) xiii. 281 My hope..is a model for all kinds of politics in village India, and beyond that for politics in all para-political situations. **1971** P. A. ALLUM *Politics & Society Post-War Naples* (1973) vi. 166 Party and para-political organisation membership is a *sine qua non* of a successful candidature. **1911** H. CARRINGTON in *Flournoy's Spiritism & Psychol.* i. 39 The most striking case of this character which I have encountered is that of Mme. Guelt, in which *parapsychic gifts and tendencies were manifested in four generations of her family. **1930** D. IBBERSON tr. *Oesterreich's Possession* II. vii. 267 Accounts of the parapsychic performances of the mediums are not susceptible of subsequent proof. **1918** D. WRIGHT in *Boirac's Psychic Sci.* p. v, Unless we choose to coin a special word for the purpose, such as '*parapsychical', as suggested by Dr. Boirac. **1957** RHINE & PRATT *Parapsychol.* i. 5 The observations and events dealt with in parapsychology—parapsychical phenomena—are associated in some central way with *living* organisms. **1893** *Syd. Soc. Lex.*, **Pararectal pouch*, a name sometimes given to the peritoneal pouch on either side of the upper part of the rectum. **1966** *New Statesman* 18 Feb. 229/2 These uncommitted people were unable to take up new religions, but they could adopt a set of *parareligious dogma if it was called scientific. **1974** *Daily Colonist* (Victoria, B.C.) 31 May 7/6 What is usually involved in 'black magic' here is not really necromancy or witchcraft, but rather 'anteria', a para-religious form of African origin and related to Macumba in Brazil and voodoo in Haiti. **1909** *Cent. Dict.* Suppl., *Parasagittal. **1925** *Jrnl. Compar. Neurol.* XXXIX. 200 (*caption*) Parasagittal section near the median line, showing the tractus olfacto-tuberalis and its connections. **1929** BRAIN & STRAUSS *Recent Adv. Neurol.* iv. 57 Parasagittal meningiomas..arise from the wall of the superior longitudinal sinus. **1969** D. SUTTON *Textbk. Radiol.* lix. 1051/2 Parasagittal tumours being in the midline, and often bilateral, are better shown by encephalography than angiography. **1975** *Nature* 6 Mar. 48/2 Parasagittal crests relatively far apart and meeting posteriorly almost at posterior border of frontoparietal. **1893** *Syd. Soc. Lex.*, **Parasinoidal spaces*, the spaces in the dura mater..which contain the Pacchionian bodies. **1909** E. B. WILSON in *Jrnl. Exper. Zool.* VI. 84 Pyrrochoris shows a close similarity to Tomopteris... This comparison has convinced me that synapsis occurs at the same period in both—whether by *parasynapsis (side to side union) or telosynapsis (end to end union). [*Note*] I have for some years made use of these terms in my lectures on cytology. **1912, 1925** [see *parasyndesis* below]. **1932** *Proc. 6th Internat. Congr. Genetics* II. 319 Parasynapsis may be demonstrated..by observation of actual side-by-side association of homologous chromosomes or chromosome-segments at zygotene. **1956** *Biol. Abstr.* XXX. II. (Index), Parasynapsis. (*See* Chromosomes; Meiosis.) **1910** *Ann. Bot.* XXIV. 727 Grégoire.., while agreeing with the *parasynaptic chromosome formation, put a different interpretation on to the 'gamosomes' and 'zygosomes' of Strasburger and Miyake. **1912** *Jrnl. Exper. Zool.* XIII. 394 Bivalent segments, each consisting of two chromosomes in parasynaptic union. **1921** *Ann. Bot.* XXXV. 386 Both the telosynaptic and the parasynaptic methods of synapsis may occur, the latter perhaps more largely in forms with long thready chromosomes and the former with short and stout chromosomes. **1929** *Jrnl. Genetics* XXI. 46 In *Prunus cerasus*..the method of pairing is parasynaptic, judging from the occurrence of diplotene chiasmata and their occasional persistence to metaphase as interstitial exchanges. **1910** *Ann. Bot.* XXIV. 752 Whether these univalent strands join with their homologous pairs telosynaptically or *parasynaptically, or by any other intermediate method between these two extremes, resolves itself merely into a question of non-essential detail. **1926** *Genetics* XI. 274 It was thought that one could differentiate in a triploid between splitting and parasynaptic union of chromosome threads, because it seemed possible that the three threads might all unite parasynaptically. **1911** *Jrnl. Morphol.* XXII. 754 The main difference between the views of *parasyndesis and metasyndesis lies in the interpretation of the longitudinal cleft of the gemini. **1912** *Jrnl. Exper. Zool.* XIII. 392 Do they [*sc.* the chromatin-elements] conjugate side by side (parasynapsis, parasyndesis), end to end (telosynapsis, metasyndesis) or in both ways? **1925** E. B. WILSON *Cell* (ed. 3) vi. 508 Evidence has steadily accumulated to show that in a large class of cases synapsis involves a side-by-side union of the synaptic mates (parasynapsis or parasyndesis) instead of an end-to-end union..as was formerly supposed. **1911** *Jrnl. Morphol.* XXII. 750 The chromosomes conjugate *parasyndetically. **1929** *Jrnl. Genetics* XIX. 171 She found a continuous spireme composed of parasyndetically paired threads alternating with single ones. **1899** *Brit. Med. Jrnl.* 25 Nov. 1483 Both tabes and general paralysis are *parasyphilitic affections. **1938** KNOPF & INGERSON *Struct. Petrology* viii. 110 Such a structure is a typical *paratectonic crystallization under conditions of differential displacement. **1956** L. V. DE SITTER *Struct. Geol.* i. 15 Paratectonic Regions contain curved folds, predominantly of concentric type without thickening of the strata in the hinges, accompanied by faulting which is secondary to the folding. **1969** *Mem. Amer. Assoc. Petroleum Geologists* XII. xxiv. 309/1 South of the fundamental Highland Boundary fault zone, inliers of the paratectonic Caledonides consist of Cambrian through Lower Devonian strata typified by simpler upright fold styles and a low degree of metamorphism. **1973** *Nature* 5 Oct. 244/2 Thickening of crust in paratectonic orogeny when two continental plates collide. **1901** G. E. SMITH in *Jrnl. Anat. & Physiol.* XXXV. 434 The..'*paraterminal body' is a structure of great morphological interest and importance, the essential unity of which has not hitherto been recognised. **1935** *Gray's Anat.* (ed. 26) 964 Immediately in front of the lamina terminalis and almost co-extensive with it, there is a narrow, triangular field of grey matter, which is termed the paraterminal gyrus (paraterminal body). **1951** O. LARSELL *Anat. Nervous Syst.* (ed. 2) xvii. 428 The septal or paraterminal area...includes the gray substance of the basal portion of the cerebral hemisphere extending from the region of the anterior commissure to the caudal end of the anterior olfactory nucleus. **1921** A. L. SMITH *Handbk. Brit. Lichens* 141/1 *Parathecium, layer surrounding the thecium (hymenium). **1973** M. A. LETROUIT-GALINOU in Ahmadjian & Hale *Lichens* ii. 76 The parathecial apparatus..comprises (1) a parathecium, often cup-shaped, flaring, and composed of filaments which..are elongated and branched [etc.]. **1895** *Jrnl. Physiol.* XVIII. p. xxx, The tissue of the *para-thyroid gland does not at all resemble that of the thyroid in its adult form. **1897** *Allbutt's Syst. Med.* III. 314 Certain bodies known as accessory thyroids and parathyroids. **1925** *Jrnl. Biol. Chem.* LXIII. 395 (*heading*) The extraction of a parathyroid hormone which will prevent or control parathyroid tetany and which regulates the level of blood calcium. **1948** MARTIN & HYNES *Clin. Endocrinol.* v. 101 Four parathyroid glands are normally situated at the posterior extremities of the lateral lobes of the thyroid. **1960** *Farmer & Stockbreeder* 1 Mar. 136/1 There are two parathyroids in the bird. **1968** *Times* 10 Feb. 5/2 Parathyroid hormone is produced by the parathyroid glands, situated in the neck. *Ibid.*, *Parathyroidal and thyroidal tissue do not play an equivalent part in preventing the development of the symptoms which follow thyroidectomy. **1847** WEBSTER *Parotomous. **1857** MAYNE *Expos. Lex., Paratomous, Mineral.* applied to cleavage when its planes are parallel with those of the fundamental figure, or are inclined to the axis. **1963** R. P. DALES *Annelids* viii. 162 In this genus [sc. *Trypanosyllis*] a series may be traced from *T. coeliaca*, in which simple paratomous stolonization occurs. **1930** J. STEPHENSON *Oligochaeta* xiii. 522 It would seem that regeneration after separation is the more primitive form; regeneration before separation a more recent development; the first is called..architomy, the second *paratomy. **1963** R. P. DALES *Annelids* viii. 161 The fragmentation of an individual into two or more parts may be referred to as 'scissiparity', either before ('architomy') or after ('paratomy') formation of heads on the parts which break away. **1908** *Paratracheal [see *metatracheal* s.v. META- 4]. **1933** *Tropical Woods* XXXVI. 9 *Paratracheal Parenchyma*, aggregated wood parenchyma in assocation with the vessels or vascular tracheids. **1965** K. ESAU *Plant Anat.* (ed. 2) xi. 258 The phylogenetic sequence among the distributional types of wood parenchyma is from the diffuse arrangement to the other apotracheal and the paratracheal types. **1835–6** TODD *Cycl. Anat.* I. 60/1 Any process of mis-nutrition or *paratrophia. **1857** MAYNE *Expos. Lex.*, *Paratrophic. **1893** *Syd. Soc. Lex., Paratrophic*, of or belonging to paratrophy. **Paratrophy*, a malnutrition; also, hypertrophy. **1897** *Allbutt's Syst. Med.* III. 879 '*Paratyphlitis' conveyed the same view of the position of the inflammatory changes. **1893** *Syd. Soc. Lex., Paravesical pouch*, the peritoneal pouch on either side of the bladder. **1935** J. C. WHITE *Autonomic Nervous Syst.* iii. 19 There is a good deal of evidence that the *paraventricular nuclei [*sic*] preside over the sympathetic system. **1942** F. A. METTLER *Neuroanat.* xiv. 321 More diffuse cells scattered about in the ventricular wall are collectively called the paraventricular nuclei..and represent what is left of a system which, in lower forms, interrelates the two thalami. **1945** *Jrnl. Compar. Neurol.* LXXXIII. 11 Here [*sc.* laterally] the anterior paraventricular nucleus becomes a thin, vertical strip of cells. *Ibid.*, Ventrally and dorsally the posterior paraventricular nucleus fades into the surrounding periventricular gray. **1972** M. L. BARR *Human Nervous Syst.* xi. 190/2 The precursors of vasopressin and oxytocin appear in the cytoplasm of cells of the supraoptic and paraventricular nuclei as neurosecretory droplets or granules.

2. In *Chemistry*, *para-* is used to form:

a. Names of substances that are (or have been supposed to be) modifications of those to the names of which *para-* is prefixed, or that have been produced along with or instead of these, or, sometimes, that merely occur with them.

This nomenclature appears to have been first used by Berzelius in 1830 (cf. Poggendorf's *Annalen* XIX. 328, where he introduces *acidum paraphosphoricum* and *paraphosphates*, also *acidum paratartaricum*, *a. parastannicum*).

In some cases the *para-* derivatives are isomers or polymers of the simply-named substance, e.g. *paraldehyde*, *paratoluene*; but in others they are neither isomeric with nor closely related to them, e.g. *naphthalene* $C_{10}H_8$, *paranaphthalene* $C_{14}H_{10}$.

para'benzene (**para'benzol**) $(C_6H_6)_n$, a hydrocarbon isomeric with benzene, occurring along with it in light coal oil. **para'buxine**, an alkaloid, $C_{24}H_{48}N_2O$, obtained from the bark of the box-tree. **paracam'phoric** *a.*, in *p. acid*, inactive camphoric acid. **para'carthamin**, a red substance allied to carthamin, contained in the bark of *Cornus sanguinea*, dogwood. **para'casein**, a phosphoprotein produced as a calcium compound in the form of a curd by the action of rennet on milk; hence **para'caseinate**, a compound of paracasein with a metal. **para'cellulose**, a supposed modification of CELLULOSE, occurring in the cellular tissue and pith of plants. **para'citric** *a.*, in *p. acid* = ACONITIC *acid*. **para'conic** *a.* [ACONIC], in *p. acid*, one of the isomeric acids of constitution $C_5H_6O_4$. **pa'raconine**, an artificial variety of CONINE, $C_8H_{15}N$, differing from it in some of its chemical reactions and physical qualities. **para'cresol**, one of the toluol alcohols found in urine; hydroxyltoluene. **para-e'llagic** *a.*, in *p. acid* = RUFIGALLIC *acid*. **para'fibrin**, a supposed modification of fibrin occurring in certain morbid conditions (*Syd. Soc. Lex.*). **parafor'maldehyde**, a polymer of formic or methyl aldehyde; also called **'paraform**. **parafu'maric** *a.*, in *p. acid* = MALEIC *acid*. **paral'bumin**, a form of albumin found by Scherer in ovarian cysts. **parama'leic** *a.*, in *p. acid* = FUMARIC *acid*. **para'malic** *a.*, in *p. acid* = Diglycollic acid, O.2 $(CH_2.COOH)$: see GLYCOLLIC. **parame'conic** *a.*, in *p. acid* = COMENIC *acid*. **parameni'spermine**, an alkaloid left as an insoluble residue after the extraction of menispermine, $C_{18}H_{12}NO_2$, of which it is an isomer. **pa'ramic** *a.*, in *p. acid*, derived from paramide. **'paramide** = MELLITIMIDE. **para'morphia**, **para'morphine** = THEBAINE, $C_{19}H_{21}NO_3$. **pa'ramylene** = DECENE, $C_{10}H_{20}$. **pa'ramylum, -one**, a carbohydrate closely allied to starch (*amylum*, AMYL[2]) of formula $(C_6H_{10}O_5)_n$, found in starch-like granules in *Euglena viridis*, a flagellate infusorian. **para'myosin**, a protein which forms the thick filaments of the contractile units of molluscan muscle; **paramyo'sinogen**, a proteid occurring in muscle-plasma. **para'naphthalene** = ANTHRACENE. **pa'raniline**, a polymer of ANILINE, $C_{12}H_{14}N_2$, obtained in long white silky needles. **pa'ranthracene**, a crystalline isomeric modification of anthracene: see quot. **para'pectic** *a.*, in *p. acid*, $C_{24}H_{34}O_{23}$, an uncrystallizable acid formed from pectic acid or pectin by long boiling, or by the action of pectose. **para'pectin**, a neutral substance, $C_{32}H_{46}O_{31}$, derived, as a translucent jelly, from pectin by boiling and precipitating with alcohol. **para'peptone**, a substance allied to syntonin, precipitated on neutralizing the action of gastric juice on egg-albumin. †**parapho'sphoric** *a.*, in *p. acid*, Berzelius's name for pyrophosphoric acid; its salts are **paraphosphates**. **para-'picoline**, an oily base, $C_{12}H_{14}N_2$, a polymer of PICOLINE, and formed from it by the action of sodium. **para'protein** [a. G. *paraprotein* (K. Apitz 1940, in *Virchows Arch.* CCCVI. 685)], any of various proteins found in the blood only in certain diseases (as myelomatosis); hence **,paraprotei'næmia** [ad. G. *paraproteinämie* (K. Apitz, loc. cit.), f. Gr. αἷμα blood], the presence of paraproteins in the blood; **pa'rarabin**, a modification of ARABIN, prepared from carrots or beet-root, not yielding sugar on treatment with dilute acids. **,pararo'saniline** [ad. G. *pararosanilin* (E. & O. Fischer 1878, in *Ann. der Chem.* CXCIV. 266)], a colourless, crystalline alcohol $(H_2NC_6H_4)_3COH$, which is used in making triphenylmethane dyes and whose red hydrochloride is used as a biological stain. **para'saccharose**, an isomeric modification of saccharose or cane-sugar, $C_{12}H_{22}O_{11}$, formed by a special fermentation of a solution of sugar-candy: see quot. **para'salicyl**, the salicylide of benzoyl, $C_{14}H_{10}O_3$; also called *spirin*. **para'sorbic** *a.*, in *parasorbic acid*, an isomer of SORBIC *acid*, $C_6H_8O_2$, a volatile oily liquid obtained from mountain-ash berries. **para'stannic** *a.*, in *p. oxide*, a name given by Berzelius to the calcined form of stannic oxide, which differs in some properties from the ordinary oxide. **paratar'taric** *a.*, in *p. acid* (Berzelius, 1830) = RACEMIC *acid*; **para'tartramide** = *racemamide* (see AMIDE 2). **para'toluene**, an isomer of TOLUENE, C_7H_8, along with which it occurs in light coal-tar oil; also **para'toluol**. **para'xanthine**, a substance, $C_{15}H_{17}N_9O_4$, having relations with the xanthine group, obtained by Salomon from urine. See also PARABANIC, PARALDEHYDE, etc.

1866–72 WATTS *Dict. Chem.* IV. 340 *Parabenzene . . has a faint alliaceous odour, less pleasant than that of pure benzene. **1857–62** MILLER *Elem. Chem.* (ed. 2) III. 654 *note*, Church found . . a hydrocarbon isomeric with benzol which he terms *parabenzol. **1906** *Paracasein [see CASEINOGEN]. **1937** A. L. & K. G. B. WINTON *Struct. Foods* III. 184 Paracasein at 5° and 23°C. has 1·5 times as much base-combining power as casein. **1959** JENNESS & PATTON *Princ. Dairy Chem.* x. 314 In view of the close similarity between the casein and paracasein, it is not surprising that the mechanism of the primary action of rennin has long remained obscure. **1961** Paracasein [see CASEINOGEN]. **1907** *Chem. Abstr.* I. 1740 Pure neutral sodium caseinate and sodium *paracaseinate solutions . . are not precipitated by saturation with pure sodium chloride. **1937** A. L. & K. G. B. WINTON *Struct. Foods* III. 185 Rennet-casein . . consists of calcium paracaseinate, formed from the calcium caseinate associated with dicalcium phosphate carried down mechanically. **1866–72** WATTS *Dict. Chem.* IV. 341 The utricular tissue forming the medullary rays of wood consists of *paracellulose. **1893** *Syd. Soc. Lex.* s.v., Paracellulose . . is characterized chemically by being insoluble in Millon's reagent, except after heating to 140° F. for several hours. **1913** *Jrnl. Industr. & Engin. Chem.* June 508/1 We have succeeded . . in producing a fusible phenol resin by heating . . paradioxydiphenylmethan with 10 grams of *paraform. **1932** I. D. GARARD *Introd. Org. Chem.* vi. 79 Paraformaldehyde is made into candles and sold for fumigating purposes under the name of *paraform*. The heat of the burning candle converts the paraform into formaldehyde. **1966** *McGraw-Hill Encycl. Sci. & Technol.* V. 472/1 It [*sc.* formaldehyde] is also sold as the solid hydrated polymer known as paraformaldehyde or paraform. **1894** *Jrnl. Chem. Soc.* LXVI. I. 487 Methylal is readily obtained by this method from *paraformaldehyde and methylic alcohol. **1913** J. WALKER *Org. Chem. for Students of Med.* 40 Paraformaldehyde is largely used as a source of formaldehyde for the purpose of disinfecting rooms, clothing, etc. **1951** KIRK & OTHMER *Encycl. Chem. Technol.* VI. 861 On heating, paraformaldehyde depolymerizes to yield a mixture of monomeric formaldehyde gas and water vapor. **1885** LANDOIS & STIRLING *Text-bk. Hum. Physiol.* I. 502 According to Hammarsten, metalbumin is a mixture of *paralbumin and other proteid substance. **1865–72** WATTS *Dict. Chem.* III. 880 *Paramenispermine has the same composition as menispermine. *Ibid.* 873 *Paramide or Mellitimide is a white amorphous powder. *Ibid.* 874 *Paramic acid. **1946** C. E. HALL et al. in *Biol. Bull.* XC. 44 Since this protein can be identified by electron microscope observation and x-ray diffraction it merits a distinguishing name and is therefore designated as *paramyosin. **1963** *Jrnl. Molecular Biol.* VII. 234 Light scattering, viscosity and sedimentation experiments on solutions of *Venus mercenaria* paramyosin show that the paramyosin molecule is a rod, 1330 Å long and 20 Å in diameter, and has a mass of 220,000 atomic mass units. **1972** *Biochemistry* (Easton, Pa.) XI. 4532/1 The paramyosin molecules align to form a bipolar core of the thick filament which is covered by a surface layer of myosin. **1838** T. THOMSON *Chem. Org. Bodies* 746 This substance was discovered by M. Dumas in 1832, in coal tar, and named by him *paranaphthalin, because from his experiments it appears in its composition to be perfectly identical with naphthalin. *c* **1865** LETHEBY in *Circ. Sc.* I. 107/1 Finally, a more solid material, named paranaphthaline, distils over. **1883** *Athenæum* 15 Sept. 343/2 Dr. D. Tommasi . . states that if anthracene is dissolved in benzol and exposed to the direct rays of the sun it becomes turbid and deposits crystals. This photogenic substance has been named *paranthracene. **1885** LANDOIS & STIRLING *Text-bk. Hum. Physiol.* I. 331 Identical with Kühne's hemial-buminose and Meissner's *parapeptone. **1877** WATTS *Fownes' Chem.* (ed. 12) I. 327 Intermediate between orthophosphates and metaphosphates, there are at least three distinct classes of salts, the most important of which are the pyrophosphates or *paraphosphates. **1866–72** —— *Dict. Chem.* IV. 354 The salts of *parapicoline are for the most part uncrystallizable. **1949** *Chem. Abstr.* XLIII. 9097 The *paraproteins have a different structural analysis than plasma protein. **1961** *Lancet* 9 Sept. 603/2 Large errors may arise if the urinary protein consists of a paraprotein, such as Bence Jones'. **1972** *Jrnl. Immunol.* CIX. 511/2 No feline paraproteins have been characterized physically or chemically. **1958** *Arch. Internal Med.* CII. 618/1 This method to this day has been used clinically as a method of evaluating dysproteinemias and *paraproteinemias in disease states. **1972** *Clin. & Exper. Immunol.* XI. 488 There were six patients whose disease was associated with an IgM paraproteinaemia . . and another six without a paraproteinaemia. **1893** *Syd. Soc. Lex.* s.v., Agar-agar, the Chinese vegetable jelly, is composed of *pararabin. **1879** *Jrnl. Chem. Soc.* XXXVI. 385 *Pararosaniline is the name applied by the authors to the colouring matter derived from paratoluidine. **1926** J. READ *Text-bk. Org. Chem.* xi. 203 By replacing six hydrogen atoms in the molecule of the magenta dye, pararosaniline, with six methyl groups, a deep violet dye, known as 'crystal violet' is produced. **1971** E. GURR *Synthetic Dyes* 81 Fuschin basic . . is, in fact a hybrid mixture of the chlorides of pararosaniline, rosaniline and new magenta. **1893** *Syd. Soc. Lex.* s.v., *Parasaccharose is more strongly dextro-rotatory than Saccharose. **1857–62** MILLER *Elem. Chem.* (ed. 2) III. 385 This new acid is identical with the *paratartaric or racemic acid. **1885** LANDOIS & STIRLING *Text-bk. Hum. Physiol.* II. 539 The crystalline body *paraxanthin occurs in traces in the urine.

b. (More systematically) Names of isomeric benzene di-derivatives in which the two hydrogen-atoms replaced by another element or radical are symmetrically disposed in the benzene ring, being separated on each side by two other atoms; as 1 and 4 in the ring 1 $^{2}{}^{3}{}_{6}{}_{5}$ 4; e.g. *paradichlorobenzene*, $C_6ClHHClHH$. So *coumaric* (1 : 2) and *paracoumaric* (1 : 4) *acids*, etc. See ORTHO- 2.

As these compound names are formed systematically, and are in number unlimited, it is not strictly necessary to give any list; cf. the following:

1876 *Jrnl. Chem. Soc.* (1) 207 Few chemists employ the terms *para-*, *meta-*, *ortho-*, in any other sense than as denoting 1 : 4, 1 : 3, and 1 : 2 compounds respectively. **1889** *Anthony's Photogr. Bull.* II. 270 We have called paradihydroxy-benzene [or quinol] *one* of the benzenes, and the prefix *para-* shows which one; there are two others, one of which is *ortho*-dihydroxybenzene, or catechol, and the other *meta*-dihydroxybenzene or resorcinol. There are thus three substances, catechol, resorcinol and quinol, all having the same composition $C_6H_4(HO)_2$ and distinguished from each other by the prefixes *ortho*, *meta*, and *para* attached to dihydroxybenzene.

para-aminosali'cylic acid, a colourless crystalline compound, $HOOC{\cdot}C_6H_3(OH)(NH_2)$, which is used (usually with isoniazid) in treating tuberculosis; **,para-dichlor(o)'benzene**, a colourless crystalline compound, $C_6H_4Cl_2$, that has a low melting point and is used as a moth-proofing agent; **parani'traniline**, a pale yellow crystalline compound, $H_2NC_6H_4NO_2$, used in making azo dyes; **para-,phenylene-'diamine**, a colourless, crystalline compound, $C_6H_4(NH_2)_2$, used as a photographic developer, for dyeing hair and fur, and for making safranine and sulphur dyes; **para'xylene**, an isomer of xylene that melts to a colourless liquid at room temperature and is now obtained from petroleum naphtha for use esp. as a source of terephthalic acid.

1946 *Lancet* 5 Jan. 15/1 (*heading*) *Para*-aminosalicylic acid in the treatment of tuberculosis. **1954** S. DUKE-ELDER *Parsons' Dis. Eye* (ed. 12) x. 120 For the common ophthalmological infections, however, the most important compounds are the sulphonamides, the sulphones and para-amino-salicylic acid. **1966** *McGraw-Hill Encycl. Sci. & Technol.* I. 320/1 *para*-Aminosalicylic acid (PAS) was synthesized in 1901. **1876** *Jrnl. Chem. Soc.* XXIX. 81 By heating equal molecules of chlorobenzenesulphonic chloride and phosphorus pentachloride to 200°–220°, paradichlorobenzene, melting at 53°, and boiling at 172°–174°, is formed. **1938** *Forum & Century* (N.Y.) Feb. 96/2 There is probably no better moth protection than para-dichlorbenzene crystals. **1965** ZIGROSSER & GAEHDE *Guide to Collecting Orig. Prints* vii. 113 Preventative measures [against microbiological infection of prints], however, can be taken by placing open containers of paradichlorobenzene crystals upon the storage shelves. **1872** WATTS *Dict. Chem.* VI. 198 A second series of bi-derivatives of benzene—the *Para-* series—is produced from dinitrobenzene. From this compound is obtained *para-nitraniline*, which may be converted into para-diazonitrobenzene, and from this may be prepared parachloronitrobenzene, parabromonitrobenzene, and para-iodo-nitrobenzene. These . . may be converted by reducing agents into parachloraniline, parabromaniline, and para-iodaniline. **1918** C. M. WHITTAKER *Applic. Coal Tar Dyestuffs* vi. 87 The first stable form of diazotized paranitraniline manufactured commercially was nitrosamine red. **1963** A. J. HALL *Textile Sci.* iv. 181 A deep bright red shade developed in the fabric as the result of formation within the fibres of an insoluble pigment by coupling of the beta-naphthol with the diazotised para-nitraniline. **1873** *Jrnl. Chem. Soc.* XXVI. 167 Dinitrobenzene was reduced by means of tin and hydrochloric acid; the bromine was eliminated by the nascent hydrogen and paraphenylenediamine was formed. **1906** *Jrnl. Soc. Dyers & Colourists* XXII. 77/1 Paraphenylenediamine is employed by furriers for dyeing pelts, and it has been used also as a hair dye. **1966** L. F. A. MASON *Photogr. Processing Chem.* i. 25 Although these para-phenylenediamine derivatives are stable in acid solution or as salts in the solid state, the free bases . . readily oxidise and are not very soluble. **1873** *Jrnl. Chem. Soc.* XXVI. 272 The author, by acting upon isoxylene and paraxylene with benzyl chloride, in presence of zinc, has obtained benzylisoxylene and benzylparaxylene. **1954** R. W. MONCRIEFF *Artificial Fibres* (ed. 2) xxi. 265 Development of a method for making large quantities of *para*-xylene proved to be difficult and delayed the manufacture of Terylene in the United Kingdom, but in America the Standard Oil Co. have developed a method of making it from petroleum. **1969** Para-xylene [see *feedstock* s.v. FEED *sb.* 7]. **1975** W. G. ROBERTS *Quest for Oil* (rev. ed.) ix. 95 Very pure aromatic compounds such as paraxylene, which is used in synthetic fibre manufacture.

c. Names of minerals having a chemical composition the same as or similar to those to the names of which *para-* is prefixed, but a different crystal structure: **para'butlerite** [f. *butlerite* (f. the name of Gordon *Butler* (1881–1961), U.S. geologist)], a basic hydrated sulphate of ferric iron, $FeSo_4(OH){\cdot}2H_2O$, found as orange orthorhombic crystals; **parahopeite** (-'həʊpaɪt), a hydrated zinc phosphate, $Zn_3(PO_4)_2{\cdot}4H_2O$, found as colourless, transparent, triclinic crystals; **para'laurionite**, a hydroxide and chloride of lead, Pb(OH)Cl, found as colourless, transparent, monoclinic crystals; **parame'laconite**, an oxide of copper, CuO, in which some of the bivalent copper (typically about a quarter) is replaced by monovalent copper and which is found as black tetragonal crystals; **para'rammelsbergite**, an arsenide of nickel, $NiAs_2$, that occurs as white, opaque, tabular crystals that alter to erythrite when exposed; **paratacamite** (,pærətə'kɑːmaɪt), a secondary mineral that is a basic chloride of copper, $Cu_2(OH)_3Cl$, and is found as green to greenish black hexagonal crystals; **para'tellurite**, an oxide of tellurium, TeO_2, found as soft, white or yellow tetragonal crystals with a waxy lustre; **para'vauxite**, a secondary mineral that is a hydrated basic phosphate of ferrous iron and aluminium $FeAl_2(PO_4)_2(OH)_2.8H_2O$, and occurs as brittle, whitish or colourless, triclinic crystals, usu. in association with vauxite and wavellite; **para'wollastonite**, the monoclinic form of the calcium silicate, $CaSiO_3$, of which wollastonite is the commoner triclinic form, both occurring as intergrowths with one another.

1938 M. C. BANDY in *Amer. Mineralogist* XXIII. 742 Parabutlerite $Fe(SO_4)(OH).2H_2O$. A basic hydrate of iron of this same composition has already been described as the mineral butlerite and as an artificial compound in the system $Fe_2O_3-SO_3-H_2-H_2O$. **1968** I. KOSTOV *Mineral.* 499 Metahohmannite, parabutlerite, and fibroferrite . . occur as yellow crusts or reniform aggregates with fibrous texture, products of weathering of pyritic deposits. **1907** *Nature* 12 Dec. 143/1 Another new species, named parahopeite, has the same chemical composition as hopeite, $Zn_3P_2O_8.4H_2O$, but is anorthic. **1908** L. J. SPENCER in *Mineral. Mag.* XV. 18 Parahopeite. This name I propose to give to a new species of hydrous zinc phosphate, identical with hopeite in chemical composition, but differing from both α-hopeite and β-hopeite in physical and crystallographic characters. **1955** *Mineral. Abstr.* XII. 479 Preliminary note on the occurrence of parahopeite and tarbuttite . . in the Kef Semmah mine [in Algeria]. **1974** *Mineral. Mag.* XXXIX. 684 Several uncommon phosphate minerals including tarbuttite, parahopeite, scholzite, and collinsite occur in near-surface gossans in the Reaphook Hill zinc prospect [in South Australia]. **1899** G. F. H. SMITH in *Mineral. Mag.* XII. 102 On some of the specimens [of lead slags from Laurium] a new mineral, paralaurionite, was found, which possesses the same chemical composition as laurionite. **1950** *Mineral. Mag.* XXIX. 341 About 1942 paralaurionite was identified in a suite of minerals from the Mammoth mine, Tiger, Arizona. **1891** G. A. KOENIG in *Proc. Acad. Nat. Sci. Philadelphia* 289 The tetragonal crystals are so unique in their appearance, that they should be accorded the rank of a very distinct species, and the name *Paramelaconite* is proposed for them. **1941** *Amer. Mineralogist* XXVI. 659 The paramelaconite occurs as stout prismatic crystals up to 3 cm. in length. **1962** *Ibid.* XLVII. 779 On a recent collecting trip to the Algomah mine [in Michigan] a few massive pieces of paramelaconite were found. **1939** M. A. PEACOCK in *Ibid.* Dec. II. 11 Recently described materials provisionally named rammelsbergite . . , from Cobalt, Ontario, and Elk Lake, Ontario, give identical *x*-ray powder photographs unlike those of from Schneeberg and Eisleben. . . The Canadian mineral is thus a distinct species for which the name *pararammelsbergite* is proposed. **1967** *Canad. Mineralogist* IX. 129 Pararammelsbergite has vacant arsenic lattice positions which are occupied in part by excess metal atoms. **1972** *Amer. Mineralogist* LVII. 1 Pararammelsbergite ($NiAs_2$) is orthorhombic.., space group *Pbca*, *Z* = 8. **1905** *Nature* 13 Apr. 574/2 This new mineral, to which the name paratacamite was given [by Prior and Smith], has the same chemical composition as atacamite. **1950** *Mineral. Mag.* XXIX. 280 It is paratacamite, not atacamite that occurs at the famous Cornish locality, Botallack mine, St. Just. **1960** SWITZER & SWANSON in *Amer. Mineralogist* XLV. 1272 Orthorhombic TeO_2 is found in nature as tellurite. The tetragonal form, well known as a chemical compound, has been found associated with tellurite and native tellurium at Cananea, Sonora, Mexico. The name paratellurite is proposed for the new mineral. **1973** *Chem. Abstr.* 8 Oct. 489/2 In an acoustooptic light deflector, frequency modulated acoustic shear waves propagate in the [110] direction in paratellurite (TeO_2). **1922** S. G. GORDON in *Science* 14 July 50/1 Preliminary notes on vauxite and paravauxite. Among the mineral specimens collected on the Vaux-Academy Andean expedition of 1921 are two that have proved to be new. **1944** *Proc. Acad. Nat. Sci. Philadelphia* XCVI. 339 Vauxite, paravauxite, metavauxite, and childrenite are secondary phosphates, derived from solution of apatite by supergene waters, and deposited usually upon wavellite. **1968** I. KOSTOV *Mineral.* 452 Paravauxite and gordonite have perfect {010} cleavage. **1935** M. A. PEACOCK in *Amer. Jrnl. Sci.* XXX. 525 It thus seems necessary to regard the triclinic modification as the normal one properly entitled to the name wollastonite; the name parawollastonite is, therefore, proposed for the rarer monoclinic modification. **1963** W. A. DEER et al. *Rock-forming Min.* II. 172 The distinction between wollastonite and parawollastonite is based on the extinction angle β:*y*, which is 3°–5° in wollastonite and 0° in monoclinic parawollastonite. *Ibid.* 173 Parawollastonite, identified by single-crystal X-ray photographs, has been recorded from Monte Somma, Vesuvius, .. from Crestmore, California.., and from Csiklova, Roumania.

3. *Physics* and *Chem.* Of, pertaining to, or designating the form of some homonuclear diatomic molecules in which (as in parahydrogen) the two nuclei have antiparallel spins (see also quot. 1940[2] s.v. ORTHO- 3); also used similarly with reference to the electronic spins of helium. Also as an independent word.

1927, etc. [see ORTHO- 3].

para-[2], a. F. *para-*, a. It. *para-*, imperative of vb. *parare* 'to ward or defend, to cover from, to shield, to shroud, to shelter' (Florio), orig. 'to make ready, prepare':—L. *parāre*; used with a sb. object, in phrases which have themselves become sbs., as *para-sole* lit. 'defend or shelter from sun', hence 'a sun-shade'; so *parafuoco* fire-guard, fire-screen, *paravento* wind-screen, *parapetto* breast-guard, parapet. (Cf. analogous Fr. and Eng. compounds, as *couvre-chef*, *couvre-feu*, *make-shift*, *spend-thrift*, *ward-robe*.) Italian *para-* has been adopted in Fr., which has added *parapluie* rain-screen, umbrella, *paracrotte* mud-guard, *parachute*, *parados*, etc. Thence English has PARAPET, PARADOS, PARASOL, PARACHUTE, with occasional humorous nonce-words, as **parabore**, defence from bores, and occasional uses of the alien (French) words, **paragrandine** [L. *grandin-em* hail], **paragrêle** [F. *grêle* hail] protection against hail, **parapluie** [F. *pluie* rain] umbrella, **paratonnère** [F. *tonnère* thunder] lightning-conductor, **paravent** [F. *vent* wind] defence against wind.

1844 LD. BROUGHAM *A. Lunel* I. i. 26 And sigh for a Bore-net, a *para-bore, to protect me, like our musquito-curtains. **1842** FRANCIS *Dict. Arts*, **Paragrandine*, an instrument, the object of which is to avert hailstones in the same manner as electric conductors avert the danger of lightning. **1886** *Cassell's Encycl. Dict.*, **Paragrêle*. **1727–41** CHAMBERS *Cycl.*, *Parasol*... The word is French.—That used against rains is sometimes called **parapluie*. **1829** MRS. SOUTHEY *Chapt. Churchyards* II. 246 Escorted by Mr. Vernon on one side and his own valet, with a *parapluie*, on the other. **1866** MRS. H. WOOD *St. Martin's Eve* xix. (1874) 234 She.. displayed an enormous crimson *parapluie*, which she held between her face and the sun.

para-[3], comb. form of PARACHUTE *sb.*

a. With sbs., denoting 'dropped by parachute', 'trained or equipped for descending by parachute', as *para-bomb*, *-cargo*, *-commando*, *-girl*, *-marine*, *-mine*, *-nurse*, *-pa(c)k* (hence *-packed* adj.), *-pooch*, *-spy*. Also PARADOCTOR, PARADROP *sb.* and *v.*, PARAFOIL, PARAGLIDER, PARAKITE, PARAMEDIC[1], PARA-RESCUE, PARASCENDING *vbl. sb.*, PARATROOPS *sb. pl.*, PARAWING. **b. parabrake**, a parachute which opens behind an aircraft and acts as a brake; **parafrag bomb**, a bomb dropped by parachute which bursts into fragments on hitting its target; **parajump** = JUMP *sb.*[1] 1 c; so **parajumping** *vbl. sb.*; **parajute**, a parachute made of jute; **parapants**, women's knickers made from parachute silk; **paraplane**, (see quot. 1942); **parasheet**, (see quot. 1951); **paraski** *attrib.*, (*a*) designating a parachute trooper trained to ski from the point where he lands; (*b*) designating a sport in which skiers ski from a place to which they have dropped by parachute; **paraskier**, a paraski trooper; **paraspotter**, a person who watches for enemy parachute landings.

1943 *Time* 18 Oct. 36/2 Parabombs burst above the ground, spray their fragments with telling effect. **1951** Parabrake [see DROGUE 3]. **1954** *Britannica Bk. of Year* 638/1 The verbal shorthand habitual to members of the armed forces produced such contractions as *parabrake*, a parachute used to slow down an aeroplane on landing. **1967** N. E. BORDEN *Jet-Engine Fund.* 97 Military fighters release a parachute, called a parabrake, from their tail as soon as their wheels contact the runway. **1951** R. MALKIN *Boxcars in Sky* 172 As for military paracargo, however, the picture is entirely different. **1965** *Britannica Bk. of Year* (U.S.) 869/2 *Para commando, n.*, a parachute commando, as in the Congolese army. **1967** *Economist* 30 Sept. 1180/1 The Israelis train Mr Mobutu's crack corps, the para-commandos. **1978** *Guardian Weekly* 18 June 16/3 The bigger white community in Likasi.. has told the Belgian Government it would leave en masse if the paracommandos go. **1944** *Tuscaloosa* (Alabama) *News* 5 Oct. 1 This.. Jap Sally plane went up in smoke a few seconds after this picture was taken—destroyed by parafrag bombs. **1972** *Courier-Mail* (Brisbane) 16 May 1/7 Lucky paragirl Jackie Smith fell from 2400 ft. into the sea when her parachute failed to open during a weekend skydiving show—and lived. **1973** *Jewish Chron.* 9 Feb. 15/2 The nearest your reporter came to hearing fighting words from Israel's paragirls. **1971** *Islander* (Victoria, B.C.) 20 June 3/4 Most parajump clubs in Canada are affiliated with the Canada Sport Parachute Association. **1977** *R.A.F. News* 30 Mar.–12 Apr. 3/3 The £16 fee (lower than that charged by similar, civilian para-jump clubs) covers the cost of membership. *Ibid.* 3/4 A halt had been called to any para-jumping that week-end. **1956** W. SLIM *Defeat into Victory* 225 In a month we had a parajute that was eighty-five per cent as efficient and reliable as the most elaborate parachute. It was made entirely of jute. **1973** J. LUCAS *Big Umbrella* x. 108 The parajutes were not intended for man-carrying, but about 100,000 of them were used for supply-dropping in the Burma campaign. *Ibid.* 107 The 'parajute'.. had no large vent in the apex, but several smaller ones all over, and it was only about one-seventh less efficient than the standard silk parachute. **1944** *Veterans' Weekly* (Lincoln, Nebraska) 15 Dec. 2 Oliver N. Magee, paramarine, son of War Dad and Mrs.. Magee [etc.]. **1969** *TV Times* (Austral.) 22 Jan. 27 He is aided by the tough leader of a group of paramarines. **1944** in *Amer. Speech* (1945) XX. 221 Nazi para-mines nearly blocked supply lines. **1942** A. M. LOW *Parachutes* p. x, A paranurse is.. a nurse dropped by parachute. **1946** *B.B.C. War Report* 234 Suddenly the pilot called our attention to the parapacks coming out from the aircraft in front of us. *Ibid.*, There go the parapacks from the formation ahead of us—yellow, brown, red, drifting down gently, dropping their containers. **1950** in *Amer. Speech* (1956) XXXI. 62 A resupply mission was flown in the afternoon—with a drop of parapaks and other supplies simulated. **1954** *N.Y. Times Mag.* 6 June 79/2 Captain Schweiter slapped the switch controlling the parapacks (belly bundles), bellowed: 'Follow me,' and jumped. **1945** *Birmingham* (Alabama) *News* 27 Mar. 1/5 Allied Airborne troops and parapacked supplies are shown as they plummeted down five miles beyond the Rhine. **1944** *Time* 10 Apr. 12/3 Parapants. In Manhattan, Mrs. Virginia Bell Jack received from her Thunderbolt-pilot husband in England a pair of real silk (German parachute) panties. **1942** A. M. LOW *Parachutes* 111 In Russia, some years ago, a young engineer, B. Pavlov, invented what he called a 'paraplane' which consisted essentially of two wings made of heavy linen stretched over a duralumin frame-work. These were strapped to the back of the parachutist and enabled him to glide before opening his parachute. **1974** *Sport Parachutist* June 18/1 Ten paraplane jumpers who are all.. experienced paraplane flyers. **1944** *N.Y. Times* 26 Apr. 5/6 St. Bernard Qualifies as 'Parapooch' for Army. Major [*sc.* a St. Bernard dog] has made seven high altitude jumps with a regular size parachute. **1951** W. D. BROWN *Parachutes* 315 *Parasheet*, a parachute constructed from one piece of fabric (or from several pieces with their warps parallel) in the form of a regular polygon, with the rigging lines attached to the apexes of the polygon. **1973** J. LUCAS *Big Umbrella* x. 110 Para-*sheets*, which acted like parachutes but were formed of strips of fabric rather than gores, were used for these [*sc.* slow-falling parachute flares]. *Ibid.*, A pair of para-sheets were used for each flare to increase stability. **1942** *Christian Science Monitor* 26 Mar. 3 Para-ski troopers of the 503rd Parachute Battalion. **1974** *Sport Parachutist* June 26 (*heading*) German Para-Ski Championships. **1942** *Christian Science Monitor* 26 Mar. 3 'Let 'Er Buck' Is War Cry of Para-Skiers. **1976** *National Observer* (U.S.) 13 Mar. 6/3 Para-skiers make 3,000-foot parachute jumps from a hovering helicopter and attempt to land precisely on a four-inch disk, then they race against the clock down a giant slalom course. **1943** *Daily Express* 10 Sept. 1/5 (*headline*) Para-spies dropped in Germany. **1940** in *Amer. Speech* (1944) XIX. 12/2, Britain has 400,000 paraspotters ready to fight parachutists.

para-aminobenzoic (ˌpærəəmiːnəʊbɛnˈzəʊɪk), *a.* [f. PARA-[1] 2 b + *aminobenzoic* s.v. AMINO-.] ***para-aminobenzoic acid***: the *para*-isomer of aminobenzoic acid, which is sometimes considered a member of the vitamin-B group, is widely distributed in plant and animal tissue, has the ability to neutralize the bacteriostatic effects of the sulphonamides, and has been used in the treatment of rickettsial infections, esp. typhus and Rocky Mountain spotted fever. Abbrev. PABA.

1906 *Proc. R. Soc.* A. LXXVIII. 82 (*heading*) Methyl derivatives of para-aminobenzoic acid. **1940** *Nature* 28 Dec. 838/2 (*heading*) Para-amino benzoic acid as a bacterial growth factor. **1963** [see PABA].

para-aminosalicylic acid: see PARA-[1] 2 b.

para-aortic (ˌpærəeɪˈɔːtɪk), *a. Anat.* [f. PARA-[1] + AORTIC *a.*] Situated beside the aorta; used chiefly (in *para-aortic body*) as an epithet of certain paraganglia.

1927 *Jrnl. Anat.* LXI. 317 The pre- and para-aortic tissue of a 16-week embryo from the region of the supra-renal glands is seen on section to contain the semilunar ganglia, collections of haemo-lymphoid tissue, and other encapsuled masses (the Zuckerkandl anlage). **1952** *Ibid.* LXXXVI. 357 Wrete (1927) observed the continuity of the chromaffin bodies of the para-aortic region with the chromaffin tissue of the adrenal glands. *Ibid.* 358 Because of the lack of uniformity in the interpretation of the 'paraganglia', it has been replaced in the present investigation by the topographical term 'para-aortic bodies'. A para-aortic body is defined as an encapsulated collection of chromaffin cells lying in intimate contact with the sympathetic nervous system and yielding a pressor substance after extraction. **1959** R. D. LOCKHART et al. *Anat. Human Body* 488/2 The paraganglia, small brownish masses,.. are similar to the suprarenal medulla... The largest masses, the para-aortic bodies, a third of an inch long at birth, lie on each side of the inferior mesenteric artery. **1965** [see PARAGANGLION]. **1973** *Gray's Anat.* (ed. 35) 144/1 Chromaffin organs are found in connection with certain.. of the secondary plexuses of the sympathetic system; the largest members of this series are the para-aortic bodies,.. commonly termed paraganglia. *Ibid.* 1381/2 The para-aortic bodies.. attain their maximum size in the first three years of post-natal life, when the largest takes the form of two elongated brownish bodies.. which lie on each side of the inferior mesenteric artery. *Ibid.*, The chromaffin cells of the paraganglia and para-aortic bodies.

parabanic (pærəˈbænɪk), *a. Chem.* [f. PARA-: see below.] In ***parabanic acid***, a dibasic acid, $CO{\cdot}2(NH{\cdot}CO)$, produced by the action of nitric acid on uric acid or alloxan; crystallizing in colourless prisms. When boiled with dilute acids, it is converted into oxalic acid and urea, whence it is sometimes called *oxalyl carbamide* or *oxalyl urea*. Hence **ˈparaban**, a proposed substitute for the name *parabanic acid*, to express its parallelism to *alloxan*. **ˈparabanate**, a salt of parabanic acid, as ***argentic parabanate***, $CO{\cdot}2(NAg{\cdot}CO)$.

1857 MILLER *Elem. Chem.* III. 635 Parabanic acid forms salts which are exceedingly unstable: parabanate of silver being the only salt which is permanent. **1866** ODLING *Anim. Chem.* 43 Paraban and alloxan are products of the oxidation of uric acid. **1873** RALFE *Phys. Chem.* p. xxviii, Kreatin is a monureide, and so are paraban and alloxan, which are obtained by the oxidation of uric acid. **1888** REMSEN *Org. Chem.* 203 Parabanic acid is formed by boiling uric acid with strong nitric acid and other oxidizing agents.

[*Note.* The term *parabanic* was introduced by Liebig and Wöhler in 1838 (*Annalen* XXVI. 285), but without any explanation of its formation. As they made parabanic acid by a reaction in which they expected to obtain alloxan, it is prob. that *para-* was used in the sense 'instead of', 'opposed to', the ending being that of *allox-an*, *-anic*, and the *b* merely euphonic. It has been suggested that the latter is a residue of *carb-*, and that the term was formed to express parallelism of constitution to urea or carbamide, $CO{\cdot}2(NH_2)$, and to alloxan, $CO{\cdot}2(NH{\cdot}CO)CO$; but as a fact, it was not till much later that the identity of urea and carbamide was discovered.]

parabaptism (pærəˈbæptɪz(ə)m). [ad. late Gr. παραβάπτισμα irregular or spurious baptism, f. παρα- aside, amiss, wrong + βάπτισμα baptism.] Uncanonical or unauthorized baptism (in the early church). So **paraˈbaptist**, **parabaptiˈzation**.

1715 BINGHAM *Orig. Eccles.* IV. 275 Such Baptisms are frequently condemned in the ancient Councils under the name of παραβαπτίσματα... Which sort of Parabaptizations are there condemned. **1890** *Cent. Dict.*, *Parabaptism*.

parabasal (pærəˈbeɪsəl), *a.* (*sb.*) [PARA-[1].]

1. *Zool.* **a.** In Crinoids: Situated next to and articulated with a basal plate. **b.** *sb.* (also in mod.L. form *parabasāle*, pl. *-ālia*). A parabasal joint.

1872 NICHOLSON *Palæont.* 125 In some cases the 'basals' are succeeded by a second row or cycle of plates.. which are sometimes regarded as something special, and are termed the 'parabasals' or 'sub-radials'. **1877** HUXLEY *Anat. Inv. Anim.* ix. 593 A calyx supported on a stem, and composed of five basalia, five parabasalia, and five radialia.

2. *Zool.* [in this sense a. G. *parabasal* (C. Janicki 1911, in *Biol. Centralbl.* XXXI. 321).] Applied to the kinetoplast (sense a) of protozoa; chiefly in ***parabasal body***. Also *ellipt.*

1912 E. A. MINCHIN *Introd. Study Protozoa* vi. 89 The ring of blepharoplasts in *Lophomonas* is supported on the edge of a membranous structure,.. which in its turn is surrounded by a peculiar striated body, the 'collar' of Grassi, or 'parabasal apparatus' of Janicki. **1924** HEGNER & TALIAFERRO *Human Protozool.* v. 127 Most of the members of the genus [*Trypanosoma*] are characterized by the possession of a more or less spindle-shaped body, a central nucleus, and a spherical or rod-shaped parabasal body, with which is closely associated a small blepharoplast and a flagellum. **1925**, etc. [see KINETOPLAST]. **1973** K. G. GRELL *Protozool.* 17 Trichomonads have only a single, though occasionally branched, parabasal body which is anchored at the base of the flagella and can either wind about an axostyle or follow a straight course to the posterior end.

3. *Med.* Applied to cells from the layers of stratified epithelium just above the deepest (basal) layer of cells.

1948 G. N. PAPANICOLAOU et al. *Epithelia of Woman's Reproductive Organs* ix. 38 The parabasal postpartum cells.. show a greater variety in size and form, somewhat larger nuclei, extensive vacuolization, and a tendency to congregate into larger groups. **1960** *Obstetr. & Gynecol.* XVI. 407/2 Deep in the layers of the epithelia are the parabasal cells, which cover the basal germinal layer of cells and are characterized by dense, thick cytoplasm with vesicular nuclei. **1972** *Acta Cytologica* XVI. 382/2 The presence [in amniotic fluid] of parabasal cells in excess of 70 per cent suggests a fetal weight of less than 500 gms.

‖**parabasis** (pəˈræbəsɪs). Pl. **-bases** (-bəsiːz). [a. Gr. παράβασις lit. a going aside, digression, stepping forward, f. παραβαίνειν to go aside, step forward.] In ancient Greek comedy, A part sung by the chorus, addressed to the audience in the poet's name, and unconnected with the action of the drama. Also *transf.*, any digression in which the author addresses the audience on personal or topical matters.

1820 T. MITCHELL *Aristoph.* I. p. cvi, What steps were used in their parabases to give effect to the rhythm. *Ibid.* p. cxiv, The play originally condemned has come down to us with part of a parabasis (or address to the audience). **1866** LOWELL *Swinburne's Trag.* Pr. Wks. 1890 II. 130 Something similar in purpose to the parabasis was essayed in one, at least, of the comedies of Beaumont and Fletcher, and in our time by Tieck. **1877** WARD in *Encycl. Brit.* VII. 407/2 The distinctive feature of Old, as compared with Middle Comedy, is the *parabasis*, the speech in which the chorus, moving towards and facing the audience, addressed it in the name of the poet, often abandoning all reference to the action of the play. **1949** *Oxf. Classical Dict.* 216/2 *Parabasis* (addresses to audience separated by brief chants). **1952** F. H. DUDDEN *Henry Fielding* I. p. v, In the frequent parabases intercalated in his novels..[Fielding] has laid open his inner-most self. **1965** *New Statesman* 30 Apr. 694/2 This is Coward's exercise in parabasis form: a lightly fictionalised justification of his way of theatre, acting and life. **1974** *Encycl. Brit. Micropædia* VII. 511/1 The *parabasis*, in which the chorus addresses the audience on the topics of the day and hurls scurrilous criticism at prominent citizens.

Parabellum (pærəˈbɛləm). Also **parabellum**. [f. L. *parā* imp. of *parāre* to prepare + *bellum* war (see quot. 1970).] The proprietary name of a make of automatic pistol or machine-gun. Also *attrib.*

1904 [see LUGER]. **1918** E. S. FARROW *Dict. Mil. Terms* 432 *Parabellum Gun*, a German aëroplane gun of small caliber. It has a belt of cartridges which contains not less than a thousand projectiles. **1924** *Blackw. Mag.* Feb. 157/1 The vessel..carried two old-pattern Maxims and a German Parabellum, mounted for anti-aircraft fire. **1962** E. AMBLER *Light of Day* ii. 46 Six Parabellum pistols. **1970** R. A. STEINDLER *Firearms Dict.* 165 Based on the Latin 'Si vis pacem, para bellum' ('If you want peace, prepare for war.'), ..the word Parabellum is the protected tradename of Mauser & D.W.M. **1973** J. WAINWRIGHT *Pride of Pigs* 127 A German gun..Official title—the German parabellum P'08, military automatic pistol...the Luger. **1974** S. GULLIVER *Vulcan Bulletins* 18 The 9mm jacketed Parabellum rounds used in..Stens and Sterlings.

‖**parabema** (pærəˈbiːmə). Pl. **-mata**. [a. mod.Gr. παράβημα, f. παρά beside + βῆμα BEMA.] In Byzantine churches, The part of the edifice on each side of the bema, when separated from the latter by a wall. Hence **parabeˈmatic** *a.*, pertaining to a parabema; supported on the parabemata.

1850 NEALE *East. Ch.* I. II. ii. 171, (3) The prothesis, (4) the diaconicon or sacristy..when divided as here by walls from the bema, are called parabemata. *Ibid.* 172 Care must be taken to recognize the parabema in cases where there is a passage through it, as it is still architecturally one. *Ibid.*, The Church of S. Theodore, given above, has a parabematic dome.

parabenzene, -benzol: see PARA-[1] 2.

†**paraˈbien**. *Obs.* [a. Sp. *parabien*, from *para* for, *bien* well, the wish 'may it be for good to you', 'I wish you joy or success', congratulation.] A congratulatory compliment, congratulation.

1622 MABBE tr. *Aleman's Guzman d'Alf.* II. I. v. 47 My Master..rendring me an account of his loue, and I giuing him the *Para-bien* thereof. **1668** LD. ARLINGTON in *Temple's Wks.* (1770) I. 516 So that now I can..give you the *parabien* of this great work. **1681** *Moores Baffled* 9 But instead of giving me the Parabien, you have disturbed my hour of Eating.

†**paraˈbility**. *Obs. rare.* [f. PARABLE *a.*] The quality of being easily procured or prepared.

1654 WHITLOCK *Zootomia* 102 He considereth not the parability, or Propriety of Medicines, it is not unusual for him to prescribe things out of use, or reach, or season.

parabiont (pærəˈbaɪɒnt). *Biol.* [f. PARA-[1] + Gr. βιουντ-, pr. pple. stem of βιοῦν to live, f. βίος life.] An animal subjected to a parabiotic union.

1935 *Proc. Soc. Exper. Biol. & Med.* XXXIII. 568 Since the serum from each parabiont agglutinated the cells of both Pearlneck and Ring dove, it would seem that cellular differences were present other than those particular to each of the 2 species. **1955** *Anatomical Rec.* CXII. 225 The lateral one-third of the adjacent kidneys in each parabiont was excised. **1970** *Nature* 19 Dec. 1186/2 The abdominal cavities of the parabionts were connnected by a common free canal.

parabiosis (pærəbaɪˈəʊsɪs). *Biol.* [mod.L., ad. F. *parabiose* (A. Forel 1898, in *Bull. de la Société Vaudoise des Sciences Naturelles* XXXIV. 380), f. PARA-[1] + Gr. βίωσις way of life (f. βίος life).] The anatomical union of a pair of organisms either natural or produced by surgery; the state of being so joined.

1908 *N.Y. Med. Jrnl.* LXXXVII. 374/1 Sauerbruch and Heyde give the name parabiosis to the new condition produced in animals which are experimented upon when they are organically connected together in an artificial manner. **1930** *Physiol. Rev.* X. 589 Parabiosis is a skin flap union, (to which is usually added peritoneal union), in which two whole organisms, instead of parts of organisms, are joined to each other. **1952** *New Biol.* XII. 46 Referring to the vascular anastomosis normally occurring between dizygotic bovine twins as 'nature's experiment in parabiosis'. **1955** *Anatomical Rec.* CXXII. 226 From parabiotic pairs formed between rats approximately 21 days of age, 12 pairs in successful parabiosis were chosen. **1962** D. J. B. ASHLEY *Human Intersex* iv. 58 Natural embryonic parabiosis has been observed in three instances in man. **1965** LEE & KNOWLES *Animal Hormones* iii. 64 If a male and a female salamander are joined by parabiosis (this allows the blood of the two animals to mix), a blood-borne substance from the male will lead to complete involution of the ovaries.

parabiotic (pærəbaɪˈɒtɪk), *a. Biol.* [f. PARA-[1] + BIOTIC *a.*] Of, pertaining to, or existing in parabiosis.

1911 *Arch. Internal Med.* VII. 396 The reaction appeared very clearly after a parabiotic union of a tuberculous and healthy guinea-pig. **1930** *Physiol. Rev.* X. 591 Each of the parabiotic individuals continues, therefore, to a certain extent, to live its own life. **1935** *Proc. Soc. Exper. Biol. & Med.* XXXIII. 568 Each member of a pair of parabiotic twins developed antibodies against the red cells of the other. **1955** [see prec.]. **1970** *Nature* 19 Dec. 1186/2 Two months later when the animals became accustomed to the parabiotic condition, they were again anaesthetized with ether and the abdominal cavities opened.

Hence **parabiˈotically** *adv.*, so as to produce parabiosis.

1915 *Arch. Internal Med.* XV. 45 Forschbach united dogs parabiotically, bringing peritoneal cavities and homologous layers of the parietes into continuity. **1961** *Lancet* 23 Sept. 707/1 If a cockroach thus rendered 'arhythmic' is joined parabiotically to a normal cockroach, its activity is restored.

parablast (ˈpærəblæst). [f. PARA- + Gr. βλαστός sprout, germ: see -BLAST.]

†**1.** *Path.* (See quot.) *Obs.*

1857 MAYNE *Expos. Lex.*, *Parablasta*..term used by Eisenmann for disease with anatomical conversion or alteration: a parablast.

2. *Embryol.* The nutritive yolk of a meroblastic ovum, as distinguished from the formative yolk or *archiblast*; also, a special layer of cells in the embryo, supposed by His to arise from the nutritive yolk, by others to belong to the mesoblast.

1876 KLEIN in *Q. Jrnl. Microsc. Sci.* XVI. 116 This quasi-extraneous portion of the germ I will call *parablast*, in contradistinction to the segmented part or blastoderm of the authors, which I will term *archiblast*... However,.. according to His, parablast is not a portion of the same substance of which the blastoderm consists, but is a part of the white yolk. **1884** *Science* IV. 341/1 The parablast of Klein, the intermediate layer of American authors. **1888** J. BEARD in *Q. Jrnl. Microsc. Sc.* Oct. 195 There are here also plenty of mesoblast—pardon, 'parablast' cells in the neighbourhood.

Hence **paraˈblastic** *a.*, pertaining or relating to the parablast (sense 2).

1885 LANDOIS & STIRLING *Text-bk. Hum. Physiol.* II. 1128 The parablastic structure of blood and connective-tissue. **1888** J. BEARD in *Q. Jrnl. Microsc. Sc.* Oct. 195 When His regards the nuclei here present as mesoblastic or 'parablastic' cells, his view is just as much a gratuitous assumption as the whole parablastic doctrine.

parable (ˈpærəb(ə)l), *sb.* Forms: 4- **parable**; also 4-7 **-bole**, 4-6 **-bil(l**, 5-6 **-byll(e**, 7 **-bile**. [ME. a. F. *parabole* (13th c. in Littré), ad. L. *parabola* comparison; in Christian L., allegory, proverb, discourse, speech, talk, a. Gr. παραβολή a placing side by side, comparison, analogy, parable, proverb. f. παρα- beside + βολή casting, putting, a throw.

From L. *parabola* came the various later forms *paravola, paraula, parola, parole, parabla, palabra, palavra*, meaning 'speech, word', in the Romanic langs. Hence *parabola, parable, parole, palaver* are all representatives of the same original word.]

a. A comparison, a similitude; any saying or narration in which something is expressed in terms of something else; an allegory, an apologue. Also vaguely extended (chiefly after Heb. or other oriental words so rendered) to any kind of enigmatical, mystical, or dark saying, and to proverbs, maxims, or ancient saws, capable of application to cases as they occur. *arch.* (exc. as in b.)

† *Parables of Solomon*, the Book of Proverbs. (*obs.*)

a **1325** *Prose Psalter* xlviii. 4 Y shal bowe myn eres in parabiles [*a* 1300 *E.E. Psalt.* forbiseninge]. *a* **1340** HAMPOLE *Psalter* ibid., Lerand me to speke in parabils, that is, in likyngis that all men kan noght vndirstand. **1382** WYCLIF *Matt.* xxiv. 32 Lerne ȝe the parable of a fyge tree. *c* **1386** CHAUCER *Wife's Prol.* 369 Been thir none othire resemblances That ye may likne youre parables to. *Ibid.* 679 And eek the Parables of Salomon. *c* **1420** LYDG. *Assembly of Gods* 1987 Hit sownyd to me as a parable, Derke as a myste, or a feynyd fable. *c* **1450** tr. *De Imitatione* I. v. 7 Lete not þe paraboles of eldir men displese þe. **1523** SKELTON *Garl. Laurel* 101 A poete somtyme..Spekyng in parablis, how the fox, the grey, The gander,..Went with the pecok ageyne the fesaunt. **1596** BACON *Max. & Uses Com. Law* Pref., All the ancient wisdom and science was wont to be delivered in that forme, as may be seen by the parables of Solomon. **1654** GAYTON *Pleas. Notes* IV. iv. 194 Accept of the Curates parabile, and his sentences in praise of a slender dyet as *Modicum non nocet.* **1671** MILTON *Samson* 500 A sin That Gentiles in their Parables condemn. **1794** SULLIVAN *View Nat.* II. 234 Moses and the Prophets wrote all in Parables. **1825** SCOTT *Talism.* x, I will reply with a parable told to me by a santon of the desert. **1881** N. T. (R.V.) *Luke* iv. 23 Doubtless ye will say unto me this parable [WYCLIF liknesse, TINDALE, 1611 proverbe, *Rheims* similitude], Physician, heal thyself.

b. *spec.* A fictitious narrative or allegory (usually something that might naturally occur), by which moral or spiritual relations are typically figured or set forth, as the parables of the New Testament. (Now the usual sense.)

c **1380** WYCLIF *Sel. Wks.* III. 352 þus spekiþ Crist..of dette in þe Pater Noster, and also in o parable. **1382** —— *Matt.* xiii. 3 And he spak to hem many thingis in parablis. **1526** TINDALE *Matt.* xiii. 10 Why speakest thou to them in parables? 13 Therefore speake y to them in similitudes. 18 Heare ye therfore the similitude [*Rheims* and **1611** parable] off the sower. **1589** PUTTENHAM *Eng. Poesie* III. xix. (Arb.) 251 Whensoeuer by your similitude ye will seeme to teach any moralitie or good lesson by speeches misticall and darke, or farre fette, vnder a sence metaphoricall applying one naturall thing to another,..the Greekes call it *Parabola*, which terme is also by custome accepted of vs... Such parables were all the preachings of Christ in the Gospell. **1688** SOUTH *Serm.* II. viii. 276 The Foundation of all Parables is..some Analogy or Similitude, between the Tropical, or Allusive part of the Parable, and the Thing couched under it. **1795** SOUTHEY *Joan of Arc* IV. 208 Or rather sing thou of that wealthy Lord, Who took the ewe lamb from the poor man's bosom,..This parable would I tell,..And look at thee and say, 'Thou art the man!' **1841** TRENCH *Parables* i. (1877) 2 The parable is constructed to set forth a truth spiritual and heavenly: this the fable, with all its value, is not.

c. *dial.* Something that may be pointed to as an example or illustration (to follow or to avoid).

[Cf. **1382** WYCLIF *Jer.* xxiv. 9 And y shal ȝyue them..in to repref, and in to parable, and in to prouerbe.] *c* **1880** *Correspondent*, Parable is used near Drumcondra, Ireland, in sense of 'An apt illustration, a case in point'. **1894** IAN MACLAREN *Bonnie Brier Bush* VI. ii. 218 'Man', says Mactavish,..'You are just a Parable, oh yes, just a Parable'. **1900** *Cent. Mag.* Feb. 601 He had his three acres in such rotation as a flower garden, his wee patch a parable to the counthry.

d. *to take up one's parable* [after Num. xxiii. 7, etc.] to begin to discourse. *arch.*

1382 WYCLIF *Num.* xxiii. 7 And takun to his parable [**1388** And whanne his parable was takun], seith. **1535** COVERDALE ibid., Then toke he [Balaam] vp his parable, & sayde [etc.]. **1868** MILMAN *St. Paul's* i. 5 In due time, the learned took up their parable.

e. *attrib.* and *Comb.*, as ***parable-art***, ***-opera***, ***-play***, ***-poem***, ***-poet***, ***-reading***, ***-writer***; ***-like*** adj., ***-wise*** adv.

1935 AUDEN in G. Grigson *Arts To-Day* 20 There must always be two kinds of art, escape-art..and parable-art, that art which shall teach man to unlearn hatred and learn love. **1976** *Listener* 8 July 27/1 Auden both devised and named the literary genre—'parable-art'—that the decade [of the 1930s] demanded. *a* **1603** T. CARTWRIGHT *Confut. Rhem. N.T.* (1618) 240 His speeches had been hitherto darke and parable-like. **1880** G. MEREDITH *Tragic Com.* (1881) 62 We Jews are a parable people. **1976** *National Observer* (U.S.) 18 Dec. 18/1 Britten composed in almost all the musical forms available to him—and even invented one, the parable opera, such as *Curlew River* and *The Prodigal Son*, in which a moral lesson was set forth in direct and easily assimilable musical terms. **1941** L. MACNEICE *Poetry of Yeats* 187 Thirdly, there are those plays which are near to fable or which might be called parable-plays—*The King's Threshold* (1904). **1884** *Athenæum* 6 Dec. 725/1 [They] can only be described as parable-poems. **1561** DAUS tr. *Bullinger on Apoc.* (1573) 149 b, It is in parablewyse, and in way of comparison, that this citie is called Sodome and Egypt. **1884** *Athenæum* 6 Dec. 727/3 The current of the story with the Western parable-writer moves too rapidly.

†**ˈparable**, *a. Obs.* [ad. L. *parābil-is* procurable, f. *parāre* to prepare, procure: see -BLE.] That can be readily prepared, procured, or got; procurable, 'get-at-able'.

1581 MULCASTER *Positions* xix. (1887) 81, I haue kept Galenes rule in chusing these exercises, and that they be all both pleasant, profitable and parable. **1621** BURTON *Anat. Mel.* II. v. I. v. (1651) 390 This of drink is a most easie and parable remedy. *a* **1691** BOYLE *Med. Exp.* Pref. (1693) 5 Receipts that being Parable or Cheap, may easily be made servicable to poor Country People. **1741** *Compl. Fam.-Piece* I. i. 60 A parable but excellent Medicine in..the Stone.

ˈparable, *v. rare.* [f. PARABLE *sb.* Cf. late and med.L. *parabolāre* to discourse, talk, whence F. *parler* to speak.]

1. *intr.* To compose or utter a parable; to speak or discourse in parables.

1571 GOLDING *Calvin on Ps.* xlix. 4 That is to say, Parable thou in parable. **1820** *Blackw. Mag.* VII. 437 My store of praise would never fail, Tho' I should parable till I were old.

2. *trans.* To represent or express by means of a parable, allegory, or similitude.

1643 MILTON *Divorce* I. vi. Wks. (1851) 32 That was chiefly meant, which by the ancient Sages was thus parabl'd. **1884** G. F. PENTECOST *Out of Egypt* iii. 54 That sign which to my mind it parables or typifies.

‖**paraˈblepsis**. [a. Gr. παράβλεψις, f. παραβλέπ-ειν to look aside at, to see wrong, to overlook, f. παρα- PARA-[1] + βλέπειν to see.] False vision; oversight. So **paraˈblepsia**; **ˈparablepsy**; **paraˈbleptic** *a.*, of or pertaining to parablepsy.

1857 MAYNE *Expos. Lex.*, *Parablepsis*, term for false vision; side vision; parablepsy. *Parablepticus*, of or belonging to *Parablepsis*: parableptic. **1886** *Athenæum* 7 Aug. 169/3 He avoids the difficulty..by supposing..the words were omitted through 'parablepsy' on the part of the scribe. **1913** F. W. HALL *Compan. Classical Texts* 154 Lipography (parablepsia), or simple omission of any kind. **1934** L. F. POWELL in G. B. Hill *Boswell's Life of Johnson* II. 370 Power.. government (*by parablepsy*).

†**'parably**, *adv. Obs. rare.* [f. PARABLE *sb.* + -LY², after advbs. from adjs. in *-ble.*] In parables, parable-wise.

1382 WYCLIF *Mark* xii. 1 And Ihesus bigan to speke parably [*gloss* or in parablis; *Vulg.* in parabolis].

parabola (pəˈræbələ). *Geom.* [a. 16th c. L. *parabola* (also *parabolē*), a. Gr. παραβολή juxtaposition, application, *spec.* in Geometry, the 'application' of a given area to a given straight line, hence also, the curve described below: for derivation and other senses, cf. PARABLE. In F. *parabole.* See note below.]

One of the conic sections; the plane curve formed by the intersection of a cone with a plane parallel to a side of the cone; also definable as the locus of a point whose distance from a given point (the focus) is equal to its distance from a given straight line (the directrix).

Sometimes distinguished from parabolas of the higher kind (see b) as the ***Apollonian*** or ***quadratic parabola***. It is approximately the path of a projectile under the influence of gravity.

[**1544** *Archimedis Opera* 142 (heading) Archimedis qvadratvra parabolæ, id est portionis contentæ a linea recta & sectione rectanguli coni. **1558** COMMANDINUS *Archimedis Opera* 18 b, (heading) Archimedis qvadratvra paraboles.] **1579** DIGGES *Stratiot.* 188, I demaunde whether then this Eleipsis shal not make an Angle with the Parabola Section equal to the distaunce betweene the grade of Randon proponed, and the grade of vttermost Randon. **1656** [see PARABOLASTER]. **1668** *Phil. Trans.* III. 876 The Spindle made of the same Parabola by rotation about its Base. **1696** WHISTON *Th. Earth* I. (1722) 14 The Orbits describ'd will be one of the other Conick Sections, either Parabola's or Hyperbola's. **1706** W. JONES *Syn. Palmar. Matheseos* 246 'Tis evident the Parabola has but one Focus. **1788** CHAMBERS *Cycl.* (ed. Rees), *Parabola, osculatory*, in *Geometry*, is used particularly for that *parabola* which not only osculates or measures the curvature of any curve at a given point, but also measures the variation of the curvature at the point. **1828** HUTTON *Course Math.* II. 136 The Area or Space of a Parabola, is equal to Two-Thirds of its Circumscribing Parallelogram. **1832** *Nat. Philos.* II. *Introd. Mech.* p. xviii. (U.K.S.), The curve-line which a ball describes, if the resistance of the air be not taken into consideration, is called in geometry a parabola. **1868** LOCKYER *Elem. Astron.* xxiii. (1870) 124 The orbit of a comet is generally best represented by what is called a parabola; that is, an infinitely long ellipse. **1881** C. TAYLOR *Anc. & Mod. Geom.* 82 The parabola was so called from the equality of the square of the ordinate of any point upon it to the rectangle contained by its abscissa and the latus rectum. .. It is reported by Proclus in his Commentaries on the first book of Euclid.. that the terms *parabola, hyperbola*, and *ellipse* had been used by the Pythagoreans to express the equality or inequality of areas, and were subsequently transferred to the conic curves.

b. Extended to curves of higher degrees resembling a parabola in running off to infinity without approaching to an asymptote, or having the line at infinity as a tangent, and denoted by equations analogous to that of the common parabola.

campaniform or ***bell-shaped parabola***: a name formerly given to cubic parabolas without cusp or node. ***Cartesian p.***: a cubic curve denoted by the equation $xy = ax^3 + bx^2 + cx + d$, having four infinite branches, two parabolic and two hyperbolic. ***cubic*** or ***cubical p.***: a parabola of the third degree. ***double p.***: a parabola having the line at infinity for a double tangent. ***helicoid p.***: see HELICOID. ***Neilian p.***: the semicubical parabola ($ax^2 = y^3$), rectified by William Neil in 1657. ***semicubical p.***: see SEMICUBICAL.

1664 *Phil. Trans.* I. 15 A Method for the Quadrature of Parabola's of all degrees. **1727-41** CHAMBERS *Cycl.* s.v., Parabola's of the higher kinds are algebraic curves, defined by $a^{m-1}x = y^m$... Some call these Paraboloids. **1765** CROKER *Dict. Arts*, Cartesian Parabola. **1795** HUTTON *Math. Dict.* II. 192 A bell-form Parabola, with a conjugate point.

[*Note.* To the earlier Greek geometers, including Archimedes, B.C. 287-212, who investigated only sections perpendicular to the surface of the cone, the parabola was known as ὀρθογωνίου κώνου τομή = sectio rectanguli coni 'the [perpendicular] section of a right-angled cone'. The use of παραβολή, 'application', in this sense is due to Apollonius of Perga, *c* 210 B.C., and, with him, referred to the fact that a rectangle on the abscissa, having an area equal to the square on the ordinate, can be 'applied' to the latus rectum, without either excess (as in the *hyperbola*), or deficiency (as in the *ellipse*). (See C. Taylor *Anct. & Mod. Geom.* 195; T. L. Heath *Apollonius of Perga*, Introd. lxxx.) But an explanation of the name, from the much more obvious property of the *parallelism* of the section to a side of the cone, is given by Eutokius of Ascalon *c* A.D. 550, and is frequent in later writers.]

‖**parabolanus** (pærəbəʊˈleɪnəs). Pl. **-ni.** [late L. (*Cod. Just., Cod. Theod.*), f. *parabol-us* reckless man, one who jeopardizes his life, a. Gr. παράβολος exposing oneself, venturesome, reckless, perilous, f. παρα- aside + βάλλειν to throw.] A sick-nurse, especially in infectious cases. In the Eastern Church from 3rd to 5th c., name of a class of lay helpers who attended upon the sick in the plague, etc.

1672 CAVE *Prim. Chr.* III. ii. (1673) 267 These Parabolani were a Kind of Clergy Physitians. **1727-41** CHAMBERS *Cycl.* s.v., The *Parabolani* were not allowed to withdraw themselves from their function, which was the attendance on the sick. **1852** HOOK *Ch. Dict.* (1871) 563. **1853** KINGSLEY *Hypatia* v, Philammon went out with the parabolani, a sort of organised guild of district visitors.

†**pa'rabolar**, *a. Geom. Obs.* [f. PARABOLA + -AR.] Of the nature of a parabola; parabolic.

1665 *Phil. Trans.* I. 105 If regular, whether Elliptick or Parabolar.

†**pa'rabolary**, *a. Obs.* [f. L. *parabola* PARABLE + -ARY.] Of the nature of a parable; parabolical.

1652 URQUHART *Jewel* Wks. (1834) 292 Allegories of all sorts, whether apologal, affabulatory, parabolary [etc.].

†**parabo'laster.** *Obs.* [f. PARABOLA: see -ASTER.] A parabola of a higher degree: = PARABOLA b. PARABOLOID 1.

1656 HOBBES *Six Lessons* Wks. 1845 VII. 185, I have exhibited and demonstrated the proportion of the parabola and parabolasters to the parallelograms of the same height and base. **1656** tr. *Hobbes' Elem. Philos.* (1839) 233 The line, in which that body is moved, will be the crooked line of the first semi-parabolaster of two means, whose base is the impetus last acquired. **1670** COLLINS in Rigaud *Corr. Sci. Men* (1841) II. 199 A pure unaffected biquadratic parabolaster.

‖**parabole** (pəˈræbəliː). [a. Gr. παραβολή comparison, analogy (see PARABLE); formerly in Latinized form *parabola.*]

1. *Rhet.* A comparison, a metaphor (in the widest sense); *spec.* a simile drawn from the present.

1589 PUTTENHAM *Eng. Poesie* III. ix. (Arb.) 251 The Greekes call it *Parabola*, which terme is also by custome accepted of vs: neuerthelesse we may call him in English the resemblance misticall. **1678** PHILLIPS (ed. 4), *Parabola*, a Similitude of a thing: In Rhetorick it is a similitudinary speech whereby one thing is uttered and another signified; as in this Example; 'As Cedars beaten with continual storms, so great men flourish'. **1828** WEBSTER, *Parabole*, in oratory, similitude; comparison.

†**2.** *Geom.* = PARABOLA. *Obs. rare.*

1684 T. BAKER *Geometr. Key* 10 Though no necessity of invoking a Parabole.. to midwife forth the two first classes of Equations.

parabolic (pærəˈbɒlɪk), *a.* and *sb.* [ad. late L. *parabolicus*, a. late Gr. παραβολικός figurative (Clemens Alex.), f. παραβολή PARABLE; in mod. use referred also to PARABOLA; cf. F. *parabolique* (14th c. in Littré).]

A. *adj.* **1. a.** Of, pertaining to, or of the nature of a parable; 'expressed by parable' (J.).

c **1449** PECOCK *Repr.* (1860) II. 533 Signified bi likenes in parabolik speche. **1669** GALE *Crt. Gentiles* I. I. ii. 11 Traditions; which he wraps up in.. parabolic.. notions. **1804** COLLINS *Scripscrap* 96 And through each parabolic tract, Pursue the trail of moral fact. **1882** A. B. BRUCE (*title*) The Parabolic Teaching of Christ, a systematic and critical study of the parables of Our Lord.

b. Of or pertaining to parabole; metaphorical.

1696 WHISTON *Th. Earth* (1722) 66 Resolving the whole into a Popular, Moral, or Parabolick Sense. **1878** G. D. BOARDMAN *Creative Week* 20 (Cent.) Creation.. transcends all experience... Hence all the words describing Creation must, in the very nature of the case, be figurative or parabolic.

2. *Geom.* Of the form of, or resembling, a parabola; of which the section is a parabola; also, having relation to the parabola.

parabolic asymptote: see quot. 1788. ***parabolic branch*** (of a curve): a branch which, like the parabola, extends to infinity without approaching an asymptote (opp. to *hyperbolic*). ***parabolic conoid***: a conoid of parabolic section, a paraboloid of revolution. ***parabolic point***: a point on a surface at which the curvature is cylindrical, the indicatrix thus being two parallel straight lines, i.e. a degenerate parabola. ***parabolic pyramidoid***: see PYRAMIDOID. ***parabolic reflector***: a reflector, usually of polished metal, made in the form of a paraboloid of circular section, so as to reflect parallel rays to a focus, or reflect in parallel lines the rays of a lamp placed at the focus. ***parabolic space***: (*a*) the space between an arc of a parabola and its ordinate; (*b*) name given by Klein to a space, of any number of dimensions, of zero curvature, as ordinary or Euclidean space (see HYPERBOLIC 2 b, quot. 1872-3). ***parabolic spindle***: a figure formed by the revolution of an arc of a parabola about its (double) ordinate. ***parabolic spiral*** = helicoid parabola: see HELICOID.

1702 RALPHSON *Math. Dict.*, *Paraboloid*.. otherwise called a Parabolick Conoid. **1704** Parabolic spiral [see HELICOID A. 1]. **1706** PHILLIPS, *Parabolick Space*, is the Area .. between the Curve.. of the Parabola and any entire Ordinate. *Ibid.*, *Parabolick Spindle.* **1748** HARTLEY *Observ. Man* I. iii. 357 The parabolic Area equal to ⅔ of the circumscribing Parallelogram. **1788** CHAMBERS *Cycl.* (ed. Rees), *Parabolic asymptote*,.. a parabolic line approaching to a curve, so that.. by producing both indefinitely, their distance from each other becomes less than any given line. **1822** IMISON *Sc. & Art* I. 19 The resistance of the air and other causes occasion projected bodies to deviate considerably from the parabolic curve. **1831** BREWSTER *Optics* xxxviii. §185. 323 Parabolic reflectors made of metal. **1842** *Penny Cycl.* XXIII. 304/1 The elliptic, parabolic, and hyperbolic cylinders are perfectly distinct. **1869** BOUTELL *Arms & Arm.* xi. (1874) 225 [They] made experiments with parabolic shot or bombs. **1872** PROCTOR *Ess. Astron.* iii. 40 Comets which sweep round the sun in parabolic or hyperbolic orbits. **1955** *Sci. Amer.* Mar. 38/1 A parabolic 'dish', either solid or made of a wire screen, reflects incoming radio waves to a focal point, where a small dipole or rod picks up the energy. **1960** *Practical Wireless* XXXVI. 391/1 The radio telescope, a parabolic mirror of 83ft diameter.. scans the sky. **1962** A. NISBETT *Technique Sound Studio* i. 23 An assembly consisting of a cardioid or omnidirectional microphone fitted at the focus of a parabolic reflector is also strongly directional. **1965** P. WAYRE *Wind in Reeds* vi. 74 Separate E.M.I. recording equipment, including.. a microphone which could be used in conjunction with a parabolic reflector. **1969** *Times* 4 Feb. 13/3 He seems to have recorded pulses of energy by means of a large array of parabolic mirrors. **1977** P. HILL *Fanatics* 38 Could we have a parabolic microphone in the control flat?

B. *sb.* †**1.** *Geom.* A parabolic figure; a parabola or paraboloid. *Obs. rare.*

1657 W. RAND tr. *Gassendi's Life Peiresc* II. 100 Whether those.. are the portions of Globes or of Parabolicks, or other figures, is truely hard to judge. **1807** SOUTHEY *Espriella's Lett.* II. 137 They were talking of parabolics and ellipticks.

2. A parabolic expression, a metaphor. *nonce-use.*

1829 *Blackw. Mag.* XXVI. 736 The grandeur of the house was above all parabolics.

parabolical (pærəˈbɒlɪkəl), *a.* [see -ICAL.]

1. Of or pertaining to parable; involving, or constituting, parable; having a figurative, as opposed to a historical or literal, existence or value.

1554 in Foxe *A. & M.* (1563) 910/2 Nothing can bee sayde more vncerteyne, or more parabolical and vnsensiblie than so to say. **1641** WILKINS *Mercury* ii. (1707) 10 The Jewish Doctors.. accustom themselves to a Parabolical Way of Teaching. *a* **1716** SOUTH *Serm.* (1717) III. 373 A Parabolical Description of God's vouchsafing to the World the Invaluable Blessing of the Gospel, by the Similitude of a King.. Solemnizing his Son's Marriage. **1827** G. S. FABER *Sacr. Calend. Prophecy* (1844) I. 6 That parabolical prophecy of our Lord: 'wheresoever the carcase is, there will the eagles be gathered together'. **1866** WHITTIER *Pr. Wks.* (1889) I. 115 The Scripture they turn unto allegory and parabolical conceits.

†**b.** Using or addicted to the use of parable. *Obs.*

1691 WOOD *Ath Oxon.* II. 265 He.. had a parabolical and allusive fancy. *c* **1817** HOGG *Tales & Sk.* (1837) IV. 9, I think aunty's unco parabolical the day.

2. *Geom.* = PARABOLIC *a.* 2. Now *rare.*

1571 DIGGES *Pantom.* Pref. A iij b, Archimedes.. (as some suppose) with a glasse framed by reuolution of a section Parabolicall, fired the Romane nauie.. comming to the siege of Syracusa. **1666** BOYLE *Orig. Formes & Qual.* (1667) 313 Not directly downwards, but in a parabolical or some such crooked line. **1728** PEMBERTON *Newton's Philos.* 234 To compare the orbits, upon the supposition that they are parabolical. *c* **1850** *Rudim. Navig.* (Weale) 111 A Parabolical Conoid.

Hence **para'bolicalness.** *rare*⁻⁰.

1727 BAILEY vol. II, *Parabolicalness*, the being of the Nature or Manner of a Parable.

parabolicalism (pærəˈbɒlɪkəlɪz(ə)m). *rare.* [-ISM.] Parabolical character; matter which is parabolical.

1854 C. WALTON *Notes Biogr. W. Law* 238 The deeply experienced spiritual man.. will be much disappointed.. at finding so much deep experience buried in such a huge mass of parabolicalism and idiocratic deformity.

para'bolically, *adv.* [f. PARABOLICAL *a.* + -LY².]

1. In a parabolical manner; with parable or allegory; according to parabole, metaphorically.

1615 BEDWELL *Moham. Imp.* II. §63 They are spoken parabolically. **1749** FIELDING *Tom Jones* II. ii, The latter was parabolically spoken. **1828** CARLYLE *Misc.* (1857) I. 148 This doctrine is to be stated emblematically and parabolically.

2. *Geom.* In the manner of a parabola. *rare.*

1755 in JOHNSON.

pa'raboliform, *a. rare.* [f. PARABOLA + -(I)FORM.] Of the form of a parabola.

1710 J. HARRIS *Lex. Techn.* II, *Paraboloids*, are Paraboliform Curves in Geometry. **1819** *Pantologia*, *Paraboliform curves*, a name sometimes given to the parabolas of the higher orders.

†**pa'rabolism.** *Alg. Obs.* [f. Gr. παραβολή in sense 'division' + -ISM.] The reduction of an equation by dividing it by the coefficient of the unknown quantity of highest degree.

1702 RALPHSON *Math. Dict.*, *Parabolism*, is the Division of the Terms of an Equation by the known Quantity (when there happens to be one) that is involved or multiplied into the first Term. Thus the following Equation $axx + 2abx = bcc$ will be reduced to this $xx + 2bx = \frac{bcc}{a}$.

parabolist (pəˈræbəlɪst). [f. Gr. παραβολή (L. *parabola*) PARABLE, PARABOLA + -IST.]

1. One who narrates, uses, or deals in any way with, parables or parabole.

1651 H. MORE *Second Lash* in *Enthus. Tri.*, etc. (1656) 196 Now my pretty Parabolist, what is there left to make your similitude good?

2. One who deals with the parabola; in quot. 'a partisan of the parabola': cf. HYPERBOLIST 2. *nonce-use.*

1831 I. TAYLOR *Logic in Theol.* (1859) 42 The partisans of the ellipsis, the parabola, and the hyperbola... The parabolists.. believing themselves qualified to act as mediators.. would gravely say much that was very plausible.

parabolize (pəˈræbəlaɪz), *v.* [See -IZE.]

1. a. *trans.* To express or represent parabolically; to set forth in a parable. Also *absol.*

1600 W. WATSON *Decacordon* (1602) 20 Otherwise could not the church Catholike be..parabolized with a net cast into the sea. *Ibid.* 34 As our Sauiour Christ rightly parabolized of such. **1623** *Doleful Even-Song* 9 Which mercifull bounty..is here parabolized vnto vs by a certaine man that was a king [etc.]. **1847** BUSHNELL *Chr. Nurt.* II. vii. (1861) 379 He [Christ] parabolizes the truth.

b. To turn into, treat, or explain as a parable.
1851 G. S. FABER *Many Mansions* 329 Some would parabolise, or rather indeed..mythise, the several statements in the Book of Job and the Vision of Micaiah.

2. To make parabolic or paraboloidal in shape.
1869 W. PURKISS in *Eng. Mechanic* 12 Nov. 208/2 Such curve being afterwards parabolised by the..polisher. **1878** LOCKYER *Stargazing* 134 M. Foucault..proceeds in a different manner in parabolising his glass mirrors.

Hence **pa,raboli'zation**, the process of making parabolic or paraboloidal. **pa'rabolizing** *vbl. sb.* and *ppl. a.*; also **pa'rabolizer**, one who parabolizes.
1691 *Search after Wit* 3 And who first shou'd Trump up, but the Parabolizers? **1702** C. MATHER *Magn. Chr.* III. II. xiv. (1852) 420 The people then perceived the meaning of the parabolizer to be that [etc.]. **1819** G. S. FABER *Dispensations* (1823) II. 302 The parabolizing Arab. **1869** W. PURKISS in *Eng. Mechanic* 12 Nov. 208/3 The shorter the focal length, the more difficult the parabolising becomes. **1903** *Sci. Amer. Suppl.* 17 Oct. 23232/3 Draper's method of 'parabolization by measure'.

paraboloid (pə'ræbəlɔɪd), *sb.* (*a.*) *Geom.* Also 7 -oeides, -oeid, 8–9 -oide. [In form, ad. Gr. παραβολοειδής a. (in a different sense), whence in 17th c. use *paraboloeides*: see PARABOLA and -OID, and cf. F. *paraboloïde.*]

† **1.** A parabola of a higher degree: = PARABOLA b.
1656 HOBBES *Six Lessons* Wks. 1845 VII. 315 The parabola is ⅔, and the cubical paraboloeides ¾ of their parallelograms respectively. **1697** EVELYN *Numism.* viii. 281 The Equated Isocrone Motion..in a Paraboloeid. **1706** W. JONES *Syn. Palmar. Matheseos* 245 Those of the Third..Order will be the Cubic Paraboloid. **1710** J. HARRIS *Lex. Techn.* II. s.v., Suppose the Parameter multiply'd into the Square of the Abscissa to be equal to the Cube of the Ordinate; that is, $pxx = y^3$. Then the Curve is called a Semicubical Paraboloid.

2. A solid or surface of the second degree, some of whose plane sections are parabolas; formerly restricted to that of circular section, generated by the revolution of a parabola about its axis, now called ***paraboloid of revolution.***
elliptic paraboloid: a paraboloid of elliptic section. ***hyperbolic paraboloid***: a curved surface of which every plane section is either a parabola or a hyperbola, the curvature being concave in one direction and convex in another (as in a saddle concave towards front and back, and convex towards each side).
1702 RALPHSON *Math. Dict.*, *Paraboloid*, is a Solid formed by the Circumvolution of a Parabola about its Ax. This is otherwise called a *Parabolick Conoid.* **1807** HUTTON *Course Math.* II. 127 The Solid Content of a Paraboloid (or Solid generated by the Rotation of a Parabola about its Axis), is equal to Half its Circumscribing Cylinder. **1829** *Nat. Philos.* I. *Optics* vii. 22 (U.K.S.) The specula, or mirrors, of all reflecting telescopes are ground into the shape of a paraboloid. **1840** *Penny Cycl.* XVII. 222/2 *Paraboloid.* The simplest form of this surface is the paraboloid of revolution. **1842** *Ibid.* XXIII. 304/2 For the elliptic paraboloid, let a parabola revolve about its principal axis, and let the circular sections become ellipses. *Ibid.*, Let two parabolas have a common vertex, and let their planes be at right angles to one another, being turned contrary ways. Let the one parabola then move over the other, always continuing parallel to its first position, and having its vertex constantly on the other: its arc will then trace out an hyperbolic paraboloid.

B. *adj.* = PARABOLOIDAL. *rare.*
1857 in MAYNE *Expos. Lex.* **1901** *19th Cent.* Oct. 586 The voice aided by a paraboloid megaphone.

parabo'loidal, *a.* [f. as prec. + -AL¹.] Of the form of a paraboloid.
1825 J. NICHOLSON *Operat. Mechanic* 575 Circular [domes] may be spherical, spheroidal, ellipsoidal, hyperboloidal, paraboloidal, &c. **1876** G. F. CHAMBERS *Astron.* 759 Using, instead of a spherical, a paraboloidal speculum.

‖**parabranchia** (pærə'bræŋkɪə). [PARA-¹.] The modified osphradium of certain gastropod molluscs, considered as a secondary branchia or gill. Hence **para'branchial** *a.*, of or pertaining to a parabranchia; **para'branchiate** *a.*, furnished with a parabranchia.
1883 E. R. LANKESTER in *Encycl. Brit.* XVI. 648/1 The right olfactory organ only is retained, and may assume the form of a comb-like ridge to the actual left of the ctenidium or branchial plume. It has been erroneously described as the second gill, and is known as the parabranchia. **1888** ROLLESTON & JACKSON *Anim. Life* 479 In some *Azygobranchia* the osphradium is large, thrown into folds, and is generally taken for a second but reduced ctenidium (parabranchia).

parabromalide (-'brəʊməlaɪd). *Chem.* [PARA-¹ 2 a.] An isomer of bromal, C_2HBr_3O, forming colourless rhombic prisms with four-sided summits.
1866 WATTS *Dict. Chem.* IV. 340.

parabutlerite, -casein(ate): see PARA-¹ 2 c, 2 a.

‖**parabysma** (pærə'bɪzmə). *Path.* [mod.L., a. Gr. παράβυσμα stuffing.] A term for swelling of the abdomen from enlargement or engorgement of the viscera. Hence **para'bysmic** *a.*
1822–34 *Good's Study Med.* (ed. 4) I. 135 Parabysmic tumours of the liver. *Ibid.* 351 On this account I have ventured to change it for Parabysma. *Ibid.* IV. 54 Thus working up a distressing parabysma or visceral turgescence. *Ibid.* 316 Parabysmic dropsy of the belly.

paracamphoric to **-cellulose**: see PARA-¹ 2.

Paracelsian (pærə'sɛlsɪən), *sb.* and *a.* [f. proper name Paracelsus (see below) + -IAN.]

A. *sb.* A follower or adherent of the celebrated Swiss physician, chemist, and natural philosopher Paracelsus (1490–1541), or of his medical or philosophical principles; in the former sense opposed to *Galenist.*
His true name was Philippus Theophrast von Hohenheim.
1574 J. JONES (*title*) Galens Bookes of Elementes..confuting..the errours..of the Paracelcians. **1654** WHITLOCK *Zootomia* 108 Our Doctor is pertinaciously either a Galenist, or Paracelsian. **1711** W. KING tr. *Naude's Ref. Politics* i. 15 The Paracelsians pervert the text of Hippocrates, to establish their visionary imaginations.

B. *adj.* Of, pertaining to, or characteristic of Paracelsus.
1617 MIDDLETON & ROWLEY *Fair Quarrel* II. ii, Can all your Paracelsian mixtures cure it? **1659** in *Burton's Diary* (1828) IV. 453 It is a paracelsian remedy, that may kill as well as cure. **1857** in MAYNE *Expos. Lex.*

Hence **Para'celsianism**, the medical principles of Paracelsus.
1668 H. MORE *Div. Dial.* v. xviii. (1713) 467 Bath..in which we all-over discover the Foot-steps of Paracelsianism and Familism.

So **Para'celsic, Para'celsical** *adjs.*, **Para'celsist** *sb.*, **Paracel'sistic** *a.*
1602 F. HERING *Anatomyes* 15 Hyperbolicall, or rather, Paracelsicall Commendations. **1625** HART *Anat. Ur.* II. x. 119 Our Paracelcists would faine feed vs with many such smoaky promises. **1653** R. SANDERS *Physiogn.* 165 The Galenick and Paracelsick Physick. **1704** J. HARRIS *Lex. Techn.* I, *Paracelsistick Medicines.* **1882** *Standard* 13 Dec. 5/5 The Galenists, the Paracelsists,..the Vitalists,..and the Anti-Hallerians had all..their followers.

‖**paracentesis** (pærəsɛn'tiːsɪs). *Surg.* Also 6 in Fr. form **paracentèse**; 7 *erron.* **-thesis, -tisis.** [L., a. Gr. παρακέντησις tapping, couching, f. παρακεντεῖν to pierce at the side, f. παρα- beside + κεντεῖν to prick, stab.] The operation of making a perforation into some cavity of the body, esp. for the removal of fluid or gas; tapping; also, couching.
1597 A. M. tr. *Guillemeau's Fr. Chirurg.* 20/1 We must make the Paracentese to drawe awaye the water out of the bellyes. **1667** FAIRFAX in *Phil. Trans.* II. 548, I had thoughts of a Paracenthesis or Tapping between the Ribs. **1779** M. CUTLER in *Life*, etc. (1888) I. 73 Rode to Chebacco, to attend the operation of paracentesis with Dr. Davis. **1874** LAWSON *Dis. Eye* 31 Paracentesis of the cornea will also be of service. **1892** *Brit. Med. Jrnl.* 1104/1.

paracentral (pærə'sɛntrəl), *a.* [f. Gr. παρα-, PARA-¹ + κέντρον centre + -AL¹.] Situated beside the (or a) centre; in *Anat.* applied to parts of the brain lying alongside the central fissure.
1878 A. HAMILTON *Nerv. Dis.* 61 The meningitis was..localized on two convolutions, the anterior and posterior marginal near the paracentral lobe. **1899** *Allbutt's Syst. Med.* VII. 715 Frequent in the parietal and temporal lobes and in the paracentral gyri.

†**para'centric,** *a.*¹ *Kinetics. Obs.* [See PARA-¹ and CENTRIC.] In ***paracentric motion,*** rendering *motus paracentricus* of Leibnitz, used by him to express that motion which, compounded with harmonic circulation, he supposed to make up the actual motion of a planet. Sometimes misunderstood by other writers, and applied to simple motion about a centre.
[**1689** LEIBNITZ *Tentamen de mot. cælest. causis*, Opera 1768, III. 216 Motu duplici, composito ex circulatione harmonica..et motu paracentrico. **1702** GREGORY *Astron. phys. elementa* I. lxxvii. 100.] **1704** C. HAYES *Fluxions* 293 Paracentric motion of Impetus is so much as the revolving Body approaches nearer to or recedes farther from the Center of Attraction. **1715** tr. *Gregory's Astron.* I. lxxvii. 175 The other Motion (namely the Paracentric) arises from a double curve, namely the excussory impression of Circulation and the Sun's attraction compounded together. **1797** *Monthly Mag.* III. 128 If a slender rod AC revolve round the point C, as a centre,..the centrifugal force arising from the paracentric velocity of the rod [etc.].

So **para'centrical** *a.* ? *Obs.* = prec.
1718 G. CHEYNE *Philos. Princ. Relig.* 32 The Paracentrical Motion is compounded of two others, viz...[that] whereby all Bodies moving in a Curve, endeavour to recede from the Center by the Tangent, and the Attraction of the Sun or the Gravitation of the Planet toward it.

paracentric (pærə'sɛntrɪk), *a.*² *Cytology.* [f. PARA-¹: cf. -CENTRIC 2.] Involving only the part of a chromosome at one side of the centromere. Opp. PERICENTRIC *a.* 2.
1938 H. J. MULLER in *Collecting Net* XIII. 187/2 If the breaks were to one side of the centromere, the inversion may be termed 'paracentric', and it will be noted that the proportions of the two arms, and hence the general shape of the chromosome as seen at mitosis, is not changed. But if the breaks included the centromere between them, being 'pericentric', the mitotic chromosome will have the relative sizes of its two arms altered, except in the special case in which the two distal sections are sensibly equal in size. **1957** C. P. SWANSON *Cytol. & Cytogenetics* xv. 485 Paracentric inversions are by far the most common type of aberration found in natural populations. **1975** *Nature* 3 July 40/1 Heterozygosity for a paracentric inversion, that is, a structural rearrangement in which a chromosome segment that does not include the centromere is rotated through 180°, results in suppression of recombination in the inversion region.

paracetamol (pærə'siːtəmɒl). *Pharm.* [f. *para-acetylaminophenol*, its chemical name.]
A white crystalline compound, $C_8H_9NO_2$, with mild analgesic and antipyretic properties; a tablet of this.
1957 *Approved Names* (Brit. Pharmacopœia Comm.), Paracetamol. **1963** *Brit. Pharmaceutical Codex* 564 Paracetamol..is a suitable alternative for patients sensitive to aspirin. **1971** *Daily Tel.* 18 June 13/4 The active ingredients of pain-killing drugs that can be bought at the chemist are only two, namely paracetamol and aspirin. **1972** J. GILL *Tenant* III. ii. 92 Denis still had his headache when he woke and he went into the bathroom and took Paracetamol. **1976** *Liverpool Echo* 23 Nov. 1/8 Open verdict recorded by Merseyside Coroner at inquest into death of A— C— (32),..who died..of paracetamol poisoning. **1977** *Listener* 28 Apr. 563/3 An obligatory late-night snack for all production staff of toasted cheese and paracetamols..and who knows what new programmes would result.

parache, parachen, var. PARISH, PARISHEN.

parachito, obs. variant of PARAKEET.

parachloralide (-'klɔərəlaɪd). *Chem.* [PARA-¹ 2 a.] An isomer of chloral, $C_2HCl_3O_2$, a pungent-smelling liquid, insoluble in water, produced by the action of chloral on wood spirit.
1866 WATTS *Dict. Chem.* IV. 341.

parachor ('pærəkɔː(r)). *Chem.* [f. PARA-¹ + Gr. χορός (= dance, but taken by the coiner, in mistake for χώρα, as = space).] A numerical quantity (found empirically to be constant over a wide range of temperature) equal to the molecular weight of a liquid multiplied by the fourth root of its surface tension and divided by the difference between its density and that of its vapour.
1924 S. SUGDEN in *Jrnl. Chem. Soc.* CXXV. I. 1178 The quantity *P* can be regarded as function of chemical composition. For saturated substances, *P* is an additive function... It is proposed to name this quantity the parachor..to signify comparative volume. **1940** GLASSTONE *Textbk. Physical Chem.* viii. 517 The mean parachor equivalent of the —NC group, in a number of alkyl and aryl isocyanides, is 66; this corresponds closely to that required for the structure $—N^+ \equiv C^-$, thus N(12·5), C(4·8), triple bond (46·6), making a total of 63·9. The alternative structure —N=C would have a parachor equivalent of only 40·6. **1956** I. L. FINAR *Org. Chem.* II. i. 9 A comparison of parachors of different liquids gives a comparison of molecular volumes at temperatures at which liquids have the same surface tension. **1974** *Nature* 22 Nov. 296/2 For a given salt, *k*, was proportional to the characteristic volume of the non-electrolyte which in $m^3\ mol^{-1}$ equals the parachor (calculated in the usual way in c.g.s units) × 10^{-6}.

parachordal (pærə'kɔːdəl), *a.* (*sb.*) *Embryol.* [f. Gr. παρα- PARA-¹ + χορδή chord + -AL¹.] Situated beside the notochord: applied to two plates of cartilage, forming the foundation of the skull in the embryo. **b.** as *sb.* = Parachordal cartilage.
1875 NEWTON in *Encycl. Brit.* III. 701/2 The hinder and front cartilages, parachordal and trabecular, are applied to each other unconformably. **1881** MIVART *Cat* 337 The basi-cranial plate or parachordal cartilage. **1892** *Syd. Soc. Lex.* s.v., The parachordals with the cephalic portion of the notochord form the basilar plate.

parachromatin, -chromatism: see PARA-¹.

parachronism (pə'rækrənɪz(ə)m). [f. Gr. παρα- PARA-¹ + χρόν-ος time + -ISM: cf. ἀναχρονισμός anachronism. Cf. F. *parachronisme.*] An error in chronology; usually taken as one in which an event, etc., is referred to a later date than the true one. (Cf. ANACHRONISM.)
a **1641** BP. MOUNTAGU *Acts & Mon.* iii. (1642) 186, I much marvaile, that..our Moderne Criticks..did not consider so great an Errour, and Parachronisme in Iustins Text. **1660** H. MORE *Myst. Godl.* v. xvi. 198 The Bride of the Lamb, he interprets of Constantine's Family and Retinue; wherein he commits a gross Parachronism. **1788** R. PORSON in *Mus. Crit.* I. 235 Parachronisms appear in the marble, respecting the age of Phidon the Argive, the assassination of Hipparchus, and the expulsion of Hippias. **1873** J. H. SMITH *Notes & Margin. Tennyson* 114 It cannot be regarded as parachronism if the poets..refrain from cutting out the very life and essence of the original tales.

So **parachro'nistic** *a.*, marked by parachronism; **pa'rachronize** *v.*
1685 H. MORE *Paralip. Prophet.* xii. 97 Though he have there over-much Parachronistick stuff. **1670** BLOUNT *Glossogr.* (ed. 3), *Parachronize*, to mistime any thing.

†**parachroous** (pə'rækrəʊəs), *a. rare*⁻⁰. [f. Gr. παράχρο-ος + -OUS.] (See quot.)
1857 MAYNE *Expos. Lex.*, *Parachroüs* (L.), of a false or altered colour; deprived of colour: parachrous.

So **parachrose** (ˈpærəkrəʊs) *a.* [irreg. as if f. χρῶσις colouring]: see quot.

1847 Webster, *Parachrose, a.* (*Min.*) changing color by exposure to the weather. *Mohs.*

para-church: see para-[1] 1.

parachute (ˈpærəʃuːt), *sb.* [a. F. *parachute*, f. para-[2] + *chute* fall.]

1. An apparatus used for descending safely from a great height in the air, esp. from a balloon or, more recently, from an aircraft; it is constructed like a large umbrella, so as to expand and thus check the velocity of descent by means of the resistance of the air.

1785 *Europ. Mag.* VII. 401 In Mr. Blanchard's late visit to this country, he brought his Parachute to England. **1837** *Gentl. Mag.* Aug. 190/2 After the parachute was divided from the car, the balloon rose rapidly. **1940** *Chambers's Techn. Dict.* 613/1 *Free parachute*, a parachute to be released or opened by the falling person. **1974** *Encycl. Brit. Micropædia* VII. 740/3 Sport parachutes have large holes that permit the air to escape and drive the parachute in the direction opposite the hole, much like a low-power jet engine.

2. *gen.* Any contrivance, natural or artificial, serving to check a fall through the air, or to support something in the air; e.g. the expansible fold of skin or *patagium* in the flying squirrel, etc. Also *transf.*

1796 Stedman *Surinam* II. 17 These [flying squirrels] have..a membrane..which when they leap, expands like the wing of a bat, and by this, like a parachute, they rest on the air. **1833** Sir C. Bell *Hand* (1834) 82 The Draco fimbriatus..dropping safely to the ground, under the protection of a sort of parachute, formed by its extended skin. **1876** Beneden *Anim. Paras.* ii. 33 The medusa, when extended, forms for them a balloon with its parachute. **1879** tr. *Semper's Anim. Life* 11 The parachutes of the flying reptiles. **1894** H. Drummond *Ascent Man* 304 The fruits and seeds when ripe are..provided with wing or parachute and launched upon the wind. **1930** R. Campbell *Adamastor* 50 The proud White gannet in his parachute of snow. **1947** Auden *Age of Anxiety* v. 112 In pelagic meadows The plankton open their parachutes.

†**3.** Name given to a broad-brimmed hat worn by women late in the 18th century. *Obs.*

1885 *Fairholt's Costume in Eng.* Gloss., *Parachute*, a ladies' hat, in fashion in 1779.

4. a. *Mining.* A contrivance, such as a safety-catch, to prevent a too rapid descent of a cage in a shaft, or of the boring-rod in a boring.

1881 in Raymond *Mining Gloss.*

b. *Watchmaking.* A contrivance to prevent injury to the balance-wheel from a shock or blow.

1884 F. J. Britten *Watch & Clockm.* 184 The idea of the parachute is that if the watch is let fall..the balance staff pivots may be saved from breaking by the yielding of the end stones.

c. *Brewing.* An apparatus made to slide up and down the side of a fermenting-vat according to the height of the fermenting wort.

1885 *Standard* 14 Mar. 7/7 Brewery fermenting tuns.. with parachutes and attemperators preferred.

5. *attrib.* and *Comb.*, as *parachute bearing* adj.; dropped by or attached to a parachute, as *parachute bomb, flare, mine, pack, rocket, signal*; designating part of a parachute, as *parachute cord, harness, ring*; using a parachute, as *parachute drop, jump* (so *jumper, jumping* vbl. sb.), *skiing* vbl. sb., *system, troops*; for, involving or consisting of parachute troops, as *parachute aircraft, attack, battalion, brigade, landing, regiment, wing*; resembling or acting as a parachute, as *parachute garment, spinnaker*; used for making parachutes, as *parachute nylon, silk*; **parachute assembly** (see quot. 1951); **parachute course**, a course of instruction in parachuting; **parachute light**, a bright light given by a burning composition contained in a small bomb (called a *parachute light-ball*) supported by a parachute so as to float in the air (the parachute being at first inclosed in the bomb, and set free by the explosion of a charge which also ignites the composition); used for observing the position or movements of an enemy; **parachute tower**, a tower from which one may make a parachute jump.

1962 G. Chatterton *Wings of Pegasus* 32 There was a very limited number of tug aircraft and *parachute air-craft. **1951** *Gloss. Aeronaut. Terms (B.S.I.)* III. 14 **Parachute assembly*, a parachute complete with all equipment for deployment and for harnessing a load. **1978** T. Allbeury *Lantern Network* iv. 36 They clambered into the thick parachute assemblies. **1941** *Hutchinson's Pict. Hist. War* 22 Jan.–18 Mar. 74 We must all be prepared to meet gas attacks, *parachute attacks, with constancy, forethought and practised skill. **1942** *Parachute battalion [see *para-ski* s.v. para-[3]]. **1883** G. Allen in *Knowledge* 22 June 367/2 Other *parachute-bearing mammals. **1912** *Sci. Amer.* 16 Nov. 422/1 A *Parachute bomb for Aeronautic Use... The bomb is provided with a small parachute which quickly destroys the horizontal velocity communicated by the airship. **1943** *Hutchinson's Pict. Hist. War* 25 Nov. 1942–16 Feb. 1943 148 Groundstaff of the R.A.F. loading parachute bombs into Hampden aircraft. **1974** *Times* 19 Apr. 15/4 The 1st *Parachute Brigade fighting in North Africa. **1941** 'R. Crompton' *William does his Bit* viii. 193 Robert's got a bit of German *parachute cord. **1976** A. White *Long Silence* xi. 101 We checked ourselves for climbing. It was very similar to checking ourselves for a parachute jump... I had taken a loop of nylon parachute cord with me. **1946** R. Capell *Simiomata* I. 13 Tzigantis, having got round rules excluding men of his age, obtained the privilege of a *parachute course. **1977** D. Seaman *Committee* 151 Like every one else in the Department, Walters had done his parachute course. **1928** *Even. News* 5 May 5/3 There will be wing walking and a *parachute drop by Miss June. **1974** 'H. Carmichael' *Motive* iii. 31 A sky-diver in a delayed parachute drop. **1918** *War Illustr.* 13 July 372/2 We saw flashes far to the south —shrapnel, star-shells, and *parachute flares. **1941** A. O. Pollard *Bombers over Reich* 46 So we dropped another parachute flare, which..showed wreckage lying all over the place. **1974** S. Gulliver *Vulcan Bulletins* 130 Wire-guided missiles, small aerial incendiaries, parachute flares. **1912** C. B. Hayward *Pract. Aeronaut.* 690 (*heading*) *Parachute garment as a safeguard. *Ibid.*, A parachute garment has been devised to ease the shock of the fall. **1929** F. P. Gibbons *Red Napoleon* 231, I made a last inspection of my *parachute harness. **1958** G. Dutton in B. James *Austral. Short Stories* (1963) 292 His shirt clung..to..the parachute harness. **1978** T. Allbeury *Lantern Network* iv. 36 He.. checked all the straps on her parachute harness. **1970** *Parachute jump [see jump *sb.*[1] 1 c]. **1977** *Listener* 28 July 104/3, I had hoped to be making my first parachute jump.. that Saturday. **1912** C. B. Hayward *Pract. Aeronaut.* 161 The *parachute jumper insisted on going up at least a thousand feet for the first trial. **1932** Auden *Orators* II. 71 The Mimosa's affair with the parachute jumper. **1952** *Chambers's Jrnl.* May 261/1 *Parachute-jumping is the field of aviation in which the monopoly belongs to the Soviet Union. **1969** *Listener* 20 Feb. 255/1, I won the Northern Junior Sky-Diving Championship, but have given up parachute-jumping at least for the time being. **1974** *Encycl. Brit. Micropædia* VII. 741/1 The sport of parachute jumping is usually governed by the parachute branch of the national aeronautic club. **1976** A. White *Long Silence* i. 14 Can he climb?.. Parachute jumping? **1940** W. S. Churchill *Into Battle* (1941) 222 If *parachute landings were attempted..these unfortunate people would be far better out of the way. **1942** E. Waugh *Put out More Flags* 247 Parachute landings were looked for hourly. **1868** *Rep. to Govt. U.S. Munitions War* 192 A *parachute light-ball..if it only burns for a few minutes, does not reveal the position of those using it. **1876** Voyle & Stevenson *Mil. Dict.* (ed. 3) 285/2 *Parachute light*, a suspended light, invented by Colonel (now General) Boxer R.A., and which is used for the same purpose as *ground light* balls..viz. to light up the enemy's works and working parties. **1918** E. S. Farrow *Dict. Mil. Terms* 432 *Parachute Lights*, rockets or flares fired electrically from the pilot's seat, through a tube. **1897** Willis *Flower. Pl. & Ferns* I. 110 Very perfect '*parachute' mechanisms. **1940** *Hutchinson's Pict. Hist. War* 20 Dec. 1939–13 Feb. 1940 2 When the '*parachute' and magnetic mines were first used in the war, many people assumed that the Allies were taken by surprise. **1961** B. Fergusson *Watery Maze* i. 44 The Germans dropped some parachute mines into the harbour. **1974** N. Freeling *Dressing of Diamond* 90 It was indeed difficult to see what a human agency could do, short of a few parachute mines. **1972** J. Poyer *Chinese Agenda* (1973) v. 42 Mountain tents of very light-weight, close-woven *parachute nylon. **1977** *New Yorker* 12 Sept. 101 Two parachute nylon traveling bags. **1975** T. Allbeury *Special Collection* iv. 20 There was ample room for..the *parachute pack. **1977** P. Way *Super-Celeste* II. 57 Bosco..pulled the green apple on the oxygen cylinder attached to his parachute pack. **1899** *Westm. Gaz.* 1 Aug. 4/1 A '*parachute' parasol with the edge fringed with lace of the style..in vogue at the period of the Crimean War. **1972** *Parachute regiment [see para[1]]. **1973** *New Statesman* 28 Sept. 410/3 Reaction against the cloistered Hampstead life drove him into the Parachute Regiment. **1977** *R.A.F. News* 11–24 May 20/6 The Dakota..stands outside the Parachute Regiment's museum at Aldershot. **1930** C. Dixon *Parachuting* 53 He will then pull out the *parachute ring in the front of his harness which will open the pack to let the parachute fly out. **1935** *Discovery* Feb. 43/2 The multi-tube *parachute rocket used for the Harz Mountain experiments. **1976** *Star-Phoenix* (Saskatoon) 23 June 52/4 Since many rescues have to be performed at night or in darkened, stormy conditions, he suggested police and other officials involved in rescues carry illuminating parachute rockets. **1937** *Discovery* June 187/2 The manufacture of marine signals, ..*parachute signals,..railway flares. **1962** M. Duffy *That's how it Was* xvi. 131 She was juggling with some pieces of *parachute silk she had been given, trying to shape them to a pair of cami-knickers. **1977** J. Cleary *High Road to China* i. 28 A length of old parachute silk was a curtain that hid..our skimpy wardrobe. **1971** *Bahamanian Rev.* Nov. 15/2 For those who like to be on the water as well as in it, water skiing is available at the larger hotel beaches. The more daring may wish to sample *parachute skiing. In this unique sport, the skiers use the wind and motion of the boat to climb on the lift of a parachute and soar perhaps a hundred feet in the air for a thrilling ride. **1932** *Yachting* Oct. 68/1 That the '*parachute' spinnaker—or 'double' spinnaker, if you prefer—has come to stay is pretty evident to those who have given it any kind of a fair trail. **1964** M. Weeks *Compl. Boating Encycl.* 398/1 *Parachute spinnaker*, a large, wide spinnaker introduced in 1927 by the Swedish yachtsman Sven Salén. **1971** *Daily Tel.* 1 July 30/6 After aerodynamically braking in the atmosphere the *parachute system was put into action and before landing the soft-landing engines were fired. **1946** A. Lee *German Air Force* 37 This stage [in training, etc.] recalls the *parachute tower in the Park of Rest and Culture at Moscow. **1938** *Jrnl. R. Aeronaut. Soc.* XLII. 840 It appears that the landing of *parachute troops will require special sighting devices. **1942** *R.A.F. Jrnl.* 18 Apr. 29, 700 parachute troops were landed. **1978** *Listener* 9 Mar. 307/1 Malthausen..held whole armies of capable men and women who hoped that Allied parachute troops..would drop on, or near enough to, the camps. **1958** P. Kemp *No Colours or Crest* xii. 264 As a further precaution we had to remove our badges of rank and *parachute wings. **1973** *Times* 18 Oct. 18 General Amin..arrived in Amman earlier this week wearing Israeli parachute wings.

Hence ˈ**parachutage**, a drop of supplies, etc. by parachute; ˈ**parachutal** *a.*; ˈ**parachutic** *a.* (sense 2).

1905 *Spectator* 14 Jan. 47/1 A parachutic arboreal serpent is not an impossible animal. **1930** *Flight* 21 Feb. 240/1 The last part of the lecture was devoted mainly to a discussion of vertical descent and to the parachutal efficiency of the autogiro. **1945** G. Millar *Maquis* iii. 38, I told myself it was risky to sleep in bed so near the parachutage. **1956** R. Braddon *Nancy Wake* xiii. 141 Whenever a parachutage was due, the B.B.C. would issue the special code phrase.

parachute, *v.* **a.** *trans.* To convey by means of a parachute. **b.** *intr.* To descend by or as if by a parachute; to use a parachute.

1807 Colman *Broad Grins, Reckoning w. Time* vi, Thy pinions next..Balloon'd me from the Schools to Town, Where I was parachuted down, A dapper Temple student. **1860** W. H. Russell *My Diary in India* II. ix. 174 And thus, with an able-bodied aborigen holding on by my tunic-tails behind,..I parachuted down. **1888** *Pall Mall G.* 28 Aug. 5/1 The lady who 'parachuted' from Clifton Suspension Bridge. **1914** G. B. Shaw *Misalliance* 46 *Tarleton*... Been up much? *Lina*. Not in an aeroplane. Ive parachuted; but thats child's play. **1930** E. W. Hendy *Wild Exmoor* 245 Meadow-pipits parachuted down to the brink. **1946** *News Chron.* 2 Mar. 3 Brig. Nicholls was parachuted into Albania in October, 1943. **1956** 'C. Blackstock' *Dewey Death* ii. 27 He was with the Resistance... They parachuted him down into France. **1971** *Sci. Amer.* Sept. 230/1 It parachuted down over the open Pacific.

c. *fig.* Const. *in* or *into*. *trans.* To appoint or elect an outsider in such a way as to disregard the existing hierarchy; *intr.* to obtain a position in such a way.

1954 [implied in parachuting *vbl. sb.*]. **1968** *Listener* 13 June 759/3 Too many of the existing hierarchy are civil servants 'parachuted' in from outside. **1968** D. Stuebing *Trudeau: Man for Tomorrow* v. 39 Trudeau was accused of parachuting into Mount Royal, the term in this sense implying that the candidate was dropped into the riding under party sponsorship and over the objections of the riding association. **1973** *Globe & Mail* (Toronto) 9 June 6/2 Mr. Roberts prudently concluded that local Liberals would resist if an officer from the Prime Minister's office parachuted into the riding to push aside a respectable candidate, and a woman at that. **1975** *Globe & Mail* (Toronto) 4 Mar. 6/2 Competent French-Canadians develop a sense of frustration and inferiority. They move more slowly and in smaller numbers up through the middle ranks. To redress the balance, the Government has to parachute French-Canadians from outside the civil service into senior positions. This parachuting produces complaints from English Canada about 'The French' taking over the Government.

Hence **parachuted** *ppl. a.*; ˈ**parachuter**, a parachutist; **parachuting** *vbl. sb.*

1893 *Westm. Gaz.* 21 Mar. 9/2 Thus Baldwin, having made a fortune by parachuting, was able to retire unscathed. **1938** *Britannica Bk. of Year* 79/1 Parachuting..seems to be considered as a kind of popular amusement for everybody in Russia and France if performed with stiff parachutes on ropes from special jumping towers. **1940** Parachuter [see chutist, 'chutist]. **1941** R. Greenwood *Mr. Bunting at War* xvi. 221, I learnt it in case I meet any parachuters. **1945** G. Millar *Maquis* xv. 316 One pair of the high brown American parachuting-boots. **1954** B. & R. North tr. *Duverger's Pol. Parties* II. iii. 357 The 'parachuting' of candidates, so developed in the first proportional elections when some deputies had never set foot in their constituency before being elected, was radically impossible in the arrondissement system. **1969** N. Freeling *Tsing Boum* xvii. 130 They came out at night to steal parachuted supplies. **1971** P. A. Allum *Politics & Society Post-War Naples* (1973) vi. 180 A controversial example of the 'parachuting' of a candidate into the constituency was the transfer and inclusion in the list in 1968 of the Parisian correspondent of *L'Unità*, Maria-Antonietta Macciocchi. **1973** *Times* 13 July 5/1 The 'parachuting in' of two young men at a relatively senior level caused some bitter feelings among existing Commission staff, who saw their promotion prospects threatened. **1974** *Times* 19 Apr. 15/4 Corporal Jackie Smith, the only girl Red Devil..[has] considerable parachuting talent... You can 'buy' the weather by paying to travel wherever it's suitable for parachuting. **1977** *R.A.F. News* 11–24 May 3/6 An instructor in high-altitude parachuting at Abingdon. **1977** *New Yorker* 20 June 90/3 The connecting roads between tanks and parachuted troops are single lanes.

parachutist. *orig.* One who descends from a balloon in a parachute, *esp.* one skilled in such descents. Now more commonly one who makes a parachute descent from an aircraft, esp. a soldier dropped by parachute.

1888 *Weekly Scotsman* 6 Oct. 4/2 Mr. Baldwin, the now well-known balloonist and parachutist. **1888** *Sci. Amer.* 13 Oct. 231/1 An American Parachutist in England. **1890** *Daily News* 21 Feb. 2/3 Narrow escape of a Lady Parachutist. **1927** *Illustr. London News* 10 Sept. 406 (*caption*) The perilous work of the parachutist. **1936** [see *ankle-boot*]. **1940** *Hutchinson's Pict. Hist. War* 10 Apr.–11 May 114 Another photograph showing large numbers of Red Army parachutists falling from troop-carrying aircraft during Soviet Army manoeuvres. **1946** *B.B.C. War Report* 78 Parachutists were to do the job, but in the darkness and bad weather the paratroops were widely scattered and only 150 men reached the rendezvous for the attack. **1972** *Daily Tel.* (Colour Suppl.) 7 Jan. 11/4 Parachutists compete in individual aerial acrobatics or accuracy work. **1974** *Times* 19 Apr. 15/5 A sports parachutist just starting out could expect to spend £500 on his kit. **1976** A. White *Long Silence* i. 14 He'll also need to be a parachutist and rock-climber.

Hence **parachutism**, the art or practice of parachuting.

1889 *Graphic* 3 Aug. 127/1 By and by, perhaps, Society may vote parachutism vulgar.

paracide, obs. erron. form of parricide.

paracitric, etc.: see PARA-[1] 2.

paracketto, obs. variant of PARAKEET.

Paraclete ('pærəkli:t). Also 5 -clit, 6 -clet. [a. F. *paraclet* (13th c. in Hatz.-Darm.), ad. eccl. L. *paraclētus* (also *paraclītus*) Tertull., etc., a. Gr. παράκλητος advocate, intercessor, one called to one's aid, f. παρακαλεῖν to call in, call to one's aid. Although a passive verbal = L. *ad-vocātus*, παράκλητος was at an early date associated by the Greek Fathers with the Hellenistic sense of παρακαλεῖν to console, comfort, and the active agent-n. παρακλήτωρ encourager, comforter. Cf. the active sense acquired by *advocate*.
In Job xvi. 2, where the LXX has παρακλήτορες κακῶν πάντες, Aquila and Theodotion have παράκλητοι.]

1. A title of the Holy Spirit (repr. Gr. παράκλητος in John xiv. 16, 26, xv. 26, xvi. 7); properly 'an advocate, one called in to one's assistance, an intercessor', but often taken as = 'comforter' (see COMFORTER 1 b). Also (rarely) repr. Gr. παράκλητος 'advocate' as applied to Christ (1 John ii. 1).

c **1450** *Mirour Saluacioun* 3616 Ffor anothere Paraclit I shalle send ȝowe nedefulle. **1582** N.T. (Rhem.) *John* xiv. 26 The Paraclete, the Holy Ghost, whom the Father will send in my name. **1659** PEARSON *Creed* viii. (1662) 361 'If any man sin we have a Paraclete with the Father, Jesus Christ the righteous'..saith S. John. *a* **1700** DRYDEN *Veni, Creator Spiritus* 8 O source of uncreated light, The Father's promised Paraclete! *a* **1714** ABP. SHARP *Serm.* (1738) V. 29 In the Te Deum, 'also the Holy Ghost the Paraclete': for that is the word in the original. **1843** NEALE *Hymns for Sick* (1863) 58 Consoler of our hearts, Blest Paraclete! **1884** J. PARKER *Larger Ministry* 21.
transf. **1871** MORLEY *Crit. Misc.*, *Carlyle* Ser. I. 238 With him [Carlyle]..The victorious hero is the true Paraclete.

†**2.** *gen.* An advocate or intercessor. *Obs.*

1550 BALE *Image Both Ch.* III. xviii. Bbv, Braggynge Winchester, the Popes paraclete in Englande, that is mayster of the Stewes at London. **1581** N. BURNE in *Cath. Tract.* (S.T.S.) 126 Your paraclet Theodore Beze is constranit to deny this pairt of the scripture. **1701** tr. *Le Clerc's Prim. Fathers* (1702) 82 [Plato] has likewise used in one place, the term Paraclete, Intercessor, in speaking of the Reason.

paraclinical (pærə'klɪnɪkəl), *a.* *Med.* [f. PARA-[1] + CLINICAL *a.*] Of or pertaining to the branches of medicine, esp. the laboratory sciences, that provide a service for patients without direct involvement in their care.

1961 *Lancet* 29 July 255/2 In each case paraclinical laboratories have been included in the main complex of buildings. **1968** *Rep. R. Comm. Med. Educ. 1965–8* 85 in *Parl. Papers 1967–8* (Cmnd. 3569) XXV. 569 A course of clinical instruction which includes..such paraclinical subjects as pathology and microbiology. **1971** *Inside Kenya Today* Mar. 15/2 The A.I.D. regional programme has given assistance to the Veterinary Faculty..including commodities necessary for the construction and equipping of a paraclinical building.

paraclose, obs. variant of PARCLOSE.

‖**paracme** (pə'rækmi:). [a. Gr. παρακμή the point at which the prime or strength is past, f. παρα- past, beyond + ἀκμή culmination, ACME.] A point or period at which the prime or highest vigour is past; the point when the crisis of a fever is past. So **parac'mastic**, †**parac'mastical** *a.* [Gr. παρακμαστικός, F. *paracmastique*, 15th c.], past the culmination or crisis.

1656 BLOUNT *Glossogr.*, *Paracmastical*, pertaining to a..feaver, wherein the heat, when it is at the greatest, by little and little diminisheth till it ceaseth. **1706** PHILLIPS, *Paracme*, the declining of a Distemper, when its Rage is abated, and the Patient judg'd beyond Danger. **1730–6** BAILEY (folio), *Paracme*, that part of life, in which a person is said to grow old, and which, according to Galen, is from 35 to 49. **1892** *Syd. Soc. Lex.*, *Paracmastic*, past the prime or the time of vigour; past the crisis. *Paracme*, the point at which the prime is past; the commencement of old age;..the period in a fever after the occurrence of the crisis.

paracolpitis to **paracresol**: see PARA-[1] 1, 2.

paracone ('pærəkəʊn). [f. PARA-[1] + CONE *sb.*[1]] An external cusp on the front, outer corner of a mammalian upper molar tooth.

1888 H. F. OSBORN in *Amer. Naturalist* XXII. 1072 (*table*) Proposed terms... Paracone. **1896** *Proc. Zool. Soc.* 563 The first two upper molars [of the hedgehog] are..provided with two well-developed external cones, the paracone and metacone. **1922** W. K. GREGORY *Origin & Evolution Human Dentition* I. 74 It seems very likely that the high apex of the upper-molar crowns [in the marsupial mole] is really the paracone. **1934** W. E. LE GROS CLARK *Early Forerunners of Man* iv. 71 The premolars of a generalized mammal would be of simple form with a single pointed cusp which in the upper teeth is called the paracone and in the lower the protoconid. **1971** W. A. CLEMENS in A. A. Dahlberg *Dental Morphol. & Evolution* x. 187 The paracone and metacone of Cretaceous marsupials were maintained at approximately equal height.

paraconformity: see PARA-[1] 1.

paraconid (pærə'kəʊnɪd). [f. PARACON(E + -ID[5].] A cusp on a mammalian lower molar tooth corresponding to the paracone on an upper molar.

1888 H. F. OSBORN in *Amer. Naturalist* XXII. 1072 (*table*) Proposed terms... Paraconid. *Ibid.* 1076 As the hypocone develops, the paraconid recedes. **1896** *Proc. Zool. Soc.* 564 The ordinal position of the paraconid in the ontogeny may seem rather strange. **1904**, etc. [see METACONID]. **1922** W. K. GREGORY *Origin & Evolution Human Dentition* I. 84 It seems probable that the paraconid, metaconid, and entoconid, arose *in situ* on the slopes of the protoconid. **1970** *Nature* 25 July 356/1 The presence of a paraconid in such a position is more characteristic of fossil lemuroids and omomyoids. **1975** [see METACONID].

†**paracood**, obs. f. BARRACUDA, a W. Indian fish.

1685 L. WAFER *Voy.* (1729) 340 They have Paracoods also,..a long and round fish, about as large as a well-grown pike.

paracrine ('pærəkri:n), *a.* *Physiol.* [ad. G. *parakrin*, f. Gr. παρα- PARA-[1] + κρίν-ειν to separate (cf. ENDOCRINE *a.* and *sb.*).] Used of the action of a hormone whose effects are only local, and of the tissues which release and respond to such a hormone.

1972 F. FEYRTER in *Endocrinol. 1971* 137 The hypothesis of the peripheral entodermal endocrine (paracrine) glands was confirmed (1) by the evidence of a pressor agent in the enteral carcinoid.., (2) by the discovery of the islet cells of the pancreatic duct with A and B cells, their endocrine function having already been established. **1976** *Nature* 8 July 92/3 The actions of this hormone are paracrine, directed that is to neighbouring cells and tissue, rather than truly endocrine. **1978** *Ibid.* 20 Apr. 730/2 Further investigations related to the possible release of other endogenous substances or peptides, such as vasopressin or those of the paracrine system of the gut, where enkephalin immunoreactivity has been demonstrated, are needed.

paracrostic (pærə'krɒstɪk). [f. PAR(A-[1] + ACROSTIC.] (See quot.)

1842 BRANDE *Dict. Sci.* etc., *Paracrostic*, a poetical composition in which the first verse contains, in order, all the letters which commence the remaining verses of the poem or division. According to Cicero (*De Divinatione*, ii. 54), the original Sibylline verses were paracrostics.

paracrystal ('pærəkrɪstəl). [f. PARA-[1] + CRYSTAL *sb.* and *a.*] An assemblage of particles that has some degree of order but is not a true crystal.

1933 *Trans. Faraday Soc.* XXIX. 1019 On addition of acetone to a cold saturated solution in acetic ester of phytosterin valerate the latter..separates out as a paracrystal. **1953** S. E. LURIA *Gen. Virol.* v. 94 In the needles, which should more correctly be called 'paracrystals', the individual rods are oriented sidewise with great regularity. **1956** *Nature* 10 Mar. 473/1 The great regularity of plant viruses is shown even more strikingly by their ability to form crystals (or paracrystals) which give good X-ray photographs. **1970** *Jrnl. Biochem.* (Tokyo) LXVIII. 885/1 Paracrystals are formed by side-by-side association of F-actin particles in the presence of an excess amount of $MgCl_2$.

Hence **para'crystalline** *a.*, of the nature of a paracrystal; ˌ**paracrysta'llinity**.

1933 *Trans. Faraday Soc.* XXIX. 1027 An especially strong paracrystallinity is to be ascribed to the paracrystalline sperm heads of Sepia officinalis. **1950** W. J. MOORE *Physical Chem.* xiv. 408 The compound ethyl-anisol-paraäminocinnamate passes through three distinct paracrystalline phases between 83° and 139°. **1964** G. H. HAGGIS et al. *Introd. Molecular Biol.* xi. 283 The haemoglobin in cells which had taken up the sickle shape was in para-crystalline, or tactoid form. **1974** *Amer. Jrnl. Anat.* CXXXIX. 135 Paracrystalline aggregates of microtubules were observed by electron microscopy in some cells of the anterior pituitary glands from ten untreated chinchillas.

paracy'anogen. *Chem.* [PARA-[1] 2.] An isomer or polymer of cyanogen, a dark brown porous substance formed in small quantity when cyanogen is prepared from cyanide of mercury. So **para'cyanate**, **paracy'anic** *adjs.*, **para'cyanide**.

1854 J. SCOFFERN in *Orr's Circ. Sc.*, *Chem.* 500 Cyanide of mercury..evolving cyanogen and metallic mercury when heated in a close vessel, and leaving a black residue termed paracyanogen. **1857** MAYNE *Expos. Lex.*, *Paracyanate*..applied by Berzelius to a fulminate. *Ibid.*, *Paracyanicus*..applied by Berzelius to fulminic acid, because, though having the same composition as cyanic acid, it widely differs in relation to its properties: paracyanic. **1864** H. SPENCER *Biol.* I. 7 In paracyanogen, formed of the same proportions of these elements in higher multiples, we have a solid which does not fuse or volatilize at ordinary temperatures. **1866** WATTS *Dict. Chem.* IV. 342 Paracyanide of silver.

paracyesis, paracystitis *Path.*: see PARA-[1].

paracyst ('pærəsɪst). *Bot.* [PARA-[1] 1.] One of a pair of sexual organs in certain Fungi.

1874 COOKE *Fungi* 175 In the middle of these [utricles] are generated elongated clavate cells..which Tulasne names paracysts. **1884** H. M. WARD in *Q. Jrnl. Microscop. Sci.* XXIV. 280 The paracyst is a club-shaped branchlet, close to the macrocyst; the apex of the paracyst and the hook-like prolongation [of the macrocyst] become united.

†**parada, -ado.** *Obs.* [app. an altered form (see -ADO 2) of F. *parade*, which at a later date was adopted unchanged. Sometimes held to be taken direct from Sp. *parada*, but the latter was not used in these senses: see PARADE *sb.*]

1. Pomp, show, display, ostentation; = PARADE I.

1621 MOLLE *Camerar. Liv. Libr.* I. x. 31 All this parado and goodly shew declineth. **1656** *Artif. Handsom.* 82 The great pomp or princely parada used by Queen Berenice, and her train of women. **1660** WATERHOUSE *Arms & Arm.* 123 No Court Paradoe, or Munificence was read of. **1689** *Def. Liberty agst. Tyrants* 137 Pompeous Paradoes and Shows.

2. A muster or display of troops; = PARADE 2.

1625 F. MARKHAM *Bk. Hon.* II. ix. §4 It may be done..in March, in Campe or on the head of a Parado. **1640** GLAPTHORNE *Wallenstein* IV. ii. Wks. (1874) II. 64 In their best furniture of Armes, all drawne Into parada.

3. Muster, 'turn-out'. *rare.*

a **1639** WOTTON *Life Dk. Buckhm.* in *Reliq.* (1651) 84 These five [Pr. Charles, Buckingham, and 3 attendants] were at the first the whole Parada of this Journey.

4. = PARADE *sb.* 4 and 5.

(In quots. 1653, 1690 applied to the *Prado* at Madrid.)
1652 EARL MONM. tr. *Bentivoglio's Hist. Relat.* 141 A large field, between Mastrick and Aquisgrane, where the Parado [*piazza d'arme*] was made. **1653** A. WILSON *Jas. I* 228 The King and Prince had some interviews in their Coaches passing to the Parada to take the Air. **1654** EARL MONM. tr. *Bentivoglio's Warrs Flanders* 383 In midst of the Parado, a Church was intended to be built. **1690** SHADWELL *Am. Bigot* I. 6 In the Evening we'l drive in the Parado.

‖**5.** = PARADE *sb.* 6.

1865 tr. *Erckmann-Chatrian's Waterloo* (1870) 98 Parada and riposte must have come like lightning.

para'dactyl. *Ornith.* [ad. mod.L. *paradactylum* (Illiger; also in Eng. use), f. Gr. παρα- beside, PARA-[1] + δάκτυλος finger]. (See quots.)

[**1811** ILLIGER *Prodrom. System. Mamm. et Avium* 178 Paradactylum, pagina lateralis digiti, pelmatis pars digitum spectans.] **1857** MAYNE *Expos. Lex.*, *Paradactylum*,..applied by Illiger to the lateral portions of the toes of birds, to distinguish it..from the inferior surface: the paradactyle. **1874** COUES *N. Amer. Birds* III. 531 Side of toes (*Paradactylum*) the sides, in any way distinguished from the toes.

Hence **para'dactylar** *a.*, of or pertaining to the paradactyl.

1890 *Cent. Dict.* s.v., The marginal lobes [etc.] of birds' toes are paradactylar.

parade (pə'reɪd), *sb.* [a. F. *parade* (15th c. in Hatz.-Darm.), 'a (boasting) apparance, or shew; a brauado, or vaunting offer' (Cotgr.); ad. It. *parata* 'a warding or defending; a dighting or garish setting forth' (Florio 1611), Sp. *parada* 'a staying or stopping, also, a standing or staying place' (Minsheu 1599); L. type **parāta*, from *parāre*.

L. parāre to make ready, procure, prepare, furnish, in late L. to deck, adorn, developed many senses in Romanic; e.g. in It. (1) 'to adorne, dight, decke, beautifie, set foorth, furnish, garnish, prouide', (2) 'to prepare to receive (a blow), to ward off, defend, cover, shield', (3) 'to teach a horse to stop and staie orderly', to make 'the stop in the action of horsemanship' (Florio). In Sp. *parar* is 'to stop, stay, rest, end, be at a non-plus, pause' (Minsheu). All the senses occur in Fr. The sb., It. *parata*, Sp. *parada*, might occur in any of the senses of the vb. used in the lang. Fr. has app. taken senses of *parade* from both. Cf. also L. *magno paratu* with great preparation, provision, or display.]

I. 1. Show, display, ostentation. ***to make a parade of***, to display ostentatiously.

1656 BLOUNT *Glossogr.*, *Parade*, an appearance or shew, a bravado or vaunting offer. **1663** COWLEY *Cromwell* Wks. 1710 II. 658 The most virtuous and laudable Deed that his whole Life could have made any Parade of. **1700** T. BROWN *Amusem. Ser. & Com.* 150 To make a fine Parade of his own good Qualities and Vertues. **1759** HUME *Hist. Eng.* (1812) IV. xxviii. 16 A new display of that state and parade to which he was so much addicted. **1789** BELSHAM *Ess.* I. xii. 217 Making an empty parade of knowledge which we do not really possess. **1812** *Gen. Hist.* in *Ann. Reg.* 22 The unseemly parade of his funeral. **1850** TENNYSON *In Mem.* xxi, Another answers, 'Let him be, He loves to make parade of pain'.

2. a. An assembling or mustering of troops for inspection or display; esp. a muster of troops which takes place regularly at set hours, or at extraordinary times to hear orders read, as a preparation for a march, or any other special purpose.

1656 BLOUNT *Glossogr.*, *Parade*..is also a term of War, and commonly used for that appearance of Souldiers in a Garrison about two or three of the clock in the afternoon, to hear prayers, and after that to recieve Orders from the Major for the Watch, and Guards next night. **1667** MILTON *P.L.* IV. 780 The Cherubim..stood armd To thir night watches in warlike Parade. **1769–72** *Junius Lett.* xxx. 138, I shall leave it to military men, who have seen a service more active than the parade. **1831** LYTTON *Godolph.* vi, He was not very much bored by drills and parade. **1859** *Musketry Instr.* 69 Permitted to be absent from afternoon parade.

b. The men appearing on parade.

1844 *Regul. & Ord. Army* 260 The Commanding Officer is then to direct the Parade to Order Arms. **1930** E. RAYMOND *Jesting Army* I. iii. 45 A medical officer..and the whole of his Sick Parade ran.

3. a. A march or procession; esp. in *U.S.*, a procession, organized on a grand scale, in support of some political object.

1673–4 DK. LAUDERDALE in *L. Papers* (Camden) III. xxiv. 36 They went up with a Parade of 9 or 10 Coaches. **1731** SWIFT *Strephon & Chloe* Misc. 1735 V. 33 The Rites perform'd, the Parson paid, In State return'd the grand Parade. **1810** CRABBE *Borough* xxiv, Not a sweet ramble, but a slow parade. **1888** BRYCE *Amer. Commw.* II. III. lxxi. 580 When a procession is exceptionally large, it is called a Parade. *Ibid.* 581 *note*, In the Cleveland Business Men's parade it was alleged that 1500 lawyers had walked.

b. An assembly of people; esp. a crowd of promenaders.

1722 DE FOE *Col. Jack* (1840) 107 We saw a great parade, or kind of meeting. *a* **1845** HOOD *Storm at Hastings* xiii, The gay Parade grew thin—all the fair crowd Vanish'd. **1871** R. ELLIS *Catullus* lv. 6 Where flocks the parade to Magnus' arches. **1873** BLACK *Pr. Thule* xvii. 265 'Did she go into that parade of people?' said Ingram.

c. Easter Parade, a crowd of promenaders in new clothes at Eastertime; a parade or pageant held at Eastertime. Hence **Easter-Parading** *vbl. sb.*

1904 'O. HENRY' in *N.Y. World Mag.* 27 Mar. 10/4 Will it tire you to be told again that Aileen was beautiful? Had she ..joined the Easter parade,..you would have hastened to say so yourself. **1933** I. BERLIN *Easter Parade* (song), In your Easter bonnet..you'll be the grandest lady In that Easter Parade. **1942** O. NASH *Good Intentions* 5 Life is an Easter Parade. **1968** *New Statesman* 26 Apr. 544/3 In a sense, I suppose, this informal Easter Parading..is a middle-class demo. **1973** *Times* 24 Apr. 12/7 Several thousand people turned up at Battersea Park for the Easter Parade.

d. *transf. spec.* of broadcasting, a sequence or recital of forthcoming programmes, events, etc.

1947 *Radio Times* (Scottish ed.) 2 May 8/1 Scottish Programme Parade. **1948** *Broadcasting in West* (B.B.C.), Listen to your regional Programme Parade at 8.10 a.m. daily. **1962** *Rep. Comm. Broadcasting 1960* 255 in *Parl. Papers 1961–2* (Cmnd. 1753) IX. 259 Broadcast of a half-hour 'parade' of new advertisements.

4. The place where troops assemble for parade; the level space forming the interior or enclosed area of a fortification; a parade-ground.

1704 J. HARRIS *Lex. Techn.* I, *Parade*, is a Military word, signifying the Place where Troops usually draw together, in order to mount the Guards, or for any other Service. **1748** *Anson's Voy.* III. x. 407 Two hundred soldiers..conducted him to the great parade before the Emperor's palace... In this parade, a body of troops..were drawn up under arms. **1844** *Regul. & Ord. Army* 240 When Barracks are occupied by Troops, the Yards and Parades are to be swept, rolled, and kept clean by them.

5. A public square or promenade; sometimes the name of a street. Freq. used of a row of shops in a town, and of the street in which they are situated.

1697 DAMPIER *Voy.* I. 219 (Leon) The Square is called the Parade. **1712** E. COOKE *Voy. S. Sea* 149 Before the Church of Santiago is a very handsome Parade. **1766** C. ANSTEY *New Bath Guide* ix. 57 Whether thou art wont to rove By Parade, or Orange Grove,..In the Circus or the Square. **1775** SHERIDAN *Rivals* I. i, We saunter on the parades [at Bath]. **1791** F. BURNEY *Jrnl.* 20 Aug. (1972) I. 35 O how I have thought..of my poor Mrs. Thrale!—I went to look..at the House on the North Parade where we dwelt. **1834** SOUTHEY *Doctor* xi. (1862) 29 In what street, parade, place, square, row, terrace, or lane..will be explained in due time. **1862** HAWTHORNE *Our Old Home* (1883) I. 85 The smart parades and crescents of the former town. **1885** *List of Subscribers, Brighton* (South of Eng. Telephone Co.) 5 Vizer E.B...154, Marine-parade. **1968** R. K. COX *Retail Site Assessment* ii. 15 Most new shopping centres..have broken away from the old strip parades which usually face each other across heavy inter-town traffic. **1970** *Times* 9 Mar. 15/2 It is convenient for the local shopper to have a compact shopping area..to provide in modern terms the facilities offered by the small local 'parades' of the 1930s. **1976** *Derbyshire Times* (Peak ed.) 3 Sept. 18/6 (Advt.), A vacant shop having a total area of 710 sq. feet, situated in a parade of shops and in a busy location. **1976** P. HILL *Hunters* viii. 95 The small parade of shops near the village hall.

II. 6. *Fencing.* = PARRY. [Fr. *parade*, It. *parata*.]

1692 SIR W. HOPE *Fencing-Master* 20 The Lessons Defensive are commonly called the Parade. *Ibid.*, Parades or wayes of defending. *Ibid.*, Two Parades, the Parade in Quart, and the Parade in Terce. **1727–41** CHAMBERS *Cycl.* s.v., There are as many kinds of Parades, as of strokes and attacks. **1834** *Encycl. Brit.* (ed. 7) VI. 502 A parade is a defence of the body, made by an opposition of one's blade to that of an adversary.

fig. **1699** LOCKE *Educ.* §94. 152 Marks, which serve best to shew, what they [men] are..especially when they are not in Parade and upon their Guard.

III. 7. *attrib.* and *Comb.* (mostly connected with sense 2), as ***parade attire, -day, -duty, horse, major, -march, officer, order, -step***; **parade drum**, a large drum played at a parade; **parade-rest**, a position of rest, less fatiguing than that of 'attention', in which the soldier stands silent and motionless, much used during reviews; also ***parade-like*** adj.

1755 *Mem. Capt. P. Drake* II. iii. 78 The Trenches were levelled,..and then I lost the Title of Parade Major. **1806** HUTTON *Course Math.* I. 149 The slow or parade-step being 70 paces per minute. **1807** W. TAYLOR in *Ann. Rev.* V. 576 They are chiefly parade letters to men of celebrity. **1813** MAR. EDGEWORTH *Patron.* (1833) I. vii. 126 A mere parade officer, who had never been out of London. **1831** CARLYLE *Sart. Res.* II. ii, Andreas too attended Church..like a parade-duty, for which he in the other world expected pay with arrears. **1888** *Century Mag.* XXXVII. 465/1 Not a man moved from the military posture of 'parade-rest'. **1894** *Rep. Vermont Board Agric.* XIV. 123 The descendants of Woodbury Morgan..possess that peculiar qualification necessary for the parade horse. **1963** M. LAURENCE in R. Weaver *Canad. Short Stories* (1968) 2nd Ser. 115 From Captain Fossey..the boy learned how to play the parade drum. **1967** W. SOYINKA *Kongi's Harvest* 64 The Big parade drum is heard. **1968** 'J. LE CARRÉ' *Small Town in Germany* ii. 21 Lieff, an empty-headed parade horse from Protocol Department, sat on his left. **1974** —— *Tinker, Tailor* xvi. 132, I refuse to bequeath my life's work to a parade horse.

parade (pəˈreɪd), *v.* [f. prec. sb.: cf. F. *parader* (1784 in Hatz.-Darm.).]

1. a. *trans.* To assemble (troops, etc.) for the sake of inspection or review: see PARADE *sb.* 2.

1686 [see PARADING *vbl. sb.*]. **1755** *Mem. Capt. P. Drake* II. iii. 73 He [the General] thought me more capable to parade the Workmen, and detach them..for the respective Works. **1799** WELLINGTON in Gurwood *Desp.* (1837) I. 26 The troops were paraded. **1887** BOWEN *Virg. Æneid* v. 550 Bid him parade his troop in his grandsire's honour.

transf. and *fig.* **1881** ROSSETTI *Ball. & Sonn.* (1882) 208 While Memory's art Parades the Past before thy face. **1890** 'R. BOLDREWOOD' *Miner's Right* (1899) 87/1 Robbing the mail, and parading every traveller on a certain line of road with almost ludicrous impartiality.

b. *intr. Mil.* Of troops, to assemble for parade. Also *transf.*

1802 C. JAMES *New Mil. Dict.*, *To parade*, to assemble in a prescribed regular manner, for the purpose of being inspected, exercised, or mustered. **1811** *Gen. Regulations* (Army) 102 All Guards are to parade with shouldered Arms. **1914** T. A. BAGGS *Back from Front* xxiv. 122 We paraded for marching at 9 a.m., and set off with two manacled prisoners ..before us. **1916** W. OWEN *Let.* 1 Feb. (1967) 377 Of course I 'paraded sick', but having no rash, I just have to crouch in my Hut. **1930** E. RAYMOND *Jesting Army* III. ii. 292 The working parties parade under the trees at nine o'clock. **1964** M. BANTON *Policeman in Community* ii. 15 He 'parades' at the beat box where he meets the constable coming off duty.

2. *intr.* To march in procession or with great display or ostentation; to walk up and down or promenade in a public place, esp. for the sake of 'showing off'.

1748 *Anson's Voy.* II. vi. 196 These troops paraded about the hill with great ostentation..practising every art to intimidate us. **1781** GIBBON *Decl. & F.* xlviii. (1869) III. 27 He paraded through the streets with a thousand banners. **1800** MRS. HERVEY *Mourtray Fam.* ix. 194 If I had my way, I would parade all the morning up and down the fashionable side of Bond Street. **1840** DICKENS *Barn. Rudge* lxvi, In this order they paraded off with a horrible merriment.

3. *trans.* To march through (a place of public resort) in procession or with great display; to walk up and down or promenade (some place) esp. for the sake of 'showing off'.

1809 W. IRVING *Knickerb.* VI. viii, Venus..in semblance of a blear-eyed trull paraded the battlements of Fort Christina. **1814** SOUTHEY *Roderick* v. 84 Have we not seen Favila's shameless wife..parade Our towns with regal pageantry? **1855** PRESCOTT *Philip II*, I. II. vi. 211 Throwing themselves into a procession, they paraded the streets of the city.

4. To march (a person) up and down or through the streets either for show or to expose him to contempt. Also *refl.*

1807 JEFFERSON *Writ.* (1830) IV. 89 The idea of a chief magistrate parading himself through the several States as an object of public gaze. **1886** R. F. BURTON *Arab. Nts.* (abr. ed.) I. 296 They set him on a camel and paraded him about the city.

5. *intr.* To make a parade; to behave, talk, or write ostentatiously; to 'show off'. Also in phr. ***to parade it***. *rare* or *Obs.*

1754 RICHARDSON *Grandison* (1766) V. 46 The whole family paraded it together. **1760–72** H. BROOKE *Fool of Qual.* (1809) III. 38 He paraded and shewed away.. concerning the divinely inherent right of monarchs. **1807–8** SYD. SMITH *Plymley's Lett.* Wks. 1859 II. 158/2 You parade a great deal upon the vast concessions made by this country to the Irish, before the Union.

6. *trans.* To make a parade of, to display or hold out to view ostentatiously, to 'show off'.

1818 LADY MORGAN *Autobiog.* (1859) 32, I thought I would amuse him a little by parading the whole Irish system of things before him. **1838** LYTTON *Alice* v. ii, A great man never loses so much as when he exhibits intolerance, or parades the right of persecution. **1865** MISS BRADDON *Sir Jasper's Tenant* ii, The very last..to parade his feelings.. before the eyes of his fellow men. **1878** BROWNING *Poets Croisic* cxl, Don't linger here in Paris to parade Your victory.

7. *nonce-use.* To provide (a town, etc.) with a parade or parades.

1889 HISSEY *Tour in Phaeton* 191 The modern part that faces the sea is..paraded, well lighted, well drained.

Hence **paˈraded** *ppl. a.*

1865 MRS. G. L. BANKS *Tried & true* in Harland *Lanc. Lyrics* 277 From paraded assistance I turn'd with disdain. **1876** BROWNING *A Forgiveness* 337 Worse than all, Each day's procession, my paraded life Robb'd and impoverished through the wanting wife.

paˈradeful, *a. rare.* [See -FUL.] Full of parade or display.

1755 RICHARDSON *Corr.* (1804) III. 224 Supper, as paradeful a one as if it were a less frugal meal than it always is at Parson's-Green, enters.

parade-ground. orig. *U.S.* [PARADE *sb.*] A place where troops parade; now the more usual term than PARADE *sb.* 4.

1724 in Temple & Sheldon *Hist. Northfield, Mass.* (1875) 200 If the enemy get within the parade ground. **1843** N. BOONE *Jrnl.* 31 July in L. Pelzer *Marches of Dragoons* (1917) 237 By one o'clock our command was formed on the parade ground of Fort Gibson. **1846** T. L. MCKENNEY *Mem.* I. v. 103 The level of the ground, and its freedom from undergrowth, were such as to give it the appearance of a parade ground. **1891** *Century Mag.* Mar. 715 The rats were so numerous that they were common sights on the parade-ground. **1933** H. H. SYMONDS *Walking in Lake District* ii. 44 Before reaching the camp you pass..the 'parade ground', a large square of cleared ground. **1975** J. CLEARY *Safe House* i. 18 Camp 93...long huts, a parade ground with a pock-marked surface. **1977** D. BEATY *Excellency* xx. 221 The Major led the way outside... The parade ground..was floodlit.

b. *transf.* and *attrib.*, esp. in phr. ***parade-ground bearing, manner, voice***, etc.

1863 'G. HAMILTON' *Gala-Days* 174 Besides abundance of food and parade ground, these happy fowls have a very agreeable prospect. **1867** A. D. WHITNEY *Summer in L. Goldthwaite's Life* vi. 129 Clothes-lines like a parade-ground of telegraphs. **1892** *Harper's Mag.* Dec. 137 Both dismounted at the parade-ground gate. **1932** *Times Lit. Suppl.* 29 Sept. 693/4 The preposterous chief constable is of no use at all, and his parade-ground manners make a suitable contrast to Colonel Gethryn's cool and gentlemanly efficiency. **1937** 'M. INNES' *Hamlet, Revenge!* I. iv. 74 The precocious bass, favoured on public-school parade-grounds. **1937** J. R. FIRTH *Tongues of Men* 41 There is a well-known Prussian parade-ground type of voice. **1944** J. D. CARR *Till Death do us Part* i. 8 Major Horace Price..had made a trumpet of his hands and was addressing them in a parade-ground voice. **1961** M. BEADLE *These Ruins are Inhabited* (1963) ii. 28 He expected the boys to have a parade-ground bearing. *a* **1963** S. PLATH *Crossing Water* (1971) 23 Pawing like paradeground horses. **1964** L. DEIGHTON *Funeral in Berlin* iv. 25 The parade ground of Europe has always been that vast area..that stretches eastward from the Elbe. **1965** *New Statesman* 9 Apr. 558/3 In a peremptory parade-ground voice Lord Balniel repeatedly bellowed the name of the current occupant of the chair ('Sir Herbert!' 'Sir Samuel!') in an effort to raise points of order. **1973** 'M. INNES' *Appleby's Answer* xvi. 138 He had a..parade-ground manner. **1976** R. CONDON *Whisper of Axe* I. xxi. 130 A spit-and-polish, parade-ground major. **1978** R. LEWIS *Uncertain Sound* vi. 189 He was all tension..no longer the stiff, military, parade ground bearing.

paradeless (pəˈreɪdlɪs), *a.* [See -LESS.] Without parade; lacking a parade.

1872 M. COLLINS *Two Plunges for Pearl* III. vi. 137 A clubless paradeless..city.

paradenitis, etc.: see PARA-[1].

parader (pəˈreɪdə(r)). [f. PARADE *v.* + -ER[1].] One who parades: in the senses of the verb.

1748 RICHARDSON *Clarissa* (1811) II. i. 3 What think you, ..rejecting both your men, and encouraging my parader? **1824** SCOTT *Redgauntlet* ch. xviii, Bring me the parader's gage. **1888** *Voice* (N.Y.) 27 Sept., The paraders marched in to swell the multitudes.

paraderm (ˈpærədɜːm). *Biol.* [f. Gr. παρα-, PARA-[1], in sense 'subsidiary', 'by-' + δέρμα skin.] The delicate membrane enclosing the pronymph of some dipterous insects.

1895 *Cambr. Nat. Hist.* V. 164 Lowne,..looking on the limiting membrane as a subsequent formation,..calls it the paraderm. **1895** in *Funk's Standard Dict.*

‖**paradiastole** (ˌpærədaɪˈæstəliː). *Rhet. Obs.* [L., a. Gr. παραδιαστολή 'putting together of dissimilar things', f. παρα- side by side + διαστολή separation, distinction.] A figure in which a favourable turn is given to something unfavourable by the use of an expression that conveys only part of the truth. **b.** (See quot. 1657.)

1586 A. DAY *Eng. Secretary* II. (1625) 84 *Paradiastole*, when with a milde interpretation or speech wee colour others or our owne faults, as when we call a subtile person, wise; a bold fellow, couragious; a prodigall man, liberall. **1589** PUTTENHAM *Eng. Poesie* III. xvii. (Arb.) 195 The figure Paradiastole, which..nothing improperly we call the Curry-fauell. **1657** J. SMITH *Myst. Rhet.* 113 Paradiastole is a dilating or enlarging of a matter by interpretation. A figure when we grant one thing that we may deny another. *Ibid.* 115 This figure paradiastole is by some learned Rhetoricians called a faulty tearm of speech, opposing the truth by false tearms and wrong names. **1706** PHILLIPS, *Paradiastole*,..a Figure which disjoyns things that seem to have one Import, and shews how much they differ.

Hence †**paradiˈastolary** *a.*

1652 URQUHART *Jewel* Wks. (1834) 292 Figurative expressions,..paradoxical, paramologetick, paradiastolary.

paradichlorobenzene: see PARA-[1] 2 b.

paradiddle (ˈpærədɪd(ə)l). *Mus.* [Echoic.] A basic drum roll, produced by alternate beating with the left-hand and right-hand drumsticks.

1927 *Melody Maker* Aug. 804/3 The ordinary paradiddle is greatly to be recommended. This is a wonderful exercise for getting out of 'one-hand' playing, and there are some variations of this beat which are invaluable to the dance drummer. **1934** *Metronome* Feb. 47 Either the single paradiddle or the flam paradiddle may be used during a marching step. **1941** *Amer. Speech* XVI. 229/2 The ramatacue and the paradiddle are advanced rhythmic drum movements, the words possibly being onomatopoeic. **1956** L. MCINTOSH *Oxford Folly* 153 Fiona thought hard for a moment of a negro Staff-Sergeant in the American Air Force whom she had once seen throwing the whole of the University Jazz Club into a prolonged ecstasy with an erotic and protracted paradiddle... But the drumsticks in her inexpert hands refused to make a smooth roll. **1960** K. AMIS *Take Girl like You* xvii. 210 A great saccharine growl came from the organ and a slow-motion paradiddle from the drums. **1961** A. BAINES *Mus. Instruments* 337 At a steady march tempo, with eight strokes on the drum in each bar, the sound of the paradiddle is fascinating. **1976** D. MUNROW *Instruments Middle Ages & Renaissance* 33/4 The specialized techniques of the side drum, such as the roll, flam, drag, and paradiddle developed in the first instance to fulfil a practical object: to encourage friend and frighten the foe.

paradidymal, -didymis: see PARA-[1] I.

paradigm ('pærədɪm, -daɪm). Also 7 **-digme.** [a. F. *paradigme*, ad. L. *paradīgma*, a. Gr. παράδειγμα pattern, example, f. παραδεικνύ-ναι to exhibit beside, show side by side. Formerly also in L. form.]

1. a. A pattern, exemplar, example.

1483 Caxton *Gold. Leg.* 208/1 We now haue none enterpretour of the parablys ne paradygmes. **1576** Fleming *Panopl. Epist.* Bj, Giue me a paradigme or example, of a deliberatiue kinde of epistle. **1669** Gale *Crt. Gentiles* I. III. iii. 45 The Universe.. was made exactly conformable to its Paradigme, or universal Exemplar. **1752** J. Gill *Trinity* v. 91 The archetype, paradigm, exemplar, and idea, according to which all things were made. **1875** Jowett *Plato* (ed. 2) IV. 133 Socrates makes one more attempt to defend the Platonic ideas by representing them as paradigms.

b. *attrib.*, as **paradigm case**, a case or instance to be regarded as representative or typical.

1955 J. L. Austin *How to do Things with Words* (1962) xi. 132 We were content to refer to 'statements' as the typical or paradigm case. **1962** *Listener* 4 Oct. 516/1 Plato's morality is supported and underlined by his theory of Forms, according to which mathematics is the paradigm case of knowledge. **1965** *Mod. Law Rev.* XXVIII. 509 The paradigm case at first instance—the core situation—appears to absorb so much attention that little concern is expended on the appeal process. **1974** *Jrnl. Philos.* LXXI. 337 Nagel employs a fairly standard 'paradigm case argument' in his analysis. **1977** *Canad. Jrnl. Linguistics* XXII. I. 13 A paradigm case is Anderson's description of Breton vowel lowering.

†**2.** *Rhet.* (In L. form.) See quot. *Obs.*

1586 A. Day *Eng. Secretary* II. (1625) 100 *Paradigma*, a manner of exhorting or with-drawing by example, as to say ..'the nature of the Dolphin is not to suffer the yong one of her kinde to straggle vndefenced'. **1589** Puttenham *Eng. Poesie* III. xix. (Arb.) 252 *margin, Paradigma*, or a resemblance by example.

3. a. An example or pattern of the inflexion of a noun, verb, or other inflected part of speech.

1599 Minsheu *Span. Gram.* 20 Now it remaineth to giue a Paradigma or example of euery Coniugation of their Moodes. **1698** Wallis in *Phil. Trans.* XX. 358 It will be convenient.. to Write him out a full Paradigm of some one Verb. **1859** Max Müller *Sc. Lang.* (1861) 81 Paradigms of regular and irregular nouns and verbs. **1892** Davidson *Hebr. Gram.* 72 Skeleton paradigm of the regular verb.

b. *transf.* and *fig.*

1929 C. Day Lewis *Transitional Poem* II. 25, I would be pædagogue—hear poplar, lime And oak recite the seasons' paradigm. **1964** *Listener* 6 Aug. 200/2 If one uses the word 'paradigm' as Wittgenstein himself used it, to denote a logical or conceptual structure serving us as a form of thought within a given area of experience. **1966** A. F. Parker-Rhodes in *Automatic Transl. of Lang.* (NATO Summer School, Venice, 1962) 173 The concept of paradigm thus enables us to approach the problem of mathematizing the process of syntactic description with greatly enhanced resources. **1970** *Eng. Stud.* LI. 18 Although Ohmann determines objective criteria to state the similarity (and at the same time the dissimilarity), there still remains a whole paradigm of related structures out of which the author has to choose the particular alternative(s) to match the marked term with. *Ibid.* 46 But, of course, for her Edwardian family life is a convenient paradigm of civilisation as a whole. **1973** C. Sagan *Cosmic Connection* (1974) xxiii. 155 There is a generation of men and women for whom.. the Moon was the paradigm of the unattainable. **1973** *Times Lit. Suppl.* 2 Mar. 238/4 The unfolding of terror and duplicity which follows is easily seen as a paradigm of the suppression of Dubček's liberalizing administration. **1973** *Nature* 6 July 59/3 The use of induced epilepsy as an 'interfering technique' in the study of learning and memory paradigms. **1975** *Language* LI. 1009 The publication of Chomsky's *Syntactic structures* provided a new paradigm for linguistics. **1976** T. Eagleton *Crit. & Ideology* i. 19 In the drive for order, proportion and propriety, the demand for socially cohesive categories of Nature and Reason,.. history once again selects criticism as both paradigm and instrument of such a project. **1976** *Language* LII. 286 As for the periods in between the quantum leaps, Kuhn contends that each period of normal science in the development of a scientific discipline corresponds to one and only one methodological framework or *paradigm*. In a nut-shell, paradigms are 'universally recognized scientific achievements that for a time provide model problems and solutions to a community of practitioners'. **1976** F. Zweig *New Acquisitive Society* II. x. 132 The television set.. is the paradigm of consumer culture, with its disarming passivity prone to desires divorced from action.

paradigmatic (,pærədɪg'mætɪk), *a.* (*sb.*) [ad. Gr. παραδειγματικ-ός, f. παραδειγματ-: see prec. and -IC.]

A. *adj.* **a.** Of the nature of a paradigm; serving as a pattern; exemplary.

1662 [see AGOGIC *a.* 1]. **1793** T. Taylor *Plato* Introd. Timaeus 372 After this, the demiurgic, paradigmatic, and final causes. **1828** in Webster. **1888** *Amer. Jrnl. Philol.* Oct. 294 The Timaeus seems at first to fit very nicely into the doctrine of the paradeigmatic idea. **1890** J. H. Stirling *Philos. & Theol.* ii. 37 All these ideas.. are not paradigmatic only but parental. **1965** M. I. Finley in *New Statesman* 11 June 926/1 The authors do not distinguish between history as a systematic discipline and Aristotle's or Machiavelli's use of the past as a quarry for data for his social and political theories ('paradigmatic history', that has been called). **1973** *Black World* Sept. 51 A violence that becomes, in Wright's vision, paradigmatic of the entire spectrum of violence Blacks experience in this country. **1974** *Nature* 16 Aug. 609/1 Most of the philosophers of science.. take the Comtean view, of physics as the paradigmatic science. **1976** *Times Lit. Suppl.* 23 Jan. 88/3 To his contemporaries Defoe was insignificant except as the paradigmatic Grub Street hack. **1977** *Church Times* 18 Feb. 6/3 Even if the (New Testament) accounts have been stylised, they have nonetheless a paradigmatic trustworthiness, an incontestable inner truth.

b. *Linguistics.* Belonging to a set of linguistically associated forms. Cf. PARADIGM 3.

1948 J. R. Firth in E. P. Hamp et al. *Readings in Linguistics II* (1966) 175 Most phoneticians.. have continued to elaborate the analysis of words... Such studies I should describe as paradigmatic and monosystemic in principle. **1953** C. E. Bazell *Linguistic Form* 43 A special instance of paradigmatic indiscreteness of phonic character is afforded by English æ. **1964** *Eng. Stud.* XLV. 388 The concept of an active selective function of what has been called a paradigmatic frame does not serve teleological explanation of linguistic history. **1964** R. H. Robins *Gen. Linguistics* 49 Paradigmatic relations are those holding between comparable elements at particular places in structures. **1972** W. Labov *Language in Inner City* v. 215 Larry is a paradigmatic speaker of black English vernacular as opposed to standard English. **1973** J. M. Anderson *Struct. Aspects Lang. Change* 124 In some cases syntagmatic influence may be the dominant force..; at other periods and under different conditions, paradigmatic forces may be stronger. **1975** *Language* LI. 665 Halle 1973 argues that paradigmatic information should be represented in the dictionary.

†**B.** *sb.* One who writes lives of religious persons to serve as examples of Christian holiness. *Obs. rare.*

1847 in Webster.

†**paradig'matical,** *a.* [See -ICAL.] = prec.

1577 tr. *Bullinger's Decades* (1592) 958 We read that some signes are paradigmaticall. **1678** Cudworth *Intell. Syst.* I. v. 733 Here therefore is there a Knowledge before the world, .. that was Archetypal and Paradigmatical to the same. **1793** T. Taylor *Plato* Introd. Timaeus 370 Primary causes, i.e. the producing the paradigmatical, and the final.

Hence **paradig'matically** *adv.*

1846 Worcester cites *Annot. Tr.* **1953** C. E. Bazell *Linguistic Form* 7 An allomorph is paradigmatically relevant. **1960** C. Geertz in J. A. Fishman *Readings Sociol. of Lang.* (1968) 283, I offer the accompanying three charts depicting paradigmatically how a single sentence alters within each of the [Javanese] dialects and among them. **1964** R. H. Robins *Gen. Linguistics* 49 The status of a particular case as a grammatical category applicable to certain word endings in a language like Latin is stated.. paradigmatically in terms of the number of different cases formally marked in the language. **1967** D. Cooper *Psychiatry & Anti-Psychiatry* p. xii, The third chapter seeks paradigmatically to make intelligible the patient-career of one young diagnosed schizophrenic in terms of the nature of his family world and the key events that have happened in it. **1971** T. F. Mitchell in *Archivum Linguisticum* II. 49 Within such a selection of phrases, *working* is definable as adjectival on the basis of the relationships it accretes paradigmatically.. and syntagmatically. **1976** *Amer. Speech 1974* XLIX. 79 These relationships are seen.. as constituting the basis for lexical sets paradigmatically.

†**para'digmatize,** *v. Obs.* [ad. Gr. παραδειγματίζ-ειν to make an example of, f. παραδειγματ-: see PARADIGM and -IZE.] *trans.* To set forth as a model, to make an example of.

1647 Hammond *Copy Papers betw. H. & Cheynell* 123 There is no question concerning any line in those Books so paradigmatized by you. **1651** Baxter *Inf. Baptism* 216 Not ..[to] go about as it were to paradigmatize, and stigmatize me throughout the whole Kingdom. **1708** *Brit. Apollo* No. 36. 2/1 To Paradigmatize and.. explain all obstupifying Quiddities.

parading (pə'reɪdɪŋ), *vbl. sb.* [f. PARADE *v.* + -ING[1].] The action of the verb PARADE; mustering of soldiers; promenading; showing off, etc. Also *attrib.*

1686 tr. *Chardin's Trav. Persia* 208 The Parading Place that is before it, serves also for a publick meeting Place. **1765** C. Smart *Phædrus* viii. 28, I value not thy gasconading, Nor all thy alamode parading. *c* **1817** Hogg *Tales & Sk.* I. 86 There was a great deal of parading, and noise.. of beating drums.

pa'rading, *ppl. a.* [f. as prec. + -ING[2].] That parades; marching up and down; showing off, given to display, etc.

1777 Mad. D'Arblay *Early Diary* July, She is parading and tolerably uncultivated as to books. **1816** Chalmers *Astron. Disc.* vii. (1830) 284 It may have been a piece of parading insignificance. **1902** *Daily Chron.* 18 Mar. 8/2 The parading bands are now passing along in silence.

Hence **pa'radingly** *adv.*

1841 W. Spalding *Italy & It. Isl.* I. 96 All that the spirit of liberty had honoured, were protected and brought paradingly forward.

‖**paradior'thosis.** *Obs. rare.* [a. Gr. παραδιόρθωσις a marginal correction, f. παρα- aside, (PARA-[1] in sense of 'improper, false') + διόρθωσις correction.] A false correction.

1658 W. Burton *Itin. Anton.* 2, I cannot choose but take notice of a Paradiorthosis, or false emendation.

,paradiplo'matic, *a.* [f. PARA-[1] I.] Aside or apart from what is strictly diplomatic or concerned with the evidence of the manuscript texts.

1854 Ellicott *Comm. Galatians* Pref. (1859) 17, I have always endeavoured, first, to ascertain the exact nature of the diplomatic evidence; secondly, that of what I have termed paradiplomatic arguments,.. by which I mean the apparent probabilities of erroneous transcription, permutation of letters, itacism, and so forth. *Ibid.* 15 The accidental omission.. seems probable on paradiplomatic considerations. **1879** Farrar in *Expositor* IX. 29 The passage is still to be retained in spite of evidence both external and internal, both diplomatic and paradiplomatic. **1882** —— *Early Chr.* II. 448 One of those cases in which the reading of the existing MSS. is outweighed by other authorities and other considerations. *Note*: To express the same thing technically, the diplomatic is outweighed by the paradiplomatic evidence.

paradisaic (pærədɪ'seɪɪk), *a.* [Arbitrarily f. PARADISE or L. *paradīs-us* (after *algebraic*, *Judaic*, *Mosaic*, *prosaic*).] = next.

1754 Shebbeare *Matrimony* (1766) I. 240 The Paradisaic Vision of excessive Love. **1843** J. B. Robertson tr. *Moehler's Symbolism* I. 34 **1898** J. P. Lilley *Princ. Protestant.* i. 16 Salvation is never represented in Scripture as a mere restoration of the paradisaic condition.

paradisaical (pærədɪ'seɪɪkəl), *a.* [f. as prec. + -AL[1].] Of, pertaining to, of the nature of Paradise; paradisiacal.

1623 R. Carpenter *Conscion. Christian* 26 This onely permanent and Paradisaicall good of an vpright conscience. **1725** Pope *Let. to E. Blount* 13 Sept., We wander in a paradisaical scene among groves and gardens. **1871** Tylor *Prim. Cult.* I. 27 The pictures drawn by some travellers of savagery as a kind of paradisaical state. **1884** *Times* (weekly ed.) 26 Sept. 5/1 The paradisaical groups of Fra Angelico.

Hence **paradi'saically** *adv.*

1832 tr. *Tour Germ. Prince* IV. 117 A singular and paradisaically luxuriant country. **1855** *Fraser's Mag.* LI. 532 How happily and almost paradisaically they seem to live.

paradisal (pærə'daɪsəl), *a.* [f. L. *paradīs-us* + -AL[1].] Of or pertaining to paradise.

c **1560** A. Scott *Poems* (S.T.S.) xv. 19, I feill no pane, I haif no purgatorye, Bot peirles, perfytt, paradisall plesour. **1723** Lady M. W. Montagu *Lett., to C'tess Mar* Apr. (1887) I. 341 The paradisal state of receiving visits every day from a passionate lover. **1839** Bailey *Festus* vi. (1852) 79 [They] each prepare His wing to poise for Paradisal flight. **1880** Webb *Goethe's Faust* Prol. in Heaven 19 To paradisal day succeedeth The awful presence of the night.

paradise ('pærədaɪs), *sb.* Forms: α. 2–4 **paradis,** (4 **-dijs, -diȝs**), 4–8 **-ice,** (5 **peradis, paradies, -yss,** 5–6 **-yce,** 6 **-ize**), 5– **paradise.** β. 2–5 **parais,** 3 **paraise,** 3–4 **parays.** [Early ME. a. F. *paradis* (also in early semi-popular form *paraïs*, *pareïs*), ad. L. *paradīs-us*, a. Gr. παράδεισος, a. OPers. *pairidaēza* enclosure, park, f. *pairi* around + *diz* to mould, form; whence also Armenian *pardez*, late Heb. *pardēs* (Neh. ii. 8 the park of the Persian king, also Eccl. ii. 5); in mod.Pers. and Ar. *firdaus* garden, paradise.

Used in Gr. (first by Xenophon) for a (Persian) enclosed park, orchard, or pleasure ground; by the LXX for the garden of Eden, and in N.T. and Christian writers for the abode of the blessed, which is the earliest sense recorded in Eng. The OE. equivalent was *neorxna wang*; cf. *Hexam. St. Basil 16 Paradisum* ðæt we hataþ on Englisc neorxna wang; called also, *Phœnix* 418, se halȝa wong (*wong* land, territory, surface of the ground).]

1. a. The garden of Eden. Also called ***earthly*** (†***terrenal, terrene, terrestre***) ***paradise***, to distinguish it from the ***heavenly paradise***.

α. *a* **1175** *Cott. Hom.* 221 God þa hine brohte into paradis. *c* **1175** *Lamb. Hom.* 129 Heo weren ipult ut of paradise. *c* **1250** *Gen. & Ex.* 291 He saȝ in paradis Adam and eue in mike[l] pris. **13..** *K. Alis.* 5685 Paradys terrene is righth in the Est. **1340** *Ayenb.* 50 Ase he did to euen and to Adam in paradys terestre. *c* **1400** *Destr. Troy* 5496 Evfraton & þe flode Tyger.. passyn out of peradis þurghe the playn Rewme. **1481** Caxton *Reynard* xxxii. (Arb.) 83 Bytwene the grete Inde & erthly paradyse. **1588** Parke tr. *Mendoza's Hist. China* 397 The riuer Ganges, one of the foure that comme foorth of paradice terrenall. **1667** Milton *P.L.* IV. 132 He.. to the border comes Of Eden, where delicious Paradise.. Crowns with her enclosure green.. the champain head Of a steep wilderness. **1885** *Encycl. Brit.* XVIII. 236/2 The *earthly* paradise, as developed by Christian fancy, is the old garden of Eden, which lay in the far East beyond the stream of Ocean, raised so high on a triple terrace of mountain that the deluge did not touch it.

β. *c* **1175** *Lamb. Hom.* 129 þet wes eorðliche parais. *a* **1225** *Ancr. R.* 66 Eue heold ine parais longe tale mid te neddre. **13..** in *Pol. Rel. & L. Poems* (1866) 230 þe ȝates of parais þoruth eue weren iloken.

b. Hence in names of plants and animals: ***apples of paradise***, the fruit of the plantain, *Musa paradisiaca*; ***bird of paradise***, see BIRD *sb.* 7; ***grains of paradise***, see GRAIN *sb.* 4.

1585 T. Washington tr. *Nicholay's Voy.* I. xvi. 17b, Apples of paradice, which they call muses.

c. *ellipt.* The plumage of a bird of paradise (cf. BIRD *sb.* 7).

1905 E. Wharton *House of Mirth* II. x. 446 Mrs. Trenor's hat? The one with the green Paradise? **1928** *Daily Express* 24 May 5/3 The same firm was responsible for wonderful curls of shaded paradise,.. toning from dark to palest beige tones.

2. a. Heaven, the abode of God and his angels and the final abode of the righteous. (Now chiefly *poetic.*)

α. [*c* **1000** *Ags. Gosp.* Luke xxiii. 43 To-dæȝ þu bist mid me on paradiso [*Hatton* on paradise; *Gr.* ἐν τῷ παραδείσῳ, *Vulg.* in paradiso; Wyclif in paradys, Tind. in paradise].] *c* **1205** Lay. 24122 þat he.. ȝefen heom his paradis, þæt heo mosten bruken blisse mid ænglen. *a* **1240** *Ureisun* in *Cott. Hom.* 191 I-brouht of helle in-to paradise. **1340** *Ayenb.* 14 þet lif wyþ-oute ende þet is þe blisse of paradis. **1484** Caxton *Fables of Æsop* v, I haue dremed that the Angels had led one of yow in to paradys or heuen. **1500–20** Dunbar *Poems* lxxvi. 4 A fre chois gevin to Paradice or Hell. **1587** FLEMING *Contn. Holinshed* III. 1352/1 If he vouchsafe to call you into paradise, how blessed shall you be. **1635** A. STAFFORD *Fem. Glory* cxxii. (1869) 122 You..shall at length arrive at the Celestiall Paradice. **1858–60** J. GARDNER *Faiths of World* II. 11 The Jewish Rabbis teach that there is an upper and a lower paradise or heaven. **1862** F. W. FABER *Hymn*, O Paradise, O Paradise..Where loyal hearts and true, Stand ever in the light..In God's most holy sight.

β. *c* **1175** *Lamb. Hom.* 61 To bon in heuene fuliwis. In touþe[?] sete of parais. *a* **1225** *St. Marher.* 13 Paraises ȝeten aren ȝarewe iopenet þe nu. *a* **1300** *Floriz & Bl.* 76 Him þuȝte he was in parais. *c* **1325** *Song Virg.* 33 in *O.E. Misc.* 195 Leuedi quene of parays.

b. The Muslim heaven or elysium.

c **1400** MAUNDEV. (1839) xii. 132 Ȝif a Man aske them [Saracens], what Paradys thei menen; thei seyn, to Paradys, that is a place of Delytes, where men schulle fynde alle maner of Frutes, in alle Cesouns [etc.]. **1702** ROWE *Tamerl.* IV. i. 1766 Prophet, take notice I disclaim thy Paradice. **1813** BYRON *Giaour* 489 *note*, The Koran allots at least a third of Paradise to well-behaved women. **1816** —— *Siege Cor.* 255 Secure in paradise to be By Houris loved immortally. **1841** LANE *Arab. Nts.* I. 20 Some assert Paradise to be in the seventh heaven, and, indeed, I have found this to be the general opinion of my Muslim friends.

c. By some theologians, the word as used in Luke xxiii. 43 is taken to denote an intermediate place or state where the departed souls of the righteous await resurrection and the last judgement. Cf. 'Abraham's bosom', Luke xvi. 23.

a **1690** BP. BULL *Serm. Acts i.* 25, Wks. 1846 I. 55 Then.. he [St. Paul] saw also the intermediate joys of paradise, wherewith the souls of the faithful are refreshed until the resurrection. *Ibid.* 59. **1703** D. WHITBY *Paraphr. N.T.* Luke xxiii. 43. **1713** A. CAMPBELL *Doctr. Mid. State* (1721) 53. **1739–56** DODDRIDGE *Fam. Expositor* (1761) IV. 523 He was also caught up into Paradise, that Garden of God, which is the Seat of happy Spirits in the intermediate State, and during their Separation from the Body. **1776** WESLEY *Let. to Miss Bishop* 17 Apr., In Paradise, in the intermediate state between death and the resurrection. *a* **1806** HORSLEY *Serm.* (1811) 395 Paradise was certainly some place where our Lord was to be on the very day on which he suffered, and where the companion of his sufferings was to be with him. It was not heaven. **1835** J. H. NEWMAN *Par. Serm.* (1837) III. xxv. 412 Paradise is not the same as Heaven, but a resting-place at the foot of it. **1885** *Catholic Dict.* (ed. 3) 518 The *Limbus Patrum* is the Paradise of Luc. xxiii. 43, so called because it was a place of rest and joy, though the joy was imperfect.

3. a. A place like or compared to Paradise; a region of surpassing beauty or delight, or of supreme bliss.

c **1300** *St. Brandan* 147 That is Foweles Parays, a wel joyful place. *c* **1386** CHAUCER *Knt.'s T.* 379 Fful blisfully in prison maistow dure. In prison? certes nay but in Paradys. **1387** TREVISA *Higden* (Rolls) VII. 215 No man schulde be i-chose pope but he were of þe paradys of Italy i-bore. **1553** EDEN *Treat. Newe Ind.* (Arb.) 15 A man woulde thinke it were a very Paradyse of pleasure. **1590** SPENSER *F.Q.* II. xii. 58 There the most daintie Paradise [the Bowre of Blisse] on ground It selfe doth offer to his sober eye. **1607** NORDEN *Surv. Dial.* v. 230, I was once in Somersetshire, about a place neere Tanton, called Tandeane... You speake of the Paradice of England. **1617** [see HELL 10]. **1745** P. THOMAS *Jrnl. Anson's Voy.* 297 Among their Buildings are many which..appear..perfect Paradises. **1814** COL. HAWKER *Diary* (1893) I. 123 These gardens are the most perfect paradise I ever saw. **1891** E. KINGLAKE *Australian at H.* 136 [Australia] is a rather overdone Paradise of the working man.

b. *fig.* A state of supreme bliss or felicity. See also FOOL'S PARADISE.

c **1386** CHAUCER *Merch. T.* 21 Wedlok is so esy and so clene That in this world it is a Paradys. *a* **1548** HALL *Chron.*, *Hen. VII* 6 This poore priest brought into this foolishe paradice through his awne fantasticall ymaginacion. **1742** GRAY *Eton* 98 Thought would destroy their paradise. **1813** MAR. EDGEWORTH *Patron.* (1833) II. xxviii. 211 As she seemed entering the paradise of love and hope. **1897** 'OUIDA' *Massarenes* xl, I shall deny him the paradise of your embrace. **1902** A. M. FAIRBAIRN *Philos. Chr. Relig.* I. ii. 79 Comfort..seems to many Englishmen the only real paradise.

c. *Assoc. Football.* (With capital initial.) A name given to Celtic Park, Glasgow, the home ground of the Celtic Football Club.

1946 C. A. OAKLEY *Second City* III. 168 Celtic Park.. seemed so palatial, in odd comparison with an adjacent graveyard, that it was described as the 'Paradise'. **1958** C. TULLY *Passed to You* xxii. 92 One of the best things about being at Paradise is that you're pretty certain to move in good company... You'll go a long way before you meet a better bunch than the Tims of Parkhead.

4. a. An Oriental park or pleasure-ground, *esp.* one enclosing wild beasts for the chase. **b.** Hence sometimes applied to an English park in which foreign animals are kept.

1613 PURCHAS *Pilgrimage* (1614) 75 Betweene Orpha and Caramit, was the Paradise of Aladeules, where he had a fortress destroyed by Selim. **1621** BURTON *Anat. Mel.* II. ii. IV. (1651) 269 A Persian Paradise, or pleasant park, could not be more delectable in his sight. **1775** R. CHANDLER *Trav. Asia M.* (1825) I. 296 He had moreover an extensive paradise or park, full of wild beasts. **1865** RAWLINSON *Anc. Mon.* III. i. 34 Semiramis built a palace, and laid out a paradise. **1900** *Daily News* 3 Aug. 5/1 A 'paradise' is the technical term for a preserve in which attempts are made with more or less success to acclimatize foreign birds and animals. The three most successful paradises in England are Haggerstone Castle, near Beale; Leonardslee, in Sussex; and Woburn Abbey.

†**5.** A pleasure-garden in general; *spec.* the garden of a convent. *Obs.*

Hence sometimes surviving in the street nomenclature of old cities or towns; e.g. 'Paradise Square', Oxford.

[**1374–5** *Durham Acc. Rolls* (Surtees) 180 In reparacione muri circa paradis'.] **1610** HOLLAND *Camden's Brit.*, *Irel.* II. 111 Minding to replant it like unto a certaine garden or Paradise. **1662** EVELYN *Diary* 9 June, [At Hampton Court] There is a parterre which they call Paradise, in which is a very pretty banquetting-house set over a cave or cellar. **1686** *Ibid.* 4 Aug., Signior Verrio..now settled in his Majesty's garden at St. James's, which he had made a very delicious Paradise. **1875** PARKER *Gloss. Archit.* (ed. 4), *Paradise*,..also the garden of a convent: the name seems originally to have been given to the open court, or area, in front of the old church of St. Peter's at Rome.

†**6.** Sometimes given (perh. orig. in jest) as a distinctive name to a particular apartment. *Obs.*

1485 *Rolls of Parlt.* VI. 372/2 The Keping of the Houses called Paradyse and Hell, within the Hall of Westminster,.. and also the Keping of the Purgatory within the said Hall, whiche Nicholas Whytfeld late had and occupied. **1538** LELAND *Itin.* (1710) I. 39, I saw in a litle studiyng Chaumber ther caullid Paradice the Genealogie of the Percys. *Ibid.* 46.

7. *slang.* The gallery of a theatre, where the 'gods' are. Cf. F. *paradis.* (*Slang Dict.* 1873.)

8. *attrib.* and *Comb.*, as ***paradise body***, ***garden***, ***weather***, etc., also ***paradise-like*** adj.; **paradise apple**, (*a*) a variety of apple: cf. *paradise-stock*; (*b*) the Forbidden Fruit or Pomello; †**paradise-bird** = bird-of-paradise: see BIRD *sb.* 7; **paradise crane**, the blue or Stanley crane, *Anthropoides paradisea*, found in South Africa and distinguished by a cluster of very long, black tail feathers; **paradise-duck**, a species of sheldrake (*Casarca variegata*) found in New Zealand; **paradise-fish**, (*a*) see quot. 1858; (*b*) a brilliantly coloured East Indian fish (*Macropodus viridiauratus*) sometimes kept in aquariums; **paradise-flycatcher**, a bird of the genus *Terpsiphone*, remarkable for the length of its middle tail-feathers; †**paradise-grain** = grain of Paradise: see GRAIN *sb.* 4; **paradise-grosbeak**, an African species of grosbeak (*Loxia erythrocephala*), grey and white, with red head and chin, often kept as a cage-bird; **paradise stock**, a hardy slow-growing apple-tree used as a stock by nurserymen for dwarfing other varieties; **paradise-tree**, a small West Indian tree, *Simaruba glauca*.

1676 WORLIDGE *Cider* 159 The *Paradice-Apple is a curious Fruit, produced by grafting a Permain on a Quince. **1699** EVELYN *Kal. Hort.* Nov. (ed. 9) 131 Stocks of the Paradise or sweet Apple-kernel. **1834** *Penny Cycl.* II. 191/2 The stocks..are the wild crab, the doucin or English paradise, and the French paradise apple. **1857** MAYNE *Expos. Lex.*, *Paradise Apple*, common name for the fruit of the *Citrus Paradisi.* **1617** K. THROGMORTON in *St. Papers Col.* (1870) 50 [Sends presents, including] a *paradise bird'. **1774** GOLDSM. *Nat. Hist.* VIII. Index Ff i b, Paradise-bird ..an inhabitant of the Molucca islands. **1690** BAXTER *Kingd. Christ* i. (1691) 10 Some think that the [resurrection body] ..is to be a *Paradise body, like Adams before he sinned. **1906** *Daily Chron.* 8 May 7/4 His consignment..included.. three *paradise cranes, five wolves and seven baboons. **1958** E. T. GILLIARD *Living Birds of World* 146/1 Other species [of crane] are named for their ornamental plumage, coloration, wattles or geographical ranges—as, for example ..the Paradise or Stanley Crane..of southern Africa; and the Crowned Crane. **1845** E. J. WAKEFIELD *Adv. N. Zealand* iii. 57 The *paradise duck..is nearly as large as a goose, and of beautiful plumage. **1882** *Pall Mall G.* 29 June 4/2 He is pretty sure of a good bag of pigeons, with as many paradise ducks as he cares to carry. **1858** SIMMONDS *Dict. Trade*, **Paradise-fish*, a species of *Polynemus*, which is esteemed excellent food in India. **1885** C. F. HOLDER *Marvels Anim. Life* 18 In Siam there is found a fish..known to science as the Macropodus or paradise-fish, on account of its curiously-shaped fins. **1893** NEWTON *Dict. Birds* 275 One of the most remarkable groups of Muscicapidæ is that known as the *Paradise Flycatchers,..the males are distinguished by the growth of exceedingly long feathers in their tail. **1910** O. LINDEMANN tr. *Delius's Village Romeo & Juliet* 178, I know another place not very far from here where we'll be quite unknown. 'Tis the *Paradise Garden. *Ibid.* 192 Der Paradiesgarten... The Paradisegarden. **1972** *Country Life* 23 Mar. 682/3 It has been suggested that such places as this, in which an attempt is made to bring together plants from all parts of the world, should be known as paradise gardens. **1977** A. WILSON *Strange Ride R. Kipling* iv. 221 The Woolsack [*sc.* their South African house] was a delight to the whole Kipling family... For the children..it was clearly a Paradise garden. **1705** BOSMAN *Guinea* xvi. (1721) 285 *Malagueta*, otherwise called *Paradice-Grains, or Guinea Pepper. **1663** GERBIER *Counsel* c vj, Your Lordships *Paradise-like Garden at Neewnem. **1706** LONDON & WISE *Retir'd Gard'ner* I. I. xvii. 82 An Apple upon a *Paradise Stock. **1834** *Penny Cycl.* II. 191/2 The doucin or English paradise stock, which is what the English nurserymen usually sell as *the* paradise stock, is intermediate in its effect between the crab and the French paradise. **1875** W. CORY *Lett. & Jrnls.* (1897) 381 Last week was a marvel of *paradise weather.

paradise (ˈpærədaɪs), *v.* [f. prec. sb.] *trans.* **a.** To make into Paradise. **b.** To place in Paradise, to imparadise; to make supremely blessed or beautiful. Hence ˈ**paradised** *ppl. a.*

1592 G. HARVEY *Pierce's Super.* in *Archaica* (1815) II. 173 Your Vertical Star that..paradiseth the earth with the ambrosial dews of his incomprehensible wit. **1594** NASHE *Unfort. Trav.* Wks. (Grosart) V. 60 If there bee anie sparke of Adams paradized perfection yet emberd vp in the breastes of mortall men. **1610** R. JONES *Muses' Gard. Delights* xii, One houre of Paradised joye Makes Purgatorie seeme a toye. **1843** E. JONES *Sens. & Event* 56 All paradised bright stars did roll.

paradisean (pærəˈdɪsiːən), *a. rare.* [f. med.L. *paradīse-us* (f. *paradīs-us*) + -AN: cf. *cærulean*, etc.]

1. Of, pertaining to, or of the nature of Paradise.

1647 J. HALL *Poems* 73 Spread those boughs, Whereon lifes grapes, those Paradisean cluster growes. **1895** *Forum* (N.Y.) Nov. 351 The paradisean years of a tender and sagacious childhood are passing.

2. Belonging to the genus *Paradisea* or family *Paradiseidæ*, which includes the Birds of Paradise.

1857 MAYNE *Expos. Lex.*, *Paradiseus*, belonging to Paradise: paradisean. *Ornithol.* Applied to a certain bird with beautiful plumage.

So **paraˈdiseid** *Ornith.*, a bird of the family *Paradiseidæ*, a Bird of Paradise. **paraˈdiseine** *a.*, of or belonging to the sub-family *Paradiseinæ*, a sub-family of *Paradiseidæ*. **paraˈdiseoid** *a.*, akin to the Birds of Paradise.

1895 *Ibis* 397 One of the most wonderful of the many new discoveries in the Paradiseine family.

paradisiac (pærəˈdɪsɪæk, -ˈdɪzɪæk), *a.* [ad. L. *paradīsiac-us*, a. Gr. παραδεισιακ-ός park-like, f. παράδεισ-ος PARADISE. In F. *paradisiaque.*] = next.

1632 LITHGOW *Trav.* v. 208 This Paradisiac [*printed* -iat] Shamma, is the..most beautiful place of all Asia. **1767** BUSH *Hibernia Cur.* (1769) 117 This most delightfully rural and paradisiac recess. **1850** KINGSLEY *Alt. Locke* xl, The paradisiac beauty and simplicity of tropic humanity. **1873** BROWNING *Red Cott. Nt.-cap.* III. 2 So slipt pleasantly away five years Of Paradisiac dream.

paradisiacal (ˌpærədɪˈsaɪəkəl, -ˈzaɪəkəl), *a.* [f. as prec. + -AL[1]]

1. Of, pertaining or belonging to Paradise; Eden-like; like that of Paradise, supremely blest; peacefully beautiful.

1649 J. ECLLISTON tr. *Behmen's Epist.* xv. § 1 (1886) In His pleasant Paradisiacal Garden. **1768–74** TUCKER *Lt. Nat.* (1834) I. 255 It would bring back the golden age or paradisiacal state again. **1840** HOWITT *Visits Rem. Places* Ser. I. 208 Ruins of Bolton Priory..; one of the most delicious and paradisiacal scenes..the heart of England holds. **1876** MRS. WHITNEY *Sights & Ins.* II. xxvi. 540 They are at the paradisiacal age; the young Adam and Eve are strong in them.

2. Of or pertaining to the heavenly Paradise; celestial.

1660 H. MORE *Myst. Godl.* I. vi. 17 Clothed with those Heavenly, Ethereal and Paradisiacal bodies which Christ will bestow upon those that belong to him. **1779** J. DUCHÉ *Disc.* (1790) II. xvii. 357 The very moment the heaven-born spirit had escaped from its tortured body, the whole Paradisiacal world was opened upon its senses.

Hence **paradiˈsiacally** *adv.*

1881 CURTISS tr. *Delitzsch's Hist. Redempt.* I. § 4. 21 That human history began and will end paradisiacally is correlated with its sinless commencement and its sanctified ending.

paradisial (pærəˈdɪsɪəl, -ˈdɪzɪəl), *a.* [irreg. f. L. *paradīs-us* PARADISE + -IAL.] = prec.

1800 W. TAYLOR in *Monthly Mag.* X. 426 Immortal men, women, and children, whose paradisial plenty..and patriarchal pleasures, are elegantly depicted. **1879** G. MACDONALD *Sir Gibbie* I. iv. 45 No..insignificant element in the paradisial character of the place.

paradisian (pærəˈdɪsɪən, -ˈdɪzɪən), *a.* [f. as prec. + -IAN.] = prec.

1657–83 EVELYN *Hist. Relig.* (1850) I. 38 O happy sovereign..whose food was paradisian; clothing, innocence; conversation, angels. *a* **1711** KEN *Hymnotheo* Poet. Wks. 1721 III. 272 The Golden Cup..is fill'd with Paradisian Wines. **1821** *Blackw. Mag.* IX. 18 A fit habitant for paradisian groves.

paradisic (pærəˈdɪsɪk, -ˈdɪzɪk), *a.* [f. Gr. παράδεισ-ος PARADISE + -IC.] = prec.

a **1745** BROOME *Ground Relig.* (R.), A life..Dead of itself to paradisic bliss. **1864** E. SARGENT *Peculiar* II. 196 Kenrick stood mute, as if a paradisic vision had dazed his senses. **1881** CURTISS tr. *Delitzsch's Hist. Redempt.* i. § 4 The condition of childish innocence is in itself paradisic.

paraˈdisical, *a. rare.* [f. as prec. + -AL[1].] = prec.

1649 J. ECLLISTON tr. *Behmen's Epist.* i. § 17 That same Image which dyed in Adam..being the true Paradisicall Image. **1728** NORTH *Mem. of Musick* (1846) 78 In the reigne of King Jac. I., and the paradisicall part of the reign of King Cha. I.

Hence **paraˈdisically** *adv.*

1894 *Outing* (U.S.) XXIV. 7/1 [His] paradisically happy years of married life.

parado: see PARADA.

paradoctor (ˈpærəˌdɒktə(r)). Chiefly *U.S.* [f. PARA-[3] + DOCTOR *sb.* 6.] A doctor who is parachuted to patients in remote areas.

1944 *Time* 10 July 92/3 He is one of six paradoctors attached to the Search and Rescue Station of the Second Air Force. **1947** *Birmingham* (Alabama) *News* 30 May 1/7 A paradoctor from Athens..parachuted into the jungle. **1949** *Ibid.* 7 Aug. 1/7 Dr...Little,..former Army para-doctor, gave first aid to the injured.

parador ('pærədɔə(r)). Pl. **paradores**. [Sp. *parador* inn, hostel.] Formerly an inn or hotel in Spain, now used as the name of a chain of hotels owned and administered by the Spanish government. Also *attrib.*

1845 R. FORD *Hand-bk. for Travellers Spain* II. 569/1 *La de Navarra*, near the Pla. Mayor, is but a mere *parador*. **1927** C. CONNOLLY *Let.* 13 Feb. in *Romantic Friendship* (1975) 257 Roach I feel was.. at home in the straw strewn venta or the noisy parador. **1960** *News Chron.* 10 Mar. 8/6 Castles in Spain have become paradores, Government run hotels. **1966** *Vogue* Nov. 182/3 Gran Canaria..here the broad terrace of a government parador looks out across a contorted volcanic landscape. **1973** *Country Life* 22 Nov. 1688/1 The needs of tourists can provide new functions..for historic buildings. Examples are the parador hotels in Spain.

parados ('pærədɒs, ‖parado). *Fortif.* [a. F. *parados*, f. PARA-² + *dos* back.] **a.** (See quots.)

1834–47 J. S. MACAULAY *Field Fortif.* (1851) 107 When the covering masses are intended to protect the defenders from reverse fire, they are called *parados*. **1853** STOCQUELER *Mil. Encycl.* 207 *Parados*, an elevation of earth which is effected behind fortified places, to secure them from any sudden attack that may be made in reverse. **1870** *Illustr. Lond. News* 29 Oct. 446 The conical top of the hill..serves as a gigantic natural parados or traverse.

b. The rear wall of a trench. Also *fig.*

1917 A. G. EMPEY *Over Top* 303 *Parados*, the rear wall of a trench which the Germans continually fill with bits of shell and rifle bullets. Tommy doesn't mind how many they put in the parados. **1938** H. G. WELLS *Apropos of Dolores* iv. 139 Much of this discourse flowed over me. I did my best to keep my head down beneath the level of parapet and parados. **1957** P. KEMP *Mine were of Trouble* iv. 79, I saw Frejo and Santo Domingo on top of the parados.

paradosis (pə'rædəsɪs). *Theol.* [Gr. παράδοσις, a handing down, a tradition.] A historical tradition, *spec.* relating to the teachings of Christ and of his disciples; teaching based on this tradition.

1950 L. S. THORNTON *Revelation & Mod. World* ix. 285 The apostolic *paradosis* was embodied, not only in the apostolic writings, but also in the accredited teachers of the Catholic Church who could show their 'didactic successions' from the apostles. **1953** *Scottish Jrnl. Theol.* VI. 117 This is a tradition, a *paradosis* which does not fall under the condemnation which Jesus pronounces with regard to the *paradosis* in general. **1956** *Ibid.* IX. 434 Cullmann's thesis is that Paul was able to accord a higher place to the *paradosis* he had received, despite the fact that Jesus had denounced the high place accorded to *paradosis* in Judaism. **1958** A. RICHARDSON *Introd. Theol. N.T.* xvi. 365 We must not make the mistake of the older NT critics who thought that what was to be interpreted was a number of ancient documents, which could be more objectively judged if they were isolated from the paradosis of the Church. **1973** *Amer. Jrnl. Philol.* XCIV. 320 Modern editors treat χειᾶ as a reasoned Triclinian conjecture. But χειᾶ proves almost certainly to be nothing but a further perversion of an already corrupt paradosis.

paradox ('pærədɒks), *sb.* (*a.*). Also 6–7 -oxe. [ad. (perh. through F. *paradoxe*, 14th c. in Hatz.-Darm.) L. *paradoxum*, *-on*, sb., properly neuter of *paradox-us*, Gr. παράδοξ-ος adj. contrary to received opinion or expectation, f. παρά past, beyond, contrary to + δόξα opinion; in Gr. and L. also used subst., esp. in pl. παράδοξα Stoical paradoxes: cf. Cicero *Paradoxa*, proœm. 4. In Fr. and Eng. the sb. is the earlier and more important.]

A. *sb.* **1. a.** A statement or tenet contrary to received opinion or belief; often with the implication that it is marvellous or incredible; sometimes with unfavourable connotation, as being discordant with what is held to be established truth, and hence absurd or fantastic; sometimes with favourable connotation, as a correction of vulgar error. (In actual use rare since 17th c., though often insisted upon by writers as the proper sense.)

1540 PALSGRAVE tr. *Acolastus* Prol. sig. Biiᵛ, We shall not wytsafe any Paradoxes in noo place i. we shall not wytsafe (to speake or make mention of, . .) any thynges, that be aboue or beyonde the common oppynyon of men. **1546** BP. GARDINER *Declar. Art. Joye* 54b, Your fonde paradox of only fayth iustifieth. **1581** MARBECK *Bk. Notes* 791 Paradox is a straunge sentence, contrarie to the opinion of the most part. Or thus: It is a straunge sentence, not easely to be conceiued of the common sort. **1602** SHAKS. *Ham.* III. i. 115 This was sometime a Paradox, but now the time giues it proofe. **1616** BULLOKAR *Eng. Expos.*, *Paradox*, an opinion maintained contrary to the common allowed opinion, as if one affirme that the earth doth mooue round, and the heauens stand still. **1653** H. MORE *Antid. Ath.* II. xii. §17 (1712) 84 That pleasant and true Paradox of the Annual Motion of the Earth. **1656** HOBBES *Liberty, Necess., & Chance* (1841) 304 The Bishop speaks often of paradoxes with such scorn or detestation, that a simple reader would take a paradox either for felony or some other heinous crime, ..whereas perhaps a judicious reader knows..that a paradox, is an opinion not yet generally received. **1697** tr. *Burgersdicius' Logic* II. xv. 65 A Paradox is said to be a Probleme true against the common Opinion..such as that, viz., the Earth moves; which, tho' it be true, yet may it be so against the common Opinion, and therefore a Paradox. **1854** DE QUINCEY *Templars' Dial.* Wks. IV. 183 A paradox, you know, is simply that which contradicts the popular opinion —which in too many cases is the false opinion. **1890** *Illustr. Lond. News* 26 Apr. 535/3 A paradox is a proposition really or apparently contradictory to a commonly received idea... It is, as its name indicates, a conceit contrary to opinion, but not..contrary to reason. A position contrary to reason is a paralogism.

†**b.** *Rhet.* [repr. L. *paradoxum*.] A conclusion or apodosis contrary to what the audience has been led up to expect. *Obs.*

1678 PHILLIPS (ed. 4), *Paradox*..In Rhetorick, it is something which is cast in by the by, contrary to the opinion or expectation of the Auditor, and is otherwise called *Hypomone*.

2. a. A statement or proposition which on the face of it seems self-contradictory, absurd, or at variance with common sense, though, on investigation or when explained, it may prove to be well-founded (or, according to some, though it is essentially true). *spec.* in *Literary Criticism*.

1569 CROWLEY *Soph. Dr. Watson* i. 187 Your straunge Paradox of Christes eating of his owne fleshe. **1607** J. NORDEN *Surv. Dial.* IV. 195, I can tell you a pretie paradoxe ..Boggy and spungy ground,..though in it owne nature it be too moist, yet if it be overflowed with water often, it will settle and become firme. **1624** HAYWARD *Suprem. Relig.* 5 Three or foure at the table; who esteemed that which I had said, not for a Paradoxe, but for an Adoxe, or flat Absurditie. **1694** BENTLEY *Boyle Lect.* 66 'Tis no less a truth than a paradox, that there are no greater fools than atheistical wits; and none so credulous as infidels. *a* **1716** SOUTH *Serm.* (1744) XI. 127 If you will admit the paradox, it makes a man do more than he can do. *a* **1806** HORSLEY *Serm.* (1811) 369 Of the two parts..of a paradox, both are often true, and yet, when proved to be true, may continue paradoxical. **1809–10** COLERIDGE *Friend* (1865) 54 The legal paradox, that a libel may be the more a libel for being true. **1885** SEELEY *Introd. Polit. Sc.* i. (1896) 3 In my opinion, to lecture on political science is to lecture on history. Here is the Paradox—I use the word in its original sense of a proposition which is really true, though it sounds false. **1902** *Daily Chron.* 30 Oct. 3/1 Perhaps the only immortal paradoxes are the divine paradoxes called Beatitudes; for each generation sees their truth, but as no one ever acts upon them, their paradox comes with perpetual freshness to every age. **1939** BROOKS & WARREN *Understanding Poetry* VI. 637 *Paradox*, a statement which seems on the surface contradictory, but which involves an element of truth. Because of the element of contrast between the form of the statement and its true implications, paradox is closely related to irony. **1942** C. BROOKS in A. Tate *Language of Poetry* 37 Few of us are prepared to accept the statement that the language of poetry is the language of paradox... Yet there is a sense in which paradox is the language appropriate and inevitable to poetry. **1947** —— *Well-Wrought Urn* 230 Paradox, as a device for contrasting the conventional views of a situation, or the limited and special view of it such as those taken in practical and scientific discourse, with a more inclusive view. **1960** *Commentary* Nov. 369 He had been instructed in *paradox*, *tension*, and *ambiguity* in a course called 'Introduction to Literature'.

b. Often applied to a proposition or statement that is actually self-contradictory, or contradictory to reason or ascertained truth, and so, essentially absurd and false.

Hence some (cf. quot. 1639) have denied statements to be paradoxes when they can be proved after all to be true, or have called them 'apparent paradoxes' (quot. 1876), when they are real paradoxes in sense 2.

1570 FOXE *A. & M.* (ed. 2) 1299 This monstrous paradoxe of transubstantiation was neuer induced or receaued publickly in the Churche, before the tyme of yᵉ Lateran Councell. **1588** SHAKS. *L.L.L.* IV. iii. 253 *Berow*..No face is faire that is not full so blacke. *Kin.* O paradoxe, Blacke is the badge of hell. **1628** WITHER *Brit. Rememb.* III. 39 Vulgar men, doe such expressions hold To be but idle Paradoxes. **1639** FULLER *Holy War* III. iv. (1840) 121 It is therefore no paradox to say, that in some case the strength of a kingdom doth consist in the weakness of it. **1645** MILTON *Tetrach.* (Matt. xix. 7–8) Wks. (1851) 215 The most grosse and massy paradox that ever did violence to reason and religion. **1777** PRIESTLEY *Disc. Philos. Necess.* ix. 110 This will be no paradox, but a most important and necessary truth. **1822** LD. JEFFREY in *Life* (1852) II. 211 The dulness is increased in proportion to the density, and the book becomes ten times more tedious by its compression. This is not a paradox now, but a simple truth. **1851** GLADSTONE *Glean.* VI. xxvi. 17 To my mind there could be no more monstrous paradox, than such a proposition would involve. **1876** L. STEPHEN *Eng. Th. 18th Cent.* II. 375 The apparent paradox that while no man sets a higher value upon truthfulness..than Johnson, no man could care less for the foundations of speculative truth.

c. *Logic.* A statement or proposition which, from an acceptable premise and despite sound reasoning, leads to a conclusion that is against sense, logically unacceptable, or self-contradictory; freq. distinguished by name, esp. of its propounder or of the type of problem it raises. Cf. LIAR 1 d, ***Russell's paradox*** s.v. RUSSELL.

1903 B. RUSSELL *Princ. Math.* xliii. 358 This paradox, which, as I shall show, is strictly correlative to the Achilles, may be called for convenience the Tristram Shandy. **1921** W. E. JOHNSON *Logic* I. iii. 45 The paradox of implication assumes many forms, some of which are not easily recognised as involving mere varieties of the same fundamental principle. **1948** H. C. BRODIE in Brodie & Coleman *Chwistek's Limits of Sci.* p. xxxiii, Typical of such paradoxes is the contradiction of Burali-Forti. **1950** R. CARNAP *Logical Found. Probability* vii. 469 This is an instance of what Hempel calls the paradox of confirmation. **1955** A. N. PRIOR *Formal Logic* III. i. 224 As with Lewis's paradoxes, these appear less startling when the definitions of the terms used are considered. **1966** W. V. QUINE *Ways of Paradox* i. 7 The paradoxes in this class are called antinomies, and it is they that bring on the crises in thought. An antinomy produces a self contradiction by accepted ways of reasoning. **1971** *Brit. Jrnl. Philos. Sci.* XXII. 337 The Nelson-Grelling paradox requires separate notice, because it can be presented with an explicit distinction between predicative phrases and what they are supposed to express. **1972** T. STOPPARD *Jumpers* I. 29 Zeno overlooked the fallacy which is exemplified at its most picturesque in his famous paradoxes, which showed in every way but experience that an arrow could never reach its target. **1973** J. L. MACKIE *Truth, Probability & Paradox* vi. 237 There is a group of paradoxes..which includes the Epimenides and other forms of the liar, heterologicality, Russell's class paradox..and so on.

3. (Without *a* or *plural*.) Paradoxical character, condition, or quality; PARADOXY.

1589 PUTTENHAM *Eng. Poesie* I. xxix. (Arb.) 71 It may be true in manner of Paradoxe. **1788** GIBBON *Decl. & F.* xliv. (ed. Milman) IV. 186 They imbibed..the love of paradox.. and a minute attachment to words and verbal distinctions. *a* **1852** WEBSTER *Wks.* (1877) II. 91 A distinguished lover of liberty of our time, said, with apparent paradox, that the quantity of liberty in any country is exactly equal to the quantity of restraint. **1869** J. MARTINEAU *Ess.* II. 88 A perpetual source of fallacy and paradox.

4. *transf.* A phenomenon that exhibits some contradiction or conflict with preconceived notions of what is reasonable or possible; a person of perplexingly inconsistent life or behaviour. ***hydrostatic paradox***: see HYDROSTATIC.

a **1625** FLETCHER *Woman's Prize* IV. ii, Not let his wife come near him in his sicknes?.. Is she refused? and two old Paradoxes, Peeces of five and fifty without faith, Clapt in upon him? *a* **1687** PETTY *Pol. Arith.* (1690) 92 The wonderful Paradox that Englishmen..pay Customs as Foreigners for all they spend in Ireland. **1706** E. WARD *Wooden World Diss.* (1708) 45 He's a down-right Paradox. **1846** LYTTON *Lucretia* II. xviii, One of those strange living paradoxes that can rarely be found out of a commercial community.

5. A shortening of the specific name *paradoxus* of the Platypus (*Ornithorhynchus paradoxus*).

1815 in O'Hara *Hist. N.S.W.* (1817) 452 The water-mole, or paradox, also abounds in all the rivers and ponds.

6. *attrib.* and *Comb.*, as ***paradox-monger***.

1642 FULLER *Holy & Prof. St.* II. iv. 62 A Paradox-monger, loving to hold strange yea dangerous Opinions. **1879** *Spectator* 23 Aug. 1069 Which made the same brilliant paradoxmonger [Prof. Clifford] enjoy saying, 'There is one thing in the world more wicked than the desire to command, and that is the will to obey'.

†**B.** *adj.* = PARADOXICAL *a.* *Obs.*

1624 CAPT. SMITH *Virginia* VI. 220 Let no man then condemne this paradox opinion. **1654** H. L'ESTRANGE *Chas. I* (1655) 61 Though paradox it may seem, and out of the rode of common beleef. **1660** BARROW *Euclid* III. xvi. *Cor.*, Many Paradox and wonderful Consectaries.

'paradox, *v. rare.* [f. prec. sb.]

†**1.** *trans.* To affect with a paradox, to cause to show a paradox or contradiction. *Obs. rare.*

1627–77 FELTHAM *Resolves* II. xv. 189 The same City that bred him a slave, for his virtues chose him a King; and to his eternal Honour, left his Statue paradox'd with Servitude and Royalty.

2. To bring or drive by paradox. *nonce-use.*

1692 R. L'ESTRANGE *Josephus, Life* (1733) 807 Paradoxing soberer Men than himself out of their Senses.

3. *intr.* To utter paradoxes. Also ***to paradox it***. Hence **'paradoxing** *vbl. sb.*

1647 WARD *Simp. Cobler* 55 If that Parliament will prescribe what they ought, without such paradoxing. **1694** R. L'ESTRANGE *Fables* lviii. (1714) 73 There must be no Paradoxing or Playing Tricks with Things Sacred. *a* **1811** R. CUMBERLAND in T. Mitchell *Aristoph.* II. 46 I could.. dogmatize..and dispute And paradox it with the best of you.

para'doxal, *a. Obs.* in gen. use. [f. L. *paradox-us* adj. (see PARADOX) + -AL¹.] = PARADOXICAL.

†***paradoxal sailing***, 'sailing on the spiral a ship would describe if she continued sailing round the world on any course except east and west, or north and south' (*Editor's note* in *Davis' Wks.* (Hakl. Soc.) 239).

1570 DEE *Math. Pref.* d iv b, Hable to vnderstand..The Proportionall, and Paradoxall Compasses (of me Inuented, for our two Moscouy Master Pilotes, at the request of the Company). **1594** J. DAVIS (*title*) The Sea-mans Secrets.. wherein is taught the 3 kindes of Sailing, Horizontall, Paradoxall, and Sayling vpon a great Circle. *Ibid.* II. Wks. (Hakl. Soc.) 315 By which motion lines are described neyther circular nor straight, but concurred or winding lines, and are therefore called paradoxall, because it is beyond opinion that such lines should be described by plaine horizontall motion. **1600** W. WATSON *Decacordon* (1602) 331 Their paradoxall, pragmaticall, and stratagemicall doctrine. **1653** MILTON *Hirelings* Wks. (1851) 338 If it suffic'd som years past to convince and satisfie the uningag'd of other Nations..though then held paradoxal. *a* **1718** PENN *Tracts* Wks. 1726 I. 678 As Paradoxal as any may please to think it. **1888** *Nature* 19 July 288/2 On paradoxal deafness..in which the patient is deaf to words uttered in the silence of a room, but not in a noisy street.

paradoxer ('pærədɒksə(r)). [f. PARADOX *v.* (or *sb.*) + -ER¹.] A propounder of paradoxes.

1863 DE MORGAN *Budget Paradoxes* (1872) 2, I shall call each of these persons a paradoxer, and his system a paradox. **1864** *Ibid.* 187 My friend Francis Baily was a paradoxer: he brought forward things counter to universal opinion. **1883** *Sat. Rev.* 21 Apr. 489 The political paradoxer is always with us. **1888** *Ibid.* 28 Apr. 515 We have known paradoxers who disputed the competence of actors as teachers of elocution.

†**paradoxial** (pærə'dɒksɪəl), *a. Obs.* [f. L. *paradoxia* PARADOX + -AL¹.] = PARADOXICAL *a.*

1624 BARGRAVE *Two Serm.* 5 Sinne, with all the paradoxiall qualities and ridling intricacy thereof.

para'doxic, *a. rare* [ad. obs. F. *paradoxique* (Cotgr.), It. *paradossico*, f. med.L. type **paradoxicus*: see PARADOX and -IC.] = next.

1632 LITHGOW *Trav.* x. 486 Shall..I..In Paradoxicke passages, Equivocate. **1888** *Science* XI. 174/1 Certain propositions of modern economic writers which are so much at variance with the current doctrines of political economy, that, if true, they are certainly paradoxic.

paradoxical (pærəˈdɒksɪkəl), *a.* [See -ICAL.]

1. Of a doctrine, proposition, etc.: Of the nature of a paradox, exhibiting or involving paradox. **a.** Contrary to common opinion.

1581 [implied in PARADOXICALLY]. **1598** FLORIO, *Paradossale*, paradoxicall, contrarie to the common opinion. **1667** PEPYS *Diary* 10 Apr., Proposing many things paradoxical to our common opinions. **1825** COLERIDGE *Aids Refl.* (1848) I. 6 Many things may be paradoxical, (that is, contrary to the common notion) and nevertheless true: nay, because they are true.

b. Apparently inconsistent with itself, or with reason, though in fact true; also, really inconsistent with reason, and so, absurd or irrational.

1638 JUNIUS *Paint. Ancients* 353 Of this point, which perchance may seem somewhat paradoxicall, we have studied elsewhere to give sufficient proofe. **1664** POWER *Exp. Philos.* I. 71, I have but one paradoxical and extravagant Quaere to make. **1678** CUDWORTH *Intell. Syst.* I. i. §34. 43 This Philosophy of the Ancients, which seems to be so prodigiously paradoxical, in respect of that Pre-existence and Transmigration of Souls. **1748** *Anson's Voy.* III. v. 342 This, however paradoxical it may appear, is evident enough. **1825** LAMB *Elia* Ser. II. *Stage Illusion*, Comedians, paradoxical as it may seem, may be too natural. **1876** FREEMAN *Norm. Conq.* V. xxiii. 65 It would be true, though it might sound paradoxical, to say that the Norman Conquest made England Saxon.

2. Of persons, etc.: Fond of or given to paradox.

1613 PURCHAS *Pilgrimage* (1614) 41 Goropius after his wont paradoxicall, holdeth it to be the Hill Paropanisus, or Paropamisus, a part of the Hill Taurus. **1708** SWIFT *Abol. Chr.* Wks. 1755 II. I. 82 This perhaps may appear too great a paradox even for our wise and paradoxical age to endure. **1875** JOWETT *Plato* (ed. 2) IV. 529 There is..a paradoxical element in the Statesman which delights in reversing the accustomed use of words. **1881** *Sat. Rev.* 23 July 101/1 Dean Stanley's paradoxical temper.

3. a. Of a phenomenon, circumstance, etc.: Exhibiting some contradiction with known laws or with itself; not in accordance with what is theoretically reasonable or possible; now said esp. of natural phenomena that deviate from the normal or are hard to reconcile with known scientific laws.

1646 SIR T. BROWNE *Pseud. Ep.* 107 Among those many paradoxicall and unheard of imitations. **1812–16** PLAYFAIR *Nat. Phil.* (1819) I. 161 A phenomenon not a little paradoxical, and not yet sufficiently examined. **1845** DARWIN *Voy. Nat.* i. (1879) 11 A most paradoxical mixture of sound and silence pervades the shady parts of the wood. **1899** *Allbutt's Syst. Med.* VI. 231 Zahn gave the name 'paradoxical embolism'..to the transportation of emboli derived from veins into the systemic arteries without passing through the pulmonary circulation.

b. Applied to sleep that is characterized by increased physiological and mental activity (e.g. rapid eye-movements and dreaming in man) and normally alternates with longer periods of orthodox sleep.

[**1959** JOUVET & MICHEL in *Compt. Rend. Soc. de Biol.* CLIII. 422 Cette phase est suivie d'une 'phase paradoxale' dont l'activité est extrêmement caractéristique.] **1962** I. OSWALD *Sleeping & Waking* i. 16 (*heading*) 'Paradoxical phase' of sleep in the cat. **1969** *Sci. Jrnl.* Dec. 78/3 The brainwaves of paradoxical sleep are more like those during normal wakefulness. **1970** *New Scientist* 23 Apr. 170/2 After about an hour of this orthodox sleep phase..paradoxical sleep begins and lasts about 10 minutes before orthodox sleep is resumed. The electrical brain waves and many other bodily functions during paradoxical sleep are different—..most muscles become quite flaccid and their reflexes are lost; the penis is erect; the heart, breathing and blood pressure are irregular; [etc.]. **1974** *Times* 4 Sept. 6/7 There was increasing evidence of a 90-minute rhythm in both sleep and waking activity. Paradoxical sleep (when dreaming) occurred every 90 minutes. **1977** D. MORRIS *Manwatching* 315 So it is safe to assume that the total of 1½ hours of Pardoxical Sleep we have each night really does represent 1½ hours of actual dreaming.

paradoxicality (pærədɒksɪˈkælɪtɪ). [f. prec. + -ITY.] Paradoxical character or quality.

1816 BENTHAM *Chrestomathia* Wks. 1843 VIII. 48 But for the apparent paradoxicality and anti-sentimentality, instead of *economizing*, *minimizing* would, in this case..have been inserted. **1889** *Ch. Times* 9 Aug. 720/1 Here comes in Ward's paradoxicality.

para'doxically, *adv.* [f. as prec. + -LY².] In a paradoxical manner; in such a way or sense as to involve a paradox.

1581 SIDNEY *Apol. Poetrie* (Arb.) 51, I aunswere paradoxically, but truely. **1606** *Sir G. Goosecappe* v. i. in Bullen *O.P.* (1884) III. 81 Divinely spoken, Sir, but verie Paradoxicallie. **1788** PRIESTLEY *Lect. Hist.* v. lxiv. 512 Some persons have paradoxically maintained that there can be no inconvenience whatever attending any national debt. **1859** GEO. ELIOT *A. Bede* v, Nevertheless, to speak paradoxically, the existence of insignificant people has very important consequences in the world.

para'doxicalness. [f. as prec. + -NESS.] The quality of being paradoxical; paradoxicality.

1668 H. MORE *Div. Dial.* III. iii. (1713) 184 The confident Ignorance of the rude and the unexpected Paradoxicalness of the skilful. **1879** H. SPENCER *Data of Ethics* vi. 77 The seeming paradoxicalness of this statement.

paradoxician (ˌpærədɒkˈsɪʃən). *rare.* [f. PARADOX *sb.* + -ICIAN.] One who deals in paradoxes; a paradoxer.

1909 W. J. LOCKE *Septimus* xvi. 186 Sypher was not convinced by the airy paradoxician.

parado'xidian, *a. Palæont.* [f. mod.L. *Paradoxides*, f. Gr. παράδοξ-ος: see PARADOX and -IAN.] Of or pertaining to the *Paradoxides*, a genus of large trilobites of Middle Cambrian age.

1882 GEIKIE *Text-bk. Geol.* 652. **1893** *Ibid.* (ed. 3) 725 Geologists have grouped the Cambrian rocks in three divisions—the lower or Olenellus group, the middle or Paradoxidian, and the upper or Olenidian.

†**paradoxion**, *a. Obs.* [app. error for *paradoxian*.] = PARADOXICAL.

1631 J. DONE *Polydoron* 40 Of all manner of People I hate the paradoxion babling wit shewers.

paradoxism (ˈpærədɒksɪz(ə)m). [f. PARADOX + -ISM. Cf. mod.F. *paradoxisme*.] The utterance or practice of paradox.

1593 NASHE *Christ's T.* (1613) 119 They would be different in paradoxisme from all the world. **1869** *Eng. Mech.* 17 Dec. 329/3 All this may seem like paradoxism of the first water, but it is fact.

paradoxist (ˈpærədɒksɪst). [f. as prec. + -IST.] A dealer in paradoxes; a paradoxer.

1673 O. WALKER *Educ.* xi. 132 For reading; verse him well in inuentive Authors, such are generally all Paradoxists, Satyrists. **1869** *Eng. Mech.* 12 Nov. 204/3 The race of paradoxists is not confined to our own country. **1871** *Athenæum* 25 Mar. 370/1 It was [De Morgan's] intention to complete his humorous exhibition of paradoxists with another series of papers.

paradoxling (ˈpærəˌdɒkslɪŋ). *nonce-wd.* [f. PARADOX *sb.* + -LING¹ 2.] A statement or tenet that is slightly paradoxical.

1863 G. M. HOPKINS *Let.* 10 July (1956) 199 Yes. You are a Fool. I can shew it syllogistically, by an Epimediculum or paradoxling.

paradoxo'graphical, *a.* [f. Gr. παραδοξογράφ-ος a writer of paradoxes + -ICAL.] Belonging or addicted to the writing of paradoxes.

1814 T. L. PEACOCK *Wks.* (1875) III. 121 Some such paradoxographical philosophaster. **1904** W. H. STEVENSON in *Eng. Hist. Rev.* Jan. 139 He assigns the younger periplus to the Alexandrian or post-Alexandrian times on account of its paradoxographical character.

paradoxology (pærədɒkˈsɒlədʒɪ). [ad. Gr. παραδοξολογία, f. παραδοξολόγος telling of paradoxes: see -LOGY.] A maintaining or putting forward of paradoxical opinions, a speaking by paradox.

1646 SIR T. BROWNE *Pseud. Ep.* To Rdr. (1650) 3 Who shall indifferently perpend the exceeding difficulty, which either the obscurity of the subject, or unavoidable paradoxologie must often put upon the Attemptor. **1856** G. F. COLLIER (*title*) Reg. v. Palmer, the Parodoxology of Poisoning. **1902** *Athenæum* 14 June 746/2 When Cicero accused Cato of political paradoxology.

paradoxure (pærəˈdɒksjʊə(r)). *Zool.* [ad. mod.L. *paradoxūrus*, f. Gr. παράδοξ-ος (see PARADOX) + οὐρά tail.] An animal of the genus *Paradoxurus*, family *Viverridæ*, or of an allied genus, so called because of its remarkably long curving tail; a palm-cat, palm-marten, or palm-civet.

1843 *Penny Cycl.* XXVI. 407/2 The Paradoxure was confounded by Buffon with the Common Genet. **1883** W. H. FLOWER in *Encycl. Brit.* XV. 436/2 The Paradoxures or Palm-Civets are less strictly carnivorous than the other members of the family. *Ibid.*, *Hemigale*, another modification of the Paradoxure type. **1886** P. S. ROBINSON *Valley Teet. Trees* 99 Paradoxures squeak and scuffle. The jerboas are wide awake.

paradoxurine (pærəˈdɒksjʊraɪn), *a.* and *sb.* [f. mod.L. *Paradoxūrinæ*: see prec. and -INE¹.]

a. *adj.* Of or pertaining to the sub-family *Paradoxurinæ*, of which *Paradoxurus* (see prec.) is the typical genus. **b.** *sb.* A member of this group.

1882 MIVART in *Proc. Zool. Soc.* 137 Professor Flower.. conclusively establishes..the Paradoxurine affinity of Arctictis. **1891** FLOWER & LYDEKKER *Mammalia* xi. 532.

paradoxy (ˈpærədɒksɪ). [ad. Gr. παραδοξία, f. παράδοξ-ος: see PARADOX.]

†**1.** A paradox. *Obs. rare*⁻¹.

1646 SIR T. BROWNE *Pseud. Ep.* 361 With industry we decline such paradoxies, and peaceably submit unto their received acceptions.

2. Paradoxical quality or character; paradoxicality.

1796 W. TAYLOR in *Monthly Mag.* II. 777 Another well-known passage..stating the paradoxy of the Christian Creed. *a* **1871** DE MORGAN *Budget Paradoxes* (1872) 186 It may be that ignorance had more to do with it than paradoxy. **1873** F. HALL *Mod. Eng.* Pref. 11 Regarding any truth whatsoever which is not of obvious perception in its fulness, paradoxy is likely to be orthodoxy.

†**'paradrome.** *Obs. rare*⁻⁰. [ad. Gr. παραδρομίς 'place for taking the air' (Liddell and Sc.).]

1656 BLOUNT *Glossogr.*, *Paradrome*, an open Gallery or walk, that has no shelter over head. **1658** in PHILLIPS.

paradromic (pærəˈdrɒmɪk), *a.* [f. Gr. παράδρομ-ος running alongside + -IC.] Running side by side; ***paradromic winding***, winding in courses that run side by side.

1883 TAIT in *Nature* 1 Feb. 317/1 The consideration of double-threaded screws, twisted bundles of fibres, etc., leads to the general theory of paradromic winding. **1884** TAIT *Scientif. Papers* II. 91 A subject treated by Listing, which he calls paradromic winding.

paradrop (ˈpærədrɒp), *sb.* and *v.* [f. PARA-³ + DROP *sb.* 12 g or DROP *v.*] **A.** *sb.* The dropping from aircraft of men or supplies by parachute. **B.** *v. trans.* To drop (men or supplies) in this way. Hence **para'dropping** *vbl. sb.*

1948 *Shell Aviation News* No. 118. 9/1 Back at the main supply base of Shell-Mera a radio message is received from this headquarters for a paradrop and feverish activity ensues. **1950** *Birmingham* (Alabama) *News* 27 Nov. 28/3 An Iuka man was one of the pilots who para-dropped more than 4,000 men of the 11th Airborne on an arc between the North Korean cities of Sukcon and Sunchow. **1952** *Time* 31 Mar. 71/2 (Advt.), Here, it paradrops vital supplies 'up front'. **1961** *Flight* LXXX. 371/2 The rear ramp allows paradropping. **1971** *Morning Star* 26 June 1 Liberation troops inspecting a U.S. ammunition paradrop captured in the far north of South Vietnam.

paradventure, obs. f. PERADVENTURE.

parael, var. PAREL *v. Obs.*

paræmiac, etc.: see PARŒMIAC, etc.

‖**parænesis, paren-** (pəˈriːnɪsɪs, -ˈɛnɪsɪs). [late L. *parænesis*, a. Gr. παραίνεσις exhortation, recommendation, f. παραινεῖν to exhort, advise, f. παρα- beside + αἰνεῖν to speak of, praise, commend. In F. *parénèse*.] Exhortation, advice, counsel; a hortatory composition.

1604 EARL STIRLING (*title*) A Paraenesis to the Prince. **1664** EVELYN *Sylva* 105 A short Parænesis touching the present ordering, and disposing of his Majesties Plantations for the future benefit of the Nation. **1716** M. DAVIES *Athen. Brit.* III. *Diss. Drama* 38 By way of Apology, or Parenesis, or both, to the Jews in general. **1866** T. HARPER *Peace thr. Truth* 229 Clement of Alexandria..in the course of a parænesis on sobriety in the drinking of wine [etc.].

Hence †**pa'rænesize** *v. Obs. rare*, to exhort.

1716 M. DAVIES *Athen. Brit.* II. To Rdr. 15, I Paranesize and endeavour to Proselyte them to [etc.].

parænetic, -enetic (pæriːˈnɛtɪk), *a.* (*sb.*) [ad. med.L. *parænetic-us*, a. Gr. παραινετικ-ός hortatory: see prec. and -IC. In F. *parénétique* (1574 in Hatz.-Darm.).] Of, pertaining to, or of the nature of parænesis; advisory, hortatory.

1656 BLOUNT *Glossogr.*, *Parenetick*. **1678** R. L'ESTRANGE *Seneca's Mor.* (1702) 393 Cleanthes allows the Parænetick, or Preceptive Philosophy, to be in some sort Profitable. **1873** W. WAGNER tr. *Teuffel's Hist. Rom. Lit.* II. 300 Of a practical and paraenetic character. **1891** DRIVER *Introd. Lit. O.T.* 32 Clauses..of a parenetic or hortatory character.

†**B.** *sb.* A hortatory composition. *Obs.*

1645 *Liberty of Consc.* 38 Let us heare no more Pareneticks for Toleration. **1656** BLOUNT *Glossogr.*, *Pareneticks*, are taken for verses full of precepts or admonitions.

paræ'netical, -e'netical, *a.* Now *rare.* [f. as prec. + -AL¹.] = prec.

1598 (*title*) A Treatise Parænetical, That is to say: An Exhortation, Wherein is shewed..the right way and true meanes to resist the violence of the Castilian king.. Translated..into the French, by I. D. Dralymont... And now Englished. *a* **1641** BP. MOUNTAGU *Acts & Mon.* vii. (1642) 435 Their writings..both Pareneticall and also Apologeticall. **1716** M. DAVIES *Athen. Brit.* II. 131 Parænetical Lectures. **1824** DIBDIN *Libr. Comp.* 466 The author..need desire nothing more parænetical than the criticism of Meuselius.

‖**paræsthesia, -esthesia** (pærɛs-, -iːsˈθiːzɪə). *Path.* [f. PARA-¹ 'disordered' + Gr. αἴσθησις perception, sensation: see ÆSTHESIS.] Disordered or perverted sensation; a hallucination of any of the senses. Also ‖**paræs'thesis**; hence **paræsthetic** (-ˈθɛtɪk), of, pertaining to, or affected with paræsthesia.

1857 MAYNE *Expos. Lex.*, Paresthetic. **1873** T. H. GREEN *Introd. Pathol.* (ed. 2) 217 They include great excitability, paræsthesiæ of sight and hearing. **1889** *Alien. & Neurol.* X. 442 A number of paræsthetic symptoms. **1897** *Allbutt's Syst. Med.* IV. 762 Chlorotic and anæmic girls..very frequently suffer from paræsthesia of the throat region. **1899** *Ibid.* VIII. 567 Various palsies and paræsthesias.

paraf, paraff: see PARAPH.

parafango (ˌpærəˈfæŋgəʊ). [f. PARA(FFIN *sb.* + FANGO.] A mixture of mud and paraffin wax used for medicinal purposes (see quots.).

1969 *Daily Tel.* 25 June 15/6 Other new treatments recently introduced at Henlow include..the parafango, a mixture of mud and paraffin wax for spot reducing, arthritis and rheumatism. **1970** *Guardian* 4 Apr. 11/7 Parafango is the technical term for warm wax or mud baths.

parafe, *v.* App. var. of PARAPH *v.* 2.

1922 JOYCE *Ulysses* 212 Farrell parafes his polysyllables.

paraffin ('pærəfɪn), *sb.* Also -ine. [f. L. *parum* too little, barely + *affinis* having affinity: so named by Reichenbach 1830 in reference to its neutral quality and the small affinity it possesses for other bodies. See *Journal f. Chem. u. Physik* LIX. 456.]

1. A colourless (or white), tasteless, inodorous, crystalline, fatty substance, solid at ordinary temperatures (chemically a mixture of hydrocarbons of the series C_nH_{2n+2}), discovered by Reichenbach in 1830; obtained by dry distillation from wood, coal, peat, petroleum, wax, and other substances, and also occurring native in coal and other bituminous strata; subsequently used for making candles, as a waterproofing material, for electrical insulators, and for various other purposes.

1838 *Penny Cycl.* XII. 396 Paraffin was discovered about the same time [1830] by Dr. Christison and Dr. Reichenbach; the former..called it *petrolin.* **1839** URE *Dict. Arts* 942 Paraffine is a..solid bicarburet of hydrogen; it has not hitherto been applied to any use, but it would form admirable candles. **1854** RONALDS & RICHARDSON *Chem. Technol.* (ed. 2) I. 374 The amount of paraffine, according to these experiments obtained from 1 ton of peat does not exceed 2½ lbs. **1868** *Q. Rev.* Apr. 345 It is not..from coal, but from certain shales, that the most abundant yield of paraffin is thus obtained. **1901** *Daily News* 10 Mar. 7/5 Until 1873 paraffin as a candle-making material had been produced almost wholly in Scotland and Germany.

2. Short for *paraffin oil*: see 4.

1861 *Ann. Reg.* 234 There has been lately introduced, for the purposes of light, an oil called 'paraffin'. **1865** *Times* 9 Mar., The hon. secretary to the River Dee Salmon Fishery had preserved a bottle of pure paraffin made from the waters of the Dee. **1880** MISS BRADDON *Just as I am* xii, [He] set his face against paraffin and the whole family of oils.

3. *Chem.* A general name, introduced by Watts 1872, for the saturated hydrocarbons of the series C_nH_{2n+2}, of which the first four members, methane, ethane, propane, quartane (see -ANE) are at ordinary temperatures gaseous, those higher in the series, oily liquids, and those higher still, solids; all are remarkable for their chemical indifference, the hydrogen being combined in the highest proportion possible with the carbon.

1872 WATTS *Dict. Chem.* VI. 705 This substance is a hydrocarbon or a mixture of hydrocarbons of the series C_nH_{2n+2};..the name paraffin may therefore be conveniently used as a generic term for the whole series. **1873** —— *Fownes' Chem.* 545 Many of the paraffins occur ready-formed in American petroleum. **1894** *Schorlemmer's Rise & Devel. Org. Chem.* 92 Henry Watts proposed to call the whole series the *paraffins*, and this name has been accepted.

4. *attrib.* and *Comb.*, as ***paraffin candle***, ***heater***, ***lamp***, ***-refiner***, ***stove***, ***tin***; **paraffin oil**, any one of several oils obtained by distillation of coal, petroleum, and other substances (chemically, liquid members of the paraffin series (see 3), or mixtures of these, often with admixture of other hydrocarbons), used as illuminants and lubricants; also called simply *paraffin* (see 2), *kerosene*, or *petroleum*; **paraffin scales**, manufacturers' name for a crude solid paraffin; **paraffin test** (see quots.); **paraffin wax**, solid paraffin (= sense 1), as distinct from *paraffin oil*.

1889 *Cent. Dict.* s.v. *Butter*, *Paraffin-butter, a crude paraffin which is used for making candles. **1862** FARADAY *Hist. Candle* 18 *Paraffin candles made of paraffin obtained from the bogs of Ireland. **1871** ROSCOE *Elem. Chem.* 294 The fatty or *paraffin group of organic bodies. **1939–40** *Army & Navy Stores Catal.* 191/3 Coleman *Paraffin Heater.. Burns ordinary paraffin oil. **1975** J. MCCLURE *Snake* iv. 59 She had dumped..that very serviceable old paraffin heater, that was only a little rusty, on her new rubbish tip. **1976** *Sunday Mail* (Glasgow) 21 Nov., It is a disgrace that people who have worked hard all their days should be forced to use paraffin heaters because they cannot afford their electricity bills. **1872** *Routledge's Ev. Boy's Ann.* 155/1 *Paraffin-lamps were not used in the house. **1874** MICKLETHWAITE *Mod. Par. Churches* 198 Paraffine lamps are now becoming much used. **1851** J. YOUNG in *Mech. Mag.* LIV. 334 Treating bituminous coal..to obtain therefrom an oil containing paraffine which the patentee calls *paraffine oil. **1866** WATTS *Dict. Chem.* IV. 1 Boghead or Bathgate Naphtha, also called Photogen and Paraffin oil. *a* **1882** SIR R. CHRISTISON *Autobiog.* (1885) I. 395 Paraffin-oil..had been found the best of all anti-friction lubricants. **1949** Paraffin oil [see KEROSENE]. **1950** *Sci. News* XV. 99 Serum from the umbilical cord can be guaranteed to increase haemoglobin production in rats only if collected under paraffin oil, that is, when protected from the oxygen of the air. **1899** *Allbutt's Syst. Med.* VIII. 521 Sulphur..in *paraffin ointment is useful. **1880** *Spons' Encycl. Manuf.* I. 586 The crude solid product separated from the light and heavy oils by the mineral oil refiners, and known as '*paraffin scales'. **1966** M. WOODHOUSE *Tree Frog* xvi. 123 There was a pressure cooker and two large *paraffin stoves. **1978** 'L. BLACK' *Foursome* ii. 18 The fug of the small wooden shed heated by a paraffin stove. **1888** *Pall Mall G.* 29 Aug. 12/1 Dinner was finished by the light of *paraffine tapers. **1950** *Ellery Queen's Mystery Mag.* Oct. 101/1 'What's a *paraffin test?' asked Nicky... 'Every gun..has a certain amount of backfire. Some of the gunpowder flashes back and is embedded in the hand of the man that fires. They coat his hand with hot paraffin and then draw it off like a glove. They then test it for gunpowder..and if it's positive, it means that the man fired the gun.' **1974** R. B. PARKER *Godwulf Manuscript* iii. 23 A paraffin test. When you fire a handgun cordite particles impregnate your skin. A lab man puts paraffin over it, lets it dry, peels it off, and tests it. The particles show up in the wax. **1935** H. EDIB *Clown & his Daughter* lv. 342 Some of them brought empty *paraffin-tins. **1937** K. BLIXEN *Out of Afr.* i. 12 The Swahili town..was built mostly out of old paraffin tins hammered flat. **1872** *Routledge's Ev. Boy's Ann.* Apr. 307/1 *Paraffine-wax candles form a good source of light. **1894** BOTTONE *Electr. Instr. Making* (ed. 6) 18 When paraffin is mentioned in this work, paraffin *wax* is understood, not paraffin *oil*.

Hence **'paraffin** *v. trans.*, to cover, impregnate, or treat with paraffin (chiefly in *ppl. a.* **'paraffined**); **para'ffinic** *a.*, *Chem.*, of paraffin, as ***paraffinic nitrite***, a compound of nitrous acid and a paraffin, having the formula $C_nH_{2n+1}NO_2$, also called *nitroparaffin*; **'paraffiˌnize** *v. trans.*, to treat with paraffin; **'paraffinoid** *a.*, of the form of or akin to paraffin.

1876 PREECE & SIVEWRIGHT *Telegraphy* 133 An apparatus composed of alternate layers of tin-foil and *paraffined paper. **1891** *Anthony's Photogr. Bull.* IV. 13 Dry them by pouring the white albumen upon a clean board which has been paraffined. **1891** *Athenæum* 14 Mar. 347/3 On the Physiological Action of the *Paraffinic Nitrites. **1888** *Amer. Nat.* XXII. 859 The *paraffinized preparation is placed on a layer of cotton to cool. **1887** *Standard* 16 Sept. 3/3 Transition from tars of the *paraffinoid to those of the benzenoid or ordinary gas tar varieties.

paraffiny ('pærəfɪnɪ), *a.* [f. PARAFFIN *sb.* + -Y¹.] Of, belonging to, or suggestive of paraffin; covered or smeared with paraffin; smelling of paraffin.

1902 CONRAD *Youth* 21 The ascending air was hot, and had a heavy, sooty, paraffiny smell. **1925** B. BEETHAM in E. F. Norton *Fight for Everest, 1924* III. vi. 368 Paraffiny fingers will taint the whole canteen. **1952** 'J. TEY' *Singing Sands* vi. 93 A large wooden tray of tuppenny buns... They were crummy and depressed-looking,..and they smelled very faintly of paraffin...the paraffiny buns and the margarine.

†**pa'raffle, pa'rafle.** *Sc. Obs.* [perh. ad. F. *parafe, paraphe* a flourish added to a signature.] 'Ostentatious display' (Jam.).

1816 SCOTT *Antiquary* xxi, Whether it is of these grand parafle o' ceremonies that Holy Writ says 'it is an abomination to me'. **1824** —— *Redgauntlet* Let. v, The subject of this paraffle of words.

parafibrin, -flagellate, etc.: see PARA-¹.

Parafilm ('pærəfɪlm). Also **parafilm.** A proprietary name for certain thermoplastic materials (see quots. 1952, 1956).

1934 *Official Gaz.* (U.S. Patent Office) 18 Sept. 520/2 Marathon Paper Mills Co., Rothschild, Wis. Filed July 23, 1934, *Parafilm.* For moistureproof, self-sealing flat wrapper, claims use July 11, 1934. **1952** *Trade Marks Jrnl.* 21 May 472/1 Parafilm... Backing cloth, being piece goods ..consisting of textile material coated with a thermoplastic substance containing rubber, the textile material predominating, for use in the manufacture of boots and shoes. Lindsay & Williams Limited,..Manchester..; manufacturers. **1956** *Ibid.* 8 Feb. 131/2 Parafilm... Electrical insulation identification tape. Lindsay & Williams Limited,..Manchester..; manufacturers. *Ibid.* 26 Sept. 947/2 Parafilm... Thermoplastic materials in the form of sheets, ribbons and tapes, none being textiles... Lindsay & Williams Limited,..Manchester..; manufacturers. **1967** K. M. SMITH *Insect Virology* xi. 214 Recently..the animal membrane has been replaced by stretched Parafilm. **1974** *Nature* 3 May 85/1 The mouth-parts of a dehydrated tick were inserted through a wax-coated parafilm membrane up to the base of the palps.

parafiscal, *a.*: see PARA-¹ 1.

parafoil ('pærəfɔɪl). Also **para-foil.** [f. PARA-³ + AERO)FOIL.] A structure of fabric designed to function as both a parachute and an aerofoil, providing lift that enables the wearer to glide.

1967 *N.Y. Times* 13 Aug. 15 A revolutionary parachute invention..known as the para-foil, would enable pilots bailing out over enemy territory to glide like birds until they reached safety. **1968** *Sunday Times* 28 Sept. 5/1 Air fills the cells of his parafoil and flows over the upper surface, creating 'lift', as with an aeroplane. **1975** *Sci. Amer.* Mar. 122/3 A major breakthrough was the invention of an inflatable multicell airfoil of fabric by D. C. Jalbert of Boca Raton, Fla... It is called the Para-Foil... Its shape in the form of a rigid, low-speed wing, is maintained entirely by air that enters openings at the leading edge to build up internal pressure. On landing the Para-Foil..can be collapsed into a manageable bundle of lines and cloth. One can also jump with it from an aeroplane. **1976** *Listener* 8 July 30/3 We sent up a parafoil instead, an amazing American invention without any rigid structure, a mixture of balloon, parachute, aerofoil and kite, which instantly climbs to the permitted height of 200 feet.

parafo'llicular, *a.* *Anat.* [f. PARA-¹ + FOLLICULAR *a.*] Situated near to, or around, a follicle: applied to cells found between the follicles of the mammalian thyroid gland, which secrete the hormone thyrocalcitonin.

1932 J. F. NONIDEZ in *Amer. Jrnl. Anat.* XLIX. 479 In the following pages the large epithelial cells with argyrophile granules will be termed 'parafollicular' cells, since they lie in the interstitial spaces in close proximity to the follicles from the epithelium of which they arose. **1968** H. RASMUSSEN in R. H. Williams *Textbk. Endocrinol.* (ed. 4) xi. 877/2 Between the follicles [of the thyroid gland] are groups of epithelial cells variously described as interstitial cells, mitochondrial-rich, or parafollicular cells. **1975** FRANCIS & MARTIN *Introd. Human Anat.* (ed. 7) viii. 267 The ultimo-branchial body, an integral part of the thyroid, in man is represented by the parafollicular or C cells.

paraform(aldehyde: see PARA-¹ 2 a.

parafovea (pærə'fəʊvɪə). *Anat.* Also with hyphen. [f. PARA-¹ + FOVEA, or as back-formation from next.] An annular area of the retina immediately surrounding the fovea centralis. Cf. PERIFOVEA.

1941 S. L. POLYAK *Retina* xvi. 211 The parafoveal region or parafovea is the intermediate belt of the central area [of the retina]. **1944** *Jrnl. Optical Soc. Amer.* XXXIV. 713/1 Rods, though absent from the fovea, appear in the parafovea and increase to a maximum density within the area of the retina to which the bright field image is projected. **1960** R. A. WEALE *Eye & its Function* v. 65 The corneo-lenticular system cannot form a sharp and undistorted image outside an area called the para-fovea. This surrounds the macula and would be covered by the image of a circular disc subtending at the eye an angular diameter of some 20°. **1970** J. A. HOWARD *Aerial Photo-Ecol.* xiii. 141 The fovea is most sensitive to green light at 0·555μ whilst in subdued light the para-fovea responds most to light at 0·515μ.

parafoveal (pærə'fəʊvɪəl), *a.* *Anat.* [f. PARA-¹ + FOVEA + -AL.] Of or pertaining to the parafovea; adjacent to the fovea.

1925 *Brit. Jrnl. Ophthalm.* IX. 53 Frequently [in macular disease] the paracentral or parafoveal elements are mainly involved. **1941** [see prec.]. **1959** S. DUKE-ELDER *Parsons' Dis. Eye* (ed. 13) xxii. 321 Central serous retinopathy..is presumably caused by exudation from the parafoveal capillaries, probably of toxic or allergic origin. **1971** *Jrnl. Gen. Psychol.* LXXXIV. 48 The considerable amount of stray light..stimulates parafoveal rods.

Hence **para'foveally** *adv.*, in a parafoveal manner; by means of the parafovea.

1960 *New Scientist* 10 Nov. 1267/2 When an object is seen parafoveally or peripherally, detail is not perceived; the object is seen as a comparatively vague shape, and the eye in these regions is sensitive mainly to motion. **1963** *Jrnl. Psychol.* LV. 394 Brightness enhancement was measurably present for part-spectrum impingements presented parafoveally under the proper conditions of intermittency.

†**parafrenesie, -frensie.** *Obs. rare.* [= OF. *parafrenasie*, ad. med.L. *parafrenēsis*, f. Gr. παρα-, PARA-¹, in sense 'false, spurious' + L. *phrenēsis* (in Celsus as a Gr. word φρένησις) madness, delirium, FRENZY.] Temporary delirium, due (as was thought) not to disorder of the brain itself, but to its being affected by the fevered state of some other part.

1398 TREVISA *Barth. De P.R.* VII. v. (Bodl. MS.), It comeþ of fumosite and smoke þat comeþ vpward to þe brayne & disturbleþ þe brayne and hatte parafrenesie, nought vrei frenesy [BARTHOL. parafrenesis, i. frenesis non vera; *OFr. version* (Godef.) parafrenasie, qui n'est pas vraye frenasye]. *Ibid.*, þanne þe brayne turneþ aȝen into his owne good state and þanne þis yuel parafrenesie is deliuered.

†**'parafront.** *Obs.* Also 7 paraphront. [f. Gr. παρα- beside, alongside of + FRONT.] A hanging for an altar, apparently a DOSSAL.

1641 *Comm. of Accommod.* in Neal *Hist. Purit.* (1733) II. 462 Advancing Crucifixes and Images upon the Parafront or Altar-cloth. *a* **1670** HACKET in Plume *Life* (1865) 129 The most curious piece that I have ever seen of purple velvet flowered with gold and silk, to be placed in the parafront above the cushion. *a* **1670** —— *Abp. Williams* II. (1692) 107 That religion might have a dialect proper to itself, as Paten, Chalice, Corporal, Albe, Paraphront, Suffront, for the hangings above and beneath the table.

paragal, variant of PAREGAL.

paragamy (pə'rægəmɪ). *Biol.* [f. Gr. παρα- beside, alongside + -γαμία marriage.] Applied to a special mode of reproduction: see quot.

1891 HARTOG in *Nature* 17 Sept. 484 Paragenesis will include the following modes, usually grouped under the term parthenogenesis, apogamy (*pro parte*), &c.:—A. True Parthenogenesis... B. Simulated Parthenogenesis... C. Metagametal Rejuvenescence... D. Paragamy or Endokaryogamy: vegetative or gametal nuclei lying in a continuous mass of cytoplasm fuse to form a zygote nucleus. 1. Progamic paragamy... 2. Apocytial paragamy.

paraganglioma (ˌpærəgæŋglɪ'əʊmə). *Path.* Pl. **-omas, -omata.** [ad. F. *paragangliome* (Alezais & Peyron 1908, in *Compt. Rend. des Séances de la Soc. de Biol.* LXV. 746): see next and -OMA.] A tumour thought to arise from a paraganglion (in its wider sense) or the adrenal medulla; *esp.* one of non-chromaffin tissue. Cf. PHÆOCHROMOCYTOMA.

1914 *Surg., Gynecol. & Obstetr.* XVIII. 209/1 Whenever a tumor of a paraganglion—a paraganglioma—is suspected, it should be fixed in a solution containing chromic acid or its salts. **1925** *Amer. Jrnl. Anat.* XXXIV. 89 By far the greater number of pathologists believe in a vascular origin for the growths of the carotid body... Some later workers would call these tumors 'paragangliomas'. **1948** MARTIN & HYNES *Clin. Endocrinol.* vii. 144 Chromaffin tumours. These uncommon tumours include the phæochromocytomata which arise from chromophile cells of the adrenal medulla, and the paragangliomata which originate from chromaffin tissue in the intrathoracic cervical chain, the carotid bodies, or the organs of Zuckerkandl. **1956** H. M. Zimmerman et al. *Atlas Tumors Nervous Syst.* 177/1 The chromaffin tumors are found most commonly in the adrenal medulla... They are called pheochromocytomas (chromaffin tumor, functionally active paraganglioma)... The term 'paraganglioma' is best used for the non-secretory and hence non-chromaffin tumors of the paraganglionic tissues. **1974** Passmore & Robson *Compan. Med. Stud.* III. I. xvii. 37/1 Glomus jugulare tumours. These are another example of non-chromaffin paragangliomata; they..grow in the connective tissue that lies between the bulb of the internal jugular vein and the floor of the middle ear.

Hence ˌ**paragangli'omatous** *a.*

1965 *Jrnl. Clin. Path.* XVIII. 291/2 Medullary carcinoma may resemble various neural or paragangliomatous tumours.

paraganglion (pærəˈgæŋglɪən). *Anat.* Pl. -ia. [a. G. *paraganglion* (A. Kohn 1900, in *Arch. f. mikrosk. Anat.* LVI. 130): see PARA-[1] and GANGLION.] Any of several highly vascular groups of chromaffin cells that are similar to those of the adrenal medulla and in position and development are closely associated with the sympathetic nerve trunks; also applied to some structures now recognized as non-chromaffin (see quots. 1940, 1962).

1907 *Med. Rec.* (N.Y.) 3 Aug. 188/2 These occur in the medullary substance of the adrenal bodies, in the so-called paraganglia of the same organs. **1930** Maksimov & Bloom *Textbk. Histol.* xxxiv. 709 These paraganglia include the carotid gland and widespread, rather small accumulations of cells in the retroperitoneum which are often spoken of as the organs of Zuckerkandl. **1937** *Contrib. Embryol.* XXVI. 17 A study of the development of the carotid body..has left me unconvinced that it can be regarded as a paraganglion in the strict sense of the term. *A priori*..the term paraganglion means a structure of which the essential cells are derived in their entirety from the nervous system. **1940** *Q. Rev. Biol.* XV. 167/2 Recently..a distinction has been made between chromaffin and non-chromaffin paraganglia. **1962** E. C. Crosby et al. *Correl. Anat. Nerv. Syst.* viii. 545/1 Small collections of cells found in relation with certain blood vessels constitute the carotid body, the aortic bodies, the jugular body..and the coccygeal body... Although sometimes referred to as paraganglia, as the term is used in its wider sense, these cell masses usually contain no chromaffin cells and are unlike the chromaffin bodies in other ways as well. **1965** Lee & Knowles *Animal Hormones* iv. 85 In mammals additional chromaffin tissue may be found in the lower part of the abdominal aorta (para-aortic glands), or in contact with sympathetic ganglia (paraganglia).

Hence ˌ**paragangli'onic** *a.*

1937 *Contrib. Embryol.* XXVI. 27 *(caption)* Reconstruction of the branchial-arch arteries in a 26-mm. human embryo to show positions in which 'paraganglionic' tissue can be found. **1959** W. Andrew *Textbk. Compar. Histol.* xiii. 530 No true carotid body is present in fishes, amphibians, and reptiles. It is only in birds and mammals that the paraganglionic cells in this region form an organ.

paragaster (pærəˈgæstə(r)). *Zool.* [f. Gr. παρα- PARA-[1] 'false' + γαστήρ belly, stomach.] The central or gastric cavity of a simple sponge. Hence **para'gastral** *a.*, of or belonging to the paragaster.

1887 Sollas in *Encycl. Brit.* XXII. 413/2 The simple paragaster of *Ascetta* may become complicated in a variety of ways. **1888** —— in *Challenger Rep.* XXV. p. xiv, The recesses, known as flagellated chambers, communicate with the cavity of the sac (paragaster) each by a single wide mouth (apopyle), and with the exterior by a small pore (prosopyle). *Ibid.* p. xxvi, If endodermal, then the cavity of the vase forming the sponge must be paragastral.

paragastric (pærəˈgæstrɪk), *a.* *Zool.* [cf. prec.]

1. [f. PARA-[1] 1.] Situated alongside the stomach or gastric cavity, as certain canals in *Ctenophora*.

1861 J. R. Greene *Man. Anim. Kingd., Cœlent.* 223 Next, radial and paragastric canals appear, the former quickly reaching the surface of the body. **1888** Rolleston & Jackson *Anim. Life* 717 These two vessels are the 'paragastric canals'.

2. [f. prec.] Pertaining to the paragaster of a sponge.

1887 Sollas in *Encycl. Brit.* XXII. 413/1 The instreaming currents bear with them into the cavity of the sac (paragastric cavity) both protoplasmic particles..and dissolved oxygen.

‖**para'gastrula.** *Embryol.* [f. PARA-[1] 1 + GASTRULA.] A kind of gastrula occurring in some sponges, produced by invagination of the flagellate cells within the granular. Hence **para'gastrular** *a.*, of or pertaining to a paragastrula; **paragastru'lation**, the formation of a paragastrula.

1887 Sollas in *Encycl. Brit.* XXII. 425/1 The two-layered sac thus produced is a *paragastrula*; its outer layer, known as the *epiblast*, gives rise to the ectoderm, the inner layer or *hypoblast* to the endoderm. **1890** *Cent. Dict.*, *Paragastrular*..*Paragastrulation*.

†'**parage.** *Obs.* Also 4 perage. [a. F. *parage* (11th c. in Hatz.-Darm.) = Pr. *paratge*, Sp. *parage*, It. *paraggio*, med.L. *parāticum*, ? f. *par* equal: see -AGE. The original sense in med.L. and Fr. was app. 'parity of condition or rank'; hence, 'noble lineage or extraction': the latter is the sense with which the word entered Eng.]

1. Lineage, descent, rank; *esp.* noble or high lineage.

a **1300** *Floriz & Bl.* 256 Þer buþ seriauns in þe stage þat serueþ þe maidenes of parage. **13..** *E.E. Allit. P.* B. 167 Aproch þou to þat prynce of parage noble. *c* **1386** Chaucer *Wife's Prol.* 250 If she be riche and of heigh parage. **1484** Caxton *Chivalry* 46 Parage is none thynge but honour auncyently acustomed. **1528** Roy *Rede me* (Arb.) 61 They.. fare moche better at their table Then lordes of worthy parage. *a* **1553** Udall *Royster D.* I. ii. (Arb.) 17 His face is for ladies of high and noble parages, With whome he hardly scapeth great mariages. **1652** Needham tr. *Selden's Mare Cl.* 281 So did the Kings of Wales of high parage.

2. Worth, value. *rare.*

1513 Douglas *Æneis* III. v. 222 Syne to my fader,.. Riche rewardis he gaif of hie parage.

3. Equality of birth or station, as in members of the same family.

1513 Douglas *Æneis* IV. Prol. 44 Thow makis febill wycht, and lawest the hie; Thow knittis frendschip quhar thar bene na parage. *a* **1670** Hacket *Abp. Williams* II. (1692) 115 He [Laud] thought it a disparagement to have a parage with any of his rank.

‖**4.** *Feudal Law.* (As Fr., paraʒ.) See quots.

[**1611** Cotgr. s.v., *Tenir en parage*, to hold part of a fief, as a coheire, or coparcener; or, younger brothers to hold of their elder by homage, and fealtie; which is therefore due vnto him, after partition, because he does homage vnto the Lord Paramount both for their parts, and his owne.] **1727–41** Chambers *Cycl.* s.v., When a fief is divided among brothers;..the younger hold their part of the elder by Parage, i.e. without any homage or service... This Parage being an equality of duty, or service among brothers or sisters. [**1875** Maine *Hist. Inst.* vii. 205 Called in French 'Parage', under which the near kinsmen of the eldest son still took an interest in the family property, but held it of him as his Peers.]

paragenesic (pærədʒɪˈnɛsɪk), *a.* *Biol.* [f. next + -IC.] Pertaining to or of the nature of paragenesis: see next, 1.

1864 *Reader* No. 94. 477/1 Observed in paragenesic hybridity. **1878** Bartley tr. *Topinard's Anthrop.* II. vii. 369 M. Broca has defined the various degrees of sexual affinity, which he calls Homogenesis, thus:—Without offspring: Abortive, Agenesic, Dysgenesic. With offspring: Paragenesic, Eugenesic.

paragenesis (pærəˈdʒɛnɪsɪs). Pl. -geneses (-ˈdʒɛnɪsiːz). [mod. f. Gr. παρα- beside, side by side + γένεσις GENESIS.]

1. *Biol.* **a.** The production in an individual organism of characters belonging to two different species, as in hybridism.

1890 in *Cent. Dict.*

b. *spec.* Hybridism in which the offspring is partially sterile.

1892 *Syd. Soc. Lex.*, *Paragenesis*: see *Paragenesia*. *Paragenesia*, a term applied by Broca to the comparative sterility of hybrids, which consists in their being sterile with similar hybrids, but fertile with members of either parent species.

c. A name for subsidiary or unusual modes of reproduction: see PARAGAMY.

2. The occurrence together of different minerals, esp. as reflecting the conditions of their formation; a set of minerals occurring together or with a given mineral; also, the sequence and periods of formation of the constituent minerals. [So named by Breithaupt in Ger. 1849.]

1853 *Edin. New Philos. Jrnl.* LIV. 324 By the paragenesis of minerals he [*sc.* Breithaupt] understands the more or less definite mode of association, by means of which he endeavours to determine their relative age. **1855** Dana *Min.* I. 239. **1865** Page *Handbk. Geol. Terms* 350 Paragenesis of Minerals. **1871** J. H. Collins *Handbk. Mineral. Cornwall & Devon* 71 A more strict paragenesis would deal with those groups of minerals which are immediately associated with each other. **1878** Lawrence tr. *Cotta's Rocks Class.* 3 What was termed by Breithaupt Paragenesis. By this is meant the law of mutual association or repulsion of certain minerals. **1894** *Thinker* V. 342 By paragenesis, or by some form of pseudomorphism, one mineral may be changed into another. **1934** *Q. Jrnl. Geol. Soc.* XC. 338 Sillimanite has been abundantly developed alongside some quartz veins... This paragenesis forms a selvedge between quartz veins and the biotite-muscovite-schist. **1951** *Mineral. Mag.* XXIX. 677 The paragenesis sylvine-halite - magnesite - quartz - anhydrite - (carnallite)..first makes its appearance in the halite zone. **1954** R. L. Parker tr. *Niggli's Rocks & Mineral Deposits* iv. 128 Another method..consists in constructing theoretical (so-called normative) mineral associations..to constitute idealized parageneses under certain physical-chemical conditions. **1966** E. W. Heinrich *Geol. of Carbonatites* vii. 233 *(caption)* Paragenesis (from oldest to youngest): (1) some cerite.., (2a) bastnäsite.., (2b) monazite, (3) parisite, (3b) sahamalite. **1974** *Nature* 22 Nov. 336/1 The mineral parageneses of alkali pegmatites are not considered in detail.

paragenetic (pærədʒɪˈnɛtɪk), *a.* [f. Gr. παρα- (see prec.) + γενετικός (see GENETIC).]

a. *Biol.* Pertaining to or originating by paragenesis; paragenesic. **b.** *Min.* Originating side by side, as in *paragenetic twin* (crystal): see quot. 1883.

1865 Page *Handbk. Geol. Terms* 350 The innate structures of granite, marble, loaf-sugar, and the like, are instances of paragenetic crystallisation. **1883** M. F. Heddle in *Encycl. Brit.* XVI. 367/1 Twins [crystals] have..been divided into 'paragenetic' and 'metagenetic'. The first term is applied to the ordinarily occurring twins, in which the compound structure is supposed..to have been compound in its very origin.

c. *Min.* Involving or pertaining to paragenesis (sense 2). Hence **parage'netically** *adv.*

1853 *Edin. New Philos. Jrnl.* LIV. 325 The paragenetic phenomena met with in druses..indicates that the deposition of some more recent minerals has taken place more readily upon certain of the pre-existing minerals than upon others. **1963** *Mineral. Abstr.* XVI. 166/1 Paragenetically, pitchblende is associated with calcite, quartz, [etc.]. **1966** E. W. Heinrich *Geol. of Carbonatites* vii. 182 All the other sulfides..are not only uncommon to very rare but, unlike most of the pyrite, are usually paragenetically late. **1974** *Nature* 15 Mar. 261/2 Miyashiro distinguishes, somewhat anomalously, some subfacies on the basis of facies series, even though paragenetic criteria may not be available.

paragenic (pærəˈdʒɛnɪk), *a.* = prec. b.

1864 Webster cites Dana.

parageosyncline, -al: see PARA-[1] 1.

paragerminal to **-glenal:** see PARA-[1] 1.

paraglider (ˈpærəglaɪdə(r)). [f. PARA-[3] + GLIDER.] A large kite-like structure composed of two flexible triangular sections joined side by side, and designed to glide with a passive load or with a pilot to control its flight.

Whether this is the sense in quot. 1942 is uncertain.

1942 A. M. Low *Parachutes* 223 There have been occasions when Russian pilots with their machines damaged have dived them straight on to their targets. No real importance attaches to these 'human bombs'... Paragliders released from aircraft may prove quite another story. **1960** F. M. Rogallo et al. *Prelim. Investigation of Paraglider* (NASA TN D-443) 4 In evaluating the para-glider concept in a practical application as a reentry vehicle, calculations were made by using equations of motion involving two degrees of freedom. *Ibid.* 8 The results of this study indicate that this flexible-lifting-surface concept may provide a lightweight controllable para-glider for manned space vehicles. **1961** *Flight* LXXX. 651/2 There are two recovery systems that are now being seriously considered for application to the Saturn system—the Rogallo or paraglider wing, and the parachute recovery. **1966** [see *low-altitude* s.v. LOW *a.* 20]. **1973** *Daily Colonist* (Victoria, B.C.) 3 May 1/7 A 27-year-old father of three was killed Wednesday when his light-weight para-glider plunged 200 feet to the ground.

para'globin. = next.

1877 Watts *Fownes' Chem.* II. 626. **1893** in *Syd. Soc. Lex.*

paraglobulin (pærəˈglɒbjuːlɪn). *Chem.* [See PARA-[1] 2.] A name given to distinguish the particular form of GLOBULIN found in blood-serum (and to a slight extent elsewhere in the tissues).

1873 Ralfe *Phys. Chem.* 31 *Para-globulin*... The globulin obtained from serum differs from that of the crystalline lens in not being precipitated from its solutions by heat or alcohol, and also by the property it possesses of coagulating certain liquids, as the pericardial, peritoneal, and hydrocele fluids... This modification of globulin has been called paraglobulin, and also fibrino-plastic substance from the power it has of forming with the above named fluids, fibrin. **1877** Foster *Phys.* I. i. (1879) 27. **1899** *Allbutt's Syst. Med.* VII. 800 The albumin is mainly paraglobulin.

‖**paraglossa** (pærəˈglɒsə). *Entom.* Pl. -æ. [f. Gr. παρα- beside + γλῶσσα tongue.] Each of two lateral appendages of the ligula in various insects.

1826 Kirby & Sp. *Entomol.* III. 359 *Paraglossæ*.. Lateral and often membranous processes observable on each side of the tongue in some Hymenoptera, etc. **1878** Bell *Gegenbaur's Comp. Anat.* 246 This has two lateral appendages, or secondary tongues (paraglossæ), at its base.

Hence **para'glossal** *a.*, of or pertaining to a paraglossa; **para'glossate** *a.*, furnished with paraglossæ. (*Cent. Dict.*)

paragnath(us to **-gnostic:** see PARA-[1] 1.

paragnathous (pəˈrægnəθəs), *a.* *Ornith.* [f. Gr. παρα-, PARA- alongside + γνάθ-ος jaw + -OUS.] Having the mandibles of equal length. Hence **pa'ragnathism**, paragnathous condition.

1872 Coues *Key N. Amer. Birds* 24 All bills..have been divided into four classes... The paragnathous, in which both [mandibles] are of about equal length, and neither is evidently bent over the other.

paragoge (pærəˈgəʊdʒiː). [a. L. *paragōgē*, a. Gr. παραγωγή a leading past, in Gram. 'addition to the end of a syllable'; f. παρα- past, beyond + ἀγωγή carrying, leading. In F. *paragoge* (*e* mute).]

1. *Gram.* The addition of a letter or syllable to a word, either inorganically as in *peasan-t*, or, as in Hebrew, to give emphasis or modify the meaning.

1656 Blount *Glossogr.*, *Paragogical*, of or pertaining to the figure Paragoge, which is when a syllable or letter is added to the end of a word. **1730–6** Bailey (folio), *Paragoge*, ..this figure is frequent with the Hebrews, *'brkh* for *'brk*. *3.10* **1883** Marsh *Comp. Gram. Anglo-Saxon* §20. 9.

fig. **1658** J. Jones tr. *Ovid's Ibis* 75 Thus Levellers by Apocope would pare off the Superfluities of long Estates; and by Paragoge add to the extremities of their short.

‖**2.** The reduction of a dislocation. [Gr.]

1730–6 in BAILEY (folio). **1893** in *Syd. Soc. Lex.*

‖**3.** A wheeling from column into line. [Gr.]

1878 *Smith's Dict. Gr. & Rom. Antiq.* 485/1 The depth of the whole body was then lessened, and these intervals filled up by the ordinary paragoge, and by the different lochi siding up nearer to each other.

paragogic (pærə'gɒdʒɪk), *a. Gram.* [ad. mod.L. *paragōgic-us*: see prec. and -IC.] Of, pertaining to, or of the nature of paragoge; *esp.* of a sound or letter: Added to a word by paragoge.

1727–41 CHAMBERS *Cycl.*, *Paragogic*, in grammar, denotes something added to a word without adding any thing to the sense thereof... In the Hebrew the ה is frequently Paragogic. **1778** BP. LOWTH *Transl. Isa.* Notes (ed. 12) 291 These are infinitives with a paragogic ה. **1827** [see ASYLLABIC *a.*]. **1837** G. PHILLIPS *Syriac Gram.* 81 In the 3rd pers. plu. præt... Peal, some verbs take the paragogic forms. **1887** A. MOREL-FATIO in *Encycl. Brit.* XXII. 349/2 The infinitives with r paragogic (*viurer*, *seurer*, *plourer*) are not used. **1968** W. S. ALLEN *Vox Graeca* iv. 95 Adding the so-called ν ἐφελκυστικόν (alias 'paragogic ν'). **1972** *Language* XLVIII. 35 The development of such 'paragogic' vowels is known also from Ukrainian and Czech dialects. **1975** *Canad. Jrnl. Linguistics* XX. 61 Portuguese phonotactics generally does not tolerate word-final stops; thus, borrowed words ending in a stop receive a paragogic final *e*: *time* 'team', *clube* 'club', etc.

paragogical (pærə'gɒdʒɪkəl), *a.* [f. as prec. + -AL[1].] = prec.

1607 HIERON *Defence* I. 88 They both read it, and that with prickes & tooke it not to be paragogical. **1641** MILTON *Animadv.* i. Wks. (1851) 188 You cite them to appeare for certaine Paragogicall contempts, before a capricious Pædantie of hot-liver'd Grammarians. **1751** WESLEY *Wks.* (1872) XIV. 154 Frequently they [Futures] assume a paragogical ה with Kamets.

Hence **para'gogically** *adv.*, by way of paragoge.

1706 A. BEDFORD *Temple Mus.* vii. 142 The Letter (ן) is Paragogically added.

'paragogize, *v. rare.* [f. PARAGOGE + -IZE.] *trans.* To add as a final syllable.

1866 BLACKMORE *C. Nowell* liv, Bob knew better than to paragogize the feminine termination.

paragon ('pærəgən), *sb.* (*a.*) Also (6 **parageon**, **peragon**, 6–7 **parragon**), 6–8 **paragone**. [a. OF. *paragon* (15th c.), now *parangon* m, in OF. also *para(n)gonne* fem., ad. It. *paragone* (also *parangone*) m., 'a triall or touch-stone to try gold, or good from bad' (so in Dino Compagni *a* 1324, and Boccaccio; also in 15th c. Fr.: see Godef.); 'a comparison or conferring together; a paragon, a match, a compare, an equal' (Florio 1611). Cf. Sp. *parangon* or *paragon* 'an equall, a fit man to match him, one comparable with' (Minsheu 1599). See below.]

A. *sb.* **I. 1.** A pattern or model of excellence.

a. A person supreme in merit or excellence.

a **1548** HALL *Chron.*, *Hen. V* 33 b, Thys prince was almost the Arabicall Phenix, and emongest his predecessors a very Paragon. **1557** *Tottell's Misc.* (Arb.) 178 But therwas neuer Laura more then one, And her had Petrarke for his paragone. **1577** B. GOOGE *Heresbach's Husb.* (1586) 168 She was the very Phenix and Parageon of all the Gentlewomen that I euer knewe. **1592** GREENE *Philom.* Wks. (Grosart) XI. 175 The peragon of Italy for honorable grace. **1689** SHADWELL *Bury Fair* II. i, Your ladyship.. has been long held a paragon of perfection. **1784** J. POTTER *Virtuous Villagers* II. 159 He is a paragon of his sex. **1833** HT. MARTINEAU *Charmed Sea* ix. 133 She will turn out a paragon of a wife. **1871** R. ELLIS *Catullus* xxxvii. 17 You chiefly, peerless paragon of the tribe long-lock'd,.. Egnatius.

b. A thing of supreme excellence.

1601 HOLLAND *Pliny* II. 372 [Magic] is at this day reputed by most nations of the earth, for the paragon & chief of al sciences. *a* **1656** BP. HALL *Rem. Wks.* (1660) 22 We came down to Antwerp, the paragon of Cities. **1756** C. LUCAS *Ess. Waters* I. Ded., The dissolved civil constitution, that paragon of perfect polity. **1861** J. RUFFINI *Dr. Antonio* x, Sir John.. pronounced it to be the paragon of easy-chairs.

†**2.** A match; a mate, companion; a consort in marriage; a rival, competitor. (Also of a thing.)

1566 PAINTER *Pal. Pleas.* I. 45 Cyrus our prince and lorde, whose paragon wee haue chosen you to bee. **1591** SPENSER *M. Hubberd* 1026 Love and Lordship bide no paragone. **1596** —— *F.Q.* VI. ix. 11 He.. her worthy deemed To be a Princes Paragone esteemed. **1594** CHAPMAN *Hymnus in Cynthiam* Wks. (1875) 15/1 Through noblest mansions, Gardens and groves, exempt from paragons. **1762** J. H. STEVENSON *Crazy Tales* 43 You cannot fish up His like and paragon again. **1824** WIFFEN tr. *Tasso* IV. xlvi, None but himself could be his paragon in vice.

†**3.** Comparison; competition, emulation, rivalry.

[Cf. **1589** PUTTENHAM *Eng. Poesie* III. xix. (Arb.) 241.] **1590** SPENSER *Muiopotmos* 274 Minerva.. deign'd with her the paragon to make. **1590** —— *F.Q.* III. iii. 54 Women valorous, Which have full many feats.. Performd, in paragone of proudest men. **1596** *Ibid.* V. iii. 24 Then did he set her by that snowy one,.. Of both their beauties to make paragone. **1664** EVELYN tr. *Freart's Archit.* Ep. Ded. 1 A Work.. worthy to go in paragon with it.

II. Specific and technical applications.

4. a. A perfect diamond; now applied to those weighing more than a hundred carats. [So in mod.F.] In quot. 1616 *fig.* of a person.

1616 B. JONSON *Devil an Ass* III. i, He is no great large stone, but a true paragon, He has all his corners. **1622** MALYNES *Anc. Law Merch.* 75 The fassets must be industriously wrought, which in great stones of 10 or 12 Carrats maketh them to be Paragons, that is to say, in all perfection. **1647** R. STAPYLTON *Juvenal* 241 That stone, which for a paragon was set. **1863** *Chambers' Bk. of Days* I. 484/1 Only six very large diamonds (called paragons) are known.

†**b.** Also *paragon-stone*. *Obs.*

1558 WARDE tr. *Alexis' Secr.* I. 94 b, Take Cristall, or paragon stone. **1573** *Art of Limming* 9 Take a beade of Christall or a Paragon stone. **1629** MAXWELL tr. *Herodian* (1635) 250 His Rings set with Paragon Stones. **1698** FRYER *Acc. E. India & P.* 213 The Diamond.. Without Spots or Foulness, is called a Paragon-stone.

†**5.** A kind of double camlet; a stuff used for dress and upholstery in the seventeenth and early eighteenth century. *Obs.* [Cf. F. *parangon de Venise*, the finest silk stuffs from Venice (Littré).]

c **1605** *Allegations of Worsted Weavers* (B.M. Add. MS. 12504, art. 64) The Paragon, Peropus, and Philiselles may be affirmed to be double chamblet; the difference being only the one was double in the warpe, and the other in the w[oo]ff. **1618** *Naworth Househ. Bks.* (Surtees) 74, xij yards of water paragon for my Lady at *vs.* viij*d*... 5 yards of French green paragon.. xxv*s.* *xd.* **1659–60** PEPYS *Diary* 8 Mar., Took my wife by land to Paternoster Row, to buy some Paragon for a petticoat and so home again. **1674** *Lond. Gaz.* No. 852/4 Hangings for a Room of Green Paragon. **1678** *Flemings in Oxford* (O.H.S.) I. 255, 7 yards & an halfe of black Paragon for a [Undergraduate's] Gowne. **1739** *Observ. Wool & Wooll. Manuf.* in Beck *Draper's Dict.* 245 Paragon.. stuff of combing wool.

attrib. **1719** D'URFEY *Pills* (1872) III. 173 The Plowman, the Squire, the Erranter Clown, At home she subdued in her Paragon Gown.

6. A kind of black marble: see quot. 1753. [F. *parangon* a kind of black marble of Egypt and Greece (Littré).] Usu. written **paragone**.

[**1632** LITHGOW *Trav.* VI. 267 The floore being curiously indented with intermingled Alabaster and black shining *Parangone*.] **1645** EVELYN *Diary* May (1879) I. 227 A niche of paragon for the statue of the Prince now living. **1753** CHAMBERS *Cycl. Supp.*, *Paragone*,.. the name given by many to the basaltes, a black marble, used as a touchstone. **1848** J. D. DANA *Man. Mineral.* vii. 349 The *Neroantico* marble of the Italians is an ancient deep black marble; the *paragone* is a modern one, of a fine black color, from Bergamo. **1888** G. H. BLAGROVE *Marble Decoration* 68 In Italy a black marble, sometimes called Paragone, is found mixed with marble of inferior quality at Castle Nuovo, in Piedmont [etc.]. **1894** H. W. PULLEN *Handbk. Anc. Roman Marbles* II. 140 The term Paragone has.. been loosely applied to several very black columns, such as those at a Tomb in the Winter Choir of St. John Lateran. **1955** M. H. GRANT *Marbles & Granites of World* 71 Paragone. [Locality.] Bergamo, Italy. [Characteristics.] A pure, fine black.

7. *Printing.* Name of a large size of type intermediate between Great Primer and Double Pica, about $3\frac{3}{4}$ lines to the inch. Now usually called 'two-line Long Primer'.

1706 *Specimen of Letters* b 1, in H. Hart *Century of Oxf. Typog.* 67 Paragon Roman (Bought 1706). Paragon Italick (Bought 1706). **1824** J. JOHNSON *Typogr.* II. 77 Paragon is the only letter that has preserved its name, being called so by all the printing nations. **1843** *Penny Cycl.* XXV. 456/1 Of types larger than those employed for book-work, the first, in an ascending series, is called *Paragon*. **1887** T. B. REED *Old Eng. Letter Foundries* 34 The first named [Trafalgar] has disappeared in England, as also has Paragon.

B. *adj.* [Perh. originating in *attrib.* use of the sb.] Of surpassing excellence, perfect in excellence. (See also 4 b.)

1601 HOLLAND *Pliny* I. 457 We may be bold to compare them with that Paragon-coronet of the Greeks, which passeth al others. **1632** WENTWORTH *Let.* 24 Sept. in Gardiner *Hist. Chas. I*, I. Pref. 14 If I do not fall square, and .. paragon, in every point of duty to my master. **1672** SIR T. BROWNE *Let. to Friend* §29 Those jewels were paragon, without flaw, hair, ice, or cloud. **1825** R. P. WARD *Tremaine* III. xv. 345 Presuming to have had opinions, which this paragon Lord does not approve.

[*Note.* This word appears first in Italian (14th c.), whence in Fr., Sp., etc. The notion of Diez that *paragon* originated in Sp., from the prep. phrase *para con* (which is sometimes = 'in comparison with') is historically untenable. But it is not certain whether the original sense of It. *paragone* was 'comparison', or 'touch-stone'; in the latter sense it might stand for *pietra di paragone*. For the etymology, Tobler (*Zeitschr. Rom. Phil.* (1880) IV. 373) suggested derivation from the Gr. vb. παρακονᾶν 'to sharpen or whet one thing against another', f. ἀκόνη 'whetstone', supposing that this may have developed the sense 'touch-stone', or that the It. vb. *paragonare* may have been formed from παρακονᾶν, with the sense of 'try or compare by rubbing together', whence *paragone* the act of doing this, *pietra di paragone* 'comparison stone, touch-stone'. A med.Gr. παρακόνη is cited as applied to a smooth hard stone used to polish the gold laid on in illuminating. But the suggestion presents various difficulties.]

paragon ('pærəgən), *v.* Also 7 **-one**, **parangon**, **parragon**. [f. PARAGON *sb.*: cf. F. *para(n)gonner*, It. *para(n)gonare* 'to equall, to paragone, to compare' (Florio), Sp. *parangonar*: see prec.]

1. *trans.* To place side by side; to parallel, compare. (Now *archaic* or *poetic.*)

a **1586** SIDNEY *Arcadia* I. (1590) L iij, The picture of Pamela.. whiche in little forme he ware in a Tablet.. purposing.. to paragon the little one with Artesias length. **1600** O. E. (? M. SUTCLIFFE) *Repl. to Libel* I. i. 1 An excellent and singular woman, to bee parangoned with the famous women of ancient time. **1606** SHAKS. *Ant. & Cl.* I. v. 71. **1667** MILTON *P.L.* x. 426 Lucifer, so by allusion calld, Of that bright Starr to Satan paragond. **1894** A. AUSTIN in *Blackw. Mag.* Sept. 312 Baby billows, mere cradles rather.. when paragoned with these monsters of the real deep.

2. To match, to mate. (Now *poetic*, etc.)

c **1615** SIR W. MURE *Sonn.* vii, My loue, my lyfe.. Bright spark of beutie, paragon'd by few. **1697** EVELYN *Numism.* vii. 239 Such proof of their Abilities.. as may rightly paragon them with.. the Ancients. **1835** LYTTON *Rienzi* VI. v, [It was] a virtue nature could not paragon, words could not repay. **1872** BROWNING *Fifine* xxiii, To join your peers, paragon charm with charm, As I shall show you may.

†**3.** To excel, surpass. *Obs.*

1604 SHAKS. *Oth.* II. i. 62 He hath atchieu'd a Maid That paragons description, and wilde Fame.

†**4.** To set forth as a paragon or perfect model.

1613 SHAKS. *Hen. VIII*, II. iv. 230 We are contented To weare our mortall State to come, with her.. before the primest Creature That's Parragon'd o' th' World.

†**5.** To serve as a paragon or model of; to typify, exemplify. *Obs.*

1617 COLLINS *Def. Bp. Ely* I. Abstr. of Contents ii, Peter the fitter to paragon the Church, because a great sinner and so apt to shew mercie.

†**6.** *intr.* To compare, compete, vie *with*. *Obs.*

1620 SHELTON *Quix.* II. IV. ix. 123 Few or none could for Feature paragon with her, and much less excel her.

paragonimiasis (ˌpærəgəʊnɪ'maɪəsɪs). *Med.* [f. mod.L. *Paragonim-us*, generic name (f. PARA-[1] + Gr. γόνιμος productive, fertile, f. root γεν-, γον- to produce) + -IASIS.] Infestation with worms of the genus *Paragonimus*, esp. the lung fluke, which results from eating infected crustacea and is marked at first by abdominal pains and later by a persistent cough and expectoration of blood.

1907 *Allbutt's Syst. Med.* (ed. 2) II. II. 861 The symptoms of paragonimiasis, or endemic hæmoptysis as it is sometimes designated, are a chronic cough—usually worst in the morning, a persistent pneumonic-like sputum in which ova abound, and recurring attacks of more or less profuse hæmoptysis. **1935** *Nature* 26 Oct. 674/1 There is fortunately no reason for anticipating that the crab will introduce into Europe the lung disease, paragonimiasis, of which it is one of the vectors in the Far East. **1961** L. E. BOLLO *Introd. Med. & Med. Terminol.* xiv. 167 Paragonimiasis (caused by the lung fluke *Paragonimus westermani*) is common in Korea, Japan, the Philippine Islands, and parts of China. **1973** KUN-YEN HUANG in J. R. Quinn *Med. & Public Health China* 258 Although careful roentgenological examinations .. may differentiate paragonimiasis from tuberculosis, the diagnosis of paragonimiasis relies primarily on the demonstration of parasite ova in the sputum or an intradermal or CF test with antigen prepared from adult worms.

paragonite ('pærəgənaɪt). *Min.* [Named 1848, from Gr. παράγων pr. pple., leading aside or astray, misleading + -ITE[1].] A hydrous mica containing sodium, and so distinguished from common or potash mica (muscovite). ***paragonite-schist***, a mica-schist in which paragonite takes the place of muscovite.

1849 J. NICOL *Min.* 163 The mica slate.. named paragonite. **1868** DANA *Min.* (ed. 5) 488 Paragonite constitutes the mass of the rock at Monte Campione.

Hence **parago'nitic** *a.*, characterized by the presence of paragonite.

1868 DANA *Min.* (ed. 5) 488 The rock.. containing cyanite and staurotide, called paragonitic or talcose schist.

†**'paragonize**, *v. Obs.* [f. PARAGON *sb.* + -IZE.]

1. *trans.* To compare, put in competition or rivalry: = PARAGON *v.* 1.

1589 PUTTENHAM *Eng. Poesie* III. xix. (Arb.) 241 Faire women whose excellencie is discouered by paragonizing or setting one to another. **1656** EARL MONM. tr. *Boccalini's Advts. fr. Parnass.* II. xxxiii. (1656) 282 Those, who presumed too much upon themselves, and dared to paragonise their privat Nobility, with his immense fortune who reigned.

2. To match, to equal: = PARAGON *v.* 2.

1606 G. W[OODCOCKE] *Lives Emperors* in *Hist. Ivstine* G g ij, He liued without al example, no man euer paragonizing him. **1635** J. HAYWARD tr. *Biondi's Banish'd Virg.* 65 If there was any accomplish'd Gentleman, that.. paragonized Perosphilo.

3. To serve as a model of, exemplify, typify: = PARAGON *v.* 5.

1586 A. DAY *Eng. Secretary* I. (1625) 147 All those excellencies, which none but her selfe can paragonize.

'paragonless, *a. rare.* [f. as prec. + -LESS.] Without a paragon, matchless, peerless.

1599 NASHE *Lenten Stuffe* (1871) 53 Whilst I loitered in this paragonless fish-town, city, town or country.

paragoric, obs. form of PAREGORIC.

†**'paragram**. *Obs.* [f. Gr. phrase τὰ παρὰ γράμμα σκώμματα, lit. 'jokes by the letter'.] A kind of play upon words, consisting in the alteration of one letter or group of letters of a word.

By some writers restricted to the change of the initial letter or letters, as in *Biberius Mero* for *Tiberius Nero*, but Aristotle included such as κολαξ for κόραξ.

a **1679** HOBBES *Rhetorick* III. x. (1681) 116 Paragrams; that is, allusions of words are graceful, if they be well placed. **1711** ADDISON *Spect.* No. 61 ¶2 Aristotle.. describes two or three kinds of Puns, which he calls Paragrams. **1753** MELMOTH tr. *Cicero's Lett.* IV. xviii, Unless it be some smart pun, or elegant hyperbole, some striking paragram, or some arch and unexpected turn. *Note*, A Paragram is a species of the pun which consists in changing the initial letters of a name.

So **para'grammatist** [Gr. *παραγραμματιστής: see prec. and -IST], a maker of 'paragrams'.

1711 ADDISON *Spect.* No. 61 ⁋3 A Gentleman whom he looked upon to be the greatest Paragrammatist among the Moderns.

paragrammatism, etc.: see PARA-¹ 1.

paragraph ('pærəgrɑːf, -æ-), *sb.* Also 6-7 -graff(e. [a. F. *paragraphe* (13th c. in Hatz.-Darm.) = It. *paragrafo*, ad. late L. *paragraphus*, a. Gr. παράγραφος orig. a short horizontal stroke drawn below the beginning of a line in which a break in the sense occurs (see Kenyon *Palæogr.* 27); also = παραγραφή, a passage so marked; f. παρα- by the side + -γραφος written.]

1. A symbol or character (now usually ¶ or ⁋) formerly used to mark the commencement of a new section or part of a narrative or discourse; now, sometimes introducing an editorial *obiter dictum* or protest, and sometimes as a reference to a marginal note or foot-note.

Its original use is common in Middle English MSS. (where the form is often a red or blue ◖, ₵ or ◗, ◗). It was retained by the early printers, and remains in the Bible of 1611 (but only as far as Acts xx), no doubt because every verse begins a new line, so that the method of indicating a paragraph by 'indenting' (as done by Tindale, Coverdale, and the Revisers of 1881-5) was not available.

1538 ELYOT *Dict.*, *Paragraphus, & paragraphum*, a paragrafe. **1565** COOPER *Thesaurus* Introd. *iv, Which he may find out by this Paragraffe ¶. **1623** COCKERAM, *Paragraph*, a note set in the margent of a booke, to obserue and marke the differing discourses therein. **1691** MIEGE *Eng. Gram.* (ed. 2) 126 Formerly..they used this Figure ¶ termed a Pilcrow, and by the Printers, Paragraph. **1824** L. MURRAY *Eng. Gram.* (ed. 5) I. 412 A Paragraph ¶ denotes the beginning of a new subject, or a sentence not connected with the foregoing. This character is chiefly used in the Old, and in the New Testaments. **1824** J. JOHNSON *Typogr.* II. iii. 52 At present, paragraphs are seen only in Bibles.

2. a. A distinct passage or section of a discourse, chapter, or book, dealing with a particular point of the subject, the words of a distinct speaker, etc., whether consisting of one sentence or of a number of sentences that are more closely connected with each other than with what stands before and after. Such a passage was at first usually indicated by the mark described above; but afterwards, as now, by beginning on a new line, which is indented or set back by the space of an 'em-quad', and ends without running on to the next passage; hence, in reference to typography or manuscript, a paragraph is a portion of the text between two such breaks; but, in a less technical sense, it is sometimes applied to any passage which, from its nature, might or ought to be so indicated in writing or printing.

1525 tr. *Jerome of Brunswick's Surg.* T vj/1 In the xxv chapytre..in the seconde paragraphe. **1545** ASCHAM *Toxoph.* I. (Arb.) 78, I call that by bookes and chapiters, whyche the greke booke deuideth by chapiters and paragraphes. **1664** H. MORE *Myst. Iniq.* 470 [He] tells us the best way..in a Paragraph worthy to be written in letters of Gold, toward the end of the first part of the Homily. **1705** R. CROMWELL in *Eng. Hist. Rev.* (1898) XIII. 122 This short paragraph hath a deal of matter in it. **1706** PHILLIPS, *Paragraph*, a Portion of Matter in a Discourse or Treatise, contained between two Breaks, *i.e.* which begins with a new Line, and ends where the Line breaks off. **1830** D'ISRAELI *Chas. I*, III. vi. 103 A chronicle which contracts many an important event into a single paragraph. **1863** MISS BRADDON *Eleanor's Vict.* (1878) I. ii. 17 The letter..was written in sharp and decisive paragraphs, and in a neat firm hand.

b. A distinct article or section of a law or legal document, usually numbered.

1552 HULOET, Paragraffe or sence in lawe wrytten, or opinion written before a sentence in lawe. **1736** BOLINGBROKE *Patriot.* (1749) 84 Our obligation to submit to the civil law is a principal paragraph in the natural law. **1813** WELLINGTON *Let. to Earl Bathurst* 3 July in Gurw. *Desp.* X. 507, I beg your Lordship's particular attention..to the 13th paragraph of the instructions. **1883** *Rules Supr. Crt.* XXXVIII. vii, Every affidavit shall be..divided into paragraphs, and every paragraph shall be numbered consecutively, and as nearly as may be shall be confined to a distinct portion of the subject.

c. *transf.* A distinct passage or section in a musical composition.

1959 *Listener* 16 July 114/2 The opening paragraph of the Fifth Symphony..takes the old-type dirge..as its model. **1975** *Gramophone* Sept. 466/3 In the slow movements and the cadenzas he shows himself to be capable of shaping long paragraphs with real discrimination. **1977** *Listener* 12 May 628/3 The opening..is one of the most difficult in the symphonic repertory..creating a tension from which the big first paragraph must be felt to spring.

3. A short passage, notice, or article in a newspaper or journal, without a heading, or having only a side heading; an item of news.

The paragraphs here are quite independent and unconnected with each other, but they constitute collectively a summary of local or general news or gossip, or of 'notes' on some special subject or department.

1769 BURKE *Corr.* (1844) I. 212 He [the newsprinter] has made a flaming paragraph of it. **1780** *Newgate Cal.* V. 202 The writer.. inserted various paragraphs in the newspapers in favour of the unfortunate men. **1833** HT. MARTINEAU *Loom & Lugger* II. v. 79 Handing the newspaper to his sister and pointing out a paragraph. **1882** PEBODY *Eng. Journalism* xi. 78 The *Morning Post*..made a name for itself by its fresh and sparkling paragraphs of Court and fashionable gossip. **1902** BESANT *Five Years' Tryst* 95 Next day there was a paragraph in the London papers [etc.].

4. In Ice-skating, used *attrib.* and *absol.* with reference to the manner in which various figures are performed in competitions.

1930 T. D. RICHARDSON *Mod. Figure Skating* xx. 184 Let me give a few suggestions of figures requiring the utmost technique; rockers and counters in eight form; three rocker three, and three counter three in paragraph form, i.e. making an eight formed figure. **1948** —— *Compl. Figure Skater* ix. 79 (*caption*) The first of the 'paragraph' figures—one foot eight forward. **1952** E. JONES *Elements Figure Skating* (ed. 2) vi. 127 The complete paragraph consists in order of a half-circle on the right outside edge, a full circle on the right inside edge, then a take-off on to the left foot, a half-circle on the left inside edge and finally a full circle on the left outside edge..this means describing three circles,..all in exact line with one another, all of equal size and symmetrically constructed. **1959** T. D. RICHARDSON *Girls' Bk. Skating* iv. 57 All you have to do..is to apply your knowledge of the components when putting figures into paragraph form. **1967** *Daily Tel.* 1 Mar. 12/6 The powerful East German later narrowed the gap with her more consistent second tracing, the backward paragraph three. **1973** *Times* 7 Feb. 15/8 On the second figure, the paragraph-loop, he was beaten.

5. *attrib.* and *Comb.* **paragraph mark** = PARAGRAPH *sb.* 1.

1769 *Middlesex Jrnl.* 14-16 Sept. 4/4 A paragraph writer shall kill you the stoutest man in the kingdom for his sixpence, and bring him to life again for another. **1798** WOLCOTT (P. Pindar) *Tales of Hoy* Wks. 1812 IV. 418 The Prince of Paragraph-makers, The Nabob of News. **1813** HAZLITT *Pol. Ess.* (1819) 9 Disposing of their government at the will of every paragraph-monger. **1855** *N. & Q.* 29 Dec. 521/2 The old paragraph mark, ¶, he [*sc.* Bilderdijk] considers to be the Roman P. **1881** *Daily News* 22 Mar. 6/4 [He] explained that paragraph advertisements were advertisements appearing in the body of the paper amongst the news. **1956** H. WILLIAMSON *Methods Bk. Design* ix. 119 If indention is not used, the typographer will have to find some other means of indicating the start of a new paragraph, such as a drop initial or a paragraph mark—¶.

paragraph ('pærəgrɑːf, -æ-), *v.* [f. prec. sb.]

†**1.** *trans.* To sign, to initial; = PARAPH *v.* 2. *Obs.*

1601 J. WHEELER *Treat. Comm.* 90 Giuen..at Praghe.. Subscribed Rudolph, Paragraphed I. D. W. Freymondt. **1652** EVELYN *St. France* Misc. Writ. (1805) 68 [They] deliver them [reports] to the Greffier or Clerk, by whom they are to be allowed, that is, Paragraphed in parchment.

2. a. To mention in a paragraph; to write a newspaper paragraph or short notice about. Also *absol.*

1764 FOOTE *Patron* III. Wks. 1799 I. 359, I will paragraph you in every newspaper. **1774** *Westm. Mag.* II. 489 We'll paragraph and puff. **1777** SHERIDAN *Sch. Scand.* I. ii, I am sneered at by all my acquaintance, and paragraphed in the newspapers. **1827** *Examiner* 749/2 The newspapers had already begun to paragraph him as a 'Nonpareil'. **1880** *Daily Tel.* 11 Nov., No one was more paragraphed and puffed.

†**b.** To treat of (a matter) in a paragraph. *Obs.*

1774 R. GOUGH *Let.* in Nichols *Lit. Anecd. 18th c.* (1814) VIII. 611 What..the menial tribe would paragraph to the newspapers.

c. With extension expressing the result achieved.

1815 in Southey *Life A. Bell* (1844) III. 573 For very little money you may be paragraphed up to the episcopal throne. **1828** *Examiner* 658/1 His enemies..squibbed, and paragraphed, and taradiddled him to death. **1830** *Ibid.* 610/2 The Politician must be quacked, paragraphed, clubbed, and coteried into notoriety.

3. To divide into or arrange in paragraphs. (Chiefly in *passive*.) Also *fig.* Cf. PUNCTUATE *v.* 3 b.

1799 C. WINTER in W. Jay *Life* (1843) 27 The whole is so injudiciously paragraphed, and so wretchedly unconnected. **1885** *Athenæum* 14 Nov. 635/2 This..contains H.M. inspectors' reports..classified, paragraphed, and summarized. **1909** H. G. WELLS *Ann Veronica* ix. 168 Ramage looked at her, and then fell into deep reflection as the waiter came to paragraph their talk again. **1959** *Vogue* Dec. 91 A soft dress in pure silk is scoop-necked and paragraphed with a lightly tying belt.

'paragraphed, *ppl. a.* [f. PARAGRAPH *v.* + -ED¹.] Mentioned or written about in a newspaper paragraph.

1898 G. B. SHAW *Plays Pleasant* Pref. p. ix, The much paragraphed 'brilliancy' of *Arms and the Man.* **1928** *Manch. Guardian Weekly* 17 Aug. 135/2 A new comedy and the first visit to Manchester of a much-paragraphed young actress brought a large and eager audience to the Palace. **1930** *London Mercury* Feb. 319 He realised..that if he ever linked his future with a member of the opposite sex, it would not be with any such perfect and paragraphed ecstasy as Dandylion or Clytemnestra.

paragrapher ('pærəgrɑːfə(r), -æ-). [f. PARAGRAPH *v.* + -ER¹.] One who writes paragraphs, a paragraphist.

1822 J. WILSON in *Blackw. Mag.* XI. 362*, I detest news-writers—paragraphers—spouting-club speechifiers. **1899** *Westm. Gaz.* 10 July 2/1 The play unheralded by the paragrapher or the Press.

‖**paragraphia** (pærə'græfɪə). *Path.* [mod.L., f. PARA-¹ 1 + Gr. -γραφία writing.] The aphasic symptom of writing one word for another.

1878 tr. *H. von Ziemssen's Cycl. Med.* XIV. 789 Morbid paragraphia, like morbid paraphasia, presents itself in mild and in severe forms. **1899** *Allbutt's Syst. Med.* VII. 442 Paraphasia and paragraphia are incoördinate rather than paretic or paralytic defects of speech.

paragraphic (pærə'græfɪk), *a.* [f. PARAGRAPH + -IC. The adj. παραγραφικ-ός was used in Greek, but not in the English senses.]

1. Of, pertaining to, or of the nature or form of a paragraph or paragraphs.

1790 *Bystander* 94 The stimulating influence of puffing spice and paragraphic Cayenne. **1813** *Edin. Rev.* XXI. 221 Some unprosperous member of the paragraphic corps. **1848** G. S. FABER *Many Mansions* Pref. (1851) 41 Translation and paragraphic division of the Cosmogony down to the end of the Fourth Day. **1866** *Athenæum* 29 Dec. 870 Sententious and paragraphic common-places.

2. *Path.* Of or pertaining to paragraphia.

1899 *Allbutt's Syst. Med.* VII. 435 The writing..of other patients may show defects of a paragraphic type. *Ibid.* 445 In persons who have been much accustomed to write, it is possible that writing (though at first of a paragraphic type) may be executed.

paragraphical (pærə'græfɪkəl), *a.* [f. as prec. + -AL¹.] = prec. 1.

1748 H. WALPOLE *Lett. to H. Mann* (1834) II. 242 Adieu! I am very paragraphical and you see have nothing to say. **1784** *New Spectator* No. 9. 8 A list of the sums paid to the Editors of six of the morning papers for the paragraphical support of a certain unpopular measure. **1785** CRUTWELL *Pref. to Bp. Wilson's Bible* b ij, The verses being numbered in the margin, and distinguished in the text by paragraphical marks. *a* **1849** POE *Marginalia* Wks. 1864 III. 577 His essays have thus only paragraphical effect; as wholes, they produce not the slightest impression.

para'graphically, *adv.* [f. as prec. + -LY².]

a. In or by means of paragraphs; paragraph by paragraph. **b.** In the style of, or by means of, newspaper paragraphs.

a **1713** ELLWOOD *Autobiog.* (1765) 293, I began the Book again, and reading it with Pen in Hand, answered it paragraphically as I went. **1727** BAILEY vol. II, *Paragraphically*, Paragraph by Paragraph, or in Paragraphs. **1793** *Sporting Mag.* II. 108 Frequently announced paragraphically in the papers. **1890** *Pall Mall G.* 18 Jan. 6/2 Writing condensedly and paragraphically.

paragraphing ('pærəgrɑːfɪŋ, -æ-), *vbl. sb.* [-ING¹.] The action of PARAGRAPH *v.* **a.** The writing of newspaper paragraphs or treating of a subject by means of these. **b.** Arrangement or division into paragraphs. Also *attrib.*

a. 1805 SURR *Winter in Lond.* (1806) II. 71 Many powerful rivals have started in the art of paragraphing, and the mystery itself has considerably sunk in its credit. **1893** J. MCCARTHY *Red Diamonds* II. 230 About whom every one in the paragraphing line wrote paragraphs.

b. 1881 *Athenæum* 23 Apr. 562/1 The arrangement is different and the paragraphing is altered, but otherwise the matter is to a large extent a reprint. **1899** F. C. CONYBEARE in *Amer. Jrnl. Theol.* Oct. 705, I have..reproduced the punctuation and paragraphing of the MS.

paragraphism ('pærəgrɑːfɪz(ə)m, -æ-). [f. PARAGRAPH *sb.* + -ISM.] The system or practice of composing or printing newspaper paragraphs.

1846 POE *Duychink* Wks. 1864 III. 64 A brevity that degenerated into mere paragraphism. **1890** *Univ. Rev.* Sept. 78 The daily newspapers..are overrun with social paragraphism.

paragraphist ('pærəgrɑːfɪst, -æ-). orig. *U.S.* [f. as prec. + -IST.] A professional writer of newspaper paragraphs.

1790 *Gazette of U.S.* 27 Nov. 655/1 A paragraphist in the General Advertiser of Thursday last. **1792** T. JEFFERSON *Writings* (1854) III. 467 One of its principal ministers enlists himself as an anonymous writer or paragraphist. **1798** in *Spirit Pub. Jrnls.* (1799) II. 350 Every paragraphist is justly noticing the immense public advantages which await the issue of the late..victory. **1805** SURR *Winter in Lond.* (1806) III. 247 A hireling pamphleteer and paragraphist. **1892** *Times* 6 Feb. 9/5 Those powers of darkness, the descriptive reporter and the sensational paragraphist.

†**paragra'phistical**, *a. Obs. rare*⁻¹. [f. as prec. + -ICAL.] = PARAGRAPHIC 1 (but purporting to be used nonsensically).

a **1625** FLETCHER *Fair Maid* III. i, Let us a little examine the severall conditions of our Paragraphisticall suitors.

'paragraphize, *v. nonce-wd.* [f. as prec. + -IZE.] *intr.* To write paragraphs for the newspapers.

1826 DISRAELI *Viv. Grey* III. viii. 123 Do you ever see the 'Age'?.. Is it true that his Lordship paragraphises a little?

†**'paragraphly**, *adv. Obs.* [f. as prec. + -LY².] Paragraph by paragraph, paragraphically.

1678 SIR A. FORRESTER in *Lauderd. Papers* (Camden) III. lxxxi. 137 That the draught of the intended Addresse might be taken paragraphly into consideration. *Ibid.* 138 The House had paragraphly and very fully heard and debated it.

paragraphy ('pærəgrɑːfɪ, -æ-). [f. PARAGRAPH: see -GRAPHY.] The writing of newspaper paragraphs; newspaper paragraphs collectively or as a class.

1896 *Critic* (N.Y.) 25 Jan. 64/2 There has been a whirl of paragraphy over the secession of Mr. P. C. from the Lyceum. *Ibid.* 17 Oct. 233 In these days of literary paragraphy..it requires some ingenuity to keep up an incognito.

paragration, obs. variant of PERAGRATION.

Paraguay (ˈpærəgweɪ, now usu. -gwaɪ). [The name of a river and Republic of South America.]

1. The South American shrub *Ilex paraguayensis*, commonly called Maté, the leaves of which are dried or roasted, and infused as a beverage in the same way as tea. Hence ***Paraguay-tea***.

1727–41 CHAMBERS *Cycl.*, *Paraguay*,..a celebrated plant of the shrub kind..better known among us under the denomination of South-Sea Tea. *Ibid.*, The use of Paraguay began lately to obtain in England; where many people seemed to like it as well as tea. **1793** B. EDWARDS *Hist. Brit. Colonies W. Indies* I. 476 Ilex Cassine. Paraguay Tea. **1802** *Brookes' Gazetteer* (ed. 12) s.v., The valuable herb called Paraguay,..the infusion of which is drank, in all the Spanish provinces of S. America, instead of tea. **1825** J. C. LOUDON *Encycl. Agric.* I. 200 Paraguay tea..is used [in Brazil] as a substitute for that of China. **1839** W. PARISH *Buenos Ayres* xv. 347 Even the yerba-maté, or Paraguay tea..is now introduced from the southern provinces of Brazil. **1856** *Househ. Words* 3 May 377/2 An eligible draught presents itself in the shape of Yerva de Paraguay, or Paraguay tea. **1858** SIMMONDS *Dict. Trade*, *Paraguay-tea*, the leaves of the South American holly, *Ilex Paraguensis*. **1924** RECORD & MELL *Timbers Trop. Amer.* II. 92 Holly bushes, the source of the famous Brazilian or Paraguay tea or 'herva mate'. **1937** A. F. HILL *Econ. Bot.* xxi. 510 Paraguay tea..is next to coffee, tea, and cocoa in importance.

2. Paraguay herb: see quots.

1748 *Earthquake of Peru* iii. 263 They make use of the Herb of Paraguay, which some call St. Bartholomew's Herb. **1887** MOLONEY *Forestry W. Afr.* 396 Paraguay Herb (*Vandellia diffusa*, L.).—Small herb. In South America this plant is used as an emetic.

Paraguayan (pærəˈgweɪən, -ˈgwaɪən), *a.* and *sb.* Also 7 **Paragueyan**, 9 **Paraguarian**. [f. PARAGUAY + -AN.] **A.** *adj.* Of or belonging to Paraguay or its inhabitants; produced in or characteristic of Paraguay. **B.** *sb.* A native or inhabitant of Paraguay.

1693 P. GORDON *Geogr. Anatomized* II. iv. 192 The Paraguayans are reported to be a people of very tall and big bodies, yet extraordinarily nimble and much given to running. **1699** *Ibid.* (ed. 2) II. ii. 283 The opposite Place of the Globe to Japan, is that part of the Paragueyan Ocean, lying between 340 and 350 Degrees of Longitude, with 30 and 40 Degrees of Southern Latitude. **1832** J. BELL *Syst. Geogr.* VI. I. 238 The Paraguarians collected an army of 6,000 men. **1856** C. KINGSLEY *Misc.* (1859) II. 18 Very interesting also..are..scattered hints as to the qualities of the Paraguayans themselves. **1884** R. G. WATSON *Spanish & Portuguese S. Amer. Colonial Period* I. xvi. 273 Two Fathers, accompanied by thirty Paraguayan disciples, set out. **1901** *Chambers's Jrnl.* Sept. 623/2 The Paraguayans are ominously polite. **1935** P. DE RONDE *Paraguay* iii. 43 From the unions between the Spanish and the natives there evolved in course of time the present Paraguayan race. **1956** G. DURRELL *Drunken Forest* iii. 62 Our housekeeper, a dark-skinned, dark-eyed Paraguayan woman. **1957** P. KEMP *Mine were of Trouble* vi. 114 He had smuggled arms to one or other of the belligerents in the Gran Chaco war—I think to the Paraguayans. **1973** G. GREENE *Honorary Consul* v. ii. 264 He does not think in terms of Paraguayans, Peruvians, Bolivians, Argentinians. **1977** *Gramophone* Dec. 1106/1 Agustin Barrios, the Paraguayan guitarist and composer.

paragutta (pærəˈgʌtə). [f. PARA-[1] + GUTTA[2].] A material derived from rubber and gutta percha used for insulating telephone cables.

1931 A. R. KEMP in *Jrnl. Franklin Inst.* CCXI. 37 An insulation called paragutta has been developed which as the name suggests is derived essentially from rubber and gutta percha. **1959** J. W. FREEBODY *Telegr.* xvii. 671/2 Paragutta, which has a specific capacitance of 2·6, eventually replaced gutta percha for the insulation of more modern cables.

paraheliotropic (ˌpærəhiːlɪəʊˈtrɒpɪk), *a. Bot.* [f. Gr. παρα- aside + ἥλιος sun + -τροπος turning + -IC: cf. HELIOTROPIC.] Of leaves: Turning their edges in the direction of incident light.

1880 C. & F. DARWIN *Movem. Pl.* 419 The leaves of some plants when exposed to an intense and injurious amount of light direct themselves, by rising or sinking or twisting, so as to be less intensely illuminated. Such movements have sometimes been called diurnal sleep... They might be called paraheliotropic. **1881** DARWIN in *Nature* XXIII. 409/2 With several species of Hedychium, a widely-different paraheliotropic movement occurs.

paraheliotropism (ˌpærəhiːlɪˈɒtrəpɪz(ə)m). *Bot.* [f. as prec. + -ISM.] A tendency in plants when exposed to brilliant light to turn their leaves parallel to the incidence of the light-rays.

1881 DARWIN in *Nature* XXIII. 409/1 This remarkable movement I have called paraheliotropism. *Ibid.*, F. Müller doubts whether so strongly marked a case of paraheliotropism would ever be observed under the duller skies of England.

parahelium (stress variable). Also **parhelium**. [f. PARA-[1] 3 + HELIUM.] The form of helium whose spectrum does not exhibit the fine structure of orthohelium, owing to the spins of the two orbital electrons being anti-parallel.

1896 RUNGE & PASCHEN in *Astrophysical Jrnl.* III. 18 We come to the conclusion that clèveite gas consists of two elements, one corresponding to the second and third series (single lines), and the other corresponding to the fifth and sixth series (double lines..). If this is true, the name *Helium* should be given only to the second element... The first element Professor Stoney has proposed to call *Parhelium*. **1903** A. M. CLERKE *Probl. Astrophysics* v. 58 'Parhelium' may then safely be treated as fictitious. **1922**, **1961** [see ORTHOHELIUM]. **1974** G. REECE tr. *Hund's Hist. Quantum Theory* iv. 60 Runge and Paschen were able to add series for O, S, Se and He in 1895–7. They discovered the two spectral systems of orthohelium and parahelium in the process.

parahippocampal, -hopeite: see PARA-[1] 1, 2 c.

parahormone (pærəˈhɔːməʊn). *Physiol.* Also †**parhormone**. [a. F. *parhormone* (E. Gley 1911, in *Rev. Scientifique* 11 Mar. 262): see PARA-[1] and HORMONE.] A product of metabolism which has a secondary hormonal role.

1918 M. FISHBERG tr. *E. Gley's Internal Secretions* 154 At most we might apply the term *parhormones* to the excretory products which play only an accessory rôle as excitants, reserving the name of hormones for the specific glandular products. **1922** R. G. HOSKINS in L. F. Barker et al. *Endocrinol. & Metabolism* I. I. 8 For nonspecific regulatory substances such as carbon dioxid, Gley has proposed the designation 'parhormones'. **1935** *Biol. Rev.* X. 440 Water.. could presumably be classified as a parahormone for renal function. **1948** C. D. TURNER *Gen. Endocrinol.* ii. 65 The synthesis, storage and release of sugar by the liver is not a true endocrine activity, since glucose is not a specific product of this organ. Sugar and such materials are important metabolites and may be designated as parahormones.

parahyal, -hypnosis: see PARA-[1].

parahydrogen (stress variable). Also **para hydrogen** and with hyphen. [f. PARA-[1] 3 + HYDROGEN, as tr. G. *parawasserstoff* (Bonhoeffer & Harteck 1929, in *Naturwissenschaften* XVII. 182/1), coined on the analogy of *par(a)helium* (see quot. 1935 s.v. ORTHOHYDROGEN).] The form of molecular hydrogen in which the two nuclei in the molecule have antiparallel spins, so that the spectrum exhibits no hyperfine structure. Cf. ORTHOHYDROGEN.

1929 *Industr. & Engin. Chem.* 10 July 6/1 At room temperatures and atmospheric pressure in glass vessels para-hydrogen is a stable gas. **1935**, etc. [see ORTHOHYDROGEN]. **1969** H. T. EVANS tr. *G. Hägg's Gen. & Inorg. Chem.* xviii. 452 The melting and boiling points of parahydrogen are approximately 0·1° lower than for ordinary hydrogen.

parail, -aile, -aille, var. PAREIL, PAREL *Obs.*

para-influenza (ˌpærəɪnfluˈɛnzə). *Biol.* Also **parainfluenza**. [f. PARA-[1] + INFLUENZA.] Any of a group of paramyxoviruses which resemble the influenza viruses and include the one causing croup; (orig. classed as myxoviruses before paramyxoviruses were recognized as a separate group). Usu. *attrib.*, esp. in ***para-influenza virus***.

1959 C. H. ANDREWES et al. in *Virology* VIII. 129 (*heading*) Para-influenza viruses 1, 2, and 3: suggested names for recently described myxoviruses. *Ibid.* 130 The following names are accordingly proposed: Sendai (including HA2). *Myxovirus para-influenzae 1* (Para-influenza 1). CA virus: *Myxovirus para-influenzae 2* (Para-influenza 2). HA1: *Myxovirus para-influenzae 3* (Para-influenza 3). **1959** *Brit. Med. Bull.* XV. 221/2 It seems.. that the Far Eastern strain of para-influenza 1 virus (Sendai) is endemic in laboratory mice and very probably pathogenic for pigs and man also. *Ibid.* 222/1 Para-influenza 2. This virus was called CA (croup-associated) by Chanock (1956). It was independently described by Beale and his colleagues as the virus of acute laryngo-tracheobronchitis of children. **1965** C. ANDREWES *Common Cold* xi. 98 Para-influenza infections are mainly seen in children in whom they cause respiratory infections of all degrees of severity up to fatal pneumonia. **1974** *Nature* 23 Aug. 650/2 As *in vivo* hybridisation seems to have permitted a human tumour to become..unusually lethal in the hamster,..similar mechanisms may be implicated in human cancer, particularly when such fusing agents as parainfluenza viruses are prevalent in man.

parais, paraison, obs. f. PARADISE, PARISON.

para'journalism. orig. *U.S.* [f. PARA-[1] past, beyond, contrary to + JOURNALISM.] A type of unconventional journalism not primarily concerned with the reporting of facts. So **para'journalist, parajourna'listic** *a.*

1965 D. MACDONALD in *N.Y. Rev. Bks.* 26 Aug. 3/1 A new kind of journalism is being born, or spawned. It might be called 'parajournalism', from the Greek *para*, 'beside' or 'against': something similar in form but different in function. **1966** *New Statesman* 4 Mar. 300/1 The second achievement is 'parajournalism'—Dwight Macdonald's word. **1966** *Atlantic Monthly* June 89 MacDonald.. castigates a Wolfe review of Mailer's latest novel and berates the reviewer as again playing para-journalist because his technique was 'to jeer at the author's private life and personality—or rather his *persona*.' **1970** *Americana Ann.* 503/1 A wave of parajournalistic publications, the so-called underground press, was mounting a serious challenge to established dailies. **1972** *Times Lit. Suppl.* 21 Apr. 444/1 (Advt.), 'What is now called para-journalism—writing it the way it happened' (Daily Mirror). **1978** *New York* 3 Apr. 81/2 Charlie, the megalomaniacal parajournalist.

parakeelya (pærəˈkiːljə). *Austral.* Also **parake(e)lia, parakilja, parakylia.** [Aboriginal name.] An annual or perennial herb belonging to the genus *Calandrinia*, of the family Portulacaceæ, native to Australia and America and bearing succulent leaves and clusters of reddish flowers. Also *attrib.*

1898 D. W. CARNEGIE *Spinifex & Sand* vii. 216 Given 'parakeelia' every second night or so a camel would never want to drink at all. **1921** *Trans. R. Soc. S. Austral.* XLV. 11 The common parakeelya at Tarcoola..appears to be this species [sc. *Calandrinia polyandra*]. **1931** I. L. IDRIESS *Lasseter's Last Ride* xii. 99 The secret was in the Parakelia grass. In appearance something like ice-plant, its thick leaves were stored with water. **1934** [see CLAYTONIA]. **1935** H. H. FINLAYSON *Red Centre* iii. 33 One can only refer to the sprightly purple and yellow flowered succulents, the parakeelia and munyeroo. **1944** F. CLUNE *Red Heart* 36 Crushed parakelia weed, broken mulga bough..—it was by signs such as these that the trackers deduced the course of the wayfarer. **1959** *Listener* 7 May 785/1 It [*sc.* the landscape] is ablaze with the scarlet of Sturt's desert pea, with cerise-coloured parakelia. **1965** *Austral. Encycl.* VI. 480/1 Parakeelya (Parakilja), the aboriginal name for several species of fleshy herbs in the genus *Calandrinia* (family Portulacaceae) which can thrive in the most arid parts of inland Australia. **1967** O. RUHEN in *Coast to Coast 1965–66* 189 A few parakeelya leaves can evoke the blessed relief of flowing saliva. **1972** Y. LOVELOCK *Vegetable Bk.* I. 193 The aborigines bake the succulent leaves of the parakilja..with bark as a food; the plant was once eaten by the early settlers.

parakeet (ˈpærəkiːt), **paroquet** (ˈpærəkɪt), **parr-.** Forms: α. 6 parroket, 7 parrocquet, parocket, 7–9 perroquet, (8 paraquet), 8– paro-, parroquet. β. 6 (? parakitie), parrachito, 6–7 paraquit(t)o, 7 parraquito, parakito, -keeto, -chito, -que(e)to; perokito, -chito; par(r)akita; parraketto, paraketo, -cketto, paroqueto, 7–8 paraquetto. γ. 7 parakeete, parrakeit, 7–8 parakite, (8 parrochite, paroqueet, 9 -keet), 7– parakeet, 8– parrakeet. [Several forms, repr. (α) OF. *paroquet* (14th c. in Hatz.-Darm.), mod.F. *perroquet* parrot; (β) It. *parrochetto*, *-ucchetto*, *perrochetto* (also in Florio, *parochito* 'a little Parret or Parochito'), Sp. *periquito* (recent); (γ) an anglicized form of this as *par(r)akeet*. The OF. *paroquet* is held by Darmesteter to be ad. It. *parrochetto*, dim. of *parroco* parson (cf. *moineau* sparrow, dim. of *moine* monk); but some think the typical It. form to be *parrucchetto*, as dim. of *parrucca* 'peruke, periwig', in reference to the plumage of the head in some species. In Sp. *periquito* is a later dim. of the much commoner name *perico*, supposed to be the same word as *Perico*, colloquial dim. of *Pedro* Peter: cf. PARROT. The relations between the Sp. and It. forms cannot be settled until the chronology is known; prob. the name has been modified by popular etymology in one or both.

As the parrot was known in Italy from Roman times downward, the name *parrochetto*, etc., may have originated there rather than (as sometimes assumed) with the Spanish and Portuguese navigators.]

A bird of the parrot kind; now *spec.* applied to the smaller birds included in the order, esp. those having long tails.

The species best known and having the widest range is the ***ring-necked parakeet*** (*Palæornis torquatus*), often kept as a cage bird; another well-known species is the ***Alexandrine parakeet*** (*P. alexandri*); the common parakeet of the United States is *Conurus carolinensis*; special genera of parrots are known as ***grass-parakeets, ground-parakeets***.

α. **1581** HAMILTON *Cath. Traict.* in *Cath. Tractates* (S.T.S.) 102 For him and sik vtheris, quha lyk parrokettis enterteneis the auditouris be clattering tellis. **1687** A. LOVELL tr. *Thevenot's Trav.* III. 38 In some places Parrocquets are taken after the same manner. **1698** FROGER *Voy.* 47 Small birds, with fine feathers: among them there are Perroquets, Cardinals, and Colibries. **1698** FRYER *Acc. E. India & P.* 71 Here were some Flocks of Parockets. **1713** BERKELEY *Guard.* No. 49 ¶7, I look on the beaus and ladies as so many paraquets in an aviary. **1718** PRIOR *Dove* 91, I would not give my Paroquet For all the Doves that ever flew. **1776** *Phil. Trans.* LXVI. 574 A perroquet..got from his master some of the boiled fish. **1796** STEDMAN *Surinam* II. xvii. 32 Beautiful paroquets, which are a species of parrots, but smaller though not less common. **1846** G. GARDNER *Brazil* 179 Parroquets,..keeping up an almost continual cry of Parroquet—Parroquet.

β. *c* **1595** CAPT. WYATT *R. Dudley's Voy. W. Ind.* (Hakl. Soc.) 38 Infinite store of parratts, parakities, and other great birds of most fine and well mixed collers. **1596** RALEIGH *Discov. Guiana* 61 They brought vs also..a sort of Paraquitos, no bigger than wrens. **1599** T. M[OUFET] *Silkwormes* 66 Millet seede wherewith Parrachitos are fed. **1603** FLORIO *Montaigne* II. viii. (1632) 214 Loved..for our pastimes, as we do apes, monkies, or perokitoes. **1644** QUARLES *Sheph. Orac.* iv, We discipline them, teach them how to prate, Like Parakitoes, words they know not what. *a* **1652** BROME *City Wit* I. i. Wks. 1873 I. 286 Madame, how does your Monckey, your Parrot, and Parraquitoes? **1652** S. S. *Secretary's Studie* 37 None of your jigging Girles, that pearch Paraquettos on their fists. **1675** *Lond. Gaz.* No. 1014/4 A Green Parraketto, with a black and red Ring about his Neck, lost. **1682** S. WILSON *Acc. Carolina* 12 In the woods great plenty of wilde..Turtle Doves, Paraquetos, and Pidgeons. **1688** R. HOLME *Armoury* II. 282/2 The

Scarlet Parakeeto, is no larger than a Black bird. **1706** PHILLIPS, *Paraquetto*, a small sort of Parret, a Bird.

γ. **1621** SIR R. BOYLE *Diary* in *Lismore Papers* (1886) II. 15 A purse of sylck lyke a parakeete. **1688** *Lond. Gaz.* No. 2341/4 A Little Parakeet with a red Head, a green, red, and black Tail.. flew out of a Window.., on Sunday last. **1700** WALLACE *Acc. New Caledonia in Darien* in *Misc. Cur.* (1708) III. 417 Parrots of many kinds, Parakites Macaws. **1705** BOSMAN *Guinea* xv. (1721) 255 Two small Parrochites, or Guinea Sparrows. **1750** G. HUGHES *Barbadoes* III. 73 The Parakite.. is of the frugivorous Kind and about the Bigness of a Thrush. **1847** L. HUNT *Men, Women, & B.* (1876) 36 What prodigious chattering and brilliant colours in the maccaws and parrakeets. **1853** KINGSLEY *Hypatia* xxii, Strange birds from India, parakeets, peacocks, pheasants. **1879** E. ARNOLD *Lt. Asia* (1889) 151 Wild fruit.. plucked By purple parokeet.

b. Applied allusively to persons, i.e. in reference to the chattering or imitative faculty of the birds, or to their gay plumage: cf. PARROT *sb.*

1596 SHAKS. *1 Hen. IV*, II. iii. 88 Come, come, you Paraquito, answer me directly vnto this question, that I shall aske. **1650** B. *Discolliminium* 41 Some young Parackettoes now nursing up in the Universities. **1661** K. W. *Conf. Charac., Cambr. Minion*, A Cambridge paraketo is an outlandish ape, whose mimick disposition makes her shape her seacole vestures into the form of the fashion. *a* **1668** DAVENANT *Man's the Master* II. i, That damsel is too pert,.. you should keep these paraqueetos in a cage. **1876** GEO. ELIOT *Dan. Der.* xxxiii, The young woman.. a sort of paroquet in a bright blue dress.

parakeratosis, -kinesia, etc.: see PARA-[1] 1.

parakite (ˈpærəkaɪt). [In sense a, f. PARA(CHUTE) + KITE; in b, f. Gr. παρά, PARA-[1] beyond + KITE.]

1. a. A kind of large kite constructed so as to be inflated by the wind like a parachute, proposed by Simmons in 1875 for military use. **b.** A kind of tailless kite devised by Woglom in 1896 for various scientific purposes.

1875 *10th Rep. Aeronaut. Soc.* 75 An attempt was made by Mr. Simmons, the aëronaut, to supplement the employment of a balloon in warfare by.. a kite, which, from the peculiar nature of its construction, he designated the parakite. It was, in fact, a combination of the parachute and kite. **1895** BADEN POWELL in *Jrnl. United Service Inst.* 888 Simmons, the aëronaut, tried in 1876 an apparatus under the name of the 'parakite' for raising a military observer. **1896** G. T. WOGLOM (*title*) Parakites; A Treatise on the Making and Flying of Tailless Kites for Scientific Purposes. *Ibid.* 25 Inasmuch as 'kite' has been the name for a toy.. it has seemed proper to distinguish therefrom these 'parakites', using the Greek prefix in its purport of *beyond the* kite—an advanced kite. **1897** *Daily News* 4 Nov. 6/4 The processes of 'Parakite Photography' are minutely described.

2. In modern use applied to a parachute kite which is towed along against the wind by a motorboat, car, or other fast vehicle. So **ˈparakiting**, the sport of soaring when harnessed to a parakite.

1962 *Aeroplane* CII. 233/2 Para kite.—First trials of the Lemoigne parachute kite have taken place in England... Mr. Walter Neumark remained at about 150 ft. for over 5 minutes while moored to the towing car. **1964** T. W. WILLANS *Parachuting & Skydiving* v. 50 The Lemoigne parakite of the 1960s—a sort of ascending parachute, a few of which had found their way from France into England. **1970** *Time* 30 Mar. 42/1 In parakiting, the water skier becomes airborne when the trailing parachute pops open. **1978** *Lancashire Life* Apr. 50 (*caption*) Instead of hang gliding's crunch-down, parakiting's finale is a splash-down: on this occasion, in an icy sea. *Ibid.*, Stan Lyons was the guinea-pig—the man setting out to make Morecambe's first parakite flight between the Stone Jetty and West End Pier.

parakite, -kitie, -kito: see PARAKEET.

paralactic (pærəˈlæktɪk), *a. Chem.* [PARA-[1] 2 a.] In *paralactic acid*, an isomeric modification of ordinary lactic acid, one of the two constituents of sarcolactic acid, existing in the animal organism, especially in muscular flesh. Its salts are **paraˈlactates**.

1877 WATTS *Fownes' Chem.* II. 328 Paralactic acid heated to 130° yields dilactic acid, convertible by water into ordinary lactic acid. **1893** *Syd. Soc. Lex.* s.v., The paralactate is.. thrown down as a mass of small, colourless crystals.

paralalia, -lampsis: see PARA-[1] 1.

paralament, obs. form of PARLIAMENT.

paralanguage (ˌpærəˈlæŋgwɪdʒ). *Linguistics.* [f. PARA-[1] alongside + LANGUAGE *sb.*[1]] The system of non-phonemic but vocal factors in speech, such as tone of voice, tempo of speech, and sighing, by which communication is assisted. Cf. KINESICS.

Some authorities also include in paralanguage such adjuncts of speech as gesture and facial expression.

1958 G. L. TRAGER in *Studies in Linguistics* XIII. 4 The vocalizations and voice qualities together are being called *paralanguage* (a term suggested by A. A. Hill). **1959** H. L. SMITH in *College English* XX. 172/2 Speech does not take place in a vacuum but is surrounded, as it were, by patterned bodily motions—the *kinesic* system—and by systematically analyzable vocalizations, or *paralanguage*. **1964** *Language* XL. 202 Trager's 1958 paper outlined a taxonomic system for the analysis of the phenomena of paralanguage. **1965** [see *morpheme-like* s.v. MORPHEME c]. **1967** *Jrnl. Eng. Linguistics* I. 28 *Paralanguage*, the non-linguistic but communicatively significant orchestration of the stream of speech, involving such phenomena as abnormally high or low pitch, abnormally fast or slow tempo, abnormal loudness or softness, drawl, clipping, rasp, openness, and the like. **1972** W. M. AUSTIN in A. L. Davis *Culture, Class, & Lang. Variety* viii. 159 We judge the dynamic and effective speaker by his use of kinesics and paralanguage as well as language. **1978** *Verbatim* May 15/2 That particular methodology called generative-transformational did not include paralanguage, kinesics, or cultural influences.

paralaurionite, -lexia: see PARA-[1] 2 c, 1.

paralax, obs. form of PARALLAX.

paraldehyde (pəˈrældɪhaɪd). *Chem.* [PAR(A-[1] 2 a.] A polymer of ALDEHYDE, $C_6H_{12}O_3$, a colourless liquid at ordinary temperatures; used as a narcotic and as a remedy against insomnia.

1857 MILLER *Elem. Chem.* III. 134 A third isomeric body termed paraldehyd, which is liquid, and boils at 257°. **1881** CAPT. ABNEY in *Nature* XXV. 191/1 Par-aldehyde has three molecules of aldehyde in its one molecule. **1885** REMSEN *Org. Chem.* (1888) 49. **1896** *Allbutt's Syst. Med.* I. 242 Paraldehyde produces few special effects other than those procuring sleep.

paralegal (ˌpærəˈliːgəl), *a.* and *sb.* Chiefly *N. Amer.* [f. PARA-[1] + LEGAL *a.*] **A.** *adj.* Of or pertaining to auxiliary aspects of the law. **B.** *sb.* One trained in subsidiary legal matters, though not fully qualified as a lawyer, etc.; a legal aide.

1972 *N.Y. Law Jrnl.* 22 Aug. 2/7 (Advt.), Para-legals (that is, legal assistants or paraprofessionals) are used by an ever-increasing number of prominent attorneys to reduce their unwanted load of paralegal matters and free up their time to render legal advice more efficiently. **1975** *Daily Colonist* (Victoria, B.C.) 23 Aug. 1/1 Miss Lissell intends to take a two-year para-legal course at one of the Vancouver colleges. **1977** *Times* 12 July 4/6 If legal aid was not available, the staff of the first-tier agency, who would have some paralegal training, would try to help. **1977** *N.Y. Rev. Bks.* 15 Sept. 55/2 (Advt.), Smith College graduate. Economics major. Financial, law and management background. Light skills. Seeks position as para-legal, office manager, social secretary, coordinator, etc.

paraleipsis, paralepsis: see PARALIPSIS.

paralerema to **paralgia**: see PARA-[1] 1.

†**paˈralian.** *Obs. rare.* [f. L. *parali-us*, a. Gr. παράλι-ος by the sea, maritime, f. παρά beside + ἅλς, ἁλ- the sea.] A dweller by the sea. So †**paˈralious** *a.*, dwelling or growing by the sea.

1654 H. L'ESTRANGE *Chas. I* (1655) 131 The Mediterraneans the Highlanders muttered at the Imposition, alledging that it being a Naval Tax, it ought.. to be born by the Paralious, the Maritime parts. **1657** TOMLINSON *Renou's Disp.* 247 The branches of paralious Tithymal. **1724** DK. WHARTON *True Briton* No. 66 II. 558 The Paralians (or those who liv'd by the Water-side).

paralic (pəˈrælɪk), *a. Geol.* [ad. G. *paralisch* (C. F. Naumann *Lehrb. d. Geognosie* (1852) II. II. vii. 452), f. Gr. παράλ-ιος by the sea (see PARALIAN): see -IC.] Formed or having occurred in shallow water near the sea.

[**1911**: see LIMNIC *a.*] **1914** H. RIES *Econ. Geol.* (ed. 4) i. 13 A distinction is, however, sometimes made between (1) limnetic coals..; and (2) paralic coals, or those derived from plant remains which collected in marshes near the sea border. **1940**, etc. [see LIMNIC *a.*]. **1963** D. W. & E. E. HUMPHRIES tr. *Termier's Erosion & Sedimentation* i. 30 There was an extension of warm marine faunas, a large distribution of paralic flora and the development of lateritic soils. **1966** *McGraw-Hill Encycl. Sci. & Technol.* XII. 142/2 The molasse is a product of paralic sedimentation. **1977** A. HALLAM *Planet Earth* 154 The seams formed from peats in coastal-swamp environments (paralic coals) are characteristically relatively thin after compaction.

paraling, variant of PARELLING *Obs.*

paralinguistic (ˌpærəlɪŋˈgwɪstɪk), *a.* and *sb. Linguistics.* [f. PARA-[1] alongside + LINGUISTIC *a.* and *sb.*; cf. PARALANGUAGE.] **A.** *adj.* Of or pertaining to paralanguage; of or pertaining to vocal communication effected non-phonemically by tone of voice, tempo of speech, etc. So **paralinˈguistically** *adv.* Cf. KINESIC *a.*

1958 A. A. HILL *Introd. Ling. Struct.* xxi. 409 The paralinguistic area investigated by Birdwhistell has been called by him kinesics. **1959** [see KINESIC *a.*]. **1964** G. L. TRAGER in D. Abercrombie et al. *Daniel Jones* 267 It has become possible to separate out paralinguistic pitch phenomena from those of language proper. **1964** CRYSTAL & QUIRK (*title*) Systems of prosodic and paralinguistic features in English. **1965** *Canad. Jrnl. Linguistics* XI. 36 This is linguistically and paralinguistically irrelevant. **1967** M. ARGYLE *Psychol. Interpersonal Behaviour* v. 89 People are often quite unaware of the emotive, paralinguistic aspects of their speech—they do not realize how cross they sound, for instance. **1971** M. L. SAMUELS in A. J. Aitken et al. *Edin. Stud. Eng. & Scots* 5 A para-linguistic feature like an unusual voice-quality is found to accompany an unusual phonetic system. **1976** *Amer. Speech 1974* XLIX. 286 Nonverbal, paralinguistic features related to male/female language involve voice pitch, body language and facial expression, and the place of silence in sex-role communication.

B. *sb.* (in form a *pl.*) [-ICS.] The study of paralanguage; non-phonemic factors of vocal communication. Cf. KINESICS.

1958 A. A. HILL *Introd. Ling. Struct.* xxi. 408 A part of communication activity which is outside the area of microlinguistics.. is what can be called paralinguistics. **1958** G. L. TRAGER in *Studies in Linguistics* XIII. 4 The words *paralinguistic* and *paralinguistics* are self-explanatory. **1962** D. H. HYMES in J. A. Fishman *Readings Sociol. of Lang.* (1968) 106 Features of speech, such as tone of voice and hesitation pauses,.. phenomena which have recently been systematized in a preliminary way under the heading of 'paralinguistics'. **1972** *Sci. Amer.* Sept. 60/1 The most probable links to investigate exist within human paralinguistics: the extensive array of facial expressions, body postures, hand signals and vocal tones and emphases that we use to supplement verbal speech. **1973** *Archivum Linguisticum* IV. 53 *Linguistic levels*.. Grammar, lexis, phonology, semantics, graphology, phonetics, paralinguistics.

‖**Paralipomena** (pærəlaɪˈpɒmənə), *sb. pl.* In 4-6 (7 in Dicts.) **paralipomenon** (also 4 -lyp-), properly gen. pl.; in 9 rarely in sing. **paralipomenon (-leip-)**. [Late L. *paralīpomena*, gen. pl. -*ōn* (Jerome), a. Gr. παραλειπόμενα (things) left out; f. παραλείπειν to leave on one side, omit.]

†**1.** (Almost always *Paralipomenon*, repr. genit. pl. Παραλειπομένων (sc. βιβλία), the title in LXX and hence in the Vulgate.) The Books of Chronicles in the Old Testament: so called as containing particulars omitted in the Books of Kings. *Obs.*

a **1340** HAMPOLE *Psalter* cxxxv. 1 Grete louyng of þis psalme is shewyd in paralypomenon. **1388** WYCLIF *1 Chron.* Prol., This book of Paralipomenon, the firste, bigynneth at Adam.. rehersinge many thingis whiche ben not writen in the book of Kingis before. *a* **1548** HALL *Chron., Hen. VIII* 227 Wyllyam Tyndale.. translated the .v. bookes of Moyses ..the bookes of the Kynges and the bookes of Paralipomenon [etc.]. **1616** BULLOKAR *Eng. Expos.*, *Paralipomenon*,.. There are two bookes in the old testament so called, because many worthy histories omitted in the bookes of Kings, are there related. **1706** PHILLIPS, *Paralipomena*, the two Books of Chronicles.

2. Things omitted in the body of a work, and appended as a supplement. (Rarely in sing. -*on*.)

1674 BOYLE *Grounds Corpusc. Philos.* 1 To reserve these thoughts, as a kind of Paralipomena to his dialogue. **1690** —— *Medic. Hydrost.* Postscr., A supplement to the first tome, containing divers historical paralipomena, that by mistake were omitted. **1887** T. A. TROLLOPE *What I Remember* I. 225 One more note.. as a paraleipomenon to that Autobiography of my brother.

‖**paralipsis** (pærəˈlɪpsɪs). *Rhet.* Also **-leipsis**; *erron.* **-lepsis, -lepsy.** [a. Gr. παράλειψις passing by omission, f. παραλείπειν to leave on one side, pass by; late L. *paralipsis* (Aquila).] A rhetorical figure in which the speaker emphasizes something by affecting to pass it by without notice, usually by such phrases as 'not to mention', 'to say nothing of'.

1586 A. DAY *Eng. Secretary* II. (1625) 95 *Paralepsis* or *Occupatio*, when in seeming to ouer-passe, omit, or let-slip a thing, we then chiefly speake thereof. **1589** PUTTENHAM *Eng. Poesie* III. xix. (Arb.) 239 *Paralepsis*, or the Passager. **1657** J. SMITH *Myst. Rhet.* 165 *Paralipsis*,.. Preterition. **1842** BRANDE *Dict. Sci.*, etc., *Paraleipsis*, in Rhetoric, the artificially exhibited omission or slight mention of some important point, in order to impress the hearers with indignation, pity, etc.

parall, variant of PAREL *v. Obs.*

parallactic (pærəˈlæktɪk), *a.* [ad. Gr. παραλλακτικ-ός of or by the parallax, f. verbal adj. *παράλλακτος, f. παραλλάσσειν: see PARALLAX.] Pertaining, relating, or due to parallax.

parallactic inequality: see INEQUALITY 4. †*parallactic instrument, telescope*, etc.: former names for an EQUATORIAL.

1630 R. N. tr. *Camden's Hist. Eliz.* 53 Thomas Digsey, and Iohn Dey.. haue learnedly prooued by Paralactic Doctrine, that it [new star in Cassiopeia] was in the celestiall, not in the Elementary Region. **1670** BLOUNT *Glossogr.* (ed. 3), *Parallactic*. **1764** *Phil. Trans.* LIV. 363 The parallactic telescope ought to be nearly of equal goodness with the transit telescope. **1789** PIAZZI *ibid.* LXXIX. 59 By the method of parallactic angles. **1834** *Nat. Philos.* III. *Astron.* iii 84/1 (U.K.S.) The diurnal, or parallactic, libration. **1887** *Pall Mall G.* 10 June 12/1 The parallactic motion of stars has been demonstrated by the Rev. Dr. Pritchard, of Oxford, under a process of making the stars photograph their position, perfected by himself.

†**paraˈllactical**, *a. Obs.* [See -ICAL.] = prec.

1671 FLAMSTEED in Rigaud *Corr. Sci. Men* (1841) II. 109 The parallactical angle. **1704** J. HARRIS *Lex. Techn.* I, *Parallactical Angle*, is an Angle made by the Oblique cutting of a Circle of Altitude, or Vertical Circle with the Ecliptick.

parallax (ˈpærəlæks). Also 6-7 **paralax**, 7 **parallaxe**; also 7 in Gr. form **parallaxis**. [a. F. *parallaxe* (1557 in Hatz.-Darm.), ad. Gr. παράλλαξις change, alteration, alternation, mutual inclination of two lines meeting in an angle, f. παραλλάσσειν to alter, alternate; in mod.L. *parallaxis*.]

1. a. (*Astron.*) Apparent displacement, or difference in the apparent position, of an object, caused by actual change (or difference) of position of the point of observation; *spec.* the angular amount of such displacement or difference of position, being the angle contained between the two straight lines drawn to the object from the two different points of view, and constituting a measure of the distance of the object. Also *transf.* (quot. 1881).

In Astronomy there are two kinds of parallax, viz. *diurnal* and *annual*, the former when a celestial object is observed from opposite points on the earth's *surface*, the latter when observed from opposite points of the earth's *orbit*. As the mean or proper position of the body is that which it would have if viewed in the one case from the earth's centre (or a point in a line with it), in the other case from the centre of its orbit, the parallax is actually calculated and stated from these central points, and called *geocentric* and *heliocentric* respectively, the base lines of these being the earth's radius and the radius of its orbit. ***horizontal parallax***: the diurnal parallax of a heavenly body seen on the horizon.

1612 SELDEN *Illustr. Drayton's Poly-olb.* xiv. 235 Those learned Mathematicians, by omitting of Paralax and refractions, deceiued themselues and posterity. **1663** BOYLE *Exp. Nat. Philos.* I. ii. 33 Which they not irrationally prove by the Parallaxis (or Circular difference betwixt the place of a Star, suppos'd to be taken by two Observations, the one made at the Centre, and the other on the surface of the Earth). **1665** *Phil. Trans.* I. 106 He hath deduced the Horizontal Parallax of this very Comet. **1696** WHISTON *Th. Earth* I. (1722) 32 The fix'd Stars..till very lately..were thought subject to no parallax at all. *a* **1711** KEN *Hymns Evang.* Poet. Wks. 1721 I. 44, I saw it moving in a Sphear so high, Scarce any Parallax I cou'd descry. **1812** WOODHOUSE *Astron.* xii. 98 The parallax of Mars was found to be about 23 seconds. **1867–77** G. F. CHAMBERS *Astron.* I. i. 2 The problem..when solved [gives] the amount of the Sun's equatorial horizontal parallax. **1881** TAIT in *Nature* XXV. 91/1 In these thermometers..no provision is made for avoiding parallax or personal equation.

b. *fig.*

1594 J. DAVIS *Seaman's Secr.* (1607) 19 To amend the parallax of false shadow of your sight. **1599** DANIEL *Musophilus* 606 Vndeceiued with the Paralax Of a mistaking eye of passion. **1682** SIR T. BROWNE *Chr. Mor.* II. §3 Many things are known, as some are seen, that is by Parallaxis, or at some distance from their true and proper beings. **1870** MAX MÜLLER *Sc. Relig.* (1873) 43 Unless we make allowance for this mental parallax [between material and spiritual]. **1892** *Nation* 7 Apr. 262/3 The sort of parallax which exhibits the light of Whitman's fame at so different an angle in his own country and in England.

†**2.** In general sense of Gr. παράλλαξις: Change, alteration. *Obs. rare*$^{-1}$.

1677 GALE *Crt. Gentiles* II. IV. 258 The Sun although it is not so variable as the Moon, yet..it has its παραλλαγας or παραλαξεις, Paralaxes and Changes: it appears otherwise at rising, otherwise at noon, otherwise at setting.

3. Special comb.: **parallax error**, error in reading an instrument caused by parallax when the scale and the indicator are not precisely coincident.

1901 C. J. LEAPER *Graduated Exercises Elem. Pract. Physics* p. iii/1 (Index), Parallax error. **1906** BOWER & SATTERLY *Pract. Physics* v. 83 The reading, especially of the burette, is very liable to parallax error. **1967** *Electronics* 6 Mar. 117/2 With analog instruments..operator and parallax errors, meter movement wear and aging often reduce their nominal accuracies.

parallel ('pærəlɛl), *a.* and *sb.* Also 6 paralelle, 6–7 -allele, -alell, -alel, 7 -allell, -alele, 7–8 parr-. [a. F. *parallele* (in Rabelais, 16th c.), ad. L. *parallēlus*, a. Gr. παράλληλος beside one another, side by side, f. παρα- beside, alongside of + ἄλληλος one another.] **A.** *adj.*

1. a. Lying or extending alongside of one another and always at the same distance apart; continuously equidistant: said of two or more lines, surfaces, or concrete things; also of one line, etc., Extending alongside another at a continuously equal distance (const. *to, with*).

In *Geom.* applied to straight lines in the same plane, or to planes, which never meet however far produced in either (or any) direction, or (according to the definition of modern geometry) which intersect at infinity; more rarely to curved lines or surfaces continuously equidistant, i.e. having common normals at all points (e.g. concentric circles or spheres); or to curves upon a curved surface (e.g. circles on a sphere) which are continuously at the same distance as measured upon that surface, or are in parallel planes.

parallel bars, a pair of bars supported on posts about 4 to 6 feet above the ground, used for gymnastic exercises; also *fig.*; ***parallel roads*** (*Geol.*), name for a series of natural terraces at different levels on the side of a hill.

1549 *Compl. Scot.* vi. 47 Cosmaghraphie..sal declair the eleuatione of the polis, and the lynis parallelis, and the meridian circlis. **1559** W. CUNNINGHAM *Cosmogr. Glasse* 37 In a Sphere the parallele or equidistant Circles, have all one Pole. **1570** BILLINGSLEY *Euclid* I. defin. 35. 5 b, Parallel or equidistant right lines are such, which being in one and the selfe same superficies, and produced infinitely on both sides, do neuer in any part concurre. **1600** HAKLUYT *Voy.* III. 56 Reuolutions..that are parallel to the equinoctiall are also parallel to the horizon. **1655** EVELYN *Diary* 24 Feb., A chrystall ball sliding on parallel wyers. **1787** G. WHITE *Selborne* i. 2 One straggling street, three quarters of a mile in length..running parallel with The Hanger. **1833** LYELL *Princ. Geol.* III. 131 The parallel roads of Coquimbo, in Chili. *Ibid.*, The analogous parallel roads of Glen Roy in Scotland. **1860** TYNDALL *Glac.* I. i. 1, I..observed that the planes of cleavage were everywhere parallel. **1868** TROLLOPE *He knew he was Right* (1869) I. iii. 17 Certain poles and sticks and parallel bars with which feats of activity might be practised. **1878** [see HORIZONTAL *a.* (*sb.*) 2 b]. **1893** LELAND *Mem.* I. 261 [He] exhibited..his skill on the parallel bars, horizontal pole, etcetera. **1962** H. C. WESTON *Sight, Light & Work* (ed. 2) viii. 225 Various objects have been suggested and used, such as the 'parallel-bar' test-object of Luckiesh. **1964** G. C. KUNZLE *Parallel Bars* 19 The parallel bars are the most interesting and varied of all the pieces of apparatus. **1973** J. FLEMING *You won't let me Finish* vii. 52 He was in the small gym giving exhibitions of walking along the parallel bars on his hands.

b. *transf.* Applied to various things involving geometrical parallelism in some way, esp. to mechanical contrivances of which some essential parts are parallel, or which are used to produce parallelism of movement, etc.

parallel bar (see quot. 1875). ***parallel coping*** (see quot. 1842–76). ***parallel file***, a file with parallel edges, not tapering. ***parallel forces*** (*Dynamics*), forces acting in parallel lines. ***parallel knife***, a knife with two blades set parallel to each other, used for cutting thin sections for the microscope. ***parallel lathe***, a small lathe bearing several grinding wheels of different sizes, besides a brush, a drill, etc., which all run simultaneously; used by jewellers, dentists, etc. ***parallel motion***, (*a*) the motion of anything which always remains parallel to itself, i.e. in the same direction; (*b*) a mechanical device by which alternating rectilinear is converted into circular motion, and *vice versa*. ***parallel perspective***, perspective in which the plane of the drawing is parallel to a principal surface of the object delineated. ***parallel rod***, the rod which connects the cranks of the driving-wheels on the same side of a locomotive so as to cause them to move together; the coupling-rod (Webster 1864). ***parallel ruler*** (or ***rulers***), an instrument for drawing parallel lines, consisting of two or more straight rulers connected by jointed cross-pieces so as to be always parallel, at whatever distance they are set. ***parallel sphere***, the celestial or terrestrial sphere in that position or aspect in which the equator is parallel to the horizon, i.e. at either of the poles; distinguished from *oblique* and *right sphere*. ***parallel text***, one of two or more versions of a literary work, etc., printed in a format which allows direct textual comparison, freq. on facing or consecutive pages of the same volume; a text of different versions of a work set out in such a way; also (with hyphen) *attrib.* ***parallel tracking***, tracking in which the pick-up is kept tangential to the record groove by a rectilinear motion of the arm; freq. *attrib.* ***parallel turn***, a swing in skiing, with the skis kept parallel to each other. ***parallel vice***, 'a vice whose jaws move in exact parallelism, a bar on one slipping in a socket on the other' (Knight *Dict. Mech.* 1875).

1594 BLUNDEVIL *Exerc.* III. I. xvii. (1636) 313 This kind of Spheare is called a parallel Spheare, in which Spheare they that dwell have six months days, and six months nights. **1664** POWER *Exp. Philos.* I. 5 Her body is..stuck all over with great black Bristles,..set all in parallel order, with their ends all pointing towards the tayl. **1704** J. HARRIS *Lex. Techn.* I, *Parallel Ruler*. **1829** *Nat. Philos.* I. *Mechanics* II. xiii. 59 (U.K.S.) The most remarkable method of converting an alternate rectilinear motion into an alternate circular one, is that known by the name of the parallel motion, invented by Watt for his double-acting steam-engine. **1830** KATER & LARDNER *Mech.* xviii. 260 Parallel motion..the name is generally applied to all contrivances by which a circular motion is made to produce a rectilinear one. **1842–76** GWILT *Archit.* (ed. 7) Gloss. s.v. *Coping*, Coping equally thick throughout is called *parallel coping*. **1857** WHEWELL *Hist. Induct. Sci.* (ed. 3) I. 381 The parallel motion of the Earth's axis. **1859** RUSKIN *Perspective* 91 The greatest masters are..fond of parallel perspective. **1870** F. J. FURNIVALL *Chaucer Soc. Six-Text Print of Chaucer's Canterbury Tales in Parallel Columns* (verso rear cover of first section), The issue for 1870 is, in the First Series, XIV. The Miller's, Reeve's, and Cook's Tales, with an Appendix of the Spurious Tale of Gamelyn, in 6 parallel Texts. **1871** —— (*title*) Chaucer Society one-text print of Chaucer's minor poems, being the best text of each poem in the parallel-text edition. **1875** KNIGHT *Dict. Mech.*, *Parallel bar*, a rod in the side-lever engine, forming a connection with the pump-rods and studs along the center line of the levers. **1877** *Trans. Philol. Soc. 1875–76* 10 The two best features of our editing are minute accuracy and fullness of material. Hence our parallel-text editions. **1878** *Lumberman's Gaz.* 5 Jan., He has successfully adopted the Austin parallel edger. **1889** C. PLUMMER *Two Saxon Chrons. Parallel* p. viii, This, the first of our two parallel texts, is commonly known as the Parker MS. **1941** *B.B.C. Gloss. Broadcasting Terms* 22 Parallel tracking unit. **1954** BRODERMAN & MCPARTLIN *Ski-ing for Beginners* ix. 77 The Parallel Turn is a speed turn. **1962** A. NISBETT *Technique Sound Studio* viii. 145 Where parallel tracking arms are used, calibration above the track is a fairly simple matter. (But parallel tracking..has not proved itself in practice.) **1963** *Amer. Speech* XXXVIII. 206 An especially fast kind of short parallel turn. **1971** (*title*) William Wordsworth: The Prelude: A parallel text. **1978** *N. & Q.* Feb. 75/2 Mrs. Bawcutt's own admirable parallel-text edition..will doubtless remain standard.

†**c.** *loosely* (with *to* or *with*): In the same parallel (of latitude) as, in a line with. *Obs.*

1634 SIR T. HERBERT *Trav.* 6 In this latitude we were paralell to [*later edd.* with] Sierra Leoon. *Ibid.* 216 On the eleuenth of Nouember, [we] were parallel to the greene Cape, and to the Gorgades.

d. *Electr.* Involving connection in parallel (cf. sense B. 6).

[**1884** *Jrnl. Soc. Telegr. Engin.* XIII. 497 These two machines..may be connected in one of two ways: they may be in parallel circuit with regard to the external conductor ..; or they may be coupled in series.] **1886** *Electrician* 19 Feb. 296/2 The three direct systems are the parallel, series, and parallel-series methods of attaching lamps to the main conductors. **1891** J. W. URQUHART *Dynamo Construction* xvi. 232 For many years this difficulty stood in the way of parallel working with series machines. **1940** *Chambers's Techn. Dict.* 614/2 *Parallel feed*, a method of connecting the anode of a thermionic valve to the high-tension supply through a high resistance or inductance, whilst the a.c. circuits are connected through a condenser. The d.c. and a.c. components of the anode current are thereby separated. **1962** [see sense B. 6].

2. *fig.* **a.** Having the same or a like course, tendency, or purport; running on the same or similar lines; resembling something else, or each other, throughout the whole extent; precisely similar, analogous, or corresponding. Const. as in 1.

1604 SHAKS. *Oth.* II. iii. 355 How am I then a Villaine, To Counsell Cassio to this paralell course, Directly to his good? **1648** STERRY *Serm. on Clouds* 22 These Parallel places make those expressions seem Parallel: Angels, Cloudes. **1664** POWER *Exp. Philos.* III. 156 Parallel and Analogical effects of Electrical with Magnetical Bodies. **1718** HICKES & NELSON *Kettlewell* III. lxxiii. 387 Sorrow, that his Prudence should not be parallel to his Zeal. **1758** J. S. *Le Dran's Observ. Surg.* (1771) 173 Having observed it to happen before in a parallel Case. **1841** MYERS *Cath. Th.* 66 There is nothing parallel to this in the history of any nation with which we are acquainted. **1875** JOWETT *Plato* III. 113 The parallel passage in the ninth book.

†**b.** Equal in amount or worth. ? *Obs.*

a **1610** HEALEY *Epictetus, Life* (1616) A vj, Then hee should haue all Epictetus his wisdome inspired into him.. and so become paralell to that admired father. **1674** S. JEAKE *Arith.* (1696) 164 If the remain be added to the Number substracted, the Total will be parallel to the Number from which Substraction is made.

c. Side by side in time; running through the same period of time; contemporary in duration.

1746–7 HERVEY *Medit.* (1818) 174 That the benefits accruing to his people..might run parallel in their duration with eternity. **1862** STANLEY *Jew. Ch.* (1877) I. xviii. 340 That Prophetical dispensation, which ran parallel with the Monarchy from the first to the last King. **1878** STUBBS *Const. Hist.* III. xviii. 131 The parallel lines of war and negotiation run on for three years more. **1953** K. REISZ *Technique Film Editing* i. 20 Porter himself developed this kind of parallel action editing further in his subsequent films. *Ibid.* 281 *Parallel action*, device of narrative construction in which the development of two pieces of action is represented simultaneously by showing first a fragment of one, then a fragment of the other, and so on alternately.

d. *Computers.* Involving the concurrent or simultaneous performance of certain operations; functioning in this way.

1948 *Math. Tables & Other Aids to Computation* III. 149 The use of plugboard facilities and punched cards permits parallel operation (as distinguished from sequence operation), with further gain in efficiency. **1963** W. H. WARE *Digital Computer Technol. & Design* II. xi. 3 Parallel arithmetic tends to be faster than serial arithmetic because it performs operations in all columns at once, rather than in one column at a time. **1974** P. H. ENSLOW *Multiprocessors & Parallel Processing* i. 1 This book focuses on..the integration of multiple functional units into a multiprocessing or parallel processing system.

e. *S. Afr.* ***parallel development*** = *separate development*.

1950 *Ann. Reg. 1949* 140 The conflict between the Southern Rhodesian policy of 'parallel development' with its emphasis on permanent European control, and the United Kingdom policy of partnership leading to self-government. **1971** *Weekend World* (Johannesburg) 9 May 3/4 Chief George agreed with an Opposition claim that parallel development in the Republic meant that the Europeans were in the sky and Africans were in the mud.

f. *S. Afr.* ***parallel-medium***, used *attrib.* to designate schooling or a school in which instruction is given through the medium of more than one language.

1958 *Cape Argus* 10 Dec. 20/5 The classroom instruction given in Afrikaans-medium classes in a parallel-medium school would be as Afrikaans as instruction given in the classes of an exclusively single-medium Afrikaans school. **1971** *Sunday Times* (Johannesburg) (Business Section) 28 Mar. 4/2 (Advt.), Separate English and Afrikaans medium primary schooling, and parallel-medium schooling to matriculation standard is available.

g. *Biol.* ***parallel evolution*** = PARALLELISM 7.

1963 E. MAYR *Animal Species & Evolution* xix. 609 There are numerous cases of..parallel evolution in the animal and plant kingdoms. **1972** *Canad. Jrnl. Earth Sci.* IX. 1032/1 The shell shape of *C*[*olus*] *brevis* closely resembles that of *A*[*tractodon*] *stonei* and provides a striking example of parallel evolution in response to parallel selective pressures.

3. *Mus.* **a.** Applied to parts which move so that the interval between them remains the same (major and minor intervals of the same name, e.g. thirds or sixths, being in this case reckoned the same); also to the movement of such parts (***parallel motion***, a particular case of similar motion; sometimes loosely used as = similar motion); and to the intervals between such parts (usually called *consecutive*). **b.** Sometimes applied to major and minor keys which have the same signature (usually called *relative*).

1864 WEBSTER, *Parallel motion*,..the ascending or descending of two or more parts in such a manner as to have constantly the same interval between the corresponding notes in the several parts. **1889** E. PROUT *Harmony* (ed. 10) iv. §93 There are three kinds of motion; *similar* (sometimes, though less frequently, called 'parallel') when two or more parts move in the same direction—up, or down; *oblique*..; and *contrary*. **1898** STAINER & BARRETT *Dict. Mus. T.*, *Parallel motion*... Parallel fifths are under certain limitations forbidden. (Consecutives.)

4. a. ***parallel cousin*** = *ortho-cousin* (ORTHO 1).

1936 R. FIRTH *We, the Tikopia* vi. 221 The differentiation between cross-cousin and parallel cousin is certainly not one of the outstanding features of the Tikopia kinship system. **1949** F. EGGAN in M. Fortes *Social Struct.* 124 Parallel cousins are treated as siblings, whereas cross-cousins are differentiated. **1970** E. LEACH *Lévi-Strauss* 121 A parallel cousin..is a cousin of the type 'mother's sister's child' or 'father's brother's child'. **1972** [see *ortho-cousin* s.v. ORTHO- 1].

5. *Comb.*, as ***parallel-edged***, ***-sided***, ***-veined*** adjs.

1859 DARWIN *Orig. Spec.* viii. (1872) 224 A little parallel-sided wall of wax. **1861** BENTLEY *Man. Bot.* 153 We apply the term parallel-veined to all leaves in which the main veins are more or less parallel. **1879** *St. George's Hosp. Rep.* IX. 515 A narrow parallel-edged opening. **1882** *Nature* XXV. 228/1 The leaves..vary..although generally parallel-nerved.

b. Forming adjectival phrases with sbs., as ***parallel-jaw(s)***, ***-plate***.

1951 *Good Housek. Home Encycl.* 325/2 The bench..having..a parallel-jaw vice at the other end. **1962** L. S. Sasieni *Princ. & Pract. Optical Dispensing* ix. 214 Parallel jaw pliers. **1971** B. Scharf *Engin. & its Lang.* viii. 60 (*caption*) Parallel jaw vice. **1926** *Encycl. Brit.* II. 331/2 The parallel plate method..for measuring the *absolute* conductivity of air. **1962** Corson & Lorrain *Introd. Electromagn. Fields* ii. 37 If one plate of a parallel-plate capacitor is charged on one face, an equal and opposite charge must exist on the opposite plate of the capacitor.

B. *sb.* **I. 1. a.** *pl.* Parallel lines (see A. 1); rarely in *sing.* A line parallel to another.

1551 Recorde *Pathw. Knowl.* I. Defin., Here might I note the error of good Albert Durer, which affirmeth that no perpendicular lines can be paralleles. **1603** Drayton *Odes* ii. 49 Those Paralels so even, Drawne on the face of Heaven. **1733** Pope *Ess. Man* III. 103 Who made the spider parallels design, Sure as Demoivre, without rule or line? **1806** Capt. Mundy in *Naval Chron.* XV. 343 Intending to steer on a parallel with the enemy. **1882** Chrystal in *Nature* XXVI. 218/1 In the modern geometrical sense, a parallel (i.e. a line intersecting another at an infinite distance) cannot of course exist in elliptic space except as an imaginary line. **1972** *Sci. Amer.* Dec. 102/1 Circles of varying radii that go around the hole or center of the torus on parallel planes are called parallels.

b. *pl.* Things running parallel, or having a parallel direction.

1589 Greene *Menaphon* (Arb.) 30 Thy aged yeres shalbe the calender of my fortunes, and thy gray haires the Paralells of mine actions. *c* **1611** Chapman *Iliad* XVII. 152 Make thy steps parallels To these of mine. **1615** H. Crooke *Body of Man* 552 As it was conuenient that the eyes should be paralels: so also the nerues, which because of the motion of the eyes might decline from the right line.

2. a. *Geog.* Each of the parallel circles imagined as traced upon the earth's surface, or actually drawn upon a map (usually at intervals of 5 or 10 degrees), in planes perpendicular to the axis, and marking the degrees of latitude: in full, ***parallel of latitude***. Also *Astron.* each of the corresponding circles on the celestial sphere (***parallels of declination***), or of similar circles parallel to the ecliptic (***parallels of latitude***), or to the horizon (***parallels of altitude***). Also *attrib.* in ***parallel sailing*** (*Naut.*), sailing along a parallel of latitude, i.e. directly east or west.

1555 Eden *Decades* 12 A hundreth leaques westwarde with-out the paralelles of the Ilandes. **1559** W. Cunningham *Cosmogr. Glasse* 37 Seyng th' Equinoctiall, the ij. tropikes, and the circles Arctike, and Antarctike, be equidistant paralleles. **1669** Sturmy *Mariner's Mag.* VI. ii. 103 Any Line drawn Parallel to the Ecliptick..represents a Parallel of Latitude of the Stars. **1704** J. Harris *Lex. Techn.* I, *Parallels of Altitude.* **1710** *Ibid.* II, *Parallel Sailing*, in Navigation, is sailing under a Parallel of Latitude. **1824** Mackintosh *Sp. S. Amer. St.* Wks. 1846 III. 463 The prodigious varieties of its elevation exhibit in the same parallel of latitude all the climates and products of the globe. **1877** G. A. Allen *Amer. Bison* 465 Along the 49th parallel they also pass north in summer and south in winter. **1900** G. Santayana *Poetry & Relig.* 261 As the parallels and meridians make a checker-board of the sea.

b. *fig.* Region, level.

1887 Mrs. A. Raleigh *Stud. in Unseen* 151 Faith, the human hand-clasp which brings God near, is only possible in another parallel than that in which the wise of this world live and move.

3. *Mil.* In a siege: A trench (usually one of three) parallel to the general face of the works attacked, serving as a way of communication between the different parts of the siege-works.

1591 *Garrard's Art Warre* 326 [They] serve for Paralell to couer the souldiours. **1710** *Lond. Gaz.* No. 4687/1 On the 6th we advanced two new Parallels. **1812** Wellington *Let.* 20 Jan. in Gurw. *Desp.* VIII. 549 On the night of the 15th we..advanced from the left of the first parallel down the slope of the hill towards the convent. **1862** F. A. Griffiths *Artil. Man.* (ed. 9) 263 *Parallels*, or *Places of arms*, thrown up at sieges, are trenches formed to connect together the several approaches to a besieged place.

fig. **1874** Lisle Carr *Jud. Gwynne* I. viii. 250 She had already undermined the parallel which she felt convinced Judith had opened against the freedom of Cousin Norman.

4. *Printing.* A reference-mark consisting of two parallel vertical lines (‖).

1771 Luckombe *Hist. Print.* 260 The Parallel is another Sign which serves for a Reference. **1861** Angus *Handbk. Eng. Tongue* xi. 342, (‖) the parallels..are used as marks of reference.

5. *fig.* A thing or person agreeing with another in essential particulars (see A. 2); something precisely analogous, comparable, or of equal worth or force; a counterpart, equal, match.

1599 B. Jonson *Ev. Man out of Hum.* III. i, Why, this is without parallel, this. **1683** Kennett tr. *Erasm. on Folly* 31 Cicero..was no less fatal to Rome, than his Parallel Demosthenes was to Athens. **1728** Theobald *Double Falseh.* III. i, None but Itself can be its Parallel. **1871** Freeman *Norm. Conq.* IV. xviii. 107 Then followed a scene to which we find several parallels in Northumbrian history.

II. 6. Parallel position; parallelism.

in parallel (*Electr.*): said of two or more circuit-wires connecting the same points; in *Electr.* also said of individual circuit components connected by such wires, so that a current is divided between them; also *transf.* Cf. A. 1 d).

1654 Gayton *Pleas. Notes* *2 a, Had thy full lines run out their Paralell, And not been charm'd in by a warie Spell. **1699** Garth *Dispens.* III. 33 Lines that from their Parallel decline. **1884** *Jrnl. Soc. Telegr. Engin.* XIII. 529 The two alternate-current generators cannot work in series;..they can work in parallel. **1892** *Gloss. Electr. Terms* in *Lightning* 7 Jan., *Abreast*, when a current is divided between two or more paths, these paths are said to be abreast or in parallel. **1943** C. L. Boltz *Basic Radio* i. 21 A voltmeter is always connected in parallel with whatever part of a circuit across which we wish to measure the electrical pressure. **1949** E. P. Abraham et al. in H. W. Florey et al. *Antibiotics* II. xv. 644 The basic unit.., of which there were six working in parallel, was a glass tube containing amyl acetate. **1962** D. F. Shaw *Introd. Electronics* iii. 51 The capacitance *C* is connected in parallel with the combination *L* and *R*. **1962** *Newnes Conc. Encycl. Electr. Engin.* 569/2 *Parallel operation.* The operation of generators or transformers in parallel implies equality of terminal voltage. **1971** *Sci. Amer.* June 31/3 This could be accomplished by using a flow rate of 2,300 gallons per minute with two pumps operating in parallel.

7. *fig.* **a.** Agreement in all essential particulars; close correspondence; analogy, parallelism.

a **1617** Daniel *To Sir T. Egerton* xvii, Maintaining still an equall paralell, Iust with th' occasions of humanity. **1628** Prynne *Cens. Cozens* 61 Thus farre you haue an exact, and perfect Paralell of our authors writings with the Papists. **1718** *Entertainer* No. 15. 105 Our Case is much upon the Parallel. **1818** Hallam *Mid. Ages* (1872) I. iii. II. 444 The two republics stand in continual parallel. **1878** Bosw. Smith *Carthage* 57 It is the Battle of Megiddo and the brook Kishon that we fancy we see... The parallel is close indeed throughout.

b. Contemporary continuance; ***in parallel with***, contemporaneously, during the same time with. Also ***in parallel*** (without *with*), concurrently, simultaneously.

1878 Stubbs *Const. Hist.* III. xviii. 124 Negotiations for a peace..going slowly on in parallel with the slow and languishing war. **1938** *New Statesman* 7 May 796/2 Nor..does it seem right to attribute to 'the scholastic tradition of the universities' of the time, the failure of social studies to grow..in parallel with the natural sciences. **1957** R. K. Richards *Digital Computer Components* viii. 365 By transmitting all bits of a word to and from storage simultaneously or 'in parallel' a great increase in the speed of operation can be obtained in comparison with the transmission of one bit at a time. **1969** P. B. Jordain *Condensed Computer Encycl.* 373 By searching all (or very many cells) in parallel, the time of the operation is greatly reduced. **1971** *Sci. Amer.* Sept. 45/1 In parallel with the increase in carbon dioxide in the atmosphere there has also been a rise in suspended particulate contamination. **1977** *New Scientist* 21 Apr. 140/1 ILLIAC IV is actually a group of 64 individual computers working in parallel and linked to a one billion bit bulk memory.

8. The placing of things mentally or descriptively side by side so as to show their correspondence; comparison, or a comparison; *esp.* a comparison of things as being alike, a statement of parallelism or analogy, a simile.

1599 *Broughton's Let.* vii. 22, I craue pardon of his Grace for abasing him in parallel with such an one as thou art. *a* **1639** Wotton in *Reliq.* (*heading*) Of Robert Devereux, Earl of Essex, and George Villiers, Duke of Buckingham: Some Observations by way of Parallel. **1646** Crashaw *Delights Muses* 107 How even thou'st drawn this faithful parallel, And match'd thy master-piece. **1710** Steele *Tatler* No. 188 ¶ 10 You are drawing Parallels between the greatest Actors of the Age. **1869** F. W. Newman *Misc.* 173 The difficulty..may be relieved..by putting in parallel the Roman armies during two full centuries of the republic.

'parallel, *v.* Forms: see prec. [f. prec. adj.]

1. *trans.* To place (one thing) beside another (const. *with*, *to*), or (two or more things) side by side mentally, so as to exhibit a likeness between them; to bring into comparison, compare; *esp.* to state or exhibit the likeness or analogy of; to represent as similar, corresponding, or of equal worth; to liken, compare as being like.

1598 Barret *Theor. Warres* v. ii. 172 To consider and paralleill his owne forces with the..powers of the aduersary. **1611** Speed *Hist. Gt. Brit.* IX. xxiv. (1623) 1236 Well may shee be parallelled with the euer-renowned Zenobia. **1693** *Humours Town* 31, I desire you to parallel the Follies and Vices of the Town with the shadows of such in the Country. **1756** Burke *Subl. & B.* III. xxv, Let us parallel this with the softness..of the beautiful in other things. **1881** *Guardian* 9 Feb. 215 [He] parallels to-day's outcry against Ritualism with yesterday's against Methodism.

†2. To make parallel, bring into conformity, equalize. *Obs.*

1603 Shaks. *Meas. for M.* IV. ii. 82 His life is paralel'd Euen with the stroke and line of his great Iustice. **1669** Sturmy *Mar. Mag.* I. ii. 16 [He] will make..use of swift-stealing Time,..that he may parallel his Art with his Valour.

3. a. To show, present, or bring forward something parallel, equal, or corresponding to; to find or furnish a match for; to match.

1606 Shaks. *Tr. & Cr.* II. ii. 162 Well may we fight for her, whom, we know well, The world's large spaces cannot paralell. **1692** Ray *Disc.* II. iv. (1732) 187 Such unknown Plants as we cannot parallel. **1841** W. Spalding *Italy & It. Isl.* I. 187 For the Italians, the Middle Ages were an era of such grandeur as even their ancient history had not paralleled. **1874** Mahaffy *Soc. Life Greece* ii. 25, I cannot parallel these facts in Homer.

†b. To bring or present as a parallel. *Obs. rare.*

1605 Shaks. *Macb.* II. iii. 67 My young remembrance cannot parallel A fellow to it.

4. To be parallel or equal to; to correspond or be equivalent to; to come up to, equal, match.

1601 Shaks. *All's Well* IV. iii. 281 For rapes and rauishments he paralels Nessus. **1644** Evelyn *Diary* 17 Oct., Of all the wonders of Italy..nothing parallels this. *a* **1718** Penn *Sandy Found. Shaken* Wks. 1726 I. 249 Whose Faction, Prejudice, and Cruelty soon parallel'd the foregoing Heathenish Persecutions. **1861** Maine *Anc. Law* ix. (1870) 306 Reluctance to admitting that..there is anything in contemporary manners which parallels the loyalty of the antique world.

5. Often in passive, in which case the distinction between senses 3 and 4 usually disappears, the subject becoming indeterminate: e.g. *it cannot be paralleled* = 'no one can parallel it' (sense 3), or 'nothing can parallel it' (sense 4).

1625 J. Williams *Gt. Brit. Salomon* 37 You neur read in your liues of two Kings more fully parallel'd amongst themselues. **1697** Potter *Antiq. Greece* I. viii. (1715) 35 A Master-piece of Architecture, not easie to be parallel'd. **1705** Bosman *Guinea* 265 This Bird is not to be parrallelled for Beauty. **1853** Bright *Sp., India* 3 June (1876) 14 A state of things..which cannot be paralleled in any other country. **1863** Tyndall *Heat* viii. §318 (1870) 243 The Phenomena of light are..also paralleled by those of sound.

6. *intr.* To be parallel; to correspond or match; to be comparable, 'compare' (*with*).

1626 Bacon *Sylva* §125 It [sound] parallelleth in so many other things with the sight and radiation of things invisible. **1637** Heywood *Dialogues* Wks. 1874 VI. 307 Will you then, Since that we parallell in number thus, Helpe us to fill a measure? **1657** in *Burton's Diary* (1828) II. 100 The case yesterday, as I apprehend, may directly parallel with this. **1907** *Smart Set* Mar. 52/2 He..recognizes the truth that so easily their paths might have paralleled if events had only favored. **1977** *Zigzag* Mar. 21/1 Then it parallels to R&B in quite a few ways.

7. *trans.* To make parallel (in space). *rare.*

1646 Sir T. Browne *Pseud. Ep.* II. ii. 63 [At the Azores] it [the needle] seemeth equally distracted by both [continents], and diverting unto neither, doth parallel and place it self upon the true Meridian.

8. To run parallel with, run alongside of, go or tend in the same direction as. (Chiefly *U.S.*)

1885 *Harper's Mag.* Apr. 695/1 Railroad Avenue has been paralleled by another..business street named Gold Avenue. **1891** *Cosmopolitan* XII. 52/2 Ribbons of greenest turf,..paralleled on both sides by shaded promenades. **1899** R. Kipling *Stalky* 257 He had then..crossed over a ridge that paralleled their rear.

9. *trans.* To connect (electrical apparatus) in parallel. Const. *with*.

1902 *Electr. Rev.* 27 June 1056/2 (*heading*) Apparatus for paralleling alternators. **1903** T. Sewell *Elem. Electr. Engin.* (ed. 2) xviii. 379 There is not so much danger in paralleling machines which have iron cored armatures, for their self-induction prevents a dangerous current from flowing. **1921** [see phase *v.* 5 a]. **1952** G. V. Mueller *Alternating-Current Machines* ix. 339 When a shunt generator is to be paralleled with an operating d-c system, it is driven at its rated speed by a prime mover. **1965** *Wireless World* Sept. 431/1 They [*sc.* thyristors] may be used singly to give a 2A d.c. output or they may be paralleled to give any desired output provided that suitable arrangements are made for simultaneous firing.

Hence **'paralleled** *ppl. a.*; **'paralleling** *vbl. sb.*

1606 Warner *Alb. Eng.* XIV. lxxxii. (1612) 344 Knowe our Weale-publiques blisse is now a paralelled Creation, Wherein Religion and our Lawes persever in their Station. **1634** Jackson *Serm. Matt.* ii. 17–18 §4 The exact paralleling of the type and antitype..they purposely leave to the industrious search of posterity.

parallelable ('pærəlɛləb(ə)l), *a. rare.* [f. prec. vb. + -able.] Capable of being paralleled.

a **1656** Bp. Hall *Rem. Wks.* (1660) 277 Such an advantage, as is not parallelable in all the World beside.

paralle'larity. *rare*⁻¹. [irreg. f. parallel *a.*, after such words as *circularity*, *similarity*, etc.] State of being parallel, parallelism.

1804 Mitford *Inquiry* 85 The exactness of the parallelarity of its lines.

parallelepiped (ˌpærəlɛl'ɛpɪpɛd). *Geom.* Earlier in Gr. form **parallelepipedon** (ˌpærəlɛlɪ'pɪpɪdɒn), pl. **-a**. Often incorrectly 6–9 **paralleli-**, 7–9 **parallelo-** (*whence* ˌpærəlɛləʊ'pɪpɪd). [ad. Gr. παραλληλεπίπεδον, f. παράλληλ-ος parallel + ἐπίπεδον plane surface, sb. use of neut. of ἐπίπεδος plane, flat (f. ἐπί upon + πέδον ground). In late L. (Boethius) *parallēlepipedus*, F. *parallélépipède* (1570 in Hatz.-Darm.), often *parallélipipède*.]

A solid figure contained by six parallelograms, of which every two opposite ones are parallel; a prism whose base is a parallelogram.

α. **1570** Billingsley *Euclid* XI. xxxi. 342 Parallelipipedons consisting vpon equall bases, and being vnder one and the selfe same altitude, are equall the one to the other. **1666** Boyle *Orig. Formes & Qual.* (1667) 42 Though Spheres and Parallelopipedons differ but in shape. **1667** Collins in Rigaud *Corr. Sci. Men* (1841) II. 479 By producing the planes of the parallelepipedons, so that their sides shall cut off (viz. each parallelepiped twelve) second segments in the whole equal. **1791** Hamilton *Berthollet's Dyeing* I. I. III. vii. 275 White crystals in flat parallelipipedons. **1857** Birch *Anc. Pottery* (1858) I. 12 These bricks are all parallelopipeda, of Nile-mud or clay of a dark loamy colour, held together by chopped straw.

β. **1663** Charleton *Chor. Gigant.* 21 Resembling Parallelipipeds, rather than Cylinders. **1667** Parallelepiped [see α]. **1744** *Phil. Trans.* XLIII. 29 This Parallelopipede Figure with oblique Angles is common to many Stones. **1812–16** Playfair *Nat. Phil.* (1819) I. 183 If a rectangular parallelepiped float in a fluid. **1868** Grove *Contrib. Sc.* in *Corr. Phys. Forces* (1874) 449 A slab of stone of a parallelopiped form. **1875** *Wonders Phys. World* I. i. 31

These most frequently are cubes or rectangular parallelepipeds.

Hence **parallelepipedal** (-ɪ'pɪpɪdəl), **parallele'pipedonal** (*irreg.*), **parallele'pipedous** *adjs.*, having the form of a parallelepiped.

1754 *New & Compl. Dict. Arts & Sci.* II. 1394/1 The capacities of all sorts of vessels.., as cubical, parallelopipedal, cylindrical,..&c. are computed. **1794** SULLIVAN *View Nat.* I. 438 Cubic..or parallelepipedal forms. **1826** KIRBY & SP. *Entomol.* IV. 267 *Parallelopipedous*, six-sided, with four parallelogramical and two quadrate sides. **1852** TH. ROSS *Humboldt's Trav.* I. xi. 368 Breaking into fragments of a parallelopipedal figure. **1890** *Century Dict.*, *Parallelepipedonal.* **1950** L. R. UNDERWOOD *Rolling of Metals* I. iv. 83 If a rectangular network of lines on the bar before rolling is still rectangular after rolling, then the total deformation may be regarded as parallelopipedal. **1974** *Chem. Physics* VI. 2/2 The term 'unit cell' will be retained here..to mean the parallelepipedal cell (whether primitive or multiple) used by crystallographers.

paralleler ('pærəlɛlə(r)). *rare.* [f. PARALLEL *v.* + -ER[1].] One who parallels; one who draws a parallel or comparison.

1641 R. B[AILLIE] *Parallel Liturg. w. Mass-bk.* 57 Many other poynts of agreement might an accurate paralleler find.

ˌparalleli'nervate, *a. Bot.* [f. after mod.L. *parallelinerv-is* and F. *parallélinervé*: see PARALLEL, NERVE, and -ATE.] Of a leaf: Having parallel nerves or veins. Also **'paralleliˌnerved**, **ˌparalleli'nervous**.

1857 MAYNE *Expos. Lex.*, Parallelinervate: parallelinervious. **1866** *Treas. Bot.*, *Parallelinerved.* **1893** *Syd. Soc. Lex.*, *Parallelinervate..Parallelinervous.*

parallelism ('pærəlɛlɪz(ə)m). [ad. Gr. παραλληλισμ-ός comparison of parallels, f. παραλληλίζ-ειν to place side by side, to parallel. Cf. F. *parallélisme* (1667 in Hatz.-Darm.).]

1. a. The state or position of being parallel; direction parallel *to* or *with* something. Rarely with *pl.*, a particular instance of this (quot. 1753).

1610 W. FOLKINGHAM *Art of Survey* II. v. 55 Proiect all Plumbe-lines in Parallelisme perpendicular to a Parallel or supposed Common Base. **1656** HOBBES *Six Lessons* Wks. 1845 VII. 263 An objection..taken from the parallelism of two concentric circles. **1753** HOGARTH *Anal. Beauty* iii. 19 To give the front of a building, with all its equalities and parallelisms. **1794** G. ADAMS *Nat. & Exp. Philos.* I. x. 408 So long as the rays preserve their parallelism. **1836** *Penny Cycl.* V. 247 The parallelism of the veins of grasses is particularly pointed out. **1880** W. B. CARPENTER in *19th Cent.* No. 38. 613 Irregularities in the general parallelism of the stratification.

b. The state or fact of remaining parallel to itself, *i.e.* of maintaining the same direction; constancy of direction, as of a moving line.

1656 tr. *Hobbe's Elem. Philos.* (1839) 430. **1660** INGELO *Bentiv. & Ur.* II (1682) 116 The Axis of the Earth being directed to keep a perpetual Parallelism. **1794** G. ADAMS *Nat. & Exp. Philos.* IV. xliii. App. 173 The axis of the earth keeps a perfect parallelism and constant inclination to the plane of the ecliptic. **1868** LOCKYER *Guillemin's Heavens* (ed. 3) 117 It is the parallelism of the axis which accounts for the nearly invariable position of the celestial pole above the horizon in each locality.

†**c.** *loosely.* The position of being in the same parallel (of latitude) *with. Obs.*

1739 *Descr. of Windward Passage* (ed. 2) 8 They fall into the Trade-Winds as soon as they arrive in that Parallelism of Latitude with Jamaica, which carries them right before it all the Way.

2. *fig.* **a.** The quality or character of being parallel (see PARALLEL A. 2); close agreement of course or tendency; similarity in details; precise correspondence or analogy.

1638 ROUSE *Heav. Univ.* vii. (1702) 99 In this parallelism, the True Internal and Mystical sense of the Mosaical Genesis doth consist. **1678** CUDWORTH *Intell. Syst.* Pref. 12 This parallelism between the ancient or genuine Platonick and the Christian Trinity might be of some use. **1790** PALEY *Horæ Paul.* i. 5 The connexion and parallelism of these with the same circumstances in the Acts. **1827** WHATELY *Logic* (1837) 235 The argument rests on the assumption of parallelism in the two cases. **1891** DRIVER *Introd. Lit. O.T.* (1892) 22 The parallelism of details which prevails between the two narratives is remarkable. **1962** *Listener* 5 Apr. 606/2 The success of *apartheid* or parallelism or separate development—call it what you will—is dependent on educating the Bantu to take over all their responsibilities themselves. **1968** *Economist* 4 May 18/2 'Parallelism' in the activities of party and state can be eliminated quite simply by emphasising that the party is the boss and the government merely its executive servant [in Romania]. **1972** *Nature* 8 Dec. 339/2 A rough parallelism between the histories of the Iceland and Hawaii plumes is noteworthy.

b. An instance of correspondence or analogy; a parallel case, passage, etc. (Usually in *pl.*)

1664 H. MORE *Myst. Iniq.* 261 Proved by Two Parallelisms of Agreements. **1794** PALEY *Evid.* I. viii. (1800) I. 153 Parallelisms in sentences, in words, and in the order of words, have been traced out between the gospel of Matthew and that of Luke. **1869** J. MARTINEAU *Ess.* II. 312 Their passages of apparent analogy are but false parallelisms. **1955** P. W. STALLMAR in *College English* XVII. 25/1 For relationships between works that are not necessarily borrowings of the one from the other, I would use the general label 'parallelism'. The differentia of the parallelism is, I suggest, that a parallelism is not necessarily a conscious borrowing.

3. *spec.* Correspondence, in sense or construction, of successive clauses or passages, esp. in Hebrew poetry; a sentence or passage exemplifying this. Also in Anglo-Saxon poetry.

1778 BP. LOWTH *Transl. Isaiah* Prelim. Diss. 10 The correspondence of one Verse, or Line, with another, I call Parallelism. When a Proposition is delivered, and a second is subjoined to it, or drawn under it, equivalent, or contrasted with it, in Sense; or similar to it in the form of Grammatical Construction. **1813** J. J. CONYBEARE in *Archaeologia* XVII. 269 The parallelism (if I may be so allowed to term it) of the Anglo-Saxon writers... The poems attributed to Cædmon afford innumerable instances of the same figure. **1816** G. GREGORY tr. *Lowth's Lect. Sacr. Poetry Hebrews* II. 39 The parallelism is sometimes formed by the iteration of the former member, either in the whole or in part. **1873** M. ARNOLD *Lit. & Dogma* 49 The very laws of Hebrew composition which make the second phrase in a parallelism repeat the first in other words. **1876** H. SWEET *Anglo-Saxon Reader* p. xcix, There is also a tendency to parallelism, or repetition of the same idea in different words. The last half of one line is often connected with the first half of the next in this way. **1935** A. C. BARTLETT *Larger Rhet. Patterns Anglo-Saxon Poetry* iii. 30 Every literary model impelled the Anglo-Saxon toward structural parallelism in pairs. **1938** A. CAMPBELL *Battle of Brunanburh* 38 The sentence structure is essentially that of the older verse, with its free use of parallelism both of expressions and sentences. **1977** J. A. CUDDON *Dict. Lit. Terms* 471 Parallelism is common in poetry of the oral tradition—for instance, in *Beowulf*.

4. A statement of correspondence or analogy; a comparison, simile: = PARALLEL B. 8. ? *Obs.*

1656 H. MORE *Enthus. Tri.* (1712) 12 Aristotle makes a long Parallelism betwixt the nature and effects of Wine and Melancholy. **1660** SHARROCK *Vegetables* 149, I shall beg leave by a parallelism to apply it to the present matter.

5. ? Levelling, or condition of being levelled.

1794 MATHIAS *Purs. Lit.* (1798) 6 France had been long looking for that, which her philosophers had taught her to term, the parallelism of the sword.

6. *Psychol.* The theory that mental (psychic) and physical processes are concomitant and that any change in the one will be correspondingly reflected in the other.

1860 J. D. MORELL tr. *Fichte's Contrib. Mental Philos.* iii. 41 How far into details this parallelism between the mind and the world reaches, it is the province of psychology to show. **1877** *Illustr. London News* 5 May 427/1 As to the relation of mind to matter, he held that there is an exact parallelism of mental and material events..as two aspects of the same thing. **1891** M. E. LOWNDES tr. *Höffding's Outl. Psychol.* ii. 64 Both the *parallelism* and the *proportionality* between the activity of consciousness and cerebral activity point to an *identity* at bottom. **1902** *Encycl. Brit.* XXXII. 66/2 The last of these [*sc.* the Monism of Spinoza, which reduced matter and mind to parallel attributes of the One Substance]—severed, however, from Spinoza's metaphysics —is now the prevailing theory, and to it the term *Psychophysical Parallelism* most properly applies. **1925** C. D. BROAD *Mind & its Place* iii. 121 Psycho-neural Parallelism has also a positive side. **1956** [see INTERACTIONISM]. **1976** *Progress in Sci. Culture* (E. Majorana Centre) Spring 11 If we are to avoid falling into parallelism with its self-stultifying philosophy of determinism, we have to develop a dualist-interactionist philosophy according to which the self-conscious mind has an identity and activity that are not entirely dependent on brain events.

7. a. *Biol.* The development of similar characteristics by two related groups of animals or plants, in response to similar environmental pressures.

1887 E. D. COPE *Origin of Fittest* ii. 98 Among the higher groups [of Lacertilia Leptoglossa] the parallelisms lie in the arrangement..of the head shields. **1898** A. S. WOODWARD *Outl. Vertebr. Palæont.* p. xxiii, The case of the horses is often cited as suggesting that such a parallelism in evolution may have occurred. **1907** V. L. KELLOGG *Darwinism To-Day* viii. 279 (*heading*) Parallelisms in variation. **1934** W. E. LE GROS CLARK *Early Forerunners of Man* i. 6 If this thesis is carried to a logical conclusion, it will necessarily demand a much greater scope for the phenomenon of parallelism or convergence in evolution. **1961** G. G. SIMPSON *Princ. Animal Taxon.* iii. 78 Parallelism is the development of similar characters separately in two or more lineages of common ancestry and on the basis of, or channeled by, characteristics of that ancestry. *Ibid.* 103 Parallelism may be difficult or practically impossible to distinguish from homology on one hand and convergence on the other. **1967** R. E. BLACKWELDER *Taxon.* iv. 139 Parallelism..differs from convergence in that the development of the similar features is the result of and is channelled by a common ancestry.

b. *Anthrop.* A similarity between the evolution and achievements of different cultures.

1937 R. H. LOWIE *Hist. Ethnol. Theory* xi. 190 Schmidt differs from Morgan mainly in denying universal parallelism, *unilinear* evolution. **1949** G. P. MURDOCK *Social Struct.* vii. 116 The extraordinary extent of parallelism, both in kinship terminology and in types of kin and local groups. **1958** E. A. HOEBEL *Man in Primitive World* (ed. 2) xxxiv. 607 Very little attention has been given to parallelism, or independent invention, in this discussion for the reason that relatively few of the total mass of cultural traits possessed and shared by the peoples of the world have been invented more than once. **1958** F. M. KEESING *Cultural Anthropol.* vi. 148 Anthropologists..have therefore been critical of attempts to read historical connections into what they regard as an instance of parallelism between Old and New World cultural elements.

parallelist ('pærəlɛlɪst). [f. PARALLEL + -IST.]

1. One who draws a parallel or comparison.

1791–1823 D'ISRAELI *Cur. Lit.*, *Literary Parallels*, The parallelist compares Erasmus to 'a river swelling its waters'. **1810** BERESFORD *Bibliosophia*, etc. 124 For the purpose of carrying on my business of a Parallelist to the last.

2. An advocate of parallelism. Also *attrib.* or as *adj.*

1883 *Daily News* 17 Apr. 5/1 Mr. L— is a strong parallelist. He insists on the hair being dressed, and whatever covering may be put upon the head being made to accord with the parallel lines of the face, and with the line of the eyebrows. **1903** C. A. STRONG *Why Mind has Body* I. i. 23 The parallelist hypothesis. *Ibid.* vii. 126 The two arguments most commonly appealed to by parallelists. **1925** C. D. BROAD *Mind & its Place* iii. 124 The orthodox Parallelist..goes much further. **1937** R. H. LOWIE *Hist. Ethnol. Theory* v. 44 McLennan was essentially a parallelist. 'All the races of men have had..a development from savagery of the same general character.' *Ibid.* 48 Apart from the parallelist faith in universal stages, we note the erroneous idea that totemism generally implies worship. **1950** R. PIDDINGTON *Introd. Social Anthropol.* I. i. 27 Obviously, claimed the parallelists, there had been no contact between these peoples, and the similarity in custom must be explained by the operation of similar psychological processes in the two widely separated areas. **1976** *Progress in Sci. Culture* (E. Majorana Centre) Spring 11 It is not in question that the happenings in the cerebral cortex are *necessary* for the experience of consciousness... However, it must not be naively assumed that these brain events are *sufficient* for the conscious experiences... This in fact is the parallelist position.

So **ˌparalle'listic** *a.* [see -ISTIC], relating to or characterized by parallelism.

1868 *Contemp. Rev.* VIII. 441 The parallelistic elucidation is nowhere applied with greater force. **1881** CHEYNE *Proph. Isa.* (1884) I. 88 A parallelistic poem. **1904** G. S. FULLERTON *Syst. Metaphysics* xxi. 341 He quite wrecks his parallelistic formula. **1934** [see INTERACTIONISM]. **1946** *Brit. Jrnl. Psychol.* Jan. 52 It was precisely because in the *Manual* Stout endeavoured to exclude philosophical discussion that his parallelistic conclusion remained, as *mere* parallelism must..remain, an exasperating mystery.

parallelity (pærə'lɛlɪtɪ). [f. PARALLEL *a.* and *sb.* + -ITY.] The state or condition of being parallel (*lit.* and *fig.*); parallelism.

1953 *Cases Court of Session, Scotl.* 290 There is no parallelity or necessary mutual dependence between the two inquiries. **1970** *Physics Bull.* Feb. 71/1 In the spaghetti, adjacent lengths tend to lie somewhere near to parallelity without achieving exact alignment.

ˌparalleli'venous, *a. Bot.* and *Entom.* [f. L. *parallēl-us* PARALLEL + *vēnōs-us*, f. *vēna* VEIN.] Of a leaf, or an insect's wing: Parallel-veined: = PARALLELINERVATE. Also **ˌparallelive'nose**.

1857 MAYNE *Expos. Lex.*, Parallelivenous. **1866** *Treas. Bot.*, *Parallelivenose.*

parallelize ('pærəlɛˌlaɪz), *v.* [ad. Gr. παραλληλίζ-ειν, f. παράλληλος PARALLEL: see -IZE.]

1. *trans.* To make parallel. †**a.** To cause to correspond; to equalize: = PARALLEL *v.* 2. *Obs.*

1620 T. GRANGER *Div. Logike* A ij, To parallelize and euen it with its obiect.

b. To place so as to be parallel; in quot., to dispose in parallel columns.

1900 FURNIVALL *E.E.T.S. Statem.* Dec. 5 If the Paris text cannot be parallelised, it will form a separate volume.

2. To place side by side, or beside something else, in contemplation; to trace a parallelism or analogy in or between; to compare: = PARALLEL *v.* 1.

1610 E. BOLTON *Elem. Armories* 59 That we should parallelize our Armes with those of the Hebrewes, Greeks, and Romans. **1669** GALE *Crt. Gentiles* I. II. iv. 42 As Apollo may be very far parallelised with Joshua in Names, so also in Things, or Exploits done. **1701** BEVERLEY *Apoc. Quest.* 28 Its Seven Mountains of Scituation are Paralelliz'd with Seven Heads, Kings. **1887** E. D. COPE *Orig. Fittest* I. ii. 95 The series among Lacertilia of Acrodonta and Iguania, parallelized by Duméril and Bibron.

†**3.** To furnish with a parallel or counterpart.

1669 GALE *Crt. Gentiles* I. II. iv. 40 We see how accurate Satan was in parallelising the Names, Attributes, and Worship of the true God.

4. To be a match for, to match (usually in *pass.*): = PARALLEL *v.* 3–5. *rare.*

1634 SIR T. HERBERT *Trav.* 208 For varietie of Gods temporall blessings..scarce to be paralellized. **1893** F. ADAMS *New Egypt* 54 The astonishing fertility of the average ox-eyed fellah woman..is parallelised by an infertility of all Europeans and their descendants.

Hence **ˌparalleli'zation**, the action of parallelizing; **'paralleˌlizer**, one who parallelizes.

1610 E. BOLTON *Elem. Armories* 59 Comparisons, or parallelisations of ancient seales. **1882–3** SCHAFF *Encycl. Relig. Knowl.* III. 1815 The attempted parallelization between Peter and Paul. **1891** E. A. ABBOTT *Philomythus* ix. 213 The Ecclesiastical Assimilator or Parallelizer *nascitur, non fit.* **1892** J. NASMITH *Students' Cotton Spinning* v. 150 Its result is to effect a much greater parallelisation of the fibres in the carded sliver. **1922** *Bull. Geol. Soc. Amer.* XXXIII. 443 From the meteorological standpoint such a far-reaching parallelization of the fluctuations of the weather from one year to the other, in Sweden and North America, is surprising. **1933** *Trans. Faraday Soc.* XXIX. 211 The process of parallelisation of long thin bodies.

parallelless ('pærəlɛllɪs), *a. rare.* [f. PARALLEL *sb.* + -LESS.] Without a parallel, unparalleled.

1611 BEAUM. & FL. *Philaster* III. i, Tell me gentle boy, Is she not parallelless?

parallelly (ˈpærəlɛllɪ), *adv.* [f. PARALLEL *a.* + -LY².] In a parallel manner or direction; so as to be parallel. (*lit.* or *fig.*)

1607 J. NORDEN *Surv. Dial.* IV. 188 Cutting them streight, from the most boggie places, to the maine brooke, euery of them as it were paralelly. **1676** GREW *Anat. Leaves* I. iv. §21 Betwixt these Ribs.. there are others much less,.. betwixt Rib and Rib, Parallelly interjected. **1804** R. JAMESON *Mineralogy* I. 154 Some rare varieties [of Quartz] shew a parallelly fibrous fracture. **1881** BENTHAM in *Jrnl. Linn. Soc.* XVIII. 296 Four collateral, more or less parallelly compressed, pollen-masses.

parallelogram (pærəˈlɛləgræm). [a. F. *parallélogramme* (1552 in Hatz.-Darm.), ad. L. *parallēlogrammum*, a. Gr. παραλληλόγραμμον sb., neut. of παραλληλόγραμμος bounded by parallel lines, f. παράλληλος PARALLEL + γραμμή line.]

1. *Geom.* A four-sided rectilineal figure whose opposite sides are parallel; sometimes *spec.* applied to a rectangle.

1570 BILLINGSLEY *Euclid* I. xxxiv. 44 There are fower kindes of parallelogrammes, a square, a figure of one side longer then the other, a Rhombus, or diamond figure, and a Rhomboides or diamondlike figure. **1611** COTGR., *Paralelogramme*, a Paralelogramme, or long Square. **1646** SIR T. BROWNE *Pseud. Ep.* 60 A parallelogram or long square figure. **1726** SWIFT *Gulliver* III. ii, Cones, cylinders, parallelograms, and several other mathematical figures. **1806** HUTTON *Course Math.* I. 288 Parallelograms.. on the Same Base, and between the Same Parallels, are equal to each other. **1846** ELLIS *Elgin Marb.* I. 71 The plan of the generality of the temples of Greece, was that of a simple parallelogram.

b. *parallelogram of forces* (*Dynamics*): a figure illustrating the theorem that if two forces acting at one point be represented in magnitude and direction by two sides of a parallelogram, their resultant will be similarly represented by the diagonal drawn from that point; hence, a name for the theorem itself. So *parallelogram of velocities*, etc. [F. *parallélogramme des forces*, Lagrange *Méc. Anal.* (ed. 2, 1811).]

1830 KATER & LARDNER *Mech.* v. 50 To verify experimentally the theorem of the parallelogram of forces is not difficult.

2. A thing shaped like the figure described in 1.

†**a.** An old name for the PANTOGRAPH *sb. Obs.*

c **1656** in Sir W. Petty *Down Survey* (1851) Pref. 16 These reducements were made by paralelagrames. **1668** PEPYS *Diary* 27 Oct. **1704** J. HARRIS *Lex. Techn.* I, *Parallelogram*, .. an Instrument made of five Rulers of Brass or Wood, with Sockets to slide or set to any Proportion, used to enlarge or diminish any Map or Draught. **1723, 1727-41** [see PANTOGRAPH *sb.*].

b. Anything of this form, or whose section is of this form, as a block of buildings, a space of ground (cf. *square*), a brick, card, domino, etc.

1820 SYD. SMITH *Wks.* (1859) I. 303/1 Mr. Owen may give his whole heart and soul to the improvement of one of his parochial parallelograms; but who is to succeed to Mr. Owen's enthusiasm? **1862** WILSON *Preh. Man* ii. (1865) 14 This [site] the original projectors of the city mapped off into parallelograms. **1873** TRISTRAM *Moab* ii. 21 Picture a parallelogram of canvas quite black, and with a roof only three or four feet above the ground.

3. *attrib.* and *Comb.*

1704 J. HARRIS *Lex. Techn.* I, *Parallelogram Protractor*, is a Semicircle of Brass, with four Rulers, in form of a Parallelogram, made to move to any Angle; one of which Rulers is an Index, which shews on the Semi-circle the Quantity of any inward or outward Angle. **1767** MONRO in *Phil. Trans.* LVII. 497 Parallelogram-shaped crystals. **1842** E. MIALL in *Nonconf.* II. 809 Communities.. shaped parallelogram-wise.

paraˈllelogramish, *a. nonce-wd.* [f. prec. + -ISH¹.] Somewhat like a parallelogram.

1839 LADY LYTTON *Chevely* (ed. 2) I. xi. 253 Handing over Monsieur de Rivoli's parallelogramish epistle.

parallelogrammatic (pærəˌlɛləʊgrəˈmætɪk), *a.* [f. late L. *parallēlogramma, -mat-* (Boethius 525, for *parallēlogrammum*, after Gr. words in -γραμμα) + -IC: so mod.F. *parallélogrammatique*.] = PARALLELOGRAMMIC.

1727-41 CHAMBERS *Cycl.* s.v. *Beam*, Not only in case of parallelogramatic, but also of elliptic bases. **1869** TROLLOPE *He Knew*, etc. xxxviii. I. 299 Turin.. is new and parallelogrammatic as an American town.

Also **paraˌllelograˈmmatical** *a.*

1890 in *Cent. Dict.*

parallelogrammic (ˌpærəlɛləʊˈgræmɪk), *a.* Also -gramic. [f. Gr. παραλληλόγραμμ-ον PARALLELOGRAM + -IC.] Pertaining to, or of the form of, a parallelogram: parallelogram-shaped.

1730 GREENWOOD in *Phil. Trans.* XXXVII. 59 There are two distinguished Parallellogramic Areæ of an intense Red. **1800** HERSCHEL *ibid.* XC. 529 The lantern has a sliding door of tin-plate, in which there is a parallelogrammic hole. **1861** J. H. BENNET *Winter Medit.* I. x. (1875) 304 The King's palace [at Athens], a factory-looking parallelogramic building surrounded by gardens.

ˌparalleloˈgrammical, *a.* ? *Obs.* Also -gramical. [f. as prec. + -AL¹.] = prec.

1647 H. MORE *Song Soul* Notes 164/2 *Rhomboides*, is a parallelogrammicall figure with unequall sides and oblique angles. **1761** STERNE *Tr. Shandy* IV. xxvii, The table being parallelogrammical, and very narrow, it afforded a fair opportunity for Yorick.. of slipping the chestnut in. **1859** W. H. GREGORY *Egypt* I. 59 The mosque.. is in the shape of a large parallelogramical hall, twice too long for its height.

ˌpalleˈlometer. [f. as PARALLEL + -OMETER.] (See quot.)

1886 *Amer. Assoc. Adv. Sc., 35th Meeting* 121 A gravity parallelometer; by J. A. Brashear,.. devised to expedite measurements of deviation from parallelism in glass plates for optical purposes.

parallelopiped, etc., erroneous spelling of PARALLELEPIPED, etc.

parallelosteric (ˌpærəlɛləʊˈstɛrɪk), *a.* [f. Gr. παράλληλο-ς PARALLEL + στερεός solid.] (See quot.)

1865-72 WATTS *Dict. Chem.* III. 432 If bodies of equal atomic volume be denominated *isosteric*, and analogous pairs of compounds exhibiting equal differences of atomic volume, *parallelosteric*, the preceding law may be more shortly stated as follows:—Pairs of compounds which are isomorphous and analogous are likewise parallelosteric.

ˈparallelˌwise, *adv.* ? *Obs.* [f. PARALLEL *a.* + -WISE.] In a parallel manner; parallelly.

1606 W. CRASHAW *Rom. Forgeries* I iij, Standing so together paralel-wise, that a man may see them both at one sight. **1763** MURDOCH in *Phil. Trans.* LIII. 188 All the sorts of rays, whether united in a pencil of light, or separated parallelwise by refraction.

†**paralling**, variant of PARELLING *Obs.*

paralog (ˈpærəlɒg). [f. PARA-¹ + Gr. λόγ-ος word.] (See quot. 1968.)

1951 TRAGER & SMITH *Outl. Eng. Struct.* 85 The instances just cited are examples of the use of different *paralogs*, a paralog being one of the forms constituting an inflectional paradigm. **1968** J. JUNG *Verbal Learning* iii. 30 Nonsense syllables and other laboratory learning materials, such as trigrams and paralogs. Trigrams are nonsense syllables, that is, a trigram is any three-letter combination which does not form a word. Paralogs or dissyllables are verbal units containing two syllables and range from meaningless units to actual words. **1970** *Jrnl. Gen. Psychol.* LXXXIII. 55 The nonsense words.. were five paralogs with approximately equal, low levels of association value.

paralogia (pærəˈləʊdʒɪə). *Med.* [f. PARA-¹ + *-logia* (see -LOGY and -IA¹).] (See quots.)

1811 R. HOOPER *Lexicon Medicum* 596/1 *Paralogia*, a delirium in which the patient talks wildly. **1857** R. G. MAYNE *Expos. Lex. Med. Sci.* (1860) 877/1 *Paralogia*,.. term for a slight degree of madness or of delirium. **1900** GOULD *Dict. Med.* (ed. 5) 973/1 *Paralogia*, difficulty in thinking logically. **1905** S. PATON *Psychiatry* xiv. 383 Another important symptom [of dementia præcox].. is the grotesque irrelevancy exhibited in replying to questions (Paralogia). **1919** R. M. BARCLAY tr. *Kraepelin's Dementia Praecox & Paraphrenia* ii. 21 Evasion or paralogia consists in this, that the idea which is next in the chain of thought is suppressed and replaced by another which is related to it. **1923** STEDMAN *Med. Dict.* (ed. 7) 737/1 *Paralogia*, false reasoning, involving self-deception. **1965** *New Scientist* 25 Nov. 605/1 The disorders of generalization are.. subdivided into lowering of the level of generalization and distortion of generalization. The.. latter seems to be the same as Kleist's 'paralogia' and Cameron's 'overinclusion'.

paralogic (pærəˈlɒdʒɪk), *a. rare.* [f. Gr. παράλογ-ος (see PARALOGY) + -IC.] = next.

1859 R. F. BURTON *Centr. Afr.* in *Jrnl. Geog. Soc.* XXIX. 329 He appears, therefore to the civilized man a paralogic being,—a mere mass of contradictions; his ways are not our ways, his reason is not our reason.

paraˈlogical, *a.* ? *Obs.* [f. as prec. + -AL¹.] Involving or characterized by paralogism or false reasoning; illogical, unreasonable.

1658 SIR T. BROWNE *Gard. Cyrus* i. 101 Whether this.. Husbandry.. had not its Originall in that Patriarch, is no such Paralogicall doubt. **1756** JOHNSON *Introd. B.'s Chr. Mor.* 54 Browne.. poured in a multitude of exotick words; many, indeed, useful.. but many superfluous, as a paralogical for an unreasonable doubt. **1826** [see *paraphysical* in PARA-¹ 1].

†**paralogician** (pærələʊˈdʒɪʃən). *Obs.* [f. PARALOGIC, after *logician*.] = PARALOGIST.

1739 *Regul. Freethinking* 31 He shall be admitted to the Degree of Paralogicians, which is the highest Honour we can possibly bestow. **1754** HILDROP *Misc. Wks.* I. 23 He would be as accomplished a Paralogician as any Man of his Talents can be supposed to be.

paralogism (pəˈrælədʒɪz(ə)m). [a. F. *paralogisme* (1556 in Hatz.-Darm.), ad. late L. *paralogismus* (Boethius), a. Gr. παραλογισμός, f. παραλογίζ-εσθαι to reason falsely: see PARALOGIZE and -ISM.] A piece of false or erroneous reasoning; an illogical argument; a faulty syllogism; a fallacy, *esp.* (as distinct from *sophism*) one of which the reasoner himself is unconscious.

1565 CALFHILL *Answ. Treat. Cross* (Parker Soc.) 4 Three kinds of paralogisms of false arguments, or fond cavils, are most familiar with you. **1641** 'SMECTYMNUUS' *Answ.* xviii. (1653) 81 It is evident that this argument is a Paralogisme, depending upon the Equivocation of the name Bishop. **1697** tr. *Burgersdicius' Logic* II. viii. 33 That the more easily true Syllogisms may be discern'd from Paralogisms, some Laws are to be observ'd. **1752** HUME *Pol. Disc.* x. 259 He is here guilty of a gross paralogism. **1877** E. CAIRD *Philos. Kant* II. xv. 541 The syllogisms of Rational Psychology are therefore paralogisms, in which the middle term is taken in two different senses.

b. Without *a* and *pl.*: False or erroneous reasoning; illogical argument. *rare.*

1691-8 NORRIS *Pract. Disc.* (1711) III. 172 Their whole life.. runs all along upon wrong principles and mistaken reasonings, and is all over Fallacy and Paralogism. **1715** CHEYNE *Philos. Princ. Relig.* II. 44 We shall run into Confusion and Paralogism. **1884** *Sat. Rev.* 5 July 11/1 A dabbler in paralogism and fallacy.

So **paˈralogist**, one who commits a paralogism, a false reasoner; **paraloˈgistic** *a.* [see -ISTIC], of the nature of a paralogism, fallacious.

1624 F. WHITE *Repl. Fisher* 47 You haue played the Paralogist. **1677** GALE *Crt. Gentiles* II. III. 92 Pagan Philosophie was not truely Logistic or discursive, but rather paralogistic and sophistic. **1757** MRS. GRIFFITH *Lett. Henry & Frances* (1767) IV. 38, I really think you equal, in this way, to Sir Marmaduke Wyvill, who they say was the best Paralogist, in the World. **1879** W. G. WARD *Ess. Philos. Theism* (1884) I. 357 We made no appeal even to Theism: which it would.. have been grossly paralogistic to do, since we are maintaining Freewill as a premise towards the establishment of Theism.

paralogize (pəˈrælədʒaɪz), *v.* [Ultimately ad. Gr. παραλογίζ-εσθαι to reason falsely, use fallacies, f. παραλογία PARALOGY: see -IZE. Perh. immediately ad. med.L. *paralogizāre* (Du Cange) or F. *paralogiser* (15.. in Godef.).] *intr.* To commit a paralogism; to reason falsely or illogically. (In quot. 1599 app. misused.)

1599 NASHE *Lenten Stuffe* 14, I had a crotchet in my head, here to haue.. run astray thorowout all the coast townes of England.. & commented and paralogized on their condition. **1624** F. WHITE *Repl. Fisher* Pref. 8 What though he paralogize in the seeming direct proposing of his argument. **1675** J. SMITH *Chr. Relig. Appeal* II. 77 The gentile proceeded, in the same way of paralogizing, to the oblation of humane blood.

†**paˈralogy.** *Obs. rare*⁻¹. [ad. Gr. παραλογία fallacy, f. παράλογ-ος aside from or beyond reason, f. παρά beside, beyond, etc. + λόγος reason.] Faulty reasoning: = PARALOGISM b.

1646 SIR T. BROWNE *Pseud. Ep.* VII. iii. 343 That Methuselah was the longest liver.. we quietly beleeve: but that he must needs be so, is perhaps below Paralogy to deny.

paralous, obs. form of PERILOUS.

paralysant (ˈpærəlaɪzənt), *a.* and *sb.* [a. F. *paralysant*, pr. pple. and sb. from *paralyser* to PARALYSE: see -ANT¹.] **a.** *adj.* Paralysing, producing paralysis. **b.** *sb.* A paralysing agent.

1875 H. C. WOOD *Therap.* (1879) 64 Heubach.. failed to prove any paralysant action of the drug. *Ibid.* 246 Atropia acts as a paralyzant to the motor nerve-trunks themselves.

paralysation (ˌpærəlaɪˈzeɪʃən). [n. of action f. PARALYSE: see -ATION.] The action of paralysing or condition of being paralysed.

a **1846** *Q. Rev.* cited in WORCESTER. **1849** JAS. GRANT *Kirkaldy of Gr.* xx. 226 The paralysation caused by the underhand intrigues of Elizabeth. **1862** *Q. Rev.* Apr. 405 The paralyzation of the only legislative organs. **1881** MRS. PIRKIS *Wanted an Heir* I. 313 Her limbs felt stiff and cramped almost to paralysation.

paralyse, -ze (ˈpærəlaɪz), *v.* Also -ize. [app. a. F. *paralyser*, found 16th c. in pa. pple. *paralysé* (Paré), f. *paralysie*: cf. ANALYSE.]

1. *trans.* To affect with paralysis; to palsy.

1804 ABERNETHY *Surg. Obs.* 188 To paralize the opposite side of the body. **1844** LD. BROUGHAM *A. Lunel* II. iii. 106 Some with their spine wounded and their limbs paralysed in consequence. **1862** DARWIN *Fertil. Orchids* v. 222 The depending right-hand antenna is almost paralysed, and is apparently functionless.

2. *fig.* To deprive of energy or power of action; to render powerless, helpless, inactive, or ineffective; to deaden, cripple. Also with constr.

1805 *London Cries* 39 (T.) Or has taxation chill'd the aguish land, And paralysed Britannia's bounteous hand? **1830** S. WARREN *Diary Physic.* (ed. Tauchn.) I. 8 My professional efforts were paralysed. **1866** G. MACDONALD *Ann. Q. Neighb.* xiii. (1878) 266 His pride paralysed his love. **1871** L. W. M. LOCKHART *Fair to See* II. xxv. 280 He saw all this, quite paralysed out of the power of surprise or wrath. **1890** *Congress. Rec.* 19 May 4933/1 You boast about what you have done for the American farmer... What audacity! It paralyzes me. **1900** *Dialect Notes* II. 47 *Paralyze*... In phrase 'to *paralyze* the professor'; to make a perfect recitation.

Hence **ˈparalysed, ˈparalysing** *ppl. adjs.*; also **ˈparalyser**, something that paralyses.

1842 MANNING *Serm.* (1848) I. 149 Under the dominion of this paralysing fault. **1855** MACAULAY *Hist. Eng.* xix. IV. 263 To brace anew the nerves of that paralysed body. **1876** BARTHOLOW *Mat. Med.* (1879) 296 Opium, aconite, lobelia, and the cardiac paralyzers. **1897** *Allbutt's Syst. Med.* II. 788 It acted.. as a paralyser of the motor nerve endings.

paralysedly (ˈpærəlaɪzdlɪ), *adv.* [f. PARALYSED *ppl. a.* + -LY².] In a paralysed manner.

1876 R. BROUGHTON *Joan* III. I. xxxiii. 48 As she so paralysedly sits the door opens softly.

†**paralysie.** *Obs.* Also 4 -asie, 5 -ise, -isy, -ysye, per-, 5-7 paralisie. [a. F. *paralysie*, in 13th c. *-isie* (Hatz.-Darm.), repr. a L. type **paralysia* for

paralysis. Hence the reduced form PALSY.] = PARALYSIS.

c **1380** WYCLIF *Serm.* Sel. Wks. II. 195 And so senewis.. weren confortid.. and paralasie was put awey. **1432–50** tr. *Higden* (Rolls) IV. 339 Criste did heale a man hauenge the peralisy. **1483** CAXTON *Gold. Leg.* 428 b/1, xiii contractes or fylled wyth paralysye were by the same restoryd in good helthe. **1581** N. BURNE *Disput.* in *Cath. Tractates* 165 Ane young man, and young voman.. had fallin in ane paralysie and trimbling of al thair membris. **1597** LOWE *Chirurg.* (1634) 292 Paralisie.. is a mollification, relaxation, or resolution of the nerues, with privation of the mooving.

'paralysingly, *adv.* [f. PARALYSING *ppl. adj.* + -LY².] In a paralysing manner.

In quot. used hyperbolically.
1926 *Socialist Rev.* Dec. 21 The paralysingly stupid 70/- a week shipping or insurance clerk.

paralysis (pə'rælɪsɪs). Also 6 -lisis, (-lices). [a. L. *paralysis*, a. Gr. παράλυσις, f. παραλύ-ειν to loose from beside, disable, enfeeble, f. παρα- beside + λύειν to loose. The word occurs already in OE. in the Gr.-L. accus. form *paralisin* (so in 12th c. Fr.); but the ME. and 16th c. form from Fr. was PARALYSIE: see PARALYSIE.]

1. *Path.* **a.** A disease or affection of the nervous system, characterized by impairment or loss of the motor or sensory function of the nerves, esp. of those belonging to a particular part or organ, thus producing (partial or total) incapacity of motion, insensibility, or functional inactivity in such part. (The earlier name, still in popular use, was PALSY.)

[*c* **1000** *Sax. Leechd.* II. 12 Læcedomas wiþ paralisin, þæt is on englisc, lyft adl.] **1525** tr. *Brunswick's Surg.* lxii. O j b/1 Paralisis of the handes. **1527** ANDREW *Brunswyke's Distyll. Waters* C ij, Good against paralisis. **1563** T. GALE *Antidot.* II. 76 Thys Oyle is moste precious in paralices. **1656** BLOUNT *Glossogr.*, *Paralysis*,.. the Palsie. **1797** M. BAILLIE *Morb. Anat.* (1807) 457 A paralysis of a part of the body. *a* **1876** HALLEY *Serm.* (1879) 50 Distorted with agony, or with convulsion or paralysis.

b. With defining word, as ***Bell's paralysis***, ***crossed paralysis***, ***crutch paralysis***, ***diver's paralysis***, etc.: see PALSY *sb.*¹; ***general paralysis***: see quots.; also called ***general paralysis of the insane*** [tr. F. *paralysie générale des aliénés* (L. F. Calmeil *De la Paralysie considérée chez les Aliénés* (1826) 9], and now recognized as a form of neurosyphilis. So ***general paralytic***, an individual with general paralysis.

1820 *Edin. Med. & Surg. Jrnl.* XVI. 373 Dissection of a case of general paralysis... The disease of the brain seemed to have originated in indolence and chagrin from the sudden loss of fortune. **1847** *Further Rep. Commissioners in Lunacy* 46 in *Parl. Papers* (Brit. Libr.) XLIX. 291 The forms of insanity, which are occasioned by extreme indigence and privation,.. are of the worst kind, and.. many of them have invariably a fatal termination. [*Note*] This is particularly observable in the very frequent form of paralysis, termed the general paralysis of the insane. **1856** *Jrnl. Mental Sci.* III. 170 General paralytics are not malignant, and although sometimes furious, their passion is gusty and transient. *Ibid.* 172 In general paralysis, the pathological conditions of which involve the whole nervous system, the excito motory sensibility is almost abolished. **1873** T. H. GREEN *Introd. Pathol.* (ed. 2) 26 This is seen in the various forms of paralysis, especially in the so-called 'essential paralysis' of children. **1893** *Syd. Soc. Lex.*, *Paralysis, general*, of insane.. a disease usually affecting persons near the prime of life, and characterised by a stage of mental excitement with exalted delusions, followed by dementia; it is accompanied by a varying amount of loss of muscular power. **1897** *Allbutt's Syst. Med.* II. 857 There are cases of general paralysis in which the bodily symptoms are present without any mental alteration. **1925** *Amer. Speech* I. 24/2 The disease 'general paralysis', also known as paresis, usually is spoken of as softening of the brain. **1930** *Daily Express* 8 Sept. 1/1 Formerly every person developing general paralysis of the insane died after a period of distressing symptoms and agony. **1941** T. WARWICK *Handbk. Venereal Dis.* v. 53 The great majority of general paralytics are men. **1964** KING & NICOL *Venereal Dis.* v. 62 In all cases of general paralysis, tests of the mental status should be carried out. **1970** W. J. BROWN et al. *Syphilis & Other Venereal Dis.* vii. 125 The common types of neurosyphilis are tabes dorsalis, general paralysis of the insane, and meningovascular neurosyphilis.

c. ***paralysis agitans*** [L. *agitans* shaking], Parkinson's disease, shaking palsy.

1817 J. PARKINSON *Ess. Shaking Palsy* in M. Critchley *James Parkinson* (1955) 153 (*heading*) Shaking palsy. (*Paralysis Agitans.*) **1845** *Encycl. Metrop.* VII. 548/2 Paralysis Agitans.. consists of a feeble trembling action of the muscles, not amounting to palsy. **1888** W. R. GOWERS *Man. Dis. Nervous Syst.* II. 594 The great characteristic of the tremor of paralysis agitans is, as Parkinson pointed out, that it continues during rest. **1909** [see PARKINSON¹]. **1941** *Brit. Jrnl. Psychol.* XXXII. 5 Only a few years after the conclusion of the peace he fell a tragic victim to that incurably fatal disease of the central nervous system, paralysis agitans. **1973** *Neurology* XXIII. 215 (*heading*) Prevalence of neoplasms and causes of death in paralysis agitans.

2. *fig.* A condition of utter powerlessness, incapacity of action, or suspension of activity; the state of being 'crippled', helpless, or impotent.

1813 J. RANDOLPH 30 Aug. in *Life of Jos. Quincy*, The whole country.. is in a state of paralysis. **1831** CARLYLE *Sart. Res.* I. ii, Let him strive to keep a free, open sense; cleared from the mists of prejudice, above all from the paralysis of cant. **1882** *Times* 13 June 11 The deeds.. by which the paralysis of law is accomplished.

paralytic (pærə'lɪtɪk), *a.* and *sb.* Forms: 4 paralitike, parlatyk, 5 paraletike, -lytyk, peralytyk, -latik, 6 paralitic, (6–7 -litick(e, -litique, 7 -lytique), 7–9 -lytick, 8– paralytic. [a. F. *paralytique* (in 13th c. *paralitike*, Littré), ad. L. *paralytic-us*, a. Gr. παραλυτικός, f. παραλύειν: see PARALYSIS.]

A. *adj.* **1. a.** Affected with, suffering from, or subject to paralysis; palsied.

13.. *E.E. Allit. P.* B. 1095 Summe lepre, summe lome, & lomerande blynde, Poysened & parlatyk & pyned in fyres. **1398** TREVISA *Barth. De P.R.* VII. xiv. (1495) p ij/1 The Palsey is somtyme in the heed.. and somtyme in the membre peralytyk. *c* **1410** LOVE *Bonavent. Mirr.* xx. lf. 47 (Gibbs MS.) Off þe paraletike man lette doune in his bedde. *a* **1425** *Langland's P. Pl.* A. v. 61 (MS. U) He was as pale as a pelat & peralatik he seemed. **1549** *Compl. Scot.* vi. 67 Morpheus.. gart al my spreitis vital ande animal be cum impotent & paralitic. **1671** SALMON *Syn. Med.* II. lvi. 340 If the Paralitick member do grow less and less.. it is hard to cure. *a* **1715** BURNET *Own Time* (1766) I. 221 He fell into a paralytick state. **1773** JOHNSON *Let. to Mrs. Thrale* 17 Aug., An old lady who talks broad Scotch with a paralytick voice. **1838** DICKENS *Nich. Nick.* xxxi, He glanced.. at his shabby clothes and paralytic limb.

b. Of a (form of) disease: characterized by paralysis.

1890 F. TAYLOR *Man. Pract. Med.* 279 (*heading*) General paralysis of the insane (paralytic dementia). **1948** O. BRELAND *Animal Facts & Fallacies* i. 45 The bats also transmit diseases... One of the worst is the frequently fatal paralytic rabies which has occasionally been transmitted to human beings. **1951** WHITBY & HYNES *Med. Bacteriol.* (ed. 5) xxiv. 408 This preparalytic stage may progress no further... On the other hand paralysis or encephalitic symptoms may appear after a few hours (paralytic poliomyelitis). **1974** H. MACINNES *Climb to Lost World* ii. 33 My first reaction was to telephone our local doctor: 'Dr. Mackenzie, have you any idea where I can get a vaccine for Paralytic Rabies?' **1976** *Yorkshire Even. Press* 9 Dec. 1/5 A seven-month-old baby from Kippax, near Leeds, is in hospital with paralytic polio according to health authorities.

2. Of the nature of or pertaining to paralysis.

1818 JAS. MILL *Brit. India* II. v. v. 529 The General, who had sustained a second paralytic attack. **1866** GEO. ELIOT *F. Holt* i. (1868) 11 The unevenness of gait and feebleness of gesture which tell of a past paralytic seizure. **1878** KINGZETT *Anim. Chem.* 53 Paralytic saliva is very thin.

3. a. *fig.* Deprived or destitute of energy or power of action; powerless, ineffective; characterized by impotency or powerlessness.

1642 NETHERSOLE *Consid. upon Affairs* 5 Without the strength of that sinew of War, his Cavaliers.. can have but paralitique Arms. **1791** BENTHAM *Draught of Code* Wks. 1843 IV. 403 Out of extortion and peculation grow inaccessible justice and paralytic laws. **1844** LD. BROUGHAM *A. Lunel* I. v. 112 The feelings of the soul, like the nerves of the body, are liable to a paralytic numbness.

b. *humorously.* Shaky, rickety.

1824 GALT *Rothelan* III. *Physiognomist* 132 A mean abode,.. furnished uncouthly with.. curiously carved cabinets, paralytic tables [etc.].

†**c.** In active sense: Having the quality of paralysing or rendering powerless. *Obs. rare.*

1649 G. DANIEL *Trinarch., Hen. IV* ccclxxxv, Richard, bound in Paraliticke Chains Vnder a Tirant's Grate.

d. Intoxicated; incapably drunk. *slang.*

a **1921** E. W. HORNUNG in *Penguin Bk. Austral. Ballads* (1964) 103 The shanty-keeper *he* was just as steady as a rock, And me as paralytic as a fool. **1927** *Daily Express* 23 Nov. 7 Woman at the Thames Court: I was not drunk. I was suffering from paralysis. Mr. Cairns: I have heard being drunk called being paralytic. **1958** [see HONKERS *a.*]. **1966** F. SHAW et al. *Lern Yerself Scouse* 76 Half-dreaming, half-par'latic on me back.

B. *sb.* A sufferer from paralysis, a palsied person. ***general paralytic***, a sufferer from general paralysis.

c **1380** WYCLIF *Serm.* Sel. Wks. II. 23 Paralitikes ben þo men þat ben siike in þe palesy. **1510** *Bonavent. Myrr. Lyfe Jhesu* xx. (ed. Pynson) G j, Oure Lorde fyrste forgave the pa[ra]letike his synnes and after he heled him of the bodely palsye. **1641** BP. HALL *Serm. Ps. lx.* 2 Rem. Wks. (1660) 77 The Paralytick was.. let down through the roof. **1757** FRANKLIN *Lett.* Wks. 1840 V. 359 A number of paralytics were brought to me.. to be electrized. **1897** *Allbutt's Syst. Med.* II. 857, 25 per cent. of the male and 20 per cent. of the female general paralytics were addicted to drink.

†**para'lytical**, *a. Obs.* [f. as prec. + -AL¹.] = prec. A.

1586 BRIGHT *Melanch.* xxiv. 138 The muscle.. receiueth a kynde of paraliticall disposition for the time. **1606** *Proc. agst. Late Traitors* 392 The state of this.. Island.. was in a manner paraliticall. **1650** ELDERFIELD *Tythes* 89 Many a paralytical or spasmatical fit. **1788** REID *Active Powers* II. i. 532 Some persons have recovered the power of speech after they had lost it by a paralytical stroke.

para'lytically, *adv.* [f. prec. + -LY².] In a paralytic manner; by or as by paralysis. Also *fig.* (see PARALYTIC *a.* 3 d.)

1710 T. FULLER *Pharm. Extemp.* 188 The Intestines.. paralytically relaxed. **1840** DICKENS *Old C. Shop* xxxii, The figure shook its head paralytically. **1899** *Allbutt's Syst. Med.* VI. 832 Paralytically disturbed ocular motility. **1969** *Sunday Times* (Colour Suppl.) 16 Feb. 38/2, I was paralytically drunk.

paralyze, etc. variant of PARALYSE, etc.

param ('pæræm). *Chem.* [f. PARA-¹ 2 + AMIDE.] A synonym of dicyanodiamide, $C_2N_2(NH_2)_2$, a white crystalline compound, a polymer of cyanamide.

1866–77 WATTS *Dict. Chem.* IV. 350 Cyanamide changes into param when left to itself for a long time. **1877** *Fownes' Chem.* II. 106 Dicyanodiamide, $C_2N_4H_4$ (*Param*).

paramagnet (pærə'mægnɪt). [Back-formation from next, after *magnet* and *magnetic*.] A paramagnetic body or substance.

1909 in *Cent. Dict.* Suppl. **1973** *Nature* 21/28 Dec. 445/1 Only above 100 K does the material become a self-respecting paramagnet, with thermally randomised spins.

paramagnetic (pærəmæg'nɛtɪk), *a.* and *sb.* [f. Gr. παρα- in sense 'alongside, parallel' + MAGNETIC.]

A. *adj.* †**1.** Having the property of being attracted by the poles of a magnet, and hence, when suspended or placed freely in a magnetic field, of taking a position parallel to the lines of the force; also *ferro-magnetic*: opp. to DIAMAGNETIC. *Obs.* (superseded by the next sense).

Faraday at first (1846) distinguished *diamagnetic* from *magnetic* bodies; afterwards (1850–51) he called the latter *paramagnetic*, using *magnetic* to include both.
1850 W. WHEWELL *Let.* (1876) II. 364 [*To Faraday.*] Hence it would appear, that the two classes of magnetic bodies are those which place their length *parallel* or *according* to the terrestrial magnetic lines, and those which place their length *transverse* to such lines. Keeping the preposition *dia* for the latter, the preposition *para* or *ana* might be used for the former; perhaps *para* would be best as the word *parallel*.. would be a technical memory for it. Thus we should have this distribution—Paramagnetic: Iron, Nickel, Cobalt, &c. Diamagnetic: Bismuth, Phosphor, &c. If you like *anamagnetic* better than *paramagnetic*, as meaning magnetic *according to* our standard, terrestrial magnetism, I see no objection. **1851** FARADAY *Exp. Res. in Electr.* No. 2790 in *Phil. Trans.* 26 As the magnetism of iron, nickel, and cobalt, when in the magnetic field is like that of the earth as a whole, so that when rendered active they place themselves parallel to its axis or lines of magnetic force, I have supposed that they and their similars (including oxygen now) might be called paramagnetic bodies, giving the following division—Magnetic: (1) *Paramagnetic*, (2) *Diamagnetic*. *Ibid.* No. 2834. 39 Masses of paramagnetic matter. **1855** MAURY *Phys. Geog. Sea* vi. (1858) §376 Faraday has shown that, as the temperature of oxygen is raised, its paramagnetic force diminishes, being resumed as the temperature falls again. **1880** [see FERROMAGNETIC *a.* 1]. **1895** STORY-MASKELYNE *Crystallogr.* i §13 Unmagnetised bodies if brought near a magnetic pole are either attracted or repelled by it, and are said to be magnetised by induction; being described in the former case as paramagnetic and as diamagnetic in the latter case.

2. a. Of a body or substance: very weakly attracted by the poles of a magnet but not retaining any permanent magnetism; having a susceptibility that is positive but small, so that the relative permeability is only slightly greater than one and hysteresis does not occur. **b.** Characteristic of or pertaining to paramagnetism. Cf. FERROMAGNETIC *a.* 2 and the note there.

1896, etc. [see FERROMAGNETIC *a.* 2.]. **1902** *Encycl. Brit.* XXX. 430/2 The magnetic susceptibility of a vacuum.. is 0, that of a diamagnetic substance.. has a negative value, while the susceptibility of paramagnetic and ferromagnetic substances.. is positive. **1903** *Proc. R. Soc.* LXXI. 239 The law of Curie, that the susceptibility of weak paramagnetic substances is inversely proportional to the absolute temperature. **1931** S. R. WILLIAMS *Mag. Phenomena* v. 159 Oxygen, palladium, air, glass, porcelain, and $FeSO_4$ were some of the paramagnetic bodies studied by Curie. **1958** N. CUSACK *Electr. & Magn. Prop. Solids* xii. 269 At a critical temperature, called the Curie point.., ferromagnetic matter undergoes a phase transition and becomes paramagnetic. **1966** C. R. TOTTLE *Sci. Engin. Materials* vi. 133 Curie.. deduced the law for paramagnetic susceptibility.

B. *sb.* A paramagnetic body or substance.

1855 *Phil. Mag.* IX. 293 The assertions I have made regarding mutual influence.. are confirmed amply by experiment for paramagnetics. **1911** *Encycl. Brit.* XVII. 324/1 Between the ferromagnetics and the paramagnetics there is an enormous gap. **1914**, **1962** [see FERROMAGNETIC *sb.*]. **1966** C. R. TOTTLE *Sci. Engin. Materials* vi. 134 The group of elements iron, cobalt, nickel demonstrates this. Below a certain critical temperature these elements remain permanently magnetized after removal of the external field... Above it, the materials behave as normal paramagnetics.

Hence **paramag'netically** *adv.*

1883 *Encycl. Brit.* XV. 248/2 By virtue of differential action, a body may behave paramagnetically or diamagnetically according as it is placed in a less or in a more permeable medium than itself. **1974** *Nature* 31 May 426/1 The reduction at 25° C of the cytochrome c_3 from *Desulfovibrio vulgaris*.. has been studied by following the paramagnetically shifted NMR resonances which lie to very low field.

paramagnetism (pærə'mægnɪtɪz(ə)m). [f. PARA-¹ 1 + MAGNETISM, after PARAMAGNETIC *a.* and *sb.*] The quality of being paramagnetic; the phenomena exhibited by paramagnetic bodies: opp. to DIAMAGNETISM. Now distinguished from FERROMAGNETISM, but formerly synonymous with it.

1850 W. WHEWELL *Let.* (1876) II. 365 [*To Faraday.*] Will it not do to talk of iron, nickel, &c., as *paramagnetic*, and glass, phosphorus, &c., as *diamagnetic*? Then this new branch of science, for so, of course, it will soon become, will be *Paramagnetism*. **1851** W. GREGORY *Lect. Anim. Magnet.* p. xv, He does indeed propose to include, under the general term Magnetism, two forms of it: viz. Para-magnetism.. and Dia-magnetism. **1877** LE CONTE *Elem. Geol.* (1879) 186 If the bar be slender, it..shows its paramagnetism by assuming the axial position. **1930** [see FERROMAGNETISM]. **1958** N. CUSACK *Electr. & Magn. Prop. Solids* xiii. 291 All matter possesses a basic diamagnetism but where there are carriers, e.g. free electrons in metals, .. the orientation of the carriers in the field direction gives a paramagnetism which usually masks the diamagnetism. **1964** J. W. LINNETT *Electronic Struct. Molecules* iii. 53 The paramagnetism of the ground state of O_2.

paramaleic, paramalic: see PARA-[1] 2.

paramastoid (pærəˈmæstɔɪd), *a.* (*sb.*) *Anat.* [f. Gr. παρα- PARA-[1] 1 + MASTOID.] Situated near the mastoid process: applied to certain processes of the occipital bone, also called *paroccipital*. **b.** as *sb.* A paramastoid process.

1847–9 TODD *Cycl. Anat.* IV. 370/2 The paramastoid apophysis is dilated into a prominent plate. **1866** HUXLEY *Preh. Rem. Caithn.* 101 None of the skulls exhibit paramastoid or pneumatic processes of the occipital bone. **1868** DARWIN *Anim. & Pl.* I. iv. 118 The paramastoids relatively..are generally much thicker than in the wild rabbit.

paramatta (pærəˈmætə). [f. Paramatta (prop. Parramatta), a town in New South Wales.

There formerly existed at Parramatta a convict establishment in which clothing materials were produced: cf. *Encycl. Brit.* (ed. 7) XVII. 65/2; perhaps the modern stuff (which according to Beck *Draper's Dict.* was invented at Bradford) was in imitation of these; there is no evidence for the assertion that the fabric was orig. made of wool imported from Parramatta.]

A light dress fabric having a weft of combed merino wool and a warp formerly of silk, but now generally of cotton.

1834 J. D. LANG *State N.S. Wales* in *Tait's Mag.* I. 410/1 Cloth, Parramatta, per yard, 1s. 8d. **1844** G. DODD *Textile Manuf.* iv. 137 There are two kinds of stuff now made, called 'Orleans' and 'Paramatta'.., apparently formed of worsted, the warp being cotton. **1846** C. P. HODGSON *Remin. Australia* Notes 367 *Paramatta*, a peculiar tweed, made in the Colony, and chiefly at Paramatta, hence the name. **1858** SIMMONDS *Dict. Trade*, *Paramatta*, a kind of bombazine, the weft of which is worsted, the warp of cotton. **1901** *Daily News* 1 Feb. 5/1 The new leaders were called, not in silk, but in paramatta, which is the proper stuff for the gown of a King's Counsel when mourning is prescribed.

‖**Paramecium** (pærəˈmiːsɪəm). *Zool.* Also erron. **-mæcium**, **-mœcium**. [mod.L. f. Gr. παραμήκ-ης oblong, oval, f. παρά against + μῆκος length: cf. L. *ob-longus*.] A genus of holotrichous ciliate Infusoria, type of the family *Parameciidæ*, of oblong shape, having the mouth near the middle of the ventral surface; also called, from their shape, slipper-animalcules. Hence **paraˈmecine** *a.*, belonging to this family.

1752 HILL *Hist. Anim.* 4 The Paramecium, with an oblong, voluble body, obtuse at each end. **1875** HUXLEY & MARTIN *Elem. Biol.* (1877) 97. **1883** H. DRUMMOND *Nat. Law in Spir. W.* (1884) 211 By the repeated subdivisions of a single *Paramecium*, no fewer than 268,000,000 similar organisms might be produced in one month.

parameconic, etc.: see PARA-[1] 1, 2.

paramedian (pærəˈmiːdɪən), *a.* *Anat.* [PARA-[1] 1.] Situated alongside of the median line, as the ***paramedian sulcus*** on the dorsal surface of the spinal cord. (*Syd. Soc. Lex.* 1893.)

1890 BILLINGS *Med. Dict.* II. 289/1 Paramedian sulcus. **1928** [see INDUCTION 9 b]. **1962** *Lancet* 19 May 1049/2 The abdomen was opened through a long left paramedian incision. **1977** *Ibid.* 28 May 1128/1 Patients in whom a midline or paramedian incision was made were not included.

paramedic[1] (pærəˈmɛdɪk). orig. *U.S.* Also **para-medic**. [f. PARA-[3] + MEDIC *a.* and *sb.*] A person trained to be dropped by parachute to give medical aid.

1951 *Sunday Mirror* (N.Y.) 8 Apr. 3 Para-medics from air-sea rescue squadrons..were in the search planes. **1957** *Time* 2 Sept. 35/2 A C-47 with a paramedic aboard started to track his flight. **1961** *Daily Tel.* 27 Feb. 18/2 The group's nucleus consists of six 'paramedics'. These are practised parachutists with a medical background. **1964** J. MASTERS *Trial at Monomoy* vii. 225 Why didn't they send a plane down with skis, paramedics, radios, food? **1974** *Spartanburg* (S. Carolina) *Herald* 25 Apr. A2/5 He hopes the state pilot, advanced course for para-medics will be available to local EMS technicians by August or September. **1974** *Courier-Mail* (Brisbane) 17 Sept. 11/4 (*caption*) Dummy United States Air Force para-medic, dressed in full gear, at the jump position of a door of a U.S.A.F. Hercules rescue aircraft.

paramedic[2] (pærəˈmɛdɪk). [f. PARAMEDIC(AL *a.*[1] and *sb.* (cf. MEDIC *a.* and *sb.*).] A paramedical worker; = PARAMEDICAL *sb.* Also *attrib.* or as *adj.*

1970 *Time* 9 Nov. 38 More than 40 training programs for doctors assistants are under way across the country. The graduates..are tagged with clumsy names—para-medic, clinical associate, health practitioner. *Ibid.*, Para-medic studies are wide-ranging—from community health to bacteriology and psychosomatic medicine, plus techniques such as regulating intravenous infusions and operating respirators. **1974** *Telegraph* (Brisbane) 27 Feb. 32/2 Paramedics tried artificial respiration, but to no avail. **1974** *Aiken* (S. Carolina) *Standard* 22 Apr. 4-A/1 Paramedic Services and the city police will provide first aid and protection during the walk. **1975** *Daily Tel.* 29 Sept. 3/1 The *Lancet* report gives details of 600 such operations, 366 performed by medical auxiliaries or 'para-medics' as they are described. The rest were carried out by qualified doctors. **1976** *Amer. Speech 1973* XLVIII. 195 Also of invaluable help to the nurse are the *paramedic personnel*, frequently shortened to *paramedics*. In their ranks we find those employees trained to read slides in the laboratory or to assist the doctor and nurse with other medical tasks. **1976** *Sci. Amer.* Sept. 72/3 (Advt.), Heart pacemakers, paramedic telecare units and ultrasonic cardioscopes—all are outgrowths of space technology. **1977** *It* May 21/2 They also have a fully-equipped ambulance, manned by State-certified paramedics and emergency medical technicians.

paramedical (pærəˈmɛdɪkəl), *a.*[1] and *sb.* [f. PARA-[1] + MEDICAL *a.* and *sb.*] **A.** *adj.* Supplementary to or supporting the work of medically qualified personnel.

1921 *Lancet* 15 Oct. 814/1 Para-medical research. The report for 1920–21 of the Committee of the Privy Council for Scientific and Industrial Research touches the fringe of several medical problems and describes work linked at several points with that being undertaken under the auspices of the Medical Research Council. **1952** C. P. BLACKER *Eugenics* 303 Marriage guidance, premarital examinations, eugenic prognosis, birth control, and treatment of infecundity have recently been described as 'para-medical services'. **1962** *Times* 2 Mar. 5/7 Nurses and other paramedical personnel. **1969** *Nature* 15 Feb. 604/1 If a student failed to complete the medical course, he would at least have a qualification that would enable him to take up a career in some non-medical or para-medical field. **1972** *Sci. Amer.* Feb. 117/1 Intended largely for paramedical students, nurses and technicians, it presents..a review of the general structure of the body. **1977** *Private Eye* 1 Apr. 7/3 New ventures in the para-medical field include Polyglot Schools (UK) limited..who canvass doctors in the Harley Street area with their scheme, 'Arabic for the Medical Professions'.

B. *sb.* A paramedical worker.

1972 *Guardian* 23 Oct. 11/1 It was suggested that abortion be delegated to paramedicals. **1974** *Financial Times* 5 July 1/8 It was announced on Wednesday that the committee, which is looking at nurses' and midwives' salaries, will also make recommendations for the 'para-medicals'. **1975** *Nature* 21 Aug. 610/3 [In China] barefoot doctors..are called 'doctors', not paramedicals or auxiliaries. **1976** *Times Lit. Suppl.* 16 July 872/5 The enlistment of para-medicals to perform the tasks of health care.

paramedical (pærəˈmɛdɪkəl), *a.*[2] [f. PARA-[3] + MEDICAL *a.* and *sb.*] Trained in parachuting and competent to give medical aid.

1962 *Flight Internat.* LXXXI. 227/1 The Near East Air Force 'para-medical' team in Cyprus. **1974** *Telegraph* (Brisbane) 17 Sept. 34/1 An American paramedical air-man will parachute into the water off Redland Bay..as part of a simulated search and rescue operation.

paramelaconite: see PARA-[1] 2 c.

paramenstruum: see PARA-[1] 1.

†ˈ**parament**. *Obs.* Also 5 **parement**. [a. OF. *parament* (10th c. in Littré), *parement* (13th c.) = It., Sp. *paramento*, late L. *parāmentum* ornament (Augustine), f. L. *parāre* to make ready, prepare, fit out, deck, adorn: see -MENT.] An ornament, a decoration. ***chamber of parament***, a richly decorated room, hung with tapestry, etc.; a state room; a presence chamber.

c **1385** CHAUCER *L.G.W.* 1106 *Dido*, To daunsynge chaumberys ful of paramentys..This Enyas is led. *c* **1386** —— *Sqr.'s T.* 261 Til he cam to his chambre of parementz. *c* **1489** CAXTON *Sonnes of Aymon* vi. 151 The chambre of paremente, whiche was hanged right rychely. **1529** MORE *Dyaloge* I. ii. Wks. 114 Woulde suffre no such superfluite in the paramentes of the church. **1589** T. L. *Advt. Q. Eliz.* (1651) 49 All the delices, the pompes and paraments of her oppressors, shall vanish as a dreame. **1654** H. L'ESTRANGE *K. Chas. I* (1655) 112 Taking away the Crucifixes, Chalices, and Paraments of the Altar. **1706** PHILLIPS, *Parament*, an Ornament for an Altar.

b. A decorated robe, a robe of state.

c **1386** CHAUCER *Knt.'s T.* 1643 Lordes in paramentz on hir courseres. **1474** CAXTON *Chesse* II. ii, One of the best parements and maketh a womman most fayr in her persone is to be shamefast. **1656** BLOUNT *Glossogr.*, *Paraments*, robes of state.

‖**paraˈmento**. *Obs.* [Sp.: see prec.] = prec. b.

a **1625** FLETCHER *Love's Pilgrim.* I. i, There were cloaks, gowns, cassocks, And other paramentos.

paramere (ˈpærəmɪə(r)). *Biol.* [f. Gr. παρα- PARA-[1] + μέρος part.]

1. One of a series of radiating parts or organs, as a ray of a star-fish; an actinomere.

1883 P. GEDDES in *Encycl. Brit.* XVI. 842/2 The former definition of the term antimere..is corrected by terming each ray a paramere, and its symmetrical halves the antimeres.

2. Each of the halves of a bilaterally symmetrical animal, or of a segment or somite of such.

1884 tr. *Claus' Zool.* I. 27 These two halves [of the body divided by the median plane], as opposed to antimeres, may be termed parameres. *Ibid.*, The antimeres of the Radiata also consist of two parameres, and are therefore bilateral. **1888** *Nature* 10 May 47/1 The primitive proximal paramere of the second visceral arch.

Hence **parameric** (-ˈmɛrɪk) *a.*, pertaining to a paramere; having parameres. (*Cent. Dict.* 1890.)

‖**paramese** (pəˈræmɪsiː). [a. Gr. παραμέση the string next the middle, f. παράμεσος next the middle, f. παρά beside + μέσος mid.] In ancient Greek music, The tone next above the mese; the lowest tone of the disjunct tetrachord.

1603 HOLLAND *Plutarch* Explan. Words, *Paramese*, next the meane or middle string. A note in musicke. **1698** WALLIS in *Phil. Trans.* XX. 250 Which was, in their Musick, that from *Mese* to *Paramese*; that is in our Musick, from A to B. **1760** STILES *ibid.* LI. 702 The paramese of the lyre, though still paramese in position, acquired the power of the mese. **1898** STAINER & BARRETT *Dict. Mus. T.* s.v. *Greek Music*, In the eight stringed lyre..Paramese took its proper place, next to Mese.

parameter (pəˈræmɪtə(r)). *Math.* [a. mod.L. *parameter*, *-metrum*, fem. (Mydorge 1631), in F. *paramètre* ('la ligne nommé ailleurs costé droit, paramètre, et icy coadjuteur' Desargues 1639); f. Gr. παρα- beside, subsidiary to + μέτρον measure.]

1. In conic sections: The third proportional to any given diameter and its conjugate (or, in the parabola, to any abscissa on a given diameter and the corresponding ordinate); this is the ***parameter of the given diameter***. *spec.* The parameter of the transverse axis (***principal parameter***, or ***parameter of the curve***), i.e. the latus rectum, or focal chord perpendicular to the axis.

[**1631** C. MYDORGE *Prodrom. Catopt. & Diopt. siue Conicorum* 3 Def. xix, Parametrum coni sectionis dicimus, rectam lineam à cuiuslibet coni sectionis, aut portionis, vertice eductam ordinatim ad contiguam diametrum applicatis æquidistantem... Quæ, si ab axis termino sit educta, recta parameter..dicetur.]

1656 HOBBES *Six Lessons* Wks. 1845 VII. 259 As much in vain..as seek for the focus or parameter of the parabola of Dives and Lazarus. **1704** J. HARRIS *Lex. Techn.* I, *Parameter*, by some..called the *Latus Rectum* of a Parabola, is a Third Proportional to the Abscissa and any Ordinate. **1795** HUTTON *Math. Dict.*, *Parameter*, a certain constant right line in each of the three Conic Sections; otherwise called also Latus Rectum..; being..a third proportional to the transverse and conjugate axes, in the ellipse and hyperbola; and, which is the same thing, a third proportional to any absciss and its ordinate in the parabola. **1798** —— *Course Math.* (1811) II. 123 The Parameter of any Diameter [of a parabola] is equal to four Times the Line drawn from the Focus to the Vertex of that Diameter. **1816** tr. *Lacroix's Diff. & Int. Calculus* 401 If..the parameter of a parabola be made to vary, a series of parabolas will be obtained. **1891** C. TAYLOR *Elem. Geom. Conics* (ed. 7) iii. §17 The Parameter of any diameter of a parabola is the focal chord which it bisects: thus the latus rectum is the parameter of the axis.

2. a. *gen.* A quantity which is constant (as distinct from the ordinary variables) in a particular case considered, but which varies in different cases; *esp.* a constant occurring in the equation of a curve or surface, by the variation of which the equation is made to represent a family of such curves or surfaces (cf. quot. 1816 in 1); also in *Computing*.

1852 B. PRICE *Infinites. Calc.* I. xiii. 409 If an equation to a curve be given, involving one or more constants, as well as the current coordinates, the position and dimensions of the curve will be changed by a change in the constants, and yet the class may remain the same... A constant that enters into an equation, and varies in the way above explained, is called a variable parameter. **1859** PARKINSON *Optics* (1866) 4 The refractive index between the two media..is a parameter which varies, (i) if the nature of the light be altered, (ii) if the relation between the two media be altered. **1879** THOMSON & TAIT *Nat. Phil.* I. I. §293. **1885** LEUDESDORF *Cremona's Proj. Geom.* 63 This anharmonic ratio is called the coefficient or parameter of the homology. **1954** *Computers & Automation* Dec. 18/1 *Parameter*, in a subroutine, a quantity which may be given different values when the subroutine is used in different parts of one main routine, but which usually remains unchanged throughout any one such use. **1958** *Communications* (Assoc. Computing Machinery) Dec. 16 A procedure..is a closed and self-contained process with a fixed ordered set of input and output parameters. **1965** [see *keyboarded* ppl. adj. s.v. KEYBOARD *v.*]. **1969** *Computers & Humanities* III. 278 Thus input parameters were included to specify page width and length, and the dictionary was photo-offset. **1973** C. W. GEAR *Introd. Computer Sci.* v. 201 A and B are input parameters, so they can be given values by any expression when the subroutine is called. **1973** MURRILL & SMITH *Introd. Computer Sci.* 585 Through the use of arguments and parameters, subroutines and functions can be used throughout a program to perform identical operations upon many different data items.

b. *Astron.* = ELEMENT 7 a.

1829 *Encycl. Metrop.* Div. 2 I. Index, Variation of Parameters. [*Ibid.* 699 Variation of elements of orbit.] **1840** *Penny Cycl.* XVII. 240/1 The parameters of the orbits are now generally called their elements. **1841** *Proc. Amer. Phil. Soc.* II. 19 Orbits having small parameters. **1963** R. H. MERSON in M. Roy *Dynamics of Satellites* 83 The values of the six basic elements at a given time..are determined from a set of observations by a differential correction technique. .. In addition to the estimates of the orbital parameters, estimates of their variances and covariances are also determined. **1967** *Technology Week* 20 Feb. 13 Orbital parameters were apogee—817·2 mi.; perigee—128 mi.; inclination—48·4 degrees, and period 100·3 minutes. **1975** *Nature* 18 Sept. 184/2 Even though a few comets with hyperbolic orbits have been seen, Whipple's calculations show that for four candidates—the only ones..with well determined parameters—the chance of any one having arrived on such an orbit from interstellar space is less than 1 in 10^4.

c. *Cryst.* Each of the intercepts made upon the axes in a crystal by the plane which is chosen for a face of the unit or primary pyramid.

1839 W. H. Miller *Crystallogr.* 2 The parameters are the portions of the axes cut off by a given face. **1878** Gurney *Crystallogr.* 18, *a, b, c* the parameters of the crystal. **1895** Story-Maskelyne *Crystallogr.* ii. §18 The ratios *a:b:c* of the intercepts [on the axes] of some one plane chosen as a standard or parametral plane are termed the parametral ratios or parameters of the system as referred to the axes *X, Y, Z.*

d. *Math.* An independent variable in terms of which each co-ordinate of a point is expressed, independently of the other co-ordinates.

1873 G. Salmon *Treat. Higher Plane Curves* (ed. 2) viii. 317 The coordinates *x', y', z'* are..expressible as quadric functions of a parameter θ. **1907** Grace & Rosenberg *Coordinate Geom.* xvi. 220 If we can find simple expressions for the coordinates of points on a conic in terms of one variable quantity, a point on the curve may be looked on as determined by a definite value of the variable, the variable being usually called the parameter. **1937** Michell & Belz *Elem. Math. Analysis* I. vii. 401 Taking $x^2/a^2 - y^2/b^2 = 1$, (*a, b* positive), as the equation of the hyperbola, we can evidently write $x = \pm a \cosh \phi$, $y = b \sinh \phi$, introducing ϕ as parameter. **1969** J. J. Stoker *Differential Geom.* iv. 75 As with curves, the surface parameters are to a considerable degree arbitrary; in fact, parameters *u, v* can be replaced by new parameters through the equations $\bar{u} = \phi_1(u, v)$, $\bar{v} = \phi_2(u, v)$, provided that the Jacobian $\partial(\bar{u}, \bar{v})/(u, v)$ is different from zero.

e. *Electr.* Any of several numerical quantities that can be used jointly to characterize a network.

1911 *Trans. Amer. Inst. Electr. Engin.* XXX. 885 The impedances required to make a normal type of network of the requisite number of parameters equivalent to the given network under specified conditions of operation. **1930** T. E. Shea *Transmission Networks & Wave Filters* iii. 71 Any network having one pair of input and one pair of output terminals may be completely represented..by a T network (or network having any form providing at least three independent parameters) as far as external current and voltage conditions are concerned. **1962** Simpson & Richards *Physical Princ. Junction Transistors* v. 82 The *h*'s define the following circuit parameters: $h_{11} = h_i$ = input impedance with output short-circuited.., $h_{12} = h_r$ = reverse voltage ratio with input open-circuited. **1966** R. H. Mattson *Electronics* ix. 381 The *y* parameters are used when discussing feedback amplifiers and pentode amplifiers. The *h* parameters are used when discussing transistor circuits.

f. *Statistics.* A numerical characteristic of a population (as distinguished from a 'statistic', which relates to a sample).

1922 R. A. Fisher in *Phil. Trans. R. Soc.* A. CCXXII. 311 The law of distribution of this hypothetical population is specified by relatively few parameters. *Ibid.* 313 These involve the choice of methods of calculating from a sample statistical derivates, or as we shall call them statistics, which are designed to estimate the values of the parameters of the hypothetical population. **1939** A. E. Treloar *Elem. Statistical Reasoning* x. 130 The true sampling error of each sample mean and standard deviation, so far as those statistics form estimates of the corresponding parameters, may be expressed as [etc.]. **1962** E. S. Keeping *Introd. Statistical Inference* v. 95 If..the population is assumed to be normal, as far as a particular variate is concerned, the density function for this variate will contain two parameters, μ and σ, which are the population mean and standard deviation respectively. **1975** Harnett & Murphy *Introd. Statistical Anal.* i. 5 The numerical characteristics of a sample are used to estimate the parameters of the parent population from which this sample was drawn. A numerical characteristic used for this purpose is referred to as a sample statistic, or usually just a statistic.

3. In extended use: any distinguishing or defining characteristic or feature, esp. one that may be measured or quantified; an element or aspect *of* anything; *loosely*, a boundary or limit.

1927 *Proc. R. Soc.* A. CXIII. 642 In the case of phenacite, the symmetry of the structure imposes no limitations on the position of the seven atoms in the molecule, so that twenty-one parameters are required to define the structure. **1934** *Ibid.* CXLVI. 570 Few of the structures of hydrated salts have as yet been found. This may be due to the large numbers of parameters usually involved, which, in the absence of any general laws concerning water of crystallization, makes the analysis very difficult. **1939** Brevoort & Joyner *Cooling on Front of Air-Cooled Engine Cylinder* (NACA Techn. Rep. No. 674) 1/1 These results are introductory to the study of front cooling and show the general effect of the several test parameters. **1950** J. C. Slater *Microwave Electronics* x. 230 The quantity, *x*.. occurs frequently in klystron theory and is called the bunching parameter. **1957** *Times* 11 Sept. 6/2 The principle that it was possible to specify the sounds of speech in terms of six parameters or factors, which might be considered as functions of time. **1961** *Jrnl. Speech & Hearing Res.* IV. 10/1 There is some evidence..that parameters other than the formant frequencies may influence human judgement of vowel qualities. **1962** *Rep. Comm. Broadcasting 1960* 335 in *Parl. Papers 1961–2* (Cmnd. 1753) IX. 259 Many Western European countries..are considering whether there would be advantage in using..the technical parameters they already use for 625-line standards in the 7 Mc/s channels of Bands I and III. **1964** A. Edel in I. L. Horowitz *New Sociol.* xiv. 220 A theory of human society is seen to involve a specific picture of the nature of man. We would then say that a social theory has a human-nature parameter. **1965** *Listener* 9 Dec. 943/2 There remains the bulk of those for whom politics is a parameter of life rather like the weather. **1967** *Economist* 16 Dec. 1157/1 A second, even bigger generator of 1,300 MW was also contracted for... With these orders, practically every existing parameter of power generating practice has been exceeded. **1970** *Time* 3 Aug. 9 The fact that Nixon was willing to make his chastisement public suggests..that the President at least understands 'the parameters of the problem'. **1971** *Jrnl. Gen. Psychol.* LXXXIV. 18 Three phenomena corresponding to the three major parameters of color—brightness, hue, and saturation. **1972** *Nature* 18 Feb. 373/2 In Fig. 2 ozone and radon concentrations together with various meteorological parameters are shown for two consecutive Saturdays. **1973** *N.Y. Times Mag.* 25 Feb. 71/4 It carries, to begin with, the liberal presumption that the mind of man can in fact comprehend the major parameters of the world we inhabit. **1975** D. M. Davin *Closing Times* p. xviii, There are parameters to these recollections which may not be immediately apparent: the world of learning..and the war. .. My chief parameter, however, is that of art. **1975** *Times* 14 Oct. 15/4 The considerable element of indeterminacy which exists within the parameters of the parole system. **1975** *Publishers Weekly* 27 Oct. 20/1 One disappointment for the publishers is that it [*sc.* the High Court decision] fails to provide any clear guidelines on the larger issue of the parameters of Government secrecy. **1976** *Listener* 30 Sept. 419/3 Carter, who has made the running so far by raising the debate beyond the orthodox economic and financial political parameters. **1976** H. Young *Crossman Affair* i. 19 At this meeting a word was first spoken and a concept first articulated which later came to dominate the Crossman Diaries case. The word was 'parameters'... Sir John Hunt, in giving guidance on the limits within which an edited version of Crossman would have to be prepared, now formalized into a set of rules his interpretation of past practice... These parameters, or limits, excluded four particular areas from detailed report or discussion.

pa͵rameteri'zation. Also **pa͵rametri'zation.** [f. as next + -ation.] The action of parameterizing; a parametric representation.

1939 H. Weyl *Classical Groups* ii. 56 (*heading*) Cayley's rational parametrization of the orthogonal group. **1964** L. Wilets *Theories Nuclear Fission* ii. 14 (*heading*) Parameterization of the nuclear surface. **1970** I. E. McCarthy *Nuclear Reactions* 1. iii. 69 To facilitate numerical calculations the following parametrization is used. **1972** A. W. F. Edwards *Likelihood* vi. 127 In view of the relatively high conformation of $\hat{x}$ and $\hat{y}$ the former parametrization in *p* and *r* is more suitable. **1975** *Physics Bull.* July 323/3 The required degree of accuracy is established at the beginning by a theoretical study using the virial co-efficients of the post Newtonian parameterization expansion for the viable gravitation theories. **1976** *European Econ. Rev.* VIII. 287 The TF form, a finite parametrization of the well-known final form, is appropriate for control and forecasting.

parameterize (pəˈræmɪtəraɪz), *v.* Also **parametrize.** [f. parameter + -ize.] *trans.* To describe or represent in terms of a parameter.

1940 E. T. Bell *Devel. Math.* xv. 322 The wave surface in optics, parametrized by elliptic functions. **1949** [see interval sb. 7b]. **1964** *Ann. Rev. Automatic Programming* IV. 125 A translation algorithm is presented, capable of being conveniently parameterized for various source language-target language pairs. **1970** *New Scientist* 9 Apr. 76/2 The nuclear charge distribution..can be parametrized directly using a suitable mathematical form which does not necessarily have fundamental significance. **1973** *Nature* 14 Sept. 61/1 Cigarette smoking is parametrized by the number smoked daily both before pregnancy and after the fourth month. **1974** *Ibid.* 20/27 Dec. 673/1 The zonal velocity (parameterised by Λ) leads to a secular change in *i* as the value of ω of the satellite orbit changes.

Hence **pa'rameterized** *ppl. a.*, **pa'rameterizing** *vbl. sb.*

1962 [see *magnetosonic* adj. s.v. magneto-]. **1964** *Ann. Rev. Automatic Programming* IV. 125 (*heading*) A parameterized compiler based on mechanical linguistics. **1971** *Physics Bull.* Jan. 24/2 Only the large scale physics of the atmosphere is well represented in our models and the subgrid scale physics..can only be included in some parametrized form.

parametral (pəˈræmɪtrəl), *a. Math.* [f. as parameter + -al^1.] = parametric *a.*^{1}

Except in *Cryst.*, *parametric* is the usual adj.

1878 Gurney *Crystallogr.* 18, *ABC* is called the parametral plane. **1880** L. Fletcher in *Phil. Mag.* Feb. 82 The parametral ratios are permanent. **1895** [see parameter 2c]. **1973** H. D. Megaw *Crystal Struct.* v. 103 The plane used to define the axial ratios *a:b:c*, the parametral plane, is (111).

parametrial: see para-^{1} 1.

parametric (pærəˈmɛtrɪk), *a.*^{1} [f. as parametral *a.* + -ic.] **a.** *Math.* Of or pertaining to a parameter. ***parametric curve***, a curve obtained by keeping constant one of the parameters in the parametric equations of a surface; ***parametric equation***, one of a set of equations each of which expresses one of the co-ordinates of a curve or surface as a function of one or more parameters (parameter 2d).

This, rather than *parametral* or *parametrical*, is the usual adj. (except in *Cryst.*: cf. parametral *a.*).

1864 Cayley in *Coll. Math. Papers* V. 552, μ is the parametric order, ν the parametric class, of the system. **1873** G. Salmon *Higher Plane Curves* 65 When the variable curve depends on a parametric point moving on a given parametric curve. **1900** *Trans. Amer. Math. Soc.* I. 461 (*heading*) Parametric representation of the fundamental quadric. **1909** L. P. Eisenhart *Treat. Differential Geom. Curves & Surfaces* i. 1 (*heading*) Parametric equations of a curve. *Ibid.* ii. 55 Upon a surface (2) there lie an infinity of curves whose equations are given by equations (2), when *u* is constant, each constant value of *v* determining a curve... In a similar way, there is an infinite family of curves $v = const.$ The curves of these two families are called the parametric curves for the given equations of the surface. **1942** C. H. Lehmann *Analytic Geom.* xi. 229 The parametric equations of a specific locus are not unique. *Ibid.* 230 Find the rectangular equation of the curve whose parametric equations are $x = 2 + 3 \tan \theta$, $y = 1 + 4 \sec \theta$. **1969** J. J. Stoker *Differential Geom.* ii. 14 Many important results in differential geometry can often be made direct and easy to achieve once a special parametric representation has been tactfully chosen.

b. *Electronics.* Applied to devices and processes in which amplification or frequency conversion is obtained by applying a signal to a non-linear device that is modulated by a pumping frequency, so that there is a transfer of power from the latter to the output, which in general can include the sum and difference frequencies.

So called because the action of the pumping frequency is to modulate the parameters of the non-linear device.

1957 *RCA Rev.* XVIII. 578 (*heading*) Theory of parametric amplification using nonlinear reactances. *Ibid.* 579 In this paper the parametric amplifier is analyzed in terms of an equivalent circuit using a nonlinear inductance. **1961** *Guardian* 14 Feb. 24/1 The so-called 'parametric amplifiers'..can increase the sensitivity of radio reception over great distances. **1968** Angelakos & Everhart *Microwave Communications* iv. 82 A parametric amplifier converts power at one frequency (from a source generally called the pump) into power at another frequency, the signal frequency... The pump voltage is mixed with the signal voltage by a nonlinear reactance, which in microwave systems is generally a varactor diode. **1971** *Physics Bull.* Aug. 464/3 Parametric conversions of waves to other frequencies are familiar in the field of non-linear optics. **1972** *Sci. Amer.* Sept. 136/3 In present-day satellite-communication terminals the maser amplifier has given way to the cooled parametric amplifier, which combines low-noise performance with an even wider bandwidth. **1972** Zernike & Midwinter *Appl. Non-linear Optics* (1973) vii. 153 The parametric up-converter is a special case of sum-frequency generation. Similarly, the parametric amplifier and the parametric oscillator are special cases of difference-frequency generation.

Also **para'metrical** *a.*

1887 R. A. Roberts *Integr. Calc.* I. 301 These angles belong to different parametrical systems.

parametric (pærəˈmiːtrɪk), *a.*^{2} *Anat.* and *Path.* [f. Gr. παρά beside + μήτρα womb, matrix + -ic: cf. mod.L. *parametrium* the organic tissue beside the uterus.] Situated beside or near the uterus, or affecting the parts so situated.

1889 J. M. Duncan *Lect. Dis. Women* viii. (ed. 4) 44 The parametric cellular tissue. *Ibid.* xiv. 101 The inflammatory disease is generally parametric.

parametrically (pærəˈmɛtrɪkəlɪ), *adv.* [f. parametric *a.*^{1}: see -ly^2.] In terms of a parameter or parameters.

1894 C. A. Scott *Introd. Acct. Plane Analyt. Geom.* v. 89 The possibility of expressing the coordinates of a point on a curve parametrically. **1940** E. T. Bell *Devel. Math.* xv. 322 Kummer's (1864) quartic surface..is the so-called singular surface of the quadratic line complex, and..is represented parametrically. **1962** W. B. Thompson *Introd. Plasma Physics* v. 86 The coordinates (*X, Y*) can be given parametrically in terms of the phase velocity $v(\theta)$ and the angle between the wave vector and the magnetic field. **1968** C. G. Kuper *Introd. Theory Superconductivity* xii. 202 The probability of occupation of a given single-particle state will depend parametrically on the *whole* distribution of quasiparticles, but not on the detailed question of whether some other particular state is occupied.

parametritic to **paramnesia**: see para-^{1} 1.

parametrize, -metrization: varr. parameterize *v.*, -meterization.

parametron (pəˈræmɪtrɒn). *Electronics.* [f. parametr(ic *a.*^{1} + -*on*; coined in Jap. by E. Goto 1955, in *Denki Tsūshin Gakkai Zasshi* XXX. 770.] A digital storage element consisting of a parametric oscillator in which the digit is represented by the phase (0° or 180°, corresponding to 1 or 0) of the output signal relative to that of an applied reference signal of the same frequency.

1956 *ETJ of Japan* June 64 A new type of electronic computer component called the 'parametron' was invented by Ei-ichi Goto of the Faculty of Science, University of Tokyo, in spring of 1954. **1957** *Jrnl. Sci. Res. Inst.* (Tokyo) LI. 59 (*caption*) A parametron unit; an exciting current is supplied from 1, causing an oscillation in the L-L'-C circuit. Input and output lines are 2 and 3 respectively. **1960** T. E. Ivall *Electronic Computers* (ed. 2) xiii. 234 The parametron requires no valves or transistors, only passive reactive elements, and being therefore extremely stable, reliable and long-lived, is ideally suited for use in digital computers. The main limitation is that because several cycles of oscillation are required to establish a binary digit,..the digit rate is necessarily low. **1967** R. K. Richards *Electronic Digital Components & Circuits* vi. 337 Parametrons quickly became very popular with Japanese computer manufacturers... However, not one computer employing parametrons is known to have been built or designed in the United States.

paramilitary (pærəˈmɪlɪtərɪ), *a.* [f. para-^{1} + military *a.*] Of or pertaining to an organization, unit, force, etc., whose function or status is ancillary or analogous to that of military forces, but which is not a professional military force. Also as *sb.* Hence **para'militarism**.

1935 *Ann. Reg. 1934* 96 A difficult problem has been raised in regard to the so-called 'para-military training', *i.e.*, the military training outside the Army of men of military age. **1936** *Punch* 1 Apr. 376/1 Let us at once impale the new and unnecessary mongrel 'paramilitary'—'paramilitary forces (S.A., S.S., Labour Corps and other organisations)'. .. Why not 'semi-military', 'quasi-military', or even 'sub-military'? **1949** F. MACLEAN *Eastern Approaches* III. xvii. 516 The military and para-military forces which they [*sc.* the quisling administrations] had raised had either surrendered or else were withdrawing northwards. **1958** *Listener* 14 Aug. 238/2 The Nazi storm-trooper is preceded by a hardly less 'heroic' communist in his paramilitary uniform. **1962** *Times Lit. Suppl.* 16 Feb. 102/1 Lawrence of Arabia was almost a paramilitary symbol as long ago as 1917. **1969** *New Statesman* 11 Apr. 499/2 The Israelis were to receive unofficial guarantees that a UN presence, or paramilitary force as it was termed, would be stationed on the Israeli-Egyptian border. **1970** *New Yorker* 14 Feb. 33 An editorial in the Times..talked about the Panthers' 'Mao-Marxist ideology and Fascist paramilitarism'. **1972** J. MCCLURE *Caterpillar Cop* xii. 199 I'd forgotten you chappies were really a para-military outfit. **1974** J. WHITE tr. *Poulantzas's Fascism & Dictatorship* III. ii. 102 Party representation was short-circuited by the formation of para-military organizations. **1976** *Times* 9 Mar. 16/8 The para-militaries are no longer prepared to be used..unless they have a say in the running of the country [*sc.* Ulster]. **1976** *Listener* 16 Sept. 325/3 To change the climate within which the paramilitaries operate. **1977** M. WALKER *National Front* i. 18 Although Mussolini had specifically warned him against building a para-military force in Britain, Mosley was convinced..that he needed a corps of tough stewards to guarantee order at his meetings.

paramnesia, -ic: see PARA-¹ 1.

†**paramo** ('paraməʊ). [Sp. *páramo*; app. from a native lang. of Venezuela or New Granada.] A high plateau in the tropical parts of South America, bare of trees, and exposed to wind and thick cold fogs.

1760–72 tr. *Juan & Ulloa's Voy.* (ed. 3) I. 422 The most remarkable paramos or deserts of Quito. **1875** *Encycl. Brit.* I. 89/2 The Indian of the Andes..through whose rude straw hut the piercing wind of the paramos sweeps, and chills the white man to the very bone. **1901** A. H. KEANE *S. Amer.* I. 193 The Venezuelan and Columbian Paramo—a narrow zone of cold bleak terraces.

paramologetic, erron. f. PAROMOLOGETIC.

paramorph ('pærəmɔːf). *Min.* [mod. f. Gr. παρα- by- (see PARA-¹ 1) + μορφή form: lit. by-form, subsidiary form.] A pseudomorph formed by a change of physical characters without a change in chemical composition.

1879 in WEBSTER *Suppl.* **1892** *Amer. Naturalist* Jan. 55 Many of the supposed paramorphs have been proven..to be due..rather to the solution of some original substance and its replacement by a new deposition.

paramorphia, -morphine: see PARA-¹ 2.

paramorphic (ˌpærə'mɔːfɪk), *a.* *Min.* [f. as PARAMORPH + -IC.] Of or pertaining to a paramorph; characterized by paramorphism.

1886 DANA in *Amer. Jrnl. Sc.* Ser. III. XXXII. 315 This type of crystal [brookite] is the one which most frequently shows the paramorphic change to rutile. **1894** *Thinker* V. 342 Phenomena like the devitrification of natural glasses oscillate from paramorphic to pseudomorphic.

paramorphism (pærə'mɔːfɪz(ə)m). *Min.* [f. as prec. + -ISM.] The change of one mineral to another having the same chemical composition but a different molecular structure.

1868 DANA *Min.* (ed. 5) 697 Aragonite..passes to calcite, through paramorphism. **1889** *Nature* 21 Nov. 49/1 Paramorphism..includes those changes within the rock-mass, involving changes in the chemical composition of the original minerals and the formation of new minerals.

paramorphosis (pærəmɔː'fəʊsɪs). *Min* [f. Gr. παραμορφό-ειν to transform, distort: see PARAMORPH and -OSIS.] = prec.

1890 in *Cent. Dict.*

paramorphous (pærə'mɔːfəs), *a.* *Min.* [f. as prec. + -OUS.] = PARAMORPHIC.

1882 in OGILVIE.

paramoudra (pærə'muːdrə). *Geol.* [Suggested by H. Norton (1881 *Proc. Norwich Geol. Soc.* I. 132) to be Anglo-Irish corruption of Erse *peura muireach* ('pɛrə 'murjəx) 'sea pears', from their shape, and occurrence on the beach below chalk cliffs.] A name given to large flints, pear-shaped, barrel-shaped, or cylindrical (sometimes 3 ft. long and 1 ft. thick), perforated with a central axial cavity, found standing erect in the chalk of the N.E. of Ireland (where the name is local) and of Norfolk (where known as *pot-stones*).

1817 BUCKLAND in *Trans. Geol. Soc.* IV. 413 These singular fossils..are known at Belfast by the name of Paramoudra, a word which I..shall adopt because I find it thus appropriated. They have, I believe, never yet been found in England, except at Whittingham near to Norwich. **1887** H. B. WOODWARD *Geol. Eng. & Wales* (ed. 2) 399 These flints are known as 'Pot-stones' or 'Paramoudras'. *Ibid.*, The most celebrated exposure of Paramoudras was in a pit at Horstead on the river Bure..in 1838.

paramount ('pærəmaʊnt), *a.* (*sb.*) Also 6–7 pera-, 7 pere-. [a. AF. *paramont, peramont* above (in place, order, or degree), f. OF. *par* by + *amont, à mont* adv., up, above (of motion or position):— L. *ad montem* to the mount or hill. In AFr. *paramont* had the simple sense 'above', e.g. in local position, on a page, or in a book:

1381 GOWER *Mirour* 10017 Il fist le mariage Jadis du Siecle a son lignage Comme je vous contay paramont.]

A. *adj.* **1.** Above in a scale of rank or authority; superior. **a.** In *lord paramount*, lord superior; overlord; *spec.* the supreme lord of a fee, from whom other feudatories hold, but who himself holds from none; hence *transf.* one who exercises supreme power or jurisdiction. So *lady paramount*, a woman in supreme authority; also *transf.* the lady who has made the highest score in an archery tournament.

[**1339** *Year-Bk. 13 Edw. III*, Trin. (Rolls) 307 La mort le chef seigneur paramont nest rien a vous. *a* **1481** LITTLETON *Tenures* ii. § 19 (1516) A iij, Autielx seruices come le donnour fait a son seignur prochaine a luy paramont [*tr.* 1544, etc., Such seruices as yᵉ donour doth vnto his lord next aboue]. **1528** J. PERKINS *Profitable Booke* v. § 430 Mes si en mesme le case le seignur paramont relees tout son droit en le tenancye al heire, par cest releas le menalte est determine [*tr.* 1642, p. 185, If in the same case the Lord paramount release unto the heire all his right in the tenancy, by this release the Menaltie is determined].]

1579 FENTON *Guicciard.* I. (1599) 5 Quarrels..betweene the vassall and the Lord Peramount. **1592** WARNER *Alb. Eng.* VIII. xliii. (1612) 207 With Scots..Who to our Kings, Lords Parramounts, not warres but vprores bring. **1628** COKE *On Litt.* 65 The King is soueraigne Lord, or Lord paramont, either mediate or immediate of all and euery parcell of Land within the Realme. **1642** CHAS. I *Answ. Declar.* 26 May in Clarendon *Hist. Reb.* v. § 287 Was not the Interest of the Lord Paramount consistent with that of the Mesne Lord? **1647** DIGGES *Unlawf. Taking Arms* xiv. 116 He..made all..feudaries to him, so that he remained ..*Lord Paramount, or overlord* in the whole Land. **1727** A. HAMILTON *New Acc. E. Ind.* I. xxiii. 275 Built, of old, by the Portugueze, when they were Lords Paramount of all the Sea-coasts of India. **1851** DIXON *W. Penn* xxiii. (1872) 202 Penn was now become the lord paramount of territories almost as large as England. **1865** LIVINGSTONE *Zambesi* v. 108 Part of the Upper Shire Valley has a lady paramount, named Nyango. **1903** *Ross Gaz.* 10 Sept. 3/4 The prizes were..given away by Lady F. who was the Lady Paramount of the afternoon.

b. *generally.* Above others in rank or order; highest in power or jurisdiction; supreme.

1531 *Dial. on Laws Eng.* II. xxxvi. 73 Thei saye that the kyng is patrone peramounte of all the benifices within the realme. **1613** PURCHAS *Pilgrimage* (1614) 406 He.. proceedeth with the gouernours of Persia, whether Paramont or deputed. **1799–1805** S. TURNER *Anglo-Sax.* I. III. iii. 170 There appears..to have been a paramount sovereign; a Pen-dragon, or Penteyrn. **1828** SCOTT *F.M. Perth* xxvii, The Clan Chattan..having for their paramount chief the powerful earl of the latter shire. **1841** MACAULAY *Ess., W. Hastings* (1851) 618 To make Britain the paramount power in India.

c. *paramount chief*, esp. in African countries, a tribal chief of the highest order, whose authority extends over an entire district.

1844 in F. Brownlee *Transkeian Native Territories: Hist. Rec.* (1923) 92 Treaty of Amity entered into..on behalf of Her Britannic Majesty, of the one part, and Faku, Paramount Chief of the Amapondo Nation. *a* **1882** G. W. STOW *Native Races S. Afr.* (1905) x. 183 They acknowledged a Bushman captain..as their great chief, who ..was succeeded by 'Khiba, or 'Kheba, who was the paramount chief over the men of the caves. **1885** in F. Brownlee *Transkeian Native Territories: Hist. Rec.* (1923) 20 Some of these clans..depended directly upon the paramount chief, others were grouped under a sub-chief. **1919** G. M. THEAL *Ethnogr. & Condit. S. Afr. before 1505* (ed. 2) x. 212 Sometimes the heads of the clans were members of the family of the paramount chief. **1928** G. P. LESTRADE in A. M. Duggan-Cronin *Bantu Tribes S. Afr.* I. I. 18 The petty chiefs, each of whom is responsible to the paramount chief for the maintenance of good order in his section of the tribe, share in..privileges at the chief's pleasure. **1948** B. G. M. SUNDKLER *Bantu Prophets S. Afr.* ii. 38 As the Queen of England was the head of the English Church, so the Paramount Chief of the Tembu should be the *summus episcopus* of the new religious organization. **1954** E. A. HOEBEL *Law of Primitive Man* viii. 193 Every village, which belongs to a subclan, has its headman... If an ordinary headman, a lesser chief..his powers extend only to the boundaries of his own village. If he is a full chief..his influence will spread over several villages and their subchiefs. If he is a paramount chief among the full chiefs, it will extend over an entire district. **1957** P. WORSLEY *Trumpet shall Sound* vi. 119 Three of the Paramount Chiefs failed to report the movement to Government. **1965** A. NICOL *Truly Married Woman* 87 His main preoccupation was to find ways of slighting the neighbouring and more powerful provincial Paramount Chief. **1971** *Rand Daily Mail* 4 Dec. 3/4 No member of your Government should consider his position to be more important and exalted than that of the Paramount Chief. **1974** *Afr. Encycl.* 505/1 The policy of 'separate development'..which led to the establishment of the Transkei has been opposed by the leader of the 'True' Thembu, Paramount Chief Saberta Dalinyebo. **1976** *Times* 26 Oct. 8/4 Dr. Nicolaas Diederichs, the President of South Africa, handed over a copy of the Transkei Act to the country's first Prime Minister, Paramount Chief Kaiser Matanzima.

2. a. In more general sense: Superior to all others in influence, power, position, or importance; pre-eminent.

1639 FULLER *Holy War* III. xix. (1840) 148 The pope that antichrist paramount. *a* **1661** FULLER *Worthies* (1840) III. 316 The Cathedral of Salisbury..is paramount in this kind. **1684** T. BURNET *Th. Earth* II. 141 He can, by a power paramount, stop the rage either of Satan or Antichrist. **1784** COWPER *Task* VI. 583 Man's..rights and claims Are paramount. **1816** COLERIDGE *Statesm. Man* 359 Sir Philip Sydney—he the paramount gentleman of Europe. **1849** GROTE *Greece* II. liv. VI. 619 The paramount feeling.. tended to peace. **1868** GLADSTONE *Juv. Mundi* iii. (1870) 74 The Achaians were paramount, and the Pelasgoi were subordinate members of one and the same community. **1877** J. D. CHAMBERS *Divine Worhsip* 229 Matters of paramount importance.

b. Const. *to.*

1625 BACON *Ess., Of Faction*, Leagues within the State are euer Pernicious to Monarchies; For they raise an Obligation Paramount to Obligation of Soueraigntie. **1690** LOCKE *Govt.* I. xi. (Rtldg.) 126 A right antecedent and paramount to all government. **1769** *Junius Lett.* xi. 47 Their first duty..is paramount to all subsequent engagements. **1844** LD. BROUGHAM *Brit. Const.* xv. (1862) 220 They regarded the title by hereditary succession as paramount to any legislative enactment.

c. With ellipsis of *to.*

1596 BACON *Max. Com. Law* i. (1636) 3 In any degree paramount the first the law respecteth not. **1636** PRYNNE *Unbish. Tim.* (1661) 29 Having no superintendent paramount them. **1643** —— *Treach. & Disloyalty* I. 6 A Generall Councell is paramount the Pope. **1882** BROWN *Scriven's Law Copyholds* (ed. 6) 25 Not..good as against a dowress, whose dower is paramount the debts.

B. *sb.* = Lord paramount; overlord; supreme ruler or proprietor.

c **1645** HOWELL *Lett.* I. v. xii. (1650) 150 (*Hymn*) Blest maid which..raignst as Paramount, And chief of Cherubins. **1667** MILTON *P.L.* II. 508 Midst came thir mighty Paramount. **1779** FORREST *Voy. N. Guinea* 327 Those paramounts claim the property of the banks, as wel as of the dry land. **1839** *Fraser's Mag.* XX. 41 The parded paramount of Rome hath rung The knell of onslaught.

Hence **'paramountly** *adv.*, pre-eminently, chiefly, above all; **'paramountship**, paramountcy.

1818 COLERIDGE in *Lit. Rem.* (1836) I. 216 Man communicates by articulation of sounds, and *paramountly by the memory in the ear. **1822** *Examiner* 185/2 Such active instinctiveness of character, as paramountly lives in the canvass of E. Landseer. **1962** S. E. FINER *Man on Horseback* v. 65 The so-called 'Free Officers'..regrouped and decided to overthrow the régime, and paramountly the king who headed it. **1971** *Country Life* 19 Aug. 464/1 The tragedy is that man..still constitutes..the paramountly weak link. **1735** J. KIRBY *Suffolk Trav.* (1764) 154 He is only the mean Lord, Sir Thomas Allen hath a *Paramountship over him. **1898** *Daily News* 23 Aug. 5/1 Four young native [Basuto] chiefs, including the heir to the paramountship.

†**'paramount**, *v.* *Obs. rare*⁻¹. [f. PARAMOUNT *a.*] *intr.* To become paramount, to rise to the highest place.

1697 POTTER *Antiq. Greece* IV. xi. (1715) 274 And dost thou think, thou dirty, servile Woman, To paramount, to cast me out?

paramountcy ('pærəmaʊntsɪ). Also **paramouncy**. [f. PARAMOUNT + -CY: *paramouncy* is formally more analogical; cf. *tenant, -ancy, frequent, -ency.*] The condition or status of being paramount.

1667 WATERHOUSE *Fire Lond.* 90 And add to her Paramouncy of renown. *a* **1834** COLERIDGE *Notes & Lect.* (1849) I. 278 If it were possible to lessen the paramountcy of Volpone himself. **1890** W. WALLACE *Life Schopenhauer* 181 That metaphysical doctrine of the essential paramountcy of the will. **1897** H. M. STANLEY in *19th Cent.* Apr. 513 British Paramouncy over the S. African Republic is acknowledged in the [Conventions of 1881 and 1884].

paramour ('pærəmʊə(r)), *adv. phr.* and *sb.* Forms: see below. [ME. a. OF. adv. phr. *par amur, amour, -s*, by or through love. From an early date the phrase was written as one word, and came to be treated (in Eng.) as a sb., both in sense of 'love' and 'beloved, lover'. This may have come partly through a mistaken analysis of the phrase *to love paramour, -s.*]

A. *adv. phr.* Forms: 3–4 **par amur, -s**, 4 **par amour, -s, per amour, -s; paramur, -s**, 4–6 **paramour, -s** (5 **paramoure, -es, -is**, 5–6 **paramor, -s, -owre**, 6 **-owris**, 5 (7) **-ore**).

†**1.** Through or by way of love; out of (your) love, for love's sake (cf. LOVE *sb.*¹ 7); sometimes in weakened sense, Of your kindness, as a favour, if you please. *Obs.*

Perh. sometimes orig. short for 'for love of God'.

13.. *Sir Beues* (MS. A.) 118 'Felawe', a saide, 'par amur: Whar mai ich finde þemperur?' **13..** *Seuyn Sag.* (W.) 1455 A! lat me in, sire, paramour! **13..** *Coer de L.* 453 Tel me the sothe, I yow prey, Off these joustes, peramours. **14..** *Recovery of Throne by Edw. IV* in *Pol. Poems* (Rolls) II. 280 He hathe deservid thancke amonge other paramour. **1611** SPEED *Hist. Gt. Brit.* IX. xxiv. § 143 The Lord Chiefe Iustice stood vp, and forbade the proceedings, alotting Paramour the Lands, with the satisfying of the Plaintifes.

†**2.** For or by way of sexual love. *Obs.* (or *arch.*)

c **1386** CHAUCER *Sir Thopas* 32 They moorne for hym paramour Whan hem were bet to slepe. **1825** SCOTT *Betrothed* xxvii, She is one I could have doated to death upon *par amours*. **1848** LYTTON *Harold* VI. vi, Some infidel, to one of whose wives he sought to be gallant, *par amours*.

†**b.** Phrase. *to love par amour* (*amours*): (Usually) To love by way of (sexual) love, to love (a person of the opposite sex), to love amorously or as a lover, to be in love with; sometimes, to have a clandestine or illicit amour with.

In some later instances *paramours* may have been taken as sb., and object of the vb.: cf. B. 2.

a **1300** *Floriz & Bl.* 486 Ho þat luueþ par amur And haþ þer-of ioye mai luue flures. *a* **1300** *Cursor M.* 52 For now is halden non in curs Bot qua þat luue can paramurs [*later MSS.* -ours, -ouris]. *a* **1310** in Wright *Lyric P.* xxxi. 91 Y lovede a clerk al par amours. **1375** BARBOUR *Bruce* XIII. 485 He his sister paramouris Lufit. *c* **1386** CHAUCER *Knt.'s T.* 297, I telle thee outrely ffor paramour I loued hire first er thow. *c* **1410** *Sir Cleges* 489 Sir Cleges..That I lovyd peramore. *c* **1430** *Syr Gener.* (Roxb.) 4553 He loueth paramoures som wight. **1430–40** LYDG. *Bochas* VIII. xxvii. (1558) 19 Aboue al women loued her peramour. **1483** CAXTON *G. de la Tour* L iij, To loue peramours eche other. **1531** ELYOT *Gov.* III. xxii, The same lady [Cleopatra] Antoni ..loued also peramours, abandonynge his wyfe. **1535** COVERDALE *Baruch* vi. 8 Like as a wench y^t loueth peramours is trymly deckte. *c* **1560** A. SCOTT *Poems* (S.T.S.) iii. 46 And swa but pane ȝe may lufe paramowris. *Ibid.* xxix. 6 For mony men ar evill to ken, þat luvis paramour, W^t fenȝeit mynd, fals and vnkynd, Bringis ȝow to dishonour. [**1652** ASHMOLE *Theat. Chem.* 200 Sche loveth him peramore and no other.]

B. *sb.* Forms: 3– paramour, 4–5 -amours (5–6 -is; 4, 6–7 -or, 4, 8 -ore, 5–6 -oure, per-).

†**1.** Love; *esp.* sexual love, an amour. *Obs.*

c **1350** *Will. Palerne* 1412 He..layked him at likyng wiþ þat faire burde Pleyes of paramours vn-parceyued longe time, So sliliche, þat no seg souched non ille. *c* **1386** CHAUCER *Cook's T.* 8 He was as ful of love & paramour As is the hyve ful of hony sweete. —— *Merch. T.* 206 By cause of leueful procreacion Of children..And nat oonly for paramour or loue. *c* **1470** HENRYSON *Mor. Fab.* iii. (*Fox & Cock*) 110 In all this warld was thair na kyndar thing; In paramouris he wald do ws plesing. *a* **1586** MONTGOMERIE *Misc. Poems* l. 27 Pigmaleon, that ane portratour Be painting craft, did sa decoir, Himself thairwith in paramour Fell suddanlie, and smert thairfoir.

†**b.** In devotional use, Divine or celestial love: cf. 2 b. *Obs.*

13.. *Salut. Our Lady* 45 in *Minor Poems fr. Vernon MS.* 135 Heil puyred princesse of paramour, Heil Blosme of Brere, Brihtest of ble.

2. A person beloved by one of the opposite sex; a 'love', a lover, a sweetheart; also of animals (quots. 1735, 1801) and *fig. arch.* and *poet.*

c **1350** *Will. Palerne* 1534 Mi perles paramours my pleye & my ioye, Spek to me spakli or i spille sone. **1393** LANGL. *P. Pl.* C. XVII. 107 A mayde for a mannes loue her moder forsakeþ,..and gooþ forth with hure paramour. *c* **1489** CAXTON *Blanchardyn* xxiii. 78 Ye knowe well my lady paramours, and that she is of your lynage. **1535** STEWART *Cron. Scot.* (1856) II. 514 Ane fair ȝoung man, Hir peramouris quhilk in the tyme wes than. ? *a* **1550** *Knight of Curtesy* 45 in Ritson *Metr. Rom.* III. 195 His paramour she thought to be, Hym for to love wyth herte and minde, Nat in vyce but in chastyte. **1590** SPENSER *F.Q.* I. i. 9 The Willow, worne of forlorne Paramours. **1629** MILTON *Nativity* 36 To wanton with the Sun her lusty Paramour. **1735** SOMERVILLE *Chase* IV. 58 Huntsman!..For ev'ry longing Dame select Some happy Paramour. **1801** SOUTHEY *Thalaba* IV. i, Pale reflection..Of glow-worm on the bank, Kindled to guide her winged paramour. **1871** R. ELLIS *Catullus* lxi. 44 Lord of fair paramours, of youth's Fair affection uniter.

†**b.** Formerly, in devotional language, applied (by men) to the Virgin, and (by women) to Jesus Christ; sometimes also to God. *Obs.*

a **1300** *Cursor M.* 69 For-þi blisce [I] þat paramour..Hyr luue is ay ilike new. *c* **1375** *Sc. Leg. Saints* l. (*Katerine*) 1118 My dere lord Ihesu criste..þat is my luf and paramor. *c* **1475** *Songs & Carols 15th C.* (Warton Club) 48 To his moder then gan he [Christ] say,..My swete moder, myn paramour. **1492** RYMAN *Poems* lxvii. 2 in *Archiv Stud. neu. Spr.* LXXXIX. 235 [Mary to Christ] Myne owne dere sonne and paramoure. **1581** MARBECK *Bk. of Notes* 1171 Thus prune and pricke vp your selues, and God himselfe shall be your paramour.

c. The lady-love of a knight, for whose love he did battle; hence, the object of chivalrous admiration and attachment. *poet.*

1503 DUNBAR *Thistle & Rose* 180 The commoun voce vpraiss of birdis small,..Welcome to be our princes of honour, Our perle, our plesans and our paramour. *c* **1590** GREENE *Fr. Bacon* vi. 37 Suffice to me he's Englands paramour. **1593** G. HARVEY *Pierce's Super.* 33 He may declare his deere affection to his Paramour [i.e. Greene] or his pure honesty to the world. **1630** B. JONSON *Chloridia* ad fin., Chloris, the queen of flowers:..The top of paramours.

3. An illicit or clandestine lover or mistress taking the place, but without the rights, of a husband or wife. Now, the illicit partner of a married man or woman.

c **1386** CHAUCER *Wife's Prol.* 454 My fourthe housbonde was a reuelour This is to seyn he hadde a paramour. *c* **1400** MAUNDEV. (1839) iv. 24 He seyde, he wolde ben hire lemman or paramour. **1483** CAXTON *G. de la Tour* L ij, Ones he was gone for to see his paramours in the wynter. *a* **1548** HALL *Chron., Edw. IV* 193 b, She might so fortune of his peramour and concubyne to be chaunged to his wyfe & lawfull bedfelow. **1598** DRAYTON *Heroic. Ep.* vii. 175, I sue not now thy Paramour to bee, But as a Husband to be link'd to thee. **1664** H. MORE *Myst. Iniq.* 257 Pranking up themselves to allure their Paramours. **1816** J. SCOTT *Vis. Paris* (ed. 5) 85 A woman can seldom possess a lover before marriage, and is as seldom without a variety of paramours after. **1832** G. DOWNES *Lett. Cont. Countries* I. 224 A Russian princess..poisoned by Catherine II, who had her husband for a paramour.

[**paramour** *v.*, 'to love' is given in some Dicts. on the strength of the subjoined passage; but prob. 'loueth' has been accidentally omitted by the scribe.

c **1450** *Merlin* 47, I knowe a faire lady that Vter paramours. [Cf. *Ibid.* 9 That she loued the holy man paramours.]

paramuthetic (pærəmjuːˈθɛtɪk), *a.* [prop. *paramythetic*, ad. Gr. παραμυθητικ-ός, f. παραμυθεῖσθαι to encourage, console, f. παρα- beside + μυθεῖσθαι to speak.] Tending to encourage, consolatory.

1854 MAURICE *Mor. & Met. Philos.* II. ii. §12. 47 The discipline of the habits or character he [Clemens] would call protreptic, of the actions hypothetic, of the passions paramuthetic.

paramylene to **-naphthalene**: see PARA-[1].

paramyxovirus (pærəˈmɪksəʊvaɪərəs). *Biol.* [f. PARA-[1] + MYXOVIRUS.] Any of a group of related viruses which includes the para-influenza viruses and those causing mumps, measles, distemper, and rinderpest, and which differ from the myxoviruses in their larger and more variable size and in being hæmolytic.

1962 [see MYXOVIRUS]. **1968** *Times* 27 Nov. 9/3 Mumps, a disease which is caused by one of the paramyxoviruses. **1969** A. COHEN *Textbk. Med. Virol.* vi. 71 Myxoviruses are characterized by particles whose size varies from 800 to 1100 Å in diameter, and whose helical internal component is 90 Å wide and lightly packed inside the envelope. Paramyxoviruses..are characterized by larger sized particles, 1000–5000 Å in diameter, whose internal component is 180 Å wide and more loosely packed within the virus envelope. Morphological differences between myxoviruses and paramyxoviruses are associated with some differences of biological activity. **1974** [see MYXOVIRUS].

Parana (pəˈrɑːnə). Also **Paraná**. The name of a river and a province in Brazil, used *attrib.*, usu. in **Parana pine**, to designate a large evergreen tree, *Araucaria angustifolia*, of the family Pinaceæ, found in the high plateau region of south-western Brazil, Paraguay, and northern Argentina; also, the light-coloured, softwood timber obtained from this tree.

1923 DALLIMORE & JACKSON *Handbk. Coniferæ* 153 Araucaria brasiliensis, Loudon. Parana Pine; Parana Wood. **1924** RECORD & MELL *Timbers Trop. Amer.* II. 92 The Paraná pine is the most extensively exploited timber in South America. **1959** *Archit. Rev.* CXXV. 333/2 Natural wood, parana pine, oak and western red cedar. **1964** *Listener* 17 Sept. 428/3 Paraná pine..—highly polished—forms the glistening verandah floor. **1971** N. E. HICKIN *Wood Preservation* 15 *Araucaria angustifolia* from Argentina and South Brazil is Parana Pine. **1977** *Irish Press* 29 Sept. 16/1 (Advt.), Unique solid Parana Pine bunk beds, £59.

paranasal: see PARA-[1] 1.

paranatal (pærəˈneɪtəl), *a. Med.* [f. PARA-[1] + NATAL *a.*[1] and *sb.*[1]] Of or pertaining to the time shortly before and after birth.

Orig. given a broader meaning (quot. 1940).

1940 F. SCHREIBER in *Jrnl. Pediatrics* XVI. 297 (*heading*) Neurologic sequelae of paranatal asphyxia. [*Note*] The term *paranatal* has been coined to designate the entire period of fetal life, the period of birth, and the neonatal period within which the results of occurrences during the first two periods may become manifest. **1954** *Jrnl. Amer. Med. Assoc.* 19 June 719/1 Proponents of the brain injury hypothesis state that in most cases anoxia during the prenatal and paranatal periods has resulted in brain damage. **1964** *Jrnl. Nerv. & Mental Dis.* CXXXIX. 357 (*heading*) Pre- and paranatal factors in mental disorders of children. **1971** C. B. COURVILLE *Birth & Brain Damage* xi. 197 (*caption*) Gliosis, the most significant tissue reaction in paranatal anoxia. **1976** *Word 1971* XXVII. 62 The developing human foetus..is 'practicing', in amniotic fluid, those neuromuscular gestures which will lead, in air, to paranatal cry and neonatal cry specifically.

paranatellon (pərænəˈtɛlɒn). *Astrol.* [f. Gr. παρα- beside + ἀνατέλλων rising.] A star that rises at the same time as another star or stars.

1811 SIR. W. DRUMMOND *Œdipus Judaicus* xxvii, Now the extra-zodiacal stars,..which rise above the horizon, or sink below it, during the time that decan takes to rise or set, are what I call its paranatellions. **1882** MARY LOCKWOOD tr. *Lenormant's Beginn. Hist.* 568 *note*, The twelve stars..are astronomically the paranatellons of the signs [of the Zodiac].

parance, parand, var. PARENCE, PARENT *a.*

paranema to **paranephritis**: see PARA-[1] 1.

paranemic (pærəˈniːmɪk), *a.* [f. PARA-[1] + Gr. νῆμα thread + -IC.] Of, pertaining to, or designating two or more like helices coiled together side by side in such a way that they may be fully separated without being unwound. Opp. PLECTONEMIC *a.*

1941 [see PLECTONEMIC *a.*]. **1950** *Biol. Rev.* XXV. 500 Until quite recently almost all observers were agreed that the plectonemic spiral was characteristic of mitosis and the paranemic of meiosis (meaning the first meiotic division). **1953** WATSON & CRICK in *Cold Spring Harbor Symp. Quant. Biol.* XVIII. 129/2 With paranemic coiling, the specific pairing of bases [in DNA] would not allow the successive residues of each helix to be in equivalent orientation with regard to the helical axis. **1974** F. CRICK in *Nature* 26 Apr. 767/2 Looking back, I think we deserve some credit..for our forthright stand against paranemic (as opposed to plectonemic) coiling.

‖**paranete** (pærəˈniːtiː). Also 7 **-neate**. [L. a. Gr. παρανήτη, f. παρα- beside + νήτη the highest in pitch of three strings.] In ancient Gr. music, The note next below the nete in either the disjunct or the upper tetrachord.

1603 HOLLAND *Plutarch* Explan. Words, *Paranete Hyperbolæan*, a treble string or note in musicke. **1660** STANLEY *Hist. Philos.* IX. (1701) 386/1. **1694** W. HOLDER *Harmony* (1731) 104 The Lichanos, Parypate, Paranete, and Trite, are changeable. **1898** STAINER & BARRETT *Dict. Mus. Terms* s.v. *Greek Music*, The scale..for the eight stringed lyre upon the Egyptian or Octave System..Upper Tetrachord. e. Nete. d. Paranete. c. Trite. b. Paramese.

‖**parang** (ˈpɑːræŋ). [Malay *pārang*.] A large heavy sheath-knife used by the Malays for various purposes, esp. as a weapon.

1839 [see KLEYWANG]. **1852** *P. Parley's Ann.* 371 He observed..in the hand of a native woodman, a parang, or wood chopper. **1882** DE WINDT *Equator* 103 Bakar..and a Malay boatman preceded us with parangs to clear the way of branches before us. **1892** *Pall Mall G.* 18 Oct. 4/2 The pirates, who were armed with spears and parangs, showed fight. **1966** D. FORBES *Heart of Malaya* v. 60 A full-blooded *amok*, slaughtering every man, woman and child in reach with the snaky kris or the curved parang. **1967** J. CLEARY *Long Pursuit* iii. 81 They cut branches from the mangroves with a parang they had found in the boat. **1972** [see JACK *sb.*[4] b]. **1976** 'G. BLACK' *Moon for Killers* ix. 109 The rent in the cloudbank..its edges as rough as a wound made with a *parang*.

Comb. **1899** W. H. FURNESS *Folk-lore Borneo* 7 This parang-handle sank deep into the rock.

parangi (pəˈræŋgɪ). Also 9 **parangy**. [Sinhalese *parangi* (*lede*), lit. '(disease of) foreigners', i.e. the Portuguese (= Skr. *phiraṅga* 'Frankish', European), f. Pg. *Frangue*, name given by the Moors to Frenchmen, Spaniards, and European Christians generally (cf. FERINGHEE).] The name given in Sri Lanka to a disease now known to be identical with yaws.

1821 H. MARSHALL *Notes Med. Topogr. Interior Ceylon* iii. 43 There is a complaint mentioned in the Kandyan medical works, called *parangy lede* (Parangy disease). *Ibid.*, *Parangy lede* seems to have been originally intended to denominate a new disease;..it may perhaps be inferred that the term meant Portuguese disease. There is, however, no tradition among the Kandyans respecting the importation of a disease. *Ibid.* 44 Many of the cutaneous affections which they denominate *parangy*, are evidently herpetic, and cannot be referred to a syphilitic origin. **1882** *Med. Times & Gaz.* 14 Jan. 30/1 The diseases which parangi resembles are syphilis and its various manifestations, lupus leprosy, and frambœsia. **1913** L. WOOLF *Village in Jungle* i. 11 There were few in the village without the filthy sores of parangi, their legs eaten out to the bone with the yellow, sweating ulcers.

paraniline, etc.: see PARA-[1] 2.

‖**paranjah** (pærənˈdʒɑː). [a. Russ. *parandzhá*, ult. f. Arabic.] A long wide robe with a (horse-)hair veil worn by Muslim women.

1928 *Daily Express* 7 Dec. 9 The women, completely covered from head to foot by the hideous 'paranjas' (veils), watch the proceedings from the far off roof-tops. **1947** *New Times* 20 June 24/2 In the streets of Sarajevo you may meet Moslem women wearing the paranja. But you needn't be surprised if the muffled figure under the black horsehair veil turns out to be a local women's leader. **1954** KOESTLER *Invis. Writing* II. xii. 141 The doors of the harems were thrown wide open; the sack-like *paranjahs* and black veils fell.

paranoia (pærəˈnɔɪə). *Path.* 9 **paranœa**. [mod.L. a. Gr. παράνοια, f. παράνο-ος distracted, f. παρα- beside + νό-ος, νοῦς mind.] Mental derangement; *spec.* chronic mental unsoundness characterized by delusions or hallucinations, esp. of grandeur, persecution, etc. The various forms of the disorder are now usu. considered as belonging to the schizophrenic group of mental illness. Also in trivial use.

1811 R. HOOPER *Lexicon Medicum* 596/2 *Paranœa*, alienation of the mind; defect of judgment. **1848** DUNGLISON *Dict. Med. Sci.* (ed. 7) 625/2 *Paranœa*, delirium, dementia. **1857** MAYNE *Expos. Lex.*, *Paranœa*. **1891** *N.Y. Tribune* 1 Dec. 3/3 (Funk), I should designate his trouble as paranoia. **1892** *Review of Rev.* 15 July 56/1 Paranoia bears fruit in delusions of persecution, or hallucinations, or delusions of grandeur. **1899** J. FISKE *Cranks* in *Atlantic Monthly* Mar., A clear instance of the megalomania which is a well-known symptom of paranoia. **1918** [see *neuropsychosis* s.v. NEURO-]. **1940** HINSIE & SHATZKY *Psychiatric Dict.* 395/2 Perhaps no term in psychiatry has undergone wider variations of meaning than the term paranoia. **1954** W. MAYER-GROSS et al. *Clin. Psychiatry* iv. 158 Much of the age-old controversy on 'paranoia' has arisen from the difficulty of distinguishing between paranoid reactions and paranoid schizophrenia. *Ibid.* vi. 256 The effort to maintain paranoia as a distinct condition has also failed. **1957** V. NABOKOV *Pnin* iv. 96 There is nothing more banal and more bourgeois than paranoia. **1970** HINSIE & CAMPBELL *Psychiatric Dict.* (ed. 4) 540/2 Several types of paranoia have been described on the basis of the type of delusion that predominates: litigious, depressed, persecutory, grandiose, erotic.., and infidelity. *Ibid.* 541/2 The patient with amorous paranoia develops delusions of marital infidelity in relation to his spouse. **1972** *Encycl. Psychol.* II. 366/1 Paranoia...was thought to be distinct from the group of schizophrenias because it did not lead to deterioration. This is not now thought to be the case. **1977** *Time* 16 May 56/3

They constitute what has become a standard trip down paranoia lane.

para'noiac, *a.* and *sb.* 9 **para'nœac.** **a.** *adj.* Afflicted with paranoia; **b.** *sb.* A paranoiac person.

1892 *Review of Rev.* 15 July 56/1 The select portion of the paranoiac race. *Ibid.*, The paranoiac suffers from a steady degeneration of the brain through hallucinations and delusions towards the delusion of grandeur. **1899** *Allbutt's Syst. Med.* VIII. 399 The paranoiac is the victim of foul wrong, he is proud, defiant, and self-centred. **1902** [see ASSOCIATION 9]. **1914** A. A. BRILL tr. *Freud's Psychopathol. Everyday Life* xii. 309 The gap between the paranoiac's displacement and that of superstition is narrower than appears at first sight. **1935** D. GASCOYNE *Short Survey Surrealism* v. 102 Dali claims that it is the paranoiac faculty that enables him to discover a head where there was, until he looked at it, only an African village. **1937** *Brit. Jrnl. Psychol.* XXVII. 245 It has frequently been suggested that those who come much in contact with paranoiacs tend themselves in time to exhibit paranoid symptoms. **1952** A. HUXLEY *Let.* 20 May (1969) 645 Boastful in an altogether childish way, mildly paranoiac, but well-meaning. **1977** A. SHERIDAN tr. *Lacan's Écrits* i. 3 The social dialectic that structures human knowledge as paranoiac. **1978** J. BLACKBURN *Dead Man's Handle* i. 20 Paranoiacs and schizophrenics like George Heath and Neville Haigh, and the Boston Strangler.

Hence **para'noiacally** *adv.*, in a paranoiac manner.

1964 P. F. ANSON *Bishops at Large* vi. 213 He continued to build castles in the air, . . paranoiacally refusing to face up to reality. **1976** *Listener* 22 Apr. 505/1 The girl next door is already out there, doing her yoga and singing paranoiacally.

para'noic, *a.* 9 **para'nœic.** = PARANOIAC *a.*

1857 MAYNE *Expos. Lex.*, *Paranoicus*, of or belonging to Paranœa: paranoic. **1952** W. J. H. SPROTT *Social Psychol.* 244 The Haida Chief whose relative has died suspects supernatural persecution; with us he would be labelled 'paranoic' and sent for 'treatment'. **1977** *Times Lit. Suppl.* 15 Apr. 462/2 His paranoic dislike not only of Robert Ferguson. *Ibid.* 1 July 799/3 The paranoic fantasies to which Bely was prey in 1916, when he believed that he was a 'human bomb', under surveillance from a 'dark-skinned man in a bowler hat'.

Hence **para'noically** *adv.*

1976 *Times Lit. Suppl.* 28 May 648/1 The outline of a paranoically hostile Soviet Union.

paranoid ('pærənɔɪd), *a.* and *sb.* [Irreg. f. PARANOIA + -OID.] **A.** *adj.* Resembling or characterized by paranoia; also used *colloq.*, *transf.*, and *fig.* So **para'noidal** *a.*

1904 *Brit. Med. Jrnl.* 15 Oct. 972 The collective grouping of hebephrenia, katanoia, and the paranoid forms makes so vast a congeries that it is impossible to perceive any connecting link between the items of the mass. **1904** tr. *Kraepelin's Lect. Clin. Psychiatry* 151 Paranoidal forms of Dementia Præcox. **1919** R. M. BARCLAY tr. *Kraepelin's Dementia Praecox & Paraphrenia* 195 Paranoid Weak-mindedness. *Ibid.* 252 Paranoid Forms. *Ibid.* 253 Delusions and hallucinations of quite the same kind, as we see them in paranoid cases, occur also in most of the remaining forms of dementia præcox. **1954** KOESTLER *Invis. Writing* xxv. 270 The paranoid tendencies inherent in the movement. **1961** L. MUMFORD *City in Hist.* ii. 39 A paranoid psychal structure was preserved and transmitted by the walled city. **1967** M. ARGYLE *Psychol. Interpersonal Behaviour* viii. 135 *Paranoid reactions* are closely related to schizophrenia. Where there is personality disintegration but with rather more systematic delusions this is called paranoid schizophrenia. **1970** *Guardian Weekly* 28 Feb. 19/1 The sort of international news letters run by paranoid ex-generals. **1974** *Guardian* 13 June 10/3 Those paranoid placards with their Red Rats and Hot Seats for Traitors and Fry 'em.

B. *sb.* A person afflicted with, or showing symptoms of, paranoia.

1922 *Brit. Jrnl. Psychol.* Oct. 113 In discussing the case of paranoids, Neisser writes, 'the patient is progressively less able to exert an independent control over the course of his presentations'. **1938** S. BECKETT *Murphy* ix. 167 Paranoids, feverishly covering sheets of paper with complaints against their treatment. **1950** T. SUGRUE in M. Hay *Foot of Pride* p. xix, The rabble-rousing race bigots who peddle hate and fear to simpletons and paranoids. **1958** *Times Lit. Suppl.* 5 Sept. 495/4 The racy blend of anecdote and psychological jargon produce . . a basic Hindu paranoid with suppressed homosexual tendencies, who is never precisely related to particular Hindus. **1967** *Listener* 9 Feb. 186/2 Naive Russian advisers might even believe that only the paranoid would see a Russian defence system as threatening the United States. **1967** M. ARGYLE *Psychol. Interpersonal Behaviour* viii. 136 Paranoids feel that they are being plotted against, spied upon, or otherwise victimized, and that this is the explanation of their failures. **1976** G. MCDONALD *Confess, Fletch* (1977) xiii. 55 Even paranoids have enemies.

paranomasia, obs. erron. f. PARONOMASIA.

para'normal, *a.* [PARA-¹.] Applied to observed phenomena or powers which are presumed to operate according to natural laws beyond or outside those considered normal or known; also *absol.* Hence **paranor'mality**, the state or character of being paranormal; **para'normally** *adv.* Cf. SUPERNORMAL *a.*

1920 WEBSTER Add., Paranormal. **1935** *Discovery* May 138 (*caption*) The paranormal displacement of a handkerchief actuated electrically the flashlight by which this photograph was taken. **1950** A. HUXLEY *Themes & Variations* 133 The general tendency of ideas to embody themselves at any price and by fair means or foul, normally or paranormally. **1955** —— *Let.* 30 June (1969) 749 Two 'sensitives', one who specializes in paranormal diagnosis, the other a 'healer'. **1958** J. BLISH *Case of Conscience* (1959) i. 82 He has no belief in the supernatural—or, as we're calling it in our barbarous jargon these days, the 'paranormal'. **1959** *Listener* 11 June 1032/3 Her judgments will be equally remote from dogmatic incredulity and uncritical acceptance of claims to paranormality. **1961** W. H. SALTER *Zoar* ii. 15 'Paranormal' has now in general use taken the place of 'supernormal'. *Ibid.* vi. 69 They were convinced that the moulds were produced paranormally by 'Ideoplasmy'. **1968** *New Scientist* 24 Oct. 209/2 The out-of-the-body or 'ecsomatic' experience has long been familiar to students of the paranormal. **1973** *Daily Colonist* (Victoria, B.C.) 19 Apr. 5/2 Critics who dislike the seemingly paranormal condemn the claims with a vehemence beyond objective scientific candor. **1973** *Daily Tel.* (Colour Suppl.) 30 Nov. 26/1 The individuals who have been at the receiving end of the paranormally-transmitted information. *Ibid.* 31/3 Jung was to claim that if he had his life over again, it would have been devoted to the study of the paranormal. **1975** *Nature* 10 Apr. 470/2 Among the claims made are that plasticity of metal was paranormally produced. **1976** 'J. Ross' *I know what it's like to Die* xxv. 157 Rogers' belief . . in the paranormality of Pybus's experiment with the two dead bodies. **1977** *N.Y. Rev. Bks.* 13 Oct. 45/2 The enormous qualitative difference between testing psychics for paranormal powers, and experimentation in *all other* branches of science.

paranotal, -notum: see PARA-¹ 1.

parant, var. PARENT *a. Obs.*

paranter: see PERADVENTURE.

paranthelion (pærænˈθiːlɪən). [mod. f. Gr. παρ(α- beside + ἀνθ' = ἀντί over against + ἥλιος sun.] A diffuse white image of the sun, due to successive reflexions from prismatic ice in the atmosphere, seen at the same altitude as the sun and at an angular distance from it varying from 90° to 140°.

1888 A. W. GREELY *Amer. Weather* xx. 262 (Cent.) There is then visible, at 120° from the sun, a white image more or less diffuse, which has received the name of paranthelion.

†**pa'ranthine.** *Min. Obs.* [f. Gr. παρανθ-εῖν to be past bloom, to wither, f. παρ(α- past + ἄνθος flower + -INE⁵.] An obsolete name for Wernerite. Also †**pa'ranthite.**

1831 BREWSTER *Optics* xvii. 149. **1837–68** DANA *Min.* (ed. 5) 319 The name *paranthine*, substituted for scapolite (and for Arendal specimens) by Haüy. **1868** *Ibid.*, The name paranthite may well be retained for this section of the Scapolite group.

paranthracene, etc.: see PARA-¹ 1, 2.

Paranthropus (pæˈrænθrəʊpəs, pærænˈθrəʊpəs). [mod.L. (R. Broom 1938, in *Nature* 27 Aug. 379/1), f. PARA-¹ + Gr. ἄνθρωπος man.] A fossil hominid first described from remains found at Kromdraai and other sites in southern Africa, formerly included in the genus so called, and now usually included in the species *Australopithecus robustus.*

1941 R. BROOM in *Nature* 5 July 13/1 We have a good lower jaw of Paranthropus. Its teeth are almost typically human. **1946** *Transvaal Mus. Mem.* II. iii. 85 In the male Plesianthropus the anterior surface of the maxilla is essentially similar to that in the female, and thus unlike that in the presumably male Paranthropus. *Ibid.* 92 The Paranthropus skull resembles the living anthropoids much more that it does man. **1953** [see AUSTRALOPITHECUS]. **1959** J. D. CLARK *Prehist. S. Afr.* iii. 62 Now, however, anatomists are agreed that only one generic form is represented in the Man-ape remains but that two specific forms exist—*Australopithecus* and a later, more specialized form, *Paranthropus.* **1961** *Lancet* 30 Sept. 768/1 The existence of a *Paranthropus*-like form at Olduvai and later at Swartkrans and Kromdraai . . seems to suggest that this genus . . was moving out peripherally from a central African habitat. **1971** S. A. BARNETT *Human Species* (ed. 5) iv. 100 There are . . some more recently discovered forms ('Paranthropus') which were probably above the average height of modern man.

parantory: see PEREMPTORY.

paranucleus (pærəˈnjuːklɪəs). *Biol.* Pl. -i. [f. PARA-¹ 1 + NUCLEUS.] A small subsidiary nucleus, of which there may be one or more, in certain *Protozoa.*

1878 BELL *Gegenbaur's Comp. Anat.* p. viii, Conjugation in the Infusoria is attended by a definite breaking-up of the nucleus and so-called nucleolus (paranucleus) of the conjugating individuals. **1888** ROLLESTON & JACKSON *Anim. Life* 255 The nucleus or endoplast, and paranucleus or endoplastule, sometimes erroneously termed nucleolus.

Hence **para'nuclear** *a.*, pertaining to or of the nature of a paranucleus; **para'nucleate** *a.*, having a paranucleus. So also **paranu'cleolus**, a body extruded from the nucleus of the mother-cell of pollen-grains or spores just before division.

1885 LANKESTER in *Encycl. Brit.* XIX. 864/1 It does not appear to be established that there is any transference of nuclear or paranuclear matter from one individual to the other in the form of solid formed particles. **1887** A. B. MACULLUM in *Q. Jrnl. Microsc. Sc.* Mar. 447.

paranym ('pærənɪm). [f. PARA-¹ + *-nym* in ANTONYM, PARONYM, SYNONYM *sb.*, etc.] **a.** A near synonym. *rare.* **b.** (See quot. 1976.)

1963 L. HOGBEN *Essential World Eng.* 11 The L.E.S.U. [*sc.* List of Essential Semantic Units] cites non-essential paranyms for new terms even if definable by reference to terms which appear earlier in the list. **1976** *Listener* 17 June 773/3 A newspaper columnist has recently been collecting what he calls 'paranyms'—words whose meaning is generally the opposite of that intended by the speaker, such as 'provisional' or 'liberation' or 'rationalise'. The writer Brian Aldiss thereupon contributed an example he had found in the New Testament: '"ever-lasting life"; in other words "death"'. **1977** *Sunday Times* 2 Jan. 32/4 What a year for paranyms. Never before can so many decent, explicit words have utterly altered their meaning to conceal an evasion or untruth.

paranymph ('pærənɪmf). Also 6–7 **-nimph.** [ad. L. *paranymphus* masc., also late L. *paranympha* fem. (Isidore), a. Gr. παράνυμφος masc. the best man, fem. the bridesmaid, f. παρα- beside + νύμφη bride. Cf. F. *paranymphe* m. and f. (15th c. in Hatz.-Darm.).]

1. *Gr. Antiq.* The 'friend of the bridegroom', who accompanied the latter when he went to fetch home the bride; also, the bridesmaid who escorted the bride to the bridegroom; hence, a modern 'best man' or groomsman, or a bridesmaid.

1600 W. WATSON *Decacordon* (1602) 204 Our blessed Ladies paranimphe Saint Gabriell. **1671** MILTON *Samson* 1020 Thy Paranymph, worthless to thee compar'd. **1771** MRS. GRIFFITH *Hist. Lady Barton* II. 274, I hope she is by this time Lady Creswell, and that my sweet little Harriet had the pleasure and honour of being her paranymph. **1829** SOUTHEY *All for Love* IV. xx, The Bride and Bride-groom side by side, The Paranymphs in festal pride Arranged on either hand. **1891** G. F. X. GRIFFITH tr. *Fouard's Christ* I. 142 By her side the paranymph, or bridesmaid, kept watch with the ten virgins.

fig. **1863** *Q. Rev.* CXIV. 530 The paranymphs of the bridal [of Mary Stuart] were to be the fiends of war.

2. *transf.* and *fig.* A person or thing that woos or solicits for another; an advocate, spokesman, or orator, who speaks in behalf of another.

1593 G. HARVEY *Pierce's Super.* Wks. (Grosart) II. 21, I would . . it had bene your fortune to haue encountred some other Paranymphes, then such as you are now to discipline. **1643** TRAPP *Comm. Gen:* xxiv. 35 Ministers, Christs Paranymphs, must likewise wo for Christ. **1656** BLOUNT *Glossogr.* [from Cotgr.], *Paranymph*, an Orator, who a little before the Commencement of Doctors, etc., makes a publick Speech in commendation of their honesty and sufficiency. *a* **1693** *Urquhart's Rabelais* III. xli. 341 To supply the place of a Paranymph, Braul broker, Proxenete or Mediator.

Hence † **para'nymphal** *a.*

1638 FORD *Lady's Trial* III. i, Saying grace As at some paranymphal feast.

parao, obs. form of *prahu*, PROA.

paraparesis to **parapeptone:** see PARA-¹ 1, 2.

parapegm ('pærəpɛm). *Gr. Antiq.* Now usually in Gr.-L. form **parapegma** (pærəˈpɛgmə). [ad. L. *parapēgma*, pl. *-pēgmata*, a. Gr. παράπηγμα, -πήγματα, a thing fixed beside or near, a tablet, calendar, etc., f. παρα- beside + πῆγμα anything fastened. Cf. mod.F. *parapegme.*] A tablet set up inscribed with some public information or announcement, as a law, a proclamation, or a calendar of annals or astronomical observations; a canon, rule, or precept; a fixed date or epoch.

α. *a* **1641** BP. MOUNTAGU *Acts & Mon.* ii. (1642) 133 From what Parapegme or root of time, these 70. weekes or 490. yeares must be current, is a thing much perplexed and involved. **1646** SIR T. BROWNE *Pseud. Ep.* IV. xiii. (1686) 182 Our fore-fathers . . set them down in their Parapegms or Astronomical Canons. **1755** JOHNSON, *Parapegm.*

β. **1662** STILLINGFL. *Orig. Sacr.* I. vi. §1 (ed. 3) 89 The want of certain parapegmata or some fixed periods of time. **1753** *Phil. Trans.* XLVIII. 225 We see here an authentic parapegma in antient history, deduced from astronomy. **1788** R. PORSON in *Museum Crit.* I. 234 Diodorus . . complains that he could find no parapegma on which he could rely, in relating the events that preceded the Trojan war.

parapet ('pærəpɪt). Also 7 **-pett, -pit.** [a. F. *parapet* (Rabelais 16th c.), or It. *parapetto*, f. PARA-² protection, defence + *petto*:—L. *pectus* breast.] *lit.* A defence breast-high, a breastwork.

1. *Mil.* A defence of earth or stone to cover troops from the enemy's observation and fire; in permanent works, a protection against shot, raised on the top of a wall or rampart; in field-works, a bank of earth high enough to screen the defenders and thick enough to resist any shot that is likely to be discharged against it. *spec.* a bank of earth in front of a military trench. Also *fig.*

[**1583** STOCKER *Civ. Warres Lowe C.* III. 83 b, The Enemie had with batterie, greatly decaied the Bulwarke, Parapetti, Maisons, houses, Cloisters and Churches.] **1590** MARLOWE *2nd Pt. Tamburl.* III. ii, It must have . . parapets to hide the musketeers, Casemates to place the great artillery. **1596** SHAKS. *1 Hen. IV*, II. iii. 55. **1655** MRQ. WORCESTER *Cent. Inv.* §73 A transmittible Gallery over any Ditch or Breach in a Town-wall, with a Blinde and Parapit Cannon-proof. **1748** *Anson's Voy.* III. x. 410 A soldier . . stalkt about on the parapet with a battle-ax in his hand. **1803** WELLINGTON in *Gurw. Desp.* I. 444 It wants . . the earth which has been washed from the parapet into the ditch to be cleared out. **1861** W. H. RUSSELL in *Times* 10 July, Higher up . . there is a breastwork and parapet, within which are six guns. **1916** J. BUCHAN *Greenmantle* xx. 266 A crump took the parapet of the trench. **1918** 'R. WEST' *Return of Soldier* i. 6 On the war-films I have seen men slip down . . from the trench parapet.

1928 BLUNDEN *Undertones of War* 317 It seems, as now I wake and brood, And know my hour's decrepitude, That on some dewy parapet The centuries' spirit gazes yet. **1929** 'C. EDMONDS' *Subaltern's War* i. 25 A head and shoulders, seen from the sniper's loophole, leaping past a gap in the enemy's parapet. **1954** W. FAULKNER *Fable* 25 He saw only a few figures crouching along his own parapet. **1975** *Times* 14 July 13/1 The Leader of the House, to whom the Prime Minister..will yield the honour of going over the parapet first. **1975** *Listener* 14 Aug. 207/1 Some TV performers..have been howitzered into the mud... A few have had the sense to learn..to keep their heads behind the parapet. **1977** H. FAST *Immigrants* III. 171 The men were leaning high on the parapet, staring out over the ruptured, wire-strewn earth that separated them from the enemy.

2. a. A low wall or barrier, placed at the edge of a platform, balcony, roof, etc., or along the sides of a bridge, pier, quay, etc., to prevent people from falling over; sometimes mainly or wholly ornamental.

1598 FLORIO, *Parapetto*,..a parapet or wall breast high. **1706** PHILLIPS, *Parapet* (Ital. in Masonry), a Wall or Balcony Breast-high, ranging about a Pillar, Tower, Steeple, or other Building. *a* **1720** SHEFFIELD (Dk. Buckhm.) *Wks.* (1753) II. 224 [The roof] defended by a parapet of ballusters. **1772** C. HUTTON *Bridges* 96. **1823** P. NICHOLSON *Pract. Build.* 310. **1866** GEO. ELIOT *F. Holt* i, The terrace surrounded with a stone parapet in front of the house. **1879** BLACK *Macleod of D.* xxxvi. 320 Sitting on the weather-worn parapet of the bridge.

b. *transf.* Anything resembling a parapet in appearance or use.

1636 B. JONSON *Discov.* Wks. (Rtldg.) 744/1 There was a wall or parapet of teeth set in our mouth, to restrain the petulancy of our words. **1823** F. CLISSOLD *Ascent Mt. Blanc* 21 After some hundred feet of ascent, we found ourselves opposed by a parapet of congealed snow, about eight feet high. **1837** SOUTHEY *Wks.* I. p. xvii, The brows of the Surrey hills bear a parapet of modern villas. **1877** BRYANT *Little People of Snow* 64 [Winter] threw Spangles of silvery frost upon the grass, And edged the brook with glistening parapets.

†**c.** *Her.* A representation of a parapet. *Obs.*

1661 MORGAN *Sph. Gentry* III. iv. 34 The Mural Crown was raised with Brectesches, parapects, and Battlements of Gold.

3. Locally, The side-walk, footpath, or pavement of a street or road.

The ordinary name in Chester, Liverpool, and the district from Crewe to Lancaster, but disappearing eastward.

1795 *Gen. Hist. Liverpool* 273 The foot paths here are called parapets. **1840** ('Well known in Liverpool.' E.L.B.). **1871** in HOPPE *Suppl. Lex.* (erron. 'North Eng. and Sc.'). **1900** ('The regular name in Ormskirk.' H.J.R.M.). **1900** M. E. FRANCIS *Daughter of the Soil* iii. 26 Occasionally, to the terror of her mistress, hoisting one wheel of the bath-chair on the parapet. [**1904** See *Manch. City News* Jan. 23—Feb. 20, '*Notes & Q.*']

4. *attrib.* and *Comb.*, as ***parapet bank***, ***mounting***, ***walk***; also **parapet line**, the line or level of the bottom of the parapet, esp. on a roof; **parapet wall**, a low wall serving as a parapet.

1739 C. LABELYE *Short Acc. Piers Westm. Bridge* 69 The Side-walks..to be six Feet in the Clear, between the Parapet-Walls. **1792** A. YOUNG *Trav. France* 77 The fence is a high broad parapet bank. **1862** T. A. TROLLOPE *Marietta* I. x. 185 A low parapet wall defended it from the edge of the rock. **1882** O'DONOVAN *Merv Oasis* I. ii. 38 The ancient chief entrance above which the parapet walk is continued. **1886** WILLIS & CLARK *Cambridge* III. 284 Wykeham's gateway-tower [at Magdalen Coll., Oxford] rises plain and square above the parapet-line of the chambers. *Ibid.* 285. **1914** *Illustr. London News* 29 Aug. 332/2 A Hotchkiss machine-gun on a parapet mounting.

Hence **'parapet** *v.*, chiefly in **'parapeted** *ppl a*, furnished with or defended by a parapet; **'parapetless** *a.*, without a parapet.

1633 T. STAFFORD *Pac. Hib.* III. vi. (1810) 548 A place naturally formed like a platforme, and parrapetted with an old ditch. **1827** SOUTHEY *Hist. Penins. War* II. 108 The housetops were parapeted to secure the defendants. **1859** *Chamb. Jrnl.* XI. 325 A perilous bridge;..high, parapetless. **1869** *Pall Mall G.* 15 July 1 A wider parapeted trench..designed for two rows of infantry.

parapetalous: see PARA-[1] I.

paraph ('pæræf), *sb.* Also 4–5 paraf, 5 -affe. [a. F. *paraphe*, *parafe*, also 15th c. *parraphe*, *-affe*, *paraffe* = It. *pa'rafo*, med.L. *pa'raphus*, shortened form of *paragraphus*: see PARAGRAPH.]

†**1.** A paragraph. *Obs.*

1395 PURVEY *Remonstr.* (1851) 15 Hostiance, in the paraf 'Quid si clericus', seith [etc.]. *c* **1440** *Promp. Parv.* 382/1 Paraf of a booke (*H.* or paragraf..), *paraphus*, *paragraphus*. **1483** *Cath. Angl.* 269/1 A Paraffe, *paragraphus*.

†**2.** (?) A paragraph mark on the margin. *Obs.*

14.. *A.B.C. Poem* 8 in *Pol., Rel., & L. Poems* (1866) 244 Wrout is on þe bok with-oute, .v. paraffys grete & stoute Bolyd in rose red. *Ibid.* 19 Grete paraffys, þat be wondis .v.

3. *Diplomatics.* A flourish made after a signature, originally as a kind of precaution against forgery.

1584 POWEL *Lloyd's Cambria* 9 That character which the Lawyers do call a *Paraph*. **1656** BLOUNT *Glossogr.* [from Cotgr.], *Paraph*, the flourish or peculiar Knot or mark set unto, after, or instead of, a name in the signing a Deed or Letter. **1727–41** CHAMBERS *Cycl.* s.v., The Paraph of the Kings of France is a grate, which the secretaries always place before their own, in all letters, etc. **1842** BRANDE *Dict. Sci.*, etc., s.v., In some countries (as in Spain) the paraph is still a usual addition to a signature. **1895** *Daily News* 17 Dec. 5/1 [*Signature of Fr. Bacon*] The paraphe is a loop-headed triangle, with a lozenge below.

paraph ('pæræf), *v.* [f. prec. sb.: cf. F. *parapher* (1565 in Hatz.-Darm.) in sense 2.]

†**1.** *trans.* To divide into paragraphs. *Obs.*

c **1440** *Promp. Parv.* 382/1 Parafyd, *paragraphatus*. Paraffyn, *paragrapho*.

2. To affix a paraph to; hence, to sign, esp. with initials; to initial.

1667 EVELYN *Publ. Employm.* To Rdr., I have yet pursued my antagonist, rightly paraff'd and compared. **1856** tr. *Draft Prelim. Peace* Vienna 1 Feb., The undersigned, after having paraphed it conformably to authorization..have agreed that [etc.].

paraphanalia, obs. erron. f. PARAPHERNALIA.

paraphasia, -phasic: see PARA-[1] I.

paraphenylenediamine: see PARA-[1] 2 b.

‖**parapherna** (pærə'fɜːnə), *sb. pl.* [L. *parapherna* pl. (in the Digest), a. Gr. παράφερνα pl., f. παρα- beside + φερνή dower.]

1. *Rom. Law.* Those articles of property held by a wife over and above the dowry she brought to her husband, and which remained under her own control; see PARAPHERNALIA I.

1706 PHILLIPS, *Parapherna* or *Paraphernalia Bona* (Gr.), those Goods that a Wife brings her Husband over and above her Dower, as Furniture for her Chamber, wearing Apparel, Jewels, etc. **1727–41** in CHAMBERS *Cycl.*

2. = PARAPHERNALIA 2.

1876 BARTHOLOW *Mat. Med.* (1879) 363 None of the parapherna of the operation..should be exhibited before the patient. **1890** *Edin. Rev.* CLXXI. 480 A succession of names and a series of disguises were of necessity part of the parapherna of every Jesuit father.

paraphernal (pærə'fɜːnəl), *a.* (*sb.*) [a. F. *paraphernal* (1575 in Hatz.-Darm.), ad. late L. *paraphernāl-is*, f. *parapherna*: see prec. and -AL[1].] Of, belonging to, or of the nature of parapherna.

1773 ERSKINE *Inst. Law Scotl.* I. vi. §15. 90 From the *jus mariti* paraphernal goods are exempted. Over these the husband has no power. **1818** COLEBROOKE *Obligations* 26 Married women may have paraphernal or other separate property.

b. as *sb.* (serving as sing. to next.)

1506 *Will of Love ats O.* (Somerset Ho.), Parapharnelles. **1839** WILSON *Tales* V. 5 (E.D.D.) Go and assign thee thy appurtenances and paraphernals. **1851** G. OUTRAM *Legal Lyrics* (1887) 95 She had fled And had not left a single paraphernal.

‖**paraphernalia** (pærəfə'neɪlɪə), *sb. pl.* [med.L., neuter pl. of *paraphernālis* (see prec.), short for *paraphernālia bona*, paraphernal goods.]

1. *Law.* Those articles of personal property which the law allows a married woman to keep and, to a certain extent, deal with as her own.

The word *parapherna* was used by the Roman jurists to indicate all property which a married woman *sui juris* held apart from her *dos* (dower). Over such property the husband could exercise no rights without his wife's consent. In most modern systems of law, based on the Roman, *paraphernalia bona* (in Fr. *biens paraphernaux*) means much the same thing, but in English and Scottish Common law, under which all personal or movable property of a wife vested *ipso jure* in the husband, the *paraphernalia* became restricted to such purely personal belongings of a wife as dress, jewels, and the like. These latter were regarded as, in a sense, appropriated to the wife, and on the husband's death they were not treated as part of his succession, and the right of a trustee over them, in the event of the husband's bankruptcy, was restricted. But in neither England nor Scotland did *paraphernalia* strictly include articles in the nature of household furniture, even though these had been marriage presents to the wife. The effect of the 'Married Women's Property Acts' of 1870, etc., was to deprive the term of all significance in English and Scottish legal practice.

[**1478–9** *Year-bk. 18 Edw. IV* 11 b, Auxy de son appareile quel est appel en nostr ley *paraphonalia* de ceo per lagreement do son baron el poet faire testament. tr. (Digby, *Real Prop.* 307) As to her apparel, which is called in our law *paraphernalia*, of this by agreement with her husband she can make a will.] **1651** W. SHEPPARD *Faithf. Counsellor* (1653) 122 The word *Paraphonalia* is used in our Law, but in the Civil Law the thing is said to be *Paraphernalia*. **1656–74** BLOUNT, *Paraphonalia*. [So **1658–78** PHILLIPS.] **1718** MACCLESFIELD in Ld. Campbell *Chancellors* (1857) VI. cxxii. 25 Paraphernalia are not devisable by the husband to the wife. **1728** VANBR. & CIB. *Prov. Husb.* To Rdr., The Ornaments she herself provided..seem'd in all Respects the *Paraphonalia* of a Woman of Quality. **1766** BLACKSTONE *Comm.* II. xxix. 435–6. **1774** MRS. DELANY *Lett., to B. Granville* in *Life & Corr.* Ser. II. II. 33 The law restored them to her as her own paraphanalia. **1845** STEPHEN *Comm. Laws Eng.* (1874) II. 266. **1876** DIGBY *Real Prop.* vi. 307 *note*.

2. Personal belongings, *esp.* articles of adornment or attire, trappings; also, the articles that compose an apparatus, outfit, or equipment; the mechanical accessories of any function or complex scheme; appointments or appurtenances in general.

1736 FIELDING *Pasquin* IV. Wks. 1882 X. 176 [Thunder and lightning] are indeed properly the paraphernalia of a ghost [on the stage]. **1746** *Brit. Mag.* 257 A Lady whose Paraphanalia fill'd up three Fourths of the Breadth of the principal Walk. **1791** 'G. GAMBADO' *Ann. Horsem.* iii. (1809) 78 Bridles, saddles, and other equestrian paraphernalia. **1809** 'M. MARKWELL' *Advice to Sportsmen* title-p., Hints in the Choice of Guns, Dogs, and Sporting Paraphernalia. **1862** TROLLOPE *Orley F.* xiii. 101 The paraphernalia of justice,—the judge, and the jury, and the lawyers. **1882** A. W. WARD *Dickens* ii. 26 Dickens, though a temperate man, loved the paraphernalia of good cheer.

b. as collective sing.

1788 *Disinterested Love* I. 14 My paraphernalia is more complete. **1822** GALT *Provost* xli. (1868) 120. **1845** DISRAELI *Sybil* III. v, A whole paraphernalia of plums. **1882** O'DONOVAN *Merv Oasis* I. 147 A ponderous paraphernalia is a concomitant of respectability.

Hence **parapher'nalian** *a.* = PARAPHERNAL.

1876 *Westm. Rev.* No. 98. 337 The Italian law, for the very reason that it regards paraphernalian of more advantage to a wife than dotal property, seizes every opportunity of construing doubts in her favour.

paraphilia (pærə'fɪlɪə). [f. PARA-[1] + Gr. φιλία affection.] Perverted sexual desires. Hence **para'philiac**, **para'philic** *adjs.* and *sbs.*

1925 J. S. VAN TESLAAR tr. *Stekel's Peculiarities of Behav.* II. 341 *Paraphilia*, interest in perversions. **1935** L. BRINK tr. *Stekel's Sadism & Masochism* I. iv. 100 If the patient can be brought to normal sexual relations, the paraphiliac impulses recede into the background. **1958** *Times Lit. Suppl.* 31 Oct. 619/2 Stekel..says that pluralistic orgies are tribal in derivation, and that frequently the paraphiliac who engages in them seeks a family combination. **1960** *Arch. Gen. Psychiatry* III. 442/1 He was allegedly heterosexually quite adequate (by using different paraphilic fantasies during coitus). **1962** C. ALLEN *Textbk. Psychosexual Disorders* I. v. 73 We regard the paraphylics [*sic*] divisible into three degrees. **1971** *Nature* 16 Apr. 433/2 Contact with urine plays little part in human relations, though it may be emphasized in paraphilias. **1977** *Proc. R. Soc. Med.* LXX. 792/2 Some patients have fantasies which involve masochistic or other paraphilic activity. **1977** E. J. TRIMMER et al. *Visual Dict. Sex* (1978) i. 12 The common paraphilias that we choose to call sexual perversions today, were defined by the Greeks as being parallel to love.

‖**paraphimosis** (ˌpærəfaɪ'məʊsɪs). *Path.* [mod.L., f. PARA-[1] I + PHIMOSIS.] Permanent retraction of the prepuce.

1693 tr. *Blancard's Phys. Dict.* (ed. 2), *Paraphimosis*,.. when the *Præputium's* too short. **1789** W. BUCHAN *Dom. Med.* (1790) 509 Paraphymosis. **1846** BRITTAN tr. *Malgaigne's Man. Oper. Surg.* 473 Paraphymosis only requires two operations—reduction—and, if that cannot be accomplished by the ordinary means, incision of the stricture. **1861** BUMSTEAD *Ven. Dis.* (1879) 114 The term Paraphimosis implies exactly the opposite of phimosis.

So **paraphi'mosed** *a.*, affected with paraphimosis; **paraphi'motic** *a.*, of, pertaining to, or of the nature of paraphimosis.

1874 VAN BUREN *Dis. Genit. Org.* 16 A paraphimosed glans penis. **1857** MAYNE *Expos. Lex.*, Paraphimotic.

†**paraphonalia**, obs. corrupt f. PARAPHERNALIA; hence †**paraphonalion**, an article belonging to a married woman's paraphernalia. *Obs.*

1599 MARSTON *Sco. Villanie* I. ii, Whether..as Paraphonalion A siluer pisse-pot fits his Lady dame?

‖**paraphonia** (pærə'fəʊnɪə). Also (in sense 1) **paraphony** (pə'ræfənɪ). [med.L., f. Gr. παράφωνος sounding beside (f. παρα- beside + φωνή sound); applied in pl. to certain harmonies: cf. παραφωνή side-sound.]

1. *Gr. Mus.* The harmony or concord of fourths and fifths: cf. ANTIPHONY I and HOMOPHONY I a.

1776 BURNEY *Hist. Mus.* I. 127 *note*, Two passages.. shew, that even in their time, thirds and sixths made no part of their *Antiphonia*, or *Paraphonia*. **1782–6** CHAMBERS *Cycl.* (ed. Rees), *Paraphonia*, in Music, is that species of concord, which results from different sounds, as the fifth and fourth: and thus it differs from *homophonia*, which is produced by the same sounds, as in the unison, and from *antiphonia*, or the replication of the same sounds, as in the octave. **1919** H. J. WATT *Found. Music* 157 The term paraphony was used by several later writers, Thrasyllus, Bacchius and Gaudentius. **1924** T. H. Y. TROTTER *Music & Mind* 154 The words 'symphony', 'paraphony', and 'diaphony' are used to express more or less complete unity and dissonance.

2. Alteration of the voice from physiological or pathological causes.

1799 HOOPER *Dict. Med.*, *Paraphonia*, alteration of the voice... A genus of disease comprehending six species. **1878** tr. *von Ziemssen's Cycl. Med.* XIV. 873 He [Mansfeld] distinguishes two varieties of defective speech [in deaf-mutes], *paraphonia* and *mogilalia*. 1. *Paraphonia*. The voice is unpleasant, rough, and even harsh.

Hence **para'phonic** *a.*, of or pertaining to paraphonia (sense 1); **para'phonically** *adv.*

1836 W. T. SPURDENS tr. *Longinus* xxviii. 113 In music, the principal sound falls more sweetly upon the ear by means of what are called paraphonic variations. **1919** H. J. WATT *Found. Music* 156 For the proper flow of simultaneous melodies intervals must either be themselves actually paraphonic or they must be used paraphonically.

paraphony, anglicized form of PARAPHONIA.

‖**paraphora** (pə'ræfərə). [a. Gr. παραφορά going aside, distraction, derangement, f. παρα- aside + φορά carrying, bearing, movement.] Slight delirium; a mild form of insanity (*Syd. Soc. Lex.*). Hence **para'phoric** *a.*, pertaining to paraphora.

1857 MAYNE *Expos. Lex.*, Paraphora, Paraphoric.

paraphosphate, -phosphoric: see PARA-[1] 2.

paraphragm (ˈpærəfræm). *Zool.* [ad. Gr. παράφραγμα breastwork, parapet, f. παραφράσσ-ειν to enclose with a breastwork.] One of the outer divisions of an endosternite in Crustacea. Hence **paraphragmal** (pærəˈfrægməl), *a.*

1877 HUXLEY *Anat. Inv. Anim.* vi. 310 The anterior horizontal uniting with its own paraphragmal apophysis, the posterior with the paraphragmal of the antecedent endosternite. **1880** —— *Crayfish* iv. 158 The outer prolongation of the capital [of the apodemes] is called..the paraphragm.

ˌparaphrasaˈbility. [f. PARAPHRASABLE *a.* + -ITY.] The capacity of being paraphrasable.

1965 *Amer. Philos. Q.* II. 185/2 Paraphrasability is generally regarded as the central issue. **1965** *Times Lit. Suppl.* 25 Nov. 1082/4 He brings the [Wittgensteinian] technique to bear on two aesthetic problems: the paraphrasability of poems and the tonality of atonal music. **1977** *Amer. Speech 1975* L. 82 Constructions in which the modifier is the author of the headword, such as *Zunser's hymn*, also vary in their paraphrasability with *have*.

ˈparaphrasable, *a.* [f. PARAPHRASE *v.* + -ABLE.] Capable of being paraphrased.

1900 *Academy* 17 Nov. 465/1 Shakespeare's text must be corrupt whenever it is not readily paraphrasable. **1936** F. R. LEAVIS *Revaluation* v. 155 It is difficult not to believe, after reading, say, Book II of *The Prelude*, that one has been reading a paraphrasable argument. **1952** *Essays in Crit.* II. 106 If it is self-sufficient (that is, if it yields a paraphrasable meaning answering the normal demands of logic and syntax). **1966** *Listener* 25 Aug. 282/1 Mr Lodge carefully demolishes the view that the novel is reducible to its paraphrasable and translatable content. **1970** *Language* XLVI. 831 The adjectives shown..are normally considered stative..and they are indeed paraphrasable with active verbs.

paraphrase (ˈpærəfreɪz), *sb.* Also 6 **perra-, parafrase.** [a. F. *paraphrase* (1525 in Hatz.-Darm.), ad. L. *paraphrasis*, a. Gr. παράφρασις, f. παραφράζειν to tell the same thing in other words, f. παρα- beside + φράζειν to declare, tell: cf. φράσις mode of speaking, speech, phrase.]

1. a. An expression in other words, usually fuller and clearer, of the sense of any passage or text; a free rendering or amplification of a passage. (Sometimes, by extension, of a musical passage.)

Chaldee Paraphrases: the TARGUM.

[**1547** *Mem. Ripon* (Surtees) III. 41 Una cum empcione diversorum librorum vocatorum paraphracez Erasmi.] **1548** UDALL *Erasm. Par.* Pref. B vj b, Thou hast here good Christian reader the paraphrase of Erasmus vpon the ghospell. *Ibid.* B vij, A paraphrase, is a plain settyng foorth of a texte or sentence more at large. **1548** HOOPER *Declar. Commandm.* vi. G iij b, A great nombre, that say not platlye and playnly there is no God, but by certayne circumloquutions and paraphresis. **1646** SIR T. BROWNE *Pseud Ep.* 2 So is it expressed in the Thargum or Paraphrase of Jonathan. **1684** N. S. *Crit. Enq. Edit. Bible* xxvii. 240 The Hebrew Text, the Chaldee paraphrase by Onkelosius, the Targum, or Arabic Paraphrase by R. Saadius. **1693** DRYDEN *Juvenal* Ded. (1697) 87 Not a literal Translation, but a kind of Paraphrase. **1791–1823** D'ISRAELI *Cur. Lit., Imprisonm. Learned*, Buchanan, in the dungeon of a monastery in Portugal, composed his excellent Paraphrases of the Psalms of David. **1874** STUBBS *Const. Hist.* I. ii. 31 This description is a mere abstract and paraphrase of the language of the Germania. **1880** GROVE *Dict. Mus.* II. 741/2 His [*sc.* Liszt's] transcriptions, paraphrases, and arrangements, comprise not only vocal and orchestral works of German, French, Italian, and Russian composers, but also the national melodies of Europe, Asia, etc. **1900** L. GODOWSKY *Let.* 24 Dec. in H. C. Schonberg *Great Pianists* (1964) xxiv. 320, I came out to play my seven Chopin paraphrases and Weber's 'Invitation'. **1944** W. APEL *Harvard Dict. Mus.* 554/1 Liszt's paraphrases on Wagnerian operas. **1963** H. C. SCHONBERG *Great Pianists* (1964) xxiv. 322 Big technicians will occasionally attempt his paraphrase on *Fledermaus*. **1976** *Gramophone* Apr. 1598/2 Liszt's *Eugene Onegin* paraphrase is not one of his most elaborate, nor his finest, but it has the authentic glitter, and a most enjoyable flair.

b. Without *a* and *pl.*, as a process or mode of literary treatment.

1656 COWLEY *Pindar. Odes* I. Notes 8 [It] could not be rendred without much Paraphrase. **1680** DRYDEN *Pref. Transl. Ovid's Epist.* Ess. 1900 I. 237 Paraphrase, or translation with latitude, where the author is kept in view.., but his words are not so strictly followed as his sense; and that too is admitted to be amplified. **1795** MASON *Ch. Mus.* iii. 177 To proceed in the way of Paraphrase. **1873** ROGERS *Orig. Bible* vi. (1875) 227 Most books need comment, explanation, illustration, but if that be the object, paraphrase is the worst way of effecting it.

†**c.** A comment. *Obs.*

1642 CHAS. I in Rushw. *Hist. Coll.* III. (1692) I. 616, I will make no Paraphrases upon what you have heard,..only this Observation. **1738** tr. *Guazzo's Art Conversation* 153 [Who] make a thousand wrong Paraphrases, and foolish Interpretations of their Actions.

d. *fig.* A practical exemplification of or commentary upon some principle, maxim, etc.

1662 SOUTH *Serm.* I. 56 All the Laws of Nations, and wise Decrees of States..were but a Paraphrase upon this standing Rectitude of Nature. **1666** —— *Serm. Tit.* ii. 15 Ded., All your After-Greatness seems but a Paraphrase upon those promising Beginnings. *a* **1670** HACKET in Plume *Life* (1865) 136 A glittering prelate without inward ornaments was but the paraphrase of a painted wall.

e. *transf.* In art, the representation of a subject in a realistic or other manner so as to convey its essential qualities.

1951 G. SUTHERLAND in *Listener* 6 Sept. 378/1, I feel that now we can perhaps enlarge the field of painting by setting our emotional paraphrases of reality—they themselves have been conceived more optically—within the ambience of optical reality. **1962** R. G. HAGGAR *Dict. Art Terms* 246/2 *Paraphrase.* The term is used by Graham Sutherland to explain the nature of his realist art, implying that he seeks to express the character and mood of the landscape or object which inspires him by other and general forms which do not constitute 'views'. **1962** *Listener* 26 July 134/1, I believe that in the case of a portrait, there are two ways of doing it. One ..is the real paraphrase such as Picasso does. **1965** *New Statesman* 14 May 775/1 His line overstates and underpraises, as in the paraphrase of a Cranach nude.

2. *spec.* In the Church of Scotland and other Presbyterian Churches: Each of the hymns contained in the 'Translations and Paraphrases, in verse, of several passages of Sacred Scripture: collected and prepared by a Committee of the General Assembly of the Church of Scotland [1745–81], in order to be sung in Churches'. These are usually appended to the Metrical Psalter in Scottish editions of the Bible or New Testament.

The first edition, entitled 'Translations and Paraphrases of several passages of Sacred Scripture, collected and prepared by a Committee appointed by the General Assembly of the Church of Scotland', was printed and issued for consideration in 1745. That finally adopted was published in 1781.

1745 *Minutes of Gen. Assembly* 18 May, The General Assembly of the Church of Scotland had laid before them.. some Pieces of Sacred Poesy, under the title of *Translations and Paraphrases of several Passages of sacred Scripture*, composed by private Persons. **1883** STEVENSON *Silverado Sq.* 51 You have to learn the paraphrases and the shorter catechism. **1889** D. J. MACLAGAN (*title*) The Scottish Paraphrases..an account of their History, Authors, and Sources. *Ibid.* 56 With all their faults..it is yet to be hoped that the time is far distant when the Scottish clergy and the Scottish people are ashamed of their Psalms and Paraphrases. **1891** BARRIE *Little Minister* iii, 'I hope', he said nervously, 'that you don't sing the Paraphrases?' **1893** *Daily News* 23 Dec. 5/2 One old Anti-Burgher used to stump out of church if a paraphrase came on last.

paraphrase (ˈpærəfreɪz), *v.* [ad. F. *paraphrase-r*, f. *paraphrase*: see prec.]

1. *trans.* To express the meaning of (a word, phrase, passage, or work) in other words, usually with the object of fuller and clearer exposition; to render or translate with latitude. Also *fig.*, *spec.* in art; cf. prec.

1630 PRYNNE *Anti-Armin.* 168 Those words of Christs.. he paraphraseth thus. **1648** BOYLE *Seraph. Love* v. (1700) 37 Which emboldened Mary to Paraphrase him [Lazarus] by a *He whom thou lov'st*. **1741** WATTS *Improv. Mind* I. ii. (1801) 21 A Tutor..when he paraphrases and explains other authors. **1841** D'ISRAELI *Amen. Lit.* (1867) 113 An ecclesiastic paraphrased the Gospel-histories. **1879** HUXLEY *Hume* ix. (1881) 173 Dr. Whately..paraphrases Hume, though he forgets to cite him.

fig. **1606** WARNER *Alb. Eng.* XIV. lxxxix. (1612) 361 To paraphrase this Painter were to Age an idle thing. **1628** JACKSON *Worthy Churchman* 45 Virgil paraphraseth the same vertue, when he compares a meeke man to a standing pool. **1961** D. COOPER *Work of Graham Sutherland* II. 14 He [*sc.* Sutherland] found that when he paraphrased what he saw he had captured more of 'the essence or the *gesture* of reality.' **1962** *Listener* 26 July 134/1, I might have wanted to paraphrase a landscape.

2. *intr.* To make a paraphrase; to comment or enlarge *upon* a passage so as to bring out the sense.

1633 PRYNNE *1st Pt. Histrio-m.* VI. iii. 339 In his Commentary on the 118. alias the 119. Psalme, verse 37..he paraphraseth thus. **1722** SEWELL *Hist. Quakers* (1795) I. III. 185 Such of the family as could make repetitions of sermons, and paraphrase thereupon. **1864** PUSEY *Lect. Daniel* (1876) 200 He paraphrased, rather than translated.

†**3.** *intr.* To comment *on*, to enlarge *upon* a subject. *Obs.*

1644–5 CHAS. I *Let. to Wife* 14 Jan., Wks. (1662) 321, I cannot but paraphrase a little upon that which he calls his superstitious observation. **1683** MOXON *Mech Exerc.*, *Printing* xxii. ¶8, I must a little digress, to paraphrase on the posture he holds the Bodkin in.

Hence ˈ**paraphrasing** *vbl. sb.*

1640 GLAPTHORNE *Wallenstein* I. iii. Wks. 1874 II. 27 May ..thy dreames Be free from paraphrasing on my memory. **1728** MORGAN *Hist. Algiers* I. Pref. 20 His Paraphrasings and mine differ.

paraphraser (ˈpærəfreɪzə(r)). Also 6 **-phryser.** [f. prec. sb. and vb. + -ER^{1}.] One who makes paraphrases or who paraphrases; a paraphrast.

1548 Q. KATERYN in Ellis *Orig. Lett.* Ser. I. II. 152, I knowe not wether ye be a paraphryser or not. **1611** COTGR., *Paraphraste*, a Paraphrast, or Paraphrasor. **1624** GATAKER *Transubst.* 94 Pachymeres the Greeke paraphraser of this Dennis. **1833** J. A. CARLYLE in *Philol. Museum* II. 624 The Paraphraser must have read ὄμματα for στρωματα.

‖**paraphrasia** (pærəˈfreɪzɪə). *Path.* [mod.L., f. Gr. παρα- PARA-^{1} 1 + φράσις speech.] Incoherent or disordered speech.

1878 tr. *von Ziemssen's Cycl. Med.* XIV. 816 This phenomenon..should be classed as paralogia and paraphrasia. *Ibid.*, We find..paraphrasia developed..in conditions of morbid hebetude and intellectual weakness.

†**paraˈphrasian,** *a.* (or *sb.*) *Obs rare*$^{-1}$. [f. L. *paraphrasi-s* PARAPHRASE *sb.* + -AN.] Given to or dealing in paraphrases (or = paraphrast).

a **1548** HALL *Chron., Hen. V* 38 b, As the logical paraphrasian and Philosophical interpreters do by a distinccion expounde this terme necessary to signifie a thyng conuenient.

‖**paraphrasis** (pəˈræfrəsɪs). [L. *paraphrasis*: see PARAPHRASE.] = PARAPHRASE *sb.* 1, 1 b.

1538 CRANMER *Rem.* (Parker Soc.) 213 (Stanf.) These words do let and interrupt the course of the paraphrasis. **1547** EDW. VI *Injunct.* in Cardwell *Docum. Ann.* (1839) I. 9 The 'Paraphrasis' of Erasmus also in English upon the gospels. *a* **1568** ASCHAM *Scholem.* II. (Arb.) 96 Paraphrasis.. is not onelie to expresse at large with moe wordes, but to striue and contend..to translate the best latin authors, into other latin wordes, as many or thereaboutes. **1609** BIBLE (DOUAY) *Ps.* xv, They repete their new text by this paraphrasis. **1776** BENTHAM *Fragm. Govt.* Wks. 1843 I. 293/1 A word may be said to be expounded by paraphrasis. **1811–31** —— *Univ. Gram.* ibid. VIII. 356/2 On this consideration the paraphrasis may be termed the development.

paraphrasist (pəˈræfrəsɪst). [f. PARAPHRASE + -IST.] = next.

1884 *Manch. Exam.* 4 July 5/3 The plan, says the paraphrasist, was evidently one for 'a military rising, directed by the General'.

paraphrast (ˈpærəfræst), *sb.* [ad. L. *paraphrast-ēs*, a. Gr. παραφραστής, f. παραφράζ-ειν: see PARAPHRASE *sb.* Cf. F. *paraphraste* (1607 in Hatz.-Darm.).] One who paraphrases; a paraphraser.

1549 COVERDALE, etc. *Erasm. Par. Thess.* Ded., Touchyng thys notable learned Paraphrast D. Erasmus. **1577** HANMER *Anc. Eccl. Hist.* To Rdr., More like a Paraphrast then a translator. *a* **1656** USSHER *Ann.* vi. (1658) 93 As Jonathan the Chaldee Paraphrast expoundeth it. **1764** *Mem. G. Psalmanazar* 55 Using all proper helps, as commentators, paraphrasts, books of controversy. **1879** FARRAR *St. Paul* I. 17 Able to understand the Bible..through the aid of a paraphrast.

†**ˈparaphrast,** *v. Obs. rare.* [f. prec. sb.] = PARAPHRASE *v.* Hence †**ˈparaphraster,** a paraphraser.

1607 HIERON *Defence* I 99 Our owne Church Bible.. Which paraphrasteth in the margin..thus. **1632** LEGRYS tr. *Velleius Paterc.* To Rdr., I do not allow either to my selfe, or any other translator the liberty of a paraphraster. **1684** N. S. *Crit. Enq. Edit. Bible* xiii. 102 It is the common Fate of Paraphrasters..to follow the freest method of translation.

paraphrastic (pærəˈfræstɪk), *a.* [ad. med.L. *paraphrastic-us*, a. Gr. παραφραστικ-ός, f. παραφραστής PARAPHRAST: see -IC. Cf. F. *paraphrastique.*] Of, pertaining to, or of the nature of paraphrase; addicted to the use of paraphrase.

1623 COCKERAM, *Paraphrasticke*, one that still keepes the sense of the Author in a translation, albe that he [etc.]. **1759** JOHNSON *Idler* No. 69 ¶9 The paraphrastic liberties have been almost universally admitted. **1836** *Penny Cycl.* V. 227/2 A paraphrastic translation of the Greek poem of Hero and Leander. **1877** SYMONDS in *Academy* 3 Nov. 419/1 The two extremes of laconic accuracy and paraphrastic freedom.

paraphrastical (pærəˈfræstɪkəl), *a.* [f. as prec. + -AL^{1}.] = prec.

1549 COVERDALE *Erasm. Par.* II. Ded. to Qn. Katerine 1 b, Erasmus..hathe by a paraphrasticall discourse playnly sette foorth the ghospelles of the fower Euangelistes. *c* **1611** CHAPMAN *Iliad* To Rdr., [Who] are ten parts more paraphrastical than I. **1685** BOYLE *Enq. Notion Nat.* 39 To ..bear with some Paraphrastical Expressions. **1779–81** JOHNSON *L.P., West* Wks. IV. 202 He is sometimes too paraphrastical. **1807** PENNINGTON *Life Eliz. Carter*, To translate such a book rather in a paraphrastical way. **1960** *Spectator* 30 Sept. 497 No don with simple-minded paraphrastical or reductive tastes [etc.]. **1977** *Archivum Linguisticum* VIII. 10 This paraphrastical relation..does not characterize the respective sentences of [examples] (67)–(72).

paraˈphrastically, *adv.* [f. prec. + -LY^{2}.] In a paraphrastic manner, by way of paraphrase.

1557 PAYNEL *Barclay's Jugurth* Ded., The whiche, because the reader shulde most redelie and plainely vnderstande and perceiue the thinge, doth paraphrasticallie so open the hole matter. *c* **1645** HOWELL *Lett.* II. III. xxi. 545 Every language hath certain idioms..which are not rendible in any other, but paraphrastically. **1778** BP. LOWTH *Isaiah* Notes (ed. 12) 135, I have been forced to render this line paraphrastically; as the verbal translation.. would have been unintelligible. **1812** L. HUNT in *Examiner* 28 Sept. 618/2 She was plain in her dress, or, more paraphrastically, in the manner of adorning herself.

paraphrenia (pærəˈfriːnɪə). [ad. F. *paraphrénie* f. PARA-^{1} + Gr. φρήν mind + -IA^{1}.] A form of mental disorder; a term sometimes used to refer to mental disorders of the paranoid and schizophrenic varieties. Hence **paraˈphrenic** *a.*

[**1846** DUNGLISON *Dict. Med. Sci.* (ed. 6) 552/1 *Paraphrénie*, insanity.] **1890** in BILLINGS *Med. Dict.* II. 290. **1917** C. R. PAYNE tr. *Pfister's Psychoanal. Method* 522 Dementia praecox (schizophrenia according to Bleuler, paraphrenia according to Freud). **1919** R. M. BARCLAY tr. *Kraepelin's Dementia Praecox & Paraphrenia* 2 It seems to me that the term 'paraphrenia', which is now no longer in common use, is in the meantime suitable as the name of the morbid forms thus delimited. **1934** WEBSTER, Paraphrenic. **1952** PURVES-STEWART & WORSTER-DROUGHT *Diagnosis of*

Nervous Dis. (ed. 10) xxii. 737 The term paraphrenia is applied to those cases of paranoidal schizophrenia who retain their personality... Paraphrenic symptoms usually develop later in life than those of the ordinary paranoidal type, often as late as the menopause. **1958** *Daily Tel.* 30 June 10/4 The effect was found to be beneficial even with some of the seriously disturbed paraphrenic patients. **1962** HENDERSON & GILLESPIE *Text-bk. Psychiatry* (ed. 9) xii. 291 We would..suggest that the term parphrenia should be discarded, as it does not serve any useful purpose. **1973** T. & R. MILLON *Abnormal Behav.* (1974) xvii. 381 The closest approximation to what we have termed paraphrenia may be found in the DSM-II descriptive text of 'schizophrenia, paranoid type'.

‖**paraphrenitis** (pærəfrɪˈnaɪtɪs). *Path.* [mod.L., f. PARA-[1] 1 + PHRENITIS.] A term for inflammation of the diaphragm, formerly thought to be invariably accompanied by delirium; hence applied to delirium supposed to be so produced. Cf. PARAFRENESIE.

1693 *Blancard's Phys. Dict.* (ed. 2), *Paraphrenitis*, Madness, accompanied with a continual Fever,..thence the Midriff and Lungs are troubled. **1727-41** CHAMBERS *Cycl.*, *Paraphrenesis*, or *Paraphrenitis*,..a secondary kind of phrenzy, supposed by the ancients, to be owing not to any immediate disorder of the brain, or meninges, but to an inflammation of the ventricle, the liver, and especially the diaphragm, whereby the brain and meninges come to be affected by consent of parts. *Ibid.*, *Paraphrenitis*, among modern physicians, is an inflammation of the mediastinum, or pleura about the diaphragm. **1876** tr. *von Ziemssen's Cycl. Med.* IV. 605 *Diaphragmatic pleuritis* is the disease of which a very expressive general description has been given by the ancient physicans, under the name of paraphrenitis.

Hence **paraphreˈnitic** *a.* (Mayne 1857).

‖**paraphronesis** (pærəfrəʊˈniːsɪs). *Path.* [mod.L., a. Gr. παραφρόνησις wandering of mind, delirium, f. παραφρονεῖν to be beside oneself.] = next. So **paraphroˈnetic** *a.*

1857 MAYNE *Expos. Lex.*, *Paraphroneticus*, of or belonging to *Paraphronesis*, or rather *Paraphrosyne*: paraphronetic.

‖**paraphrosyne** (pærəˈfrɒsɪniː). *Path.* [mod.L., a. Gr. παραφροσύνη, f. παράφρων out of one's wits, f. παρα- beside + φρήν mind.] A mild form of delirium or temporary mental derangement.

1693 tr. *Blanchard's Phys. Dict.* (ed. 2), *Paraphrosyne*, a slight sort of Doting in the Imagination and Judgment. **1818-20** E. THOMPSON *Cullen's Nosol. Meth.* (ed. 3) 230 The symptomatic species of Mania are, (a) Paraphrosyne from poison, (b) Paraphrosyne from passion, (c) Febrile Paraphrosyne. (In mod. Dicts.)

paraphyllum to **paraphysical**: see PARA-[1] 1.

‖**paraphysis** (pəˈræfɪsɪs). *Bot.* Also **ˈparaphyse**. Pl. **-physes**. [mod.L., f. Gr. παρα- PARA-[1] 1, in sense 'by-' or 'subsidiary' + φύσις growth; so F. *paraphyse.*] A sterile filament accompanying the reproductive organs in certain cryptogams.

1857 BERKELEY *Cryptog. Bot.* 270 Abortive asci, known under the name of paraphyses. **1858** CARPENTER *Veg. Phys.* §759 Among the spore-cases lie sterile filaments, termed *paraphyses*, which serve to bind them together. **1870** BENTLEY *Man. Bot.* (ed. 2) 367 Among the antheridia there are..found slender cellular jointed threads called paraphyses.

Hence **paraphysate** (pəˈræfɪsət) *a.*, having or producing paraphyses (*Cent. Dict.* 1890); **paraphyˈsiferous**, bearing paraphyses (Mayne 1857).

parapicoline, etc.: see PARA[1] 2.

paraplasm (ˈpærəplæz(ə)m). [ad. mod.L. *paraplasma*, f. Gr. παρα- PARA-[1] 1 + πλάσμα: see PLASM]

1. *Biol.* **a.** Kupffer's name for the more fluid part of a cell-substance; called by Flemming *paramitom*. **b.** See quot. 1891.

1887 SCHAFER *Essent. Histol.* (ed. 2) 2 Paraplasm is often present in sufficient amount to reduce the protoplasm to the condition of a fine sponge-work or net-work. **1891** *Quain's Elem. Anat.* (ed. 10) I. II. 174 *note*, The terms 'deutoplasm' and 'paraplasm'..have sometimes been applied to materials contained within a cell, which are not considered to constitute a part of the actual protoplasm.

2. *Path.* **a.** Morbid tissue; a neoplasm. **b.** A malformation. (*Syd. Soc. Lex.* 1893.)

Hence **paraˈplasmic** *a.*, pertaining to or of the nature of paraplasm.

1902 *Brit. Med Jrnl.* 29 Mar. 786 Aërobic germs find [a suitable resting-place] in paraplasmic tissue.

paraplastic (pærəˈplæstɪk), *a.* [f. PARA-[1] 1 + PLASTIC: cf. prec.] Of, pertaining to, or connected with paraplasm; neoplastic.

1853 DUNGLISON *Med. Lex.*, *Paraplastic*, possessed of depraved formative powers, as Carcinoma. **1893** HYATT in *Proc. Boston Soc. Nat. Hist.* XXVI. 97 The stages..could be collectively spoken of as paraplastic with relation to the ontogeny of others of their own type or allied types.

paraplectic (pærəˈplɛktɪk), *a.* [ad. Gr. παραπληκτικ-ός, f. παραπλήσσ-ειν: see PARAPLEGIA.]

1. Affected with paraplegia: = PARAPLEGIC.

1661 LOVELL *Hist. Anim. & Min.* 13 Those that are vertiginous, epileptick, apoplectick, paraplectick. **1857** in MAYNE *Expos. Lex.*

2. *paraplectic weevil*, a species of weevil (*Lixus paraplecticus*, Linn.) inhabiting a plant the eating of which causes the staggers in horses.

1802 BINGLEY *Anim. Biog.* (1813) III. 135 The larvæ of the Paraplectic Weevil inhabit the interior part of the stems of an umbelliferous plant, the *phellandrium aquaticum.*

‖**paraplegia** (pærəˈpliːdʒɪə). *Path.* [mod.L., a. Gr. παραπληγία = παραπληξία a stroke on one side, hemiplegia, f. παραπλήσσ-ειν to strike at the side, f. παρα- beside, aside + πλήσσειν to strike.] Paralysis of the lower limbs and a part or the whole of the trunk, resulting from an affection of some part of the spinal cord.

1657 *Physical Dict.*, *Paraplegia*, the same with paralysis. **1693** tr. *Blancard's Phys. Dict.* (ed. 2), *Paraplegia*, a Palsy which seizeth all the parts of the Body below the Head. **1802** *Eng. Encycl.* VI. 9/1 When it [palsy] happens to all the parts below the head, or to the lower half of the body, it is called paraplegia. **1869** GEO. ELIOT in Cross *Life* III. 102 He had an attack of paraplegia.

paraplegic (pærəˈplɛdʒɪk, -ˈpliː-), *a.* and *sb.* [ad. Gr. παραπληγικός, dial. form of παραπληκτικός: see PARAPLECTIC.]

A. *adj.* Marked by or characteristic of paraplegia; affected with paraplegia.

1822-34 *Good's Study Med.* (ed. 4) III. 478 Paraplegic palsy. The disease affecting and confined to the lower part of the body on both sides or any part below the head. **1880** GARROD & BAXTER *Mat. Med.* 325 Incontinence of urine in children and paraplegic patients. **1899** *Allbutt's Syst. Med.* VII. 708 The contraction may have a hemiplegic or a paraplegic distribution.

B. *sb.* A person with paraplegia.

1890 W. JAMES *Princ. Psychol.* I. ii. 16 Paraplegics draw up their legs when tickled. **1950** *Time* 31 July 39/1 The story of war-wounded paraplegics makes a powerful and moving salute to the human spirit. **1970** C. HAMPTON *Philanthropist* iii. 26 Like realizing that Socialism is about as much use to this country as—a pogo-stick to a paraplegic. **1975** *Oxford Times* 12 Dec. 4/4 Her son had been a paraplegic since he injured his spine in a fall four years ago.

†ˌ**paraplero'matically**, *adv. Obs. rare*[−1]. [f. Gr. παραπληρωματικ-ός expletive + -AL[1] + -LY[2].] Expletively, as an expletive.

1698 C. BOYLE *Bentley's Dissert.* 205, 30 or 40 Instances.. where the Particle ἂν is us'd Parapleromatically.

‖**parapleura** (pærəˈplʊərə). *Entom.* Pl. **-æ**. Also **paraˈpleurum**, pl. **-a**. [mod.L., f. Gr. παρα- beside + πλευρά, πλευρόν rib, side.] (See quot.)

1826 KIRBY & SP. *Entomol.* III. 382 The *Parapleuræ*. Two pieces, one on each side of the *Postpectus*, included between the *Scapularia*, *Mesostethium*, and *Pleuræ*. *Ibid.* IV. 372 Their scapulæ and parapleuræ are parallel and placed obliquely.

‖**parapleuritis** (pærəplʊəˈraɪtɪs). *Path.* [mod.L. f. Gr. παρα- PARA-[1] 1 + PLEURITIS pleurisy.] 'A slight degree of pleuritis; also, applied to pleurodynia' (*Syd. Soc. Lex.* 1893).

‖**parapluie** (paraplɥi). [Fr.] An umbrella.

The word had wide literary currency in the 19th c.

1781 H. NEWDIGATE *Let.* 30 Sept. in A. E. Newdigate-Newdegate *Cheverels* (1898) iii. 35 It has poured all this Day ..but with yᵉ help of Pattins & Parapluies we got to yᵉ Well. **1790** E. HELME tr. *Le Vaillant's Trav. Afr.* I. ii. 32 He that takes the East side of the mountain should carry his *paraplue* [sic], while he that takes the West would have occasion for his *parasol*. **1813** M. EDGEWORTH *Let.* 31 May (1971) 69 A shower came on and all the dressed groups were forced to take shelter under trees and parapluies. **1827** M. WILMOT *Jrnl.* 21 Aug. in *More Lett.* (1935) 291 Both wet, but not very bad as they had paraplius [*sic*]. **1847** *Punch* 6 Feb. 62/2 Our umbrellas..bear no announcement of some new pill... The *parapluie* is destined to become a tremendous vehicle for information. **1970** T. S. CRAWFORD *Hist. Umbrella* viii. 158 In the 1880s, the French author, Uzanne, was implying that certain French 'gentlemen' armed with *parapluies* were in the habit of preying on girls..on rainy evenings.

ˈ**parapod**, anglicized form of PARAPODIUM.

1890 in *Cent. Dict.*

parapodial (pærəˈpəʊdɪəl), *a.* [f. next + -AL[1].] Of or pertaining to a parapodium.

1877 HUXLEY *Anat. Inv. Anim.* v. 245 Marine vermiform animals without distinct external segmentation or parapodial appendages.

‖**parapodium** (pærəˈpəʊdɪəm). *Zool.* [mod.L., f. PARA-[1] 1 in sense 'subsidiary', 'false' + Gr. ποδ- foot (cf. Gr. παραπόδιος at the feet).] One of the jointless lateral processes or rudimentary limbs of annelids, which serve as organs of locomotion, and sometimes of sensation or respiration.

1877 HUXLEY *Anat. Inv. Anim.* v. 227 Those parapodia which lie in the vicinity of the mouth may be specially modified in form and function, foreshadowing the jaws of the Arthropoda. **1878** BELL *Gegenbaur's Comp. Anat.* 134 The foot-stumps or parapodia. *Ibid.* 237 The parapodia.. found in the higher Annulata.

†ˈ**parapoint**. *Obs. rare*[−1]. [f. PARA-[1] 1 over against + POINT.] ? A corresponding point.

1647 WARD *Simp. Cobler* 46 The crazie world will crack, in all the middle joynts, If all the ends it hath, have not their parapoynts.

parapolar, etc.: see PARA-[1] 1.

parapolitical: see PARA-[1] 1.

‖**parapophysis** (pærəˈpɒfɪsɪs). *Anat.* [mod.L., f. Gr. παρ(α- beside + APOPHYSIS.] An anterior or ventral transverse process of a vertebra, in some animals greatly developed and serving as articulation for the head of a rib.

1854 OWEN *Skel. & Teeth* in *Circ. Sc.*, *Organ. Nat.* I. 168 The haemal arch..sometimes includes..bones called 'parapophyses'. **1872** MIVART *Elem. Anat.* vi. 220 One made up of tubercular processes (or diapophyses) and ribs, the other made up of capitular processes (or parapophyses) and ribs.

Hence **parapoˈphysial** *a.*, of or belonging to a parapophysis.

1857 in MAYNE *Expos. Lex.* **1887** *Amer. Naturalist* XXI. 565 Three cervical vertebræ, with large parapophysial fossæ looking downwards and outwards.

parapoplexy to **paraproctium**: see PARA-[1] 1.

parapos, an obsolete fabric: see PEROPUS.

parapraxia (pærəˈpræksɪə). Also **paraˈpraxis**, *pl.* **-es**. [f. PARA-[1] + -PRAXIA.] The faulty performance of an intended act; in psychoanalysis, a minor error said to reveal a subconscious motive.

1912 STEDMAN *Med. Dict.* (ed. 2) 657/2 *Parapraxia*, a condition..in which there is a defective performance of certain purposive acts. **1937** tr. *Freud's Gen. Sel. Wks.* i. 25 That group of everyday mental phenomena whose study has become a technical help for psycho-analysis. These are the bungling of acts (parapraxes) among normal men as well as among neurotics. **1953** M. CRITCHLEY *Parietal Lobes* v. 160 The patient, requested to make a particular movement, may do something quite different (parapraxia or parakinesis). **1959** *Observer* 1 Feb. 19/4 Such forces in scientists may produce quite unpredictable parapraxes in their experimental work. **1969** P. ANDERSON in Cockburn & Blackburn *Student Power* 261 No appeal to the conventions of drawing-room conversation can controvert the parapraxes of the couch. **1975** *Times Lit. Suppl.* 4 July 713/1 Have we recognized a bit of the Latin Mass?.. An astronomical reference? A Freudian parapraxis? **1975** *New Society* 11 Sept. 600/3 All too many malapropisms and misprints (or are they parapraxes? We get, for instance, 'He apostasises', followed by a quotation from Mill, for 'He apostrophises'.).

paraprofessional (ˌpærəprəʊˈfɛʃənəl). [f. PARA-[1] + PROFESSIONAL *a.* (*sb.*).] A person without professional training to whom a particular aspect of a professional task is delegated. Also as *adj.*, of or pertaining to such a person.

1967 *Maclean's Mag.* May 64 There is some talk now of using para-professional help, trained on the job like interns. In some schools, mothers already are supervising lunch hours and study periods. **1968** *Bull. Council for Basic Educ.* (U.S.) June 2 The future student..would discover other quaint educational terms which are currently fasionable... 'Paraprofessional' is one, meaning a mother who helps the kindergarten teacher in putting on children's overshoes. **1971** *Harvard Business Rec.* Nov.-Dec. 39/2 The understandable reluctance of the physician to delegate tasks to paraprofessionals. **1972** *N.Y. Law Jrnl.* 22 Aug. 3/5 Another paraprofessional in our office is a retired police officer, presently responsible for..important trial preparation functions. **1974** *Yale Law Jrnl.* LXXXIII. 806 In many professions greater use of paraprofessional employees could help to solve problems in the delivery of professional services. **1975** *Publishers Weekly* 22 Sept. 89/1 A paraprofessional's view of how to survive breast cancer. **1976** *Maclean's Mag.* 17 May 26/1 Basford also stressed the need for developing native lawyers and para-professional court workers for small settlements. **1976** *Times Lit. Suppl.* 16 July 872/4 The personal service ideologies of medical professionals, para-professionals, indigenous non-professionals.

paraprotein(æmia: see PARA-[1] 2 a.

parapsidal (pəˈræpsɪdəl), *a.* [f. next + -AL[1].] Of or pertaining to the parapsis of an insect.

‖**parapsis**[1] (pəˈræpsɪs). Pl. **-apsides**. [mod.L., f. Gr. παρ(α- beside + ἀψίς, ἁψίς, in sense 'circle, arch, vault'. In mod.F. *parapside.*] Each of the two lateral pieces of the mesoscutum of the thorax of an insect, by means of which it is articulated with the wing.

1830 MACLEAY in *Zool. Jrnl* V. 177 *note*, The lateral pieces of the scutum of the mesothorax, which I call *parapsides*.

‖**paˈrapsis**[2]. *Path.* [mod.L., f. Gr. παρ(α- PARA-[1] 1 + ἅψις touch] Disordered touch.

1822 GOOD *Study Med.* III. 272 Parapsis. Morbid Touch. Sense of touch or general feeling vitiated or lost. **1842** in DUNGLISON *Med. Lex.*

parapsoriasis (ˌpærəsɒˈraɪəsɪs). *Med.* [mod.L. (coined in Fr. by L. Brocq 1902, in *Ann. de Dermatol. et de Syphiligr.* III. 446), f. PARA-[1] + PSORIASIS.] Any of various rare chronic diseases of the skin which resemble psoriasis and are characterized by red scaly patches, resistance to treatment, and lack of subjective symptoms.

1906 DORLAND *Med. Dict.* (ed. 4) 526/1 *Parapsoriasis*, a chronic skin-disease resembling psoriasis and lichen. **1920** J. M. H. MACLEOD *Dis. of Skin* xxvii. 844 Brocq has divided the parapsoriasis group into three varieties namely: Parapsoriasis en gouttes, P. lichénoïde, P. en plaques. **1936** *Practitioners Libr. Med. & Surg.* X. vi. 617 Much of the confusion that has been occasioned by parapsoriasis is attributable to its widely differing clinical types and its multitudinous nomenclature. **1956** D. M. PILLSBURY et al. *Dermatol.* xxxii. 744 The original definition of parapsoriasis was a chronic eruption resembling psoriasis and having no acute manifestations. *Ibid.*, Lichenoid parapsoriasis is the parapsoriasis analogue of lichen planus. **1961** R. D. BAKER *Essent. Path.* xx. 540 There are other histologically identifiable noninfectious dermatoses in addition to psoriasis and pityriasis rosea. These include parapsoriasis, lichen planus and several other rare conditions. **1968** A. J. ROOK et al. *Textbk. Dermatol.* I. 804/2 The terms guttate parapsoriasis and varicelliform parapsoriasis are still frequently used as synonyms for pityriasis lichenoides chronica and pityriasis lichenoides acuta, respectively.

parapsychic(al: see PARA-[1] 1.

parapsy'chology. [PARA-[1].] The science or study of phenomena which lie outside the sphere of orthodox psychology. Cf. METAPSYCHICS *sb. pl.* Hence **parapsycho'logical** *a.*, **parapsycho'logically** *adv.*; **parapsy'chologist.**

1924 *Times Lit. Suppl.* 10 Jan. 27/2 Its inherent merit.. renders the publication a noteworthy and welcome contribution to parapsychological literature. **1927** H. DRIESCH in C. Murchison *Case Psychical Belief* 164 The philosophic importance of Parapsychology. **1936** *Discovery* Dec. 396/1 The book [sc. *The Modern Dowser*]..should be useful to the would-be dowser and of interest to the parapsychologist. **1954** M. LOWRY *Let.* 10 May (1967) 369 You were so sporting as to write us para-psychologically suspecting some Lowry misery-grisery. **1957** RHINE & PRATT *Parapsychol.* i. 12 The term parapsychology was adapted from the German word *Parapsychologie*... It means the same as the older English expression, *psychical research*, and the French, *métapsychique*. **1967** A. WILSON *No Laughing Matter* I. 12 Alas for the limits of our parapsychological knowledge. **1973** *Daily Tel.* (Colour Suppl.) 30 Nov. 33/1 The Russians, who had previously persecuted parapsychologists as bourgeois deviationists, began to encourage research, doubtless with their space communications system in mind. **1975** *Sci. Amer.* Oct. 117/3 Whenever a major experiment, such as the SRI test of Targ's ESP machine, is a conspicuous failure, parapsychologists themselves become strongly motivated to give reasons for the failure. **1976** *Listener* 3 June 698/3 Once you postulate psychic communication..you are really committed to a whole new dimension... You can't sell parapsychology by the yard. **1977** *Church Times* 7 Apr. 6/1 They accept the reality of the 'Easter experience' understood psychologically, perhaps parapsychologically.

‖**pa'rapterum, -on.** [mod.L., f. Gr. παρα- beside + πτερόν wing. In mod.F. *paraptère*.] (See quot.) Hence **pa'rapteral** *a.*, pertaining to a parapterum.

1857 MAYNE *Expos. Lex.*, *Parapterum. Entomol.* Applied to a piece..in the lateral parts of each segment of the thorax of hexapodous insects, which has relation with the *episternum* and wing... *Ornithol.* Applied by Illiger to the long feathers directed backwards, which are inserted in the arm near the *axilla*, and which cover more or less of the wings.

†**para'pyclite,** variant of BARA-PICKLET. *Obs.*

1731 MRS. DELANY *Life & Corr.* I. 287 M'Donnellan, his sister, and I breakfast together on coffee and parapyclites.

paraquat ('pærəkwɒt, -kwæt). [f. PARA-[1] 2 b + QUAT(ERNARY *a.* and *sb.*

So called from the fact that the bond between the two pyridyl groups is in the *para* position with respect to their quaternary nitrogen atoms.]

Any salt, esp. the dichloride or dimethylsulphate (both crystalline and water-soluble), of the 1,1′-dimethyl-4,4′-bipyridylium ion, $(-C_5H_4\overset{+}{N}\cdot CH_3)_2$, a quick-acting contact herbicide that is rendered inactive by the soil.

1961 *Weed Abstr.* X. 572 *Paraquat di(methyl sulphate), previously PP.910, a new herbicide.* Publ. Plant Protection Ltd., 1961 pp. 6. Paraquat (1,1′-dimethyl-4,4′-bipyridylium) is the name given to the free radicle. Two salts are currently under test, the di(methyl sulphate) (PP.910) and the dichloride (PP.148)... Paraquat salts are very rapidly absorbed into the aerial parts of plants. **1962** *New Scientist* 6 Sept. 490/1 The active ingredient—paraquat—is a member of a family of herbicidal chemicals (quaternary salts of bipyridyls). **1962** *Listener* 15 Nov. 836/1 A new family of weed-killing substances based on 'paraquat' may herald a new agricultural revolution. Paraquat is almost a total weed-killer but is especially useful in killing grasses. **1965** *Economist* 5 June 1193/2 The 'Paraquat' herbicides, used in ploughless cultivation. **1968** *Times* 17 Dec. 10/5 The weedkiller paraquat..is highly poisonous but is swiftly broken down to harmless components by bacteria in the soil. **1972** *Country Life* 20 Jan. 169 The advent of paraquat was one of the most important developments in British farming in the 1960's. **1974** *Daily Tel.* 2 Feb. 1/1 The weedkiller paraquat has been officially declared a poison... Only registered pharmacists or firms will be able to sell paraquat, and only people engaged in agriculture or horticulture will be able to buy it. **1974** *Times* 2 Feb. 4/2 At least twenty deaths in Britain in the past 10 years are known to have been caused by paraquat. In almost all cases death followed the decanting of agricultural paraquat solutions into soft drink bottles. Granular preparations containing less than 5 per cent of paraquat salts are not affected by the new controls. **1977** *Jrnl. R. Soc. Arts* CXXV. 567/2 Paraquat acts..by killing the green top growth of all plants and is inactivated by soil.

paraqueeto, -quet, -quetto: see PARAKEET.

pararabin to **-salpingitis**: see PARA-[1] 1, 2.

para-rescue ('pærə,rɛskjuː). [f. PARA-[3] + RESCUE *sb.*] A rescue carried out by a parachutist or parachutists. Chiefly *attrib.* and *Comb.*

1950 *N.Y. Times* 30 Jan. 20/2 A para-rescue crew is being held in readiness here and will be sent out at once if the ground party finds any trace of the missing transport. **1961** *Aeroplane* C. 458/1 A ground search party and 12 trained pararescue men are included. **1968** *Washington Post* 4 July A 11/6, I realized there was a guy in green bending over me. .. He was the chopper's para-rescueman. **1973** *Maclean's Mag.* July 58/3 Gathercole..told Mooddy to direct..a helicopter and a Hercules with a pararescue team, piloted by Captain Neil Toby.

para-rhyme, pararhyme ('pærəraɪm). [f. PARA-[1] + RHYME *sb.*] A half-rhyme, with the same consonant pattern but vowel variation.

In English poetry particularly associated with Wilfred Owen (1893–1918).

1931 E. BLUNDEN in W. Owen *Poems* 28 Having discovered and practised this para-rhyme, Owen became aware that it would serve him infinitely in the voicing of emotion and imagination... By means of it he creates remoteness, darkness, emptiness, shock, echo, the last word. **1939** *Eng. Stud.* XXI. 99 He [sc. Wilfred Owen] had invented what has been called pararhymes. Choosing words built upon the same framework of consonants but different vowels, he played with this blend of similarity and dissimilarity..placating the ear while disturbing it. **1951** [see DISSONANTAL *a.*]. **1961** *Listener* 23 Nov. 863/1 Owen muted the rhythms of the romantics by the use of para-rhyme. **1975** *Ibid.* 9 Jan. 69/1[Wilfred] Owen had taught him pararhyme, but [Keith] Douglas uses both pararhyme and assonance.

pararosaniline, -sagittal: see PARA-[1] 2 a, 1.

parasang ('pærəsæŋ). See also FARSANG. [ad. L. (It., Sp.) *parasanga*, ad. Gr. παρασάγγης, of Persian origin, the corresponding mod.Pers. word being FARSANG, Arab. *farsaχ*; in mod.F. *parasange, farsange*.] A Persian measure of length, usually reckoned as equal to between 3 and 3½ English miles. Also *fig.*

Reckoned by Herodotus, and app. also by Xenophon, as equal to 30 stadia, which, taking the stadium at 610 ft., would make the Parasang less than 3½ miles. The Arab geographers according to Freytag reckon the *farsakh* at 3 (Haschemite) miles. But according to Pliny and Strabo the length of the parasang was reckoned differently by authors, some making it = 40 or even 60 stadia. See also Grote *Greece* IX. II. lxix. 20 *note.*

[**1555** EDEN *Decades* 315 The lake conteyneth fortie Persian myles cauled *Parasange*.] **1594** BLUNDEVIL *Exerc.* III. II. vi. (1636) 382 The Grecians did measure the distances ..by furlongs,..and the Persians by parasanges. **1623** BINGHAM *Xenophon* 9 From hence..hee marched fiue Parasangs, euen to the streights of Cilicia. **1821** BYRON *Sardan.* II. i, Sloth..moves more parasangs in its intents Than generals in their marches. **1847** GROTE *Greece* II. xxxvi. IV. 418 He [Artaphernes] caused the territory of each [Ionian] city to be measured by parasangs (each parasang was equal to thirty stadia, or about three miles and a half). **1882** FLOYER *Unexpl. Baluchisian* 376 A farsakh or parasang varies in length from three to four and a half and even five miles in different parts of Persia.

fig. **1621** BURTON *Anat. Mel.* II. iii. III. (1651) 325 Thou art many parasanges before me in means, favour, wealth, honour. **1836** LANDOR *Peric. & Asp.* Wks. 1846 II. 382 If there are paces between Sculpture and Painting there are parasangs between Painting and Poetry. **1880** *Daily Tel.* 9 Dec., Between a canary and a cook there is distance of many parasangs.

parascending ('pærəsɛndɪŋ), *vbl. sb.* [f. PARA-[3] + ASCENDING *vbl. sb.*] A sport in which participants, wearing open parachutes, are towed behind a vehicle to gain height before release for a conventional parachute descent, usu. towards a predetermined target area. Hence '**parascender**, one who takes part in this sport.

1970 *Policy, Organisation & Rules of Scout Assoc.* III. 169 In order to ensure the safe control of the sport of Parascending within the Scout Movement the following safety regulations must be applied. **1973** J. LUCAS *Big Umbrella* xiii. 137 The advent of multiple aerofoil parachutes has led to a challenging new kind of fun-jumping —parascending, which is enjoying increasing popularity among children as well as adults. Parascending is practised at sea as well as on land. One girl, towed by a motor boat, travelled more than half-way across the English Channel by parachute. On land, the parachutist takes off with the aid of a towing vehicle, such as a Land-Rover. *Ibid.*, Parascending made its first appearance in Britain in 1962, and has gained a firm foothold in the sporting world. **1973** *Daily Tel.* 28 Feb. 16/4 (*heading*) Parascenders split from parent group. *Ibid.*, Parascending..has become independent of the British Parachute Association. *Ibid.* 16 July 12/4 The parascender ..chooses the point of release and tries to hit the centre of the target, five and a half inches across. **1975** *Valiant* 30 Aug. 1 Parascending is a new all-action sport. **1978** *Observer* (Colour Suppl.) 9 Apr. 43/4 Two helpers hold the parachute open, the Land-Rover moves forward and the parascender soars into the air.

parascene ('pærəsiːn). *Gr.* and *Rom. Antiq.* Also in L. form **para'scenium.** [a. F. *parascène*, mod.L. *parascēnium*, a Gr. παρασκήνιον, one of the side-entrances to the stage, a side-scene, f. παρα- side + σκηνή stage.] The part of an ancient theatre on either side of the stage, comprising rooms to which the actors retired; the side-scene.

1706 PHILLIPS, *Parascenium*,..the back part of the Scene or Stage in a Play-house. **1842** *Penny Cycl.* XXIV. 295/1 There was no other architectural exterior than that formed by the Parascene (Παρασκήνη) and colonnade behind the stage.

†**parasceu'astic,** *a. Obs. rare.* [ad. Gr. παρασκευαστικός (cf. next).] Preparatory.

1672 *Corah's Doom* 128 The Latine and Greek, and those other Learned Languages..are the Parasceuastick part of Learning.

†**parasceuo'logical** *a. Obs. rare.* In 7 -scu-. [f. Gr. παρασκευή preparation (see next) + -(O)LOGY + -ICAL.] Relating to preparation.

1671 SALMON *Syn. Med.* III. xxxiv. 504 The Parascuological Instruments, wherewith Medicines are prepared.

Parasceve ('pærəsiːv, ‖pærə'siːviː). Also 7–8 parascue. [ad. late L. *parascēvē* day of preparation, day before the Sabbath, a. Gr. παρασκευή preparation, in Jewish use the 'day of preparation'; f. παρα- against + σκευή equipment, outfit, attire, etc. Cf. F. *parascève* (15–16th c. in Godef.).]

1. The day of preparation for the Jewish sabbath, the eve of the sabbath, Friday; *spec.* Good Friday (from Mark xv. 42, etc.). *Obs.* exc. in *R. C. Ch.*

[**1391** *Earl Derby's Exp.* (Camden) 117 In die parasseue.] **1548** UDALL *Erasm. Par. Luke* xxiii. 167 b, The same lorde finished yᵉ redempcion of the worlde on the sixth daie, which is the parasceue daie). **1582** N. T. (Rhem.) *Mark* xv. 42 It was the Parasceue, which is the Sabboth-eue. —— *John* xix. 14 It was the Parasceue of Pasche. **1613** PURCHAS *Pilgrimage* (1614) 123 The fourteenth day being the Parascue, or preparation. **1697** BP. PATRICK *Comm. Exod.* xvi. 5 From which Preparation this Day was called the Parascue.

†**2.** Preparation (with allusion to sense 1). *Obs.*

1612 R. SHELDON *Serm. St. Martin's* 5 Preparing and making a Quadragesime, or fortieth, as a parasceue of Christ his death and passion. **1647** HERRICK *Noble Numbers, Parasceve*, Let's go, my Alma, yet, e're we receive, Fit, fit it is, we have our Parasceve. **1654** H. L'ESTRANGE *Chas. I* (1655) 195 This Treaty at Rippon was but the Parasceue, the preparation to another of higher import.

parasche, -en, obs. forms of PARISH, -EN.

paraschematic (,pærəskiː'mætɪk), *a. rare.* [mod. f. Gr. type *παρασχηματικός: cf. παρασχηματίζειν to transform, to form by a slight change.] Formed by slight change of an existing element.

1868 MAX MÜLLER *Rede Lect.* II. Sel. Ess. 1881 I. 98 The growth of these early themes may have been very luxuriant, and, as Prof. Curtius expresses it, chiefly paraschematic.

parascience ('pærəsaɪəns). [f. PARA-[1] + SCIENCE.] The study of phenomena assumed to be beyond the scope of scientific inquiry or for which no scientific explanation exists. So **,parascien'tific** *a.*, **-'scientist.**

1953 *Mind* LXII. 360 [The fallacy] that I know about thinking by 'observing' myself thinking, whereby thought is transformed into a paraphysical object studied by a parascience of introspection. **1961** *Times Lit. Suppl.* 1 Sept. 577/3 Time Travel, like hyperspace, is one of the classical Science-Fiction presumptions which, though abstruse mathematical discussion may give it para-scientific justification, is essentially a basis for fantasy. **1974** *Nature* 8 Nov. 129/1 So much of the interpreting, let alone the theorising, of parascientists and parathinkers is based on seemingly natural occurrences which either cannot be fully corroborated according to the rules of evidence, or cannot be properly repeated according to the rules of experiment. **1975** *Ibid.* 6 Nov. 22/1, I lumped them all [sc. telepathy, telekinesis, parapsychology, etc.] under the title 'parascience'. **1976** *Word 1971* XXVII. 77 As we know very little about human language (a fact..little known to most parascientists..), any approach toward its analysis may contribute something to our understanding of the subject.

parasecretion: see PARA-[1] 1.

‖**paraselene** (,pærəsɪ'liːniː). Pl **paraselenæ** (-niː). [In form, mod.L. *paraselēnē*, f. Gr. παρα- in sense 'subsidiary, false' + σελήνη moon (after PARHELION): cf. F. *parasélène* (1547 in Hatz.-Darm.).] A bright spot on a lunar halo, somewhat resembling the moon itself; a mock moon.

1653 [see PARASTER]. **1670** *Phil. Trans.* V. 1071 Observed together with the Paraselene's or Mock-moons by M. Hevelius. **1790** UMFREVILLE *Hudson's Bay* 24 Paraselenes or mock moons appear, when the vapours arising from open water become condensed by the frost. **1835** SIR J. ROSS *Narr. 2nd Voy.* xxxvi. 501 A large and beautiful halo round the moon, with four paraselenæ. **1878** A. H. MARKHAM *Gt. Frozen Sea* xv. 206 Paraselenæ, or mock moons, and auroras were of frequent occurrence.

Hence **paraselenic** (,pærəsɪ'lɛnɪk) *a.*, pertaining to or of the nature of a paraselene. In mod. Dicts.

parasexual (pærə'sɛksjuːəl), *a. Genetics.* [f. PARA-[1] + SEXUAL *a.*] Involving, exhibiting, or being a process by which recombination of genes from different individuals occurs without meiosis.

1954 G. PONTECORVO in *Proc. 9th Internat. Congr. Genetics* 192 In the last ten years, processes other than standard sexual reproduction, and yet resulting in recombination of hereditary properties, have come to light in microorganisms of widely different groups.. The purpose of the present paper is to give a summary of the work which has led, in our Laboratory, to the discovery in the filamentous fungi of another of these mechanisms, which could be called 'para-sexual'. This mechanism, based on *mitotic* segregation and recombination, occurs side by side with a standard sexual cycle in one of the three species investigated. **1962** *Ann. Rev. Microbiol.* XVI. 39 Using parasexual processes, 40 markers have been assigned to eight linkage groups in *A[spergillus] nidulans*. **1962** G. DALLDORF *Fungi & Fungous Dis.* x. 135 Even in asexual fungi, recombinant types may arise through a parasexual process. **1970** J. WEBSTER *Introd. Fungi* 161 The occurrence of parasexual recombination explains how variation can occur in Fungi Imperfecti. **1974** *Nature* 27 Sept. 321/2 Genetic analysis of their development [*sc.* that of cellular slime moulds] has been hampered by the apparent absence of a true sexual cycle, although progress has been made in parasexual genetic analysis. **1977** P. B. & J. S. MEDAWAR *Life Sci.* iii. 39 In some bacteria..the sexual process is restricted to something that amounts to hardly more than the infection of one bacterium by nucleic acid from another—the 'parasexual' process that lies at the root of the enormously important phenomenon of bacterial transformation.

Hence ˌ**parasexu'ality**, the parasexual process.

1959 *Mycologia* LI. 109 Somatic recombination or parasexuality..reassorts genetic characters of heterokaryotic components in a vegetative system to yield products that are comparable to the meiotic products of the sexual process. **1974** *Nature* 18 Jan. 142/1 Using an improved version of the methods employing parasexuality.., we have selected axenic resegregants carrying various markers from non-axenic strains.

‖**parashah** ('pærəʃɑː). Also 7 (**parashioth**, from Heb. pl.), **parash**, 8–9 **parascha**, 9 **parasha**. [Heb. *pārāshāh* division, f. *pārash* to divide.] Each section of the Pentateuch read as the weekly Sabbath lesson in the synagogue. Also, more loosely, any section, chapter, or passage of the Old Testament.

In mod. Jewish use, applied spec. to the section of the weekly lesson publicly recited in the Synagogue by a Jewish youth at the age of 13, when he becomes *Bar-mitsvah* ('Son of, or heir to, the Commandment'). In this sense colloquially called '*Parshā* or '*Persha*: 'the boy read his *Parsha* well'.

? **1624** R. SKYNNER in *Ussher's Lett.* (1686) 352 They have told us that there be 54 Parashioths or Sections in Moses's Law. **1723** MATHER *Vind. Bible* 362 Read instead of the Paraschas of the law. **1853** J. CUMMING *Script. Read. Gen.* vi. 59 One parasha was read each Sabbath.

parashoot ('pærəʃuːt), *sb. rare.* [Alteration of PARACHUTE *sb.* after SHOOT *sb.*[1], SHOOT *v.*] (See quot.)

1940 [see CHUTIST, 'CHUTIST].

parashot ('pærəʃɒt). [f. PARA-[3] + SHOT *sb.*[1]] In the war of 1939–45, a member of the British Home Guard whose task was to shoot down enemy parachutists. Also *attrib.* So '**parashoot** *v. trans.*; '**parashooter**.

1940 *Star* 14 May 8/5 (*caption*) 'What are you doing with that gun?' 'I'm practising-to-parashoot Germans!' **1940** *Daily Mirror* 17 May 5/2 Over a quarter of a million had applied to join Britain's parashooters by midnight on Wednesday, the War Office stated last night. **1940** Parashot [see PARATROOPS *sb. pl.*]. **1940** *Star* 22 May 8/2 Clubs' part in fight against parachute troops... The appeal for parashooters has brought rifle shooting into the news. Clubs are offering free instruction to applicants. **1940** *Economist* 8 June 1005/2 Air-raids will precede invasion; and the transfer of wardens and other civil defence workers to become Ironsides and parashooters..should be stopped immediately. **1940** *New Yorker* 29 June 46/3 A movement to provide parashots with hand grenades. **1941** A. CHRISTIE *N or M?* vi. 85 I've got to go to a meeting about this Parashot business, raising a corps of local volunteers. **1942** A. M. LOW *Parachutes* p. x, Parashot, the word coined by the newspapers in the summer of 1940 to describe gentlemen with shotguns seeking enemy parachutists. **1944** *Ourselves in Wartime* 129 The village men lined up..to join the local Defence Volunteers. The 'Parashooters' they called themselves in those days, when everyone thought the enemy might drop on us from the sky just in the same way as he had done over the Low Countries.

parasinoidal: see PARA-[1] 1.

parasitæmia (ˌpærəsaɪ'tiːmɪə). *Path.* Also (chiefly *U.S.*) **-emia**. [f. PARASIT(E *sb.* + Gr. αἷμα blood: see -IA[1].] The presence of demonstrable parasites in the circulation.

1947 DORLAND & MILLER *Med. Dict.* (ed. 21) 1066/2 *Parasitemia*, the presence of parasites (especially malarial parasites) in the blood. **1956** *Nature* 21 Jan. 133/1 In December 1952, N'Dama 151 was challenged with a strain of *T[rypanosoma] vivax*..; a low-grade intermittent parasitæmia persisted until August 1953, after which time no parasites were detected in the blood. **1972** *Ann. Trop. Med. & Parasitol.* LXVII. 390 A direct counting technique for estimating high parasitaemias of *Babesia argentina* is described. **1973** B. J. WILLIAMS *Evolution & Human Origins* v. 80/2 He confirmed Beet's observation that the incidence of parasitemia was less in *AS* individuals than it was in *AA* individuals.

parasital ('pærəsaɪtəl), *a.* [f. PARASITE *sb.* + -AL[1]] = PARASITIC.

1839 J. E. READE *Deluge* 24 Idle thoughts..Which, like the parasital plants, cling round. **1862** LYTTON *Str. Story* II. 344 Round the sides..clustered parasital plants.

†**parasi'taster.** *Obs. rare*[−1]. [L. (Terence): see next and -ASTER.] A mean or sorry parasite.

1606 MARSTON (*title*) Parasitaster, or the Fawne.

parasite ('pærəsaɪt), *sb.* Also 6 **parrasite, parasyte, paresite,** 6–7 **parasit.** [ad. L. *parasīt-us, -a*, a. Gr. παράσιτος lit. one who eats at the table of another, hence one who lives at another's expense and repays him with flattery, etc.; orig. an adj. = feeding beside; f. παρα- beside + σῖτος food. Cf. F. *parasite* (Rabelais 1535).]

1. a. One who eats at the table or at the expense of another; always with opprobrious application: 'One that frequents rich tables and earns his welcome by flattery' (J.); one who obtains the hospitality, patronage, or favour of the wealthy or powerful by obsequiousness and flattery; a hanger-on from interested motives; a 'toady'.

1539 TAVERNER *Erasm. Prov.* (1552) 71 It is the fashion of a flatterer and parasyte to lyue of an other man's trencher. **1542** UDALL *Erasm. Apoph.* 199 Parasites, were called suche smellefeastes as would seeke to bee free geastes at riche mennes tables. **1568** GRAFTON *Chron.* II. 397 He.. distributed the Dukes landes to his Parasites, and flatteryng folowers. **1607** SHAKS. *Timon* III. vi. 104 You knot of Mouth-Friends:..Most smiling, smooth, detested Parasites. **1736** BOLINGBROKE *Patriot.* (1749) 139 Crowds of spies, parasites and sycophants, will surround the throne under the patronage of such ministers. **1862** THACKERAY *Four Georges* iii, The good clergy not corrupted into parasites by hopes of preferment.

fig. **1597–8** BP. HALL *Sat.* I. Prol. 10 Hath made his pen an hired parasite. **1602** *2nd Pt. Return fr. Parnass.* v. iv. 2160 This fond earth..Where most mens pens are hired parasites.

b. *Gr. Antiq.* One admitted to the table kept up for a public officer, or to the feast after a sacrifice.

(This is a sense given by the Greek grammarians and late writers, which was app. obs. in B.C. 400; it comes nearer to the etymological sense, but stands quite apart from the general current of meaning in Gr., L., and Eng.)

1697 POTTER *Antiq. Greece* I. xxvi. (1715) 147 The βασιλεύς is to take care that the Parasites be created out of the People, whose duty 'tis, each of them to reserve out of his allowance an Hecteum of Barly,..for the maintenance of the Genuine Citizens Feast. **1706** PHILLIPS, *Parasite* (among the Ancients) was the Priest's Guest, whom he invited to eat part of the Sacrifice: whence the word is taken for a smell-feast [etc.]. **1770** LANGHORNE *Plutarch* (1879) I. 106/1 *note*, In the first ages the name of parasite was venerable and sacred, for it properly signified one that was a messmate at the table of sacrifices. **1791–1823** D'ISRAELI *Cur. Lit., Confus. Words.* **1807** ROBINSON *Archæol. Græca* I. xxiii. 100, III. iii. 202. **1868** SMITH *Smaller Dict. Ant.*, s.v.

2. a. *Biol.* An animal or plant which lives in or upon another organism (technically called its *host*) and draws its nutriment directly from it. Also extended to animals or plants that live as tenants of others, but not at their expense (strictly called *commensal* or *symbiotic*); also to those which depend on others in various ways for sustenance, as the cuckoo, the skua-gull, etc. (see PARASITIC 2 b); and (inaccurately) to plants which grow upon others, deriving support but not nourishment from them (*epiphytes*), or which live on decaying organic matter (*saprophytes*).

See note s.v. PARASITIC 2 a.

1727–41 CHAMBERS *Cycl.*, *Parasites*..in botany, a kind of diminutive plants, growing on trees, and so called from their manner of living and feeding, which is altogether on others. .. Such is moss,..which, with the lichens and mistletoe's, make the family of parasite plants. **1826** KIRBY & SP. *Entomol.* xliv. IV. 209 The great body of insect parasites.. belong to the *Hymenoptera* Order. **1835** HENSLOW *Phys. Bot.* §234 Certain plants..obtain their nourishment immediately from other plants to which they attach themselves, and whose juices they absorb. Such plants are true 'Parasites'. **1871** DARWIN *Desc. Man* I. I. i. 12 Man is infested with internal..and is plagued by external parasites. **1892** J. A. THOMSON *Outlines Zool.* 151 The Trematodes are leaf-like or roundish external or internal parasites.

b. Applied, loosely or poetically, to a plant that creeps or climbs about another plant or a wall, trellis-work, etc., by which it is supported.

1813 SHELLEY *Q. Mab* I. 43 Like tendrils of the parasite Around a marble column. **1843** PRESCOTT *Mexico* II. vii. (1864) 114 The branches of the..trees were..festooned with clustering vines of..variegated convolvuli, and other flowering parasites. **1876** BROWNING *A Forgiveness* 77 Helpless as the statue..Against that strangling bell-flower's bondage: tear Away..the parasite.

c. *fig.* A person whose part or action resembles that of an animal parasite.

1883 H. DRUMMOND *Nat. Law in Spir. W.*, *Parasitism* (1902) 95 Instead of having learned to pray the ecclesiastical parasite becomes satisfied with being prayed for. His transactions with the Eternal are effected by commission. **1898** *Westm. Gaz.* 18 Jan. 3/1 If the employer who gives less than the equivalent of work in wages is a parasite, so also is the labourer who gives less than the equivalent of wages in work.

d. *Philol.* A parasitic vowel or consonant: see PARASITIC 3 b.

1888 SWEET *Eng. Sounds* 40 The quality of the parasite is often determined by that of the nearest accented vowel.

3. *Min.* A mineral developed upon or within another; *spec.* [ad. Ger. *parasit*] a plumose variety of BORACITE, the result of alteration.

1868 DANA *Min.* (ed. 5) 596 Parasite of Volger is the plumose interior of some crystals of boracite. **1896** A. H. CHESTER *Dict. Names Min., Parasite*..(Parasit), because formed as a parasite at the expense of the original mineral. The plumose interior of certain crystals of boracite.

4. *attrib.* often passing into adj. = parasitic; ***parasite-vowel, -consonant, -sound, -letter***: see 2 d; **parasite-diphthong**, a diphthong formed by the development of a parasite beside the original vowel; **parasite drag** *Aeronaut.*, the drag of all parts of an aircraft other than that induced by the lift or due to the lifting surface (quot. 1927 represents a broader use); **parasite (jet) fighter** *Aeronaut.*, an aircraft carried by and operating from another aircraft; **parasite resistance** *Aeronaut.* = *parasite drag*.

1875 F. S. HADEN *Earth to Earth* 60 Not the respectable tradesman..but a *parasite class which interposes itself. **1888** SWEET *Eng. Sounds* 40 E. *fear*..from OE. *fēr* shows how *parasite-diphthongs begin. **1927** V. W. PAGE *Mod. Aircraft* (1928) iv. 134 The *parasite drag results from friction of the air on the parts of the airplane, including the wings, tail, fuselage, landing gear, etc., and from the eddies set up by these parts when in motion. **1934** *Jrnl. R. Aeronaut. Soc.* XXXVIII. 459 For aeroplanes of normal design, the ratio of induced drag to parasite drag was very low at high speeds. **1958** *Guided Missiles* (U.S. Dept. Air Force) ii. 24/2 Both parasite and induced drag vary as the square of the velocity. **1965** C. N. VAN DEVENTER *Introd. Gen. Aeronaut.* iv. 59/1 The resistance of parts that do not contribute to lift is called parasite drag. **1948** *Daily Progress* (Charlottesville, Va.) 2 Jan. 10/1 A new jet fighter plane is expected soon to start and end a flight high in the sky for the first time in history. This is the McDonnell XP-85, known as a '*parasite' fighter because it is based on a larger craft. **1948** *Shell Aviation News* No. 121. 6/3 The Air Force has announced the building by McDonnell of a parasite jet fighter..designed to be carried in the front bomb-bay of Consolidated's B-36. It has no landing gear and is launched and picked-up by means of a retractable hook which engages in an eye on the mother plane. **1977** *New Scientist* 25 Aug. 489/4 In the immediate post-war years the US Army Air Force test launched the diminutive McDonnell XF-85 Goblin parasite fighter from the bomb bay of a Boeing B-29 bomber. **1727–41** CHAMBERS *Cycl.* s.v. *Moss*, A little plant of the *parasite kind. **1817** COLERIDGE *Biog. Lit.* I. i. 6 These *parasite plants of youthful poetry. **1918** WEBSTER Add., *Parasite resistance. **1921** *Flight* XIII. 509/2 Great reduction in parasite resistance..is brought about by the cantilever construction. **1929** *Aircraft Engineering* Mar. 10 Giant seaplanes are another story... Aerodynamically they are disappointingly full of parasite resistance. **1888** *Parasite vowel [see PARASITE *v.* 3]. **1809–10** COLERIDGE *Friend* (1865) 37 The *parasite weeds, that fed on its very roots.

5. *Comb.*, as ***parasite-containing, -covered, -infested, parasite-like*** adjs.

1897 *Outing* (U.S.) XXX. 163/2 Fish..with thin, parasite-covered bodies. **1897** *Pop. Sci. Monthly* Nov. 70 Which effect their dispersal in this parasitelike way. **1898** P. MANSON *Trop. Diseases* iii. 74 Parasite-containing red blood corpuscles. *Ibid.* 75 Effete parasite-infested corpuscles.

'**parasite**, *v. rare.* [f. prec. sb.]

1. *intr.* To act the parasite or sycophant.

1609 BP. W. BARLOW *Answ. Nameless Cath* 41 Popes testifying of themselues; or Canonists Paraziting to Popes. **1932** [see GAZUMP *v.*].

2. *trans.* To infest as a parasite, to parasitize. Also *fig.*

1868 *Amer. Naturalist* May 128 Parasited cocoons and eggs of insects, or living insects and other animals infested by parasites. **1882** *Amer. Naturalist* XVI. 150, I had the opportunity of examining a larva..parasited by an allied species. **1963** *Guardian* 14 June 10/2 The cuckoo bees Psithyrus..parasite the Bombex. **1968** *Daily Tel.* (Colour Suppl.) 8 Nov. 12/3 Viruses are incomplete cells. They exist by parasiting 'proper' cells, and getting into them. **1969** K. GILES *Death cracks Bottle* vii. 83 The only worry I had was that he might be parasiting the business stone dry. **1976** *Eastern Daily Press* (Norwich) 19 Nov. 12/2 Beds of pelargoniums..heavily parasited by this rust.

3. *intr.* (*Philol.*) To develop a parasitic sound.

1888 SWEET *Eng. Sounds* 40 (*Parasiting*) The development of parasite-vowels before and after certain consonants... The first stage in parasiting..is seen in such words as E. *bower*, German *bauer* from older *būr*, in which the glide to the (r) has been exaggerated into an independent (ə).

parasitic (pærə'sɪtɪk), *a.* and *sb. pl.* [ad. L. *parasīticus*, a. Gr. παρασιτικ-ός, f. παράσιτ-ος: see PARASITE *sb.* and -IC. Cf. F. *parasitique* (Littré).]

A. *adj.* **1.** Of, pertaining to, or characteristic of parasites; having the nature of a parasite, sycophantic.

1627 HAKEWILL *Apol.* (1630) 3rd Advt., The Bishop received small thankes for his parasiticke presentation. **1648** *Eikon Bas.* xx. 197 Some parasitick Preachers. **1654** VILVAIN *Epit. Ess.* VI. 79 Parasitic Panegyrics. **1855** KINGSLEY *Westw. Ho!* viii. (1869) 150 Somewhat of a gnathonic and parasitic soul.

2. *Biol.* Of, belonging to, or having the nature of a plant or animal parasite.

a. Living, as an organism, in or upon another from the body of which it derives its nourishment; pertaining to or of the nature of such an organism; also, by extension =

SYMBIOTIC. In *Path.* applied to diseases caused by parasites.

Earlier naturalists included plants which grow upon others but are now known not to derive nourishment from them, e.g. polypody, moss, lichens.

1731–3 MILLER *Gard. Dict.* s.v. *Hedera*, Ivy..is a parasitick Plant. **1760** J. LEE *Introd. Bot.* III. iv. (1765) 169 *Parasitic*, when they grow not out of the Ground, but on some other Plant. **1799** HOOPER *Med. Dict.*, *Parasitic*, animals..that receive their nourishment in the bodies of others, as worms, polypes, hydatids, &c. **1826** KIRBY & SP. *Entomol.* xliv. IV. 213 The Ichneumons that are parasitic upon larvæ. **1851** H. SPENCER *Social Statics* IV. 449 In certain states of body, indigenous cells will take on new forms of life, and by continuing to reproduce their like, give origin to parasitic growths, such as cancer. **1861** MISS PRATT *Flower. Pl.* IV. 80 Lesser Broom-rape..occurs chiefly on..clover, [but] is..parasitic on various other plants. **1899** *Allbutt's Syst. Med.* VIII. 853 Parasitic diseases of the skin. *fig.* **1874** H. R. REYNOLDS *John Bapt.* i. §6. 58 Some parasitic untruth which criticism was competent to cut away. **1878** GEO. ELIOT *Coll. Breakf. P.* 564 A parasitic growth on the vast real and ideal world of man and nature.

b. Applied to animals which do not provide for themselves, but depend in some way upon others for sustenance, *e.g.* by robbing them of their food, as the skua-gull, or by laying their eggs in others' nests, as the cuckoo.

1837 SWAINSON *Nat. Hist. Birds* II. 196 The parasitic gulls (*Lestris*)..derive their chief supply of food by robbing their more feeble congeners. **1838** *Encycl. Brit.* (ed. 7) XVI. 648 *Lestris parasiticus*, Ill. Parasitic Gull. **1860** *All Year Round* No. 63. 296 Many bees are parasitic, and always lay their eggs in the nests of bees of other kinds. **1889** GEDDES & THOMSON *Evol. Sex* xix. 278 The American cuckoo..is occasionally parasitic.

c. Used loosely or poetically of climbing plants, which depend on other plants or on something external for support. Now *rare* or *Obs.*

1830 HOOD *Haunted H.* I. ix, Vagrant plants of parasitic breed Had overgrown the Dial. *a* **1845** —— *Ode to R. Wilson* xxiii, Faith is a kind of parasitic plant, That grasps the nearest stem with tendril-rings.

3. *transf.* (from 2.) **a.** Applied to something subsidiary growing upon or attached to something else; *spec.* in *Min.* to minerals found upon or within other minerals; in *Phys. Geog.* to subordinate volcanic cones developed on the sides of the principal cone.

1811 J. PINKERTON *Petralogy* I. 208 The most usual parasitic stones of granitel are schorl and garnets. **1878** HUXLEY *Physiogr.* 194 Mount Etna..having its flanks studded with parasitic cones. **1891** FREEMAN *Sk. Fr. Trav.* II. ii. 112 A number of parasitic buildings on the south side [of a church].

b. *Philol.* Applied to a non-original vowel, consonant, or element, attached to an original phonetic element, out of which it has been developed, or to which it has been added; e.g. the *d* in *thunder*, the *e* in *flower*, the second element in the 'parasite-diphthongs' (eɪ, ɛə, əʊ, ɔə).

1870 MARCH *Compar. Gram. Anglo-S. Lang.* 20 The consonants most difficult to make, the trills *l*, *r*, and the gutturals *c*, *g*, *h*, are often accompanied by an involuntary sympathetic movement of other parts of the organs, which produces what may be called a parasitic sound. **1871** *Pub. Sch. Lat. Gram.* 8 Parasitic *u* or *v* follows *q*, *ng*, and *s*; as, *sequor* or *seqvor*; *lingua* or *lingva*; *suavis* or *svavis*.

c. Applied to trades: †(*a*) see quot. 1909; (*b*) non-productive.

1909 *Q. Rev.* Jan. 83 The so-called parasitic trades—that is, trades in which it is alleged that workers who have incomes or maintenances derived from sources other than their wages underbid those who live entirely on their wages. **1926** *Spectator* 19 June 1032/1 Far too much still goes in what we may call parasitic middlemen's profits.

4. Applied to unwanted subsidiary phenomena and effects in physical apparatus, esp. in electronic devices and electrical machinery.

1889 *Telegraphic Jrnl.* 1 Nov. 497/1 If..the iron core were solid, the E.M.Fs. induced in it would..cause enormous currents to flow... They are currents which could not be utilised... By suitably dividing the iron core..these so-called parasitic currents may be rendered almost negligible. **1921** *Wireless World* 15 Oct. 437/1 The..parasitic noise which abounds in amplifiers wired on the usual principle. **1927** V. W. PAGÉ *Mod. Aircraft* (1928) vi. 206 (*heading*) Reduction of parasitic resistance. **1943** F. E. TERMAN *Radio Engineers' Handbk.* VI. 498 Parasitic oscillations..are very likely to occur when large tubes are employed because of the long leads, large interelectrode capacities, and relatively high values of transconductance involved. **1958** NAYLER & SAUNDERS *Handbk. Aircraft Industry* viii. 125 In modern aircraft the 'parasitic' drag due to extraneous items..has been largely eliminated. **1959** *Listener* 25 June 1109/1 They are electric insulators and therefore do not carry parasitic electric currents (so-called eddy currents) when their magnetization changes rapidly. **1967** *Electronics* 6 Mar. 251/1 With discrete components, parasitic capacitance from the diodes' packages increased the over-all capacitance. **1972** *Sci. Amer.* Aug. 19/2 The Wankel operates with less friction than a conventional engine... The lower friction alone means decreased parasitic losses and can be translated directly into an increase in fuel economy.

5. ***parasitic bronchitis*** = HOOSE; ***parasitic gastritis, gastro-enteritis***, in cattle, horses, or other domesticated animals, a gastric inflammation caused by parasitic nematode worms.

1925 *Vet. Rec.* 19 Dec. 1137/1 Parasitic bronchitis is also known as husk, hoose, verminous bronchitis, or paper skin. It is a bronchial irritation, arising from the presence in the air passages of nematode parasites. **1942** *Skandinavisk Veterinär-Tidskrift* XXXII. 488 (*title*) On parasitic gastritis in the horse. **1947** *New Biol.* III. 49 The inflammation of the alimentary tract of sheep (and of that of other farm animals also) which is caused by parasitic roundworms is called by the veterinarian parasitic gastro-enteritis. **1951** *Vet. Rec.* 22 Dec. 864/2 The literature presents certain references to the occurrence of parasitic bronchitis in adult cattle. **1965** *Ibid.* 9 Oct. 1196/1 Field investigations into parasitic gastro-enteritis in the west of Scotland showed that *Ostertagia ostertagi* was the predominant parasite. *Ibid.*, In Great Britain, outbreaks of bovine parasitic gastritis have been reported for many years. **1967** W. R. KELLY *Vet. Clin. Diagnosis* vi. 27/2 (*caption*) Moderate degree of dyspnoea in a yearling heifer suffering from parasitic bronchitis.

6. Applied to an aerial that is not electrically connected to a transmitter or receiver.

1936 L. S. PALMER *Wireless Engin.* xii. 469 Antenna B is not directly energised from the power source, but receives its current through the induction and radiation field of the directly energised antenna A. Antenna B..is sometimes called a parasitic antenna. **1947** C. E. TIBBS *Frequency Modulation Engin.* vi. 114 When the parasitic aerial is at resonance.., and the separation between it and the energised aerial is held at 0·1λ, maximum radiation is in the direction of the parasitic aerial, which is then called a 'director'. **1970** J. EARL *Tuners & Amplifiers* v. 113 When a reflector and directors (called parasitic elements because they are not electrically connected to the dipole) are added to the system the centre impedance of the dipole falls well below 75Ω.

B. *sb. pl. Electronics.* Parasitic oscillations.

1943 F. E. TERMAN *Radio Engineers' Handbk.* VI. 498 Parasitics cause reduction in the power at the desired mode of operation, introduce spurious frequencies, give rise to distortion in linear amplifiers and modulators,..etc. **1967** *Electronics* 6 Mar. 177/2 (Advt.), 'Strays', 'streaks', 'parasitics'..you may forget them all.

parasitical (pærəˈsɪtɪkəl), *a.* [f. as prec. + -AL[1].]

1. = prec. 1.

1577–87 HOLINSHED *Chron.* III. 1400/2 This is the parasiticall and flattering sermon of a popeling. **1652–62** HEYLIN *Cosmogr.* I. (1682) 72 Courteous enough to strangers, and Parasitical enough to their superiours. **1728** MORGAN *Algiers* I. iv. 93 [He] has faith and credulity enough to believe their parasitical Protestations. **1862** MERIVALE *Rom. Emp.* (1865) VII. lvi. 65 Poppaea..had entertained a parasitical brood of astrologers about her.

2. *Biol.* = prec. 2.

1646 SIR T. BROWNE *Pseud. Ep.* 98 Such as living upon the stock of others, are termed Parasiticall plants, as Polypody, Mosse..and many more. **1682** GREW *Anat. Pl.* Pref., I intended to have subjoyned the Description..of Parasitical, Marine, and Sensitive Plants. **1776** WITHERING *Brit. Plants* (1796) II. 209 Cuscuta... This plant is parasitical, without seed-lobes. **1826** KIRBY & SP. *Entomol.* xliv. IV. 228 When hatched..they cease to be parasitical. **1875** B. MEADOWS *Clin. Observ.* 25 The parasitical disorder removed, the skin was left in an unnaturally irritable state. **1879** V. BALL *Jungle Life India* i. (1880) 41, I observed a species of *Viscum*, or Mistletoe, parasitical on a *Loranthus*, which was itself parasitical on *Sal* (*Shorea robusta*).

b. = prec. 2 c. Now *rare* or *Obs.*

1827 SCOTT *Chron. Canong.* Introd. vi, Iron railing, twined round with honeysuckle and other parasitical shrubs. **1834** MRS. SOMERVILLE *Connex. Phys. Sc.* xxvii. (1849) 300 Interlaced by creeping and parasitical plants.

3. *Min.* = prec. 3.

1811 J. PINKERTON *Petralogy* II. 22 The slits of a marble, or of a slate, filled with spar or quartz..these foreign bodies, or parasitical, as Linnæus calls them, have been [etc.].

Hence **paraˈsiticalness**.

1727 BAILEY vol. II, *Parasiticalness*, fawningness, flatteringness. **1838** JACKSON tr. *Krummacher's Elisha* xii. 277 Our unworthy parasiticalness with respect to the higher ranks.

parasitically (pærəˈsɪtɪkəlɪ), *adv.* [f. prec. + -LY[2].] In the manner of a parasite.

1635 PAGITT *Christianogr.* 229 Boniface..parasitically insinuated with the Emperour Phocas. **1705** HICKERINGILL *Priest-cr.* II. iv. 46 Priests..devoted to Ambition, are apt enough Parasitically to give to Princes more than their due. **1864** *Chambers' Encycl.* VI. 203/2 The species [of Louse]..live parasitically on human beings,..mammalia, and birds. *fig.* **1860** TYNDALL *Glac.* I. xiv. 95 Minor oscillations..cover parasitically the large ones of a vibrating string.

parasiticide (pærəˈsɪtɪsaɪd). *Med.* [f. L. *parasitus* PARASITE + -CIDE[1].] An agent that destroys parasites, e.g. such as infest the skin.

1864 W. T. FOX *Skin Dis.* 14 What means its cure by the action of parasiticides? **1875** H. C. WOOD *Therap.* (1879) 86 Oil of Cajeput..is exceedingly destructive to low forms of life, and consequently has been used as a parasiticide. **1899** *Allbutt's Syst. Med.* VIII. 771 The destruction of the parasite by means of parasiticides.

attrib. **1869** T. H. TANNER *Practice of Med.* (ed. 6) II. 426 To form an opening through which the parasiticide lotion can soak. **1899** *Allbutt's Syst. Med.* VIII. 517 Antiseptic and parasiticide properties.

Hence **paraˈsiticidal** *a.*, parasite-destroying.

1892 DALZIEL *Dis. Dogs* (ed. 3) 79 Almost inaccessible to parasiticidal remedies. **1897** *Allbutt's Syst. Med.* II. 729 Due directly to the parasiticidal action of the drug.

parasitism (ˈpærəsaɪˌtɪz(ə)m). [f. PARASITE *sb.* + -ISM. Cf. F. *parasitisme* (Littré).]

1. The practice of living on or at the expense of another; sycophancy, servile complaisance.

1611 COTGR., *Escornifierie*,..base Parasitisme, ieasting, or tale-carrying, for victuals. **1659** GAUDEN *Serm.* etc. (1660) A iv b, Parasitisme differs as much from just and comely praise, as Divels do from good Angels. **1860** A. L. WINDSOR *Ethica* v. 221 Nor was venality and parasitism less its characteristic than at the worst times of the Restoration. **1874** COUES *Birds N.W.* 181 Among mammals we have pure parasitism in the asserted relations of the jackal and lion. **1899** *Westm. Gaz.* 28 Nov. 2/2 Accepting the conditions of parasitism imposed by his time upon the poet and the preacher. **1974** *Times* 19 June 16/5 One of them [*sc.* Russian Jews], Vitali Rubin, was..told that he had 15 days to get a job, otherwise he would be tried for parasitism, a charge entailing a heavy prison sentence. **1975** *Nature* 17 Apr. 554/3 Methods mentioned include the issue of call-up papers for retraining in the Soviet Army.., prosecution for 'parasitism' (being without employment, although the scientists concerned have been deprived of their jobs as a result of applications for exit visas), [etc.]. **1976** *Ibid.* 3 June 363/1 Some 20 scientists called in to regional police headquarters in Moscow were told that if they did not commence working within two weeks they would be charged under the 'parasitism' law, which covers such offences as prostitution, drug addiction, and alcoholism.

2. *Biol.* The condition of being a (plant or animal) parasite; parasitical quality or habits.

1853 G. JOHNSTON *Nat. Hist. E. Bord.* I. 258 Numerous microscopic Algae deform the cleanness of the stems by their excessive parasitism. **1870** ROLLESTON *Anim. Life* p. xix, The special habit of parasitism..must be regarded as entailing a true morphological degradation.

3. *Path.* Parasitical infestation; disease caused by the agency of parasites.

1884 *Public Opinion* 12 Sept. 335/1 Vegetarians..flattered themselves..they escaped the ills of parasitism. **1898** H. W. CONN *Story Germ Life* v. 172 The severity of the disease will depend upon the extent of the parasitism.

parasitization (pærəsɪtaɪˈzeɪʃən, pærəsaɪtaɪˈzeɪʃən). [f. PARASITIZ(E *v.* + -ATION.] The infestation of a plant or animal by a parasite.

1932 J. S. HUXLEY *Probl. Relative Growth* i. 38 Parasitization of Inachus with Sacculina..actually increases the growth-ratio of the female abdomen. **1946** *Nature* 3 Aug. 174/1 A team of workers is co-operating on different aspects of the work, namely, rate of growth, parasitization-rates and mortality. **1950** *Hilgardia* XIX. 422 There was a slight drop in the population (probably due to *Apanteles* parasitization). **1953** *New Biol.* XIV. 100 Parasitization of the larvae [of wheat blossom midges] does not prevent them from feeding. **1962** GORDON & LAVOIPIERRE *Entomol. for Students of Med.* xxxii. 201 A few days after parasitisation has occurred the site occupied in the skin by the larva assumes the appearance of a boil-like swelling. **1975** *Nature* 29 May 403/1, I examined the effects of parasitisation on tumorigenesis by parasitising *vg* tu^{28} larvae.

parasitize (ˈpærəsaɪˌtaɪz, ˈpærəsɪˌtaɪz), *v.* [f. PARASITE *sb.* + -IZE.] *trans.* and *intrans.* To infest as a parasite. Chiefly in *pa. pple.*, infested with parasites. Also *fig.*

a **1890** in *Cent. Dict.*, Fish parasitized are termed lanthorn-sprats. [Cf. F. Day *Brit. Fishes* (1880–4) II. 233 These fishes [sprats] infested by parasites [i.e. Lernea, luminous at night-time]..being termed lanthorn-sprats.] **1895** HART in *Illinois Bulletin Nat. Hist.* IV. 253 The nymphs of that species (*Stratyomyia norma*) and of *Odontomyia* are parasitized by large chalcids of the genus *Smicra*. **1899** *Speaker* 5 Aug. 124/1 The mosquito which has become parasitised from the blood of a malarial patient. **1915** W. B. HERMS *Med. & Vet. Entomol.* ii. 7 That an animal is parasitized does not necessarily involve it in death. **1922** W. M. WHEELER *Social Life Insects* v. 197 Our bodies, our domestic animals and food plants, dwellings, stored foods, clothing and refuse support such numbers of greedy organisms, and we parasitize on one another to such an extent that the biologist marvels how the race can survive. *Ibid.* 198 The thoroughly parasitized host must abandon all hope of being an end in itself. **1934** J. S. HUXLEY *Sci. Res. & Social Needs* vii. 111 New suburbs, almost all in ribbon development, have been allowed to parasitize the road. **1955** *Sci. Amer.* Apr. 98/3 Viruses..used to be thought of solely as foreign intruders—strangers to the cells they invade and parasitize. **1956** T. W. M. CAMERON *Parasites* 235 In some cases (*Leishmania*) the phagocytic cells themselves are parasitized. **1970** *Nature* 25 July 382/1 Mice were infected with..erythrocytes parasitized with the NK 65 strain of *Plasmodium berghei*. **1974** *Sci. Amer.* Oct. 98/3 The estrildid finches parasitized by these two related widow-bird species are also two species of the same genus, *Uraeginthus*. **1977** *N.Z. Jrnl. Agric.* Jan. 21/3, 90 per cent of the caterpillars were parasitised.

parasitoid (ˈpærəsɪtɔɪd), *sb.* and *a.* [a. mod.L. *Parasitoïdea* (O. M. Reuter *Lebensgewohnheiten und Instinkte der Insekten* (1913) v. 53), f. PARASIT(E *sb.* + -OID.] An insect, esp. one belonging to the orders Hymenoptera or Diptera, whose larva lives as an internal parasite which eventually kills its host. Also as *adj.*, of or pertaining to an insect of this kind.

1922 W. M. WHEELER *Social Life Insects* ii. 46 Recent studies of the parasitic, or as I prefer to call them with O. M. Reuter, the 'parasitoid' Hymenoptera. *Ibid.*, The parasitoids exhibit another peculiarity. **1941** J. S. HUXLEY *Uniqueness of Man* v. 135 There exist fully formed adult insects—a beetle or two, and several parasitoid wasplike creatures—of smaller bulk than the human ovum. **1971** *Nature* 12 Feb. 508/1 Many viruses, bacteria, fungi and insect parasitoids can attack insects. **1972** L. E. CHADWICK tr. *Linsenmaier's Insects of World* 300/1 Since most 'parasites' of the Hymenoptera destroy the host, they are not true parasites. Instead they are more accurately called parasitic predators or parasitoids. *Ibid.*, Although it is important to know the distinction between parasites and parasitoids, in actual practice even entomologists tend to use the word parasite for both. **1974** *Nature* 22 Feb. 572/1 A parasitoid fly was suspected as the cause of death.

parasitology (pærəsaɪˈtɒlədʒɪ). [f. Gr. παράσιτο-ς PARASITE + -(O)LOGY.] That branch of biology, and of medical science, which treats of parasites and parasitism.

1882 in OGILVIE (Annandale). **1893** *Times* 15 May 7/1 The well-known Director of the Laboratory of Parasitology in Paris. **1901** *Daily Chron.* 9 Sept. 3/5 A paper on Tropical Parasitology.

Hence **parasitoˈlogical** *a.*, of or pertaining to parasitology; **parasitoˈlogically** *adv.*; **parasiˈtologist**, one who studies or is versed in parasitology.

1890 *Cent. Dict.*, *Parasitological. **1921** H. G. PONTING *Gt. White South* 125 On the south side..was Dr. Atkinson's parasitological laboratory. **1962** J. D. SMYTH *Introd. Animal Parasitol.* ii. 8 The question of the part played by environmental conditions in controlling the development of the parasite is..one scarcely touched on by modern parasitological research. **1971** *Nature* 16 July 209/2 Both these organisms have been widely used in parasitological research. **1976** *Nature* 15 Apr. 608/2 Our experimental group consisted of 100 male and female white laboratory mice, strain ICR, from 3 weeks to 3 months old, which had been standardised both microbiologically and *parasitologically (specific pathogen-free). **1977** *Lancet* 21 May 1095/1 Stool samples can be negative for *Giardia lamblia* even in parasitologically confirmed cases of giardiasis. **1862** T. S. COBBOLD in *Intell. Observ.* No. 1. 30 It affords the *parasitologist a ready mode of ascertaining to what genus the entozoon belongs. **1901** *Brit. Med. Jrnl.* No. 2098. 622 Forms..which the parasitologists regard as indicating stages in the life-history of one or other microbic forms.

parasitopolis (ˌpærəsaɪˈtɒpəlɪs). [f. Gr. παράσιτο-ς PARASITE *sb.* + πόλις city; see -POLIS.] A parasite city; a city that is over-developed and economically non-productive.

1927 P. GEDDES in A. Defries *Interpreter* viii. 199 In all the great cities..you have in progress the history of Rome in its decline and fall. Beginning as Polis—the city, it developed into Metro-polis—the capital; but this into Megalo-polis—or city overgrown... Next, with its ample supply of 'bread and shows' (nowadays called 'budget') it was Parasito-polis, with degeneration accordingly. Thus, all manner of diseases, bodily, mental, moral: hence Patholo-polis, and finally,..Necro-polis—city of the dead. **1945** L. MUMFORD in *Archit. Rev.* XCVII. 7/1 But one outstanding fact must first be frankly acknowledged: the Parasitopolis of the late nineteenth century has already become the spectral Necropolis of the mid-twentieth century. **1961** —— *City in Hist.* viii. 234 Parasitopolis had become Patholopolis; and even further, Patholopolis had turned into Psycho-pathelopolis, with a Nero or a Caligula as absolute ruler.

†**ˈparasitry.** *Obs. rare.* [f. PARASITE *sb.* + -RY. Cf. F. *parasiterie* (16th c. in Littré).] The practice of a parasite; sycophancy.

1638 MAYNE *Lucian* (1664) 312 *Tychiades.* But is Parasitry say you, Simo, an Art then? *Ibid.* 313 As if one should aske, What Art 'tis, and we should answer as we doe of Grammer, or Physicke, 'tis Parasitry.

parasol (pærəˈsɒl, ˈpærəˌsɒl), *sb.* [a. F. *parasol* (1580 in Hatz.-Darm.), ad. It. *parasole*, f. PARA-² + *sole* sun. Smart, 1836, pronounces (ˌpærəˈsəʊl), which was still said by some *c* 1904.]

1. A light portable screen or canopy carried as a defence from the sun; a sunshade: used by persons of high rank in the East, and hence, by women in Europe, etc., in the form of a small light umbrella, often ornamental or gaily coloured.

1660 F. BROOKE *Le Blanc's Trav.* 52 The Portugais..have their Parasols carried by them. **1675-6** LOCKE *Jrnl. Trav. France* in *Life* (1876) I. vii. 351 Parasols, a pretty sort of cover for women riding in the sun, made of straw, something like the fashion of tin covers for dishes. **1765** *Meretriciad* 50 And two more bore an Indian parasol. **1803** JANE PORTER *Thaddeus* (1826) III. iii. 49 She took her parasol and descended the stairs. **1838** DICKENS *Nich. Nick.* xviii, 'You naughty creature', said the lively lady, poking the peer with her parasol. **1871** ALABASTER *Wheel of Law* 84 Suthawat, the great Brahma, brought his great royal parasol and extended it. **1883** F. M. CRAWFORD *Dr. Claudius* ii. 21 A dainty lace-covered parasol.

2. *transf.* **a.** Anything serving as a defence from the rays of the sun. Now *rare* or *Obs.*

1616 DRUMM. OF HAWTH. *Madrig. & Epigr.* Wks. (1856) 95 Love suffereth no parasol... Sweet I would you advise To choose some other fan than that white hand. **1678** SANCROFT *Serm.* (1694) 127 While the World is all on fire about them, they journey through that torrid Zone, with their mighty Parasol, or Umbrella over their Heads, and are all the while in the Shade. **1798** FERRIAR *Cert. Var. Man* in *Illustr. Sterne*, etc. 200 Feet so large as to shelter the whole body—these were the first parasols. **1801** SOUTHEY *Thalaba* IV. Notes, Wks. 1838 IV. 163 This was a greater miracle than that of the cloud with which God defended his chosen people in the wilderness from the heat of the sun, inasmuch as it was a more elegant and fanciful parasol.

b. An aircraft having wings raised above the fuselage. Also *attrib.* and *Comb.*

1914 *Aeroplane* 29 Jan. 110/1 M. Gilbert has been flying another 'parasol', 60-h.p. *Ibid.*, The 'parasol' monoplane..has been fitted with a new..Gnome [engine]. **1930** *Flight* 8 Aug. 896/1 The machine used by Lombardi was a Fiat 'A.S.1' parasol monoplane. **1940** *Jrnl. R. Aeronaut. Soc.* XLIV. 661 Outboard tanks were employed with the Junkers J.21/22 parasol fighters. **1952** A. Y. BRAMBLE *Air-Plane Flight* xi. 161 The high-wing type was sometimes known as the 'parasol' type, especially when the wing was carried on struts rising above the main structure of the fuselage. **1969** K. MUNSON *Pioneer Aircraft 1903–14* 131/1 A few R.E.P. parasol-winged monoplanes were in French and R.N.A.S. service during the early part of the war.

3. *attrib.* and *Comb.*, as *parasol-handle*, *parasol-shaped* adj.; **parasol ant**, a leaf-carrying ant, esp. *Œcodoma cephalotes* of S. America (see quots.); **parasol fir**, a fir-tree of the Japanese genus *Sciadopitys*, so called from the form of its tufts of leaves; also called *umbrella-fir* or *-pine* (Miller *Plant-n.* 1884); **parasol mushroom**, a species of mushroom (*Agaricus procerus*) with a broad reddish-brown pileus (Miller); **parasol pine**, (*a*) the stone-pine (*Pinus Pinea*), from the form of its head of branches; (*b*) = *parasol-fir*; **parasol probang**, a probang with an attachment at the end capable of being opened like a parasol; **parasol skirt**, a spreading skirt worn by ballet-dancers.

1781 SMEATHMAN in *Phil. Trans.* LXXI. 175 *note* 35 Those..called, in Tobago, *Para-sol-Ants, because they cut out of the leaves of certain trees and plants pieces almost circular,..which..give a very good idea of people walking with para-sols. **1871** KINGSLEY *At Last* v, The parasol ants..walk in triumphal processions, each with a bit of green leaf borne over its head. **1877** 'OUIDA' *Puck* x. 90 Little Cosmo..had told me, that *parasol handles could rap fearfully hard. **1864** W. J. HIGGINS in *Cornh. Mag.* Aug. 179 Gardens and public walks, adorned with tall *parasol pines, dark cypress and ilex. **1882** M. MACKENZIE *Dis. Throat & Nose* II. 103 In two cases..polypi were removed with the *parasol-probang. **1896** *Westm. Gaz.* 27 Jan. 3/2 Her dress was the ballet dress of 1845, with the skirts longer than the '*parasol' skirt now in fashion. **1850** R. G. CUMMING *Hunter's Life S. Afr.* (1902) 66/2 Scattered through a grove of the picturesque *parasol-topped acacias.

Hence **paraˈsol** *v. trans.*, to serve as a parasol for, to shade from the sun; **paraˈsoled** *a.*, having a parasol; **parasoˈlette**, a small parasol.

1799 SOUTHEY *Nondescripts* iii, And if no kindly cloud will parasol me,..I shall be negrofied. **1843** CARLYLE *Misc. Ess.*, *Dr. Francia* (1872) VII. 24 Frondent trees parasol the streets. *a* **1851** MOIR *Daisy* iii, The parasol'd Chinese. **1883** *Century Mag.* XXVI. 418 The crowd of parasoled ladies. **1842** *Fraser's Mag.* XXVI. 223 What a 'rush' there was when the first 'parasollette' made its appearance. **1847** WEBSTER, *Parasolette*, a small parasol or sunshade.

parasorbic: see PARA-¹ 2.

parasphenoid (pærəsˈfiːnɔɪd), *a.* (*sb.*) *Zool.* and *Comp. Anat.* [f. PARA-¹ 1 + SPHENOID.] Lying alongside the sphenoid bone; epithet of a bone extending in the median line along the base of the skull in birds, reptiles, amphibians, and fishes. **b.** as *sb.* The parasphenoid bone.

1872 MIVART *Elem. Anat.* 137 The para-sphenoid bone encloses it below. **1875** HUXLEY in *Encycl. Brit.* I. 754/2 The parasphenoid has the form of a dagger with a very wide guard and short handle. **1884** *Athenæum* 13 Dec. 775/1 Mr. Sutton came to the conclusion that the parasphenoid of fishes was the homologue of the vomer of mammals.

Hence **paraspheˈnoidal** *a.*, of the nature of or pertaining to the parasphenoid.

parastacine (pəˈræstəsaɪn), *a. Zool.* [f. mod.L. *Parastacus* (see defin.) + -INE¹.] Belonging to the genus *Parastacus* or family *Parastacidæ* of fresh-water Crustacea of the Southern Hemisphere.

1880 HUXLEY *Crayfish* v. 253 Diagram, Parastacine Plan.

parastannic, *Chem.*: see PARA-¹ 2.

‖**paˈrastas**, in pl. **parastades** (pəˈræstədiːz). *Arch.* [a. Gr. παραστάς, -άδες, door-posts, gateposts, antæ, f. παρα- beside + root στα- standing.] In *pl.* Pilasters, antæ.

1706 PHILLIPS, *Parastades*,..the Posts or Pillars, on both sides of a Door, call'd Jaumbs. **1884** SCHLIEMANN *Troja* iii. 80 The *parastades* or *antæ*..have been used here principally for constructive reasons.

para-state (ˈpærəsteɪt). [f. PARA-¹ + STATE *sb.* IV.] An institution or body which takes on some of the roles of civil government or political authority; an agency through which the state works indirectly. Also *attrib.* Hence **paraˈstatal** *a.* and *sb.*

1959 *Listener* 5 Feb. 245/2 He [*sc.* Lenin] described the proletarian dictatorship as a sort of a para-state.., a state progressively dissolving in society and working towards its own extinction. **1966** *Economist* 24 Sept. 1233/3 Since the [Tunisian] government is only too keen to load off its shares.., there is developing a group of what are called para-state industries, with both government and private capital. **1969** *Nationalist* (Dar es Salaam) 25 Jan. 1/4 The Vice-President told the workers that the aim of opening TANU branches in industries and parastatal organisations was to strengthen the political role of the Party. **1969** *Reporter* (Nairobi) 13 June 20/3, 65 per cent of parastatal investment would also come from within the country. **1971** *Guardian Weekly* 23 Oct. 6 The parastatals were still almost wholly outside central control. **1971** P. A. ALLUM *Politics & Society Post-War Naples* (1973) i. 38 The public administration groups a plethora of institutions and para-state agencies... prefecture, field offices of ministries, municipalities, state banks (Bank of Naples) ISVEIMER, IRI, ENI, etc. **1974** J. WHITE tr. *Poulantzas's Fascism & Dictatorship* III. i. 74 A whole series of hidden parallel networks, operating as the channels of real communication of real power and decisions, varying from the emergence of pressure groups and private militia..to the setting up of virtual para-state networks. **1974** *Daily News* (Tanzania) 13 Sept. 5/6 Employees of hotels, bars and parastatal organisations in Shinyanga Region who fail to enrol in adult education courses by the end of this month will be sacked. **1976** *Nigerian Herald* 20 July 5/1 In terms of depth of investigation and the sheer volume of assignment, the Odje Commission of Inquiry, which probed parastatals in the Bendel State, is remarkably unprecedented.

parastatic (pærəˈstætɪk), *a.*¹ *rare.* [ad. Gr. παραστατικός presentative, impelling, f. παριστά-ναι to set before, etc.: see PARA-¹ 1 and STATIC.]

†**1.** Having the function of impelling to action.

1656 STANLEY *Hist. Philos.* v. (1701) 191/1 The souls of the Gods have a dijudicative faculty, called Gnostic, and impulsive to some action, called Parastatick.

2. Having the quality of presenting something before the mind.

1866 LIDDON *Bampt. Lect.* (1869) 70 The Shekinah [etc.] only involve a parastatic appearance of God, are symbols of His presence.

†**paraˈstatic**, *a.*² *Obs.* [f. Gr. παραστάται testicles + -IC. Cf. *Parastates* in Phillips.] Seminal.

a **1693** *Urquhart's Rabelais* III. xxxi. 264 The Parastatick Liquor. [**1696** PHILLIPS (ed. 5), *Parastates*, two little Purses full of winding Nooks..where the Seed remains in Reserve.]

parastemon: see PARA-¹ 1.

paˈraster, paˈrastron. *nonce-wd.* [f. Gr. παρα- beside, etc. (see PARA-¹ 1) + ἀστήρ, ἄστρον star, after *parhelion*, *paraselene*.] A (supposed) image of a star, analogous to a parhelion.

1653 H. MORE *Antid. Ath.* III. xvi. §9 It should seem a hundred times more easy for natural Causes to hit upon a *Paraster* or *Parastron* (for let Analogy embolden me so to call these seldom or never seen Phænomena..) than upon a *Parelios* or *Paraselene*.

parasternal (pærəˈstɜːnəl), *a. Anat.* [f. PARA-¹ 1 + STERN-UM + -AL¹: cf. STERNAL.] Lying alongside the sternum or breast-bone.

parasternal line, a line drawn vertically down the surface of the chest from a point in the collar-bone distant one-third of its length from its inner end. *parasternal region*, the space between this line and the edge of the sternum.

1870 S. J. GEE *Auscult. & Percuss.* ii. §1. 13 Parasternal (i.e. midway between the side-sternal and nipple lines). *Ibid.* I. ii. (1893) 39 The position of the impulse [of the heart] is the fifth left interspace midway between the nipple and the parasternal lines. **1899** *Allbutt's Syst. Med.* VI. 16.

parastichy (pəˈræstɪkɪ). *Bot.* [f. PARA-¹ 1 + Gr. -στιχία, from στίχ-ος row, rank: cf. ORTHOSTICHY.] A secondary spiral or oblique rank of lateral members, as leaves or scales, around the stem or axis, in a phyllotaxis in which the leaves, scales, etc. are close together, as in certain leaf-rosettes, pine-cones, etc.

1875 BENNETT & DYER tr. *Sachs' Bot.* I. iii. 173 When the members of a spiral phyllotaxis with a constant angle of divergence stand sufficiently close to one another, spiral arrangements are easily seen and followed to the right and left which more or less conceal the genetic spiral. These rows are called Parastichies, and are particularly clear in the cones of species of Pinus. **1884** BOWER & SCOTT *De Bary's Phaner.* 285 Two bundles..come into contact—that from the one side following the parastichies composed of every third leaf, that from the other the parastichies composed of every fifth leaf.

‖**paraˈstigma.** *Entom.* [mod.L., f. Gr. παρα- beside + στίγμα prick, point, spot: see STIGMA.] A chitinous spot situated beside the stigma on the wings of certain insects, as dragon-flies. So **parastigˈmatic** *a.*, situated beside the stigma; pertaining to the parastigma.

1826 KIRBY & SP. *Entomol.* III. 377 The Parastigma. A corneous spot between the costal and postcostal nervures, distinct from the Stigma, observable in the *Libellulina*.

parasymbiosis (ˌpærəsɪmbaɪˈəʊsɪs, -bɪˈəʊsɪs). *Biol.* [a. G. *parasymbiose* (W. Zopf 1897, in *Ber. Deutsch. Bot. Ges.* XV. 90), f. PARA-¹ + SYMBIOSIS.] The relationship between a free-living lichen and an organism (either a fungus or another lichen) which infests it and establishes a symbiotic relationship with the algæ of the lichen. So **ˌparasymbiˈotic** *a.*, of or pertaining to such an association; **paraˈsymbiont**, an organism involved in an association of this kind.

1897 *Jrnl. R. Microsc. Soc.* 228 Prof. W. Zopf finds fresh confirmation of his theory that many of the fungi which grow on lichens are not true parasites, but have a kind of symbiotic relationship to the host, which he terms parasymbiosis, the hyphæ of the 'parasite' enveloping the algal constituent of the lichen, without inflicting any injury upon it. **1921** A. L. SMITH *Lichens* vi. 264 Zopf found several instances of such parasymbiosis in his study of fungal parasites. *Ibid.*, There occur in lichens, certain parasites classed as fungi which at an early stage are more or less parasymbionts of the host. *Ibid.* 265 Tobler has added two more of these parasymbiotic species on the border line between lichens and fungi. **1952** Parasymbiont [see LICHENIZED *ppl. a.* b]. **1967** M. E. HALE *Biol. Lichens* x. 155 This [*sc.* the order Lecanorales] includes..the parasymbiotic lichen fungi. *Ibid.*, Other parasymbionts are classified under appropriate fungal families.

ˌparasympaˈthetic, *a.* *Anat.* [PARA-[1].] Of, pertaining to, or designating one of the major divisions of the autonomic nervous system, distinguished from the sympathetic system by its place of origin, its use of acetylcholine as a transmitter, and its general association with rest and recuperation rather than alertness. Also *absol.*, the parasympathetic system.

1905 J. N. LANGLEY in *Jrnl. Physiol.* XXXIII. 403, I use the word para-sympathetic for the cranial and sacral autonomic systems. **1920** *Gray's Anat.* (ed. 21) 768 The peripheral part [of the autonomic system] is..arranged in two subsidiary systems—the parasympathetic system and the sympathetic system. **1925** *Jrnl. Physiol.* LX. p. ix, The absence of effect of pilocarpine and atropine on muscle tonus indicates that the parasympathetics do not control the tonus of voluntary muscle. **1940** [see MUSCARINE]. **1946** *Nature* 10 Aug. 207/1 Most internal organs have a double nerve supply of which one is excitatory (sympathetic) and the other inhibitory (parasympathetic), that is, they work against each other. **1948** A. BRODAL *Neurol. Anat.* xi. 340 From the anatomical arrangement of the sympathetic and parasympathetic it is also to be inferred that the former must be involved predominantly as a whole in diffuse reactions, affecting the entire organism, whereas in the latter, the structural organization permits more restricted, localized effects. **1954** S. DUKE-ELDER *Parsons' Dis. Eye* (ed. 12) v. 68 A second type of drug acts as a parasympathetic stimulant. **1967** G. M. WYBURN et al. *Conc. Anat.* iii. 92/1 Branches from the sympathetic and the vagus (the parasympathetic) form plexuses in relation to the arch of the aorta and the bifurcation of the trachea. **1968** PASSMORE & ROBSON *Compan. Med. Stud.* I. xxiv. 90/2 Overall parasympathetic activity corresponds roughly to the picture of an old man asleep after dinner, i.e. slow heart, small pupils, constricted bronchioles and noisy breathing, salivary secretion, vigorous peristalsis. **1972** J. A. WILSON *Princ. Animal Physiol.* xi. 416/2 That part of the autonomic nervous system originating in the thorocolumbar portion of the spinal cord is the sympathetic division; that part originating in the other three segments of the central nervous system is the parasympathetic system. **1977** D. MORRIS *Manwatching* 166 Whenever we are called upon to perform some intense, violent activity, the sympathetic system takes over and pours adrenalin into the blood, temporarily dominating the keep-calm parasympathetic system.

Hence **ˌparasympaˈthetically** *adv.*

1957 *Jrnl. Nerv. & Mental Dis.* CXXV. 463/1 For the most part a situation in which the sympathetic nervous activity is high inhibits parasympathetically innervated consummatory reactions. **1978** A. WINGATE in M. U. Barnard et al. *Human Sexuality for Health Professionals* iii. 18 The first phase [of the male sexual response]..is parasympathetically mediated.

ˌparasympathoˈlytic, *a.* (*sb.*) *Pharm.* [f. prec. + -O + -LYTIC.] Annulling or opposing the physiological action of the parasympathetic nervous system. Also as *sb.*, a substance which does this.

1949 *Jrnl. Pharmacol. & Exper. Therap.* XCV. 53 There is need for a simple *in vivo* assay for the study of parasympatholytic agents. **1960** A. BURGER *Medicinal Chem.* (ed. 2) liii. 1147/2 Diphemanil methylsulfate is a parasympatholytic agent which blocks the cholinergic impulse to the eccrine sweat glands. **1969** *Scand. Jrnl. Gastroenterol.* IV. 641/1 The following parasympatholytics were applied: atropine, Isopropamide.., and Gastrixone. **1973** *Jrnl. Pharmacol. & Exper. Therap.* CLXXXVII. 293/2 The mechanism for this parasympatholytic augmentation of dopamine's pressor and inotropic actions is not clear and may involve an interaction between dopamine and acetylcholine within the central nervous system.

paraˌsympathomiˈmetic, *a.* (*sb.*) *Pharm.* [f. as prec. + -O + MIMETIC *a.* (and *sb.*).] Producing physiological effects characteristic of the action of the parasympathetic nervous system by promoting stimulation of parasympathetic nerves. Also as *sb.*, a substance which does this, either by mimicking the action of acetylcholine or by interfering with that of cholinesterase.

[**1940** *Q. Jrnl. Med.* IX. 239 Observations on the effect of parasympathetic-mimetic drugs have been made.] **1946** *Jrnl. Pharmacol. & Exper. Therap.* LXXXVII. 31 A range of doses of eleven parasympathomimetic drugs (acetylcholine, mecholyl, [etc.]..) was administered subcutaneously. **1968** W. C. BOWMAN et al. *Textbk. Pharmacol.* xxviii. 702 In addition to their important muscarinic actions, many parasympathomimetic drugs exert other actions at different sites. For example, acetylcholine itself..stimulates ganglion cells and striated muscle. **1972** *Exper. Neurol.* XXXIV. 355 (*heading*) The central activity of parasympathomimetics on gastric secretory function. **1974** *Ann. Internal Med.* LXXXI. 49/1 All parasympathomimetic maneuvers and drugs affect arrhythmias by causing local release of acetylcholine in cardiac tissues. **1974** M. C. GERALD *Pharmacol.* v. 103 Analogous terms are used for drugs modifying cholinergic activity, that is, cholinergic or parasympathomimetic agents and cholinergic blocking agents.

parasynapsis to **-tacamite**: see PARA-[1].

‖**parasynesis** (pærəˈsɪnɪsɪs). *Philol.* [a. Gr. παρασύνεσις misunderstanding, f. παρα- in sense 'amiss, wrong' + σύνεσις understanding.] Misunderstanding or misconception of a word, resulting in an alteration or corruption of it. Hence **parasynetic** (-sɪˈnɛtɪk) *a.*, pertaining to or due to parasynesis.

1877 HALDEMAN *Outlines Etymol.* 31 Parasynesis, a misunderstanding or misconception of a word all of which is present, as when 'Chinese' is supposed to be a plural, and capable of furnishing 'Chinee' in the singular number. **1885** *Trans. Amer. Philol. Assoc.* XVI. App. 32 Such parasynetic forms as 'sparrer-grass' for 'asparagus', due to.. misconception of a word, are common enough in Negro.

parasynovitis, -syphilitic, etc.: see PARA-[1] 1.

‖**parasynthesis** (pærəˈsɪnθɪsɪs). *Philol.* [mod. a. Gr. παρασύνθεσις, f. παρα- beside, alongside + σύνθεσις composition, SYNTHESIS.] Derivation from a compound; conjoint combination and derivation, as a process of word-formation: see next.

1862 CHANDLER *Grk. Accentuation* Pref. xii, It is said that synthesis does, and parasynthesis does not affect the accent; which is really tantamount to saying, that when the accent of a word is known..we shall be able to judge whether a Greek grammarian regarded that word as a synthetic or parasynthetic compound. **1884** *Amer. Jrnl. Philol.* July 193 The principle of parasynthesis..is more regularly and extensively developed here [in Portuguese] than in any other one of the Romance group of languages.

parasynthetic (pærəsɪnˈθɛtɪk), *a.* (*sb.*) *Philol.* [mod. f. Gr. παρασύνθετος 'formed from a compound' (f. παρα- beside + σύνθετος put together, compounded) + -IC. In mod.F. *parasynthétique.*] Formed from a combination or compound of two or more elements; formed by a conjoint process of combination and derivation. **b.** *sb.* A parasynthetic formation or derivative.

Applied, esp. in Romanic Philology, to verbs derived from a combination of preposition and object, with the addition of a verbal ending, as *aborder* from phr. *à bord*, *aboutir* from *à bout*, *endosser* from *en dos*, etc.; also to the derivatives of these, as *en-table-ment*, etc. Many of these parasynthetic derivatives have entered Eng. from French, e.g. *accost, embark, endorse, imprison*; but native formations of this kind are rarely if ever made in Eng. Our parasynthetic derivatives chiefly consist of adjs. and sbs. formed by combining two words in some grammatical relation, and adding to the combination a formative suffix; e.g. from *black eye, black-eyed*, from *silk hat, silk-hatted*, from *all ages, all-aged*, from *big end, big-ender*, from *free trade, free-trader*, from *at home, at-homeish, at-homeishness, at-homeness*, from *get at, get-at-able*, etc. Thus *black-eyed, big-ender*, etc., notwithstanding the hyphen, are not formed from *black + eyed, big + ender*, etc., but from *black eye + -ed, big end + -er*, etc., the suffix indicating a formation not upon the element next to it, but upon the combination of the two elements, which, of themselves, without the suffix, are only in grammatical collocation.

1862 [see prec.]. **1884** (April) *N.E. Dict.* s.v. *Ash* sb.[2], 8. *Comb.* a. In a similative relation..passing into parasynthetic compounds, as *ash-bellied..ash-coloured.* **1884** A. M. ELLIOT in *Amer. Jrnl. Philol.* July 186 (*heading*), Verbal parasynthetics in *a-* in the Romance languages. *Ibid.* 187 That species of word-creation commonly designated as parasynthetic covers an extensive part of the Romance field, both in its noun and verb-development, and is usually found more abundant in the later than in the earlier periods of these languages. *Ibid.* 192. *Ibid.* 194.

So ‖**paraˈsyntheton**, pl. **-eta** [a. Gr. παρασύνθετον, neut. used subst.], a parasynthetic formation.

[Cf. Chœrob. C. 477. 21 in Chandler *Grk. Accent.* (ed. 2) §417 *Παρασύνθετον δέ τὸ ἀπὸ συνθέτου γιγνόμενον, ὡς ἀπὸ τοῦ Ἀντίγονος συνθέτου γίνεται τὸ ἀντιγονίζω παρασύνθετον.*] Used in German by Diez *Gramm. Rom. Spr.* (ed. 3. 1869) and in the French transl. by G. Paris and Morel Fatio 1874 (II. 388). **1870** MARCH *Compar. Gram. Anglo-S. Lang.* 134 Parasyntheta are derivatives from compounds. **1884** A. M. ELLIOTT in *Amer. Jrnl. Philol.* July 198 The Neo-Latin parasyntheta in their origin are independent so far as form is concerned, having, however, models in the Latin literary and especially Folk language that would suggest them, e.g. *similare, assimilare.*

parat, -ate, obs. forms of PARROT.

paratactic (pærəˈtæktɪk), *a.* *Gram.* [mod.f. Gr. παρα- PARA[1] 1 + τακτικός pertaining to arrangement, from τάσσειν: see PARATAXIS.] Pertaining to or involving parataxis; co-ordinative.

1871 tr. *Lange's Comm., Jer.* 49 We change the paratactic mode of expression into the syntactic. **1883** tr. *Godet's Comm. John* Prol. iii. 376 The paratactic form characteristic of the Hebrew. **1898** *Amer. Jrnl. Philol.* July 215 The use of *licet* as a conjunction developed from the paratactic construction.

So **paraˈtactical** *a.*; **paraˈtactically** *adv.*

1886 MEYER in *Proc. Philol. Soc.* 18 June p. xliv, Old phenomena..preserved in Teutonic... Such are the paratactical arrangement of sentences, in preference to hypotaxis, which where it appears is of the simplest form. **1884** tr. *Lotze's Logic* 362 We distrust any practical project which instead of co-ordinating side by side, paratactically, to use a phrase of syntax, independent conditions of success, lets them depend hypotactically on a web of mutually conditioning presuppositions. **1890** J. S. REID *Cicero, Pro Balbo* Notes 50 All the clauses from *fatetur* to the end of the sentence are paratactically, not syntactically arranged, that is, they are merely put side by side, and not linked together by particles.

paratarsial, -tartaric, etc.: see PARA-[1] 1, 2.

parataxic (pærəˈtæksɪk), *a.* *Psychol.* [f. PARA- 1 + TAX(IS 6 + -IC.] A term used mainly by H. S. Sullivan to describe the mode in which subconscious attitudes or emotions affect overt interpersonal relationships. See also PROTOTAXIC *a.*, SYNTAXIC *a.*

1938 H. S. SULLIVAN in *Psychiatry* I. 125/2 A *parataxic* situation, a much more complicated entity in that two of the *four* or more persons now concerned, while illusory, are real antagonists to any collaboration of A and Mrs. A. Our Mr. A has become multiplex. **1945** P. MULLAHY in *Ibid.* VIII. 184/1 With the development of the parataxic mode of symbol activity, the original undifferentiated wholeness, oneness, of experience is broken. **1961** J. A. C. BROWN *Freud & Post-Freudians* ix. 168 By a process of what Sullivan describes as 'parataxic distortion' one may attribute to others traits taken from significant people in one's past. **1970** HINSIE & CAMPBELL *Psychiatric Dict.* (ed. 4) 222/2 One way to learn what is true and what is parataxic in thinking or feelings about another is to compare one's evaluations with those of others. **1973** *Jrnl. Genetic Psychol.* CXXIII. 338 The extent to which a person distorts his perception of the norm for self-acceptance by attributing his own high or low acceptance of self to the average person is termed 'parataxic distortion'.

‖**parataxis** (pærəˈtæksɪs). *Gram.* [mod.a. Gr. παράταξις a placing side by side, f. παρατάσσ-ειν to place side by side, f. παρα- PARA-[1] 1 + τάσσειν to arrange, τάξις arrangement.] The placing of propositions or clauses one after another, without indicating by connecting words the relation (of co-ordination or subordination) between them.

1842 in BRANDE *Dict. Sci.* etc. **1883** B. L. GILDERSLEEVE in *Amer. Jrnl. Philol.* IV. 420 Now to make hypotaxis out of parataxis we must have a joint. **1888** W. LEAF *Iliad* II. 414 A good instance of primitive parataxis, two clauses being merely set side by side.

paratectonic to **-terminal**: see PARA-[1].

paratha (pɑrɑːthɑː). [Hindi *parāṭhā*.] In India and among Indian communities outside India: a variety of unleavened bread fried in butter, ghee, etc., on a griddle.

1935 M. MORPHY *Recipes of All Nations* 691 *Paratha* (Indian bread)..as Chapati, but the dough..is..fried in butter on the griddle. **1960** R. P. JHABVALA *Householder* i. 46 Her eyes were modestly lowered and she appeared intent on preparing dough for parathas. **1964** S. M. SADEEK *Windswept & Other Stories* (1969) 13 The wife and two daughters of the East Indian headman were busy with the cooking of the curry-mutton..the rice and paratha rotie. **1971** *Hindustan Times Weekly Rev.* (New Delhi) 4 Apr. p. iv/5 Have you ever tried mashing up leftover *gobhi, aloo*, or *matar bhujia* and using it as a filling for stuffed *parathas*? **1977** *New Society* 3 Feb. 242/1 While others were still wondering whether chapatis were folded or flat, I was boldly ordering poppadoms and parathas.

parathecial, -ium: see PARA-[1] 1.

paratherian (pærəˈθɪərɪən), *a.* *Zool.* [f. mod.L. *Parathēria* pl., f. Gr. παρα- PARA-[1] 1 + θήρ, θηρίον beast.] Belonging to the *Paratheria*, a name proposed (after Huxley's *Prototheria, Metatheria*, and *Eutheria*) for the Edentate Mammals.

1887 OLDFIELD THOMAS in *Phil. Trans.* II. 462 On the left, above, is the Paratherian (Edentate), and below, the continued Metatherian branch.

parathermic (pærəˈθɜːmɪk), *a.* [f. Gr. παρα- PARA-[1] 1 + θερμός warm, hot + -IC.] Name given by Sir J. Herschel to invisible rays accompanying the orange and red rays in the spectrum, and having the quality of discharging the colour from paper tinted with certain vegetable juices: so called in reference to the neighbouring thermic or heat rays.

1843 SIR J. HERSCHEL in *Phil. Trans.* I. 5 Certain rays, which..accompany in the spectrum the red and orange rays, and are also copiously emitted by heated bodies short of redness..I would propose the term *parathermic rays* to designate them. **1849** MRS. SOMERVILLE *Connex. Phys. Sc.* xxiv. (1858) 217 A new set of obscure rays in the solar spectrum, which seem to bear the same relation to those of heat that the photographic or chemical rays bear to the luminous.

‖**parathesis** (pəˈræθɪsɪs). [mod.L., a. Gr. παράθεσις a putting beside, apposition, juxtaposition, f. παρατιθέναι to place beside, f. παρα- beside + τιθέναι to place, θέσις placing, position, THESIS.]

†**1.** *Gram.* = APPOSITION[2] 6. *Obs.*

1657 J. SMITH *Myst. Rhet.* 190 *Parathesis,..appositio*, apposition, or a putting of one thing to another... Apposition is a continued or immediate Conjunction of two Substantives of the same case, by the one whereof the other is declared: as, *Vrbs Roma*, the City Rome. **1678** PHILLIPS (ed. 4), *Parathesis*..is a Grammatical figure of Construction.

b. In Greek and Latin grammar: Simple composition of two words without change, as in *Διόσκυροι, res-publica*: opp. to *synthesis* and *parasynthesis.*

1862–81 CHANDLER *Grk. Accentuation* (ed. 2) §416 Retention of [the accent was held by the Greek grammarians to be] a distinctive mark of Parasynthesis and Parathesis.

†**2.** *Rhet.*, etc. The insertion or interpolation of a clause, phrase, or word in the midst of a sentence or discourse by way of explanation or

exposition; a parenthesis or parenthetic remark. *Obs.*

1668 WILKINS *Real Char.* II. i. §6. 45 Discourse... i... Elements... Parenthesis. Parathesis, Exposition. **1706** PHILLIPS, *Parathesis*,..a Figure in Rhetoric, when a small hint of a thing is given to the Auditors, with a Promise to inlarge on it at some other convenient Time. **1711** J. GREENWOOD *Eng. Gram.* 226 Parathesis or Exposition, is used for Distinction of such Words as are added by Way of Explication.

†**b.** *Printing.* = PARENTHESIS 3. *Obs.*

1685 BOYLE *Veneration Man's Intellect owes to God* Advt., Those passages included in Paratheses. **1706** PHILLIPS s.v., In the Art of Printing, Parathesis signifies the Matter contain'd within two Crotchets, thus marked [ ]. **1711** J. GREENWOOD *Eng. Gram.* 226.

3. *Philol.* The juxtaposition of primary elements of a language, as the monosyllabic roots in Chinese; supposed by some to characterize an early stage in the development of language, prior to the formation of inflexions and connective particles.

1882 in OGILVIE (Annandale).

4. *Gr. Ch.* A prayer pronounced by a bishop over converts or catechumens.

1864 WEBSTER cites WRIGHT.

So **parathetic** (pærəˈθɛtɪk) *a.*, pertaining to or characterized by parathesis (in quot. in sense 1 b or 3).

1869 FARRAR *Fam. Speech* iv. (1873) 126 These are *parathetic* compounds, i.e. there is only a juxtaposition not a fusion. *Ibid.* 127 Such a parathetic compound as *house-top* or *sister-in-law*.

parathion (pærəˈθaɪən). [f. the elements PARA-[1] 2 b and THIO- in its chemical names + *-n*.] An organophosphorus insecticide which is also highly toxic to mammals and is available in commercial preparations similar to those of malathion; diethyl-*p*-nitrophenylthiophosphate, $(C_2H_5O)_2{\cdot}PS{\cdot}O{\cdot}C_6H_4NO_2$.

1947 *Jrnl. Econ. Entomol.* XL. 915/2 (*heading*) Parathion for control of green peach aphid. *Ibid.*, Parathion may be formulated into emulsions, dusts and wettable powders. **1953** *Sci. Amer.* July 62/2 A slow-acting insecticide—e.g., parathion—may have a devastating effect on a bee colony. **1958** E. HYAMS *Taking it Easy* II. 198, I noticed Red Spider mite on some newly-budded peach trees... I went to my small store of parathion. **1960** *Jrnl. R. Hort. Soc.* LXXXV. III. 127 A parathion smoke was used and..200 dead beetles were collected from the floor and staging. **1970** *Daily Tel.* 22 Aug. 3/1 On the fruit and vegetable farms of California..it is not uncommon for workers coming in contact with parathion to faint, become nauseated, or go into convulsions. **1977** *Jrnl. R. Soc. Arts* CXXV. 566/2 In 1950 parathion, the first of many powerful organic phosphorus materials, gave positive control of Red Spider Mites.

parathormone (pærəˈθɔːməʊn). *Physiol.* [Blend of *parath(yroid* (s.v. PARA-[1] 1) and HORMONE.] A polypeptide hormone secreted by the parathyroid glands of higher vertebrates, which increases the amount of calcium in the blood by its action on bones, kidneys, and gut.

Registered in the U.S.A. as a proprietary name, although its protection lapsed in 1966.

1925 *Official Gaz.* (U.S. Patent Office) 17 Nov. 591/1 Eli Lilly & Company, Indianapolis, Ind. Filed Oct. 1, 1925. *Para-thor-mone*... Medicine or Pharmaceutical Preparation. Claims use since Sept. 1, 1925. **1926** *Encycl. Brit.* III. 147/2 Collip prepared from the [parathyroid] glands an extract, parathormone, which is capable, when injected subcutaneously into parathyroidectomised dogs, of promptly removing the symptoms of tetany. **1948** MARTIN & HYNES *Clinical Endocrinol.* v. 101 Parathormone is a protein substance obtainable in solid, but not crystalline, form by acid extraction of fresh parathyroid tissue. **1965** LEE & KNOWLES *Animal Hormones* vi. 104 It would appear that the rate of secretion of parathormone is controlled by the level of the blood calcium.

parathyroid, etc.: see PARA-[1] 1.

ˌparathyroiˈdectomy. [f. *parathyroid* s.v. PARA-[1] 1 + -ECTOMY.] Excision of the parathyroids, or a portion of them.

1903 *Med. News* (Philadelphia) 31 Oct. 823/2 Various detailed studies of the results of complete and partial parathyroidectomy have..been made. **1921** *Times Lit. Suppl.* 12 Nov. 898/2 The primary effect in both parathyroidectomy and guanidine poisoning is an abnormal breakdown of tissue proteins. **1971** *New Scientist* 19 Aug. 437/3, I recently had a parathyroidectomy, which was followed, 48 hours later, by acute hypocalcaemia. The effects of this were according to the text book—tingling limbs and fuzzy-headedness. **1974** F. ELLIS in R. M. Kirk et al. *Surgery* viii. 171 Correction of calcium metabolism defects by the use of vitamin D for rickets and osteomalacia, and by parathyroidectomy for hyperparathyroidism.

Hence **ˌparathyroiˈdectomize** *v. trans.*, to deprive of the parathyroids; **ˌparathyroiˈdectomized** *ppl. a.*

1903 *Med. News* (Philadelphia) 31 Oct. 823/2 The condition into which these parathyroidectomized animals fall after a few days is..as follows. **1922** *Endocrinology* VI. 222 When a litter of eight pure black rats 75 days old..was parathyroidectomized all but two survived the 48 hour period. **1965** LEE & KNOWLES *Animal Hormones* vi. 107 In the female duck oestrogen administration leads to an elevation of the blood calcium, but it is without effect in the parathyroidectomized animal. **1972** *Jrnl. Endocrinol.* LIV. 107 Bone loss did not occur in parathyroidectomized dogs.

†**paˈration.** *Obs. rare*[−1]. [ad. L. *parātiōnem*, n. of action from *parāre* to make ready.] A making ready, preparation.

a **1617** BAYNE *On Eph.* i. (1643) 357 If a man fall out of a dead palsy, into a light phrenzy, phrenzy of itself, is no paration to health.

†**ˈparatitle.** *Obs.* [ad. med.L. *paratitla* pl., f. Gr. παρα- PARA-[1] 1 + L. *titulus* TITLE: in mod.F. *paratitle* (Littré).] In *pl.* A short explanation of the titles of the Digest and the Code, to make known the subject and connexion. In *sing.* An abstract of any section of the Code: see quot. 1781.

1610 HOLLAND *Camden's Brit.* I. 263 James Cuiacius readeth Gynæcij and in his Paratitles upon the Code interpreteth it *Sacrum textrinum*. [**1781** GIBBON *Decl. & F.* xvii. II. 47 *note*, Consult, however, the copious *paratitlon* or abstract, which Godefroy has drawn up of the seventh book, de Re Militari, of the Theodosian Code.]

paratoluene to **paratomial**: see PARA-[1] 1, 2.

paratomy: see PARA-[1] 1.

paratonal (pærəˈtəʊnəl), *a. Linguistics.* [f. PARA-[1] + TONAL *a.*] Ancillary to tone; *spec.* of or pertaining to a range of features, excluding pitch, associated with a particular tone.

1966 H. L. SHORTO in C. E. Bazell *In Memory of J. R. Firth* 399 The paratonal register distinction is broadly similar to that described for Cambodian by Henderson. Its exponents are distributed throughout the articulatory complex but exclude pitch features.

paratone (ˈpærətəʊn). *Linguistics.* [f. PARA-[1] + TONE *sb.* 1.] A postulated tonal unit of a sequence of simple tone-groups, in which information concerning sentence-type, the speaker's attitude, etc. is conveyed. Also *attrib.* Hence **paratoˈnality; paratoˈnicity**.

1973 A. FOX in *Archivum Linguisticum* IV. 21 As far as the paratone-group is concerned, we may identify three kinds of choice which parallel exactly those applicable to the tone-group. By the side of tonality we may have 'paratonality', which is concerned with the number of paratone-groups in the utterance. Since the position of the major tone-group within the paratone-group is variable, we must also have a 'paratonicity' system to locate it..; and parallel to the choice of tone we may have a choice of 'paratone', that is, of the specific tone-sequence to be used.

paratonic (pærəˈtɒnɪk), *a.* [f. Gr. παρα- PARA-[1] 1 + TONIC; cf. Gr. παράτον-ος stretched beside or beyond.]

1. *Path.* Relating to overstrain.

1857 MAYNE *Expos. Lex.*, *Paratonia*,..an overstraining. *Paratonicus*, of or belonging to *Paratonia*: paratonic.

2. *Bot.* **a.** [First formed in this sense as G. *paratonisch* (J. Sachs *Lehrb. der Bot.* (1868) III. i. 517).] Applied by Sachs to the effect of the varying intensity of light in causing the movements of 'waking' and 'sleeping', *i.e.* opening and closing of the leaves, etc. in certain plants; in general, applied to plant movements caused by external stimuli (e.g. tropisms and kineses). **b.** Applied to movements of leaves, or of growing organs, caused by external stimuli, as light or mechanical irritation. **c.** Applied to the effect of light in retarding growth in most growing organs, as district from its stimulating effect on leaves.

1875 BENNETT & DYER tr. *Sachs' Bot.* 677 In most leaves endowed with periodic movements the paratonic influence of light is so strong that it neutralises them. *Ibid.* 678 Both the periodic and paratonic movement..is lost when they [the plants] have remained in the dark for a considerable time, such as a whole day; in other words, they become rigid by long exposure to darkness. **1878** McNAB *Bot.* 136 In other cases the nutations are due to the action of external causes on growth. Such nutations are called paratonic or kinetic. **1910** J. M. COULTER et al. *Textbk. Bot.* I. II. 454 The terminal leaflet of *Desmodium gyrans*, like leaves of other members of the bean family, exhibits paratonic movements (i.e. those due to special stimuli, not tonic; opposed to autonomic). **1973** A. CRONQUIST *Basic Bot.* xxvi. 412/2 Some growth movements are self-controlled (autonomic); others are induced by external stimuli (paratonic)... Paratonic movements are further classified as tropisms and nasties.

Hence **paraˈtonically** *adv.*, in a paratonic manner (in quot. in sense 2 a).

1880 C. & F. DARWIN *Movem. Pl.* 123 But cotyledons, besides being heliotropic, are affected paratonically (to use Sachs' expression) by light.

‖**paratonnerre** (paratɔnɛr). [Fr., f. PARA-[2] + *tonnerre* thunder.] An apparatus for protection against 'thunder-stroke'; a lightning-conductor.

1827 *London Encycl.* xv. 74 The stem of a paratonnerre effectually defends a circle of which it is the centre. **1879** NOAD *Electricity* (ed. 3) 112 Paratonnerres or Lightning Conductors for the Protection of Telegraph Lines.

paratopism (pəˈrætəpɪz(ə)m). *nonce-wd.* [f. PARA-[1] 1 + Gr. τόπος place + -ISM: cf. PARACHRONISM.] (See quot.)

1851 *Fraser's Mag.* XLIII. 89 We want some word which will bear the same relation to place as *anachronism* does to time—for his *paratopisms*, let us say.

parator, var. PARITOR, aphetic f. APPARITOR.

ˈparatory. *rare*[−0]. [ad. L. *parātōrium*, f. L. *parāt-*, ppl. stem of *parāre* to prepare: see -ORY.] A place of preparation; *e.g.* a vestry or sacristy.

1877 LEE *Gloss. Liturg. Terms*, *Paratory*.—An old English term for a vestry.—See *Paratorium*. *Paratorium*.—1. A place of preparation. 2. Hence, a vestry, sacristy, or robing-chamber for ecclesiastics.

paratory, var. PARIETARY *Obs.*, pellitory.

paratracheal: see PARA-[1] 1.

†**paratraˈgediate**, *v. Obs.* [irreg. f. L. *paratragœdāre*, f. Gr. παρατραγῳδεῖν, f. παρατραγῳδος pseudo-tragic, bombastic: see PARA-[1] 1.] *intr.* To speak or write in mock-tragic style; to use bombastic language.

1656 BLOUNT *Glossogr.*, *Paratragediate*. **1659** HICKMAN *Justif. Fathers* 4 How doth Mr. Pierce paratragædiate? How doth he tumble in his ugly tropes, and rowle himselfe in his rayling eloquence? **1683** E. HOOKER *Pref. Pordage's Mystic Div.* 19 In regard of their so paratragœdiating.

‖**paratragœdia** (pærətrəˈdʒiːdɪə). [mod.L., f. Gr. παρατραγῳδ-ος: see prec.] Mock-tragedy.

1891 A. T. MURRAY (*title*) On Parody and Paratragoedia in Aristophanes. **1897** T. G. TUCKER in *Class. Rev.* XI. 344/1 The paratragoedia of comedy.

para-transit (ˈpærəˌtrænzɪt). Also as one word. [f. PARA-[1] + TRANSIT *sb.*] Public transport of a flexible, informal kind (see quots.). Also *attrib.*

1973 *Technology Rev.* July-Aug. 46/2 Modes such as taxis, jitneys, dial-a-ride, car pools, subscription buses, and minicars, the modes we collectively call 'para-transit'. **1974** R. KIRBY et al. (*title*) Para-transit: neglected options for urban mobility. **1977** *Chicago Tribune* 2 Oct. XII. 37/7 (Advt.), Transit manager to implement and supervise innovated public paratransit system in growth suburb NW of Chicago. System will consist of subscription mini-bus and dial-a-ride van service. **1978** *Para-transit: Rep. 40th Round Table Transport Econ.* (Europ. Conf. Ministers of Transport) i. 9 'Paratransit'..embraces a series of transport modes, organisational procedures and services falling broadly *midway* between two pre-eminent types of conventional transport, i.e. private cars and public transport services.

paratripsis: see PARA-[1] 1.

paratriptic (pærəˈtrɪptɪk), *a.* (*sb.*) *Med.*, etc. [f. Gr. παρα- PARA-[1] beside, alongside of, against, etc. + τριπτ-, deriv. stem of τρίβειν to rub: cf. Gr. παρατρίβειν to rub on or against.]

1. Of or pertaining to friction or chafing.

1857 in MAYNE *Expos. Lex.*

2. Having the property of preventing waste of bodily tissue. Also as *sb.* A substance having this property.

1887 W. S. SEARLE in *N. Amer. Rev.* CXLV. 150 The paratriptic effect persists and daily continues to manifest itself. *Ibid.*, The so-called paratriptics—or preventers of waste in the body. Of these the most common and best known are wine, tea, coffee, and tobacco. **1891** T. CHILD *Delicate Dining* xi. 116 Tea, coffee, and tobacco come under the heading to which scientific men have given the name of *Paratriptics*.

paratroops (ˈpærətruːps), *sb. pl.* [f. PARA-[3] + TROOP *sb.* 2.] A body of soldiers dropped by parachute from aircraft flying over enemy territory. Also, in the singular, = PARATROOPER below. Also *attrib.* and *fig.*

1940 *Daily Express* 16 May 3/1 Parashots—the new Local Defence Volunteers now being enrolled to deal with paratroops dropped from planes—will have uniforms of overall material. **1940** *N. & Q.* 29 June 459/1 Parachutists dropped as troops, or to establish themselves in the enemy's country..have now been shortened to 'paratroops'. **1940** *English Digest* Sept. 43 Copford, East Anglia, has a nasty lesson in store for any paratroops who may land there. **1941** *Aeronautics* Apr. 41/1 Paratroops. Better late than never! Parachute troops, originally developed by the Russians.. were used by the British early in February. **1941** *Time* 14 July 19/2 Boys and girls..were organized as paratroop detectors. **1942** in *Amer. Speech* (1943) XVIII. 64/2 George Hopkins had made 2,300 parachute jumps..before enlisting as a paratroop. **1942** *Time* 17 Aug. 38 He was transferred to paratroop service. **1943** *Illustr. London News* 17 July 71 (*caption*), A paratroop about to land, with feet together and knees bent ready to take the shock. **1944** *Times* 18 Mar. 4/7 A big-scale exercise with paratroops..was in progress at one point. **1946** A. R. D. FAIRBURN in Chapman & Bennett *Anthol. N.Z. Verse* (1956) 106 Love's paratroops have hit the ground. **1956** *Nature* 4 Feb. 218/1 During the Second World War he [*sc.* Dr. P. B. Walker] was responsible at the Ministry of Aircraft Production for the supervision of the design of gliders and paratroop aircraft. **1958** *Spectator* 20 June 807/2 The attitude of many French paratroop officers towards General Raoul Salan. **1966** *New Scientist* 22 Sept. 659/3 Emotional sweating..has been reported in paratroops before jumping. **1973** 'R. MACLEOD' *Burial in Portugal* i. 18 She'd been young, she'd married a pair of paratroop wings. **1977** *R.A.F. News* 27 Apr.–10 May 13/1 To give them a detailed refresher course on formation flying and paratroop dropping, the film company enlisted the help of the RAF.

Hence **ˈparaˌtrooper**, a soldier of this kind; also, an aeroplane transporting paratroops.

1941 *Time* 4 Aug. 20/1 The paratroopers..had never been in an airplane when it was landed. **1943** J. STEINBECK *Once there was a War* (1959) 228 The lieutenant wanted to look back to see whether any of the paratroopers were in sight. **1945** *Times* 12 Jan. 8/3 The trial of..an American paratrooper..has been fixed for Tuesday next. **1946** *R.A.F.*

Jrnl. May 180 There were..three distinct types of *Halifax* Glider Tugs and Paratroopers. **1956** *Flight* 8 June 748/2 As a paratrooper the Beverley carries 70 soldiers. **1957** *Economist* 5 Oct. 39/1 The dispatch of paratroopers to Little Rock was a painful blow to Americans. **1962** *Times* 29 Mar. 15/5 For the paratroopers the sheer luck of their landing place meant..the difference between a swift regrouping or death in the air.

paratrophia to **paratyphlitis**: see PARA-[1] 1.

paratrophic (pærəˈtrəʊfɪk), *a. Biol.* [ad. G. *paratroph* (A. Fischer *Vorlesungen über Bakterien* (1897) v. 47), f. PARA-[1]: see TROPHIC *a.* (*sb.*).] Needing live organic matter for nutrition.

1900 A. C. JONES tr. *Fischer's Struct. & Functions Bacteria* v. 49 The paratrophic group includes all those bacteria that can exist only within the living tissues of other organisms. **1902** [see METATROPHIC *a.*]. **1919** F. O. BOWER *Bot. Living Plant* xxx. 460 On the basis of nutrition Bacteria have been classified into three groups:..(iii) Paratrophic, those which develop normally only within the living tissues of other organisms, and are true, and obligatory parasites, such as the germs of Tubercle or Diphtheria. **1930** S. THOMAS *Bacteriol.* (ed. 2) xiv. 228 The paratrophic organisms..must have living organic matter from which to get all or part of their food requirements.

† **ˈparature.** *Obs. rare*$^{-0}$. [ad. L. *parātūra* preparation.]

1656 BLOUNT *Glossogr.*, *Parature*, the matter whereof any thing is made.

paratype (ˈpærətaɪp). *Taxonomy.* [f. PARA-[1] + TYPE *sb.*[1]] A specimen from a group that includes the one designated as the nomenclatural type of a species in its first description, but not the type itself.

1893 O. THOMAS in *Proc. Zool. Soc.* 242 Since the other specimens mentioned or enumerated.. in the original description are of unquestionably great value in a typical sense, they ought also to have a name and might be called 'para-types' (or side-types). *Ibid.*, A Para-type is a specimen belonging to the original series but not the type, in cases where the author has himself selected a type. It should, however, be one of the specimens mentioned or enumerated in the original description. **1914** *Brit. Mus. Return* 171 in *Parl. Papers* LXXI. 193 Two paratypes of a new species of River-crab from Cochin. **1933** *Jrnl. R. Soc. W. Austral.* XIX. 15 The type specimen is being presented to the Western Australian Museum and a paratype to the British Museum. **1943** [see ISOTYPE 3]. **1951** G. H. M. LAWRENCE *Taxon. Vascular Plants* ix. 204 A paratype is a specimen cited with the original description, other than the holotype. **1956** *Internat. Code Bot. Nomencl.* ii. 15 A paratype is a specimen cited with the original description other than the holotype or isotype(s). **1962** GORDON & LAVOIPIERRE *Entomol. for Students of Med.* liii. 325 Specimens other than the holotype which the author used when describing the species are known as the 'paratypes'. **1964** *Internat. Code Zool. Nomencl.* xvi. 79 After the holotype has been labelled, each remaining specimen (if any) of the type-series should be conspicuously labelled 'paratype', in order clearly to identify the components of the original type-series. **1971** *Nature* 30 July 311/2 It [*sc.* the skull of a fossil hominid] resembles the paratype from Bed II (Olduvai H. 13) in both cranial and dental characters.

paratyphoid (pærəˈtaɪfɔɪd), *sb.* (*a.*) *Path.* [f. PARA-[1] + TYPHOID *a.* (*sb.*).] A fever similar in symptoms to, but generally milder than, typhoid fever, from which it can be distinguished bacteriologically. Freq. *attrib.* or as *adj.*, esp. in ***paratyphoid fever***.

1902 *Amer. Jrnl. Med. Sci.* CXXIII. 977 Paratyphoid fever closely resembles typhoid in its course, temperature curve, and abdominal symptoms. **1904** *Jrnl. R. Microsc. Soc.* June 369 If there is suspicion of para-typhoid (or dysentery) the agglutination of the colonies in question must be investigated with the specific serum of this disease. **1948** MORGAN & CHEEVER in R. J. Dubos *Bacterial & Mycotic Infections of Man* xvii. 384/2 *Salmonella paratyphi* is found only in man where it has been described as one cause of paratyphoid fever. **1965** HARGREAVES & MORRISON *Pract. Trop. Med.* ii. 91 Paratyphoid infections are caused by *S*[*almonella*] *paratyphosus A.*, *S. paratyphosus B* and *S. paratyphosus C.* In general paratyphoid A occurs in the tropics whilst B infections are met with more frequently in temperate zones. Paratyphoid C occurs in the Indian subcontinent, the Middle East and the Balkans. **1972** HOOK & JOHNSON in P. D. Hoeprich *Infectious Dis.* lv. 588/2 Members of the genus *Salmonella* other than *S. typhi* can produce an illness with all the clinical characteristics of typhoid fever—paratyphoid fever.

† **paˈraunce.** *Obs.* [Aphetic f. *aparaunce*, APPARENCE 2.] = APPARENCE 2: in ***heier of paraunce***, heir of apparency, heir apparent.

c **1450** *Bk. Curtasye* 497 in *Babees Bk.* (1868) 315 No mete for mon schalle sayed be, Bot for kynge or prynce or duke so fre; For heiers of paraunce also y-wys.

† **paˈraunt,** *a. Obs. rare*$^{-1}$. [a. OF. *parant* apparent, visible, of eminent or distinguished appearance, pr. pple. of *paroir*:—L. *pārēre* to appear.] Apparent, prominent, distinguished.

c **1450** *Merlin* 356 These foure were paraunt a-bove alle the tother, ffor these dide soche prowesse with her owne bodyes that it was wonder.

paraunter, -tre, -tur, obs. ff. PERADVENTURE.

parautochthonous (pærɔːˈtɒkθənəs), *a. Geol.* [f. PARA-[1] + AUTOCHTHONOUS *a.*; prob. orig. formed in Ger.] Intermediate in character between autochthonous and allochthonous.

1927 L. W. COLLET *Struct. Alps* I. vi. 20 The Morcles Nappe and similar parautochthonous folds. **1935** E. B. BAILEY *Tectonic Ess.* iii. 34 In parautochthonous folds and thrust-masses (Arnold Heim) the travel of the rock has been considerable or great, according to ordinary standards, but small in the Alpine scale of magnitudes. **1962** READ & WATSON *Introd. Geol.* I. x. 580 Parautochthonous granites have travelled only a short distance from their place of origin. **1963** J. G. RAMSAY in Johnson & Stewart *Brit. Caledonides* vii. 166 It is not certain where these pieces have their roots. They might be parautochthonous folds, but some evidence seems to indicate that a few might represent the noses of nappes.

paravaginitis: see PARA-[1] 1.

† **paraˈvail,** *adv.* (*a.*) *Obs.* exc. *Hist.* Also 6 parаual, 6–7 -availe, 7 peravall(e. [a. OF. *par aval* down (of direction or position), f. *par* through, by (often = Eng. *be-*) + *aval*, *à val*, adv. and prep., 'down':—L. *ad vallem* to the valley, as opposed to *amont*, *ad montem* to the hill, up.] Down below or beneath; below one in position; as ***tenant paravail***, one who holds under another who is himself a tenant; *spec.* with English legal writers since 16th c., the lowest tenant, he who actually worked or occupied the land, etc. Opposed to PARAMOUNT.

The English view of a *tenant paravail* was prob. influenced by the erroneous notion which connected the word with *avail*, because the lowest tenant or actual holder was he who made his avail or profit out of the land. Cf. *a* **1634** COKE *On Litt.* II. (1642) 296 The Tenant of the land is called Tenant *per availe*, because it is presumed, that he hath availe and profit by the land.

[**1531** FITZHERB. *Nat. Brev.* 80 b, Et le seignur paramount destreigne le tenant paravale pour lez seruicez dont [etc.].] **1579** J. STUBBES *Gaping Gulf* D iij, In respect whereof al other the greatest castelles, honors, and manors, are but mesnalties or rather very messuages and tenancyes parаual. **1585–6** HOOKER *Serm. Justif.* §28 Let the Pope..no longer count himself Lord Paramount over the Princes of the earth, no longer use Kings as his tenants [*ed.* 1613 servants] paravaile. *a* **1625** SIR H. FINCH *Law* (1636) 156 The Lord grants his seigniory, the Mesne must atturne, and not the tenant parauaile: for the Mesne is Tenant to the Lord. **1647** N. BACON *Disc. Govt. Eng.* I. lix. (1739) 114 All degrees.. from the Lord paramont to the Tenant paravale. **1766** BLACKSTONE *Comm.* II. v. 60 The king therefore was stiled lord paramount; A was both tenant and lord, or was a mesne lord; and B was called tenant paravail, or the lowest tenant.

b. ***court paravail***, the court below; a lower or inferior court of law.

a **1650** BEAUMONT *Poems* (N.), But though there lie writs from the courts paramount, To stay the proceedings of the courts paravaile.

paravane (ˈpærəveɪn). [f. PARA-[2] + VANE.] An apparatus, fitted with vanes to keep it at a constant depth, designed to be towed at the bows of a vessel in order to clear its path from mines, cut the moorings of submerged mines, or destroy hostile submarines. Also *attrib.* Also *Aeronaut.*, a towing device (see quot. 1959).

1919 *Daily Mail* 6 Jan. 6/2 Like many other great conceptions, the paravane seems a quite simple thing. *Ibid.*, On one occasion last year a flotilla of light cruisers found themselves in a minefield, and by using the paravane they were able to cut their way safely through it. *Ibid.*, The paravane was invented by Lieut. Dennis Burney, R.N. **1920** *Rep. Brit. Assoc. Adv. Sci. 1919* 273 The Paravane has been developed as a weapon to fulfill two purposes:—(1) To attack a submarine. (2) To protect vessels from moored mines. **1920** [see OTTER *sb.* 4 c]. **1920** *Glasgow Herald* 8 Oct. 10 Nor was part of the manufacturing profits in respect of paravane systems supplied to the Navy paid by the Government. *Ibid.* 5 Nov. 11 The 'paravane' is a name invented in or about 1916 to denote a particular kind or type of water kite of special shape and material and with special appliances. It was evolved and developed and in 1916 was adopted by the naval authorities as standard. **1922** *Encycl. Brit.* XXXII. 33/1 Paravane, a naval device used in the World War first for attacking submerged submarines and subsequently for protecting vessels against mines and for cutting up hostile minefields. The name of Acting-Comm. C. D. Burney is especially associated with its design and development. **1948** R. DE KERCHOVE *Internat. Maritime Dict.* 519/2 Two paravanes are towed, one on each side of the ship, by means of specially constructed wire towropes. **1959** J. L. NAYLER *Dict. Aeronaut. Engin.* 186 *Paravane*, a kite-shaped device by means of which a wire is kept at an angle from a towing vehicle. This device is used at Woomera, towed behind an aircraft, in snatch recovery methods for intercepting guided missiles towards the end of their flights.

† **paravant, -aunt,** *adv. Obs.* [a. OF. *paravant* adv. and prep., 'before' in time or place, f. *par* 'through, by, be-' + *avant* before:—L. **abante* from before.

In mod. F. retained only in the archaic *paravant que* before that, and the compound *auparavant* before, in time, formerly. The latter has heaped up successive elements, until it has, for the expression of the simple L. adv. *ante*, the representatives of *ad illud per ab ante*.]

Before; in front; before the rest, pre-eminently.

1590 SPENSER *F. Q.* III. ii. 16 Tell me some markes by which he may appeare, If chaunce I him encounter paravaunt. **1595** —— *Col. Clout* 941 Yet that I may her honour paravant, And praise her worth, though far my wit above. **1596** —— *F. Q.* VI. x. 15 But that faire one, That in the midst was placed paravaunt.

paraventricular: see PARA-[1] 1.

paraventure, obs. form of PERADVENTURE.

paravertebral (pærəˈvɜːtɪbrəl), *a. Med.* [f. PARA-[1] + VERTEBRAL *a.*] Situated or occurring beside the vertebral column or a vertebra.

1893 DUNGLISON *Dict. Med. Sci.* (ed. 21) 822/1 *Paravertebral*, situate beside or in the vicinity of the vertebral column. **1923** R. E. FARR tr. H. Braun in *Pract. Local Anesthesia* v. 123 Paravertebral anesthesia had been employed quite extensively in abdominal surgery. **1934** *Practitioners Libr. Med. & Surg.* V. xiii. 854 The sympathetic nerves pass from the higher centers in the midbrain down the spinal cord and then out into the paravertebral sympathetic chain. **1963** *Lancet* 12 Jan. 85/2 The patient was given..paravertebral block with 1% procaine. **1967** J. J. BONICA *Princ. & Pract. Obstetr. Analgesia & Anesthesia* I. xxxvii. 643/2 Each thoracic paravertebral space contains loose areolar and fatty tissue.

paravesical, -xanthine, etc.: see PARA-[1] 1, 2.

paravisual (pærəˈvɪʒjuːəl, -ˈvɪzjuːəl), *a.* [f. PARA-[1] + VISUAL *a.*] Conveying information visually but not requiring a person's direct gaze.

1960 *Aeroplane* XCVIII. 764/1 Airborne experience with the Smiths Para-Visual Director system will leave the newcomer with a strong conviction that this new flight-director/instrument-flying concept must inevitably alter present ideas about weather minima and automatic-landing prospects. **1964** M. ALLWARD *Inside Jet Airliner* vii. 53 Three little instruments called Para-Visual Directors mounted in line along the top of the instrument panels in front of each pilot. **1968** G. D. P. WORTHINGTON *Airline Instrument Flying* xvi. 256 The Para-visual Director is designed to apply command information in regard to pitch and bank through a rotating 'barber's pole' display which is so located that it is within the pilot's general field of vision but outside the limits of his direct field of vision. The direction of rotation of the pole applies a signal in the pilot's peripheral field of vision which demands fly up or fly down in the case of the pitch bars, or fly left or fly right in the case of the bank presentation.

parawing (ˈpærəwɪŋ). *Aeronaut.* Also **para wing.** [f. PARA-[3] + WING *sb.*] A parachute device having a flat inflatable wing in place of the more usual umbrella, allowing greater manœuvrability.

1960 R. L. NAESETH *Exploratory Study of Parawing as High-Lift Device for Aircraft* (NASA TN D-629) 1 A wind-tunnel investigation was made of the high-lift capabilities of two supersonic airplane configurations equipped with auxiliary parawings which are lightweight, stowable, fabric wings of parachute-like construction that may be used for take-off and landing. **1964** *Engineering* 7 Feb. 237/1 All of these gliders make use of the fact that the parawing is simple and cheap enough to be expendable. **1966** *Guardian* 12 May 14/5 Inflated triangular 'parawings' are being tested by the US army for possible use in place of parachutes. The parawing, which can be folded, packed and released like a parachute, inflates on opening into a flattened triangular dirigible that glides and maneuvres through the air. **1973** D. POYNTER *Hang Gliding* ii. 54 The idea of a limp para wing was presented to NASA as a reentry vehicle and millions of dollars were spent in research and tests... Stiffened Para Wings have performed much better than the limp models.

parawollastonite: see PARA-[1] 2 c.

paraxial (pəˈræksɪəl), *a.* [f. PARA-[1] 1 + L. *axi-s* AXIS: cf. *axial*.] **a.** *Anat.* and *Zool.* Lying alongside, or on each side of, the axis of the body.

1861 J. R. GREENE *Man. Anim. Kingd., Cœlent.* 228 The oral extremities of the paraxial canal system. **1870** NICHOLSON *Man. Zool.* 113 The 'paraxial system', comprising the paragastric canals. **1893** *Syd. Soc. Lex.*, *Paraxial muscles*, the muscles developed by the side of the vertebral column.

b. *Optics.* Situated close to the axis of an optical system, and (if linear) virtually parallel to it; of or pertaining to such a region.

1906 H. D. TAYLOR *Syst. Appl. Optics* iv. 55 The ultimate or paraxial rays. **1930** L. C. MARTIN *Introd. Appl. Optics* I. i. 17 Imagine..that the point P is brought so close to the axis that the inclination of the ray to the axis becomes very small; these conditions are characteristic of a 'paraxial' ray. **1934** W. H. A. FINCHAM *Optics* v. 83 For light in the paraxial region the angles of incidence and refraction will be very small, and may be considered as proportional to their sines in applying the law of refraction. **1974** W. T. WELFORD *Aberrations Symmetr. Optical Systems* iii. 17 We..define the domain of paraxial or Gaussian optics to be close enough to the axis to ensure that all terms of higher order of magnitude than quadratic in *x* and *y* are to be neglected.

Hence **paˈraxially** *adv.*, adjacent to or virtually parallel to an axis.

The 1905 reference given in quot. 1909 is incorrect and has not been traced.

1909 *Cent. Dict.* Suppl., *Paraxially*, in *zoöl.*, in such a way as to lie on each side of the long axis (of the body). *Proc. Roy. Soc.* (London), Feb., 1905, p. 318. **1927** V. T. SAUNDERS *Light* iii. 38 If a single ray is incident on the mirror through the principal focus it is seen to be reflected paraxially. **1950** H. H. HOPKINS *Wave Theory of Aberrations* 162 The paraxial equations..refer to rays which are limitingly close to the axis. Since, however, the equations are linear in the angles *u*, *a*, *i* rays at finite apertures may be traced paraxially.

paraxylene: see PARA-[1] 2 b.

parayl(e, variant of PAREIL, PAREL *Obs.*

parays, obs. variant of PARADISE.

‖**parazoa** (pærə'zəʊə), *sb. pl. Zool.* [mod.L. neut. pl., f. Gr. παρα- PARA-[1] + ζῷον animal; after PROTOZOA, METAZOA.] In some classifications, a name for the Sponges considered as a division co-ordinate with *Protozoa* and *Metazoa*. Hence **para'zoan** *a.*, belonging to the *Parazoa*; *sb.*, a member of the *Parazoa*.

1887 SOLLAS in *Encycl. Brit.* XXII. 421/1 The phylum *Parazoa* or *Spongiæ* consists of two main branches.

‖**parazonium** (pærə'zəʊnɪəm). *Gr. Antiq.* Also 7 anglicized as **parazon, -zone**. [L. (Martial), ad. Gr. παραζώνιον = παραζωνίδιον a dagger worn at the girdle, from παραζωνίδιος at the girdle, f. παρά beside + ζώνη girdle, belt.] A small sword or dagger worn at the girdle by the ancient Greeks; also applied by mediæval writers to similar weapons.

1623 COCKERAM, *Parazon*, a wood-knife. [So **1658** in PHILLIPS.] **1674** BLOUNT *Glossogr.* (ed. 4), *Parazone* (*parazonium*), a Dagger, Fauchon, or Short Sword. **1850** LEITCH tr. *C. O. Müller's Anc. Art* §414 (ed. 2) 579 The Athenian Anakes..in chlamydes with parazonia, on a sardonyx as amulet. **1874** BOUTELL *Arms & Arm.* iii. 49 A weapon..in general use by all classes of Greek soldiers, is a short sword or dagger, called *parazonium* (belt-companion), which sometimes was reduced to the proportions of a knife.

'par,bake, *v. nonce-wd.* [f. *par-* in PARBOIL, taken as = 'part' + BAKE.] *trans.* To bake partially, half bake.

1885 MRS. RITCHIE *Mrs. Dymond* I. vi, Everything was so hot and so glaring that very few people were about; a few par-baked figures went quickly by.

‖**parbleu** (parblø), *int.* Now only as Fr. In 8 **parblew**. [F. *parbleu* (La Fontaine, Molière 17th c.), a deformation of *pardieu* 'by God', PARDIE.] An exclamation or minced oath.

1709 PRIOR *Thief & Cordelier* x, Parblew, I shall have little Stomach to eat. **1813** SOUTHEY *March to Moscow* i, The fields were green, and the sky was blue, Morbleu! Parbleu! **1836** W. IRVING *Astoria* I. 313 The poor Canadians [ejaculated]..'Parbleu! this is a sad scrape we are in, brother!'

parboil ('pɑː,bɔɪl), *v.* Forms: α. 5 **parbuille**, **-boylyn**, 5–7 **-boyl(e**, (7 *erron.* **part-boil**), 6– **parboil**. β. 5 **perbuille**, 6–7 **-boyl(e**, **-boile**. [a. OF. *parboill-ir*, *parbouillir*, *parbouyllyr* (Godef.) (*pourbouiller* Cotgr.):—late L. *perbullīre* (Theod. Prisc.) to boil thoroughly, f. *per* through, thoroughly + *bullīre* to bubble, BOIL. The prefix has been erron. identified with *part*, whence sense 2.]

†**1.** *trans.* To boil thoroughly. *Obs.*

c **1430** *Two Cookery-bks.* 6 Take fayre caboges..parboyle hem in fayre water, an þanne presse hem on a fayre bord. *c* **1450** *Douce MS.* 55, xxx. lf. 19 Lete parbuille hem ryȝth well. **1565** STAPLETON tr. *Bede's Hist. Ch. Eng.* 122 It might all be perboyled out by the fire of long tribulation. **1611** COTGR., *Pourbouiller*, to parboile throughly. *a* **1655** SIR T. MAYERNE *Archimagirus* v. (1658) 2 Take the Hare and parboyl him, then take all the flesh from the bone.

2. To boil partially, half boil.

c **1440** *Promp. Parv.* 382/1 Parboylyn mete, *semibullio*, *parbullio*. **1530** PALSGR. 652/1 It muste be parboyled first and than baken: *il le fault parbouyllyr premier et puis le mettre cuyr au four*. **1555** EDEN *Decades* 183 Flesshe can not bee preserued..excepte it be rosted, sodden or perboylde. **1613** PURCHAS *Pilgrimage* VIII. iii. 623 Sometimes they will perboile their meate a little. **1670** BLOUNT *Glossogr.* (ed. 3), *Part-boil*, to boil in part not fully. **1769** MRS. RAFFALD *Eng. Housekpr.* (1778) 151 Parboil a calf's-head, when cold cut it in pieces. **1853** KANE *Grinnell Exp.* xvii. (1856) 130 Rub with soda; wash out the soap thus freely made; parboil and pickle.

3. In figurative or hyperbolical use (from 1 or 2); usually in reference to overheating.

1566 DRANT *Horace, Sat.* ix. E iij b, My harte in choller perboylde was. **1598** B. JONSON *Ev. Man in Hum.* IV. i, They should haue beene perboyl'd, and bak'd too, euery mothers sonne. **1642** HOWELL *For. Trav.* (Arb.) 74 When hee sees the same Sun which only cherisheth and gently warmes his Countrey men, halfe parboyle and tanne other people. **1682** N. O. *Boileau's Lutrin* IV. 12 He..parboil'd in his mellow Sweat lay frying. **1807** W. IRVING *Salmag.* viii. *On Style*, Being squeezed, and smothered, and parboiled at nightly balls. **1879** H. GEORGE *Progr. & Pov.* v. ii. (1881) 263 To get four dollars a day for parboiling themselves two thousand feet underground.

Hence **parboiled** ('pɑː,bɔɪld) *ppl. a.*, †thoroughly boiled (*obs.*); partly boiled, half-boiled; also *fig.*; hence **parboiledness**; **'parboiling** *vbl. sb.* and *ppl. a.*

c **1440** *Promp. Parv.* 382/1 *Parboylyd, *parbullitus*. **1559** *Mirr. Mag.*, *Jack Cade* xxi. 5 Than were on poales my parboylde quarters pight. *c* **1644** CLEVELAND *Mixt Assembly* Wks. (1687) 33 Strange Scarlet Doctors these; they'll pass in Story For Sinners half refin'd in Purgatory; Or parboyl'd Lobsters. **1844** TUPPER *Twins* xxiv. 180 My fellow passengers..were lying about as weak as parboiled eels. **1862** *Temple Bar Mag.* VI. 154 Sweltering heat and *parboiledness seem to be the fashion. *c* **1440** *Promp. Parv.* 382/1 *Parboylynge, *parbullicio*. *a* **1560** R. HALL *Life Bp. Fisher* (1655) 211 The parboyling in hot water. **1727–41** CHAMBERS *Cycl.*, *Parboiling*, in pharmacy, etc. a term applied to fruits, herbs, etc. which are boiled a little while, to draw out the first juices. *c* **1450** *Two Cookery-bks.* 84 Take faire parcelly, and parboyle hit in a potte, & *parboylingge broþe.

parbreak ('pɑːbreɪk), *sb. Obs.* or *arch. rare.* [f. next.] Vomit, spewing.

1586 MARLOWE *1st Pt. Tamburl.* v. ii, Loathsome parbreak of the Stygian snakes. **1590** SPENSER *F.Q.* I. i. 20 Her filthie parbreake all the place defiled has. **1884** SYMONDS *Shaks. Predec.* x. 374 The very parbreak of a youthful poet's indigestion.

†**parbreak** (pɑː'breɪk), *v. Obs.* Forms: α. 5–7 **parbrake**, 6 **-breke**, **-brack**, 6–7 **-break(e**. β. 6–7 **perbrake**, **-break**. *Pa. pple.* 6 **-braked**, **-brak'd**, **-brackt**, **-breakt**, 7 **-brak't**, **-breaked**. [A compound of BRAKE *v.*[6], of which it is a synonym; subseq. referred to the more common BREAK *v.* The prefix is identical in form with F. *par-*, and, like it, in Eng. occas. spelt *per-*; cf. PERBREAK *v.* to break through or thoroughly. By Sylvester, and in recent Dicts., stressed '*parbreak*.]

1. To spew, vomit; = BRAKE *v.*[6] **a.** *intr.*

c **1440** *Promp. Parv.* 47/2 Brakynge or parbrakynge, *vomitus*. **1519** HORMAN *Vulg.* 39 b, He wyll nat cease fro surfettynge, tyll he be redy to parbrake. *a* **1529** SKELTON *Duke of Albany* 322 And virulently dysgorgyd, As though ye wolde parbrake [*rime* to make]. **1530** PALSGR. 478/1, I cast my gorge, as a haulke doth, or a man that parbraketh. **1587** LEVINS *Pathway to Health* (1632) 27 b, It will cause a man for to cast or perbreake. *a* **1610** HEALEY *Theophrastus* (1616) 14 Yesterday, hee sayth, I was wamble-cropt, and (sauing your presence) parbrak't.

b. *trans.*

1545 RAYNOLD *Byrth Mankynde* 128 Marke that the which the chylde doth perbrake, whether it sauer sharpely lyke vyneger. **1573** TWYNE *Æneid* x. (1584) P v b, His goldbright shield fire perbrakes. **1589** *Mar Martine* 5 Thou hast parbrackt out thy gorge, and shot out all thy arrowes. **1598** SYLVESTER *Du Bartas* II. i. III. *Furies* 253 Come, parbreak here your foul, black, banefull gall.

2. *fig.* (*trans.*) To utter or pour forth recklessly or offensively; to vomit forth.

1401 *Pol. Poems* (Rolls) II. 63 That semeth the beter than with sotil sillogismes to parbrake thi witt. **1523** [COVERDALE] *Old God & New* (1534) R, Many there are now a daies, which in yᵉ pulpit do..perbrake forth theyr priuate braulles, hatredes, & pryde. **1597–8** BP. HALL *Sat.* I. v. 9 And when he hath parbrak'd his grieued mind. **1599** *Broughton's Lett.* i. 6 Your virulent letters (parbreakt from a poysonfull stomacke). **1629** Z. BOYD *Last Battell* 165 One of those in whom Satan hath parbreaked and spewed the spawne of all sorts of sinne.

Hence †**par'breaking** *vbl. sb.* and *ppl. a.*

c **1440** [see 1 a]. **1530** PALSGR. 251/2 Parbrekyng, *vomissement*. **1590** BARROUGH *Meth. Physick* 293 Miserably tormented with perbraking and continuall vomiting. **1656** RIDGLEY *Pract. Physick* 61 It [Cholic] is eased by parbreaking. **1746** *Exmoor Scolding* (E.D.S.) 148 A wud ha' had a coad, riggelting, parbeaking, piping Body in tha!

†**par'bruilyie**, *v. Sc. Obs.* Erron. f. BARBULYE, to confuse, perplex.

1600 J. MELVILL *Diary* (Wodrow Soc.) 411 Maist confusedlie parbruilyied.

parbuckle ('pɑːbʌk(ə)l), *sb.* Also 7 **-bunkel**, **-bunkle**, 8–9 **-buncle**. [Orig. *parbunkle*, *-buncle*, of unknown origin; about 1760 associated by popular etymology with *buckle*] A device for raising or lowering heavy objects, either vertically or in an inclined plane, by means of a rope of which both ends are passed round the object. **a.** A sling formed by passing the two ends of a rope round the object and through a bight of the rope, and tightening, the weight of the object serving to keep it tight. (See also quot. 1627.) **b.** A rope having a bight looped round a post, etc., at the level to or from which the object is to be raised or lowered, and the two ends passed round the object, and hauled in or paid out to raise or lower it, the object acting as a movable pulley; used in hoisting casks or other cylindrical bodies, also in Capt. Cunningham's method of furling a sail by hoisting the yard in the bight of the chain.

1626 CAPT. SMITH *Accid. Yng. Seamen* 13 The canhookes, slings, and parbunkels. **1627** —— *Seaman's Gram.* v. 21 A Parbunkel is two ropes that haue at each end a noose or lumpe [? loope] that being crossed, you may set any vessell that hath but one head vpon them, bringing but the loopes ouer the vpper end of the caske, fix but the tackle to them, and then the vessell will stand strait..to heaue out, or take in without spilling. **1658** PHILLIPS, A *Parbunkle* (in Navigation), a roap seased together at both ends; and so put double about the Cask to hoise it in by. **1704** J. HARRIS *Lex. Techn.* I, *Parbuncle*,..a Rope in a Ship, almost like a pair of Slings; 'tis seized both Ends together, and then put double about any heavy thing that is to be hoised in or out of the Ship; having the Hook of the Runner hitched into it to hoise it up by. **1731–1800** BAILEY, *Parbuncle* (*Sea Term*). **1769** FALCONER *Dict. Marine* (1776), Parbuckle. **1823** CRABB *Technol. Dict.*, Parbuckle. **1831** JANE PORTER *Sir E. Seaward's Narr.* II. 65 By means of planks, and tackles, and parbuckles, they succeeded in dragging the gun up to the flag-staff. **1838** *Encycl. Brit.*, *Parbuncle* [same as quot. 1704]. **1867** SMYTH *Sailor's Word-bk.* s.v., The parbuckle is frequently used in public-house vaults.

attrib. **1779** in Almon *Remembrancer* VIII. 372, 50 fathoms of skid and parbuckle rope.

'parbuckle, *v.* [f. prec. sb.] *trans.* To raise or lower (a cask, gun, etc.) by the device of a parbuckle: see prec. b.

1831 TRELAWNEY *Adv. Younger Son* xcvi, We parbuckled Louis into his shore-grave. **1833** MARRYAT *P. Simple* xliii, You might parbuckle it up to the very top. **1859** F. A. GRIFFITHS *Artil. Man.* (1862) 110 To parbuckle a gun is to roll it so as to cause it to move in either direction from the spot on which it rests. **1890** *Daily News* 19 Aug. 3/2 The gun ..has then to be dismounted down the rear on watered skids, moved then on rollers, and parbuckled across a ditch.

Hence **'parbuckling** *vbl. sb.* (also *attrib.*).

1859 F. A. GRIFFITHS *Artil. Man.* (1862) 131 Where there is a swell, parbuckling is not to be attempted. *Ibid.*, The ends of the parbuckling skids should rest on the dunnage.

parc, obs. or alien form of PARK.

parca, var. PARKA.

parcaas, parcas(e, variant of PERCASE *Obs.*

†**'parcage**. *Sc. Obs.* [a. F. *parcage*, f. *parquer* to PARK.] Enclosure, shutting up (of stray beasts).

1453 *Truce w. Scotl.* in Rymer *Foedera* (1710) XI. 337 Without Pynding, Parcage or other Distourbing. **1576** *Reg. Privy Council Scot* Ser. I. II. 523 To doubill the pane of the parcage or poindage.

parcar(e, Parcee, obs. ff. PARKER[1], PARSEE.

parceit, parceive, obs. ff. PERCEIT, PERCEIVE.

parcel ('pɑːsəl, 'pɑːs(ə)l), *sb.* Forms: α. 4–6 **parcelle**, 5–6 **-cele**, 4–8 **-cell**, (5–7 **passell**, 9– *dial.* **passel** ('pæsəl), **pasel**, **passle**, **pazil**), 6 **parsel**, **-syll**, 4– **parcel**. β. 4–7 **percel(l**, 6 **persell**. [a. F. *parcelle* = Pr. *parcela*, Pg. *parcella*, It. *particella*:—L. type **particella*, dim. of *particula*, dim. of *pars*, *part-em* PART.]

A. *sb.* **I. 1. a.** *gen.* A part, portion, or division *of* anything (material or immaterial), considered separately, as a unit; a small part, a particle. *arch.*

by parcels: by parts, a part at a time, piecemeal.

c **1368** CHAUCER *Compl. Pite* 106 What nedeth to shewe parcel of my peyne? *c* **1391** —— *Astrol.* I. §12 A certein parcelle of the body of a man. **1412–20** LYDG. *Chron. Troy* I. vii, Where as Naso recordeth..But percell eke of the vnkyndnesse Of this Jason. **1459** in *Somerset Medieval Wills* (1901) 193 Chargyng my said sonne..that he never clayme parcell ne part thereof. **1523** FITZHERB. *Surv.* Prol. (1539) 2 That there be no parcell thereof loste. **1628** PRYNNE *Lovelockes* 9 Those onely suffer a little part and parcell of their Haire to growe long. **1692** RAY *Disc.* II. v. (1732) 226 A great Parcel of the Earth is every year carried into the Sea. **1794** GODWIN *Cal. Williams* 242 They took up the detached parcels of my miserable attire. **1873** M. ARNOLD *Lit. & Dogma* (1876) p. xxxi, Truth more complete than the parcel of truth any momentary individual can seize. **1879** RUSKIN *Lett. to Clergy* 37 The insinuation of having committed the smallest parcel of them [sins].

b. A constituent or component part, one of the parts or members (*of* something), something included in a whole: emphasizing comprehension in the whole, rather than partitive character. (Often without article.) *arch.* (exc. as in c.)

of a parcel with: of a piece with, consonant with.

1414 *Rolls of Parlt.* IV. 60/1 The fees of his seal, which is parcel and partie of his sustenance. **14..** 26 *Pol. Poems* (E.E.T.S.) 51/16 Þe leste lygeman wiþ body and rent, He is a parcel of þe crowne. **1570** T. NORTON tr. *Nowel's Catech.* (1853) 204 To praise and magnify God's goodness..is parcel of the worshipping of God. **1605** BACON *Adv. Learn.* I. i. §3 That nothing parcel of the world is denied to man's inquiry and invention. **1784** COWPER *Task* v. 247 Being parcel of the common mass. **1818** CRUISE *Digest* (ed. 2) III. 275 Franchises..which were originally parcel of the royal prerogative. **1871** SWINBURNE *Songs bef. Sunrise, Litany of Nations* 95 Till the soul of man be parcel of the sunlight.

c. Phrase *part and parcel*: see PART *sb.* 18.

†**d.** Share, allotted portion. *Obs.*

1362 LANGL. *P. Pl.* A. XI. 50 Luyte [B. litel] loueþ he þat lord þat leneþ him þat Blisse, þat þus parteþ with he pore A parcel whon him neodeþ. **1393** *Ibid.* C. XXIII. 289 Þei shal ȝeue þe freres A parcel to preye for hem and maken hem murye With þe remenant of þe good. *a* **1400–50** *Alexander* 4318 Þe pouert of oure persons for plente we hald, Þe quilke is part vs, all þe pake be parcells euyn.

†**e.** A part of the world, of a country, etc.: = PART *sb.* 13. *Obs. rare.*

1582 STANYHURST *Æneid*, etc. III. (Arb.) 85 How beyt theese parcels in sayling must be refused. *Ibid.*, *Conceits* ii. 136 Wheare barcks haue passed, with cart's that parcel is haunted [in winter].

†**f.** Part (in a play, etc.), rôle. *Obs. rare.*

c **1412** HOCCLEVE *De Reg. Princ.* 3055 In lordes courtes þou pleyest þi parcel.

2. *spec.* **a.** A portion or piece of land; *esp.*, in Law of Real Property, as part of a manor or estate. (Often without article.)

[**1321** *Rolls of Parlt.* I. 387/1 Tenant de dis parceles de terre.] ? **1449** *Paston Lett.* I. 93 On lese then that he sel a parcel of his land. **1539** BIBLE (Great) *1 Chron.* xi. 13 And there was there a parsell of grounde full of barleye. **1604** in *Eng. Gilds* (1870) 433 For that parcell he shall agree with the lord for his years rent. **1611** BIBLE *John* iv. 5 A city of Samaria..neere to the parcell of ground that Iacob gaue to his sonne Ioseph. **1642** tr. *Perkins' Prof. Bk.* iii. §226. 100 A parcell of an acre of land. **1720** *Col. Rec. Pennsylv.* III. 108 Owners of certain parcels of Land. **1778** *Eng. Gazetteer* (ed. 2) s.v. *Twiford*, In this town is a parcel of ground, said to be in the county of Wilts. **1883** C. SWEET *Law Dict.*, *Parcel*, in the Law of Real Property, signifies a part or portion of land. Thus, every piece of Copyhold land forms parcel of the manor to which it belongs. **1897** *Act 60 & 61 Vict.* (*Land Transfer Act*) c. 65. §14 (2) Regard being had to ready identification of parcels.

b. A small portion, item, instalment, *of* a sum of money; a small sum. Now *rare* or *Obs.*

1491 HEN. VII. in Ellis *Orig. Lett.* Ser. II. I. 172 The said summe of ten pounds and every parcell therof. **1524** *Churchw. Acc. St. Giles, Reading* 20 For the bequest of Pokeriges wife in parcel of a more Smª.. vjs. viijd. **1586** A. DAY *Eng. Secretary* I. (1625) 110 To credite him with a small parcell of money in dispatch of a iourney. **1590** RECORDE, etc. *Gr. Artes* (1646) 202 The parcels of these foure Merchants made in one summe 240 pounds. **1755** in Fowler *Hist. C.C.C.* (O.H.S.) 287[The College received the] last Parcel of Lord Coleraine's Legacy.

†**c.** A small portion or passage of a book, esp. a sacred book, as the Bible or the Koran. *Obs.* (or merged in 1.)

1570 T. NORTON tr. *Nowel's Catech.* (1853) 173 This parcel, 'the communion of saints', doth somewhat more plainly express [etc.]. **1577** HANMER *Anc. Eccl. Hist.* (1663) 120 He.. took the Bible, opened it, and happened upon this parcel of Scripture. **1636** FEATLY *Clavis Myst.* xiv. 185 The parcell of Scripture whence I have taken my text. **1655** E. TERRY *Voy. E. Ind.* 264 The Mahometan priests.. read some parcells out of their Alcoran, upon Frydays.

†**d.** *Arith.* A term of a progression. *Obs. rare.*

1542 RECORDE *Gr. Artes* (1575) 213 Tell how many numbers there are (whiche numbers here [in progression] wee call places or parcels).

†**e.** *Gram.* A particle. *Obs.*

1571 GOLDING *Calvin on Ps.* viii. 4 This parcell (*Chi*) among the Hebrewes importeth as much as (*Quia*) in Latin, which signifyeth (by cause) in English.

†**3.** Each of the definite parts or units which make up a complex whole (material or immaterial); an item, detail, particular, point; *esp.* an item of an account. *Obs.*

c **1330** R. BRUNNE *Chron.* (1810) 135 Liste and I salle rede þe parcelles what amountes If any man in dede wille keste in a countes. **1393** LANGL. *P. Pl.* C. XIV. 38 Þe parcels of hus paper and oþer pryuey dettes Wol lette hym. *c* **1468** *Paston Lett.* II. 332 Ples yow to send me passels of costes and expences ȝe bere and pay for the said causez. **1509** FISHER *Fun. Serm. Hen. VII* Wks. (1876) 279 The fourth percell of his complaynt. **1596** SHAKS. *1 Hen. IV*, III. ii. 159. *a* **1641** BP. MOUNTAGU *Acts & Mon.* viii. (1642) 513 No Herald could drawe downe a better Pedegree, were it possible to prove the parcels.

4. a. A separate portion *of* a material or substance (rarely of something immaterial); a small piece, particle; a (small or moderate) quantity or amount; a lot. *Obs.* exc. as in b and c.

1413 *Pilgr. Sowle* (Caxton) I. iii. (1859) 4 The Centre was veray derke, withoute ony parcel of clereness. *c* **1548** HALL *Chron. Hen. VIII* 51 We finde in a corner.. a great persell of bloud. **1684** T. BURNET *Th. Earth* II. 67 Such undiscover'd parcels of fire, as lie fix'd and imprison'd in hard bodies. **1734** SWIFT *Let.* Wks. 1824 XVIII. 255, I prophesied a fine parcel of weather from yesterday: but I was deceived. **1757** A. COOPER *Distiller* I. ii. (1760) 15 Being thus loosely mixed with a moderate Parcel of the Liquor. **1830** KATER & LARDNER *Mech.* iii. 32 An inanimate parcel of matter is incapable of changing its state of rest or motion.

b. *Mining*: see quots.

1881 RAYMOND *Mining Gloss., Parcel*, Corn., a heap of dressed ore ready for sale. **1883** GRESLEY *Gloss. Terms Coalmining, Parcel* (S. Staff), an old term for a ton; really 27 cwts. **1887** R. HUNT *Brit. Mining* (ed. 2) 911/2 A parcel of ore is a pile or heap of copper or lead ore dressed for sale. **1898** *Barrier Weekly Post* 29 Oct. 13 [They] received satisfactory prices for their parcels. **1903** *Eng. Dial. Dict., Parcel* (Cornw.), a quantity of tin stone of a certain weight and uniform quality. **1958** M. D. BERRINGTON *Stones of Fire* 20 They gradually collected a 'parcel' of choice stones. **1965** G. T. WILLIAMS *Econ. Geol. N.Z.* viii. 119/1 Increase in the price of gold resulted in renewed activity in 1935 and a certain amount of prospecting and development ensued for over a decade, though apparently only one parcel of 400 tons was treated.

c. *dial.* A small quantity of new-mown hay spread out to dry.

1863 BARNES *Gloss. Dorset* s.v. *Haÿmeäken*, On the following morning the.. cocks are thrown abroad in passels—parcels—which, after being turned, are in the evening put up into large ridges—weäls.

†**5. a.** One of several parts into which a thing is broken or divided; a fragment, piece. *Obs.*

1686 BURNET *Trav.* ii. (1750) 94 They piece their broken Pots so close.. without any Cement, by sowing with Iron Wire the broken Parcels together. **1688** STRADLING *Serm.* (1692) 186 To join and re-unite the scattered parcels. **1783** AINSWORTH *Lat. Dict.* (Morell) IV. s.v. *Absyrtes*, Being busied in gathering up the parcels of his son's body.

†**b.** *fig.* (Usually contemptuous.) *Obs.*

1598 B. JONSON *Ev. Man in Hum.* III. vii, I muse, your parcell of a souldier returnes not all this while. **1599** —— *Cynthia's Rev.* II. i, What parcel of man hast thou lighted on for a Master? **1609** DEKKER *Gull's Horn-bk.* v. (1862) 27 Get some fragments of French, or small parcels of Italian, to fling about the table.

6. a. A small party, company, collection, or assemblage (of persons, animals, or things); a detachment; a group, lot, set; a drove, flock, herd. *Obs.* exc. *dial.* and *U.S. colloq.*, or as in b.

In earlier instances prob. always implying a *portion* of a larger body or of a whole, but eventually losing this implication.

[*c* **1449** PECOCK *Repr.* (Rolls) II. 438 Ech Apostle was heed of oon certeyn parcel of peple.] **1588** SHAKS. *L.L.L.* v. ii. 160 A holy parcell of the fairest dames that euer turn'd their backes to mortall viewes. **1615** SIR T. ROE *Jrnl.* in Churchill *Voy.* (1704) I. 767/2 [Penguins] do not fly, but only walk in parcels. **1689** LUTTRELL *Brief Rel.* (1857) I. 604 When the English horse went, they went but in parcells. **1712** STEELE *Spect.* No. 326 ¶5 A parcel of Crows.. heartily at Break-fast upon a piece of Horse-flesh. **1775** ROMANS *Florida* App. 34 A parcel of dangerous sunken heads called the Hen and Chickens. **1780** A. YOUNG *Tour Irel.* I. 96 Sheep are kept in small parcels. **1841** CATLIN *N. Amer. Ind.* (1844) II. xlviii. 128 One day, a parcel of them were run upon so suddenly by the Choctaws. **1895** EMERSON *Man & Nat.* 89 (E.D.D.) The arrival and passing over of a parcel of linnets.

dial. and *U.S. colloq.* **1835** A. B. LONGSTREET *Georgia Scenes* 195 'How did you come on raisin' chickens this year, Mis' Shad?' 'La Messy, honey! I have had mighty bad luck. I had the prettiest pasel you most ever seed till the varment took to killin 'em.' **1865** W. B. FORFAR *Kynance Cove* vii. 43 She ax'd about 'n a fine passle more than she wud ef he'd ben a stranger. **1871** E. EGGLESTON *Hoosier Schoolmaster* 169 A passel of thieves. **1881** *Atlantic Monthly* June 740/1 A passel o' folks. **1889** T. E. BROWN *Manx Witch* 16 She knocked two dishes And a pazil of plates there off the dresser. **1890** S. S. BUCKMAN *John Darke's Sojourn in Cotteswolds* ii. 6 Lor, thur wur quite a passel o' volk altogither. **1893** H. A. SHANDS *Some Peculiarities of Speech in Mississippi* 49 *Passle* (pæsel). Used to some extent by all classes, but principally by the uneducated, to mean a *parcel*, not in the sense of a small bundle or a small quantity, but in that of a considerable number; as, 'There was a whole *passle* of hogs in the yard'; i.e. there were a good many. The word has, perhaps, a somewhat larger meaning than *a good many*, but denotes less than a multitude. This word is used in Kentucky, but is becoming rare there. **1903** K. D. WIGGIN *Rebecca* xix. 202 Then you can explain, if you can, who gave you any authority to invite a passel of strangers to stay here overnight. **1906** KIPLING *Puck of Pook's Hill* 264 'Twas a passel o' nonsense talk. **1935** Z. N. HURSTON *Mules & Men* I. vii. 151 A man had a wife and a whole passle of young 'uns. **1936** [see NO-'COUNT *a.*]. **1948** *Sun* (Baltimore) 3 Dec. 14/2 Who wants to gamble that a passel of bureaucrats in a planned economy could have shown similar bounce in the face of adversity? **1957** W. C. HANDY *Father of Blues* vi. 80 We had to absorb a 'passel' of oratory of the brand served by some Southern politicians just this side of the turn of the century. **1972** M. J. BOSSE *Incident at Naha* iii. 134 'He'll forget,' I declared, thinking of the wives and the passel of kids. **1973** *Science* 12 Jan. 162/1 But the AAAS did succeed in having a passel of young activists evicted from the meeting's main registration area. **1973** D. WESTHEIMER *Going Public* iv. 54 How'd you like to make yourself a passel of money without hardly havin' to do any work? **1977** *Time* 20 June 47/2 She plays a small rancher who pools her resources with neighboring Land-owner James Caan to fight off greedy Cattle Baron Jason Robards and a passel of oil companies lusting after their range land.

b. In depreciative or contemptuous use: A 'lot', 'set', 'pack'.

1607 MIDDLETON *Michaelm. Term* III. i. 167 You parcel of a rude, saucy, and unmannerly nation. **1702** ADDISON *Dial. Medals* iii. Wks. 1721 I. 533 Of great use.. to let posterity see their forefathers were a parcel of blockheads. **1758** L. TEMPLE *Sketches* (ed. 2) 76 Born Lyars; who tell you every Day very seriously a Parcel of insipid unmeaning Lies. **1778** MISS BURNEY *Evelina* xiv, I think the English a parcel of brutes. **1818** HAZLITT *Eng. Poets* vii. (1870) 172 Making a parcel of wry faces over the matter. **1881** 'RITA' *My Lady Coquette* i, I'm not going to be lectured by a parcel of girls.

7. a. A quantity of anything or a number of things (esp. goods) put together or wrapped up in a single package (usually of moderate or small size); an item of goods in carriage or postage; a package: now chiefly used of packages wrapped in brown paper. ***bill of parcels***: see BILL *sb.*³ 6.

[*a* **1562** G. CAVENDISH *Wolsey* (1893) 148 Basketts with old plate,.. and bokes conteyning the valewe and wayte of every parcell. *c* **1645** HOWELL *Lett.* IV. xlvi, I Receiv'd that choice parcel of Tobacco your servant brought me.] **1692** *Oxford Almanack* in *Wood's Life* (1848) 162 For the carriage of the greatest parcel, (all being to be esteemed parcels under one quarter of an hundred weight,) one shilling. **1715** *Lond. Gaz.* No. 5330/3 The General Penny-Post-Office.. where Letters and Parcels will be taken in as usual. **1745** *De Foe's Eng. Tradesman* i. (1841) I. 6 He sees the bills of parcels of goods bought. **1820** W. HUNTINGDON in *Q. Rev.* (1821) XXIV. 484 A shoemaker.. told me a parcel was left there for me... I opened it, and behold there was a pair of leather breeches. **1844** DICKENS *Mart. Chuz.* ii, The youngest Miss Pecksniff ran out again to pick up his hat, his brown-paper parcel, his umbrella, his gloves. **1897** Paper parcels [see PAPER *sb.* 10 a].

b. *transf.* and *fig.* Cf. BUNDLE 3.

1785 REID *Intell. Powers Man* II. x. 285 What I call a father, a brother, or a friend, is only a parcel of ideas in my own mind. **1822** HAZLITT *Table-t.* Ser. II. xii. (1869) 246 It is true I can.. rake up a parcel of half-forgotten observations. **1842** A. COMBE *Physiol. Digestion* (ed. 4) 73 A continuation of the circular fibres of the gullet, which divide into two parcels.

c. *Comm.* A quantity (sometimes definite) of a commodity dealt with in one transaction; *esp.* in the wholesale market: a 'lot'.

1832 MCCULLOCH *Comm. Dict.* (1852), *Parcel*, a term indifferently applied to small packages of wares, and to large lots of goods. In this latter sense, 20 hogsheads of sugar or more, if bought at one price, are denominated 'a parcel of sugar'. **1882** *Times* 19 July 13 At to-day's cloth market.. considerable parcels of winter stock were taken for Italy, Austria [etc.]. **1897** *Daily News* 17 Feb. 11/4 Cocoa.—At public sale to-day the parcels offered went off freely at dearer prices.

d. A large amount of money gained or lost. *slang.*

1903 A. M. BINSTEAD *Pitcher in Paradise* vii. 172 'Aye, it's a pinch for t'pair of 'em, y'r Graace', roared Old Jack, with much warmth; 'an' what's moo-re, if y'r Graace doesn't *pack oop a reglar parcel* over 'em, why—why, A'al *never* speak to y'r Graace on a racecourse agin!' **1922** E. WALLACE *Flying Fifty-Five* x. 56 In the argot of his kind he had 'packed up a parcel' over the disqualification of Fifty-Five. **1923** WODEHOUSE *Inimitable Jeeves* xii. 131 'But if you haven't dropped a parcel over the race,' I said, 'why are you looking so rattled?' *Ibid.* xiv. 162, I think I can put you in the way of winning a parcel on the Mothers' Sack Race.

8. *Law.* (*pl.*) The name given to that part of a conveyance, lease, or other deed dealing with property, which follows the operative words, and contains the description of the property dealt with; in the case of lands, generally beginning with such words as 'All that piece or parcel of land', etc.; forming the last of the clauses called the PREMISSES.

1766 BLACKSTONE *Comm.* II. App. No. ii. (margin). **1837** T. MARTIN *Conveyancing* II. 84 Of Parcels. **1844** DAVIDSON *Conveyancing* Introd. §7 *Of Parcels.* The word 'parcel'.. seems to have been originally applied, in the sense of 'a piece', to land only [see sense 2], but in modern usage the expression 'parcels' is used to signify the description of the property, be it what it may. **1882** C. SWEET *Law Dict.*

9. *Naut.* = PARCELLING *vbl. sb.* 4 b.

1875 KNIGHT *Dict. Mech.* 1632/2 *Parcel* (*Nautical*), a wrapping of tarred canvas on a rope to prevent chafing.

II. *attrib.* and *Comb.*

10. Ordinary attributive uses and combinations, chiefly in sense 7, as ***parcel book, boy, company, lift, man, office, porter, van***; ***parcel-carrying, -packing, -tying*** sbs. and adjs.; **parcel bomb**, a bomb wrapped up so as to resemble a parcel; **parcel-carrier**, one who or that which carries a parcel; *spec.* a basket or case slung from a cable, etc. for transporting parcels; **parcel(s) delivery**, the action of, or an agency for, delivering parcels (also *attrib.*); †**parcel ground**, a 'parcel' of land (see 2 a); †**parcel-like** (**-lyk**), *adv.*, ? in part, partly (= PARCELLY *adv.* 2); **parcel paper**, stout paper, usually brown and unsized, made or used for wrapping parcels; **parcel(s) shelf, tray**, a shelf or tray upon which parcels may be placed, esp. in a motor vehicle; **parcel tanker**, a vessel designed to carry various liquids with separate piping and tanks; **parcel-wise** *adv.*, by 'parcels' or portions, bit by bit, piecemeal. See also PARCEL-MAKER, PARCEL POST.

1950 *Times* 22 Aug. 3/1 Injured by *parcel bomb. A small parcel addressed to Mr. Thomas Rose.. blew up when he opened it on Sunday night. **1966** 'A. HALL' *9th Directive* iv. 44 There's a dozen ways—prussic acid.. the parcel bomb. **1974** *Guardian* 25 Jan. 24/5 Police scientific experts are examining the remains of a parcel bomb which exploded in an Israeli bank in the City of London yesterday. **1977** *New Society* 27 Jan. 163/3 The weekend parcel-bomb murder of Jason Moyo. **1858** SIMMONDS *Dict. Trade*, **Parcel-book*, a merchant's register book of the dispatch of parcels. **1897** *Daily News* 13 Dec. 8/4 By day these Boys are errand boys, *parcel boys, van boys, office boys. **1893** *Westm. Gaz.* 19 Sept. 3/1 The railway companies.. fancied.. that this new development of Post Office enterprise would destroy their *parcel-carrying business. **1878** JEVONS *Prim. Pol. Econ.* xv. 125 At present there are a great number of *parcel companies. **1844** MRS. CARLYLE *Lett.* I. 291 Send me some books by the *parcels delivery. **1858** SIMMONDS *Dict. Trade, Parcels Delivery Company*, a company in London which receives, and delivers by vans, packages and small parcels over the metropolis. **1892** *Daily News* 14 Oct. 5/3 Tips to omnibus men and parcels delivery men are unknown in London. **1632** LITHGOW *Trav.* IV. 166 If these Timariots were not rewarded, with such absolute possessions of *parcell grounds. **1884** KNIGHT *Dict. Mech.* Suppl., **Parcel Lift*, a dumb waiter used in stores and warehouses. **1426** LYDG. *De Guil. Pilgr.* 9759 Ffor, ffyrst, the sowle pryncypally Susteneth & bereth the body; And *parcel-lyk .. The body bereth by accident The sowle. **1567** MAPLET *Gr. Forest* 26 The rest of time hath he in part and parcell like so disposed and ordred of Nature to lay holde on.. the other life above this. **1882** OGILVIE, **Parcel-office*, a place where parcels are received for delivery. **1827** *Edin. Rev.* XLV. 429 Some have a.. *parcel-packing action. **1951** *Motor* 2 May 386/3 There are two useful *parcel shelves unobtrusively located beneath the front seat cushions. **1953** *Motor* 9 Dec. 728/3 Large cases.. have to be lifted over a somewhat high rear bulkhead, and then slid forward into place below the rear parcels shelf. **1973** *Country Life* 31 May 1547/2 Stowage capacity is also good for a large car.... There is.. a useful parcel shelf. **1974** 'J. ROSS' *Burning of Billy Toober* i. 9 He placed the pipe in the parcels shelf. **1976** *Chrysler World of Motoring* '77 15/4 With the parcel shelf folded away, and the rear seat folded flat, you've suddenly got 49 cu. ft. **1973** *Sea Breezes* May 297/1 The typical modern purpose-built *parcel tanker is a complex and expensive investment. **1974** *Times* 31 May (Poseidonia Suppl.) p. iii/4 Parcel tankers have been developed which have the ability to carry incompatible chemicals in separate tanks. **1950** *Motor* 19 Apr. 372/3 There is a *parcel tray of generous size below the instrument panel. **1956** *Motor* 24 Oct. 525 (*caption*) Air for de-misting this window is blown through the slots seen here on the parcel tray. **1866** GEO. ELIOT *F. Holt* (1868) 59 A pence-counting, *parcel-tying generation, such as mostly fill your chapels. **1647** TRAPP *Comm. Heb.* ix. 8 The mystery of Christ was manifested piecemeal and *parsel-wise. **1876** GEO. ELIOT *Dan. Der.* II. xxi. 45 Looking at life parcel-wise.

B. *adv.* or quasi-*adv.* or *adj.* [Cf. similar use of *part, part-*.]

1. In part, partly, partially, in some degree, to some extent. †**a.** qualifying vb. or phrase. *Obs.*

c **1402** LYDG. *Compl. Bl. Knt.* 224 The salte teres that fro myn eyen falle, Parcel declare grounde of my peynes alle. *c* **1420** —— *Thebes* Prol., Chaucer's Wks. (1561) 356 b/1 To morowe early.. we will forthe, parcell afore prime. **1430–40** —— *Bochas* VIII. xxvii. (1558) 13 b, Parcell for pride, parcel for gladnesse.

b. qualifying adjs., as *parcel blind, deaf, drunk, Greek, guilty, Latin, mad, Popish,* etc. Also PARCEL-GILT. *Obs.* since 17th c., but revived by Scott and used by later writers.

In these often hyphened; but properly so only when the adj. is used *attrib.* Cf. *part-, half-.*

1465 [see PARCEL-GILT]. **1601** B. JONSON *Poetaster* v. iii, Parcel-guilty, I. **1609** DEKKER *Gull's Horn-bk.* II. (1862) 12 Their parcel-Greek, parcel-Latin gibberish. **1618** FLETCHER *Chances* IV. iii, She is parcell drunke. *a*1661 FULLER *Worthies, Somerset.* (1662) 19 The Author.. being parcel-popish. **1826** SCOTT *Woodst.* iv, The worthy dame was parcel blind, and more than parcel deaf. **1854** *Athenæum* 1 Apr. 399 The humour, parcel jocose, parcel stupid. **1873** F. HALL *Mod. Eng.* i. 23 Penny-a-liners and such parcel-learned adventurers have had their fellows in every age. **1897** W. C. HAZLITT *Ourselves* 26 Our Church is a mixed institution, parcel-divine, parcel-terrestrial.

c. qualifying sbs., as *parcel ass, bawd, broker, devil, heresy, lawyer, poet, Protestant, soldier,* etc. Also with vbl. sbs. *Obs.* since 17th c., till revived by Scott.

Often hyphened, but properly so only when it has an adj. force, as in quots. 1602, *a* 1661, *c* 1665, 1672, 1867.

1602 DEKKER *Satirom.* Wks. 1873 I. 235 Nay and thou dost, the Parcell-poets shall sue thy Wrangling Muse. **1603** SHAKS. *Meas. for M.* II. i. 63 He Sir: a Tapster Sir: parcell Baud: one that serues a bad woman. **1608** DAY *Hum. out of Br.* I. i, True, shee's parcell poet, parcell fidler already. **1610** B. JONSON *Alch.* IV. vi, That parcell-broker, and whole-bawd, all raskall. **1611** BARREY *Ram Alley* I. i. in Hazl. *Dodsley* X. 275 Parcel lawyer, parcel devil, all knave. **1640** HABINGTON *Queen of Arragon* 1, Who vents him For ought but parcell-asse may be in danger. *a*1661 FULLER *Worthies, Yorksh.* (1662) 213 He was at the least a Parcell-Protestant. *c*1665 MRS. HUTCHINSON *Mem. Col. Hutchinson* (1848) 135 He.. then, I know not how, got to be a parcel-judge in Ireland. **1672** SIR C. WYVILL *Triple Crown* 70 Friar Pedro has mark'd them with the black Coal of parcel Heresie. **1820** SCOTT *Abbot* iv, He was a jester and a parcel poet. **1829** —— *Jrnl.* 25 Apr., A ventriloquist and parcel juggler came in. **1849** TICKNOR *Span. Lit.* I. 242 *note,* The principal personage is Marcelia,—parcel witch, wholly shameless. **1867** LOWELL *Study Wind.* (1870) 95 Gilbert, Hawkins, Frobisher and Drake, parcel-soldiers all of them. **1867** [see PARCEL-GILDING]. **1902** A. H. HIORNS *Metal-Colouring & Bronzing* (ed. 2) III. 243 (*heading*) Parcel coppering or bronzing as applied to fine zinc castings. **1907** *Handbk. Electro-Plating* (W. Canning & Co.) (ed. 3) 64 (*heading*) Parcel-plating. Plating articles in two or three colours. **1911** S. FIELD *Princ. Electro-Deposition* xii. 175 Partial deposition.. is, in the case of copper, called parcel coppering. **1925** FIELD & BONNEY *Chem. Coloring of Metals* xiii. 166 'Parcel plating'.. is applicable to all deposited metals. **1971** T. C. COLLOCOTT *Dict. Sci. & Technol.* 855/2 *Parcel plating,* the electrodeposition of a metal over a selected area of an article, the remainder being covered with a nonconductor in order to prevent deposition.

†**2.** *ellipt.* = PARCEL-GILT. (Nares.) *Obs.*

1613 BEAUM. & FL. *Coxcomb* IV. iii, The Turkey carpet, And the great parcel salt, Nan, with the cruets.

parcel ('pɑːsəl, 'pɑːs(ə)l), *v.* [f. PARCEL *sb.* Cf. mod.F. *parceller* to divide into parcels or very small portions. The connexion of sense 3 is not apparent, and it is perhaps a distinct word.]

1. *trans.* To divide or distribute into 'parcels' or (small) portions. (Usually with *out.*)

1584–5 in T. West *Antiq. Furness* (1774) 160 Devydinge, percellinge, and porcioninge of tenements. **1610** WILLET *Hexapla Dan.* 319 H. Broughton.. doth thus parcell out the yeares. **1639** FULLER *Holy War* v. iii. (1840) 245 Whose verdict we will parcel into these several particulars. **1727** POPE, etc. *Art of Sinking* 114 Divided into several branches, and parcelled out to several trades. **1796** MORSE *Amer. Geog.* II. 532 The empire.. was parcelled into twelve grand divisions. **1840** DICKENS *Old. C. Shop* xv, The mean houses parcelled off in rooms. **1885** *Act* 48 & 49 *Vict.* c. 77 §16 Tracts of land to be parcelled out in allotments.

b. To distribute in parcels or lots.

1699 BURNET 39 *Art.* xxii. (1700) 242 St. Stephen's and St. James's Bones might have been then parcelled about. **1863** LD. LYTTON *Ring Amasis* I. I. i. 21 Before nightfall we shall be parcelled off to our different destinations.

†**c.** To put asunder or separate as parts; to part, divide. *Obs.*

1652 J. HALL *Height Eloq.* p. lxxii, Things being scatter'd and parcell'd one from another can never close into any Height.

2. To make into a parcel or parcels, to put up in parcels.

1775 ASH, *Parcel,*.. to make up into a small bundle. *c*1887 J. CROLL in J. C. Irons *Autobiog. Sk.* (1896) 70 Learned in the mechanical art of weighing and parcelling up the tea. **1898** *Daily Chron.* 24 Sept. 10/6 Girls.. wanted for parcelling card-board boxes.

3. *Naut.* **a.** To cover (a caulked seam, etc.) with canvas strips and daub with pitch. **b.** To wrap (a rope) round with canvas strips or *parcelling* (to be then bound with spun yarn).

1627 CAPT. SMITH *Seaman's Gram.* ii. 13 Parsling is most vsed vpon the Decks and halfe Decks; which is, to take a list of Canuas so long as the seame is you would parsell, being first well calked, then powre hot pitch vpon it, and it will keepe out the water. **1691** T. H[ALE] *Acc. New Invent.* p. xx, The Bolt-heads, &c., being fairly parcelled. **1775** FALCK *Day's Diving Vessel* 54 These rings were parcelled with canvas, and served with inch rope. **1842** BRANDE *Dict. Sci.,* etc., *Parcel a rope,* in Naval language, to cover it smoothly with tarred canvass, which is then bound over with spun-yarn. **1875** KNIGHT *Dict. Mech.* 1632/2 Usually, the rope is wormed, then parcelled, and then served. **1875** BEDFORD *Sailor's Pocket Bk.* x. (ed. 2) 360 Three men can worm, parcel, and serve 2 fathoms of 12-inch in an hour.

¶ In the following passage the vb. has been variously but not satisfactorily explained. Johnson took it as 'To make up into a mass'; Schmidt, 'To enumerate by items, specify'. Cf. quot. 1594 in *parcelled* below.

1606 SHAKS. *Ant. & Cl.* v. ii. 163 O Cæsar, what a wounding shame is this,.. that mine owne Seruant should Parcell the summe of my disgraces, by Addition of his Enuy.

Hence **parcelled, parceled** ('pɑːsəld) *ppl. a.,* divided into parcels, parts, or portions, distributed, etc.: see the verb. In first quot. opposed to *general*: Schmidt explains it as 'particular'.

1594 SHAKS. *Rich. III,* II. ii. 81 Was neuer Mother had so deere a losse. Alas! I am the Mother of these Greefes, Their woes are parcell'd, mine is generall. **1649** G. DANIEL *Trinarch., Hen. V,* ccxxxiv, Not liveing Men, but as fixt Statues grew; Polisht by English Swords; cut into halfes And parcell'd faces. *a*1716 SOUTH *Serm.* (1744) XI. 289 There was no building any solid confidence upon a parcelled, curtailed obedience. **1887** W. G. PALGRAVE *Ulysses* 162 The waving emerald of the parcelled rice-field.

parcel, parcelay, obs. forms of PARSLEY.

'parcel-gilt, *a.* (*sb.*) Forms: see PARCEL *sb.* and GILT *ppl. a.*; and 7 *Sc.* **persyall gylt,** *erron.* **partial-gilt.** [f. PARCEL *sb.* B + GILT *ppl. a.*] Partly gilded; *esp.* of silver ware, as bowls, cups, etc., having the inner surface gilt.

a. In participial construction, after the substantive. (Usually as two words.)

1465 in Heath *Grocers' Comp.* (1869) 424, ii Basens and ij ewers of sylver parcell gylte. **1482** MARG. PASTON *Will* in *Lett.* III. 286 My standing cuppe chased parcell gilt. **1546** *Inv. Ch. Goods Yorksh.,* etc. (Surtees) 87 Juelles all gylte.. juelles, parcell gylte. **1604** *Deed of Mortif., Arbuthnot of that Ilk* (Jam.), Twa fair syluer salt fattis, ane dubill ourgilt, maid in the stypell fessone, the other on the bel fassone persyall gylt. **1884** KNIGHT *Dict. Mech.* Suppl., *Parcel-gilt.* Meaning partly gilt. Silver ware gilt inside.

b. In attributive construction (hyphened).

1576 BAKER *Jewell of Health* 101 b, Into which if you put parsyll or doubble gylt cuppes or pottes, the Sylver shortly after wyll be dissolved. **1597** SHAKS. *2 Hen. IV,* II. i. 94. **1620** BRATHWAIT *Five Senses* in *Archaica* (1815) II. 12 Desiring rather a direction in her way to eternity, than to have partial-gilt corruption her best solicitor in this vale of misery. **1894** *Times* 7 Apr. 9 Art Sales... A parcel-gilt beaker, engraved with scroll, foliage, and strap ornament.

c. quasi-*sb.* Parcel-gilt ware. Also *fig.*

1610 B. JONSON *Alch.* III. ii, Or changing His parcell guilt to massie gold. **1614** C. BROOKE *Ghost Rich. III,* Poems (1872) 60 Fortune's favorites, Whose percell guylt, my touch will not endure.

So **'parcel-gilder, parcel-gilding.**

1867 A. BARRY *Sir C. Barry* ii. 55 Parcel-gilding was gaudy. **1884** *B'ham Daily Post* 23 Feb. 3/4 Advertisem., Wanted, an experienced Parcel Gilder and Oxydiser.

parcelization (ˌpɑːsəlaɪˈzeɪʃən). Also **parcellization.** [f. PARCEL *sb.* + -IZATION.] = PARCELLATION.

1960 E. R. GOODMAN in J. A. Fishman *Readings Sociol. of Lang.* (1968) 725 The treatment of the Moslem peoples of the Soviet Union provides the clearest illustration of this policy of parcelization. In an effort to avoid the creation of a large Moslem state in the Volga-Urals area, the Soviet regime created separate Bashkir and Tartar ASSRs. **1963** *Listener* 21 Feb. 322/1 Parcelization gets worse and worse. *Ibid.* 322/2 Even such an obvious reform as a change in the law which permits parcelization seemed to be viewed with suspicion. **1975** DJURFELDT & LINDBERG *Behind Poverty* 124 The parcellization of land among many small owners.

'parcellate, *v. rare.* [f. PARCEL *v.* + -ATE[3] or as back-formation from next.] *trans.* To divide into separate parcels or portions. So **'parcellated** *ppl. a.*

1934 WEBSTER, Parcellate. **1971** *Country Life* 3 June 1374/1 About 50 [vine] growers among the 1,700 whose heavily parcellated strips dominate the district. **1978** *Ibid.* 7 Sept. 642/1 The 100 growers concerned.. now have an average of 800 square metres of consolidated vineyard in place of the 200 square metres of parcellated terraces they formerly had to work.

parce'llation. *rare.* [f. PARCEL *v.* + -ATION.] Division into separate parcels or portions.

1885 *American* IX. 350 Rash as such a parcellation of his troops might seem. **1965** K. H. CONNELL in Glass & Eversley *Population in Hist.* xvii. 429 Connaught.. was.. the province where parcellation of the land was most acute.

parcelle, obs. form of PARCEL, PARSLEY.

'parceller. *rare.* [f. PARCEL *v.* + -ER[1].] One who or that which 'parcels', divides, or distributes.

1664 *Spelman's Gloss., Parcener.* Quasi *parceller,* id est, rem in parcellas dividens. Hence **1670** in BLOUNT *Law Dict.* **1672** in *Cowell's Interpr.*

'parcelling, 'parceling, *vbl. sb.* Also 7–8 (in sense 4) **parsling.** [f. PARCEL *v.* + -ING[1].] The action of the verb PARCEL, or its result, etc.

†**1.** A part, portion. *Obs. rare.*

*c*1449 PECOCK *Repr.* III. xviii. 400 Tithis and offringis and suche othere smale parcellingis of paymentis.

2. Division into parcels or portions; partition.

1584–5 [see PARCEL *v.* 1]. **1803** JANE PORTER *Thaddeus* (1826) I. xi. 236 He did not observe the parcelling out of his temperate meal; one bringing in the fowl, another the bread. **1834** SIR W. NAPIER *Penins. War* XIV. viii, The parcelling of an army before a concentrated enemy. **1866** GEO. ELIOT *F. Holt* xxix, An ingenuity of device fitting them to make a figure in the parcelling of Europe.

3. The action of putting up in a parcel or parcels.

1876 MRS. WHITNEY *Sights & Ins.* vi. 31 The buying and selling and crowding and parceling and callings of 'Cash!'

4. *Naut.* **a.** The putting of a canvas strip over a caulked seam, bolt, etc., and covering it with hot pitch; also, the wrapping of a rope round with canvas strips.

1627 [see PARCEL *v.* 3]. **1668** WILKINS *Real Char.* II. xi. §4. 283 Parsling. **1691** T. H[ALE] *Acc. New Invent.* 25 The parcelling, or laying with Tarr and Hair all the Iron-work under water. *c*1860 H. STUART *Seaman's Catech.* 28 To begin serving, you should begin where you leave off parcelling.

b. *concr.* A strip of canvas (usually tarred) for binding round a rope, in order to give a smooth surface and keep the interstices water-tight.

1769 FALCONER *Dict. Marine* (1776), *Parcelling,* certain long narrow slips of canvas, daubed with tar, and frequently bound about a rope. **1879** N. H. BISHOP *4 Months in Sneak-Box* (1880) 13 There were piles of old rigging, iron bolts and rings, tarred parcelling.

5. *attrib.,* as **parcelling machine,** (*a*) a machine for making up parcels of yarn, cloth, etc.; (*b*) a machine for making parcelling (4 b).

1875 KNIGHT *Dict. Mech.* 1632/2.

†**'parcellize,** *v. Obs. rare*[-1]. [f. PARCEL *sb.* + -IZE.] *trans.* To subdivide; = PARCEL *v.* 1.

1605 SYLVESTER *Du Bartas* II. iii. IV. *Captaines* 1154 That same Majesty.. Is not extinguisht nor extenuate, By being parcelliz'd to a plurality Of petty Kinglings.

†**'parcelly,** *adv. Obs.* [f. PARCEL *sb.* + -LY[2].]

1. By parcels or portions; in detail, item by item.

?**1469** *Paston Lett.* II. 334 Folowyng apperith, parcelly, dyvers and soondry maner of writyngs. **1525** in W. H. Turner *Select. Rec. Oxford* 54 As hereafter parcelly followeth.

2. In part, partly: *parcelly gilt* = PARCEL-GILT.

1509 in *Suss. Archæol. Coll.* XLI. 27, ij chalices of siluer parcelly gylt.

parcelly, obs. form of PARSLEY.

†**parcel-maker** ('pɑːsəlˌmeɪkə(r)). *Obs.* exc. *Hist.* In *pl.* Two officers in the Exchequer, who formerly made the parcels of the escheators' accounts, in which they charged these with everything they had levied for the use of the Sovereign during their period of office, delivering the same to the auditors to make up their accounts therewith.

1617 in MINSHEU *Ductor.* **1642** C. VERNON *Consid. Exch.* 111 The decree lately procured by the parcell makers for Sheriffs.. to accompt before them for.. Escheats, etc. **1658** SIR T. FANSHAW *Pract. Excheq.* 100 They be *Veter. Escaet. & nova Escaet.*: totalled up by themselves by the parcell-makers, which be the whole Charge of the Escheator. **1704** J. HARRIS *Lex. Techn.* I.

†**'parcelmeal,** *adv. Obs.* [f. PARCEL *sb.* + -MEAL.] By 'parcels' or portions; in small portions at a time; bit by bit, piecemeal.

1362 LANGL. *P. Pl.* A. III. 72 Men.. þat most harm worchen, To þe pore people þat percel-mel buggen. **14..** *Chaucer's Pars. T.* ¶932 (Petw. MS.) þow shalt schryve þe of alle þi synnes to oo man and nouȝt parcell mele [*so Lansd. MS.; other MSS.* a parcel] to oon man and parsel mele to a noþer man. **1476** *Will of Crosby* (Somerset Ho.), Ley down the said C li. parcelemele as the werkes thereof go forthward. **1548** UDALL *Erasm. Par. Matt.* ii. 26 Which in time and by parsel meale, should be promulgated. **1596** BP. W. BARLOW *Three Serm.* ii. 64 We will.. examine them parcell meale.

'parcelment. *rare.* [f. PARCEL *v.* + -MENT.] Division into parcels (of land).

1847 *Tait's Mag.* XIV. 560 That [small holdings].. have succeeded in the Channel Islands.. is owing not so much to the plan of parcelment, as to the state of tenure.

parcel post. (At first called erroneously **parcels post.**) [f. PARCEL *sb.* 7 + POST *sb.*] That branch of the postal service which undertakes the carriage and distribution of parcels.

1837 *9th Rep. Comm. Managem. Post-Office* 28 in *Parl. Papers* XXXIV. 431 Would it not occasion great delay if you made a parcel-post of it to that extent? **1843** *Rep. Sel. Comm. Postage* 41 in *Parl. Papers* VIII. 1 The Banghy post of the East Indies is a parcel post; the maximum of weight appears to be about 15 lb. [**1859** *Househ. Words* XIX. 393 They urge that a small parcels-post ought to be forthwith organised.] **1883** *P.O. Guide* 1 Oct. 3 Inland Parcels Post... In order that a packet may go by Parcels Post, it must be tendered for transmission as a parcel, and should bear the words 'Parcels Post' [so up to 1 July 1884; 1 Oct. 1884 'Parcel Post']. **1884** *Whitaker's Almanack* 278 *Remarkable Occurr.* 1883 August 1, New Parcel Post first in operation. **1902** *Daily Chron.* 4 Aug. 5/1 The parcel post was recommended by Rowland Hill just sixty years ago. It was proposed to Parliament with success by Mr. Fawcett twenty years ago, and came into force in 1883.

parcelye, obs. form of PARSLEY.

†**'parcen,** *v. Obs. rare*[-1]. [app. repr. an AF. *parcener, for OF. parçoner:—L. type *part(it)iōn-āre to divide.] *trans.* To divide among parceners.

*a*1641 BP. MOUNTAGU *Acts & Mon.* ii. (1642) 111 Be it, that such estates, entire or parcenned, might lawfully be by Femals dismembred.

parcenary ('pɑːsənərɪ). *Law.* Also 7 -cin-. [a. AF. *parcenarie* = OF. *parçonerie*, *personnerie*, etc. (med.L. type *partionaria), f. *parçonier*: see -ERY, -ARY.] Joint heirship: = COPARCENARY 1.

[*a* **1481** LITTLETON *Tenures* xxiii. (1516) D j b, Les autres poient tener le remenaunt en parcenarie & occupier en comen sans particion.] **1544** transl. H vij b, The other may holde the remenaunt in parcenary and occupy in common without partycion. **1658** PHILLIPS, *Parcinarie*, in Common-law, is a holding of Land, by two, or more *pro indiviso*, or by Joynt-Tenants, otherwise called Copartners. **1821** JEFFERSON *Autobiog.* Wks. 1859 I. 43, I proposed to abolish the law of primogeniture, and to make real estate descendible in parcenary to the next of kin.

† '**parcenel**, *sb. Obs.* Also 5 **parsonal.** [Corruption of PARCENER.] A sharer, partaker. Hence † '**parcenel** *v.*, to share, partake.

a **1340** HAMPOLE *Psalter* x. 8 *comm.*, þe rightwisnes of god, in the whilk all rightwismen ere parcenel [*v.r.* partiner]. *Ibid.* lxxxi. 6 ȝe ere ayres & percenels in þe bliss of heuen. *Ibid.* cxxi. 3 Ierusalem þe whilke is made as cite whas parsenelynge [Vulg. *participacio*] of it in it selfe. This is ierusalem.. as cite in sere degres of honur and meryt, and parsenel of godis stabilnes. **1438** *Bk. Alexander Gt.* (Bann. Cl.) 94 Baith he & he Suld parsonalis & lordis be.

parcener ('pɑːsənə(r)). Forms: 3-4 **parciner**, 4 **parsener, -sainer, -saner, -soner(e, -conner, -cenar, -cyner, -cner, personer**, 4-5 **parcenere, parceynere**, 5 **-senere**, 4- **parcener**. [a. AF. *parcener* = OF. *parçonier*, *parsuner*, *parsonier*, etc. = med.L. *partiōnārius*, for *partītiōnārius*, f. *partītiōn-em*, in OF. *parçon*, PARTITION: see -ER².]

†**1.** One who shares, or has a part in, something with another or others; a partner; a sharer, partaker. *Obs.* in *gen.* sense.

1297 R. GLOUC. (Rolls) 6309 And ich mot ek of engelond be þi parciner. *a* **1300** *Cursor M.* 27207 (Cott.) O sin þan es he parsainer [*Fairf.* parcenere]. *c* **1374** CHAUCER *Boeth.* v. pr. v. 132 (Camb. MS.) As we ben parsoneres of Reson. *c* **1375** *Sc. Leg. Saints* vi. *Thomas* 139 ȝe ar now Parsaneris of lestand lyfe. *c* **1380** WYCLIF *Sel. Wks.* III. 152 þei ben parcyneres of þis grete synne. *c* **1440** LOVE *Bonavent. on Sacram. Christ's Body* 124 (Gibbs MS.) Desirynge þat þe kynge schulde be partyner or parceynere of þat grete and so worthy a syghte. **1621** BP. MOUNTAGU *Diatribæ* 178 To diuide betwixt Partners, or Parceners.

2. *Law.* One who shares equally with another or others in the inheritance of an estate from a common ancestor; a coheir: = COPARCENER.

[**1292** BRITTON III. iv. §23 Mes nul parcener ne sa issue ne jurge feauté a autre si noun a soen eynznee parcener. **1865** NICHOLLS *tr.*, But no parcener or his issue shall swear fealty except to the eldest parcener.] **1574** tr. *Littleton's Tenures* III. i. §241 And if there be two daughters to whom the land descendeth, then they be called two parceners. **1647** N. BACON *Disc. Govt. Eng.* I. xli. (1739) 66 It equally concerned all, both Sons and Daughters, as Parceners. **1883** JESSOPP in *19th Cent.* Feb., What had been hitherto a single lordship became 3 lordships, each of the parceners looking very jealously after his own interest.

† '**parcery.** *Obs. rare*⁻¹. [Erroneous form of PARCENARY.] Apportionment, division.

1582 STANYHURST *Æneis* III. (Arb.) 81 This part was to Helenus by wylled parcerye lotted.

parceve, -cew, -ceyve, obs. ff. PERCEIVE.

parch (pɑːtʃ), *v.* Forms: 5-6 **perch, parche**, 6 **partch(e**, 7 **pearch**, 6- **parch.** [Evidenced since *c* 1400; origin unknown. See note below.]

1. *trans.* To dry by exposure to great heat; to roast or toast slightly (corn, pease, and the like); 'to burn slightly and superficially' (J.). (The subject is usually a person.)

1398 TREVISA *Barth. De P.R.* XVII. cxxxi. (Bodl. MS.) lf. 223 b/1 Saresines put peper into an Ouen whan is new igadered and percheþ it so & benemeþ þe vertu of burginge & of springinge. *c* **1440** *Promp. Parv.* 382/2 Paarche pecyn, or benys, *frigo.* **1530** PALSGR. 652/2, I parche pesyn, as folkes use in lent. **1551** TURNER *Herbal* I. H vj b, Chestnuts.. if they be perched, or dryed. **1583** STUBBES *Anat. Abus.* II. (1882) 37 To make the sooles stiffe, and harde, they must be parched before the fire. **1601** HOLLAND *Pliny* XVIII. vii, After they haue pearched them all well, they blend them together and grind them in a quern. **1693** SIR T. P. BLOUNT *Nat. Hist.* 115 The Goodness of Coffee chiefly consists in an exact way of Parching and managing the Berries. **1853** SOYER *Pantroph.* 41 Dry, near the fire or in the oven,.. barley flour, then parch it. **1900** *Daily News* 4 May 5/4 Parching the oats, as is done in some parts of Scotland.

2. To dry to extremity, to make hot and dry; to 'scorch': said esp. of the action of the sun's heat, or of fever or thirst.

1555 W. WATREMAN *Fardle Facions* I. ii. 30 The earth beyng more parched by the heate of the sonne,.. ceased to bring furthe any mo greate beastes. **1573-80** BARET *Alv.* P 97 The feuer parcheth him. *Ibid.* P 98 Thirst parcheth them. **1697** DRYDEN *Virg. Past.* VII. 79 Parch'd are the Plains, and frying is the Field. **1707** *Curios. in Husb. & Gard.* 126 To hinder the.. extream Heats of Summer from parching them up. **1875** W. S. HAYWARD *Love agst. World* 95, I am parched with thirst.

b. *transf.* To dry, shrivel, or wither with cold.

1573-80 BARET *Alv.* P 95 Parcheth, *adurit Solis calor, adurit etiam frigus. Ibid.* P 98 They suffer themselues to be bitten, or parched in the cold hilles, *pernoctant venatores in niue, in montibus vri se patiuntur.* **1667** MILTON *P.L.* II. 594 The parching Air Burns frore, and cold performs th' effect of fire. **1793** SOUTHEY *Triumph of Woman* 6 Who.. felt the storm Of the bleak winter parch his shivering form. **1888** SWINBURNE in *19th Cent.* XXIII. 320 The live woods feel not the frost's flame parch.

3. *intr.* To become very dry and hot; to shrivel up with heat.

1530 PALSGR. 653/2, I partche by heate of the sonne, or the fyre, *je me retire.* **1606** SHAKS. *Tr. & Cr.* I. iii. 370 We were better parch in Affricke Sunne. **1756** P. BROWNE *Jamaica* 162 New coffee will never parch or mix well. **1825** COBBETT *Rur. Rides* 16 The grass never parches upon these downs. **1877** BLACK *Green Past.* xx. (1878) 160 He would sooner parch with thirst.

[*Note.* Koch suggested the identity of *parch* with OF. *perchier*, *parchier*, now *percher*, Picard form of F. *percer* to pierce. Phonologically this would be possible, but the difficulties involved in respect of the chronology and sense seem insuperable, esp. when the history of PIERCE is compared. A more plausible conjecture would see in it a repr. of L. *persiccāre* to dry thoroughly; cf. obs. F. *parseicher* (Godef.); but here also the historical and other difficulties appear to be too great.]

parch, *sb.*¹ [f. prec. vb.]

1. The action of parching or the condition of being parched. *rare.*

1874 MRS. WHITNEY *We Girls* xi. 232 The summer had not gone.. only the parch and the blaze were over. **1900** S. PHILLIPS *Paolo & Franc.* II. ii, I love not, I, the long road and the march, With the chink, chink, chinking, and the parch.

2. *attrib.*, as **parch mark** *Archæol.*, a localized discoloration of the ground in dry weather over buried remains.

1947 *Antiquity* XXI. 82 The crop's growth had not improved matters, and curiously enough there did not seem to be any 'parch-marks'. **1977** *Times* 19 Sept. 3/2 The latest discovery emerged partly through last summer's drought. Parch marks on the ground disclosed regular lines of Roman trench work.

‖**parch** (pɑːx), *sb.*² *rare.* [W. *parch* reverence, *parchedig* reverend.] In Wales: a clergyman.

1944 DYLAN THOMAS *Let.* 21 Sept. (1966) 267 Hearing rise slimy from the Welsh lechered Caves the cries of parchs and their flocks. **1953** —— *Under Milk Wood* (1954) 20 A beer-tent black with parchs.

parchable ('pɑːtʃəb(ə)l), *a. rare*⁻⁰. [f. PARCH *v.* + -ABLE.] Capable of being parched.

1611 COTGR., *Adustible*,.. burneable,.. parcheable.

parchance, obs. form of PERCHANCE.

parched (pɑːtʃt, 'pɑːtʃɪd), *ppl. a.* [f. PARCH *v.* + -ED¹.]

1. Dried by exposure to great heat; roasted: said esp. of the effect of fire upon farinaceous substances.

c **1440** *Promp. Parv.* 382/2 Parchyd, as pesys, or benys. **1539** BIBLE (Great) *1 Sam.* xxv. 18 Fyue measures of parched corne. **1562** TURNER *Herbal* II. 93 The perched or burstled peasen.. called in Northumberland carlines. **1634** SIR T. HERBERT *Trav.* 213 The Hens in eating taste like parched Pigs. **1682** *Lond. Gaz.* No. 1750/4 Fine Coffee-Powder, from 2*s.* 6*d.* to 3*s.* per Pound, or the Parched Berries at the same rate. **1841** EMERSON *Lect., Man Reformer* Wks. (Bohn) II. 243 Parched corn eaten to-day that I may have roast fowl to my dinner on Sunday, is a baseness.

2. Deprived of natural moisture, by the sun's heat, fever, etc.; dried up, 'scorched': see PARCH *v.* 2.

1552 HULOET, Parched with heate, or the sunne, *retorridus.* **1560** BIBLE (Genev.) *Jer.* xvii. 6 He.. shal inhabit the partched places in the wildernes. **1595** SHAKS. *John* v. vii. 40 To make his bleake windes kisse my parched lips, And comfort me with cold. **1709** STEELE *Tatler* No. 92 ⁋ 2 A parched Soil and a burning Climate. **1853** C. BRONTË *Villette* xxii, As good to me as the well is to the parched wayfarer.

Hence **parchedly** ('pɑːtʃɪdlɪ), *adv.*; '**parchedness.**

1598 FLORIO, *Aridamente*, barrenlie, dryly, parchedly. **1653** H. MORE *Conject. Cabbal.*, *Def. Mor. Cab.* i. 206 A waste silent Solitude, and one uniform parchednesse and vacuity. **1887** CLARK RUSSELL *Frozen Pirate* II. iv. 95 A dryness and parchedness of old age.

‖**parcheesi, parchesi** (pɑ'tʃiːsiː). Also 8 **pacheess**; 9 **pachchisi** (erron. *-chisi*), 9- **pachisi.** [ad. Hindī *pach(ch)īsī*, lit. 'of *pach(ch)īs*', i.e. twenty-five; the standard form outside India now includes an intrusive *r*.] A four-handed game played in India and subsequently also elsewhere, on a cruciform board or (more often) cloth, with six cowries for dice: so named from the highest throw, which is twenty-five. Also *attrib.* (A simplified form is known in Europe as *ludo.*)

1800 *Asiatic Ann. Reg., Misc. Tracts* 314/2 In one square court the pavement is worked with squares, in the manner of the cloth used by the Indians for playing the game called Pacheess. **1867** A. F. BELLASIS in E. Falkener *Games Anc. & Orient.* (1892) 258 There is a gigantic pachisee board at the palace at Agra where the squares are inlaid with marble on a terrace. **1892** KIPLING & BALESTIER *Naulahka* 78 It seemed to him no extraordinary mark of court favour to play pachisi with the King. **1892** E. FALKENER *Games Anc. & Orient.* 257 Pachisi is the national game of India. **1892-3** *T. Eaton & Co. Catal.* Fall & Winter 67/2 Games... Parcheesi, linen board, 50c. **1895** *Montgomery Ward Catal.* 235/3 Royal Game of Parchesi complete.. including.. folding board,.. 8 dice,.. and 16 counters. *a* **1910** 'O. HENRY' *Rolling Stones* (1916) 37 John Tom Little Bear, in full Indian chief's costume, drew crowds away from the parchesi sociables and government ownership conversaziones. **1948** C. MCCULLERS *Discovery of Christmas* in *Mademoiselle* Sept., Budge.. was too little to count straight, to play Parcheesi, to wipe himself. **1950** O. NASH *Family Reunion* (1951) 15 They can't pass it in bridge or parchesi or backgammon. **1969** L. KENNEDY *Very Lovely People* i. 35 The first night we were there two girls came over with a parcheesi board, and for the next two months we played nothing but parcheesi. **1972** *Jrnl. Social Psychol.* LXXXVII. 108 This procedure was chosen over Vinacke's parchesi game and Gamson's simulated political convention to emphasize the relative importance of the subjects [*sic*] initial resources. **1972** *Listener* 13 July 51/3, I was playing a lot of board games at home. We had Pachisi, Monopoly.. Chinese chequers and what-not.

parchemen, -mener, obs. ff. PARCHMENT, -ER.

parchemin ('pɑːʃəmɪn), *v. rare.* [ad. F. *parchemine-r*, f. *parchemin* PARCHMENT.] = PARCHMENTIZE *v.*

1884 EISSLER *Mod. High Explos.* I. v. 123 The more readily a fibre is parchemined by the action of sulphuric acid.

parchemin(e, -myn(e, obs. ff. PARCHMENT.

parchemyner, obs. f. PARCHMENTER.

parcher ('pɑːtʃə(r)), *rare.* [f. PARCH *v.* + -ER¹.] One who or that which parches.

1593 BARNES *Parthenoph.* xl. in Arb. *Garner* V. 361 That proud, commanding, and swift-shooting Archer;.. which.. more than Phœbus, is an inward parcher!

parcheryte: see PAR *prep.* 1 b.

† '**parchfully**, *adv. Obs. rare*⁻¹. ? In a parched or burning state.

1582 STANYHURST *Æneid* etc., (Arb.) 137 In the den are drumming gads of steele, parchfulye sparckling; And flam's fierclye glowing from fornace flasshye be whisking.

parching ('pɑːtʃɪŋ), *vbl. sb.* [f. PARCH *v.* + -ING¹.] The action of the verb PARCH.

1398 TREVISA *Barth. De P.R.* XVII. cxxxi. (Bodl. MS.) lf. 223/2 Somme peper.. is blacke and ryuely wiþ perchinge and rostinge of hete of the fire. **1573-80** BARET *Alv.* P 98 A burning, or parching, *ambustio.* **1760** tr. *Juan & Ulloa's Voy.* (1772) I. 288 They have several methods of preparing the maize; one is by parching. **1898** *Allbutt's Syst. Med.* V. 11 A severe cold in the chest, with deep-seated rawness, soreness and parching.

'**parching**, *ppl. a.* [f. PARCH *v.* + -ING².] That parches; drying to excess; scorching.

1565 COOPER *Thesaurus* s.v. *Acer*, *Sol acer*, parchyng hoate. **1591** SHAKS. *1 Hen. VI*, I. ii. 77 Whilest I.. to Sunnes parching heat display'd my cheekes. **1707-12** MORTIMER *Husb.* (1721) II. 206 Having of water at hand.. especially in dry parching Times. **1827** LYTTON *Pelham* xxi, Then will this parching thirst be quenched at last.

b. Becoming excessively dry and hot.

1697 DRYDEN *Virg. Georg.* III. 844 The slow creeping Evil.. Consumes the parching Limbs. **1819** KEATS *Ode Grecian Urn* iii, A burning forehead, and a parching tongue.

Hence '**parchingly** *adv.*, '**parchingness.**

1847 WEBSTER, *Parchingly*, scorchingly. **1727** BAILEY vol. II, *Parchingness*, burning &c. Quality.

parchment ('pɑːtʃmənt), *sb.* Forms: *α.* 3-4 **parchemin**, 4 **-men**, 4-6 **-myn(e, -mine**; 4 **parchymene**; 5 **perchymyn, perchemyn(e, -men**, 6 **-meyne, -mine**; 4 **parchmen**, 5-6 **perchmyne**, 6-7 **parchmine.** *β.* 5-6 **perchement**, 5-7 **parche-**, (7 **partch-**), 6- **parchment.** [ME. a. F. *parchemin*, in 11th c. north. F. *parcamin*: cf. Pr. *pergamen*, *-mi*, Cat. *pergami*, Sp. *pergamino*, Pg. *pergaminho*; It. *perga'mena*, *perga'mina* (Florio), ad. L. *pergamēna*, in Isidore *pergamīna*, abs. use (sc. *charta*) of *Pergamēna*, fem. of *Pergamēnus* adj., of or belonging to *Pergamum*, a city of Mysia in Asia Minor. The Romanic forms (exc. It.) point to a L. neuter form *pergamēnum*, *-mīnum* (both in med.L.); OFr. shows a further change, evidenced in med.L. *percamīnum*, and in Du., of original *g* to *c*, which before *a* became *ch-* in Fr. and thence in Eng. The later Eng. form in *-ment* corresponds to a med.L. by-form *pergamentum* (11th c. in Wright-Wülcker) with falsified suffix, seen also in OHG. *pergement*, *perment*, Ger. *pergament*, MDu. *parca-*, *parkement*, Du. *perka-*, *perkement.*]

1. a. The skin of the sheep or goat, and sometimes that of other animals, dressed and prepared for writing, painting, engraving, etc.

α. *a* **1300** *Cursor M.* 8503 Als written es in parchemin. **13..** *E.E. Allit. P.* B. 1134 Polysed als playn as parchmen schauen. *c* **1375** *Sc. Leg. Saints* xxiv. (*Alexis*) 337 Sone askyt he.. pene, Ink, and parchemyne. *c* **1400** tr. *Secreta Secret., Gov. Lordsh.* 113 [þei] peyntyd his figure in perchemyn. **1483** CAXTON *Gold. Leg.* 316/1 Brynge to me perchymyn & ynke. **1512** *Act 4 Hen. VIII*, c. 19 §10 The seid Commissioners shall delyver by one parte of theyr wrytyng in parchemyn triplicate.. the hole some. **1594** R. ASHLEY tr. *Loys le Roy* 21 Thicker then double parchmine.

β. *a* **1400-50** *Alexander* 5305 þar in perchement depayntid his person scho schewid. ? **1456** *Paston Lett.* I. 405, I sende yow the copie of your patentes, in parchement. **1560** in W. H. Turner *Select. Rec. Oxford* 279 The drum is covered with parchment. **1578** in *Maitl. Cl. Misc.* I. (1833) 4 Foure volumes.. coverit with quhite perchement. **1602** SHAKS. *Ham.* v. i. 123 *Ham.* Is not Parchment made of Sheep-skinnes? *Hor.* I my Lord, and of Calue-skinnes too. *a* **1634** CHAPMAN *Alphonsus* Plays 1873 III. 257 Mine Entrals shrink together like a scrowl Of burning parchment. **1875** SCRIVENER *Lect. Text N.T.* 17 [The vellum] is often no better than coarse parchment made from sheep's skins.

b. With defining word, applied to substances resembling parchment, as ***cotton parchment***, a parchment-like material made by soaking cotton fibre in a solution of sulphuric acid, glycerin, and water, and then rolling it into sheets; ***vegetable parchment*** = parchment-paper (see 5 b).

1838 *Mech. Mag.* XXX. 192 M. Pelouze states that if.. paper be plunged into nitric acid.. and immediately washed .. a species of parchment is produced. **1860** *Edin. Phil. Jrnl.* XII. 324 Vegetable parchment.—Papyrine. **1860** HOFMANN in *Ure's Dict. Arts* III. 406 In its appearance, vegetable parchment greatly resembles animal parchment.

2. a. A skin, piece, scroll, or roll of parchment; a manuscript or document on parchment.

13.. *Seuyn Sag.* (W.) 3011 The knight toke vp the parchemyne, And red the Franche, ful fayre and fyne. *c* **1374** CHAUCER *Boeth.* v. met. iv. 129 (Camb. MS.) Thilke stoyciens wenden þat the sowle hadde ben naked of it self as a myroure or a cleene parchemyn. **1483** *Cath. Angl.* 269/1 A Parchement, *membrana, pergamenum.* **1557** N.T. (Genev.) *2 Tim.* iv. 13 Bryng with thee.. the bokes, but specially the parchementes [so 1611; WYCLIF parchemyn, TINDALE partchement]. **1595** SHAKS. *John* v. vii. 33, I am a scribled forme drawne with a pen Vpon a Parchment. **1786** tr. *Beckford's Vathek* 29 Carathis was privately drawing from a filigreen urn, a parchment that seemed to be endless. **1865** KINGSLEY *Herew.* x, He glanced with awe at the books, parchments [etc.].

b. A certificate; *spec.* (see quot. 1962).

1888 C. M. YONGE *Our New Mistress* ii. 14 She had been two years from her training college, and had an excellent parchment and report from the place she had left. **1914** 'BARTIMEUS' *Naval Occasions* xxii. 206 The sailor him-self.. describes his Certificate as his 'Discharge'. In Accountant circles in which the thing circulates it is known as a 'Parchment'. A Service Certificate.. is a double sheet of parchment with printed headings, foolscap size. **1962** GRANVILLE *Dict. Sailors' Slang* 86/1 *Parchment*, naval rating's service certificate on which his character and abilities are assessed by the commanding officer of each ship in which he has served.

3. A skin or membrane resembling parchment; *spec.* the husk of the coffee-bean; in quot. 1879 short for *parchment-beaver*; in 1883 for *parchment-coffee.*

1677 GREW *Anat. Fruits* v. §13 The Case is lined with a dry and thin Parchment, as smooth as Glass. **1791** *Trans. Soc. Arts* IX. p. xiii, Coffee brought over in the inner skin or parchment only. **1879** D'ANVERS tr. *J. Verne's Fur Country* I. xvi, The beavers' skins were.. labelled as 'parchments' or 'young beavers' according to their value. **1883** *Cassell's Fam. Mag.* Aug. 528/1 The 'parchment', as it is called, is sewn up in stout bags and dispatched by bullock carts to the nearest railway station. **1893** *Kew Bulletin* No. 78. 129 The husk or parchment protects the [coffee] bean from atmospheric influences which affect the colour.

4. A colour resembling that of parchment.

1934 *Dict. Colour Standards* (Brit. Colour Council) 58 Parchment. B.C.C. 165. General representation of samples submitted by Textile and other Colour Using Industries. **1947** J. H. BUSTANOBY *Princ. Color & Color Mixing* IV. 68 Parchment. A pale tint of brown, resembling the prepared and polished skin of sheep, goats, lambs, young calves, and other animals, used for writing, painting, engraving, etc. **1970** P. WEST *Words for Deaf Daughter* vi. 117 Old golds, and parchments (the tone, not the stuff). **1974** *Simpson (Piccadilly) Catal.* Christmas 15 Cable cardigan... Parchment, vicuna colour or light green.

5. *attrib.* and *Comb.* **a.** *attrib.* or as *adj.* Made of, pertaining to, or of the nature of parchment; existing only on parchment, i.e. in writing; parchment-coloured.

1593 SHAKS. *Rich. II*, II. i. 64 England.. is now bound in with shame, With Inky blottes, and rotten Parchment bonds. **1679** E. PYCKERING in *Buccleuch MSS.* (Hist. MSS. Comm.) I. 331 The parchment deed I delivered to Mr. Pack. **1821** J. MARSHALL *Const. Opin.* (1839) 231 Its effects cannot be restrained by parchment stipulations. **1886** G. R. SIMS *Ring o' Bells*, etc. I. i. 14 A look of pity overspread his parchment features. **1939–40** *Army & Navy Stores Catal.* 637/2 Satin, marocain, etc... in Oyster, Pearl and Parchment shades. **1959** *Sears, Roebuck Catal.* Spring/Summer 1224/1 Vitrous china Bathroom Fixtures.. Frosty pink, Parchment beige, Sage green. *Ibid.* 618/3 Rayon Fortisan [curtains].. Frosty pink, Parchment ivory. **1977** *Times* 29 Dec. 17/7 (Advt.), Mercedes-Benz.. Magnetic blue/parchment velour.

b. *Comb.* Instrumental, parasynthetic, etc., as ***parchment-coloured, -covered, -faced, -like, -skinned, -spread*** adjs.; **parchment-beaver**, name for beaver skins taken in summer after the hair has been shed; 'dry beaver' or 'dry castor'; **parchment-coffee**, the coffee-bean while still enclosed in its husk: cf. sense 3; **parchment-glue**, a glue made from parchment cuttings; **parchment-maker**, a maker of parchment; **parchment-paper**, a tough, translucent, glossy kind of paper resembling parchment, made by soaking ordinary unsized paper in dilute sulphuric acid; **parchment size** = *parchment-glue*; **parchment-skin**, a piece of parchment; also *fig.*; also, a disease of the skin in which it becomes dry and rough so as to resemble parchment; **parchment window** *Obs. Canad.*, a window-pane made of parchment. Also PARCHMENT-LACE.

1781 PENNANT *Hist. Quad.* II. 386 *Parchment Beaver, because the lower side resembles it. **1819** REES *Cycl.* s.v. *Castor*, Beaver skins are distinguished by the name of coat beaver and parchment beaver, by traders. **1864** in WEBSTER. **1894** J. M. WALSH *Coffee* 62 The best seed being what is known as '*parchment' coffee. **1932** W. FAULKNER *Light in August* vi. 115 Always against her eyelids was that ..*parchmentcolored face watching her. **1936** —— *Absalom, Absalom!* viii. 335 The slight dowdy woman.. with parchment-colored skin. **1979** *Country Life* 9 Aug. 431/3, I have included photographs.. of two intarsia sweaters... I particularly like the parchment-coloured one. **1799** G. SMITH *Laboratory* I. 209 Then, with *parchment-glue, mix it into a mass. **1884** BOWER & SCOTT *De Bary's Phaner.* 231 The remarkable white '*parchment-like' skin of the Orchids. **1899** J. HUTCHINSON in *Arch. Surg.* X. Descr. Plate xvii, It was quite impossible to pinch the skin up anywhere, as it was tight and parchment-like. *c* **1483** CAXTON *Dialogues* 47/9 Iosse the *parchemyn maker solde me a skyn of parchemyn. **1609** D. ROGERS *Harl. MS.* 1944 lf. 25 b in *Digby Myst.* (1882) p. xxii, Glouers and Parchment makers. **1851** in *Illustr. Lond. News* (1854) 5 Aug. 119/2 (Occup. of People) Parchment maker. **1860** HOFMANN in *Ure's Dict. Arts* (ed. 5) III. 406, I have carefully examined the new material, called vegetable parchment, or *parchment paper. **1899** CAGNEY tr. *Jaksch's Clin. Diagn.* i. (ed. 4) 84 Spread in a thin layer on a parchment-paper dialyser. **1758** [R. DOSSIE] *Handmaid to Arts* 411 It is better to employ the glover's or the *parchment size. **13..** *Minor Poems fr. Vernon MS.* 501/308 He wrot se faste til þat he want, Ffor his *parchemyn-skin was so scant. **1859** H. KINGSLEY *G. Hamlyn* (1900) 65/2 Good-night, old bat, old parchment skin, old sixty per cent. **1893** *Syd. Soc. Lex., Parchment skin*, see Xeroderma. **1859** CORNWALLIS *New World* I. 295 A dried-up looking, *parchment-skinned attorney, styled Eldon. *a* **1847** ELIZA COOK *Room of a Household* iii, The *parchment-spread battledore. **1775** HEARNE & TURNOR *Jrnls.* (1934) 182 The Carpenter Employed nailing on a set of new *Parchment windows. **1882** *Royal Readers* (Canada) v. 435 He [*sc.* Robert Campbell] and his companions were forced to use for food the parchment windows of their hut.

parchment, *v.* [f. prec. sb.] = PARCHMENTIZE *v.* So **'parchmented** *ppl. a.*: see quot., and cf. *parchment-skin* (PARCHMENT *sb.* 5 b).

1893 *Syd. Soc. Lex., Parchmented*,.. applied to a hard, tough condition of the skin in certain diseases. **1899** *Ibid.* s.v. *Xeroderma*, The skin is parchmented, and the epidermis is wrinkled and thinned out.

parchmen'tarian. *nonce-wd.* Applied to a book bound in parchment.

1808 SOUTHEY *Lett.* (1856) II. 58 The parchmentarians have all been rubbed and scrubbed. *Ibid.* 63 Brackets in my study.. support the parchmentarians.

†**parchmenter.** *Obs.* Forms: 5 parche-, perchy-, 5–6 perch(e)-; 5 -myner(e, -mener, -menter, 6 -mentier. [a. OF. *parcheminier* (13th c. in Hatz.-Darm.), in med.L. *pergamēnārius, -inerius.*] A maker or seller of parchment. (In quot. 1576, a maker of parchment-lace.)

1415 in *York Myst.* Introd. 20 Parchemyners Bukbynders. **14..** *Nominale* in Wr.-Wülcker 685/14 *Hic membrarius*, a perchmenter. **1576** GASCOIGNE *Steele Gl.* (Arb.) 80 When drapers draw, no gaines by giuing day, When perchmentiers, put in no ferret Silke.

parchmentize ('pɑːtʃməntaɪz), *v.* [f. PARCHMENT *sb.* + -IZE.] *trans.* To convert into parchment; to make parchment-like in texture. Hence **'parchmentized** *ppl. a.*, **'parchmentizing** *vbl. sb.*

1878 ABNEY *Photogr.* (1881) 44 Sulphuric acid parchmentises paper when it is immersed in it,.. that is, renders it tough and of close texture. **1882** J. SWAN in *Nature* 10 Aug. 357 A carbon filament produced from parchmentised cotton thread. **1883** *Hardwick's Photogr. Chem.* (ed. Taylor) 153 The ..effect of the previous parchmentizing.

parchment-lace. *Obs.* exc. *Hist.* A kind of lace (LACE *sb.* 5), braid, or cord, the core of which was parchment. (See Mrs. Palliser's *Hist. Lace*, ed. 1902, 37–8, and quots. there given.)

1542–3 *Privy Purse Exp. P'cess Mary* (1831) 97, ij payr of Sleves wherof one of gold w^{t} parchemene lace. *c* **1570** *Pride & Lowl.* (1841) 19 Of xx^{s} a yard, as I beleeve, And layd upon with parchment lace without. *c* **1645** R. HARPER *Mock-beggar Hall* in *Roxb. Ball.* (1874) II. 133 No gold, nor silver parchment lace Was worne but by our nobles. [**1678–9** *Wardrobe Acc. Chas. II* (in Palliser (1902) 38) [$19\frac{1}{2}$ yds.] aureæ et argenteæ pergamenæ laciniæ.] **1900** MRS. F. N. JACKSON & E. JESURUM *Hist. Lace* 65 The parchment lace, as it was called.. when silk, gold or silver thread was twisted over the thin strips of cartisane or cardboard which formed the main lines of the design. **1902** M. JOURDAIN & ALICE DRYDEN *Palliser's Hist. Lace* 37. **1905** N. H. MOORE *Lace Bk.* II. 62 The English term for this old Guipure was 'Parchment Lace'. **1930** P. G. TRENDELL *Guide to Collection of Lace* (Victoria & Albert Mus.) 6 In England there was frequent mention of 'parchment lace' in Queen Mary's reign. **1960** C. W. CUNNINGTON et al. *Dict. Eng. Costume* 268/1 *Parchment lace.* 16th and 17th c.'s. A lace usually of gold or silver but occasionally of coloured silks.

parchmenty ('pɑːtʃməntɪ), *a.* [f. PARCHMENT + -Y.] Of the nature of parchment.

1856 W. B. CARPENTER *Microsc.* §396 The wings are usually of parchmenty consistence. **1867** F. H. LUDLOW *Little Briggs* 207, I look back with a shudder upon the number of parchmenty sandwiches which I ate. **1889** G. GISSING *Nether World* II. ii. 18 Parchmenty cheek and lack-lustre eye.

†**parchy** ('pɑːtʃɪ), *a.* *Obs.* *rare*$^{-1}$. [irreg. f. PARCH *v.* + -Y.] Dried up, parched.

1746 *Brit. Mag.* 156 When minute show'rs refresh the parchy ground.

parcial(l, etc., obs. form of PARTIAL, etc.

parci'dentate, *a.* *Zool.* [f. L. *parcus* sparing + DENTATE.] Having few teeth or tooth-like processes.

1890 in *Cent. Dict.*

†**par'ciloquy.** *Obs.* *rare*$^{-0}$. [ad. L. *parciloquium* speaking sparingly, f. *parcus* sparing + *loqui* to speak.] (See quot.)

1656 BLOUNT *Glossogr.*, *Parciloquy* (*parciloquium*), a sparing or niggarly speech. **1658** PHILLIPS, *Parciloquy*, a moderation in words, a speaking little.

parcimonious, -ony, var. PARSIMONIOUS, -ONY.

parcinary, -iner, obs. ff. PARCENARY, -ENER.

†**'parcity.** *Obs.* Also 6 -cyte, -cite. [ad. L. *parcitās* sparingness, f. *parc-us* sparing: see -ITY.] Sparingness, frugality; scantiness, smallness.

1509 BARCLAY *Shyp of Folys* Argt. (1874) I. 17 As nere as the parcyte of my wyt wyl suffer me. **1526** *Pilgr. Perfect.* (W. de W. 1531) 52 These morall vertues, mekenes.. abstynence, sylence, & discrete parcite or scarsenes. **1620** VENNER *Via Recta* viii. 175 If they shall at any time exceed .., they must make amends with a following parcity. **1658** PHILLIPS, *Parcity*, thrift, sparingnesse, frugality.

parclose ('pɑːkləʊz), **perclose** ('pɜːkləʊz), *sb.* Forms: α. 4–6 **parclos**, (5 -cloos, -klos); 5 **perclos**, -cloos; β. 4–7, 9 **parclose**, (6 -close, 7 -cloese, 9 para-); 5–8 **perclose**, (6 -clowse). [ME. *parclos, parclose*, a. OF. *parclos* m., *parclose* fem., pa. pple. of *parclore* (see next) used subst.]

†**1.** Close, conclusion (esp. of a sentence, discourse, or writing). *Obs.*

13.. *Minor Poems fr. Vernon MS.* 611/75 Now þis schal beo þe parclose, No more to speken of þis prose. **1602** WARNER *Alb. Eng.* Epit. (1612) 377 Omitting the particulars of King Harolds answere.. the Parcloese was, that by his Sword he would maintaine his Scepter. **1645** QUARLES *Sol. Recant.* vii. 97 Let the Perclose of her thoughts be this, To study what Man was, and what Man is. **1671** F. PHILLIPS *Reg. Necess.* 174 The perclose of that Law.

2. A partition, screen, or railing, serving to enclose or shut off a space in a building; *esp.* (now only) a screen or railing in a church enclosing an altar, a tomb, etc., or separating a chapel, etc. from the main body of the church.

c **1400** *Laud Troy Bk.* 11281 Thei made afftir a parclos That al a-boute that fair werk gos. *c* **1412** HOCCLEVE *De Reg. Princ.* 4231 By-twix hem nas þer but a parclose Of borde. *c* **1440** *Promp. Parv.* 382/2 Parcloos, *pargulum.* **1504** *Nottingham Rec.* III. 314 For makyng of a parclose in the Shomaker Both. **1513** in Madox *Formul. Anglic.* 440 My body to be beryed.. before the rode within the new perclowse. **1530** PALSGR. 251/2 Parclos to parte two roumes, *separation.* **1611** FLORIO, *Vacerra*, a raile or perclose of timber wherein something is closed. **1867** ELLACOMBE in *Trans. Exeter Dioc. Archit. Soc.* Ser. II. I. 105 The nave is separated from the tower by a parclose of three bays.

†**3.** An enclosed space, enclosure, cloister, closet; *esp.* one in a building, separated from the main part by a screen or railing. *Obs.*

1445–6 in Willis & Clark *Cambridge* (1886) I. 394 Pro.. ij fenestris de lez parcloses Regis et Regine. **1516** *Ibid.* II. 244 A doore into the perclose there. **1523** LD. BERNERS *Froiss.* I. cccvi. 460 The other Englysshemen were on the felde, and the Constable styll in his perclose. **1571** in Nicolson & Burn *Cumberland* (1777) 90 A decent perclose of wood, wherein morning and evening prayer shall be read.

4. *Her.* (*perclose*). See quot.

1780 EDMONDSON *Heraldry* II. Gloss., *Per close*, or *Demigarter*, is that part of the garter that is buckled and nowed.

[*Parclose* = 'limber-hole', in Smyth *Sailor's Wd.-bk.*, is an error, founded on F. *parcloses* limber-boards: see Littré.]

par'close, per'close, *v.* [ad. OF. *parclore*, pa. pple. *parclos, -close*, f. *par-*, L. *per-* through, thoroughly, quite + *clore*:—L. *claudĕre* to CLOSE.]

†**1.** To bring to a close, close, conclude. *Obs.*

1610 GUILLIM *Heraldry* III. xxi. (1660) 230, I purpose.. so to perclose this Treatise. **1626** BOYLE in *Lismore Papers* (1886) II. 187 Raphe Curteis.. this day perclosed all accompts with me for the same. **1667** *Ormonde MSS.* in *10th Rep. Hist. MSS. Comm.* App. v. 52 Orders to satisfy.. your petitioner the remaining £120, after perclosing their worke.

2. *trans.* To enclose; to fence in or shut off with a parclose (see prec. 2). *rare.*

1577 STANYHURST *Descr. Irel.* in Holinshed *Chron.* (1807–8) VI. 30 The towne was not perclosed either with ditch or wall. **1855** *Ecclesiologist* XVI. 113 The sanctuary is parclosed, the organ standing on its north side.

par-cook ('pɑːkʊk), *v.* *rare.* [After PARBOIL *v.* 2.] *trans.* To cook partially.

1927 *Daily Express* 17 Nov. 5/2 The chicken was par-cooked and cooled, the stock being set aside for next day.

parcoure, parcullis, obs. ff. PARKER[1], PORTCULLIS.

parcy in *draw parcy*: see PERSUE *sb.*

parcyal, parcyl, obs. var. PARTIAL, PARSLEY.

pard[1] (pɑːd). Also 4 parde, (5 perde). [a. OF. *pard, part, parde,* ad. L. *pard-us* (male) panther, a. Gr. πάρδος (later formation from πάρδαλις fem.), panther, leopard, or ounce, an Eastern word; cf. Pers. *pārs* panther.] A panther or leopard. (Now only an archaic or poetic name.)

a **1300** *Cursor M.* 11629 Leon yode þam als Imid, And pardes als þe dragons did. **1382** WYCLIF *Jer.* v. 6 A parde wakynge on the citees of hem. **1398** TREVISA *Barth. De P.R.* XVIII. lxxxiii. (1495) 834 The perde varieth not fro the pantera, but the pantera hath moo white speckes. **1600** SHAKS. *A.Y.L.* II. vii. 150 Then, a Soldier, Full of strange oaths, and bearded like the Pard. **1657** W. MORICE *Coena quasi Κοινή* Def. xxiv. 240 As mute.. as a.. Dogg bitten by a Pard. **1725** POPE *Odyss.* IV. 616 Sudden, our band a spotted pard restrain. **1817** J. F. PENNIE *Royal Minstrel* II. 409 Has the fierce mountain pard assail'd the flock? **1820** KEATS *Ode Nightingale* iv, I will fly to thee, Not charioted by Bacchus and his pards.

b. *Comb.* **1821** SHELLEY *Adonais* xxxii, A pard-like Spirit beautiful and swift.

pard[2] (pɑːd). *slang,* chiefly *U.S.* [Abbreviation of PARDNER.] A partner, mate.

1872 'MARK TWAIN' *Roughing It* (1900) II. vi. 68 He was the bulliest man in the mountains, pard! **1883** *Longm. Mag.* Nov. 97 Here's success, pard! **1887** A. A. HAYES *Jesuit's Ring* 300 Don't go back on your old pard.

pard, obs. f. PART; obs. f. *pared,* pa. t. of PARE *v.*

parda, pardah, var. spellings of PURDAH.

†**'pardal.** *Obs.* Also -ale. [ad. L. *pardalis* a female panther, a. Gr. πάρδαλις fem. a panther; cf. obs. F. *pardalide* (Godef.): see PARD[1].] Another name for the panther or leopard; more commonly identified with the leopard when this was supposed to be distinct from the panther.

1553 BRENDE *Q. Curtius* v. K viij b, Great nombres of horses wyth Lyons, and Pardalles caried in cages. **1590** SPENSER *F.Q.* I. vi. 26 The spotted Panther, and the tusked Bore, The Pardale swift, and the Tigre cruell. **1594** BLUNDEVIL *Exerc.* v. ix. (1636) 551 Spotted with many spots, as is the Pardale or Leopard. **1661** LOVELL *Hist. Anim. & Min.* 84 They are enimies to the Pardal.

b. In L. form **pardalis.**

1687 DRYDEN *Hind & P.* III. 667 The Pardalis [*old edd.* Pardelis] replied.

pardalote ('pɑːdələʊt). *Ornith.* [ad. mod. Zool. L. *Pardalōtus* (L. J. P. Vieillot *Analyse d'une nouvelle Ornithologie* (1816) 31), a. Gr. παρδαλωτός spotted like a pard, f. πάρδαλις PARD.] A bird of the Australian genus *Pardalotus,* consisting of small birds allied to the flycatchers; = *diamond-bird* s.v. DIAMOND *sb.* 12.

[**1826** J. F. STEPHENS in G. Shaw *Gen. Zool.* XIII. II. 252 Olive-green Pardalotus, with the back spotted with fulvous.] **1848** J. GOULD *Birds Australia* II. 35 *Pardalotus punctatus,* Temm. Spotted Pardalote. *Ibid.* 36 *Pardalotus rubricatus,* Gould. Red-lored Pardalote. **1894** A. NEWTON *Dict. Birds* III. 684 *Pardalote,* see *Diamond-bird.* **1901** A. J. CAMPBELL *Nests & Eggs Austral. Birds* I. 441 The Red-tipped Pardalote occasionally breeds underground. **1961** *Coast to Coast 1959–60* 63 He pointed to where some pardalotes and sitellas were fluttering about the drooping branch of pepper-tree. **1965** *Austral. Encycl.* VI. 481/1 Pardalotes, a group of very small, insectivorous, tree-haunting birds (genus *Pardalotus*)... Most are brightly coloured and liberally spotted, hence the term 'pardalote' and the alternative name 'diamond-bird'. **1975** I. ROWLEY *Bird Life* iii. 40 Pardalotes and shrike-tits may turn to bark searching.

‖**par'dao.** *E. Ind. Obs.* Forms: 6 **pardaw, perdao, 7 pardawo, perdaw, -au, pardai, pardain, 6–7 pardao, (9 pardo).** [Pg. *pardao,* ad. 15th c. Western Indian form *partāb,* ultimately:—Skr. *prātāp* splendour, majesty (Yule).] A coin circulating in Goa, worth at the end of the 16th c. about 4*s.* 6*d.*, but afterwards diminshing in value to 10½*d.*; used also as a money of account.

1582 N. LICHEFIELD tr. *Castanheda's Conq. E. Ind.* I. lv. 117 In ready money there was found two hundred thousand Perdaos. **1598** W. PHILLIPS tr. *Linschoten* I. (1885) II. 222 Every Quintall standeth them in twelve Pardawes. **1613** PURCHAS *Pilgrimage* (1614) 473 A brother of his.. offered one hundred and fiftie thousand Pardawos. **1653** H. COGAN tr. *Pinto's Trav.* iv. 9 Two hundred Pardaos, which are worth three shillings and nine pence a piece of our coyn. **1662** J. DAVIES tr. *Mandelslo's Trav.* 107 Six Tanghes make a Pardai. **1858** SIMMONDS *Dict. Trade, Pardo,* a money of account of Goa.. of 4 or 5 tangas, and worth about 2*s.* 6*d.*

parde, pardee: see PARDIE.

parded ('pɑːdɪd), *a.* [f. PARD[1] + -ED[2].] Spotted like a pard.

1806 J. GRAHAME *Birds Scot.* 39 How prettily, upon his parded breast, The vividly contrasted tints unite. **1870** ROCK *Text. Fabr.* I. 225 Giraffes.. with their long necks and parded skins.

[**pardelun,** a little pard (Wyclif *Deut.* xiv. 5); an error; see s.v. CAMELION.]

pardenystour: see PARDONISTER.

‖**pardessus** (pardəsy). [F., 'a man's overcoat', sb. use of *par-dessus* adv., 'over-above'.] †**1.** A name for a kind of lady's cloak, worn *c* 1850–60. *Obs.*

1843 *Godey's Lady's Bk.* Nov. 240 *Pardessus.*—At the present moment this most useful appendage to a lady's out-door costume, is more than ever in request. **1850** *Harper's Mag.* I. 575 Pardessus of pink glacé silk.. edged with a narrow silk fringe. **1862** *Eng. Wom. Dom. Mag.* IV. 237/2 The pardessus is composed of black corded silk, trimmed with narrow velvet.

2. Mus. *pardessus de viole* (də vjɔl) [F. *par-dessus* adv.], a small treble viol, played esp. in France during the eighteenth century; also *ellipt.* as *pardessus.*

1889 GROVE *Dict. Mus.* IV. 277/2 The five-stringed Treble Viol survived longest in France where it was called 'Quinton' or 'Pardessus de Viole'. **1893** J. S. SHEDLOCK tr. *Riemann's Dict. Mus.* 832/2 The violin quietly took the place of the 'Pardessus de viole' in the band of viols, for the highest part. **1941** N. BESSARABOV *Anc. Europ. Mus. Instruments* IV. 303 The *quinton* is very often confused with the *pardessus de viole,* which also has five strings. These instruments belong to different families: the *quinton* is a true violin, and the *pardessus de viole* (the high treble) is a viol. **1954** *Grove's Dict. Mus.* (ed. 5) VIII. 804/2 A small sopranino viol was evolved, called a *pardessus de viole,* which was in all respects a true viol, but suited to a tuning a fourth above the treble. *Ibid.,* All sizes of viols, even the smallest *pardessus*.., must be held downward resting on or between the knees. **1961** T. DART in A. Baines *Mus. Instruments* vii. 189 A tiny viol—the *pardessus de viole*—found an admirer or two among the court ladies of France. **1974** *Early Music* Jan. 75/3 Several pardessus de viole, the smallest of the viols, cultivated by court ladies of the time. **1976** *Ibid.* July 361/1 The pardessus is built like a small treble viol, with deep ribs, flat back and frets.

pardie (pɜː'diː), **perdie** (pɜː'diː), *int.* or *adv. arch.* Forms: α. (3 par deu), 4–6 **parde,** (5 **pardee**), 5– **pardie,** 7–9 **pardi,** (5 **par dy,** 6 **pardye,** 6, 9 **pardy,** 9 **pardieu**). β. 4–6 **perde,** (5 **per dieu**), 6 **per de,** (**per dee, perdee, perdye**), 6– **perdie** (**perdy**). [a. OF. *par dé* (13th c.), mod. *pardieu* (also colloq. *pardi*), by God.] A form of oath: = 'By God!'; hence as an asseveration: Verily, certainly, assuredly, indeed.

α. *c* **1290** *Becket* 2046 in *S. Eng. Leg.* I. 165 Nai par deu, nouȝt a fote. *c* **1386** CHAUCER *Merch. Prol.* 22 A good sire hoost I haue ywedded bee Thise monthes two and moore nat pardee [*v.r.* parde]. **1413** *Pilgr. Sowle* (Caxton) I. xv. (1859) 12 Parde, some wyght wyl haue vpon me routhe. *c* **1475** *Rauf Coilȝear* 168 The hous is myne, pardie. *c* **1540** J. HEYWOOD *Four P.P.* B iij b, In that ye palmer as debyte May clerely dyscharge him parde. **1630** WADSWORTH *Pilgr.* ii. 10, I pardi demanding.. how they could take such an oath.., they answered. **1754** FIELDING *Fathers* III. ii, Pardie! Sir, your most humble servant. **1841** THACKERAY *2nd Fun. Napoleon* iii. 66 Not their deeds of arms alone, *pardi.* **1842** TENNYSON *Day Dream, Revival* iv, 'Pardy', return'd the king, 'but still My joints are somewhat stiff or so.' [**1843** LYTTON *Last Bar.* I. i, But, pardieu, he.. knows all the Neviles by eye.]

β. **1375** BARBOUR *Bruce* v. 545 Bot how that euir it fell, perde, I trow he sall the varrar be. **1470–85** MALORY *Arthur* I. cxxxvi, Perdé a twelve-moneth will be soone gone. **1548** UDALL, etc. *Erasm. Par. John* xix. 115 A place perdye detestable. *c* **1550** BALE *K. Johan* (Camden) 81 Symon of Swynsett my very name is per dee. **1602** SHAKS. *Ham.* III. ii. 305 For if the King like not the Comedie, Why then belike he likes it not perdie. **1748** THOMSON *Cast. Indol.* I. xxi, Not to move on, perdie, is all they can. **1858** KINGSLEY *Red King* 32 There's Tyrrel as sour as I, perdie.

pardine ('pɑːdaɪn), *a. rare.* [f. L. *pard-us* PARD[1] + -INE.] Of or pertaining to the pard.

1859–63 WOOD *Illustr. Nat. Hist.* I. 182 The Marbled Cat partakes more of the proverbial pardine spotted character.

pardner ('pɑːdnə(r)). *colloq.* (orig. *U.S.*). Also †**pardener.** Var. PARTNER *sb.* Cf. PARD[2].

1795 B. DEARBORN *Columbian Gram.* 137 Improprieties, commonly called Vulgarisms... Pardener for Partner. **1837** A. SHERWOOD *Gazetteer Georgia* (ed. 3) 71 *Pardner,* for partner. **1847** F. A. BUCK *Let.* 23 Feb. in *Yankee Trader in Gold Rush* (1930) 4 Mr. Johnson has taken a pardner, a Mr. Hollister, who appears to be a very smart man. *Ibid.* 5 The young lady who was my pardner gave me a private lesson beforehand so that I walked through it pretty well. **1857** *Observer* 12 Apr. 2/4 The Punch and Judy man.. cleared from £2 to £3 a week, he and his 'pardner'. *a* **1861** T. WINTHROP *John Brent* (1862) vii. 71, I don't mean sech. I mean jolly dogs, like me and my pardener. *Ibid.* xiii. 140 'Pardners for a kerdrille!' cried Jake. **1864** DICKENS *Mut. Fr.* (1865) I. I. i. 4 'Arn't been eating nothing as has disagreed with you, have you, pardner?' 'Why, yes, I have,' said Gaffer. 'I have been swallowing too much of that word, Pardner. I am no pardner of yours.' **1875** J. MILLER *First Fam'lies Sierras* (1876) v. 55 That evening Limber Tim.. told.. what a hero his 'pardner' had become. **1882** D. PIDGEON *Engineer's Holiday* I. xvii. 200 The mine is worked by two 'pardners' who dig and wash by turns. **1907** S. E. WHITE *Arizona Nights* I. xi. 178 It's money I haven't got, and can't get unless I let somebody in as pardner. **1926** *Ladies' Home Jrnl.* Nov. 24 'There', she added as she crouched once more beside her pardner. **1952** M. ALLINGHAM *Tiger in Smoke* xiii. 196 'Now, pardner,' he said. They were both great readers of Westerns. **1973** R. PERRY *Nowhere Man* iv. 59 'Well, pardner,' he said.. overdoing both the western accent and the sarcasm, 'it seems I'm stuck with you.'

pardo: see PARDAO.

pardon ('pɑːd(ə)n), *sb.*[1] Forms: 3–4 **perdun, pardun,** 3– **pardon;** also 4 **perdune,** 4–5 **per-, pardone,** 4–6 **perdon; per-, pardoun, -e,** 5 **pardown, -e.** [ME. a. OF. *perdun, pardun, pardon* = Pr. *perdo,* Cat. *perdó,* Sp. *perdon,* Pg. *perdão,* It. *perdono,* med.L. *perdōnum,* f. *pardonner,* late L. *perdōnāre* (see next), assimilated in form to *dōnum* gift.] *gen.* The act of pardoning or fact of being pardoned; forgiveness.

†**1. a.** Remission of something due, as a payment of any kind, a debt, tax, fine, or penalty. *Obs.*

1390 GOWER *Conf.* I. 115 Thei.. His grace scholden go to seche And pardoun of the deth beseche. **1444** *Rolls of Parlt.* V. 121/2 To rere the peyne or peynes of him or of hem so forfeted,.. withouten eny pardon. **1449** *Ibid.* 146/2 If eny suche persone.. accept or take eny pardon of you, of the said Subsidie. **1461** *Ibid.* 492/1 Grauntes, Relefis, amenisshingez and pardons of Feefermes. **1536** *Act 27 Hen. VIII,* c. 42 §4 His mooste gracious pardonne and releasce of the said firste frutes and tenthe.

b. Remission of sentence, granting of mercy, sparing. (So in F.) *Obs. rare.*

1555 W. WATREMAN *Fardle Facions* II. viii. 176 Withoute pardon, they kille him, and make a feaste with him.

2. a. The passing over of an offence without punishment; the overlooking of an offence and treatment of the offender as if it had not been committed; forgiveness (but often more formal than this, and coloured by sense 4).

a **1300** *Cursor M.* 1168, I am ouertan wit sli treson þat i agh not to haf pardon. *c* **1470** HENRY *Wallace* v. 975 Pardown he ast off the repreiff befor. **1590** SPENSER *F.Q.* I. xii. 18 Therefore I ought crave pardon, till I there have beene. **1603** SHAKS. *Meas. for M.* III. i. 173 Let me ask my sister pardon. **1646** CRASHAW *Delights of Muses* 109 Speak Her pardon or her sentence; only break Thy silence! speak. **1754** HUME *Hist. Eng.* (1812) I. 275 [Robert] craved pardon for his offences, and offered to purchase forgiveness by any atonement. **1875** J. P. HOPPS *Princ. Relig.* xv. 47 Pardon, or forgiveness, is an act or feeling which frees the wrong-doer from the resentment of an offended person, or from outward penalty. **1887** BOWEN *Virg. Æneid* II. 184 To invoke Pardon for great transgressions.

b. *Theol.* Forgiveness of sins.

a **1300** *Cursor M.* 11002 þe annunciaciun O crist, þat broght vs al pardun. *c* **1400** *Ywaine & Gaw.* 857 Of his sins do him pardowne. **1513** DOUGLAS *Æneis* III. iv. 100 Bot, with offerandis and eik devote prayer, Thai wald we suld perdoun and pece requier. **1699** BURNET *39 Art.* xvi. (1700) 142 Our Saviour has made our pardoning the offences that others commit against us, the measure upon which we may expect pardon from God. **1742** YOUNG *Nt. Th.* IV. 322 A Pardon bought with Blood! **1836** J. GILBERT *Chr. Atonem.* Notes (1852) 370 Pardon supposes law and sin.

3. *Eccl.* **a.** = INDULGENCE 3 a, b.

c **1290** *Becket* 2421 in *S. Eng. Leg.* I. 176 þe pope ȝaf alle pardon þat þudere wolden gon, þat men nusten in Engelonde suuych pardon non. *a* **1300** *Cursor M.* 21614 (Edin.) þe quene wiþ hir menie [went] apon þe fridai eftirwarde Of perdun [*v.rr.* pardun, -doun] for to serue hir parte. **1340** HAMPOLE *Pr. Consc.* 3926 þus pardon in purgatory availles, Als I tald. **1362** LANGL. *P. Pl.* A. II. 198 And ȝaf pardun for pons poundmele a-boute. *c* **1380** WYCLIF *Sel. Wks.* III. 331 þis bischop of Rome.. stireþ men bi grete perdon to breke opynly Goddis hestis. **1481** CAXTON *Reynard* (Arb.) 17, I gyue to hem alle pardon of her penance and relece all theyr synnes. **1560** DAUS tr. *Sleidane's Comm.* I b, Lamenting that the ignoraunt people, should be so far abused as to put the whole trust of their salvation in pardons. **1840** tr. *D'Aubigné's Hist. Ref.* (ed. 3) I. 268 The penitent was himself to drop the price of his pardon into the chest.

b. A church festival at which indulgence is granted; the festival of the patron saint.

1477 EARL RIVERS (Caxton) *Dictes* 1 The Jubylee & pardon.. at the holy Appostle Seynt James in Spayne. *c* **1483** CAXTON *Dialogues* 28/28 The procession of couentre; The pardon of syon shall be at the begynnyng of august. *a* **1578** LINDESAY (Pitscottie) *Chron. Scot.* (S.T.S.) I. 339 [The king] passit to Sanctandrois.. and thair remanit quhill the Michallmas perdoun. **1840** T. A. TROLLOPE *Summ. Brittany* II. 300 Many of these are situated in villages where Pardons are held. **1859** JEPHSON *Brittany* v. 62 To-day was the village 'Pardon', and the whole population were assembled in the church to celebrate it.

4. *Law.* A remission, either free or conditional, of the legal consequences of crime; an act of grace on the part of the proper authority in a state, releasing an individual from the punishment imposed by sentence or that is due according to law.

general pardon, a pardon for offences generally, or for those committed by a number of persons not named individually.

[**1328** *Act 2 Edw. III,* c. 2 De ceo que chartres de pardoun ont este si legierment grantees avant ces heures, des homicides, etc.] **1450** *Rolls of Parlt.* V. 202/2 Your Letters of pardon under your grete Seale. **1473** *Ibid.* VI. 73/1 Lettres of prive Seale, of Pardon generall or speciall. **1559** *Mirr. Mag., J. Cade* xviii, With generale pardon for my men halfe gone. **1600** E. BLOUNT tr. *Conestaggio* 314 Offering to all such as were in the Iland a generall pardon in his Maiesties behalfe, if they woulde yeeld. **1603** SHAKS. *Meas. for M.* IV. ii. 75, I hope it is some pardon, or repreeue For the most gentle Claudio. **1611** *Collection of Statutes* 292 b (anno 43 Eliz.), A generall pardon with many exceptions, as followeth. **1761** HUME *Hist. Eng.* (1812) VI. liv. 373 The farmers and officers of the customs.. were afterwards glad to compound for a pardon by paying a fine of 150,000 pounds. **1772** *Junius Lett.* lxviii. 356 He might have flattered himself .. with the hopes of a pardon. **1809** TOMLINS *Jacob's Law Dict.* s.v., A Pardon, if pleaded, must be averred to be under the Great Seal: except a Statute Pardon, or what amounts thereto.

5. The document conveying a pardon: **a.** in sense 3; **b.** in sense 4.

a. *c* **1386** Chaucer *Prol.* 687 His walet [lay] biforn hym in his lappe Bret ful of pardon comen from Rome al hoot. **1542–5** Brinklow *Lament.* (1874) 100 Their pardons, and other of their tromperye, hath bene bought and solde in Lombard strete. **1667** Milton *P.L.* iii. 492 Then might ye see..Indulgences, Dispenses, Pardons, Bulls, The sport of Winds.

b. **1603** Shaks. *Meas. for M.* ii. iv. 152 Signe me a present pardon for my brother. **1879** Dixon *Windsor* II. xxii. 231 The king sent him a full pardon for his past offences.

6. a. (In weakened sense, from 2.) The excusing of a fault or what the speaker politely treats as one; courteous forbearance or indulgence; allowance; excuse; acquittance of blame. Often in phrases of polite apology, esp. in *I beg your pardon*, a courteous form of expressing dissent or contradiction, = 'Excuse me'; e.g. 'I beg your pardon, it was not so'; and interrogatively = 'I do not catch what you say', or 'what you mean'.

1548 Forrest *Pleas. Poesye* 62 Perdon I haue askte for my symplenes. **1607** Middleton *Michaelm. Term* ii. iii. 283 Yet, under both your pardons, I'd rather have a citizen. **1676** Wycherley *Pl. Dealer* ii. i. Wks. (Rtldg.) 116/2 Captain, I beg your pardon: you will not make one at ombre? **1806–7** J. Beresford *Miseries Hum. Life* (1826) vii. xxviii, Endeavouring in vain to hear a person's..question addressed to you; and after repeatedly saying 'I beg your pardon, Sir', &c...still not hearing him. **1873** 'L. Carroll' *Thr. the Looking-Gl.* vii, 'I beg your pardon?' said Alice. 'It isn't respectable to beg', said the King. 'I only meant that I didn't understand', said Alice.

†**b.** Leave, permission. *Obs.*

1548 Udall, etc. *Erasm. Par. Acts* xxvi. 84 Thou haste pardon to speake for thy selfe. **1602** Shaks. *Ham.* iv. vii. 46, I shall (first asking your Pardon thereunto) recount th' Occasions of my..returne. **1606** —— *Ant. & Cl.* iii. vi. 60 My Lord Marke Anthony..acquainted My greeued eare withall: whereon I begg'd His pardon for returne.

†**c.** Allowance for defect, toleration. *Obs.*

1607–12 Bacon *Ess., Beauty* (Arb.) 212 Noe youth can be comely, but by pardon and by considering the youth, as to make vpp the comelynes. *a* **1639** Wotton *Surv. Educ.* Ep. Ded., A slight Pamphlet, about the Elements of Architecture..hath been entertained with some pardon among my Friends.

d. Ellipt. for *I beg your pardon* (see sense 6 a). *colloq.*

1898 G. B. Shaw *Man of Destiny* 161 *Giuseppe* (coming to the foot of the couch) Pardon. Your excellency is so unlike other great men. **1914** —— *Fanny's First Play* iii. 221 *Knox*. .. You sit there after carrying on with my daughter, and tell me coolly youre married... *Duvallet.* Pardon. Carrying on? What does that mean? **1930** J. Cannan *No Walls of Jasper* xv. 277 Julian said, 'That's all nonsense. You're drunk.'.. 'Pardon?' said Eric. **1930** A. P. Herbert *Water Gipsies* xiii. 178 To gain time she said 'Pardon?' and Mr. Baxter had to repeat his question. **1951** [see grant *v.* 4 e]. **1954** A. S. C. Ross in *Neuphilol. Mitt.* LV. 45 *Pardon!* is used by the non-U in three main ways:—1) if the hearer does not hear the speaker properly; 2) as an apology (e.g. on brushing by someone in a passage; 3) after hiccupping or belching. **1978** I. Murdoch *Sea* 211 'Did you destroy the letter?' 'Pardon?' 'Did you destroy the letter?' 'Yes.'

†**7.** 'A plea in law by which land was claimed under a gift special' (Editor *Plumpton Corr.*). *Obs.*

1489–90 *Plumpton Corr.* (Camden) 91 Fech your pardon & my ladyes, & send them both. *Ibid.* 146 They have made search in the Escheker for the perdon that was pledet. **1500** *Ibid.* 147, I pled for your mastership x yere agoo a Perdon for Wolfe-hunt lands about Maunsefeild in Shirwood; by which plee ye clamed the land by fefement of my master, yore father.

8. *attrib.* and *Comb.* (chiefly in sense 3), as *pardon-bull*, *-monger*, *office*, *-pedlar*; †**pardon-beads** = pardoned beads: see pardon *v.* 4; **pardon-bell**, a name for the angelus-bell (because special pardons were formerly granted to those who on hearing it recited the angelus correctly); **pardon-chair**, a confessional; **pardon-screen**, a screen around or in front of a confessional; **pardon-stall**, a stall from which pardons are read, or in which confessions are heard (Lee *Gloss. Liturg. Terms* 1877).

1516 *Will of R. Simpson* (Somerset Ho.), A pair of *pardon beades. **1538** Bp. Shaxton *Injunct.* in Burnet *Hist. Ref.* (1829) III. ii. 202 That the bell called the *Pardon, or Ave Bell,..be not hereafter in any parte of my diocesse any more tollyd. **1872** Ellacombe *Bells of Ch.* ix. in *Ch. Bells Devon* 433 The Pardon Bell was silenced by Shaxton, Bishop of Sarum, in 1538. **1556** *Olde Antichrist* 74 The *pardon bulls which they offre to sell for large money to men. **1570** Foxe *A. & M.* (ed. 2) 971/2 The vnordinate outrage of those hys *pardonmongers, whiche so excessiuely did pyll and pole the simple people. **1874–7** Wylie *Hist. Protestant.* (1899) 257 The whole population of the place..had come out to welcome the great pardon-monger. **1681** Flavel *Right. M. Ref.* 209 Gods faithfulness..is as it were that *pardon-office from whence we fetch our discharges. **1653** Urquhart *Rabelais* i. i. 10 Porters and *pardon-pedlars [*pardonnaires*].

†**pardon**, *sb.*[2] *Obs.* [app. corr. of a native name.] The wine obtained from a species of palm on the Guinea Coast, app. *Raphia vinifera*, the wine from which is called by P. Beauvois (*Flore d' Oware et de Benin*, I. 77) *Bourdon.* Hence **pardon-tree, -wine.**

1705 Bosman *Guinea* xvi. 286 The third sort is drawn at Ancober, Abokroe, Axim..and goes by the name of *Pardon. Ibid.* 288 The Pardon-Trees grow like the Coco-nuts, though on a much thinner Stalk. *Ibid.* xxi. 438 Their Drink Water and Pardon-Wine.

pardon ('pɑːdən, 'pɑːd(ə)n), *v.* Also 5 **pardone, -donne, perdoun,** 6 **perdon.** [a. OF. *pardoner, perduner* (11th c.), F. *pardonner* = Pr., Sp. *perdonar*, Pg. *perdoar*, It. *perdonare*, late L. *perdōnāre* (Carolingian Capit.) to grant, concede, remit, condone, indulge, f. L. *per-* through + *dōnāre* to present, give, perh. after OHG. *forgeben*, forgive.]

†**1.** *trans.* To remit or condone (something due, a duty, obligation, debt, fine, or penalty). Sometimes with indirect (dative) obj. of the person. *Obs.*

1433 *Rolls of Parlt.* IV. 478/1 That the Bailliffs.. abbregge ne pardon no maner of duty that longeth to the seid Cominalte. *c* **1465** *Eng. Chron.* (Camden 1856) 10 The kyng pardoneth the thy drawyng and hankyng, but thyn hed shalle be smyte of atte tourhille. **1547** Gardiner in Burnet *Hist. Ref.* (1829) II. ii. 163, I am by nature already condemned to die, which sentence no man can pardon. **1596** Shaks. *Merch. V.* iv. i. 374, I pardon thee thy life before thou aske it. **1605** —— *Lear* iv. vi. 111. **1639** Fuller *Holy War* iii. xxv. (1840) 165 Who had their lives pardoned on condition to cleanse the city. **1643** Prynne *Sov. Power Parl.* ii. 75 The King cannot pardon nor release the repairing of a Bridge or Highway, or any such like publike charges.

2. To remit the penalty of (an offence); to pass over (an offence or offender) without punishment or blame; to forgive.

Pardon is a more formal term than *forgive*, being that used in legal language; also often in theology.

a. With the offence as *obj.*: sometimes with the offender as *indirect obj.*, or governed by *to*.

c **1489** Caxton *Sonnes of Aymon* i. 47 Pardone theym the dethe of your sone. **1535–6** *Act 27 Hen. VIII*, c. 24 §1 No personne..shall have any power..to pardon or remitte any tresons..or any kyndes of felonnyes what so ever they be.. but that the Kinges Highnesse..shall have the hole and sole power and auctoritie therof. **1602** *How to choose good wife* v. iii. in Hazl. *Dodsley* IX. 90 On my knee I beg Your angry soul will pardon me her death. **1611** Bible *Exod.* xxiii. 21 Provoke him not; for he will not pardon your transgressions. **1759** Hume *Hist. Eng.* (1812) V. xliv. 418 Her father would never have pardoned so much obstinacy. **1861** J. A. Alexander *Gospel Chr.* xxvii. 369 God pardons nothing or He pardons all.

b. With the offender as *obj.*

c **1430** *Syr Gener.* (Roxb.) 3239 And he pardoned Generides thoo Of al the wrathe betwix hem twoo. **1450** Marg. Paston in *Lett.* I. 115 The Duke of Suffolk is pardonyd,..and is in the Kyngs gode grase. **1459** *Paston Lett.* I. 499 My maistr, whom Iesu for his mercy pardonne. **1484** Caxton *Fables of Æsop* ii. x, I praye the that thow wylt pardonne me of thoffense that I have done to the. *a* **1533** Ld. Berners *Huon* lxxxiv. 266, I holde you quyt..& pardon you of all myn yll wyll. **1611** Bible *2 Kings* v. 18 In this thing the Lord pardon thy seruant. **1741** Richardson *Pamela* (1824) I. 103 Pardon you! said he, What! when you don't repent? **1754** Hume *Hist. Eng.* (1812) I. vi. 321 That the adherents of each should be pardoned. **1841** Lane *Arab. Nts.* I. 82 Pardon me, and kill me not, and so may God pardon thee.

c. *absol.* To grant pardon or forgiveness.

a **1450** *Knt. de la Tour* (1868) 138 But for no amonestement..she wolde not pardone. **1611** Bible *Isa.* lv. 7 Hee will abundantly pardon.

d. To put *away* by pardon. (*nonce-use.*)

1875 J. P. Hopps *Princ. Relig.* xv. 48 We cannot pardon away a wound or forgive away a disease.

3. To make courteous allowance for; to excuse: **a.** a fact or action.

1526 *Pilgr. Perf.* (W. de W. 1531) 2, I beseche you to pardon my boldnes. **1605** Chapman *All Fooles* Plays 1873 I. 136 Ladie, youle pardon our grosse bringing up? **1648** *Hamilton Papers* (Camden) 194 Pardon my impatience. **1761** Hume *Hist. Eng.* (1812) VI. 405 You will be pleased to pardon my infirmity. **1847** Tennyson *Princess* ii. 289 My needful seeming harshness, pardon it.

b. a person; formerly esp. in asking to be excused from doing something (now *excuse me*: see excuse *v.* 7).

1509 Hawes *Past. Pleas.* xx. (Percy Soc.) 98 To pardon me of my rude wrytyng. **1570** Foxe *A. & M.* (ed. 2) 2291/1 Her graces Cooke aunswered: my Lord, I will neuer suffer any straunger to come... He [Ld. Chamberlain] sayd they should. But yᵉ Cooke said, his Lordship should pardon hym for that matter. **1599** Shaks. *Much Ado* ii. i. 131 *Beat.* Will you not tell me who told you so? *Bene.* No, you shall pardon me. **1603** —— *Meas. for M.* iii. ii. 142 *Duke.* What (I prethee) might be the cause? *Luc.* No, pardon: 'Tis a secret must bee lockt within the teeth and the lippes. **1764** Foote *Patron* iii. Wks. 1799 I. 359 My hand! what, to a poet hooted, hissed, and exploded! You must pardon me, Sir. **1795** Anna Seward *Lett.* (1811) IV. 81 Pardon me from dwelling so long on this sad theme. **1849** Macaulay *Hist. Eng.* vi. II. 46 Men who had been so long..oppressed might have been pardoned if they had eagerly seized the first opportunity of obtaining..revenge.

†**4.** *Eccl.* To hallow (beads) so that pardon or indulgence for sins was attached to their use. *Obs.*

1524 *Will of R. Hallay* (Somerset Ho.), Beads &c. pardoned at Sion. **1553** Becon *Reliq. Rome* Wks. (1564) iii. 358 b, To all good christen people disposed to say our Ladyes psaulter..on any of these beades, the which bene pardoned at the holye place of Shene, shal haue ten thousande yeres of pardon.

Hence '**pardoned** *ppl. a.*; '**pardoning** *vbl. sb.* and *ppl. a.*

1530 Palsgr. 251/2 Pardonyng, *pardonnance.* **1547** *Homilies* i. *Good Wks.* iii. (1859) 59 All things which they had were called holy, holy cowls, holy girdles, holy pardoned beads. **1678** South *Serm.* II. x. 379 That solid and substantial Comfort..which Pardoning-grace,..for the most part, never gives. **1692** Luttrell *Brief Rel.* (1857) II. 347 One of the witnesses against him, being a pardoned robber. **1828** Scott *F.M. Perth* xxii, Thou thyself shalt preach up the pardoning of injuries. **1896** *Academy* 12 Dec. 520/1 Reformers..whose essential integrity of intention wins for them at last a pardoning respect.

pardonable ('pɑːdənəb(ə)l), *a.* [a. F. *pardonnable* (12th c. in Hatz.-Darm.), f. *pardonner*: see pardon *v.* and -able.] That can be pardoned or forgiven, admitting of pardon; excusable.

a. Said of an offence.

1548 Udall, etc. *Erasm. Par. Mark* iii. 23 Erroure and ignoraunce are pardonable. **1712** Addison *Spect.* No. 285 ¶3 Such little Blemishes..we should..impute to a pardonable Inadvertency. **1800** *Med. Jrnl.* III. 361 It is a very pardonable error. **1876** Tennyson *Harold* iii. i, Of all the lies that ever men have lied, Thine is the pardonablest.

b. Of an offender (or his condition). Now *rare.*

1638 Baker tr. *Balzac's Lett.* (vol. III) 118 The Italian women are more pardonable than the French. **1803** Jane Porter *Thaddeus* (1826) III. iii. 68, I dare say your daughter is pardonable. **1846** Trench *Mirac.* vii. (1862) 195 To bring the culprit to a free confession, and so to put him in a pardonable state.

Hence '**pardonableness**; '**pardonably** *adv.*

a **1643** Ld. Falkland, etc. *Infallibility* (1646) 48 This difficulty of using this meanes, (and so pardonablenesse of erring). **1674** Boyle *Excell. Theol.* i. i. 23 The Stoicks absurdly..(but much more pardonably than..Mr. Hobbs) would have men to spring up like mushrooms out of the ground. **1871** L. Stephen *Playgr. Eur.* (1894) v. 132 Our thoughts pardonably concentrated themselves on the.. question of food. **1892** *Chamb. Jrnl.* 13 Aug. 514/2 A conviction of that neighbour's pardonableness.

†'**pardonance.** *Obs. rare*⁻¹. [a. OF. *pardonance* (12th c.), *-aunce* (Gower), f. *pardonner* to pardon: see -ance.] Pardoning; a pardon.

1413 *Pilgr. Sowle* (Caxton) i. xxxiv. (1859) 40 This present pardonaunce is my yeft.

pardonee (pɑːdə'niː). [f. pardon *v.* + -ee.] One who is pardoned; the recipient of a pardon.

1895 in *Funk's Stand. Dict.*

pardoner[1] ('pɑːdənə(r)). Now only *Hist.* Also 4–6 **perdon-,** (5 **perden-**); 5 **-eer,** 5–6 **-are, -air, -ar.** [In AF. *pardoner*; F. *pardonnier* (Palsgr.); f. pardon *sb.* + -er[2] 2: cf. *garden-er*; also obs. F. *pardonnaire* in Rabelais.] A person licensed to sell papal pardons or indulgences.

1362 Langl. *P. Pl.* A. Prol. 65 Þer prechede a pardoner, As he a prest were. *c* **1380** Wyclif *Eng. Wks.* (1880) 154 þere comeþ a pardoner wiþ stollen bullis & false relekis. *c* **1386** Chaucer *Prol.* 670 With hym ther was a gentil Pardoner..That streit was comen from the court of Rome. **1486** *Bk. St. Albans* F vij, A Lyeng of perdeneris. *a* **1500** *Colkelbie Sow* i. 120 A peruerst perdonair, And practand palmair. **1536** *Proclam.* in *Elyot's Gov.* (1883) Life 124 Light persons called pardoners and sellers of indulgences. **1672** R. Wild *Declar. Lib. Consc.* 13 The old Pardoner will never get Peter-pence enough here to buy him a pair of breeches. **1706** tr. *Dupin's Eccl. Hist. 16th C.* II. iii. ii. 18 The Complaints which the Faithful made of the Pardoners. **1808** Scott *Marm.* i. xx, Or pardoner or travelling priest.

'**pardoner**[2]. [f. pardon *v.* + -er[1] 2: cf. F. *pardonneur.*] One who pardons or forgives.

1581 Fulke in *Confer.* ii. (1584) N, Be present as a pardoner of our excesse. **1675** Traherne *Chr. Ethics* 388 An injury forgiven is forgotten by him that did it, and the friendship continues at the expence, and to the honour and comfort of the pardoner. **1866** Miss Mulock *Noble Life* xiii. 220 [He] who is at once the Judge and the Pardoner of sinners.

†**pardonister.** *Obs.* Forms: 4–5 **pardonystre, -ter, pardenystour.** [ME. *pardonistre*, app. repr. an Anglo Fr. **pardonistre*, by-form of **pardoniste*: see -ister.] = pardoner[1].

c **1380** *Antecrist* in Todd *Three Treat. Wyclif* (1851) 147 Bi pardenystours & procuratours. **1401** *Pol. Poems* (Rolls) II. 78, I trowe thou menys the pardonystres..that rennen so fast aboute. **1496** *Dives & Paup.* (W. de W.) vii. xix. 306/2 Bothe the preest & the pardonyster be bounde to restytucyon.

pardonless ('pɑːdənlıs), *a.* [f. pardon *sb.* + -less.] Without pardon; unpardonable.

1567 Drant *Horace, Arte Poetrie* B iij b, He..In one thinge ofte is perdonles. **1630** Heywood *Rape Lucrece* Wks. 1874 V. 218 My example Might in my seruants breed encouragement So to offend..which were pardonlesse. **1867** J. B. Rose tr. *Virgil's Æneid* 83 If that offence be pardonless, then cast The living in yon main.

†'**pardonous,** *a. Obs. nonce-wd.* [f. pardon *sb.* + -ous.] Abounding in pardon.

1610 Marcellini *Triumphs Jas. I* 94 Thy Pardons are too pardonous, and thy Indulgences, have too much indulgence.

pardriche, -yche, obs. ff. partridge.

pardure, -durable, obs. ff. perdure, -able.

pardy(e: see pardie.

†**pare,** *sb.*[1] *Obs. rare.* [f. pare *v.*[1]]

1. That which is pared off; the paring or parings collectively.

c **1430** *Two Cookery-bks.* 30 Take a part of Applys, & do a-way þe corys, & þe pare.

2. A piece of turf, a sod.

1651 tr. *Beza's Fun. Verses on Calvin* in Fuller *Abel Rediv.* 284 How happens it that this is Calvins share, To lye under this little, unknowne pare? Is not this he who living did appeare, Decaying Romes continued dread and feare?

‖**pare** ('pɑre), *sb.*² *N.Z.* [Maori.] A lintel in a Maori building.

1897 A. HAMILTON *Maori Art* (1901) II. 156 The small doorway has the usual *pare* or *korupe* over it with a single figure in the centre, and the bird-headed monsters at the ends. **1911** *Dominion Museum Bull.* (N.Z.) No. 3. 106 From the Salem Museum comes also the photograph of a *pare* or door-lintel.. This *pare* can be definitely located, from the style of carving, as having been made in the Bay of Plenty District. **1927, 1949** [see KORUPE]. **1950** *N.Z. Jrnl. Agric.* May 501 The dark-brown pare or korupe framing the window..is a modern totara carving. **1962** N. DAVIS in Davis & Wrenn *Eng. & Medieval Stud.* 324 The central group on a lintel (*pare*) from Porangahau, Hawke's Bay.

pare (pɛə(r)), *v.*¹ Also 4–6 payre, 6 paire, 7–8 pair. [a. F. *pare-r* to prepare, trim, dress, etc., 'also, to pare the hoofe of a horse' (Cotgr.):—L. *parāre* to make fit or ready: see PREPARE.]

I. †**1.** *trans.* To get ready, to prepare; to adorn, deck out. *Obs.*

1392, 1444 [see PARING *vbl. sb.* 1]. *a* **1400–50** *Alexander* 4208 Quen it [a boat] was done at his diuyse & draȝen ouer with hidis, Pared & Parreld at his pay, pickid & taloghid. *a* **1450** *Knt. de la Tour* (1868) 67 It is synne to haue so mani diuerse clothes, and to do so moche coste to pare the foule body. **1617** MINSHEU *Ductor*, To Pare, to make readie.

†**2.** To form, shape (or ? to cut). *Obs.*

13.. *E.E. Allit. P.* B. 1408 Lyfte logges þer-ouer & on lofte coruen, Pared out of paper & poynted of glolde [? golde]. *Ibid.* 1536 A fust faylaynde þe wryst, Pared on þe parget, purtrayed lettres. **13..** *Gaw. & Gr. Knt.* 802 Pared out of papure purely hit semed.

II. 3. To trim by cutting off projecting, irregular, or superficial parts; to cut close to the edge so as to make even or neat; to cut away the outer edge or outside of (something), *e.g.* the skin or rind of (a fruit), in thin layers, slices, or flakes.

c **1320** *Sir Tristr.* 542 Bred þai pard and schare, Ynouȝ þai hadde at ete. *c* **1375** *Sc. Leg. Saints* xxxvi. (*Baptista*) 1099 To payre ane apil & til eete. **1377** LANGL. *P. Pl.* B. v. 243 To wey pens with a peys, and pare þe heuyest. *c* **1420** *Pallad. on Husb.* VII. 2 At Iuyn a floor for thresshing thus thei make: They pare hit first, and lightly after gete Hit doluen smal. *c* **1530** H. RHODES *Bk. Nurture* 171 in *Babees Bk.* 76 Your hands cleane, your nayles parde. **1530** PALSGR. 252/1 Paryng yrone to pare a horsehofe with. **1563** GOLDING *Cæsar* VII. (1565) 199 b, A littel hill..notably fortified, and on all sides, pared stepe. **1626** MIDDLETON *Anything for Quiet Life* IV. ii, What a cursed wretch was I to pare my nails to-day! a Friday. **1686** *Lond. Gaz.* No. 2124/4 Stolen.., about 350 of the best Kids, some ready pared. **1769** MRS. RAFFALD *Eng. Housekpr.* (1778) 215 Take some pippins, pare, core, and boil them. **1855** MACAULAY *Hist. Eng.* xxi. IV. 620 The practice of paring down money..was far too lucrative to be so checked.

b. Phrase *to pare to the quick*, to cut away the epidermis, or other superficial part, so deep as to reach the 'live' or sensitive parts; to pare so as to hurt. Also *fig.* So *to pare too close* or *near*.

1538 ELYOT, *Resecare ad viuum*, to pare to the quicke, to touche the quicke in a mater. **1573** TUSSER *Husb.* (1878) 8 Great fines so neere did pare me. **1598** CHAPMAN *Iliad* To Rdr. (1865) 91, I entreat my..Reader, that all things to the quick he will not pare. **1683** BURNET tr. *More's Utopia* (1685) 14 Whom, to raise their Revenues, they pare to the Quick. **1708** SWIFT *Sacram. Test* Wks. 1755 II. I. 134 His claws pared to the quick. **1790** HAN. MORE *Relig. Fash. World* (1791) 49 The prevailing mode of living has pared real hospitality to the very quick. **1846** J. BAXTER *Libr. Pract. Agric.* (ed. 4) I. 452 The smith..proceeds at once to 'pare the corn out to the quick, till the blood starts'.

c. To prune by cutting off superfluous shoots (*obs.*); to reduce the thickness of (a hedge, etc.).

1398 TREVISA *Barth. De P.R.* XVII. xcviii. (Bodl. MS.) lf. 214 b/1 The apple tree waxiþ bareyne but he be pared and ischred. **1598** SYLVESTER *Du Bartas* II. i. I. *Eden* 86 He plants, he proins, he pares, he trimmeth round Th' ever green beauties of a fruitful ground. **1633** G. HERBERT *Temple, Paradise* iv, When thou dost..with thy knife but prune and pare, Ev'n fruitfull trees more fruitfull are. **1884–5** *Act* 48 & 49 *Vict.* c. 13 §2 It shall be lawful..to cut, prune, or pare the said hedge.

4. To slice off the turf or other vegetation covering the surface of the ground. **a.** with the ground or land as object; esp. in phr. *pare and burn*, to cut the turf to the depth of two or three inches, and burn it, in order to use the ashes as manure, as is done in denshiring or burn-beating.

1530 PALSGR. 652/2 He hath pared his grounde, he loketh to have saffrone shortly. **1761** STERNE *Tr. Shandy* IV. xxxi, The..expense of paring and burning and fencing in the Ox-moor. **1789** *Trans. Soc. Arts* VII. 40 Seventeen acres were pared and burned in 1779. *c* **1830** *Glouc. Farm Rep.* 14 in *Libr. Usef. Knowl., Hubs.* III, When the saintfoin plants begin to fail, which is about the sixth year, the land is pared, and burned, and sown to turnips.

b. with the turf as obj. (cf. 6).

1577 B. GOOGE *Heresbach's Husb.* (1586) 20 They cast into their Foldes suche Turues pared from the grounde. **1704** *Dict. Rust. et Urb.* s.v. *Burning*, With a Breastplayt to pare off the Turff. **1846** in J. Baxter *Libr. Pract. Agric.* (ed. 4) II. 181 This system of culture consists in paring off the grassy sward or surface of the land, with an instrument called a breastplough,..the turf..pared off being burnt.

5. To reduce (a thing) by cutting or shaving *away*; hence, to reduce or diminish little by little; to bring *down* in size or amount. Also *absol.*

1530 PALSGR. 701/2, I shave, I pare away any thing by thynne portions. **1643** MILTON *Divorce* II. xx. Wks. (1851) 119 We never leave subtilizing and casuisting till we have straitn'd and par'd that liberall path into a rasors edge to walk on, between a precipice of unnecessary mischief on either side. **1721** RAMSAY *Poet's Wish* i, Tay and Tweed's smooth streams, Which gently, and daintily, Pare down the flow'ry braes. **1825** in Cobbett *Rur. Rides* (1885) II. 16 They pare down the wretched souls to what is below gaol allowance. **1864** BOWEN *Logic* iii. 57 To pare down the complexity and redundance of rhetorical expression.

6. To cut, shave, or shear *off* or *away* (an outer border, surface, rind, or skin, a projection; formerly also, any part on the outside of something).

1387 TREVISA *Higden* (Rolls) IV. 47 Þere the Affres closed hym [Regulus] in a streiȝt tree..and parede of his yȝe liddes. *c* **1400** *Laud Troy Bk.* 13407 He pared her chekes al aboute, That al here tethe fellen oute. *c* **1420** *Pallad. on Husb.* III. 532 Now is to repare Rosayres olde & drynesse of to pare. **14..** *Sir Beues* 197/3939 (MS. M) Halfe the helme he can pare: Than myght men se his hede bare. **1530** PALSGR. 652/2 Pare your crust away, *parés la crouste de vostre payn.* **1613** HEYWOOD *Silver Age* I. i. Wks. 1874 III. 90 Whose head wee by Mineruaes aide par'd off. **1686** HORNECK *Crucif. Jesus* xviii. 536 Let them pare away that poysonous rind. **1787** WINTER *Syst. Husb.* 105 Where ants inhabit, their hills should be pared off. **1855** MACAULAY *Hist. Eng.* xxi. IV. 623 To pass a halfcrown, after paring a pennyworth of silver from it. **1885** *Manch. Weekly Times* Suppl. 20 June 4/3 The edges are pared off by the old-fashioned bookbinders' plough.

b. *fig.* To cut off or remove.

1549 COVERDALE, etc. *Erasm. Par. Col.* ii. 5 b, Nor haue ye a litle piece onlye of the carnall man pared awaye. *c* **1610** SIR J. MELVIL *Mem.* (1735) 401 Conditions and Articles might be added and pared at the Pleasure of their Friends. **1649** JER. TAYLOR *Gt. Exemp.* Pref. §47, I was diligent to remarke such doctrines, and to pare off the mistakes. *a* **1677** BARROW *Serm.* Wks. 1716 I. 10 Paring away the largest uses of wealth. **1883** ANNIE THOMAS *Mod. Housewife* 32, I did not see how it was possible for me to pare and prune off any more of our expenses.

c. To make or form by paring or cutting away.

1708 J. PHILIPS *Cider* I. 27 Slow house-bearing snails, that creep O'er the ripe fruitage, paring slimy tracts In the sleek rinds. **1713** WARDER *True Amazons* (ed. 2) 121 To pare away with a sharp Chizel a place for the Slider.

Hence **pared** (pɛəd, *poet.* 'pɛərɪd) *ppl. a.* (also with *down*).

c **1440** *Promp. Parv.* 384/1 Paryd, as breede, *decrustatus.* *c* **1500** *For to serve Ld.* in *Babees Bk.* 367, iiij or v loves of paryd brede. **1597–8** BP. HALL *Sat.* IV. iii. 89 Not his pared nayle will he forego. **1855** MACAULAY *Hist. Eng.* xxi. IV. 643 Huge heaps of pared and defaced crowns and shillings. **1974** *Country Life* 21 Feb. 398/2 The pared-down practicality of mini skirts and boots. **1977** *Rolling Stone* 30 June 98/2 The arrangements are just pared-down versions of the originals.

†**pare,** *v.*² *Obs.* [Shortened from *compare.*] *intr.* To 'compare', admit of comparison.

c **1430** *Pilgr. Lyf Manhode* II. civ. (1869) 114 Þat j haue prys of alle, and þat noon be paringe to me.

pare, obs. form of PAIR *sb.*¹ and *v.*², PEAR.

parea, obs. form of PARIAH.

pareable ('pɛərəb(ə)l), *a. rare.* [f. PARE *v.*¹ + -ABLE.] That can be pared or cut off.

c **1449** PECOCK *Repr.* II. iv. 160 The yuel..is pareable and kutteable awey.

‖**pareccrisis** (pə'rɛkrɪsɪs). *Path.* [mod.L., f. PARA-¹ 1 + Gr. ἔκκρισις secretion. In mod.F. *pareccrise.*] Improper or disordered secretion.

1857 in MAYNE *Expos. Lex.*

[**parechasis, parecnasis, parecuasis.** Errors for *parecbasis*, Gr. παρέκβασις deviation, digression. Also **parectbaticall** *a.*

1584 SCOT *Disc. Witchcr.* XV. xxiii. 438 *marg.*, A parecuasis or transition of the author to matter further purposed. **1589** *Arte Eng. Poesie* III. 195 *marg.*, *Parecnasis*, or the Stragler. **1625** *A. Day's Eng. Secretary* II. 100 *Pareonasis* [sic], or *Digressio*, a speech beside the matter in present spoken on, as to say, But here let me remember vnto you something of the deserts and eternized memory of your worthy and most vertuous parents. **1659** *Quæres Prop. Officers Armie to Parlt.* 4 The first instrument together with a new fangled advice, have proved parectbaticall botcheries, or meer peccant forms of Polity, without any patterne or president in the Chequer Rolle of politicall Records. **1678** PHILLIPS (ed. 4), *Parechasis* [so 1696–1706], a digression, in Rhetorick, it is a wandering in discourse from the intended matter.]

pareche, -chen, obs. form of PARISH, -EN.

†**pa'redrial.** *Obs. rare.* [f. Gr. παρεδρία a sitting beside + -AL¹: cf. next.] = next.

1652 GAULE *Magastrom.* 270 He had a devil his paredrial or assessor.

‖**pa'redrus.** *Obs. rare.* [late and med.L., a. Gr. πάρεδρος sitting beside, one who sits beside, an assessor, f. παρ(α- beside + ἕδρα seat.] One who sits beside; a familiar spirit.

[**1603** HOLLAND *Plutarch* Explan. Wds., Assistants he had twaine, named *Paredri*, who sat in commission with him.] *a* **1641** BP. MOUNTAGU *Acts & Mon.* iii. (1642) 161 Witches ..having Familiar Spirits, Paredros, Assisters to..them.

Paree (pæ'ri:). *colloq.* [Repr. the Fr. pronunc. of *Paris.*] Paris; esp. in phr. *gay Paree.*

1848 F. A. DURIVAGE *Stray Subjects* 116 Walk in, gentlemen, and see the collection.., which beats the Zoological Gardens all holler, and can't be come over by the Gardens des Plantys in Par-*ee!* **1903** MRS. G. DE H. VAIZEY *Pixie O'Shaughnessy* xvi. 171 The Major..revived recollections of an old visit to 'Paree'. **1930** E. WAUGH *Labels* 21 There are good young men saving up their money for a beano in 'Gay Paree'. **1964** 'P. LORAINE' *Day of Arrow* i. 12 The porter, putting on a weary archness reserved for British and American visitors to *Paree.* **1974** *Times* 9 Feb. 10/5 The prize: a second honeymoon in—guess where? You've got it —Gay Paree.

†**paregal, peregal,** *a.* and *sb. Obs.* Forms: *α.* 4 parigal, -agal, (paringal(le, -ingale, paruyngal, parmyngalle), 5–6 paregall, 6 -egale, 7 -egal. *β.* 4 perigal(e, 4–7 peregal(l, 5–6 -egalle, (5 perengale, peringall), 6 perigall, (perregal). [a. OF. *parigal*, *paringal*, *paregal*, *peringal* (12th c. in Godef.):—L. type *peræquāl-em, f. *per-* through, thoroughly + *æquāl-is* EQUAL. Britton, III. xx. §4, has the deriv. sb. *perigalté.* With *peringale*, cf. *nightingale* from OE. *nihtegale.*]

A. *adj.* **1.** Fully equal; equal (esp. in power, rank, value, or the like).

a **1300** *Cursor M.* 776 (Cott.) He dos it for he ne wald ȝee were Parigal [*Gött.* paringale] til him ne pere. *Ibid.* 2096 Þof þe werld es..Delt..in thrin parteis principale, þe partes er noght perigale. *c* **1374** CHAUCER *Troylus* v. 840 His herte ay wiþ þe firste and wiþ þe beste Stod peregal to dorre don that hym leste. *c* **1400** tr. *Secreta Secret., Gov. Lordsh.* 64 Alexander, kepe þy most noble saule hegh, and to angeles perengale. *c* **1450** *Merlin* 163 Thei heilde hem peryngall. **1513** DOUGLAS *Æneis* VI. xiv. 50 Schynand with elyk armes paregale. *a* **1548** HALL *Chron., Hen. VII* 44 Although in degree they were not peregall with these great lordes. **1636** *Fascic. Florum* §273. 63 All goodly fair, in years, all Peregall.

b. Adequate; adequately qualified, worthy.

14.. HOCCLEVE *Aungeles Song* ii. Wks. (E.E.T.S.) III. p. xlvii, No praisyng is, þat may be peregall. *c* **1560** A. SCOTT *Poems* (S.T.S.) vii. 20 Wald God þat I wer perigall, Vnder þat redolent ross to rest!

¶**2.** *catachr.* Equal to any other; of the highest rank or standing.

1600 W. WATSON *Decacordon* (1602) 274 Our noble Elizabeth, prince peregall, paramount and paragon. *Ibid.* 236 An absolute statesman paramount, peregall [**1612** T. JAMES *Jesuits' Downf.* 66 Paregal].

B. *sb.* One who is fully equal to another in some respect; an equal, peer, match.

c **1395** *Plowman's Tale* 130 That holdeth no man his peringall. **1399** LANGL. *Rich. Redeles* I. 71 Þoru partinge of ȝoure powere to ȝoure paragals. **14..** *Sir Beues* 104/2138 (MS. S.) At hoom y am his parmyngalle [*N.* paruyngal; *C.* In hys contre y am hys pere]. **1513** DOUGLAS *Æneis* IX. x. 152 Nor na disdene at the sal haue, suythly, To be hys peregall into archery. *a* **1555** LYNDESAY *Tragedy* 45 Duryng my tyme, I had no perigall. **1602** MARSTON *Ant. & Mel.* III. Wks. 1856 I. 39 *Bal.* How lik'st thou my suite? *Cat.* All, beyond all, no peregal.

‖**pa'regmenon.** *Rhet.* [mod.L., a. Gr. παρηγμένον derived, neuter of perf. pple. pass. of παράγειν to lead aside, change.] (See quot.)

1678 PHILLIPS (ed. 4), *Paregmenon*..in Rhetorick, is a Figure in which are words conjoyned, which are derived one of another, as *Discreet, Discretion.*

paregoric (pærɪ'gɒrɪk), *a.* and *sb.* Also 8 **para-**. [ad. late L. *parēgoric-us*, a. Gr. παρηγορικ-ός encouraging, soothing, f. παρήγορος consoling, soothing, f. παρα- PARA-¹ beside, on the side of + -αγορος in sense 'speaking', cf. ἀγορά assembly of the people; cf. ἀγορεύειν to speak in the assembly. In F. *parégorique.*]

A. *adj.* Of medicines: Assuaging pain, soothing.

1684 tr. *Bonet's Merc. Compit.* VI. 190 The fury of the bloud is restrained..by a paregorick draught of Diacodium. **1744** BERKELEY *Siris* §75 It [tar-water] is..both paregoric and cordial. **1784** T. COLBY in *Med. Commun.* II. 18, I directed a paregoric draught to be taken at night.

b. spec. *paregoric elixir*, a camphorated tincture of opium flavoured with aniseed and benzoic acid.

Formerly, also, the ammoniated tincture of opium (*Scotch paregoric elixir*); see Buchan *Dom. Med.* ed. 1790, App. 698.

1751 STARK tr. *Mead's Med. Precepts* v. 113 Of all this tribe [anodynes] I know no better medicine than the paragoric elixir. **1857** MAYNE *Expos. Lex.*, *Paregoric Elixir*, name for the *Tinctura opii camphorata*, or English paregoric elixir, to distinguish it from the *Tinctura opii ammoniata*, which was formerly also called paregoric elixir. **1893** in *Syd. Soc. Lex.*

B. *sb.* A medicine to assuage pain, an anodyne.

1704 J. HARRIS *Lex. Techn.* I, *Anodynes*..are sometimes also called Paragoricks. **1780** GRANT in *Phil. Trans.* LXX. 129 Taking only a paregoric at night. **1815** *Mr. John Decastro* I. 36 This acted like a paregoric for a little time.

b. *spec.*, in the British Pharmacopœia = *paregoric elixir*: see A. b.

1875 tr. *von Ziemssen's Cycl. Med.* I. 457 The above mentioned mixture of paregoric and wine of opium. **1885** 'F. ANSTEY' *Tinted Venus* xv. 180, I never sell paregoric to children. **1892** *Daily News* 1 Nov. 6/5 In the third reprint of the [British Pharmacopœia], issued in November, 1888, the Council drew attention in a prefatory notice to their insertion of paregoric—on page 411. **1898** *Allbutt's Syst. Med.* V. 154 We endeavour..to relieve cough, particularly at night, by paregoric and other anodynes.

† **pare'gorical**, *a. Obs.* [See -ICAL.] = prec. A.
1657 TOMLINSON *Renou's Disp.* 113 Some are Paregoricall or leniating. **1657** B. W. *Expert Phisician* 66 Diaphoretical and Paregorical Medicines.

pareiasaur (pəˈraɪəsɔː(r)). Also (erron.) **pariasaur.** [f. mod.L. name of suborder *Pareiasauria*, f. generic name *Pareiasaurus*: see following entry.] A herbivorous fossil reptile of the group once included in the suborder Pareiasauria, known from Permian remains found in southern and eastern Africa, eastern Europe, and Russia, now classified as the superfamily Pareiasauroidea of the suborder Procolophonia. So **pareia'saurian** *sb.* Also as *adj.*, of or pertaining to an animal of this type.
1905 E. R. LANKESTER *Extinct Animals* v. 220 These Pariasaurs were about as big as well grown cattle, but not so high on the legs. **1927** HALDANE & HUXLEY *Animal Biol.* xi. 242 (*caption*) Primitive type [of reptile] (Pareiosaurian [*sic*]). **1933** A. S. ROMER *Vertebr. Paleont.* vi. 129 A more advanced type..is that of the pareiasaurs of the Middle and Upper Permian of Europe and Africa. **1966** E. PALMER *Plains of Camdeboo* vi. 105 The great 'Cheek-Lizards', the Pareiasaurs,..were found..in the lowest and oldest zone of the Beaufort series. **1971** E. C. OLSON *Vertebr. Paleozool.* viii. 315 The main link between procolophons and pareiasaurs is provided by *Rhipaeosaurus*. *Ibid.*, *Rhipaeosaurus* has a dentition that appears somewhat like that to be expected in an ancestral pareiasaurian. *Ibid.*, The skull..has a somewhat pareiasaurian and somewhat procolophonian look. **1975** *Nature* 3 Apr. 415/1 The first..is an exposure of the Madumabisa Mud-stones yielding abundant therapsid and some pareiasaur remains. **1977** A. HALLAM *Planet Earth* 270 The second group were the pareiasaurs, which were up to 3m..long.

pareiasaurus (pəˌraɪəˈsɔːrəs). Also (erron.) **pariasaurus.** [mod.L. (R. Owen *Descr. & Illustr. Catal. Fossil Reptilia S. Afr.* (1876) 7), f. Gr. παρειά cheek + σαῦρος lizard.] = prec.
1876 R. OWEN *Descr. & Illustr. Catal. Fossil Reptilia S. Afr.* 10 (*caption*) A vertebra from the hinder part of the dorsal, or from the lumbar, region of a *Pareiasaurus*. **1905** E. R. LANKESTER *Extinct Animals* v. 218 (*caption*) Photograph of a skeleton of Pariasaurus. **1959** *Times* 19 June 7/5 Those [animals] like the pareiasaurus..have gradually become extinct.

† **pareil**, *a.* and *sb. Obs.* Forms: 5 **pareille, -eile, -eylle, parelle, parail, parayl, -le, -lle, 6 pareyl, 7 pareil.** [a. F. *pareil* adj. and sb., like, equal (12th c. in Hatz.-Darm.) = Pr. *parelh*, Sp. *parejo*, It. *parecchio* 'equal, euen, like' (Florio):—late pop.L. **pariculum* dim. of *par* equal.]
A. *adj.* Equal.
1470–85 MALORY *Arthur* v. ii, Vnto yow is none lyke ne pareylle in Crystendome. **1483** CAXTON *Gold. Leg.*, Who is he that is founde paraylle or lyke to thys sacrefyse. **1610** G. FLETCHER *Christ's Vict.* I. lxxviii, Was never sight of pareil fame.
B. *sb.* **a.** Equality. **b.** A mate, fellow, companion. **c.** An equal, a match.
a **1450** *Knt. de la Tour* (1868) 61 She beleuid for to haue pareille to God. *c* **1460** J. RUSSELL *Bk. Nurture* 343 Suffere youre parelle to stond stille to þe botom. *c* **1495** *Epitaffe*, etc. in *Skelton's Wks.* (1843) II. 392 Whos paryl alyue thou can not fynde. **1512** *Helyas* in Thoms *Prose Rom.* (1828) III. 51 He ne knew his pareyl in prudence of understanding. **1638** JER. TAYLOR *Serm. Anniv. Gunpowder Tr.* 7 We shall quickly finde out more then a pareil for S. Iames and S. Iohn the Boanerges of my Text.

pareil, obs. form of PARREL.

pareira (pəˈrɛərə). [ad. Pg. *parreira* vine trained against a wall; whence *parreira brava* wild climbing vine, the name given to the Brazilian plant.] A drug made of the root of a Brazilian shrub, used in disorders of the urinary passages. Originally understood to be the root of the climbing shrub *Cissampelos Pareira* or 'Velvet-leaf', the *parreira brava* of the Portuguese, whence the name: now said to be that of a different shrub, *Chondrodendron tomentosum*; the 'Velvet-leaf' being distinguished by some as ***spurious pareira.***
(The fact is that, historically, the latter is the *real* pareira, 'pareira' of pharmacy being a misnomer.)
1715 *Phil. Trans.* XXIX. 365 The *Pareira Brava* is a Root which comes to us from Brazil by the way of Lisbon. **1876** HARLEY *Mat. Med.* (ed. 6) 721 Pareira Brava is a climbing shrub indigenous in Brazil. **1880** GARROD & BAXTER *Mat. Med.* 187 Pareira is a bitter tonic, like calumba, but scarcely ever used as such; it is thought to act as a diuretic. **1887** MOLONEY *Forestry W. Afr.* 514 *Pareira brava* (*Cissampelos Pareira*) Velvet-leaf or spurious Pareira.

pareis, pareiss, obs. ff. PARISH, PARIS.

† **'parel, parail**, *sb. Obs.* Forms: 4 **parail, -aille, 4–5 -aile, -ayl(e, 5 -ayll, -eylle, 6 parrelle, 6–7 parrell, -el, parel, -ell.** [Aphetic form of ME. *aparail*, APPAREL, q.v.]
1. Preparation, equipment: = APPAREL *sb.* 1.
c **1400** *Laud Troy Bk.* 17501 We schal come on suche parayle That..Off his purpos schal he be rent. *c* **1450** *Cov. Myst.* xxv. (Shaks. Soc.) 246 Jewgys that knowyth the parayl ..this matere to amende.
2. A body of troops: = ARRAY *sb.* 4.
13.. *Coer de L.* 1644 Kyng Rychard wente, with hys parayle, To Marcyle they ganne ryde. **1511–12** *Act 3 Hen. VIII*, c. 3 *Preamble*, Much partey of the cominalte and parell of the Realme..be not of power nor abilitie to bye theym longbowes.
3. Apparatus, outfit, furniture, tackle: = APPAREL *sb.* 2, 3.
c **1420** *Chron. Vilod.* 448 þis chapelle..wᵗ alle þe pareylle þᵗ longede þerto. **14..** in *Tundale's Vis.* (1843) 114 Or of hur bed was ther any perayle of gold or sylke. **1532** in Weaver *Wells Wills* (1890) 120 All the parell belongyn to the plowe.
b. Clothing, array, attire: = APPAREL *sb.* 5.
1377 LANGL. *P. Pl.* B. XI. 228 For his pore paraille and pylgrymes wedes. **1393** *Ibid.* C. XIII. 131 In þe parail of a pilgrim. *a* **1400** *Octouian* 1680 Melk whyte armes, yn ryme I rede, Was here parayle. *a* **1547** SURREY *Æneid* IV. 337 A shining parel..of Tirian purple. **1647** WARD *Simp. Cobler* 14 Fling all his old parrell after him.
4. Ornament, decoration: = APPAREL *sb.* 7, 7 b; cf. PARURE I.
1546 *Inv. Ch. Goods Yorksh.*, etc. (Surtees) 138 Two albes and parrelles [*MS. transcript* parrettes] of ymagerye. **1554** *Ludlow Churchw. Acc.* (Camden) 58 Item, for porrelz for albis..vjd. **1698** *Lond. Gaz.* No. 3370/4 Stole.., one piece of..Cloth,..marked in the Parrel, I O H.
b. A chimney-piece, mantelpiece.
1532–3 in Bayley *Hist. Tower London* (1821) I. App. Pt. I. xxix, The settyng of vij. new parells in vij. chymneys..ev'y parell' v. fote in wydnes. **1541** in Rogers *Agric. & Prices* III. 571/2 (Dartford) Parells of stone for chimneys. **1845** PARKER *Gloss. Archit.* (ed. 4), *Parrell*,..a chimney-piece; A set of dressings or ornaments for a fire-place.
5. A preparation of eggs, etc. put into wine to refine it (see quots.).
1594 PLAT *Jewell-ho.* III. 66 Which parrell for the most part in one night will cause them [the wines] to fine. *a* **1700** B. E. *Dict. Cant. Crew*, *Parell*, Whites of Eggs, Bay-Salt, Milk and Conduit-Water beat together, and poured into a Vessel of Wine..in order to Fine it. **1703** *Art & Myst. Vintners* 14 They make a Parell of burn'd Alum, Bay-Salt, and Conduit Water.
6. (?) Cf. APPAREL *sb.* 6.
a **1330** *Roland & V.* 196 Fele þousand of sarazines, Swiþe heyȝe of parail. **1390** GOWER *Conf.* III. 119 Lich to tuo twinnes of mankinde..So be thei bothe of o parail. *c* **1400** *St. Alexius* (MS. Laud 622) 27/165 To þe chirche of seint Bonefas Wiþ þis maiden þai token þe pas, þat heiȝe was of paraile. *Ibid.* 56/810 He hidde þere noman shulde ywite, His book of gode paraile. **1528** PAYNEL *Salerne's Regim.* H, The ruddier wines of the same parell are more nouryshyng than white.
7. *Naut.* See PARREL.

† **'parel, parail**, *v. Obs.* Forms: 4 **parayle, 4–5 parail, 5 parael, parrail, -aille, parell, parele, parrel, 6 parall, 7 parel.** [Aphetic form of ME. *aparail, -ayle*, APPAREL *v.*, q.v.]
1. *trans.* To prepare, get ready, put in order: = APPAREL *v.* 1.
a **1400–50** *Alexander* 480 þis dere kyng..Had parreld him a proude feste. *Ibid.* 765 (Ashm.) He parrails [*Dubl.* apperels] him a proude ost of princes & oþire.
b. To give a 'parel' to (wine): see prec. 5.
1615 MARKHAM *Eng. Housew.* II. iv. (1668) 113 Parel it with six Eggs, yolks and all, one handfull of bay salt, and a pint of conduit water to every parel.
2. To clothe, dress, array, attire: = APPAREL *v.* 5.
c **1350** *Will. Palerne* 1990 Al þe pepul is parayled and passed to cherche. **1393** LANGL. *P. Pl.* C. III. 224 Ac marchauns metten with hym [Guile]..And parailed hym lyke here prentys. **14..** *Thomas of Erceldoune* (ed. 1875) 94 But I am a lady of anoþer cuntre, If I be parellid moost of price.
3. To adorn, embellish: = APPAREL *v.* 7.
a **1510** DOUGLAS *K. Hart* I. ix, And said he suld it parall all with fyn And fresche delyt, with mony florist floure.

parel, -e, obs. forms of PERIL.

‖**pa'relcon.** *Gram. Obs.* [mod.L., a. Gr. παρέλκων, pr. pple. of παρέλκειν to draw aside or along, spin out, prolong.] (See quot.)
1678 PHILLIPS (ed. 4), *Parelcon*, Protraction, a figure wherein a word or syllable is added to the end of another, as *Numnam, Etiamnum*.

parelectronomy (pærɪlɛkˈtrɒnəmɪ). *Physiol.* [ad. F. *parélectronomie*, f. Gr. παρ(α- PARA-[1] against + ELECTRO- electric + -νομία, f. νόμος law, etc.] (See quot. 1893.) Hence **parelectro'nomic** *a.*, pertaining to or marked by parelectronomy.
1877 ROSENTHAL *Muscles & Nerves* 208 Called parelectronomy by E. du Bois-Reymond, because it differs from the usual electric action of muscles. **1878** FOSTER *Phys.* I. ii. §2. 52 It is not until this parelectronomic layer, as he calls it, has been removed..that the natural current can manifest itself in its proper strength. **1893** *Syd. Soc. Lex.*, *Parelectronomy*, name applied by Du Bois Reymond to the weakened condition of the electrical current of muscle, while the natural transverse section at the tendinous ends is maintained. The condition is due to the presence of an opposite current across the natural transverse section.

parelie, parelion: see PARHELION.

parell, -e, var. PAREIL, PAREL *Obs.*; obs. f. PERIL.

parellic (pəˈrɛlɪk), *a. Chem.* [f. Bot. L. *parella*, f. F. *parelle*, formerly *pareele*, ad. med.L. *paratella*, name of a plant.] In ***parellic acid*** ($C_9H_6O_4$), obtained from a crustaceous lichen, *Lecanora Parella*; also called **pa'rellin.** Hence **pa'rellate**, a salt of parellic acid.
1866–77 WATTS *Dict. Chem.* IV. 355 *Parellic acid* or *Parellin*... Parellic acid forms colourless needles, very slightly soluble in cold water, soluble in alcohol and in ether. .. Parellate of barium..is a white powder insoluble in water.

† **'parelling**, *vbl. sb. Obs.* Also 5 **parral-, 5–7 paral-.** [f. PAREL *v.* and *sb.* + -ING[1].] The action of the verb PAREL; preparation, equipment, arraying, etc.; also *concr.* equipage, furniture, apparatus (= PAREL *sb.* 3).
1496 *Acc. Ld. High Treas. Scot.* I. 322 For xxxᵗⁱ sparris, to mak a paraling of ak for the gunnys. **1505** *Ibid.* III. 142, viij dosan of rauchteris to be coyis in the schip and paraling gif tha com to ony segis. **1665** J. WEBB *Stone-Heng* (1725) 88 The upright Stones..retain their Angles, Arras, and a Shew of paralling, conspicuous, fair, and perfect even to Admiration.
b. *attrib.* in **parelling staff**, a stick used by vintners in 'parelling' (see PAREL *v.* 1 b).
1594 PLAT *Jewel-ho.* III. 68 A hazell sticke of the bignesse of a good cudgell,..(the Vintners call it their parrelling staffe). **1703** *Art & Myst. Vintners* 16 They add more Wine, and stir them together in a Half-tub, with a Parelling staff.

paremayn, obs. f. PEARMAIN, kind of apple.

‖**parembole** (pəˈrɛmbəliː). *Rhet.* [a. Gr. παρεμβολή insertion, interpolation, parenthesis, etc., f. παρ(α- PARA-[1] I + ἐμβολή throwing in, insertion.] A kind of parenthesis: see quot. 1753.
[**1658** HARRINGTON *Prerog. Pop. Govt.* Wks. (1700) 236 In which is contain'd the Parembole or Courses of Israel before the Captivity.] **1753** CHAMBERS *Cycl. Supp.*, *Parembole*, Παρεμβολή, in rhetoric, a figure wherein something relating to the subject is inserted in the middle of a period. All the difference between the *parembole* and *parenthesis*, according to Vossius, is, that the former relates to the subject in hand, whereas the latter is foreign to it.

parement, variant of PARAMENT *Obs.*

‖**paremp'tosis.** *Rhet.* [a. Gr. παρέμπτωσις irruption, insertion, f. παρ(α- beside + ἔμπτωσις falling in, incidence.] = PAREMBOLE.
[**1706** PHILLIPS (Kersey), *Paremptosis*..a Grammatical Figure when a Letter is added in the middle of a Word.] **1842** BRANDE *Dict. Sci.* etc. s.v. *Parembole*, It is also called *paremptosis*, and is a species of parenthesis.

parence, obs. f. *parents*, pl. of PARENT *sb.*

‖**parencephalon** (pærɛnˈsɛfəlɒn). *Anat.* [mod.L., f. Gr. παρ(α-, PARA-[1] I + ἐγκέφαλον, -ος brain, ENCEPHALON; cf. Gr. παρεγκεφαλίς cerebellum.] The cerebellum. Hence ‖**parencephalitis** (-ˈaɪtɪs) [-ITIS], inflammation of the cerebellum; **paren'cephalocele** (-siːl) [Gr. κήλη tumour], hernia of the cerebellum.
1704 J. HARRIS *Lex. Techn.* I, *Parencephalos*, the same as the *Cerebellum*. **1706** PHILLIPS, *Parencephalos*. **1842** DUNGLISON *Med. Lex.*, *Parencephalocele*, hernia of the cerebellum; a very rare disease. **1857** MAYNE *Expos. Lex.*, *Parencephalitis*.

parenchym, -me (pəˈrɛŋkɪm). [ad. next, or a. F. *parenchyme* (1546 in Hatz.-Darm.).] = next.
1669 W. SIMPSON *Hydrol. Chym.* 67 Obstructions in the very parenchym of that bowel. **1811** PINKERTON *Petral.* II. 514 Fossile beds of a light marl, which contains leaves.. whose fibres are in the most beautiful preservation, but whose parenchyme is black and carbonised. **1835** LINDLEY *Introd. Bot.* (1848) I. 50 Cellular tissue is frequently called *Parenchym*. **1880** R. C. DRYSDALE in *Med. Temp. Jrnl.* Oct. 3 In the parenchyme of the organs.

parenchyma (pəˈrɛŋkɪmə). Pl. **paren'chymata.** [a. Gr. παρέγχυμα, -ματ-, lit. 'something poured in beside' (f. παρα- beside + ἔγχυμα infusion), used by Erasistratus in sense 1 a below; the substance of the liver, lungs, etc. being anciently supposed to be formed of blood strained through the blood-vessels and coagulated.]
1. *Anat.* and *Zool.* **a.** The special or proper substance of a gland or other organ of the body, as the liver, spleen, kidneys, lungs, etc., as distinguished from the connective tissue or *stroma*, and from muscular tissue or *flesh* proper. (In quot. 1682 applied to the connective tissue forming the true skin, as distinguished from the nerve-fibres distributed through it.)
1657 S. PURCHAS *Pol. Flying-Ins.* 115 Physitians.. determine the Parenchyma of the Liver to bee a certain flowing of blood, as if nothing else were there but coagulated blood. **1664** ETHEREDGE *Com. Revenge* v. i. I..fear that the parenchyma of the right lobe of the lungs..is perforated. **1682** T. GIBSON *Anat.* (1684) 13 The true skin..is made up of nervous fibres..closely interwoven..and of a parenchyma that fills up the interstices. **1783** W. CULLEN *First Lines* §293 Wks. 1827 II. 32 An inflammation of the parenchyma, or substance of viscera. **1893** *Syd. Soc. Lex.* s.v., The parenchymata of glandular organs are vascular.
b. The soft tissue composing the general substance of the body in some invertebrates, as sponges and certain worms; *spec.* the undifferentiated cell-substance or protoplasm of unicellular animals.

1665 R. HOOKE *Microgr.* xxii. 138 In a Sponge, the Parenchyma, it seems, is but a kind of mucous gelly. **1878** BELL *Gegenbaur's Comp. Anat.* 106 The calcareous bodies (spicula) always lie in the connective tissue of the parenchyma. *Ibid.* 131 The body-parenchyma of this sporocyst becomes differentiated. **1881** MIVART *Cat* 9 Histology enables us to understand the structure and nature of the ultimate substance or parenchyma of the body.

2. *Bot.* Tissue consisting of cells of approximately equal length and breadth placed side by side, usually soft and succulent, and often with intercellular spaces; found in all the systems of tissues, but chiefly and typically in the fundamental or ground tissue, as in the softer parts of leaves, the pulp of fruits, the bark and pith of stems, etc.; hence sometimes used as a synonym for 'fundamental tissue'. (Distinguished from PROSENCHYMA.)

1651 BIGGS *New Disp.* ¶79 Beginners must learn to distinguish the bloud of plants, from their gore and Parenchyma or garbage. **1671** GREW *Anat. Plants* i. §18 Next to the Cuticle [in a bean], we come to the *Parenchyma*. ..I call it the *Parenchyma*. Not that we are so meanly to conceive of it, as if..it were a meer concreted Juyce. For it is a Body very curiously organiz'd. *Ibid.* iv. §7 The Parenchyma of the Leaf, which lies betwixt the Nerves, and ..fills all up. **1786** *Gentl. Mag.* LVI. I. 456 They make corks of the parenchyma, the second bark of the black poplar. **1870** H. MACMILLAN *Bible Teach.* vii. 144 The green cellular substance, called parenchyma, which fills up all the interspaces in..leaves. **1875** BENNETT & DYER tr. *Sachs' Bot.* 78.

3. *attrib.* and *Comb.*, as *parenchyma-cell*.

1899 *Allbutt's Syst. Med.* VI. 249 Emboli of air, of fat and of parenchyma-cells.

Hence **pa'renchymal**, **parenchy'matic** *adjs.*, of, pertaining to, or consisting of parenchyma, parenchymatous; **parenchyma'titis** *Path.*, inflammation of the parenchyma of an organ.

1839-47 TODD *Cycl. Anat.* III. 485/2 The bloodvessels.. remain on the..*parenchymal aspect of the mucous tissue. **1897** *Allbutt's Syst. Med.* II. 1111 Probably they are actually derived from the parenchymal layer. **1651** BIGGS *New Disp.* ¶213 The *parenchymatick Laboratorie of the Liver. **1822-34** *Good's Study Med.* (ed. 4) IV. 300 Inflammation of the brain, and particularly..parenchymatic inflammation. **1857** MAYNE *Expos. Lex.*, **Parenchymatitis.*

parenchymatous (pærɛŋ'kɪmətəs), *a.* [f. Gr. παρέγχυμα, παρεγχυματ- (see prec.) + -OUS.]

1. *Anat.* and *Zool.* **a.** Consisting of or having the nature of parenchyma (sense 1); *spec.* applied to intestinal worms whose bodies are composed of solid parenchyma with no visceral cavity.

1667 *Phil. Trans.* II. 498 Their Liver is of a dark Green, inclining to black, and Parenchymatous. **1766** UNDERWOOD *ibid.* LVII. 5 Under this kind of parenchymatous substance ..was a muscular mass. **1835** KIRBY *Hab. & Inst. Anim.* I. xi. 319 The Parenchymatous intestinal worms of Cuvier. **1835-6** TODD *Cycl. Anat.* I. 19/2 The abdominal viscera may be subdivided into the membranous and the parenchymatous.

b. Of or belonging to the parenchyma of an organ; occurring in or affecting the parenchyma.

1822-34 *Good's Study Med.* (ed. 4) II. 88 Parenchymatous or deep-seated inflammation..distinguished from meningic. **1866** A. FLINT *Princ. Med.* (1880) 54 The cells in inflamed parts undergo parenchymatous degeneration. **1876** tr. *Wagner's Gen. Path.* 210 Parenchymatous hæmorrhages.

2. *Bot.* Consisting, or having the nature, of parenchyma (sense 2); of or belonging to the parenchyma.

1791 HAMILTON *Berthollet's Dyeing* II. II. III. i. 112 The.. ligneous parts are more easily pounded than the parenchymatous parts. **1861** BENTLEY *Man. Bot.* (ed. 2) 7 Cells have been divided into parenchymatous and prosenchymatous; parenchymatous being..applied to those cells which are placed end to end; and prosenchymatous to those which are attenuated, and overlap one another,..but various transitional states occur which render it impossible to draw..a distinct line of demarcation between them. **1884** BOWER & SCOTT *De Bary's Phaner.* 517 Narrow ligneous bundles are separated..by broad parenchymatous medullary rays.

Hence **paren'chymatously** *adv.*

1834 *Therapeutic Gaz.* VIII. 555 The injection of tincture of iodine parenchymatously is dangerous in cases where the growth is very vascular.

parenchyme: see PARENCHYM.

‖**parenchy'mella.** *Embryol.* [mod.L. dim. of PARENCHYMA.] = PARENCHYMULA.

1887 METSCHNIKOFF in *Amer. Naturalist* XXI. 419 There finally arose a two-layered parenchymella, which, by abbreviation of the embryonic process..became changed into a gastrula. *Ibid.* 421 How does the Parenchymella theory agree with the facts of embryology in general?

parenchymous (pə'rɛŋkɪməs), *a.* Now *rare.* [f. PARENCHYM + -OUS.] = PARENCHYMATOUS.

1666 J. SMITH *Old Age* (ed. 2) 185 The flesh of the body is of three sorts, Parenchymous, Glandulous, or Musculous. **1671** GREW *Anat. Plants* iv. §7 The Cortical Body, or Parenchymous part of the Barque. **1706** BAYNARD in Floyer *Hot & Cold Bath.* II. (1709) 381 The parenchymous Substance of the Liver. **1826** KIRBY & SP. *Entomol.* III. xxix. 91 [The eggs] are usually deposited in the parenchymous substance of the leaves. **1868** E. P. WRIGHT *Ocean World* vi. 121 Among the Gorgonidæ the polypier ceases to be parenchymous—that is, spongy and cellular.

‖**parenchymula** (pærɛŋ'kɪmjʊlə). *Embryol.* [mod.L. dim. of PARENCHYMA.] (See quot.)

1884 A. HYATT in *Proc. Boston Soc. Nat. Hist.* (1885) I. 91 It [Sycandra] is a form with concentrated development, in which the gastrula appears without the parenchymula. **1886** —— in *Amer. Jrnl. Sci.* Ser. III. XXXI. 341 (*Orig. Tissue*), The Parenchymula is a recently discovered stage of the embryo immediately succeeding the closed blastula..A differentiated colony, like the amphiblastula, with the cells at one end becoming better fitted to take in food, could be transformed into a parenchymula by the migration of differentiated feeding cells into the interior, and the parenchymula could then have been transformed into a true gastrula.

parenesis, parenetic: see PARÆNESIS, etc.

‖**parens patriæ** (ˌpærɛnz 'pætriː). *Law.* [mod.L., lit. 'parent of the country'.] The sovereign, or some other authority, regarded as the guardian or protector of citizens who are unable to protect themselves.

1764 T. CUNNINGHAM *New & Compl. Law-Dict.* II. s.v. Ideots and Lunaticks §2, It seems to be agreed at this day, that the King as *parens patriæ* hath the protection of all his subjects, and that in a more particular manner he is to take care of all those who, by reason of their imbecillity and want of understanding, are incapable of taking care of themselves. **1883** *Wharton's Law Lexicon* (ed. 7) 593/2 *Parens patriæ*, the sovereign, as *parens patriæ*, has a kind of guardianship over various classes of persons, who, from their legal disability, stand in need of protection, such as infants, idiots, and lunatics. **1955** *Times* 25 May 15/2 Was it prepared, as regarded a subject of her Majesty and having regard to the jurisdiction which they exercised on her Majesty's behalf as *parens patriae*, to send the child away to become a citizen of another country? **1973** *N.Y. Law Jrnl.* 20 July 1/1 A Court of Appeals has upheld the right of a state to sue to enjoin antitrust violations as parens patriae for its citizens. **1976** *Howard Jrnl.* XV. I. 51 A legal rational was discovered in the ancient doctrine of parens patriae. **1976** *Washington Post* 19 Apr. A22/4 These bills contain a so-called *parens patriae* provision permitting state attorneys general—directly or by hiring outside attorneys—to bring a class action for alleged anti-trust infractions.

parent ('pɛərənt), *sb.* [a. OF. *parent* (11th c. in Littré, pl. *parenz*, *parens* (cf. Eng. pl. *parence* in 16–17th c.) = Pr. *parent*, *paren*, Sp. *pariente*, Pg., It. *parente*:—L. *parent-em* (nom. *parens*), sb. use of old pr. pple. of *parĕre* to produce, bring forth, beget; prop. a father or mother, or by extension, an ancestor; in mod. Romanic langs. any kinsman.]

1. a. A person who has begotten or borne a child; a father or mother. Also *parent-in-law*, a father-in-law or mother-in-law.

c **1450** *Mirour Saluacioun* 901 To Nazareth was sho had home vntil hire parentes house. **1557** SEAGER *Sch. Vertue* 294 in *Babees Bk.* 341 In thy parence presence Humbly salute them with all reuerence. **1568** GRAFTON *Chron.* II. 397 He..seased without right or title all the goodes of the sayde Duke Iohn his parent. **1623** BP. HALL *Contempl.*, *O.T.* XVIII. iv, Children are but the pieces of their Parents in another skin. **1647** *Husbandman's Plea. agst. Tithes* 61 From our Ancestors, and naturall parence. **1741** RICHARDSON *Pamela* i, He was not undutiful to his parents. **1827** JARMAN *Powell's Devises* (ed. 3) II. 335 The bequest was not made by a parent or person standing in *loco parentis*. **1883** H. DRUMMOND *Nat. Law in Spir. W.* (ed. 2) 257 No man can select his own parents. **1899** EARL ROSEBERY in *Daily News* 6 May 4/2 The crusty old parent-in-law. **1932** E. E. EVANS-PRITCHARD in *Sociologus* VIII. 411 There may be difficulty later with his parents-in-law because he has taken no steps to protect their daughter from the perils of child-birth. **1937** R. H. LOWIE *Hist. Ethnol. Theory* vii. 78 This typical parallelist cites many instances of African, American, Australian, and Asiatic parent-in-law avoidance. **1972** D. BLOODWORTH *Any Number can Play* ix. 71 An agent..with parents-in-law in Peking was obviously open to pressure. **1976** *Southern Even. Echo* (Southampton) 10 Nov. 24/7 His wife Josephine and five-year-old son Simon, were at Heathrow Airport yesterday, together with his parents-in-law.

b. By extension (already in L.): A progenitor, a forefather; esp. in *our first parents*, Adam and Eve.

1413 *Pilgr. Sowle* (Caxton 1483) v. xiv. 105 There myght thou beholde thyn owne parentes Adam and Eue. **1592** DAVIES *Immort. Soul* Introd. ii, God's Hand had written in the Hearts Of our First Parents all the Rules of Good. **1667** MILTON *P.L.* III. 65 On Earth he first beheld Our two first Parents, yet the onely two Of mankind. **1805** SOUTHEY *Madoc in W.* VIII. Wks. 1838 V. 65 The glad promise, given To our first parent, that at length his sons..Should form one happy family of love.

c. *transf.* A person who holds the position or exercises the functions of a parent; a protector, guardian; sometimes applied to a father- or mother-in-law. *spiritual parent*: a sponsor, god-parent; also, a person to whom one owes one's spiritual life or conversion.

1526 *Pilgr. Perf.* (W. de W. 1531) 9 In the fayth of theyr spirituall parentes. **1570** *Homilies* II. *Rebellion* III. (1859) 570 The rebels do not only dishonour their prince, the parent of their country, but also do dishonour and shame their natural parents. **1700** DRYDEN *Sigism. & Guisc.* 358 A publick parent of the state. **1888** in *Charity Organ. Rev.* May 231 The 'house parents' receive their fixed salary.

†**2.** A relative; a kinsman or kinswoman. [So in Fr. and other Romanic langs.] *Obs.* or *alien.* (Common in 16th c.)

a **1450** *Knt. de la Tour* (1868) 150 Fulle goodly thei reuerenced and obeyed eche to other as louyng cosynes and parentys. **1490** CAXTON *Eneydos* xi. 41 The man..ys nyghe kynne and parent of yᵉ goddis. **1541** R. COPLAND *Guydon's Quest. Chirurg.* Q ij b, As bretherne, and cosyns, or other parentes. **1585** T. WASHINGTON tr. *Nicholay's Voy.* IV. xxvii. 145 b, Being by her next parents brought vnto..her husband. **1621** J. REYNOLDS *God's Revenge* I. 131 Hee sends the chiefest of his Parents to Vermandero. **1745** ELIZA HEYWOOD *Female Spect.* No. 10 (1748) II. 172 She should be saluted with the frowns and upbraidings of a wronged husband and incensed parent [her uncle]. **1771** MRS. GRIFFITH *Hist. Lady Barton* I. 267, I had many times thought of returning to Briançon, of throwing myself at my only surviving parent's feet, and of endeavouring to obtain her pardon.

3. Any organism (animal or plant) considered in relation to its offspring.

1774 GOLDSM. *Nat. Hist.* (1776) V. 182 The parent began to change her note, and send forth another cry. **1841-71** T. R. JONES *Anim. Kingd.* (ed. 4) 366 The ultimate derivation of every animal is from an egg. Mediately, or immediately, there is always not merely a parent but a mother. **1877** DARWIN *Forms of Fl.* v. 212 Out of the above 211 seedlings, 173 belonged to the same two forms as their parents, and only 38..to the third form distinct from either parent.

4. *fig.* **a.** That from which another thing springs or is derived; a source, cause, origin. (Usually of things; less commonly of persons, in relation to their 'productions'.)

1590 SHAKS. *Mids. N.* II. i. 117 And this same progeny of euills, Comes from our debate, from our dissention, We are their parents and originall. **1597** HOOKER *Eccl. Pol.* v. i. §4 We have reason to think that all true virtues are to honour true religion as their parent. **1646** CRASHAW *Steps to Temple* 8 Hail sister springs, Parents of silver-forded rills! **1754** GRAY *Poesy* 14 Parent of sweet and solemn-breathing airs. **1841** MIALL in *Nonconf.* I. 1 The evils of which it is the parent. **1877** J. D. CHAMBERS *Div. Worship* 243 It [the Liturgy of St. James] is undoubtedly the parent of the Armenian Rite.

b. *Nuclear Sci.* A nuclide that becomes transformed into another nuclide (the 'daughter') by nuclear disintegration.

1905 E. RUTHERFORD in *Phil. Mag.* X. 294 The experiment..was also utilized to prove that radium E was the parent of the α ray product radium F. **1950** [see DAUGHTER 6 d]. **1961** G. R. CHOPPIN *Exper. Nucl. Chem.* vi. 82 If the parent is shorter lived than the daughter, the daughter activity will grow to some maximum value, then decay with its own characteristic half life. **1972** SMITH & STOKES *Princ. Atomic & Nucl. Physics* xii. 364 The number of atoms of the daughter nuclide decays with either the daughter's or the parent's half-life, whichever is the larger.

5. *attrib.* and *Comb.* **a.** Appositive (with or without hyphen), chiefly in sense 4; cf. *mother-country*. (Unlimited in number.)

1646 CRASHAW *Steps to Temple* 3 Such the maiden gem.. Peeps from her parent stem. **1672** DRYDEN *2nd Pt. Conq. Granada* IV. iii, Speak, holy shade; thou parent-form, speak on. *a* **1721** PRIOR *To C'tess Devonshire* 37 When the parent sun with genial beams Has animated many goodly gems. **1735** SOMERVILLE *Chace* IV. 26 New blooming Honours to the Parent-Tree. **1784** COWPER *Task* VI. 446 To let the parent bird go free. **1787** SIR J. HAWKINS *Johnson* 500 In the contentions between a parent-state and its offspring. **1821** SHELLEY *Adonais* xlvi, So long as fire outlives the parent spark. **1868** DARWIN *Anim. & Pl.* I. iv. 105 The parent-form must have been a burrowing animal. **1870** MARCH *Compar. Gram. Anglo-S.* 2 Theoretical roots..given by grammarians as those of the Parent Speech. **1878** GUTHRIE *Pract. Physics* 46 To find with what pressure the vapour separates itself from the parent liquid. **1896** [see DIVISION 1 f]. **1903** *Edin. Rev.* Oct. 380 The parent-substance can scarcely have been used up or annihilated. **1905** E. RUTHERFORD in *Phil. Mag.* X. 295 The activity of the successive product, when in equilibrium with the parent substance, can be utilized to determine the period of a substance which itself does not emit rays. **1909** J. JOLY *Radioactivity & Geol.* iii. 57 Detrital sediments are 67 per cent. of the total parent igneous rocks. **1914** *Phil. Mag.* XXVIII. 837 It is possible from the disintegration equations of uranium and thorium, and the atomic weights of the parent elements, to calculate the atomic weights of the end products. **1934** M. BODKIN *Archetypal Patterns in Poetry* 329 In the psychological study of poetry it seems to me to have value, partly because it helps us to relate to the facts of poetic experience, those facts which Freud has formulated under the hypothesis of the parent-imago, or super-ego. **1955** [see *daughter atom* s.v. DAUGHTER 7 c]. **1956** *Nature* 11 Feb. 248/1 The fact that the chief expressive movements are the same throughout the world he regards as affording an argument that we are descended from a single parent-stock. **1957** G. E. HUTCHINSON *Treat. Limnol.* I. xv. 829 One of these isotopes, mesothorium 1, has a half life.. long enough for it to undergo some geochemical migration with radium, independently of the parent element thorium. **1967** H. HELLMAN *Controlled Guidance Syst.* vi. 158 The 'parent' aircraft can carry a larger transmitter and transmitting antenna than the missile can. **1971** I. G. GASS et al. *Understanding Earth* viii. 121/1 The abundance of the common chondrites indicates that most of the parent bodies must have had similar compositions. **1978** *Jrnl. R. Soc. Arts* CXXVI. 686/1 In many cases the mechanical properties of EB welds remain unchanged from those of the parent metal.

b. Other combinations. (*a*) attrib. (*b*) instrumental, as *parent-blest* adj.; also *parent-like* adj. (adv.); **c. parent-cell** (*Biol.*), a cell from which other cells are derived; a cytula; **parent-child**, used *attrib.* of or pertaining to both a parent and a child, esp. in phr. *parent-child relationship*; **parent company**, a company of which other companies are subsidiaries; **parent figure**, one who is regarded as having some of the characteristics of a parent; **parent-kernel**, the nucleus of the fertilized egg-cell; a cytococcus; **parent language**, a language from which certain other languages are derived; **parents' day**, a day on which parents visit their children's school; **parent ship**, a ship which protects smaller vessels or which acts as a base for ships or aircraft; **parents' meeting**, a meeting of parents with their children's teachers at a school; **parent-teacher**, used *attrib.* of or pertaining to parents and the teachers of their children, chiefly in phr. **parent-teacher association**, a local organization of parents and teachers established to promote closer relations and improve educational facilities; *abbrev. P.T.A.* s.v. P II.

1880 G. MEREDITH *Trag. Com.* (1881) 150 He was bent on winning a *parent-blest bride. **1810** LEE *Odes of Pindar* (1810) 486 Forth from thy *parent-bosom swarm'd Thy Dorian sons, to lead the way. **1842** S. LOVER *Handy Andy* iii. 36 He earthed himself under his mother's bed in the *parent cabin. **1879** tr. *Haeckel's Evol. Man* I. 176, I therefore assign a peculiar name to the new cell, from which the child really proceeds.. usually inaptly called 'the fertilized egg-cell'.. I shall call it the *parent-cell (*cytula*), and its kernel (*nucleus*) the *parent-kernel (*cytococcus*). **1928** in *Smith Coll. Stud. Social Work* (1931) I. 411 (*title*) A study of *parent-child dependency. **1939** AUDEN in *I Believe* (1940) 26 The family is based on inequality, the parent-child relationship. **1942** H. NICOLSON *Diary* 28 Aug. (1967) 239 Will that child not come to.. lose that atmosphere of sacrifice-gratitude which is the best parent-child relationship? **1965** M. MORSE *Unattached* i. 70 Strained parent-child relationships were characteristic of the unattached in all areas. **1972** *Guardian* 11 Aug. 9/6 The idea is.. for parent-child involvement in getting the maximum from the material. **1869** *Bradshaw's Railway Manual* XXI. 5 They would soon be enabled to declare a dividend equal to that of the *parent company. **1943** J. D. DAWSON *Tunisian Battle* i. 21 Six Simcas, small cars similar to Fiats but manufactured in France for the parent Italian company. **1970** T. LUPTON *Managem. & Social Sci.* (ed. 2) ii. 47 The American parent company.. had taken steps to reduce labour costs. **1976** *Times* 1 Mar. 12/4 The British Government did not bind the American parent company [of Chrysler] to continue its operations in Britain for any specific period. **1960** I. BENNETT *Delinquent & Neurotic Children* i. 11 The same process that occurs in the rearing of every child, i.e. that of identifying with the *parent-figure and incorporating his ideals. **1976** S. HYNES *Auden Generation* ii. 51 In the war, young men.. were faced with a real challenge which was yet like a school game: highly competitive.. and earning.. the approval of parent-figures. *a* **1835** MRS. HEMANS *Return Poems* (1875) 453 The holy prayer Of the child in his *parent-halls. **1905** O. JESPERSEN *Growth & Struct. Eng. Lang.* ii. 19 The Arian language.. was in course of time differentiated into all these languages, or as the same fact is generally expressed in a metaphor of dubious value, was the *parent-language from which all these languages have descended. **1933** L. BLOOMFIELD *Language* xviii. 298 In the case of the Romance languages, we have written records of this parent language, namely, Latin. **1965** H. A. GLEASON *Linguistics & Eng. Gram.* 33 This reconstructed parent language is now generally called Proto-Indo-European,.. abbreviated PIE. **1971** D. CRYSTAL *Linguistics* 154 This parent language (*Ursprache*) was probably more inflected than any of the attested languages. **1608** DOD & CLEAVER *Expos. Prov.* xi–xii. 75 Marueilous is the efficacy of a *parentlike blessing. **1735** THOMSON *Liberty* I. 371 He my great Work Will Parent-like sustain. **1973** *Times* 31 Oct. 10/4 This was certainly *parents' day with a difference. Small groups were escorted round the buildings and shown classrooms stacked with books on Marxism, on Russian geography and on Cuba. **1973** *Listener* 15 Nov. 675/3 Parents' Day at their son's prep school. **1976** C. STORR *Unnatural Fathers* v. 60 She and Martin.. always appeared together at the parents' days at their children's schools. **1933** *Jane's Fighting Ships* 148/3 Beskytteren... Cruising speed is 9 kts... Serves as *parent ship for aircraft. **1961** F. H. BURGESS *Dict. Sailing* 157 *Parent ship*, a mother ship to several smaller ones. **1972** *Guardian* 17 Oct. 19/8 The parents who never come to a *parents' meeting or try.. to help or influence their children's school. **1973** 'J. Patrick' *Glasgow Gang Observed* viii. 79 He simulated the voice of a form teacher at a parents' meeting. **1899** E. PHILLPOTTS *Human Boy* 197 With fathers or women he [the master] had an expression known as the '*parent-smile'. **1915** (*title*) *Parent-teacher associations in the rural and village schools of Oregon. **1916** *Ann. Amer. Acad. Pol. & Social Sci.* LXVII. 139 The Congress [of Mothers and Parent-Teacher Associations] assumed the task of organizing Parent-Teacher Associations in every school. **1951** M. MCLUHAN *Mech. Bride* (1967) 126/2 There is in the parent-teacher relationship a basic violation of the idea of equality. **1957** *Times* 16 Sept. 11/5 The National Federation of Parent-Teacher Associations, formed last year, seeks to promote closer relations between parents and teachers mainly by practical means. **1968** *Daily Tel.* 12 Nov. 21 (*heading*) Parent-teacher link guide for schools. **1973** *Times* 10 Apr. 3/2 In an ideal world all schools would have parent-teacher associations.

†**parent**, *a.*[1] *Obs.* Also 5 -ant, -aunt, 7 -and. [Either a. OF. *parant* apparent, visible, pr. pple. of *paroir*:—L. *pārēre* to appear, or aphetic form of *aparant*, APPARENT.] = APPARENT *a.* 4: in *parent heir*, *heir parent*.

1490 CAXTON *Eneydos* xxix. 112 The mooste parent heyre of the lynage. **1494** FABYAN *Chron.* VII. ccxxxiii. 268 The sayd Henry shulde be proclaymed.. for heyre parant. *Ibid.* 533 By auctoryte of the same parliament syr Roger Mortymer, erle of the Marche.. was soone after proclaymyd heyer paraunt vnto yᵉ crowne of Englonde. [*a* **1677** *Lovers Quarrel* IV. in Child *Ballads* IV. cix. B. (1886) 447/1 My heir and parand thou shalt be.]

†'**parent**, *a.*[2] *Obs. rare*⁻⁰. [ad. L. *pārēns*, *pārēnt-em* obedient, pr. pple. of *pārēre* to obey.]

1656 BLOUNT *Glossogr.*, *Parent*, obedient, dutiful, serviceable.

parent ('pɛərənt), *v.* [f. PARENT *sb.*: cf. OF. *parenter* (14–15th c. in Godef.) in same senses.] **1.** *trans.* **a.** To be the parent of, beget, produce. **b.** To be or act as a parent to; to 'father' or 'mother'. Hence '**parented** *ppl. a.* (cf. PARENTED *a.*).

1663 SIR G. MACKENZIE *Relig. Stoic* ii. (1685) 23 Churlishness and Close-handedness parented by Avarice. **1884** W. F. CRAFTS *Sabb. for Man* (1894) 192 Even a republican government is compelled to parent such of its people as are not capable of self-government. **1904** BELLOC *Avril* I. 4 Literary.. epochs.. are.. definitely parented. We know their special stuff and harmony. We can show.. the parts meeting and blending. **1954** E. H. W. MEYERSTEIN *Verse Lett. to Five Friends* 2 One so quick, so parented, as you Needed but *time*, to feed her fancies new. **1957** *Times* 7 May 6/5 It is almost heaven-sent that the Suez Canal Company, with its position and its money, should be wanting to parent the idea [of a Channel tunnel]. **1975** *Listener* 13 Mar. 340/3 Over 75 couples.. have already been approved as adoptive or foster-parents... Many.. are most suitable candidates to parent the child in question.

2. *intr.* To be a parent. Hence '**parenting** *vbl. sb.*; also *attrib.*

1959 *Britannica Bk. of Year* 547/1 *Parenting*, the supervision by parents of their children. **1970** F. DODSON (*title*) How to parent. **1970** L. B. AMES in *Ibid.* p. xi, New parents have a great deal to learn from those already experienced in what Dr. Fitzhugh Dodson calls the art of parenting. **1972** *Times* 30 Oct. 8/3 The single-minded, unconditional desire.. to provide a loving, caring home, which is the hallmark of good parenting. **1973** A. E. WILKERSON *Rights of Children* 305 While making available to parents the range of resources necessary for effective parenting, we need to be more explicit about the social expectations of parents. *Ibid.* 308 The price of waiting indeterminably for parents who cannot or will not develop acceptable parenting requirements is paid by the child. **1975** *N.Y. Times* 16 Sept. 84 Because of all the changes in American society, we are losing our intuitive ability to parent. **1976** *Guardian* 16 Aug. 9/3 Energy gone, parenting is handed over to the parent-substitute, the teak box in the corner.

parentage ('pɛərəntɪdʒ). [a. F. *parentage* (12th c. in Littré), f. *parent* PARENT + -AGE.]

1. Exercise of the functions of a parent; parental conduct or treatment. *rare.*

c **1489** CAXTON *Sonnes of Aymon* iv. 123 Our fader.. sholde have slayne vs, if it hadde not be our lorde that kepte vs therfro.. Sore harde parentage dyd he shewe to vs, our naturell fader. **1623** WODROEPHE *Marrow Fr. Tongue* 478/2 Good Amitie is a second Parentage. **1867** LEWES *Hist. Philos.* (ed. 3) I. 269 Plato ordains community of wives, and interdicts parentage.

†**2.** Parents collectively. *Obs. rare.*

1513 BRADSHAW *St. Werburge* I. 1851 This blessed Audry from her yonge aege Was.. Obedyent lowly vnto her parentage. **1590** SPENSER *F.Q.* II. x. 27 He.. Inquyrd, which of them most did love her parentage?

3. Derivation or descent from parents, esp. in reference to the particular parent or parents; 'birth', lineage.

1565 COOPER *Thesaurus*, *Parentela*.. Parentage: auncestrie. **1593** SHAKS. *2 Hen. VI*, IV. ii. 152 The elder [child],.. ignorant of his birth and parentage, Became a Bricklayer, when he came to age. **1664** POWER *Exp. Philos.* Pref. 18 That doubly Honourable (both for his parts and parentage) Mr. Boyle. **1765** BLACKSTONE *Comm.* I. ix. 363 Settlements by parentage.. all legitimate children being really settled in the parish where their parents are settled. **1870** FREEMAN *Norm. Conq.* (ed. 2) I. App. 714 The alleged parentage of her son Harold was generally doubted.

b. *fig.* Derivation from an author or source, origin.

1581 MULCASTER *Positions* v. (1887) 35 This worde, γραμματικη, with.. γραφικη, both the two of one parentage and petigree. **1641** WILKINS *Math. Magick* I. ii. (1648) 9 We shall find it to spring from honourable parentage. **1833** L. RITCHIE *Wand. by Loire* 153 The superstition.. is of very ancient and respectable parentage. **1882** FARRAR *Early Chr.* II. 436 Sin.. shows by ethical likeness its Satanic parentage.

4. *spec.* Derivation or descent from parents in relation to inherited rank or character; hereditary degree or quality; 'family', 'birth'. Usually with qualifying adj.; in quot. 1608 *absol.* good birth, high rank.

1490 CAXTON *Eneydos* xi. 41 They whiche ben borne of basse parentage. *a* **1548** HALL *Chron.*, *Hen. VII* 38 Cicile Duches of Yorke.. a woman of small stature, but of muche honour and high parentage. **1568** GRAFTON *Chron.* II. 649 Heyres of great parentage in the South part. **1600** SHAKS. *A.Y.L.* III. iv. 39 He askt me of what parentage I was; I told him of as good as he. **1608** DOD & CLEAVER *Expos. Prov.* xi–xii. 49 Poore women which neither haue parentage, nor beauty, nor riche apparel to set them forth. **1754** SHERLOCK *Disc.* (1759) I. iii. 95 They upbraided him with the Meanness of his Parentage. **1838** LYTTON *Alice* I. xi, Born of humble parentage.

†**5.** Relationship, kinship; *concr.* relations collectively, kindred. *Obs.*

1548 LD. SOMERSET *Epist. Scots* A iv b, By mariage.. one bloude, one lignage and parentage, is made of twoo. **1587** FLEMING *Contn. Holinshed* III. 1001/1 By equalitie and loue, which is by parentage and mariage. **1657** EARL MONM. tr. *Paruta's Pol. Disc.* 56 If Cato had not despised the Parentage offered him by Pompey. **1693** TATE in *Dryden's Juvenal* xv. Notes (1697) 382 The Souldier is also priviledg'd to make a Will, and to give away his Estate, which he got in War.. without consideration of Parentage, or Relations. **1768** BOSWELL *Corsica* ii. (ed. 2) 93 Signor Luiggi Giafferi.. who had a numerous parentage.

6. The condition or status of a parent; parenthood. Also *fig.*

1876 GLADSTONE *Homeric Synchr.* 165 This supposes that Tyre, since it had reached the age of political parentage, must have come into possession of considerable power some time before. **1877** MRS. PHELPS *Story of Avis* xv. 275 Romances, in which parentage is represented as a blindly deifying privilege, which it were an irreverence to associate with teething.. or an insufficient income. **1887** BLACKMORE *Springhaven* III. 54 Another race.. with doubts whether marriage could make parentage between them.

7. = PARAGE 4.

1727–41 CHAMBERS *Cycl.* s.v. *Parage*, This Parage being an equality of duty, or service among brothers and sisters, some have called it *Fratriage* and *Parentage*.

parental (pə'rɛntəl), *a.* [ad. L. *parentāl-is*: see PARENT and -AL[1]. Cf. obs. F. *parental* (16th c. in Godef.).]

1. Of or pertaining to a parent; characteristic of or resembling a parent; fatherly or motherly.

1623 COCKERAM, *Parentall*, of or belonging to the parents. **1646** SIR T. BROWNE *Pseud. Ep.* 143 It overthrows the carefull course, and parentall provision of nature. **1798** MALTHUS *Popul.* (1806) II. IV. vii. 399 One of the most delightful passions in human nature—parental affection. **1826** DISRAELI *Viv. Grey* IV. vi, The finger pressed on the parental lip warned him to silence. **1856** FROUDE *Hist. Eng.* (1858) II. vii. 159 The early English held almost Roman notions on the nature of parental authority.

2. Of the nature of a parent; *fig.* that is the source or origin from which something springs.

1647 WARD *Simp. Cobler* 15 If I can but finde the parentall root, or formall reason of a Truth, I am quiet. **1727–46** THOMSON *Summer* 577 To Parental Nature pay The tears of grateful joy. **1813** W. TAYLOR in *Monthly Rev.* LXXI. 477 The first appendix.. attempts to shew that it [Sanscrit] is parental to the Low-Dutch and other Gothic Dialects of Europe. **1877** OWEN *Mrq. Wellesley's Desp.* p. xxiii, The principal, and (so to speak) parental agent in that scheme. **1904** H. BRIERLEY in *Chr. World* 11 Feb. 22/5 When the nesting season is over, the parental robins retire to the thickest woods and copses.

Hence **parentality** (pærən'tælɪtɪ), the state or condition of being a parent, parenthood; **pa'rentally** *adv.*, in the manner of a parent.

1780 BENTHAM *Princ. Legisl.* xvi. §50 It involves in it divestment of parentality; to wit, of paternity, or of maternity, or of both. **1801** W. TAYLOR in *Monthly Mag.* XII. 578 He absolves debauchery from the cares of parentality. **1791** BURKE *App. Whigs* Wks. VI. 197 Whatever rights the king enjoys as elector, have been always parentally exercised. **1837** SIR F. B. HEAD 19 Dec. in *Narrative* ix. (1839) 319, I parentally called upon them [the Canadian rebel leaders], as their Governor, to avoid the effusion of human blood.

‖**parentalia** (pærən'teɪlɪə). *pl.* [L. *parentālia* lit. parental things or rites.] Among the ancient Romans, Periodical observances in honour of dead parents or relations; also *transf.* as title of a work (so L. in Ausonius).

1706 in PHILLIPS. **1750** WREN (*title*) Parentalia, or Memoirs of the Family of the Wrens. **1801** SHAW in *Southey's Thalaba* VIII. *note*, For.. two or three months after any person is interred, the female relations go once a week to weep over the grave, and perform their parentalia upon it.

parentalism (pə'rɛntəlɪz(ə)m). [f. PARENTAL *a.* + -ISM.] The character or quality of a parent.

1878 W. L. BLACKLEY in *19th Cent.* Nov. 838 What some folk sneer at under the name of 'parentalism'. **1923** *Daily Mail* 4 Oct. 7/2 The parentalism of our laws, with their mixture of foolish prohibitions and foolish laxities.

†**pa'rentate**, *v. Obs.* [f. L. *parentāt-*, ppl. stem of *parentāre*, f. *parent-em* PARENT: see -ATE[3]. Cf. F. *parenter* in same sense.] *intr.* To celebrate the funeral rites of parents or relations; hence in general sense, to offer funeral obsequies.

1620 BARRET *Ded. Southwell's Poems* (Turnbull) 246 Not to perish unrevenged, they parentated to themselves, with the blood of the Senate. **1623** COCKERAM, *Parentate*, to celebrate ones parents funerals. **1654** R. CODRINGTON tr. *Iustine* XI. 159 He did parentate to the Tombs of those who fell in the Trojan war. *Ibid.* XXXIX. 470 By her death [he] did parentate to the Ghosts of his wife.

parentation (pɛərənt-, pærən'teɪʃən). ?*Obs.* [ad. L. *parentātiōn-em*, n. of action from *parentāre*: see prec. So F. *parentation* (16th c.).] The performance of the funeral rites of parents or relatives; hence, any memorial service for the dead.

1627 MAY *Lucan* IV. 867 Let Fortune this new parentation make For hated Carthages dire spirits sake. **1772** NUGENT tr. *Hist. Fr. Gerund* II. 265 An happy voyage over the procellous ocean of your funeral parentation. **1807** ROBINSON *Archæol. Græca* I. xxxiv. 124 Children and heirs were to perform the accustomed rites of parentation.

parentcraft ('pɛərəntkrɑːft, -æ-). Also with hyphen. [f. PARENT *sb.* + CRAFT *sb.*] The 'craft' or business of a parent; knowledge of, and skill in, the rearing of children.

1930 *Lancet* 22 Mar. 672/1 (*heading*) The teaching of parentcraft. **1945** *Times* 10 Mar. 8/2 The Ministry were discussing various schemes regarding children under two, and they had lately set up a committee to go into the question of parentcraft. **1958** *Times* 7 July (National Health Service Suppl.) p. xii/1 It [*sc.* maternity care] should also include guidance in parent-craft and in problems associated with infertility and family planning. **1973** *Guardian* 3 Apr. 18/2 A school can teach good parentcraft, both explicitly and implicitly. **1976** *Oxford Times* 10 Dec. 17/1 This state of affairs has certainly been fostered by the voluntary parentcraft classes organised by doctors, midwives and health visitors.

'parentdom, *nonce-wd.* [f. PARENT *sb.* + -DOM.] The realm, domain, or body of parents.

1840 *New Monthly Mag.* LIX. 168 All parentdom is up in arms against it.

'parented, *a. rare.* [f. as prec. + -ED².] Having parents.

1902 *Daily Chron.* 30 Oct. 5/1 The best parented children have to suffer exile at times. **1974** *Times Lit. Suppl.* 11 Oct. 1109/1 The orphan..tearfully watching his parented friends go off to camp.

parentela (pærən'tiːlə). *Biol.* [a. L. *parentēla* relationship, f. *parent-*, stem of *parens* parent.] The set of all descendants of a particular pair of individuals.

1927 J. F. VAN BEMMELEN in *Proc. Sect. Sci. Kon. Akad. Wetensch. Amsterdam* XXX. 772 The pedigree itself forms a so-called Parentela, which means a survey of all the descendants of a certain pair. **1932** *Proc. 6th Internat. Congr. Genetics* II. 7 The Table of Descendants is better called the parentela. There are two kinds: the definite or closed parentela and the indefinite or open parentela. Only the latter is important for research in heredity. **1946** R. R. GATES *Human Genetics* II. xxix. 1320 The members of this parentela were also small as children.

†**paren'tele.** *Obs.* [a. F. *parentèle* (15th c. in Hatz.-Darm.), ad. L. *parentēla* relationship.]

1. Kinship, relationship; kindred.

c **1385** CHAUCER *Pars. T.* ¶834 Certes parentele is in two maneres outher goostly or flesshly. **1422** tr. *Secreta Secret., Priv. Priv.* 163 Honestly hym he Prayed..wyth his grete Perentele awhyle hym dysporte. **1541** *St. Papers Hen. VIII*, III. 346 The Juges..inclyned to parcialitie and unlaufull favor unto their parentile and affynytie.

2. = PARENTAGE 3, 4.

1491 CAXTON *Vitas Patr.* (W. de W. 1495) I. xl. 54b/2 They ben comen of grete parentele and lygnage in worldly honour. *c* **1530** L. COX *Rhet.* (1899) 57 He hath spoken of his parentele and bryngynge vp in youth. *a* **1734** NORTH *Exam.* I. iii. §156 (1740) 223 Not so many..as there were Cities strove for the Parentele of Homer.

parentelic (pærən'tɛlɪk), *a.* [f. as PARENTELA + -IC.] Of or pertaining to relationship based on common ancestry.

1895 POLLOCK & MAITLAND *Hist. Eng. Law* II. 294 In a parentelic scheme my great-nephew, since he springs from my father, is nearer to me than my first cousin. **1957** *Jrnl. R. Anthrop. Inst.* Jan. 40 The other entrenched law, åsetasrett, shows the same emphasis but it operates in close conjunction with the law of inheritance which is based on quite different principles, namely the equality of spouses, bilateral affiliation, and equality of siblings. A full discussion of this law and of the parentelic system that it employs is out of place here.

parenteral (pə'rɛntərəl), *a. Med.* [f. PARA-¹ + Gr. ἔντερ-ον intestine + -AL.] Involving the introduction of a substance into the body other than by the alimentary tract. Also as *sb.*, a preparation for parenteral administration. Hence **pa'renterally** *adv.*

1910 *Lippincott's New Med. Dict.* 692/1 *Parenteral, -ly*, not by way of the digestive tract. **1912** A. E. TAYLOR *Digestion & Metabolism* viii. 467 The secretions of the intestine and of the pancreas are toxic on parenteral introduction. **1916** A. J. SMITH tr. *O. von Fürth's Probl. Physiol. & Path. Chem. of Metabolism* ii. 48 The toxic effect of the parenterally introduced trypsin. **1949** E. P. ABRAHAM et al. in H. W. Florey et al. *Antibiotics* II. xv. 639 Such a test could scarcely be expected to give an accurate forecast of the effect of a drug administered by mouth or parenterally for the treatment of a generalized infection. **1957** *Obstetr. & Gynecol.* X. 261/2 Esterification of the different steroid preparations resulted in longer-acting, oil-soluble, nonirritating parenterals being made available for clinical use. **1971** *Nature* 12 Nov. 101/2 Excitatory effects of amphetamine administered parenterally in other regions of the brain. **1974** R. M. KIRK et al. *Surgery* iii. 38 When it cannot be given into the gut, it must be administered parenterally. **1974** PASSMORE & ROBSON *Compan. Med. Stud.* III. II. l. 11/1 In experienced hands, complete parenteral nutrition is a safe if time-consuming form of therapy.

parenter'linarie, -lignarie: see PAR *prep.* 1 g.

†**pa'renthese,** *v. Obs. rare.* [f. PARENTHES-IS or its F. form *parenthèse.*] *trans.* To intersperse as with parentheses.

1635 J. HAYWARD tr. *Biondi's Banish'd Virg.* 226 A faint voyce, whose..lamentations were often parenthesed with sighes and teares. *Ibid.* 228 Shee (parenthesing her words with greedy kisses) thus bespake him.

parenthesis (pə'rɛnθɪsɪs). Pl. **-theses** (-siːz). [a. med.L., a. Gr. παρένθεσις, f. παρεντιθέναι to put in beside, f. παρ(α- beside + ἐν in + τιθέναι to place, θέσις placing. Cf. F. *parenthèse* (15th c.), It. *parentesi.*]

1. a. An explanatory or qualifying word, clause, or sentence inserted into a passage with which it has not necessarily any grammatical connexion, and from which it is usually marked off by round or square brackets, dashes, or commas.

1568 GRAFTON *Chron.* II. 811 The Duke somwhat marueylyng at his sodaine pauses, as thoughe they were but Parenthesis, with a high countenaunce sayde. **1586** A. DAY *Eng. Secretary* II. (1625) 83 *Parenthesis*, an intercluding of a sentence..commonly set betweene two halfe circles, as thus, I am content (not in respect you deserue so much at my hands) onely for pittie sake to hearken vnto you. **1631** R. BYFIELD *Doctr. Sabb.* 218 Note M. Breerwoods Parenthesies. **1659** in *Burton's Diary* (1828) IV. 283 You see the inconveniency of a long parenthesis; we have forgot the sense that went before. **1762** STERNE *Tr. Shandy* V. xvi, The phenomenon had not been worth a parenthesis. **1880** MUIRHEAD *Gaius* Introd. 12 What is illegible.., but.. obvious from the context.., is in italics, within marks of parenthesis ( ).

†**b.** A passage introduced into a context with which it has no connexion; a digression. *Obs.*

1600 HEYWOOD *1st Pt. Edw. IV* Wks. 1874 I. 29 Away with this parenthesis of words. **1654** GATAKER *Disc. Apol.* 4 But let this go for a Parenthesis; return we to our task. **1757** H. WALPOLE *Lett. H. Mann* 5 May (1846) III. 288, I thought you would prefer this parenthesis of politics.

c. As a grammatical or rhetorical figure.

1589 PUTTENHAM *Eng. Poesie* III. xii[i.] (Arb.) 180 Your first figure of tollerable disorder is (Parenthesis) or by an English name the (Insertour). **1836** H. ROGERS *J. Howe* xi. (1863) 333 He is..full of involution, parenthesis, and awkward transposition. **1902** *Daily Chron.* 5 May 4/3 That essential quality of the amusing storyteller, the art of parenthesis, the dropping in of the appropriate and unexpected word, the swift and illuminating phrase.

2. *transf.* An interval; an interlude; a hiatus.

1599 B. JONSON *Ev. Man out of Hum.* III. iii, I ne're knew tabacco taken as a parenthesis, before. **1628** EARLE *Microcosm., Antiquary* (Arb.) 29 A Manuscript he pores on euer-lastingly, especially if the couer be all Moth-eaten, and the dust make a Parenthesis betweene euery Syllable. **1654** R. CODRINGTON tr. *Iustine* III. 62 In the Parenthesis of time whiles the Infant grew up, he..made Laws for the Spartans. **1796** BURNEY *Mem. Metastasio* II. 162 Rural amusements usually serve as a parenthesis to music. **1899** STOPF. BROOKE *Eng. Lit.* 152 During that parenthesis of bad government and national tumult which filled the years between the death of Aldfrith..and the renewed peace and order under Ceolwulf.

3. a. The upright curves ( ) collectively, used to include words inserted parenthetically; now usually in pl. *parentheses*; 'round brackets'.

Also extended to the 'square brackets' or crotchets [ ].

1715 in Somers *Tracts* II. 436 Our old Bibles..had these Words..in small Letters, and sometimes in a Parenthesis. **1771** LUCKOMBE *Hist. Printing* 274 The Parenthesis serves to inclose such parts of a Period as make no part of the subject. **1823** H. J. BROOKE *Introd. Crystallogr.* 238 This symbol is placed in a parenthesis to distinguish it from a combination of three simple or mixed decrements. **1824** [see PARENTHETIC 1]. **1831** CARLYLE *Sart. Res.* I. iv, Sentences.. in quite angular attitudes, buttressed-up by props (of parentheses and dashes). *Mod.* The words in parentheses.

b. *transf.* A pair of curved lines or figures resembling 'round brackets'.

1608 DAY *Law-Trickes* III. Ej, Doost see Vulcan with the horning parenthesis in his fore-head! **1820** LAMB *Elia* Ser. I. *Christ's Hosp.* 35 *Yrs. ago*, Weaving those ingenious parentheses called cat-cradles.

c. *Logic.* Such curved lines (brackets) or other symbols used in the notation of formal logic to punctuate a proposition or to indicate that the expression they contain forms a unit within the whole proposition; also *attrib.* and *comb.* as **parenthesis-free** *a.*, a term referring to notation, esp. that of Łukasiewicz, which eliminates the need for such symbols.

1918 C. I. LEWIS *Survey Symbolic Logic* iv. 233 For any function of one variable we here omit any parenthesis around the variable. **1940** W. V. QUINE *Math. Logic* i. 40 The parenthesis notation formulated at the beginning of the section is retained. **1954** I. M. COPI *Symbolic Logic* viii. 253 (*heading*) A parenthesis-free notation. **1959** O. BIRD tr. *Bocheński's Precis of Math. Logic* v. 82 In this it is better to use the Peano-Russell notation with parentheses, since its similarities to algebra facilitate the 'multiplication'. **1963** O. WOJTASIEWICZ tr. *Łukasiewicz's Elem. Math. Logic* p. ix, I enumerate here the more important new results whose authorship, I think, I may ascribe to myself. They are as follows: 1. The parenthesis-free notation of expressions in the sentential calculus and in Aristotle's syllogistic. **1965** DICKOFF & JAMES *Symbolic Logic* Pref., The parenthesis-free Lukasiewicz notation was especially convenient. **1976** H. LEBLANC *Truth-Value Semantics* i. 11 When no ambiguity threatens, we shall omit the outer parentheses of conditionals, conjunctives..and biconditionals.

parenthesist (pə'rɛnθɪsɪst). [f. PARENTHESIZE: see -IST.] One who introduces a parenthesis.

1901 *Q. Pioneer* Dec. 27 His poverty is here put to silence ..by this parenthesis—('but thou art rich')... No doubt, the parenthesist had in his eye Polycarp's riches towards God exclusively.

parenthesize (pə'rɛnθɪsaɪz), *v.* [f. PARENTHES-IS + IZE: cf. *emphas-ize.*]

1. a. *trans.* To insert as a parenthesis; to express or state in parenthesis. (Usually with obj. clause.)

1837 SOUTHEY *Doctor* cxix. IV. 181 Sir Kenelm Digby observes..that 'it is a common speech (but', he parenthesizes, 'only amongst the unlearned sort) *ubi tres medici duo athei*'. **1854** LOWELL *Jrnl. in Italy* Pr. Wks. 1890 I. 167 Speaking of Italian quarrels, I am tempted to parenthesize here another which I saw at Civita Vecchia. **1940** W. V. QUINE *Math. Logic* i. 39 It may be bounded at its other end by the limit of that parenthesized expression. **1971** *Amer. Jrnl. Physics* XXXIX. 501/1 The first parenthesized term in the final member of [equation] (29). **1973** A. H. SOMMERSTEIN *Sound Pattern Anc. Greek* i. 6 A schema with parentheses abbreviates a sequence of rules with and without the parenthesized elements, the longest first.

b. *intr.* To introduce a parenthesis, to say something in parenthesis.

1880 BRIGHT *Sp. at B'ham* 19 Mar., I was going to observe —but your friendly interruptions forced me to parenthesise.

2. *trans.* To insert a parenthesis in; to interlard or intersperse with parentheses.

1889 *Lancet* 22 June 1277/1 The amount of constant practice that is required to take a verbatim report of a complicated and much parenthesised speech.

3. To put between marks of parenthesis; to bracket.

1866 *Contemp. Rev.* III. 470 If our parenthesized question admit of a negative answer. **1866** *Sat. Rev.* XXI. 26 Each word or member of a phrase, with its explanation appended in parenthesized clauses.

4. To curve into the shape ( ). *humorous.*

1879 *Scribner's Mag.* XIX. 771/1 Legs somewhat parenthesized by usage to the saddle.

Hence **parenthesized** *ppl. a.*

1866, etc. [see senses 1 a, 2, 3 above].

parenthetic (pærən'θɛtɪk), *a.* [ad. med.L. *parenthetic-us*, a. Gr. *παρενθετικ-ός, f. παρένθετος 'put in beside', f. παρεντιθέναι: see PARENTHESIS.]

1. Of, pertaining to, or of the nature of a parenthesis; inserted as a parenthesis.

1776 G. HORNE *Comm. Ps.* lxxiii. 11, I would rather suppose the foregoing verse (to whomsoever it may belong) to be parenthetic. **1824** L. MURRAY *Eng. Gram.* (ed. 4) I. 410 The parenthesis itself does not supply the place of a point between the parenthetic clause, and the words immediately preceding it. **1883** J. PARKER *Apost. Life* II. 6 They speak of him with many parenthetic qualifications.

b. *fig.* Interposed in the course of something else.

1876 GEO. ELIOT *Dan. Der.* xxxiv, Deronda took in these details by parenthetic glances. **1881** MASSON *De Quincey* 61 About a year..of parenthetic peace and happiness.

2. = next, 2. *rare.*

1782 TYERS *Rhapsody on Pope* 33 Cleland (whom he describes as a man of sense,..and, to be very parenthetic, who was the Will Honeycomb of the Spectator's club).

paren'thetical, *a.* [f. as prec. + -AL¹.]

A. *adj.* **1.** = prec. 1.

1624 T. SCOTT (*title*) Votivæ Angliæ: or the Desires and Wishes of England, in a Parenthetical Discourse. **1638** ROUSE *Heav. Univ.* ix. (1702) 128 The three first verses.. being a Parenthetical Interposition. **1855** H. SPENCER *Princ. Psychol.* (1872) II. VI. vi. 62 Returning from this parenthetical discussion. **1868** E. EDWARDS *Ralegh* I. xxii. 508 It had many times found parenthetical employment in urging upon Salisbury yet one expedition more.

2. Characterized by parenthesis; addicted to or using parenthesis.

1837–9 HALLAM *Hist. Lit.* III. iii. §141 We call it levity, when the mind is easily diverted, and the discourse is parenthetical. **1846** POE *A. S. Stephens* Wks. 1864 III. 62 [Style] involved, needlessly parenthetical. **1859** HELPS *Friends in C.* Ser. II. II. v. 112 Then there is the parenthetical talker.

3. Curved like ( ); bandy. *nonce-use.*

1856 R. F. BURTON *El-Medinah* xxvii. III. 217 An Indian woman, with her semi-Tartar features..and her thin parenthetical legs.

B. as *sb.*

1957 *Publ. Amer. Dial. Soc.* XXVIII. 73 We may divide the segmental tentations according to position into three groups: initials, parentheticals, and finals. **1977** *Canad. Jrnl. Linguistics* 1976 XXI. II. 166 Parentheticals containing 'do'.

parenthetically (pærən'θɛtɪkəlɪ), *adv.* [f. prec. + -LY².] In a parenthetical manner; in a parenthesis; by way of parenthesis or interlude.

1664 H. MORE *Myst. Iniq.* 390 If we referre ὅπου to the great City, and read (which is spiritually called Sodom and Ægypt) Parenthetically. **1803** BRYANT *Observ. Script.* III. 163 The intelligence is certainly mentioned parenthetically. **1859** HAWTHORNE *Marble Faun* xxxii. (1883) 339 Many of whom are parenthetically devout. **1874** H. R. REYNOLDS *John Bapt.* v. §3. 337 The clause..is brought in parenthetically, and is not the main point of the statement.

parenthood ('pɛərənthʊd). [f. PARENT *sb.* + -HOOD.] The state or position of a parent; fatherhood or motherhood.

1856 MISS MULOCK *J. Halifax* xxv, Those on whom the Father of all men has bestowed the holy dignity of parenthood. **1873** H. SPENCER *Stud. Sociol.* xv. (1874) 371 Parenthood produces a mental exaltation not otherwise producible.

parenticide¹ (pə'rɛntɪsaɪd). [f. L. *parent-em* PARENT *sb.* + -CIDE 1.] One who murders his parent.

1656 in BLOUNT *Glossogr.* *a* **1834** COLERIDGE in Cottle *Early Recoll.* (1837) II. 249 Pain, dark Error's uncouth child, Blameless parenticide!

pa'renticide². *rare*⁻⁰. [f. as prec. + -CIDE 2.] The murder of a parent.

1658 PHILLIPS, *Parenticide*, a killing of ones Parents.

parentile, variant of PARENTELE *Obs.*

†**'parentine.** *Obs. rare.* [Derived in some way from PARENT: cf. OF. *parenté* (AF. *parentee*), *parentesse, parentois* parentage.] Parentage.

c **1400** *Beryn* 841 Noriture & connyng, bewte & parentyne. *Ibid.* 3241 3it for his parentyne, to pipe, as doith a mowse, I woll hym tech.

parent-in-law: see PARENT *sb.* 1

parentless (ˈpɛərəntlɪs), *a.* [f. PARENT *sb.* + -LESS.] Without parents; fatherless and motherless; orphaned. Also *fig.* Having no (known or traceable) parents, author, or source.

1561 T. NORTON *Calvin's Inst.* II. xvi. (1634) 245 He will not leave them as parentlesse, but will come againe to them. **1610** *Mirr. Mag., Eng. Eliza* Induct. 778 Thy Orphans left poore parentlesse alone. *c* **1800** H. K. WHITE *Wand. Boy*, I am a parentless wandering boy. **1862** MERIVALE *Rom. Emp.* (1865) VII. lx. 289 Thus it is that the Colosseum, the most conspicuous type of Roman civilization,.. is nameless and parentless.

parentship (ˈpɛərənt-ʃɪp). [f. as prec. + -SHIP.] The office or position of a parent.

1849 *Tait's Mag.* XVI. 510 In the sphere of parentship there are two human providences. **1895** J. KIDD *Moral. & Relig.* viii. 337 The ideas that flow from it are not kingship and citizenship, but parentship and sonship.

pareo, var. PAREU.

pareœan (pæreɪˈiːən), *a.* and *sb.* *Anthrop.* [f. PARA-[1] + Gr. ἑῴ-ος dawn, eastern + -AN.]

A. *adj.* Designating a Southern Mongol people, esp. those found in and near China, perhaps to distinguish them from the older Chinese stock whose myths spoke of themselves as the people of the dawn. **B.** *sb.* A member of this people.

1904 T. W. KINGSMILL in *Jrnl. R. Asiatic Soc.* (North China Branch) XXXV. 95 In the Mantses, and in a less degree in.. the Lolos, the yellow pigment, characteristic of the Pareæan [*sic*] races, is either altogether absent or at most slightly developed. **1909** A. C. HADDON *Races of Man* 18 (*heading*) Indo-Chinese, Pareœans or Southern Mongols. **1929** L. H. D. BUXTON *China* iii. 44 The Chinese belong to the southern or 'Pareoean' branch of that great group of humanity which is usually called 'Yellow Man' or 'Mongolian'. *Ibid.* 45 Pareoean (παρηοῖος), 'from beside the east', is a term originally proposed by T. W. Kingsmill and now definitely adopted by Haddon for the group frequently known as 'southern Mongols'. **1931** C. G. SELIGMAN in W. Rose *Outl. Mod. Knowl.* 443 The Southern Mongols, who in recent literature are tending more and more to be called Pareoean. **1957** *Encycl. Brit.* XVIII. 866/2 In Korea there is a narrow belt which forms a connecting link between the northern and the Pareoean peoples. The latter differ most strikingly from their northern neighbours in having less prominent cheek-bones and a broadish nose.

‖**parepididymis** (pærɛpɪˈdɪdɪmɪs). *Anat.* [mod.L., f. PAR(A-[1] I + EPIDIDYMIS.] The organ of Giraldes, a mass of convoluted tubules just above the epididymis. Hence **parepiˈdidymal** *a.*, pertaining to the parepididymis.

1831 [see PAROOPHORON]. **1888** ROLLESTON & JACKSON *Anim. Life* 355 Remnants of the non-sexual part of the mesonephros may persist (par-epididymis, par-oophoron, of Mammalia). **1890** *Cent. Dict., Parepididymal.*

parepigastric (pærɛpɪˈgæstrɪk), *a.* *Anat.* [f. PAR(A-[1] I + EPIGASTRIC.] Situated or occurring beside or about the epigastrium.

1876 tr. *von Ziemssen's Cycl. Med.* VI. 30 This pulsation is designated in general terms 'epigastric'... But still to avoid confusion with another form.. it is better to designate the first-mentioned as 'parepigastric'.

‖**parepithymia** (pærɛpɪˈθɪmɪə). *Path.* [mod.L., f. PAR(A-[1] I + Gr. ἐπιθυμία desire.] A mental disorder characterized by perverted desires. Hence **parepiˈthymic** *a.*, relating to parepithymia.

1857 MAYNE *Expos. Lex.*, Parepithymia, Parepithymic.

pareplum, obs. form of PEAR-*plum*.

†**paˈrepochism.** *Obs.* [f. PAR(A-[1] I + EPOCH + -ISM: cf. *parachronism.*] An error of date.

1685 H. MORE *Paralip. Prophet.* x. 63 A gross Parepochism committed by Josephus. *Ibid.* xi. 81 And so fairly committed a Parepochism, the taking one Epocha for another.

parer (ˈpɛərə(r)). [f. PARE *v.* + -ER[1].] **a.** An instrument for paring.

1573 TUSSER *Husb.* (1878) 98 A hone and a parer, like sole of a boote, to pare away grasse and to raise vp the roote. **1600** HAKLUYT *Voy.* III. 271 The women with short peckers or parers,.. doe onely breake the vpper part of the ground to raise vp the weeds, grasse, and olde stubbes of corne stalks. **1828** MOIR *Mansie Wauch.* xiii. (1833) 89 A sharp shoemaker's parer. **1883** LOVETT in *Proc. R. Geog. Soc.* 29 Jan. 68 The shoeing-smith.. drawing this parer or gouge over the hoof.

b. A person that pares, in various senses.

1862 MRS. H. WOOD *Mrs. Hallib.* I. xx, There were parers, grounders, leather sorters, dyers, cutters, makers-up, and else. **1887** GISSING *Thyrza* III. iii. 62 The old man must have.. friends about him, and not cold-blooded pinchers and parers.

parer, obs. form of PARURE.

parera (ˈparera). [Maori.] A New Zealand name for the grey duck, *Anas superciliosa*, found in many islands of the South Pacific region.

1835 W. YATE *Acct. N.Z.* (ed. 2) ii. 57 *Parera*, or Wild Duck—These birds exactly resemble the common English wild-duck. They are of a fine flavour. **1855** R. TAYLOR *Te Ika a Maui* xxv. 407 Parera, turuki.. the duck; very similar to the wild duck of England. **1894** C. W. RICHMOND *Let.* 22 Mar. in *Richmond-Atkinson Papers* (1960) II. x. 597 Your Uncle James got a pot-shot at a lot of parera (grey duck) and knocked over *seven.* **1930** W. R. B. OLIVER *N.Z. Birds* 215 Grey Duck. Parera. **1966** R. A. FALLA et al. *Field Guide to Birds N.Z.* 90 Grey Duck *Anas superciliosa*... Maori name: Parera.

parergal (pəˈrɜːgəl), *a.* [f. PARERG-ON + -AL[1].] Of the nature of a parergon; subsidiary, supplementary. So †**parerˈgetic, -ical** [cf. *energetic*] *adjs.*, in same sense.

1827 G. S. FABER *Sacr. Calend. Prophecy* (1844) I. 53 On the morrow of this parergal sabbath, as being the beginning of the barley-harvest, they were directed to bring a sheaf of the first-fruits for a wave-offering. **1643** R. BAILLIE *Lett., to Spang* 2 June (1841–2) II. 72, I take Wednesday, either before or afternoon for some parergetick Diatribes. **1607** WALKINGTON *Opt. Glass* xv. 159 If there be any parergeticall clauses, not suiting true judgement.

†**parerˈgastical**, *a.* *Obs. rare.* [f. PARERGON, after Gr. ἐργαστικ-ός working + -AL[1].] Of the nature of a parergon, done as by-work.

1597 G. HARVEY *Trimming Nashe* Wks. (Grosart) III. 15 But to leaue these parergasticall speeches and to come to your trimming, because I will deale roundly with you.

parergic (pəˈrɜːdʒɪk), *a.* *rare.* [f. as PARERGON + -IC.] Pertaining to by-work.

1900 G. W. E. RUSSELL *Conferences* Ded. 27 Tame spirits of a parergic pen.

‖**parergon** (pəˈrɜːgɒn). Pl. **parerga** (in 7 *erron.* **parergas**). [L. *parergon* an extra ornament in art, a. Gr. πάρεργον by-work, subordinate or secondary business, etc., sb. use of neuter of πάρεργος beside or in addition to the main work, f. παρά beside + ἔργον work.]

1. In Painting: Something subordinate or accessory to the main subject; hence, generally and *fig.*, ornamental accessory or addition, grace, embellishment. ? *Obs.*

1601 HOLLAND *Pliny* II. 542 He painted among those by-works (which painters call *Parerga*) certaine small gallies and little long barks, to show therby the small beginnings of his art. **1612** PEACHAM *Graphice* 45 For your *Parergas* or needlesse graces, you may set forth the same with Farm-houses, Water-mills, Pilgrims travelling, &c. **1656** BLOUNT *Glossogr.* s.v. *Landskip*, All that which in Picture is not of the body or argument thereof is Landskip, Parergon, or by-work. **1658** PHILLIPS s.v. *Lantskip*, The persons are called the Argument, the Landskip the Parergon or By-work. **1724** R. WODROW *Life J. Wodrow* (1828) 68 These were the proper parerga to and the gentlemanly learning of a minister.

2. By-work, subordinate or secondary work or business; work apart from one's main business or ordinary employment. Also a work, composition, etc., that is secondary to or a derivative of a larger or greater work; an opusculum.

c **1618** E. BOLTON *Hypercrit.* IV. iv, For that the Subject.. is rather *Parergon*, then the thing it self I write of. **1673** O. WALKER *Educ.* xiv. 197, I advise to, but onely as a parergon, not an employment. **1897** *Athenæum* 9 Jan. 51/3 [He] pursued astronomy as a parergon (to use his own favourite phrase). **1928** W. M. WHEELER *Foibles of Insects & Men* p. vii, For some time friends have been urging me to republish in book form some of my papers which have appeared in various scientific journals. The continued demand for these parerga.. suggests that they may, perhaps, be of interest to readers who do not habitually consult scientific journals. **1957** H. NICOLSON *Let.* 2 Oct. (1968) 339, I don't think that you [*sc.* Vita Sackville-West] will really go down to posterity as a writer of gardening articles. You will be remembered as a poet... So your gardening things will be regarded as a mere *parergon* ('a bye-work'), like the flute-playing of Frederick the Great. **1963** *Times* 15 Feb. 6/6 At the end of the programme he and his orchestra played the suite of Symphonic Dances from *West Side Story*, a parergon of the musical show, and a very distinguished one. **1975** A. MIMS tr. N. Kazantzakis *Let.* in *Nikos Kazantzakis* IV. 526, I think that my whole soul.. is crystallized in the *Odyssey*. All the other works are parergons. **1975** *Times Lit. Suppl.* 16 May 531/2 Henry Bradley's *The Making of English*.. is what it is only because it arose as an inspired parergon to its author's main work as co-editor of the great Oxford Dictionary.

†**3.** A supplemental work. (As title of a book.)

1726 AYLIFFE (*title*) Parergon Juris Canonici Anglicani: or, a Commentary by Way of Supplement to the Canons and Constitutions of the Church of England.

†**ˈparergy.** *Obs.* [f. prec. with change of suffix.] A thing beside the purpose in hand.

1646 SIR T. BROWNE *Pseud. Ep.* VII. xvi. 373 The Scriptures being serious, and commonly omitting such Parergies, it will be unreasonable from hence to condemne all laughter. **1650** CHARLETON *Paradoxes* Prol. 12 Whether Roman Vitriol may not be justly referred to the Classis.. must be a parergy here to dispute it. **1656** BLOUNT *Glossogr.*, *Parergy*, *Parergon* or *Parergum*,.. any thing that is besides the principal question, point or purpose in hand.

pares, paresche, pareshe, obs. ff. PARISH.

pareschatology (ˌpærɛskəˈtɒlədʒɪ). *Theol.* [f. Gr. παρέσχατο-ς penultimate + -LOGY.] A term introduced for theories about human life after physical death and before the final resolution.

1976 J. HICK *Death & Eternal Life* i. 22 Whereas eschatology is the doctrine of the *eschata* or last things, and thus of the ultimate state of man, pareschatology is, by analogy, the doctrine of the *para-eschata*, or next-to-last things, and thus of the human future between the present life and man's ultimate state. *Ibid.* iv. 34 The rather rare Greek word *pareschatos* means 'penultimate' or 'next-to-last', and enables us to coin 'pareschatology' as the study of the next-to-last things, on analogy with 'eschatology', the study of the last things. I am grateful to my colleague Michael Goulder for this useful word. **1977** *Theol. Today* XXXIV. 182 His own constructive proposal for a 'pareschatology' is a form of the doctrine of resurrection expanded to include what he calls 'vertical' as opposed to 'horizontal' reincarnation. **1977** *Times Lit. Suppl.* 1 Apr. 390/4 He examines in detail Western and Eastern pareschatologies (ie, pictures of what happens between death and an ultimate state).

paresi: see PARISIS, a French coin.

‖**paresis** (ˈpærɪsɪs). [mod.L., a. Gr. πάρεσις letting go, slackening of strength, paralysis, f. παριέναι to let go, let fall, relax, etc., f. παρα- by + ἱέναι to let go.]

1. *Path.* Partial or incomplete paralysis, paralysis affecting muscular motion but not sensation. ***general paresis***, a term used by some for progressive paralysis of the insane.

1693 tr. *Blancard's Phys. Dict.* (ed 2), *Paresis*, a sort of Palsie. **1790** J. C. SMYTH in *Med. Commun.* II. 491 He had.. been subject to.. paresis or palsy. **1822–34** *Good's Study Med.* (ed. 4) I. 144 The paresis of the olfactory nerves. **1867** FLINT *Princ. & Pract. Med.* 645. **1874** ROOSA *Dis. Ear* 108 The form of insanity was general paresis in eight cases. **1899** *Allbutt's Syst. Med.* VII. 301 There was paresis of the left side of the face, paresis of the arm, and complete paralysis of the hand and foot.

fig. **1896** HOWELLS *Impressions & Exp.* 208 The slowly-creeping desolation, the gradual paresis, that was seizing upon the late full and happy life of our hotel.

2. The 'letting go' or 'dropping' of elements of a word.

1885 *Trans. Amer. Philol. Assoc.* App. p. xxxi, He [the Negro] has simply taken the principle of *paresis*, or word-neglect,—a principle by which *maculate* becomes *mote* (a spot)—and worked it out to its ultimate consequences.

paressh, paresshe, obs. forms of PARISH.

paresthesia, variant of PARÆSTHESIA.

Paretan (pəˈreɪtən, -ˈiːtən), *a.* and *sb.* Also **Paretian** (-ʃən). [f. PARET(O + -AN, -IAN.] **A.** *adj.* Of or pertaining to Pareto or his economic or sociological theories or methods. **B.** *sb.* A follower of Pareto or someone who adheres to his theories or methods. Hence **Paˈretanism.**

1936 WIRTH & SHILS tr. *Mannheim's Ideology & Utopia* v. 279 From Nietzsche the lines of development lead to the Freudian and Paretian theories of original impulses. **1949** R. K. MERTON *Social Theory* viii. 219 Not only ideological analysis.. but also.. Marxism, semanticism, propaganda analysis, Paretanism and.. functional analysis have.. a similar outlook on the role of ideas. **1965** *McGraw-Hill Dict. Mod. Econ.* 369 A situation is not a Paretian or social optimum if it is possible.. to make one person better off without making another person (or persons) worse off. **1969** D. MACRAE in Ionescu & Gellner *Populism* 153 For over a century ideologies have been regarded as epiphenomena by sociologists and political scientists. As such Marxists have 'unmasked' them, Paretans treated them as the verbal derivations of non-logical sentiments,.. Freudians psycho-analysed them, and so on. **1969** R. WOLLHEIM *Family Romance* 170 A pupil asked me a question about Paretan *optima.*

paretic (pəˈrɛtɪk), *a.* and *sb.* *Path.* [ad. mod.L. *paretic-us*, f. Gr. πάρετ-ος relaxed, palsied: see -IC.] **A.** *adj.* Of or pertaining to paresis; affected with or characterized by paresis.

1822–34 *Good's Study Med.* (ed. 4) III. 480 A debilitated and paretic state of the liver. **1888** *Forum* (U.S.) Sept. 101 The increase of paretic dementia, and the increase of alcoholic insanity. **1896** *Allbutt's Syst. Med.* I. 350 The use of the kathode for paralytic or paretic states.

B. *sb.* A person affected with paresis.

1881 *Brit. Med. Jrnl.* 12 Mar. 394/1 Local anæsthesia seems.. the rule with paretics. **1924** [see CONFABULATE *v.* 2]. **1957** J. KEROUAC *On Road* (1958) II. vi. 142 An old college schoolmate whose father, a mad paretic, had died and left a fortune. **1972** *Brit. Jrnl. Psychiatry* CXXI. 146/1 Quite a few paretics can be rehabilitated following a complete treatment.

Hence **paˈretically** *adv.*

1878 *Smithsonian Inst. Rep.* 361 He proved that.. currents [of galvanism] travelling in both directions act paretically.

Pareto (pæˈreɪtəʊ, -ˈiːtəʊ). The name of the Italian economist and sociologist, Vilfredo *Pareto* (1848–1923), used *attrib.* and in the possessive to indicate his theories or methods and esp. the law, or mathematical formula, in which he claimed that the distribution of income for any society could be expressed.

1920 A. C. PIGOU *Econ. of Welfare* v. ii. 699 When these points are conceded, the general defence of 'Pareto's law' as a law of even limited necessity rapidly crumbles. **1930** E. R. A. SELIGMAN in *Political Sci. Q.* XLV. 341. His *Cours d'economie politique*.. contained among other notable contributions the first formulation of the principle which subsequently became known as Pareto's law. This was a generalization which attempted to express the relation between the amount of income and the number of its recipients. **1937** YULE & KENDALL *Introd. Theory Statistics* (ed. 11) vi. 100 In economic statistics this form of distribution [*sc.* the extremely asymmetrical] is particularly characteristic of the distribution of wealth in the population at large.., and the curve to which it gives rise has been called the 'Pareto line', after Vilfredo Pareto. **1949** [see ERGODICITY]. **1962** *Times Lit. Suppl.* 24 Aug. 634/1 The Pareto coefficients measuring such interspatial and intertemporal differentials of remuneration show 'a very considerable consistency'. **1967** [see IMPOSSIBILITY 4]. **1968**

Internat. Encycl. Social Sci. XI. 406/1 Thus, Pareto's law is nothing else than the ordinary negative exponential distribution, truncated at the left to log *h*. **1971** I. J. Good in *Public Choice* X. 99 The definition of a Pareto-optimal set is a set such that every point outside it is dominated by at least one point inside it, whereas no point inside it is dominated by any other point in it. **1974** *Encycl. Brit. Macropædia* XIX. 680/1 The right-hand tail of the Pareto curve for *disposable* income distribution is curved downward considerably by taxation. **1974** *Times* 25 Mar. 17/8 We were warned of the dangers of Pareto's law—to spend 80 per cent of the time on 20 per cent of the people.

pareu (ˈpɑːreɪuː). Also **pariu, pareo.** [Native Polynesian name.] A skirt worn by men and women in Polynesia, made of a single straight piece of cloth, usu. of printed cotton. So **pareu cloth**, the cloth of which this and other Polynesian garments are made.

1860 Mayne Reid *Odd People* 211 There is but one 'garment' to be described, and that is the 'pareu', which will be better understood, perhaps, by calling it a 'petti-coat'. **1894** Stevenson & Osbourne *Ebb-Tide* I. i. 13, I saw a man in a *pariu*, and with a mat under his arm, come along the beach from the town. **1914** R. Brooke *Let.* 5 Apr. (1968) 574 I'll wind my parea [*sic*] tighter round my middle & go & pull out the canoes & we'll all jump in. **1914** —— *Let.* 24 May (1968) 588 Raymond Buildings must be littered with dropped smocks. May I add a well-worn *paréo* to the heap on Friday week—a day or two after you get this? **1919** *Century Mag.* Aug. 452/2 The light fell upon..the men,.. catching ruddy gleams from red *pareus*. **1919** W. S. Maugham *Moon & Sixpence* liii. 230 The *pareo* is a long strip of trade cotton... It is worn round the waist and hangs to the knees. **1932** —— *Narrow Corner* ix. 46 In a little while a blackfellow, wearing nothing but a pareo, came along. **1949** P. H. Buck *Coming of Maori* (1950) II. v. 158 The women's skirt, termed *pareu* in the Cook and Society Islands, was a wider piece of material wound around the waist and descending to above the knees for single girls and below the knees for married women. **1961** *Sunday Express* 26 Nov. 21/1 A gorgeous young Polynesian girl..was wearing a native *pareu*,—a sort of wrap-around costume of flowered cloth. **1969** R. T. Wilcox *Dict. Costume* (1970) 259/2 *Pareu, pareo*, a Polynesian skirt or loincloth of standard size and colors, a rectangle printed with conventional flower designs. **1972** *Islander* (Victoria, B.C.) 16 Apr. 2/1 The children also discovered..pareu cloth at 89c a yard. This brightly colored, boldly designed cloth is used all over the Pacific for virtually all clothing, as well as for bed-covers, drapes, room dividers and tablecloths. **1974** T. Heyerdahl *Fatu-Hiva* i. 41 To walk in the woods and hills of Papenoo was sheer pleasure, for there we wore only an airy *pareu*, and the temperature felt like a pleasant dream.

par excellence: see PAR *prep.* II b.

pareyll, obs. f. PERIL.

pareylle, var. PAREL.

parfait (ˈpɑːfeɪ). [a. F. *parfait* sb., absolute use of *parfait* PERFECT *a.*] A rich iced pudding of whipped cream, eggs, etc.; also, ice cream, fruit, syrup, whipped cream, etc., arranged in layers and served in a tall glass. Also *attrib.*

1894 C. Ranhofer *Epicurean* 994 Parfait with Nougat and with Almonds. **1906** [see MOUSSE]. **1932** 'N. Shute' *Lonely Road* iv. 67 The parfaits came, and proved to be a tinned peach and ice mixed up together in a cup. **1936** G. Greene *Gun for Sale* i. 11 He stared with distaste at the long list of sweet iced drinks, of *parfaits* and sundaes and *coupes* and splits. **1948** *Good Housek. Cookery Bk.* II. 490 A Parfait..is usually understood to be a rather rich form of Mousse, light for the reason that it contains whipped whites of eggs. **1953** E. Taylor *Sleeping Beauty* ix. 161 Sundaes, shakes, parfaits, whips, melbas. **1969** R. & D. De Sola *Dict. Cooking* 168/2 *Parfait*, dessert made of alternate layers of ice cream, fruit, syrup, and whipped cream. *Ibid.*, *Parfait glass*, tall narrow glass used for serving parfaits. **1978** *Monitor* (McAllen, Texas) 25 June 1E Mayan Parfait is a smooth, rich mix of vanilla ice cream layered between a banana-nut frozen confection. *Ibid.*, Parfait glasses are perfect for showing off this pretty dessert.

parfait, -ayt, -ect, -et, -it, -ite, etc., obs. ff. PERFECT.

‖**Parfait Amour** (ˌpɑːfeɪt æˈmʊə(r)). [Fr., lit. 'perfect love'.] A sweet, spiced liqueur.

1818 T. Moore *Fudge Fam. Paris* 25 A neat glass of *parfait-amour* which one sips Just as if bottled velvet tipp'd over one's lips! **1862** C. Schultz *Manual for Manuf. Cordials &c.* 183 *Parfait Amour*... 8 ounces of cedrat rinds. 4 do. lemon peels. ½ do. cloves. Ground; macerate for 24 hours with 3 gallons of alcohol, 95 per cent, and 3½ gallons of water.. distil from off the water 3 gallons of flavored alcohol; add 30 lbs. of sugar dissolved in 5¼ gallons of water; color deep red, and filter. **1877** [see *orange bitters* s.v. ORANGE *sb.*[1] 7 a]. **1950** O. A. Mendelsohn *Earnest Drinker* xvii. 130 The bright purplish tint of such a liqueur as *Parfait Amour* is.. as artificial an effect as possible. **1965** *House & Garden* Dec. 90/3 *Parfait Amour*. Sweet and heavy taste and colouring. **1972** N. Freeling *Long Silence* II. 156 She..was being given a choice between crème de cacao, crème de banane and a mauve concoction known to Holland as Parfait Amour.

parfay: see PERFAY.

‖**parfilage** (parfilaʒ). [F., f. *parfiler* to unravel thread by thread: in OF. *pourfiler*, f. *pour* for + *fil* thread.] The unravelling of gold or silver thread from laces, epaulets, tassels, etc.; fashionable as a pastime among ladies, esp. in France, in the latter part of the 18th century.

1894 A. Dobson *18th Cent. Vignettes* Ser. II. 256 Of the Austrian Court and its decorums, of its *parfilage* and its card-parties, Lady Mary has much to say. **1896** *Godey's Mag.* Feb. 177/2 The business was known as parfilage, and the thread-pickers (called *parfileuses*), when they went to court, took large bags to hold whatever they received from the men. *Ibid.*, The countess introduces a scene in one of her novels ridiculing parfilage.

‖**parfleche** (parflɛʃ). Also **-flesh, -flash.** [app. Canadian Fr.] Among some tribes of North American Indians: A hide, usually of a buffalo, deprived of the hair and dried by stretching on a frame; an article made of such hide. Occas. *fig.* Hence **par'fleched** *a.*, made or covered with parfleche.

1827 E. Ermatinger in *Trans. R. Soc. Canada 1912* (1913) VI. II. 110 We embarked with crews and cargoes as follows: viz..1 pack Parfleches. **1845** J. C. Frémont *Rep. Exploring Expedition* 237 Some of us had the misfortune to wear moccasins with parflêche soles, so slippery that we could not keep our feet. **1850** L. H. Garrard *Wah-to-Yah* vii. 106 With a sole of *par-fleche*, lapping over on top of the foot. **1867** *Harper's Mag.* Oct. 584/2 The *teet-sock* or *parfleche* is generally made of a dried buffalo hide, the hair of which has been beaten off with a stone..; it is then cut in the shape of an envelope. **1870** Keim *Sheridan's Troopers* 168 Opposite the chief..lay several very fine robes and parfleshes finely painted. **1882** R. I. Dodge *Our Wild Indians* xix. 254 *note*, Among almost all the Plains tribes, the common name for a skin so prepared is 'parfleche', and almost everything made of it is also 'parfleche'. **1899** G. B. Grinnell in *Atlantic Monthly* LXXXIII. 25/2 In an Indian village..the hand that scrapes the parfleche rules the camp. *a* **1918** G. Stuart *40 Yrs. on Frontier* (1925) II. 40 [The medicine man] usually had a highly ornamental parflash, in which he kept one or more fetishes. **1938** P. H. Godsell *Red Hunters of Snows* 33 Here braves..stored..commodities in painted parfleche bags for the forthcoming journey to York Factory. **1940** F. Niven *Mine Inheritance* 61, I saw her bending over another parflèched box in front of the tent and taking out two long, gleaming knives. **1952** *Beaver* June 6/1 The hides were manufactured into robes or were divested of their hair and made into tepee covers, clothing, moccasins, *parfléche* trunks and shields. **1956** V. Fisher *Pemmican* 199 The old man's face was a parfleche of seams. **1972** D. Kennedy *Recoll. Assiniboine Chief* 92 These parfleches were made from flint hides with the hair scraped off. They were decorated with colours in geometric designs. **1973** A. H. Whiteford *N. Amer. Indian Arts* 78 Parfleches are large envelopes of rawhide used in the Plains to pack dried food and other things. **1974** *Sci. Amer.* Jan. 129/1 These modern ingenuities do not overshadow the photographs within: a parfleche, a yurt or an old folding feather-bed-in-a-chest.

parfocal (pɑːˈfəʊkəl), *a.* [f. PAR *sb.*[1] + FOCAL *a.*] Having or pertaining to the property that corresponding focal points of different lenses lie in the same plane, so that they may be interchanged without the need to adjust the focus. Const. *with.*

1886 *Microsc. Bull. & Sci. News* Aug. 31/1 Referring to the article in the April issue..on 'changing eye-pieces without altering focus, etc.', we announce that we are prepared to furnish eye-pieces, as there described... We have named these eye-pieces *parfocal*, meaning 'of equal focus'. **1944** C. P. Shillaber *Photomicrography* iii. 234 The objectives are said to be parfocal with each other when one setting of the microscope will serve to focus all four objectives. **1955** *Sci. Amer.* Feb. 122/2 This is called 'parfocal' mounting, and it saves a lot of time when, for example, you are searching your collection for a specific type of crystal, surface texture or color to match an unknown mineral. **1965** J. R. Benford in R. Kingslake *Appl. Optics & Optical Engin.* III. iv. 167 The 3·5 × objective is a comparatively recent 'telephoto' construction, designed to be parfocal with the high-power objectives. **1970** R. P. Loveland *Photomicrography* I. iii. 114 The rotating objective holder is the most convenient in use when the objectives are parfocal. **1976** *Physics Bull.* Nov. 511/1 To meet the recently increased demand for low magnification objectives, a parfocal distance of 45 mm has been employed. **1979** *Nature* 1 Mar. p. xxiii, All optical components are parfocal and permanently centred.

Hence **parfo'cality**, the property of being parfocal; **par'focally** *adv.*

1965 J. R. Benford in R. Kingslake *Appl. Optics & Optical Engin.* III. iv. 165 Tightening one of these and loosening the other provide a precise means of moving the objective lens up and down to bring about the desired parfocality setting, so that objectives on a multiple nose-piece can be interchanged without losing focus. **1971** J. H. Richardson *Optical Microscopy for Materials Sci.* i. 41 Parfocality is not an inherent property of an objective, but is rather a convenience often provided on the more modern microscopes. **1974** *Physics Bull.* May 197/2 For optical measurements the instrument has a high pressure xenon arc lamp and six pairs of matched condenser and objective lenses mounted parfocally in turrets.

parfocalize (pɑːˈfəʊkəlaɪz), *v.* [f. prec. + -IZE.] *trans.* To make parfocal. So **parˌfocali'zation**, the action or result of parfocalization.

1944 C. P. Shillaber *Photomicrography* iii. 234 As a rule parfocalization can be attained for all microscope objectives except those of great focal length. **1958** G. H. Needham *Pract. Use Microscope* xv. 234/2 On the modern, routine stands these three or four objectives are parfocalized on the revolving nosepiece so that after focusing with the low dry, the high dry may be swung into position without racking the body tube up. **1965** J. R. Benford in R. Kingslake *Appl. Optics & Optical Engin.* III. iv. 165 The second adjustment is to parfocalize the objective.

parforce, obs. f. PERFORCE.

parforme, -fourme, -fourne, obs. ff. PERFORM.

parfornysshe, var. PERFURNISH *Obs.*

‖**parfumerie** (parfymǝri). [Fr.] A factory which produces, or a (department of a) shop which sells, perfume.

1842 Poe *Mystery of Marie Rogêt* in *Ladies' Compan.* (N.Y.) Dec. 97/2 The disappearance of..Marie Rogêt from the *parfumerie* of Monsieur Le Blanc. **1855** S. Whiting *Heliondé* iii. 125 The department of parfumerie would have used up a whole continent of 'sweet gul',..steppes of lavender, [etc.]. **1951** W. Sansom *Face of Innocence* 138 In Eve's parfumerie shadowy with scent and cool with pale attendants. **1970** 'S. Troy' *Blind Man's Garden* vi. 63 They were sitting in André's office at the *parfumerie*. **1977** *Time* 11 Apr. 29/3 They are fellow clerks in the same Budapest *parfumerie*.

parfyght, parfyt, obs. ff. PERFECT.

pargana, -ganna, variants of PERGUNNAH.

pargasite (ˈpɑːgəsaɪt). *Min.* [ad. Ger. *pargasit* (Steinheil 1814), f. *Pargas* in Finland, where found: see -ITE[1] 2 b.] A green or greenish variety of HORNBLENDE.

1818 T. Thomson *Ann. Philos.* XI. 469 A new mineral called pargasite has been sent to this country. **1868** Dana *Min.* (ed. 5) 235 Pargasite is usually made to include green and bluish-green kinds, occurring in stout lustrous crystals, or granular.

parge (pɑːdʒ), *v.* [? Shortened from PARGET *v.*] = PARGET *v.* 1.

1701 in *New Eng. Hist. & Gen. Reg.* (1879) XXXIII. 176 *note*, To point the garret and to Parge the chimnyes with good Lime morter. **1703** T. N. *City & C. Purchaser* 31 They do not Parge, or (which is all one) Plaster their Garrets. **1805** R. W. Dickson *Pract. Agric.* I. 57 The thatch should be properly parged with lime-mortar on the inside, to prevent any dust falling upon the milk. **1908** G. P. Bankart *Art of Plasterer* vi. 77 'Lambert's Farm', in the parish of Great Tey, Essex, has a parged front.

So **parge-work** = PARGET *sb.* 2, PARGETING 2. Hence **'parge-worker.** Also *parge decoration*, etc.

1649 in *Archæologia* X. 403 Above which [waynscot] is a border of freet or parge worke wrought..the seeling is of the same fret or parge worke. **1906** *Essex Rev.* XV. 162 The unique designs in parge-work on its front. **1908** G. P. Bankart *Art of Plasterer* vi. 58 One form of parge decoration consisted of a simple type of incising, or cutting patterns through the top layer of plaster down to the coating underneath. *Ibid.* 79 The favourite spots of the parge-worker were over-mantels, gable ends, and lunettes, [etc]. **1940** *Chambers's Techn. Dict.* 617/1 *Parge-work* (*Build.*), an ancient form of external plastering with a mixture similar to that used in *pargetting*..chimneys. **1951** Lambert & Marx *Eng. Popular Art* iii. 48 This 'parge work' ornament was very popular in the sixteenth, seventeenth and eighteenth centuries. At Ipswich there are numerous examples of external parge decorations from about 1557.

'parge-board. = BARGE-BOARD.

1845 Parker *Gloss. Archit.* (ed. 4) I. 42 Barge-board, Berge-board, Verge-board, or Parge-board.

†**'pargen**, *v. Obs.* Altered form of PARGET *v.* Hence †**pargener (-ur).** = PARGETER.

1449–50 *Durham Acc. Rolls* (Surtees) 239 Pro le pargenynge eccl. par. supradicte. **1489** *Priory of Finchale* in Parker *Gloss. Archit.* (1845) I. 272 Pro le pergenyng et weschyng ecclesiæ de Fynkhall.

parget (ˈpɑːdʒɪt), *sb.* Also 5–7 pariet (*i* = *j*), 6 -ette, 6 pergit, 7 parjet. [app. f. PARGET *v.* (or from same source).]

1. Plaster spread upon a wall, ceiling, etc.; whitewash; roughcast; in mod. dial. *spec.* a plaster made of lime and cow-dung with which the flues of chimneys are lined.

13.. *E.E. Allit. P.* B. 1536 A fust faylaynde þe wryst, Pared on þe parget, purtrayed lettres. *c* **1420** *Pallad. on Husb.* I. 414 The parget of thi wough be strong & bryght. *c* **1440** *Promp. Parv.* 383/2 Pa[r]get, or playster for wallys, *gipsum*,..*litura*. **1530** Palsgr. 252/1 Pariette for walles, *blanchissevre*. **1545** Joye *Exp. Dan.* v. 69 Wrytinge..in the whight parget of the wall of the kynges palace. **1639** Horn & Rob. *Gate Lang. Unl.* xlviii. (1643) §526 Wih his trovell hee roughcasteth all over the plastering; to wit, with slaked lime..and with parjet. **1789** M. Madan tr. *Persius* (1795) 120 *note*, The plaster, parget, or rough cast of a wall. **1842–76** Gwilt *Archit.* (ed. 7) Gloss., *Parget*, a name given to the rough plaster used for lining chimney flues, and formed of lime and cow's dung.

fig. **1597** J. King *On Jonas* (1618) 162 Wipe out the parget of thy flitting honours, and take a naked view of thy naked selfe. **1657** W. Morice *Coena quasi Κοινὴ* Def. xx. 172 With what parget soever men may daub.

2. *spec.* Ornamental work in plaster; a facing of plaster with ornamental designs in relief or indented, used for decoration of walls: also called *pargeting*. (†Also applied to other wall-decoration, as gilding: cf. next, 1 c.) *Obs.* or *Hist.*

[*a* **1400–50** *Alexander* 5285 A chambre,..parraillid all of plate-gold, pariet and opire.] **1569** Spenser *Visions Bellay* ii, Golde was the parget: and the sielyng eke Did shine all scaly with fine golden plates. **1606** Sylvester *Du Bartas* II. iv. II. *Magnificence* 1162 All the Parget carv'd and branched trim With Flowers and Fruits, and winged Cherubim. **1726** Leoni *Alberti's Archit.* II. 17/1 Unless you will grant the name of painting to a parget of various colours... This parget may be made of red oker burnt.

†**3.** Gypsum used for making plaster; plaster-stone.

1657 Tomlinson *Renou's Disp.* 27 Many Poysons are drawn from Minerals..as Quicksilver, red-Lead, Parget.

1762 tr. *Busching's Syst. Geog.* III. 56 Near Bardi, among the parget and chalk-veins, are found sexangular crystals.

†**4.** *transf.* Paint (for the face): cf. next, 2. *Obs.*

1593 DRAYTON *Eclogues* iv. 77 And Beauties selfe.. Scorn'd Paintings Pergit, and the borrowed Haire.

parget ('pɑːdʒɪt), *v.* Also 4 **parchet**, 5–6 **pargett(e, pergette, (5 pergete, 6 pargytt), 6 pariet** (*i* = *j*), 7 **pariete, perget,** 7–8 **pargit.** [app. a. OF. *pargeter, parjeter* to throw or cast over a surface, in Liège *pârjeter* = *jointoyer* (Godef.) ('a term of masonry, to fill up the joints of stones with mortar or plaster' Littré), f. *par* through, all over + *jeter* to throw or cast: cf. (1557) 'they cast it all over with claie, to keepe out the wind', CAST *v.* 57, and see ROUGHCAST.

The synonym *spargette* (found only in *Promp. Parv.*) has suggested to some a connexion with L. *spargĕre*, or a med.L. frequentative *spargitare*; the spelling *pariet* (i.e. *parjet*) has been by others ineptly connected with L. *pariet-em* partition-wall.]

1. *trans.* To cover or daub with parget or plaster, to plaster (a wall, etc.); to adorn with pargeting or ornamental plaster-work.

1382 WYCLIF *Ezek.* xiii. 10 And he bildide a wal, forsothe thei dawbeden [*gloss* or pargetiden] it with fen with oute chaffis. **1398** TREVISA *Barth. De P.R.* XVI. xxiv. (Bodl. MS.), Cement..to ioyne stones togedres and to pargette and to whitelyme walles. **1555** W. WATREMAN *Fardle Facions* II. xii. 301 The walles to be parieted without, and within, and diuersly paincted. **1632** LE GRYS tr. *Velleius Paterc.* 125 Quintus Catulus..shut himselfe up in a place lately pergetted with lime and sand,..and withall suffocating his owne breath, died. **1726** LEONI *Alberti's Archit.* I. 101/2 Let the floor of your Vault be pargetted. **1869** *Latest News* 5 Sept. 7 That no iron chimney bars supporting the arch are absent, and that the flues are pargeted.

†**b.** To daub or plaster over *with* (anything).

1398 TREVISA *Barth. De P.R.* XVIII. xii. (Bodl. MS.), Beene..pergetteth þe rof off her huyues wiþ wose and gomme. **1594** PLAT *Jewell-ho.* III. 31 Then parget ouer whatsoeuer thou wilt with this composition. **1656** EARL MONM. tr. *Boccalini's Advts. fr. Parnass.* I. lxxvii. (1674) 104 They saw the Wretch pargeted with apparances four inches thick, all over his body. **1698** FRYER *Acc. E. India & P.* 424 The continual confluence of Flocks of Water-Fowl..having paved or pargetted the whole Rock [Ascension] with their Filth.

†**c.** To cover or decorate (a surface) with ornamental work of any kind, as gilding, precious stones, etc. *Obs.*

a **1400–50** *Alexander* 3673 All pargestis [? pargettid] of plate as pure as þe noble. **1576** BAKER *Jewell of Health* 34 b, The vessels of Glasse are pargetted and fenced. **1634** SIR T. HERBERT *Trav.* 61 Their outside tyling pargetted with azure stones resembling turquoises. **1694** MOTTEUX *Rabelais* v. xxxviii, The Roof and Walls of the Temple..all pargetted with Porphyry and Mosaick Work. **1886** R. F. BURTON *Arab. Nts.* (abr. ed.) I. 85 The couch of juniper-wood, pargetted with gold and silver.

†**2.** *transf.* To daub or plaster (the face or body) with paint; to paint. Also *intr.* for *refl. Obs.*

1581 PETTIE *Guazzo's Civ. Conv.* III. (1586) 125 b, Those dawbed, pargetted, and vermilion died faces. **1609** B. JONSON *Sil. Wom.* v. ii, She's aboue fiftie too, and pargets! **1660** F. BROOKE *Le Blanc's Trav.* 192 They delight much to parget their bodies with a reddish earth.

3. *fig.* To cover with a fair appearance; to 'whitewash', to smooth or gloss over. ? *Obs.*

1592 *Conspir. Pretended Ref.* 6 The sinke of these sinnes in him, hee alwayes smoothlie couered and parieted ouer.. with a very rare outward earnestnesse. **1640** BASTWICK *Lord Bps.* ii. C, Thus they did..parget, or roughcast their vices. **1824** CARLYLE *Wilhelm Meister* II. xii. 237 If one did not try to parget-up the outward man as long as possible.

Hence '**pargeted** *ppl. a.*

1538 ELYOT, *Calcatus*, pergetted or whyte lymed. **1552** HULOET, Pargetted house, *calcata.* **1645** BURGESSE *Serm. Ho. Comm.* 30 Apr. 51 With faire, (specious, pargetted, glozing words). **1888** *Athenæum* 16 June 760/2 Some charming pictures of old pargeted houses.

pargeter ('pɑːdʒɪtə(r)). Forms: 6 **pargetour(e, pergeter,** 6– **pargetter,** 7 **-gettor, -jetter,** 9 **-giter,** 8– **-geter.** [orig. *pargetour* = OF. *parjetteur, agent-n. from *parjet-er*: see prec.]

1. A plasterer; a whitewasher.

1538 ELYOT, *Cementarii*, daubers, pargetters, rowghe masons, whiche do make onely walles. **1658** BROMHALL *Treat. Specters* I. 8 Not far from the Town, he met 10 Pargettors..carrying with them their tools. **1826** J. BAILEY *Forcellini, Dealbator*, one who white-washes, a pargeter. **1936** S. R. JONES *Eng. Village Homes* vi. 96 Men who dabbed on the clay were 'daubers', and those responsible for working the plaster were 'playsterers' or 'pargetters'. **1951** LAMBERT & MARX *Eng. Popular Art* iii. 48 In the nineteenth century the pargeter sometimes turned his hand to making plaques for inn signs. **1968** J. ARNOLD *Shell Bk. Country Crafts* iii. 55 This includes millwrights, masons, thatchers, sawyers, drystone-wallers and pargetters.

2. *fig.* One who 'bedaubs' with flattery; a sycophant.

a **1656** USSHER *Power Princes* I. (1683) 71 Let those parjetters of great men now come forth.

pargeting ('pɑːdʒɪtɪŋ), *vbl. sb.* [-ING[1].]

1. The action of PARGET *v.*; plastering; adorning with plaster-work; †*transf.* painting (of the face).

1396 *Compotus Will. Chert Custodis Coll. Cantuar. Oxon.* (1881) 33 Item pro carecta calcis pro parchetting vjs. viijd. *c* **1440** *Promp. Parv.* 384/1 Pargettynge (or spargettynge of wallis), *gipsacio, gipsatura.* **1588** T. THOMAS *Dict.* (1606), *Incrustatio*, a laying over, a pargetting,..a rough-casting. **1661** RUST *Origen's Opin.* in *Phœnix* (1721) I. 42 If the House be ruinous..all the external Painting and Pargetting imaginable..can neither secure the Inhabitants from its Fall. **1703** T. N. *City & C. Purchaser* 218 Pargeting.. signifies the Plastering of Walls. **1853** TURNER *Dom. Archit.* II. ii. 45 Impressed on the plaster in the same manner as pargetting was performed.

fig. **1657** W. MORICE *Coena quasi Κοινὴ* Diat. v. 247 Much pargetting there is, to shew a disparity between the Word and Prayer and the Sacraments.

2. *concr.* Plaster or plaster-work, often ornamental: = PARGET *sb.* 1, 2.

1388 WYCLIF *Ezek.* xiii. 12 Where is the pargetyng [1382 dawbynge], which ȝe pargetiden? **1538** ELYOT, *Tectorium*, the playstrynge or pariettynge of a house. **1603** KNOLLES *Hist. Turks* (1621) 543 The wals glistered with red marble, and pargeting of divers colours. **1756** BP. POCOCKE *Trav.* (1889) II. 228 All the old houses in Herefordshire are built with frames of wood and cage work between, call'd pargiting. **1838** *Civil Eng. & Arch. Jrnl.* I. 212/2 The practice is to coat the inside of the flue with a composition of lime-mortar with cow-dung, called 'pargetting'. **1885–94** R. BRIDGES *Eros & Psyche* May 9 The pargeting of ceiling and of wall Was fresco'd o'er with figures manifold.

3. *attrib.*

1613 PURCHAS *Pilgrimage* VII. i. 550 They annoynt it with a kinde of pargetting mortar.

'**pargeting,** *ppl. a.* [f. as prec. + -ING[2].] That pargets; †that 'whitewashes', glosses or smooths over.

1637 GILLESPIE *Eng. Pop. Cerem.* Ep. A ij b, You must not acquiesce in the pargetting verdict of those who are wealthy and well at ease.

'**pargetry.** [f. PARGET *sb.* + -RY]. = PARGET *sb.* 2.

1908 G. P. BANKART *Art of Plasterer* vi. 64 (*caption*) Pargetry on House in High Street, Maidstone, now pulled down. **1936** S. R. JONES *Eng. Village Homes* vi. 97 Thought in design, and capacity to invent suitable tools for working, brought a good deal of variety to pargetry, as may be seen in roughcast and those numerous pricked, combed and scratched arrangements once known as arrowheads, tortoise-shell, zig-zag, herring-bone, basket-work, scallops, interlacing squares and wavy lines.

† '**pargety,** *a. Obs. rare.* [f. PARGET *sb.* + -Y.] Of the nature of plaster, sticky.

1684 tr. *Fambresar. Art Physick* I. 42 Four sorts [of flegm]; the Watery..and the Pargetty.

parging ('pɑːdʒɪŋ), *vbl. sb.* [f. PARGE *v.* + -ING[1].] = PARGETING *vbl. sb.*

1897 F. C. MOORE *How to build Home* iii. 34 The parging or plastering of the inside of the flue is permitted. **1903** *Eng. Dial. Dict.* IV. 423/2 *Parging*..(1) the lining of a chimney ..(2) a ceiling. **1940** *Chambers's Techn. Dict.* 617/1 *Parge-work*... Also called *parging.* **1964** J. S. SCOTT *Dict. Building* 224 Pargetting or parging or pargeting.

pargo, pargie: see PORGO, PORGY.

pargyline ('pɑːgɪliːn). *Pharm.* [Etym. unkn.] A monoamine oxidase inhibitor used in the treatment of benign hypertension, usu. in the form of the hydrochloride, a white crystalline powder; *N*-methyl-*N*-prop-2-ynylbenzylamine, $C_6H_5CH_2N(CH_3)CH_2C{:}CH$.

1961 *Current Therapeutic Res.* III. 381 Pargyline hydrochloride appears to be a potent antihypertensive agent, the maximal effect of which is manifested slowly. **1963** *Yearbk. Drug Therapy* 85 (*heading*) Antihypertensive properties of pargyline hydrochloride (Eutonyl): new nonhydrazine monoamine oxidase inhibitor. **1970** PASSMORE & ROBSON *Compan. Med. Stud.* II. viii. 10/2 Pargyline, a nonhydrazine compound, possesses modest anti-hypertensive potency and its effect begins several days after the drug is given and continues for 2–3 weeks after treatment is stopped. **1972** [see *methyldopa* s.v. METHYL c]. **1977** *Lancet* 6 Aug. 275/1 Plasma-prolactin levels doubled in depressive patients treated with the monoamine-oxidase inhibitors, clorgyline and pargyline.

parhedral (pɑː'hɛdrəl), *a. rare.* [f. Gr. πάρεδρος adj., sitting beside, sb. an associate, coadjutor + -AL[1]; cf. PAREDRIAL.] Attendant, subsidiary.

1884 *Guide to Exh. Gall. Brit. Mus.* 94 Besides the principal gods, inferior or parhedral gods, personifications of the faculties, senses, and others.

parhelion (pɑː'hiːlɪən). Pl. **parhelia** (-ɪə), rarely **-ions.** Also 7 **parelion,** (*pl.* (*erron.*) **-elias, -helia's**), 8 **parelium, -helium;** also *β.* 7 **parelius, -elios, -helius,** *pl.* **-elii, -helii;** *γ.* 7 **parelie.** [a. L. *parēlion*, a. Gr. παρήλιον, also παρήλιος, f. παρα- beside + ἥλιος sun. Early forms represent also the latinized *parēlius, parēlium*, and F. *parélie* (1547 in Hatz.-Darm.). The insertion of *h*, after Gr. ἥλιος *hēlios*, is later.]

1. A spot on a solar halo at which the light is intensified (usually at the intersection of two halos or bands of light), often prismatically coloured, and sometimes dazzlingly bright, formerly supposed to be a reflected image of the sun; a mock sun.

Two or more parhelia are usually seen at once, on a level with and on opposite sides of the sun, and sometimes vertically above and below it.

1647 H. MORE *Song of Soul* II. i. III. xxv, Glistring Parelies or other meteors. **1648** BOYLE *Seraph. Love* xii. (1700) 61 As absurd as it were for a Persian to offer his Sacrifice to a Parhelion (as the Greeks call that Meteor) instead of adoring the Sun. **1649** JER. TAYLOR *Gt. Exemp.* I. ii. 71 The Sunne reflecting upon a cloud produces a Parelius, or a representation of his owne glory. **1661** BOYLE *Style of Script.* 259 As parhelions [**1675** parrhelions] to the sun. **1665–6** *Phil. Trans.* I. 220 At the two extremities..appeared two Parhelia's or Mock-suns. **1706** PHILLIPS, *Parelium* or *Parhelium*, a Mock Sun. **1721** W. WHISTON in *Phil. Trans.* XXXI. 213 Two plain Parhelia, or Mock-Suns. **1780** VON TROIL *Iceland* 55 The parhelions are observed in Iceland chiefly at the approach of the Greenland ice. **1878** NARES *Polar Sea* I. xii. 301 A fine circular prismatic halo was seen round the sun with a distinct prismatic parhelion at the usual distance on each side and above it.

2. *fig.* Applied to a fainter image or reflection of something else.

1647 T. GOODWIN *Wks.* (1861) III. 277 Parhelii, and resemblances, and shadows of those thoughts the mind secretly conceives and forms. **1683** J. SCOTT *Chr. Life* (1699) V. 341 Only the parhelius or reflection of the visible glory of him. **1867** DRAPER *Amer. Civ. War* I. xxxiii. 563 The sky was full of parhelions of delusive glory.

Hence **parheliacal** (pɑːhiː'laɪəkəl), **parhelic** (pɑː'hiːlɪk or -'hɛlɪk) *adjs.*, pertaining to or resembling a parhelion.

parheliacal ring or ***parhelic circle***, a horizontal circle of light passing through the sun, seen in connexion with halos, with parhelia at certain points on it.

1839 BAILEY *Festus* xxxii. (1852) 546 Parheliacal gods which mocked men's minds. **1890** *Chambers' Encycl.* V. 524/2 The Parhelic circle, which is a white circle passing through the sun and parallel with the horizon.

parhelium, obs. var. PARHELION, var. PARAHELIUM.

‖**parhi'drosis.** Also **parid-.** [f. PAR(A-[1] 1 + Gr. ἱδρώς sweat: see -OSIS.] 'Secretion of sweat of an abnormal kind' (*Syd. Soc. Lex.* 1893).

1890 in *Cent. Dict.*

parhomologous (pɑːhəʊ'mɒləgəs), *a. Comp. Anat.* [f. PAR(A-[1] 1 + HOMOLOGOUS.] Applied to parts apparently but not really homologous: see quot. So **parho'mology** (pɑːhəʊ'mɒlədʒɪ), the condition of being parhomologous.

1888 H. GADOW in *Nature* 13 Dec. 151/2 Two plexuses may be homodynamous, although, strictly speaking, not homologous. This is expressed by the term 'imitatory homodynamy', more happily by parhomology. *Ibid.*, The muscles..together with the nerves, undergo metameric changes until they..are only parhomologous.

parhormone, obs. var. PARAHORMONE.

‖**parhypate** (pɑː'hɪpətiː). Also 8 **parypate.** [a. Gr. παρυπάτη (sc. χορδή), f. παρ(α- beside + ὕπατος uppermost.] In ancient Greek music, The name of the lowest note but one in either of the lowest two tetrachords.

1603 HOLLAND *Plutarch* Explan. Wds., *Parhypate hypatôn*,..Subprincipall of principals. A string or note in Musicke: C, FA, UT. *Parhypate Mesôn*,..Subprincipall of meanes: a string or note in Musicke: F, FA, UT. **1706** PHILLIPS, *Parhypate*,..the Sound of the String next the Bass. **1753** CHAMBERS *Cycl. Supp.*, *Parypate*, in antient music,..that note or chord of a tetrachord which lay next to the hypate.

pariah (pə'raɪə, 'pɛərɪə, 'pɑːrɪə). Forms: 7 **parea, (piriawe, parrier,** 8 **parrear, bareier),** 8–9 **paria, (pariar, parriar,** 9 **pareiya),** 8– **pariah.** [ad. Tamil *paṛaiyar*, pl. of *paṛaiyan* name of the largest of the lower castes in Southern India, lit. '(hereditary) drummer', f. *paṛai* 'the large drum beaten at certain festivals'. (Yule & Burnell.)]

1. *prop.* A member of a very extensive low caste in Southern India, especially numerous at Madras, where its members supplied most of the domestics in European service.

1613 PURCHAS *Pilgrimage* (1614) 494 The Pareas are of worse esteeme,..reputed worse than the Diuell. **1626** *Ibid.* (ed. 4) 998 The worst whereof are the abhorred Piriawes. **1717** J. T. PHILLIPS *Acc. Malabar* xxxii. 127 Bareier (or a sort of poor People that eat all sort of Flesh). **1807** F. BUCHANAN *Mysore* I. i. 20 The Parriar, and other impure tribes..would be beaten, were they to attempt joining in a procession of any of the gods of the Bráhmans. **1856** R. CALDWELL *Dravidian Gram.* App. 494 The Pariars [*ed.* 2 Pareiyas] constitute a well defined, distinct, ancient caste,.. and..has subdivisions of its own,.. its own traditions, and its own jealousy of the encroachments of the castes which are above it and below it. **1886** YULE & BURNELL *Anglo-Ind. Gloss.* s.v., There are several castes in the Tamil country considered to be lower than the *Pariahs*, *e.g.* the caste of shoemakers, and the lowest caste of washermen. And the *Pariah* deals out the same disparaging treatment to these that he himself receives from higher castes.

2. Hence, extended to a member of any low Hindu caste, and by Europeans even applied to one of no caste, an outcaste.

This extension of application began among the higher castes of Hindus, because the Pariahs are lower than the lowest caste of the Brahmanical system, by whom they are shunned as unclean and thus, practically, *outcasts.*

1711 in J. T. Wheeler *Madras in Old. Time* (1861) II. 125 A resort of basket makers, Scavengers,..and other Parriars, to drink Toddy. **1798** W. TAYLOR in *Monthly Mag.* VI. 550 As little..[to] be looked for..as a brave heroic spirit among the outcast Parias of the Hindoos now. **1816** SINGER *Hist. Cards* 317 To shew that Gipsies..were of the lowest and most degraded cast of Parias or Suders. **1823** BYRON *Juan* XII. lxxviii, They lose their caste at once, as do the Parias.

1842 PRICHARD *Nat. Hist. Man* 164 This may be true with respect to the Parriahs, or outcasts.

3. *fig.* **a.** Any person (or animal) of a degraded or despised class; a social outcast.

1819 SHELLEY *Lett.* Pr. Wks. 1888 II. 286 Such remembrances..as an exile and a Pariah may be permitted to address to an acknowledged member of the community of mankind. **1834** L. RITCHIE *Wand. by Seine* 245 A king's daughter..thrown forth to prowl with the Pariahs of society. **1884** *Expositor* Feb. 106 The sparrow, a very Pariah amongst the feathered tribes! **1901** *Academy* 23 Mar. 244 Ibsen is the supreme pariah of the English stage.

b. = *pariah dog*: see 4 b.

1816 'QUIZ' *Grand Master* 39 But soon some Paria's appear. *Note*, The Paria puppies of Bombay. **1895** MRS. B. M. CROKER *Village Tales* (1896) 58 I'll get you an old pariah out of the bazaar, and give you fifty rupees to buy him a collar!

4. a. *attrib.* That is a pariah; consisting of or belonging to pariahs; also applied to animals of low breed or things of base quality (see also b).

1711 C. LOCKYER *Acc. Trade India* i. 20 The Company allows two or three Peons to attend at the Gate, and a Parrear Fellow to keep all clean. **1716** in J. T. Wheeler *Madras in Old. Time* (1861) II. 230 A Pariah woman of the Right hand castes. **1837** *Lett. fr. Madras* (1843) 121 People here talk of high-caste and Pariah horses, Pariah dogs, &c. **1860** EMERSON *Cond. Life, Behaviour* Wks. (Bohn) II. 387 Some men appear to feel that they belong to a Pariah caste.

b. †**pariah-arrack**, a deleterious native spirit made in India (*obs.*); **pariah brig**, a sea-vessel built in India; **pariah-dog**, a yellow vagabond dog of low breed which frequents towns and villages in India and the East; **pariah-kite**, the Scavenger-kite of India (*Milvus govinda*).

1671–2 SIR W. LANGHORNE in J. T. Wheeler *Madras in Old. Time* (1861) III. 422 The unwholesome liquor called *Parrier arrack. **1929** F. C. BOWEN *Sea Slang* 101 **Pariah brigs*, deep-sea native vessels in India. **1935** M. H. BEATTIE *On Hooghly* 116 She was what was termed a pariah brig, or native craft, which would find her way to Kedgeree and there pick up a native pilot. **1946** 'SHALIMAR' *Ships & Men* 122 Indian pariah brigs were taken up to replace coasting steamers. **1780** I. MUNRO *Narr. Milit. Operat.* IV. (1789) 36 A species of the common cur, called a *pariar dog. **1878** E. ARNOLD *Pref. P. Robinson's In my Ind. Gard.* 9 The very pariah-dogs are classic to those who know Indian fables. **1877–78** V. BALL *Jungle Life* xiv. (1880) 655 The scavenger or *pariah kites (*Milvus govinda*)..though generally to be seen about the tents, are not common in the jungles.

Hence '**pariahdom**, the condition of a pariah; also '**pariahhood**, '**pariahism**, '**pariahship**.

1878 SYMONDS *Sonn. M. Angelo & Campanella* 16 The men of whom I speak were conscious of Pariahdom. **1887** *Globe* 22 Oct. 1/4 It is astonishing that any person..should regard the national uniform as a badge of pariahism. **1894** *Work & Workers* June 258/2 Ostracism from the class carries with it..hopeless, entire pariahdom. **1897** W. J. LOCKE *Derelicts* xx. 256 Forgetful of the gaol and his pariahdom. **1906** —— *Beloved Vagabond* (1908) vi. 68 They walked on together, and I dropped behind, suddenly realising my pariahdom. **1920** *Edin. Rev.* Jan. 18 The possibility of intermarriage is the crucial test of equality of consideration; its absence sets a stamp of servility and pariahship on the proscribed caste. **1936** W. FAULKNER *Absalom, Absalom!* 334 Rode the two horses through that night..in something very like pariah-hood. **1945** R. HARGREAVES *Enemy at Gate* 19 This choice aggregation of desperadoes and 'poor masterless men', welded into that solidarity of pariahdom which is the outlaws' primary source of strength. **1967** H. ARENDT *Orig. Totalitarianism* (new ed.) iii. 68 Disraeli..discovered the secret of how to preserve luck, that natural miracle of pariahdom. **1977** *New Yorker* 15 Aug. 70/2 Moynihan is the strongest force in the attempt to shift New York out of the congressional pariahdom to which it has long been consigned.

parial ('pɛərɪəl), *a.* *rare*$^{-1}$. [f. L. *pari-* equal, in pl. *paria* pair + -AL[1].] Belonging to or constituting a pair; paired.

1854 OWEN *Skel. & Teeth* in *Circ. Sc., Organ. Nat.* I. 215 [The plastron..consists..of nine pieces,—one median and symmetrical, and the rest in pairs]. *Ibid.* 216 The parial pieces of the plastron are the 'hæmapophyses' [etc.].

parial, obs. form of PAIR-ROYAL.

Parian ('pɛərɪən), *a.* (*sb.*) [f. L. *Pari-us* of Paros + -AN: in F. *parien.*] **A.** *adj.*

1. Belonging to the island of Paros, one of the Cyclades, famed for a white marble highly valued among the ancients for statuary.

Parian Chronicle, a famous chronicle of Grecian history from the reign of Cecrops B.C. 1450 to the archonship of Diotimus B.C. 354, engraved on marble; formerly kept in the island of Paros, and now preserved among the Arundel Marbles at Oxford; a further fragment was found in 1897 and is kept on Paros.

1638 JUNIUS *Paint. Ancients* 46, I had rather have a good piece of rough Parian marble. **1700** PRIOR *Carmen Sec.* 370 The King shall there in Parian Marble breathe. **1762–9** FALCONER *Shipwr.* III. 278 The port an image bears of Parian stone. **1847** EMERSON *Poems, Snow Storm*, Mockingly, On coop or kennel he hangs Parian wreaths.

2. Name given to a fine white kind of porcelain. Usually *absol.* as *sb.*; also *attrib.* made of parian.

1850 *Jrnl. of Design* IV. 45 Messrs Minton and Copeland almost simultaneously introduced the new 'body' in pottery ..called Parian, statuary porcelain, carraran, &c. **1894** *U. S. Tariff* in *Times* 16 Aug. 6/3 China, porcelain, parian, bisque, earthen, stone, and crockery ware.

3. ***Parian cement***, a plaster similar to Keene's cement but prepared with borax in place of alum.

1858 P. L. SIMMONDS *Dict. Trade Products* 276/1 *Parian-cement*, a fine or coarse cement, according to the purpose for which it is to be used. **1880** *Encycl. Brit.* XI. 351/2 Parian cement is plaster hardened with water containing 10 per cent. of borax. **1949** KIRK & OTHMER *Encycl. Chem. Technol.* III. 443 Keene's cement is the best known of the hard-plaster group, others, differing only slightly, being Parian cement and Martin's cement.

B. *sb.* **1.** A native or inhabitant of Paros.

1550 T. NICOLLS tr. *Thucydides' Hystory* [*Peloponnesian War*] IV. xiii. sig. U6 Being nyghe the towne of Thase, whyche was a colonie of the Paryans, distante frome Amphipolis aboute one journey by sea. **1629** HOBBES tr. *Thucydides' Hist. Peloponnesian Warre* IV. 270 Thasus (which is an island, and a colonie of the Parians, distant from Amphipolus, about halfe a dayes sayle). **1753** W. SMITH tr. *Thucydides' Hist. Peloponnesian War* II. IV. 85 Thasus is an island, a colony of the Parians, and distant about half a day's sail from Amphipolis. **1845** *Encycl. Metrop.* XVII. 487/2 Themistocles made the Parians pay severely for their perfidy to Aristides. **1911** *Encycl. Brit.* XX. 861/1 So high was the reputation of the Parians that they were chosen by the people of Miletus to arbitrate in a party dispute. **1960** R. CARPENTER *Greek Sculpture* i. 14 The Parians..had acquired the craft in Egypt. **1978** CARSON & CLARK *Paros* (rev. ed.) 5 Campers have established a good reputation among Parians.

2. (See sense A 2.)

3. = *Parian cement.*

1886 H. C. SEDDON *Builder's Work* vi. 238 Parian is a white cement. **1967** A. G. GEESON *Building Sci. Materials* (ed. 2) II. i. 56 Adhesion on Keene's or Parian is notoriously poor.

†**pari'ation.** *Obs.* [ad. L. *pariātiōn-em*, n. of action from *pariāre* to make equal, balance.] The action of making equal; equalization, balancing.

1623 COCKERAM, *Pariation*, Euennesse of account. *a* **1656** HALES *Gold. Rem.* III. *Serm.* (1673) 17 Nothing clears our accounts with God but pariation of Expences with Receipts.

paribuntal (pærɪ'bʌntəl). [f. *Pa*racale, *Par*añaque, *Par*ang or *Par*asan, places in the Philippines + BUNTAL.] A fine straw.

1926 *Vogue* May 105 An attractive summer model is carried out in paribuntal, a new fine straw. **1935** *Times* 17 June 11/3 For a tall girl there is a charming wide brimmed hat in brown paribuntal. **1963** *Harper's Bazaar* May 47 The hat..in cream paribuntal. *Ibid.* 49 The hat..in white paribuntal overlaid with toast paillasson straw.

parich, obs. f. PARISH, PERISH.

parichnos (pə'rɪknɒs). [a. F. *parichnos* (C. E. Bertrand 1891, in *Trav. & Mém. Facultés de Lille* II. VI. 84), f. PARA-[1] + Gk. ἴχνος track, trace.] A strand of tissue found beside the leaf traces in fossil plants of the family Lepidodendraceæ. Also *attrib.*

1893 W. C. WILLIAMSON in *Phil. Trans. R. Soc.* B. CLXXXIV. 10 Since I agree with M. Bertrand on this point, I shall accept and employ his name of parichnos. **1906** *Ann. Bot.* XX. 269 (*title*) On the presence of a parichnos in recent plants. *Ibid.*, The term Parichnos was used by Bertrand to designate the thin-walled parenchymatous strand of tissue, occurring in *Lepidodendron Harcourtii*, which accompanies the leaf-trace on the posterior side during its outward journey. **1935** F. O. BOWER *Primitive Land Plants.* xii. 234 These lateral pits are connected internally with the parichnos. **1969** F. E. ROUND *Introd. Lower Plants* xi. 135 Two structures entirely unknown in modern lycopods occur on either side of the leaf trace—these are the parichnos scars. *Ibid.*, There may be two other scars beneath the leaf scar which are also parichnos strands branching off those entering the leaf.

parichone, -oner, -yngher, obs. ff. PARISHEN, PARISHIONER.

paricidal, paricide, obs. ff. PARRICIDAL, -CIDE.

paridigitate (pærɪ'dɪdʒɪtət), *a. Zool.* [f. *pari-*, stem of L. *par* equal + DIGITATE.] Having an even number of toes on each foot; artiodactyl.

1864 WEBSTER cites OWEN.

paridrosis, variant spelling of PARHIDROSIS.

†'**parient**, *a. Obs. rare*$^{-0}$. [ad. L. *parient-em*, pr. pple. of *parĕre* (*pari-*) to bring forth.]

1656 BLOUNT *Glossogr.*, *Parient* (*pariens*), travelling with yong, lying in travel, bringing forth yong.

‖**paries** ('pɛərɪi:z). *Anat.*, *Nat. Hist.*, etc. Pl. **parietes** (pə'raɪɪti:z). [L. *pariēs, parietem* wall, partition-wall.] A part or structure enclosing, or forming the boundary of, a cavity in an animal or plant body or other natural formation; a wall (of a hollow bodily organ, a cavity of the body or of a shell, an abscess, or wound, an ovary or capsule of a plant, a cell of a honey-comb or wasp's nest, etc.). Chiefly in *pl.*

1727–41 CHAMBERS *Cycl.* s.v., The parietes of the two ventricles of the heart are of unequal strength and thickness. **1808** BARCLAY *Muscular Motions* 543 Between this membrane and the dorsal parietes, are situated all the various convolutions of the intestine. **1830** LINDLEY *Nat. Syst. Bot.* 191 In the opposite parietes of the ovarium of Brunonia. **1872** NICHOLSON *Palæont.* 150 A central portion, which is termed the 'paries', which is attached by its base to the 'basis' of the shell.

pariet, -ette, obs. forms of PARGET.

parietal (pə'raɪɪtəl), *a.* (*sb.*) [a. F. *pariétal* (*c* 1560 in Paré), ad. L. *parietāl-is*, f. *paries*: see PARIES and -AL[1].]

A. *adj.* **1. a.** *Anat.* and *Zool.* Belonging to or connected with the wall of the body or of any of its cavities.

Applied *esp.* to a pair of bones (***parietal bones***), right and left, forming part of the sides and top of the skull, between the frontal and occipital bones; and to structures connected with these, or situated in the same region (***parietal region***) of the head, as the ***parietal eminence***, ***protuberance***, or ***tuber***, a central elevation on the outer surface of the parietal bone, corresponding to a depression (***parietal fossa***) on the inner surface; ***parietal eye***, in the tuatara and many lizards, a structure of unknown function, resembling an eye and situated in the upper part of the skull beneath an opening in the parietal bone; ***parietal lobe***, the middle lobe of each hemisphere of the brain, composed of the three ***parietal convolutions*** or ***lobules***; etc. Also applied to those parts of the peritoneum and pleura which line the body-wall (***parietal peritoneum***, ***p. pleura***), as distinct from the parts investing the viscera and lungs.

1597 A. M. tr. *Guillemeau's Fr. Chirurg.* lf. xv b/2 The two bones, the Foreheade, and the Parietale. **1704** J. HARRIS *Lex. Techn.* I, *Parietal* [*printed* pariental] *Bones.* **1706** PHILLIPS, *Parietals*, or *Parietal Bones.* **1854** OWEN *Skel. & Teeth* in *Circ. Sc., Organ. Nat.* I. 177 The penultimate segment of the skull..is called the 'parietal vertebra'. **1866** HUXLEY *Prehist. Rem. Caithn.* 120 The parietal sutures are somewhat full. **1872** MIVART *Elem. Anat.* 77 At the side of the head we have..the parietal region. **1886** W. B. SPENCER in *Nature* 13 May 35/1 In formation of the paired eyes [of *Hatteria punctata*] invagination to form an optic cup takes place, whilst apparently it does not do so in the case of what may be called the parietal eye. **1911** *Phil. Trans. R. Soc.* B. CCI. 264 The pineal or parietal eye in Sphenodon is..the left-hand member of the original pair of pineal outgrowths. **1937** *Discovery* May 135/1 The so-called third eye of the tuatara..is sometimes known as the parietal or pineal eye. **1969** A. BELLAIRS *Life of Reptiles* I. vi. 232 In many lizards the parietal eye seems to play some part in regulating the amount of time spent basking.

b. *Bot.* Belonging to, connected with, or attached to the wall of a hollow organ or structure, esp. of the ovary, or of a cell: see quots.

1830 LINDLEY *Nat. Syst. Bot.* 158 They differ in their parietal exalbuminose comose seeds. **1835** —— *Introd. Bot.* (1848) I. 364 Botanists call anything *parietal* which arises from the inner lining, or wall of an organ. **1875** BENNETT & DYER *Sachs' Bot.* 5 The nucleus..approaches..the circumference of the sap-cavity, and becomes parietal. *Ibid.* 342 A rapid absorption of water in the parietal cells.

2. In U.S., Pertaining to residents and order within the walls of a college, as in ***Parietal Board***, ***P. Committee***, at Harvard College: see quot. 1837.

1837 *Orders & Reg. Harvard Univ.* 12 The Officers resident within the College walls shall constitute a permanent standing Committee of the Faculty, to be called the Parietal Committee. This Committee shall have particular cognizance of all offences against good order and decorum within the walls. **1878** *N. Amer. Rev.* CXXVI. 15 One instance in which the Parietal Board [Harvard College] took him in hand. **1893** *Nation* (N.Y.) 5 Jan. 16/1 One might call it, in college phrase, a style of parietal admonition. **1968** 'E. LATHEN' *Come to Dust* (1969) xiv. 140 Two young women had been discovered at a time and in circumstances all too clearly proscribed by the parietal rules and Brunswick's honor system. **1972** A. ULAM *Fall of Amer. Univ.* iii. 106 In any case in most schools, certainly at Harvard, the formerly idiotically strict parietal rules had been eroded by the sixties to sensibly hypocritical proportions. **1973** E. TAYLOR *Serpent under It* (1974) xxi. 177 The kinds of things that stir them [*sc.* students] up these days are parietal hours and open admissions and black studies. **1977** *National Observer* (U.S.) 1 Jan. 10/4 Parietal rules were ignored and, later, abandoned.

3. *gen.* Of or belonging to a wall. *rare.*

1845 *Ecclesiologist* IV. 257 The man..who surrounds with parietal deal a space belonging to twenty others. **1874** LOWELL *Lett.* (1894) II. xii. 134 They were much our betters in parietal wit. **1916** [see MURAL *a.*[1] 2].

B. *sb.* **1.** = Parietal bone: see 1 a.

1706 [see 1 a]. **1758** J. S. *Le Dran's Observ. Surg.* (1771) 57 A Blow upon the posterior Part of the left Parietal. **1855** OWEN *Skel. & Teeth* in *Circ. Sc., Organ. Nat.* I. 192 The constant coalescence of the parietals with one another.

2. *pl.* (see quot.) *U.S. slang.*

1967 *N.Y. Times* 17 Dec. IV. 9 Yale students..have rejoined the nationwide battle for liberalized 'parietals'—campus term for women's visiting hours in male dormitories, or vice-versa.

†**parietary** ('pærɪətərɪ), *sb. Obs.* Forms: α. 4–5 **paritorie**, 5 **paritarie**, (**paratory**, **pyritorie**), 5–6 **peritorie**, (**-yt-**, **-ye**), 6 **paritory**; β. 6 **parietary**, **-orie**, **-ory**, 6–7 **-arie**. [ME. and AF. *paritarie* = OF. *paritaire* (13th c.), mod.F. *pariétaire*, ad. L. *parietāria* i.e. *herba parietāria*, from *parietāri-us*: see next.] The herb Pellitory (*Parietaria officinalis*).

c **1386** CHAUCER *Can. Yeom. Prol. & T.* 28 Ful of Plantayne and of Paritorie [*v.rr.* peritorie, permytorye, Pyritorie]. *c* **1400** *Lanfranc's Cirurg.* 219 Leues of malue..& peritorie. **14..** *Voc.* in Wr.-Wülcker 602/10 *Peritoria*, Perytorye. *c* **1475** *Pict. Voc.* ibid. 787/26 *Hoc colitropium*, a paratory. **1538** TURNER *Libellus. Helxine*, Latinis parietaria dicitur, vulgo Paritory. **1578** LYTE *Dodoens* I. xxxiv. 50 Parietorie is singuler against cholerike inflammations. **1696** PHILLIPS (ed. 5), *Parietarie*..commonly called Pellitory of the Wall.

parietary (pə'raɪɪtərɪ), *a.* *rare*⁻¹. [ad. L. *parietāri-us*, f. *paries*, *pariet-em* wall: see PARIES and -ARY.] = PARIETAL *a.* 2.

1881 *Nation* (N.Y.) XXXII. 442 The snuffing out of the school by a parietary regulation of President Wayland's.

parietes, pl. of PARIES.

parietin (pə'raɪɪtɪn). *Chem.* and *Bot.* [f. L. *parietinus* of or belonging to walls (f. *pariēs*, *pariet-* wall), in the fem. a specific epithet of the lichen *Xanthoria parietina* from which the compound was obtained; see -IN[1].] An anthraquinone derivative present as an orange-yellow pigment in some lichens; 1:8-dihydroxy-3-methoxy-6-methylanthraquinone, $C_{16}H_{12}O_5$.

1844 R. D. THOMSON in *Proc. Philos. Soc. Glasgow* I. IX. 187, I have succeeded in obtaining the colouring matter, or *Parietin*, as I propose to term it, in the form of needles. **1894** *Jrnl. Chem. Soc.* LXVI. I. 541 The colouring matter.. may be extracted by means of benzene without destroying the lichen. It crystallises in small, golden-yellow needles which are soluble in alkalis with blood-red coloration... The authors consider this colouring matter to be a dihydroxyanthraquinone, and propose for it the name *chrysophyscin*... The colouring matter was termed parietin by Thomsen [*sic*]. **1921** A. L. SMITH *Handbk. Brit. Lichens* 44 The species [of *Xanthoria*] grow most freely in maritime districts, and are bright-yellow in the open where the acid substance parietin.. is freely formed. *Ibid.*, Parietin is produced in more or less abundance in the thallus of most species [of *Placodium*], and in the apothecia of all except *Pl. repellens* which is probably an impoverished form. **1966** *New Phytologist* LXV. 211 Unlike the species of *Peltigera*, those of *Xanthoria* are relatively rich in 'lichen acids' such as parietin and atranorin. **1967** M. E. HALE *Biol. Lichens* viii. 105 The following four pigments are also common to non-lichenized fungi: endocrocin and parietin, both anthraquinones, and polyporic and thelephoric acids, both terphenylquinones.

†**parietines**, *sb. pl.* *Obs.* *rare*⁻¹. [ad. L. *parietinæ*, pl. fem. of *parietinus* of or belonging to walls: see PARIETES and -INE[2].] Fallen or ruined walls; ruins.

1621 BURTON *Anat. Mel.* II. ii. II. (1651) 238 We have many ruines of such bathes found.. among those parietines and rubbish of old Romane townes.

parieto- (pə,raɪɪtəʊ), used as combining form (not on L. type) of PARIES or PARIETAL, in several terms of Anatomy, denoting **a.** Belonging to or connected both with the parietal bone, or lobe, and (the structure indicated by the second element): as **pa,rieto-'frontal** *a.* and *sb.*, **pa,rieto-'jugal**, **pa,rieto-'mastoid**, **pa,rieto-oc'cipital**, **pa,rieto-'quadrate**, **pa,rieto-sphe'noidal**, **pa,rieto-squa'mosal**, **pa,rieto-'temporal** *adjs.* **b.** Belonging to or connected with the wall of (a cavity), or of the body and (some structure): as **pa,rieto-'splanchnic** (-'splæŋknɪk) *a.* [Gr. σπλάγχνα viscera], belonging to the walls of the viscera, visceropleural; **pa,rieto-va'ginal** *a.* [L. *vagina* sheath], connected with the body-wall and the tentacle-sheath (applied to certain muscles in Polyzoa); **pa,rieto-'visceral** *a.* = *parieto-splanchnic*.

1875 HUXLEY & MARTIN *Elem. Biol.* 208 (The Frog) Two long flat bones, the *parieto-frontals, one on each side of a median suture which answers to the sagittal and frontal sutures in man. **1893** *Syd. Soc. Lex.*, **Parieto-jugal index*, the ratio of the greatest transverse diameter of the skull, or maximum parietal diameter, to the bizygomatic diameter. *Ibid.*, **Parieto-mastoid suture*, the.. suture between the inferior border of the parietal bone.. and the superior border of the mastoid portion of the temporal bone. **1879** CALDERWOOD *Mind & Brain* ii. 16 Towards the back part of the brain.. is the *Parieto-occipital fissure, which indicates a two-fold subdivision of the upper portion of the brain behind the fissure of Rolando. **1897** *Trans. Amer. Pediatric Soc.* IX. 185 Abscess of both parieto-occipital lobes and the cerebellum. **1893** *Syd. Soc. Lex.*, **Parieto-sphenoidal artery* .. *P. notch*. **1870** ROLLESTON *Anim. Life* 50 (Edible Snail), The upper or *parieto-splanchnic portion of the sub-oesophageal mass. **1893** *Syd. Soc. Lex.*, **Parieto-temporal suture*, the suture between the parietal and temporal bones. **1856** ALLMAN *Fresh-w. Polyzoa* (Ray Soc.) 27, 28 *Parieto-vaginal. **1878** BELL *Gegenbaur's Comp. Anat.* 144 The retractors of the anterior part of the body (parieto-vaginal muscles). **1888** ROLLESTON & JACKSON *Anim. Life* 236 A pair of parieto-vaginal muscles attached to the base of the fold surrounding the tentacle-sheath.

†**pari'formal**, *a.* *Obs.* *rare*⁻¹. [f. L. *pār*, *pari-* equal + *forma* form + -AL[1]: cf. *formal*. Improperly for **pariform*, med.L. *pariformis*, whence *pariformiter* adv. = 'pariter, similiter' (Du Cange).] Of equal form; equiform.

1651 BIGGS *New Disp.* ¶ 180 The Isonomy or pari-formall lawes of Re-publiques.

So †**pari'formity** *Obs. rare*, similitude of form.

1436 *Libel Eng. Policy* in *Pol. Poems* (Rolls) II. 193 Now see wee welle than that this rownde see To oure noble by paryformytee [*v.r.* parformyté], Undere the shypp, shewyd there the sayle.

†'**parify**, *v.* *Obs. rare.* [a. OF. *parifi-er* (15th c. in Godef.), or ad. med.L. *parificare* (1285 in Du Cange), f. *pār*, *pari-* equal: see -FY.] *trans.* To make, or represent as, equal; to compare, liken. So †**parifi'cation** *Obs.*

c **1425** WYNTOUN *Cron.* v. Prol. 2 Orosius apon syndry wys tyll Babylone Rome paryfyis. **1537** *Let.* in *Cranmer's Misc. Writ.* (Parker Soc.) II. 352 Subsequently ye parify me unto them. **1537** CRANMER *ibid.* 354 Where you say, that I parify you to the false traitors in Lincolnshire. *Ibid.*, When I write this parification (as you call it) of the rebels of Lincolnshire, I nothing thought less than to compare any man hereabout to them.

parigal, var. PAREGAL *Obs.*

pariglin, var. PARILLIN.

‖**parigot** (parigo), *a.* *colloq.* [Fr.] Of an accent, etc.: Parisian. Also as *sb.*, Parisian French.

1974 N. FREELING *Dressing of Diamond* 175 'What sort of accent would you call that, Johnny?' 'Overlaid,' said the technician stolidly. 'Predominance parigot.' 'Parigot hell, that's peasant... Peasant who went up to Ivry and acquired the rhythms.' *Ibid.* 202 A young or youngish woman who speaks with something of a parigot accent. **1977** *Times Lit. Suppl.* 6 May 546/5 French, in this case the most idiomatic 1977 Parigot French.

paril, obs. f. PERIL.

†'**parile**, *a.* *Obs.* [ad. L. *paril-is* equal, like, f. *par* equal: cf. *similis* like.] Equal, like.

1650 CHARLETON *Paradoxes* 11 Otherwise, I shall by a parile argument of ignorance, conclude, that [etc.]. **1686** GOAD *Celest. Bodies* I. xviii. 116 Doubts.. why the First Sextile should not be parile to the Later.

So †**pa'rility** *Obs.* [L. *parilitās*], equality.

1610 HEALEY *St. Aug. Citie of God* 425 His beauty consisting more of proportion and parilyty of parts. **1634** T. JOHNSON *Parey's Chirurg* I. v. (1678) 4 The temperature.. is a little absent from the exact and severe parility of mixed qualities.

parillin (pə'rɪlɪn) *Chem.* Also **pariglin** (pə'rɪljɪn). [f. Sp. *parilla* (see SARSAPARILLA), Pg. *parrilha*, It. *pariglia* + -IN[1].] A white or colourless, inodorous, crystalline substance ($C_{40}H_{70}O_{18}$) obtained from sarsaparilla-root; also called **pa'rillic acid**, *salsaparin*, *sarsaparillin*, *sarsaparilla-saponin*, or *smilacin*.

1831 J. DAVIES *Manual Mat. Med.* 234 *Parilline, Pariglium*, a peculiar proximate principle, discovered by Pallota. **1838** T. THOMSON *Chem. Org. Bodies* 278. **1881** WATTS *Dict. Chem.* VIII. 1780 Parillin does not excite sneezing like saponin.

‖**pari mutuel** (pari mytɥɛl). *Orig.* usu. in pl. **paris mutuels** (with same pronunciation). Now usu. **pari-mutuel**. [Fr., = mutual stake or wager.] **a.** A form of betting 'in which those who have put a stake on the winning horse divide among themselves the total of the stakes on the other horses' (less the percentage of the managers—i.e., in France, the Government).

1881 *Standard* 7 Sept. 5/2 That the accounts of their horseracing should sometimes puzzle English readers by the mention of 'pools' and 'Paris mutuals' is possible. **1888** [see FAR-EASTERN *a.*]. **1891** *Harper's Mag.* Mar. 511/1 For this rough horde of human beings the only interest that the races offered was the betting.. by means of the mutual pool or *pari mutuel* system. **1894** *Daily News* 13 Oct. 5/3 The Minister of the Interior has prohibited throughout France the opening of pari mutuel offices at cycle races... As for morality, there is little to be said for private pari mutuels. Bad as they are, however, they are better than the Government-instituted ones. **1931** E. WAUGH *Remote People* 12 There had been a horse-race.. with a pari-mutuel. **1955** 'S. RANSOME' *Deadly Bedfellows* xiii. 123 The legislature.. will choose to legalise *pari-mutuel* horse-racing. **1964** A. WYKES *Gambling* viii. 191 The pari-mutuel system (which was devised in 1872 by a French chemist named Pierre Oller). **1969** C. DRUMMOND *Odds on Death* ii. 43 The big market is not the parimutuel —totaliser, call it what you will—but book-making, legal and illegal. **1971** L. KOPPETT *N.Y. Times Guide Spectator Sports* x. 172 Pari-mutuel betting refers to a system in which all the participating bettors are betting against each other. **1976** *Maclean's Mag.* 12 Jan. 34/1 The state bicentennial commission raised $845,000 from the taxes on one extra day of betting at pari-mutuel outlets.

b. The booth at which such bets are placed, or the machine which issues tickets recording such bets.

1913 'F. SUMMERVILLE' *Spirit of Paris* v. 38 But there is a great keenness on the animals too, and men and women bet at the *pari-mutuel* with much earnestness. **1923** E. HEMINGWAY *Three Stories & Ten Poems* 43 The gong going for dear life and the pari mutuel wickets rattling down. **1934** 'A. BRIDGE' *Ginger Griffin* xvi. 200 They strolled towards the *pari-mutuel* windows, which extended in a long row between the paddock and the grand-stand. **1973** D. FRANCIS in *Winter's Crimes* 5 115 It meant hanging around the pari-mutuel with your eyes open.

parine ('pɛəraɪn), *a.* *Ornith.* [f. mod.L. *Parīnæ*, f. L. *parus* titmouse, in mod.L. the name of the typical genus.] Belonging to or having the characters of the subfamily *Parinæ* of passerine birds (the true titmice).

paring ('pɛərɪŋ), *vbl. sb.* [f. PARE *v.*[1] + -ING[1].] The action of PARE *v.*[1], or the result of this.

†**1.** The action of preparing, preparation. *Obs.*

1392 *Earl Derby's Exp.* (Camden) 156/6 Et pro bulting et paring dicti frumenti. **1444** *Rolls of Parlt.* V. 114/1 The saide Wyne hat his true makyng, and trewe boillyng and paryng.

2. The action of pruning, or cutting off the edge or surface, or anything superficial. *lit.* and *fig.*

1398 TREVISA *Barth. De P.R.* XVII. cxvii. (Bedl. MS.) lf. 220/1 Euerich ȝere þe spraie [of a vyne] nedeþ kuttinge and paringe. **1607** MIDDLETON *Michaelm. Term* II. iii, For all his cleansing, pruning, and paring, he's not worthy a broker's daughter. **1866** ROGERS *Agric. & Prices* I. xxi. 528 The hoofs of horses have become less solid in consequence of continual paring. **1881** E. J. WORBOISE *Sissie* viii, That one is never the better for mere scraping, and paring, and saving.

3. *concr.* A thin portion pared off the surface of anything, usually as refuse or superfluous matter; a shaving.

1382 WYCLIF *1 Cor.* iv. 13 We ben maad, the paringis [*gloss* or outcastinge] of alle thingis til ȝit. **1413** *Pilgr. Sowle* (Caxton 1483) IV. vii. 61 The rynde or the paryng of this appel. **1602** *Narcissus* (1893) App. i. 25 What is left for mee but the paringes, when I have given others the peares? **1698** FRYER *Acc. E. India & P.* 140 Never was more truly verified that Proverb, Half the King's Cheese goes away in Parings. **1793** GOUV. MORRIS in Sparks *Life & Writ.* (1832) II. 278 To take her islands is to possess but the paring of her nails. **1856** MISS MULOCK *J. Halifax* i, Sailing thereon a fleet of potato parings.

4. *attrib.* and *Comb.*, as **paring-bee**, *N. Amer.* (BEE[1] 4), **-chisel**, **frolic**, **gouge**, **-iron**, **-knife**, **-mattock**, **-plough**, **-shovel**, **-spade**, etc.; **paring-place**, ? the castor (of a horse).

1830 J. PICKERING *Emigration* 72 A paring 'bee', or 'be', [is] an assemblage of neighbours invited to one house, to prepare apples for drying. **1845** *Lowell* (Mass.) *Offering* V. 269 When we were about to have a paring bee we sent our invitations a day or two previous. **1850** *Knickerbocker* XXXV. 24 Give me the real paring-bee reels and jigs before all your waltzes and Spanish dances. **1857** *Quinland* I. 191 Went this evening.. with the young people to a paring-bee at Squire Carter's. **1888** J. Q. BITTINGER *Hist. Haverhill* (N.H.) 359 Quite an incident was the paring-bee in bringing young folks together. The.. young men mounted the paring machines and peeled the apples, whilst the.. young ladies quartered and cored them. **1933** E. C. GUILLET *Early Life Upper Canada* 195 A paring bee produced large numbers of strings of dried apples, and these were suspended from the ceiling of kitchen or attic. **1703** MOXON *Mech. Exerc.* 76 The Paring-Chissel.. must have a very fine and smooth edge. **1895** *Montgomery Ward Catal.* Spring & Summer 365/2 Barton's paring chisels. **1940** *Chambers's Techn. Dict.* 617/1 *Paring chisel* (*Carp.*, *Join.*), a long chisel with a thinner blade than a firmer tool, used for finishing off work by hand. **1964** W. L. GOODMAN *Hist. Woodworking Tools* 33 Plate I of the 'Charpente' article shows a workman using the paring-chisel end of this tool. **1968** J. ARNOLD *Shell Bk. Country Crafts* 287 Each blade produced may be compared very roughly to a carpenter's paring-chisel in having a bevel along its two sides. **1974** P. W. BLANDFORD *Country Craft Tools* v. 76 A longer and thinner chisel for hand pressure only was called a 'paring' or 'heading' chisel. **1931** V. P. SEARY *Romance Marit. Provinces* 177 Another sort of frolic was the 'paring frolic', when young men and girls gathered to pare and slice apples, that they might be dried out and kept throughout the winter. **1909** WEBSTER, Paring gouge. **1940** *Chambers's Techn. Dict.* 617/2 *Paring gouge* (*Carp. etc.*), a gouge having the bevel ground upon the inside or concave face of the cutting edge. **1966** A. W. LEWIS *Gloss. Woodworking Terms* 39 A paring gouge is a long thin scribing gouge. **1530** PALSGR. 652/2, I pare a saffrone grounde, or aley with a paryng yron. **1591** PERCIVALL *Sp. Dict.*, *Tranchete*, a shoemakers paring knife. **1908** *Sears, Roebuck Catal.* 768/1 Kitchen or paring knives... Length of blade, 3 inches. **1925** *Scribner's Mag.* Oct. 430/1 She was rubbing the paring-knife across her fingers to free them from dirt and water. **1968** J. ARNOLD *Shell Bk. Country Crafts* 139 The box contains hammer, pritchel, buffer, paring-knife, pincers and, of course, a supply of nails. **1693** *Lond. Gaz.* No. 2935/4 A black [Gelding].. with a swelling on the Paring place of the far hind Leg. **1805** R. W. DICKSON *Pract. Agric.* I. 12 The Paring-Plough is a necessary instrument.. in bringing into cultivation heath, moor, and other waste lands. **1552** HULOET, Paring shouell, or instrument to pare flores, *valgium*. **1888** *Sheffield Gloss.*, *Paring-spade*, an instrument used for clearing stubble from land after harvest.

paringal, -ale, -alle, var. PAREGAL *Obs.*

‖**pari passu** ('pɛəraɪ 'pæsjuː, 'pɑːriː 'pæːsuː), *advb. phr.* [L. = 'with equal step'.] With equal pace; at an equal rate of progress; side by side; simultaneously and equally. In *Law*, On an equality, equally, without preference.

1567 SIR N. THROKMORTON *Let.* in Robertson *Hist. Scot.* Wks. 1826 I. 378 *note*, They think it convenient to proceed with yow both for a while pari passu. **1642** SIR E. DERING *Sp. on Relig.* xvi. 88 Let both these bils go *pari passu*, hand in hand together. **1775** J. ADAMS *Wks.* (1854) IX. 356 To.. proceed with warlike measures and conciliatory measures *pari passu*. **1827** JARMAN *Powell's Devises* II. 139 Copyholds are now placed *pari passu* with freeholds. **1890** GLADSTONE *Sp. Ho. Commons* 19 Feb., The only method of describing *pari passu* was that adopted by Mr. John Bright.. when he said that, when people were content with a *pari passu* progress, it was like driving six omnibuses abreast down Park-lane.

paripatecian, erron. f. PERIPATETIAN *Obs.*

paripinnate (pærɪ'pɪnət), *a.* *Bot.* [ad. mod. Bot. L. *paripinnāt-us*, f. *pār*, *pari-* equal: see PINNATE.] Pinnate with an even number of leaflets, i.e. without a terminal leaflet.

1857 HENFREY *Elem. Bot.* §95 When there is no end leaflet, the leaf is abruptly- or pari-pinnate. **1870** BENTLEY *Man. Bot.* (ed. 2) 163.

Paris ('pærɪs), the name of the capital of France, used in various collocations: e.g. in names of materials or articles made in Paris, as ***Paris †crisp, cup, net***; in names of measures or weights used at Paris, differing from the corresponding English ones, as ***Paris foot, inch, line, pint***. Also, in names of articles associated with or designed in Paris, esp. with an implication of being fashionable, exclusive, or expensive, as ***Paris cloth, cut, dress, felt, gown, hat, net, shirt***; **Paris baby** = *Paris doll* (*Cent. Dict.* 1890); † **Paris ball**, a tennis ball; **Paris basin** (*Geol.*), the area of Tertiary strata on which Paris is situated; **Paris binding** (see quot. 1964); † **Paris black**, ? name of some black stuff used for garments; **Paris blue**, (*a*) a bright shade of Prussian blue; (*b*) a bright blue colouring matter obtained from aniline; † **Paris candle**, a kind of large wax-candle; **Paris cap** (see quot.); **Paris daisy**, the plant *Chrysanthemum frutescens* from Teneriffe, cultivated also as *Marguerite*; **Paris doll**, a doll or lay-figure dressed in the latest fashion, used by dress-makers as a model; **Paris embroidery** (see quots.); **Paris green**, a vivid light green pigment composed of aceto-arsenite of copper, and used as an insecticide; **Paris gypsum**, gypsum from the Paris basin; † **Paris head**, a head-dress from Paris; **Paris lake** = carmine lake (Watts *Dict. Chem.* 1866–77); **Paris plaster** = PLASTER-OF-PARIS; hence † **Paris-plasterer**; **Paris-red**, †(*a*) a shade of red; (*b*) ferric oxide, finely divided, used as a polish for glass, gold and silver, etc.; **Paris violet**, a coal-tar colour, called also methyl-violet; **Paris white**, a fine kind of whiting used in polishing.

1471 RIPLEY *Comp. Alch.* v. xxxi. in Ashm. (1652) 155 Ther Pauteners be stuffed wyth *Parrys balls. **1530** PALSGR. 240/1 Lytell paresball, *estevf.* **1599** SHAKS. *Hen. V*, II. iv. 131 To that end..I did present him with the Paris-Balls. **1832** DE LA BECHE *Geol. Man.* 233 Comprised within what is commonly termed the *Paris basin. **1918** E. & M. WALLBANK *Dress Cutting & Making* x. 65 For binding skirt seams, use ¼" lute or *Paris binding with one edge folded over rather less than half the width. **1964** C. PENTON *ABC of Sewing* 64/1 *Paris binding*, a braid ½" wide used for covering raw edges cut on the straight, and slip-stitched to the fabric beneath. *a* **1568** R. SEMPLE *Jonet Reid* 4 Bayth *Pareiss blak and Inglis broun. **1864–72** WATTS *Dict. Chem.* II. 227 The pure ferric ferrocyanide..is sometimes called *Paris blue. **1900** *Daily News* 4 June 2/6 Manufacturers of Paris blue, starch, and black lead. [**1401–2** *Mem. Ripon* (Surtees) III. 209, ij lib. *candel, de Parys.] **1480** *Wardr. Acc. Edw. IV* (1830) 121, iij dosen and ix lb' of paris candell'. **1512** *Northumbld. Househ. Bk.* (1827) 2 Of Parisch Candle viij dosson x lb. **1547** SALESBURY *Welsh Dict.*, *Kanwyll baris*, a pares candel. **1966** J. S. COX *Illustr. Dict. Hairdressing* 109/1 **Paris cap*, a woman's head-dress of the mid-sixteenth century. It fitted the head closely with a jewelled band running over the top of the head and ending in a point on the cheeks. **1960** C. W. CUNNINGTON et al. *Dict. Eng. Costume* 268/1 **Paris Cloth, Toile de Paris.* Med. and 17th c. Originally a fine white linen; later a woollen cloth. **1401** in Frost *Notices rel. Hull* (1827) App. 3 Pro x dus[enis] *paris crisp. **1479** *Paston Lett.* III. 270, iiij *Parys cuppis with a cover. **1748** SMOLLETT *R. Random* II. xlv. 80 In the evening, [I] dressed myself in a plain suit of the true *Paris cut. **1884** MILLER *Plant-n.*, *Chrysanthemum frutescens*, Marguerite, *Paris Daisy. **1959** J. BRAINE *Vodi* xiv. 195 The rather cold-eyed girl with the *Paris dress and the real pearls. **1973** H. MCCLOY *Change of Heart* ii. 17 The black dress was Paris and so at least four years old... Yet old as it was that Paris dress made every other dress in the room look shapeless. **1882** CAULFEILD & SAWARD *Dict. Needlework* 378/1 **Paris Embroidery*.—This is a simple variety of Satin Stitch worked upon Piqué with fine white cord for washing articles, and upon coloured rep silk, or fine cloth with filoselles for other materials. **1957** M. B. PICKEN *Fashion Dict.* 243/2 *Paris embroidery*, white cord embroidery on piqué. **1969** R. T. WILCOX *Dict. Costume* (1970) 259/2 *Paris embroidery*, a fine white cord embroidery appliquéd in satin stitch on piqué. Used in washable linens and garment accessories. **1853** J. B. FELT *Customs New Eng.* 119 They were at first called *sombreros*,..*slouches*, and *California hats*,..but latterly, by some, **Paris felts*. **1742** *Phil. Trans.* XLII. 188 The *Paris Foot..contains 12·785 English Inches. **1839** F. A. KEMBLE *Jrnl. Residence Georgian Plantation* (1863) 346 A *Paris gown and bonnet might have been in equal danger of shocking his prejudices. **1896** E. TURNER *Little Larrikin* xiii. 141 The commanding presence in the Paris gown. **1913** A. BENNETT *Regent* II. viii. 219 Elegant women wearing Paris or almost-Paris gowns. **1965** ROACH & EICHER *Dress, Adornment, & Social Order* 396 Writer sees Hollywood fashions beginning to take some of the prestige away from Paris gowns in the 1930's. **1868** *Amer. Agriculturist* XXVII. 321 The following is going the rounds of the press 'Sure death to Potato Bugs: Take 1 lb. *Paris green, 2 lbs. pulverized lime. Mix together, and sprinkle the vines.' We consider this unsafe, as..Paris green is a compound of arsenic and copper, and a deadly poison. **1882** HOWELLS in *Longm. Mag.* I. 44 Saffron, with Paris-green shutters. **1902** *Encycl. Brit.* XXVIII. 530/2 The best fruit farmers spray fruit trees regularly in the early spring..with quassia and soft soap and paraffin emulsions, and a very few with Paris green only. **1966** LOCKHART & WISEMAN *Introd. Crop Husbandry* vii. 231 Baits such as Paris green. **1885** *Lyell's Elem. Geol.* (ed. 4) Index, Fossil footprints in *Paris gypsum. **1845** G. DODD *Brit. Manuf.* 5th Ser. 172 The plush for the larger number of silk hats is woven in Lancashire; but for '*Paris hats', as they are called, it is woven in France. **1906** E. DYSON *Fact'ry 'Ands* vii. 87 A man in a long frock coat, a high, glittering, Paris hat. **1951** C. PORTER *Kiss me Kate* 108 Mr. Harris, plutocrat, Wants to give my cheek a pat, If the Harris pat Means a Paris hat—Bé-bé. **1957** M. B. PICKEN *Fashion Dict.* 165/2 *Paris hat*, high silk hat worn by men. *c* **1596** in *Gentl. Mag.* (1819) LXXXIX. I. 23 Next after them came the Lady Strange.. in her *paris head. **1791** BOSWELL *Johnson* 28 Apr. an. 1778, A *Paris-made wig. **1759** *Newport* (Rhode Island) *Mercury* 26 June 4/3 To be sold by Jacob Richardson,..plain Gauze, *Parisnets, gimp and floss Garland. **1766** C. ANSTEY *New Bath Guide* iii. 23 Stomachers and Parisnets. **1882** CAULFEILD & SAWARD *Dict. Needlework* 378/1 *Paris net*, a description of Net employed in Millinery. **1795** *Gentl. Mag.* LXV. II. 925 Ten quarts (or *Paris pints). **1855** *Ecclesiologist* XVI. 336 Mortar, *Paris-plaster, sulphur, and even lead. *c* **1515** *Cocke Lorell's B.* 10 *Parys plasterers, daubers, and lyme borners. **1600** in *Hakluyt's Voy.* (1811) III. 289 [The Captaine] bestowed vpon him a cloake of *Paris red. **1937** N. COWARD *Present Indicative* I. 28, I can smell the eau-de-Cologne, see..the stripes on his *Paris shirt. **1588** *Reg. Privy Council Scot.* IV. 322 Ane quarter of an unce *Pareis wecht. **1434** in *E.E. Wills* (1882) 101, I towell of *parys werk.

paris: see HERB PARIS; obs. form of PARISH.

† **parisant**, *a. Obs. rare*$^{-1}$. [a. OF. *parissant*, f. *parir* to appear.] Seemly, of good appearance.

c **1400** *Laud Troy Bk.* 8599 Eche man now his harneis rubbes, That thei be clene and Parisaunt.

parische, parise, obs. ff. PARISH, PERISH.

parisee: see PARISIS.

† **Paris garden.** *Obs.* Also 6–7 **Parish garden**. [See quot. 1674.] Name of a place at Bankside, Southwark, where a bear-garden was kept in Elizabethan and later times; hence, 'a bear-garden', a noisy disorderly place. Also *attrib.*

1589 NASHE *Pasquil's Return* Wks. (Grosart) I. 109 Strange trickes, and deuises, betweene the Ape and the Owle, the like was neuer yet seene in Paris-garden. **1592** GREENE *Upst. Courtier* Wks. (Grosart) XI. 253 Eager to catch him, as a dog to take a beare by the eares in Parish-garden. **1663** BUTLER *Hud.* I. ii. 172 Bred up, where Discipline most rare is, In Military Garden-Paris. **1672** R. WILD *Poet. Licent.* 31 Their Churches Paris-Gardens are become. **1674** BLOUNT *Glossogr.* (ed. 4), *Paris Garden*, is the place on the Thames Bank-side at London, where the Bears are kept and baited; and was antiently so called from Robert de Paris, who had a House there in Richard the second's time.

parish ('pærɪʃ), *sb.* Forms: α. 3–7 **paroche**, 4–8 **paroch**, (4 **proche**, 6 **parroch(e)**. β. 4 **parosche**, **-osshe**, **-osse**, 5 **-oish**, **-ossh**, **-os**; 4–5 **parizs**, **-yzsh**, (**-ise**, **parshe**, **persche**), 4– **parish**, (5 **parisch(e**, **-isshe**, **-issche**, **-isse**, **-esche**, **-essh**, **-es**, **-eche**, **-ysch(e**, **-ysh(e**, **-yssh**, **-ysse**, **parresche**, **-ych**, **peresche**, **parsche**, 5–6 **parishe**, **-issh**, **-asche**, **-esshe**, *Sc.* **paris**, **-eis**, **parriche**, **-ish**). [Two forms: (α) *paroche*, a. AF. *paroche*, OF. *par(r)oche*, app. a learned form, ad. late. L. *parochia*; (β) *parosshe*, etc.:—OF. *paroisse*:—popular L. **parocia* for *parochia*. The latter (in Sidonius, *c* 472) was a form substituted for Christian L. *parœcia* (Augustine, Jerome), a. Gr. παροικία, in Christian use, the charge of a bishop, a diocese, later the charge of a presbyter, a parish: see Note below. With *parochia*, *parocia*, *paroisse*, cf. *brachia*, *bracia*, F. *brasse*. With Eng. *parosshe* from *paroisse*, cf. ME. *marish*, *marsh*, from OF. *mareis*, *marois*; also *brush*, etc. The stress was already *c* 1300 on *par-*; whence the *o* was weakened to *e* and *i*, giving *paresche*, *parisshe*, *parish*.]

1. In the United Kingdom, and some of the Colonies, the name of a subdivision of a county: applied to it primarily in its ecclesiastical aspect, but also as an area recognized for various purposes of civil administration and local government.

The name occurs in Norman French in the Laws of William I, *c* 1075, but has not been found in Eng. before the 13th c. Although the parochial system was more or less developed in many (perhaps most) parts of England before the year 1000, there is no word formed from *parochia*, nor any directly answering to it, in OE.; the nearest equivalents being *preost-scír* 'priest-shire' (*Eccles. Inst.* xiv in Thorpe *Laws*), and *scrift-scír* 'shrift-shire' (*Canons of Edgar* vi, *Eccl. Laws of Cnut* xiii), both of 11th or late 10th c., the latter rendered *parochia* in the 13th c. L. version.

a. *orig.* A township or cluster of townships having its own church, and ministered to by its own priest, parson, or parish clergyman, to whom its tithes and ecclesiastical dues are (or originally were) paid. **b.** A later division of such an original parish for ecclesiastical purposes only, having its own church and clergyman.

The latter includes the ancient ***parochial chapelries*** of some of the large northern parishes (CHAPEL 3 b, CHAPELRY 1), and the more recent ecclesiastical districts constituted under the powers given by the various Church Building Acts, distinguished as ***new ecclesiastical parishes***. In Scotland these are called ***parishes quoad sacra***, while the original parishes which remain such for all purposes are ***parishes quoad omnia***. The original parish when retained for civil, although subdivided for ecclesiastical purposes, is commonly distinguished as the ***civil parish***, in Scotland a ***parish quoad civilia***.

Most of the older territories colonized from Great Britain have parishes, both for ecclesiastical and civil purposes, frequently as electoral districts or divisions; in the newer territories where there is no established church the parish has often no official existence, though the Church of England (and, in some cases, other Churches) has applied the name to areas formed for the organization of its own work; and the term is used in the same way by the Protestant Episcopal Church in the United States.

α. [**1292** BRITTON II. xix. §4 Car en une vile porrount estre plusours paroches, et en une paroche plusours maners, et hameletz plusours porrount apendre a un maner. **1865** NICHOLS *tr.*, For in one town there may be several parishes, and in one parish several manors, and several hamlets may belong to one manor.] **13..** *Cursor M.* 29501 If þou did a sin Anoþer preistes paroch in. **1464** *Rolls of Parlt.* V. 542/1 In the paroche of Cleobury. **1533** CRANMER *Let. to Cromwell* in *Misc. Writ.* (Parker Soc.) II. 269 My friend..was born in the same paroche. **1681** in *Lond. Gaz.* No. 1649/2 The Ministers of each Paroch. **1742** CAMPBELL in *Phil. Trans.* XLII. 240 John Ferguison, a Native of the Paroch of Killmellfoord in the Shire of Argyle.

β. [*c* **1075** *Laws of William I.* I. i. 1 E de mere iglise de parosse [*v.r.* paroisse] xx souz, e de chapele x souz.] **1340** *Ayenb.* 42 Ine ham þet be yefþes..yeueþ þe prouendres and þe parosses oþer oþre benefices of holy cherche. *c* **1380** WYCLIF *Wks.* (1880) 413 þis shulde teche siche persones to take more hede to þer paryzshis. *c* **1386** CHAUCER *Prol.* 449 In al the parisshe [*v.rr.* parysshe, -ich, -issche, -isch(e) wif ne was ther noon That to the offrynge bifore hire sholde goon. **1387** TREVISA *Higden* (Rolls) V. 89 Denys..to deled parisches [*v.rr.* parsches, paryshes, **1432–50** paresches] and chirche hawes, and assigned to everich a preost. **1393** LANGL. *P. Pl.* C. XXIII. 263 Pilours and pyke-herneys in eche parshe [*v.r.* paresche] a-corsede. *c* **1440** *Promp. Parv.* 384/2 Paros, or parysche (*S.* pares, or parych), *parochia*. **1511–12** *Act 3 Hen. VIII*, c. 17 §17 Medowes..in the parriche of Ewherst. **1526** TINDALE *1 Pet.* v. 3 Nott as though ye were lordes over the parisshes. **1549** *Compl. Scot.* 167 Nocht ane boroustone nor landuard paris vitht in the realme. **1589** GREENE *Menaphon* (Arb.) 45 A heards-mans daughter of the same parish. **1642** FULLER *Holy & Prof. St.* III. xxiv. 220 Otherwise Palestine was a great Parish, and some therein had an hundred miles to Church. **1739** WESLEY *Wks.* (1872) I. 201, I look upon all the world as my parish. **1758** JOHNSON *Idler* No. 29 ¶9, I am going to settle in my native parish. **1846** MCCULLOCH *Acc. Brit. Empire* (1854) I. 141 Parishes are frequently intermixed with one another. This seems to have arisen from the lord of the manor having had a parcel of land detached from the main part of his estate, but not sufficient to form a parish of itself. **1875** STUBBS *Const. Hist.* I. viii. 227 The parish, then, is the ancient *vicus* or tún-scipe regarded ecclesiastically. As many townships were too small to require or to support a separate church and priest, many parishes contain several townships. **1885** C. I. ELTON in *Encycl. Brit.* XVIII. 296/1 Under the powers given by the Church Building Acts, many populous parishes have been subdivided into smaller ecclesiastical parishes.

c. Used as the English name for the corresponding ecclesiastical areas in ancient times or in foreign countries.

1839 *Encycl. Brit.* (ed. 7) XIX. 432/1 There are in Rome 54 parishes and 300 churches. **1880** E. HATCH in *Dict. Chr. Antiq.* 1560/1 In Gaul and Spain a single presbyter or a single deacon was sometimes put in charge of a parish. That a deacon might be 'rector' of a parish is clear from many instances, e.g. Conc. Illib. c. 77.

d. As many as would fill a parish; a parishful.

1611 SHAKS. *Cymb.* IV. ii. 168 I'ld let a parish of such Clotens blood.

2. A district, often identical with an original parish, but often having quite different limits, constituted for various purposes of civil government, and thus designated a ***civil parish***: **a.** primarily, Such an area constituted for the administration of the Poor-law, and sometimes distinguished as a ***poor-law parish***; legally defined by Act 52 & 53 Vict. c. 63 §5 as 'a place for which a separate poor-rate is or can be made, or for which a separate overseer is or can be appointed'. (This area at first coincided with the original parish in sense 1.) Hence the phrase ***on the parish***, in receipt of parochial relief; so ***to go on the parish, to be brought up by the parish, buried by the parish***, etc.

b. An original parish, or other area, separately assessed for land-tax; a ***land-tax parish***. 'They are described in the series of land-tax accounts from 1692 to the present time, and are also defined in the Taxes Management Act of 1880' (Elton in *Encycl. Brit.* XVIII. 296).

c. An area treated as a parish for the purpose of the Burial Acts, from 1852 onward; a ***Burial Acts parish***.

d. A district, larger or smaller than an original parish, which constituted a unit for the maintenance of its own highways; a ***highway parish***.

[**1601** *Act* 43 *Eliz.* c. 2 Ouerseers of the Poore of the same Parish.] **1632** N. FERRAR *Story Bks. Little Gidding* (1899) 219 That a Father should leave his children on the Parish through..unthriftines. **1830** *Examiner* 803/2 He shall either go upon the parish or starve. **1846** MCCULLOCH *Acc. Brit. Empire* (1854) II. 653 The selection of the 'parish' as the territorial division likely to prove the most convenient for the purposes of poor-law administration, was, no doubt, fully justified by the circumstances of the country in Queen Elizabeth's reign. But..the 13 and 14 Car. II., c. 12, enabled townships, under certain circumstances, to erect themselves into parishes for poor-law purposes. **1885** SIR W. B. BRETT in *Law Rep.* 15 *Queen's Bench Div.* 385 An ordinary parish may..be conterminous with and practically the same thing as a highway parish. **1885** SIR C. DILKE in

Daily News 14 Oct. 6/1 The township, the hundred, and the county... In place of the three sets of districts which never overlap we have..overlapping areas,..highway parishes and land-tax parishes, as distinguished from poor-law parishes, and other anomalies. **1890** F. W. ROBINSON *Very Strange Fam.* 6 The boy will certainly be sent to the parish, if you don't pay for him. **1893** *Daily News* 22 Mar. 4/6 There are..civil parishes and ecclesiastical parishes, which do not exactly coincide either in number or in extent.

e. *transf.* and *fig.* (also influenced by sense 1).

1940 AUDEN *Another Time* 52 The ape Is really at home in the parish Of grimacing and licking. **1941** —— *New Year Let.* I. 25 However miserable may be Our parish of immediacy. **1951** *Times* 1 Jan. 7/6 Covering the whole of the F.E.A.F. [*sc.* Far East Air Force] area,..two impressions stand out..the vastness of its 'parish' and of its commitments..and the slenderness of the aircraft resources at its disposal. **1958** P. KEMP *No Colours or Crest* viii. 153 My parish includes not only the old frontiers of Albania, but the new regions incorporated into the country by the Axis. **1976** *Shooting Times & Country Mag.* 16–22 Dec. 13/2 Others—in the north—consider they are too far south, while in the south some consider they are too far north! In fact, WAGBI is based almost equally between their interests, bordered by the 'parish' of Northern Ireland; the North of Scotland; Cornwall and Kent. **1977** D. BEATY *Excellency* ii. 25 From British Embassies and High Commissions all over the world came messages reporting reactions of their parishes to the recent events.

3. a. The inhabitants of a parish; parishioners collectively.

c **1290** *Becket* 1845 in *S. Eng. Leg.* I. 159 Ech preost somonede is paroche [*v.r.* (Percy Soc.) parosche]. *c* **1325** *Pol. Songs* (Camden) 157 Everuch a parosshe heo polketh in pyne, Ant clastreth with heore colle. *c* **1325** *Poem Times Edw. II* 102 ibid. 328 And thus shal al the parish for lac of lore spille. *c* **1380** WYCLIF *Wks.* (1880) 418 þey harmen hem silf & þer parizs & oþer puple. *a* **1450** MYRC 678 Whan thi parisse is togidir mette. **1583** *Leg. Bp. St. Androis* 102 Sic preist, sic pariche: what suld mair? **1680** BAXTER *Answ. Stillingfl.* xxxiv. 54 Not the..Tenth Part of the Parish can come to Hear him in the Church. **1750** GRAY *Long Story* 42 By this time all the Parish know it. **1876** BARING-GOULD *R. S. Hawker* ix. 220 The parish offered to give the church a roofing of the best Delabole slate.

b. *U.S.* The body of people associated for Christian worship and work in connexion with a particular local church; a congregation; hence, a denomination.

1851 HAWTHORNE *Twice-Told T., Minister's Black Veil*, All the busybodies and impertinent people in the parish. **1858** —— *Fr. & It. Note-Bks.* (1883) 25 Being of another parish, I looked on coldly, but not irreverently. **1875** H. JERSON *Lamson's Ch. First Three Cent.* VII. ii. 308 The term 'parish' is applied in America to congregations, considered as the minister's 'cure of souls' without the reference to local limits with which in England it is associated.

4. *U.S.* **a.** In colonial times, and still in some of the southern States: A subdivision of a county made for purposes of local self-government. **b.** In Louisiana, the name of the (64) territorial divisions corresponding to the counties of other States. Cf. COUNTY *sb.* 3.

1772 *Amherst* (Mass.) *Rec.* (1884) 60/1 The Vote taken respecting the Dividing of the District into two Districts or parishes was past in the Negative. **1839** *Penny Cycl.* XIV. 174/1 For political and civil purposes Louisiana is divided into thirty-one parishes. **1856** OLMSTED *Slave States* 639 In the parish of Opelousas (parish, in Louisiana, is equivalent to county) there were many.

5. *Hist.* In sense of Gr. παροικία: A diocese, or district under the spiritual charge of a bishop.

1709 J. JOHNSON *Clergym. Vade M.* II. 10 Let not a Bishop be allowed to leave his own parish, and leap into another. **1898** JESSOPP in *19th Cent.* Jan. 50 Parish indicated originally the geographical area over which the jurisdiction of a bishop extended.

6. *Curling.* The ring with the tee in the centre.

1893–4 *R. Caled. Curling Club Ann.* 104 (E.D.D.) He has plenty of running to win into the parish.

7. *attrib.* and *Comb.*: often = 'parochial' *adj.* **a.** Of, belonging, or pertaining to a parish, as ***parish altar, bell, bounds, constable, drudge, dungeon, duty, feast, knell, living, meeting, officer, parson, preacher, pulpit, rate*** (so ***parish-rated*** adj.), ***school, vestry, wall***; for the service or use of the parish, as ***parish doctor, mag, magazine, mill, nurse, pound, pump, room***, etc.; maintained or provided by the parish, as the recognized unit of poor relief (see 2 a), as ***parish-boy, -child, -coffin, -girl, -house, poor, relief, shell, workhouse***; characteristic of a parish, parochial, as ***parish-jest, -wit***; also ***parish-pensioned*** adj. **b.** Special Combs.: **parish blue**, cloth supplied as a pauper dress (see BLUE *sb.* 3); **parish-book** = *parish-register* (b); **parish communion, Eucharist**, a communion service held as the principal service of the day (usu. Sunday), and at which most of the congregation communicate; **parish lands**, landed property belonging to a parish, and administered by the churchwardens; **parish lantern** (*dial.* and *slang*), the moon; **parish mass**, a mass celebrated in a parish church, *spec.* = *parish communion* (quot. 1763 is a fortuitous collocation); **parish pump**, used allusively (often *attrib.* or as *adj.*) to denote political speakers and their speeches, and other matters, that are limited in scope, outlook, or knowledge, or of local importance only; hence **parish pumper**, one who is concerned with parish-pump politics; **parish pumpery**, concern with local matters only, parochialism; **parish-pumpish** *a.*, limited in outlook and interests, parochial; **parish-register**, † (*a*) the registrar of a parish; (*b*) a book recording the christenings, marriages, and burials which take place at the parish church; **parish rig** (see quots.); **parish-rigged** *a.*, cheaply rigged; **parish school** *Sc.* and *N. Amer.*, = *parochial school* (PAROCHIAL *a.* (*sb.*) 1 a); so ***parish schoolmaster*** (the collocation in quot. 1788 may be fortuitous); †**parish-top**, a top kept for the use of the parishioners; †**parish-watch**, a parish constable; **parish work**, the work or duty of attending to the poor and sick of a parish; pastoral work in a parish. See also PARISH CHURCH, CLERK, etc.

1481 *Peebles Charters* (1872) 188 Chaplanis and serwandis at the *paroche alter in Sant Andros kyrk, as pleban and curat. **1864** TENNYSON *En. Ard.* 616 Though faintly, merrily—far and far away—He heard the pealing of his *parish bells. **1830** GEN. P. THOMPSON *Exerc.* (1842) I. 212 A mark and a suit of *parish blue. **1594** GREENE & LODGE *Looking Glasse* G.'s Wks. (Rtldg.) 131/2 For proof he was my child, search the *parish book. **1861** J. BRENT in *Archæol. Cant.* IV. 36 Approaching St. George's *parish-bounds. **1749** FIELDING *Tom Jones* II. iii, Who, together with seven *Parish-boys, was learning to read and write. **1663** PEPYS *Diary* 20 Aug., A good likely girle, and a *parish child of St. Bride's, of honest parentage. **1715** NELSON *Addr. Pers. Qual.* 187 They will rather take a Child, who hath been educated in a way of Industry,..than any other Parish-Child. **1936** *Church Q. Rev.* Oct.–Dec. 103 There will naturally be no later Solemn Eucharist, and only provision earlier for those who cannot possibly attend the *Parish Communion. **1937** A. G. HEBERT *Parish Communion* i. 3 By 'the Parish Communion' is meant the celebration of the Holy Eucharist, with the communion of the people, in a parish church, as the chief service of the day, or, better, as the assembly of the Christian community for the worship of God. **1953** [see MORCELLATED *ppl. a.*]. **1968** L. DEWAR *Outl. Anglican Moral Theol.* vii. 171 The rise of the ' Parish Communion' in the last thirty or forty years..is one of the most remarkable phenomena in the history of the Church of England. **1972** C. STEPHENSON *Merrily on High* ii. 36 It was his custom to go to Holy Communion on the first Sunday in the month, but when a new vicar started a parish communion..my father felt it his duty to back him up and became a weekly communicant. **1975** *Church Times* 8 Aug. 6/5 The Sunday Parish Communion at 9.15 a.m. had been pioneered, though not originated, by St. John's Newcastle, in 1927. **1897** RHOSCOMYL *White Rose Arno* 195 Playing *parish constables and apprehending vagrants. **1848** *Punch* 12 Feb. 59 (*caption*) Well, young man. So you wish to be engaged as *Parish Doctor? *c* **1875** 'BRENDA' *Froggy's Little Brother* (new ed.) ix. 115 It turned out to be only the parish doctor come to see little Deb Blunt. **1977** R. L. WOLFF *Gains & Losses* viii. 425 The parish doctor is a rich man, a scientist. **1796** H. HUNTER tr. *St.-Pierre's Stud. Nat.* (1799) II. 580 A simple and obscure *parish-drudge, to whom no one pays any manner of attention. **1681** OTWAY *Soldier's Fort.* v. i, Ye Night-Toads of the *Parish-Dungeon. **1798** SOUTHEY *Old Mansion-ho.* i, Old friend! why you seem bent on *parish duty, Breaking the highway stones. **1936** E. UNDERHILL *Worship* v. 94 The choral *Parish Eucharist, the Roman Catholic rite of Benediction,..or any other truly congregational service where the general movement is understood, and hymns, chants, and actions are familiar to all. **1965** C. E. POCKNEE *Parson's Handbk.* (ed. 13) p. xii, The whole trend of Sunday morning worship as manifested today in the Parish Eucharist had been foreshadowed by John Wordsworth in *The Ministry of Grace* (1901). **1715** GAY *What d'ye Call it* Pref., The Ghost of the Embryo and the *Parish-Girl are entire new Characters. **1762** GOLDSM. *Cit. W.* xxvi, In every *parish-house..the poor are supplied with food, clothes, fire, and a bed to lie on. **1869** BLACKMORE *Lorna D.* xliii. (1889) 273 The *parish-knell, which begins when all is over. **1896** POLLOCK *Land Laws* ii. 40 Sometimes these *parish lands are within the modern boundaries, but by no means always. **1847–78** HALLIWELL, *Parish lantern. **1887** J. ASHTON *18th Cent. Waifs* 235 *note*, The link-boy's natural hatred of 'the Parish Lantern', which would deprive him of his livelihood. **1827** COBBETT *Prot. Ref.* II. §47 The Bishopricks, the *Parish-livings, the Deanships,..are all in their gift. *a* **1966** M. ALLINGHAM *Cargo of Eagles* (1968) xii. 140 The vicar called to leave 'is compliments and a *parish mag. **1888** C. M. YONGE *Our New Mistress* ii. 14 As had been put into the '*Parish Magazine', she had been two years from her training college. **1926** S. T. WARNER *Lolly Willowes* I. 67 The parish magazine said: 'The vicar had scarcely left East Bingham when war was declared.' **1955** M. ALLINGHAM *Beckoning Lady* ii. 19 He'd ploughed down there through the snow to take her the parish magazine. **1974** *Times* 8 Mar. 16/8 The editor of *The Shoreham Gazette*, a parish magazine, boasts that he is the first to get into print with a prayer for the new government. **1976** *Deeside Advertiser* 9 Dec., In his parish magazine the Vicar of Shotton has warned parishioners to be prepared for disturbances during Midnight Mass on Christmas Eve. **1763** C. CORDELL *Divine Office for Use of Laity* I. p. vi, The prayers, publications, and familiar instructions used at the *Parish-Mass, on Sundays. **1929** S. LESLIE *Anglo-Catholic* xx. 275 The following morning Jasper did not return from saying the Parish Mass in time for his early breakfast. **1958** S. NEILL *Anglicanism* xiv. 403 In many parishes the 'Parish Mass' is followed by a parish breakfast. **1965** C. E. POCKNEE *Parson's Handbk.* (ed. 13) ii. 22 The parson must think out whether he intends to develop the Parish Mass with a choir as his chief act of Sunday morning worship. **1970** H. BRAUN *Parish Churches* xvii. 206 While the sermon has always played a part in the parish Mass, no architectural provision for its delivery appears to have been made until late in the Middle Ages. **1712** PRIDEAUX *Direct. Ch.-Wardens* (ed. 4) 55 They..have a Vote in the *Parish-meetings. **1765** *Goody Two-Shoes* (1766) I. Introd., He stood up for the Poor at the Parish Meetings. **1894** [see PARISH COUNCIL]. **1676** WORLIDGE *Cider* (1691) 96 Carry your fruit to a *parish-mill. **1716** M. DAVIES *Athen. Brit.* II. 345 Venerable Alms-women and experienc'd *Parish-Nurses. **1689** S. JOHNSON *Rem. on Sherlock's Bk.* 37 Without a Constable or *Parish-officer. **1746** LOCKMAN *To 1st Promoter of Cambrick & Tea Bills* 23 Bad tenants, and the '*parish-pension'd band. **1693** C. DRYDEN in *Dryden's Juvenal* vii. (1697) 179 And shew his Tally for the Dole of Bread, With which the *Parish-Poor are daily fed. **1709** STEELE *Tatler* No. 56 ¶3 Nicolas de Boutheiller, *Parish-Preacher of Sasseville. **1915** *Truth* 21 Apr. 620/1 They are the last word in parochialism; but the table is their *parish pump and the croupier is the beadle. **1923** *Daily Mail* 12 Mar. 5 Parish pump politicians distort every word they [*sc.* statesmen] utter. **1923** U. L. SILBERRAD *Lett. J. Armiter* x. 211 The to-dos we make over our own parish pump matters. **1961** A. WILSON *Old Men at Zoo* i. 11 The Treasury job..had called for a good measure of toughness; after it, Regent's Park affairs smelt a little of the parish pump. **1962** *Punch* 14 Feb. 285/1 Parish Pump radio, when it comes, may be the biggest draw yet. **1962** *Radio Times* 22 Nov. 40/2 In 'Talking Point' we introduce a bit of controversy to avoid being too parish-pump. **1963** *Times* 27 Feb. 8/6 Resistance from parish-pump politics is clearly being encountered; hostility to fresh ideas seems inevitable in a country that has some 38,000 communes containing fewer than 500 people. **1973** *Times* 6 June 18/2 Graham Tope, a Liberal, swept to victory..on a platform of community politics, or the politics of the parish pump. **1977** *N.Y. Rev. Bks.* 9 June 32/4 The news they brought did nothing to still those local manifestations around the parish pumps which had been the very essence of the Old Republic in its Golden Age. **1978** G. GREENE *Human Factor* I. i. 14, I don't think I've voted since the war. The issues nowadays so often seem—well, a bit parish pump. **1963** *Economist* 29 June 1387 Worthy *parish-pumpers would do well on the enclave councils. **1962** *Economist* 5 May 425/1 The rest of the country may simply shrug its shoulders at London's enduring *parish-pumpery. **1979** G. POTTINGER *Secretaries of State for Scotland 1926–76* xv. 163 To combat apathy at local elections it was hoped that the top tier would offer an avenue to aspiring politicians, while parish-pumpery would find their satisfaction in the second one. **1968** *Listener* 29 Feb. 283/2 It all sounds incredibly *parish pumpish, but..the parish pump is extremely important when you live next door to it. *a* **1721** PRIOR *Epit., Interr'd beneath this marble stone* 33 They paid the Church and *Parish Rate. **1653** *Acts & Ordin. Parl.* c. 6 (Scobell) 237 Some able and honest person..to have the Keeping of the said Book [a Register of Marriages, Births, and Burials], and the person so elected, approved and sworn, shall be called the *Parish-Register. **1712** PRIDEAUX *Direct. Ch.-Wardens* (ed. 4) 96 The Parish-Register is a Parchment Book, in which all the Christnings, Marriages, and Burials of the Parish are Recorded. This was first ordered by the Lord Vicegerent Cromwell,..1538. **1816** MRS. MARCET *Convers. Pol. Econ.* x. (1861) 151 *Parish relief thus became the very cause of the mischief which it professed to remedy. **1864** R. A. ARNOLD *Hist. Cotton Famine* vi. 179 One or two members of the Manchester Committee..evidently considered that all subscriptions should be applied to supplement parish relief. **1949** N. MITFORD *Love in Cold Climate* xiii. 134 Uncle Matthew.. was quite certain in his own mind that he would end up on parish relief. **1937** PARTRIDGE *Dict. Slang* 606/1 *Parish-rig*, a poorly found ship or an ill-clothed man. **1958** J. BISSET *Sail Ho!* 36 These men [*sc.* pierhead jumpers] usually had nothing except the clothes they stood up in—known as a 'parish rig'. **1899** F. T. BULLEN *Log Sea-waif* 163 She was what sailors call '*parish rigged', meaning that all her gear was of the cheapest. **1933** P. A. EADDY *Hull Down* 135 A couple of the new hands who had been shipped just before we left Portland had come aboard pretty well 'parish rigged', to use an old sailor term for a man going to sea short of clothes. **1962** A. G. COURSE *Dict. Naut. Terms* 145 When a seaman joins a ship with few clothes and little working gear he is said to be 'parish rigged'... The term came to be used afterwards with reference to the ships themselves, so that if they had a minimum of sails, spares and gear to start a voyage they were said to be 'parish rigged'. **1968** L. MORTON *Long Wake* i. 15, I joined *Beeswing* in what in those days was called 'Parish rigged' [*sic*], in other words with little or no kit. **1794** J. MUIRHEAD in J. Sinclair *Statist. Acct. Scotl.* XI. 81 A *parish school is now a momentary, or at least a temporary employment, for some necessitous person of ability. **1812** W. TENNANT *Anster F.* II. xix, That day the doors of parish-school were shut. **1875** G. MACDONALD *Malcolm* I. vii. 67 A cottage rather larger than the rest, which stood close by the churchyard gate. It was the parish school. **1910** J. KERR *Scottish Educ.* 196 The name, parish schools, conveys no definite idea of the very varied character of the work done in them. **1964** *Winnipeg Tribune* 27 Feb. 1/5 Parish schools deserve a measure of public support, in keeping always with the overall resources of the community and without detriment to the public school system. **1788** P. M. FRENEAU *Misc. Wks.* 371 She would have killed the *parish schoolmaster with the cluva-stick. **1929** J. B. PHILIP *Weelum* 11 More than a hundred years ago, the Parish Schoolmaster, who was also a poet, often wandered here. **1879** BROWNING *Halbert & Hob* 24 Save the sexton the charge of a *parish shell. **1847** EMERSON *Poems, Monadnoc*, Rallying round a *parish steeple. **1601** SHAKS. *Twel. N.* I. iii. 44 A Coward and a Coystrill that will not drinke to my Neece, till his braines turne o'th toe, like a *parish top. *c* **1616** FLETCHER & MASS. *Thierry & Theod.* II. iii, A boy of twelve Should scourge him hither like a parish-top, And make him dance before you. *c* **1400** *Rowland & O.* 284 Lete Duke Naymes lenge at hame To kepe *pareche walles fro schame. *a* **1745** SWIFT *Story Injured Lady*, I must maintain a *parish watch against thieves and robbers. **1864** TENNYSON *Aylmer's Field* 521 To him that fluster'd his poor *parish wits. **1873** MRS. H. WOOD in *Argosy* XVI. 133 *Parish work is not to everyone's taste. **1885** C. M. YONGE *Nuttie's Father* I. xiv. 163 She had a practical soul for parish work, and could appreciate..the exertions made for people of the classes she had always supposed too bad or else too well off to come under clerical supervision. **1911** W. OWEN *Let.* 18 June (1967) 75 To become the 'assistant' of some hard-worked or studiously inclined parson, helping in parish work, correspondence etc.

[*Note.* (1) Gr. παροικία was the abst. sb. from πάροικος adj. (f. παρά by, beside + οἶκος house, dwelling), in cl. Gr. 'dwelling beside or near, neighbouring, a neighbour'; in LXX, N.T., and Christian writers, 'dwelling temporarily or sojourning in a foreign land, a sojourner'. As to which of these notions was present, when παροικία passed into ecclesiastical use, opinions differ; the earlier etymologists (Diez, etc.) have taken it as 'the body of persons dwelling beside, and hence, the district lying about, a church or ecclesiastical centre'; but more recent writers, founding their conclusions upon the usage of the LXX and N.T., take it as = 'the body of sojourners', holding the appellation to have been primarily applied to colonies of Jews of the Dispersion sojourning in Alexandria and other Gentile cities, and to have been from them continued or adopted as a name for 'the Christian brotherhood sojourning in a town or district', perh. not without reference to the spiritual use of πάροικοι, παροικία (1 Pet. i. 17, ii. 11): see Lightfoot *S. Clement* II. 6, Hatch in *Dict. Chr. Antiq.* s.v. *Parish.* (2) According to Lightfoot, παροικία was at first used in a much more general sense than διοίκησις, diocese, of which it was later a synonym, as were its L. representatives *parœcia, parochia* down even to the 12th c. The modern sense 'parish' appears already in St. Basil *a* 379. Although *parochia* was used in the wider sense at the Councils of Celchyth A.D. 816, and Clovesho 825, and is so rendered even in 12th c. glossaries (cf. Wr.-Wülcker 537/10 *Diocesis* vel *parochia*, biscopriche), *parish*, as an English word, is found only with the modern meaning (exc. when used by later writers as a literal rendering of the Gr. or L. word: sense 5). (3) The relation to the original παροικία, *parœcia*, of later and med.L. *parochia*, presents difficulty. The latter could not arise out of the former by any normal phonetic process; and it has been suggested by various scholars independently that *parochia* is really a derivative from L. *parochus* (Gr. πάροχος), the name of a local official in the country parts of Italy who supplied public personages with entertainment, etc., when they came into his district; and that this familiar term was popularly substituted for the unfamiliar *parœcia*. Cf. what is said under PARROCK, as to the OHG. rendering of *parochia* by the apparently native *pharra, pfarre.*]

Hence **'parished** *a.* (in comb.), having parishes.

1864 *Life H. Airay* in *Comment. Bible* 1 The county is somewhat wide and many-parished.

parish ('pærɪʃ), *v. dial.* [f. PARISH *sb.*] *intr.* **a.** To belong *to* or go *with* as part of a parish.

1833 *Drakard's Stamford News* 8 Oct., A village that parishes with one adjoining. **1886** *S. W. Linc. Gloss.* s.v., It is said of an hamlet or township that it parishes to some other place, that is, forms one ecclesiastical parish with it. Thus Whisby parishes to Doddington, and Morton to Swinderby.

b. Of a clergyman: to do parish work. *rare.*

1880 J. GOTT *Lett.* (1918) 132 The growth and gymnastics of the mind, the which one prays and parishes.

‖**parishad** (pɑːriː'ʃad). [Bengali and Hindi, f. Skr. *pariṣhad* an assembly, council, f. *pári* around, about + *sad, sídati* to sit down.] In India and Bangladesh: an assembly, group, or council; also *attrib.* Also *zil(l)a parishad*, a district council.

1919 R. MOOKERJI *Local Govt. Anc. India* i. 29 The communal life of ancient India..sought to express itself through a variety of institutions, civic and municipal, industrial and commercial, political and religious... The following, for example, are the terms we generally come across in our literature, viz. *kula*,..*pariṣat, charana.* **1932** V. R. R. DIKSHITAR *Mauryan Polity* iii. 97 This passage only corroborates our view that the *pariṣad* (Council) exercised real executive powers. **1959** R. S. SHARMA *Aspects Polit. Ideas & Inst. Anc. India* xiii. 191 The influence of caste is to be also seen in some of the collective institutions such as the *pariṣad.* **1963** B. A. SALETORE *Anc. Indian Polit. Thought & Inst.* v. v. 417 The term *pariṣad*, which was confined originally in the Vedic days only to a congregation or assembly of learned men, seems to have been used in a wider sense of a council or assembly of ministers by the time of Pāṇini. **1971** *National Herald* (Lucknow) 1 Apr. 3/6 The commission will also go into the wage structure of employees of local bodies, zila parishads, town areas, notified areas, municipalties, [etc.]. **1975** *Bangladesh Times* 23 July 2/3 One Nagoruddin Mondal, member Bilasbari union parishad under Badalgaehi Police station has been suspended for selling relief goods in black market and the misuse of test relief fund. **1976** *CRC Jrnl.* July 5/3 There was a very wide representation, from Trade Unions.. Vishwa and Parishad groups. **1976** D. HIRO *Inside India Today* 50 What then emerged was a three-tiered system whereby the old district boards..were replaced by zilla parishads (i.e. district councils) with responsibility for co-ordinating development plans to be channelled through panchayat samitis (i.e. council committees). **1977** *Bangladesh Times* 20 Jan. 1 The district-wise break-ups of the Union Parishads where polls took place on Wednesday are Dacca and Sylhet 18 each.

parish church. Forms: see PARISH, CHURCH, KIRK. The church of a parish.

c **1380** WYCLIF *Wks.* (1880) 14 Axe hem what charite it is to laten parische chirchis fallen doun. **1448** *Paston Lett.* I. 72 Being at messe in one Parossh Chirche. **1563** *Reg. Privy Council Scot.* I. 248 The parochinaris of the paroche kirk within this realm. **1584** FENNER *Def. Ministers* (1587) 49 Diuers..haue made men paye twelue pence a Saboth for being absent from their parishe Church. **1600** SHAKS. *A.Y.L.* II. vii. 52 The why is plaine, as way to Parish Church. **1732** BERKELEY *Alciphr.* I. §1 Crito, whose parish-church is in our town. **1841** MACAULAY *Ess., W. Hastings* (1863) II. 243/2 Behind the chancel of the parish church of Daylesford,..was laid the coffin of [Warren Hastings]. **1890** STUBBS *Study Med. & Mod. Hist.* (1900) 457 The parish church where for generations their fathers have been baptized, married and buried.

parish clerk. An official appointed by the incumbent of a parish to assist in various duties connected with the church and its services: before the Reformation usually a member of one of the five minor orders; after the Reformation a layman, the office being often conjoined with that of sexton; by the Act of 1844, which at present regulates the office, the duties may be undertaken by a curate. See CLERK *sb.* 2 b.

One of his most prominent duties in former times, that of leading the responses (often without any following) is now generally given up (being performed by the choir and congregation), except at baptisms, funerals, etc.

c **1386** CHAUCER *Miller's T.* 126 Now was ther of that chirche a parissh clerk. **1439** *E.E. Wills* (1882) 114 The brederhede of seynt Nicholas founded by paressh clerkes in London. **1591** SPENSER *M. Hubberd* 557 And craftie Reynold was a Priest ordained, And th' Ape his Parish Clarke procur'd to bee. **1674** PLAYFORD *Skill Mus.* I. 71 Parish-Clerks,..being the Leaders of those Tunes in their Congregations. **1774** WARTON *Hist. Eng. Poetry* xxxiv. (1775) II. 395 Plays acted by the society of the parish-clerks of London. **1778** *Eng. Gazetteer* (ed. 2) s.v. *Plymouth*, This town has..two churches, which..have each so large a cure of souls, that the parish-clerks were, till very lately, in deacon's orders, to enable them to perform all the sacerdotal functions. **1840** DICKENS *Barn. Rudge* i, The little man.. was the parish-clerk and bell-ringer of Chigwell. **1857** TOULMIN SMITH *Parish* 197 The 'Parish Clerk' is not the clerk to the Parish, in the modern sense of the word 'clerk'. **1885** C. I. ELTON in *Encycl. Brit.* XVIII. 296/1 It is said that the only civil function of the parish-clerk now remaining is to undertake the custody of maps and documents.. deposited under the provisions of the Railway Clauses Act, 1845.

Hence **parish-'clerkly** *a.*, characteristic of a parish clerk; **parish-'clerkship**, the office of parish clerk.

1513 in *Trans. R. Hist. Soc.* VI. 361 The parroch clerkschip beand vacand be the deceiss of Thomas Wemys. **1886** G. R. SIMS *Ring o' Bells*, etc. I. i. 8 In a..parish-clerkly way he swore to humble the lady's pride.

'parish 'council. A council of a parish; *spec.* the local administrative body created in rural civil parishes of more than three hundred inhabitants by the Act of 1894. Hence **'parish 'councillor**, a member of this body.

1772 NUGENT tr. *Hist. Friar Gerund* II. 350 All royal councils..must prove their descent to have been from parish-councils. **1893** *Daily News* 22 Mar. 4/6 Every one.. which has a population of three hundred and upwards will have a Parish Council. **1894** *Act* 56 & 57 *Vict.* c. 73 §1 There shall be a parish meeting for every rural parish, and there shall be a parish council for every rural parish which has a population of three hundred or upwards. *Ibid.* §3 (5) The parish councillors shall be elected by the parochial electors of the parish.

†**parishen**[1], **parishion.** *Obs.* Forms: α. 3 paroschian, 4 -oschien, -oschen, 4–5 -oisshien, 5 -oshyn; β. 4–5 parischien, -isshien, 4–6 parishen, (4–5 -izschen, 4–6 -iscen, is(s)chen, -is(s)hen, -ysshen, -yschen, -in, -yn, -ene, -ion, -in, -ing, -yn, -on, 5 paraschen, -es(s)chen(e, -eshon, -echen, -ishon, -yshchon, parschen, -one, par-, perrishen, -yshyn, 6 paryschoon, -yn, -esshen, -achen, perishen. [ME. *paroschien, -oisshien*, etc., a. OF. *paroissien*, f. *paroisse* PARISH, after med.L. *parochiān-us*: see PAROCHIAN. Subsequently, following *parosshe, parish*, it became *parishen*, with many variations of spelling, and sometimes phonetic reduction to *parschen.* OF. had a parallel form *parochien*, a closer adaptation of the med.L., whence also ME. *parochien, parochen*, etc.; these forms are treated under PAROCHIAN, though they often show a mixture of the two types, *ch* not being distinguished from *sh* or *sch.*] One of the community of a parish; = PARISHIONER.

α. *a* **1225** *Ancr. R.* 198 Þet child þet ne buhð nout his eldre, vnderling his prelat, paroschian his preost. *c* **1325** *Metr. Hom.* 87 Quen paroschenis com him to. **1377** LANGL. *P. Pl.* B. Prol. 89 Þat þei sholden shryuen here paroschienes. **14..** *Lett. Marg. Anjou & Bp. Beckington* (Camden) 46 The paroisshiens of the said paroish.

β. **13..** *Cursor M.* 26292 (Cott.) Alsua if þi parischen [*Fairf.* parochin] In sin lang has ligand bene. *Ibid.* 26315 (Cott.) Alsua þou preist, if þou ha ben In plight wit þi pariscen [*Fairf.* parochien]. *c* **1386** CHAUCER *Prol.* 482 Hise parisshen [*v.rr.* parischiens, -isshiens, -isschens, -isshins] devoutly wolde he teche. **1393** LANGL. *P. Pl.* C. I. 82 Persones & parshepreestes pleyned..Þat hure parshens [*v.rr.* parschone, paresschene, -ischene, parshen] ben poore. *c* **1449** PECOCK *Repr.* (Rolls) II. 391 That the paraschens so ȝaue. **1482** *Monk of Evesham* (Arb.) 49 Whoys pareshon also y was. **1533** MORE *Debell. Salem* Wks. (1557) 1018/1 If the person woulde take it of his perishen by force. **1536** WRIOTHESLEY *Chron.* (1875) I. 55 The curates should preach and teatch their parishiones the 'Pater noster', 'Avee', and 'Creede'. **1566** *Three 15th Cent. Chron.*, etc. (Camden) 138 Suche quarylynge..was between yᵉ mynystars and parishoners that to quyat yᵉ mattar yᵉ churche dores wer fayn to be closyd, and yᵉ paryschyns to departe.

parishen[2]. *Sc. dial.* In 6 parichoun, -schone. [f. PARISH *sb.*: the suffix is obscure: cf. PARISHING and PAROCHIN in same sense.] = PARISH.

a **1555** LYNDESAY *Tragedy* 367 Mak hym..Persone, quhilk his parischoun can teche. **1596** DALRYMPLE tr. *Leslie's Hist. Scot.* VIII. 90 Robert Schau, quha pastour was of the parischone of Minto. **179.** BURNS *The Cardin' o't* ii, Yet I hae seen him on a day, The pride of a' the parishen. **1896** *Shetland News* 6 Aug. (E.D.D.).

†**parishenant.** *Obs.* (See quot.)

1534 *Test. Ebor.* (Surtees) VI. 44 Every clerke officer ijd., and every odre clerke paryshenaunte jd.

Parish garden: see PARIS GARDEN.

†**'parishing.** *north. Eng. Obs.* [f. PARISH *sb.* + (app.) -ING[1]; but nature and function of the suffix not clear.] = PARISH. (Chiefly Yorksh.)

(It is not certain that quot. *c* 1450 belongs here.)

c **1450** *Bidding Prayer* in *Lay Folk's Mass Bk.* 71 We sall pray also for all women þat er bun with childer in þis parichin. **1486** in *Surtees Misc.* (1888) 48 A gentilman borne in the parishing of Estrington. **1511** *Test. Ebor.* (Surtees) V. 24 To the well of my parishyng iij.*s.* iiij.*d.* **1524** *Knaresborough Wills* (Surtees) I. 19, I, William Hall of the paryshynge of Pannall. **1584** *Ibid.* 145 My neighbours and poure of the parishing.

†**pa'rishional,** *a. Obs.* Also 7 **parrishonall** [f. PARISHION(ER + -AL[1].] Of or pertaining to a parish; parochial; of parishioners.

1604 H. JACOB *Reas. Ref. Ch. Eng.* 7 A Parishionall Bishop, who is a Pastor of one ordinary Congregation only. **1614** J. ROBINSON *Relig. Communion* 20 These parrishonall assemblyes want not onely all such power. **1641** in 'Smectymnuus' *Vind. Answ.* §13. 153 By Congregation.. cannot be meant a parishionall meeting. **1786** in F. Chase *Hist. Dartmouth Coll.* (1891) I. 526 The town..have for a considerable time past indulged one parishional division of about 3,000 acres, round and near the College. **1803** W. TAYLOR in *Ann. Rev.* I. 419 Various parishional experiments were tried to employ them [the poor] profitably.

Hence **pa'rishionally** *adv.*, as a parish or body of parishioners.

a **1617** P. BAYNE *Dioces. Tryall* (1621) 2 That which was more numbersome then could meet Parishionally, was no Parishional but Diocesan church.

parishionate (pə'rɪʃəneɪt). [f. PARISHION(ER + -ATE[1].] Body of parishioners.

1910 *Tablet* 3 Sept. 363 The archiepiscopal diocese with its parishionate of nearly four million souls.

parishioner (pə'rɪʃənə(r)). Forms: 5 parisshoner, 6 parysshoner, -issyoner, -ischoner, pari-, perishoner, parishener, -iner, -ner, -nore, parichyngher, 6– parishioner. [f. *parishion*, PARISHEN[1] + -ER[1]: for the form cf. *practitioner*, etc. See also the doublet PAROCHINER.] One of the inhabitants or community of a parish.

1471 in *Somerset Medieval Wills* (1901) 221 Item, I bequeath to the chirche werkes of the church of Brewton where I am parisshoner of 20s. **1523** *Visitation Dean & Chapter York* (MS.), With the mynds & holle consent of the Parichynghers of the same. **1540** *Act* 32 *Hen. VIII*, c. 44 Beyng parisheners of the said fiue parrish churches. **1546** in *Eng. Gilds* (1870) 221 Ffor the..Comffort of alle the parissyoners there. **1561** T. HOBY tr. *Castiglione's Courtyer* II. (1577) L iv b, A Priest of the Countrey saying Masse to his parishioners. **1567** HARMAN *Caveat.* 19 Your poore, indygente, and feable parishnores. **1591** SPENSER *M. Hubberd* 561 Th' euill will Of all their Parishners they had constraind. **1617** MORYSON *Itin.* I. 193 The King..was the chiefe Parishioner. **1726** AYLIFFE *Parergon* 407 A man is said to be a Parishioner in respect of his Dwelling or Habitation ..in such a Parish. **1857** TOULMIN SMITH *Parish* 1 The practical duties and rights of every Parishioner.

Hence **pa'rishionership**, the status of a parishioner.

1842 CARLYLE in *Daily News* 5 May (1899) 6/3 Shocked to admit that, after seven years of parishionership, I did not know the face of him. **1882** *Ch. Times* 6 Apr. 245 A shorter sojourn would have created sufficient parishionership for purposes of banns.

parish priest. The priest in charge of a parish.

a **1300** *Cursor M.* 26173 (Cott.) To þi pariche preist þou þe bede. *c* **1491** *Chast. Goddes Chyld.* 29 Neyther to the pope.. ne to the parysshe prest. **1504** in *Eng. Gilds* (1870) 282 Who-so-euer be person, vycary, or parasche prest. **1659** HOWELL *Lexicon, Eng. Prov.* 1 The Parish-Priest forgot that he was ever a Clark. **1865** SARAH AUSTIN *Ranke's Hist. Ref.* II. 83 The parish priest of Cronach was one of the first who married.

Parisian (pərɪ'zɪən, -'rɪʒ(ɪ)ən), *sb.* and *a.* Also 6 -ien. [a. F. *parisien*, med.L. *parisiān-us*, f. *Parisiī* Paris: see -AN.]

A. *sb.* **a.** A native or inhabitant of Paris.

1530 PALSGR. 34 In this worke I moost folowe the Parisyens. **1683** *Apol. Prot. France* iv. 48 During that rage the Parisians were then stirred up to. **1779** J. ADAMS in *Fam. Lett.* (1876) 355, I admire the Parisians prodigiously. **1831** SIR J. SINCLAIR *Corr.* II. 95 The Parisians, as usual, had a number of novelties.

b. The French spoken in or associated with Paris.

1841 M. EDGEWORTH *Let.* 23 Mar. (1971) 587 Educated at Paris and all proper—'hors les p-s and b-s and c-s' which could not pass surely..for true Parisian. **1846** R. FORD *Gatherings from Spain* xi. 119 Their silly grandees murder the glorious Castilian tongue, by substituting what they fancy is pure Parisian. **1909** W. J. LOCKE *Septimus* xii. 177 Peculiar vocables which she had learnt at school, and which Hégisippe declared to be the purest Parisian he had ever heard an Englishwoman use. **1932** KIPLING *Limits & Renewals* 322 His speech—to suit his hearers—ran From pure Parisian to gross peasant. **1969** [see GRENADIAN *a.* and *sb.*]. **1976** 'TREVANIAN' *Main* (1977) iii. 59 Guttmann speaks up in his precise European French, the kind Canadians call 'Parisian', but which is really modelled on the French of Tours.

B. *adj.* Of or pertaining to Paris; resembling Paris or that of Paris. Special collocations: **Parisian cloth** (see quot.); **Parisian French** = *sb.* b. above; **Parisian ivory**, an early type of celluloid; **Parisian pattern** (see quot.); **Parisian stitch** (see quot.).

1614 in *Crt. & Times Jas. I* (1848) I. 346 For fear a Sicilian vespers, or Parisian matins, did ensue. **1688** SOUTH *Serm.* I. 477 Perhaps the Cut-Throat may rather take his Copy from the Parisian Massacre. **1828** *Lights & Shades* II. 72 No gown sat well that was not of Parisian make. **1921** *Daily Colonist* (Victoria, B.C.) 26 Oct. 9/1 (Advt.), A new display of Parisian ivory. **1934** M. THOMAS *Dict. Embroidery Stitches* 157 *Parisian stitch*.., a Canvas Stitch, consisting of upright stitches worked alternately over one and three horizontal threads of the canvas. **1960** C. W. CUNNINGTON et al. *Dict. Eng. Costume* 268/1 *Parisian Cloth*, 19th c., an English textile of cotton warp and worsted weft. **1962** P. O'BRIAN tr. *Erlanger's St. Bartholomew's Night* iv. 162 At four o'clock in the morning the tocsin in Saint-Germain l'Auxerrois had begun ringing for what history was to call the Parisian matins. **1964** W. L. GOODMAN *Hist. Woodworking Tools* 34 This tool [*sc.* twybill] is 2ft. 6in. long, has no handle, and is described as the 'Parisian pattern'. **1974** E. AMBLER *Dr. Frigo* I. 20 He speaks Parisian French. **1976** E. BERCKMAN *Be All & End All* v. 59 Cecil spoke Parisian French and he himself hated the English.

Hence **Pa'risianism**, Parisian character, habit, or practice; **Pa'risianize** *v. trans.*, to make or render Parisian (whence **Pa,risiani'zation**), also *refl.*; hence also **Pa'risianized** *ppl. a.*; **Pa'risianly** *adv.*, in a Parisian fashion or manner.

1892 *Athenæum* 25 June 821/3 All his good points—his gaiety, his shrewdness,..his Parisianism—appear excellently. **1851** *Fraser's Mag.* XLIII. 415 He has become irreparably Parisianized. *Ibid.*, A considerable amount of Parisianization. **1876** G. MEREDITH *Beauch. Career* I. x. 139 Where folly had danced Parisianly of old. **1897** [see BOULEVARDED *a.*]. **1913** E. WHARTON *Custom of Country* xii. 156 Mrs. Harvey Shallum, a showy Parisianized figure. **1916** W. J. LOCKE *Wonderful Year* xv. 220 The last thing a solid and virtuous citizen of Central France desires to do in Paris is to Parisianize himself. **1962** *Punch* 28 Nov. 783/1 This fashion should not be a Parisianised version from Bond Street.

‖**Parisienne** (parizjɛn). [F. fem. of *Parisien* Parisian.] A female Parisian.

1886 *Illustr. Lond. News* Summer No. 22/2 A..black-eyed, red-cheeked *Parisienne*. **1887** *Contemp. Rev.* May 718 She is a Parisienne, if you will, but a very exceptional Parisienne.

†**parisis, parisee.** *Obs.* Also 5 -ysee, -esi, 6 -yse, 8 -isis. [a. F. *parisis*:—L. *parisiens-em* Parisian, f. *Parīsiī* Paris.]

1. A word, orig. *adj.*, meaning 'of Paris'; used to distinguish deniers struck at Paris, which were worth one-fourth more than those struck at Tours; hence *sb.* a denier of Paris.

1426 LYDG. *De Guil. Pilgr.* 17664 To tourne, by hys sotylte, A Tourneys to A parysee. *c* **1430** *Pilgr. Lyf. Manhode* III. xix. (1869) 145 Bi enchauntementes she maketh it [*denier tournois*] in to paresis. **1528** SIR R. WESTON in Dillon *Calais & Pale* (1892) 93 Forfeytes for every soche tree cut x li. paryses. [**1901** SHARPE *Cal. Let. Bk. C.* 230 In part payment of the value of £58 9*s.* 4*d.* parisis.]

‖**2.** In the old French Custom-house practice, etc.: A surtax of one-fourth upon the duties fixed by the tariffs and pancartes.

1714 *Fr. Bk. of Rates* 17 The Augmentations of Anno 1644, 1647, 1654, and the Parisis 12 and 6 Peny, of all the said Duties. *Ibid.* 265 The Duties of the Parisis, the 12th and 6th Deniers, shall be levied and collected by the said Measurers in the accustomed Manner.

parisite ('pærɪsaɪt). *Min.* [Named 1845 after the discoverer, J. J. Paris: see -ITE[1].] A fluocarbonate of the metals of the cerium group, found in small brownish-yellow crystals in the emerald mines of Colombia.

1846 *Amer. Jrnl. Sci.* Ser. II. II. 415 Parisite was discovered..in the valley of the Musso. **1899** *Ibid.* Ser. IV. VIII. 21 Crystals of pyrite and parisite.

paris mutuels: see PARI MUTUEL.

pari'sology. *rare.* [f. Gr. πάρισος almost equal, evenly balanced + -λογια speaking: see -LOGY.] The use of ambiguous language.

18.. CAMPBELL cited in WORCESTER (1846).

‖**parison**[1] ('pærɪsən). *Rhet.* Pl. **parisa.** [a. Gr. πάρισον, neuter of πάρισος exactly or evenly balanced, f. παρ(α- beside + ἴσος equal.] An even balance in the members of a sentence.

1586 A. DAY *Eng. Secretary* II. (1625) 86 *Membrum* or *Parison*, when one or more members doe follow in equall sentences. **1589** PUTTENHAM *Eng. Poesie* III. xix. (Arb.) 222 *Parison*, or the Figure of euen... In this figure we once wrote..these verses. The good is geason, and short is his abode, The bad bides long, and easie to be found: Our life is loathsome, our sinnes a heauy lode, Conscience a curst iudge, remorse a priuie goade. **1603** HOLLAND *Plutarch's Mor.* 988 His *parisa*, standing upon equall weight and measure of syllables. **1894** C. G. CHILD *Lyly & Euphuism* 52 As Lyly's first thought is evidently to be antithetical, the use of parison, though constant, enters as a secondary matter.

Hence (irreg.) †**pa'risonal, pari'sonic** *a.*, characterized by 'parison' or exact balance of clauses.

1652 URQUHART *Jewel* Wks. (1834) 293 The harmony of a well-concerted period, in its isocoletick and parisonal members [cf. DIODORUS xii. 53 ἰσόκωλα και πάρισα]. **1884** SYMONDS *Shaks. Predecess.* xiii. 512 [Euphuism] is characterised..by antithesis of thought and diction,.. enforced by alliterative and parisonic use of language. **1894** RALEIGH *Eng. Novel* ii. (1903) 33 Almost every sentence being balanced in two or more parisonic parts.

parison[2] ('pærɪsən). *Glass-blowing.* Also 9 **paraison.** [a. F. *paraison*, deriv. of *parer* to prepare, corresp. to L. *parātiōn-em* from *parāre*.]

1. *orig.* The rounded mass into which the molten glass is first gathered and rolled when taken from the furnace. Also *attrib.* as *parison-hole*.

1832 G. R. PORTER *Porcelain & Gl.* 169 By this means the particles of glass are agglomerated in a cylindrical form, which is then called by the workmen a *paraison*. **1903** K. A. MACAULAY (Chance Bros.) *Let.*, The word 'parison' survives among our workmen, not as directly applied to the piece of glass, but to the 'hole' or opening into a furnace for reheating the glass after moulding it, which they call a 'parison-hole'.

2. Hence, in a bottle-making machine: see quot.

1888 *Daily News* 14 Feb. 6/6 The present machine consists first of a receptacle, called a 'parison', in which the exact quantity of molten metal required to form a bottle is placed, there being no overplus or waste. At the lower part of the 'parison' is the collar mould which forms the lip.

parissyoner, obs. form of PARISHIONER.

paristhmic (pə'rɪsθmɪk), *a. Anat.* [f. Gr. παρίσθμιον tonsil (f. παρ(α- by + ἰσθμός neck, narrow passage or connexion) + -IC.] Pertaining to the tonsils. So **pa'risthmiotome** [Gr. -τομος cutting] (see quot.); **paristhmitic** (pærɪsθ'mɪtɪk) *a.*, pertaining to paristhmitis; ‖**paristhmitis** (-'aɪtɪs), inflammation of the tonsils.

1822–34 *Good's Study Med.* (ed. 4) II. 322 In the second or Paristhmitic variety, the morbid virus is chiefly directed to the fauces. *Ibid.* (1822) II. 339 The common quinsy of the present day, the paristhmitis tonsilaris of the system before us. **1857** MAYNE *Expos. Lex.* 884/1 Of or belonging to the *Paristhmia* or tonsils: paristhmic. *Ibid.*, An old instrument with which the tonsils were cut or scarified: a paristhmiotome. *Ibid.*, *Paristhmitis*,..inflammation of the tonsils; the same as *Tonsillitis*.

parisyllabic (,pærɪsɪ'læbɪk), *a.* and *sb. Gram.* [f. L *par*, *pari-* equal + *syllaba* (a. Gr. συλλαβή) syllable + -IC: cf. *syllabic*.]

A. *adj.* Of Greek and Latin nouns: Having the same number of syllables in the nominative as in the oblique cases of the singular.

1656 BLOUNT *Glossogr.* s.v. *Parisyllabical*, We say in Grammar, the first declension of Nouns is Parisyllabique, because all the cases of such Nouns in the singular number especially have even syllables, as *Gemma, gemmæ, gemmæ, gemmam, gemma, gemma*, etc. **1775** in ASH. **1876** KENNEDY *Pub. Sch. Lat. Gram.* (ed. 4) 104 I-nouns come under four chief Heads: (A) Parisyllabic I-nouns with Nom. Sing. ĭ-s ..(B) Parisyllabic I-nouns in ē-s (ĭ-s).

B. *sb.* A parisyllabic noun.

1893 *Athenæum* 5 Aug. 189/2 The classification..cannot be commended. The distinction of parisyllabics and imparisyllabics is barely indicated.

†**parisy'llabical,** *a. Obs. rare*[−0]. [f. as prec. + -AL[1].] = prec. adj.

1656 BLOUNT *Glossogr.*, *Parasyllabical*, that hath equal syllables. **1658** PHILLIPS, *Parisyllabical Nounes*.

paritarie, variant of PARIETARY *sb. Obs.*

†**paritor** ('pærɪtə(r)). *Obs.* Also 6 parritour, -ator, 7 -itor, 8 -ettor, -otter; 6 perritore, 6–7 parator, 8 -iter. [Aphetic f. APPARITOR.] An apparitor or summoning officer of an ecclesiastical court.

1530 PALSGR. 252/1 Parytorie [? parytor] somoner, *bedeau*. **1587–8** in Swayne *Sarum Churchw. Acc.* (1896) 135 Sparkes the parritour for smoke fardinges to the vse of o[r] Ladie church. **1600** HEYWOOD *2nd Pt. Edw. IV*, Wks. 1874 I. 161 We are the Bishops Parators, my friend. **1614** J. ROBINSON *Relig. Commun.* 19 The greatest part from the Prelate to the Paritour are..irreligious. **1671** EACHARD *Observ. Answ. Contempt Clergy* (1705) 16 Unless I should have..turned Parrettor or Informer. **1682** N. O. *Boileau's Lutrin* III. 187 Where Doctors, Proctors, Paritors together Shaun't leave upon thy Naked back one Feather. **1716** *Finghall Churchw. Acc.* (MS.), Paid To the Pariter 1*s.* 9*d.* **1794** *Pilton Churchw. Acc.* in *Notes and Gleanings* (Exeter) II. 38/1 Paid the Parrotter 1*s.* 6*d.* **1825** SCOTT *Betrothed* xvii, A paritor, or summoner of the ecclesiastical court.

paritorie, -ory, variant of PARIETARY *sb. Obs.*

parity[1] ('pærɪtɪ). [ad. L. *paritās* equality, f. *par* equal. Cf. F. *parité* (14th c. in Hatz.-Darm.).]

1. a. The state or condition of being equal, or on a level; equality.

1613 R. CAWDREY *Table Alph.* (ed. 3), *Paritie*, equalitie, likenesse. **16..** WEBSTER & ROWLEY *Cure for Cuckold* I. i, Equality in birth, parity in years. *c* **1656** BRAMHALL *Replic.* v. 190 For the clearing of which point, I shewed that there was a parity of power among the Apostles. **1783** W. F. MARTYN *Geog. Mag.* II. 326 Men and women [in marriage] are obliged to pay a proper regard to the parity of years. **1842** GROVE *Corr. Phys. Forces* 101 The bodies in which this parity of force has been discovered..are small compared with the exceptions.

b. A state in which two countries potentially hostile to one another have equal strategic resources, used *spec.* of the capacities in nuclear weapons of the U.S. and the U.S.S.R.

1955 *Bull. Atomic Sci.* Mar. 100/2 To try to achieve parity in conventional weapons would mean such a regimentation of our industry and manpower that we would lose the freedom we seek to preserve. **1965** H. KAHN *On Escalation* 295 The term 'parity' is shorthand for 'nuclear parity' or 'strategic parity'. Parity exists when neither side obtains any important strategic technical advantages..from its central war forces. **1971** *Human World* Nov. 20 In the last five or six years the Russians have achieved nuclear-missile parity with the United States.

c. In phr. ***parity of esteem***, the state or condition of being regarded as equal, used *spec.* of the status of administratively comparable educational institutions.

1961 D. JENKINS *Equality & Excellence* vi. 112 The authors of the 1944 [Education] Act..enunciated their principle..that there should be 'parity of esteem' for all forms of secondary education. **1961** *Guardian* 3 Apr. 3/2 The training colleges must aim high... Parity of esteem with the universities must be earned. **1966** D. JENKINS *Educated Society* ii. 63 There has to be 'parity of esteem' as between the various sections of the community. **1966** *Rep. Comm. Inquiry Univ. Oxf.* I. 117 We are convinced that undergraduate and postgraduate education should enjoy parity of esteem. **1974** *Listener* 23 May 661/3 If they [*sc.* polytechnics] could accept the challenge that they can offer a different kind of degree from well-established universities, they might get something like parity of esteem.

2. Equality of rank or status, social, political, or ecclesiastical; *esp.*, equality among the members, or among the ministers, of a church.

1572 in Neal *Hist. Purit.* (1732) I. 284 There ought to be a Parity among the ministers in the Church. **1593** BILSON *Govt. Christ's Ch.* 413 What conflictes and uproares your paritie of Presbyters will breede. **1642** CHAS. I *Answ. 19 Prop.* 22 The Common people..grow weary of Journey-work, and set up for themselves, call Parity and Independence, Liberty. **1709** HEARNE *Collect.* 5 Mar. (O.H.S.) II. 173 To..introduce Presbyterian parity.. among our Clergy. **1841** D'ISRAELI *Amen. Lit.* (1867) 442 With the disciples of parity, a free election..was a first state principle. **1903** F. W. MAITLAND in *Camb. Mod. Hist.* II. xvi. 594 A call for 'parity', for an equality among all the ministers of God's Word, and consequently for an abolition of all 'prelacy'.

3. Equality of nature, character, or tendency; likeness, similarity, analogy; parallelism; as in ***parity of reason*** or ***reasoning***. (Cf. L. *pari ratione*.)

1620 VENNER *Via Recta* iii. 55, I thinke that there is a neerer parity of nature betweene the flesh of Fallow-Deere, and of the Red. **1646** P. BULKELEY *Gospel Covt.* I. 33 Argument..from the paritie and likenesse between the covenant of works, and the covenant of grace. **1652** NEEDHAM tr. *Selden's Mare Cl.* 23 Truly there is a paritie of Reason also for this. **1692** BENTLEY *Boyle Lect.* ix. 325 We may infer by parity of Argument. **1734** BERKELEY *Hylas & Phil.* (ed. 3) iii. Wks. 1871 I. 329 There is..no parity of case between Spirit and Matter. **1834** MUDIE *Brit. Birds* (1847) I. 172 By parity of reasoning that house on which the magpie perches is in no danger of falling.

4. † **a.** Of numbers: The fact of being even and not odd; evenness. *Obs.*

a **1619** FOTHERBY *Atheom.* II. x. §4 (1622) 308 It [unity] is not variable, by parity; or imparitie. **1646** SIR T. BROWNE *Pseud. Ep.* 115 If we survey the totall set of animals, we may in their legs..observe an equality of length, and parity of numeration; that is, not any to have an odde leg.

b. The oddness or evenness of a number, or of the number characteristic of something.

1915 P. A. MACMAHON *Combinatory Analysis* I. III. vi. 139 (*heading*) The parity of the greater index. **1949** G. & R. C. JAMES *Math. Dict.* 258/1 If two integers are both odd or both even they are said to have the same parity; if one is odd and the other even they are said to have different parity. **1960** G. N. LANCE *Numerical Methods for High Speed Computers* i. 10 The extended word should always have odd parity unless binary digits have been lost or gained during the transfer of the word from one part of the machine to another. **1966** R. R. ARNOLD et al. *Introd. Data Processing* xiv. 268/2 Codes that use an odd number of bits are said to have an odd parity. Codes that use an even number of bits are said to have an even parity. **1971** HUNTER & MONK *Algebra & Number Syst.* ii. 28 Let us..say that *b* is related to *a*, when the positive integer *b* has the same parity as the positive integer *a*, that is when *a* and *b* are either both odd or both even. **1975** J. FINKEL *Computer-Aided Experimentation* xvii. 374 Parity is computed by adding the total number of 'ones' in a word. If the total is an even number and even parity is desired, the parity bit is stored as a 'zero'.

c. *Physics.* The property of having or being a spatial wave function that remains the same (has even parity) or changes sign (has odd parity) when a change of sign is applied to the co-ordinates; also (*charge parity*, *G-parity*), the same property with respect to certain other symmetry operations (see quots. 1964, 1970); the value of the quantum number (eigenvalue) representing such a property (+1 for even parity, −1 for odd parity).

1939 *Physical Rev.* LVI. 526/2 Only the selection rules for *J* and parity would remain valid ($\Delta J = \pm 1$ or 0, no change in parity allowed). **1953** *Ann. Rev. Nuclear Sci.* II. 240 Means are available..for determining the angular momentum and parity change carried off by the emitted radiation. **1955** R. D. EVANS *Atomic Nucleus* iv. 174 The parity of an isolated system is a constant of its motion and cannot be changed by any internal processes. Only if radiation or a particle enters or leaves the system..can the parity change. **1956** *Canad. Jrnl. Physics* XXXIV. 1110 There is..evidence for spin and parity assignment of $\frac{1}{2}(+)$ for the C^{15} ground state. **1957** *Times* 11 Nov. 11/5 The launching of an Earth satellite is of less fundamental importance than..the failure of the law of parity conservation. **1964** G. Källén *Elem. Particle Physics* xii. 316 We can describe the *G*-operation as a charge conjugation followed by a rotation [in isospin space] through the angle π around the 1-axis. The eigenvalue of this operator is usually referred to as '*G*-parity'. *Ibid.* 317 *G*-parity is a conserved quantum number in all reactions involving strong interactions. **1968** M. S. Livingston *Particle Physics* vii. 134 The parity of a wave function representing a system of particles includes the intrinsic parities of each of the individual particles and also depends on the relative angular momemtum of the several particles. **1969** *Observer* 13 Apr. 2/6 Certain particles do not obey.. the parity (or P) principle. This P principle says, in effect, that nature does not 'know' the difference between left and right. **1970** Martin & Spearman *Elem. Particle Theory* v. 237 We define an operation *C* as the mapping of a physical system into another physical system in which each particle has been replaced by one with the opposite value of charge, baryon number, (lepton number) and strangeness... The eigenstates of *C* have eigenvalue either +1 or −1, that is they have either even or odd charge parity. **1973** L. J. Tassie *Physics Elem. Particles* iii. 32 When discussing the parity of the π^-, we assumed that the proton and the neutron have the same intrinsic parity. If we assume that the proton and the neutron have opposite intrinsic parities, then we find that the π^- and the π^0 have opposite intrinsic parities... We choose the parities for different charge states to give the simplest scheme.

5. *Comm.* **a.** Equivalence in another currency; a standard of price expressed in another currency.

1886 *Wool Report* 22 June, Public sales of wool..were held in Berlin..1800 bales..are reported to have been all sold at full London parity. **1886** *Times* 7 July, Prices generally soon advanced above the parity of Saturday night's closing quotations in New York. **1894** *Ibid.* 8 Dec. 5/2 The London parity will be about £94·50.

b. = par *sb.*[1] 2 b, 3 b.

1900 *Stock Market Report*, Buying on days when the market is weak and below parity, and selling when prices are put above parity by the operations of local speculators.

c. An agreed price for agricultural produce, relative to other commodities.

1941 *Time* 2 June (Air Exp. Ed.) 2/3 'Parity' is a political concept which holds that the farmer should receive prices for his products which will give him a purchasing power (in terms of other commodities) equal to that which he had in the period 1909–14. **1977** *Askov* (Minnesota) *American* 31 Mar. 1/2 The milk price support increase to 83 percent of parity will have a positive impact on Minnesota dairy farmers.

d. The value of one currency in terms of another or others, as agreed by the procedures of the International Monetary Fund, which became effective on 1 March 1947.

1945 *Ann. Reg. 1944* I. ii. 41 All transactions between the Fund and members were to be at par, and all transactions in member currencies at rates within an agreed percentage of parity. **1949** *Britannica Bk. of Year* 254/2 Mexico temporarily suspended exchange transactions by the Central bank on July 22, 1948, pending the establishment of a new parity. Although the new parity had not been announced, the Bank of Mexico was authorized to engage in free market transactions. **1971** *Daily Tel.* 10 May 14 The major countries agree..that if..the price of their own currency in relation to any other foreign exchange moves to more than 1 p.c. away from the fixed price (called parity), they will intervene. **1971** *Ibid.* 11 May 1/3 The Swiss franc closed below its new parity of 4·08 to the dollar. **1976** *Shooting Times & Country Mag.* 18–24 Nov. 28/2 Doubtless the parity of the pound sterling against other currencies is leaning..in favour of the visitor.

6. In Monetary parlance: Equality, as legal tender or money, between coins of one metal and coins of another in certain definite proportions of weight and fineness, fixed by law.

1895 *Spectator* 2 Feb. 157 Convinced..that silver can be raised by legislation to a 'parity' with gold. **1900** Ld. Aldenham *Colloquy on Currency* 280 The object..was to maintain the parity between Gold and Silver money... The parity which they have in the United States is a National parity between the coins, not between the metals... What I desire is International parity.

7. *attrib.* and *Comb.*, as ***parity level, price***; ***parity-preaching***; **parity bit** *Computers*, a bit that is automatically made 1 or 0 so as to make the parity of the word or set containing it either odd or even, as previously determined; **parity-canton**, a canton in Switzerland where the Catholic and Protestant Churches are on an equal footing in their relations with the State; **parity check** *Computers*, a check on the correctness of a set of binary digits that involves ascertaining the parity of a number derived from the set in a predetermined way; so **parity checking** *vbl. sb.*; **parity digit** *Computers* = *parity bit* above.

1957 D. D. McCracken *Digital Computer Programming* xii. 151 A common system is to assign six bits to each character... The six bits and the parity bit are then recorded in a row, which requires a seven-channel tape. **1975** J. Finkel *Computer-Aided Experimentation* xvii. 373 The parity bit is computed by the memory write hardware before storing a word. When a word is fetched from storage the parity bit is recomputed, and if it does not agree with the parity bit appended to the word an interrupt is issued. **1899** *Westm. Gaz.* 27 July 3/3 In the 'Parity-Cantons' of the Swiss Confederation, where two *Landeskirchen* are established—a Catholic and an Evangelical Church. **1950** R. W. Hamming in *Bell Syst. Techn. Jrnl.* XXIX. 150 The type of check used ..will be called a parity check. The above was an even parity check; had we used an odd number of 1's to determine the setting of the check position it would have been an odd parity check. **1958** *IRE Trans. Electronic Computers* VII. 207/1 If the specified number of ONE digits is even the parity check digit is a zero. If the number of ONE digits is odd the parity check digit is a one. **1970** N. R. Scott *Electronic Computer Technol.* v. 220 'Digital' parity checks.. depend upon the digits of the number and not upon the significance attached to the digits by virtue of their position. .. The numerical parity check..is a function of the number represented by the digits but not a function of the digits themselves. **1972** *Computers & Humanities* VI. 149 One channel is reserved for the internal control, the parity check. **1958** *IRE Trans. Electronic Computers* VII. 207/1 Parity checking usually is defined for the binary system in terms of the odd or evenness of the number of ONE digits in a specified block of binary digits. **1966** R. R. Arnold et al. *Introd. Data Processing* xiv. 268/1 Parity checking is a built-in self-checking feature utilized in most magnetic tape as well as paper tape coding methods. **1954** *Computers & Automation* Dec. 18/1 *Parity check*, use of a digit (called the 'parity digit') carried along as a check. **1959** S. H. Hollingdale *High Speed Computing* ii. 27 Some computers are designed to deal with numbers which contain an extra digit, known as the parity digit. **1970** N. R. Scott *Electronic Computer Technol.* v. 217 The correct parity digit is attached to the digit group at the source, and then the augmented group is tested upon reception to determine whether the parity digit and the message digits are still in agreement. **1907** *Daily Chron.* 3 Oct. 2/1 Opening under the parity level prices continued to lose ground every hour up to the close. **1659** W. Brough *Schism* 549 Have all doors shut upon you for your parity-preaching. **1909** *Westm. Gaz.* 20 May 12/4 The parity price of Amalgamated was 85 3-16. **1937** McIntosh & Orr *Pract. Agric. for High Schools* 15 Show the actual and parity prices of the major farm products. **1955** *Times* 24 Aug. 7/2 American farm prices are kept relatively high and often above world prices by the arrangements whereby the Government must buy certain produce for stock when its price falls to certain specified percentages of so-called 'parity prices'.

parity[2] ('pærɪtɪ). *Obstet. Med.* [f. par-ous *a.* + -ity.] The condition of being parous; the fact of having borne children.

1878 Sir J. Williams in *Obstet. Trans.* (1879) XX. 173 Diagnosis of Parity. *Ibid.*, Circumstances..in which proof of parity or nulliparity may turn out to be proof of innocence or guilt. **1889** J. M. Duncan *Clin. Lect. Dis. Women* (ed. 4) Index 535 Signs of Parity. **1898** G. E. Herman *Dis. Women* ix. 87.

pariu, var. pareu.

parizs, -chen, obs. ff. parish, parishen.

parjet, obs. form of parget.

†**parjetory.** *Obs.* [? f. parget.] ? = parget *sb.* 2.

1642 Milton *Apol. Smect.* Introd., Wks. (1851) 263 This prevaricator of America..brought us home nothing but a meer tankard drollery, a venereous parjetory for a stewes.

parjure, parjuri, obs. ff. perjure, perjury.

park (pɑːk), *sb.* Also 3–4 parc, (also 9 in senses 5, 6), 3–7 parke, 5 paark, perke, 8– *Sc.* perk. [ME. a. OF. *parc* preserve for beasts of the chase, etc. The OF. was ultimately identical with WGer. **parruk*, whence OE. *pearruc*: for the history see parrock. The Welsh *parc* and Gael. *pàirc* are from Eng. In senses 5 and 6 from later uses of F. *parc*. The Fr. word has also passed into Du. and Ger., where it is used alongside of the native forms descended from WGer. **parruk*.]

1. a. *Law.* An enclosed tract of land held by royal grant or prescription for keeping beasts of the chase. (Distinguished from a *forest* or *chase* by being enclosed, and from a *forest* also by having no special laws or officers.)

c **1260** *Charter of Friðuuald of Surrey* (dated *a* 675) in Kemble *Cod. Dipl.* V. 18 Bitwiene ðe shrubbes and Winebriȝt goinde adun norðriȝte binuðe ða parkes gate. *c* **1275** Lay. 1432 Ʒe honteþ in þis kinges parc [*c* 1205 friðe] þar fore ȝe solle deȝe. **1297** R. Glouc. (Rolls) 12 Engelonde is vol inoȝ of frut & ek of tren, Of wodes & of parkes. *c* **1350** *Will. Palerne* 2845 A pris place was vnder þe paleys a park as it were þat whilom wiþ wilde bestes was wel restored. **1436** *Rolls of Parlt.* IV. 498/2 To make a Park in Grenewyche. *a* **1440** *Sir Degrev.* 362 Have ye nat perkus and chas? **1542** Boorde *Dyetary* iv. (1870) 239 A parke repleted with dere & conyes is a necessarye and a pleasaunt thyng to be anexed to a mansyon. **1617** Moryson *Itin.* iii. 139 Wood-stocke Towne is famous for the Kings House and large Parke, compassed with a stone wall, which is said to haue been the first Parke in England. **1781** S. Peters *Hist. Connecticut* 249 There are only two small parks of deer in Connecticut. **1818** Cruise *Digest* (ed. 2) III. 255 To a park three things are necessary: 1. A grant from the King. 2. Inclosures by pale, wall, or hedge. 3. Beasts of park, such as buck, doe, &c. And where all the deer are destroyed, it shall no more be accounted a park.

b. Hence extended to a large ornamental piece of ground, usually comprising woodland and pasture, attached to or surrounding a country house or mansion, and used for recreation, and often for keeping deer, cattle, or sheep.

In these the name has either come down from a time when the ground was legally a park in sense 1, or has been more recently given to a ground laid out in imitation of such as were originally parks. It is thus not possible to separate the quotations accurately.

1715 De Foe *Fam. Instruct.* i. iii. (1841) I. 63 Nor walk out in the park or fields any more on the Lord's-day. **1813** Mar. Edgeworth *Patron.* (1833) I. xvi. 256 Hungerford Castle —a fine old place in a beautiful park. **1850** Lyell *2nd Visit U.S.* II. 326 Having never remarked this splendid tree in any English shrubbery or park. **1872** Raymond *Statist. Mines & Mining* 226 Giving to the pine woods..the aspect of beautiful natural parks. **1890** 'R. Boldrewood' *Miner's Right* (1899) 175/1 One of those natural forest-parks peculiar to Australia.

c. In this sense now often forming part of the name of a country house or mansion; and thence of suburban districts, as Addington Park, Osterley Park; Clapham Park.

1848 Miss Sewell *Amy Herbert* viii. (1858) 92 She felt a little unwilling to acknowledge that her home was neither a park nor a hall. *Ibid.* x. 127, I daresay you have been dreaming of having a large house like Rochford Park.

d. *fig.*

1579 Tomson *Calvin's Serm. Tim.* 899/1 Wee must bee so much the more watchfull, and keepe our selues still within the parke wherein God inpaled vs with his worde. **1606** Sir W. Harbert *Proph. Cadwallader* clxxvi, Wolsey..did erect those glorious towres of yore [Christ Church, Oxford], Learning's receptacle, Religion's parke. **1898** H. M. Stanley *Introd. Capt. Burrows' Land Pigmies* p. xi, This vast slave park whence Dongolawi and Arab, Bakongo and Portuguese half-caste slave traders culled their victims.

2. a. An enclosed piece of ground, of considerable extent, usually within or adjoining a city or town, ornamentally laid out and devoted to public recreation; a 'public park', as the various 'parks' in and around London, and other cities and towns. Also, an enclosed piece of ground, of considerable extent, where animals are exhibited to the public (either as the primary function of that 'park' or as a secondary attraction); see also ***safari park, zoological park. the Park*** (in London): in 17th c. St. James's Park, later esp. Hyde Park, as the place of fashionable promenade.

This application has its origin in some of the royal parks (in sense 1) near London (i.e. St. James's, etc.) developing into ornamental grounds to which the public were conditionally admitted.

[**1661**: see pall-mall 2 and 3 b.] **1663** Pepys *Diary* 15 May, I walked in the Parke, discoursing with the keeper of the Pell Mell. **1666** *Ibid.* 15 July, Walked..to the Park; and there..lay down by the canalle. **1706–7** Farquhar *Beaux' Strat.* iv. ii, There will be Title, Place and Precedence, the Park, the Play, and the Drawing-Room. **1727** Fielding *Love in Sev. Masq.* ii. ii, Come, my dear, by this, I believe, the park begins to fill. **1820** Byron *Blues* ii. 150 But 'tis now nearly five, and I must to the Park. **1855** *London as it is* 112 Victoria Park..was first opened in 1847, for the recreation of the inhabitants of the east side of London... The park has been most admirably laid out. **1894** Ralph in *Harper's Mag.* Aug. 332 To create there a charming park filled with summer cottages for themselves and other wealthy New Yorkers. **1897** *Daily News* 25 Feb. 6/4 It is not etiquette to bow or curtsey to Royalty in the parks. **1897** *Westm. Gaz.* 25 June 2/3 The Jubilee celebrations..included among other things the opening of a new park. **1909** Elliot & Thacker tr. *Hagenbeck's Beasts & Men* ii. 40, I wished my new park to be a great and enduring example of the benefits that can be wrought by giving the animals as much freedom and placing them in as natural an environment as possible. **1914** E. Velvin *From Jungle to Zoo* xxiii. 336 There are 139 employees engaged in taking care of the ground and collections of this Park [*sc.* the New York Zoological Park]. **1976** W. Blunt *Ark in Park* i. 15 William the Conqueror established or perhaps took over an already existing animal park at Woodstock, near Oxford. **1977** *Belfast Tel.* 22 Feb., The initiation of compulsory safety programmes at wild life parks and circuses.

b. An extensive area of land of defined limits set apart as national property to be kept in its natural state for the public benefit and enjoyment or for the preservation of wild life, as the ***Yellowstone Park*** (65 miles long by 55 broad) in the United States.

Up to Jan. 1903, seven such *National Parks* had been established by Act of Congress in the United States.

[**1841** Catlin *N. Amer. Ind.* (ed. 2) I. 262 What a beautiful and thrilling specimen for America to preserve and hold up to the view of..future ages! A *nation's Park*, containing man and beast, in all the wild and freshness of their nature's beauty.] **1871** N. P. Langford (in *N.Y. Tribune* 28 Jan.), This new field of Wonders [the Yellowstone Park] should be at once..set apart as a public National Park for the enjoyment of the American people for all time. **1872** *Rep. Regents of Smithsonian Inst.* (1873) 28 A proposition, originally made by Mr. Catlin as early as 1832, has been revived and presented to Congress, to reserve the country around these geysers as a public park. **1872** *U.S. Statutes* XVII. 32 An Act to set apart a certain Tract of Land lying near the Head-waters of the Yellowstone River as a public Park. **1895** Roosevelt & Grinnell *Hunting in Many Lands* 400 The preservation of elk, deer, antelope and the carnivora is assured... Their wide distribution within the Park,..added to the danger attendant on killing them within the Park, is a sufficient protection. **1903** *U.S. Statutes* XXXI. 765 An Act To set apart certain lands in the State of South Dakota as a public park to be known as the Wind Cave National Park. **1922** *Baedeker's Dominion of Canada* (ed. 4) vii. 309 About 3M. to the S. of Lamont lies the pretty Elk Island Park..., one of the Canadian National Parks.., 16 sq. M. in area and including elk, deer, moose, and buffalo. **1926** *Encycl. Brit.* II. 1020/1 In Canada since 1910 the following national game preserves, bearing the name of parks, have been established... Nemiskam National Park.., an antelope preserve in southeastern Alberta [etc]. **1957** *Ibid.* XXIII. 603/1 The Serengeti National park..preserves the finest remaining assembly of the plains game of Africa. **1959** *Chambers's Encycl.* IX. 705/1 In African parks the emphasis is on wild life conservation and public access is strictly controlled. **1974** *Afr. Encycl.* 362/1 *National parks* are areas of land where large numbers of wild animals live in natural surroundings.

1975 *Islander* (Victoria, B.C.) 31 Aug. 4/1, I got to see the first of the wild animals for which Africa is famous. This was in the Game Park at Lake Nakuru. **1978** K. TURNER *Serengeti Home* i. 1 This was my first visit to the Serengeti, a vast wildlife park in Tanganyika, now Tanzania.

c. A sports ground or stadium; *spec.* (*a*) in the U.S., a baseball field (cf. *ball park* s.v. BALL *sb.*[1] 21); (*b*) a football field or stadium; also in the names of football teams.

1867 *Chicago Times* 25 July 5/2 These cars connect with the stock-yards dummy, which runs to within a short distance of the park. **1880** *Times* 8 Nov. 11/3 Notts v. Glasgow Queen's-Park. This match was played at Nottingham on Saturday, and ended in favour of Queen's-park by four goals to three. **1892** J. HIGSON *Hist. Salford Football Club* 18 Our first ground was the Peel Park cricket ground. *Ibid.* 96 The first game they played with us was against Birkenhead Park. **1902** '*Golden Penny*' *Football Album 1901–2* 32/3 The record gate at an International match is £4,387 9s. 6d. for Scotland v. England, at Celtic Park, Glasgow, in 1900. **1917** C. MATHEWSON *Second Base Sloan* 217 Which way is the park from here, please? **1948** S. MATTHEWS *Feet First* xii. 66 The first thought that flashed through my anxious mind was Hampden Park. Would this injury keep me out of the England team to play Scotland? **1974** *Linlithgowshire Jrnl. & Gaz.* 16 Aug. 12/5 Old favourite Paddy Buckley led the Bo'ness team on to the park on Saturday. **1974** *Sunday Tel.* 8 Sept. 33/6 Middlesbrough began as if they were going to sweep Chelsea off the park. **1976** E. DUNPHY *Only a Game?* i. 31 He'd been troubled by knee injuries ever since Palace kicked us off the park the year they got promotion. **1976** *Scotsman* 27 Dec. 10/5 The sad sight of fighting on the terracing and terrified youngsters spilling on to the park.

d. ***industrial park***: see INDUSTRIAL *a.* e.

3. a. In Ireland, Scotland, and north of England: An enclosed piece of ground for pasture or tillage; a field; a parrock or paddock.

town parks (Ireland), small fields or plots of ground lying round a town or village, usually let for tillage or pasture to the townsmen or villagers.

1581 *Inv.* in *Gentl. Mag.* Sept. (1861) 257 The foure parkes by the greene which Richard and John Shanighaine holdeth of me for years. **1701** *Scotl. Charac.* in *Harl. Misc.* (ed. Park) VII. 379 Upon inquiry how many deer his father had in his perk, the truth will out,..that they call an inclosure a perk, in his country. *c* **1802** MAR. EDGEWORTH *Ennui* viii, Many a ragged man had come..with the modest request that I would let him one of the parks near the town. *Ibid.*, Just what would feed a cow is sufficient in Ireland to constitute a *park*. **1887** *Pall Mall G.* 19 Aug. 11/1 Mr. Healy ..explained in a graphic way that a 'town park' was accommodation land, by means of which in the wretched villages, misnamed towns, scattered throughout Ireland, the hucksters..eked out a miserable business by growing potatoes or feeding stock for early slaughter. **1899** *Westm. Gaz.* 13 Mar. 1/3 Kodaks from the Kingdom [i.e. Fife] ..'Old Kirsty'..lived all alone, far up in the 'parks', as we say of the wide stretches of old pasture which reach away inland till they merge into gorse and heather.

†**b.** Any enclosed piece of ground. *Obs. rare.*

1658 EVELYN *Fr. Gard.* (1675) 138 In what manner you should inclose your melon ground. In this park (which may be of what extent you think good) you shall make beds of horse-dung.

c. *U.S.* An enclosure into which animals are driven for slaughter; a corral. *Obs.*

c **1797** in L. F. R. Masson *Les Bourgeois de la Compagnie du Nord-Ouest* (1889) I. 280 The chief of the park thinks that if he were to eat any of this meat thus killed, it would be out of his power to make buffaloes enter his park ever after; so he must have meat killed in the open field for his own use. **1805** M. LEWIS in Lewis & Clark *Orig. Jrnls. Lewis & Clark Expedition* (1904) I. 313 There was a park which they had formed of timber and brush, for the purpose of taking the cabrie or antelope. **1820** D. W. HARMON *Jrnl. Voy. & Trav. Interior N. Amer.* 99 The Natives..killed upwards of eighty [buffalo] by driving them into a park, made for that purpose. **1839** Z. LEONARD *Adventures* (1904) 224 After travelling a short distance we arrived at a large pen, enclosing about three-fourths of an acre, which they call a park or correll.

4. a. Applied in some parts of the United States, esp. Colorado and Wyoming, to a high plateau-like valley among the mountains.

1808 PIKE *Sources Mississ.* (1810) II. 123 Passed the Park, which is ten miles round, and not more than three quarters of a mile across. **1851** MAYNE REID *Scalp Hunt.* xix. 137 Hence the oases, such as the 'parks' that lie among these mountains. **1877** J. A. ALLEN *Amer. Bison* 560 Adventurers and miners..exterminated them [bisons] in the parks and valleys of the mountains. **1890** *Century Mag.* Feb. 523/1 Then it had descended into a great 'park', crossed it, and begun a new ascent.

b. (See quots.)

1950 *Amer. Speech* XXV. 163 The meaning of *park* as 'any grassy piece of level land enclosed by trees, hills, or mountains' has become, or at least is fast becoming, the central meaning of the word [in Colorado]. **1961** *Ibid.* XXXVI. 269 *Park* means either 'mountain meadow' or 'clearing', from the foothills communities westward; especially in the northwest it is likely to mean both.

5. a. *Mil.* The space occupied by the artillery, wagons, beasts, stores, or the like, in an encampment; these objects themselves when thus placed together; a complete set or equipment of artillery, of tools, etc.

1683 SIR J. TURNER *Pallas Armata* III. xx. 294 As to these Oblong Quadrangles, wherein are encamped several bodies, .. you may if you please, call them as the French do, Parks, and that properly enough. **1704** J. HARRIS *Lex. Techn.* I, *Park of the Artillery*, is a certain Place in a Camp without Cannon-shot of the Place besieged, where the Cannon, Artificial Fires, Powder, and other Warlike Ammunition are kept. *Ibid.*, *Park of Provisions*, is another Place in the Camp, on the Rear of every Regiment, which is taken up by the Suttlers, who follow the Army with all sorts of Provisions, and sell them to the Soldiers. **1755** WASHINGTON *Writ.* (1889) I. 160 The whole park of artillery were ordered to hold themselves in readiness to march. **1799** STUART in Owen *Mrq. Wellesley's Desp.* (1877) 113 The main body of the army, with the park and provisions, remained at Seedapore. **1827** NAPIER *Penins. War* VI. iv, A vast parc of carriages. **1836** ALISON *Europe* (1849–50) V. xxxi. §29 Kray ..despatched his grand park, consisting of one hundred and sixty pieces and eight hundred caissons. **1859** MARCY *Prairie Trav.* vi. 221 If..a small party be in danger of an attack from a large force of Indians, they should seek the cover of timber or a park of wagons. **1884** *Mil. Engineering* (ed. 3) I. II. 8 Sites for the artillery, engineer, and grand magazine parks should now be prepared. **1900** *Westm. Gaz.* 19 Mar. 5/1 There is no reserve of boots in the supply column or supply-park.

b. An open space, a building, or underground accommodation, in or near a city or town, where cars and other vehicles can be left; = *car-park* (CAR *sb.*[1] 6). Also *transf.* See also *caravan park*.

1916 A. BENNETT *Lion's Share* xxiii. 162 Audrey's motor-car..was waiting in the automobile park outside the principal gates. **1925** *Times* 14 Apr. 8/5 The Automobile Association..has put forward a scheme for the construction of motor parks below ground. **1929, 1944** [see *air park* s.v. AIR *sb.*[1] III. 7]. **1970** *Times* 9 Feb. 13/4 Underground there will be a park for up to 2,200 cars. **1972** R. HILL *Fairly Dangerous Thing* I. i. 11 The park was quite full and he would probably never have noticed the two-tone Consul if it hadn't begun to move.

c. [f. the vb., 2 b.] In a motor vehicle with automatic transmission: the position of the selector lever in which the gears are locked, preventing the vehicle from moving.

1963 *Which? Car Suppl.* Oct. 116/1 P meant *Park*. This position could only be engaged with the car at rest and it served as a transmission brake which would hold the car on a hill. *Ibid.* 116/2 If the engine was started with the lever at *Park* and it was running quickly, the car would tend to jerk backwards as the lever was passed through *Reverse* on its way to *Drive*. **1965** PRIESTLEY & WISDOM *Good Driving* v. 40 In *Park* the gearbox is locked and thus the car is completely immobilized. **1967** *Times* 31 Mar. 3/7 It is obvious that in using a car with automatic transmission it is of the utmost importance that drivers should ensure that the lever is in the 'park' position, while they use the handle. **1972** D. E. WESTLAKE *Cops & Robbers* (1973) i. 15 He shifted into drive, caught up, and shifted back into park. **1977** J. CLEARY *Vortex* viii. 208 Stenhouse moved the gear-lever from *Park* to *Drive* and the car started to move forward.

6. An enclosed area in which oysters are bred, communicating with the sea so as to be overflowed at every high tide; an oyster-park. (In quot. 1603, applied to a similar enclosure for fish.)

[**1603** OWEN *Pembrokeshire* (1891) 117 They haue ready at their call..sault water fishe as yt were in a parke of wild fish.] **1867** *Times* 15 Oct. 5/6 In the shallowest of these parcs..not one of the young oysterlings..was known to have been killed. **1882** *Standard* 18 Feb. 5/2 In some of the French 'parks' the water is renewed every tide. **1883** F. G. SOLA *Fisheries Spain* 5 The Government..is laying down..a model park for oyster culture.

7. *attrib.* and *Comb.*, as ***park deer, -fence, -gate, -hound, -land, -lodge, -pale, -paling,*** †***-palis, -robber, -wall; park-like*** adj.; **park bench**, a bench in a park provided for the public; also *attrib.*; †**park-bote**, the repair of the fence or wall of a park; the impost levied for this; **park-breaker**, one who breaks into a park (cf. *house-breaker*); so **park-breaking; park-hack**, a horse for riding in the park: see HACK *sb.*[3] 1 b; **park-ranger, -warden**, an official responsible for the patrolling and maintenance of a national park; **park-time** (*nonce-wd.*, after *dinner-time*, etc.), time for riding in the park; **parkway** (*a*) (orig. *U.S.*) (see quot.); (*b*) a name given to a railway station with extensive parking facilities, situated on the outskirts of a city for the use of travellers into the city centre. Also PARK-KEEPER.

1906 *Daily Chron.* 6 Sept. 3/2 When a *Park-bench orator has shouted at you for a quarter of an hour, you cease to be able to attend. **1908** *Busy Man's Mag.* Mar. 63/2 So amiably and with gusto he economized, sleeping in the moonlight upon a park bench and following the marvels of the water front by day. **1946** A. CLARKE *Second Kiss* 14 That park bench in the rain, the dredge of leaves, I sat there wrapped in miserable sleeves. **1965** *Listener* 11 Nov. 763/1 Those tendencies of sloth and indolence which..have marked me out as a friend of park-bench philosophers. **1976** 'O. BLEECK' *No Questions Asked* xii. 137 If I weren't here, you could find a priest or a psychiatrist or just somebody on a park bench. *a* **1634** COKE *Inst.* IV. 308 **Parkebote*, to be quit of enclosing of a Park or any part thereof. **1821** SCOTT *Kenilw.* v, If you take him for a house-breaker, or a *park-breaker, is it not most natural you should welcome him with cold steel or hot lead? **1834** LANDOR *Exam. Shaks.* Wks. 1846 II. 267 Venerable laws..against *park-breaking and deer-stealing. **1898** *Daily News* 26 Jan. 9/5 Animals held more or less in confinement..whether they be *park-deer, rabbits, pigeons, or animals in menageries. **1901** *Daily Chron.* 7 Aug. 6/4 Legislation for the suppression of park-deer hunting. **1856** EMERSON *Eng. Traits, Aristocr.* Wks. (Bohn) II. 84, I pardoned high *park-fences, when I saw that besides does and pheasants, these have preserved Arundel marbles, Towneley galleries. *c* **1400** *Master of Game* (MS. Digby 182) xxxv, If the huntynge shall be in a parke, alle men shulden abyde at þe *parke gate. **1644** MILTON *Areop.* (Arb.) 48 The exploit of that gallant man who thought to pound up the crows by shutting his Parkgate. **1848** THACKERAY *Van. Fair* li, *Park-hacks and splendid high-stepping carriage-horses. **1851** MAYNE REID *Scalp Hunt*, i, 11 Views *park-like and picturesque. **1890** 'R. BOLDREWOOD' *Col. Reformer* (1891) 266 Green park-like woodlands. **1837** LYTTON *E. Maltrav.* ix, The chaise.. stopped at the gates of a *park lodge. *a* **1550** *Image Ipocr.* II. in *Skelton's Wks.* (1843) II. 434 He cane tell many tales, Of many *parke pales, Of butgettes and of males. **1846** GREENER *Sci. Gunnery* 14 Birmingham is the emporium of the world for guns, from the..'*park paling' so called, of the slave-trade..up to the elaborately-finished gun of the peer. **1899** R. KIPLING *Stalky* 12 The high Lodge gate in the split-oak park palings. *c* **1475** *Pict. Voc.* in Wr.-Wülcker 812/21 *Hoc vallum*, a *parke palys. **1713** SWIFT *Cadenus & Vanessa* 46 From equipage, and *Park-parades. **1912** J. B. BICKERSTETH *Let.* 20 June in *Land of Open Doors* (1914) 150 Next day, after seeing the *park ranger about the burial place, the doctor and I went down..to a place where there is a flat stretch of land. **1940** E. FERGUSSON *Our Southwest* 144 Park rangers now assiduously police almost two million acres of land. **1963** *Weekly News* (Auckland) 15 May 30/2 The maintenance of bush tracks and huts is almost a full-time occupation for the park rangers [at the Fiordland National Park]. **1972** G. DURRELL *Catch me a Colobus* ix. 192, I felt that, if we talked to the park rangers, they would be sure to give us information about the whereabouts of the Teporingoes. **1977** *Borneo Bull.* 7 May 4-A/1 Park rangers, who have continued to look for him, found some traces. **1881** MRS. O'DONOGHUE (*title*) Ladies on Horseback; Learning, *Park-riding and Hunting. **1688** R. HOLME *Armoury* II. 184/2 The Blood-hound..hunts Beasts, or Men ..that are *Park Robbers. **1439** *Rolls of Parlt.* V. 15/1 They came by a *Parke side, called ye Park of Prys. **1672** WYCHERLEY *Love in Wood* I. ii, Pray Mr. Ranger, let's go ..'tis *Park-time. **1673** DRYDEN *Marr. à la Mode* IV. iv, What a clock does your lordship think it is?.. It is almost park-time. **1936** D. MCCOWAN *Animals Canad. Rockies* vii. 62 Bill Hartley..is *Park Warden at Glacier in British Columbia. **1964** C. WILLOCK *Enormous Zoo* ix. 159 The park warden is more than an impresario. **1973** *Times* 9 Feb. 9/1 In the party will be..an Ethiopian Government minister, and national park wardens. **1887** *Visit to States* (ser. 1) xxix. 378 This broad *parkway has a magnificent drive on either side of a central walk for pedestrians. **1896** *Godey's Mag.* (U.S.) Apr. 350/1 The right to travel upon the public roads and *park-ways. **1898** *19th Cent.* Apr. 585 'Park-ways', to connect the great outlying woodlands..with the Metropolitan Parks of Boston and the surrounding townships. These park-ways are broad boulevards with margins of grass, wood, and river. **1929** *Times* 23 Jan. 20 Parkway system near New York City. **1937** *Times* 13 Apr. (Suppl.) p. x/2 The plan may provide for orbital and radial roads, parkways, viaducts and tunnels, communications to aerodromes, railway stations, and docks. **1938** *Archit. Rev.* LXXXIV. 238/3 The city of Stockholm, which has had the foresight to buy up large tracts of land in its neighbourhood, has been able to plan a system of 'Parkways'. Initially an American development the 'Parkway' represents a form of planning which might with advantage be extensively used in the English countryside. **1939**, etc. Parkway [see *clover-leaf* s.v. CLOVER *sb.* 4]. **1944** *Ann. Reg. 1943* 58 An easy flow of open space from..parkway to green wedge, and from green wedge to Green Belt. **1958** *Listener* 23 Oct. 642/1 The development of the Wythenshawe estate by the City of Manchester..with its beautifully landscaped parkway—the first, I think, in this country. **1972** *Modern Railways* July 271 The Western Region recently commissioned two new stations, one completely new at Bristol Parkway. **1973** *Bulletin* (Sydney) 25 Aug. 11 Canberra's major new freeway-type road which is the subject of a major 'environmental impact investigation' is now styled the Molonglo Parkway. **1976** P. R. WHITE *Planning for Public Transport* viii. 155 The 'parkway' stations opened by British Rail in recent years, notably that at Bristol, offer undoubted evidence of cars being abandoned by their users in favour of a rail journey. **1977** *Evening Gaz.* (Middlesbrough) 11 Jan. 1/4 The route of their return to the Royal Yacht will be made by the Mandale Interchange and the new Parkway. **1672** WYCHERLEY *Love in Wood* II. i, Then you are a *Park-woman, certainly.

park (pɑːk), *v.* [f. PARK *sb.*]

1. a. *trans.* To enclose in, as in, or as, a park.

1526 [see PARKING 1]. **1559** W. CUNNINGHAM *Cosmogr. Glasse* 144 A certayne hyll, whiche they must nedes go ouer that go by land from Egipte to Arabia Petrea, that parketh them. **1580** HOLLYBAND *Treas. Fr. Tong, Enclore*,..to enclose and parke in. **1591** SHAKS. *1 Hen. VI*, IV. ii. 45 How are we park'd and bounded in a pale! **1856** MRS. BROWNING *Aur. Leigh* III. 456 We fair fine ladies, who park out our lives From common sheep-paths.

b. ***park about***, to surround with a park.

1876 BROWNING *Shop* vi, Some suburb-palace, parked about And gated grandly, built last year.

c. To lay out or plant in the manner of a park: see PARKING 2.

2. a. *Mil.*, etc. To arrange compactly (artillery, wagons, etc.) in a park: see prec. 5.

1812 *Examiner* 30 Nov. 756/2, 6000 Cossacks..took six pieces of cannon, which were parked. **1844** *Regul. & Ord. Army* 180 At night..the waggons are to be parked, so as to occupy as little space as possible. **1883** *Army Corps Orders* in *Standard* 22 Mar. 3/3 The Artillery will be parked to the east and west of the south end of the Race-course.

b. To place or leave (a vehicle or the like), usu. temporarily, in a park (sense 5 b), at the side of the road, or elsewhere. orig. *U.S.*

1864 J. S. BILLINGS in F. H. Garrison *John Shaw Billings* (1915) 95 The trains are parked along the edge of the river. **1867** A. D. RICHARDSON *Beyond Mississippi* 79 At night the wagons are parked in a circle. **1887** *Police Arrangem. Jubilee Process.* 21 June, The area..is reserved for parking carriages belonging to the Procession. **1900** *Congress. Rec.* 2 Feb. 1445/1 No part of said street..shall be used for depot purposes, or railroad yard, or for the purpose of switching, shifting, or parking cars. **1911** *N.Y. Even. Post* 29 Nov. 16 The train was parked near the Union Station and was visited by hundreds of townsfolk and countrymen. **1921** *Daily Colonist* (Victoria, B.C.) 13 Mar. 6/2, I am now in the position of fearing to leave my car anywhere at all in the central part of the city lest I should be parking it where it should not be. **1925** WODEHOUSE *Carry on, Jeeves!* vi. 156 It was about an hour later that I shoved my way out to where

I had parked the car. **1929** J. B. PRIESTLEY *Good Companions* I. iv. 139 They were not able to keep the van with them, but had to.. park it up a side-street in a line of other cars and carts and caravans. **1938** *Times* 25 Feb. 15/2 The Chinese.. state that over 40 Japanese aeroplanes were observed parked on the air-field. **1969** *Highway Code* 22 Make sure you always park your vehicle safely. **1974** *Nature* 15 Nov. 185/3 Down by the river, in the specially built loop for parking punts, the economic crisis seemed a thousand light years away.

c. *transf.* To place or leave (a person or thing) in a suitable or convenient place until required; to put aside for a while. Also *refl.*

1908 *St. George's Rev.* July 282 The children being 'parked' in their own schoolyards. **1922** *Atlantic Monthly* June 773 High-school girls..'park' their corsets when they go to dances. **1923** WODEHOUSE *Inimitable Jeeves* iv. 40 At this point the brother, who after shedding a floppy overcoat and parking his hat on a chair had been standing by..gave a little cough. *Ibid.* ix. 94 The policeman, having retrieved a piece of chewing-gum from the underside of a chair, where he had parked it against a rainy day, went off into a corner. **1927** *Evening Standard* 7 Dec. 19/1 Then I suppose I park myself here. **1938** E. WAUGH *Scoop* I. v. 81 A voice said in English, 'Anyone mind if I park myself here?' and a stranger stood at the table. **1949** R. HARVEY *Curtain Time* 66 So for Hattie the Grand Opera House, Daly's Theatre, Wallack's, Booth's, Tony Pastor's Variety Theatre and Niblo's Garden became familiar enchanted night nurseries where her father would park her, safe and amused, until his meeting was over. **1960** E. W. HILDICK *Jim Starling & Colonel* xv. 137 Come on, dad! Park yerself! **1968** [see BOOSTER 2c]. **1971** 'A. BURGESS' *MF* xiv. 158 His companion had parked his black lenses on his brow. **1972** J. PHILIPS *Vanishing Senator* (1973) III. iii. 139 Peter crawled round to the other side of the bed where his aluminium leg was parked. **1978** G. GREENE *Human Factor* III. ii. 117 The girl was parking her gum on the back of the telephone directory while she got down to a long satisfactory conversation.

d. *intr.* To take up a position in or as in a park; to place a vehicle in a park or elsewhere; to occupy a suitable or stationary position; to stay where one is.

1865 O. W. NORTON *Army Lett.* (1903) 255 The wagons parked behind the stables to wait orders. **1926** G. FRANKAU *My Unsentimental Journey* xi. 149 There, Stidger put on his brakes, 'parked', took out the inevitable keys to lock his gear-lever and ignition-switch. **1929** *Strand Mag.* Feb. 183 'I want them' persisted the other 'and I guess I'm parking right here until I do get 'em'. **1948** *Democrat* 1 Jan. 4/2 Drivers now can park or back into alleys or up to loading platforms with much greater ease. **1959** *Daily Tel.* 24 Mar. 9/3 Besides asking motorists not to park on main roads, he urged them to use alternative routes. **1966** P. MOLONEY *Plea for Mersey* 51 Not hardened junkies, when deprived of dope, Ere felt such anger..As Scouseville driver seeking space to park.

3. *intr.* To walk or drive in a park.

a **1783** H. BROOKE *Love & Vanity* Poems (1810) 416/2 Then all for parking, and parading, Coquetting, and dancing, masquerading.

Hence **parked** (pɑːkt) *ppl. a.*

1807 J. BARLOW *Columb.* VI. 375 Deep squadron'd horse.. And park'd artillery. **1841** MIALL in *Nonconf.* I. 57 A residence..compassed round with parked and shaven acres. **1919** C. P. THOMPSON *Cocktails* 176 The old farm where the V.A.D. drivers were cleaning their parked ambulances. **1932** *Daily Tel.* 23 May 8/6 In view of..the parked cars using the park, it was felt that it was an injustice that the horse-rider should be solely blamed for damage to the turf. **1962** [see DOUBLE-PARK *v.*]. **1973** *Daily Tel.* 19 June 3/1 A visitor to Gatwick Airport complained yesterday that he had been able to walk unchallenged up to a parked airliner. **1976** C. BERMANT *Coming Home* II. i. 113 One can hardly move for tourists and traffic and parked cars.

parka ('pɑːkə). Also **parkha**; (all †) **parca, parkee, parki.** Pl. **parkas** (northern Canada **parki**). [Aleutian, from Russ. *párka* skin jacket.] An outer garment or long jacket with a hood attached, made of skins and worn by Eskimos; a similar garment, usu. of wind-proof fabric, worn by mountaineers, skiers, etc. Also *attrib.*

1780 W. COXE *Acct. Russ. Discoveries* 256 The inhabitants of Alaxa, Umnak, Unalaksha..wear coats (parki) made of bird skins. **1813** G. H. VON LANGSDORFF *Voy. & Trav.* II. ii. 37 They are called *parka*, and are worn some-times with one side outwards sometimes with the other. **1818** V. M. GOLOVNIN *Narr. Captivity in Japan* I. i. 32 The women wore parkis made of the skin of birds with the feathers outward. **1851** J. RICHARDSON *Arctic Searching Exped.* II. 379 (*heading*) Eskimo vocabulary. English... *Parka*... Kuskutchewak... atkuk. **1907** R. W. SERVICE *Songs of Sourdough* 56 Talk of your cold! through the parka's fold it stabbed like a driven nail. **1910** —— *Ballads of Cheechako* 25 My eyes were seared, yet thralled I peered through the parka hood nigh blind. **1922** *Chambers's Jrnl.* Feb. 137/1 He had no snowshoes, no parki, and he did not see the dense black blizzard sweeping up from the north-west. **1922** *19th Cent.* Feb. 269 They changed their drill parkees for coats of caribou fur. **1926** *Spectator* 18 Sept. 408/2 The woodsman of the north..wears no fur, unless it be a little trimming round the neck of the 'parca'. **1934** *Sun* (Baltimore) 31 Jan. 3/3 Stocky Indians and Eskimos, fur-trimmed parkas and mukluks, miners with violent red and green plaid shirts,.. —these characterized the simpler functions at crossroad taverns. **1948** *Manch. Guardian Weekly* 1 Jan. 9 Your correspondent will now buckle on his parka, latch his skis, and take off. **1955** E. HILLARY *High Adventure* 37 We took possession of our own equipment—..double-layered windproof parkas. **1958** *Tararua* XII. 31 *Parka.* This name is the only one used in New Zealand for the hooded garment based on that of the Eskimos. *Anorak* seems to be common in England. **1958** L. WHISHAW *As far as You'll take Me* vii. 94, I spent a wonderful couple of hours trying on fabulous parkas (pronounced parkees in the North). **1963** *Times* 25 Feb. (Canada Suppl.) p. xv/1 Eskimo children..Huddled inside their sealskin *parkhas* and warmed by the low flame of a blubber lantern,..may listen spellbound to stories of the powers of Talluliyuk the seal-goddess. **1968** *Globe & Mail* (Toronto) 17 Feb. 1/7 Busloads of parka-clad workers.. arrived almost hourly yesterday at Elliot Lake's two hotels. **1973** *Guardian* 10 Apr. 13/2 Fox-trimmed parka with shirred waist. **1973** A. H. WHITEFORD *N. Amer. Indian Arts* 86 The Kutchin made fine tailored skin skirts, parkas, and one-piece leggings and moccasins. **1976** *Evening Post* (Nottingham) 14 Dec. 1/6 A boy's parka coat worth £4·50 was stolen from the cloakroom of the Chaucer Junior School, Ilkeston. **1978** *Times* 23 Feb. 13/6, I wore a silk Chinese padded jacket under my parkha.

park-and-ride (ˌpɑːkənd'raɪd), *a.* [f. PARK *v.* + AND *conj.* + RIDE *v.*] Designating or pertaining to a system whereby commuters and other visitors travel by private car to car-parks situated on the outskirts of a city, and continue their journey to the centre of the city by means of public transport. Also as *sb.*

1966 *Leicester Mercury* 30 Dec. 24/3 Park 'n' Ride was the success of the year. **1968** *Economist* 20 Apr. 48 Public transport to those facilities, largely by rail (incorporating park-and-ride stations), must be built up. **1971** *Sunday Times* (Johannesburg) (Business Section) 28 Mar. 7/4 He wants to attract shoppers to the city centre by way of off-street parking and establish 'park-and-ride' schemes outside the city with a speedy bus service to the downtown area. **1973** *Times* 28 Feb. (Victoria Centre, Nottingham Suppl.) p. iii/3 (*heading*) 'Park-and-ride' can beat the traffic problem. **1974** *Drive* Autumn 110/1 Public transport improvements now in operation include a park-and-ride service, catering for the parking of 250 cars..and distribution of the occupants from a site $1\frac{1}{4}$ miles south of the city centre. **1977** *Modern Railways* Dec. 461/3 Perhaps we can hope for improved road/rail interchange or even park-and-ride facilities to woo potential rail commuters.

Park Avenue. Name of a street in New York City, U.S.A., used *attrib.* and as *adj.* to designate the fashionable and luxurious style of life for which it is noted.

1956 R. MACAULAY *Towers of Trebizond* vi. 59 Mrs. Van Damm looked very handsome and bland, with blue hair and eyes and Park Avenue clothes. **1971** M. BABSON *Cover-up Story* vi. 67 Lou-Ann isn't Park Avenue Hillbilly material. .. Hillbilly, yes. Park Avenue, no. **1975** J. HONE *Sixth Directorate* iv. 149 She had all the rare finesse of a Park Avenue debutante. **1976** *National Observer* (U.S.) 13 Mar. 7/1 They know we run a Park Avenue operation at Marquette, that we SRO the joint. The kids realize that by playing at Marquette they'll be constantly in the limelight and get good pro contracts.

parker[1] ('pɑːkə(r)). Also 4 **parkere**, 5 **-are, parcare, -oure**, 5–6 **-ar**, 6 **perker.** [a. Anglo-F. *parker* (= OF. type **parquier*), in med.L. *parcārius*, f. PARK *sb.*: see -ER[2] 2.]

1. A man who has charge of a park; a park-keeper. *Obs.* exc. *Hist.*

[**1321–2** *Rolls of Parlt.* I. 397/2 Ses geentz, c'est a savoir Johan soun Parker, & Richard [etc.].] **1395** in *E.E. Wills* (1882) 8, I bequethe to Roger, my parkere,..c.s. *c* **1430** LYDG. *Lyke thyn Audience* 28 in *Pol. Rel. & L. Poems* 26 Mawgre the wache of fosters and parkerrys. *c* **1440** *Promp. Parv.* 382/2 Parcare, *indagator.* **1483** *Cath. Angl.* 269/2 A Parcoure (*A.* Parkare), *parcarius.* **1530** PALSGR. 458/1 This parker blodyeth his clothes. **1643** PRYNNE *Sov. Power Parlt.* III. 17 If the Parker negligently suffer the Deere to be killed, or kill the Deere himselfe..it is a direct forfaiture of his Office. **1818** CRUISE *Digest* (ed. 2) III. 147 An annual fee of 40*l.* had been given to the parker, issuing out of the king's manors in the county of Surry.

2. A rabbit that lives in a park.

1846 *P. Parley's Ann.* VII. 325 Gamekeepers give various names to rabbits: with them they are warreners, parkers, sweethearts, and hedgehogs... The parker's favourite haunt is in gentlemen's pleasure grounds. **1870** BLAINE *Encycl. Rur. Sports* (ed. 3) §2683.

Hence †'**parkership** *Obs.*, the office of parker.

1461 *Rolls of Parlt.* V. 473/1 The Offices of Constableship ..and Parkership of the same Castell. **1574** tr. *Littleton's Tenures* 81 b, The office of a Parkershippe of a Parke. **1671** BRYDALL *Law Eng. relating to Nobility & Gentry* (1675) 35 As if a Parkership be granted to an Earl.

parker[2] ('pɑːkə(r)). [f. PARK *v.* + -ER[1].] **1.** One who parks a vehicle.

1930 M. MCCLINTOCK *Rep. Parking & Garage Probl. Washington 78* (*caption*) Street obstruction by a desperate parker. **1959** *Encounter* Aug. 32/2 He's used to pinching parkers on the broad highway. **1959** *Times* 8 Dec. 5/6 Mr. Marples gave an example of the immunity these all-day parkers have enjoyed. **1974** W. GARNER *Big enough Wreath* xi. 151 Smith had the luck to find a car leaving the meter. He reversed fast..cutting out another would-be parker.

2. *Austral. colloq.* = *parking light.* Usu. *pl.*

1967 S. H. COURTIER *Murder's Burning* xiii. 187 Mr. Proctor switched on his tail lights and parkers. **1971** R. DENTRY *Encounter at Kharmel* x. 179 Keep out of the way as soon as you see me switch the parkers on. **1971** *Southerly* XXXI. 71 A prowl car told us to switch our parkers on.

'**Parker**[3]. [Name of the manufacturing company.] The proprietary name of a pen made by the Parker Pen Company.

1906 *Official Gaz.* (U.S. Patent Office) 2 Oct. 1507/2 Parker Pen Company, Janesville, Wis... Used ten years Parker..for Fountain-pens. **1914** *Trade Marks Jrnl.* 5 Aug. 1229 'Parker' Fountain Pens, not of Precious Metal or imitation thereof. The Parker Pen Company..Wisconsin, United States of America. **1923** *Official Gaz.* (U.S. Patent Office) 2 Jan. 18/1 The Parker Pen Co., Janesville, Wis... Parker..Fountain Pens and Mechanical Pencils. Claims use since 1891 on fountain pens; since 1921 on mechanical pencils. **1935** *Trade Marks Jrnl.* 5 June 718/1 Parker... Fountain pens and propelling pencils (none being of precious metal or of imitation precious metal) and desk stands (not of precious metal or imitation precious metal) for pens. The Parker Pen Company..Wisconsin, United States of America. **1959** I. JEFFERIES *Thirteen Days* (1961) x. 143, I reckon I'll get a Parker 51, a gold one. **1974** 'E. ANTHONY' *Malaspiga Exit* ii. 44 An assortment of pens from ball-point to gold-nibbed Parkers. **1976** 'Z. STONE' *Modigliani Scandal* I. iv. 38 He filled up the form with the gold Parker in his pocket.

parkerite ('pɑːkəraɪt). *Min.* [f. the name of R. L. *Parker* (b. 1893) of Zurich + -ITE[1].] A sulphide of nickel, bismuth, and lead, $Ni_3(Bi,Pb)_2S_2$, occurring as orthorhombic crystals with a metallic lustre.

1936 D. L. SCHOLTZ in *Publ. Univ. Pretoria* 2nd Ser. I. 186 The new minerals F and G were first recognised towards the end of the year 1932..when the writer benefited greatly by the valued advice and criticism of Professors P. Niggli and R. Parker. The author, therefore, proposes the name 'Niggliite' for the former (F), and 'Parkerite' for the latter (G). **1943** *Amer. Mineralogist* XXVIII. 345 Single grains of parkerite..are bright bronze coloured with brilliant metallic lustre on fresh fractures, becoming darker and dull on tarnished surfaces. **1969** *Canad. Mineralogist* IX. 610 The parkerite in the Great Slave Lake area occurs as small inclusions in niccolite and is associated with native bismuth.

Parkerizing ('pɑːkəraɪzɪŋ), *vbl. sb.* [f. the name of the *Parker* Rust-Proof Co. of America (incorporated 1915), which introduced the process.] A rust-proofing process in which iron or steel is given a protective coating of phosphate by immersing it for a short time in a hot acidic solution of a metal phosphate (usu. manganese dihydrogen phosphate).

A proprietary name in the U.S.A.

1919 *Chem. & Metall. Engin.* 31 Dec. 787/2 Messrs. Allen and Richards were mainly responsible for changes in the Coslett process, which made its present modification one of the most simple methods of rust prevention. Their patented modification in use today is known as 'Parkerizing'. **1932** *Metal Industry* XL. 369/2 The basis of the Parkerizing process is a solution of a prepared powder, which consists essentially of manganese dihydrogen phosphate. **1949** *Official Gaz.* (U.S. Patent Office) 24 May 984/1 Parker Rust Proof Company, Detroit, Mich...Certification mark. 'Protected by Parkerizing for rust resistance.'.. Claims use since Mar. 15, 1936. **1954** E. MOLLOY *Electro-Plating & Corrosion Prevention* xiii. 213 'Parkerising' is applied to cameras and instruments, rifles, typewriters, chains, bolts, nuts, tacks, and so on. **1976** J. A. VON FRAUNHOFER *Basic Metal Finishing* xiii. 147 The original Coslett process, based on phosphoric acid containing zinc phosphate, has been superseded by the accelerated Parkerising, Bonderising and similar processes.

So '**Parkerize** *v. trans.*, to treat in this way; '**Parkerized** *ppl. a.*, a proprietary name applied to articles so treated.

1922 *Raw Material* V. 438/2 Heavy castings of intricate shape, containing irregular cavities, can be completely Parkerized. *Ibid.* 439/1 On structural iron work, heavy Parkerized coatings can be produced. **1932** *Metal Industry* XL. 369/2 The Parkerized surface is..excellent for absorbing and retaining paint, lacquer or enamel. **1939** BURNS & SCHUH *Protective Coatings for Metals* xvi. 375 It is possible to Parkerize zinc coatings. **1942** *Trade Marks Jrnl.* 20 May 205/2 Parkerized... Hand tools and side arms. The Pyrene Company Limited,..Brentford, Middlesex; manufacturers. *Ibid.* 2 Dec. 505/2 Parkerized... Small domestic utensils and containers, non-electric instruments for cleaning purposes..all being goods of common metal; steel wool. The Pyrene Company Limited,..Brentford, Middlesex; manufacturers and merchants. **1961** *Chem. Abstr.* LV. 8883 (*heading*) The resistance of parkerised iron in polar marine climatic conditions.

†**ˌParker's ce'ment.** *Obs.* except *Hist.* [Named after James *Parker*, who patented it in England in 1796.] = *Roman cement* s.v. ROMAN *a.*[1] 16 c.

1814 *Trans. Geol. Soc.* II. 193 This place is particularly known on account of its furnishing abundance of the septaria, from which that excellent material for building under water and for stucco is made, known by the name of Parker's cement. **1839** *Penny Cycl.* XV. 420/1 The mortars made with them are called hydraulic mortars. Of these, Parker's cement is a well known kind. **1889** W. A. TILDEN *Watts' Man. Chem.* I. 337 Parker's or Roman cement is made in this manner from the nodular masses of calcareo-argillaceous ironstone found in the London clay. **1917** E. A. DANCASTER in G. Martin *Industr. & Manuf. Chem.: Inorg.* II. 85 The first of the natural cements was prepared by James Parker towards the end of the eighteenth century. It was known at first as Parker's cement, but was afterwards called Roman cement, by which name it is still known.

Parkes (pɑːks). *Metallurgy.* [Name of Alexander *Parkes* (1813–90), English chemist and inventor, who first patented the process in 1850 (*Brit. Pat. 13,118*).] *Parkes* (or †*Parkes'*, ¶*Parke's*) *process*: a process for removing silver and gold from lead by adding zinc to the molten lead, so that the precious metals form an alloy with the zinc and collect on the surface.

1857 PHILLIPS & DARLINGTON *Rec. Mining & Metalurgy* 180 (*heading*) Parkes' process for desilverizing lead. **1892** W. CROOKES tr. *R. von Wagner's Man. Chem. Technol.* II. 180 A further advantage of the Parkes process is that a minimum proportion of gold, present in the work-lead, can be first extracted by a small addition of zinc..whilst the subsequent main quantity of silver extracted..is free from gold. **1912** J. W. MELLOR *Mod. Inorg. Chem.* xxi. 382 Lead can be desilverized by means of Pattinson's or Parkes' process. **1923** U. R. EVANS *Metals & Metallic Compounds* IV. 268 Parke's process..only serves to remove silver and gold, and would leave the objectionable impurities in the lead. **1940** *Chambers's Techn. Dict.* 617/2 Parke's process. **1969** R. F. Lang tr. *Henglein's Chem. Technol.* 531 The refining of crude lead takes place in two steps: 1. refining proper... 2. desilvering by the aid of Zn (Parkes process).

Parkesine ('pɑːksiːn). Now *Hist.* [f. prec. + -INE[5].] A substance more or less identical with celluloid, based on pyroxylin and castor oil or camphor.

1862 *Chem. News* 9 Aug. 75/2 Parkesine.—A number of pretty and useful articles, formed of a material which the inventor, Mr. Parkes, has named after himself, are exhibited in Case 1112, Class IV. The basis of this material is the mixture of collodion and castor oil. **1868** *Chambers's Encycl.* X. 679/1 Parkesine was first shewn in quantity at the International Exhibition of 1862. **1911** E. C. Worden *Nitrocellulose Industry* I. xi. 364 Lewthwaite utilized the patented product of A. Parkes (called Parkesine) by ornamenting, embossing, and printing, and treated it in a manner similar to real leather. **1958** *Times* 25 Mar. (Careers in Industry Suppl.) p. xii/3 'Parkesine' was the forerunner of 'xylonite' and is identical with 'celluloid', the American article which in the 1870's was the first commercially satisfactory plastics product. **1964** V. E. Yarsley et al. *Cellulosic Plastics* xv. 181 The celluloid of the Parkesine process was produced by squeezing out the dough between rolls and subsequently removing the residual volatile solvent.

parkie, parky ('pɑːkɪ). *colloq.* (chiefly *Sc.* and *north.*). [f. PARK *sb.* 2 + -Y[6], -IE.] A park-keeper.

[**1939** Joyce *Finnegans Wake* 587 Touching our Phoenix Rangers' nuisance at the meeting of the waitresses,..and those pest of parkies, twitch, thistle and charlock.] **1953** *Scottish Jrnl. Theol.* VI. 424 [Schopenhauer] one day sat hunched up on a seat in the Tiergarten, sunk in profound reflection. A *Parkaufseher*, or as we should say 'parky', saw him and not unnaturally put him down as at least a suspicious character. **1957** J. Kirkup *Only Child* 124 We lived in mortal terror of being caught by the parky. **1965** *Listener* 4 Nov. 720/1 The Parkie's usually an auld man and he cannie climb the poles. **1971** *Sunday Times* 9 May 34 It's just coats on the ground and the parkies chase us at least once a month for doing something wrong. **1975** *Scottish Field* Apr. 4/3 You had to be on the lookout for the Parky if, as was likely, you had nipped on [to the Alexandra Park golf course] without paying.

parkin ('pɑːkɪn). *north. dial.* Also **-en, perkin.** [Origin unknown: perh. from proper name *Perkin* or *Parkin.*] A kind of gingerbread or cake made of oatmeal and treacle.

1800 D. Wordsworth *Jrnl.* 6 Nov. (1941) I. 71, I was baking bread, dinner, and parkins. **1828** *Craven Gloss.* (ed. 2), *Parkin*, a cake made of treacle and oat meal, commonly called a treacle-parkin. **1884** Mrs. G. L. Banks *Sybilla*, etc. III. 145 Bribed by a cake of parkin from Dame Dorothy's capacious pockets. **1887** *Suppl. to Jamieson, Addenda*, Perkins. **1896** *Allbutt's Syst. Med.* I. 404 The diet should be varied, and should include..whole-meal bread, 'parkin', gingerbread and molasses. **1968** E. R. Buckler *Ox Bells & Fireflies* xix. 268 Two women had brought oatmeal parkins on cake plates that were exactly alike. **1973** *New Society* 20 Dec. 709/3 The re-birth of interest in regional specialities like parkin (a rich, dark gingerbread, eaten with cheese).

parking ('pɑːkɪŋ), *vbl. sb.* [f. PARK *v.* + -ING[1].]

1. The action of PARK *vb.* (in various senses).

1526 in Dillon *Calais & Pale* (1892) 82 If he dunge it with parkinge of shepe or of bests, he to have ijs. viijd. for evry acre. **1607** J. Milwarde *Jacobs Gt. Day* (1610) I iv b, The parking in of beasts, and the depopulating Townes, to shut out Christians.

2. *concr.* Ground laid out in the style of a park. Also, in U.S., a strip of turf, with or without trees, in the centre of a street; in some regions of the U.S., a strip of grass between the footpath and the curb. Also **parking strip**.

1885 *Johns Hopkins Hist. Studies* Ser. III. Mar. 109 Spaces were left for a market-place, court-house green and parking for the palace. **1888** H. Gannett in *Encycl. Brit.* XXIV. 382/2 In some cases, similar parking has been left in the middle of the streets. **1888** *Appleton's Cycl. Amer. Biog.* IV. 578/1 In 1871 he [F. L. Olmsted] urged..the so-called 'parking system' for the broad streets of Washington. **1945** *Amer. Speech* XX. 154/1 *Parking*, the grassed area between curbing and sidewalk. The term is used by some Minnesotans instead of *Boulevard*, by others as an alternate. **1963** R. I. McDavid *Mencken's Amer. Lang.* 667 In the Minneapolis area it [sc. *boulevard*] designates the grass strip between the sidewalk and the curb, elsewhere called a *tree lawn* or a *parking strip*. **1964** *Amer. Speech* XXXIX. 293 That strip of grass and weeds between the sidewalk and the curb..seems to be most commonly called *tree lawn* or *parking strip*... I use the colorless *parking* from the language of relatives in Iowa. **1966** *Inland* (Inland Steel Co., Chicago) Autumn 16/2 For the grass strip between sidewalk and street there is a bewildering array of local terms:..*parking* in Illinois. **1969** *Better Homes & Gardens* (U.S.) Apr. 85 They look best when used in a formal manner, such as in pairs on front parkings or equally spaced along property lines.

3. a. The placing or leaving of a vehicle or vehicles in a park (PARK *sb.* 5 b), at the side of the road, or elsewhere. Also *transf.*

1926 *Rep. Commissioner Police Metropolis 1925* 17 in *Parl. Papers* (Cmd. 2660) XV. 239 Parking of Cars.—The arrangements tentatively made by Police for parking cars on certain highways have been given statutory effect. **1929** *Minnesota Alumni Weekly* June 619 The new space along with a lot now used for parking will be seeded. **1931** *Times Lit. Suppl.* 15 Oct. 789/2 Let off with a caution at Marlborough-street for improper parking of his car. **1959** *Daily Tel.* 24 Mar. 9/2 A possible ban on parking on main roads was hinted at yesterday. **1961** *Product Engineering* 14 Aug. 34/1 Additional symbols of status are granted, such as reserved parking, distinctive badge passes..., and a difference in the treatment of financial progress through merit. **1970** *R.A.C. Guide & Handbk. 1970–71* 63/2 Where unexpired time is shown on the meter at the time of parking this period may be used without payment. **1977** 'M. Underwood' *Fatal Trip* i. 7 A re-arrangement of her domestic routine including the parking of Simon on a good-natured neighbour.

b. *attrib.* and *Comb.*, as *parking apron, area, attendant, fee, fine, garage, offence, place, space*; **parking bay**, a recess at the side of a road or other space allocated for parking a vehicle; **parking brake**, a brake provided on a motor vehicle or trailer for holding it at rest; **parking deck** [DECK *sb.*[1] 3 b], a floor of a building used as a parking place for vehicles; also, a multi-storey car park; **parking disc**: see DISC *sb.* 2 f; **parking lamp, light**, a small (often detachable) light on a motor vehicle for indicating its position when parked at night; = SIDE-LIGHT; **parking lot** orig. *U.S.*, a plot of ground used for the parking of vehicles; **parking meter** orig. *U.S.*, a coin-operated meter which registers the time a vehicle has been parked; **parking orbit**, an orbit around the earth or some other planet from which a space vehicle can be launched farther into space; **parking strip** (see quots.); **parking tag, ticket** orig. *U.S.*, a ticket attached by an official to a vehicle which has violated parking regulations; **parking warden** = *traffic warden*.

1974 Hawkey & Bingham *Wild Card* i. 20 The mile-long journey to the parking apron. **1961** R. A. Futterman *Future of our Cities* iii. 62 Less ambitious freeway plans may be more successful—especially when the roadways and interchanges are raised, allowing for cross access at many points and providing parking areas below the ramp. **1966** 'A. Hall' *9th Directive* vii. 63 A car had come into the parking area. **1977** E. Leonard *Unknown Man No. 89* xxi. 212 He..crossed the parking area to the front entrance. **1941** B. Schulberg *What makes Sammy Run?* iii. 48 He was on speaking terms with everybody, the parking attendant, the hat-check girl. **1962** J. Brierley *Parking of Motor Vehicles* 298 *Parking attendant*, a person authorized by or on behalf of a council or parking authority to supervise a parking place. **1973** A. Mann *Tiara* ix. 87 He handed the Maserati over to a parking attendant of the Automobile Club. **1962** J. Brierley *Parking of Motor Vehicles* v. 49 A parking bay 18 feet long will be long enough for the majority of modern cars. **1972** *Times* 26 Jan. 6/1 The notice was given to comply with the provisions for rent revision contained in an underlease for a flat on the seventh and eighth floors of Ambassador House and a parking bay. **1976** T. Heald *Let Sleeping Dogs Die* viii. 167 The van ahead berthed in a parking bay. **1944** L. D. Kitchin *Road Transport Law* 41/4 It is an offence to leave a vehicle without stopping the engine ..and applying the parking brake. **1959** E. K. Wenlock *Kitchin's Road Transport Law* (ed. 12) 20/1 On all trailers exceeding 2 cwt unladen the braking system must also be capable of acting as a parking brake to prevent at least two wheels from revolving. **1967** *Gloss. Caravan Terms* (*B.S.I.*) 2 *Parking brakes*, brakes for holding the caravan when at rest, usually the overrun brakes or power brakes provided with additional means of manual application. **1974** *New Yorker* 25 Feb. 44/3 He went into a double-parking maneuver that culminated as, with a flourish, he pulled at the parking-brake handle. **1970** Parking deck [see DECK *sb.*[1] 3 b]. **1972** *Graphic* (Tuscaloosa, Alabama) 30 Nov. 12/3 The County Commission Tuesday formally adopted a multi-level parking deck to be constructed adjacent to the County Jail. **1972** *Birmingham* (Alabama) *News* 17 Dec. 4A/1 With two parking deck sites assured..the property surrounding the station could be purchased and the proposed seven-story structure built in an L-shape. **1974** *Tuscaloosa* (Alabama) *News* 17 Feb. 3D/2 The authority was to build a parking deck for the downtown area. **1932** *Autocar* 9 Sept. 469, I have only once, in two years, been asked to pay a parking fee. **1963** P. Hall *London 2000* v. 111 One exception, which parking fees do not meet, is the extra congestion in the very short morning and evening rush periods. **1971** 'S. Smith' *Grave Affair* ix. 134 Horsham Police were surprised to receive payment of the £2 parking fine on the Cortina... It came in a plain manilla envelope,..and inside were two pound notes and the parking ticket. **1972** P. D. James *Unsuitable Job* iv. 117 She daren't risk a parking fine nor the impounding of the car. **1977** D. Williams *Treasure by Degrees* xviii. 166 Miss Stopps was not the type of citizen who would ignore a parking fine demand. **1948** *Sun* (Baltimore) 18 Feb. 10/2 There will undoubtedly be debates as to whether the commission should build and operate parking garages as public enterprises. **1974** M. G. Eberhart *Danger Money* (1975) xi. 118 Greg drove..to a parking garage where he left the car and hailed a taxi. **1976** *Billings* (Montana) *Gaz.* 1 July 3-B/2 Bids to construct Billings first municipally owned parking garage have all been rejected as being at least $300,000 too high. **1926–7** *Army & Navy Stores Catal.* 1134/1 Motor lamps..parking lamp... Burns very small amount of current. **1957** E. K. Wenlock *Kitchin's Road Transport Law* (ed. 11) 60/1 Parking lamps which can be used only on certain vehicles..must show a 1 in diameter white light to the front and a 1 in diameter red light to the rear. **1972** *Daily Tel.* 27 Apr. 19/6 Motorists will be able to discard their clip-on auxiliary parking lamps after Sunday next, when standardised regulations for parking without lights come into effect throughout the country. **1938** H. A. Tripp *Road Traffic & its Control* III. ix. 160 'Parking lights' of extremely low power (in order to economise current) are fitted to some cars. **1943** R. Chandler *Lady in Lake* (1944) xxiv. 136 A motor purled gently in the car with the parking lights on it. **1973** 'B. Mather' *Snowline* xiv. 171 It was a car running on its parking lights. **1924** H. Croy *R.F.D. No. 3* 172 Some of the people still lingered under the arc light, with its summer collection of bugs still in it, waiting for the two to come from the parking lot. **1930** M. McClintock *Rep. Parking & Garage Probl. Washington* 19 Parking lot rates average substantially lower than those for garages. **1958** *New Statesman* 1 Nov. 590/3 Partial over-building of these parking lots would do little to disguise the inherent visual bleakness of conception. **1972** *Times* 18 Mar. 8/7 People who in Leeds, for instance, will have stepped across the parking lot from rehearsals in the Playhouse to others in the studio. **1976** H. Nielsen *Brink of Murder* ix. 81 Simon found the restaurant..and drove into the parking lot. [**1935** *Pop. Sci. Monthly* Aug. 33/3 (*heading*) Curb-parking meter times autoist's stay.] **1936** *Amer. City* Jan. 95/3 In July.. there came to the attention of the officials in Dallas a device known as the parking meter. **1938** *Encycl. Brit. Bk. of Year* 649/2 Many cities have installed parking meters, usually requiring the deposit of five cents per hour for permission to park at the kerb. **1949** *Chicago Daily News* 11 Aug. 3/4 A runaway horse and wagon collided with a parking meter. **1956** *Planning* XXII. 210 There has been much discussion of the merits of coin-in-slot parking meters as a means of enforcing time limits. **1958** *Observer* 13 July 7/8 Six hundred parking meters, the first in Britain, came into operation in Mayfair on Thursday morning. **1966** *New Scientist* 24 Nov. 447/1 The psychological effect of the parking meter is always diluted by the element of gambling involved. **1974** *Guardian* 24 Jan. 28/4 Increases in parking meter charges. **1959** M. Summerton *Small Wilderness* i. 21 Once..he'd let me off a parking offence. **1960** G. Mikes *How to be Inimitable* 60 The most heinous offence known to the Police is officially called 'obstructing the Queen's Highway'. The Queen is brought into it to underline the close connection between a parking offence and high treason. **1960** *Aeroplane* XCIX. 496/1 Such a satellite could be launched for immediate interception, or placed in a 'parking' orbit, always ready to intercept, interrogate or inspect in detail another object orbiting in space. **1961** *Flight* LXXIX. 426/1 Injection into 'parking orbit', which places the vehicle at the proper location in space for departure into the desired lunar trajectory. **1970** *New Scientist* 2 July 21 The spacecraft goes on into a parking orbit and the two boosters coast down to land. **1925** *Act 15 & 16 Geo. V* c. 71 §68 (9) In this section the expression 'parking place' means a place where vehicles, or vehicles of any particular class or description, may wait. **1941** Parking-place [see BINDI-EYE]. **1975** N. Luard *Robespierre Serial* ii. 6 It's the residents coming back from work; they've got permits for the parking-places. **1924** *Collier's* 5 Jan. 17/2 Secretary Mellon has asked permission to move the Washington Monument so as to get more parking space. **1926** Parking space [see *car-park* s.v. CAR *sb.*[1] 6]. **1941** G. Marx *Let.* 25 July (1967) 29 Parking space is at a premium around this ramshackle building. **1971** A. Price *Alamut Ambush* iii. 35 His mind on a parking space thirty yards ahead. **1961** *New Left Rev.* July–Aug. 57/2 In front of the garages and kitchens are cobbled parking strips which absorb oil stains and from which moving traffic is kept by low bollards. **1966** *Inland* (Inland Steel Co., Chicago) Autumn 16/2 For the grass strip between sidewalk and street there is a bewildering array of local terms:..*parking strip*..in Illinois. **1956** 'E. McBain' *Cop Hater* (1958) iii. 28 Anybody who ever got a parking tag is automatically a cop hater. **1968** *Globe & Mail* (Toronto) 17 Feb. 5/8 More than $6-million of this amount came from the magistrates' courts. About $1,850,000 came from parking tags. **1977** *Time* 22 Aug. 34 (*caption*) The telltale parking tag and Deputy Craig Glassman with hate letters from his neighbor. **1947** *Denver Post* 2 Mar. A1/2 Parking tickets no longer could be fixed. **1951** T. Sterling *House without Door* vii. 80 These old bastards haven't even read a parking ticket for the last twenty years. **1959** W. R. Bird *These are Maritimes* x. 300 He took an old parking ticket out of his pocket. **1971** [see *parking fine* above]. **1973** H. Gilbert *Hotels with Empty Rooms* xvi. 137 The car stood where they had left it. A parking ticket had been inserted under the right-hand windscreen-wiper. **1966** P. Moloney *Plea for Mersey* 51 This sentinel your chariot will keep Till Parking Wardens, roused up from their sleep, Espy the yellow in the monster's face, And mark the car, with symbol of disgrace. **1974** L. Deighton *Spy Story* xiii. 130, I watched two parking wardens clobber a delivery van.

Parkinson[1] ('pɑːkɪnsən). The name of James *Parkinson* (1755–1824), English surgeon and palæontologist, used in **Parkinson's disease** [tr. F. *maladie de Parkinson* (J. M. Charcot 1876, in *Progrès médical* 2 Dec. 838/2)], a chronic, slowly progressive disorder of the central nervous system that occurs chiefly in later life as a result of degenerative changes in the brain and produces tremor, rigidity of the limbs, and slowness and imprecision of movement (described by Parkinson, under the names *shaking palsy* and *paralysis agitans*, in *An Essay on the Shaking Palsy* (1817)); **Parkinson syndrome** = PARKINSONISM.

1877 G. Sigerson tr. D.-M. Bourneville in *Charcot's Lect. Dis. Nervous Syst.* (ser. 1) v. 144 This man, aged 50 years, was attacked by 'Parkinson's disease' in consequence of a strong emotion occasioned by the attempts of the Federalists, during the time of the Commune, to incorporate him in their battalions. **1888** W. R. Gowers *Man. Dis. Nervous Syst.* II. 589 From the fact that it was first fully described by Parkinson in 1817, it has been called 'Parkinson's disease', but the name which he gave to it of 'shaking palsy' is both apt and adequate. **1909** *Practitioner* Feb. 290 In Parkinson's disease (paralysis agitans), the drug produced considerable decrease in all the cases. **1933** [see HOFFMANN 3]. **1950** A. Huxley *Let.* 19 July (1969) 627 Poor Osbert [Sitwell] has got Parkinson's disease and has started to tremble. **1955** *Sci. News Let.* 20 Aug. 120/2 A drug of the antihistamine class has helped almost half of a group of patients suffering with the Parkinson syndrome, best known to the layman as shaking palsy. **1970** [see DOPA]. **1973** *Sci. Amer.* July 98/3 Symptoms of Parkinson's disease..include active features such as tremor and muscular rigidity and negative features such as slowness in the initiation of movement and loss of the usual facial expression of emotions.

Parkinson[2] ('pɑːkɪnsən). The name of Cyril Northcote *Parkinson* (b. 1909), historian and journalist, used in the possessive to denote the 'law' propounded by him, that work expands to fill the time available for its completion. Also *transf.*

1955 *Economist* 19 Nov. 635/1 Before the discovery of a new scientific law—herewith presented to the public for the first time, and to be called Parkinson's Law—there has.. been insufficient recognition of the implications of this fact in the field of public administration. **1957** C. N. PARKINSON (*title*) Parkinson's law. **1957** *N.Y. Times* 5 May III. 1/7 Parkinson's Law is that British Government employes multiply by about 5 per cent a year even though their total work output does not increase in proportion. **1958** C. N. PARKINSON *Parkinson's Law* (U.K. ed.) 4 Parkinson's Law or the Rising Pyramid. Work expands so as to fill the time available for its completion. **1958** N. MACKENZIE *Conviction* 15 Our civil servants are bureaucratic slaves to Parkinson's Law. **1958** *Times* 3 July 11/6 An extension of Parkinson's Law to the parliamentary system establishes that the British instinct 'is to form two opposing teams, with referee and linesmen, and let them debate until they exhaust themselves'. **1960** *Guardian* 22 July 10/4 There is some 'Parkinson's law' that cars increase in numbers to fill..any space made available. **1962** *Lancet* 28 Apr. 898/2 The transportation of anything to high camps is subject to Parkinson's law: the greater the weight, the greater the number of porters; the greater the number of porters, the greater the weight of supplies; the greater the weight of supplies, the greater the number of porters. **1964** M. ARGYLE *Psychol. & Social Probl.* xiv. 172 Studies of factories, hospitals and school districts of different sizes show that larger ones have if anything a lower proportion of administrators, so that Parkinson's law is by no means generally true. **1966** R. H. ROBINS *Gen. Linguistics within Liberal Educ.* 15 A sort of Parkinson's Law applies in vocabulary: the meaning range of a word expands to fill the available space. **1972** *Daily Tel.* 3 Feb. 14 The engineers will tell you that, once it is built, the traffic will be there; and this, alas, is true, for Parkinson's Law ensures that traffic expands to fill the space available. **1974** L. DEIGHTON *Spy Story* xiii. 127 Before we had the security cards, there had been no delays. I was a victim of some Parkinson's law of proliferating security. **1978** *Cornish Guardian* 27 Apr. 3/1 Having spent the money, they then see the need to take on scores of new planners and technical officers. It was Parkinson's Law gone mad.

Hence **Parkin'sonian** *a.*², of or pertaining to Parkinson or his law; also as *sb.*², a believer in this law; **'Parkinsonism²**, the principle or doctrine reflected in Parkinson's law; an instance of this.

1957 *Life* 15 Apr. 57/1 Maybe where the squeeze ought to be applied hardest is on 'Parkinsonism', that trend for every bureau to proliferate. **1959** *Times* 3 Mar. 3/7 A port scene by Seurat, compounded of a thousand 'pointillist' dots must seem to Parkinsonians like a troupe of typists at £12 a week and 10 clerks at £20 and a dozen 'high executives' at £5,000 a year all busily employed in the composition and dispatch of a 'Yours of the 9th to hand'. *Ibid.* 5 May 11/5 They seem, perhaps, to be in some danger of falling into the (Parkinsonian?) trap of treating theoretical maxima as practical minima. **1960** *N.Y. Times* 31 Jan. 56/3 Professor Parkinson's book, 'Parkinson's Law', expounding this and other Parkinsonisms, was published in 1957. **1962** *Daily Tel.* 14 Mar. 12/2 The LCC has built up some efficient teams, with high status and pay at the top, for supervising its many services. Though some of these may smack of Parkinsonian internal empire building, many are good. **1964** R. BRADDON *Year Angry Rabbit* iv. 33 Committees of otherwise useless Civil Servants (whose numbers had swollen to quite terrifying and parkinsonian proportions since World War II). **1964** *New Society* 29 Oct. 6/2 In spite of the charges of Parkinsonism, Mr. Wilson's administration is fairly orthodox in its size and structure. **1968** A. DIMENT *Bang Bang Birds* ii. 15 At the outset it was just a little sub-department but by inevitable Parkinsonian growth it had assumed an identity of its own. **1971** C. RUSSELL *Crisis of Parliaments* III. i. 110 The Parkinsonian process by which people administering particular subjects under the Chamber acquired subordinates and a formal organization was accelerated by the increase in government business. **1975** M. SINCLAIR *Long Time Sleeping* xiv. 166 The best of all Parkinsonian models—when he had little to do he did nothing; when overstretched he always managed to fit extra into the day.

Parkinsonian (pɑːkɪn'səʊnɪən), *sb.*¹ and *a.*¹ *Med.* Also **parkinsonian.** [f. PARKINSON¹ + -IAN.] **A.** *sb.* A person affected with Parkinsonism.

1899 CHURCH & PETERSON *Nervous & Mental Dis.* VII. iii. 516 The gait of Parkinsonians is strikingly peculiar. **1949** *Lancet* 26 Feb. 364/2 The parkinsonian has difficulty in starting to walk, and in stopping when once started. **1973** M. RIKLAN *L-Dopa & Parkinsonism* iii. 185 In the usual therapeutic dosages, L-Dopa has a wide variety of behavioral effects, both positive and negative, on the behavior of the parkinsonian.

B. *adj.* Characteristic of or affected with Parkinsonism.

1906 P. STEWART *Diagnosis Nervous Dis.* xvii. 243 The posture and gait of *paralysis agitans* are diagnostic... In a well-marked case the patient stands with the trunk stooping forwards, the face appearing 'starched' and expressionless —the so-called 'Parkinsonian mask', in which there is little or no emotional play of features. **1930** *Arch. Ophthalm.* IV. 364 Neurologic examination revealed a characteristic postencephalitic parkinsonian facies, gait and attitude. **1933** W. R. BRAIN *Dis. Nervous Syst.* viii. 447 The Parkinsonian gait..is usually slow, shuffling, and composed of small steps. **1970** *Nature* 4 Apr. 23/2 It is likely..that at least 50 per cent of the total Parkinsonian population may obtain benefit from L-dopa.

Parkinsonism¹ ('pɑːkɪnsənɪz(ə)m). *Med.* Also **parkinsonism.** [f. PARKINSON¹ + -ISM.]

a. The group of symptoms seen esp. in Parkinson's disease, but occurring also in other cerebral disorders. **b.** = *Parkinson's disease.*

1923 *Brain* XLVI. 268 Post-encephalitic Parkinsonism is usually due to degeneration of the substantia nigra. **1949** *Lancet* 12 Feb. 258/1 A patient with advanced parkinsonism ..was bedridden owing to extreme rigidity. **1954** H. H. MERRITT in L. J. Doshay *Parkinsonism & its Treatment* i. 3 Two striking characteristics of the symptoms of parkinsonism are their relationship to emotional tension and their disappearance in sleep. **1966** WRIGHT & SYMMERS *Systemic Path.* II. xxxiv. 1292/2 Tremor and rigidity may develop in other diseases, and it is usual to refer to this syndrome as Parkinsonism. Postencephalitic Parkinsonism ..is the most familiar example of this disability; it also occurs in chronic manganese poisoning and in patients who have survived severe carbon monoxide or nitrous oxide intoxication. **1970** *Times* 29 Apr. 2/3 There are about 60,000 sufferers from Parkinsonism in England and Wales. **1974** E. AMBLER *Dr. Frigo* II. 110 If you can catch Parkinsonism in the early stages treatment nowadays can do a lot to help the patient.

Parkinsonism²: see under PARKINSON².

parkish ('pɑːkɪʃ), *a.* [f. PARK *sb.* + -ISH¹.] Resembling a park; somewhat park-like.

1813 J. FORSYTH *Rem. Italy* 86 The immediate approaches..are planted in the open parkish style. **1824** SCOTT *St. Ronan's* xx, A rage to render their place 'parkish', as was at one time the prevailing phrase. **1838** *Fraser's Mag.* XVIII. 148 A parkish-looking sort of pleasure-ground.

'park-ˌkeeper. The keeper of a park.

1624 MIDDLETON *Game at Chess* IV. ii, Some falconers, some park-keepes, and some huntsmen. **1785** BARKER in *Phil. Trans.* LXXV. 354. **1855** MACAULAY *Hist. Eng.* xvii. IV. 34 All that the Queen could do was to order the parkkeepers not to admit Sir John again within the gates.

So **'park-ˌkeeperess** (*nonce-wd.*), a female park-keeper, or park-keeper's wife.

1852 JAMES *Pequinillo* III. 161 They had been park-keeper and park-keeperess to the Westwood family thirty years and six months.

parkland ('pɑːklænd). [PARK *sb.* 7.]

1. An area of grassland scattered with occasional clumps of trees. Also *attrib.*

1907 H. A. KENNEDY *New Canada* 182 Very soon the parklands of the north were all behind us. **1909** E. WARMING *Oecol. Plants* lxxxix. 325 We may cite the 'park-lands' of eastern Asia, where grassland has become occupied by trees and shrubs. **1920** H. G. WELLS *Outl. Hist.* 84/2 They were forest and parkland peoples without horses. *Ibid.* 267/2 A slow change in climate..was replacing the swamps and forests and parklands of South Russia..by steppes. **1926** TANSLEY & CHIPP *Study of Vegetation* x. 209 Parkland.. aptly describes the great stretches of country which in Africa almost completely surround the Closed Forest... The characteristic feature of the Parkland is grass, interspersed with trees. **1948** A. L. RAND *Mammals E. Rockies* 110 The parklands of central Alberta. **1953** *Canad. Geogr. Jrnl.* XLVI. 240/1 This fact would seem to urge caution in the extension of irrigation northward into the parkland belt. **1960** N. POLUNIN *Introd. Plant Geogr.* xiv. 441 Savanna-woodlands or 'parklands' are often found where the rainless period is more prolonged and the annual rainfall less heavy than in true closed forest. **1968** R. M. PATTERSON *Finlay's River* 3 It [*sc.* a relief map] has been carefully painted with the varying greens and yellows that indicate the different kinds of forest, parkland and tundra.

2. Land given over to the cultivation of a park or parks (PARK *sb.* 1 b).

1937 *Proc. Prehist. Soc.* III. 73 The edges of the barrow are turfed and merge into undisturbed parkland. **1952** *Antiquity* XXVI. 161 The houses of Stowe or Wimpole or Castle Howard were being absorbed into their parklands. **1954** M. BERESFORD *Lost Villages* i. 28 The parkland..was both attractive to the eye and useful to the pocket. **1959** *Geogr. Rev.* XLIX. 28 A thousand acres of parkland was deliberately left unaltered. **1977** *Times* 26 Nov. 28/5 (Advt.), Enjoy a weekend in the country at a beautiful Georgian Rectory in 26 acres of parkland.

3. *Canad.* **a.** A parcel of land required by law to be set aside for public recreation and wildlife conservation.

1957 *Financial Post* (Toronto) 29 June 23/3 Every major Canadian city knows it should be providing 10 acres of parkland for every 1,000 people. **1977** *Little Cataraqui Environment Assoc. Newsletter* Nov. 1 The [conservation] authority will maintain this land as a natural parkland, paying both taxes to the city and maintenance costs.

b. A national or provincial park.

1958 *Maclean's Mag.* 10 May 8/1 We do, of course, sometimes set aside tracts of country for recreation and so forth—and we say these are in perpetuity; but this phrase only seems to mean until the parkland is needed for logging, or mining. **1971** *Weekend Mag.* (Montreal) 21 Aug. 9/2 Quebec..now has an accelerated program attending to some 25,000 square miles of developed and partially developed parkland.

Park Lane (pɑːk leɪn). The name of a fashionable London street used as a symbol of wealth and breeding and the social attitudes they imply. Hence **Park Lane-ite.**

1880 TROLLOPE *Duke's Children* II. vii. 78 Park Lane was sweeter than the Fifth Avenue. Lord Silverbridge was nicer than the bank clerk. **1906** *Westm. Gaz.* 27 Apr. 1/3 The attitude of this lady of the ballad is a common one among the Park-lanes of every land. **1936** 'J. TEY' *Shilling for Candles* vii. 73 What I'd like to know is if that method goes in Pimlico or if you keep it for Park Lane. **1944** M. LASKI *Love on Supertax* ii. 27 Would you yourself be quite happy to see your children playing with scrubbed little brats from Park Lane? **1961** A. SMITH *East-Enders* ii. 29 If they want to live like Park Lane-ites they should live in Park Lane.

'park-ˌleaves. ? *Obs.* [app. f. PARK *sb.* + *leaves*, pl. of LEAF.] A name for the shrub Tutsan (*Hypericum Androsæmum*). Also, with early herbalists, the tree *Vitex Agnus castus*: the name *agnus castus* having app. been applied to both (see Turner *Names of Herbes*, A viij b).

a **1400-50** *Stockh. Med. MS.* 157 Totsane or parkleuys: *agnus castus.* **1545** ELYOT, *Agnos*, is a tree..commonly called *Agnus castus*, in englysshe parke leaues, it hathe leaues lyke to wyllowe. **1578** LYTE *Dodoens* I. xlv. 66 If Androsemon be Tutsan or Parke leaues, it groweth plentifully in woodes and parkes, in the west partes of England. **1611** COTGR., *Amerine*, Agnus castus,..chast or hempetree, Parke-leauis. **1682** WHELER *Journ. Greece* II. 205 On the top..succeedeth a large yellow Flower, much bigger than Parks-Leaves. **1857** MAYNE *Expos. Lex.*, *Park Leaves*, the *Hypericum androsæmum*, All-heal, or St. Peter's-wort.

parklet ('pɑːklɪt). [dim. of PARK *sb.*] A small park in an urban area.

1966 *Listener* 27 Jan. 135/1 The charming little 'parklets' ..have real herbaceous borders. **1968** MRS. L. B. JOHNSON *White House Diary* 2 Oct. (1970) 715 These two small parklets on Hobart Street in a low-income area were a gift to the city by David Lloyd Kreeger.

parklos, obs. form of PARCLOSE.

parkly ('pɑːklɪ), *a. rare.* [f. PARK *sb.* + -LY¹.] Of the nature or character of a park; park-like.

1541 *Act 33 Hen. VIII*, c. 37 The same..with goodli & parkely parkes..to beautifie adorne and decorite. **1886** RUSKIN *Præterita* I. v. 164 Among the gentry of that town and its parkly neighbourhood.

'parkward, *adv.* [f. as prec. + -WARD.] Towards the park. Also **'parkwards.**

1598 SHAKS. *Merry W.* III. i. 5 Marry Sir, the pittie-ward, the Parke-ward: euery way: olde Windsor way, and euery way but the Towne-way. **1886** G. ALLEN *Maimie's Sake* xxi, She..took a stroll..out parkwards.

parky ('pɑːkɪ), *a.*¹ [f. as prec. + -Y.] Of the nature of a park, or abounding in parks.

1831 M. EDGEWORTH *Let.* 11 Apr. (1971) 517 We came to a beautiful parky place where Dr. Fitton flourishes for the summer. **1850** *Tait's Mag.* XVII. 613/1 Some of the parky purlieus of London. **1955** R. P. HOBSON *Nothing too Good for Cowboy* v. 43 Cow tracks fanned out through the parky poplar country leaving a messy swath many yards wide. **1973** R. D. SYMONS *Where Wagon Led* III. x. 181 The country around Turtleford was parky, with aspen bluffs and just the odd spruce.

parky, *a.*² *slang.* Cold, chilly.

1895 *Sporting Times* 9 Feb. 1/4 A toff came and ordered a pint of hot, As he said that the weather was parkey. **1898** *Pink 'un & Pelican* 273 (Farmer), 'Morning William; cold s'morning?'..'It is a bit parky', assented William. **1900** G. SWIFT *Somerley* 109 Oh! stars! this water is parky. **1916** 'TAFFRAIL' *Pincher Martin* xi. 191 'Strewth!..it's a bit parky, ain't it? **1969** J. CLARKE *Foxon's Hole* xxv. 153 Gawaine ventured to say that it was a fine day... 'Ah. Parky, though. Shouldn't wunner if we 'ad a bit o' snow.' **1970** *Kenya Farmer* Feb. 36/3 All our visitors seem to labour under the delusion that it should be warm and sunny all twenty four hours... They are utterly demoralised by our parky nights on the farm. **1975** T. HEALD *Deadline* v. 99 'Cold isn't it?' 'Pretty parky.'

parky: see PARKIE.

parl: see PARLE.

†**'parlage,** *a. Sc. Obs. rare*⁻¹. [app. a. F. *parlage* babbling, palaver, useless talk.] ? Babbling, full of empty talk; yelping.

c **1615** SIR W. MURE *Sonn.* xi, A parlage cur, a brokin staffe for stay.

parlament(e, -mentt, obs. ff. PARLIAMENT.

parlance ('pɑːləns). Also 7 -ence. [a. AngloFr. and OF *parlance -launce*, f. *parler* to speak. (Not in mod. French.)]

1. Speaking, speech; *esp.* debate, parleying, parley. *arch.*

[**13..** LANGTOFT *Chron.* I. 147 Le ray William le Rous.. A countes et barouns..Par lettre maunde et prie venir a sa parlaunce [R. BRUNNE 87 parlement].] **1579-80** NORTH *Plutarch, Crassus* (1595) 614 Word was brought to Crassus, and he accepted parlance. **1611** SPEED *Hist. Gt. Brit.* IX. xii. 575/2 King Edward..signifies..to the Pope, that Battel and not Parlance should determine his right, and title. **1701-2** *Case of Schedule Stated* 26 The Place of that Common Parlance was call'd the Parliament Chamber. **1824** *Examiner* 585/1 He was not disposed to let him pass without further parlance. **1830** TENNYSON *Isabel* ii, A hate of gossip parlance and of sway. **1879** BOULTBEE *Hist. Ch. Eng.* 45 After some parlance, the stranger foretold deliverance.

2. Way of speaking, mode of speech, language, idiom. Usually with defining words, as *in common, legal, ordinary, vulgar parlance*, etc.

[*a* **1481** LITTLETON *Tenures* vi. (1516) A v, Mes per comune parlaunce [1544-1608 *tr.* language] celuy qui tient pur terme de sa vie demesne est appelle tenaunt pur terme de vie.] **1787** BENTHAM *Def. of Usury* xiii. 180 Birmingham ..claims in common parlance, the title of a projecting town. **1798** BAY *Amer. Law Rep.* (1809) I. 183 In common law parlance an execution is not an action. **1829** SOUTHEY *Sir T. More* (1831) II. 267 A wise woman, by which I do not mean in vulgar parlance one who pretends to prophecy. **1841** L. HUNT *Seer* II. (1864) 70 A curious specimen of English parlance. **1844** DISRAELI *Coningsby* II. vii, The political opinions..were what in ordinary parlance are styled Tory. **1884** SIR W. B. BRETT in *Law Rep. 14 Q. Bench Div.* 191 In legal parlance there might be a debt.

‖**parlando** (pɑː'lændəʊ), *a., adv.*, and *sb. Mus.* [It.] A direction that a passage is to be played or sung 'as if speaking', in an expressive or declamatory manner.

1876 STAINER & BARRETT *Dict. Mus. Terms* 342/2 *Parlando, Parlante (It.)*, in a declamatory manner, as if speaking. **1880** GROVE *Dict. Mus.* II. 650/2 *Parlando, Parlante*, 'speaking'. A direction allowing greater freedom in rendering than *cantando* or *cantabile*, and yet referring to the same kind of expression. **1930** *Time & Tide* 7 June 745/1 Against a dissonant pianoforte accompaniment, the voice disclaims monotonously in the 'parlando' style. **1944** W. APEL *Harvard Dict. Mus.* 554/1 Parlando occurs particularly in rapid tempo when the syllables of the text change with every note... In connection with instrumental music, parlando (*parlante*) calls for an expressive declamation, suggestive of speech or song. **1955** *Times* 27 May 13/4 Miss Nancy Evans sang 'The Water Mill' too slowly and with too much tone—this is a *parlando* song. **1960** *Times* 23 May 16/7 A..lyrical setting of the Bible story, involving..choral parlando. **1970** *Daily Tel.* 28 Sept. 11/3 Where he perhaps carried relaxation a shade too far.. was in a habit, during less important recitative-like passages, of lapsing occasionally into a toneless parlando of too vaguely defined pitch. **1977** *Gramophone* Dec. 1098/3 Brahms to them is a romantic to the hilt, and they go out of their way to extract the maximum *parlando*-type expression from every phrase.

† **'parlant.** *Obs.* [a. F. *parlant* speaking, pr. pple. of *parler* to speak.] One who parleys or takes part in a conference.

1586 WARNER *Alb. Eng.* III. xix. (1589) 79 The place appointed, Parlantes him in simple meaning meet Farre from their Armie all vnarm'd.

parlary, var. PARLYAREE.

parlasy, parlatyk, obs. ff. PALSY, PARALYTIC.

parlatory ('pɑːlətəri). [ad. med.L. *parlātōrium*, It. *parlatorio (-toio)* parlour, f. *parlāre* to speak; L. type **parabolātōrium*.] The reception-room or room for conversation in a convent.

1651 HOWELL *Venice* 185 What he had overheard in a Parlatory of Nunnes. **1768** J. BARETTI *Acc. Mann. Italy* II. 12 They were shown into the parlatory. *Ibid.* 17 Both in the morning and afternoon they are allowed some hours of parlatory, as they call it. **1772** NUGENT tr. *Hist. Fr. Gerund* I. III. vi. 557 The drawing-rooms of the ladies, or the parlatories of nuns. **1890** in *Cent. Dict.*

parlay ('pɑːleɪ), *sb.* *U.S.* Also parley. [Corruption of PAROLI *sb.*]

1. *Faro.* = PAROLI.

1904 *American Corresp.*, In horse-racing the parley must be for the whole 'card' of races. In faro, and in rouge-et-noir, one lays a bet and, winning, leaves it on the table once more only.

2. *Betting.* A cumulative series of bets in which winnings accruing from one transaction are transferred to the next. Also *attrib.*

1904 [see sense 1 above]. **1927** *National Turf Digest* (U.S.) Jan. 19/1 From the standpoint of the bookmaker..no money coming from a winning horse can be 'iffed' to a parlay on that same horse and another. **1928** *Ibid.* Feb. 91/1 A parlay player cannot protect himself against a changed track condition, a change of jockeys, or added starters. **1932** D. RUNYON in *Collier's* 26 Mar. 40/2 He has a dispute with Sorrowful about a parlay on the races the day before. **1946** *Sun* (Baltimore) 2 Apr. 26/4 A $2 parlay would have paid $10,906.70. **1957** *New Yorker* 2 Nov. 105/1 Colonel Martingale..has figured out that a parlay on the same horses would have paid $4,045.58. **1963** T. PYNCHON *V.* vii. 158 Both, together, were like a parlay of horses, capable of a whole arrived at by some operation more alien than simple addition of parts. **1976** *New Yorker* 23 Feb. 85/2 Well, all the players who made parlays on the Proud horses—Birdie and Delta—clicked.

parlay ('pɑːleɪ), *v.* *U.S.* Also parley, parlee. [Corruption of PAROLI *v.*]

1. In faro and horse-racing, To apply the money staked, together with the money won on a bet, in continuing to bet on the same card, or as a further stake on another horse or combination of horses. *trans.* and *intr.*

1890 J. P. QUINN *Fools of Fortune* II. ii. 194 Almost all [faro] bankers will allow a player to 'parlee' as the percentage is largely in favor of the bank. **1895** *How to Make Money on Small Cap.* 63 Were he, however, to what is termed 'parley' his money—that is to say, if..he put his $5 on his choice on the first race, and, if the horse should win, put all the winnings and his original $5 on the next race, and so on. *Ibid.* Gloss. 126. **1895** *Funk's Stand. Dict.* s.v., To parlay one's bet. **1903** ADE *People you Know* 110 He wanted to parlee a $2 Silver Certificate and bring home enough to pay the National Debt.

2. *trans.* To increase (capital) by means of gambling; more generally, to exploit (a circumstance) for gain, to transform (an asset, advantage, etc.) *into* something considerably greater or more valuable. Also *absol. colloq.*

1942 *San Francisco Examiner* 5 May 18/5 As far as the girl who was kicked off the '36 Olympic team and parlayed it into a million dollars or so, is concerned, water these days is strictly for drinking and bathing. **1947** *Life* 20 Jan. 89/2 Only 25 years ago trucking firms consisted of a few men with strong backs and iron nerves who parlayed their savings into creaky trucks and did their bookkeeping on backs of envelopes. **1949** *Sat. Even. Post.* 25 June 32 H. J. Heinz.. parlayed a pickle into one of the most valuable family heirlooms in America. **1952** *Sun* (Baltimore) 8 Oct. 11/2 She would like to parlay an original 'People's Union' fund of $100 into lots more and start in motion her mailing plan for errant politicians. **1956** B. HOLIDAY *Lady sings Blues* (1973) vi. 57, I hoped he could shoot enough dice to parlay it into a bill big enough I didn't have to feel ashamed to send home. **1964** 'E. MCBAIN' *Axe* v. 78 Cards... Dice. Anything where he can parlay a small stake into some quick cash. **1972** *Publishers' Weekly* 17 Jan. 56/3 His family had parlayed the sum awarded him by the court into millions. **1973** *Times Lit. Suppl.* 28 Sept. 1131/3 Parlaying his genuine physical tragedy, by unspoken comparison, into a certificate of literary genius. **1975** *High Times* Dec. 106/2 (Advt.), I have parlayed $146 into $90,000. **1976** *Wood Sci.* VIII. 180 These findings may be parlayed into savings in sample size in future experiments on the strength of lumber. **1977** *New Society* 5 May 236/3 Former pupils who had parlayed a third-class degree into £7,000 a year and ten minutes' teaching a week. **1977** *Time* 27 June 15/1 Rainer Werner Fassbinder, 31, the *Wunderkind* of low-budget West German cinema,..is about to parlay his critical acclaim into box office success as an international director.

parle (pɑːl), *sb. arch.* and *dial.* Also 7 parl. [app. f. PARLE *v.* Cf. also F. *parole* word, speech.]

1. Speech; talk; conversation.

1587 *Mirr. Mag., Brennus* xxvi, There could no parle of peace preuayle. **1611** CORYAT *Crudities* 2 After this familiar parle, [he] dismissed us to our lodging. **1641** J. TRAPPE *Theol. Theol.* Ep. Ded. A v, I..have learned from our Saviours parle with Peter, not (childishly) to strive for the last word. **1814** CARY *Dante, Paradise* IX. 109 But fully to content Thy wishes..Demands my further parle. *a* **1850** ROSSETTI *Dante & Circ.* I. (1874) 213 There with dames and maids hold pretty parles.

b. Speech, language, parlance. *nonce-wd.*

1793 BURNS *Meg o' the Mill* iv, A tocher's nae word in a true lover's parle, But, gie me my love, and a fig for the warl!

2. A conference, discussion, debate; *spec.* a meeting to discuss terms (between enemies or opposed parties) under a truce; a truce; = PARLEY *sb.*[1] 2. † *to break parle*: see BREAK *v.* 24.

1575 CHURCHYARD *Chippes* (1817) 123 Cloking pretensed mallice vnder a parle and communication of peace. **1585** T. WASHINGTON tr. *Nicholay's Voy.* I. xix. 23 A whyte banner should..call the enemies too a Parle. **1592** KYD *Sol. & Pers.* III. iv, Drum, sound a parle to the Citizens. **1602** SHAKS. *Ham.* I. i. 62 When in an angry parle He smot the sledded Pollax on the Ice. **1650** HUBBERT *Pill Formality* 204 There is no cessation of Assaults, no parle to be admitted. **1671** MILTON *Samson* 785 Let weakness then with weakness come to parl. **1702** ROWE *Tamerl.* I. ii. 618. **1807** J. BARLOW *Columb.* v. 284 When sudden parle suspended all the field. **1868** WHITTIER *Dole of Jarl Thorkell* 50 'So be it!' cried the young men, 'There needs nor doubt nor parle.'

3. *Comb.* **parle-hill** = *parley-hill* (PARLEY *sb.*[1] 3).

1664 *Spelman's Gloss., Parle hill*, Collis..ubi convenire olim solebant Centuriæ, aut viciniæ incolæ ad lites inter se tractandas & terminandas.

† **parle** (pɑːl), *v.* *Obs.* or *arch.* and *dial.* Also 6–7 parl. [a. F. *parle-r* to speak = Pr. *parlar*, Sp. *parlar*, It. *parlare*, med.L. *parlāre*, late pop. L. *parabolāre* to discourse, talk, f. *parabola* PARABLE, discourse, speech.]

1. *intr.* To speak; to talk in conference.

1377 LANGL. *P. Pl.* B. XVIII. 268 Patriarkes and prophetes han parled her-of longe, þat such a lorde & a lyȝ te shulde lede hem alle hennes. **1573** G. HARVEY *Letter-bk.* (Camden) 31, I wuld be loth to have sutch an orator to parl for me in a weitier matter. **1582** STANYHURST *Æneis* I. (Arb.) 36 Brieflye then heere Dido, with downe cast phisnomye, parled. *Ibid.* IV. 106 At length thus briefly dyd he parle. **1641** J. TRAPPE *Theol. Theol.* iii. 43 His delights were with the sonnes of men..with whom he parled in Paradise. **1706** BAYNARD in Sir J. Floyer *Hot & Cold Bath.* II. 229 He parled with them, and told them, that if any Body came in, he would certainly Drown 'em.

2. *intr.* To treat, discuss terms, parley (*with* an opponent); to hold a parley.

1558 in *9th Rep. Dep. Kpr. Irel.* 84 Commission to Sir Henry Radclif..to parle with, take pledges from..the Irish of the said counties. **1587** in *Hakluyt's Voy.* (1600) III. 816 They..within 5 or 6 houres fight set out a flagge of truce and parled for mercy. **1643** TRAPP *Comm. Gen.* iii. 1 When the Spaniard comes to parle of peace, then double bolt the door. **1675** J. EASTON *Narr.* (1858) 25 Thay had demanded the Indians' Armes, and went againe to parrell with them. **1709** DE FOE *Hist. Union* in Arnot *Hist. Edinb.* I. v. (1788) 188 The Jacobite and the presbyterian..parled together.

b. *trans.* To treat with, parley with. (Cf. PARLEY *v.* 2 b.)

1635 PAGITT *Christianogr.* II. vii. (1636) 65 Whilst the Bishop of Rome parleth a faction which receiveth union from himselfe onely. **1838** S. BELLAMY *Betrayal* 94 To throw the gate, already jarring on its mutinous hinge, To the parl'd foe.

c. To discuss, debate.

1631 HEYWOOD *2nd Pt. Maid of West* II. Wks. 1874 II. 360 Where kings affaires are questioned, Or may be parled.

parle, obs. f. PARREL.

parlecue, parleycue (*Sc.*): see PURLICUE.

parlement, obs. f. PARLIAMENT.

‖**parlementaire** (parləmɑ̃tɛr). [Fr., f. *parlementer* to discuss terms, to parley.] = PARLIAMENTARY *sb.* 3.

1918 E. S. FARROW *Dict. Mil. Terms* 434 *Parlementaire*, in the French services the term meaning a bearer of a flag of truce. **1931** *Economist* 14 Nov. 892/2 The Japanese expeditionary force..began by sending parlementaires to the local Chinese military commander..who agreed to withdraw his troops ten kilometres. **1945** R. HARGREAVES *Enemy at Gate* 230 Terms having been refused his *parlementaires*, Osman was left with no option but to submit in unconditional surrender. **1945** C. S. FORESTER *Commodore* xxii. 253 'French or Russian, sir,' said the parlementaire 'they will die unless they receive speedy aid.' **1950** W. S. CHURCHILL *Second World War* (1951) IV. II. xxiv. 376 At dawn on the 21st General Klopper sent out a parlementaire with an offer to capitulate, and at 7.45 a.m. German officers came to his headquarters and accepted his surrender.

parlence, parler, obs. ff. PARLANCE, PARLOUR.

parlesie, etc., obs. ff. PALSY.

parley ('pɑːlɪ), *sb.*[1] Also 6–7 parlye, -lie, -lee, (7 -le, -lé), 6–9 parly. [Either from PARLEY *v.*, F. *parler* vb. inf. taken sbst., or a. OF. *parlée*, fem. sb. from pa. pple. of *parler* to speak.]

1. Speech, speaking, talk; conversation, discourse, conference; debate, argument. (Now usually coloured by 2.)

1582 STANYHURST *Æneis* IV. (Arb.) 97 Her bye tale owt hauking amyd oft her parlye she chocketh. **1583** W. FLEETWOOD in Ellis *Orig. Lett.* Ser. I. II. 292, I know not what other parlee Mr. Nowell can pled. **1589** GREENE *Menaphon* (Arb.) 46 They did frolicke amongst themselves with manie pleasaunt parlies. *c* **1645** HOWELL *Lett.* (1650) III. 25 Admiration..that..you should com to be so great a Master of those Languages both for the Pen and Parley. **1717** PRIOR *Alma* I. 330 They meet each evening in the grove; Their parley but augments their love. **1791** COWPER *Iliad* XXII. 148 A nymph and swain soft parley mutual hold. **1860** HOLLAND *Miss Gilbert* vi. 105 Arthur..without further parley commanded him to be silent. **1887** BOWEN *Virg. Æneid* III. 481 Why with longer parley the rising breezes delay?

† **b.** A public discussion or disputation in a University. *Obs.*

1577 FULKE *Confut. Purg.* 441 This were a pretty question for a Sophister in Oxford to demand in their parleis.

2. A conference for the debating of points in dispute; *esp. Mil.*, an informal conference with an enemy, under a truce, for the discussion of terms, or the mutual arrangement of matters, as the exchange of prisoners; a discussion of terms. *to beat* or *sound a parley*, to call for or request a parley by sounding a drum or trumpet.

1581 PETTIE *Guazzo's Civ. Conv.* III. (1586) 138 b, Castles that come to parley, are commonlie at the point to render. **1607** DEKKER *Hist. Sir T. Wyatt* Wks. 1873 III. 97 *stage-direct.*, The Herald soundes a parlee, and none answers. **1607** *Schol. Disc. agst. Antichr.* I. i. 38 Sound for Parlé, and thinke vpon conditions of peace. **1682** BUNYAN *Holy War* (Cassell) 262 When this drummer had beaten for a parley he made this speech to Mansoul. **1720** DE FOE *Capt. Singleton* xvi. 278 Carrying a white flag, and offering a parley. **1838** PRESCOTT *Ferd. & Is.* (1846) II. xiv. 60 We find them proposing a parley for arranging terms of capitulation.

b. *Sc. dial.* A truce or armistice in certain games; the place of truce. Cf. BARLEY *int.*

1723 MESTON *Knight* Poet. Wks. (1767) 7 On it [his skull] you might thresh wheat or barley, Or tread the grape ere he cry'd parley.

c. (See quot.) Cf. *beat a parley* in a.

1867 SMYTH *Sailor's Word-bk.*, *Parley*, that beat of drum by which a conference with an enemy is desired. Synonymous with *chamade*.

3. *Comb.* † **parley-hill**, in Scotland and Ireland, formerly, a mound, usually fortified, where the local disputes of neighbouring districts were debated and settled.

1641 in D. Beveridge *Culross & Tulliallan* (1885) I. vi. 196 Those who stand in the kirkyard or parlyhill discoursing. **1664** *Spelman's Gloss.* s.v. *Mallobergium*, Quæ in Hibernia *parly hills*, i. placitandi vel interloquendi montes appellantur.

'parley, *sb.*[2] *Sc.* and *dial.* Also parly. [Short for *parliament*.] A thin cake of gingerbread; a parliament-cake.

1825 JAMIESON s.v. *Parliament-cake*, Here's a bawbee taw ye: awa' an' buy parleys wi't. **18..** MCGILVRAY *Poems* (1862) 108 (E.D.D.) Pies, parlies, tarts, and butter bakes. **1891** BARRIE *Little Minister* (1892) 3 A little boy..pressed forward and offered him a sticky parly.

'parley, *sb.*[3] *humorous.* [Short for PARLEYVOO.] A Frenchman.

1831 LADY GRANVILLE *Lett.* (1894) II. 78 The girls are led out by unknown parleys, who caper by their sides and then give them back to my care.

parley ('pɑːlɪ), *v.* Also 6–7 -lie, 6–8 -ly, (7 -lee). [Either f. F. *parler* to speak, *parlez* speak!, or f. PARLEY *sb.* (if the latter was earlier).]

1. *intr.* To speak, talk; to converse, discourse, confer (*with*). Now *arch.* (and tending to be coloured with 2).

1591 SYLVESTER *Du Bartas* I. iii. 963 As bashfull Suters, seeing Strangers by, Parley in silence with their hand or eye. **1610** HOLLAND *Camden's Brit., Irel.* II. 116 Ulisses, when hee went down to parlee with those in hell. **1791** COWPER *Iliad* XXII. 147 It is no time..With him to parley, as a nymph and swain. **1847** DISRAELI *Tancred* III. i, Is it not the land upon whose mountains the Creator of the Universe parleyed with man?

b. *trans.* To speak, utter; *esp.* to speak a foreign or strange language.

1570 J. PHILLIP *Frendly Larum* in Farr *S.P. Eliz.* (Parker Soc.) II. 526 Not basshing suche pernitious talke To parley and reporte. **1691** WOOD *Ath. Oxon.* I. 257 That Beauty in Court which could not parly Euphuism, was as little regarded as those now there that cannot speak French. **1873** DIXON *Two Queens* II. IX. ix. 147 An Italian, who could parley French and Spanish.

2. *intr.* To treat, discuss terms; *esp.* to hold a parley (*with* an enemy or opponent); to come to parley. Also *fig.*

1600 DYMMOK *Ireland* (1843) 34 The Lord Lieutenant sent the Lord of Cayre to parly with him. **1613** HEYWOOD *Silv. Age* III. Wks. 1874 III. 143 Vpon them, when we parlee with our foes. **1719** DE FOE *Crusoe* II. xi, We..offered a truce to parley. **1823** SCOTT *Peveril* vii, Major Bridgenorth advanced, as if to parley. **1866** DK. ARGYLL *Reign Law* ii. (ed. 4) 53 And so we see the men of Theology coming out to parley with the men of Science.

b. *trans.* To grant a parley, or an interview for discussion, to (a person); to hold discussion with, speak to, address.

1611 HEYWOOD *Gold. Age* III. Wks. 1874 III. 48 Beare Saturne first to prison, Wee'l after parly them. **1631** —— *Maid of West* V. Wks. 1874 II. 321 Conduct him safe where we will parly him. **1676** ROW *Contn. Blair's Autobiog.* xi. (1848) 347 They parlied Lambert. **1839** BAILEY *Festus* vi. (1852) 79 Would'st parley Luniel on her silver seat?

Hence ˈ**parleying** *vbl. sb.* and *ppl. a.*

1692 *Diary Siege Lymerick* 16 The Cessation which began yesterday upon the Besieged's Parlying, continued till Ten a Clock the next Morning. **1803** WORDSW. *Sonn., to Men of Kent*, No parleying now! In Britain is one breath. **1887** BROWNING (*title*) Parleyings with certain People of Importance in their Day.

parley: see PARLAY *sb.* and *v.*

parleyvoo (pɑːlɪˈvuː), *sb. humorous.* Also 8 parle-vous, 9 parlez-vous, parlyvoo. [f. F. *parlez-vous* (parlevu) in *parlez-vous français?* do you speak French?]

1. The French language, French; school-study of French; *pl.* French utterances or talk.

1754 FOOTE *Knights* II. Wks. 1799 I. 76 In comes a French fellow..with his muff and parle-vous. **1813** SOUTHEY *March to Moscow* viii, But he look'd white and he look'd blue, Morbleu! Parbleu! When parlez-vous no more would do. **1822** GALT *Steam-boat* xii. 290 But the bodies hae a civil way with them for a' that, and it's no possible to be angry at their parleyvoos. **1889** LOWELL in *Atlantic Monthly* LXIV. 148 No words to spell, no sums to do, No Nepos and no parlyvoo!

2. A Frenchman.

1815 *Sporting Mag.* XLV. 164 Jockies, Jews, and Parlezvous, Courtezans and Quakers. **1884** PAE *Eustace* 91 You'll have the honour of going to fight the frog-eating parleyvoos.

3. *attrib.* or as *adj.* = French, or foreign.

1828 MOIR *Mansie Wauch* xi. 95 His waistcoat was cut in the Parly-voo fashion.

parleyˈvoo, *v. slang* or *humorous.* Also 8 parler vous, 9 parlez-vous, parleyvous. [Formed as prec. sb.] *intr.* To speak French; to speak a foreign tongue; to palaver.

1765 FOOTE *Commissary* II. Wks. 1799 II. 28 You know I can't parler vous. **1813** SOUTHEY *March to Moscow* viii, He would rather parlez-vous than fight. **1823** GALT *Entail* II. xxviii. 265 Me and your honest grandfather..had no foistring and parleyvooing, like your novelle turtle-doves. **1824** MACAULAY *Gt. Lawsuit* Misc. Writ. 1860 I. 94 He kept six French masters to teach him to parleyvoo. **1881** *Sat. Rev.* 9 July 44/2 They will be tempted to ask, with their grand-fathers, where is the use of all this parleyvooing?

parliament (ˈpɑːlɪmənt), *sb.*[1] Forms: 3-8 parlement, (4-5 perle-), 4 parly-, (perly-), 4-6 parlea-, 5 parli-, 5-7 parla-, (5-6 perla-), 5- parliament, (5 perlia-, 5-7 parlya-, 7 parleement); also occas. 4-6 -mente. [ME. a. OF. *parlement* speaking (*Chans. Roland* 11th c.), f. *parler* to speak + *-ment*, in It. *parlamento*, med.L. *parlāmentum*, whence also 15-16th c. *parlament*; the form *parliament* corresponds to an Anglo-Lat. *parliamentum*, found in 13th c., founded perhaps on the ME. forms in *parly-*, *parli-*.]

†**1. a.** The action of speaking; a 'spell' or 'bout' of speaking; a speech; a talk, colloquy, conversation, conference, consultation; a discussion or debate. *Obs.*

[**1216-59** MATT. PARIS *Hist. Angl.* (Rolls) II. 197 Quod [Lodowicus] voluit habere per intermedios parlamentum pacificum cum eo [Huberto de Burgo].] **1297** R. GLOUC. (Rolls) 3519 Þere he hulde is parlement wat were best to done. *c* **1320** *Cast. Love* 896 Gret perlyment they han i-nomen. *a* **1375** *Lay Folks Mass Bk.* App. iv. 282 Takeþ good tent þat ȝe holde no parlyment Wiþ no cristen mon Whon ȝe come þe Churche with-Inne. **1413** *Pilgr. Sowle* (Caxton 1483) I. ix. 5 Thenne herde I within the curteyne a longe parlament. *c* **1450** *Merlin* 521 Thus ended the parlement betwene the fader and the sone. *c* **1489** CAXTON *Sonnes of Aymon* vi. 136 After Bourgoyns hadde taken Tholouse, he made a grete parliamente to his folke, And sayd to theym, 'Lordes, ye knowe well [etc.]'. **1542** *St. Papers Hen. VIII*, IX. 219 Who wil shortely..comme to Bononye to be at parlement with thEmperour.

b. = PARLEY *sb.*[1] 2. *Obs.*

c **1330** R. BRUNNE *Chron. Wace* (Rolls) 7844 Þorow trist of trues, of on assent, Þey sette a day of Parlement, Opon þe Playne of Salesbury. *Ibid.* 16226 Til Cadwalyn his sonde he [Oswy] sent, þat he wolde com til parlement. **1596** DANETT tr. *Comines* (1614) 169 Wherefore they fell to parlament and yeelded it by composition. **1610** HOLLAND *Camden's Brit.* II. 194 In Carbry, after a certain Parliament ended betweene the Irish and English, there were taken prisoners.

†**2.** A formal conference or council for the discussion of some matter or matters of general importance; *spec.* the name applied in the early times of the French monarchy to the assembly of the great lords of the kingdom, and in England, in the course of the 13th c. to great councils of the early Plantagenet Kings; hence, retrospectively applied to those of earlier kings before and after the Norman Conquest, and in ME. widely and vaguely, or allusively, to any similar councils of ancient times or foreign nations. (Now only *Hist.* and as an earlier stage of sense 3, into which, in use, it passed without any break.)

[**12..** in Stubbs *Const. Hist.* I. xiii. 570 Parliamentum Runimedæ. **1237-59** MATT. PARIS *Hist. Angl.* (Rolls) II. 393 De magno parlamento habito Londoniis in octavis Epiphaniæ ubi rex exigebat tricesimum regni. [*Before this, the word is* colloquium.] **1246-59** *Ibid.* III. 5 Convenit ad parlamentum generalissimum regni Anglicani totalis nobilitas, tam prælatorum quam militum.] *c* **1290** *Beket* 531 in *S. Eng. Leg.* I. 121 Þo heo comen to þe parlement [to clarindone] þe king axede heom a-non ȝweþur heo wolden holde þe lawes ase heore Auncestres heolden ech-on. *a* **1300** *Cursor M.* 5497 He [Pharaoh] gedir[d] him a parlement. *c* **1330** R. BRUNNE *Chron.* (1810) 214 Þe barons..To mak disturbaunce þei held a parlement. [This was the Mad Parliament.] *c* **1374** CHAUCER *Troylus* IV. 115 (143), Pryam þe kyng ful soone in general Let here-vpon his Parlement to holde. *c* **1400** *Destr. Troy* 9379 Palomydon a perlement puruait anon, And the grete of þe grekes gedrit he somyn. **1432-50** tr. *Higden* (Rolls) VII. 111 After that he kepede a parliament [**1387** TREVISA, made a parlemente] at Oxenford, where Ynglische men and Danes were acorded to observe the lawes of kynge Edgarus. *c* **1440** *Boctus* (Laud MS. 559 lf. 10), A noon forthe they wente And kepte a grete perliamente. **1563** GOLDING *Cæsar* I. (1565) 22 They made request that it might be lawfull for them to sommon a Parlament of Gallia at a certain day. **1570** LEVINS *Manip.* 68/14 A Parlament, *senatus consultus.* **1762** HUME *Hist. Eng.* II. xii. 9 In a parliament, summoned at Oxford (for the great councils began about this time [1222] to receive that appellation). **1863** H. COX *Instit.* I. iii. 15 In the reign of Edward I the word 'Parliaments' was frequently applied to the assemblies of the four great courts as well as to the Great Council of the realm. **1875** STUBBS *Const. Hist.* II. xiv. §175 *marg.*, Parliament of 1242. First report of a debate.

3. The Great Council of the nation, which forms, with the Sovereign, the supreme legislature of the United Kingdom (formerly of the Realm of England), consisting of the three Estates, namely the Lords Spiritual and Temporal (forming together the House of Lords), and the representatives of the counties, cities, boroughs, and universities (forming the House of Commons). By some legal writers, the Sovereign, as part of the Legislature, is included in the Parliament; but this is not usual.

a. Viewed as a temporary assemblage of persons, summoned by the Sovereign, and after a time (the length of which is now limited) again dissolved, to be succeeded (formerly at an uncertain and often distant interval, but now within a very short period) by another assemblage similarly constituted.

This is, in its origin, merely a development of sense 2, corresponding to the gradual evolution of the modern parliament from the Great Council. Stubbs *Const. Hist.*, following the chroniclers, uses 'parliament' from 1242 onwards; but the 'parliaments' previous to 1275 belong rather to our sense 2, with progressive approaches to this sense.

In this sense the word may be preceded by *a* or *the*, and have a plural; so we speak of a new parliament, or of the first, second, or third parliament of Edward I, or of Queen Victoria, and historians individualize many parliaments by distinctive appellations: see 8.

[**1275** *Act 3 Edw. I* (*Statute of Westm.*) Preamble, Ces sunt les Establisemenz le Rey Edward, le fiz le Rey Henry, fez a Weymoster a son primer parlement general apres son corounement..par son Conseil e par le assentement des Erceveskes, Eveskes, Abbes, Priurs, Contes, Barons, & la Cōmunaute de la tere ileokes somons.] *c* **1330** R. BRUNNE *Chron.* (1810) 244 To London he [Edw. I: 1286] went..He sent to his barouns, a parlement to hold. **1424** *Paston Lett.* I. 17 Be billes in the too last parlementz holden at Westminster and at Leycestre. **1459** *Rolls of Parlt.* V. 372/2 By th' advyce of his Lords Spirituell and Temporell, and by you his Commons in this his presente Parleamente assemblyd. **1546** *Suppl. Commons* (E.E.T.S.) 65 They were not all sturdy beggers that were in the Parlament when this lawe was stablished. **1659-60** PEPYS *Diary* (1875) I. 2 To acquaint him [Monk] with their desires for a free and full Parliament. **1665** BOYLE *Occas. Refl.* IV. xvii. (1848) 268 Grievances..for whose prevention or redress, Parliaments are wont to be assembled and Laws to be enacted. **1765** BLACKSTONE *Comm.* I. ii. 160 These are the constituent parts of a parliament; the king, the lords spiritual and temporal, and the commons. **1818-48** HALLAM *Mid. Ages* (1871) III. viii. III. 19 As to the meeting to which knights of shires were summoned in 38 Hen. III, it ought not to be reckoned a parliament. *Ibid.* 37 The usual object of calling a parliament was to impose taxes. **1860** C. INNES *Scot. Mid. Ages* vii. 213 The earliest Parliament that can be proved..to have resembled the present legislative constitution of England by summons of citizens and burgesses is 49 Hen. III, A.D. 1265. **1875** STUBBS *Const. Hist.* II. xiv. 92 The famous parliament of Simon de Montfort was called together by a writ issued on the 14th of December, to meet at Westminster on the 20th of January, 1265. **1885** GLADSTONE *Sp. Ho. Commons* 16 Nov., After sitting in 12 Parliaments a man begins to have, if he has any brains at all, the capacity and faculty of knowing what a particular Parliament can do and is likely to do.

b. Viewed as a permanent or continuous institution, the composition, character, and size of which have changed from time to time, but which has itself a continuous history. In this sense usually without *a* or *the*, or *plural* (except in speaking of such institutions in different countries, as, 'the Scottish and Irish Parliaments are now incorporated in that of Great Britain').

Act of Parliament, a law made by the Sovereign with the advice of his Parliament; a statute passed by both Houses of Parliament and ratified by the royal assent. ***Clerk of the Parliaments*** (†***Parliament***), the chief official of the House of Lords, who reads the royal assent to bills before Parliament assembled as a corporate body in the House of Lords. ***Imperial Parliament***: see IMPERIAL A. 2 b. ***Member of Parliament***: see MEMBER. ***Writ of Parliament***: see WRIT.

1362 LANGL. *P. Pl.* A. IV. 34 Þene Pees com to parlement and put vp a Bille, Hou þat Wrong aȝeyn his wille his wyf hedde I-take. *c* **1380** WYCLIF *Sel. Wks.* III. 329 Þes worldly prelatis þat sitten in Perlement. **1393** LANGL. *P. Pl.* C V. 185 Þow shalt nat ryden hennes, Bote be my chyf chaunceler in chekyr and in parlement, And conscience in alle my courtes. **1454** *Rolls of Parlt.* V. 239/2 If the said Thomas shuld be relessed by Privelegge of Parlement. **1455** *Ibid.* 317/2 The Office of Clerk of oure Parlement. **1526** *Pilgr. Perf.* (W. de W. 1531) 16 By acte of parlyament. **1628** COKE *On Litt.* II. x. §164. 109b, Parliament is the highest and most honourable and absolute court of justice in England, consisting of the king, the lords of parliament, and the commons. **1647-8** (18 Jan.) CHARLES I *Declar. fr. Carisbrooke Castle*, Which I would have rather done, by the way of my two Howses of Parlament. **1680-1** WOOD *Life* 5 Mar. (O.H.S.) III. 84 Providing convenience for the lords to sit in parliament in the schools [at Oxford]. **1706** *Act 6 Anne* c. 11. §3 That the United Kingdom of Great Britain be represented by One and the same Parliament to be stiled The Parliament of Great Britain. **1765** BLACKSTONE *Comm.* I. i. 102 The privileges of parliament. *Ibid.* ii. 161 Some have not scrupled to call its power, by a figure rather too bold, the omnipotence of parliament. **1774** PENNANT *Tour in Scot. in 1772.* 161 This Shire and that of Cathness send a Member to Parlement alternatly. **1800** *Act 39 & 40 Geo. III* c. 67 Art. iii, That the said United Kingdom be represented in one and the same Parliament, to be called the Parliament of the United Kingdom of Great Britain and Ireland. **1839** KEIGHTLEY *Hist. Eng.* II. 57 Parliament was prorogued on the 24th. **1896** *Law Q. Rev.* July 201 We are pretty sure it is not the law Parliament intended to make.

c. ***High Court of Parliament***, a name formerly applied collectively (as in Bk. of Common Prayer) to the two Houses of Parliament in session; now mostly said of Parliament in its judicial capacity.

1450-1662 [see COURT *sb.*[1] 10].

d. *transf.* The place where Parliament meets; the Parliament House. *rare.*

1628 EARL MANCH. in *Buccleuch MSS.* (Hist. MSS. Comm.) I. 268 Werden tells me he hath provided you [with a lodging] not far from the Parliament.

e. ***Act of Parliament clock***, a type of wall clock produced in the 18th century for use in inns and taverns and characterized by a black or green dial with gold numerals over which there was no glass. The name arose from the popular belief that such clocks were acquired by innkeepers in order to attract custom after Parliament imposed a tax on clocks and watches in 1797.

1899 F. J. BRITTEN *Old Clocks & Watches* 337 In country inns and other places Act of Parliament clocks may still occasionally be seen. **1917** A. HAYDEN *Chats on Old Clocks* iv. 124 It is supposed that these clocks suddenly came into being when private clocks were taxed. Owing to such a deep-seated belief they are always known throughout the country as 'Act of Parliament' clocks. But they were used earlier than the Act of 1797, and were probably ordinary inn clocks in common use about that time. **1952** J. GLOAG *Short Dict. Furnit.* 191 *Coaching Inn Clock*..Such clocks have been misnamed Parliament or Act of Parliament clocks, on the assumption that they were introduced and used extensively by innkeepers after Pitt's Act of 1797 (under which clocks and watches were taxed) presumably to save customers..buying a watch or clock and then paying tax on it—not a plausible theory. **1960** *House & Garden* Apr. 100/1 The round-faced Act of Parliament clock..is two feet across. **1962** *Kent & Sussex Courier* 19 Oct. 6/6 The Rose and Crown Hotel boasts the town's oldest public clock. A fine example of an Act of Parliament clock, it was made in 1797 and now stands in the entrance hall.

4. The title of the corresponding legislative bodies which formerly existed in Scotland and Ireland, and of the existing legislative bodies of certain former British colonies or dependencies, as the Dominion of Canada, the Australian Commonwealth, the separate colonies of New South Wales, Victoria, and Tasmania; also popularly applied to the legislative assemblies of other colonies, and to those of foreign countries, as the French Chambers, the German Reichstag, the Spanish Cortes, etc.

In Scotland and Ireland, as in England, the earliest use was that of a meeting or session of the legislature, as in 3 a.

a. [**1292** *Acts Parl. Scot.* I. 445 Coram ipso Rege et consilio in parliamento suo primo. **1296** Entry in *Liber Niger* of Chr. Ch., Dublin, 26 Edw. I, Justiciarius..ordinavit et statuit generale parliamentum hic ad hunc diem.] **1398** *Acts Parl. Sc.* I. 573 Item it is ordanyt þat ilke yhere þe kyng sal halde a parlement. **1428** *Close Roll of Ireld.*, 7 Hen. VI, Ye lordes spiritual and temporels, & communes of your land of Ireland, at your parlement last holden at your citie of Dyvelin [Dublin]. **1617** MORYSON *Itin.* II. 7 In an Irish Parliament he put vp his petition, that..he might there haue the place and title of the Earle of Tyrone. **1621** in *Crt. & Times Jas. I* (1849) II. 267 The King of Denmark..is gone back to a Parliament in Denmark.

b. **1424** *Sc. Acts Jas. I* (1597) §29 It is statute and ordaned, that the breakers of the actes of Parliament be punished. **1596** SPENSER *State Irel.* Wks. (Globe) 671/1 Howe will those be redressed by Parliament, when as the Irish which sway most in Parliament.. shall oppose them-selves agaynst them? **1706** (*title*) Speech in the Scotch Parliament concerning the Union. **1707** *Acts Parl. Scot.* XI. 407 (Act of Union 16 Jan.) At the time of ratifying the Treaty of Union in the Parliament of Scotland. **1778** MISS BURNEY *Evelina* xxxii, A senator of the nation! a member of the noblest parliament in the world! **1800** GRATTAN *Speech* 26 May, Connexion is a wise and profound policy; but connexion without an Irish Parliament is connexion without its own principle.. without the pride of honour that should attend it. **1896** LECKY *Liberty & Democr.* (1899) I. i. 14 The system of direct election of members of Parliament was not established in France till 1817. *Ibid.* II. vi. 44 A law was carried through the Prussian Parliament giving the Government a discretionary power. **1902** J. E. C. BODLEY in *Encycl. Brit.* XXVIII. 491/1 The [French] opportunist minister of War understood the feeling of parliament.

5. Applied to various consultative assemblies.

a. In the Stannaries, a representative assembly or convocation of tinners for Devon, or for Cornwall, formerly held for the redress of grievances, and general regulation of the stannaries. Now only *Hist.*

1574 in T. Pearce *Laws & Customs Stannaries* (1725) 240 The Great Court, or Parliament, of our Sovereign Lady Elizabeth.. of the Dutchy of Cornwall holden at Crockerrentorre.. before.. Frances Earl of Bedforde.. Lord Warden of the Stannaries of Devon and Cornwall. *c* **1630** RISDON *Surv. Devon* §215 (1810) 223 A high rock, called Crocken-Torr, where the parliament for stannary causes is kept. **1686** in *Calr. Treas. Pap.* (1868) 18 His Lordship's letter for the speedy calling a convocation or parliament of tinners. **1752** in *Laws of Stannaries* (1808) 14 We, the above-said four and twenty stannators being duly elected.. to serve in this present convocation, or parliament of Tinners, do agree that [etc.]. **1842** *Penny Cycl.* XXII. 444/1 These assemblies were called parliaments, or convocations, of tinners, and were summoned by the lord warden of the stannaries, under a writ, issued by the duke of Cornwall, or by the king, when there was no duke, authorizing and requiring him to do so. The last convocation was held in 1752.

b. A consultative assembly of the members of the Middle or the Inner Temple.

1583 *Cal. Inner Temple Recds.* (1896) I. 102 Parliament-house. **1681** LUTTRELL *Brief Rel.* (1857) I. 94 Last week there was a parliament held in the Inner Temple.. to debate the affaires of the house. **1706** PHILLIPS s.v., The Societies of the two Temples, or Inns of Court, do likewise call that Assembly a Parliament, wherein they consult about the common Affairs of their respective Houses. **1861** *Illustr. Lond. News* XXXIX. 480/1 The Treasurer.. conducted him [Prince of Wales] to the new Parliament Chamber.. A Parliament was then formed of the Masters of the Bench present.

c. *fig.* and *transf.* uses.

a **1400** CHAUCER *Epil. Cant. T.*, The book of seint Valentynes day of the parlement of briddes. *c* **1430** LYDG. *Min. Poems* (Percy Soc.) 23 The royall lyon lete call a parlement, All beestes aboute hym every on. *a* **1592** H. SMITH *Serm.* (1622) 22 A man neuer abandoneth euill, untill hee abandon euill company: for no good is concluded in this Parliament. **1640** DAY (*title*) The Parliament of Bees. **1727** FIELDING *Love in Sev. Masq.* II. i, I sometimes look on my drawing-room as a little parliament of fools, to which every different body sends its representatives. **1741** RICHARDSON *Pamela* (1883) II. 100 This would bear a smart debate, I fancy, in a parliament of women. **1842** TENNYSON *Locksley Hall* 128 Till.. the battle flags were furl'd In the Parliament of man, the Federation of the world. **1893** J. H. BARROWS (*title*) The World's Parliament of Religions.. held in Chicago in connection with the Columbian Exposition of 1893. **1903** *Daily Chron.* 9 Dec. 4/4 The Cricket Parliament at Lord's. **1905** R. B. SMITH *Bird Life* x. 386 Two such 'Parliaments of rooks' I have had the opportunity of watching, from early times. **1939** C. E. HARE *Lang. Field Sports* xxiii. 192 The modern accepted rook term is believed to be *parliament*, but no authority for this can be traced. **1968** J. LIPTON *Exaltation of Larks* 57 (*caption*) A parliament of owls.

†d. *Pimlico Parliament*: see quot. *Obs.*

1799 *Hull Advertiser* 2 Feb. 2/4 One thousand citizens, with a sprinkling of what is here [Dublin] called the Pimlico Parliament, or mob.

6. Foreign uses:

a. In France (before the Revolution of 1789), the name given to a certain number of supreme courts of justice, in which also the edicts, declarations, and ordinances of the king were registered. Of these there were twelve, of which the Parliament of Paris was of greatest importance in French history. [= F. *parlement.*]

1560 DAUS tr. *Sleidane's Comm.* 454 The Senate of Paris, whiche they cal the Parliament. **1626** in *Crt. & Times Chas. I* (1848) I. 84 The French king, by sentence of the parliament of Rouen and Rennes hath arrested and in his possession above the worth of £300,000 of our merchants' goods. **1656** BLOUNT *Glossogr.* s.v., In France, those high Courts of Justice.. are called Sedentary Parlements; and their Assembly of States General is onely equivalent to our Parliament. **1727–41** CHAMBERS *Cycl.* s.v., The parliament of Paris is the principal, and that whose jurisdiction is of the greatest extent. This is the chief court of justice throughout the realm. **1771** *Ann. Reg.* 82 His majesty has thought fit to branch the parliament of Paris into five different parliaments, under the denomination of superior courts. **1877** MORLEY *Crit. Misc.* Ser. II. 228 The parlements took up their judicial arms in defence of abuses and against reform.

b. In Florence. [= It. *parlamento.*]

1832 tr. *Sismondi's Ital. Rep.* i. 22 This meeting of all the men of the state capable of bearing arms was called a parliament. **1900** E. G. GARDNER *Florence* ii. 56 The State was reorganised, and a new constitution confirmed in a solemn Parliament held in the Piazza.

7. Short for *parliament-cake*: see 9.

1812 H. & J. SMITH *Rej. Addr., Tale Drury Lane*, Crisp parliament with lollypops, And fingers of the Lady. **1828** MOIR *Mansie Wauch* iii. 30 As for the gingerbread I shall not attempt a description:.. roundabouts, and snaps,.. and parliaments. **1848** THACKERAY *Van. Fair* xxxviii, Gorging the boy with apples and parliament. **1881** *Proc. Geog. Soc.* III. 515 They [walls] look exactly as if they were made of the sort of gingerbread called 'parliament'.

8. With qualifying words, in the names applied to various parliaments, chiefly in sense 3 a (but also in senses 2 and 4). Many of these are not contemporary, being due to later chroniclers or historians.

addled (†addle) Parliament, that of 1614: see quots. 1614, 1862. **Barebone's P.**, a nickname given to the *little P.* (q.v.), from the name of Praise God Barbon, one of the members for London. **cavalier P.** = *pensioner P.* **convention P.**: see CONVENTION 5 a. **devil's P.** (*Parliamentum diabolicum*), that held by Henry VI at Coventry in 1459, which attainted the Duke of York, his son the Earl of March, afterwards Edward IV, and their chief followers. **drinking** or **drunken P.**, the Scottish parliament which met after the Restoration on 1 Jan. 1661. **good P.**, that which met in 1376, and endeavoured to reform abuses. **great P**: see quots. **lack-learning** or **lay P.** = *unlearned P.* **little P**, the assembly of 120 members, nominated by Cromwell and his Council of Officers, which sat from 4 July to 12 Dec. 1653. **long P.**, that which met on 3 Nov. 1640, commenced the Civil War, and brought about the death of Charles I; being 'purged' by Col. Pride and the Republicans in 1648, dispersed by Cromwell in 1653, and twice restored in 1659, it was finally dissolved in March 1660, after restoring Chas. II; also the Parliament of Chas. II, which continued from 1661 to 1679. **mad P.** (*Parliamentum insanum*), name given to the meeting of the barons at Oxford in 1258, which passed the 'Provisions of Oxford'. **marvellous, merciless, unmerciful,** or **wonderful P.**, that of 1388, which condemned the favourites of Richard II. **nominated P.** = *little P.* **pension, pensionary,** or **pensioner P.**, a nickname of the long Parliament of Charles II. **rump P.**, the remnant of the long Parliament, in its later history: see RUMP. **running P.**, name for the Parliament of Scotland, from its being shifted from place to place (Brewer). **short P.**, that which sat from 13 April to 5 May 1640, before the long Parliament. **unlearned P.**, **P. of dunces** (*Parliamentum indoctorum*), that convened by Hen. IV at Coventry in 1404, from which all lawyers were excluded. **unmerciful P.**: see *merciless P.* **unreported P.**, that which sat from 1768 to 1774. **useless P.**, the first parliament of Chas. I, 18 June to 12 Aug. 1625. **wonderful** or **wonder-working P.**: see *marvellous P.*

1614 in *Crt. & Times Jas. I* (1849) I. 323 The parliament is dissolved, without the ratification of so much as any one act;.. thereby rendering it, as they term it here, an *addle parliament. **1862** *Ann. Eng.* II. 353, A.D. 1614 The parliament meets April 5, and is dissolved June 7, without passing a single act... It was in consequence nicknamed the 'addled parliament'. **1657** LD. SAY & SEALE *Let.* 29 Dec. in *Eng. Hist. Rev.* (1895) X. 107 'A *barbones Parliament', as they call it, without choyce of the people att all, is not worse than this. **1663** J. HEATH *Brief Chron. Civil Wars* 648 It was better known.. by the name of Barebones Parliament, whose Christian name was Praise God, a Leatherseller in Fleet Street. **1900** [see *little P.*] **1849** MACAULAY *Hist. Eng.* ii. (1871) I. 95 The *Cavalier Parliament, chosen in the transport of loyalty which had followed the Restoration. *c* **1690** KIRKTON *Hist. Ch. Scot.* iii. (1817) 114 This parliament [1662] was called the *Drinking Parliament. **1580** STOW *Chron.* 467 (an. 1376) A Parliament, commonly called the *good Parliament, was holden at Westminster [*c* 1440 WALSINGHAM *Hist. Angl.* I. 324 Parliamenti quod Bonum merito vocabatur]. **1705** HICKERINGILL *Priest-cr.* II. v. 54 We meet.. with a Parliament, called the *good Parliament*, in the 50th Year of Edw. III, and the *great Parliament*, and the *marvellous Parliament*, both in the Reign of Rich. II. **1875** STUBBS *Const. Hist.* II. xvi. §262. 433 The impeachment of the great offenders, and the substitution of a new council, were however only a small part of the business of the Good Parliament. *c* **1465** *Eng. Chron.* (Camden 1856) 9 In the xxj. yeer of King Richard [II], he ordeyned and held a parlement at Westmynstre, that was callid the *grete parlement. **1705** [see *good P.*] **1886** F. YORK POWELL *Hist. Eng. to* 1509 IV. i. 198 The Great Parliament of 1295, which was afterwards acknowledged as the model for such gatherings, as the three Estates were all present regularly summoned. **1765** BLACKSTONE *Comm.* I. ii. 177 Our law books and historians have branded this parliament with the name of *parliamentum indoctum*, or the *lack-learning parliament. **1886** F. YORK POWELL *Hist. Eng. to* 1509 v. i. 294 In October 1404 the *Lay or Unlearned Parliament was called. **1653–76** WHITELOCKE *Mem.* 14 Aug. (1732) 563/2 They [Cromwell and his Officers] had appointed the *little Parliament whom they chose, and commanded them. **1900** MORLEY *Cromwell* 359 The company of men so constituted stands in history as the Little Parliament, or, parodied from the name of one of its members, Barebones' Parliament. **1654** R. WILLIAMS in *Mass. Hist. Coll.* Ser. III. X. 2 Major G. Harrison was the 2d in the nation.. when the Lord Genl and himselfe joined against the former *long Parliament and dissolved them. **1659** *Englands Conf.* 8 Their old hackney drudges of the Long Parliament. **1837** W. WALLACE *Contn. Mackintosh's Hist. Eng.* VII. vii. 225 Thus ended the long or pensionary parliament of Charles II., after having sat seventeen years! **1873** EDITH THOMPSON *Hist. Eng.* xxxiv. 165 Thus ended that famous 'Long Parliament' which, twice expelled and twice restored, had existed for twenty years. **1878** S. R. GARDINER in *Encycl. Brit.* VIII. 348/2 When the Long Parliament of the Restoration met in 1661. **1884** —— *Hist. Eng.* IX. xiv. 218 On November 3 [1640] that famous assembly which was to be known to all time as the Long Parliament met at Westminster. **1580** STOW *Chron.* (1631) 191/1 The Lords.. held a Parliament at Oxford, which was after called the *mad Parliament [1274 *Lib. de Antiq. Leg.* (Camden) 37 Hoc anno fuit illud insane Parliamentum apud Oxoniam.] **1875** STUBBS *Const. Hist.* II. xiv. §176. 74 On the 11th of June [1258], at Oxford, the Mad Parliament, as it was called by Henry's partisans, assembled. **1705** *Marvellous P. [see *good P.*]. **1875** STUBBS *Const. Hist.* II. xvi. §266. 482 The '*merciless' parliament sat for 122 days. Its acts fully establish its right to the title [*a* 1500 in *Knighton's Chron.* (Rolls) II. 249 Parliamentum sine misericordia]. **1901** S. R. GARDINER *Hist. Commw.* (1903) III. xxxv. 175 One of the advanced members of the *Nominated Parliament. *a* **1735** E. HARLEY in *Portland MSS.* (Hist. MSS. Comm.) V. 642 During the whole reign of Charles II. he [sir R. Harley] was a member of that Parliament called the *Pension Parliament. **1837** *Pensionary P. [see *long P.*]. **1681** NEVILE *Plato Rediv.* 20 The Evil Counsellors, the *Pensioner-Parliament, the Thorow-pac'd Judges, the Flattering Divines. *c* **1641** EVELYN *Diary* 11 Apr. an. 1640, His Majesties riding through the City in state to the *Short Parliament. [**1782** PENNANT *Journ. Chester to Lond.* 141 Stiled **Parliamentum indoctorum*; not that it consisted of a greater number of blockheads than parliaments ordinarily do.] **1878** STUBBS *Const. Hist.* III. xviii. §634–5 In October at Coventry the 'Unlearned Parliament' met. This assembly acquired its ominous name from the fact that in the writ of summons, the king.. directed that no lawyers should be returned as members. **1853** J. W. CROKER in *C. Papers* (1884) III. xxviii. 291 There is a *lacuna* in our Parliamentary debates.. from 1768 to 1774. That Parliament is commonly called the '*unreported Parliament'. **1841** (*title*) Sir Henry Cavendish's Debates of the House of Commons during the thirteenth Parliament of Great Britain, commonly called the unreported Parliament [from 10th May 1768 to 13 June 1774]. **1580** STOW *Chron.* (1631) 303/1 This Parliament was named the Parliament that wrought *wonders [*a* 1500 in *Knighton's Chron.* (Rolls) II. 258 *note*, Parliamentum apud Westmonasterium operans mira]. **1878** FREEMAN in *Encycl. Brit.* VIII. 319/2 A parliament known as the *Wonderful and the Merciless.

9. *attrib.* and *Comb.* Of or belonging to a or the parliament, sometimes = parliamentary; as ***parliament army, barge, book, buildings, business, censure, day, diary, fee, gentleman, journal, knight, news, people, robe, time***; made or ordained by Parliament, as ***parliament church, faith, law, religion***, (hostile terms); also **parliament-cake, -gingerbread**, a thin crisp rectangular cake of gingerbread; **Parliament-chamber**, the room in which a parliament meets, *spec.* that in the Old Palace of Westminster; **Parliament Christmas**, a hostile name for Christmas according to New Style, at the introduction of the latter; **parliament-heel** (*Naut.*): see quot.; **parliament hinge**, a hinge with so great a projection from the wall or frame as to allow a door or shutter to swing back against the wall; **parliament ordinance**: see ORDINANCE *sb.* 7; **Parliament Roll**: see ROLL *of Parliament*. Also PARLIAMENT-HOUSE, -MAN.

[The reason of the name in some of the special combs. has not been ascertained.]

1771 GOLDSM. *Hist. Eng.* III. 277 One of the generals of the *parliament army. **1606** *Progr. Jas. I* (1828) II. 53 The King of Great Britain passed in the *Parliament-barge to Gravesend. **1640** J. BAILLIE *Lett. & Jrnls.* (1841) I. 281 The Cancelling.. was registrate in the *Parliament-books of that second session. **1821** GALT *Ann. Parish* xix. 182 A general huxtry, with *parliament-cakes, and candles, and pin-cushions, as well as other groceries, in their window. **1454** *Rolls of Parlt.* V. 239/2 The Lordes Spirituelx and Temporelx beyng in the *Parlement Chambre. *c* **1543** W. CLEBE *MS. Add.* 4609 lf. 409 in the Parker *Dom. Archit.* III. 79 At Westminster the grete chamboure for your gracioуse personne, & the quenes logging, with the parlement chambre & paynted chambre. **1896** *Law Times* CII. 123/2 A Parliament chamber [Inns of Court] is close tiled, except for purposes of discipline affecting character. **1837** SOUTHEY *Doctor* cix. IV. 71 There were people.. who refused to keep what they called *Parliament Christmas. **1711** HICKES *Two Treatises* (1847) I. 318 We have a parliament religion.. parliament bishops, and a *parliament Church. **1726** TRAPP *Popery* I. 63 They call our Church and Religion.. a Parliament-church, and Religion. **1738** BIRCH *Milton* I. App. 70 Lord Altham declar'd, That he had been turning over his Father's Papers, amongst which he found a *Parliament-Diary, written by himself. **1581** *Reg. Privy Council Scot.* Ser. I. III. 428 Certane small custumes, callit of auld the *Parliament fee or archearis wyne. **1629** in *Crt. & Times Chas. I* (1848) II. 35 What passed between the judges and our *parliament gentlemen upon their appearance the first day of the term, the enclosed will inform you. **1861** C. M. YONGE *Stokesley Secret* iii. 39 A stall full of *parliament gingerbread. **1769** FALCONER *Dict. Marine* (1789), **Parliament-heel*, the situation of a ship, when she is made to stoop a little to one side, so as to clean the upper part of her bottom on the other side. **1782** *Ann. Reg.* 225 * The Royal George.. should receive a sort of slight careen, which the seamen.. call a parliament heel. **1841** C. CIST *Cincinnati in 1841* 247 The lighter castings kept in hardware stores—butt and *parliament hinges, for example—will be made here. **1609** BIBLE (Douay) *2 Kings* v. comm., Those that.. goe to church, to shew them selves obedient to the *Parliament law. **1845** JAMES *A. Neil* i, Have you seen any of the *parliament people there? **1629** in *Crt. & Times Chas. I* (1848) II. 15 Proceedings against the *parliament prisoners in the Star Chamber. **1565** HARDING *Confut. Jewel's Apol.* VI. ii. 278 Let vs not be blamed, if we call it *parlament religion, parlament gospell, parlament faith. **1711–26** [see *Parliament-church*]. **1533** WRIOTHESLEY *Chron.* (Camden) I. 19 The Lordes going in their *Parliament roabes. **1414** *Rolls of Parlt.* IV. 57/2 Enacted in the *Parlement Rolle. **1454** *Rolls of Parlt.* V. 239/2 In tyme of vacation.. and not in *Parlement tyme.

†**parliament**, *sb.*[2] Error for PARAMENT b or PALLIAMENT.

1539 *Inv. R. Wardr.* (1815) 32 Ane gowne of freis claith of gold bordourit with perle of gold lynit with crammasy satyne the hude and parliament of the samyn. **1584** R. W.

Three Ladies London in Hazl. *Dodsley* VI. 312 Wouldst know whither with this parliament I go?

parlia'ment, *v. rare.* [Late ME. *parlement*, a. OF. *parlementer* (14th c. in Littré): cf. It. and med.L. *parlamentare* (1297 in Du Cange) to parley or speak together.]

†**1.** *intr.* To talk, converse; to confer, parley. *Obs.*

1491 CAXTON *Vitas Patr.* (W. de W. 1495) I. xlviii. 91/2 After that they hadde longe parlemented togyder in theyr langage. **1543** *St. Papers Hen. VIII*, IX. 465 [They] wolde have parlamentidde withe the capteyns of the towne for the rendringe of it. **1596** DANETT tr. *Comines* (1614) 301 Who brought word that they were content to parlament. *Ibid.* 302, 308. **1610** J. MELVILL *Diary* (1842) 223 The King.. resolved to Parliament.

†**2.** *trans.* ? To assemble, gather together. *Obs.*

1589 NASHE *Almond for Parrat* 2 The full sinode of Lucifers ministers angells assembled, did parlament all their enuy to the subuersion of our established ministry.

3. *intr.* To attend Parliament; to discharge the duties of a member of Parliament. Also with *it.*

1642 R. HARRIS *Sermon* Ep. Ded., My worke was to Mourne, to Preach; not to Parliament-it. **1786** BURNS *Twa Dogs* 147 Wha, aiblins, thrang a parliamentin, For Britain's guid his saul indentin.

4. *fig.* (*humorous*) To vociferate, gabble.

1893 *Field* 20 May 714/1 A great phalanx [of geese], which stood loudly 'parliamenting' on the mud beyond.

Hence **parlia'menting** *vbl. sb.*

1596 DANETT tr. *Comines* (1614) 309 But waiting for this parlamenting I had begun. **1830** GALT *Lawrie T.* I. iv. (1849) 11 There was a pleasure in.. our sederunts which I doubt if wiser parliamenting often furnishes.

†**parlia'mental,** *a. Obs.* [See -AL[1].] Of or pertaining to Parliament; parliamentary.

1570 FOXE *A. & M.* (ed. 2) 611/1 A summary recapitulation of such parlamentall notes and proceedinges, as then were practised by publike parlament. **1627–77** FELTHAM *Resolves* I. xxiii. 41 Against the Parliamental Acts of the two Houses. **1649** PRYNNE *Vind. Liberty Eng.* 17 Deriving their Parliamental Authority onely from the people. **1775** T. LYNCH in Sparks *Corr. Amer. Rev.* (1853) I. 83 The destruction of the Parliamental army in America will certainly produce peace.

,parliamen'tarian (-'ɛərɪən), *sb.* and *a.* Also 7 parla-. [f. as PARLIAMENTARY + -AN.]

A. *sb.* †**1.** One who accepts a religion or church ordained or ruled by parliament. *Obs.* Cf. *parliament church*, PARLIAMENT *sb.*[1] 9.

1613 SIR E. HOBY *Countersnarle* 72 Yet doth hee make no other reckoning of you, then of so many Parlamentarians, whose Religion is steared by the Helme of the State.

2. *Hist.* One who took the side or was in the service of the Parliament, as against the King, during the contests and Civil War of the 17th c.

[WHITELOCKE *Mem.* (1682) 57/2, *sub anno* 1642: And now came up the Names of Parties, Royallists, and Parliamentarians; Cavaliers, and Roundheads.] **1644** in Rushw. *Hist. Coll.* III. II. 746 The Parliamentarians were forced to retreat in haste. **1648** *Petit. of East. Assoc.* 19 Under the titles of Malignants, and Parliamentarians. **1649** *Bounds Publ. Obed.* (1650) 40 So many here were insnared, both Royallists and Parliamentarians. **1736** NEAL *Hist. Purit.* III. 39 His Majesty.. gave directions to seize the lands and goods of the Parliamentarians. **1831** R. VAUGHAN *Mem. Stuart Dynasty* II. 121 The parliamentarians were found chiefly in the metropolis and its neighbourhood.

3. One versed and skilful in parliamentary usages and tactics; a skilled and experienced parliamentary debater.

1834 *Oxford Univ. Mag.* I. 39 A veteran parliamentarian. **1894** *Westm. Gaz.* 15 Mar. 5/1 Parliamentarians were proud of the greatest Parliamentarian of the century.

4. Applied to a member of a French *parlement*, or of a foreign 'parliament'.

1893 A. OGLE *Marq. D'Argenson* 33 He took refuge, like many an irate, but thrifty parliamentarian, in the Rue Quincampoix.

B. *adj.* = PARLIAMENTARY *a.*, esp. in sense 1 b.

1691 WOOD *Ath. Oxon.* II. (R.), Being in a manner undone by the severities of the parliamentarian visitors in 1648. **1823** SCOTT *Peveril* ii, The parliamentarian Major was considerably embarrassed by this proposal. **1856** R. A. VAUGHAN *Mystics* (1860) I. 25 The Parliamentarian soldier was often seen endeavouring to adapt his life to a mistaken application of the Bible. **1882–3** in Schaff *Encycl.* I. 381 Canada is a self-governing country, with a parliamentarian system.

Hence **parliamen'tarianism**, the parliamentary principle or system.

1879 M. PATTISON *Milton* 137 The Greeks of Constantinople.. were not more infatuated than these pedantic common-wealth men with their parliamentarianism when Charles II. was at Calais. **1884** *Athenæum* 27 Dec. 831/2 M. Hubert proves that the Belgian constitution of 1831 was drawn.. partly also from English parliamentarianism.

parlia'mentarily, *adv.* [f. PARLIAMENTARY + -LY[2].] In a parliamentary way; in accordance with parliamentary procedure; in connexion with parliament.

1768 GRENVILLE in Bancroft *Hist. U.S.* (1876) IV. xxxviii. 134 How do we know, parliamentarily, that Boston is the most guilty of the colonies? *a* **1797** H. WALPOLE *Mem. Geo. II* (1822) I. 48 He disliked proceeding parliamentarily in this business. **1888** G. GISSING *Life's Morning* III. xix. 113 Mr. Baxendale was in London, parliamentarily occupied.

parlia'mentariness. *rare*—[0]. [f. as prec. + -NESS.] 'The being according to the Rules, Method or Authority of a Parliament' (Bailey vol. II. 1727).

parliamentarism (pɑːlɪ'mɛntərɪz(ə)m). [f. as prec. + -ISM: cf. *militarism.*] A parliamentary system of government.

1870 *Daily News* 14 Jan., There is not one.. who, if left alone, would not, in a given time, bring Parliamentarism into discredit. **1884** *American* VIII. 295 He cannot stay.. the onward sweep of parliamentarism in Germany. **1890** *Harper's Mag.* June 79/2 A procedure similar to English parliamentarism.

,parliamentari'zation. [f. PARLIAMENTARY *a.* + -IZATION.] The act or process of becoming parliamentary in character or in means of government.

1924 *Contemp. Rev.* Aug. 256 The book deals.. with the progress of the ideas of Parliamentarisation and racial self-determination under the stress of war. **1974** J. WHITE tr. *Poulantzas's Fascism & Dictatorship* III. iii. 132 The peace pact and the parliamentarization of the fascist movement were resented. **1975** *Times Lit. Suppl.* 12 Sept. 1028/2 *Gesellschaft, Parlament und Regierung* is concerned with the painful evolution of German parliamentarism and its weaknesses both before and after the First World War. More specifically, Dr Ritter's own introduction asks why those forces that might, on the strength of their economic resources, have pressed for parliamentarization.. failed to mount an effective challenge to the traditional elites.

parliamentary (pɑːlɪ'mɛntərɪ), *a.* (*sb.*). Also 7 parla-, 7–8 parle-. [f. PARLIAMENT or med.L. *parliament-um* + -ARY[1]: cf. mod.F. *parlementaire.*]

A. *adj.* **1. a.** Of, belonging or relating to a parliament, or to parliament as an institution; of the nature of a parliament.

parliamentary agent, a person professionally employed to take charge of the interests of a party concerned in or affected by any private legislation of Parliament; ***Parliamentary Commissioner (for Administration)*** = OMBUDSMAN; ***Parliamentary Counsel***, barristers employed as established civil servants to draft government bills and amendments; ***Parliamentary Private Secretary***, a member of Parliament who acts as assistant to a government minister; the post has no official status and is unpaid.

1626 SIR S. D'EWES *Autobiog. & Corr.* (1845) II. 179 Ordinarie newes I omitt, such I call Parliamentarie, of the Lower House, and forraine. **1644** VICARS *God in Mount* 134 That forementioned.. inclination of our Parliamentary Senators. **1813** MAR. EDGEWORTH *Patron.* (1833) III. xxvii. 29, I know.. as a minister what must be yielded to parliamentary influence. **1819** J. DEAN in McAdam *Rem. Road Making* (1823) 187 Would you, as a parliamentary agent, undertake to prepare and conduct an ordinary road bill through parliament? **1833** *Rep. Select Comm. Establ. House of Commons* 163 in *Parl. Papers* XII. 341 You are Parliamentary Counsel to the Treasury?—I am. **1850** *Rep. Sel. Comm. Official Salaries* 8 in *Parl. Papers* XV. 179 Both the Secretaries to the Treasury.. are most responsible officers. With regard to the Parliamentary secretaryship, which I once held myself, I do not know so difficult or so disagreeable office in the Government. **1858** H. G. G. GREY *Parliamentary Govt.* vi. 90 Our whole system of Parliamentary Government rests.. upon the Ministers of the Crown possessing such authority in Parliament as to enable them generally to direct its proceedings. **1872** DISRAELI in *Times* 4 Apr. 5/2, I believe that, without party, Parliamentary government is impossible. **1886** GLADSTONE 21 Jan. in *Hansard* Ser. III. CCCII. 112, I will venture to recommend them, as an old Parliamentary hand, to do the same. **1886** *Whitaker's Almanack 1887* 156/1 Office of Parliamentary Counsel,—Spring Gardens. *Parliamentary Counsel*, Hen. Jenkyns, C.B. **1917** *H.M. Ministers & Heads of Public Departments* (Stationery Office) 1 Parliamentary Private Secretary... Capt. Hon. W. Ormsby-Gore, M.P. **1918** *Act 8 Geo. V* c. 3 §1 (1) A Secretary who shall discharge the functions both of a parliamentary secretary to the Board and a parliamentary under-secretary to the Secretary of State. **1930** W. K. HANCOCK *Australia* x. 210 The practice of the Australian Labour party makes England's classic philosophy of parliamentary government appear strangely artless and out of date. **1930** A. J. BALFOUR *Chapters of Autobiogr.* viii. 103 On taking his new post, he [*sc.* Salisbury in 1878 when he became Foreign Secretary] asked me to become his Parliamentary Private Secretary. **1939** W. I. JENNINGS *Parliament* vii. 229 A department official and the draftsman are seated in the 'box' and communications pass through his parliamentary private secretary or 'fetch-and-carry' man. **1954** H. MORRISON *Govt. & Parliament* iv. 66 The life of the Parliamentary Secretary can be interesting and fairly full, or, on the other hand, uninteresting and rather empty. **1966** *Listener* 11 Aug. 194/2 Sir Edmund Compton, Comptroller and Auditor-General, is to be Britain's first Parliamentary Commissioner, or Ombudsman. **1968** T. STOPPARD *Real Inspector Hound* 11 I dream of champions chopped down by rabbit-punching sparring partners while eternal bridesmaids turn and rape the bridegrooms over the sausage rolls and parliamentary private secretaries plant bombs in the Minister's Humber. **1969** *Times* 2 May 22/1 The work of the Parliamentary Counsel is not widely known. They draft the Government's Parliamentary Bills. *a* **1974** R. CROSSMAN *Diaries* (1975) I. 42 What was a bit crazy was to put Charles Snow in as his Parliamentary Secretary. *Ibid.* 239 Whereas the parliamentary draftsman who has worked on my Bill is superb, in the Ministry I feel we could have got a far stronger team together if we hadn't relied so entirely on the administrative class. **1976** *Daily Tel.* 20 July 1/2 An issue which has split both Ministers and the different wings of the Parliamentary Labour party. **1976** B. KEMP *Sir Robert Walpole* iv. 79 Walpole and the other ministers cannot be called the 'executive'... Their relation to parliament cannot be called 'parliamentary government', if by this is meant a state of affairs where the 'executive power and the power of legislation are virtually united in the same hands'. **1976** H. WILSON *Governance of Britain* ii. 32 When choosing ministers of state and parliamentary under-secretaries, the prime minister would naturally consult—or at least inform—the Cabinet minister concerned.

b. Of, belonging or adhering to, the Parliament in the Civil War of the 17th c.

1761 HUME *Hist. Eng.* III. lxi. 319 He.. inspired that spirit which rendered the parliamentary armies in the end victorious. **1778** PENNANT *Tour in Wales* (1883) I. 16 His house, which in September 1643 was surrendered to the parlementary forces. **1843** *Penny Cycl.* XXVII. 560/1 In 1642 Worcester was besieged by the parliamentary forces.

c. Of or belonging to the Parliament of Paris.

1620 BRENT tr. *Sarpi's Council Trent* v. 463 There was a fame that the French-men, though Catholikes, came with Sorbonicall and Parlamentarie minds, fully bent to acknowledge the Pope no further then they pleased. **1791** MRS. RADCLIFFE *Rom. Forest* i, The proceedings in the Parliamentary Courts of Paris during the 17th century.

d. *allusively.* Slow or deliberate like the procedure of Parliament.

1835 J. M. GULLY *Magendie's Formul.* Pref. 3 Beholding the parliamentary pace of our British Pharmacopœias in the official recognition and adoption of the numerous and active remedies which the chemists of France are continually sending forth.

2. a. Enacted, ratified, or established by Parliament.

parliamentary minister (Ch. of Scot.), a minister of a church having an endowment, but which is not a parish church.

1616 CHAMPNEY *Voc. Bps.* 161 Not onlie this parlementarie fashion of ordination but the verie order of Bishops it selfe. **1622** BACON *Hen. VII* Wks. 1879 I. 734/2 To the first three titles.. were added two more, the authorities parliamentary and papal. *c* **1702** *Rem. Reign Will. III* in *Select. fr. Harl. Misc.* (1793) 493 Thus the prince of Orange.. mounted the imperial throne of England, Scotland, and Ireland, by a parliamentary title. **1772** PRIESTLEY *Inst. Relig.* (1782) I. Ded. 7 Chearfully pay all parliamentary taxes. **1854** H. MILLER *Sch. & Schm.* xxii. (ed. 4) 461 When.. the General Assembly admitted what were known as the Parliamentary ministers, and the ministers of chapels of ease, to a seat in the church courts. **1855** MACAULAY *Hist. Eng.* xvii. IV. 106 To obtain a Parliamentary ratification of the treaty.

b. ***parliamentary train***: A train carrying passengers at a rate not exceeding one penny a mile, which, by Act of Parliament (7 & 8 Vict. c. 85), every railway company was obliged to run daily each way over its system. So ***parliamentary carriage, fare, ticket***, etc.

1845 *Bradshaw's Railway Guide* Aug. 5 Fares between London and Brighton—Passengers by 1st class 1½ hour trains, 14*s.* 6*d.*;.. 2nd class.. by 2¼ hour trains, 8*s.*; third class, 5*s.*; parliamentary trains, 4*s.* 3*d.* **1849** ALB. SMITH *Pottleton Leg.* (repr.) 65 In a parliamentary carriage, very like a rabbit-hutch. **1880** MISS BRADDON *Clov. Foot* xxxviii, He went early on Tuesday morning by the parliamentary train. **1893** G. ALLEN *Scallywag* I. 178 A parliamentary ticket by the slow train from Dorsetshire to Hillborough.

c. (See quot.)

1886 J. BARROWMAN *Gloss. Scotch Mining Terms* 49 *Parliamentary pit*, an outlet pit required by statute.

3. a. Consonant with the usages or agreeable to the practice of Parliament; according to a parliamentary constitution.

1625 *Commons' Debates* (Camden) 94 His Majestie promis'd a more particular, and, as I may terme it, a more Parliamentary answere, article to article. **1628** in *Crt. & Times Chas. I* (1848) I. 354 We now sit in parliament, and therefore must take his majesty's word no otherwise than in a parliamentary way. **1656** in *Burton's Diary* (1828) I. 206 It is not parliamentary, under colour of a petition, to bring in a Bill. **1711** *Fingall MSS.* in *10th Rep. Hist. MSS. Comm.* App. v. 116 He desired money in a parliamentary way from his people.

b. Of language: Such as is permitted to be used in parliament; hence *allusively*, Admissible in polite conversation or discussion; civil, courteous. Sometimes, of a peculiar or novel word or phrase: that has been used by some one in Parliament.

1818 *Parl. Debates* 1409 Mr. Brougham asked, whether the last expression ['totally false'] of the hon. gentleman was intended in a parliamentary sense? **1824** BYRON *Juan* XVI. lxxiii, He was 'free to confess'—(whence comes this phrase? Is't English? No—'tis only parliamentary) [i.e. used by the Younger Pitt, 1788–9]. **1824** GALT *Rothelan* I. II. vii. 205 The taste and discrimination with which we so give them the go-by, to use an elegant parliamentary phrase. **1854** EMERSON *Lett. & Soc. Aims, Eloquence* Wks. (Bohn) III. 192 The speech of the man in the street is invariably strong, nor can you mend it by making it what you call parliamentary. **1866** GEO. ELIOT *F. Holt* xxx, The nomination-day was a great epoch of successful trickery, or, to speak in a more Parliamentary manner, of war stratagem. **1885** *L'pool Daily Post* 7 May 5/3 Two gentlemen politely and in strictly Parliamentary language calling one another incompetent administrators.

B. *sb.* **I. 1. a.** A member of Parliament.

1626 in *Crt. & Times Chas. I* (1848) I. 116 The eight parliamentaries who gave their charge against him to the Lords will not accuse him in that court. *a* **1825** MRS. SHERIDAN *Let. to Parr* 13 Dec. in *P.'s Wks.* (1828) VIII. 468 An unlucky word.. has made some little confusion in the heads of a few old Parliamentaries. **1878** MORRIS in Mackail *Life* I. 362 On Monday our Parliamentaries began to quake.

b. = PARLIAMENTARIAN *sb.* 2.

1649 *Declar. Bps. & Clergy at Clonmacnoise* 4 Dec. in J. C. Monahan *Rec. Dioceses Ardagh & Clonm.* (1886) 101 The Commander in Chief of the Rebel Forces commonly called Parliamentaries.

2. Short for *parliamentary train*: see 2 b above.

1864 TRAFFORD (Mrs. Riddell) *G. Geith* (1865) II. vi. 54 Our pleasures travel by express: our pains by parliamentary. **1866** DICKENS *Mugby Junction*, She's a Parliamentary, sir.

II. 3. A person sent to parley with the enemy, to make or listen to proposals. [F. *parlementaire*.]

1865 MAFFEI *Brigand Life* I. 155 On the 29th of May he sent..a parliamentary to the Piedmontese garrison, summoning them to surrender. **1898** in *Columbus* (Ohio) *Disp.* 15 Apr. 1/2 The colonial government..is to send Senors Giberga, Dolz and Viondi in the character of parliamentaries, to treat with the insurgents.

Hence **parlia'mentaryism** = PARLIAMENTARISM.

1839 *Blackw. Mag.* XLVI. 105 They have no taste for.. the journalism, the budgetism, the parliamentaryism of the 19th century. **1898** *Edin. Rev.* Apr. 531 The inharmonious working of parliamentaryism.

†**parliamen'tation.** *Obs. rare*⁻¹. [a. F. *parlementation* (16th c.), f. *parlementer*: see PARLIAMENT *v.* and -ATION.] The holding of a parliament or council; conference.

1622 E. MISSELDEN *Free Trade* 4 With the Parliamentation and Consultation of all the Parts together about these Causes and Remedies.

parliamenteer (pɑːlɪmən'tɪə(r)), *sb.* Also 7 -eir, 7-8 -ier. [f. PARLIAMENT *sb.* + -EER[1].]

1. *Hist.* = PARLIAMENTARIAN *sb.* 2.

1642 *Pr. Rupert's Jrnl.* 10 Nov. in *Eng. Hist. Rev.* (1898) XIII. 731 The Parliamentiers came to treate at Colebrooke. **1643** *Ibid.* 21 Sept. ibid. 735. **1643** PRYNNE *Popish R. Favourite* 73, I..beseech all protestant cavaliers, and Anti-parliamenteers whatsoever. **1691** WOOD *Ath. Oxon.* I. 463 He left five sons..who all (one excepted) proved zealous Parliamenteers. **1738** BIRCH *Life Milton* App., M.'s Wks. 1738 I. 84 The very Destroyers of the King (whom the first Parliamentiers call'd Rebels). **1845** CARLYLE *Cromwell* (1885) I. 175 A Committee of Parliamenteers went with him.

2. = PARLIAMENTARIAN *sb.* 3. *rare.*

1893 *National Observer* 15 Apr. 543/2 Novelist or play-wright, painter or parliamenteer.

Hence **parliamen'teership** *nonce-wd.*

1840 CARLYLE *Heroes* vi, If my Protectorship is nothing; what in the name of wonder is your Parliamenteership?

parliamen'teer, *v.* [f. prec. sb.] Rarely used exc. in **parliamen'teering** *vbl. sb.*, engagement in parliamentary affairs, electioneering; *ppl. a.* occupied with parliamentary affairs. (Cf. *mountaineering*, etc.)

1711 *Brit. Apollo* III. No. 151. 2/2 A Parliamenteering to Chelmsford..I lately rid down. **1722** (*title*) The Art of Parliamenteering. **1789** GOUV. MORRIS in Sparks *Life & Writ.* (1832) II. 63 All are engaged in parliamenteering. **1871** CARLYLE in *Mrs. C.'s Lett.* II. 374 William Harcourt, the now lawyering, parliamenteering, &c.; loud man.

†**parlia'menter.** *Sc. Obs.* [f. PARLIAMENT + -ER[1].] A parliament-man, a member of Parliament.

1787 TAYLOR *Poems* 9 (E.D.D.) Some Parli'mentars may tak bribes. **1834** *Tait's Mag.* I. 11/1 Ye are aye complaining o' the parliamenters, Robin. **1842** VEDDER *Poems* 120 If I'd been fluent, do you see, I'd been a parliamenter.

parliament-house, parliament house. The building in which a parliament meets.

Formerly applied to the (Old) Houses of Parliament at Westminster; still used of the building in Edinburgh in which the Scottish Parliament met (now used as the general waiting-room and lounge of persons engaged in the business of the Court of Session), and of those of various Colonial Legislatures.

c **1394** *P. Pl. Crede* 202 Y-set on lofte; As a Parlement-hous. **1525** LD. BERNERS *Froiss.* II. cxxviii. 363 The constable hath entred his quarell and plee agaynst you in the parlyament house of Parys. **1545** BRINKLOW *Compl.* 27 Ye that be lordes and burgessys of the parlament house. **1605** in *Crt. & Times Jas. I* (1849) I. 36 There was placed under the Parliament House, where the King should sit, some thirty barrels of powder. **1706** *Lond. Gaz.* No. 4270/3 His Grace ..was attended in his going to the Parliament-House [Edinburgh] by most of the Nobility. **1771** GOLDSM. *Hist. Eng.* III. 165 Their first intention was to bore a way under the parliament-house from that which they occupied. **1818** SCOTT *Hrt. Midl.* v, The haill Parliament House..was speaking o' naething else. **1836** GEN. P. THOMPSON *Exerc.* 23 July, A wearisome and fruitless debate on the plans for the new Parliament-houses.

'parliament-,man, parliament man. Now *Hist.* or *dial.* Also 8 **parliamentman.**

1. A member of the Parliament, orig. of England, also of Scotland and Ireland, later of the United Kingdom; occasionally applied to a member of the House of Lords, but usually, like 'Member of Parliament' now, to a member of the House of Commons.

1605 SIR E. HOBY in *Crt. & Times Jas. I* (1849) I. 35 Sundry parliament men are dead since the last session, as Sir Thomas Atye, Sir Edward Stafford,..young Sir Henry Beaumont, &c. **1621** J. MEAD *ibid.* II. 265 We talk here as though the Earl of Southampton should refuse to answer the commissioners..because he is a Parliament man. **1622** R. BRUCE in *Serm.* etc. (1843) 131, I spoke not with a [Scottish] Parliament-man, except the Lord Kilsyth. **1660** EVELYN *Diary* 5 July, All the Parliament-men, both Lords and Commons. **1668** PEPYS *Diary* 5 Dec., My great design..is to get myself to be a Parliament-man. **1766** GOLDSM. *Vic. W.* xviii, I set him down in my own mind for nothing less than a Parliament-man at least. **1802** ANDERSON *Cumbld. Ball.* 22 Our squire's to be parliament man. **1818** SCOTT *Hrt. Midl.* iv. **1889** TENNYSON *Owd Roä* vii, Fur 'e's moor good sense na the Parliament man 'at stans fur us 'ere.

†**b.** Applied loosely to members of other legislative bodies. *Obs.*

c **1729** W. BYRD *Hist. Dividing Line* (1866) I. 36 Letting us know he was a Parliament Man [described as 'one of the Senators of N. Carolina'].

2. = PARLIAMENTARIAN *sb.* 2. *rare.*

1853 WHITTIER *Prose Wks.* (1889) II. 419 The pious enthusiasm of the old Cameronians and Parliament-men of the times of Cromwell.

†**'parliance, 'parleance.** *Obs.* [Altered from PARLANCE after *parley*.] Parleying, parley.

1599 HAKLUYT *Voy.* I. 229 If you shall be inuited into any Lords or Rulers house, to dinner, or other parliance. **1615** HEYWOOD *Foure Prent. Lond.* I. Wks. 1874 II. 212 Ile sound my Drumme To drown his voyce, that doth for parleance come. **1632** HEYWOOD *2nd Pt. Iron Age* IV. i. Wks. 1874 III. 399 After some amorous parliance.

†**par'lier,** *v. Obs. rare*⁻¹. [ad. F. *parler* after *parley*: cf. Ger. *parlieren*.] *intr.* To speak French.

1666-7 DENHAM *Direct. Paint.* IV. vi, Then draw..Not homewards, but for Flanders, or for France; There to parlier a while.

parlimente, obs. form of PARLIAMENT.

'parling, *vbl. sb.* [f. PARLE *v.* + -ING[1].] The action of the vb. PARLE. **a.** Speaking, conversing.

1582 STANYHURST *Æneis* IV. (Arb.) 104 In myd of his parling from gazing mortal he shrincketh. **1650** J. REYNOLDS *Flower Fidel.* 155 Their melodious parling.

b. Parleying; a parley; a conference.

1537 *St. Papers Hen. VIII*, II. 492 The Judges..shuld be dyschargeid from hosteinges, parlings, roodes, and jornayes. **1644** PRYNNE & WALKER *Fiennes's Trial* 61, I followed the Enemy..fell from fighting, to Parling.

c. *Comb.* **parling-hill:** = PARLEY-*hill*.

1664 in *Spelman's Gloss.* s.v. *Parlamentum*.

'parling, *ppl. a.* [f. PARLE *v.* + -ING[2].] Speaking; parleying.

1593 SHAKS. *Lucr.* 100 But she that neuer cop't with straunger eies, Could picke no meaning from their parling lookes. *c* **1605** ROWLEY *Birth Merl.* I. i, The king..calls a council for return of answer Unto the parling enemy.

‖**parloir** (parlwar). [Fr.: see PARLOUR.] A room in a monastery or convent used for conversation with people from outside, or among the inmates; = PARLOUR B. 1. Also, a similar room in a prison.

1728 CHAMBERS *Cycl.* II. 354/2 *Parloir, Parlour*, in Nunneries, a little Room, or Closet, where People talk to the Nuns, thro' a kind of grated Window... Antiently, there were also Parlours in the Convents of Monks, where the Novices used to converse together at the Hours of Recreation. **1924** A. D. SEDGWICK *Little French Girl* III. vi. 276 She might have sat, in her early convent days, giving an account of herself in the *parloir*..to the relative who had come to pay her a weekly visit. **1927** J. RHYS *Left Bank* 43 The old man and the little boy were the last of the queue of people waiting..to be admitted to the *parloir*—a row of little boxes where on certain days prisoners may speak to their friends through a grating. **1955** J. THOMAS *No Banners* xxv. 248 His camp bed had been installed in the narrow, steel-barred passage dividing the two sections of the *parloir* or visiting cell.

parlour, parlor ('pɑːlə(r)). Forms: 3-5 parlur, (5 -lure), 4-6 parlore, 4-5 perlowr, 5 parlowr(e, -lere, 5-7 parler, -loure, (6 perler, -lour, parlar(e); 4- parlour, 6- parlor. *Parlour* is now usual in Britain, *parlor* in America. [ME. *parlur*, etc. a. AF. *parlur*, from OF. *parleor*, *parleur* (12th c.), *parleour* = Pr. *parlador*, It. *parlatorio*, *-toio* = med.L. *parlātōrium* (L. type **parabolātōrium*), f. *parlāre*:—*parolāre*:—*parabolāre* to speak. Cf. the more usual med.L. *locūtōrium*, f. *loquī*, *locūt-us* to speak.]

A. Forms.

a **1225** Parlur, *c* **1330** Parlour [see B. 1]. *c* **1290** *South Eng. Leg.* I. 286 'Ʒwat In þe parlore?' seint Domenic seide. **14..** in *Tundale's Vis.* (1843) 114 Fresch perlowres glased as bryght as day. *c* **1440** *Promp. Parv.* 384/2 Parlowre, *locutorium*. **1445** AGNES PASTON in *Lett.* I. 59 The parler and the chapelle at Paston. **1483** *Somerset Medieval Wills* (1901) 242 The hall parlur chambers Chapell Kechin and other houses of my maner of Assheton. **1509** *Nychodemus Gospell* (W. de W. 1518) 4 Than wente our lorde Ihesu out of the parlore. **1535** COVERDALE *2 Sam.* xviii. 33 Then was the kynge sorouful1, and wente vp in to the perler vpon the gate, and wepte. **1554** HOOPER *Breafe Treat.* in Strype *Eccl. Mem.* (1721) III. App. xxiv. 69 Mr. Hales came into the parlare. **1610-** Parlor, Parlour [see B. 2]. **1676** D'URFEY *Mad. Fickle* II. ii, I've led him into the Parler.

B. Signification. **I. 1.** An apartment in a monastery for conversation with persons from outside, or among the inmates.

a **1225** *Ancr. R.* (Camden) 68 Nimeð oðer hwules..þeo oðre men & wummen to þe parlurs þurle, speken uor neode. *c* **1330** R. BRUNNE *Chron. Wace* (Rolls) 7066 He asked leue atte priour To speke wyþ Constant y þe parlour. *c* **1425** *Eng. Voc.* in Wr.-Wülcker 670/5 *Hoc locutorium*, parloure. **1593** *Rites of Durham* (Surtees) 52 Thorowgh yᵉ parler, a place for merchaunte to vtter ther waires. **1727-41** CHAMBERS *Cycl.*, *Parlour, Parloir*, in nunneries, a little room, or closet, where people talk to the nuns, through a kind of grated window... Anciently there were also parlours in the convents of the monks, where the novices used to converse together at the hours of recreation. **1886** RUSKIN *Præterita* I. 421 A chat with us in the parlour. **1903** J. T. FOWLER in *Rites of Durham* (Surtees) 238 The utter or outer Parlour, Locutorium, or Spekehouse, was usually on the western side of the cloister. .. There was always an inner parlour for more strictly monastic conversation.

2. a. In a mansion, dwelling-house, town-hall, etc., *orig.* A smaller room apart from the great hall, for private conversation or conference (e.g. a banker's parlour, the Mayor's Parlour in a town-hall). Hence, in a private house, the ordinary sitting-room of the family, which, when more spacious and handsomely furnished, is usually called the drawing-room. Formerly often simply = 'room' or 'chamber', sometimes a bedchamber.

c **1374** CHAUCER *Troylus* II. 33 (82) Two oþere ladyes sette and she, Wiþ-Inne a paued parlour. *a* **1400-50** *Alexander* 5304 In-to a preue parlour þai passe bathe to-gedire. *a* **1425** *Cursor M.* 16093 (Trin.) Anoon pilate vp he roos:..And ȝede in to þe parlour [*earlier MSS.* pretori]. *c* **1460** *Towneley Myst.* iii. 133 Make in thi ship also, Parloures oone or two, And houses of offyce mo. **1486** *Nottingham Rec.* III. 253 þe Counsell House and þe Parlour vnder hit. **1549-62** STERNHOLD & H. *Ps.* lv. 16 For mischiefe raigneth in their hall and parlour where they dwell. **1589-90** in Willis & Clark *Cambridge* (1886) III. 382 A forme for the College parler. **1598** *Ibid.*, The parlor all seeled with waynscott. **1595** *Lanc. Wills* (1857) II. 129 [To] permit my wife to have two parlers or other conveniente places to her use. **1610** BP. HALL *Recoll. Treat.* (1614) 780 Extemporarie devotions in your Parlors. **1625** BACON *Ess.*, *Building* (Arb.) 549 To haue, at the further end, a Winter, and a Summer Parler, both Faire. **1787** M. CUTLER in *Life*, etc. (1888) I. 235 The Parlor, Drawing-room, and Dining-hall are in the second story. **1798** WASHINGTON *Writ.* (1893) XIV. 130 *note*, Mr. Lear.. informed me that a gentleman in the parlour below desired to see me. **1884** J. QUINCY *Figures of Past* 367 He stood at one end of the low parlor of the President's house. **1886** MORLEY *Crit. Misc.*, *Geo. Eliot* III. 106 Jane Austen bore her part in the little world of the parlour that she described.

b. Used as a dining or supper room.

1377 LANGL. *P. Pl.* B. x. 97 To eten bi hym-selue In a pryue pa[r]loure..and leue þe chief halle. **1526** TINDALE *Mark* xiv. 15 He wyll shewe you a greate parlour, paved, and prepared. **1542** UDALL *Erasm. Apoph.* 69 b, Neither could he wishe..a more galaunte parloure to eate in. *a* **1586** SIDNEY *Arcadia* I. (1629) 15 To the Parler where they used to sup. **1689** in Taylor *Wakefield Manor* (1886) 126 Duas cœnaculos, anglice parlors. **1796** *Hist. Ned Evans* I. 199 In the parlour was a table elegantly covered, and a servant in a laced livery behind every chair. **1823** RUTTER *Fonthill* 63 The Oak Parlour was the only room for the service of dinner. **1904** LD. ALDENHAM *Let. to Editor*, In my youth [1830-50] the room on the ground floor which is now called the Dining Room was always called the Parlour.

c. In different parts of England, the inner or more private room of a two-roomed house, cottage, or small farm-house, variously used according to locality, kind of household, etc., as the living-room of the family distinct from the kitchen, or as the 'best room' distinct from the ordinary living room (or sometimes as a bedroom). See *Eng. Dialect Dict.* s.v.

[**1469** *Bury Wills* (Camden) 45, I will that the seid Denyse haue the new hows callyd a parlure, wyth the kechyn, and the chamberys parteynyng to the seid parlure and kechyn. **1482** MARG. PASTON *Will* in *Lett.* III. 286 My fetherbedde ..in my parlour at Mauteby. **1599** *Acc.-bk. W. Wray* in *Antiquary* XXXII. 243 In the chamber over the hawle and parloure.] **1825** MACKINNON *Acct. Messingham* 25 (E.D.D.) The cottages had only a house and parlour, the parlour being used as a dormitory for the whole family, both male and female.

d. *transf.* and *fig.* = 'chamber', 'inner chamber'.

1561 T. NORTON *Calvin's Inst.* v. (1634) 8 He hath framed his Parlours in the waters, that the clouds are his chariots. **1670** COTTON *Espernon* I. IV. 156 He had also discover'd that the Duke every afternoon us'd to play at Cards in the Parlour of his Tent. **1866** G. MACDONALD *Ann. Q. Neighb.* v. (1878) 63 Forgetful to entertain strangers, at least in the parlour of his heart.

e. In *attrib.* use with the names of outdoor games which have been adapted to a smaller scale for use indoors.

1872 A. ELLIOT *Within Doors* 45 Numerous Parlour Games have recently been introduced... Such are Parlour Croquet,..Parlour Billiards, [etc.]. **1881** *Cassell's Bk. In-Door Amusem.* 74 The game described in this book as German Balls is sometimes also known as Parlour Bowls. **1887** E. CUSTER *Tenting on Plains* xv. 501 A game of parlor croquet was proposed. **1895** *Montgomery Ward Catal.* 235/3 Parlor Tennis. This new and fascinating game is arranged for parlor or lawn use and is played with 12 light rubber balls... Parlor Quoits..consists of two turned posts..and four quoits five inches in diameter. **1899** BEERBOHM *More* 140 Playing parlour-golf with his only child. **1901** Parlour cricket [see DART *sb.* 1 d]. **1926-7** *Army & Navy Stores Catal.* 854/3 The parlour golf hole... For practising 'putting' indoors.

f. In *attrib.* use applied to persons of comfortable or prosperous circumstances who profess support, usu. of a non-participatory nature, for radical, extreme, or revolutionary political movements, as ***parlour Bolshevik, communist, socialist***, etc. Hence ***parlour Bolshevism, socialism***.

1910 *Ann. Library Index 1909* 273 (*title*) Parlour socialists. **1915** T. DREISER *Let.* 26 Apr. in *Lett. H. L. Mencken* (1961) 68, I hold no brief for the parlor radical. **1918** [see BOLSHEVISM]. **1922** R. NEVILL *Yesterday & Today* i. 14 What may be called 'Society Socialism' is an entirely modern development, pretty well limited to England and

America where the 'Parlour Socialist' has become recognized as a regular type. **1926** G. Frankau *My Unsentimental Journey* iv. 56 The audience..were only 'parlour Bolsheviks'. **1929** F. P. Gibbons *Red Napoleon* 67 Margot was more than a parlour pink; she was an ardent internationalist. **1930** H. G. Wells *Autocracy of Mr. Parham* II. i. 86 Don't imagine we are that mysterious unseen power, the Money Power, your parlour Bolsheviks talk about. **1938** G. T. Garratt *Shadow of Swastika* 201 Mr. Neville Chamberlain remained..invincible because of his backing amongst the very wealthy and influential parlour fascists outside. **1939** C. Isherwood *Goodbye to Berlin* 105 Wasn't I a bit of a sham..with my arty talk..and my newly-acquired parlour-socialism? **1954** Koestler *Invis. Writing* iii. 40 The most fashionable poet among the snobs and parlour-Communists of the period was Bertold Brecht. **1960** *News Chron.* 22 June 6/5 A wonderfully reactionary view of country life. It makes John Buchan look a 'parlour pink'. **1969** *Times* 24 Mar. 7/7 Cripps..had just come into notoriety before the war as a 'parlour Bolshevist' of a high intellectual order. **1973** K. Giles *File on Death* vi. 156 A parlour pink! Did he have anything to contribute? **1976** S. Hynes *Auden Generation* x. 367 The stock notion of the 'thirties writer as a *New Country* parlour-communist.

3. A room in an inn more private than the taproom, where people may converse apart.

1870 E. Peacock *Ralf Skirl.* II. 146 A private entrance.. led to the back parlour or inner room. **1883** *Harper's Mag.* Nov. 818/1 He was sitting in the 'parlor'. **1899** *Westm. Gaz.* 12 Apr. 7/2 A tavern consisted of three open rooms, freely inviting class distinctions—the saloon, the parlour, and the tap-room.

4. a. orig. *U.S.* (Commercial cant.) An elegantly or showily fitted apartment, for some special business or trade use, as a ***misfit parlor***, ***oyster p.***, ***photographer's p.***, ***tonsorial p.***, etc.

1884 Ice cream parlor [see ice-cream *attrib.*]. **1890** in *Cent. Dict.* **1908**, etc. Beauty parlour [see *beauty parlour* s.v. beauty *sb.* III]. **1912** Manicure parlor [see manicure *sb.* 2]. **1913**, etc. Massage parlour [see massage *sb.* b]. **1927** E. Glyn *'It'* xiii. 122 'The Oak Parlour', a new little restaurant. **1928** *Daily Express* 22 Oct. 1/3 The bodies of the boys will be kept in sealed caskets in an 'undertaking parlour' until the mother is well enough to attend the funeral. **1942** H. C. Bailey *Dead Man's Shoes* xxvi. 100 Pat's Parlour, a tea shop for holiday visitors. **1952** S. Selvon *Brighter Sun* iv. 63 He was listless and dull, and attracted very little business, though his was the only well-stocked parlour in that part of Barataria. **1963** H. Garner in R. Weaver *Canad. Short Stories* (1968) 2nd Ser. 41, I tried a couple of beer parlours, but couldn't stand the noise and laughter. **1973** W. McCarthy *Detail* ii. 115 Stuart..went to the adjoining pizza parlour. **1974** *Listener* 8 Aug. 168/3 Model industrial communities, with sun-lamp parlours.

b. *ellipt.* form of ***milking-parlour*** s.v. milking *vbl. sb.* 4.

1950 *N.Z. Jrnl. Agric.* June 541/1 Near Davis [California] I visited some dairies using the 'parlour' system of milking. **1973** *Country Life* 28 June 1904/1 Development work on milking machinery..directed at speeding the movement of cows through the parlour.

II. †**5.** Conversation, colloquy, conference. *Obs.*

[Cf. OF. *parloir*, 'ce qu'on dit dans une assemblée' (Godef.).]

1483 *Cath. Angl.* 269/2 A Parlowr, *colloquium, colloquotorium.* **1501** Douglas *Pal. Hon.* II. xxvi, Vprais the court, and all the parlour ceist.

III. 6. *attrib.* and *Comb.*, as ***parlour art***, ***casement***, ***cat***, ***door***, ***fire***, ***game***, ***novel***, ***pastime***, ***politics***, ***sofa***, ***table***, ***wall***, ***window***; **parlour-boarder**, a boarding-school pupil who lives in the family of the principal and has other privileges not shared by the ordinary boarders; **parlour-car** (*U.S.*), a luxuriously fitted railway carriage, a 'drawing-room' car; so ***parlour cattle-car***; **parlour child**: see quot.; **parlour-floor**, the floor of a parlour; the floor or story of a house which contains the parlour; **parlour-girl** *U.S.*, = parlour-maid; **parlour-house**, (*a*) a house having a parlour; (*b*) *U.S. slang*, an expensive type of brothel; **parlour-jumper** *slang*, one who robs rooms (see quot. 1938); **parlour-jumping**, *slang*, robbing of rooms by entering at a window; so **parlour-jump** *v.*; **parlour-magic**, feats of legerdemain, etc., performed in and suited to a parlour; **parlour man**, a male domestic servant; = *house-parlourman* s.v. house *sb.*[1] 24; (the sense in quot. 1851 is uncertain); **parlour match**, 'a friction match which contains little or no sulphur' (Webster *Suppl.* 1902); **parlour melodeon** *U.S.*, a kind of parlour organ; **parlour-organ**, a reed-organ suitable for a private room; **parlour-palm**, the aspidistra; **parlour pew**, a family pew in a church, furnished like a small parlour, sometimes occupied by the lord of the manor or squire with his household; **parlour-piece**, a slight entertainment suitable for performance in a parlour; †**parlour-preacher**, a preacher who preaches to a private congregation; so †**parlour-sermon**, †**-worship**; **parlour-skate**, a roller-skate (Knight *Dict. Mech.* 1875); **parlour social** *U.S.*, = *house-rent party* s.v. house *sb.*[1] 24; **parlour trick**, (*a*) (in *pl.*) society arts or accomplishments; (*b*) an amusing 'turn' or trick performed, often by an animal, as entertainment; †**parlour trimmer**, a parlour servant. See also parlour-maid.

1777 P. Thicknesse *Year's Journey* I. ii. 12 The Prieure of this convent..had received, as *parlour boarders, some English ladies of very suspicious characters. **1812** *Theatrical Inquisitor* I. 211, I am a parlour boarder at Mrs. Twizzle's school. **1817** *Crit. Rev.* Apr., Romantic enough to satisfy all the parlour-boarders of ladies' schools in England. **1848** Thackeray *Van. Fair* xx, Surely it must be Miss Swartz, the parlour boarder. **1882** Sala *Amer. Revis.* (1885) 88 A couple of fauteuils in the Pullman '*parlour-' or, as it is called in England, 'drawing-room car'. **1902** E. L. Banks *Newspaper Girl* 302, I saved that amount to pay my parlour-car fee..and a late dinner on the train. **1881** *Chicago Times* 30 Apr., The first *parlor cattle-car left to-night for New York. **1874** *Temple Bar* Oct. 346 Such an only child used to be called 'a *parlour child', to denote that there was more intercourse between child and parent than exists in a 'nursery child', to whom the nurse seems his natural guide and ruler. **1560** Daus tr. *Sleidane's Comm.* 209 b, Streyght waies cometh one of the women to the *parlour dore. **1596** Shaks. *Tam. Shrew* v. ii. 102 They sit conferring by the *Parler fire. **1828** Scott *F.M. Perth* xvi, Simon Glover.. placed him in a chair by his parlour fire. **1780** Mrs. Harris in *Lett. Earl Malmesbury* (1870) I. 453 We illuminated the *parlour floor and the drawing-room floor. **1872** *Parlour game [see sense 2 e above]. **1894** I. Zangwill in *Critic* (N.Y.) 24 Nov. 342/2 In the parlor-game of 'Consequences'. **1923** W. de la Mare *Riddle* 127 She *talks* to you; but it's all make-believe. It's all a 'parlour game'. **1958** Wodehouse *Cocktail Time* xviii. 157 The television set..was now deep in one of those parlour games designed for the feeble-minded trade. **1975** *Listener* 28 Aug. 279/1 At this season of the year, the listener to Radio 4 cannot expect much more than.. parlour games. **1863** A. D. Whitney *Faith Gartney's Girlhood* iii. 9 The *parlor-girl made her appearance with her mop and tub. **1875** Mrs. Stowe *We & Neighbors* xxxiv. 323 Maggie was parlor-girl and waitress, and a good one too. **1872** E. Crapsey *Nether Side N.Y.* 142 A most deplorable change..greatly decreasing the number of *parlor houses, while houses of assignation have multiplied. **1924** in Henderson & Maddock *Housing Acts* (1930) 431 Appropriate normal rents may be fixed for different classes of houses, *e.g.* parlour and non-parlour. **1926** J. Black *You can't Win* iv. 28 Women who kept 'parlor houses' until the Tenderloin district. **1927** St. John Ervine *Wayward Man* I. i. 3 Three shops, four parlour-houses... The front of his house looked like that of any other parlour-house, but if a passer-by had peeped through the window he would have seen, not, as he might have expected, a small d'oyley-covered table, bearing a pot of geraniums or [etc.]. **1927** F. E. Fremantle *Housing of Nation* 40 At Roehampton the cost of a parlour house rose to £1,750. **1975** J. Gores *Hammett* (1976) v. 38 The parlor houses, cribs, brothels and bagnios had disappeared..and a thousand prostitutes had been thrown out of work. **1977** *Belfast Tel.* 19 Jan. 25/3 (Advt.), Parlour house, off Newtonards Rd., good condition. **1894** A. Morrison *Mean Streets* 260 No boy would *parlour-jump nor dip the lob for him. **1898** *Daily Tel.* 4 Aug. 3/2 A constable explained that the prisoner.. was known as a '*parlour-jumper'... He went in for robbing rooms. **1938** F. D. Sharpe *Sharpe of Flying Squad* xv. 170 'Parlour Jumpers'.. went round knocking on doors until they found a temporarily unoccupied house or flat, when they would force a way in and collect everything of value.., put it in the table cloth..and walk out. **1879** *Autobiog. of Thief* in *Macm. Mag.* XL. 500, I palled in with some older hands at the game, who used to take me *parlour-jumping. **1851** H. Melville *Moby Dick* II. xiv. 121 Beale's.. frontispiece, boats attacking Sperm whales, though no doubt calculated to excite the civil scepticism of some *parlour men, is admirably correct..in its general effect. **1922** *Glasgow Herald* 31 Oct. 7/1 The men who have disappointed as 'housemen' and 'parlourmen' are for the most part ex-Service men..prepared to do anything to get a job. **1960** *Times* 5 Jan. 3/3 (Advt.), Cook and Butler/House Parlourman required for Surrey;..excellent kitchen; own redecorated flat. **1909** 'O. Henry' *Roads of Destiny* vii. 107 The natives were panning out enough from the beach sands to buy all the rum, red calico, and *parlour melodeons in the world. **1845** in C. Cist *Cincinnati Misc.* I. 179/1 'I was on a visit to Vermont, a few weeks since,' said he, 'and intended to buy a *parlor Organ.' **1943** A. G. Powell *I can go Home Again* 96 There was an ordinary parlor organ, but on the days in which Old Lady McCan..attended services the organ in the Baptist Church could not be used. **1904** *Amateur Gardener's Diary* 145 *Aspidistra* (*Parlour Palm), one of the hardiest of indoor plants, as it will survive dust and even the fumes of gas. **1876** G. M. Hopkins *Poems* (1967) 65 And ever, if bound here hardest home, You've *parlour-pastime left. **1896** *Daily News* 30 May 8/5 The village church, lately in possession of a 'squire's pew', carpeted, with fireplace, chairs, and tables; a snuggery wherein the great man snored unobserved,..now the *parlour pew is gone. **1938** *Amer. Speech* XIII. 255 Most of the music..played on these many pianos was..'light classical', and in anthologies the terms 'salon music' and '*parlor pieces' were used. **1957** T. Hughes *Hawk in Rain* 20 (*title*) Parlour-piece. **1940** H. G. Wells *New World Order* § 1. 18 This is no small affair of *parlour politics we have to consider. **1589** Nashe *Pasquils Returne* Wks. (Grosart) I. 100 In the tippe of the tongue of some blind *Parlor-preacher. **1646** Crashaw *Delights Muses* 131 His *parlour-sermons rather were Those to the eye, than to the ear. **1552** Huloet, *Parlour seruaunte or trimmer, *triclinarius.* **1956** *Parlour social [see *house-party* s.v. house *sb.*[1] 24]. **1966** W. T. E. Kirkeby *Ain't Misbehavin'* iv. 39 Another and popular way to meet expenses was the parlour social or, as it later became familiarly known, the 'rent-party'. **1663** P. Henry *Diary* (1882) 128 Agreed to give me 30s. for yᵉ *Parler table. **1805** W. Taylor in *Ann. Rev.* III. 56 This book..has lain for exhibition on the parlour-table of all our polished families. **1922** R. Leighton *Compl. Bk. Dog* vii. 99 He [*sc.* the Chow Chow]..often has a clever gift for *parlour tricks. **1961** *Times* 7 Jan. 7/7 The art of skiing is.. gradually suffering conversion into a gigantic outdoor parlour trick. **1839** Longf. *Footst. Angels* ii, Shadows.. Dance upon the *parlour wall. **1700** Dryden *Cock & Fox* 15 Her *parlour window stuck with herbs around Of savoury smell. **1623** T. Scott *Highw. God* 72 He will haue a *parlor-worship, a religion by himselfe.

†**'parlouring.** *Obs. rare*[−1]. [f. prec. + -ing[1].] Tapestry for the walls of a parlour: cf. halling.

1496 *Will of Brice* (Somerset Ho.), My two hallinges & ij parlourynges..one of theme peynted with..fenne Countreys & bourdred with historyes of the bible.

'parlour-maid. A female domestic servant who waits at table in houses where indoor men-servants are not kept.

1840 Dickens *Old C. Shop* xxxi, Miss Monflather's parlour-maid inspected all visitors before admitting them. **1887** I. R. *Lady's Ranche Life* 112 Here am I, cook, parlour-maid, house-maid, and scullery-maid all rolled into one.

Hence **'parlourmaiding**, parlourmaid's work.

1885 G. Allen *Babylon* xv, I'd go back again willingly to the parlour-maiding. **1887** I. R. *Lady's Ranche Life Montana* 17, I do all the housemaiding and parlourmaiding.

parlous ('pɑːləs), *a.* (*adv.*) *arch.* and *dial.* Forms: α. 4–6 perlous, (4–5 -louse, 5 -lewse, 7 -les). β. 4– parlous, (4 -lows, 5–6 -louse, 6–7 -les, 9 *dial.* -lish). γ. 4–5 perlious, -laous, 5–6 parlious, (6 -yous, -yus). [A syncopated form of perilous (ME. also *perelous*, *peralous*, *parelous*), found from 14th c. alongside of the fuller forms, but since 17th c. more or less arch. in literary use; common dialectally from Durham to Hampshire.]

1. Perilous, dangerous; hazardous.

α. *a* **1400–50** *Alexander* 3949 Out of þis perlaous place he past with his ost. *c* **1440** *Gesta Rom.* xxviii. 108 (Harl. MS.) Then hit shall be to the a perlewse case. **1535** Coverdale *Micah* ii. 3 It will be a perlous tyme. **1596** Drayton *Legends* iii. 165 His course was per'lous to be stayd. **1613** Beaum. & Fl. *Coxcomb* v. i, Upon a Perles ground too.

β. **1380** *Lay Folks Catech.* 1225 (Lamb. MS.) Sum men þynke þat þis is a ful parlows heresy. **1512** *Nottingham Rec.* III. 340 Thoro the which the hye wey shall be parles both for man and beest. **1589** *Hay any Work* (1844) 11 Cards I tel you though they bee without hornes, yet they are parlous beasts. *a* **1677** Barrow *Serm.* Wks. 1716 I. 181 The tongue is a sharp and parlous weapon. **1825** Brockett *N.C. Gloss.*, *Parlous*, perilous, dangerous, wonderful,—also acute, clever, shrewd. An old word.—*Parlish*, a variation in dialect. **1885** *L'pool Daily Post* 11 Apr. 4/8 Suggestions which in these parlous days ought to receive..practical attention. **1886** Chamberlain *Sp. Ho. Comm.* 26 Aug., Their position is very perilous. They are in a very parlous state. **1892** M. C. F. Morris *Yorks. Folk-Talk* 259 The word parlous.. forms one of the very commonest components of our dialectic vocabulary—parlous roads, parlous weather, a parlous tahm, &c.

γ. *c* **1400** Maundev. (Roxb.) vii. 24 Many perlious hauens er þerin. **1447** Bokenham *Seyntys* (Roxb.) 169 Thou stondyst in a ful perlyous caas. **1512** *Act 4 Hen. VIII*, c. 19 *Preamble*, Whiche..ys..parlyous and terrible example to all Cristen fayth. **1536** Boorde *Let.* in *Introd. Knowl.* (1870) Forewds. 59 Persons..þat be hys aduersarys, & speketh parlyus wordes.

b. Risky to deal with; ticklish, awkward, precarious.

1658 Cokaine *Obstinate Lady* III. ii, This London wine is a parlous liquor. **1868** Browning *Ring & Bk.* I. 269 Mother Church; to her we make appeal By the Pope, the Church's head.—A parlous plea, Put in with noticeable effect it seems. **1882** H. C. Merivale *Faucit of B.* II. 106 Snipe—a parlous bird to hit, at the best of times.

2. Dangerously cunning, clever, eager, etc.; keen, shrewd; capable of harming, mischievous; very bad, 'shocking'; surprising, extraordinary, excessive, 'terrible', 'awful'. (In later use *colloq.* and *dial.*)

a **1400** *Pistill Susan* 53 Whon þeos parlous [*v.r.* perlous] prestes perceyued hir play. **1590** Shaks. *Mids. N.* III. i. 14 Berlaken, a parlous feare. **1594** —— *Rich. III*, II. iv. 35 A parlous Boy: go too, you are too shrew'd. *c* **1620** Fletcher & Massinger *Trag. Barnavelt* II. ii, He is a Scholler and a parlous Scholler. **1641** Milton *Animadv.* i. 6 Sure some Pedagogue stood at your Elbow, and made it itch with this parlous Criticisme. **1658** Cokaine *Obstinate Lady* v. vi, You have a parlous wit. **1696** Phillips (ed. 5), *Parlous*, a kind of made Word, signifying shrewd, notable. *a* **1700** B. E. *Dict. Cant. Crew*, *Parlous*, or *Perillous Man*, a notable shrew'd Fellow. **1730** Fielding *Coffee Ho. Polit.* Ep., Oh! may our youth whose vigour is so parlous, To Italy be wafted with Don Carlos! **1839** Bailey *Festus* xviii. (1848) 176 Oh! you are a parlous little infidel.

B. as *adv.* Excessively, 'terribly', 'awfully', 'desperately', 'precious'.

1599 Massinger, etc. *Old Law* III. ii, I am old, you say, Yes, parlous old, kids, an you mark me well! **1796** *Hist. Ned Evans* I. 135 The night is parlous cold. *Ibid.* 136 He's a parlous rich man. **1817** Keats *Lett.* Wks. 1889 III. 54 'Twould be a parlous good thing. **1843** Lytton *Last Bar.* I. iv, There's parlous little care from the great. **1870** Edgar *Runnymede* 81 She is parlous handsome, and bewitching to look upon.

Hence **'parlously** *adv.*; **'parlousness**.

1450–1530 *Myrr. our Ladye* 45 How moche more *perlously are they traytours to god. **1535** Coverdale *2 Macc.* iv. 16 For the which they stroue perlously. **1663** Killigrew *Parson's Wed.* I. ii. in Hazl. *Dodsley* XIV. 395 Scorning me, who (by this hand) lov'd her parlously. **1713** C. Johnson *Generous Husb.* v. 51 How parlously he talks. Well, he is a sweet Gentleman. **1840** Barham *Ingol. Leg.*, *Leech of Folkest.*, Thou art parlously encompassed. **1563** Golding *Cæsar* VIII. (1565) 265 Our soldiers..were hindred both with the *perlousenes of thencounter, & wyth the disaduauntage of yᵉ place. **1727** Bailey vol. II, *Parlousness*, uncapableness of being equalled, spoken commonly in an ill Sense. **1755** Johnson, *Parlousness*, quickness; keenness of temper.

†**parls, parles.** *Sc. Obs. rare.* Paralysis, palsy.
*a***1585** MONTGOMERIE *Flyting* 324 With parles and plurisies opprest, And nipd with nirles. *c***1615** SIR W. MURE *Sonn.* xii. Wks. I. 58 Puir, perjurd palliard, plaged wt the parls.

parlsy, parlune, parly(a)ment, obs. ff. PALSY, PURLOIN, PARLIAMENT.

parly, colloquial abbreviation of *parliamentary* (train).

parlyaree (pɑːlɪ'ɑːriː). Also **parlary.** [f. It. *parlare* to speak, talk.] A form of slang used by actors and showmen, particularly in the 18th and 19th centuries, and characterized by Italianate vocabulary. Cf. PALARIE *v.*

The word appears to be related to *nanty parnarly* recorded in Barrère & Leland *Dict. Slang* (1890) II. 81/2.

1933 PARTRIDGE *Slang To-day & Yesterday* iii. 223 Until about the end of the eighteenth century, actors were so despised that, in self-protection, they had certain words that, properly, should be described as cant and were actually known as Parlyaree. **1933** *Times Lit. Suppl.* 15 June 412/3 Circus slang is a nineteenth-century offshoot from the Parlyaree of the seventeenth and eighteenth centuries. **1950** PARTRIDGE *Here, There & Everywhere* 117 It was among showmen and strolling players that parlyaree originated. *Ibid.* 122 Most parlyaree-speakers prefer a *carser* or *carsey*, i.e. a house, when they can get it. *Ibid.* 125 Parlyaree..is a glossary, a vocabulary, not a complete language. **1952** GRANVILLE *Dict. Theatr. Terms* 132 *Parlyaree* (occasionally *parlary*). Little is known about this language which has neither accidence nor syntax of its own but is built on a base of Italian words and phrases, whereon cant terms and illiteracies are piled. **1960** J. FRANKLYN *Dict. Rhyming Slang* 106/1 The term [*sc.* parlamaree] is obviously a mispronunciation of Parlyaree, the language of the Circus. **1960** *Spectator* 11 Mar. 355 The canting jargon of the Victorian fairgrounds known as 'parlyaree'.

parm (pɑːm). Colloq. contraction of *pardon* (*me*).
1945 A. KOBER *Parm Me* 180 Parm me fa contердicting. **1957** J. BLISH *Fallen Star* vii. 101, I was hun'ry. Parm me. **1967** C. DRUMMOND *Death at furlong Post* xiv. 171 'Piss off,' said Hart. 'Parm?' **1973** K. GILES *File on Death* v. 144 Parm me, sir, but I've got me good name to consider.

Parma[1] ('pɑːmə). The name of a city in northern Italy, used *attrib.* or *absol.* to designate products associated with the region, as **Parma ham,** a local type of ham which is eaten uncooked; **Parma violet,** (*a*) a cultivated violet with double, scented flowers, usually light or deep purple, belonging to a group of cultivars of *Viola alba*; a crystallized flower of this kind; (*b*) a perfume manufactured from a flower of this type or imitating its scent; (*c*) a deep or medium shade of purple.

[**1960** E. DAVID *French Provincial Cooking* 134 It is a common misconception that all hams eaten raw, including that of Parma, are smoked.] **1964** A. LAUNAY *Caviare & After* vii. 54 The Bayonne and Parma hams are served raw. **1966** 'J. MELVILLE' *Nell Alone* i. 21 She's doing a lot of eating..Parma ham, tinned stuff, the best coffee. **1971** *Sunday Times* (Colour Suppl.) 27 June 50/3 Parma ham..and Westphalian smoked ham, all eaten raw, have always been popular with gourmets. **1976** E. WARD *Hanged Man* xx. 118 Eggs and Parma ham and oven-hot bread and coffee. **1856, 1880** Parma violet [see VIOLET *sb.*[1] 2 a]. **1907** *Yesterday's Shopping* (1969) 521/1 Perfumes... Opoponax. Parma Violet. Peau d'Espagne. **1919** K. MANSFIELD in *Art & Lett.* II. 155 A stout lady in blue serge, with a bunch of artificial 'parmas' at her bosom. **1922** *Weekly Dispatch* 10 Dec. 15 A leather set in the new shade of violet. Something between purple and parma, this hue will soon be the rage. **1923** *Daily Mail* 7 Feb. 1 (Advt.), Black, Navy,..Parma. *Ibid.* 12 Feb. 1 (Advt.), Shades: Fawn, Grey, Lovat, Parma, Browns. **1932** *New Flora & Silva* IV. 190 The origin of the Parma Violet has never been satisfactorily elucidated... There are many violets growing round Naples, but none..which I have seen suggest themselves as parents of the Parma. **1938** G. L. ZAMBRA *Violets* vii. 62 The family of Parma violets gives the sweetest perfume, the longest flowering season, and the handsomest foliage of all the double violets. **1954** 'M. COST' *Invitation from Minerva* 96 A frock..parma-violet in colour. **1956** *Punch* 23 May 626/1 If the modest violet is employed it must be..a shameless bunch of Parmas. **1963** R. D. MEIKLE *Garden Flowers* 105 The delicious Parma Violet, with smaller, rather glossy leaves, and slender-stalked flowers, is probably a form of *Viola alba* Bess., found wild (with innumerable variations) over most of the Mediterranean area and Asia Minor. **1970** *Observer* 1 Feb. 32/7 Dior: Parma violet coat. **1970** I. ORIGO *Images & Shadows* ii. 60 The ladies in summer gowns..leaving behind them a faint aroma of lavender and Parma violet. **1974** *Country Life* 25 Apr. 1025/2 Using parma violet or electric blue, she sprinkles these vibrating colours through the wardrobe. **1977** *Times* 14 June 18/6 Women in the chocolate factory..place walnuts and Parma violets on to the store's handmade confectionery.

parma[2] ('pɑːmə). *Geol.* (See quots.)
1888 *Encycl. Brit.* XXIV. 4/1 The section [of the Urals] between the 64th and 61st parallels has..a wholly distinct character... From the broad plateaus, or *parmas*, which stretch towards the north-west, it might be conjectured..that the structure is more complicated. **1904** *Amer. Jrnl. Sci.* CLXVIII. 469 This may mean that no true axis or 'parma' was in existence during Richmond time, but it does seem to show that the Wabash parma at least indicates the strike for the then highest land. **1904** tr. *Suess' Face of Earth* I. II. xii. 601 We see great folded chains merge with gradually flattening undulations into the similar foreland, where they form secondary folds, or 'parmas'—this is the case in the Urals and the Appalachians. **1913** A. W. GRABAU *Princ. Stratigr.* xx. 808 Many of the low-dipping domes are perceptible as such only by the erosion which has removed their central portion, often leaving a topographic depression. Such low domes have also been called parmas. **1957** *Gloss. Geol.* (Amer. Geol. Inst.) 212/2 *Parma*, a low dome or quaquaversal.

†**parma'cety.** *Obs.* Forms: 6 **parmacete, -citie, -sitie,** 6–7 **-cetie,** 7 **-cety, -city,** 7–8 **-sity,** 7–9 **-cetty, -citty;** 7 **permacetty, -ceti.**

1. A popular corruption of SPERMACETI.
1545 *Rates of Customs* c iij, Parmacete the pounde iiis. iiiid. **1577–87** HOLINSHED *Chron.* III. 1259/2 The oile being boiled out of the head was parmasitie. **1596** SHAKS. *1 Hen. IV*, I. iii. 58 The Soveraign'st thing on earth Was Parmacity, for an inward bruise. **1624** *Althorp MS.* in Simpkinson *Washingtons* App. 56 Metridate, Dies cordin, and permacetty of every one of them a little. *c***1720** W. GIBSON *Farrier's Dispens.* II. i. (1734) 34 *Parmasity*, or Sperma Ceti. **1828** *Craven Gloss.* (ed. 2), *Parmacitty*, Sperma-ceti..now considered vulgar or antiquated.

b. *poor man's parmacety*: a name for the plant Shepherd's Purse (*Capsella Bursa-pastoris*).
1597 GERARDE *Herbal* II. xxiii. §2. 215 Shepheardes purse or Scrip: of some..poore mans Parmacetie. **1657** COLES *Adam in Eden* xxxv. 71 Shepherds pouch and poor mans Parmacety, it being in some sort effectual for the same things that Parmacety is.

2. In full *parmacety whale*: The Cachalot, or Sperm whale.
1730 S. DALE *S. Taylor's Hist. & Antiq. Harwich* 413 The Parmacitty-Whale, or Pot-Wall-fish. **1851** H. MELVILLE *Whale* xvi. 80 Chewed up, crunched by the monstrousest parmacetty that ever chipped a boat.

parmanable, parmayn: see PERMANABLE, PEARMAIN.

parmeliaceous (pɑːmiːlɪ'eɪʃəs), *a. Bot.* [f. mod.L. *Parmēlia* (f. Gr. πάρμη, L. *parma* small round shield) + -ACEOUS.] Belonging or allied to the lichens of the genus *Parmelia*, repr. by the Common Yellow Wall-lichen. So **par'melioid** *a.* [-OID], resembling the genus *Parmelia* (*Cent. Dict.* 1890).

Parmenidean (pɑːmɛnɪ'diːən), *a.* (*sb.*) Also 7 **-ian.** [f. Gr. prop. name Παρμενίδης + -AN.] Belonging or relating to Parmenides of Elea, a Greek philosopher of the 5th century B.C., or his philosophy. **b.** *sb.* A follower or disciple of Parmenides.
1678 CUDWORTH *Intell. Syst.* I. iv. §21. 387 That Controversie, betwixt the Heracliticks and Parmenideans. *Ibid.* §36. 580 The most Refined Platonick and Parmenidian or Pythagorick Trinity. **1845** MAURICE *Mor. & Met. Philos.* in *Encycl. Metrop.* (1847) II. 576/1 This search after an organ or instrument for the Parmenidean philosophy.

†'**parmenter.** *Obs.* [a. OF. *parmentier*, in med.L. *parmentārius* (1148 in Du Cange), of uncertain origin.
Sometimes assumed to be f. L. *parāmentum*, F. *parement*, PARAMENT; but the *a* of the second syllable would not be lost in med.L. and Fr.]

A tailor. So †**parmentery, -try** *Obs.* [OF. *parmenterie*], ? the trade of a tailor.
[**1301** *Rolls of Parlt.* I. 246/1 Nich[ola]s le Parm[en]ter h[ab]uit die [prædicto]..11s... In furratura et pellibus agninis 1 marc.] *a***1307** in Riley *Liber Albus* (1861) 198 Parmentery. [*a***1400** in Gross *Gild Merch.* II. 206 Item nul parmenter estraunge neyt cuue ne counfite en sa mesone.] **14..** *Voc.* in Wr.-Wülcker 601/39 *Penularius*, a parmenter (or a scynnere). *a***1695** WOOD *City of Oxford* (O.H.S.) I. 492.

Parmentier (pɑː'mɑ̃tiːeɪ), *a.* [f. the name of Antoine A. *Parmentier* (1737–1813), French agriculturalist, who popularized potatoes in France.] In cookery, made with or accompanied by potatoes.
1906 *Mrs. Beeton's Bk. Househ. Managem.* 1314 *Parmentier eggs*... Poach the eggs in salted water flavoured with lemon-juice, and place them carefully in the halved potatoes. **1929** A. E. HOUSMAN *Let.* 14 Sept. (1971) 284 Food not varied or inventive, especially soup: I do not mind Santé twice in ten days, but Parmentier I do. **1951** *Good Housek. Home Encycl.* 580/2 *Parmentier*, the name of the man who introduced the potato into France... The term is now applied to a number of potato dishes... Parmentier soup. **1963** A. L. SIMON *Guide Good Food & Wines* 38/1 In culinary parlance *Parmentier* always means potatoes; it is the homage of French cooks to Parmentier, who introduced potatoes in France. **1965** *House & Garden* Dec. 84/2 *Parmentier*. Named after the man who did so much to improve the cultivation of potatoes in France..and so, naturally, means potatoes.

Parmesan (pɑːmɪ'zæn), *a.* and *sb.* Forms: 6 **parmeson, parmasen, -zen, -sine, -sian,** 7 **parmezan, parmazan, -zine, parmisan,** 7–9 **parmasan,** 8 **-zene,** 7– **parmesan;** also 7 **parmesant, (-is-, -iz-), parmasent, (permoysaunt).** [a. F. *parmesan*, It. *parmegiano*, f. *Parma*.]

A. *adj.* Of or belonging to Parma, a city and province (formerly a duchy) of Northern Italy; *esp.* applied to a celebrated cheese made there and elsewhere in North Italy.
1519 HORMAN *Vulg.* xvii, Ye shall eate parmeson chese. **1660** F. BROOKE tr. *Le Blanc's Trav.* 328 It becomes firm as Parmasan cheese. **1883** STEVENSON *Treas. Isl.* IV. xix. (1886) 155 In my snuff-box I carry a piece of Parmesan cheese..very nutritious. **1885** [see EDAM]. **1946** G. MILLAR *Horned Pigeon* iii. 47 Denis Patchett..stole a large lump of Parmesan cheese from one of our guards.

B. *sb.* **1.** Parmesan cheese: see A.
1556–68 WITHALS *Dict.* 49 b/1 Parmeson, *caseus parmensis.* **1577** B. GOOGE *Heresbach's Husb.* (1586) 147 b, The best Cheeses are counted the Parmasines. **1621–3** MIDDLETON & ROWLEY *Changeling* I. ii, A mouse that spoiled him a parmesant. **1633** FORD *'Tis Pity* I. iv, He loved her almost as well as he loved parmasent. **1705** HICKERINGILL *Priest-cr.* I. Wks. 1716 III. 26 Whilst Men live like Rats and Mice, only to eat Parmazene, and run squeaking up and down. **1842** E. FITZGERALD *Lett.* (1889) I. 84, I mean to take down a Thucydides, to feed on: like a whole Parmesan. **1876** [see BRIE]. **1960** [see CANNELLONI *sb. pl.*]. **1971** *Sunday Times* (Colour Suppl.) 28 Mar. 39/2 Parmesan is a cheese with remarkable keeping qualities.

†**2.** Some Italian fashion of drinking. *Obs.*
1606 DEKKER *Sev. Sinnes* I. (Arb.) 12 Drunke, according to all the learned rules of Drunkennes, as *Vpsy-Freeze, Crambo, Parmizant.* **1617** T. YOUNG *Eng. Bane* D j b, [To] quaffe Vpsey-freese crosse, Bowse in Permoysaunt, in Pimlico, in Crambo.

†**3.** The duchy or territory of Parma. *Obs.*
1702 *Lond. Gaz.* No. 3822/1 Some of our Men..being seized in the Parmesan. **1707** *Ibid.* No. 4396/1 Those Troops which lie in the Mantuan and Parmesan.

parmyngalle, corrupt form of PAREGAL *Obs.*

parmytte, parmyxtiue, obs. ff. PERMIT, PERMIXTIVE.

parnas(s (pɑː'nɑːs). Pl. **parnassim** (pɑːnə'siːm). [Heb.] The lay head of a Jewish synagogue congregation.
1831 [see MAHAMAD]. **1892** I. ZANGWILL *Childr. Ghetto* I. 97 Michael Birnbaum was a great man in the little local synagogue... He had been successively *Gabbai* and *Parnass*, or treasurer and president. **1907** —— *Ghetto Comedies* 76 The Great Synagogue..struck a note of modern English gaiety,..looking towards the box of the *Parnass* and *Gabbai*, she saw it was occupied by officers with gold sashes. *Ibid.* 122 The *Parnass* proffered his presidential hand in pious congratulation. **1932** C. ROTH *Hist. Marranos* 247 The community boasted a model organisation. The power of the *Parnasim*, the elected Wardens, was autocratic, as offenders like Benedict Spinoza or Uriel Acosta learned to their cost. **1949** *Spectator* 4 Nov. 595/2 The *Parnas Presidente*, the President of the Wardens of the Synagogue. **1962** B. ABRAHAMS tr. *Life Glückel of Hameln* ii. 18 My father has been *parnass* for many years. [*Note*] In Glückel's time the office of *parnass* (president or warden [of the synagogue]) was a monthly one. **1967** D. T. KAUFFMAN *Dict. Relig. Terms* 346/1 *Parnas steward*, lay president of a synagogue congregation.

parnassia (pɑː'næsɪə). [mod.L. (Linnæus *Hortus Cliffortianus* (1737) 113), f. PARNASS(US + -IA[1].] A small perennial herb of the genus so called, belonging to the family Saxifragaceæ, native to temperate or cold regions of the northern hemisphere, and bearing radical ovate or cordate leaves and white or pale yellow flowers; = *grass of Parnassus* s.v. PARNASSUS c.
1772 R. WESTON *Universal Botanist* II. 546 Parnassia, Grass of Parnassus. **1793** J. E. SMITH *Eng. Bot.* II. 82 The Parnassia agrees with Saxifraga in the wonderful œconomy of its impregnation. **1883** W. ROBINSON *Eng. Flower Garden* 207/2 In many of our moist heaths and bogs the Marsh Parnassia..is not unfrequently met with. **1941** W. A. PERCY *Lanterns on Levee* ix. 97 In the streams where the iris forgathered there are parnassia, the snowdrop's only kin. **1951** *Dict. Gardening* (R. Hort. Soc.) III. 1485/1 The Parnassias are hardy, and succeed in moist, peat soils.

Parnassian (pɑː'næsɪən), *a.* and *sb.* Also 7 **Parnassean, Pernassian.** [f. L. *Parnās(s)i-us, -ē-us* (f. *Parnāsus*, PARNASSUS) + -AN. Cf. F. *Parnassien*.]

A. *adj.* **1. a.** Of or belonging to Parnassus; of or belonging to poetry, poetic.
*a***1644** QUARLES *Sol. Recant.* Sol. xi. 49 Hadst thou what strength the Parnassean Muse Can blesse thy fancy with. **1734** POPE *Ess. Man* IV. 11 Twin'd with the wreaths Parnassian laurels yield. **1875** E. C. STEDMAN *Victorian Poets* (1876) 272 Its composer holds a place in the Parnassian hemicycle as legitimate as that of Robin Goodfellow in Oberon's court. **1884** *Harper's Mag.* Feb. 335/1 What Parnassian flowerets have strewn its course.

b. *spec.* Epithet of a school of French poetry of the latter half of the 19th c., from the title *Parnasse contemporain* of a collection of their poems published in 1866; also *transf.* Cf. B. 1 b.
1902 E. GOSSE in *Daily Chron.* 20 May 3/1 This school was that of the Parnassian poets, who ruled French verse from about 1850 to 1890. **1902** —— in *Encycl. Brit.* XXVIII. 256/1 The name of the 'Parnassian School' has been given to a group of poets who belonged to the generation succeeding that of the Rossettis and Wm. Morris.

c. Of or pertaining to sense B. 1 c.

2. *Entom.* Belonging to the genus *Parnassius* of butterflies, found in mountainous regions of the northern hemisphere.

B. *sb.* **1. a.** A poet: cf. A. 1.
1659 *Elegy on Cleveland* 49 C.'s Wks. (1687) 278 Such was this pure Pernassian, whose clear Nature To gain a World could never brook to flatter. **1899** *Q. Rev.* July 90 There are two souls in these Parnassians.

b. *spec.* A French poet of the Parnassian school.
1882 J. CLARETIE in *Athenæum* 9 Dec. 774/2 He does not speak the tortured language of the Parnassians, but the free and clear *langage gaulois* of Mathurin Régnier. **1893** *Nation*

(N.Y.) 9 Feb. 101/2 Leconte de Lisle..is the head of the Parnassians.

c. *spec.* In the writings of G. M. Hopkins, a second kind of poetry, which can only be written by poets but which is not the language of inspiration.

1864 G. M. HOPKINS *Let.* 10 Sept. (1956) 216 *Parnassian* then is that language which genius speaks as fitted to its exaltation, and place among other genius, but does not sing ..in its flights. Great men, poets I mean, have each their own dialect as it were of Parnassian, formed generally as they go on writing, and at last,—this is the point to be marked,—they can see things in this Parnassian way and describe them in this Parnassian tongue, without further effort of inspiration. *Ibid.* 217 In Parnassian pieces you feel that if you were the poet you could have gone on as he has done, you see yourself doing it, only with the difference that if you actually try to find you cannot write his Parnassian. *Ibid.* 218, I believe that when a poet palls on us it is because of his Parnassian.

2. *Entom.* A butterfly of the genus *Parnassius* or subfamily *Parnassiinæ*.

Parnassianism (pɑːˈnæsɪənɪz(ə)m). [f. PARNASSIAN *a.* 1 b + -ISM.] The Parnassian style in poetry.

1905 *Times* 4 Oct. 6/2 He began to write the sonnets which attracted the attention of the most expert connoisseurs in Parnassianism. **1922** *Freeman* (N.Y.) 26 Apr. 105 Parnassianism means objectivity, impassivity, attention to line and image rather than to colour and music and vague suggestiveness. **1927** *Observer* 11 Sept. 7/3 Parnassianism, Symbolism, and the Ecole Roman have all had their day. **1967** *Guardian* 19 May 7/2 Some of the poems are too deliberate, Parnassian... And very splendid, too, parnassianism at that level.

Parnassus (pɑːˈnæsəs). Also formerly: 6 **Pernasse, Parnasse,** 7 **Parnass.** [a. L. *Parnāsus, Parnassus*, a Gr. *Παρνᾱσός*, later *Παρνασσός*; in Fr. *Parnasse*.] Name of a mountain in central Greece, anciently sacred to Apollo and the Muses; hence used allusively in reference to literature, esp. poetry. (Cf. CASTALIA.)

c **1386** CHAUCER *Franklin's Prol.* 49, I sleepe neuere on the Mount of Pernaso Ne lerned Marcus Tullius Scithero. **1557** GRIMALD *Funeral Song* in *Tottel's Misc.* (Arb.) 116 With ioyes at hert, in this pernasse [Cambridge] I bode. **1579** SPENSER *Sheph. Cal.* Apr. 41 And eke you Virgins, that on Parnasse dwell. **1591** —— *Tears of Muses* 58 Our Syre, that raignst in Castalie And mount Parnasse. **1597** (*title*) The Returne from Parnassus. **1735** POPE *Prol. Sat.* 4 All Bedlam, or Parnassus, is let out. **1850** S. DOBELL *Roman* vii, There are good feet that do not walk Parnassus.

b. As the title of a collection of poems.

1600 ALLOT (*title*) England's Parnassus or choysest Flowers of our English Poets. **1657** J. POOLE (*title*) The English Parnassus: or, a Helpe to English Poesie. **1810** (*title*) Gammer Gurton's Garland: or, the Nursery Parnassus.

c. ***Parnassus grass, grass of Parnassus***, a white-flowered marsh plant, *Parnassia palustris*: also extended to other species of the same genus.

1578–1854 [see GRASS *sb.*[1] 2 b].

Parnate (ˈpɑːneɪt). *Pharm.* A proprietary name for the drug tranylcypromine.

1960 *Official Gaz.* (U.S. Patent Office) 17 May TM112/2 Smith Kline & French Laboratories, Philadelphia, Pa. Filed Oct. 19, 1959. *Parnate* for anti-depressant. First use Oct. 6, 1959. **1960** *Trade Marks Jrnl.* 29 Dec. 1681/1 Parnate... Preparations and substances in capsule or tablet form for use in medicine and pharmacy. Smith Kline & French Laboratories Limited,..Welwyn Garden City, Hertfordshire; manufacturing chemists. **1964** *New Statesman* 6 Mar. 354/1 An American anti-depressant drug —Parnate or tranylcypromine—has been declared unsafe by the US Food and Drug Administration. **1965** J. POLLITT *Depression & its Treatment* iv. 56 The monoamine oxidase inhibitors include several members, among them phenelzine (Nardil), iproniazid (Marsilid),..and tranylcypromine (Parnate). **1970** *Daily Tel.* 7 July 3/3 The result of eating cheese with the drug Parnate was to trigger off fatal side-effects. **1976** *Ibid.* 11 Mar. 19/4 She was taking Parnate, which is a very strong drug. If mixed with alcohol it could have a most terrible effect.

†**parnel.** *Obs.* exc. *dial.* Forms: 4 **pernele, purnele,** 6 **peronall,** 7 **parnell, pernel,** 7–8 **parnel,** (9 *dial.* **panel**). [a. OF. *Peronele, Pernele*:—L. *Petronilla* a woman's name, a saint so named; popularly viewed as a feminine deriv. of *Petrus*, Peter.] A priest's concubine or mistress; a harlot; a wanton young woman.

1362 LANGL. *P. Pl.* A. IV. 102 Til lordes and ladies louen alle treuþe, And perneles porfyl be put in heore whucche. **1393** *Ibid.* C. XVIII. 71 Of þat þat holychurche of þe olde lawe cleymeþ, Priestes on aparail and on purnele spenen. **1508** DUNBAR *Tua Mariit Wemen* 231 A tender peronall, that myght na put thole. **1560–4** BECON *Display. Popish Mass* Wks. III. 41 b, Your noppy Ale and Toste, which your pretty Parnel hath ful louingly prepared for you against your Masse be done. **1606** *Choice, Chance*, etc. (1881) 70 His dainty Parnell hath no paragon. **1678** PHILLIPS (ed. 4), *Parnel*,..an Appellation, particularly applied to any kind of wanton Woman. *a* **1800** *Old Lincolnshire Ballad* (Halliw.), Panels march by two and three, Saying, Sweetheart, come with me.

b. ***prattling parnel***: an old name for the plant London Pride (*Saxifraga umbrosa*).

1597 GERARDE *Herbal* II. ccxlxiii. 645 Of our London dames pratling Parnell.

Parnellism (ˈpɑːnɛlɪz(ə)m). [See -ISM.] The principles or policy of the party of Irish members in the House of Commons led by Charles Stewart Parnell from 1880 to 1891, whose aim was to establish Home Rule in Ireland. So **ˈParnellite**, a member of this party, a follower of C. S. Parnell.

1881 E. W. HAMILTON *Diary* 26 Jan. (1972) I. 102 This nettled the Parnellites, and they intimated they would fight to the death. **1882** *Ibid.* 30 Apr. 259 Wednesday was quite an important day, as it was taken up by the discussion of the bill brought in by the Parnellite party, with the name of Parnell himself on the bill. **1885** *Spectator* 20 June 808/2 We desire ..to see the Liberal party win at the next elections, and win so completely that both Toryism and Parnellism will be powerless. **1887** *Ibid.* 28 May 723/1 The shameless and persistent obstruction of the Parnellite members. **1892** W. B. YEATS *Lett.* (1954) 222 Parnellite Dublin and the Parnellite young men in the country parts. **1931** *Times Lit. Suppl.* 17 Sept. 708/1 His anecdote of the Parnellite in an Irish theatre. **1936** W. B. YEATS *Poems* (1957) 586 Come gather round me, Parnellites, And praise our chosen man. **1939** JOYCE *Finnegans Wake* 307 Are Parnellites Just towards Henry Tudor?

parnor, obs. form of PERNOR.

†**ˈparnter.** *Obs. rare*[−1]. Perh. a contracted form of PARMENTER.

c **1400** *Destr. Troy* 1591 Parnters, painters, pynners also.

paro: see PROA.

paroccipital (pærɒkˈsɪpɪtəl), *a.* (*sb.*) *Anat.* and *Zool.* [f. PAR(A-[1] 1 + OCCIPITAL.] Situated at the side of the occiput, or beside the occipital bone; applied *spec.* to certain bones, or processes of bone (also called *paramastoid*), as the jugular process of the occipital bone. **b.** as *sb.* A paroccipital bone or process.

1854 OWEN *Skel. & Teeth* in *Circ. Sc.*, *Organ. Nat.* I. 205 The transverse processes..are called the 'paroccipitals'. **1881** MIVART *Cat* 62 External to each condyle is an expanded process of bone called the par-occipital process.

paroch (ˈpærək). *rare.* [ad. 16th c. L. *parochus* parish priest, for earlier *parochiānus* (12th c.): cf. It., Sp. *parroco*, Romanian *paroh*, parish priest.] A parish clergyman.

1900 DIXON *Hist. Ch. Eng.* (1902) VI. xxxviii. 106 *note*, It was as much as to say, You nonconforming parochs,..at least you must put on a surplice.

parochial (pəˈrəʊkɪəl), *a.* (*sb.*) Also 5 **per-.** [a. OF. *parochial, parr-, perr-*, in AF. *parochiel* (Britton, etc.), ad. late L. *parochiāl-is* (S. Greg. *Ep. a* 600), f. late L. *parochia* diocese, PARISH. In ME. the *ch* was prob. (tʃ).]

A. *adj.* **1.** Of, belonging, or pertaining to a parish, or parishes in general. **a.** Of the ecclesiastical parish. ***parochial school*** (*Sc.* and *N. Amer.*): a school established and maintained by a religious body. Hence ***parochial schoolmaster***. (See also *parish school* s.v. PARISH *sb.* 7 b.)

[**1292** BRITTON I. xix. § 1 De eglises cathedrales parochieles et religiouses. **1314–15** *Rolls of Parlt.* I. 297/1 L'Eglise de Bosham, q'est parochiele.] **1393** *Complaint* in *Peasant's Rising* (1899) 47 After thoffertorie the masse parochiell. **1426** *Pol. Poems* (Rolls) II. 137 But in his chirche than parochialle Of Seint Johan he came with good entent. **1628** COKE *On Litt.* III. xi. §648. 344 A church parochiall may be donative and exempt from all ordinary jurisdiction. **1641** MILTON *Ch. Govt.* I. vi. Wks. (1851) 122 The poore dignity or rather burden of a Parochial Presbyter. **1704** NELSON *Fest. & Fasts* x. II. (1739) 598 Tithes..are the main legal Support of the Parochial Clergy. **1755** in *Sc. Nat. Dict.* (1968) VII. 37/2 How great importance it would be both to the College and the Parish to have a Parochial School. **1791** A. MURRAY in J. Sinclair *Statist. Acct. Scotl.* I. 457 The parochial schools are by no means supplied with such enlightened teachers as those that were formerly instrumental in diffusing this knowledge. **1792** D. MCDOUGAL in *Ibid.* III. 188 The parochial schoolmaster teaches Latin, English, Gaelic, [etc.]. *a* **1817** T. DWIGHT *Trav. New Eng.* (1821) I. 16 In these countries what may be called parochial schools are everywhere established. **1832** *Chambers's Edin. Jrnl.* I. 226/2 Acts of Parliament..have considerably enlarged the salaries of the parochial schoolmasters. **1842** *Burn's Eccl. Law* (ed. 9) I. IV. 299 A parochial chapel is that which hath the parochial rights of christening and burying; and this differeth in nothing from a church, but in the want of a rectory and endowment. **1851** C. CIST *Sk. Cincinnati in 1851* 58 Parochial Schools. The Catholic schools are the only ones which are strictly parochial. **1860** *Nor' Wester* (Red River Settlement) 14 Feb. 2/1 The Parochial Schools of our Protestant population speak for themselves, and I am sorry that they should have found disparagement at the hands of your correspondent. **1876** J. GRANT *Hist. Burgh & Parish Schools Scotl.* 100 The teacher of the burgh and parochial school was invariably session clerk and precentor. **1904** F. CRISSEY *Tattlings Retired Politician* 263 When he [*sc.* the Governor] was renominated the parochial school teachers camped on his trail and made it some hot for him. **1926** J. B. RITCHIE *Forres* 74 It was held that the Grammar School of Forres had never been a parochial school. **1955** *Western Star* (Corner Brook, Newfoundland) 10 Mar. 2/3 An amendment to the Municipal Act..would allow municipalities to exempt parochial schools from taxation. **1964** *Calgary Herald* 11 Feb. 15 Premier Roblin Monday proposed a partial solution to the dilemma of Manitoba's parochial schools. **1972** *Lebende Sprachen* XVIII. 35/2 US *parochial school*—BE/US *denominational school*. **1976** *Globe & Mail* (Toronto) 16 Jan. 29/8, I attended parochial school in Winnipeg. That meant I was Roman Catholic, that I ate fishcakes on Friday and smelled of candle wax and incense. **1978** *Times* 30 Jan. 12/5 As soon as you get more than half black in a school then the whites..put their youngsters in to private and parochial schools.

b. Of or pertaining to the civil or poor-law parish.

parochial board: in Scotland, an elective board charged with the administration of the Poor Law in a parish (later merged in the Parish Council).

1765 BLACKSTONE *Comm.* I. ix. 361 The statute of queen Elizabeth; in which the only defect was confining the management of the poor to small, parochial districts. **1836** DICKENS *Sk. Boz* (C.D. ed.) 4 It was at this period that he applied for parochial relief. **1861** W. BELL *Dict. Law Scot.* 641/1 Assessments [for the relief of the poor] are imposed by the parochial boards of the several parishes. **1894** *Act 56 & 57 Vict.* c. 73 §2 (2) Every parochial elector may, at any parish meeting..give one vote and no more.

2. *fig.* Pertaining or confined to a narrow area or region, as if within the borders of one's own parish; narrow, provincial. (Said of affairs, interests, etc.)

1856 EMERSON *Eng. Traits, Literature* Wks. (Bohn) II. 113 Parochial and shop-till politics..betray the ebb of life and spirit. **1867** LOWELL *Wks.* (1890) II. 276 The larger part of contemporary fame is truly parochial everywhere. **1899** C. TREVELYAN in *Daily News* 21 Feb. 5/1 Many Conservatives call social reform 'parochial'. We claim that it is the first duty of an imperial people.

3. *Ch. Hist.* Of or pertaining to the *parochia* or charge of a bishop in the early Church.

1861 J. G. SHEPPARD *Fall Rome* xii. 644 To the parochial cities were attached bishops, to the provinces metropolitans, to the dioceses patriarchs.

B. *sb.* (*rare.*) (elliptical uses of the adj.) **a.** A parish church. **b.** A parish clergyman.

1637 C. DOW *Answ. H. Burton* 189 Cathedrals have ever had certaine rites..which have not beene used in parochials. **1853** R. W. CHURCH in *Life Dean Lake* (1901) 184 In all the matters that happier parochials are so full of, and find the work and enjoyment of their lives in.

Hence **paˈrochially** *adv.*; **paˈrochialness.**

1690 STILLINGFLEET *Charge* 40 By the Fourth Council of Toledo, the Bishop was to Visit his whole Diocess, Parochially, every Year. **1840** J. H. NEWMAN *Let. to F. Rogers* 21 Mar., I have little or nothing to do at Oxford parochially, and a great deal at Littlemore. **1866** G. DAWSON *Addr. Open. Free Libr.*, Histories..minute in their parochialness, large in their amplitude. **1929** S. LESLIE *Anglo-Catholic* xiii. 182 He could never tell the truth to his father, since the Canon had parochially decreed that his cryptic daughter-in-law was no fit person to live in the parish. **1971** *Daily Tel.* 19 June 15/1 This [tax] relief has been very limited in its scope and I doubt whether its passing will be more than parochially mourned. **1977** *Ibid.* 19 Apr. 12 For a flower festival to open its golden jubilee celebrations at Addington Palace, Croydon, next month the Royal School of Church Music plans to have desert flowers from Southern California, orchids from Singapore and proteas from South Africa to demonstrate its ecumenism. More parochially, though, displays from this country will be the responsibility of the Surrey Flower Arrangers' Association.

parochiˈalic, *a. nonce-wd.* [See -IC.] = prec.

1848 *Tait's Mag.* XV. 490 Eloquent speeches were made to precede patriotic or parochialic resolutions.

parochialism (pəˈrəʊkɪəlɪz(ə)m). [See -ISM.]

1. 'Parochial' character or tendency; confinement of one's interests to a narrow sphere, with indifference to the world outside; local narrowness of view; petty provincialism.

1847 *Fraser's Mag.* XXXVI. 369 The narrow and jealous spirit of parochialism. **1881** *Athenæum* 30 July 141/2 A natural impatience of the parochialism of the petty Greek state. **1894** *Times* 7 Mar. 3/3 Able to..reconcile the conflicting claims of parochialism and nationalism.

2. Absorption in parish duties.

a **1884** M. PATTISON *Mem.* ii. (1885) 91 They took pains with their sermons—were, in short, steeped in parochialism.

parochiality (pərəʊkɪˈælɪtɪ). [f. late L. *parochiāl-is* PAROCHIAL + -ITY.]

1. The quality or state of being parochial. In *pl.* Parochial matters, affairs of the parish.

1769 SIR J. MARRIOTT *On Rights Univ.* 32[This] would be for the justices to take upon themselves in effect to determine the parochiality of colleges. **1871** CARLYLE in *Mrs. C.'s Lett.* II. 237 Neighbour Chalmers, great in parochialities, did his best. **1889** *Ch. Times* 28 June 587/2 A rigid parochiality is a thing of the past.

2. *fig.* Absorption in petty local interests; also *pl.* narrow or restricted interests or affairs.

1887 *Athenæum* 25 June 829/2 Her limited knowledge of real life, her intense strain of 'parochiality',..form a rather depressing combination. **1892** C. RHODES in *Pall Mall G.* 25 June 3/2 Home Rule..will lessen that absorption in trivialities and parochialities.

parochialize (pəˈrəʊkɪəlaɪz), *v.* [f. PAROCHIAL + -IZE.]

1. *trans.* To make parochial.

a **1846** *Brit. Crit.* cited in WORCESTER. **1870** GOULBURN *Cathedral System* i. 15 Do not parochialise [the Cathedrals], or turn them into vast parish churches. **1886** G. L. GOMME *Lit. Local Instit.*, A private act..to enclose, allot, and parochialise and make it chargeable to the poor.

2. *intr.* To do parish work; to work a parish.

1871 EARLE *Philol. Eng. Tongue* §310 Young ladies who helped the parson in any way were said to *parochialize*. **1881** *Ch. Times* 10 June 382 There are crowds of people who have not the very slightest aptitude for parochializing.

Hence **paˈrochializing** *vbl. sb.* and *ppl. a.*; **paˈrochialiˈzation.**

1877 T. SINCLAIR *Mount* (1878) 5 It can well be put, whether the parochialising of great men may not be in some way an immoral kind of pursuit. **1884** *Nonconf. & Indep.* 11 Dec. 1179/2 The new constituencies.. ought to be able to rise above parochialising influences. **1884** *Pall Mall G.* 4 Dec. 11/2 The 'parochialization' of our borough contests. A man who is nobody out of his own ward.. is often within his proper district a great gun. **1896** *Antiquary* June 171 The scheme.. included the parochialization of the cathedral.

†**pa'rochian**, *sb.* and *a.* *Obs.* Also 4–6 **parochien**, (4 **-ochin**, 6 **-ochen**, **perrochioun**). [(*a*) In ME. form, a. OF. *parochien*, ad. med.L. *parochiān-us* f. *parochia*; (*β*) in early mod.Eng. conformed to the med.L.: see PARISH and -AN. The ME. forms are not always separable from the parallel series *parosshien*, etc., which gave at length PARISHEN, *parishion*.]

A. *sb.* **1.** An inhabitant of a parish, a parishioner.

a. **1357** *Lay Folks Catech.* 61 Enioygne thair parochiens and thaire sugettes. [**13..** *Cursor M.* 26292 (Fairf.) Alsqua if at þi parochin [*Cott.* parischen] In synne lange lyande has bene. **1377** LANGL. *P. Pl.* B. v. 426, I kan.. Construe oon clause wel and kenne it to my parochienes [*v.r.* parisshens].] **1503–4** *Act 19 Hen. VII*, c. 29 *Preamble*, Amongeste the poure parochens of the paryche Churche aforeseid. **1552** LYNDESAY *Monarche* 4692 Bot he is oblyste, be resoun, To preche on tyll perrochioun.

β. **1502** *Will of Bartelet* (Somerset Ho.), Wheras I am parochian. **1529** CROMWELL in Merriman *Life & Lett.* (1902) I. 62, I gyue and bequeth to the poure parochians. **1765** BLACKSTONE *Comm.* I. xi. 387 In this act a pension is directed to be distributed among the poor parochians.

2. A parish clergyman. *rare.*

1621 BP. MOUNTAGU *Diatribæ* 401 For payment of the Tenth of a Tenth, from the Parochian vnto the Diocesan. **1715** M. DAVIES *Athen. Brit.* I. 177 Edward Brown, Parochian of Sandwich in Kent.

B. *adj.* Of or pertaining to a parish, parochial.

13.. *Cursor M.* 28429 Til oþer men þan to my right priest parochen. **1604** BACON *Consid. Ch. Eng.* Wks. 1879 I. 357/2 A computation taken of all the parochian churches. **1644** MAXWELL *Prerog. Chr. Kings* 72 The Parochian Pope, or independent Soveraigne in every Parish.

parochianar, -or: see PAROCHINER.

parochien, -in: see PAROCHIAN.

†'**parochin, -ine.** *Sc. Obs.* Also 6 **parr-.** [f. late L. *parochia*, OF. *paroche*, or ME. *paroch(e*, doublet of PARISH: the suffix is obscure; cf. PARISHING.] = PARISH.

1500–20 DUNBAR *Poems* xvi. 56 Sum givis parrochynins ful wyd, Kirkis of Sanct Barnard and Sanct Bryd. *Ibid.* lviii. 24. **1563** *Reg. Privy Council Scot.* I. 246 The toun and parochin of Dunfermling. *a* **1578** LINDESAY (Pitscottie) *Chron. Scot.* (S.T.S.) I. 159 [He] preichit to the said parochin him self. **1637** GILLESPIE *Eng. Pop. Cerem.* IV. viii. 35 The generall Confession of Faith, sworne and subscribed ..by the severall Parochines in the Land. **1819** W. TENNANT *Papistry Storm'd* I. (1827) 11 The tither.. In landwart parochins gaed stretchin'. **1824** SCOTT *Redgauntlet* Let. xi, He was lying in the auld kirkyard of Redgauntlet parochine.

†**pa'rochinal**, *a.* *Sc.* *Obs.* *rare*$^{-1}$. [? f. PAROCHIN + -AL[1].] = PAROCHIAL *a.* 1 a.

1636 W. SCOT *Apol. Narr.* (1846) 65 The Parochinall and Classicall Elderships.

†**pa'rochiner.** *Obs.* Chiefly *Sc.* and *north. Eng.* Forms: 5 **parochoner, -anar**, 6 **-ianar, -ianor**, 6–7 **-inar, -iner, -ener.** [f. PAROCHIAN (in its ME. forms) + -ER[1].] A doublet of PARISHIONER.

c **1450** *Cov. Myst.* (Shaks. Soc.) 71 So xulde every curat in this werde wyde ȝeve a part.. to his parochoneres that to povert slyde. **1481** *Peebles Charters*, etc. (1872) 188 Parochanaris. **1534** CRANMER *Misc. Writ.* (Parker Soc.) II. 278 A Controversy.. between you and divers of your parochinars. **1552** *Inv. Ch. Goods Yorksh.*, etc. (Surtees) II. 89 The sayd curate and parochianors. **1552** ABP. HAMILTON *Catech.* (1884) 5 That ye reid the samyn Catechisme to your awin parochianaris. **1561–2** *Reg. Privy Council Scot.* Ser. I. I. 205 All and sindrie parrochinaris, takkismen,.. possessouris and byaris. **1578–9** *Ibid.* III. 95 Quhen the parochinneris war absent. *a* **1651** CALDERWOOD *Hist. Kirk* (1843) II. 46 The parochiners of Restalrig.

†'**parochrie.** *Sc.* *Obs.* [f. *paroch*, PARISH + -RY.] A parochial area; a parish.

1581 *Sc. Acts Jas. VI* (1814) 211/1 That euerie paroche kirk and samekle boundis as salbe found to be a sufficient and a competent parochrie [*ed.* 1597 §100 Parochin] sall have þair awin pastoure wth a sufficient and Ressonable stipend.

parock, parocket: see PARROCK, PARAKEET.

parode ('pærəʊd). [ad. Gr. πάροδ-ος passage, entrance from the side, esp. that of the chorus in the orchestra, also the first song sung after entrance, f. παρ(α- by, by the side + ὁδός way.] In the ancient Greek drama, The first ode sung by the chorus after its entrance.

1869 SWINBURNE *Ess. & Stud.* (1875) 206 Between the opening speech of Silenus and the parode. **1870** R. C. JEBB *Sophocles' Electra* (ed. 2) 49/1 The parode or entrance-chant.

parode, obs. variant of PARODY *sb.*[1]

parodiable ('pærədɪəb(ə)l), *a.* [f. PARODY *v.* + -ABLE.] Capable of being parodied.

1888 *Sat. Rev.* 20 Oct. 467/1 Plenty of things.. which, if criticizable and parodiable.. are as unmistakably poetry as anything that was ever written. **1895** SAINTSBURY *Corr. Impress.* viii. 73 It is when a thing is imitable, not when it is parodiable, that it stands confessed as second-rate.

parodial (pə'rəʊdɪəl), *a.* [f. L. *parōdia*, a. Gr. παρῳδία PARODY *sb.*[1] + -AL[1].] Pertaining to or of the nature of a parody.

1807 E. S. BARRETT *Rising Sun* III. xii. 124 This parodial jeu d'esprit raised the glow of the company. **1856** *Titan Mag.* Dec. 496 A specimen.. of the parodial banter to which their productions are subject.

†**pa'rodic**, *a.*[1] *Math.* *Obs.* *rare.* [ad. Gr. παροδικ-ός passing, f. πάροδος a passing, a passage: see -IC.] Applied to any one of the series of degrees or powers of the unknown or variable below the highest that occurs in an equation.

1684 T. BAKER *Geometr. Key* 18 Of the Construction.. of Cubic Equations, affected under no Parodic Degree; or of Quadrato-quadratic, affected under the first Parodic Degree. **1710** J. HARRIS *Lex. Techn.* II, A Cubick Equation where no Term is wanting; but having all its Parodick Degrees. **1775** ASH, *Parodic*, regularly ascending or descending as the indices of the unknown quantity in adfected equations.

So †**pa'rodical** *a.*[1] *Obs.* = prec.

1674 JEAKE *Arith.* (1696) 336 All Magnitudes under the Power proposed, are called Parodical to the Power. **1710** J. HARRIS *Lex. Techn.* II. s.v., Parodical Degrees in an Equation in Algebra.

parodic (pə'rɒdɪk), *a.*[2] [ad. Gr. παρῳδικ-ός burlesque: see PARODY *sb.*[1] and -IC.] Of the nature of a parody, burlesque.

1828–32 in WEBSTER. **1873** WAGNER tr. *Teuffel's Hist. Rom. Lit.* II. 583 A parodic poem in derision of Pan. **1962** D. LESSING *Golden Notebk.* IV. 529 The word *correct* had an echoing parodic twang. **1974** C. A. PATRIDES *Eng. Poems George Herbert* 9 Herbert looked beyond the Bible for parodic purposes. **1976** *Archivum Linguisticum* VII. 27 H. B. Richardson.. follows Meyer-Lübke in suggesting *escuerzo* < *scorteum*, 'made of leather', meaning in 1544c 'toad'; this is possible, given the parodic context (the mock planctus for Urraca).

So **pa'rodical** *a.*[2] = prec.

1774 T. WARTON *Hist. Eng. Poetry* lviii. (1840) III. 343 This version [Drant's Horace] is very paraphrastic, and sometimes parodical. **1832** *Examiner* 227/1 Profane, parodical muse of Hone, Be pleased to keep your distance!

†**pa'rodious**, *a.* *Obs.* *rare*$^{-1}$. [f. L. *parōdia* PARODY *sb.*[1] + -OUS.] Of the nature of a parody, parodial.

a **1704** T. BROWN *Sat. Antients* Wks. 1730 I. 21 The Silli of the Greeks were parodious from one end to the other, which cannot be said of the Roman Satires.

parodist ('pærədɪst). [ad. F. *parodiste* (1723 in Hatz.-Darm.), f. Gr. παρῳδία: see -IST.] The author of a parody.

1742 MELMOTH *Fitzosb. Lett.* xlix. (1749) II. 18, I have observed in most of the modern Latin poems.. a remarkable barrenness of sentiment, and have generally found the poet degraded into the parodist. **1794** MRS. PIOZZI *Synon.* II. 276 Numberless have.. been the parodists of Johnson. **1889** J. JACOBS *Æsop's Fables* I. 197 Æsop's Fables have suffered too from the parodist.

parodistic (pærəʊ'dɪstɪk), *a.* [f. prec. + -IC.] Of the nature of a parody; that parodizes. So **paro'distically** *adv.*

1840 G. S. FABER *Christ's Disc. Capernaum* viii. 234 *note*, That gorgeous and seductive adulteress.. whom the stern voice of inspiration parodistically denounces as the mother of harlots and abominations of the earth. **1881** *Daily Tel.* 11 July 2/2 The concert included some curious parodistic variations by Ernst Scherz on the 'Carnival of Venice'. **1937** *Scrutiny* VI. 298 His [*sc.* Lord Berners']..measure is by no means summed up in his satirical and parodistic pieces. **1949** KOESTLER *Insight & Outlook* 427 Freud distinguished between the comic effects of imitation as such, and the parodistic attitude which usually accompanies it. **1975** *Times Lit. Suppl.* 21 Oct. 1305/1, I must record my partial disappointment, both at the parodistic and the confessional level. **1977** *Gramophone* June 106/3 The parodistic 'Danzon' is also, I think, the most entertaining of the three dances from Bernstein's ballet *Fancy Free.*

parodize ('pærədaɪz), *v.* [f. Gr. παρῳδία PARODY *sb.*[1] + -IZE.] = PARODY *v.* (*trans.* and *intr.*)

1658 BURTON *Itin. Anton.* 76 If first you will give me leave a little to parodize. **1681** BLOUNT *Glossogr.* (ed. 5), *Parodize*, to change the signification of a Verse, by altering some words. **1834** T. HOOK *G. Gurney* (1836) I. 52 At that period it was the rage to parodize tragedies.

parody ('pærədɪ), *sb.*[1] Also 7 **parode.** [ult. ad. Gr. παρῳδία a burlesque poem or song, f. παρ(α- beside, in subsidiary relation, mock-, etc. + ᾠδή song, poem; perh. immed. from L. *parōdia* or F. *parodie* (1622 in Hatz.-Darm.).]

1. A composition in prose or verse in which the characteristic turns of thought and phrase in an author or class of authors are imitated in such a way as to make them appear ridiculous, especially by applying them to ludicrously inappropriate subjects; an imitation of a work more or less closely modelled on the original, but so turned as to produce a ridiculous effect. Also applied to a burlesque of a musical work.

1598 B. JONSON *Ev. Man in Hum.* V. v, *Clem.* [reads some poetry]. How? this is stolne! *E. Kn.* A Parodie, a parodie! to make it absurder then it was. **1607** T. WALKINGTON *Opt. Glass* v. 35 All which in a parode, imitating Virgil wee may set downe. **1693** DRYDEN *Juvenal* Ded. (1697) 34 From some Fragments of the *Silli*,.. we may find, that they were Satyrique Poems, full of Parodies; that is, of Verses patch'd up from great Poets, and turn'd into another Sence than their Author intended them. **1774** J. BRYANT *Mythol.* II. 132 *note*, The history of Aristæus is nearly a parody of the histories of Orpheus and Cadmus. **1875** JOWETT *Plato* (ed. 2) IV. 134 The derivations in the Cratylus.. are a parody of some contemporary Sophist.

2. *transf.* and *fig.* A poor or feeble imitation, a travesty.

1830 COLERIDGE *Table-t.* 5 Oct., The Brussels riot.. is a wretched parody on the last French revolution. **1841** W. SPALDING *Italy & It. Isl.* II. 106 Tuscanella,.. now a petty hamlet, had a government whose complication looked like a parody on the Lombard republics. **1900** W. M. RAMSAY in *Expositor* Mar. 210 Such a parody of justice could be paralleled only by the very worst acts attributed to the Inquisition.

¶['A popular maxim, adage or proverb' (Bailey 1730–6). *Some error.*]

†**parody**, *sb.*[2] *Obs.* *rare.* [Only in Chaucer, and (after him) in Lydgate; app. a distorted form of F. *période* (14th c.), PERIOD (not found in Eng. in its proper spelling till later).] A period; a term of duration, life, etc.

? *c* **1374** CHAUCER *Troylus* v. 1548 Among al þis þe fyn of þe parodye [*gloss* (*Harl. MS.* 2280) duracion] Of Ector gan approchen wonder blyue. **1412–20** LYDG. *Chron. Troy* III. xxvii. (MS. Digby 230) lf. 129 b/2 When þe parodie of þis worþi knyȝt [Hector] Aprochen shal. *Ibid.* v. xxxviii. lf. 190/2 And howe þat he [Ulysses] myȝte not escape The Parodye þt was for him y shape; For Parchas han his laste terme set. **1430–40** —— *Bochas* IV. x. (MS. Bodl. 263) lf. 227/2 Parodie [*ed.* 1554 periody] of pryncis may nat chaungeed be The terme sette fro which thei may nat flee.

parody ('pærədɪ), *v.* [f. PARODY *sb.*[1]; perh. after F. *parodier* (1690 in Furetière).]

1. *trans.* To compose a parody on (a work or author); to turn into parody; to ridicule (a composition) by imitating it.

a **1745** POPE (J.), I have translated, or rather parodied, a poem of Horace, in which I introduce you advising me. **1763** J. BROWN *Poetry & Mus.* 149 The best Men, as well as the best Tragedies, were parodied or ridiculed more commonly than the worst. **1850** L. HUNT *Autobiog.* II. x. 24 He parodied music as well as words. **1894** LOWELL in *Century Mag.* May 24/2 [Milton] is easily parodied and easily imitated.

b. *intr.* To write or compose a parody.

1875 BROWNING *Aristoph. Apol.* 3365 Archippos punned, Hegemon parodied.

2. *trans.* In general sense: To imitate in a way that is no better than a parody.

1801 SOUTHEY *Thalaba* IX. *note*, I could show that it is the trick of Beelzebub to parody the costume of religion. **1869** ROGERS *Adam Smith's W.N.* I. Pref. 20 After his death, his [Pitt's] finance was parodied by incapable successors. **1878** MISS J. E. A. BROWN in *Sunday Mag.* Dec. 42 Children of the period, who parody the ways and the worldliness of men and women.

paroe, obs. form of *prahu*: see PROA.

†**parœce.** *Obs.* *rare.* [ad. L. *parœcia*, a. Gr. παροικία: see PARISH.] A parish. (A re-formation of the word after L. and Gr.)

1564 *Brief Exam.* ****** ij b, As yf you saw in one of your paroeces, what is conuenient for the whole Realme. *Ibid.* ******* ij, It shall not be lawefull for you to vse them before your paroeces.

†**pa'rœcian.** *Obs.* *rare*$^{-1}$. [f. L. *parœcia* (see prec.) + -AN.] A parish priest.

1725 tr. *Dupin's Eccl. Hist. 17th C.* I. v. 85 The Priests ordained for the Government of these Churches.. were call'd also.. Priests of a Parish, or Paroecians, and in fine, Rectors or Curates, a name which is become most common.

parœcious (pə'riːʃ(ɪ)əs), *a.* *Bot.* [f. Gr. πάροικος dwelling side by side, παροικία the condition of so dwelling (see PARISH) + -OUS; after *diœcious*, etc.] Having the male and female reproductive organs growing beside or near each other, as in certain cryptogams. Hence **pa'rœciously** *adv.*, **pa'rœciousness**; so **parœcism** (pə'riːsɪz(ə)m), the condition of being parœcious.

1882 *Encycl. Brit.* XIV. 718/2 They [*sc.* the antheridia] are usually seated in the axils of modified leaves (perigonial), sometimes appearing.. on special branches of the same plant (parœcious). **1890** in *Cent. Dict.* **1912** S. M. MACVICAR *Student's Handbk. Brit. Hepatics* p. xix, In some cases they [*sc.* the antheridia] occur below the female inflorescence,.. usually making this 'paroicous' [*sic*] form of inflorescence easy to recognize. **1968** E. V. WATSON *Brit. Mosses & Liverworts* (ed. 2) 34 Paroecious, bearing antheridia and archegonia close together, but not mixed, the antheridia being in the axils of bracts below those that surround the archegonia.

‖**parœmia** (pə'riːmɪə). *Rhet.* [L., a. Gr. παροιμία by-word, proverb, f. πάροιμ-ος by the way, f. παρ(α- by + οἶμος way, road.] A proverb, adage. Hence †**pa'rœmial** *a.* = PARŒMIAC *a.* 1.

1586 A. DAY *Eng. Secretary* II. (1625) 80 Parœmia, called amongst vs an Adage, or common saying, as thus: Who so toucheth pitch, shal be defiled therewith. **1589** PUTTENHAM *Eng. Poesie* (Arb.) 199 Parimia, or Prouerb, or, as we vse to call them, old said sawes, as thus: As the olde cocke crowes so doeth the chick: A bad Cooke that cannot his owne fingers lick. **1652** URQUHART *Jewel* Wks. (1834) 292 Allegories.. parabolary, ænigmatick or parœmial. **1716** M. DAVIES *Athen. Brit.* II. To Rdr. 1, I take these eighteen Parœmial Effata's for unquestionable Axioms.

parœmiac (pə'riːmıæk), *a.* (*sb.*) [ad. Gr. παροιμιακ-ός (in both senses), f. παροιμία: see prec.]

1. *prop.* Of the nature of a proverb, proverbial; in quot. = PARABOLIC 1 (after παροιμία = παραβολή in St. John's Gospel).

1820 A. KNOX in *Corr. w. Jebb* (1834) II. 451 It is a transcendant piece of parœmiac composition.

2. *Gr. Pros.* Applied to a form of verse: see B.

1699 BENTLEY *Phal.* 133 The Anapæst Feet run on to the Parœmiac, that is, to the end of the Sett, as if the whole had been a single Verse. **1778** BP. LOWTH *Prelim. Diss. Isaiah* p. xxxii, Somewhat like the parœmiac verse of the Greeks.

B. *sb. Gr. Pros.* That short line (anapæstic dimeter catalectic) with which an anapæstic system usually ends.

1803 R. PORSON *Let. Dalzel* in *Mus. Crit.* I. 334 The proportion of paroemiacs to other anapaests is scarcely one in ten.

parœmiographer (pəriːmı'ɒgrəfə(r)). [f. Gr. παροιμία: see PARŒMIA, -O¹, and -GRAPHER.] A writer of proverbs. So **parœmi'ography**, the writing of proverbs; a collection of proverbs.

1791–1823 D'ISRAELI *Cur. Lit., Philos. Proverbs*, The royal parœmiographer classes among their studies, that of 'understanding a proverb and the interpretation'. *Ibid. note*, England may boast of no inferior parœmiographers. **1818** W. TAYLOR in *Monthly Mag.* XLVI. 404 It seems to have been the model of the Parœmiography of Howell.

parœmiology (pəriːmı'ɒlədʒı). [f. as prec: see -LOGY.] The subject of proverbs. So **parœmi'ologist**, one who treats of proverbs.

1832 *Fraser's Mag.* VI. 501 A faithful historian of the parœmiology of his country. **1861** W. K. KELLY *Prov. all Nat.* (ed. 2) 93 That is all that Scotch parœmiologists condescend to tell us.

paroicious, *a. Bot.* = PARŒCIOUS.

1890 in *Cent. Dict.*

paroish, -ien, obs. ff. PARISH, PARISHEN.

paroke, parokeet, obs. ff. PARROCK, PARAKEET.

parol ('pærəl), *sb.* and *a.* Forms: 5–8 **parole,** 6 **parrall,** 6–7 **paroll,** 7 **parroll,** 6– **parol.** [Orig. *parole*, a. AF. and F. *parole*:—late pop. L. *paraula* :—*paravola*:—*parabola* word, speech, orig. story, PARABLE.]

A. *sb.* **1.** Something said or spoken; an oral statement or declaration; an utterance; a word. Chiefly in *Law*; now only in the legal phrase ***by parol***, by word of mouth.

[**1377** LANGL. *P. Pl.* B. xv. 113 ȝe aren enblaunched with *bele paroles* and with clothes also.] **1474** CAXTON *Chesse* 12 The symple parole or worde of a prynce. **1567** T. PAYNELL tr. *Amadis de Gaula* To Rdr., The dulcet and sweete parolls of his paramour. **1594** WEST *2nd Pt. Symbol.* §43 If the submission were by paroll. **1652** BENLOWES *Theoph.* XIII. cix. 250 But Saints with an attentive hope from high On Heav'ns Paroll do live and die. **1714** SCROGGS *Courts-leet* (ed. 3) 160 A Lease for three Years by Parol is a Forfeiture. **1844** WILLIAMS *Real Prop.* (1877) 389 A tenancy at will may be created by parol, or by deed.

2. *Law.* The pleadings filed in an action (formerly presented by word of mouth).

[**1598** KITCHIN *Le Court Leete et Court Baron* 193 b, Parol fuit mise sauns iour in precipe vers prior.] *a* **1625** SIR H. FINCH *Law* (1636) 360 If the tenaunt plead a warrantie with assets against him, the parroll shall demurre. **1741** T. ROBINSON *Gavelkind* vi. 108 And the youngest Son.. shall have his Age, or the Parol shall demur. **1768** BLACKSTONE *Comm.* III. 300. **1772** *Jacob's Law Dict.*, *Parol*, or *Pleadings*, are the mutual altercations between the plaintiff and the defendant; which at present are set down and delivered into the proper office in writing, tho' formerly they were usually put in by their counsel *ore tenus*, or *viva voce*.

B. *adj.* [attrib. use of the sb.]

1. Expressed or given orally; verbal, oral. Now only in *Law*, in such phrases as ***parol evidence***, as distinguished from documentary evidence.

1601 HOLLAND *Pliny* (1634) II. 31 Topping the heads of the highest Poppies there growing, without any answere parole, [he] dispatched them away. **1627–77** FELTHAM *Resolves* II. lxxxii. 334 He gave him a Law Parole; and inscribed it in his heart. **1706** PHILLIPS s.v. *Will*, *Will Parole* or *Nuncupative Will*, a Will only by Word of Mouth. **1768** BLACKSTONE *Comm.* III. xxiii. 367 Proofs, (to which.. the name of evidence is usually confined,) are either written, or parol, that is, by word of mouth. **1876** DIGBY *Real Prop.* x. §1. 379 The other terms of the tenancy may be proved by parol or verbal evidence without writing.

2. *Law.* Made (as a contract or lease) by word of mouth or in a writing not sealed.

1590 *Acts Privy Council* (1899) XIX. 178 A lease parol for three yeares of certaine growndes. **1600** *Manchester Court Leet Rec.* (1885) II. 158 Adam Smythe houldeth a Dunghill ..of James Radclyffe by lease parrall. **1717** *N. Riding Rec.* VIII. 35 Let to Ralph Wilson by paroll-lease.. for seven years. **1834** *Penny Cycl.* II. 195/1 Binding by deed poll, or by an agreement to execute an indenture, or a parol binding, have been held not to constitute an apprenticeship.

parole (pə'rəʊl), *sb.* Also 7 -ol, -oll. [a. mod.F. *parole* (parol) word (see prec.), in sense 'formal promise, engagement,' *parole d'honneur* word of honour, honourable engagement.]

1. (*a*) In full, ***parole of honour***: Word of honour given or pledged; *esp. Mil.* the undertaking given by a prisoner of war that he will not try to escape, or that, if liberated, he will return to custody under stated conditions, or will refrain from taking up arms against his captors for a stated period, generally for so long as the war then going on shall last. (*b*) Now generally used for a system of conditional release of selected prisoners before they have completed their sentences. (*c*) A person so liberated is said to be ***on parole***.

a **1616** BEAUMONT *Antiplatonic* iii, Loves Votries inthrale each others soule, Till both of them live but upon Parole. *c* **1648** *Short Abridgem. Britane's Distemper* 93 Upon his word of honour, or upon his paroll, as soldiers now call it. **1658–9** in *T. Burton's Diary* (1828) IV. 6 Mr. Turner and Mr. Trevor moved that his parole might be taken. Sir Arthur Haslerigge: The word parole is a new word; I move that the Sergeant take his bond. Sir George Booth: Seeing that we all understand not French, let us take his word; that is English... Sir Richard Temple: His word is sufficient. **1658** WILLSFORD *Secrets Nat.* 198 Licens'd to go upon their Paroles. **1662** J. DAVIES tr. *Mandelslo's Trav.* 130 Finding means to make an escape, contrarie to their parole. **1700** ASTRY tr. *Saavedra-Faxardo* I. 235 Aspersions.. upon him for the Breach of his Parole. **1722** DE FOE *Col. Jack* (1840) 315, I.. took their paroles of honour for my safety. **1776** R. J. MEIGS in Sparks *Corr. Amer. Rev.* (1853) I. 265, I arrived here the 22d instant, from Quebec, on my parole of honor, to return when called for. **1837** LOCKHART *Scott* xxvii. *note*, A good many French officers, prisoners of war, had been living on parole in Melrose. **1880** DIXON *Windsor* IV. xxviii. 259 They had broken their parole and fled. **1908** J. M. SULLIVAN *Criminal Slang* 18 *Parole*, released from prison, not a pardon. **1939** JOYCE *Finnegans Wake* 246 So they must have their final since he's on parole. **1966** *Listener* 3 Mar. 301/2 Parole was introduced in the United States—at the Elmira Reformatory in New York—in 1876; today some form of parole is in use in all the fifty States, as well as in the separate Federal prison system. **1972** J. GORES *Dead Skip* (1973) xvi. 116 We go see his parole officer. If he was sent up two years ago and is out now, he's on parole. **1974** *Times* 17 Apr. 14/1 Only a minority of the prisoners are getting a parole. *Ibid.* 14/2 Since the parole system began on April 1, 1968, about 14,000 prisoners have been paroled and about 1,550 are on parole at any one time.

b. *ellipt.* The condition of being on parole.

1667 ANNE WYNDHAM *King's Concealm.* (1681) 76 They had lately obtained their Paroles. **1855** MACAULAY *Hist. Eng.* xii. (1871) I. 735 This man [Rich. Hamilton] had violated all the obligations,.. had forfeited his military parole.

2. *Mil.* The password used only by the officers or inspectors of the guard; distinguished from the *countersign* given to all the men on guard.

1777 W. DALRYMPLE *Trav. Sp. & Port.* xliii, The governor of Madrid, having received the parole, he enters the room to the ambassadors. **1844** *Regul. & Ord. Army* 260 The Officers.. to be formed about forty paces in front of the centre, in two Ranks, facing the Line where they are to receive the old Parole.

fig. **1781** JOHNSON 8 May in *Boswell*, Classical quotation is the *parole* of literary men all over the world.

3. *Linguistics.* With pronunc. (parɔl). [f. *parole* in sense '(spoken) word, utterance'.] The actual linguistic behaviour of individuals, in contrast to the linguistic system (opp. LANGUE 3).

1935 W. F. TWADDELL in *Lang. Monogr.* XVI. 40 The utterance occurs, it is speech, 'parole'; the form exists, so to say, it is a part of the language 'langue'. **1939** L. H. GRAY *Foundations of Lang.* ii. 18 The third part of our definition of language.. is obviously concerned almost exclusively with *langage* rather than with *langue* or *parole*. **1953**, etc. [see LANGUE 3]. **1959** W. BASKIN tr. *F. de Saussure's Course in Gen. Linguistics* (1960) 13 Execution is always individual, and the individual is always its master: I shall call the executive side *speaking* (*parole*). **1968** J. LYONS *Introd. Theoret. Linguistics* i. 51 Let us follow de Saussure, and say that all those who 'speak English' (or are 'speakers of English') share a particular *langue* and that the set of utterances which they produce when they are 'speaking English' constitute instances of *parole*. **1971** D. CRYSTAL *Linguistics* 162 This leads to the correlative Saussurean concept of *parole*, the actual, concrete act of speaking. **1974** R. QUIRK *Linguist & Eng. Lang.* iii. 47 Every individual has a unique *parole*, a unique realization of what is possible in the language of his time and place. But at the same time this is not to deny that the *parole* of some individuals is more interesting than that of others. **1976** *Language* LII. 93 The particular contextual variant of the adjective may vary for each parole application.

4. *attrib.* and *Comb.* ***parole board, -breaker, clinic, engagement, matron, officer, scheme, sponsor, system.***

[**1908** *Charities & Commons* 26 Sept. 730/2 Clearly the Board of Parole is acting adversely to its own rule.] **1916** *N.Y. Times* 9 Jan. IV. 19/4 There will be weekly meetings.. of the Parole Board. **1938** C. HIMES *Black on Black* (1973) 163 He beseeched God to bless the warder and the deputy warder and the chaplain and the guards and the parole board and the outside judges and the governor and the sovereign state itself. **1956** B. HOLIDAY *Lady sings Blues* (1973) xix. 158 If I had been a booster or a petty thief I'd have the parole board helping me to get a job. **1972** 'W. HAGGARD' *Protectors* v. 63 Jack would be out in around five years, even less if the Parole Board were helpful. **1974** *Times* 17 Apr. 14 Prisoner's cases are considered by the local review committee.. and are then referred.. to the Parole Board for England and Wales. **1900** *Westm. Gaz.* 19 Sept. 4/2 It is difficult to see how we can with any show of fairness inflict any severe punishment on the parole-breakers. **1939** *Sun* (Baltimore) 22 Nov. 9/2 The State hospital system will institute an extensive program of parole clinics within the next few weeks to provide a follow-up service for furloughed and discharged patients which authorities believe may tend to curtail readmissions. **1812** *Chron.* in *Ann. Reg.* 89/2 A considerable number of officers have.. been ordered into confinement, for.. breaches of their parole engagements. **1907** *Charities & Commons* 24 Aug. 609/2 Three parole officers and one parole matron have been added to the police department. **1949** *Times-Picayune* (New Orleans) *Mag.* 13 Nov. 23/3 He became chief probation and parole officer for the federal court. **1970** G. JACKSON *Let.* Apr. in *Soledad Brother* (1971) 51 Parole officers have sent brothers back to the joint for selling newspapers. **1974** *Guidelines to Volunteer Services* (N.Y. State, Dept. Correctional Services) 36 *Parole officer*, title. A law enforcement officer, peace officer specifically charged with the supervision, and other related duties, of inmates who are released from correctional facilities via parole or some other form of conditional release. They are professional caseworkers in a law enforcement setting. **1973** *Daily Tel.* 20 June 8/6 During the five years of the parole scheme, only 36 of the 11,055 paroled from sentences for crimes of sex or violence had been further convicted of similar offences. **1973** *Philadelphia Inquirer* (Today Suppl.) 7 Oct. 14/3 The Rev. Anthony Velasquez, his parole sponsor, insists that 'Tony has never had a fair trial.' **1900** *Congress. Rec.* 24 Jan. 1130/2 We have in that State what is known as the parole system. Prisoners are put out on their good behavior. **1952** *Manch. Guardian Weekly* 8 May 4 The parole system should be reformed and speeded up. **1973** *Guardian* 31 Jan. 6/1 Lord Hunt.. said the parole system had been operating for five years and had shown a low failure rate in terms of recalling of prisoners.

parole (pə'rəʊl), *v.* [f. PAROLE *sb.*]

† **1.** *intr.* To pledge one's word. *Obs.*

1716 BP. NICOLSON in Ellis *Orig. Lett.* Ser. I. III. 392, I dare parole for him, if the Government sends him back.. he'll never petition for another return into his native country.

2. a. *trans.* To put (a prisoner) on his parole, to liberate on parole.

1790 D. FANNING *Narrative* (1861) 33, I then parolled the prisoners, except 30, which I sent to Wilmington. **1863** EMERSON *Emanc. Proclam.* (Cent.), The President by this act has paroled all the slaves in America; they will no more fight against us. **1893** LELAND *Mem.* II. 100 If you get [him], don't parole him. Shoot him at once. **1948** *Chicago Daily News* 27 Feb. 1/6 Another of those parolled.. put up $5,000 as a fee. **1973** *Publishers' Weekly* 2 Apr. 61/2 The murders took place in 1934. Mrs. Judd was parolled in 1971. **1974** [see PAROLE *sb.* 1]. **1975** *Daily Tel.* 3 Apr. 3/4 The two Great Train robbers paroled from jail yesterday had each served more than their legal minimum sentences.

b. *U.S.* To liberate (a prisoner) on his own recognizances.

1888 *Troy Daily Times* 7 Feb. (Farmer *Amer.*), The defendant was paroled on his own recognisance. **1888** *N.Y. Herald* 29 July (ibid.), He was paroled until August 8.

Hence **pa'roled** *ppl. a.*, put upon parole.

1865 L. N. BOUDRYE *Hist. Rec. Fifth N.Y. Cavalry* 196 It is remarkable how readily paroled Rebel soldiers affiliate with us. **1898** *Daily News* 7 June 5/4 The Spanish are already in American debt for paroled prisoners. **1908** *Independent* (N.Y.) 16 Jan. 146/2 Of his one thousand and seven or eight paroled men, up to this evening, seventy-seven have fallen. **1925** *Scribner's Mag.* Oct 410/1 A large proportion of paroled prisoners have been reclaimed from their evil ways by this judicious system. **1966** *Listener* 4 Aug. 155/1 There may be one or more conditions attached to it, and failure to observe them may cause the paroled prisoner to be returned to prison to finish his sentence. **1972** J. GORES *Dead Skip* (1973) xviii. 131 I'm looking for a paroled con named Howard Odum.

parolee (pərəʊ'liː). [f. PAROLE *sb.* or *v.* + -EE¹.] One who is released on parole.

1916 *Dialect Notes* IV. 327 *Parolee*.., one to whom parole is granted, esp. one sentenced to jail or reformatory or penitentiary who is released 'on parole'. **1934** *Sun* (Baltimore) 3 Dec. 8/3 One of the defects in the system in Baltimore is obvious—lack of supervision of parolees because of inadequate funds. **1937** *Ibid.* 9 Feb. 15/7 (*headline*) Parolee held in murder. **1938** *Yale Rev.* XXVIII. 157 The large majority of parolees are out to-day under such conditions as those which have just been described. **1957** V. NABOKOV *Pnin* 46 The Nansen Passport (a kind of parolee's card issued to Russian émigrés). **1964** M. ARGYLE *Psychol. & Social Probl.* v. 72 Shaw also organized a good deal of local support and sympathy for parolees and ex-convicts. **1973** *Publishers Weekly* 3 Dec. 40/1 In 1971, Long Island University opened its doors to young parolees. The ex-prisoners lived with the other students.. except that they were closely supervised by their parole officer. **1975** *Times Lit. Suppl.* 26 Sept. 1100/2 The process of making parole decisions, and the subsequent supervision of parolees, must be looked at from the viewpoint of all the various participants—prisoners, prison staff, paroling authority and parole supervisors.

parolein ('pærəliːn). *Pharm.* Also -oleine. [f. PAR(AFFIN *sb.* + L. *ole-um* oil + -IN¹, -INE⁵.] = *liquid paraffin* s.v. LIQUID *a.* 7.

Formerly a proprietary name in the U.K.

1892 MARTINDALE *Extra Pharmacopœia* (ed. 7) 311 Paroleine, a still more fluid odourless petroleum, or Adepsine Oil.. are used.. more especially as bases for Laryngeal and Nasal Spray Solutions or Pigments. **1908** *Practitioner* Apr. 441 A parolein spray containing a little oil of eucalyptus. **1964** S. DUKE-ELDER *Parsons' Dis. Eye* (ed. 14) xv. 184 Local treatment consists in relieving the dryness with methycellulose, parolein or weak alkaline solutions.

paroli ('pɑːrəliː), *sb.* [a. f. *paroli* (Oudinot 1653), a. It. *paroli* 'a grand part, set, or cast, at dice': cf. *parolare* 'to set or play at a grand part at dice' (Florio 1611); ? deriv. of *paro* pair, couple.] In faro and similar card games, the leaving of the money staked and the money won as a further stake; the staking of double the sum before staked. Cf. PARLAY *v.*

1701 FARQUHAR *Sir H. Wildair* II. i, I can dance a minuet, ..play at picquet; or make a paroli, with any Wildair in Christendom. *Ibid.* II. ii, The capot at picquet, the paroli at basset. **1709** COTTON *Compl. Gamester* (ed. 3) 179 The Paroli is..having won the Couch or first Stake, and having a mind to go on to get a *Sept-et-le-va*, you crook the Corner of your Card, letting your Mony lie without being paid the vallue of it by the *Talliere*. **1762** H. WALPOLE *Lett., to Montagu* clxxx, My friendship goes to sleep like a paroli at Pharoah, and does not wake again till their deal is over. **1794** *Sporting Mag.* IV. 43 That no parolis stand which are lost, and should retire. **1835** *Hoyle's Games* 46 At Rouge et Noir ..Paroli. Double the sum staked the first time. **1844** THACKERAY *B. Lyndon* ix. (1886) 127 When I turned up the ace of hearts and made Paroli.

Hence **'paroli** *v.*, to stake one's money over again, plus that gained by it.

1835 *Hoyle's Games* 61 When a punter gains, he may either take his money or paroli..should he again prove successful, he can paroli for quinze and le va.

parolist (pəˈrəʊlɪst). *rare.* [In sense 1, f. PAROL *sb.*; in 2, f. PAROLE *sb.* + -IST.]

†**1.** A user of affected words. *Obs.*

1604 T. WRIGHT *Passions* IV. i. 112, I heard once one of these worthy parolists who had got by the end the word 'intricat'; he..tould..that such a gentleman and he did beare most 'intricat' loue one to another: [meaning] intier.

2. One released on parole.

1901 *Scotsman* 16 Apr. 8/3 Parolists..admit..that further resistance signifies daily increasing misery for all.

parolivary (pəˈrɒlɪvərɪ), *a. Anat.* [PARA-¹ I.] Adjacent to the olivary body of the brain.

1893 *Syd. Soc. Lex., Parolivary body*, the Root-zone, anterior.

‖**paromœon** (pærəʊˈmiːɒn). *Gram.* [mod.L., a. Gr. παρόμοιον, neuter of παρόμοιος closely resembling, f. παρ(α- PARA-¹ + ὅμοιος like.] The beginning of two or more words in a sentence with the same letter; alliteration.

1706 PHILLIPS, *Paromœon*, a Figure in Grammar when all the Words of a Sentence begin alike, or with the same Letter; as *O Tite, tute, Tati, tibi tanta Tyranne tulisti.* **1793** HELY tr. *O'Flaherty's Ogygia* II. 74 In every fourth part of a distich, there should be a paromæon of two words.

paromology (pærəʊˈmɒlədʒɪ). *Rhet.* Chiefly in L. form **paromologia**. [ad. Gr. παρομολογία partial admission, f. παρ(α- subsidiary + ὁμολογία agreement, admission, HOMOLOGY.] A rhetorical figure in which something is conceded to an adversary in order to strengthen one's own position.

1586 A. DAY *Eng. Secretary* II. (1625) 97 *Paramologia*, where we grant one or more things meet to be marked or alledged, and forthwith doe inferre thereupon sufficient whereby to ouerthrow it. **1657** J. SMITH *Myst. Rhet.* 115 Sometimes we confesse that which will not prejudice us; and this is called *Paromologia*, confession: as, I grant that they are resolute, but..to their own undoing. **1864** WEBSTER, *Paromology*: so in later Dicts.

So †**paromoloˈgetic** *a.* [f. Gr. παρομολογεῖν to admit], of the nature of an admission.

1652 URQUHART *Jewel* Wks. (1834) 292 Figurative expressions..paradoxical, paramologetick, paradiastolary.

paromomycin (ˌpærəʊməʊˈmaɪsɪn). *Pharm.* [f. Gr. παρόμοιος closely resembling (f. παρ- (see PARA-¹) + ὅμοιος resembling): see -MYCIN.] A broad-spectrum antibiotic that is a mixture of the sulphates of certain substances (chemically related to neomycin) produced by some strains of the bacterium *Streptomyces rimosus*, and is given orally in the treatment of intestinal infections. Also called *paromomycin sulphate*.

1956 *Brit. Pat.* 797,568 Paromomycin is a stable amorphous white substance which is very soluble in water, moderately soluble in methanol and sparingly soluble in absolute ethanol. **1964** M. HYNES *Med. Bacteriol.* (ed. 8) x. 138 Kanamycin..and paromomycin..are chemically similar to neomycin (and streptomycin) and have much the same properties. **1969** J. H. THOMPSON in J. A. Bevan *Essent. Pharmacol.* li. 545 Paromomycin sulphate (Humatin) is usually prescribed as 10 to 25 mg per kilogram per day. *Ibid.*, Paromomycin has been used in the treatment of intestinal amebiasis, trichomoniasis, some types of bacterial dysentery, preoperatively to suppress the colonic flora, and in hepatic coma and precoma. **1974** *Indian Jrnl. Med. Res.* LXII. 495 Streptomycin and paromomycin were selected for treatment of cholera carriers at Hong-kong.

paromphalocele (pəˈrɒmfələʊsiːl). *Path.* [f. PAR(A-¹ + Gr. ὀμφαλός navel + κήλη tumour.] 'A hernia near the umbilicus' (*Syd. Soc. Lex.* 1893). Hence **paˌromphaloˈcelic** *a.*

1857 MAYNE *Exp. L.*, Paromphalocele, Paromphalocelic.

‖**paronomasia** (pərɒnəʊˈmeɪzɪə, -sɪə). Also *erron.* 7–8 **paran-**. [L., a. Gr. παρονομασία, f. παρ(α- PARA-¹ I + ὀνομασία naming, after παρονομάζειν to alter slightly in naming.] A playing on words which sound alike; a word-play; a pun.

1579 E. K. *Spenser's Sheph. Cal.* Jan. Gloss., A Paronomasia or playing with the word, where he sayth *I loue thilke lasse, alas* etc. **1666** DRYDEN *Ann. Mirab.* Let. Sir R. Howard, The jingle of a more poor paranomasia. **1727** POPE, etc. *Art of Sinking* 97 The Paranomasia, or Pun, where a word, like the tongue of a jackdaw, speaks twice as much by being split. **1820** SCOTT *Monast.* xxxiii, A most idle paronomasia. **1879** *Expositor* X. 20 Both classes of paronomasia are found in St. Paul.

Hence **paronoˈmasial, paronoˈmasian, paronomasiˈastic** *adjs.*, of or pertaining to paronomasia; characterized by paronomasia; so **paronoˈmastic, -ical** *adjs.*, **paronoˈmastically** *adv.*

1823 *New Monthly Mag.* VIII. 108 [This] raised..a ludicrous *paranomasial association in the minds of some of the audience. **1890** *Sat. Rev.* 13 Sept. 309/2 The playful, *paronomasian method of the poet. **1902** *Speaker* 4 Jan. 400/1 The finesses allusive, *paronomasiastic, and the like of the Erasmian Latin. *c***1810** COLERIDGE in *Lit. Rem.* (1838) III. 266 The very letter of the famous *paronomastic text proves that Peter's confession, not Peter himself, was the rock. **1664** H. MORE *Exp. 7 Epist.* Pref. b ij, The sound of Θυάτειρα and θυγάτειρα are near enough for *paronomasticall Allusion in any indifferent man's judgement whatsoever. **1888** *Bookworm* I. 273 Cleverly paronomastical is 'A Cursory History of Swearing' by Julian Sharman. **1846** TREGELLES *Gesenius' Hebr. Lexicon* s.v. [*aˈbîw*], For the purpose of *paronomastically answering to the words.

†**paroˈnomasy**. *Obs.* Also 7 *erron.* **paran-**. [a. F. *paronomasie* (1557 in Hatz.-Darm.).] = PARONOMASIA.

1601 B. JONSON *Poetaster* III. i, A kind of paranomasie, or agnomination. *a* **1677** BARROW *Serm.* Wks. 1716 I. 142 Some elegant figures and tropes of rhetorick.. paronomasies, oxymorons and the like, frequently used by the best speakers.

‖**paronychia** (pærəʊˈnɪkɪə). Also 7 **paˈronychie**. [L., a. Gr. παρωνυχία a whitlow, f. παρ(α- PARA-¹ I beside + ὄνυξ, ὀνυχ- nail. In F. *paronychie* (Paré *c* 1560). Cf. also PANARICIUM.]

1. *Path.* An inflammation about the finger-nail; a whitlow.

1597 [See PANARICIUM] callede *Panaris* or *Paronichia.* **1663** BOYLE *Usef. Exp. Nat. Philos.* II. v. xi. 229 Tormented with a *Paronychia* for four daies together. **1696** PHILLIPS (ed. 5), *Paronychie*, a preternatural swelling in the Fingers ends, very troublesome. **1741** A. MONRO *Anat.* (ed. 3) 5 The deep-seated kind of *Paronychia.* **1874** ROOSA *Dis. Ear* 120 The pain will be intense, like that from a paronychia.

2. *Bot.* A genus of herbaceous plants (N.O. *Illecebraceæ*), with narrow leaves, and conspicuous silvery stipules usually concealing the minute apetalous flowers; whitlow-wort.

1666 LOCKE *Let. to Boyle* 24 Feb., B.'s Wks. 1772 VI. 537, I have endeavoured to provide paronychia, and I think I shall be able to forward pretty good store of it..it begins to be in flower..about a fortnight hence. **1861** MISS PRATT *Flower. Pl.* II. 315.

Hence **paroˈnychial, paroˈnychic** *adjs.* (*Path.*), pertaining to or of the nature of paronychia.

1857 MAYNE *Expos. Lex.*, Paronychic. **1890** *Cent. Dict.*, Paronychial.

paronym (ˈpærənɪm). [ad. Gr. παρώνυμον, from neuter of παρώνυμος 'formed by a slight change of the word, derivative'.] A word which is derived from another, or from the same root; a derivative or cognate word.

1846 SMART Suppl., *Paronyme*, a paronymous word. **1888** P. SHOREY in *Amer. Jrnl. Philol.* Oct. 290 Plato was determined to preserve the dignified associations of Being and its paronyms for the abstract studies he delighted to honor.

b. 'A word of one language which translates a word of another with only a difference of termination or other slight change' (*Cent. Dict.* 1890): cf. PARONYMIZE, PARONYMY 3.

Hence **paroˈnymic** *a.* = PARONYMOUS.

1890 in *Cent. Dict.*

paronymize (pəˈrɒnɪmaɪz), *v.* [f. prec. + -IZE.] *trans.* To convert into a paronym; to adapt (a foreign word) by giving it a native form. So **paronymiˈzation**.

1885 B. G. WILDER in *Proc. Amer. Assoc. Adv. Sc.* XXXIII. 529 *note*, I have suggested that, in English works, so far as possible, the names be given an English aspect by paronymisation. **1889** *Nation* (N.Y.) 18 July 58/3 The Latin words are commonly paronymized rather than translated into inelegant or misleading heteronyms; e.g. *pedunculus* is Anglicised as *peduncle*, not *footlet*.

paronymous (pəˈrɒnɪməs), *a.* [f. Gr. παρώνυμ-ος (see PARONYM) + -OUS.]

1. Of words: Derived from the same root; radically connected, cognate.

1661 BLOUNT *Glossogr.* (ed. 2), *Paronymous* (Gr.), pertaining to words or terms that have denomination from the same thing, but differ in case or termination. **1697** tr. *Burgersdicius his Logic* I. xxv. 100 A Paronymous is a Concrete Word, and so deriv'd from the Primitive, as that it differs only from it in Termination. **1827** WHATELY *Logic* III. viii. 157 The Fallacy..that paronymous words (i.e. those belonging to each other, as the substantive, adjective, verb, &c. of the same root) have a precisely correspondent meaning; which is by no means universally the case. **1832** AUSTIN *Jurispr.* (1879) I. xxiv. 482 The term 'delitum' is exactly coextensive with the..paronymous expression 'delitor'.

b. Derived from a word in another language with the same or similar form.

1890 in *Cent. Dict.*

†**2.** (See quots.)

1836 SMART, *Paronymous*, near to another word in meaning, as distinguished from *synonymous*..it may be said that there are few if any synonymous words in a language, but many that are *paronymous.* **1846** WORCESTER, *Paronymous*, alike in sound, but differing in orthography and signification; as, *air* and *heir*.

paronymy (pəˈrɒnɪmɪ). [f. Gr. παρώνυμ-ος (see PARONYM) + -Y. (Gr. παρωνυμία = a by-name, a surname.)]

†**1.** = PARONOMASIA. *Obs.*

1627 W. SCLATER *Exp. 2 Thess.* (1629) 29 *Tribulation to them that trouble.* The paranomasie, or paronymie, I thinke is not casuall,..but intended to point at the *Talio* God holds in recompencing.

†**2.** The family of words derived from one root.

1682 *Weekly Mem. Ingen.* 375 The Paronymie or derivatives from thence.

3. Formation from a word in another language with but slight change; adaptation of a foreign word to native word-types.

1885 B. G. WILDER in *Jrnl. Nervous & Ment. Dis.* July (*title*) Paronymy versus Heteronymy as Neuronymic Principles. **1885–9** *Buck's Handbk. Med. Sc.* VIII. 519 (Cent.) The relation between the Latin *pons* and the French *pont* is one of paronymy; but between *pons* and the English *bridge* it is one of heteronymy.

paroo, obs. var. *prahu*: see PROA.

‖**paroophoron** (pærəʊˈɒfərɒn). *Anat.* [mod.L., f. PAR(A-¹ + *oöphoron* ovary.] **a.** = PAROVARIUM. **b.** A small remnant of the Wolffian body in the female, corresponding to the parepididymis in the male. So ‖**paroophoˈritis** *Path.*, inflammation of the parts adjacent to the ovary.

1872 PEASLEE *Ovar. Tumors* 12 The paroophoron, or parovarium, is a rule of embryonic life. **1881** BALFOUR *Comp. Embryol.* II. xxiii. 597 Remnants of the anterior non-sexual parts of the Wolffian bodies have been called by Waldeyer parepididymis in the male, and paroophoron in the female. **1893** *Syd. Soc. Lex., Paroöphoritis.*

paropa, -pos, a fabric: see PEROPUS.

parophite (ˈpærəfaɪt). *Min.* [Named 1852, f. PAR(A-¹ I + OPHITE, from its resemblance to ophite or serpentine.] A variety of PINITE, allied to agalmatolite, of various colours (greenish, yellowish, reddish, or greyish).

1862 DANA *Man. Geol.* §67. 61 The Parophite of Hunt is a rock of similar composition, from Canada.

‖**paˈropsis**. *Path.* [mod.L., f. Gr. παρα- PAR(A-¹ + ὄψις sight, vision.] (See quot.)

1822 GOOD *Study Med.* III. 198 Paropsis is literally 'diseased or depraved vision'... The ophthalmic monographists..have most unmercifully enlarged the list under this genus. **1857** MAYNE *Expos. Lex.*

paroquet (ˈpærəkɪt). [Another form of PARAKEET.]

1. = PARAKEET, q.v. for forms and quotations.

2. *Comb.* **paroquet (perroquet) auk**, a small auk, *Ombria psittacula* (*Cyclorhynchus psittaculus*), inhabiting the coasts and islands of the northern Pacific; **paroquet-bur**, a name in Jamaica of the plants of the genus *Triumfetta*: see quot.

1802 BINGLEY *Anim. Biog.* (1813) II. 345 The Perroquet Auk..is found in flocks in Kamtschatka, in the isles towards Japan, and on the western shores of America. **1835** *Penny Cycl.* III. 101/1 The Perroquet Auk is about eleven inches in length... The head, neck, and upper parts are black, blending into ash-colour on the fore-part of the neck; the under parts from the breast are white; the legs are yellowish. **1866** *Treas. Bot.* 1176 In Jamaica the name Paroquet Burr is ..given to them [species of *Triumfetta*], on account of the green paroquets feeding on their ripe fruits or burrs.

paroral (pəˈrɔːrəl), *a. Zool.* [f. PAR(A-¹ I + ORAL *a.*] Situated beside the mouth: applied to a series of cilia in certain infusorians.

1882 W. SAVILLE KENT *Infusoria* II. 762 A fourth, but as yet rarely observed, series [of cilia]..obtaining in Gastrostyla..he proposes to distinguish as the 'paroral' one.

parorchid (pəˈrɔːkɪd). *Anat.* Also in L. form **parorchis**. [ad. mod.L. *parorchis*, f. PAR(A-¹ + Gr. ὄρχις testicle: cf. *orchid*.] The epididymis.

1878 BELL *Gegenbaur's Comp. Anat.* 614 The vasa efferentia pass to a parorchis. *Ibid.* 617 The primitive kidneys are partly united with the testes, and there form the parorchids (epididymes).

‖**parorexia** (pærɒˈrɛksɪə). *Path.* [mod.L., f. PAR(A-¹ + Gr. ὄρεξις appetite.] Perverted appetite.

1898 *Allbutt's Syst. Med.* V. 500 In neurasthenia this anorexia or parorexia leads to emaciation.

paros, parosche, (-osse, -ossh(e,) -en, -ian, obs. ff. PARISH, -EN.

paroschen, ? scribal error for *parosche*, PARISH.

c **1330** R. BRUNNE *Chron. Wace* (Rolls) 5774 To a dyocise langed a cite, & ordened paroschens [*v.r.* parisches, WACE parosces] for to be.

‖**parosmia** (pəˈrɒzmɪə). *Path.* [mod.L., f. PAR(A-¹ I + Gr. ὀσμή smell.] Perverted sense of smell. Also (irreg.) **paˈrosmis.**

1822 GOOD *Study Med.* III. 254 *Parosmis.* Morbid Smell. Sense of smell vitiated or lost. This is the *parosmia* and *anosmia* of many writers. **1884** M. MACKENZIE *Dis. Throat & Nose* II. 472 Parosmia is often met with in lunatics. **1897** *Allbutt's Syst. Med.* IV. 695 Parosmia, or perversion of the sense of smell, in which imaginary or subjective perceptions of odours are present.

parosteal (pəˈrɒstiːəl), *a. Anat., Zool., Path.* [f. Gr. παρ(α- PARA-¹ I + ὀστέον bone: see OSTEAL.] = PAROSTOTIC.

1854 JONES & SIEV. *Pathol. Anat.* (1874) 146 Osseous tumours,..and especially articulations, called by Virchow parosteal tumours. **1870** ROLLESTON *Anim. Life* 36 Those 'parosteal' bones which are developed from the skin and the subcutaneous and aponeurotic tracts underlying it.

So **parostic** (pəˈrɒstɪk), *a. Path.* [f. mod.L. *parostia*], pertaining to or characterized by *parostia* or defective ossification.

1822–34 *Good's Study Med.* (ed. 4) IV. 248 A parostic diathesis seems from some cause or other to have existed.

‖**parostosis** (pærɒˈstəʊsɪs). *Anat., Zool., Path.* [f. as prec. + -OSIS.] The formation of bone outside the periosteum, as in the integument or connective tissue, or the sheaths of blood-vessels. (*Syd. Soc. Lex.* 1893.) Hence **paroˈstotic** *a.*, of or formed by parostosis.

1870 ROLLESTON *Anim. Life* Introd. 63 No 'parostotic' bones are ever developed in relation with either limb-girdle.

parot, obs. form of PARROT.

parotic (pəˈrɒtɪk), *a. Anat.* and *Zool.* [ad. mod.L. *parōtic-us*, F. *parotique*, f. PAR(A-¹ I + Gr. οὖς, ὠτ- ear, ὠτικός of the ear.] Situated beside or near the ear; parotid.

1857 MAYNE *Expos. Lex.*, The parotic region in birds is the turn of the ear. **1871** HUXLEY *Anat. Vert. Anim.* v. 220 The parotic apophysis on the posterior face. **1893** *Syd. Soc. Lex.*, *Parotic process*, in the skull of the *Teleostei*, formed by the union of the *Pterotic* and *Epiotic* bones.

parotid (pəˈrɒtɪd), *a.* and *sb.* Also 7–8 **-ide**. [a. F. *parotide* (1545 in Hatz.-Darm.), or ad. L. *parōtis, parōtid-*: see PAROTIS.]

A. *adj.* (*Anat., Zool., Path.*) Situated beside or near the ear; applied esp. to a lobulated racemose gland (in man, the largest of the three salivary glands), situated one on each side, just in front of the ear, and having a duct (***parotid duct*** or *Stenson's duct*) opening into the mouth opposite the second upper molar tooth; also to the arteries, nerves, veins, etc. belonging to the same region, and to inflammation, tumours, etc. occurring in it.

1687 *Phil. Trans.* XVI. 486 Neither was there any swelling formed in the Maxillary or Parotide Glandules. **1758** J. S. *Le Dran's Observ. Surg.* (1771) 10 The Parotide is not a single Gland. **1807–26** S. COOPER *First Lines Surg.* iv. (ed. 5) 311 The parotid duct passes beneath the integuments of the cheek over the masseter muscle. **1877** ROBERTS *Handbk. Med.* (ed. 3) I. 178 Mumps is chiefly characterized anatomically by inflammation of one or both parotid glands. **1878** KINGZETT *Anim. Chem.* 53 Parotid saliva is alkaline and viscous.

B. *sb.* **1.** *Anat.* and *Zool.* The parotid gland.

1770 T. PERCIVAL *Ess.* (1777) I. 383 Indurated parotids, and deafness have ensued. **1841–71** T. R. JONES *Anim. Kingd.* (ed. 4) 835 The parotids vary principally in their proportionate size.

†**2.** *Path.* A parotid tumour. *Obs.*

1747 tr. *Astruc's Fevers* 214 Parotids, which are nothing else but tumified lymphatic, not salival glands, situated about the neck, ears, etc. These tumours have given occasion to two different systems for their explication. **1808** *Med. Jrnl.* XIX. 450 We saw some parotids, but almost all were mortal, notwithstanding the stimulating topicks.

So **parotiˈdeal, parotiˈdean** *adjs.* = PAROTID *a.*; ‖**parotiˈditis** [see -ITIS] = PAROTITIS.

1831 R. KNOX *Cloquet's Anat.* 99 The breadth of the face is..limited on each side by the parotideal edge of the inferior maxillary bone. **1842** E. WILSON *Anat. Vade M.* (ed. 2) 275 The Parotidean Arteries are 4 or 5 large branches ..given off from the external carotid. **1878** T. BRYANT *Pract. Surg.* I. 520 Parotiditis, or 'Mumps', is a simple, although an infectious disease.

parotidectomy (pəˌrɒtɪˈdɛktəmɪ). *Surg.* [f. PAROTID *sb.* + -ECTOMY.] Excision of the parotid gland.

1893 DUNGLISON *Dict. Med. Sci.* (ed. 21) 825/1 *Parotidectomy*, operation for excision of the parotid gland. **1951** MARSHALL & MILES in *Surg. Pract. Lahey Clinic* 122 The operation may be altered to extensive subtotal parotidectomy. **1974** *Lancet* 7 Dec. 1353/2 The patient's left parotid gland was explored, found to contain a mixed tumour in the deep lobe and a total parotidectomy was performed. **1974** J. D. MAYNARD in R. M. Kirk et al. *Surgery* ix. 201 Intraoral duct ligation may lead to parotid atrophy and cessation of symptoms in some cases, otherwise conservative parotidectomy must be considered.

‖**parotis** (pəˈrəʊtɪs); usually in pl. **parotides** (pəˈrəʊtɪdiːz). [L., a. Gr. παρωτίς, παρωτιδ-, f. παρ(α- PARA-¹ I beside + οὖς, ὠτ- ear: see -ID.]

1. The parotid gland.

1615 H. CROOKE *Body of Man* 823 Vnder the eares and behind them there are many glandules called Parotides. **1747** tr. *Astruc's Fevers* 246 When the parotis begins to suppurate, let the suppuration continue for some time.

†**2.** A parotid tumour. *Obs.*

1693 tr. *Blancard's Phys. Dict.* (ed. 2), *Parotides*,..also a preternatural Swelling of those Glandules. **1720** QUINCY tr. *Hodges' Loimologia* 148 Deafness joined with Drowsiness were signs the Parotides would soon appear. **1813** T. BUSBY tr. *Lucretius* II. 25 (Jod.) The hard dry parotides induced mortification. **1893** *Syd. Soc. Lex.*, *Parotis*,..Also, an old term for a swelling of the parotid gland.

parotitis (pærəʊˈtaɪtɪs). *Path.* [irreg. for PAROTIDITIS, f. prec.: see -ITIS.] Inflammation of the parotid gland, or of neighbouring structures; usually constituting the disease called *mumps*. Hence **parotitic** (-ˈtɪtɪk) *a.*, pertaining to or affected with parotitis.

1822 GOOD *Study Med.* II. 337 In advanced life parotitis is sometimes apt to run into a chronic form. **1857** MAYNE *Expos. Lex.*, Parotitic. **1880** J. W. LEGG *Bile* 469 Such symptoms as..a parotitis, and injection of the conjunctivæ. **1897** *Allbutt's Syst. Med.* III. 358 Though it [i.e. Mumps] is called Parotitis, the other salivary glands as well as the parotid are usually affected.

parotoid (pəˈrəʊtɔɪd), *a.* (*sb.*) *Zool.* [irreg. f. PAROTIS + -OID.] Applied to certain glands of the skin forming warty excrescences near the ears in some batrachians, as toads. Also as *sb.*

1873 MIVART *Elem. Anat.* xii. 488 The so-called 'parotoid' glands, as in the common Toad. **1875** HUXLEY in *Encycl. Brit.* I. 762/1 In many Anura and Urodela these glandular structures attain a greater complication of structure,..and constitute what are termed the 'parotoid' glands.

parott(e, parour, obs. ff. PARROT, PARURE.

parous (ˈpærəs), *a. Obstet. Med.* [f. L. element *-par-us* bearing; see next. Cf. PARITY².] Having brought forth offspring.

1898 G. E. HERMAN *Dis. Women* ix. 87 In text-books of anatomy it is stated that the parous uterus is normally larger than the virgin uterus.

-parous, *suffix*, f. L. *-parus* bearing, producing (belonging to *par-ĕre* to produce, bring forth; in Fr. *-pare*) + -OUS, as in *oviparus* oviparous, *viviparus* viviparous; so in numerous later and modern formations, as *albuminiparous, biparous, criniparous, larviparous, multiparous, uniparous*, etc.

Parousia (pəˈruːzɪə). *Theol.* Also **parousia.** [ad. Gr. παρουσία presence, in N.T. (Matth. xxiv. 27, etc.) used as below.] The Second Coming or Advent of Christ. Also *transf.*

1875 *Expositor* May 385 The feverish expectation of a visible *parousia* was requiring modification. **1895** *Dublin Rev.* Apr. 334 The date of Our Lord's second coming, the Parousia. **1910** W. MONTGOMERY tr. *Schweitzer's Quest Historical Jesus* xix. 360 The Parousia of the Son of Man is to be preceded according to the Messianic dogma by a time of strife and confusion. **1918** J. H. LECKIE *World to Come* ii. 66 The Church has held its belief in the Parousia in varying forms throughout the ages. **1927** A. H. MCNEILE *Introd. New Testament* 112 At the end of his [*sc.* St. Paul's] life, the thought of the Parousia..had practically faded from his mind. **1936** A. M. RAMSEY *Gospel & Catholic Ch.* iii. 42 Christ is in us—yet the Parousia is in the future. **1941** AUDEN *New Year Let.* 39 Thus *Wordsworth*..Saw in the fall of the Bastille The Parousia of liberty. **1964** *Listener* 27 Feb. 352/1 Your personal Parousia, the Biggest Show on Earth! **1969** A. T. HANSON in A. Richardson *Dict. Christian Theol.* 113/2 The complaint that the *parousia* (coming) had not arrived as expected. **1977** *Illustr. London News* Nov. 50/4 A pale yellow cross is just visible against a background of deeper yellow... Austin Winkley [the architect] calls it a Parousia cross, significant of the mysterious end of a mysterious journey. **1977** G. W. H. LAMPE *God as Spirit* iii. 65 The presence of the Spirit is..a substitute for the early *parousia* that had at first been expected.

Hence **Paˌrousiaˈmania**, excitement or frenzy aroused by the thought of the Parousia.

1904 *Amer. Jrnl. Relig. Psychol. & Educ.* May 40 Men chanted, raved, spoke in unknown tongues, prophesied, gazed up into heaven all day, longed for vision, with a real parusiamania.

‖**parovarium** (pærəʊˈvɛərɪəm). *Anat.* [f. PAR(A-¹ I + OVARIUM.] A remnant of the Wolffian body in the female, consisting of a group of closed tubules lying between the ovary and the Fallopian tube; corresponding to the *epididymis* in the male. (Also called *organ of Rosenmüller*.)

1859 TODD *Cycl. Anat.* V. 594/1 The parovarium is formed out of the Wolffian body. **1872** [see PAROOPHORON]. **1888** ROLLESTON & JACKSON *Anim. Life* 426 The anterior portion of the mesonephros is in this case converted into epididymis in the male, parovarium in the female.

So **paroˈvarian** *a.*, pertaining to the parovarium.

1878 T. BRYANT *Pract. Surg.* (1879) II. 269 The majority of the pure unilocular cysts are broad ligament cysts or parovarian. **1897** *Allbutt's Syst. Med.* III. 585 The variety of tumour most likely to be mistaken for free fluid in the peritoneum is the parovarian cyst. *Ibid.* IV. 432 Ascitis or parovarian cystoma.

Parowax (ˈpærəʊwæks). Also **parowax.** [f. *paro-* (f. PARA(FFIN *sb.*) + WAX *sb.*¹] A proprietary name in the U.S. for paraffin wax.

1909 *Official Gaz.* (U.S. Patent Office) 7 Dec. 301/2 Standard Oil Company... *Parowax*. Particular description of goods.—Paraffin. **1926** *Daily Colonist* (Victoria, B.C.) 4 July 2/1 (Advt.), Parowax, for sealing, lb. 15c. **1945** *Industr. & Engin. Chem.* June 518/2 To extend the series of *n*-paraffins into the range of higher paraffins, Parowax was used. Fractional crystallization..showed the composition to be substantially normal paraffins... The paraffins ranged from C_{20} to C_{28}, with an average number of 23·8 carbon atoms. **1974** J. E. UNDERHILL *Wild Berries Pacific Northwest* 23 Cook until thick, then pour into hot sterilized jars, and seal promptly, with parowax or tight lids.

parowre, obs. form of PARURE.

paroxysm (ˈpærəksɪz(ə)m). Also 7 **-isme, -ysme, -im(e,** 7–8 **-ism.** [a. F. *paroxysme* (16th c.), earlier *peroxime* (13–14th c. in Hatz.-Darm.), ad. med.L. *paroxysmus* irritation, exasperation, a. Gr. παροξυσμός, f. παροξύνειν to goad, exasperate, irritate, f. παρ(α- PARA-¹ I + ὀξύν-ειν to sharpen, goad, render acute. In 16th c. used in Greek or L. form.]

1. *Path.* An increase of the acuteness or severity of a disease, usually recurring periodically in its course; a violent temporary access of disease; a fit.

[**1577** FRAMPTON *Joyfull Newes* II. 86 When thei bee in their traunce, or *paroxismos* the smoke of it maketh theim to awake.] **1604** THO. WRIGHT *Passions* v. §2. 161 When the paroxime was vpon them. **1605** B. JONSON *Volpone* III. v, Againe, I feare a Paroxisme. **1654** WHITLOCK *Zootomia* 83 If they can..go but so far, as to call the fit of an Ague, a *Paroxysme*,..my admiring Patient taketh him to be a great Schollard. **1704** F. FULLER *Med. Gymn.* (1711) 34 They may give wonderful Relief in the Paroxism. **1802** *Med. Jrnl.* VIII. 409 In the course of the paroxysm she felt great aversion to water. **1876** tr. *Wagner's Gen. Pathol.* (ed. 6) 16 The period in which the symptoms make their appearance is called the paroxysm or attack.

2. A violent access of action or emotion; a fit, convulsion (*e.g.* of laughter, excitement, rage, terror, etc.; also said of physical processes, as earthquakes or volcanic eruptions).

1641 MILTON *Reform.* I. Wks. (1851) 30, I will not run into a paroxism of citations again on this point. **1762** STERNE *Tr. Shandy* VI. xxiii, In one or two of the more violent paroxysms of the siege. **1839** JAMES *Louis XIV*, IV. 42 He was cast into paroxysms of rage and despair which were frightful to behold. **1869** PHILLIPS *Vesuv.* iii. 48 In this violent paroxysm the whole top of the mountain is believed to have been swept away.

b. (Without *pl.*) The extreme height or violence, the acute stage (of any action, etc.). Now *rare*.

1650 FULLER *Pisgah* IV. v. 84 And four-score [Years]..in the Paroxysme of their [Egyptian] bondage. **1693** R. FLEMING *Disc. Earthquakes* 110 By a falling down of the greatest Darkness, he brings their case to some higher Paroxism. **1821** J. Q. ADAMS in Davies *Metr. Syst.* III. (1871) 145 At the very moment of fanatical paroxysm of the French revolution.

c. Violent or convulsive (physical) action.

1893 A. W. MOMERIE in J. H. Barrows *World's Parlt. Relig.* I. 271 It is manifest that the species themselves..have been created not by paroxysm but by evolution.

†**3.** A violent outburst; an open quarrel. *Obs.*

1650 FULLER *Pisgah* IV. i. 13 The greatest contention happening here, was that Paroxysme betwixt Paul and Barnabas. **1655** —— *Ch. Hist.* II. ii. §88 The paroxisme continued and encreased betwixt the Scotish Bishops..and such who celebrated Easter after the Roman rite. **1702** C. MATHER *Magn. Chr.* III. II. iii. (1852) 372 The misunderstanding did proceed so far as to produce a paroxism.

paroxysmal (pærəkˈsɪzməl), *a.* [f. prec. + -AL¹.] Pertaining to or of the nature of a paroxysm; marked by paroxysms; violent, convulsive.

1651 BIGGS *New Disp.* 144 The cruel Tertian did not forget to keep its paroxysmal course and return. **1811** SHELLEY *St. Irvyne* x. Pr. Wks. 1888 I. 200 In a paroxismal frenzy of contending passions. **1866** A. FLINT *Princ. Med.* (1880) 253 Asthma is essentially a paroxysmal disease. **1878** BAYNE *Purit. Rev.* 488 A risk of their being elected in some paroxysmal mood of feeling.

b. *spec.* in *Geol.* Of or pertaining to a violent natural convulsion; sometimes = CATASTROPHIC, CATACLYSMIC. (In quot. 1877, Holding the theory of paroxysmal or catastrophic changes.)

1830 LYELL *Princ. Geol.* I. 463 Paroxysmal convulsions.. are usually followed by long periods of tranquillity. **1841** TRIMMER *Pract. Geol.* 469 These paroxysmal disturbances which have hitherto occurred at intervals from the remotest geological periods, may be renewed. **1877** A. H. GREEN *Phys. Geol.* xi. §4. 524 The Paroxysmal School of Geologists. **1882** J. GEIKIE in *Nature* XXVII. 44/2 We have had experience of paroxysmal changes of level.

Hence **paroˈxysmalist** *Geol.* = PAROXYSMIST; **paroˈxysmally** *adv.*, in a paroxysmal way, by or in paroxysms or fits.

1833 LYELL *Princ. Geol.* III. 149 A line of shoals, therefore, or reefs, consisting of shattered and dislocated rocks,..ought first to have been pointed out by the paroxysmalist. **1859** SEMPLE *Diphtheria* 85 The hæmorrhage..is suspended and paroxysmally renewed.

paroxysmic (pærək'sɪzmɪk), *a. rare.* [f. as prec. + -IC.] = PAROXYSMAL.

1850 KINGSLEY *Alt. Locke* xv. (1874) 130 They fancy that they honour inspiration by supposing it to be only extra-ordinary and paroxysmic. **1889** A. W. TOURGEE in *Chicago Advance* 7 Feb. 114 The slender figure writhed with the paroxysmic effort [of coughing].

paroxysmist ('pærəksɪzmɪst). *Geol.* [f. as prec. + -IST.] One who attributes certain phenomena to paroxysms or sudden and violent natural convulsions; a catastrophist.

1865 LUBBOCK *Preh. Times* xi. 357 The argument of the Paroxysmist would probably be something like the following.

paroxytone (pə'rɒksɪtəʊn), *a.* and *sb. Gram.*, chiefly *Gr. Gram.* [ad. mod.L. *paroxyton-us*, a. Gr. παροξύτον-ος, f. παρ(α- beside, past + ὀξύτονος OXYTONE. In F. *paroxyton* (1570 in Hatz.-Darm.).] **a.** *adj.* Having an acute accent on the last syllable but one. **b.** *sb.* A word so accented.

1764 W. PRIMATT *Accentus redivivi* 106 The Ionians.. when they turned proparoxytone nouns of the second declension in εια into ιη, at the same time they made them paroxytones. **1881** CHANDLER *Greek Accent.* (ed. 2) 2 A word with the acute on the last syllable is called Oxytone; on the penultimate, Paroxytone.

Hence **paroxytonic** (-'tɒnɪk) *a.*, characterized by paroxytone accent or stress; **pa'roxytone, pa'roxytonize** *vbs.*, to accent on the penultimate syllable.

1887 A. MOREL-FATIO in *Encycl. Brit.* XXII. 349/2 As regards the tonic accent and the treatment of the vowels which come after it, Castilian may be said to be essentially a paroxytonic language, though it does not altogether refuse proparoxytonic accentuation. **1890** *Cent. Dict.*, *Paroxytone* vb.

paroxytonization (pə,rɒksɪtənaɪ'zeɪʃən). [f. PAROXYTONIZE *v.* + -ATION.] The rule which places stress on the penultimate syllable.

1973 A. H. SOMMERSTEIN *Sound Pattern Anc. Greek* v. 177 This rule.. changes all properispomenon words ending in *-ks* to paroxytones: (221) Paroxytonization. [+ sharp]→[-falling]/–C₀Vks[+ WB.].

paroyall, obs. form of PAIR-ROYAL.

parp (pɑːp), *sb.* [Echoic.] A honking noise, *spec.* that of a car horn. Hence as *v. intr.*, to make such a noise; also *trans.*

1951 E. BLYTON *Big Noddy Bk.* 51 Noddy had a good little hooter on his car. When he pressed it it said 'Pip-Pip', and sometimes 'Poop-Poop', and sometimes 'Parp-Parp'. **1953** —— *Noddy at Seaside* 14 'Parp-parp-parp!' Yes, that was Noddy's little car, longing to be taken out into the sunshine for a drive. *Ibid.* 16 'Parp-parp!' said the little car excitedly. **1958** [see BLEEP *sb.*]. **1968** S. CHALLIS *Death on Quiet Beach* v. 69 Outside his hotel, a horn suddenly parped. **1973** M. AMIS *Rachel Papers* 124 To break her reverie I parped the horn.

parpal, perpal. *Sc.* In mod.Sc. pairple. [app. var. of PARPEN.] In full ***parpal wall***, partition-wall, partition. Hence **parpalling.**

c **1470** HENRYSON *Mor. Fab.* II. *Town & C. Mouse* xxvii, I thank yone courtyne and yone perpall [*v.r.* parpane] wall Of my defence now fra yone crewell beist. *Ibid.* xxvi, Vp in haist behind ane parpaling [*MSS.* parraling, perr-, *ed.* 1621 parpelling] Scho clam sa hie. **1558** *Acts Council Edin.* (Jam.), The counsellors.. did.. give order to the Dean of Guild to big within the said church [St. Giles's] parpall walls of stone. **18..** JAMIESON, *Perple*, a wooden partition. *Mod. Sc.* (Roxb.), Ye can hear the mice ahint the pairple.

parpen, parpend, parpent ('pɑːpən, -ənd, -ənt). Forms: 5-8 **perpend**, (5 **perpoynt**), 6-8 **parpen**, (**parpin(e**, 6-9 **parpan(e**, 9 **parpoint**), 6-9 **perpen**, (7-8 **perpin**, 7-9 **perpent**, 9 **perpeyn**). [a. OF. *parpain* (1304-1550 in Godef.), *perpain* (1306), *parpin* (1394), *parpan* (1498), *parpoin* (16th c.), *perpin* (Cotgr. 1611), mod.F. *parpaing* (Littré), in med.L. *parpanus* (1402 in Littré). Of doubtful origin (see Note below); hence the etymological spelling is unsettled. In OFr. the word was used as an adj. with fem. *parpaigne* *-paigne*, *-peigne*, also ellipt. as sb. (for *pierre parpeigne*): see also *parpine* in Littré.]

1. In Masonry, A stone which passes through a wall from side to side, having two smooth vertical faces; a stone squared or dressed for this purpose. In quot. 1579-80, perh. adj. 'with perpendicular faces'.

c **1429** in Willis & Clark *Cambridge* (1886) II. 445 Pro xxxiij ped' de perpoynt' xvijᵈ. **1579-80** NORTH *Plutarch* (1676) 88 The pillars of this temple are cut out of a quarry of marble called pentlike marble, and they were squared parpine, as thick as long. **1688** R. HOLME *Armoury* III. 111/1 *Perpin*, are less than the size of Ashlers. *Ashler*, is a Stone a Yard long, and 8, 9, or 10 inches square. **1712** J. JAMES tr. *Le Blond's Gardening* 208 Lay here and there Stones that reach the whole Thickness of the Wall, that is to say, such as make the Surface on both Sides, which Workmen call Making a Parpin. **1890** *Tablet* 28 June 1026 The church is .. built of brick-faced Yorkshire parpoints.

2. Short for *parpen-wall*: A wall built of parpens; a partition-wall. Also *fig.*

1591 BRUCE *Serm.* I. viij b, Sinne.. casteth a balk and a mist betuixt the sight of God and vs; and therefore the Prophet calleth it a parpane. *Ibid.* T v b, Gif thou build vp an perpen of thine awin making betuixt thee and him. **1624** —— in *Serm.*, etc. (Wodrow Soc.) 10, That I should take the full burden upon me, until this parpan was demolished. **1825** JAMIESON s.v., 2 The parapet of a bridge is called a *parpane*, or *parpane-wa'*, Aberd. **1828** *Craven Gloss.* (ed. 2), *Parpoint*, a thin wal, the stones of which are built on the edge. *Ibid.*, The parapet of a bridge is called in Scotland, *parpane*, which, in general, consists of a single stone in width.

3. *attrib.* and *Comb.*: ***parpen ashlar, stone, work.***

c **1429** in Willis & Clark *Cambridge* (1886) II. 445, lxxxij et di' fott of *perpendaschler vjᵈ. **1756** *Ibid.* 529 The ashler under the Plinth of the Ballustrade.. is parpin ashler. **1781** J. WOOD *Cottages* (1806) 8 The freestone is sawed out with a common hand-saw into what is called perpen-ashlar, that is, stone of four, six, eight or ten inches thick. **1721** BAILEY, **Perpend-stone*, (among Builders), a stone fitted to the Thickness of a wall, so as to shew its smoothed ends on both sides. **1845** PARKER *Gloss. Archit.* (ed. 4), *Perpent-stone*.., a large stone reaching through a wall so as to appear on both sides of it; the same as what is now usually called a bonder, bond-stone, or through, except that these are often used in rough-walling, while the term perpent-stone appears to have been applied to squared stones, or ashlar;.. in Gloucestershire, ashlar thick enough to reach entirely through a wall, and shew a fair face on both sides, is called *Parping ashlar.* **1600** HOLLAND *Livy* XLIV. xi. 1177 A new wall, not built to the thickenesse of the old, but with *perpend worke, laid with one course of bricke and no more.

b. parpen wall, a thin wall built of parpen stones or of single bricks, as commonly in interior partition-walls; hence, a thin partition-wall of any kind; also locally, a parapet wall, as of a bridge.

1554-5 *Burgh Rec. Edinb.* (1871) II. 297 Ane braid daill to be ane porpen-wall to the litill hous of the portell in the counsall-hous. **1688** R. HOLME *Armoury* III. 457/1 A perpin wall, is a Single stone wall. **1720** WODROW *Life R. Bruce* in *B.'s Serm.*, etc. (Wodr. Soc.) 80 The King.. discharged the taking down of a parpan wall in the Great Kirk, to enlarge the East Kirk. **1860** G. E. STREET in *Archæol. Cant.* III. 126 The altar set on a foot pace about three feet from the east wall, with a low stone perpeyn wall at its back. **1903** J. T. FOWLER in *Rites of Durham* (Surtees) 195 At Rievaulx the five eastern altars were divided by perpent walls of stone.

[*Note.* For the derivation of the French word, M. Antoine Thomas suggested in *Romania* XXVI. 437, 442 a L. type **perpāginem* (f. L. *per* through + radical of *compāginem, pro-pāginem*), with the notion of 'something fastened or driven through'. M. Gaston Paris, *ibid.* XXVII. 481, indicated some difficulties in this, and suggested a popular L. **perpendium*, related to *perpendiculum*, referring to the smooth vertical faces of the parpend stone. He admitted however the difficulty of thus accounting for the corresp. Sicilian *parpagnu*, Engadine *parpaun*, and Sp. *perpiaño*, unless these are more or less altered adaptations of the Fr. word.]

parpetrat, etc., obs. f. PERPETRATE, etc.

parquet ('pɑːkeɪ, pɑː'kɛt, ‖parkɛ), *sb.* [a. (in specific senses) F. *parquet*, OF. *parchet* (14th c.) a small compartment, part of a park, theatre, court, etc., wooden flooring; dim. of *parc* PARK: see -ET¹.]

1. A flooring; *spec.* a wooden flooring composed of pieces of wood, often of different kinds, arranged in a pattern; a flooring of parquetry.

1816 TINGRY *Painter & Varnisher's Guide* (ed. 2) 384 Distemper for parquets, or floors of inlaid work. *Ibid.*, The name of parquets is given to boards of fir intersected by pieces of walnut-tree, or disposed in compartments of which the walnut-tree forms the frame or border. **1832** tr. *Tour Germ. Prince* II. xiii. 254 The large blocks of wood on the fire; the tile parquet,—all recall vividly to my mind that I am in France, and not in England. **1867** 'OUIDA' *C. Castlemaine* (1879) 10 None such as these could cross the inlaid oak parquet of Lilliesford.

2. (Also erroneously **parquette.**) Part of the auditorium of a theatre, the front part of the ground-floor nearest the orchestra, or sometimes the whole of it. Chiefly *U.S.*

1848 W. IRVING *Life & Lett.* (1864) IV. 34 Ladies.. with their gay dresses, make what is the parquette in other theatres look like a bed of flowers. **1883** M. SCHUYLER in *Harper's Mag.* Nov. 880/1 No actual hardship is attached to a seat in the parquet. *Ibid.* 884/2 The partition which runs from the floor of the parquette to the floor of the gallery is of fire-proof blocks. **1896** *Daily News* 10 Feb. 6/6 In New York the stalls occupy the whole of the parquet.

‖**3.** In France, etc.: The branch of the administration of the law concerned with the prevention, investigation, and punishment of crime.

1892 *Pall Mall G.* 30 Sept. 6/3 The orgies reported last week as having taken place in a Paris restaurant have attracted the attention of the parquet. **1902** *Encycl. Brit.* XXVII. 289 The head of the whole Parquet in France is the Procureur-Général. **1903** *Speaker* 19 Sept. 556/1 An unwise economy in the pay of the native Parquet or prosecuting body.

4. *attrib.* and *Comb.*, as ***parquet-flooring, -work***; **parquet carpet**, a patterned square of carpet.

1902 Parquet carpet [see *art square* s.v. ART *sb.* 18]. **1819** M. WILMOT *More Lett.* (1935) 20 Fruit and flowers dirt cheap—parqué flours—*Carpits* if you chuse to give a daughters dowery for them. **1833** PRINCESS ELIZABETH *Let.* 28 Dec. (1898) 213 And the doctor said with those shoes she might now walk about the parquet floors. **1865** M. EYRE *Lady's Walks S. of France* xxxi. 330 The *parquet* floors are undusted, unwaxed, and unswept. **1874** LADY HERBERT tr. *Hübner's Ramble* II. ii. (1878) 245 The lacquered borders of the parquet floor. **1899** *Allbutt's Syst. Med.* VII. 5 A polisher of parquet-flooring. **1901** *Westm. Gaz.* 14 Mar. 4/2 Scottish tweeds are some of the herring-bone pattern;.. others, again, what is called 'parquet', imitating a parquet flooring. **1886** WILLIS & CLARK *Cambridge* I. 116 A dais in parquet-work for the high table.

parquet ('pɑːkɪt, ‖parkɛ), *v.* [a. F. *parqueter* (1382 in Hatz.-Darm.), f. *parquet*: see prec.]

trans. To provide (a room) with a floor of parquet-work; to construct (a flooring) of parquetry; to make of inlaid wood-work.

1678 EVELYN *Diary* 23 Aug., The roomes are wainscotted, and some of them parquetted with cedar, yew, cypresse, &c. **1865** J. C. BELLEW *Blount Tempest* I. 58 The flooring was parqueted very curiously, and so highly polished, that.. it was as unsafe as ice. **1873** M. COLLINS *Squire Silchester* III. xxii. 239 From the parqueted floor to the open oaken-raftered roof.

b. To turn into, or make like, a parquet floor.

1875 R. F. BURTON *Gorilla L.* (1876) II. 277 We ascended a path greasy with drizzle, parquetted by negro feet.

parquetage ('pɑːkɪtɪdʒ). [a. F. *parquetage* (1676 in Hatz.-Darm.) flooring, wooden mosaic, f. *parqueter*: see prec. and -AGE.] = PARQUETRY.

1845 *Art-Union Jrnl.* June 169 Twelve different patterns of parquetage, or inlaid wood flooring. **1847** *Illustr. Lond. News* 11 Sept. 170/2 Carved oak, stained glass, parquetage.

parquetry ('pɑːkɪtrɪ). Also ‖**parqueterie** (parkɛtriː). [a. F. *parqueterie* (1835 in *Dict. Acad.*), f. *parquet*: see -ERY¹.] Inlaid work of wood, in which a pattern is formed by different kinds of wood; esp. in flooring: cf. PARQUET *sb.* 1.

1842 FRANCIS *Dict. Arts, Parquetry.* **1877** *Gd. Words* XVIII. 19/1 The floors are in parqueterie. **1879** *Cassell's Techn. Educ.* III. 184/2 Parquetry is a beautiful species of flooring, consisting of various patterns formed of different woods. **1883** J. PAYN *Thicker than Water* xx, The floor.. left a free opportunity for parquetry round its margin.

attrib. **1883** *Times* 19 Nov. 4 The floor.. is.. a parquetry floor. **1895** *Daily News* 10 May 9/2 A Louis XVI. parqueterie secretaire of tulip and rosewood.

parr¹, par (pɑː(r)). [app. of Scottish origin; derivation unknown.]

1. A young salmon before it becomes a smolt; distinguished by the parallel transverse bands on its side; = BRANDLING *sb.* 2.

Formerly supposed to be a distinct species.

1715-22 PENNECUIK *Descr. Tweeddale* Wks. (1815) 107 Salmo salmulus, Samlet, or Par. *a* **1771** SMOLLETT *Ode to Leven-Water*, The scaly brood In myriads cleave thy crystal flood;.. The salmon, monarch of the tide, The ruthless pike, intent on war; The silver eel and motled par. **1820** SCOTT *Abbot* xxiv, Par, which some suppose infant salmon. **1827** —— *Jrnl.* 9 May, Warm dispute whether par are or are not salmon trout. **1844** *Zoologist* II. 527 *note*, Brandling-trout, fingerling, par, smolt, &c. all denote the same fish. **1862** *Act 25 & 26 Vict.* c. 97 §2 'Salmon' shall.. include.. bull trout, smolts, parr, and any other migratory fish of the salmon kind. **1868** PEARD *Water-farm.* x. 103 The ova deposited in our boxes have long since become parr.

2. A young coal-fish or black cod, less than a year old (see BILLET³); a sillock. *local.*

1769 PENNANT *Brit. Zool.* III. 153 *Coal Fish*, The fry.. are called at Scarborough *Parrs*, and when a year old, *Billets.* About nine or ten years ago such a glut of Parrs visited that part, that for several weeks it was impossible to dip a pail into the sea without taking some. **1832** J. COLE *Scarborough Guide* 108 The principal fish brought to Scarborough for sale are.. herrings, whiting, parr, billits, colefish.

3. *attrib.* and *Comb.*, as ***parr-fishing***; **parr-marks**, the dark transverse bands which characterize the salmon in the parr stage; **parr-tail**, an artificial fly used in salmon fishing.

1889 *Daily News* 9 July 5/3 What better means of diminishing the population of salmon can be invented than free *parr-fishing? **1867** F. FRANCIS *Angling* ix. (1880) 305 With bands or marks on the sides known as *parr-marks. **1866** CRICHTON *Ramble in Arcades* 129 Though we spun the *parr-tail assiduously we did not succeed in moving one [salmon]. **1867** F. FRANCIS *Angling* v. (1880) 294.

parr². *dial.* Also parre, par. (See quot.)

1847 HALLIWELL, *Parre*, a young leveret (Devon). [Thence in WEBSTER, etc.]

parrachite, -chito: see PARAKEET.

parrah: see PARA, Eastern coin.

parrail(le, var. PAREL.

parrakeet, -ket, variants of PARAKEET.

†'**parraketism.** *Obs. nonce-wd.* [f. prec. + -ISM.] Acting like a parrot, i.e. speaking without understanding what one says.

1658 HARRINGTON *Prerog. Pop. Govt.* Wks. (1700) 254 Did you ever hear such a Parraketism? for to speak a word without understanding the sense of it, is like a Parrat.

parral, parraling, var. PARREL, PARELLING.

parrall, obs. f. PARLE, PAROL.

parramatta: see PARAMATTA.

parraquito: see PARAKEET.

† **par-rational**, *a. nonce-wd. Obs.* [f. L. *pār* equal (see PAR *sb.*[1]) + RATIONAL.] Equally rational or reasonable.
1647 WARD *Simp. Cobler* 50, I know no difference in these Essentialls, between Monarchies, Aristocracies, or Democracies; the rule will bee found par-rationall say Schoolmen and Pretorians what they will.

parrator, obs. f. PARITOR.

parre: see PAIR, PAR *v.*[1], PARR[2].

parrear, obs. f. PARIAH.

parree, parreiall, obs. ff. PARRY, PAIR-ROYAL.

parrel, parral ('pærəl), *sb. Naut.* Forms: 5 perell, 6 parle, 7 parel, parrell, (8 pareil), 7– parrel, 9 parral. [app. the same word as PAREL *sb.* Cf. OF. *parail* rigging (1345 in Godef.).] A band of rope, chain, or iron collar by which the middle of a yard is fastened to a mast.
1485 *Naval Accts. Hen. VII* (1896) 37 Layners for the truss perell. **1591** PERCIVALL *Sp. Dict.*, *Racamenta*, the parle of a ships yard, *Aplustre*. **1627** CAPT. SMITH *Seaman's Gram.* v. 20 Parrels are little round Balls called Trucks, and little peeces of wood called ribs, and ropes which doe incircle the Masts, and so made fast to the Yards, that the Yards may slip vp and downe easily vpon the Masts. **1720** DE FOE *Capt. Singleton* xi. (1840) 192 The pareil of the mizen topsail yard ..giving way. **1764** VEITCH in *Phil. Trans.* LIV. 286 From the parrel of the main-yard down to the upper deck of the ship. *Ibid.* 288. **1867** SMYTH *Sailor's Word-bk.* 518 *Parrals*, or *Parrels*. Those bands of rope, or sometimes iron collars, by which the centres of yards are fastened at the slings to the masts, so as to slide up and down freely.
b. *Comb.*, as *parrel-lashing, -rope, -truck*.
1711 W. SUTHERLAND *Shipbuild. Assist.* 142 Parrel Rope, as big as the Pendants of the Brace. **1867** SMYTH *Sailor's Word-bk.*, *Parrel-rope*. **1875** KNIGHT *Dict. Mech.* s.v., The parral..has strung upon it parral-trucks, that is, small wooden globes to prevent friction..in hoisting or lowering.
Hence '**parrel, parral** *v.*, to fasten by means of a parrel (in quot. 1895 *intr.* for *refl.*).
c **1860** H. STUART *Seaman's Catech.* 49 The masthead men parrel the yard. **1895** *Outing* (U.S.) Apr. 46/1 Hook them on to the trysail gaff, the jaws of which parral on to the mast.

parrel(l, parrer, parresche, parret, parrettor, obs. ff. PAREL, PERIL, PARURE, PARISH, PARROT, PARITOR.

[**parrett**, copyist's error for *parrell*: see PAREL.
1546 in *Inv. Ch. Goods Yorksh.* etc. (Surtees) 138–9.]

‖**parrhesia** (pə'riːzɪə, -'riːsɪə). *Rhet.* Also 6 parresia, parisia; in 7 anglicized as '**parrhesy**. [Late L. *parrhēsia* (Isidore *Orig.* ii. 20), a. Gr. παρρησία free-spokenness, frankness, f. παρα- beside, beyond + ῥῆσις speech.] Frankness or freedom of speech.
1586 A. DAY *Eng. Secretary* II. (1625) 90 *Parresia*, or liberty to speake, when by winning of curtesie to our speech we seeke to auoide any offence therein, as thus: Pardon if I be tedious. **1589** PUTTENHAM *Eng. Poesie* III. xix. (Arb.) 234 *Parisia*, or the Licentious. **1659** GAUDEN *Tears of Ch.* III. iv. 274 An honest and innocent parrhesy, or freedome of speaking, such as becomes the Messenger of heaven. **1678** PHILLIPS (ed. 4), *Parrhesia*, liberty in speaking; in Rhetorick it is a figure in which we speak boldly, and freely, in things displeasing, and obnoxious to envy. **1893** *Ch. Times* 27 Oct. 1090, I..do not the less admire the womanly sweetness and beauty of characters like Perdita and Miranda because of their occasional parrhesia.

parrhesiastic (pəriːsɪ'æstɪk), *a. rare.* [ad. Gr. παρρησιαστικ-ός free-spoken, f. παρρησιαστ-ής (L. *parrhesiastēs*), ult. f. παρρησία: see prec.] Bold and open in speech; free-spoken, outspoken.
1835 WHATELY *Commpl.-Bk.* (1864) 120 The supposed superiority of wisdom attributed to cautious, reserved.. characters, as compared with the more open, unreserved, energetic and parrhesiastic.

parriah, -iar, -ier, obs. ff. PARIAH.

parrial, -all, parriche, obs. ff. PAIR-ROYAL, PARISH.

parricidal (pærɪ'saɪdəl), *a.* [ad. L. *parricīdālis*: cf. obs. F. *parricidal* (16th c. in Godef.), f. *parricīda* PARRICIDE[1].] Of, pertaining to, of the nature of a parricide; guilty of parricide.
1627 MAY *Lucan* VII. N vj, On brothers, and on fathers empty bedds The killers lay their parricidall heads. **1850** BLACKIE *Æschylus* II. 194 The parricidal Oedipus. **1867** FREEMAN *Norm. Conq.* (1876) I. v. 270 Swegen's parricidal war with his father.
Hence **parri'cidally** *adv.*, in a parricidal manner.
1856 MISS MULOCK *J. Halifax* xxiv, Dust of the dead ages ..never parricidally profaned by us the living age.

parricide[1] ('pærɪsaɪd). Also 6–8 pari-, (6 para-, 7 parra-). [a. F. *parricide* (13th c. in Hatz.-Darm.), ad. L. *parricīda*, *pāricīda*, of doubtful derivation; by Quintilian thought to be for **patricīda*, f. *patr-em* father: see -CIDE I. See also PATRICIDE.] One who murders his father or either parent, or other near relative; also, the murderer of any one whose person is considered specially sacred as being the ruler of the country or in some position of trust; one guilty of the crime of parricide: see next; *transf.* one who commits the crime of treason against his country.
1554 W. PRAT *Africa* v. G iv, They haue a sharpe punishement for the paradices [*sic*] and mansleers. **1555** EDEN *Decades* 270 The Romans were accustomed to sowe paricides in sackes. **1560** DAUS tr. *Sleidane's Comm.* 64 b, Luther..exhorteth all men that they would come to destroye these wycked theves and paracides. **1563** FOXE *A. & M.* (1583) 755/2 Thus was Solyman murderer & parricide of hys owne sonnes. **1613** PURCHAS *Pilgrimage* (1614) 812 Parricides, which slew their Parents, or which slew their wives or children. **1633** T. ADAMS *Exp. 2 Peter* ii. 5 If a woman murder her husband, she is judged by the civil law a parricide. **1638** R. BAKER tr. *Balzac's Lett.* (vol. III) 170 They lend the Spaniard their blood, and their hearts, to make a slave of their country, and are parricides of their Mother. **1644–58** CLEAVELAND *Gen. Poems* (1677) 171 My Compassion to my Country must not make me a Parricide to my Prince. *c* **1696** PRIOR *Cupid Mistaken* 11 Parricide! Like Nero, thou hast slain thy mother. **1703** ROWE *Fair Penit.* v. i. 1810 This Parricide..Shortens her Father's Age, and cuts him off. **1853** MERIVALE *Rom. Rep.* i. (1867) 5 Should a victorious general dare to turn his arms against his own country, where was the nation which should rise and overwhelm the parricide?
b. *attrib.* or as *adj.* = PARRICIDAL.
1686 tr. *Chardin's Trav. Persia* 58 Persons that had.. dipp'd their Parricide Hands in his Blood. **1796** ANNA SEWARD *Lett.* (1811) IV. 295 To exalt the French character, and, with parricide impulse, to depreciate that of England?

'**parricide**[2]. Also 7–8 pari-. [a. F. *parricide* (15th c. in Littré), ad. L. *parricīdium*: see prec. and -CIDE 2.] The murder of a father, parent, near relative, ruler, etc.; the crime of a parricide: see prec.; *transf.* the crime of treason against one's country.
Parricīda and *parricidium* had already in Latin a very wide application, including all uses found in English. In Codes in which distinctions are or were made between different kinds of murder, *parricide*, besides meaning the murder of parents and near relatives, has been variously extended; English Common Law distinguishes 'in no respect between the crime of parricide or that of killing a husband, wife, or master, and the crime of simple murder' (Wharton *Law Lex.* 1848).
1570 T. NORTON tr. *Nowel's Catech.* (1853) 132 If it be for every private man..parricide to kill his private parents. **1654** R. CODRINGTON tr. *Iustine* XXXII. 405 The Father being compelled to parricide, did make sad all the Court with the execution of his Son. *a* **1674** CLARENDON *Hist. Reb.* XI. §244 This unparalleled murder and parricide was committed upon the 30th of January. **1782** COWPER *Let. to J. Newton* Wks. 1837 XV. 126 The Americans..seem to me to have incurred the guilt of parricide, by renouncing their parent, by making her ruin their favourite object. **1866** R. LOWE *Sp. Reform.* 31 May (1867) 212 To precipitate a decision..is parricide in the case of the Constitution, which is the life and soul of this great nation. **1879** FROUDE *Cæsar* viii. 87 They denied that they had themselves killed Sextus Roscius. They said the son had done it, and they charged him with parricide.
b. *attrib.* or as *adj.* = PARRICIDAL.
1806 JEFFERSON *Writ.* (ed. Ford) VIII. 473 Persons who may reject..parricide propositions.
Hence '**parricided** *ppl. a.*, killed by parricide.
1858 CARLYLE *Fredk. Gt.* II. ix. (1872) I. 106 The parricided Albert's son.

† **parri'cidial**, *a. Obs.* [ad. L. *parricīdiāl-is*, f. *parricīdium* PARRICIDE[2]: see -AL[1]. Cf. obs. F. *parricidial* (*c* 1600 in Godef.).] Of, pertaining to, or of the nature of parricide; parricidal.
1598 SYLVESTER *Du Bartas* II. i. III. *Furies* 797 Who..in all humane lives In cold bloud bath their parricidiall knives. *a* **1656** USSHER *Ann.* (1658) 337 Partly by parricidial acts committed in his own family. **1692** WASHINGTON tr. *Milton's Def. Pop.* (1851) Pref. 9 The news of Salmasius Parricidial Barbarisms.

† **parri'cidious**, *a. Obs.* [f. L. *parricīdi-um* PARRICIDE[2] + -OUS.] = PARRICIDAL.
1609 BP. W. BARLOW *Answ. Nameless Cath.* 241 The vngratious and vnnaturall despight of a Parricidious Vsurper. *Ibid.* 246 A parricidious Murder. **1779** *Hist. Mod. Europe* I. xix. 228 This parricidious Zealot. **1807** J. BARLOW *Columb.* v. 397 Arrest, my son, thy parricidious hate.

'**parricidism.** *rare*$^{-1}$. [See -ISM; cf. *libertinism*.] The practice of parricide.
1797 W. TAYLOR in *Monthly Rev.* XXIV. 193 An inflexible and severe magistrate, accused of incest and parricidism.

† **parricidous**, *a. Obs. rare*$^{-1}$. [f. PARRICIDE + -OUS.] = PARRICIDIOUS. (Perh. a misprint.)
1646 SIR T. BROWNE *Pseud. Ep.* III. xvi. 143 The men of Melita when they saw a viper upon the hand of Paul, said.. the parricidous animall and punishment of Murtherers is upon him.

† '**parricidy.** *Obs.* In 6 paracidie, 7 pari-. [ad. L. *parricīdi-um*; cf. *homicidy*.] = PARRICIDE[2].
1560 DAUS tr. *Sleidane's Comm.* 339 For committing Paracidie, that is to wit, for poysoning thy Mother and a Nephew of thine. **1602** WARNER *Alb. Eng.* x. liv. (1612) 242 How they wrought Paricidie. **1610** HOLLAND *Camden's Brit.* I. 113 Aurelius Conanus..defiled with Paricidies or murthers of his owne Kinred.

parrier ('pærɪə(r)). [f. PARRY *v.*[1] + -ER[1].] One who parries.
1809 ROLAND *Fencing* 45 To understand that it is very possible to hit these kind of windmill parryers.

parrier, obs. form of PARIAH.

parrish, -en, etc., obs. ff. PARISH, PARISHEN, etc.

parritch, Sc. and north. dial. f. PORRIDGE.

parritor, -our, obs. forms of PARITOR.

par-roast, *v. nonce wd.* [f. ROAST *v.*, after PARBOIL 2.] *trans.* To roast partially.
1847 DE QUINCEY in *Tait's Mag.* XIV. 576 Martin, the man that parboiled, or par-roasted York Minster.

parroche, -in, -yn, obs. ff. PARISH, PARISHEN.

parrochite, -ocquet: see PARAKEET.

parrock ('pærək), *sb.* Now chiefly *dial.* (see PADDOCK). Forms: 1 pearroc, pear(r)uc, 5 parrok, 6 -ocke, 6– parrock, (7 parock, *dial.* purrock, 9 *dial.* parrack, -ick). [OE. *pearroc*, *-ruc* masc., corresp. to OHG. *pfarrih*, *pferrih*, MHG. *pferrich* 'fencing about, enclosure, enclosed space', mod.Ger. *pferch* 'fold (for sheep, etc.)'; MLG. *perc* masc. and neut.; MDu. *perc*, *parc*, Du. *perk*, *park* neut., 'pen', and (after Fr.) 'park'; all pointing back to a com. WGer. **parruk*, *-ik*. Found also in early med.L. as *parricus*, *parcus* (8th c. in *Ripuar. Laws*), and in mod. Romanic langs.: It. *parco*, Sp., Pg. *parque*, Pr. *pargue*, *parc*, F. *parc*, whence ME. *parc* PARK, and mod.Ger. *park*, Du. *park* (in part). Also in Welsh *parwg* (from ME. *parrock*), *parc* (from Eng.), Gael. *pàirc* (from Eng.), Bret. *park* (from Fr.).
The ulterior origin and relations are disputed: see Diez, Körting, Kluge, Franck. The OE. and cognate Ger. forms show that the word must have been in WGer. as early as the 4th c. The oldest sense in OE. and OHG. appears to be 'the enclosing fence or hurdles, *clathri*', rather than 'the enclosed space'. Diez and Körting favour a Romanic origin, and possible connexion with L. *parcĕre*, *parcus* adj., but Darmesteter rejects this, because Prov. *pargue* (with *pargou*, *pargade*, *pargagi*) requires orig. *parric-* not *parc-*. A Celtic origin is out of the question (Thurneysen); all the Celtic forms are late borrowings from Eng. and Fr. It is thus not improbable that **parruk*, **parrik*, was a dim. of a WGer. **parra*, OHG. *pharra*, Ger. *pfarre*, in an original sense 'circuit, compass, precinct, district' (taken in Christian times as a convenient equivalent for med.L. *parochia* parish); cf. mod. dial. PAR *sb.*[3] 'enclosure for beasts', and ME. *parren*, PAR, PARR *v.*[1] 'to enclose, confine'.]
1. † **a.** A fence, or hurdles, with which a space is enclosed. (*O.E.*) **b.** An enclosed space of ground; a small enclosure or field, a paddock.
a **700** *Epinal Gloss.* 224 (so Erf. 224) *Clat(h)rum*, pearroc. *a* **725** *Corpus Gloss.* 486 *Clatrum* (*clathri*), pearuc. *c* **888** K. ÆLFRED *Boeth.* xviii. §2 On ðisum lytlum pearroce [L. *saeptum*, CHAUCER clos, i.e. the earth] þe we ær ymbe spræcon buʒiaþ swiþe maneʒa ðeoda. *c* **918** *O.E. Chron.* an. 918 [Hie] him wið ʒefuhton..and bedrifon hie on anne pearruc and besæton hie þær utan. *c* **1000** ÆLFRIC *Gloss.* in Wr.-Wülcker 140/8 *Clatrum*, pearruc. *c* **1000** in Kemble *Cod. Dipl.* V. 277 Ðis sindon ða landʒemæro. Ærest..on Boʒeles pearruc; of Boceles pearruce. *a* **1400–50** *Alexander* 4702 Pyned þar in a parroke inparkid as bestis. **1530** PALSGR. 252/1 Parrocke a lytell parke, *parquet*. **1582** SIR T. HENEAGE *Let.* in Nicolas *Life Hatton* (1847) 277 To kill a doe in the parrock of the great park. **1589** NASHE *Martins Months Minde* 49 My parrock of ground..abutting vpon three high waies, wherevpon standeth a Cottage, built triangle wise [i.e. the gibbet at Tyburn]. **1729** *N. Riding Rec.* IX. 107 The paddock or parrock called Butt-paddock. **1825** BROCKETT *N.C. Gloss* s.v. *Paddock*, In Westmorland *parruck*..is a common name for an inclosure near a farmhouse. **1886** ELWORTHY *W. Som. Word-bk.* s.v., They cows mus'n bide in the parrick no longer.
2. A small apartment or narrow cell in a building; a stall, coop, or pen for animals.
c **1440** *Promp. Parv.* 384/2 Parrok, or cowle, *saginarium*, .. *cavea*, ..*pargulus*. *Ibid.*, Parrok, or caban, *preteriolum*, *capana*. **1818–80** JAMIESON, *Parrock, Parrok*, 1. A small inclosure, a little apartment, *Dumfr.*.. 2. A very straight enclosure in which a ewe is confined, that she may take with her own lamb, or with that of another when her own is dead. *Roxb.*
† **3.** (See quot.) *Obs.* [Perh. a different word.]
a **1700** *Kennett MS.* in Halliwell s.v., When the bayliff or beadle of the Lord held a meeting to take an account of rents and pannage in the weilds of Kent, such meeting was calld a parock.

'**parrock**, *v. Obs.* exc. *dial.* [f. prec.] *trans.* To enclose, shut up, confine within narrow limits.
1377 LANGL. *P. Pl.* B. xv. 281 Poule *primus heremita* had parroked hym-selue, þat no man miʒte hym se. **1393** *Ibid.* C. VII. 144 Ich am ywoned sitte Yparroked in puwes. *c* **1440** *Promp. Parv.* 384/2 Parrokkyn, or speryn in streyte place (*K.* speryn in strey(t)ly, *S.* closyn in streythly). **1825–80** JAMIESON s.v., Sheep are said to be parrach'd in a fold, when too much crowded. *Ibid.*, *To parrock a ewe and lamb*, to confine a strange lamb with a ewe which is not its dam, that the lamb may suck. *Roxb.* **1894** *Northumbld. Gloss.*, *Pairock, parrick*, to shut up..in a paddock.
Hence '**parrocked** *ppl. a.*, shut up, closed.
c **1520** *Treat. Galaunt* 116 in Hazl. *E.P.P.* III. 156 For all ..thy parrocked pouche that thou so fast doest brace.

parroket, -quet: see PARAKEET.

parroll, obs. form of PAROL *sb.*

parrot ('pærət), *sb.* Also 6–7 **parot, parat,** 6–8 **parrat, -et,** (6 **parrote, -otte, parott(e, parate**). [Known first *c* 1525; of uncertain origin, there being no cognate form of the name in other langs.; conjectured to be = F. *Perrot* 'a mans proper name, being a diminutive or derivative of Pierre' Peter (Cotgr.): cf. *Pierrot*, diminutive of Pierre, in mod.Fr. a name of the house-sparrow.

The chief difficulty in this is that the sense 'parrot' is not recorded for F. *Perrot* (although Littré has *pérot* as a modern Fr. familiar name given to the parrot), while *Perrot* does not appear as a man's name in 16th c. Eng., so that points of contact are wanting. Cf. however the suggested origin of Sp. *perico, periquito*, under PARAKEET.]

1. a. A bird of the order *Psittaci*, or family *Psittacidæ*, and spec. of the genus *Psittacus*; these are scansorial and zygodactyl, and have a short hooked bill and naked cere; many of the species have very beautiful plumage, and some of the fleshy-tongued ones can be taught to repeat words and sentences with great perfection; hence, much valued as cage-birds, the species most commonly kept being the Grey Parrot (*Psittacus erythacus*) of West Africa.

The order includes many genera and species chiefly inhabiting tropical and semi-tropical regions; a few are found in the temperate zones in N. America, Australia, and New Zealand. As differentiated from *parakeet*, 'parrot' is applied to the moderate-sized and larger species of the order. Various families, genera, and species have distinct names, as *cockatoo, kea, lory, macaw*, etc.

c **1525** SKELTON *Sp. Parrot* 1 My name is Parrot, a byrd of paradyse. *Ibid.* 9 Parot must haue an almon or a date. *Ibid.* 15 Speke, Parrot, I pray you, full curtesly they say; Parrot is a goodly byrd, a prety popagey. **1564–78** BULLEYN *Dial. agst. Pest.* (1888) 61 Our Parate will saie, Parate is a minion, and beware the Catte, and she will call me Roger as plaine as your Maistership. **1581** RICH *Farew. Milit. Prof.* H iij b, Haue you founde your tongue now pretie peate, then wee must haue an Almon for Parrat. **1600** J. PORY tr. *Leo's Africa* Introd. 52 Heere be likewise gray parots. **1601** HOLLAND *Pliny* I. 146 The Island Gagandus: where they began first to haue a sight of the birds called Parats. **1617** MORYSON *Itin.* III. 2 Children like Parrats, soone learne forraigne languages, and sooner forget the same. **1656** EARL MONM. tr. *Boccalini's Advts. fr. Parnass.* I. x. (1674) 13 Seeing a beautiful Indian Parret..[he] delighted to hear her speak. **1727** POPE *Th. Var. Subj.* Swift's Wks. 1755 II. I. 230 A very little wit is valued in a woman, as we are pleased with a few words spoken plain by a parrot. **1781** COWPER *Convers.* 7 Words learned by rote a parrot may rehearse. **1884–5** *Stand. Nat. Hist.* (1888) IV. 363 The gray parrots, forming the family *Psittacidæ*, are few in number and are confined to Africa and Madagascar.

b. A figure of the bird; esp. one used as a mark for shooting at; a popinjay.

1578 T. N. tr. *Conq. W. India* 198 They will make a Parret or Popin Jay of mettall, that his tongue shall shake, and his heade move, and his wings flutter. **1662** J. DAVIES tr. *Olearius' Voy. Ambass.* 262 You passe through a place appointed for tilting..and in the midst, a high Pole for shooting at the wooden Parrat.

2. Applied contemptuously to a person; esp. in reference to an unintelligent mechanical repetition of speech, or imitation of the action of others.

1581 J. BELL *Haddon's Answ. Osor.* II. 107 Speake out Parrotte, in what place doth Luther subuerte the dueties of vertue? Where doth hee blotte out honesty and godly carefulnesse of good men? **1656** W. D. tr. *Comenius' Gate Lat. Unl.* §595. 181 To make a parrot of a man, a rehearser of other men's sayings. *c* **1802** MAR. EDGEWORTH *Ennui* ix, The mere puppets and parrots of fashion. **1837** EMERSON *Addr., Amer. Schol.* Wks. (Bohn) II. 175 He tends to become a mere thinker, or, still worse, the parrot of other men's thinking.

3. sea-parrot. a. The coulterneb or puffin, so called on account of the peculiar shape of its bill.

1694 *Acc. Sev. late Voy.* II. 88 Amongst all web-footed Birds..this hath a peculiar Bill; and because it seem'd to those that gave him this Name to be like that of a Parret, therefore they called him also a Parret. **1772–84** *Cook's Voy.* (1790) VI. 2126 We saw numbers of sea parrots, and small ice-birds. **1865** GOSSE *Land & Sea* (1874) 30 These are known by the fishermen as sea-parrots or coulternebs; but are more generally designated in books as puffins.

b. Some kind of fish: see PARROT-FISH.

1706 PHILLIPS, *Sea-Parret*, a Fish that has very sparkling and beautiful Eyes, the Balls of which are as clear as Crystal [etc.]. **1883** *Fisheries Exhib. Catal.* (ed. 4) 105 Sea Wolf.. Sea Parrot..Sea Sow, Cock Peddle..Sea Mouse.

4. *attrib.* and *Comb.*, as ***parrot cage, family, form, -pie, -shooting, species, story, teacher,*** etc.; of the nature of or resembling that of a parrot, esp. with reference to the mechanical repetition of words or phrases in the manner of the bird, as ***parrot-cry, -echo, -faculty, -fury, -lawyer, -learning, -phrase, -player, -prate, -prating, teaching, -voice, way, -work,*** etc.; ***parrot-billed, -bright, -learnt, -nosed, -plumed, -sharp*** adjs.; ***parrot-fashion, -like*** adjs. and advs., ***parrot-wise*** adv.; **parrot-beak** = next (*a*); **parrot-bill,** (*a*) a New Zealand plant, *Clianthus*, Kaka-bill or Glory pea (Morris *Austral Eng.*); (*b*) a war-hammer with a point like a beak (*Cent. Dict.*); (*c*) applied *attrib.* and *absol.* to a type of cutting-tool the blades of which resemble a beak; **parrot-bullfinch,** an Indian bird of the genus *Paradoxornis*; **parrot-crossbill,** a species of crossbill, *Loxia pytiopsittacus*, having a larger bill than the common species; **parrot disease, fever** = PSITTACOSIS; **parrot-finch,** (*a*) = *parrot-crossbill*; (*b*) one of the *Ploceidæ* or Weaver-birds, *Erythrura psittacea*, from New Caledonia (*List Anim. Zool. Gard.* (1896) 252); **parrot-green,** a yellowish green like the colouring of some parrots; **parrot mouth,** a malformation of a horse's mouth, in which the upper incisors project beyond the lower, so as to prevent grazing; **parrot-perch** = PARROT-FISH b (Morris *Austral. Eng.*); **parrot's bill,** †(*a*) a form of surgeon's pincers; (*b*) = *parrot-bill* (*a*); **parrot's corn**: see quot.; **parrot snake** (see quot. 1931); **parrots' plague, rinderpest,** a contagious disease to which parrots are subject; **parrot-toed** *a.*, intoed, pigeon-toed; **parrot tongue,** a tongue like that of a parrot; *spec.* a dry shrivelled condition of the human tongue in typhus, etc.; **parrot tulip,** a variety of tulip with fringed and ruffled petals, often of variegated colours; **parrot-weed,** the Tree Celandine, *Bocconia frutescens*, a tropical American plant; **parrot-wrasse** = PARROT-FISH a. Also PARROT-COAL, -FISH.

1971 *Power Farming* Mar. 46/4 Stem cutting...*parrot bill shears may be used. **1972** *Country Life* 23 Mar. 690/3 After this major excitement a willow lapses into hum-drummery and can be lopped with the parrot-bill. **1838** *Encycl. Brit.* XVI. 581/2 The *parrot-billed species. **1920** E. SITWELL *Wooden Pegasus* 24 From her fan, sliding slow, *Parrot-bright fire's feathers. **1937** —— *I live under Black Sun* 89 Giving a little girl a forbidden parrot-bright apple. **1825** P. J. SELBY *Illustr. Brit. Ornith.* I. 254 *Parrot-Crossbill. **1843** YARRELL *Hist. Brit. Birds* II. 35 Specimens of the Parrot Crossbill are frequently brought from Germany..by dealers in birds' skins. **1894** R. B. SHARPE *Handbk. Birds Gt. Brit.* (1896) 58 The so-called 'Parrot' Crossbill..is an inhabitant chiefly of Northern Europe, whence it ranges occasionally into the British Islands. **1837** J. S. MILL in *Westm. Rev.* XXVIII. 3 There would be an end to the *parrot cry of 'Do not endanger the Ministry'. **1898** *Daily News* 2 June 7/6 An old parrot-cry which had been exploded long ago. **1956** [see EYEBROW 1 c]. **1963** *Times* 20 Feb. 4/7 Such attacks are only worth noticing because they have tended to become a parrot cry. **1977** *Socialist Press* 2 Mar. 7/5 'If you have a case, why don't you go to an industrial tribunal', has become the favourite parrot cry of every barrack room lawyer crossing the picket line. **1908** *Spratt's Parrot Culture* 29 Should a room have become infected with the *parrot disease..it will be needful to have it fumigated with sulphur. **1930** *Daily Express* 6 Feb. 11/5 They [*sc.* alarming facts] concerned that dread illness, psittacosis, or parrot disease, of which a number of cases have occurred lately in London and Birmingham. **1955** *Times* 8 June 6/4 A case of psittacosis (parrot disease) has occurred in the aircraft-carrier Centaur, which berthed here to-day on her return from the Mediterranean. **1884** J. TAIT *Mind in Matter* (1892) 238 False miracles or *parrot-echoes of real ones. **1901** *Daily News* 5 Feb. 6/3 A *parrot-faculty for picking up languages. **1951** *Mind* LX. 346 People just know it by heart and recite it *parrot-fashion. **1956** D. ABERCROMBIE *Probl. & Princ.* 25 Parrot-fashion teaching is apt to result from regarding reasoned explanation as 'unnatural'. **1977** 'F. CLIFFORD' *Ten Minutes on June Morning* 111 Reassurances..were passed on, parrot-fashion, without knowledge or understanding. **1955** *Sci. News Let.* 3 Sept. 148/2 Viral hepatitis, better known to the layman as jaundice; psittacosis or *parrot fever; rabies; smallpox; yellow fever; the common cold,..are other of the virus diseases. **1957** O. BRELAND *Animal Friends & Foes* ii. 63 This malady has also been called parrot fever, because the first known human cases were traced to sick parrots. **1973** 'D. SHANNON' *No Holiday for Crime* (1974) i. 9 The stolen goods had been..tropical parrots, and..one of the San Diego detectives had subsequently succumbed to parrot fever. **1885** NEWTON *Dict. Birds* (1896) 686 The home of the vast majority of *Parrot-forms is..within the tropics. **1627** *Peele's Merry Jests* C iv b, At which shee biting her lip, in a *parrat fury went downe the staires. **1646** SIR T. BROWNE *Pseud. Ep.* 138 The little Frogge of an excellent *Parrat-green, that usually sits on trees and bushes. **1885** STEVENSON *Child's Gard. Verses, Trav.* 4 Where below another sky *Parrot islands anchored lie. **1616** T. ADAMS *Pol. Hunting* Wks. 1862 I. 16 Their ban-dogs, corrupt solicitors, *parrot-lawyers, that are their properties and mere trunks. **1901** G. G. COULTON *Public Schools & Public Needs* 312 We cannot prevent..mere *parrot-learning, from counting somewhat ..against real culture. **1977** *Observer* 20 Mar. 13/3 There seem to be two potent reasons why memorising (or 'parrot-learning', as people ignorant of the mental capacities of parrots sometimes call it) should once more become a staple component of curricula. **1856** MISS MULOCK *J. Halifax* xxvi, His lips moved in a paroxysm of prayer—helpless, *parrot-learnt, Latin prayer. **1847** CARPENTER *Zool.* §458 The horny *parrot-like beaks of Cuttlefish. **1888** F. HUME *Mme. Midas* I. v, Why do I repeat them, parrot-like? **1899** *Allbutt's Syst. Med.* VIII. 246 In the education of mentally feeble children, parrot-like repetition should be carefully avoided. **1891** O. WILDE *Pict. Dorian Gray* v. 89 'Foolish child! foolish child!' was the *parrot-phrase flung in answer. **1958** *People* 4 May 4/2, I can get no comment except the parrot-phrase: 'The Home Secretary is still considering this case.' **1907** P. FOUNTAIN *Rambles Austral. Naturalist* ii. 8 *Parrot-pie is as much esteemed in Australia as rook-pie in England. **1923** E. SITWELL *Bucolic Comedies* 25 Who came from the *parrot-plumed sea. **1804** WOLCOTT (P. Pindar) *Epist. to Ld. Mayor* Wks. 1812 V. 206 Despise his mind and *parrot-prate. **1582** STANYHURST *Æneis* I. (Arb.) 26 His prittye *parat prating. **1597** A. M. tr. *Guillemeau's Fr. Chirurg.* lf. xv b/2 The pinsers which are callede '*parates billes'. **1866** *Treas. Bot.* 298 C[lianthus] *puniceus*, called Parrot's-Bill..from the resemblance of the keeled petal to the bill of that bird. **1857** MAYNE *Expos. Lex.*, **Parrot's Corn*, common name for the seeds of the *Carthamus tinctorius*, or bastard saffron. **1936** E. SITWELL *Victoria of Eng.* ii. 33 Her dark *parrot-sharp face. **1907** P. FOUNTAIN *Rambles Austral. Naturalist* ii. 8 *Parrot-shooting is a favourite sport in Australia. **1931** R. L. DITMARS *Snakes of World* Pl. 19 (*caption*) Green Tree Snake; Chocoya or *Parrot Snake, *Leptophis occidentalis*. Found from Guatemala to northern South America. Uniform leaf-green with two hair-like strips on the back. **1958** J. CAREW *Wild Coast* ii. 28 A green parrot-snake slithered down a coconut tree. **1895** *Daily News* 19 Dec. 5/4 Spoken of as the *parrots' plague..called by Laics *parrots' rinderpest... One of the persons who died..at Versailles of the distemper was an officer's wife. She caught it by feeding the bird with sugar from her mouth. **1599** SHAKS. *Much Ado* I. i. 139 You are a rare *Parrat teacher. **1887** MOLONEY *Forestry W. Afr.* 255 Too much time devoted in the past to the exercise of memory, to '*parrot' teaching. **1849** W. F. LYNCH *Exped. Jordan* v. 91 Most of the Turks walk what is termed *parrot-toed, very much like our Indians. **1860** READE *Cloister & H.* lviii. (1896) 179 If you would but..hold your *parrot tongues. **1897** *Allbutt's Syst. Med.* II. 357 Dry, brown-crusted, shrivelled tongue—'the parrot-tongue' of typhus. **1774** GOLDSM. *Nat. Hist.* V. 283 The *parrot-tribe might be an instance. [**1829** J. C. LOUDON *Encycl. Plants* 266 One of the latest London catalogues (Mason's) enumerates six sorts of early blowing tulips; four perroquets or middle blowers; twenty-two double sorts.] **1856** C. M. YONGE *Daisy Chain* II. xxi. 586 She was nothing better than a *parrot-tulip, stuck up in a parterre. **1882** *Garden* 13 May 333/3 A bunch of Parrot Tulips..in a tall Dutch jar. **1890** O. WILDE *Pict. Dorian Gray* iii, in *Lippincott's Monthly Mag.* July 22 Some large blue china jars, filled with parrot-tulips, were ranged on the mantel-shelf. **1897** *Westm. Gaz.* 11 May 2/1 That marvel of red and gold and green and terra-cotta, with its fantastic jagged petals and its sharp spur, which goes by the name of the parrot tulip. **1911** J. WEATHERS *Bulb Bk.* 441/2 Parrot or Dragon Tulips. These curious-looking and remarkable Tulips are believed to be derived from *T*[*ulipa*] *viridiflora*. **1932** A. J. MACSELF *Bulbs* v. 58 The Cottage, Darwin, and Parrot tulips..require similar general treatment. **1971** R. GENDERS *Collecting Antique Plants* viii. 191 Early Parrot tulips are depicted in a water colour drawing about 1700... The artist is Herman Henstenburg. **1925** R. FRY *Let.* 1 May (1972) II. 568 A lady with a *parrot voice screaming that she wanted a Picasso of the blue period. **1975** C. FREMLIN *Long Shadow* v. 37 'Very well, thank you,' she heard her parrot voice saying..to the two or three people who rang up. **1828** *Lights & Shades* I. 318 Their notions are in all cases alike infused in the true *parrot way. **1856** J. W. WARTER in *Southey's Lett.* (1856) II. 292 In what way Southey wished the Catechism taught,..not *parrotwise, but Christianwise. **1806** *Edin. Rev.* VII. 468 Avoiding..what he calls *parrot-work. **1884** *Longm. Mag.* Mar. 529 Certain tropical species of herrings and *parrot-wrasses.

Hence (*nonce-wds.*) **parro'tese** [see -ESE], parrot-language; **'parrothood.**

1889 MAX MÜLLER *Nat Relig.* xiv. 361 The parrot never speaks parrotese. **1894** *Daily Tribune* (N.Y.) 5 July, From early parrothood the lost one displayed a keen sense of the conventionalities of polite speech.

parrot ('pærət), *v.* [f. prec., q.v. for Forms.]

1. *intr.* To chatter like a parrot; to repeat words or phrases in a mechanical manner, like that of a parrot taught to speak. Also ***to parrot it.*** Now only as *absol.* use of next.

1596 NASHE *Saffron Walden* 136 Hee would do nothing but crake and parret it in Print, in how manie Noble-mens fauours hee was. **1612** CHAPMAN *Widow's T.* Plays 1873 III. 82 If you Parrat to me long. **1647** TRAPP *Comm. 1 Cor.* xiv. 15 It is not praying but parotting. I have read of a Parot in Rome, that could..say over the whole Creed. **1970** C. HAMPTON *Philanthropist* iv. 49 Will you please stop parroting on about breakfast?

2. *trans.* To repeat (words) mechanically or by rote like a parrot; to iterate to weariness; to repeat or imitate without understanding or sense.

1649 HEYLIN *Relat. & Observ.* II. 202 If the Ministers will not parret forth the new States Doctrine to you, they shall be starved out of their Pulpits. **1805** T. HOLCROFT *Bryan Perdue* I. 132 Boys parrot what they hear. **1823** DE QUINCEY *Lett. Educ.* v. (1860) 94 To parrot the *ipsissima verba* of Kant. **1872** F. HALL *False Philol.* 31 The verb *experience* is, to Mr. White, parroting Dean Alford, altogether objectionable. **1880** *Grove's Dict. Mus.* I. 225/2 An idea.. which has been parrotted by incapable..critics. **1965** *Austral. Women's Weekly* 20 Jan. 48/1 'I'll wait,' he said. 'He'll wait,' she parroted. **1968** *Language* XLIV. 204 School textbooks..had simply parroted a series of rules. **1971** *Nature* 13 Aug. 456/2 Thus a child who produces the correct response when asked the AC question may do so by parroting a verbal label picked up during the initial comparisions. **1976** *Amer. Speech 1973* XLVIII. 259 She quickly muddies the water when she parrots the creed that all languages and dialects are equally fit to express 'concepts such as time or relativity'. **1977** *Spare Rib* Jan. 11/1 The catechism, which we had to be able to parrot, went into the different sorts of sins at great length.

3. *trans.* To teach to repeat in a mechanical parrot-like manner; to drill like a parrot.

1775 S. J. PRATT *Liberal Opin.* III. (1783) I. 9 The most sensible people are frequently parrotted; they think as they are bid to think, and talk the dull dialect of their teachers, from the cradle to the coffin. **1827** LAMB *Let.* in Hazlitt *Mary & C. Lamb* (1874) 278 We are parroted into delicacy. **1890** *Sat. Rev.* 15 Feb. 196/2 The rank and file are tutored and parroted by author, by manager, or by state-manager.

Hence **'parroting** *vbl. sb.* and *ppl. a.*; **'parroter,** one who mechanically repeats something learned by rote.

a **1603** T. CARTWRIGHT *Confut. Rhem. N.T.* (1618) Pref. 5 Which had been liker vnto the prating, pratling, and parating of birds. ? *a* **1700** in D'Israeli *Cur. Lit., Hist. Thea. during Suppression*, Those proud parroting players, a sort of superbious ruffians. **1840** DE QUINCEY *Style* iii. Wks. 1890

X. 208 Passages of great musical effect..vulgarized by too perpetual a parroting. **1861** MILL *Autobiog.* i. (1874) 31 Mere parroters of what they have learnt. **1934** E. POUND *Let.* 30 Dec. (1971) 263 Mr. Croft seems to me an idiot... His kind of parroting seems to me exactly what does keep people from studying the classics. **1951** G. HUMPHREY *Thinking* iii. 223 Much 'parroting' is not entirely meaningless. **1971** *Daily Tel.* 1 Nov. 5/7 Rote learning—learning something by constant repetition or 'parroting'—free recall and other memory tests were included.

ˈparrot-coal. *Sc.* and *north. dial.* [Origin of *parrot* uncertain. (Quot. 1853 offers a fanciful guess.)] The Scotch and northern name of cannel coal.

a **1789** BLACK in Brand *Hist. Newcastle* (1789) II. 242 *note*, Parrot, or kennel coal. **1793** *Statist. Acc. Scot., Fifesh.* VIII. 451 There is, on the north parts of Torry, a fine parrot coal, in thickness 4 feet, which is very valuable. **1801** *Encycl. Brit.* (ed. 3) Suppl. II. 231/1 Cannel coal..is found in Lancashire, and in different parts of Scotland, where it is known by the name of *parrot coal.* **1853** FLEMING in *Pharmac. Jrnl.* XIII. 124 'Parrot'..might be applied to them, from the fact that, when burning, they 'chattered' somewhat like a parrot. **1877** LE CONTE *Elem. Geol.* v. (1879) 343 Cannel or parrot coal is a dense, dry, structureless, lustreless, highly-bituminous variety, which breaks with a conchoidal fracture.

ˈparroted, *ppl. a.* [f. PARROT *v.* + -ED[1].] That is repeated mechanically in the manner of a parrot.

1927 M. SADLEIR *Trollope: a Comm.* 295 Wherever he appears as..waverer from their parrotted idealisms, Sir Thomas Underwood is Trollope himself. **1966** *Listener* 30 June 949/1 This romanticism is probably a reaction from thousands of inane, parroted essays. **1969** *Daily Tel.* 5 Sept. 17 Underpaid teachers whose mission it was to hammer into my brain..the parroted conjugations of Latin verbs.

ˈparrot-fish. A name given to several fishes on account of their brilliant colouring, or as having a strong hard mouth resembling the bill of a parrot; *spec.* **a.** A fish of the family *Scaridæ* found in tropical seas and having a very strong jaw. **b.** A fish of the Australian labroid genus *Labrichthys*, esp. L. *psittacula*. **c.** One of the gymnodonts.

1712 E. COOKE *Voy. S. Sea* 28 We also took here that they call the Parrot-Fish. **1735** MORTIMER in *Phil. Trans.* XXXIX. 113 *Psittacus Piscis, viridis, Bahamensis*: The Parrot-Fish; so called from the Shape of the Head, and its beautiful Variety of Colours, green, blue, red, and yellow. **1756** P. BROWNE *Jamaica* 446 The Parrot-fish. This fish has the most beautiful lustres of any I have ever seen... The jaws thick and strong resembling the beak of a parrot. **1885** C. F. HOLDER *Marv. Anim. Life* 1 The gorgeous parrot-fishes are the sun-birds of the sea. **1902** SIR W. KENNEDY in *Daily Chron.* 13 Oct. 3/1 A very curious specimen, known in the tropic seas as the parrot-fish, from its formidable beak, like a macaw's.

parrot-house. A building in a zoological garden in which parrots are kept; freq. in *transf.* or *fig.* use *esp.* with reference to loud or raucous noise.

1872 GEO. ELIOT *Middlem.* I. II. xv. 251 Our chat would be thin and eager, as if delivered from a camp-stool in a parrot-house. **1923** H. C. BAILEY *Mr Fortune's Practice* vii. 186 It is an old-fashioned orphanage..as noisy as the parrot house. **1929** J. BUCHAN *Courts of Morning* I. 35 Yanqui youth..is chronically alcoholic and amorous, and its manners are a brilliant copy of the parrot-house. **1945** E. WAUGH *Brideshead Revisited* II. i. 216 The parrot-house fever of my wife's party. **1959** *Times* 2 Mar. 3/3 Without Mias to coordinate them, there was the tell-tale, parrothouse chatter of half a dozen leaders. **1967** 'S. WOODS' *And shame Devil* 126 A clamour in many ways reminiscent of the Parrot House at the Zoo. **1977** 'M. UNDERWOOD' *Murder with Malice* xxiii. 209 The courtroom became a parrot-house of chatter as people pushed towards the exits.

parrotism (ˈpærətɪz(ə)m). *rare.* [f. PARROT *sb.* + -ISM.] Action like that of a parrot; mechanical repetition or imitation; parrotry.

1773 MRS. GRANT *Lett. fr. Mount.* (1813) I. xxi. 170 You have traced all this premature reflection to its true..source; and you will possibly call it parrotism. **1877** M. WALLACE *Russia* 413 The 'monkeyism' and 'parrotism' of those who indiscriminately adopted foreign manners and customs.

ˈparrotize, *v. rare.* [f. PARROT *sb.* + -IZE.] *intr.* To act or speak like a parrot, to repeat parrot-like, to parrot.

1647 WARD *Simp. Cobler* 24 That Language be adapted to the Theme, He that to Parrots speaks, must parrotise. **1789** MRS. GRANT *Lett. fr. Mount.* (1813) II. xxxi. 156 You will hear many people..parrotizing about enthusiasm, when they mean bigotry or fanaticism.

parrotry (ˈpærətrɪ). [f. PARROT *sb.* + -RY.] The mechanical or servile repetition or imitation of the sayings, language, etc., of others.

1796 COLERIDGE *Watchman* No. 3. 93 *note*, This sentiment is so lugged into every debate, that it has degenerated into mere parrotry. **1847** J. STERLING *Ess.*, etc. (1848) I. p. xliii, To render the ordinary religious confidences little more than parrotry or gibberish.

parrotter, var. PARITOR *Obs.*, apparitor.

parroty (ˈpærətɪ), *a. rare.* [f. PARROT *sb.* + -Y.] Like or characteristic of a parrot.

1822 *New Monthly Mag.* V. 45 Terence reckons it, together with cat's eyes and a parrotty nose, as an insurmountable objection to a proposed bride. **1890** A. LANG *Old Friends* (1892) 158 You will have a parroty time.

parry (ˈpærɪ), *sb.* Also 8 parree. [f. PARRY *v.* Substituted for PARADE, a. F. *parade*, ad. It. *parata* (to which Fr. has no answering **parée*).]

1. The act of warding off or turning aside a blow or weapon by opposing one's own weapon or other means of defence; = PARADE *sb.* 6.

1705 H. BLACKWELL *Eng. Fencing-Master* 7 The Parry for Carte and Tierce is both from the Wrist. **1779** SHERIDAN *Critic* III. i, O cursed parry! that last thrust in tierce Was fatal. **1828** SCOTT *F.M. Perth* xxxiv, You were taught the thrust, but not the parry. **1863** WHYTE MELVILLE *Gladiators* 31 A fatal thrust.., and irresistible by any parry yet discovered.

2. *gen.* The warding off of any attack.

1709 SACHEVERELL *Serm.* 15 Aug. 11 We may..observe many..Politicians..to act always..on the Reserve,..and hold their Adversaries at a parry. **1801** MRS. PIOZZI *Let.* (in *Sotheby's Sale Catal.* (1899) 24 Nov. 122), This must be a Severe Parry [Battle of Copenhagen] to the Chief Consul.

†**3.** A fencing-bout; hence, an encounter of wits.

a **1734** NORTH *Exam.* III. vii. §11 (1740) 589 Sir George Jeffries, and one of the Prisoner's Witnesses, had a Parree of wit.

parry (ˈpærɪ), *v.* Also 7 **parie**, 8 **pary**. [app. repr. F. *parez* from *parer*, ad. It. *parare* 'to ward or defend a blow' (Florio), a development of the sense 'to prepare, make ready':—L. *parāre*.

Probably an echo of the F. imperative *parez!* as a word of command, constantly used in giving fencing lessons.]

1. *intr.* To ward off or turn aside a weapon or blow by opposing to it one's own weapon or other means of protection.

1672 MARVELL *Reh. Transp.* I. 139 Excellent at parrying and fencing. **1692** SIR W. HOPE *Fencing Master* 4 To Parie is to put by a thrust or blow, so that you are not touched with it. **1727–41** CHAMBERS *Cycl.* s.v., Good fencers push and parry at the same time... The Spaniards parry with the poniard. The ancients parried with their bucklers. **1872** BAKER *Nile Tribut.* viii. 116 They never parry with the blade.

fig. **1717** PRIOR *Alma* III. 382, I could..With learned skill, now push, now parry, From Darii to Bocardo vary. **1813** MAR. EDGEWORTH *Patron.* (1833) II. xxxiv. 327 Too angry to parry, as she usually did, with wit. **1878** BROWNING *La Saisiaz* 404 Fancy thrust and Reason parry!

2. *trans.* To stop, ward off, or turn aside (a weapon, a blow, etc.) in this way.

1692 SIR W. HOPE *Fencing Master* 26 After you have *Paried* him, you are readier to go to the *Parade* again. **1705** H. BLACKWELL *Eng. Fencing-Master* 7 Carte must be parried partly by the Edge of the Foile or Sword: Tierce must be parried with the Flat. **1824** W. IRVING *T. Trav.* I. 290, I might as well have attempted to parry a cudgel with a small sword. **1857** HUGHES *Tom Brown* II. iii, He now fights cautious,..parrying the Slogger's lunging hits.

b. *gen.* and *fig.* To avert or turn aside from oneself (anything threatened); to meet and turn aside (an awkward question, demand, etc.) by an adroit reply; to avoid, evade.

1718 *Free-thinker* No. 90 ¶5 They..retort upon the Aggressour the Injury, which they parry from themselves. **1766** CHESTERF. *Lett. Godson* (1890) 196 Nothing is more usefull either to put off or to parry disagreable and puzzling affairs. **1803** *Med. Jrnl.* X. 472 The effects of moisture must have been, in a great degree, parried by his labour. **1859** W. COLLINS *Q. of Hearts* (1875) 32, I parried her questions by the best excuses I could offer.

Hence **ˈparried** *ppl. a.*, **ˈparrying** *vbl. sb.*

1680 HICKERINGILL *Meroz* 13 I'le warrant there has been ..Parrying and Fencing. **1815** CHALMERS *Posth. Wks.* (1849) VI. 306 He would not trifle or delay or make any parrying with temptation. **1867** CARLYLE *Remin.* II. 26 Argumentative parryings and thrustings. **1878** BROWNING *La Saisiaz* 165 Estimating what was come of parried thrust.

†**parry,** app. obs. form of PERRY.

1490–1 *Durham Acc. Rolls* (Surtees) 100 Pro ij trowez pro strenyng del parry, viij*d.*

parrych, obs. form of PARISH.

†**pars,** *sb. pl. Obs.* [a. OF. *pars*, pl. of *part* PART.] Parts; parts of speech, grammar.

a **1300** *St. Gregory* 480 in Herrig *Archiv* LVII. 64 Gregorye can ful wel his pars, he can ful muche also of lawe. [Cf. *Vie du pape Grégoire* 41 (Godef.) Que a douze ans sot bien ses pars Lire et entendre des ars.] **13..** *K. Alis.* 665 The sevethen maister taught his pars, And the wit of the seoven ars. *c* **1412** HOCCLEVE *De Reg. Princ.* 480 O lordes, yeue vnto your men hir pars.

parsable (ˈpɑːsəb(ə)l, -zəb(ə)l), *a.* [f. PARSE *v.* + -ABLE.] Capable of being parsed.

1889 W. G. JENKINS in *Amer. Ann. Deaf* Apr. 105 A sentence or phrase..perfectly parsable.

parsainer, parsaner, obs. ff. PARCENER.

parsche, -en, -one, obs. ff. PARISH, PARISHEN.

parse (pɑːs, pɑːz), *v.* Also 6 peirse, 7 parce, pearce. [app. f. PARS, or f. L. *pars* part. (The pronunciation (pɑːs) is historical, and accords with the analogy of all words in *-rse*.)] **a.** *trans.* To describe (a word in a sentence) grammatically, by stating the part of speech, inflexion, and relation to the rest of the sentence; to resolve (a sentence, etc.) into its component parts of speech and describe them grammatically. In extended use in computational linguistics, to analyse (a string) into syntactic components to test its conformability to a given grammar.

a **1553** COXE *Let.* in Foxe *A. & M.* (1583) 1395/2 He [Prince Edward] hath learned almoste foure bookes of Cato to construe, to parse, and to say wythout booke. *a* **1568** ASCHAM *Scholem.* I. (Arb.) 27 Let the childe, by and by, both construe and parse it ouer againe. **1658** GURNALL *Chr. in Arm.* verse 14. II. ii. (1669) 12/2 The child reads, construes, and pearces his Lesson as the Master saith. **1797** *Monthly Mag.* III. 200/2 The important rule, that we should scrupulously parse every word we use. **1881** F. G. LEE *Reg. Barentyne* I. v. 59 Joram himself, they say,..can't parse his own sentences which never scan. **1962** J. J. ROBINSON *Prelim. Codes & Rules Automatic Parsing of English* (Rand Corp. Memo. RM-339-PR) p. v, This Memorandum presents a set of grammar codes and rules for analyzing, or 'parsing', English sentences automatically on a digital computer. *Ibid.* iii. 34 All the words in the string being parsed have been accounted for. **1963** *Communications Assoc. Computing Machinery* VI. 669/1 It will parse strings describable in essentially Backus Normal Form. **1967** D. G. HAYS *Introd. Computational Linguistics* viii. 148 First, we transcribe the grammar, omitting all context restrictions. Obviously, the new grammar parses every string acceptable to the old one and if the restrictions are not vacuous it either assigns extra structures to some acceptable strings or accepts some additional strings, and may do both. **1975** J. S. ROHL *Introd. Compiler Writing* xiii. 226 For syntax analysis it is convenient to have the definitions in an analytic form, so that we can analyse or parse a string of characters to see whether they conform to the grammar.

b. *intr.* or *absol.*

1575 LANEHAM *Let.* (1871) 61, I coold my rulez, coold conster & pars with the best of them. **1596** NASHE *Saffron Walden* 75 His Schoole-master neuer heard him peirse or conster, but he cryde out, *O acumen.* **1799** HAN. MORE *Fem. Educ.* (ed. 4) I. 241 Why in parsing is he led to refer every word to its part of speech?

fig. **1824** MISS FERRIER *Inher.* xxv, The Earl, therefore, parsed and prosed away to good Mrs. B. **1965** P. KAEL *I lost it at Movies* 9 A movie had to tell some kind of story that held together: a plot had to parse.

c. *intr.* for *pass.* To admit of being parsed.

1880 GRANT WHITE *Every-day Eng.* Pref. 13 Anxious.. whether his sentences will parse.

d. *trans.* To put (one) through his parsing; to examine minutely.

1867 FITZGERALD 75 *Brooke St.* II. 77 Look here, Mrs. Archbold, parse him well on that.

e. *transf.* To examine or analyse minutely.

1788 F. GROSE *Rules for drawing Caricaturas* 14 When a caricaturist wishes to delineate any face..he may commit it to his memory, by parsing it in his mind (as the school-boys term it). **1860** *Leisure Hour* 9 Aug. 507/2 Let him soak and remove the leather covering, parsing his way, as it were, by minute examination. **1931** *Times Lit. Suppl.* 7 May 353/3 Reade's biographer is confronted with the necessity of, as it were, 'parsing' a character which..does not make sense. **1962** P. TOMPKINS *Spy in Rome* xxxi. 307 Franco spoke Italian with a slightly foreign (or aristocratic) accent—depending on which way the listener chose to parse it.

Hence **parsed** *ppl. a.*; **ˈparsing** *vbl. sb.* (also *attrib.* or as *ppl. a.*).

a **1568** ASCHAM *Scholem.* I. (Arb.) 28 Plaine construinge, diligent parsinge. **1871** EARLE *Philol. Eng. Tongue* §211 What is called Parsing, or assigning words to their parts, is a juvenile exercise. **1962** J. J. ROBINSON *Prelim. Codes & Rules Automatic Parsing of English* (Rand Corp. Memo. RM-339-PR) i. 2 The English codes and parsing rules being developed at RAND are essentially a machine grammar. **1963** *Communications Assoc. Computing Machinery* VI. 669/1 The automatic parsing algorithms..simplify compiler construction but contribute little to the production of 'optimized' machine code, for example. **1964** *Ibid.* VII. 131/2 The right side of the algorithm..in effect runs the input string backwards..until the tentatively parsed word is reached. *Ibid.*, An example of a syntactically ambiguous phrase is 'medical schools and hospitals of Boston' which actually has five possible parsings: ((MS)AH)OB; (MS)A(HOB); (M(SAH))OB; M((SAH)OB); M(SA(HOB)). **1967** D. G. HAYS *Introd. Computational Linguistics* vi. 107 A systematic answer to questions like this, determining the exact sequence in which reductions will be made to any particular string, is the basis for a parsing strategy. *Ibid.* 114 Only complete parsing of a string reveals that any part of a tentative parsing is correct. **1971** E. WILSON in R. A. Wisbey *Computer in Lit. & Ling. Res.* v. 210 This definition it attempts to transform into an equivalent definition which can be parsed by a one-track algorithm. If it succeeds, SID can be made to generate this parsing algorithm. **1972** J. A. N. LEE *Computer Semantics* v. 273 The form of text which is generated by the analyzer, we shall name the parsed text, which may take the form of a syntactic tree or a phrase marked string.

parse (pɑːz, -s), *sb.* [f. the vb.] The action or result of parsing.

1963 *Communications Assoc. Computing Machinery* VI. 670/1 In the algorithm presented here, all possible parses are carried along as shown below in the progressing parse of *abce* according to the syntax of the earlier example. When the symbol *e* is encountered, Parse 1 cannot be continued and is dropped, leaving Parse 2 as the correct one. **1973** W. M. WAITE *Implementing Software for Non-Numeric Appl.* viii. 292 Both pattern-directed and string-directed scans have been used for parsing algorithms. If a pattern-directed scan is used, the procedure is known as a 'top-to-bottom' or 'top-down' parse; a string-directed scan yields a 'bottom-to-top' or 'bottom-up' parse.

parsec (ˈpɑːsɛk). *Astr.* [f. PAR(ALLAX + SEC(OND *sb.*[1]] A unit of length equal to the distance at which a star would have a heliocentric parallax of one second of arc, viz. $3{\cdot}09 \times 10^{16}$ metres ($19{\cdot}2 \times 10^{12}$ miles, $3{\cdot}26$ light-years), approximately.

1913 F. W. DYSON in *Monthly Notices R. Astron. Soc.* LXXIII. 342 There is need for a name for this unit of distance... Professor Turner suggests *Parsec*, which may be taken as an abbreviated form of 'a distance corresponding to a parallax of one second'. **1921** *Glasgow Herald* 11 July 4 He estimates the distance of the object as 140 parsecs or four times the distance of the Hyades cluster. **1955** *Sci. News Let.* 29 Jan. 71/2 These hydrogen clouds have diameters of several parsecs, one parsec being the distance light travels in 3·26 years. **1962** F. I. ORDWAY et al. *Basic Astronautics* vi. 290 Within 5 parsecs (16·5 light years) of the Sun, 53 individual stars have been counted, the nearest of which is Proxima Centauri, 25 trillion miles away. **1974** S. V. M. CLUBE in R. H. Stoy *Everyman's Astron.* viii. 309 The nearest star clusters are the Pleiades and Hyades which are at distances of 130 and 40 parsecs respectively and therefore beyond the reach of trigonometric parallax determinations. **1977** *Time* 30 May 42/2 The four of them are even now setting out to deliver the secret plans to rebel headquarters, light-years and parsecs away.

parsecucion, parsecut: see PERSECUTE, etc.

Parsee (pɑːˈsiː). Forms: 7 Persie, Parcee, -sie, -sey, -sy, 7–9 -si, Persee, 8– Parsee. [a. Pers. *Pārsī* Persian, f. *Pārs* Persia.

In earlier use, *Persees, -seis, -ceys*, occur as variants of *Perses, -is*, F. *Perses*, L. *Persas*, Persians.

1398 TREVISA *Barth. De P.R.* xv. cxviii. (Harl. MS. 644, lf. (131/2), þe first Perceys weron clepyd Elamytes. **1495** *Ibid.* XVIII. civ, The Persees callen an arowe Tigris.]

1. One of the descendants of those Persians who fled to India in the seventh and eighth centuries to escape Muslim persecution, and who still retain their religion (ZOROASTRIANISM); a Guebre.

1615 TERRY in Purchas *Pilgrims* (1625) II. 1479 There is one sect among the Gentiles.. called Parcees. **1630** LORD (*title*) The Religion of the Persees, As it was Compiled from a Booke of theirs. **1662** J. DAVIES tr. *Mandelslo's Trav.* 74 The Parsis believe that there is but one God, preserver of the Universe. **1698** FRYER *Acc. E. India & P.* 197 The Parsies .. are of the old stock of the Persians, worship the Sun and Adore the Elements. **1727** A. HAMILTON *New Acc. E. Ind.* I. xiv. 158 The Parsees are numerous about Surat. **1808** A. PARSONS *Trav.* xii. 260 The Mahometans are the next in number, and the Persees the least. **1881** MONIER-WILLIAMS in *19th Cent.* March 500 The Pārsīs, who are merely colonists in India, derive their name from Pārs (in Arabic, Fārs), the proper name of a particular province of their mother-country.

b. *attrib.* or as *adj.*

1698 FRYER *Acc. E. India & P.* Table, Parsy-Tombs in Persia the same as in India. **1864** PUSEY *Lect. Daniel* ix. 555 Daily objects of Parsee-worship. **1894** R. H. ELLIOT *Gold, etc. in Mysore* 224 A Parsee gentleman, whose unceasing efforts to aid the progress of India entitle him to be placed in the very highest rank.

2. The language of Persia under the Sassanian kings.

1840 *Penny Cycl.* XVII. 479/2 As to the Derí or Parsí, after it became the language of the court, it was very much cultivated by the Sassanian kings. **1881** MONIER-WILLIAMS in *19th Cent.* Jan. 160 Pārsī is merely a form of vernacular Persian, later than Pahlavī.

parsee, parsie, in hunting: see PERSUE *sb.*

Parseeism (pɑːˈsiːɪz(ə)m). Also **Parsiism**. The religion of the Parsees, Zoroastrianism.

1843 R. NESBIT in *Mem.* viii. (1858) 212 Constrained to make himself acquainted with Parsiism. **1882–3** SCHAFF *Encycl. Relig. Knowl.* II. 877/2 Parseeism with its fully-developed idea of God as light.

parsel(l, parsely(e, obs. forms of PARSLEY.

‖**parsemé** (pɑːrsəmeɪ), *a.* [Fr., pa. pple. of *parsemer* to sprinkle, strew f. L. *per-* through + *sēmināre* to sow.] Sprinkled or strewn (with); used *esp.* in embroidery with reference to the decoration of fabrics and costumes.

1814 M. BIRKBECK *Notes Journey through France* App. 14 The numerous longitudinal ridges.. with which this charming country is, 'parsemé', appear to be the venerable remains of the ancient surface. **1832** F. TROLLOPE *Dom. Manners Amer.* I. vi. 74 She was preparing to set to work in a yellow dress parsemé with red roses... I thought it was a pity to spoil so fine a gown. **1883** H. C. DENT *Jrnl.* 9 June in *Year in Brazil* (1886) i. 4 The country on the north bank has a low coastline, *parsemé* with red-roofed white houses. **1890** O. WILDE *Pict. Dorian Gray* ix, in *Lippincott's Monthly Mag.* July 71 A skull-cap *parsemé* with pearls. **1905** *Athenæum* 17 June 760 The rise of a new conception of design, with figures and ornaments parsemé on a velvet ground,.. in the fifteenth century.

parsenep, -nip, obs. forms of PARSNIP.

parsener, obs. form of PARCENER.

parser (ˈpɑːsə(r), -zə(r)). [f. PARSE *v.* + -ER[1].] One who parses; a book on parsing; a computer program for parsing.

1864 in WEBSTER. **1869** MARCH (*title*) A Parser and Analyzer for Beginners. **1882** *Mrs. Raven's Tempt.* II. 99 An expert parser need not be an intelligent reader. **1965** *Communications Assoc. Computing Machinery* VIII. 688/1 In testing the program on 300 basic English sentences Knowlton's parser produced 137 correct parsings and 44 incorrect ones. **1967** D. G. HAYS *Introd. Computational Linguistics* vi. 116 Whereas the other parsers considered.. have generally operated more or less from left to right on the string, or from right to left, this one operates by choosing.. the top of the dependency structure, and working downward. **1970** *Computers & Humanities* v. 25 More computational parsers are being written following the generative-transformational model than any other. **1977** E. VON GLASERSFELD in D. M. Rumbaugh *Lang. Learning by Chimpanzee* v. 121 The parser, however, can handle a lexicon of 250 items.

parser, obs. f. PIERCER.

parsettensite (pɑːˈsɛtənzaɪt). *Min.* [ad. G. *parsettensit* (J. Jakob 1923, in *Schweiz. min. und petrogr. Mitt.* III. 227), f. Alp *Parsettens*, name of the locality in Val d'Err, Graubünden, E. Switzerland where it was first found: see -ITE[1] 2 b.] A basic silicate of manganese that often contains appreciable potassium and occurs as copper-red masses.

1924 *Mineral. Abstr.* II. 251 Parsettensite.. occurs as a filling in rather thick veins. **1962** W. A. DEER et al. *Rockforming Min.* III. 103 Parsettensite.. was shown by Fankuchen.. to be a manganese stilpnomelane, and it is proposed to retain this name to describe varieties rich in manganese. **1968** I. KOSTOV *Mineral.* 362 Transitional towards the vermiculite group are stilpnomelane, ekmanite, and parsettensite, with formulas similar to those of the illites but as a rule without aluminium in tetrahedral co-ordination.

parseue, -seyue, obs. ff. PERCEIVE.

Parseval (ˈpɑːsɪvəl). Also **Parsefal**. [The name of the inventor, the German engineer August von *Parseval* (1861–1942).] A type of non-rigid dirigible airship formerly in use in Germany.

[**1908** W. H. STORY tr. *Hildebrandt's Airships* viii. 85 (*caption*) Major Parseval's dirigible balloon.] **1909** *Chambers's Jrnl.* Oct. 660/2 At present the airship fleet consists of three Zeppelins, three Parsefals, and two Gross dirigibles. *Ibid.*, It is of the Parsefal type. **1910** C. C. TURNER *Aerial Navig. To-day* xxiv. 295 The 'Parseval' is a non-rigid balloon with a cubic capacity of 190,000 cubic feet... It is rounded at the front and pointed at the rear. **1931** C. ST. J. SPRIGG *Airship* viii. 106 In its final form the Parseval was not much smaller than the early Zeppelins, and was of a good streamline shape. *Ibid.* 110 Two of the Parseval type were built by Messrs. Vickers under licence. **1957** *Encycl. Brit.* I. 465/1 Maj. August von Parseval in 1906 constructed for the German army the first in a series of some 28 Parseval pressure type airships which were built from that date until 1929. **1959** J. A. SINCLAIR *Famous Airships of World* iii. 30 In Germany, Major von Parseval.. in 1911 constructed the *Parseval No. 3*... The steel tube car carried 12 passengers. **1971** R. JACKSON *Airships* v. 112 On the outbreak of war, the Astra-Torres and the Parseval were immediately allocated to coastal patrol duties.

parshe, obs. f. PARISH.

Parsi, Parsiism, var. PARSEE, PARSEEISM.

Parsic (ˈpɑːsɪk), *a.* [f. Pers. *Pārs* Persia (see PARSEE) + -IC.] Pertaining to the Parsees.

1876 tr. *Keil's Ezek.* I. 126 The seven Parsic amschaspands.

parsil, dial. form of PARSLEY.

parsimonious (pɑːsɪˈməʊnɪəs). *a.* Also 7 perci-, 7– parci-. [f. L. *parsimōnia* PARSIMONY + -OUS. Cf. It. *parsimonioso* (Florio 1598), F. *parcimonieux* (1788 in Hatz.-Darm.).] Characterized by parsimony; careful in the use or disposal of money or resources; sparing, saving; 'close'. Said of persons, their expenditure, etc.

1598 DALLINGTON *Meth. Trav.* H, Such a parsimonious sparer was Lewes 11. **1601** R. JOHNSON *Kingd. & Commw.* (1603) 238 Being so percimonious and sparing in his expences. **1655** FULLER *Ch. Hist.* III. i. §28 Afterward he proved most parcimonious. **1769** ROBERTSON *Chas. V*, XI. III. 315 He husbanded the provisions.. with the most parsimonious economy. **1874** GREEN *Short Hist.* vii. §3. 364 Her expenditure was parsimonious and even miserly.

b. *fig.* Sparing or niggardly in the use or disposal of immaterial things.

a **1716** SOUTH *Serm.* (1744) IX. vii. 212 These are those inexorable spiritual Cato's, those parsimonious dispensers of mercy. **1745** J. MASON *Self Knowl.* I. v. (1853) 46 Nature .. deals out her Favours in the present State with a parcimonious Hand. **1865** SEELEY *Ecce Homo* i. (ed. 8) 4 They asked, is God so little parsimonious of his noblest gift.

c. Of things: Yielding sparingly, unproductive; meagre, scanty; showing parsimony, poor, mean.

1713 C'TESS WINCHELSEA *Misc. Poems* 169 T'allay thy envy'd Gains, Unthought of, on the parcimonious Plains. **1782** MISS BURNEY *Cecilia* I. ix, Her dress, though parsimonious, was too neat for a beggar. **1830** S. WARREN *Diary Physic.* (ed. Tauchn.) I. 11 Our parsimonious fare hardly deserved the name of food.

Hence **parsiˈmoniously** *adv.*, **parsiˈmoniousness**.

1671 L. ADDISON *W. Barbary* v. 130, I find them.. without Parsimoniousness, and placing no Character of good House-keeping in abundance of Viands. *a* **1745** SWIFT (J.), Our ancestors acted parsimoniously, because they only spent their own treasure for the good of their posterity; whereas we squandered away the treasures of our posterity. **1822–56** DE QUINCEY *Confess.* (1862) 161, I continued.. to live most parsimoniously in lodgings. **1859** HELPS *Friends in C.* Ser. II. II. v. 110 It should tend to.. generosity rather than to parsimoniousness.

parsimony (ˈpɑːsɪmənɪ). Also 5– parci-, (7 percemonie). [ad. L. *parsimōnia* or *parcimōnia*, f. *parc-ĕre*, ppl. stem *pars-* to spare, save. Cf. It. *parsimonia* (Florio 1598), F. *parcimonie* (1567 in Hatz.-Darm.), *parsimonie* (Cotgr. 1611); adm. in Dict. Acad. 1798 as *parsimonie*, altered 1835 to *parcimonie*. Latin scholars appear to agree that *parsimonia* was the actual spelling in classical L.] Carefulness in the employment of money or material resources; saving or economic disposition. **a.** In good or neutral sense.

1432–50 tr. *Higden* (Rolls) III. 35 The nowble man Ligurgus.. movenge that parcimony scholde be hade of alle men, leste the labore of cheuallry scholde faile thro plente. *c* **1540** tr. *Pol. Verg. Eng. Hist.* (Camden No. 36) I. 90 A prince of great parsimonie, and in noe respecte ambitious. **1604** R. CAWDREY *Table Alph.*, *Parsimonie*, thriftines, sparing. **1623** COCKERAM, *Parsimonie*, thriftinesse, good husbandrie. **1631** T. POWELL *Tom All Trades* (1876) 170 Without profusenesse, or too much percemonie. **1642** AMES *Marrow Div.* 378 Parsimony is a vertue whereby we make only honest and necessary expences. **1776** ADAM SMITH *W.N.* v. iii. (1869) II. 509 The want of parsimony in time of peace, imposes the necessity of contracting debt in time of war. **1865** TYLOR *Early Hist. Man.* ix. 268 In.. all domestic matters, they use the ancient parsimony.

b. In dyslogistic sense: Stinginess, niggardliness.

1561 EDEN *Arte Nauig.* Pref., By miserable couetousnes and parcimonie. **1673** *Lady's Call.* II. iii. §5 This is one of the most pernicious parsimonies imaginable. **1697** DRYDEN *Virg. Georg.* III. 281 Nor be with harmful Parsimony won. **1712** ARBUTHNOT *John Bull* III. vii, It is impossible to march up close to the frontiers of frugality, without entering the territories of parsimony. **1782** MISS BURNEY *Cecilia* v. viii, By parsimony, vulgarity and meanness [he should] render riches contemptible. **1871** *Daily News* 3 Jan., What is not just economy may fairly be charged with the opprobrious name of parsimony. **1896** *Times* 1 Sept. 7/4 Due to ill-judged Parliamentary interference and to the misplaced parcimony of the Treasury.

c. *fig.* With reference to immaterial things. Also, the principle that organisms tend towards economy of action in learning or in fulfilling their needs.

1656 BLOUNT *Glossogr.*, *Parsimony*,.. brevity or sparingness in the use of words. **1667** SOUTH *Serm.* I. 286 That Parsimony in God's Worship were the worst Husbandry in the World. **1876** LOWELL *Among my Bks.* Ser. II. 40 Dante's parsimony of epithet. **1931** D. K. ADAMS in *Brit. Jrnl. Psychol.* XXII. 153 This economy upon repetition or, better, the property (we shall call it parsimony) of which it is simply one manifestation, is a fundamental property of a certain class of bodies. *Ibid.*, I think that parsimony is a property of all organisms. **1948** E. R. HILGARD *Theories of Learning* xi. 295 The process of need satiation is regulated by a principle called 'parsimony'. That is a preference for short-cuts, described by others as the principle of least action. **1955** *Sci. Amer.* June 68/1 This is the grand overriding law of the parsimony of nature: every action within a system is executed with the least possible expenditure of energy.

d. ***law of parsimony***: the logical principle that no more causes or forces should be assumed than are necessary to account for the facts. Also *parsimony*, ***principle of parsimony***.

1837 SIR W. HAMILTON *Metaph.* xxxix. (1870) II. 395 The law of Parcimony, which forbids, without necessity, the multiplication of entities, powers, principles, or causes; above all, the postulation of an unknown force, where a known impotence can account for the effect. **1864** BOWEN *Logic* i. 17 By the law of parsimony.. language makes up its millions of names or designations out of comparatively few words. **1890** C. L. MORGAN *Anim. Life & Intell.* (1891) 174 We do not know enough about the causes of variation to be rigidly bound by the law of parcimony. **1933** J. C. FLÜGEL *Hundred Years Psychol.* ii. 124 The 'law of parsimony', according to which we must always explain animal behaviour in terms of the simplest mental processes that will account for the facts. **1957** R. K. MERTON *Social Theory* (rev. ed.) viii. 259 The theoretical objective of *parsimony*, found whenever several empirical generalizations are derived from a more general formulation. **1970** M. H. MARX *Learning: Theories* I. i. 16/2 The principle of parsimony, often called William of Occam's razor or Lloyd Morgan's canon,.. is a rough guideline to the acceptability of hypotheses and principles. *Ibid.* 17/1 The failure to accept the principle of parsimony results in the overloading of relatively untested.. ideas. **1972** *Encycl. Psychol.* I. 202/2 The essential similarity between classical and operant conditioning has led students to pose questions about the parsimony or necessity of more than one principle to account for this type of learning.

pars intermedia (pɑːz ɪntəˈmiːdɪə). *Anat.* [mod.L., = 'middle part'.] A layer of tissue in the hypophysis between the anterior and posterior lobes (sometimes regarded as a part of the anterior lobe).

1908 P. T. HERRING in *Q. Jrnl. Exper. Physiol.* I. 132 It is convenient to consider as the anterior lobe only that portion of it which has already been distinguished from the 'pars intermedia'. **1912** H. CUSHING *Pituitary Body & its Disorders* i. 4 The posterior lobe comprises the pars nervosa .. and its epithelial investment (pars intermedia of Herring). **1926**, etc. [see *neuro-intermediate* adj. s.v NEURO-]. **1932** [see INTERMEDIN]. **1962** E. C. CROSBY et al. *Correl. Anat. Nerv. Syst.* vi. 323/2 From Rathke's pouch, an embryonic diverticulum from the roof of the stomadeum, are derived the pars distalis, pars intermedia, and pars tuberalis. **1968** W. C. BOWMAN et al. *Textbk. Pharmacol.* xiv. 365 The hormone of the pars intermedia (the melanocyte stimulating hormone, MSH) stimulates dispersion of the melanin granules in melanocytes of the skin of fish, amphibia and reptiles, with a resulting darkening of the skin.

Parsism (ˈpɑːsɪz(ə)m). [f. *Parsi*, PARS-EE + -ISM.] = PARSEEISM.

1849 FROUDE *Nemesis of Faith* 89 It was the development of Parsism in settling finally the vast question of the double principle. **1892** T. K. CHEYNE *Orig. Psalter* viii. 437 Inconceivable on the principles of Parsism.

parsley ('pɑːslɪ). Forms: α. 1 petersilie, 4–5 petrosilye, -sili. β. 3–5 percil, 4–5 peresil, persil, -sel, -cel, -cyl(l, -sile, -syle, -sylle, -cile, -cyle, -cell(e, -cylle, 4–7 -cell; 5 parcyl, -celle, 6 *Sc.* -sell, 8 *Sc.* -sel, 8–9 *dial.* -sil, -cel. γ. 4–6 percely, 4–7 persely, 5 -selye, -selee, -celi, -celli, -cyly, -sol(e)y, 5–6 -celly, 6 -seley, -celey, 6–7 -selie; 5 parcel(l)y, 6 -selye, -celye, -celay, 6–7 -sely. δ. 5 persle, 5–7 (8 *dial.*) persley, 6 -lie, 7 -ly; 6 parslye, 6–8 parsly, 6– parsley. [In α forms (cf. OHG. *petarsile*, MHG. *petersîl*, Ger. *petersilie*, MDu. *petersilie*, Du. *peterselie*), ad. late L. *petrosilium*, an unexplained alteration of cl. L. *petroselinum*, a. Gr. πετροσέλῑνον 'rock-parsley', f. πέτρα rock, or πέτρος + σέλῑνον parsley. In β forms. a. OF. *peresil* (13th c. in Hatz.-Darm.), later *persil*:—late L. *petrosīlium*; in It. *petrosillo* (Florio), now *petrosellino*. In γ and δ, *perselye*, etc., app. a mixture of the OF. forms with the ending of the OE.]

1. A biennial umbelliferous plant (*Petroselinum sativum*, sometimes classed as *Apium* or *Carum Petroselinum*), a native of the Mediterranean region, having white flowers, and aromatic leaves which in the commonly cultivated variety are finely divided and curled, and are used for seasoning and garnishing various dishes; in another variety (***Hamburg parsley***) the large spindle-shaped root is dressed and eaten. Hence, the leaves of this plant, or the plants collectively. (Not used with *a* or in *pl.*, exc. as = kind of parsley.) Also extended to the genus *Petroselinum*.

α. *c* **1000** *Sax. Leechd.* I. 240 Hy sume men..petersilie hateþ. **1398** TREVISA *Barth. De P.R.* XVII. cxxx. (MS. Bodl.) lf. 223/1 Petrosilye [**1495** Petrosili] hatte Petrosilium and is an herbe þat groweþ in gardynes wiþ goode smel.

β. [*c* **1265** *Voc. Plant.-n.* in Wr.-Wülcker 556/11 *Petrosillum* i. peresil, i. stoansuke.] **1362** LANGL. *P. Pl.* A. VII. 273, I haue porettes and percyl [*v.rr.* persil(e, persely]. *a* **1400** *Pistill Susan* 107 þe persel, þe passenep, poretes to preue. *c* **1440** *Anc. Cookery* in *Househ. Ord.* (1790) 427 Take sage and parcyl. **14..** *Nom.* in Wr.-Wülcker 710/14 *Hoc petrocillum*, persylle. *c* **1450** *Alphita* (Anecd. Oxon) 169 Persile. **1483** *Cath. Angl.* 270/1, 275/2 Parcelle, Percelle, *petrocillum*. **14..** *Treat. Gardening* in *Archæologia* LIV. 1. 164/126 The kynde of percell. **1595** DUNCAN *App. Etymol.*, *Petroselinum*, parsell. **1828** *Craven Gloss.* (ed. 2), *Parsil*.

γ, δ. *c* **1386** CHAUCER *Cook's Prol.* 26 Of thy percely [*v.rr.* persle, -sele, -sely, -celly] yet they fare the wors. **1393** LANGL. *P. Pl.* C. IX. 310 Ich haue porett-plontes perselye [*v.r.* percile] and scalones. *c* **1420** *Liber Cocorum* (1862) 31 Take persoley and sage and grynde hit wele. *c* **1440** *Promp. Parv.* 393/2 Persley, herbe (*K.* percyly, *S.* percyle, *P.* percyll), *petrocillum vel petrocilium*. *c* **1450** *Two Cookery-bks.* 72 Take parcelly, Sauge, Isoppe, Rose Mary. **1530** PALSGR. 252/1 Parcelay, *parsil*. **1542** BOORDE *Dietary* xix. (1870) 278 The Rootes of percelly soden tender. **1570** LEVINS *Manip.* 99/32 Parcelye. **1584** COGAN *Haven Health* xxxi. (1636) 50 The chiefe vertue of perselie is in the roote. **1594** LYLY *Moth. Bomb.* III. iv, Me thought his hose were cut and drawen out with parsly. **1617** MINSHEU *Ductor*, *Parsley*, ..*Perselie*,..*Persly*. **1620** VENNER *Via Recta* vii. 133 Sodden with Orgaine and Parsely. **1699** EVELYN *Acetaria* 8 Fried in fresh Butter crisp with Persley. **1747** WESLEY *Prim. Physick* (1762) 39 A Plaister of chopt Parsley mixt with Butter. **1876** HARLEY *Mat. Med.* (ed. 6) 581 Parsley yields an aromatic volatile oil.

2. Applied, with defining words, to various plants (almost all umbelliferous), mostly with finely-divided leaves; as **bastard parsley**, the genus *Caucalis*, esp. *C. daucoides*; **beaked parsley**, the genus *Anthriscus* (from its beaked fruit); **black parsley**, (*a*) Stone-Parsley, *Sison Amomum*; (*b*) a shrubby umbelliferous plant of Madeira, *Melanoselinum* (*Thapsia*) *decipiens*; **corn parsley**, a cornfield weed, *Petroselinum segetum*, allied to the common parsley; **garden parsley, Hamburg parsley** (see 1); †**great parsley**, an old name for Alexanders, *Smyrnium Olusatrum*; **hedge parsley**, †(*a*) = Bastard Parsley; (*b*) *Torilis Anthriscus* (see HEDGE *sb.* 10), or the genus *Torilis*; **Macedonian parsley**, *Seseli* (*Bubon* L.) *macedonicum*; also identified by Lyte, etc. with various other umbellifers; **marsh parsley**, †(*a*) an old name for smallage or wild celery, *Apium graveolens*; (*b*) '*Œnanthe Lachenalii* and the genus *Elæoselinum*' (Miller *Plant-n.* 1884); **milk, milky parsley**, a name for species of *Peucedanum* and *Selinum* with milky juice; **mountain parsley**, (*a*) an umbelliferous plant, *Peucedanum Oreoselinum*; (*b*) the Parsley Fern, *Allosorus crispus* (*Cryptogramme crispa*); **pig's parsley**, 'probably *Anthriscus sylvestris*', Cow-parsley (Britten & Holland); **rock parsley**, †(*a*) Stone-parsley; (*b*) the Parsley Fern; †**rose parsley**, a name suggested by Turner for the garden anemone; **square parsley**, †(*a*) applied by Turner to *Carum Bulbocastanum*; (*b*) now usually applied to *Ptychotis heterophylla* (*Carum heterophyllum*); †**thorough-bored parsley**, 'an old name for *Smyrnium apiifolium*' (Miller), from its hollow stem; **wild parsley**, name for various wild umbellifers with finely-divided leaves. See also ASS[1] *parsley*, BUR *parsley*, COW-PARSLEY, *dog's parsley* (DOG *sb.*[1] 20 d), *fool's parsley* (FOOL *sb.*[1] 7 c), HEMLOCK *parsley*, HORSE *parsley*, SHEEP'S *parsley*, STONE-PARSLEY, WATER-PARSLEY.

1548 ELYOT, *Caucalis*,..an herbe like fenel with a white flowre and short stalke, and is supposed to come of naughtye persely seede. It is also called *bastarde persely. **1578** LYTE *Dodoens* v. xlviii. 612. **1841** *Withering's Arr. Brit. Pl.* (ed. 5) 143 Common *Beaked-parsley. Fruit egg-shaped. **1562** TURNER *Herbal* II. 139 b, Sison..is called of som *black perselye. **1861** MISS PRATT *Flower. Pl.* III. 3 A shrubby plant of this Order..called the Black Parsley. **1633** JOHNSON *Gerarde's Herbal* II. cccc. 1017 Of *Corne Parsley, or Hone-wort. **1640** PARKINSON *Theatr. Bot.* 931. **1760** J. LEE *Introd. Bot.* App. 321 Parsley, Corn, *Sison*. **1578** LYTE *Dodoens* v. xli. 605 *Garden Parsely hath greene leaues, iagged, and in diuers places deepe cut, and snypt. **1712** tr. *Pomet's Hist. Drugs* I. 2 A Plant which resembles..our Garden-Parsley. **1578** LYTE *Dodoens* v. xlv. 608 Of *great Parsely or Alexander. *Ibid.* 609 The seede of great Parsely is of lyke vertue to the seede of the garden Parsely. **1796** C. MARSHALL *Garden.* xv. (1813) 245 Parsley broad leaved, as an esculent root, is commonly called *Hamburgh parsley and is eat as carrots. **1633** JOHNSON *Gerarde's Herbal* II. ccccciii. 1022 *Caucalis minor flosc. rub.*..I haue thought good to call *Hedge, or field Parsley. **1683** SALMON *Doron Med.* I. 7 Hedge, or Bastard Parsly. **1578** LYTE *Dodoens* v. xliv. 607–8 Of stone Parsely..The whiche..is the true Parsely, called by the name of the place, where as it groweth most plentifully, *Parsely of Macedonie. **1640** PARKINSON *Theatr. Bot.* 924–5. **1706** PHILLIPS, *Macedonian Parsley*, otherwise called *Alisanders*, one of the Furnitures of Winter-Sallets. **1746** WATSON in *Phil. Trans.* XLIV. 230 Two Persons, who had eaten these roots, mistaking them for Macedonian Parsley. **1578** LYTE *Dodoens* v. xlii. 606 Of *Marish Parsely, March or Smallache. **1657** W. COLES *Adam in Eden* 290. **1866** *Treas. Bot.* 849/1 Parsley, Marsh, *Elæoselinum*. **1806** GALPINE *Brit. Bot.* 131 *Milk parsley (Selinum). **1884** MILLER *Plant-n.*, *Peucedanum palustre*, Brimstone-wort, Milk-Parsley. **1640** PARKINSON *Theatr. Bot.* 928, I have entituled it in English, Wild *milkie Parsley. **1760** J. LEE *Introd. Bot.* App. 321 Parsley, Milky, *Selinum*. **1578** LYTE *Dodoens* v. xliii. 607 The Auncientes haue alwayes described a kinde whiche they name *Mountayne Parsely..albeit it be nowe growen out of knowledge. **1760** J. LEE *Introd. Bot.* App. 321 Parsley, Mountain, *Athamanta*. **1861** MISS PRATT *Flower. Pl.* VI. 168 Curled Rock-brake, Mountain Parsley, or Rock Parsley. **1866** *Treas. Bot.* 849/1 Parsley, Mountain, *Peucedanum Oreoselinum*. *a* **1697** AUBREY *Wilts.* (R. Soc. MS. p. 120) (Br. & Holl. s.v. *Pig's Parsley*), The taylor's wife ..made a pultesse of *Pigges-Parseley stampt with oatemeale grutts, and tooke of the swelling in a very short time. **1611** COTGR., *Persil de roc*..*Rocke Parseley, stone Parseley. **1861** [see *mountain parsley*]. **1548** TURNER *Names of Herbes* 13 Anemone groweth muche about Bon in Germany..it may be called in english *rose perseley. *Ibid.* 22 Bunium..may be called in englishe *square perseley. **1866** *Treas. Bot.* 849/1 Parsley, Square, *Ptychotis heterophylla*. **1597** GERARDE *Herbal* II. ccclxxxvii. 869 Smyrnium..in English..*Thorowbored Parsley. *c* **1265** *Voc. Plant-n.* in Wr.-Wülcker 556/12 *Closera*, i. alisaundre, i. *wilde percil. *a* **1450** *Stockh. Med. MS.* ii. 783 in *Anglia* XVIII. 326 Wylde persyle most is he lyk. **1548** TURNER *Names of Herbes* 74 Sison...Ther groweth a kinde of this besyde Shene, and it maye be called in englishe wylde Perseley. **1611** COTGR., *Persil aigrun*, Wild Parseley, great water Parseley, sallade Parseley. **1760** J. LEE *Introd. Bot.* App. 321 Parsley, Wild, of America, *Cardiospermum*. **1861** MISS PRATT *Flower. Pl.* III. 23 *Petroselinum segetum* (Corn Parsley)...This is the truly Wild Parsley.

3. *attrib.* and *Comb.*, as ***parsley-crown, -leaf, -pie, -root, -wreath***; ***parsley-dark, -flavoured, -like*** adjs.; †**parsley apple**, a (? green-skinned) variety of apple; **parsley-bed**, (*a*) a bed of parsley; (*b*) see quot. 1622 [cf. Gr. σέλινον]; **parsley break-stone** = PARSLEY-PIERT (see BREAKSTONE); **parsley butterfly** *U.S.*, the black swallowtail butterfly, *Papilio polyxenes asterius*; **parsley camphor** = APIOL; **parsley caterpillar** *U.S.*, the larva of the anise swallowtail butterfly, *Papilio zelicaon*, which is a pest of umbelliferous plants in western North America; **parsley fern**, name for the Rock Brake (*Allosorus crispus* or *Cryptogramme crispa*), also applied to a variety of the Lady Fern (*Athyrium Filix-femina*), from their finely-divided fronds; **parsley frog**, a spadefoot toad, *Pelodytes punctatus*, found in western Europe; **parsley green**, a colouring additive used in cookery; **parsley haw**, a species of hawthorn (*Cratægus apiifolia*) of Southern U.S., with finely-cut leaves; **parsley-leaved elder**, a cultivated variety of the elder, *Sambucus nigra* var. *laciniata*, distinguished by its cut leaves; †**parsley-more**, parsley-root; **parsley sauce**, a white sauce flavoured with parsley; †**parsley vine**, some variety of grape-vine; **parsley-worm** *U.S.*, the larva of the parsley butterfly, which is a pest of umbelliferous plants.

c **1440** *Alph. Tales* (E.E.T.S.) xxiv. 18 þer come so swete a savur oute of his *parcell bed & his erbis. *a* **1592** GREENE *Jas. IV*, IV. iii, She is like a frog in a parsley-bed. **1622** MABBE tr. *Aleman's Guzman d'Alf.* I. 25 *margin*, That phrase which we vse to little children, when we tell them they were borne in their mothers Parsly-bed. **1687** SETTLE *Refl. Dryden* 51 Little less Poetical, then Parsly-beds for the conception of Children. **1796** PEGGE *Anonym.* I. §91 (1809) 52 The child, when new-born, comes out of the persley bed, they will say in the North. **1892** T. HARDY *Well-Beloved* III. iii. **1633** JOHNSON *Gerarde's Herbal* App. iii. 1594 In the West countrey about Bristow they call this Herbe Percepier; but our herbe women in Cheapside know it by the name of *Parsley Breakestone. **1825–80** JAMIESON, *Parslie Break-stone*, Parsley-Piert. **1889** S. H. SCUDDER *Butterflies Eastern U.S.* II. 1353 Papilio Polyxenes.—The black swallow-tail. .. *Parsley butterfly (Emmons). **1879** WATTS *Dict. Chem.* VIII. 118 *Apiol*, or **Parsley Camphor*, is a crystalline substance, extracted..by distilling parsley-seeds with water. **1926** E. O. ESSIG *Insects Western N. Amer.* xxvii. 634 The western *parsley caterpillar, *Papilio zelicaon*,..is yellow or orange and black. **1962** METCALF & FLINT *Destructive & Useful Insects* (ed. 4) xiv. 598 In the West it [*sc.* the parsleyworm] is replaced by the western parsley caterpillar. **1648** HERRICK *Hesper.*, *Epigr. to Larr*, No more shall I from mantle-trees hang downe, To honour thee, my little *parsly crown. **1693** G. STEPNEY in *Dryden's Juvenal* viii. (1697) 212 The poor Renown Of putting all the Grecian Actors down, And winning at a Wake their Parsley-Crown. **1920** E. SITWELL *Wooden Pegasus* 31 Face as white as any clock's Cased in *parsley-dark curled locks. **1777** LIGHTFOOT *Flora Scot.* II. 655 *Osmunda crispa*... Crisped Fern. *Parsley Fern. **1866** *Treas. Bot.* 489/2 Fern, Parsley, *Allosorus crispus*; also sometimes applied to *Athyrium Filix-fœmina crispum*. **1897** *Proc. Zool. Soc.* 577 (*title*) On the structure and development of the hypobranchial skeleton of the *Parsley-Frog. **1934** J. FLETCHER tr. *Rostand's Toads* vii. 72 In a pond near Paris..the larvae of the Common Frog were in the North and West;..those of the Parsley Frog, the South-east. **1960** R. MERTENS *World of Amphibians & Reptiles* ii. 34 The parsley frog (*Pelodytes*)..occurs only in south-western Europe and the Caucasus. **1845** E. ACTON *Mod. Cookery* iv. 151 (*heading*) *Parsley green, for colouring sauces. Gather a quantity of young parsley,..pound it in a mortar,..set it into a pan of boiling water. *c* **1400** *Master of Game* (MS. Digby 182) xii, Take þe leues of leekes..and of *persle leues. **1731** P. MILLER *Gardener's Dict.* s.v. Sambucus. The Cut or *Parsley-leav'd Elder. **1838** J. C. LOUDON *Aboretum* II. 1028 The Parsley-leaved Elder; has the leaflets cut into fine segments. **1904** E. STEP *Wayside & Woodland Trees* 125 An Elder with its leaflets deeply cut into very slender lobes...is an escape from cultivation—a garden variety (*laciniata*) known as the Cut-leaved or Parsley-leaved Elder. **1486** *Bk. St. Albans* B iij, Take the Juce of *percelly Moris otherwise calde percelly Rootis. **1866** *Treas. Bot.* 79/2 In Cornwall it is..largely used in *parsley pies, which are peculiar to that part of England. **1876** MISS BRADDON *J. Haggard's Dau.* vii. 93 A parsley-pie ..in which tender young chickens nestled in a bed of parsley and cream. *a* **1450** *Stockh. Med. MS.* i. 429 in *Anglia* XVIII. 306 Take..sawge and *percely-rotys. **1836** E. COPLEY *Cook's Compl. Guide* II. v. 359 **Parsley Sauce.* Boil a bunch of green parsley in salt and water for five minutes; when done, chop it fine, put in half a pint of bechamel sauce, or good melted butter. **1877** E. S. DALLAS *Kettner's Bk. of Table* 329 *Parsley Sauce*..is generally in England given to what in the French kitchen is known as maître d'hôtel sauce. **1965** R. CARRIER *Cookbk.* ii. 90 (*heading*) English parsley sauce. **1978** *Listener* 23 Mar. 366/1, I've just dialled for the weather... There was a slight crossed line. The outlook is warm with parsley sauce, Regulo 7. **1657** AUSTEN *Fruit Trees* I. 59, I know none so good, and fit for our Climate as the *Parsley Vine. **1842** T. W. HARRIS *Insects Injurious to Vegetation* 211 In the month of June, there may be found, on the leaves of the parsley and carrot, certain caterpillars, more commonly called *parsley-worms. **1972** SWAN & PAPP *Common Insects N. Amer.* 204 Black Swallowtail (Parsleyworm). *Papilio polyxenes asterius*.

parsley-piert (-pɪət). Also **parsley pert.** [app. a popular corruption of F. *perce pierre*, lit. 'pierce-stone', according to Littré, one of the Fr. names of this plant: cf. BREAKSTONE.] A dwarf annual herb (*Alchemilla arvensis*), allied to the Lady's Mantle, growing on dry barren ground, hedge-banks, etc., with jagged leaves and minute green axillary flowers. (Erron. applied to the Knawel, *Scleranthus annuus*: see quot. 1597.)

1597 GERARDE *Herbal* II. clxii. 454 Knawel, which herbe is called (as I saide before) Parsley Piert. **1640** PARKINSON *Theatr. Bot.* IV. xvi. 449, I shewed you before that the word Parsly pert, was but a corruption of time in the vulgar sort, and Percepier also, derived from the French word *Percepierre*, which..signifieth as much as pierce stone, or breakestone in English. **1829** *Glover's Hist. Derby* I. 105 *Aphanes vulgaris*, parsley piert. **1882** G. ALLEN *Colours Flowers* v. 96 *Alchemilla arvensis* (parsley-piert) is an extremely debased moss-like descendant.

parsling, obs. form of PARCELLING.

†**parsment.** *Sc. Obs.* app. = PARTIMENT.

1513 DOUGLAS *Æneis* v. x. 31 Twise sax childer followis ilkane about In thair parsmentis [L. *agmine partito*] arrayit in armour brycht.

parsnip ('pɑːsnɪp). Forms: α. 4 passenep, 4–6 pasnepe, 5 pastnep, 5–6 pasnep, 6 pasneppe. β. 6 parsnepe, -neppe, -nebb, parsenep, persnepe, perseneppe, 7 parsenip, parsneip, 8 parsneep, 6– parsnep, parsnip. [Corrupted from ME. *passenep*, *pasnep(e*, ultimately repr. L. *pastināca* 'parsnip', a name connected with *pastināre* to dig and trench the ground, *pastinum* a two-pronged digging-fork. Thence OHG. *pastinak*, *-naga*, Ger. *pastinak*, *-nake*, Du. *pastinak*; in It. *pastinaca*, OF. *pasnaie*, *panaie*, also *pasnaise*, *panaise*, mod.F. *panais*. The ME. form may have been derived from OF. *pasnaie*, with the second syllable changed to *nep*, after ME. **nēp* (in 15th c. *nep*, *nepe*, *neppe*):—OE. *nǽp* turnip, ad. L. *nāpus*, the parsnip being considered a kind of *nepe*. Cf. the later word *turnep*, TURNIP.

Other (mostly 16th c.) French forms were *pastenée*, *pastenaye*, also the deriv. forms *pastenade*, *-tinade*, *-tonade*, *pastenague, -aque, -aille*; but these were too late to affect the Engl. word. The OE. Glossaries render *pastinaca*, 'feldmora, walhmore, wealmora, more', in 12th c. 'walmore'.]

1. a. A biennial umbelliferous plant (*Pastinaca sativa*), a native of Europe and part of Asia, having pinnate leaves, yellow flowers, and a pale yellow root which in the cultivated variety is fleshy, sweet, and nutritious, and has been used from ancient times as a culinary vegetable; a kind of beer and a wine are also locally made from it. Hence, the root or edible part of this plant. Also extended to the genus *Pastinaca*.

1398 Trevisa *Barth. De P.R.* xvii. cxxxvii. (MS. Bodl.) lf. 225 b/2 Eueriche herb wiþ a rote of meche norissching haþ seede þat is nouȝt norisschinge: as it fareþ in Pasnepis and in rapis. *a* **1400** *Pistill of Susan* 107 þe persel, þe passenep, poretes to preue. *c* **1420** *Pallad. on Husb.* ix 56 Also this mone is sowyng of pasnepe. *a* **1450** *Stockh. Med. MS.* 95 Pastnepys erroles. **1530** Palsgr. 252/1 Pasneppe an herbe. **1533** Elyot *Cast Helthe* (1539) 25 Parsnepes and carettes. **1562** Turner *Herbal* ii. 138 b, Of Persnepes. **1570** Levins *Manip.* 140/42 A parsnip, *pastinaca.* **1594** R. Ashley tr. *Loys le Roy* 28 Leekes, chibols, carrets, parsnebbs. **1699** Evelyn *Acetaria* 51 Parsnep..is by some thought more nourishing than the Turnep. **1762** *Gentl. Mag.* 261 To sow parsneps in the open fields. **1846** J. Baxter *Libr. Pract. Agric.* (ed. 4) II. 189 The Parsnip is..extensively cultivated in Jersey and Guernsey for feeding milch cows.

b. Prov. ***fine (fair, soft) words butter no parsnips*** (see also butter *v.* 1 c).

a **1625** Fletcher *Woman's Prize* i. iii, I shall rise again, if there be truth In eggs, and butter'd parsnips. **1639** Clarke *Paroemiologia* 12 Faire words butter noe parsnips, *verba non alunt familiam.* **1797** G. Colman *Heir at Law* iii. iii, Business is business; and fine words, you know, butter no parsnips. **1867** Trollope *Chron. Barset* II. xii, I often tell 'em how wrong folks are to say that soft words butter no parsnips, and hard words break no bones.

c. In various colloq. or slang expressions: ***before you can say parsnips***, very rapidly, 'in the twinkling of an eye'; ***to look parsnips***, to look sour or displeased; ***I beg your parsnips***, joc. alteration of 'I beg your pardon'.

1803 G. Colman *John Bull* ii. ii. 18 'You'll come back again,' says she—'That's what I will, before you can say, parsnips, my darling,' says he. **1837** J. Hook *Jack Brag* II. iv. 167 'I'm delighted,' said Jack, looking parsnips. **1886** H. Baumann *Londinismen* 131/2 *Parsnip*,..I beg ~s (statt pardon) bitt' um Entschuldigung. **1922** Joyce *Ulysses* 297 Who said Christ is good?—I beg your parsnips, says Alf.—Is that a good Christ, says Bob Doran, to take away poor little Willy Dignam?

2. Applied, with defining words, to various umbellifers, allied to or resembling the common parsnip; as **giant parsnip**, 'the genus *Heracleum*' (Miller *Plant-n.* 1884); **meadow parsnip**, (*a*) cow-parsnip, *Heracleum Sphondylium*; (*b*) the N. American genus *Thaspium*; **prickly parsnip, sea parsnip**, names for the genus *Echinophora*, esp. *E. spinosa*, growing on sea-shores, with prickly inflorescence; **rough parsnip**, (*a*) cow-parsnip, *Heracleum Sphondylium*; (*b*) the Opopanax plant, *Opopanax Chironium* (*Pastinaca Opopanax*); **Victorian parsnip**, *Trachymene australis* (Miller); **wild parsnip**, the wild form of *Pastinaca sativa* (see 1). See also cow-parsnip, water-parsnip.

1562 Turner *Herbal* ii. 145 Spondilion..maye be called in Englishe Kow persnepe or middow persnepe. **1866** *Treas. Bot.* 1140 *Thaspium*, a genus of North American orthospermous *Umbelliferæ*... Its popular American name is Meadow Parsnip. **1760** J. Lee *Introd. Bot.* App. 321 Parsnep, *Prickly, *Echinophora.* **1548** Turner *Names of Herbes* 76 Sphondilium..may be called in englishe Cowpersnepe or *rough Persnepe. **1640** Parkinson *Theatr. Bot.* 1286 The *Sea Parsneppe. **1538** Elyot, *Staphilinus*, *wylde parsnyppe. **1747** Wesley *Prim. Physick* (1762) 41 A Poultis of Wild Parsnips flowers, leaves, and stalks.

3. *attrib.* and *Comb.*, as ***parsnip beer, culture, pie, seed, soup, tint, wine***; ***parsnip-coloured*** adj.; **parsnip butterfly, swallowtail** = *parsley butterfly* s.v. parsley 3; **parsnip-chervil**, *Anthriscus bulbosus* (*Chærophyllum bulbosum*), cultivated for its esculent root; **parsnip web-worm** *N. Amer.*, the larva of a moth, *Depressaria pastinacella*, a pest of parsnips and related plants.

1897 *Daily News* 24 Mar. 7/3 Parsnip beer contained nearly 14 per cent. [of proof spirit]. **1867** *Amer. Naturalist* I. 220 The Parsnip butterfly (*Papilio Asterias*) may be seen flying over the beds of parsnips. **1866** *Treas. Bot.* 74/1 The Parsnip Chervil..is a native of France... In size and shape the root attains the dimensions of a small Dutch carrot. **1617** Middleton *Witch* i. i. 65 I'll send you venison, custard, parsnip-pie. **1845** E. Acton *Mod. Cookery* i. 25 (*heading*) Parsnip soup. Dissolve,..four ounces and a half of good butter,..and slice in directly two pounds of sweet tender parsnips. **1942** E. O. Essig *College Entomol.* xxxi. 503 *Papilio ajax* Linn. Parsnip swallowtail. **1897** *Allbutt's Syst. Med.* IV. 375 The pale or parsnip tint which belongs to nephritis. **1888** *Insect Life* I. 94 The Parsnip Web-worm... We found this insect extremely common in the stems of Wild Parsnips. **1928** Metcalf & Flint *Destructive & Useful Insects* xvi. 509 Parsnip Webworm... The flower heads of parsnip and celery are webbed together with silk and devoured by small yellow, greenish or grayish caterpillars covered with small black spots. **1954** Borror & DeLong *Introd. Study Insects* xxvi. 536 The parsnip webworm..attacks parsnips, celery, and related plants. **1834** J. Baxter *Libr. Pract. Agric.* (1846) II. 417 March is the month for making parsnip wine.

parson (ˈpɑːs(ə)n). Forms: α. 3-6 **persone**, 3-7 **person**, (4-5 **-oun**, 5 **-un**, 6 **-onne**). β. 4 **parsonne**, **-oun**, 4-6 **-one**, 4- **parson**. [ME. *persone*, a. OF. and AF. *persone* (12th c. in Littré, 1292 in Britton), later OF. (Picard) *parsoune* (1466 in Godef.), AF. *parsone, parson* (Littleton):—L. *persōna* (see person), in med.L. 'rector of a parish': see Note below.]

1. a. *Eccl.* A holder of a parochial benefice in full possession of its rights and dues; a rector. ***parson imparsonee***: see imparsonee. ***parson mortal, p. immortal***: see β. quot. 1706.

α. *c* **1250** *Lutel Soth Serm.* 51 in *O.E. Misc.* 188 þes persones ich wene ne beoþ heo noȝt for-bore. *c* **1290** *Beket* 561 in *S. Eng. Leg.* I. 122 Person, preost, oþur ȝwat-so he beo. *Ibid.* 176/2425 Of priores and of persones: and manie oþur clerkes al-so. **1362** Langl. *P. Pl.* A. Prol. 80 Persones [*B.* parsons] and parisch prestes playneþ to heore Bisschops, þat heore Parisch haþ ben pore seþþe þe Pestilence tyme. *c* **1386** Chaucer *Prol.* 478 A good man was ther of Religioun And was a poure Person [*v. rr.* persoun, -one, parson] of a toun. *c* **1449** Pecock *Repr.* 394 That the louȝen curatis as persouns and vikers of paraschenis ben stabili endewid in her riȝt. **1553** T. Wilson *Rhet.* 20 A patrone of a benefice wil have a poore yngrame soule to beare the name of a persone for xx marke. **1625** Burges *Pers. Tithes* 61 The Person of Whitwell being sued for taking away a Horse for a Mortuary.

β. [**1314-15** *Rolls of Parlt.* I. 313/1 Au Priour de Launseton, Parsone de la dite ville.] *c* **1325** *Poem Times Edw. II* 55 in *Pol. Songs* (Camden) 326 Sone so a parsoun is ded and in eorthe i-don, Thanne shal the patroun have ȝiftes anon. **1377** Langl. *P. Pl.* B. v. 422, I haue be prest and parsoun passynge thretty wynter. **1449** *Paston Lett.* I. 87, j scholere of Cambryg, qweche is parsone of Welle. **1560** Daus tr. *Sleidane's Comm.* 119 b, The parson and vicar wyll have for a mortuary, or a coarse present, the best thynge that is about the house. *c* **1630** Risdon *Surv. Devon* § 192 (1810) 205 Whose prior was parson thereof, and had a vicar endowed there. **1691** *Case of Exeter Coll.* 40 If a meer Layman be inducted into a Benefice, he is, whilst he continues in possession, a Parson *de Facto.* **1691** Bp. Stillingfl. *Charge* 15 A Vicar cannot appoint a Vicar, but a Parson may. And altho that Name among some be used as a Term of Reproach, yet in former Ages *Personatus* and *Dignitas* were the same thing; and so used here in England in the time of Henry II. **1706** Phillips, *Parson Mortal*, the Rector of a Church, made for his own Life, was formerly so call'd,..but a Collegiate or Conventual Body, to whom the Church is for ever appropriated, was styled *Persona Immortalis*, or *Parson Immortal.* **1709** *Ord. in Counc.* 13 Jan. in *Lond. Gaz.* No. 4508/1 All Parsons, Vicars and Curates within this Realm. **1765** Blackstone *Comm.* I. xi. 384 A parson..is one that hath full possession of all the rights of a parochial church... He is sometimes called the rector..of the church: but the appellation of *parson*, (however it may be depreciated by familiar, clownish, and indiscriminate use) is the most legal, most beneficial, and most honourable title that a parish priest can enjoy. **1901** Sprott *Bk. Com. Order* Introd. 49 *note*, The word parson is used in lists of clergy till 1645 to mark those who had the whole tithes of a parish, like Rector.

†**b.** ***grey*** (***grey-coated, grey-coat***) ***parson***: an impropriator or farmer of the parish tithes. *Obs.*

1785 Grose *Dict. Vulg. T.* **1830** in *Cobbett's Rural Rides* (1886) I. 123 *note.* **1847-78** in Halliwell.

2. Extended successively, in popular use, so as to include a vicar, or any beneficed clergyman; a chaplain, a curate, any clergyman; a nonconformist minister or preacher. In the more extended sense only *colloq.*, and (exc. in rural use) usually more or less depreciatory or dyslogistic.

1588 Shaks. *L.L.L.* v. ii. 932 When all aloud the winde doth blow, And coffing drownes the Parsons saw. **1591** Spenser *M. Hubberd* 480 The Foxe was well induc'd to be a Parson. **1616** R. C. *Times' Whistle* vi. 2383 The country parson may, as in a string, Lead the whole parish vnto anything. **1666** South *Serm.* I. 204 Call a man Priest or Parson, and you set him in some Mens Esteem, ten Degrees below his own Servant. **1691** Luttrell *Brief Rel.* (1857) II. 311 Mr. Baxter, the famous nonconformist parson, is lately dead. **1720** Gordon & Trenchard *Independ. Whig* (1728) 187 After a Coach and Six, the next Trappings of Domestick Grandeur, are a Page, Plate, and a Parson. **1771** Horne in *Junius Lett.* li. 264 Popular prejudice..is violent against the parson. **1799** Han. More *Fem. Educ.* (ed. 4) I. 15 The clergy are spoken of under the contemptuous appellation of The Parsons. **1825** Jefferson *Autobiog.* Wks. 1859 I. 9 This information I had from Parson Hunt, who happened at the time to be in London. **1827** *Sporting Mag.* XX. 59 The interruption [of a prize fight]..through the intervention of a grocer at Hungerford, and a Methodist parson. **1859** Geo. Eliot *A. Bede* i, Which was ye thinkin' on, Seth,..the pretty parson's face or her sarmunt? **1899** *Daily News* 29 May 5/4 'Mr. C.! He ain't a parson. He's a Man', with great emphasis on the 'man'. 'He's a downright Christian man. That's what he is.'

3. *transf.* **a.** From the black coat of a clergyman, applied to animals with black fur or markings, as a black lamb, a black rabbit, or to birds with black feathers, as the ***Isle of Wight parson***, the cormorant. See also parson-bird.

1806 *Guide to Watering Places* 176 The cormorant, called by the sailors 'the Isle of Wight Parson'. **1827** Col. Hawker *Diary* (1893) I. 312 The chase we had with the shag, alias cormorant, alias 'parson'. **1853** W. D. Cooper *Sussex Gloss.*, *Parson*, the hake... So called from the black streak on its back. **1881** *Leicester Gloss.*, *Parson*, a large black beetle; a cockroach. **1886** Elworthy *W. Som. Word-bk.*, *Parson*,..a black rabbit... A farmer when rabbiting cried out to me..there's a parson! shoot thick for God's sake.

b. 'A tiny finch of Brazil, *Spermophila minuta*' (*Cent. Dict.* 1890).

4. *Angling.* A kind of artificial fly.

1867 F. Francis *Angling* x. (1880) 344 The Parson..is a very showy fly.

5. *fig.* A finger-post: see quots. Chiefly *dial.*

1785 Grose *Dict. Vulg. T.*, *Parson*, a guide post, hand or finger post by the road side for directing travellers;..because..it sets people in the right way. **1819** *Banquet* 59* Like the rude guide post some a parson call That points the way but never stirs at all. **1889** in *N.W. Lincs. Gloss.*

6. *attrib.* and *Comb.* **a.** appositive, as ***parson-editor, -magistrate, -peer, -physician***, etc.; **b.** attrib., as ***parson-power, -premium***; **c.** obj. gen., etc., as ***parson-baiting, -fighter, -hunting, -worship***; ***parson-like*** adj. **d.** Special Combs.: **parson-and-clerk**, (*a*) a children's game: see quot. 1863; (*b*) = *parson-in-the-pulpit* (*a*); **parson-grey** *sb.* and *a.*, dark grey, priest-grey; **parson-gull**, a local name of the great black-backed gull (*Larus marinus*); **parson-has-lost-his-coat**, name of some game; **parson-in-the-pulpit**, a popular name, from the form of the flowers, of two plants, (*a*) cuckoo-pint, (*b*) monkshood; **parson's-nose**, the rump of a fowl, etc.; **parson's table** *U.S.*, a small, simple, wooden table with a square top supported at each corner by straight legs; **parson's-week**, the time taken as a holiday by a clergyman who is excused a Sunday, lasting (usually) from Monday to the Saturday week following. Also parson-bird.

1788 H. Walpole *Let. to Mrs. H. More* 22 Sept., Let my snuff of life flit to the last sparkle of folly, like what children call the *parson and clerk in a bit of burnt paper. *a* **1800** Cowper *On observing some names in Biog. Brit.* **1863** Barnes *Dorset Dial.* Gloss., *Passons an' clarks*, the running fiery spots on burning paper. **1882** *Gloss. Devon. Plant-n.* (E.D.S.), Parson-and-Clerk, *Arum maculatum.* **1826** W. E. Andrews *Exam. Fox's Cal. Prot. Saints* 473 The *parson-editor of the folio edition of the *New Book of Martyrs.* **1821** *Blackw. Mag.* VIII. 620 His bonnet blue, a coat of *Parson gray. **1885** Swainson *Prov. Names Brit. Birds* 208 Greater Black-backed Gull..*Parson gull, or mew. **1889** Doyle *Micah Clarke* 163 Saturday night game of 'kiss-in-the-ring', or '*parson-has-lost-his-coat'. **1742** Fielding *J. Andrews* iii. vi, Some of them declaring that *parson-hunting was the best sport in the world. **1856** F. E. Paget *Owlet Owlst.* 145, I don't see why we are to assume that *parson-husbands have more sense than other husbands. **1882** *Gloss. Devon. Plant-n.* (E.D.S.), *Parson-in-the-Pulpit, (1) *Arum maculatum*..(2) *Aconitum Napellus.* **1625** Hart *Anat. Ur.* ii. i. 55 No lesse then three..*Parson-Physitians had administered to him. **1841** Lever *C. O'Malley* lxvii. 319 Not ..pronounced doubly hazardous by the Insurance Companies, nor acceptable under a '*Parson-premium'. **1839** Longfellow *Hyperion* vii, An epicurean morsel—a *parson's nose. **1873** *Slang Dict.*, *Parson's nose*, the hind part of a goose—a savoury mouthful. Sometimes called the Pope's nose. **1969** *Sears Catal.* Spring/Summer 1385/1 *Parson's Tables. Avocado green. **1973** R. Hayes *Hungarian Game* xlvi. 271 Except for a matched set of Sheraton chairs, a salon mirror and a parson's table, the landing was empty. **1976** *Billings* (Montana) *Gaz.* 24 June 7-F/6 (Advt.), 16 × 16″ parsons tables. **1790** Cowper *Let. to Lady Hesketh* 28 June, Wks. 1836 VII. 39 If they come..they will stay..a *parson's week, that is to say, about a fortnight and no longer. **1856** Kingsley *Let. to T. Hughes* in *Life* xiv. (1879) II. 3, I wish you would..go with me to Snowdon..for a parson's week, *i.e.* twelve days. **1897** W. C. Hazlitt *Ourselves* 4 Persons who identify piety with churchgoing and *parson-worship.

Hence (mostly *nonce-words*) **ˈparsonarchy**, rule by parsons, a body of ruling parsons. **parsoˈnese** *a.*, parsonic. **ˈparsonhood**, the state or condition of a parson. **parˈsonify** *v. trans.*, (*a*) to make parsonic; (*b*) in passive, to be married by a parson; (*c*) to make into a parson. **ˈparsonish** *a.*, like or characteristic of a parson, parsonic. **parˈsonity** = *parsonhood.* **ˈparsonize** *v.*, (*a*) *trans.* to make parsonic; (*b*) *intr.* to play the parson, do parson's work. **ˈparsonly** *a.*, belonging to or befitting a parson. **parsoˈnolatry**, parson-worship. **parsoˈnology**, lore about parsons. **ˈparsonry**, parsons collectively. **ˈparsonship**, the office or position of parson, rectorship.

1830 *Examiner* 789/1 A pampered squirarchy, and a magnificent *parson-archy. **1860** Huxley in L. Huxley *Life* (1900) I. 212 Sunk, as nine tenths of women are, in mere ignorant *parsonese superstitions. **1834** *Tait's Mag.* I. 632/1 The perquisites of *parsonhood are of a more solid and tangible nature. **1737** J. Thomson *Let.* 12 Jan. in W. Goodhugh *Eng. Gentl. Libr. Man.* (1827) 262, I have not yet seen the round man of God to be. He is to be *parsonifyed a few days hence. **1880** W. S. Gilbert *Pirates of Penzance*, You shall quickly be parsonified..By a doctor of divinity. **1926** tr. *William II's Early Life* iii. 19 He..left all dogmas and creeds severely alone. They were, in his view,..apt to 'parsonify' the grand and simple outline of the Christian Faith. *a* **1834** Lamb cited in Worcester (1846), **Parsonish.* **1884** *Punch* 11 Oct. 178/2 A proper parsonish style. **1844** J. T. Hewlett *Parsons & W.* vi, All the duties of *parsonity. **1880** in *Congregationalist* (U.S.) 21 June (Cent.), The hope that lay evangelists will not 'presently become *parsonized'. **1892** Stevenson in *Illustr. Lond. News* 6 Aug. 171/2 Now, it seems, he's parsonising down Somerset way. **1775** S. J. Pratt *Liberal Opin.* lxxxv. (1783) III. 129 [Attire] prig, prim, prue, and *parsonly. **1776** —— *Pupil of Pleas.* (1777) I. 82 Whining passages about pity, and virtue, and all the etcætera of parsonly cant. **1852** *Tait's Mag.* XIX. 342 *heading*,

The *Parsonolatry of Dissent. **1815** BYRON *Let. to Moore* 10 Jan., Which proves..your proficiency in *parsonology. **1886** P. FITZGERALD *Fatal Zero* xxix. (1888) 185 D.'s ready sneer about preaching or 'parsonology'. **1876** G. MEREDITH *Beauch. Career* I. xvii. 259 The *parsonry are a power absolutely to be counted for waste, as to progress. **1680** R. WARE *Foxes & Firebrands* II. (1682) 35 The Convert continued not fully two years in his *Parsonship or Parish before he died.

[*Note.* The ecclesiastical use of L. *persōna* does not appear before the 11th c. It was app. still new at the Council of Clermont 1096, when it was said, c. iii 'Ecclesiæ vel decimæ ..sæpius ab Episcopis sub palliata avaritia venduntur: mortuis nimirum, seu mutatis Clericis, quos Personas vocant' (Mansi *Concilia* XX. 902). Various views have been taken of its genesis. English legal writers, Coke, Blackstone, etc., have referred it to the Civil Law sense of *persōna*, the parson being viewed as the legal 'person' by whom the property of God, the Patron Saint, or the church, in the parish, was actually held; the person to sue and be sued in respect of this property. Du Cange (ed. 1762), pointing to the early equivalent use of *persōna* and *dignitās*, would start from the sense 'personage, great or dignified person, dignitary'. Dr. H. Schaefer, *Pfarrkirche und Stift im Deutschen Mittelalter* (1903) §19, shows that *persōna* was primarily applied to the holder of a parochial living who was non-resident, being either a conventual body, a chapter, or member of one, or often a mere layman, the spiritual duties being in either case discharged by a *vicārius* or substitute, who received a small portion of the revenues. He refers the designation to the fact that the holder of the living merely figured in the character or rôle (cl. L. *persōna*) of parish clergyman, without actually discharging the duties. He explains the frequent early equivalence of *persōna* and *dignitās*, adduced by Du Cange, in the case of conventual or collegiate rectors, by the usual application of *dignitās* to the superior personages or 'dignitaries' of a chapter, and the fact that it was by these that the parochial parsonages were held. It would appear however that in England the appellation must have been early interpreted in the Civil Law sense; else how should it have been extended from the *persōna immortālis* to the *persōna mortālis* or resident rector, and have become in England his legal designation?]

parson, obs. form of PERSON.

parsonage ('pɑːsənɪdʒ). Forms: see PARSON; also 6 -edge, -ige, 7 -adge. [Altered form, as in prec., of *personage*, a. AF. *personage*, OF. *person(n)age*, ecclesiastical dignity or benefice, = late L. *persōnāticum*, med.L. (from Fr. or Eng.) *personāgium*: see PERSONAGE.]

1. The benefice or living of a parson; a rectory. *Obs.* exc. in *Law.*

α. [**1292** BRITTON IV. iii. §7 II. 179 A prendre garde lequel ele est de tut voide, ou soulement le personage. Nichols *tr.* It must be observed whether it [the church] is entirely vacant, or the parsonage only.] *c* **1380** WYCLIF *Wks.* (1880) 433 þe fourþe part shulde be dispendid to kepe þe housis of þe personage. **1425** *Rolls of Parlt.* IV. 290/2 Noun residens of Persons of holy Chirche, upon theire Personages. **1482** *Monk of Evesham* (Arb.) 93 A certen knyght that was patron of a chyrche solde..a personage to a certen clerke for xxvij. marke. **1544** *Supplic. to Hen. VIII* (E.E.T.S.) 34 Other patrons haue presented theyr clerckes to personagyes & vicaragyes. **1642** MILTON *Apol. Smect.* iii. Wks. (1851) 288 Whether..a good Personage, or Impropriation bought out for him would not improper him.

β. **1377** LANGL. *P. Pl.* B. XIII. 245 And I hadde neuere of hym..Noither prouendre ne parsonage ȝut of þe popis ȝifte. **1450** *Rolls of Parlt.* V. 206/1 Churches, Parsonages, and other Possessions. **1588** FRAUNCE *Lawiers Log.* Ded. ¶iv b, Their fathers haue either compounded with their Landlord for some pelting vicaredge, or payd ready money for a better parsonage. **1646** *Royalist Comp. Papers* (Yorksh. Rec. Ser.) II. 57 He offers the parsonage of Hornsey worth £100 for £1000. *a* **1704** T. BROWN *Two Oxford Scholars* Wks. 1730 I. 5, I cannot exercise the Office..without some Curacy, Vicarage, or Parsonage. **1818** CRUISE *Digest* (ed. 2) III. 60 The rectory or parsonage, which comprises the parish church with all its rights, glebes, tithes, and other profits whatsoever.

2. (= *parsonage-house*). The house attached to a parson's living, the rector's house. Also, in later use, the house of a vicar, perpetual curate, or other incumbent of a parish or parochial district; sometimes (esp. in U.S. and Colonies) applied to the residence provided for any minister of religion.

1472 *Will* in *Rec. St. Mary at Hill* (E.E.T.S.) 16 The parsonage & Chirchyerd of seynt Botolphes Chirche. **1523** FITZHERB. *Surv.* xx. (1539) 41 The syte of the personage standeth..between the sayd hye way. **1628** EARLE *Microcosm., Surgeon* (Arb.) 62 It is ofter out of reparations, then an old Parsonage. *a* **1704** T. BROWN *Two Oxford Scholars* Wks. 1730 I. 10 An old rotten Parsonage or Vicarage-house. **1806** BOWLES *Banwell Hill* ii. 34 Where the white parsonage, among the trees, Peeped out.

†**3.** The parson's or rector's tithe. *Sc. Obs.*

1818 SCOTT *Hrt. Midl.* viii, What have I been paying stipend and teind, parsonage and vicarage for, ever sin' the aughty-nine, and I canna get a speil o' a prayer for't?

4. *attrib.*, as ***parsonage-garden, -house, -land.***

1566 *Eng. Ch. Furniture* (ed. Peacock) 145 Burnte by the said Churchwardens at the said parsonedge house. **1610** *Burford Reg.* (Hist. MSS. Comm.) *Var. Collect.* I. 82 The buildinge of the said cottage..uppon the parsonadge land of Calne. **1796** MRS. M. ROBINSON *Angelina* I. 26 We have but few houses of any note, and please your honour—only three. .. The parsonage-house, the poor-house, and the public-house. **1838** D. F. STRAUSS *Lutheran Clergym.* III. 273 The door of the parsonage garden opened.

parsonage, obs. form of PERSONAGE.

'**parson-bird.** [See PARSON 3.]

1. A New Zealand bird (*Prosthemadera novæzelandiæ*), so called from its dark plumage and white neck-feathers; also called *poe-bird* or *tui.*

1857 C. HURSTHOUSE *N. Zealand* I. 118 (Morris), The most common, and certainly the most facetious, individual of the ornithology is the tui (parson-bird). **1866** LADY BARKER *Stat. Life N. Zeal.* 93 (ibid.), The tui, or parson-bird, most respectable and clerical-looking in its glossy black suit..and white wattles of very slender feathers.

2. Applied to the Rook.

1902 *Westm. Gaz.* 7 Jan. 2/3 Entirely devoted to the glorification of our friend Mr. Rook, the parson-bird. *Ibid.* 14 Feb. 12/1 We have no doubt that the 'parson birds' will keep up the ancient tradition and celebrate their weddings to-day.

parsondom ('pɑːsəndəm). [f. PARSON + -DOM.] The state or quality of a parson; the domain of parsons, parsons collectively.

1850 P. CROOK *War of Hats* 3 All parsondom is up. **1860** TROLLOPE *Framley P.* xiv, His sins against parsondom were grievous.

parsone, -elly, obs. ff. PARSON, PERSON, -ALLY.

parsoned ('pɑːsənd), *ppl. a.* [f. PARSON + -ED[2].]

1. Made or penned by a parson.

1742 YOUNG *Nt. Th.* IV. 840 Ye Deaf to Truth! peruse this Parson'd Page, And trust, for once, a Prophet, and a Priest.

2. Furnished with a parson, as a parish.

1882 in OGILVIE.

3. Married in church or chapel. *colloq.*

1886 *Cassell's Encycl. Dict., Married and Parsoned*: A colloquial expression, signifying that all the necessary rites have been performed. **1892** EMERSON *Son of Fens* 154 (E.D.D.) Don't you wish you was married?.. Don't you wish you was passoned?

parsoner(e, obs. form of PARCENER.

parsoness ('pɑːsənɪs). *colloq.* or *humorous.* [See -ESS[1].] The wife of a parson.

1784 *Unfortunate Sensibility* I. 121 The few good ladies,.. such as the parsoness,..were extremely concerned. **1873** M. COLLINS *Squire Silchester* II. i. 3 A lady who was parsoness of the parish. **1898** *Contemp. Rev.* 75 The parson reigned supreme in the church, and the parsoness in the school.

parsonet (pɑːsə'nɛt). *colloq.* or *humorous.* [f. PARSON + -ET[1].]

1. A parson's child.

1812 G. COLMAN *Br. Grins, Two Parsons* xxv, The Parson dearly lov'd his darling pets, Sweet, little, ruddy, ragged, Parsonets.

2. A petty or newly-fledged parson.

1834 GEN. P. THOMPSON *Exerc.* III. 15 This is all 'hay, straw, stubble';—the stuff..to make over to hireling preachers and fashionable parsonets. **1877** P. BROOKS *Lect. Preach.* ii. (1895) 45 The people in the neighbourhood dubbed us 'parsonnettes'.

Parsonian (pɑː'səʊnɪən), *a. Sociol.* [f. the name of Talcott *Parsons* (1902–), Amer. sociologist + -IAN.] Of or relating to the theories of action and change within a society or culture put forward by Parsons, or to his structural-functional method of analysing a social system. Hence **Par'sonianism**, the views or theories of Parsons.

1961 A. HACKER in M. Black *Social Theories of Talcott Parsons* 298 One obstacle to a Parsonian theory of class and power may not be easy to overcome. **1970** TOURAINE & PÉCAUT in I. L. Horowitz *Masses in Lat. Amer.* iii. 68 If the Parsonian categories are to be directly applied, it should be possible to define a system of values. **1973** J. REX *Discovering Sociol.* ix. 117 As Parsonianism developed, and as the attack upon it and its ideological offspring rumbled on. **1974** R. JESSOP *Traditionalism, Conservatism & Brit. Polit. Culture* i. 23 In addition to the well-known Parsonian pattern-variables, there are others developed specifically for political analysis and relevant to the problems in hand. **1977** *Times Lit. Suppl.* 25 Feb. 198/3 The family thus functioned, in the best Parsonian fashion, as the principal agent of 'socialization'. *Ibid.*, Mr. Gutman never does tell us what he means by 'socialization', and his implicit Parsonianism hardly does justice to Talcott Parsons.

parsonic (pɑː'sɒnɪk), *a.* [f. PARSON + -IC (after words from Gr.).] Of or pertaining to a parson; resembling or characteristic of parsons.

1785 MRS. S. BOYS *Coalition* II. 74 He felt himself bold, not entertaining any great idea of parsonic valour. **1847** C. BRONTE *J. Eyre* xxxvii, His manners..are not to your taste?—priggish and parsonic? **1891** E. PEACOCK *N. Brendon* I. 284 A secular as well as a parsonic view of life.

parsonical (pɑː'sɒnɪkəl), *a.* [f. as prec. + -ICAL.] = prec. So **par'sonically** *adv.*, after the manner of a parson.

1750 CHESTERF. *Lett.* (1774) III. 14, I am not stoically advising, nor parsonically preaching to you. **1834** LD. SHERBROOKE in *Life* I. 97 Please to let me know how your parsonical duties go on. **1902** *Irish Rosary* VI. 77/2 His (*sc.* Herrick's) verse..is on the whole more poetical than *parsonical.* **1972** *Times* 13 Oct. 3/6, I never wear a parsonical collar unless someone asks me to. **1976** *Church Times* 20 Aug. 7/3 The advent of the tape-recorder has, one hopes, eradicated the worst aberrations of the parsonical voice.

'**parsoning,** *vbl. sb.* [f. PARSON + -ING[1].] Acting as a parson; doing parson's work.

a **1792** WOLCOTT (P. Pindar) *Parson-dealer*, Meaning by pars'ning to support a table. **1887** T. E. KEBBEL *Eng. Country Life* (1891) 8 There were..many very bad clergymen, to whom what they called 'parsoning' was a simple bore.

parsonsite ('pɑːsənzaɪt). *Min.* [a. F. *parsonsite* (A. Schoep 1923, in *Compt. Rend.* CLXXVI. 173), f. the name of Arthur L. *Parsons* (b. 1873), Canadian mineralogist: see -ITE[1] 2 b.] A hydrated phosphate of lead and uranium, $Pb_2(UO_2)(PO_4)_2.2H_2O$, found as crusts and powdery aggregates of transparent or translucent, minute, lath-like crystals.

1923 *Chem. Abstr.* XVII. 1776 (*heading*) Parsonsite, a new radioactive mineral. **1950** *Amer. Mineralogist* XXXV. 247 Parsonsite occurs at the Ruggles pegmatite near Grafton Center, Grafton County, New Hampshire, as crusts of microscopic spicular or lath-like crystals... The parsonsite is associated with autunite and phosphuranylite and all of these have ultimately been derived from the alteration of the primary uraninite. **1964** *Bull. U.S. Geol. Survey* No. 1064. 233 Parsonsite probably is monoclinic, but the possibility of triclinic symmetry cannot be ruled out.

parsoure, obs. variant of PIERCER.

‖**pars pro toto** (pɑːz prəʊ 'təʊtəʊ). [L., = 'a part for the whole'.] A part considered as representative of the whole. Also *attrib.*

1702 [see SYNECDOCHICAL *a.*]. **1958** W. STARK *Sociol. of Knowl.* 156 The fallacy of *pars pro toto*—taking the part for the whole. **1965** *Eng. Stud.* XLVI. 55 It is a *pars pro toto* figure, just as *rand* is used to refer not only to the metal border or ring round the wooden board but also to the shield as such. **1970** *Jrnl. Gen. Psychol.* LXXXIII. 66 The tendency to combine areas of questionable form into strange or absurd entities or the *pars pro toto* effect.

parsuadable, -suasion, obs. ff. PERSUADABLE, -SUASION.

Parsy, obs. form of PARSEE.

part (pɑːt), *sb.* (*adv.*) Forms 1, 3- **part**; also 4-5 **paart, (pard),** 4-6 **pert,** 4-7 **parte,** 5 **perte,** 6 **partt,** 6- *Sc.* **pairt.** [In OE. ad. L. *pars, part-em* (in sense 2 a); in 13th c. a. F. *part* = Pr. *part*, Sp., It. *parte*:—L. *part-em* part. The pl. in ME. was sometimes PARS, after OF. pl. *pars*, earlier *parz.*]

A. *sb.* **I.** Portion or division of a whole.

1. a. That which together with another or others makes up a whole (whether really separate from the rest, or more often only separated in thought); a certain amount, but not all, of any thing or number of things (material or immaterial); any one of the smaller things into which a thing is or may be divided (in reality or in idea); a portion, division, section, element, constituent, fraction, fragment, piece. (Now the ordinary word for this; in OE., and usually in ME., expressed by DEAL *sb.*[1])

When denoting a number of persons or things, often construed as a noun of multitude, with plural verb.

[*c* **1050** *Byrhtferth's Handboc* in *Anglia* (1885) VIII. 317 Rabanus cwyð þæt se dæg hæfð partes, þæt synt dælas.] *a* **1300** *Cursor M.* 2096 þof þe werld es..Delt..In thrin parteis principale, þe partes er noght perigale. *c* **1380** WYCLIF *Sel. Wks.* III. 339 Christis chirche..hath þree partis. þe first part is in blis, wiþ Crist... The secounde part ..ben seintis in purgatorie. *c* **1400** MAUNDEV. (1839) ii. 13 O part is at Parys, and the other part is at Constantynoble. *c* **1440** *Promp. Parv.* 385/1 Paart, or deele, *porcio.* **1535** STEWART *Cron. Scot.* (1858) I. 37 In equall pairtis this kinrik to diuide. **1538** STARKEY *England* I. ii. 51 One louyng one a nother as membrys and partys of one body. **1570** BILLINGSLEY *Euclid* I. Post. ix. 8 The whole is equal to all his partes taken together. **1574-5** *Reg. Privy Council Scot.* Ser. I. II. 426 With all..partis pendicles and pertinentis thairof. **1609** BIBLE (Douay) *Deut.* vii. 22 He wil consume these nations in thy sight by litle and litle and by partes. **1638** JUNIUS *Paint. Ancients* 292 Of all parts of the countenance the eyes are most powerfull, being as the soule's window. **1726** tr. *Gregory's Astron.* I. 392 Let the Diameter *AB* of the Circle..be divided into two equal Parts in the Point *C.* *a* **1774** GOLDSM. *Hist. Greece* II. 264 The greatest part of the Indian cavalry were cut to pieces. **1794** *Rigging & Seamanship* I. 168 *Leading-part*, that part of a tackle which is hauled upon. **1836-7** SIR W. HAMILTON *Metaph.* xxxvii. (1870) II. 338 Whatever is the part of a part, is a part of the whole. **1875** JOWETT *Plato* (ed. 2) I. 443, I agree, Socrates, in the greater part of what you say. **1882** *Times* 25 Sept. 8 They formed but a small part of deaths caused by infectious fevers.

b. Often idiomatically used without article: ***part of*** = a part of, some of; so ***great part of*** = a great part of, much or many of; ***most part of,*** the majority or greater part of, most of.

c **1375** *Cursor M.* 3534 (Fairf.) Gif me part of þat þou grayde. *a* **1425** *Ibid.* 19049 (Trin.) A mon croked in þe palesy And had ben moost part of his dayes [*so Laud MS.*; *Cott. & Gött.* mast all]. **1450** *Paston Lett.* I. 107 And part therof sold, and part ther of yaffe, and the remenaunt thei departed among them. **1531** TINDALE *Expos. 1 John* Wks. (Parker Soc.) II. 524 Part of his laws are ceremonies. **1611** BIBLE *Isa.* xliv. 16 He burneth part thereof in the fire: with part thereof he eateth flesh. **1760** JOHNSON *Idler* No. 97 ¶5 The road was passable only part of the year. **1778** *Learning at a Loss* I. 155, I shall probably spend great Part of the Summer with him. **1827** SOUTHEY *Hist. Penins. War* II. 705 Great part perished before they could reach the wall. **1847** TENNYSON *Princ.* Prol. 47 Part were drown'd within the whirling brook. **1860** WHEWELL in *Life* (1881) 512 We were at Oxford great part of last week, for the meeting of the British Association.

c. *spec.* An essential or integral portion; something essentially belonging to a larger whole; a constituent, element. (Also without article.)

1732 Law *Serious C.* i. (ed. 2) 9 They must be made parts of our common life. 1742 Young *Nt. Th.* ix. 413 'Tis a prime Part of Happiness, to know How much Unhappiness must prove our Lot. 1816 Scott *Bl. Dwarf* vi, The rider sate as if he had been a part of the horse. 1863 Fr. A. Kemble *Resid. in Georgia* 14 That formed no part of our discussion. 1879 Mozley *Serm.* 276 Affection is part of insight.

2. Specialized uses of sense 1.

†**a.** = *part of speech*: see 19. *Obs.* (The earliest use in English.)

*c*1000 Ælfric *Gram.* xvi. (Z.) 107 þry eacan synd *med, pte, ce,* þe man eacnað on leden-spræce to sumum casum þises partes. *Ibid.* xvii. 108 Anfeald ʒetel byð on ðisum parte *ego* ic, *tu* ðu, *ille* he. *Ibid.* xxxix. 242 þes part mæg beon ʒehaten dælnimend. *a*1300 [see pars]. *c*1483 Caxton *Dialogues* viii. 38 Donettis, partis, accidents. 1615 Brinsley (*title*) The Posing of the Parts. *a*1637 B. Jonson *Eng. Gram.* ix. Wks. (Rtldg.) 777–8 In our English speech we number the same parts with the Latins... Only we add a ninth, which is the article.

b. The name of a division or section of a book, play, poem, or other literary work; in mod. use also *spec.* Each of the portions of a work issued at intervals, at a uniform price, and in thin covers, and intended to be afterwards bound up into one or more volumes.

*c*1450 tr. *De Imitatione* 64 Here begynneþ þe third parte of inwarde conuersacyon.. Capitulum primum. 1551 Turner *Herbal* i. Prol., I haue set one part of a great herball. 1562 (*title*) The seconde parte of Guilliam Turners herball. 1594 (*title*) The First Part of the Contention betwixt the two famous houses of Yorke and Lancaster. 1677 Lady Chaworth in *12th Rep. Hist. MSS. Comm.* App. v. 44, I have presented your Lordship with the last part of *Hudibras*, to help to heighten your mirth this Christmasse. 1742 Young *Nt. Th.* vii. 12 Thro' various Parts our glorious Story runs; Time gives the Preface. 1873 Ruskin *Stones Ven.* I. Pref. 7 The architect had read his third part of the Stones of Venice to purpose. 1901 *Daily Chron.* 27 Dec. 3/3 The new Dickens would have to find a second Cruikshank to illustrate any novel issued in separate weekly parts. *Mod.* The work is now coming out in monthly parts.

†**c.** An element or constituent *of* some quality or action, considered by itself (and with no stress on its being merely a part); a point, particular. (Usually in *pl.*) Hence *absol.* Point; matter, affair; respect (= party *sb.* 3). *Obs.*

1563 *Homilies* ii. *Repentance* iii. (1859) 545 Ye heard of the true parts and tokens of repentance. 1589 Puttenham *Eng. Poesie* iii. xxiv. (Arb.) 295 But at all insolent and vnwoonted partes of a mans behauiour we find many times cause to mislike or to be mistrustfull. *a*1639 W. Whateley *Prototypes* ii. xxvi. (1640) 43 Perfection of parts, is when all the parts of goodnesse are found in a man. 1692 Locke *Educ.* §142 Nothing can cure this Part of Ill-breeding but Change and Variety of Company. 1719 Bp. Robinson in Perry *Hist. Coll. Amer. Col. Ch.* I. 200 If we neglect our duty in that part.

d. Each of the separate or separable pieces that go to make up a machine or the like. Also *attrib.* in *pl.*

1886 D. Clerk *Gas Engine* 5 Fig. 3 is a sectional elevation of the first engine, showing the principal working parts. *Ibid.* 8 Barnett's second engine.. is double-acting, and therefore requires a greater number of parts. 1890 W. Robinson *Gas & Petroleum Engines* ii. 11 The wearing parts can be easily taken out and, when worn, replaced by duplicates. 1897 *Trans. Inst. Naval Archit.* XXXVIII. 217 Set of accessories, spare parts, and securing gear. 1923 *Radio Times* 28 Sept. 6 (Advt.), The user of the 'Gecophone'.. may desire to purchase in his own locality spares and replacement parts. 1939 G. W. Stubbings *Diseases Electr. Machinery* iii. 60 A.C. transformers.. are entirely static and have no moving parts. 1939 H. R. Simonds *Industr. Plastics* (1940) ix. 244 The average household refrigerator has more than 20 important plastics parts. 1947 W. W. McCullough *Electr. Motor Maintenance* ii. 13 Worn parts should be replaced promptly. 1968 *Amer. Speech* 1967 XLII. 40 Owner's manuals, parts catalogues, motoring publications from abroad. 1971 *Good Motoring* Sept. 4/1 It was driven by Billy Mackay, a VW Motor parts manager in Scotland. 1974 *Daily Tel.* 4 Dec. 12/3 On average, parts for a Renault 12TL are 77 per cent. more expensive than for the Austin Allegro 1300. 1975 *Sci. Amer.* Feb. 25/2 Industry mass-produces parts in great variety and number. 1976 *Nature* 1 Apr. 391/3 Two fibres, called Kevlar and Kevlar 49 by Dupont,.. look likely to be used in tyre belting and in composites for body armour and aircraft parts.

3. A portion of an animal body: either definitely, a particular member or organ; or indefinitely, a 'spot', 'place' (cf. 13). Usually *pl.*; often with defining adj., as ***hinder parts, inward parts***; also *absol.* (*euphem.*) = privy parts.

*c*1400 *Destr. Troy* 884 Iason.. anoyntide hym anon.. Bothe the face and þe fete, & all þe fore perte. 1526 *Pilgr. Perf.* (W. de W. 1531) 3 God hath no lineamentes nor partes corporall. 15.. *Sir A. Barton* in *Surtees Misc.* (1888) 73 In a previe place and a secrete pert, He shoote hime in at the left oxtere, The arrowe quiett throughe harte. 1535 Back parts [see back *a.* 1]. 1590 Spenser *F.Q.* i. ii. 41 Her neather partes misshapen, monstruous. 1598 B. Jonson *Ev. Man in Hum.* iv. i. 1617 Moryson *Itin.* iii. 115 The inner parts of Goates.. are esteemed great dainties, especially in Toscany. 1634 Sir T. Herbert *Trav.* 41 A cloth which should couer those parts, made to be priuate. 1747 Wesley *Prim. Physic* (1762) 80 Wash the parts with Juice of Calamint. 1799 M. Underwood *Treat. Dis. Children* (ed. 4) II. 136, I had occasion to examine the parts [of a child] very attentively at the birth. 1899 *Allbutt's Syst. Med.* VIII. 558 The patches in such parts may then assume a salmon tinge. 1942 Berrey & Van den Bark *Amer. Thes. Slang* §121/37 *Genitals*,.. parts. 1958 S. A. Grau *Hard Blue Sky* 152 The young girls giggled and felt a hot touch in their parts. 1968 J. Updike *Couples* ii. 141 'Oh you have big—' 'Parts?' 1977 'J. Le Carré' *Hon. Schoolboy* ii. 41 The devil's red-hot wind would burn his parts to a frazzle.

†**4.** A minute portion of matter, a particle. *Obs.*

1707 *Curios. in Husb. & Gard.* 31 The Entrance of some such small aqueous Parts, as may excite the Fermentation. 1709 F. Hauksbee *Phys.-Mech. Exp.* ii. (1719) 36 Woollen impregnated with saline and spirituous parts. *a*1774 Goldsm. *Surv. Exp. Philos.* (1776) II. 88 Now the parts of the air,.. being to this case driven asunder by some external interposition, such as fire, or any other agent. 1800 tr. *Lagrange's Chem.* II. 278 The earthy principle, which is confounded with the indigo and some mucilaginous parts.

5. *spec.* **a.** (with a numeral): Each of a number of equal portions into which a whole may be divided; an aliquot part, exact divisor, submultiple.

(*a*) With an ordinal numeral indicating the number of such portions in the whole, as *a third part, two third parts*: now more usually omitted by ellipsis, the ordinal thus becoming a sb., as *a third, two thirds.* (*b*) With a cardinal numeral, implying a number of portions one less than the number which constitutes the whole, as *two parts* = two thirds, *three parts* = three quarters. (Formerly also as collective sing., as *two part.*)

*c*1290 *St. Michael* 665 in *S. Eng. Leg.* I. 318 ȝeot nis þare, to wonien Inne, onneþe þe seueneþe part. *a*1300 *Cursor M.* 973 þe half parte gladli or þe thrid We wil þe giue, if þou it bid. 1375 Barbour *Bruce* v. 47 Mair than twa part of his rout War herbreit in the toune tharout. *c*1386 Chaucer *Sqr.'s T.* 545 Ne koude man by twenty thousand part Countrefete the Sophymes of his Art. *c*1475 *Rauf Coilȝear* 123 He tyt the King be the nek, twa part in tene. 1603 Owen *Pembrokeshire* ii. (1891) 11 Ffoure partes of five of this sheere is compassed with the sea. *c*1611 Chapman *Iliad* x. 223 Two parts of night are past, the third is left t' employ our force. 1660 Barrow *Euclid* v. Def. i, A part is a magnitude of a magnitude, a less of a greater, when the less measures the greater. 1706 E. Ward *Wooden World Diss.* (1708) 12 The Queen allots him three Parts in eight for his singular Hazards. 1813 Mar. Edgeworth *Patron.* (1833) III. xli. 130 Possession.. being nine parts of the law. 1878 Bosw. Smith *Carthage* 319 He was himself only three parts Roman.

†**b.** Used by confusion or error as if = 'times', as in (*by*) ***a thousand part(s)*** = a thousand times, a thousandfold; ***by the seventh part*** = seven times, sevenfold. *Obs.* (Cf. deal *sb.*[1] 1 e.)

*a*1400–50 *Alexander* 2157 þai pleyne more þe pouirte.. of þar horsis þan þe soroȝe of þam-selfe by þe seuynt parte [*Dubl. MS.* dele]. 1460–70 *Bk. Quintessence* 7 ȝe schule haue ȝoure licour by an hundrid part bettir gilt. 1528 Tindale *Wks.* (Parker Soc.) I. 149 A thousand parts better may it be translated into the English, than into the Latin. 1590 Spenser *F.Q.* ii. ix. 48 Not he.. Might be compar'd to these by many parts. *c*1611 Chapman *Iliad* To Rdr. (1865) 88 They.. are ten parts more paraphrastical than I. 1625 B. Jonson *Staple of N.* iii. ii, I have better news from the bake-house, by ten thousand parts, in a morning.

c. In expressing the proportion of the ingredients of a mixture or compound: One of a number of equal portions of indeterminate amount.

1615 Chapman *Odyss.* ix. 298 It was so strong,.. twas before allaid With twentie parts in water. 1756 C. Lucas *Ess. Waters* III. 298 Two parts of this water poured into one part boiling milk. 1811 A. T. Thomson *Lond. Disp.* (1818) 512 Take of pure sulphate of copper, two parts; subcarbonate of ammonia, three parts. 1854 Ronalds & Richardson *Chem. Technol.* (ed. 2) I. 183 One part of carbon consumes in burning to carbonic acid $2\frac{2}{3}$ parts of oxygen.

†**6.** A mediæval measure of time, equal to $\frac{1}{15}$ of an hour, or 4 minutes: see atom *sb.* 7. *Obs.*

1844 Lingard *Anglo-Sax. Ch.* (1858) II. xi. 158 Each.. admits of four different subdivisions, into four points, ten minutes, fifteen parts or degrees, and forty moments.

II. Portion allotted, share.

7. a. A portion of something (material or immaterial) allotted or belonging to a particular person; a share. Sometimes almost in abstract sense: Sharing, participation; interest, concern.

to have part: to share, partake (*in*, †*of*). ***to have neither part nor lot in***: to have no share or concern in, to have nothing to do with (see lot *sb.* 2 b). See also *art and part*: art *sb.* 16.

*a*1300 *Floriz & Bl.* 522 He moste kunne muchel of art þat þu woldest ȝeue þer-of part. *a*1300 *Cursor M.* 19585 Has þou na part, coth petre, here. 1382 Wyclif *Rev.* xx. 6 Blessid and holy he, that hath paart in the first aȝen risyng. 1390 Gower *Conf.* III. 104 Cham Upon his part Aufrique nam. *c*1449 Pecock *Repr.* iii. i. 277 The preestis and dekenes of the Oold Testament schulden not haue part and lott in the firste parting of the lond of Iewry. 1477 Earl Rivers (Caxton) *Dictes* 1 Aduersitees, Of the whiche I.. haue had my parte. 1538 Bale *John Bapt.* in *Harl. Misc.* (Malh.) I. 216 My ways.. with mennys ways haue no part. 1601 Barlow *Serm. Paules Crosse* 23 We haue no part in Dauid, nor inheritance in the son of Isay. 1611 Bible *Acts* i. 17. 1760–72 H. Brooke *Fool of Qual.* (1809) I. 151 We had neither art or part, concern or interest therein. 1850 S. Dobell *Roman* i. Poet. Wks. 1875 I. 14 Death Can have no part in Beauty. 1891 Dougall *Beggars All* (ed. 2) 271 That she would have neither part nor lot in his dishonest career.

b. Allotted portion (without definite notion of division or sharing); possession (*concr.* or *abstr.*); one's lot in life. *Obs.* or *arch.*

1382 Wyclif *Ps.* lxii. 11 [lxiii. 10] Thei shul be taken in to the hond of swerd, the partis of foxis thei shul be. *c*1386 Chaucer *Clerk's T.* 594, I haue noȝht had no part of children tweyne But first siknesse, and after wo and peyne. *c*1500 *Three Kings Sons* 66 To obeie and abide the wille of oure lord, & to take suche part yn pacience, as he wol sende. 1609 Bible (Douay) *Hos.* v. 7 Now shal a moneth devoure them with their partes. 1858 Neale *Bernard de M.* (1865) 36 The Lord shall be thy part.

8. A person's share in some action; what one has to do; function, office, business, duty. Formerly in *pl.* when referring to a number of persons.

1375 Barbour *Bruce* xi. 245 Be liklynes the mast cowart Semyt till do richt weill his part. 1451 Marg. Paston in *P. Lett.* I. 201 He seyd itt was not his parte to do itt. 1542 Udall *Erasm. Apoph.* 297 The partes of menne is, to reioyce in the behalf of the commenweale. 1563 *Homilies* ii. *Repentance* ii. (1859) 544 It is therefore our parts.. to pray unto our heavenly Father. 1611 Bible *Ruth* iii. 13 But if hee will not doe the part of a kinseman to thee, then will I doe the part of a kinseman to thee, as the Lord liueth. 1667 Milton *P.L.* viii. 561 Accuse not Nature, she hath don her part. 1712 Addison *Spect.* No. 418 ¶7 It is the part of a Poet to humour the Imagination. 1865 Trollope *Belton Est.* xxii. 254 Was it not a brother's part to go to a sister in affliction? 1882 *Times* 23 Sept. 4 The artillery did its part with its usual devotion.

9. a. *Theatr.* The character assigned to or sustained by an actor in a dramatic performance; a rôle. Also, the words assigned to or spoken by an actor in such a character; hence, a written or printed copy of these.

1495 in Sharp *Cov. Myst.* (1825) 36 Payd for copyyng of the ij knyghts partes, & demons. 1584 *Ibid.* 38 To Jhon Copestake, for playenge of Esron his parte xxd. 1600 Shaks. *A.Y.L.* ii. vii. 142 All the world's a stage.. And one man in his time playes many parts. 1622 Mabbe tr. *Aleman's Guzman d' Alf.* i. 264 Let every man take his Qu and perfect his owne part. 1710 Steele *Tatler* No. 180 ¶6 They must be called off the Stage, and receive Parts more suitable to their Genius. 1809 Malkin *Gil Blas* ii. viii. ¶2, I was sent on the boards in children's parts. 1882 H. C. Merivale *Faucit of B.* I. 145 Minna in the 'Pirate' would be more the line of part to fall to you.

b. *fig.* A character sustained by any one, either as a special office or function (nearly = 8), or as assumed or feigned.

to play (act) the part of: to act as or like; to perform the function of. ***to play (act) a part***: to perform a function, or pursue a course of action; also, to sustain a feigned character, make a pretence, act deceitfully.

*a*1400–50 *Alexander* 361 þan þe figour of a freke he sall take eftire, And preualy in þat part a-pere ȝowe be-forne. *a*1548 Hall *Chron., Rich. III* 50 Homfrey Cheiny pleiyng the parte of a good blood hounde, foloed the tract of ye flyer. 1590 Spenser *F.Q.* ii. iv. 27 Where left, he went, and his owne false part playd. 1663 Butler *Hud.* i. ii. 205 None ever acted both Parts bolder, Both of a Chieftain and a Soldier. *a*1732 Gay *Fables* ii. vi. 2 The man of pure and simple heart Thro' life disdains a double part. 1886 Baring-Gould *Court Royal* xxxv, He was unskilled to act a part and speak half the truth. 1891 *Speaker* 11 July 36/2 The Referendum and the Initiative.. have a great part to play in the future of Switzerland.

†**c.** *transf.* One who performs a part, an actor.

*a*1643 W. Cartwright *Commend. Verses Fletcher's Dram. Poems*, That some who sat spectators haue confessed.. [they] felt such shafts steal through their captiued sense, As made them rise Parts, and go Lovers thence.

10. *Mus.* The melody assigned to a particular voice or instrument in concerted music, or a written or printed copy of this for the use of a particular performer; each of the constituent melodies or successions of notes which make up a harmony. Hence *transf.* Each of the voices or instruments which join in a concerted piece.

1526 Skelton *Magnyf.* 1481, I synge of two partys without a mene. *c*1586 C'tess Pembroke *Ps.* lvii. vi, Thou my harp the consort make, My self will beare a part. 1597 Morley *Introd. to Mus.* 1 Musicke bookes.. being brought to the table: the mistresse of the house presented mee with a part, earnestly requesting mee to sing. 1674 Playford *Skill Mus.* iii. 1 The Parts of Musick are in all but four, howsoever some skilful Musicians have composed songs of twenty, thirty, and forty parts. 1706 A. Bedford *Temple Mus.* iii. 55 This one Voice or Part is mentioned as the greatest Excellency of the Temple Musick. 1889 E. Prout *Harmony* (ed. 10) iv. §94 Most music is written in four-part harmony, and the parts are generally named after the four varieties of the human voice... The highest part is called the *treble*, or *soprano*, the next below this, the *alto*, the third part.. the *tenor*, and the lowest part the *bass*.

†**11.** A piece of conduct, an act (usually with qualification expressing praise or blame). *Obs.*

1561 T. Hoby tr. *Castiglione's Courtyer* ii. (1577) Mj, Alonso Garillo.. hauing committed certaine youthfull partes.. was by the Kings commaundement carried to prison. 1579–80 North *Plutarch* (1895) III. 333 Pausanias.. committed many insolent partes by reason of the great authority he had. 1596 Raleigh *Discov. Gviana* A ij, For your Honors many Honorable and friendlie parts, I have hitherto onely returned promises. *a*1632 T. Taylor *God's Judgem.* i. ii. i. (1642) 155 He.. after shewed him many other unkinde and unchildly parts.

12. A personal quality or attribute, natural or acquired, esp. of an intellectual kind (? as a constituent element of one's mind or character, or ? as allotted to one by Providence: cf. *gift, talent*); almost always in *pl.* Abilities, capacities, talents. Usually with an adj. expressing excellence; also *absol.* = high intellectual ability, cleverness, talent. Now *arch.*, rare in speech.

1561 T. Hoby tr. *Castiglione's Courtyer* ii. (1577) G vij b, To set his delite to haue in himselfe partes and excellent qualities. 1598 B. Jonson *Ev. Man in Hum.* iii. i, I ne'er saw any gentlemanlike part [in him]. *Ibid.* iv. i, A gentleman.. of very excellent good partes. 1599 Shaks. *Much Ado* v. ii.

64 For which of my bad parts didst thou first fall in loue with me? **1627–77** FELTHAM *Resolves* I. xxxiv. 88 We magnifie the wealthy man, though his parts be never so poor. **1678** BARCLAY *Apol.* (1841) 283 Three things go to the making up of a minister. 1. Natural parts, that he be not a fool. 2. Acquired parts, that he be learned in the languages [etc.]. **1710** STEELE *Tatler* No. 197 ¶5 Courage is the natural Parts of a Soldier. **1710** HEARNE *Collect.* (Oxf. Hist. Soc.) II. 351 A man of Parts, but a most vile, stinking Whigg. **1806** G. CANNING *Poet. Wks.* (1827) 49 But if, amongst this motley crew, One man of real parts we view. **1844** MACAULAY *Ess., Earl Chatham* (1887) 818 Some of them were indeed, to do them justice, men of parts. **1894** 'IAN MACLAREN' *Bonnie Briar Bush* (1899) 5 A Lad o' Pairts. *a* **1901** BESANT *Five Years' Tryst*, etc. (1902) 196 At school the son was a steady lad, of good, not brilliant parts.

III. Region; side.

13. a. A portion of a country or territory, or of the world; a region, quarter. (Usually in *pl.*; often with a vague collective rather than plural sense.)

(When the words *of the world* or the like are added, the sense is 1 above: e.g.

c **1400** MAUNDEV. (Roxb.) i. 4 If a man come fro þe west partys of þe werld. **1535** BOORDE in *Introd. Knowl.* (1870) Forewds. 53 Few frendys ynglond hath in theys partes of Europe. **1560** DAUS tr. *Sleidane's Comm.* 132 Going into the foure partes of the worlde.)

c **1400** *Destr. Troy* 217 And all prouyns and pertes þi pes shall desyre. **1558** KNOX *First Blast* (Arb.) 20 Women in those partes, were not tamed nor embased by consideration of their own sex and kind. **1607** MIDDLETON *Michaelm. Term* III. iii. 52, I am a mere stranger for these parts. *a* **1674** CLARENDON *Surv. Leviath.* (1676) 2 One who ha's spent many years in foreign parts. **1725** BERKELEY *Proposal Supplying Ch. in For. Plant.* Wks. III. 215 To propagate the Gospel in foreign parts. **1833** *Rep. Sel. Committee on Munic. Corporat.* 334 The mixed jurisdiction in the Parts of Kesteven. **1861** E. FITZGERALD *Lett.* (1889) I. 277 Let me know when you come into these parts.

b. ***Part of Fortune*** (Astrol.): that point of the heavens in which the moon is when the sun is in the ascendant or 'horoscope'.

1696 in PHILLIPS (ed. 5). **1819** WILSON *Dict. Astrol.* *a* **1836** SMEDLEY *Occult Sc.* in *Encycl. Metrop.* (1855) XXXI. 311 *The Part of Fortune*, is the distance of the moon's place from the sun, added to the degrees of the ascendent.

14. †**a.** Side (*lit.*); hence, direction in space. *Obs.*

c **1380** *Sir Ferumb.* 3517 Y schal take out to anoþer pard & prykie fro hem anon. *a* **1548** HALL *Chron., Hen. IV* 30 Made a bridge over the river on the part of saint Denis strete, and so escaped. **1551** ROBINSON tr. *More's Utop.* I. (1895) 34 Sume here and sume there; yea, verye manye of bothe partes. **1574** BOURNE *Regiment for Sea* (1577) Introd. 5 b, If that the Sonne..be unto the North part, or Southe part of the Equinoctiall. **1611** BIBLE *Luke* xvii. 24 As the lightning that lighteneth out of the one part vnder heauen, shineth vnto the other part vnder heauen. **1774** T. HUTCHINSON *Diary* 7 Sept., [Norwich] is on every part walled in.

b. = HAND *sb.* 32 i. Now *rare*.

1485 CAXTON *Paris & V.* 67 On that other parte he had grete drede. **1534** CROMWELL *Let.* 17 Nov. in Merriman *Life & Lett.* (1902) I. 391 Neglecting of thone parte the kinges highnes honour to be preserued..of thother parte as it were contempnyng all frieendeship in giving place to a litle Lucre. **1587** GOLDING *De Mornay* iv. 40 On the contrary part, his mind seeth not itself, but only turneth into itself. **1882** STEVENSON *New Arab. Nts.* (1884) 135 On the other part, I judged that I might lose nearly as much.

†**c.** *fig.* (Father's or mother's) Side (in genealogy). (Cf. HALF *sb.* 2.) *Obs.*

1558 in Strype *Ann. Ref.* (1709) I. II. App. v. 398 All other your majesty's ancestors..of the part of your said mother [cf. L. *ex parte materna*].

15. a. Side (*fig.*), in a contest, dispute, question, contract, or any relation of opposite persons or bodies of people; party; cause.

1375 BARBOUR *Bruce* VII. 624 Clyffurd and wauss maid a melle, Quhar cliffurdraucht him a cole, And athir syne drew to partis. *c* **1380** WYCLIF *Sel. Wks.* III. 363 þe fend haþ þe strenger part here þan þe part of treuþe. **1396** in *Scott. Antiq.* XIV. 217 This indenture made..betwx..Scher Henry Synclar..on the ta part and..Scher Jone of Dermounde on the tother part. *c* **1489** CAXTON *Blanchardyn* xlvii. 179 Of that other part, they marked well that wyth subyon were grete fuson of men. **1526** TINDALE *Mark* ix. 40 Whosoeuer is not agaynste you is on youre parte. **1565–73** COOPER *Thesaurus* A j b/1 *A Senatu stat*..he is on the senates part. **1592** KYD *Sp. Trag.* I. ii. 64 The victory to neither part inclinde. **1700** PRIOR *Carmen Seculare* 356 Betwixt the Nations let her hold the Scale, And, as she wills, let either Part prevail. **1882** H. C. MERIVALE *Faucit of B.* I. 107 No word had been spoken on either part. **1884** *Bythewood & Jarman's Prec. in Conveyancing* (ed. 4) I. 402 An agreement made..Between ——..(the vendor) of the one part, and ——..(the purchaser) of the other part.

b. *concr.* A party; a body of adherents or partisans; a faction. Now *rare* or *Obs.*

c **1330** R. BRUNNE *Chron. Wace* (Rolls) 10455 When boþe partis come to þe fight. *c* **1386** CHAUCER *Knt.'s T.* 1724 Arcite & eek the hondred of his parte. **1534** in *Lett. Suppress. Monasteries* (Camden) 9 Bothe the seyde partes hathe ben more ardente now..then they were before. **1560** DAUS tr. *Sleidane's Comm.* 409 He in dede would gladly have pleased both parts. **1596** SPENSER *F.Q.* IV. iv. 25 Then gan the part of Chalengers anew To range the field, and victorlike to raine.

†**c.** *pl.* ? = *part-fray* (see 29). *Obs. rare.*

1600 *Look About You* I. iii. in Hazl. *Dodsley* VII. 401 Shift for thyself, good Skink; there's gold, away: Here will be parts. **1616** B. JONSON *Epigrams* cx, [Cæsar] lived scarce one just age, And that midst envy and parts.

IV. [f. PART *v.*] Parting.

†**16.** Parting, separation, leave-taking. *Obs. rare.*

1605 *1st Pt. Ieronimo* II. vi. 27 O cruell part; Andreas bosome bears away my hart.

17. The parting of the hair. *U.S.*

1871 'MARK TWAIN' in *Galaxy* Aug. 284/1 He..brushed his hair with elaborate care,..accomplishing an accurate 'part' behind. **1890** in *Cent. Dict.* **1895** *Century Mag.* Aug. 489/1 His straight, smooth hair, with its definite part. **1933** J. STEINBECK *To God Unknown* (1935) viii. 61 He raked a nervous hand through his hair and destroyed the careful part. **1970** *Globe Mag.* (Toronto) 26 Sept. 19/2 (Advt.), Balding! So you moved your part down over your ear. **1972** D. RAMSAY *Little Murder Music* 123 A shoulder-length fall of blue-black hair divided by a snow-white part in centre. **1976** 'R. MACDONALD' *Blue Hammer* xxiv. 126 The part in her hair was white and straight.

V. Phrases.

18. part and (or) parcel. (The addition of *parcel* emphasizes the sense of *part.*)

a. ***part and parcel***, emphasizing sense 1 c: cf. PARCEL *sb.* 1 b.

[**1414**: see PARCEL *sb.* 1 b.] **1535–6** *Act 27 Hen. VIII*, c. 11 This present Act, and euery part and parcel therof, shall extend [etc.]. *Ibid.* c. 26 The..Lordships..to be part and parcell of the same hundred [of Wesebery]. **1592** WEST *1st Pt. Symbol.* (1647) 100 [To] suffer the same and every part and parcell thereof to descend come and remaine according to the true meaning of this Indenture. **1664** *Compleat Clark* 795 The said Capital Messuage, Lands, Tenements, Hereditaments, and Premisses, and every part and parcel thereof. **1837** GORING & PRITCHARD *Microgr.* 106 This being part and parcel of my present subject. **1846** MCCULLOCH *Acc. Brit. Empire* (1854) I. 194 The places referred to are, to all intents and purposes, part and parcel of the metropolis. **1856** DOVE *Logic Chr. Faith* v. i. §2. 272 The moral law of the conscience is part and parcel of man himself.

b. ***part or (nor) parcel.***

1459 [see PARCEL *sb.* 1]. **1535–6** *Act 27 Hen. VIII*, c. 11 Vnited,..to and with the countie of Hereford, as a member, part, or parcell of the same. **1539** *Act 31 Hen. VIII*, c. 13 All such Right [or] Title..to the premisses, or to any part or parcell therof. **1576** FLEMING *Panopl. Epist.* 64 Neuer a part or parcel thereof left vndiscouered. **1664** *Compleat Clark* 6 As often as it shall happen the said annuity of a hundred pounds or any part or parcell thereof to be behind and unpaid. **1867** LADY HERBERT *Cradle L.* iv. 126 The Protestants alone have no part or parcel in the sacred inheritance.

19. a. part of speech (*Gram.*) [L. *pars orationis*]. Formerly also *part of reason* (REASON *sb.*[1] 3 c), or simply *part* (sense 2 a). Each of the grammatical categories or classes of words as determined by the kind of notion or relation which they express in the sentence. Also (with hyphens) attrib.

Usually reckoned as eight, viz. noun or substantive, adjective, pronoun, verb, adverb, preposition, conjunction, interjection (sometimes as nine, the article being reckoned separately from the adjective). Formerly the participle was often reckoned as a distinct 'part'.

1481–1530 [see REASON *sb.*[1] 3 c]. **1509** HAWES *Past. Pleas.* v. (Percy Soc.) 24 For as much as there be Eight partes of speche, I would knowe ryght fayne, What a noune substantive is in hys degre. **1530** PALSGR. Introd. 24 They have also a nynth part of reason whiche I call article, borowyng the name of the Grekes. **1612** BRINSLEY *Lud. Lit.* (1627) 56 *Q.* How many parts of speech have you? Or how many parts are there in Speech? *A.* Eight. **1711** J. GREENWOOD *Eng. Gram.* 62, I have not made the Article (as some have done) a distinct Part of Speech. **1866** J. MARTINEAU *Ess.* I. 277 We..must have the parts of speech before we can predicate anything. **1933** L. BLOOMFIELD *Language* i. 17 Even the fundamental features of Indo-European grammar, such as, especially, the part-of-speech system, are by no means universal in human speech. **1964** *Language* XL. 167 One-syllable words, graphemically defined, have the same part-of-speech assignments when checked against standard dictionaries.

b. ***principal parts*** (of a verb): those from which the other parts can be derived, or which contain the different stems in the simplest forms.

In Latin Grammar, applied to the first pers. sing. pres. indic., the infinitive mood, the first pers. sing. perfect indic., and the supine (or in deponent verbs, instead of the two last, the perf. pple.); in English, and Teutonic langs. generally: see quot. 1870.

1870 MARCH *Comp. Gram. Ags. Lang.* 78 The Principal Parts [of a verb] are the present infinitive, the imperfect indicative first person, and the passive participle.

20. a. most part: the greatest part, most; as *adv.* mostly; †***most part all***, almost all; †***the more part***, the greater or major part, the majority.

13.. *K. Alis.* 5390 þe mest parte þereof hy slowen. *c* **1400** *Destr. Troy* 13308 The most parte of my pepull put to þe dethe. **1523** LD. BERNERS *Froiss.* I. 772 The towne was than mooste parte all the houses covered with strawe. **1526** TINDALE *Acts* xix. 32 The moare parte knewe not wherefore they were come togedder. **1567** *Gude & Godlie B.* (S.T.S.) 166 [Mankynde] leuand maist part in all vice. **1693** *Humours Town* 48 Their Spendthrift Sons..have dipt most part of their Estates in Judgements, Bonds, and Warrents. *Mod.* He lives there most part of the year.

b. ***for (the) most part, the most part***, †***for the more part***: as concerns the greatest part, in most cases, mostly.

c **1386** CHAUCER *Reeve's Prol.* 4 For the moore part they loughe & pleyde. *c* **1400** MAUNDEV. (1839) xix. 213 þei ben alle, for the moste part, alle Pygmeyes. **1594** R. ASHLEY tr. *Loys le Roy* 13 They ride the most part, without sadles, spurs, or shoes on their horses. **1685** LOVELL *Gen. Hist. Relig.* 123 Bishopricks and Monasteries,..for most Part, in great Disorder. **1833** HT. MARTINEAU *Berkeley Banker* I. viii. 166 The shops were for the most part closed.

†**21. some part**: as *adv.*, in some parts; to some extent; somewhat. *Obs.*

1456 SIR G. HAYE *Law Arms* (S.T.S.) 14 It [the vision] be sum part subtile to understand. **1569–70** *Tragedie* 140 in *Satir. Poems Reform.* x, Lord Darlie, Of quhais rair bewtie scho did sumpart farlie.

22. bear a part: to sustain a part (as in acting); to take part: = 23 b.

c **1611** CHAPMAN *Iliad* Anagram (1865) 73 No spirit in our blood But in our soul's discourses bears a part. **1712** ARBUTHNOT *John Bull* III. i, John Bull's mother..bears a part in the following transactions. **1782** PRIESTLEY *Corrupt. Chr.* II. IX. 186 The king himself..bore a part in it.

23. take part. a. To share, partake *of* or *in* (cf. sense 7); **b.** To participate *in* (some action), to assist, co-operate (cf. 8).

1382 WYCLIF *Hebr.* ii. 14 Therfore for children comuneden to fleisch and blood, and he also took part of the same. *a* **1533** LD. BERNERS *Huon* lxxxi. 245 Such as regarded her were constrayned to take parte of her sorow. **1596** SPENSER *F.Q.* IV. ix. 24 Each one taking part in others aide. **1875** JOWETT *Plato* (ed. 2) IV. 19 Philebus..takes no further part in the discussion.

c. ***to take part with***, to side with, range oneself on the side of (see sense 15). ***to take the part of***, to espouse the side of, to support, second, back up.

c **1420** LYDG. *Assembly of Gods* 1058 Vertu was full heuy, when he sy Frewyll Take part with Vyce. *Ibid.* 1220, I haue gret meruayll Ye durst be so bolde Vyces part to take. **1545** BRINKLOW *Lament.* (1874) 80 The Iewes cried out agaynst Christ, takynge parte with the highe prestes. **1560** DAUS tr. *Sleidane's Comm.* 34 They shall doubtles have mo to take their parts. *c* **1611** CHAPMAN *Iliad* I. 570 To take part Against Olympius. **1732** LEDIARD *Sethos* II. IX. 338 He took your part in this war. **1850** *Tait's Mag.* XVII. 559/1 Some took part with him, some with Carrol. **1875** JOWETT *Plato* (ed. 2) III. 251 Zeus sent him flying for taking her part when she was being beaten.

†**24. a part, on part**, early analytical ways of writing APART, q.v. *Obs.*

1470–85 MALORY *Arthur* I. xv, We wille go on parte.

25. for my part: as regards *my* share in the matter; as far as I am concerned (cf. *on my part*, etc., 28): so *for his, our, your part*, etc.

c **1440** *Generydes* 3013 Syr Anasore the knyght, and ser Darell,..Eche for his parte quyte hym self full wele. **1450–1530** *Myrr. our Ladye* 137 We oughte to offer yt vp vnto hym with thankeynges for his parte, and meke our selfe for our parte. **1552** *Bk. Com. Prayer, Communion*, I for my part am here present. **1663** BUTLER *Hud.* I. ii. 35 But as for our Part, we shall tell The naked Truth of what befell. **1762** WHITEHEAD *School for Lovers* IV. i, I wish all the women were in the bottom of the sea, for my part. **1818** M. G. LEWIS *Jrnl. W. Ind.* (1834) 185 For my own part, I have no hope of any material benefit.

26. a. in part: partly.

c **1380** WYCLIF *Sel. Wks.* III. 351 It may be purgid in part. **1568** GRAFTON *Chron.* II. 663 The lawes of the realme, in part he reformed, and in part he newely augmented. **1611** BIBLE *1 Cor.* xiii. 9 For we know in part, and we prophesie in part. **1642** J. EATON *Honey-c. Free Justif.* 374 To make himselfe righteous by his own works, either in whole or in part. **1878** HUTTON *Scott* iii. 30 The lady herself was in part responsible for this impression.

b. in good part: favourably or without offence; ***in ill*** or ***evil part***, unfavourably; so ***in better, best, worse part***, etc. Chiefly with *take*, or the like. (Cf. L. *in bonam partem accipere*, or *interpretari*.)

1559 KNOX *Let. Q. Eliz.* in *First Blast* (Arb.) App. 60 Interpret my rude wordis in the best part. **1560** DAUS tr. *Sleidane's Comm.* 35 b, Fearinge lest the duke should it take in evyll part. *Ibid.* 107 Thus verely doe they frendly counsell them, and requyre them to take it in that parte. *c* **1566** J. ALDAY tr. *Boaystuau's Theat. World* A iij, Accepting [it] in good part. **1585** T. WASHINGTON tr. *Nicholay's Voy.* I. xxii. 28 b, Bread, wine, and sweet water..were accepted in better parte then the answeare of the grand maister. **1594** SHAKS. *Rich. III*, III. iv. 21 Which I presume hee'le take in gentle part. *c* **1611** CHAPMAN *Iliad* XXIV. 124 And myself take that wrong..To Hector in worst part of all. **1761–2** HUME *Hist. Eng.* (1806) IV. lx. 544 The parliament took this remonstrance in ill part. **1867** TROLLOPE *Chron. Barset* I. xviii. 160, I am sure that he will take it in good part.

†**27. of the part of, of my part**, etc.: = on the part of (see 28); also, *of my part*, from my side, from me. *Obs.*

c **1530** *To My Heart's Joy* 9 in *Pol. Rel. & L. Poems* 40 Yf ye liste to haue knoweliche of my part, I am in hel [= health], god thanked mote he be, As of body. **1565–73** COOPER *Thesaurus* A j b/1 All this is of my part, or maketh for me. **1585** T. WASHINGTON tr. *Nicholay's Voy.* I. vi. 4 b, [The] Moores, to whom of our partes was made good cheere. **1595** SHAKS. *John* v. vi. 2 Of the part of England. *a* **1626** BACON *New Atl.* (1627) 6 We of our parts saluted him in a very lowly and submissive manner.

28. on the part of (any one, *on his part*, etc.): on the side of; as regards (his, etc.) share in the action, as far as (he, etc.) is concerned (cf. *for my part*, 25). Also, Proceeding from (the person or party mentioned) as agent; made or performed by; by.

c **1400** *Destr. Troy* 11836 Priam on his part, & his prise knightes,..no swyke thoghtyn. *c* **1420** LYDG. *Assembly of Gods* 460 On my part no defaute hath be. **1526** TINDALE *1 Pet.* iv. 14 On their parte he is evyll spoken of: but on youre parte he is glorified. **1631** GOUGE *God's Arrows* III. §2. 183 Without any cause, or provocation on Israels part. **1667** MILTON *P.L.* IX. 7 Foul distrust, and breach Disloyal on the part of Man,..On the part of Heav'n Now alienated, distance and distaste. **1849** MACAULAY *Hist. Eng.* iv. I. 503 The conclusion, that no excess of tyranny on the part of a prince can justify active resistance on the part of a subject. **1875** Jowett *Plato* I. 20 No objection on my part, I said.

VI. 29. Combinations and attributive uses: **part-book**, a book containing one part (or a number of parts printed separately) of a harmonized musical composition (see 10); †**part-fray**, a conflict between two parties or factions (*obs.*); **part-music**, music in parts (esp. vocal); **part-playing**, playing in parts (sense 10); **part-score** *Bridge* (see quot. 1936); **part-singing**, singing in parts; **part-whole** *a.*, of or pertaining to the relationship of a part or parts to a whole; **part-work**, (*a*) used *attrib.* to designate a system of part-time work; (*b*) a book or the like published in parts; also *attrib.*; **part-writing**, composition of music in parts, combination of parts in musical composition (see 10). See also part-song.

1864 A. McKay *Hist. Kilmarnock* (ed. 4) 278 A complete set of *part-books of Handel's 'Joshua'. **1889** W. S. Rockstro in Grove *Dict. Mus.* IV. 739 Separate volumes, well known to students of mediaeval Music as 'the old Part-Books'. **1631** Heywood *Maid of West* ii. Wks. 1874 II. 282 Pox of these *part-frayes. **1880** H. F. Frost in Grove *Dict. Mus.* II. 658 When secular *part-music again occupied the attention of composers, it took the form of the glee rather than that of the madrigal or part-song. **1946** R. Blesh *Shining Trumpets* (1949) i. 18 *Tempo*: I. Strict tempo or controlled acceleration. II. Moderate, never too fast. Relaxed, and with room for improvised *part-playing. **1960** *Times* 29 Feb. 15/1 Balanced part-playing and clear harmonic progression appeared to dominate his intentions to the detriment of artistic communication. **1899** *Daily News* 2 Nov. 6/3 Once the craze was all for issuing volumes in parts; to-day *part publication is almost unknown. **1932** *Official Syst. Contract Bridge* 187 (*heading*) Bidding against a side which has a *part score. **1936** E. Culbertson *Contract Bridge Complete* 17 *Part-score*, (1) A contract of less than game; (2) the points earned for the making of such a contract. **1973** *Times* 20 Oct. 11/3 You then run the risk of missing a game unless you have a part-score. **1859** Geo. Eliot *A. Bede* xix, It had cost Adam a great deal of trouble ..to learn his musical notes and *part-singing. **1949** M. Mead *Male & Female* iii. 73 The Balinese child..develops a *part-whole relationship to the world, in which each part of his body is a whole, and yet each is part of the whole. **1953** C. E. Bazell *Linguistic Form* 107 It is likely that, as soon as the part-whole rather than the member-class terminology is used, the ostensible criteria for phonemic analysis should be transferred to the analysis of phonemic parts. **1972** *Language* XLVIII. 452 Semantic analysis based on a strict part-whole conception of meaning. **1966** *Economist* 26 Mar. 1231/1 One of the aims of the *part-work system is to increase the sum of technically trained people in the rural areas. **1969** *Times* 13 Mar. 20/7 (Advt.), Part work publishing. *Ibid.*, Part-works now account for more than 10 per cent of all money spent on periodicals. **1971** *Guardian* 22 Oct. 9/2 'World of Wildlife' is the latest in a string of partwork publications... Partworks began in the mid-eighteenth century when the 'Encyclopaedia Britannica' found itself unable to raise sufficient funds to publish all the volumes in one go. **1975** *Nature* 24 Jan. 227/2 Dr. Magnus Pyke..currently to be seen on British television, advertising the appearance of a new partwork about science. **1889** E. Prout *Harmony* (ed. 10) iv. §95 Rules which the student must observe in *part-writing.

B. *adv.* or quasi-*adv.* or *adj.* [Cf. similar use of parcel *sb.* B.] In part, partly, in some degree, to some extent. **a.** qualifying vb. or phrase.

1513 More in Grafton *Chron.* II. 787 The king made his mother an answere part in earnest and part in play. **1535** Coverd. *Dan.* ii. 33 His fete were parte off yron, and parte of earth. **1591** Sylvester *Du Bartas* i. vi. 517 To th' end each Creature might..Part-sympathize with his own Element. **1604** Shaks. *Oth.* v. ii. 296 This wretch hath part confest his Villany. **1647** Trapp *Comm. 2 Tim.* i. 12 The ship that is part in the water, and part in the mud. **1704** Pope *Windsor For.* 18 Waving groves..part admit, and part exclude the day. **1828** *Craven Gloss.* (ed. 2) s.v., 'It rains part', it rains a little. **1864** Tennyson *Grandmother* viii, A lie which is part a truth is a harder matter to fight.

b. qualifying adj. or pple.

Properly hyphened when the adj. is used *attrib.*

1597 Shaks. *2 Hen. IV*, i. iii. 60 One..who (halfe through) Giues o're, and leaues his part-created Cost A naked subiect to the Weeping Clouds. **1832** Motherwell *Poems* (1847) 266, I watched those cold part-opened lips. **1891** *Mail* 14 Dec. 3/6 A part-heard case of alleged dealing in bogus cheques.

c. qualifying sb. With agent-nouns and nouns of action, still of adverbial character, as in ***part-payment***, payment in part, action of partly paying, part-owner; but with other sbs. functioning as an adj. In part-time, part-way, etc. often = part of (the time, the way): cf. *half-time*, *half-way*. Usually hyphened to the sb., and the combination may be used *attrib.*, as in ***part-mine pig-iron***, absol. ***part-mine***, pig-iron partly from native ore. **part-exchange**, a transaction in which the owner of an article exchanges it for another (usu. new) article and pays a sum of money to cover the difference between the value of the two articles; hence as *v. trans.*, to exchange (something) in this way; also *fig.*; **part-load** (see quot. 1971); **part-pay**, a part of one's pay; *spec.* that part paid to whalemen before the start of a voyage.

1818 Hallam *Mid. Ages* (1872) I. i. 122 A part performance of Gregory II.'s engagement. **1833** Ht. Martineau *Fr. Wines & Pol.* i. 1 An excursion of part business, part pleasure. **1850** H. Melville *White Jacket* II. xxxvii. 234 There were instances of men in the Neversink receiving money in part pay for work done for private individuals. **1851** —— *Moby Dick* III. xlix. 309, I hope my poor mother's drawn my part-pay ere this. **1862** H. Spencer *First Princ.* ii. xx. §159 (1875) 447 A part-cause of the transformation of the Earth's crust. **1878** Bosw. Smith *Carthage* 238 It was part payment only, payment in full was still to come. **1878** C. Read *On Theory of Logic* 130 It is certain that C is a Cause or Part-Cause of E. **1893** *Daily News* 20 Nov. 2/6 Staffordshire part-mines are 45*s* 6*d* to 46*s* 6*d* and 47*s*, according to mixture; common, 35*s* to 36*s*; and all mine hot-blast forge iron, 60*s* to 62*s* 6*d*. **1896** *Westm. Gaz.* 29 Jan. 1/2 The part-authors, and part-condoners, of the horrors in the Armenian provinces. **1901** H. H. Joachim *Study Ethics of Spinoza* 169 In our ignorance we attribute these qualities of sensation directly to the external bodies, which are at most their part-causes. **1926** *Punch* 10 Nov. 505/3 A correspondent writes to know if, when the new wave-lengths come into force, the old ones will be accepted in part-exchange. **1929** *Melody Maker* Jan. 18 (Advt.), Your present instrument in part exchange. **1931** D. L. Sayers *Five Red Herrings* xx. 218 He had something to do with the second-hand motor trade and was taking the bike in part-exchange for something. **1932** H. H. Price *Perception* viii. 270 One needs..to know that any material thing is a part-cause of the sense-data belonging to it. **1961** *Guardian* 12 June 2/3 The urge to part-exchange my car comes upon me. **1964** M. Argyle *Psychol. & Social Probl.* v. 61 Different part-causes combine together, so that if one is very strong, or if several of them add together, the result is a delinquent. Each part-cause has a known statistical weight over a large sample, so that it is possible to estimate the chances that a given person will be a delinquent. **1968** *Listener* 30 May 711/1 One way is to resolve to *part-exchange* an idea long before it has been driven down to the rims. **1969** *Jane's Freight Containers 1968–69* 315/1, 20% will go to wagon-load and 80% to LCL, or part-load. **1971** M. Tak *Truck Talk* 115 *Part load*, a consignment to a destination that is less than a complete trailer load. **1972** *Daily Tel.* 10 Oct. 3/3 He part-exchanged his old power-boat for the Carnation in 1970. **1973** *Times* 25 Oct. 38/7 (Advt.), Steinway and Sons ..are prepared to purchase or take part exchange pianos of their own or other makes. **1976** *Leicester Trader* 24 Nov. 21/2 They do part-exchanges, offer an excellent after-sales service and an insurance repair service.

part (pɑːt), *v.* Also 4–5 pert, 4–6 parte, 6– *Sc.* pairt. Pa. pple. **parted**, in 4–5 (8–9) part. [a. F. *part-ir* (pr. pple. *part-ant*, 3 sing. pres. indic. *part*, pres. subj. *parte*), formerly 'to part, sunder, divide, sever; also' (in mod.Fr. now only) 'to part, depart, remoue, or goe from' (Cotgr.) = Pr. and Sp. *partir*, It. *partire*:—L. *partīre* (in cl. L. usually *partīrī*) to part, divide, distribute, share, f. *pars, part-em*, stem *parti-* part *sb.*]

I. 1. a. *trans.* To divide into parts (by actual local separation, or by marking or assigning boundaries, or merely in thought); to divide, break, cleave, sever. Now somewhat *rare*.

to part the hoof: to have cloven hoofs (cf. divide *v.* 1 b).

c **1275** *On Serving Christ* 27 in *O.E. Misc.* 91 And Adames eyres beoþ parted on pre. *c* **1330** R. Brunne *Chron.* (1810) 49 Knoute..parted þe lond in foure parties. *a* **1340** Hampole *Psalter* xxi. 18 þai partid his clathes in foure partis. *c* **1440** *Promp. Parv.* 385/1 Partyn a-sundyr, or clevyn,..*divido*. **1483** *Cath. Angl.* 270/2 To Parte in thre, *tripartiri*. **1594** Willobie *Avisa* xlv, A heavy burden wearieth one, Which being parted then in twaine, Seemes very light. **1611** Bible *Lev.* ii. 6 Thou shalt part it in pieces, and powr oyle thereon. —— *Deut.* xiv. 6 Euery beast that parteth the hoofe, and cleaueth the clift into two clawes. **1650** Trapp *Comm. Exod.* xiv. 21 That torrent of fire..yet parted it self; making a kinde of a lane. **1874** Green *Short Hist.* ii. §9. 112 The besiegers were parted into two masses by the Seine.

†**b.** *Arith.* = divide *v.* 9 a. *Obs.*

1579 Digges *Stratiot.* 8 To deuide or parte, is ingeniously to finde how oftentimes the diuisor is conteined in the number to be diuided.

c. To separate (the hair), as with a comb, on each side of a dividing line or *parting*.

1615 G. Sandys *Trav.* 68 The haire of their heads..They part it before in the midst, and pleate it behind. *a* **1822** Shelley *Pr. Wks.* (1888) I. 405 The hair delicately parted on the forehead. **1839** Yeowell *Anc. Brit. Ch.* iii. (1847) 30 The hair of his upper lip being parted on both sides lay upon his breast.

d. *Naut.* To break, or suffer the breaking of (a rope) so as to get loose from an anchor, a mooring, a vessel in tow, etc. Also *absol.* to get loose in this way.

1793 Smeaton *Edystone L.* §149 In the attempt, it parted the grappling rope. **1800** Nelson 26 Feb. in Nicolas *Disp.* (1845) IV. 200 She having split her maintopsail and foresail, parted the cable, let go another anchor. **1854** G. B. Richardson *Univ. Code* v. (ed. 12) §3746, I have parted, sweep for my anchor when I am gone. **1892** *Pall Mall G.* 9 Apr. 6/2 He did not think that three of the best ocean tugs could have taken the Federation through the cyclonic seas without parting their hawsers.

2. *intr.* To suffer division, be divided or severed, to divide, break, cleave, come in two or in pieces.

1579 W. Wilkinson *Confut. Familye of Love* 16 b, The clouen ayre, which parteth in sunder at the end of his arrow. **1716** B. Church *Hist. Philip's War* (1865) I. 111 They came into the Country Road, where the track parted. **1801** Southey *Thalaba* xi. xxxviii, The gentle waters gently part In dimples round the prow. **1830** Marryat *King's Own* liv, The frigate parted amidships. **1898** *Daily News* 24 Nov. 5/5 The cord parted, and he was dashed to the pavement lifeless.

3. a. *trans.* To dissolve (a connexion, etc.) by separation of the persons or parties concerned: in special phrases, as ***to part company***, to dissolve companionship, take leave, separate (= sense 6); ***to part a fight, fray***, to put an end to a fight by separating the combatants (see 4); †***to part beds***, to cease to live together in wedlock (*obs.*). Also ***to part brass-rags***: see brass *sb.* 7.

1426 Lydg. *De Guil. Pilgr.* 9168 Truste ek trewely, Ye partë neuere company. *c* **1586** C'tess Pembroke *Ps.* cvii. xi, Of seas and winds he partes the fight. **1599** Shaks. *Much Ado* v. i. 114 Welcome signior, you are almost come to part a fray. **1698** Fryer *Acc. E. India & P.* 46 The Vice-Admiral ..left not off till Night parted the Fray. **1710** Steele *Tatler* No. 150 ¶4, I could name Two, who after having had Seven Children, fell out and parted Beds upon the boiling of a Leg of Mutton. **1844** Dickens *Mart. Chuz.* xxxvii, They parted company at the gate of Furnival's Inn. **1875** Jowett *Plato* (ed. 2) IV. 380 He parts company from the vain and impertinent talker. **1883** H. Drummond *Nat. Law in Sp. W.* ii. (1884) 76 The point at which the scientific man is apt to part company with the theologian.

b. To dissolve, break up (an assembly). *rare*.

13.. *Cursor M.* 13850 (Gött.) Wid þis þai partid þair semble. **1720** Ozell *Vertot's Rom. Rep.* II. ix. 132 The Night coming on, parted the Assembly, before anything was decided.

4. a. To put asunder, separate, sunder (two or more persons or things, or one *from* another); to separate (combatants) so as to stop the combat; to make a separation between (companions, lovers, etc.). Also *fig.* to separate in thought, to put in a different class or category, to distinguish.

c **1315** Shoreham i. 2089 Eche hordom ne parteþ nauȝt þe mane al fram hys wyfe. **13..** *Cursor M.* 390 (Gött.) To part þe dai fra þe night. *c* **1440** *Generydes* 2295 The kyng of kynggez partyd them twayn. **1588** Shaks. *L.L.L.* i. ii. 7 How canst thou part sadnesse and melancholy? **1602** —— *Ham.* v. ii. 312 Part them, they are incens'd. **1611** Bible *Ruth* i. 17 The Lord doe so to me, and more also, if ought but death part thee and me. —— *Luke* xxiv. 51 While he blessed them, hee was parted from them, and caried vp into heauen. *c* **1645** Howell *Lett.* (1650) I. 242 A fool and his money is soon parted. **1758** R. Brown *Compl. Farmer* ii. (1760) 87 [Horse-beans and tares] are easily parted with a riddle. **1830** Tennyson *Isabel* ii, To part Error from crime. **1853** Kingsley *Hypatia* iii. 35 The women shrieked to their lovers to part the combatants.

b. To keep asunder or separate; to separate, as a boundary; to form a boundary or interval between.

1575 Laneham *Let.* (1871) 50 Each windo arched in the top, and parted from oother..by flat fayr bolted columns. **1632** Lithgow *Trav.* ii. 56 Which Riuer parteth also Dacia, from Mysia. **1781** Cowper *Charity* 20 Where seas or deserts part them from the rest. **1859** Tennyson *Geraint & Enid* 1118 As..two wild men supporters of a shield, Painted, who stare at open space, nor glance The one at other, parted by the shield. **1874** Green *Short Hist.* i. §1. 1 The peninsula which parts the Baltic from the Northern seas.

c. *spec.* in technical uses: (*a*) *Metallurgy*. To separate (gold and silver) from each other by means of an acid. (*b*) *Paper Manuf.* To separate (the damp sheets) after pressing. (*c*) *Comb-making*. To cut (a pair of combs, or their teeth) from one piece of material by a special method, so that the teeth of each correspond to the spaces between the teeth of the other. (*d*) *Turning* (usu. ***to part off***), to separate (a piece) from the block, as with a ***parting-tool***: see parting *vbl. sb.* 2, quot. 1879.

1487 *Act 4 Hen. VII*, c. 2 *Preamble*, It was of old Time used..to fine and part all Gold and Silver..needful for the said Mints. **1825** J. Nicholson *Operat. Mechanic* 766 The gold and silver to be parted ought previously to be granulated. **1839** Ure *Dict. Arts* 927 Fine papers are often twice parted and pressed. *Ibid.* 1061 The one space..is allotted to the processes of dissolving the silver, and parting the gold. **1875** *Ibid.* (ed. 7) I. 905 The teeth of the larger descriptions of comb are *parted*, or cut one out of the other with a thin frame saw; then the shell, equal in size to two combs with their teeth interlaced, is bent like an arch in the direction of the length of the teeth... Smaller combs of horn and tortoise-shell are parted whilst flat, by an ingenious machine with two chisel-formed cutters, placed obliquely, so that every cut produces one tooth. **1923** C. M. Linley *Lathe Users' Handbk.* vii. 118 In bar work, as each piece is finished, it is parted off. **1945** W. C. Durney *Capstan & Turret Lathes* iii. 78 Mount a parting off tool in one of the remaining stations of the rear square turret and locate a longitudinal stop to part off the bar ½ in. from the collet face. **1948** L. H. Sparey *Amateur's Lathe* x. 126/1 When work of large diameter must be parted-off, it is not advisable to make the part in one cut. **1958** C. T. Bower *Aids to Workshop Pract.* viii. 94 The parting-off tool shown..has been designed for use on a 3½-in. centre lathe to enable work gripped in the chuck to be parted off without jamming.

d. *intr.* or *absol.* To make or cause separation, division, or distinction.

1611 Bible *Prov.* xviii. 18 The lot causeth contentions to cease, and parteth betweene the mighty [Coverd., parteth the mightie asunder]. **1750** *Boston Rec.* (1887) XVII. 252 In a range with the Fence and Trees which parts between John Richardson Esqrs. Land..and Samuel Wells Esqrs. Land. **1850** Tennyson *In Mem.* xlviii, Her care is not to part and prove.

II. 5. *intr.* To become or be separated or sundered (*from* something); to be liberated or detached; to proceed, emanate; to come off. *rare*.

a **1300** *Cursor M.* 20755 þan parted his hend fra þe bere. **1594** Constable *Diana* vi. ix, But from his bow a fiery arrow parteth. **1679** *Establ. Test* 13 A stolen smile will part from me. **1717** Pope *Eloisa* 95 Ev'n thought meets thought, ere from the lips it part. **1862** Borrow *Wild Wales* III. xv. 168 The sheep caught the disease and the wool parted.

6. a. In reciprocal sense: To go or come apart or asunder, to separate. Of persons: To go away from each other, quit one another's company.

1297 R. GLOUC. (Rolls) 6153 þe kinges & muche of hor folc aliue partede atuo. *a* **1300** *Cursor M.* 20264 Allas! hou sal we part in tua. **13..** *Gaw. & Gr. Knt.* 2473 þay acolen and kyssen..and parten ryȝt þere. *c* **1400** MAUNDEV. (Roxb.) xiii. 57 þare þare it and Iordan partes es a grete brigg. *c* **1475** *Rauf Coilȝear* 572 Thus partit thay tua. **1596** SPENSER *F.Q.* VI. i. 10 So both tooke goodly leave, and parted severall. **1602** SHAKS. *Ham.* I. v. 18 A Tale..Would..Make..Thy knotty and combined locks to part, And each particular haire to stand on end. **1646** CRASHAW *Delights of Muses* 119 And, when life's sweet fable ends, Soul and body part like friends. **1725** GAY *Black-eyed Susan* iv, We only part to meet again. *a* **1732** —— *Hare & Friends* 61 But dearest friends, alas! must part. **1817** SHELLEY *Rev. Islam* I. xviii, Her lips grew pale, Parted, and quivered. **1842** TENNYSON *Edwin Morris* 70 We met to part no more. **1897** MARY KINGSLEY *W. Africa* 392, I give my guides buttons, reels of cotton,..fish-hooks, and matches, and we part friends. *Mod.* Here our roads parted.

b. *part from*: (*a*) to separate from, go away from, leave (see also 7); (*b*) = next *b* (now *rare*).

a **1225** *Ancr. R.* 64 Hwon he parteð urom ou. *Ibid.* 406 Bute ȝif ich parti urom ou, þe Holi Gost..ne mei nout kumen to ou. *a* **1300** *Cursor M.* 13033 Herodias..wend to part fra herod. **1375** BARBOUR *Bruce* VI. 492 The hwnd hym lufit swa, That he vald part na vis hym fra. *c* **1400** *Laud Troy Bk.* 10692 For al his myȝt & his prowes He partied neuere fro him harmles. **1509** HAWES *Past. Pleas.* XVI. (Percy Soc.) 60 Fare well, she sayde, for I must parte you fro. **1591** SHAKS. *Two Gent.* IV. iv. 102 This Ring I gaue him, when he parted from me. **1727** C. COLDEN *Hist. Five Ind. Nat.* 3 This extremity obliged the Adirondacks to part from those of the Five Nations. **1863** GEO. ELIOT in *Life* (1885) II. 365 Our poor boy Thornie parted from us to-day. **1596** SHAKS. *Merch. V.* III. ii. 174, I giue them with this ring, Which when you part from, loose, or giue away, Let it presage the ruine of your loue. **1640** GLAPTHORNE *Wallenstein* III. iii, That jewell which you seeme To part from so unwillingly. **1793** *Minstrel* III. 30 Grasping the shadow of power, whilst their poverty constrained them to part from the substance. **1860** GEO. ELIOT in *Life* (1885) II. 166 His precious bag, which he would by no means part from.

c. *part with*: (*a*) = prec. *a* (now *rare*); (*b*) to let go, give up, surrender; to get rid of, send away, dismiss; in mod. use also of a body or substance: to lose, give off (heat, or a constituent or element).

to part with child (*bairn*): to be delivered prematurely, to suffer abortion (*Sc.*).

13.. *Cursor M.* 17022 (Cott.) Kynd na saul suffers ar to part wit [so *Gött.*; *Trin. & Laud* parte fro] man o-liue. **1590** SHAKS. *Com. Err.* V. i. 221 He was with me then, Who parted with me to go fetch a Chaine. **1600** —— *A.Y.L.* III. ii. 235 How parted he with thee? **1643** TRAPP *Comm. Gen.* xiii. 14 Abram had now parted with Lot, to his great grief. **1766** GOLDSM. *Vic. W.* ix, The ladies seemed very unwilling to part with my daughters. **1871** M. ARNOLD *Friendship's Garl.* 97 Just after I had parted with him at his lodgings.

c **1350** *St. John Evang.* 290 in Horstmann *Altengl. Leg.* (1881) 38 He dredes his gude sal fro him fall, So þat he dar noght part with all. **1581** PETTIE *Guazzo's Civ. Conv.* I. (1586) 28 b, The Dutches was driuen to part with one of her chiefe women. *c* **1592** MARLOWE *Jew of Malta* IV. 411 Oh, that I should part with so much gold! **1663** BOYLE *Exp. Hist. Colours* III. xlix. Annot. ii, Lixiviate salts..dispose them [vegetables] to part readily with their tincture. **1718** *Freethinker* No. 92 ¶3, I would part with all my Jewels, to be but Twenty. **1800** *Asiat. Ann. Reg., Misc. Tr.* 327/1 Such substances as are known to contain oxygen in the greatest abundance, and to part with it with the greatest facility. **1878** DALE *Lect. Preach.* v. 131 Men will not part with what they have until you give them something better.

a **1578** LINDESAY (Pitscottie) *Chron. Scot.* (S.T.S.) I. 61 The ȝeir following the quene pairtit witht bairne... The bairne was born quick and deceissit witht in schort space thairefter. **1722** WODROW *Hist. Ch. Scot.* II. III. viii §7. 432 All which put her to such Fright that she parted with Child, and never recovered. **1883** GRAHAM *Writings* II. 20 (E.D.D.) Maggy had parted wi' bairn.

d. *absol.* To part with something, esp. money; to give or pay money. *slang* or *colloq.* Also (*Austral.* and *N.Z. colloq.*) const. *up*.

1864 HOTTEN *Slang Dict.* 196 *Part*, to pay, restore, give up; 'he's a right un, he is; I know he'd part.'.. The term is in general use in *Sporting* circles. **1873** *Slang Dict.* s.v., 'He's a right un, he is; I know'd he'd part'. **1889** *Bulletin* (Sydney) 21 Sept. 20/1 An' then they reckoned I'd been usin' 'em [*sc.* double-headed pennies in a game of two-up] all the time, and they made me part up. **1894** 'J. S. WINTER' *Red-Coats* 107 The master of Dorien was wily—what the country folk call 'unwilling to part'. At least, he would only part for a consideration. **1913** E. WHARTON *Custom of Country* II. xiv. 202 People said of him that he 'didn't care to part'. **1933** A. G. MACDONELL *England, their England* xv. 267 Might squeeze another hundred [pounds]... Not more. He doesn't part easily. **1943** *Amer. Speech* XVIII. 92 Words and phrases..which deserve to be recorded in any attempt to convey something of the flavour of the colloquial speech of the country [*sc.* New Zealand]...*to part up*, to pay up. **1946** F. SARGESON *That Summer* 152 Ted got more but of course there was his wife, and he had to part up. **1952** WODEHOUSE *Barmy in Wonderland* viii. 81 Fanny won't part. She's so tight she could carry an armful of eels up two flights of stairs and not drop one. **1953** K. TENNANT *Joyful Condemned* iv. 39, I guess Rene might part up to know who her mum was. **1966** WODEHOUSE *Plum Pie* i. 17 Uncle Tom ..had to foot the bills. He has the stuff in sackfuls, but he hates to part. **1970** J. AIKEN *Embroidered Sunset* x. 209 'So where are all the old girl's pictures?' 'Scattered all over the village. Nobody will part; they are thought to be lucky.'

7. a. *intr.* To take one's leave or departure; to depart, go away; to set out. *arch.* [Cf. F. *partir*.]

In perfect tenses, it often took *be*: 'he is parted from Rome'.

a **1300** *Cursor M.* 12975 Sum oþir ansuar sal þou sai, Ar I fra þe yitt part a-wai. *c* **1300** *Havelok* 2962 Hwan he wore parted alle samen, Hauelok bi-lefte wit ioie and gamen In engelond. **1382** WYCLIF *Mark* i. 42 Anoon the lepre partide [Vulg. *discessit*] awey fro hym. *c* **1400** *St. Alexius* (Laud 622) 384 For to dye it were my riȝth, And hennes to party. *c* **1489** CAXTON *Blanchardyn* iv. 20 Who moued you to leue me, and to parte soo? **1591** SHAKS. *Two Gent.* I. i. 71 But now he parted hence to embarque for Millain. **1622** J. BOROUGH in *Lett. Lit. Men* (Camd.) 129 Mr. Norgate is parted from Rome..for England. *c* **1642** TWYNE in *Wood's Life* 1 Sept. (O.H.S.) I. 58 They desisted and parted awaye quietly. **1676** *Lond. Gaz.* No. 1151/2 The Queen of Poland was parted from Janowits, to go and meet the King at Leopol. **1724** DE FOE *Mem. Cavalier* (1840) 44, I parted from Vienna the middle of May. **1814** CARY *Dante, Paradise* VI. 142 Aged and poor He parted thence. **1885–94** R. BRIDGES *Eros & Psyche* Aug. xxiii, 'But ere he parted', said she, 'he confer'd On thee the irrecoverable boon'.

b. *to part* (*hence, out of this life*, etc.): to die.

c **1325** *Spec. Gy Warw.* 297 Whan þeih sholen parten henne, Ful wel þeih sholen here weie kenne Riht to þe blisse of paradys. **13..** *Chron. Eng.* 422 (Ritson) Er he partede of thisse live. **1599** SHAKS. *Hen. V*, II. iii. 12 A [= he] parted eu'n iust betweene Twelue and One. **1616** B. JONSON *Epigr.* I. xxii, At six months' end, she parted hence. **1816** J. WILSON *City of Plague* I. iii. 50 An angel sent from pitying heaven To bid him part in peace. **1878** *Masque of Poets* 14, I know it well and yet in peace I part.

8. †**a.** *trans.* To depart from, go away from, take leave of, leave, quit, forsake: = DEPART *v.* 8. *Obs.*

In quot. 1609, app. a mixture of 'had parted this life' and 'had been parted from this life'. Cf. PASS *v.*

a **1529** SKELTON *Epit. Dk. Jaspar* Wks. 1843 II. 398 But or I parte the place, Up his hede he caste. **1587** TURBERV. *Trag. T.* (1837) 39 That I should part my countrey, to avoide My monstrous charge. **1593** SHAKS. *Rich. II*, III. i. 3 Since presently your soules must part your bodies. **1609** BIBLE (Douay) *2 Macc.* v. 5 As though Antiochus had bene parted this life. **1787** *Minor* IV. vi. 222 My regret at parting this second Eden. *c* **1802** MAR. EDGEWORTH *Ennui* xiv, Though loth to part his country, he could rather part that nor me. **1812** *Examiner* 14 Sept. 588/1 One of the transports, ..having parted the convoy, was captured.

b. To part with, give up: = 6 b (*b*), c (*b*). *dial.*

1823 SHARPE *Ballad Bk.* (1868) 2 (E.D.D.) O we maun part this lore, Willie. **1899** MACMANUS *Chim. Corners* 73 (E.D.D.) He wouldn't part his wife Molly at home for all the princesses in the world.

III. 9. *trans.* To divide to or among a number of recipients; to distribute in shares, apportion. (With various const.) Somewhat *arch.*

13.. *K. Alis.* 4678 He nam Daries tresour, And pertid hit among his kynne. *c* **1330** R. BRUNNE *Chron.* (1810) 296 He parted his wynnyng tille his men largely. *a* **1400–50** *Alexander* 4318 þe quilke is part vs, all þe pake, be parcells euyn. **1579** SPENSER *Sheph. Cal.* Apr. 153, I will part them all you among. *c* **1586** C'TESS PEMBROKE *Ps.* CVIII. iii, Let me part out Sichems fields. **1609** BIBLE (Douay) *1 Macc.* v. 20 And there were parted to Simon three thousand men, to goe into Galilee. *a* **1661** FULLER *Worthies* (1840) II. 503 She parted herself, whilst living..betwixt these three places. **1715** POPE *2nd Ep. Miss Blount* 15 To part her time 'twixt reading and bohea. **1809** BAWDWEN *Domesday Bk.* 332 This land was parted between 41 Burgesses who have 12 ploughs. **1876** FREEMAN *Norm. Conq.* IV. xviii. 209 Lands which seem to have been parted out among the magistrates and chief burghers.

10. a. To share with another or others; (of one person) to give a share of to another; (of a number of persons) to take each a share of, divide among themselves. Now rare or *Obs.* exc. *dial.*

13.. *Seuyn Sages* (W.) 2053 Yif thou wilt half parte with ous, Thou sschalt hit have, Sire Cressus. **1362** LANGL. *P. Pl.* A. XI. 50 Luyte loueþ he þat lord..þat þus parteþ with þe pore a parcel whon him neodeþ. **1382** WYCLIF *John* xix. 24 Their partiden my clothis to hem, and in to my cloth thei senten lott. *c* **1386** CHAUCER *Merch. T.* 386 [He] thanked god ..That no wight his blisse parten shal. **1484** CAXTON *Fables of Æsop* II. xviii, Ye shalle parte to gyder your good. **1500–20** DUNBAR *Poems* lviii. 5 Giff thame the pelffe to pairt amang thame. **1588** SHAKS. *L.L.L.* V. ii. 249 *Long.* Let's part the word. *Mar.* No, Ile not be your halfe. **17..** POPE (J.), Jove himself no less content wou'd be To part his throne, and share his heav'n with thee. **1840** DICKENS *Old C. Shop* xliv, Her friend parted his breakfast..with the child and her grandfather.

†**b.** *to part stakes* (also *to part shares*): to share, partake, participate, 'go shares' (*with* a person, *in* a thing). In quot. 1581, to make division or distribution (*of* a thing *between* persons).

1553 T. WILSON *Rhet.* (1580) 133 The Deuill and thei.. shall parte stakes with theim one daie. **1581** J. BELL *Haddon's Answ. Osor.* 406 b, To make Invocation to the dead, to part stakes of honour betwixt God and his Saincntes. **1622** MABBE tr. *Aleman's Guzman d'Alf.* II. 304, I might part shares with my wife. **1628** GAULE *Pract. The. Panegyr.* 7 To share the Honour with him, and part stakes in the Prayse. **1665** BRATHWAIT *Comment Two Tales* 42 This was before they parted Stakes.

†**11.** *intr.* To make division into shares; to give or impart a share; to take or have a share; to share, 'go shares', participate, partake (*with* a person; *of* or *in*, rarely *with*, a thing). *Obs.*

c **1290** *St. Brandan* 264 in *S. Eng. Leg.* I. 226 Heo wollez party þar-of mid us. *a* **1330** *Otuel* 1658 And ȝef we ani good winne, For soþe þou schalt parten þer inne. **1340** *Ayenb.* 38 þe þyeues be uelaȝrede byeþ þo þet parteþ of þe þyefþe. **1426** LYDG. *De Guil. Pilgr.* 4706, I ffeede folk that hongry be, And parte with hem off my plente. *a* **1578** LINDESAY (Pitscottie) *Chron. Scot.* (S.T.S.) I. 254 Lat me and the Frinchemen pairt amang ws. **1611** BIBLE *1 Sam.* xxx. 24 As his part is that goeth downe to the battel, so shall his part bee that tarieth by the stuffe: they shall part alike. **1670** WALLIS in Rigaud *Corr. Sci. Men* (1841) II. 519 Who longs to hear of some here willing to part in the impression of my things at Leyden.

†**12.** *trans.* and *absol.* To give a part or share of; hence, To give away, bestow, impart. *Obs.*

1362 LANGL. *P. Pl.* A. I. 156 Bote ȝe..loue þe pore, And such good as God sent Treweliche parten, ȝe naue no more merit [etc.]. **1382** WYCLIF *Baruch* vi. 27 [Thei] nether parten to seeke man, nether to beggynge. *c* **1430** LYDG. *Min. Poems* (Percy Soc.) 219 With glad herte parte thyn almesse. **1522** *World & Child* in Hazl. *Dodsley* I. 243 For poverty I part in many a place To them that will not obedient be.

†**13.** To mix or temper (wine) with other liquors or substances. *Obs.* [Cf. F. *couper le vin.*]

a **1700** B. E. *Dict. Cant. Crew*, *Freeze*, a thin..Cyder.. us'd by Vintners..in parting their Wines, to lower the Price of them. **1703** *Art & Myst. Vintners* 67 To part a Butt of Muskadel. Draw half your Wine into another Butt; then take your Lags of all sorts that do not prick, and so much Syrup as will not prick;..beat them up, and let it rest after you have blown the froth from off it [etc.].

IV. †**14.** *trans.* To side with, take part with. (Cf. PARTY *v.* 2 a.) *Obs. rare.*

1652 [see PARTING *vbl. sb.* 6]. **1669** MACFARLANE *Genealog. Collect.* (1900) I. 58 Alexander Earl of Argyle parted the Baliol. **1715** *Wodrow Corr.* (1843) II. 89 The influence of High Church in England, who parted our disaffected party, and stopped all prosecution of them.

†**part**, *ppl. a. rare.* Obs. pa. pple. of prec. vb. = PARTED. *part per pale* = party per pale; as *sb.* = an escutcheon party per pale.

1708 *Brit. Apollo* No. 3. 2/2 He, that selleth Ale, Hangs out a Chequer'd Part per Pale. Part per Pale sells Ale and Beer. **1862** LONGF. *Wayside Inn* Prel. 107 A Wyvern part-per-pale addressed Upon a helmet barred.

†**partable** ('pɑːtəb(ə)l), *a.* *Obs.* [a. OF. *partable*, f. *partir*, *partant* to divide, to PART.]

1. Capable of being parted or divided; = PARTIBLE.

[**1292** BRITTON III. viii. §5 Soit acune foiz le cors del eglise divisible ou partable de antiquité.] *c* **1380** WYCLIF *Sel. Wks.* III. 63 Watris..remuynge, freele, and partable. *c* **1400** tr. *Secreta Secret., Gov. Lordsh.* 88 It ys partable in ffoure. **1503–4** *Act 19 Hen. VII*, c. 33 §1 To be parteable amonges the seid Robert Dymmok, Thomas Laurence, and Kateryn. **1632** I. L. *Womens Rights* 5, I have some kind of doubts.. whether..it bee partable as among coheires.

2. Capable of having a part or share *in*; able to partake *of*; participant.

1426 LYDG. *De Guil. Pilgr.* 9928 Ffor he wyl also be partable Off thy merytes & guerdouns. *a* **1450** *Knt. de la Tour* (1868) 61 He shalle be partable in the synne. **1527** *Golden Legend* in *Docum. St. Paul's* (Camden) 188 Vouchesafe..to make hym partable of thyn excellent ioye.

partack, obs. form of PARTAKE.

Partaga (pɑː'tɑːgə). The proprietary name of a brand of Havana cigar.

1862 *Illustr. Catal. Internat. Exhib., Industr. Dept., Brit. Div.* I. No. 869 The exhibitors are manufacturers of the following Cigars:—..Cubas. Partagas. Salvadoras. **1865** *Dublin Univ. Mag.* Apr. 378/1 By-and-by, after smoking two or three Partagas, I may recollect some lunatic who would do such an absurd thing. **1871** M. LEGRAND *Cambridge Freshman* 145 The O'Higgins was accommodated with a prime Partaga. **1878** *Trade Marks Jrnl.* 17 Apr. 264/1 Design patent. Partagas... Juan Antonio Bances, of and on behalf of the firm of Bances and Co.,..Havana, Cuba; manufacturers of cigars, cigarettes, and picadura. **1908** *Ibid.* 3 June 921 Partagas... Cigars. Cifuentes, Fernandez y Ca.,..Havana, Cuba; cigar manufacturers. **1930** A. BENNETT *Imperial Palace* xvi. 100 Evelyn took a cigar out of a box of Partagas. *Ibid.* xxiii. 145 Oldham handed Partaga cigars, and, the table having been cleared of all but finger-bowls, ash-trays and cigars,.. disappeared. **1973** J. M. WHITE *Garden Game* 115 Our cigars..were Partagas, and merited careful attention.

‖**partage**, *sb.* [a. F. *partage* = It. *partaggio*, med.L. *partāgium* (13th c. in Du Cange), f. F. *partir*, It. *partire*, to PART: see -AGE. Formerly naturalized ('pɑːtɪdʒ); but, since 18th c., treated as F. (partaʒ). ('A word merely French' J.)]

1. The action of dividing; division; partition; esp. division into shares. Also *attrib.*

1598 DALLINGTON *Meth. Trav.* F iv, The Comfrerie were against the Leaguers, for their partage. **1599** DANIEL *Let. Octavia* Wks. 1717 I. 75 Unequal Partage, to b'allow'd no share Of Power to do of Life's best Benefit. *a* **1656** USSHER *Ann.* (1658) 335 In the partage of the kingdom..she seemed a little inclined to her youngest son. **1751** T. DICEY *Hist. Acc. Guernsey* 61 The Fief Noble goes directly to the Eldest, unless he will put it into Partage with the rest. **1857** MUSGRAVE *Pilgr. into Dauphiné* I. iii. 58 The *partage* system, which parcels out the land into these infinitesimal patches.

2. A part, portion, share, lot.

1456 SIR G. HAYE *Law Arms* (S.T.S.) 160 Thir pure folk has na charge, na takis na lyfing, na partage of the weris. **1502** *Ord. Crysten Men* (W. de W. 1506) v. ii. 370 Deth eternall unto hym is his partage & propre herytage. **1598** DALLINGTON *Meth. Trav.* E iij b, That the yonger sonnes of the King cannot have partage with the Elder. **1623** tr. *Favine's Theat. Hon.* II. i 67 [Such] as should fall to their lot and partage. *a* **1661** FULLER *Worthies* (1840) III. 388 Divine Providence..stopped the flowing of those salt-springs..till the poor were restored to their partage therein. **1763** H. WALPOLE *Let. to H.S. Conway* 21 May, Vivacity is by no means the *partage* of the French. **1843** MRS. ROMER *Rhone, Darro*, etc. I. 281 Exempt from the cruel pounding that is the *partage* of inside places.

¶ Mistrans. L. *compāgēs*.

1593 Q. ELIZ. *Boeth.* II. pr. v. 31 What is there that wantes a spirit and lymmes partage [CHAUCER jointure], that Justly may seeme fayre to the myndes and Reasons nature?

So † **ˈpartage** *v. trans.* [F. *partager, a* 1400], to divide into parts. *Obs. rare.*

c **1586** C'TESS PEMBROKE *Ps.* XLV. viii, Children thou shalt bring, Of partag'd earth the kings and lords to bee.

partakable, -takeable (pəˈteɪkəb(ə)l, pɑː-), *a. rare.* [f. next + -ABLE.] †**a.** Capable of partaking. *Obs.* **b.** Capable of being partaken.

1632 J. HAYWARD tr. *Biondi's Eromena* 96 He neither saw his favours participated, nor any person partakeable of them. **1701** NORRIS *Ideal World* I. v. 256 Seeing in what degrees his Divine essence was imitable or partakable.

partake (pəˈteɪk, pɑː-), *v.* Also 6-7 **pertake,** 7 *Sc.* **partack.** [Back-formation (after 1550) from PARTAK-ING, PARTAKE-R, which were 16th c. syncopated forms of the earlier regular combinations *part-taking, part-taker,* repr. L. *particeps, -cipium.* Cf. *housekeep* vb. from *housekeeping, housekeeper.*

As a direct formation, a vb. *part-take* would have been against Eng. idiom. In 16-17 c., the feeling of connexion with *take* vb. was so weak, that the pa. t. and pple. were often *partaked.*]

I. *trans.* **1. a.** To take a part in, to share in.

1589 GREENE *Menaphon* (Arb.) 32, I lent you sighes to partake your sorrowes. **1594** CAREW *Huarte's Exam. Wits* vii. (1596) 96 The propertie of the generall is equally partaked by the special. *c* **1611** CHAPMAN *Iliad* IX. 362, I never will partake his works, nor counsels, as before. **1751** JOHNSON *Rambler* No. 153 ⁋3, I had never..partaken one triumph over a conquered fox. **1805** SOUTHEY *Madoc in W.* XIII. The old man Partook that feeling. **1863** KINGLAKE *Crimea* (1876) I. xiv. 234 Adventurers who were willing to partake his fortunes.

b. To share (a meal); to take (food or drink) in company with others; hence (without the idea of sharing), To eat or drink of, to take some of, to 'take'. (Cf. 4 b.) Now *rare* or *Obs.* exc. *absol.*

1617 SIR W. MURE *Misc. Poems* xxi. 114 Thou may partack such as this soyle affords. **1725** POPE *Odyss.* IV. 298 Alternate all partake the grateful springs. **1795** SOUTHEY *Joan of Arc* III. 29 They..reclined Beside him, and his frugal fare partook. **1837** TICKNOR in *Life,* etc. (1876) II. iv. 71 When the cardinal had partaken the sacrament he administered it to her. **1844** D. B. REID *Illustr. Theory & Pract. Ventilation* 181 Nor was any of the members aware.. that they had partaken more heartily than usual. **1870** J. P. SMITH *Widow Goldsmith's Daughter* ix. 144 Chris could not touch anything, but the widow partook with the particular relish which a well-spent morning gave her. **1974** J. MCCLURE *Gooseberry Fool* v. 80 He hardly ever drank... He didn't often partake, but then it was also bloody hot.

†**c.** To share in (a communication or news), to be informed of, be made acquainted with. *Obs.*

c **1592** MARLOWE *Jew of Malta* v. 296 And, Gouernour, now partake my policy. **1605** *1st Pt. Ieronimo* II. iv. 70 But has the King pertooke your embassy? **1607** DEKKER *Northw. Hoe* I. Wks. 1873 III. 5 May we without offence pertake the ground of it? **1667** MILTON *P.L.* XII. 598 Let her with thee partake what thou hast heard.

†**2.** To give a part of (something) *to* to share it *with* another or others; to impart, communicate; *esp.* to communicate information about (something), to make known. *Obs.*

1561 T. HOBY tr. *Castiglione's Courtyer* (1577) K v, A liberall man that partaketh his goods in common with his friends. *c* **1585** CARTWRIGHT in R. Browne *Answ.* 87 Christ, who..hath partaked vnto them his holy spirite. **1594** MARLOWE & NASHE *Dido* IV. ii, If you would partake with me the cause Of this.., I would be thankfull for such curtesie. **1611** SHAKS. *Wint. T.* v. iii. 132 Go together..your exultation Partake to euery one.

†**3.** To make (a person) a sharer or partaker (*of* information or news); to make acquainted with something; to inform *of. Obs.*

1565 *MS. Cott. Cal.* B. IX. lf. 218 Your lordship, I am sure, is partaken of such letters as I write to Mr. Secretary. **1590** SPENSER *F.Q.* II. iv. 20 My friend, hight Philemon, I did partake Of all my love and all my privitie.

II. *intr.* **4. a.** To take a part or share in some action or condition; to have a portion or lot in common with others; to participate. Const. *in, of* (†*with*) the thing; *with* the person sharing.

c **1585** R. BROWNE *Answ. Cartwright* 69 Howe then should the people partake with them in the sacrifices? **1597** BEARD *Theatre God's Judgem.* (1612) 412 As for Cleopatra,..as she partaked of the sin, so shee did of the punishment. **1640** HABINGTON *Edw. IV* 105 The King having even after death partaked with the troubles and disgraces of his life. **1664** MARVELL *Corr.* Wks. 1872-5 II. 161 The King my Master has sent me..to congratulate in His stead, and partake of Your Majestie's present felicity. **1708** STANHOPE *Paraphr.* (1709) IV. 244 This Care you have partook of. **1771** GOLDSM. *Hist. Eng.* IV. 308 Bred in a luxurious court, without partaking in its effeminacy. **1838** WHITTIER *Quaker of Old. Time* iii, He felt that wrong with wrong partakes, That nothing stands alone. **1882** SPURGEON *Treas. Dav.* Ps. cxix. 74 We do not only meet to share each others' burdens, but to partake in each other's joys.

b. *esp.* (with *of*) To receive, get, or have a share or portion of. Often used without any notion of sharing with others, esp. in reference to eating and drinking, = to take some of, take of, take.

1601 R. JOHNSON *Kingd. & Commw.* (1603) 122 There is no cittie that doth more absolutely inioy her owne commodities, and doth more freely pertake of others. **1615** G. SANDYS *Trav.* 14 The streets do almost all the night long partake of their musicke. **1635** J. HAYWARD tr. *Biondi's Banish'd Virg.* 34 If it..partaked of its substance and colour. **1656** BLOUNT *Glossogr., Parasite,* a flatterer,..one that is still hanging on some rich man..to the end to pertake of his good cheer. **1795** *Gentl. Mag.* 543/1 Nonjuring clergymen and their families partook very largely of his benevolence. **1805** EMILY CLARK *Banks of Douro* III. 41 Her solitary meals she partook of in the apartment next the eating room. **1818** CRUISE *Digest* (ed. 2) II. 254 He would of course have no right to partake of the money, till their claims were satisfied. **1865** DICKENS *Mut. Fr.* III. iv, Your papa invited Mr. R. to partake of our lowly fare.

†**c.** To share the nature *of;* to have some of the qualities or characteristics *of. Obs.*

c **1585** R. BROWNE *Answ. Cartwright* 64 They did partake with such watchemen. **1620** T. GRANGER *Div. Logike* 104 So truce partaketh more of warre then of peace.

d. To have something *of,* possess a certain amount *of* (a quality or attribute); †formerly also, To contain some *of,* have an admixture *of* (a material substance) (*obs.*).

c **1615** BACON *Adv. Sir G. Villiers* ii. §16 The attorney of the duchy of Lancaster..partakes of both qualities, partly of a judge, and partly of an attorney-general. **1627-77** FELTHAM *Resolves* I. xvi. 28 For that which doth partake on both: it makes Just God, a friend to unjust man, without being unjust. **1776** G. SEMPLE *Building in Water* 40 Where the Gravel partook of Mud. *Ibid.* 43 Sea-water that partook of putrid Water, running from a foul Sewer. **1858** O. W. HOLMES *Aut. Breakf.-t.* iii. 21 Scientific knowledge, even in the most modest persons, has mingled with it a something which partakes of insolence.

†**5.** To take part *with* a person, take sides. *Obs.*

c **1600** SHAKS. *Sonn.* cxlix, When I against my selfe with thee pertake.

†**parˈtakener.** *Obs. rare.* Erroneous variant of PARTAKER.

1565 STAPLETON tr. *Bede's Hist. Ch. Eng.* 48 And it is mete suche men were partakeners, and inheretors with the Angels in heauen. —— *Fortr. Faith* 113 b, I am partakner of all those that feare thee and kepe thy commaundements.

partaker (pəˈteɪkə(r), pɑː-). Forms: *α.* 5-7 **part taker,** (5-6 **parte taker,** 6 **parte-taker, partetaker, parttaker,** 6-7 **part-taker**). *β.* 6- **partaker,** (6-7 **per-**). [Comb. of PART *sb.* + TAKER (perh. after *part-taking;* rendering L. *parti-ceps*). In 16th c the combination of the two *t*'s in *parttaker* began to be simplified, giving *partaker.*]

1. One who takes a part or share, a partner, participator, sharer. (Now viewed as agent-noun from PARTAKE *v.*: = one who partakes.)

α. c **1400** *Destr. Troy* 2183 (MS. after 1500) And part taker of my payne with prickyng in hert. **1483** *Cath. Angl.* 270/2 A Parte taker (*A.* Partitakere), *particeps.* **1526** TINDALE *Luke* v. 10 James and Jhon the sonnes of Zebedei which were partetakers with Simon. —— *1 Cor.* ix. 10 He which throssheth in hope shulde be part taker of his hope. **1561** EDEN tr. *Cortes' Arte Navig.* Pref., All the other are part-takers therof more or lesse. **1602** DEKKER *Satiromastix* Wks. 1873 I. 244 Thou shouldst have been hang'd, but for one of these part-takers. **1611** SPEED *Hist. Gt. Brit.* (1632) 1024 You wolde make them part takers off your myscheffe.

β. **1547** BOORDE *Brev. Health* xxii, Partaker of good or euyll. **1565** COOPER *Thesaurus, Coniurationis particeps,* a partaker of the conspiracie. **1630** PRYNNE *Anti-Armin.* 125 All men are pertakers of it. **1631** SIR S. D'EWES *Autobiog.* 26 Apr. (1845) II. 31 Went to Lavenham, where I was a partaker of a good sermon. **1672** PETTY *Pol. Anat.* Ded., To ..be partaker with him in new Scenes of Action. *a* **1774** HARTE *Boecius to Rusticiana* 14 Joint partner of my life, my heart's relief; Alike partaker of my joys or grief. **1866** G. MACDONALD *Ann. Q. Neighb.* viii. (1878) 129 Man must be a partaker of the Divine nature.

†**2.** One who takes another's part or side; a supporter, adherent, partisan. *Obs.*

? *a* **1500** *Chester Pl.* viii. 321 (MS. *c* 1600) And all his partackers I shall slea and beate downe.

α. **1545** *Reg. Privy Council Scot.* I. 4 To command..the said Donald and all utheris his part takeris. **1593** *Tell-Troth's N. Y. Gift* (1876) 8 When a woman distrustes of any helpe to come from any part-taker, shee will bee glad to please hir husband. **1653** *Nissena* 66 That they would not want assistants and part-takers even in the very Court it self.

β. a **1548** HALL *Chron., Hen. IV* 20 To the great displeasure and long unquieting of kyng Henry and his partakers. *a* **1656** USSHER *Ann.* iv. (1658) 35 There grew a long war between his partakers and the partakers of David. **1700** TYRRELL *Hist. Eng.* II. 844 The Partakers of Lewis were to be indemnified.

partaking (pəˈteɪkɪŋ, pɑː-), *vbl. sb.* Forms: *α.* 4-6 **part(e taking,** 6-7 **part-taking, parttaking;** also *β.* 6-7 **parts-, parts taking.** *γ.* 6- **partaking.** [Comb. of PART *sb.* + TAKING *vbl. sb.* (perh. orig. a literal rendering of L. *participātio*). As in prec., simplified in 16-17th c. to *partaking;* in which modified form it gave rise to the vb. PARTAKE, of which it is now viewed as the vbl. sb.]

1. The taking of a part or share; sharing, participation.

1382 WYCLIF *1 Cor.* x. 16 The breed which we breken, wher it is not the delynge [*gloss* or part takynge; *v.r.* parting; *Vulg.* participatio] of the body of the Lord? *c* **1400** *Apol. Loll.* 12 In part takyng of þe defaut. **1483** *Cath. Angl.* 270/2 A Part takynge, *participacio.* **1526** TINDALE *1 Cor.* x. 16 Ys not the breed which we breake partetakynge of the body of Christ? *a* **1714** SHARP *Wks.* (1754) IV. Serm. vi. 108 In order to the partaking of his benefits.

†**2.** The taking the part of some one; the action of taking sides (in a dispute or contest). *Obs.*

α. **1548** UDALL, etc. *Erasm. Par. Matt.* ii. 27 No nede of helpes, riches, power, parte taking. **1611** SPEED *Hist. Gt. Brit.* IX. xx. (1623) 976 Remembring withall the mischiefes of part-takings. **1646** EARL MONM. tr. *Biondi's Civil Warres* VII. 84 Hearing that there was part-taking, and tumults raised in the City.

β. **1539-40** ABP. PARKER *Corr.* (Parker Soc.) 11 We should by our disagreement..cause a murmur and parts taking among themself. **1593** ABP. BANCROFT *Daung. Posit.* I. i. 3 To draw them into partes-taking. **1598** DALLINGTON *Meth. Trav.* R iv, The ambition of the house of Guise, and the parts-taking with them, and those other of Burbon, is guilty thereof.

γ. a **1548** HALL *Chron., Hen. VII* 2 b, Forgettynge clerely the diuersite of faccions & voyce of partakyng. *a* **1618** RALEIGH *Maxims St.* (1651) 23 Joyning with them in their partakings and Factions. **1657** EARL MONM. tr. *Paruta's Pol. Disc.* 50 There was no siding nor partaking studied amongst them.

parˈtaking, *ppl. a.* [orig. *part-taking:* cf. prec.] That takes part, or partakes; †taking another's part or side (*obs.*); sharing.

1639 LD. DIGBY, etc. *Lett. conc. Relig.* (1651) 113 Mens part-taking subtilties have given to God's Word many various acceptions. *Ibid.* 131 Through any partaking passion, or forelaid designe. **1756** H. JONES *Earl of Essex* 52 The kind condoling comfort of a dear Partaking friend.

partan (ˈpɑːtən). *Sc.* and *north. dial.* Also 6 **partane, pertane,** 7-9 **parten,** 9 **partin, parton.** [app. from Celtic: in Gael. *partan,* Manx *partan,* Ir. *partón, portán* crab; ulterior history unknown.]

1. A crab; esp. the common crab, *Cancer pagurus.*

c **1425** WYNTOUN *Cron.* I. 813 In to þe watyr of Ganges.. wormys als of hugis strenythe, Lyk to partanys heyr ar þa, And on þar cors has armys twa. **1549** *Compl. Scot.* xix. 159 Plutarque rehersis ane exempil of the partan, quhilk repreuit ane of hyr ȝong partans, be cause the ȝong partan vald nocht gang euyn furtht, bot rather sche ȝeid crukit, bakuart, and on syd. **1693** WALLACE *Descr. Orkney Isl.* ii. 14 Lobsters, Partens, Mussels. **1710** SIBBALD *Fife* II. ii. [iii.] 55 *Cancer marinus Vulgaris,* the Common Sea-Crab; our Fishers call it a Partan. **1816** SCOTT *Antiq.* xi, A half-a-dozen o' partans to make the sauce. **1894** CROCKETT *Raiders* (ed. 3) 75 Progressing, as the partan..is said to do, backwards.

b. The shore crab, *Carcinus mœnas.*

1790 GROSE *Provinc. Gloss.* MS. add. (C.) (E.D.D.), *Partan,* a kind of small crab..not eaten, as it is said to be poisonous. **1880** *Antrim & Down Gloss., Parten,* the shore crab, *Carcinus mœnas.*

2. *fig.* An ill-favoured or ill-natured person.

1896 BARRIE *Tommy* iv. 45 Tak' that, you glowering partan! **1899** CROCKETT *A. Mark* xx. 163 A silly partan o' a bairn like this.

3. *attrib.* and *Comb.* **partan-cage,** a crab-trap; **partan-crab** = sense 1; **ˈpartan-face,** an ill-favoured or sour-faced creature, a term of abuse: cf. sense 2; **ˌpartan-ˈfull** *a.,* as full as a crab is of meat; **ˈpartan-ˌhanded** *a.,* close-fisted, stingy; **ˈpartan-ˈtoe,** a crab's claw.

1899 CROCKETT *A. Mark* xviii. 140 To set his *partan cages in Byness Bay. **1893** STEVENSON *Catriona* xxii, A boat, that was backed like a *partan-crab. **1895** ROY *Horseman's Wd.* xii. (E.D.D.), Answer yoursell, *parten-face, gin you're grown sic a wonder o' wisdom. **1787** TAYLOR *Poems* 56 (E.D.D.) She was sae *partan-fu' o' pride. **1823** GALT *Entail* xci, Ye *partan-handit,..Mammon o' unrighteousness. *a* **1568** *'Listis Lordis, I sall yow tell'* 57 (Bannatyne MS.) With ten *partane taes, And nyne knokis of windil strais.

partargo, obs. form of BOTARGO, POTARGO.

c **1640** [SHIRLEY] *Capt. Underwit* III. iii. in Bullen *Old Pl.* (1883) II. 371 Oh the Neats tongues and partargoes that I haue eaten.

partch(e, parte, obs. ff. PARCH *v.,* PART, PARTY.

parted (ˈpɑːtɪd), *ppl. a.*

I. [*pa. pple.* of PART *v.*: see -ED[1].]

1. Divided into parts; severed, cloven; divided, as the hair, by a parting.

1590 SHAKS. *Mids. N.* IV. i. 194 Me-thinks I see these things with parted eye, When euery thing seemes double. **1667** MILTON *P.L.* IV. 302 Hyacinthin Locks Round from his parted forelock manly hung Clustring. **1817** KEATS *'Woman! when I behold thee'* ii, Light feet, dark violet eyes, and parted hair.

b. *Bot.* Divided or cleft nearly to the base, as a corolla or calyx; esp. with a numeral indicating the number of divisions, as 3-*parted,* tripartite.

1880 GRAY *Struct. Bot.* vi. §5 (ed. 6) 245 The calyx or corolla..is said to be parted (3-parted, 5-parted, etc.).

c. *Her.* = PARTY *a.* 3; hence of cloth, trappings, etc.: cf. PARTY *a.* 2.

1482 CAXTON *Chron. Eng.* ccxli. S ij, A mylk whyte stede ..trapped with cloth of gold and rede parted [*ed.* 1520 partyed] to geder. **1486** *Bk. St. Albans, Heraldry* D iij, Armys partit aftir the long way. *Ibid.* D vj, In armys partit it is requyrit alway that the partys of the colouris be equall. **1562** LEIGH *Armorie* 44 Parted per Pale. **1568** GRAFTON *Chron.* II. 383 Two fayre steedes, trapped in riche cloth of Golde, parted of red and white. **1823** RUTTER *Fonthill* p. xxi, Beckford, Parted per Pale Gules, and Azure.

†**d.** Of diverse kinds or colours intermixed; parti-coloured, pied. *Obs.* (Cf. PARTY *a.* 2.)

c **1380** WYCLIF *Wks.* (1880) 471 Herfore biddiþ God in his lawe þat his men shulden not be cloþid in wollun & lynnun partid to-gidere. **1570** NORTH *Doni's Philos.* (1888) 70 So goodly a beaste..with his parted hide (halfe blacke, halfe white) and blased starre in the foreheade.

2. Separated, sundered; placed or standing apart.

c **1611** CHAPMAN *Iliad* v. 898 So soon his wound's parted sides ran close in his recure. **1727** GAY *Fables* I. xxxiv. 38 Awhile the parted warriors stood. **1879** BLACK *Macleod of D.* xli. 372 With her saucy eyes and her laughing and parted lips.

3. Departed, gone away; deceased, dead. *arch.*

1593 SHAKS. *2 Hen. VI*, III. ii. 161 A timely-parted Ghost, Of ashy semblance, meager, pale, and bloodlesse. **1597** WARNER *Alb. Eng.* I. i. 3 Their parted fathers Ghost. **1795** SOUTHEY *Joan of Arc* VIII. 93 And hymn the requiem to his parted soul. *a* **1838** CAMPBELL *Last Man*, Yet mourn I not thy 'parted sway, Thou dim discrowned king of day!

4. Divided between two or more; shared.

1596 SPENSER *F.Q.* VI. ii. 48 So off he did his shield, and ..him up thereon did reare, And twixt them both with parted paines did beare.

II. [f. PART *sb.* + -ED².]

†**5.** (Usually with qualifying word.) Furnished with or having (good, mean, etc.) 'parts' or abilities (see PART *sb.* 12); gifted, talented, accomplished. *Obs.*

1599 B. JONSON *Ev. Man out of Hum.* Pref. 7 A Man well parted, a sufficient Scholler. —— *Cynthia's Rev.* v. ii, A man rarely parted, second to none in this court. **1628** EARLE *Microcosm., Detractor* (Arb.) 43 A detractor..commonly some weak parted fellow. *a* **1668** DAVENANT *News fr. Plymouth* II. Wks. 1873 IV. 126 Better parted, more polite and vers'd in The rules of courtship.

6. Charged with a dramatic part or character. (See also OVER-PARTED.)

1612 HEYWOOD *Apol. Actors* (1841) 28, I have seen Tragedyes, Comedyes,..publicly acted, in which the graduates..have been specially parted. *Mod. Newsp.*, I have seen Sir Henry better 'parted' a score of times, and Miss Ellen Terry a hundred times.

Hence **ˈpartedness** (in quot., in sense 5).

1654 WHITLOCK *Zootomia* 12 Wisdome, though but knavery, men afford so many grains of esteem, as to term partednesse, and cunning.

partee, parteiner, obs. ff. PARTY, PARTNER.

parteis, obs. pl. of PARTY.

[**partel,** spurious word; mis-reading of PARCEL. (*Reliq. Antiq.* II. 57.)]

parteless(e, -let, obs. ff. PARTLESS, PARTLET².

†**ˈparten,** *v. Obs.* [f. PART *sb.* (?) + -EN⁵ 2: in sense a synonym of PART *v.*; perh. in b associated with *partener*, PARTNER.]

a. *intr.* To bestow a part or share, impart some *of*: = PART *v.* 11. **b.** *trans.* To share, partake (*with* a person): = PART *v.* 10.

1397 TREVISA *Barth. De P.R.* VIII. xxix. (Bodl. MS.), And soo fattenes of þe matere lettith distribucioun and partenynge of þe schynyng þat is ifonge. *c* **1400** *Pol. Poems* (Rolls) II. 98 And also the pore man..praiede to the apostlis to parten of her almes. *c* **1470** *Golagros & Gaw.* 1104 Ane wounder peralous poynt, partenyng grete plight. **1561** T. HOBY tr. *Castiglione's Courtyer* I. (1577) C j b, That if any blame happen..it may be also partned with you. *Ibid.* IV. (1577) X viij b, A shyning beame of that light, whiche is the true image of the Angelike beautie partened wyth hyr, whereof shee also partneth with the body a feeble shadowe.

parten, var. PARTAN, crab.

partenar, -er, partene, obs. ff. PARTNER, PERTAIN *v.*

parter (ˈpɑːtə(r)). Now *rare.* [f. PART *v.* + -ER¹.] One who or that which parts; a divider, separator, distributor, etc.: see the verb.

c **1380** WYCLIF *Serm.* Sel. Wks. II. 231 Who made me juge and partere among ȝou? **1470–85** MALORY *Arthur* XVIII. vii, The knyȝtes parters of the lystes toke vp sire Mador. **1487** *Act 4 Hen. VII*, c. 2 (*Preamble*), Finers and Parters of Gold and Silver by Fire and Water. **1567** MAPLET *Gr. Forest* 62 b, To be a defence and a partour of our neighbour his ground and ours. **1612** CHAPMAN *Widow's T.* Plays 1873 III. 40 Not we Sir, we are no parters of fraies.

parteriche, obs. form of PARTRIDGE.

parterre (pɑˈtɛə(r), pɑː-). Also 7 **parterra, parter, parterr.** [a. F. *parterre* (1549 in R. Estienne); absolute use of the adverbial phrase *par terre* on or over (the surface of) the ground.]

1. A level space in a garden occupied by an ornamental arrangement of flower-beds of various shapes and sizes.

a **1639** CAREW *Coel. Brit.* Wks. (1824) 188 A delicious garden, with severall walkes and parterra's set round with low trees. **1661** COWLEY *Prop. Exper. Philos., College*, A Parterre of Flowers. **1663** GERBIER *Counsel* d ij b, Paradise like gardens..with Parters. **1699** LISTER *Journ. Paris* 181 Large Parterrs in the middle, and large Fountains of Water, which constantly play. **1717** LADY M. W. MONTAGU *Let. C'tess Bristol* 1 Apr., Like a parterre of tulips. *a* **1839** PRAED *Poems* (1864) II. 53 A paling, cleaned with constant care, Surrounds ten yards of neat parterre. **1857** C. BRONTE *Professor* ix, A parterre of rose-trees.

fig. **1709** MRS. MANLEY *New Atl.* (ed. 2) II. 197 See! that Chamber! are you not, as you look round, in a beautiful Parterre? **1872** GEO. ELIOT *Middlem.* I. i, The casket was soon open before them, and the various jewels spread out, making a bright parterre on the table. **1889** *Illustr. Lond. News* 16 Mar. 322, I cull these flowers from two parterres of opposite politics.

2. A level space on which a house or village stands.

1677 J. P. tr. *Tavernier's Trav.* (1684) II. 79 (Stanf.) Moreover it is required for the beauty of an House, that it be seated in the midst of some great *Parterre.* **1876** *Cornh. Mag.* Sept. 318 The village stands upon a small *parterre.*

3. The part of the ground-floor of the auditorium of a theatre behind the orchestra; later, in U.S., that part beneath the galleries. Also, The occupants of this part of a theatre.

1711 ADDISON *Spect.* No. 29 ¶8 The Chorus..gives the Parterre frequent Opportunities of joining in Consort with the Stage. **1753** MURPHY *Gray's Inn Jrnl.* No. 41 (1756) I. 263 The *Parterre*..turned their Backs to the Stage, and blew their Noses. **1756–7** tr. *Keysler's Trav.* (1760) III. 373 The parterre or pit is likewise adorned with several statues. **1883** *Harper's Mag.* Nov. 884/1 The parterre and the ..'first' tier are distributed among the stockholders.

4. *attrib.* and *Comb.*, as ***parterre-like*** adj.

1849 CLOUGH *Dipsychus* I. iii. 66 The brilliant season's gay parterre-like room. **1901** *Westm. Gaz.* 31 July 6/3 The American parterre system, which has been so successful at the Theatre Royal.

Hence **parˈterred** *a.*, laid out in parterres.

1816 J. SCOTT *Paris Revisit.* (ed. 3) 203 What must have been the beautiful Hougomont,—with its wild orchard, its parterred flower garden, its gently-dignified chateau.

partesant, partezan, obs. ff. PARTISAN².

partey, parteyn, parteynge, obs. ff. PARTY, PERTAIN.

parteyner, parthenare, -ere, obs. ff. PARTNER.

partheniad (pɑːˈθiːnıæd). ? *Obs.* [f. as next + -AD c.] A poem or song in honour of a virgin (in quot. 1589, of Queen Elizabeth).

1589 PUTTENHAM *Eng. Poesie* III. xix. (Arb.) 224 In another Partheniade..insinuating her Maiesties great constancy in refusall of all marriages offred. **1591** HARINGTON *Orl. Fur., Apol. Poetrie* ¶ iij, Diuerse pieces of Partheniads and hymnes in praise of the most praisworthy.

parthenian (pɑːˈθiːnıən), *a. rare.* [f. Gr. παρθένιος (f. παρθένος virgin) + -AN.] Of or pertaining to a virgin.

1656 BLOUNT *Glossogr.*, *Parthenian*..belonging to virginity, or to a Maid. **1892** W. W. PEYTON *Memorab. Jesus* iv. 88 Nature is not cheated of her rights when a parthenian birth takes place in the human family.

parthenic (pɑːˈθɛnık), *a.*¹ *rare.* [ad. Gr. παρθενικ-ός, f. παρθένος virgin.] Of or belonging to, or of the nature of, a virgin; *fig.* unviolated, 'virgin', 'maiden'.

1834 DISRAELI *Rev. Epick* III. xvii, The virgin towers Of Coni, whose parthenic crest a flag Hostile ne'er sullied! **1869** J. EADIE *Comm. Galatians* 91 Through her parthenic maternity, the mystery of mysteries realized—God manifest in the flesh.

parˈthenic, *a.*² *Chem.* [f. L. *parthenium*, a name of several plants; in the herbalists a species of camomile (*Matricaria Parthenium*); now, in Botany, a genus of Compositæ: see -IC 1 b.] In ***parthenic acid***: see quots.

1866–77 WATTS *Dict. Chem.* IV. 357 *Parthenic acid*, the name given by Peretti to the acid which forms in distilled chamomile water after long keeping. **1893** *Syd. Soc. Lex.*, *Parthenic acid*, a non-crystallisable acid occurring in combination with *Parthenine* in the *Parthenium hysterophorus.*

So **parthenine** (ˈpɑːθənaın), *Chem.* [-INE⁵], an alkaloid, $C_{19}H_{28}NO_6$, obtained from *Parthenium Hysterophorus*, an American composite plant, used as a remedy for fever and neuralgia. Also called **parthenicine** (pɑːˈθɛnısaın) [f. L. *parthenicē* = *parthenium*].

1885 *Lancet* 11 July 86/2 Parthenine..has recently been studied..as a remedy for facial neuralgia. **1888** *Ibid.* 30 June 1312/2 The physiological and clinical trials that have been made with 'parthenicine'.

parthenism (ˈpɑːθənız(ə)m). *rare*⁻¹. [f. Gr. παρθένος virgin + -ISM.] = PARTHENOGENESIS.

1892 W. W. PEYTON *Memorab. Jesus* iv. 88 These creatures show parthenism or sexless generation.

parthenocarpy (ˈpɑːθənəʊkɑːpı). *Bot.* [a. G. *parthenocarpie* (F. Noll 1902, in *Sitzungsber. d. Niederrheinischen Ges. für Natur- und Heilkunde* 160), f. Gr. παρθένο-ς virgin + καρπός fruit + -Y³.] The development of a fruit without fertilization having taken place in the plant producing it. Hence **ˌparthenoˈcarpic** *a.*, of a fruit, produced without prior fertilization; **ˌparthenoˈcarpically** *adv.*

1911 J. M. COULTER et al. *Textbk. Bot.* II. 917 In striking contrast to ordinary fruit production is parthenocarpy, or the development of fruit without the fusion of gametes. *Ibid.*, Plants with parthenocarpic fruits are..propagated vegetatively. **1924** M. SKENE *Biol. Flowering Plants* v. 406 An embryo may develop without fertilisation having occurred. Corresponding to this parthenogenesis we have parthenocarpy, where a fruit is produced without any seeds. **1929** *Nature* 13 July 63/2 Triploids occur..with partial parthenocarpy in the cultivated apples. **1949** *Endeavour* VIII. 191/1 Even in plants which normally produce seeded fruits, parthenocarpy may occur spasmodically. *Ibid.* 191/2 Parthenocarpic fruits often differ from seeded fruits of the same variety, not only in size and shape but in chemical composition. **1951** *New Biol.* XI. 72 There is virtually no fertilization in the seedless edible varieties [of banana], the fruits being formed parthenocarpically. **1960** *New Scientist* 11 Feb. 322/3 Such parthenocarpic fruits contain no viable seed. **1965** K. ESAU *Plant Anat.* (ed. 2) xix. 586 Formation of a fruit may also occur without seed development and without fertilization, a phenomenon known as parthenocarpy.

parthenogenesis (ˌpɑːθənəʊˈdʒɛnısıs). *Biol.* [f. Gr. παρθένο-ς virgin + γένεσις origin, birth, nativity, GENESIS.] Reproduction without concourse of opposite sexes or union of sexual elements.

Now usually restricted to reproduction by the development of a single sexual cell (as an ovum or ovule) without fertilization by union with one of the opposite sex (which occurs, normally or occasionally, in certain insects and other invertebrates, and in rare instances in plants); formerly used more widely to include asexual reproduction, as by fission or budding (cf. AGAMOGENESIS).

1849 OWEN (*title*) On Parthenogenesis, or the Successive Productions of Procreating Individuals from the Single Ovum. **1859** DARWIN *Orig. Spec.* xiv. (1878) 387 The term parthenogenesis implying that the mature females..are capable of producing fertile eggs without the concourse of the male. **1875** BENNETT & DYER *Sachs' Bot.* 805 *note*, *Parthenogenesis*..is a phenomenon of very rare occurrence in the vegetable kingdom. **1879** tr. *Haeckel's Evol. Man* I. ii. 28 The so-called parthenogenesis, or virginal generation, of Bees has been proved..by the meritorious zoologist, Siebold, of Munich, who also showed that male Bees develop from unimpregnated, and female bees only from impregnated eggs. **1886** VINES *Physiol. of Plants* xxiii. 674 When..these gametes, having failed to conjugate, germinate independently, it must be assumed that both male and female parthenogenesis takes place. **1889** GEDDES & THOMSON *Evol. of Sex* xiii. §1 In 1701, Albrecht observed that a female silkmoth, which had been isolated in a glass case, laid fertile eggs... The occasional parthenogenesis of this insect has been repeatedly confirmed by competent observers. **1902** D. H. CAMPBELL *Univ. Text-bk. Bot.* v. 122 In one species of Chara, *C. crinita*, the oöspores are developed without fertilization—one of the few well-authenticated cases of parthenogenesis. **1936** [see EUTELEGENESIS]. **1950** *Adv. Genetics* III. 195 In vertebrata normal parthenogenesis is unknown (with the possible exception of certain fish hybrids). **1965** BELL & COOMBE tr. *Strasburger's Textbk. Bot.* 203 There are exceptions in which a sexual cell will germinate and undergo development without fertilization. This phenomenon is referred to as parthenogenesis. Habitual parthenogenesis is that occurring when egg cells germinate regularly without fertilization.

fig. **1870** LOWELL *Among my Bks.* Ser. I. (1873) 223 How one sin involves another, and forever another, by a fatal parthenogenesis.

parthenogenetic (ˌpɑːθənəʊdʒıˈnɛtık), *a.* [f. as prec. + -GENETIC.]

1. *Biol.* Pertaining to, of the nature of, or characterized by parthenogenesis; reproducing by parthenogenesis.

1872 DARWIN *Orig. Spec.* xiv. (ed. 6) 387 To accelerate parthenogenetic reproduction by gradual steps to an earlier and earlier age. **1877** HUXLEY *Anat. Inv. Anim.* vii. 446 The terms arrenotokous and thelytokous have been proposed by Leuckart and Von Siebold to denote those parthenogenetic females which produce male and female young respectively. **1884** *Q. Jrnl. Microsc. Sci.* XXIV. 266 In certain cases, the oospores become normally developed and capable of germination without any male organs being formed at all... Pringsheim himself termed these oospores parthenogenetic. **1889** GEDDES & THOMSON *Evol. of Sex* iv. §1. 46 In the artificial environment of a greenhouse, equivalent to a perpetual summer.., the parthenogenetic succession of females [aphides] has been experimentally observed for four years. **1936** [see AMPHIDIPLOID *a.* and *sb.*]. **1950** *Adv. Genetics* III. 195 Some big animal groups are wholly (or almost wholly) characterized by parthenogenetic reproduction. **1965** B. E. FREEMAN tr. *Vandel's Biospeleol.* ix. 110 *E*[*laphoidella*] *bidens*, a species with parthenogenetic reproduction, is cosmopolitan.

2. Born of a virgin. *nonce-use.*

1871 TYLOR *Prim. Cult.* II. 279 The enigmatic nature of this inextricable compound parthenogenetic deity.

ˌparthenogeˈnetically, *adv.* [f. prec.: see -ICALLY.] In a parthenogenetic manner; in the way of or by means of parthenogenesis.

1875 tr. *Schmidt's Desc. & Darw.* 48 Ova developing parthenogenetically, without fecundation. **1884** *Q. Jrnl. Microsc. Sci.* XXIV. 281 *Ascobolus furfuraceus* probably produces its fructification parthenogenetically. **1890** *Q. Rev.* Apr. 382 Amongst the creatures which are parthenogenetically produced is the male, or drone, of the hive-bee. **1895** *Ann. Bot.* IX. 638 In *S*[*aprolegnia*] *mixta*.. we conclude that fertilization frequently takes place, but in default of its occurrence the oosphere may develop parthenogenetically. **1924** *Jrnl. Agric. Res.* XXVII. 513 The stem-mother is always wingless and gives birth to living young parthenogenetically. **1938** [see APOMICT]. **1950** *Adv. Genetics* III. 195 Some vertebrata have been artificially induced to reproduce parthenogenetically. **1972** *Nature* 28 Jan. 196/1 Microtubule proteins are still synthesized in parthenogenetically activated, nucleated half-eggs.

ˌparthenoˈgenic, *a.* [Cf. Gr. παρθενογενής virgin-born.] = PARTHENOGENETIC 1. So **partheˈnogenous** *a.* in same sense; **partheˈnogeny** = PARTHENOGENESIS.

1890 in *Century Dict.*

parthenogenone (ˌpɑːθənəʊˈdʒɛnəʊn). *Zool.* [f. PARTHENOGEN(ESIS + *-one.*] An organism of parthenogenetic origin, having only one parent.

1957 R. A. BEATTY *Parthenogenesis & Polyploidy in Mammalian Devel.* i. 4 Parthenogenesis will be considered here as a term applicable not only to born young but also to embryos and foetuses, the parthenogenetic organism being called a parthenogenone. **1970** *Sci. Jrnl.* June 42/3 The human population, by virtue of its enormous size, could indeed contain a few parthenogenones. **1973** *Nature* 13 Apr.

475/2 [Mouse] eggs were examined under the ×50 magnification of a Wild dissecting microscope to determine the overall frequency and types of parthenogenones induced. **1977** *Ibid.* 6 Jan. 53/2 Diploid and haploid parthenogenones evidently possess the capacity to form teratomas and give rise to differentiated tissues.

‖**ˌparthenogoˈnidium.** *Bot.* [mod.L., f. Gr. παρθένος virgin + GONIDIUM.] A gonidium in certain algæ, as *Volvox*, by which they are reproduced asexually.

1895 KERNER & OLIVER *Nat. Hist. Plants* II. 634 Daughter-colonies [of *Volvox Globator*] are developed from special cells, usually eight in number, called *parthenogonidia*, .. larger than the ordinary vegetative cells.

parthenolatry (-ˈɒlətrɪ). [f. Gr. παρθένο-ς virgin + λατρεία worship, -LATRY.] Virgin-worship.

1818 COLERIDGE in *Lit. Rem.* (1838) III. 174 Frippery patches, cribbed from the tyring Room of Romish Parthenolatry.

partheˈnology. [f. as prec. + -LOGY.] The part of physiology which deals with virginity.

1853 in DUNGLISON *Med. Lex.*

Parthenopean (ˌpɑːθənəˈpiːən), *a.* [ad. It. *Partenopea*, f. L. *Parthenopēi-us* belonging to Naples (f. *Parthenopē* Naples) + -AN.] Of or belonging to Naples; applied *esp.* to the shortlived republic established in Naples by French revolutionary forces in 1799.

1799 NELSON *Let.* 19 Jan. (1845) III. 236 The Parthenopien Republic is forming. **1858** S. HORNER tr. *Colletta's Hist. Kingdom of Naples* I. IV. ii. 341 The day had arrived when the Parthenopean Republic was to be abandoned to her own resources. **1879** *Encycl. Brit.* IX. 79/1 The French, entering the city after a furious but undisciplined resistance by the lazzaroni, established with the aid of the citizens and nobles the 'Parthenopean Republic'. **1894** C. E. CLEMENT *Naples* vi. 156 Vesuvius.. sent forth a brilliant flame, which the Neapolitans regarded as an omen of future prosperity. Thus was the Parthenopean Republic established. **1900** P. ORSI *Mod. Italy* ii. 45 It was then that the Parthenopæan Republic—so-called from the ancient name of the city—was proclaimed at Naples. **1903** C. GIGLIOLI (*title*) Naples in 1799: an account of the revolution of 1799 and of the rise and fall of the Parthenopean Republic. **1915** C. MACKENZIE *Guy & Pauline* 284 They would travel farther south and perhaps come to that Parthenopean shore calling to him still now from the few days he had spent upon its silver heights and beside its azure waters. **1921** *Q. Rev.* Apr. 365 The relationship of the Parthenopean Republic to the Mother-Republic of France, could not be safely dealt with in a public print. **1925** L. V. BERTARELLI *S. Italy* 262 Burdensome taxation.. aroused the Neapolitans to insurrection under Masaniello in 1647, but his 'Parthenopean Republic' endured only a few months... In 1799.. Gen. Championnet, at the head of a Napoleonic army, founded the second Parthenopean Republic. **1956** H. ACTON *Bourbons of Naples* xvii. 333 The Parthenopean Republic was installed by conquest, and the French army of occupation was its only solid prop. **1974** *Encycl. Brit. Macropædia* IX. 1156/1 Thus was born the Parthenopean Republic, which.. was the most democratic of the Italian states set up between 1796 and 1799.

parthenopian (pɑːθəˈnəʊpɪən), *a.* and *sb.* [f. mod.L. *Parthenopē*, a. Gr. Παρθενόπη, name of one of the Sirens.] **a.** *adj.* Pertaining to the genus *Parthenope* or family *Parthenopidæ* of crabs. **b.** *sb.* A crab of this genus or family. So **parˈthenopine** *a.* and *sb.*

1840 *Penny Cycl.* XVII. 289 (heading) Parthenopians.

parthenospore (ˈpɑːθənəʊˌspɔə(r)). *Bot.* [f. Gr. παρθένο-ς virgin + SPORE.] A reproductive cell resembling a zygospore, but produced without conjugation, in certain algæ. Also called **ˈparthenosperm** [see SPERM].

1889 BENNETT & MURRAY *Cryptog. Bot.* 261 (*Mesocarpaceæ*) In Gonatonema.. parthenosperms are said to be formed closely resembling zygosperms. *Ibid.* 292 (*Volvocineæ*) The non-sexual propagative cells, zoospores or parthenospores.

Parthian (ˈpɑːθɪən), *a.* and *sb.* [See -AN.]

A. *adj.* Of or pertaining to Parthia, an ancient kingdom of western Asia.

The Parthian horsemen were accustomed to baffle the enemy by their rapid manœuvres, and to discharge their missiles backward while in real or pretended flight: hence used allusively in ***Parthian fight, shaft, shot, glance***, etc.

1590 C'TESS PEMBROKE *Antonie* 107 Thou car'st no more for Parth nor Parthian bow. *c* **1640** WALLER *Phillis* 26 To look upon this Parthian Fight Of Love. **1848** LYTTON *Harold* VII. iv, The fugitive Britons.. performed their flight with the same Parthian rapidity that characterised the assault. **1874** LISLE CARR *Jud. Gwynne* I. i. 31 Casting back Parthian glances of scornful hostility. **1902** GREENOUGH & KITTREDGE *Words* 380 A 'Parthian shot' was very literal to Crassus.. : to us it is only an elegant and pointed synonym for our method of 'having the last word'.

B. *sb.* **1.** A native or inhabitant of Parthia.

1526 TINDALE *Acts* ii. 9. **1611** SHAKS. *Cymb.* I. vi. 20 Or like the Parthian I shall flying fight. **1678** BUTLER *Hud.* III. Heroic. Ep. 173 You wound, like Parthians, while you fly, And kill, with a Retreating Eye. **1742** YOUNG *Nt. Th.* II. 335 Whose Yesterdays look backward with a Smile; Nor, like the Parthian, wound him as they fly.

2. The Iranian language of the Parthians; = PAHLAVI *a.* and *sb.* Also as *adj.*

1932 W. L. GRAFF *Lang.* x. 373 For a time Armenian was deemed to be an Iranian dialect on account of the large number of Parthian (Persian) words in its vocabulary. **1933** L. BLOOMFIELD *Language* iv. 63 Discoveries of manuscript fragments in Chinese Turkestan gave us knowledge of other medieval Iranian languages, which have been identified as Parthian, Sogdian, and Sakian. **1939** L. H. GRAY *Foundations of Lang.* 320 We have a fair amount of material in some other Middle Iranian dialects, notably *Middle Parthian* north of Persia. **1944** *Trans. Philol. Soc. 1942* 44 Scripts used in Iran in ancient times.. derive from the Aramaic script of twenty-two letters (not counting.. Chinese for Middle Persian and Parthian). **1954** M. BOYCE *Manichaean Hymn-Cycles in Parthian* 1 There are in Parthian three long texts which are divided into sections known as *handāms* or 'limbs'. **1972** W. B. LOCKWOOD *Panorama Indo-European Lang.* 236 The Manicheans borrowed the Estrangelo Syriac script and used it to write other Middle Iranian languages as well, i.e. Parthian and Sogdian.

‖**parti** (parti). [Fr., = party; side, match, resolution taken for oneself.]

1. A marriageable person considered in reference to means or position, or what kind of a 'match' he or she may be.

1814 BYRON *Let. to Moore* Oct., It is likely she will prove a considerable *parti*. **1873** MISS BROUGHTON *Nancy* II. 278 He was looked upon as quite a *parti*. **1899** MRS. DYAN *All in a Man's K.* 72 He was an eligible parti in every way.

2. ***parti pris***, side taken, mind made up, bias. Also *attrib.* and as *pred. adj.*

1871 MORLEY *Crit. Misc.* Ser. I. *Carlyle* (1878) 189 That fatal spirit of *parti-pris* which has led to the rooting of so much injustice, disorder, immobility and darkness in English intelligence. **1880** 'OUIDA' *Moths* I. 60 Lady Dolly scanned the garment with a critical air and a *parti pris*. **1885** [see FAUTE DE MIEUX]. **1905** R. BROUGHTON *Waif's Progress* xxiv. 268 It can be no *parti pris* that has dwindled her to half her size. **1923** H. CRANE *Let.* 18 Feb. (1965) 125 In his letter his partis pris emotionalism was too evident to convince his readers properly. **1958** L. DURRELL *Mountolive* v. 103 Personally I think we both have made a mess of it, and I have no *parti-pris* in the matter. **1959** *Times* 31 Dec. 11/3 Professor Brinton is not *parti pris* as Lecky and Westermarck were. **1973** *Times Lit. Suppl.* 15 June 660/5 With none of the characters in Lawrence's life is he *parti-pris*. **1974** *Broadcast* 9 Dec. 17/2 Most discussion about advertising is conducted on a basis of *parti pris*. **1977** *N.Y. Rev. Bks.* 9 June 21/2 The ideological *parti-pris* of these last two sources does not invalidate their generally rigorous and sound historical documentation.

parti, obs. form of PARTY.

parti-[1] (also †partie-), extended use of the first element in PARTI-COLOURED, earlier ***partie-coloured***, after which Shakspere has †**ˈpartie-coated**, having a **party-coat**, i.e. a parti-coloured or motley coat. So, in later use: **ˈparti-ˌdecorated**, decorated part in one way, part in another; †**ˈparti-ˌmembered**, having members or limbs of two kinds; †**ˈparti-named**, having diverse names.

1638 SIR J. BEAUMONT in *Jonsonus Virbius*, When heretofore, the Vice's only note, And sign from virtue was his *party-coat. **1588** SHAKS. *L.L.L.* v. ii. 776 As Loue is.. Varying in subiects as the eie doth roule, To euerie varied obiect in his glance: Which *partie-coated presence of loose loue Put on by vs [etc.]. **1894** *Westm. Gaz.* 3 Oct. 7/1 One finds the drawing-room *parti-decorated: one half is adorned with sporting pictures.. the other presents a Scriptural text and other signs of sanctity. **1641** MILTON *Ch. Govt.* I. v. Wks. (1851) 119 So was Jereboams Episcopacy partly from the patterne of the law, and partly from the patterne of his owne carnality; a parti-colour'd and a *parti-member'd Episcopacy. **1634** SIR T. HERBERT *Trav.* 149 Though the meat be particoloured, or *party named, yet the ground and meate is Pelo and no other.

parti-[2], combining form of L. *pars, part-em*, PART; as in **parti-ˈpartial** *a.* (*Logic*), applied by Sir W. Hamilton to a proposition in which both terms are partial or particular; **parti-ˈtotal**, in which one term is particular and the other universal.

1833 SIR W. HAMILTON *Discuss.* (1852) 162, iii. Parti-total—Some is all. *Ibid.* 162, iv. Parti-partial—Some is some.

partial (ˈpɑːʃəl), *a.* (*sb.*) Forms: 5 **parcial, -cyale**, 5–6 **-cyal(l, -ciall**, (6 **perciall, -cyall**), 6–7 **partiall**, (6 *Sc.* **pertiall**), 6– **partial**. [a. OF. *parcial* (14th c. in Godef.), F. *partial*, and in sense 2 *partiel*, It. *parziale*, Sp., Pg. *parcial*, ad. late L. *partiāl-is* (S. Gregory); cf. *partiāliter* adv. in Cælius Aurel., 5th c.

Fr. now distinguishes *partial* in our sense 1 (Amyot 16th c.), from *partiel* in our sense 2 (*Dict. Acad.* 1762), but this distinction is recent, for *parcial* was used by Oresme *a* 1400, and *partial* by Calvin 16th c., = mod.F. *partiel*.]

A. *adj.* **I. 1. a.** 'Inclined antecedently to favour one party in a cause, or one side of the question more than the other' (J.); unduly favouring one party or side in a suit or controversy, or one set or class of persons rather than another; prejudiced; biased; interested; unfair. (The opposite of *impartial*.)

partial counsel (*Sc. Law*), improper advice or communication to one of the parties in a cause.

c **1420** LYDG. *Assembly of Gods* 153 Yef ye in thys matyr be nat parciall. **1442–3** *Rec. Coldingham Priory* (Surtees) I. 148 For the qwilk thai war pursewit be process of a parcyale Juge. **1526** TINDALE *Acts* x. 34, I perseaue, that God is not parciall. *a* **1548** HALL *Chron., Hen. V* 36 A perciall interpretour marreth the sentence. **1660** SOUTH *Serm.* I. 97 Your Worldliness, your Luxury, your sinister partial Dealing. **1693** STAIR *Inst.* (ed. 2) IV. xliii. §9 Witnesses become Inhabile, by giving partial Council. **1715–20** POPE *Iliad* XVIII. 582 The witness is produced on either hand: For this or that the partial people stand. **1861** W. BELL *Dict. Law Scot.*, *Partial counsel*; is one of the circumstances which throws discredit upon a witness's testimony. *Ibid.*, Partial counsel is a ground of declinature of a judge. **1861** MILL *Utilit.* v. 67 It is inconsistent with justice to be partial. **1872** BLACKIE *Lays Highl.* 54 Who sits supreme in righteous state Above man's partial mood.

b. Favouring a particular person or thing excessively or especially; prejudiced or biased in some one's favour; hence in weakened sense: Favourably disposed, favourable, kindly, sympathetic. Const. *to*. Now *rare*, or merged in prec. or next.

c **1585** *Faire Em* III. 1326 And never could I see a man, methought, That equalled Manvile in my partial eye. **1586–7** Q. ELIZ. *Let. Jas. VI*, 14 Feb., Who shall other-wise perswade yow, judge them more partiall to others then to yow. **1699** BENTLEY *Phal.* 148 So obliging, so partial to our Sophist. **1759** HUME *Hist. Eng.* (1812) V. xli. 275 Men naturally believed she had been influenced by an affection still more partial than that of friendship. **1771** *Junius Lett.* xlix. 253, I am not so partial to the royal judgment as to affirm [etc.]. **1804** M. G. LEWIS *Bravo of Venice* (1856) I. vi. 280 Rosabella, a creature in whose formation partial nature seemed to have omitted nothing which might constitute the perfection of female loveliness. **1852** ROBERTSON *Serm.* Ser. III. xv. 192 Not the partial Father, loving one alone.

c. With *to*: Having a liking for, fond of. *colloq.*

1696 PRIOR *Secretary* 16 Athens.. Where people knew love, and were partial to verse. **1747** H. WALPOLE *Lett.* (1846) II. 189, I am not partial to the family. **1827** LYTTON *Pelham* lxxxvi, I am not more partial to my arm chair, nor more averse to shaving than of yore. **1889** A. LANG *Prince Prigio* xvii. 133 He brought out some cold sausage (to which Alphonso was partial).

†**d.** Inclined, apt (*to do* something). *Obs. rare*$^{-1}$.

1615 in *Crt. & T. Jas. I*, I. 363 They are too partial to think themselves *sacro sancti*, that they may not be touched.

e. *Comb.*, as ***partial-eyed***.

1593 NASHE *Four Lett. Confut.* Wks. (Grosart) II. 248 A discontented Scholler.. tragicallie exclaiming vpon his partial-eid fortune.

II. 2. a. Pertaining to or involving a part (not the whole); 'subsisting only in a part; not general or universal; not total' (J.); constituting a part only; incomplete. ***partial cause***: see quot. 1697.

1641 H. L'ESTRANGE *God's Sabbath* 22 A total Prolepsis of an entire story before another there may be, and yet no partial of one part of that story before another. **1643** BURROUGHES *Exp. Hosea* iv. (1652) 225 Idols are content with a partiall obedience, because they are but partiall in bestowing of good things. **1697** tr. *Burgersdicius his Logic* I. xv. 51 That [cause is] Partial which, joyned with the other Causes of its own Species causes the Caused only in Part. **1734** POPE *Ess. Man* IV. 114 Or partial Ill is universal Good. **1781** GIBBON *Decl. & F.* xxvi. (1869) II. 35 This partial defeat was balanced, however, by partial success. **1861** W. BELL *Dict. Law Scot.* s.v. *Insurance*, A partial loss is one short of a total loss; or, where the articles insured are actually landed at the port of delivery, the injury will amount to a partial loss. *Ibid.*, In all cases.. between the insurers and the insured, there is no question as to the legality of the capture or the change of property, but simply whether it be a total or a partial loss, and whether it admits of an abandonment. **1864** BOWEN *Logic* iv. 61 Our representation.. is necessarily partial, as not including all its Marks. **1886** W. A. HARRIS *Techn. Dict. Fire Insurance*, Partial damage to merchandise.

b. *spec.* That is one of the parts which make up a whole; constituent, component.

1481 CAXTON *Myrr.* I. xiii. 40 Who that myght haue the parfayt science therof [of astronomy], he myght wel knowe how the world was compassed and plente of other parcyal sciences. **1834** MRS. SOMERVILLE *Connex. Phys. Sc.* iii. (1849) 17 The whole force which disturbs a planet is equivalent to three partial forces.

†**c.** *spec.* Particular, individual, personal. *Obs.*

1489 CAXTON *Faytes of A.* I. xx. 63 A true counseiller seeth more to the comyn wele than to his owne parcyall proffit. **1560** ROLLAND *Crt. Venus* Prol. 224 Ilk man takis his proper part partiall. *a* **1578** LINDESAY (Pitscottie) *Chron. Scot.* (S.T.S.) I. 87 The iniuries done to ony of them.. sould be equall pertiall to thame all.

†**d.** Using or dealing with only a part, not the whole, of something; sparing. [? associated with L. *parcus*.] *Obs. rare.*

1576 FLEMING *Panopl. Epist.* 81, I thought good, first not to touche, secondly to be parciall of my pen. *Ibid.* 245 Howe parciall and sparing in diet, how moderate in apparel.

3. In several technical uses.

a. *Astron.* Applied to an eclipse in which part only of the disk of the luminary is covered or darkened.

1704 in J. HARRIS *Lex. Techn.* I. s.v. *Eclipse*. **1857** MAYNE *Expos. Lex.*, Partial eclipse occurs when the moon enters but in part into the shade of the earth, or when it covers a part of the disc of the sun.

b. *Math.* (*a*) Applied to differentials, differentiation, etc. relative to only one of the variables involved, the rest being for the time supposed constant. (*b*) ***partial determinant*** = MINOR *determinant*; (*c*) ***partial fractions***: the simpler fractions as the sum of which a compound fraction can be expressed; (*d*) ***partial product***: (i) the product of one term of a multiplicand and one term of its multiplier; (ii) the product of the first *n* terms of a series, where *n* is a finite integer (including 1); (*e*) ***partial sum***: (see quot. 1973); (*f*) ***partial ordering*** or

order: a transitive antisymmetrical relation among the elements of a set, which is not necessarily informative about each pair of elements; *(g)* ***partial pivoting***: see PIVOTING *vbl. sb.* 2.

1816 tr. *Lacroix's Diff. & Int. Calculus* 146 Usually expressed by saying that one is the partial differential relative to *x*, and the other the partial differential relative to *y*. **1823** J. MITCHELL *Dict. Math. & Phys. Sc.* 346/1 Theory of Partial Differences. **1889** W. W. JOHNSON *Treat. Ordinary & Partial Differential Equations* xi. 288 An equation..giving the value of a single partial derivative, or more generally an equation giving a relation between the several partial derivatives of a function of two or more independent variables, is called a partial differential equation. **1898** *Cayley's Coll. Math. Papers* Index, Partial Differential Equations; system of. **1975** F. G. HAGIN *First Course Differential Equations* i. 32 Another important concept is the partial derivative... Recall that this can be computed simply by treating *y* as a constant and differentiating *F* as a function of *x*.

1816 PEACOCK & HERSCHEL tr. *Lacroix's Elem. Treat. Differential & Integral Calculus* II. 186 The general method of integrating differentials of the above form, consists in decomposing them into others, whose denominators are more simple, which we designate by the name of partial fractions. **1908** G. H. HARDY *Course Pure Math.* vi. 198 It is very often convenient, in differentiating a rational function, to employ the method of partial fractions. **1975** FLANDERS & PRICE *Algebra* vi. 207 In general, $\frac{ax+b}{(x-r)(x-s)} = \frac{A}{x-r} + \frac{B}{x-s}$ for suitable constants *A* and *B*. This expression is called the partial fraction decomposition of the given rational function.

c **1823** *New Pract. Builder* 554 The sum of all the partial products will be the answer. **1959** G. & R. C. JAMES *Math. Dict.* 285/1 *Partial product*, the product of the multiplicand and one digit of the multiplier, when the latter contains more than one digit. **1977** *Sci. Amer.* Sept. 82/2 Since each digit of the multiplier must be either a 0 or a 1, each partial product formed must be equal either to zero or to the multiplicand.

1966 W. RUDIN *Real & Complex Analysis* xv. 290 The p_n are the partial products of the infinite product. **1972** A. G. HOWSON *Handbk. Terms Algebra & Anal.* xxviii. 145 Given a sequence (a_n) of non-zero real or complex numbers we form a second sequence (P_n) whose terms are the partial products $P_n = \prod_{k=0}^{n} a_k = a_0 a_1 \ldots a_n$.

1926 BROMWICH & MACROBERT *Introd. Theory Infinite Series* (ed. 2) 540 (Index), Partial Sum of Fourier Series. **1928** R. C. YOUNG tr. *Knopp's Theory & Appl. Infinite Series* ii. 99 An infinite series is a new symbol for a definite sequence of numbers deducible from it, namely the sequence of its partial sums. **1973** D. BALL *Introd. Real Anal.* iv. 71 The sum of the first *n* terms of a series $a_1 + a_2 + a_3 + a_4 + a_5 + \ldots$ is called the *n*th partial sum.

1941 BIRKHOFF & MACLANE *Survey Mod. Algebra* xi. 326 (*heading*) Partial orderings. **1964** T. O. MOORE *Elem. Gen. Topology* vii. 126 Many writers require that a partial ordering be reflexive; some do not. We choose not to do so in this book. **1972** A. G. HOWSON *Handbk. Terms Algebra & Anal.* iii. 18 A binary relation on a set *X* which is reflexive, transitive and antisymmetric is called a partial order of *X*. A set with a partial order is known as a poset.

c. *Bot.* Forming one of the parts or divisions of a compound structure; secondary, subordinate: as ***partial umbel***, each of the smaller umbels of a compound umbel; so ***partial involucre***, the involucre of a partial umbel, an involucel.

1760 J. LEE *Introd. Bot.* I. viii. (1765) 17 The Umbellula which proceeds from the universal Umbel, a partial Umbel. **1819** *Pantologia*, *Partial umbel*, in botany; otherwise called umbellule... The involucre at the foot of this is called the partial involucre..a partial peduncle, is a subdivision of a common peduncle. **1872** OLIVER *Elem. Bot.* I. vii. 82 The entire inflorescence forms a compound umbel; the umbels of single flowers being the partial umbels.

d. *Acoustics* and *Mus.* Applied to any one of the simple tones which together form a complex tone. ***upper partial tones*** (or ***upper partials***): those higher in pitch than the fundamental tone, produced by the vibrations of the aliquot parts of the sonorous body; also called *harmonics* or *overtones*: see HARMONIC B. 2.

1879 G. PRESCOTT *Sp. Telephone* 96 That characteristic of a musical note or clang, which is called its quality, depends upon the number and relative intensities of the partial tones which go to form it. **1880** *Grove's Dict. Music* II. 654/1 Notwithstanding the difficulty of hearing the upper partial tones, many musicians have been able to do so by their unaided ears.

e. *R.C. Ch.* Of an indulgence: see quots.

1885 *Cath. Dict.* (ed. 3) s.v. *Indulgence, Divisions of Indulgences.*—Plenary remit all, partial a portion of the temporal punishment due to sin. **1890** W. J. B. RICHARDS *Catech. Indulgences* 2 Indulgences are..Plenary and Partial; the former take away the whole of temporal punishment to which the power of the Church extends; the latter take away a greater or less part only of the punishment.

f. ***partial pressure***: the pressure that would be exerted by a gas in a given mixture if it alone occupied the space.

1857 H. E. ROSCOE tr. *Bunsen's Gasometry* 131 The quantity of each constituent gas absorbed, is proportional to the pressure on that constituent part..; and these pressures may be distinguished as 'partial pressures', in contradistinction to the 'total pressures' of the whole mixture. **1899** J. WALKER *Introd. Physical Chem.* vii. 55 When a mixture of gases dissolves in a liquid, each component dissolves according to its own partial pressure. **1968** *Brit. Med. Bull.* XXIV. 249/2 The changes in composition of the body when the CO_2 partial pressure..is raised or lowered. **1971** *Physics Bull.* Feb. 83/3 The UKAEA's pulsed electrolytic hygrometer..can measure water in a gas down to a partial pressure of 10^{-7} atm.

g. Dentistry. ***partial denture***: a denture that replaces one or more, but not all, of the natural teeth of one set.

1860 J. RICHARDSON *Pract. Treat. Mech. Dentistry* xv. 374 (*heading*) Partial dentures constructed in a base of vulcanizable gums. **1921** D. GABELL *Prosthetic Dentistry* ix. 206 Partial dentures should slide smoothly and tightly into place and rest evenly on their supports. **1975** H. THOMSON *Occlusion* xi. 215 With the exception of the canine an abutment tooth for a partial denture should have two roots.

h. Chem. ***partial valency*** [tr. G. *partialvalenz* (J. Thiele 1899, in *Ann. d. Chem.* CCCVI. 89)]: a partially unsatisfied valency formerly attributed to some atoms in unsaturated compounds to account for the addition reactions of olefins and the stability of the benzene ring.

1899 *Jrnl. Chem. Soc.* LXXVI. I. 554 The author holds the view that, in unsaturated compounds, whilst two affinities of every atom which participates in the double linking are occupied with those of the contiguous atom, the combining energy is not completely absorbed, so that the atoms in question still possess valency (*Partialvalenz*), and it is in this partial valency that the source of additive capacity is to be found. **1937** H. B. WATSON *Mod. Theories Org. Chem.* viii. 105 The reactivity of the olefinic linkage was attributed to the incomplete saturation of the affinities of the doubly bound carbon atoms, which were thus regarded as possessing free 'partial valencies'. **1964** N. G. CLARK *Mod. Org. Chem.* xix. 394 When applied to a conjugated system, such as occurs in buta-1,3-diene, Thiele postulated the union of the centre pair of partial valencies, thus creating a relatively inert type of double bond between C_2 and C_3, and leaving reactive partial valencies only at C_1 and C_4.

i. Dentistry. ***partial veneer***: used *attrib.* to designate a crown consisting of a covering of three or more, but not all, of the surfaces of a tooth (the labial or buccal enamel being left exposed).

1928 *Jrnl. Amer. Dental Assoc.* Oct. 1919/2 The cast restoration is indicated in most other locations where esthetics will permit its use... One of the greatest fields of usefulness is in the construction of abutment pieces of the inlay, partial and full veneer types. **1940** S. D. TYLMAN *Theory & Pract. Crown & Bridge Prosthesis* xxvii. 332 (*heading*) The preparation of anterior teeth for partial veneer crowns. *Ibid.*, The partial veneer retainer is indicated primarily in bridge prosthesis when two or more missing teeth are restored. **1963** C. R. COWELL et al. *Inlays, Crowns, & Bridges* ix. 98 Although a well-constructed partial veneer crown shows little gold, an alternative preparation should be undertaken if a patient is anxious to avoid showing any gold.

j. ***partial title*** (see quots.).

1938 L. M. HARROD *Librarians' Gloss.* 113 *Partial title*, one which consists of only a part of the title as given on the title-page. **1967** *Anglo-Amer. Catal. Rules: Brit. Text* 267 *Partial title entry*, an added entry made under a secondary part of the title as given on the title page, e.g. a catchword title, subtitle, or alternative title.

k. *Cryst.* Of a dislocation: such that the displacement involved, as represented by the Burgers vector, is not an integral multiple of the lattice spacing.

1951 F. C. FRANK in *Phil. Mag.* XLII. 816 Unlike an ordinary twin-boundary, a translation-twin-boundary need not go right through the crystal. When it does not, its edge in the interior of the crystal is a dislocation. It will be called an imperfect dislocation (alternatively, a partial dislocation) in contrast with perfect dislocations which are surrounded entirely by good crystal. **1960** [see GLIDE *sb.* 5]. **1966** C. R. TOTTLE *Sci. Engin. Materials* iv. 101 Metals such as copper, silver, and gold have low values of this stacking-fault energy, and so readily form partial dislocations. **1976** M. T. SPRACKLING *Plastic Deformation Simple Ionic Crystals* iv. 51 A strip of stacking fault extending through a crystal has two opposite sides terminated by partial dislocations.

l. Physics. ***partial wave*** (see quot. 1971).

1953 R. G. SACHS *Nuclear Theory* iv. 65 The straightforward analysis of a scattering problem involving a short-range potential makes use of the method of partial waves. **1970** I. E. MCCARTHY *Nuclear Reactions* I. i. 13 Large values of *l* correspond to trajectories which miss the nucleus. Therefore the effect of the nuclear forces is noticeable only in the first few partial waves. **1971** *Physics Bull.* Sept. 516/2 Any wavefunction describing a quantum mechanical system can be expanded in terms of eigenfunctions of angular momentum ('partial waves') characterized by an integer *l* ranging from zero to infinity; usually only a finite number of partial waves is required to specify the system.

m. ***partial drought***: see DROUGHT 2.

B. *sb.* **1.** *Acoustics* and *Mus.* Short for ***partial tone***: see 3 d above.

1880 *Grove's Dict. Music* II. 654/2 From the mass of compound tone each resonator singles out and responds to that partial which agrees with it in pitch, but is unaffected by a partial of any other pitch. **1881** BROADHOUSE *Mus. Acoustics* 312 Those combinational tones which result from the union of the upper partials.

2. *Cryst.* A partial dislocation (see sense 3 k above).

1952 READ & SHOCKLEY in W. Shockley et al. *Imperfections in nearly Perfect Crystals* ii. 85 It was first pointed out by Heidenreich and Shockley that a dislocation having a ½ [110] slip vector (taking the lattice constant as unit length) in a face-centered cubic crystal could lower its energy by dissociating into two partials (Shockley partials) having slip vectors ⅙ [211] and ⅙ [121], respectively, and connected by a stacking fault. **1967** A. H. COTTRELL *Introd. Metall.* xvii. 280 The more widely the partials are separated initially, the more the energy required to bring them together to form the constriction and the more rare is the cross-slip. **1969** tr. *Kubo & Nagamiya's Solid State Physics* v. iii. 752 The characteristic of Shockley partials is that they together with their stacking faults can move and slip freely inside the slip planes.

partial ('pɑːʃəl), *v.* *Statistics.* [f. PARTIAL *a.* (*sb.*)] ***partial out*** (trans.): to eliminate (a factor or variable) during analysis so as to remove its influence when considering the relationship between other variables.

1932 *Brit. Jrnl. Psychol.* XXIII. 184 This figure [for mean concrete imagery] is reduced..when the influence of visual verbal imagery is 'partialled out'. **1940** G. H. THOMSON *Anal. Performance Test Scores* ii. 9 The form of distribution of age is not very important since age was partialled out. **1949** BRUNER & POSTMAN in J. S. Bruner *Beyond Information Given* (1974) iv. 73 We cannot partial out the differential effect of serial position of a card, whether first or third or fifth in the series, independently of the kinds of experience the subject had before being presented any given card. **1972** *Visible Language* Winter 57 For eighth graders there is no relation between linear spatial ability and either word or nonsense anagram performance when decentration is partialled out. **1976** *Nature* 24 June 689/1 When the effect of air temperature was partialled out..a rise in adjusted oral temperature was found in the 6 d following.

† **partial-gilt**, obs. erron. form of PARCEL-GILT.

1573 *Reg. Privy Council Scot.* Ser. I. II. 269 Twa silver saltfattis, ane thairof partiall gilt with gold.

partialism ('pɑːʃəlɪz(ə)m). [See -ISM.]

1. A partial theory or view, which does not take into account the whole of the facts or subject.

1872 H. W. BEECHER *Lect. Preach.* i. 25 Your mode of presenting the truth will be imperfect, your partialisms are full of danger. **1897** C. A. BERRY in *Chicago Advance* 2 Dec. 779/3 The Gospel also is in danger. In danger from partialism, because men do not fully realize what Christ is in his three offices of prophet, priest and king.

2. *Theol.* = PARTICULARISM I.

1864 in WEBSTER. Hence in later Dicts.

partialist ('pɑːʃəlɪst). [f. PARTIAL *a.* + -IST.]

1. *gen.* A partial, prejudiced, or biased person; one who favours one party or side unduly; a partisan.

1597 DANIEL *Philotas* IV. ii, To satisfie The most stiffe partialist that will not see. **1654** VILVAIN *Theol. Treat.* iii. 89 Which dissent..cannot..falsify their consent and harmony ..as partialists infer. **1788** MME. D'ARBLAY *Diary* 11 Jan., I have not been willing to deny myself the pleasure of letting my equally blind partialists hear. **1892** *Chicago Advance* 22 Dec., How all these things came to be..is not a matter to be settled by partialists.

2. One who holds a partial view or theory; one whose knowledge or outlook is limited.

1841–4 EMERSON *Ess.* Ser. II. viii. (1876) 198 Very fitly, therefore, I assert, that every man is a partialist. **1874** H. W. BEECHER in *Chr. World Pulpit* VI. 239/1 We are all of us ignorant; we know in part; we are partialists.

3. *Theol.* = PARTICULARIST.

1864 in WEBSTER. In later Dicts.

Hence **partia'listic** *a.*, belonging to partialists; characterized by partialism.

1896 W. GLADDEN in *Papers Ohio Ch. Hist. Soc.* VII. 141 The whole partialistic scheme of a rulership which is for a portion of mankind and against the rest.

partiality (pɑːʃɪ'ælɪtɪ). Forms: α. 5 **parcialte, -tee, -cyalte, partialte.** β. 5–6 **parcialite, -tialite,** (6 **-cialyte, -cyalite, -tye, -tie; parsealyte, percialitee, persealytie,** etc.), 6– **partiality.** [In α, a. OF. **parcialté, -aulté* (15th c. in Godef.); in β, a. OF. *parci-, partialité*, in Pr. *parcialitat*, Sp. *parcialidad*, It. *parzialità*, med.L. *partiālitās*, f. *partiālis* PARTIAL: see -ITY.]

I. 1. The quality or character of being partial (see PARTIAL 1); 'unequal state of the judgment and favour of one above the other, without just reason' (J.); prejudicial or undue favouring of one person or party, or one side of a question; prejudice, bias, unfairness; an instance of this.

α. **1422** *Rolls of Parlt.* IV. 176/1 With oute favour or eny maner parcialtee or fraude. **1461** *Ibid.* V. 464/1 Abusion of the Lawes, partialte, riotte..rape and viciouse lyvyng. **1451** *Paston Lett.* I. 212 Whiche myght weel by knowe for open parcialte.

β. *c* **1430** LYDG. *Min. Poems* (Percy Soc.) 120 Injuste promocioune and parcialité. **1526** in *Archæol.* (1891) LIII. 374 Empanell a queste withoute partialite or maintenance. *a* **1533** LD. BERNERS *Huon* lxxxi. 250 Gyue trew iugement without ony fauoure or parsealyte. **1589** *Acts Privy Council* (1898) XVII. 112 Without partyallytie, indyrect dealinge or prejudice to anie partie. **1648** NETHERSOLE *Problems* I. 5 Whether Neutrality or Partialitie be more agreeable to the duty of good subjects, in such a Warre. **1739** CIBBER *Apol.* (1756) II. 2 We had our partialities, our prejudices, our favourites of less merit. **1878** R. W. DALE *Lect. Preach.* viii. 249 Rebekah's treatment of Jacob may bring home to parents the sin of partiality.

b. Excessive or especial preference for, or prepossession in favour of, a particular person or thing; hence, Favourable disposition, predilection, fondness, or affection for some one or something. Const. *to, for, towards.*

1581 G. PETTIE tr. *Guazzo's Civ. Conv.* III. (1586) 120 b, If he shall euer vnderstand this your partialitie, I doubt me ..that he will beshrew me for it. **1669** R. MONTAGUE in *Buccleuch MSS.* (Hist. MSS. Comm.) I. 425, I have no partiality in the world towards him. **1759** HUME *Hist. Eng.* (1812) V. xlii. 330 Another favourite who at this time received some marks of her partiality. **1833** HT. MARTINEAU *Loom & Lugger* II. iv. 66 Miss Storey had always more partiality for our people. **1871** H. AINSWORTH *Tower Hill* II.

x, Henry's partiality for St. John's Chapel had prevented it from being desecrated by the Vicar-General.

†**2.** Party-spirit, rivalry; factiousness. *Obs.*

1480 CAXTON *Chron. Eng.* III. (1520) 25 b/1 Hircanus after the decesse of his moder succeded in the kyngdom, in the which he had lytel prosperyte for parcyalte of the people. **1583** STOCKER *Civ. Warres Lowe C.* IV. 38 There was greate partialitie betweene the Citie of Groenyng, and the Countrey men, by reason of certain Rightes and Priuiledges. **1595** DANIEL *Civ. Wars* IV. v, His State being turbulent, Factious, and full of partialitie. **1752** HUME *Ess. & Treat.* (1777) I. 427 What domestic confusion, jealousy, partiality, revenge, heart-burnings, must tear those cities.

†**b.** A party, a faction. *Obs.*

a **1533** LD. BERNERS *Gold. Bk. M. Aurel.* (1546) B ij, There is greatte nombre of parcialities, Cinitiens, Catoniens, Peripaticiens, Academiens, and Epicuriens. **1578** T. N. tr. *Conq. W. India* 165 Mutezuma hath environed them about, because they were of the parciality of Tlaxcallan. **1623** tr. *Favine's Theat. Hon.* VII. xv. 287 The Inhabitants..were in former times past deuided into two Leagues and partialities.

II. †**3.** A political division, a province. *rare.*

[Cf. Du Cange, '*Parcialidad*, vox Hispanica, Patria, regio', with quot. of 1585 'nomina, cognomina, parentes, .. et regionem, vulgo Parcialidad, et oppidum.']

1601 R. JOHNSON *Kingd. & Commw.* (1603) 198 They [Japan Islands] are in number sixty sixe, diuided into three partialities.

III. 4. The quality of being partial as opposed to universal; relation to a part and not to the whole; partialness. *rare.*

1822–34 *Good's Study Med.* (ed. 4) III. 49 Without any attention to the universality or partiality of the disease.

partialize (ˈpɑːʃəlaɪz), *v.* [ad. F. *partialis-er* (Amyot 1559), f. *partial*: see PARTIAL and -IZE.]

†**1.** *intr.* To take a part or side; to favour one side unduly or unjustly. *Obs.*

1592 DANIEL *Delia*, etc. *Compl. Rosamond* K iij, Thus stood I ballanc'd equallie precize..Till world and pleasure made me partialize. **1656** S. H. *Gold. Law* 15 But yet fully to clear it, that I partialize not in my plea in behalf of his Highness.

2. *trans.* To render partial or one-sided; to bias; †to divide into parties (*obs.*).

1593 SHAKS. *Rich. II*, I. i. 120, I make a vow, Such neighbour-neerenesse to our sacred blood, Should nothing priuiledge him, nor partialize The vn-stooping firmenesse of my vpright soule. *a* **1618** SYLVESTER *Mirac. Peace* xxxvi, O how I hate these partializing words, Which show how wee are in the Faith devised. **1627–77** FELTHAM *Resolves* II. lxii. 289 His hate will partialize his Opinion. **1802–12** BENTHAM *Ration. Judic. Evid.* (1827) V. 642 The fact..may have influenced, perverted, and partialized, the perceptions presented by it.

†**3.** *intr.* ? To concern oneself with a part and not the whole. *Obs. rare.*

1594 *Zepheria* vi, My tears, my sighs all haue I summ'd in thee, Conceit the total, do not partialize.

4. *trans.* To make partial as opposed to universal.

1882 *Chicago Advance* 13 Apr., To confine, to partialize, is to destroy. **1889** *Tablet* 30 Nov. 856 Such a unification.. is only partialised knowledge.

partially (ˈpɑːʃəlɪ), *adv.* [f. PARTIAL + -LY[2].]

I. = F. *partialement.* **1. a.** In a partial or biased manner, with partiality; so as unduly to favour one side, or a particular person; unfairly, unjustly. Now *rare.*

1495 *Act 11 Hen. VII*, c. 24 *Preamble*, Officers..making panelles parcially for rewardes to theym geven. **1526** TINDALE *1 Tim.* v. 21 Do nothinge parcially [**1611** by partialitye]. **1576** *Reg. Privy Council Scot.* Ser. I. II. 516 Intending partiallie under cullour of justice to put thame to deith. **1593** SHAKS. *Lucr.* 634 Their own transgressions partially they smother. **1643** PRYNNE *Sov. Power Parl.* III. 124 Nor are Noble-mens crimes to be more partially censured, then ignoble ones. *a* **1716** SOUTH *Serm.* V. xii. 562 We act partially, in gratifying one Sect, who can pretend to no more Favour than what others may as justly claim. **1755** JOHNSON, *Partially*; with unjust favour or dislike [no quot.].

b. With special favour or affection. Now *rare.*

1633 T. STAFFORD *Pac. Hib.* II. vi. (1821) 283 All which for feare of their estates, were partially affected to the English. **1718** J. HUGHES in J. Duncombe *Lett.* (1773) I. 193 May you always persist in thinking so partially of me. **1800** MAR. EDGEWORTH *Will* iii, One of whom you lately appeared to think so partially.

II. = F. *partiellement* (14th c. in Hatz.-Darm.).

2. a. In a partial way or degree, as opposed to totally; to some extent; in part; incompletely, restrictedly; partly.

1460–70 *Bk. Quintessence* 24 Sikirly alle oþere maner of feueris pestilence..may be curid partialy wiþ oure 5. essence. **1579** G. HARVEY *Letter-bk.* (Camden) 59 They were hudlid and..bunglid upp in more haste then good speede partially at the urgent and importune request of a honest good-naturid and worshipfull yonge gentleman. **1646** SIR T. BROWNE *Pseud. Ep.* 112 Which was but partially true. **1794** U. PRICE *Ess. Picturesque* 21 Those obstacles themselves, either wholly or partially concealing the former ones. **1827** G. S. FABER *Sacr. Calend. Prophecy* (1844) II. 12 The two feet, branching out into ten toes, are partially of iron, and partially of clay. **1889** SWINBURNE *Stud. B. Jonson* 11 As to whether *The Case is Altered* may be wholly or partially or not at all assignable to the hand of Jonson.

b. *Comb.* (usually with pa. pples.) ***partially ordered*** (Math.), having a partial ordering (see PARTIAL *a.* (*sb.*) 3 b (*f*)).

1813 T. BUSBY *Lucretius* I. I. Comm. 17 A progressive, partially-potent, and finite being, like man. **1833** LYELL *Princ. Geol.* III. 311 Layers of partially-rolled and broken flints. **1895** *Educat. Rev.* Sept. 112 Science is..only partially-unified knowledge. **1941** BIRKHOFF & MACLANE *Survey Mod. Algebra* xi. 326 Partially ordered systems with a finite number of elements can be conveniently represented by diagrams. **1949** Partially-sighted [see *dark-ground* s.v. DARK *a.* 14 c]. **1971** *Optometry Today* (Amer. Optometric Assoc.) 15 Partially-sighted and legally-blind persons must first be located. **1974** HILTON & WU *Course in Mod. Algebra* 2 *Zorn's lemma.* Every inductive partially ordered set has a maximal element.

ˈ**partialness.** [f. PARTIAL *a.* + -NESS.] The quality of being partial as opposed to total or universal; incompleteness.

1701 NORRIS *Ideal World* I. ii. 23 He..did as truly view and contemplate it as I do now, only with an intireness instead of my partialness. **1898** H. C. KING in *Chicago Advance* 24 Mar. 388/1 The many-sidedness of truth, and the necessary partialness of one's own view.

†ˈ**partian.** *Obs. rare*[−1]. [f. L. *pars, part-em* PART (or f. *parti* PARTY) + -AN.] = next, A.

1624 BP. MOUNTAGU *Gagg* 41 He is not of that desert or esteeme to be ranked with the Fathers of the Primitive times: being..a Partian many wayes: for which cause I answere him not.

partiary (ˈpɑːʃ(ɪ)ərɪ), *sb.* and *a. rare.* [In form ad. L. *partiāri-us* adj., F. *partiaire*, that shares, or is shared, with another, sb. a sharer. But in sense A. 1, app. f. F. *parti* PARTY + -ARY.]

†**A.** *sb. Obs.* **1.** One who supports a particular side or party, esp. in a narrow or prejudiced way; a partisan.

1624 BP. MOUNTAGU *Gagg* Pref. 24 The Councels of Trent, of Florence, of Laterane, are not all Councels. We refuse them as factions, as bastards, as partiaries, as having nothing but the names of Councels. **1625** —— *App. Cæsar* 14 Not any man but Partiaries would have taken them spoken Dogmaticè.

2. (See quot.)

1656 BLOUNT *Glossogr.*, *Partiary* (*partiarius*), a partaker, a follower, a copartner: It may also be used adjectively for partial, or that hath respect to persons.

B. *adj.* That shares something with another; taking or having a share. In quot. 1654, ? Having only a portion or part of the office; that is so in part, partial.

1654 HAMMOND *Answ. Animadv. Ignat.* iii. §4. 74 The Epistles of Ignatius are the best records..on which to build this second Order of Secundarie, or Partiarie Presbyters. **1880** MUIRHEAD *Gaius* II. §254 He..is in the position of a partiary legatee, i.e. a legatee to whom a share of the estate is legated.

partibility (pɑːtɪˈbɪlɪtɪ). [f. next: see -ITY.] The quality of being partible; divisibility.

1644 DIGBY *Nat. Bodies* xi. §10. 97 Water when it is in a payle..hath the effect of grauity predominating in it; but if it be poured out, it hath the effect of partibility more. **1741** T. ROBINSON *Gavelkind* i. 4 The partibility of lands in other countries. **1869** *Pall Mall G.* 22 July 10 The substitution of partibility for primogeniture in cases of intestacy of real property would work very little alteration in the first instance at all events.

partible (ˈpɑːtɪb(ə)l), *a.* [ad. post-cl. L. *partibilis*, f. *partīrī* to part, divide: see -BLE.] Capable of being parted or separated; capable of being divided or distributed among a number; subject to partition; divisible; separable.

1540 *Act 32 Hen. VIII*, c. 29 Landes..by a custom.. partible betwen and amongest heyres males. **1586** FERNE *Blaz. Gentrie* 293 That their land should be partible, as in Gauelkind. **1626** BACON *Sylva* §502 It were best to make the Moulds partible, glued, or cemented together, that you may open them when you take out the Fruit. **1767** T. HUTCHINSON *Hist. Mass.* (1768) II. 66 The principal point in view was to make real estates partible among the children of an intestate. **1863** W. BEAMONT tr. *Domesday Bk., Cheshire* 13 For more than a century after this Survey,..a father's land was partible among all his children.

b. That involves partition of inheritance.

1653–4 WHITELOCKE *Jrnl. Swed. Emb.* (1772) I. 218 The like partible law takes place generally in Germany, Denmarke, and other..countryes, both for goods and lands. **1835** REEVE *De Tocqueville's Democr.* I. iii. 55 The law of partible inheritance.

particate (ˈpɑːtɪkət). *Sc. Obs.* exc. *Hist.* Also **pertícat.** [ad. med.L. *pertĭcāta* (also *particāta*), f. *pertica* a PERCH: cf. *bovate, carrucate.*] A Scotch rood (as a measure of land); one fourth of the Scotch acre, containing 40 square falls, rods, or raips, each of 36 sq. ells; or 13,690 sq. ft.

(The Imperial rood contains 10,890 sq. ft.)

[**1597** SKENE *De Verb. Sign.*, Particata vel perticata terræ ..ane ruid of land.] **1673** in Macfarlane *Genealog. Collect.* (1900) II. 368 Four Several Tennements of Land with a Particat of Land and Kiln and house built thereon. **1793** *Statist. Acc. Scotl.* VIII. 526 *note*, Taxed with one penny of the kingdom of Scotland, upon the ground of his half particate. **1864** JEFFREY *Hist. Roxburgh.* IV. viii. 272 Each tenant is named in the charter [to the Burgh of Hawick], with the number of particates which he was possessed of.

b. *Comb.*, as **particate-man**, the holder of a particate of land.

1864 JEFFREY *Hist. Roxburgh.* IV. viii. 283 The bestial belonging to the particate man.

partice, obs. pl. of PARTY.

partician, -on, -oun, obs. forms of PARTITION.

participable (pəˈtɪsɪpəb(ə)l, pɑː-), *a.* [a. OF. *participable*, f. *participer* to PARTICIPATE: see -BLE.]

†**1.** Liable or entitled to participate or share. *Obs.*

a **1450** *Mankind* (Brandl 1898) 16 Þat ȝe may be partycypable of hys retribucyone.

2. Capable of being participated or shared.

1610 W. FOLKINGHAM *Art of Survey* I. vi. 11 Communicate Matter is that which is participable to the Plot together with other Places. *Ibid.* II. ii. 50 A mutuall propertie or duety participable to the Conterminants, as bancking, balking, dyking. **1701** NORRIS *Ideal World* I. iii. 246 According as the essence of God is..in this or that degree participable by things without. **1822** T. TAYLOR *Apuleius* 296 An union with that which is participable.

Hence **parˌticipaˈbility**, capability of being shared.

1701 NORRIS *Ideal World* I. v. 254 So far as it states the ideality of God upon his imitability or participability.

†**parˈticipal**, *a. Obs. rare.* In 5 pertycypall. [ad. L. *participālis* partaking, f. *particip-em* a partaker.] = next, A. 1.

1497 BP. ALCOCK *Mons Perfect.* C iij b, And also setteth hym amonge angels there to be pertycypall of the eternall beatytude.

participant (pəˈtɪsɪpənt, pɑː-), *a.* and *sb.* [ad. L. *participānt-em*, pr. pple. of *participāre*: see PARTICIPATE *v.* Cf. F. *participant* (13–14th c.).]

A. *adj.* **1. a.** Participating, partaking, sharing.

1549 *Compl. Scot.* 131 To reueil it til diuerse men to gar them be participant vitht vs. **1551** GARDINER *Explic., Presence* 54 In this Sacrament, we be made participaunt, of his Godhode. **1607** *Schol. Disc. agst. Antichr.* I. ii. 79 It maketh the Church participant with the popish superstition. **1687** EVELYN *Diary* 20 Mar., The Communion followed, at which I was participant. **1795** SOUTHEY *Joan of Arc* VII. 101 In the ills of that defeat Participant. **1865** CARLYLE *Fredk. Gt.* XII. vii. (1872) IV. 170 Of which..we propose to make the reader participant before going farther.

†**b.** Having a share in the knowledge *of*; cognisant, informed. *Obs.*

1527 W. KNIGHT in Ellis *Orig. Lett.* Ser. I. I. 280 The Kyngs Highnesse wolde that your Grace shulde be participant of that that occurreth or is..doone here. **1568** in H. Campbell *Love Lett. Mary Q. Scots* (1824) App. 54 In this sort, they were now made participant of the whole state of the cause, even as largely as the rest of Hir Majestie's Privy Counsel were.

†**c.** Sharing the nature of something. *Obs.*

1634 SIR T. HERBERT *Trav.* 12 [The penguin] is rather participant with the water then land.

†**2.** Giving out, imparting. *Obs.*

a **1595** SOUTHWELL *Hundred Medit.* (1873) 215 O my God, Who art infinitely more noble and more participant than any other creature.

B. *sb.* **1. a.** One who participates in anything; one who takes part in, possesses, or experiences something in common with others; a sharer, partaker, participator. Also *attrib.* and *Comb.*; **participant democracy** = *participatory democracy*; **participant observer**, a research worker (esp. in the social sciences) who, while apparently belonging to the group under observation, is gathering information about it for the study team; hence **participant observation, observing**, this method of research.

1562 *Reg. Privy Council Scot.* I. 216 Thai sal be reknyt as participantis with the saidis thevis. **1579** FULKE *Heskins's Parl.* 445 Christe instituted a communion of many participantes. **1679** J. GOODMAN *Penitent Pardoned* III. v (1713) 348 That none of the participants may go away without full measures of what is desirable to them. **1839** STONEHOUSE *Axholme* 74 He [Vermuyden] sold shares to several of his countrymen, who thus became Partners, or Participants, with him in this great undertaking, by which latter demonstration the holders of these lands have ever since been distinguished. **1891** *Leeds Merc.* 25 May 5/2 The chief participants in the recent massacre are now in custody. **1924** E. C. LINDEMAN *Social Discovery* II. viii. 191 For experimental purposes the coöperating observers have been called '*participant observers*'. The term implies, not that the observers are participating in the study but that they are participating in the activities of the group being observed. **1933** HADER & LINDEMAN *Dynamic Social Res.* x. 147 (*heading*) Participant observing as a technique for psycho-social research. *Ibid.* 148 *Participant Observation* is based on the theory that an interpretation of an event can only be approximately correct when it is a composite of two points of view, the *outside* and the *inside.* **1948** *Mind* LVII. 510 Anthropologists, psychologists and administrators will all offer their contributions, making use of social surveys, opinion polls, official statistics, time-budgets, interviews of various types, 'participant-observers', and new techniques of self-observation. **1971** G. K. ROBERTS *Dict. Polit. Analysis* 144 Ethical and practical problems are raised connected with the concealed 'dual role' of the participant observer. *Ibid.*, Several advantages are served by participant observation rather than external observation or interview techniques. **1971** *Sci. Amer.* Mar. 72 These 'alternative institutions' frequently emphasize values similar to those of a therapeutic community: group cohesion and commitment; ..and 'participant democracy', meaning involvement of the entire group in decision-making. **1976** *Word 1971* XXVII. 421 Classical anthropological techniques were used in our research: participant observation, interviews, sociological data surveys, questionnaires, and so on. **1977** *Jrnl. R. Soc. Arts* CXXV. 198/1 Some concern is also paid to academic ethics; and research involving, for example, joining a political or aberrant social group so that one can be a participant observer—the new academic name for *snoop*—or the manipulation of people as subjects for research purposes, may not get very far.

†**b.** With *poss. pron.* One who takes part with another; a partisan, adherent; a partner. *Obs.*

1562 *Reg. Privy Council Scot.* I. 222 He and his saidis sonnis and utheris thair participantis. **1650** HOLLINGWORTH *Exerc. Usurped Powers* 66 Abraham..rescued Lot..from Chederlaomer and his participants. **1675** G. R. tr. *Le Grand's Man without Passion* 145 All her Participants take share in her Grandeur.

†**c.** A sharer of information; one to whom news is communicated. *Obs.*

1639 SIR T. STAFFORD in *Lismore Papers* Ser. II. (1888) IV. 37, I beseech you make me a participant of their safe accession to the Army.

†**d.** That which has something of the quality, or contains some amount, of something else. *Obs.*

1686 GOAD *Celest. Bodies* II. iv. 201 Fog being a Participant of both Dryth and Moisture.

†**2.** *Mus.* In the ecclesiastical modes: A particular note in each mode, constituting one of the 'Regular Modulations'; normally, in the authentic modes, either between the Final and Mediant or between the Mediant and Dominant, and in the plagal modes the lowest note of the scale. *Obs.*

1889 W. S. ROCKSTRO in Grove *Dict. Mus.* IV. 592 [A close] may terminate upon the Dominant, or Participant of the Mode.

Hence **par'ticipance, par'ticipancy**, the fact or quality of participating.

1869 MRS. WHITNEY *Hitherto* xiv. 191 An Infinite Participance and Sympathy. **1883** *Longm. Mag.* July 263 That sense of long participancy which is one of the pleasures of age.

participate (pə'tɪsɪpət), *ppl. a.* (*sb.*) Now *rare* or *Obs.* [ad. L. *participāt-us* made to share, pa. pple. of *participāre*: see next.]

†**1.** Made to share; = prec. A. 1. *Obs.*

a **1450** *Mankind* (Brandl 1898) 181 Oneto hys blysse ye be all predestynatt. Euery man for hys degre, I trust, xall be partycypatt. **1657** HAWKE *Killing is M.* 20 To be participate of the fraude of the Fox as well as the force of the Lion.

2. as *pa. pple.* = PARTICIPATED.

†**a.** Communicated. *Obs.*

1567 in Robertson *Hist. Scot.* (1759) II. App. 37, I have participat the contents thereof to such as I thought meet.

b. Shared, participated.

1850 MRS. JAMESON *Leg. Monast. Ord.* (1863) 399 Well has he been named Il Beato and Angelico whose life was participate with angels even in this world!

†**B.** *sb.* One made to participate; a participant: = prec. B. 1 b. *Obs.*

1648 in H. Cary *Mem. Gt. Civ. War* (1832) II. 19 The committee of estates, which I supposed did consist of the earl of Lanerick and his participates.

participate (pə'tɪsɪpeɪt, pɑː-), *v.* [f. L. *participāt-*, ppl. stem of *participāre*, f. *particeps*, *particip-em* partaking, a partaker, f. *parti-* PART + *-cip-*, weak form of *cap-*, stem of *capĕre* to take. As with many other vbs. in *-ate*, the L. pa. pple. in *-ātus* was adapted as *-at*, *-ate*, before any other part of the vb.: see prec. and -ATE³.]

I. *trans.* **1.** To take or have a part or share of or in; to possess or enjoy in common *with* others; to share: = PARTAKE 1.

1531 ELYOT *Gov.* III. xxiv, The one [the soul] we participate with goddes, the other [the body] with bestes. *c* **1611** CHAPMAN *Iliad* IX. 579 Since half my honour and my realm thou mayst participate. **1756** WASHINGTON *Lett.* Writ. 1889 I. 249, I see their situation, know their danger, and participate their sufferings. **1807** ROBINSON *Archæol. Græca* III. viii. 233 Dione..is said to have participated with Jupiter the incense burnt at the temple of Dodona. **1847** R. W. HAMILTON *Disq. Sabbath* iv. (1848) 118 This 'general assembly' is not called to behold or to participate combat.

†**2.** To give (a thing) to be shared; to share (a thing) *with* others; to give a share or portion of (it) *to* or *unto* another; hence, to communicate, impart; to impart (information), make known; = PARTAKE 2. *Obs.*

c **1540** tr. *Pol. Verg. Eng. Hist.* (Camden No. 36) I. 92 [He] didde participate his whole councell with her. **1588** KYD *Househ. Phil.* Wks. (1901) 245 A friende and neighbor ..who often time participates the profit of his sports with my Son. *Ibid.* 251 A matter which my Father..participated vnto me a fewe yeeres before his death. *a* **1677** HALE *Prim. Orig. Man.* IV. iv. 323 God Almighty must be called in to distribute and participate the portions of this Mental Nature. **1707** FREIND *Peterborow's Cond. Sp.* 203, I have resolved..to write and participate to you this Opportunity.

†**b.** To impart, give. *Obs.*

1597 A. M. tr. *Guillemeau's Fr. Chirurg.* b iv b/1 The Ingravere hath participated some propre and perpolite fashone to the handle.

†**3.** To make (a person) partaker. *Obs.* (Cf. PARTAKE 3.)

1597 BEARD *Theatre God's Judgem.* (1612) 376 He used.. to maintaine heards of whores, with whom he participated his friends and servants.

II. *intr.* **4.** To take part; to have a part or share; to share: = PARTAKE 4 (but not now said of sharing in material things). Const. *with* a person, *in* (†*of*, †*with*) a thing.

1565 *Reg. Privy Council Scot.* I. 362 To draw in strangearis..to participat with thame in thair attemptattis. **1577** HARRISON *England* II. xxii. (1877) I. 339 Our red and fallow deere will not let to participat thereof [mast] with our hogs. **1699** LUTTRELL *Brief Rel.* (1857) IV. 548 His aunt, who participated of the same dose,..is like to recover. **1777** ROBERTSON *Hist. Amer.* I. II. 97 Their eagerness to participate of the same favours, removed all their fears. **1809** SYD. SMITH *Serm.* I. 64 Fourteen or fifteen youths, who have long participated of your bounty. **1873** HOLLAND *Arth. Bonnic.* xii. 207 Millie and I talked of many things..and participated very little in the general conversation. **1876** MOZLEY *Univ. Serm.* v. (ed. 2) 106 One member of the human body has to bear the burden and participate in the grief of another.

†**b.** To share the nature, have some of the qualities or characteristics *of*, have a common character or something in common *with* (another thing or person): = PARTAKE 4 c. *Obs.*

1533 ELYOT *Cast. Helthe* (1541) 37 The sprynge tyme dothe participate the fyrste parte with wynter, the later parte with sommer. **1652–62** HEYLIN *Cosmogr.* III. (1682) 143 The people..in their persons, habit, and Religion, participate somewhat of the Arabians. **1670** CAPT. J. SMITH *Eng. Improv. Reviv'd* 32 All Earth simple or compound doth participate with the Clime wherein it lieth.

c. To have something (of a quality); †also (quot. 1594) to contain some (of a substance): = PARTAKE 4 d. Const. *of*, †*with*.

1578 BANISTER *Hist. Man* VIII. 103 This fift Muscle, participating with the propertie of euery action. **1589** *Pasquil's Ret.* B iv, Your abode in England hath made you participate with the nature of an Englishman. **1594** PLAT *Jewell-ho.* I. 10 Not any one thing in the worlde, which dooeth not participate of this salt. **1678** CUDWORTH *Intell. Syst.* I. iii. §33. 139 Such a force as participating of order, proceeds as it were methodically. **1751** JOHNSON *Rambler* No. 90 ¶14 Both members participate of harmony. **1824** L. MURRAY *Eng. Gram.* (ed. 5) I. 113 The participle..derives its name from its participating, not only of the properties of a verb, but also of those of an adjective.

Hence **par'ticipated** *ppl. a.*, **par'ticipating** *vbl. sb.* and *ppl. a.* (*spec.* profit-sharing), **par'ticipatingly** *adv.*

1561 in Strype *Ann. Ref.* (1709) I. I. xxiv. 244 A great part ..forbear coming to church, and participating of the Sacraments. **1614** JACKSON *Creed* III. xxix. §7 Any inherent or participated splendor. **1646** SIR T. BROWNE *Pseud. Ep.* 294 Absurdities of a middle and participating nature. **1704** NORRIS *Ideal World* II. xiii. 520 A certain participated similitude of the increated Light. **1762** R. GUY *Pract. Obs. Cancers* 15 Signs of their participating of the Disease. **1881** *19th Cent.* May 805 The great majority of participating houses combine the two systems. **1845** *Blackw. Mag.* LVII. 385 As if [Shakspere] had stood personally, confidentially, participatingly present in the heart of all human transactions. **1930** *Daily Express* 6 Nov. 14/3 The dividend on the Participating Preferred Ordinary shares is again made up to the maximum of 9 per cent. by the recommendation of a final dividend of 5½ per cent. **1952** *Prentice-Hall Encycl. Dict. Business* 458/1 Participating insurance is a plan of insurance under which the policyholder receives dividends from his insurance company. *Ibid.* 626/1 *Participating* preferred stock gives the stockholder the right to receive dividends beyond the fixed rate. *Ibid.* 626/2 A company with two kinds of preferred stock might have one class participating, and the other non-participating. **1957** CLARK & GOTTFRIED *Dict. Business & Finance* 268/2 Practically all mutual insurance company policies, and some stock insurance company policies, are participating policies. *Ibid.* 337/1 Typically the participating stock receives dividends at a fixed rate, after which the common stock receives the excess up to a given amount. **1959** L. E. DAVIDS *Dict. Insurance* 158 *Participating insurance*, insurance on which the policyholder is entitled to share in the surplus earnings of the company through dividends which reflect the difference between the premium charged and actual experience. **1964** *Lebende Sprachen* IX. 100/2 Participating bonds share in the profits of the insuring company in addition to receiving a fixed rate of interest. **1974** *Terminol. Managem. & Financial Accountancy* (Inst. Cost and Managem. Accountants) 61 *Participating preference shares*, shares which usually entitle the holder to a fixed dividend, and to participate in any surplus profits after payment of dividends at a specified rate on the ordinary share.

participation (pətɪsɪ'peɪʃən, pɑː-). [a. F. *participation* (13th c. in Littré), ad. L. *participātiōn-em*, n. of action from *participāre* to PARTICIPATE.] The action or fact of participating.

1. The action or fact of partaking, having or forming part *of*; †the partaking of the substance, quality, or nature *of* some thing or person (*obs.*).

c **1374** CHAUCER *Boeth.* III. pr. xi. 75 (Camb. MS.) But alle thing þat is good quod she grauntisthow þat it be good by the participacioun of good or no? *a* **1450** *Mankind* (Brandl 1898) 199 Of þe very wysdaum ȝe haue partycypacyone. **1490** CAXTON *Eneydos* iv. 20 Eneas..abode a longe tyme ynough lyke a corps..wythoute partycypacyon of sensityf moeuynge. **1555** EDEN *Decades* 320 The sea Mediterraneum so named bycause it is in the mydlande as is the Caspian sea withowt participacion of the great Ocean. **1561** T. NORTON *Calvin's Inst.* IV. xvii. (1634) 696 *marg.*, This Sacrament being instituted for the participation of Christ by faith. **1631** GOUGE *God's Arrowes* I. §67. 112 As for the other Sacrament, make conscience of a frequent participation thereof. *a* **1742** BENTLEY (J.), Convince them that brutes have the least participation of thought, and they retract. **1796** MORSE *Amer. Geog.* II. 324 They first conquered Glaris and Zug, and admitted them to an equal participation of their rights. **1866** J. G. MURPHY *Comm. Exod.* xii. 8 The eating of it is a figure of the participation of pardon, acceptance, and full blessedness.

2. a. The fact or condition of sharing in common (*with* others, or with each other); association as partners, partnership, fellowship; profit-sharing.

1432–50 tr. *Higden* (Rolls) III. 477 God wille me to haue communion and participacion with his creatures and werkes. **1570** DEE *Math. Pref.* 2 A straunge participation betwene thinges supernaturall and thynges naturall. **1596** SHAKS. *1 Hen. IV*, III. ii. 87 For thou hast lost thy Princely Priuiledge, With vile participation. **1604–5** BACON *Certif. Commiss. Union* Wks. 1879 I. 460 The communion and participation by commerce. **1709** STEELE *Tatler* No. 49 ¶6 Their Satisfactions are doubled, their Sorrows lessen'd by Participation. **1812** L. HUNT in *Examiner* 14 Sept. 578/1 Participations of empire have long been out of fashion. **1881** *19th Cent.* May 809 Sharing in whatever surplus profits are realised by the more efficient labour which participation calls forth.

b. A taking part, association, or sharing (with others) *in* some action or matter; *spec.* the active involvement of members of a community or organization in decisions which affect their lives and work. Cf. *audience participation* s.v. AUDIENCE 7 d.

1667 DIGBY *Elvira* I. in Hazl. *Dodsley* XV. 11 Of all this I have not only had knowledge, But great participation in your joys. **1789** JEFFERSON *Writ.* (1859) II. 567 It is probable the States General will obtain a participation in the legislation. **1858** BRIGHT *Sp., Reform* 27 Oct. (1876) 279 Many persons..are shut out from any participation in political power. **1875** GLADSTONE *Glean.* VI. li. 135 Will it increase..the active participation of the flock in the service? **1939** *Amer. Speech* XIV. 254 *Teacher placement,..pupil participation,..language usage* are a few typical examples of the monstrosities I refer to. **1944** H. P. FAIRCHILD *Dict. Sociol.* 213/2 *Participation*, entry into, identification with, as through communication or common activity, some defined social situation. **1948** A. L. KROEBER *Anthropol.* (rev. ed.) ix. 347 The second mechanism making for participation of the young in their culture, and their putting into society, is education. **1964** M. ARGYLE *Psychol. & Social Probl.* viii. 113 One way of allowing greater participation is through the use of democratic techniques of supervision. **1968** *Guardian* 13 July 9/2 General de Gaulle's social reform programme, summed up by the slogan 'Participation'. *Ibid.* 10 Sept. 8/5 Participation begins when employees at all levels feel that their own supervisors enlist their help to get what has to be done at their own level performed expeditiously. **1970** *Ibid.* 5 May 13/2 Students have shown no more enthusiasm for 'participation' than did French workers when General de Gaulle proposed it to them. **1974** *Listener* 28 Feb. 276/3 Publicity for proposals is easy, but..effective participation is much more difficult..there is a need to involve all sectors of the community in any debate on proposals. **1976** *Which?* May 110/3 So it's important to make sure that the major issues that you think affect your area do get discussed, and one of the purposes of the public participation legislation is that the public should be involved at the formative stage. **1977** *Times* 25 Feb. 1/7 The unions had an essential role in any system for developing participation.

c. A participating bond or share.

1931 *Economist* 5 Dec. 1057/1 In Germany, foreign exchange (by which is meant foreign notes, claims, bills of exchange, cheques and gold in any form, but not foreign bonds or shares or other industrial participations, except bonds acquired after July 12th) must, within three days after acquisition, be sold to the Reichsbank. **1968** *Globe & Mail* (Toronto) 13 Feb. B2/4 In addition to long-term bonds with call provisions, the new mortgage bank would sell participation certificates on the mortgage holdings in its secondary market operations portfolio.

d. participation mystique, imaginative identification with people and objects outside oneself, regarded as an attribute of primitive peoples by the French anthropologist Lucien Lévy-Bruhl (1857–1939); merging of the individual consciousness with that of a group or with the external world.

Discussed by Lévy-Bruhl in *Les fonctions mentales dans les sociétés inférieures* (1910) I. ii. 78, etc.

1927 A. HUXLEY *Proper Stud.* 77 A subjectivized world, with which the observer lives in a state of what Lévy-Bruhl calls '*participation mystique*', is unamenable to scientific treatment. **1933** DELL & BAYNES tr. *Jung's Mod. Man in Search of Soul* viii. 198 The secret of artistic creation and of the effectiveness of art is to be found in a return to the state of *participation mystique*—to that level of experience at which it is man who lives, and not the individual, and at which the weal or woe of the single human being does not count, but only human existence. **1949** D. MACARDLE *Children of Europe* I. i. 20 Powerful, also, is a deeper source of unrest—a *participation mystique*—the craving, much stronger in some races than in others, which makes individuals long to merge in the herd. **1956** F. HERBERT *Dragon in Sea* (1960) 36 *Religious services*, thought Ramsey. .. *Participation Mystique!* **1957** N. FRYE *Anat. Crit.* 295 College yells, sing-songs, and similar forms of *participation mystique*. **1966** J. B. PRIESTLEY *Moments* 228 In our early childhood..we exist in a state that a French anthropologist has called *participation mystique*. **1974** *Times* 23 May 10/5 As one who has never visited the Indian sub-continent, nothing I have read has..given me so much the sense of *participation mystique* in a civilisation..the antithesis of our own.

¶The alleged sense 'Distribution, division into shares' (Johnson), appears to arise from a misunderstanding of the passage cited; that of 'Community, fellowship' (Schmidt) to be merely a contextual use of sense 2.

participational (pɑːtɪsɪ'peɪʃənəl), *a.* [f. PARTICIPATION + -AL.] Involving or requiring participation.

1959 *Times* 18 June (Queen in Canada Suppl.) p. xv/4 Recreational pursuits turn to swimming, fishing and 'participational' outdoor life. **1964** M. MCLUHAN *Understanding Media* ix. 82 Electric technology seems to favor the inclusive and participational spoken word over the specialist written word. *Ibid.* xvii. 168 This participational and do-it-yourself aspect of the electric technology. **1970** *Americana Ann.* 687 The $30 million Ontario Science

Center opened in September in Toronto. The Center features hundreds of 'participational' exhibits that are operated by push buttons. **1971** *Guardian Weekly* 19 June 12 In spite of its premature closing, the participational section of the Morris exhibition was valuable because of the discussion and thought it provoked among artists and public alike.

participative (pə'tɪsɪpeɪtɪv, pɑː-), *a.* [f. med.L. type **participātīv-us* (f. *participāre*, *-āt-*: see -IVE): cf. F. *participativement*.] **a.** Having the quality of participating.

1651 [implied in PARTICIPATIVELY *adv.*]. **1818** TODD, *Participative*, capable of partaking. **1975** *Church Times* 22 Aug. 13/4 (Advt.), Many Clergy have benefited from our open consultations on running the local church... Ecumenical and participative methods of learning. *Ibid.* 3 Oct. 6/3 Those who are not so high-minded..might be dedicated to sabotage a new system as it staggered forward to achieve a new, different and participative venture.

b. In business administration: pertaining to or characterized by the sharing of the decision-making process with either (*a*) the lower grades of management, or (*b*) the workers.

1961 B. VON H. GILMER *Industrial Psychol.* v. xiv. 303 Gradually industrial organizations moved towards *participative management*, still leaving the worker in the position of having someone else plan for him... Participative management aimed higher, giving increased status to the people in middle management. **1965** R. C. SAMPSON *Mangaging the Managers* xii. 193 In participative coaching, a manager works with the executive, both in problem-solving and learning situations, in such a way that the subordinate retains the decision-making function and learns as the result of the experience. **1966** *New Statesman* 19 Aug. 255/3 There is growing interest in 'participative' and even democratic styles of management. **1972** *Jrnl. Social Psychol.* LXXXVII. 100 They [*sc.* Blake and Mouton] indicate that..participative leadership..can create conditions where work group standards are high. **1973** *Nature* 6 Apr. 381/1 The view that a boss-and-minion society can be replaced by something more cooperative and participative. **1976** *Birmingham Post* 16 Dec. 6/6 Another important feature of such improvements programmes is participative training to change attitudes, open minds and spread awareness and knowledge of control and improvement techniques. **1977** *Jrnl. R. Soc. Arts* CXXV. 671/2, I think we have now moved out of the participative area, in terms of management; I think Bullock is maybe ten years out of date.

Hence **partici'patively** *adv.*

1651 C. CARTWRIGHT *Cert. Relig.* I. 32 The word Catholick is taken in three severall sences, formally, casually, and participatively:..Participatively, because particular Churches agree, and participate in Doctrine and Communion with the Catholick.

participator (pə'tɪsɪpeɪtə(r), pɑː-). Also 8 **-er**. [a. late L. *participātor*, agent-n. from *participāre* to PARTICIPATE. (In earlier L. supplied by *particeps*, in F. by *participant*.)] One who participates; one who takes or has a part; a partaker, sharer.

1796 CHARLOTTE SMITH *Marchmont* I. 106 Leaning on the faithful participater of her grief. **1876** E. MELLOR *Priesth.* vi. 281 The sacrament will remain a witness and a warning, even if its participators should eat and drink unworthily. **1880** McCARTHY *Own Times* III. 141 Four persons were put on trial as participators in the attempt.

Hence **partici'patress**, a female participator.

1827 CARLYLE *Germ. Rom.* I. 97 Not in the selfish view of becoming participatress in a large fortune.

participatory (pə'tɪsɪpətərɪ), *a.* [f. L. *participātor* or stem *participāt-*: see -ORY.] Characterized by participation or profit-sharing. *spec.* in government, etc., involving members of the community in decisions; allowing members of the general public to take part, as ***participatory art***, ***broadcasting***, ***democracy***, ***radio***, ***television***, ***theatre***.

1881 *19th Cent.* May 803 A..survey of the ground already covered by participatory operations abroad. **1968** *N.Y. Times* 6 May 46 Both the Negroes and the antiwar groups have made use of the politics of marches, sit-ins and mass demonstrations. But those who practice this 'participatory democracy' can ultimately achieve their objectives only if they work through electoral processes and win control of Congress and the Presidency. **1968** *N.Y. Rev. Bks.* 11 July 31/2 Those who really are committed to 'participatory democracy' and hence insist on participating directly and fully in all forms of social life that can rightly command their allegiance, are separated by an ideological abyss from those traditional representatives of 'representative democracy'. **1968** *Guardian* 10 Oct. 2/5 The prevailing catechism.. requires all 'dialogue' to be 'meaningful' and democracy itself to be 'participatory'. **1970** *Time* 23 Feb. 68 These ventures in dramatic exploration are also intimately related to an attempt to bridge the we-they gap in the actor-audience relationship—what is popularly called 'participatory' theater. **1970** *Sat. Rev.* (U.S.) 30 May 9/2 The most dramatic action of the early New Left was the journey hundreds of young people took in the summer of 1963 to live and work in Mississippi, helping Negroes organize themselves... The main slogan of that movement ..was 'participatory democracy'. **1972** *Listener* 17 Aug. 197/3 Participatory broadcasting could be seen as a threat to the impartial provision of facts on the air. **1972** *Guardian* 2 Sept. 10/3 The best of BBC participatory local radio. *Ibid.* 6 Nov. 10/6 The BBC is to start 'participatory' television... A trial run of 50 weekly programmes, each devised by community or pressure groups on their own terms. **1977** *Times* 10 Aug. 14/7 That most trendy of activities, participatory art.

†**par'ticipe**, *v.* *Obs. rare.* [a. F. *participe-r* (14th c.), or ad. L. *participāre* to PARTICIPATE.] *intr.* To participate.

1508 *Kalender of Sheph.* T j, Prayers..and orysons in whiche yu mayste rendre partycypynge thy frendes and kynnesmen. *c* **1510** *Ibid.* xlii. L viij, He is called the lytel worlde, for he partycypeth of all, or he is called all creatures, for..he partycipeth and hath condycion of all creatures.

participial (pɑːtɪ'sɪpɪəl), *a.* and *sb.* *Gram.* [ad. L. *participiāl-is*, f. *participi-um* PARTICIPLE. Cf. mod.F. *participial*.]

A. *adj.* Of the nature of a participle; of, pertaining to, or involving a participle. ***participial adjective***, an adjective that is a participle in origin and form.

1591 PERCIVALL *Sp. Dict.* D iv b, You shall sometime finde a participiall voice of the present tense, as *Amante*..but they are rather nounes adiectiues then participles. **1612** BRINSLEY *Pos. Parts* (1669) 83 Do all Nouns Participials require a Genitive Case? **1755** JOHNSON *Dict.* Pref. ¶36 A *thinking* man, a man of prudence; a *pacing* horse, a horse that can pace; these I have ventured to call *participial adjectives*. **1882** FARRAR *Early Chr.* I. 213 *note*, In the participial constructions of this chapter..the sentences sometimes have an unfinished look.

B. *sb.* A verbal derivative of the nature of, or akin to, a participle.

1570 LEVINS *Manip.* 89 *Mete* is also the signe of some uerbals in *bilis*, and of participials in *dus*, as, Mete to be loued. **1590** STOCKWOOD *Rules Construct.* 47 A participial.. is taken for an adiectiue like a participle, but yet in deede no participle, bicause he doth not signifie time. **1696** PHILLIPS (ed. 5), *Participial*..an Adjective derived from a Verb, though not an absolute Participle. *a* **1861** GIBBS (Ogilvie), The new philology embraces the participle, the infinitive, the gerund, and the supine, all under the general name of participials.

Hence **participi'ality**, participial character; in quots. (*nonce-use*) addiction to the use of participles; **parti'cipialize** *v. trans.*, to make participial, turn into a participle; **parti'cipially** *adv.*, in a participial manner, as a participle.

1632 SHERWOOD, Participially, *Participialement*. **1730-6** BAILEY (folio), Participially. **1786-1805** H. TOOKE *Purley* II. iii. (1829) 93 Their most usual method of speech was to employ the past tense itself without *participializing* it, or making a participle of it by the addition of *ed*, or *en*. **1885** GILDERSLEEVE *Pindar's Odes* Ol. ix. 111 A good specimen of Pindar's terse participiality. **1888** —— in *Amer. Jrnl. Philol.* IX. 144 A well participialized or eumetochic sentence. **1902** *Ibid.* XXIII. 259 Nothing could be more exotic than Caxton's participialities. His Eneydos (1490) begins thus: 'After dyverse werkes made, translated and achieved, having no werke in hande, I sitting in my studye' [etc.].

participle ('pɑːtɪsɪp(ə)l), *sb.* (*a.*) [a. OF. *participle* in Grammar (13th c. in Hatz.-Darm.), by-form of *participe*, ad. L. *participium* a sharing, partaking, in Grammar a participle.]

†**1.** A person, animal, or thing that partakes of the nature of two or more different classes. *Obs.*

1432-50 tr. *Higden* (Rolls) II. 167 The peple of the sowthe is meke and quiete, the peple of þe northe is more moveable and cruelle, the peple of the myddelle partes be in maner as a participulle [HIGDEN *participii vicem tenet*]. **1605** BACON *Adv. Learn.* II. v. §2 In all Diuersities of things there..bee certaine Participles in Nature, which are almost ambiguous to which kinde they should bee referred. **1613** PURCHAS *Pilgrimage* (1614) 78 In the mountaines dwelt the Curdi, that were Participles or Mungrels in Religion, professing partly Christ, partly Mahumet. **1665** SIR T. HERBERT *Trav.* (1677) 385 Bats, flying fish and Seals be participles of nature and species of a doubtful kind, participating both of Bird and Beast. **1694** R. BURTHOGGE *Reason* 248 Extreams are Knit and United by Participles that partake of Both.

2. *Gram.* A word that partakes of the nature of a verb and an adjective (or 'noun adjective'); a derivative of a verb which has the function and construction of an adjective (qualifying a noun), while retaining some of those of the verb (*e.g.* tense, government of an object); a verbal adjective. Formerly often reckoned a separate part of speech.

1388 WYCLIF *Prol.* 57 A participle of a present tens, either preterit, of actif vois, eithir passif, mai be resoluid into a verbe of the same tens, and a coniunccioun copulatif. **1530** PALSGR. 65 In the frenche tong be ix partes of speche, article, ..verbe, participle, adverbe [etc.]. **1590** STOCKWOOD *Rules Construct.* 16 There are three kinds of adiectiues, a noune adiectiue, a pronoune adiectiue, and a participle adiectiue. **1681** FLAVEL *Meth. Grace* i. 12 *To whom coming as unto a living stone*: the participle notes a continued motion. **1751** HARRIS *Hermes* I. x. (1786) 184 If we take away the assertion, and thus destroy the Verb, there will remain the Attribute and the Time, which make the Essence of a Participle. **1866** MASON *Eng. Gram.* (ed. 2) 38 Participles are verbal adjectives, differing from ordinary adjectives in this, that the active participle can take a substantive after it as its object.

†**B.** *adj.* Participating in the nature of two things or classes; belonging partly to one and partly to another. *Obs. rare*$^{-1}$.

1694 R. BURTHOGGE *Reason* 141 By the Gradation of Shades, or Participle intermediate Colours.

†**participled** ('pɑːtɪsɪp(ə)ld), *a.* *Obs.* [f. PARTICIPLE *sb.* 2 + -ED^2.] Euphemism for 'damned' or 'confounded'.

1887 *Sat. Rev.* 17 Dec. 815 Thucydides.., by the way, was a participled Tory, like Clarendon, Gibbon, Tacitus, and all the greatest historians.

par'tickler, *sb.* and *a.* (*adv.*) Also **partiklar**, **partic'lar**. ¶ With distortion of spelling to indicate an uneducated pronunciation of PARTICULAR *a.* and *sb.* (*adv.*)

1833 DICKENS *Let.* ? Jan. (1965) I. 14, I am so anxious to hear the *particklers*. **1837** —— *Pickw.* xv. 147 He wants you partickler; and no one else'll do. *Ibid.* xliv. 482 Vich is your partickler wanity? **1871** *Harper's Mag.* Oct. 690 Ef Pat Role, or any other consarned Irishman, kicks up a muss 'bout these yer diggins, he'll kotch *par*tic'lar lightnin'. *c* **1875** 'BRENDA' *Froggy's Little Brother* (new ed.) ii. 22, I feels quite well, sir..and I wants to go home partiklar. **1901** M. FRANKLIN *My Brilliant Career* xvii. 150 The boss is so dashed partickler too.

particle ('pɑːtɪk(ə)l), *sb.* Also 4 **-ycle**, 4-6 **perticle**, 5 **-ykyll**, 6 **-ikcle**. [ad. L. *particula*, dim. of *pars*, *part-em* PART: cf. PARTICULE.]

1. a. A small part, portion, or division of a whole. Now *rare* or *Obs.*, or merged in 2.

1380 *Lay Folks Catech.* (Lamb. MS.) 243 Eche on of þese thre partyes contenys many partyclys. *c* **1400** *Lanfranc's Cirurg.* 192 Also blood leting is good þerfore, if oþere particlis acordiþ þerfore. **1567** *Earl Mar's Househ. Bk.* in Chalmers *Mary* (1818) I. 178 Ane particle of beif. **1613** PURCHAS *Pilgrimage* (1614) 66 Persians..accounted the Sunne the greatest God, and worshipped the Fire as a particle thereof. **1664** POWER *Exp. Philos.* I. 7 (*Horse Fly*) You shall most fairly see..a pulsing particle (which certainly is the heart). **1745** tr. *Columella's Husb.* XI. ii, One particle or degree of the Ecliptic. **1836** EMERSON *Nature* i, I am part or particle of God. **1881** 'MARK TWAIN' *Prince & Pauper* xxxi. 374 Now began a movement of the gorgeous particles of that official group.

b. A very small part of any proposition, statement, writing, or composition; a clause; an article of a formula.

1526 *Pilgr. Perf.* (W. de W. 1531) 199 The thyrde particle of this first article of our fayth, is *Creatorem celi et terre*. **1563** *Ressoning Crosraguell & Knox* E iij b, Of the formar pertikcle I mark twa heidis in speciall. **1634** SIR T. HERBERT *Trav.* 156 Just when they are praying that particle. **1789** T. TAYLOR *Proclus' Comm.* II. 102 Those who enunciated this proposition, and at the same time omitted the particle, *having one side produced*.

c. A small piece or plot of ground. *local.*

[**1540**: see PARTICULE I.] **1839** WILSON *Tales Borders* V. 330/2 Confiscation o' a' gudes, gear, chattels, particles, and pendicles. **1890** A. W. MOORE *Surnames Isle Man* 318 Small portions of land which, though not intacks, were, for some unknown reason, not included in the designation of *Quartirland*, are called *Particles*..they are now on the same footing as the Quartirlands.

2. a. A very minute portion or quantity of matter; the smallest sensible, component part of an aggregation or mass; formerly often = atom or molecule; in *Dynamics*, a minute mass of matter which while still having inertia and attraction is treated as a point, i.e. as having no magnitude. In *Physics* now applied esp. to the constituents of atoms and to other sub-atomic entities (some of which are now regarded as likely to be composite in nature). Cf. *alpha particle* s.v. ALPHA 3 e, *elementary particle* s.v. ELEMENTARY *a.* 6.

1398 TREVISA *Barth. De P.R.* x. iii. (Bodl. MS.) lf. 101 b/1 An element is semple and leste perticle of a bodie þat is compowned [*orig.* Elementum est..simpla & minima corporis compositi particula]. *Ibid.* VIII. i. (1495) 295 Pertykyll. **1661** GLANVILL *Van. Dogm.* x. 88 The different effects, which fire and water have on us, which we call heat and cold, result from the so differing configuration and agitation of their Particles. **1664** POWER *Exp. Philos.* I. 57 Camphire (which spends it self by continually effluviating its own Component Particles). **1743** EMERSON *Fluxions* 263 To find the Motion of any Particle of the String as suppose of *X* the middle Point. **1756** C. LUCAS *Ess. Waters* I. 43 It is impossible..to comprehend the size or form of an elementary particle of water. **1800** tr. *Lagrange's Chem.* II. 271 The oxide of copper combines easily with the greater part of the colouring particles precipitated by acids. **1871** TYNDALL *Fragm. Sc.* (1879) I. xiii. 373 Every particle of matter attracts every other particle. **1878** ABNEY *Photogr.* (1881) 11 When we say particle we mean to convey the idea of the smallest visible quantity of matter. **1880** CLEMINSHAW *Wurtz' Atom. Th.* 39 The particle..is a collection of a definite number of molecules in a definite situation, occupying a space incomparably greater than that of the volume of the molecules. **1898** J. J. THOMSON *Discharge Electr. through Gases* 189 The other theory..regards the cathode rays as marking the course of a stream of negatively electrified particles. *a* **1901** BESANT *Five Years' Tryst*, etc. (1902) 117 Through the open windows..were borne black particles and a smell as of a bonfire. **1942** H. DINGLE *Sub-Atomic Physics* i. 12 We next assume that the atoms of all bodies are constructed from three kinds of particles—one positively electrified (the proton), one negatively electrified (the electron), and one unelectrified (the neutron). **1968** M. S. LIVINGSTON *Particle Physics* iv. 77 By this time [*sc.* 1947] the definition of elementary particles had expanded to include more than the components of atoms. It now included particles created in nuclear decay processes, such as pions and muons..; it also included antiparticles, although the positron was the only example which had been observed... The list of elementary particles jumped to over 30 within the next 8 years. **1969** *Times* 8 Jan. 12/2 This star ..would consist entirely of the nuclear particles called neutrons. **1970** P. H. A. SNEATH *Planets & Life* i. 24 Modern physics has demonstrated the existence of a large number of 'smaller' subatomic particles, some of them very short-lived, and it has recently been suggested that they are all composed of yet 'smaller' particles, called quarks.

b. A very small or the smallest conceivable portion or amount of something immaterial.

1620 T. GRANGER *Div. Logike* 32 Performed by and in all actions, and things, to the least particle. **1742** YOUNG *Nt. Th.* VII. 824 This Particle of Energy divine. **1794** PALEY *Evid.* (1825) II. 384 They had never entertained a particle of doubt. **1875** JOWETT *Plato* (ed. 2) I. 361 No one who has a particle of understanding.

c. *R.C. Ch.* The portion of the Host given to each lay communicant.

1727–41 CHAMBERS *Cycl.* s.v., Particles is also..used in the Latin church for the crums or little pieces of consecrated bread, called Μερίδες in the Greek church. **1847** CDL. WISEMAN *Unreal. Anglican Belief* Ess. 1853 II. 406 The word 'particle' being equally applied to the Host given in lay-communion, and to the smallest visible fragment. **1853** DALE tr. *Baldeschi's Ceremonial* 104 After which he receives the Sacred Particle.

3. *Gram.* **a.** A minor part of speech, esp. one that is short and indeclinable, a relation-word; also, a prefix or suffix having a distinct meaning, as *un-*, *-ly*, *-ness*.

1533 UDALL *Flowres* 107 Compowned with theym selfes, they sygnifye as moche as if they were compowned with this partycle *cumque*, as *quisquis*, i. *quicunque*. **1535** JOYE *Apol. Tindale* (Arb.) 38 There thys particle (*and*) expowneth what yt is to come to Crist. **1611** FLORIO, *In*, a Particle or Preposition locall and of priuation. **1668** WILKINS *Real Char.* IV. vi. 452 Their words are not declined by Terminations, but by Particles, which makes their Grammar much more easie than that of the Latin. **1711** STEELE *Spect.* No. 147 ⁋3 Emphasis..improperly..placed on some very insignificant Particle, as upon *if*, or *and*. **1762** KAMES *Elem. Crit.* xviii. (1833) 305 Conjunctions, prepositions, articles, and such like accessories, passing under the name of *particles*. **1845** STODDART *Gram.* in *Encycl. Metrop.* (1847) I. 65/1 These inferior Parts of speech have been called *particles*: and, as such, are sometimes distinguished from *words*, and sometimes treated only as a separate class of words. **1868** GLADSTONE *Juv. Mundi* ii. (1870) 54 To hold that it attains its initial vowel by junction with the particle *a* in its intensive or any other sense. **1924** O. JESPERSEN *Philos. Gram.* 87, I therefore propose to revert to the old terminology by which these four classes [*sc.* adverbs, prepositions, conjunctions, and interjections] are treated as one called 'particles'. **1933** O. JESPERSEN *Essent. Eng. Gram.* vii. 69 Some particles can be used in one capacity only, others may be used now as adverbs, now as prepositions, and now as conjunctions, others again in two of these capacities. **1935** H. STRAUMANN *Newspaper Headlines* 56 Particles, then, are all those words which cannot be looked upon as nominals, verbals, and neutrals. **1964** A. S. C. ROSS *Essent. Eng. Gram.* 18 English consists of *words* and *particles*. The main difference between these two things is that the class of words is very numerous and can be added to at will, whereas the class of particles is rather small and cannot be added to at will. **1965** *Eng. Stud.* XLVI. 439 By 'particles' he [*sc.* A. S. C. Ross] means, not only prepositions, articles, indefinite pronouns, etc., but also prefixes, suffixes and inflectional endings. **1977** M. COHEN *Sensible Words* i. 40 Particles..are the grammatical functions that serve what Arnaud called the reasoning and ordering operations of the mind.

b. The preposition-like word which forms part of a complex (phrasal) verb and which can be optionally separated from the verb in certain constructions. Also *attrib.*

1925 GRATTAN & GURREY *Our Living Lang.* xii. 80 When, therefore, such words [as in He has run *up* a bill] differ clearly from the ordinary adverb, it is advisable to give them a more precise label: Verbal Particles. **1957** N. CHOMSKY *Syntactic Struct.* vii. 76 Further investigation of the verb phrase shows that there is a general verb + complement.. construction that behaves very much like the verb + particle construction. **1964** KATZ & POSTAL *Integr. Theory Ling. Descr.* (1965) iii. 41 The particle inversion transformation.. inverts the particle of a certain set of complex verbs with their Noun Phrase objects. **1968** JACOBS & ROSENBAUM *Eng. Transformational Gram.* xiii. 102 Some sentences contain words known as *verb particles* in their verb phrases. *Ibid.* 103 When question sentences containing verb particles are generated, the particle *must* remain in its original position. *Ibid.* 104 The transformation responsible for introducing a particle segment into the structure is called the *particle segment transformation*, or more simply, the particle transformation. *Ibid.* 106 The particle movement transformation is normally optional. **1968** R. W. LANGACKER *Lang. & its Struct.* 118 The Particle Shift rule ..separates a verb and a particle by placing the particle after the following direct object noun phrase. **1974** MCARTHUR & ATKINS *Dict. Eng. Phrasal Verbs* 5 Phrasal verbs..are, usually, combinations of simple, mono-syllabic verbs (put, take, get etc.) and members of a set of particles (on, up, out etc.).

4. *attrib.* and *Comb.*, as ***particle-size***; ***particle-accelerating***, ***-like*** adjs.; **particle accelerator** = ACCELERATOR e; **particle physics**, the branch of physics concerned with the properties, relationships, and interactions of sub-atomic particles; so **particle physicist**. See also sense 3 b above.

1947 *Electronics* Dec. 82/1 An electrostatic particle-accelerating machine called a Van de Graaf generator. **1959** *Sunday Times* 5 Apr. 8/6 The particle-accelerating machines of the nuclear physicist. **1975** *Nature* 2 Oct. 360/2 Work has thrived on the use of pulsed sources, including particle-accelerating machines, for neutron diffraction experiments. **1946** *Physical Rev.* LXX. 91/1 (*heading*) Particle accelerators as mass analyzers. **1968** *Times* 21 Dec. 13/7 Bubble chambers..are used in conjunction with powerful particle accelerators—machines that produce beams of high energy particles—to study how subatomic particles interact. **1977** D. BAGLEY *Enemy* xvii. 145 Microbiology isn't like atomics; you don't need a particle accelerator costing a hundred million. **1959** G. TROUP *Masers* ii. 14 The 'wave-like' aspects of radiation have been stressed rather more than the 'particle-like' aspects. **1973** *Sci. Amer.* Oct. 104/2 Dirac called his hypothetical particlelike holes positrons. **1977** *Ibid.* Apr. 116/1 Allowance must be made for wavelike properties, such as interference, diffraction and polarization, and for particlelike properties, such as the momentum carried by a beam of light. **1969** *New Scientist* 24 Apr. 171/1 What the high-energy particle physicists are witnessing..is evidently a yet further spectrum of some kind. **1971** *Ibid.* 5 Aug. 334 Even particle physicists and molecular biologists would be hard put to point to new discoveries, insights and ideas rivalling those in the field of astronomy..since 1961. **1946** *Proc. Amer. Philos. Soc.* XC. 44/2 Some of the outstanding experimental problems in elementary particle physics—problems concerned with electrons and positrons, nuclear explosions, neutrino physics, and most of all with the meson. *Ibid.* 47/1 Elementary particle physics..will get sources of energetic particles and use these sources to study the transformations of the elementary particles. **1962** LIVINGSTON & BLEWETT *Particle Accelerators* p. v, Phenomena in nuclear physics and high-energy particle physics. **1969** *New Scientist* 24 Apr. 171/1 In 20th century particle physics there has been a continuous progression from the world of the atom,..through the MeV world of nuclear physics..to the present perplexing phenomena of the GeV world created by the big particle accelerators. **1946** *Nature* 21 Dec. 908/2 Particle-size in silts and sands. **1966** D. G. BRANDON *Mod. Techniques Metallogr.* v. 249 There is very little to be said about the quantitative analysis of particle-size or grain-size distributions.

Hence (*nonce-wds.*) †**'particle** *v. trans.*, to connect by a particle or conjunction; **'particled** *a.*, composed of particles, particulate.

1650 HOLLINGWORTH *Exerc. Usurped Powers* 48 If they be not the same persons, how come they to be thus particled together? **1883** C. MORRIS in *Nature* 14 June 148/2 An ether whose condensation yields particled matter.

particle board. [f. PARTICLE *sb.* 2 + BOARD *sb.* I.] (See quot. 1957.)

1957 *Brit. Commonwealth Forest Terminol.* II. 29 *Board, particle*, a board (sheet) constituted from fragments of wood (chips, shavings, sawdust, etc.) and/or other vegetable materials that have been partly or wholly comminuted and then consolidated by pressure, heat, etc., with or without binders and supplementary material. **1959** *Times Rev. Industry* Apr. 91/3 Particle board is a building board made by bonding woodflakes or shavings under heat and pressure with the aid of a resin adhesive. **1966** A. W. LEWIS *Gloss. Woodworking Terms* 55 Manufactured boards..include hardboard, chipboard or particle board, plywood, and laminboard. **1973** *Time* 25 June 29/1 (Advt.), We manufacture and distribute building materials, including plywood, particleboard, sidings, prefinished paneling, and adhesives. **1973** *Globe & Mail* (Toronto) 4 Aug. 8/4 In 1970 a lumber company owned by New Brunswick industrialist K. C. Irving obtained cutting rights in the area and was expected to put up a particle-board plant. **1977** *36 Home Handyman Projects* (Austral. Home Jrnl.) 6/1 Here we show how to make some great seating from particle board—it's simple to make, can look elegant or casual and..it's so comfortable.

'parti-colour, particolour, *a.* (*sb.*) Shortened from PARTI-COLOURED, esp. in reference to a dog's coat, marked in patches of two distinct colours. Cf. *rose-colour*, etc. Also as *sb.*, esp. a dog whose coat is coloured in this way.

1610 HEALEY *St. Aug. Citie of God* XII. xxv. 466 For he [Jacob] liking the particolours [i.e. sheep] cast white straked rods into the watring places. **1662** GLANVILL *Lux Orient.* ii. (1682) 15 The divine way of working is not parti-colour or humoursome. **1945** C. L. B. HUBBARD *Observer's Bk. Dogs* 113 Pekingese... Colour red, tricolour, parti-colour. **1961** C. H. D. TODD *Popular Whippet* vi. 90 Like most judges.. I dislike a 'butterfly nose', but it is permissible in a parti-colour. **1971** F. HAMILTON *World Encycl. Dogs* 200 Colors [of Tibetan terriers] are white, golden, cream, gray or smoke, black particolor and tricolor. *Ibid.* 262 In particolors [*sc.* cocker spaniels], the contrasting color must be ten per cent or more.

parti-colour, party-colour, *v. rare.* [Back-formation from next.] *trans.* To make particoloured, colour variously. So **'parti-,colouring** *vbl. sb.*

1610 W. FOLKINGHAM *Art of Survey* I. x. 28 Being.. intermedled by the plow with the soyle, it puffie-lights and party colours the same. **1649** JER. TAYLOR *Gt. Exemp.* III. Disc. xiv. 27 A bubble which himself hath made and the sun hath particoloured. **1880** BURTON *Reign Q. Anne* I. i. 38 In the feminine element there was relief in a party-colouring of rich costumes. **1971** F. MEYNELL *My Lives* xi. 168 A man.. can paint..or decorate a room or parti-colour a motor-car.

parti-coloured, party-, particoloured ('pɑːtɪ,kʌləd), *a.* Also 6 partye-, 6–7 partie-. [The first element appears to be *parti*, PARTY *a.*, which itself occurs from *c* 1380, in the sense 'particoloured', and in such phrases as 'party red and white': see PARTY *a.* 2. Of the three spellings current from late in the 16th c., Johnson admitted only *party-coloured*, which still remains the main form in dictionaries; but *parti-coloured* or *particoloured* is now more prevalent, at least in Great Britain.]

a. Partly of one colour and partly of another; variegated in colour, diversicoloured; esp., in reference to dogs, having a coat marked with two or more colours in distinct patches.

†α. ***partie-coloured*** (***partye-***). *Obs.*

1535 COVERDALE *Gen.* xxx. 35 The speckled and partye coloured goates, and all the spotted and partye coloured kyddes. **1577** B. GOOGE *Heresbach's Husb.* (1586) 139 The policie of Iacob..in procuring of partie coloured Lambes. **1630** *R. Johnson's Kingd. & Commw.* 143 A Guard of Swisse, attired in partie-coloured-Cloth. **1693** J. EDWARDS *Author. O. & N. Test.* 178 A rich partie-coloured vest.

β. ***party coloured, party-coloured.***

1593 T. WATSON *Teares Fancie* vi, Beames..That welnigh burnt loues party coloured wings. **1684** LUTTRELL *Brief Rel.* (1857) I. 296 The new serjeants..putt on their party coloured robes. **1712** ADDISON *Spect.* No. 265 ⁋5, I looked..on this little party-coloured Assembly, as upon a Bed of Tulips. **1805** WORDSW. *Waggoner* IV. 31 Party-coloured garments gay. **1858** HAWTHORNE *Fr. & It. Note-bks.* I. 80 A party-colored dress, striped with blue, red and yellow, white and black. **1875** LOWELL *Under Old Elm* IV. i, All party-coloured threads the weaver Time Sets in his web.

γ. ***parti-coloured.***

1590 GREENE *Orl. Fur.* (1599) 48 Iuno..mounted on her parti-coloured Coach. **1688** R. HOLME *Armoury* III. 127/2 A Barber is always known by his Cheque parti-coloured Apron. **1822** W. IRVING *Braceb. Hall* xxi. 183 Making garlands of parti-coloured rags. **1879** G. MEREDITH *Egoist* xxxi. (1889) 305 The Pope's parti-coloured body guard. **1893** E. B. HEATON in *Chicago Advance* 23 Nov., The slopes ..are parti-colored. **1879–81** V. SHAW *Illustr. Bk. Dog* xxvi. 185 Parti-coloured dogs [*sc.* Pomeranians] are much objected to. **1922** R. LEIGHTON *Compl. Bk. Dog* 285 All colours [of Pekingese] allowable, red, fawn, black, black and tan, sable, brindle, white and parti-coloured.

δ. ***particoloured.***

1598 DALLINGTON *Meth. Trav.* I iv b, A Gard of Swisse, attired in particoloured Cloth. **1600** J. PORY tr. *Leo's Africa* II. 72 This kinde of particoloured marble. **1706** ADDISON *Rosamond* I. vi, The particolour'd gay Alcove. **1839** BAILEY *Festus* xix. (1852) 274 Double and triple particoloured suns. **1852** R. S. SURTEES *Sponge's Sp. Tour* (1893) 373 Broad-backed particoloured jockeys.

b. *fig.* Varied, diversified, 'chequered'.

1622 S. WARD *Life of Faith in Death* (1627) 110 Their delights..particoloured and spotted with mixture of sorrow. *c* **1710** PRIOR *Own Monument* 12 In life party-colour'd, half pleasure, half care. **1803** *Edin. Rev.* II. 96 By their quaintness and party-coloured learning. **1885** R. L. & F. STEVENSON *Dynamiter* 184 He got to bed with these parti-coloured thoughts.

particular (pə'tɪkjʊlə(r)), *a.* and *sb.* (*adv.*) Forms: 4–7 partic(u)ler, (5 -ere), 5–6 par-, pertyculer, 6 partycular, 6–7 perticuler, (6 -ar, -ere), 6– particular, (6 *Sc.* -air, 6–7 -are). [a. OF. *particuler* (mod.F. -*ier*), ad. L. *particulār-is*, of or concerning a part, partial, particular, f. *particula* PARTICLE: see -AR[1]; in 16th c. conformed in spelling to the L.] **A.** *adj.*

I. † **1.** Belonging to, or affecting, a part, not the whole, of something; partial; not universal. *Obs.* (exc. as implied in 2).

1387 TREVISA *Higden* (Rolls) II. 325 þe þridde particuler flood [orig. *tertium diluvium particulare*] in Thessalia. **1542** BOORDE *Dyetary* xxxvi. (1870) 297 They the whiche haue the Palsye, vnyuersall or pertyculer, must beware of anger. **1625** BACON *Ess., Viciss. Things* (Arb.) 569 The Three yeares Drought, in the time of Elias, was but Particular, and left People Aliue. **1643** SIR T. BROWNE *Relig. Med.* I. §22 'Tis ridiculous to put off, or drowne, the generall Flood of Noah, in that particular inundation of Deucalion.

2. a. Pertaining or relating to a single definite thing or person, or set of things or persons, as distinguished from others; of or belonging to some one thing (etc.) and not to any other, or to some and not to all; of one's (its, etc.) own; special; not general.

Often preceded by a *poss. pron.*, as 'its particular advantages' = the advantages which it, as distinct from other things, possesses; 'my particular sentiments' = sentiments which are my own, not those of some one else.

particular average: see also AVERAGE *sb.*[2] 4.

c **1386** CHAUCER *Frankl. T.* 394 As yonge clerkes..Seken ..Particuler sciences for to lerne. —— *Clerk's Prol.* 35 Or lawe or oother Art particuler. **1465** *Rolls of Parlt.* V. 535/2 To be perceyved..by the handes of the particuler Resceyvour of the Lordship of Heigham Feres for the tyme beyng. **1553** (*title*) The xiii. Bukes of Eneados..Translatet ..bi..Gawin Douglas..Euery Buke hauing hys perticular Prologe. **1559** in Strype *Ann. Ref.* (1709) I. II. App. viii. 423 The first byshopps of Rome were particular byshopps of a certein precinct. **1651** J. GOODWIN *Redempt. Red.* v, There are conscientious and learned men..who either deny universal or assert particular redemption. **1656** EARL MONM. tr. *Boccalini's Advts. fr. Parnass.* I. lv. (1674) 71 We ..prohibit..the writing particular Histories of any whatsoever City. **1677** MARVELL *Corr.* Wks. 1872–5 II. 554 This was..reported to the House, who..named a particular Committee to that purpose. **1709** STEELE *Tatler* No. 83 ⁋1 We live in an Age wherein Vice is very general, and Virtue very particular. **1773** *Encycl. Brit.* I. 506/1 The simple or particular average..consists in the extraordinary expences incurred for the ship alone, or for the merchandizes alone. **1780** BURKE *Let. to W. Watts* in *Athenæum* (1893) 27 May 672/1 These are not my particular Sentiments..they are the unanimous Sentiments of all who are distinguished in this Kingdom, for learning, integrity, and abilities. **1850** MCCOSH *Div. Govt.* (1852) 176 There have been disputes.. in all ages as to whether the providence of God is general or particular. Philosophers, so called, have generally taken the former view, and divines the latter. **1895** W. GOW *Marine Insurance* xii. 208 The repairs of damage of the nature of particular average are confined to what will put the vessel in the same state of efficiency as she was in before the accident which rendered these repairs necessary. **1960** DOVER & CALVER *Banker's Guide Marine Insurance of Goods* 287 If incurred as a consequence of a peril insured against, particular average is made good by underwriters subject to the conditions of the policy. **1974** L. E. DAVIDS *Dict. Insurance* (ed. 4) 203 *Particular average*, loss borne by one of a number of carriers in marine insurance, such as partial loss of cargo, hull, or freight, falling entirely on the interest concerned.

†**b.** Belonging only *to* (a specified person or thing): proper, peculiar, restricted (*to*). *Obs.*

1597 MORLEY *Introd. Mus.* 179 The light musicke particular to vs in England. *c* **1703** LORD GODOLPHIN in

Buccleuch MSS. (Hist. MSS. Comm.) I. 352 What the Queen has commanded..is not particular to that office, but general to all others. **1725** tr. *Dupin's Eccl. Hist. 17th C.* I. vi. ii. 228 His System upon Original Sin..was particular to him.

c. *Logic.* Applied to a proposition in which something is predicated of some, not all, of a class of things: opp. to *universal.*

1551 T. Wilson *Logike* (1580) 27 Whereby euery Proposition is knowne, either to be vniuersall or particular, affirmatiue, or negatiue. **1697** tr. *Burgersdicius his Logic* II. 27 *A*, denotes a Universal Affirming..*I*, a Particular Affirming. *Ibid.*, A Proposition Universal or Particular. **1843** Mill *Logic* I. iv. §4 (1846) 115 A particular proposition is that of which the subject is undistributed. **1860** Abp. Thomson *Laws Th.* §74 (ed. 5) 127 A judgment about part of a conception as 'Some lakes have an outlet' is a particular judgment.

d. ***Particular Baptists***: a body of Baptists holding the Calvinistic doctrines of ***particular election*** and ***particular redemption***, i.e. the Divine election and redemption of some, not all, of the human race. Opp. to *General Baptists.*

1717 [see baptist 3 b]. **1738** T. Crosby *Hist. Baptists* I. 173 Those that have followed the Calvinistical scheme of doctrines, and from the principal point therein, personal election, have been termed Particular Baptists. **1796** Morse *Amer. Geog.* I. 276 The leading principles of the regular or particular baptists. **1847** Particular redemption [see particularism 1]. **1876** Besant & Rice *Gold. Butterfly* (1877) 210 A face which..conveyed the impression of a Particular Baptist who was also in the oil trade.

†**3. a.** Belonging to, concerning, or known to an individual person or set of persons and no other; private, personal, not public. *Obs.*

1456 Sir G. Haye *Law Arms* (S.T.S.) 265 Bataill particulere is ay for hid caus that may nocht be kyd opynly. **1459** *Paston Lett.* I. 499 There be many and diverse particuler billes put inne, but noon redde. **1472** *MS. Reg. N. Cant. Cath. Libr.* lf. 236 Youre gramerscole in Canterbury ..send your commaundment that noon othir particler scole be kept nygh by. **1563** *Reg. Privy Council Scot.* I. 244 Personis without ony particular interest, and voyd of all passioun. **1565** *Ibid.* 414 Untrew and groundit upoun particular malice. **1605** Shaks. *Lear* v. i. 30 For these domesticke and particular broiles, Are not the question heere. **1662** J. Davies tr. *Mandelslo's Trav.* 3 They about the Court..procured me a particular audience. **1703** Moxon *Mech. Exerc.* 240 Houses, both Publick and Particular. **1768** Boswell *Corsica* ii. (ed. 2) 120 Their want of union; which made particular animosities take up their attention.

b. Of persons: Not occupying a public office or position; private. *Obs.*

1583 Stocker *Civ. Warres Lowe C.* iv. 4 b, All the rest of the Nobilitie, Knights, perticuler Gentlemen, and Subjects. **1663** Gerbier *Counsel* a viij, Not onely to particular but to Publique Builders. **1748** *Anson's Voy.* II. x. 238 Enriching the Jesuits and a few particular persons besides.

†**4.** ***particular numbers***, the individual components or factors of a number. *Obs. rare.*

1460 Capgrave *Chron.* (Rolls) 3 This noumbir eke of sex is prayed for his particuler noumberes, whech be on, too, thre.

5. ***particular estate*** (Law): see quot. 1876. So ***particular tenant***, the tenant of a particular estate.

1628 Coke *On Litt.* 251 b, A particular estate of any thing that lies in grant cannot be forfeited by any grant in fee by deed. **1642** *Perkin's Prof. Bk.* viii. §495. 217 Upon which particular estate the remainder is expectant. **1766** Blackstone *Comm.* II. xviii. 274 Alienations by particular tenants, when they are greater than the law entitles them to make, and devest the remainder or reversion, are also forfeitures to him whose right is attacked thereby. **1876** Digby *Real Prop.* v. §3 (1) 225 Where a tenant in fee simple has created an estate in tail, for life, or for years, he has left in him a present estate, which will come into possession or enjoyment on the expiration or sooner determination of the estate tail, the estate for life, or the estate for years. The smaller estate thus granted is called the 'particular' estate.

6. a. That is a unit or definite one among a number; taken or considered by itself, apart from the rest; individual, single, separate.

1529 More *Dyaloge* iv. Wks. (1557) 261/2 Who was there euer that laid vnto another all the perticulere euill dedes of any one other man. **1538** Starkey *England* I. ii. 64 Euery man particular and also the hole commynalty. **1601** Shaks. *All's Well* I. i. 97 That I should loue a bright particuler starre, And think to wed it. **1602** —— *Ham.* I. v. 19 Make.. each particular haire to stand an end. **1688** R. Holme *Armoury* III. 401/2, I shall set down each perticular Letter. **1763** J. Brown *Poetry & Mus.* xii. 207 Particular and well attested Facts are stubborn Things. **1868** Freeman *Norm. Conq.* II. vii. 125 This particular tax was a painful and hateful badge of national disgrace. **1893** Liddon, etc. *Life Pusey* I. xviii. 417 The Ancient Fathers..bring the thought of particular Churches into communion with the thought of the Universal Church, when outwardly united.

†**b.** Existing by itself apart from others; standing alone; actually separate or distinct; independent.

1547 Boorde *Brev. Health* Pref 3 b, Dylygentlye to consyder yf the syckenes..or impediment, be perticuler by hym selfe, or els that it haue any other infirmitie concurrant with it. **1585** T. Washington tr. *Nicholay's Voy.* I. vii. 6 Alger is as it were ordered as a particular common wealth. **1655** E. Terry *Voy. E. Ind.* 78 Thirty and seven several and large Provinces, which antiently were particular Kingdomes.

7. a. Distinguished in some way among others of the kind; more than ordinary; worth notice; marked; special.

1485 Caxton *Chas. Gt.* 195 Al creatures resonable owen to gyue synguler honour & pertyculer loue to hym that hath gyuen to them beyng. **1599** B. Jonson *Cynthia's Rev.* v. iii, Particular pains particular thanks do ask. **1622** Bacon *Hen. VII*, Wks. 1879 I. 785/1 Of this prince [Arthur]..there is little particular memory: only..that he was very studious and learned. **1797** *Monthly Mag.* III. 200 The politician takes up the paper..and tells his friend that it contains nothing *particular*, when he means that it has nothing important. **1838** Dickens *Nich. Nick.* xxxv, He was a sturdy old fellow..with no particular waist. **1861** M. Pattison *Ess.* (1889) I. 35 To tender particular thanks to Anne..for the felicitous suggestion.

†**b.** Remarkable, noteworthy; peculiar, singular.

1665 Bunyan *Holy Citie* 27 They were men of a particular and peculiar Spirit. **1713** A. Bayne in J. Duncombe *Lett.* (1773) I. 109 There is something very particular in my story. **1774** Goldsm. *Nat. Hist.* (1862) I. vii. viii. 544 The nylghau's manner of fighting is very particular. **1791** Boswell *Johnson* an. 1737, Johnson's mode of penmanship, which at all times was very particular.

†**c.** Peculiar so as to excite surprise or wonder; singular, strange, odd. *Obs.*

1712 Arbuthnot *John Bull* III. iii, Peg..loved anything that was particular..Jack was her man! for he neither thought, spoke, dressed, nor acted like other mortals. **1771** Wesley *Wks.* (1872) V. 322 Do we not many times dispense with religion and reason together, because we would not look particular? *c* **1817** Hogg *Tales & Sk.* V. 75 His gait was very particular: he walked as if he had been flat-soled.

d. In *Hymns*, used in the names of certain modifications of ordinary iambic metres, viz. ***common particular metre*** (8.8.6.8.8.6), ***long particular metre*** (8.8.8.8.8.8), ***short particular metre*** (6.6.8.6.6.8). Now chiefly *U.S.*

e. ***in a particular condition***, pregnant. (Cf. interesting *ppl. a.* 3.)

1922 Joyce *Ulysses* 411 All these little attentions would enable ladies who were in a particular condition to pass the intervening months in a most enjoyable manner.

8. Relating to or concerned with the separate parts, elements, or details of a whole; describing or setting forth something in detail; detailed, minute, circumstantial.

a. Of a narrative, account, etc.

1450 *Paston Lett.* I. 173 The avertisementes of you and my frendz that have more particuler knowlege yn such maters. *a* **1548** Hall *Chron., Hen. VIII* 223 A more playne and perticuler declaracion of the malicious & trayterous intentes of the sayd Elizabeth. **1669** Sturmy *Mariner's Mag.* II. i. 47 The particular Description of the several Instruments. **1786** Jefferson *Writ.* (1859) I. 536 It is as particular as the four-sheet maps from which it is taken. **1798** in *Times* 28 June 1/4 To be prepared..true and particular Lists, signed by them or their Agents, to be made out in the form prescribed. **1813** Jane Austen *Let.* 26 Oct. (1952) 359 Your Saturday's Letter..was quite as long & as particular as I could expect.

b. Of a person in giving a description or account.

1607 B. Jonson *Volpone* Ded., Where have I been particular? where personal? except to a mimic, cheater [etc.]? **1727** Swift *What passed in Lond.* Wks. 1755 III. I. 179, I think my self obliged to be very particular in this relation, lest my veracity should be suspected. **1803** Jane Porter *Thaddeus* i. (1831) 6, I am thus particular in the relation of every incident.

9. †**a.** Specially attentive to a person; bestowing marked attentions; familiar in manner or behaviour. *Obs.*

1610 B. Jonson *Alch.* iv. i, *Mam*... Sweet madame, le'me be particular— *Dol.* Particular, sir? I pray you, know your distance. **1694** Congreve *Double Dealer* III. vi, So unaffected, so easy, so free, so particular, so agreeable. **1749** Fielding *Tom Jones* xi. iv, Never suffer this Fellow to be particular with you again. **1771** Smollett *Humph. Cl.* 31 May, I must tell you, in confidence, he was a little particular; but perhaps I mistake his complaisance; and I wish I may, for his sake.

b. Closely acquainted, familiar, intimate. (Now associated or identified with 7.)

1706 Phillips, *Particular*,..intimate, familiar. *a* **1713** Ellwood *Autobiog.* (1714) 3, I became an early and particular Play-fellow to her Daughter Guli. **1779** Sheridan *Critic* II. ii, These are particular friends of mine. *a* **1817** Jane Austen *Lady Susan* xi. in *Mem.* (1871) 223 On terms of the most particular friendship. **1848** Dickens *Dombey* i, Paul, my dear, my very particular friend Miss Tox.

10. Attentive to details of action; specially careful; precise, exact, scrupulous; hence, exacting in regard to details, nice in taste, fastidious.

1814 Wellington 11 June in Gurw. *Desp.* (1838) XII. 50, I am very particular about the appointment of my chaplains. **1865** H. Kingsley *Hillyars & Burtons* xxviii, More particular over their rations than any corn-stalk cockatoo. **1879** Black *Macleod of D.* xviii, People who have to work for their living must not be too particular. **1932** *Punch* 2 Nov. 488/1 He was rather particular what he ate and drank. **1933** D. C. Peel *Life's Enchanted Cup* xiv. 176 Mothers who were 'particular' used to see to it that their girls went to dances with other girls well known to them.

11. ***particular integral*** (Math.): **a.** A solution of a differential equation obtained by assigning values to the arbitrary constants of the complete primitive of the equation. Also called ***particular solution.***

1814 P. Barlow *New Math. & Philos. Dict.*, *Particular Integral*, in the Integral Calculus, is that which arises in the integration of any differential equation, by giving a particular value to the arbitrary quantity or quantities that enter into the general integral. **1885** A. R. Forsyth *Treat. Differential Equations* iii. 49 The primitive then consists of two parts: First, the quantity η, which is called the Particular Integral and is any solution whatever (the simpler the better) of the original equation; Second, the quantity Y, which is called the Complementary Function. **1897** D. A. Murray *Introd. Course Differential Equations* i. 6 The solution which contains a number of arbitrary constants equal to the order of the equation, is called the general solution or the complete integral. Solutions obtained therefrom, by giving particular values to the constants, are called particular solutions. **1958** G. E. H. Reuter *Elem. Differential Equations & Operators* i. 5 General solution = particular solution plus complementary function. **1966** S. Ross *Introd. Ordinary Differential Equations* iv. 95 Consider the differential equation $\frac{d^2y}{dx^2} + y = x$... A particular integral is given by $y_p = x$.

†**b.** A solution of a differential equation which cannot be obtained by assigning values to any or all of the arbitrary constants of the complete primitive; now called *singular solution. Obs.*

1820 G. Peacock *Coll. Examples Appl. Differential & Integral Calculus* II. xi. 477 A particular integral of the original equation, involving only one arbitrary function. **1845** *Encycl. Metrop.* II. 23 This value of y satisfies the proposed equation; but as it cannot be derived from the complete integral we have obtained above by assuming a particular value for one of the arbitrary constants, it ought to be considered as a particular integral.

II. Absolute uses.

12. the particular. That which is particular (see the prec. senses); †the individual (*obs.*).

1551 T. Wilson *Logike* (1580) 73 This argument is from the particular, to the vniuersall. **1632** Sir T. Hawkins tr. *Mathieu's Unhappy Prosperitie* 259 It is the interest both of the particular, and publike, that the wicked perish, and the good prosper. **1635** R. Bolton *Comf. Affl. Consc.* vi. (ed. 2) 36 Thou mightest have been that, either for the kinde, or for the particular.

13. in particular. a. (Each) by itself, one by one, individually, separately, severally; in detail. ? *Obs.*

1502 *Ord. Crysten Men* (W. de W. 1506) I. vi. 49 For to declare what is to be seen of euery artycle in pertyculer. **1611** Bible *1 Cor.* xii. 27 Now ye are the body of Christ, and members in particular [*R.V.* severally members thereof]. **1737** [S. Berington] *G. di Lucca's Mem.* (1738) 18 Every Thing in General and Particular, we could think of.

b. As one of a number distinguished from the rest; in distinction from others; particularly, especially. †***in more particular*** (quot. 1628), more particularly (*obs.*).

1502 *Ord. Crysten Men* (W. de W. 1506) I. ii. 13 It apperteyneth in particular & in especyal unto the godfaders & godmoders. **1628** W. Sclater *Three Serm.* (1629) Ep. Ded., The other is, your vndeserued fauours towards my selfe in more particular. **1732** Wesley *Wks.* (1830) I. 163, I observing the tears run down the cheeks of one of them in particular. **1859** Mrs. Carlyle *Lett.* III. 16 Ready to swear at 'things in general', and some things in particular. **1879** J. Payn in *19th Cent.* Dec. 994 The Bar, with its high road leading indeed to the woolsack, but with a hundred by-ways leading nowhere in particular.

†**c.** Privately, in private. *Obs.*

1585 T. Washington tr. *Nicholay's Voy.* III. xxii. 112 b, They are waged either publikely, or of som in particular. **1702** *Eng. Theophrast.* 162 Preachers who offering us the kingdom of Heaven in publick, sollicit in particular a small benefice with the utmost importunity.

†**14. in the particular.** In the particular or special case; with regard to the individual instance: opp. to *in the general* (see general A. 11 d). *Obs.*

1639 Ld. Digby, etc. *Lett. conc. Relig.* (1651) 41, I doe not think him more in the wrong in the particular, then I beleeve him right in the generall. **1827** Fonblanque *Eng. under 7 Administr.* (1837) I. 44 Though Mr. Canning was often in the general the avowed enemy of oppression, we never in any one single instance found him so in the particular.

III. 15. *Comb.*

1767 S. Paterson *Another Trav.* I. 318 Rail at the believer, wrapt up in a particular-fashioned habit.

B. *sb.*

†**1.** A part, division, or section of a whole; a constituent part or element; *spec.* a division or 'head' of a discourse or argument; in quot. 1494, a part-payment or instalment. ? *Obs.*

1494 Fabyan *Chron.* VII. 320 For the which..he payed vnto the archebisshop iii. M. marke, and to the other, by partyculers xv. M. marke. **1601** R. Johnson *Kingd. & Commw.* (1603) 36 Let us devide the discourse..into foure particulars. **1630** *Ibid.* 496 The ancient Provinces were divided into three particulars. **1650** Weekes *Truth's Confl.* ii. 54 If you please to minde the first particular in the 11. Verse (*For*) which is a Rationative Particle. **1660** Mrq. Worcester *Water-Comm. Engine* 14 The Engine consisteth of the following Particulars. **1694** Salmon *Bate's Dispens.* (1713) 168/1 This done, put in the several Particulars into the Liquor. **1859** W. Anderson *Disc.* (1860) 17 In constructing the systematic argument, a 'particular', as it is called, will be bestowed on the Divine mercy.

2. a. A minute or subordinate part of a thing, statement, or whole of any kind, considered apart from the rest; a detail, item, point, circumstance.

1533–4 *Act 25 Hen. VIII*, c. 12 As by the particulers therof here after..shalbe expressed. **1555** Eden *Decades* 176 This particular of the mynes of gold, is a thing greatly to bee noted. **1596** Shaks. *1 Hen. IV*, II. iv. 414 Examine mee vpon the particulars of my Life. **1622** J. Borough in *Lett. Lit. Men* (Camden) 130 A private Library..to be sold, and [I] am promised a Catalogue of the particulars. **1683** Robinson in *Ray's Corr.* (1848) 137 The *Seseli pratense Monspeliens* agrees with our English Meadow Saxifrage in every particular. **1790** Paley *Horæ Paul.* Rom. i. 10 Turn..to the second epistle..and you will discover the particular which remains to be sought for. **1844** Ld. Brougham *A. Lunel* I.

iii. 67 Every particular of it remains deeply engraven on my memory.

b. *spec.* (*pl.*) Items or details of statement or information; information as to details; a detailed account. In the textile industry, Detailed specifications, subsequently given, as to the manner in which an inclusive or general order or contract is to be carried out.

1606 SHAKS. *Ant. & Cl.* I. ii. 57 But how, but how, giue me particulars. **1687** A. LOVELL tr. *Thevenot's Trav.* I. 74 A French man..told me all the particulars, and the order of it very exactly. **1716** *Lond. Gaz.* No. 5445/3 Particulars of the said Estate may be had. **1830** SYD. SMITH *Mem. & Lett.* (1855) II. 305, I have not heard the particulars of Jeffrey becoming Lord Advocate. **1891** *Daily News* 23 Oct. (Bradford), There is an absence of orders, but 'particulars' come to hand without delay and keep spinners fully employed. *a* **1901** BESANT *Five Years' Tryst*, etc. (1902) 197, I shall be prepared to give you further particulars as to the persons to whom this sum is due.

†**3.** A statement setting forth the several points or details of a thing or matter; a minute account, description, or enumeration; a minute. *Obs.*

1600 DYMMOK *Ireland* (1843) 26 A perticuler of such strengths and fastness of woode and bogge as are in every province of Irelande. **1630** *R. Johnson's Kingd. & Commw.* 521, I have seene a particular of his daily expences. **1693** *Mem. Cnt. Teckely* III. 82 A loose Sheet..in which they made a Particular of the Cruelties which had been practised against several Persons of Note. **1786** LD. NORTH *Let.* 6 Jan. (in *Davey's Catal.* (1895) 28), I send you the descriptive Particular of Cudworth corrected according to my last letter from the country and as I believe perfectly accurate.

†**4. a.** A single thing among a number, considered by itself; each one of a number or group of things; an individual thing or article. *Obs.*

1586 A. DAY *Eng. Secretary* II. (1625) 78 *Synecdoche*, when by one particular we vnderstand a number. **1660** SHARROCK *Vegetables* 3 The ways of increasing the particulars of each kinde. **1691** RAY *Creation* II. (1692) 57 That they [vertebres] should be all perforated in the middle ..and each particular have a hole on each side. **1743** *New Jersey Archives* XII. 190 The above Particulars were stolen by one Robert Fryar.

b. An individual person, an individual; sometimes *spec.* a private person, one not holding a public position. *Obs.*

1599 B. JONSON *Cynthia's Rev.* v. ii, And, for your spectators, you behold them what they are; the most choice particulars in court. **1656** EARL MONM. tr. *Boccalini's Advts. fr. Parnass.* II. vi. (1674) 142 [This] was publickly praised by all, and in private abhorr'd by every particular. **1741** WARBURTON *Div. Legat.* II. 30 Ahimelech is described without his guards..as a simple particular. **1766** *Museum Rusticum* VI. 75 In the case of a few particulars, who have public spirit, and private ability sufficient to lead them.

5. a. More vaguely: A particular case or instance; an individual thing in relation or contrast to the whole class. (Usually in *pl.*; opp. to *generals* or *universals*.)

c **1600** SHAKS. *Sonn.* xci, But these perticulers are not my measure, All these I better in one general best. **1651** HOBBES *Leviath.* I. vi. 29 Reasoning is in generall words; but Deliberation for the most part is of Particulars. **1722** WOLLASTON *Relig. Nat.* iii. 41 We reason about particulars, or from them; but not *by* them. **1773** MONBODDO *Language* (1774) I. I. i. 5 These conceptions are either of particulars, viz. individual things, or of generals. **1874** W. WALLACE *Hegel's Logic* Introd. §13. 18 When the universal is made a mere form and coordinated with the particular, as if it were on the same level, it sinks into a particular itself.

b. *Logic.* = *particular proposition* (see A. 2 c).

1551 T. WILSON *Logike* (1580) 24 b. **1553** EDEN *Treat. Newe Ind.* (Arb.) 9 *margin*, A perticuler proueth no vniuersall. **1697** tr. *Burgersdicius his Logic* II. 27 Now Indefinite Propositions are all here taken for Particulars.

†**6. a.** (One's) individual case; personal interest or concern; part. Chiefly in phr. *for, in, as to,* etc. (*one's*) *particular* = in (one's) own case, for (one's) own part, as far as (oneself) is concerned. *Obs.*

1580 *Reg. Privy Council Scot.* Ser. I. III. 324 Nawyis willing to impeid the publick peax for his particular. **1623** HEMING & CONDELL *Wks. Shaks.* Ep. Ded., Whilst we studie to be thankful in our particular, for the many fauors we haue receiued. **1657** W. RAND tr. *Gassendi's Life Peiresc* II. 281 This losse..concerns the whole Common-wealth, as much as mine own particular. **1724** WARBURTON *Tracts* (1789) 12 To return from the common Cause to what concerns our Particular. **1790** COWPER *Let. to Mrs. King* 31 Dec., We have all admired it..and for my own particular, I return you my sincerest thanks.

b. In stronger sense: Personal or private interest, profit, or advantage. *Obs.*

1597 HOOKER *Eccl. Pol.* v. Ded. §9 Such, as doth not propose to itself τὸ ἴδιον our own particular, the partial and immoderate desire whereof poisoneth wheresoever it taketh place. *c* **1610** SIR J. MELVIL *Mem.* (1735) 297 Some of the Lords whose Particulars he promised to set forward. **1653** in *Nicholas Papers* (Camden) II. 17 If the gentleman had kept all the allowance for his own particular, I should have doubted his affection.

c. Private matter or business. *Obs.*

c **1610** SIR J. MELVIL *Mem.* (1735) 66 My Companion told the Emperor, that I had a Particular with his Majesty. **1653** in *Nicholas Papers* (Camden) II. 22 Going to England in about a fortnight upon some particulars of his own.

d. Personal relation, close acquaintance, intimacy; personal interest, regard, or favour. *rare.*

1607 SHAKS. *Cor.* v. i. 3 He..Which was sometime his Generall: who loued him In a most deere particular. **1631** WEEVER *Anc. Fun. Mon.* 797 Out of his particular to their Towne, hee procured of Queene Elizabeth a Charter of Incorporation.

7. *colloq.* or *slang.* **a.** Something specially belonging to, or characteristic of, a place or person; one's special choice or favourite.

London particular: (*a*) a special quality of Madeira wine as imported for the London market (? *obs.*); (*b*) a humorous name for a London fog.

1807 W. IRVING *Salmag.* ii. *Acc. Friends*, I uncorked a bottle of London particular. **1852** DICKENS *Bleak Ho.* iii, This is a London particular... A fog, miss. **1901** *Scotsman* 6 Nov. 10/6 'The London particular', the fog which, four or five years ago, assumed the consistency of peasoup. **1902** FARMER *Slang*, *Particular*..a special choice: *e.g.* to 'ride one's own particular', 'a glass of one's particular', etc.

b. A special friend, a favourite.

1828 *Craven Gloss.* (ed. 2), *Particulars*, old particulars, very old friends. **1830** GEN. P. THOMPSON *Exerc.* (1842) I. 285 Except you and your particulars, who are living on the taxes. **1902** FARMER *Slang*, *Particular*, subs. (old), a favorite mistress: Fr. *une particulière*.

†**C.** *adv.* Particularly, individually. *Obs. rare.*

1600 NASHE *Summers last will* Wks. (Grosart) VI. 146 Innumerable monstrous practises,..Which t'were too long particuler to recite.

†**par'ticular,** *v. Obs. rare.* [f. prec.] *trans.* To mention particularly, to particularize.

1605 *Nottingham Rec.* IV. 274 Slanderinge all the Company, but being vrged, would not particuler any thinge. **1646** SIR T. BROWNE *Pseud. Ep.* 340 The Text, wherein is only particulared that it was the fruit of a tree good for food and pleasant unto the eye.

†**particu'larian,** *a. Obs. rare.* [f. L. *particulāri-s* + -AN.] Relating to particles of matter: = CORPUSCULAR 2.

1674 BOYLE *Excell. Theol.* II. iv. 169 Those..things, which are..alledged in the praise of the corpuscularian philosophy..established by the inventors and promoters of the Particularian hypothesis.

particularism (pəˈtɪkjʊlərɪz(ə)m). [a. F. *particularisme* (Bossuet, 17th c., in sense 1), or ad. mod.L. *particularismus*, Ger. *partikularismus*: see PARTICULAR and -ISM.]

1. *Theol.* The doctrine of particular election or particular redemption (see PARTICULAR A. 2 d); the dogma that Divine grace is provided for or offered to a selected part, not the whole, of the human race.

a **1828** MURDOCK cited in Webster. **1847** BUCH tr. *Hagenbach's Hist. Doctr.* II. 255 The Calvinists..adopted the notion of particular redemption (*Particularism*). **1969** J. E. DITTES in Lindzey & Aronson *Handbk. Social Psychol.* (ed. 2) V. 633 Religious ideology tends to promote a concept of social exclusiveness or 'particularism'..especially with notions of..special election as a member of a divinely chosen group.

2. Exclusive attachment or devotion to one's particular party, sect, nation, etc.; exclusiveness.

1824 COLERIDGE in *Lit. Rem.* (1838) III. 82 A jealous spirit of monopoly and particularism, counterfeiting catholicity by a negative totality. **1828** PUSEY *Hist. Enq.* I. 144 The sole object of the Epistle to the Romans was to oppose the particularism of the Jews. **1845** GEO. ELIOT in Cross *Life* (1885) I. 135 'Habits of thought' is not a translation of the word *particularismus*... If he decidedly objects to *particularism*, ask him to be so good as substitute *exclusiveness*. **1875** JOWETT *Plato* (ed. 2) IV. 36 An abstract principle..strong enough to override all the particularisms of mankind. **1955** *Bull. Atomic Sci.* Apr. 142/2 The humanitarian theme of the two preceding centuries certainly persisted, but universalism yielded step by step to national particularism which was in many respects naïve but which became increasingly noticeable among European scientists and scholars. **1964** *Welsh Hist. Rev.* II. 147 The break-down of local particularisms in general elections.. was resented in some quarters. **1973** *Daily Tel.* 4 May 18 He attacks the concept of youth particularism, stating that as a group youth has few common interests or problems. **1975** *New Left Rev.* Nov.–Dec. 1 The intrinsically uneven and combined development of capitalism and imperialism were bound to intensify..national particularism and antagonism.

3. *Politics.* The principle of leaving each state in an empire or federation free to retain its own government, laws and rights, and to promote its own interests, without reference to those of the whole; esp. in German politics after *c* 1850. Also *transf.*

1853 *Tait's Mag.* XX. 387 The other..protests against all centralization, seeks to confederate the estates, to establish universal independence, separation and extreme division of powers; which has lately been denominated *particularism* in Germany. **1869** *Daily News* 22 Apr., The faults and excesses of 'particularism'—weakness abroad, discord at home, and obstacles in the way of trade and traffic. **1891** *Spectator* 4 July, The majority returned at recent elections [in New South Wales] is believed to be opposed to Federation, and in favour of particularism. **1893** *Times* 15 May 9/5 The old particularism has again attained formidable proportions [in the German Empire]. **1912** *Q. Rev.* Jan. 212 A recognition of Albanian particularism would create a precedent of which all other nationalities would take advantage. **1965** *Mod. Law Rev.* XXVIII. v. 616 He may well be right in affirming that regional particularism..call[s] for a redrawing along provincial lines. **1976** M. A. JONES *Old World Ties Amer. Ethnic Groups* 13 Particularism..had for centuries kept the German states apart.

4. Exclusive attention to a particular subject; specialism.

1872 E. TUCKERMAN *Genera Lichenum* 1 The marked particularism which has characterized the study of Lichens for the last thirty years. **1936** *Nature* 25 Apr. 681/1 The advance of science is along two roads: the first is in the direction of greater intensity, particularism and of empiricism, and the second, from intensity, particularism and empiricism, towards extensity, generalisation and synthesis.

5. a. *Philos.* The fact or quality of being concerned with elements that have a particular (as opposed to universal) application, or to which no general standard is applicable.

1939 J. DEWEY in P. A. Schilpp *Philos. J. Dewey* 544 In philosophy there is also the need to find an alternative for that combination of atomistic particularism with respect to empirical material and Platonic *a priori* realism with respect to universals. **1943** *Mind* LII. 140 Almost every philosophical term which connotes a tendency to particularism may be predicated of the Berkeley of this early period. **1963** R. M. HARE *Freedom & Reason* ii. 19 Such a philosopher could indeed embrace..the extremest form of particularism.

b. *Sociol.* and *Econ.* In some analyses of social and economic organization, a name that characterizes the particular or fixed nature of a role or element, as contrasted with the universal, general, or mobile nature of other elements or roles.

1949 T. PARSONS *Ess. Sociol. Theory* viii. 197 In all these cases though in different ways and degrees, particularism tends to replace universalism. **1951** PARSONS & SHILS *Toward Gen. Theory of Action* II. i. 98 The pattern variables most relevant to the description of the normative patterns governing roles..are achievement-ascription and universalism-particularism. **1959** B. F. HOSELITZ *Sociol. Aspects Econ. Growth* (1960) ii. 32 We must not expect the principle of particularism in assigning economic roles to appear in complete purity in all societies on a low level of economic advancement. **1964** T. PARSONS *Ess. Sociol. Theory* (rev. ed.) 16 On the level of the research techniques he [*sc.* Weber] used, the broad contrasts, e.g. as between Chinese traditionalistic particularism and Western universalistic 'rationalism', were unmistakable. **1969** I. DEUTSCHER *Marxism in our Time* (1971) 190 The growth of bureaucracy was further stimulated by the breaking down of feudal particularism and the formation of a market on a national scale.

particularist (pəˈtɪkjʊlərɪst), *sb.* (*a.*) [f. as prec. + -IST. Cf. F. *particulariste* (1701 in Furetière).] **A.** *sb.* An advocate or adherent of particularism (in any sense: see prec.).

1727–41 CHAMBERS *Cycl.*, *Particularist*, among polemical divines, a person who holds for particular grace, i.e. teaches, or believes that Christ died for the elect only. **1842** BRANDE *Dict. Sci.* etc., *Particularists*... As a party name, it seems to date from the Synod of Dort. **1870** *Daily News* 27 Sept., They are known as 'Particularists', that is men who would maintain unaltered the..petty governments which still hinder Germany from..displaying the strength of a united country. **1872** *Spectator* 7 Sept. 1128 We do not..believe.. that the unity of Germany..has anything serious to fear from the particularists of Bavaria. **1889** *Ibid.* 5 Oct., The desire of the scientific particularist. **1935** *Jrnl. Gen. Psychol.* XII. 55 For the same reason we cannot accept the definition proposed by the extreme particularist. **1939** E. MUIR *Present Age* 160 But he remained an inveterate particularist; his philosophy is not an organic whole, but is made up of a number of peculiar ideas. **1963** R. M. HARE *Freedom & Reason* ii. 18 A particularist (if I may use that name for the opposite of a universalist). *Ibid.* 20 It is quite impossible for a naturalist to be, consistently, any sort of particularist.

B. *adj.* = next.

1876 *N. Amer. Rev.* CXXIII. 338 During the administration of Washington the particularist tendencies were mostly quiet. **1888** G. W. SMALLEY *Lond. Lett.* I. 5 The German analogue for parochial is Particularist. **1968** D. M. MURPHY tr. *Gelin's Concept of Man in Bible* iv. 63 In the Bible there is a universalist outlook and a particularist outlook.

particula'ristic, *a.* [f. prec. + -IC: see -ISTIC.] Pertaining to, characterized by, or upholding particularism (in any sense).

1881 *Fortn. Rev.* Mar. 375 To overcome the particularistic tendencies of the single States. **1886** C. P. TIELE in *Encycl. Brit.* XX. 369/1 Buddhism, Islâm, and Christianity were neither national nor particularistic. **1937** T. PARSONS *Struct. Soc. Action* III. xv. 551 The whole Chinese social structure accepted and sanctioned by the Confucian ethics was a predominantly 'particularistic' structure of relationships. **1955** M. GLUCKMAN *Custom & Conflict in Afr.* v. 123 She also brings out the particularistic nature of their answer to the problem, what is man? **1956** *Jrnl. Theol. Stud.* VII. 99 Both the universalistic and the particularistic strands in their teaching. **1964** GOULD & KOLB *Dict. Social Sci.* 489/1 He may decide to be particularistic, treating them 'in accordance with their standing in some particular relationship to him or his collectivity, independently of the objects' subsumibility under a general norm'. **1970** J. COTLER in I. L. Horowitz *Masses in Lat. Amer.* xii. 426 Through the..particularistic pattern in which juridical and political authorities are designated, the Pisac mestizos become political figures. **1972** *Science* 9 June 1094/3 The differentiation of scholarship within a field into a variety of highly particularistic specialties reduces the potential for the type of behavior associated with intellectuality. **1974** tr. *Wertheim's Evolution & Revolution* i. 51 Popular emancipation movements do not stress an abstract universalism as their main ideology, but rather strike a note of particularistic loyalties.

So **particula'ristically** *adv.*

1951 PARSONS & SHILS *Toward Gen. Theory Action* 260 A specific situation vis-à-vis particularistically designated persons. **1963** R. M. HARE *Freedom & Reason* ii. 20 The particularistically inclined non-naturalist.

particularity (pətɪkjʊˈlærɪtɪ). [a. F. *particularité*, ad. late L. *particulāritāt-em* (Cassiodorus, Boethius), f. *particulār-is* PARTICULAR: see -ITY.] The quality of being particular; something that is particular.

1. a. The quality of being particular as opposed to general or universal; the fact of being or relating to one or some (not all) of a class; relation to an individual thing, individuality; *spec.* in *Theology*, with ref. to Christ as the incarnation of God as a particular human being at a particular time and place.

1587 FLEMING *Contn. Holinshed* III. 1027/1 So also was it generallie doone throughout all England, in which generalitie this city was of a particularitie. **1647** H. MORE *Song Soul* II. ii. III. vi, Not wedg'd in strait particularity, But grasping all in her vast active spright. **1656** tr. *Hobbes' Elem. Philos.* (1839) 22 A common name set by itself with-out any note either of universality or particularity, as *man, stone*,.. is called an indefinite name. **1725** WATTS *Logic* I. iv. §4 Any common name whatsoever is made proper by terms of particularity added to it. **1865** MOZLEY *Mirac.* ii. 41 That.. does not alter the particularity of the fact, or make it at all the more a universal. **1930** E. HOSKYNS in Bell & Deissmann *Mysterium Christi* 89 The philosopher should.. make sense of it [*sc.* revelation] by some other means than by obscuring the particularity of the Old Testament and by refusing to recognize that in the end the particularity of the Old Testament is only intelligible in the light of its narrowed fulfilment in Jesus, the Messiah, and of its expanded fulfilment in the Church. **1966** G. W. H. LAMPE in Lampe & Mackinnon *Resurrection* vii. 92 The Incarnation necessarily involves particularity. If the Word was truly made flesh then he had to be incarnate as a certain individual man in a particular time and place. **1969** T. F. TORRANCE *Theol. Sci.* iii. 140 God reveals Himself in the contingent particularity and sheer singularity of Jesus Christ. **1975** *Listener* 17 July 92/2 She seems to lack awareness of individuals in the particularity of each. **1979** B. HEBBLETHWAITE in M. Goulder *Incarnation & Myth* iv. 93 The inevitable limitations of that particularity are overcome .. by his spiritual and sacramental presence and activity, by means of which God's personal self-revelation in Jesus is universalized.

†**b.** A particular or individual matter or affair; a particular case or instance. *Obs.*

1593 SHAKS *2 Hen. VI*, v. ii. 44 Now let the generall Trumpet blow his blast, Particularities, and pettie sounds To cease. **1598** MANWOOD *Forest Lawes* i. §3 (1615) 22 There is no principle or ground so generall, that there is not some particularity exempted out of it.

2. a. The quality of being special or of a special kind; the fact of being in some way distinguished or noteworthy; speciality, peculiarity. Now *rare*.

1570 DEE *Math. Pref.* C iv, Sufficient to notifie, the particularitie, and excellency of the Arte. **1711** STEELE *Spect.* No. 142 ¶8 To.. have the Esteem of a Woman of your Merit, has in it a Particularity of Happiness. **1793** SMEATON *Edystone L.* Contents 7 Further augmented by the particularity of the Tide.

†**b.** Peculiarity such as to excite surprise, singularity, oddity; an instance of this, an odd action or characteristic. *Obs.*

1712 STEELE *Spect.* No. 438 ¶4 An habitual Humour, Whim, or Particularity of Behaviour. **1754** RICHARDSON *Grandison* (1781) VI. xxiii. 132 Mr. Greville.. has frequently surprised us with his particularities. *a* **1791** REYNOLDS in *Boswell's Johnson* an. 1739, One instance of his absence of mind and particularity, as it is characteristick of the man, may be worth relating.

3. An attribute belonging particularly to the thing in question; a special or distinctive quality or feature; a peculiarity. Now *rare*.

1588 PARKE tr. *Mendoza's Hist. China* 343 It is thought that they doo descend of the tartares, by some particularities that is found amongst them. **1604** E. G[RIMSTONE] tr. *D'Acosta's Hist. Indies* III. xii. 159 To speak what we know of the particularities of the Antartike straight. **1713** STEELE *Guard.* No. 10 ¶7 Some particularities in the garb of their Abbés may be transplanted hither to advantage. **1779** SIR W. HAMILTON in *Phil. Trans.* LXX. 75 The particularity of this last eruption was, that the lava.. was now chiefly thrown up from its Crater. **1844** LD. BROUGHAM *A. Lunel* III. viii. 231 He has, however, some of the particularities of the family. **1863** E. V. NEALE *Anal. Th. & Nat.* 75 Seeking for the general conception through the particularities of the individual.

†**4.** Personal interest or advantage: = PARTICULAR B. 6 b; also, regard to personal or private interest, an act dictated by this. *Sc. Obs.*

1549 *Compl. Scot.* 158 The quhilk gracis and propreteis ar nocht grantit be god for thy particularitie, but rather.. to be ane dispensatour of his gyftis amang the ignorant pepil. **1578–9** *Reg. Privy Council Scot.* III. 79 The correctioun of his thevis is nather done for gredines nor ony kynd of particularitie. **1585–6** *Ibid.* IV. 47 Mair respecting thair awne particulariteis nor the commounweill of the said citie.

5. A particular point or circumstance, a detail: = PARTICULAR B. 2. (Common in 16–17th c.)

1528 GARDINER in Pocock *Rec. of Ref.* I. l. 103 And so from such good words entered into the particularities of the matter. **1536** CROMWELL 14 May in Merriman *Life & Lett.* (1902) II. 12, I write noo particularities, the thinges be soo abhomynable, that I thinke the like was neuer harde. **1632** SANDERSON *Serm.* 302 In this particularity whereof we now speake. **1717** LADY M. W. MONTAGU *Let. to Abbé Conti* 29 May, When I spoke of their religion, I forgot to mention two particularities. **1796** MORSE *Amer. Geog.* II. 19 The particularities related of this animal would be incredible, were they not attested upon oath. **1961** W. HERBERG in *Webster* s.v., Fixing exclusively on the particularities of the current situation. **1977** *Times Lit. Suppl.* 11 Feb. 148/3 Sociologists are notorious for their use of generalizing terms that ride roughshod over the particularities of history.

6. Minuteness or detailedness of description, statement, investigation, etc.; treatment of the particulars of a matter.

1638 A. READ *Chirurg.* xviii. 130 Fomentations.. for a gangrene, whereof I meane to discourse in a particularity. **1699** BURNET 39 *Art.* ii. (1700) 53 There is no part of the Gospel writ with so copious a Particularity, as the History of his Sufferings and Death. **1790** PALEY *Horæ Paul.* i. 5 The very particularity of St. Paul's Epistles. **1844** GLADSTONE *Glean.* V. xix. 95 Charges which, ponderous as they are, are so deficient in particularity. **1883** SIR A. HOBHOUSE in *Law Rep.* 9 App. Cases 180 It is necessary to examine the proceedings with some particularity.

†**7.** Special attentiveness to a person; an instance of this, a particular attention; familiarity. *Obs.*

1709 STEELE *Tatler* No. 47 ¶2 All the remarkable Particularities which are usual for Persons who admire one another. **1734** FIELDING *Univ. Gallant* III. ii. Wks. 1882 X. 76 Sister, I am surprised at you. This particularity with a young fellow is very indecent. **1815** JANE AUSTEN *Emma* III. xiv. 380 Behaving one hour with objectionable particularity to another woman.

8. Attentiveness to details of action; special carefulness; preciseness, fastidiousness.

1671 WOODHEAD *St. Teresa* II. 255 With great weight, and much particularity, I heard internally that Verse of the Psalm. **1753** RICHARDSON *Grandison* (1781) I. viii. 36 Sir Rowland himself, as you will guess by his particularity, is an old bachelor. **1832** J. P. KENNEDY *Swallow B.* (1860) 14 It [the letter] flouted my opinions, laughed at my particularity. **1882** MISS WOOLSON *Anne* 96 A particularity as to the saving of string.

†**9.** Phr. ***in particularity***: in detail; individually; specially: = *in particular* (PARTICULAR A. 13 a, b).

1559 PARKER in Burnet *Hist. Ref.* (1681) II. Collect. Rec. 362 Which mine disability I might alleadg at length in particularity. **1569** *Act 11 Eliz.* in Bolton *Stat. Irel.* (1621) 317 Your Majesties title in generalitie to the whole Realme of Ireland, and in particularitie to the dominion and territories of Ulster. **1588** FRAUNCE *Lawiers Log.* Ded. ¶¶b, There is no Law-maker so provident, as that hee can in particularity foresee and.. prevent the infinite variety of future inconveniences.

particularization (pəˌtɪkjʊləraɪˈzeɪʃən). [f. next + -ATION.] The action of particularizing.

1. Individual or detailed mention, description, or treatment; specification.

1657 J. SERGEANT *Schism Dispach't* 410 With such allusion to his name, and other particularisations, as.. are apt to breed an expectation of something particular in the thing promised. **1798** W. TAYLOR in Robberds *Memoir of W. Taylor* I. 217 Enterprises, for the particularization of which they afford ample materials. **1876** LOWELL *Among my Bks.* Ser. II. 240 This power of particularization is what gives such vigor and greatness to single lines and sentiments of Wordsworth.

2. The action of making particular as opposed to general; restriction to a particular thing. *rare*.

1836 DE MORGAN *Diff. & Integr. Calculus* 583 *note*, The difficulty arises from the particularization of the meaning of δ being made a little too early in the process.

particularize (pəˈtɪkjʊləraɪz), *v.* [a. F. *particularise-r* (15th c. in Littré): see -IZE.]

1. *trans.* To render particular (as opposed to general); to apply, appropriate, or restrict to a particular thing or class. *rare*.

1588 J. HARVEY *Disc. Probl.* 44 And who can directly discusse, or particularize the æquiuocation, and ouer-great generalitie of Interregni, and Auiti sanguinis propago? **1677** G. HICKES in Ellis *Orig. Lett.* Ser. II. IV. 41 To particularise the general information.. I have sent you the names of the most considerable and mischievous of them. **1876** F. H. BRADLEY *Eth. Stud.* iv. 135 You can not particularize a definition so as to exhaust any sensible object.

2. To mention or describe particularly; to name or state specially, or one by one; to speak or treat of individually, or in detail; to specify. (The usual sense.)

1593 G. HARVEY *Pierce's Super.* Wks. (Grosart) II. 321, I dare not Particularise her Description according to my conceit. **1596** NASHE *Saffron Walden* 154 Except he particularize and stake downe the verie words. **1674** *Essex Papers* (Camden) I. 161, I doe beleeve the Howse of Commons will Vote the King a Supply..but not particularise the sume. **1741** EARL ORRERY 7 July in *Swift's Lett.* (1768) IV. 241 In mentioning your friends, I must particularize Mr. Pope. **1842** S. LOVER *Handy Andy* Pref. 6 Various causes, needless to particularise here. **1884** SIR J. BACON in *Law Times Rep.* L. 345/1 The plaintiffs.. might particularise more distinctly the grounds on which they claim.. relief.

b. *intr.* To mention, speak or treat of, or attend to, particulars or details; to go into detail.

1601 HOLLAND *Pliny* XXXVI. xiv. 580 They would require many volumes to.. particularize upon them. **1626** C. POTTER tr. *Sarpi's Hist. Quarrels* 196 It sufficed.. to say they had many Reasons, being not able to particularize in any. **1670** CLARKE *Nat. Hist. Nitre* 68 But to a little more particularise. **1709** E. WARD tr. *Cervantes* 34 He took such Pains to particularize upon every Point of his Happiness. **1834** W. H. AINSWORTH *Rookwood* III. xiii, In our hasty narrative of the fight, we have not paused to particularize.

3. *trans.* To place or represent apart as an individual thing; to render distinct or separate; to individualize, distinguish, differentiate. *rare*.

1643 DIGBY *Observ. Relig. Med.* (1644) 84 Particularize a few drops of the Sea, by filling a glasse full of them; then that glasse-full is distinguished from all the rest of the watery Bulke. *a* **1661** FULLER *Worthies* (1840) III. 203 The place.. not sufficiently particularized to his memory in so wide a common. **1893** *Black & White* 24 June 764/2 In dress, in manner.. he particularises himself from his fellows.

†**b.** *intr.* To be distinguished. *Obs. rare*.

1637 EARL MONM. tr. *Malvezzi's Romulus & Tarquin* 45 Beyond the common equalitie amongst brethren, they did particularise in being equally.. at the same time borne.

Hence **parˈticularized** *ppl. a.*; **parˈticularizing** *vbl. sb.* and *ppl. a.*

1611 COTGR., *Particularisé*, Particularized,.. distinguished. **1632** G. HERBERT *Priest to Temple* xiv, If the Parson were ashamed of particularizing in these things, he were not fit to be a parson. **1657** J. SERGEANT *Schism Dispach't* 394 If then it were spoken.. after a particularizing way. **1841** BORROW *Zincali* I. xii. I. 207 We may be well excused from particularizing. **1851** KITTO *Bible Illustr.* (1867) VIII. 440 He dwelt with particularizing emphasis on his persecution of the believers in Jesus. **1860** MAURY *Phys. Geog. Sea* (Low) xx. §840. 462 Irrespective of the particularized facts and phenomena which we have been considering.

particularly (pəˈtɪkjʊləlɪ), *adv.* [f. PARTICULAR *a.* + -LY².] In a particular manner, or with a particular reference.

1. a. In the case of, or in respect of, each one of a number; one by one, severally, singly, individually. Now *rare* or *Obs.*

1398 *St. Paper* 26 Oct. in Rymer *Foedera* (1709) VIII. 56/1 The qwhilkis the said Commissairs ne may noght, for faut of laisure,.. particularly ger be refourmyd and amendit. **1472–3** *Rolls of Parlt.* VI. 59/1 Every such somme and sommes of money,.. that in their said accompt.. shal be particulerly expressed. **1526** *Pilgr. Perf.* (W. de W. 1531) 44 And euery hand and fote hath his fyngers & toos particularly distinct. **1567** MAPLET *Gr. Forest* 30 Treating of Plants as of Herbes, Trees, and Shrubs, perticulerly and Alphabetically. **1630** PRYNNE *Anti-Armin.* 146 They are all particularly redeemed by his death. **1766** GOLDSM. *Vic. W.* xvi, He.. amused them by describing the town with every part of which he was particularly acquainted. **1877** W. BRUCE *Comm. Rev.* 100 The different images that are used also particularly agree with each other.

b. In relation to, or in the case of, some one thing, person, or class, as distinct from any other; individually, personally; specifically, in particular; in a particular case, for a particular purpose, etc.

1547 BOORDE *Introd. Knowl.* vii. (1870) 146 Also I do not, nor shal not, dispruue no man in this booke perticulerly. *c* **1592** MARLOWE *Jew of Malta* I. ii, No, Jew, we take particularly thine To save the ruine of a multitude. **1625** BACON *Ess., Regim. Health* (Arb.) 59 It is hard to distinguish, that which is generally held good, and wholesome, from that, which is good particularly, and fit for thine owne Body. **1774** J. BRYANT *Mythol.* I. 319 It signified a lord or prince: and was particularly assumed by the sons of Chus. **1868** LOCKYER *Elem. Astron.* iii. x. (1879) 61 There is still much more to be learnt, both about the system generally, and the planets particularly.

c. *Logic.* In the manner of a particular proposition; in relation to some, not all, of a class.

1860 ABP. THOMSON *Laws Th.* §65. 105 Such an image is a conception, used particularly, i.e. only some part of it is called up. **1864** BOWEN *Logic* v. 139 Equivalent to quantifying the Predicate particularly.

2. With respect to the several parts of a whole; in relation to particulars or details; minutely, circumstantially, in detail.

1489 CAXTON *Faytes of A.* II. xx. 133 It semeth me gode to adde.. more partyculerly thoo thinges that be goode and propyce to assaylle Cytees, Castelles and Townes. **1553** EDEN *Treat. Newe Ind.* (Arb.) 5 Albeit it do not so largely or particularlye entreate of euery parte. **1638** CHILLINGW. *Relig. Prot.* I. vii. §18. 398 My purpose of answering them more punctually and particularly. **1765** *Act 5 Geo. III*, c. 26 *Preamble*, Their.. appurtenances.. more particularly described. **1885** SIR J. BACON in *Law Times Rep.* LII. 569/1 It becomes necessary to consider more particularly the facts out of which those issues arise.

3. In a special degree; more than others, or more than in other cases; especially, notably, markedly; *colloq.* more than usual, much, very.

1676 tr. *Guillatiere's Voy. Athens* 270 In matters of Commerce, he is particularly intelligent. **1697** DRYDEN *Eneid* Ded., Ess. (Ker) II. 207 By some passages in the Pastorals, but more particularly in the Georgics, our poet is found to be an exact astronomer. **1711** ADDISON *Spect.* No. 255 ¶10 Thus is Fame a thing difficult to be obtained by all, but particularly by those who thirst after it. **1813** MAR. EDGEWORTH *Patron.* (1833) I. vii. 123 What I particularly admire in him is his candour. **1862** BORROW *Wild Wales* i, Which.. he would have been very unwilling to do, more particularly as he had a wife and family. **1885** *Spectator* 30 May 714/2 One does not feel.. particularly drawn towards the heroine.

†**4.** Personally, familiarly, intimately. *Obs.*

1680 BURNET *Rochester* Pref. (1692) 7 He was particularly known to few of the clergy. **1723** STEELE *Consc. Lovers* III. i, Admitting Mr. Cimberton as particularly here, as if he were married to you already. **1749** FIELDING *Tom Jones* XI. viii, Her Lady, with whom he was very particularly acquainted.

†**parˈticularment.** *Obs. rare.* [f. as prec. + -MENT.] A particular or individual thing; a particular, a detail.

1647 H. MORE *Song Soul* I. II. xv, Upon this universall Ogdoas Is founded every particularment. *Ibid.* II. iii. III. xxx, With straight line It binds down strongly each partic'larment Of every edifice.

par'ticularness. *rare.* [f. as prec. + -NESS.] The quality of being particular (in any sense); in quot. 1859, Preciseness, fastidiousness.

1727 BAILEY vol. II, *Particularness*..peculiarness, singularness. **1859** GEO. ELIOT *Adam Bede* l, You're getting to be your aunt's own niece, I see, for particularness.

†**par'ticulary,** *adv.* Obs. Sc. form of PARTICULARLY.

1473–4 *Acc. Ld. High Treas. Scot.* I. 66 As his bill beris, particulary examinit at the Chakkere. **1567** *Reg. Privy Council Scot.* I. 551 The dayis particularie abonespecifit. **1571–2** *Ibid.* II. 179 Under the panis particularie undermentionat. **1589** *Excheq. Rolls Scotl.* XXII. 22.

particulate (pə'tɪkjʊlət), *a.* and *sb.* Only in scientific use. [ad. med. or mod.L. *particulāt-us* divided into particles: see next.]

A. *adj.* **a.** Existing in the condition of minute separate particles.

1871 *Q. Jrnl. Microsc. Sci.* XI. 325 It may be supposed either that the germinal substance is universally and equally distributed, *i.e.* dissolved in such liquids, or that it is unequally distributed or particulate. **1874** SIMON *Rept. of Med. Deptmt. P.C.* 30 July 6 [In] the common septic contagium or ferment..particulate, as above described, there seems now to be identified a force..acting disintegratively upon organic matter. **1880** *Lancet* 17 Jan. 85 The contagium..is particulate—that is, consists of definite particles of organic nature. **1885** KLEIN *Micro-Organisms* 46 Chauveau was the first to prove experimentally that in vaccinia and in variola the active principle is a particulate non-diffusible substance. **1891** A. CARPENTER in *Pall Mall G.* 2 June 1/3 Showing that particulate matter can be conveyed many thousands of miles in the higher regions of the atmosphere. **1962** F. I. ORDWAY et al. *Basic Astronautics* iv. 120 Interstellar and interplanetary particulate matter. **1966** *McGraw-Hill Encycl. Sci. & Technol.* IX. 197/2 Beta rays are particulate radiation consisting of electrons or positrons emitted from a nucleus during β-decay. **1974** *Environmental Conservation* I. 16 The addition of carbon dioxide and particulate matter to the atmosphere by mankind.

b. Of or relating to minute separate particles. ***particulate inheritance***, the manifestation in offspring of discrete characters each inherited from one or other of the parents.

1881 E. R. LANKESTER in *Jrnl. Microsc. Sc.* Jan. 121 The ingestion of fats in a particulate form by Vertebrata. **1886** F. GALTON in *Rep. Brit. Assoc. Adv. Sci. 1885* 1213 To express this aspect of inheritance, where particle proceeds from particle, we may conveniently describe it as 'particulate'. **1888** *Times* 20 Jan. 10/2 The particulate and undulatory theories of smell are not exclusive of each other. **1889** F. GALTON *Nat. Inheritance* ii. 8 The exact meaning of Particulate Inheritance, namely, that each piece of the new structure is derived from a corresponding piece of some older one. **1930** R. A. FISHER *Genetical Theory Nat. Selection* i. 1 The need for an alternative to blending inheritance was certainly felt by Darwin, though probably he never worked out a distinct idea of a particulate theory. *Ibid.* 8 Apart from dominance and linkage,..all the main characteristics of the Mendelian system flow from assumptions of particulate inheritance of the simplest character, and could have been deduced *a priori.* **1971** J. Z. YOUNG *Introd. Study Man* xxviii. 392 (*heading*) Genes and their mutations. Particulate inheritance.

B. *sb.* A particulate substance; particulate material. Also *attrib.*

1960 *New Scientist* 13 Oct. 1001/3 The future will see the ultra-centrifuge used more and more as a tool to determine the physical structure of specific parts of such macromolecules as the nucleoproteins, coenzymes and cell particulates. **1971** *Nature* 20 Aug. 553/2 Airborne particulate was collected on 0·45 μm 'Millipore' membrane filters. **1973** *Physics Bull.* May 314/3 Methods for the elemental analysis of air particulates. **1974** *Post-Herald* (Birmingham, Alabama) 29 June A7/3 The Jefferson County particulate count has exceeded the 260 level 82 times during the past year. **1976** *Sci. Amer.* July 77 The emission of particulates is reduced by the liberal use of filters.

†**par'ticulate,** *v. Obs.* [f. ppl. stem of med.L. *particulāre* (cf. late L. *particulātio* division into particles, Mart. Capella *c* 425), f. *particula* PARTICLE.] *trans.* = PARTICULARIZE 2.

1579 FENTON *Guicciard.* Ded., I am bolde to leave to particulate in my epistle any part of the argument. **1610** HOLLAND *Camden's Brit.* I. 605 If I should particulate the scufflings and skirmishes. **1656** HEYLIN *Surv. France* 140 Many acts..which I will not stand here to particulate.

b. *intr.* = PARTICULARIZE 2 b.

1602 WARNER *Alb. Eng.* XI. lxiv. (1612) 277 But why particulate we thus, that much in few would write? **1605** CAMDEN *Rem.* (1637) 14 That I may not particulate of Alexander of Hales, the Irrefragable Doctor. *Ibid.* 27, I could particulate in many more.

'particule. *Obs.*, exc. in sense 2 b, as Fr. (partikyl). Also 6 **perticule.** [a. F. *particule* (1484 in Hatz.-Darm.), ad. L. *particula* PARTICLE.]

†**1.** A small part or portion (in quot. 1540, of land); a particle. *Obs.*

1540 *Sc. Acts Jas. V* (1814) 376/2 þe landis and barony of Estwemis..aduocatioun and donatioun of kirkis tenentis tenandrijs particulis pendiculis..and pertinentis parof. **1647** LILLY *Chr. Astrol.* xxix. 193, I ever tooke..that very particule of hour when it was proposed.

†**2.** *Gram.* = PARTICLE *sb.* 3. *Obs.* exc. as in b.

c **1620** A. HUME *Brit. Tongue* (1865) 33 *Ane* is a noun of number,..*an* a particule of determination preceding a voual.

‖**b.** *spec.* Applied to the French preposition *de* used as a prefix of nobility in personal names.

1889 *Blackw. Mag.* CXLVI. 270/1 We..generously add a 'de' where no particule is, with no consciousness that we are thus conferring nobility. **1898** BODLEY *France* I. 191 Of the 1500 boys 200 have names prefixed with the particule, signifying that they claim to be of gentle birth.

‖**partie.** [mod.F. *partie* (parti).] A match in a game; a game. ***partie carrée,*** †***quarrée*** [F., = square or quadrate party] a party of four.

1678 DRYDEN *Limberham* IV. ii, Well, I have won the partie, and revenge. **1816** SINGER *Hist. Cards* 16 The parties at Cards are doubled. **1848** THACKERAY *Van. Fair* li, Champignac was very fond of écarté, and made many *parties* with the Colonel of evenings. **1876** A. CAMPBELL-WALKER *Correct Card* (1880) Gloss. 13 *Partie*, the same players playing two rubbers consecutively, or, should it be necessary, a third rubber, to decide which is the best of the three rubbers.

1739 CIBBER *Apol.* (1756) I. 186 Very often in a *tete à tete* and sometimes in a *partie quarrée.* *a* **1845** BARHAM *Ingol. Leg.* Ser. III. *Ld. Thoulouse*, The *partie quarrée* had like aldermen fed. **1890** 'R. BOLDREWOOD' *Col. Reformer* (1891) 130 A *partie-carrée* composed of George..his mother, sister, and Mr. John.

partie-coated: see PARTI-[1].

partier ('pɑːtɪə(r)). *colloq.* [f. PARTY *sb.* 9 + -ER[1].] One who likes to give or attend parties.

1965 J. HART *File for Death* xii. 94 Jinsie most certainly did not care for the 'partiers'. **1973** *Daily Colonist* (Victoria, B.C.) 16 Sept. 13/3 Thor said he understood the hesitancy of many landlords to rent to male rather than female students. Women are generally neater than men, he concedes, and are not partiers.

†**parti-'fellow.** *Obs.* In 5 partifelewe, 6 partie-. [f. *parti* PARTY *sb.* + FELLOW.] One who shares, a partner: cf. *parting fellow* s.v. PARTING *ppl. a.* 4.

1422 tr. *Secreta Secret., Priv. Priv.* 219 [In] the Passions of that oone, that other is Parcenere, or Partifelewe. **1530** PALSGR. 252/1 Partie felowe, *parsonnier.*

'partified, *ppl. a. colloq.* [f. PARTY *sb.* 9 + -FY + -ED[1].] Dressed up for a party.

1928 *Sunday Express* 13 May 16/4 He couldn't quite get over the queerness of seeing Bobs with feathers on her head and white gloves up to her shoulders—and that strip of train on the ground..the thought of a word used by his childhood's nurse to denote a certain standard of sartorial tribute to 'occasions'. 'You look so frightfully "partified",' he added. **1969** A. CHRISTIE *Hallowe'en Party* i. 9 They look good and partified.

†**'partify,** *v. Obs. rare.* [f. PARTY *sb.* + -FY.] *trans.* To render partisan; to give a party complexion to, or imbue with party spirit.

1715 M. DAVIES *Athen. Brit.* I. Pref. 8 Adulterations of partify'd Collectors and additional Refiners of the perverted Text. **1716** *Ibid.* III. 67 Publications manag'd, and partify'd by the respective Romanists.

parti-generic ('pɑːtɪdʒɪ'nɛrɪk), *a. Linguistics.* [f. PARTI-[2] + GENERIC *a.* (*sb.*)] Referring to an indefinite amount or sub-set of a whole.

1939 P. CHRISTOPHERSEN *Articles* ii. 33 Continuate-words have only zero-form and *the*-form. The former is used when the thing meant is viewed as unlimited or having indefinite limits. We can distinguish three different significations of the zero-form: (1) The whole genus everywhere and at all times (*toto-generic sense*)... (2) An indefinite amount of the genus (*parti-generic sense*)... (3) (In negative phrases) nothing of the genus (*nulli-generic sense*). **1962** J. SÖDERLIND in F. Behre *Contrib. Eng. Syntax* 103 They [*sc.* 'uncountables and plural countables' in zero-form] then refer either to the whole genus of their content (toto-generic sense) or to some indefinite amount or number of it (parti-generic sense).

partile ('pɑːtaɪl, -tɪl), *a.* Also 7 partil(l. [ad. L. *partilis* divisible. f. root of *partire* to divide: see -ILE; also, partial (in adv. *partiliter* partially, in part). In mod. Fr., in sense 2, *partil.*]

†**1.** = PARTIAL *a.* II. *Obs.*

1576 FLEMING *Panopl. Epist.* 178 The light of my renowne, shal not suffer a partile eclipse, but it shal be in maner, wholy darkned. **1588** J. HARVEY *Disc. Probl.* 116 Being but a Partile not a Totall Eclipse. **1678** W. ADAMS *Didham Pulpit* 67 There are many beginnings of fulfilling them, partile accomplishments. **1695** E. HALLEY in *Phil. Trans.* XIX. 18 The *Penumbra* or Partile shade of the Sun. **1697** *Ibid.* 445 A partile Account of a Book long since published.

2. *Astrol.* Of an aspect: Exact to the same degree and minute, or, at least, within a degree; e.g. ***partile conjunction***, exact conjunction; so ***partile opposition***; ***partile trine***, positions exactly 120° apart. Opposed to PLATIC.

1610 HEALEY *St. Aug. Citie of God* 199 Mars..being in the seventh house in a partile aspect with the Horoscope. **1674** JEAKE *Arith.* (1696) b ij, His Fiery Partil Trine, to actuate The Active House to a more Active Fate. **1701** MOXON *Math. Dict.* s.v., The Sun in one Degree of Taurus and the Moon in one Degree of Cancer make a Partile Sextile. **1819** J. WILSON *Dict. Astrol.* s.v., An aspect is partile when it falls in the same degree and minute, both with respect to longitude and latitude... This can seldom happen, but a few minutes can make no difference. **1839** BAILEY *Festus* ix. (1852) 121 Your aspects, dignities, ascendances, Your partile quartiles, and your platic trines.

†**'partily,** *adv. Obs. rare.* [app. f. PARTY *a.* + -LY[2].] With respect to a part; partly.

1497 HEN. VII in Ellis *Orig. Lett.* Ser. I. I. 57 That the said Kings of Fraunce and Spayne..be in this behalf contributory, partilie in men, and partly in money.

†**'partiment.** *Obs. rare.* Also 6 **partyment.** [ad. med.L. *partīmentum* (1292 in Du Cange) partition, division; f. *partīre* to PART: so It. *partimento.*] **a.** A part or division; a company. **b.** ? A constituent part or element.

1513 DOUGLAS *Æneis* XII. iii. 39 And eftir that the trumpet blew a sing, Than euery partyment bownys to thar stand. **1641** LD. BROOKE *Eng. Episc.* vii. 40 Estates and Revenues.. which are the Partiments and Supporters of Noble Honours.

partin, partinar, -er, obs. ff. PARTAN, PARTNER.

parting ('pɑːtɪŋ), *vbl. sb.* [f. PART *v.* + -ING[1].] The action of the verb PART, partition; the result, or place, of this action; something that parts.

1. a. The action of dividing or fact of undergoing division into parts; division, breaking, cleaving: see PART *v.* 1, 2.

1530 PALSGR. 252/1 Partyng of any thyng, *partaige.* **1555** ADAMO (*title*) An Anatomi, that is to say a parting in peeces of the Mass. **1748** *Anson's Voy.* II. iii. 146 There being great danger of the ship's parting. **1875** KNIGHT *Dict. Mech.*, *Parting*..(*Nautical.*) Breaking cable, leaving the anchor in the ground.

b. The division or dividing line of the hair when combed: see PART *v.* 1 c.

1698 FARQUHAR *Love & Bottle* III. i, Does the parting of my fore-top show so thin? **1862** MRS. H. WOOD *Mrs. Hallib.* I. i. (1864) 6 Smoothing the parting of the glossy brown hair on her well-shaped head. **1887** J. ASHBY STERRY *Lazy Minstrel* (1892) 193 My hair is getting thin,..Old Time has made my parting wide, And sunk my hopes to zero.

2. a. (*a*) The action of separating or putting asunder, or fact of being separated; separation. (*b*) *spec.* in technical uses: see PART *v.* 4 c. ***parting off***: the separation of a piece from a longer length (cf. PART *v.* 4 c (*d*)). Freq. *attrib.*

c **1315** SHOREHAM *Poems* (E.E.T.S.) 66/1855 ȝef he by wyl seruep þat flesch, Ryȝt partyng worthe hym none. **1340** HAMPOLE *Pr. Consc.* 1803 Dede es noght elles..Bot a partyng of þe saul and body. *c* **1440** *Promp. Parv.* 385/1 Partynge a-sundyr.., *separacio.* **1710** J. HARRIS *Lex. Techn.* II, *Parting*, is one of the Refiner's ways to separate Gold and Silver. **1839** URE *Dict. Arts* 1059 In parting by nitric acid, the gold generally retains a little silver. **1879** H. NORTHCOTT in *Cassell's Techn. Educ.* IV. 71/2 Tools..chiefly for 'parting', or cutting off pieces of work from the main cylinder or log. **1905** J. HORNER *Tools for Engineers & Woodworkers* v. 60 Tools for parting off..have clearance both behind and below. Being generally very thin at the cutting end, this is commonly reduced from a bar of greater width, in order to afford sufficient width and rigidity for clamping in the tool-holder. **1923** C. M. LINLEY *Lathe Users' Handbk.* v. 88 In capstan work where parting-off tools are in continual use..I have used milling cutters or slitting saws as tools with great success. **1950** C. T. BOWER in A. W. Judge *Machine Tools & Operations* II. viii. 186 The parting-off saw shown..has been evolved for cutting off non-ferrous extrusions or bars up to 4 in. by 2½ in. deep. **1977** C. R. SHOTBOLT *Technician Workshop Processes & Materials* I. vii. 84/1 The draw tube and the back end of the collet are hollow to permit bars to be fed through the spindle for repetition turning and parting-off of workpieces.

b. (*a*) That part in which separation is realized; the place at which two or more things separate or are separated: as ***the parting of the ways***, the place or part at which a road divides into two or more that proceed in different directions (often *fig.* in reference to a choice between courses of action); ***water-parting***, the line separating two river-systems, a WATERSHED. (*b*) *spec.* in *Founding*, the division or meeting-surface of two parts of a mould (see also c).

c **1400** *Master of Game* (MS. Digby 182) xxxv, Whan he is passed þe partynge of þe quarter and entered into a newe quarter, he shulde blowe iii. moot and seke forth. **1611** BIBLE *Ezek.* xxi. 21 The king of Babylon stood at the parting of the way, at the head of the two wayes, to vse diuination. **1869** LOWELL *Parting of the Ways* i, Who hath not..Stood doubtful at the Parting of the Ways? **1875** KNIGHT *Dict. Mech.* 1460/1 An exact *parting* is now made with the trowel along the median line, if the casting be symmetrical. *Ibid.* 1634/2 *Parting*..4. (*Founding.*) The meeting surfaces of the sand rammed up in the *cope* and in the *drag.* **1888** *Pall Mall G.* 20 Dec. 5/2 Take the Nile valley and the water partings on each side from Berber. **1897** MARQ. SALISBURY *Sp. Ho. Lords* 19 Jan., For the difficulties in which we find ourselves now, the parting of the ways was in 1853, when the Emperor Nicholas's proposals were rejected.

c. *concr.* Something that parts or separates two things; *esp.* in technical uses, as (*a*) *Mining* and *Geol.* A layer of rock, clay, etc. lying between two beds of different formations; (*b*) *Founding.* Fine sand (*parting-sand*) or other powdery substance used to prevent adhesion of the surfaces of the parts of a mould (cf. b).

1708 J. C. *Compl. Collier* (1845) 23 A sort of bad foul Air, or Fume exhaling out of some Minerals, or partings of Stone. **1839** MURCHISON *Silur. Syst.* I. xxxv. 466 The laminae..are occasionally marked by very thin carbonaceous partings. **1874** J. H. COLLINS *Metal Mining* (1875) 67 The partings of the shafts consist of strong beams of wood..longitudinal timbers are nailed to these so as to form the shaft parting. **1875** KNIGHT *Dict. Mech.* 1461/2 The charcoal-dust of the black-wash acts as a parting.

3. a. Mutual separation of two or more persons; esp. the action of quitting one another's company; leave-taking.

c **1330** *Amis & Amil.* 325 Gret sorwe thai made at her parting. *c* **1410** LOVE *Bonavent. Mirr.* xlviii. (Gibbs MS.) lf. 101 A my dere sone a byttre partynge was thys. **1592** SHAKS. *Rom. & Jul.* II. ii. 186 Good night, good night, Parting is such sweete sorrow, That I shall say good night, till it be morrow. **1667** MILTON *P.L.* IV. 1003. **1773** JOHNSON *Let. to Mrs. Thrale* 20 Mar., The last parting is very afflictive. **1875** JOWETT *Plato* I. 70, I said..a few words to the boys at parting.

b. With *with*: see PART *v.* 6 c.

1620 BARRET *Ded. Southwell's Poems* 149 To purchase it by parting with their Armes. **1705** STANHOPE *Paraphr.* III. 482 The parting with a beloved Child is at any time an Affliction. **1804** MAR. EDGEWORTH *Ennui* xxi, The parting with a watch and some other trinkets..enabled me to pay this money.

4. The action of going away or setting out, departure; also *fig.* (*euphem.*) Decease, death. *arch.*

a **1300** *Floriz & Bl.* 684 He droȝ forþ a riche ring His moder him ȝaf at his parting. **1377** LANGL. *P. Pl.* B. VII. 57 Her pardoun is ful petit at her partyng hennes. **1489** CAXTON *Faytes of A.* I. xiv. 37 He shal be purueied bifore his partyng. **1603** JAS. I in Ellis *Orig. Lett.* Ser. I. III. 78 My sonne, that I see you not before my pairting impute it to this great occasion. **1656** HEYLIN *Extraneus Vapulans* 64 To let him know, that the Company was upon the parting. **1719** DE FOE *Crusoe* II. ii, Nothing troubled me at my parting from the island. **1857** HEAVYSEGE *Saul* (1869) 194 Who can, at parting, picture his return?

†**5. a.** Division into shares; division among a number, distribution; the giving of a share to another, imparting. *Obs.*

c **1380** WYCLIF *Sel. Wks.* III. 342 Chesyng of cardenalis, & parting of beneficis. *c* **1440** *Promp. Parv.* 385/1 Partynge, or delynge, *particio, distribucio.* **1560** DAUS tr. *Sleidane's Comm.* 80 b, They fell out about the partyng.

†**b.** The taking or having of a share; sharing, participation. *Obs.*

1382 WYCLIF *2 Cor.* vi. 14 Sothli what partynge [*gloss* or comunynge] of riȝtwysnesse with wickidnesse?

†**6.** The action of taking parts or sides. *Obs.*

1652 W. BROUGH *Sacr. Princ., Preserv. agst. Schisme* 31 With them there will be Siding and Parting. There cannot be Unity and Order.

7. *attrib.* and *Comb.* **a.** *attrib.* Of or pertaining to parting, *i.e.* leave-taking, departure, or (*euphem.*) death; *esp.* (in adjectival construction) Given, taken, performed, etc. at parting; 'farewell', concluding, final; esp. ***parting shot*** (cf. *Parthian shot* s.v. PARTHIAN *a.*). (See also PARTING-CUP.)

1592 GREENE *Upst. Courtier* Wks. (Grosart) XI. 219 Thus much I must say for a parting blow. **1611** SHAKS. *Cymb.* I. iii. 34 Ere I could Giue him that parting kisse. **1646** CRASHAW *Steps to Temple* 77 Hark! she is call'd, the parting hour is come. **1779** SHERIDAN *Critic* II. ii, If you go out without the parting look you might as well dance out. **1794** SOUTHEY *Frederic* 6 That deep cry..seems to sound My parting knell. **1875** JOWETT *Plato* (ed. 2) I. 266 This seems to be indicated by his parting words. **1894** HALL CAINE *Manxman* 75 With this parting shot..Nancy flung into the house. **1898** FLO. MONTGOMERY *Tony* 19 Forgetful of his mother's parting injunctions. **1906** GALSWORTHY *Man of Property* III. ix. 372 He could not resist a parting shot. 'H'mm! All flourishing at home? Any little Soameses yet?' **1957** P. WORSLEY *Trumpet shall Sound* iii. 67 Dasiga.. finally left with a parting-shot of 'unintelligible gibberish'. **1962** P. VAN GREENAWAY *Crucified City* xiii. 136 Still Creston permitted himself a parting shot. 'I suppose we're going through the whole farce again?' **1963** *Daily Tel.* 19 Aug. 8/6 It was also something of a parting shot, following a 100 yards victory in 9·9 sec. **1967** T. STOPPARD *Rosencrantz & Guildenstern* II. 57 He smiles briefly at them without mirth, and starts to back out, his parting shot rising again.

b. Of or pertaining to parting or separation, as '***parting-,point***; *esp.* in names of various technical appliances used for separating something, etc., as **parting-assay** (see quot. and ASSAY *sb.* 6); **parting-bead** = *parting-strip*; **parting-glass**, a glass flask used in 'parting' gold and silver (see PART *v.* 4 c (*a*)), esp. in assaying; **parting-line** (*Founding*), the line in which the 'parting' of a mould (see 2 b (*b*)) meets the surface of a pattern as it lies in the mould; **parting-rail** (see quot.); **parting-sand** (*Founding*), fine dry sand, free from admixture of clay, used to prevent adhesion of the parts of a mould at the 'parting' (see 2 b (*b*)); **parting-shard** (*Pottery Manuf.*), a thin piece of baked clay placed between pieces of unbaked ware to prevent adhesion; **parting-strip**, a strip of material used for separating two parts, e.g. the vertical strip of wood inserted at the side of the frame of a sash window to keep the sashes apart when raised or lowered; **parting-tool**, name of various tools used in different kinds of work for separating pieces of material, or for trimming, cutting fine outlines and markings, etc.; †**parting water**, nitric acid as used in 'parting' gold and silver (*obs.*).

In some of these, e.g. *parting bead, rail, shard, strip*, the attrib. use of the vbl. sb. can hardly be separated from that of the ppl. adj. (see next). Thus a *parting strip* may be viewed either as a strip used for parting, or as a strip that parts. When the hyphen is used, the former is implied: cf. a *walking-stick*, a *walking leaf*.

1758 REID tr. *Macquer's Chym.* I. 56 This method..is called the *Parting Assay. **1842–76** GWILT *Archit.* Gloss., *Parting Bead, the beaded slip inserted at the centre of the pulley style of a sash window, to keep the two sashes in their places. **1885** LOCK *Workshop Rec.* IV. 349/1 The washing may be performed in one of the conical precipitating or '*parting' flasks. **1594** PLAT *Jewell-ho.* III. 79 Water in a *parting glasse vpon warme imbers. **1825** J. NICHOLSON *Operat. Mechanic* 766 Parting glasses..ought to be very well annealed, and chosen free from flaws. **1875** KNIGHT *Dict. Mech.* 1460/1 The *parting-line is..that line upon the pattern, as it lies in the sand, above and below which the sides of the pattern run inward from the perpendicular. **1835** in Liddon etc. *Life Pusey* (1894) I. xv. 350 Mr. Maurice ..made up his mind that it represented the *parting-point between him and the Oxford School. **1884** KNIGHT *Dict. Mech.* Suppl., **Parting Rail*... A rail intermediate between the bottom and top rails of a door or partition. **1864** WEBSTER, **Parting sand*. **1875** KNIGHT *Dict. Mech.* 1460/1 Some dry parting-sand is next scattered over the surface. **1686** PLOT *Staffordsh.* 123 Haveing only *parting-shards, i.e. thin bits of old pots put between them, to keep them from sticking together. **1881** YOUNG *Ev. Man his own Mechanic* §648. 297 The *parting-tool is a sort of gouge or grooving tool, with an angular edge. **1895** *Mod. Steam Eng.* 90 Side tools to cut at the side, Parting tools, narrow and sharp for parting work. **1662** MERRETT tr. *Neri's Art of Glass* xxxviii. 62 (*heading*) How to make Aqua-fortis call'd *parting water, which dissolves silver and quick-silver.

parting, *ppl. a.* [f. as prec. + -ING².] That parts (in various senses of the verb).

(See also prec. 7 b.)

1. Separating, dividing; forming a boundary or interval between two things.

1699 *Boston Rec.* (1881) VII. 233 The gate in the parting line between Mr. Winthrops land and Major Townsends farm. **1733** TULL *Horse-Hoeing Husb.* xi. 121 The Parting Space is that Distance which the Drill leaves betwixt the Row it plants in going one Way, and that Row which it makes in returning back. **1833** LYELL *Princ. Geol.* III. 239 Occasionally there is a parting layer of pure flint.

2. Undergoing division; dividing, breaking, going to pieces.

1719 S. SEWALL *Diary* 14 Dec., At the parting way came up with Col. Quincey. **1736** GRAY *Statius* II. 21 Parting surges round the vessel roar. **1762** FALCONER *Shipwr.* III. 511 The parting ship that instant is no more!

3. Going away, departing; *fig.* dying.

a **1577** GASCOIGNE *In praise Gentlewoman* Wks. (1587) 284 And she to quyte hys loue..dyd yeeld her parting breath. **1591** SHAKS. *1 Hen. VI*, II. v. 115 And Peace, no Warre, befall thy parting Soule. **1667** MILTON *P.L.* IX. 276 Both by thee informd I learne, And from the parting Angel overheard. **1750** GRAY *Elegy* i, The curfew tolls the knell of parting day. **1866** NEALE *Sequences & Hymns* 127 To fortify the parting soul.

†**4.** Sharing, participating; ***parting fellow***, sharer, partner: = PARTI-FELLOW. *Obs.*

1377 LANGL. *P. Pl.* B. XIII. 206 If pacience be owre partyng felawe, And pryue with vs bothe. *c* **1386** CHAUCER *Pars. T.* ¶563 Thise scorneres been partyng felawes with the deuel. **1514** *Will of Stanyng* (Somerset Ho.), Partyng feloo.

'parting cup. **a.** A drinking-cup with two handles on opposite sides, used by two persons in taking a draught of liquor at parting. (Cf. LOVING CUP.) **b.** A kind of 'cup' or compound beverage, made with ale and sherry, sweetened, and with soda-water added just before drinking.

1868 J. MARRYAT *Pottery* (ed. 3) 484 Marshal de Bassompierre, when about to return..had called his friends together that he might drink their health in a parting cup.

†**'partion.** *Obs. rare*⁻⁰. [ad. L. *partiōn-em* a bringing forth, f. *parĕre, part-* to bring forth.]

1656 BLOUNT *Glossogr.*, *Partion*, a birth, a breeding, a lying in travail of children or yong; a laying of Eggs, a sitting on brood.

parti pris: see PARTI 2.

‖**Parti Québecois** (parti kebɛkwa). *Canad.* [Fr., f. PARTI + QUÉBECOIS *a.*] A French-Canadian political party which advocates greater autonomy for Quebec. Also *attrib.*

1968 *Times* 30 Oct. 4/7 After many years as the first official champions of the separatist cause in Quebec, Le Rassemblement pour l'Indépendence Nationale (R.I.N.) has decided to join forces with Mr. Rene Levesque's new Parti Québecois which until recently was Le Mouvement Souveraineté-Association (M.S.A.). **1970** *Globe & Mail* (Toronto) 27 Apr. 4 Rene Levesque, the Parti Quebecois leader. **1972** *Maclean's Mag.* Mar. 8/2 It is interesting to note that the Parti Québecois..has managed to affect the terrorist movement. **1976** *Southern Even. Echo* (Southampton) 16 Nov. 1/2 Parti Quebecois won a clear majority of seats in the Quebec National Assembly. **1978** *Times* 20 Mar. 5/6 On the Parti Québecois social policies, Mr. Lévesque said that it was a left-of-centre party.

partisan, partizan ('pɑːtɪzæn, pɑːtɪ'zæn), *sb.*¹ (*a.*) Also 6 **partisen, -sann, -sant,** 7 **partizant, -zen, -zane.** [a. F. *partisan* sb. and adj. (15th c. in Littré), ad. It. dial. form = Tuscan *partigiano*: cf. Roman and Neapol. *partiśano, -eśano*, Upper Italian *parteźan, partźan*; f. *parte* part: cf. *courtesan, parmesan*.

Flecchia, in *Archivio Glottolog. Ital.* II. (1876) 12–17, finds the origin of the Italian suffix in the adj. ending *-ese*:—L. *-ensis, -ēsis*, whence a derivative (originally sb.) *-esiano*, as in *cortese, cortesiano, corteg-, cortigiano, Parmese, Parmesiano, Parmigiano*; on the analogy of these, derivatives of the same type were subseq. formed directly from their primitives, without the intermediate adj. in *-ensis, -ese*. Adaptations of these have passed from It. into Fr. and other Romanic languages.]

A. *sb.* **1.** One who takes part or sides with another; an adherent or supporter of a party, person, or cause; *esp.* a devoted or zealous supporter; often in unfavourable sense: One who supports his party 'through thick and thin'; a blind, prejudiced, unreasoning, or fanatical adherent.

1555 EDEN *Decades* 62 Theyr newe capitayne..placed his souldiers as pleased hym in the forwarde and rereward, and sume as pertisens abowt his owne person. **1569** STOCKER tr. *Diod. Sic.* I. iv. 6 [To] haue a number of men in euery citie to be his Pertisannes or garde. **1595** DANIEL *Civill Wars* II. iv, These partizanes of factions, often tride. **1600** E. BLOUNT tr. *Conestaggio* 292 The Portugals, pertisants vnto Anthonie. **1602** *Archpriest Controv.* (Camden) II. 198 The partizants and fauorers of the late seditious puritaine Erle. **1603** KNOLLES *Hist. Turks* (1621) 1298 They made themselves partisans to the one to oppresse the other. **1779** J. MOORE *View Soc. Fr.* (1789) II. xcvi. 429 Why the inhabitants of every other country should..become partizans of America, is not so apparent. **1780** BENTHAM *Princ. Legisl.* ii. §4 A partizan of the principle of asceticism. **1866** G. MACDONALD *Ann. Q. Neighb.* xii. (1878) 234 The clergy-man must never be a partisan. **1874** GREEN *Short Hist.* vi. §1. 274 The Duke of Gloucester..had now placed himself at the head of the partizans of the war.

2. *Mil.* **a.** A member of a party of light or irregular troops employed in scouring the country, surprising the enemy's outposts and foraging parties, and the like; a member of a volunteer force similarly engaged, a guerilla.

1692 LUTTRELL *Brief Rel.* (1857) II. 523 Leiutenant collonel Manwaring..brought in 50 French partizans, with excellent arms. **1810** WELLINGTON in Gurw. *Desp.* (1838) VI. 319 The numerous bands of partizans which are carrying on a destructive warfare. **1827** SCOTT *Napoleon* VII. 36 The qualities of a partizan or irregular soldier are inherent in the national character of the Spaniard.

b. A leader of such a party of light or irregular troops; a guerilla chief or captain.

1706 PHILLIPS s.v., In the Art of War, *a good Partisan* is an able Soldier well skill'd in commanding a Party. **1731** BAILEY vol. I, *Partisan* (in *Military Affairs*) a Commander of a Party. **1760** *Hist.* in *Ann. Reg.* 26/2 This march would have been thought an astonishing exploit in a partizan at the head of a small and disencumbered corps. **1837** W. IRVING *Capt. Bonneville* II. 38. **1853** STOCQUELER *Milit. Encycl.*, *Partisan*, ..also means an officer sent out upon a party, with the command of a body of light troops, generally under the appellation of the partisan's corps.

c. In the war of 1939–45, a guerrilla, esp. one working in enemy-occupied territory in Eastern Europe and the Balkans, *spec.* in Yugoslavia. Also *attrib.*

1939 C. GUBBINS (*title*) Partisan leader's handbook. **1942** *Daily Tel.* 22 May 1/3 Behind the fighting front the Russian 'partisan front' in the German rear forms a skeleton army. **1944** *Hutchinson's Pict. Hist. War* 27 Oct. 1943–11 Apr. 1944, 414 In the autumn of 1941 Marshal Tito's partisans began a wild and furious war for existence against the Germans... The partisan movement soon out-stripped in numbers the forces of General Mikhailovitch. **1958** P. KEMP *No Colours or Crest* vi. 100 He arrived with thirty Partisans, saying he intended to lay an ambush in exactly the same place as ours. **1965** B. SWEET-ESCOTT *Baker St. Irreg.* vii. 191 Maclean and Velebit were mainly concerned to obtain British training for a Yugoslav tank regiment and a fighter squadron, and to get a fleet of light craft for a partisan navy. *Ibid.* 193 His assignment had been to make contact with the Bulgarian partisans. **1968** *New Left Rev.* Jan.–Feb. 67 During the Second World War I had no doubts about which side I was on in the struggle, let us say, between the Yugoslav Partisans and the Nazi occupation forces. **1974** tr. *Sniečkus's Soviet Lithuania* 47 The Lithuanian people gave every possible aid to the partisans, whom they regarded as true patriots. **1978** A. PRICE *'44 Vintage* xix. 220 He got back in..in 1939... France in '40, then the Middle East... And finally Yugoslavia as a weapons adviser to a big Partisan outfit.

3. *Comb.*, as ***partisan-like*** adj.

1841 I. TAYLOR *Spir. Chr.* 190 None commands our servile or partisanlike support.

B. *attrib.* or as *adj.* [cf. F. *partisan*, adj.].

1. Of, pertaining to, or characteristic of a partisan; supporting a party, esp. zealously or blindly; biased, prejudiced, one-sided.

1842 AGNES STRICKLAND *Queens Eng.* II. 380 Nothing but partisan malice could blame such hospitality. **1882** HINSDALE *Garfield & Educ.* II. 363 One spot..across which the shadow of partisan politics has never fallen. **1885** *L'pool Daily Post* 1 June 5/3 Every obstacle which partisan malevolence could create.

2. *Mil.* Of or pertaining to military partisans (see A. 2); pertaining to irregular or petty warfare. ***partisan ranger***: = RANGER *sb.*¹ 3.

1708 *Lond. Gaz.* No. 4447/3 Our Partisan Parties have lately been very successful. **1731** BAILEY vol. II, *Partisan Party*, a small body of Infantry commanded by a Partisan, to make an incursion upon the enemy, to lurk about their camp to disturb their foragers, and to intercept their convoys. **1827** SCOTT *Napoleon* VII. 35 The system of guerilla or partizan warfare [in Spain]. **1855** MACAULAY *Hist. Eng.* xii. III. 226 The Enniskilleners had never ceased to wage a vigorous partisan war against the native population.

Hence **'parti,saning** *a.*, supporting a party zealously or blindly; **'partisanism**, the practice of partisanship; partisan spirit; **'partisanize** *v. trans.*, to render partisan; **'parti,sanly** *adv.*, in the manner of a partisan; **'parti,sanry** (rarely *partisanery*), partisanship, a partisan feeling or act.

1790 in Dallas *Amer. Law Rep.* I. 319 Violent attacks..to gratify partisaning and temporising resentments. **1866** H.

SIDGWICK *Let.* 7 Nov. in A. & E. M. Sidgwick *Henry Sidgwick* (1906) 153 To ensure no..votes be lost, partisanly speaking. **1882** *Daily News* 18 Aug. 5/5 The 'World', which is partisanly Irish, calls the sentence outrageous. **1889** BRUCE *Plant. Negro* 67 Whose partisanry conforms..to the seductions of bribery. **1890** *Columbus* (Ohio) *Disp.* 29 Mar., As long as partisanism continues rampant in the legislature. **1896** *Ibid.* 28 Sept., Loyal Prohibitionists are neither partisanized old men, nor spoiled children. **1911** G. B. SHAW *Getting Married* Pref. 119 Such paltry follies and sentimentalities, snobberies and partisaneries, as ignorance can understand and irresponsibility relish. **1976** *Church Times* 9 July 12/4, I wish I could understand why so many Christians feel so strongly—or so partisanly—about events in South Africa. **1977** *Times Lit. Suppl.* 27 May 644/3, I may be partisanly over-optimistic about the ability of the Sussex Constabulary to stand up to Mother Ancilla.

partisan, partizan ('pɑːtɪzæn), *sb.*² Also 6 **partyzyne, partesant, partison,** 6–7 **partezan, pertison,** 7 **partizane,** 7–8 **pertuisan(e,** 8 **partuisan(e,** 9 *arch.* **pertuizan.** *Obs.* from *c* 1700, till revived by Scott and 19th c. antiquaries. [a. 16th c. F. *partizane, parti-, parthisane,* ad. It. *partesana, partigiana,* in med.L. *partesana, pertixana*; in Sw. *bardisan.*

The origin of the It. word is disputed. Diez associates it with *partigiano* PARTISAN¹, as if the weapon carried by partisans; others would identify the first part with OHG. *parta, barta* halberd, leaving the rest of the word unexplained. In Fr., popularly corrupted in 15–16th c. to *pourtisaine, pertuisegne, pertusaine,* mod.F. *pertuisane,* as if from *pertuis* a hole, *pertuiser* to bore, pierce.]

1. A military weapon used (under this name) by footmen in the 16th and 17th c., consisting of a long-handled spear, the blade having one or more lateral cutting projections, variously shaped, so as sometimes to pass into the gisarme and the halberd; in some of its forms used also in boar-hunting.

1556 J. HEYWOOD *Spider & F.* lii. 25 Byls, bowes, partisance, pikes. **1557** *Will of W. Oliver* (Somerset Ho.), A staffe called a Partyzyne. **1573–80** BARET *Alv.* P 138 A Partison, a iaueline to skirmish with, *hasta velitaris.* **1583** *Rates of Customs* D vj, Partesants or Bore speares vngilt the dosen xxvis. viijd. **1596** *Lanc. & Chesh. Wills* III. 4 A pertison and a leadinge staffe. **1604** E. G[RIMSTONE] *D'Acosta's Hist. Indies* VII. xxiv. 570 Shewing their swordes, lances, pertuisans, and other armes. **1606** SHAKS. *Ant. & Cl.* II. vii. 14, I had as liue haue a Reede that will doe me no seruice, as a Partizan I could not heaue. **1625** MARKHAM *Souldiers Accid.* 5 Their weapons..shall be faire Partizans of strong and short blades. **1688** CAPT. J. S. *Art of War* 40 The Pike and Partisan are the onely Arms proper to stop the fury of the Cavalry. **1706** PHILLIPS, *Partisan* or *Pertuisan,* a Weapon like a Halbard, sometimes us'd by Lieutenants of Foot. **1805** SCOTT *Last Minstr.* IV. xx, On battlement and bartizan Gleam'd axe and spear and partizan. **1855** MOTLEY *Dutch Rep.* II. ix. (1866) 317/2 Others had the partisans, battle-axes, and huge two-handed swords of the previous century. **1874** BOUTELL *Arms & Arm.* viii. 145 The terms *partizan, halberde,* and *guisarme,* denote the same class of weapon, which admitted various modifications... In all these examples a lance-head and an axe are present.

b. Used as a leading-staff, and borne as a halberd by civic and other guards.

1611 COTGR., *Pertuisane,* a Partisan, or leading staffe. **1667** CHAMBERLAYNE *St. Eng.* I. (1684) 213 Of the Yeomen of the Guard..One half..bear in their hands..partizans. **1681** *Lond. Gaz.* No. 1661/3 His Royal Highness was received by the Provost, Magistrates and Council, and by a Band of the Young Men of the Town, bearing Gilded Partisans. [**1828** SCOTT *F.M. Perth* viii, They have brought two town officers with their partizans, to guard their fair persons, I suppose. **1860** FAIRHOLT *Costume* 277 One of King Charles II.'s yeomen of the guard has been here copied... He carries a partisan in his right hand and a sword by his side.]

2. *transf.* A soldier or civic guard armed with a partisan.

1693 *Lond. Gaz.* No. 2869/2 First marched the City Partizanes in new Liveries bare-headed. [**1820** SCOTT *Abbot* xviii, They..were fighting hard, when the provost, with his guard of partizans, came in thirdsman, and staved them asunder with their halberds, as men part dog and bear.]

partisanship (see PARTISAN¹). [f. PARTISAN¹ + -SHIP.] The state, condition, or practice of a partisan; zealous or blind support of one's party.

1831 CARLYLE *Sart. Res.* III. i, Not out of blind sectarian partisanship. **1867** FREEMAN *Norm. Conq.* I. iv. 268 The frenzy of religious partizanship.

partise, obs. pl. of PARTY.

† **'partising.** *Sc. Law. Obs.* Also 6 pairt-. [app. corrupt. of OF. *partison, -isson, -eisun* partition, separation, departure (:—L. *partitiōn-em*); the ending being confused with Sc. *-in, -ene, -ing,* of vbl. sbs.] Legal parting or separation; formal divorce. ***libel of partising,*** bill of divorce.

1552 ABP. HAMILTON *Catech.* 165 b, Sumtyme a man haffand displesure at his wife wald geue to hir a libel of partising and put hir fra him. *c* **1568** in H. Campbell *Love-lett. Mary Q. Scots* (1824) App. 47 April..26, the first precept for the partising of the Erle of Bothwell and his wyif was direct furth from the Commissarys of Edinburgh. *a* **1578** LINDESAY (Pitscottie) *Chron. Scot.* (S.T.S.) II. 217 To adwyse of the pairtising of the quein and my lord bothwell.

partisman: see PARTSMAN.

partison, obs. form of PARTISAN².

partita (pɑː'tiːtə). *Mus.* [It.] An air with variations; a suite.

1880 GROVE *Dict. Mus.* II. 656/1 He [*sc.* Bach] also wrote three Partitas (in the Suite-form) for the lute. The name has very seldom been used since Bach... But in the modern rage for revivals it may possibly reappear. **1925** *Chambers's Jrnl.* 31 Oct. 755/1 In such a week Mr Samuel has played sixteen preludes and fugues, ten French suites, partitas and English suites. **1948** *Times* 30 July 7/3 Mr. Vaughan Williams's most recent work, a Partita for strings, was given its first concert performance at the Albert Hall last evening. **1967** I. SPINK *Hist. Approach Mus. Form* iii. 67 Bach clearly distinguishes the forms in his six sonatas for violin alone by calling those in church style 'sonatas' and those in chamber style 'partitas'.

partite ('pɑːtaɪt), *a.* [ad. L. *partīt-us* parted, divided. Cf. BIPARTITE, QUINQUEPARTITE, etc.]

a. Divided into parts or portions.

1570 LEVINS *Manip.* 151/40 Partyte, *partitus, a.* **1680** MORDEN *Geogr. Rect., Spain* (1685) 170 Spain fell into a 12-partite division.

b. *Bot.* and *Entom.* Divided to the base, or nearly so, as a leaf, corolla, or insect's wing.

[**1753** CHAMBERS *Cycl. Supp.* s.v. *Leaf, Quinquepartite Leaf,* one which is separated into five parts down to the very base... In the same manner a leaf is said to be *bipartite,* etc.] **1760** J. LEE *Introd. Bot.* III. v. (1765) 179 *Partite,* divided; when they are separated down to the Base. **1826** KIRBY & SPENCE *Entomol.* IV. 296 Partite (*Partita*), divided to the base. **1861** BENTLEY *Man. Bot.* 232 The corolla may be partite, cleft, toothed, or entire. **1880** GARROD & BAXTER *Mat. Med.* 180 The leaves are..palmate, five-partite.

† **par'tited,** *ppl. a. Her. Obs. rare.* [f. as prec. + -ED.] Divided into parts: said of a cross used as a bearing, having each arm doubled, or tripled (TRIPARTITED).

1486 *Bk. St. Albans, Heraldry* c vij, He berith Sable and a cros dowble pertitid of Siluer. *Ibid.* c vij b, Then hit is called a cros dowble partitid florishid, as here.

partition (pə'tɪʃən, pɑː-), *sb.* Also 5–6 **per-.** [a. F. *partition* (Oresme, 14th c.), in 12th c. *particion,* ad. L *partītiōn-em,* from *partīre* to PART.]

1. a. The action of parting or dividing into parts; the fact of being so divided; division; esp. the division of a country into two or more nations; *spec.* (*a*) the division of Ireland into Northern Ireland and the Irish Republic; (*b*) the division of the Indian sub-continent into India and Pakistan in 1947. Hence **par'titionist,** one who advocates partition; also as *adj.*

1509 HAWES *Past. Pleas.* I. (Percy Soc.) 5 An ymage.. With two fayre handes stretched out along, Unto two hye wayes there in particion. **1552** HULOET, Deuision or particion of a praye or spoyle in warre. **1567** MAPLET *Gr. Forest* 28 Some..ioynted or deuided as the Reede: some without any such particion. **1571** DIGGES *Pantom.* II. xiv. O j, Certayne questions for the partition and diuision of grounde. **1591** PERCIVALL *Sp. Dict., Creēncha,* the partition of the haire, *comæ diuisio. c* **1620** A. HUME *Brit. Tongue* (1865) 16 Quhen a word fales to be divyded at the end of a lyne, the partition must be made at the end of a syllab. **1741** MIDDLETON *Cicero* xi. II. 436 The partition of the Empire. **1855** BAIN *Senses & Int.* II. i. §8 (1864) 88 The threefold partition of mind into Feeling, Volition, and Intellect. **1919** *Times* 25 Jan. 9/5 (*headline*) Irish Unionist breach. New League against Partition. *Ibid.* 27 Jan. 9/4 The principles of the [Anti-Partition] League were defined as follows:—To maintain the legislative union of Great Britain and Ireland, to secure Ireland against partition, and to safeguard the liberties and interests of Irish Unionists. **1919** P. S. O'HEGARTY *Ulster* 1 In North Down the Independent vote was counted as Partitionist. **1921** *Spectator* 4 June 713/2 Partition has come to be reckoned the unforgivable sin by the Sinn Feiners. The worst thing a man can be called is a partitionist. **1938** *Ann. Reg. 1937* 256 The World Zionist Executive, sitting in Jerusalem, formally resolved that the Zionist Organization would resist any attempt to curtail the rights of the Jews as defined in the Mandate, either by Partition or any other measure. **1941** K. CHANDRA *Tragedy of Jinnah* xv. 220 Many schemes of partition of India on communal basis [*sic*] were put forward by a few fanatics, off and on. **1945** *Ann. Reg. 1944* 164 This weakening of Mr. Gandhi's hitherto uncompromising opposition to partition was denounced by the Hindu Mahasabha and the Sikhs and caused much misgiving in Congress circles. **1948** *Ann. Reg. 1947* 153 The Muslims having voted for partition of India, the Hindus and Sikhs then voted for the partition of two Provinces, and the frontiers of Pakistan were thus drawn in the midst of the Punjab and Bengal. **1955** R. P. JHABVALA *To whom she Will* vi. 43 Hari Sahni's family..were Punjabi Indians who in 1947, at the time of Partition, had had to leave their native Lahore. **1959** P. COLUM *Arthur Griffith* II. iv. 121 The Irish people were now shown that this claim would be countered by a move for Partition. **1967** P. M. HUBBARD *Custom of Country* (1969) vii. 81, I agreed I was English, and he said, 'Ah, then you will have been a government servant out here before Partition.' **1971** R. DENTRY *Encounter at Kharmel* iii. 58 There hasn't been a tribal rising..since the Partition troubles died down. **1972** A. BOYD *Brian Faulkner* i. 12 The issue, as in all previous elections, was partition. **1973** *Archivum Linguisticum* IV. 42 In the Indo-Pakistan sub-continent before partition..Delhi and Lucknow were recognized as the places where 'they spoke the best Urdu'. **1975** *Guardian* 24 Feb. 9/6 Just as in every other country that has fallen for the silly expedient of Partition—Ireland, Korea, Vietnam— nobody profits but the politicians.

b. Division into shares or portions; distribution.

c **1430** LYDG. *Min. Poems* (Percy Soc.) 170 Al tho that make suche a particioune Amonge theyr subjettis. **1580** SIDNEY *Ps.* XXII. xi, Of my poore weedes they do partition make. **1653** H. COGAN tr. *Pinto's Trav.* xxii. 71 He spent out of the general booty, before the partitions were made. **1751** *Affect. Narr. of Wager* 102 A final Partition was this Day made of the remaining Flour. **1799** W. TOOKE *View Russian Emp.* I. 327 At the first partition of Poland in 1773. *a* **1832** MACKINTOSH *Fr. War of* 1793 Wks. 1846 III. 179 We cannot ..imagine that a greater evil could befall the human race than the partition of Europe among the spoilers of Poland. **1901** *N. Amer. Rev.* Feb. 275 The partition of sovereignty between..the State governments that the people created, and the government of the United States.

c. *fig.* (Cf. 2 *Tim.* ii. 15.)

1641 J. JACKSON *True Evang. T.* I. 7 It is a safe rule in the partition of holy Scripture, not to churne the sincere milk thereof till butter come. **1684** WILLARD *Mercy Magn.* 9 We may briefly take partition of this parable.

d. *Physical Chem.* The distribution of a solute between two immiscible or slightly miscible solvents in contact with one another, in accordance with its differing solubility in each. Cf. *partition coefficient* (sense 10).

1861 *Nat. Philos. for Use of Schools: Chem. & Chemical Analysis* ii. 44 Partition of Elements.—Affinities are sometimes modified by circumstances which might not be supposed likely to produce any effect: thus, the more difficult solubility of one of the compounds present in a solution. **1898** C. L. SPEYERS *Text-bk. Physical Chem.* v. 119 (*heading*) Partition of substance between two solvents. **1950** F. HAUROWITZ *Chem. & Biol. Proteins* iii. 21 Synge..has made use of the partition of amino acids between water and ..organic solvents which are immiscible with but partly soluble in water. **1970** SHERMA & ZWEIG in G. Zweig et al. *Paper Chromatogr. & Electrophoresis* (1971) II. ii. 11 The paper..acts by a combination of partition, adsorption, and ion exchange.

2. The action of parting or separating two or more persons or things; the fact or condition of being separated; separation, division.

1530 PALSGR. 165 *Separaisón,* a particion. **1562** TURNER *Baths* 1 b, We make no partition betwen yᵉ men and the weomen whilse they are in bathing. **1611** SHAKS. *Cymb.* I. vi. 38 Can we not Partition make..Twixt faire, and foule? **1766** FORDYCE *Serm. Yng. Wom.* (1767) II. xiii. 233 Every wall of partition..it throws down. **1872** BLACKIE *Lays Highl.* 104 Walls of ancient, harsh partition 'Twixt the people, and the crown.

3. Something that separates (either a material structure, or more rarely an immaterial boundary or dividing line); *esp.* that which separates one part of a space from another; *e.g.* a structure separating rooms or parts of a room (*esp.* when of slighter nature than a wall proper); a septum or dissepiment in a plant or animal body; etc.

1545 ELYOT, *Dissepimentum,* the particion in a wall nutte, wherwith the kernell is deuided. **1571** DIGGES *Pantom.* II. xv. O j b, A hedge dyke or other partition runnyng from.. the fountayne to..the marke espyed. **1617** in Willis & Clark *Cambridge* (1886) I. 205 All the particians shall bee maide with good and sufficient groundesills. **1681** DRYDEN *Abs. & Achit.* I. 164 Great wits are sure to madness near allied, And thin partitions do their bounds divide. **1687** A. LOVELL tr. *Thevenot's Trav.* I. 82 The High Altar is divided from the rest of the Church by a wooden partition with three doors in it. **1763** BICKERSTAFF *Love in Village* 56 Did I not overhear your scheme..through the partition? **1844** LD. BROUGHAM *A. Lunel* I. iii. 85 The thin partition that divided his mirth and good humour from his anger. **1846** *P. Parley's Ann.* VII. 235 One shaft divided by a brattice or partition in two. **1878** MACALISTER *Vertebr. & Inv.* 46 The red organ-pipe coral of the Indian Ocean, with its table-like partitions and its green polyps. **1892** J. A. THOMSON *Outl. Zool.* 138 A number of partitions or mesenteries extend from the body-wall towards this gullet. Some of the partitions are 'complete'.

4. Each of the parts into which any whole is divided, as by boundaries or lines; a portion, part, division, section.

a. *gen.* (Formerly applied to the divisions of a book or literary work.) Now *rare.*

1561 T. NORTON tr. *Calvin's Inst.* I. xiii. (1634) 56 He.. affirmeth, that there be part, and partitions in the essence of God, of which every portion is God. **1571** (*title*) Toxophilus, The Schole, or partitions of shooting contayned in ij bookes written by Roger Ascham. **1608** R. NORTON tr. *Stevin's Disme* D iv, The Yard, Ell, &c., with his tenne partitions. **1621** BURTON *Anat. Mel.* I. i. III. iv. (1651) 36 Of this last..I will speak..in my third Partition. **1727** POPE, etc. *Art of Sinking* 115 The vituperative partition will as easily be replenished. *a* **1854** REED *Lect. Eng. Lit.* vii. (1878) 235 In each partition of our earth's time.

b. One of a number of actual superficial or cubic spaces into which an object is divided; a compartment; a pane, a panel; a pocket (of a bag); an apartment, chamber, room.

1578 T. N. tr. *Conq. W. Ind.* 66 Of a faire and straunge workemanshippe inwardes, with many great partitions, some full of pottes of honey, and maiz. **1697** DAMPIER *Voy.* (1729) I. 412 The Hold was divided in many small Partitions. **1756** MRS. BROOKE *Old Maid* No. 37 (1764) 300 The temple was divided into two noble partitions. **1783** WESLEY *Wks.* (1872) IV. 250 The garden before the house was in three partitions. **1900** G. SWIFT *Somerley* 58 She walked straight up to the window, which was divided into three partitions.

5. *Law.* A division of real property, esp. of lands, between joint-tenants, tenants in common, or coparceners, made either by private agreement, a judicial decree, or private act of parliament, by which their co-tenancy or co-ownership is abolished and their individual interests in the land are separated; a division into severalty.

1474 *Rolls of Parlt.* VI. 100/1 That the seid Dukes and their seid wyfes..may make particion of all the premisses and every part therof [the premisses were real estate]. **1512** *Act 4 Hen. VIII*, c. 13 *Preamble*, Particion was made be twyne theyme of the sayd Maners. **1696** Phillips (ed. 5) s.v., Partition of Lands descended by the Common Law, or by Custom among Coheirs or Parceners. **1741** T. Robinson *Gavelkind* i. 7 To shew an actual partition of the Lands. **1818** Cruise *Digest* (ed. 2) II. 521 The third mode of voluntary partition is, where the eldest makes the division of the lands; in which case she shall choose last. **1845** *Act 8 & 9 Vict.* c. 106 §3 A partition and an exchange of any tenements or hereditaments, not being copyhold..shall also be void at law, unless made by deed.

6. a. *Logic.* Analysis by systematic separation of the integrant parts of a thing; enumeration of parts. (Distinguished from *division*: see division 6.)

1551 T. Wilson *Logike* (1580) 15 A manne is diuided into bodie and soule, and this kinde of diuidyng is properlie called a partition. **1697** tr. *Burgersdicius his Logic* II. v. 17 When Man or Human Body is divided into its three Regions and Limbs; or the Year into 12 Months... It is a Definition of the Integrate, or Mathematical, and is called Partition. **1725** Watts *Logic* I. vi. §8. **1866** Fowler *Elem. Deduct. Logic* viii. (1887) 59 As a test of a logical division..the term divided must be predicable of each dividing member... In this manner it is distinguished from *partition* of a whole into its parts. **1870** Jevons *Logic* xii. 108 Logical division must not be confused with physical division or Partition.

b. *Math.* A collection of non-empty subsets of a given set such that each element of the latter is a member of exactly one of the subsets; a way of dividing a set thus.

1905 J. Pierpont *Lect. Theory Functions Real Variables* I. ii. 82 Let α be any number of $\mathfrak{R}$; we can use it to throw all numbers of $\mathfrak{R}$ into two classes A, B. In A we put all numbers $< \alpha$; in B all numbers $> \alpha$. The number α we may put in A or B. This division of the numbers of $\mathfrak{R}$ into two classes we call a partition. **1937** Michell & Belz *Elem. Math. Analysis* II. xxi. 1051 The notion of partitions of the rationals forms the basis of Dedekind's treatment of real numbers. **1968** E. T. Copson *Metric Spaces* i. 12 If $\sim$ is an equivalence relation on a set E, two equivalence classes are either identical or have no common member; the collection of all equivalence classes is a partition of E. **1972** A. G. Howson *Handbk. Terms Algebra & Anal.* xxiv. 118 A finite set of points $P = \{a_0, \ldots, a_n\}$ satisfying the above requirements, i.e. $a = a_0 < a_1 < a_2 < \ldots < a_n = b$, is known as a partition of the interval $\leqslant a, b \geqslant$.

7. *Math.* †**a.** = division 5 a. *Obs.*

1571 Digges *Pantom.* I. xii. D iij b, Augment by the parts, and make particion by 12. **1709–29** V. Mandey *Syst. Math., Arith.* 3 Division, or Partition, is the finding of a Number which shews..how often the Number Dividing..is contained in the Dividend.

b. Any one of the ways of expressing a number as a sum of positive integers (*e.g.* the partitions of 4 are 1 + 1 + 1 + 1, 1 + 1 + 2, 1 + 3, 2 + 2).

1855 Cayley *Coll. Math. Papers* II. 235 (*heading*) Researches on the Partition of Numbers. **1859** Sylvester (*title*) Lectures on the Partitions of Numbers, delivered at King's College, London.

8. *Mus.* An arrangement of the several parts of a composition one above another on the same stave or set of staves; a score. Now *rare* or *Obs.*

1597 Morley *Introd. Mus.* 97 Here it is set downe in partition, because you should the more easilie perceiue the conueiance of the parts. **1727–41** Chambers *Cycl.*, *Partition*, in music, the disposition of the several parts of a song, set on the same leaf; so as upon the uppermost ranges of lines are found the treble; in another the bass [etc.]. **1891** *Daily News* 24 Oct. 5/4 Here are to be found original scores and partitions, MSS. interesting not only to the musician but to the collector of autographs.

9. *Her.* **a.** The division of a shield into two parts of different tinctures by one of the dividing lines (see parted, party *a.*). ? *Obs.* †**b.** An ordinary which separates or lies between common charges on a shield. *Obs.* **c.** Each of the divisions or compartments of a parted or quartered shield.

1486 *Bk. St. Albans, Heraldry* d iij, The first particion forsoth is of ij colouris in armys after the long way in the playne maner. *Ibid.* d v, The.. particion ouerwart is made as mony wyse as is the partycion on length. **1610** Guillim *Heraldry* III. ii. (1660) 108 Whensoever there is a separation of common charges..by reason of the Interposition of some ..Ordinaries, then they are not termed Ordinaries, but most worthy Partitions. **1725** Coats *Dict. Her.*, *Partitions*, or *Compartiments*, as the French call them, as also *Quarterings* of the Escutcheon, according to the Number of Coats that are to be on it, are the several Divisions made in it, when the Arms of several Families are born altogether by one.

10. *attrib.* and *Comb.*, as *partition-balk*, *-beam*, *fence*, *-line*; **partition chromatography**, chromatography which utilizes the differing solubilities of the components of a mixture in a liquid sorbent (chosen to be immiscible with the carrier if this is a liquid); *spec.* that in which the sorbent is a polar liquid and the carrier a less polar liquid; hence **partition-chromatogram**, **-chromatographic** *a.*; **partition coefficient** *Physical Chem.* [tr. F. *coefficient de partage* (Berthelot & Jungfleisch 1872, in *Ann. de Chim. et de Physique* XXVI. 398)], the ratio of the concentrations of a solute in each of two immiscible or slightly miscible liquids, or two solids, when it is in equilibrium across the interface between them; **partition function** *Physics*, a sum of the form $\sum_i \Omega_i \exp(-E_i/kT)$ (where Ω_i is the degeneracy of the state with energy E_i, k is Boltzmann's constant, and T the absolute temperature), or an analogous integral, which enters into the expression for the distribution of the particles of a system among different energy states and other thermodynamic quantities; symbol Z; **Partition treaty**, name given to each of the two treaties (of 11 Oct. 1698 and 11 Oct. 1700) attempting 'to settle from outside the complex question of the Spanish Succession on the death of the king, Charles II' (Low and Pulling *Dict. Eng. Hist.* 1884, 804). See also partition-wall.

1581–90 in Willis & Clark *Cambridge* (1886) II. 412 A particion balke..of .16. foote breadthe. **1944** *Biochem. Jrnl.* XXXVIII. 286/2 On paper strip partition chromatograms ..a number of free peptides travel as reasonably narrow bands whose presence can be revealed by treatment with ninhydrin. *Ibid.* 65/1 We record here some technical aspects of the experience which we have gained in the use of our partition chromatographic method..for the quantitative analysis of amino-acid mixtures. **1968** *Jrnl. Chromatogr.* XXXVII. 97 Partition systems..are much less likely to hinder complete recovery of unchanged, separated components. Hence there is an interest in developing practically useful liquid partition chromatographic systems. **1943** A. H. Gordon et al. in *Biochem. Jrnl.* XXXVII. 79/1 In the present paper we report new applications and developments of partition chromatography* (Martin & Synge, 1941*b*) in the study of amino-acids and peptides. [*Note**] We employ the term 'partition chromatography' at the suggestion of Dr. E. Lester Smith, to distinguish it from the classical adsorption chromatography. Our earlier term 'liquid-liquid chromatography' was liable to confusion with the fractional elution procedure sometimes called 'liquid chromatography'. **1966** *McGraw-Hill Encycl. Sci. & Technol.* III. 94/2 Volatile, nonpolar substances such as hydrocarbons may be examined by gas adsorption or gas partition chromatography... Weakly polar substances such as alcohols..are examined by adsorption or partition chromatography. *Ibid.* 95/2 With the phases reversed, that is with the polar phase as the wash liquid and the less polar phase fixed in the support, the method is known as reversed phase partition chromatography. It provides a chromatographic sequence the inverse of that produced by partition chromatography. **1967** M. E. Hale *Biol. Lichens* viii. 130 It is only in the past 15 years that the development of partition chromatography has brought a rapid and sure means of identifying plant products within the reach of taxonomists and physiologists. **1891** *Jrnl. Chem. Soc.* LX. II. 1148 (*heading*) Relation between affinity and partition coefficients in immiscible solvents. **1925** *Jrnl. Iron & Steel Inst.* CXII. 492 Variations in the concentration of cementite can be studied by means of the position of the Curie point, which allows of ascertaining variations in the partition coefficient of manganese between the carbide and the ferrite according to the annealing temperature. **1964** G. I. Brown *Introd. Physical Chem.* xxi. 235 Suppose that 100 cc. of benzene is available for extracting a solute, X, dissolved in 100 cc. of water, and that the partition coefficient of X between benzene and water is 5. **1639** *Early Rec. Dedham, Mass.* (1892) III. 51 A pticon [*sc.* partition] fence in the same. **1748** *New Hampsh. Probate Rec.* (1916) III. 608 [This land is] to be possess'd and enjoy'd by them..as ye partition fence between them now stands. **1870** *Rep. Comm. Agric. 1869* (U.S. Dept. Agric.) 395 Partition fences must be proof against sheep. **1927** Fisher & Hartree tr. *Born's Mech. Atom* 3 The so-called partition function (Zustandsintegral). **1970** P. W. Atkins *Molecular Quantum Mech.* x. 392 The proportion of molecules in the rotational state J is given by $Z^{-1}(2J + 1) \times \exp\{-E(J)/kT\}$, where Z is the rotational partition function. **1796** Morse *Amer. Geog.* I. 465 The partition line between New York and Connecticut as established Dec. 1, 1664. **1838** Prescott *Ferd. & Is.* (1846) II. xviii. 165 The removal of the partition line was followed by important consequences to the Portuguese. **1711** Swift *Conduct of Allies* 15 The Violation of the Partition-Treaty, by the French. **1779–81** Johnson *L. P.*, *Prior* Wks. III. 134 The impeachment of those lords who had persuaded the king to the Partition-treaty. *a* **1859** Macaulay *Hist. Eng.* xxiv. (1880) II. 693 It was said, when first the terms of the Partition Treaty were made public..that the English and Dutch governments..were guilty of a violation of plighted faith.

partition (pəˈtɪʃən, pɑː-), *v.* [f. prec. sb.]

1. a. *trans.* To make partition of; to divide into parts or portions; to dismember and deal *out*.

1741 Richardson *Pamela* (1824) I. 52 She mentions his concealing himself to hear her partitioning out her clothes. **1821** *Examiner* 420/1 He never sullied his conquests by partitioning and dividing the conquered. **1828** D'Israeli *Chas. I*, I. vi. 162 We have witnessed, in our own times, this political artifice of partitioning a great kingdom.

b. *spec.* To divide (land) into severalty.

1880 Muirhead *Gaius* Dig. 442 The *actio familiae erciscundae* for partitioning an inheritance. **1883** *Law Times Rep.* XLIX. 162/2 They claimed..that the estate should be sold in lieu of being partitioned.

c. *Math.* To subdivide by means of a partition (sense 6 b).

1943 K. Mather *Statist. Anal. Biol.* xi. 180 A compound χ^2 can be partitioned into simple components each dependent on a single comparison and each taking 1 degree of freedom. **1959** Perfect & Petersen tr. *Alexandroff's Introd. Theory of Groups* vi. 67 Every group may be partitioned into classes of mutually conjugate elements. **1966** S. Beer *Decision & Control* vi. 106 The set of commercial responsibilities is partitioned, for example, into home sales (heavy), home sales (light) and export sales. **1968** E. T. Copson *Metric Spaces* v. 68 We can partition this set into two separated sets.

2. To separate by a partition; to divide *off*.

1832 Ht. Martineau *Hill & Valley* iv. 67 Paul had partitioned off half his little room to serve as a workshop. **1851** Dickens *Lett.* III. 131, I dream that I am a carpenter and can't partition off the hall. **1884** Bower & Scott *De Bary's Phaner.* 217 The internodes and petioles..are partitioned by diaphragms.

parˈtitional, *a.* Now *rare*. [f. partition *sb.* + -al[1].] Of, pertaining to, or of the nature of a partition.

1669 *First Cent. Hist. Springfield, Mass.* (1898) I. 379 The Towne order says that partitionall ffences betweene Lot and Lot..shal be ordered by ye Select men. *a* **1693** *Urquhart's Rabelais* III. l. 401 A separating and partitional Work. **1764** Grainger *Sugar Cane* IV. 456 *note*, The pods..contain from three to five seeds in partitional cells.

parˈtitionary, *a. rare.* [f. as prec. + -ary[1].] Of or concerned with the partition of lands.

1897 Maitland *Domesday & Beyond* 489 The loss of acres due to partitionary arrangements.

partitioned (pəˈtɪʃənd, pɑː-), *ppl. a.* [f. partition *sb.* and *v.* + -ed.] Having partitions; divided or separated by partitions. (Also with *off*.)

1625 Bacon *Ess.*, *Buildings* (Arb.) 549, I vnderstand both these Sides..to be vniforme without, though seuerally Partitioned within. **1838** Dickens *Nich. Nick.* xxxv, A little partitioned-off counting-house. **1866** S. B. James *Duty & Doctrine* (1871) 7 Your special studies, your divided and partitioned duties. **1875** Bedford *Sailor's Pocket Bk.* v. (ed. 2) 189 Partitioned spaces for their reception.

parˈtitioner. [f. partition *v.* + -er[1].] One who partitions; one who divides land.

1799 S. Turner *Anglo-Sax.* (1836) I. iv. iii. 275 Their first occupiers or partitioners transmit them [cultivated lands] to their descendants. **1888** *Archæol. Rev.* Mar. 23 As each partitioner might in course of time be represented by a group of persons, his heirs, each of these fields might be again partitioned into smaller enclosures.

parˈtitioning, *sb.* [f. partition *sb.* and *v.*]

1. [f. the sb.] Work consisting of partitions inside a house; material for partitions.

1663 Gerbier *Counsel* 80 The selings and Partitionings at one shilling two pence a yard. **1703** T. N. *City & C. Purchaser* 141 The Carcase, Flooring, Partitioning, Roofing, Ceiling-beams. **1811** *Self Instructor* 135 Roofing, flooring, and partitioning by the principal carpenters.

2. [f. the vb.] The action of the verb partition.

1890 *Daily News* 8 July 5/1 The most stupendous business in territorial partitioning known to history.

parˈtitioning, *ppl. a.* [f. partition *v.* + -ing[2].] That partitions: see the verb.

1795 Burke *Regic. Peace* iv. Wks. IX. 35 Revolution has not..taught the three..partitioning powers..moderation. **1815** *Ann. Reg.* 110 The former annexations of the three partitioning Powers.

parˈtitionment. [f. partition *v.* + -ment.]

1. The action or fact of partitioning; division into parts or shares; separation.

1864 in Webster. **1875** Bryce *Holy Rom. Emp.* xix. (ed. 5) 348 That greatest of public misfortunes, the partitionment of Poland. **1879** Tyler *Amer. Lit.* xvii. II. 272 The.. definite partitionment from Virginia of land that once belonged to it.

2. *concr.* A partition; a compartment.

1851 I. Taylor *Wesley* (1852) 105 As to these partitionments within which soulless religionists are content to be penfolded, he walked over them unconsciously.

parˈtition-wall. A wall forming a partition; *esp.* a wall dividing one room or portion of a building from another, an internal wall. Also *fig.*

1633 G. Herbert *Temple, Ch. Milit.* 26 But to the Gentiles he bore crosse and all, Rending with earthquakes the partition-wall. **1667** S. Primatt *City & C. Build.* 67 Partition-walls you may have Lathed, Plaistered, and Rendered for one shilling a yard. **1742** Young *Nt. Th.* IV. 658 Oh when will Death This mould'ring, old Partition-wall throw down? **1849** James *Woodman* vii, A partition wall, with a rude door in it, crossed the building at about one third of its length.

partitive (ˈpɑːtɪtɪv), *a.* and *sb.* [ad. L. *partītīv-us* (perh. through F. *partitif*, *-ive*, 1550 in Hatz.-Darm.), f. L. *partīt-us* divided: see -ive.]

A. *adj.* Having the quality or function of dividing into parts; characterized by or indicating partition. **a.** *spec.* in *Gram.* Denoting or indicating that only a part of a collective whole is considered or spoken of: esp. applied to a noun, pronoun, or adjective denoting such a part; also to the 'genitive of the divided whole' (Roby) used with such words (*partitive genitive*), in Greek, Latin, etc. (represented in Eng. by *of* with the sb.: see of *prep.* XIII).

1520 Whitinton *Vulg.* (1527) 5 b, The nowne partityue, as *aliquis, quisquam*: & euery nowne set as a nowne partityue. **1530** Palsgr. Introd. 29 Nownes partityves and distributyves as *tout, nul*. **1590** Stockwood *Rules Construct.* 33 Somtime of a noune partitiue or distributiue. **1828** in Webster. **1876** B. H. Kennedy *Pub. Sch. Lat. Gram.* II. (ed. 4) 417 The Plural Genitive of the Thing Distributed is a divisible Whole, and depends on Partitive Words indicating that one or more Parts (or no Part) of such Whole are taken. **1899** E. Anwyl *Welsh Gram.* §380 After the adjective *llawn*, 'full', what was probably an old Partitive Genitive, has survived in the dependent noun.

b. *partitive judgement* in *Logic*: see quot.

1895 *Funk's Stand. Dict.*, *Partitive judgment*, a judgment that, under form of a disjunctive, predicates of a genus its several species; as 'Indians are either North-American or South-American'.

B. *sb.* *Gram.* A partitive word; a word denoting a part of a whole.

1530 PALSGR. 74 Pronownes, unto which I joyne, by cause of lykenesse in nature, partityves. **1591** PERCIVALL *Sp. Dict.* E iv, Partitiues will haue a Genitiue case. **1609** SIR E. HOBY *Let. to T. H[iggons]* 28 So that Matthewes partatiue, and Markes collectiue doe note one thing. **1612** BRINSLEY *Pos. Parts* (1669) 133 This order is changed in the oblique cases of the Relative *qui*, of Interrogatives, Indefinites, and Partitives. **1876** B. H. KENNEDY *Pub. Sch. Lat. Gram.* II. (ed. 4) 418 Partitives sometimes take the Gen. of a Collective Noun: 'Plato totius Græciæ doctissimus fuit'.

'partitively, *adv.* [f. prec. + -LY[2].] In a partitive way; in the way of partition or division; *spec.* in *Gram.* In a partitive sense.

1520 WHITINTON *Vulg.* (1527) 5 b, Nownes y[t] be set partityuely be these. **1590** STOCKWOOD *Rules Construct.* 46 Nounes of the comparatiue and the superlatiue degree being put partitiuely.. require a genitiue case. *a* **1828** *Ruddiman's Rudiments* (ed. 2) 99 Partitives, and words placed Partitively, Comparatives, Superlatives, Interrogatives, and some Numerals, govern the Genitive Plural. **1870** *Contemp. Rev.* XIV. 416 The unperplexed steadiness with which, partitively employed, in hundreds, he carries on a multitude of difficult and complicated operations at the same time.

partizan: see PARTISAN.

partless ('pɑːtlɪs), *a.* Now *rare.* [f. PART *sb.* + -LESS.]

†**1.** Having no part or share (*of*, *in*); not sharing or participating *in* (= L. *expers*). *Obs.*

a **1340** HAMPOLE *Psalter* v. 7 God sall.. make þam partles of heuen. **13..** *E.E. Allit. P.* A. 335 Now rech I neuer for to declyne,.. When I am partlez of perlez myne. *c* **1374** CHAUCER *Boethius* IV. pr. iii. 93 (Camb. MS.) Who is he þat nolde deme þat he that is ryht myhty of good weere partles of the Meede. **1432–50** tr. *Higden* (Rolls) II. 251 Heber.. was partelesse [*immunis*] in the confusion of the langage of theyme. **1515** BARCLAY *Ecloges* ii, It were a great wonder among the women all, If none were partles of luste venerall. **1570** LEVINS *Manip.* 91/11 Partlesse, *expers.*

2. Destitute of parts or talents (see PART *sb.* 12).

1603 J. DAVIES *Microcosm.* (1878) 72/2 For Men of woorth (say they) with parts indow'd The tymes doe not respect, nor wil relive, But wholly vnto partlesse Spirits giue.

3. Having no parts; indivisible.

a **1696** SCARBURGH *Euclid* (1705) 4 As indivisible and partless as a point. **1766** G. CANNING *Anti-Lucretius* IV. 273 How much more easily, and surely, breeds Our Æther Motion, than your partless Seeds. *a* **1868** G. M. HOPKINS *Poems* (1967) 36 Your parley was not done and there! You went into the partless air. **1904** G. S. FULLERTON *Syst. Metaphysics* xxv. 410 An unanalyzable and part-less thing like the percept. **1972** *Sci. Amer.* Aug. 8/2 Democritus.. desired that his atoms be partless, a property they were to have in common with geometrical points.

Partlet[1] ('pɑːtlɪt). Forms: 4–5 **Pertelot(e**, 5 **Pertilot(e**, 7– **Partlet**. [a. OF. *Pertelote*, a female proper name.] A word used as the proper name of any hen, often ***Dame Partlet***; also applied, like 'hen', to a woman.

c **1386** CHAUCER *Nun's Pr. T.* 50 Seuene hennes.. Of whiche the faireste hewed on hire throte Was cleped faire damoysele Pertelote. **1481** CAXTON *Reynard* (Arb.) 31 Chantecler the cock, pertelot wyth alle theyr children. **1513** DOUGLAS *Æneis* XII. Prol. 159 Phebus red fowle.. Hys wifis, Toppa and Pertelok, hym by. **1607** W. YONGE *Diary* 11 June (Camden) 14, I saw a partlet slain therewith [by a thunder shower]. **1611** SHAKS. *Wint. T.* II. iii. 75 Thou dotard, thou art woman-tyr'd: vnroosted By thy dame Partlet heere. **1746** H. WALPOLE *Let. to G. Montagu* 22 May, The partlets have not laid since I went. *a* **1845** HOOD *Tale of Trumpet* xliii, Like the call of Partlett to gather her young. **1885** *Punch* 13 June (*Forward Boy*), Do you think an old Partlet who's taken to preaching Is like to be heard?

partlet[2]. *Obs.* exc. *Hist.* Forms: 6–7 **partelet**, 6–8 **partlet**, (6 **-lett(e**, **pertelet**). [app. a corrupted form of *patelet*, PATLET.] An article of apparel worn about the neck and upper part of the chest, chiefly by women: orig. a neckerchief of linen or the like; a collar or ruff; also, a kind of habit-shirt.

1519 *Harl. MS.* 2284 lf. 42 b, x yerdes of russet satten for a Jaquet & a partelet for the kinges grace. **1526** *Lanc. Wills* I. 13 To Emme my doughter myne other bonett and a partlett. **1526** TINDALE *Acts* xix. 12 From his body were brought unto the sicke napkyns and partlettes. **1528** —— *Obed. Chr. Man* Wks. (1573) 131 Paul sent his pertelet or jerkyn to the sicke, and healed them also. **1580** HOLLYBAND *Treas. Fr. Tong*, *Vn collet, ou gorgias de quoy les femmes couvrent leurs poictrines*, a partlet. *a* **1586** SIDNEY *Arcadia* III. (1629) 274 Parthenia.. tearing off her linnen sleeves and partlet to serve about his wounds. **1617** COLLINS *Def. Bp. Ely* II. ix. 364 To see Lazarus come forth bound about with his partlets. **1658** PHILLIPS, *Partlet*, a word used in some old Statutes, signifying the loose collar of a dublet to be set on or taken off by it self without the bodies, also a womans neckercheif. **1786** CUMBERLAND *Observer* III. No. 65. 44 A close-bellied doublet coming down with a peake behind as far as the crupper, and cut off before by the breastbone like a partlet or neckercher. [**1834** PLANCHÉ *Brit. Costume* 245. **1843** LYTTON *Last Bar.* I. iv, She turned aside, and took off the partelet of lawn.]

attrib. or *Comb.* **1597–8** BP. HALL *Sat.* IV. vi. 9 Tyr'd with pinned ruffs, and fans, and partlet strips. **1641** *Dial. Rattle-h. & Round-h.* 8 Let Lawn-sleeves serve instead of Buffe, And for your Arms your partlet ruffe.

†**'partlike**, *adv.* *Sc.* *Obs.* *rare.* [f. PART *sb.* + LIKE.] Proportionally.

1538 *Aberdeen Regr.* XVI. (Jam.), And suld haff pait thair part partlyk and he had tynt. *Ibid.*, Thair part partlyk of thre crovnis. *Ibid.* XV, Partlyik.

†**'partlings**, *adv.* *Sc.* *Obs.* *rare.* [f. PART *sb.* + *-lings*: see -LING[2].] = PARTLY.

1578–9 *Reg. Privy Council Scot.* Ser. I. III. 78 Partlingis according to thair naturall ewill inclinatioun.

partly ('pɑːtlɪ), *adv.* [f. PART *sb.* + -LY[2].]

1. With respect to a part; in part; in some measure or degree: not wholly. (Usually repeated in reference to each of the parts considered.)

1523 SKELTON *Garl. Laurel* 1054 Partly by your councell, .. Was my fresshe coronell. **1563** SHUTE *Archit.* B ij, Partelye for their beautye,.. partelye for their fortitude and strength. **1570** LEVINS *Manip.* 101/5, 6 Partly redde, *rubicundus.* Partly fayre, *pulchrellus.* **1613** PURCHAS *Pilgrimage* (1614) 78 The Curdi, that were Participles or Mungrels in Religion, professing partly Christ, partly Mahumet. **1712** ADDISON *Spect.* No. 269 ¶12 Hearing the Knight's Reflexions, which were partly private, and partly political. **1873** *Act 36 & 37 Vict.* c. 85 §8 Every such agreement shall be in writing or in print, or partly in writing and partly in print.

b. Usually hyphened to a participial adjective when preceding its substantive.

1888 J. PAYN *Myst. Mirbridge* xxiv, A partly-heard conversation. **1891** T. HARDY *Tess* lvi. (1900) 137/2 Within the partly-closed door. **1898** *Westm. Gaz.* 18 July 8/1 The whole of the partly-paid shares of the new company.

†**2. partly-coloured**, parti-coloured. *Obs.*

1582 in W. H. Turner *Select. Rec. Oxford* (1880) 430 Scottyshe cappes partelie colored.

partly, obs. form of PERTLY.

†**'partment.** *Sc.* *Obs.* In 7 **pairtment**. [f. PART *v.* + -MENT.] Departure.

1663 T. MAKDOWELL *Let.* in J. Russell *Haigs* x. (1881) 276 To express what grief your mother doth sustain since your pairtment from hence.

partner ('pɑːtnə(r)), *sb.* Forms: 3–8 **partener**, (4 **parteneer**, **parthenare**, **-ere**, 4–5 **partenere**, **pertener**, **-yner(e**, 4–6 **partenar**, **-iner**, **-yner(e**, 5 **partoner**, **perteynor**, 5–6 **pertiner**, **-eyner**, 6 **parteiner**, **-eyner**, **-inar**, 7 *Sc.* **pairtenar**), 6– **partner**. [In 13th c. *partener*, app. an alteration of PARCENER under the influence of PART *sb.*

In the earliest examples it appears as a variant MS. reading of *parcener*; it has been suggested that, in some cases at least, this was due to a scribal confusion of *c* and *t*; but, as *parcener* was in 14th c. very commonly written *parsener*, it is evident that such a scribal error could not have been perpetuated but for sense-association with *part*.]

1. a. One who has a share or part with another or others; one who is associated with another or others in the enjoyment or possession of anything; a partaker, sharer. (Before 1600 of much wider application than now.) Const. *with*, rarely *of* (a person); *of*, *in*, †*to* (a thing).

1297 R. GLOUC. *Chron.* (Rolls) 6313 Ich as þi parciner [*v.rr.* partiner, -yner(e] half engelond mid þe. *a* **1340** HAMPOLE *Psalter* x. 8 In þe whilk all rightwismen ere parcenel [*MS.S.* partiner]. *c* **1340** —— *Prose Tr.* 15 þe flesche is pertynere of þe payne. *c* **1375** *Sc. Leg. Saints* xxi. (*Clement*) 808 God has [send] me til ȝow here of ȝoure crone to be parthenere. **1387** TREVISA *Higden* (Rolls) I. 87 At þe laste þey were partyners wiþ the Romayns, and deled lordschipe wiþ hem. **1477** EARL RIVERS (Caxton) *Dictes* 15 He shal be partenar to the Ignoraunse of froward folke. **1480** in *10th Rep. Hist. MSS. Comm.* App. v. 316 He.. shall desire and require his partener, to whom half the gutter appartained, to repaire and amende his half of the same. **1567** SIR N. THROGMORTON *Let. to Leicester* in Robertson *Hist. Scot.* (1759) II. App. 47 It may please your lordship to make my lord Stuard partner of this letter. *c* **1585** CARTWRIGHT in R. Browne *Answ. C.* 95 Parteners of impietie. **1590** SPENSER *F.Q.* II. iv. 24 A groome of base degree, Which of my love was partener Paramoure. **1617** MORYSON *Itin.* I. 43 He intreated a gentleman of Friesland to admit me partner of his bed. **1718** ROWE tr. *Lucan* I. 174 No Faith, no Trust, no Friendship, shall be known Among the jealous Partners of a Throne. **1840** THIRLWALL *Greece* VII. lvi. 131 Acknowledged as partner of Arridæus Philip in the empire. **1870** FREEMAN *Norm. Conq.* I. App. 716 A wife worthy to be the partner of his Empire.

†**b.** With the notion of participation with others weakened or lost: One who has a part or share in something, a partaker. *Obs.*

c **1290** *S. Eng. Leg.* I. 380/126 Blessede eov for þat ȝe scholden of heouene beo parteners. **1398** TREVISA *Barth. De P.R.* II. ii. (Add. MS.), Aungel is.. partiner of immortalite. **1535** FISHER *Ways Perf. Relig.* Wks. (1876) 382 You shall be partener to the more plentuous abundance of his loue.

2. a. One who is associated in any function, act, or course of action; one who takes part with another or others in doing something; an associate, colleague (sometimes merely = companion). Formerly often in reference to evil deeds: An accomplice. Now *rare*, exc. in specific senses: see 3.

a **1325** *Prose Psalter* x. 7 [xi. 6] þe gost of tempestes ys partener [*v.r.* parcener] of her wyckednesse. **13..** *Cursor M.* 26677 (Cott.) Bot þai be samen partener sekand til an sakful dede. *c* **1386** CHAUCER *Pars. T.* ¶894 They þat eggen or consenten to the synne been parteners of the synne. *c* **1430** *Syr Gener.* (Roxb.) 9724 Think wel,.. How that ye ar partenere Of that we haue doon to king Aufris. **1503–4** *Act 19 Hen. VII*, c. 34 §2 The seid Erle was not prevy nor partener to the offens of his seid sonne. **1602** MARSTON *Antonio's Rev.* v. i, The Florence Prince.. Is made a partner in conspiracie. **1611** BIBLE *Prov.* xxix. 24 Who so is partner with a thiefe hateth his owne soule. **1660** MARVELL *Corr.* Wks. 1872–5 II. 39, I suppose this day my good partner Mr. Ramsden will arrive at Hull. **1875** JOWETT *Plato* (ed. 2) I. 99 Laches and I are partners in the argument.

†**b.** One who takes part in some action. *Obs.*

1513 MORE *Rich. III* Wks. (1557) 64/1 He wyth other pertiners of that counsayle, drew aboute the duke. *c* **1565** NORTON (*title*) A Warning agaynst the dangerous practises of Papistes, and specially the parteners of the late Rebellion.

3. *spec.* **a.** *Comm.* One who is associated with another or others in the carrying on of some business, the expenses, profits, and losses of which he proportionately shares.

sleeping (or ***dormant***) ***partner***, a partner who has capital in a business and shares in its profits without taking any part in the management. ***predominant partner***: see PREDOMINANT.

1523 *Act 14 & 15 Hen. VIII*, c. 4 §1 (2) They occupie here .. not onely for them selfe, but also colourably for other straungers, their frendes, and partners. **1534** TINDALE *Luke* v. 10 Iames and Iohn.. which were partners [1526 partetakers] with Simon. **1613** *Compt. Bk. D. Wedderburne* (Sc. Hist. Soc.) 240 Tua puncheounis Wyne perteining to Walter Kynnereis & pairtenaris. **1660** F. BROOKE *Le Blanc's Trav.* 4 Which losse broak my fathers partner, Robert Pontoine. **1817** SELWYN *Law Nisi Prius* (ed. 4) II. 1055 How far the Acts of one Partner are binding on his Co-partners. **1828** WEBSTER s.v. *Dormant*, *Dormant partner*, in commerce and manufactories, a partner who takes no share in the active business of a company or partnership... He is called also sleeping partner. **1833** HT. MARTINEAU *Berkeley the Banker* I. i. 18 In Scotland, there are a great many partners in a bank, which makes it very secure. **1870** LOWELL *Study Wind.* 196 He has been the sleeping partner who has supplied a great part of their capital. **1891** *Daily News* 30 Sept. 7/1 On attaining his majority he was elected partner in the firm, of which at the present moment he is sole partner.

b. One associated in marriage, a spouse; more frequently applied to the wife.

1749 SMOLLETT *Regicide* II. vii, What means the gentle partner of my heart? **1816** SOUTHEY *Poet's Pilgr.* I. I. viii, So forth I set.. And took the partner of my life with me. **1879** FARRAR *St. Paul* II. 69 The believing wife or husband might win to the faith the unbelieving partner.

c. One's companion in a dance.

1613 SHAKS. *Hen. VIII*, I. iv. 104 Lead in your Ladies eu'ry one: Sweet Partner, I must not yet forsake you. **1712** STEELE *Spect.* No. 515 ¶3, I at first Entrance declared him my Partner if I danced at all. **1837** DICKENS *Pickw.* vi, Isabella Wardle and Mr. Trundle 'went partners'.

d. In various games, e.g. whist, tennis, etc.: A player associated on the same side with another.

1680 COTTON *Compl. Gamester* x. 84 If he can have some petty glimpse of his Partners hand. **1778** C. JONES *Hoyle's Games Impr.* 60 It appears to you that your Partner has the last Trump. **1870** *Mod. Hoyle* 1 (*Whist*), The players are divided into a couple of groups, each group being partners, and therefore winning or losing together. Partners sit opposite each other. **1875** J. D. HEATH *Croquet Player* 49 He never thinks of his partner at all, but places himself in front of his own hoop!

e. *Biol.* Each of a pair or group of symbiotically associated organisms.

1924 J. A. THOMSON *Sci. Old & New* xxvii. 147 The fungus partners, which supply the water and salts, sometimes get the upper hand and absorb their partner algae, without which, however, they cannot continue to live. **1925** R. S. LULL *Ways of Life* ii. 39 Both partners [of a lichen] combine, when they come to the formation of sexual reproductive bodies. **1970** *Canad. Jrnl. Zool.* XLVIII. 371 (*heading*) The association of *Calliactis tricolor* with its pagurid, calappid, and majid partners in the Caribbean.

f. partners' (also **partner's**, **partners**) **(pedestal) desk** (see quot. 1952).

1946 *Connoisseur* Dec. p. i (Advt.), Mahogany Partners' Pedestal Desk in style of William Kent. *Circa* 1745. **1950** *Apollo Misc.* p. ix (*caption*) A fine mahogany pedestal partners' desk. **1952** J. GLOAG *Short Dict. Furnit.* 351 *Partners' desk*, a large flat-topped kneehole desk, at which two people may sit, facing each other. The term is probably of 19th century origin. **1971** J. LEASOR *Love-All* iii. 36 His eighteenth-century partner's desk was covered with polished leather. **1974** *Country Life* 11 Apr. (Suppl.) 70 Handsome Partners Desk... The Desk is fitted with five drawers each side.

†**4.** One who is on the side (of any one); a partisan. *Obs.*

1388 WYCLIF *Hos.* iv. 17 Effraym is the partener [1382 parcener] of idols, leeue thou him. **1395** PURVEY *Remonstr.* (1851) 58, I am parteneer [1382 WYCLIF *Ps.* cxviii. 63 parcener] of alle that dreden thee.

5. *Naut.* (in *pl.*) A framework of timber fitted round any hole or scuttle in a ship's deck, through which a mast, capstan, pump, etc. passes, and serving to strengthen the deck and to relieve strain.

a **1608** SIR F. VERE *Comm.* (1657) 48 My main mast being in the partners rent to the very spindell. **1727** A. HAMILTON *New Acc. E. Ind.* II. l. 219 Our Main mast breaking in the Parteners of the Upper-deck, disabled both our Pumps. **1869** SIR E. REED *Shipbuild.* xv. 273 In some ships the partner-plates have been cut away in order to allow corner chocks of the wood partners to pass down through in one length. **1874** THEARLE *Naval Archit.* 47 The mast holes of a ship with wood beams are framed with a series of carlings termed fore and aft partners, cross partners, and girder chocks.

6. *attrib.*: formerly quasi-*adj.* = associated.

1639 FULLER *Holy War* IV. x. (1840) 195 This great overthrow, to omit less partner causes, is chiefly imputed to the Templars.. breaking the truce with the sultan of Babylon. **1647** TRAPP *Comm. Heb.* i. 6 The manhood.. hath a partner-agency..in the work of redemption and mediation. **1902** *Daily Chron.* 5 Aug. 3/2 He calls them [Colonies] rather happily 'Partner-States'.

partner ('pɑːtnə(r)), *v.* [f. prec. sb.]
1. *trans.* To make a partner, to join or associate.
1611 SHAKS. *Cymb.* I. vi. 121 A Lady, So faire,..to be partner'd With Tomboyes. **1819** *Blackw. Mag.* V. 592 A respectable accompaniment of lads and 'lasses free'; with whom it is time to partner ourselves on the green. **1898** *Times* 10 June 11/4 Harry Vardon, who was partnered with Bob Simpson.
2. To be or act as the partner of; to associate oneself with as a partner.
1882 *Daily Tel.* 24 June, The Colonials had scored 192 for the loss of four wickets,..on resuming Bonnor partnered Giffen. **1890** *Daily News* 16 July 3/6 Prince George, partnered by one of his officers, proved himself a most skilful player at tennis. **1894** *N.B. Daily Mail* 4 Sept. 3 Golf. .. The Right Hon. A. J. Balfour..had a couple of rounds, partnering Mr. A. M. Ross against Mr. R. M. Harvey and Mr. Ben Sayers.
3. *intr.* (cf. next). **a.** To associate or work as partners. **b.** To associate or join *with* as a partner.
1961 A. B. MAYSE in *Webster* s.v., Him and me, we partnered once. **1961** R. O. BOWEN in *Ibid.*, He still partnered with Tom on the piers. **1968** *Globe & Mail* (Toronto) (Mag.) 17 Feb. 9/2 In 1929 he partnered with a U.S. businessman, Ben Raeburn, to publish a series of 'forbidden' sex books. **1977** *Bangladesh Times* 19 Jan. 5/1 Partnering with Habib against Tipu and Haroon, the foursome played perhaps the most evenly contested matches in Bangladesh tennis to date.

partnering ('pɑːtnərɪŋ), *vbl. sb.* [f. PARTNER *v.* + -ING[1].] Association as partners; the action or work of a partner.
1897 S. & B. WEBB *Industr. Democr.* II. 475 Occasionally the employer has tried to have only one boy-piecer to two spinners. This system, called ' joining' or 'partnering', is always resisted by the union. **1963** *Times* 8 Jan. 4/1 His partnering proved adequate and his dancing showed vitality and breadth. **1975** 'M. FONTEYN' *Autobiogr.* I. iv. 41 This impromptu lesson stood me in good stead after I joined the ballet and sometimes danced with boys as new to partnering as I was. **1976** U. HOLDEN *String Horses* vii. 80 Wait until you try my partnering. I'll take a turn with you both.

'partnerless, *a.* [-LESS.] Without a partner.
1852 MISS YONGE *Two Guard.* xiii. (1861) 241 That rosy tall boy standing partnerless. **1869** LADY BARKER *Station Life N. Zealand* vi. (1874) 37 Some of the pretty and partnerless groups of a London ball-room.

partnership ('pɑːtnəʃɪp). [See -SHIP.]
1. The fact or condition of being a partner; association or participation. Now esp. of relationships in industry and politics.
1576 FLEMING *Panopl. Epist.* 23 Shee..might runne the race of her age in his pleasaunt partenership. **1741** MIDDLETON *Cicero* II. viii. 196, I have faithfully performed to him..every duty which our partnership in office.. required. **1769** BIBLE *2 Kings* xv. 1 *marg.*, This is the 27th year of Jeroboam's Partnership in the kingdom with his Father. **1877** FREEMAN *Norm. Conq.* (ed. 3) I. App. 786 A scandal which charged Emma herself with a partnership in the deed. **1933** *Planning* 25 Apr. 2 It aims at giving labour effective partnership in industry and at creating a new attitude of mind to replace sterile hostilities. **1941** *Ann. Reg. 1940* 140 The attainment by India of free and equal partnership in the British Commonwealth. **1959** *Times Lit. Suppl.* 31 July 449/2 It has been a cardinal principle in Rhodesia that the way should be open not for *apartheid* but for partnership, and that the new State will avoid the racial impasse of the Union. **1976** *Star* (Sheffield) 30 Nov. 14/7 Dennis Amiss and Brearley, the opening partnership which England hope will serve them throughout the forthcoming Test series with India, made a quiet start to their alliance when they launched the innings. **1977** *World of Cricket Monthly* June 31/2 He and Kallicharran set about repairing the damage with a fourth-wicket partnership of 90 in 85 minutes and 20 overs.
2. *Comm.* **a.** An association of two or more persons for the carrying on of a business, of which they share the expenses, profit, and loss.
a **1700** L'ESTRANGE (J.), A necessary rule in alliances, partnerships, and all manner of civil dealings. **1801** MAR. EDGEWORTH *Irish Bulls* xiv. 276 His brother took him into partnership. **1849** FREESE *Comm. Class-bk.* 117 An entry to the debit or credit of each Partner, in the proportions agreed upon in the articles of Partnership. **1861** DICKENS *Lett.* (1880) II. 145 He has been for some time seeking a partnership in business.
b. The persons collectively composing such a business association.
1802–12 BENTHAM *Ration. Judic. Evid.* (1827) IV. 74 The rate at which business is done, when the partnership are ashamed or afraid to put it off any longer. **1813** MAR. EDGEWORTH *Patron.* (1833) II. xxi. 20 He had..obtained the partnership's permission to go over to the Dutch merchants.
3. *Arith.* The rule or method for the calculation of a partner's share of gain or loss in proportion to his share of the capital or other determining conditions; = FELLOWSHIP 9.
1704 J. HARRIS *Lex. Techn.* I, *Partnership*, a Rule in Arithmetick; the same with the *Rule of Fellowship*, which see. **1859** BARN. SMITH *Arith. & Algebra* (ed. 6) 508 Fellowship or Partnership.
4. *attrib.*
1770 FOOTE *Lame Lover* II. Wks. 1799 II. 70 The charge must be made for partnership-profit. **1817** W. SELWYN *Law Nisi Prius* (ed. 4) II. 1058 A general partnership agreement ..under seal. **1818** JAS. MILL *Brit. India* II. v. v. 487 The sort of partnership sovereignty, which the Nabob and the Company had established in the Carnatic.

partness ('pɑːtnɪs). Also **part-ness.** [f. PART *sb.* + -NESS.] The fact or quality of being partial or incomplete.
1925 D. H. LAWRENCE *Let.* ? 26 Jan. (1962) II. 828 Any relation based on the one half—say the delicate spiritual half alone—inevitably brings revulsion and betrayal. It is halfness, or partness, which causes Judas. **1945** KOESTLER *Yogi & Commissar* 240 Isolation destroys their very character of 'part-ness'. *Ibid.* 253 A 'vertical' approach which brings to the dry concepts of part-ness, love and all-oneness the igniting spark of experienced reality.

†**'partnit, -nyt.** *Obs. rare.* [app. f. PART *sb.* 3 + NIT.] The pubic louse or CRAB-LOUSE.
1530 PALSGR. 252/1 Partnyt that bredeth under ones arme, *mortpou.* **1547** SALESBURY *Welsh Dict.*, *Krankleuen*, a partnyt.

parton ('pɑːtɒn). *Nuclear Physics.* [f. PART(ICLE *sb.* + -ON[1].] Each of the hypothetical point-like constituents of the nucleon that were invoked by R. P. Feynman to explain the way the nucleon inelastically scatters electrons of very high energy.
The printed coinage was published after the term had been given currency by Feynman in discussions.
1969 *New Scientist* 26 June 679/2 A similar 'current bun' concept of the proton is implied by the so-called 'parton' theory of Feynmann [*sic*]. **1969** R. P. FEYNMAN in C. N. Yang et al. *High Energy Collisions* 241, I call the fundamental bare particles of my underlying field theory 'partons'. **1973** *Sci. Amer.* Aug. 34/3 There is some evidence that partons and quarks are the same, although they have been postulated in different ways. **1974** M. L. PERL *High Energy Hadron Physics* xx. 482 We take the partons to be point particles with fixed mass and fixed internal quantum numbers... The quark model discussed in Ch. 14 is a particular form of the parton model in which the partons have been assigned a particular set of internal quantum numbers.

parton, partoner: see PARTAN, PARTNER.

partoriche, obs. form of PARTRIDGE.

'part-,owner. (Also stressed ,*part-'owner.*) [f. PART *adv.* c + OWNER: = owner in part.] One who owns something in common with another or others; each of two or more joint-owners or tenants in common. Hence (stress variable) **part-own** *v. trans.*; **part-ownership.**
1562 *Act 5 Eliz.* c. 5 §8 Bottoms whereof..Strangers born then be Owners, Shipmasters or Part-owners. *c* **1677** in Marvell *Growth Popery* (1678) 62 The *John and Elizabeth*, English built, Thomas Rising, Master and part-Owner. **1817** W. SELWYN *Law Nisi Prius* (ed. 4) II. 1273 If one of two part-owners of a chattel sue alone for a tort, and the defendant do not plead in abatement, the other part-owner may after-wards sue alone. **1884** SIR W. B. BRETT in *Law Rep. 16 Queen's Bench Div.* 65 A part-owner might be compelled to incur expense against his will. **1890** *Act 53 & 54 Vict.* c. 39 §2 Joint tenancy, tenancy in common, joint property, common property, or part ownership does not of itself create a partnership as to anything so held or owned. **1969** R. ESSER *Hot Potato* 42 He..part-owned a night club. **1974** *Listener* 10 Oct. 460/3 A mainly middle-class constituency was told of his part-ownership of a factory. **1975** D. BLOODWORTH *Clients of Omega* iv. 31 This mighty organization..covers two thousand factories, banks and businesses... It part-owns a high percentage of them. **1977** M. T. BLOOM *Thirteenth Man* (1978) ii. 26 Now he was wealthy enough to have..part-ownership of a private bank.

partridge ('pɑːtrɪdʒ). Forms: see below. [ME. *pertrich, partrich*: cf. OF. *perdriz, pertriz* (mod.F. *perdrix*), alteration of *perdiz* (= Pr. *perditz*, Sp. *perdiz*, It. †*perdice* (Florio), now *pernice*):—L. *perdix, perdīc-em*, a. Gr. πέρδιξ, πέρδῑκ-α (the Greek) partridge.
The change of orig. *perd-* to *pert-* is occasional also in OF. (*pertris, petris, pertrisel, pertriset*, Godef.); the further change to *part-* is as in *clerk, heart*, and also occurs in OF. *pardix*; that of *-ich, -itch*, to *-idge* is as in *cnowleche, knowledge*, etc. The change of *perdix* to *perdrix* (perh. from a mixture of *perdis* and **pedris, petris*) occurred in French, the second *r* being present in Eng. from the first. But no explanation has been found of the representation of the Fr. *-riz, -ris*, by Eng. *-rich*, nor of the notable fact that this became *-rik* in northern Eng., like the final element in *hevenriche, hevenrik, kingriche, kingrik*, etc.]
A. Forms. (The collective *pl.* is often like *sing.*)
a. α. 3–8 (9 *dial.*) **partrich**, 4–6 **-riche**, 5 **-eriche**, **-oriche**, (**parthyryd**), 5–6 **partrych(e**, **-ricche**, **-rytche**, **-reche**; **pardriche**, **-dryche**; 6– **partridge**, (6 **-rydge**, **-rege**, **-yrege**, **-erige**, 7 **-rige**, **-ridg**, **-rage**). β. 4–6 **pertrich(e**, **-ry(t)che**, 5 **-erych**, 6 **-rige**. γ. *dial.* 6–9 **patrich**, 7–9 **-ridge**.
c **1290** *S. Eng. Leg.* I. 411/316 A ȝong partrich he bar on his hond. *c* **1386** CHAUCER *Prol.* 349 A fat partrich [*v.rr.* partrych, perterych, partriche]. *c* **1400** *Master of Game* (MS. Digby 182) xvi. 73/15 Of þe parteriche and þe quayle. *Ibid.* 73/17 A goode goshauke..for þe pertriche. **1422** tr. *Secreta Secret., Priv. Priv.* 245 Pardriches, culueres. **14..** *Metr. Voc.* in Wr.-Wülcker 625/2 Perdix [*glossed*] parthyryd. **1432–50** tr. *Higden* (Rolls) I. 339 Partricche and fesaunte, pyes, nyȝtegales. *c* **1440** in *Househ. Ord.* (1790) 450 Rosted pejons, egretys, partoriches. *c* **1440** *Promp. Parv.* 395/1 Pertryche, byrd, *perdix.* **1526** SKELTON *Magnyf.* 484 A plummed partrydge all redy to flye. **1530** PALSGR. 164 *Pardris*, a partrytche. *Ibid.* 253/2 Pertrytche a byrde, *pardris.* **1542** UDALL *Erasm. Apoph.* To Rdr. 3 b, One y[it] serueth his stomake with a Pertrige. *a* **1550** in Ellis *Orig. Lett.* Ser. III. III. 71, I sende yowe by this bringer half a dossen partterigs... I sende owte my hawke this day to kyll yowe parterige for super on Monday. **1550** J. COKE *Eng. & Fr. Heralds* iii. (1877) 57 Pardryche, quayles,..and other wylde fowle. **1578** COOPER *Thesaurus*, *Cacabo*,..to call like a patrich. **1579** E. K. *Gloss. Spenser's Sheph. Cal.* Apr. 118 A Couey of Partridge. **1585** T. WASHINGTON tr. *Nicholay's Voy.* II. v. 34 b, xij. couple of quick partriges. **1616** B. JONSON *Forest* ii. 29 The painted Partrich lyes in every field. *a* **1674** CLARENDON *Hist. Reb.* XIV. §76 (1704) 404 To see a Dog set patridge. **1892** HEWETT *Peas. Sp.* 12 (E.D.D.) Zo plump's a pattridge.
b. *north. Eng.* and *Sc.* α. 4–6 **partryk**, (4–5 **-ryke**, 5 **-rike**), 4, 9 **-rick**. β. 4–6 **pertrik**, (4–5 **-ryke**, 4–6 **-rike**, 5–6 **-ryk**, **-rycke**, 6 **-rek**, 6–7 **-rick**, 6–9 **pairtrick**, 8 **peartrick**). γ. 8–9 **paitrick**, **patrick**, 9 **paitric**, **paetrick**.
13.. *E.E. Allit. P.* B. 57 My polyle þat is penne-fed & partrykes boþe. *c* **1375** *Sc. Leg. Saints* v. (*Johannes*) 457 A fule..quhilk we ane partryk cal. **1388** *Durham Acc. Rolls* (Surtees) 47 In v pertrikis..emptis. **1408** *Ibid.* 53, xv pertrykes. *c* **1425** *Voc.* in Wr.-Wülcker 640/41 *Hic perdix*,.. pertrycke. **1438** *Bk. Alexander Grt.* (Bann. Cl.) 14 Sparhalk, Pertrik, or Quailȝe. **1609** SKENE *Reg. Maj.*, *Pecun. Crimes* 139 b, Pertricks, Plovers, Black-cocks. **1728** RAMSAY *Lure* 12 Peartricks, teals, moor-powts, and plivers. **1784** BURNS *Ep. to J. Rankine* vii, I..brought a paitrick to the grun'. **1807** TANNAHILL *Poems* (1817) 229 (E.D.D.) The paitrick sung his e'ening note. **1824** MACTAGGART *Gallovid. Encycl.* (1876) 176 Wha had..shot a paitric or hare. **1838** HOGG *Tales* (1866) 63 Shooting moor-cocks, an' paetricks.
B. Signification.
1. a. The name of certain well-known game-birds; specifically the British and Central European species *Perdix cinerea*, also called distinctively ***common*** or ***grey partridge***. More widely, used to include all species of the genus *Perdix*, and some allied genera: see 2.
c **1290**, etc. [see A. a and b]. **1382** WYCLIF *Jer.* xvii. 11 The partrich nurshede that she bar not. **1447** BOKENHAM *Seyntys* (Roxb.) 48 Lyche to lyche evere doth applie As scheep to scheep and man to man Pertryche to pertryche and swan to swan. **1513** *Bk. Keruynge* in *Babees Bk.* 275 Wynge that partryche. *c* **1592** MARLOWE *Jew of Malta* IV. iv, Hee hides and buries it vp, as Partridges doe their egges, vnder the earth. **1611** BIBLE *1 Sam.* xxvi. 20 The king of Israel is come out to seeke a flea, as when one doeth hunt a partridge in the mountaines. **1629** SYMMER *Spir. Posie* I. iv. 14 The Partridges of Paphlagonia have two hearts. **1774** GOLDSM. *Nat. Hist.* (1776) V. 206 The partridge is now too common in France to be considered as a delicacy. **1844** DICKENS *Mart. Chuz.* xxv, Plump as any partridge was each Miss Mould.
b. In former British Colonies and U.S., popularly applied to several birds of the *Tetraonidæ* or Grouse Family and *Phasianidæ* or Pheasant Family, esp. in New England, the Ruffed Grouse (*Bonasa* or *Tetrao umbellus*), in Pennsylvania, etc. the Virginian Quail, Colin, or Bob-white (*Ortyx virginianus*): see also 2.
By some earlier naturalists extended to include the Tinamous of S. America (*perdizes* of Spanish and Portuguese).
1634 *Relat. Ld. Baltimore's Plant.* (1865) 16 Euery day they are abroad after squirrells, partridges, turkies, deere, and the like game. **1637** T. MORTON *New Eng. Canaan* (1883) 194 Partridges there are, much like our Partridges of England. **1808** PIKE *Sources Missis.* (1810) 73 My Indians killed fifteen partridges, some nearly black,..called the Savanna partridge. **1809** A. HENRY *Trav.* 53 The neighbouring woods abounded in partridges, and hares. [*Note*] The birds, here intended, are red grouse. *a* **1813** A. WILSON *Amer. Ornith.* (1832) II. 230 The food of the Partridge [*Ortyx virginianus*] consists of grain, seeds, insects, and berries. **1840** *Penny Cycl.* XVII. 440/1 This, the *Quail* of the inhabitants of New England, the *Partridge* of the Pennsylvanians, has the bill black. **1849** BRYANT *Old Man's Counsel* v, The grouse, that wears A sable ruff around his mottled neck; Partridge they call him by our northern streams, And pheasant by the Delaware. **1854** THOREAU *Walden* xii. (1863) 243 In June the partridge (*Tetrao umbellus*)..led her brood past my windows. **1894** NEWTON *Dict. Birds* 696 By English colonists the name Partridge has been very loosely applied, and especially so in North America. There is sometimes a difficulty at first to know whether the Ruffed Grouse (*Bonasa umbellus*) or the Virginian Colin (*Ortyx virginianus*) is intended. **1895** *Ibid.* 964 Buffon and his successors saw that the Tinamous, though passing among the European colonists of South America as 'Partridges', could not be associated with those birds.
c. The bird, or its flesh, as used for eating.
13.. *Coer de L.* 3526 There is no flesch so noryssaunt,.. Partrick, plover, heroun, ne swan. ? *c* **1475** *Sqr. lowe Degre* 318 With deynty meates that were dere, With partryche, pecoke, and plovere. **1584** COGAN *Haven Health* clix, Partrich of all foules is most soonest digested. **1715** S. SEWALL *Diary* 19 Sept., Din'd with Fry'd Lamb and Partridge.
2. *Ornith.* With defining words, applied to particular species of the genus *Perdix*, or of the sub-families *Perdicinæ*, *Odontophorinæ*, and *Caccabineæ*, of family *Phasianidæ*, also to some species of *Tetraonidæ*, all of Order *Gallinæ*; in S. Africa, to some of Order *Pterocletes* (Sand-grouse). The following are the chief species:
African or **Barbary p.**, of N. Africa, *Caccabis petrosa*; **bamboo p.**, of North China, *Bambusicola thoracica*; **bearded p.**, of E. Siberia, *Perdix barbata*; **blackheaded p.**, of Arabia and Abyssinia, *Caccabis melanocephalus*; **Bonham's p.**, of W. Asia, *Ammoperdix Bonhami*; **buff-breasted p.**, of W. Africa, *Ptilopachys ventralis*; **California p.** (or Quail), *Callipepla californica*; **capoeira p.**, of Brazil, *Odontophorus dentatus*; **chukar p.**, of India, *Caccabis Chukar*; **French p.** = *red-legged p.*; **Gambel's p.**, of California, *Callipepla Gambelli*;

Greek p., of Southern Europe (the original Gr.-L. πέρδιξ, *perdix*), *Caccabis saxatilis*; **grey p.** (*a*), the *common p.* (sense 1); (*b*) the Indian genus *Ortygornis*; **Guiana p.**, of S. America, *Odontophorus guianensis*; **Hey's p.**, of Arabia, *Ammoperdix Heyi*; **hill-p.**, the genus *Galloperdix*, esp. *G. lunulatus* of India; **Himalayan p.** = *snow p.*; **Hodgson's p.**, of Bhutan, *Perdix hodgsoniæ*; **Massena p.**, of New Mexico, *Callipepla montezumæ*; **mountain** or **plumed p.**, of California, *Oreortyx pictus*; **Namaqua p.**, of S. Africa (Sand-grouse), *Pterocles namaqua*; **painted p.** (or Francolin), of S. Africa, *Francolinus pictus*; **redlegged p.**, of Europe, *Caccabis rufa*; **rock p.**, a synonym of *Greek p.* and *Barbary p.*; **sanguine p.**, of China, Geoffroy's Blood-Pheasant, *Ithaginis geoffroyi*; **snow p.**, *Lerwa nivicola*; also *Tetraogallus Himalayensis*; **spruce p.** = *Canada grouse* s.v. GROUSE *sb.*[1]; **tree** or **white-browed p.**, of Central America, *Dendrostyx leucophrys*.

Also, **night partridge**, a name locally given in U.S. to the American woodcock, *Philohela minor* (Webster, 1890).

1894 NEWTON *Dict. Birds* 696 The French Partridge has several congeners, all with red legs... In Africa north of the Atlas there is the *Barbary Partridge. **1611** COTGR., *Perdrix gaille*..the great browne-bodied, and red-legd Partridge, the *French Partridge. **1894** NEWTON *Dict. Birds* 695 The common Red-legged Partridge of Europe, generally called the French Partridge,..was introduced into England toward the end of the eighteenth century. **1884–5** *Stand. Nat. Hist.* (1888) IV. 204 A genus of *gray partridges, styled *Ortygornis*,..is found in India and Ceylon. **1894** NEWTON *Dict. Birds* 692 *note*, In India the name Grey Partridge is used for *Ortygornis ponticerianus*, which is perhaps a Francolin. **1753** CHAMBERS *Cycl. Supp.* s.v., **Indian Partridge*, the name given by the Spaniards to a bird of the West Indies, of which there are three or four species; all which, Nieremberg says, are properly of the partridge kind. **1850** R. G. CUMMING *Hunter's Life S. Afr.* (ed. 2) I. 161 The *Namaqua partridges..every morning and evening visit the vleys and fountains in large coveys for the purpose of drinking... By watching the flight of these birds mornings and evenings I have discovered the fountains in the desert. **1611** COTGR., *Perdrix rouge*..the great *red-legd Partridge. **1678** RAY *Willughby's Ornith.* 167 The Red-leg'd Partridge, *Perdix ruffa* Aldrov. called in Italy Coturnice and Coturno. **1753** CHAMBERS *Cycl. Supp.* s.v., *Red-legged Partridge*..is not found in England, but is sometimes shot in the islands of Guernsey and Jersey. **1840** *Penny Cycl.* XVII. 443/1 The *Sanguine Partridge..may be considered as uniting the Partridges with the *Pheasants* and the *Polyplectrons*. **1894** NEWTON *Dict. Birds* 696 The group of birds known as Francolins and *Snow-partridges are generally furnished with strong but blunt spurs,..the genus *Lerwa* contains but a single species, *L. nivicola*, which is emphatically the Snow-Partridge of Himalayan sportsmen. **1895** *Outing* (U.S.) XXVII. 218/1 The *spruce partridge abounds here.

†**3.** *Mil.* **a.** A kind of charge for cannons consisting of a number of missiles fired together, similar to langrage or case-shot; also *partridge-shot*: see 5. See also quot. 1788. *Obs.*

1678 *Lond. Gaz.* No. 1361/1 He Steered from us, falls a Stern, loaded his Guns with double Head and round Partridge. **1697** *Ibid.* No. 3318/3 We had time enough to give her four entire Broad-sides with Round and Partrage from Aloft. **1726** SHELVOCKE *Voy. round World* 262 We had no more ammunition than two round shot, a few chain bolts and bolt-heads, the clapper of the Speedwell's bell, and some bags of beach stones to serve for partridge. **1751** SMOLLETT *Per. Pickle* ii. **1788** GROSE *Mil. Antiq.* Descrip. of Plates II. 5 *The Partridges.* A mortar that threw thirteen grenadoes and one bomb at the same time; the bomb representing the old hen, and the grenadoes the young partridges. **1867** SMYTH *Sailor's Word-bk.*, *Partridges*, grenades thrown from a mortar.

b. (See quot.)

1823 CRABB *Technol. Dict.*, *Partridge* (*Gunn.*), large bombards which were formerly used. [So in later Dicts.]

This is app. an error, due to a misunderstanding of Grose, quot. 1788 above. But cf. OF. *perdriau* 'an engine for throwing stones' Guiart 1304, in Du Cange and Littré.

4. sea partridge. †**a.** A name of the sole. [Cf. F. *perdrix de mer* 'the sole-fish' (Cotgr.).] **b.** A local name of the Golden Wrasse or Gilt-head, *Crenilabrus melops* (Webster 1890).

1633 HART *Diet of Diseased* I. xxi. 89 The Sole is without exception a good and dainty Fish..it is for this cause called the Sea-partridge. **1740** R. BROOKES *Angling* II. xv. 120 The Sole..in some Countries, they stile it the Sea-Partridge.

5. *attrib.* and *Comb.* **a.** simple attrib., as ***partridge brood, chick, dance, drive*** (see DRIVE *sb.* 1 c), ***eye, fillet, ground, hackle, mew, net, pie, poult, prairie, season, wing***. **b.** objective, etc., as ***-breeder, -driving, -hawking, -killer, -shooter, -shooting***; also ***partridge-like*** adj. **c.** Special Combs.: **partridge-bird**: see quot.; **partridge-breast, -breasted (aloe)**, the name of an American species of aloe (*Aloe variegata*); **partridge bush** = PARTRIDGE-BERRY b; **partridge-cane**: see PARTRIDGE-WOOD 1; **partridge cochin**, a variety of cochin-china fowl (*Cent. Dict.*); **partridge-dove**, a local name given to a ground-dove of Jamaica (*Geotrygon cristata*), also called mountain-witch (ground-dove); **partridge-hawk**, the North-American goshawk (*Astur atricapillus*); **partridge-legged clover**: see quot.; **partridge pea**, (*a*) a speckled or mottled variety of field pea; (*b*) a yellow-flowered leguminous plant (*Cassia Chamæcrista*) of U.S.: called also *sensitive pea*; (*c*) a plant (*Heisteria coccinea*, N.O. *Olacineæ*) having red fruits enclosed in an enlarged fleshy calyx; **partridge-pigeon**, an Australian pigeon (*Geophaps scripta*), one of the bronzewings; **partridge plum**, the fruit of the partridge-berry; **partridge-shell**, a large univalve shell (*Dolium perdix*) with partridge-like mottlings, a *partridge tun*; **partridge-shot**, (*a*) = sense 3 a; (*b*) shot suitable for shooting partridges; †**partridge tun**, *Conch.*, a shell of one of the two groups into which Cuvier divided the genus *Dolium* (see TUN, TUNSHELL); **partridge-vine**, = PARTRIDGE-BERRY a. (Funk 1895). Also PARTRIDGE-BERRY, -WOOD.

1871 J. BURROUGHS *Wake-Robin, Adirondac* (1884) 120 Here..I met my beautiful singer, the hermit-thrush... A boy..said it was the '*partridge-bird', no doubt from the resemblance of its note, when disturbed, to the cluck of the partridge. **1825** *Greenhouse Comp.* I. 103 *Aloe variegata*, *partridge-breast. **1858** GLENNY *Gard. Every-day Bk.* 191/1 The various Aloes, of which the *Partridge-breasted..is at the head. **1864** TENNYSON *Aylmer's F.* 382 These *partridge-breeders of a thousand years. **1843** *Amer. Pioneer* II. 125 The vivid green leaves and bright scarlet berries of the '*partridge bush', or 'Checker-berry'. **1843** HOLTZAPFFEL *Turning* I. 19 Some of the smallest palms are imported..for walking-sticks, under the names of *partridge and Penang canes, etc. **1852** C. W. HOSKYNS *Talpa* 127 The *partridge-chick had found cool midday covert under the young turnip-leaf. **1829** COL. HAWKER *Diary* (1893) II. 3 This is not a professed *partridge country. **1871** DARWIN *Desc. Man* II. xiii. (1890) 380 In these *Partridge-dances,..the birds assume the strangest attitudes. **1892** GREENER *Breech-Loader* 223 In *partridge-driving the stations are frequently changed, and the object is to break up the coveys as early as possible in the day. *c* **1470** HENRYSON *Mor. Fab.* IX. (*Wolf & Fox*) xxvi, It is ane side of salmond, as it wair, And callour, pypand like ane *pertrik ee. **1867** F. FRANCIS *Angling* vi. (1880) 244 The *Partridge Hackle. Dressed similarly to the last fly. **1781** LATHAM *Gen. Synopsis Birds* I. I. 78 This bird..was sent from Severn River, Hudson's bay, where it was called Speckled *Partridge Hawk. **1807** YOUNG *Agric. Essex* I. 8 It [the 'red' land] yields clover, but the plant will fatten nothing,..they call it *partridge-leg'd clover, with red stalks and small leaves. **1840** *Penny Cycl.* XVII. 438/2 The *Partridge-like ..plumage..of the..Quails. **1900** *Westm. Gaz.* 23 June 8/2 The tinamous, a partridge-like bird of South America. **1749** FIELDING *Tom Jones* IV. iv, I must take care of my *partridge mew. I shall have some..man or other set all my partridges at liberty. **1759** H. WALPOLE *Lett. H. Mann* 13 Dec. (1846) IV. 7 Fourteen thousand soldiers and nine generals taken, as it were, in a *partridge-net! **1812** SIR J. SINCLAIR *Syst. Husb. Scot.* I. 225 The *partridge pea may be sown in May, but no other field variety. **1844** H. STEPHENS *Bk. Farm* II. 370 The *partridge*, *grey maple*, or *Marlborough pea*, is suited for light soils and late situations. **1866** *Treas. Bot.* 574/1 *Heisteria coccinea*..is a native..particularly of Martinique, where the French call it Bois perdrix, which is a corruption of Pois perdrix, signifying partridge pea, the fleshy red fruits forming a favourite food of pigeons and other birds. **1723** J. NOTT *Cook's & Confectioner's Dict.* sig. y7 (*heading*) To make a *Partridge Pye. **1757** EARL OF BUCKINGHAM *Let.* Sept. in *Lett. to & from Henrietta, Countess of Suffolk* (1824) II. 239 If the partridge-pie gives you as much pleasure as your letter did to me. **1963** A. L. SIMON *Guide Good Food & Wines* 579/2 Partridge pie. **1847** L. LEICHHARDT *Overland Exped.* i. 8 The *partridge pigeon (*Geophaps scripta*) abounded in the Acacia groves. **1872** MRS. STOWE in *Christian Union* 3 Jan. 32/3 Little Love gathered stores of bright checker berries and *partridge plums. **1855** KINGSLEY *Westw. Ho* iii, [They] felt like a brace of *partridge-poults cowering in the stubble. **1840** *Penny Cycl.* XVII. 436/1 The well known object of every European *partridge-shooter. **1683** R. D. *State of Turkey* 153 Laden with..pieces of iron, and *partridg-shot. **1769** FALCONER *Dict. Marine* (1789), *Sachets de mitrailles*, grape-shot, or partridge-shot. **1833** G. A. MCCALL *Lett. fr. Frontiers* (1868) 263 A load of partridge-shot. **1837** *Penny Cycl.* IX. 456/1 *Dolium*... Cuvier has separated the species into two sections, viz. the Tuns (*Dolium*) and the *Partridge Tuns (*Perdix* of de Montfort). **1880** *Harper's Mag.* Nov. 864/1 Here are soft beds of rich green moss studded with scarlet berries of wintergreen and *partridge vine. **1940** *Sun* (Baltimore) 9 Dec. 8/4 In Christmas seasons when holly berries are comparatively scarce, the berries of the smoke bush come as a substitute, and often of the dogwood and of the partridge vines in the woodlands. **1599** SHAKS. *Much Ado* II. i. 155 There's a *Partridge wing saued, for the foole will eate no supper that night.

Hence **'partridging** *vbl. sb.*, shooting partridges; (cf. *blackberrying* and -ING[1] 1 c).

1894 STEEL *Potter's Thumb* (1895) 108, I don't.. remember how it happened. We were partridging, I suppose.

'partridge-,berry. Name of two North American plants, and their fruit: **a.** *Mitchella repens* (N.O. *Cinchonaceæ*), a trailing evergreen herb with edible but insipid scarlet berries; also called *partridge(-berry)-vine*. **b.** *Gaultheria procumbens* (N.O. *Ericaceæ*), the CHECKER-BERRY or WINTERGREEN, whose red berries furnish food for partridges and other animals.

1714 *Phil. Trans.* XXIX. 63 Another Plant,..Partridge-berries, excellent in curing the Dropsy. **1748** H. ELLIS *Hudson's Bay* 169 Shrubs bearing red and black Berries, which the Partridges feed on, therefore called Partridge Berries. **1868** H. W. BEECHER *Norwood* 91 Here the little queen took on airs, and sent her Ethiop..[for] some partridge-berry vines from the edge of the wood. **1871** J. BURROUGHS *Wake-Robin, Hemlocks* (1884) 79 At the foot of a rough, scraggy yellow birch, on a bank of club-moss, so richly inlaid with partridge-berry and curious shining leaves. **1875** T. HILL *True Ord. Stud.* 81 Our American plant Gaultheria is called in some sections Winter-green,.. in others Partridge-berry. **1913** W. P. EATON *Barn Doors & Byways* 245 We have come upon ferns still flaunting through the snow and partridge berry vines; scratched up into sight by some hungry bird.

†**'partridger.** *Obs.* Also 7 **partringer.** [a. AF. **perdrichour*, *perdrigeour*, in OF. *perdriseur* partridge-hunter, f. *perdrich*, *-ris* partridge.] One who hunts or catches partridges.

1601 F. TATE *Househ. Ord. Edw. II* §59 (1876) 45 A partringer. **1611** COTGR., *Perdriseur*, a Partridger, or Partridge-taker; also, an Officer that hath the command of that Game, in France.

'partridge-wood.

1. A hard red wood, much prized for cabinet work, also used for walking and umbrella sticks, obtained from the W. Indies, having darker parallel stripes, once thought to be the wood of the partridge-pea, *Heisteria coccinea*, now supposed to be (at least in part) obtained from the leguminous tree *Andira inermis*; called also *pheasant-wood*.

1830 LINDLEY *Nat. Syst. Bot.* 78 The wood of *Heisteria coccinea* is the Partridge wood of the cabinet-makers. *c* **1865** J. WYLDE in *Circ. Sc.* I. 172/2 [Descr. of a machine] These tubes are terminated by circular knobs, which enclose jets of partridge-wood, shaped of a cylindrical form, and having a jet somewhat resembling a bats-wing gas-burner. **1898** MORRIS *Austral Eng.*, *Partridge-wood*, another name for the Cabbage-Palm.

2. A name for the appearance of wood when attacked by the saprophytic fungus *Stereum frustulosum*, on account of its speckled colour.

1894 SOMERVILLE & WARD tr. *Hartig's Dis. Trees* 203 Thelephora Perdix. A form of disease which is very common in the oak throughout the whole of Germany is known as 'partridge wood', on account of the peculiar discoloration which it induces in the wood. **1899** MASSEE *Text-bk. of Plant Diseases* 172.

partschinite ('pɑːtʃɪnaɪt). *Min.* [f. Ger. *partschin*, as named 1847 after Prof. Partsch of Vienna + -ITE[1].] A silicate of iron, aluminium, and magnesium, occurring in auriferous sand.

[**1854** DANA *Min.* 501 Partschin..found in grains in small monoclinic crystals.] **1868** *Ibid.* 293 Partschinite.

†**'partsman.** *Sc. Obs.* In 6 **partisman.** [f. *partis* = *part's*, possessive of PART *sb.*: cf. *daysman.*] One who has a part or share; a partaker, sharer.

1513 DOUGLAS *Æneis* XII. vii. 132 To mak the partisman of gret senȝeory. **1563** WINȜET *Wks.* (1890) II. 45 *marg.*, Obserue guid Christiane, that you be partisman of thir blissingis.

'part-,song. [f. PART *sb.* 10 + SONG.] A song for three or more voice-parts, usually without accompaniment, and in simple harmony (not with the parts independent as in the *glee*, or contrapuntally treated as in the *madrigal*).

[**1597** J. DOWLAND (*title*) The first Booke of Songes or Ayres of fowre partes with Tableture for the Lute. **1698** PURCELL *Orpheus Britann.* 39 A Two Part Song, in *Epsome-Wells.*] **1850** (*title*) Novello's Part-Song Book..No. 1. *Ibid.* p. i, It is intended to select some of the most striking of these German choruses and part-songs, for insertion. **1894** HALL CAINE *Manxman* IV. vi. 221 He went over to the piano and they sang a part song.

parts-taking: see PARTAKING 2 β.

partterig, obs. f. PARTRIDGE.

part-time (,pɑːt'taɪm), *a.* [PART *adv.* c.] Employed, occurring, lasting, etc., for part of the time or for less than the customary time. Also as *adv.* Cf. FULL TIME.

1891 *East. Daily Press* 26 Aug. 2/1 Wanted, a Part-time Girl, (15), for housework. **1896** *Daily News* 30 Oct. 10/5 Gentleman..open to part-time engagement to manage the advertising of a cycle firm. **1931** *Times Lit. Suppl.* 14 May 380/3 The legislation of 1919..has put some 10,000 small farmers and 20,000 men upon part-time and spare-time holdings. **1955** *Times* 1 July 10/7 The chairman need devote only part of his time to the board. Most of the members should be part-time. **1959** *New Statesman* 23 May 710/2 Are married women who worked part-time for years after the war, but are now being squeezed out, to be compensated? **1965** M. MORSE *Unattached* i. 33 She began studying part-time for G.C.E. 'O' levels. **1973** *Fisheries Fact Sheet* (Environment Canada Fisheries & Marine Service) No. 1. 4/3 Winter fishing..is carried on by teams of men, many of whom are only part-time fishermen.

Hence **part-'timer**, a part-time worker, student, or the like.

1927 *Daily Tel.* 3 May 3 (*heading*) Part-timers employed. **1936** A. G. STREET *Gentleman of Party* vii. 134 The dairyman's eldest son, George, went to work as a part-timer at ten years of age. **1939** *Rostrum* (N.Z.) 7 Some grove of Academe where part-timers will have no place. **1952** G. WILSON *Julien Ware* 19 The part-timers were a handful of men engaged by John Cecil for a couple of months at the peak of each year. **1972** *Daily Tel.* 25 Apr. 7/2 Places for at least one million full-time students in 1980 would be planned, with a comparable provision for part-timers. **1976** *Listener* 2 Dec. 712/2 What is often seen as a part-time job is further split among several part-timers: the *Times* has four people who review [TV] programmes.

partuisan, obs. f. PARTISAN[2].

parturb, obs. f. PERTURB.

† 'parture¹. *Obs.* [? f. PART *v.* + -URE, after *departure*; but cf. OF. *parteure*, *parture* division, separation, from *partir*: see PART *v.*] Departure.
 1567 TURBERV. *To his Loue, long absent* Epit., etc. 65 b, For since your parture I haue lead a lothsome state. 1587 T. HUGHES *Misfort. Arthur* v. i. in Hazl. *Dodsley* IV. 335 Yet let my death and parture rest obscure. 1622 C. FITZ-GEFFRY *Elisha* 1 Elisha his complaint at the parture or rapture of Elijah from him into Heauen.

† 'parture². *Obs.* [ad. L. *partūra*, f. *parĕre*, *part-* to bring forth: see -URE.] The bringing forth of young, or bearing of fruit; that which is brought forth, offspring, produce.
 1588 J. HARVEY *Disc. Probl.* 67 The flowers, seedes, berries, fruits, gums, or other parture of trees or shrubs. 1597 A. M. *Guillemeau's Fr. Chirurg.* 35 b/2 Some woemen are to much affrighted of the parture or Childbirth.

parturiate (pɑː'tjʊərɪeɪt), *v. rare.* [irreg. f. L. *parturī-re* + -ATE³.] **a.** *intr.* To bring forth young; to bear fruit. **b.** *trans.* To bring forth.
 1660 HICKERINGILL *Jamaica* (1661) 33 This Tree Parturiates every Moneth, and will have fifty or sixty Nuts at a burthen. 1866 J. B. ROSE tr. *Ovid, Met.* 18 And then did mother earth parturiate Spontaneously. *Ibid.* 161 The goddess great, parturiating twins. —— *Fasti* I. 669 The matrons vowed not to parturiate, And slew their offspring in its embryo state. 1922 JOYCE *Ulysses* 206, I am big with child.. Let me parturiate!

parturience (pɑː'tjʊərɪəns). *rare*⁻¹. [f. L. *parturient-em*: see PARTURIENT and -ENCE.] The action of giving birth; parturition.
 1822 *New Monthly Mag.* V. 361 His helpmate in annual parturience is seen.

parturiency (pɑː'tjʊərɪənsɪ). [f. as prec. + -ENCY.] Parturient condition or quality. (Usually *fig.* in reference to ideas, etc.)
 1652 URQUHART *Jewel* Wks. (1834) 210 From whose brains have already issued offsprings every whit as considerable, with parturiencie for greater births. 1686 H. MORE *Real Pres.* vii. 49, I believe in the Authors thereof there was a kind of Parturiency, and more confused Divination of that Truth. 1736 BERKELEY *Querist* App. ii. §253 A more general parturiency with respect to politicks and public counsels.

parturient (pɑː'tjʊərɪənt), *a.* and *sb.* [ad. L. *parturiens*, *-ent-*, pr. pple. of *parturīre* to be in labour, to travail, to be pregnant, desiderative of *parĕre*, *part-* to bring forth.]
 A. *adj.* **1.** About to bring forth or give birth; travailing; *transf.* bearing fruit.
 1592 G. HARVEY *Four Lett.* iii. Wks. (Grosart) I. 199 More ..then the whole Supplication of the Parturient Mountaine. 1597 A. M. *Guillemeau's Fr. Chirurg.* 35 b/2 Of the parturient woman. 1657 HAWKE *Killing is M.* 56 Thus have ..Allen's parturient mountaines produced a pittiful and ridiculous Mouse. 1667 JER. TAYLOR *Serm. for Year, Suppl.* iii. 37 The plant that is ingrafted, must also be parturient and fruitful. 1861 W. B. BROOKE *Out w. Garibaldi* iii. 26, I saw Annita Garibaldi, the now parturient mother, lie down ..to die.
 2. *fig.* Ready to bring forth or produce something; big or 'in travail' with (a discovery, idea, principle, etc.).
 1599 NASHE *Lenten Stuffe* Wks. (Grosart) V. 248 Not the diminutiuest nooke or creuise of them but is parturient of the like superofficiousnes. 1668 M. CASAUBON *Credulity* (1670) 121 That the whole world in a manner, since the Creation, hath been parturient, or in travel of this great truth, and mystery, till the birth of Christ. 1807 J. BARLOW *Columb.* VIII. 144 Freedom, parturient with a hundred states, Confides them to your hand. 1850 GROTE *Greece* II. lxviii. VIII. 621 The fresh and unborrowed offspring of a really parturient mind.
 3. Of or pertaining to parturition.
 1748 RICHARDSON *Clarissa* (1810) VII. xcii. 382 Describing the parturient throes. 1860 TANNER *Pregnancy* i. 40 Because the parturient process in domesticated animals is easy or difficult, in proportion as they are subjected to a life of toil. 1893 *Syd. Soc. Lex.*, *Parturient apoplexy*, a puerperal disease occurring in cows.
 B. *sb.* A parturient woman.
 1956 *Amer. Jrnl. Obstetr. & Gynecol.* LXXI. 1251 A clinical program was set up to evaluate the effects of chlorpromazine on the parturient during the first and second stages of labor. 1958 R. LIDDELL *Morea* II. viii. 192 No birth or death might take place in the sacred enclosure, and the dying or parturient had to be carried hastily on to the hills. 1974 R. WINSTON tr. *Wunderlich's Secret of Crete* xxv. 334 Many highborn young ladies brought children into the world in this way; the infants were ascribed to the god in whose sanctuary these women had been temple servants or whose medical men had taken care of the parturient.

parturifacient (pɑːtjʊərɪ'feɪʃ(ɪ)ənt), *a.* and *sb.* [f. L. *parturīre* to travail + -FACIENT.]
 a. *adj.* Serving to accelerate parturition. **b.** *sb.* A medicine having this property. = OXYTOCIC *a.* and *sb.*
 1853 DUNGLISON *Med. Lex.*, *Parturifacient*, parturient. 1867 C. H. HARRIS *Dict. Med. Terminol.*, *Parturifacient*, in *Obstetrics*, that which promotes or causes parturition. 1886 *Brit. Med. Jrnl.* 27 Mar. 614/2 [He] calls attention to the value of mistletoe as a parturifacient.

† 'parturing, *ppl. a. Obs. rare.* [After L. *parturiens*.] Parturient.
 1597 A. M. *Guillemeau's Fr. Chirurg.* 35 b/2 Certifyed heereof, as wel of the parturinge woman, as of the Midwyfe.

parturiometer (pɑːtjʊərɪ'ɒmɪtə(r)). [irreg. f. L. *parturīre* (see next) + -OMETER.] (See quot.)
 1890 in *Cent. Dict.* 1893 *Syd. Soc. Lex.*, *Parturiometer*, *Leaman's*... An instrument for indicating the effective movement of the advancing part of the ovum or fœtus at any moment during parturition.

† par'turious, *a. Obs. rare.* [irreg. f. L. *parturīre* to bring forth, or *partūra* bearing + -OUS.] Of or pertaining to parturition.
 1604 DRAYTON *Moses* II. Poems (1810) 482/1 Stirring with pain in the parturious throes.

† par'turitie. *Obs. rare.* In 5 parturite. [f. L. *partūr-us* about to bring forth (or f. stem of *parturī-re*) + -ITY.] = PARTURITION 1.
 c 1440 LONELICH *Merlin* 924 Swich as to mester scholde be That longeth to wommans parturite.

parturition (pɑːtjʊə'rɪʃən). [ad. L. *parturītiōn-em*, n. of action f. *parturīre*: see PARTURIENT.]
 1. The action of bringing forth or of being delivered of young; childbirth. (Chiefly in technical use; also *fig.*)
 1646 SIR T. BROWNE *Pseud. Ep.* 116 The conformation of parts is necessarily required..also unto the parturition or very birth it selfe. 1799 *Med. Jrnl.* I. 157 Case of difficult Parturition. 1877 SHIELDS *Final Philos.* 127 What Rospe termed Nature in the act of parturition.
 †**2.** That which is brought forth; a 'birth'; offspring. In quot. *fig. Obs. rare.*
 1659 O. WALKER *Oratory* viii. 117 The ardency of love, which we have to any new parturition, is by some space of time abated, after that we have diverted to some other imployment.

parturitive (pɑː'tjʊərɪtɪv), *a. rare.* [f. ppl. stem of L. *parturīre* + -IVE.] Inclined or tending to parturition; in quot. *catachr.* Relating to parturition; obstetric.
 1852 LYTTON *My Novel* XII. xi, According to the prophecies of parturitive science.

part-way (,pɑːt'weɪ), *adv.* Also **part way**, **partway**. [PART *adv.* c.] Part of the way; a certain distance along the way; to some extent; partly.
 1859 MRS. GASKELL *Lett.* (1966) 530 Flossy is gone to school..at Knutsford. I took her part way on Tuesday last. 1875 KINGLAKE *Crimea* V. iv. II. 70 He moved some battalions part-way towards the frowning Sapounè Heights. 1930 BLUNDEN *De Bello Germanico* 15 Half-ruined houses, with sacks stretched partway over some windows. 1954 *Essays in Crit.* July 320 It is unbearable for a man or woman to be faced with anything less than a person—and thus, tragically, even part-way unbearable to be faced only with other human persons, where the personal relationship is inevitably enmeshed in material situations. 1968 C. HELMERICKS *Down Wild River North* I. ii. 22 Starting off toward Billings, we learned partway there that the road was blocked. 1976 I. LEVIN *Boys from Brazil* i. 34 He stopped and rewound part-way and replayed a few bits. 1978 *Sci. Amer.* Feb. 68/1 When a peg is partway into a hole, it can wobble back and forth a good deal farther than the clearance itself.

party ('pɑːtɪ), *sb.* Forms: 3-7 partye, (3-4 partiȝe), 4-5 parti, (4 perti, 4-5 -y, 5 parte, perte (?); *pl.* 4 partijs, 4-5 parteis, -eys, partise, -yse, 5 partice, -yce), 4-7 partie, (5, 7 pertie, 6 *Sc.* pairtie, -y, 7 partee), 4- **party**. [ME. *partie*, *partye*, a. F. *partie* (12th c. in Littré) = Pr., Sp. *partida*, It. *partita* lit. a parting or division, from fem. pa. pple. of L. *partīre*, It. *partire*, F. *partir*: see PART *v.* This sb. (analogous to those in *-ata*, *-ada*, *-ade*, *-ée*, *-y*) in some senses coincided with or superseded *part*, PART *sb.* But in some uses the Eng. sb. answers to F. *parti*, It. *partito*:—L. *partītum* that which is divided, shared, or allotted.
 Final mute *e* in Eng. being often dropped or added without reference to derivation, it is not possible to separate the senses belonging to *parti* from those belonging to *partie*; and the arrangement here is in many points provisional.]
 I. Part, portion, side. [= F. *partie*.]
 †**1.** A division of a whole; a part, portion, share; an aliquot part; a part or member of the body; cf. PART *sb.* 1-7. *Obs.*
 c 1290 *S. Eng. Leg.* I. 231/418 Þat he for-clef is foule bouk in þre partyes at þe laste. 1297 R. GLOUC. (Rolls) 8112 Hii departede verst hor ost as in vour partye. a 1300 *Cursor M.* 2094 Þe werld es..Delt in thrin parteis [*v.r.* partijs] sere. *Ibid.* 13583 O godd him semes ha na perti. 1362 LANGL. *P. Pl.* A. I. 7 Þe moste parti of þe peple. 1387 TREVISA *Higden* (Rolls) I. 103 Iudea is a kyngdom of Syria a party of Palestyna. 1433 *Rolls of Parlt.* IV. 475/2 In party of payment of the said l *li.* 1497 BP. ALCOCK *Mons Perfect.* E ij b/1 Bewteuous in colour of al partyes of theyr bodyes. 1526 TINDALE *Matt.* xxvii. 51 The vayle of the temple was rent in two parties. 1541 R. COPLAND *Guydon's Quest. Chirurg.*, In what partye of the sholdre is it? 1628 COKE *On Litt.* 47 Out of a generall, a party may be excepted, as out of a manor an acre. 1654 GATAKER *Disc. Apol.* 69 To prov the truth concerning an over-great partie of them.
 b. Phr. ***a party*** (see A-PARTY), ***in party***: in part, partly; somewhat, a little. Also (15-17th c.) simply *party* (ellipt. or advb.), in part, partly (= PART *sb.* (*adv.*) B). So ***for the more party***, etc.: ***a great party***, in great part, to a large extent; (cf. PART *sb.* V). *Obs.*
 c 1330 R. BRUNNE *Chron. Wace* (Rolls) 11749 When þei were stilled a party, ffirst spak sire Ohel. 1375 BARBOUR *Bruce* III. 292 He sall eschew It In party. c 1380 WYCLIF *Wks.* (1880) 389 In sum londis hooly, & in ynglonde for þe more party. *Ibid.*, Þe lordis ben vndo in grete party. 1382 —— *1 Cor.* xiii. 12 Now I knowe of party, thanne forsooth I schal knowe as and I am knowyn. c 1400 *Gamelyn* 392 Now I haue aspied thou art a party fals. c 1440 CAPGRAVE *Life St. Kath.* IV. 859 Thus party with witte, party wyth nygramauncy She peruerteth oure lond in wonder wise. c 1450 *Merlin* 21, I knowe thynges that be for to come a grete partye. 1450-1530 *Myrr. our Ladye* 58 Like to this in party. 1473 WARKW. *Chron.* (Camden) 11 Alle Englonde for the more partye hatyd hym. 1578 LYTE *Dodoens* II. lxxvii. 251 Sometimes all white, and sometimes partie white. 1688 R. HOLME *Armoury* III. 197/1 Their [Deacon's] Office..is party Humane, party Divine.
 †**2.** A part of the world, region, district (usually *pl.*): = PART *sb.* 13. *Obs.*
 13.. *K. Alis.* 4910 Thoo that woneth in the est partie. c 1400 *Destr. Troy* 305 Mony prouyns and perties were put out of helle. c 1400 *Three Kings Cologne* 123 In all þe partyes & kyngdoms of þe eest. 1538 STARKEY *England* I. i. 2 Dyuerse partyes beyond the see. 1578 T. NICHOLAS tr. *Cortes' Hist. W. Ind.* (1596) 17 Freely to goe and trafficke into those parties.
 b. Side; direction, 'quarter' of the compass: = PART *sb.* 14. *Obs.*
 c 1400 MAUNDEV. (Roxb.) xx. 91 And a man þare take a spere and sett it euen in þe erthe at midday,..it makez na schadowe till na party. 14.. *Tundale's Vis.* 1973 Thay hanged thykke on ilke party. 1547 BOORDE *Introd. Knowl.* xxii. (1870) 177 Marchauntes passeth from both parties by the water of Tiber. 1585 T. WASHINGTON tr. *Nicholay's Voy.* II. xviii. 51 The Northeast wind..comming from the party of Arctus whiche in greek signifieth a she Bear. 1588 J. MELLIS *Briefe Instr.* D iv, In the Debitor partie. And..in the Creditor party of the Leager.
 †**3.** ? A part of a matter, a point, particular; matter, affair; respect. (Cf. PART *sb.* 2 c.) *Obs.*
 1390 GOWER *Conf.* III. 46 His houres of Astronomie He kepeth as for that partie Which longeth to thinspeccion Of love and his affeccion. 1439 *E.E. Wills* (1882) 115 Y bequeth to eche of my seide executours for his labor in this party to be had, Cs. 1509 HAWES *Past. Pleas.* XI. (Percy Soc.) 47 Nowe after this, for to make relacyon Of famous rethoryke so in this party, As to the fourth part, Pronouncyacyon, I shal it shew anone ryght openly.
 †**4.** ? State, condition, plight, predicament. *rare.*
 c 1440 *Generydes* 3518 'If thu', quod he, 'had done after my rede, Thu shuldest not now haue ben in this parte' [*rimes* vterly, trewelly]. 1485 CAXTON *Paris & V.* 5 Ye see..in what party we be now.
 5. Side in a contest, in a dispute, a contract, or the like; cause, interest: = PART *sb.* 15. ? *Obs.* or merged in 6. † ***on*** (in) ***a party***: on one side. † ***to draw to parties***: to take sides.
 a 1300 *Cursor M.* 729 Bath ar now on a partie to confund [him] wit trecherie. *Ibid.* 7470 And her i bede mi-self redi, For to fight for vr parti [*v.r.* party]. 1393 LANGL. *P. Pl.* C. II. 95 And for no lordene loue leue þe trewe partye. 1411 *Rolls of Parlt.* III. 650/1 The ordenance..made betwen William Lord the Roos on that oon partie and Robert Tirwhit..on that other partie. c 1450 *Merlin* 113 And whan thei were alle assembled to-geder, thei were well vijᵐˡ on his partye. 1512 *Act 4 Hen. VIII*, c. 10 A paire of Indentures made betwen your Highnes on the oon partie and William Courteney..on the other partie. 1548 UDALL, etc. *Erasm. Par.* Pref. 16, I cannot tell on whose partie first to commence. 1568 GRAFTON *Chron.* II. 289 Manye feates of armes were there done on both parties. c 1586 C'TESS PEMBROKE *Ps.* CXVIII. vi, Jehova doth my party take. 1649 in J. Harrington *Def. Rights Univ. Oxford* (1690) 32 What hath been said on either party. 1754 FIELDING *Jon. Wild* I. xi, By the contrary party men often made a bad bargain with the devil. 1854 MILMAN *Lat. Chr.* VII. v. (1864) IV. 153 Rome was on that party which at the time could awe her with the greatest power or win her by the most lavish wealth.
 †**b.** ***on*** (or ***of***) ***my party***: on my behalf, on my part (OF. *de ma partie*, F. *de ma part*). ***for, on*** (***in, of***) ***my party***: as far as I am concerned, as for my part, on my part: so ***for, on, his party***, etc. (cf. PART *sb.* 25, 27, 28). *Obs.*
 a 1300 *Cursor M.* 12810 (Cott.) Tell þam soth, o [*Gött.*, *Trin.* on, *Fairf.* of] mi parti. *Ibid.* 15196 (Cott.) Til þe lauerd o þat hus Yee sai on mi parti, þat he yow wald len sum place. 1390 GOWER *Conf.* III. 196, I thenke also for mi partie Upon the lawe of Juerie. c 1430 *Freemasonry* (Halliw.) 29 They schul enquere every mon On his party, as wyl as he con. 1502 ATKYNSON tr. *De Imitatione* III. xi. 206 Thou, good lorde, fulfyll that I want of my partye. 1542 UDALL *Erasm. Apoph.* 101 If they beleved any offense on their partie against the Goddes.
 c. † ***to hold party*** (obs.), ***to make one's party good***: to make good one's cause, or position.
 c 1350 *Will. Palerne* 3643 His men miȝt nouȝt meyntene here owne, Prestly to hold party to puple þat hem folwed. 1631 HEYLIN *St. George* 53 To make good his party, against these severall Squadrons. 1662 J. DAVIES tr. *Olearius' Voy. Ambass.* 6 A man hath much ado to make his party good against them [gnats]. 1809-12 MAR. EDGEWORTH *Vivian* xii, Julia has made her party good with him, for he writes me word he cannot part with her.
 †**d.** A league, confederacy; a conspiracy, plot.
 1624 CAPT. SMITH *Virginia* 88 Hee had such parties with all his bordering neighbours. 1640 in *Hamilton Papers* (Camden) App. 261 The said Marques made many proffers of great parties within the Realme of Scotland.
 II. A company or body of persons.
 6. a. *concr.* Those who are on one side in a contest, etc., considered collectively; a number of persons united in maintaining a cause, policy, opinion, etc., in opposition to others who maintain a different one; a body of partisans or

adherents. In early instances (usually), One of the two 'sides' or bodies of combatants arrayed against each other, as in a battle or tournament.

1297 R. GLOUC. (Rolls) 1445 He sei þat hor partie [*v.r.* partiȝe] ibroȝt was nei to ssame. *c* **1350** *Will. Palerne* 1150 Boþe parties here place pertiliche had chosen. *c* **1380** WYCLIF *Wks.* (1880) 372 If þe clergi gete þis swerde oonys fully in her power, þe seculer party may go pipe wiþ an yuy lefe for eny lordeschipis þat þe clerkis wille ȝeue hem aȝen. *c* **1430** LYDG. *Min. Poems* (Percy Soc.) 4 The meyer.. Made hem hove in rengis twayne, A strete betwene eche party lyke a walle. **1502** *Ord. Crysten Men* (W. de W. 1506) Prol. 5 Taking part yt suche prechers weren of ye party of Ihesu cryst. **1584** POWEL *Lloyd's Cambria* 284 Euerie partie returned home. *a* **1625** FLETCHER *Chances* v. iii, My end is mirth, And pleasing, if I can, all parties. **1714** POPE *Let. to Jervas* 27 Aug., I expect no greater from the Whig-party, than the same Liberty.—A Curse on the Word Party, which I have been forced to use so often in this Period! **1769** ROBERTSON *Chas. V*, VI. Wks. 1826 IV. 84 Thus ended a war ..in which both parties exerted their utmost strength. **1813** SOUTHEY *March to Moscow* v, It was through thick and thin to its party true; Its back was buff, and its sides were blue. **1871** FREEMAN *Norm. Conq.* (1876) IV. xviii. 126 A party of order had sprung up among all classes of Englishmen.

b. *abstr.* The system of taking sides on public questions, the system of parties; attachment to or zeal for a party, party feeling or spirit: partisanship.

1729 BUTLER *Serm. Love Neighb.* ii. Wks. 1874 II. 165 The spirit of party, which unhappily prevails amongst mankind. **1774** GOLDSM. *Retal.* 32 Here lies our good Edmund [Burke] ..Who, born for the universe, narrowed his mind, And to party gave up what was meant for mankind. **1821** J. W. CROKER *Diary* 22 June, Party is in England a stronger passion than love, avarice, or ambition. **1841** GEN. P. THOMPSON *Exerc.* (1842) VI. 32 Party.. means being of any but the right party, which is every man's own. For when it is the right, then none will call it party. In fact it is the ill-natured, or as Jeremy Bentham called it, the dyslogistic word, for everybody except a man's self and friends. **1893** *Westm. Gaz.* 1 Feb. 1/3 Party is the embodiment of certain principles, beliefs, persuasions, which are commonly held by all who belong to it as essential to the right conduct of public affairs.

c. *spec.* (freq. with capital initial) ***the party***: the Communist Party.

1920 *Times* 5 Oct. 14/3 (*heading*) Realities of Russia. Iron Rule of 'The Party'. **1922** E. P. OPPENHEIM *Great Prince Shan* iv. 38 'Her father at present represents the shipping interests of Russia and England. He is one of the authorised consuls.' 'Is he of the party?' **1928** E. & C. PAUL tr. *Stalin's Leninism* I. 168 The central unit of organisation is the Party. **1936** A. HUXLEY *Eyeless in Gaza* xxii. 316 One joined the Party, one distributed literature. **1943** KOESTLER *Arrival & Departure* I. 18 He had courage, but he could not adapt himself to changes in the tactics of the movement. That's why he had to leave the Party. **1959** *Times Lit. Suppl.* 11 Sept. 575/4 The recent dramatic dismissal of the Kerala Government by the President of India.. is certain to influence the attitude of the Party towards legally constituted authority. **1975** *New Left Rev.* Nov.–Dec. 65 A whole series of import–export co-operatives.. pay a tithe of their profits to the party.

7. *Mil.* A detachment or small body of troops selected for a particular service or duty.

1645–6 *Pr. Rupert's Jrnl.* in *Eng. Hist. Rev.* (1898) XIII. 740 March 1, Sunday, a partie from Oxford, surprise Abingdon; but were beaten out. **1647** CLARENDON *Hist. Reb.* VI. §250 Sir John Berkley.. with a good party volant, of horse and dragoons,.. visiting all places in Devon,.. took many prisoners of name. **1772** *Ann. Reg.* 73*/2 Surprizing several of their posts, routing their parties, and destroying their magazines. **1853** STOCQUELER *Milit. Encycl.* s.v., *Recruiting Parties* are a certain number of men, under an officer or non-commissioned officer, detached from their respective battalions for the purpose of enlisting men.—*Firing Parties* are those who are selected to fire over the grave of any one interred with military honours.—*Working Parties* consist of small detachments of men.. who are employed on fatigues which are not purely of a military nature. **1900** *Westm. Gaz.* 2 June 7/2 A few minutes after they had passed our demolition party destroyed the line.

†**b.** ***upon party***, on the service upon which such a detachment is sent. *Obs.*

1709 STEELE *Tatler* No. 18 ¶6 They have been upon Parties and Skirmishes, when our Armies have lain still. **1756** WASHINGTON *Lett.* Writ. 1889 I. 334 Complaint.. that the officers and soldiers upon party, take up the strays they find in the woods.

c. *transf.* A gang of prisoners working together.

1896 *Daily News* 28 Dec. 6/3 There are numbers of gangs or 'parties', as they are officially termed, working in the open... There is the quarry party, which works about two hundred yards from the prison.

8. A company of persons (rarely of animals); esp. a company formed or gathered together for a temporary purpose; a body of persons travelling together or engaged in any common pursuit; a number of persons met together for amusement or entertainment.

Thus, a hunting or fishing party, a reading party, a house party; to form a party to go to Switzerland, etc.

1773 G. WHITE *Selborne* xxxviii. (1789) 97, I.. have found these birds in little parties in the autumn cantoned all along the Sussex downs. **1797** MRS. RADCLIFFE *Italian* Prol. (1826) 3 One of the party pointed him out to the friar. **1805** LD. COLLINGWOOD 16 Dec. in Nicolas *Disp.* (1846) VII. 242 Truly sorry am I that Calder was not of the party. **1827** LYTTON *Pelham* xxi, A bench, which.. one might appropriate to the entire and unparticipated use of one's self and party. **1860** TYNDALL *Glac.* I. xxi. 150 A party of gentlemen.. had started at three o'clock for the summit. **1870** E. PEACOCK *Ralf Skirl.* III. 141 When the party were once more on their horses.

9. A gathering or assemblage for social pleasure or amusement; a social gathering or entertainment, esp. of invited guests at a private house.

Thus, a dinner, tea, or supper party, a garden or picnic party, to give a party, go to parties, etc.

1716 LADY M. W. MONTAGU *Let. to Mrs. Smith* 5 Aug., I rather fancy myself upon parties of pleasure. **1728** ELIZA HEYWOOD tr. *Mme. de Gomez' Belle A.* (1732) II. 99 To entreat we would favour her with our Company, to make a Party of Pleasure, which her Daughter had put her in mind of. **1754** CHATHAM *Lett. Nephew* iv. 24 Decline their parties with civility. **1809** MALKIN *Gil Blas* VIII. ix. ¶6 After the example of his excellency,.. I determined to give parties of my own... Scipio, too, had his parties in the servants' hall. **1827** LYTTON *Pelham* xv, The party was as stiff and formal as such assemblies invariably are. **1902** *Westm. Gaz.* 20 Nov. 7/3 The luncheon-party included four or five of Lord Rosebery's personal guests.

b. Phrases: ***the party is over***: enjoyment must stop; the happy or easy times are at an end; ***to keep the party clean***: to act responsibly; to conform to accepted patterns of behaviour.

1937 M. ALLINGHAM *Dancers in Mourning* xxvii. 328 'You've made up yer mind to go to-day? It's a lovely day.' His wistfulness was pathetic, and Campion felt sudden sympathy for him. 'I'm afraid so,' he murmured. 'The party's over. Sorry.' **1938** E. WAUGH *Scoop* III. 210 'The party's over,' said Bannister... 'From tomorrow onward, I shall get a daily pile of bumf from the Ministry.' **1959** *Times* 7 Nov. 7/4 Then they [*sc.* young people] should be invited to cooperate in keeping the party clean and so ensuring that the letting off of fireworks is kept within bounds. **1965** D. FRANCIS *For Kicks* vi. 91 'Do your dress up,' I said. 'Why? Are you impotent after all, Danny boy?' 'Do your dress up,' I repeated. 'The party's over.' **1975** *Times* 10 May 1/1 Local government.. is coming to realize that, for the time being, the party is over. **1977** *Time* 22 Aug. 5/1 Now in the '70s, the party is over. **1977** PARTRIDGE *Dict. Catch Phrases* 131/1 *Keep the party clean!*.. Don't talk smut or tell dirty stories; don't act loosely or indelicately. A correspondent.. commented thus: 'But the speaker often does not quite mean it. "Give me my hat and knickers," she said. "I thought you were going to keep the party clean."' **1978** D. MURPHY *Place Apart* xi. 243 To them [*sc.* Provos] their campaign is ..a conventional war, and they want to keep the party clean.

c. An attack, a combat, or fight; an operation, or a unit engaged in an operation. *Armed services' slang.*

1942 'B. J. ELLAN' *Spitfire!* v. 23, I just fired when something came into my sights and then turned like hell as something fired at me! What a party! **1942** *R.A.F. Jrnl.* 27 June 7 Confirmation came through that the big party was on. And that the target was Cologne. **1943** P. BRENNAN et al. *Spitfires over Malta* 18 This party is about 40 miles North, coming South. **1946** J. IRVING *Royal Navalese* 131 A good example of naval understatement for, in one sense, a 'party' can mean quite a tough fight while it lasts. **1959** *Times Lit. Suppl.* 7 Aug. p. iii/3 Classic understating metaphors like 'having a party'.. had their value in time of war when men had to accept as steadfastly and as mildly as they could the possibility of their own violent and horrible deaths.

†**10.** A game or match, esp. at piquet: = PARTIE. (F. *partie.*) *Obs.*

1726 [see QUADRILLE *sb.*[1]]. **1727** GAY *Beg. Op.* I. iv, He hath promis'd to make one this evening.. at a party of quadrille. **1731** FIELDING *Mod. Husb.* III. xi, I am confident ..that he lost the last party designedly. **1770** C. JENNER *Placid Man* I. III. vii. 188 Sir Isaac was within a few points of winning the party. **1796** MRS. M. ROBINSON *Angelina* II. 33 Let's play a party at back-gammon.

III. A single person considered in some relation.

11. a. Each of the two or more persons (or bodies of people) that constitute the two sides in some proceeding, as the litigants in an action at law, the persons who enter into a contract, who contract marriage, etc.

c **1290** *Beket* 577 in *S. Eng. Leg.* 123 ȝif bi-twene tweie lewede men were ani striuinge, Oþur bi-tuene a lewed man and a clerk.. þe king wolde þat in his court þat plai scholde beon i-driue, For ase muche ase a lewed man þe o partye was. **1377** LANGL. *P. Pl.* B. XIV. 268 A mayden.. þat is maried þorw brokage, As bi assent of sondry partyes. *c* **1420** LYDG. *Assembly of Gods* 146 Euenly dele twene these partyes tweyn. **1467** *Waterf. Arch.* in *10th Rep. Hist. MSS. Comm.* App. v. 305 There shal none of the saide counsaile.. passe in no jure betwene party and party. **1489** CAXTON *Faytes of A.* IV. x. 257 The party playntyf that is to saye he that calleth that other whiche is party deffendaunt. *a* **1568** *Satir. Poems Reform.* xlvii. 100 Becauss their bandis wer reddy to be proclamit The pairteis mett and maid a fair contrack. **1596** DANETT tr. *Comines* (1614) 190 The King.. neuer meant to accomplish this marriage, because there was no equalitie between the age of the two parties. **1704** J. HARRIS *Lex. Techn.* I. s.v., Those that make any Deed, and they to whom it is made, are called *Parties in the Deed.* **1726** AYLIFFE *Parergon* 158 If a Bishop be a Party to a Suit, and excommunicate his adversary; such Excommunication.. shall not disable or bar his Adversary from his Action. **1853** MAURICE *Proph. & Kings* xx. 343 It appears to be a narrative written by a third party. **1857** BADEN POWELL *Chr. without Judaism* 139 The word διαθήκη.. signifies, generally, any legal act or deed; whether of one party, as a will or 'testament', or of two, as a covenant.

Hence *attrib.*, ***party-and-party***, as between the two parties in an action at law.

1895 *Daily News* 31 Oct. 5/6 The levelling down of solicitor and client costs to the party-and-party scale. **1898** *Westm. Gaz.* 4 May 1/3 The distinction which is known as 'party and party' costs and 'solicitor and client' costs.

†**b.** Hence, An opponent, an antagonist. *Obs.* (Cf. F. *forte partie*, a powerful antagonist.)

c **1500** *Melusine* 262, I doubte me to haue shortly a strong werre & to haue a doo with a strong partye. **1513** DOUGLAS *Æneis* VII. iv. 38 Ilk ane besy his party for to irk. **1572** tr. *Buchanan's Detect.* E iij b, He is denyit of his freindis and seruandis quha suld haue accompanyit him to his honour and suretie of his lyfe, in respect of the greatnes of his partie.

12. One who takes part, participates, or is concerned in some action or affair; a participator; an accessory. Const. *to*, formerly also *in*.

1399 THIRNYNG in *Rolls of Parlt.* III. 451/2 That he was nevere partie, no kaster, no willyng ne assentyng to the dethe of the Duc of Gloucestre. **1512** *Act 4 Hen. VIII*, c. 9 *Preamble*, The said Edward was not previe ne partie to the offence of his Sonne. **1604** SHAKS. *Oth.* v. i. 86, I do suspect this Trash To be a party in this Iniurie. **1630** *R. Johnson's Kingd. & Commw.* 244 He also made himselfe a partie in the present quarrell. **1760–72** H. BROOKE *Fool of Qual.* (1809) II. 158, I would willingly have been a party in any kind of wickedness. **1844** DICKENS *Mart. Chuz.* lii, He was a party to all their proceedings. **1891** *Law Rep.* Weekly Notes 138/1 The defendant was a party to the making of the codicil.

†**13.** One associated with another as counterpart; a fellow; a partner (esp. in marriage), a mate. *Obs.* (chiefly *Sc*). [OF. *partie* (Godefroy).]

1562 A. SCOTT *Poems* (S.T.S.) i. 198 Thow.. wes King Frances pairty maik and peir. **1563** WINȜET *Four Scoir Thre Quest.* Wks. 1888 I. 110 Quhiddir gif a man or woman being lang absent fra thair party, or haifand thair party impotent throw seiknes,.. may mary an vthir? **1651** tr. *De-las-Coveras' Don Fenise* 249 They fell upon this discourse of marriage, saying that it was necessary for every one, to take a party conformable to his disposition.

b. An equal in a contest; a match. *Sc. Obs.*

a **1578** LINDESAY (Pitscottie) *Chron. Scot.* (S.T.S.) I. 118 Thinkand.. he sould be pairtie to the king and gif him battell. *Ibid.* II. 20 The governour nor cardinall durst nocht ..gif thame battell becaus thay mycht nocht be pairtie at that tyme to thame.

14. In extended sense: The individual person concerned or in question; more vaguely, the person (defined by some adjective, relative clause, etc.). (Formerly common and in serious use; now shoppy, vulgar, or jocular, the proper word being *person*.)

In the plural, *the parties*, meaning 'the persons', is more tolerable, being susceptible of explanation as 'the groups of persons'.

c **1460** FORTESCUE *Abs. & Lim. Mon.* xv. (1885) 145 To make hem also ffauorable and parcial, as were the same seruantes, or the parties þat so moved hem. **1541** *Act 33 Hen. VIII*, c. 12 §9 The sergeant of the pantrie.. shall.. giue bread to the partie that shal haue his hande so striken of. **1579** W. WILKINSON *Confut. Familye of Love* 12 [They] thought the parties baptized of heretiques, ought to be rebaptized agayne. **1597** BP. ANDREWES *Serm. Zach.* xii. 10 Serm. (1631) 341 Not onely, it is we that have pierced the Party thus found slaine; but, that this Party, whom we have thus pierced, is.. even the Only begotten Sonne of the most High God. **1611** B. JONSON *Catiline* II. ii. 111 'Tis the party, madame. What party? Has he no name? **1621** BURTON *Anat. Mel.* III. iv. I. ii. (1651) 655 [As] used by such parties as Moses, Elias, Daniel, Christ, and as his Apostles made use of it. **1631** HEYLIN *St. George* 303 That the partie nominated, bee a Gentleman of name and armes. **1684** R. JOHNSON *Man. Physick* I. iii. 33 When the fit is coming or upon the Party, blow up some sneezing-powder into the Nostrils. **1772** COLLIGNON in *Phil. Trans.* LXII. 467 If done immediately after the party's death. **1823** WORDSW. *Prose Wks.* III. 206 The party was not known to me, though she lived at Hawkshead. **1843** J. H. NEWMAN *Miracles* 59 St. Paul's supernatural power.. was doubted at Corinth by the very parties who had seen his miracles and been his converts. **1888** BURGON *Lives 12 Gd. Men* II. v. 63 'Do you know, my Lord', (said the old party solemnly).

b. With *a*: A person. Now *low colloquial* or *slang*. (In early examples from sense 11.)

[**1650** EARL MONM. tr. *Senault's Man bec. Guilty* 191 She should be innocent, if she were not fastened to so guilty a Party. *a* **1654** GATAKER *Antid. Errour* (1670) 14 A partie offends and wrongs his Neighbor.] **1686** *Lond. Gaz.* No. 2149/4 A Red Scarlet Cloak.. delivered to a wrong Party by Mr. Capers at the Bells of Osney. **1770** FOOTE *Lame Lover* III. Wks. 1799 II. 81 There is, likewise, another party, for whom a place ought to be kept. **1855** BAGEHOT *Lit. Stud.* I. 304 'From what you tell me, sir, said an American,.. 'I should say he was a go-ahead party'. **1859** HELPS *Friends in C.* Ser. II. I. iv. 185 Calumny herself has been a most calumniated 'party', to use the mercantile slang word of the day. **1870** M. COLLINS *Vivian* II. vi. 116 She was a professedly pious party.

c. A telephone subscriber; a person using a telephone.

At first used only with reference to party lines (PARTY LINE 2), *subscriber* being the usual term.

1912 J. POOLE *Pract. Telephone Handbk.* (ed. 5) xxxii. 531 Party lines up to 4 stations on a line can be worked on the automatic by giving each of the parties on the line a separate number and multipleing the lines on four sets of connectors. **1938** C. W. WILMAN *Automatic Telephony* (ed. 2) xix. 185 All incoming calls are received at one of the ordinary telephones, from which they can be transferred to the wanted party. **1955** W. GADDIS *Recognitions* II. v. 508, I think we got a crossed wire, would the other parties mind hanging up. **1973** *Times* 23 May 8/7, I heard him say: 'I am receiving a report on that right now' to the party on the other end.

IV. Senses of doubtful affinity, mostly repr. F. *parti*.

†**15.** A decision on one side or the other, a determination, resolution: *esp.* in ***to take a party*** (cf. F. *prendre son parti*). *Obs.*

1585 T. WASHINGTON tr. *Nicholay's Voy.* I. xix. 23 The souldiers.. setting al honor aside,.. concluded together to take some party. **1702** VANBRUGH *False Friend* I. Wks. (Rtldg.) 398/1, I am not come to ask counsel.. my party is taken. **1760** *Hist.* in *Ann. Reg.* 6–7 He had two parties to take; either to keep within the town,..or to march out... He resolved on the latter party.

†**16.** A person to marry, considered in respect of desirability; a (good or bad) match or offer. (See PARTI.)

The first quot. is quite uncertain.

[**1423** JAS. I *Kingis Q.* xlviii, Now gif there was gud partye, god It wote.] **1655** *Theophania* 169 She easily condescended to so advantagious a party. **1789** CHARLOTTE SMITH *Ethelinde* (1814) V. 200 Try..to make him look upon either of your daughters as a desirable party for him. **1855** THACKERAY *Newcomes* I. 296 A girl in our society accepts the best party which offers itself.

†**17.** A proposal, an offer. *Obs.*

1653 H. COGAN tr. *Pinto's Trav.* xlix. 241 As such a one I accept of the party thou dost present me with, obliging myself to render thee the two passages of Savady free. **1765** H. WALPOLE *Otranto* v. (1834) 241 Manfred accepted the party, and, to the no small grief of Isabella, accompanied her to her apartment.

V. 18. *attrib.* and *Comb.* †**a.** *attrib.* or as *adj.* (with sbs.) or as *adv.* (with adjs.), in sense 1 b: In part, partial (or partially): = PART B, PARCEL B: as ***party-bawd***, ***-fulfilling***, ***-halting***, ***-payment***; †***party-gilt*** adj. = PARCEL-GILT. Also **party-verdict**, one person's share or part of a joint verdict.

1473 in *Somerset Medieval Wills* (1901) 226 A couple of salt salers party gilt. **1497** *Naval Acc. Hen. VII* (1896) 140 In partie payment of the sayd warraunt. **1593** SHAKS. *Rich. II*, I. iii. 234 Thy sonne is banish'd vpon good aduice, Whereto thy tongue a party-verdict gaue. **1610** B. JONSON *Alch.* III. iii, My deare Delicious compeere, and my partie-bawd. **1633** FORD *Love's Sacr.* III. iii, Unfold What by the party-halting of thy speech Thy knowledge can discover. **1691** BEVERLEY *Thous. Years Kingd. Christ* 30 For all the swelling Rhetorick and seeming Hyperboles,..had but Party-fulfillings before.

b. *attrib.* or as *adj.* with sense as in PARTY-WALL, q.v.; as ***party arch***, ***fence-wall***, ***structure***.

1812–16 J. SMITH *Panorama Sc. & Art* I. 267 They must have a party-wall, with a party-arch or arches of the thickness of a brick and a half at the least, to the first and second rate. **1823** P. NICHOLSON *Pract. Build.* 363 Proprietors of houses and grounds must..give three months' notice to pull down old party-walls, party-arches, party fence-walls, or quarter partitions. **1842–76** GWILT *Archit.* (ed. 7) Gloss., *Party Fence Wall*, a wall separating the open ground in one occupation from that in another; each owner having a right up to the centre of such wall. **1855** *Act 18 & 19 Vict.* c. 122 §3 'Party structure' shall include party walls, and also partitions, arches, floors, and other structures separating buildings, stories, or rooms which belong to different owners.

19. Ordinary attributive uses (often hyphened) and combinations, chiefly in sense 6 (often = PARTISAN *sb.*[1] B.), as ***party-administration***, ***-author***, ***boss***, ***card***, ***caucus***, ***cell***, ***-chief***, ***conference***, ***congress***, ***-contest***, ***convention***, ***-cry***, ***discipline***, ***-division***, ***-feeling***, ***-fury***, ***-government***, ***hack***, ***image***, ***label***, ***-leader***, ***-lie***, ***-list***, ***loyalty***, ***machine***, ***-making***, ***-malice***, ***manager***, ***-measure***, ***meeting***, ***member***, ***membership***, ***-mindedness***, ***-monger***, ***-pamphlet***, ***-paper***, ***passion***, ***platform***, ***point***, ***politician***, ***-politics*** (hence ***party-political*** adj.; also ellipt., a party-political broadcast), ***prejudice***, ***press***, ***quarrel***, ***question***, ***rage***, ***rally***, ***secret***, ***-state***, ***system***, ***woman***, ***worker***, ***writer***, ***zeal***, ***zealot***, etc.; ***party-bound*** adj.; also (sense 1 or 5) †***party-taker*** (= PARTAKER); (sense 7) ***party-making***, ***-war***; (sense 8) ***party-boat*** (N. Amer.) (hence as *v. intr.*); (sense 9) ***party call***, ***dress***, ***frock***, ***game***, ***girl***, ***-giving***, ***-goer***, ***-going***, ***mood***, ***piece***, ***record***, ***thrower***, ***trick***; ***party-frocked***, ***-like*** adjs.; (11) ***party-hunting***, ***-witness***; **party manners**, good manners, best behaviour; **party piano**, a boogie-woogie or barrel-house style of piano-playing; **party plan**, a sales strategy by which goods are displayed or demonstrated at a party in a private house; also *attrib.*; **party poop**, **pooper** *U.S. slang*, one who throws a gloom over social enjoyment; **party spirit**, (*a*) feeling of solidarity with and support for one's political party; (*b*) feeling or atmosphere of festivity; hence ***party-spirited adj.***

1735 BOLINGBROKE *On Parties* vi. 56 The Abettors of a *Party-Administration. **1712** ADDISON *Spect.* No. 457 ⁋4 Our *Party-Authors will also afford me a great Variety of Subjects. **1937** E. HEMINGWAY *To have & have Not* I. i. 14 You *party-boat captains. *Ibid.* 28, I..went party-boating and broke out this sword-fishing in Cuba. **1963** J. T. ROWLAND *North to Adventure* i. 27 She [*sc.* a sloop] had a long, open cockpit and a small cuddy, since it was his intention to rent her as a party boat. **1909** *Times* 27 Apr. 4/5 There would thus be a good chance of undermining the '*party boss'. **1938** *Ann. Reg. 1937* 320 The men and the movement, the party and the party bosses, the national aims of the Third Reich. **1977** J. CLEARY *Vortex* ii. 32 He had never been able to make his mark with any of the state's party bosses. **1908** *Westm. Gaz.* 30 Dec. 4/3 The one honest solution which is constantly shirked by those who are either *party-bound or who..hope for a secular solution. **1936** WIRTH & SHILS tr. *Mannheim's Ideology & Utopia* iii. 136 Those whose standpoints are party-bound are finding it necessary to have a broader perspective. **1910** J. W. TOMPKINS *Mothers & Fathers* 144 They only came twice, and those were *party calls. **1935** N. MITCHISON *We have been Warned* II. 209 He had very few papers..his trade union card, and his *Party card. **1970** *Guardian* 10 Mar. 13/1 Union leaders must talk to Ministers, whatever the shade of their party cards. **1977** P. JOHNSON *Enemies of Society* xiv. 185 Such a brutal division can only be maintained by laws of status and privilege—a nobility by birth, or by party card. **1882** W. M. THAYER *From Log Cabin to White House* 300 Garfield..was nominated by acclamation at the *party caucus, and unanimously elected. **1977** *N.Z. Herald* 5 Jan. 1-6/3 The party caucus has long functioned as part and parcel of New Zealand politics. **1949** *Ann. Reg. 1948* 285 There were 25,635 *party cells in all sections of the country's structure and economy. **1978** F. MACLEAN *Take Nine Spies* iv. 132 The Party..[was] using him to organize Party cells and cadres and study-groups. **1935** N. MITCHISON *We have been Warned* IV. 381 It was the best *Party Conference he'd been at. **1969** *Listener* 12 June 827/1 The Party Conference defeated Gaitskell..on the question of nuclear weapons. **1954** B. & R. NORTH tr. *Duverger's Pol. Parties* II. i. 273 After 1935 the army played a part of first-rate importance in the *party Congresses at Nuremberg. **1977** W. WEAVER tr. *Morante's Hist.* (1978) 341 The Party Congress had been held in Rome. **1881** *Nation* (N.Y.) XXXIII. 4 The slipshod method in which the Vice-President is commonly chosen by *party conventions. **1976** *National Observer* (U.S.) 1 May 4/5 The rural followers of William Jennings Bryan fought Al Smith's city legions at the party convention in New York City. **1865** LOWELL *Wks.* (1890) V. 274 Mr. Johnson has chosen to revive the paltry *party-cries. **1830** *Deb. Congress U.S.* 9 Feb. 149/2 The provisional power of removal from office by a President ..[should not] be exercised..in the corrupting spirit of '*party discipline'. **1909** H. ZIMMERN tr. *Nietzsche's Human, All-too-human* I. 181 The old obsequiousness..still survives in party-feeling and party-discipline. **1933** *Discovery* Feb. 64/1 The English party system has many advantages, but it also has the disadvantage that party-discipline and party-loyalty do sometimes exercise a prejudicial, cramping or numbing effect on the mind and actions of individual members of the House of Commons. **1961** W. A. SWANBERG *Citizen Hearst* IV. iii. 213 He..came to be regarded..as a professional radical leading a small pack of obedient terriers whose constant snapping was demoralizing to party discipline. **1735** BOLINGBROKE *On Parties* i. 2 Maintaining, or renewing our *Party-Divisions. **1770** *Gentl. Mag.* XL. 121 The Earl of Bute..had not for a great while gone out of his own house, without being followed by one of those *party-doggers. **1873** 'S. COOLIDGE' *What Katy did at School* (1874) x. 175 Elsie is much excited over the *party dresses which Mrs. Hall is having made for her. **1960** [see COVER-UP *attrib.* or quasi-*adj.*]. **1973** G. GREENE *Honorary Consul* IV. ii. 195 A pale-faced child of three..dressed in a blue party dress. **1791–1823** D'ISRAELI *Cur. Lit.*, *Suppressors of MSS.*, All *party feeling is the same active spirit with an opposite direction. **1883** S. C. HALL *Retrospect* I. 130 Party feeling ran frightfully high. **1898** *Daily News* 10 Dec. 6/3 *Party frocks for girls aged from 11 to 16 years. **1960** *Times* 3 Aug. 5/2 A juvenile delinquent cousin who appears..*party-frocked in the second [act]. **1718** BLACKMORE *Alfred* XI. (1723) 400 And *Party-Fury took the Rebells Side. **1929** G. MITCHELL *Mystery of Butcher's Shop* xvii. 192 Idiotic invitations to play silly *party games with pencils and paper. **1972** *Guardian* 14 Mar. 14/6 Party game time. What do the following have in common? **1936** *Sun* (Baltimore) 20 Apr. 3/1 A '*party girl's' flat was hunted by police today as the probable scene of the slaying of Arthur P. Hewitt, rich retired contractor. **1960** A. WEST *Trend is Up* vii. 298 He had never thought of asking himself what she was, inside of the hard shell of her disguise as the party girl who would go the limit for fun. **1968** *Globe & Mail* (Toronto) 11 July 5/2 The prostitutes and partygirls who hang around the beer parlors are having poor pickings, police say. **1977** *Time* 26 Dec. 36/1 He characterized Sylvia Miles as a 'party girl and gate crasher'. **1864** TROLLOPE *Small House at Allington* II. xxiii. 242 Nor had they any ground on which to stand, except the *party-giving ground. **1879** F. W. ROBINSON *Coward Conscience* II. vii, It did not seem a time for party-giving. **1963** *Times Lit. Suppl.* 10 May 345/2 A sensible guide to party-giving of every sort. **1831** *Society* I. 257 That young woman has the manners of a practised *party-goer. **1864** TROLLOPE *Small House at Allington* II. xxvi. 274, I knew it wasn't to be all *party-going and that sort of thing. **1973** *Listener* 14 June 805/2, I am probably..cloistered.. when it comes to party-going, but I do hear a lot of talk and gossip. **1977** M. HINXMAN *One-Way Cemetery* xvi. 119 She didn't feel up to party-going and I sympathized. **1869** R. F. D. PALGRAVE *House of Commons* 22 This system is called *party government. **1879** FROUDE *Cæsar* iii. 28 Party government turns on the majorities at the polling places. **1899** BEERBOHM *More* 89, I should be glad to see..his office held by an artist, not by a *party-hack. **1974** E. AMBLER *Dr. Frigo* II. 73 Your father's party needed a Cavour... All they had were party hacks. [**1908** G. WALLAS *Human Nature in Politics* iii. 84 A party..is primarily a name, which, like other names, calls up when it is heard or seen an 'image' that shades imperceptibly into the voluntary realisation of its meaning.] **1960** BUTLER & ROSE *Brit. Gen. Election 1959* iii. 17 In the two years before the 1959 election the Conservative party engaged in a public relations campaign ...the term '*party image' was continually invoked. **1962** *Listener* 19 Apr. 702/2 In the discussion of the Party Image in the same programme, the Liberals appeared to me to come out best. **1931** G. B. SHAW *Fabian Ess. Socialism* Pref. p. xiv, Candidates with a *party label, pledged to vote for their party right or wrong. **1718** ROWE tr. *Lucan* I. 492 And bring the Potent *Party-Leaders low. **1882** A. BAIN *John Stuart Mill* ii. 60 That his father would have made an able minister or party-leader, we must cheerfully allow. **1974** E. AMBLER *Dr. Frigo* I. 56 The loss of our Party leader..was a demoralizing blow. **1976** *Encounter* June 78/2 The party leader believes in himself, and his supporters believe in him because he is *their* leader. **1712** ADDISON *Spect.* No. 507 ⁋2 That abominable Practice of Party-lying:..a *Party-lie is grown as fashionable an Entertainment, as a lively Catch or a merry Story. **1832** DICKENS *Let.* 30 July (1965) I. 7, I give you this early notice not because there is anything formal or *party like in the arrangements. **1875** *Encycl. Brit.* III. 291/2 This voting..carried on by *party-lists on differently coloured cards is practically open. **1968** *Listener* 20 June 806/2 Freedom and participation in one's place of work are to replace constituency or 'party list' democratic choice. **1882** A. BAIN *John Stuart Mill* iv. 125 He set a good example of perfect *party loyalty, combined with the assertion of difference of opinion on particular questions. **1968** W. SAFIRE *New Lang. Politics* 321/1 'Sometimes party loyalty asks too much,' said John F. Kennedy to a Democratic friend, excusing him for supporting Republican Leverett Saltonstall for Senator of Massachusetts. **1891** 'O. THANET' *Otto the Knight* 266 He can't be trusted to run the office as a *party machine, and Milton Bedford can! **1918** *Observer* 29 Sept. 6/2 No serious citizen..can doubt..what is imperatively demanded by the interests of the nation, no matter what may be the interests of some caucuses and party-machines. **1939** *War Illustr.* 2 Dec. 375/3 Even in Germany itself there are millions who stand aloof from the seething mass of criminality and corruption constituted by the Nazi party machine. **1972** *Guardian* 8 June 12/2 The wholehearted support of the party machine rather than just a resigned tokenism. **1977** *Cleethorpes News* 6 May 7/4 It is a moot point whether they do much good because, like other party machines, the Conservative local unit functions day-in and day-out pretty successfully. **1702** C. MATHER *Magn. Chr.* VII. i. (1852) 490 Little piques..have misled all the neighbors..into most unaccountable *party-making. **1881** *Bradstreet's* IV. 305 The voters of Kings county have usually been relied upon by *party managers. **1885** W. HARRIS *Hist. Radical Party* ii. 19 That great body of the people who were too frequently regarded by placemen and party managers as machines to be used and property to be disposed of. **1930** A. HARRIS tr. *P. Cohen-Portheim's England, the Unknown Isle* iv. 45 When we get into our party clothes we put on our *party manners and party conversation with them. **1931** R. R. MARETT in W. Rose *Outl. Mod. Knowledge* 422 After much steam has been blown off, all cheerfully assume their party-manners. **1969** 'J. MORRIS' *Fever Grass* ii. 22 A child suddenly remembering its party manners. **1974** G. JENKINS *Bridge of Magpies* xii. 178 Judging from what I've seen of their party manners, it won't be a pretty operation. **1931** H. NICOLSON *Diary* 22 Sept. (1966) 91 *Party-meeting at 11.30. **1976** S. HYNES *Auden Generation* v. 138 *It's a Battlefield*..is full of Communists, and a long scene is devoted to a Party meeting. **1920** S. LEWIS *Main St.* x. 116 He's a socialist..a regular old-line *party-member. **1942** [see FELLOW-TRAVELLER 2]. **1974** 'J. LE CARRÉ' *Tinker, Tailor* xvii. 147 His father was a docker..and a Party member. **1972** *Listener* 20 July 69/2 According to the proposed Democratic Party charter, there would be a national dues-paying *party membership. **1976** S. HYNES *Auden Generation* ix. 317 For Upward, Party membership seems to have been a mode of salvation in a desperate time. **1957** R. N. C. HUNT *Guide to Communist Jargon* xxxii. 110 **Party-mindedness* ('Partiinost') was given its classical formulation by Lenin in his polemic with Peter Struve of the middle 'nineties, when he laid down that 'Materialism involves party-mindedness, since it compels us in evaluating anything which takes place openly and directly to adopt the standpoint of a specific social group'. **1958** *Ann. Reg. 1957* 209 Leading writers..were reminded that negative features of Soviet life could be criticized only from the standpoint of 'Party-mindedness' (*partiynost*) i.e. recognition that all defects were being successfully overcome by the Party. **1724** RAMSAY *Tea-t. Misc.* (1733) III. 280 If any is so zealous To be a *party-minion. **1727** DE FOE *Syst. Magic* I. ii. (1840) 59 The magic of the *party-mongers. **1973** H. MCCLOY *Change of Heart* ix. 104 I'm hardly in a *party mood. My father is still unconscious. **1976** G. SIMS *End of Web* xvii. 116 Being quite sober and not in a party mood they shared a feeling of detachment. **1751** *Pope's Wks.* V. 164 He began under twenty with furious *Party-Papers. **1838** J. S. MILL in *Westm. Rev.* XXXII. 246 The 'Standard'..on this occasion has merged the *party passions..in the sympathy of talent for talent. **1945** W. S. CHURCHILL *Victory* (1946) 193 If party passions, doctrines, and ambitions were to dominate our life for any lengthy period, [etc.]. **1942** C. E. SMITH *Jazz Record Bk.* 81 The '*party piano' style, a growth that owes more to oldtime blues playing than to any other one source, was already a flourishing development in the 1930's. **1946** R. BLESH *Shining Trumpets* xiv. 337 A number of gifted Harlem pianists in the 'party-piano' tradition. **1962** *Listener* 6 Sept. 367/1 A late-night series of *party pieces. **1967** 'P. LORAINE' *W.I.L. One to Curtis* i. 20 It's been my party piece for over a year now: not *family* parties, I hasten to add. **1969** E. H. PINTO *Treen* 86 Although all these spoons could be used,.. one feels that they were very much 'party pieces'. **1973** *Times* 25 Apr. 10/1 (Advt.), Scott James of Westminster distribute a superb range of family clothing direct to the consumer, through *party plan and catalogue selling techniques. **1976** *Billings* (Montana) *Gaz.* 30 June 5-D/3 (Advt.), Montana owned firm looking for party plan representatives in Billings area. Work your own hours for good commission. **1977** *Evening Gaz.* (Middlesbrough) 11 Jan. 10/2 (Advt.), Party Plan demonstrators, car available for ambitious applicant. **1848** J. R. LOWELL *Biglow Papers* 1st Ser. 111 It gives a *Party Platform, tu, jest level with the mind Of..honest folks thet mean to go it blind. **1964** GOULD & KOLB *Dict. Social Sci.* 484/1 A *party platform* is a general statement of principles, policies, and issues, and a programme of promises which the party pledges to enact into legislation. **1972** *Jrnl. Social Psychol.* LXXXVII. 46 Public opinion should not be a major concern of political leaders in writing party platforms. **1957** *Times* 14 May 11/2 There was an admirable absence of rancour or effort to make *party points when the decision to afford British ships the facilities for using the Suez Canal again was announced in the House of Commons yesterday. **1886** G. WHETENALL *Echetlus* i. 60 Let us consider shortly some of these results, the common phenomena of our *party-political life. **1910** Party-political [see CARTOON *sb.* 2]. **1947** *Radio Times* 14 Mar. 1/1 Party political broadcasts of a controversial character are to be resumed. **1966** *New Statesman* 4 Mar. 289/1, I am..unable to watch party-politicals at all. **1974** *Guardian* 23 Jan. 1/1 A plan to shorten 'News at Ten' to make way for a party political broadcast. **1977** *Jrnl. R. Soc. Arts* CXXV. 467/1 Such questions are..essentially political, though not necessarily party-political. **1831** J. S. MILL in *Examiner* 9 Jan. 20/2 They who prefer the ravings of a *party politician to the musings of a recluse, may consult a late article in Blackwood's Magazine. **1773** MELMOTH *Rem. on Cato* 142 The narrow and polluted channels of *party-politicks. **1922** *Brit. Jrnl. Psychol.* Oct. 116 The 'party politics complex' in the mind of the party politician. **1942** L. B. NAMIER *Conflicts* 200 It is of paramount importance that the extent to which our present constitutional system is bound up with party organisations and party politics should be fully understood. **1961** *Middle*

East Jrnl. XV. 6 The bulk of the preparation had.. proceeded under the supervision of the Ministry of the Interior, whose officials are barred from party activity and probably generally disinterested in party politics. **1969** *New Yorker* 11 Oct. 53/1 They pecked the hostess farewell, apologized in unison for being *party poops. **1954** *Amer. Speech* XXIX. 293 Such comic master-pieces as *lounge lizard* and **party pooper* are of American origin. **1956** in Wentworth & Flexner *Dict. Amer. Slang* (1960) 377/1 No one can call Mr. Bulganin and Mr. Khrushchev party poopers... The Russian leaders demonstrated their suavity and cleverness at the party. **1788** SHERIDAN in *Sheridaniana* 99 Every *party-prejudice has been overcome by a display of genius. **1842** DICKENS *Let.* 1 Apr. (1974) III. 176 The silly, drivelling, slanderous, wicked, monstrous *Party Press. **1950** *Middle East Jrnl.* Apr. 168 With one full-fledged *journal d'information*..a party press..Egyptian journalism can look to an interesting future. **1705** STANHOPE *Paraphr.* I. 50 By such profitable Condescensions on either side.. they would lay down all *Party-quarrels. **1803** *Deb. Congress U.S.* 6 Jan. (1851) 337 This ought not to be made a *party question. **1885** A. CRUMP *Formation Polit. Opinion* 152 The position was now far too grave to be treated as a party question. **1711** ADDISON *Spect.* No. 57 ¶4 That *Party-Rage which of late Years is very much crept into their Conversation. **1813** SCOTT *Rokeby* VI. viii, Brute and blind-fold party rage. **1941** 'G. ORWELL' *Lion & Unicorn* I. 16 No *party rallies, no Youth Movements. **1959** I. JEFFERIES *Thirteen Days* vi. 75 A single truck stuck out like a top hat at a Party rally. **1964** *Amer. Folk Music Occasional* I. 10 Under-the-Counter '*party' records provide a traditional version of *The Eddystone Light.* **1968** P. OLIVER *Screening Blues* vi. 175 The cheapened styles of the party records which have a large illicit sale in the white society. **1855** TENNYSON *Maud* XXV. 91 And another, a statesman there, betraying His *party-secret, fool, to the press. **1711** ADDISON *Spect.* No. 125 ¶3 A furious *Party Spirit..exerts it self in Civil War and Bloodshed. **1882** FARRAR *Early Chr.* II. 87 Any lie, however often refuted, is good enough for party-spirit. **1941** N. MARSH *Death & Dancing Footman* (1942) viii. 151 He's gone into a huddle over the fire and does *not* exactly manifest the party spirit. **1971** S. JEPSON *Let. to Dead Girl* xix. 218 I'm not ungregarious but I'm quite incapable of the party spirit in a roomful of people busy smoking themselves into lung cancer. **1974** J. WHITE tr. *Poulantzas's Fascism & Dictatorship* III. ii. 113 It is unnecessary to go into details of the continuous contradictions between big capital and the Nazi *party-state. **1977** P. JOHNSON *Enemies of Society* vi. 78 Nazi Germany was equally frank in imposing control of labour and eliminating all foci of political and economic power other than the party-state. **1824** J. S. MILL in *Westm. Rev.* I. 530 Here..the evils of the *party system are most clearly shown. **1959** B. & R. NORTH tr. *Duverger's Pol. Parties* (ed. 2) II. 203 With the exception of the single-party states, several parties coexist in each country: the forms and modes of their coexistence define the 'party system' of the particular country being considered. **1483** *Cath. Angl.* 270/2 A Parte taker (*A.* *Partitaker), *particeps.* **1961** *How-to-do-it-Encycl.* (Mechanix Illustr.) I. 12 If you are a *party thrower, you may need added capacity. **1962** *Listener* 22 Feb. 347/3 One friend of mine, a compulsive party thrower, had four flats in five months. **1929** *Radio Times* 8 Nov. 390/1 Tony Monke..has been persuaded to execute his best *party trick of standing on his head. **1722** DE FOE *Col. Jack* (1840) 229 The latter part of the campaign we made only a *party war. **1829** BENTHAM *Justice & Cod. Petit., Abr. Petit. Justice* 33 Say accordingly *party-witnesses, or testifying parties. **1725** SWIFT in *Pope's Wks.* (1751) IX. 55 Fortune is both blind and deaf, and a Court-lady, but then she is a most damnable *Party-woman. **1892** *Courier-Jrnl.* (Louisville, Kentucky) 2 Oct. 1/7 The '*party workers'.. were well represented. **1935** N. MITCHISON *We have been Warned* I. 51 The thick sense of urgency and seriousness which was beginning to show among the Party workers. **1974** *Listener* 14 Mar. 330/2 On election day, my wife and I..did the traditional tour.. to thank and encourage the party workers. **1714** ADDISON *Spect.* No. 567 ¶3 Our *Party-writers are so sensible of the secret Vertue of an Innuendo to recommend their Productions. **1836** H. ROGERS *J. Howe* i. (1863) 12 *note*, That splenetic party-writer Anthony Wood. *a* **1746** HOLDSWORTH *On Virgil* (1768) 401 Passion and spleen may so far blind an Historian..as to make him prostitute his character to *party zeal. **1711** POPE *Temp. Fame* 464 Priests, and *party-zealots, num'rous bands.

Hence **'partyism**, the system of parties; excessive attachment to a party, party spirit; so **'partyist**, a partisan; **'partykin**, a small party; †**'partyship**, the being of a party, partisanship.

1842 *Amer. Pioneer* I. 278 *Partyism or love of party is the vibratory motion. **1844** MARY HENNELL *Soc. Syst.* 191 It [human nature] persists in living in industrial incoherence and family partyism. **1886** GOLDW. SMITH in *Macm. Mag.* Aug. 247 Allowance being made for all the partyism..by which the great issue was obscured. **1903** *Dial* (Chicago) 16 Mar. 194/2 The vast canvas whereon he has painted American partyism with all its deformities. **1889** *Voice* (N.Y.) 10 Jan., The temperance men in the Republican party outnumber the 'third *partyists seven to one'. **1855** THACKERAY *Let.* in *Virgin.* (1903) Introd. 19, I had a very pleasant *partykin last night. **1650** HOLLINGWORTH *Exerc. Usurped Powers* 5 The Kingdom is divided by *partieship with them, on the one side or the other.

party ('pɑːtɪ), *a.* Also 4–7 -i, 5 -ye, 5–8 ie. [a. F. *parti*:—L. *partīt-us* divided, pa. pple. of *partir*, L. *partīre* to part, divide.]

†**1.** Parted, divided; separate; *fig.* separate in character, different. *Obs.*

a **1400–50** *Alexander* 668 Oft storbis me þi statour and stingis me ȝerne, þat þi personale proporcion sa party is to myne.

b. ***gold party, party gold***: beaten gold, gold leaf. *Sc. Obs.*

1496 *Acc. Ld. High Treas. Scot.* I. 293 For ijᶜ of gold party to the Duke of Ȝorkis banar. **1507** *Ibid.* III. 404, iiij quaris parti gold.

†**2.** Parti-coloured, variegated. *Obs.*

c **1386** CHAUCER *Knt.'s T.* 195 She gadereth floures party white & rede. **1390** GOWER *Conf.* I. 312 Juno let bende hire parti bowe. *c* **1440** *Promp. Parv.* 385/1 Party clothe, or clothe made of dyuers colowrys. **1494** *Acc. Ld. High Treas. Scot.* I. 225, v½ quarteris of crammesyn satyne to be half a party dowblat. **1513** DOUGLAS *Æneis* VIII. iv. 201 The party popill grane Heildit his heid wyth skug Herculeane. **1594** PLAT *Jewell-ho.* III. 38 Partie letters and other fansies. **1707** MORTIMER *Husb.* (1721) II. Q, Some [Hyacinths] are more double, as well White as Blew, and therefore are to be esteemed because of their Party-flowering.

b. *fig.* Combining two different qualities; of composite character. *Obs.*

c **1420** LYDG. *Assembly of Gods* 316 Fortune, the goddesse, with her party face. **1563** WINȜET *Vincent. Lirin.* Wks. 1890 II. 6, I hef præparit..a litle, partie, handsum, instrument that may suffice ws,..bayth for a waippin and werk-lume, for a speir or a spade.

3. *Her.* Said of a shield divided into parts of different tinctures, usually into two such parts by a line in the direction of an ordinary (indicated by *per*); thus ***party per pale***, divided by a vertical line through the middle; ***party per fess***, by a horizontal line through the middle; so ***party per bend, party per chevron***: see PALE, FESS *sb.*, etc.

(In blazoning now usually omitted, *per pale*, etc. being used instead of *party per pale*, etc.) Also PARTED, q.v.

1486 *Bk. St. Albans, Heraldry* F ij, He berith party after the longe way of ij colouris golde and goules. **1562** LEIGH *Armorie* 43 b, Party per Fesse, Argent, and Vert. *Ibid.* 45 Partye per Cheuron, Or, and Geules. **1605** CAMDEN *Rem.* (1637) 225 Iohn Beauford..bare party per pale Argent and Azure a bend of England with a labell of France. **1725** COATS *Dict. Her., Partie*, or *Party*, signifies in French divided, but their Heralds use it only to denote what we call *Party*, or *Parted per pale.* **1882** CUSSANS *Handbk. Her.* iv. (ed. 3) 72 A Shield is never *party* of any of the Diminutives, or of the Chief or Bar.

†**b.** ***party per pale*** (*fig.*): Having two different, esp. opposite or contrasted, qualities; of mixed or composite character; half-and-half. (Cf. 2 b.) *Obs.*

1616 B. JONSON *Epigr.* lxxiii, Your *partie per pale* picture one half drawn In solemn cypres, the other cob-web-lawne. *a* **1652** BROME *Covent Garden* I. i Wks. 1873 II. 13 O thou party perpale, or rather parboild Bawd. **1717** HEARNE in *Relig.* (1857) I. 376 It was, as I hear, a party per pale sermon, viz. both for the whiggs and for the tories. **1781** H. WALPOLE *Let. to C'tess Ossory* 18 Dec., A grandee hopping with one foot on the *haut du pavé*, and t'other in the kennel, *partie per pale*, ermine and mud!

4. *Comb.*, as †**party-livered**, of divided loves; see also PARTI-, PARTI-COLOURED.

1601 CHESTER *Love's Mart.* etc. (1878) 180 Not like that loose and partie-liuer'd Sect Of idle Louers, that..Change their Affections with their Mistris Sights.

'party, *v.* [f. PARTY *sb.*]

†**1. a.** *trans.* To take the part of, side with. **b.** *intr.* To side (*with*). = PART *v.* 14. *Sc. Obs. rare.*

a **1639** SPOTTISWOOD *Hist. Ch. Scot.* VI. (1677) 412 The Lords Levingston and Elphinston did party the committers. **1644** HUME *Hist. Doug.* 16 This house of Abernethie..did assist and party them in all their enterprises. **1734** R. KEITH *Hist. Ch. Scot.* I. xi. 121 The Earl of Huntly..had, it seems, an unfix'd Resolution what Side to party with.

†**2.** ***to party it***: to take sides; to form a party. *Obs. rare.*

1656 S. H. *Gold. Law* 72 To incense the people to faction or party it against him. *Ibid.* 81.

3. *N. Amer.* **a.** *intr.* To give a party; to attend a party; to have a good time. **b.** *trans.* To entertain (someone) at a party; to accompany to a party.

1922 E. E. CUMMINGS *Let.* 5 Dec. (1969) 91 Haven't seen Vanity All is Fair in? but have extensively partyed with Er former Heditor. **1948** *Penguin New Writing* XXXV. 106 Between times, when they were not drinking at the cafés, partying, writing, or making love, they talked a lot and did a certain amount of thinking. **1953** *N.Y. Times Bk. Rev.* 12 July 8/1 The delegates and guests..were partied to a crisp. **1957** M. MILLAR *Soft Talkers* 97 All those times when I was so ill I could scarcely move and he went off partying. **1963** D. B. HUGHES *Expendable Man* (1964) ii. 30 You can't imagine the entertainment she's had..every club on the campus has partied her. **1967** [see JOINER *sb.* 1 b]. **1971** J. PHILIPS *Escape a Killer* (1972) I. iii. 34 You're to drive into New York..stay there a few days... Peter will party you around. **1973** *Islander* (Victoria, B.C.) 25 Feb. 6/3 Everybody crowded in, the home brew arrived and we partied until 4 in the morning. **1976** H. NIELSEN *Brink of Murder* xx. 177 A small crowd..who had been partying on another boat. **1977** *Time* 31 Jan. 31/1 Outgoing Democratic National Committee Chairman Robert Strauss partied along with singer Helen Reddy and actor Alan Alda. *Ibid.* 25 Apr. 48/3 Los Angeles rockers do not lack for private places in which to party.

Hence **'partying** *vbl. sb.* and *ppl. a.*

1681 *Whole Duty Nations* 37 Such kind of partyings in Religion..are like the *Hetæriæ* or Cabals in Civil Government. **1717** *Wodrow Corr.* (1843) II. 323 And you'll scarce now meet with a case, but..in ten minutes' time, you'll see a partying of ministers and great men. **1953** W. P. MCGIVERN *Big Heat* iv. 54 A woman..waiting up for a partying teen-age daughter. **1970** N. ARMSTRONG et al. *First on Moon* ii. 42 There was so much partying that not a few people wondered about the size of the national hangover. **1977** *Daily Tel.* 9 Apr. 15/6 Mrs Trudeau returned to Ottawa after a weekend of partying in Toronto with the Rolling Stones.

party, *adv.*: see PARTY *sb.* 1 b.

partycion, obs. f. PARTITION.

party-coat, party-coloured: see PARTI-¹, PARTI-COLOURED.

†**'party-,jury.** *Obs.* [f. PARTY *a.* + JURY.] = *jury de medietate*: see JURY *sb.* 2 e.

1662 *Act 14 Chas. II*, c. 11 §13 There shall not be any Party Jury but such only as are the natural and free born Subjects of the King. **1704** J. HARRIS *Lex. Techn.* I, *Mediatus Linguæ*, or *Party-Jury*,..whereof the one half consists of Denizens, the other of Strangers, and is used in Pleas, where one Party is a Denizen, and the other Stranger.

partyless ('pɑːtɪlɪs), *a.* [f. PARTY *sb.* + -LESS.] Not having or not belonging to a political party.

1896 *N.Y. Voice* 9 July 2/4 This means..a reign of straight-out, inexorable, sectless, seminaryless, partyless righteousness in citizenship. **1909** *Westm. Gaz.* 15 Mar. 2/1 In 1901 Francis Ferdinand was practically alone, partyless. **1963** *Times* 2 Feb. 9/2 Mr. Nkomo, the partyless but undoubted African Nationalist leader. **1966** N. NICOLSON in H. Nicolson *Diaries & Lett.* 66 Harold Nicolson, being partyless, was one of the first to join him. **1977** *Times* 15 Nov. 15/2 Nepal will stick to its 'partyless panchayat' rather than risk..one man one vote.

party line. [f. PARTY *sb.* + LINE *sb.*²] **1.** A policy adopted by a political party; an area of policy or 'line' separating the policy of one political party from that of another. Also *transf.* and (with hyphen) *attrib.*

1834 T. H. BENTON *30 Years' View* (1854) I. 431/2 Look at the vote in the Senate upon the adoption of the resolution, also as clearly defined by a party line as any party question can ever be expected to be. **1904** G. B. SHAW *Common Sense of Municipal Trading* xi. 105 A councillor selected on strict party lines. **1915** MRS. H. WARD *Eltham Ho.* xiv. 268 The dogged adherence to the traditional party lines and shibboleths on the part of the average British voter. **1937** C. CONNOLLY in L. Russell *Press Gang!* 95 The kind of bullets they keep for reviewers who step across the party line. **1942** Z. N. HURSTON in A. Dundes *Mother Wit* (1973) 32/2, I am a mixed-blood,..but I differ from the party line in that I neither consider it an honor nor a shame. **1948** *Daily Ardmoreite* (Ardmore, Okla.) 2 May 5/4 On party-line votes, this will give the democrats guarantee of a two-thirds majority. **1957** *Times Lit. Suppl.* 27 Dec. 782/3 Mr Dawson's party-line pronouncements on such subjects as contraception or the mediative role of the Church. **1966** *Listener* 10 Mar. 357/2 When any of his whig friends deviated from the party-line, the old pedant laid into them. **1975** J. P. MORGAN *House of Lords & Labour Govt.* iv. 134 It can be safely concluded that, for whatever reason, there is such a phenomenon as party-line voting in the Lords. **1976** S. HYNES *Auden Generation* vi. 171 This party-line definition of proletarian art. **1977** A. ECCLESTONE *Staircase for Silence* v. 88 He was well aware of the faith-destroying outcome of the dogmatism of the party-line, whether in Church or State.

2. [PARTY *sb.* 18 b.] A telephone line shared by two or more subscribers. Also *transf.* and (with hyphen) *attrib.*

1893 W. J. HOPKINS *Telephone Lines* i. 4 When 'party lines', so called, are used, they should be connected according to the 'bridging-bell' method. **1901** *Ann. Rep. Amer. Telephone & Telegr. Co. 1900* The general adoption of..party lines..has attracted many thousands of subscribers. **1930** *Telegraph & Telephone Jrnl.* XVI. 115/2 The 'party line' is not so rife in this country as in America. *Ibid.* 119/2 The number of rural party lines at Dec. 31, 1929 was 10,322. **1933** *Punch* 10 May 508/1 If you take a real personal interest in your fellow-beings as I do, I should advise all those living in the country to have a party-line. **1959** *Ibid.* 19 Aug. 30/3 The new 'party-line' electronic stethoscope..allows up to four doctors to listen to a patient's heart simultaneously. **1973** M. RUSSELL *Double Hit* vi. 44 He overheard things on our party line.

Hence ,**party-'liner**, one who follows the line adopted by a political party; also *transf.*; so ,**party-'lining** *vbl. sb.*

1940 *Common Sense* (N.Y.) Feb. 21/2 Right now a Communist Party-liner does not have a ghost of a chance in the A.F. of T. **1943** *Sun* (Baltimore) 28 Sept. 12/2 The speech he [*sc.* Earl Browder] has just made at Chicago is fully as brash as anything he said before Marshal Stalin disowned him and other party-liners outside of Russia by liquidating the Communist Internationale in May of this year. **1948** *Daily Mail* 7 Feb. 2/6 When the party-liner squawks an indignant protest he is at once knocked off his perch. **1949** *Virginia Q. Rev.* Winter 44 For the past eleven years he has allied himself with, and never broken on any significant issue from, the 'party-liners'. **1958** *Spectator* 27 June 846/3 Large immigrant colonies of Poles, Lithuanians and others who were not easily taken in by Soviet party-lining. **1966** *Economist* 1 Oct. 39/3 The Chinese here—Nationalists and party-liners alike..are clearly confused. **1969** *Guardian* 31 July 5/3 The..gulf..between..party-liners and deviationists. **1973** C. MULLARD *Black Brit.* ix. 106 Good councillors who find themselves in disagreement with their party's views on race can be removed and replaced with party-liners.

'party-,man. [f. PARTY *sb.* + MAN.]

†**1.** *Mil.* A soldier belonging to, or officer commanding, a party (PARTY *sb.* 7). *Obs.*

1693 *Mem. Cnt. Teckely* II. 112 The Male-contents, much better Party-Men than the Imperialists. **1724** DE FOE *Mem. Cavalier* (1840) 186 Prince Rupert, a most active vigilant party-man, and fitter for such than for a general.

2. A man belonging to, or devoted to, a party (PARTY *sb.* 6): = PARTISAN *sb.*¹ 1.

1701 SWIFT *Contests Nobles & Comm.* v. Wks. 1755 II. I. 49 Bibulus the party-man is persuaded, that Clodius and Curio do really propose the good of their country as their chief end. **1741** RICHARDSON *Pamela* (1824) I. 187, I am no party-man... I think the distinctions of *whig* and *tory* odious. **1798** *Char.* in *Ann. Reg.* 327 Mr. Burke became a professed party-man. **1874** L. STEPHEN *Hours in Library*

(1892) I. i. 12 Although a party man, he was by no means a man to swallow the whole party platform. **1933** *Discovery* Feb. 64/1 M. Briand, not at all a 'party' or 'group' man in his later career, also had his own personal following of deputies. **1938** W. S. CHURCHILL *Into Battle* (1941) 15 The Fascists of Italy, the Party-men, are asking themselves whether all this is to the permanent safety.. of their native land. **1946** 'G. ORWELL' *Crit. Ess.* 136 The young G.P.U. man..is the typical 'good party man'.

3. One who frequently attends or gives parties.

1936 *Mademoiselle* Apr. 20/1 The true Party Man possesses a *je ne sais quoi* which lends a rich grace to the most distinguished party. **1963** *Times* 14 Jan. 9/4 The non-party man (speaking in the social rather than the political sense) is saddened by the occasional receipt of invitations... How does one become a successful party man?

partyner(e, obs. form of PARTNER.

partyness ('pɑːtɪnɪs). Also **party-ness**. [f. PARTY *sb.* + -NESS.] **a.** Party-mindedness (see quot. 1976). **b.** The state or condition of being a political party.

1952 *Mind* LXI. 120 It is, of course, a principle of Marxism-Leninism that philosophy should be written in a 'party spirit', with 'partyness'. This principle..originated with Lenin. **1969** P. WORSLEY in Ionescu & Gellner *Populism* 228 Professor Brough Macpherson has described ..the United Farmers of Alberta,..and its successor, Social Credit... Macpherson..labels this a 'quasi-party' system: not 'non-party', because institutionalized opposition and other..manifestations of 'party-ness' still persisted. **1976** *Russ. Rev.* (N.Y.) XXXV. 69 Lenin advocated the principle of *partiinost*, a concept roughly translatable as 'partyness', the constant referral to party policy as the inspiration and guide to action.

partyrege, obs. form of PARTRIDGE.

'party-,wall. [f. PARTY *a.* + WALL.] A wall between two buildings or pieces of land intended for distinct occupation, in the use of which each of the occupiers has a partial right.

The primary and most common meaning in law is 'a wall of which the two adjoining owners are tenants in common'; but three other cases are included under the term in Elphinstone, etc. *Interpr. Deeds* (1885) Gloss. The structure of party-walls between houses, and the rights and duties of their owners have been the subject of much legislation.

1667 S. PRIMATT *City & C. Build.* 93 The Builder is to receive of his next Neighbor, if they have the benefit of all his Party-walls and Peer-stones, sixty five pounds and ten-pence. **1677–1703** MOXON *Mech. Exerc.* 145 No Light can be placed in the Stair-Case, because of the Party-walls. **1853** WHARTON *Pennsylv. Digest* II. 405 The moiety of the cost of a party wall is a personal charge against the builder of the second house and lien upon the house itself. **1855** *Act 18 & 19 Vict.* c. 122 §3 'Party wall' shall apply to every wall used or built in order to be used as a separation of any building from any other building, with a view to the same being occupied by different persons.

fig. **1870** J. H. NEWMAN *Gramm. Assent* I. v. 95 Not as if there were in fact, or could be, any line of demarcation or party-wall between these modes of assent.

Hence **'party-,walled** (-wɔːld) *a.*, having a party-wall.

1703 MOXON *Mech. Exerc.* 145 Our Party-walled Houses in London.

partyzyne, obs. form of PARTISAN *sb.*[2]

partzite ('pɑːtsaɪt). *Min.* [Named 1867 after Dr. A. Partz.] A hydrous oxide of antimony containing other metallic oxides, and varying in colour from yellowish-green to blackish-green.

1867 *Amer. Jrnl. Sci.* XLIII. 362 Partzite occurs together with argentiferous galena. **1868** DANA *Min.* (ed. 5) 188. **1877** RAYMOND *Statist. Mines & Mining* 411 This was the partzite..ore of which so much has been said.

parumbilical (pærʌm'bɪlɪkəl), *a.* *Anat.* [f. PAR(A-[1] + L. *umbilic-us* navel + -AL[1].] Situated around or close to the umbilicus or navel.

1890 in *Century Dict.* **1893** *Syd. Soc. Lex.*, *Parumbilical veins.* **1897** *Allbutt's Syst. Med.* IV. 178 The passage of blood from the portal vein, by the parumbilical vein to the epigastric system.

‖**parure.** *Obs.* or *alien.* Also 5 parowre, -ur, perur, 5–6 parour, 6 parrer, parer. [a. OF. *pareure*, *parer* paring, peeling:—L. *parātūra*, f. *parāre* to prepare, make ready, F. *parer* to PARE. In sense 3 an alien word from mod.F. (paryr).]

†**1.** An ornament for an alb or amice. *Obs.* Cf. PAREL *sb.* 4 a, APPAREL *sb.* 7 b.

c **1425** WYNTOUN *Cron.* IX. vi. 596 The Byschape Waltyr ..Gave twa lang coddis off welwete.. Albis wyth parurys to tha lyk. *c* **1440** *Promp. Parv.* 384/2 Parowre of a vestyment, *paratura*, vel *parura*. **1449–50** in Nicolas *Test. Vetust.* 267 One coope, chesible diacones, for decones; with the awbes and parures. **1519** *Churchw. Acc. St. Giles, Reading* 7 For wasshyng of the churche gere and settyng on the parours ijs. viijd. **1527** in Fiddes *Wolsey* (1726) II. 104, 7 payer of odde parrers for children [choristers].

†**2.** A paring, peeling. *Obs.*

1499 *Promp. Parv.* 384/2 (Pynson) Parour of frute, *idem quod paringe* (*H.* parowre). **1587** TURBERV. *Trag. T.* (1837) Ded. 4 Dedicating to you these few Poeticall parers, and pensive Pamphlets.

‖**3.** A set of jewels or other ornaments intended to be worn together; a set of decorative trimmings or embroideries for a dress.

1818 LADY MORGAN *Autobiog.* (1859) 47 A red leather case containing a beautiful *parure* of amethysts. **1860** O. W. HOLMES *Elsie V.* iv. (1891) 51 The women whom ornaments of plain gold adorn more than any other *parures*. **1875** R. F. BURTON *Gorilla L.* (1876) I. 223 Wrists and ankles were laden with heavy rings of brass and copper, the *parure* of the great in Fán-land. **1877** MRS. FORRESTER *Mignon* II. 49 Sir Tristram has given her a *parure* of diamonds.

‖**paruria** (pə'rʊərɪə). *Path.* [f. Gr. παρ(α- PARA-[1] I + οὖρον URINE.] 'Disordered micturition, or dysuria' (*Syd. Soc. Lex.*). Hence **pa'ruric** *a.*, pertaining to paruria.

1822 GOOD *Study Med.* IV. 438 Paruria. Mismicturition. Morbid secretion or discharge of urine. **1857** MAYNE *Expos. Lex.*, Paruric.

paruyngal, corrupt form of PAREGAL *Obs.*

parvanimity (pɑːvə'nɪmɪtɪ). [f. L. *parv-us* small + *anim-us* mind: a suggested antithesis to *magnanimity*.] Littleness of mind, meanness; also, an instance of this, or *transf.* a person characterized by it.

a **1691** BOYLE *Disc. agst. Swearing* Plea xiii, They will justly esteem your parvanimity so great that you deserve derision. **1829–30** DE QUINCEY *Sk. Prof. Wilson* Uncoll. Writ. 1890 I. 260 The meanness and parvanimity of Bonaparte. *Note.* I coin this word *parvanimity* as an adequate antithesis to *magnanimity*. **1840** —— in *Tait's Mag.* VII. 37 Memorably connected with the parvanimities of the English government at one period. **1873** F. HALL *Mod. Eng.* 33 *note*, Persons..of the class of hopeless parvanimities of the true insular stamp.

‖**parvenant** (parvənɑ̃). [F., pr. pple. of *parvenir*: see PARVENU.] A person who is acquiring a position, or on the way to being a parvenu.

1843 tr. *Custine's Empire of Czar* III. 184 A specimen of the worst kind of emulation—that of the *parvenant* already giving himself the airs of the *parvenu*!

parvenke, obs. form of PERIWINKLE[1].

‖**parvenu** (‖parvəny, 'pɑːvənjuː), *sb.* and *a.* Also in fem. form **parvenue**. [F., 'said of an obscure person who has made a great fortune' (Littré), sbst. use of pa. pple. of *parvenir* to arrive (at a destination), to rise to a position, make a fortune:—L. *pervenīre* to arrive, attain.]

A. *sb.* A person of obscure origin who has attained wealth or position beyond that of his class; *esp.* such a one when unfitted for his position, or when making large assumptions for himself on account of his wealth; an upstart. Also *transf.*

1802 W. GIFFORD tr. *Juvenal* v. 228 *note*, His patronage,.. like that of many other *parvenus*, was so burdensome, that the poet, in a fit of spleen, threatens to shake it off entirely. **1826** DISRAELI *Viv. Grey* II. xiv. 'Ah! there is nothing like old families!' remarked Mrs. Million, with all the awkward feelings of a parvenue. **1834** L. RITCHIE *Wand. by Seine* 68 The Bonaparte people were parvenus, and clung to all the prestiges of the preceding dynasty. **1848** THACKERAY *Van. F.* xxxvi, The ladies their wives, who could not bear the parvenue [Rebecca]. **1891** M. O'RELL *Frenchm. in Amer.* 209 The parvenu is a person who makes strenuous efforts to persuade other people that he is entitled to the position he occupies. **1944** PARTRIDGE *Here, There & Everywhere* (1950) 54 A word begins its career as a *parvenu*. **1955** *Times* 20 Aug. 7/7 To such a man the Jews are not only aggressors and common thieves but parvenus too. **1978** P. VAN GREENAWAY *Man called Scavener* vii. 95 Genealogy.. attracts a growing body of parvenus.

B. *adj.* That has but recently risen to wealth or position; like or characteristic of a parvenu in manners, vulgar display, etc.

1828 J. S. MILL in *Westm. Rev.* IX. 290 No one licked the dust before the *parvenu* emperor with greater *gusto* than the abbé Maury. **1839** POE *W. Wilson* Wks. 1874 I. 347 A young *parvenu* nobleman. **1879** *Q. Rev.* July 14 Other monarchs had treated the *parvenu* ruler of France with distant arrogance. **1897** *Harper's Mag.* Apr. 746 There was nothing *parvenu* in the penniless lad. **1958** *Times* 12 Nov. 3/5 She sounds a *parvenu* proletarian, if such a fancy be comprehended. **1978** *Amer. N. & Q.* XVII. 31/2 Some of the parvenu universities are rapidly approaching maturity.

Hence **parve'nudom**, the domain of parvenus; **'parvenuism**, the habits or practices of parvenus, parvenu character.

1854 LOWELL *Jrnl. Italy* Prose Wks. 1890 I. 205 A Roman column standing near..satirizes silently their tawdry parvenuism. **1868** W. R. GREG *Lit. & Soc. Judgm.* 280 [A] piece of inflated affectation in the richest style of parvenuism. **1891** *Star* 12 Dec. 4/3 The servile grovelling of parvenudom. **1900** *Westm. Gaz.* 31 Jan. 3/2 How far it is true as a study of Berlin parvenudom, few..could say.

parvenuess (,pɑːvənjuː'ɛs). *rare.* [-ESS[1].] A female parvenu.

1903 'O. HENRY' in *Everybody's Mag.* July 59/2 As proud and satisfied as a prince that's abjured a two-hundred-dollar crown for a million-dollar parvenuess.

parvers, obs. form of PERVERSE *a.*

parvi- (pɑːvɪ), comb. form of L. *parvus* small, as in **parvi'folious** *a.* (*Bot.* L. *parvifolius*), having small leaves; †**,parvi'pension** [L. *pensio* a weighing, cf. phr. *parvi pendĕre* to esteem little], slight estimation; **par'vipotent** *a.* [POTENT], having little power; **parvi'psoas** [Gr. ψόα lumbar muscle], a name applied by Coues to the *psoas parvus* or small psoas muscle; hence **parvipso'atic** *a.*; **parvi'rostrate** *a.* [L. *rostrum* beak], having a slender beak; **par'viscient** *a.* [L. *scient-em* knowing], knowing little.

1857 MAYNE *Expos. Lex.*, *Parvifolius*, having small leaves, ..*parvifolious. **1893** in *Syd. Soc. Lex.* **1675** R. BURTHOGGE *Causa Dei* 44 When we consider in it that Contempt, Scorn, and *Parvipension of God, which does compose it. **1678** PHILLIPS (ed. 4) *List Barbarous Words*, *Parvipension*, a setting litely by, an esteeming at a small rate. **1862** F. HALL *Hindu Philos. Syst.* (1897) 152 The ignorance of a single soul ..keeps it *parviscient, *parvipotent. **1857** MAYNE *Expos. Lex.*, *Parvirostris*, having a slender beak,..*parvirostrate. **1884** T. J. SCOTT in J. M. Reid *Doomed Relig.* 160 Brahma alone..is neither parviscient nor omniscient.

parvis ('pɑːvɪs). Also 5 **parvys**, **per-**, **par-vyce**, 5–9 *erron.* **parvise**. [a. F. *parvis*, 'place in front of the principal door of a church, particularly of a cathedral, as the Parvis of Notre Dame', in OF. *parevis* (12–13th c. in Hatz.-Darm.), earlier *pareïs* (*paraïs*, *-aÿs*, *parewis*) (Godef.):—L. *paradīs-um* PARADISE (a name given in the Middle Ages to the atrium or court in front of St. Peter's at Rome, and to the courts before other churches: see Du Cange). From F. also a med.L. form *paravīsus*, *paravīsius*.]

1. The enclosed area or court in front of a building, esp. of a cathedral or church; in some cases, surrounded as a cloister with colonnades or porticoes; whence, sometimes applied to a single portico or colonnade in front of a church, and (in dictionaries) explained as a church-porch.

The parvis of St. Paul's in London was a noted place of resort, esp. for lawyers.

c **1386** CHAUCER *Prol.* 310 A Sergeant of the Lawe war & wys That often hadde been at the Parvys. *c* **1440** *Promp. Parv.* 385/2 Parvyce, *parlatorium*. **1476** J. PASTON in *P. Lett.* III. 156, I prey yow as ye se hym at the parvyse and ellys where, calle on hym for the same letter. *c* **1485** in *Digby Myst.*, *Mor. Wisd.* (1882) 167 At the parvyse I wyll be A' Powlys, be-twyn two and three. **1687** A. LOVELL tr. *Thevenot's Trav.* II. 80 Before this Mosque there is a Parvis or Walk of many Angles, and in the middle of it a Bason of Water likewise Polygone. **1706** PHILLIPS, *Parvis*, a Court before a Church-Porch, or any Palace or stately House. **1745** BLOMEFIELD *Norfolk* II. 748 In 1300, I find Mention of a Publick School for Children to learn to read and sing, kept in the Parvis of this Church [St. Martin's, Norwich]. **1864** LONGF. *Div. Commedia* ii, Canopied with leaves Parvis and portal bloom like trellised bowers. **1875** H. JAMES *Trans. Sk.*, *Rom. Neighb.* 179 It stands perched on a terrace as vast as the parvise of St. Peter's. **1881** *Daily News* 1 Apr. 3/1 Its illuminating power was clearly proved by the two lamps on the parvis of St. Paul's Cathedral. **1886** [see sense 2]. **1895** H. RASHDALL *Universities* II. II. xii. §5. 448 *note*, The word 'Parvis' is used of the Cloister of Notre Dame at Paris, the Palace Yard at Westminster, etc.

¶**b.** By some 19th c. writers applied in error to 'a room over a church-porch'.

App. originating in a misunderstanding of quot. 1745 above. See *Penny Post* 1868, pp. 159, 213.

1836 PARKER *Gloss. Archit.*, *Parvis*, a small room over the porch, formerly used as a school. **1838** *Ibid.* ed. 2 s.v. **1842** GWILT *Archit.* Gloss., *Parvis*..It seems also to have signified a room over the church porch, where schools used to be held. **1848** *Rickman's Archit.* p. xlvi, A plain porch.. with a room over it (commonly but erroneously called a parvise). **1852** HOOK *Ch. Dict.* (1871) 568. **1856** J. ALLEN *Liskeard* viii. 120. **1867** *Gwilt's Archit.* (ed. 6) 956 A Norman porch, with an upper story or *parvise*, a chamber which appears to have been variously appropriated. **1881** *Archit. Publ. Soc. Dict.*, *Parvise* or *Parvis*... Modern writers have applied this term, but apparently without any good authority, to a room often found over church porches. **1888** *N. & Q.* 7th Ser. VI. 203/1.

†**2.** A public or academic conference or disputation. (So called from being originally held in the court or portico of a church.) *Obs.*

1496 *Dives & Paup.* (W. de W.) III. vi. 142/1 There [in chirche] they holde theyr peruys of many wronges whiche they thynke to doo. *c* **1530** MORE *Answ. Frith* Wks. 841/2 Whan he was a young sophister he would I dare say haue been full sore ashamed so to haue ouerseene himselfe at Oxforde at a peruise. **1579** FULKE *Heskins's Parl.* 296 M. Hesk. will set..a boy in the Paruis to answere the Bishop. **1706** PHILLIPS, *Parvis*, a Court before a Church-Porch,.. whence that Disputation at Oxford, call'd *Disputatio in Parvisiis*. It is also apply'd to the Mooting or Law-Disputes among young Students at the Inns of Court. **1886** H. C. MAXWELL LYTE *Univ. Oxford* 205 A 'general sophister'.. was required to attend the logical 'variations' that were held 'in the parvise' for at least a year, 'disputing, arguing, and responding' on sophisms... The parvise being a cloister, paved platform, or other open space, immediately adjoining a church. A curious instance of the survival of old names is to be found in the 'testamur'..which is nowadays [down to 1893] issued by the examiners at 'Responsions', to the effect that a successful candidate has answered to the questions of the Masters of the Schools 'in parviso'.

parvitude ('pɑːvɪtjuːd). *rare.* [f. L. *parv-us* small, after *magnitude*. (The L. derivative was *parvitās*.)] Littleness, smallness.

1657 TOMLINSON *Renou's Disp.* 34 Magnitude, Parvitude, and Number. **1661** GLANVILL *Van. Dogm.* 59 Because of its parvitude it cannot reach to the same floor with them. **1788** T. TAYLOR *Proclus* I. 89 They differ in magnitude and parvitude. **1903** *Edin. Rev.* Jan. 59 A continued preference for the slum..would confess parvitude in the point of view.

†**b.** An absolutely small or minute thing, an atom. *Obs.*

1653 H. MORE *Conject. Cabbal.* (1713) 189 These perfect Parvitudes..which are so infinitely subtile, that no Touch can perceive them. **1659** —— *Immort. Soul* II. i. 115 By a meer point of Matter I doe not mean a meer Mathematicall point, but a perfect Parvitude, or the least reality of which Matter can consist. **1678** CUDWORTH *Intell. Syst.* I. v. 777 To suppose Incorporeal Substances, Unextended and Indivisible, is to make them Absolute Parvitudes.

†ˈ**parvity.** *Obs.* [ad. L. *parvitās* smallness, f. *parv-us* small: see -ITY.] = prec.
1620 VENNER *Via Recta* viii. 190 Through paruity of exercise..many crude..humours are bred. **1650** BULWER *Anthropomet.* i. 4 Such a kind of turbinated figure represents a certain parvitie. **1691** RAY *Creation* I. (1692) 159 But what are these for their fineness and parvity?

parvoline (ˈpɑːvəlaɪn). *Chem.* [f. L. *parv-us* small, little + *-oline*, after *quinoline*.] A ptomaine $C_9H_{13}N$, = $C_5H_2N(CH_3)_2(C_2H_5)$ dimethylethylpyridine, obtained as an oily liquid with a disagreeable odour, from decaying mackerel and horse flesh, and also from certain shales and bituminous coals.
1855 GREV. WILLIAMS in *Q. Jrnl. Chem. Soc.* VII. 106, I propose to assign it the name of Parvoline in allusion to its small volatility as compared with its associated bases. *c* **1865** LETHEBY in *Circ. Sc.* I. 118/2 Of the alkaline matters there are leucoline,..and parvoline $C^{18}H^{13}N$). **1887** A. M. BROWN *Anim. Alkal.* 31 Parvoline $C^9H^{13}N$.—This was the first ptomaine chemically analysed and defined. It was discovered by MM. Gautier and Etard in the putrefactive products of the mackerel and horse flesh.

parvovirus (ˈpɑːvəʊˌvaɪrəs). *Microbiol.* [f. L. *parv-us* small + -O[1] + VIRUS.] Any of a group of very small animal viruses consisting of single-stranded DNA in an icosahedral capsid without an envelope and occurring in a wide variety of vertebrates.
1965 *Proposals & Recomm. Provisional Committee Nomencl. Viruses* in *Ann. de l'Inst. Pasteur* CIX. 629 (*table*) Parvovirus. **1968** RHODES & VAN ROOYEN *Textbk. Virol.* (ed. 5) III. 352/2 Johnson..has isolated and identified the virus of feline panleukopenia (or feline enteritis) as a parvovirus. **1974** J. A. ROSE in Fraenkel-Conrat & Wagner *Comprehensive Virol.* III. i. 50 The biological significance of most of the parvoviruses is still obscure. Only the feline and related viruses are known to cause disease naturally, but the pathogenicity of rodent viruses under experimental conditions indicates that other disease potentials may exist. .. Because of their latency and hardiness, parvoviruses must always be considered as potential contaminants of cells, other virus stocks, and certain vaccines. **1976** FENNER & WHITE *Med. Virol.* (ed. 2) xxii. 424 There is current controversy about whether two important human pathogens, hepatitis A virus and the Norwalk agent of gastroenteritis, are parvoviruses or picornaviruses, but the former seems more likely.

parvule (ˈpɑːvjuːl). *U.S.* [f. L. *parvul-us, -um* very small, dim. of *parvus* small.] (See quot.)
1890 in *Cent. Dict.* **1893** *Syd. Soc. Lex.*, *Parvules*, an American speciality, similar in all respects to 'granules'; made up with a fixed, but very small, quantity of some active drug.

parwanah, -wanna, variants of PURWANAH.

parwynke, obs. form of PERIWINKLE[1].

†**pary,** *v. Obs. rare.* [ad. F. *parier* or L. *pariāre*, to be equal, to tally, f. *pār, par-em* equal.]
1. *intr.* To tally.
1716 BENTLEY *Let. to Abp. Wake* 15 Apr. in Monk *Life* (1833) I. 399 When I came to try Pope Clement's Vulgate, I soon found the Greek of the Alexandrian, and that would by no means pary.
2. *trans.* To bet, stake.
a **1462** HENRYSON *Practysis of Med.* 84 (Bann. MS.) Sir, minister this medecyne at evin to sum man, And, or pryme be past, my powder I pary, They sall bliss yow or ellis bittirly yow ban.

pary, obs. f. PARRY.

parylene (ˈpærɪliːn). Also **Parylene.** [f. *par(ax)ylene* s.v. PARA-[1] 2 b.] Any of several transparent thermoplastic polymers of paraxylene or its substituted derivatives that are obtained as thin films or particles by condensation of the vapour of the monomer.
1965 *N.Y. Times* 18 Feb. 43 The product, named parylene, has been successfully used as a dielectric..on capacitors. **1965** *Mod. Plastics* Mar. 113/2 The simplest member of the family is parylene N. A chlorinated member, designated parylene C, is also available. **1969** C. A. HARPER *Handbk. Electronic Packaging* vii. 43 The basic member of the series, called Parylene N, is poly-para-xylylene, a completely linear, highly crystalline material. *Ibid.*, The parylenes are produced by vapor-phase deposition in a variety of forms. **1975** J. A. BRYDSON *Plastics Materials* (ed. 3) xxi. 470 With both Parylene materials the polymers have molecular weights of the order of 500,000.

paryll, obs. f. PERIL.

parysch(e, parysse, -yzsh, obs. ff. PARISH.

paryschoon, -shchon, var. PARISHEN[1] *Obs.*

paryse(e: see PARISIS.

parytory, obs. f. PARIETARY *sb.*

‖**pas** (‖pa, pɑː). [F. *pas* step, precedency, etc.]
1. The right of going first; precedence. Phrases, *to dispute, give, take, yield, the pas* [F. *prendre, céder le pas*, etc.] Also *fig.*
1707 *Vulpone* 23 It appears they have always fiercely contended for the *pas* among themselves. **1712** ADDISON *Spect.* No. 529 ¶7 Aristotle would have the latter yield the *Pas* to the former. **1771** SMOLLETT *Humph. Cl.* 8 Nov., My aunt and her paramour took the *pas*. **1848** THACKERAY *Bk. Snobs* xvi, He takes the *pas* of dukes. **1885** *Spectator* 22 Aug 1109/2 It is difficult to give any one portion of it the *pas* of the others.
2. A step in dancing; a kind of dance; mostly in names of special dances, as *pas d'action*, a thematic dance or mime; *pas de basque*, a dance step derived from Basque national dances; *pas de bourrée*: see BOURRÉE 2; *pas de chat* (see quot. 1957); *pas de cheval* (see quots.); *pas de deux*, a dance or figure for two persons; also *transf.* and *fig.*; *pas de quatre*, a dance or figure for four persons; *pas de trois*, a dance or figure for three persons; also *transf.* and *fig.*; *pas grave*, a slow or solemn dance; *pas seul*, a dance or figure for one person.
1775 SHERIDAN *Rivals* III. iv, Mine are true-born English legs, they don't understand their curst French lingo! their *pas* this, and *pas* that, and *pas* t'other. **1868** *Daily News* 3 Nov., The father of some 'young phenomenon' of a minor theatre fiddling in an ecstacy of admiration at his little daughter's rehearsal of her 'pas' before going on.
1951 *Ballet Ann.* V. 25 He has a superb plastic imagination which he showed even in that wickedly conceived **pas d'action* to the music of Tristan. **1957** G. B. L. WILSON *Dict. Ballet* 206 *Pas d'action*, lit. action dance. A dance expressive of a theme or telling a story, in opposition to absolute dance—e.g. the Rose Adagio in *Sleeping Beauty*. **1818** T. WILSON *Quadrille & Cotillion Panorama* 100 **Pas de basque*, a Step used in Quadrille Dancing. **1865** MRS. GASKELL *Lett.* (1966) 748 The neat maid servant had performed a sort of 'pas-de-basque', hopping & sliding with more grace than security to the dishes she held. **1892** E. SCOTT *Dancing* ix. 119 Remember, in performing a *gavotte*, that the French *pas de basque* is employed, in which the first two movements are made to one count of the music. **1948** *Ballet Ann.* II. 144 To see a Basque dancer perform the *pas de basque* is to realise the true nature of that step. The soft, cat-like landing gives an impression of immense strength and of power in reserve. **1964** J. F. & T. M. FLETT *Trad. Dancing in Scotl.* viii. 190 In reel tempo the commonest setting step was the pas de Basque. **1968** J. WINEARLS *Mod. Dance* (ed. 2) iii. 88 The pas de basque lends itself to many rhythmic and expressive variations. **1914** T. & M. W. KINNEY *Dance* iv. 90 In this group might appropriately be included **pas de bourrée dessus-dessous* (i.e., in front and behind); *glissades*; *petits battements*; and the devilish-looking little **pas-de-chat*. **1916** *Dancing Times* Sept. 327 [Espinosa's] 'Syllabus of Dancing.'..Steps. — .. pas de basque, pas de chat, pas de cheval. **1922** BEAUMONT & IDZIKOWSKI *Man. Classical Theatr. Dancing* II. v. 197 *Pas de chat.* This *pas* is composed of *three* movements, generally executed *en diagonale*. **1953** E. TAYLOR *Sleeping Beauty* vi. 114 The staggered thumps of children practising a *pas de chat*. *Ibid.* 116 She was still humming the *pas de chat* tune. **1957** G. B. L. WILSON *Dict. Ballet* 207 *Pas de chat*, lit. a cat's step. A springing movement in which one foot jumps over the other, executed on the diagonal. A jumping step in which the feet are one after the other drawn up to the knee of the opposite leg... Also called pas de papillon. **1976** *New Yorker* 15 Nov. 111/1 The pas-de-chat/pirouette ending of the second variation, nowadays done at the New York City Ballet as a line of brisés, gave her no difficulty. **1916** *Pas de cheval [see *pas de chat* above]. **1930** CRASKE & BEAUMONT *Theory & Pract. Allegro in Classical Ballet* 41 Pas de cheval. Stand erect in the centre of the room and face 2, with the head upright [etc.]. **1957** G. B. L. WILSON *Dict. Ballet* 207 *Pas de cheval*, a pawing movement of one foot while the dancer hops on the other. **1762** G.-A. GALLINI *Treat. Art Dancing* 282 Venus and Adonis form a **pas-de-deux*, or duet-dance. **1775** H. WALPOLE *Let.* 23 Aug. in *Corr.* (1965) XXXII. 255, I was not so struck with the dancing as I expected, except with a *pas de deux* by the Marquis de Noailles and Madame Nolstein. **1802** [see ENSEMBLE *sb.* 1]. **1806** E. FREMANTLE in *Wynne Diaries* (1940) III. 265 The grand Ballet..has fine effect... Des Hayes pas de deux with his wife quite beautiful. **1808** T. ASHE *Trav. Amer.* III. xxxv. 118 The Waltz had most votaries; the *Pas de deux* next. **1819** T. HOPE *Anastasius* (1820) I. vii. 136 A *pas-de-deux* which we performed together as a lover and his mistress. **1955** *Times* 5 July 14/1 The choreography is designedly adventurous,..particularly in the long central section which is set as a *pas de deux*. **1960** [see *pas de trois* below]. **1962** *Listener* 13 Sept. 380/2 Dr Adenauer would have to go faster and further in the *pas de deux* to convince himself and his people that 'the Franco-German alliance is what counts'. **1973** *Times Lit. Suppl.* 26 Oct. 1324/1 Between them they perform a ritual examination of conscience, a *pas de deux* in which they are painfully at cross-purposes. **1978** *Times* 27 May 14/7 This was no ordinary *debut* performance in the *corps de ballet*, but was a solo performance in a *pas de deux* specially introduced for her. **1978** *Country Life* 27 July 220/2 She..rode side-saddle in the pas-de-deux dressage with David Hunt. **1882** *Standard* 26 Dec. 5 The famous **pas de quatre* which had the effect of killing the Ballet in England. **1890** [see GAIETY 4]. **1897** G. BELL *Let.* 28 Jan. (1927) I. iii. 42 There is a rather nice sort of variant of the 'pas de quatre' which they call the 'pas de patineur' which I quickly learnt. **1902** CHESTERTON *Twelve Types* 43 His metre is a bounding 'pas de quatre'. **1978** *Times* 9 Mar. 13/6 Ashton's *pas de quatre* and Neapolitan dance. **1762** G.-A. GALLINI *Treat. Art Dancing* 280 A **pas-de-trois* or trio-dance follows. **1773** H. WALPOLE *Let.* 3 Apr. in *Corr.* (1965) XXXII. 116 Lord Delawar's two eldest daughters and the Ancaster infanta performed a *pas de trois* as well as Mlle Heinel. **1794** [see DIVERTISSEMENT 2]. **1823** T. CREEVEY *Let.* 14 Feb. in *Creevey Papers* (1963) xi. 190 We went to our *own* play-house, where we saw 1st a *pas de trois* between Wilson, Hobhouse and Canning, and then a *pas de deux* between Broughman and Canning. **1957** G. B. L. WILSON *Dict. Ballet* 208 *Pas de trois* (de quatre, de cinq, de six, etc.), a dance for three (four, five, six, etc.) persons. **1960** A. PODHAJSKY *Spanish Riding School Vienna* 40 The 'Pas de Deux' or 'Pas de Trois' demands perfectly trained horses which allow themselves to be led by the rider both as regards keeping time and performing the steps with great precision. **1976** *New Yorker* 9 Feb. 95/1 There is a gracious and supple, long-limbed pas de trois..in which the boy holds an invisible lute or mandolin. **1977** D. WILLIAMS *Treasure by Degrees* vi. 55 The Dean's violent about-turn led him straight into the arms of Amelia Hatch... She, in turn, recoiled on to Witaker so that all three had momentarily become engaged in a curious *pas de trois* for ill-matched performers. **1804** CHARLOTTE SMITH *Conversations*, etc. I. 140 She..shewed a new **pas grave*, which her dancing-master had lately introduced. **1813** BYRON *Waltz* 14 Not decent David, when, before the ark, His grand *pas-seul excited some remark. **1830** R. BARTON tr. *Blasis's Code of Terpsichore* v. 354 From time to time these bacchanalia are interrupted by *pas seuls* and *pas de deux*. **1832** F. TROLLOPE *Dom. Manners Amer.* I. xiii. 188 Had Mercury stepped down, and danced a *pas seul* upon earth, his godship could not have produced a more violent sensation. **1839** DICKENS *Nickleby* xlviii. 473 A castanet pas seul by the Infant Phenomenon. **1849** THACKERAY *Pendennis* I. xxvii. 260 Now the young ladies went over to Pen's side, and Cornet Perch performed a *pas seul* in his turn. **1863** MRS. GASKELL *Sylvia's Lovers* I. xiii. 291 Philip hardly knew what he said in reply, the mention of that *pas-seul* lifted such a weight off his heart. **1870** MISS BRIDGMAN *Rob Lynne* I. viii. 165 Fanny ..performed a..*pas de seul* up the garden path. **1939** JOYCE *Let.* 28 Jan. (1966) III. 436, I am afraid the traditional *pas seul* with high kicking effects..will be beyond my powers this year of grace. **1955** *Times* 29 Aug. 10/5 If Mr. Ashton has not succeeded in making the love-duet the climax of his work he has almost compensated for it in Juliet's pas seul after the marriage in Friar Laurence's cell. **1978** S. ROSENFELD *Temples of Thespis* iv. 71 Little Chatterley, as the black slave, was admired for his *pas seul*.
3. *pas-de-souris.* (*Fortif.*) [F. lit. 'mouse-steps'.] A staircase from the ravelin to the ditch.
1704 J. HARRIS *Lex. Techn.* I, *Pas de Souris.* **1859** F. A. GRIFFITHS *Artil. Man.* (1862) 268 *Stairs*, or *Pas de souris*. These steps of masonry are made at the gorges of the several works, and at the salient, and re-entering angles of the counterscarp.

pas, obs. form of PACE, PASS.

pasa doble: see PASO DOBLE.

pasan, pasang (ˈpɑːzən, -əŋ). Also 8 **pazan,** 9 **pazun, paseng.** [a. Pers. *pāzan* the mountain goat; erron. analysed as f. *pā* foot + *sang* stone.]
A species of wild goat (*Capra Ægagrus*), found in Western Asia and Crete; the bezoar-goat.
1774 GOLDSM. *Nat. Hist.* III. 74 The eighth is called the pazan; or, by some, the bezoar goat. **1834** J. B. FRASER *Persia* xii. 470 Two of the most interesting creatures to be met with in these countries are the..Pazun (the mountain goat) and the Argali. **1838** *Penny Cycl.* XI. 282/2 Cuvier..considers the Paseng (*Capra Ægagrus*) to be the parent-stock of all the varieties of the domestic goat. **1893** LYDEKKER *Horns & Hoofs* 107 The bezoar stone..is a concretion obtained from the stomach of the pasang.
¶ Mistakenly identified by Buffon (1764, XII. 212) with the oryx or gemsbok, a S. African antelope; the error was formerly followed by some English compilers, and is reproduced in some 19th c. dictionaries.

‖**pasar** (ˈpæsɑː(r)). [Indonesian *pasar*, perh. f. Pers. *bāzār* market.] A market in Indonesia and Malaysia. So **pasar gelap** [Indonesian *gelap* dark], black market; **pasar malam** [Indonesian *malam* night], a fair.
1958 H. FORSTER *Flowering Lotus* ii. 26 The women.. walked miles from their villages.. to the big *pasar*, the covered market. **1959** 'M. DERBY' *Tigress* iv. 154 The *pasar gelap* or black market trade with Sumatra was risky but profitable. **1961** CONYN & MARTEN *Bali Ballet Murder* xvi. 175, I shall ask the cook to go to the *pasar*. **1972** *Malay Mail* (Kuala Lumpur) 25 May 4/5 The pasar malam in Gurney Drive will end on Tuesday.

pasc, pasce, obs. ff. PASCH, PASS.

pascage, pascal, obs. ff PASCUAGE, PASCHAL, PASCUAL.

Pascal (pæˈskɑːl). [The name of Blaise *Pascal* (1623–62), French scholar and scientist.]
1. *Math. Pascal's triangle*: a triangular array of numbers in which those at the ends of the rows are 1 and each of the others is the sum of the nearest two numbers in the row above, the apex, 1, being at the top. [Described in Pascal's *Traité du Triangle Arithmetique* (1665).]
1886 G. CHRYSTAL *Algebra* I. iv. 65 (*heading*) Pascal's triangle generalised. **1977** R. E. MEGILL *Introd. Risk Analysis* vii. 67 You can construct a triangle, called Pascal's triangle, from the binomial expansions just reviewed.
2. Written **pascal** (ˈpæskəl). The unit of pressure in the M.K.S. system (now incorporated into the International System of Units), equal to one newton per square metre (approximately 0·000,145 p.s.i., 9·9 × 10^{-6} atmosphere, or 0·102 kilogramme-force per sq. cm.). Abbrev. Pa.
1956 KAYE & LABY *Tables Physical & Chem. Constants* (ed. 11) 7 (*table*) Pascal. **1964** H. S. HVISTENDAHL *Engin. Units* iii. 29 In the French decree of May 3rd, 1961, the name pascal (Pa), is adopted for the N/m^2,..although that name has not yet received international recognition. **1972** *Physics Bull.* Jan. 40/1 The 14th General conference of Weights and Measures (CGPM) met in Paris on 4–7 October 1971... Amongst the main decisions taken by the conference were the final adoption..of the 'pascal' (Pa) as the SI unit of pressure (Nm^{-2}) and the 'siemens' (S) as the

SI unit of conductance (Ω^{-1}). **1974** *B.S.I. News* Sept. 12/2 The pascal is advised by the aircraft industry.. as the best unit to use in their fields. **1975** *Sci. Amer.* Feb. 110/2 The manual uses the MKS pressure unit, the pascal, almost throughout. **1976** *Nature* 29 Apr. 745/3 A Pascal of pressure on top of your head Is the same push that butter exerts on sliced bread.

3. *Computing.* Also **PASCAL**. A high-level programming language used esp. for teaching purposes. [Named after Pascal because he devised and built a calculating machine *c* 1642.]

1971 N. WIRTH in *Acta Informatica* I. 35 The development of the language *Pascal* is based on two principal aims. The first is to make available a language suitable to teach programming as a systematic discipline... The second is to develop implementations of this language which are both reliable and efficient on presently available computers. **1971** —— in *Software Pract. & Experience* Oct.–Dec. 323 Work on implementation of an earlier version of PASCAL was started in 1968. **1972** *Computing Rev.* XIII. 224/2 PASCAL is a simple algorithmic language patterned after ALGOL 60 with an elegant facility for describing and manipulating data structures. **1979** *Personal Computer World* Nov. 73/2 This feature is included in PASCAL as a safety measure to guard against the tendency of some programmers to re-use a loop counter at a later stage of the program, without assigning a new value to it. **1984** J. GARDNER *Pole of Honour* vi. 46 Bond started to learn.. more complex languages like.. the high-level Pascal.

Pascalian (pæ'skɑːlɪən), *sb.* and *a.* [f. prec. + -IAN.] **A.** *sb.* An admirer or adherent of Pascal (see prec. (etym.)); an interpreter of his works. **B.** *adj.* Of or pertaining to Pascal or to his ideas and philosophy.

1929 A. HUXLEY *Do What you Will* 235, I now propose to write of Pascal. As a positivist first of all... More sympathetically next, in the guise of a Pascalian. **1930** tr. *Chevalier's Pascal* i. 26 Charron's work contained, as it were, the germ of Pascalian apologetics; at any rate we find in it a great deal of material that Pascal was to utilize after changing its order. **1937** A. HUXLEY *Ends & Means* xv. 304 There is, however, an element of truth in the Pascalian doctrine. **1937** *Sunday Times* 25 Apr. 8/3 The truth is Pascalian Christianity is only fit for heroes and saints; it is not a possible life for ordinary men. **1948** *Scottish Jrnl. Theol.* I. 98 A full length study of Pascal by an established Pascalian scholar. **1971** G. STEINER *In Bluebeard's Castle* iii. 64 We are forced now to return to an earlier, Pascalian pessimism, to a model of history whose logic derives from a postulate of original sin. **1973** *Listener* 6 Sept. 298/1 The man who finds himself suddenly independent in this way will then fall prey to Pascalian despair, existential anguish, dereliction. **1977** *N.Y. Rev. Bks.* 14 Apr. 26/4 Sennett is thus an atheist about social science, but a Pascalian about society.

Pascarete, var. PAXARETE.

pascent ('pæsənt), *a. rare*⁻¹. [ad. L. *pāscent-em*, pr. pple. of *pāscĕre* to feed, graze.] Feeding.

1763 GOLDSM. *Misc. Wks.* (1837) II. 538 The pascent creature finds a bed which at once supplies food and protection.

pasch (pɑːsk, -æ-). Now *arch.* or *Hist.* Forms: 2–4 *pl.* **pasches**, 3 (*Orm.*) **passke**, 3–7 **pasche**, 4–6 **paske**, **pask**, 5, 9 **pasque**, 4– **pasch**, (4 **pasck**, 5 **pasc**, **pasce**, **pache**, **passh**, 5–6 **passe**, 6 **paasse**, *Sc.* 5 **paisch**, 6 **pashe**, **pess**, **peice**, 7 **peace**: see also PACE *sb.*²; in L. form, 4, 9 **pascha**). [a. OF. *pasche* (Phil. de Thaun, etc.) and *pasque* (mod.F. *pâque*), ad. L. *pascha*, a. Gr. πάσχα, ad. Heb. *pesakh*, in Aramaic emphatic state *paskhā* a passing over, the Passover; f. *pāsakh* to pass over. The OF. pl. *pasches*:—L. *paschas* (acc. pl.) occurs already in the OE. Chron. *a* 1131. Cognate forms from L. were OS., OFris. *pascha* (MDu. *paeschen*, Du. *paaschen*, MLG. *pasche(n*, LG. *pâschen*, *pâsken*), Icel. *páskar* (Sw. *påsk(a*, Da. *paaske*); the Northern Eng. forms in *paske*, *pask* (whence *pass*, *pace*, etc.), were perh. from Scandinavian. Formerly often *pl.* with *sing.* sense, as in F., Du., LG., Icelandic, etc.]

1. The Jewish feast of the Passover.

c **1200** ORMIN 15850 Forr Passke,—ȝiff þu turrnenn willt þatt word till Ennglissh spæche, þa taccneþþ itt tatt uss birrþ aȝȝ Uss flittenn towarrd Criste. *c* **1250** *Gen. & Ex.* 3157 Ðat niȝt sal ben fest pasche, forð-for, on engle tunge, it be. *a* **1300** *Cursor M.* 6164 (Cott.) Quat wise þai suld þair paskes [*later MSS.* pask, paske] hald. *Ibid.* 16814 + 2 If ani man At paschez to ded wore broght. **1382** WYCLIF *Exod.* xii. 43 This is the religioun of phask [*Vulg.* phrase]; ech alien shal not ete therof. —— *Mark* xiv. 14 Wher is my fulfilling [*gloss* or etyng place] where I schal ete pask [1582 *Rhem.* the Pasche] with my disciplis. *c* **1400** MAUNDEV. (1839) viii. 92 There made our Lord his Pask with his Disciples. *c* **1440** *York Myst.* xxvii. 29 Þe lambe of Pasc. **1609** BIBLE (Douay) 1 *Esdras* i. 1 Josias made a Pasch in Ierusalem. **1745** A. BUTLER *Lives Saints, James* 1 May (1847) V. 16 In the second year of Christ's preaching, soon after the Pasch, in the year 31. [**1850** NEALE *Med. Hymns* (1867) 114 Hail our Pascha, That wast dead! **1885** *Catholic Dict.* (ed. 3) 284/2 The Churches of Asia Proconsularis.. kept the feast of Passover or Pasch at the same time as the Jews—viz. 14 Nisan.]

2. The Christian festival of Easter. *arch.* or *local*: cf. PACE *sb.*² (In ME. often in *pl.* with collective sense = Easter-tide: cf. F. *les Pâques.*)

a **1131** *O.E. Chron.* an. 1122 On þis ȝeare wæs se king Heanri on Cristes mæssan on Northwic and on Pasches he weas on Norhthamtune. **13..** *Coer de L.* 6475 Hys brother Ihon, Wolde do corowne hym anon, At the Pask. *c* **1330** R. BRUNNE *Chron. Wace* (Rolls) 9267 At Londone his Pasches he [Uther] held. **1357** *Lay Folks Catech.* 321 Anes in the yhere, That is at sai, at paskes. *c* **1450** *Merlin* 104 Syr, we pray yow that the swerde be suffred yet in the ston to Passh. **1481** CAXTON *Godeffroy* clxiii. 241 There helde they the feste of ester or pasque, the x day of Apryll. **1535** LYNDESAY *Satyre* 2004 And halds me ȝit vnder that same proces, That gart me want the Sacrament at Pasche [*v.r.* pess]. **1557** TUSSER 100 *Points Husb.* lxviii, Spare meddowes at shroftide, spare marshes at paske. **1596** DALRYMPLE tr. *Leslie's Hist. Scot.* IV. 234 To grant the ryᵗ celebratione of the Pashe. **1638** CHILLINGW. *Relig. Prot.* I. vi. §30. 349 Who had assigned the fourteenth of the Moneth of March for the observation of the *Pasche.* **1722** S. SEWALL *Diary* 21 Dec., They kept not Yule nor Pasch. **1885** *Catholic Dict.* (ed. 3) 284/2 The great majority of Christians celebrated the Pasch on the Sunday after Nisan 14.. because on that day Christ rose again.

3. *attrib.* and *Comb.* in many collocations = Easter-, as ***pasch-even***, ***-lamb***, ***-mass***, ***-morn***, ***-tide***, ***-week***. Also PASCH-DAY, -EGG.

c **1200** ORMIN 15849 Þa frellsenn þeȝȝ, þatt witt tu wel, Gastlike Passkemesse. *a* **1300** *Cursor M.* 18617 Þe seuend dai in paske tide, He ras arli, wit-vten bide. **1375** BARBOUR *Bruce* XV. 101 Quhill the tysday in pask-owk [*v.rr.* payss wouk, Pasche Oulk] On athir half thai trowis tuk. *Ibid.* 105 Apon paske evin all richt To the castell.. come schippis xv. *c* **1460** *Towneley Myst.* xxiii. 666 That Lord that.. rose on pasche morne. **1533** TINDALE *Supper of Lord* C vj b, I wyll compare circumcision wyth baptysme: and the passe lambe wyth Christes supper. **1605** SYLVESTER *Du Bartas* II. iii. III. *Law* 583 Th' Israelites, whose doores were markt before, With sacred Pass-Lambs Sacramental gore.

paschal ('pɑːskəl, -æ-), *a.* and *sb.* Also 5–6 **paskal**(l, 6 **pascal**(l, **pascquall**, 8 **pasqual**. [a. F. *pascal* (12th c. in Hatz.-Darm.), ad. late L. *paschāl-is* (Codex Theod.), f. *pascha* PASCH: see -AL¹.]

A. *adj.*

1. Of or pertaining to the Jewish Passover.

paschal lamb, the lamb slain and eaten at the Passover; applied to Christ, hence also to various symbolic representations of Christ: = AGNUS DEI b and c.

c **1430** LYDG. *Hors, Sheep & G.* 1 in *Pol. Rel. & L. Poems* 15 This pascalle Lambe with-owte spott, alle whyte. **1526** TINDALE *Mark* xiv. 12 The first daye of swete breed, when they offered the pascal lambe. **1658** LIGHTFOOT *Horæ Hebraicæ* (1859) II. 336 That Judas after the paschal supper ..could make his agreement with the priests, and get his blades.. together ready to apprehend our Saviour. *a* **1714** SHARP *Wks.* (1754) VII. Serm. xii. 223 The paschal-feast, from whence our Saviour took his sacrament of the Lord's supper. **1845** H. J. ROSE in *Encycl. Metrop.* (1847) II. 891/1 The paschal lamb they called the body of the Passover.

2. Of or pertaining to Easter; used in Easter celebrations.

paschal candle, a large candle blessed and lighted in the service of Holy Saturday and placed on the gospel side of the altar there to remain till Ascension day.

1432–50 tr. *Higden* (Rolls) V. 377 The grete cicle of the terme Paschalle is finischede or complete in this vᵗʰᵉ yere of Iustinus, whiche is of v.ᶜ. yere and xxxijᵗⁱ from the passion of Criste, and after Marianus v.ᶜ. and lx. yere. **1477–9** in *Rec. St. Mary at Hill* (E.E.T.S.) 92 For makyng of the paschall tapre.. weyng xxx lb. **1506** in Glasscock *Rec. St. Michael's Bp. Stortford* (1882) 31 For the paskal sylver at Ester eve. **1519** in Nash *Churchw. Acc. St. Giles, Reading* 6 For mending and scouring of the Pascall cansticke. **1653** JER. TAYLOR 25 *Serm.* 39 They then thought that when the Paschall taper burn'd, the flames of hell could not burn, till the holy wax was spent. **1670** BLOUNT *Law Dict.*, *Paschal Rents*, are rents or yearly tributes paid by the inferior Clergy to the Bishop or Arch-Deacon at their Easter-Visitation. **1772** NUGENT tr. *Hist. Fr. Gerund* I. 61 At the time of confession and pasqual communion. **1875** LIGHTFOOT *Comm. Col.* 56 Polycarp.. visited Rome, hoping to adjust the Paschal controversy.

B. *sb.* Various absolute uses of A. 1 and 2.

1. A great candle lighted at Easter: see A. 2. **b.** A candlestick to hold the same. Cf. JUDAS 2.

1427 in *Rec. St. Mary at Hill* (E.E.T.S.) 64 A pece of tymbre to þe newe Paschall. *Ibid.*, A dysch of peuter for þe Paskall. **1519** in Nash *Churchw. Acc. St. Giles, Reading* 5 For wax and making of the Pascall. **1590** MUNDAY *Eng. Romayne Life* in *Harl. Misc.* (Malh.) II. 186 After the Iewes ..be baptized, they be brought into the church, and there they see the hallowing of the paschall, which is a mightie great wax taper. **1593** in *Rites & Mon. Ch. Durh.* (Surtees 1903) 11 On the height of the sᵈ candlestick or pascall of lattine was a fair large flower.. wherein did stand a long peece of wood.. wheron stood a great long square tap of wax called the pascall. **1826** HONE *Every-day Bk.* I. 436 The paschal or great Easter taper at Westminster Abbey was three hundred pounds' weight. *Ibid.*, The paschal in Durham cathedral was square wax, and reached to within a man's length of the roof.

2. The Passover celebration, Passover supper, or Passover lamb.

1579 FULKE *Heskins's Parl.* 46 He did desire to eat the Pascall of the lawe. **1581** R. GOADE in *Confer.* III. (1584) T iij, There was some distance of time betweene the Pascall and the Supper. *a* **1655** VINES *Lord's Supper* (1677) 16 The Levites killed the paschals. **1670** G. H. *Hist. Cardinals* I. II. 34 To suffer them [Jews].. to Celebrate their Paschal with all possible Solemnity.

† **'Paschalist.** *Obs. rare*⁻¹. [f. prec. + -IST.] An adherent of (the Greek or Roman) Easter.

1641 MILTON *Prel. Episc.* Wks. (1851) 89 That which Church Histories report of those East, and Western Paschalists.

'Paschaltide. [f. PASCHAL *a.* + TIDE *sb.*] The period following Easter Sunday, esp. Easter Week.

1894 G. F. X. GRIFFITH tr. *Fouard's St. Paul* xv. 349 The octave of Paschal-tide, a rite of Jewish origin. **1974** *Oxf. Dict. Chr. Ch.* (ed. 2) 1038/1 *Paschaltide*, the period in the ecclesiastical year immediately after Easter.

† **'pasch-day.** *Sc.* and *north. dial. Obs.* Forms: see PASCH, PACE *sb.*² Easter-day. (Sometimes applied to Good Friday.)

c **1200** ORMIN 15552 Forr þatt Judisskenn Passkedaȝȝ þa shollde cumenn newenn. *a* **1300** *Cursor M.* 13227 (Cott.) Sant ion.. was slan in pasch daus [*F.* paske dawes]. **1472** in *Surtees Misc.* (1888) 25 The Lord sall reperell be Passe day. **1596** DALRYMPLE tr. *Leslie's Hist. Scot.* IV. 227 Anent the celebratione of the Pasche day. *a* **1670** SPALDING *Troub. Chas. I* (1850) I. 262 No preiching nor commvnion.. wes vsit and wont, nor yit givin on pash day.

pasch-egg ('pask,ɛg). *Sc.* and *north. dial.* Forms: see PASCH, PACE *sb.*²; also corruptly paste-egg. An Easter egg: an egg dyed of various colours, and boiled hard, as an Easter gift.

1579, **1611**, etc. [see PACE *sb.*²]. **1677** COLES *Eng.-Lat. Dict.*, Pasch-eggs, Eggs given at Easter, *Ovum paschale croceum* or *luteum*. **1777** BRAND *Pop. Antiq.* 310 Of Pasche, or as they are commonly called, Paste Eggs. **1825** BROCKETT *N.C. Gloss.*, *Paste-eggs.* **1847** MARY HOWITT *Ballads* 80 And kindly country-women, yet, Their Pasch-eggs ready make, Of divers colours beautiful, To give for Jesus' sake. **1898** *Dublin Rev.* July 153 In France it is, or was until recently, usual to eat the Pasch-egg before any other food was partaken of on Easter Day.

Paschen¹ ('pæʃən). *Physics.* The name of L. C. H. Friedrich *Paschen* (1865–1947), German physicist, used *attrib.* and in the possessive to designate certain phenomena he discovered, as **Paschen('s) curve**, a graph of the breakdown voltage in a gas against the product of pressure and interelectrode distance; **Paschen's law**, the law that at a constant temperature the breakdown voltage in any given gas depends only on the product of the pressure and the interelectrode distance (formulated by Paschen in *Ann. d. Physik und Chem.* (1889) XXXVII. 90); **Paschen series**, a series of lines in the infra-red part of the spectrum of atomic hydrogen, with wave numbers represented by $R(1/3^2 - 1/m^2)$ (where R is the Rydberg constant and m = 4, 5, . . .), of which the first line has a wavelength of 1857 nanometres and the series limit is at 821 nanometres.

1903 *Proc. R. Soc.* LXXI. 375 A general application of Paschen's law demands that the minimum spark potential must be a physical constant for each gas. **1922** Paschen series [see LYMAN]. **1957** A. F. MONYPENNY tr. *Penning's Electr. Discharges in Gases* vi. 32 (*caption*) Paschen curves for breakdown between flat iron plates in various gases and gas mixtures. **1967** *IEEE Trans. Electr. Insulation* II. 82/1 In accordance with Paschen's curve, equally large discharge voltages could also result for very small voids. **1967** Paschen series [see LYMAN]. **1968** J. F. WESTON *Cold Cathode Glow Discharge Tubes* ii. 59 For the case of a non-uniform field Paschen's law relating breakdown to gap width and pressure no longer holds.

Paschen² ('pæʃən). *Med.* The name of Enrique *Paschen* (1860–1936), Mexican-born bacteriologist, used *attrib.* in **Paschen body**, each of the particles making up one of the cytoplasmic inclusions found in epithelial cells in cases of smallpox (described by Paschen in *Münch. med. Wochenschr.* (1906) 4 Dec. 2391).

1931 *Jrnl. Path. & Bacteriol.* XXXIV. 122 A preparation is shown which demonstrates the presence of elementary bodies precisely similar to the Paschen and Borrel bodies. **1974** J. D. ACTON et al. *Fund. Med. Virol.* xi. 167 Although the poxviruses are DNA viruses, they replicate in the cytoplasm and produce characteristic cytoplasmic inclusions called Guarnieri bodies; the inclusions are composed of a dense aggregation of many virus particles. Virus particles are also referred to as 'elementary bodies' or Paschen bodies.

Paschen-Back effect (,pæʃən 'bæk). *Physics.* [f. PASCHEN¹ + the name of Ernst E. A. *Back* (1881–1959), German physicist, who jointly published a description of the effect in 1913 (*Ann. der Physik* XXXIX. 897).] An effect observed when a source of spectral lines is in a magnetic field so strong that the resultant splitting of each line is comparable in magnitude to the separation of the lines in a multiplet, the spacing of the lines corresponding to the normal Zeeman effect rather than the anomalous Zeeman effect generally observed at lower field strengths.

1923 H. L. BROSE tr. *Sommerfeld's Atomic Struct. & Spectral Lines* vi. 389 The Paschen-Back effect links together only such lines as belong together in a series as multiplicities. **1964** G. W. KING *Spectrosc. & Molecular Struct.* iii. 109 A magnetic field that would be strong enough to produce a resolvable splitting of nuclear Zeeman lines is usually more than sufficient to uncouple **I*** from **J*** and cause them to precess independently around the *z* axis, giving a nuclear Paschen-Back effect instead. **1970** G. K. WOODGATE *Elem. Atomic Struct.* viii. 150 This strong-field limit of the Zeeman effect is called the Paschen-Back effect.

pasch-flower: see PASQUE-FLOWER.

paschite ('pæskaɪt). [f. Gr. πάσχα, PASCH + -ITE.] One who observed Easter on the date of the Jewish Passover, the fourteenth of Nisan; a quartodeciman.
1890 in *Cent. Dict.*

pascible ('pæsɪb(ə)l), *a. rare.* [ad. L. type **pascibilis*, f. *pascĕre* to feed: see -IBLE.] Capable of serving as pasture.
1795 J. BILLINGSLEY *Agric. Somerset* (1798) 52 Land.. when pascible for the remaining months, of little value from being overstocked.

pascioun, pasck, obs. ff. PASSION, PASCH.

'**pascuage.** *rare*⁻⁰. Also 7 **pascage**. [a. OF. *pascuage* (14th c. in Godef.), ad. late L. *pascuāticum* (med.L. *pascuāgium*), f. L. *pascuum* pasture, neuter of *pascuus* adj., PASCUOUS, f. *pascĕre* to feed: see -AGE.] The grazing of cattle.
1656 BLOUNT *Glossogr.*, *Pascage*, grazing, feeding or pasturing of Cattle. **1848** in WHARTON *Law Lex.*

pascual ('pæskjuːəl), *a.* (and *sb.*) Also 7 **pascal**. [a. OF. *pascual*, *pascuel*, ad. med.L. *pascuāl-is*, f. *pascu-um* grazing: see -AL¹. Cf. med.L. *pascuale* sb.] Of or pertaining to pastures; growing in pastures; esp. describing plants growing in pasture or grassland. Also as *sb.*, a pascual plant.
1656 BLOUNT *Glossogr.*, *Pascal*, feeding here, and there abroad, belonging to pasture. **1847** H. C. WATSON *Cybele Britannica* I. 65 The proposed series of terms runs thus:—1. Pratal... 2. Pascual.—Plants of pastures and grassy commons, where the herbage is usually less luxuriant than in the meadow-lands, [etc.]. *Ibid.* 67 The pratal plants are occasionally pascual plants, as Phleum pratense; the pascuals are in turn ericetals, as Prunella vulgaris. **1863** J. G. BAKER *N. Yorks. Stud.* 183 We may employ a series of adjectives such as sylvestral, pratal, pascual, ericetal [etc.]. **1883** A. FRYER in *Jrnl. Bot., Brit. & For.* XXI. 375 No hard and fast line can be drawn between Pascual and Pratal plants. **1926** G. C. DRUCE in J. J. Walker *Nat. Hist. Oxf. Distr.* 96 *Carex tomentosa* L., usually classed as a paludal, is a pascual in its only known Oxford locality near Burford.

Pascuan ('pæskjuːən), *a.* and *sb.* [a. F. *Pascuan* (H. Lavachery 1935).] **A.** *adj.* Of or pertaining to Easter Island in the South Pacific, its inhabitants, or its script. **B.** *sb.* **a.** A native or inhabitant of Easter Island. **b.** The script used by the inhabitants of Easter Island. So **Pascuense** *a.* and *sb.*
[**1935** H. LAVACHERY *Ile de Pâques* i. 16 Ici la naiveté des Espagnols apparaît non moins admirable que l'ingéniosité des Pascuans.] **1940** B. BONNERJEA in *N. & Q.* 17 Feb. 110/2, I have used the term 'Pascuans'—following Lavachery—in place of the more cumbersome English expression 'Easter Islanders'. *Ibid.* 111/1 It is an undeniable fact that the Pascuans are Polynesians. *Ibid.*, Since the.. discovery of the Pascuan script, numerous articles have been written on the subject. **1948** D. DIRINGER *Alphabet* 137 According to local traditions, Hotumatua, an ancestor of the Pascuans..came to the island..and brought with him 67 inscribed wooden tablets. **1960** J. FUENTES *Dict. & Gram. Easter Island Lang.* 591 The spoken language keeps some of the old Pascuense characteristics, that is to say, the Pascuense before assimilating modern foreign expressions.

pascuant ('pæskjuːənt), *a. Her.* [f. L. *pascu-um* pasture, grazing + -ANT.] Said of deer, oxen, etc. represented as grazing.
c **1828** BERRY *Encycl. Herald.* I, *Pascuant*, or *Pasquant* (French *paissant*), is a term used for sheep, cows, &c. when feeding. **1882** CUSSANS *Her.* vi. (ed. 3) 90 *Pascuant*: Applied to Deer, Oxen, etc., when grazing.

pascuous ('pæskjuːəs), *a.* [ad. L. *pascuōs-us* abounding in pasture, f. *pascuum* pasture, grazing: cf. OF. *pascueux*.] = PASCUAL.
1656 BLOUNT *Glossogr.*, *Pascuous*, serving for pasture, or for feeding, or grazing of Beasts. **1866** *Treas. Bot.*, *Pascuous*, growing in pastures.

‖**pas devant les enfants** (pɑ dəvɑ̃ lezɑ̃fɑ̃). [F.] Not in front of the children, used of an expression or action that requires discretion. Also *transf.* and *ellipt.*, ***pas devant***, and as *adj.*
1951 N. MITFORD *Blessing* I. xv. 153 'Adultery is for when you're older, darling.' 'Oh I see. A sort of pas devant thing?' **1953** D. PARRY *Going Up—Going Down* i. 21 Mrs. Tyndale was holding forth in that extraordinary *pas-devant* French which the upper-class English used to speak so confidently. **1955** L. P. HARTLEY *Perfect Woman* vii. 65 'There's something I want to say to you. *Mais pas devant les enfants*,' he went on heavily. **1958** M. SPARK *Robinson* v. 51 'Pas devant,' said Tom Wells, casting his eyes towards the child. **1962** *Listener* 7 June 975/2 There is a sickening folklore of *pas devant*—'not in front of the children'—which excludes children from some of the very conversations that would show their parents as people with strong interests. **1962** *Times* 6 Aug. 9/3 It will be a mistake for the War Office to adopt a *pas devant les enfants* attitude. **1968** J. FLEMING *Kill or Cure* vii. 87 *Pas devant les enfants*; such bad form having rows before one's—friends. **1971** O. NORTON *Corpse-Bird Cries* v. 85 '*Pas devant les opérateurs*,' I said. I knew what manual [telephone] exchanges can be. **1974** J. JOHNSTON *How Many Miles to Babylon?* 7 'Dr. Desmond is an ass.' 'Frederick, pas devant—.' **1978** D. BLOODWORTH *Crosstalk* xxxix. 311 You mean *pas devant les enfants terribles*.. Not in front of the CIA?

pase, obs. form of PACE, PASS.

‖**pasear** (pase'ar), *v.* and *sb. slang* and *U.S. dial.* [See PASEO.] **A.** *vb. intr.* To take a paseo or walk. **B.** *sb.* = PASEO. Also *attrib.*
1840 R. H. DANA *Two Yrs. before Mast* xxviii. 313 He was going to paseár with our captain a little. **1847** *Calif. Star* (San Francisco) 24 July 2/3, I am told this *pasear* over the mountains, will cost the Commodore [Stockton] five thousand dollars. **1878** B. HARTE *Man on Beach* 112, I was reck'nin' on taking a little *pasear* with you. **1892** STEVENSON & OSBOURNE *Wrecker* xii. 192, I tell you, Mr. Dodd, it was a queer thing to see me and the old lady taking a *pasear* in the garden, and the old man scowling at us over the pickets. **1903** CONRAD & HUEFFER *Romance* III. iii. 141, I just come from taking a pasear that way. **1914** *Sunset* July 64/1 It was the pasear madness that made despairing feet give way to auto tires—it is the undiminishing nature of pasear joys that is stretching the eighteen-million-dollar highway through the state. **1948** *Popular Western* June 16/2 Yuh're takin' a little *pasear* to the penitentiary in Walla Walla.

pasel, dial., etc. var. PARCEL.

pasement, obs. f. PASSEMENT.

paseng, var. PASANG.

‖**paseo** (pa'seo). [Sp. *paseo* walk, *pasear* to walk.] In Spain and southwestern parts of the United States, a walk taken at a leisurely pace for exercise, amusement, or the like; any trip or outing of a similar nature; (concretely) a street or promenade; a parade, a procession, *spec.* at a bull-fight.
1832 W. IRVING *Leg. Alhambra* 111 An alameda, or public walk..not so fashionable as the more modern and splendid paseo of the Xenil. **1840** R. H. DANA *Two Yrs. before Mast* xxii. 219 The theme of..conversation..in our afternoon's *paséo* upon the beach, was the ship. **1897** 'H. S. MERRIMAN' *In Kedar's Tents* xviii. 205 He..proposed to Julia that they should take a 'paseo' in the garden. **1902** *Out West* Dec. 683 Such bosoming of motherly hills, knee-deep with winter wild flowers, as you may have unrolled to you in an afternoon's *paseo* from the metropolis. **1920** *Glasgow Herald* 22 Sept. 8/5 The greater companies..have built model towns, intersected with finely laid-out paseos and plazas, for their employees. **1927** E. HEMINGWAY *Men without Women* (1928) 29 They formed up for the paseo as soon as the bull had gone through. **1950** G. BRENAN *Face of Spain* ix. 187 It was the hour of the evening *paseo*: the girls were in their best frocks; the young men had oiled and smoothed their hair. **1967** MCCORMICK & MASCAREÑAS *Compl. Aficionado* iii. 72 You will now show me how to walk in the *paseo*. **1974** *Times* 2 May 17/2 Less than a decade ago, the *paseos* and boulevards were crowded on sunny days with strollers... Madrid has sacrificed these shady strolling places. **1976** E. P. BENSON *Bulls of Ronda* iv. 25 The stewards..led the *paseo*; the matadors were next, followed by the *bandilleros*... The bull..came charging into the arena. **1977** P. SOMERVILLE-LARGE *Eagles near Carcase* v. 91 Evening was being heralded..by the emergence of the *paseo*, if the three youths..and the four fat girls in black could be so described.

paseporte, pase-tyme, pas-flower, pasgarde: see PASSPORT, PASTIME, PASQUE-FLOWER, PASS-GUARD.

pash (pæʃ), *sb.*¹ *Obs.* exc. *dial.* A head.
1611 SHAKS. *Wint. T.* I. ii. 128 Thou want'st a rough pash, & the shoots that I haue, To be full like me. **1674–91** RAY *N.C. Wds.*, *Pash*, 'a mad pash', a mad-brain. *Chesh.* *a* **1697** CLELAND *Poems* 66 Some turning up their gay Mustachoes, And others robbing [i.e. rubbing] their dull pashes. **1719** RAMSAY *To Arbuckle* 118, I [wig-maker and poet] theek the out, and line the inside Of mony a douce and witty pash. **1836** J. STRUTHERS *Dychmont* II. 6 Where's Jock Arneil's lang witty pash? [In E.D.D. as *Scotch* and *Cheshire*.]

pash (pæʃ), *sb.*² Now chiefly *dial.* [f. PASH *v.*]
1. A smashing or crushing blow or stroke. *rare.*
1611 COTGR., *Gourmade*, a cuffe on the mouth, a pash on the nose.
2. A crashing blow or fall; a crash. Now *dial.*
1677 O. HEYWOOD *Diaries*, etc. (1883) III. 149 There was suddenly a pash of a chamber-floore. **1781** J. HUTTON *Tour to Caves* (ed. 2) Gloss., *Pash*, a sudden crash. **1828** *Craven Gloss.* (ed. 2), *Pash*. 'I fell wi sike a *pash*'.
3. A heavy fall or dash of rain or snow. *dial.*
1790 MARSHALL *Midl. Counties* (1796) II. Gloss. (E.D.S.), *Pash* (of rain), a heavy fall of rain. **1828** *Craven Gloss.* (ed. 2), *Pash*. 'We hev hed a sad pash last week'. **1885** *Q. Rev.* Apr. 350 The soil would have been run together like lime by a 'pash' of rain.
4. *transf.* 'The fragments produced by a smash' (E.D.D.), debris; hence, a collection, a medley, a great quantity or number.
1790 GROSE *Prov. Gloss.* Suppl., *Pash*, a great many. *North.* **1894** *Sat. Rev.* 14 Apr. 386 (*title of Article*) A Pash of Heraldry.

pash, *sb.*³ Aphetic form of CALIPASH.
1764 FOOTE *Patron* I. i, Not the meanest member of my corporation but can distinguish the pash from the pee.

pash (pæʃ), *sb.*⁴ and *a. colloq.* **A.** *sb.* Abbreviation of PASSION; esp. in phr. ***to have a pash for***, to be infatuated with, to have a 'crush' on; *transf.* a person who is the object of an infatuation. **B.** *adj.* Abbreviation of PASSIONATE *a.*
1914 *N.Y. World Mag.* 1 Nov. 5/6 There wasn't much 'pash' about it. **1920** F. SCOTT FITZGERALD *This Side of Paradise* (1921) 52 That isn't as pash as some of them. **1922** C. E. M. JOAD *Highbrows* iii. 102, I have met such a duck of a man. You'll never believe! I've quite a pash for him. **1924** P. MARKS *Plastic Age* 24 Let's go the movies... Gloria Nielsen is there and she's a pash baby. **1930** A. HUXLEY *Brief Candles* 217 Miss Figgis, the classical mistress, had been her pash for more than a year. **1930** WODEHOUSE *Very Good, Jeeves!* x. 257 The last bloke in the world..who you would think would ever fall a victim to the divine pash. **1934** G. GREENE *It's a Battlefield* 168 When you've got a pash for someone like I have, anybody's better than nothing. **1937** AUDEN & MACNEICE *Lett. from Iceland* 17 Sometimes containing frank demands for cash, Sometimes sly hints at a platonic pash. **1952** [see CRUSH *sb.* 2 d]. **1955** AUDEN *Shield of Achilles* i. 30 As when past Iseult's tower you floated The willow pash-notes of wanted Tristram. **1972** J. MCCLURE *Caterpillar Cop* xiii. 209 'You know her then?' 'Oh sure. Had a pash for her big sister once.' **1975** J. HITCHMAN *Such a Strange Lady* iii. 36 In her efforts to get over her 'pash' on Dr. Allen she became extremely bossy.

pash (pæʃ), *v.* Also 4 **passche**, 4–6 **pas(s)he**. [app., like many other vbs. in *-ash*, of onomatopœic origin: cf. BASH, SMASH. In sense 5 doubtfully related to Sw. dial. *paska*; see PASK.
A much used word (esp. in sense 2) from *c* 1575 for some 60 years; but now chiefly *dial*: see *Eng. Dial. Dict.*]
1. *trans.* To hurl or throw (something) violently, so as either to break it against something, or smash something with it; to dash. *Obs.* exc. *dial.*
1362 LANGL. *P. Pl.* A. v. 16 Piries and Plomtres weore passchet to þe grounde. **1590** GREENE *Orl. Fur.* (1599) 17 As the sonne of Saturne in his wrath Pasht all the mountaines at Typheus head. **1628** FORD *Lover's Mel.* I. i, And in that sorrow, As he was pashing it [the lute] against a tree, I suddenly stept in. **1876** *Mid Yorksh. Gloss.* s.v., To pash a thing is..to hurl or dash it violently, from a short distance.
2. To break or dash (a thing) in pieces or to atoms; to crush or smash by blows.
1377 LANGL. *P. Pl.* B. xx. 99 Deth cam dryuende after and al to doust passhed [*v.rr.* paschte, passhte] Kynges & kynȝtes kayseres and popes. *c* **1540** J. REDFORD *Mor. Play Wit & Sc.* (Shaks. Soc.) 8 Pash head, pash brayne, The knaves are slayne. **1628** GAULE *Pract. The.* (1629) 9 One should ryse from her Loynes..and pash that wily Serpents head. *a* **1693** *Urquhart's Rabelais* III. xxxiii. 282 It pasheth into pieces the Steel Sword. *a* **1825** FORBY *Voc. E. Anglia*, *Pash*, to beat any thing brittle into small fragments. **1875** BROWNING *Aristoph. Apol.* 843 Planed and studded club Once more has pashed competitors to dust.
3. To strike or knock violently, usually so as to bruise or smash. Also *absol.*
c **1440** *York Myst.* xlvi. 38 þei dusshed hym, þei dasshed hym,..þei pusshed hym, þei passhed hym. **1570–83** FOXE *A. & M.* 295/2 In the meane while the Christians..were pelted and pashed with stones by them which stood aboue. **1606** SHAKS. *Tr. & Cr.* II. iii. 213 If I goe to him, with my armed fist, Ile pash him ore the face. **1611** COTGR., *Gourmé*..cuffed on the mouth, pashed on the nose, or face. **1791** COWPER *Odyss.* XVIII. 119 His adversary on the neck Pash'd close beneath his ear; he split the bones. **1863** COWDEN CLARKE *Shaks. Char.* xiv. 362 Never wouldst thou ..have pashed that venerable face with the rude flint-stones.
b. With obj. of cognate meaning.
1602 *How man may chuse good wife* II. iii, *Per Jovem et Junonem! hoc* Shall pash his coxcomb such a knock.
4. To drive *out* by a violent blow, to dash *out* (brains, etc.).
1530 PALSGR. 653/2 He passhed out his braynes with a stone. **1587** HOLINSHED *Chron.* III. 79/2 They left him [Becket] not till they had cut and pashed out his braines. **1647** H. MORE *Song of Soul* Quot. xxiv. 199 So may their scattered Brain Pash'd from their cursed Sculls the Pavement stain. **1828** *Craven Gloss* (ed. 2) s.v., I'll pash thy brains out. **1855** BROWNING *Childe Roland* xii, 'Tis a brute must walk Pashing their [dock-leaves'] life out.
5. *intr.* Said of the dashing action of sudden heavy rain (now *dial.*); also of that of a wave upon a rock; and of the action of beating or striking water as by the feet of a horse (*rare*).
[With the last of these cf. ME. PASK, to dabble; but this sense does not appear to have come down dialectally, and Browning's use is prob. due to the exigency of rime.]
1589 [see PASHING below]. **1855** BROWNING *Up at a Villa* vii, There's a fountain to spout and splash!..horses with curling fish-tails, that prance and paddle and pash Round the lady atop in her conch. **1892** STOPF. BROOKE *Early Eng. Lit.* II. xvi. 87 The black sea waves pash and push upon it. **1903** in *Eng. Dial. Dict.* s.v., It [the rain] fair pash'd doon. The water was pashing out of the broken spout. The rain came pashing against the windows.
Hence '**pashed**, '**pashing** *ppl. adjs.*
1589 NASHE *Anat. Absurd.* 24 Yᵉ watrie clowdes with pashing showres vncessantlie, sending down their vnreasonable moysture. **1593** —— *Christ's T.* (1613) 39. **1606** SHAKS. *Tr. & Cr.* V. v. 10 Wauing his beame, Vpon the pashed courses of the Kings. **1828** *Craven Gloss.* (ed. 2), *Pashed*, dashed. **1847** *Bairusla Ann.* 12 (E.D.D.) Pashin' rain.

‖**pasha, pacha** ('pɑːʃə, 'pæ-, pə'ʃɑː). Forms: 7–8 **pascha**, 7 **passa**, 9 **pashaw**, **pacha**, 8– **pasha**. [Turkish *pāshā*, generally held to be the same as *bāshā* from *bāsh* head, chief, in some Eastern Turkish dialects *pāsh*. The form with *b* was app. the earlier, being that first adopted in Western languages: see BASHAW.
In Turkish there is no hard-and-fast line between the breath and voice stops; and in the case of *p*, *b*, the confusion is increased by the absence of *p* in Arabic and the occasional replacement of Persian and Turkish *p* by *b* (cf. *papoosh*, *pabouch*, *babouche*, etc): this may have conduced to interchange of *b*, *p*, and survival of the *p* in *pasha*. Some however think *pāshā* and *bāshā* originally distinct words (cf. quot. 1687); Zenker distinguishes *bāshā*, the officer of the Janizaries, from *pāshā*, which is now largely a civil title; but Barbier says that the title, in either form, was under the ancient régime exclusively a military one. The best Turkish scholars think there is no ground for connecting the word in

any way with Pers. *pādshah* king or emperor, Turkish *pādishah* the Sultan.]

Hist. A title formerly borne in Turkey by officers of high rank, as military commanders, and governors of provinces. Formerly, esp. in the case of military commanders, written BASHAW.

There were three grades of pashas, formerly distinguished by the number of horse-tails displayed as a symbol in war; the highest grade (of three tails) corresponding to a commanding general, admiral, or governor of equivalent rank; the second (of two tails) to a general of division or vice-admiral, etc.; the third (of one tail) to a general of brigade, rear-admiral, or naval officer of corresponding rank.

[For earlier quotations (1534–1860) see BASHAW.]

1646 CRASHAW *Deo Nostro* (1652) 193 The aged Pascha pleads not years, But spies love's dawn, and disappears. **1687** *Lond. Gaz.* No. 2219/2 The Chiaus Bassa is made a Passa, which is a Preferment to his Loss. **1717** LADY M. W. MONTAGU *Let. to Abbé Conti* 17 May, Every pasha has his Jew, who is his *homme d'affaires*. **1808** A. PARSONS *Trav.* i. 4 The price of bread..is fixed by the pashaw of the province. **1822** SHELLEY *Hellas* 565 The freedman..has beat back the Pacha of Negropont. **1848** THACKERAY *Bk. Snobs* iv, I am like the Pasha of three tails. **1867** LADY HERBERT *Cradle L.* i. 3 The rest of the party went on to see the Pacha of Egypt's Palace.

Hence **pasha-like** *a.*, like or after the manner of a pasha. **pashadom**, the domain, realm, or estate of pashas.

1849 E. B. EASTWICK *Dry Leaves* 172, I..began to feel quite supreme and Pashá-like. **1883** *Pall Mall G.* 24 Nov. 1/2 On the 23rd of October last year I was at Cairo... Pashadom seemed fairly ablaze with decorations and ribbons. **1885** *Manch. Exam.* 24 July 5/3 The Sultan and all pashadom have been filled with growing anxiety and concern.

pashalic, pachalic (ˈpɑːʃælɪk, pəˈʃɑːlɪk), *sb.* (*a.*) Also -lick, -lik. [Turkish *pāshālik*, from *-lik*, suffix of quality or condition.] The jurisdiction of a pasha; the district governed by a pasha.

1745 POCOCKE *Descr. of East* II. I. 76 The place of residence of the pasha of this country, on which account it was called the pashalic of Saphet. **1802** *Edin. Rev.* I. 52 A pachalic is divided, for military purposes, into certain districts, called sangiacs, or standards. **1813** BYRON *Br. Abydos* II. xv, Abdallah's Pachalick was gain'd. **1894** *Times* 11 Oct. 10/6 In September, 1877, he was appointed Consul for the pashalics of Adana, Aleppo, and Tripoli, residing at Aleppo.

B. as *adj.* Of or pertaining to a pasha.

1863 WOOLNER *Beautiful Lady* 129 Seizing pachalic power by a swift blow. **1884** *Manch. Exam.* 16 Feb. 4/7 There is to be an end to military exactions and Pashalic oppression [in the Soudan].

†**pashe.** *Obs.* Also 6 paishe. App. short for *passion*, in the asseveration 'for the pashe of God': cf. the full 'for the passion of God', by the same speaker in IV. iii.

a **1553** UDALL *Royster D.* IV. iii, Nay for the paishe of God, let me now treate peace. *Ibid.* vii, Backe for the pashe of God, backe sirs. *Ibid.* viii, *R. Royster.* Away, or else die we shall. *M. Mery.* Away for the pashe of our sweet Lord Iesus Christ. *Ibid.* v. v.

pashe, pashion, obs. ff. PASCH, PASSION.

‖**pashm** (ˈpæʃ(ə)m). [Pers. *pashm* wool, down.] The under-fur of hairy quadrupeds in the elevated lands north of the Himalayas, esp. that of the goat, which is the material of Cashmere shawls. So ‖**pashmina** (pæʃˈmiːnə) [Pers. *pashmīn* adj., woollen].

1880 MRS. A. G. F. E. JAMES *Ind. Indust.* xxxi. 364 The *pashm*, or shawl-wool, is a downy substance, growing next to the skin and under the thick hair of those goats found in Thibet and in the elevated lands north of the Himalayas. **1885** BALFOUR *Cycl. India* III. 154 Pashm and pashmina are specially applied to the fine shawl-wool of Turfan and Changthan. **1893** *R. Nat. Hist.* (ed. Lydekker) I. 7 This under-fur is greatly developed in Mammals of all groups inhabiting Tibet, where it is locally known as 'pashm'; and it is this pashm of the goat of these regions which affords the materials for the celebrated Kashmir shawls.

‖**Pashto** (ˈpaʃtoː), **Pushtoo, -tu** (ˈpʌʃtuː), *sb.* and *a.* Also **Pakhto, -tu, Pushto.** [a. Pers. *paʃtō*, Afghan *păχtō*.

(The second consonant, written as *sin* with dot above and below, is pronounced by Western Afghans nearly as Pers. *shin* (ʃ or *sh*), by Eastern Afghans nearly as (x or *kh*); hence the name has been also transliterated as *Pukhto*, *Pakhtu*, *Pukshto*, and in many other ways. See Lepsius *Standard Alphabet*, and the Grammars and Dictionaries of Raverty, Trumpff, Bellew, Lorimer, etc.)]

The native name of the language of the Afghans, intermediate in character between the Iranian and Sanskritic families of the Aryan languages.

1784 H. VANSITTART *Let.* 3 Mar. in *Asiatick Researches* (1790) II. 67 A book written in the Pushto language by Husain. *Ibid.* 68, I also submit a specimen of their language, which is called by them Pukhto; but this word is softened in Persian into Pushto. **1790** *Asiatick Researches* II. 76 The Pushto language, of which I have seen a dictionary, has a manifest resemblance to the Chaldaick. **1815** ELPHINSTONE *Acc. Caubul* II. ii. 168 The principal person present.. repeats a Pushtoo verse, importing that 'Events are with God, but deliberation is allowed to man'. **1841** J. WILSON in G. Smith *Life* vii. (1878) 153 He talks nothing but Persian and Pushtoo. **1859** C. FORSTER *New Key for Recov. Lost Ten Tribes* 242 *note*, The Dictionary of the Pushtoo language. **1878** R. N. CUST *Lang. E. Indies* 29 The Pushtu, or Pakhtu, is the Language of the Afghans or Putáns. **1933** L. BLOOMFIELD *Lang.* 62 *Afghan* (*Pushto*), with some 4 million speakers. **1939** L. H. GRAY *Found. Lang.* 320 Besides Persian, the Modern Iranian dialects are Kurdish.., Balōčī and Afghān or Puštū, each with two principal sub-divisions, and..Ossetic. **1955** *Times* 25 May 10/3 The demand for the independence of the Pakhto- (or Pushtu-)speaking people could possibly assume some apparent validity. **1956** J. WHATMOUGH *Language* 29 In the Pamirs dialects of Persian proper and some related dialects as Kurdish, Pashtu (in Afghanistan).., also have maintained their hold. **1962** CHAVARRIA-AGUILAR & PENZL in Householder & Saporta *Probl. Lexicogr.* 238 Pashto is taught in the elementary schools of West Pakistan's Pashto-speaking areas. **1964** H. H. PAPER tr. *Shafeev's Short Gramm. Outl. Pashto* Introd., Pashto is the language of the people who inhabit Afghanistan and the northwest part of Pakistan. The Afghans themselves call their language paṣ̌tó (in the east paxtó). **1965** *Language* XLI. 529 Only very rarely is there a discrepancy between the Pashto examples and the English translations. **1973** *Times* 22 Mar. (Pakistan Suppl.) p. ii/2 In Karachi, the provincial capital, Urdu-speakers probably account for about 70 per cent of the population, with Punjabis and Pashto-speakers—the latter mainly members of an itinerant Pathan labour force—making up a further 20 per cent. **1974** *Times* 30 Apr. 7/7 It should be ascertained whether the Pushto-speaking people wanted to stay with Pakistan, merge with Afghanistan or have an independent country.

Pashtun, var. PAKHTUN.

pasigraphy (pəˈsɪgrəfɪ). [irreg. f. Gr. πᾶσι for all + -GRAPHY.] A name given to a system of writing proposed for universal use, with characters representing ideas instead of words, so as to be (like the ordinary numerals 1, 2, 3, etc.) intelligible to persons of all languages. Applied originally to a system proposed in 1796; subsequently to others having a similar object.

1796 in *Monthly Rev.* XIX. 357 *Pasigraphy*, from πᾶσι *to all* and γράφω *I write*, will not explain the sounds of any known language but the sense of the words of every language, even of that which people have never learnt. **1797** T. BROWN in Welsh *Life* i. (1825) 35. **1801** *Sk. Paris as it was* II. xl. 45 It is also in contemplation to teach a blind pupil pasigraphy, or universal language, invented by Demaimieux. **1805** *Med. Jrnl.* XIV. 189 Essay on geological Pasigraphy, or on the manner of representing the phenomena of the stratification of the rocks, by perfectly simple signs. **1870** BACHMAIER *Pasigraph. Dict. & Gram.* Introd., Pasigraphy teaches people to communicate with one another in writing by means of numbers, which convey the same ideas in all languages.

Hence **ˈpasigraph** *v. trans.*, to express or represent in pasigraphy; **pasiˈgraphic, -ical** *adjs.*, of or pertaining to pasigraphy.

1796 in *Monthly Rev.* XIX. 357 At the end of a very few hours, any intelligent person may pasigraph his own idiom, by consulting the method, characters, and the twelve invariable rules. **1797** W. TAYLOR in *Monthly Rev.* XXIV. 563 Over each column is stationed one letter of the pasigraphic alphabet. **1804** —— in *Crit. Rev.* Ser. III. I. 382 The figures of arithmetic are already pasigraphic. **1839** *Proc. Amer. Philol. Soc.* I. 121 The Chinese alphabet forms a sort of pasigraphic system. **1852** JERDAN *Autobiog.* II. 221. **1870** BACHMAIER (*title*) Pasigraphical Dictionary and Grammar.

pasilaly (ˈpæsɪlælɪ). *rare.* [irreg. f. Gr. πᾶσι for all + -λαλια speaking.] A spoken language for universal use.

1805 W. TAYLOR in *Ann. Rev.* III. 14 It appears that the Indians have invented, what a recent French writer calls a *pasilaly*, a method of talking to people of all languages, without understanding theirs. **1864** in WEBSTER.

†**pask**, *v. Obs.* [Appears to be cognate with mod.Sw. dial. *paska* to dabble in water (Rietz); cf. Norw. *baska* in same sense: cf. also PASH *v.*, PLASH *v.*] *intr.* To dabble or plash (in water).

c **1305** *St. Andrew* 8 in *E.E.P.* (1862) 98 Here nettes gonne forsake And suede him.. Hem was so betere þan to pasken in þe water iwis While oure louerd an vrþe was.

pask, -e, pasmain, obs. ff. PASCH, PASSEMENT.

†**pasme.** *Obs. rare.* [a. OF. *pasme* (Godef.) swoon, faint = Pr. *pasme*, Sp., Pg. *pasmo* (and *espasmo*), It. *spasimo*:—L. *spasmus* SPASM *sb.*, treated as *ex-pasmus*, *pasmus*, and with altered meaning; cf. mod.F. *pâmer* to faint.] A swoon.

1591 GREENE *Farew. Folly* Wks. (Grosart) IX. 315 Semyramis no sooner heard of the death of hir husbande, but she fell into a pasme, and was hardly brought to life.

pasment, obs. f. PASSEMENT.

pasmo (ˈpæzməʊ). [Amer. Sp., f. Sp. *pasmo* spasm.] A disease of flax, first reported from the Argentine in 1911, caused by the fungus *Mycosphaerella linorum*, and distinguished by circular brown or yellowish lesions on the leaves and stems of the plants affected. Also *attrib.*

1926 W. E. BRENTZEL in *Jrnl. Agric. Res.* XXXII. 25 (*title*) The pasmo disease of flax. *Ibid.*, The disease of flax called 'pasmo' in South America..caused great injury to flax in Argentina. **1942** *N.Z. Jrnl. Sci. & Technol.* A. XXIV. 102 Pasmo disease of flax is of almost world-wide occurrence. **1946** *Nature* 16 Nov. 723/1 The dreaded Pasmo disease was first described from the Argentine in 1911, reached Europe in 1936, and spread to five countries by 1942. **1958** *New Biol.* XXVII. 21 A number of fungi responsible for causing diseases of flax are seed-borne. The principal parasites in this group and the diseases they cause are..*Botrytis cinerea* Fr. (grey mould),..and *Sphaerella linorum* Wollenw. (pasmo). **1974** E. C. STACEY *Peace Country Heritage* ii. 121 They [*sc.* flax varieties] had been bred for resistance to pasmo and other diseases.

pasmond, obs. f. PASSEMENT.

pasnep(pe, -nepe, obs. ff. PARSNIP.

paso (ˈpaso). [Sp.] An image, or group of images, representing Passion scenes, carried in procession as part of Holy Week observances in Spain.

1923 *Chambers's Jrnl.* Apr. 213/1 Away goes the paso across the square. **1939** SPENDER & GILI tr. *Lorca's Poems* 19 (*title*) Paso. *Ibid.* 141 [Note] *Paso*, image, or group of images, representing a scene from the Passion of Christ, carried in procession during Holy Week, particularly in Andalusia. **1950** G. BRENAN *Face of Spain* viii. 178 Making our way into another church, we found the *pasos*, or floats holding images, pulled out into the nave in preparation for the Easter processions. *Ibid.*, One particularly large *paso*, supported on cart wheels, showed the scene of Christ being whipped by Roman soldiers. **1970** 'D. HALLIDAY' *Dolly & Cookie Bird* x. 155 The procession..got moving again...the paso of the poor hunting bishop [*sc.* St. Hubert] came rollicking past.

paso doble (ˌpaso ˈdoble). Also (erron.) **pasa doble**, and as one word. [f. Sp. *paso* step + *doble* double.] A quick Spanish dance-step; the music for such a dance.

1927 V. SILVESTER *Mod. Ballroom Dancing* 121 The *Paso Doble* is danced very little in this country, but it is popular in certain parts of the Continent. It is often referred to as the Spanish one-step. The walk is short and springy, not unlike a very modified Quickstep. **1934** C. LAMBERT *Music Ho!* II. 94 The Russian folk dance gives way to the pasodoblé of the street band. **1939** E. AMBLER *Mask of Dimitrios* vi. 101 An accordion band was playing a *paso-doble*. **1948** F. BORROWS *Theory & Technique Lat.-Amer. Dancing* iv. 156 Paso Doble music is in march time. **1955** W. GADDIS *Recognitions* III. iii. 771 An old man with a battered guitar..had two tunes, one a vaguely recognizable pasa doble. **1959** *Listener* 18 June 1059/2 The band plays a tinny *paso doble*. **1971** *New Scientist* 22 Apr. 219/1 The only sensuality indulged.. would be a quick routine or two from the pas a doble [*sic*] or the slow foxtrot. **1973** *Times* 23 Apr. 6/2 The baby-faced couples who dance the samba..and Pasodoble..are sometimes a bit short of Latin-American fire. **1974** *Times* 7 Jan. 5/8 There is Italian smooch-song and Spanish light music, pasadoble and tango. **1975** 'M. FONTEYN' *Autobiogr.* I. iii. 35 At every tea-dance in the..Hotel we waltzed and fox-trotted and danced the *paso-doble*, he so tall and me a little shrimp of eleven years.

paspalum (ˈpæspələm). [mod.L. (Linnæus *Systema Naturæ* (ed. 10, 1759) II. 855), f. Gk. πάσπαλος a kind of millet.] An annual or perennial grass of the genus so called, native to warm regions, especially South America, and cultivated elsewhere for fodder. Also *attrib.*

1772 R. WESTON *Universal Botanist* III. 547 Round-flowered American Paspalum. **1857** *Ann. Rep. Mass. Board Agric.* IV. 84 Hairy Slender Paspalum..has an erect or decumbent, slender culm, from one to two feet high. **1884** G. VASEY *Agric. Grasses U.S.* 31 *Paspalum laeve.* (Smooth paspalum.) This species grows from 2 to 4 feet high... *Paspalum dilitatum.* (Hairy-flowered paspalum.) **1906** *Chambers's Jrnl.* 24 Feb. 207/2 Paspalum Grass..has been known in the United States since 1880, where it is called hairy and flowered paspalum. **1926** *Brit. Weekly* 12 Aug. 392/3 There's a corner of paspalum down there on the creek that would do your two eyes good to see. **1929** *Contrib. U.S. Nat. Herbarium* XXVIII. I. 4 Paspalum-grass..was introduced into the southern United States from Uruguay or Argentina about the middle of the last century. *Ibid.* 5 The seeds of paspalum are eaten by a large number of birds. **1940** A. UPFIELD *Bushranger of Skies* x. 111 Bony stepped off the veranda..and..trod the yielding paspalum grass lawn to arrive at the bottom fence. **1962** *Coast to Coast 1961–62* 94 In no time weeds and paspalum had hidden the grave. **1970** A. T. SEMPLE *Grassland Improvement* 381/2 Brownseed paspalum. **1977** *N.Z. Jrnl. Agric.* Jan. 52/3 Rhizomatous grasses—such as paspalum..—are not controlled with paraquat.

paspy, var. PASSEPIED.

pasque, var. PASCH, Easter.

pasque-flower (ˈpɑːskˌflaʊə(r), -æ-). Forms: α. 6–7 Passe-, 7 Pas-flower. β. 6- pasque-, 7–8 pasch-flower. [Orig. *passeflower*, a. F. *passefleur* (1539 R. Estienne) 'a variety of anemone' (Hatz.-Darm.); changed by Gerarde to *pasque-flower*, after *pasque*, PASCH, Easter.] A species of Anemone (*A. Pulsatilla*) growing on chalk downs in England, and elsewhere in Europe, blossoming in April, with bell-shaped purple flowers clothed with silky hairs. Called also *pasque-anemone*.

With distinctive adjuncts the name is applied to other species of Anemone, as the **American pasque-flower**, *A. patens*, var. *Nuttaliana*; **Japanese p.**, the Autumnal Anemone, *A. Japonica*.

α. **1578** LYTE *Dodoens* III. lxxv. 422 Passeflower or the first Anemone, hath leaves like Coriander. **1597** GERARDE *Herbal* II. lxxiii. 309 Passe flower is called..after the Latin name Pulsatill, or Flawe flower. **1611** COTGR., *Passe-fleur*, the Passeflower, bastard Anemone, or Windflower. **1651** J. F[REAKE] *Agrippa's Occ. Philos.* 39 Poisonous things delight in the Plant called Pas-flower. **1658** PHILLIPS, *Passe-flower*, a certain kind of flower, otherwise called Pulsatil.

β. **1597** GERARDE *Herbal* II. lxxiii. 309 They flower for the most part about Easter, which hath moved me to name it Pasque flower, or Easter flower. **1629** PARKINSON *Paradisus*

201 The yellow Pasque flower... Red Pasque flower... White Pasque flower. **1785** MARTYN *Rousseau's Bot.* xxi. (1794) 301 The Pasque-flower, so called from its flowering about Easter,..adorns some of our dry chalky hills, with its beautiful bell-shaped purple flowers. **1854** S. THOMSON *Wild Fl.* III. (ed. 4) 175 The pasque-flower, purple anemone.

pasquil ('pæskwɪl), *sb.* Also 6 **pasqual**, 7 **pasquell**. [ad. med.L. *Pasquillus*, ad. It. *Pasquillo*, dim. of *Pasquino*; in F. *Pasquille*: see PASQUIN.

The L. form is known as early as 1509: see PASQUIN. The Fr. appears in *Les Visions de Pasquille*, 1547 (Ebert).]

†**1.** = PASQUIN 1. *Obs.*

1533 ELYOT *Wise Man* Proheme A v, For there be Gnathos in Spayne as wel as in Grece, Pasquilles in Englande as welle as in Rome. —— *Pasquil the playne* A ij, Pasquille is an olde Romane, but by longe sittinge in the strete, and hering market men chat, he is become rude and homely. **1551** T. WILSON *Logike* (1580) 67 These two verses were written to the Pope, as worthie such a one, and sette upon Pasquillus in Roome. **1609** DEKKER *Gvlls Horne-bk.* I. (1862) 9 I'm the Pasquil's madcap that will do it. **1616** R. CARPENTER *Past. Charge* 66 Making the Pulpit often-times a Pasquill to ease their spleenes. **1651** WELDON *Crt. K. Chas.* 205 The Councell Table was growne more like a Pasquil then a grave Senate.

2. A lampoon posted up in a public place; any circulated or published lampoon; a pasquinade.

1542 *St. Papers Hen. VIII*, IX. 12 Here hathe been also after the maner of Rome, a pasqual set up upon Sainct Marques day laste, tantynge thEmperour. **1589** COOPER *Admon.* 56 The Libeller to set out his *Pasquill*, raketh all things. **1612** T. JAMES *Jesuits' Downf.* 38 They blame others for Libells and verie vnpriestly Pasquils, and yet write themselues. **1709** STEELE *Tatler* No. 92 ¶1 All the Pasquils, Lampoons and Libels, we meet with now-a-days. **1865** WRIGHT *Hist. Caricature* xix. 315 The pasquils formed a body of satire which struck indiscriminately at everybody within its range.

3. *attrib.* and *Comb.*, as ***pasquil-maker***, ***-pulpit***.

c **1642** A. BROME *On Death J. Shute* 35 Nor such as into pasquill pulpits come With thundering non sence, but to beat the drum To civil wars. **1770** BARETTI *Journ. Genoa* II. 1 They only put one in mind of the Pasquil-makers of Rome or the Monthly and Critical Reviewers of England.

Hence **pa'squillic** *a.*, of the nature of a pasquil.

1833 CARLYLE *Misc.* (1872) V. 66 Verse (be it heroic, be it pasquillic).

†**'pasquil**, *v. Obs.* [f. prec. sb.] **a.** *intr.* To compose pasquils. **b.** *trans.* To libel or satirize in a pasquil; to lampoon.

1621 BURTON *Anat. Mel.* I. ii. IV. iv. (1651) 148 Princes.. are grievously vexed with these pasquelling libels and satyrs. **1643** HOWELL *Twelve Treat.* (1661) 268 In Holland and other places he was pasquill'd at. *a* **1648** LD. HERBERT *Hen. VIII* (1683) 609 There wanted not some, who took occasion to pasquil it.

So **'pasquillant** *sb.*, the writer of a pasquil; *adj.* lampooning; **'pasquiller**, the composer of a pasquil or pasquils.

1817 COLERIDGE *Biog. Lit.* (1870) 204 [The character] of a gossip, backbiter and pasquillant. **1833** CARLYLE *Misc.* (1872) V. 125 A Pasquillant verse. **1597–8** BP. HALL *Sat.* V. i. 14 Or Lucile's muse.. Or Menips old, or Pasquillers of late. *a* **1659** OSBORN *Luther Vind.* Wks. (1673) 408 This favour..did so work with him, and the rest of the Pasquillers of the time, that..none used the like Invectives.

Pasquin ('pæskwɪn), *sb.* [ult. ad. It. *Pasquino*, in L. *Pasquinus*, F. *Pasquin*.

Pasquino or *Pasquillo* was the name popularly given to a mutilated statue, or piece of ancient statuary, disinterred at Rome in the year 1501, and set up by Cardinal Caraffa at the corner of his palace near the Piazza Navona. Under his patronage, it became the annual custom on St. Mark's Day to 'restore' temporarily and dress up this torso to represent some historical or mythological personage of antiquity; on which occasion professors and students of the newly restored Ancient Learning were wont to salute Pasquin in Latin verses which were usually posted or placed on the statue. In process of time these *pasquinate* or pasquinades tended to become satirical, and the term began to be applied, not only in Rome, but in other countries, to satirical compositions and lampoons, political, ecclesiastical, or personal, the anonymous authors of which often sheltered themselves under the conventional name of Pasquin. According to Mazocchi, in the preface to the printed collection of the *pasquinate* of 1509, the name Pasquino or Pasquillo originated in that of a schoolmaster ('*literator seu magister ludi*') who lived opposite the spot where the statue was found; a later tradition given by Castelvetro, 1558–9, made Pasquino a caustic tailor or shoemaker; another of 1544 calls him a barber. See L. Morandi in *Nuova Antologia* 1889 I. 271, 755, D. Gnoli *ibid.* 1890 I. 51, 275, *Storia di Pasquino*. The latinized form *Pasquillus* was already *a* 1544 applied both to the author and the pasquinade, in which extended application it was subseq. followed also by *Pasquin*.]

1. The Roman Pasquino (man or statue), on whom pasquinades were fathered; hence, the imaginary personage to whom anonymous lampoons were conventionally ascribed.

1566 (*title*) Pasquine in a Traunce. A Christian and learned Dialogue.. Wherunto are added certayne Questions then put forth by Pasquine, to haue beene disputed in the Councell of Trent. **1581** ALLEN *Apol. Eng. Colleges* 97 b, Neither the Old Comedie, nor Pasquino, nor any ruffian or Carneuall-youth in Rome. **1592** WOTTON in *Reliq.* (1685) 680 The Gabell of Sixtus's time, which Pasquin told him of. **1617** MORYSON *Itin.* I. 135 At one end of this market place, in a corner of a street opposite to a publike Pallace, is the statua of Pasquin, vpon a wall of a priuate house. **1670** LASSELS *Voy. Italy* II. 229 This Pasquin is an old broken statue..jeering wits set up here, and father upon poore Messer Pasquino, their Satyrical jeasts, called from him, Pasquinades. **1686** DRYDEN *Addr. Higden* 2 The Grecian wits, who Satire first began, Were pleasant Pasquins on the life of man. *a* **1797** H. WALPOLE *Mem. Geo. II*, I. 283 If Pasquin has seen wittier, he never saw more severe or less delicate lampoons. **1885** *Encycl. Brit.* XVIII. 341 The 16th century was indeed Pasquin's palmy time, and in not a few of the rare printed collections of his utterances Protestant polemic..is mingled.

attrib. **1582** T. WATSON *Centurie of Loue* lxxxi, A Pasquine piller erected in the despite of Loue.

†**2.** = PASQUINADE, PASQUIL 2. *Obs.*

1611 FLORIO, *Pasquino*, an old statue in Rome on whom all Satires, Pasquins, rayling rimes or libels are fastned and fathered. **1653** A. WILSON *Jas. I* 53 On him some unhappy Wit vented this Pasquin. **1692** LUTTRELL *Brief Rel.* (1857) II. 371 Wrote from Rome, the French had caused a pasquin to be fixt reflecting on the pope for conniving at the protestant alliance against his eldest son. *a* **1745** SWIFT *Answ. Sheridan* 32 Wks. 1841 I. 761/1 But enough of this poetry Alexandrine; I hope you will not think this a pasquine.

Hence **'pasquin** *v. trans.* [= It. *pasquinare* (Florio); F. *pasquiner*], to lampoon, pasquinade.

1682 DRYDEN & LEE *Duke of Guise* Ded., Not..that any Man delights to see himself pasquin'd and affronted by their inveterate Scriblers.

pasquinade (pæskwɪ'neɪd), *sb.* [ad. It. *pasquinata*: cf. F. *pasquinade*, and see PASQUIN and -ADE.] A lampoon affixed to some public place; a 'squib', libel, lampoon, or piece of satire generally.

[**1592** WOTTON in *Reliq.* (1685) 656 A *Pasquinata* set forth against him in form of a Prophesie.] **1658** PHILLIPS, *Pasquinade*, a Satyrical Invective or Libel, savoring of the Pasquin at Rome. **1711** ADDISON *Spect.* No. 23 ¶4 This Pasquinade made a great Noise in Rome. **1760–72** H. BROOKE *Fool of Qual.* (1809) III. 136 The very person who ..contrived the honour of the pasquinade on my back this day. **1843** PRESCOTT *Mexico* VII. i. (1864) 411 The white walls of the barracks were covered with epigrams and pasquinades levelled at Cortez. **1934** W. GERHARDI *Resurrection* xv. 43 A man famous for his evil tongue came up and..delivered himself of a long pasquinade at the expense of my friend. **1946** W. S. MAUGHAM *Then & Now* xxxv. 204 A cold shiver ran down his spine at the thought of the pasquinades, the epigrams that his misadventure would suggest. **1977** *Times Lit. Suppl.* 6 May 572/1 The famous pasquinade: 'quod non fecerunt barbari fecerunt Barberini'.

attrib. **1858** BORROW *Rom. Rye* I. 10 A pasquinade picture was stuck up at Rome.

pasquinade (pæskwɪ'neɪd), *v.* [f. prec. sb.] *trans.* To satirize or libel in a pasquinade.

1796 *Sporting Mag.* VII. 312 One of the candidates..has already been pasquinaded. **1880** DISRAELI *Endym.* i. 5 We dined and voted together, and together pasquinaded our opponents.

pasquinader (pæskwɪ'neɪdə(r)). [f. prec. sb. or vb. + -ER[1].] **a.** A writer of pasquinades. **b.** (*nonce-use*). A collector of pasquinades.

1862 BURTON *Bk. Hunter* (1882) 19 He was not a black-letter man..or a pasquinader. **1888** *N. & Q.* 7th Ser. V. 511/1 Pasquinaders often maintained that the more hidden the allusion the more terrible the import.

†**pasqui'nado.** *Obs. rare*[−1]. [See -ADO.] = PASQUINADE *sb.*

1600 O. E. *Rep. Libel* III. Pref. 2 His great practise and skill in Pasquinadoes.

pa'squinian, *a. rare.* [See -IAN.] Of, pertaining to, or characteristic of Pasquin; pertaining to a pasquin, satirical.

1796 BURNEY *Mem. Metastasio* I. 189 You have exhausted all your..friendship, in transports of true Pasquinian passion in my defence.

pass (pɑːs, -æ-), *sb.*[1] Also 4 **pas**, **pase**, 5 **paas**, 5–6 **passe**. [In ME. *pas*, *paas*, a. F. *pas*:—L. *passus* step, pace, track, trace, etc. Orig. the same word as PACE; in later use often associated with PASS *v.*, and thus in some senses not easily separated from PASS *sb.*[2], F. *passe*.]

I. Obs. senses: = PACE, PASSUS.

†**1.** Occasional spelling of *pas*, PACE *sb.*[1] (in various senses), q.v.

a **1300** *Cursor M.* 10970, I and mi wijf on ald tas, Of barns er we passed þe pass [*v.r.* pas]. **1375** BARBOUR *Bruce* VII. 203 Till hym thai ȝeid a full great pass. *c* **1400** MAUNDEV. (Roxb.) xi. 41 Fra þe kirke of þe sepulcre..ane aght score passez es þe temple *Domini*. **1615** CHAPMAN *Odyss.* IX. 734 A little pass Beyond our fore-deck from the fall there was.

†**2.** A passage (in a narrative or writing); a canto of a poem, a chapter, section, or division of a book; = PACE *sb.*[1] 12, PASSUS.

c **1350** *Will. Palerne* 161 þus passed is þe first pas of þis pris tale. *a* **1400–50** *Alexander* 2845 Here a passe endes. **1546** GARDINER *Declar. Art. Joye* 27 So as in thys passe of saynt Paule, saynte Chrisostome is verye dylygente to note and conferme vnto vs. **1553** KENNEDY *Compend. Tract.* iii, It is to be notit of this pas of Scripture abone rehersit. **1573** *Reg. Privy Council Scot.* Ser. I. II. 275 In quhilk Act, besyde mony utheris passis and claussis,..it is statute and ordanit [etc.]. **1633** *Sc. Acts Chas. I* (1817) V. 152/1 Dispenssis for ever In all..heades articles claussis obleisments pointes passis..of the samyn. **1647** N. BACON *Disc. Govt. Eng.* Prol. ¶7 A summary view of the cardinal passes of the government of this Kingdom.

II. A passage.

3. A way or opening by which one passes through a region otherwise obstructed or impassable, or through any natural or artificial barrier. *esp.* **a.** A narrow and difficult or dangerous passage through a mountainous region or over a mountain range; also (less usually) through a forest, marsh, bog, or other impassable ground.

In ME. applied to a road or passage in a wood, over a heath, etc., such as was exposed to ambush, robbery, etc.; in its later application prob. a re-adoption from mod.F. *pas*.

a **1300** *Cursor M.* 2519 þan he broght þam til a pase [*G.* pas] þat men cald in þ[at l]and temase [*v.r.* themas]. *c* **1325** *Metr. Hom.* 52 In our gat lis Satenas Wit his felawes, als thef in pas. **1340** HAMPOLE *Pr. Consc.* 1239 Thefs and out-lawes, ..þat hald pases, and robbes and reves Men of þat þai have. **1377** LANGL. *P. Pl.* B. XIV. 300 þe sexte is a path of pees: ȝe, þorw þe pas of altoun Pouerte myȝte passe withoute peril of robbynge. **1390** GOWER *Conf.* III. 208 Into the pas whanne he was falle, Thembuisschementz tobrieken alle. **1538** *St. Papers Hen. VIII*, III. 7, I have cut divers pases, and made suche smothe wayes. **1680** MORDEN *Geog. Rect.*, *Piedmont* (1685) 205 Pignerol..a Commodious Pass from France to Italy. **1703** MAUNDRELL *Journ. Jerus.* (1732) 35 Having gone thro' a very rugged and uneven Pass. **1806** *Gazetteer Scotl.* (ed. 2) 226 Glentilt; a pass in the Highlands of Athol, famous for..the dangerous road which runs through it. **1810** SCOTT *Lady of L.* V. iii, The guide, abating of his pace, Led slowly through the pass's jaws. **1833** *Penny Cycl.* I. 388/2 The chief pass of the Lepontian Alps is that of the St. Gothard... The height of the pass is 6890 feet. **1851** TURNER *Dom. Archit.* I. 106 The wooded pass of Alton on the borders of Surrey and Hampshire, which was not disafforested until the end of Henry's reign, was a favourite ambush for outlaws, who there awaited the merchants and their trains of sumpter-horses travelling to or from Winchester.

fig. *c* **1500** *Melusine* 31 But ones as he said he shuld passe the cruell paas of the deth. **1864** TENNYSON *Aylmer's F.* 209 But Edith's eager fancy hurried with him Snatch'd thro' the perilous passes of his life.

b. esp. in *Mil.* Such a passage viewed strategically as commanding the entrance into a country or place; hence, by extension, any place which commands or holds the key to such entrance. Also *fig.*, and in various phrases, as ***to gain, hold, keep the pass***. †***pass of arms*** [F. *pas d'armes*]: see quot. 1727–41. ***to sell the pass***: see SELL *v.* 7 g.

1683 KENNETT tr. *Erasm. on Folly* 98 They would be able to keep their Pass and fence off all assault of Conviction. **1684** *Scanderbeg Rediv.* v. 108 The City Mohilow on the Dniester, a place of great Importance, as being the pass into Moldavia. *a* **1704** T. BROWN *Sat. agst. Woman* Wks. 1730 I. 56 Thus all the unguarded passes of his mind she'll try. **1727–41** CHAMBERS *Cycl.*, *Pass of arms*, in chivalry, a place which the ancient knights undertook to defend, *e.gr.* a bridge, road, &c. which was not to be passed without fighting the person who kept it. **1751** JOHNSON *Rambler* No. 165 ¶2 The passes of the intellect are barred against her by prejudice and passion. **1774** *Chesterfield's Lett.* I. xvii. 74 Horatius Cocles, who alone defended the pass of a bridge against the whole Tuscan army. **1838** THIRLWALL *Greece* V. 283 When Philip reached Thermopylæ, he found the pass strongly guarded.

c. More generally: A way by which to pass or get through; a passage, road, route. Also *fig.*

1608 CHAPMAN *Byron's Trag.* Plays 1873 II. 294 Let your Armie Have the directest passe, it shall goe safe. *a* **1674** CLARENDON *Hist. Reb.* IX. §92 The force of both counties.. should be drawn to Tiverton, and upon that pass, to fight with the rebels. **1689** LUTTRELL *Brief Rel.* (1857) I. 617 The Danish horse..are ordered to march for Scotland, being the shortest passe for Ireland. **1787** M. CUTLER in *Life*, etc. (1888) II. 395 Through the Sandusky and Scioto lies the most common pass from Canada to the Ohio and Mississippi. **1798** BLOOMFIELD *Farmer's Boy*, *Spring* 302 [He] Sees every pass secur'd, and fences whole.

fig. **1651** N. BACON *Disc. Govt. Eng.* II. xvi. (1739) 84 The King and Council seemed to have the sole power..to open and shut the passes of Trade.

d. A passage across a river; a place at which a river can be crossed by ford, ferry, or, *rarely* a bridge. Now *rare*.

1649–50 CROMWELL *Let. to Lenthall* 15 Feb. in *Carlyle*, Desirous to gain a Pass over the Suir; where indeed we had none but by boat, or when the weather served. **1650** *Ibid.* 2 Apr., By which means we have a good pass over the Barrow, and intercourse between Munster and Leinster. *a* **1661** FULLER *Worthies* (1840) III. 384 The royalists chiefest strength consisted in two passes they possessed over the river of Severn. **1718** ROWE tr. *Lucan* I. 815 To guard the Passes of the German Rhine. **1862** STANLEY *Jew. Ch.* (1877) I. iii. 55 The watch-tower of Peniel, which years afterwards guarded the passes of the Jordan.

e. A navigable channel, esp. at a river's mouth, or in a delta.

1698 FRYER *Acc. E. India & P.* 123 The next Morning, with only sending my Servant ashore to acquaint the Rendero, I quitted the Pass. **1704** ADDISON *Italy* (1733) 56 Passes that lead to the City from the Adriatic. **1758** *Ann. Reg.* 109 The greatest part [of the vessels] escaped by running into the pass of Toulinquet. **1817** J. W. HEUSTIS *Phys. Observ. Topog. & Dis. Louisiana* 23 The main branch of the Mississippi has three mouths, or, as they are called, passes. **1895** J. WINSOR *Mississ. Basin* 154 A fort was soon built at the Balize,..on the edge of the Gulf, but which to-day is nine miles up the pass.

f. Applied to other narrow passages: e.g. in a road or street.

a **1710** POPE *Alley* 2 A narrow pass there is with Houses low. **1712** STEELE *Spect.* No. 454 ¶4 While he whipped up James-Street, we drove for King-Street, to save the Pass at St. Martin's Lane. *Ibid.* No. 498 ¶2 Till he came to the Pass, which is a Military Term the Brothers of the Whip have given the Strait at St. Clement's Church. **1902** *Daily Chron.* 16 Apr. 7/2 How Royal and Coronation processions got through the Pass is a secret which our London fore-fathers have taken to their graves.

g. A passage or alley in a church. *Sc. dial.*

1871 W. ALEXANDER *Johnny Gibb* xi. (1892) 68 He was going along the pass to shut the door. **1873** GILMOUR *Pen-Flk.* 51 (E.D.D.) William McLerie.. steps noiselessly up the 'pass', asking kindly for each as he slips along.

h. A passage for fish over or past a weir.

1861 *Act 24 & 25 Vict.* c. 109 §23 Any Proprietor of a Fishery with the written Consent of the Home Office may attach to every Dam.. a Fish Pass, of such Form and Dimensions as the Home Office may approve. **1867** *Lond. Rev.* 22 June 696/1 To restore our rivers to their former prolific condition, it is indispensable that salmon-passes should be provided. **1899** *Daily News* 4 May 11/2 In 1863 a salmon pass or ladder was made at Wood Mill, with the result that fish were enabled to ascend into the non-tidal waters.

4. *Mining.* (See quots.)

[May perh. belong to PASS *sb.*[2]]

1671 *Phil. Trans.* VI. 2108 After the Ore is landed,.. 'tis brought.. and unloaded at the head of the Pass (*i.e.* 2 or 3 bottom-boards with 2 side-boards sloping-wise) in which the Ore slides down into the Coffer. **1710** J. HARRIS *Lex. Techn.* II. s.v., A Frame of Boards consisting of 2 or 3 bottom Boards and two side ones set slope-wise, thro' which the Ore slides down into the Coffer of the Stamping-Mill, for the Tin-works, is called by the Workmen *the Pass.* **1881** in RAYMOND *Mining Gloss.*

pass (pɑːs, -æ-), *sb.*[2] Forms: 4-7 passe, (6 pas), 7- pass. [Partly a. F. *passe*, f. *passer* to pass; partly immed. from PASS *v.* Not always clearly separable from PASS *sb.*[1], with which, since 1600, and occasionally earlier, it has been identified in spelling.]

I. 1. a. An act or the fact of passing; passage.

[*a* **1400-50** *Alexander* 2978 þe pepill of þe palais quen þai his passe [*D.* hym passe] saȝe, Rusches vp in a res rynnes in-to chambres.] **1599** SHAKS. *Hen. V*, II. Chor. 39 Charming the narrow seas To giue you gentle Passe. **1600** W. WATSON *Decacordon* (1602) 45 In the passe and repasse out of England into Fraunce. *c* **1611** CHAPMAN *Iliad* III. 242 Out of his ample breast, he gave his great voice pass. *Ibid.* IV. 406 He went, and safely had his pass Back to Asopus' flood. *Ibid.* XX. 422 One ear it enter'd, and made good his pass to th' other ear. **1647** N. BACON *Disc. Govt. Eng.* I. xx. (1739) 38 This privilege of Safe Pass being.. ancient and fundamental,.. resteth still in force. **1671** GREW *Anat. Plants* ii. §31 The Sap moving in the Barque, towards the Pith, through the Insertions, thereinto obtains a pass. **1820** J. CLELAND *Rise Glasgow* 121 There are four or five hundred passes and repasses in the same period. **1844** D. WELSH *Serm.* 186 How dread must be the pass from the unsubstantial fabric of this earthly state to those abodes. **1966** *B.B.C. Handbk.* 53 Previously we had to snatch in a hit or miss fashion at 'passes' as *Telstar* or one of its cousins streaked from horizon to horizon. **1967** *Technology Week* 23 Jan. 28/2 Primary function of the subsystem is to correct the flight trajectory to assure a close pass by Mars. **1968** M. WOODHOUSE *Rock Baby* xvi. 153, I don't say it was impossible to spot, but.., short of an overhead pass by a very low-flying helicopter, I thought it would pass muster. **1974** *Nature* 4 Jan. 24/1 The orbit is near-polar with the north-going passes on the nightside at about 2230 LT, and the south-going passes on the dayside at about 1030 LT. **1977** *Offshore Engineer* Apr. 28/1 It is followed up by an external welder or 'bug', which completes a 3 mm weld thickness in one pass over wall thicknesses above 9·6 mm.

b. Departure from life, death. Also *fig.*

a **1645** FEATLY in *Fuller's Abel Rediv., Reynolds* (1867) II. 238 Whose happy pass, agreeable to his godly life, God forbid that any should deplore. **1742** YOUNG *Nt. Th.* III. 134 For Man you smile; Why not smile *at* him too? You share indeed His sudden Pass; but not his constant Pain. **1827** POLLOK *Course T.* III, This pass of human thought, This wilderness of intellectual death.

c. *Bridge.* The act of declining to make a bid.

1923 M. C. WORK *Auction Bridge of 1924* 497 Business Pass, a pass which indicates to the partner, who has made an Information Double, that the existing declaration will be remunerative. **1927** [see AUCTION *sb.* 2 c]. **1958** *Listener* 25 Dec. 1094/3, I agree with West's opening pass and with his next bid of Two No Trumps. **1959** *Ibid.* 15 Jan. 146/1 After two passes, South opened Three Spades. **1959** REESE & DORMER *Bridge Player's Dict.* 165 West's double is for a take-out and East's pass is a penalty pass. **1977** *Times* 14 May 12/7 Hands which were so freakish that an unorthodox pass was the only road to safety.

d. *Computers.* A passage of data through a computer for processing; a single cycle of reading, processing, and writing; the performance of a particular kind of operation on each in turn of a set of data.

1954 *Jrnl. Assoc. Computing Machinery* I. 151/1 A single pass of the data through the 702 may be enough to carry out .. a statistical analysis. **1961** *Ibid.* VIII. 46 Passes are continued until no item is exchanged during a given pass... This signals that all items have been sorted. **1968** *Amer. Documentation* Jan. 78/1 During one pass all elements which have already been classed in a particular category are retrieved. A second retrieval pass is then made to retrieve all remaining elements which have headwords or definitions which match those of items retrieved on the first pass. **1968** G. EMERY *Electronic Data Processing* ii. 10 Figure 1.5 shows a single job, made up of three separate runs... Runs are sometimes subdivided further into separate passes—sorting runs are an example. **1975** H. LORIN *Sorting* i. 6 A pass of Linear Selection involves selecting the element with the lowest key on the list to be sorted and placing it on a growing output list. Additional passes are made until the output list is complete.

†**2.** (?) Demeanour, 'walk'; (?) course of action.

1555 W. WATREMAN *Fardle Facions* II. xii. 269 To be honestly appareiled, and accordyngly to vse their passe and conuersacion. **1603** SHAKS. *Meas. for M.* v. i. 375 When I perceiue your grace, like powre diuine, Hath look'd vpon my passes.

†**3.** The fact of passing as approved; reputation, estimation; currency. *Obs.*

1598 B. JONSON *Ev. Man. in Hum.* v. i. 442 Or that their slubbered lines haue currant passe, From the fat iudgements of the multitude. **1601** SHAKS. *All's Well* II. v. 58, I do know him well, and common speech Giues him a worthy passe.

4. The passing of an examination; *esp.* in a university examination, the attainment of such a standard as satisfies the examiners without entitling the candidate to honours. Often *attrib.*: see 18.

1838 ARNOLD *Let.* in *Life & Corr.* (1844) II. viii. 127 A pass little *go*, or even great *go*, is surely a ridiculous thing, as all that the University expects of a man after some twelve or fourteen years of schooling and lecturing. **1860** M. BURROWS (*title*) Pass and Class: an Oxford Guide-Book through the Courses of Literæ Humaniores, Mathematics, Natural Science, and Law and Modern History. **1874** BURNAND *My time* xxxvi. 388 Honours were out of the question, and a pass we most of us obtained. **1882** J. SOUTHWARD *Pract. Print.* (1884) 199 If, however, there are only three marks or less, there is 'no pass'.

II. That in which the fact of passing is embodied; the condition to or through which anything passes.

†**5.** Event, issue; completion, accomplishment.

[**1481**: see 6 b.] **1542** UDALL *Erasm. Apoph.* I. *Socr.* §93 n., 38 a, [He] shall easily bryng the same to suche ende, and to such passe and effecte, as he would dooe. **1579** TOMSON *Calvin's Serm. Tim.* 287/2 God will bring all to good passe. *c* **1600** SHAKS. *Sonn.* ciii, To no other passe my verses tend Then of your graces and your gifts to tell. **1611** BIBLE *Transl. Pref.* 11 Wee haue at the length, through the good hand of the Lord vpon vs, brought the worke to that passe that you see. **1649** MILTON *Eikon.* ix. 86 By this reckning his consents and his denials come all to one pass.

6. Phrases. (Now somewhat *arch.*)

(Here *to pass* is often regarded as infinitive of the vb.; but see quot. 1549 in a, 1542 in b, and cf. prec.)

a. *to bring to pass* (rarely †*unto pass*): to bring to accomplishment, fulfilment, or realization; to carry out; to accomplish, produce, bring about.

1523 SKELTON *Garl. Laurel* 1228 A tratyse he deuysid & browght it to pas, Callid *Speculum Principis.* **1530** TINDALE *Gen.* xli. 32 That the thynge is certanly prepared of God, and that God will shortly brynge it to passe. **1538** STARKEY *England* II. ii. 195 Thys were a commyn remedy, yf hyt myght be brought to passe. **1539** BIBLE (Great) *Ps.* xxxvii. 5 Commytte thy waye vnto the Lorde, and put thy trust in hym, & he shall brynge it to passe. **1549** LATIMER *1st Serm. bef. Edw. VI* B viij b, Many hath taken in hande to brynge manye thynges vnto passe [*printed* paste]. *c* **1592** MARLOWE *Jew of Malta* v. iii, Doe but bring this to passe which thou pretendest. *a* **1634** CHAPMAN *Alphonsus* Plays 1873 III. 225 Huge wonders will Alphonsus bring to pass. **1651** HOBBES *Leviath.* II. xxix. 169 They [faith and sanctity] are not Miracles, but brought to passe by education.

b. *to come to pass*: to come to the event or issue; to be carried out, accomplished, or realized; to turn out in the event, to eventuate; to issue, come about. Also, †*to go to pass.* †*to come well to* (*our*) *pass, to come evil to pass*, to turn out well (for us), to turn out ill.

1481 CAXTON *Reynard* xl. (Arb.) 108 The wulf.. threw the foxe al plat vnder hym, whiche cam hym euyl to passe. [*Leeu's text*, 1479, xli, dat hem seer misuiel]. **1526** SKELTON *Magnyf.* 2134 *Magn.* I am Magnyfycence, that somtyme thy mayster was. *Lyb.* What, is the worlde thus come to passe? **1526** TINDALE *John* xiii. 19 Nowe tell I you before it come: that when yt is come to passe, ye myght beleve that I am he. *a* **1533** LD. BERNERS *Huon* lxvi. 226 Alas! why dyd not Huon knowe his entente? if he had, the mater had not gone so to passe. **1542** UDALL *Erasm. Apoph.* 336 'A man that fleeth will renewe battaill again' is a prouerbiall verse.. by whiche we are warned not.. to be brought in despaire, if some thyng have not well come to our passe. —— in *Lett. Lit. Men* (Camden) 2 If it had succeded and cum to passe accordyng to my request. **1611** BIBLE *Num.* xi. 23 Thou shalt see now whether my word shall come to passe vnto thee [COVERD. shall be fulfilled in dede], or not. **1662** STILLINGFL. *Orig. Sacr.* II. vi. §5 When therefore any Prophets did foretell things.. and those things did not come to pass, it was a certain evidence of a false Prophet. **1887** LECKY *Eng. in 18th C.* VI. 121 If the projects foreshadowed by De Maulde had come to pass.

c. quasi-*impers.*, with *it*, and subord. clause. To come to be the fact, to come about, to turn out, to happen (esp. in Scriptural lang.).

1526 TINDALE *Matt.* xi. 1 And it came to passe when Iesus had ended his preceptes.. he departed thence. **1611** BIBLE *Gen.* xxii. 1. **1628** HOBBES *Thucyd.* (1822) 49 After this it came to pass that the Athenians and their confederates fought against the Medes. **1712** ADDISON *Spect.* No. 418 ¶3 But how comes it to pass, that we should take delight in being terrified or dejected by a Description. **1796** H. HUNTER tr. *St.-Pierre's Stud. Nat.* (1799) III. 44 It comes to pass, that those places only, which are situated in the point of divergence.. experience two tides a day.

7. a. A position or situation in the course of any affair; *esp.* a position, qualified in some way; a critical position, a juncture, a predicament. Also phr. (*to come to*) *a pretty pass*, (to reach) a regrettable state of affairs.

Cf. F. *être en belle passe, dans une mauvaise passe*, etc.: see Littré, *Passe* 5. But in Eng. app. sometimes associated with PASS *sb.*[1] as if a fig. use of sense 3 a.

1560 DAUS tr. *Sleidane's Comm.* 58 Yet all thynges lyke to come to suche a passe. **1581** PETTIE tr. *Guazzo's Civ. Conv.* II. (1586) 49 b, The worlde is come to this passe, that it counteth anie thing to bee lawfull which is delightfull. **1596** SPENSER *F.Q.* VI. iii. 14 Him seemed fit that wounded Knight To visite, after this nights perillous passe. **1596** SHAKS. *Tam. Shr.* v. ii. 124 Lord let me neuer haue a cause to sigh, Till I be brought to such a sillie passe. **1610** R. ABBOTT *Old Way* 27 To that desperate passe they are brought by the writings of the authors. **1732** LAW *Serious C.* iv. (ed. 2) 66 To such a pass are we now come. **1822** SHELLEY *Triumph Life* 302 How and by what paths I have been brought To this dread pass. **1833** HT. MARTINEAU *Fr. Wines & Pol.* vi. 98 Where is the patriotism of bringing things to this pass? **1842** [see PRETTY *a.* 3 c]. **1843** DICKENS *Mart. Chuz.* (1844) xiv. 178, I need be departing, with all speed, for another country; for I have come to a pretty pass in this! **1876** H. MELVILLE *Clarel* II. IV. xvi. 501 'Was ever Saracen so bold!' 'Well, things have come to pretty pass —The mysteries slobbered by an ass!' **1894** C. N. ROBINSON *Brit. Fleet* 9 Neglecting, at this critical pass, to secure the maritime approaches to his realm. **1909** *Dialect Notes* III. 359 *Pretty pass*,.. a peculiar or astounding situation, as abnormal condition: used in derogatory sense. **1955** *Times* 5 Aug. 10/4 Things, one felt, must have reached a pretty pass if the big banks, or any one of the big banks, had run into the same squalid staffing problems as the National Coal Board or the chain groceries. **1970** *Brewer's Dict. Phr. & Fable* (rev. ed.) 808/1 *A pretty pass*, a difficult or deplorable state of affairs.

†**b.** *to pass.* (?) To (proper) position; in position. [Cf. Du. *te passe.* But see WELL *to pass.*]

c **1595** CAPT. WYATT *R. Dudley's Voy. W. Ind.* (Hakl. Soc.) 58 Her ordinance lyinge well to pass, shee went as upright as a church. **1644** NYE *Gunnery* II. (1670) 5 If the first shot had struck under the Mark, then bring the Peece in all points as before to passe.

III. Permission or authorization to pass.

8. a. 'Permission to go or come anywhere' (J.); *esp.* a written permission to pass into, out of, or through a country or place, or between places within a country; a passport; also, a document authorizing the holder to pass, *e.g.* through the lines of an army; authorization or leave to pass.

1591 SPENSER *M. Hubberd* 936 He cast to leave The Court, not asking any passe or leave. **1598** HAKLUYT *Voy.* I. 472 They shall haue a letter of passe giuen vnto them. *a* **1604** HANMER *Chron. Irel.* (1633) 120 To give him Passe to seek adventures in some forraigne country. **1647** CLARENDON *Hist. Reb.* II. §44 He had given passes to many obscure persons, to go into and return out of that kingdom. **1667** PEPYS *Diary* 3 Apr., The Dutch have ordered a passe to be sent for our Commissioners. **1722** DE FOE *Plague* (1754) 9 To get Passes and Certificates of Health.. for, without these, there was no being admitted to pass thro' the Towns. **1798** NELSON *Let.* 27 Oct. in Nicolas *Disp.* (1845) III. 163, I am much displeased that you should grant Passes to the Ships of any Power with whom we are at War. **1867** SMYTH *Sailor's Word-bk.*, *Pass*, or *Passport*, a permission granted by any state to a vessel, to navigate in some particular sea without molestation. **1900** [see 18 a].

b. *Mil.* (See quots.)

1617 MORYSON *Itin.* II. 253 No souldier should bee discharged but by Passe from the Lord Deputie, Principall Gouernour, or chiefe Commanders. **1853** STOCQUELER *Mil. Encycl.*, *Pass*,.. also a certificate of leave of absence to a soldier for a short period. **1887** *Times* 28 Sept. 7/3 Passes to remain out after hours for well-conducted soldiers. **1919** [see LEAF *sb.*[2]]. **1939** JOYCE *Finnegans Wake* III. 507 Such my billet. Buy a barrack pass. **1955** 'N. SHUTE' *Requiem for Wren* iii. 67 Before she had been a year at Ford Janet came to look forward to her next pass with something close to apprehension. **1955** [see BIND *v.* 23].

†**c.** An order passing a pauper to his or her parish; 'an order by which vagrants or impotent persons are sent to their place of abode' (J.). *Obs.*

1646-7 in Swayne *Sarum Church-w. Acc.* (1896) 325 Pore woman traveling from Ireland by passe, 4*d.* **1743-4** *Act 17 Geo. II*, c. 5 Incorrigible rogues.. who being apprehended .. refuse to go before a magistrate, or to be examined on oath, or to be conveyed by a pass. **1786** *Pilton Churchw. Acc.* in *Notes & Gleanings* (Exeter) II. 37/2 Paid a woman that had a Pass to Wexford in Ireland 0*s.* 6*d.*

d. A document or ticket authorizing the holder to travel free on a railway, etc. Usually *free pass.* **e.** A ticket or order giving free admission to a theatre or the like.

1838 *Actors by Daylight* I. 141 Give the Mounseer a pass to the pit. **1858** SIMMONDS *Dict. Trade*, *Pass*.. a free journey-ticket on a railway; an unpaid admission to a place of amusement. **1871** M. COLLINS *Mrq. & Merch.* II. ix. 270 He has.. railway-passes. **1894** [see FREE *a.* 32]. **1944** J. W. KRUTCH *Samuel Johnson* (1945) viii. 210 Johnson.. complained that Garrick had just refused him a pass to the theater for Miss Williams because.. he saw no reason why he should give away a ticket to what he knew was going to be a full house. **1961** BOWMAN & BALL *Theatre Lang.* 250 *Pass*, a permit to admit a person into a theatre without a ticket. British: *complimentary ticket.* **1977** *Times* 22 Apr. 11/1 Forging free passes to movie theatres.

f. In South Africa and (formerly in) Rhodesia, a document issued to non-white residents (now usu. one which it is obligatory for them to carry), authorizing and regulating their movement and residence in particular areas.

Pass laws were repealed in S. Africa in 1986.

1828 J. PHILIP *Res. S. Afr.* I. 167 Among the many hardships to which the Hottentot is subject by this proclamation, one must advert to the Law of Passes, contained in the 16th article. **1899** W. J. K. LITTLE *Sk. & Stud. S. Afr.* II. i. 127 It was required that he [*sc.* a Hottentot] should have.. a 'pass' or certificate when moving from place to place, and should be fined or punished as a vagrant if unable, when required, to produce this pass. **1901** *Natives S. Afr.* x. 165 Every native on entering a district, being in possession of the pass required by the existing Pass Law, was directed to repair to the district office and get a pass and badge. **1902** in *Statute Law of Transvaal* (1910) II. 871 Any native found in any street public place or thoroughfare.. between the hours of nine pm. and four am. without a written pass or certificate.. shall be liable to a fine. **1914** in *Statute Law of S. Rhodesia* (1923) II. 273 Every native shall be bound, on demand made by any Pass Officer, to state all the particulars required to be entered upon his pass or certificate. **1914** in *Ibid.* (1939) II. 286 To amend and consolidate the law relating to native's passes. *Ibid.*, 287 Every male native within the Colony over the apparent age of fourteen years shall register himself at the proper pass office. **1928** R. R. R. DHLOMO *Afr. Tragedy* 21 There was no necessity for him to go to the Pass Office and spend half a day there waiting for his pass to be endorsed. **1941** C. W. DE KIEWIET *Hist. S. Afr.* 45 They were naturally inclined to arrest the Hottentot as a vagabond and compel him to take service or achieve the same result by refusing him the pass or certificate without which he could not move from one district to another. **1948** *Rep. Native Laws Comm. 1946–48* (Dept. Native Affairs, S. Afr.) 26/1 It is not always clear whether a particular document can rightly be described as a pass or not. Neither from European nor from Native witnesses did we receive a satisfactory definition, but we think it would be correct to say that in the mind of the Natives a document is a pass, to which they object, if it is a document—(*a*) which is not carried by all races, but only by people of a particular race; and which either (*b*) is connected with restriction of the freedom of movement of the person concerned; or (*c*) must at all times be carried by the person concerned on his body, since the law lays the obligation on him of producing it on demand to the police and certain other officials and the mere failure to produce it is by itself a punishable offence. **1949** *Handbk. Race Relations S. Afr.* 275 The tendency was to equate a pass with a document controlling movement. Clearly however, the pass has acquired a wider connotation to-day. **1952** *Statutes Union S. Afr.* 1013 To repeal the laws relating to the carrying of passes by natives; to provide for the issue of reference books to natives. **1956** D. JACOBSON *Dance in Sun* 51 I've been to the police and told them to chase him away, but they looked at his passes and said his passes were in order. **1964** *Ann. Reg. 1963* 327 All adults were entitled to vote, provided that they had registered and that this fact had been recorded on their identity cards or 'passes'. **1968** R. GRIFFITHS *Man of River* 137 But they must! At all times they must carry their passes! **1971** T. SHARPE *Riotous Assembly* ii. 10 The milk delivery boy was charged with being out without a Pass. **1972** P. DRISCOLL *Wilby Conspiracy* (1973) iii. 40 The black man shuffled forward, reaching automatically for his pass, and the constable paged through the green booklet. **1977** *Times* 5 Nov. 15/1 The tribal homelands are henceforth to issue travel documents to their nationals, a more dignified card of identity. But these, even if upgraded to passport status upon independence, will serve the police and the Ministry of Bantu Affairs as well as the passes. Possession of one will be needed to apply for a job in white South Africa.

IV. The causing of something to pass.

9. a. *Fencing.* The act of passing the sword or rapier; a lunge, a thrust; a round or bout of fencing.

1598 SHAKS. *Merry W.* II. i. 233 In these times you stand on distance: your Passes, Stoccado's, and I know not what. **1602** —— *Ham.* v. ii. 173 In a dozen passes between yourself and him, he shall not exceed you three hits. **1678** OTWAY *Friendship in F.* I. i, I put by his Pass, clos'd with him and threw up his Heel's. **1692** SIR W. HOPE *Fencing Master* (ed. 2) 79 A Pass is that with which a man goeth quite by, and behind his adversary; the second kind which is called a Pass (but improperly) is that with which a Man goeth only close to his Adversary, and commandeth his Sword. **1692** WASHINGTON tr. *Milton's Def. Pop.* vii. M.'s Wks. (1851) 173 You lie every where so open to blows, that if any one were.. to make a Pass at any part of you, he could hardly miss. **1752** YOUNG *Brothers* IV. i, Thy bloody pass cleave thro' thy brother's breast. **1840** THACKERAY *Catherine* vi, He drew his.. sword and made a pass at Mr. Sicklop.

†**b.** *fig.* A sally of wit; a witty thrust or stroke: in phrases *pass of pate, wit. Obs.*

1610 SHAKS. *Temp.* IV. i. 244 Steale by line and leuell is an excellent passe of pate. **1822** HAZLITT *Table-t.* Ser. II. viii. (1869) 173 This is a curious pass of wit.

10. The manipulation of a juggler; the transference or changing of the position of anything by sleight of hand, or the like; a trick.

to make the pass (in card tricks), to alter the position of the cards in the pack, by dexterously bringing the lower cards to the top, or shifting the top or bottom card.

1599 MINSHEU *Span. Dict.*, *Passa*, as *juego de Passa*, iuglers playing passe and repasse. **1814** BYRON *Diary* 8 Apr., He will yet play them a pass. *c* **1821** *Philosoph. Recreations* 97 No. 151 How to make the Pass [i.e. with cards—a full description]. **1836** MARRYAT *Japhet* xi, For hours and hours was I employed by his directions in what is called 'making the pass' with a pack of cards, as almost all tricks on cards depend upon your dexterity in this manœuvre. **1859** WRAXALL tr. *R. Houdin* iv. 38 He performed the most difficult 'passes' with a coolness no one would expect him to possess. **1861** *Boy's Own Conj. Bk.* 94 As.. a friend is not always present who can perform the pass, I will endeavour to describe it. **1872** *Routledge's Ev. Boy's Ann.* 346/1 To make the Pass (*sauter la coupe*).

11. a. A passing of the hands over or along anything; manipulation; esp. in Mesmerism.

1848 THACKERAY *Van. Fair* xxiii, Alexis, after a few passes from Dr. Elliotson, despises pain, reads with the back of his head. **1851** H. MAYO *Pop. Superstit.* (ed. 2) 180 The employment of mesmeric passes.. as a local means of tranquillising the nervous sensibility. **1874** CARPENTER *Mental Phys.* II. xiv. (1879) 553 The delusion was kept up by a frequent recourse to 'passes', resembling those of the Mesmerists.

b. An amorous advance, esp. in phr. *to make a pass at* (someone). *colloq.*

1928 J. P. MCEVOY *Show Girl* 27 Almost all parties look alike at the takeoff—a few high balls, a few dunces, and the boys getting merry and making preliminary passes. **1936** D. PARKER *Not so Deep as a Well* 70 Men seldom make passes At girls who wear glasses. **1938** G. GREENE *Brighton Rock* I. i. 21 He made no immediate pass at Ida in the taxi. **1939** C. R. COOPER *Designs in Scarlet* ii. 14 The girl sipped idly at her drink, swallowing with it her disgust that she should be forced to stick with a dedo when she might be making a pass at a 'gentleman'. **1942** E. WAUGH *Put out More Flags* 173 What are you doing now besides making passes at Susie? **1944** AUDEN *For Time Being* ii. 31 His progress from outrage to outrage would not relent before the gross climax of His making, horror unspeakable, a pass at her virgin self. **1945** J. STEINBECK *Cannery Row* xxix. 190, I been over there. He never made a pass at me. **1952** W. PLOMER *Museum Pieces* ix. 68 Since my visit to the painting room he had almost completely hidden from me the feelings which seemed to have driven him to make a pass at me. **1957** J. BRAINE *Room at Top* vii. 70 A little gentle flirtation, even a discreet sort of pass, would have changed her attitude entirely. **1959** 'D. BUCKINGHAM' *Wind Tunnel* xv. 127 Male passes were nothing new to Janet. **1972** J. GORES *Dead Skip* (1973) xiii. 89 As for making a pass at her, he'd as soon have made one at his five-year-old daughter. Sex was for home. **1973** 'D. SHANNON' *No Holiday for Crime* (1974) iv. 58 If he started to get fresh, threw a pass, she could just walk off. **1978** D. DEVINE *Sunk without Trace* ii. 23 He cast round for ulterior motives. Was she perhaps making a pass at him?

12. a. *Football, Lacrosse, Hockey,* etc. A transference of the ball by one of the players to another on his own side.

1891 *Lock to Lock Times* 24 Oct. 16/2 L. who took the ball well from a difficult pass by C. secured a try after a capital run. **1894** *Badminton Libr., Football (Assoc.)* 109 Inside forwards.. must, like the outsides, be on the look-out for making a pass to the opposite wing. *Ibid. (Rugby)* 332 Some of the leading clubs soon discovered that for a 'pass' to be accurate it must be short. **1944** N. MAILER *Calculus at Heaven* in E. Seaver *Cross-Section* 345 Sergeant! Did I ever tellya how I got to throw a pass in the Red Bank game one year? **1961** J. S. SALAK *Dict. Amer. Sports* 319 *Pass* (baseball, softball), base on balls. **1970** *Washington Post* 30 Sept. D4/3 Shugars.. has been very accurate this year, completing 37 of 78 passes for 376 yards and a 47 per cent average. **1972** *N.Y. Times* 4 June 5/2 He has been throwing passes in casual workouts.

b. In real tennis, a service which drops in the pass-court; in lawn tennis, a shot which succeeds in passing the racket of an opponent.

1888 *Encycl. Brit.* XXIII. 179/2 A pass counts for nothing but annuls a previous fault. **1900** in A. E. T. Watson *Young Sportsman* 614 A 'pass' shall not neutralise a previous fault. **1911** *Encycl. Brit.* XXVI. 627/2 'Pass': a service in which the ball drops beyond the passline; the service in this case does not count, but a 'pass' does not annul a previous fault, as was once the case. **1961** F. C. AVIS *Sportsman's Gloss.* 259/2 *Pass* .. Passing shot. **1962** *Times* 27 Apr. 4/1 A mixture of lobs and angled passes. **1975** *Oxf. Compan. Sports & Games* 825/1 The remainder of the winning area is the 'pass court' and, if the ball falls there, 'pass' is called and a let played. **1978** *Times* 4 July 19/4 Newcombe actually reached set point with a glorious backhand cross-court pass off second service.

13. In a rolling-mill: 'A single passage of a plate or bar between the rolls' (Knight *Dict. Mech.* 1875).

1881 RAYMOND *Mining Gloss.*, *Pass*.. When the bar passes 'on the flat' it is called a *flatting-pass*; if 'on the edge', an *edging-pass*. **1939** [see LAP *sb.*³ 2 e]. **1967** A. H. COTTRELL *Introd. Metall.* xxii. 439 For the first few passes the draught (i.e. reduction of cross-section) is light... Reductions of 10–50 per cent per pass are then used.

14. In full, *food-pass*. Among certain birds of prey, the habit of passing food from one bird to another while in flight.

1931 D. NETHERSOLE-THOMPSON in *Brit. Birds* XXV. 147 During the early stages of incubation the food 'pass' of the Hobbies may be occasionally witnessed. **1940** H. F. WITHERBY et al. *Handbk. Brit. Birds* III. 19 During this period [of incubation] male feeds hen both by food pass and by calling hen off to adjoining perch. **1948** B. H. RYVES *Bird Life in Cornwall* vi. 93 The aerial 'pass' of a kill is spectacular. **1956** D. A. BANNERMAN *Birds Brit. Isles* V. 182 Excellent views of the food-pass of the cock to the hen [marsh harrier] were also witnessed. *Ibid.* 195 Some account of the serious business of the 'pass' will be given. **1970** E. HOSKING *Eye for Bird* xi. 157 They [*sc.* a pair of hobbies] rolled over, swung up their feet and passed food from one to the other. It is the speed and precise flight control which makes the hobby's food-pass so exhilarating to watch.

V. †**15.** An iron ring through which the ball was driven in the game of PALL-MALL. [F. *passe.*]

1611 COTGR., *Leve*, a Mallet.. wherewith the bowle is raysed, and cast through the Passe at Palemaille. **1727** BAILEY vol. II. s.v. *Mall*, The Ball is struck.. so as to run through an iron Arch at the End of a long Alley.. This Arch is call'd the Pass.

16. The aperture formed by the corresponding grooves in a rolling-mill.

1875 KNIGHT *Dict. Mech.* 1635/1 The pass is so formed as to give the required shape to the metal rolled therethrough. **1930** *Engineering* 12 Dec. 759/2 The drawing of the strip through the pass of the rolls. **1939** [see LAP *sb.*³ 2 e]. **1960** D. J. O. BRANDT *Manuf. Iron & Steel* (ed. 2) xxxiii. 249 The most commonly used passes in bar and rod rolling are the diamond, the diagonal, the oval, and to finish with, the round.

17. More fully *pass-hemp*: the third quality of Russian hemp, next to *outshot*.

1744–50 W. ELLIS *Mod. Husbandm.* V. III. 87 There is another Sort from Russia,.. called Pass-hemp, which is a very shaggy, coarse, cheap Sort, used altogether for Roping. **1812** [see OUTSHOT 3]. **1858** SIMMONDS *Dict. Trade*, *Pass*, a name for the third classification or quality of Russian hemp. **1886** W. A. HARRIS *Techn. Dict. Fire-Insurance*, *Pass-hemp*.

VI. 18. *attrib.* and *Comb.* **a.** *attrib.*: (*a*) relating to the passing of an examination (sense 4), ***pass class, coach, degree, divinity, examination, mark, moderations*** (colloq. ***mods***), ***rate, schools***, etc.; (*b*) relating to the issue of passes (sense 8), ***pass-form, inspector, law, office, regulation, system, warrant***, etc; ***pass-bearing*** adj.

a. 1838 [see 4]. **1853** 'C. BEDE' *Verdant Green* xii, He had gone to a farewell pass-party. **1861** MILL *Repr. Govt.* xiv. 259 A mere pass examination never, in the long run, does more than exclude absolute dunces. **1868** M. PATTISON *Academ. Organiz.* vi. §2. 236 When a pass-examination was instituted. *Ibid.* 238 The university should cease the pass-business altogether. *Ibid.* 239 It is not possible, nor is it proposed, that such a measure as the abolition of the pass-degree should be taken at once. **1883** *Times* 1 June 4 Some pass-examiner.. set a continuity of traps.. whereby the unwary examinee was brought to grief. **1890** *Spectator* 5 Apr., We quite see the use of a pass examination in health for all appointments, because the State does not want to be burdened with invalids. **1891** *Daily News* 8 Dec. 3/2 The pass-schools are once more upon us, and the pass-men in their white ties monopolize the High-street after breakfast and lunch. **1908** E. M. SNEYD-KYNNERSLEY *H.M.I.* xi. 110 He had taken refuge in a Hall. There he exhausted the pass-coaches of Oxford. **1911** W. OWEN *Let.* Sept. (1967) 79 Have I passed? I do think so! even in Arith. & Geometry. At least I have done enough right to score pass marks. **1912** *Rep. Brit. Assoc. Adv. Sci. 1911* 219 The opinion has been expressed that Pass Mods. is not a bad thing. **1915** W. S. MAUGHAM *Of Human Bondage* xxvi. 109 When he only got a pass degree his friends were astonished. **1919** MENCKEN *Amer. Lang.* 105 His [*sc.* an English university man's] daily speech is full of terms unintelligible to an American student, for example, *wrangler, tripos, head, pass-degree* and *don*. **1948** M. LASKI *Tory Heaven* i. 5 After reading for a Pass Degree at Oxford, James had.. been sent to.. an uncle's rubber-plantation in Malaya. **1953** K. AMIS *Lucky Jim* viii. 82 Of course, their problems down there are very different. .. The Pass classes in particular. **1957** *Economist* 12 Oct. 104/1 It is often assumed that there is a common pass mark for the whole of each county, but there can hardly be that until the school bus is replaced by each child's own jet propelled transport. **1969** G. SMITH in *Lett. Aldous Huxley* 11, 1913... October: H. enters Balliol and prepares for Pass Moderations. **1973** *Morning Star* 18 May 4/2 In the schools in the countryside the average pass rate was more than 95 per cent. **1976** *Daily Mail* (Hull) 16 Dec., Their pass rate of 79 per cent from 77 entries was better than most he had seen. **1977** P. STREVENS *New Orientations Teaching Eng.* ii. 34 In many countries.. the effective criterion for success in an English-language course has been to achieve the pass mark in an examination set and marked in Britain.

b. 1859 *Queenstown Free Press* 2 Mar. (Pettman), Upon more occasions than one I have endeavoured to bring to the notice of the public the evils of the Pass system. **1900** *Daily News* 23 Feb. 6/4 He also bribed the 'pass inspectors', whose business it was to see natives had proper passes. **1928** Pass office [see sense 8 f above]. **1936** *New Statesman* 11 July 46/1, I badly wanted to know whether God approved of the colour bar and the Pass system for natives. **1939** J. S. MARAIS *Cape Coloured People* p. viii, The pass system as applied to the Coloured north of the Orange, was abolished by the Natives (Urban Areas) Act of 1923. **1943** E. H. BROOKES *Bantu in S. Afr. Life* v. 11 The provisions of the Act under which Industrial Councils are formed do not apply to 'pass-bearing Natives'. **1948** *Rep. Native Laws Comm. 1946–48* (Dept. Native Affairs, S. Afr.) 66/2 Any Native *entering* the Province must proceed to the nearest Pass Office (or to the nearest Pass Office to his destination if entering by rail) and take out an *Inward Pass*. *Ibid.* 33/1 If in course of time, as matters develop, the pass regulations fall into entire disuse, the laws authorising their application may well disappear from the statute book. **1953** P. ABRAHAMS *Return to Goli* IV. ii. 129 He was soon picked up outside the Pass Office by one of the touts or 'runners' who look out for unemployed Africans. **1972** P. DRISCOLL *Wilby Conspiracy* (1973) vi. 74 A national campaign among Africans against the pass system.

b. Special combs.: **passband**, a frequency band within which signals are transmitted by a filter without attenuation; †**pass-bank, pass-boat**, see quots.; **pass-box**, a box for transferring cartridges from the magazine to the guns on the field; **pass-burner** *Southern Africa*, an African who burns his pass in protest against the pass laws; hence **pass-burning** *vbl. sb.*; **pass check**, a ticket of admission to a place of entertainment allowing the holder to withdraw and re-enter (Simmonds *Dict. Trade* 1858); **pass court** *Real Tennis* (see quots.); **pass door**, a door of communication between the stage and the house in theatres; **pass duty**, a duty levied on goods entering a territory; †**pass-gilt** (*Sc.*), 'current money'; **pass-hemp**, see sense 17; **pass-holder**, one who holds a 'pass' to a theatre, etc. (Simmonds 1858); **pass lamp**, a lamp on a motor vehicle for use in fog; **pass law** *Southern Africa*, a law regulating the carrying of passes (see sense 8 f above); **pass light** = *pass lamp*; so **pass-lighting**; **pass line** *Real Tennis*, the line between the pass-court and the service court; **pass-note**, 'a certificate from an employer that the bearer has regularly left his last employment' (Webster Suppl. 1879); **pass pawn**, a passed pawn; †**pass-penny**, the obolus placed by the ancient Greeks on the tongue of the dead to pay their fare over the Styx; **pass play** *Amer. Football*, a sequence of passes between members of the same team; **pass raid**, in South Africa, a raid on African premises by the white authorities to check that passes are in order; **pass-shooting** (*U.S.*), the shooting of wild ducks as they pass to and from the feeding-grounds in autumn; **pass-ticket**, a ticket empowering the holder to pass in (or out); **pass-**

warrant, see quot; **pass-woman**, a woman-student who passes an examination without honours: cf. PASSMAN. Also PASS-MASTER.

1922 G. A. CAMPBELL in *Bell Syst. Techn. Jrnl.* Nov. 15 The *pass band and stop band characteristics of wave-filters are concretely illustrated.. by the curves of Figs. 8–13. *Ibid.* 26 Each state holds for one or more continuous bands of frequencies; these bands have been distinguished as stop bands and pass bands. 1965 *Wireless World* Sept. 459/1 The low-frequency passband of the filter. 1970 J. EARL *Tuners & Amplifiers* v. 102 A BBC station at ±75kHz deviation with a modulation frequency of 15kHz.. would call for a passband of about 180kHz for the best results. 1970 *Nature* 12 Dec. 1069/2 A 30 Å passband Faby-Perot type filter was used to isolate the line. a1700 B. E. *Dict. Cant. Crew*, *Pass-bank, the Stock or Fund thereto belonging [i.e. to the game of passage]; also the playing Place Cut out in the Ground almost Cock-pit waies. 1721 in BAILEY. 1875 KNIGHT *Dict. Mech.*, *Pass-boat, a broad, flat-bottomed boat. A *flat* or *punt*. 1953 P. ABRAHAMS *Return to Goli* VI. i. 190 Strikers and *pass-burners were jailed and shot down in large numbers. 1961 *Economist* 4 Nov. 415/1, 2,072 [Northern Rhodesians] were convicted on charges of stoning, *pass-burning, arson, road-blocking, and the like. 1844 J. COWELL *30 Yrs. among Players* I. xi. 27 We agreed to pay the extra three and sixpence and go into the boxes; but as to obtaining a *pass check, it was impossible. 1858 G. A. SALA *Twice round Clock* in *Welcome Guest* 22 May 60/1 There is a theatrical pass-check, and the thumb of a white kid glove, very dirty, lying.. at the back [of the hansom]. 1961 BOWMAN & BALL *Theatre Lang.* 250 *Pass check*, a re-admission pass for a spectator who leaves the theatre temporarily. British: *pass-out check.* 1900 G. E. A. Ross in A. E. T. Watson *Young Sportsman* 608 The *pass-court is the area enclosed by the pass-line, the service-line, the end-wall and the main-wall. 1961 J. S. SALAK *Dict. Amer. Sports* 320 *Pass court* (court tennis)—the part of the floor on the hazard side that lies between the main wall, the grille wall, the pass line (but not including the pass line), and the service line (including the service line). 1975 Pass court [see sense 12b above]. 1856 DICKENS *Lett.* (1880) I. 431 The wall dividing the front from the stage still remained, and the iron *pass-doors stood ajar. 1937 N. COWARD *Present Indicative* VIII. 313 At the final curtain there was booing... I dashed through the pass door and on to the stage as quickly as I could. 1939 JOYCE *Finnegans Wake* I. 146 The little passdoor, I go you before, so, and you're at my apron stage. 1950 'J. TEY' *To love & be Wise* xviii. 233 Marta.. came down to the edge of the stage... 'Come through the pass door, will you?' 1970 A. MORICE *Death in Grand Manor* x. 103 Be an angel, Annie, and show Miss Crichton to the pass door. 1909 *Daily Chron.* 20 Feb. 4/4 Opium.. is grown in the Native States, the Government levying a heavy *pass duty on its entrance to British territory. 1657 *Records of Elgin* (New Spald. Cl.) I. 300 Money not *pasguilt. The officers are ordained.. to advertise the inhabitants not to receive this newe brought in base couper coyne. 1659 W. GUTHRIE *Chr. Gt. Interest* II. (1724) 169 His Prayers, his other Service done to God, his Alms-deeds, &c. are not Pass-gilt before God, since they came not from a right Principle in his Heart.. his sacrifices have been an abomination. 1948 *Times* 14 Jan. 2/5 It has been found that the low-mounted *passlamp is especially liable to cause dazzle. 1897 A. MILNER *Let.* 12 Aug. in C. Headlam *Milner Papers* (1931) I. vi. 194 If they do exempt Cape Boys from the degrading provisions of the *Pass Law. 1901 Pass law [see sense 8f above]. 1921 *Outward Bound* May 46/2 Soon after that, all my own boys cleared one night... I would not report them, that was not my way, let the pass-law say what it pleased. I don't hold with pass-law slavery. 1948 *Rep. Native Laws Comm. 1946–48* (Dept. Native Affairs, S. Afr.) 26/1 They regard even the certificates of exemption, which are issued to them as evidence of exemption from the pass laws, as passes; for only Natives require them, and they must be produced at any time on demand by an authorised official. 1956 T. HUDDLESTON *Naught for your Comfort* ii. 30 Another consequence of the pass laws—a consequence known to every intelligent South African at all interested in penal reform—is that it leads to an absolute contempt for the law. 1960 *Observer* 27 Mar. 16/4 Throughout South Africa's history, the pass laws have caused more bitter resentment than any other grievance. 1971 *Rand Daily Mail* 4 Dec. 1/1 It is where family life—the very basis of stability in traditional African societies—is being devastated by the pass laws and other apartheid regulations. 1974 A. WILLIAMS *Gentleman Traitor* xiii. 213 Two African youths had been arrested for breaking the Pass Laws. 1977 *Times* 16 Feb. 8/3 Legislation tabled in Parliament [in South Africa] today proposes the doubling of fines for violations of the country's pass laws. 1977 *Time* 2 May 22/3 The 'pass laws'—which control the movement of blacks into white areas—cost South Africa no less than $130 million a year to administer. 1938 *Times* 20 July 12/5 A rubber footrest for the clutch foot in which is the switch to cut out the head-lamps and put on a *pass-light. 1948 *Times* 14 Jan. 2/5 Three-quarters of the cases of dazzle are caused by dipped headlights and pass lights. 1959 *Motor Manual* (ed. 36) vi. 181 The so-called spotlight.. provides a concentrated beam, but of more general use is the pass-light or fog-lamp, which is designed to throw a broad, flat beam with a fairly sharply defined top edge. 1965 PRIESTLEY & WISDOM *Good Driving* ii. 21 Many cars are fitted with 'fog' or 'pass' lights. 1938 *Times* 14 Oct. 11/1 Radio sets, permanent jacking systems, and an arrangement of *pass-lighting which conduces to safety are outstanding features in standardization this year. 1888 *Encycl. Brit.* XXIII. 179/2 A 'pass' [is called] if the ball has gone beyond the *pass line. 1911 *Ibid.* XXVI. 627/1 The pass-line is drawn 7 ft. 8 in. from the main wall. 1935 *Encycl. Sports* 619/2 On the 'hazard side' of the court.. is traced the 'service line'.. and at right angles to this again is the 'pass line'. 1961 J. S. SALAK *Dict. Amer. Sports* 321 *Pass line* (court tennis)—the line on the floor nearest the grille and extending from the service line to the grille wall. 1908 *Daily Chron.* 29 Sept. 1/6 Lasker has a *pass pawn, but.. a draw appears probable. 1657 W. RAND tr. *Gassendi's Life Peiresc* II. 50 Whether the Ægyptians also were wont to put a *Passe-penny in the mouth of the dead. 1968 *Globe & Mail* (Toronto) 11 July 32/5 Turek scored on a 71-yard *pass play with Joe Zuger. 1969 *Official Playing Rules Canad. Football* 29 For interference on a forward pass play see Rule 6, Section 4. 1970 *Toronto Daily Star* 24 Sept. 17/7 Eckman added Ticats' clinching touchdown a few minutes later when he shook off a blitzing B.C. lineman and ran seven yards on a broken pass play. 1958 *New Statesman* 8 Nov. 619/3 '*Pass raids' are so commonplace in Johannesburg that even few liberal whites experience any real shock when they see a group of 10 or 20 Africans under police guard on a street corner, waiting to become part of the more than a thousand of their kind who, every day of the year, spend at least a day in custody because their papers are not in order. 1971 *Rand Daily Mail* 27 Mar. 1/1 To this is added perpetual insecurity, the harassment of pass raids and the miseries of life below the poverty datum line. 1877 C. HALLOCK *Sportsm. Gaz.* 204 Another method is *pass shooting; that is, standing.. in belts of woods, over which the birds fly when travelling in their afternoon flights to the roosting and feeding grounds. 1761 *Ann. Reg.* 229 The friendship of Mr. Rolles, who had procured me a *pass ticket, as they call it, enabled me to be present both in the hall and the abbey. 1840 *Penny Cycl.* XVIII. 401/2 Paupers who have no settlement must be maintained by the parish in which they happen to be, as casual poor, unless they were born in Scotland or Ireland, or in the islands of Man, Jersey, or Guernsey, in which case they are to be taken under a *pass-warrant of two justices to their own country. 1896 *Westm. Gaz.* 13 Feb. 1/3 One of the resolutions.. proposes that only women who have taken honours.. shall be eligible for the degree, a diploma being offered to the '*passwoman' in lieu thereof. 1900 G. C. BRODRICK *Mem. & Impressions* 349 If there should ever be a large influx of pass-women of the same type as pass-men.. difficulties of discipline will be greatly aggravated.

†**pass**, *sb.*³ *Obs. rare.* Also 5 **passe**. [ad. L. *passum* raisin-wine, made from dried grapes, neuter of *passus* spread out, (of fruit) spread out to dry, dried, pa. pple. of *pandĕre* to spread: cf. *uvæ passæ* raisins.] Raisin-wine; also attrib. **pass-wine**. Now in L. form **passum**.

c1420 *Pallad. on Husb.* XI. 491 Now passe is maad that Affryk vseth make Aforn vyndage. 1671 CHARENTE *Lett. Customs Mauritania* 37 They.. are forc'd to make use of Pass-wine, or Raisin-wine, for they call Raisin of the sun Pass,.. it is a white Wine, but muddy. [1811 HOOPER *Med. Dict.*, *Passum*, Raisin-wine. 1841 SPALDING *Italy & It. Isl.* I. 381 The passum was made from raisins.]

pass (pɑːs, -æ-), *v.* Forms: 3–5 **passe(n**, (3 **passi**, 3–5 **-y**, 4 **paci**, **pasi**, **-ye**, 4–5 **passyn**, **pacyn**), 3–7 **passe**, (4 **pasce**, 4–6 **pas**, **pase**, **pace**), 4– **pass**. Pa. t. and pple. **passed**, **past** (now rarely as pa. t.); also 4 **paced**, **pased**, 4–6 *Sc.* **passit**; 3–5 **ipassed**, **ipast**, 4–6 **ypassed**, **ypast**. [a. F. *pass-er* (11th c. in Littré, Hatz.-Darm.), a Com. Romanic vb.; in Pr. *passar*, Sp. *pasar*, It. *passare*:—late pop.L. *passāre (med.L. in Du Cange, with derivs. of 11th c.), f. *pass-us* step, pace, track (PASS *sb.*¹). The primary signification was thus 'to step, pace, walk', but already in 11th c. OF. it had come to denote progression or moving on from place to place. *Pass* and *pace* are the same word, the forms having been in later times differentiated, and *pace* restricted to those senses which are akin to or derived from PACE *sb.*, while *pass* has been retained for the other original senses and the newer ones developed from them.]

In Eng. *pass* has become the most general verb expressing onward motion; *passing* may consist in going, running, riding, flying, swimming, sailing, floating, gliding, or in being carried, drawn, driven, impelled, or moved on, in any way. In many cases the intrans. sense can be expressed by *go*, especially when construed with, or extended by, prepositions or adverbs expressing varieties of direction, etc.; but it can be used in many transferred senses in which *go* is inapplicable; e.g. to *pass* into a new state or condition, or to a new subject. It differs from *move* in expressing the effect rather than the action. Without any prepositional or adverbial extension, the original and intrans. use is now chiefly confined to senses 12 and 18, being otherwise less frequent than the derived trans. and causal uses in branches II and III.

As in other intrans. vbs. of motion (*go*, *come*, *depart*, etc.), the perfect of resultant condition had originally the auxiliary *be* (*he is* passed, they *were* passed): cf. sense 1, quot. c1380, 1b, 14.., 2, c1400, etc. This was sometimes retained even when *pass* was transitive: cf. sense 34, quot. 1375; 38, quots. 14.., 1526, etc. Hence arose the later PAST *prep.*, q.v.

I. Intransitive uses.

* To go, proceed, move onward.

1. a. To go on, move onward, proceed; to make one's way. Now usually with some preposition, adv., or advb. extension = *go* (with same extension).

1297 R. GLOUC (Rolls) 4498, & vor to passy vorþ þe mouns he ȝarkede uaste is route. c1320 *Sir Beues* 2043 (MS. A) Euer a was pasaunt, Til a com to Mombraunt. c1380 *Sir Ferumb.* 2026 Wan þay weren alle yn y-paste.. Floripe het schitte þe dore faste. 1423 JAS. I *Kingis Q.* xxii, Out of my contree.. Be se to pas, tuke I myn auenture. 1456 SIR G. HAYE *Law Arms* (S.T.S.) 178 He understude nocht that he suld pas be see.. and thare sa mony.. that may pas land gate. 1549 *Compl. Scot.* Ded. 6 Ther durst none of that grit companye pas bakuart nor forduart. 1593 SHAKS. *1 Hen. VI*, II. i. 69 Most part of all this Night.. I was imploy'd in passing to and fro, About relieuing of the Centinels. 1667 MILTON *P.L.* II. 1031 A Bridge.. by which the Spirits perverse With easie intercourse pass to and fro. 1727 GAY *Fables* I. xv. 7 But where he past, he terror threw.

b. With advb. accusative, expressing route or distance, as *to pass that way*, *to pass a mile*, etc.

a1300 *Cursor M.* 8806 Quen he moght pass nanoþer gatt. 14.. *Sir Beues* 89/1725 + 7 (MS. C) When he was paste a myle fro Damaske. c1475 *Rauf Coilȝear* 570 Sir gaitis pas thay, Baith to Paris in fay. 1596 SPENSER *F.Q.* V. ii. 6 For never wight he lets to passe that way Over his Bridge,.. But he him makes his passage-penny pay. 1611 CORYAT *Crudities* 93 After I was passed a few miles from Vercellis, I came into the Dukedome of Milan. 1847 TENNYSON *Princ.* I. 183 She once had past that way.

c. Of something inanimate or involuntary: To move on under any force, to be moved, carried, conveyed, transported, impelled onward; to flow as water, a stream, etc.

1340–70 *Alex. & Dind.* 140 From perlese paradis passeþ þe stronde. 1585 T. WASHINGTON tr. *Nicholay's Voy.* III. vii. 80 If the water do.. passe aboue the gyrdlesteed, they haue a hundred Aspres. 1617 MORYSON *Itin.* I. 146 A bridge.. with three Arches, vnder which the boates passe. 1703 MOXON *Mech. Exerc.* 177 That the Pole may.. pass from one Puppet to the other, as the Work may require. 1794 MRS. RADCLIFFE *Myst. Udolpho* xv, The river was gay with boats passing to that city. 1846 McCULLOCH *Acc. Brit. Empire* (1854) II. 11 No official accounts having been kept of the quantity or value of the articles passing between the two countries. 1899 *Allbutt's Syst. Med.* VIII. 23 While the rheophore is thus placed and the current still passing, the patient should be made to exercise these muscles.

d. Of a line, string, path, etc.: To extend or be continued, to have its course, 'run'.

1703 MOXON *Mech. Exerc.* 220 Each two Centers.. shall have an imaginary Axis pass between them. 1726 tr. *Gregory's Astron.* I. 439 A Diameter of the Ellipse.. passing thro' the given Points *B* and *A*. 1793 SMEATON *Edystone L.* §254 *note*, Two strong.. ropes, one passing from the head of the shears.. to the rocks. 1813 HOBHOUSE *Journey* 485 The path passes round a bay, where there is a solitary cottage. 1884 BOWER & SCOTT *De Bary's Phaner.* 297 Branch bundles passing down through the cortex.

e. To proceed or go on in narration, consideration, or action. Now usually *pass on*: see 65a.

c1384 CHAUCER *H. Fame* III. 265 But hit were alle to longe to rede The names and therefore I pace. c1386 —— *Prol.* 36 Er that I ferther in this tale pace. 1563 SHUTE *Archit.* F ij, The whiche pillor of .60. foote in height shalbe deuided into .9. partes, where of the Epistilium occupieth.. one such part, and so passing forward as necessitie shall requyre in order as is before mencioned. 1585 T. WASHINGTON tr. *Nicholay's Voy.* II. viii. 42, I will not passe further without first making a.. description of the yle. 1620 T. GRANGER *Div. Logike* 309 One being finished, we immediately passe to another. 1899 F. HARRISON *Tennyson, Ruskin, Mill*, etc. i. 10 So far we have been considering the lyrical form of the *In Memoriam*... We pass to its substance.

2. a. With reference to place or object of destination. Chiefly with *to* (*unto*, *into*).

c1350 *Leg. Rood* (1871) 75 Till araby sone gan he pas. 1362 LANGL. *P. Pl.* A. VII. 77 To Penaunce and to pilgrimage I wol passe with þis oþure. c1384 CHAUCER *H. Fame* II. 212 [It] stant eke in so Juste a place That every soune mot to hyt pace. c1400 *Laud Troy Bk.* 5606 Now ben thei alle to batayle paste. a1425 *Cursor M.* 1034 (Trin.) A welle.. þat renneþ out of foure stremes Passynge into dyuerse remes. 1589 GREENE *Menaphon* (Arb.) 21 Democles.. elected two of his chiefe Lordes to passe vnto Delphos. 1600 J. PORY tr. *Leo's Africa* IX. 334 This riuer taking his originall from mount Atlas.. passeth southward. 1782 A. MONRO *Anat. Bones, Nerves*, etc. 15 The marrow passes into the articular cavities. 1864 TENNYSON *En. Ard.* 326 She rose.. And past into the little garth beyond.

b. Of spiritual destination; esp. in *to pass to God, heaven*, etc.

a1225 *Ancr. R.* 330 Þet we moten þuruh rudi scheome passen to þe heouene. c1375 *Sc. Leg. Saints* xxxviii. (*Adrian*) 150, I sal cume.. & cal þe.. to pas to God quhen we are bone. 1453 *Paston Lett.* I. 256 He passyd to God on Monday last past, at xj. of the clok befor none. 1517 *Knaresborough Wills* (Surtees) I. 6 All my good freindes passyd to the mercie of God. 1602 SHAKS. *Hamlet* I. ii. 73 All that liues must dye, Passing through Nature, to Eternity. 1859 TENNYSON *Guinevere* 690 She.. past To where beyond these voices there is peace.

** To go about, circulate, have currency (in some capacity or character).

†**3. a.** To go about, to travel; to move about, be astir, be alive and active. *to pass on earth* (*mold*), to have one's active being, to exist: cf. GO *v.* B. 1b.

1340–70 *Alex. & Dind.* 741 Whi fauure ȝe þanne falce godus, and folliche seggen þat þei han power of peple þat pacen on molde? 1362 LANGL. *P. Pl.* A. I. 7 þe moste parti of þe peple þat passeþ nou on eorþe. 1393 *Ibid.* C. VII. 67 Hadde he wysshes at wille, Sholde no lyf lyuye, þat on hus londe passede. 1561 *Reg. Privy Council Scot.* I. 162 That na skipparis, marineris, nor utheris pass in company with thame. 1567 *Gude & Godlie B.* (S.T.S.) 45 He did his Apostillis teiche, Throw all the warld for to pas, And till all Creature for to preiche. 1585 T. WASHINGTON tr. *Nicholay's Voy.* IV. i. 114 Yong men.. passyng as I haue said, in the nightes to goe about the streetes.

†**b.** *well to pass*, well to do, well off (cf. †*well to live*) *Obs.*: see WELL *adv.*

4. To be handed round or about; to circulate, be in circulation, be current, have currency. *to pass current* (†*for current*): see CURRENT *a.* 8.

1589 NASHE *Anat. Absurd.* Wks. (Grosart) I. 65 Vpstart reformers.. coueting to haue newe opinions passe vnder their names. 1639 T. BRUGIS tr. *Camus' Moral Relat.* 248 This foolish and false rule of honour, which passeth.. among the Nobility and Gentry of France. a1715 BURNET *Own Time* VI. (1734) II. 161 Our money they thought would not pass, and so the Markets would not be furnished. 1731 SWIFT *On Death Dr. Swift* 189 And then, to make them pass the glibber, Revised by Tibbalds, Moore, and Cibber. 1777 SHERIDAN *Sch. Scand.* III. iii. *song*, Let the toast pass, drink to the lass. 1810 SIR A. BOSWELL *Edinburgh* xiii, From hand to hand the whirling halfpence pass. 1872 E. W. ROBERTSON *Hist. Ess.* I. i. 3 The coinage of Constantinople passed.. over the greater part of the Eastern world. 1886 *Manch. Exam.* 13

Mar. 5/2 A certain quantity of paper engraved and signed so as to pass instead of gold.

5. a. *to pass for, as*: to be accepted as equivalent to; to be taken for; to be accepted, received, or held in repute as. Often with the implication of being something else.

1596 SHAKS. *Merch. V.* I. ii. 61 God made him, and therefore let him passe for a man. 1607 MIDDLETON *Michaelm. Term* II. iii. 289, I might make my bond pass for a hundred pound i' th' city. 1662 STILLINGFL. *Orig. Sacr.* III. ii. §17 Had Lucretius been only a Poet, this might have passed for a handsomly described Fable. 1688 R. HOLME *Armoury* III. 29/1 The Double Rose Noble..passes for thirty nine or Forty shillings. 1711 ADDISON *Spect.* No. 1 ¶5, I..sometimes pass for a Jew in the Assembly of Stock-jobbers at Jonathan's. 1809 MALKIN *Gil Blas* IX. vii. ¶1 You pass for a kind-hearted gentleman. 1870 FREEMAN *Norm. Conq.* (ed. 2) I. App. 664 Something happened..which at least passed for a regular election. 1884 H. SPENCER *Man v. State, New Toryism* 1 Most of those who now pass as Liberals, are Tories of a new type. 1933 M. GRANT *Conquest of Continent* 269 This enables some of these light Negroes to 'pass' as Whites. 1948 *Time* 16 Feb. 25/1 Possibly as many as 5,000,000 people with 'a determinable part' of Negro blood are now 'passing' as whites.

b. *to pass by*: to be currently known by (a name or appellation).

1761 HUME *Hist. Eng.* II. App. iii. 518 Davis..discovered the Straits which pass by his name. *Ibid.* (1806) IV. lix. 460 A low room, which passed by the appellation of 'hell'. 1894 HUXLEY *Evol. & Ethics* Prolegom. 13 That progressive modification of civilisation which passes by the name of the 'evolution of society'.

c. *to pass on, upon*: to impose upon; to gain credit with.

1678 BUTLER *Hud.* III. i. 1202 'Tis true, I thought the Trick would pass Upon a Woman well enough. *a* 1680 —— *Rem.* (1759) I. 229 Illiterate Dunces undiscern'd Pass on the Rabble for the learn'd. 1738 tr. *Guazzo's Art Conversation* 192, I am now sensible that you have passed upon me very pleasantly. 1781 C. JOHNSTON *Hist. J. Juniper* I. 193 This imposition was too gross to pass upon him. 1802–12 BENTHAM *Ration. Judic. Evid.* (1827) V. 60 Such modes of speaking as would not pass for reasons upon any body. 1895 *Century Mag.* Sept. 676/2 It was a poor thing for the Bruce boys to do, to try to pass upon him like this.

d. To be held or accepted as a member of a religious or ethnic group other than one's own. Used esp. of a person of Negro ancestry who is held to be or regards himself as a white person.

1935 H. W. HORWILL *Dict. Mod. Amer. Usage* 224/2 In Am. there are many persons with a strain of Negro blood in whom this heritage of colour is so inconspicuous that they might easily be supposed to be of pure white lineage. If such persons leave their Negro associations and succeed in becoming accepted as Whites, they are said to *pass*. 1938 I. GOLDBERG *Wonder of Words* vi. 118 There are other Jews who resembling, psychologically, the troubled Negro—try to 'pass', which is the Negro term for being taken as a White. 1952 M. STEEN *Phoenix Rising* vii. 170 Coloured people who hide their origin and live as whites are said to 'pass'. 1953 E. H. BROOKES *S. Afr. in Changing World* vii. 147 Because of the permutations of nature, a coloured man white enough to 'pass' can have children or grandchildren who look 'Coloured'. 1955 D. VIKLUND tr. *Tingsten's Probl. S. Afr.* xiii. 148 There are two coloured brothers. One of them manages to 'pass' and becomes a barrister, a respectable member of white Cape society. 1960 D. JACOBSON *Evidence of Love* 92 He could 'pass' in the Transvaal, very easily, she thought. 1963 M. MCCARTHY *Group* xiv. 319 'Freddy's parents were trying to pass,' she went on sombrely. 'Like so many rich German Jews.' 1966 K. L. MORGAN in A. Dundes *Mother Wit* (1973) 606/2 The children used to love to come to Philadelphia with Caddy because there they could pass and have fun. 1971 *Encycl. Judaica* X. 60 At the height of 19th-century liberalism in Europe and America, it was possible for some Jews to 'pass' without doing anything more than simply ceasing to function in any Jewish association. 1976 *Wilson Q.* Autumn 87 Acceptable pigmentation plus wealth and influence were necessary for persons who hoped to obtain the *limpeza-de-sangue* document. But how dark one could be and still 'pass' varied from region to region.

*** To go from one to another, be transferred.

6. To go or be transported from one place or set of circumstances to another. (Usually with prep.) *hey pass!* a conjurer's exclamation, professing to order something to go from one place to another.

c 1340 HAMPOLE *Prose Tr.* 8 Fowheles..þat passes fra a land to a-nothire. 1573–80 BARET *Alv.* P 163 A griefe passed from the side into the heart. 1727 GAY *Fables* I. xlii. 35 'See this bank-note: observe the blessing: Breathe on the bill'. Heigh! pass! 'tis gone. 1860 TINDALL *Glac.* II. iv. 248 Nothing..is more common than to pass, in descending a mountain, from snow to rain.

7. To undergo transition from one form or state to another, 'to be changed by regular gradations' (J.); to undergo chemical, mineralogical, structural, or other gradual conversion *into*.

c 1385 CHAUCER *L.G.W.* 1583 *Hypsip.*, And from forme in to forme it [matter] passyn may. 1618 CHAPMAN *Hesiod* I. 197 Jove's will was, The good should into heavenly natures pass. 1674 PLAYFORD *Skill Mus.* III. 5 That which is a fifth shall pass into a third. 1710 BERKELEY *Princ. Hum. Knowl.* §124 Ancient and rooted prejudices do often pass into principles. 1813 BAKEWELL *Introd. Geol.* (1815) 197 It is said that peat has been discovered passing into mineral coal. 1851 WRIGHT *Richardson's Geol.* 126 Thus granite passes through syenite and greenstone into basalt, and this last to pitchstone. 1854 BREWSTER *More Worlds* xv. 228 Our Earth passed from a state of chaos into an orderly world. 1855 PRESCOTT *Philip II*, I. II. iii. 179 The hatred of theologians has passed into a proverb. 1871 B. STEWART *Heat* (ed. 2) §84 A substance passes from the solid to the liquid state. 1899 *Allbutt's Syst. Med.* VIII. 595 The patient then passes into a severe general lichen, after the ordinary type.

8. *Law.* Of property: To be conveyed *to* a person; to go by conveyance, or come by inheritance *to, into the hands of*.

1429 *Rolls Parlt.* IV. 344/1 Neyther be colour or occasion of feffement or of yeft of gode moeble passede be Dede, nor other wyse. *c* 1449 PECOCK *Repr.* II. 404 The ȝifte so mad to him passid into him fulli and hooli. 1574 tr. *Littleton's Tenures* 47 Al the rente and service..bee incidences to the reversion and passe by the graunte of reversion. 1611 BIBLE *Num.* xxvii. 7 Thou shalt cause the inheritance of their father to passe vnto them. 1642 tr. *Perkins' Prof. Bk.* iii. §204. 91 If liverie and seisin bee made unto the Monke..nothing shall passe thereby. 1818 CRUISE *Digest* (ed. 2) V. 51 The advowson passed, because it was clearly referred to in the grant. 1883 *Law Times Rep.* XLIX. 337/1 There is no case in which the benefit of a personal covenant, not assignable on the face of it, has been held to pass by assignment.

9. To be uttered between two (or more) persons mutually; to be interchanged or transacted, as discourse, communications, letters, mutual offices.

1568 T. HOWELL *Arb. Amitie* (1879) 91 Remember yet the friendly wordes, ypast betweene vs twaine. *c* 1592 MARLOWE *Jew of Malta* II. 462 Here must no speeches passe, nor swords be drawne. 1598 SHAKS. *Merry W.* III. v. 63 Now M. Broome, you come to know What hath past betweene me, and Fords wife. 1712 STEELE *Spect.* No. 263 ¶5 Two Letters which passed between a Mother and Son very lately. 1773 GOLDSM. *Stoops to Conq.* v, I know what has past between you. 1819 SHELLEY *Julian & Maddalo* 158 The Count entered. Salutations passed. 1885 *Gd. Words* 258/2 Then, by-and-by, the vesper bells at ten ring out from the steeple, ..some moral reflections pass.

**** With reference to place left: To go away.

10. a. To go away; to go forth, depart, remove *from* (†*of, off*) a place, thing, or person. Of a thing: To be taken away or removed (*from*).

a 1300 *Cursor M.* 13731 Giue vs þi dome, and lat vs pas. *c* 1330 *King of Tars* 49 That schul ye witen ar ye pase. 13.. *Cursor M.* 4001 (Gött.) If þu will þai sal pasce, And cum nohut in his hand percas. *c* 1384 CHAUCER *H. Fame* I. 239 And shortly of this thyng to pace. *c* 1400 *Destr. Troy* 1896 Pas fro my presens on payne of þi lyffe. *c* 1435 *Torr. Portugal* 1483 Fro the wyld bestis gan he passe To an hye hyll. 1456 SIR G. HAYE *Law Arms* (S.T.S.) 147 To pas of the contree. 1530 PALSGR. 653/2, I passe, I go forthe or away, *je passe*. 1611 BIBLE *Matt.* xxvi. 39 If it be possible, let this cup passe from me. 1819 BYRON *Juan* II. cx, The sand Swam round and round, and all his senses pass'd. 1879 E. ARNOLD *Lt. Asia* III. (1883) 66 The holy man..made The eight prostrations,..Then turned and passed.

†**b.** *to pass one's way*: to depart. *Obs.*

c 1375 *Sc. Leg. Saints* xi. (*Symon & Iudas*) 384 þane þe apostolis can assay owt of þe land to pass þar vay. *Ibid.* xxxiii. (*George*) 346[He] lape one horse & passit his way. 1375 BARBOUR *Bruce* IX. 184 In pess lete thame pass thar vay. *c* 1386 CHAUCER *Miller's T.* 387 That we may frely passen forth oure way. *c* 1435 *Torr. Portugal* 771 And hys way fast ageyn dyd pase.

c. *fig.* To depart, diverge *from* a course, practice, principle; *to pass from* (†*of*) = to leave, abandon, forsake; †*to pass of wit*, to go out of one's wits.

c 1400 *Destr. Troy* 8685 Sum walt into wodenes, & of wit past. *c* 1449 PECOCK *Repr.* I. 176 A man leueth..and passith fro that that he hath toke upon him to kepe as lawe of God. 1497 BP. ALCOCK *Mons Perfect.* C iij, As a henne yᵗ passeth fro her egges & suffre them to be colde. 1777 WATSON *Philip II*, I. x. 285 Intreating him..to pass from the other taxes.

11. To depart from this life, decease, die. **a.** with various extensions, as *to pass hence*, etc.

a 1300 *Cursor M.* 17019 þe..wittes five..all sal be tint er saul pas. *a* 1330 *Roland & V.* 130 To sende him miȝt & space,..Er he hennes passe. *c* 1375 *Lay Folks Mass Bk.* 295 (MS. B) And for þo soules þat hethen are past. 1482 *Monk of Evesham* (Arb.) 72 The sowlys that passyn hens out of this world. 1583 *Leg. Bp. St. Androis* Pref. 74 Lyk to our faythfull pastoris past befoir. 1613 SHAKS. *Hen. VIII*, IV. ii. 162 His long trouble now is passing Out of this world. 1871 R. ELLIS *Catullus* lxiv. 153 No handful of earth shall bury me, pass'd to the shadows. 1874 L. STEPHEN *Hours in Library* (1892) I. vii. 237 There passed from among us a man who held a high..position in English literature.

b. *simply.* Now *arch.* or *dial.*

1340 *Ayenb.* 214 Non ne wot huanne he ssel sterue ne huanne he ssel paci. *c* 1386 CHAUCER *Sqr.'s T.* 486 Myn harm I wol confessen er I pace. 1418 in *E.E. Wills* (1883) 38 3yf þat I passe Rather þan sche. 1593 SHAKS. *2 Hen. VI*, III. iii. 25 Disturbe him not, let him passe peaceably. 1605 —— *Lear* v. iii. 314 Vex not his ghost, O let him passe. 1850 TENNYSON *In Mem.* lx, He past; a soul of nobler tone. 1878 SEELEY *Stein* III. 560 About 6 o'clock [he] was seen to turn on his left side, breathe a deep sigh, and pass.

***** To go by, move past.

12. a. To go by. Now the leading intransitive sense of the simple verb. (Not in J.)

c 1320 *Sir Beues* 849 (MS. A) A wende pasi in griþ & pes, þe stiward cride; 'Leiþ on & sles'. *c* 1430 *Syr Tryam.* 219 An olde knyȝt that may hur lede, Tylle sche be paste. 1477 EARL RIVERS (Caxton) *Dictes* 99 Ther passed a theef byfore alexandre. 1549 *Compl. Scot.* Ded. 6 The hagbutaris past neir to the camp of ther enemeis. 1611 BIBLE *1 Sam.* xvi. 10 Againe Iesse made seuen of his sonnes to passe before Samuel. 1708 *Lond. Gaz.* No. 4445/3 The Right of the Foot .., pass'd yesterday in Review before his Grace. 1842 TENNYSON *Voyage* vi, And hills and scarlet-mingled woods Glow'd for a moment as we past. 1878 B. TAYLOR *Deukalion* III. ii. 105 At a distance I Have seen thee pass. *Mod.* Allow me to pass, please. Looking on as the procession passed.

b. Of things: To be moved, conveyed, impelled past; to flow past. Also *fig.*

13.. *K. Alis.* 2192 That launce paced without harme: Ac Alisaundre him smot thorugh the brest. 1585 T. WASHINGTON tr. *Nicholay's Voy.* I. xii. 14 At the beginning of the valley passe two smal riuers. 1590 SPENSER *F.Q.* I. ii. 22 And high hath set his throne where Tiberis doth pas. 1594 SHAKS. *Rich. III*, I. ii. 38 My Lord stand backe, and let the Coffin passe. 1596 —— *1 Hen. IV*, IV. i. 95 The nimble-footed Mad-Cap, Prince of Wales,..that daft the World aside, And bid it passe. *a* 1689 MRS. BEHN *Dream*, The grove was gloomy all around, Murmuring the stream did pass. 1748 THOMSON *Cast. Indol.* I. vi, Gay castles in the clouds that pass. 1836 J. H. NEWMAN *Prayer* ii. in *Lyra Apost.* (1849) 65 The pageant of a kingdom vast, And things unutterable, past Before the Prophet's eye.

c. With various complementary adjs., mostly of negative meaning, as *to pass unheeded, unnoticed*, etc. *lit.* and *fig.*

1607 MIDDLETON *Michaelm. Term* II. i. 109 Do I pass altogether unnoted, think you? 1624 QUARLES *Div. Poems, Sion's Sonn.* (1717) 382 Those crimes Which past unthought of in my prosp'rous times. 1766 FORDYCE *Serm. Yng. Wom.* (1767) I. i. 13 It is done every day, and passes unregarded. 1784 COWPER *Task* I. 317 Nor unnoted pass The sycamore, capricious in attire. 1809 BYRON *Eng. Bards & Sc. Rev.* 255 Shall gentle Coleridge pass unnoticed here?

13. Of time and temporal things, conditions, etc.: **a.** Of time: To elapse, glide by, come to an end.

13.. R. GLOUC. (Rolls) App. XX. 578 Twelf hundred & sixtene þer to ȝeres were ipassed, ar þis were ido. 1377 LANGL. *P. Pl.* B. v. 416 And vigilies and fastyng dayes alle þise late I passe, And ligge abedde in lenten. 1388 WYCLIF *Job* xvii. 11 Mi daies ben passid. 1523 LD. BERNERS *Froiss.* I. 84 The first day passed without any thing doyng. 1697 DRYDEN *Virg. Georg.* III. 82 More Ages..Than have from Tithon past to Cæsar's Days. 1736 BUTLER *Anal.* I. ii. Wks. 1874 I. 42 If the husbandman lets his seedtime pass without sowing, the whole year is lost to him. 1826 DISRAELI *Viv. Grey* v. x, The first few days..appear to pass very slowly. 1856 SIR B. BRODIE *Psychol. Inq.* I. iv. 148 As we advance in age so do the years pass more rapidly. *Mod.* Make haste; time passes!

b. Of things in time.

13.. *Cursor M.* 27630 If þou be fair, it passes sone. 1382 WYCLIF *Luke* xxi. 33 Heuene and erthe schulen passe: but my wordis schulen not passe. 1502 ATKYNSON tr. *De Imitatione* I. xx. 169 The worlde passeth with all his plesaunt delites. 1590 SPENSER *F.Q.* II. xii. 75 So passeth, in the passing of a day, Of mortall life the leafe, the bud, the flowre. 1667 MILTON *P.L.* v. 453 Not to let th' occasion pass. 1697 DRYDEN *Virg. Past.* II. 20 Beauty's a Charm, but soon the Charm will pass. *a* 1771 GRAY *Song* 10 Skies serene Speak not always winter past. 1841 JAMES *Brigand* i, Thus passed the earlier part of the day's journey. 1882 TENNYSON *To Virgil* vii, Kings and realms that pass to rise no more.

****** To go or get through.

14. a. To go or get through (esp. by a narrow or contracted passage, or in face of obstructions and difficulties); to have, obtain, or force passage, to make one's way. Also of things.

c 1320 *Sir Beues* 4417 (MS. A) To Iesu he made his praiere ..þat he moste pase wiþ is lif, To sen is children and is wif. *c* 1325 *Metr. Hom.* 70 What thyng sall passe qwyte, And be noght in this snarres tane. *c* 1400 *Destr. Troy* 11149 The yates..þai stake,..Neuer in purpos with prise to pas at hom efte. 1509 *Act 1 Hen. VIII*, c. 9 *Preamble*, The Kynges Subgiectes shal nott..passe on horsebacke..nor on fote by that way. 1585 T. WASHINGTON tr. *Nicholay's Voy.* IV. xv. 129 Through which narrow streights, Alexander..made his armie to passe. 1588 SHAKS. *Tit. A.* I. i. 290 *Mut.* My Lord you passe not heere. *Tit.* What villaine Boy, bar'st me my way in Rome? 1667 MILTON *P.L.* III. 480 And they who to be sure of Paradise Dying put on the weeds of Dominic Or in Franciscan think to pass disguis'd. *a* 1700 B. E. *Dict. Cant. Crew* s.v., [At] Billiards, when the Ball goes through the Court or Porch, it is said to pass. 1879 E. ARNOLD *Lt. Asia* III. (1883) 80 At the gates he set A triple guard, and bade no man should pass By day or night, issuing or entering in.

fig. 1563–7 BUCHANAN *Reform. St. Andros* Wks. (1892) 12 No man salbe admittit..to the philosophie that has nocht passit be the first or second classe of humanite.

†**b.** To make the passage of a channel or sea.

1588 B. C. in Ellis *Orig. Lett.* Ser. II. III. 135 From Dunkerke is lately come to Lisbone a small shipp..having passed in vij daies. 1662 J. DAVIES tr. *Mandelslo's Trav.* 102 A hundred small vessels..which came from Cananor and the coasts of Malabar, and had pass'd, notwithstanding the blockhouse of Dutch vessels.

c. Of things: e.g. to be admitted through a customs barrier.

1637 *Star Chamb. Decree* §6 in *Milton's Areop.* (Arb.) 12 Nor shall any Searcher, Wayter, or other Officer belonging to the Custome-house,..suffer the same to passe. 1849 MACAULAY *Hist. Eng.* vi. II. 115 The officers of the customs allowed the superstitious garments and trinkets to pass.

d. To go through a duct; to be voided.

1731 ARBUTHNOT *Aliments* I. vi. (1735) 17 Such [substances], whose Tenacity exceeds the Powers of Digestion, will neither pass nor be converted into Aliment. 1801 *Med. Jrnl.* V. 480 When a bougie can readily pass, there is no necessity for using any other method. 1869 E. A. PARKES *Pract. Hygiene* (ed. 3) 181 If large quantities are given, much passes by the bowels. 1897 *Allbutt's Syst. Med.* IV. 233 The patient was progressing satisfactorily, save that ..the button had not passed.

15. To be allowed or not stopped by a censor, to go uncensured; to go without check or challenge; to be tolerated or allowed to serve the purpose; to be successful as an expedient or trick; to 'go down', to 'do'; to pass muster.

13.. *Cursor M.* 28707 (Cott.) For quen a sin was wroken sua, Hu sal he passe has hundret ma. 1565 ABP. PARKER in *Lett. Lit. Men* (Camden) 28 We thinke it maye so passe well ynoughe. 1613 SHAKS. *Hen. VIII*, Prol. 11 Those that come to see Onely a show or two, and so a gree The Play may passe. 1672 WYCHERLEY *Love in a Wood* v. iii, Indeed and indeed, the trick will not pass, Jonas. 1781 COWPER *Wks.*

(1837) XV. 92, I never suffer a line to pass till I have made it as good as I can. *a* **1850** ROSSETTI *Dante & Circ.* I. (1874) 108 This sonnet..might be divided yet more nicely, and made yet clearer; but this division may pass. **1876** OUIDA *Winter City* vi. 130 Pranks that pass in a palace, though the police would interfere in a dancing garden. **1907** G. B. SHAW *Major Barbara* II. 222 Youd pass still. Why didnt you dye your hair. **1962** J. BRAINE *Life at Top* xv. 191 She said: 'He's a lovely little boy.' 'He'll pass,' I said absently.

16. To be allowed and approved by a court, legislature, or deliberative body; to 'get through'; to receive legislative sanction; to be ratified.

1568 GRAFTON *Chron.* II. 110 Vpon him onely whome the king nominated, he compelled most commonly the election to passe. **1579** FULKE *Heskins's Parl.* 376 The bill will passe neuer the sooner. **1672** MARVELL *Corr.* Wks. 1872-5 II. 409, I tell him that we must get the Patent passe before Parliament. **1711** ADDISON *Spect.* No. 72 ¶5 This Resolution passed in a general Club *Nemine Contradicente.* **1765** *Chron.* in *Ann. Reg.* 154/2 A motion was lately made in the Irish house of commons to address his majesty..But it passed in the negative. **1790** BURKE *Fr. Rev.* Wks. V. 61 That great body or our statute law which passed under those whom they treat as usurpers. **1880** MCCARTHY *Own Times* IV. lviii. 285 The bill passed without substantial alteration.

17. To go or get through any trial successfully; *spec.* to be successful in an examination, to reach or satisfy the required standard. ***to pass master***, etc., to graduate as master, etc. (in some faculty).

1600 O. E. (? M. SUTCLIFFE) *Repl. Libel* I. viii. 217 Parsons is not onely a practitioner, but also has passed master in this facultie. **1727-41** CHAMBERS *Cycl.* s.v. *Degree*, To pass bachelor of divinity, the candidate must have been seven years master of arts. **1833** MARRYAT *P. Simple* xxxviii, If I pass, which I trust I shall be able to do. **1840** *Encycl. Brit.* (ed. 7) XXI. 498/2 The candidate for mathematical honours must, in the first instance, 'pass' in classics. **1843** *Penny Cycl.* XXVI. 29/2 Candidates will pass who show a competent knowledge in any two of the subjects. The list of the candidates who have passed is to be published. **1872** in *Athenæum* 11 May 583/2 Lest it should be supposed that no Lawrence could pass for the artillery. **1876** LUBBOCK *Elem. Educ.* in *Contemp. Rev.* June 79 Only 62,000 passed in any extra subject.

†**18.** To succeed, to be successful. *Obs.*

c **1400** *Destr. Troy* 8295 Than Troiell..Wold haue led the lord o-lyue to þe towne; But..Thai pullid hym with pyne, but passid þai noght. **1481** CAXTON *Godeffroy* ccviii. 304 They ansuerd that it shold be hard to be had, not withstondyng they muste essaye, ffor they myght passe in none other maner. **1589** NASHE *Martins Months Minde* Wks. (Grosart) I. 161 Howe they meane than to proceede (if they passe) shall bee a Mumchaunce for me.

******* To go beyond, exceed, excel, surpass.

†**19. a.** To excel, to surpass: to go to excess. *Obs.*

c **1380** WYCLIF *Wks.* (1880) 392 þouȝ þai be lesse in oo chirche, þai passen in an-oþer. *c* **1394** *P. Pl. Crede* 846 Paraunter y miȝte Passen par auenture, & in som poynt erren. *c* **1440** *Ipomydon* 916 In alle the feld was none so wight, But if it were my lord the kynge, For he is passand in euery thynge. **1526** SKELTON *Magnyf.* 1401 So dyd he excede & passe. *a* **1529** —— *Ph. Sparowe* 151 Because that she dyd pas In poesy to endyte. **1573-80** BARET *Alv.* P 169 Onely Demosthenes passeth, or excelleth. **1602** *Life T. Cromwell* v. iii. 123 My faith compar'd with thine as much shall pass As doth the diamond excel the glass. *c* **1611** CHAPMAN *Iliad* II. 594 The fairest man..Of all the Greeks, save Peleus' son, who pass'd for gen'ral frame.

b. *quasi*-impersonal, ***it passes***: it exceeds all ordinary limits, passes description, 'beats everything'. *Obs.*

1549 CHALONER tr. *Erasm. on Folly* K ij, It passeth, to see what sporte and passetyme the Godds them selues haue, at suche folie of these selie mortall men. **1599** PORTER *Angry Wom. Abingd.* in Hazl. *Dodsley* VII. 352, I, hearing her,..led her such a dance in the dark as it passes. **1606** SHAKS. *Tr. & Cr.* I. ii. 178 There was such laughing, and Hellen so blusht, and Paris so chaft, and all the rest so laught, that it past. *a* **1658** CLEVELAND *Wks.* (1687) 376 You keep such Hurly-burly that it passes. **1689** SHADWELL *Bury F.* I. i, And were as merry as pass'd.

******** **20.** Of events: To go on or proceed in the course of things; to take place, occur, happen. Formerly with indirect obj.: see quot. *a* 1542.

a **1542** WYATT *Let.* in *Wks.* (1861) p. xix, That I should write and declare such thinges as haue passed me whilst I was in the Emperor's Court. **1590** SPENSER *F.Q.* I. i. 30 If he did know Of straunge adventures, which abroad did pas. **1667** MILTON *P.L.* VIII. 173 Heav'n is for thee too high To know what passes there. **1732** BERKELEY *Alciphr.* II. §25, I am attentive to all that passes. **1802** MAR. EDGEWORTH *Moral T.* I. iii. 17 Reflect coolly upon what has passed. **1855** MACAULAY *Hist. Eng.* xvi. III. 726 Intelligence of what was passing was conveyed to the Lord President.

********* Used in reference to process of law.

[AF. *passer*, orig. to proceed, go on: cf. the legal sense of 'process', 'proceedings'.]

21. a. Of a jury (assize, inquest): To sit in inquest *on* or *upon*; to decide or adjudicate *between* parties; to give a verdict *for* or *against*. *arch.*

[**1293** *Yearbks. 20 & 21 Edw. I* (Rolls) 399 Lassise passe, ke dyt ke Willem sun pere..ne morut poynt seysy. *Ibid.* 401 [see 22 below]. *a* **1377** *Liber Assisarum* (Repts. of Edw. III, ed. 1679) 5 Si l'assise passe pur le demandant. *Ibid.* 46 Et l'assise passa sur le point contre le barun et la feme.] **13..** *Evang. Nicod.* 243 in Herrig *Archiv* LIII. 396 He chesed a quest, on him to pas. **1437** *Rolls of Parlt.* IV. 509/2 If the seid Thomas Stamford, perceyve that eny enquest woll not passe with his entent. **1442** T. BECKINGTON *Corr.* (Rolls) II. 215 We avis..not lightly to passe upon suche graunts of your demaynnes. **1454** *Rolls of Parlt.* V. 239/2 By the Jurre that passed betwene the said Duke and the said Thomas, it was founde that the same Thomas was gylty. **1473** SIR J. PASTON in *P. Lett.* III. 84 The jurye that passyd again Saundre. **1495** *Act 11 Hen. VII*, c. 21 Such persones as passen and ben impanelled upon issues joined between partie and partie in the Courtes of the same Citie. **1599** *Warn. Faire Wom.* II. 1209 Master Shiriff, ye shal not need to returne any Iury to passe upon him, for he hath pleaded guilty. **1688** *Jrnl. Ho. Comm.* (1803) X. 22 Jurors, which pass upon Men in Tryals for High Treason, ought to be Freeholders. **1752** J. LOUTHIAN *Form of Process* (ed. 2) 203 The Clerk saith to the Prisoner '..these Men which you shall hear called..are to pass between our Sovereign Lord the King and you, upon Trial of your Life and Death'. **1887** *Pall Mall G.* 4 Nov. 2/1 Judge Stephen has decided that a jury could not be trusted to pass upon the question of Endacott's good faith. **1901** *N. Amer. Rev.* Feb. 248 Sheriffs' juries should never be asked to do more than pass upon the estates of the alleged lunatics.

b. To serve or 'sit' *on* (*upon*, † *in*) a jury, assize, or trial.

1574 *Waterf. Arch.* in *10th Rep. Hist. MSS. Comm.* App. v. 333 Thinhabitanntes..used to passe in juries of triall. **1597** in Ferguson & Nanson *Munic. Rec. Carlisle* (1887) 277 Yf thes [slander] may goe unpunished, it is not for noe honest man..to pass upon any jury. **1752** J. LOUTHIAN *Form of Process* (ed. 2) 40 With a List of the Assizers Names and Designations, that are to pass upon his Assize. *Mod. Juryman's Oath* (Sc. Criminal Cases), You fifteen swear by Almighty God..you will truth say and no truth conceal, in so far as you are to pass on this assize.

c. Of a court, a judge, the law: To adjudicate, pass sentence *upon*, *on*. Also *transf.* (With *indirect passive.*)

1532 TINDALE *Pathw. Script.* Wks. (Parker Soc. 1848) 11 When the law hath passed upon us, and condemned us to death. **1545** RAYNOLD *Byrth Mankynde* Prol. C ij, Yf euery thynge in this wourdle shold be wayed and passyd vpon after this sorte. **1586** A. DAY *Eng. Secretary* I. (1625) 137 The laws must further passe vpon him. **1605** SHAKS. *Lear* III. vii. 24 We may not passe vpon his life Without the forme of Iustice. **1640** D. CAWDREY *Three Serm.* (1641) 12 A Commission of Oyer and Terminer, which passes upon life and death. **1680** HICKERINGILL *Narr. Tryal* Wks. 1716 II. 208 The wicked World..cannot pass upon it..till they have first defiled it with Lies and Slanders. *a* **1863** C. P. DALY in *Ct. Comm. Pleas, New York* in *Herald & Genealog.* (1863) 345 It does not fall within the sphere of my judicial duty to pass upon that question. **1896** *Law Times* C. 491/1 The conception of a judge to pass on questions of law, and a jury to pass on questions of fact. **1917** ADE *Let.* 29 July (1973) 68 If you want me to pass upon the sub-titles, I shall be glad to do so and if I change them it will be to make them more compact and not more intricate.

22. a. Of a verdict, sentence, or judgement: To be rendered, given, or pronounced; of justice: To be executed; †(rarely) of a case or suit: To be determined or decided (quot. 1453).

[**1293** *Yearbks. 20 & 21 Edw. I* 401 Unkes jugement ne passa sur le verdyt de le assise: kar, apres le Assise passe, les partyes aveyent jour pur oyer lur jugement; e la partye demandant ne voleyt pluys venyr en Court. *Ibid.* 411 Entre ky e ky passa le jugement?] *a* **1380** in Horstmann *Altenglische Legenden* (1878) I. 32/2 þe sentence, mayden, asoyleþ þe, Whon þat hit passeþ on me. **1453** *Rolls of Parlt.* V. 267/2 If..the mater pleded passe or be demed for the Pleintif therin. **1580** SIDNEY *Ps.* XVII. ii, O, let my sentence passe from thine own face. **1647** N. BACON *Disc. Govt. Eng.* I. xxxix. (1739) 59 After Verdict, Judgment passed according to the letter of the Law. **1771** GOLDSM. *Hist. Eng.* II. 82 A similar sentence passed against some of his adherents. **1818** JAS. MILL *Brit. India* II. IV. v. 199 Before his arrival, unlimited condemnation had passed on the whole of his proceedings. **1891** *Law Rep.* Weekly Notes 78/2 The verdict and judgment passed for the plaintiff.

†**b.** Of the accused: To undergo trial and sentence; to be sentenced. *Obs. rare.*

a **1533** LD. BERNERS *Huon* lxxxii. 254 To dyssymell the matter vayleth not, syn that Huon must passe by iugement; howe saye you, shall he be hangyd or drawen?

********** †**23.** To care, to reck. (Usually with negative.) *Obs.* **a.** Const. *for*: ***to pass for***, to care for, regard, mind.

1548 UDALL, etc. *Erasm. Par. Acts* 60 Paule and Sylas, not passyng for theyr whyppyng..prayed and song hymnes. **1565-73** *Durh. Depos.* (Surtees) 109 She..said that she dyd not passe yf all ropers were hanged. *a* **1568** ASCHAM *Scholem.* I. (Arb.) 82 They passe for no Doctores: They mocke the Pope: They raile on Luther. **1606** G. W[ODCOCKE] *Hist. Ivstine* XIV. 61 Neither doe I passe greatly for my life. **1633** G. HERBERT *Temple, Forerunners* vi, Yet if you go, I passe not; take your way. **1671** H. M. tr. *Erasm. Colloq.* 292, I do not so much pass for the body.

b. Const. *of* (cf. *to reck of*), *on*, *upon*. *Obs.*

1542 UDALL *Erasm. Apoph.* 24 The scoldying of brathels is no more to bee passed on then the squekyng of welle wheles. *a* **1548** HALL *Chron., Edw. IV* 212 For he passed litle, either of the pein of his seruaunt, or of his charge and expence. **1555** EDEN *Decades* 12 Thinhabitantes passe not on them. **1561** T. HOBY tr. *Castiglione's Courtyer* II. (1577) Hj, In our countrey of Lumbardy these matters are not passed vpon. **1590** GREENE *Never too late* (1600) 47, I passe of my honour more than life. **1598-9** [see d].

c. Const. with *infin.* or *at.* To care, concern oneself, trouble oneself; to scruple, hesitate, stickle; to take any heed; to 'mind', object. *Obs.*

1548 UDALL *Erasm. Par. Luke* 4 Y[e] couetous Phariseis passed lesse at the violacion or breakyng of gods preceptes, then of their tradicions. **1549-62** STERNHOLD & H. *Ps.* lv. 22 Of frendship to neglect the bandes they passe or care no whit. **1563** *Homilies* II. *Place Prayer* II. (1859) 349 Much wicked people pass nothing to resort to the church. **1578** J. STOCKWOOD *Serm. 24 Aug.* A ij b, I passe very little to be iudged of them. *a* **1625** E. CHALONER *Six Serm.* (1629) 149 To retaine it, it passeth not to forgoe halfe her controversies.

d. Const. with clause, becoming at length object of *pass*; in later use with obj. sb. = care for, regard. *Obs.*

Cf. 'I care not who he is'. 'Not regarding his entreaties'.

1549 in *Disc. Common Weal Eng.* (1893) p. lii, He passythe not what he saythe, nor what he dothe, so that he may satisfie his vngodlie desires. **1551** ROBINSON tr. *More's Utop.* II. viii. (1895) 255 Nor the Vtopians passe not how many of them they bring to distruction. **1573** TUSSER *Husb.* (1878) 104 Three poles to a hillock (I pas not how long). *a* **1617** BAYNE *On Coloss.* (1634) 340 Passe not you who doth give sentence against you. **1633** G. HERBERT *Temple, Forerunners* ii, I passe not, I, what of the rest become.

1598-9 B. JONSON *Case is Altered* v. *ad fin.*, Signiors, for you, I pass you not, though I let you pass; for in truth I pass not of you. *a* **1641** BP. MOUNTAGU *Acts & Mon.* iv. (1642) 270 Not passing his much and often intreaties she continued her refusall. **1647** H. MORE *Song of Soul* I. II. xliii, [He] deemed it no small disgrace That that bold youngster should so little passe His learned speech.

e. With emphatic expansion: ***to pass nothing at all, not to pass a fly, pin, straw, whit.*** *Obs.*

1556 OLDE *Antichrist* 132 They passe not a pynne of the Magistrates. **1572** J. JONES *Bathes of Bath* Pref. 5 So for the reprochfull words of the backbiting Zoilus I passe not a strawe. **1573** G. HARVEY *Letter-bk.* (Camden) 27 He..said he passid not ani thing at al of there displeasure. **1579** TOMSON *Calvin's Serm. Tim.* 54/2 We passe not a flie for it. *a* **1592** GREENE *Alphonsus* I. Wks. (Rtldg.) 228 Whoe'er it be, I do not pass a pin. **1610** DAY *Festivals* iii. (1615) 63 Nor doe we passe a whit what Iew or Gentile can say against it.

*********** Elliptical or absolute uses of II. or III.

24. *Fencing.* To make a pass; to thrust, lunge. Const. *on*, *upon*.

1595 SAVIOLO *Practice* ***j, You may suddenly passe with your left foot..and turne your point vnder his Rapier. **1598** B. JONSON *Ev. Man in Hum.* I. v. (1616) 17 *Bob.* A well-experienc'd hand would passe vpon you, at pleasure. *Mat.* How meane you, Sir, passe vpon me? *Bob.* Why, thus Sir (make a thrust at me) come in. **1601** SHAKS. *Twel. N.* III. i. 48 Nay, and thou passe vpon me, Ile no more with thee. **1602** —— *Ham.* v. ii. 309 Laertes, you but dally, I pray you passe with your best violence. **1602** MARSTON *Antonio's Rev.* I. iii, And if a horned divell should burst forth, I would passe on him with a mortall stocke. **1700** DRYDEN *Palamon & Arc.* II. 196 They lash, they foin, they pass, they strive to bore Their Corslets.

25. *Conjuring.* To cause any object to pass, as by magic, from one person or place to another.

1589 *Pasquil's Ret.* D iij, No body knowes how it came or how it went, for, since she was deliuered, (passe and repasse) the childe was neuer heard of. **1627** H. BURTON *Bait. Pope's Bull* Ep. Ded. 19 They are like cunning Iugglars, that can passe and repasse at pleasure.

26. *Cards* and *Dice.* **a.** In primero, poker, etc.: To throw up one's hand, retire from the game.

1599 MINSHEU *Sp. Dict., Dial.* iii. 26, I am come to passe againe. **1717** PRIOR *Alma* I. 284 As in a luckless gamester's place, She would not play, yet must not pass. **1816** SINGER *Hist. Cards* 246 When the first player says *Pass*, every one is obliged to discard, notwithstanding any one may have an ace or a six in hand. *a* **1889** *American Hoyle* in Farmer *Americanisms*, 'I pass' is a term used in draw poker, to signify that a player throws up his hand, and retires from the game.

b. In euchre, napoleon, etc.: To decline or voluntarily forgo one's opportunity (as of making the trump): see EUCHRE *sb.* 1. Also, in Bridge and other card games, to decline to make a bid. Also *fig.*

1869 'MARK TWAIN' *Innoc. Abr.* xxxiv. 375 Jack said, 'I pass'—he plays euchre sometimes—and we all passed in turn. **1884** *Encycl. Brit.* (ed. 9) XVII. 229/1 The eldest hand may decline to play, when he says 'I pass'. If the eldest hand passes, the next player to the left has a similar option of standing or passing, and so on all round... If all pass, the hand is not played. **1908** R. F. FOSTER *Auction Bridge* 29 The player on his left must either pass, or make a better declaration, or 'double'. **1918** [see GO *v.* 80 k]. **1929** M. C. WORK *Compl. Contract Bridge* 42 South..bids one No Trump: North..passes. **1959** REESE & DORMER *Bridge Player's Dict.* 163 North, not being obliged to keep the bidding open, might pass. **1964** *Official Encycl. Bridge* 414/2 *Pass*, a call by which a player indicates that, at that turn, he does not choose to contract for a number of odd tricks at any denomination, nor does he choose, at that turn, to double a contract of the opponents or redouble a contract by his side that opponents have already doubled. **1976** L. SANDERS *Hamlet Warning* (1977) xxv. 216 'If you want to run up and take a look..' 'I'll pass. If you've seen one cannonball, you've seen them all.' **1976** *Washington Post* 15 Oct. A 23/3 The Washington Post passed. It made no mention whatsoever of what the committee had to say about the news media.

†**c.** To win in the game of PASSAGE, q.v. *Obs.*

1600 MUNDAY & DRAYTON *Sir J. Oldcastle* F iv, *Hunt.* I must haue the dice, What do we play at? *Suff.* Passage if ye please... *Har.* George, You are out. Giue me the dice, I passe for twentie pound. **1680** [see PASSAGE 15]. *a* **1700** B. E. *Dict. Cant. Crew, Passage*, a Camp-Game, with three Dice, Doublets, making up Ten or more, to *Pass* or Win, any other Chances lose. **1725** in *New Cant. Dict.*

d. In dominoes, to miss a turn when one does not have a suitable number.

1960 R. C. BELL *Board & Table Games* I. 169 When one player has drawn all but the last two dominoes from the pool, and can neither make a ten, nor play a matador, he says, 'pass'. *Ibid.* 170 When a player is unable to make a match he calls 'pass', and the next player tries.

27. a. To pass the ball at Football, etc.: see 46 b.

1888 [see sense 46 b].

b. (*U.S.*) To throw and catch a ball: see quot.

1889 *Jrnl. Amer. Folk-lore* II. No. 5 In New England the ordinary term used to express the throwing and catching of a ball by two or more persons is *pass*. 'Let's go out and pass'.

II. Transitive uses. (From I 12–19.)

* To go by (something). Trans. of I 12–13.

28. a. To go by, to proceed past (a person or thing); to leave behind or on one side as one goes on.

c 1290 *S. Eng. Leg.* I. 273/50 Þo heo þe croiz i-passede hadden: a-ȝein to þe weie he cam. 13.. *Relig. Pieces fr. Thornton MS.* 39 Swa þat nan houre passe the þat þou ne sall be swetely ocupyed. c 1400 *Destr. Troy* 564 The perlouse pointtes þat passe you behoues, Hit is vnlike any lede with his liffe pas. 1461 J. Paston in *P. Lett.* II. 3 There have not passid Thetford, not passyng cccc. 1585 T. Washington tr. *Nicholay's Voy.* II. ii. 31 b, [We] followed on along the coast ..to passe the cape Malee. 1615 Chapman *Odyss.* VI. 306 Thus, passing him, she to the virgins went. 1784 Cowper *Task* IV. 211 Time, as he passes us, has a dove's wing, Unsoil'd, and swift, and of a silken sound. 1842 Tennyson *Sir Galahad* 81 So pass I hostel, hall, and grange. *Mod.* Many carriages passed the door. I never pass the spot without thinking of him.

b. To get the other side of; to avoid, escape. *Obs.* or *dial.*

c 1450 *St. Cuthbert* (Surtees) 4603 To passe þat persecucioune. 1894 R. Reid *Poems* 88 (E.D.D.) The herds wad gang five mile aboot Tae pass this lanely brae.

29. †**a.** *fig.* To go by without attending to; to leave unnoticed; to neglect, disregard, omit. *Obs.*

c 1380 Wyclif *Wks.* (1880) 448 Wedding wiþ þes newe bilawis, passinge þe wedding wiþ goddis lawe, makiþ þes newe rotun sectis. 1595 Shaks. *John* II. i. 258 If you fondly passe our proffer'd offer. 1607 —— *Cor.* II. iii. 207 You should haue ta'ne th' aduantage of his Choller, And pass'd him vnelected. 1643 Sir T. Browne *Relig. Med.* I. §29, I wonder how the curiosity of wiser heads could pass that great and indisputable Miracle, the cessation of Oracles. 1645 Evelyn *Diary* 21 May, We dined at Sienna, where we could not passe admiring the great church.

b. To omit in narration, to leave unmentioned.

1585 T. Washington tr. *Nicholay's Voy.* IV. xxxiii. 156 Other goodly ordinances, which I passe with silence. 1616 R. C. *Times Whistle* I. 469 To passe the papist and the Lutheran, Their trans and consubstantiation. 1697 Dryden *Virg. Georg.* I. 239 Nor must we pass untold what Arms they wield. *Ibid.* III. 415, I pass the Wars that spotted Linx s make With their fierce Rivals, for the Females sake. 1890 *Times* 6 Dec. 12/4 We may pass the cleaning-rod and the downhill position; they are not of much consequence.

c. *U.S.* To omit payment of (a dividend, etc.).

1870 J. K. Medbery *Men & Mysteries Wall St.* 137 To 'pass' a dividend... A dividend is said to be passed when the directors vote against declaring it. 1890 *Financial News* 7 July, A few days ago the National Bank of —— passed its interim dividend, and now..the Banco Nacional of —— has suspended specie payments. 1903 *Forum* (N.Y.) Oct. 209 Concerns which not only passed dividends..but went bankrupt. 1965 Perry & Ryder *Thomson's Dict. Banking* (ed. 11) 422/2 *Passing a dividend*, a term used when a company decides not to pay a dividend.

†**d.** ***to pass one's flag*** (*Naval*), to decline promotion to flag rank, and become a retired Captain. *Obs.*

1805 Nelson in Nicolas *Disp.* (1846) VII. 41 When you passed your Flag, I wrote my regret that the Service was to lose your abilities at Sea.

** To go through, across, or over (something).

30. a. To go from side to side of, or across, to cross (a sea, channel, river, barrier, frontier, mountain-range); also (less frequently), to go through, traverse (a forest, way, street).

to pass the pikes: see PIKE.

c 1290 *Beket* 1773 in *S. Eng. Leg.* I. 157 For godes loue: ne passe nouȝt þe se. a 1300 *Cursor M.* 12375 Þan he yode þe flum to pass. c 1380 *Sir Ferumb.* 3523 So þat god me graunty grace, þe brigge of Mantrible saf to pace. 1430–40 Lydg. *Bochas* VIII. ii. (1558) 3 b, They of Almayne the Alpes dyd pace. 1526 *Pilgr. Perf.* (W. de W. 1531) 14 The fyrst people ..so entred & passed the reed see. 1579 Gosson *Sch. Abuse* (Arb.) 36 They..are..pointed at commonly as they passe the streetes. 1590 Spenser *F.Q.* I. v. 33 They pas the bitter waues of Acheron. 1591 Shaks. *Two Gent.* IV. iii. 24 The waies are dangerous to passe. 1667 Milton *P.L.* II. 776 To keep These Gates for ever shut, which none can pass Without my op'ning. 1673 Ray *Journ. Low C.* 23 They.. measure their way in these countreys, by the time they spend in passing it. 1743 T. Jones in *Buccleuch MSS.* (Hist. MSS. Comm.) I. 405, 15,000 men..had passed the bridge at Aschaffenburg. 1819 Byron *Juan* II. cv, He could, perhaps, have pass'd the Hellespont, As once..Leander, Mr. Ekenhead, and I did. 1871 Freeman *Norm. Conq.* IV. xviii. 221 At Cambridge the river and the marshy ground beyond had to be passed.

b. Of a book or printed work: To go through (the printing-press, or successive editions). ? *Obs.*

1665 *Phil. Trans.* I. 104 Which hath already so far passed the Press. 1792 *Munchausen's Trav.* Pref. 4 This Work..has passed several editions within a short period.

†**31.** To pierce, to penetrate: said of a spear or other weapon, also of the person driving it. *Obs.*

1588 Parke tr. *Mendoza's Hist. China* 331 Their weapons are strong bowes and arrowes..wherwith they will pierce and passe a shirt of mayle or plate coate. 1630 Capt. Smith *Trav. & Adv.* 12 At the sound of the charge, he passed the Turke throw the sight of his Beaver, face, head, and all. 1715–20 Pope *Iliad* XVI. 567 From strong Patroclus' hand the javelin fled, And pass'd the groin of valiant Thrasymed.

32. a. *fig.* To go or come through in the way of a course of study or treatment, experience or suffering; *esp.* to experience, undergo, endure, put up with, suffer. Now usually *pass through* (58 b).

a 1340 Hampole *Psalter* cxxiii. 1 Þaim þat ere passid þe perils of þis warld. c 1400 *Destr. Troy* 12704 Thies passet the perellis of the pale ythes, Houit on the hegh sea, held hom o ferre. 1563–7 Buchanan *Reform. St. Andros* Wks. (1892) 12 In thre ȝeris thyr regentis sal pas be degreis the hail cours of dialectic, logic, physik, and metaphysik. 1582 N. Lichefield tr. *Castanheda's Conq. E. Ind.* I. xv. 39 b, Hauing past many troubles and daungers upon the sea. 1588 Parke tr. *Mendoza's Hist. China* 252 The Spaniardes.. remained a good while, and passed great heate. 1604 Shaks. *Oth.* I. iii. 132 The Storie of my life, From yeare to yeare: the Battaile, Sieges, Fortune, That I haue past. 1652 J. Wright tr. *Camus' Nat. Paradox* v. 249 Withdrawing himself secretly out of that Province (where he had passed so many perills). 1755 J. Shebbeare *Lydia* (1769) II. 191 After having past the previous ceremonies. 1849 M. Arnold *Consolation* ii, And countless beings Pass countless moods.

b. ***to pass one's time, life***, etc.: see 44.

33. To get through the process of being considered, examined, and approved. **a.** Said of a measure approved by or carried in Parliament; hence, to be agreed to, accepted, sanctioned by (anybody). ***to pass the seals***, to receive royal (or other) sanction or ratification expressed by sealing.

1429 *Rolls of Parlt.* IV. 343/2 In alle thynges that owith to passe and be agreed be the seide Counseill. 1607 Shaks. *Cor.* III. i. 29 Hath he not pass'd the Noble, and the Common? 1667–8 Pepys *Diary* 5 Feb., An Act of Comprehension is likely to pass this Parliament, for admitting of all persuasions in religion to the public observation of their particular worship. 1670 Ld. Roos in *12th Rep. Hist. MSS. Comm.* App. v. 14 My Bill hath passed the Lords House and was this day read in the House of Commons. 1710 *Lond. Gaz.* No. 4728/3 Their Commissions are passing the Seals accordingly. 1725 Berkeley *Let. to Prior* 3 June Wks. 1871 IV. 111 Yesterday the Charter passed the Privy Seal. 1771 *Junius Lett.* lxiv. 327 These bills passed the house of lords..such bills could never have passed the house of commons without his knowledge. 1793 Smeaton *Edystone L.* §335 Estimates..were approved, and passed the common seal of the Corporation.

b. Said of a person or thing that goes satisfactorily through a test, trial, or examination: to undergo and come out successfully; to come up to the standard required by (the examiners or examination); to be allowed by.

1536 Cromwell *Let.* 6 Dec. in Merriman *Life & Lett.* (1902) II. 38 This maner of dealing..is suche as I am right sory to see pass you that shuld be a man of honestie. 1599 Chapman *Hum. Days Mirth* Plays 1873 I. 63 Then have you passed the full list of experiment. 1653 H. More *Antid. Ath.* II. iii. (1712) 47 There is nothing in Nature but what passes the Approbation of a Knowing Principle. 1712 Steele *Spect.* No. 438 ¶3 All things among Men of Sense and Condition should pass the Censure, and have the Protection, of the Eye of Reason. 1832 Austin *Jurispr.* (1879) II. xlvi. 808 On the bales..being weighed over or 'passing the scale'. 1858 Hogg *Veg. Kingd.* 616 All [Russian Rhubarb] that does not pass this examination is burned. 1885 *Manch. Exam.* 11 Nov. 3/1 Very few..could pass even the most elementary examination. a 1901 Besant *Five Years' Tryst* (1902) 26 You'll pass your exams with distinction; you'll get appointments.

c. ***to pass muster***: see MUSTER.

*** To go beyond, surpass, exceed. (fr. I. 19.)

34. To go beyond (a point or place); to overshoot (a mark); to outrun, outstrip in a race; to rise above, surmount.

1362 Langl. *P. Pl.* A. II. 164 Soþnesse..seide bote luyte, Bote prikede on his palfrey and passede hem alle. 1375 Barbour *Bruce* xx. 432 The lord dowglass..passit wes All the folk that wes chassand then. c 1386 Chaucer *Knt.'s T.* 2231 Ffor gentil mercy oghte to passen right. c 1400 Maundev. (Roxb.) iii. 8 In þis ile es þe mount Caucase þat passez þe clowdes. a 1425 tr. *Higden* Harl. Contin. (Rolls) VII. 505 The see overflowide and passide the clyves. 1585 T. Washington tr. *Nicholay's Voy.* IV. xxiv. 140 Mount Athos is so high, that it passeth the skies. 1871 R. Ellis *Catullus* iv. 4 Nor yet a timber o'er the waves alertly flew She might not aim to pass it.

35. To go beyond or outside of; to overstep (bounds, limits); to transgress. *fig.* To go beyond (one's province, warrant, knowledge, etc.).

c 1320 *Cast. Love* 1057 Þat hose passede Godes heste, He scholde be myn. 1362 Langl. *P. Pl.* A. I. 102 He þat passeþ þat poynt is a-postata in þe ordre. c 1380 Wyclif *Sel. Wks.* III. 346 Þis stiward passiþ his power, & failiþ in governaunce of þe Chirche. 1456 Sir G. Haye *Law Armys* (S.T.S.) 119 And haldis it nevertheles in his rycht reule, that is, pas nocht his mesure. 1560 Daus tr. *Sleidane's Comm.* 111 b, Let hym loke..that in no wyse he doe passe the boundes of his commission. 1604 T. Wright *Passions* (1620) 114 Let not the cobler passe his pantofle. 1607 Chapman *Bussy d'Ambois* Plays 1873 II. 6 A poore staid fisherman, that neuer past His countries sight. 1754 Gray *Progr. Poesy* 98 He pass'd the flaming bounds of Place and Time. 1784 Cowper *Task* VI. 192 He marks the bounds which Winter may not pass, And blunts his pointed fury.

36. To exceed or be beyond the compass or range of (any faculty or expression); to be too great for, transcend.

1382 Wyclif *Phil.* iv. 7 And the pees of God, that passith al witt, kepe ȝoure hertis and vndirstondingis in Crist Jhesu oure Lord. 1413 *Pilgr. Sowle* (Caxton) v. i. (1859) 73 Hit passed his wytte, thenne muste hit nedes passen the power of his speche. 1589 R. Robinson *Gold. Mirr.* (1851) 6 It passeth all my skill the halfe for to indite. 1624 R. Davenport *City Nightcap* I. i. in Hazl. *Dodsley* XIII. 106 Where each word stands so well-plac'd, that it passes Inquisitive detraction to correct. 1701 Norris *Ideal World* I. vi. 364 It passes all comprehension to conceive such a thing. 1820 W. Irving *Sketch Bk.* I. 229 To express..that grief which passes show.

37. a. To surpass or excel in some quality; to surpass or exceed in degree. *arch.*

c 1230 *Hali Meid.* 43 Alswa passeð meiden onont te mihte of meidenhad, widewen & iweddede. c 1300 *Beket* 1031 For gold ne passeth noȝt in bounté so moche leode iwis, As dignité of preosthod passeth the lewed man þat is. 1380 *Lay Folks Catech.* 61 (Lamb. MS.) Þis pater noster..passys oþer prayers. c 1386 Chaucer *Prol.* 448 Of clooth makyng..She passed hem of ypres & of Gaunt. c 1450 tr. *De Imitatione* I. i. 2 The doctrine of crist passiþ þe doctrine of all seintes & holy men. a 1533 Ld. Berners *Huon* lxxxi. 244 None coulde passe hym in beaute. 1539 Bible (Great) *2 Sam.* i. 26 Thy loue to me was wonderfull, passyng the loue of wemen. 1604 E. G[rimstone] *D'Acosta's Hist. Indies* II. ii. 83 Ethiopia passeth Affrike and Barbarie in heat. 1704 *Collect. Voy.* (Churchill) III. 25/2 The Milk..has a sweetness..which passes ordinary Milk. 1850 Neale *Med. Hymns* (1867) 17 Of rival towns thou passest all.

b. To exceed in number, measurement, or amount. Now *rare*.

a 1300 *Cursor M.* 1237 Adam had pastd nine hundret yere, Nai selcut þof he wex vnfere. 1375 Barbour *Bruce* v. 198 Thai in hy assemblit then, Passand, y trow, a thousand men. c 1440 *Generydes* 5954 Ffrom hens it passith not a myle or twayne. 1468 Sir J. Paston in *Lett.* II. 329 The utter-most pryse had not passyd v. mark. 1592 Davies *Immort. Soul* VIII. xx. (1714) 54 Tho' they in Number pass the Stars of Heav'n. 1618 Chapman *Hesiod* 183 Let Jove steep the grass Three days together, so he do not pass An ox's hoof in depth. 1874 Micklethwaite *Mod. Par. Churches* 164 The whole chest should not much pass four feet in height.

†**38. a.** To get beyond (a stage or condition of life or existence). *Obs.* (exc. as *fig.* from 34).

c 1315 Shoreham *Poems* (E.E.T.S.) 74/2111 On wenddeþ, Þoþer abyde schel [H]wet oþer passeþ age By kende. 14.. *Tundale's Vis.* 1464 A blissed soule y may þe calle For þou art passed thy paynes alle. c 1450 *Gesta Rom.* x. 33 (Harl. MS.) Withoute dowte, whenne we shul passy þis life,..he shal ȝelde to vs þe fowrefold. c 1510 Barclay *Mirr. Gd. Manners* (1570) E vj b, When he passed childe, And come to mannes estate. 1526 *Pilgr. Perf.* (W. de W. 1531) 20, I am passed my purgatory, and I am saued. 1552 Huloet, Passe boyes age, *ex ephæbis, uel pueris excedere*. 1611 Bible *1 Cor.* vii. 36 If she passe the floure of her age. 1685 Evelyn *Diary* 15 Sept., On purpose that they might whilst young pass that fatal disease.

b. To go beyond or exceed (a defined time).

c 1384 Chaucer *H. Fame* I. 392 How he forswore hym ful falsly,..And falsly gan hys terme pace. 1607 Middleton *Mich. Term* II. iii. 342, I never pass my month, you know.

**** **39.** ***to pass the lips***, †***the mouth of***: to come out of the mouth of, be spoken or uttered by.

1526 *Pilgr. Perf.* (W. de W. 1531) 115 b, Kepe it in the, that it passe not thy mouth. c 1611 Chapman *Iliad* I. 493 Iove at this sat silent; not a word In long space pass'd him. 1755 H. Walpole *Lett. to Mann* 15 June, I will describe him to you, if I can, but don't let it pass your lips. 1819 Shelley *Prom. Unb.* I. 219 Mother, let not aught Of..evil pass again My lips.

III. Causative uses.

* **40. a.** To cause or enable (a person or thing) to go, proceed, or make his way anywhere; to carry, convey, send: usually with prep. or adv. specifying the direction, etc.; *esp.* to convey across a river, a ferry, etc., to transport.

a 1533 Ld. Berners *Huon* clvi. 597 Me thynke ye be none of the fayrey, wherfore I am not contente that I haue passed you ouer. 1585 T. Washington tr. *Nicholay's Voy.* IV. xxiv. 140 The way whereby Xerxes passed his army. 1600 E. Blount tr. *Conestaggio* 30 The most of them were barkes to passe horse and munition. 1611 Cotgr., *Pile trigone*, a triangle peece of yron to be thrown at a ring, through which he that passes it wins the game. 1698 Fryer *Acc. E. India & P.* 126, I sent to the Havaldar, to know when he would Pass us up the Gaot. 1722 De Foe *Plague* (Rtldg.) 164 Every vagrant Person may..be..pass'd back to their last legal Settlement. 1798 I. Allen *Hist. Vermont* 254 A canal.. sufficient to pass boats of 25 tons burthen into said lake.

†**b.** *refl.* = *intr.* to pass, proceed, depart, cross.

c 1500 *Lancelot* 362 So the king proponit And for to pas hyme one the morne disponit. 1615 Chapman *Odyss.* XIV. 260 He pass'd him for the Pylian shore to find His long-lost father.

†**c.** With double object: To send or convey (a thing) over or across (a place). *Obs. rare.*

1512 W. Knight in Ellis *Orig. Lett.* Ser. II. I. 199 Which can shew yow..with what besynes thei [the Spaniards] haue passyd thaire Artiliarie the grete mountaynys.

41. a. To make (a thing) go in any specific manner or direction; to move, draw, push (a thing); as ***to pass one's hand over, to pass one's eye over*** (to glance rapidly or cursorily over), ***to pass a wet sponge over*** (often *fig.* to obliterate the memory of), ***to pass the sweeper over*** a floor, ***to pass a rope*** or ***string round*** anything.

1705 Addison *Italy* 434, I had only time to pass my Eye over the Medals, which are in great Number. 1853 M. Arnold *Sohrab* 94 O'er his chilly limbs his woollen coat He passed. 1859 Jephson *Brittany* ii. 21 Washing their hands by having water passed over them. 1867 Smyth *Sailor's Word-bk.*, *To pass*,..to take certain turns of a rope round a yard, etc. 1868 Yates *Rock Ahead* II. ii, He had passed the wet sponge over the slate containing any records of his early life. 1896 *Allbutt's Syst. Med.* I. 437 If..the nurse cannot pass the catheter into the orifice at once. *Mod.* Pass a rope round its hind legs.

†**b.** = ***pass through***: to pass through a sieve, etc.

1530 PALSGR. 654/2, *Je sasse*.... I left hym passynge of synnamon. **1639** J. W. tr. *Guibert's Char. Physic.* II. 66 Two ..searses or sieves to passe bitter things.

42. To cause to pass or go by. ***to pass in review***: (*orig.*) *Mil.* To cause (troops) to march by for inspection; hence *fig.* to cause writings or proceedings to pass before the eye or mind for examination or scrutiny.

1852 GROTE *Greece* II. lxix. IX. 24 Here..Cyrus, halting three days, passed the army in review. **1865** M. ARNOLD *Ess. Crit.* ii. (1875) 52 The works of other writers..might also.. be passed under the Academy's review. **1878** BROWNING *La Saisiaz* 162 Passing lightly in review What seemed hits and what seemed misses in a certain fence-play.

43. To cause or allow (a person or thing) to go past or through some barrier or obstruction.

1611 SHAKS. *Wint. T.* II. ii. 57 Madam, if't please the Queene to send the babe, I know not what I shall incurre, to passe it, Hauing no warrant. **1867** MACGREGOR *Voy. Alone* (1868) 39, I had letters..for the highest authorities to pass the Rob Roy as an article entered for the Paris Exhibition. **1884** *Graphic* 30 Aug. 215/1 The men who pass tobacco, wine, and spirits into England..by contraband.

44. a. To cause or allow to pass or go by, to spend (time, or any portion of time, one's life, a season, etc.): sometimes merely in reference to staying through or to the end, as *to pass the winter at a place*; but oftener with reference to occupation or mode, as *to pass one's time in sleep, pass a pleasant evening, pass an anxious day*. Cf. *pass away* (60 f), *pass forth* (62 c).

1390 GOWER *Conf.* I. 115 Thus passen thei that wofull nyht. *Ibid.* III. 316 Thus passen thei a day or tuo. **1594** SHAKS. *Rich. III*, I. iv. 2 O, I haue past a miserable night, So full of fearefull Dreames, of vgly sights [etc.]. **1674** BOYLE *Excell. Theol.* I. i. 35 A very pleasant way of passing one's time. **1709–10** ADDISON *Tatler* No. 153 ¶15 A Friend.. invites me to pass the Evening at his House. **1779** J. MOORE *View Soc. Fr.* II. lvi. 63 He generally passes the summer in the country. **1859** GEO. ELIOT *A. Bede* xxiv, Those whose lives are passed in humble everyday work. **1860** THACKERAY *Round. Papers, Lazy Idle Boy* (1876) 1, I had occasion to pass a week in the autumn in the little old town of Coire. **1878** J. C. MORISON *Gibbon* 2 The longest period he ever passed at school were two years at Westminster.

†**b.** ? To cause to pass away, dispel. *Obs. rare.*

1565 COOPER *Thesaurus, Acquiescere in re aliqua*,..to take delight and pleasure in: to passe his sorow and phantasies.

** †**45. a.** To carry through its stages, transact; to bring to an end, to accomplish or execute (a matter, a business); to complete (a voyage). *Obs.*

c **1450** *Cov. Myst.* 89 We beseche ȝow of ȝoure pacyens, That we pace these materes so lythly away. **1473** *Rolls of Parlt.* VI. 66/1 In cas all other things were thoroughly passed and concluded betwixt his Highnes and theym. **1596** SHAKS. *Tam. Shr.* IV. iv. 57 Then at my lodging,..there this night Weele passe the businesse priuately and well. **1602** MARSTON *Antonio's Rev.* IV. i, If you but meditate of what is past, And what you plot to passe. **1605** B. JONSON *Volpone* III. v, I told his son, brought, hid him here, Where he might hear his father pass the deed. **1748** *Anson's Voy.* III. x. 403 The contract being past, it was some satisfaction..to be certain that his preparations were now going on.

b. To cause or allow (anything proposed) to proceed, esp. after examination or scrutiny; to carry or get carried (a measure in Parliament, a resolution in a meeting); to agree to, declare correct, confirm, sanction, endorse.

1549–62 STERNHOLD & HOPKINS *Ps.* cxix. III. 24 They serve in stead of councellours my matters for to passe. **1624** CAPT. SMITH *Virginia* 185 The greatest matter passed, was a Proclamation against the spoile of Cahowes. **1666–7** MARVELL *Corr.* Wks. 1872–5 II. 206 His Majesty came yesterday to the Lords' House, and there past five publick Bills. **1669** in *10th Rep. Hist. MSS. Comm.* App. v. 104 Severall rectoryes and impropriations..have been passed into patent in the name of his Grace. **1705** S. SEWALL *Diary* 12 Nov., Brooklin is pass'd to be a Township by the Council. **1707** WATTS *Hymn, 'Life is the time'* vi, There are no acts of pardon pass'd In the cold grave to which we haste. **1799** JEFFERSON *Writ.* (1859) IV. 263 Their majority will pass the bill. **1836** *Penny Cycl.* V. 296/2 Boyle..clearly proved that he passed his accounts in an irregular and dishonest manner. **1863** H. COX *Instit.* III. vi. 663 He was required to pass under the Great Seal the requisite authority to Commissioners. **1868** FREEMAN *Norm. Conq.* II. x. 483 They began..to pass decrees in utter defiance of the royal authority. **1878** MONTAGU BROWNE *Pract. Taxidermy* ii. 21, I have submitted the foregoing to a practical birdcatcher,..and he has 'passed' it as correct. **1885** *Law Rep.* 29 Ch. Div. 796 A scheme of arrangement passed by the shareholders. **1892** A. S. WILKINS in *Bookman* Oct. 26/2 He had already passed for the press all the sheets of the present volume.

c. To allow or enable (a person) to pass an examination; to get (him) through.

1833 MARRYAT *P. Simple* xxxviii, Come Mr. Simple, stand up again... Don't be afraid, we wish to pass you. **1844** DICKENS *Mart. Chuz.* xxvii, I'll pass you..I can conscientiously report you a healthy subject. **1889** *Nature* 18 Apr. 577 His first duty..is *to pass* his men; and as our systems of examination are at present ordered, the passing is more a question of the facts than of the principles.

†**d.** To allow (something) to pass or go unchecked or without notice; to overlook, excuse, pass over. *Obs.*

c **1611** CHAPMAN *Iliad* III. 114 An old man will consent to pass things past, and what succeeds He looks into. **1768** *Woman of Honor* II. 212 Pass me this digression. **1802** H. MARTIN *Helen of Glenross* I. 247, I tell you, I will not, cannot pass that boy's bravado.

*** **46. a.** To cause to go from one to another; to hand over, hand round, hand, transfer. ***to pass the buck***: see BUCK *sb.*[9]; ***to pass the word*** (colloq., orig. *Naut.*), to convey information orally; to issue an oral order or instruction.

1596 SHAKS. *Tam. Shr.* IV. iv. 45 If..like a Father you will deale with him, And passe my daughter a sufficient dower, The match is made, and all is done. *a* **1716** SOUTH *Serm.* (1727) IV. 75 When God makes a Man wealthy and potent, he passes a double Obligation upon him. **1824–8** T. HOOK *Sayings & Doings* 222 (Stratm.) Shall I pass you a spoon? **1833** MARRYAT *P. Simple* xxvii, Desire the sentry to pass the word for the butcher; I want to speak with him. *Ibid.* xxxv, Pass the word to reduce the cartridges. **1843** S. LEECH *30 Yrs. from Home* ix. 186 Her officer..so exasperated our captain that he passed the word to fire into her. *Ibid.* x. 218, I heard the order from an officer, of 'Pass the word for the boy Leech'. **1849** THACKERAY *Pendennis* ii, The intelligence was 'passed round'..in an instant. **1884** *Naval Encycl.* 636/2 *To pass the word* for a man is to summon him by name, the cry being repeated by the boatswain's mates on all decks. *a* **1901** BESANT *Five Years' Tryst*, etc. (1902) 117 They passed buckets of water from hand to hand. **1901** G. B. SHAW *Caesar & Cleopatra* II. 133 Pass the word to the guard; and fetch my armor. **1910** H. Y. MOFFAT *From Ship's-Boy to Skipper* iii. 39 He called to the sentry: 'Pass the word for the boy Moffat.' **1924** J. BUCHAN *Three Hostages* vi. 96, I will visit it as a man..to see about the meter... Macgillivray will pass the word for me. **1946** E. O'NEILL *Iceman Cometh* III. 184 They know I was framed. And once they've passed the word, it's as good as done, law or no law. **1961** *Sat. Even. Post* 3 June 60/2 Hundreds of men are required to pass the word to the button pushers and to push the buttons.

b. *Football*, etc. To transfer (the ball) to another player on the same side. Also *absol.* (sense 27 a). Cf. PASS *sb.*[2] 12.

c **1865** F. WOOD *Beeton's Football* [*Assoc.*] Rules 36 No player shall carry the ball, hold it, throw it, pass it to another with his hands, or lift it from the ground with his hands. **1888** IRVINE, etc. *Football, Laws Rugby* 9 It is lawful for any player who has the ball to throw it back towards his own goal, or to pass it back to any player of his own side who is at the time behind him. *Ibid.* 71 Never pass blindly, and be very chary of passing at all near your own goal. Never throw forward, for it is illegal. **1889** *Pall Mall G.* 4 Oct. 3/1 Seven years ago hockey was an utterly unscientific game... The Moulsey Club was the first to adopt a passing game. **1900** FEGAN, etc. *Football* etc., *Hockey* 135 The ball may often be passed as usefully from forwards to halves, or from halves to backs, as in the contrary direction.

c. To put into circulation, give currency to (coin, or the like): esp. used of putting base coin into circulation. Also *fig.*

1589 PUTTENHAM *Eng. Poesie* III. xix. (Arb.) 237 One whom his mistresse burdened with some vnkinde speeches which he had past of her. **1634** WOOD *New Eng. Prosp.* (1865) To Rdr., There hath beene many scandalous and false reports past upon the Countrey. **1802** MAR. EDGEWORTH *Moral T.* (1816) I. xix. 155 This bank-note.. he was afraid to pass, till all inquiry had blown over. **1864** *Daily Tel.* 28 Nov., Utterers of base coin have a trick of passing a bad shilling between two good ones.

47. *Law.* To convey, make over, in legal form or with legal effect.

1587 LD. BURLEIGH in *Collect.* (O.H.S.) I. 204 You passe ..a lease to the Ladie Stafford. **1690** LOCKE *Govt.* II. xvi. §186 Nor does it at all alter the Case..no more than it excuses the Force, and passes the Right, when I..deliver my Purse myself to a Thief, who demands it with a Pistol at my Breast. **1891** *Law Rep.* Weekly Notes 201/1 The delivery of the key of a trunk was held to pass the trunk and its contents.

48. a. To give in pledge (one's word, promise, oath); †to pledge (one's faith, honour, etc.).

1469 SIR J. PASTON in *Lett.* II. 369 Ȝe wryteth in your letter that ye durst not passe your credens. **1528** WRIOTHESLEY in Pocock *Rec. Ref.* I. xli. 79 To pass his promise on such sort..might make much broylery. **1588** SHAKS. *L.L.L.* I. i. 49 Your oath is past, to passe away from these. **1601** —— *Twel. N.* I. v. 86 Sir Toby will be sworn that I am no Fox, but he wil not passe his word for two pence that you are no Foole. **1724** DE FOE *Mem. Cavalier* I. 114 He [King of Sweden] had passed his Honour to the Norembergers, that he would not leave them. **1837** KEBLE *Chr. Y.* 2 Sun. Lent viii, That Name, by which Thy faithful oath is past. **1855** MACAULAY *Hist. Eng.* xiii. III. 329 Half the sum was raised,..and Dundee is said to have passed his word for the remainder. **1896** EDITH THOMPSON in *Monthly Packet* Christm. No. 97 He had passed his word of honour ..that he would report himself at the fort of Haraf.

†**b.** To give or tender (a vote). *Obs.*

1642 G. MOUNTAGU in *Buccleuch MSS.* (Hist. MSS. Comm.) I. 298 These are the votes.., which passed shall be published in a Declaration to the kingdom. **1685** in Picton *L'pool Munic. Rec.* (1883) I. 266 Everie person..shall.. passe his vote when required,..the town clerke shall.. proceed from person to person till the whole Councell have passed their votes.

**** †**49.** To send forth or out, to emit. ***to pass the ghost***: to give up the ghost, to die. *Obs. rare.*

c **1400** *Destr. Troy* 8216 Tha he gird to the ground & the gost past. **1602** MARSTON *Antonio's Rev.* II. iii, Here is a vent to passe my sighes. **1621** QUARLES *Argalus & P.* (1678) 46 She past a sigh, and said, O ask not who.

50. To discharge from the body by excretion.

1698 SIR R. SIBBALD in *Phil. Trans.* XX. 266 He hath past none by the Yard since he past these the other way. **1799** *Med. Jrnl.* II. 264 She passes her stools naturally. **1822–34** *Good's Study Med.* (ed. 4) I. 192 He..was incapable of passing a motion by any means. **1899** CAGNEY tr. *Jaksch's Clin. Diagnosis* vii. (ed. 4) 292 Hairs have been known to be passed with this fluid.

†**51.** To discharge (a volley). *Obs.*

1681 *Lond. Gaz.* No. 1628/1 One of them..shooting a-head and passing his Broad-side,..fell a stern, by her Lee side.

52. a. To give utterance or expression to; to utter, pronounce (speech, criticism, censure); rarely, to put (a question). Sometimes, to exchange (words). ***to pass a*** (or ***the***) ***remark*** (*colloq.*): to make an observation or comment, esp. one that is gratuitously sarcastic or depreciatory; freq. *pl.*

1615 CHAPMAN *Odyss.* I. 274 On him again the grey-eyed Maid did pass This kind reply. **1617** MORYSON *Itin.* II. 38 Tyrone..saluted his Lordship standing on the other banke, and there they passed many speeches. **1654** tr. *Scudery's Curia Pol.* 35 To passe a censure, or to whisper seditiously against the Actions of Princes. **1694** ATTERBURY *Serm.* (1726) I. 186 A Way of exposing Things sacred and serious, by passing a bold Jest upon them. *a* **1698** SOUTH *Serm.* III. i. 30 By all this (it seems) our Saviour was only teaching those about Him, how to pass Complements upon Almighty God. **1828** SCOTT *F.M. Perth* xi, No man shall brook life after he has passed an affront on Douglas. **1875** JOWETT *Plato* (ed. 2) V. 6 They are dissatisfied with the free criticisms which the Athenian passes upon the laws of Minos. **1899** R. WHITEING *No. 5 John St.* xxi. 218, I didn't sye I 'ad nothin' to sye to 'im. I only passed the remark. **1924** KIPLING *Debits & Credits* (1926) 157 ''E *could* pass remarks, too!' Humberstall recited..a fragment..ending with, 'You lazy-minded, lousy-headed, long-trousered, perfumed perookier.' *Ibid.*, Macklin had a wonderful way o' passing remarks on a man's civil life; an' he put it about that our B.S.M. had run a dope an' dolly-shop with a Chinese woman. **1929** J. B. PRIESTLEY *Good Companions* II. v. 370 'Dewn't you be so personal', said Mr. Jerningham... 'You're always passing remawks.' **1933** C. MACKENZIE *Water on Brain* x. 142, I only passed the remark to Mr Wigmore yesterday, 'Mr Wigmore,' I said, 'people are getting pre-war again.' **1934** R. FERGUSON *Celebrated Sequels* 134 Were they or were they not laughing and passing remarks? **1939** JOYCE *Finnegans Wake* 463 He is looking aged with his pebbled eyes, and johnnythin too, from livicking onpidgins' ifs with puffins' ands, he's been slanderising himself, but I pass no remark. **1941** E. BOWEN *Look at Roses* 103, I merely passed the remark. There's no harm in my passing a remark occasionally. **1958** J. CANNAN *And be a Villain* iii. 70 I'll tell him you've broken off your engagement and not to pass any remarks. **1962** —— *All is Discovered* ii. 43, I passed a remark about her being indoors. I don't like her. **1975** C. STORR *Chinese Egg* xxvi. 168 He called her Fatty..and passed remarks about her figure.

b. To utter or pronounce judicially. (Cf. 21, 22.)

1590 SHAKS. *Com. Err.* I. i. 148 Thou art adiudged to the death, And passed sentence may not be recal'd. **1600** —— *A. Y. L.* I. iii. 86 Firm and irreuocable is my doombe, Which I haue past vpon her. **1700** DRYDEN *Palamon & Arcite* I. 266 If our doom be past in bonds to lie. **1820** W. IRVING *Sketch Bk.* II. 265 When sentence of death was passed upon him. **1894** HALL CAINE *Manxman* VI. viii, The Deemster in the half-lit court was passing sentence.

c. In various phrases, as ***to pass the time of day*** (*dial.* or *colloq.*), to exchange salutations or gossip in passing; so, ***to pass (a) good morning, the good day, the compliments of the day***.

1836 A. A. PARKER *Trip to West* 165 Two Indians..halted within a few rods of us, stared a moment, and then civilly passed the time of day. **1851** [see TIME *sb.* 28 b]. **1875** *Sussex Gloss.* s.v. *Time of Day*, 'I doänt know any more of him than just to pass the time o' day'. **1882** B. HARTE *Flip* iii, 'Dropping in to pass the time of day' with her father. **1890** L. C. D'OYLE *Notches* 180 She had simply passed him a pleasant 'Good morning'. **1894** *Outing* (U.S.) XXIV. 10/1 Nothing has happened to prevent my passing the compliments of the day with Mrs. Crombie. **1936** 'F. GERALD' *Millionaire in Memories* xii. 316, I was riding home after doing some work on my racecourse and I pulled up at Swanson's swagger camp to pass the time of day. **1960** G. DURRELL *Zoo in Luggage* viii. 192, I was passing the time of day with the garage man. **1965** N. GULBENKIAN *Pantaraxia* xi. 230 Joe Boyle, one of the directors of the Royal Dutch Shell..went to see my father, as though merely to pass the time of day. **1965** *Listener* 23 Sept. 453/2 The English chaps would pretend..to be very friendly and jovial and pass the time of day and that sort of thing. **1978** M. GIROUARD *Life in Eng. Country House* v. 147 The King..was then conveyed to the prince's bedchamber, where *he* passed the time of day for a few minutes.

***** †**53.** *Fencing.* To make or execute (a thrust).

1598 SHAKS. *Merry W.* II. iii. 26 To see thee fight, to see thee foigne, to..see thee passe thy puncto, thy stock, thy reuerse, thy distance, thy montant.

54. To perform the pass on a pack of cards: see PASS *sb.*[2] 10.

1859 L. WRAXALL tr. *Mem. J. E. Robert-Houdin* I. viii. 157 He also said, in allusion to the ace of hearts, which he had 'passed' on one of the most beautiful women in the room: 'Will you be kind enough, madam, to lay your hand on your heart?' **1884** *St. James's Gaz.* 5 Dec. 5/2 [To] prevent him from watching the operator too closely when engaged in 'readying' and 'passing' the cards. *Ibid.*, Striking feats of dexterous 'readying' and 'passing' which his companion performed.

IV. With prepositions and adverbs.

* With prepositions.

Pass (intrans., trans., or causal) may be followed by any preposition of motion or direction, with its object, both words having their own senses. Sometimes the prep. appears to be more closely united with the verb, so as to form with it a verbal phrase, often expressible by a single verb with its object. Thus *pass across* = cross, traverse, *pass down* = descend, *pass into* = enter, *pass up* = ascend, etc. Of these, the following are the more important:

pass at ——. See 23 c.

55. pass beyond ——. **a.** See simple senses and BEYOND *prep.*

b. To pass the limits of, exceed, transcend.

1819 KEATS *Lamia* II. 32 His spirit pass'd beyond its golden bourn Into the noisy world. **1875** JOWETT *Plato* (ed. 2) IV. 257 No effort of reflection will enable us to pass beyond the limits of our own faculties.

56. pass by ——.

†**a.** To go through or by way of. *Obs.*

13.. *K. Alis.* 1320 Anon they..Passith by Tire, and by Cidoyne,..Alle til they come to Babiloyne. **1390** Gower *Conf.* III. 63 Wher as sche passeth be the strete. *a* **1548** Hall *Chron., Hen. VIII* 61 [They] assauted the Alyens as they passed by the stretes. **1573–80** Baret *Alv.* P 162 As we came to this Citie, we passed by Lions, where we soiourned two daies.

b. To go past; to pass; = 28.

13.. *K. Alis.* 6658 Heo passeden by a quenes lond, That hette Candace, Y undurstond. *c* **1386** Chaucer *Merch. T.* 340 Thanne sholde he se ful many a figure pace By his Mirour. **1481** Caxton *Reynard* xxiii. (Arb.) 54, I supposed to haue passed by hym peasibly toward this feste. **1550** Crowley *Epigr.* 34 b, As he paste by a pasture most pleasaunte to se. **1606** Shaks. *Tr. & Cr.* iii. iii. 39 Please it our Generall to passe strangely by him, As if he were forgot. **1711** Addison *Spect.* No. 63 ¶6, I heard several double Rhymes as I passed by them. **1850** S. Dobell *Roman, Chamouni*, If Thou..hast..passed by The sleeping savage dreadful still in sleep.

c. To pass without stopping, or without notice; to take no notice of, disregard, omit: see 61 c.

***pass for* ——.** See 5, 23. ***pass into* ——.** See 7. ***pass of* ——.** See 10, 10 c, 23 b. ***pass on* ——.** See 5 c, 21 b, c, 24.

57. pass over ——.

a. To cross above or on the surface of (a sea, river, or expanse); to cross, to traverse; = 30.

c **1275** Lay. 1341 Seyles drawe to toppe, leten lade þane wind, passi ouer bieres. **1297** R. Glouc. (Rolls) 228 Suþþe he ssulde mani lond over passi & wende. *a* **1300** *Cursor M.* 10120 Do me to passe þe dikes [*v.r.* diches] ouer. *c* **1325** *Lai le Freine* 141 The maide..passed ouer a wild heth. *c* **1400** *Melayne* 878 To Charls now will I torne agayne þat passes ouer Mountayne & playne. *c* **1440** *Promp. Parv.* 376/2 Pacyn ovyr, *transgredior.* **1600** Shaks. *A.Y.L.* v. iii. 19 It was a Louer, and his lasse,..That o're the greene corne feild did passe. **1600** J. Pory tr. *Leo's Africa* Introd. 39 A man must beware how he passe ouer deepe riuers with them. **1749** *Apol. Life B.-M. Carew* 125 Passing over this Ferry they came into Rhode Island. **1874** J. W. Draper *Hist. Conflict Relig. & Sci.* vi. 161 The distance passed over in a voyage from Italy to the Gulf of Guinea.

fig. **1887** Bowen *Virg. Æneid* ii. 284 O'er thy people and city, alas! what sorrows have passed. *a* **1905** *Mod.* A change passed over his countenance.

b. To pass the hand over.

1805 Southey *Madoc in W.* xiv, He took a harp..and passing o'er its chords Made music. **1879** Sir E. Arnold *Lt. Asia* iii. (1883) 52 So sigh we, passing o'er the solemn strings.

†**c.** *trans.* To spend (time); = sense 44. *Obs.*

1390 Gower *Conf.* III. 64 The queene..passeth over thilke nyht, Til it was on the morwe liht. **1548** Udall, etc. *Erasm. Par. Matt.* i. 20 So that the reste of the life be passed ouer after the rule of Christ. **1577** *F. de L'isle's Legendarie* A viij, He neuer medled with matters of estate but passed ouer his time in pleasure. **1662** J. Davies tr. *Olearius' Voy. Ambass.* 198 Many times he pass'd over the Winter therein.

d. To pass a thing without dwelling upon it, or without notice or remark, to omit: see 67 e.

58. pass through ——.

a. To go from side to side of, to cross, traverse.

a **1300** *Cursor M.* 6265 þe see on aiþer side þam stod,..Til þai war passed thoru þat flod. **1375** Barbour *Bruce* xvi. 319 That he wes passit throu all Irland Fra end till end. *c* **1385** Chaucer *L.G.W.* 746 *Thisbe*, And with a soun as softe as ony shryfte They lete here wordis thour the clift pace. **1526** *Pilgr. Perf.* (W. de W. 1531) 12 b, Ye people of god passyng through the same see drye fote. **1530** Palsgr. 653/2 He shall passe thorowe fyre and water or he get it. **1613** Purchas *Pilgrimage* (1614) 62 Not cause their children to passe through the fire. **1709** Steele *Tatler* No. 44 ¶4 On Saturday last he passed through Staines. **1885** Leudesdorf *Cremona's Proj. Geom.* 237 If two conics which are inscribed in a given quadrilateral pass through a given point.

fig. **1639** T. Brugis tr. *Camus' Mor. Relat.* 318 All the Idea's which passe thorow our mindes. **1722** Wollaston *Relig. Nat.* i. 11 Abimelek gave greater credit to that information which passed through his eye.

b. In reference to times, stages, states, conditions, processes, actions, experiences, etc.

c **1320** *Sir Beues* (MS. A.) 1035 Erst þow schelt pase þour3 min hond And þour3 Morgelay, my gode brond! **1362** Langl. *P. Pl.* A. viii. 11 [Thei] Han pardoun þorw Purgatorie to passen ful sone. **1604** E. G[rimstone] *D'Acosta's Hist. Indies* iv. iv. 211 Golde which hath often passed through the fire, keepes his colour. **1660** F. Brooke tr. *Le Blanc's Trav.* 128 Men having passed thorough all sorts of animalls at last became Gods. **1711** Addison *Spect.* No. 115 ¶5 How many Hands must they pass through before they are fit for Use? **1747** *Gentl. Mag.* XVII. 325 Having pass'd thro' his Degrees in Arts, he became domestick Chaplain to Dr Tho. Smith. **1865** R. W. Dale *Jew. Temp.* xxi. (1877) 233 We..are passing through times of speculative unbelief.

c. To make or force a passage through; to penetrate; to pierce through; to shoot through, send a shot through.

14.. in *Tundale's Vis.* (1843) 133 And thorow thi sowle schall a scharp swyrd pace. **1412–20** Lydg. *Chron. Troy* iv. xxx, For he felte thorugh his herte pace The persyng stremys of hir eyen two. *c* **1470** *Gol. & Gaw.* 708 Throw platis of polist steill thair poyntis can pase. **1530** Palsgr. 654/2 He passed thorowe his harnesse and his bodye at one shotte, *il transpassa son harnoys et son corps a vng traict. Mod.* The bullet passed through his shoulder.

fig. **1638** Junius *Paint. Ancients* 211 No man is able to passe through the secrets of Art,..unlesse he first overcome the pompe of vaine glorie.

d. *causal.* To cause (a thing) to pass or go through; to put, thrust, or impel through.

1530 Palsgr. 654/2, I passe thorowe, as spyce..thorowe a sarce, or pepyr thorowe the querne, or meale thorowe a boulter. **1731** Medley *Kolben's Cape G. Hope* II. 67 The ground becomes frequently so hard, that twenty oxen are not sufficient to pass a plough through it. **1853** Soyer *Pantroph.* 288 Take a flour sieve, and pass the cheese through it. **1857** Borrow *Rom. Rye* xxxix, The principal component parts were burnt wine and rosemary, passed through an alembic. **1885** *Law Rep.* 15 Q.B.D. 316 A catch ..which prevented the pin, when passed through a slit, from repassing. **1898** Florence Montgomery *Tony* 20 Passing his arm through the strap of the window. **1899** *Allbutt's Syst. Med.* VIII. 848 The preparations being much reduced in virulence by passing the culture through rabbits. *a* **1905** *Mod.* A dragoon passed his sword through him.

e. To follow a ritual of going through a narrow opening in a natural object such as a cleft tree or rock, etc., in the belief that the object will prove a barrier to evil or will absorb illness. Also *trans.*, in causal senses. Hence **passing-through** *sb.*

1804 *Gentl. Mag.* Oct. 909/1 Rowe's son was passed through the present tree in 1792, at the age of one or two. **1846** *Athenæum* 5 Sept. 909/1 A second point arises upon the 'passing through'... The passing through a cleft or aperture in a rock is a medical superstition..found in many countries. **1900** C. Hose in *Geogr. Jrnl.* XVI. 45 The funeral procession climbed the mound on which the ceremony was situated, passing through the V of the cleft stick in single file. **1913** J. G. Frazer *Golden Bough: Balder the Beautiful* (ed. 3) II. xi. 176 The words uttered by the mourners in passing through the cloven stick shew clearly that they believe the stick to act as a barrier or fence, on the further side of which they leave behind the ghost. *Ibid.* 184 In Scotland children who suffered from hectic fever and consumptive patients used to be healed by passing thrice through a circular wreath of woodbine. **1961** C. Hole *Encycl. Superstitions* 21 A young ash-sapling was split, and the child was passed through it, three or nine times. **1968** *Proc. Amer. Philos. Soc.* CXII. 388/1 Passing-through rituals in the earth usually involved grassy terrain, where sod could be cut, piled, and arched to make a passageway. *Ibid.* 391/1 Prevention of disease by passing through seems more pronounced in passing through stones than in other kinds of rituals involving passing through.

***pass upon* ——.** See 5 c, 21 c.

†**59. pass with ——**: to have done with, take no notice of. *Obs. rare.*

1641 *Nicholas Papers* (Camden) 27 Neither have they gratifyed the kinge with the release of the lo. Montrosse or with the passing with the Ea. of Traquaire.

** With adverbs.

60. pass away. a. See simple senses and away *adv.* **b.** *intr.* Of persons: To depart; also, to get or break away (as from restraint).

a **1425** *Cursor M.* 12975 (Trin.) Somme oþere vnswere shaltou say Ar I passe from þe away. *c* **1430** *Syr Tryam.* 317 The quene passyd awey & fledd On fote. **1590** Spenser *F.Q.* i. vi. 48 But, when he saw the Damsell passe away, He left his stond, and her pursewd apace. **1879** E. Arnold *Lt. Asia* iv. (1883) 88 But that ox-king..Trampled the warders down, and passed away.

c. To die, expire.

c **1375** *Lay Folks Mass Bk.* (MS. B) 112 God lord graunt ..rest and pese þat lastis ay to cristen soules passed away. **1806** Southey *Lett.* (ed. Warter) I. 366 Immediately as he uttered the words he passed away. **1892** *Law Times* XCII. 144/2 Mr. Richard Williams..passed away on the 21st ult., at the great age of ninety years.

d. Of time: To elapse, come to an end.

a **1425** *Cursor M.* 20858 (Trin.) Tyme passeþ faste awey. **1711** Addison *Spect.* No. 93 ¶2 The Moments that are to pass away before the happy Meeting. **1847** Marryat *Childr. N. Forest* iv, Thus passed the winter away so rapidly, that [etc.].

e. Of things: To pass out of existence, come to an end, cease to be, be dissolved, perish.

13.. *S. Paula* in Horstm. *Altengl. Leg.* (1878) 4/1 Precious stones þat wiþ þis world and eorþe here Passen awey al in fere. **1539** Bible (Great) *2 Pet.* iii. 10 The heauens shall passe awaye. **1557** N. T. (Genev.) *Matt.* xxiv. 35 Heauen and earth shall passe awaye [Wyclif passe, Tindale perisshe], but my wordes shal not passe awaye. **1814** Southey *Ode War Amer.* xiii, Dominion passeth like a cloud away. **1845** M. Pattison *Ess.* (1889) I. 26 His anger passed away. **1856** Froude *Hist. Eng.* (1858) I. i. 59 All the ..convictions of the old world were passing away, never to return. **1884** *Manch. Exam.* 20 May 5/2 The fears of a general crisis are passing away.

f. *trans.* To spend (time, etc.); to while away, to pass: emphatic of 44.

c **1550** *Lusty Juventus* in Hazl. *Dodsley* II. 46 What shall I do now to pass away the day? **1560** Daus tr. *Sleidane's Comm.* 139 Going than to Wittemberge, they passed away the rest of the wynter there. **1594** Shaks. *Rich. III*, i. i. 25 Why I..Haue no delight to passe away the time. **1665** Earl Dorset *Song Written at Sea* vii, To pass our tedious hours away. **1711** Addison *Spect.* No. 106 ¶1 An Invitation..to pass away a Month with him in the Country. **1848** Thackeray *Lett.* 12 Aug., One day is passed away here very like its defunct predecessor.

†**g.** To transfer away; to relinquish, surrender (rights, etc.); to convey away (property). *Obs.*

1651 Hobbes *Leviath.* ii. xxi. 111 What Rights we passe away, when we make a Common-wealth. **1690** Locke *Govt.* ii. viii. §116 Because our Fathers or Progenitors passed away their natural Liberty. *a* **1692** Pollexfen *Disc. Trade* (1697) 28 A Man that is to pass away Lands, or Goods. **1781** Cowper *Hope* 11 Riches are passed away from hand to hand.

61. pass by.

a. *intr.* To go or proceed past; to move on without stopping; to flow past.

c **1430** *Syr Tryam.* 278 There the quene schulde passe by. **1568** Grafton *Chron.* II. 301 The Englishmen passed by without anye approchyng. **1611** Bible *Lam.* i. 12 Is it nothing to you, all ye that passe by? **1712** Steele *Spect.* No. 398 ¶1 He saw Robin the Porter..passing by. **1799** Southey *Ruined Cottage* Wks. 1838 III. 32 The countrymen..leaning o'er the bridge,..would all look up When she pass'd by. **1850** Tennyson *In Mem.* xix, There twice a day the Severn fills; The salt sea-water passes by.

b. *fig.* and in reference to time.

c **1386** Chaucer *Man of Law's T.* 1026 But I lete all his storie passen by, Of Custance is my tale specially. *a* **1821** Keats *Sonn., Human Seasons*, To let fair things Pass by unheeded, as a threshold brook. **1885** *Manch. Weekly Times* 20 June 5/5 A generation would pass by before the adversaries..would find their way back to power.

c. *trans.* To go past (a thing or person) without stopping, or without taking notice; to fail to notice, to overlook; to omit; to take no notice of, dismiss from consideration, disregard, ignore; = *pass over*, 67 e, f.

When the object is a sb., it usually comes after *by*, so that the construction can be analysed as that of an intrans. vb. with a preposition and its object, as in *to pass by his eldest son*: cf. *to pass him by*.

[*a* **1300** *Cursor M.* 15634 Quer i sal þis calice drinc, or i sal pass þar-bi?] **1560** Bible (Genev.) *Prov.* xix. 11 His glorie is to passe by an offence. **1611** Ld. T. Howard in *Harington's Nugæ Ant.* (ed. Park 1804) I. 393 He was overcharged with confusion, and passed by admiring the dressing of the horse. **1621** T. Williamson tr. *Goulart's Wise Vieillard* 77 Better to wink at, and passe by an iniurie. **1658–9** in *Burton's Diary* (1828) IV. 3, I would hear him first, and then pass it by... He must come as a delinquent on his knees. **1677** Horneck *Gt. Law Consid.* v. (1704) 297 These observables are passed by as things out of his element. **1869** J. Martineau *Ess.* II. 76 Instances..which legislation passes by in silence. **1869** Freeman *Norm. Conq.* III. xiii. 278 That Eadward might rightly pass by an incompetent minor. **1871** R. H. Hutton *Ess.* (1877) I. 71, I pass them by with the remark.

62. pass forth.

a. *intr.* To go out or away (*arch.*). †*to pass forth of use*, to go out of use, become obsolete (*obs.*).

1297 R. Glouc. (Rolls) 2910 He sey þe contreys as he passede vorþ & destrued & bar in eche half. *c* **1394** *P. Pl. Crede* 96 Leue nou3t on þo losels but let hem forþ pasen. **1530** Palsgr. 654/1, I passe forthe, I go forthe, as an armye whan it is removynge, or a company byfore a great estate. **1565** *Reg. Privy Council Scot.* I. 332 Understanding the privilegis of the Scottis merchantis..to decay and pas furth of use in the partis of Flanderis. **1596** Spenser *F.Q.* vi. iii. 16 He passed forth with her in faire array.

†**b.** To go forward, advance, go on, continue.

c **1386** Chaucer *Miller's T.* 184 This passeth forth..ffro day to day..this..Absolon So woweth hire. *c* **1450** *St. Cuthbert* (Surtees) 7505 He was wele paste forthe in age. **1568** Grafton *Chron.* II. 391 The yongest..say their opinions first, and so passe foorth in order vntill it come to the highest.

†**c.** *trans.* To spend or pass (time). *Obs.*

1509 Hawes *Past. Pleas.* xvi. (Percy Soc.) 73 She wyll wyth love her grene flouryng age Passe forth in joye, pleasure, & courage. **1552** Huloet, Passe forth the day or tyme, *agitare diem, exigere tempus.* **1573–80** Baret *Alv.* P 158, I will passe forth this day by little and little [*paulatim hunc producam diem*] with sipping and drinking.

63. a. pass in. *trans.* To hand in (e.g. a cheque to a bank). ***to pass in one's cheques***, to die (*slang*): see also check *sb.*[1] 15; ***to pass in one's chips***: see chip *sb.*[1] 2 e; also *absol.*; ***to pass in one's marble***: see marble *sb.* 4 b.

1872 'Mark Twain' *Roughing It* 332 (Farmer) One of the boys has passed in his checks, and we want to give him a good send-off. **1894** H. Nisbet *Bush Girl's Rom.* 108 The best thing I can do for you is to give you a cheque of my own made payable to yourself at sight, with an introduction to the bank as well, and I will pass in the form myself next time I am down there. **1900** *W. Lond. Observ.* 4 May 3/7, I see that young M. has passed in his checks. **1904** *N.Y. Even. Jrnl.* 3 May 2 'I may die' he told friends, 'and I want to breathe American air again before I pass in.'

b. *trans.* To withdraw from an auction sale because of failure to reach the reserve price. *Austral.* and *N.Z.*

1973 *Sun-Herald* (Sydney) 26 Aug. 23/2 The house was passed in at $37,000—the reserve was $42,000. **1977** *N.Z. Herald* 5 Jan. 1-11/10 What seemed to be unrealistic prices asked for by vendors in general resulted in 60 of the 99 lots on offer at a thoroughbred sale at Alexandra Park yesterday being passed in.

64. pass off.

a. *intr.* To go off or disappear gradually: said of sensations, physical conditions, moisture, etc.

1845 Budd *Dis. Liver* 266 In the presence of some medicines that pass off in the bile. **1861** Headland *Med. Handbk.* 160 Remittent fever instead of intermitting at distinct periods, passes off after a variable time, and then recurs. *a* **1905** *Mod.* After a little the feeling of faintness passed off. The hydrogen unites with the oxygen to form water, which passes off in steam. The smell of the paint will pass off in a few days.

b. *intr.* Of a proceeding: To be carried through and completed (with more or less success).

1787 J. Woodforde *Diary* 4 Dec. (1926) II. 356 Everything passed of [*sic*] as agreeable as one might expect from such a Meeting. **1788** E. Sheridan *Jrnl.* (1960) 107 All pass'd off very well—My Father a little stately at first but soon thoroughly cordial with his Son. *Ibid.* 141 Our day pass'd off very well—no awkwardness or unpleasantness of any kind. **1886** *Times* 23 Nov. 9 In every sense the festival passed off as its promoters must have desired. **1891** *Leeds Merc.* 2 May 6/3 The Labour Demonstrations throughout Europe yesterday passed off on the whole more peaceably than was anticipated. *a* **1905** *Mod.* How did the wedding pass off? Everything passed off very well.

c. *trans.* To put into circulation, or dispose of (esp. deceptively); to palm off; to impose; *spec.*

in *Law*, to represent (goods, etc.) as those of another.

1799 HAN. MORE *Fem. Educ.* (ed. 4) I. 297 They might be tempted to pass off for their own what they pick up from others. **1857** BORROW *Rom. Rye* xvii, And other customers came in, who..also passed off their jokes upon me. *Ibid.* xli, [He] sometimes shortened money, and at other times passed off what had been shortened by other gentry. **1865** M. ARNOLD *Ess. Crit.* ii. 65 Trying to pass off their wares as excellent. **1884** *Law Times Rep.* LI. 222/2 The applicants.. pass off their goods for those of the Baron de Geer. **1900**, etc. [see PASSING *vbl. sb.* 2 b]. **1902** *Encycl. Brit.* XXXIII. 388/1 No trader is entitled to 'pass-off' his goods as those of another... Even if the 'passing-off' is done innocently it will be restrained. **1972** WHITE & JACOB *Kerly's Law of Trade Marks* (ed. 10) xvi. 362 The question whether the use of particular words or badges is calculated to pass off the defendant's goods as those of the plaintiff is often one of difficulty.

d. To cause (a person) to be accepted in some false character; *esp. refl.* (with *for* or *as*), to give oneself out as what one is not, to pretend to be.

1809 MALKIN *Gil Blas* v. i. ¶12 He passed himself off for my servant. *Ibid.* ¶18 The insolence of this scoundrel who fancies to pass me off for a highwayman. **1871** SMILES *Charac.* vi. (1876) 181 He does not seek to pass himself off as richer than he is. **1885** H. CONWAY *Family Affair* I, A child still young enough to be passed off as a child in arms.

e. To ward off or adroitly put aside (a remark, etc.) without seriously meeting it: to parry.

1890 A. GISSING *Village Hampden* III. xi. 238 The young man passed off lightly all such reference.

65. pass on.

a. *intr.* See simple senses and ON *adv.*; *esp.* to proceed on one's way, in one's course, in one's discourse or writing; to continue one's course; to proceed or advance, as a transaction or progressive state; to pass, as time.

a **1300** *Cursor M.* 17288 + 395 Þe day is passed on, no farrer may þou wyn. **1470–85** MALORY *Arthur* XVIII. xx, Soo this paste on alle that wynter with alle manere of huntynge and haukyng. **1573–80** BARET *Alv.* P 163 The more time that passed on, the more [etc.]. **1611** BIBLE *Gen.* xviii. 5, I will fetch a morsell of bread; and comfort ye your hearts, after that ye shall passe on. **1626** C. POTTER tr. *Sarpi's Hist. Quarrels* 46 The Pope spake all this with so great heat, that the Ambassador did not iudge fit at that time to passe on further. **1634** MILTON *Comus* 430 Yea there, where very desolation dwels..She may pass on with unblench't majesty. **1842** TENNYSON '*Come not when I am dead*' ii, Pass on, weak heart, and leave me where I lie. **1899** *Allbutt's Syst. Med.* VII. 651 The optic neuritis is passing on to post-neuritic atrophy. *a* **1905** *Mod.* Pass on, please, and do not obstruct the way. The preacher passes on to his second head. But we have said enough on this point; we pass on.

b. *trans.* To send or hand (anything) to the next member of a series.

1791 'G. GAMBADO' *Ann. Horsem.* xvii. (1809) 139 No Vagrants past on. **1877** SPURGEON *Serm.* XXIII. 357 Getting rid of a case by saving your own pocket and passing the applicant on to another. *Mod.* Please read this and pass it on.

c. *intr.* To proceed from one existence or activity to another; *spec.* to die.

1804–1820 W. BLAKE *Jerusalem* III, in *Compl. Writings* (1972) 714 So Men pass on: but States remain permanent for ever. **1884** *150th Anniv. Settlement of Boscawen & Webster, New Hampsh.* 44 They have all passed on to become soldiers of the unseen army. **1920** R. MACAULAY *Potterism* III. ii. 131 If I have to pass on before Percy, he will be left bereaved indeed. **1923** *Amer. Mag.* June 15/1 The murderer took poison and so the two passed on. **1925** *Nat. Geogr. Mag.* XLVII. 489/2 His mother now dwells in comfort..while his father has passed on. **1928** L. NORTH *Parasites* 77 When my dad passed on there was just enough insurance to have let me finish up. **1930** 'E. QUEEN' *French Powder Myst.* xxxv. 274 Bernice [should] come in for a good share of Cyrus's estate when Cyrus should pass on. **1945** A. HUXLEY *Time must have Stop* vi. 66 'They don't die,' said Mrs. Gamble. 'They pass on.' **1946** E. O'NEILL *Iceman Cometh* I. 89 Too late! The old Doc has passed on to his Maker. **1960** S. KAUFFMAN *If it be Love* i. 12 'Margaret passed on.' William winced.. when someone used a euphemism for 'died'. **1973** A. BROINOWSKI *Take One Ambassador* i. 14 I'm Mrs Bert Norrice, well, Mrs Fern Norrice these days, since Mr Norrice passed on last year. **1977** B. PYM *Quartet in Autumn* i. 10 Old Snowy had long since died, 'passed on' or 'been taken', however one liked to put it.

66. pass out.

a. *intr.* See simple senses and OUT *adv.*; chiefly, to go out through a passage. ***to pass out of***, to issue from, leave; ***to pass out of sight***, to go beyond the reach of sight.

13.. *K. Alis.* 6246 Ther no schal schip out passe. *c* **1375** *Cursor M.* 12127 (Fairf.) How lange þi life sal laste or þou passe out of þis werde. *a* **1425** *Ibid.* 17350 (Trin.) Þei sent aspies also aboute þat he shulde not passen oute. **1574** tr. *Marlorat's Apocalips* 3 That he should passe out of Asia into Macedonia. *a* **1711** KEN *Art. Visit.* Wks. (1838) 492 When any one is passing out of this life. **1833** KEBLE *Serm.* (1848) I. 147 He may..pass out of this world, before he see any abatement in the triumph of disorder and irreligion. **1842** TENNYSON *Locksley Hall* 34 Love..Smote the chord of Self, that, trembling, pass'd in music out of sight.

†**b.** *trans.* To spend the whole of (a time).

1603 KNOLLES *Hist. Turks* (1621) 55 The poore Sultan utterly discouraged, returned againe to Constantinople, and there..passed out the rest of his dayes.

c. *intr.* (*a*) to die; (*b*) to faint, become unconscious; also, ***to pass out cold***. *colloq.*

1899 *Westm. Gaz.* 6 Mar. 2/1 Another [spirit] who 'passed out' with consumption is heard coughing. **1924** P. MARKS *Plastic Age* i. 12 He left us a whole lot of jack when he passed out. **1927** *Hutchinson's Myst. Story Mag.* Feb. 80 First, the name of the dead relative or friend, then when they passed out. **1939** JOYCE *Finnegans Wake* 627, I am passing out. O bitter ending! **1968** *Publ. Amer. Dial. Soc.* 1966 XLVI. 28 *Pass out*, die—'When he passed out, he was buried with his dogs.' **1915** C. MATHEWSON *Catcher Craig* i. 9 They sure do work you hard over there. I worked in the stock-room one summer and nearly passed out! **1918** J. M. GRIDER *War Birds* (1927) 97 We..carried him home after he passed out. **1924** P. MARKS *Plastic Age* xxii. 254 A man 'passed out cold' and had to be carried from the gymnasium. **1935** J. T. FARRELL *Guillotine Party* 191 Young Johnny Herbert had gotten drunk for the first time in his life and he'd passed out like a light. **1936** WODEHOUSE *Laughing Gas* ii. 26, I broke off here, because she had fainted... She slid sideways along the seat and quietly passed out. **1939** J. B. PRIESTLEY *Let People Sing* vii. 167 He's a big success in the cocktail bar... Does a few little tricks now and then, an' they nearly pass out. **1942** D. POWELL *Time to be Born* (1943) x. 245 'What'll we do if he passes out in your place?' Corinne asked. 'I'll look after him,' said Vicky. **1947** 'N. SHUTE' *Chequer Board* i. 3, I suddenly passed out cold... I passed out cold and fell down..on the floor. *a* **1953** E. O'NEILL *Hughie* (1962) 22, I got scared he'd pass out with excitement. **1974** D. GRAY *Dead Give Away* ix. 95 'How has she taken it?' 'Badly... She passed out when I told her.'

d. *trans.* To knock unconscious. *Austral. slang.*

1906 E. DYSON *Fact'ry 'Ands* xii. 151 He promised to show Feathers a 'boshter knack for passing out gazobs'.

e. *intr.* To complete a course of instruction, etc., successfully; to graduate. Also *trans.*, to undergo (a course of instruction); to allow or enable (someone) to pass out.

1916 *Daily Colonist* (Victoria, B.C.) 28 July 4/7 Midshipman Robert W. Wood..passed out first in 1914 both in the college and in ships. **1920** *Discovery* Mar. 77/2 Airship pilots..are required to pass-out a course in free ballooning, which includes a night flight and a solo flight. *a* **1968** S. FAESSLER in R. Weaver *Canad. Short Stories* (1968) 2nd Ser. 335 My plan, after being passed out of Grade VIII, was to go..to Harbord Collegiate. **1968** J. SANGSTER *Touchfeather* ii. 8, I romped through the training, passing out with the highest marks anyone could remember.

f. To hand out or distribute.

1926 *Publishers' Weekly* 10 July 116 Librarians..are eager and willing to pass out catalogs that have won their confidence. **1927** *Ibid.* 12 Feb. 599 On that day she had passed out 130 books. **1964** MRS. L. B. JOHNSON *White House Diary* 5 June (1970) 154, I was impressed that Charlotte Ford said, 'I'll do anything you want me to do. Type, pass out cards, anything.' **1973** R. HILL *Ruling Passion* III. iii. 179 He passed out some photostatted sheets. **1978** *Detroit Free Press* 2 Apr. 8E/1 Allow the ATF to lift licenses from dealers at any time in the future for the most minor of errors in complicated bookkeeping procedures, as well as pass out $10,000 fines.

g. *Bridge.* Of the players: to make three consecutive passes following (a bid), the auction thus ending and this bid becoming the contract; to make no positive bid at all in (a hand). Usu. in *passive*.

1959 *Listener* 19 Mar. 530/3 The fourth hand bid Three Spades which was passed out. **1960** T. REESE *Play Bridge with Reese* 91 Partner now surprises me by going five hearts. That is passed out. **1969** A. TRUSCOTT *Gt. Bridge Scandal* 307 A two notrump opening bid that has been passed out.

67. pass over.

a. *intr.* To go across; to cross to the other or opposite side. In *Chemistry*, said of the volatilized substances which pass from the retort in distillation, and are condensed in the receiver.

a **1330** *Otuel* 707 Ouer þe brugge þei wenten ifeere,..& þo þei ouer passed were, Such auntres þei funden þere. **1611** BIBLE *Deut.* iii. 18 Ye shall passe ouer armed before your brethren the children of Israel. **1641** FRENCH *Distill.* vi. (1651) 196 Adde the tartarizated quintessence, yet so that.. that passe over with it. **1849** MACAULAY *Hist. Eng.* v. I. 601 The hope that some of those regiments which he had formerly commanded would pass over to his standard. **1863–72** WATTS *Dict. Chem.* I. 10 That which passes over towards the middle must be redistilled to free it from copper mechanically carried over. **1864–72** *Ibid.* II. 337 Some organic compounds boil at so low a temperature that, when heated in a retort, they pass over unchanged. **1875** BENNETT & DYER tr. *Sachs' Bot.* 802 The contents of one of the conjugating cells pass over into the other which remains stationary. **1879** HARLAN *Eyesight* ii. 25 After lining the inner surface of the lids, it [mucous membrane] passes over to the ball, forming a loose fold.

b. Of a period of time: To go by, elapse, be spent, come to an end.

c **1470** HENRY *Wallace* I. 271 This passit our, quhill diuers dayis war gane. **1659** H. PLUMPTRE *Let.* in *12th Rep. Hist. MSS. Comm.* App. v. 6 Wishing that all your yeares yet to come may passe over with mirth and jollityes. **1794** W. BLAKE *Urizen* IV, in *Compl. Writings* (1972) 228 And a second Age passed over, And a state of dismal woe. **1795–1804** —— *Vala* v, in *Compl. Writings* (1972) 307 Till many a morn & many a night pass'd over in dire woe. **1840** R. H. DANA *Two Yrs. before Mast* xxiv. 250 The night passed over without any trouble. **1878** R. L. STEVENSON in *London* 6 July 10/1 The journey passed over without much incident.

†**c.** With compl., as ***to pass over unpunished***, to go unpunished. *Obs.*

1566 *Reg. Privy Council Scot.* I. 470 Wordis of dishonour ..quhilk aucht nocht to pas owir untryit and unpuneist.

d. *trans.* To hand over *to* another; to transfer.

1560 DAUS tr. *Sleidane's Comm.* 306 b, [They] leauing behinde them no children, passed ouer the gouernment to their yongest brother. **1577** HARRISON *England* II. xxiii. (1877) I. 355 But then I should exceed the limits of a description. Wherefore I passe it ouer to others [etc.]. **1631** WEEVER *Anc. Fun. Mon.* 687 This house..satisfied the said Sir Richard; who thereupon past it ouer to Q. Mary. *a* **1686** T. WATSON *Body Divin.* (1692) 460 The Covenant of Grace ..by vertue of which God passeth himself over to us to be our God. **1862** DANA *Man. Geol.* 583 Geology here passes over the continuation of the history of man to Archaeology.

e. To pass (a thing) without touching it, or without remark or notice, esp. in narration; to omit, to skip, to disregard; to ignore the claims of (a person) to promotion, etc., to pass by in selection for a special post or duty.

As in *pass by* 61 c, when the object is a sb., it usually comes after *over*, so that the construction can then be analysed as that of an intrans. vb. followed by a preposition with its object; as in the literal *he passed over the bridge*. Cf. also the vb. OVERPASS, of which *pass over* was formerly the decomposed form used in certain verbal constructions.

c **1380** WYCLIF *Serm.* Sel. Wks. II. 226 Paul passiþ over þes two vertues, and praieþ after charite. *c* **1386** CHAUCER *Pard. Prol.* 17 This is a pitous tale for to heere But nathelees passe ouer is no fors. **1526** SKELTON *Magnyf.* 646, I wyll passe ouer the cyrcumstaunce, And shortly shewe you the hole substaunce. **1530** PALSGR. 654/2, I have many mo thynges to saye..but, for faulte of tyme, I passe them over. **1573** G. HARVEY *Letter-bk.* (Camden) 8, I pas mani sutch misusagis over. **1621** ELSING *Debates Ho. Lords* (Camden) 54 The matter of Yelverton is of such ymportaunce as yt cannot be paste over. **1711** ADDISON *Spect.* No. 1 ¶3 As for the rest of my Infancy... I shall pass it over in Silence. **1839** JAMES *Gentl. Old Sch.* xiv, This gross offence..was not to be passed over. **1890** W. E. NORRIS *Misadventure* viii, He does not think it would be right to pass over his son. **1890** T. W. REID *Monckton-Milnes* (1891) I. viii. 360 He had again been disappointed of his..expectation of office, Peel having once more passed him over.

f. To let go unpunished, to overlook (an offence).

1388 WYCLIF *Prov.* xix. 11 His glorie is to passe ouere wickid thingis. **1611** BIBLE *ibid.*, It is his glory to passe ouer a transgression. **1814** WELLINGTON 16 May in Gurw. *Desp.* (1838) XII. 21 If conduct such as that..be passed over, it will be impossible to maintain the necessary discipline of the army. **1877** SPURGEON *Serm.* XXIII. 662 The sin..was not to be winked at and passed over as a mere trifle.

†**g.** To surpass = OVERPASS *v.* 7.

1390 GOWER *Conf.* II. 264 A goddesse..what hir liste.. Sche dede, That passeth over manneskinde.

h. To convey across; to transport.

1832 N. WYETH *Jrnl.* 18 June in *Corr. & Jrnls.* (1899) 157 Reached the place for fording the platte. 19th, Passed over my goods during a severe wind without accident.

i. *intr.* To die.

Associated esp. with spiritualism.

1909 *Review of Reviews* Feb. 123/2 His automatic writing ..came..through the same friend through whom he has constantly communicated ever since he passed over. **1928** *Daily Mail* 7 Aug. 16/5 This doctor was now with my mother, who had recently passed over. **1930** D. L. SAYERS *Strong Poison* xvi. 209, I have had the most marvellous talks with the dear ones who have passed over. **1938** AUDEN & ISHERWOOD *On Frontier* III. i. 89 Those who have passed over are all very happy. He said the Other Side was difficult to describe. **1958** C. WATSON *Coffin scarcely Used* ii. 18 If the living's good and bad mixed, then those who've passed over are two sorts as well. **1974** J. STUBBS *Painted Face* vii. 108, I wonder if her poor husband ever read those diaries, after she passed over?

68. pass through: emphatic of sense 14.

c **1400** *Ywaine & Gaw.* 15 Thurgh I past, with mekyl payn. *a* **1693** SOUTH *Serm.* II. v. 176 His Heart lies open.. for all the Sin and Villainy in the World freely to pass through. **1801** BLOOMFIELD *Rural T., Fakenham Ghost* xi, So long it [the gate] swung That Ghost and all pass'd through. **1832** TENNYSON *Dream Fair Women* 83 Pass freely thro': the wood is all thine own.

69. pass up. To give up or abandon (a course of action, etc.); to decline or refuse to have (further) dealings with (someone or something); to reject (something) on the terms offered; to renounce or forgo (an opportunity, prospect, etc.). orig. *U.S.*

1896 ADE *Artie* i. 5 If he gets on a street-car where I am, I get off and walk. That ain't no lie. I pass him up. *Ibid.* xii. 112 Well, I guess I'll pass up the whole thing. **1906** H. D. PITTMAN *Belle of Bluegrass Country* vii. 108 'I know,' he continued, 'when I've got enough. I pass this little town up.' **1923** R. D. PAINE *Comrades of Rolling Ocean* ii. 33 My duty is to stand by the family... That is why I passed up college. **1926** *N.Y. Times Mag.* 13 Aug. 1 He was sent to the U.S. Senate, but on his own terms, having previously passed up the Senatorship rather than take it on the terms of others. **1931** W. G. MCADOO *Crowded Yrs.* xxxii. 503 This would have been congenial work..but I had to pass it up. **1932** WODEHOUSE *Hot Water* xi. 188 And those jewels? You're really going to pass them up? **1939** —— *Uncle Fred in Springtime* i. 19 Your name..will be mud if you pass up an excellent bet like old Horace Davenport. **1943** R. FROST *Let.* Feb. (1972) 241, I am lucky to be getting lectures still at here and there a college and feel I mustn't pass any of them up. **1948** L. A. G. STRONG *Trevannion* v. 98, I don't like to see a good man waste himself. Pass up his opportunities. **1951** E. PAUL *Springtime in Paris* xvi. 310 'You mean that miserable bookworm turned her down, when she offered herself? He's a cad.' 'Don't say that... He didn't pass her up.' **1956** 'A. GILBERT' *And Death came Too* xiv. 146 Eventually he agreed to take the case (his heel of Achilles being an inability to pass up a chance of wiping the official eye). **1962** *Listener* 26 Apr. 722/2 They passed up opportunities of wealth and property. **1964** MRS. L. B. JOHNSON *White House Diary* 6 July (1970) 175 When Lyndon insisted that I go over to the Scharnhorst Ranch with him, it was one last chance that I couldn't pass up. **1969** AUDEN *City without Walls* 48 If you pass up a dame, you've yourself to blame, For shame is neurotic, so snatch! **1972** J. POTTS *Trouble-Maker* (1973) x. 72 All false leads so far, but they can't afford to pass any of them up. **1975** *Times Lit. Suppl.* 11 Apr. 401/1 When the book does put reproductions of two states of the same etching side by side..Mr Passeron passes up the opportunity to discuss the meaning of the changes made. **1976** *Daily Tel.* 26 Oct. 17/1 He had passed up a job offer with a large accounting firm to cruise the South Seas.

pass-, the vb.-stem or imper. of PASS *v.*, used in a few combinations, mostly nonce-words: †**'pass-dice** = PASSAGE 15 [cf. It. *passa-dieci*: see quot. 1598 s.v.]; †**'pass-man** *a.*, surpassing man, superhuman; †**'pass-praise** *a.*, transcending praise, beyond praise.

1805 T. HOLCROFT *Bryan Perdue* II. 56 To..idle away..part of the four and twenty hours at hazard, pass-dice, picquet [etc.]. **1606** SYLVESTER *Du Bartas* II. iv. II. *Magnif.* 1254 The passe-man Wisedome of th' Isaacian Prince, A light so bright, set in such eminence. *a* **1586** SIDNEY *Astr. & Stella* lxxvii, That skin, whose passe-praise hue scornes this poor tearm of white.

passable ('pɑːsəb(ə)l, -æ-), *a.* (and *sb.*) Also 5–6 -yble, 7 passeable. [a. F. *passable* (13th c. in Hatz.-Darm.), f. *passer* to PASS: see -ABLE. Cf. It. *passabile*. In OF. the word had most of the senses retained in Eng.; mod.F. retains only sense 4.]

1. That may be passed, crossed, or traversed.

1413 *Pilgr. Sowle* (Caxton) I. iii. (1859) 4 Ryght as the fletyng ayer geuyth place to the flyght of byrdes..right so was al this erthe passyble to spirites. **1527** KNIGHT in Pocock *Rec. Ref.* I. xxviii. 57 The rivers not being always passable. **1576** *Act 18 Eliz.* c. 10 §7 For the better keeping of the Highways passable for her Majesty's People. **1593** R. HARVEY *Philad.* 4 Since Brutes time the Alpes haue been passable enough. **1614** RALEIGH *Hist. World* III. (1634) 106 To leave at their backs a wood scarce passeable. **1685** *Lond. Gaz.* No. 2080/3 The Streets were hardly passable. **1722** DE FOE *Col. Jack* (1840) 104 The ford was not passable. **1841** W. SPALDING *Italy & It. Isl.* I. 38 The river is passable for boats..to the Mediterranean, a distance of nearly sixty miles. **1880** GEIKIE *Phys. Geog.* iv. 302 The last time that the Thames at London was passable on ice was in 1814.

†**2.** Able to pass or have passage. *Obs.*

1555 EDEN *Decades* 121 Forasmuche as they [sunbeams] are not passyble in them selues, as doth manyfestly appeare by the snowe lyinge contynually vnmolten vpon certeyne hygh montaynes. **1664** H. MORE *Antid. Idolatry* x. 131 So that a Soul otherwise passable of her self would be necessarily drown'd in this one foul Deluge of Guilt. **1745** HALES in *Phil. Trans.* XLIII. 502 All passable Stones which have lately fallen from the Kidneys into the Bladder,..might readily and easily be brought out thence. **1762** DUNN *ibid.* LII. 464 The Sun's rays become passable through such a length of medium.

3. Of money: That may be circulated, that has valid currency, current; of a book: qualified or fit for circulation. Also *fig.*

1590 GREENE *Neuer Too Late* Wks. (Grosart) VIII. 26 Sterling coyne passable from man to man in way of exchange. **1607** SHAKS. *Cor.* v. ii. 13 The vertue of your name, Is not heere passable. **1674** HICKMAN *Hist. Quinquart.* (ed. 2) 196 He would have prevailed with some of them to authorize his Book, that it might have been more passable. **1702** *Eng. Theophrast.* 188 It is with Men, as it is with false Money; One piece is more or less passable than another, as it happens to have more or less Sense or Starling in the Mixture. **1888** B. W. RICHARDSON *Son of Star* III. xi. 186 The coin may cease to be of value as a passable thing, as money, but as a relic it must always live.

4. That can pass muster; tolerable, fairly good, fair; moderate, sufficient, presentable.

1489 CAXTON *Faytes of A.* I. xii. 33 Take gode hede that noon be reteyned but he be passable so that noo fawte be in his persone. **1597** MORLEY *Introd. Mus.* 122 At that time I thought it excelling, but nowe I feare it will bee found scant passable. **1637** LAUD *Sp. in Star-Chamb.* 14 June 6 Our maine Crime is..that we are Bishops; were we not so, some of us might be as passable as other men. **1748** RICHARDSON *Clarissa* (1811) I. ii. 8 There were many women deemed passable who were inferior to herself. **1838** SOUTHEY *Doctor* cxlv. (1862) 398 A passable knowledge of living languages. **1893** *Times* 12 June 4/2 Potatoes appear in eight departments very good, 13 good, 17 satisfactory, 18 passable, six mediocre, and three bad.

†**5.** Passing, transient, ephemeral. *Obs. rare*$^{-1}$.

1627–77 FELTHAM *Resolves* I. xx. 36 Things acted..are too more retainable, than the passable tones of the tongue.

6. [f. PASS *v.* 46 b + -ABLE.] Capable of passing or being passed by a deliberating assembly.

1831 WHATELY in *Life* (1866) I. 66 It is a task of double difficulty to frame what shall be at once an improvement and passable in Convocation [of Oxford University].

7. quasi-*adv.* = PASSABLY.

1581 SAVILE *Tacitus, Hist.* I. lxxviii. (1591) 43 Things which the..cares at hande made passable good. **1675** MARVELL *Wks.* (1872–5) II. 431, I have a passable good estate. **1706** E. WARD *Wooden World Diss.* (1708) 41 But for him, the Ship's Crew would be passable good Christians.

8. as *sb.* A person or thing that is passable.

1908 *Westm. Gaz.* 26 June 2/1 Among such offspring there would be a small class of 'desirables', a large class of 'passables', and a small class of 'undesirables'.

Hence **'passableness**, the quality of being passable.

1727 BAILEY vol. II, *Passableness*..capableness of being passed. **1779** WOLFF *Dansk Ord-bog, Temmelighed*, mediocrity, passableness. **1834** *Blackw. Mag.* XXXV. 176 There was a river to cross, the passableness of which was very questionable. **1888** J. Q. BITTINGER *Hist. Haverhill* (N.H.) 191 The roads of Haverhill will average in passableness and comfort with the roads of neighboring towns.

passable, obs. erroneous form of PASSIBLE.

passably ('pɑːsəblɪ, -æ-), *adv.* [f. PASSABLE *a.* + -LY².] Tolerably, sufficiently well to pass; fairly well, moderately.

a **1610** HEALEY *Theophrastus* To Rdr. (1636) I ij b, The French is elegant enough, passably copious, happie in composition. **1741** RICHARDSON *Pamela* (1824) I. xlix. 379 [She] is mighty pretty, and passably genteel. **1801** MAR. EDGEWORTH *Gd. French Governess* Wks. 1832 III. 175 Miss Fanshaw had learned to speak French passably. **1874** MRS. H. WOOD *Mast. Greylands* xxvii. 315 The night was passably bright.

‖**passacaglia** (passa'kaʎa). [It., a. Sp. *pasacalle* (pasa'kaʎe), f. *pasar* to pass + *calle* street; because often played in the streets.] An early kind of dance tune (of Spanish origin) having a movement slower than the CHACONNE, generally constructed on a ground bass and written in triple time; also the dance to this.

1659 HOWELL *Vocab.* Sect. 50 Giggs, salibrands, chaconas, passingalias, galiards. **1668** DRYDEN *Evening's Love* II. i, Pray let me hear it: I hope it will go to the tune of one of our *Passa-calles*. **1724** *Short Explic. For. Wds. Mus. Bks.*, *Passacaglio*, or *Passacaille*, or *Passagillio*, is a Kind of Air somewhat like a Chacoone, but of a more slow or graver Movement. **1880** GROVE *Dict. Mus.* II. 660/1 The feature which, in common with the Chaconne, has elevated the Passacaglia above the majority of dance forms, is the construction of the music on a ground bass, generally consisting of a short theme of two, four, or eight bars. **1898** G. B. SHAW *Perf. Wagnerite* 3 There are passacaglias on ground basses, canons ad hypodiapente.

‖**passacaille** (pæsə'kaɪ). [a. F. *passecaille* (Furetière 1690), ad. Sp. *pasacalle*: see prec.] = prec.

1711 E. PEMBERTON (*title*) Essay for the Further Improvement of Dancing,..to which is added Three Single Dances: a Chacone, a Passacaille, and a Jig. **1862** E. PAUER *Progamme* 8 Mar., The origin of the Passacaille is Spanish.

passade (pə'seɪd). [a. F. *passade*, ad. Pr. *passada* or It. *passata* (Sp. *pasada*), f. *passare* to PASS: see -ADE, -ADA, -ATA.]

1. *Horsemanship.* (See quots.) *rare.*

1656 BLOUNT *Glossogr.* [from Cotgr.], *Passade*,..the manage of a Horse, backward and forward. **1727–41** CHAMBERS *Cycl.*, *Passade*, in the manage, signifies a turn, or course of a horse backwards or forwards on the same plot of ground; passing or repassing from one end to the other. **1892** B. HINTON *Lord's Return* 214 The action of Sir Walter was like the passade in the manege, a turn backward, forward, without being able to extricate himself.

†**2.** An alms given to a passer-by. *Obs. rare.*

1656 BLOUNT *Glossogr.* [from Cotgr.], *Passade*, an alms, benevolence or entertainment given by, or to a Passenger. **1658** in PHILLIPS. **1727–41** in CHAMBERS *Cycl.*

†**3.** = next, 1. *Obs. rare.*

1706 PHILLIPS, *Passade* or *Passado*, a Pass or Thrust in Fencing. **1727–41** in CHAMBERS *Cycl.*

4. (With pronunc. ‖pasad). A transitory love affair; a passing romance.

1931 *Times Lit. Suppl.* 19 Feb. 134/2 His [*sc.* Mérimée's] singular *passade* with George Sand. **1934** H. G. WELLS *Exper. Autobiogr.* II. vii. 465 The French..distinguish between the *passade*, a stroke of mutual attraction that may happen to any couple, and a real love affair. In theory, I was now to have *passades*. *Ibid.* 466 For women even more than for men, the frequent *passade* seems unattractive. **1937** —— *Brynhild* ix. 176 This lady had experienced two *grand passions* and a vast number of minor *passades*... The term *passade* was new to Brynhild. She tried to imagine the technique of a *passade*. **1938** —— *Apropos of Dolores* iv. 158 She has a wonderful French word 'passades'. She may have *passades*. Possibly with rather scared youngish men. **1973** WODEHOUSE *Bachelors Anonymous* viii. 88 'Sure I did, the first moment I got here,' said Mr Llewellyn, feeling it unnecessary to complicate things by mentioning his *passade* with Miss Vera Dalrymple.

‖**passado** (pə'sɑːdəʊ). *Obs.* [Altered from F. *passade*, or Sp. *pasada*, It. *passata* (both of these also in early use): see prec. and -ADO.]

1. *Fencing.* A forward thrust with the sword, one foot being advanced at the same time.

1588 SHAKS. *L.L.L.* I. ii. 184 The Passado hee [Cupid] respects not, the Duello he regards not. [**1595** SAVIOLO *Practise* K ij, You may with much sodainenesse make a passata with your lefte foote.] **1598** B. JONSON *Ev. Man in Hum.* IV. v, I would teach these 19 the special tricks [*ed.* 1616 rules], as your Punto, your Reverso, your Stoccato, your Imbroccato, your Passado [*ed.* 1616 passada], your Montanto. **1636** DEKKER *Wond. Kingd.* I. i. Wks. 1873 IV. 222, I have my Passees Sir: and my Passadoes. **1830** JAMES *Darnley* xv, We'll have no crowd..to criticise our passados.

attrib. **1648** *Merc. Acad.* No. 1. 6 After a Passado complement with his Chancellorship.

2. = PASSAGE 13 b.

1606 *Sir G. Goosecappe* I. iii. in Bullen *O. Pl.* III. 19, I am sure I past one Passado of Courtship upon her. **1656** HEYLIN *Surv. France* 39 In the Passados of their court-ship, they [the French] expresse themselves with much variety of gesture.

3. Way, going, passage. *rare.*

1599 NASHE *Lenten Stuffe* (1871) 89 Angelo went off, and all wind instruments blew..in his passado to the Pope's ordinary or dining-chamber.

passage ('pæsɪdʒ), *sb.* [a. F. *passage*, *pasage* (11th c. in Hatz.-Darm.) = Pr. *passatge*, Sp. *pasage*, It. *passaggio*, a Romanic formation from *passer*, *passare* to PASS: see -AGE.]

I. The action of passing, and cognate senses.

1. a. The action of passing; a going or moving onward, across, or past; movement from one place or point to another, or over or through a space or medium; transition, transit.

Const. *of* (or with possessive) indicating the person or thing that passes; more rarely *of* = objective genitive.

c **1290** *Beket* 682 in *S. Eng. Leg.* I. 126 He wende eft in-to þe se, þe passage for-to fonde. **1390** GOWER *Conf.* I. 233 He wolde..The passage of the water take. **1526** *Pilgr. Perf.* (W. de W. 1531) 1 The passage of the children of Israel from Egypte. **1558** GRAFTON (*title*) The Passage of our most drad Soveraigne Lady Queen Elyzabeth through the City of London to Westminster. **1582** STANYHURST *Æneis* I. (Arb.) 19 Yeeld to the wynds passadge, duck downe theire fleete with a tempest. **1615** W. LAWSON *Country Housew. Gard.* (1626) 4 So as the Water may be staied from passage. **1702** ROWE *Tamerl.* II. i 546 Not far from hence The Captives were to wait the Emperor's Passage. **1768** *Ann. Reg.* 67 To observe..the passage of Venus over the sun's disk on the 3d of June 1769. **1869** TYNDALL *Notes Lect. Light* 20 In the passage from one medium to another of a different refractive index, light is always reflected. **1885** WATSON & BURBURY *Math. Th. Electr. & Magn.* I. 236 A cell in which no chemical actions can take place on the passage of the current.

b. The passing of people; hence nearly = people passing, passers. *rare.*

1590 SHAKS. *Com. Err.* III. i. 99 If by strong hand you offer to breake in Now in the stirring passage of the day. **1604** —— *Oth.* v. i. 37 What hoa? No Watch? No passage? Murther, Murther. **1886** STEVENSON *Dr. Jekyll* 4 Even on Sunday, when it [the street] lay comparatively empty of passage.

c. The 'passing' or extending of a line, string, or the like, from one point to another.

1615 CROOKE *Body of Man* 485 They are like to nerues in their passage, colour and vse. **1831** R. KNOX *Cloquet's Anat.* 247 It divides, after a short passage, into four very distinct bundles.

d. The migration or migratory flight of birds. See also quot. 1879.

1774 GOLDSM. *Nat. Hist.* (1776) V. 267 At the approach of winter, it totally disappears, and its passage can be traced to no other country. **1879** E. D. RADCLIFFE in *Encycl. Brit.* IX. 7/2 The line herons take over a tract of country on their way to and from the heronry when procuring food in the breeding season is called a 'passage'.

e. *of passage* (= F. *de passage*): †(*a*) That passes through a place or state, without continuing in it; transitory. *Obs.* exc. as in (*b*) ***bird of passage***, a bird that migrates from one region to another at a particular season and returns at another, a migratory bird; esp. = *passage-migrant* (sense 16 b below); also *fig.* (*slang*), a tramp; so ***fish of passage***.

1673 TEMPLE *Ess. Trade Irel.* Wks. 1720 I. 120 The poorer Traders, or the young Beginners, or those of Passage. **1727–41** CHAMBERS *Cycl.* s.v., *Birds of Passage*... There are also fishes of passage, as herrings, mackerel, etc. **1728** CHAMBERS *Cycl.* II. 758/2 Birds of Passage, are such as only come at certain Seasons, and then disappear again. **1732** POPE *Ep. Cobham* 97 In Man, the judgment shoots at flying game, A bird of passage! gone as soon as found. **1763** J. BELL *Trav. from St. Petersburg* I. 188 As for water-fowl..they are also birds of passage. **1771** SMOLLETT *Humph. Cl.* I. 150 The ..entertainments of Bath are over for this season; and all our gay birds of passage have taken their flight to Bristol-well, Tunbridge..&c. **1785** E. SHERIDAN *Jrnl.* (1960) 52 Our young Man is I find only a Bird of passage so the lady will be our only dinner companion. **1789** G. WHITE *Selborne* I. x. 29 Mr. Stillingfleet makes a question whether the blackcap (*motacilla atricapilla*) be a bird of passage or not. **1797** HOLCROFT *Stolberg's Trav.* (ed. 2) III. lxxxiv. 348 The sword fish is a fish of passage. **1853** DICKENS *Bleak Ho.* xl. 398 My Lady has been but poorly..when she was here as a bird of passage—like. **1879** MISS BRADDON *Cloven Foot* xxviii, I am only in town as a bird of passage. **1879** MRS. C. COOK *Comic Hist. N.S.W.* 49 It was a speculation by a bird of passage, one (poor little) Sparrow. **1893** A. NEWTON *Dict. Birds* II. 550/1 Others again—and these are strictly speaking the 'Birds of Passage'—which shew themselves but twice a year, passing through the country without staying long in it. **1896** E. DOWSON *Let.* c 4 June (1967) 366 People arrive daily; most of them, however, birds of passage. **1945** BAKER *Austral. Lang.* 103 *Traveller* and *commercial traveller*, together with *food inspector, bird of passage, wallaby tracker, tourist, footman* and *professional pedestrian*, are often applied to itinerants. **1960** *Guardian* 13 Oct. 12/3 As a 'bird of passage' the graduate tended to be supernumerary in the various departments. **1963** *Times* 20 Apr. 5/4 There is a need to differentiate between the birds of passage and those who give a lifetime to the profession.

2. a. In various *fig.* senses: Transition from one state or condition to another (*spec.* from this life to the next, by death); the passing or lapse of time; the going on, course, or progress of events, etc., or of a person through a course of action; a passing in thought or speech from one point, idea, or subject to another. †*in passage*, in passing, by the way (*obs.*).

c **1430** *Life St. Kath.* (1884) 67 Wyth good passage out of thys lyf. **1516** *Life St. Bridget* in *Myrr. our Ladye* p. lii, A lytel before hir blessyd passage out of this world. **1579** W. WILKINSON *Confut. Familye of Love* 52 The bookes of H. N. do make a more easie passage..to the vnderstandyng thereof. **1605** BACON *Adv. Learn.* II. Ded. §8 These fundamental knowledges have been studied but in passage. **1769** SIR J. REYNOLDS *Disc.* ii. (1876) 317 Students..this day rewarded for their happy passage through the first period. **1830** LYELL *Princ. Geol.* I. 206 There is a passage between this and ordinary travertin. **1839** MURCHISON *Silur. Syst.* I. xxxiv. 450 The passage of the red marl into the lias is here well exposed. **1871** B. STEWART *Heat* §85 The passage of bodies from the solid to the liquid state.

†**b.** *absol.* 'Departure', death. *Obs.*

1390 GOWER *Conf.* I. 261 Bot ate laste of thi passage Thi deth was to the houndes like. **1507** in Wood *Oxford* (O.H.S.) III. 116 By pestilence I had my passage. **1602** SHAKS. *Ham.* III. iii. 86 When he is fit and season'd for his passage. **1693** *Humours Town* 13 A perpetual Requiem for your Soul before its Passage.

c. ***rites of passage***: see RITE 1 d.

3. a. Possibility, power, or opportunity of passing; liberty, leave, or right to pass. (*lit.* and *fig.*)

*c*1330 R. BRUNNE *Chron.* (1810) 30 þei purueied hir passage, And led hir vnto France, spoused forto be. **1417** in Ellis *Orig. Lett.* Ser. IV. I. 63 That ye oure Chanceller doo make unto thaim soufficeant Writtes of passage. **1589** GREENE *Menaphon* (Arb.) 68 She made passage to her choller in these termes of contempt. **1667** MILTON *P.L.* XI. 122 All approach farr off to fright, And guard all passage to the Tree of Life. **1844** H. H. WILSON *Brit. India* II. 79 The refusal to give a passage through Nepal to a British force intended to take possession of Lassa.

†**b.** Admission or permission. *Obs.*

1622 BP. HALL *Contempl., O.T.* XVII. vii, He [Solomon] gave not passage onely to the Idolatry of his heathenish wives, but furtherance.

4. a. A definite passing or travelling from one place to another, by sea, or formerly sometimes by land; a journey; a voyage across the sea from one port to another, a crossing.

*a*1300 *Cursor M.* 19990 þis it was þe first passage þat þe apostels in parti Mad mang þe folk o paeni. **13..** *E.E. Allit. P.* C. 97 þus he passes to þat port, his passage to seche, Fyndez he a fayr schyp to þe fare redy. *a*1529 SKELTON *Sp. Parrot* 324 Prepayre yow, Parrot, breuely your passage to take, Of Mercury undyr the trynall aspecte. **1582** STANYHURST *Æneis* III. (Arb.) 87 Foorth we take oure passadge, oure sayles ful winged vp hoysting. **1776** *Hist. Eur.* in *Ann. Reg.* 8/2 Nor was the march by land more eligible than the passage by water. **1815** *Chron.* ibid. 108/1 A vessel is arrived in the Thames from New South Wales after an extraordinarily short passage of less than five months. **1836** MARRYAT *Midsh. Easy* xi, He had suffered all the horrors of a passage in a slave ship. **1877** TALMAGE 50 *Serm.* 16 You have found a rough passage.

b. Right of transit or conveyance as a passenger, esp. by sea; accommodation of a passenger. ***to work one's passage***: see WORK *v.* 12 h.

1632 J. HAYWARD tr. *Biondi's Eromena* 6 Carasio..having agreed with the mariners for their passage, acquainted therewith Polemiro. **1743** BULKELEY & CUMMINS *Voy. S. Seas* 199 That the Governor would give us a Pass, and that we would work for our Passage. **1782** JOHNSON *Let. to Mrs. Thrale* 8 June, I have this day taken a passage to Oxford. **1864** TENNYSON *En. Ard.* 646 And clothes they gave him and free passage home.

†**5.** A charge or custom levied upon passengers: a toll. *Obs.*

[**1200** *Charter K. John* in *Reg. S. Osmundi* (Rolls) I. 212 Sint quieti..de theoloneo, pontagio, passagio.] ?*c*1525 *Robyn Hode* in Child *Ballads* (1857–9) V. 425 Yet was he never so curteyse a potter, As one peny passage to paye. **1610** W. FOLKINGHAM *Art of Survey* III. iv. 70 Immunities and Exemptions from Theolonie, Pontage,..Passage, Tranage,..Cariage, &c. **1710** J. HARRIS *Lex. Techn.* II, *Passage, Passagium*, was a Tribute or Toll paid by Passengers or Travellers for the Repair or Maintenance of some Road or Passage. **1812** SEYER *Bristol Charters Engl.* 1 My burgesses of Bristol..shall be quit both of toll and passage, and all custom, throughout my whole land. **1883** PICTON *L'pool Munic. Rec.* I. 6 They claim to be quit of.. passage, pontage and lastage.

†**6.** The fact of 'passing current' or being generally accepted, as coins, customs, etc.; currency, general reception. *Obs.*

1545 *Reg. Privy Council Scot.* I. 10 Double dukatis.. quhilkis commonly hes course in France for lxxx and xvis. and ar worth samekle to have passage in this realm. **1605** BACON *Adv. Learn.* I. v. §3 As if the multitude..were not ready to give passage rather to that which is popular and superficial. **1644** DIGBY *Nat. Bodies* viii. 53, I would.. render this treatise intelligible to euery rationall man ..(among whom I expect it will haue a fairer passage, then among those that are already deepely imbued with other principles).

7. The passing into law of a legislative measure.

1587 HARRISON *England* II. viii. (1877) I. 178 This is the order of the passage of our lawes. **1668** MARVELL *Corr.* Wks. 1872–5 II. 249 It is a businesse of that weight that I scarce believe it can have a passage this session. **1669–70** *Ibid.* 311 [The Bill] had but a narrow passage, there being only 100 for it against 99. **1856** C. BECK *Age Petronius Arbiter* 73 Soon after,..for the precise time of its passage is not known—the lex Furia Caninia was enacted. **1893** *Times* 2 May 10/1 The passage of any measure resembling this would be a deadly blow at landed property in Ireland. **1931** J. T. ADAMS *Epic of Amer.* ix. 240 The passage of a more stringent fugitive-slave law. **1968** *Globe & Mail* (Toronto) 3 Feb. 3/5 She rejected a request from Edward Schreyer (NDP, Springfield) that passage of the clause be postponed until members had had a chance to think about it. **1974** *Encycl. Brit. Macropædia* VII. 875/2 He could not prevent the passage of the bill.

8. *Horsemanship.* See quots. (= F. *passage.*)

1727–41 CHAMBERS *Cycl., Passage*, in the manage, an action wherein the horse raises two legs together, a hind and a fore leg, in form of St. Andrew's cross; when, setting those two on the ground again, he raises the other two; and thus alternately. **1884** E. L. ANDERSON *Mod. Horseman.* II. xvii. 146 The Passage..is a slow brilliant trot, in which the horse brings each pair of diagonal legs to the ground at exactly the same moment... Usually employed in traversing.

9. *Med.* An evacuation of the bowels, a 'motion'; also *concr.*

1778 PR. OF WALES in *Buccleuch MSS.* (Hist. MSS. Comm.) I. 416 He took medicine three or four times during the day in order to procure a passage. **1809** *Med. Jrnl.* XXI. 480 He..has been repeatedly from eighteen to twenty-five days without a passage. **1875** H. C. WOOD *Therap.* (1879) 106 Late in the attack the passages are in most cases very light clay-colored, or even whitish.

10. a. The action of causing something to pass (in various senses: see PASS *v.*); transmission, transference, etc. *rare.*

1860 TYNDALL *Glac.* I. ii. 20 As fine as if produced by the passage of a rake. **1890** in *Financial News* 31 July 1/4 The passage of the preferred dividend by the directors of the St. Louis and San Francisco Railway is regarded as consistent with policy. **1890** *Spectator* 16 Aug. 197/1 The passage of a great measure has become as difficult to effect as the passage of a cannon-ball through earthworks. **1899** *Allbutt's Syst. Med.* VI. 73 The unskilful passage of an œsophageal bougie.

b. *Med.* and *Biol.* A stage in the maintenance of a strain of micro-organisms or cells, from inoculation into a host organism or culture medium, through a period of multiplication, to extraction; the process of passing micro-organisms or cells through a series of hosts or cultures in this way, so as to maintain them or modify their virulence. Freq. with pronunc. (pæ'sɑːʒ).

1896 *Allbutt's Syst. Med.* I. 531 The virulence of many organisms may..be permanently or temporarily increased ..by passing the organisms through a series of animals (a process which is called 'passage'). **1926** G. H. SMITH tr. *F. d'Herelle's Bacteriophage* iv. 160 The virulence of a bacteriophage may be exalted by successive passages in suspensions of a susceptible bacterium. **1945** *Jrnl. Immunol.* LI. 390 A chorio-allantoic suspension of the 259th chick embryo passage. **1947** *Jrnl. Exper. Med.* LXXXV. 24 The virus was maintained by occasional lung passage in albino Swiss mice. **1973** *Nature* 18 May 163/1 These tumours are transplantable and have been transplanted for up to six consecutive passages.

II. 11. a. That by which a person or thing passes or may pass; a way, road, path, route, channel; a mountain pass; an entrance or exit.

Locally a name for a narrow entry or lane in a town, etc., serving as the approach to a row of houses, or as a thoroughfare for foot-passengers; e.g. *Norman Passage, St. Helen's Passage* (Oxford), *All Saints' Passage* (Cambridge).

*c*1290 *Beket* 56 in *S. Eng. Leg.* I. 108 Heo cam to þe se: and redi fond hire passage. *a*1300 *K. Horn* 1323 To kepe þis passage, Fram horn þat is of age. **1340** HAMPOLE *Pr. Consc.* 1394 þis world es þe way and passage, þurgh whilk lyes our pilgrimage. *c*1350 *Will. Palerne* 2139 And loke þat hirde-men wel kepe þe komune passage, And eche brugge þer a-boute þat burnes ouer wende. **1480** CAXTON *Chron. Eng.* ccxxiii. 222 At an hongyng bought of the more in a streit passage. **1540** *Act 32 Hen. VIII*, c. 41 In any towne or village being a thoroughfare or common passag within this realme. **1553** EDEN *Treat. Newe Ind.* (Arb.) 8 Into the frosen sea..and so forth to Cathay (yf any suche passage may be found). **1585** T. WASHINGTON tr. *Nicholay's Voy.* I. xxii. 29 Doria..was tarrying for vs at the passage with 5 principal gallies. **1601** R. JOHNSON *Kingd. & Commw.* (1603) 6 Inuironed with mountaines which hath fewe and secret passages. **1627–8** in Swayne *Sarum Church-w. Acc.* (1896) 187 The open passadge in the middell of the Church. **1725** DE FOE *Voy. round World* (1840) 6 He had already sent one ship..for a new attempt upon the North-West or North-East passages. **1801** SOUTHEY *Thalaba* VI. xiv, Was it the toil of human hands Had hewn a passage in the rock? **1812** *Gen. Hist.* in *Ann. Reg.* 137/2 They weighed anchor, and made sail through the passage Taigneuse. **1828** [see PASSENGER 1]. **1856** STANLEY *Sinai & Pal.* iv. (1858) 217 As the passage of Beth-horon led up to Gibeon, so the passage of Michmash and Ai led up to Bethel. **1897** *Allbutt's Syst. Med.* IV. 22 Freeing the liver and its bile passages from their injurious presence.

b. *spec.* A place at which a river or strait is or may be crossed; a crossing; a ford, ferry, or bridge. ? *Obs.*

*c*1330 R. BRUNNE *Chron. Wace* (Rolls) 14012 An heremitage Bysyde Chymoun, at a passage. **1470–85** MALORY *Arthur* VII. vi, There was a grete ryuer and but one passage. **1477** *Paston Lett.* III. 203 Wherefore my lord hath do brokyn all the passages except Newham bryge. *a*1533 LD. BERNERS *Huon* lii. 176 When I cam to ony passage of water he wolde caste me in his necke..& bere me ouer. **1611** BIBLE *Judg.* xii. 6 Then they tooke him, and slewe him at the passages of Iordan. **1779** S. RUDDER *Gloucestershire* 492 In this parish are two ferries over the Severn. The uppermost, or *Old Passage*, is in the Tything of Aust... The *New Passage* is at Redwick. **1853** KANE *Grinnell Exp.* vii. (1856) 50 Its several 'crossings' have been divided into the South, the Middle, and the Northern passages.

c. A way giving access to the various apartments or divisions of a building, or affording communication from one apartment to another; a corridor or gallery; a lobby or hall.

1611 CORYAT *Crudities* 202 At the West end of this glorious Councell hall..there is a passage into another most stately roome. **1663** GERBIER *Counsel* 23 By convenient passages about or under them. **1707** MORTIMER *Husb.* (1721) I. 371 In Building of Houses long, the use of some Rooms will be lost, in that the more room must be allowed for Entries and Passages. **1722** DE FOE *Col. Jack* (1840) 207, I was in the passage, or entry of the house. **1810** CRABBE *Borough* xx. 66 Hark to the winds! which through the wide saloon And the long passage send a dismal tune. **1835** G. A. MCCALL *Lett. fr. Frontiers* (1868) 280 The house..was one of those structures called in the West 'two pens and a passage'.

†**12.** ? A means of passing; a vessel or vehicle in which a person or thing may pass; a conveyance. Cf. CARRIAGE. *Obs. rare.*

1473 *Paston Lett.* III. 94, I praye yow wrycht ageyn, and sende it by the next passage.

III. 13. a. Something that 'passes', goes on, takes place, occurs, or is done; an occurrence, incident, event; an act, transaction, proceeding. *Obs.* or *arch.* (exc. as in b and c).

1568 GRAFTON *Chron.* II. 731 Surely it was a daungerous passage to conuey a prince in a straunge realme, by such a strayte. **1601** SHAKS. *Twel. N.* III. ii. 77 There is no christian ..can euer beleeue such impossible passages of grossenesse. **1612** WOODALL *Surg. Mate* Wks. (1639) B vj b, Observing the whole passages of the diseased people, considering both when they began to bee sicke,..what hath been applyed [etc.]. **1624** DK. BUCKHM. in Ellis *Orig. Lett.* Ser. I. III. 180 [It] will facilitate..those passages of favors, grace, and goodnes which his Majesty hath promised for the ease of the Romaine Catholickes. **1671–2** SIR C. LYTTELTON in *Hatton Corr.* (Camden) 76 There has lately happened a very strange passage upon occasion of [etc.]. **1710** STEELE *Tatler* No. 198 ¶1 Her Life has lately met with Passages very uncommon. *a*1741 T. CHALKLEY *Jrnl.* an. 1734 Wks. (1751) 265 A remarkable and dismal Passage he related to me. **1820** LAMB *Elia* Ser. I. *Old Benchers*, I remember a pleasant passage, of the cook applying to him..for instructions how to write down *edge* bone of beef. **1866** KINGSLEY *Herew.* xvi, The magnificent young Scot sprang to him,..talked over old passages.

b. Something that passes between two persons mutually; a negotiation; an interchange of communications, confidences, or amorous relations.

1612 N. FIELD *Woman is Weathercock* II. i. in Hazl. *Dodsley* XI. 33 And such strange passages and mutual vows. **1647** SPRIGGE *Anglia Rediv.* III. vi. (1854) 165 Several passages between the prince and his excellency, and between his excellency and Goring. **1649** MILTON *Eikon.* viii. 68 The King..gives..order to stop all passages between him [the Governor of Hull] and the Parlament. **1845** R. W. HAMILTON *Pop. Educ.* vi. (1846) 138 Would not both parties profit in these passages of confidence? *a*1901 BESANT *Five Years' Tryst*, etc. (1902) 108 She was by no means ignorant of certain passages and rumours of passages between Will Stephen and this simple country maid. **1920** *Brit. Mus. Return* 115 in *Parl. Papers* XXXVI. 673 The threatened extermination of the Elephants in the Addo Bush ..has led to the passage of a number of letters between the Museum and various writers.

c. (Now usually ***passage of*** (or ***at***) ***arms***.) An exchange of blows between two combatants, a fight; also *fig.* a verbal altercation or dispute; an amorous fence or encounter.

1599 B. JONSON *Cynthia's Rev.* v. ii, You have your passages and imbrocatas in courtship; as the bitter bob in wit. **1612** *Two Noble K.* v. iv. 114 The conquerd triumphes, The victor has the losse; yet in the passage The gods have beene most equall. **1856** FROUDE *Hist. Eng.* (1858) I. iii. 267 Luther..had not forgotten his early passage at arms with the English Defender of the Faith. **1876** TREVELYAN *Macaulay* I. iii. 136 That passage of arms against the champions of the Utilitarian Philosophy. **1879** STEVENSON *Trav. Cevennes* (1886) 12, I returned it to its maker, with whom I had so contumelious a passage that the street outside was crowded..with gossips..listening. **1885** *Manch. Exam.* 21 Mar. 6/2 The most interesting part of the debate was a smart passage at arms between his Grace and Lord Bramwell.

14. a. An indefinite portion of a discourse or writing, usually of small or moderate length, taken by itself; a part of a speech or literary work relating to some particular matter.

*c*1611 CHAPMAN *Iliad* II. Comm. (1865) 57 His interpreters must needs come [short] of him in his strait and deep places, when in his open and fair passages they halt and hang back so. **1686** SOUTH *Serm.* (1697) II. ix. 386, I shall give you the whole Passage in his own Words. **1711** STEELE *Spect.* No. 2 ¶1 He..gained universal Applause by explaining a Passage in the Game-Act. **1802** MAR. EDGEWORTH *Mor. T.* (1816) I. xv. 130 To look for the passage in the original author. **1891** *Speaker* 2 May 533/1 The paper contains brilliant passages, notably an admirable estimate of Gautier.

†**b.** A part of a discourse or writing in which the author passes or turns aside for a time to some other subject; a digression. *Obs.*

1625 BACON *Ess., Dispatch* (Arb.) 247 Prefaces, and Passages,..and other Speeches of Reference to the Person, are great wasts of Time. **1663** GERBIER *Counsel* 102 The first discourse, was..intermixt with recreative passages.

†**c.** The 'passing' or utterance of an opinion or the like; a remark, observation (in speech or writing); a phrase, expression. *Obs.*

*a*1649 WINTHROP *Hist. New Eng.* (1853) I. 247 One of the assistants using some pathetical passages of the loss of such a governour in a time of such danger. **1651** W. LILLY (*title*) Monarchy or No Monarchy in England. Grebner his Prophecy... Passages upon the Life and Death of the late King Charles. *a*1657 BRADFORD *Plymouth Plant.* (1856) 307, I would..deliver yᵉ truth..as nere as I can, in their owne words and passages. **1660** *Trial Regic.* 44 Being there, I did observe some Passages fall from the Prisoner at the Bar; the words were to this purpose.

d. *Mus.* (*a*) ? *orig.* A progression from one note to another by intermediate notes (*passing-notes*); ? hence, A short series of such notes, or of small notes in general; a run or flourish; a figure or phrase. *Obs.* exc. as applied (rarely) to ornamental runs or flourishes introduced for display. (*b*) In mod. use (associated with 14): A portion of a composition, of indefinite but

moderate length, and forming more or less of a unity.
1674 PLAYFORD *Skill Mus.* I. xi. 39 Observing the same Rule in making the passages of Division by some few Quavers to Notes and to Cadences, not exceeding the Value of half a Semibreve at most. **1727–41** CHAMBERS *Cycl.*, *Passage*, or *Passo*, in music, a portion of an air, or tune, consisting of several short notes, as quavers, demi-quavers, etc. lasting one, two, or at most three measures. **1767** *Ess.* in *Ann. Reg.* 199/2 The Italians solfa'd our most pathetic airs, without discovering either passage or tune. **1776** BURNEY *Hist. Mus.* (1789) I. v. 62 In no one of the seven treatises upon ancient music is a single air or passage of Greek melody come down to us. **1859** TENNYSON *Lancelot & Elaine* 891–2 As a little helpless innocent bird, That has but one plain passage of few notes, Will sing the simple passage o'er and o'er For all an April morning. **1880** C. H. H. PARRY in *Grove's Dict. Mus.* II. 661.

e. In the phraseology of art criticism: A particular part or detail in a picture; *spec.*, an area of a picture where one tone merges into another; the technique of achieving this effect.
1861 THORNBURY *Turner* I. 142 In the earliest Saxon and Old English MSS. are to be found passages of transparent colour. **1897** *Mag. Art* Nov. 39 There are passages which represent the original with curious felicity. **1961** M. LEVY *Studio Dict. Art Terms* 84 *Passage*... Also used to describe the transition from one tone to another, by means of a half-tone. **1962** *Listener* 15 Feb. 304/1 They [*sc.* the Cubists] exaggerated his [*sc.* Cézanne's] use of his device known as *passage* by which the near end of a plane is clearly defined while the far end dissolves into space. **1962** R. G. HAGGAR *Dict. Art Terms* 247/2 *Passage*, a term used to describe a certain area of paint on a picture where one color or tone merges into another, where some special technique has been used, or where there may be over-painting by another hand. **1967** J. N. BARRON *Lang. of Painting* 143 These passages are used to relate volumes or three-dimensional forms to the two-dimensional picture frame.

f. *gen.* An indefinite portion of a course of action; an episode. (Cf. 13.) *rare.*
1848 W. H. BARTLETT *Egypt to Pal.* xiv. (1879) 315 The track to-day was an easy one, and indeed the whole route from Sinai offered no passages of extreme difficulty. **1897** LD. TENNYSON *Life Tennyson* I. ii. 40 Despite such passages of gloom he worked on.

IV. [The *passing* or exceeding of ten = It. *passa-dieci*, F. *passe-dix*, i.e. pass-ten.]

†**15.** An obsolete game at dice: see quot. 1680.
1426 LYDG. *De. Guil. Pilgr.* 11194 And affter pleyn at the merellys, Now at the dees, in my yong age, Bothe at hassard & passage. **1522** *World & Child* in Hazl. *Dodsley* I. 266 And then we will with lombards at passage play. **1598** FLORIO, *Passa dieci*, a game at dice called passage or aboue ten. **1602** *2nd Pt. Return fr. Parnass.* Prol. 12 You that knowe what it is to play at primero, or passage. **1680** COTTON *Compl. Gamester* 119 Passage is a Game at dice to be played at but by two, and it is performed with three Dice. The Caster throws continually till he hath thrown Dubblets under ten, and then he is out and loseth; or Dubblets above ten, and then he *passeth* and wins. **1739–40** *Act 13 Geo. II*, c. 19 §9 A certain game called Passage is now daily practiced and carried on, to the ruin and impoverishment of many of his Majesty's subjects. **1755** *Mem. Capt. P. Drake* II. xvi. 262, [1740] The Games of Rowly Powly and Passage.. all these Games were suppressed by Parliament, and, on severe Penalties, not to be played after the 25th of March 1745.

V. 16. *attrib.* and *Comb.* **a.** Used or serving for the passage or conveyance of passengers, esp. across the sea or a river, as ***passage-barge***, ***-bark***, ***-canoe***, ***-hoy***, ***-ship***, ***-wagon***; of transition, transitional, as ***passage-form***, ***-time***; also in other senses, as ***passage-bell***, ***-gallery*** (11 c), ***-work*** (14 d). **b.** Special combs.: **passage-bed** (*Geol.*), a stratum showing transition from one formation to another; **passage-bird**, (*a*) = *bird of passage* (see 1 e); (*b*) = *passage-hawk*; **passage-board**, a board placed between the parts of an organ to make them accessible for tuning or repairs; †**passage-book** = PASS-BOOK 1; **passage-free** *adv.*, free of charge for passage or conveyance; †**passage-gelt**, **-gilt** [see GELT *sb.*^{2}] = PASSAGE-MONEY; **passage grave** *Archæol.*, an underground burial chamber connected with the surface by a passage; also *attrib.*; **passage-hawk**, a falcon taken when full-grown, during its 'passage' or migration, for the purpose of training (opp. to *eyas*); †**passage-house**, a privy; **passage-migrant**, a bird that stays for a short time in an area on the route of its migration to summer or winter quarters; also *fig.*; **passage-penny**, a penny charged for passage or fare; **passage-room**, a room serving as a passage to another, or through which one passes to another; †**passage-thermometer** (see quot.); **passage-work** *Mus.*, a passage of a composition which calls for virtuosic display; the execution of such a passage. Also PASSAGE-BOAT, -MONEY, -WAY.
1804 *Europ. Mag.* XLV. 443/1 Going from Fontainbleau to Dijon, in the *passage barge. **1865** *Reader* No. 147. 465/1 The *passage-beds of Herefordshire. **1825** *Eng. Life* II. 231 The *passage-bell rung loudly. **1852** R. F. BURTON *Falconry in Valley of Indus* iv. 41 Hawks.. are of two kinds, the 'eyess' (or nyess), and the '*passage-bird'. **1878** C. STANFORD *Symb. Christ* v. 139 The passage bird is never lost. High over the waves of the Atlantic it strikes a right path to its home a thousand leagues away. **1880** C. A. EDWARDS *Organs* (1881) 59 A *passage-board for the use of the tuner. **1816** in Merivale *Rep. Cases Chancery* I. 535 A book, called a *passage-book, is opened by the bankers, and delivered by them to the customer. **1901** *Nature* 3 Jan. 234/2 He finds that.. *passage-forms prove to be the rule, while sharply-defined and typical species are the exception. **1928** *Daily Express* 28 Aug. 3/7 She.. brings to Canada almost *passage-free any man of good health and physique who is an experienced agriculturist. *a* **1615** SIR S. D'EWES *Autobiog.* (1845) II. 334 My Lord.. laid it in a *passage-gallery, in several papers. **1712** THORESBY *Diary* (1830) II. 164 Baldock-lanes, notorious for their badness, as the neighbourhood for exaction of *passage-gelt through the enclosures. **1727** A. HAMILTON *New Acc. E. Ind.* I. xxxii. 388 In the whole, it cost me about 1£. Sterl. for Passage-gilt. **1745** [see GELT *sb.*^{2}]. **1888** F. H. WOODS tr. *Montelius's Civilisation of Sweden* i. 30 The graves of this period are commonly described as 'dolmens' (*stendösar*), '*passage-graves' (*gånggrifter*), and 'stone cists' (*hällkistor*). **1919** [see *boat-axe* s.v. BOAT *sb.* 3]. **1934** *Discovery* Mar. 66/2 Soon after 4,000 B.C. began the neolithic civilization marked by great stone tombs, first dolmens then passage-graves, and lastly long stone cists. **1943** J. & C. HAWKES *Prehist. Brit.* ii. 45 The men who introduced passage-grave architecture and art seem to have reached Ireland from Portugal and south-west Spain. **1958** F. E. ZEUNER *Dating Past* (ed. 4) 81 This leaves only something like 200 years for that part of the Neolithic in Denmark which is clearly anterior to the arrival of the Bronze Age Beaker folk in Britain, namely all that preceding the middle of the Passage Grave period. **1963** E. S. WOOD *Collins Field Guide Archaeol.* I. iv. 57 Passage Graves have a chamber, round, square or with side chambers, connected by a narrow passage to the outside of the usually round mound or cairn which covers it. **1970** *Canad. Antiques Collector* Nov. 19/1 The shape of Knowth differs from other known passage graves in Ireland. **1828** SIR J. S. SEBRIGHT *Observ. Hawking* 30 The falconers are obliged to keep the *passage-hawks somewhat low, from the fear of losing them. **1852** R. F. BURTON *Falconry in Valley of Indus* iv. 42 The birds when taken up are as wild as passage-hawks. **1727** SWIFT *Further Acc. E. Curll* Wks. 1755 III. I. 161 And thence be drawn.. bit by bit, to the *passage-house. **1705** *Lond. Gaz.* No. 4141/4 Employed in the *Passage-Hoys between London and the Nore. **1934** INGRAM & SALMON *Birds in Brit. To-day* xiii. 115 Records of small parties [of Scandinavian lesser black-backed gulls].. occurring as *passage-migrants, especially in spring, should be considered extremely doubtful. **1940** H. F. WITHERBY et al. *Handbk. Brit. Birds* III. 12 Distribution [of peregrine falcon].—British Isles.—Resident and passage-migrant. **1964** *Oxf. Bk. Birds* 74/1 Ruffs and reeves used to breed in Britain, but now they are mainly passage migrants..; a few spend the winter and summer. **1976** N. ROBERTS *Face of France* iv. 47 In the past they [*sc.* the French] did indeed accept Black immigrants, and particularly passage migrants, happily enough. **1977** *Times* 18 Aug. 14/6 Formby Point is a haunt of passage-migrants. **1596** SPENSER *F.Q.* v. ii. 6 But he him makes his *passage-penny pay. **1665–6** PEPYS *Diary* 25 Feb., I and my wife in a *passage-room to bed, and slept not very well because of noise. **1838** *Gentl. Mag.* IX. 255/2 A passage-room and staircase. **1734** BERKELEY *Let. to Prior* 30 Apr., Wks. 1871 IV. 227 You can tell what *passage-ships are on this side of the water. **1792** SIR B. THOMPSON in *Phil. Trans.* LXXXII. 51 As this instrument is calculated merely for measuring the passage of heat in the substance whose conducting power is examined, I shall give it the name of **passage-thermometer*. **1873** M. ARNOLD *Lit. & Dogma* (1876) 352 There will be a *passage-time of confusion first. **1774** J. ADAMS *Diary* 29 Aug., Here we saw two or three *passage wagons, a vehicle with four wheels, contrived to carry many passengers and much baggage. **1865** *Athenæum* No. 1968. 89/2 The *passage-work in Astrofiammante's two airs. **1920** *Musical Times* LXI. 159 The Fantasia is mere passage-work of the most desolating description. **1931** G. JACOB *Orchestral Technique* iii. 25 Of course arpeggios and passage-work generally can freely *pass through* this part of the compass. **1959** *Times* 13 Nov. 15/4 Some of his faster passage-work (notably in Beethoven's semi-quavers) tended to sound scratchy. **1966** *Listener* 10 Feb. 219/1 The passage work sounded anything but assured and intonation was distinctly impure. **1972** *Daily Tel.* 11 Jan. 9/4 The choral singing.. was sonorously centred and admirably articulated in quickfire passage-work. **1977** *Gramophone* Sept. 423/1 All three of these concertos are well constructed and melodious, sometimes with brilliant passage-work for the soloist.

passage (ˈpæsɪdʒ), *v.*^{1} *Horsemanship.* Most freq. in vbl. sb. **passaging.** [a. F. *passager*, altered by pop. etymol. from *passéger*, ad. It. *passeggiare* to walk, pace (cf. *passeggio* walk), deriv. of L. *passus*: see PASS, PACE.] **a.** *intr.* To move sideways in riding, by pressure of the rein on the horse's neck and of the rider's leg on the opposite side: said of the horse, or of the rider. **b.** *trans.* To cause a horse to 'passage'.
1796 *Cavalry Instr.* (1813) 220 These doublings of ranks are performed by reining back, and passaging. **1832** *Regul. Instr. Cavalry* II. 18 The.. men passaging right, or left, as may be necessary. **1833** *Ibid.* I. 81 The motion of the horse's legs in 'Passaging' is the same as that in 'Shoulder-in', but the head is turned differently. **1891** *Blackw. Mag.* May 647 He [the pony] should be able even to 'passage' at a canter.
transf. **1893** STEVENSON *Catriona* 263 The ship.. plunging and passaging upon the anchor cable.

ˈ**passage**, *v.*^{2} [f. PASSAGE *sb.*: cf. *voyage.*]
1. *intr.* To make a passage, as in a ship or boat; to move across, pass, cross.
1824 GALT *Rothelan* I. I. xv. 141 Few pastimes are more soothing to a wounded spirit than easy passagings, at that delicious season, on the bosom of the generous river Thames. **1826** *Blackw. Mag.* XX. 21 Low stifled growling, and rapid passaging to and fro against the bars of the dens. **1833–40** J. H. NEWMAN *Ch. of Fathers* (1842) 79, I earnestly desired to find some brother.. who might passage with me over the brief wave of this life. **1834** MAR. EDGEWORTH *Helen* xvii. (Rtldg.) 161 Beauclerc passaged to Lady Davenant.
2. To carry on a passage of arms; *fig.* to fence with words, etc. (cf. PASSAGE *sb.* 13 c).
1798 COLERIDGE *Nightingale* 59 They answer and provoke each other's song, With skirmish and capricious passagings. **1862** CARLYLE *Fredk. Gt.* XII. ix. (1872) IV. 188 There was diplomatic passaging in these weeks. **1895** CROCKETT *Men Moss Hags* 45 It was a curious sight to see them passaging with little airs and graces, like fighting cocks matched in a pit.
3. *Med.* and *Biol.* To subject a strain of (micro-organisms or cells) to a passage (sense 10 b). In *Med.* usu. with pronunc. (pæˈsɑːʒ).
1927 *Brit. Jrnl. Dermatol.* XXXIX. 7 Although the herpetic strain has been submitted to intracerebral passages for 4 years, it is still far from being as virulent or 'neurotropic' as the lethargica strain which has been passaged for 18 months only. **1952** *Jrnl. Exper. Med.* XCV. 260 All [influenza strains] were prepared from allantoic fluid passaged in 10 to 11 day old embryos. **1973** R. G. KRUEGER et al. *Introd. Microbiol.* xix. 514/1 The higher the donor species lies on the evolutionary scale, the more times one can passage that species' tissue *in vitro*. **1973** *Nature* 18 May 163/2 Non-infected, non-transformed hamster cells passaged *in vitro* fifteen times failed to develop tumours in 1-day-old hamsters.

†ˈ**passageable**, *a. Obs.* [f. PASSAGE *sb.* + -ABLE.] Affording passage, passable.
1574 BOURNE *Regiment for Sea* (1580) 75 To discourse the third way, that is not known, but supposed that it may be passageable. **1611** SPEED *Hist. Gt. Brit.* VI. xvi. (1623) 96 In making ways passageable from place to place.

ˈ**passage-**ˌ**boat.** A boat for the conveyance of passengers, plying regularly between two places, upon the sea, or a river or canal.
1598 FLORIO To Rdr. bj, They were many to steere a passage-boate. **1662** J. DAVIES tr. *Mandelslo's Trav.* 281 Being to passe in the ordinary passage boat from England to Dublin.., they were taken by a French Pirate. **1738** *N. Jersey Archives* XI. 529 He also keeps a Passage-Boat to ply between New-York and Amboy. **1840** DICKENS *Barn. Rudge* xxxi, The party embarked in a passage-boat bound for Gravesend.

ˈ**passage-**ˌ**money.** Money charged for passage; fare; †a payment for permission to pass.
1591 PERCIVALL *Sp. Dict.*, *Fletar*, to pay passage money. **1686** tr. *Chardin's Trav. Persia* 347 Those Thorow-fairs are a sort of Places for the skinning of strangers... They must alway there pay Passage-money. **1833** *Chambers's Edin. Jrnl.* 25 May 140/3 Hereabout the captain collects the passage-money. **1842** DICKENS *Amer. Notes* xvi, Others had sold their clothes to raise the passage-money. **1889** F. D. LUGARD *Diary* 31 Dec. (1959) I. i. 60 Rs. 300 is I think very moderate. He asks no passage money &c. and speaks the language. **1966** *Times* (Australia Suppl.) 28 Mar. p. xv/1, I am not talking about cultural encouragement, only passage money.

†**passager.** *Obs. rare*$^{-1}$. [app. a. F. *passagère* fem., passing, a female passer or passer-by.] A name for a curled lock on the temples.
1690 EVELYN *Mundus Muliebris* 6 Nor Cruches she, nor Confidents, Nor Passagers nor Bergers wants. *Ibid.* 19 (*Fop Dict.*) *Passagere*, a Curl'd Lock next the Temples.

passager(e, obs. form of PASSENGER.

ˈ**passage-**ˌ**way**, ˈ**passageway.** A way affording passage; a path by which a person or thing may pass through, in, or out; a passage, esp. in a building: = PASSAGE *sb.* 11 c. (Until 19th c., *U.S.*)
1649 *Rec. Early Hist. Boston* (1877) II. 98 Wm. Franklin is fined 20s. for disablinge the passage way. **1715** in *Cambridge* (Mass.) *Reg. Bk.* (1896) 276 It is Neither Needfull nor convenient for to have a passage Way thro' Said Dickson's lot. **1846** T. L. MCKENNEY *Mem.* I. ix. 191 On reaching the War Department I was met in the passage-way by the Hon. James Barbour. **1851** HAWTHORNE *Ho. Sev. Gables* vii, There was a step in the passage-way, above stairs. **1876** *N. Amer. Rev.* CXXIII. 64. **1878** W. PATER *Wks.* (1901) VIII. 177 The realities.. of the greater world without steal in upon us, each by its own special little passage-way. **1894** R. H. DAVIS *Eng. Cousins* 227 A net-work of narrow passageways and blind alleys. **1897** *Westm. Gaz.* 1 Oct. 7/1 The deceased was lying in the passage way bleeding from the mouth.

passaging: see PASSAGE *v.*^{1}, ^{2}.

passagour, -iour, -jour, obs. variants of PASSENGER.

passalid (ˈpæsəlɪd), *a.* (*sb.*) *Ent.* [f. mod.L. family name *Passalidæ*, f. the generic name *Passalus* (J. C. Fabricius *Entomologia Systematica* (1792) I. II. 240), f. Gr. πάσσαλος peg, in allusion to the shape of the insect: see -ID^3.] Belonging to the family Passalidæ, which includes black or dark brown beetles with slightly flattened bodies, found in decaying wood in warm forest regions. Also as *sb.*, a beetle belonging to this family.
1904 G. J. ARROW in *Trans. Entomol. Soc. London* 748 The Passalid beetle stridulates by the opposition of certain stout spines upon the wings to other spines.. upon the antepenultimate dorsal segment. **1916** *Records Indian Museum* XII. 138 Madame Merian's larva can no longer be regarded as a Passalid. **1927** *Chambers's Jrnl.* 20 Aug. 601/1 The whole Passalid family lives in rotten tree-stumps. **1959** E. F. LINSSEN *Beetles Brit. Isles* I. 44 The Passalid beetles are so interesting and of such exceeding importance to the comparative study of the social behaviour of insects that the reader may wish to know more about them. **1972** L. E. CHADWICK tr. *Linsenmaier's Insects of World* 155/2 Famous for their family life are the passalid beetles.

Passamaquoddy (ˌpæsəmə'kwɒdɪ). Also 8 **Passamaquoda, Pesmaquady.** [Micmac, = 'place where pollack are plentiful', with reference to Passamaquoddy Bay.] (A member of) a tribe of North American Indians nearly identical in language and culture to the Maliseet and inhabiting parts of south-east Maine and (formerly) south-west New Brunswick; the Algonquian language of this tribe. Also *attrib.* or as *adj.*

1726 J. GYLES in *Maine Hist. Soc. Coll.* (1853) III. 357 Memorandom of ye No of Indians in each tribe from 16 years of age... Pesmaquady Indians 30. **1759** T. POWNALL in *Ibid.* (1857) V. 371 Zacharie was asked what Tribe he was of, ans[d] Passamaquoda. **1842** *Wasp* (Nauvoo, Illinois) 3 Sept. 3/1 Our Passamaquoddy Indians are divided into two political parties, between which a good deal of acrimonious feeling exists. **1857** *Porter's Spirit of Times* 11 July 292/2 Much interest was felt in the birch canoe race, between some Indians of the Passamaquoddy, Penobscot and Micmac tribes. **1910** F. W. HODGE *Handbk. Amer. Indians* II. 207/2 Passamaquoddy... A small tribe belonging to the Abnaki confederacy... They formerly occupied all the region about Passamaquoddy bay and on St Croix r and Schoodic lake, on the boundary between Maine and New Brunswick. **1912** *28th Ann. Rep. U.S. Bureau Amer. Ethnol. 1906–7* 259 The consonantic clusters of Passamaquoddy. *Ibid.* 285 The Passamaquoddy independent mode. **1917** *Internat. Jrnl. Amer. Linguistics* I. 58/1 The Passamaquoddies live about four hundred strong at Pleasant Point... It is safe to estimate that about a thousand persons still speak Passamaquoddy. *Ibid.* 58/2, I intend to publish shortly a complete chrestomathy of Passamaquoddy tales. **1935** *Explorations & Field Work Smithsonian Inst. 1934* 85 Probably all the Passamaquoddy have white blood in varying degrees. *Ibid.* 88 Passamaquoddy (as is the case with other Eastern Algonquian languages) has deviated from the normal type. *Ibid.* (*caption*) Alexander Spain, a Passamaquoddy. **1957** *Encycl. Brit.* I. 49/2 They [*sc.* the Abnaki] included the.. Passamaquoddy. **1974** *Encycl. Brit. Micropædia* VII. 786/1 In 1969 there were two Passamaquoddy reservations in Maine. **1977** C. F. & F. M. VOEGELIN *Classification & Index World's Lang.* 17 Passamaquoddy... D[ialect] also Malecite... 9,000–10,000 [speakers]. New Brunswick, Maine, and adjacent Quebec. **1978** *Times* 11 Jan. 7/3 In Maine, the Passamaquoddy and Penobscot Indians are claiming.. nearly two thirds of the entire state.

passameasure, -meso, -meze, -mezzo: see PASSEMEASURE.

†**passance.** *Obs. rare*⁻¹. [f. PASSANT: see -ANCE.] Journey.

1580 SAKER *Narbonus* I. 131 Thus passed they their passance, and wore out the weerie way with these pleasant discourses.

passand, -e, obs. pr. pple. of PASS *v.*

passant ('pæsənt), *a.* (*sb.*) Also 4–5 -aunt, -e, 7 -ent. [a. F. *passant*, pr. pple. of *passer* to PASS.]

†**1.** Surpassing, exceeding; excelling; = PASSING *ppl. a.* 3. *Obs.*

c **1386** CHAUCER *Knt.'s T.* 1249 Ffor euery wight that.. wolde his thankes han a passant name Hath preyd þat he myghte been of that game. **1413** *Pilgr. Sowle* (Caxton 1483) v. v. 76 The stones sholde nought haue kept them fro syngynge, for the passaunt ioye. *c* **1485** *Digby Myst.* v. 612 *Mynde.* Coryous aray I wyll euer haunt. *Vnderstondyng.* And I, ffal[s]nesse, to be passaunt.

†**2.** Passing, transitory, transient, fugitive. *Obs.*

c **1400** tr. *Secreta Secret., Gov. Lordsh.* 57 Coueyte noght þinges coruptibles & passant. **1604** WEBSTER *Ode* in *Arch's of Triumph*, For pleasure's stream Is like a dream, Passant and fleet, as is a shade. *a* **1677** BARROW *Wks.* (1686) II. Serm. xvi. 223 Our actions (even our passant words, and our secret thoughts). **1715** JANE BARKER *Exilius* II. II. 55 All the Glories of this World are passant.

†**3.** Passing, going on, journeying; proceeding.

1608 HIERON *Defence* III. 56 So as it be with an honor passant and transcurrent from and through it to the Creator. **1609** *Nottingham Rec.* IV. 291 Richard Parkyns to be passant to and fro. *a* **1618** SYLVESTER *Job Triumphant* IV. 472 When they [Lionesses].. watch For passant Heards. **1686** GOAD *Celest. Bodies* I. iii. 10 Fiery Trajections, and Passant Meteors. *c* **1710** CELIA FIENNES *Diary* (1888) 124 It was a fine thing and would have delighted me severall dayes but I was passant.

4. *Her.* Of a beast: Walking, and looking toward the dexter side, with three paws on the ground and the dexter fore-paw raised.

passant guardant: see quot. 1787. *passant reguardant*, passant with head contourné or looking backwards. *passant repassant*, walking as above in opposite directions.

c **1500** *Sc. Poem Heraldry* 128 in *Q. Eliz. Acad.* 98 A lionne ..Third saliant; the four, passand I-wis. **1590** SPENSER *F.Q.* III. i. 4 His goodly shield That bore a Lion passant in a golden field. **1594** KYD *Cornelia* v. 207 Passant regardant softly they [two lions] retyre. **1610** GUILLIM *Heraldry* III. xii. (1660) 156 A Leopard or Wolfe, must be portrayed going ..step by step; which..is termed Passant. **1787** PORNY *Elem. Her.* (ed. 4) Dict. Techn. Terms, *Passant-gardant*, is when an Animal is in the same posture as passant, but with his face turned, so that his eyes are both distinctly seen. **1864** BOUTELL *Her. Hist. & Pop.* xxi. §2 (ed. 3) 359 An ox of the second, passant over a ford ppr.

†**5.** Current, in general use, in vogue. *Obs.*

1611 COTGR., *Passant*.. Passing..; also, passant, currant, verie tollerable. **1619** HALES *Gold. Rem.* II. (1673) 90 This as yet is all the Newes that is passant. **1646** SIR T. BROWNE *Pseud. Ep.* 118 Many opinions are passant concerning the Basilisk. **1680** in Howell *St. Trials* (1816) VII. 1195 Ay, said she,.. I believe thou hast no hand in the plot (a casual word that was passant at that time). **1844** C. MACFARLANE *Camp of Refuge* I. 67 It came to be a passant saying with men who would describe anything that was super-excellent.

†**6.** Cursory, done in passing. *Obs.*

1685 J. SCOTT *Chr. Life* II. I. iv. (1686) I. 185 He doth not inspect our Actions with a passant and cursory View, as things of little or no Moment. **1693** SIR P. PETT in *Bp. Barlow's Rem.* Ep. to Rdr. A iv, On a Passant review of what ..I wrote to the Bp.

†**7.** quasi-*adv.* = EN PASSANT, in passing. *Obs.*

1600 W. WATSON *Decacordon* (1602) 162 As is euident by sundrie bookes written, and to be written..and may be gathered passant in these Quodlibets. *a* **1617** BAYNE *Lect.* (1634) 112 The eye of the body taketh a double view, the one passent in *transitu*, the other fixed. **1653** H. MORE *Antid. Ath.* II. xii. *Schol.* §1 (1712) 160 Johnston briefly and as it were passant tells the same story.

‖**B.** *sb.* (pasɑ̃). [French uses.]

1. One who passes; a passer.

1890 *Athenæum* 18 Jan. 89/2 A constant stream of [Huguenot] refugees passed through the town [Dover]... Amongst the 'passants' appears the name of 'Severin Durfy'.

2. 'The French term denoting a piping without a cord running through it' (Caulfeild & Saward *Dict. Needlework* 1882).

†'**passantly,** *adv. Obs.* [f. prec. + -LY².] **a.** Exceedingly, very greatly. **b.** Cursorily, passingly, in passing.

c **1440** *Gesta Rom.* xxvi. 98 (Harl. MS.) This knyght lovid passantly þe grehounde, with the faucon. **1600** W. WATSON *Decacordon* (1602) 330 As before hath beene passantly touched here and there.

†**passa'rado.** *Naut. Obs.* Also 7 pasarado, passerado. [Cognate with next: the ending -ADO (q.v.) for *-ada* in Sp. and Pg. = *-ée* in Fr. Known only in Capt. J. Smith, or as cited from him.] = next.

1626 CAPT. SMITH *Accid. Yng. Seamen* 27 Bend your passerado to the mayne sayle, git the sailes to the yeards. **1627** —— *Seaman's Gram.* ix. 42 They hale them downe.. with a Pasarado, which is any rope wherewith wee hale downe the sheats blockes of the maine or fore saile. **1658** in PHILLIPS. **1704** in HARRIS *Lex. Techn.* I. **1867** [see next].

†**passaree** (pæsə'riː), *sb. Naut. Obs.* Also 7 pass-a-ree, 9 pazaree. [Origin obscure. Littré has F. *passeresse*, fem. of *passeur* 'passer', applied to small ropes serving to supplement the brails; but connexion is uncertain.] A rope or tackle used to spread the clews and haul down the sheet-blocks of the foresail and mainsail when sailing large before the wind: see quot. 1867.

1669 STURMY *Mariner's Mag.* I. ii. 18 Hawl aft the fore-Sheet, bring him down to the Cat-head with a pass-a-ree. **1769** FALCONER *Dict. Marine* (1776), *Passaree*, a rope used to fasten the main-tack down to the ship's side, a little behind the chess-tree,..very rarely used,..in light breezes of wind. **1867** SMYTH *Sailor's Word-bk.*, *Passaree*, or *Passarado*, a rope..to haul out the clues of the fore-sail to tail-blocks on the booms, so as to full-spread the foot of that sail.

Hence †**passa'ree** *v. trans.*, to spread the clews of the foresail and mainsail with a passaree.

1884 LUCE *Text-bk. Seamanship* 435 (Cent.) With stun'sails both sides, passaree the foresail, by means of a rope on each side, secured to the clew of the foresail, and rove through a bull's eye on the lower boom.

passata, variant of PASSADO 1.

‖**passa'tempo.** *Obs.* [It. *passatempo* 'a pastime, a solace, a sport' (Florio 1598): see PASSETEMPS.] = PASTIME *sb.*

1632 T. REVELL in *J. Hayward's tr. Biondi's Eromena*, No, th'are thy Passatempos fruits, and they Tasted by a judicious palat may Have a good relish.

passback ('pɑːsbæk, -æ-). [f. PASS *v.* + BACK *adv.*] **a.** *Amer. Football.* = SNAP-BACK. **b.** *Association Football*, etc. A defensive pass directed backwards to a team-mate, usu. the goalkeeper.

1934 in WEBSTER. **1947** *Richmond* (Virginia) *Times-Dispatch* 16 Nov. 8B/7 For the first time in the game Filer called play No. 43. The passback came directly to the big fullback. **1976** *Scottish Daily Express* 23 Dec. 12/5 Goalkeeper Ted McPheat dropped a passback at the feet of Mike Lafnach. **1976** *Sunday Post* (Glasgow) 26 Dec. 35/3 If there's a better fetch-and-carry midfield man in the country than Lex Richardson (as long as he doesn't attempt passbacks) I'd like to see him.

'**pass-book.** [app. = book passing to and fro between bank (or tradesman) and customer.]

1. The account-book supplied by a bank to a person having a current or deposit account, in which entries are made of all sums deposited and drawn, so that the customer may at any time see what is his balance at the bank: = BANK-BOOK b.

Formerly app. called *passage-book*.

1828 GILBART *Banking* (ed. 2) §3 The person is supplied ..with..A cash-book, called in some houses a Pass-book. **1847** *Minutes Crt. Direct. Bank Eng.* 6 May, Resolved.. That the following notice be inserted in the Pass Books. [*Similar entry of 11 Jan. 1827 had* Bank Books.] **1855** *Ann. Reg.* 366 He was credited with the dividends in his pass-book. **1866** CRUMP *Banking* i. 35 A banker's pass-book affords a complete history of the expenditure for the year. *a* **1901** BESANT *Five Years' Tryst* (1902) 91 Your pass-book ..shall be made up to-day, and you shall have the book to-morrow morning, when you can draw your balance. **1902** G. MEREDITH *Let.* ? 20 Apr. (1970) III. 1441, I do not see in my pass-book the Swedish £15. **1916** *Banking Publicity* Oct. 1/1 It is not more necessary for the banker to advertise who would have men and women leave their money with nothing more than a passbook to carry home in place of it? **1922** JOYCE *Ulysses* 707 A bank passbook issued by the Ulster Bank, College Green branch showing statement of a/c for halfyear ending 31 December 1903. *Ibid.* 710 The endowment policy, the bank passbook, the certificate of the possession of scrip. **1949** G. B. SHAW *Buoyant Billions* III. 30 What money I need appears to my credit in my bank passbook as cash or dividends on the few investments my stockbroker has advised. **1954** R. GITTINGS *John Keats: Living Year* v. 49 A small red leather wallet with a tuck-in flap, rather like a bank pass-book. **1977** *Time* 28 Feb. 38/1 If the salesman had $2,000 or more in a savings account, he could borrow on his passbook and pay 1% more in interest on his loan than he received in interest on his savings.

2. A book in which a merchant or trader makes an entry of goods sold on credit to a customer, for the information of the latter.

1833 *Chambers's Edin. Jrnl.* II. 321/1 [Are there] no unheard-of overcharges in those pass-books I see flying about like evil spirits? **1839** BOUVIER *Law Dict. U.S.* **1861** MRS. BEETON *Bk. Househ. Managem.* 1108 The 'pass-books' employed backwards and forwards between bakers, butchers, and the like domestic traders, and their customers. **1972** *Lebende Sprachen* XVII. 34/1 US passbook—BE credit sales book, roundsman's book.

3. *S. Afr.* = PASS *sb.*² 8 f.

Usu. written as two words without hyphen.

1961 T. MATSHIKIZA *Chocolates for my Wife* 88 The sergeant..thumbed querulously through each ninety-six paged pass book. **1963** K. MACKENZIE *Dragon to Kill* xvi. 181 The police came to know about the evidence he could give in this case when they arrested him again, on a charge involving forged pass books. **1971** *Post* (Golden City, S. Afr.) 21 Mar. 7 Bishop Alpheus Zulu, who was arrested a week ago for not carrying his pass book. **1972** P. DRISCOLL *Wilby Conspiracy* (1973) vi. 74 People were advised..to destroy the pass books which the law required them to carry. **1973** *Times* 21 Sept. 15/5 Sizwe appropriates the dead man's name and pass book.

pass-by ('pɑːsˌbaɪ, -æ-). [f. PASS *v.* + BY *adv.*]

†**1.** The act of passing by. *Obs. rare.*

1550 CRANMER *Defence* 73 This is the Lordes Passeby, or Passeouer, euen so sayth Christ in the newe Testament. **1661** GLANVILL *Van. Dogm.* 66 We see the face of Truth, but as we do one anothers, when we walk the streets, in a careless Pass-by.

†**2.** ? = Passer by, by-passer. *Obs. rare.*

1600 W. WATSON *Decacordon* (1602) 135 There is alwaies some dogge in the dorter of Gods Church waking, readie to barke at euerie passe-by out of the way.

3. *Mining.* **a.** A siding in a working, where trucks, etc. can pass one another.

1883 GRESLEY *Gloss. Terms Coal Mining* s.v., A plan of a pass-by as sometimes constructed upon a self-acting inclined plane. **1892** *Daily News* 3 Mar. 5/7 'Pass-bys', as they are called, have to be placed at short intervals along all passages in which there is less than about 4½ feet of clear space between the rails and the wall. **1911** *Act 1 & 2 Geo. V* c. 50 §43(3) Where, in the case of any mine, sets or trains of tubs are coupled or uncoupled at the face, or at the pass-bye next the face. **1967** *Gloss. Mining Terms* (*B.S.I.*) x. 11 *Pass-by*, 1. A siding in an underground haulage track having a turnout at both ends to the main line... 2. A loop of track around the shift at the pit bottom.

b. A place on a plate-rail (PLATE *sb.* 8) where vehicles can pass. Also *attrib.*

1797 J. CURR *Pract. Coal Viewer* 26 Pass bye plates. Useful for 2 horses going contrary ways and passing each other with a draught of corves. *Ibid.* 27 Supposing a branch of road is required to be made to a new pit, one end of the above described pass bye..will accommodate such purpose.

pass-dice: see PASS- in comb.

‖**passé** (pɑse), *a.* and *sb.*¹ Also (in fem. form) **passée.** [F. *passé, passée*, pa. pple. of *passer* to PASS, used as adj., in same sense.] **A.** *adj.* Past, past the prime; *esp.* of a woman: past the period of greatest beauty; also, out of date, behind the times, superseded.

1775 MME. D'ARBLAY *Early Diary* (1889) II. 101 Others say that she is passée. **1823** BYRON *Juan* XIII. lxxx, The passport shrouds The 'passée' and the past; for good society Is no less fam'd for tolerance than piety. **1853** LYTTON *My Novel* v. viii, Even a Frenchman would not have called her *passée*—that is for a widow. For a spinster, it would have been different. **1865** 'OUIDA' *Strathmore* I. viii. 133 Malice is for *passées* women. **1886** F. HARRISON *Choice Bks.* 71 They ..pronounce Fielding to be low, and Mozart to be *passé*.

B. as *sb.* In Ballet (see quot. 1948). Also *attrib.*

1948 A. CHUJOY tr. *Vaganova's Basic Princ. Classical Ballet* vi. 65 Passé corresponds to its French meaning (passed). It is an auxiliary movement which transfers (passes) the leg from one position into another. If you are standing in développé effacé forward and you wish to bring the leg back into arabesque without doing a grand rond de jambe, you bend the leg at the knee, leaving it at a height of 90°, brush the toe of that foot past the standing leg and bring it out into arabesque. The passing the leg through this path is called passé. **1957** T. MARA *Second Steps in Ballet* 41 *Passé*... This means to pass the foot to a position at the knee in preparation for opening it in the *développé*. The right foot is strongly pointed at the little hollow of the supporting knee. **1959** B. & P. FLETCHER *How to improve your Ballet Dancing* ix. 100 Relevé to passé position on left toe with right toe touching inside supporting knee. **1967** G. GRANT *Tech. Man. & Dict. Classical Ballet* (ed. 2) 75 *Passé*,..is an auxiliary movement in which the foot of the working leg passes the knee of the supporting leg from one position to another (as, for example, in développé passé en avant) or one leg passes the other in the air (as in jeté passé en avant) or one foot is picked up and passes in back or in front of the supporting leg (as in chassé passé).

‖**passe** (pɑs), *sb.*² [Fr., f. *passer* to pass: see quot. 1903.] In roulette, the section of the cloth covering the numbers 19 to 36; a bet placed on this section.

1850, etc. [see NOIR 2 a]. **1902** *Encycl. Brit.* XXXII. 304/1 *Pair* indicates even numbers, *impair* odd numbers; *manque* includes the numbers from 1 to 18; *passe*, from 19 to 36. **1903** 'L. HOFFMANN' *Card & Table Games* (ed. 3) 649 So called because in this event the ball 'fails' (Fr. *manque*) to fall into a higher number than 18. *Passe* is so called because the ball 'passes' that number. **1923**, etc. [see MANQUE]. **1937** G. FRANKAU *More of Us* vii. 76 By plying rake on impair, manque, passe, parity, or any number you might put your fish on. **1971** P. O'NEIL-DUNNE *Roulette for Millions* iv. 38 The roulette table is divided into six areas which, starting from the top nearest the wheel, are labelled: *manque* for low; *passe* for high; *impair* for odds; *pair* for evens.

‖**passe-**, repr. F. *passe*, vb.-stem, orig. imp. of vb. *passer* to PASS; used in a few words more or less naturalized from Fr., chiefly in 16th and 17th centuries, as PASSE-PAROLE, PASSE-PARTOUT *sb.*, etc. Not a living prefix in English: cf. PASS- in comb. ‖**passe-pierre**: Parsley-piert. ‖**passe-pomme** [obs. F., 1544, Godef.], name of a rich table-apple. **Passe Colmar**, a variety of pear; ? = COLMAR 1.

1664 EVELYN *Kal. Hort.* (1729) 232/1 Fruit Trees..for a moderate Plantation. Apples..*Passe-pome, Pome Apis, Cour pendue* [etc.]. **1706** PHILLIPS, *Passe-pierre*, or *Pierce-pierre*, a sort of Stone-Parsley, an Herb. **1837** *Amer. Q. Rev.* XXI. 377 We could speak of others just coming into notice, such as the passe colmar. **1860** R. HOGG *Fruit Manual* 204 Passe Colmar... An excellent pear. Ripe during November and December. **1882** *Garden* 14 Jan. 18/1 The most useful of all Pears which we have is Passe Colmar. **1928** H. B. TUKEY *Pear* x. 108 Passe Colmar..and other winter sorts sometimes shrivel and rot before reaching an edible condition.

passe, obs. f. PACE *sb.*², PASCH, PASS, PEISE.

passea fleminco: see PASSER-FLAMINGO.

passeboard, obs. corrupt or erron. f. PASSPORT.

passed (pɑːst, -æ-), *ppl. a.* See also PAST *ppl. a.* [Pa. pple. of PASS *v.*]

1. a. That has passed or has been passed, in the various senses of PASS *v.* Also with advbs. ***passed pawn*** (Chess): see quot. 1837.

1512 *Will of Riswyk* (Somerset Ho.), As is accustomed for people passed to God. **1797** *Encycl. Brit.* (ed. 3) IV. 640/2 The advantage of a passed pawn is this: for example, if [etc.]. **1837** *Penny Cycl.* VII. 51/2 *Passed Pawn*, a pawn is called *passed* when it is no longer obstructed by any adverse pawn on its own file, or either of the adjoining ones. **1885** O. CRAWFURD *Woman's Reput.* I. i. 4 Such a condition of society as this, with..its passed-away modes of life. **1902** *Recollect. Dublin Castle & Soc.* 17 Another of these regularly 'passed on' veterans was Everard.

†**b.** *spec.* Dead, passed away, 'gone', deceased.

1449 J. METHAM *Amor. & Cleop.* (E.E.T.S.) 307 But nowe thei bothe be pasyd; & affter schal I. **1555** W. WATREMAN *Fardle Facions* I. v. 79 Yᵉ kindesfolke of the deade signefie to..the friendes of this passed, yᵉ day of yᵉ burial.

2. That has passed an examination; qualified by examination, esp. *Naut.*, in ***passed midshipman***, etc.

1829 MARRYAT *F. Mildmay* xii, One of the passed midshipmen. **1867** SMYTH *Sailor's Word-bk.*, *Passed boys*, those who have gone through the round of instruction given in a training-ship. **1879** *Spectator* 31 May 680 Dr. Colenso, who is a passed expert in Zulu matters. **1898** *Westm. Gaz.* 17 Dec. 8/2 They..concluded that there was more promise in that plucked student than in many a passed man.

3. ***passed-out***: unconscious, *spec.* through alcoholic drink. *colloq.*

1927 *Amer. Speech* II. 277 *Passed out*, intoxicated. **1939** G. GREENE *Lawless Roads* iii. 95 The blue soda-water bottles and the passed-out Mexican.

passe-day, variant of PASCH-DAY.

passed-master. One who has passed as a master; a qualified or accomplished master: cf. *to pass master*, PASS *v.* 17, and see PAST-MASTER.

1563-7 BUCHANAN *Reform. St. Andros* Wks. (1892) 13 Ane of profession of medecine passit maister, and ane regent in humanite. **1882** H. C. MERIVALE *Faucit of B.* I. vi, Faucit was a passed master as a guide to the classics. **1894** *Athenæum* 24 Mar. 383/1 We praise ourselves, rather than such a passed-master of the art, by saying 'ditto' to his axiom. *Mod.* A passed master in the art of swindling.

passe-flemingo: see PASSER-FLAMINGO.

passe-garde: see PASS-GUARD.

‖**passeggiata** (passed'dʒata). [It., = walk, promenade.] A leisurely walk; a regular stroll.

1967 *Listener* 30 Mar. 434/2 They step out together like a mother and children on a walk, or an Italian family making a *passeggiata*. **1969** HURD & OSMOND *Smile on Face of Tiger* v. 141 In the canyons of the Chinese town the deafening *passegiata* [*sic*] of the poor, dressed in their holiday best. **1971** N. FISHER *Rise at Dawn* viii. 137 We drove into Viareggio one evening. It was the hour of the *passeggiata*... The pavements thronged with strolling families. **1973** *Sat. Rev. Society* (U.S.) Feb. 19/3 The *passeggiata* after working hours of citizens along the Via dei Caizaiuoli. **1978** 'A. STUART' *Vicious Circles* 4, I found myself peacefully watching the flow of people..taking their passegiata, or shopping.

‖**passéisme** (paseizm). [Fr.] Adherence to and regard for the traditions and values of the past, esp. in the arts. So **passéist(e)**, a traditionalist, one who is backward-looking (also *attrib.* or as *adj.*).

1914 WYNDHAM LEWIS *Let.* 14 June (1963) 62 There are certain artists in England who do not belong to the Royal Academy nor to any of the passéist groups, and who do not on that account agree with the futurism of Sig. Marinetti. **1927** R. FRY *Let.* 4 Aug. (1972) II. 603 I've never been a Passéist—I was a Futurist but I have gradually trained myself to be a Presentist. **1943** WYNDHAM LEWIS *Let.* 15 Oct. (1963) 368, I remember that clown Marinetti (the 'father of fascism') and his bellowings about 'passéisme' and his proposal to destroy all the pictures and buildings reminding people of the Past in Italy. **1953** —— *Let.* 23 Nov. (1963) 552 In editing *Blast* I regarded the contributions of Ezra as compromisingly passéiste. **1962** *Times* 12 Apr. 18/5 Delacroix was far more of a *passéiste* than the author suggests. **1968** *Listener* 29 Feb. 259/1 The old conflict between *passéiste* faculty and *antipasséiste* students is over.

passel, dial., etc. var. PARCEL.

†**passe'measure.** *Obs.* Forms: α. 6 **passe-, passameze, -meso**, 8 **passamezzo**. β. 6 **passa-measure**, 7 **passy-, passe-, pace-measure.** [Perversion of It. *passe-, passa-mezzo*: see quots. 1776, 1880.] A slow dance of Italian origin, app. a variety of the pavan; the music for this, in common time. Also called ***passemeasures paven, passy measures pavyn*** = It. *passemezzo pavana*.

α. **1568** *Alford's Instruct. for Lute*, Passameze. **1597** MORLEY *Introd. Mus.* 180 *Pastorellas* and *Passamesos* with a dittie and such like. **1776** SIR J. HAWKINS *Hist. Music* IV. 386 As a Galliard consists of five paces or bars in the first strain, and is therefore called a Cinque Pace; the Passamezzo, which is a diminutive of the Galliard, has just half that number, and from that peculiarity takes its name. **1880** W. B. SQUIRE in Grove *Dict. Mus.* II. 662/1 Tabourot in his *Orchésographie* [1589] says that when the Pavan was played less solemnly and more quickly, it was called a *Passemezzo*..It is probable that the name *Passemezzo* (in which form it is found in the earliest authorities), is simply an abbreviation of *Passo e mezzo*, i.e. a step and a half, which may have formed a distinctive feature of the old dance.

β. **1597** BRETON *Wits Trenchmour* (1879) 15/1 With a *Passa* measure pace comming toward her sweet presence. **1601** SHAKS. *Twel. N.* v. i. 205 Then he's a Rogue, and a passy measures Pauyn: I hate a drunken rogue. [**1607** *Lingua* III. vii. G iij b, Thou must dance nothing but the passing measures.] **1611** FLORIO, *Passo mezzo*, a cinque-pace, or pace-measure. **16..** *MS. Camb.* Dd. 2. 11 Passe-mezures Pauen. **1623** MIDDLETON *More Dissemblers Besides Wom.* v. i. 162, I can dance nothing but ill-favouredly, A strain or two of passa-measures galliard. **1847-78** HALLIWELL, *Passamezzo*... The long-disputed phrase *passy-measures pavin*..is in fact the name of an ancient dance, thus described in a MS. quoted by Mr. Collier in the Shak. Soc. Papers, i. 25, 'two singles and a double forward, and two singles syde, reprynce back.' It is only necessary to read this, and have seen a drunken man, to be well aware why Dick is called a 'passy-measures pavin'.

passement ('pæsmənt), *sb. Obs.* exc. *Hist.* Forms: α. 6 **pasmond, pastment**, 6-8 **pasment**, 7-9 **pass-**, 8 **pace-, pesment**, 6- **passa-, passement.** β. 6 **passemain, -mayne, -min, passamen, -maine, pasmain.** [a. F. *passement* (in this sense in 16th c.), pl. *-mens*, f. *passer* to pass: see -MENT. The forms in *-main*, etc., appear to correspond to It. and Sp. *passamano*, app. f. *passare* to pass + *mano* hand: the reason of this name, and the relations between this and the Fr. form in *-ment* are not clear.] Gold or silver lace, gimp or braid of silk or other material, for decorative trimming; = LACE *sb.* 5.

α. **1539** *Inv. R. Wardr.* (1815) 31 Ane uthir gowne of purpour satyne with ane braid pasment of gold & silvir. **1542** *Ibid.* 70 Item ane hat of velvott with ane pasmond of silver. **1589** PUTTENHAM *Eng. Poesie* III. i. (Arb.) 150 As the embroderer [setteth]..passements of gold vpon the stuffe of a Princely garment. **1619** in Ritchie *Ch. St. Baldred* 115 He had broun claiths and black passaments on him. **1756** MRS. CALDERWOOD *Jrnl.* (1884) 66 The finest liveries quite covered over with pacements. **1869** MRS. PALLISER *Lace* iii. 21 Many of the earlier laces were made by the threads being passed or interlaced one with the other; scarcely more than a white braid; hence they derived the name of passament. **1902** M. JOURDAIN & ALICE DRYDEN *Mrs. Palliser's Hist. Lace* 26 The earlier laces, such as they were, were defined by the word 'passament'—a general term for gimps and braids as well as for lace. Modern industry has separated these two classes of work, but their being formerly so confounded renders it difficult in historic researches to separate one from the other.

β. **1565-6** *Roy. Procl. as to Apparel* 12 Feb., Any fringe, lace, or passemayne, of gold, syluer, or silke.

fig. **1637** RUTHERFORD *Lett.* (1671) I. xlvi. 104 These broad passements and buskings of religion. *Ibid.* clxvi. 326 This love would be fair and adorning passements.

†**b.** *attrib.*, as ***passement lace, silk.*** *Obs.*

α. **1546** *Aberdeen Regr.* (1844) I. 239 Half ane pund of black pastment silk. **1585** T. WASHINGTON tr. *Nicholay's Voy.* II. xxv. 66 Gownes of veluet..set with passament lace and buttons of golde or siluer. **1613** T. MILLES tr. *Mexia's*, etc. *Treas. Anc. & Mod. T.* 960/1 Lacing their Cloakes, Doublets, and Hose, with passement laces of fine Gold.

β. **1548** W. PATTEN *Exped. Scot.* C viij b, Hemmed round about very sutably with pasmain lace of grene caddis. **1549** *Egerton Papers* (Camden) 11 That no man under the degree of an Erle, weare any cloth of gold, silver, tissue, or purple silke, any embroderye, passamen lace [etc.]. **1583** *Rates of Customs* D vj, Passemin lace of Cruell the dosen xiijs. iiijd. **1600** in Nichols *Progresses* (1823) III. 509 Item, one cloake of blacke taphata..with passamaine lace of Venice golde and silver.

passement ('pæsmənt), *v.* [f. PASSEMENT *sb.*, perh. after F. *passementer* (Rabelais, 16th c.).] *trans.* To adorn with passement or lace; to edge (a garment) with decorative braiding or trimming.

1539 *Inv. R. Wardr.* (1815) 32 Item ane gowne of quhite velvot all droppit oure with gold wyre pasmentit with the samyne. **1629** Z. BOYD *Last Battell* 620 Ashamed to be seene among these who are pasmented with gold. **1818** SCOTT *Hrt. Midl.* xxiv, The doomster..arrayed in a fantastic garment of black and grey, passmented with silver lace. **1828** —— *F.M. Perth* iv, The Flemish hose and doublet..were.. passamented (laced, that is) with embroidery of black silk. *a* **1894** STEVENSON *St. Ives* xxviii. (1898) 212, I mind I had a green gown, passementit.

fig. **1640** RUTHERFORD *Lett.* (1671) II. xxix. 490 Your cross is..pasmented over with the faith and comforts of the Lords faithful Covenant with Scotland.

‖**passementerie** (pɑsmɑ̃tri). Also **pasmentier.** [F. (16th c. in Hatz.-Darm.), f. *passement*: see above and -ERY.] Trimming of gold or silver lace, or (in later use) of gimp, braid, or the like, or of jet or metal beads.

1794 A. YOUNG *Trav. France* (ed. 2) I. xix. 550 They assert their *pasmentiers* of silk and cotton mixed, to be cheaper than any similar fabric in England. **1851** *Harper's Mag.* II. 431/1 A cloak..having three rich..fastenings of *passementerie*. **1879** MISS BRADDON *Vixen* x. 76 The purchase of an artistic arrangement in black silk and jet, velvet and passementerie. **1882** *Daily News* 30 Aug. 3/1 Open-worked boots..made of a kind of passementerie or gimp. **1893** *Daily Tel.* 6 Oct. 5/2 The Duchess..wore a velvet and passementerie mantle. **1903** [see DANGLY *a.*]. **1933** M. DE LA ROCHE *Master of Jalna* viii. 100 'Put a frill on it,' he suggested. 'A frill! A frill of what?' 'Would *passementerie* do?' he asked. **1936** M. MITCHELL *Gone with Wind* xii. 232 Her stout bosom heaved violently beneath its glittering passementerie trimmings.

†**passen**, *ppl. a. Obs. rare*⁻¹. [Erroneously f. PASS *v.* after strong pa. pples., e.g. *washen, waxen*.] = PASSED.

1624 CAPT. SMITH *Virginia* Pref. 4 And know both passen and vnpassen road.

'**passen** *v.*, pseudo-archaic for PASS.

1748 THOMSON *Cast. Indol.* I. lvi, These I passen by, with nameless numbers moe.

passenep, obs. form of PARSNIP.

passenger ('pæsɪndʒə(r)). Forms: α. 4-7 **passager**, (5 **-agour**, 6 **-agere**). β. 5 **passyngere**, 6 **-anger**, *Sc.* **-ingeoure**, 6-8 **passinger**, 6- **passenger.** [ME. *passager*, a. F. *passager*, *-ier* a passer by, a sojourner, a passenger on a ship, sb. use of *passager*, *-ier* adj., passing, fleeting, temporary, sojourning, f. *passage* + *-ier* (= L. *-āris*). In late ME. *n* was phonetically inserted before *-ger* (-dʒər) as in some other words, including *harbinger*, *messenger*, *ostringer*, *porringer*, *scavenger*, *wharfinger*, etc.: cf. also *popinjay*. (See Jespersen in *Engl. Studien* XXXI. 239.)]

1. a. A passer by or through. **b.** A traveller (usually on foot), a wayfarer. Now unusual, exc. in ***foot-passenger***: see FOOT 34 b.

α. *c* **1330** R. BRUNNE *Chron. Wace* (Rolls) 16593 By passagers wel herde he seye þe venimouse eyr was al a-weye. **1426** LYDG. *De Guil. Pilgr.* 16539 A Pylgrym or a passagour that kometh ffro fforeyne Cuntres.

β. *a* **1450** MYRC 845 Of scoler, of flotterer, or of passyngere Here schryft lawfully þou myȝt here. **1538** H. MEDWALL *Nature* (Brandl) 41/96, I let the wyt thou arte a passanger That hast to do a great and longe vyage. **1538** STARKEY *England* I. ii. 60 Not as a passenger only. **1583** STUBBES *Anat. Abus.* I. (1879) 87 To beholde the passengers by. **1593** SHAKS. *2 Hen. VI*, III. i. 129 A bloody Murtherer, Or foule felonious Theefe, that fleec'd poore passengers. **1615** CHAPMAN *Odyss.* I. 266, I cannot think you a foot passenger. **1633** T. ADAMS *Exp. 2 Peter* i. 3 The passengers in mockery bad Christ come down from the cross. **1684** *Contempl. St. Man* I. vii. (1699) 74, I have nothing to do with this World; ..I am only a Passenger. *a* **1710** POPE *Alley* 19 The snappish cur (the passenger's annoy) Close at my heel with yelping treble flies. **1828** SCOTT *F.M. Perth* xix, She avoided the High Street..and reached the wynd by the narrow lanes... Even these comparatively lonely passages were now astir with passengers. **1875** EMERSON *Lett. & Soc. Aims* iv. 123 Every passenger may strike off a twig with his cane.

†**c.** *Rhet.* Puttenham's name for the figure PARALIPSIS. *Obs. rare*⁻¹.

1589 PUTTENHAM *Eng. Poesie* III. xix. (Arb.) 239 *marg.*, *Paralepsis*, or the Passager.

2. One who travels or is carried in some vessel or vehicle, esp. on board ship or in a ferry- or passage-boat; later applied also to travellers by coach, and by railway, tramway, or the like; now always with the implication of a public conveyance entered by fare or contract. (The prevailing sense.)

1511 GUYLFORDE *Pilgr.* (Camden) 72 Syr Christopher Palusyn and the best passengers aforesayde lefte and forsoke oure galye. **1611** CORYAT *Crudities* 168 There are..ferries or passages..where passengers may be transported in a Gondola. **1726** SHELVOCKE *Voy. round World* 129 They brought with them the Spanish Captain, and some of the chief Passengers. **1796** BURKE *Regic. Peace* ii. Wks. VIII. 239 They were then only passengers in a common vehicle. **1841** *Penny Cycl.* XIX. 248/2 The experiment of forming a railway for passengers as well as general merchandise traffic, had scarcely been tried. *a***1901** BESANT *Five Years' Tryst*, etc. (1902) 246 We stood on deck watching the arrival of the passengers.

3. †**a.** A vessel that carries passengers; a passage-boat; a ferry-boat. *Obs.*

[**1392** *Earl Derby's Exp.* (Camden) 279 Et pro vj passaiours et j balinger conductis de Caleys vsque Douer.] **1473** SIR J. PASTON in *P. Lett.* III. 98 Yisterdaye ij passagers off Dovr wer takyn. **1513** DOUGLAS *Æneis* VI. vi. 18 Vnleful war, and ane forbodin thing Within this passinger our Stix to bring Ony leifand wycht. **1525** LD. BERNERS *Froiss.* II. lvii. 197 He..toke the see in a passagere, & aryued at Calays. **1630** *R. Johnson's Kingd. & Commw.* 113 Three great ships and fifteene gallies, layed purposely..to intercept all English passengers.

b. Ellipt. for *passenger train. colloq.*

1886 H. BAUMANN *Londinismen* 132/1 *Passenger*,.. passenger-train. **1920** 'O. DOUGLAS' *Penny Plain* xxiii. 259 He could spend ecstatic days watching every 'passenger' and every 'goods' that rushed..along the permanent way. **1962** 'D. SHANNON' *Extra Kill* ix. 145 I'd just taken a couple to the Union Station, I guess to make the Owl for San Francisco—only passenger I know of leaving about then.

†**4.** A ferryman, a ford-keeper. *Obs. rare.*

*a***1533** LD. BERNERS *Huon* clvi. 597 When they wer ouer, the passanger, who was named Clarimodes,..demaunded of Huon what he and his wyfe were. **1534** *Act 26 Hen. VIII*, c. 5 §1 Oneles the said passangers..haue good knowledge of such person. **1573–80** BARET *Alv.* P 167 A passenger, one that conueigheth ouer manie, *conuector*.

5. a. A bird of passage. Also *attrib. Obs.*

1579–80 NORTH *Plutarch* (1595) 26 Which hath giuen some occasion to holde..that the vulters are passagers, and come into these partes out of straunge countries. **1624** CAPT. SMITH *Virginia* 171 Sometimes are also seene Falcons..but because they come seldome, they are held but as passengers. **1672** SIR T. BROWNE *Let. Friend* §4 Passager and migrant Birds..whom no Seas nor Places limit.

b. *spec.* An adult hawk caught on its migration, a passage-hawk; also, a name for the Peregrine falcon; in full, ***passenger falcon***. *Obs.*

1575 TURBERV. *Faulconrie* 176 Many times our happe is to haue Haggardes or Passengers, or Lentiners, the which haue flowen either to the Riuer, or prayed for themselues. **1611** COTGR., *Pelerin*,..the Faulcon tearmed a Passenger. **1615** LATHAM *Falconry* Contents, Of the Passenger, or soare hawke. **1617** MINSHEU *Ductor*, A Passenger faulcon. **1694** MOTTEUX *Rabelais* IV. lvii. (1737) 236 Merlins, Hagards, Passengers, wild rapacious Birds.

6. *colloq.* One of the crew of a racing-boat who adds to the weight without contributing his share to the work; hence, an ineffective member of a football team, etc. Also, in extended uses, one who takes a passive role in a group activity, enterprise, etc., making no personal contribution and requiring the continuous support of the rest.

1852 J. F. BATEMAN *Aquatic Notes* iii. 23 Some University scratch Four-oared Races were rowed... Here would be seen three good oars endeavouring to row along a 'passenger', of some eleven stone weight. **1885** [Remembered at Oxford]. **1892** *Guardian* 25 May 791/3 In the ordinary amateur band there are always several 'passengers'. **1900** *Westm. Gaz.* 27 Feb. 4/3 The two inside men on the amateur side were practically 'passengers'. **1908** *Animal Managem.* 297 A sick or lame ox should be removed from the span at once, as he..is in fact 'a passenger', and has to be dragged along by the others. **1914** *Daily Mail* 6 Apr. 9/4 There was not a passenger in any division of the winning team. **1932** AUDEN *Orators* I. 19 We simply can't afford any passengers or skrimshankers. **1932** *Times Educ. Suppl.* 6 Aug. 301/2 It is a lucky school that has no passenger on its staff. **1946** D. HAMSON *We fell among Greeks* iv. 47 We nearly had to shoot both of them later on at different times, because they were lazy and untrustworthy and we had no room for 'passengers'. **1948** 'N. SHUTE' *No Highway* xi. 288 As a scientist from Farnborough I was expected to be a passenger, useless in the woods. **1949** 'J. TEY' *Brat Farrar* xx. 185 You cannot expect to carry two adults as passengers in the estate... They are both capable of earning their own living. **1951** J. B. PRIESTLEY *Festival at Farbridge* II. ii. 319 Theodore plodded on, like a man walking on a hot afternoon to some place he hated. 'I'm beginning to feel I'm almost a passenger.' **1957** *Listener* 28 Nov. 882/2 More women have had to learn to become self-reliant in the mountains, or at least not to be mere passengers. **1961** A. WILSON *Old Men at Zoo* ii. 79 If you haven't any appreciation at all for serious research work, then the sooner you get out..the better. We're carrying enough passengers already. **1964** J. MASTERS *Trial at Monomoy* vii. 219 I'd want to do my share of work. I don't want to be a passenger. **1971** L. P. DAVIES *Shadow Before* v. 49 The scheme was really yours in the first place. Jack Latham wasn't much more than a passenger. **1971** R. J. WHITE *Second-Hand Tomb* vii. 72 It was..an affection born of patronage. Pamela was so obviously a passenger.

7. a. *attrib.* and *Comb.* Of or pertaining to passengers, esp. by ship, railway, or other mode of conveyance; carrying passengers, paid by a passenger, etc.: as ***passenger automobile, boat, cabin, car, carriage, coach, department, depot, door, elevator, fare, jetty, lift, liner, list, lounge*** (spec. in an airport), ***manifest, pier, plane, seat, service, ship, side, station, steamer, terminal, ticket, trade, traffic, train, vehicle, way, window***, etc.; of a passenger train, as ***passenger engine, guard, line, locomotive***, etc; ***passenger-carrying*** adj.; ***passengerless*** adj. and adv.

1858 SIMMONDS *Dict. Trade*, *Passenger-agent*, a broker, licensed to engage passages in ships for emigrants. **1900** *Engineering Mag.* XIX. 764/1 The passenger automobile is an accepted and rapidly-increasing institution. **1839** *Encycl. Brit.* (ed. 7) XIX. 50/1 The passenger boats, going 10 miles an hour, charge from 1*d.* to 1½*d.* per passenger, per mile. **1946** R. A. MCFARLAND *Human Factors Air Transport Design* xi. 492 The general arrangement of the passenger cabin will naturally vary with the type of service for which the plane will be used. **1952** *Shell Aviation News* No. 166. 24 (*caption*) Cutaway drawing showing interior arrangement of the 44-passenger Convair-Liner 340. Forward of the passenger cabin is a large compartment for baggage and cargo. **1832** *Amer. Railroad Jrnl.* I. 305/3 Arrived, 9 passenger cars with 71 passengers. **1847** *Hunt's Merchants' Mag.* XVI. 211 Attached to this station, are also..two wood and water stations..a brass foundry, passenger car house, passenger rooms, offices &c. **1881** *Chicago Times* 4 June The passenger-cars..rival all competing lines in the magnificence of their finish. **1968** *Globe & Mail* (Toronto) 3 Feb. B 3/3 Extensive absenteeism by members of local 444 of the United Auto Workers forced a shutdown of the passenger car lines yesterday at the Windsor plant of Chrysler Canada Ltd. **1975** A. BERGMAN *Hollywood & LeVine* xiv. 211 Some Indian children waved at the train. They..stopped to stare at the silver blur of passenger cars. **1977** *Reinforced Plastics* XXI. 22/3 Engineering plastics materials have been used for many years for the production of cooling fans for passenger car engines. **1838** *Mechanics' Mag.* 13 Oct. 32/1 The *passenger carriages* of the American railways are extremely large and commodious. They are seated for 60 passengers, and are made so high in the roof, that the tallest person may stand upright in them without inconvenience. **1879** *Harper's Mag.* July 165 A bustling little locomotive with one passenger-carriage comes whistling down the valley. **1978** N. MARSH *Grave Mistake* vii. 210 A slow train with a passenger carriage. **1909** *Daily Chron.* 8 Sept. 1/6 He was placed third in the speed contest, fourth in the Gordon-Bennett Cup contest, and second in the passenger-carrying competition. **1928** *Manch. Guardian Weekly* 21 Sept. 224/4 It is with this passenger-carrying airship that the Germans hope to fly across the Atlantic. **1937** *Discovery* Sept. 270/2 The ultimate aim of all such experiments is the production of a passenger-carrying rocket plane. **1967** *Jane's Surface Skimmer Systems 1967–68* 87/2 The PT 20, a 27-ton boat for 75 passengers, is considered by Supramar to be the smallest size hydrofoil suitable for passenger-carrying coastal services. **1841** *Penny Cycl.* XIX. 258/2 The weight of the ordinary passenger-coaches, when empty, is mostly from three to five tons. **1849** *Hunt's Merchants' Mag.* XX. 342 A spacious freight and passenger depot..has been completed in the lower part of Detroit. **1958** *Amer. Speech* XXXIII. 145 Though both units are likely to be in the same building, separate reference is sometimes made to the *freight depot* and the *passenger depot*. **1952** *Shell Aviation News* No. 165. 24 It is authorized that 87 occupants may be carried in aircraft with six exits, and one passenger door in the passenger area. **1968** K. BIRD *Smash Glass Image* xii. 149 The dark-green Seat swung into the kerb... The passenger door opened. **1974** 'J. LE CARRÉ' *Tinker, Tailor* xxxv. 311 In one of these blaring side-streets..Ricki Tarr would unlock the passenger door and hold him up at gun-point. **1886** J. A. PORTER *New Stand. Guide Washington* 205 The building.. is furnished with passenger-elevator, steam-heating, deposit-vaults, speaking tubes. **1919** C. MORLEY *Haunted Bookshop* iv. 87 Maybe he had no right to be riding in the passenger elevator. **1926** *Scribner's Mag.* Aug. 196/1 We ain't no trunks. Take us up in a passenger-elevator. **1839** *Encycl. Brit.* (ed. 7) XIX. 49/2 Expense for some coals drawn by passenger engines. **1882** DE WINDT *Equator* 13 It is to be wondered how the passenger fares of this line can even be made to cover the outlay. **1906** *Westm. Gaz.* 11 Dec. 6/3 One would almost imagine that the running of a passengerless train from station to station,..would 'grow' on the conductors. **1952** R. FINLAYSON *Schooner came to Atia* 110 He was soon back, passengerless. **1907** *Shipping World* 16 Jan. 111 (Advt.), S.S. 'Lusitania' is being fitted with Passenger Lifts. **1931** *Times* 16 Mar. 21/7 An unique and beautifully-fitted flat, ideally situated and equipped with constant hot water, central heating, passenger and service lifts. **1938** M. ALLINGHAM *Fashion in Shrouds* xv. 248 They came up in a small handworked passenger lift to a front door. **1975** D. BLOODWORTH *Clients of Omega* xxii. 207 Dr. Moondance..will take the fast number one passenger lift to the fiftieth floor. **1851** *Min. Proc. Inst. Civil Engin.* X. 255 Owing to the different value now put upon the resistances to railway trains at high velocities,..good gradients had become relatively of less importance on passenger lines. **1843** DICKENS *Mart. Chuz.* (1844) xvi. 196 I've just now sent a boy up to your office with the passenger-list. **1869** 'MARK TWAIN' *Innoc. Abr.* xx. 199 We had the whole passenger list for company. **1928** KIPLING *Bk. of Words* 268 H.M.S. Great Britain carries a passenger list..of forty-five millions. **1931** —— *Limits & Renewals* (1932) 189 It's on the back of the passenger-list. **1958** B. HAMILTON *Too Much of Water* ii. 23 A copy of the Passenger List which he had found in his cabin. **1973** A. PRICE *October Men* ii. 31 He was on the passenger list... It was an ordinary scheduled flight. **1969** D. BARRON *Man who was There* i. 14, I..was considering looking for Gregory beyond the confines of the passenger lounge when they began to broadcast the announcement of our impending departure. **1970** M. PEREIRA *Pigeon's Blood* viii. 95 The Hall..for obvious reasons, was the only way of leaving the Passenger Lounge. **1971** Passenger manifest [see MANIFEST *sb.* 3]. **1976** B. JACKSON *Flameout* (1977) ix. 149 I've..got the list of cargo. .. And the passenger manifest. **1931** W. L. SMITH *Air Transport Operation* i. 5 The cost per passenger mile is about 7 cents for the largest passenger planes. *Ibid.* 4 In about the same period [12 yrs.], the capacity of passenger planes has increased from 2 to 30 passengers. **1937** *Discovery* May 164/1 The Pan-American Grace Company converted one of its passenger planes into a cargo plane. **1970** 'D. HOLLIDAY' *Dolly & Cookie Bird* viii. 124 Every now and then a big passenger plane would come droning in. **1975** S. JOHNSON *Urbane Guerilla* III. 114 The US..has banned shipment of nuclear material by passenger plane. **1844** *Act 7 & 8 Vict.* c. 85 §6 All Passenger Railway Companies..shall..provide for the Conveyance of Third Class Passengers to and from the terminal and other ordinary Passenger Stations of the Railway. **1878** F. S. WILLIAMS *Midl. Railw.* 264 Some discrepancy in the account of the passenger receipts per train mile. **1937** M. ALLINGHAM *Dancers in Mourning* xxiv. 299 The body lay doubled up on the floor with..its head jammed against the front of the passenger seat. **1962** D. FRANCIS *Dead Cert* xvii. 187 Pete himself poked his big bald head out of the passenger seat and called to me. **1972** *Guardian* 5 Dec. 7/2 Travel organisers..[must] keep within the terms and conditions of their licences... The licence will cost £250 a year plus 2p for each one-way passenger seat authorized by it. **1977** B. PYM *Quartet in Autumn* x. 91 Ken stuck in the passenger seat of a car on test. **1836** *Backwoods of Canada* 7 The 'Laurel' is not a regular passenger-ship. **1969** J. GARDNER *Compl. State of Death* x. 216 He removed the bar, gently placed it on the passenger-side floor. **1972** *Country Life* 15 June 1577/2 A large glove box on the passenger side and a smaller one for the driver. **1844** Passenger station [see *passenger railway* above]. **1900** *Westm. Gaz.* 2 May 19/1 On the Clyde they manage things better in the way of passenger-steamer service than is done on the Thames. **1841** *Penny Cycl.* XIX. 260/2 The passenger-tax ..amounts to one-eighth of a penny per mile for every passenger carried. **1976** *New Yorker* 16 Feb. 76/2 More personnel are needed at passenger terminals than at freight terminals relative to the value of their respective services. **1780** A. YOUNG *Tour in Ireland* II. vi. 30 At the ports of Belfast, Derry, &c. the *passenger trade* as they called it, had long been a regular branch of commerce, which employed several ships, and consisted in carrying people to America. **1866** 'MARK TWAIN' *Lett. from Hawaii* (1967) 21 The sailing vessels..[are] too slow and uncertain to build up the passenger trade. **1972** 'G. BLACK' *Bitter Tea* (1973) vii. 110 The public is held back by a long counter..only we don't have much public really, not being in the passenger trade. **1836** *Mechanics' Mag.* 15 Oct. 30/1 No credit whatever was taken in the Eastern Counties Railway estimates for any of the passenger-traffic from *transmarine* sources, as that traffic was, at best, of a contingent character. **1846** *Penny Cycl.* Suppl. II. 670/1 Coupled wheels..are now largely and increasingly employed for passenger traffic. **1883** W. H. MAW *Recent Pract. Marine Engin.* I. 117/2 In the case of a larger launch 40 ft. long fitted with engines of twenty indicated horse-power, and employed for passenger traffic on the River Dart, the average [fuel] consumption per week is but 10 cwt. **1933** S. L. MILLER *Inland Transportation* xxi. 361 Efforts to increase the volume of railway passenger traffic have been in the past decade increasingly active. **1963** N. WYMER *Behind Scenes at London Airport* i. 17 The 'Short-haul' Building, opened in 1955, is for passenger traffic to and from Europe. **1976** Passenger traffic [see *private motoring* s.v. PRIVATE *a.* (*sb.*) 4c]. **1836** *Mechanics' Mag.* 5 Nov. 83/1 What is the usual weight you carry in one of your trains; your passenger train?—Forty or fifty tons; no, not more than thirty to forty tons, carriages and passengers together. **1846** *Penny Cycl.* Suppl. II. 660/2 One third-class passenger train..all along the line, on every day [etc.]. **1937** *Discovery* Mar. 88/2 Each [van]..is vacuum fitted and fully equipped for working on fast passenger trains. **1976** *Daily Tel.* 20 July 4/1 Last Thursday he left Nairobi in a passenger train for Kampala. **1908** *Westm. Gaz.* 14 Mar. 2/1 Using the parallel of the street..he claimed that the river should be regarded as a passenger way. **1971** R. PETRIE *Thorne in Flesh* xiv. 175 There was a large, dark saloon parked at the kerb... The nearside passenger window slid down and Tina called to him. **1977** P. HILL *Fanatics* 145 Dice..wound down the passenger window.

b. Special Comb., as **passenger-mile**, a unit of measurement representing one passenger travelling a distance of one mile; hence ***passenger-mileage***; also ***passenger-kilometre*** (abbrev. *km.*).

1900 *Geogr. Jrnl.* XVI. 221 The number of passengers carried in 1898 was 126 millions, the number of passenger-kilometres amounting to 4439 millions. **1903** E. JOHNSON *Amer. Railway Transportation* x. 140 An equal mileage of road accommodates a much greater traffic in Europe than in the United States. This is shown by dividing the total number of miles traveled by all passengers (the 'passenger miles') by the miles of railroad. **1930** *Flight* 28 Nov. 1381/2 Taking paying passengers only, the figure becomes 41 passenger-miles. **1936** *Jrnl. R. Aeronaut. Soc.* XL. 850 The criterion then being the number of passenger miles flown per period. **1943** *Ibid.* XLVII. 249 An expectation that the accident rate can..be reduced to a long-term average of no more than 1·0 fatality per 100,000,000 passenger-miles. **1962** R. B. FULLER *Epic Poem on Industrialization* 219 Passenger miles per capita per annum By all modes of transport Represents a smoothly ascending Curve. **1971** *Guardian* 13 July 2/2 TWA on its own rates as the world's second largest airline—in terms of passenger-miles—behind United, the American domestic operator. **1974** *State* (Columbia, S. Carolina) 1 Apr. 2-A/2 (Advt.), If your carpool cars average, say, 13 miles to the gallon and you share costs with three others, you are paying for only one gallon in four, and you're getting 52 passenger miles-per-gallon. **1976** P. R. WHITE *Planning for Public Transport* viii. 175 Of the 29000 million or more passenger-km generated on the BR system each year about 45 per cent are classified as intercity. **1978** *Jrnl. R. Soc. Arts* CXXVI. 427/1 In London Transport, we have adopted as our corporate aim the maximization of passenger-mileage within the financial resources available to us from fares and grants.

ˈpassengered, *a. rare.* [f. PASSENGER + -ED[2].] Of a vehicle, ship, etc.: carrying or occupied by passengers.

1929 R. GRAVES *Poems* 27 That was the hospital-boat of twelve years back, Passengered as before with doubt and dying. **1955** W. GADDIS *Recognitions* III. i. 723 Traffic often consists only in the gay orange garbage carts, passengered by black vultures.

ˈpassenger-ˌpigeon. [See PASSENGER 5: in F. *pigeon de passage*.] The 'Wild Pigeon' of North America (*Ectopistes migratorius*), noted for its exceptional powers of long and sustained flight, and formerly for the countless numbers in which it passed from place to place. The bird became extinct in 1914.

1802 BINGLEY *Anim. Biog.* (1813) II. 225 Passenger Pigeons visit, in enormous flocks, the different parts of

North America. **1837** *Penny Cycl.* VII. 366/2 The passenger-pigeons..have their first quill-feather as long as any of the others—a sure indication of that rapid and long-continued power of flight they are known to possess. **1894** NEWTON *Dict. Birds, Passenger-pigeon*, so called in books, but in North America commonly known as the 'Wild pigeon',.. famous in former days for its multitude, and still occasionally to be found plentifully in some parts of Canada and the United States. **1907** W. B. MERSHON *Passenger Pigeon* p. ix, As recently as 1880 the Passenger Pigeon was thronging in countless millions through large areas of the Middle West. **1955** A. W. SCHORGER *Passenger Pigeon* ix. 229 The passenger pigeon became extinct through such constant persecution that it was unable to raise sufficient young to perpetuate the race. **1967** D. GOODWIN *Pigeons & Doves of World* 203 The Passenger Pigeon shares with the Dodo the doubtful fame of being one of the two best known species that have been exterminated by man. **1972** G. DURRELL *Catch me a Colobus* x. 213 It was impossible, everyone thought, that the Passenger pigeon (so delicious to eat and so plentiful) could ever be exterminated... The last Passenger pigeon in the world died in the Cincinnati zoo in 1914. **1975** *New Yorker* 7 Apr. 45/1, I saw the last passenger-pigeon flocks in Iowa.

passent, erron. form of PASSANT.

‖**passe-parole.** *Obs. rare.* Also pass-parole. [F. (1642 in Hatz.-Darm.), ad. It. *passaparola*, lit. 'pass-word': see PASSE-.] (See quots.)

[**1591** *Garrard's Art Warre* 172 And as they say, according to the word *Passà Parola*, aduance the word.] *Ibid.* 11 Those words..which the Captaine giues ouer to be pronounced from mouth to mouth, as to *Passe Parole* appertaines. **1727–41** CHAMBERS *Cycl., Pass-parole*, a command given in the head of an army, and thence communicated to the rear, by passing it from mouth to mouth.

‖**passe-partout, passepartout** (pɑspartu), *sb.* (*v.*) [F *passe-partout* (16th c. in Littré), f. *passe* vb. imp. (PASSE-) + *partout* everywhere.]

1. That which passes, or permits to pass, everywhere; *spec.* a key that opens any or many doors, a master-key; also *fig.*, and *attrib.*

[*c* **1645** HOWELL *Lett.* IV. xix. 52 A travelling warrant is call'd *Passeport*, wheras the Original is *passe par tout*.] **1675** WYCHERLEY *Country Wife* I. i, Now may I..be, in short, the *Pas par tout* of the town. **1680** DRYDEN *Kind Keeper* V. i. 55 With this *Passe par tout*, I will instantly conduct her to my own Chamber. **1700** CONGREVE *Way of World* III. vii, Why this wench is the *passe-partout*, a very master-key to everybody's strong-box. **1709** MRS. MANLEY *Secret Mem.* (1720) III. 279 One of my Servants, who is gone with two of Monsieur le Envoy's, and his *Passe par toute* to Nova. **1749** LADY M. W. MONTAGU *Let. to C'tess Bute* 30 Nov., He opened his door with the *passe-partout* key. **1760** FOOTE *Minor* I. Wks. 1799 I. 237 My art, Sir, is a *pass-par-tout*. I seldom want employment. **1831** *Edin. Rev.* Sept. 46 Their master-key was allegory, a *passe-partout* to all difficulties. **1833** C. MACFARLANE *Banditti & Robbers* (1837) 365 Shortly after the prior went with a *passe-partout*, and opened the door of his cell.

2. a. An engraved plate or block with the centre cut out for the insertion of some other plate or block, thus forming a fixed engraved border to receive any engraving or picture of suitable size. (Used largely in illustrated books of 16th–17th c.) Also a fixed typographical border for a printed page. (So in Fr.; English use doubtful.)

1842 BRANDE *Dict. Sci.*, etc., *Passepartout*, in Engraving, a plate or wood block, whose centre part is entirely cut out round the outer part, whereof a border or ornamental design is engraved, serving as a frame to what may be placed in the centre. **1875** KNIGHT *Dict. Mech., Passe-partout*... This is common in wood-engraving, where an ornamental border may be made to do duty with changing central advertisements or labels.

b. An ornamental mat or plate of cardboard or the like, having the centre cut out so as to receive a photograph, drawing, or engraving, to which when framed it serves as a mount or border. Hence ***passe-partout frame***, a frame ready made with such a mount for reception of photographs, etc.

1867 MRS. WHITNEY *L. Goldthwaite* vi. 120 There were engravings and photographs in *passe-partout* frames. **1870** *Eng. Mech.* 4 Feb. 514/2 Information as to gilding cardboard for gold passe partouts. **1873** ALDRICH *Marjorie Daw* vii, There is an exquisite ivorytype of Marjorie in *passe-partout*, on the..mantle-piece. **1889** *Anthony's Photogr. Bull.* II. 60 A plain passe-partout greatly assists in 'setting off' a picture which otherwise would be but a plain print. **1898** *Daily News* 17 Oct. 5/4 Reproductions in colour and autolithographs printed on choice Dutch, Japanese, and Chinese paper, and very handsomely mounted with a passe-partout to each work.

c. A kind of adhesive tape or paper used for framing photographs and for other purposes. Also *attrib.* and as *vb. trans.*

1909 *Cent. Dict.* Suppl. 952/1 *Passepartout*,..to place in a passe-partout frame. **1910** V. TREE *Let.* 13 Nov. in *Castles in Air* (1926) 54, I have found a manufacturer of *passe-partouts* for my flower and French costume prints. **1910–11** *T. Eaton & Co. Catal.* Fall & Winter 144/1 Passepartout binding, black, green, brown, grey, red and white. **1928** *Daily Express* 17 May 9/4 A favourite occupation is evidently to 'passe-partout' their pictures. **1954** *Paper Terminol.* (Spalding & Hodge) 44 *Passe-partout*, a strong embossed paper, gummed on one side and sold in coils about 1 in. wide. It is made in many colours and is used for picture mounting and the binding of lantern slides. **1969** R. BLYTHE *Akenfield* viii. 136 *Passe-partout*-ed photographs of their sons and daughters..hang on long strings from the picture rail. **1978** J. GOODMAN *Last Sentence* iii. 112 Haphazardly hung photographs, all framed amateurishly with passe-partout.

‖**passe-passe.** *Obs.* [F., f. *passe* vb. imperative, as said by conjurors.] Juggling, sleight of hand, skilful deception. ***tour of passe-passe*** [F. *tour de passe-passe*] a turn or feat of adroit manipulation or clever trickery.

1687 R. L'ESTRANGE *Brief Hist. Times* I. 82 After this, and in the Next Parliament, they had Another Tour of Passe-Passe.

‖**passepied** (ˈpɑspje), †**paspy** (ˈpɑːspɪ, -æ-). [F. *passe-pied* (16th c. in Hatz.-Darm.), f. *passe* vb. imp. (see PASSE-) + *pied* foot, *lit.* pass (the) foot.] A French dance, resembling the minuet, but quicker, which became popular in England towards the beginning of the 18th c. (Grove); also, the music for this dance, in triple rhythm.

Said to be of Breton origin, and to have been first danced in Paris by street-dancers in 1587. (Grove *Dict. Mus.*)

a **1695** PURCELL in Stainer & Barrett *Dict. Mus. Terms* (*title of piece*), Paspy. *c* **1700** CROFT *ibid.* (*title of piece*), The English Paspy. **1696** tr. *Du Mont's Voy. Levant* 284 A kind of *Gavote* or *Branle*, in which the Men and Women are mingl'd, as at *Passepied* in France. **1724** *Short Explic. For. Wds. in Mus. Bks., Passepied*, is an Air very much like a Minuet in all Respects, only to be play'd more brisk and lively. **1898** STAINER & BARRETT *Dict. Mus. Terms, Paspy*, the English name for the dance *Passe-pied*. Hawkins says it 'is said to have been invented in Bretagne, and it is in effect a quick minuet'... From the fact that examples exist by writers as late as Purcell and Croft, it could not have been out of fashion in their time.

passer (ˈpɑːsə(r), -æ-). [f. PASS *v.* + -ER[1].]

1. One who passes, travels, or goes by; a passer-by.

1382 WYCLIF *Jer.* xxii. 20 Crie to the passeres, for to-trode ben alle thi loueres. **1552** HULOET, Passer by the contrey, *viator.* **1602** CAREW *Cornwall* 133 Without troubling the passer, or borrowing Stentors voyce, you may..conferre with any in the..towne. **1800** SOUTHEY *Lett.* (1856) I. 112 This must exclude the great body of passers and repassers. **1886** F. HARRISON *Choice Bks.* i. 11 Men who surrender their time to the first passer in the street.

2. One who passes an examination.

1898 *Weekly Reg.* 26 Nov. 680 Successful passers of the London University B.A. [Examination].

3. a. One who causes to pass, in the various senses of the verb. (See PASS *v.* III.)

1832 LEWIS *Use & Ab. Pol. Terms* Introd. 10 The passers of bad money. **1871** MAURICE in *Life* (1884) II. xii. 178 The passer of the Roman Catholic Bill.

b. In ball games, a player who passes the ball to another player (cf. PASS *v.* 46 b).

1905 *Westm. Gaz.* 12 Dec. 9/2 From a clever pass—the 'passer' could not be distinguished in the fog—Parker feinted and swerved cleverly, scored behind the posts, and an easy goal resulted from Nesbitt's kick. **1970** *Washington Post* 30 Sept. D 4/3 If he played the whole season, he would rank among the top passers in the country. **1972** J. MOSEDALE *Football* ii. 18 Clark was his team's leading passer. **1973** *Times* 25 Jan. 12/8 Ian's a much better passer of the ball on the ground.

c. In various trades, a person who examines materials or manufactures to ensure that they are of the required quality, workmanship, etc. (see PASS *v.* 45 b).

1921 *Glasgow Herald* 21 June 9/7 The proposed reduction is 3d. per hour in respect of measure cutters,..fitters-up, tailors' pressers, machinists, passers, etc.

d. One who receives and passes on counterfeit money. *slang.* (Cf. PASS *v.* 46 c.)

1929 *Detective Fiction Weekly* 25 May 683/1 The dealer calls the carrier..they meet..and..a few bills are handed out as a sample. The carrier calls the 'shovers', sometimes known as 'passers' or 'pushers' who begin to operate. To this class belong the men who actually place the bogus money in circulation. **1955** W. GADDIS *Recognitions* II. v. 490 I'm going out to meet a passer, to hand this stuff over to him. It's all arranged and paid for. *Ibid.*, It's always trouble with the middleman and the passers that get you pulled in.

4. One who 'passes' as a member of an ethnic group other than his own. (Cf. PASS *v.* 5 d.)

1953 P. ABRAHAMS *Return to Goli* II. iv. 64 If the passing is successful even the parents of the passer cease to know him or her. **1956** L. KUPER *Passive Resistance in S. Afr.* I. ii. 66 The psychology implicit in apartheid legislation is the psychology of the coloured man who has successfully 'passed' into the white group. Over the generations, there would have been inculcated into the successful 'passer' the dominant value that 'whiteness is all'.

5. One who sells drugs illicitly.

1955 [see MEET *sb.* 1 b]. **1956** *Sun* (Baltimore) 26 July 14/1 This is an Act of the utmost severity, even providing the death penalty for 'passers' under certain circumstances.

†ˈ**passerage.** *Obs. rare.* [a. F. *passerage* cress (16th c. in Littré), f. *passe* (see PASSE-) + *rage* madness, from its supposed property of curing madness.] The French name of Garden-Cress. ***wild passerage*** (F. *passerage sauvage*), a synonym in Lyte of the Cuckoo-flower or Meadow Cress, *Cardamine pratensis.*

1578 LYTE *Dodoens* VI. lx. 626 The wild Passerage or Coccow flowers. **1879** PRIOR *Plant-names* (ed. 3) 178 *Passerage*, the garden cress.

ˌ**passer-ˈby.** [f. *pass by*: see PASS *v.* 61.] One who passes or goes by, *esp.* a casual passer.

1568 *Manch. Crt. Leet Rec.* (1884) I. 117 Placed..to the Displeasure of Neighbours and passers by. **1650** *Sc. Metr. Ps.* lxxxix. 41 He to all passers by [*earlier versions* commers by] a spoil, to neighbours is a scorn. **1799** SOUTHEY *Ruined Cottage* Wks. 1838 III. 32 Methinks I see her Raising her eyes and dark-rimm'd spectacles To see the passer-by. **1876** BESANT & RICE *Gold. Butterfly* iv, The steps of the passers-by kept her awake.

‖**Passeres** (ˈpæsəriːz), *sb. pl. Ornith.* [L. pl. of *passer* sparrow.] An order of Birds typified by the genus *Passer*, including the perchers generally, and comprehending more than half of existing birds: see quot. 1894.

1872 NICHOLSON *Palæont.* 395 The 6th order of Birds is that of the Insessors, or Perchers—often spoken of as the Passeres, or 'Passerine' Birds. **1894** NEWTON *Dict. Birds* 697 *Passeres*, the name given by Linnæus to his Sixth Order of Birds, which though for a time set aside in favour of other designations, *Insessores* and the like, or modified into such a form as *Passerinæ*, has been restored to use of late years, and approximately in its author's sense—the genera *Certhia*, *Sitta*, *Oriolus*, *Gracula*, *Corvus*, and *Paradisea*, which he had placed in his *Picæ*, being added, while *Caprimulgus*, the portion of *Hirundo* containing the Swifts, and *Columba* have been removed. **1894** R. B. SHARPE *Handbk. Birds Gt. Brit.* I. 1 The deep plantar tendons of the Passeres are of the simplest kind.

†ˈ**passer-flaˈmingo.** *Obs.* Forms: see quots. [app. f. L. *passer* sparrow, also ostrich + FLAMINGO.] The Flamingo.

1625 PURCHAS *Pilgrims* I. III. 275 Wild-geese, Duckes, Pellicans, Passea, Flemincos [*sic*], and Crowes. *Ibid.* IV. 536 Larks, Wild-geese, Ducks, Passerflannugos [*sic*], and many others. **1630** CAPT. SMITH *Trav. & Adv.* 54 The best and greatest is a Passer Flaminga, which walking at her length is as tall as a man. **1634** SIR T. HERBERT *Trav.* 18 (Engraving) Pasche-Flemingo. *Ibid.* 212 Passe-flemingoes, Geese, Powts, Swallowes.

passeriˈcidal, *a. nonce-wd.* [f. L. *passer* sparrow + -CIDE + -AL[1].] Sparrow-killing.

a **1876** M. COLLINS *Th. in Garden* (1880) I. 32 They will be glad to bring back the exiled birds, after the manner of certain passericidal villagers whom Longfellow has immortalised.

passeriform (ˈpæsərɪfɔːm), *a. Ornith.* [f. L. type **passeriformis*, f. *passer* sparrow: see -FORM.] Sparrow-like in form or structure; *spec.* of or pertaining to the *Passeriformes* or Oscinine group of the *Passeres* or passerine birds.

In mod. Dicts.

passerine (ˈpæsəraɪn), *a.* (*sb.*) *Ornith.* [f. L. *passer* sparrow + -INE[1].]

1. Of or belonging to the *Passeres* or Perchers, an order of birds.

1776 PENNANT *Zool.* (ed. 4) I. 254 Order V. Passerine. **1825** WATERTON *Wand. S. Amer.* II. ii. 165 A bird..of the passerine tribe and very common about the houses. **1880** A. R. WALLACE *Isl. Life* ii. 15 Among passerine birds the raven has the widest range. **1894** R. B. SHARPE *Handbk. Birds Gt. Brit.* I. 1 Passerine or Perching Birds.

2. Of about the size of a sparrow. In various bird-names, as ***passerine ground-dove*** (*Chamæpelia passerina*), ***passerine owl*** (*Glaucidium passerinum*), ***passerine parrot*** (*Psittacula passerina*).

1883 *List Animals Zool. Soc.* (1896) 343 Passerine Parrot. *Ibid.* 379 Passerine Owl. *Ibid.* 465 Passerine Ground-Dove.

B. *sb.* A passerine bird.

1842 BRANDE *Dict. Sci.*, etc. s.v., All the Passerines have short and slender legs, with three toes before and one behind. **1893** NEWTON *Dict. Birds* Introd. 57 The *Aves Passerinæ*, divided [by Gloger] into two Suborders:—Singing Passerines (*melodusæ*), and Passerines without an apparatus of Song-muscles (*anomalæ*).

passe-temps, pastemps. ? *Obs.* [F. *passetemps* (pɑstɑ̃), 15th c. in Littré = It. *passatempo*, f. *passe*, *passa* vb. imp. (PASSE-) + *temps*, *tempo* time. Cf. PASTANCE.] = PASTIME *sb.*

1542 UDALL *Erasm. Apoph.* 151 The incommoditees or displeasures..it easeth with honeste passetemps & recreacion. **1548** —— *Erasm. Par. Luke* Pref. 2 Contemnyng prouocacions of all vayne pastemps. **1649** JER. TAYLOR *Gt. Exemp.* Ep. Ded. 8 Such Meditations which are..the *passe-temps* of your severest hours. **1840** GEO. ELIOT *Let.* 20 July (1954) I. 60 It [sc. *Don Quixote*] is a charming passe-temps (a word by the bye that I ought to have outlawed long ago). **1848** T. ARNOLD *N.Z. Lett.* (1966) 27 One cannot be always reading and this sail-making forms a very agreeable passe-temps. **1891** W. FRASER *Disraeli & his Day* 344 After many dreary weeks of solitude at the 'Three Cups' hotel, the only *passe-temps* being to watch the corpses, removed from the sunk-fort, of soldiers who died daily of small-pox, the Election took place.

passetime, -tyme, obs. forms of PASTIME.

‖**passe-velours.** *Obs.* [F. *passe-velours* (pɑsvəlur), lit. 'surpass velvet', 16th c. in Hatz.-Darm.: see PASSE-.] A former name for the COCK'S-COMB (*Celosia cristata*), called also by Cotgrave *Flower valure, Velvet flower*; cf. FLORAMOUR.

1597 GERARDE *Herbal* II. xl. §3. 254 *Amaranthus Tricolor.* Floramor and Passeuelours. **1601** HOLLAND *Pliny* XXI. x. 92 The Passe-veleur or Flower-gentle. **1611** FLORIO, *Amarànto*,..the flowre gentle or Passeuelours. **1706** in PHILLIPS.

†**passe-volant.** *Obs.* Also 6 pasuolan, *Sc.* paswolent, -voland, 7 pas-, pass-, passevolant. [a.

F. *passe-volant* (pɑsvɔlɑ̃), 1529 in Hatz.-Darm., It. *passauolante* (Florio), f. F. *passe*, It. *passa* (see PASSE-) + *volant*, *volante* flying.]

1. A small cannon used in the 16th and 17th centuries; = BASE *sb.*[6]

1513 *Acc. Ld. High Treas. Scot.* IV. 487 Item, to Alexander Routh for vij new paswolentis, the price of the pece iij *li.* greit. **1524** in Hakluyt *Voy.* (1599) II. I. 79 The meane shot, as sacres and pasuolans, were in great number. **1566** *Inv. R. Wardr.* (1814) 172 Item ane pasvoland of brace upone ane traist. **1656** BLOUNT *Glossogr.*, *Pasvolant*, the Artillery called a Base. [**1867** SMYTH *Sailor's Word-bk.*, *Passe-volant*, a name applied by the French to a Quaker or wooden gun on board ship; but it was adopted by our early voyagers as also expressing a movable piece of ordnance.]

2. (See quots.) (So in Fr.)

[**1611** COTGR., *Passevolant*,..also, a hireling whom a Captaine, on Muster dayes, foisteth into his companie; and generally, any such skipiacke, or base nimblesbie.] **1617** MORYSON *Itin.* II. 105 Letters from the Lords in England, requiring that no Captain should supply his Company with Passe-volants at pleasure. **1727-41** CHAMBERS *Cycl.*, *Pass-volant*, or *passe-volant*, a faggot, or a pretended soldier,.. whom the captain or colonel makes pass in review, or muster, to shew that his company is compleat, or to receive pay thereof to his own profit... In France the passe-volants are condemned to be marked on the cheek with a flower de luce.

pass-fail (equal stress), *a.* [f. PASS *v.* 17 + FAIL *v.* 14.] Of or pertaining to passing and failing (in an examination or the like); applied *spec.* to methods of assessing examination performance in terms simply of success or failure, without further reference to the individual standards attained.

1959 *Psychol. Rev.* LXVI. 62/2 Using a pass-fail scoring on all eighteen tests, the test-subject matrix was 91.8 per cent reproducible. **1963** *Times* 2 Dec. 11/7, I would like to suggest a Use of English paper on a five-point scale with no pass-fail line drawn. **1966** *Crimson-White* (Univ. of Alabama) 1 Dec. 4/3 On the last SRI poll, students were asked to give their opinion on a system known as 'pass-fail electives'. Under this system a student could take 2 or 3 electives while he was here at the University and not have to worry about his grade. **1970** *Times* 20 Apr. 2, I believe we have gained a great deal in suggesting grading instead of somewhat more rigid pass-fail standards. **1972** *Sat. Rev.* (U.S.) 4 Mar. 49/2 All courses are given on a pass/fail basis. **1973** *Harvard Law School Bull.* Apr. 18/2 A strictly pass-fail grading system.

‖**passglas** ('pasglas). Also **pass glas**, and in anglicized form **pass glass** (pɑːs glɑːs, pæs glæs). Pl. ‖**passgläser**, **pass glasses**. [Ger.] A tall, cylindrical drinking glass decorated with parallel rings or a spiral down its length.

1897 A. HARTSHORNE *Old Eng. Glasses* 68 Touching the Passglas, its usual type was a tall cylindrical vessel..spaced, by fine wheeled stringings, into divisions for measuring and controlling the drinking. *Ibid.*, Rembrandt,..in his portrait by himself at Dresden, holds up exactly such a Rhine-land Passglas. *Ibid.* 81 Certain rare Pass glasses are ornamented with figures of knaves from playing cards, painted in enamel on white grounds. **1907** E. DILLON *Glass* xvi. 273 The tall *pass*-glass..is dated 1662. **1926** W. BUCKLEY *European Glass* 54 The Pass-glas is a typical German form which was made chiefly during the 17th century. It is always cylindrical, and is decorated by a stringing which sometimes encircles the glass spirally and at other times forms a number of rings more or less equidistant from one another. **1942** *Burlington Mag.* Dec. 299/1 The vessels depicted in Dutch still-life paintings are in fact as often of German as of Italian form —the *Roemer*, the *Passglas*,..are as commonly seen as the Italianate 'winged' goblets. **1960** H. HAYWARD *Antique Coll.* 211/1 *Passglas*,..a German glass beaker encircled by a notched spiral thread dividing it into equal parts so that the glass could be passed from guest to guest allowing each his allotted share. **1965** A. VON SALDERN *German Enameled Glass* 145 Cylindrical Stangen with horizontal rings in multicolored enamel—so-called Pass glasses..are derived from similar glasses with applied rigaree bands or spirals; each horizontal ring is called a Pass... In drinking, the trick was to bring the wine or beer down exactly to the level of one of the rings.

'pass-guard. *Obs.* exc. *Hist.* Forms: 6–9 **pacegard(e, 7 pace-guard, 7– passguard, 8– pass guard, pass-guard,** (9 **passegarde, passgard**). [app. f. PASS *sb.*[2] 9 + GUARD *sb.* (Littré has F. *passe-garde* only as a neologism of 19th c.)

If *passe-garde* were Fr. it would necessarily mean 'that which is used to pass a guard' (see PASSE-); as an Eng. compound it would naturally mean 'the guard of a pass'.]

An item of ancient tilt armour; according to Hewitt, a separate piece provided to accompany the grandguard, being screwed upon the left elbow as an additional defence in the tournament; also called by recent writers *elbow-shield*.

a **1548** HALL *Chron., Hen. IV* 12 One sorte had the vambrases the pace gardes the grandgardes..parted with golde and azure. **1660** *Tower Survey* in *Archæol. Jrnl.* (1847) IV. 346 Sundry parcells of Tilt Armour..Pace-guards, viz. Russet, 7, White, 3:10. Granguards, viz. Russet, 7, White, 2:9. **1668** *Tower Survey* (in Hewitt) One compleat arm^r capape engraven with the ragged staffe with a maine-guard and passguard—made for the Earle of Leicester. **1876** J. HEWITT in *Stothard's Monum. Effigies Gt. Brit.* 190 This would seem to fix the name of passguard to the additional elbow-defence. **1898** VISCT. DILLON in *Archæol. Jrnl.* Ser. II. V. 313 The pasguard is also linched on a pin.

¶ By some writers on armour, followed by dictionaries, French and Eng., the name has been erroneously applied to the *garde-collet*, a raised ridge-like projection of the pauldron or shoulder-piece, to turn aside the blow of a lance, used on armour before and after 1500. See **1786** GROSE *Anc. Armour* 24; **1824** MEYRICK *Antient Armour* II. 228, III. Gloss.; **1846-60** FAIRHOLT *Costume* 225-6, and Glossary s.v. [corrected in ed. 1885]; **1874** BOUTELL *Arms & Arm.* ix. 155; Littré *Dict. Française* s.v. *Passe-garde*; and recent Dicts.

passh, passhion, obs. ff. PASCH, PASSION.

‖**pas si bête** (pɑ si bɛt). [Fr.] Not so foolish; 'not that stupid' (said of the speaker or of someone other than the speaker). Also (in quot. 1924), not so bad.

1840 THACKERAY in *Fraser's Mag.* June 727/2, I am not holding up the whole affair as a masterpiece—*pas si bête*. **1849** —— *Pendennis* I. xxix. 283 'Emily was always as stupid as an owl,' said Miss Blenkinsop. 'Eh! pas si bête,' the old Peer said. **1862** W. COLLINS *No Name* II. 82, I am not fool enough to open it. *Pas si bête*, as we used to say in the English circle at Zurich... *Pas si bête!* **1923** GALSWORTHY *Captures* 247 Why suppose one's family superior to other people's? *Pas si bête!* **1924** J. BUCHAN *Three Hostages* xii. 179 'What about the weather?' I asked anxiously. '*Pas si bête*,' he said, sniffing. 'The wind is pretty sure to go down.' **1939** N. MARSH *Overture to Death* xvi. 183 'Try us,' suggested the young man. 'Pas si bête,' said Alleyn, ' I want my lunch.' **1965** N. FREELING *Criminal Conversation* II. i. 102 You see how the parallel fails?.. *Pas si bête*.

passibility (pæsɪ'bɪlɪtɪ). [ad. late L. *passibilitās* (Arnobius), f. *passibilis*: see -ITY. Cf. F. *passibilité* (15th c.), OF. *passibleté*.] The quality of being passible; capability of suffering, or of receiving impressions from external agents.

a **1340** HAMPOLE *Psalter* lxv. 10 þou led vs in til þe snare of passibilite. **1398** TREVISA *Barth. De P. R.* VIII. i. (Bodl. MS.), þis worlde..schal passe touchinge þis passibilitie and kinde and schappe þat it haþ now3e, butte it schal abide euer-more touchinge þe substaunce. **1555** BONNER *Homilies* 69 The fourmes and qualities sensible, which in dede are subiecte to passibilitie. **1622** DONNE *Serm.* i. (1640) 2 He was defective in nothing; not in Power, as God, not in passibility, as man. **1893** FAIRBAIRN *Christ in Mod. Theol.* II. III. ii. 483 The very truth that came by Jesus Christ may be said to be summed up in the passibility of God.

†**b.** Passiveness; inaction; sloth. *Obs. rare.*

1456 SIR G. HAYE *Law Arms* (S.T.S.) 119 Sa kepis the vertu cardinale the activitee, or passibilitee of mannis governaunce in his lyf. **1526** *Pilgr. Perf.* (W. de W. 1531) 228 b, Shall brynge with them theyr olde grosnes, heuynes, & passibilite.

passible ('pæsɪb(ə)l), *a.* Also 7 *erron.* **-able.** [a. OF. *passible* (12th c. in Hatz.-Darm.), ad. late L. *passibilis* capable of feeling or suffering (Tert.), f. *pass-*, ppl. stem of *patī* to suffer: see -IBLE.]

1. Capable of suffering, liable to suffer; liable to impressions or feelings; susceptible of sensation or of emotion. (Chiefly *Theol.*)

a **1340** HAMPOLE *Psalter* lxxi. 5 He is in generations in passybles, þat ar of generations passiblis. **1382** WYCLIF *Acts* xxvi. 23 Whiche thingis the prophetis and Moyses spaken for to be comynge, if Crist passible [*gloss* or able to suffre]. **1491** CAXTON *Vitas Patrum* v. xi. (1495) 341/2 For the loue of the, he was made man passyble & mortall; whiche was Immortall & Impassyble. **1594** R. ASHLEY tr. *Loys le Roy* 101 Pythagoras was of opinion, that the first cause was not sensible, nor passible. **1691** BAXTER *Repl. Beverley* 6 The Paradise Saints have bodies of flesh, passible, and such as must have food. **1719** WATERLAND *Vind. Christ's Divinity* xxvi. (1720) 414. **1872** BUSHNELL *Serm. Living Subj.* 425 God is a being morally passible.

†**2.** Liable to suffer change or decay. *Obs.*

1390 GOWER *Conf.* II. 153 The Sonne and Mone eclipse bothe, That be hem lieve or be hem lothe, Thei soffre; and what thing is passible To ben a god is impossible. **1601** DEACON & WALKER *Spirits & Divels* 83 The aire is both passible, and corruptible, and may easily be corrupted and changed. **1655** STANLEY *Hist. Philos.* I. I. 15 That Bodies are passible and divisible, in infinitum, and continuous as are also a line, superficies, place, and time.

3. Capable of being suffered or felt. ? *Obs.*

1558 BP. WATSON *Sev. Sacram.* xv. 92 Although God doth punishe and afflict vs, yet he doth it not with passible anger. **1621** BURTON *Anat. Mel.* I. i. II. vi. (1651) 21 His [the Sensible Faculty's] object in general is a sensible or passible quality, because the sense is affected with it.

†**4.** = PASSIVE. *Obs. rare.*

c **1532** DU WES *Introd. Fr.* in *Palsgr.* 1057 What it is of understandyng actyve & passyble.

Hence **'passibleness** = PASSIBILITY. *rare.*

1614 BREREWOOD *Lang. & Relig.* xxv. 181 It [heresy of Eutiches and Dioscorus] drew after it, the heresie of the passiblenesse of the deitie. **1858** BUSHNELL *Serm. New Life* 347 After all there must be some kind of passibleness in God, else there could be no genuine character in him.

‖**Passiflora** (pæsɪ'flɔərə). *Bot.* [mod.L., f. L. *pass-* as stem of *passio* PASSION + *-flōrus* flowering. Formed by Linnæus, 1737, on the earlier L. name *flos passionis*, flower of the Passion.] The genus of plants containing the Passion-flower.

1763 *Chron.* in *Ann. Reg.* 105/2 The fruit of the Passiflora was cut in high perfection, at Castle-Howard, in Yorkshire ..the best of the tropical fruits. **1869** DARWIN in *Life & Lett.* III. 279 The elaborate series of *chevaux-de-frise*, by which the nectary of the common Passiflora is guarded.

Hence **passiflo'raceous** *a.*, pertaining to the *Passifloraceæ*, the Natural Order containing the Passion-flower. **passi'floral** *a.*, applied to the alliance (*Passiflorales*) of Natural Orders allied to *Passifloraceæ*. **passi'florine** *Chem.*, an alkaloid obtained from the root of the Passion-flower.

1846 LINDLEY *Veg. Kingd.* 333 *Passiflora quadrangularis* ..is said to owe its activity to a peculiar principle called Passiflorine. **1857** MAYNE *Expos. Lex.*, *Passiflorin*,..term for an alkali little known, which Ricord-Madiana has obtained from the roots of the *Passiflora*.

‖**passim** ('pæsɪm), *adv.* [L., = 'scatteredly', f. *passus* spread abroad, scattered; hence 'here and there, at random, anywhere, everywhere'.] A Latin word, used chiefly after the name of a book or author, to indicate the occurrence of something in various places throughout the book or writings. Rarely *attrib.* or quasi-*adj.*

1803 *Edin. Rev.* July 474 Our readers may find abundance of this..in these volumes, *passim*. **1821** BYRON *Juan* III. cxi, I'll prove that such the opinion of the critic is, From Aristotle *passim*. **1895** *Westm. Gaz.* 4 Sept. 2/3 In these *passim* allusions one often 'nods'.

passimeter (pə'sɪmɪtə(r)). Also (erron.) **passimetre.** [f. PASS *v.* or PASS(ENGER + -METER.] An automatic machine for supplying public transport passengers with tickets and recording the number of people who pass through.

1921 *Railway Gaz.* 2 Dec. 860/2 There are three separate registering cyclometers... The first registers the dating and cancellation of each ticket, setting the passenger free to proceed through the 'passimeter', whereby another cyclometer automatically records his passage. **1923** *Westm. Gaz.* 11 Aug. 6/4 Fifteen passimeters will be installed, and ..it is hoped..to eliminate booking queues. **1927** *Observer* 16 Jan. 18/2 The work of substituting passimeters for the booking offices is now in progress. **1928** *Daily Express* 10 May 9 What a contrast with the modern 'passimetre', the glitter of green and white tile, the silent motion of escalators! **1928** J. P. THOMAS *Handling London's Undergr. Traffic* xii. 156 The first passimeter booking-office was introduced at Kilburn Park in 1921. **1964** *Guardian* 26 June 5/2 Central London is to have six experimental 'standee' buses, on which a single coin fare will be placed in a 'passimeter'. *Ibid.* 1 Dec. 4/2 On the six fast 'standee' buses which London Transport hopes to introduce next year..the fare..will be placed in a 'passimeter'.

passing ('pɑːsɪŋ, -æ-), *vbl. sb.* [f. PASS *v.* + -ING[1].]

1. a. The action of the vb. PASS in various senses: going, going on, going by, going away, departing, dying; getting through an examination, going beyond, surpassing, etc.

in passing, by the way; in the course of some procedure, narrative, speech, etc.; parenthetically, = F. *en passant*.

a **1325** *Prose Psalter* cxv. 2 [cxvi. 11], Y said in my passing, Ich man is li3er. *a* **1340** HAMPOLE *Psalter* cxviii. [cxix.] 136 Passyngis of watirs led myn eghyn. **1387** TREVISA *Higden* (Rolls) I. 335 þere is no3t gret passynge and exces in [c]hele noþer in hete. *c* **1400** *Destr. Troy* xxxv. *heading*, Of Pyrrus and of his passyng ffrom Troy. **1512** in *Southwell Visit.* (1891) 115, I wyll that at the howre of my passyng the grettist bell in the church be rongen. **1691** T. H[ALE] *Acc. New Invent.* p. l, Mens passing about their Affairs in the Night. **1753** *Scots Mag.* Nov. 542/2 The question for the bill's passing was put. **1849** C. BRONTE *Shirley* vi, It may be remarked, in passing. **1869** TENNYSON (*title*) The Passing of Arthur. **1926** C. VAN VECHTEN *Nigger Heaven* 286 *Passing*, passing for white. **1952** L. MARQUARD *Peoples & Policies S. Afr.* iii. 77 Though..it is impossible to say how many coloured have succeeded in 'passing'—that is, in being fully accepted as European—'passing' has certainly occurred. **1952** M. STEEN *Phoenix Rising* vii. 176 Those who succeed in 'passing' live their lives in mortal terror of being found out. **1953** [see PASSER 4]. **1958** S. E. HYMAN in A. Dundes *Mother Wit* (1973) 46/2 The account of lynching, passing, discrimination, or varieties of resistance. **1961** *Guardian* 4 May 10/4 'Passing', the word used to describe Negroes merging indistinguishably into a white community in America. **1973** G. D. BERREMAN *Caste in Mod. World* 10/2 The response of *Burakumin* to their birth-ascribed status is that common to all low castes: accommodation on the most part, and occasional 'passing'... As in all societies passing is difficult and stressful, for the fear of discovery and the necessary loss or attenuation of family contacts are traumatic.

b. In causative senses: Causing or allowing to pass, carrying over, transportation, transference, carrying into law, uttering, pronouncing, etc.; *spec.* in ball games, the action of transferring (the ball) to another player (see sense 46 b of the vb.). Also *absol.*

1565 *Act 8 Eliz.* c. 13 §5 The Ordinary Passing and Carrying of the Queen's Majesty's People to and from as other Watermen..do. **1674** *Essex Papers* (Camden) I. 276 Neglecting to take any Securities upon ye passing of Wooll. **1692** SIR W. HOPE *Fencing-Master* (ed. 2) 79 My next Lesson is of Passing, or making of a Pass. **1739** LABELYE *Short Acc. Piers Westm. Bridge* p. iii, Before the passing the first Act for Building the Bridge. **1821** *Act 1 & 2 Geo. IV*, c. 64 §1 The passing of any Rogue, Vagabond,..or other idle and disorderly Person, to his or her Place of legal Settlement or Place of Birth. **1855** MACAULAY *Hist. Eng.* xv. III. 602 The passing of the sentence was therefore deferred. **1882** *Blackburn Times* 1 Apr. 6/3 While the Rovers worked their way towards their opponents' goal by passing, the Etonians did so by rushes. **1889** *Pauline* VIII. 38 Carter got in once more, owing to a good piece of passing between himself, Stokoe, and Browne. **1892** F. MARSHALL *Football* 121 For a time, passing was confined to the forwards exclusively, and was what is termed 'short' passing. **1906** GALLAHER & STEAD *Compl. Rugby Footballer* 85 A player's object in passing the ball is to give possession of it to a colleague who is in a better position for making further headway with it than he is himself. **1952** J. B. PICK *Phoenix Dict. Games* I. 63 This.. ensures that the passing will be precise. **1960** E. S. & W. J.

HIGHAM *High Speed Rugby* 5 A method of passing the ball in which the outside elbow is bent upwards.

c. A means of passing; a passing-place; a ford.

1872 TENNYSON *Gareth & Lynette* 597–8 O'er it [the river] are three passings, and three knights Defend the passings.

2. a. With advbs.: see PASS *v.* IV.

1387 TREVISA *Higden* (Rolls) VII. 193 Of whos ende and passing forþ it is expressid in þinges þat gooþ bifore. *c* **1410** LOVE *Bonavent. Mirr.* xliv. lf. 95 (Gibbs MS.) He þurstede bodyly by cause of þe gret passynge out of blode. **1573–80** BARET *Alv.* P 161 A passing ouer,..or carrieng ouer, *traiectio.* **1597** A. M. tr. *Guillemeau's Fr. Chirurg.* 48/1 These remedyes, which in passinge by, it seemed convenient vnto me to rehearse. **1726** LEONI *Alberti's Archit.* I. 74 Ants, with constant passing up and down, will wear traces even in flints. **1882–3** SCHAFF *Encycl. Relig. Knowl.* III. 1812 The passing-away of the educational enthusiasm.

b. With *off*: see sense 64 c of the vb.

1900 *Rep. Patent Cases* (Patent Office) 15 Aug. 482 In the *Yorkshire Relish* case the inference was drawn that the mere use of a name implied passing off. **1902** [see PASS v. 64 c]. **1908** *Westm. Gaz.* 30 Apr. 9/2 Damages were claimed by the plaintiff for alleged libel, and the passing off of a story written by her in 1895 and 1896. Defendants denied that there was any libel or passing off. **1959** *Times* 6 Feb. 17/1 His action against them for alleged libel and passing off. **1960** *Times* 20 Sept. (Pure Food Suppl.) p. i/5 There still remains ..the possibility of verbal passing-off at the time of sale. **1962** *Listener* 15 Mar. 457/1 We might..be called upon to change our law in respect of 'passing-off'. Broadly speaking, this is selling one's own goods or services in a way which deceives the public into thinking that they are those of some other trader. **1970** WHITE & JACOB *Patents* III. viii. 65 In an action for passing-off the plaintiff must in practice prove that he has extensive enough goodwill for his goods to be recognised by members of the public.

3. *concr.* A gold or silver thread made by winding a thin strip or ribbon of the metal about a core of silk. Cf. PASSEMENT.

1848 E. C. P. in C. H. Hartshorne *Eng. Medieval Embroidery* 113 A rich gold thread, called passing, or tambour. **1880** L. HIGGIN *Handbk. Embroidery* i. 8 *Gold and silver passing*, a very fine kind of thread. **1882** in CAULFEILD & SAWARD *Dict. Needlework*. **1899** W. G. P. TOWNSEND *Embroidery* iv. 73 A diaper in string worked over in gold passing. *Ibid.* v. 82 Gold and Silver Passing and Tambour. **1901** LEWIS F. DAY & MARY BUCKLE *Art in Needlework* xxix. (ed. 2) 245 Japanese gold does not tarnish so readily as 'passing'. **1957** M. B. PICKEN *Fashion Dict.* 349/2 *Passing*, smooth, flattened thread made by twisting strands of gold or silver around a strand of silk. **1960** B. SNOOK *Eng. Hist. Embroidery* 48 A very fine flexible metal thread called 'passing' was known to the Elizabethans.

4. a. *attrib.* and *Comb.*, as *passing knell*, †*peal*, *rule*; **passing-braid** (see quot.); **passing certificate**, a certificate of having passed an examination or the like; †**passing-close**, *Mus.*, an interrupted cadence; **passing door** *Mining*, an arrangement of doors in a gallery that enables people to pass through while preventing the free passage of air currents; **passing nippers** (see quot.); **passing novel** (see quot.); †**passing-penny** = *pass-penny* (PASS *sb.*[2] 18 b); hence allusively, a passport to the future world; **passing place**, a place where persons or things may pass; *spec.* (*a*) a ford, (*b*) a railway siding; (*c*) on a narrow or single track road; **passing-stroke**, *Croquet* (see quot.). Also PASSING-BELL.

1882 CAULFEILD & SAWARD *Dict. Needlework*, **Passing Braid*, a description of Braid employed in Embroidery, made with gold or silver thread, such as used on military uniforms. **1787** NELSON 20 July in Nicolas *Disp.* (1845) I. 248, I transmit to you a *Passing Certificate, with two Warrants, for Mr. James Ballentine. **1833** MARRYAT *P. Simple* xxxviii, My passing certificate was signed, and the captains did me the honour to shake hands with me, and wish me speedy promotion. **1597** MORLEY *Introd. Mus.* 127 They be *passing closes, which we commonly call false closes, being deuised to shun a final end and go on with some other purpose. **1839** URE *Dict. Arts* 989 *Passing doors.. may be substituted in any place for a passage where there is a stopping. **1798** SOUTHEY *Bishop Bruno* i, The sound it gave was his *passing knell. **1884** KNIGHT *Dict. Mech.* Suppl., **Passing Nippers* (Nautical), a strong hank of untwisted but mailed yarn used in binding the messenger to the cable. **1964** J. H. CLARKE *Harlem* 345 James Weldon Johnson..wrote '*passing' novels, i.e. novels about Negroes who were able to pass as whites. **1533** *Nottingham Rec.* IV. 202 For a *passyng pele xij *d.* **1651** JER. TAYLOR *Holy Dying* iv. §9 (1727) 178 It is good so to carry our *Passing-penny in our hand. **1716** B. CHURCH *Hist. Philip's War* (1867) II. 89 Maj. Church..ask'd the French men where their *passing Place was? **1841** *Penny Cycl.* XIX. 257/2 The manner in which switches are applied at passing-places and crossings. **1951** N. M. GUNN *Well at World's End* xxiv. 210 The lorry swung into a 'passing place' with squealing brakes. **1963** P. MACTYRE *Fish on Hook* v. 73 He pulled ponderously into the next passing-place, to allow the vehicle behind to overtake. **1972** *Times* 16 Oct. 13/6 It's a single track road, with passing places not very close together—and of course heavy lorries can't back. **1973** G. MOFFAT *Lady with Cool Eye* vii. 74 A narrow tarred track..only wide enough for one vehicle. At intervals there were passing-places. **1900** *Westm. Gaz.* 30 Apr. 8/1 The competing cars..streamed off in single file with strict injunctions as to observance of the *passing rule. **1901** *Scotsman* 16 Sept. 10/4 The '*passing stroke' is used when it is necessary that the player's ball should go further than the ball which has been roqueted.

b. With advbs., as *passing-off action*; *passing-out examination, inspection, parade*; *passing-through ritual.*

1925 F. I. SCHECHTER *Hist. Found. Law Trade-Marks* i. 10 Lord Chancellor Halsbury, in analyzing the plaintiff's pleadings in a 'passing-off' action, stated that such an action 'has been a well recognized cause of action, certainly for the last two hundred and fifty years'. **1946** *Nature* 2 Nov. 604/1 Traders were obliged to rely on cumbersome and expensive passing-off actions to protect their name and goods. **1970** WHITE & JACOB *Patents* III. viii. 66 Many businesses do not keep their trade marks fully and validly registered, so that resort to a passing-off action may always be necessary to cover flaws in the trade-mark position. **1976** *Century of Trade Marks* (Patent Office) i. 2/2 In France..there is at least one recorded instance in the 16th Century of what would be called today a passing-off action, in which the defendant was subjected to a perpetual injunction and made to pay heavy costs. **1916** *Daily Colonist* (Victoria, B.C.) 28 July 4/7 He came out first in the recent passing-out examinations. **1973** *Soviet Weekly* 5 May 2/3 Moscow School of Choreography..has begun its passing-out examinations. **1930** *Times Educ. Suppl.* 2 Aug. 340/3 The passing-out inspection of aircraft apprentices..was held on Tuesday. **1955** *Times* 11 Aug. 6/5 The Sudan defence force to-day held the first passing-out parade of officer cadets since the Sudanization of the force. **1971** B. W. ALDISS *Soldier Erect* 156 The C.O. of Kanchapur spoke to us on passing-out parade. **1973** 'S. HARVESTER' *Corner of Playground* I. v. 38 Officer cadets due to receive their commissions at the passing-out parade. **1969** *Times* 19 Mar. 4/4 The wedding ring and the custom of the groom carrying his bride over the threshold may be relics of the 'passing through' rituals.

'passing, *ppl. a.* (*adv.* and *prep.*) [f. PASS *v.* + -ING[2].]

A. *ppl. adj.* **1.** That goes or passes by.

c **1330** R. BRUNNE *Chron. Wace* (Rolls) 3297 Al day of passande men þey herd. **1398** TREVISA *Barth. De P.R.* XVII. cxlii. (Bodl. MS.), Passinge men comeþ: and beþ ispoyled and robbed and ofte slayne. **1697** DRYDEN *Virg. Georg.* IV. 679 Th' Infernal Troops like passing Shadows glide. **1794** SOUTHEY *Wat Tyler* II. i, The green corn waves to the passing gale. **1850** TENNYSON *In Mem.* Concl. xxvi, The shade of passing thought. **1874** L. STEPHEN *Hours in Library* (1892) I. i. 26 Some passing traveller from distant lands.

2. a. That passes away or elapses; of time or things measured by time: transient, transitory, temporary, fleeting; ephemeral, vanishing.

a **1340** HAMPOLE *Psalter* v. 14 Þis luf is noght passand bot lastand. **1387–8** T. USK *Test. Love* II. viii. (Skeat) l. 102 How passing is the beautie of flesshly bodyes, more flyttinge than mouable floures of sommer. **1398** TREVISA *Barth. De P.R.* IX. ii. (Bodl. MS.), Noþinge is..more passinge þanne tyme, for tyme resteþ neuere. **1567** HARMAN *Caveat* xi. 55 When they had thus wrong water out of a flint in spoyling him of his euyl gotten goods, his passing pens, and fleting trashe. **1709** STEELE *Tatler* No. 15 ¶ 1 The History of the passing Day. **1899** A. AUSTIN in *Daily News* 16 Nov. 4/5 The confounding of the Passing with the Permanent.

b. Done, given, etc., in passing; cursory.

1750 GRAY *Elegy* 80 Some frail memorial..Implores the passing tribute of a sigh. **1806** CALLCOTT *Mus. Gram.* vi. 66 The Passing Shake is expressed in Germany by a particular character. **1819** *Pantologia, Passing-shake*, a short trill, made *en passant*, in flowing passages of quavers or semiquavers, without..interrupting the natural course of the melody. **1828** SCOTT *F. M. Perth* xxvii, Few opportunities..of exchanging even such passing greetings. **1862** MILL *Utilit.* 8 A passing remark is all that needs be given.

c. *passing show*, the spectacle of contemporary life; an entertainment using as material current events and interests, a revue.

1908 *Sears, Roebuck Catal.* 1047/3 A whole passing show. .. Your friends grotesquely photographed... By getting a focus on passing pedestrians, horses, cars, etc., the most ludicrous pictures are witnessed. **1915** (*title of journal*) The passing show. **1915** A. WIMPERIS (*title of revue*) Passing show. **1956** *B.B.C. Handbk.* 1957 31 To keep the listener fully in touch with the 'passing show' of contemporary life. **1968** *N.Y. City* (Michelin Tire Corp.) 81 In 1864, Tony Pastor's Opera House made vaudeville fashionable...the 'revue' or 'passing show' caught on in the 90's. **1976** *Scottish Rev.* Summer 9 Reason tends to be hostile to the passing show, tends to view reality as an eternity of fixed types amenable to the eye of reason.

3. Surpassing, pre-eminent; transcendent; extreme. *Obs.* or *arch.*

c **1375** *Sc. Leg. Saints* xxxi. (*Eugenia*) 342 Quhat passand luf til hym scho had. *c* **1386** CHAUCER *Can. Yeom. Prol.* 61 He is a man heigh of discrecioun I warne yow wel he is a passyng man. **1523** SKELTON *Garl. Laurell* 841 The passynge bounte of your noble astate. **1577** HARRISON *England* II. xiii. (1877) I. 254 Tokens..of passing workemanship. **1591** SHAKS. *Two Gent.* I. ii. 17 Pardon deare Madam, 'tis a passing shame. **1632** J. HAYWARD tr. *Biondi's Eromena* 195 To the passing content of her grandparents.

4. Having the charge of testing and passing candidates; examining.

1788 NELSON 26 Dec. in Nicolas *Disp.* (1845) I. 277 On his going to be Examined..the Passing Captains had refused to examine him. **1840** MARRYAT *Olla Podr.* III. 28 The passing captains..suffered from the heat of the weather.

B. *adv.* **a.** (= PASSINGLY). In a passing or surpassing degree; surpassingly, pre-eminently, in the highest degree; exceedingly, very. (With adjs. or advbs. only.) Now somewhat *arch.*

1387 TREVISA *Higden* (Rolls) II. 411 Þan Menelaus.. gadrede passyng strong men. **1465** *Paston Lett.* II. 216 He gave the baly of Cossey..a passyng gret rebuke. **1470–85** MALORY *Arthur* VII. xviii, Hee hath done passyng ylle and shamefully. **1510–20** *Everyman* in Hazl. *Dodsley* I. 128 It pleaseth God passing well. **1596** HARINGTON *Metam. Ajax* (1814) 66 Vitellius who is noted to haue been a passing great eater. **1770** GOLDSM. *Des. Vill.* 142 A man he was..passing rich with forty pounds a year. **1786** MME. D'ARBLAY *Diary* 8 Nov., I liked them all passing well. **1837** DISRAELI *Venetia* II. i, Strange, passing strange indeed, and bitter! **1891** T. HARDY *Tess* xli. (1900) 100/2 It would be passing mean to enrich herself by a legal title to them which was not essentially hers at all.

†**b.** *passing old*: of advanced age, superannuated.

1456 SIR G. HAYE *Law Arms* 96 Quhethir a passand alde ancien man be law of armes may be haldin prisoner.

C. quasi-*prep.* Uses in which the pr. pple. (governing an object) through some ellipsis approaches the character of a preposition with its object. (The participial character remains more perceptible in 2, 3, than in 1.)

†**1.** Beyond (some definite measure or number), more than. After 1500 app. only with negative: *not passing*, not more than. *Obs.* or *arch.*

1377 LANGL. *P. Pl.* B. v. 422, I haue be prest and parsoun passynge thretti wynter. **1393** *Ibid.* C. XXIII. 218 Proude preostes cam with hym passend an hundred. **1418** *26 Pol. Rel. & L. Poems* (E.E.T.S.) 63 Þat borweþ moche he geteþ hate, Spende waste passyng his rent. *c* **1483** *Chron. London* (1827) 116 The whiche hadde nought passyng ye fytynge men with them. **1545** RAYNOLD *Byrth Mankynde* 68 To a woman geue neuer passyng a drame at once of safrane. **1585** T. WASHINGTON tr. *Nicholay's Voy.* I. xix. 22 The trenches of the Salaris beeing not passing 150. paces from the Castle. **1685** H. MORE *Paralip. Prophet.* ix. 57 He was not passing fifty nine years when he died. **1767** *Woman of Fashion* I. 24 It is not passing four Month's ago, that I must needs..let my Girl go to an Assembly.

†**2.** Beyond in degree, to a greater degree than, more or better than; also, in preference to, rather than. *Obs.*

c **1386** CHAUCER *Frankl. T.* 201 He syngeth, daunceth, passynge any man That is or was sith þat the world bigan. *c* **1400** MAUNDEV. (Roxb.) xi. 44 He gert sla his wyf, whilk he luffed passand all oþer creatures. **1539** [see PASS *v.* 37].

†**3.** Beyond the limit, range, or compass of; so as to surpass; as in *passing measure*, beyond measure. *Obs.*

c **1449** PECOCK *Repr.* (Rolls) I. 36 Thenne he dide a maistrie passing his power. **1561** T. HOBY tr. *Castiglione's Courtyer* III. (1577) Q v, Men paste feare, and hardie passing measure. **1830** TENNYSON *Talking Oak* 58 The slight sheslips of loyal blood, And others, passing praise.

passingalia: see PASSACAGLIA.

'passing-,bell. [f. PASSING *vbl. sb.* (cf. PASS *v.* 11) + BELL *sb.*[1]] 'The bell which rings at the hour of departure, to obtain prayers for the passing soul: often used for the bell which rings immediately after death' (J.); = DEATH-BELL.

The name still survives, but only in rare cases is the bell now rung until after death. See *N. & Q.* 10th ser. I. 308, 350, 3rd ser. II. 246. For the original use, cf. *Constit. & Canons* (1603) lxvii, And when any is passing out of this life, a bell shall be tolled, and the Minister shall not then slack to do his last duty. And after the party's death, if it so fall out, there shall be rung no more than one short peal, and one other before the burial, and one other after the burial.

1526 in Ellacombe *Ch. Bells Devon* (1872) 463 The clerke to have for tollynge of the passynge belle,..if it be in the day, *os.* 4*d.* ? *c* **1600** *Distracted Emp.* v. i. in Bullen *O. Pl.* III. 243 If I but chaunce to toule his passinge bell And give the parryshe notyce who is dead. **1604** DONNE *To Sir H. Wotton going to V.* iv, As prayers ascend To Heaven in troops, at a good man's passing-bell. **1691** NORRIS *Pract. Disc.* 149 If his Senses hold out so long, he can hear even his Passing-Bell without disturbance. **1731** SWIFT *On his Death*, Before the passing-bell begun, The news through half the town has run. **1795** SOUTHEY *Joan of Arc* I. 332 More mournfully than dirge or passing bell, The joyous carol came. **1866** MONSELL *Passing Bell* i Listen! it is the Passing Bell. Lift up thy heart to God and pray. A soul is passing,—who can tell How prayer may help it on its way.

b. *fig.* That which forebodes or signalizes the death or passing away of anything; the 'knell'.

1577 WHETSTONE *Remembr. Gascoigne* xxv, The Swan in songs, dooth knolle her passing bel. **1696** BROOKHOUSE *Temple Open.* 62 The Sounding of the Seventh Angel, Is the worlds Passing Bell. **1819** KEATS *Lamia* II. 39 Knowing well That but a moment's thought is passion's passing bell. **1821** SHELLEY *Hellas* 669 And my solemn thunder knell Should ring to the world the passing bell Of tyranny!

'passing-by. *rare.* [See PASSING *vbl. sb.* 2.]

†**a.** = PASSOVER. *Obs.*

1533 TINDALE *Supper of Lord* D iij b, Where is this geste chamber where I myghte eate the passing by with my disciples?

b. The action of ignoring or neglecting.

1909 *Westm. Gaz.* 6 May 8/3 The ousting of home-bred meat, and the passing-by of the market by the great importers.

passingeoure, -ger, obs. forms of PASSENGER.

passingly ('pɑːsɪŋlɪ, -æ-), *adv.* [f. PASSING *ppl. a.* + -LY[2].] In a passing manner. **a.** For the time, temporarily (*obs.*); in passing, cursorily.

a **1340** HAMPOLE *Psalter* xlviii. 1 Þat ȝe here not passandly, all þat wonnys þe warld. **1340** *Ayenb.* 172 Þe zeneȝere ssel guo in-to his house..naȝt pasindeliche ase þe iogelour þat ne bleſþ naȝt bleþeliche in his house. **1530** PALSGR. 383 All these actes be but passyngly brought in. **1684** in Wodrow *Hist. Ch. Scot.* (1722) II. III. viii. 388 Not having been for several Years there, but passingly. **1836** *Fraser's Mag.* XIV. 633 They are passingly noticed in the last stanza. **1891** G. MEREDITH *One of our Conq.* II. xii. 289 Victor commented passingly on the soundness of them.

b. In a surpassing degree or manner, surpassingly; pre-eminently, exceedingly; = PASSING *adv.* (qualifying adj., adv., vb.). *arch.*

c **1380** WYCLIF *Wks.* (1880) 315 Þei ben passyngliche holy. **1387** TREVISA *Higden* (Rolls) VII. 483 Oon preysed hym in metre passingliche in þis manere. *c* **1450** *St. Cuthbert*

(Surtees) 2537 Passandly sho loued cuthbert. **1470–85** Malory *Arthur* iii. iii, He was passyngly wel vysaged and passyngly wel made. **1587** M. Grove *Pelops & Hipp.* (1878) 56 She loues their wisdome passinglie. **1638** Ford *Fancies* iv. i, You, forsooth,.. were contented, Passingly pleased. **1887** *Harper's Mag.* June 37, I, who thought myself so strong, am passingly weak.

passing-measure, var. passemeasure *Obs.*

ˈpassingness. [f. passing *ppl. a.* + -ness.] Passing quality; transitoriness.

1839 Bailey *Festus* vi. (1852) 68 Feelings so serene and sweet,.. That they can make amends for their passingness. **1865** Neale *Hymns Glor. Parad.* (1866) 10 Here they live in endless being, Passingness hath passed away.

ˈpassing-ˌnote. *Mus.* A note not belonging to the harmony, interposed between two notes essential to it, for the purpose of passing smoothly from one to the other. Sometimes also applied to *auxiliary notes* (see auxiliary *a.* 2 b).

1730 *Short Treat. Harmony* v. 28 We make use of the Second, the Seventh, and of the Fourth as Discords or Passing Notes. **1776** Burney *Hist. Music* (1789) I. ii. 39 Merely.. a passing-note serving only to lead more smoothly to the sixth. **1875** Ouseley *Princ. Harmony* xviii. 199 'Passing notes' should be regarded as nothing more than embellishments. **1898** Stainer & Barrett *Dict. Mus. Terms* s.v., It is a necessary characteristic of a passing-note, that it should have a degree of the scale on each side of it.

passion (ˈpæʃən), *sb.* Also 2–6 -iun, -ioun, -yo(u)n, etc., 4 pascioun. [a. OF. *passiun, passion*, ad. L. *passiōn-em* suffering (Tertullian, etc.), n. of action f. *patī, pass-* to suffer. In L. chiefly a word of Christian theology, which was also its earliest use in Fr. and Eng., being very frequent in the earliest ME.]

I. The suffering of pain.

1. a. (Now usually with capital.) The sufferings of Jesus Christ on the Cross (also often including the Agony in Gethsemane). Formerly also in *pl.*

Cross of Passion, in Heraldry: see quots. ***Instruments of the Passion***, the cross, the crown of thorns, the nails, scourge, etc.

c **1175** *Lamb. Hom.* 119 Vre drihtnes halie passiun, þet is his halie þrowunge þe he for mancunne underfeng. *a* **1225** *St. Marher.* 1 Efter ure louerdes pine, ant his passiun. *c* **1290** *S. Eng. Leg.* I. 15/472 Riȝt þane wei þat ore louerd ȝeode toward is passioun. **1340** *Ayenb.* 12 Þe uerthe article belongeþ to his passion. **1382** Wyclif *Acts* i. 3 To which and he ȝaf [1388 schewide] hym silf alyue after his passioun. [So all 16–17th c. versions.] **1526** Tindale *1 Pet.* i. 11 The passions that shulde come vnto Christ. **1547** Boorde *Introd. Knowl.* xxxix. (1870) 220 The mount of Caluery, where Iesu Chryst did suffer his passions. **1548–9** (Mar.) *Bk. Com. Prayer, Litany*, By thy crosse and passion,.. Good lorde deliuer us. **1666** Pepys *Diary* 3 Nov., This morning comes Mr. Lovett, and brings me my print of the Passion, varnished by him. **1682** J. Gibbon *Introd. ad Lat. Blason.* 76 A long Cross: Bara makes it like a Cross of Passion, that is, the Traverse beam a pretty deal below the top of the palar part. **1725** Coats *Dict. Her.* s.v., *Cross of the Passion*.. not crossed in the Middle but somewhat below the Top, with Arms short in proportion to the Length of the Shaft. **1754** Sherlock *Disc.* (1759) I. vii. 211 As if the Remission of our Sins was to be ascribed peculiarly to the Passion. **1839** *Encycl. Brit.* (ed. 7) XIX. 428/1 Pictured representations of the fourteen stages of our Lord's passion. **1845** G. A. Poole *Churches* vi. 48 The font of North Somercoats, Lincolnshire, has on two of its sides shields charged with the instruments of the passion.

†b. Used allusively in asseverations; also *transf.* applied by persons to themselves, as in ***passion of me, my heart, my soul***. Obs.

c **1386** Chaucer *Shipman's Prol.* 13 A-bide for godis digne passion. *c* **1530** *Hickscorner* in Hazl. *Dodsley* I. 168 Help, help, for the passion of my soul. **1570** Preston *Cambyses* I. 180 O' the passion of God, I have done. **1601** B. Jonson *Ev. Man in Hum.* (Q.) iii. iii. 127 Gods passion, and I had twise so many cares, as you haue, I'ld drowne them all in a cup of sacke. **1601** Shaks. *All's Well* v. ii. 43 Cox my passion, giue me your hand. **1684** Meriton *Yorksh. Dial.* 477 Pashions a Life! here'st Land-lord just at deaur. **1738** tr. *Guazzo's Art Conversation* 24 Passion o' me! Who will then carry my Corn to Mill?

c. The narrative of the sufferings of Christ from the Gospels; also, a musical or dramatic setting of this; cf. *passion-play*.

a **1300** *Cursor M.* 8844 Þus sais sum opinion, Bot sua sais noght þe passion. *a* **1533** Ld. Berners *Huon* cxlix. 566 After that your deuyne seruyce be done, and the passyon of our lorde Iesu Chryste red. **1823** W. Hone *Anc. Mysteries Described* 169 In 1298, the passion was played at Friuli. **1844** Lingard *Anglo-Sax. Ch.* (1858) II. ix. 64 That every deacon read two passions. **1880** in Grove *Dict. Mus.* II. 664/2 Until the latter half of the 16th century the Passion was always sung.. by the three Deacons alone. *Ibid.* 666/1 Bach['s] .. 'Passion according to S. Matthew' is.. the finest work of the kind. **1903** E. K. Chambers *Mediæval Stage* II. xxii. 129 There were performances of Passions in Reading in 1508, in Dublin in 1528, [etc.]. **1962** R. Southern *Seven Ages of Theatre* 107 The *Passion* of Mons may well have run to ninety-eight separate representations of 'scenes'.

†d. Passion-tide or Passion Week. *Obs.*

1297 R. Glouc. (Rolls) 10178 Þe Sonenday of þe passion. *Ibid.* 11330 Wiþinne þe passion Wiþ is ost he wende uorþ & arerde is dragon.

2. a. The sufferings of a martyr, martyrdom. *arch.*

a **1225** *St. Marher.* 1 Her beginneð þe liflade & te passiun of seinte margarete. **1377** Langl. *P. Pl.* B. xv. 265 What penaunce and pouerte and passioun þei [the saints] suffred. *c* **1440** Capgrave *Life St. Kath.* v. 1668 The emperour commaunded.. Thei shulde be led on-to her passyon. **1503** *Gold. Leg.* Colophon, The lyues passyons and myracles of many other sayntes. **1672** Cave *Prim. Chr.* i. vii. (1673) 160 The great reverence they had for Martyrs. Their passions stiled their Birthday. **1754–8** T. Newton *Observ. Proph., Dan.* xii. 204 Cyprian ordered the passions of the Martyrs in Africa to be registred. **1901** T. R. Glover *Life & Lett. 4th Cent.* 250 With the martyrs came their relics, the tales of their passions, their tombs and their images.

transf. **1598** B. Jonson *Ev. Man in Hum.* iii. iv, A fasting-day no sooner comes, but.. poore cobs they smoke for it, they are made martyrs o' the gridiron, they melt in passion.

b. A narrative account of the passion of a martyr.

1904 T. Shearman *Veneration of S. Agnes* 90 Helen of Rossow, or Roswitha, a Benedictine nun of the Convent of Gandersheim, Saxony, wrote poems in the 10th century, 'to replace,' as she says in her preface, 'the pagan passions which dishonour the profane drama, by the triumphs of the Christian heroines, the chaste spouses who are admitted to the Nuptials of the Lamb.' **1913** E. R. Barker *Rome of Pilgrims* xiii. 183 In an eighth-century manuscript there is a note that Passions are to be read at Office in the Church of S. Peter. *Ibid.* xiv. 192 It is always the conventional version of a Passion which is reproduced in numerous manuscripts. *Ibid.* 195 For this saint.. there exists not only the contemporary Passion, but also a series of records. **1927** F. J. E. Raby *Hist. Christian-Latin Poetry* ii. 56 His poem was used as a basis for later prose passions of Cassian.

†3. Suffering or affliction generally. *Obs.*

a **1225** *Ancr. R.* 188 In all ower passiuns, þencheð euer inwardliche up o Godes pinen. *a* **1340** Hampole *Psalter* xv. 7 In wrangis & temptaciouns & passions. **14..** in *Tundale's Vis.* (1843) 130 Sche was exempt from all such passyon [of travail]. **1509** Hawes *Conv. Swearers* xliv, The wounde of synne to me is more passyon Than the wounde of my syde for thy redempcyon. **1606** Shaks. *Ant. & Cl.* v. i. 63 Giue her what comforts The quality of her passion shall require. **1656** H. Vaughan *Thalia Rediv., Nativ.* 15 Great type of passions! Come what will, Thy grief exceeds all copies still.

4. a. A painful affection or disorder of the body or of some part of it. *Obs.* exc. in certain phrases, as ***colic, hysteric(al, iliac, sciatic passion***, for which see the adjs.

1382 Wyclif *Lev.* xv. 13 If he were helid, that suffreth siche a maner passioun [L. *hujusmodi passionem*]. **1398–1856** [see iliac 1]. **1460** Capgrave *Chron.* (Rolls) 40 Asa, Kyng of Juda.. had sore feet, whech passioune our bokys sey it was podegra. **1529** Wolsey in *Four C. Eng. Lett.* 10 Beyng entereyd into the passyon of the dropsy. **1547** Boorde *Brev. Health* (1557) 33 In latyn it is named *Ventralis passio*. In English.. the belly ache, or a passion in the belly. **1563** T. Gale *Antidot.* ii. 29 It is of ryght good effecte in the passions of the ioyntes. **1684** tr. *Bonet's Merc. Compit.* xvi. 566 Thirst is a Passion of the Mouth of the Stomach. **1822–34** [see hysteric 1].

†b. A violent access, attack, or fit of disease.

1390 Gower *Conf.* III. 7 As a drunke man I swerve, And suffre such a Passion. **1641** Hinde *J. Bruen* xlvii. 150 His fits and passions were much after this manner.

II. The fact of being acted upon, the being passive. [Late L. *passio*, used to render Gr. πάθος.]

5. a. The fact or condition of being acted upon or affected by external agency; subjection to external force: = affection *sb.* 1; †an effect or impression produced by action from without. Now *rare* or *Obs.*

c **1374** Chaucer *Boeth.* v. met. iv. 130 (Camb. MS.) The passion, þat is to seyn þe suffraunce or the wit in the qwyke body goth byforn exitinge and moeuynge the strengthis of the thoght. **1413** *Pilgr. Sowle* (Caxton 1483) v. xiv. 108 Al that is done withouten might, it lacketh the dignyte and the name of dede, but it is cleped passion. **1530** Palsgr. 111 Verbes meanes.. betoken neyther action nor passion. **1610** Guillim *Heraldry* iii. iii. (1660) 109 The.. brightnesse of these [Sun and Moon] is.. subject to the passion of darkning or eclipsing. **1668** Wilkins *Real Char.* iii. i. 303 That kind of word.. adjoyned to a Verb, to signifie the quality and affection of the Action or Passion, is stiled an Adverb. **1725** Watts *Logic* i. iv. §7 The word passion signifies the receiving any action, in a large philosophical sense. **1846** Trench *Mirac.* xxxiii. (1862) 470 That work shall be the work of passion rather than of action.

†b. A way in which a thing is or may be affected by external agency; a passive quality, property, or attribute; = affection 11, 12. *Obs.*

1570 Billingsley *Euclid* i. xxxiv. 44 In this Theoreme, are demonstrated three passions or properties of parallelogrammes. **1610** B. Jonson *Alch.* ii. v, What's the proper passion of mettalls? **1657** W. Morice *Coena quasi Κοινή* Diat. iii. 139 Frigidity is the proper passion of water, which is sometime accidentally hot. **1690** Leybourn *Curs. Math.* 330 Of certain Passions and Properties of the Five Regular Bodies. **1707** Floyer *Physic. Pulse-Watch* 209 The different Manners.. produc'd by a particular hot or cold Diet, or Air, Exercise, and Passions peculiar to each Nation.

III. An affection of the mind. [L. *passio* = Gr. πάθος.]

6. a. Any kind of feeling by which the mind is powerfully affected or moved; a vehement, commanding, or overpowering emotion; in psychology and art, any mode in which the mind is affected or acted upon (whether vehemently or not), as ambition, avarice, desire, hope, fear, love, hatred, joy, grief, anger, revenge. Sometimes personified.

c **1374** Chaucer *Troylus* iv. 676 (704) As she þat al þis mene while brende Of oþer passion þan þat þey wende. **1526** *Pilgr. Perf.* (W. de W. 1531) 118 He wyll stere vp in his soule yͤ passyons of ire & impacyency. **1528** Tindale *Obed. Chr. Man* Wks. (Parker Soc.) I. 246 A poor woman with child, which longed, and, being overcome of her passion, ate flesh on a Friday. **1591** Shaks. *1 Hen. VI*, v. ii. 18 Of all base passions, Feare is most accurst. **1611** Bible *Acts* xiv. 15 We also are men of like passions with you. **1647** Cowley *Mistr., Passions* i, From Hate, Fear, Hope, Anger, and Envy free, And all the Passions else that be. **1710** Norris *Chr. Prud.* vii. 323 By the Passions I think we are to understand certain Motions of the Mind depending upon and accompanied with an Agitation of the Spirits. **1732** Pope *Ep. Bathurst* 154 The ruling Passion conquers Reason still. **1791** Mrs. Radcliffe *Rom. Forest* i, A man whose passions often overcame his reason. **1797** *Encycl. Brit.* (ed. 3) XIV. 2/1 The common division of the passions into *desire* and *aversion*, *hope* and *fear*, *joy* and *grief*, *love* and *hatred*, has been mentioned by every author who has treated of them. *Ibid.* 14/2 Passions, in painting, are the external expressions of the different dispositions and affections of the mind; but particularly their different effects upon the several features of the face. **1843** Prescott *Mexico* vi. viii. (1864) 401 It were as easy to curb the hurricane in its fury, as the passions of an infuriated horde of savages. **1872** Ruskin *Eagle's N.* §169 Their reverence for the passion, and their guardianship of the purity, of Love.

b. Without article or *pl.*: Commanding, vehement, or overpowering feeling or emotion.

1590 Spenser *F.Q.* i. v. 1 Such restlesse passion did all night torment The flaming corage of that Faery knight. **1604** Shaks. *Oth.* iv. i. 277 Is this the Nature Whom Passion could not shake? **1678** South *Serm.* (1697) II. x. 434 Passion is the Drunkenness of the Mind. **1724** De Foe *Mem. Cavalier* (1840) 3 He told me, with a great deal of passion, that he loved me above all the rest. **1770** Wesley *Lett., to J. Benson* 5 Oct., Passion and prejudice govern the world. **1901** H. Black *Culture & Restraint* iv. 106 Philosophy is a feeble antagonist before passion.

c. A fit or mood marked by stress of feeling or abandonment to emotion; a transport of excited feeling; an outburst of feeling.

1590 Spenser *F.Q.* i. i. 49 In this great passion of unwonted lust, Or wonted feare of doing ought amis, He starteth up. **1599** Chapman *Hum. Day's Mirth* Plays 1873 I. 92 Come, come, leave your passions, they cannot moove mee. **1628** Hobbes *Thucyd.* (1822) 119 They sent these men thither in passion. **1725** Pope *Odyss.* iv. 150 From the brave youth the streaming passion broke. **1854** Milman *Lat. Chr.* vii. ii. (1864) IV. 98 Henry fell on his knees and in a passion of grief entreated her merciful interference. **1856** W. Collins *After Dark* (1862) 214 She burst into an hysterical passion of weeping.

d. A poem, literary composition, or passage marked by deep or strong emotion; a passionate speech or outburst. *Obs.* or *arch.*

1582 T. Watson *Centurie of Loue* i. *heading*, The Authour in this Passion taketh.. occasion to open his estate in loue. **1590** Shaks. *Mids. N.* v. i. 321 Heere she comes, and her passion ends the play. **1599** Massinger, etc. *Old Law* i. i. Wks. (Rtldg.) 416/1 These very passions I speak to my father. [Gifford *note* These pathetic speeches.] **1614** Tomkis *Albumazar* ii. i. in Hazl. *Dodsley* XI. 327 Not a one shakes his tail, but I sigh out a passion. **1871** Browning *Balaustion* 193 Now it was some whole passion of a play.

7. a. *spec.* An outburst of anger or bad temper.

1530 Palsgr. 320/1 Passyonate, inclyned sone to be in a passyon. **1590** Spenser *F.Q.* ii. iv. 11 It's eath.. to.. calme the tempest of his passion wood. **1688** Miege *Fr. Dict.* s.v. *Bring*, To bring a Man in a passion [*transporté de colère*] to himself. **1731** *Gentl. Mag.* I. 391/1 This put Bluster into such a Passion, that he quitted the Surgery in a Pet. **1773** Johnson in *Boswell* 28 Aug., Warburton kept his temper all along, while Lowth was in a passion. **1819** *Metropolis* II. 212 She chose, woman-like,.. to fly in a passion and to abuse the sheriff's officer. **1842** Browning *Pied Piper* x, And folks who put me in a passion May find me pipe after another fashion.

b. Without *a*: Impassioned anger, angry feeling.

1524 Wolsey *Let. to Knight* in Strype *Eccl. Mem.* (1721) I. i. iv. 57 Whatsoever they might speak in passion or otherwise. **1605** Chapman *All Fooles* iv. i. 125, I pray you good Gostanzo, Take truce with passion. **1628** Hobbes *Thucyd.* (1822) 37 [To] undergo the danger with them and that without passion against you. **1729** Butler *Serm. Resentm.* Wks. 1874 II. 98 Passion; to which some men are liable, in the same way as others are to the epilepsy. **1798** Southey *Cross Roads* xviii, Passion made his dark face turn white. **1882** J. Parker *Apost. Life* I. 143 We can stifle the hot word of passion.

8. a. Amorous feeling; strong sexual affection; love; †also in *pl.*, amorous feelings or desires. Often ***tender passion***.

1588 Shaks. *Tit. A.* ii. i. 36 My sword.. shall.. plead my passions for Lauinia's loue. **1590** Spenser *F.Q.* iii. v. 30 But, when shee better him beheld, shee grew Full of soft passion and unwonted smart. **1592** Shaks. *Rom. & Jul.* ii. Prol. 13 Passion lends them Power, time, meanes to meete. **1658** Phillips, *Passion*,.. an affection of the mind,.. in Poems and Romances it is more peculiarly taken for the passion of love. **1710** Steele *Tatler* No. 128 ¶4 Fairest Unknown.. I have conceived a most extraordinary Passion for you. **1752** Fielding *Amelia* ii. i, I declared myself the most wretched of all martyrs to this tender passion. **1855** Milman *Lat. Chr.* ix. viii. (1864) V. 413 Seized with a poetic passion for Eudoxia, wife of William.

b. *transf.* An object of love, a beloved person.

1783 Lady Suffolk in *Lett. C'tess S.* (1824) II. 275 Lord Buckingham's former passions go off very quickly: poor Lady Northampton is dead. **1842** Thackeray *Fitz-Boodle Papers* Wks. (Biogr. ed.) IV. 295 Whenever one of my passions comes into a room, my cheeks flush.

9. Sexual desire or impulse.

1641 Wilkins *Math. Magick* i. i. (1648) 2 Which set a man at liberty from his lusts and passions. **1667** Milton *P.L.* i. 454 Sions daughters.. Whose wanton passions in the sacred Porch Ezekiel saw. **1798** Malthus *Popul.* iii. iii. (1806) II. 132 Delaying the gratification of passion from a sense of duty. **1842** Longf. *Quadroon Girl* x, He knew whose passions gave her life, Whose blood ran in her veins.

10. a. An eager outreaching of the mind towards something; an overmastering zeal or enthusiasm for a special object; a vehement predilection.

1638 BAKER tr. *Balzac's Lett.* (vol. II.) 70 Concerning his passion of horses, which he calls his malady.. never counsell him to cure it. **1671** tr. *Frejus' Voy. Mauritania* 1 A passion of meriting the esteem of a considerable Company of Merchants. **1708** SWIFT *Sentiments Ch. Eng. Man* Wks. 1755 II. I. 61 That mighty passion for the church, which some men pretend [etc.]. **1780** COWPER *Lett.* 8 May, The passion for landscape-drawing. **1838** MISS MITFORD in L'Estrange *Life* (1870) III. vi. 89 My present passion is for indigenous orchises. **1874** GREEN *Short Hist.* iv. §2. 169 The growing passion for the possession of land.

b. *transf.* An aim or object pursued with zeal.

1732 POPE *Ess. Man* II. 261 Whate'er the Passion, knowledge, fame, or pelf. **1856** FROUDE *Hist. Eng.* (1858) I. i. 69 The drama was the passion of the people. **1874** BANCROFT *Footpr. Time* i. 81 To rule was her passion. **1883** H. DRUMMOND *Nat. Law Spir. W.* I. i. (1884) 4 The pursuit of Law became the passion of science. *Mod.* Golf has become a passion with him.

11. *attrib.* and *Comb.* **a.** simple attrib., as ***passion-fever***, ***-fit***, ***-monger***, ***-pitch***, ***-verse***, ***-wave***; objective and instrumental, as ***passion-blazing***, ***-breather***, ***-kindling***, ***-thrilling***, and esp. with any pa. pple. of suitable sense, as ***passion-clouded***, ***-coloured***, ***-dimmed***, ***distracted***, ***-driven***, ***-filled***, ***-frantic***, ***-guided***, ***-kindled***, ***-led***, ***-pale***, ***-pastured***, ***-plunged***, ***-ridden***, ***-shaken***, ***-smitten***, ***-stirred***, ***-stung***, ***-swayed***, ***-torn***, ***-tossed***, ***-wasted***, ***-wearied***, ***-winged***, ***-worn***; also ***passion-like***, ***-proud*** adjs.; ***passion-wise*** adv.

1894 *Outing* (U.S.) XXIII. 362/1 Then turns his *passion-blazing eye and stamps impotently with shackled feet. **1925** W. B. YEATS *Vision* III. 183 Aristophanes' *passion-clouded eye. **1899** —— *Wind among Reeds* 26 Because your crying brings to my mind *Passion-dimmed eyes and long heavy hair. **1899** CROCKETT *Kit Kennedy* 406 Curious freaks of violent and *passion-driven men. **1877** M. ARNOLD *Last Ess. on Ch. & Relig.* 22 The *Passion-filled reasoning and rhetoric of Pascal. **1842** FABER *Styrian Lake*, etc. 105 When in a *passion-fit I spoke. **1916** A. HUXLEY *Burning Wheel* 29 So, troubled, *passion-frantic, The poet's mind boils gold and amethyst. *a* **1644** QUARLES *Sol. Recant.* Sol. iv. 63 A self-conceipt may bribe Thy *passion-guided Will to take up Arms 'Gainst soveraign Reason. *a* **1835** MRS. HEMANS *Poems, Genius singing to Love*, The *passion-kindled melody Might seem to gush from Sappho's fervent heart. **1799** CAMPBELL *Pleas. Hope* I. 121 Congenial Hope! thy *passion-kindling power, How bright, how strong, in youth's untroubled hour! **1893** F. GREENWOOD *Lover's Lex.* 275 Then we shall be at peace from the *passion-mongers. **1889** O. WILDE in *19th Cent.* Jan. 47 The *passion-pale face of Andromeda. *c* **1865** G. M. HOPKINS *Voice from World* in *Poems* (1967) 125 How turn my *passion-pastured thought To gentle manna and simple bread? **1879** BLACK *Macleod of D.* xxxvii, Your feelings supposed to be always up at *passion-pitch. **1876** G. M. HOPKINS *Wreck of Deutschland* xxxiii, in *Poems* (1967) 62 Our *passion-plungèd giant risen, The Christ of the Father compassionate, fetched in the storm of his strides. **1592** GREENE *Disput.* Wks. (Grosart) X. 241, I began to waxe *passion-proud. **1606** SYLVESTER *Du Bartas* II. iv. II. *Magnificence* 510 O why is my Minde More *passion-stirred, then my hand is strong? **1605** *Ibid.* II. iii. IV. *Captains* 1070 What Sea more apt to swell Then is th' unbridled Vulgar, *passion-toss't? **1880** O. CRAWFURD *Portugal* 369 Modern *passion-verse generally in its lyric form. **1799** COLERIDGE *Lines in Concert Room* ii, Nature's *passion-warbled plaint. **1881** O. WILDE *Poems* 4 With *passion-wearied face. **1821** SHELLEY *Adonais* ix, The *passion-wingèd ministers of thought. **1814** SOUTHEY *Roderick* xiv, One countenance So strongly mark'd, so *passion-worn.

b. Special Combs.: †**passion-banner**, a banner inscribed with the tokens of Christ's Passion; **Passion cross**, see quot. and *Cross of Passion* in 1; †**passion-day**, the day on which a martyr suffered; **passion-fruit**, the edible fruit of some species of Passion-flower, esp. *Passiflora edulis*, the granadilla, which produces egg-shaped fruit with reddish-purple, slightly wrinkled skin and sweet yellow pulp surrounding small black seeds; **passion killers** *slang* (see quots.); **passion-lettuce**, an early kind of spring lettuce; **passion-music**, music to which the narrative of the Passion is set (cf. 1 c); so **passion-oratorio**; **passion play**, a mystery-play representing the Passion of Christ; also *transf.*; **passion-tide**, a tide or flow of passion; see also PASSION-TIDE; **passion-tree**, a species of Passion-flower cultivated for its fruit; **passion vine** = PASSION-FLOWER; **passion wagon** *slang* (see quot. 1948). Also PASSION SUNDAY, PASSION WEEK;

1552 *Inventory* in *Ecclesiologist* XVII. 125 A *passion banner of red sarsnet. **1780** EDMONDSON *Her.* II. Gloss., **Passion Cross*, the same as the *Cross Calvary*. *Cross Calvary*,.. the *Cross of the Passion*. **1882** CUSSANS *Hand-bk. Her.* iv. 60 The Latin Cross is sometimes called a *Passion Cross*; but in the latter, all the limbs should be couped, that is the top and bottom of the Cross should not touch the extremities of the shield while still retaining the distinctive features of the Latin Cross. **1672** CAVE *Prim. Chr.* I. vii. (1673) 204 We celebrate the *passion days of the Martyrs. **1752** H. WALPOLE *Lett.* (1846) II. 454 A garden of Eden, from which.. my sister-in-law long ago gathered *passion-fruit. **1867** R. HENNING *Let.* 18 Feb. (1966) 234, I have also been making some passionfruit jelly. **1881** MRS. C. PRAED *Policy & P.* I. 145 A high fence.. overgrown with passion-fruit. **1908** E. J. BANFIELD *Confessions of Beachcomber* I. vi. 192 There may be some who do not know that the humble papaw.. belongs to the passion-fruit family. **1934** T. WOOD *Cobbers* xvii. 217 Passion fruit, squeezed into a wineglass, mixed with cream and sugar and a spoonful of sherry, has a rich smoothness. **1961** L. VAN DER POST *Heart of Hunter* I. ii. 27 His old lady, dark and wrinkled with age like a passion fruit about to fall. **1969** *Oxf. Bk. Food Plants* 98/1 Passion Fruit or Purple Granadilla (*Passiflora edulis*). A perennial climbing plant, originally native to Brazil but now widely planted in the tropics, it is also sufficiently hardy to be grown in some Mediterranean countries. **1974** *Herald* (Melbourne) 5 Apr. 23/1 Pavlova,.. a crusty meringue-like sweet-cake made from egg whites and sugar and topped with whipped cream and, usually, passionfruit. **1976** *Observer* 17 Oct. 36/3 (Advt.), Easy to grow delicious passion fruits. Our own specially cultivated pot-grown species of Granadilla for fruiting in Britain. **1977** 'E. CRISPIN' *Glimpses of Moon* xii. 235 The infant Grand Duchess.. lisps a request for a glass of.. passion-fruit juice. **1943** C. H. WARD-JACKSON *Piece of Cake* 47 **Passion killers*, service knickers issued to airwomen. **1946** J. IRVING *Royal Navalese* 136 An elastic-bound bifurcated undergarment said to be worn in the women's Services and known.. as 'passion-killers'. **1974** *Times* 17 Dec. 12/5 Stout fleecy lined drawers.. which would have been called by this generation 'passion-killers'. **1707** MORTIMER *Husb.* (1721) II. 148 Another sort of Lettices, called *Passion Lettice, prosper well in light Ground. **1880** W. S. ROCKSTRO in *Grove's Dict. Mus.* II. 665 Here then we have the first idea of the '*Passion Oratorio'. **1870** in J. Brown *Lett.* (1912) 378 I was very much touched by the *Passion-play, and wrote some very bad verses at Ammergau. **1873** *Baedeker's South. Germany* (ed. 3) 128 Ober-Ammergau, celebrated for the passion-plays performed there every ten years. **1965** B. SWEET-ESCOTT *Baker St. Irreg.* iii. 90 It turned out to be.. the ritual passion play on the 10th of the month of Muharram which commemorates the death of Hassan. **1975** *Listener* 10 Apr. 472/3 Going to Oberammergau to the Passion Play. **1825** D. L. RICHARDSON *Sonn.* 27 While its *passion-tides serener flow. **1741** *Compl. Fam.-Piece* II. iii. 362 If you now plant, and make Layers of the *Passion-tree, in most Places, it will make it bear Fruit. **1853** 'P. PAXTON' *Stray Yankee in Texas* 57 The '*passion vine' with its singular flower and luscious fruit. **1862** R. HENNING *Let.* 23 Sept. (1966) 100 A veranda covered with passion-vine and a garden full of petunias in most brilliant flower. **1892** *Daily News* 27 Aug. 3/1 A dish of the edible fruit of the passion vine. **1946** *Coast to Coast 1945* 64 Let his girls dig in the orchard or chip around the passion-vines. **1957** M. WEST *Kundu* ii. 19 A passion vine trailing over a bamboo summer-house. **1969** *West Australians* 5 July 41/7 (Advt.), Nellie Kelly the amazing grafted passion vine. **1948** PARTRIDGE *Dict. Forces' Slang* 137 **Passion waggon*, truck taking men for a day's, or part of a day's, leave, into a town or place of entertainment. **1961** *New Left Rev.* Jan.-Feb. 24/2 He knows every girl who comes out the base on Saturday on the passion-wagon.

passion ('pæʃən), *v.* [a. OF. *passionner* (Godef.), f. *passion* PASSION *sb.*]

1. *trans.* To affect or imbue with passion.

c **1468** *Paston Lett.* II. 324 The seyd Fastolf, mevyd and passyoned gretely in his soule, seyd and swar by Cryst ys sides [etc.]. **1567** FENTON *Trag. Disc.* Ded., To see the follye of a foolishe lover passioninge himselfe uppon creditt. **1590** SPENSER *F.Q.* II. ix. 41 Great wonder had the knight to see the mayd So straungely passioned. **1818** KEATS *Endym.* I. 248 For whose soul-soothing quiet, turtles Passion their voices cooingly. **1886** W. ALEXANDER *St. August. Holiday* 214 The land where Jordan passioneth His poetry of waterfalls night and day.

†**b.** To move or impel by passion. *Obs. rare*$^{-1}$.

1502 *Ord. Crysten Men* (W. de W. 1506) I. vii. 67 That he be inclyned and passyoned to take vengeaunce.

c. To express with passion or deep feeling.

1884 W. C. SMITH *Kildrostan* I. iii. 6 In the old home.. She sits alone, and passions her sharp pain.

†**2.** To affect with suffering, to afflict. *Obs.*

1491 CAXTON *Vitas Patr.* (W. de W. 1495) II. 205/1 A dyscyple of his that was sore passyoned & tourmented of a greuous maladye. **1576** BAKER *Jewell of Health* 125 b, It especially helpeth the strangurie and those passioned with the stone. *a* **1626** BP. ANDREWES *Serm., Passion* i. (1661) 221 Whom.. in body and soul.. they have pierced and passioned.. on the Cross.

3. *intr.* To show, express, or be affected by passion or deep feeling; formerly *esp.* to sorrow.

1588 SHAKS. *L.L.L.* I. i. 264. **1591** —— *Two Gent.* IV. iv. 172 'Twas Ariadne, passioning For Theseus periury, and vniust flight. **1598** CHAPMAN *Bl. Beggar Alex.* Plays 1873 I. 33 How now Queene, what art thou doing, passioning over the picture of Cleanthes? **1610** SHAKS. *Temp.* v. i. 24 Shall not my selfe, One of their kinde.. Passion as they? **1819** KEATS *Lamia* I. 182 She stood.. By a clear pool, wherein she passioned To see herself escaped from so sore ills. **1870** *Gd. Words* 418 Larks passioning hung o'er their brooding wives. **1887** W. SHARP *Shelley* 98 There can be few of us who.. so passion for this passion as did Shelley.

Hence **'passioning** *vbl. sb.*

1844 MRS. BROWNING *Vis. Poets* cxxxv, Burns, with pungent passionings Set in his eyes. **1900** S. PHILLIPS *Paolo & Francesca* 102 Your blood is crimson with my passioning.

†**'passionable,** *a. Obs. rare.* [a. F. *passionnable*, f. *passion.*] Subject to passion; passionate.

1571 CAMPION *Hist. Irel.* II. ix. (1633) 106 Kildare was open and passionable, in his moode desperate. **1575** G. HARVEY *Letter-bk.* (Camden) 92 An inflamid passionable minde.

passional ('pæʃənəl), *sb.* (Also in L. form.) [ad. med.L. *passiōnāle*, neuter of *passiōnālis* (see next) of or pertaining to passion, to the Passion, used as sb. = *liber passionalis* (Du Cange).]

1. A book containing accounts of the sufferings of saints and martyrs, for reading on their festival days.

1650 G. LANGBAINE in *Ussher's Lett.* (1686) 552 A good old Book, which was sometime the Passional of the Monastery of Ramesey. **1849** [see PASSIONARY]. **1882** *Ch. Q. Rev.* 276 Missals, Troparies, Passionals, Hymnaries, Collectaria, and Benedictionals. **1887** *Chicago Advance* 27 Oct. 674, 53d chap. [of Isaiah] known since the days of Polycarp.. as the Golden Passional. **1901** A. C. WELCH *Anselm & his Wk.* v. 89 The Archbishop.. ordered Osbern .. to have a passionale composed to his memory.

†**b.** *fig.* A story of suffering or woe. *Obs. rare.*

a **1500** *Colkelbie Sow* Prohem. 19 Quhat is the warld without plesance or play Bot passionale?

2. 'A manuscript of the four Gospels, upon which the kings of England, from Henry I. to Edward VI., took the coronation oath' (Shipley *Gloss. Eccl. Terms* 1872).

passional ('pæʃənəl), *a.* [ad. late L. *passiōnāl-is* (Tertullian), f. *passiōn-em* PASSION: see -AL[1]. Cf. OF. *passionnel*, *-al*, inspired by passion, causing suffering.] Of or pertaining to passion or the passions; inspired by or imbued with passion; characterized by passion.

1700 J. WODROW in R. Wodrow *Life* (1828) 35 This is rational, the other passional. **1845** O. A. BROWNSON *Wks.* VI. 37 The Fourierists.. place.. the passional nature.. at the summit of the psychical hierarchy. **1857** MAYNE REID *War-Trail* xiv, Three elements or classes of feeling: the moral, the intellectual, and what I may term the passional. **1867** F. PARKMAN *Jesuits N. Amer.* xiv. (1875) 175 A mystic of the intense and passional school.

†**'passionar.** *Obs.* [a. OF. *passion(n)er*, *-ier*, ad. med.L. *passiōnārium*, *-ārius*: see next. (Med.L. *passionerius* was from the Fr.)] = next.

14.. *Nominale* in Wr.-Wülcker 720/6 *Hic passionerius*, a passyonar.

passionary ('pæʃənərı). [ad. med.L. *passiōnārium*, *-us*, f. *passiōn-em* PASSION: see -ARY. Cf. mod.F. *passionnaire.*] = PASSIONAL *sb.* 1.

c **1475** *Pict. Voc.* in Wr.-Wülcker 755/16 *Hoc passionari[um]*, a passionari. **1513** BRADSHAW *St. Werburge* I. 694 As declareth the true Passyonary A boke wherin her holy lyfe wryten is. **1774** WARTON *Hist. Eng. Poetry* xxvii. (1840) II. 371 The passionaries of the female saints, Werburgh, Ethelred, and Sexburgh, which were kept for public edification in the choir of the church. **1853** ROCK *Ch. of Fathers* IV. xii. 212 The Passional, or Passionary, had in it the lives of martyrs and saints.

passionate ('pæʃənət), *a.* (*sb.*) [ad. med.L. *passiōnātus*, corresponding to F. *passionné* (Pr. *passionado*, It. *passionato*), pa. pple. of *passionner*: see PASSION *v.*]

1. Easily moved to angry passion or wrath; prone to anger, hot-tempered, irascible.

c **1450** tr. *De Imitatione* II. iii. 43 A passionat man turniþ good into euel... A gode pesible man drawiþ all þinges to good. **1530** PALSGR. 320/1 Passyonate, inclyned sone to be in a passyon. **1613** CHAPMAN *Bussy D'Ambois* Plays 1873 II. 142 Homer made Achilles passionate, Wrathfull, revengefull, and insatiate In his affections. **1781** COWPER *Friendship* 64 A temper passionate and fierce May suddenly your joys disperse At one immense explosion. **1841** MACAULAY *Ess., L. Hunt* (1887) 614 Though passionate and often wrong-headed, he [Collier] was a singularly fair controversialist.

†**b.** Possessed by angry passion, enraged, angry.

a **1500** *Colkelbie Sow* 903 Susan angrit heirat, as oft woman is, Quhile passionat that all consaitis kennis, Tuk in disdane this gift. **1628** HOBBES *Thucyd.* (1822) 39 Men.. are more passionate for injustice than for violence. *c* **1817** HOGG *Tales & Sk.* I. 278 He was violently passionate when he conceived himself wronged.

c. Of language, etc.: Marked by angry passion, angry, wrathful.

1590 SHAKS. *Mids. N.* III. ii. 220, I am amazed at your passionate words. **1693** J. EDWARDS *Author. O. & N. Test.* 240 This passionate expletive. **1711** STEELE *Spect.* No. 107 ¶1 To vent peevish Expressions, or give passionate or inconsistent Orders. **1879** MCCARTHY *Own Times* II. xx. 93 The debates were long, fierce, and often passionate.

2. Of persons: Affected with passion or vehement emotion; dominated by intense or impassioned feeling; enthusiastic, ardently desirous; †zealously devoted, attached, or loyal (*obs.*).

1526 *Pilgr. Perf.* (W. de W. 1531) 51 To renne hedlynge without feare vpon all ieopardyes, as communly passionate persones doth. **1650** JER. TAYLOR *Holy Living* ii. §2 (1727) 65 That by enkindling thy desire to heavenly banquets, thou may'st be indifferent and less passionate for the earthly. **1651** HOBBES *Leviath.* II. xxiv. 127 Cicero, (a passionate defender of Liberty). **1671** tr. *Frejus' Voy. Mauritania* 15, I am.. Your Majesties most Humble, most Obedient, and Passionate Servant. **1805** SOUTHEY *Madoc in W.* x. ii, He.. swept with passionate hand the ringing harp. **1845** S. AUSTIN *Ranke's Hist. Ref.* III. 573 Her husband's house and garden were daily thronged with her passionate admirers. **1879** FROUDE *Cæsar* xiv. 215 The army was now passionate for an engagement.

b. Of language, etc.: Imbued with passion, marked or characterized by strong emotion; expressive of strong emotion, impassioned.

1581 SIDNEY *Apol. Poetrie* (Arb.) 22 Their passionate describing of passions. **1655** FULLER *Ch. Hist.* IV. iii. §42 To these he made a passionate speech, to exhort them to unite. **1771** *Junius Lett.* lviii. 303 Forgive this passionate language. **1845** STODDART in *Encycl. Metrop.* (1847) I. 174/1 The interjection rises from a scarcely articulate sound to a passionate, and almost to an enunciative sentence.

c. Of an emotion: Vehement.

1567 DRANT *Horace* To Rdr., The one thicke powdered wyth manly passionat pangs, the other watered wyth wominishe teares. **1589** GREENE *Menaphon* Ded. (Arb.) 3 By such passionate sorowes. **1660** F. BROOKE tr. *Le Blanc's Trav.* 243 They bear a passionate affection to their Princes. **1813** MAR. EDGEWORTH *Patron.* vi, His declaration of passionate attachment to Caroline. **1818** SOUTHEY *Ode Death Q. Charlotte* iii, With a passionate sorrow we bewail'd Youth on the untimely bier.

3. Subject to passion; swayed by the passions or emotions; easily moved to strong feeling; impressible, susceptible; of changeful mood.

1589 PUTTENHAM *Eng. Poesie* I. xii. (Arb.) 44 To make him [God] ambitious of honour,..angrie, vindicatiue,.. indigent of mans worships: finally so passionate as in effect he shold be altogether *Anthropopathis*. *a* **1619** FLETCHER *Wit without Money* II. iv, Thou art passionate; Hast thou been brought up with girls? *c* **1622** FORD, etc. *Witch Edmonton* II. ii, You..have the power To make me passionate as an April day; Now smile, then weep; now pale, then crimson red. **1685** SOUTH *Serm.* (1697) I. 466 God will not..admit of the Passionate man's Apology, That he has so long given his Unruly Passions their Head, that he cannot now Govern or Controul them. **1877** MRS. OLIPHANT *Makers Flor.* iii. 78 Those hot and sudden friendships which men of passionate temper rush into.

†4. *spec.* Affected with the passion of love, dominated or swayed by the 'tender passion'. *Obs.*

1589 GREENE *Menaphon* (Arb.) 32 Seeing by the shepheards passionate lookes, that the swain was halfe in loue. **1632** SHIRLEY *Changes* I. ii, My wife is passionate and affects this Knight. **1704** STEELE *Lying Lover* I. (1747) 18 Judge..what the condition of a passionate Man must be, that can approach the hand only of her he dies for.

†5. Moved with sorrow; grieved, sad, sorrowful.

1586 A. DAY *Eng. Secretary* I. (1625) 118 These things.. permit you not, for such losse of riches, possessions, children or friends to become passionate. **1595** SHAKS. *John* II. i. 544 She is sad and passionate at your highness Tent. **1613** CHAPMAN *Bussy D'Ambois* Plays 1873 II. 157 Be not so passionate; rise, cease your tears. **1665** SIR T. HERBERT *Trav.* (1677) 71 Ecbar (who loved him dearly) becomes so passionate, that for..some time [he] refused to be comforted.

b. Inclined to pity, compassionate. Now *dial.*

1594 SHAKS. *Rich. III*, I. iv. 121, I hope this passionate humor of mine, will change, It was wont to hold me but while one tels twenty. **1658** GURNALL *Chr. in Arm.* verse 16. iii. (1679) 190/2 Them that have had the longest and passionatest treaty of mercy. **1903** *Eng. Dial. Dict.*, (Dorsetshire) Master's very good to his workpeople, he's so pash'nate.

†c. That moves to compassion, pitiful. *Obs.*

a **1586** SIDNEY *Arcadia* III. (1590) 294b, Melting with compassion at so passionate a sight. **1595** SPENSER *Col. Clout* 427 In tragick plaints and passionate mischance.

B. *sb.* (elliptical use.) One who is influenced by passion, †*esp.* one who is in love (*obs.*).

1651 tr. *De-las-Coveras' Don Fenise* 78 It came into my fancie to give a serenade to my wife, counterfeiting the amorous passionate. **1751** RICHARDSON *Corr.* (1804) III. 182 When the passionates (forgive the word) break fences, leap from windows, climb walls, swim rivers. **1819** J. HODGSON in J. Raine *Mem.* (1857) I. 234, I could..have joined the passionates in clapping.

†**'passionate**, *v. Obs.* [f. F. *passionner* = It. *passionare*, f. *passion* PASSION *sb.*: see -ATE[3] 6.]

1. *trans.* To excite or imbue with passion, or with a particular passion, as love, fear, wrath, etc.

1566 PAINTER *Pal. Pleas.* I. 107b, This traitour.. passionated not with Loue, but rather with rage and fury. **1612** CAPT. SMITH *Proc. Virginia* 88 It shall not so much passionate me, but I will doe my best for my worst maligner. **1652** BENLOWES *Theoph.*, *Pestill for Author*, Beaumont and Fletcher coyn'd a golden Way T'expresse, suspend, and passionate a play. **1658** tr. *Bergerac's Satyr. Char.* xi. 38 Thaile passionate an elegie by interrupted sobbs.

2. To express or perform with passion.

1567 PAINTER *Pal. Pleas.* II. 330 Nowe leaue we this amorous Hermite, to passionate & plaine his misfortune. **1588** SHAKS. *Titus A.* III. ii. 6 Thy Neece and I..want our hands And cannot passionate our tenfold griefe, With foulded Armes. **1615** G. SANDYS *Trav.* 246 Play-houses, where the parts of women are acted by women, and too naturally passionated.

3. To desire passionately.

1652 LOVEDAY tr. *Calprenede's Cassandra* I. 2 The Knight ..whom powerfull Reasons obliged to passionate the others Ruin.

4. To compassionate.

1638 BAKER tr. *Balzac's Lett.* (1654) II. 48, I finde more contentment in your passionating me.

Hence **'passionating** *vbl. sb.* (in quot. exciting of angry passions).

1598 BARRET *Theor. Warres* II. i. 28 If there be any banding, secting or passionating among them, he is to appease and compound the same.

passionately ('pæʃənətlı), *adv.* [f. PASSIONATE *a.* + -LY[2].] In a passionate manner.

1. With passion or intensity of feeling; enthusiastically, ardently; †zealously, with zealous attachment (*obs.*).

1590 GREENE *Never too late* (1600) 18 As I begun passionately, I breake off abruptly. **1624** DK. BUCKHM. in Ellis *Orig. Lett.* Ser. I. III. 180 Being pasionatelie in love. **1667** FLAVEL *Saint Indeed* (1754) 111 David was so passionately moved for Absalom. **1711** STEELE *Spect.* No. 168 ¶5 Many a..Hand, which the fond Mother has passionately kissed. **1801** FOSTER in *Life & Corr.* (1846) I. 135 Passionately fond of conversation. **1856** FROUDE *Hist. Eng.* (1858) I. ii. 139.

†2. With sorrowful emotion, sadly. *Obs.*

1599 MASSINGER, etc. *Old Law* III. i. Wks. (Rtldg.) 426/2 *Gnoth.* Oh, wife, wife! *Aga.* What ail you, man, you speak so passionately? *Gnoth.* 'Tis for thy sake, sweet wife.

3. With angry feeling, wrathfully; with heat.

1665 SIR T. HERBERT *Trav.* (1677) 334 They saved some ..but those our Boats took up resented our dealing so passionately as they seem'd more willing to be drown'd. **1692** LOCKE *Educ.* §67 They lay the Blame on the poor little Ones, sometimes passionately enough. *a* **1901** BESANT *Five Years' Tryst* (1902) 41 'Man! I must be paid for the risks I run!' He spoke passionately. He raised his voice.

passionateness ('pæʃənətnıs). [f. as prec. + -NESS.] The quality or condition of being passionate; susceptibility to passion; intensity or vehemence of emotion; susceptibility to anger; wrathfulness, irascibility.

1648 BOYLE *Seraph. Love* i. Wks. 1772 I. 249 To love even with some passionateness the person you would marry, is not only allowable but expedient. *Ibid.* iv. 255 Seraphic Love (whose passionateness is its best complexion). **1868** E. EDWARDS *Ralegh* I. Introd. 33 A passionateness of self-assertion. **1884** J. PARKER *Apost. Life* III. 51 This man concerns himself burningly, and with passionateness and fanaticism, respecting things that are not of the earth and of time.

†**'passionative**, *a. Obs. rare.* [f. PASSIONATE *v.* or *a.* + -IVE: see -ATIVE.] Having the character of passionating: a. Subject to passionate desire; b. Of impassioning nature or tendency.

1593 NASHE *Christ's T.* G ij b, God forbid I shold be so Luciferous passionative-ambitious. *a* **1678** WOODHEAD *Holy Living* (1688) 185 The more enjoying and passionative part performed chiefly by the will.

passion-dock. *local.* [app. f. PASSION *sb.* + DOCK *sb.*[1]: but cf. PATIENCE 4.] The plant Bistort (*Polygonum Bistorta*): see PASSIONS.

1828 *Craven Gloss.* s.v. *Patience Dock*, The leaves of the passion dock were a principal ingredient in herb puddings, which were formerly made..in this district, about the season of the passion. **1870** HAZLITT *Brand's Pop. Antiq.* I. 89 (*Good Friday*), In the North of England, they [used to] make a herb-pudding, composed, among other ingredients, of the passion-dock, on this day.

passioned ('pæʃənd), *ppl. a.* [f. PASSION *v.* or *sb.* + -ED. Cf. F. *passionné*, med.L. *passiōnātus*.]

1. Affected with or possessed by passion; marked by or indicating passion; = PASSIONATE *a.* 2.

1587 *Sir F. Drake's W. Ind. Voy.* in *Hakluyt's Voy.* (1811) IV. 17 Wherewith the Generall being greatly passioned, commaunded the Prouest Martiall to cause a couple of Friers then prisoners..presently to be hanged. **1589** *Reg. Privy Council Scot.* Ser. I. IV. 424 We have nocht shawne oure selff..rashe passioned. **1818** KEATS *Endym.* II. 201 Nor sigh of his, nor plaint, nor passion'd moan. **1824** J. GILCHRIST *Etym. Interpreter* 76 All words that have any import..are obviously distinguishable into passioned and unimpassioned..: the one indicate thoughts, the other sentiments. **1866** RUSKIN *Eth. Dust* 211 The purest and most mightily passioned human souls.

†2. Affected with suffering or sorrow; grieved, sad; = PASSIONATE *a.* 5. *Obs.*

1591 PERCIVALL *Sp. Dict.*, *Apassionado*, sicke, greeued, passioned. **1633** T. ADAMS *Exp. 2 Pet.* i. 17 Between the passioned powers of his soul, and whatsoever might refresh him, there was a traverse drawn.

Hence **'passionedly** *adv.*, passionately.

1611 COTGR., *Passionnément*, passionately, passionedly.

'passion-flower. [f. PASSION *sb.* 1 + FLOWER; in 16th c. L. *flos passionis*, Sp. *flor de la pasion*, F. *fleur de la passion*: see quot. 1885.] The name of plants of the genus *Passiflora*, consisting mostly of climbing shrubs, many of which have an edible fruit; so called because the parts of the flower, etc., were fancifully thought to resemble the instruments of Christ's Passion, or suggest its attendant circumstances.

[**1582** MONARDES *Simplic. Medicament. ex Novo Orbe* 16-17. **1613** PURCHAS *Pilgrimage* VIII. ii. 616 The flower of the Granadille they say..hath the marks of the Passion, Nailes, Pillar, Whippes, Thornes, Wounds.] **1633** JOHNSON *Gerarde's Herbal* (1636) 1591 Maracoc or Passion Floure. The Spanish Friers for some imaginarie resemblances..first called it *Flos Passionis*. **1792** MAR. RIDDELL *Voy. Madeira* 100 Three species of passion flowers are found in this island. **1833** WHITTIER *Toussaint L'Ouverture* 17 The passion-flower, with symbol holy, Twining its tendrils long and lowly. **1885** *Encycl. Brit.* XVIII. 343/1 The name passionflower—*flos passionis*—arose from the supposed resemblance of the corona to the crown of thorns, and of the other parts of the flower to the nails, or wounds, while the five sepals and five petals were taken to symbolize the ten apostles,—Peter..and Judas..being left out of the reckoning.

passionful ('pæʃənfʊl), *a. rare.* [f. PASSION *sb.* + -FUL.]

†1. Full of suffering, sorrowful. *Obs. rare*$^{-1}$.

1605 A. WOTTON *Answ. Pop. Articles* 55 In this passionful agony and agonizing griefe.

2. a. Full of passion, passionate.

1881 FAIRBAIRN *Stud. Life Christ* v. 86 A queen..strong, passionful, pitiless. **1885** *Blackw. Mag.* July 138 Shaking the senate with peals of passionful thunder.

b. Subject to or susceptible to passion.

1902 *Amer. Anthropologist* Jan.-Mar. 33 The savage man conceived the diverse bodies collectively constituting his environment..to be living, thinking, willing, passionful beings.

3. Full of anger, wrathful.

1901 'ZACK' *Tales Dunstable Weir* 187 'You mustn't go like that', she burst out, passionful.

Hence **'passionfulness**, the state or quality of being passionful.

1922 *Glasgow Herald* 16 Dec. 10/6 Several members..by their passionfullness of heart and uncontrollable spirit had ..broken the order and decorum of the House of Commons.

Passionist ('pæʃənıst), *sb.* (*a.*) [= F. *passionniste*, Sp. *pasionista*, f. PASSION *sb.*: see -IST.]

1. a. *R.C. Ch.* A member of 'The Congregation of the Discalced Clerks of the most Holy Cross and Passion of our Lord Jesus Christ', founded in Italy by Paolo della Croce in 1720.

In addition to the usual vows, they take an obligation that they will do their utmost to keep alive in the hearts of the faithful the memory of Christ's passion.

1832 G. SPENCER *Let.* 7 June in C. R. Leetham *Luigi Gentili* (1965) iii. 40 The General of the Passionists. **1839** LD. SHREWSBURY *Let.* 16 Apr. in E. S. Purcell *Life & Lett. A. P. de Lisle* (1900) I. vi. 105, I have seen Lord Clifford, Father Glover and the Passionists. **1847** *Nat. Encycl.* I. 363/1 The monastery of the Passionists. **1862** MERIVALE *Rom. Emp.* (1865) VI. lii. 296 The oblong platform..now occupied by the garden of the Passionists. **1885** *Catholic Dict.* (ed. 3) s.v., The life of a Passionist is very austere. **1957** *Oxf. Dict. Chr. Ch.* 1022/2 In 1841 the Passionists came to England, where they were the first religious after the Reformation to lead a strict community life and wear their habit in public. **1967** D. T. KAUFFMAN *Dict. Relig. Terms* 347/1 Passionists wear black garments and heart-shaped badges symbolizing the Passion. **1975** R. PLAYER *Let's talk of Graves* iii. 89 Father Dominic the Passionist who received our dear Newman into Christ's Church.

b. *attrib.* or as *adj.*

1844 A. P. DE LISLE *Jrnl.* 8 July in E. S. Purcell *Life & Lett. A. P. de Lisle* (1900) I. vii. 118 The Superior of the Passionist Monks called upon us. **1885** *Daily News* 13 Feb. 3/1 The English and Irish Passionist clergymen of the Avenue Friedland confraternity. **1885** *Cath. Dict.* (ed. 3) s.v., There are now five Passionist houses in England..two in Ireland..and one in Scotland. **1911** *Encycl. Brit.* XX. 887/1 The order of Passionist Fathers,..was founded by St Paul of the Cross..in 1720. **1975** *Irish Times* 30 May 16/1 The fact that in Ireland strong religious piety coexists with fierce sectarian hatreds is lamentable and points to a need for a questioning of the reality of religious beliefs, President O Dalaigh states in an interview in the current issue of the Passionist magazine, the Cross.

2. *Eccl. Hist.* = PATRIPASSIAN.

1874 in J. H. BLUNT *Dict. Sects.*

passionless ('pæʃənlıs), *a.* [See -LESS.]

1. Void of passion; unimpassioned.

1612 SHELTON *Quix.* IV. vi. 346 An Honest, Noble, Warie, Retired, and Passionlesse woman. **1659** O. WALKER *Oratory* 98 The stricter examination of a now passion-less judgment. **1844** MRS. BROWNING *Grief*, Hopeless grief is passionless. **1855** MACAULAY *Hist. Eng.* xxi. IV. 574 An excellent digest of evidence, clear, passionless, and austerely just.

2. Without suffering, painless. *rare.*

1858 NEALE *Hymn*, '*Brief life is here our portion*' iii, The crown Of full and everlasting And passionless renown.

Hence **'passionlessly** *adv.*; **'passionlessness**.

1847 LEWES *Hist. Philos.* (1867) II. 185 The intense disinterestedness and passionlessness of his system. **1868** LIGHTFOOT *Comm. Philipp.* (1885) 273 Passionlessness (ἀπαθία) was the sovereign principle of [Zeno]. **1876** G. MEREDITH *Beauch. Career* III. xviii. 294 How passionlessly pure the little maidenly sentiment was. **1899** A. B. BRUCE *Moral Ord. World* iv. 130 The apathetic sage, passionlessly yet passionately following reason, is the *beau idéal* of Stoicism.

passio'nometer. *nonce-wd.* [f. PASSION *sb.* + -OMETER.] An (imaginary) barometer for registering the rise and fall of passion.

1758 H. WALPOLE *Let. to G. Montagu* 24 Oct., While I have so much quicksilver left, I fear my passionometer will be susceptible of sudden changes.

†**'passions.** *Obs.* Also 6 **pationes**, 6-7 **pas(s)hions**. [app. in origin a corruption of PATIENCE, name of a dock, *Rumex Patientia*, early cultivated for its leaves eaten as spinach; subseq. associated by popular etymology with *Passiontide*, and transferred locally to the Bistort, also in some parts used as a pot-herb, which, says Lyte p. 22, 'hath long leaues, like Patience, but smaller, and not so smooth or playne'.]

A name given in the north and north-west of England to the Bistort, *Polygonum Bistorta*. (See also PASSION-DOCK, PATIENCE 4, PATIENCE-DOCK.)

1568 TURNER *Herbal* III. 12 Bistorta is called in some places..Astrologia, and in some places Pationes, but there is no general name for it. **1597** GERARDE *Herbal* II. lxxxi. §2. 323 Bistorta is called..in Cheshire Passhions,..and there

vsed for an excellent potherbe. **1611** COTGR., *Britanique*, Brittannica..Snakeweed, Pashions, Oisterloite. **1706** PHILLIPS, *Bistort* or *Snake-weed*, an Herb..otherwise call'd Adders-wort, English Serpentary, Oisterich and Pastions.
[*Note*. Mod. Ital. has '*Lapazio*, sorrel, an herb so called' (Baretti); Florio (1611) has '*Lapato*, the wild Docke or Patience'. These names represent L. *lapathum*, *-ium*, Gr. λάπαθον, sorrel, a kind of rumex. Some have conjectured that the name 'passions' or 'passion-dock' arose from a corruption of It. *lapazio* to *la passio* the Passion (of Christ); but this takes no note of the chronological sequence of the names *patientia*, *patience*, *pationes*, *passions*, *passion dock*.]

Passion Sunday. [tr. med.L. *Dominica in Passione*.] The fifth Sunday in Lent; reckoned as the beginning of Passion-tide. (In the R.C. Ch. suppressed as a separate observance in 1969.)
a **1400** *Wyclif's Bible* IV. 686 (Table of Lessons, etc.) Passioun Sonday..Palme Sonday..Estir day. **1517** TORKINGTON *Pilgr.* (1884) 2 Passion Sonday, the xxix Day of Marche. [Easter Sunday was 12 April.] **1559-60** *Croscombe Church-w. Acc.* (Som. Rec. Soc.) 48 Paid for bred and wyne from passyng Sonday. **1623-4** LAUD *Diary* 14 Mar., Passion Sunday I preached at Westminster. [Easter Sunday was 28 Mar.] **1657** SPARROW *Bk. Com. Prayer* 154, 5. Sunday [in Lent]. This is called Passion Sunday. **1777** BRAND *Pop. Antiq.* 327 Durand tells us, that on Passion Sunday the Church began her public Grief, remembering the Mystery of the Cross, the Vinegar, the Gall, the Reed, the Spear, &c. **1903** *Ch. Times* 9 Apr. 476/4 The fifth Sunday in Lent is Passion Sunday, and marks the commencement of Passiontide. Holy Week, also called Passion Week, commences with Palm Sunday.

'Passion-tide. The season immediately before Easter, in which Christ's Passion is commemorated: see prec.
1847 *Dublin Rev.* Mar. 25 The physical cause of our Lord's death is a subject..adapted to the season of Lent and Passion-tide. **1849** J. H. NEWMAN *Discourses to Mixed Congreg.* xv. 323 Though at this season [*Note* Passion-tide] many words would be out of place. **1861** MRS. BROCK (*title*) Daily Readings for Passion-Tide. **1876** (*title*) Sermons for the Church Year. Vol. I. From Advent to Passion-tide... By..J. M. Neale. **1891** *Daily News* 18 Mar. 5/5 'Passion Week' is the second week before Easter..and commences on the fifth Sunday in Lent. The fortnight which includes Passion Week and Holy Week is commonly termed 'Passiontide'.

Passion Week. [f. PASSION *sb.* 1 + WEEK; cf. med.L. *hebdomada passionis*, *hebd. pœnalis* (Du Cange).] The week immediately before Easter, in which the Passion of Christ is commemorated, also (more recently) called Holy Week.
c **1400** *Beryn* 3804 Oppon a tuysday In the passion-woke, when men leven play, And vse more devosioune, fastyng & preyer, Then in othir tyme or seson of þe ȝeer. **1489** *Acc. Ld. High Treas. Sc.* I. 151 Item, in Passion Wolk again Payce, for vj elne of smal braid clayth to be fut scheytis. **1530** PALSGR. 252 Passyon weke, *sepmaine penevse*. **1560** DAUS tr. *Sleidane's Comm.* 334 b, On Maundy thursday in the passion weke. **1662** PEPYS *Diary* 24 Mar., I went to see if any play was acted, and I found none upon the post, it being Passion week. [Easter Sunday was 30 March.] **1706** PHILLIPS, *Passion-Week*, the Week next before the Festival of Easter. **1727-1812** [see HOLY WEEK]. **1797** *Encycl. Brit.* (ed. 3) X. 687/1 Maundy Thursday is the Thursday in Passion week. **1845** S. AUSTIN *Ranke's Hist. Ref.* II. 157 On Palm-Sunday no palms were strewed; and in Passion-Week the ceremony of laying down the cross and raising it again, was omitted. **1854** MILMAN *Lat. Chr.* IV. iii. (1864) II. 246 Palm Sunday, the commencement of Passion week.
b. The fifth week in Lent, beginning with PASSION SUNDAY.
1449 PECOCK *Repr.* 200 What is red..in the ympne *Vexilla Regis prodeunt* sungun in the Passion Weke in Lent.
1852 HOOK *Ch. Dict.* s.v., Some persons call the week, of which Passion Sunday is the first day, Passion Week; and the real Passion Week they call Holy Week. This is, however, a piece of pedantry, founded on a mistake. **1891** [see PASSION-TIDE.].

'passionwort. *Bot.* [f. PASSION (-FLOWER) + WORT.] A plant of the N.O. *Passifloraceæ*.
1846 LINDLEY *Veg. Kingd.* 332 *Passifloraceæ*. — Passionworts. *Ibid.* 333 Smeathmannia forms a connecting link between Passionworts and Samyds.

passi'uncle. *nonce-wd.* [f. PASSION, with dim. ending *-uncle*, after Hartley's *vibratiuncle*.] A petty or contemptible passion.
1834 DE QUINCEY *Autobiog. Sk.* Wks. 1889 I. 174 Now, of men and women generally, parodying that terminology, we ought to say—not that they are..at all capable of passions, but of passiuncles. **1840** —— *Soc. of Lakes* ibid. II. 385 Many..of whom I have already said, borrowing the model of the word from Hartley, that they have not so much passions as passiuncles.

passival (pæ'saɪvəl), *a. Gram.* [f. L. *passīv-us* PASSIVE + -AL[1]; cf. *adjectival*, *subjunctival*.]
a. Pertaining to or used with the passive voice. *rare*.
1880 EARLE *Philol. Eng. Tongue* (ed. 3) §523 Our ears are still familiar in Bible English with this passival *of*.
b. Semantically passive, *spec.* ***passival verb***, an intransitive verb with a quasi-passive meaning.
1892 H. SWEET *New Eng. Gram.* I. 90 *The book sells well, meat will not keep in hot weather*... We call *sells* and *keep* in such constructions passival verbs. **1926** H. POUTSMA *Gram. Late Mod. Eng.* II. II. xlvi. 64 Sweet..calls the verbs thus used passival verbs. **1950** *Eng. Stud.* XXXI. 156 It is generally said that in a sentence like *His books don't sell* the verb is active in form, but passive in meaning, what is 'really' meant being *His books are not sold*. In accordance with this theory verbs used in this way are sometimes called active-passive or passival. **1961** Y. OLSSON *On Syntax Eng. Verb* vii. 180 That article, which..rightly rejects the analysis of such collocations as 'active-passive or passival'. **1963** F. T. VISSER *Hist. Syntax Eng. Lang.* I. ii. 152 (*heading*) Intransitive verbs used to represent the action as quasi-automatic, or self-originated. (Sweet's 'passival verbs'; Jespersen's 'activo-passive' use.)

passivate ('pæsɪveɪt), *v.* [f. PASSIV(E *a.* and *sb.* + -ATE[3].] **a.** *trans.* To render (metal) passive (PASSIVE *a.* 7 b), e.g. to prevent corrosion.
1913 *Chem. News* 28 Nov. 259/1 We assume the passive state of metals (which can be passivated) to be the normal state. **1916** *Jrnl. Chem. Soc.* CIX. 1365 Hittorf has passivated chromium by anodic treatment in hydriodic acid. **1961** *Flight* LXXIX. 747/1 All surfaces that are to be in contact with HTP [*sc.* High Test Peroxide] must be 'passivated' to prevent surface decomposition. **1967** *Times Rev. Industry* Apr. 80/1 Unpainted non-stainless steel parts are cadmium plated and passivated for use at temperatures below 200 degrees centigrade. **1973** *Sci. Amer.* June 119/2 The brass or iron piping and fittings you use must be degreased, nitrogen-purged and passivated in a dilute stream of the fluorine, allowed to enter slowly enough to form a metal-fluoride film on the surface.
b. To give (semiconducting material) a protective coating of some relatively inert material in order to protect it from contamination.
1964 *IBM Jrnl. Res. & Devel.* VIII. 368 (*heading*) Space-charge model for surface potential shifts in silicon passivated with thin insulating layers. **1969** GRAY & SEARLE *Electronic Princ.* v. 176 The oxide layer is said to passivate the semiconductor surface. **1972** PLANER & PHILLIPS *Thick Film Circuits* xi. 123 Active devices..are passivated with a layer of glass or silicon monoxide.
Hence **'passivated** *ppl. a.*, **'passivating** *vbl. sb.* and *ppl. a.*
1914 *Trans. Faraday Soc.* IX. 261 The amount of hydrogen..is too small to counteract the passivating action of the potassium hydroxide. **1919** H. P. TIEMANN *Iron & Steel* (ed. 2) 364 Iron in this condition has been termed passive, passivated, passivified, inactive, altered, or prepared. **1941** *Nature* 28 June 803/1 An electro-formed nickel-surfaced mould is..made and a coat of nickel..applied to the outer passivated nickel face. **1959** C. F. CORFE in *Control in Electroplating* iii. 57 (*heading*) Passivating dips. **1963** *Engineering* 27 Dec. 814/1 Passivated and hardened stainless steel is used for the housings. **1967** *Electronics* 6 Mar. 281/2 The silicon planar passivated construction employed provides long-term parameter stability. **1974** J. A. VON FRAUNHOFER *Concise Corrosion Sci.* viii. 79 Nitrates are poor passivating agents since they..are only sluggishly reduced. **1978** *Gramophone* Jan. 1334/3 The main chassis is constructed from passivated steel.

passivation (pæsɪ'veɪʃən). [f. as prec. + -ATION.] The process of passivating.
1912 *Trans. Faraday Soc.* VIII. 234 (*heading*) Direct experiments on the passivation of metals. **1925** *Jrnl. Iron & Steel Inst.* CXI. 601 The anodic passivation of iron in sodium sulphate solution is demonstrated experimentally. **1956** *Nature* 17 Mar. 508/1 The mechanism of metallic corrosion, oxidation and passivation processes. **1964** *IBM Jrnl. Res. & Devel.* VIII. 385/1 Films..used for surface passivation of semiconductor devices. **1969** *Jane's Freight Containers 1968–69* 484/1 Approximate cost £1,450, depending on optional customer requirements for:—separate compartments,..passivation, fork-lift pockets, etc. **1972** PLANER & PHILLIPS *Thick Film Circuits* xi. 123 Passivation with silicon nitride yields a considerably increased protection against ionic contamination.

passivator ('pæsɪveɪtə(r)). [f. as prec. + -OR.] A passivating agent.
1935 F. N. SPELLER *Corrosion* (ed. 2) ix. 378 Passivators may be used effectively to retard corrosion in refrigerating systems or anti-freezing mixtures. **1951** *Engineering* 28 Dec. 819/3 The oxidation, which causes sludging and the formation of acids, may be prevented by using an inhibited oil. The substances employed for this purpose include catalyst passivators and de-activators. **1974** J. A. VON FRAUNHOFER *Concise Corrosion Sci.* viii. 79 Passivators or Type IIIA inhibitors... Generally these substances are oxidising agents with redox potentials that are more noble than that of the metal and they are readily reduced.

passive ('pæsɪv), *a.* and *sb.* [ad. L. *passīv-us* capable of suffering or feeling, f. *patī*, *pass-* to suffer: see -IVE. Cf. F. *passif* (Oresme 14th c.).]
A. *adj.* †**1.** Suffering; exposed to suffering, liable to suffer. *Obs.*
(Quot. *c* 1400 is of doubtful sense.)
[*c* **1400** *Apol. Loll.* 14 God may not autorise þat actyfe cursyng..But passyue cursyng, þat is peyn be it self wiþ synne folowand, is iust.] *c* **1485** *Digby Myst.* IV. 962 For man diete the maker of all, By his manhed passyve. **1611** COTGR., *Patible*, patible, passiue, sufferable. **1655** H. VAUGHAN *Silex Scint.*, *Resurr. & Immort.* ii, His passive Cottage; which (though laid aside)..Shall one day rise.
2. a. Suffering action from without; that is the object, as distinguished from the subject, of action; acted upon, affected, or swayed by external force; produced or brought about by external agency.
1413 *Pilgr. Sowle* (Caxton) II. lx. (1859) 57 Thou were in me actyf as fire is in the wood, and I in to the passyf as woode is in the fyre. **1613** PURCHAS *Pilgrimage* (1614) 750 Their Canoas are of the barke of birch,..fit for actiue or passiue carriage. **1662** SOUTH *Serm.* (1697) I. 66 The Active informations of the Intellect, filling the Passive reception of the Will. **1709** STEELE *Tatler* No. 10 ¶2. **1773** MONBODDO *Language* (1774) I. I. iv. 46 The mind is to be considered as merely passive, receiving like wax the impressions of external objects. **1842** J. WILSON *Chr. North* (1857) I. 245 Such passive impressions are deeper than we can explain. **1867** SWINBURNE *Ess. & Stud.* (1875) 173 Receptive and passive of her [Nature's] influences and forces.
b. Of movements or physical states of an animal or plant: Produced by external agency.
1845 TODD & BOWMAN *Phys. Anat.* I. 171 Passive contraction is that which every muscle is continually prone to undergo. **1857** MAYNE *Expos. Lex.*, *Passive Motion*, term for motion exerted not by the patient himself but gently by another person. **1893** A. S. ECCLES *Sciatica* 71 The patient is directed to resist the passive movements practised by the attendant.
3. *Gram.* An epithet of voice in verbs used transitively: opposed to ACTIVE 3. Applied to that form of, or mode of using, the verb, in which the action denoted by it is treated as an attribute of the thing towards which the action is directed; or, in which the logical object of the action is made the grammatical subject of the assertion.
1388 WYCLIF *Prol.* 57 A participle of a present tens, either preterit, of actif vois, eithir passif, mai be resoluid into a verbe of the same tens, and a coniunccioun copulatif. **1530** PALSGR. 124 Verbes passyves be suche as..betoken suffring. **1563-7** BUCHANAN *Reform. St. Andros* Wks. (1892) 8 The verbes actives, passives, and anomales. *c* **1620** A. HUME *Brit. Tongue* (1865) 32 The passive verb adheres to the person of the patient. **1678** PHILLIPS (ed. 4), *Passive Voice of a Verb*..is that which betokeneth suffering or a being acted upon, as *Doceor*, I am taught. **1845** STODDART in *Encycl. Metrop.* (1847) I. 33/1 It often becomes necessary to state the object of a verb active, or the agent of a verb passive. Hence arises the necessity for two other cases, which have been called the accusative and the ablative. **1904** C. T. ONIONS *Adv. Eng. Syntax* §27 In the Passive Construction of Verbs taking one Object, what was the Object in the Active becomes the Subject.
4. *Sc. Law.* Of a title to an estate: Under a liability. Of an heir or executor: Liable for the debts of an estate. Also in general sense: Of the nature of a liability.
1576-7 *Reg. Privy Council Scot.* Ser. I. II. 664 In the saidis Margaret Dundas as relict executrice..and hir said spous for his interes passive. **1693** STAIR *Inst.* (ed. 2) III. vi. §3 The Reason of introducing this passive Title, is in favour of Creditors, that they be not un-satisfied, or shifted by the Heirs of the defunct Creditors. **1727-41** CHAMBERS *Cycl.* s.v. *Debt*, *Active Debts* are those whereof a person is creditor: *Passive Debts*, those whereof he is debtor. **1773** ERSKINE *Inst.* III. viii. §87 That apparent heirs might not, upon gratuitous dispositions from their ancestors, enjoy their estates without being liable for their debts, the passive title of *præceptio* was introduced, by which an heir, if he accepts of a grant from his ancestor, of any part, however small, of that estate to which he would have succeeded as heir, is subjected to the payment of all such debts due by the ancestor as were contracted previously to the grant. **1861** W. BELL *Dict. Law Scot.* 615 A passive title, by which the heir, without acquiring an active title, as by service or confirmation, tacitly and by implication subjects himself to the responsibilities belonging to the character of heir. **1875** POSTE *Gaius* III. (ed. 2) 350 A curator was appointed,..and instead of selling the active and passive universality of the insolvent's estate,..merely sold the active residue.
5. Suffering or receiving something without resistance or opposition; readily yielding or submitting to external force or influence, or the will of another; submissive.
passive obedience, ***prayer***, ***righteousness***: see the substantives. See also PASSIVE RESISTANCE.
1626 JACKSON *Creed* VIII. xii. §7 All passive obedience doth properly consist in patient suffering such things as are enjoyned by lawfull authority. *a* **1634** CHAPMAN *Revenge for Honour* Plays 1873 III. 311 Your Soft passive nature do's like jet on fire When oyls cast on't, extinguish. **1691** *New Disc. Old Intreague* iii. 42 While passive Zealots their Harangues applaud; Their Dictates swallow. **1732** FIELDING *Mock Doctor* i, You know my temper is not over and above passive, and that my arm is extremely active. **1858** CARLYLE *Fredk. Gt.* VI. iii. (1872) II. 163 Passive she, all the while, mere clay in the hands of the potter. **1873** H. ROGERS *Orig. Bible* i. (1875) 28 The passive virtues—those of patience, humility, meekness, forgiveness of injuries.
6. Not active, working, or operating; not exerting force or influence upon anything else; quiescent, inactive, inert.
1477 NORTON *Ord. Alch.* v. in Ashm. (1652) 54 Heate, and Cold, be qualities Active; Moisture, and Drines, be qualityes Passive. **1604** BACON *Apol.* Wks. 1879 I. 436, I am merely passive, and not active in this action. **1704** J. HARRIS *Lex. Techn.* I, *Passive Principles*, so the Chymists call Water and Earth, because either their Parts are at rest, or else at least not so rapidly moved as those of Spirit, Oil, and Salt, and so do serve to stop and hinder the quick Motion of the *Active Principles*. ?**1710** LADY M. W. MONTAGU *Lett.*, *to Mrs. Hewet* (1887) I. 30, I am passive in their disputes, and endeavour to study my Italian in peace. **1902** *Westm. Gaz.* 10 June 4/3 Passive loyalty being, under the circumstances, to my mind, as great a virtue in a Dutchman as active loyalty in an Englishman.
7. In various technical uses related to sense 6.
a. *Path.* Of an inflammation, congestion, or the like: Characterized by sluggish or diminished flow of blood.
1813 J. THOMSON *Lect. Inflam.* 129 The change from active to passive, or from acute to chronic inflammation, is frequently seen in the progress of ophthalmia. **1842** DUNGLISON *Med. Lex.*, *Passive*, an epithet for diseases, which seem owing to a greater or less diminution of strength, or which are without apparent reaction. **1871** W. A. HAMMOND *Dis. Nerv. Syst.* 41 Passive Cerebral Congestion. **1886** *Syd. Soc. Lex.*, *H*[*æmorrhage*], *passive*, hæmorrhage occurring without any increase in the activity

of the circulation..; also, hæmorrhage occurring with impeded circulation.

b. *Chem.* Not possessing active chemical properties; not readily entering into chemical combination; inert, inactive. Also, applied to substances that are normally reactive.

1836 *Phil. Mag.* IX. 54 The third wire can make indifferent or passive a fourth one, and so on. *Ibid.*, Direct contact between the two wires..is not an indispensably necessary condition for communicating chemical activity from the active wire to the passive one; for any metal.. renders the same service. **1849** NOAD *Electricity* (ed. 3) 183 A voltaic battery, consisting of zinc and passive iron, or of active and passive iron. **1864-72** WATTS *Dict. Chem.* II. 430 This effect is evidently due to the formation of a thin coating of oxide. The iron thus treated is no longer attacked by strong nitric acid, but may be preserved in it for any length of time without change; it is said to be *passive*... Iron may ..be rendered passive..by holding it for a few seconds in the flame of a spirit-lamp, whereby it becomes superficially oxidised. **1940** *Nature* 19 Oct. 506/1 The addition of a sufficient amount of chromium to iron confers upon the iron the property of producing spontaneously upon its surface a passive and resistant film as a result of contact with the atmosphere or with certain aqueous environments. Such passive films, if mechanically damaged, are self-repairing. **1965** D. ABBOTT *Inorg. Chem.* x. 447 Nitric acid renders some metals completely passive, e.g. iron and nickel are rendered passive by the concentrated acid.

c. *Law* and *Comm.* Of a debt, bond, or share: On which no interest is paid. Of a trust: On which the trustees have no duty to perform; nominal. Of a trade balance: unfavourable; with debits greater than credits. ***passive commerce***: commerce in which the productions of one country are transported by the people of another; opposed to *active commerce*, in which a country transports as well as produces its own goods. ***passive rate*** (see quot. 1972). ***passive use***: a use in which one person had possession of the estate while another enjoyed the profits arising from it: a permissive use.

1837 W. HAYES *Conveyancing* (ed. 3) 83 The right of the wife of a sole owner of the legal inheritance to be endowed of one-third of the land at his death, also gave occasion..to passive trusts. **1848** WHARTON *Law Lex.* s.v., In order to guard against the forfeiture of a legal estate for life, passive trusts, by settlement, were resorted to..and passive trusts were and are created in order to prevent dower. **1882** BITHELL *Counting-ho. Dict.*, *Passive Bonds or Shares*, Bonds or Shares issued by a Government or by a commercial company, on which no interest is paid, but entitling the holder to some future benefit or claim. **1883** LELY *Wharton's Law Lex.* (ed. 7), *Passive debt*, a debt upon which, by or without agreement..no interest is payable. **1930** *Economist* 15 Mar. 587/2 The passive balance of Kr. 25 million was quite normal for the time of the year, as there is always an excess of imports during the winter months. **1936** K. A. H. EGERTON *Bower's Dict. Econ. Terms* (ed. 10) 119 *Passive trade balance*, a balance of imports in excess of exports—another term for 'unfavourable trade balance'. **1940** G. CROWTHER *Outl. Money* viii. 298 Following the usual terminology we can say that the balance of trade between the two countries was unfavourable (or 'passive') to Switzerland. **1972** *Times* 29 Dec. 15/1 It has also been accepted that the annual rate of monetary growth should be curbed gradually rather than suddenly until it reaches a 'passive' rate—the planned rate of economic growth plus the going rate of inflationary expectations.

d. *Immunol.* [tr. G. *passiv* (given this sense by P. Ehrlich 1892, in *Zeitschr. f. Hygiene und Infectionskrankheiten* XII. 189).] Produced by or involving the introduction into the body of antibodies of external origin.

1895 *Science Progress* III. 204 'Passive immunity', a term first employed by Ehrlich. **1898** R. T. HEWLETT *Man. Bacteriol.* v. 123 'Passive immunity' is soon lost, but..is transmitted to the fœtus. **1935** F. P. GAY et al. *Agents of Dis.* xxii. 450 Passive transfer occurs naturally from immune mothers to their offspring. **1970** W. H. PARKER *Health & Dis. in Farm Animals* ix. 114 Natural passive immunity is acquired from the first meals of colostrum. **1974** R. M. KIRK et al. *Surgery* ii. 33 Passive immunity is often transmitted to humans by using the serum from a highly immunised horse.

e. *Chess.* Designating a sacrifice (*a*) in which a piece or pawn attacked by an opponent's move is left to be captured; (*b*) that an opponent need not accept.

1907 S. S. BLACKBURNE *Terms & Themes Chess Probl.* 87 *Sacrificing*, offering a White man to be captured. If a man or men already *en prise* be left so, this may be called a 'passive sacrifice'. **1924** A. EMERY *Chess Sacrifices & Traps* II. 40 In general, 'passive' sacrifices like that in No. 1—where, the Queen being attacked, Alekhine calmly allows it to be taken —are more pleasing than the 'active' variety. **1935** J. DU MONT tr. *Spielmann's Art of Sacrifice in Chess* I. 2 Under the heading 'form', there are two types, namely active and passive. In making a distinction between these two types, the deciding factor, from a scientific point of view, would be whether the sacrifice arises from a move made for the purpose, or from a raid by the enemy... For reasons of practicability, however, it has seemed to me better to make the distinction a different one, namely, whether acceptance of the proffered sacrifice is compulsory or not. Those which must be accepted I call active, the others passive. **1968** P. H. CLARKE tr. *Vuković's Chess Sacrifice* i. 12 Passive sacrifices have the drawback that they can be declined; they can, as it were, be ignored.

f. *Psychol.* Of, relating to or characteristic of the female or the inactive role in a sexual relationship, freq. associated with masochism in psychoanalytic theory; that fails or refuses to respond with, or shows an abnormal lack of, activity.

1916 A. A. BRILL tr. *Freud's Leonardo da Vinci* ii. 39 Strangely enough this phantasy is altogether of a passive character; it resembles certain dreams and phantasies of women and of passive homosexuals who play the feminine part in sexual relations. **1921** *Internat. Jrnl. Psycho-Anal.* II. 439 The author comes to the conclusion that masochism has to be considered as the result and expression of the primacy of passive partial impulses. **1935** *Ibid.* XVI. 337 The sexual aims of the little boy's incestuous wishes are clearly passive. **1940** HENDERSON & GILLESPIE *Text-bk. Psychiatry* (ed. 5) 312 Predominantly inadequate or passive, this again is an important and numerous group. **1969** R. L. KELLEY in Solomon & Patch *Handbk. Psychiatry* xlii. 521 Severe characterologic problems such as sexual perversion, alcoholism..and passive dependent personality. **1973** L. C. KOLB *Mod. Clin. Psychiatry* (ed. 8) vi. 93/1 In this type the personality contains a considerable element of aggression.. expressed by passive measures, such as sullenness, stubbornness, procrastination [etc.].

g. *Electronics.* Containing no source of e.m.f.

1924 K. S. JOHNSON *Transmission Circuits Teleph. Communication* xi. 121 The transmission properties of passive networks may often be best determined by considering them as equivalent to lines having smoothly distributed constants. **1930** T. E. SHEA *Transmission Networks & Wave Filters* ii. 43 A network composed only of inductances, capacitances, and resistances is a passive network. **1965** *Wireless World* July 332/1 In the so-called hybrid circuit,..the active elements..are formed in the silicon slice by the normal planar process, but..the passive elements (resistors, capacitors and conductors) are deposited as thin films on to the thermally grown silicon dioxide protective coating. **1970** J. EARL *Tuners & Amplifiers* ii. 29 A junction diode is equivalent to the thermionic valve diode, a transistor to a thermionic valve and an IC to a multiplicity of active and passive devices and components.

h. *Linguistics.* Of vocabulary, etc.: that is recognized and understood but through inability, lack of assurance, or for some other reason, is not used by the auditor or reader himself.

1935 G. K. ZIPF *Psycho-Biol. of Lang.* (1936) v. 220 The auditor's passive vocabulary (i.e. the words which the auditor can understand). **1966** J. DERRICK *Teaching Eng. to Immigrants* ii. 99 Most stories will contain far more material than the pupils are expected to reproduce themselves (i.e. relying on and helping to build up their 'passive' or recognition vocabulary). **1976** *Word 1971* XXVII. 85 Grammont reported and demonstrated that 'passive language' precedes 'active language'.

i. Of radar, homing systems, etc.: relying on radiation generated by the target. Of a satellite, space relay station, etc.: not generating any signal.

1954 K. W. GATLAND *Devel. Guided Missile* (ed. 2) iii. 67 A missile can be homed on to its target..by..'passive' homing (whereby the missile homes on to a source of energy radiated by the target). **1960** *N.Y. Times* 9 Oct. E 9/6 Echo, a 'passive' satellite, reflects or bounces radio signals sent from one station back to another point on the earth. **1962** J. CLEMOW *Missile Guidance* ii. 45 It is possible to have a passive radar system where a receiver carried in the missile detects the direction of the source of radar signals from the target. **1966** *McGraw-Hill Encycl. Sci. & Technol.* XII. 504/2 Modern submarines carry passive sonar apparatus which is believed to be capable of detecting ships as far away as 100 miles. **1967** H. HELLMAN *Controlled Guidance Syst.* vi. 161 Additional advantages of passive systems are that they emit no telltale signals to aid the enemy, and the guidance equipment is kept to a bare minimum. **1969** *Proc. IEEE* LVII. 427/1 Passive remote sensing at microwave frequencies has applications which range from meteorology to oceanography and geology.

j. ***passive smoking*** [cf. G. *passivrauchen*], the inhalation of smoke involuntarily from the tobacco being smoked by others, considered as a health risk; hence ***passive smoker***, one who suffers this.

1971 G. RICHARDSON *2nd World Conf. Smoking & Health* 217 Some studies give attention to the fact that non-smokers cannot avoid inhaling smoke when breathing smoky air, the so-called 'passive smoking'. **1974** *Lancet* 2 Nov. 1031/1 (*heading*) Influence of passive smoking and parental phlegm on pneumonia and bronchitis in early childhood. **1976** *Med. Jrnl. Aust.* II. 68 This type of smoker is known as a passive or second-hand smoker. **1978** *N.Y. Times* 22 Nov. C1/5 'Passive smokers' are beginning to speak out. **1986** *Scotsman* 16 June 11/2 The passive smoker is exposed mainly to 'sidestream' smoke given off directly from a cigarette, pipe or cigar. **1987** *Sunday Tel.* 9 Aug. 20/6 A report of the Independent Scientific Committee on Smoking and Health ..goes out of its way to deny that any causal association between passive smoking and lung cancer has yet been established.

B. *sb.* [Elliptical uses of the adj.]

1. a. That which is the object of the action of something else; a passive thing, quality, or property. Now usually in *pl.*

1387-8 T. USK *Test. Love* I. ii. (Skeat) l. 12 Euery actiue woorcheth on his passiue. **1584** R. SCOT *Discov. Witchcr.* XIV. vi. (1886) 308 The artificiall applieing of the actives and passives of gold and silver. **1646** SIR T. BROWNE *Pseud. Ep.* 44 A due conjunction of actives and passives. *a* **1677** HALE *Prim. Orig. Man.* IV. v. 338 Man..by applying Actives to Passives, may do things of not unlike a nature; as the acceleration of the growth of Seeds by Mineral Preparations.

b. *pl.* In pillow-lace making, the bobbins holding the threads which correspond to the warp threads in weaving.

1907 MINCOFF & MARRIAGE *Pillow Lace* vii. 89 The other pairs which these [*sc.* the wefts] must cross are called the 'passives'. **1953** M. POWYS *Lace & Lace-Making* iv. 20 This makes the connection and the worker bobbins pass back again across the passives. *Ibid.* xi. 186 The bobbins hanging straight down are called the 'passives'.

2. *Gram.* The passive voice; a passive verb.

1530 PALSGR. Introd. 34 Changyng the gendre and nombre of the participle..lyke as thoughe they were passyves. **1533** UDALL *Floures* 104 b, *Induo* is one of the verbes that gouerne a double accusatife after them, and of al suche verbes their passiues require the later accusatife of both. **1669** MILTON *Accedence* Wks. (1851) 450 The Passive signifieth what is done to one by another. **1755** JOHNSON *Dict.* Gram. (1765) M ij, The passive is formed by the addition of the participle preterite, to the different tenses of the verb *to be*. **1894** O. F. EMERSON *Hist. Eng. Lang.* §35 The place of this old inflected passive has been supplied in the Teutonic languages by a compound passive using auxiliaries.

3. A passive, unresisting, or submissive person or creature. Now *unusual*.

1626 JACKSON *Creed* VIII. i. §3 His patience in all His sufferings did farre exceed the patience of dumb creatures, of lambs themselves, of wormes, or meaner sensible passives. **1749** RICHARDSON *Corr.* (1804) II. 215 Poor Passives! not allowed to have wills of their own! **1755** *Ibid.* III. 223 Down goes the passive; finds them, either tired with their walk, or discontented with the want of variety in the neighbouring fields or lanes.

†**'passiveless**, *a. Obs. rare*$^{-1}$. [irreg. f. PASSIVE *a.* + -LESS.] Not passive, impassive.

1602 J. DAVIES *Mirum in Modum* G iij b, Wert [= were it] in him, as in vs, a passiue moode, He were not God, for God is Passiuelesse.

passively ('pæsɪvlɪ), *adv.* [f. PASSIVE *a.* + -LY².] In a passive way or manner: **a.** In various senses corresponding to those of PASSIVE *a.*

1590 SWINBURNE *Testaments* 203 He..is intestable, both actiuely and passiuely..he can neither make a testament, nor receiue anie benefite by a testament. **1643** PRYNNE *Sov. Power Parl.* III. 5 The whole State and Kingdome..may lawfully..not only passively, but actively resist their Prince, in such his violent, exorbitant, tyrannicall proceedings. **1775** JOHNSON *Tax. no Tyr.* 68 Incendiaries, that..toss brands among a rabble passively combustible. **1837** WHEWELL *Hist. Induct. Sc.* (1857) III. 40 Soft iron is only passively magnetic. **1864** BOWEN *Logic* I It [the mind] is passively receptive of any impressions that may be made upon it. **1875** BENNETT & DYER tr. *Sachs' Bot.* 713 The tissues which are passively distended may be said to be in a state of negative tension.

b. *Gram.* In the sense or with the construction of the passive voice; in a manner asserting the undergoing of some action.

1530 PALSGR. 302 All..whose signifycacion may serve bothe actyvely and passively, as *muable*, apte or mete or able to chaunge, or apte or mete or able to be chaunged. **1571** GOLDING *Calvin on Ps.* xxxvii. 3 (Ragna) should be taken passively, (to be fed). **1685** *Case Doubt. Conscience* 63 Sometimes it is taken Passively, and then the Signification of it is this, to be Divided.

passiveness ('pæsɪvnɪs). [f. as prec. + -NESS.] The quality or condition of being passive, passivity; in *Grammar*, the being in the passive voice.

a **1652** J. SMITH *Sel. Disc.* iv. 75 Mere body, which will be recoiling back perpetually into its own inert and sluggish passiveness. **1678** R. BARCLAY *Apol. Quakers* v. §17. 149 In him that is saved, the working is of the Grace and not of the Man; and it's a Passiveness, rather than an Act. **1798** WORDSW. *Expost. & Reply* 24, I deem that there are Powers Which of themselves our minds impress; That we can feed this mind of ours In a wise passiveness. **1832** HT. MARTINEAU *Ireland* v. 78 Dora's passiveness arose from a sense of the uselessness of opposition. **1845** STODDART in *Encycl. Metrop.* (1847) I. 41/1 It signifies activity with actives, and passiveness with passives..but indeed it always savours, in some degree, of passiveness.

passive resistance. [cf. RESISTANCE 1.] Simple refusal to comply with some demand, without active opposition, now mostly used of refusal to comply with demands or legal requirements imposed by a government or other authority.

In *spec.* use, refusal to pay voluntarily the education rate imposed by the Education Act of 1902.

1819 SCOTT *Ivanhoe* xxiii, In this humour of passive resistance..Isaac sat in a corner of his dungeon. **1844** H. H. WILSON *Brit. India* I. 467 Their conduct was uniformly peaceable; passive resistance was the only weapon to which they trusted. **1869** FREEMAN *Norm. Conq.* (1875) III. 58 The resistance was probably passive. **1883** *Encycl. Brit.* XX. 147/2 The student of English constitutional history will observe the success with which they [*sc.* the Quakers] have, by the mere force of passive resistance, obtained from the legislature and courts indulgence for all their scruples and a recognition of the legal validity of their customs. **1909** J. J. DOKE *Indian Patriot in S. Afr.* ii. 5 The Passive Resistance movement had come into prominence [in 1907]. **1927** C. BERGMANN *Hist. Reparations* xxiii. 173 (*heading*) Force and passive resistance. *Ibid.* 180 The military invasion of the Ruhr District was met by the German people and the German Government with an attitude which has become generally known as passive resistance. **1928** V. G. DESAI tr. *Gandhi's Satyagraha in S. Afr.* xii. 172 None of us knew what name to give to our movement. I then [*sc.* in 1906] used the term 'passive resistance' in describing it. **1930** *Economist* 22 Mar. 631/1 The Education Bill, which was the cause of the bitter religious controversy that gave rise to the passive resistance movement. **1936** [see CONSCIENTIOUS *a.* 2]. **1942** E. PAUL *Narrow St.* vi. 46 Unable to collect reparations, on account of German poverty and 'passive resistance' which became spasmodically impassive, Poincaré declared an embargo on iron and steel into Germany. **1950** G. BRENAN *Face of Spain* vii. 167 The land is difficult to legislate for, and those who own it are past masters in passive resistance. **1974** J. WHITE tr. *Poulantzas's Fascism & Dictatorship* IV. ii.

170 In July 1923, with..the failure of passive resistance in the Ruhr,..there was a situation of open crisis.
attrib. **1845** LD. CAMPBELL *Chancellors* xc. (1857) IV. 227 By a partial scrutiny Pritchard, his passive-resistance competitor, was placed in the civic chair.

Hence **passive-re'sistant, -re'sister**, one who practises passive resistance; **passive-re'sistful** *a.*, expressive of passive resistance. Also **passive-resist** *v. intr.* (*rare*), to practise passive resistance.

1903 *Westm. Gaz.* 29 May 5/1 At Hastings, where the Passive Resisters are numbered by hundreds. **1904** G. B. SHAW in *Daily Mail* 27 Feb. 4/4 They look at me with volumes of reproach in their earnest, passive-resistful eyes. **1906** Passive resister [see LIPPY *a.* 2]. **1907** G. B. SHAW *John Bull's Other Island* Pref. p. xxx, The warcry of the Passive Resisters is Voltaire's warcry, 'Écrasez l'infâme'. **1936** M. PLOWMAN *Faith called Pacifism* 86 It was as a passive resister that the greatest revolutionary in the world became the greatest social force in the world. **1949** KOESTLER *Promise & Fulfilment* I. xii. 131 The soldiers were confronted with the grotesque task of dragging the passive resistants..into barbed-wire cages for interrogation. **1952** B. WOLFE *Limbo* (1953) xvii. 255 Couldn't you just lie down and passive-resist? **1968** *Punch* 2 Oct. 474/1 He incurred much unpopularity as a Passive Resister, which is what people called those who refused to pay their rates towards the upkeep of Church Schools.

†**passivication** (pæsɪvɪˈkeɪʃən). *Obs.* [Irreg. f. PASSIVE *a.* and *sb.* + *-ication*, after nouns of action like *application, publication.*] = PASSIVATION.

1922 *Trans. Faraday Soc.* XVIII. 4 (*heading*) Anodic passivication. **1942** R. T. ROLFE *Steels for User* (ed. 2) x. 300 Owing to passivication of the surface by nitriding, no corrosion was found to occur.

†**passivification** (pæˌsɪvɪfɪˈkeɪʃən). *Obs.* [f. as prec.: see -FICATION.] = PASSIVATION.

1907 *Jrnl. Soc. Chem. Industry* 31 Aug. 900/2 Retardation of passivification is brought about..by making the liquid in question less oxidizing. **1937** *Jrnl. Iron & Steel Inst.* CXXXV. 301A (*heading*) Passivification and activation of chromium-iron alloys.

†**passivifier** (pæˈsɪvɪfaɪə(r)). *Obs.* [f. next + -ER[1].] = PASSIVATOR.

1911 J. N. FRIEND *Corrosion of Iron & Steel* 298 Passivifiers are oxidizers. **1921** *Jrnl. Chem. Soc.* CXIX. 946 All passivifiers are not oxidisers, hydronitric acid being a case in point.

†**passivify** (pæˈsɪvɪfaɪ), *v.* *Obs.* [f. PASSIV(E *a.* and *sb.* + -IFY.] *trans.* = PASSIVATE *v.* a.

1907 *Jrnl. Soc. Chem. Industry* 31 Aug. 902/1 All the solutions enumerated above that passivify iron contain an oxy-anion. **1934** *Jrnl. Iron & Steel Inst.* CXXIX. 619 The addition of easily passivified metals, such as chromium and nickel, to iron yields alloys which are more easily passivified than iron itself.

Hence **pa'ssivified** *ppl. a.*, **pa'ssivifying** *vbl. sb.* and *ppl. a.*

1907 *Jrnl. Soc. Chem. Industry* 31 Aug. 903/2 The passivifying of an iron anode. **1911** J. N. FRIEND *Corrosion of Iron & Steel* xii. 189 (*heading*) The characteristic properties of passivified iron. **1915** *Jrnl. Physical Chem.* XIX. 644 It is..possible that both nitrous acid and nitrogen peroxide may be passivifying agents. **1919** [see PASSIVATED *ppl. a.*]. **1934** [see above]. **1934** *Jrnl. R. Aeronaut. Soc.* XXXVIII. 425 An alkaline pigment, such as zinc oxide or a passivifying pigment, like zinc chromate. **1938** *Jrnl. Iron & Steel Inst.* CXXXVIII. 404A, Strong nitric acid acted primarily as a cleaner, but had some value as a passivifying agent.

passivism (ˈpæsɪvɪz(ə)m). [f. PASSIV(E *a.* and *sb.* + -ISM.] An abnormal state of passivity, esp. that of a male who accepts or desires the passive role in a sexual relationship.

1903 H. ELLIS *Stud. Psychol. Sex* III. 93 Stefanowsky, who also discussed this condition [*sc.* masochism]..termed it passivism. **1940** HINSIE & SHATZKY *Psychiatric Dict.* 403/2 *Passivism*, a form of sexual perversion in which the subject, usually male, is submissive to the will of the partner in the unnatural sexual practices. **1961** *Brit. Med. Dict.* 1060/1 *Passivism*, a type of sexual perversion characterized by submission of one partner (usually the male) to unnatural sexual practices desired by the other partner, who may be of either sex.

passivist (ˈpæsɪvɪst). [f. PASSIV(E *a.* and *sb.* + -IST.] One who or that which is characterized by passivity, *spec.* (*a*) a (male) person who abnormally accepts or desires a passive sexual role (see PASSIVISM); (*b*) an opponent of active participation in war. Also *attrib.* or as *adj.*

1895 [see MASOCHIST]. **1942** PARTRIDGE *Usage & Abusage* (1947) 222/2 There is, in cultured usage, a tendency to make *pacifist* an active, *passivist* an inactive, indeed a negatively passive, opponent of war. **1945** K. R. POPPER *Open Society* II. xxiii. 201 It continues on the lines of Kant's criticism of what we may term the 'passivist' theory of knowledge. **1955** *Bull. Atomic Sci.* Sept. 265/3 But if armaments are not acceptable to the pacifist, does this mean that he will submit to the aggressor and meekly resign himself to what he considers evil? The answer is emphatically no. This is to confuse pacifism with appeasement. The pacifist is definitely not a passivist. **1957** P. WORSLEY *Trumpet shall Sound* 236 The basic division,..is not between millenarian and non-millenarian movements but between activist and passivist movements. **1961** *Brit. Med. Dict.* 1060/1 *Passivist*, anyone who is the subject of passivism.

passivity (pæˈsɪvɪtɪ). [f. L. *passīv-us* PASSIVE + -ITY: cf. F. *passivité, passiveté* (17th c.).]

†**1.** Capability of suffering; passibility. *Obs.*

1664 H. MORE *Synopsis Proph.* 517 The passivity of that divinity lodging in Christ. **1680** BAXTER *Cath. Commun.* (1684) 20 As Man, his knowledge and will must have somewhat of Passivity, though not of Pain.

2. a. The quality or condition of being subject to external force; the state of being affected or acted upon by an external cause or agent. Also, with *a* and *pl.*, an instance of this, a passive quality or affection; *transf.* a thing that is merely passive.

1659 H. MORE *Immort. Soul* II. ii. 128. *a* **1667** JER. TAYLOR *Serm.* III. x. (R.), God in the creation of this world first produced a mass of matter, having nothing in it but an obediential capacity and passivity. **1722** WOLLASTON *Relig. Nat.* ix. (1724) 187 These..affections of matter..are proofs of its passivity, deadness, and utter incapacity of becoming cogitative. **1865** MASSON *Rec. Brit. Philos.* iii. 184 The mind must be more than a mere passivity or receiving-surface. **1885** J. MARTINEAU *Types Eth. Th.* I. I. ii. §2. 156 The liability of matter to be shaped, and the liability of the mind to have perceptions and ideas, are pure passivities. **1958** T. D. WELDON *Kant's Critique of Pure Reason* (ed. 2) iv. 132 Thus there really is a marked distinction between the activity of the understanding and the passivity of sensibility. **1967** G. H. VON WRIGHT in N. Rescher *Logic of Decision* 130 He [*sc.* the agent] can do nothing to produce a change..or to prevent a change which independently of him happens. We may call this case [of impotence] (forced) passivity.

b. *Gram.* Passive meaning or construction.

1871 EARLE *Philol. Eng. Tongue* §523 This *of* as the instrument of passivity has given place to *by*. *Ibid.* §525 The preposition *with*..in the fourteenth century..was used like the *by* of passivity.

3. Submission or tendency to submit to external force or to another's will; submissiveness.

1681 H. MORE *Exp. Dan.* v. Notes 155 The purity, mildness and passivity of their Spirits. **1849** ROBERTSON *Serm.* Ser. I. ii. (1866) 33 The soul resigns itself in pure passivity. **1871** R. ELLIS *Catullus* xxviii. 10 You did aptly finger My passivity, fool'd me most supinely.

4. a. Want of activity, quiescence, inertness: †inertia.

1667 WATERHOUSE *Fire Lond.* 115 The passivity of a potent Army and Party formerly against him. **1740** CHEYNE *Regimen* 311 Its Passivity or Inertia cannot be infinit, but lessens as its Density does. **1826** GOOD *Bk. Nat.* (1834) I. 69 Passivity, inertia, or vis inertiæ, is the tendency in a body to persevere in a given state, whether of rest or motion.

b. *Chem.* The state of chemical inactivity that is produced in some normally reactive metals following a slight initial attack.

1866 R. M. FERGUSON *Electr.* (1870) 140 The passivity of iron can be produced in various ways. **1881** *Jrnl. Chem. Soc.* XL. 344 Passivity may be induced in a rod of iron by the immersion of a part only in concentrated nitric acid. **1940** GLASSTONE *Text-bk. Physical Chem.* xii. 1010 The resemblances between a metal rendered passive by chemical and electrochemical methods is very marked, and there is little doubt that the fundamental cause of passivity is the same in each case. *Ibid.* 1011 In certain cases the dissolution of an anode is prevented by a visible film, e.g., lead dioxide on a lead anode in dilute sulfuric acid: this effect has been called 'mechanical passivity', but it is probably not fundamentally different from electrochemical passivity. **1966** *McGraw-Hill Encycl. Sci. & Technol.* III. 488/1 Passivity is usually due to surface films which act as barriers between the metal and its environment... Aluminum is a reactive metal, but it is widely used for corrosion applications because of protection by a stable aluminum oxide film.

5. *Psychol.* The state or condition of being abnormally inactive or lacking in normal responsiveness (see PASSIVE *a.* 7f); also *attrib.*

1927 HENDERSON & GILLESPIE *Text-bk. Psychiatry* 88 In other cases the patient believes that someone reads his thoughts... These later conditions are examples of 'passivity'. **1952** W. WOLFF *Threshold of Abnormal* xviii. 436 Passivity may appear as apathy, as anxiety, as helplessness. **1955** *Psychiatric Q.* XXIX. 604 Nowhere is it more difficult to decide whether passivity is an ego defense mechanism or an instinctual gratification than in the study of masochism. **1958** M. E. SPIRO *Children of Kibbutz* IV. vii. 146 Play among the two younger groups is marked by an aimlessness and passivity that are two of its most characteristic features. **1968** W. WEISS in Lindzey & Aronson *Handbk. Social Psychol.* (ed. 2) V. 113 Television may reinforce withdrawal and passivity when these pre-existed or are latent, but does not create them. **1969** W. MAYER-GROSS et al. *Clin. Psychiatry* (ed. 3) v. 270 The passivity phenomena in which this loss of [self] is best seen are indeed very characteristic of schizophrenia.

passivizable (ˌpæsɪˌvaɪzəb(ə)l), *a.* *Gram.* [f. as next + -ABLE.] Able to undergo passivization; meeting the structural analysis for the passive transformation. So ˌ**passivizaˈbility**.

1970 N. CHOMSKY in Jacobs & Rosenbaum *Readings Eng. Transformational Gram.* 203 Passivizability is a property of verbs. **1972** A. MAKKAI *Idiom Struct. Eng.* 152 The tournure *kick the bucket*, per se, is not passivizable. **1978** *Language* LIV. 172 Phrases are apt to be passivizable if 'they perform the same function as single verbs'.

passivization (ˌpæsɪvaɪˈzeɪʃən). *Gram.* [f. next + -ATION.] Conversion into the passive form.

1965 N. CHOMSKY *Aspects of Theory of Syntax* ii. 104 It accounts automatically for the restriction of passivization to Verbs that take Manner Adverbials freely. *Ibid.* 229 The sentences 'I regard John as pompous', 'it struck me blind', ..are freely subject to passivization. **1968** *Language* XLIV. 230 The syntactic motivation for this treatment comes from the fact that the verbs that can undergo passivization are restricted to those that take manner adverbials freely. **1970** *Ibid.* XLVI. 466 Whatever the machinery may be to handle these cases, it can clearly also handle constraints on the passivization of verbs like *condescend*. **1971** J. M. ANDERSON *Gram. of Case* ix. 132 Both 'primary' and 'secondary' passivization.., as well as the two kinds of object ('direct' and 'indirect') are allowed for in this way. **1976** J. S. GRUBER *Lexical Struct. Syntax & Semantics* I. iv. 98 The deletion of *for* in certain complement constructions apparently applies after passivization.

passivize (ˈpæsɪvaɪz), *v.* [f. PASSIV(E *a.* and *sb.* + -IZE.] †**1.** = PASSIVATE *v.* a. *Obs.*

1910 *Jrnl. Physical Chem.* XIV. 731 When the current is interrupted after the anode has been passivized, the potential of the anode rises slowly. **1912** *Trans. Faraday Soc.* VIII. 279 One of the slabs was 'passivized' and then allowed to regain its normal state.

2. *Gram.* **a.** *trans.* To convert into the passive form. **b.** *intr.* To be subject to conversion into the passive.

1965 N. CHOMSKY *Aspects of Theory of Syntax* 229 Such sentences as 'John strikes me as pompous', 'his remarks impress me as unintelligible' do not passivize. **1972** R. A. PALMATIER *Gloss. Eng. Transformational Gram.* 120 The application of the passive transformation, by which the sentence is said to have been passivized. **1973** *Amer. Speech 1969* XLIV. 212 There are certain transitive combinations which are phrasal verbs although they do not passivize. **1977** *Verbatim* Feb. 10/1 Thus, transitive verbs in idiomatic expressions frequently will not passivize (*the cowboy kicked the bucket*, but not *the bucket was kicked by the cowboy*). **1978** *Language* LIV. 93 Causation is a transitive process which can be passivized.

Hence ˈ**passivized** *ppl. a.*, ˈ**passivizing** *vbl. sb.*

1975 *Language* LI. 792 Under Hasegawa's analysis, the passivized clause originates as an object complement. **1977** *Trans. Philol. Soc. 1975* 219 It is clear that the passivized/intransitivized sense continued for some. *Ibid.* Assuming that both reflexive and passivizing/intransitivizing functions passed into the Suffix verbs.. we have a source for the four functional types having middle-voice forms which are found in Lowland Eastern Cushitic now. **1978** *Amer. Speech* LIII. 25 Between the passivized versions of the following sentence, only the one in which the deep-structure subject has been deleted can be interpreted impersonally.

pass-key (ˈpɑːsˌkiː, -æ-). [f. PASS *v.* or *sb.* + KEY *sb.*[1]] A key (other than the ordinary key) of a door or gate, with which a person can let himself in or out at times when the door or gate is shut: *spec.* **a.** A key that will open any of a number of locks, a master-key; also *fig.*; **b.** a private key to a gate, etc.; **c.** a latch-key.

c **1817** HOGG *Tales & Sk.* (1837) IV. 164, I gained the gate; but..it was fast locked, the Countess having the pass-key. **1835** *Court Mag.* VI. 31/2 The baron, by means of a pass-key, entered the chamber of his son. **1846** MRS. GORE *Eng. Char.* (1852) 26 Deprecation, whether in tone, manner, or phraseology, is an universal pass-key. **1861** M. ARNOLD *Pop. Educ. France* 152 The Nancy inspector who went round the schools of that town with me, had a pass-key by which he let himself into any one of them when he pleased. **1872** H. W. BEECHER *Lect. Preaching* x. 184 There is only one pass-key that will open every door, and that is the golden key of love. **1881** J. HAWTHORNE *Fort. Fool* I. xxxi, If she returned late, she would let herself in with her pass-key.

pass-lamb, paschal lamb: see PASCH 3.

passle, dial., etc. var. PARCEL.

passless (ˈpɑːslɪs, -æ-), *a.* [f. PASS *sb.* + -LESS.]

1. That cannot be passed, impassable. *poetic.*

1656 COWLEY *Pindar. Odes, Plagues Egypt* xvii, Behold what passless Rocks on either hand Like Prison walls about them stand! **1794** COLERIDGE *Lines on a Friend* 47 Is this piled earth our Being's passless mound? **1881** G. B. SMITH *Life Bright* I. ii. 19 Prejudices which formed an almost passless barrier.

2. Without a pass or passport (PASS *sb.*[2] 8).

1900 *Daily News* 1 Jan. 3/3 To the discomfort of the passless and the terror of the suspect.

passman (ˈpɑːsmən, ˈpæs-). [f. PASS *sb.*[2] + MAN.] **a.** In some universities: A student who reads for and takes a 'pass' degree; opposed to *honour-* or *honours-man, class-man.*

1860 BURROWS *Pass & Class* i. 6 A place in either Class List will distinguish him from the Pass-men. **1888** BRYCE *Amer. Commw.* III. VI. cii. 446 That separation which has grown up in Oxford and Cambridge between pass or poll men and honour men. **1894** J. C. JEAFFRESON *Bk. of Recoll.* I. iv. 56 More scholarship than a mere Oxford passman usually possesses.

b. A prisoner who is allowed to leave his cell. *slang.*

1965 B. KNOX *Taste of Proof* iii. 49 The passmen, the privileged, trusted prisoners. **1973** J. PATRICK *Glasgow Gang Observed* ix. 82 He had envied the 'passmen', boys who in the afternoon were permitted to leave their cells to scrub floors and polish shoes.

†ˈ**pass-ˌmaster.** *Obs.* [f. PASS *v.* or *sb.* + MASTER *sb.*]

1. One who has passed as a master: = PASSED-MASTER.

1599 JAS. I *Βασιλ. Δῶρον* (1603) 58, I would haue you reasonably versed in them, but not preassing to bee a passe-maister in any of them.

2. = PAST-MASTER 1.

1785 W. O. V——N *Three Knocks at Door of Free-Masonry* 2 The Pass-Master hath the Compasses and Sun, with a Line of Cords about his Neck, viz. 60 Degrees.

3. An officer of a poor-law district having the charge of passing on paupers to their own parish or union.

1818 ALD. WOOD in *Parl. Debates* 1010 There was a penalty of £20 upon the pass-master who suffered vagrants to escape. **1887** RIBTON-TURNER *Vagrants & Vagrancy* x. 241 The Pass Master for the City of London.

† **'passock.** *Obs. rare.* Also 7 pessock. [Cf. *pess* 'a hassock to kneel on at church' (Forby); also *hassock.*] ? = HASSOCK. Cf. BASS *sb.*[2] 2.

1680 in Glasscock *Rec. St. Michael's, Bp. Stortford* (1882) 79 Pd for passocks for the church. **1687** *Ibid.*, Payd for two Pessocks for the Pullpett and Deske.

passo-porto, obs. form of PASSPORT, q.v.

pass-out ('pɑːsaʊt, -æ-). [PASS-.]

a. (A document giving) permission to leave and re-enter a theatre, etc.; also *attrib.* in ***pass-out check, ticket.***

1894 A. CHEVALLIER *Record by Himself* 191 An attendant proffering her a pass-out check respectfully asked if she intended to return. **1896** *Westm. Gaz.* 24 Nov. 1/3 The agitation for pass-out checks at the variety theatres. **1907** *Daily Chron.* 29 Aug. 5/6 He begged for a pass-out ticket to see how his old friends were doing down below. **1922** JOYCE *Ulysses* 106 No fear of anyone getting out, no passout checks. **1952** GRANVILLE *Dict. Theatr. Terms* 133 *Pass-out checks*, a ticket given by the usher to permit a patron to re-enter the theatre if he, or she, leaves during the interval. **1959** K. WATERHOUSE *Billy Liar* xii. 159 The Roxy was unguarded. They dodged in, giggling... 'Where's yer pass-outs, you two?' yelled Stamp. 'Hey, mister, they're getting in for nix!' **1962** J. WAIN *Strike Father Dead* 60, I stuck to Lucille till the dance ended. At one point she suggested that we should get pass-outs and go out for a drink. **1968** C. DRUMMOND *Death & Leaping Ladies* iii. 61 No need for pass-outs... I'm the Manager. The pub's okay.

b. A fit of unconsciousness. Also, one who has become unconscious (cf. PASS *v.* 66c).

1946 E. O'NEILL *Iceman Cometh* II. 115 He puts his head back on his arms and closes his eyes, but this time his habitual pass-out has a quality of hiding. **1949** *Esquire's Handbk. for Hosts* 272 There is small pleasure to be derived from finding yourself with an eighteen-year-old passout on your hands. **1967** E. FENWICK *Passenger* iv. 31 She slept like a pass-out, a total, never making a sign of any kind of consciousness.

passover ('pɑːsəʊvə(r), 'pæs-). [f. verbal phrase *pass over*: see PASS *v.* 67e.]

I. (With capital initial.) **1. a.** The name of a Jewish feast, held on the evening of the fourteenth day of the (first) month Nisan, commemorative of the 'passing over' of the houses of the Israelites whose door-posts were marked with the blood of a lamb, when the Egyptians were smitten with the death of their firstborn. Extended to include the seven following days, the whole making the 'days of unleavened bread' (*Exod.* xii. 8).

1530 TINDALE *Exod.* xii. 11 And ye shall eate it in haste, for it is the Lordes passeouer. **1535** COVERDALE *Exod.* xii. 43 This is the maner of the kepynge of Passeouer. **1662** GURNALL *Chr. in Arm.* verse 19. iv. §4 (1679) 495/1 Baptism is clearer than Circumcision, Lords Supper than Passover. **1797** *Encycl. Brit.* (ed. 3) XIV. 17/2 The modern Jews observe in general the same ceremonies which were practised by their ancestors, in the celebration of the passover. **1840** *Penny Cycl.* XVII. 304 *Passover*..also called the feast of unleavened bread.

b. *transf.*

1726 AYLIFFE *Parergon* 236 Thus the Lord's Passover, which we commonly call Easter, was order'd by the Canon-Law to be celebrated every year on a Sunday, otherwise stiled the Lord's-Day.

2. a. *Contextually*, The lamb sacrificed at the Passover, the Paschal lamb. **b.** *fig.* Applied to Christ, of whom the Paschal lamb was regarded as typical (1 *Cor.* v. 7).

1530 TINDALE *Exod.* xii. 21 Chouse out and take to euery housholde a shepe, and kyll passeouer. **1539** BIBLE (Great) 1 *Cor.* v. 7 For Christ oure passeouer is offered vp for vs. **1581** R. GOADE in *Confer.* III. (1584) Xj b, The Pascall lambe is called the passeouer. *a* **1680** CHARNOCK *Christ our Passover* Wks. (1849) 266 The lamb was called the passover. The sign for the thing signified.

3. *attrib.*, as ***Passover-bread, -cake, lamb, offering.***

1545 BRINKLOW *Lament.* 16 The passeouer lambe was a sygne, a token, and a remembraunce. **1611** BIBLE 2 *Chron.* xxxv. 7 Iosiah gaue to the people, of the flocke, lambes and kiddes, all for the Passeouer-offerings. **1858** SIMMONDS *Dict. Trade, Passover-bread, Passover-cake*, a thin unleavened cake, used among the Jews at the festival of the Passover.

II. ('pɑːs,əʊvə(r), 'pæs-). In general senses from the verbal phr. *pass over* (PASS *v.* 67).

4. a. A passing or going over; a passing from this world to the next; a going over from one religion to another.

a **1662** HEYLIN *Laud* (1668) 530 On the Evening before his [Laud's] Passover, the night before the dismal Combate betwixt him and Death. **1889** S. J. EALES *St. Bernard* I. 35 When he made his passover, that is when he was converted from Judaism to Christianity.

b. A path or pass over hills.

1839 Z. LEONARD *Adventures* (1904) 230 We..continued all day without any interruption, and in the evening encamped at the foot of the passover.

5. *Sc.* An act of passing over something, or something passed over, in speech or writing; an intentional omission.

1822 SCOTT *Nigel* xiv, I wish to Heaven I was mair worthy of the name; but let that be a pass-over. **1830** GALT *Lawrie T.* I. i. (1849) 4 A passage in my history that should not be a passover. **1833** *Fraser's Mag.* Oct. 396, I could master the tenth chapter of Nehemiah, without making above a dozen pass-overs.

'passoverish, *a.* [f. PASSOVER + -ISH[1].] Suggestive of the passover.

1921 A. HUXLEY *Crome Yellow* xxviii. 299 The disorganized, passoverish meal that took the place of dinner on this festal day. **1930** H. G. WELLS *Autocracy of Mr. Parham* II. iii. 106 After an exceptionally passoverish dinner at Marmion House.

pass-parole, variant of PASSE-PAROLE.

passport ('pɑːspɔːt, -æ-), *sb.*[1] Forms: 6 passe-, passporte, (pase-, paspourte), 6–7 passeport, pasporte, (*erron.* 6 paspote, pastport, 7 passeboard), 6–8 pasport, 6– passport, (7 pass port, 7–8 pass-port). *β.* 7 passo-porto. [a. F. *passeport* (15th c. in Littré) = It. *passaporto*, f. *passe, passa*, imper. of *passer, passare* (see PASSE-) + *port, porto*, PORT, seaport.]

† **1.** Authorization to pass from a port or leave a country, or to enter or pass through a country. ***letters of passport***, a letter or document giving such authorization; = sense 2. *Obs.*

? *c* **1500** *Cov. Corp. Chr. Plays* (E.E.T.S.) 23/670 Youre pase-porte for a C deyis Here schall you haue of clere cummand, Owre reme to labur any weyis. **1521** DK. ALBANY in Ellis *Orig. Lett.* Ser. III. I. 287 Send me 3[or] lettres of passe-port for my said secretaire. *c* **1540** tr. *Pol. Verg. Eng. Hist.* (Camden No. 36) 276 His sowldiers, covenauntinge with the Normans for free pasporte. **1555** EDEN *Decades* 237 To cary theym [cloues] frome thense into other regions, they paye for pasporte .xviii. fanans the bahar. **1585** in Tolstoy *1st 40 Yrs. Interc. Eng. & Russ.* (1875) 266 [He] sent certein his folkes owte of our countrey..without our princelie knowledge or lycence, and without pasport letters. **1606** in *Capt. Smith's Wks.* (Arb.) Introd. 37 Suffer no man to return but by pasport from the President and Counsel.

2. a. A formal document authorizing a person to pass out of or into a country or state, or to pass through a foreign country; in the latter case orig. = safe-conduct, and granted usually with defined limitations of destination, time, and purpose; but gradually extended in use, until it now means a document issued by competent authority, granting permission to the person specified in it to travel, and authenticating his right to protection.

1546 EARL OF SURREY in Ellis *Orig. Lett.* Ser. III. III. 286 Now ther resteth nothing to be don, but their paspourte and redy dispatch from you. *a* **1548** HALL *Chron., Edw. IV* 227b, Aduisinge the Frenche kyng..to send to him an Herault, to fetche a saue conduyte & pasport. **1551** T. WILSON *Logike* (1567) 43 In time of warre it is euill trauailing without a passeport [**1580** pasport]. **1573–80** BARET *Alv.* P 172 A Passport, or safe conduct to passe. **1633** T. STAFFORD *Pac. Hib.* I. viii. (1821) 111 To graunt mee..your passeport and Safe-conduct through all your Garrisons. **1655** DIGGES *Compl. Ambass.* 326 The Lord Levingston desireth most earnestly to have a passport to pass through England. **1665** EVELYN *Diary* 24 Apr., I was commanded to go with him to the Holland Ambassador, where he was to stay for his passport. **1727–41** CHAMBERS *Cycl.*, *Pass-port*, a licence, or letter from a prince, or governor, granting liberty and safe-conduct to travel, enter, and go out of his territories, freely and without molestation. The pass-port is, properly, given to friends; and the safe-conduct to enemies. **1840** *Penny Cycl.* XVII. 304/2 *Passport*, a printed permission signed by the secretary of state of the home department of a country, which allows a subject of that country to leave it and go abroad. When he has obtained this, the bearer must have his passport signed by the minister or agent of the state to which he intends to proceed... Such a document states the name, surname, age, and profession of the bearer, and serves as a voucher of his character and nation... The system of passports..has become much more rigid and vexatious during the last half century. The only civilised countries in which passports are not required are the British Islands and the United States of North America. **1842** BRANDE *Dict. Sci.*, etc. s.v., In France, and in many continental countries, home passports are necessary for the native traveller. **1845** FORD *Handbk. Spain* I. 7 The French, during their intrusive occupation of Spain, introduced the severe machinery of police and passports.

† **b.** A permit for discharged inmates of a hospital, soldiers, paupers, etc. to proceed to a specified destination, and (often) to ask alms on the way. *Obs.*

1548 *Act 2 & 3 Edw. VI*, c. 2 §10 No Captain..shall give to any of his Soldiers..any Licence or Passports to depart from his Service. **1552** in *Vicary's Anat.* (1888) App. xvi. 308 At their departure [as cured], to geue vnto them a passe-porte. *Ibid.* 336 [Form of] A passeport to be deliuered to the Poore [to pass them to their place of nativity]. **1574** in *N. & Q.* 9th Ser. (1903) XII. 414/2 To a pore man having a paspote to go to the Cytie of Bathe, vj[d]. **1575** *Nottingham Rec.* IV. 158, iij. sodyors havyng a pasport to pase frome Oxford to New Castyll'. **1591** SPENSER *M. Hubberd* 196 Ere we farther passe I will devise A pasport for us both in fittest wize, And by the names of Souldiers us protect: That now is thought a civile begging sect. **1597** *1st Pt. Return fr. Parnass.* I. i. 184 Thou migh[t]st betake thyselfe in *forma pauperis* to a boxe and a passporte. **1601** CORNWALLIS *Ess.* (1632) v, Counterfaits [which]..begge under the Passe-port of Love.

c. *transf.* (See quots.)

1696 BROOKHOUSE *Temple Open.* 2 These Marks confirm and ratifie their Claim, and give them a *Passo-porto* to enter into the Millennium, which is the promised Land of the Christians. **1717** LADY M. W. MONTAGU *Let. to Pope* 12 Feb., They are heirs-general to all the money of the laity; for which, in return, they give them formal passports, signed and sealed for heaven. **1796** MORSE *Amer. Geog.* II. 79 (Russian funeral) The priest produces a ticket, signed by the bishop and another clergyman, as the deceased's passport to heaven. **1839** E. D. CLARKE *Trav. Russia* 36/1 This is what all you foreigners call the passport; and you relate, in books of travels, that we believe no soul can go to Heaven without it..it is nothing more than a declaration, or certificate, concerning the death of the deceased.

3. *Naval.* A document granted to a neutral merchant-vessel, esp. in time of war, by a power at peace with the state to which it belongs, authorizing it to proceed without molestation in certain waters; a sea-letter.

1581 L. ALDERSEY in Hakluyt *Voy.* (1589) 183 Our captaines pasport and the gift of 100 chekins discharged all. **1642** *Ord. & Declar. Lords & Comm.* 20 Oct. 3 Other Vessels,..not having on board them a Pasport or Licence from the Commissioners of the Admiralty. **1798** NELSON 25 Oct. in Nicolas *Disp.* (1845) III. 158 You will grant Passports for all Vessels which the Inhabitants may wish to send to Sicily. **1838** *Encycl. Brit.* (ed. 7) XVII. 112 *Passport*, or *Pass*,..is also a permission granted by any state to navigate some particular sea, without hindrance or molestation. **1867** in SMYTH *Sailor's Word-bk.*

4. A licence to import or export dutiable goods without paying the usual duties, or contraband goods on payment of the duties.

1715 *Lond. Gaz.* No. 5344/2 The Pass-port..granted to the Prussian Minister for sending from this Country 14225 Cannon Balls. **1727–41** CHAMBERS *Cycl.* s.v., *Pass-port*..a licence granted by a prince for the importing, or exporting merchandizes, &c. without paying the duties... *Pass-port* is also a licence obtained for the importing or exporting of merchandizes deemed contraband, and declared such by tariffs.

5. *fig.* **a.** An authorization or permission to pass or go anywhere; †a dismissal (*obs.*).

15.. in *Rel. Ant.* I. 250 Kepe hym as longe as he cann lyve, And at hys ende hys paseport geve. **1579** SPENSER *Sheph. Cal.* Epil. 7 Goe lyttle Calender, thou hast a free passeporte. *c* **1586** C'TESS PEMBROKE *Ps.* LXXII. vi, Without his praise No nights, no daies Shall pasport have to go. **1631** *Celestina* XVIII. 182, I will give him his passe-port, I warrant you, unlesse hee betake him to his heeles, and runne away from me. **1634** W. WOOD *New Eng. Prosp.* (1865) 108 This little Pappouse travells about with his bare footed mother to paddle in the Icie Clammbankes after three or foure dayes of age have sealed his passeboard and his mothers recoverie. **1691** J. WILSON *Belphegor* v. iii, I made his passport for t'other world about four years since. **1706** BAYNARD in Sir J. Floyer *Hot & Cold Bath.* II. 318 She told me that she was in a dying condition, and..I wished her a comfortable passport to the other World. **1831** LYTTON *Godolphin* iii, Give me free passport hereafter to come and go as I list. **1837** SOUTHEY *Wks.* I. p. xxx, The approbation of the reviewers served as a passport for the poem to America. **1878** BOSW. SMITH *Carthage* 47 The Phoenicians, true to their general policy..to trade with those countries only where trade was its own passport and its own security.

b. That which gives the right or privilege of entry into some society, state, or sphere of action; a warrant of admission.

1581 SIDNEY *Apol. Poetrie* (Arb.) 22 Neyther Phylosopher nor Historiographer, coulde..haue entred into the gates of populer iudgements, if they had not taken a great passport of Poetry. *a* **1700** DRYDEN *Death of Anyntas* 76 His pass-port is his innocence and grace. **1715** SOUTH *Serm.* (1727) IV. viii. 339 Without a Passport from the Judgment, it [Religion] will never gain a full and free Admittance into the Affections. **1826** DISRAELI *Viv. Grey* I. vii, In England personal distinction is the only passport to the society of the great. **1827** LYTTON *Pelham* xlvi, If you are rich enough to afford it,..there is no passport to fame like eccentricity. **1883** S. C. HALL *Retrospect* I. 185 The man to whom intellectual ability was the surest passport for attention.

c. A certificate intended to introduce, or secure admission; a voucher.

1578 WHETSTONE *Promos & Cassandra* I. iii. Bij b, *La.* Thou shalt haue a Pasporte. *Ros.* Yea, but after what sorte? *La.* Why, that thou wart my man. **1596** NASHE *Saffron Walden* 5 For a more ratefied pasport..that I haue read it and digested it, this title it beareth. **1601** SHAKS. *All's Well* III. ii. 58 Looke on his Letter Madam, here's my Pasport. **1676** TOWERSON *Decalogue* 124 Looking upon their images as..fit passports of his worship. **1757** FOOTE *Author* II. Wks. 1799 I. 153 What apology can you make me, who was your passport, your security? **1875** FORTNUM *Majolica* v. 50 A few of these forgeries..have found their way into public museums under a false passport.

† **d.** Authorization (*to do* something). *Obs.*

1597 *1st Pt. Return fr. Parnass.* II. i. 783 When ragged pedants have there pasports sealde To whip fonde wagges for all there knaverie. **1605** CHAPMAN *All Fools* Ded., Plays 1873 I. 111 Least by others stealth it be unprest, Without my passport, patcht with others wit.

6. *attrib.* and *Comb.*, as ***passport clerk, holder, letter*** (see 1), ***number, office, officer, official***; **passport control**, (*a*) regulation of the issuing and inspecting of passports; (*b*) the department or office at a port, airport, etc., which checks passports; † **passport-maker** (*humorous*), a maker of 'passports' to another world, a halter-maker; **passport photo(graph)**, (*a*) the identification photograph in a passport; (*b*) a photograph of the size required for passports; **passport port**, a port for the entrance of which by foreigners a passport is required.

1862 F. A. TROLLOPE *Marietta* I. ii. 32 Drawn with an accuracy which..might move the envy of a passport clerk. **1947** AUDEN *Age of Anxiety* I. 17 An ordered world Of planned pleasures and passport-control. **1948** M. LASKI *Tory Heaven* i. 6 A lifetime of devoted service in Passport Control. **1960** 'R. EAST' *Kingston Black* vi. 60 Passport control would report when she left the country and returned. **1966** C. MACKENZIE *My Life & Times* V. 43 We were lucky to have a Minister like Sir Francis Elliot..; he agreed to this experiment in passport control. **1973** W. MCCARTHY *Detail* iii. 150 He walked across the airport towards passport control. **1976** *CRC Jrnl.* July 3/2 The UK passport holders from East Africa have a right to settle in Britain. **1788** *Lond. Mag.* 136 The gentleman..was a very eminent passport or halter-maker. **1971** M. KELLY *25th Hour* i. 15 He opened the other page..closed the passport and held it out... He took a pen..and wrote something down. I said, 'What's that?' 'Your passport number.' **1976** 'M. BARAK' *Secret List H. Roehm* xiv. 139 He checked names, addresses, and passport numbers. **1849** I. SPENCER *Let.* 14 Aug. in U. Young *Life Fr. Ignatius Spencer* (1933) III. ii. 165, I write from the Belgian passport office. **1975** *Times* 14 June 6/3 Long queues form at passport offices [in Angola] and 40,000 passports are already on order from Lisbon. **1950** P. BOTTOME *Under Skin* i. 16 The passport officers are in the dining saloon. **1958** L. VAN DER POST *Lost World of Kalahari* viii. 193 There was a group of vigilant painted animals assembled on a ledge rather like passport officers at a frontier. **1975** D. BLOODWORTH *Clients of Omega* xxiv. 235 The Passport Officer said..'May I see your passport, please?' **1922** M. ARLEN *Piracy* III. vi. 89 The passport officials at the ports. **1961** J. BARLOW *Term of Trial* I. vi. 127, I got my passport photo to show you. **1975** 'A. HALL' *Mandarin Cypher* x. 150 Passport photos are only ever good for a giggle. **1935** J. BUCHAN *House of Four Winds* iii. 84 The passport photograph isn't unlike him. **1939** G. GREENE *Confid. Agent* I. ii. 50 Life seemed determined to make him look less and less like his passport photograph. **1965** G. LYALL *Midnight plus One* ii. 17 There is one passport photograph only. **1966** N. FREELING *King of Rainy Country* 85 Switzerland confirmed that nobody would bother checking such well known passport photographs. **1898** *Westm. Gaz.* 12 May 2/2 Talien-Wan has now been at different times 1. A free port. 2. An open port. 3. A treaty port. 4. A passport port.

†**'pass-,port**, *sb.*² *Obs. rare*⁻¹. [? f. PASS- + PORT *sb.*¹] A port by which to pass, an outlet.
1676 GREW *Anat. Leaves* iv. §2 The Skins, of at least many Plants, are formed with several Orifices or *Pass-ports*.

'passport, *v.* [f. PASSPORT *sb.*¹] *trans.* To furnish (or trouble) with a passport.
1824 *Blackw. Mag.* XV. 473 Parched, passported,.. plundered, starved, and stenched, for 1200 miles. **1885** G. W. CABLE *Creoles of Louisiana* xii. 81 Their ships must be passported.

'passportless, *a.* [f. as prec. + -LESS.] Without a passport, unprovided with a passport.
1595 CHAPMAN *Ovid's Banquet of Sence* Ded., Wandering like passportless men. **1877** D. M. WALLACE *Russia* xxix. 481 Regarding fugitives or passportless wanderers in general. **1919** J. BUCHAN *Mr. Standfast* v. 96 It seemed to me that, in spite of being passportless, I might be able somehow to make my way. **1968** *Punch* 16 Oct. 525/2 The Common Market..envisages a common nationality and a passportless society for most of Western Europe. **1970** *Guardian* 24 Mar. 11/3 Europe's airport lounges are still littered with passportless Kenyan Asians. **1973** *Daily Tel.* 5 Apr. 8/3 Passportless, on the run, he escapes into the Connecticut woods.

pass-through ('pɑːsθruː, -æ-), *a.* and *sb.* [f. vbl. phr. *to pass through*: s.v. PASS *v.* 58.]
A. *adj.* 1. Through which something may be passed.
1955 *Sun* (Baltimore) 24 Aug. 12/4 An arm length's [*sic*] away via the 'pass-through' window is the kitchen range. **1976** C. LARSON *Muir's Blood* (1978) xxix. 153 The phone rang..while Blixen was lifting it from his crowded breakfast table to the pass-through bar.
2. Of costs, etc.: that are passed on to the buyer; that are chargeable to the customer.
1972 *Time* 17 Apr. 44/1 The commission may order an end to 'pass-through' profits. At present, businessmen are allowed to pass along to customers not only their increases in costs, but also to tack on their standard profit margins. **1976** *National Observer* (U.S.) 14 Feb. 17/3 'Political' ads are also excluded from pass-through expenses in most states, such as those that promote offshore oil and gas drilling.
B. *sb.* 1. A passage; a means of passing through; *spec.* a hatch through which food, etc., is passed.
1958 *Washington Post* 16 Aug. B3/2 (Advt.), Over-size dining-family room served by louvered pass-through from kitchen. **1959** 'S. RANSOME' *I'll die for You* iii. 37 Anne.. began piling the breakfast dishes in the pass-through to the kitchen. **1971** *Daily Colonist* (Victoria, B.C.) 21 Oct. 15/1 Como sawed through two vertical bars in his cell into the passageway, and then 'enlarged a food pass-through' to get into an outside corridor. **1976** C. WESTON *Rouse Demon* (1977) xx. 94 Through the bar-type pass-through into the kitchen they could see a rusty stove. **1977** *Austral. House & Garden* Jan. 58/1 Above the stove the pass-through overlooks the informal dining room.
b. *fig.* A route for money, profits, or investments. *N. Amer.*
1968 *Economist* 18 May 77/2 Last March Ottawa promised to make sure that its banks and other financial intermediaries here would not permit American investors to use Canada as a pass-through for funds destined for the Euro-dollar market.
2. An act of passing through or passing on.
1975 *Sci. Amer.* June 55/1 The beams collide at two regions on the perimeter of the ring... The probability of even a single e^-e^+ annihilation in any one pass-through of the bunches is quite low. **1976** *Billings* (Montana) *Gaz.* 16 June 5-A/3 O'Leary took the position that a Supreme Court decision of last Dec. 30, which permitted a temporary pass-through of Montana Power's higher Canadian-gas costs, has the effect of also authorizing reduced rates on an interim basis.

pass-time, obs. form of PASTIME.

passulate ('pæsjʊlət), *a. rare*⁻⁰. [f. med. or mod.L. *passulātus* for It. *passolato* dried (as raisins) in the sun, f. *passola*, *passola uva* dried grape, raisin, f. L. *uva passa* raisin: see PASS *sb.*³] (See quot. 1857.) So **passulate** ('pæsjʊleɪt) *v. trans.*, to make into raisins, to dry (grapes); **passu'lation**, the drying of grapes into raisins.
1857 MAYNE *Expos. Lex.*, *Passulatus*, applied to certain medicines of which raisins formed the chief ingredient: passulate. **1873** THUDICHUM *Cantor Lect. Wines* 20/1 Grapes which had been strongly passulated in the sun. **1884** —— *Alcoholic Drinks* 14 These grapes..have the peculiar faculty of becoming very sweet without passulation, or shrivelling to raisins.

‖**passus** ('pæsəs). [L. *passus* step, pace; in med.L. passage of a book, etc.] A section, division, or canto of a story or poem. (Used in reference to mediæval works in which it was used as Latin.) Cf. PACE *sb.*¹ 12, PASS *sb.*¹ 2.
[*a* **1400-50** *Alexander* p. 7 Secundus passus Alexandri. *a* **1400** *Langland's P. Pl.* C. p. 15 (MS. Cott. Vesp. B. xvi.) Hic incipit secundus passus de uisione Willelmi de petro plouhman.] **1575** LANEHAM *Let.* (1871) 42 At this, the minstrell made a pauz & a curtezy, for *Primus passus*. **1885** SKEAT *Langland's P. Pl.* Gen. Pref. p. xi, MS. Rawl. Poet. 137 contained a complete copy of the A-text, and preserved the whole of Passus XII. *Ibid.* p. xv, Prefixed to the Notes on each Passus of the C-text is a Scheme of Contents.

passvolant, obs. form of PASSE-VOLANT.

passway ('pɑːsweɪ, -æ-). [PASS *sb.*¹] **a.** A means of passing; a passage or gangway. **b.** = PASS *sb.*¹ 3.
1825 *Mechanics' Mag.* IV. 203/1, I hope we shall have a better passway than the present, otherwise we shall have the bridge down again. **1835** A. B. LONGSTREET *Georgia Scenes* 99 These were the only passways to the interior. **1874** J. W. LONG *Amer. Wild-Fowl Shooting* 161 There is a good passway for flight shooting. *Ibid.* 245 Good sport may then be had on the passways. **1889** 'C. E. CRADDOCK' *Despot of Broomsedge Cove* xiv. 267 Through the broad passways he could see the white frost gleam responsive upon the expanse of the fields. **1889** *Harper's Mag.* Aug. 390/2 Our family carriage..is left out in the streets along with many others to block up the passway. **1920** *Blackw. Mag.* June 817/1 There is only one pass-way through the wild hills at the back.. —a narrow defile.

password ('pɑːswɜːd, -æ-). [f. PASS *sb.*² + WORD *sb.*] A word authorizing the utterer to pass; a word appointed as a token to distinguish friends from enemies; *esp. Mil.* a parole, a watchword.
c **1817** HOGG *Tales & Sketches* I. 293 The other retaliated the blame on the wounded youth, for his temerity in coming without the pass-word. **1855** MACAULAY *Hist. Eng.* xv. III. 555 Ferguson..longed to be again the president of societies where none could enter without a pass-word. **1862** SALA *Seven Sons* II. viii. 206 [He] gave the pass-word to the sentinel, and was admitted.
b. *fig.* = Watchword; secret of admittance.
1836 *Backwoods of Canada* 127 My pass-words are 'Hope! Resolution! and Perseverance!' **1890** 'R. BOLDREWOOD' *Colonial Reformer* (1891) 142 That fresh, unspoiled, girlish heart to which he alone had the password.

†**passwort**. *Obs.* = PALSYWORT, the Cowslip.
1671 SKINNER *Etymol. Botan.*, *Passworts*, Flores Primulæ veris, contr. à Palsy-worts (i.e.) Paralyseos.

passyble, obs. form of PASSABLE, PASSIBLE.

passy-measure: see PASSEMEASURE.

passyngere, obs. form of PASSENGER.

Passyng Sunday, corrupt f. PASSION SUNDAY.

past (pɑːst, -æ-), *ppl. a.* and *sb.* Forms: α. 3-9 **passed**, (4 y-, 5 -id, -yd, i-, 5 *Sc.* **passit**, 7 **pass'd**); β. 3- **past**, (4-6 **paste**). [Pa. pple. of PASS *v.*: cf. F. *passé*, L. *præteritus.*] A. *ppl. a.*
I. 1. Predicatively after *be*: Gone by in time; elapsed; done with; over. (L. *præteritus.*)
This was really the perfect tense of resultant condition, (cf. PASS *v.* 13), formed, as in other vbs. of motion, with *be* instead of *have*: cf. he *is* come, he *is* gone, the sun *was* risen, Babylon *is* fallen. Also *past and gone*.
13..-1388 [see PASS *v.* 13]. **1377** LANGL. *P. Pl.* B. XVIII. 133 Sith þis barn was bore ben xxxᵗⁱ wynter passed. **1387** TREVISA *Higden* VIII. 59 When þe ȝere were i-passed he sent to Rome. *c* **1400** *Destr. Troy* 10133 When paste was the pes, parties were gedirt. *c* **1430** *Syr Tryam.* 799 The nyȝt was paste, the day was come. **1526** TINDALE *Rom.* iii. 25 He forgeveth the synnes thatt are passed [*mispr.* passhed]. **1592** SHAKS. *Ven. & Ad.* 380 My day's delight is past, my horse is gone. **1611** BIBLE *1 Sam.* xv. 32 Agag said, Surely the bitternesse of death is past. **1784** COWPER *Task* I. 639 The dream is past; and thou hast found again Thy..homestall thatched with leaves. **1842** TENNYSON *Vision of Sin* iv. 69 What! the flower of life is past.
II. *attrib.* (orig. after its sb.)
2. That is gone, passed away, bygone; elapsed (of time); belonging to or having existed or occurred in former days, or before the time current.
a **1340** *Ayenb.* 59 On is preterit, þet is to zigge; of þinge ypased. **1387-8** T. USK *Test. Love* I. Prol. (Skeat) l. 77 Al the vaineglory that the passed Emperours, Princes, or Kinges hadden. **1390** GOWER *Conf.* I. 5 Long tyme in olde daies passed. **14..** *Voc.* in Wr.-Wülcker 604/43 *Præteritus*... ypassyd. *c* **1400** tr. *Secreta Secret., Gov. Lordsh.* 63 Repent þe noght of þinges passyd. **1568** GRAFTON *Chron.* II. 761 Things passed cannot be called agayne. **1678** WALTON *Life Sanderson* 53 This Relation of my pass'd thoughts. **1781** COWPER *Truth* 256 While danger passed is turned to present joy. *a* **1821** KEATS *In a drear-nighted December* iii, But were there ever any Writhed not at passed joy?
β. **13..** *Cursor M.* 12125 Noght allan þe time past [*MS. F.* paste] Bot elles hu lang þi life sal last. *a* **1450** *Cov. Myst.* viii. (Shaks. Soc.) 70 Fro perellys past, present, and future. **1585** T. WASHINGTON tr. *Nicholay's Voy.* I. viii. 8 b, [The city] in times paste was by the Emperours of Rome honoured. **1611** SHAKS. *Wint. T.* III. ii. 34 My past life Hath been as continent, as chaste, as true, As I am now vnhappy. **1623** WEBSTER *Duchess Malfi* III. ii, Past sorrows, let us moderately lament them. **1781** COWPER *Truth* 491 Past indiscretion is a venial crime. **1875** JOWETT *Plato* III. 266 A narration of events, either past, present, or to come.
3. Gone by immediately before the present time; just passed. Often strengthened by LAST, q.v. (B. 2 b).
a. Following words expressing a space of time, and indicating a date removed by this space: Passed away, gone by, bygone, agone, ago.
a **1300** *Cursor M.* 6716 If his lauerd kneu [þe ox] kene o horn Thre dais passed [*Gött.* pascid] þar be-forn. [**1377** LANGL. *P. Pl.* B. Prol. 189, I herde my sire seyn is seuene ȝere ypassed, þere [etc.].] **1393** *Ibid.* C. XVII. 368 As ich tolde þe with tonge a lytel tyme passed. **1444** *Rolls of Parlt.* V. 117/2 As thay used to bye hem a xx or xxx yere past. **1572** J. JONES *Bathes of Bath.* I. 2 More then two thousande yeares passed. **1653** SCLATER *Fun. Serm. 25 Sept.* Ep. Ded., Above twenty years last past..you erected, and ever since continued, at your own proper cost, an Arabick Lecture. **1670** WALTON *Lives* III. 156 About forty years past. **1747** *Mem. Nutrebian Crt.* I. 170 Some time past. **1790** *Bystander* 153 Some numbers past it was announced in this publication, that [etc.]. **1830** PUSEY *Hist. Enq.* II. 135 According to a plan prescribed a hundred or more years past.
b. with *for*: = during the space just gone by.
1732 BERKELEY *Alciphr.* I. §1 For several months past, I have enjoyed such liberty. **1756** AMORY *Buncle* (1770) II. 164 He has been for a year and a half last past in Italy. **1803** *Med. Jrnl.* X. 212 Drier..than it has been for some years past. **1894** G. MOORE *Esther Waters* 179 Esther admitted that she had for some time past neglected her religion.
c. Following a date of month or week: = preceding this, last. Cf. LAST B. 2 b.
1411 *Rolls of Parlt.* III. 650/1 The Saturday neghst after the fest of Seint Michael last passed. *c* **1475** *Partenay* 6182 The tewisday passed Aforne penticost, The yere A thousand four hundred & seuyn wend. **1583** STOCKER *Civ. Warres Lowe C.* I. 36 The fifth of Aprill the yeere last past. **1626** C. POTTER tr. *Sarpi's Hist. Quarrels* 37 In the Moneth of May last past.
d. *ellipt.* Of the past month, last month, *ultimo*.
1711 *Lond. Gaz.* No. 4893/2 Our Letters of the Thirty-first past..bring an Account. **1751** WARBURTON in *Lett. w. Hurd* (1809) 93, I have yours of the 28th past to acknowledge. **1766** CHESTERF. *Lett.* (1774) IV. 246, I received yesterday your letter of the 30ᵗʰ past.
e. *generally.* Of time or order: That has just passed, bygone; foregoing, preceding. (Usually preceding its sb.)
c **1450** *Mirour Saluacioun* 4283 The passid Chapitle shewed vs the last examynacionne. **1588** PARKE tr. *Mendoza's Hist. China* 176 Of whom wee made mention in the Chapter past. **1665** BOYLE *Occas. Refl.*, *Disc. Occ. Med.* IV. v, If you should imagine, that in the passed discourse I have [etc.]. **1803** *Edwin* I. xv. 241 On the past day Adelfrid ..had departed into Deïri. **1902** *Westm. Gaz.* 24 Feb. 12/1 Famous in the religious history of the past century.
4. Of or relating to bygone time; in *Grammar*, Expressing past action or state, preterite: as in ***past tense*** (also *attrib.* and in extended uses), ***past participle*** (also ***past-participial*** adj.).
past imperfect: see IMPERFECT A. 5 and B. ***past perfect*** = PLUPERFECT. ***past tenses***, applied to the aorist, imperfect, perfect or preterite, and pluperfect tenses.
1530 PALSGR. Introd. 32 The thre generall distinctions of tyme, present, parfytly past, and to come. *c* **1620** A. HUME *Brit. Tongue* (1870) 31 Tyme is an affection of the verb noating the differences of tyme, and is either present, past, or to cumm... Tyme passing befoer, quhilk we cal imperfectlie past..I was writing, or did wryte. **1772** PRIESTLEY *Inst. Relig.* (1782) II. 113 There is nothing past or future in his ideas. **1798** J. H. TOOKE *Diversions of Purley* (ed. 2) I. viii. 263 The adjective *Less* and the comparative *Less* are the imperative..; and the superlative *Least* is the past participle. **1813** *Examiner* 12 Apr. 230/2 Mine, alas!.. has long ago been all of it, in the *past* tense. **1823** BYRON *Juan* XIII. xl, The past tense, The dreary '*Fuimus*' of all things human. **1839** *Penny Cycl.* XIII. 314/1 The past-imperfect and aorist tenses of the Greek verb. **1889** *Academy* 23 Nov. 343 The form 'scripsi', the traditional 'past-perfect', was now called 'present perfect'; 'scripseram' was called past-perfect. **1892** W. W. SKEAT *Primer Eng. Etym.* ix. 104 The suffix so common in Lat. past participles, as in *amā-tus*.., loved. The corresponding past participial suffix in E. is *-d*, as in *dea-d*.., orig. a past participle. **1937** *Jrnl. Eng. & Gmc. Philol.* XXXVI. 474 The strong vowel is divided into classes..according to the vowel of the past and ignoring the past participle vowel. **1961** R. B. LONG *Sentence & its Parts* vii. 167 Where main predicators are past-tense forms, common-mode predicators in subordinate clauses..are likely to be past-tense too if a choice between past forms and presents is possible. *Ibid.* xviii. 406 Latin past-participial stems are commonly marked..by the use of either the letter *t* or the letter *s*. **1961** B. MALAMUD *New Life* (1962) 290, I did—ah—see one but that's all past tense. **1976** H. MACINNES *Agent in Place* xxviii. 286 No need to think anything. It's all past tense now. **1976** *National Observer*

(U.S.) 27 Mar. 19/3 Vidal's spicy past-tense peep show adds seasoning to this year's version. **1976** G. L. Brook *Lang. Shakespeare* iii. 110 The present participle is normally active and the past participle is normally passive. **1977** *Word 1972* XXVIII. 98, 89·5 percent of all past-tense environments preserve lenition.

5. In the usage of various societies: Having served one's term of office. Cf. PAST-MASTER.

B. *sb.* [elliptical uses of A.]

1. a. ***the past***: The time that has gone by; all time before the present; bygone times or days collectively, past time. Phr. ***a thing of the past.***

1590 Spenser *F.Q.* I. iii. 30 She speakes no more Of past: true is, that true love hath no powre To looken backe. *c* **1600** Shaks. *Sonn.* cxxiii, Not wondering at the present and the past. **1732** Pope *Ess. Man* II. 52 Then see how little the remaining sum, Which serv'd the past, and must the times to come. **1832** Tennyson *Love thou thy Land* 2 Love thou thy land, with love far-brought From out the storied Past, and used Within the Present. **1871** Smiles *Charac.* vii. (1876) 201 Men of a comparatively remote past.

Phr. **1863** *Athenæum* 15 Aug. 200/3 Even in America the woman-doctor is an eccentricity, and most probably will in a few years be a thing of the past. **1903** G. B. Shaw *Man & Superman* III. 92 Do not ask me how old I was—as if I were a thing of the past. I am 77. **1952** E. O'Neill *Moon for Misbegotten* I. 43 Who told you I fall for the dainty dolls? That's all a thing of the past. **1961** New Eng. Bible *Luke* xvi. 9 When money is a thing of the past. **1977** C. Allen *Raj* i. 21/2 By the 1880s the discomfort of travelling by *palkee* (palanquin)..was already becoming a thing of the past.

b. That which was done or happened in the past.

1665 G. Thomson (*title*) Loimotomia; or the Past Anatomized. **1811** W. R. Spencer *Poems* 7 Oh, Mother! past is past! 'tis o'er. **1892** Westcott *Gospel of Life* 18 No repentance on earth can undo the past.

2. A past life, career, or history; a stage that one has passed through; *esp.* in pregnant sense, a past life over which a veil is drawn.

1836 J. H. Newman *Par. Serm.* (1837) III. xxii. 366 Is it never maintained, that a Christian Minister is off his past? **1855** Trench *Eng. Past & Pr.* i. (1870) 6 Why we should occupy ourselves with the past of our language. **1876** Ouida *Winter City* v. 86 In real truth a woman is easier to manage who has had a past. **1890** R. Kipling in *Contemp. Rev.* July 28 The Lords of Life and Death would never allow Charlie Mears to speak with full knowledge of his pasts.

3. *Gram.* (*ellipt.*) = *past tense*: see A. 4.

1783 Blair *Rhet.* (1812) I. ix. 187 An aörist, or indefinite past. **1845** Stoddart in *Encycl. Metrop.* (1847) I. 57/1 The present imperfect implies something of the past, and something of the future.

C. *attrib.* and *Comb.* (from A), as **past-future** *a.* (Gram.), of a tense: expressing an action or a state viewed as future in relation to a given past time; **past-president**, one who has been a president; **past-profit** *a.*, concerning past profits; **past-time** *a.*, belonging to a bygone time, ancient, antique, old-fashioned. Also from B, as ***past-coloured, -dissecting, -done*** adjs.

1939 S. Spender *Still Centre* 24 In the past-coloured pigment of the mind's eye They feed and fly and dwell. **1939** L. MacNeice *Autumn Jrnl.* 18 The final cure is not in his past-dissecting fingers. **1762** Sterne *Tr. Shandy* VI. xxi. 89 Chatting..upon past-done deeds. **1925** Grattan & Gurrey *Our living Lang.* 230 The Past-Future Tense (a)..(a) He said he should (would) write, etc. *Ibid.*, The Past-Future-Continuous Tense (b)..(b) He said he should (would) be writing, etc. *Ibid.*, The Past-Future-Perfect Tense (c)..(c) He said he should (would) have written, etc. *Ibid.*, The Past-Future-Perfect-Continuous Tense (d)..(d) He said he should (would) have been writing, etc. **1961** R. B. Long *Sentence & its Parts* v. 127 Progressive-aspect forms..sometimes emphasize..in past-perfect and past-future tenses closeness to a past time that is central in the attention at the moment. **1903** *Nature* 12 Feb. 348/2 James Glaisher..was also a past-president of the Royal Meteorological Society. **1961** *Newark* (New Jersey) *Even. News* 22 Mar. 25 He regretted Hughes had made a personal attack on a past president. **1899** *Westm. Gaz.* 15 Mar. 6/1 There will be no valuation or past profit statement. **1889** Hissey *Tour in Phaeton* 89 These past-time inns..how they delight the eye of the nineteenth century traveller.

past (pɑːst, pæst), *prep.* and *adv.* Also 4 **ipassed,** 4-6 **passed, passit.** [The prepositional use appears to have arisen out of the perfect tenses of PASS *v.*, formed with *be* instead of *have* in the statement of resultant condition (see prec.); *be* was illogically used even when the vb. was transitive, as in the following examples:

c **1305** *St. Cristoph.* 52 in *E.E.P.* (1862) 61 þo he þe croice ipassed was, he tournde aȝe to þe clene. **1387** Trevisa *Higden* (Rolls) VII. 487 Whanne þey were unneþes i-passed A reden [*v.r.* reedy] marys. *c* **1400** *St. Alexius* (Laud 622) 283 þe Cee of grece he passed is. *c* **1430** *Syr Tryam.* 61 Now ys the kyng passyd the see. *c* **1460** *Towneley Myst.* x. 168, I am old..passed I am all preuay play. **1600** Abp. Abbot *Exp. Jonah* 273 Ionas was passed the pikes, and now entering upon a victory, when [etc.].

In these we can substitute for *i-passed, passed,* or *past*, the prep. *beyond* (as expressing the result of passing); whence it was natural to treat *past* as = 'beyond' in other contexts.]

A. *prep.* **1. a.** Beyond in time (as the result of passing); after; beyond the age for or time of.

a **1300** *Cursor M.* 10970 (Cott.) Of barns [*Gött.* child] er we passed þe pass [*Trin.* [We] are past tyme childe to welde]. *c* **1386** Chaucer *Friar's T.* 176 The day is short and it is passed pryme. *c* **1391** —— *Astrol.* II. §3 It was passed 8 of the clokke the space of 2 degrees. **1432-50** tr. *Higden* (Rolls) VI. 343 Noon of theym lyvede passede oon yere. **1509** Hawes *Past. Pleas.* xxvii. (Percy Soc.) 119, I thought me past al chyldly ygnoraunce. **1526** Tindale *Heb.* xi. 11 Sara..was delivered of a childe when she was past age. **1573-80** Baret *Alv.* P 162 Old houndes past hunting. *Ibid.* 177 A disease Past the worst. **1613** Purchas *Pilgrimage* (1614) 119 When it was halfe an houre past the sixt houre. **1655** Fuller *Ch. Hist.* x. iv. §15 Children not yet come to, and old men past, helping of themselves. **1709** Hearne *Collect.* (O.H.S.) II. 309 After he was past the Age of one hundred Years. **1760-72** H. Brooke *Fool of Qual.* (1809) III. 68 This horse is quite passed mark of mouth. **1885** *Truth* 28 May 833/2 Dancing was kept up till past two. *Mod.* The time is half past three.

b. In stating age *past* sometimes follows. Cf. PAST *ppl. a.* 3 c.

1676 *Lond. Gaz.* No. 1153/4 A light gray Gelding..five years old past. **1720** *Ibid.* No. 5898/9 Lost.., a black Mare, ..aged three Years past.

c. *ellipt.* Beyond the age of (so many years).

1560 Daus tr. *Sleidane's Comm.* 33 The Emperour beyng now past one and twenty yeres of Age. **1718** *Entertainer* No. 20. 132 Augustus..injoin'd Marriage to all past 25 Years of Age. **1767** Warburton in *Lett. w. Hurd* (1809) 406 His being able, at past eighty, to perform this expedition on foot. **1838** Lytton *Alice* I. i, The elder lady, the guest of her companion, was past seventy. **1967** M. Forster *Trav. Maudie Tipstaff* I. v. 98 In Maudie's opinion, no woman could get past forty and still have those needs.

†**d.** Of time measured backwards: Going back beyond, of older date than. Cf. BEYOND *prep.* 5.

1575 *Reg. Privy Council Scot.* Ser. I. II. 472 [This] hes bene in use..within the said Burgh past memor of man.

2. a. Beyond in place (as the result of passing); further on than; at or on the farther side of.

past sight, (gone) out of or beyond the reach of sight.

c **1305-1430** [see above in Etymology]. **1523** Ld. Berners *Froiss.* I. 154 When he was past the ryver, he thanked God. **1594** Shaks. *Rich. III*, v. iii. 345 My Lord, the Enemy is past the Marsh. **1611** Bible *Num.* xxi. 22 Until we be [*R.V.* have] past thy borders. **1615** Chapman *Odyss.* v. 459 She..again Turn'd to a cormorant, dived, past sight, the main. *Mod.* He lives in the first house past the corner. [**1870** W. Morris *Earthly Par.* Prol. (1890) 6/2 When we are passed the French and English strait.]

b. Of motion: By (in passing). ***to go past***, to pass, go by; so ***to flow, ride, run, hurry***, etc. ***past*** (a person or place). spec. ***to get past***, to pass, to overtake.

1542 Udall *Erasm. Apoph.* 137 He..behelde hir after that she was gon past hym. **1808** Scott *Marm.* III. xii, He drew his mantle past his face. **1818** Shelley *Rev. Islam* III. xxxiv, As past the pebbly beach the boat did flee. **1836** Marryat *Japhet* vii, Crowds of people were running past our shop. **1857** T. Hughes *Tom Brown's School Days* I. v. 109 They're the bounds. As soon as the ball gets past them, it's in touch, and out of play. **1863** Mrs. Oliphant *Salem Ch.* xv. 256 He pushed in past the pails. **1906** Gallaher & Stead *Compl. Rugby Footballer* xix. 262 We don't think Scoular was to blame for allowing Smith to get past him and score. **1971** *Croquet Gaz.* July 14/2 The..Singles..were won by Lady Ursula Abbey who just got past Mrs. Temple in a close and protracted final. **1977** *Daily Express* 29 Mar. 32/4 England put nine goals past Luxemburg 16 years ago in the away leg of a World Cup qualifier.

3. a. Beyond the reach, range, or compass of; not within the scope or reach of; incapable of: chiefly with nouns of action or mental state. Sometimes with some notion of time: = No longer capable of, or within the scope or reach of.

In more or less permanent combinations with various sbs., many of which survive in literature, chiefly as Shaksperian or Biblical echoes, as ***past belief, compare, comprehension, (all) cure*** (cf. CURE *sb.* 6b), ***doubt, endurance, finding out, grace, hope, mending, question, recovery, redress, remedy, saving, shame***, etc. Others have become colloquial, as ***past praying for*** also loosely, beyond hope (of cure, recovery, etc.), etc. (See BEYOND *prep.* 5, 6.)

1509 Barclay *Shyp of Folys* (1874) II. 55 Some ar so past shame in theyr langage So fowle and lothly, that [etc.]. **1526** Tindale *Eph.* iv. 19 Beynge past repentaunce [1611 past feeling]. **1534** —— *Rom.* xi. 33 How vnserchable are his iudgementes and his wayes past findyng out. **1560** Daus tr. *Sleidane's Comm.* 5 Lest in proces of tyme..it be paste remedy. **1590** Shaks. *Mids. N.* IV. i. 211, I had a dreame, past the wit of man, to say, what dreame it was. **1593** —— *Rich. II*, II. iii. 171 Things past redresse, are now with me past care. **1596** —— *1 Hen. IV*, II. iv. 211 Nay, that's past praying for; I have pepper'd two of them. **1599** Q. Eliz. *Let. to Essex* 14 Sept. in Moryson *Itin.* II. (1617) 41 It is to Us past comprehension. *c* **1600** Shaks. *Sonn.* cxxix, Past reason hunted, and no sooner had, Past reason hated. **1607** Middleton *Mich. Term.* II. iii. 384 Nay, 'tis done now, past mending. *a* **1661** Fuller *Worthies* (1840) III. 494 It is past my power to compromise a difference betwixt two so great persons. **1708** Swift *Death Partridge* Wks. 1755 II. I. 258 Yesterday..word was brought me, that he was past hopes. **1782** Cowper *Mutual Forbearance* 25 Well, I protest 'tis past all bearing. **1827** Carlyle *Germ. Rom.* II. 289 He now saw nothing past common. **1881** G. M. Hopkins *Lett. to R. Bridges* (1955) 126, I have become very musical of late... I could make great progress—not in execution: that is past praying for—but in composition and understanding. **1897** *Cornh. Mag.* June 830 The man who can deliberately set aside his own personal knowledge and the gift of reason and commonsense with which God has endowed him,..is indeed 'past praying for'. *a* **1901** Besant *Five Years' Tryst*, etc. (1902) 129 'I cannot help your face', said the herb-woman; 'that is past my skill'. **1902** H. James *Wings of Dove* I. i. 5 The precious name..in spite of the harm her wretched father had done it..was not yet past praying for. **1909** Kipling *Rewards & Fairies* (1910) 46 I've seen her walk to her own mirror by bye-ends, and the woman that cannot walk straight *there* is past praying for. **1939** C. Day Lewis *Child of Misfortune* III. i. 264 Everything's past praying for. **1962** J. Ludwig in R. Weaver *Canad. Short Stories* (1968) 2nd Ser. 255 Sidney was past praying for, she herself couldn't have kids.

b. *colloq.* Beyond the ability or power of. Esp. in phr. ***not to put it*** (or ***anything***) ***past*** (***someone***), to think (a person) quite capable of performing a specific action, or behaving in a specified way.

1611 Beaum. & Fl. *King & No K.* III. i, You are welcome, sir, I think; but if you be not, 'tis past me To make you so; for I am here a stranger Greater than you. **1859** G. Meredith *Juggling Jerry* ix, It's past parsons to console us. **1870** G. M. Hopkins *Jrnls. & Papers* (1959) 198 Br. Yates gave me the following Irish expressions—*I wouldn't put it past you* or *I wouldn't doubt you* = It is just what I should expect of you. **1894** Somerville & 'Ross' *Real Charlotte* I. v. 63, I wouldn't put it past Charlotte to be trying to ketch Mr. Dysart. **1912** J. N. McIlwraith *Diana of Quebec* xvii. 259, I did not put it past her to have a desire to meet the scoundrel once more, since I had assured her he was really a Green Mountain Boy. **1916** H. L. Wilson *Somewhere in Red Gap* vi. 272, I wouldn't put it past him that he had old Jerry kicked on purpose to-day! **1922** Joyce *Ulysses* 733, I wouldn't put it past him. **1929** W. Faulkner *Sound & Fury* 251 I'm not surprised though... I wouldn't put anything past you. **1930** J. B. Priestley *Angel Pavement* v. 214, I believe he waits until he has the tickets, then rings you up that morning and makes it up... I wouldn't put it past him. **1946** K. Tennant *Lost Haven* (1947) xv. 240 'Bracewell is a boy any mother could trust.' 'Don't you be too sure... I wouldn't put anything past that little devil.' **1953** S. Beckett *Watt* 16 Poor woman, God forgive her, said Telty. Faith I wouldn't put it past him, said Mr Hackett. **1961** 'E. Lathen' *Banking on Death* (1962) i. 5, I wouldn't put it past him to do this deliberately. **1976** M. Birmingham *Heat of Sun* ix. 159 'Do you think she could possibly consider killing justified for the sake of her deprived flock?' 'I wouldn't put it past her'.

c. ***past it*** (slang), incompetent through senility, etc., no longer competent, ineffective after long use; (quot. 1864) dead. Also (with hyphen) *attrib.*

1864 C. M. Yonge *Trial* II. xi. 197 'He is almost past it,' said Tom, 'but..he may be roused by my voice.' **1928** E. Wallace *Flying Squad* xv. 130 He was a handy old chap—but he was getting rather past it. **1950** 'J. Guthrie' *Is this what I Wanted?* ii. 37 One never dreamed of going to them for advice. The fact was they were past it; they had lived their lives. **1959** *Listener* 22 Jan. 154/1 They never knew much about it anyway... Ramsay was past it then. **1972** K. Bonfiglioli *Don't point that Thing at Me* xiv. 118 The faded allure of portly, past-it Mortdecai. **1974** M. Babson *Stalking Lamb* xix. 138 'You're getting past it, Ma.' Aaron seemed obscurely satisfied by her display of weakness. **1978** *Times Lit. Suppl.* 1 Dec. 1388/2 Not for him the slumped envy of the past-it fantasizer.

†**d.** Beyond the limits of; without. *Obs.* or *arch.* ***past himself***, beside himself (now *dial.*).

1470-85 Malory *Arthur* VII. xxi, So he brenned in loue that he was past hym self in his reason. **1600** W. Watson *Decacordon* (1602) 132 He was so vexed, lacerated, and calumniated..that he became almost past himselfe. *c* **1611** Chapman *Iliad* II. 331 But Jove hath..cast My life into debates past end. **1618** —— *Hesiod* (Hooper) 180 That man, put To his fit task, will see it done past talk With any fellow. **1870** W. Morris *Earthly Par.* (1890) 156/2, I..Am nowise God to give man bliss Past ending. **1903** *Eng. Dial. Dict.* (Durham), Past hissel.

†**4. a.** More than, above (in number or quantity). (Cf. also 1 c.)

1469 Marg. Paston in *Lett.* II. 385, I have sent to Hary Halman..and he canne not gette passyd v. or viij. at the most. **1470-85** Malory *Arthur* IV. iv, Ther were founde but lytel past two honderd men slayne. *a* **1533** Ld. Berners *Huon* iv. 7 They..departyd fro Parys without restynge past one night in a plase. **1598** B. Jonson *Ev. Man in Hum.* I. iii. 191 Faith I have not past two shillings, or so. **1608** Topsell *Serpents* (1658) 744 Their egges are not past so big as pease. **1627** Capt. Smith *Seaman's Gram.* x. 47 They haue it not past once in fiue..yeeres. **1668** Sedley *Mulb. Gard.* II. i. Wks. 1722 II. 22 The Portion I can give with you does not deserve a Man of past half his Fortune.

†**b.** Above in rank or degree. *Obs.*

1551 Crowley *Pleas. & Payne* 168 But spent all..in rayment past your degree. **1598** Chapman *Blind Beg. Alexandria* Plays 1873 I. 27 My husband is a Lord, and past a Lord.

c. Beyond in manner or degree. Now *rare.* Also *dial.*, in negative sentences.

c **1611** Chapman *Iliad* I. 284 He affects, past all men, height. *Ibid.* xv. 105 His greatness past all other Gods, and in fortitude, And ev'ry godlike pow'r, he reigns past all endu'd. **1847** C. Brontë *J. Eyre* xxxvi, He set store on her past every thing. **1897** *Bromyard Rec.* 9 Dec. (E.D.D.), Fortunately, past a profusion of soot and water, no damage was done.

B. *adv.* (absolute use of the prep.; = past the speaker, or the person, point, or place spoken of.)

1. So as to pass or go by; by.

1805 Wordsw. *Fidelity* 32 The sounding blast, That, if it could, would hurry past. **1836** Marryat *Japhet* iv, We had watched her past. **1846** Worcester s.v., Sometimes incorrectly used for *by*; as 'to go past'. **1855** M. Arnold *Balder Dead* 96 Painfully the hinds With goad and shouting urge their cattle past. **1862** Longf. *The Cumberland* 4 The alarum of drums swept past. **1884** W. C. Smith *Kildrostan* 43 The tread of time as it hastens past.

2. On one side, aside; as ***to lay past***, to put aside or away, to lay by or save up. *Sc.* and *north Irel.*

1830-2 Carleton *Traits Irish Peasantry* (1843) 260 (E.D.D.) It is not to lay them past to rust. **1847** *Jrnl. R. Agric. Soc.* VIII. II. 377 It is stacked past until the following year. *Ibid.* 388 It enables the farmer to store past his crop. **1891** *Blackw. Mag.* Oct. 570, I hed to pit it past in the attic.

1894 STEVENSON *Puddin* iii. 65 I'm prood to think ye're layin' past siller.

C. *Comb.* (of *prep.* or *adv.*) **a.** Esp. by 16–17th c. poets, rarely by prose-writers, phrases consisting of *past* prep. with object (A. 3), which predicatively are written as two words, were frequently used *attrib.*, and then necessarily hyphened to make the syntax clear: thus 'a malady past cure', but 'a past-cure malady'. Among such syntactical combinations are: ***past-comfort, -cure, -feeling*** (whence ***-feelingness***), ***-good*** (whence ***-good*** sb.), ***-helping, -hoping, -prayer*** (as *sb.*), ***-price, -saving, -shame*** (whence ***-shame*** sb.); also **past-human** *adj.*, superhuman; **past-proportion** *sb.*, immeasurableness, immensity. Also more recently, **past-pointing** *Med.* [tr. G. *vorbeizeigen* (R. Bárány 1910, in *Wien. med. Wochenschr.* LX. 2036)], pointing to one side of an object that a person intends to point at, e.g. after being spun round, as a diagnostic test.

1553 ASCHAM in *Lett. Lit. Men* (Camden) 15 Thei judge bashfull men to be rude, and past-shames to be well manered. 1553 T. WILSON *Rhet.* (1567) 107 The extreme wickednes of some pastgood roisters. *a* 1586 SIDNEY *Arcadia* III. Wks. 1724 II. 445 Sorrowing not only his own sorrow, but the past-comfort sorrow which he foreknew his mother would take. 1601 SHAKS. *All's Well* II. i. 124 To prostitute our past-cure malladie To empericks. *Ibid.* IV. iii. 158 What a past-sauing slaue is this? 1602 J. DAVIES *Mirum in Modum* (1878) 6 The Soule is such a precious thing, As cost the price of past-price deerest bloud. 1606 SHAKS. *Tr. & Cr.* II. ii. 29 Will you with Counters summe The past proportion of his infinite? 1614 SYLVESTER *Parl. Vertues Royall* 1257 Immortall Beauties of past-humane Soules. 1631 CHAPMAN *Caesar & Pompey* Plays 1873 III. 143, I be forc't To helpe my Countrey, when it forceth me To this past-helping pickle. 1767 S. PATERSON *Another Trav.* I. 332 Enable me..to rejoice the past-hoping heart. 1876 FARRAR *Marlb. Serm.* xiii. 124 The past-feelingness of a miserable despair. 1876 G. M. HOPKINS *Wreck of Deutschland* xxxiii, in *Poems* (1967) 62 A vein for the visiting of the past-prayer, pent in prison, The-last-breath penitent spirits. 1916 *N.Y. Med. Jrnl.* 15 July 100/2 Movement of the endolymph in the semicircular canals in a given direction, stimulates the sensitive hair cells in these canals, and produces definite phenomena. These phenomena are: 1, A twitching of the eyes or nystagmus of a certain type; 2, vertigo; 3, so-called 'past pointing'; 4, falling reactions. 1934 R. R. GRINKER *Neurology* xiii. 372 In cerebellar disturbances if a past pointing does occur it is outward, no matter where the lesion. 1977 J. MACLEOD *Davidson's Princ. & Pract. Med.* (ed. 12) xiv. 662 If a movement is attempted with the eyes closed the finger overshoots towards the side of the cerebellar lesion ('past-pointing').

b. In various nonce-wds. (adjs.), as ***past-prime, past-the-middle-age***; **past-due**, overdue; **past-gone**, bygone, former, late; **past-meridian** (*fig.*), past one's prime, elderly; **past-ordinar** *Sc.*, extraordinary, exceptional, uncommon, 'by-ordinar'.

1896 *Harper's Mag.* XCIII. 158/1, I wrote out the *past-due subscription bill. 1784 R. BAGE *Barham Downs* I. 199 When you reflect upon your *past-gone occupation. 1898 G. MEREDITH *Odes Fr. Hist.* 14 Like dotage of the *past-meridian dame For some bright Sungod adolescent. 1823 GALT *Entail* lxiv, A man o' *past-ordinar sense. 1826 —— *Lairds* xii, The Doctor is a past ordinar young man. 1883 J. GREENWOOD *Odd People in Odd Places* xxiv. 204 These *past-prime belles of the garden. 1844 J. T. HEWLETT *Parsons & W.* x, A *past-the-middle-age college bed-maker.

pasta ('pæstə). [It., = PASTE *sb.*] A generic name for various forms of Italian dough mixtures or 'pastes', as macaroni, spaghetti, vermicelli, etc. Also *attrib.* and *Comb.*

[1673 J. RAY *Observations Journey Low-Countries* 405 *Paste* made into strings like pack-thread or thongs of whit-leather (which if greater they call *Macaroni*, if lesser *Vermicelli*) they cut in pieces and put in their pots as we do oat-meal to make their *menestra* or broth of.] 1874 R. H. BUSK *Folk-Lore of Rome* 118 There was a dish of 'pasta' heaped up like a mountain. 1927 F. STARK *Lett. from Syria* (1942) i. 13 They were preparing us a gigantic *pasta asciutta*. 1934 *Discovery* Aug. 215/1 What these country folk do not know about the preparation of *pasta* in its various forms of macaroni, spaghetti, tagliatelli and so on,..is not worth knowing. 1946 C. P. STEWART *Her Husband's House* xx. 134 She slapped a sheet of pasta down upon the..table. 1958 *Woman* 8 Feb. 23/1 British manufacturers are now successfully making pasta products. 1959 *Sunday Times* 22 Mar. 5/4 Pasta-loving Italian girls carry too much weight around the hips. 1973 *Times* 1 Dec. 6/5 The pasta-makers have stopped delivering spaghetti and other products to the shops. 1974 *Guardian* 31 Jan. 12/4 Trials have been made here to grow the durum or 'pasta' wheat, from which macaroni is made. 1976 *New Yorker* 15 Nov. 51/3 'George would be pleased to hear that,' Lenore says, lifting a small piece of pasta to her lips.

pastaique, var. PASTEQUE *Obs.*, water-melon.

pastall, obs. form of PASTEL[1].

ˈ**pastance.** *Obs.* exc. *arch.* Also 6 **pastaunce.** [app. a phonetic repr. of F. *passe-temps* (in 15–16th c. also *passetamps, passetans*, Godef.), f. *passe* vb. imper. (PASSE-) + *temps* time, in It. *passatempo*. For the final *-ce*, cf. TENSE, in early use also *tence*. See also PASSE-TEMPS and PASTIME.] Recreation; = PASTIME *sb.* 1.

1501 DOUGLAS *Pal. Hon.* I. 409 Quhat gudlie pastance? and quhat menstralie? 15.. SKELTON *P. Sparowe* 1095 To haue in remembraunce Her goodly dalyaunce, And her goodly pastaunce. *c* 1525 HEN. VIII *Pastance vitht gude companye* i, For my pastance, hunt, syng, & daunce, my hart is sett! *Ibid.* ii, Youthe must haue sum daliance Off good or yll, sum pastance. 1598 YONG *Diana* I. i, They haue no kind of pastaunce Which you think not to excuse. 1873 DIXON *Two Queens* II. XII. iii. 298 His fine ballad, 'Pastance with good company', rank[s] among the better known. 1906 *Outlook* 7 Apr. 471/2 During the dog-days..the grouse, the pheasant, and the fox are..withdrawn by the needs of Nature from their altruistic task of providing pastance for the gentlemen of England.

pastay, obs. form of PASTY *sb.*

paste (peɪst), *sb.* Also 4–8 **past**, 5–6 **paast**, 6 **payst(e**, 6–7 **paist**. [a. OF. *paste* (13th c. in Littré), mod.F. *pâte* = Pr., Sp., It. *pasta*:—Com. Romanic *pasta* (instanced in L. in a medical sense 'a small square piece of a medical preparation', Marc. Empir. *c* 400), generally supposed to be ad. Gr. πάστη, also pl. παστά, πασταί barley porridge, sb. uses of παστός sprinkled.]

1. *Cookery.* **a.** Flour moistened with water or milk and kneaded, dough; *esp.* (now only) with addition of butter, lard, suet, or the like, as used in making pastry, etc.

1377 LANGL. *P. Pl.* B. XIII. 250 þanne wolde I be prest.. paste [*v. rr.* past, paast] for to make, And buxome and busy aboute bred and drynke. 1390 GOWER *Conf.* I. 294 The levein of the bred, Which soureth all the past. *c* 1430 *Two Cookery-bks.* 45 Make fayre past..and keuere þin cofyns with þe same past. 1526 *Pilgr. Perf.* (W. de W. 1531) 39 b, Mixtynge water with floure, & werkynge it in to paste. 1582 N.T. (Rhem.) *1 Cor.* v. 6 A litle leauen corrupteth the whole paste. 1605 SHAKS. *Lear* II. iv. 124 Cry to it Nunckle, as the Cockney did to the Eeles, when she put 'em i' th' Paste aliue. 1769 MRS. RAFFALD *Eng. Housekpr.* (1778) 144 To make crisp Paste for Tarts. 1888 MRS. BEETON *Bk. Househ. Managem.* §1676 Common Paste for Family Use... $1\frac{1}{2}$ lb. of flour, $\frac{1}{2}$ lb. of butter, rather more than $\frac{1}{2}$ pint of water.

b. Name for various sweet confections of doughy consistence. † ***paste royal***, a confection of sugar and spices: see quot. 1676.

1389–90 *Durham Acc. Rolls* (Surtees) 596 In iij Coffins de pastreall. *c* 1440 *Anc. Cookery* in *Househ. Ord.* (1790) 455 A half pounde of past roiale. 1591 in *Lyly's Wks.* (1902) I. 449 Preserues,..iellies,..marmelats, pasts, comfits, of all sorts. 1653 W. I. *True Gentlew. Delight* 53 To make Paste-royal in Sauces. Take Sugar..four ounces, very finely beaten and searced, and put into it an ounce of Cinnamon and Ginger, and a grain of Musk, and so beat it into paste, with a little Gum-Dragon. 1662 *Stat. Irel.* (1765) II. 461, Past of Jean, the pound 7*s.* 6*d.* 1796 MORSE *Amer. Geog.* II. 635 Making marmalades and perfumed pastes, which exceed those of Genoa. 1853 SOYER *Pantroph.* 285 Oublies..were thin sheets of paste composed of flour and honey. 1858 SIMMONDS *Dict. Trade* s.v., The term paste is applied to the inspissated juice of liquorice, and some other vegetables.

c. Applied to compositions of this consistence (usually sweet) used as baits in angling.

1653 WALTON *Angler* viii. 169 The Carp bites either at wormes or at Paste. *Ibid.* 170 As for Pastes, there are almost as many sorts as there are Medicines for the Toothach. 1704 (*title*) The Compleat Fisher..Being a Clear..way of Taking all Sorts of Fresh-Water Fish with the Worm, Fly, Paste, and other Baits. 1898 *Westm. Gaz.* 5 Oct. 9/3 Salmon-roe is his favourite and usual lure, and with this bait—the 'paste' he calls it—he works sad havoc.

d. A relish made of some fish or crustacean cooked, pounded, and seasoned; as ***anchovy-paste, shrimp-paste***.

1817 KITCHINER *Cook's Oracle* (1823) 320 [Receipt for making] Anchovy Paste or le Beurre d'Anchois. 1836 *Guide to Worcester* Advt., A stock of anchovies and anchovy paste. 1855 HASSALL *Food & its Adulterat.* 505 One of the samples of bloater paste was adulterated..with starch or flour. 1902 *Daily Chron.* 28 Aug. 3/2 The pots were first made for the shrimpers of Pegwell Bay—to contain the shrimp-paste prepared there.

2. a. A mixture of flour and water (sometimes strengthened with starch) boiled together, used as a cement for sticking paper and other substances.

1530 PALSGR. 250/2 Paast or glewe, *cole.* 1601 HOLLAND *Pliny* I. 393 The common past that wee vse, made with the finest floure of wheat. 1710 HEARNE *Collect.* (O.H.S.) III. 46 Small bits of Paper sticking with some of the Past with w[ch] 'twas fix'd. 1879 *Print. Trades Jrnl.* No. 29. 47 Brush paste, not gum, lightly over the back.

†**b.** = PASTEBOARD 2. *Obs.*

1548–9 (Mar.) *Bk. Com. Prayer* (Colophon), The same bounde in paste or in boordes. 1562 in *Comm. Ld. Grey of Wilton* (Camden) 59 A schoocheon of armes wrowght on payste.

3. a. *gen.* Any composition or mixture containing just enough moisture to render it soft and plastic: see quots., and b, c below.

1604 E. G[RIMSTONE] *D'Acosta's Hist. Indies* v. xx. 383 An idoll made of paste of wheate and mays mingled with hony. 1727–41 CHAMBERS *Cycl.* s.v. *Porcelain*, With the sediment, collected at bottom in form of a paste, [they] fill a kind of moulds. 1774 GOLDSM. *Nat. Hist.* (1776) VIII. 92 The egg is involved in a sort of paste, which serves at once for the young animal's protection and nourishment. 1800 tr. *Lagrange's Chem.* II. 30 Forming corrosive muriate of mercury into a paste with water. 1839 URE *Dict. Arts* 631 A species of rapid crystallization ensues, and the thin paste soon acquires a solid consistence.

b. A mixture of clay and water (sometimes with other ingredients) of which earthenware or porcelain is made; distinguished as ***hard paste*** or ***soft paste*** according to its consistence and power of resisting heat.

1735 *Dict. Polygraph.* s.v. *China*, To make your paste of this powder, first dissolve an ounce of very white gum arabic in a pail of water [etc.]. 1753 CHAMBERS *Cycl. Supp.* s.v. *Porcelain*, The china-ware being made of a paste, part of which is made of a substance in itself scarce possible to be vitrified. 1879 J. J. YOUNG *Ceram. Art* 55 There is..very little difference in hardness between the hard-paste and the soft-paste.

c. A soft composition applied to the skin, medicinally or as a cosmetic (or taken internally).

1765 GOLDSM. *Double Transform.* 85 In vain she tries her paste and creams, To smooth her skin, or hide its seams. 1842 DUNGLISON *Med. Lex.*, *Paste*, a compound medicine like the pastil, but less consistent, flexible, less saccharine, and more mucilaginous. 1863–76 CURLING *Dis. Rectum* (ed. 4) 48 The confection of black pepper..known as Ward's Paste..in great repute as a remedy for piles... The usual dose is a drachm three times a day. 1901 *Brit. Med. Jrnl.* No. 2097. 39 A variety of pastes are also useful in this stage [of eczema].

4. *fig.* The material of which a person is figuratively said to be made (in reference to quality).

c 1645 HOWELL *Lett.* I. I. xliv. (1655) 69 The Inhabitants of that Town [Geneva], methinks, are made of another paste. 1700 DRYDEN *Fables* Ded., Others were more sweet and affable, made of a more pliant paste. 1865 M. ARNOLD *Ess. Crit.* v. 174 To us..with the German paste in our composition. 1868 BROWNING *Ring & Bk.* VI. 329 But you, who are so quite another paste Of a man,—do you obey me?

5. A hard vitreous composition (of fused silica, potash, white oxide of lead, borax, etc.), used in making imitations of precious stones; a factitious or artificial gem made of this. Also called STRASS. Also *attrib.* Made of, or adorned with, paste.

1662 MERRETT tr. *Neri's Art of Glass* xcii. 143 This past imitates all Jewels and colours, and hath a wonderful shining and lustre, And in hardness too it imitates the jewels. 1718 LADY M. W. MONTAGU *Let. to C'tess Bristol* 10 Apr., That paste with which they make counterfeit jewels. 1753 CHAMBERS *Cycl. Supp.* s.v., Pastes, in the glass trade, a sort of compositions of the glass kind, made from calcined crystal, lead, and metallic preparations, to imitate the several natural gems. 1796 BURNS *Poem on Life* iii, Tho' fiction out may trick her, And in paste gems and fripp'ry deck her. 1824 W. IRVING *T. Trav.* I. 28 High-heeled shoes ..with paste or diamond buckles. 1827 LYTTON *Pelham* i, The diamonds went to the jeweller's, and Lady Frances wore paste.

6. *Min.* A mineral substance in which other minerals are imbedded.

1828 in WEBSTER.

†**7.** Some kind of ornamental head-dress (app. made with a foundation of pasteboard) worn by women. *Obs.*

1529 MORE *Suppl. Soulys* Lijb, Wyth partelettes and pastis garneshed wyth perle. 1530 PALSGR. 183 *Vnes paces*, a payre of pastes for the attyre of a womans heed. *Ibid.* 252 Paste for a lady or woman, *unes paces.* 1541–2 *Act 33 Hen. VIII*, c. 5 Every other..person..whos Wiff shall were any Frenche hood or bonett of Velvet, w[t] any habiliment, past, or egge, of golde, perle or stone. 1570 BILLINGSLEY *Euclid* XI. 320 If ye draw the like formes in matter that wil bowe and geue place, as most aptly ye may do in fine pasted paper, such as paste-wiues made womens pastes of. 1592 GREENE *Vision* Wks. (Grosart) XII. 227 The Bride..was very finelie dizond in a little Cappe, and a faire paste. [1853 ROCK *Ch. of Fathers* IV. xii. 174 The bride, when a maiden, wore her hair flowing..and nothing but a wreath of jewels, called a 'paste', or flowers, about her head.]

8. *Comb.*, as (sense 2) ***paste-bowl, -brush*** (also in sense 1), ***-pot***; (sense 3) ***paste-blacking***; **paste-bodied** *a.*, of porcelain (see quots.); **paste-cutter**, an instrument for cutting paste into shapes for pastry; **paste-eel**, a small nematoid worm (*Anguillula glutinis*) found in sour paste; **paste-fitter**, a workman who fits together with paste the parts of boot-uppers for the machine; †**paste-god**, an idol made of paste; **paste grain**, split sheep-skin with paste put on the back to harden it and give a better grain; also, occas. used of morocco; **paste-horn**, a cow's horn used as a receptacle for paste; †**paste-house**, a building where pastry is made; **paste-kettle**, a kettle for boiling paste; **paste-maker**, (*a*) a person employed in making paste; (*b*) a machine for mixing the ingredients of paste; †**paste-meat**, pastry; †**paste-pin**, a wooden pin for rolling paste, a rolling-pin; **paste-point** (*Printing*): see quots., and POINT *sb.*; **paste-rock** (*Geol.*), a shaly formation found in Wales, also called *Tarannon shales*; †**paste-roller**, a rolling-pin = *paste-pin* (*obs.*); **paste-wash**, paste much diluted with water, used in bookbinding; hence **paste-wash** *v.*, to apply a mixture of paste and water to leather bindings, in order to improve the surface before lettering or decoration is applied; hence ***paste-washing*** vbl. sb.; **paste-water** = *paste-wash*; †**paste-**

wife, a woman who made and sold 'pastes' (sense 7) and other articles of female attire (*obs.*).

1915 R. L. HOBSON *Chinese Pott. & Porc.* II. ix. 141 Steatitic porcelain,..with the body..composed of *hua shih* ..is light to handle, and opaque; and the body has a dry, earthy appearance, though it is of fine grain and unctuous to touch. It is variously named by the Chinese *sha-t'ai* (sand bodied) and *chiang-t'ai* (*paste bodied). **1936** *Burlington Mag.* Jan. 10/1 Many fine specimens of a 'soft paste' white porcelain (paste-bodied the Chinese call it). **1964** M. MEDLEY *Handbk. Chinese Art* 63/1 *Chiang-t'ai*, 'paste bodied' wares made from a fine-grained white firing clay, often miscalled 'soft paste'. These wares occur mainly from the 18th century onward. **1873** E. SPON *Workshop Receipts* Ser. I. 394/1 Tools for small work..*paste-bowl. **1846** *Jewish Manual, or Pract. Information Jewish & Mod. Cookery* vi. 106 Beat the yolk of an egg, dip a *paste-brush into it, and lay it on the crust before baking. **1845** E. ACTON *Mod. Cookery* i. 5 Divide the bread into dice, or cut it with a deep *paste-cutter into any other form. **1893** BARING-GOULD *Cheap Jack Zita* II. 84, I sold a box of paste-cutters at one and nine. **1857** C. E. OTTÉ tr. *Quatrefages' Rambles* I. 282 Certain *Paste-eels which belong to the Helminthes. **1883** *B'ham Daily Post* 11 Oct., Boot Trade.—Wanted, an experienced *Pastefitter for General Men's Work. **1626** PURCHAS *Pilgrimage* (ed. 4) Table, *Paste-god of the Mexicans [cf. 880 the Religious Virgins or Nuns mingled a quantity of Beets with rosted Maiz, and moulded it with Hony, making an Image of that paste]. **1880** *Bookseller* 3 May 471 Cruden's Concordance..in limp *Paste-grain and Morocco. **1885** *Ibid.* 5 Mar. 236 Books in padded paste grain and German calf. **1923** H. A. MADDOX *Dict. Stationery* 59 Pastegrain.—Also abbreviated to P.G., but more correctly specified as pastegrain roan. Comprises the thin grain side of a split sheepskin, mechanically grained with a cracked or fissured pattern and stiffened slightly by pasting on the back... In the fancy trade P.G. roan is elaborately but erroneously described as French morocco. **1963** B. C. MIDDLETON *Hist. Eng. Craft Bookbinding Technique* xi. 122 In the 30s and 40s of the nineteenth century hard- and paste-grain morocco replaced straight-grain morocco and russia for use on fine bindings. **1834** CARLYLE *Sart. Res.* III. i, Working on tanned hides, amid pincers, *paste-horns, rosin, swine-bristles. **1471-2** *Durham Acc. Rolls* (Surtees) 94 Pro nova construccione unius *Pastehous juxta ostium Coquinæ. **1480-1** *Ibid.* 97, j pipa et j tubba in le Pastehous. **1824** GALT *Quadr.* in *Rothelan* III. 187, I..showed the *paste-impression of the seal. **1825** *Sporting Mag.* XVII. 36 A somewhat truant disposition..coupled him to a *paste-kettle. **1875** KNIGHT *Dict. Mech.*, **Paste-maker*, a stirring-machine for mixing the components of paste. **1598** *Epulario* D ij, These *past meates would..be yellow with Saffron. **1611** FLORIO, *Pasticciami*, all manner of pyes or paste-meates. **1769** MRS. RAFFALD *Eng. Housekpr.* (1778) 145 Roll it up tight, then with your *paste-pin roll it out again. **1825** HANSARD *Typographia* 912 The blocks being..inked with the requisite colours in proper succession, and united..by means of those sheet-anchors of pressmanship called points, three or even four of which are fixed (by what a printer calls *paste-points) upon the tympans, so as to act upon the margins of the print. **1888** JACOBI *Printer's Vocab.* s.v., Paste-points: very fine points—usually drawing-pins—used for very closely registered work on a hand-press. **1845** *Ainsworth's Mag.* VII. 27 Elliston now demanded the *paste-pot. **1857** N. W. T. ROOT *School Amusements* 207 A large scrap-book is prepared, a committee of selection is chosen, a paste-pot made ready, and contributions are invited. **1881** F. G. LEE *Reg. Baront.* v. 51 There was little furniture..except a desk, a deal counter, and a paste-pot. **1885** *Lyell's Elem. Geol.* xxvii. (ed. 4) 431 A..set of beds of fine light grey or blue shales, termed '*paste-rock', which overlie the Upper Llandovery strata. **1660** HEXHAM *Dict.*, *Een Rol-stock*, a *Past-roler to make Pyes with. **1880** J. W. ZAEHNSDORF *Art of Bookbinding* 116 The porous varieties [of leather] must be *paste-washed carefully. *Ibid.* 174 Paste-wash.—Paste diluted with water. **1946** E. DIEHL *Bookbinding* II. xxii. 327 When leathers such as calf, sheep, or russia are used, they should be paste-washed before tooling, in order to fill up the many fine pores. *Ibid.*, Calf and other very porous leathers require a heavier paste wash than morocco or levant. **1963** B. C. MIDDLETON *Hist. Eng. Craft Bookbinding Technique* xiv. 211 Paste-wash, glaire, glue-size, yolk of egg and boot and furniture polishes have been used on leather, but mainly to improve the surface. **1921** *Librarian* Nov. 74 *Pastewashing and varnishing tends to crack and destroy the leather, and does not soften or preserve it in the slightest degree. **1946** E. DIEHL *Bookbinding* II. xxii. 327, I do not approve of paste-washing or sizing leather if it can be avoided. **1875** *Ure's Dict. Arts* I. 424 (*Bookbinding*) The leather..is..softened by..the application of *paste-water to make it pliable. **1880** J. W. ZAEHNSDORF *Art of Bookbinding* 116 The non-porous leathers need only be washed with thin paste water or vinegar. **1901** D. COCKERELL *Bookbinding* xiv. 198 Paste-water is paste and water well beaten up to form a milky liquid. **1550** CROWLEY *Epigr.* 32 Her mydle braced in, as smal as a wande..some b[u]y wastes of wyre at the *paste wyfes hande. **1570** Paste-wife [see 7].

paste (peɪst), *v.* [f. PASTE *sb.* 2, 3.]

1. a. *trans.* To make to adhere or stick by means of paste; to fasten with paste. ***to paste up***, to stick up (on a wall, etc.) with paste. ***to paste down***, to line the cover of a book by attaching half the endpaper to it.

1561-2 in Willis & Clark *Cambridge* (1886) II. 142 For pastinge yᵉ table of the x commandementes ijd. **1592** NASHE *P. Penilesse* (ed. 2) 18 b, Such as paste vp their papers on euery post. **1665** *Phil. Trans.* I. 80 With Parchment pasted or glewed upon them. **1687** A. LOVELL tr. *Thevenot's Trav.* I. 136 Several pieces of Cloth pasted together. **1710** SWIFT *Baucis & Phil.* 94 The ballads pasted on the wall. **1804** M. G. LEWIS *Bravo of Venice* (1856) II. 310 The following address was..pasted against the corners of the principal streets. **1835** 'J. A. ARNETT' *Bibliopegia* I. 67 When dry, the end papers are pasted down, and the work finished. **1843** PRESCOTT *Mexico* (1850) I. I. v. 122 The feathers, pasted on a fine cotton web, were wrought into dresses. **1880** J. W. ZAEHNSDORF *Art of Bookbinding* viii. 35 When the book is to be pasted down, the ends [*sc.* end-papers] are lifted from the book. **1901** D. COCKERELL *Bookbinding* xvii. 254 To paste down end papers, the book is placed on the block with the board open. **1963** B. C. MIDDLETON *Hist. Eng. Craft Bookbinding Technique* xiii. 203 Until, roughly, the end of the first quarter of the nineteenth century the endpapers of all grades of bindings were pasted down without being trimmed.

b. *transf.* and *fig.* To cause to adhere closely or firmly (as if by pasting).

1863 *N. Syd. Soc. Year-bk. Med. for 1862.* 387 General diffuse peritonitis, many coils of intestine being pasted together by adherent lymph. **1883** H. W. V. STUART *Egypt* 425 A perfect tempest of wind, which..drove the Era against the western bank, where she remained hopelessly pasted.

2. To cover by (or as by) pasting on or over.

1609 DEKKER *Gvlls Horne-bk.* IV. (1862) 24 [A] door, pasted and plastered up with serving-mens' supplications. **1669** STURMY *Mariner's Mag.* II. xii. 79 Paste it well with good Paper. **1697** DRYDEN *Æneid* IX. 1099 With driving dust his cheeks are pasted o'er. **1849** MRS. CARLYLE *Lett.* II. 38, I have been busy..pasting a screen..all over with prints.

3. To incorporate with or into a paste, as a colour in dyeing.

1862 C. O'NEILL *Dict. Calico Print. & Dyeing* s.v. *Resists*, Resist compositions intended for this latter purpose are usually called pastes, and the colour so preserved is said to be 'pasted'.

4. *slang.* To beat, thrash: cf. BASTE *v.*³ Also, to inflict heavy damage on by bombing or shelling; in *Cricket*, to hit (a ball, the bowling) hard.

1846 *Swell's Night Guide* 58 They pasted his nibs, and scarpered rumbo. **1851** [see PASTING 3]. **1873** *Slang Dict.*, *Paste*, to beat, to thrash vigorously. **1882** *Daily Tel.* 6 Oct. 2/2 No matter how he punches her and 'pastes' her. **1896** A. MORRISON *Child of Jago* 132 'Is ribs is goin' black where father pasted 'em. **1911** *Daily Colonist* (Victoria, B.C.) 30 Apr. (Mag.) 10/1 As the ducks kept coming round the point the shooters in the canoes had a great opportunity of pasting them. **1924** A. C. MACLAREN *Cricket Old & New* xiii. 128 Many and many a short ball bowled by Gregory in the Test Matches of 1921, would have been pasted to the square leg boundary in the days 'when Plancus was consul'. **1930** *Strand Mag.* May 348/1 The Major was gazing at Trout's forehead, where the stick had pasted him. **1934** D. L. SAYERS *Nine Tailors* III. 275 Deacon..pastes the fellow one. **1942** *Hutchinson's Pict. Hist. War* 18 Mar.–9 June 23 (*caption*) The nose of a Westland Whirlwind single-seater fighter... The Whirlwind has been used with much success for 'pasting' enemy aerodromes. **1955** M. ALLINGHAM *Beckoning Lady* ix. 127 He came to this part of the country in 1942 when London was being pasted. **1973** A. MANN *Tiara* ii. 17 [He] used to play for Yorkshire. Let's go down and watch him paste the bowling. **1977** *New Yorker* 25 July 70/3 She guessed correctly each time just where Mrs. King, in charge of the forecourt, would be pasting her volley.

5. The verb-stem in *Comb.*: see PASTE-DOWN and PASTE-IN *a.* and *sb.*

Hence **pasted** *ppl. a.*, fastened or covered with paste; † ***pasted paper***, pasteboard.

1570 [see PASTE *sb.* 7]. **1601** HOLLAND *Pliny* I. 393 Long streaks..between the pasted places. *a* **1693** *Urquhart's Rabelais* III. xxxvii. 314 Ears of pasted Paper. *c* **1790** IMISON *Sch. Art* II. 53 The pasted side of the paper.

paste, obs. form of PASTY *sb.*

pasteboard ('peɪstbɔəd), *sb.* (*a.*) [f. PASTE *sb.* or *v.* + BOARD *sb.* (I and II are really of distinct formation.)]

A. *sb.* **I.** †**1.** A substitute for a thin wooden board made by pasting sheets of paper together; *esp.* a board of a book so made (cf. BOARD *sb.* 4). *Obs.*

1548-9 (Mar.) *Bk. Com. Prayer, Consecr. Abps.* etc. (Colophon), Bounde in lether, in paste bordes or claspes. **1612** STURTEVANT *Metallica* (1854) 66 The superficiall [model] describeth only the..lineaments in paper, bordes or past-bords. **1726** SWIFT *Gulliver* II. vii, It was as thick and stiff as a Past-board. **1796** WITHERING *Brit. Plants* (ed. 3) I. 32 Put it upon a dry fresh pasteboard, and, covering it with fresh blossom paper, let it remain in the press [etc.].

2. a. As a material: A stiff firm substance made by pasting together, compressing, and rolling, three or more sheets of paper.

These sheets consist of 'outsides' and 'middles'; in ordinary pasteboard, the 'middle' is of inferior quality, and generally of a greyish colour. *Cardboard* is pasteboard made of superior paper, and of the same quality and colour throughout; a finer and more highly-finished form made with starch paste is called *ivory board*. The name 'pasteboard' is sometimes improperly given to *pulpboard*, made not by pasting, but of compressed paper pulp.

1562 in *Comm. Ld. Grey of Wilton* (Camden) 59 Item iiij. greate schoocheons wrowght with metall on payste boorde. **1606** PEACHAM *Graphice* (1612) 94 Take of the fairest and smoothest pastboord you can get. **1793** BEDDOES *Math. Evid.* 21 A model of each triangle cut out in pasteboard. **1858** LARDNER *Hand-bk. Nat. Phil., Hydrost.*, etc. 196 A conical reflecting shade, the best material for which is paper or paste-board.

b. *fig.* As the type of something flimsy, unsubstantial, or counterfeit: cf. B. b.

1829 CARLYLE *Misc.* (1857) I. 270 Doings in the world of pasteboard. **1838** EMERSON *Addr. Cambridge, Mass.* Wks. (Bohn) II. 203 The new worship..to the goddess of Reason,—to-day, pasteboard and fillagree, and ending to-morrow in madness and murder.

3. *slang.* A card. **a.** A visiting-card. **b.** A playing-card; also, playing-cards collectively. **c.** A railway-ticket.

a. 1837 T. HOOK *Jack Brag* i, They lodge their pasteboard and away they go. **1849** THACKERAY *Pendennis* xxxvi, 'We shall only have to leave our pasteboards, Arthur'. He used the word 'pasteboards', having heard it from some of the ingenious youth of the nobility about town, and as a modern phrase suited to Pen's tender years. **1889** 'J. S. WINTER' *Mrs. Bob* (1891) 70 The unutterable fag of paying calls and leaving pasteboards.

b. 1859 THACKERAY *Virgin.* xv, Three honours in their hand, and some good court cards,..hour after hour.. delightfully..spent over the pasteboard. **1896** FARJEON *Betrayal J. Fordham* III. 277 I'm that neat with the pasteboards. I can shuffle 'em any way I want.

c. 1856 'OCKSIDE' & 'DOESTICKS' *Hist. & Rec. Elephant Club* 29 Putting his physiognomy before the seven by nine aperture through which the money goes in and the pasteboard comes out. **1873** J. H. BEADLE *Undevel. West* xxxvi. 771 The call of 'Tickets, gents', showed one man without the pasteboard. **1901** *Daily Chron.* 11 Nov. 5/2 Season ticket holders may not travel indefinitely without producing their 'pasteboards'.

II. 4. *Cookery.* (Usually with hyphen.) A board on which paste or dough is rolled out for making pastry, etc. (Cf. BOARD *sb.* 2.)

1858 SIMMONDS *Dict. Trade*, *Paste-board*, a wooden board on which dough is rolled out for pastry. **1888** MRS. BEETON *Bk. Househ. Managem.* §1674 Make the paste, using a very clean pasteboard and rolling-pin. **1894** A. ROBERTSON *Nuggets* 51 She dropped the rolling-pin on the paste-board.

5. The board used by a paper-hanger in cutting and pasting wall-paper.

1901 *J. Black's Carp. & Build., Home Handicr.* 41 The lengths of paper should be laid..on the pasteboard supported by the trestles.

B. *attrib.* (or as *adj.*) **a.** Made of pasteboard.

1599 B. JONSON *Cynthia's Rev.* I. Wks. (Rtldg.) 76/2 As if we practised in a paste-board case. **1641** MILTON *Reform.* II. Wks. (1851) 42 To blow them down like a past-bord House built of Court-Cards. **1668** WOOD *Life* Mar. (O.H.S.) II. 131 Bound with a past-board cover and vellum over it. **1707** MORTIMER *Husb.* (1721) I. 290 Put them into a Paste-board Box. **1885** J. K. JEROME *On the Stage* xii. 105 The pantomime was still running, and Mat played a demon with a pasteboard head.

b. *fig.* Unsubstantial; unreal, counterfeit, sham.

1659 TORRIANO, *Signóre Cartóne*, a pastboard Lord, a Lord of Clouts. **1764** GOLDSM. *Trav.* 150 The pasteboard triumph and the cavalcade. **1898** WYNDHAM *Poems Shaks.* p. lxx, The alarums and excursions of these paste-board hostilities.

C. *Comb.*, as ***pasteboard-cutter***, ***-maker***; ***pasteboard-like***, ***-looking*** adjs.; **pasteboard-wasp**, a species of wasp which makes a nest resembling pasteboard (cf. *paper-wasp*).

1875 KNIGHT *Dict. Mech.* 1636/1 **Pasteboard-cutter*,..for grooving and cutting pasteboard strips employed for making boxes. **1662** GERBIER *Principles* 18 Nor are the wooden Shutters such *Pastboard-like things, as are..put on the..London..Houses. **1849** E. B. EASTWICK *Dry Leaves* 195 The Agency..was a large *pasteboard-looking house. **1669-96** AUBREY *Lives*, *Cavendish* (1898) I. 153 His wife..sold this incomparable collection..to the *past-board makers for wast paper. **1864-5** WOOD *Homes without H.* xiv. (1868) 259 The nest..of the *Pasteboard Wasp (*Chartergus nidulans*).

Hence **'pasteboardy** *a.* (*nonce-wd.*)

1878 *Scribner's Mag.* XV. 574/2 The construction is of the thinnest, most pasteboardy kind.

pastec, var. PASTEQUE *Obs.*, water-melon.

paste-down ('peɪstdaʊn). [f. PASTE *v.* 5 + DOWN *adv.* 1.] In modern bindings, that part of the end-paper which is pasted to the inside of the cover of a book; in earlier bindings, a piece of paper or parchment used as a lining inside a cover.

1888 C. T. JACOBI *Printers' Vocab.* 97 *Paste-downs*, the blank flyleaves, sometimes coloured, at either end of a book which are pasted down on the covers. **1901** D. COCKERELL *Bookbinding* xvii. 254 One of the paste-down papers is then stretched over the board. *Ibid.* 256 All rubbing down must be done through paper, or the 'paste-down' will be soiled. **1934** *Yorkshire Archæol. Jrnl.* XXXI. 338 The paste-down and recto of the fly-leaf are blank. **1954** N. R. KER (*title*) Fragments of medieval manuscripts used as pastedowns in Oxford bindings. **1963** *Times* 11 June 5/7 A collection of leaves and fragments from manuscripts..which had been used as pastedowns in later bindings went to Quaritch. **1972** P. GASKELL *New Introd. Bibliogr.* 148 Then the endpapers were sewn on... Their purpose was, as paste-downs, to reinforce the joints of the covers.

pastee, obs. form of PASTY *sb.*

paste-egg, corrupt. of *pasch-egg*: see PASCH *sb.* 3.

paste-in ('peɪstɪn), *a.* and *sb.* [f. PASTE *v.* 5 + IN *adv.* 1.] **A.** *adj.* Pasted in, inserted by pasting. Also, of a scrapbook, etc., containing blank paper on which cuttings or pictures may be pasted. **B.** *sb.* A correction or illustration printed separately from the main text of a book, and attached to the relevant page by its inner edge being pasted to the margin.

1902 *Daily Chron.* 30 June 3/3 Seeking the cause of this paste-in fly leaf. **1907** *Yesterday's Shopping* (1969) 436A (*heading*) Paste-in Albums for Photographs, &c. **1939** *Library* XIX. 486 When, more than a month after the publication of the *Lyrical Ballads*, 1800, Wordsworth received copies of Volume II, he was greatly irritated to find that the lower half of page 210..was blank... There exist at least two specimens of a paste-in supplying the fifteen missing lines... Each of the two specimens is pasted to the inner margin of page 211 to open out onto the blank on page 210. **1960** *Times* 13 Oct. 15/7 Where paste-ins have become puckered, wavy lines must be expected. **1971** L. M. HARROD

Librarians' Gloss. (ed. 3) 488 Paste-in. 1. A correction or addition to the text supplied after the sheets have been printed, and tipped into the book opposite the place to which it refers... 2. A separately printed illustration or map, cut to the size of the book, and the inner edge pasted into the text before gathering.

pastel[1] ('pæstəl). Also 6 -all. [a. F. *pastel* (1510 in Hatz.-Darm.), a. Pr. *pastel*, It. *pastello* 'woad to dye blew with' (Florio); dim. from *pasta* paste; 'the name having been applied first to the colouring matter obtained by reducing to a paste the twigs of the plant, then to the plant itself' (Hatz.-Darm.).

OF. had *pastel* in the senses 'paste, plaster, cake', etc.]

The plant Woad, *Isatis tinctoria*; also, the blue dye obtained from it.

1578 LYTE *Dodoens* I. xlvi. 66 This herbe is called..in English Woad, or Pastel: in French *Guesde* or *Pastel*: in Spanish also *Pastel*: in Italian *Guado*. **1696** PHILLIPS (ed. 5), *Pastel*, otherwise called Woad... It is of great use among the Dyers. **1783** JUSTAMOND tr. *Raynal's Hist. Indies* VI. 13 Indigo, when mixed with pastel,..rendered the colours..more lasting. **1838** T. THOMSON *Chem. Org. Bodies* 382 Thus prepared, pastel has a yellow or greenish-yellow colour.

b. *Comb.* **pastel-vat**: see quots.

1838 T. THOMSON *Chem. Org. Bodies* 382 To prepare the pastel vat, 4 parts of indigo, 50 parts of pastel, 2 parts of madder, and 2 parts of potash are employed. **1875** KNIGHT *Dict. Mech.* 1636/1 *Pastel*,..woad. It gives its name to the vat in which pastel and indigo are used, the *pastel-vat*.

pastel[2] ('pæstəl). Also 7-9 -il, (9 *erron.* -elle). [a. F. *pastel* (1676 in Hatz.-Darm.), ad. It. *pastello*: see PASTEL[1].]

1. A kind of dry paste made by grinding pigments and compounding them with gum-water, used as a crayon or for making crayons. *in pastel*, drawn with pastels: cf. CRAYON *sb.* 1 b.

1662 EVELYN *Chalcogr.* v. Misc. Writ. (1805) 314 Rubbing in the shades with pastills and dry compositions. **1688** R. HOLME *Armoury* III. 144/2 Pastils are rouls of Plaster or Clay ..to draw withal. **1696** in PHILLIPS (ed. 5). **1727-41** CHAMBERS *Cycl.*, *Pastil*, or *Pastel*,..a sort of paste made of several colours, ground up with gum-water, either together or separately; in order to make crayons to paint with on paper, or parchment. **1735** *Dict. Polygraph.* s.v., Also the crayons themselves, are call'd pastils. **1859** GULLICK & TIMBS *Paint.* 316 Coloured crayons, or pastels, are made by the mixture of colour with a colourless base. **1866** GEO. ELIOT *F. Holt* i, Portraits in pastel of pearly-skinned ladies with hair-powder.

2. a. A drawing in pastel; also, the art of drawing with pastels.

1855 THACKERAY *Newcomes* lxiii, What awfully bad pastels there were on the walls! **1882** HAMERTON *Graphic Arts* xviii. 152 The principle of pastel is that the colours, when on the paper, are in a state of dry powder, most of which is slightly adherent. **1884** *Century Mag.* XXIX. 205 It is a question among artists..whether pastel should be called a process of drawing or of painting. **1893** F. ADAMS *New Egypt* 154 Two charming portraits,..two pastels standing in all the piquant incompleteness of a rapid reality.

b. *transf.* to a kind of literary sketch.

1893 *Critic* (U.S.) 22 Apr. 249/1 The French pastel is really a little study (without a very definite beginning or end) of a trifling topic which lacks complexity, and needs little more than a very moderate space.

3. Applied to certain soft tints of dress-material and to soft or subdued shades used generally in textiles, interior decoration, etc. Usu. *attrib.*

1899 *Westm. Gaz.* 9 Mar. 3/1 A gown in the new pale blue we call pastel. **1899** *Daily News* 21 Oct. 7/7 The soft, wraith-like tints..are now in fashion again. The modern name for them is 'pastels',..for these soft, half-faded tones bear the same relation to real colours as pastels do to oil-paintings. *Ibid.* 4 Nov. 7/6 Pastel blue or pink, hydrangea blue or pastel green. **1900** *Westm. Gaz.* 8 Mar. 3/1 Pastel tones are ubiquitous in both silks and woollens. **1926-7** *Army & Navy Stores Catal.* 678/1 Gloves..washable suède, light grey, pastelle, or white. **1934** *Archit. Rev.* LXXV. 14/2 There is, for instance, a stone known as Quartzite, which.. when worked to a rough surface provides an everlasting wall lining in a variety of cool pastel shades. **1951** *Good Housek. Home Encycl.* 19/1 Upholstered fibre furniture..is available in various pastel shades. **1970** H. RATCLIFFE *Home Decorating* xiii. 84/2 White plus a colour is a tint, white plus colour plus grey or black is a pastel shade. **1974** N. FREELING *Dressing of Diamond* 96 A glimpse of pastel green tiles. **1976** *Star* (Sheffield) 26 Nov. 24 (Advt.), 1976 (P) Cavalier 1600 L 4-door. In pastel beige. Fitted radio.

4. *attrib.* and *Comb.*, as ***pastel painter, picture***; ***pastel-coloured, -like, -tinted*** adjs. (See also 3.)

1884 *Century Mag.* XXIX. 207/1 The pastel painters of to-day. **1889** *Pall Mall G.* 15 Oct. 2/3 His 'Leisure Hour' is very decorative and pastel-like. **1900** *Westm. Gaz.* 10 Feb. 3/1 The strongest hues of the pastel-box. **1922** H. CRANE *Let.* 2 Mar. (1965) 80 Delicate pastel tinted flowers. **1932** *Daily Tel.* 25 Apr. 4/4 Pearls on Pastel Gowns. Pearls are to be worn even more than usual this season. The reason is the vogue for pastel coloured gowns. **1952** *Granta* 29 Nov. 8/1 We find it agreeable to place a Victorian chair or print among the blond woods and foam rubber, or to hang pastel-tinted antlers on the wall near a mobile. **1978** B. FREEMANTLE *Clap Hands* iv. 26 A fine-featured..man who affected pastel coloured shirts with matching socks.

Hence **ˌpastelle'teer** (*nonce-wd.*) [after *pamphleteer*], a writer of literary pastels (2 b); **'pastelling**, the production of pastel-pictures.

1893 *Critic* (U.S.) 22 Apr. 249/1 Mr. Harrison S. Morris, who has given to *Arcadia*..a neat parody-burlesque of the pastel, adds a few pungent sentences upon it... He calls it Ollendorfian; and the 'pastelleteer' the seeker after 'odd similitudes'. **1899** *Daily News* 1 Aug. 6/4 The Artistic Ghost moves in higher circles than those of pavement pastelling.

†**paste'lade.** *Obs.* Also **pystelade, petelade.** [app. repr. an OF. **pastellade*, deriv. of OF. *pastel* paste, etc., or *pastelle* a dish: see PASTEL[1].] A dish in old cookery.

c **1430** *Two Cookery-bks.* 59 Spaulde de Motoun. Capoun Rostyd. Pastelade. *Ibid.* 62 Pystelade chaud. Pystelade fryid... Petelade Fryid.

pastelar, -ler(e, variants of PASTLER.

pastellist, pastelist ('pæstəlɪst). [f. PASTEL[2] + -IST: in mod.F. *pastelliste*.] An artist who works with pastels or coloured crayons.

1881 *Times* 9 Feb. 4/1 Mr. Whistler..succeeds in combining something of the brilliancy and purity of the pastellist with the general effect..of the oil and water-colour painter. **1888** *Academy* 3 Nov. 294/2 M. Machard, who may be accounted the Rubens of the French Society of Pastelists. **1889** *Pall Mall G.* 18 July 6/1 The Shah has become quite a pavement favourite. The open air pastellist has taken him up and is doing a roaring trade in the last novelty.

pastemaker: see PASTE *sb.* 8, PASTY *sb.* c.

pastemps, var. PASSE-TEMPS *Obs.* = PASTIME *sb.*

‖**pasteque.** *Obs.* Also 6-7 **pateque**, 7 **pastique, -aique**, 9 **pastec.** [a. F. *pastèque* (pastɛk), †*pateque* (1512 in Hatz.-Darm., 1610-79, Pyrard de Laval in Yule) = Pg. *pateca*, Sp. *albudeca, badea*, ad. Arab. *al-baṭṭīkha*, vulgar form of *-biṭṭīkha*; cf. Heb. *ăbaṭṭiakh*, Syr. *paṭṭīkh* (Numbers xi. 5).] The Water-melon.

1585 T. WASHINGTON tr. *Nicholay's Voy.* I. xviii. 21 Ther grow good Melons, Raues, and pateques. **1660** F. BROOKE tr. *Le Blanc's Trav.* 184 A little kernell..like that of a Pastique, or Pumpion. **1677** J. P. tr. *Tavernier's Trav.* (1684) II. 80 There are also *Pateques*, or Water-Melons in abundance. **1696** tr. *Du Mont's Voy. Levant* 131 The Pastaique is a Fruit very much resembling a Citrul, but not quite so big... There are two sorts of it, one red and the other white. **1826** [J. R. BEST] 4 *Yrs. France* 321 Melons and pastecs, or water-melons.

paster ('peɪstə(r)). [f. PASTE *v.* + -ER[1].]

1. One who pastes: see PASTE *v.*

1737 J. CHAMBERLAYNE *St. Gt. Brit.* II. III. 86 Three Paisters for fixing on the said Labels, at 50*l.* per *ann.* each. **1885** *Ann. Rep. Camb. Univ. Libr. Syndicate* 2 The wages of R. F—, Senior Paster, were raised from 38*s.* to £2 a week.

2. orig. *U.S.* (See quot. 1888.) Also, a piece of adhesive paper used for various other purposes.

1870 *Congress. Globe* 13 Apr. 2659/3 There were ten tickets..which were scratched and had pasters with the name of Caleb N. Taylor. **1882** *Nation* (N.Y.) 6 July 7/2 The Erie and Central Railroads have made the attempt to rid themselves of all liabilities..by putting a 'paster' on their bills of lading. **1888** BRYCE *Amer. Commw.* II. III. lxvi. 494 Small slips of paper gummed at the back..are called 'pasters' or 'stickers', because the independent voter pastes them over the name or names..he objects to on the ticket which he is about to place in the box. **1889** *Columbus* (Ohio) *Disp.* 19 Sept., Persons may paste slips over names, providing the names so substituted by pasters are printed or written in red ink. **1906** *World's Work* (N.Y.) May 7511/1 You may read upon its label that it has been 'U.S. Government Inspected'. The paster on the box from which it came assures us again of that fact.

paster, obs. form of PASTURE.

†**'pasterer.** *Obs.* Also 6 **paistrer, paisterer.** [f. *pasterie*, PASTRY + -ER[1]: cf. *fripperer*.] A pastry-cook, confectioner.

1552 HULOET, Paistrer, *ceragius*. **1586** T. B. *La Primaud. Fr. Acad.* (1589) 193 Sobrietie..caused Alexander the Great to refuse those Cookes and Paisterers which Ada Queene of Caria sent unto him. **1600** SURFLET *Countrie Farme* v. xx. 709 The flower of meale..whereof the pasterers or cookes for pastrie, doe make wafers. **1660** HOWELL *Lexicon*, A pasterer, *pasteleur, ou pastier, pastissier, pasticier*.

pastern ('pæstən), *sb.* Forms: 4 **pastron**, 6 **pastren**, 7 **pastrone**; 6 **pasto(u)rne, -tour**, 6-7 **pasterne**, 8 **pastorn**, 6- **pastern.** [ME. *pastron* = OF. *pasturon* (1530 in Palsgr.), mod.F. *paturon*, deriv. of OF. *pasture* used in sense 2, also a shackle or cord with which a horse is tethered by the pastern-joint (mod.Norman dial. *pâture* clog, shackle); held by French etymologists to be the same word as OF. *pasture*, F. *pâture* PASTURE, transferred first to the tether of a horse at pasture, and then to the joint. Cf. It. *pastora, pastoia* (Florio), a shackle for a horse, also a pastern, part of a horse's foot (Baretti); *pastura* pasture.]

†**1.** A shackle fixed on the foot of a horse or other beast at pasture, or of an unruly horse to confine his movements; a tether; a hobble. *Obs.*

c **1343** *Durham Acc. Rolls* (Surtees) 543 In lxiiij capistris.. iij paribus de pastrons [etc.]. **1347-8** *Ibid.* 545 Et in vj par. de Pastronnes novis. **1469** *Ord. Dk. Clarence* in *Househ. Ord.* (1790) 97 Sadelles, harnesse,..halters, turnelles, pastrons,..and all suche other. **1570** NORTH *Doni's Philos.* (1888) 258 A tying Coller, a paire of Pastornes, and a Cranell. **1607** MARKHAM *Caval.* II. ix. 104 [Some] will..put a verie strong pasterne vpon one of the horses hinder feete, then passing the other end of the corde thorowe the pasterne, bring it againe to the saddle pommell. *Ibid.* VII. lxxxii. 78 Shackle gall is any sore got by wearing pasternes, shackls, or other fetters. **1611** COTGR., *Empas*, shackles, fetters, or pasternes for vnrulie, or vnbroken horses. *a* **1625** FLETCHER *Chances* I. ix, Ye found an easie foole that let you get it [a child]; Sh' had better have worne pasternes. [**1824** BARETTI *Ital.-Eng. Dict.* (ed. 7), *Pastoja*, a pastern, a shackle for a horse.]

2. That part of a horse's foot between the fetlock and the hoof, corresponding in extent to the two pastern-bones.

1530 PALSGR. 252/2 Pastron of an horse, *pasturon*. Pastren, *pasturiau*. *a* **1533** LD. BERNERS *Huon* cxxx. 477 The bloode of them that were slayne, ranne in the strettes to the horse pastours. **1636** MASSINGER *Gt. Dk. Flor.* III. i. Wks. (Rtldg.) 177/2 He treads weak in his pasterns. **1774** GOLDSM. *Nat. Hist.* (1862) I. III. i. 347 A tail which hangs down to the pastern. **1843** LEVER *J. Hinton* vii. (1878) 43 A strong hackney, whose flat rib and short pastern showed his old Irish breeding.

b. The corresponding part in other quadrupeds; also *transf.* the human ankle.

1555 EDEN *Decades* 260 There are also Alces muche lyke vnto hartes, with..longe legges withowt any bowinge of theyr houx or pasternes. *a* **1625** FLETCHER *Hum. Lieut.* II. iii, Let me see your leg;—she treads but low in the pasternes. *a* **1700** DRYDEN *Wife of Bath's T.* 52 So straight she walk'd, and on her pasterns high. **1845** YOUATT *Dog* ii. 33 The low placing of the pastern.

3. = Pastern-bone (see 4 b).

1656 BLOUNT *Glossogr.*, *Pastern* (*talus*), the ankle or huckle-bone of a Beasts foot. **1840** BLAINE *Encycl. Rur. Sports* (1870) §633 The lesser pastern or coronary bone.. receives the great pastern below.

4. *attrib.* and *Comb.*, as ***pastern artery***; **pastern-deep** *adv.*, so deep as to cover the pasterns; **pastern-joint**, the joint or articulation between the cannon-bone and the great pastern-bone.

1682 *Lond. Gaz.* No. 1747/4 A black Gelding,..standeth cripled with his pastern joynts. **1846** J. BAXTER *Libr. Pract. Agric.* (ed. 4) I. 451 There is a dryness of the hoof, throbbing of the pastern arteries. **1863** MISS BRADDON *J. Marchmont* II. vi. 135 Pools of water through which the wretched animals floundered pastern-deep.

b. pastern-bone, each of the two bones (***upper*** or ***great***, and ***lower*** or ***small*** ***p.***) between the cannon-bone and the coffin-bone, being the first and second phalanges of the foot of a horse.

1601 HOLLAND *Pliny* I. 351 The Once..hath that which somewhat resembles a pasterne bone. **1726** POPE *Odyss.* xx. 367 Where to the pastern-bone..The well-horn'd foot indissolubly join'd. **1855** HOLDEN *Hum. Osteol.* 170 The three joints of this finger answer to those called 'great pastern bone', 'little pastern bone', and 'coffin bone' in the horse.

Hence †**'pastern** *v.*: see quot.; **'pasterned** *a.* [-ED[2]], furnished with or having pasterns: in parasynthetic compounds, as ***short-, thick-pasterned***.

1598 FLORIO, *Pastoiare*, to fetter, to clog, to shackle, to pastern, to giue. **1614** MARKHAM *Cheap Husb.* I. i. (1668) 2 Short pastern'd, strong joynted. **1898** MISS YONGE *Founded on Paper* xxi, Poor broken-kneed, thick-pasterned Jack [an old horse].

pastery, obs. form of PASTRY.

†**'pasteth.** *Obs.* Also **pastyth, pasthethe.** [perh. an alteration of OF. *pasté*, mod.F. *pâté*, PASTY: cf. *bounteth, dainteth*, etc.] = PASTY *sb.*

c **1425** *Voc.* in Wr.-Wülcker 661/22 *Hic pastillus*,.. pastyth. **1483** *Cath. Angl.* 271/1 A Pasteth, *pastellus*.

paste-up ('peɪstʌp). [f. PASTE *v.* 5 + UP *adv.*[1] 21.] **1.** A plan of a page or group of pages, with the position of text, illustrations, etc., indicated. Also *attrib.*

1930 FRESHWATER & BASTIEN *Pitman's Dict. Advertising & Printing* i. 186/2 A proof with blocks, blue prints, or odd pieces of type matter pasted up in position is termed a paste-up. **1948** H. MISSINGHAM *Student's Guide Commercial Art* II. 76 Paste-up. The various components of the complete layout pasted together on a card to form the complete advertisement. **1949** MELCHER & LARRICK *Printing & Promotion Handbk.* 202/1 Extreme neatness is not necessary on a paste-up dummy. *Ibid.*, There are many tricks to paste-up technique. **1967** E. CHAMBERS *Photolitho-Offset* iii. 35 This key drawing or paste-up, as it is often called, should at least include all type pulls. **1975** J. BUTCHER *Copy-Editing* v. 61 In the paste-up the illustrations are represented by photocopies, rough sketches or just empty rectangles. **1977** *Sci. Amer.* Sept. 95/3 (Advt.), In May, 1977 we announced KODAK MX-929 Resist, for use in an arrangement for translating a paste-up of a newspaper page to metal by scanning with a He-Ne laser and modulating an argon ion laser to expose the resist.

2. A piece of paper or cardboard with a newspaper or book clipping, etc., pasted to it. Also *transf.*

1944 *Daily Progress* (Charlottesville, Va.) 11 Mar. 8/6 Simple paper paste-ups a child could do. **1953** *Amer. Speech* XXVIII. 81 The *D*[*ictionary of*] *A*[*mericanisms*]..had the benefit of but a mere 300,000 quotation slips... Nor did this number represent fresh materials only, for it included thousands of paste-ups from its predecessors. **1972** D. H. LAURENCE *Coll. Letters G. B. Shaw* II. p. xviii, Making paste-ups of previously published correspondence. *a* **1974** R. CROSSMAN *Diaries* (1975) I. 401 The following weekend my red box contained the paste-up of all the extracts and they included one or two absolutely unequivocal statements. **1977** *Times Lit. Suppl.* 3 June 682/1 His novel is a carefully constructed, defiantly random paste-up of *faits divers*.

Pasteur (pastœr, pɑːˈstɜː(r), pæ-), *v.* [From the name of the French scientist Louis Pasteur (1822–95).] *trans.* = PASTEURIZE 1.

1892 *Chambers' Encycl.* X. 685 This effect of time may.. be imitated by art—by Pasteuring the wine.

Pasteur (pastœr, pɑːˈstɜː(r), pæ-). The name of *Pasteur* (see PASTEUR *v.*) used *attrib.* and †in the possessive to designate apparatus he devised and effects he discovered, as **Pasteur effect**, the effect of oxygen of inhibiting fermentation in favour of respiration in certain organisms and tissues; formerly called the *Pasteur reaction*; **Pasteur('s) flask**, a glass flask with an elongated neck bent downwards so that micro-organisms in the air cannot contaminate its contents; **Pasteur('s) pipette**, a sterile pipette which at one end has a plug of cotton-wool or the like and a rubber bulb and at the other terminates as a capillary tube whose end is sealed at the time of drawing and not broken until the pipette is to be used; also, in mod. use, a pipette bought for similar purposes but not sterilized, plugged, or sealed; **Pasteur reaction** [after G. *Pasteursche reaktion* (O. Warburg 1926, in *Biochem. Zeitschr.* CLXXII. 435)] = *Pasteur effect.*

1935 *Nature* 15 June 995/2 (*heading*) Mechanism of the Pasteur effect. **1942** O. MEYERHOF et al. *Symposium Respiratory Enzymes* 48 Most doubly equipped organisms possess in the Pasteur effect a regulatory device that enables them to use, as occasion demands, either their aerobic or their anaerobic systems. **1953** FRUTON & SIMMONDS *Gen. Biochem.* xx. 483 Under anaerobic conditions the rate of consumption of carbohydrate by muscle tissue is approximately six to eight times that observed under aerobic conditions... This inhibition, by oxygen, of the rate of carbohydrate breakdown is frequently termed the Pasteur effect. **1971** I. G. GASS et al. *Understanding Earth* x. 146/2 In many primitive organisms, the change-over from fermentation to respiration occurs when oxygen reaches about 1 per cent of its present concentration in the atmosphere. Pasteur pointed out this effect..during his study of the spoilage of wines, so it is known as the 'Pasteur effect'. [**1876** tr. *Schützenberger's On Fermentation* II. iii. 327 (*heading*) M. Pasteur's flask to deprive the air of its germs.] **1882** W. W. CHEYNE *Antiseptic Surg.* i. 17 Mr. Lister has found that in Pasteur's flasks with the long open necks, no floating dust is present after what was originally there has settled. **1913** G. MARTIN *Industr. & Manuf. Chem.: Organic* v. i. 231 A pure culture in sterilised wort is obtained by inoculating from each separate colony nutrient sterilised wort contained in a Pasteur's flask. *Ibid.*, A small amount of pure yeast culture from a Pasteur flask. **1969** R. K. DAS *Industr. Chem.* II. xvi. 221 The sterile wort is inoculated with pure culture (from the Pasteur flask). **1902** J. W. H. EYRE *Elem. Bacteriol. Technique* i. 21 (*heading*) Capillary pipettes or Pasteur's pipettes. **1903** SWITHINBANK & NEWMAN *Bacteriol. of Milk* 547 (*heading*) Method of making a Pasteur pipette. **1972** *Jrnl. Endocrinol.* LIV. 108 Fluid from control and test dishes was removed with a sterile Pasteur pipette. **1930** *Biochem. Jrnl.* XXIV. 1302 Ethyl *iso*cyanide is therefore said to be a specific inhibitor of the Pasteur reaction, *i.e.* of the reaction between respiration and fermentation, using the latter term to include glycolysis. **1966** IRVINE & JAMES tr. *Lundegårdh's Plant Physiol.* iv. 193 The exact position of the Pasteur reaction in the glycolysis chain..cannot be very easily determined.

pasteurella (pɑːstəˈrɛlə, -æ-). Pl. **-ellæ, -ellas.** [mod.L. (V. Trevisan 1887, in *Rendiconti Reale Istituto Lombardo di Scienze e Lettere* XX. 94), f. prec. + *-ella*, diminutive ending.] A bacterium of the genus so called, which includes those causing plague and other acute infectious diseases in man, other mammals, and birds.

1913 H. J. HUTCHENS tr. *Besson's Pract. Bacteriol.* xxviii. 446 Lignières..came to the conclusion that varieties of the Pasteurella could be distinguished by means of their pathogenic properties. *Ibid.* 447 Organisms of the pasteurella group are..very pleomorphic. **1929** G. F. PETRIE in *Syst. Bacteriol.* (Med. Res. Council) III. 139 The plague bacillus..is generally considered to be a member of the Pasteurella group. **1929** H. SCHÜTZE in *Ibid.* IV. 447 (*heading*) Pasteurellas in man. **1949** *Vet. Rec.* 5 Feb. 64/1 (*title*) Pneumonia in sheep associated with infection by a pasteurella-like organism. **1961** *Lancet* 7 Oct. 812/2 Organisms of the pasteurella group are non-motile aerobic gram-negative rods. **1963** JUBB & KENNEDY *Path. Domestic Animals* I. iii. 172/1 A complete separation of the different strains of the pathogenic pasteurellae has still to be determined. **1974** Q. N. MYRVIK et al. *Fund. Med. Bacteriol. & Mycol.* xxiv. 309 The pasteurellae..are parasites and pathogens for an unusually wide range of animal species.

pasteurellosis (ˌpɑːstərɛˈləʊsɪs, -æ-). *Med.* and *Vet. Sci.* Pl. **-oses.** [ad. F. *pasteurellose* (J. Lignières 1901, in *Ann. Inst. Pasteur* XV. 734), f. prec. + -OSIS.] An infection produced by a bacterium of the genus *Pasteurella.*

1902 *Nature* 29 May 120/1 The name pasteurelloses is applied to a group of diseases of the same type, including typhoid fever and pneumonia of the horse, chicken cholera and hæmorrhagic septicæmia of the sheep, ox, and pig. **1913** H. J. HUTCHENS tr. *Besson's Pract. Bacteriol.* xxviii. 447 (*heading*) The pasteurelloses and plague in animals. **1925** *Jrnl. Hygiene* XXIV. 66 Deaths due to Pasteurella and deaths in which no evidence of pasteurellosis was found.. were grouped together. **1929** [see BARBONE]. **1963** JUBB & KENNEDY *Path. Domestic Animals* I. iii. 172/1 In the various hosts, pasteurellosis may take a variety of forms. **1966** *Daily Tel.* 4 Nov. 13/4 He has pasteurellosis too, or 'pseudo-tuberculosis', also found in voles, sparrows, magpies, wrens, swallows, and, especially, wood pigeons. More important, children can be affected—it causes a swelling of the glands that may be mistaken for appendicitis.

Pasteurian (pɑːˈstɜːrɪən, -æ-), *a.* [See PASTEUR *v.* and -IAN.] Of or belonging to Pasteur.

1888 *Scott. Leader* 23 Aug. 4 The latest extension of the Pasteurian system. **1898** P. MANSON *Trop. Diseases* vii. 138 Protective inoculations..prepared on the Pasteurian system of attenuation.

Pasteurism (ˈpæstərɪz(ə)m, ˈpɑːst-). [f. the surname *Pasteur* (see above) + -ISM.] A method of treatment, devised by Pasteur for preventing or curing certain diseases, esp. hydrophobia, by successive inoculations with attenuated virus gradually increasing in amount.

1883 J. H. CLARKE (*title*) Physiological Fallacies. The Millennium of Pasteurism. **1894** CANON WILBERFORCE in *Westm. Gaz.* 26 Feb. 2/1, I do not believe in Pasteurism. On the contrary, I think it is the greatest delusion of the age.

pasteurize (ˈpɑːstɜːraɪz, ˈpɑːstjʊə-, -æ-), *v.* [f. as prec. + -IZE.]

1. *trans.* To prevent or arrest fermentation in (milk, wine, etc.) by exposure to a high temperature so as to destroy contained microbes or germs; to kill most but not all of the micro-organisms present in (food) so as to render its consumption safe and to improve its keeping quality (as by heat treatment or irradiation).

Distinguished from *sterilize*, which implies the killing of all the micro-organisms.

1881 *Pharmaceut. Jrnl.* 29 Oct. 358 Beer..previously 'pasteurized'—and exposed to direct sunlight... At the end of three weeks the non-pasteurized beer..commenced to lose its clearness; but the pasteurized sample remained quite bright. **1896** *19th Cent.* Sept. 458 Cream should be pasteurised before being sent out from the dairy. **1945** *ABC of Cookery* (Ministry of Food) vi. 19 Unless milk has come from a herd of tuberculin tested cows or has been pasteurized it should be scalded or boiled before drinking. **1959** *Internat. Jrnl. Appl. Radiation & Isotopes* VI. 205/2 Packaging does not present a problem for foods 'pasteurized' by radiation. **1966** *Proc. Internat. Symp. Food Irradiation* (Internat. Atomic Energy Agency) 842 The cost of pasteurizing food (300 000 to 500 000 rads) should be less than one-tenth the cost of radio-sterilization. **1970** *Preservation of Fish by Irradiation* (United Nations F.A.O.) 3 A test was..developed for evaluating whether or not there exists a botulinum Type E hazard in fish fillets pasteurized with gamma radiation.

2. To treat by the method of PASTEURISM.

1886– [implied in PASTEURIZATION: see below].

Hence **ˈpasteurized** *ppl. a.* (also *fig.*); also **ˈpasteurizing** *ppl. a.*; **pasteuriˈzation**, the action or process of pasteurizing (in sense 1 or 2); **ˈpasteurizer**, an apparatus for pasteurizing milk.

1886 *Times* 21 Oct. 4/6 Hydrophobia mortality fluctuates widely... What value then for or against Pasteurization can attach to the returns of a single year? **1895** *Westm. Gaz.* 30 Sept. 1/3 The Pasteurisation of beer has..become a phrase. **1897** *Melbourne Argus* 2 Mar. 6/7 The pasteuriser is a circular tank of tin into which the milk is received. **1957** *Jrnl. Appl. Bacteriol.* XX. 286 For meat processing, two different types of treatment have been envisaged. One is complete sterilization... The other process, which is becoming known as 'pasteurization', consists in decreasing the bacterial numbers sufficiently to give a substantial increase in storage life, usually under refrigeration. Doses from 5×10^4 to 5×10^5 rads have been suggested as giving useful results. **1959** *Internat. Jrnl. Appl. Radiation & Isotopes* VI. 143/1 Some species of fish stand up better to irradiation than others and..these when subjected to only pasteurizing levels suffer none of the undesirable changes produced by sterilization. **1962** *Listener* 13 Sept. 406/2 After Mr Kokoschka's verve and spontaneity our average spoken word sounds pasteurized and insipid both in substance and expression. **1966** *Proc. Internat. Symp. Food Irradiation* (Internat. Atomic Energy Agency) 527 With the exception of thiamine, no significant changes occurred in the water-soluble vitamins of haddock fillets and clam meats subjected to pasteurizing doses of radiation. *Ibid.* 549 (*heading*) Investigations on pasteurization of cold marinades by ^{60}Co gamma rays. **1973** STEWART & AMERINE *Introd. Food Sci.* v. 203 Radiation dosages for pasteurization are only about a tenth of that [*sic*] required for sterilization. **1976** *National Observer* (U.S.) 19 June 20/5 The pasteurised, homogenised, tanned, toothy, breasty, false-lashed, make-up-larded, honey cascade-haired beings thrust upon us as representatives of young womanhood. **1976** N. FREELING *Lake Isle* vi. 38 Castang, though a youngish cop with a university degree, didn't think much of his more pasteurized colleagues.

pastey(e, obs. form of PASTY *sb.*

‖**pasticcio** (paˈstittʃo). [It. *pasticcio* 'any manner of pastie or pye' (Florio), in med.L. *pastīcium*, deriv. of Com. Romanic *pasta* PASTE.] A medley of various ingredients; a hotchpotch, farrago, jumble; *spec.* **a.** In the orig. It. sense, a pie containing numerous ingredients, of which macaroni and some form of meat are the chief constituents. **b.** An opera, cantata, or other composition, made up of various pieces from different authors or sources, a pot-pourri. **c.** A picture or design made up of fragments pieced together or copied with modification from an original, or in professed imitation of the style of another artist; also, the style of such a picture, etc.

[**1706** *Art of Paint.* (1744) 67 Those pictures that are neither originals nor copies, which the Italians call *Pastici*.. because as the several things that season a pasty are reduc'd to one taste, so counterfeits that compose a *pastici* tend only to effect one truth.] **1752** H. WALPOLE *Lett. to Mann* 1 Nov., Our operas begin to-morrow with a pasticcio, full of most of my favourite songs. **1785** R. CUMBERLAND *Natural Son* I. i. 7 What a pasticcio of gauzes, pins, and ribbons go to compound that multifarious thing, a well-dress'd woman. **1787** P. BECKFORD *Lett. Italy* (1805) I. 7 My Letters will be a *pasticcio*, a mere hotch potch. **1880** W. S. ROCKSTRO in Grove *Dict. Music* II. 668 *Pasticcio*... A species of Lyric Drama, composed of Airs, Duets, and other movements, selected from different Operas, and grouped together..in such a manner as to provide a mixed audience with the greatest possible number of favourite Airs in succession. **1893** *Nation* (N.Y.) 11 May 349/2 His pasticcio, or remembrance, rather, of Ronsard, is fairly delightful. **1907** JOYCE *Let.* 18 Feb. (1966) II. 216, I have made a lovely pasticcio, it seems. **1923** *Mrs. Beeton's Bk. Househ. Managem.* 1326 *Pasticcio Maccharóni.* (*Macaroni Pie*). *Ingredients.*—¾ of a lb. of cold beef or mutton, ½ an onion, 3 or 4 tomatoes, ¼ of a lb. of macaroni, breadcrumbs, grated cheese, stock, salt, pepper, nutmeg. **1937** M. MORPHY *Good Food from Italy* 63 Pasticcio di maccheroni (Ferrara). **1967** *Listener* 19 Jan. 107/1 The *pasticcio*, the medley of movements contributed by different composers. **1973** *Guardian* 14 Apr. 5/4 Anyone at sea among unfamiliar Italian dishes would be well rewarded by going straight for such specialities as Pasticcio. **1973** J. WAINWRIGHT *Touch of Malice* 63 Fernlea Autumn Fair..had ended up as a crummy, screaming pasticcio of brash lights and belching noise. **1974** *Listener* 28 Feb. 282/3 Next year Handel supplied..*Deborah*, largely a *pasticcio* over which he took little trouble. **1976** *Survey* Summer–Autumn 322 The contents turn out to be a pasticcio of themes rather tenuously connected.

‖**pastiche** (pæˈstiːʃ), *sb.* [F. ad. It. *pasticcio*: see prec.] = prec. Now in more general use than *pasticcio.*

1878 SWINBURNE *Poems & Ball.* Ser. II. 129 (*title*) Pastiche. **1892** *Nation* (N.Y.) 24 Nov. 396/2 Mr. Burne-Jones is not accused..of plagiarism, but of *pastiche*, which is a very different thing. **1899** E. GOSSE *Life Donne* I. 62 It was left to his [Donne's] Caroline disciples to introduce..a trick of pastiche, an alloy of literary pretence. **1902** *Westm. Gaz.* 22 Nov. 3/1 It is an extraordinarily clever and unabashed lightning-pastiche of Sir Thomas Lawrence. **1934** C. LAMBERT *Music Ho!* I. 20 The illogicality of some of the present-day pastiches may give you 'a rare turn'. **1955** *Times* 11 May 7/5 At the Players' we are still basking in the glory of having started *The Boy Friend* on its historic career, and to attempt *pastiche* again would have been an affront to the theatrical gods. **1961** *Listener* 7 Sept. 335/1 The subject that lies at the back of popular writing on contemporary themes is sociology: it is the Americans who have sold best—Whyte, Riesman, Galbraith, the pastiche merchants Wright Mills and Vance Packard. *Ibid.* 5 Oct. 508/1 The new examination is *not* conceived as a pastiche of the G.C.E. **1964** *Ibid.* 16 Apr. 649/1 Henze is sometimes called an eclectic composer ..an inference that he is the worse for being a pasticheur... Henze's interest in pastiche has long since died a natural death. **1978** *Listener* 2 Feb. 158/2 Such genre pastiches as the recent film, *Chinatown.*

paˈstiche, *v.* [f. the sb.] **a.** *intr.* To create pastiches. Also const. *about.* **b.** *trans.* To copy or imitate the style of. Hence **paˈstiching** *vbl. sb.*

1957 *Listener* 26 Dec. 1082/2, I pastiche of course and exaggerate, but that is the kind of thing. **1962** D. LESSING *Golden Noteb.* III. 375 Well, Anna, and how do you describe all this pastiching about? **1965** R. G. COHN *Toward Poems of Mallarmé* 6 Rimbaud..'pastiched' Mallarmé's *Les Fleurs.* **1970** *Times* 17 Oct. 20 The unfortunate Victorian habit of 'reviving', that is, pastiching, the Renaissance, the Baroque and just about every other style of the past. **1973** *Nature* 11 May 49/2 A device for selecting as university students only those who have already demonstrated that they can survive a university course as pastiched at school.

‖**pasticheur** (pastiʃœr). [Fr., f. PASTICHE.] An artist who imitates the style of another artist.

1912 R. FRY *Let.* 3 Feb. (1972) I. 353 One doesn't like to be called a *pasticheur*... I've always been searching for a style to express my *petite sensation* in. **1913** *Nation* 2 Aug. 676 A skill which might lead him [*sc.* C. Brancuzi], in default of any overpowering imaginative purpose, to become a brilliant *pasticheur.* **1934** C. LAMBERT *Music Ho!* v. 329 The dog-Latin classicism of the post-war pasticheurs. **1944** *Burlington Mag.* Mar. 71/2 Steer, on the other hand, was a *pasticheur* and to say of him that he 'was beyond doubt the greatest of our landscape painters since Turner and Constable'..is as meaningless as it is ridiculous. **1958** *Observer* 7 Dec. 16/4 The obvious accusation against Betjeman is that he is a pasticheur—and it is certainly true that he has scarcely ever written a poem which was not, quite consciously, in the manner of someone else. **1964** [see PASTICHE *sb.*]. **1973** *Daily Tel.* 9 Apr. 5 For many he [*sc.* Picasso] was one of the great creators of his age. To others he was at best an accomplished pasticheur and at worst a mountebank. **1976** *Gramophone* Apr. 1643/3 Karg-Elert (1877–1933) was a pasticheur, too, and even a consciously humorous parodist in some of his miniatures.

pastie (ˈpeɪstɪ). [f. PASTE *v.* + -Y⁶, -IE.] (Chiefly *pl.*) A covering for the nipple of a strip-teaser's breast.

1961 *Washington Post* 17 May A3/6 Miss Mason was lying on the floor with nothing on except the scantiest of brassieres, known in the trade as 'pasties'. **1964** *Punch* 29 July 164/3 The young ladies [of the *Folies Bergère*] have been bidden [in New York]..to wear, in the cause of innocence, two 'pasties'. **1969** *Sunday Truth* (Brisbane) 23 Nov. 10/4 Stripper Sharon was promoting a Valley nightclub, wearing nothing on top but a couple of pasties to keep her modest. **1973** 'E. MCBAIN' *Let's hear It* viii. 123 Topless dancing, in this city, was something more than topless—the something more being pasties or filmy brassieres. **1975** *New Society* 23 Oct. 198/3 Go-go dancers in New York are not allowed to dance completely nude; they wear G-strings and mini bras or nipple-covering 'pasties'... For the dancers to get a tip, the 'pasties' usually have to come off.

‖**pastiglia** (pa'stiʎa). *Art.* Also pastiglio. [It., = paste.] A kind of stucco (see quots.). Also *attrib.*

1927 EBERLEIN & RAMSDELL *Pract. Bk. Ital., Span., & Portuguese Furnit.* 36 The process of *pastiglia* decoration.. consisted in covering the *cassone*, cabinet, or whatever the piece of furniture might be with coarse linen or fine canvas, strained or glued over both the moulded and flat surfaces. Over this were painted successive coats of *pastiglia*, a thick creamy mixture of *gesso*, which dried and hardened rapidly. **1938** L. E. COTCHETT *Evol. Furnit.* ii. 21 Canvas was.. painted with several coats of *pastiglia* or gesso. **1959** L. A. BOGER *Compl. Guide Furnit. Styles* iii. 27/2 Pastiglia work as a form of decoration is chiefly identified with the 15th century. **1969** R. MAYER *Dict. Art Terms & Techniques* 284/2 (*caption*) Italian casetta (casket) of the latter half of the 15th century, ornamented in pastiglia relief. **1977** *Technical Bull.* (National Gallery) Sept. 3/2 The top corners of the eight panels.. were decorated in pastiglio.

pastil, pastille ('pæstɪl, pæ'stiːl), *sb.* Also 7 pasteel, 7–8 pastill, 8 pastel, 8–9 pastile. [a. F. *pastille* (1561 in Hatz.-Darm.), ad. L. *pastillus*, *-um* a little loaf or roll of bread, a round lozenge, a troche, esp. an aromatic lozenge: a word of dim. form of which the primitive is uncertain, but which in Romanic was app. associated with *pasta* PASTE; cf. It. *pastilli* 'little pasties, pastelets, chewets' (Florio 1611); Sp. *pastillas* 'kindes of mixtures or pastes for to perfume withal' (Minsheu 1599).]

1. A small roll of aromatic paste prepared to be burnt as a perfume, now esp. as a fumigator, deodorizer, or disinfectant.

[**1616** B. JONSON *Devil an Ass* IV. iv, To know how to make Pastillos of the Dutchesse of Braganza, Coquettas.] **1658** tr. *Porta's Nat. Magic* VI. ii. 179 Artificers call those pellets which are made of the salts, and the forenamed powder and water, Pastils. **1690** SHADWELL *Am. Bigot* III, I'le get some Pasteels and stiffen my Whiskers. **1704** J. HARRIS *Lex. Techn.* I, *Pastills*, are Odoriferous Tablets, or Trochisks made up of Perfumes or Odorous Bodies, with Mucilage of Gum Tragacanth. **1715** tr. *C'tess D'Aunoy's Wks.* 422 Certain Spanish Pastils spread a fragrant Odour round the Room. **1835** MRS. CARLYLE *Lett.* I. 19 Burning pastilles before a statue of Jupiter. **1897** *Allbutt's Syst. Med.* IV. 791 Pastilles of benzoic acid or of the chloride of ammonium are also of service.

2. a. A kind of sugared confection of a rounded flat shape (often medicated); a troche, lozenge.

a **1648** DIGBY *Closet Open.* (1677) 104 Put into the sack some ambergreece or ambered-sugar or Pastils. *a* **1691** BOYLE *Hist. Air* (1692) 205 Divers pastils or lozanges that he was wont to carry in his pockets. **1706** PHILLIPS s.v., Among Confectioners, Pastils are a kind of perfum'd Sugar-paste of several Colours,.. as Apricot-Pastils, Cinnamon-Pastils, Orange-flower-Pastils, etc. **1888** F. ANSTEY *Black Poodle* etc., *Sugar Prince* 47 Rows of glass jars, containing pastilles and jujubes of every colour, shape, and flavour.

b. *Med.* A small disc of barium platinocyanide whose gradual change of colour when exposed to X-rays was formerly used as an indication of the dose delivered.

1906 *Sci. Abstr.* A. IX. 49 (*heading*) Use of platinocyanide pastilles in radiotherapy. **1922** G. W. C. KAYE *Pract. Appl. X-Rays* iv. 71 Of all the various intensity measurers, the pastille finds the most favour with medical men in this country. *Ibid.*, The pastille is placed at a specified distance from the anticathode of the bulb, and the colour is matched against one of a number of standard tints. **1956** C. W. WILSON *Radium Therapy* (ed. 2) iv. 74 Sabouraud.. made use of the fact that a pastille of barium platinocyanide turns from apple green to reddish brown when irradiated by X-rays.

3. = PASTEL² 1, q.v.

4. A paper tube containing the composition which, when ignited, causes a pinwheel or similar firework to rotate.

In recent Dicts.

5. *attrib.* and *Comb.* as *pastille box*, *paper*, etc.; *pastille-burning* adj.; **pastille-burner** = CASSOLETTE 2; **pastille dose** *Med.*, an obsolete unit of radiation dose corresponding to a change from one standard colour to another of a pastille (sense 2 b).

1853 MISS E. S. SHEPPARD *Ch. Auchester* i. (1875) 7 The bronze pastille-box. **1904** A. HAYDEN *Chats on Eng. China* i. 11 Crown Derby Pastille-Burner. **1957** MANKOWITZ & HAGGAR *Conc. Encycl. Eng. Pott. & Porc.* 32/2 There is.. a red script mark 'P. Bradley 1828' on a pastille burner probably of Coalport manufacture in the National Museum of Wales. **1971** *Country Life* 7 Oct. 922/2 The larger sizes [of pottery model houses] have a hole in their back, being intended for use as nightlights or pastille burners. **1833** T. HOOK *Parson's Dau.* I. ix. 95 His pastille-burning dragons. **1909** *Lancet* 15 May 1380/1 A Sabouraud pastille dose with the anticathode at 6½ inches from the nearest point of the scalp is given to the vertex, occiput, lower occiput, right side and left side in succession. **1935** *Nature* 14 Dec. 960/2 The ionisation unit of X-ray quantity, the röntgen, has practically replaced the older arbitrary standards such as the pastille dose. **1950** WALTER & MILLER *Short Textbk. Radiotherapy* x. 243 The 'pastille dose'.. has now been completely superseded and there is no justification for its continued use. **1835** WILLIS *Pencillings* II. xlv. 58 Incense-wood for my pastille lamp. **1884** KNIGHT *Dict. Mech.* Suppl., *Pastille Paper*, paper prepared with an odoriferous composition.

Hence **pastil, pastille** *v. trans.*, to fumigate with pastils.

1846 in WORCESTER (citing *Q. Rev.*).

†**pa'stilicate**, *v. Obs. rare*⁻⁰. [f. L. **pastillicāre*, inferred from *pastillicans* of globular shape.] (See quot.) Hence †**pastili'cation**.

1656 BLOUNT *Glossogr.*, *Pastilicate* (*pastilico*), to make in form of little round Balls, to minister Pills. **1658** PHILLIPS, *Pastilication*, a making any thing into the form of a pill or round ball.

pastillage ('pæstɪlɪdʒ, ‖pastijaʒ). [Fr., lit. compression of paste into blocks.] **1.** *Pottery.* (See quot. 1940.)

1901 W. P. RIX tr. *Bourry's Treat. Ceramic Industries* II. ix. 427 This method of decoration is known as 'pastillage'. **1940** *Chambers's Techn. Dict.* 619/2 *Pastillage*, dot and dribble designs made with coloured slip, which is dribbled from a container with a flexible base and a spout. **1947** *Horizon* June 369 There must be hundreds of years difference between the coarse idols obtained by a process of *pastillage* and the delicately coloured and modelled figures of the kind reproduced here. **1962** G. KINNELL tr. *Lehmann's Pre-Columbian Ceramics* I. ii. 19 The *pastillage* technique used in the decoration. *Ibid.* II. i. 40 The eyes, almost always slanted, are indicated by incisions or *pastillage*. **1974** SAVAGE & NEWMAN *Illustr. Dict. Ceramics* 214 *Pastillage*.., slip applied by trailing through a quill.

2. A type of icing.

[**1951** *Good Housek. Home Encycl.* 499/1 The special stiff royal icing.. (called pastillage in French).] **1963** *Times* 20 Apr. 10/3 The cake is decorated with 46 lb. of marzipan and 25 lb. of royal icing and pastillage.

pastilled ('pæstɪld), *a. rare.* [f. PASTIL, PASTILLE *sb.* + -ED².] Subjected to the effect of a medicated pastille.

1935 E. M. FORSTER *Abinger Harvest* (1936) 101 The clearing of pastilled throats.

pastime ('pɑːstaɪm, 'pæ-), *sb.* Forms: 5 pase tyme, 5–6 passe tyme, 6 passe-tyme (past-tyme, paste-time, past-time), 6–7 passe-time, 7 pas-time, 7–9 pass-time; 5– pastime (5–6 passetyme, passetime, pastyme). [f. PASS *v.* + TIME: in sense 1, tr. F. *passe-temps*: see PASTANCE. Sense 2 may be an independent formation.]

1. *gen.* That which serves to pass the time agreeably; recreation, diversion, entertainment, amusement, sport; occas. †occupation (*obs.*). (No *pl.*)

1490 CAXTON *Eneydos* xii. 43 The fayr pase-tyme that they take therat. **1491** —— *Vitas Patr.* (W. de W. 1495) I. li. 104 b/1 [They] came thyder euery daye in maner of passe tyme. **1526** TINDALE *Heb.* xiii. 9 Which have not proffeted them that have had their pastyme in them. **1572** *Nottingham Rec.* IV. 139 For pastyme in beyttyng of a bulle. **1635** QUARLES *Embl.* I. x. (1718) 41 Brave pastime, readers, to consume that day, Which without pastime flies too swift away. **1709** ADDISON *Tatler* No. 119 ¶2 Huge Leviathans.. take their Pastime as in an Ocean. **1870** FREEMAN *Norm. Conq.* (ed. 2) I. App. 746 On the road, seemingly by way of pastime, he ravages Gaul.

b. With *a* and *pl.*: A specific form of diversion or amusement; a recreation; a sport, a game.

c **1489** CAXTON *Blanchardyn* xxiii. 76 Tournoynge and behourdyng are my passe tyme. **1513** BRADSHAW *St. Werburge* I. 1052 The elder prynce.. Vsed haukynge, huntynge, for a past-tyme. **1562** ROWBOTHUM *Playe Cheasts* * iij b, The same game being a pastime wᵗout all tediousnes, malice,.. gyle, or deceit. **1634** MILTON *Comus* 121 The Wood-Nymphs deckt with Daisies trim, Their merry wakes and pastimes keep. **1722** SEWEL *Hist. Quakers* (1795) I. III. 204 He could not go to bowls or any other pastime. **1843** LYTTON *Last Bar.* I. i, The sports and pastimes of the inhabitants.

†**2.** A passing or elapsing of time; a space of time; an interval between two points of time. *Obs.*

1494 FABYAN *Chron.* VII. 645 In whiche passetyme the kynge sent.. vnto the forenamed John and hym by many meanys instaunsyd to leue the company of the lordys. *Ibid.* 666 In the whiche passetyme dyed innumerable people in the sayd cytie. **1529** RASTELL (*title*) The pastyme of people. The Cronycles of dyuers realmys and most specyally of the realme of Englond. *Ibid.* (1811) 161 In this pastyme [*i.e.* during this campaign] dyed Geffrey Plantagenet. [**1875** PARISH *Sussex Gloss.*, *Passtime*, time passed.]

3. *attrib.*, as *pastime-ground*, *-reading*, *-student*.

1843 LYTTON *Last Bar.* III. iv, The stranger of the pastime-ground was before her. **1902** *Daily Chron.* 22 Jan. 7/2 No sensible person in search of pastime-reading will waste time and attention upon the ponderous problem-novels.

'**pastime**, *v.* Now *rare.* [f. prec. sb.]

†**1.** *intr.* To pass one's time pleasantly; to take one's pleasure; to divert, entertain, or amuse oneself; to play. *Obs.*

1523 *IX Drunkardes* title-p., Storyes ryght plesaunte and frutefull for all parsones for to pastyme with. **1548** LATIMER *Ploughers* (Arb.) 25 They pastyme in theyr prelacies with galaunte gentlemen. **1567** MAPLET *Gr. Forest* 77 The Cat.. vseth to pastime or play with the Mouse ere she deuoureth hir. **1592** KYD *Sol. & Pers.* I. ii. 6 When did Perseda pastime in the streetes, But her Erastus ouer-eied her sporte?

†**b.** *trans.* To divert, amuse. *Obs.*

1577 HANMER *Anc. Eccl. Hist.* (1663) 162 He being.. linked with malefactors to pastime and sport the people. **1579** TOMSON *Calvin's Serm. Tim.* 324/1 Then must they goe to play & pastime them selues.

2. *trans.* (*nonce-use.*) To make a diversion of, to amuse oneself with, to find amusement in.

a **1860** J. A. ALEXANDER *Gosp. of Jesus* iv. 50 The man who pastimes Christ and His religion, who allows the Church a place among his sources of amusement.. may imagine that he really respects religion.

Hence †'**pastiming** *vbl. sb.* and *ppl. a.*; also †'**pastimer**, one given up to pastimes, one engaged in sport.

1573–80 BARET *Alv.* P 179 Pastiming, or sporting, ..*esbatement*. **1580** HOLLYBAND *Treas. Fr. Tong*, *Esbatement*, pastiming. **1606** BIRNIE *Kirk-Buriall* Ded., In all campestrial prowes and pas-tyming exploits. **1608** SIR J. HARINGTON *Nugæ Ant.* (1804) I. 382 Some idle pastimers did diverte themselves with huntinge mallards in a ponde.

†**pasti'naceous**, *a. Obs. rare.* [f. L. *pastināca* parsnip + -EOUS.] Of the nature of or akin to the parsnip.

1657 TOMLINSON *Renou's Disp.* 246 Its root is carnous.. of a pastinaceous sapour.

pastinacine (pæstɪ'neɪsaɪn). *Chem.* [f. L. *pastināca* parsnip + -INE⁵.] The name given by Wittstein to a volatile alkaloid distilled from the seeds of the parsnip; also found in the root of the broad-leaved water-parsnip (*Sium latifolium*).

1866–77 WATTS *Dict. Chem.* IV. 357. **1881** *Ibid.* 3rd Suppl. 1497.

†'**pastinate**, *ppl. a. Obs.* [ad. L. *pastināt-us*, pa. pple. of *pastināre* to dig: see PASTINE *v.*] Of land: Dug, prepared for planting.

c **1420** *Pallad. on Husb.* III. 50 This mon ek al thy soyles pastynate With wynes wold be filde. *Ibid.* IV. 177 Now melon seed.. is sette In places wel ywrought or pastynate.

So †'**pastinate** *v. trans.*, to dig, loosen by digging; †'**pastinated** *ppl. a.*, dug, delved; †**pasti'nation** [ad. L. *pastinātiōn-em*], digging.

c **1420** *Pallad. on Husb.* III. 130 In thi pastinated lond. **1623** COCKERAM II, To Delue, *Pastinate*. A Deluing, *Pastination*. **1656** BLOUNT *Glossogr.*, *Pastinate*, to delve or dig in a Garden. **1708** KERSEY, *Pastination* (in *Husbandry*), the opening, breaking fine, and laying loose of earth in order to be planted. **1721** in BAILEY. **1745** tr. *Columella's Husb.* III. xvi, The pastinated ground is proper for planting, when it is a little moist.

†'**pastine**, *sb. Obs. rare.* [ad. L. *pastinum* a two-pronged dibble; the digging and trenching of ground; also *pl.* ground so prepared (Palladius 4th c.).] Ground prepared for planting by digging and trenching.

c **1420** *Pallad. on Husb.* III. 429 This mone in places temporate, oliue In pastine or in tables brynkes sette. *Ibid.* XII. 86 Now ther is hoot.. The pechis boon in pastyne is to sette.

†'**pastine**, *v. Obs. rare.* [ad. L. *pastin-āre* to prepare ground (for planting) by digging and trenching (Pliny, Columella).] *trans.* **a.** To dig and trench (ground) for planting, etc. **b.** To plant in prepared soil. Hence †'**pastining** *vbl. sb.*

c **1420** *Pallad. on Husb.* I. 772 Lete delue hit deepe Thre foote or iiij in wise of pastynyng, That hit may in hit silf his moystour kepe. *Ibid.* II. 77 With diche or forgh to pastyne hit, no drede is. *Ibid.* III. 651 Pasneppes seed or plauntes faat & rare, Pastined depe, ysette in this mone are.

pastiness ('peɪstɪnɪs). [f. PASTY *a.* + -NESS.] Pasty quality, condition, or consistence.

1608 TOPSELL *Serpents* (1658) 783 Insnarled with the binding pastinesse, and tenacious glewish substance of the Web. **1854** J. SCOFFERN in *Orr's Circ. Sc.*, *Chem.* 433 They ..assume the condition of intermediate pastiness. **1872** *Echo* 4 Oct. 6 Their diamonds were conspicuous by their pastiness.

pasting ('peɪstɪŋ), *vbl. sb.* [f. PASTE *v.* + -ING¹.] The action of the verb PASTE.

1. Sticking or fastening with paste. Also *attrib.*, esp. as *pasting-lace* (see quot. 1882).

1596 *Vestry Bks.* (Surtees) 271 For making a new borde, and pasting on of the table of Consanguinitie and Affinitie set up in the church, iiijd. **1669** STURMY *Mariner's Mag.* v. xii. 63 Allow.. more than 3 diameters for the pasting. **1846** G. DODD *Brit. Manuf.* 6th Ser. v. 132 Coach-trimmings.. 'Pasting-lace', about half an inch broad.. is employed to cover and hide rows of tacks. **1871** G. MACDONALD *Wilf. Cumb.* I. vii. 47 There I carried on my pasting operations. **1882** CAULFEILD & SAWARD *Dict. Needlework*, *Pasting Lace*, a narrow kind of Coach Lace, used to conceal rows of tacks. **1883** *Goole Weekly Times* 14 Sept. 5/2 A patent paper pasting machine.

2. The process of reducing to a paste.

1884 WATT *Soap-making* v. 42 Well-prepared soft soda.. is employed to produce the pasting in the first operation.

3. *slang.* A beating, a basting. Also *fig.*

1851 MAYHEW *Lond. Labour* I. 415 He.. gave me a regular pasting. **1922** G. B. SHAW *Let.* in *To a Young Actress* (1960) 24 There is nothing for your soul in Shakespear.. but there is plenty of pasting for your ear; and you need an exquisite ear for tragedy. **1930** *Collier's* 1 Feb. 44/2 Instead of being mad at Lillian and giving her a pasting for such goings on, Wilbur is somewhat pleased. **1942** *R.A.F. Jrnl.* 3 Oct. 33 We were getting a pasting. Everything going up in smoke and everything coming down with a bang. **1950** J. D. MACDONALD *Brass Cupcake* (1955) x. 105 Fictional heroes.. can bounce back from a pasting that should have put them in hospital beds. **1953** in Wentworth & Flexner *Dict. Amer.*

Slang (1960) 377/2 [The] Philadelphia A's took a 13–10 pasting from the Washington Senators. **1974** *Times* 14 Jan. 3/7 Some managers have taken a real pasting when things have gone wrong. **1976** *Listener* 1 Apr. 409/2 'More embarrassing interviews..and more feeble comedy sketches.'.. Was it fair to give a show such a pasting in advance?

pastique, var. PASTEQUE *Obs.*, water-melon.

pastis ('pæstɪs). [Fr.] An aperitif made from aniseed.

1926 'C. BARRY' *Detective's Holiday* vi. 51 'Have your tea if you like, but I will drink a "*pastis*".' 'A matter of taste, *mon ami*,' Gilmartin replied. 'To me your terrible aniseed smells like a pharmacy.' **1942** W. SANSOM in *Penguin New Writing* XIV. 72 Jean was saying, 'Damn that waiter! Why must he bring me quinquina instead of pastis?' **1955** *Times* 8 Aug. 8/7 No longer the friendly gossip at the pump, no longer the fraternal glass of pastis on the terrace of the Auberge de la Pageole. **1958** X. FIELDING *Corsair Country* viii. 165 Even obvious Europeans like the pastis-drinkers in the bar. **1959** *Encounter* Oct. 53/1 Spain for the bull-fights, Provence for the *pastis*. **1967** A. LICHINE *Encycl. Wines* 396/2 *Pastis*, the aperitif of Marseilles. Pastis is made on an alcohol base with herb flavourings, notably liquorice. **1973** P. O'DONNELL *Silver Mistress* ii. 24 He had called at the auberge to drink a pastis.

pastisar, var. PATISSER *Obs.*, pastry-cook.

pastism ('pɑːstɪz(ə)m, 'pæ-). [f. PAST *sb.* + -ISM.] Memory of, nostalgia for, the past.

1921 W. DE MORGAN *Old Man's Youth* xxvii. 258 The late fifties were still under the spell of Pastism. **1962** *Listener* 30 Aug. 326/3 The *Jugendbewegung* was sterile 'past-ism' by contrast with contemporary futurism.

†'**pastle.** *Obs. rare.* [corrupt or altered form of *pastour*, PASTERN. (Cf. PESTLE.)] = PASTERN.

1552 ELYOT, *Astragalus*,.. the pastle bone in a beast. **1611** COTGR., *Clapponniere*, the huckle, pastle, or pasterne, bone of a beast.

†'**pastler.** *Obs.* Forms: 4–5 **pasteler(e**, 5 **pastlere, -iller**, 6 **pastlar, pastelar, paistler**, 6–7 **pastler**. [ME. and AF. *pasteler* = OF. *pastellier, pastiler* (Godef.), Sp. *pastelero* 'a man that maketh pies or pasties' (Minsheu 1599), in med.L. *pastillārius*; f. OF. *pastel* little pie, pasty.

OF. *pastel* was cognate with Sp. *pastel* 'a little pie made of small meat' (Minsheu), It. *pastello*, in pl. *pastelli, -egli* 'fine little pasties or paste-meates, tartes, pyes' (Florio); all:—L. *pastillus* (see PASTEL[1], PASTIL), but in sense associated with Com. Romanic *pasta* paste.]

A maker of pastry; a pastry-cook; a baker.

1390–1 *Earl Derby's Exp.* (Camd.) 64 Pro xliij shephell farine frumenti..emptis..de Hankyn Edeyne, pasteler, pro diuersis pastelleriis in domo suo factis. *c* **1420** *Liber Cocorum* (1862) 1 Pasteler. **1426** LYDG. *De Guil. Pilgr.* 5442 Charyte gan neyhen ner, And wolde be-come a pasteler,.. Off that flour to make her bred. *c* **1440** *Promp. Parv.* 385/2 Pastlere, ..*pastillarius*. **1530** PALSGR. 252/2 Pastler that baketh, *pastisier*. **1552** HULOET, Paistler, or maker of fyne paist, *dulciarius*. **1598** STOW *Surv.* x. (1603) 82 Cookes or Pastelars for the more part in Thames streete. **1657** HOWELL *Londinop.* 307 Which Cooks (or Pastlers) were admitted to be a Company.

pastless ('pɑːstlɪs, 'pæ-), *a.* [f. PAST *sb.* + -LESS.] Without a past; having no history.

1954 W. FAULKNER *Fable* 21 The perfect soldier: pastless, unhampered, and complete. **1965** P. ROGERS in *Granta* Summer 12/1 It's all very well being pastless in a moment of existential dilemma. **1971** S. CAVEL *World Viewed* 97 His people are without fantasy (hence pastless and futureless, hence presentless).

past-master, past master ('pɑːst,mɑːstə(r), 'pæ-).

1. One who has filled the office of 'master' in a guild, civic company, freemasons' lodge, club, etc.

1762 *Key to Free-Masonry* (1785) 7 (*Plan*) Past-Master, with the Sun and Compasses, and a String of Cords. **1786** *Laws Soc. Royal Arch Masons* 15 That the three Principals, and all Past-masters are stiled, *most excellent*. **1858** SIMMONDS *Dict. Trade*, *Past-master*, one who has been master of a civic company, or has filled the chair of freemason's lodge. *Past-master's Jewel*, a freemason's honorary distinction or decoration, worn..by one who has filled the master's chair. **1874** *Fraser's Mag.* 245 Past-master of the Alpine Club.

2. One who is thoroughly proficient or has ripe experience in any subject or sphere of action; a thorough 'master' (of a subject). Const. *in*, *of*.

App. this use has arisen partly in allusion to the efficiency which results from having passed through such an office as that of master of a freemasons' lodge, etc.; sometimes it alludes to the efficiency resulting from having 'passed' the necessary training or examination to qualify as 'master' in any art, science, or occupation; see also PASSED-MASTER.

1868 [implied in PAST-MISTRESS]. **1877** BESANT & RICE *Son of Vulc.* I. xiv. 149 He was Past-Master, Right Worshipful Grand, *Frère Venérable*, in every kind of vice. **1882** H. C. MERIVALE *Faucit of B.* I. 42 He was a past master in the art. **1890** *Spectator* 13 Sept. 334 A past-master of electioneering tactics. **1892** E. REEVES *Homeward Bound* 46 They are past masters in extras at some of the largest hotels. **1894** LD. WOLSELEY *Life Marlborough* II. lvi. 117 Marlborough was a 'Past-Master' in fluency of speech.

'**past-,mistress.** Also **past mistress** [After prec.] A woman well skilled in some accomplishment or study.

1868 MISS BRADDON *Dead Sea Fr.* (ed. Tauchn.) II. vi. 90 The lovely proprietress..was past-mistress in the art. **1892** *Athenæum* 23 July 129/1 Her portrayal of Grimalkin in his fiercer mood proves her a past-mistress of cat character. **1915** [see COCK-AND-BULL 3]. **1939** A. THIRKELL *Before Lunch* iii. 56 Mrs. Middleton was a past mistress in the art of keeping a staff. **1974** G. BUTLER *Coffin for Canary* vi. 72, I would meet reproachful gazes from Sarah. She was a past mistress in the art of giving me such a look.

'**pastness.** [f. PAST *ppl. a.* + -NESS.] The state or condition of being past.

1829 JAS. MILL *Hum. Mind* (1869) II. 119 To our conclusion, that 'Time' is the equivalent of Pastness, Presentness, and Futureness, combined, it may be objected, that the word 'Time' is applicable to all three cases. **1873** WHITNEY *Orient. Stud.* 260 He will thus at a blow..reduce to a state of irretrievable pastness, a host of..philosophical systems. **1890** W. JAMES *Princ. Psychol.* I. xv. 605 They are associated with other things which for us signify pastness. But how do these things get *their* pastness? What is the *original* of our experience of pastness, from whence we get the meaning of the term? **1919** T. S. ELIOT *Sel. Essays* (1951) 14 The historical sense involves a perception, not only of the pastness of the past, but of its presence. **1925** C. D. BROAD *Mind & its Place* v. 262 The very same characteristic..we took to be 'pastness' in other situations. **1941** F. MATTHIESSEN *Amer. Renaissance* XIV. iv. 654 He did not so often think of the presentness of the past as of the pastness of the present, of its illimitable shadowy extensions backward to the roots of history. **1954** K. TILLOTSON *Novels of Eighteen-Forties* I. 111 The Brontës..turn from the present, emphasizing their choice by a specified..'pastness'. **1973** A. H. SOMMERSTEIN *Sound Pattern Anc. Greek* ii. 63 The verb whose pastness brings the rule into operation may be in the infinitive or participial form. **1977** *Theology* LXXX. 201 The faith of the communion of saints..confers on the death of Jesus at least one kind of capacity to survive 'pastness' and to become in a valid sense objectively present for us.

pastophor ('pæstəfɔː(r)), ‖**pastophorus** (pæ'stɒfərəs). *Archæol.* [a. F. *pastophore*, ad. L. *pastophor-us*, pl. *-phori*, a. Gr. παστοφόρος, f. παστός a shrine, + -φόρος carrying. More usually in L. form.] One of the order of priests who carried shrines of the gods in procession, as frequently represented in Egyptian art.

1658 PHILLIPS, *Pastophories*, (Greek) the most honourable order of Priests among the Egyptians. **1706** —— (ed. Kersey), *Pastophori*, certain Priests, whose Business it was, at solemn Festivals, to carry the Shrine of the Deity. **1753–97** [see below]. **1891** tr. *De La Saussaye's Hist. Sc. Relig.* l. 437 Singers, pastophores, hierodules and others.

So ‖**pasto'phorium** [L., a. Gr. παστοφόριον or παστοφορεῖον], the apartment of the pastophori in the temples of the gods; applied to a similar division of the Temple at Jerusalem (LXX, Jer. xlii. 4). Hence, each of the two apartments, one on each side of the bema, in ancient churches, retained in the Greek Church.

1753 CHAMBERS *Cycl. Supp.*, *Pastophoria*, in antiquity, the apartments near the temples where the *pastophori* were lodged. **1797** *Encycl. Brit.* (ed. 3) XIV. 6/1 The cells or apartments near the temples, where the pastophori lived, were called *pastophoria*. **1839** YEOWELL *Anc. Brit. Ch.* xii. (1847) 133 It has an outbuilding which accords with the descriptions of the ancient pastophorium.

pastor ('pɑːstə(r), 'pæ-), *sb.* Forms: 4–7 **pastour**, 6 **-oure, -ure**, 6– **pastor.** [ME. and AF. *pastour*, = OF. *pastor*, *pastur* (12th c. in Littré), ad. L. *pastōr-em* shepherd, lit. 'feeder, giver of pasture', agent-n. from *pasc-ĕre* to feed, give pasture to. In 16th c. the ending was changed to *-or* after L.]

1. A herdsman or shepherd. Now *unusual*.

1362 LANGL. *P. Pl.* A. xi. 300 Pore peple as plouȝmen and pastours of bestis. **1484** CAXTON *Fable of Æsop* III. i, Of the pastour or herdman. **1596** FITZ-GEFFREY *Sir F. Drake* (1881) 19 Above the pitch of pastors rurall reede. **1609** BIBLE (Douay) *Ezek.* xxxiv. *comm.*, Pastors do lawfully eate of the milke of their flock. **1774** PENNANT *Tour Scot. in 1772*. 107 Flocks of sheep, attended by little pastors. **1885** A. H. KEANE in *Jrnl. Anthrop. Inst.* XV. 225 Of these nomad pastors there are two classes: 1. Those who always stay with their herds... 2. Those who..migrate to the coast.

2. A shepherd of souls; one who has the spiritual oversight over a company or body of Christians, as bishop, priest, minister, etc.; *spec.* the minister in charge of a church or congregation, with particular reference to the spiritual care of his 'flock'.

1377 LANGL. *P. Pl.* B. xv. 488 þei wil[ne] a name, To be pastours and preche. *c* **1450** HOLLAND *Howlat* 80 Fayne wald I wyte,.. Quha is fader of all foule, pastour and pape. **1548–9** (Mar.) *Bk. Com. Prayer, Catech.*, To submitte my selfe to all my gouernours, teachers, spirituall pastours, and maisters. *Ibid.*, *Order. Priests*, To be the messengers, the watchemen, the Pastours, and the stewardes of the Lorde, to teache, to premonisshe, to feede, and prouyde for the Lordes famylye. **1557** N.T. (Genev.) *Eph.* iv. 11 He..gaue some to be Apostles,..and some Pastours [*earlier versions* shepherds] and Teachers. **1596** DALRYMPLE tr. *Leslie's Hist. Scot.* VIII. 90 Robert Schau, quha pastour was of the parischone of Minto. **1627** *Cosin's Collect. Priv. Devot.*, *Prayer Ember Weeks* 356 So rule and gouerne the hearts and minds of thy seruants, the Bishops and Pastors of thy Flocke, that they may lay hands suddenly on no man, but [etc.]. **1641** MILTON *Ch. Govt.* I. iv. Wks. (1851) 112 Wherein..is the office of a Prelat excellent above that of a Pastor? **1782** PRIESTLEY *Corrupt. Chr.* III. x. 233 Each city was to have its own pastor. **1833** HT. MARTINEAU *Three Ages* II. 36 A young Presbyterian clergyman, the beloved pastor of a large congregation. **1878** R. W. DALE *Lect. Preach.* viii. 224 Most of you..are to be pastors of churches, not missionaries or evangelists.

3. One who exercises protecting care or guidance over a number of people.

c **1400** tr. *Secreta Secret.*, *Gov. Lordsh.* 94 Kynge ys þe Pastour of Barouns. *a* **1529** SKELTON *Bk. Three Fooles* Wks. 1843 I. 203 Romulus and Remus..were pastours, for they establyshed lawes in the citie. **1605** BACON *Adv. Learn.* II. xxi. §8 A Moses or a David, pastors of their people. **1715–20** POPE *Iliad* XIV. 612 His people's pastor, Hyperenor fell. **1897** *Daily News* 6 July 4/1 Two good 'Unionists' told against their pastors and masters on the Treasury bench.

4. *Ornith.* A genus of starlings (Temminck, 1815) of which the species *Pastor roseus* (see OUZEL 2 b) is an occasional visitor to the British islands.

1825 SELBY *Illustr. Brit. Ornith.* I. 94 The Rose-coloured Pastor, the Rose-coloured Ouzel..of different ornithologists. **1837** SWAINSON *Nat. Hist. Birds* II. 100 In the genus Pastor..the bill..is compressed. **1894** R. B. SHARPE *Handbk. Birds Gt. Brit.* I. 26 In addition to its brilliant plumage, the Pastor has an enormous crest.

5. 'A small tropical fish (*Nomeus Gronovii*) that lives among the tentacles of the hydrozoan *Physalia* or Portuguese man-of-war; hence called Portuguese man-of-war fish' (Webster *Suppl.* 1902).

6. *Comb.*, as *pastor-like* adj.

1641 MILTON *Reform.* II. Wks. (1851) 68 The Pastorlike and Apostolick imitation of meeke and unlordly Discipline. **1670** —— *Hist. Eng.* III. ibid. 97 To the ignominy and scandall of thir pastorlike profession. **1851** I. TAYLOR *Wesley* (1852) 240 The less skillful, or the less pastor-hearted, minister.

Hence '**pastoress**, a female pastor; '**pastorhood**, a body of pastors: = PASTORATE 2; '**pastorize** *v. trans.*, to provide with a pastor or pastors; '**pastorless** *a.*, lacking a pastor; '**pastorling**, a feeble or incompetent pastor.

1887 *Amer. Missionary* (N.Y.) Mar. 75 The industrial training is now under the direction of the *pastoress, Mrs. M——. **1839** *Times* 15 July, The political brawlings of the dissenting *pastorhood. **1882** *Guardian* 5 July 933/3 Difficulties of *pastorising small scattered bodies. *a* **1711** KEN *Hymnotheo* Poet. Wks. 1721 III. 30 *Pastorless the Flock remain'd. **1624** R. HALL tr. *Bp. Hall's Noah's Dove* 7 Negligent *pastorlings..which haue more heed to their owne hides, than to the soules of their people.

pastor ('pɑːstə(r), 'pæ-), *v.* [f. prec. sb.: cf. *to herd, to shepherd.*]

†**1.** *trans.* To take care of (beasts); to shepherd.

1587 CHURCHYARD *Worth. Wales* (1876) 97 Nor heard of Beasts, to pastor and to feede.

2. To take charge of (a spiritual flock) as pastor.

1872 J. ROSS *Ministry of Reconcil.* 47 When any church is pastored by a minister as his sole work. **1884** *Regions Beyond* Mar., The flock..which he lovingly pastored.

Hence '**pastoring** *vbl. sb.* and *ppl. a.*

1623 AILESBURY *Serm.* 5 But I..repaire, for the Catholike veritie, to the Church, where the pastoring eagles are. **1894** *Kingdom* (Minneapolis) 20 Apr., Having given half his life to pastoring and preaching.

pastor, obs. form of PASTURE.

‖**pa'stora.** *Obs.* [It., Sp. *pastóra*, in OF. *pastore* shepherdess; fem. of *pastore*, *pastor*.] A shepherdess.

1612 SHELTON *Quix.* II. iv. (1620) 81 She that goes vp and downe these plaines and hils among vs in the habite of a *Pastora*. **1621** LADY M. WROTH *Urania* 354 The Princesse of Rhodes was like a Pilgrime, of Lemnos like a Pastora.

pastorable, variant of PASTURABLE.

pastorage ('pɑːstərɪdʒ, 'pæ-). *rare.* [See -AGE.]

†**1.** The function of a pastor, spiritual oversight or guidance. *Obs.* *rare*$^{-1}$.

1662 PETTY *Taxes* in *Tracts*, etc. (1769) 2 A third branch of the public charge is that of the pastorage of men's souls.

2. A pastor's house: a parsonage or manse.

1883 B. HARTE *Carquinez Woods* ii. 39 The 'pastorage', as it was..called,..[was] built of brick. **1897** P. WARUNG *Tales Old Regime* 226 The Protestant chaplain in the pastorage.

pastoral ('pɑːstərəl, 'pæs-), *a.* and *sb.* Also 7 *erron.* **pastural**. [ad. L. *pastōrāl-is*, f. *pastōr-em*: see PASTOR *sb.* and -AL[1]. Cf. F. *pastoral*, in 12–13th c. *pastural*, Sp. *pastoral*, It. *pastorale*.]

A. *adj.*

I. 1. Of or pertaining to shepherds or their occupation; of the nature of a shepherd; relating to, or occupied in, the care of flocks or herds.

1432–50 tr. *Higden* (Rolls) II. 229 Tubal exercisede firste musike to alleuiate the tediosenes pastoralle [L. *tædium pastorale*]. **1549** *Compl. Scot.* vi. 43 Pastoral and rustical occupatione. **1600** HOLLAND *Livy* IX. xxxvi. 340 They were clad in pastoral weeds like heardmen. **1634** MILTON *Comus* 345 Or sound of pastoral reed with oaten stops. **1794** MRS. RADCLIFFE *Myst. Udolpho* vi, Fruits, cream, and all the pastoral luxury his cottage afforded. **1841** ELPHINSTONE *Hist. Ind.* II. 613 Inhabited by pastoral tribes, who live in tents. **1849** H. STEPHENS *Bk. of Farm* (ed. 2) I. 532/1 Pastoral farms, devoted to sheep. **1859** CORNWALLIS *New World* I. 108 The Green Hills, a pastoral station, and twenty-five miles from Melbourne.

2. a. Of land or country: Used for pasture. Hence of scenery or its features: Having the simplicity or natural charm associated with such country.

1790 COWPER *Mother's Pict.* 53 Once we call'd the past'ral house our own. **1794** MRS. RADCLIFFE *Myst. Udolpho* i, The pastoral landscapes of Guienne and Gascony. **1814** WORDSW. *Yarrow Visited* vi, The grace of forest charms decayed, And pastoral melancholy. **1847** GROTE *Greece* II. xxiv. III. 564 Epirus is essentially a pastoral country. **1872** JENKINSON *Guide Eng. Lakes* (1879) 42 The scenery round Esthwaite Water is purely pastoral.

b. ***pastoral lease***, in Australia and New Zealand, a lease of land for sheep or cattle farming.

1850 *Papers Rel. Crown Lands in Austral. Colonies* 95 in *Parl. Papers* XXXVII. 287 You are empowered to grant pastoral leases for eight years... No leases..whether pastoral or tillage leases, are to convey a perpetual right of renewal. **1894** W. EPPS *Land Syst. Australasia* 154 In the event of a renewal of any pastoral lease being determined upon, it must be offered at auction 12 months before the expiry of the term. **1924** S. H. ROBERTS *Hist. Austral. Land Settlement* 293 Thus, after ten years of waste, the resumed areas of 1884, both in the centre and the west, were again placed under pastoral lease. **1948** V. PALMER *Golconda* iii. 18 Nominally the country around was held on pastoral lease by an old cattleman named Gourlay. **1950** *N.Z. Jrnl. Agric.* Nov. 413/2 At this period of Canterbury's development it would not have been possible for many of the so-called squatters to make a profit out of grazing sheep if they had been required to freehold the land. Though the pastoral lease was a partial answer, it did not give any security of tenure. **1953** A. UPFIELD *Murder must Wait* xix. 169 Prospecting pastoral leases in the far north of South Australia. **1959** A. MCLINTOCK *Descr. Atlas N.Z.* 38 With the growth in sheep numbers, regulations covering the granting of pastoral leases were laid down.

3. Of literature, music, or works of art: Portraying the life of shepherds or of the country; expressed in pastorals.

1581 SIDNEY *Apol. Poetrie* (Arb.) 43 Is it then the Pastorall Poem which is misliked? **1641** MILTON *Ch. Govt.* II. Introd., Wks. (1847) 43/2 The Scripture..affords us a divine pastoral drama in the Song of Solomon. **1751** MRS. DELANY in *Life & Corr.* (1861) III. 52 Pretty pastoral music. **1779–81** JOHNSON *L.P., Phillips* Wks. IV. 193 The Italians soon transferred Pastoral Poetry into their own language.. and all nations of Europe filled volumes with Thyrsis and Damon, and Thestylis and Phyllis. **1860** RUSKIN *Mod. Paint.* V. IX. i. 198 Pastoral,..consisting usually of simple landscape,..with figures, cattle, and domestic buildings. **1895** C. H. HERFORD *Spenser's Sheph. Cal.* Introd. 27 Drama and romance, dialogue and lyric, satire and epigram, had all..invested themselves in pastoral disguise. Nay, there were examples even of the pastoral sermon and the pastoral prayer.

II. 4. Of or pertaining to a pastor or shepherd of souls; having relation to the spiritual care or guidance of a 'flock' or body of Christians.

pastoral epistles, a collective name given to the epistles of Paul to Timothy and Titus, which deal largely with the work of a pastor. ***pastoral letter*** = PASTORAL *sb.* 5 b. ***pastoral staff*** = CROZIER 3.

1526 BP. TUNSTALL *Proclam.* in Foxe *A. & M.* (1583) 1017/2 By the duty of our pastorall office. **1548–9** (Mar.) *Bk. Com. Prayer* Cert. Notes Ministr. Thinges, His pastorall staffe in his hande. **1607** *Statutes* in *Hist. Wakefield Gram. Sch.* (1892) 63 Not called..to a pastorall charge. **1640** WHITE in R. Baillie *Canterb. Self-Convict.* 75 Some private forme of pasturall collation with their flock. **1781** GIBBON *Decl. & F.* xxxii. III. 184 The pastoral labours of the archbishop of Constantinople. **1836** ARNOLD in Stanley *Life* (1845) II. 22, I am..engaged upon the three Pastoral Epistles. **1858** J. PURCHAS *Direct. Angl.* 18 The Pastoral Staff in form somewhat resembles a shepherd's crook. **1885** *Encycl. Brit.* XVIII. 351/2 *Pastoral letter*, a letter addressed, in his pastoral capacity, by a bishop to his clergy, or the laity of his diocese, or both. **1957** *Oxf. Dict. Chr. Ch.* 1023/2 *Pastoral letters*,..official letters addressed by a bishop to all members of his diocese.

B. *sb.* (Elliptical uses of the adj.)

I. †**1.** A person of pastoral occupation, a shepherd or herdsman. *Obs. rare*⁻¹.

1607 *Barley-Breake* (1877) 5 Old Elpin with his sweete and louely May Would oft prepare (as Pastorals vie to doe) To keepe their sheep.

†**2.** *pl.* Pastoral games or pastimes. *Obs. rare*⁻¹.

a **1586** SIDNEY *Arcadia* I. (1590) M v, To know whether it were not more requisite for Zelmanes hurt to rest, then sit vp at those pastimes; and she..earnestly desiring to haue Pastorals, Basilius commanded it should be at the gate of the lodge.

3. a. A poem, play, or the like, in which the life of shepherds is portrayed, often in an artificial and conventional manner; also extended to works dealing with simple rural and open-air life.

1584 in Cunningham *Accts. Revels* (Shaks. Soc.) 188 A pastorall of Phillyda and Choryn presented and enacted before her Maᵗᵉ by her highnes servauntes on Sᵗ. Stephens daie. **1589** FLEMING (*title*) The Bvcoliks of Pvblivs Virgilivs Maro,..otherwise called his Pastoralls, or Shepherds Meetings. *c* **1620** ROBINSON *Mary Magd.* Ded. 5 Some.. Cronicles and Warlicke strains admire; Others a deepe conceited Pastorall. **1706** WALSH *Let. to Pope* 24 June, In looking over my old Italian Books, I find a great many Pastorals and Piscatory Plays. **1838** LYTTON *Alice* v. viii, Persons of our rank do not marry like the Corydon and Phyllis of a pastoral. **1949** *Poetry* (Chicago) LXXXIII. 245 Pastoral. In Empson, a frequent literary device 'of putting the complex into the simple' by a process of inversion; e.g., the last shall be first, a little child shall lead them, etc. 'The essential trick of the old pastoral, which was felt to imply a beautiful relation between rich and poor, was to make simple people express strong feelings (felt as the most universal subject, something fundamentally true about everybody) in learned and fashionable language (so that you wrote about the best subject in the best way).' **1957** N. FRYE *Anat. Crit.* 43 The pastoral of popular modern literature is the Western Story.

b. A pastoral picture or scene in art.

1819 KEATS *Ode Grecian Urn* 45 O Attic shape! Fair attitude! with brede Of marble men and maidens overwrought, With forest branches and the trodden weed; Thou silent form... Cold Pastoral! **1903** *Westm. Gaz.* 23 Nov. 2/2 The most striking of the Gainsboroughs..is the large 'pastoral' which hangs in the middle of the North Wall.

c. *Mus.* = PASTORALE I.

1851 THACKERAY *Eng. Hum.* iv. (1853) 176 The pretty little personages of the pastoral..dance their loves to a minuet-tune played on a bird-organ.

4. Pastoral poetry as a form or mode of literary composition.

1598 MERES *Pallad. Tamia* 284 As Theocritus in Greeke, Virgil and Mantuan in Latine, Sanazar in Italian..are the best for pastorall. **1602** SHAKS. *Ham.* II. ii. 416 The best Actors in the world, either for Tragedie, Comedie, Historie, Pastorall. **1713** POPE *Guard.* No. 40 ¶2 The first rule of pastoral, that its idea should be taken from the manners of the golden age, and the moral formed upon the representation of innocence. **1829** HOOD in *The Gem* 181 The Golden Age is not to be regilt; Pastoral is gone out, and Pan extinct. **1895** C. H. HERFORD *Spenser's Sheph. Cal.* Introd. 36 Pastoral, from Vergil onward, has been persistently allegorical.

II. 5. a. 'A book relating to the cure of souls' (J.).

Cf. the title of St. Gregory's *Cura Pastoralis*.

1395 PURVEY *Remonstr.* (1851) 3 This article is taught bi seynt Gregori in his morals and in his pastoralis. **1526** *Pilgr. Perf.* (W. de W. 1531) 87 b, So sayth saynt Gregory in his pastoralles. **1632** HERBERT *Country Parson* To Rdr., Others ..may..add to those points which I have observed, until the Book grow to a complete Pastoral. **1824** WATT *Bibl. Brit.* I. s.v. *St. Gregory*, A Pastoral, or a Treatise on the Duties of a Pastor. **1892** C. G. M'CRIE *Publ. Worship Presb. Scot.* i. 20 Among the books are a Pastoral [etc.].

b. A letter from a spiritual pastor to his flock; *esp.* a letter from a bishop to the clergy or people of his diocese.

1865 LECKY *Ration.* (1878) I. 143 The pastorals of French bishops occasionally relate apparitions of the Virgin. **1885** *Manch. Exam.* 17 Feb. 5/6 The Lenten pastoral..was read in the Roman Catholic churches of the archdiocese of Dublin on Sunday.

c. *pl.* The pastoral epistles: see A. 4.

1901 DODS in *Expositor* July 71 In considering the authorship of the Pastorals. **1902** DENNEY *Death of Christ* III. 115 Leaving out the Pastorals, Paul wrote his other epistles within the space of ten years.

6. A pastoral staff, a crozier.

1658 *Hist. Queen Christina* 407 They showed her the rod of Moses, the pastorall of Aaron, *Arca Foederis* [etc.]. **1672** *Lond. Gaz.* No. 670/4 The Officers at Arms carrying the Pastoral and Mitre. **1903** *Westm. Gaz.* 15 July 1/2 Twenty-eight tiaras ornamented with precious stones,..sixteen pastorals in gold and precious stones.

7. *Comb.*, as ***pastoral-maker***, ***-monger***.

1713 STEELE *Guard.* No. 30 ¶2 The generality of pastoral-writers. *a* **1720** SHEFFIELD (Dk. Buckhm.) *Wks.* (1753) I. 146 Whose simple profession's a pastoral-maker. **1783** BLAIR *Rhet.* (1812) III. 113 Our common Pastoral-mongers.

Hence **'pastorally** *adv.*; **'pastoralness**.

1752 NEWTON *Milton, Lycidas* 193 *note*, Mr. Richardson conceives that by this last verse the poet says (pastorally) that he is hastening to, and eager on new work. **1887** 'SARAH TYTLER' (Miss H. Keddie) *Disappeared* iv. 72 There was a curious sort of gentle pastoralness tempering its profundity. .. There was not a don..that did not appear..intimate with wild flowers and wild birds. **1899** SOMERVILLE & ROSS *Irish R.M.* 232 A life pastorally compounded of Petty Sessions and lawn-tennis parties.

pastoral ('pɑːstərəl, 'pæ-), *v.* [f. prec.] *intr.* in phr. ***to pastoral it***, To play the shepherd or shepherdess.

1828 *Lights & Shades* II. 298 Misses pastoraling it in their ..sausage curls. **1891** J. W. HALES in *Athenæum* 1 Aug. 159/3 Simichidas proposes that they shall pastoral it together:—Βουκολιασδώμεσθα.

pastoral, obs. variant of PASTURAL.

‖**pastorale** (pasto'rale, pæstə'rɑːlɪ). Pl. **-ali** (-'rali), **-ales**. [It., sb. use of *pastorale* adj. PASTORAL.]

1. *Mus.* **a.** An instrumental composition in pastoral or rustic style, or in which pastoral sounds and scenes are represented; usually a simple melody in 6–8 time. **b.** An opera, cantata, or other vocal work, the subject of which is pastoral.

1724 *Short Explic. For. Wds. Mus. Bks.*, *Pastorale*, is an Air composed after a very sweet, easy, gentle Manner, in Imitation of those Airs which Shepherds are supposed to play. **1782** *Char.* in *Ann. Reg.* 11/2 In Christmas time, all quarters of Naples resound with *Pastorali* or *Siciliane*, a kind of simple rural music, executed by..shepherds, upon a species of bagpipes. **1866** ENGEL *Nat. Music* i. 9 The theme of the Pastorale in Handel's 'Messiah' has been derived from the Pifferari, Italian peasants. **1880** W. B. SQUIRE in *Grove's Dict. Mus.* II. 670 Pastorales had their origin in Italy, where..the study of the Eclogues of Theocritus and Virgil led to the stage representation of pastoral dramas.

2. = PASTOURELLE.

1864 TREVELYAN *Compet. Wallah* (1866) 197 When one couple is dancing 'Trélise', and another 'Pastorale'.

pastoralia (pɑːstə'reɪlɪə, pæst-). [L., neut. pl. of *pastōrālis*, PASTORAL *a.*] Things having relation to spiritual care or guidance; the duties of a pastor.

1959 *Listener* 26 Feb. 379/3 Mr. McCulloch seems,..to be reaching towards not a blank rejection but..towards an existential theology and pastoralia. **1962** G. LAWTON *John Wesley's English* 261 It is..a little classic of pastoralia. **1973** *Church Times* 20 July 2/2 The Rev. John Elford..specialises in ethics, philosophy and pastoralia. **1975** M. SULLIVAN *Watch how you Go* iii. 57 The new Warden lectured in Church History and Doctrine and gave us a full course in Pastoralia. **1977** *Church Times* 7 Apr. 11/5 Pastoralia was the soft edge of the traditional three-year course [for ordinands].

pastoralism ('pɑːstərəlɪz(ə)m, 'pæs-). [See -ISM.] Pastoral quality or character; the action or practice of dealing with pastoral or rural life; the pastoral style in literature; a pastoral trait or affectation.

1854 RUSKIN *Lect. Archit.* iii. 167 Claude embodies the foolish pastoralism. **1873** MASSON *Drumm. of Hawth.* iv. 38 There is something of the same sustained pastoralism, the same poetical tact. **1880** VERN. LEE *Stud. Italy* iii. 148 The effeminate pastoralisms of the dying seventeenth century. **1959** *Economist* 7 Feb. 489/2 The economy of West Germany today is something very different from the 'pastoralism' of the Morgenthau Plan. **1973** *Nature* 28 Sept. 194/2 The human response to the low and highly variable rainfall..is nomadic pastoralism, which is a very functionally adapted form of life. **1974** F. EMERY *Oxfordshire Landscape* i. 36 Neolithic settlers..liked to graze their cattle, pigs and sheep in the woods and clearings; together with this strong pastoralism they retained a high degree of skill in hunting and snaring wild animals. **1976** *Sci. Amer.* Sept. 170/2 In traditional agriculture and pastoralism ruminants also represent a means of storing and transporting food supplies.

pastoralist ('pɑːstərəlɪst, 'pæs-). [See -IST.]

1. A writer of pastorals.

1793 *Drayton's Wks.* 588 Spenser is the prime Pastoralist of England. **1882** GROSART *Spenser's Wks.* III. p. liv, Quotations from representative 'Pastoralists' (if the name be allowable).

2. One who lives by keeping flocks of sheep or cattle; *spec.* (*Australia*) a sheep-farmer, a squatter.

1880 *Gentl. Mag.* CCXLVI. 62 The outside districts, occupied only by pastoralists. **1890** *Times* 14 Oct. 7/1 Representatives of the newly formed Pastoralists' or Squatters' Union. **1911** J. COLLIER *Pastoral Age in Australasia* iii. 16 The pastoralist, however, needs something more than level and spacious lands; he needs water and grass. **1926** *Daily Colonist* (Victoria, B.C.) 10 Jan. 1/5 A sheep calendar is to be issued, illustrating the various acts to be engaged in by the pastoralist in care of his flock. **1941** I. L. IDRIESS *Great Boomerang* v. 35 Coastal pastoralists [in Australia] generally speak of a beast or beasts to the acre. **1973** *Sci. Amer.* July 74/3, I obtained more responses from the herders of Kapsirika than from the farmers of Sasur. This was partly because polygamous marriages are twice as common among the pastoralists. **1975** *Nature* 15 May 180/2 A highland ridge, supporting an agricultural population of some 2.2 million, cuts into a semi-desert lowland ('Issa and Ogaden) which is seven times greater in area, with a population in normal times of up to 0.5 million pastoralists. **1977** *Caravan World* (Austral.) Jan. 107/1 The road..proved a lifeline to the pastoralists of the west.

pastorality (pɑːstə'rælɪtɪ, 'pæ-). [ad. med.L. *pastōrālitās*, f. *pastōrālis* PASTORAL: see -ITY.] Pastoral quality or character; *transf.* something pastoral; a little pastoral figure.

1821 T. G. WAINEWRIGHT *Ess. & Crit.* (1880) 190 Little china pastoralities. **1844** R. P. WARD *Chatsworth* I. 17 The cockney pastoralities of Wiesbaden. **1875** W. CORY *Lett. & Jrnls.* (1897) 383 Even sentiment has a touch of natural pastorality in it.

pastorali'zation. [f. PASTORALIZE *v.* + -ATION.] The fact or process of pastoralizing land, *spec.* the restoration of an industrial area to agriculture.

1949 I. DEUTSCHER *Stalin* 501 Even as late as September 1944 both Roosevelt and Churchill were still to favour plans for the 'pastoralization' of Germany which were to deprive Germany of her heavy industry. **1964** F. CROUZET in *Jrnl. Econ. Hist.* Dec. 573 Because of the permanent injury inflicted on many Continental industries by interruption of overseas trade, the war brought about a lasting de-industrialization or pastoralization of large areas. **1975** T. BALOGH in *Times Lit. Suppl.* 10 Oct. 1212/2 Reparations based on dismantling factories—pastoralization—a policy on which the Russians and Americans at first agreed, could of course not really be pursued.

pastoralize ('pɑːstərəlaɪz, 'pæ-), *v.* [See -IZE.]

1. *trans.* To make pastoral or rural.

1825 *Examiner* 34/1 A pretty little pastoralized edition of Kensington Gardens.

2. To put into or celebrate in a pastoral.

1839 *Blackw. Mag.* XLV. 536 It would never have answered to pastoralize the prattle which was heard in the streets and forums of Syracuse. **1842** *United Service Mag.* II. 6 Izaak Walton pastoralized the art into popularity. **1895** C. H. HERFORD *Spenser's Sheph. Cal.* Introd. 43 A somewhat clumsy attempt to pastoralise Bion's dainty myth.

3. To guide or take charge of pastorally.

1870 TYERMAN *J. Wesley* I. 420 The time of the two Wesleys was now employed in pastoralizing the societies they had formed.

4. *intr.* To 'do' the pastoral; to occupy oneself with pastoral music. *colloq.*

1828 *Blackw. Mag.* XXIII. 39 A second set.. pastoralising over the little musical pieces of the 'Vaudeville'.

pastorate ('pɑːstərət, 'pæ-). [ad. med.L. *pastōrātus* office of pastor; in mod.F. *pastorat* (Littré).]

1. The office or position of a pastor; the tenure of such office.

a **1795** EZRA STILES cited in Webster 1828. **1828** WEBSTER, *Pastorate*, the office, state or jurisdiction of a spiritual pastor. **1852** MISS YONGE *Cameos* (1877) IV. xi. 124 They insisted on his assuming the pastorate. **1901** *Scotsman* 9 Mar. 8/8 Recollections from a Border pastorate of twenty years.

2. A body of pastors, pastors collectively.

1846 WORCESTER, *Pastorate*, the office or body of pastors. *Ec. Rev.* **1878** BAYNE *Purit. Rev.* i. 23 The pastorate of Scotland, dependent.. for its existence on its representing the.. national feeling. **1894** *Times* 14 Aug. 15/3 It is not.. a question of celibate brotherhoods *versus* a married pastorate.

†**pastorel.** *Obs. rare*⁻¹. [a. OF. *pastorel*, in mod.F. *pastoureau*, L. *pastōrālis*: see PASTORAL.] A shepherd, a herdsman.

?*a* **1400** *Morte Arth.* 3121 Pouералle and pastorelles passede one aftyre, With porkes to pasture at the price ȝates.

‖**pastorela, -ella** (pastə'rɛlə). [Prov., Pg.: see PASTOREL, PASTOURELLE.] = PASTOURELLE b.

1878 F. HUEFFER *Troubadours* I. viii. 77 Guiraut Riquier is the Provençal representative of the 'Pastorela', or 'Pastoreta', the shepherd's song. **1885** *Encycl. Brit.* XIX. 555/2 The effects of Diniz's influence pervade the whole of Portuguese poetry, for not only was he in his pastorellas the forerunner of the great pastoral school, but.. he.. perpetuated.. lyric forms of great beauty. **1899** J. H. SMITH *Troubadours at Home* II. 451 The *pastorela*, *alba*, and *balada* were popular forms, and for that reason pretty much ignored by the troubadours. **1910** E. POUND *Spirit of Romance* iii. 58 The Pastorella has a peculiar interest in so far as it is one of the roots of modern drama. **1925** A. F. G. BELL *Portuguese Lit.* ii. 53 Airas Nunez.. wrote a *pastorela* in the manner of the trouvères. **1931** [see next]. **1960** BECKSON & GANZ *Reader's Guide to Lit. Terms* (1961) 159 *Pastourelle* (*Pastorella*), a type of medieval lyric in dialogue form in which a knight or a man of equivalent social rank attempts to court a shepherdess. **1976** M. BOGIN *Women Troubadours* 40 The refrain.., common in some of the more popular song forms such as.. the *pastorela*.

pastoress: see PASTOR *sb.*

‖**pastoreta** (pasto'rɛta). [Prov.] = PASTORELA, -ELLA.

1867 *Chambers's Encycl.* IX. 560/2 They [*sc.* the troubadours] even descended to depict the life of the peasantry, and sang their adventures with shepherdesses, &c. in *pastoretas* and *vaqueyras*. **1878** [see prec.]. **1931** W. P. JONES *Pastourelle* i. 6 The pastourelle takes its name.. from its principal actor, the shepherdess herself... The name was perhaps applied first to the Provençal specimens, the *pastorela* or *pas*[*t*]*oreta*.

pastorhood, pastorize: see PASTOR *sb.*

†**pa'storical,** *a. Obs. rare.* [f. PASTOR, after *oratorical*, etc.] = PASTORAL *a.*

1569 J. SANFORD tr. *Agrippa's Van. Artes* 97 b, Pastorical songes of loue. **1603** H. CHETTLE *Eng. Mourn. Garm.* C iv, Euer to heare Pastoricall song againe.

‖**pastorie** (pastu'ri). *S. Afr.* [Afrikaans, = Du. *pastorie*, ad. med.L. *pastoria*.] The dwelling of a pastor of the Dutch Reformed Church or one of its sister churches: a parsonage.

[**1856** E. M. MURRAY *Let.* 20 Sept. in J. Murray *Young Mrs. Murray* (1954) 11 Bloemfontein Parsonage (or Pastorie as the Dutch call it).] **1934** E. A. WALKER *Gt. Trek* vii. 217 A house was provided for public worship at the capital, and granted an erf for the metropolitan church and another alongside it for the *pastorie*. **1944** L. SMIT *Sudden South-Easter* 8 He had received a telephone call asking him to supper at the Pastorie. **1946** *Cape Times* 26 Jan. 11/7 Smoke was.. seen coming from the thatched roof of the Dutch Reformed Pastorie. **1958** *Ibid.* 19 Nov. 5/6 On the site.. a second pastorie will be built.

†'**pastorist.** *Obs. rare*⁻¹. [f. PASTOR + -IST.] An actor of pastoral plays.

1626 MIDDLETON *Mayor Queenborough* v. i. 77 Comedians, tragedians,.. pastorists, humourists.

†**pasto'ritial,** *a. Obs. rare.* [f. L. *pastōrīci-us*, *-itius* (f. *pastor* PASTOR) + -AL¹.] Of a pastoral sort or kind; pastoral.

1654 GAYTON *Pleas. Notes* III. xiii. 160 Such rare straines, and so exactly sung, rais'd their opinion, (that it was not pastoritiall, nor any Dorus that sang). **1728** NORTH *Mem. Music* (1846) 8 Considering how usefull singing was in the pastoritiall life.

†**pasto'ritious,** *a.* [f. as prec. + -OUS.] = prec.

1656 BLOUNT *Glossogr.*, *Pastoral*, *Pastoritious*, belonging to a Shepherd, or Pastor, Shepherdly, Rural.

pastorless, pastorling: see PASTOR *sb.*

pastorly ('pɑːstəlɪ, 'pæ-), *a.* [f. PASTOR + -LY¹.] Of, pertaining to, or befitting a pastor; pastor-like.

1616 CHAMPNEY *Voc. Bps.* 222 A fatherly, or pastorlie admonition to the Emperour. **1641** MILTON *Reform.* II. Wks. (1851) 62 How he can reject the Pastorly Rod, and Sheep-hooke of Christ,.. and not feare to fall under the iron Scepter of his anger. **1859** BUSHNELL in *Life* xx. 423, I shall look back.. with longings.. on these pastorly works and cares.

pastorn, obs. form of PASTERN.

pastorship ('pɑːstəʃɪp, 'pæ-). [f. PASTOR + -SHIP.] The dignity, office, or function of a pastor; a pastorate.

1563 FOXE *A. & M.* 1353/1 He [Latimer] dyd of his own fre accorde resigne.. his Pastorship. **1657** J. SERGEANT *Schism Dispach't* 53 The Pope's Universal Pastorship. **1684** BAXTER *Par. Congreg.* 32 They null not the Parochial Pastorship. **1821** W. TAYLOR in *Monthly Mag.* LI. 35 It.. occasioned his being invited to a pastorship at Riga. **1882–3** W. M. TAYLOR in Schaff *Encycl. Relig. Knowl.* II. 932/1 An office which he held in conjunction with his assistant pastorship.

†'**pastory,** *a.* [ad. L. *pastōri-us* of or belonging to a shepherd, f. *pastor*: see -Y.] Pastoral.

1752 THYER in *Newton's Milton*, *Lycidas* 163 *note*, So the Pastory Elegy on Sir Philip Sidney.

pastose (pæ'stəʊs), *a. Painting.* [ad. It. *pastoso* pasty, 'full of paste, plum-fat; also soft and yet full in handling' (Florio), 'soft, plump, fat' (Baretti). Cf. IMPASTO.] Charged or loaded with paint. So **pa'stosity.**

1784–98 J. BARRY in *Lect. Paint.* vi. (1848) 223 To have a greater degree of pastosity or charging of colour on those parts. **1893** *Mag. Art* 237 That pastosity peculiar to the master. **1901** *Athenæum* 31 Aug. 293/2 The rich and liquid handling of the paint, the luminous shadows and pastose lights.

pastour, obs. form of PASTOR, PASTURE.

‖**pastourelle** (pasturɛl). [Fr., = little shepherdess, shepherdess's song, fourth figure in a quadrille; fem. of *pastoureau*; = It. *pastorella* 'a prettie Shepheardesse' (Florio), fem. of *pastorello*, dim. of *pastore* shepherd.]

a. A medieval lyric whose theme is love for a shepherdess. Also *attrib.*

1882 A. B. GROSART *Spenser's Compl. Wks.* III. p. li, Equally vital to an adequate apprehension and comprehension of Spenser as a pastoral poet, is a like vision and grasp of the mediæval *pastourelle*, or courting of a shepherdess by a man of rank. **1908** *Mod. Philol.* VI. 33 A *pastourelle* is a simple poem set in a rustic scene, graceful and trifling in tone, describing the meeting of a man of culture and an *ingenue*, generally a shepherdess. **1929** C. R. BASKERVILL *Elizabethan Jig* I. i. 26 The dominance of the pastourelle figure Marian in the Robin Hood cycle would argue for song drama. *Ibid.* I. viii. 253 The rôle of the Gentleman, recalling that of the gentleman or knight of the pastourelles who pursues the sweetheart of the shepherd or clown. **1933** R. TUVE *Seasons & Months* iv. 97 The lady is the one figure in the spring landscape that we may come to expect.. in *aube*, *pastourelle* or *chanson de danse*. **1965** P. DRONKE *Med. Latin & Rise Europ. Love-Lyric* I. iv. 214 The motif of the young girl scolded or beaten by her parents.. on account of her lover is most frequent in the *pastourelle*.

b. One of the figures in a quadrille, resembling the dance of shepherds and shepherdesses.

1890 in *Cent. Dict.*

pastport, obs. corrupt form of PASSPORT.

pastrami (pæ'strɑːmɪ). [Yiddish, f. Rum. *pastramă*, f. *păstra* to preserve.] A smoked beef, usu. prepared from a shoulder cut, highly seasoned and eaten hot or cold. Also *attrib.*

1940 G. MARX *Groucho Lett.* (1967) 45 The catering was delegated to Levitoff, the demon pastrami prince. **1941** L. G. BLOCHMAN *See you at Morgue* (1946) xxiv. 164 The hot pastrami sandwich on rye. **1945** A. KOBER *Parm Me* 110 Mr. Freidkin was.. eating a plate of pastrami and eggs. **1953** W. P. MCGIVERN *Big Heat* ix. 111 He liked Jewish food.. sour red cabbage, pastrami, cheese cake. **1961** E. HUNTER *Mothers & Daughters* II. 160 She.. unwrapped the pastrami sandwich. **1962** J. LUDWIG in R. Weaver *Canad. Short Stories* (1968) 2nd Ser. 239 The air inside was like a home-made mist—garlic pickles, pastrami, salami. **1967** M. WALDO *Internat. Encycl. Cooking* II. 477/2 *Pastrami* (Jewish), a cut of beef, usually the shoulder, highly seasoned (especially with garlic) and smoked. Cut into thin slices, it is served either hot or cold. **1973** *New Yorker* 24 Feb. 114/2 The sandwich makers at the counter always maintain rigid queue discipline while hand-slicing a high-quality pastrami on rye. **1976** *Time* 27 Dec. 31/1 One child conquered her stage fright by downing a quick pizza and a hot pastrami.

pastren, -on, -one, obs. forms of PASTERN.

pastry ('peɪstrɪ). Also 6 **pastrye, paistrie,** 6–7 **pasterie, -tery(e, -trie,** 7 **pastree,** 8 **paistrey.** [app. f. PASTE *sb.* + -ERY, -RY. Cf. OF. *pastaierie*, *-oierie*, *-eirie* in same sense, f. *pastaier*, *-oier*, *-eier*, *-eer* pastry-cook (L. type **pastātiārius*, f. *pastāta*: see PASTY *sb.*).]

1. a. The collective term for articles of food made of paste (see PASTE *sb.* 1), or of which paste forms an essential part; now only applied to such articles when baked, as pies, tarts, etc.

1539 [see *pastry-house* below]. **1544** PHAER *Regim. Lyfe* (1553) H iij, Beware of.. spicery, pastry, and bread not very well leuened. **1648** HERRICK *Hesper.*, *To his Booke* xiii, Lest rapt from hence, I see thee lye Torn for the use of pasterie: .. Or see the grocers in a trice, Make hoods of thee to serve out spice. **1671** MILTON *P.R.* II. 343 Meats of noblest sort .. In pastry built. **1841** LANE *Arab. Nts.* I. 124 The diet.. includes a large variety of pastry. **1844** DICKENS *Mart. Chuz.* xii, Tarts wherein the raspberry jam coyly withdrew itself.. behind a lattice-work of pastry.

b. = PASTE *sb.* 1.

1845 E. ACTON *Mod. Cookery* xvi. 402 This glazing answers also very well,.. if used before the pastry is baked. **1892** A. B. MARSHALL *Larger Cookery Bk.* xiv. 528 Prepare a pastry fleur case with paste as below and cook it as for Fleur of Apples. **1906** *Mrs. Beeton's Bk. Househ. Managem.* xxxi. 883 The pastry may be used at once, but it will be lighter if allowed to stand for 1 hour in a cool place before being used. **1948** *Good Housek. Cookery Bk.* II. 408 Fold the pastry in three, folding the first lap away from you and the second one towards you. *Ibid.* 409 Roll the pastry about ½ inch thick. **1952** F. DALE *Ambitious Cook* 51 Roll out the pastry thinly into a strip 4 in. wide. **1970** SIMON & HOWE *Dict. Gastron.* 290/1 *Pastry*, a paste, usually a fat-and-flour mixture with water or other liquid added to make a dough for shaping and baking. Also the product of the baking.

c. A small confection made wholly or partly of pastry.

1906 *Mrs. Beeton's Bk. Househ. Managem.* xxxi. 879 Since the dinner *à la Russe* banished almost everything of an edible nature from the table, any talent in this direction has been chiefly expended on small pastries. **1929** E. J. KOLLIST *French Pastry* ii. 15 This cream is used for various pastries (Tartelettes), gâteaux, petits-fours, etc. **1935** D. L. SAYERS *Gaudy Night* xix. 395 A plateful of synthetic pastries in Ye Olde Worlde Tudor Tea-Shoppe. **1938** H. ROBERTSON *Cassell's New Cookery Bk.* 420 Pastries are baked in a hot oven. **1957** S. STRONG *Good Food from Vienna* 181 (*heading*) How to enter earthly heaven by way of Viennese pastries, cakes, bakery and torten. **1960** E. DAVID *French Provincial Cooking* 435 The ingredients of good pastries.. are very expensive. **1972** 'M. YORKE' *Silent Witness* vi. 125 They carried a box of cream pastries.. and said they had come to tea. **1973** 'J. ASHFORD' *Double Run* viii. 60 In a café.. he ate a stale pastry and half drank a cup of very peculiar-tasting coffee.

†**2.** A place where pastry is made. *Obs.* exc. *Hist.*

1570 LEVINS *Manip.* 105/21 A Pastrye, *pistorium*. **1577** B. GOOGE *Heresbach's Husb.* I. (1586) 10 b, Hereby is a Backhouse and a Pastrie with two Ouens. **1592** SHAKS. *Rom. & Jul.* IV. iv. 2 They call for Dates and Quinces in the Pastrie. **1667** PRIMATT *City & C. Build.* 150 A Pastery or Larder. *c* **1710** CELIA FIENNES *Diary* (1888) 66 Their kitching, pastry, and pantry. **1883** A. DOBSON in *Eng. Illustr. Mag.* Nov. 81/2 To the right.. were.. inferior buildings and offices,—kitchens, cellars, pastries, spiceries, bakehouses.

†**3.** The art and business of a pastry-cook. *Obs.*

c **1710** [see *pastry-school* below]. **1712** STEELE *Spect.* No. 314 ⁋ 13 The whole Art of Paistrey and Preserving. **1752** J. MIDDLETON & H. HOWARD (*title*) Five Hundred New Receipts in Cookery, Confectionery, Pastry [etc.].

4. *attrib.* and *Comb.*, as ***pastry-board*** (= PASTE-BOARD 4), ***-brush, chef, -cutter, -deity*** (cf. *bread-god*, BREAD *sb.*¹ 10), ***-house***, (cf. sense 2 above), ***-making, -man*** (= PASTRY-COOK), ***-meat, -school, -scraper, -shop, -slab, -vendor, -work.***

1902 *Daily Chron.* 25 Jan. 8/4 Strew fine bread crumbs over the *pastry-board. **1907** *Yesterday's Shopping* (1969) 115/1 Brushes, &c., *Pastry, tin bound or boxwood. **1948** P. HARBEN *Way to Cook* (rev. ed.) x. 203 Moisten right round the edge of your sheet of paste (a pastry brush is the best tool for this job). **1976** M. PATTEN *Barbecue* 25/2 Glaze (brush) with beaten egg; use a pastry brush for this. **1961** *N.Y. Times* 3 July 13/5 A dedication to decoration worthy of a *pastry chef creating a wedding cake for [etc.]. **1971** R. THOMAS *Backup Men* ix. 82 Check out the new pastry chef. **1974** *John O'Groat Jrnl.* (Wick) 6 Sept. 8/1 *Pastry chef*, Post House Hotel, Aviemore, requires a Pastry Chef. **1902** *Daily Chron.* 25 Jan. 8/4 Stamp them into fancy shapes with a *pastry cutter. *c* **1625** BP. HALL *Serm. Def. Cruelty* Wks. 1837 V. 229 They fall down upon their knees, and thump their breasts; as beating the heart, that will not enough beleeve in that *pastry-deity. **1539** CROMWELL *Let.* 24 Apr. in Merriman *Life & Lett.* (1902) II. 220 Jennyns sergeant of your graces *pasterye house. **1742** SHENSTONE *Schoolmistress* xxxii, In *pastry kings and queens th'allotted mite to spend. **1682** G. ROSE (*title*) Perfect School of Instructions.. shewing the Whole Art of a Master of the Household,.. Master Cook, and Master *Pastryman. **1711** ADDISON *Spect.* No. 251 ⁋ 10 The Pastry-man, commonly known by the Name of the Colly-Molly-Puff. **1691** tr. *Emilianne's Frauds Romish Monks* 222 Confects, Neats-Tongues, Bononia Sausages, and fine *Pastry-meat. *c* **1710** in Ashton *Soc. Life Q. Anne* (1882) I. 24 To all Young Ladies at Edw. Kidder's *Pastry School in Little Lincoln's Inn Fields, are taught all Sorts of Pastry and Cookery [etc.]. **1809** *Sporting Mag.* XXXIII. 281 The sewing-school, the pastry-school, were then essential branches of female education. **1962** *Listener* 22 Nov. 887/1 *Pastry scraper, mixing spoon, and pastry brush. **1656** EARL MONM. tr. *Boccalini's Advts. fr. Parnass.* I. xliv. (1674) 59 The *Pastry-Shop in the corner of the Herb-market. **1782** J. WOODFORDE *Diary* 25 May (1926) II. 26, I dined at a pastry shop on 3 Cheese Cakes. **1977** 'S. LEYS' *Chinese Shadows* (1978) ii. 68 The local pastry shop.. sells.. strudels and little pink marzipan pigs. **1837** DICKENS *Pickw.* ii, The propriety of enforcing the heated *pastry-vendor's proposition. **1565** COOPER *Thesaurus*, *Opus pistorium*, *pasterie woorke. **1705** *Pastry-Cook's Vade Mecum* title-p., Receipts for making all sorts of Pastry-work.

'**pastry-cook.** One whose occupation it is to make pastry or articles of food in which pastry is an essential part; now *esp.* one who makes such articles for public sale.

1712 STEELE *Spect.* No. 304 ⁋ 4 He may be allowed to sell them.. to his good Customers the Pastry-Cooks. **1855** KINGSLEY *Westw. Ho!* viii, As a ragged boy eyes the cakes in a pastrycook's window.

attrib. **1802** *Med. Jrnl.* VIII. 159 They.. ought to give place to lac amygdalæ, pastry-cook-whey, or even common water. **1897** *Westm. Gaz.* 4 Feb. 3/3 One of the most successful new notions for the toque is suggested by a chef's cap... The pastrycook crown is the name to which this very *seyant* toque answers.

Hence ˈ**pastry,cookery.**
1860 SALA in *Cornh. Mag.* I. 275 This Arabian Nights' pastrycookery.

pasttime, past-tyme, obs. forms of PASTIME.

pasturable (ˈpɑːstjʊərəb(ə)l, ˈpæ-), *a.* Also 7 pastorable. [f. PASTURE *sb.* or *v.* + -ABLE: cf. obs. F. *pasturable* (1534 in Godef., also in Cotgr.).] That may be pastured; fit for pasture; affording pasture.
1577 HARRISON *England* I. viii. in Holinshed *Chron.* I. 14/1 The South part is pasturable and breedeth Conyes. **1632** LITHGOW *Trav.* VI. 292 We pitched our Tents in a pastorable plaine. **1766** BLACKSTONE *Comm.* II. iii. 34 All these species, of pasturable common, may be and usually are limited as to number and time. **1840** *Fraser's Mag.* XXII. 605 Some forty or fifty acres, arable or pasturable.
Hence **pastura'bility.**
1879 *Athenæum* No. 2696. 817 According to the arability, or, if we may coin a new word, pasturability of the land.

pasturage (ˈpɑːstjʊərɪdʒ, ˈpæ-). Also 7-8 pastorage. [a. OF. *pasturage* (12-13th c. in Godef. *Compl.*), mod.F. *pâturage*, f. *pasturer* to PASTURE: see -AGE.]
1. The action or occupation of pasturing; grazing.
1579-80 NORTH *Plutarch* (1656) 377 That they should.. make the Countrey a Desart: so that it should never after serve for other thing, but for pasturage of Beasts. *a* **1656** BP. HALL *Rem. Wks.* (1660) 257 The grasse in the Church-yard may not be used to any pasturage. **1751** JOHNSON *Rambler* No. 161 ¶2 For the shelter of woods or convenience of pasturage. **1883** HT. MARTINEAU *Vanderput & S.* vi. 100 [He] lamented that this soil was not already fit for pasturage.
2. Grass or other herbage for cattle to feed on; = PASTURE *sb.* 3.
1540 *Act 32 Hen. VIII*, c. 7 §1 Tithes of cornes, hay, pasturages. **1632** LITHGOW *Trav.* II. 47 Abounding in cornes, wines, bestiall and pasturage. **1702** ADDISON *Dial. Medals* ii. 124 The riches of the Country consisted chiefly in flocks and pasturage. **1887** RUSKIN *Præterita* II. xi. 379 A waste of barren rock, with pasturage only for a few goats.
transf. and *fig.* **1821** LAMB *Elia* Ser. I. *Mackery End*, She was tumbled..into a spacious closet of good old English reading,..and browsed at will upon that fair and wholesome pasturage. **1846** J. BAXTER *Libr. Pract. Agric.* (ed. 4) I. 92 Pasturage.—Those who are desirous of profiting by their bees should plant, to a certain degree, for their provision.
3. Pasture-land; a piece of grazing land; = PASTURE *sb.* 4.
a **1533** LD. BERNERS *Huon* cv. 351 A, ye vyllaynes, this pasturage is myn,..in an yll houre ye put your beestes here to pasture. *a* **1623** W. PEMBLE *Zachary* in *Serm. 1 Cor.* xv. 18-19, etc. (1629) 159 Within their proper grounds and pasturages. **1732** ARBUTHNOT *Rules of Diet* in *Aliments*, etc. 254 The Flesh of Oxen, Sheep, and Deer in different Pasturage. **1820** SCOTT *Monast.* i, The sheep-walks and hills ..annexed to the township, to serve as pasturage to the community. **1900** G. C. BRODRICK *Mem. & Impressions* 291 They are greatly inferior in forests, pasturages, and picturesque *châlets*.
4. *Sc. Law.* The right of pasture.
1693 STAIR *Inst.* (ed. 2) II. vii. §14 Common Pasturage is ordinarily Constitute by the Charter of the Dominant Ground, expressing the Clause with common Pasturage. **1872** *Bell's Princ. Law Scot.* (ed. 6) 446 Pasturage is the right to feed cattle or sheep on another's ground, or on a common.
5. *attrib.* and *Comb.*, as ***pasturage-land, -right.***
1897 PULLEN-BURRY *Blotted Out* xv. 98 Lovely woodland and pasturage land.

†**pastu'ragious,** *a. Obs. rare.* [f. prec., or med.L. *pastūrāgi-um* + -OUS.] Devoted to pasturage.
1632 LITHGOW *Trav.* I. 14 Playne and pastoragious fields.

pastural (ˈpɑːstjʊərəl, ˈpæs-), *sb.* and *a.* Also 6 *erron.* pastorall. [f. L. *pastūra* PASTURE + -AL¹.]
†**A.** *sb.* Pasture, pasture-ground. *Sc. Obs.*
1596 DALRYMPLE tr. *Leslie's Hist. Scot.* I. 12 Baith abundes in fertilitie of the ground, and nobill pastorall. *Ibid.* 19 Ane ample and plesand pastural called the forest.
B. *adj.* Of or pertaining to pasture.
1725 *MS. Indenture* (Rotherham, co. York), All pastural tithes. **1854** CLOUGH *Poems*, etc. (1869) I. 221 The pastural eminence of Primrose Hill. **1886** *Pall Mall G.* 2 Oct. 4 Our most common pastural ornaments the daisy, buttercup, and primrose.
¶ An occasional error for PASTORAL, q.v.

pasture (ˈpɑːstjʊə(r), ˈpæs-), *sb.* Also 4-6 -ur, -our, 5 -urre, 5-6 -or, -er. [a. OF. *pasture* (12th c. in Littré), mod.F. *pâture* = Pr. and It. *pastura*:—late L. *pāstūra*, lit. feeding, grazing, f. *pāst-*, ppl. stem of *pāsc-ĕre* to feed, graze, attend to the feeding of (beasts): see -URE.]
1. The action of feeding (said of animals); *spec.* the grazing of cattle. *rare.*
c **1386** CHAUCER *Nun's Pr. T.* 365 Leue I this Chauntecleer in his pasture. **1486** *Bk. St. Albans* E v b, Iff ye se where the haare at pasture hath bene. **1530** PALSGR. 252/2 Pasture fedyng, *pasture*. **1658** PHILLIPS, *Pasture*, a feeding. **1878** BROWNING *La Saisiaz* 318 The leaf, its [the worm's] plain of pasture.
†**2.** Food, nourishment, sustenance. *lit.* and *fig.*
?*c* **1400** LYDG. *Æsop's Fab.* I. 119 Among rude chaffe to scrape for my pasture. *c* **1430** —— *Chichevache & B.* Min. Poems (Percy Soc.) 133 By cause that pasture I fynde none, Therfor I am but skyn and boon. **1590** SPENSER *F.Q.* III. x. 59 Todes and frogs, his pasture poysonous. **1646** SIR T. BROWNE *Pseud. Ep.* III. xxi. 162 Unto its conservation there is required a solid pasture, and a food congenerous unto the principles of its nature. **1786** JEFFERSON *Writ.* (1859) II. 60 What effect changes of pasture and temperature would have on the fisheries.
3. The growing grass or herbage eaten by cattle.
common pasture, the use of such by the cattle of a number of owners. *common of pasture*: see COMMON *sb.* 6.
a **1300** *Cursor M.* 2445 (Cott.) To pastur commun þai laght þe land [*Trin.* To commune pasture þei took þe lond] þe quilk þam neiest lay to hand. *Ibid.* 2448 (Gött) Bot fra þair stor bigan to sprede þair pastur gan to wax al nede [*Cott.* bigan to knede]. **1480** CAXTON *Descr. Brit.* 45 Her londe is fruytefull ynough in pasture. **1526** TINDALE *John* x. 9 He shalbe safe and shall goo in and out and fynde pasture. **1687** A. LOVELL tr. *Thevenot's Trav.* II. 28 We entered a Plain, which..abounds in Pasture. **1700** PRIOR *Robe's Geog.* 17 Twenty acres..For pasture ten, and ten for plough. **1842** BISCHOFF *Woollen Manuf.* II. 283 Pasture has a great influence on the fineness of the fleece.
4. a. A piece of land covered with grass used or suitable for the grazing of cattle or sheep; grass land; a piece of such land.
c **1330** R. BRUNNE *Chron.* (1810) 310 þorgh pastours forto fare, for bestes to lardere. **14..** in *Tundale's Vis.* (1843) 97 To bryng the lost schepe ageyn Owt of desert unto hys pasture. *a* **1550** *Vox Populi* 718 in Hazl. *E.E.P.* III. 293 Suche lyke comonwelthe wasters, That of erable groundes make pasters. **1595** SPENSER *Col. Clout* 238 And where may I the hills and pastures see, On which she useth for to feed her sheepe? **1776-96** WITHERING *Brit. Plants* (ed. 3) II. 432 Wild white Campion... Pastures, hedges, and fallow fields. **1816** J. SMITH *Panorama Sc. & Art* II. 618 Grass lands..for the growing herbage, to support cattle, in which state they are called pastures. **1862** WHYTE MELVILLE *Ins. Bar* xi. 388 A low swampy pasture patched with rushes.
b. *fig.*, esp. in ***pastures new.***
13.. *Cursor M.* 18449 (Gött.) þat pastur es cald heuen blis, þar till vs bring iesus wid his! *a* **1340** HAMPOLE *Psalter* xciv. 7 Folke of his pasture & shepe of his hend. **1579** W. WILKINSON *Confut. Familye of Loue* 42 They will..driue vs to poysoned pastures. [**1638** MILTON *Lycidas* in *Iusta Eduardo King* II. 25 To morrow to fresh woods and pastures new.] **1712** ADDISON *Hymn*, The Lord my Pasture shall prepare. **1901** *Scotsman* 5 Mar. 9/3 The pleasant literary pastures of Oxford's bookshops. **1906** G. ADE (*title*) In pastures new. **1922** JOYCE *Ulysses* 645 Wrapped in the arms of Murphy, as the adage has it, dreaming of fresh fields and pastures new. **1975** L. GILLEN *Return to Deepwater* i. 6 He had always resolutely refused to leave his native heath..and ..had never felt the need to seek pastures new. **1977** *It* June 5/2 Some of this third group came to London to lead the winos and the rejects out to pastures new and they used 66 as a clearing house.
5. *U.S.* (*a*) That part of a deep-water weir which the fish first enter (*Cent. Dict.* 1890). (*b*) An inshore spawning-ground for cod-fish (*Funk's Standard Dict.* 1895).
6. *attrib.* and *Comb.*, as ***pasture-field, -grass, -ground, -man, -master, -right, -sheep, -sod.***
c **1830** *Glouc. Farm Rep.* 17 in *Libr. Usef. Knowl., Husb.* III, The dry *pasture-field. **1874** G. M. HOPKINS *Jrnls. & Papers* (1959) 251, I sat down in the lap or fold of a steep slanting pasturefield. **1922** JOYCE *Ulysses* 407 A region where grey twilight ever descends, never falls on wide sage-green pasturefields. **1949** K. M. WELLS *Owl Pen Reader* (1969) II. 196 Even the mill-pond is vanished. The old pond bottom is now part of a tree-spangled pasture field. **1806** FORSYTH *Beauties Scotl.* IV. 53 Alternate frosts and thaws.. greatly injure the *pasture-grass. **1890** 'R. BOLDREWOOD' *Miner's Right* (1899) 130/1 The pasture grasses..burgeon with tropical rapidity of growth. **1578-9** *Reg. Privy Council Scot.* III. 79 Scotland upoun that Marche is ane *pastour ground. **1668** in *Connecticut Hist. Soc. Coll.* (1912) XIV. 21 All that percell of pasture Ground lyeing on the east Side. **1733** TULL *Horse-Hoeing Husb.* x. 104 One Acre of Turneps will then maintain more than Fifty of Meadow or Pasture-Ground. **1775** J. NOURSE in *Jrnl. Amer. Hist.* (1925) XIX. 351 Water enough for Cattle may be kept all year here for pasture grounds. **1789** J. MORSE *Amer. Geogr.* 381 On the north end it subsides gradually into extensive pasture-grounds. **1841** H. S. FOOTE *Texas & Texans* I. 14 The tide of indiscriminate havoc..[marked] its dreadful course with ..the spoliation of her fair plantations and pasture-grounds. **1621** CADE *Serm.* 11 Bootes, the heard or *pastureman. **1833** *MS. Indenture* (York city), *Pasture-master of Walmgate Ward. **1549-62** STERNHOLD & H. *Ps.* c. ii, We are his owne flocke and *pasture sheepe.

pasture (ˈpɑːstjʊə(r), ˈpæs-), *v.* [a. OF. *pasturer* to feed flocks (12th c. in Littré), mod.F. *pâturer*, f. *pasture*: see prec.]
1. †**a.** *intr.* To feed, to eat (said of animals). *Obs.*
1474 CAXTON *Chesse* 118 The cok..began to crowe and pasture.
b. *spec.* Of cattle, sheep, etc.: To graze.
1390 GOWER *Conf.* I. 140 So that he lich an Oxe schal Pasture. *c* **1400** MAUNDEV. (1839) xxx. 302 Thei sende forth tho Mares, for to pasturen aboute tho Hilles. **1587** FLEMING *Contn. Holinshed* III. 1003/1 Such cattell as were found pasturing abroad neere to the wals. **1694** ADDISON *Poems, Virgil* Misc. Wks. 1726 I. 16 Nor sheep nor goats must pasture near their stores. **1786** tr. *Beckford's Vathek* 53 The steeds that pastured in his uncle's domains. **1850** R. G. CUMMING *Hunter's Life S. Afr.* (ed. 2) I. 67 The springboks and wildebeests pastured before the door.
fig. **1590** SPENSER *Muiopot.* 176 He..pastures on the pleasures of each place. **1861** LYTTON & FANE *Tannhäuser* 56 Who hath embraced thee..And pastured on thy royal kiss.
2. †**a.** *trans.* To feed, supply with food. *Obs.*
a **1400-50** *Alexander* 5425 3it ware þai pasturde of pepir.. Of gyloffre & of gingere. *c* **1440** *Gesta Rom.* I. xxvi. 98 (Harl. MS.) To fede or to pasture him with pappe.
b. *spec.* To feed (cattle) by letting them graze on a pasture; to lead or put to pasture.
1413 *Pilgr. Sowle* (Caxton 1483) IV. xxxvii. 84 Alle suche labourers that trauaylen..in pasturynge of beestes. **1585** T. WASHINGTON tr. *Nicholay's Voy.* I. xii. 14 [The country] pastoureth in the valley a great number of oxen. **1639** FULLER *Holy War* I. xxi. 33 Here Uzziah pastured his cattel. **1776** ADAM SMITH *W.N.* I. xi. III. (1869) I. 231 The land is manured..by pasturing the cattle upon it. **1877** BRYANT *Sella* 332 Whose flocks Were pastured on the borders of her stream. **1976** L. SANDERS *Hamlet Warning* (1977) iv. 39 The ranch seems in good shape. He pastures about four hundred head of cattle on it.
transf. **1864** LOWELL *Fireside Trav.* 103 The coach leaves W. at five..and one must breakfast..at..four,..the passengers being pastured gregariously.
†**c.** *intr.* To afford pasture. *Obs. rare.*
1651 R. CHILD in *Hartlib's Legacy* (1655) 156 That the place might pasture the better for their young Cattle.
3. *trans.* Of sheep or cattle: to graze upon (herbage, grass-land), to eat down. Of persons: to put sheep or cattle on (grass-land, etc.) to graze; also, to use (land) as pasture; to feed cattle on (land).
1533-4 *Act 25 Hen. VIII*, c. 13 §10 They shall permitte.. the..lessees..to manure and pasture the saide quillettes. **1550** SIR R. BOWES in Hodgson *Hist. Northumbld.* (1828) III. II. 211 Theire Cattell doe pasture & eate the said ground. **1604** in *Eng. Gilds* (1870) 435 No man shall pasture the stubbell while the corne is upon the ground. **1789** *Trans. Soc. Arts* (ed. 2) II. 68 Do not mow it, but pasture it every summer. **1850** R. G. CUMMING *Hunter's Life S. Afr.* (ed. 2) I. 178 The plains..were pastured short and bare by the endless herds of game. **1901** J. MUIR *Our National Parks* 5 The great Central Valley of California..is ploughed and pastured out of existence, gone forever.
Hence ˈ**pastured** *ppl. a.*; ˈ**pasturing** *vbl. sb.*, the action of the verb, also *concr.* pasturage, pasture-land; ˈ**pasturing** *ppl. a.*, grazing.
1552 HULOET, *Pastured, *pastus*. **1777** R. POTTER *Æschylus* I. 28 Thy woes, beneath the sacred shade Of Asia's pastur'd forests. **1837** BOWEN *Virg. Ecl.* v. 24 None..their pastured oxen did lead,..to drink of the cold clear rivulet. **1538** ELYOT, *Pastio, onis*, *pasturinge, or fedinge of catell. **1759** T. SMITH *Jrnl.* (1849) 273 A fruitfull summer, especially in pasturing and hay. **1819** REES *Cycl.* s.v. *Pasture-land*, An increase of fertility is produced..by the pasturing of lands with sheep. **1667** MILTON *P.L.* IX. 1109 The Indian Herdsman shunning heate..tends his *pasturing Herds. **1842** J. AITON *Domest. Econ.* (1857) 183 A wholesome and acceptable food for every kind of pasturing animal.

pasture land. Also **pasture-land, pastureland.** Grass land used or suitable for the grazing of cattle or sheep; pasturage. Also *fig.*
1591 in A. McKay *Hist. Kilmarnock* (1880) 361 We give and grant all the meadows, pastures, and pasture-lands. **1669** J. WORLIDGE *Systema Agriculturae* 15 Meadow and Pasture Lands are of..considerable use and advantage to the Husband-man. **1718** *New Hampsh. Probate Rec.* (1914) II. 4, I give and bequeath unto my son..two thirds of my pasture lands. **1786** G. WASHINGTON *Diaries* (1925) III. 108, I..directed the best plowman at it to break up about 10 Acres of Pasture land. **1867** 'T. LACKLAND' *Homespun* I. 65, I believe in my heart that this same huckleberry field..is a real pasture-land for the spirit of the boy. **1875** SWINBURNE in *Examiner* 6 Nov., The green pasture lands and golden harvest fields of that noble book of songs. **1885** *Outing* VII. 58/1 Fortunately I live within a mile of real pasture-land and forest. **1920** W. D. HOWELLS *Vacation of Kelwyns* 146 They all struck through the woods into a piece of pasture-land beyond. **1922** JOYCE *Ulysses* 124 Of bosky grove and undulating plain and luscious pastureland of vernal green. *Ibid.* 290 Sheep and pigs and heavyhooved kine from pasturelands of Lush and Rush and Carrickmines. **1966** *New Statesman* 23 Dec. 928/2 The pasturelands of higher output and industrial efficiency and competitiveness.

ˈ**pasturer.** *rare.* [f. PASTURE *v.* + -ER¹.] One who pastures cattle, a herdsman or grazier.
1558 in Hakluyt *Voy.* (1598) I. 327 The people..are all men of warre, and pasturers of cattel. **1619** SIR J. SEMPILL *Sacrilege Handled* App. 38 Will any man say, that this one, or all Pharisees, were labourers or Pasturers? **1904** C. EDWARDS *Hammurabi Code* 69 If a man hire a pasturer for cattle and sheep.

pasty (ˈpæstɪ, ˈpɑːstɪ, ˈpeɪstɪ), *sb.* Forms: 4-5 pastee, paste, 4-6 pastey, 5 -eye, -ay, 5-7 pastie, 6 -ye, 5- pasty. [ME. *pastee*, a. OF. *pastée* adj. of ppl. form (L. type **pastāta*), from Rom. *pasta* PASTE, i.e. something made of or with paste. OF. had also the corresp. masc. *pasté* (L. type **pastātum*), whence perh. ME. *pasté*.]
a. Formerly, a pie, consisting usually of venison or other meat seasoned and enclosed in a crust of pastry, and baked without a dish; a meat-pie. Now usu. a small pastry turnover containing meat and vegetables (see *Cornish pasty*), or fruit. Also *transf.*
a **1300** *Land Cokayne* 54 in *E.E.P.* (1862) 157 Al of pasteiis beþ þe walles, Of fleis, of fisse, and rich met. *c* **1300** *Havelok* 644 Bred an chese, butere and milk, Pastees and flaunes. *c* **1386** CHAUCER *Cook's Prol.* 22 Many a pastee hastow laten blood. **1390** GOWER *Conf.* II. 208 And bad ordeine for here mete Tuo Pastes. *c* **1460** J. RUSSELL *Bk. Nurture* 490 Venesoun bake,..Kut it in þe pastey. **1525** LD. BERNERS *Froiss.* II. cxiii. 325 Botelles of wyne..and pastyes of samonde, troutes, and eyls. **1659-60** PEPYS *Diary* 6 Jan., The venison pasty was palpable beef, which was not handsome. **1717** LADY M. W. MONTAGU *Let. to Abbé Conti* 17 May, Bakers..with cakes, loaves, pasties. *a* **1839** PRAED *Poems* (1864) II. 432 A pasty of game and a flagon of hock. **1877** *N. & Q.* 14 Apr. 297 *The Divisions of an Orange*... The

word 'pasty' is used in Cornwall, from the likeness to the shape of the Cornish pasty baked without a dish. **1880** MISS BRADDON *Barbara* xliii. 295, I sold my comforter to Billy Blake for a whortleberry pasty. **1880** M. A. COURTNEY in Courtney & Couch *Gloss. Words Cornwall* 41/2 *Pasty*, a meat and potatoe or fruit turnover. **1906** J. H. HARRIS *Cornish Saints & Sinners* (ed. 2) xx. 194 When small, a pasty is a snack; when large, it's a meal... The home of the pasty is Cornwall. **1966** *Times* 28 Dec. 9/7 Cornwall is as protective about its pasties as Devon is about its cream. **1972** K. STEWART '*Times' Cookery Bk.* xvi. 213 (*heading*) Chicken liver and bacon pasties. **1978** R. BUSBY *Garvey's Code* x. 119 Cooper collected a couple of pasties in a paper bag.

†**b.** ? A confection; cf. PASTE *sb.* 1 b. *Obs.*

1398 TREVISA *Barth. De P.R.* XVIII. cxvii. (Bodl. MS.) Of þis serpente Vipera beth made pasties þat beþ icleped Crosisti tiriaci of þe whiche is made triacle þat remedy aȝens venym.

c. *Comb.*, as ***pasty-crust, -lid, -maker, -wench.***

1311 *Letter Bk. D City of London* lf. 133 b, Ricardus filius Gregorii le Pastemakere attachiatus..pro eo quod indictatur in Warda de Bisshoppesgate quod ipse est noctivagus. *c* **1460** J. RUSSELL *Bk. Nurture* 631 Open þe pastey lid. **1562** TURNER *Baths* 14 Beware of..pies and pasticrustes and all vnleuened breade. **1584** COGAN *Haven Health* iv. (1636) 27 Hard crusts, and Pasticrusts, doe engender adust choller. **1631** *Celestina* xv. 166 That old pasty-wench.

pasty ('peɪstɪ), *a.* [f. PASTE *sb.* + -Y.] **a.** Like or resembling paste; of the consistence, appearance, or colour of paste; *esp.* of the complexion: pale and dull.

1659 H. MORE *Immort. Soul* II. vii. §13. 197 Supposing that the Soul's Centre of perception..could be..seated in such dull pasty Matter as the Pith of the Brain is. **1793** SMEATON *Edystone L.* §185 A soft pasty substance. **1864** H. AINSWORTH *John Law* III. iii. (1881) 163 His fat, pasty face. **1878** HUXLEY *Physiogr.* 193 Little cavities..formed by the disengagement of gas or vapour when the matter is in a pasty condition. **1897** *Allbutt's Syst. Med.* III. 388 A white pasty fur on the tongue is looked upon as a sign of atony and weakness.

fig. **1884** *Pall Mall G.* 12 Apr. 2 His pasty sophistries concerning prison discipline. **1909** *Westm. Gaz.* 28 Jan. 4/1 The pasty feeling of exhaustion usually experienced at the end of a long [railway] journey. **1926** E. O'NEILL *Great God Brown* 100 A little dab of pasty resignation here and there —and even broken hearts may be repaired to do yeoman service!

b. Of or pertaining to paste jewellery.

1865 DICKENS *Mut. Fr.* I. x, A pasty sort of glitter.

c. *Comb.*, as ***pasty-faced*** adj.

1607 DEKKER & WEBSTER *Northw. Hoe* I. D.'s Wks. 1873 III. 10 You pasty-footed Rascalls. **1878** E. YATES *Wrecked in Port* vi. 51 Fat, pasty-faced, straight-haired.

pastyme, pasuolan, paswax, obs. ff. PASTIME, PASSEVOLANT, PAXWAX.

pat (pæt), *sb.*[1] Also 5 patte, 7–8 patt. [Late ME. *pat, patte*, was prob. onomatopœic, as an instinctive expression of the action by 'vocal gesture'. The later uses are to a great extent nouns of action from PAT *v.*[1] in its various applications.]

I. The action.

1. A stroke or blow with a flat or blunt surface. *Obs.* exc. *dial.*

(Perh. formed anew from the vb. in 17th c.)

c **1400** *Laud Troy-Bk.* 8841 He gaff hem aȝeyn suche pattis That thei fel doun as dede cattis. *Ibid.* 16777 Sche ȝaff him certis suche a pat That doun to grounde he fel flat. *a* **1440** *Sir Eglam.* 1241 Syr Egyllamowre turnyd hys swerde flatt, And gafe hys sone soche a patte, That to the erthe he ys gone. **1642** FULLER *Holy & Prof. St.* II. v. 66 The flat hand of Rhetorick..rather gives pats than blows. **1676** ETHEREDGE *Man of Mode* IV. i, Hit her a pat for me there. *a* **1764** LLOYD *Fam. Ep. to J. B. Esq.* Poems (1790) 207 He ..would not for the World rebuke, Beyond a pat, the school-boy Duke. **1823** E. MOOR *Suffolk Words* s.v., A pat..is..the punishment inflicted by a pedagogue on the palm of unruly boys. **1886** ELWORTHY *W. Som. Word-bk.* s.v., Hares and rabbits when caught..are..killed by a pat on the poll.

2. a. A stroke or tap with a flat surface, so as to flatten or smooth.

Mod. Give the earth a pat with your trowel.

b. *spec.* A gentle stroke or tap with the hand or fingers, esp. as a caress or in expression of soothing or approbation. Also *fig.*, esp. in phr. ***a pat on the back*** (also ***head.***)

c **1804** LADY HAMILTON in *G. Rose's Diaries* (1860) I. 241 Sir William..never got even a pat on the back. *c* **1850** *Arab. Nts.* (Rtldg.) 214 She..frequently gave him gentle pats with her hand. **1865** DICKENS *Mut. Fr.* I. iv, To give him a kiss and a pat or two on the cheek. **1881** DORAN *Drury Lane* II. 213 A pat on the head from a master's hand is the supreme delight of the ever-faithful dog. **1898** QUILLER-COUCH *Stevenson's St. Ives* 306 A word of approbation—a little pat on the back, as I may say. **1933** E. O'NEILL *Ah, Wilderness!* (1934) I. 41 He gives him an approving pat on the back. **1952** M. ALLINGHAM *Tiger in Smoke* iv. 81 He had liked the boy. .. The present assignment had been in the nature of a personal pat on the head for him. **1969** *Listener* 15 May 698/2 A pat on the back for the regional bulletin *South-East*, which gave Eastbourne's maligned medical officer a chance to explain..what he really meant about the artificial prolongation of life into living death. **1973** L. MEYNELL *Thirteen Trumpeters* vi. 100 If I could dive like that—well, I'd give myself a big pat on the back.

II. That which is formed by patting.

3. a. A small mass of some soft substance (*e.g.* butter), formed or shaped by patting.

1754 WHITAKER in *World* No. 83. III. 116 He has produced a clap of thunder which blew out a candle..with a flash of lightening which made an impression on a pat of butter. **1788** COWPER *Let.* (*Sotheby's Catal.* (1897) 29 Apr. 20), One ounce of Castile soap scraped fine..with as much honey as will bring it to a consistency for rolling into pills. Liquorice powder is very proper to dust the patts with while forming it into pills. **1844** J. T. HEWLETT *Parsons & W.* iii, The butter is served up in such very diminutive pats. **1891** LD. HOBHOUSE in *Law Times Rep.* LXV. 562/2 Butterine.. was made up into pats and sold from the retail shop.

b. *transf.* Something of the shape and size, or appearance, of a pat of butter (or the like).

1852 R. S. SURTEES *Sponge's Sp. Tour* (1893) 93 Both volumes richly bound and lettered, with the Jawleyford crests studded down the backs, and an immense pat of arms plastered on the side. **1888** C. F. WOOLSON in *Harper's Mag.* Oct. 776/1 It was raining..in torrents, with great pats of water coming over, almost like stones.

c. = *cow-pad, -pat.* Also of other animals.

1940 F. SARGESON *Man & Wife* (1944) 22 On cold mornings we'd watch out, and whenever a cow dropped a nice big pat we'd race for it, and the one who got there first wouldn't let the others put their feet in. **1957** V. NABOKOV *Pnin* iii. 63 The bright pat of dog dirt somebody had already slipped upon. **1959** C. T. M. HERRIOT tr. *Voisin's Grass Productivity* II. 115 The scattering of dung pats over the whole area of a pasture could make the cattle anything but willing to graze. **1966** 'J. HACKSTON' *Father clears Out* 181 A cow,..will,..in a most flagrant manner, deposit a pat fair bang in the bail. **1973** G. MITCHELL *Murder of Busy Lizzie* iv. 51 The rough road..was muddy with the tramplings of cattle and plentifully endowed with large pats of cow-dung.

III. The sound. (Cf. PAD *sb.*[5])

4. a. The sound made by striking lightly with something flat; *esp.* that made by a light foot in walking or running; hence, rate of walking or running, pace.

1697 COLLIER *Ess. Mor. Subj.* I. vi. 219 The least Noise is enough to disturb the Operation of his Brain... The Patt of a shittle Cock, or the creaking of a Jack will do his Business. **1833** T. HOOK *Widow & Marquess* vii, Up hill and down hill ..all at the same pat. **1889** MRS. OLIPHANT *Poor Gentleman* xvi. I. 295 No sound but..the pat of those footsteps which scarcely touched the ground.

b. Reduplicated, to express repetition.

1876 J. SAUNDERS *Lion in Path* xvii, The peculiar wooden-sounding pat-pat of a lady's fashionable boot. **1899** WERNER *Capt. of Locusts* 67 The pat-pat of bare feet on the matting.

Pat (pæt), *sb.*[2] [Abbreviation of the Christian name *Patrick.*] A nickname for an Irishman; cf. PADDY *sb.*[2]. Hence **'Patess**, an Irishwoman.

1806 *Port Folio* (Philad.) 11 Oct. 221/2 A company of honest Pats in the purlieus of St. Giles's. **1825** SCOTT *Let. to Morritt* 3 Aug. in *Lockhart*, The habit of the more youthful Pats and Patesses is decent and comely. **1857** HUGHES *Tom Brown* I. iv, Here's fun! let the Pats have it about the ears.

‖**pát, paut** (pɑːt), *sb.*[3] [Hindī *pāt* leaf, indigo plant, jute.] An East Indian name for **a.** Jute fibre; **b.** The leafy part of the indigo-plant, as cut off a foot from the ground, and made into bundles for delivery.

1801 *Trans. Soc. Arts* XIX. 235 Specimen of Paper from Paut fibre. **1881** JAS. PATON in *Encycl. Brit.* XIII. 798/2 Importations of the substance [jute] had been made at earlier times under the name of *pát*, an East Indian native term by which the fibre continued to be spoken of in England till the early years of the 19th century.

pat, on one's: see PAT MALONE.

pat (pæt), *v.*[1] [Related to PAT *sb.*[1], and perh. directly formed from it in senses 1 and 2.]

†**1.** *trans.* To cause (something) to strike or hit *upon* any surface; to throw (something) *upon* anything so as to strike it. *Obs. rare.*

1567 GOLDING *Ovid's Met.* XII. 508 Like haylestones from a tyled house, or as a man should pat Small stones vppon a dromslets head.

2. To hit, to strike, properly with a flat or blunt implement; also, to drive or impel by so striking, as a ball with the hand. *Obs.* exc. *dial.*

In later use, perh. ironical from 5.

1591 R. TURNBULL *Exp. St. James* 196 Thus was the pryde of Goliah resisted, when..David..with his sling stone patted him on the pate. *a* **1604** HANMER *Chron. Irel.* (1633) 166 One takes a sticke, and pats the Irish man on the pate, another..pricks him behinde with a pinne. *a* **1825** *Jew's Daughter* i. in Child *Ballads* v. (1888) 251/1 And all the boys and girls to-day Do play at pat the ball. *Ibid.* ii, They patted it into the Jew's garden. **1886** ELWORTHY *W. Som. Word-bk.*, *Pat on the poll*, phr., to kill by a blow such as would dislocate the neck.

3. *intr.* To tap or beat lightly (*upon* any surface).

1601 HOLLAND *Pliny* XII. i. 358 To heare the showers of raine to pat drop by drop, and rattle over his head upon the leaves. **1626** BACON *Sylva* §63 It is Childrens sport, to proue whether they can rub vpon their Brest with one hand, and pat vpon their Fore-head with another. **1771** LUCKOMBE *Hist. Print.* 447 Patting upon the Face of the Letter where it Hangs, with the Balls of the Fingers. **1861** G. F. BERKELEY *Sportsm. W. Prairies* xxi. 349 Asked them who could 'pat' as an accompaniment to a dance and song. **1902** J. S. PHILLIMORE *Poems, Rain at Naples*, On dusty road and tree Drops, kicking up the faint smells where they pat.

4. *trans.* To strike (something) more or less gently with a flat surface, so as to flatten or smooth; to flatten down by such action.

1607 WALKINGTON *Opt. Glass* xii. (1664) 127 The Hyacinth..patted down to the Earth with suddain drops of Rain. **1676** WORLIDGE *Cyder* (1691) 67 Cover the loose ground about the tree, and pat it smooth with the back of your spade. **1801** in *Southey's Thalaba* III. Notes, Wks. 1838 IV. 111 After they have kneaded the cake..they pat it a little. **1901** H. MCHUGH *John Henry* 48 Clara Jane..patted her hat-pins and grabbed her gloves.

b. *Brickmaking.* To remove the rough edge of (green bricks) with a stamper.

1895 in *Funk's Stand. Dict.*

5. *esp.* To strike or clap gently with the inner surface of the fingers, esp. as an expression of approbation, encouragement, soothing, or sympathy; hence *fig.* to express such feeling to (any one), esp. in ***to pat on the back.***

[**1668** DRYDEN *Even. Love* II. i, We love to get our mistresses..and let them go a little way; and..to pat them back again.] **1714** BYROM *Phœbe* v. in *Spect.* No. 603 Phœbe ..to my dog said, Come hither, poor Fellow, and patted his Head. **1791** R. CUMBERLAND *Observer* No. 143. V. 198 'Brava!' quoth he, patting the neck of his mule. **1813** MAR. EDGEWORTH *Patron.* xiii, The child patted Caroline's cheek, played with her hair. **1821** *Examiner* 770/1 Thus is the already inflated faction patted up against the irritated majority. **1821** M. EDGEWORTH *Let.* 18 Nov. (1971) 270 Sydney Smith who wrote the review..first patted his friend Holford on the back and then cut him up. **1866** *Galaxy* I. 750 It seems as if John Bull would never have done patting us on the back for our performance of a very plain and simple duty. **1874** GREEN *Short Hist.* vii. §3. 363 She [Elizabeth] patted handsome young squires on the neck when they knelt to kiss her hand. **1884** *Chr. Commw.* 14 Feb. 424/3 We..pat every man on the back who has the courage of his convictions. **1946** E. O'NEILL *Iceman Cometh* (1947) III. 148 Dey all pat me on de back and say, 'Joe, you sure is white.' **1973** *Washington Post* 13 Jan. B 8/6 'We broke our arm, trying to pat ourselves on the back,' is the way Wood now describes the ad.

6. *intr.* To tap or strike lightly so as to produce a characteristic sound; *esp.* to walk or run with a light step emitting such sound. Cf. PAD *v.*[1] 2. Also reduplicated, ***pat-pat.***

1760–72 H. BROOKE *Fool of Qual.* (1809) III. 135 A humming of mixed voices, and patting feet was heard. **1767** E. JERNINGHAM *Alisia* ix, She fondly cried—Oh that is he! While patted fast her heart. **1801** BLOOMFIELD *Rural T., Fakenham Ghost* vi, A short quick step she hears Come patting close behind. **1803** MARY CHARLTON *Wife & Mistress* IV. 91 It makes a body shiver to hear you pat-patting in those tiny slippers. **1889** *Spectator* 2 Nov., A small, white dog pats along..we can hear the beat of the four light paws upon the country-road.

b. *trans.* To beat with light-sounding steps.

1798 LANDOR *Gebir* VII. 205 When ye heard My feet in childhood pat the palace-floor.

7. The vb. stem used advb. or as an interj.

1681 OTWAY *Soldiers Fort.* V. i, What's that upon the Stairs?.. Hist, hark, pat, pat, pat. **1801** BLOOMFIELD *Rural T., Fakenham Ghost* xiii, Still on, pat, pat, the Goblin went, As it had done before. *a* **1849** HOLMES *Spectre Pig* xxii, Little mincing feet were heard Pat, pat along the floor.

Hence **'patting** *vbl. sb.* and *ppl. a.*

1611 COTGR., *Marchis*,..a path beaten out by often patting, or treading. **1726–31** WALDRON *Descr. Isle Man* (1865) 65 Smiles, pattings on the cheek, and all the marks of a most sincere and tender passion. **1727** GAY *Fables* I. xiii. 22 He stands, To feel the praise of patting hands. **1885** L. MALET *Col. Enderby's Wife* (ed. 3) II. III. vi. 44 She..slowly settled her mantle into its place, with sundry dainty pattings and smoothings.

†**pat**, *v.*[2] *Obs. nonce-wd.* [f. PAT *adv.*] *trans.* To bring out 'pat'.

1575 R. B. *Appius & Virg.* B j b, *Mansipulus.* By the gods how vngraciously the vicksen she chatteth. *Mansipula.* And he euen as knauishly my answer he patteth.

pat (pæt), *adv.* and *a.* Also 6 patte, 7 patt. [app. closely related to PAT *sb.*[1], *v.*[1]: perh. immediately from the vb. stem, as in the expressions *to fall crash, come pop, go bang*, etc. A frequent early use was to *hit pat*, as if to hit with a pat, i.e. with a flat blow; hence with *fall, lie, come*, etc.

The predicative use (sense 2) was in origin adverbial; cf. *to lie pat, come pat, be pat*; but after *be* it had the same function as an adj. in the predicate; hence the transition to the attrib. or adj. use (sense 3), at first after a sb. was easy.]

1. *adv.* In a way that hits, and does not miss its object or aim; in a manner that fits or agrees to a nicety with the purpose or occasion; so as exactly to suit the purpose; appositely, aptly; in the very nick of time, opportunely; so as to be ready for any occasion, readily, promptly.

1578 WHETSTONE *1st Pt. Promos & Cass.* IV. vi, I chaunst to light on one, Hyt me as pat as a pudding Pope Ione. **1580** LYLY *Euphues* (Arb.) 296 When I heard my Physition so pat to hit my disease. **1581** *Confl. Consc.* II. iii. in Hazl. *Dodsley* VI. 62, I will pay them home pat. **1589** NASHE *Almond for Parrat* 6 b, Haue not I hit your meaning patte in this comparison? **1592** GREENE *Art Conny Catch.* III. Wks. (Grosart) X. 151 Seeing things fadge so pat to his purpose. **1596** NASHE *Saffron-Walden* Wks. (Grosart) III. 52 If they will hit the nayle on the head pat. **1602** SHAKS. *Ham.* III. iii. 74 Now I might do it pat, now he is praying. **1639** FULLER *Holy War* IV. xxi. (1840) 218 An unhappy nation whose heads lie pat for every one's hands to hit. **1658** W. BURTON *Itin. Anton.* 176 Camden..seems..to have lighted pat upon the place. **1665–6** PEPYS *Diary* 20 Feb., I came just pat to be a godfather. **1733** SWIFT *On Poetry* 61 And here a simile comes pat in. **1882** MRS. RIDDELL *Pr. Wales's Garden-Party* 259 He..had the whole story pat enough.

2. *predicatively*: as *adv.* or *adj.* (as in 1 or 3).

1638 WILKINS *New World* v. (1707) 41 Whose Words are more pat to the purpose. **1656** SANDERSON *Serm.* (1689) 80 A passage..very pat to his purpose. **1710** in Hearne *Collect.* 7 Mar. (O.H.S.) II. 355 A Mitre may be pat to his Mind. **1820** W. IRVING *Sketch Bk.* II. 124 To tell a rather broad story out of Joe Miller, that was pat to the purpose. **1903** *Sat. Rev.* 17 Oct. 482 He has pat..the denunciations of sacerdotalism with which the same deputed ones will attack the Church of England.

3. *attrib.* or as *adj.* That comes or lies exactly to the purpose; exactly suitable or to the purpose, apposite, apt; ready or suitable for the occasion, opportune. (Said esp. of things spoken.)

1646 J. Hall *Poems, To young Authour,* With phansies queint and gay expressions pat. **1648** 'Mercurius Pragmaticus' *Plea for King* 3 Having a pat occasion offered them. *a* **1677** Barrow *Wks.* (1687) I. Serm. xiv. 195 Sometimes it [facetiousness] lieth in pat allusion to a known story. **1698** Fryer *Acc. E. India & P.* 47 Concerning..these Winds, perhaps some others may give patter Guesses than my self. **1788** Cowper *Pity for Africans* 18 A story so pat, you may think it is coined. **1852** Thackeray *Esmond* III. ii, Backing his opinion with a score of pat sentences from Greek and Roman authorities.

b. ***pat hand*** (in the game of Poker): see quot. 1889.

c **1868** *How Gamblers Win* 51 When quick work is to be made with a victim, 'pat hands', in other words, hands which fall complete,..are given out. **1889** Farmer *Americanisms, Pat Hand* (in poker), an original hand not likely to be improved by drawing, such as full, straight, flush, or pairs. **1903** *Architect* 24 Apr., Suppl. 28/2 Anybody's liable to play a pat hand too strong.

pat, obs. f. PATE; var. PATTE; dial. f. POT; obs. or dial. pa. t. of PUT.

pata ('pʌtə). *Indian Art.* [Skr. *pata.*] Cloth, canvas; a picture painted on a scroll of canvas.

1948 T. Bhattacharyya *Study on Vāstuvidyā* 261 A mere representation of a temple, building, idol and the like, either in sculpture..or a painting on pata. **1963** —— *Canons of Indian Art* xxx. 373 The Kātyāyana Saṁhitā prescribes worship of image (Pratimā) or drawings on Pata (paint on canvas). *Ibid.* 382 Paintings on canvas having the form of a scroll were known as patas. *Ibid.* 383 Such patas were commonly shown along with explanatory songs in East Bengal fairs. **1970** *Centennial Acquisitions Mus. Fine Arts, Boston* 43 (*caption*) Mandala of Eight Bodhisattvas.. probably the earliest known example of Nepali painting of the type known as pata. **1974** *Times* 30 Apr. 18/6 The top price was paid for..a Nepalese pata depicting the mandala of a Tantric deity. **1976** *Sunday Standard* (Bombay) 5 Sept 9/7 The patas, or painted scrolls, are specimens of folk-art in Bengal.

pataca (pə'tɑːkə). [Sp. and Pg.] **1.** = PATACOON. *Obs.* except *Hist.*

1875 C. Schreiber *Jrnl.* (1911) I. 415 We found him to be a stupid old man,..selling bars of iron to people who paid him in heavy patacas. **1948** C. R. Boxer *Fidalgos in Far East 1550–1770* vi. 102 The 1625 Voyage..netted Dom Francisco Mascarenhas a personal profit of 26,000 *patacas* (silver dollars).

2. The monetary unit of Macao, and, formerly, of Timor; also, a coin of this value; also *attrib.*

1928 *Whitaker's Almanack 1929* 804/2 *Macao,* in China, on the Canton River..total trade 1926–27, *Patacas* 25,057,898. *Portuguese Timor*..(the budget includes a loan to be realized of *Patacas* 1,120,074); total trade 1926–27, *Patacas* 3,178,439. **1967** 'A. Cordell' *Bright Cantonese* x. 109 One..came over..with his girl..a pataca woman... For her the big black Mozambiques would pay about two or three patacas a night. **1968** *Economist* 16 Nov. 39/2 In exchange for the grant of..franchises to import gold, the government now charges the syndicate a tax of 7.60 patacas an ounce. **1977** *Times* 16 Apr. 11/3 The Macanese *pataca* is at par with the Hongkong dollar... But get rid of any *patacas* before returning to Hongkong, where they are not generally accepted.

'pat-a-cake. The first words of a nursery rime, said or chanted to accompany the action of patting or gently clapping together the child's hands; hence, the game which the nurse plays with the child in doing this.

A usual form of the rime is: 'Pat a cake, pat a cake, baker's man! Bake me a cake as fast as you can, Shape it and prick it, and mark it with [B], And put it in the oven for [Baby] and me!'

1897 Ld. Tennyson *Life Tennyson* I. xviii. 371 [He] would play pat-a-cake with them.

Hence **pat-a-cake** *v.*, *nonce-wd.*, to superintend or direct any one's action as the nurse does the baby's hands in this game.

1874 Mrs. Whitney *We Girls* ii. 42, I can be contrary. I don't like to be pat-a-caked.

‖**pa'tache.** Forms: (6 pataxo, 6–8 patacho), 7–8 **patach, petach, pattache,** 6– **patache.** [F. *patache* (pataʃ), or Sp. *patache* (pa'tatʃe), in Pg. *patacho,* †*pataxo,* It. *patacchia, patascia, patazzio,* Du. and Ger. *patas;* of uncertain origin.]

†**1.** A small ship used for communication between the vessels of a fleet; an advice-boat. *Obs.* exc. *Hist.*

1589 Greene *Span. Masq.* Wks. (Grosart) V. 274 Hee had in his Fleete, of Gallions, Hulkes, Pataches, Zabres, Galeasses, and Gallies 130. **1596** in *Cecil Papers* (Hist. MSS. Comm.) VI. 61 By the help of two patachoes which they had with them, they took a small English bark. *Ibid.* 62 Patacheoes. **1598** W. Phillip *Linschoten* 192/2 Other smal ships Pataxos, yᵗ came to serue as messengers from place to place. **1633** T. Stafford *Pac. Hib.* III. vii. (1821) 551 There was a Spanish patach landed the night before. **1666** *Lond. Gaz.* No. 98/3 A Genouese Petach is arrived here with Oyls. **1704** *Collect. Voy.* (Churchill) III. 729/2, 6 *Patacho's* or Yachts. **1748** *Anson's Voy.* I. iii. 20 A Patache of twenty guns. **1887** R. Welford *Hist. Newcastle* III. 321 The St. Peter, a Spanish patache,..entered the harbour of the Tyne.

2. *transf.* A small kind of public conveyance used in France.

1833 L. Ritchie *Wand. by Loire* 20 Little country carriages..called pataches (which in general are nothing more than a cart covered with leather, like a cabriolet).

†**pata'coon.** *Obs.* Also 6 **patachine,** 7 **patagon,** 7 **pattacoone, -coon.** [a. Sp. *patacon,* in It. *pataccone,* also *patacchina,* a. Pg. *patacão,* augment. of *pataca* piece of eight, dollar.] A Portuguese and Spanish silver coin, worth, in the 17th c., about 4*s.* 8*d.* English.

1584 in *Hakluyt's Voy.* (1811) II. 411 There is also a sort of siluer money, which they call Patachines and is worth 6 Tangas. *c* **1645** Howell *Lett.* (1650) II. 31 Unless souldiers would be contented to take cloves and peppercorns for patacoons and pistolls. **1665** G. Turnbull *Diary* (S.H.S.) 315 We hired two wagons for 10 patagons. **1679** Oates *Narr. Popish Plot* 5 The Letter..was carried by a special messenger, for which he had 10 Pattacoones. **1749** *Wealth Gt. Britain* 30 The Dutch oblige themselves to pay.. 800,000 patacoons.

‖**patagium** (pætə'dʒaɪəm). *Zool.* Pl. **-ia.** [med.L., from ancient L. *patagium* a gold edging or border on a Roman lady's tunic = Gr. παταγεῖον.] **a.** A fold of skin or membrane extending along the side of the body of certain flying mammals and reptiles, capable of expansion so as to act as a parachute; the wing-membrane of a bat or similar animal. **b.** *Ornith.* The fold or integument occupying the angle between the upper arm and the forearm of birds. **c.** *Entom.* The name for each of a pair of processes or appendages on the pronotum and thorax of certain Lepidoptera.

1826 Kirby & Sp. *Entomol.* III. 368 *Patagia*... Two corneous scales observable in Lepidoptera, fixed on each side of the trunk, just behind the head, and covered with a long tuft of hair. *Ibid.* IV. 381 The patagia or tippets that adorn their evanescent thorax. **1872** Nicholson *Palæont.* 374 An expanded flying membrane or 'patagium'. **1899** *Cambridge Nat. Hist.* VI. 311 The patagia.. are of some interest in connection with the question of wing-like appendages on the prothorax of Palaeozoic insects, and they have been considered by some writers to be the equivalents of true wings. *Ibid.* 312 These appendages are frequently erroneously called patagia, but have also been called scapulae, pterygodes, paraptera, and shoulder-tufts, or shoulder-lappets.

Hence **patagial** (pə'teɪdʒɪəl) *a.*, of, pertaining to, or connected with a patagium; **pa'tagiate** *a.*, formed into or furnished with a patagium.

1887 *Science* 5 Aug. 71/1 Dorsal View of the Patagial Muscles of a Woodpecker. **1894** Newton *Dict. Birds* 607 Garrod devoted much labour to the elucidation of these patagial muscles. **1890** *Cent. Dict.*, Patagiate.

†**'Patagon.** *Obs.* [a. Sp. *patagon* large clumsy foot.] A member of a tribe of South American Indians, whence Patagonia received its name.

1579 in *Hakluyt's Voy.* (1812) IV. 257. **1605** Sylvester *Du Bartas* II. iii. III. *Law* 211 A Pagan (a proud Infidell, A Patagon, that tasted nought so well As Israel's bloud). **1698** Froger *Voy.* 75 The famous Patagons whom some Authers avouch to be eight or ten feet high..: How-ever..the tallest among them was not above six Foot high. **1773** Johnson *Hebrides, Ostig in Sky,* If we have not searched the Magellanick regions, let us however forbear to people them with Patagons. [**1871** G. C. Musters *At Home w. Patagonians* 162 Hide overshoes are worn besides, and the footprints thus made are really large enough to convey the idea of giants' feet, and partly explain the term 'Patagon', or large feet, applied to these Indians by the Spanish discoverers.]

patagon, obs. form of PATACOON.

Patagonian (pætə'gəʊnɪən), *a.* and *sb.* [See PATAGON and -AN.]

A. *adj.* **1.** Of or pertaining to Patagonia or its inhabitants (see B); hence, formerly, †Gigantic, huge, immense.

1767 *Jrnl. Byron's Voy. rd. World* 24 + 5 The Patagonian system of education is quite gymnastic. **1786** Wolcott (P. Pindar) *Farew. Odes R. Acad.* viii. 26 This year, of picture, Mister West Is quite a Patagonian maker. **1818** Kirby & Sp. *Entomol.* II. 101 Seeing a number of ants carrying off a Patagonian centipede. **1856** Kane *Arct. Expl.* I. xvii. 202 Their numbers were not as great, nor their size as Patagonian as some of us had been disposed to fancy.

2. ***Patagonian cavy, hare,*** a large rodent, *Dolichotis patagona,* belonging to the cavy family and found in southern parts of South America; = MARA[1].

1833 [see MARA]. **1910** *Encycl. Brit.* V. 586/2 A very different animal is the Patagonian cavy, or mara.., the typical representative of a genus characterized by long limbs, comparatively large ears, and a short tail. **1961** G. Durrell *Whispering Land* i. 43 Small, desert-like areas seemed to be favoured by that curious animal, the Patagonian hare... They had blunt, rather hare-like faces, small, neat, rabbit-shaped ears, neat forequarters with slender forelegs. But the hindquarters were large and muscular in comparison, with powerful hind-legs. **1965** D. Morris *Mammals* 226 The Mara, or Patagonian Cavy, is the most hare-like of all the rodents. **1971** L. H. Matthews *Life of Mammals* II. vii. 205 When they run..they hop with a gait much resembling that of a rabbit—this gait, and the long ears and legs, have earned them the misnomer of Patagonian hare.

B. *sb.* A South American Indian of a race inhabiting southern Patagonia, said to be the tallest known people (their stature, however, being much exaggerated by 17th and 18th c. travellers and romancers); hence, *fig.* †a giant, a gigantic specimen.

1767 *Jrnl. Byron's Voy. rd. World* 24 + 15 A petty Patagonian, not seven and a half feet high. **1786** Wolcott (P. Pindar) *Ep. to Boswell* 63 Two huge Patagonian pockets ..Which Patagonians..Would fairly both his Dictionaries hold. **1871** G. C. Musters (*title*) At Home with the Patagonians.

patail, obs. form of PATEL.

pataka ('pɑːtɑːkɑː). [Maori.] In New Zealand, a Maori storehouse for food, raised off the ground on poles.

1842 W. R. Wade *Journey N. Island N.Z.* vi. 151 In the pa, a large elaborately carved pataka, or kumara store, supported on four strong wooden pillars, attracted my attention. **1843** E. Dieffenbach *Trav. N.Z.* II. v. 70 A third sort of structure are the provision-houses (pataka), which are built on poles to prevent rats from entering them. **1949** P. H. Buck *Coming of Maori* (1950) II. i. 106 In order to store the preserved food, special storehouses (*pataka*) had to be built. *Ibid.* ii. 132 The best *pataka* were much more extensively carved than the meeting houses, to outward appearance. **1950** *N.Z. Jrnl. Agric.* May 502/3 The carved pile of a pataka, a storehouse, [is a] choice example of age-old Native arts. **1967** A. & D. Reid *Paddle Wheels on Wanganui* 33 A few other scattered cottages, whares, and patakas belonging to the Maori residents and a few odd ancillary sheds and outbuildings completed the layout.

patamar(e, patan(d: see PATTAMAR, PATTEN.

‖**patana** ('patana). Also *erron.* **patena, -ina.** [Sinhalese *patana,* f. Skr. *pat* to descend, fall.] A glade in the jungle-covered mountainous districts of Ceylon, usually with sloping sides.

1854 Baker *Rifle & Hound in Ceylon* viii. 218 Instead of taking across the patinas (plains), she [the elk] doubled back to an immense pathless jungle. **1859** Tennent *Ceylon* I. 24 These verdant openings to which the natives have given the name of patenas generally occur about the middle elevation of the hills. **1880** Mrs. E. H. Edwards *Pezazi* in *Macm. Mag.* No. 253. 79 In a small store standing alone on the patina.

patant, obs. f. PATENT.

pataphysics (pætə'fɪzɪks), *sb. pl.* (const. as sing.) Also **'pataphysics.** [ad. Gr. τὰ ἐπὶ τὰ μεταφυσικά 'the (works) imposed on the Metaphysics' (see METAPHYSICS *sb. pl.*).] The study of a realm additional to metaphysics, a concept introduced by Alfred Jarry (1873–1907), French writer and dramatist of the absurd. Hence **pata'physical** *a.*, **pataphy'sician.**

[**1911** A. Jarry (*title*) Gestes et opinions du docteur Faustroll, pataphysicien.] **1945** C. Connolly tr. *Jarry's Ubu Cocu* in *Horizon* Dec. 375 What's all this? Monsieur Ubu, sometime King of Poland and Aragon, Professor of Pataphysics? That makes no sense at all. *Ibid.* 376 Remember that you are conversing with a famous pataphysician... Pataphysics is a branch of science which we have invented and for which a crying need is generally experienced. **1960** *Evergreen Rev.* May–June 131 'Pataphysics..is the science of that which is superinduced upon metaphysics... 'Pataphysics is the science of imaginary solutions. **1971** Lennon & McCartney in A. Aldridge *Beatles' Illustr. Lyrics* II. 106 Joan was quizzical studied pataphysical Science in the home Late night all alone with a test-tube. **1973** *Times Lit. Suppl.* 13 Apr. 415/4 That dogged pedantry which is perversely common among 'pataphysicians like himself. **1975** *Physics Bull.* Feb. 61/1 Perhaps it should also be mentioned here the existence of another 'physics'—'pataphysics', an invention of Alfred Jarry, probably the father of the Dada movement.

patararo, -r(r)ero, obs. var. PEDRERO, a small gun.

Patarin, -ene ('pætərɪn, -riːn), *sb.* and *a.* Also 9 **Paterin(e.** [ad. med.L. pl. *Patarīnī, Patarēnī,* F. *Patarin, Paterin* (13th c. in Littré), commonly understood to be derived from *Pattaria,* name of a low quarter of Milan (see Du Cange s.v. *Paterini*), or to be identical with It. *pat(t)arino* 'a Porter or day-labourer, a base mecanicall fellow' (Florio 1611), which had prob. the same origin.]

A. *sb.* A name which began to be applied at Milan in the middle of the 11th century to the deacon Arialdi and his followers who opposed the marriage of priests; also applied in the 12th c. and later to the Albigenses, Cathari, and others; and generally employed as a term of opprobrium, identified with Manichæan, etc.

1727–41 Chambers *Cycl.* s.v. *Albigenses,* They were also known by various other names; as..Arnoldists, Cathari, Patarins, Publicans,..Passagers, etc. **1854** Milan *Lat. Chr.* VI. iii. III. 63 The Lombard Clergy affected to treat their adversaries as Paterines or Manicheans. **1855** *Ibid.* IX. viii. IV. 189 In the twelfth century Manicheism is rampant... Everywhere are Puritans, Paterines, Populars. **1867** H. C. Lea *Sacerdot. Celibacy* 221 The meetings of Landolfo and Arialdo [at Milan 1044] were held in a spot called Pataria, whence they soon became known as Paterins—a term which for centuries continued to be of fearful import as synonymous with Manicheans.

B. *adj.* Of or pertaining to the Patarins.

1926 A. L. Maycock *Inquisition* iv. 89 In February 1231 a number of Patarin heretics were arrested in Rome. **1934** R.

MACAULAY *Going Abroad* ii. 33 It was odd how those dear people inclined to the Patarine heresy. **1968** *Trans. R. Hist. Soc.* XVIII. 25 After 1056, its [*sc.* Milan's] order and independence were rudely challenged when the Patarene movement gave rise to nineteen years of civil strife.

Hence **'Patarinism**, the doctrine of the Patarins.

1854 MILMAN *Lat. Chr.* VI. iii. III. 84 The lowest rabble, infected with Paterinism,.. furtively placed female ornaments in the chambers of priests.

†**pa'tart.** *Obs.* [a. OF. *patart, patard*, med.L. *patardus, patarus* (Du Cange.).] A former coin of Flanders, Picardy, etc.: see quots.

1583 STOCKER *Civ. Warres Lowe C.* III. 85 b, A Proclamation made, that no Butcher shoulde sell a pounde of the best Beefe aboue a patart. **1656** BLOUNT *Glossogr.*, *Patart*, a Low-countrey coyn worth a *Sol tournois*, or the Stiver. **1658** PHILLIPS, *Patart*, a Dutch coin, five whereof amount to six pence. **1727–41** CHAMBERS *Cycl.* s.v. *Coins*, Flemish Coins.. those of copper, patards. *Ibid.*, Patard or penny.

‖**patas** (pə'tɑː). [F. *patas*, from a dialect of Senegal.] The red monkey (*Cercopithecus patas*) of West Africa.

1745 *New Collect. Voy.* (Astley) II. 68 The Sieur Brue, on his anchoring at Tuabo [in 1698], found a new kind of monkeys, of so lively a red, that they seemed painted.. The Negros called them Patas. **1774** GOLDSM. *Nat. Hist.* (1862) I. VII. i. 505. **1790** BEWICK *Quadrupeds* (1824) 466 The Patas, or Red Monkey,.. inhabits the same country [Guinea, Congo, &c.]. **1893** *Royal Nat. Hist.* (Lydekker) I. 98 The West African patas, or red monkey, from Senegambia.

patata, obs. f. BATATA, POTATO.

Patau ('pætaʊ). *Path.* [Name of K. *Patau* of Germany, who with others described the condition in 1960 (*Lancet* 9 Apr. 790).] ***Patau('s) syndrome***: a syndrome due to trisomy and marked by mental retardation, seizures, cleft lip and palate, and other congenital anomalies, and usu. resulting in death soon after birth.

1964 GORLIN & PINDBORG *Syndromes of Head & Neck* xvii. 80 (*heading*) Trisomy 13–15 syndrome (Patau's syndrome, trisomy D_1). **1971** LEVITAN & MONTAGU *Textbk. Human Genetics* iii. 76 (*caption*) The shortness of the neck and low-set malformed ears are also found frequently in the Patau (D_1) syndrome. **1976** W. L. L. REES *Short Textbk. Psychiatry* (ed. 2) xxviii. 255 Patau's syndrome is due to an extra chromosome of the D group. **1978** D. A. P. EVANS in R. B. Scott *Price's Textbk. Pract. Med.* (ed. 12) IV. 354/2 Mongolism (Down's syndrome) is caused by trisomy 21 and the much rarer Edwards and Patau syndromes.. by trisomy 18 and 13 respectively.

Patavinian (pætə'vɪnɪən). [f. L. *Patavīn-us* (see PATAVINITY) + -IAN.] A native or inhabitant of Padua (formerly Patavinium); *spec.* Livy. Also †**'Patavin(e** *obs.*

1611 CORYAT *Crudities* 129 The Romanes.. priviledged them.. that the Patauines should giue their suffrages in the election of the Romane Magistrates. *Ibid.* 131 Three [statues] are of that famous Historian Titus Livius, who was borne and brought vp in Padua: the other three of other worthy Patauins. **1771** C. BURNEY *Present State of Mus. France & Italy* 124 He died universally regretted by the Patavinians. **1924** *Glasgow Herald* 6 Sept. 4/2 Livy.. does not make the actual route clear, for among the Patavinians excellent geographical accuracy is not included. **1932** E. WEEKLEY *Words & Names* 149 Virgil the Mantuan, Livy the Patavinian.

Patavinity (pætə'vɪnɪtɪ). [ad. L. *patavīnitās*, f. *Patavīn-us* of or pertaining to *Patavium*, now Padua, the birth-place of the Roman historian Livy.] The dialectal characteristics of Patavium or Padua, as shown in Livy's writings; hence *gen.* Provincialism in style; also an instance of this, a provincial word or usage. (Cf. PADUANISM.)

1607 R. C[AREW] tr. *Estienne's World of Wonders* ¶iij b, Find Solœcismes in Tullie, and I know not what Patauinitie in Livie. **1661** BLOUNT *Glossogr.* (ed. 2) s.v., Livy was censured by Asinius for Patavinity in his writings, by which was meant that he had too much used the phrases or affectations of Padua, and neglected those of Rome. **1745** H. WALPOLE *Lett.* (1846) II. 54 None of the critics could make out what Livy's Patavinity is. *a* **1814** J. RAMSAY *Scot. & Scotsmen in 18th C.* (1888) II. xvi. 544 If a few Patavinities in phraseology or pronunciation.. escaped them. **1830** MACKINTOSH *Eth. Philos.* Wks. 1846 I. 140 Such critics as those who exulted over the Patavinity of the Roman historian.

pataxo, patayn, obs. ff. PATACHE, PATTEN.

pat-ball ('pætbɔːl). [f. PAT *v.*[1] + BALL *sb.*[1]] A game in which a ball is hit back and forth between two players. Also used as a contemptuous name for lawn tennis, especially when not played vigorously; also, tactical slow and gentle play in lawn tennis. Also *fig.*

1775 S. J. PRATT *Liberal Opin.* vii. (1783) I. 96, I might go home, and play at pat-ball with my sister. **1890** S. W. GORE in *Tennis, Lawn Tennis, Rackets, Fives* (Badminton Libr.) 282 This derisive name of 'pat-ball' was applied to lawn tennis by tennis and racket players, who maintained that, from the absence of back- or side-walls, it was impossible to hit hard without sending the ball out of court. *Ibid.* 285 The final blow to the 'pat-ball' game was given by the brothers Renshaw when they discovered that they could stand back at the service-line, and.. volley. **1891** F. W. NEWMAN *Cdl. Newman* 3 We had cricket and rounders,.. patball and trapball,.. and multiform games of marbles. **1896** *Westm. Gaz.* 9 May 3/1 Facetious Undergrad (at tennis, to his partner): Our opponent isn't much good at pat-ball, I take it. **1900** *Captain* IV. 26/1 In the summer, a great form of 'eccer' is 'patters', a corruption of 'patball', *i.e.* tennis. **1904** J. P. PARET *Lawn Tennis* ii. 13 The next three years have been aptly described by an English historian as 'the era of pat-ball'. **1923** *Daily Mail* 28 Apr. 11 At this stage Mishu played 'pat ball'.. and Norton wisely did likewise, for in slowing the pace he affected Mishu's game. **1927** *Daily Tel.* 21 June 12/3 No one would have guessed.. that the mild game derisively nicknamed 'pat-ball'.. would develop so rapidly into this highly exacting and arduous exercise. **1944** C. DILKE in *Wine & Food* No. 41. 16 He might have been back at the Eureka tennis club.. watching the nymphs who played patball on summer evenings. **1955** *Times* 20 June 9/4 Lawn tennis was still known as pat-ball when I was an undergraduate. **1959** *Economist* 18 July 150/3 An astonishing amount of rather owlish erudition and a no less astonishingly patball standard of controversy. **1963** *Times* 23 Apr. 13/4 No contestant.. at Wimbledon would care to have his sport spoken of as pat-ball. **1973** P. GEDDES *Ottawa Allegation* xii. 160 When they spoke during the journey, it was like pat-ball. **1977** J. WAINWRIGHT *Do Nothin'* vi. 102 A kiosk means a telephone call. Where to go next. Maybe another kiosk, for another call. A crazy, pat-ball game that could stretch forever.

patch (pætʃ), *sb.*[1] Forms: 4 pacche, 4–6 patche, 5 pahche, pacch, 5–6 pache, pachch(e, 6– patch. [ME. *pacche, patche*, of unascertained origin. If native, its OE. form would be **pæcce*.

Some have conjectured an earlier **platche*, with subsequent loss of *l*, comparing mod.Sc. PLATCH, q.v., but for this there is no evidence. Ger. dial. *patsche* puddle, mire, 'mess', also instrument of striking, hand, *patschen* to splash, dabble, dash, clap, tap, suits the form but not the sense.]

1. a. A piece of cloth, leather, wood, metal, or other material put or fastened on to mend a hole or rent in something, or to strengthen a weak place.

1382 WYCLIF *Mark* ii. 21 No man seweth a pacche [1388 patche] of rude.. clothe to an old clothe. **1426** LYDG. *De Guil. Pilgr.* 17172 A garnement.. Wych she werede vp-on hyr bak: Gret noumbre ther-on I tolde Off cloutys and off pachchys olde. **1481** in *Eng. Gilds* (1870) 320 A brasen krocke of ij galons and more, a pache clowted in the brem w[t] laten. **1595** SHAKS. *John* IV. ii. 32 As patches set vpon a little breach, Discredite more.. Then did the fault before it was so patch'd. **1675** HOBBES *Odyssey* (1677) 294 A foul coat full of patches. **1787** JEFFERSON *Writ.* (1859) II. 152 The hole and the patch should be commensurate. **1875** HELPS *Ess., Pract. Wisd.* 6 To prefer a good open visible rent to a time-serving patch. **1898** *Sun* 23 Mar. 4/1 The 'patch' included in the 'ordinary [bicycle] outfit' is by no means large enough for an ordinary burst.

b. A piece of court-plaster or the like put over a wound or scar.

1591 LODGE *Catharos* (Hunter. Cl.) 6 Better to weare patches on my cloake, than to beare the patch on my head. **1599** SHAKS. *Hen. V*, V. i. 93 Patches will I get vnto these cudgeld scarres. **1875** HAZLITT *Dodsley's Plays* XI. 140 *note*, Feesimple alludes also to the patch on the face of Tearchaps.

c. A pad or piece of cloth worn to protect an injured eye.

1598 CHAPMAN *Blind Beggar* Wks. 1873 I. 10 Though he.. want an eye, Wearing a veluet patch upon the same. **1702** *Lond. Gaz.* No. 3847/4 [He] had a Patch on his right Eye. **1812** H. & J. SMITH *Rej. Addr., Fire & Ale* ix, Over the horse's left eye was a patch, To keep it from burning the manger. *a* **1901** BESANT *Five Years' Tryst*, etc. (1902) 221 You can change your face,.. put a patch over one eye.

d. A piece of cloth sewn upon a garment as an ornament, badge, etc.

1898 *Daily News* 22 Oct. 6/3 Spots.. such as black silk on scarlet velvet, black or coffee-brown on blue, pale blue on green... These 'patches' are now the very height of the fashion. **1900** *Ibid.* 22 Aug. 5/1 One juvenile wearer of the 'patch', belonging to H.M.S. Aurora, was in the thick of the fire carrying messages to and fro. **1912** 'AURORA' *Jock Scott* i. 4 He passed out of the *Britannia* a midshipman and was wearing his patches the day he left... Naval cadets wear a little bit of white twist on their coat collars, while a full-blown midshipman has a patch of white cloth about two inches square instead. **1970** N. ARMSTRONG et al. *First on Moon* v. 107 John Young's wife.. designed a handsome red Roman numeral X for the patch he and Mike Collins wore on Gemini 10. **1974** R. B. PARKER *Godwulf Manuscript* i. 8 A fatigue jacket with a staff sergeant's stripes, a Seventh Division patch.

e. ***not a patch on*** (*colloq.*), in no way comparable to, nowhere near.

1860 READE *Cloister & H.* xxxvii, He is not a patch on you for looks. **1880** MISS BRADDON *Just as I am* xii. 85 A fine handsome-looking young man,.. but not a patch upon his father. **1880** *Sat. Rev.* 18 Dec. 779 The adventures with savages.. and so on, are, to speak familiarly, not a patch upon the adventures which Captain Mayne Reid would have made out of the same materials. **1889** *Westm. Gaz.* 20 Feb. 10/1 We have some strange weather in England.. but it is doubtful whether we are a patch upon Australia. On December 6 the thermometer in many places there fell over 40 deg. within six hours.

2. A small piece of black silk or court-plaster, often of fanciful shape, worn on the face either to hide a fault, or, more usually, to show off the complexion by contrast. (Fashionable, esp. among women, in 17th and 18th centuries; cf. PATCH-BOX.)

1592 LYLY *Midas* III. ii, *Licio.* Take Masticke else. *Pet.* Mastick's a patch. Masticke does many a foole's face catch. **1601** ? MARSTON *Pasquil & Kath.* v. 220 Blacke patches are worne, Some for pride, some to stay the Rhewme, and Some to hide the scab. **1611** COTGR., *Moucheron*,.. the little blacke patch thats glued by Masticke, etc., on the faces of many. *a* **1625** FLETCHER *Elder Bro.* III. v, Your black patches you wear variously, Some cut like stars, some in half moons, some lozenges. *c* **1706** PRIOR *Phillis's Age* 6 Her patches, paint, and jewels on. **1715** LADY M. W. MONTAGU *Town Ecl., Saturday* 49 Hours.. pass'd in deep debate, How curls should fall, or where a patch to place. **1876** PLANCHÉ *Cycl. Costume* I. 388. **1897** RHOSCOMYL *White Rose Arno* 23 The patch that lent piquancy to the cheek of beauty.

3. a. A portion of any surface markedly different in appearance or character from what is around it; a large or irregular spot.

1573 TUSSER *Husb.* (1878) 118 Reward not thy sheepe (when ye take off his cote) With twitchis and patches, as brode as a grote. **1701** *Lond. Gaz.* No. 3745/4 A Patch near the Flank on the near Side [on a horse]. **1810** *Edin. Rev.* XVII. 196 Those detached and unmeaning patches of different colours, which compose what opticians call an *anamorphosis*. **1873** HAMERTON *Intell. Life* II. i. (1875) 50 The sky will not come right.. it is all spots and patches. **1894** NEWTON *Dict. Birds* 818 The Surf-Duck.. with a white patch on the crown and another on the nape.

b. A small piece or area of undefined shape, of ground, or of anything lying or growing on it.

1577 HARRISON *England* II. iv. (1877) I. 98 In.. Buckinghamshire.. there is a piece of Hartfordshire.. this patch is not aboue three miles in length, and two in breadth. **1602** SHAKS. *Ham.* IV. iv. 18 We go to gain a little patch of ground That hath in it no profit but the name. **1684** *Contempl. St. Man* II. iii. (1699) 154 Why doth he content himself with some patch of the Earth, when he may be Lord of the whole Heavens? **1742** SHENSTONE *Schoolmistress* v, A patch so green, On which the tribe their gambols do display. **1807** WORDSW. *Wh. Doe Ryl.* IV. 66 Like a patch of April snow. **1847** GROTE *Greece* II. xxvi. IV. 35 Patches of cultivable soil. **1894** HOWELLS *Trav. fr. Altruria* 103 The chief crop was hay, with here and there a patch of potatoes or beans.

c. An area of floating pieces of ice, joining and overlapping one another, of more or less circular or polygonal form.

1817 SCORESBY *Nat. Hist.* in *Ann. Reg.* 531/1 If it assume a circular or polygonal form, the name of patch is applied. **1820** *Ibid.* II. 1324 A *patch* is a collection of drift or bay-ice of a circular or polygonal form. In point of magnitude, a pack corresponds with a field, and a patch with a floe. **1850** *Natural Phenomena* 106 If the field [of ice] is broken up into a number of pieces, none of which are more than forty or fifty yards across, the whole is called a *pack*; if the pieces are broad they are called a *patch*; and when long and narrow a *stream*.

d. *Anat.* and *Path.* A small well-defined area of the skin, etc. distinct in colour or appearance.

Peyer's, Peyerian patches, the agminate glands in the small intestine.

1797 *Monthly Mag.* III. 153 In other cases, there are many circular gangrenous patches, on the surface of the intestines. **1809** *Med. Jrnl.* XXI. 132 As the patch expands, the centre of it gradually assumes the natural colour of the skin. **1849–52** TODD *Cycl. Anat.* IV. 839/1 Each Peyerian patch consists of but a single layer of gland-vesicles. **1878** HUXLEY *Physiogr.* 226 It undergoes a process of division whereby it is converted into the embryonic patch or cicatricula. **1899** *Allbutt's Syst. Med.* VII. 296 A patch of softening was found in each hemisphere.

e. The area which is assigned to a policeman as his responsibility; a policeman's 'beat'. Also *transf.*

1963 *T.V. Times* (Austral.) 18 Apr. 10/2 *Patch*, a police area: as in 'It's on my patch'. **1965** 'W. HAGGARD' *Hard Sell* xii. 126 I'm a foreign official on another man's patch. I'm quite without standing. **1965** J. WAINWRIGHT *Death in Sleeping City* II. 123 My patch in the city. I'm not like you—a county officer. **1969** D. DEVINE *Death is my Bridegroom* xi. 113 Smith was from the south and had never before turned up in Christie's patch. **1975** J. SYMONS *Three Pipe Problem* xvi. 157 Either he gets off your patch or he finds his reputation as an art dealer ruined.

4. A piece of cloth sewed together with others of varying shape, size, and colour to form patchwork or to adorn a garment.

a **1529** SKELTON *Bowge of Courte* 358 His cote was checked with patches rede and blewe. **1560** DAUS tr. *Sleidane's Comm.* 424 The other two.. had as it were sowed together certen fragmentes and patches. **1628** EARLE *Microcosm., Pot-poet* (Arb.) 45 His Verses are like his clothes, miserable Cento's and patches. **1690** LOCKE *Hum. Und.* IV. xix. (1695) 400 A pie-bald Livery of coarse Patches and borrowed Shreds.

5. a. A small scrap, piece, or remnant of anything.

a **1529** SKELTON *Replyc.* 3 A lytell ragge of rethorike.. A pece or a patche of philosophy. **1579** FULKE *Heskins's Parl.* 81 They reade but patches out of other mens notes. **1602** SHAKS. *Ham.* III. iv. 102 A King of shreds and patches. **1633** T. ADAMS *Exp. 2 Peter* ii. 9 And fills up the time with.. some.. patch of poetry. **1782** MME. D'ARBLAY *Lett., to Mrs. Thrale* Apr., This letter is written by scraps and patches. **1835** ARNOLD *Let.* in Stanley *Life & Corr.* (1845) I. 435 Much of ancient history consists apparently of patches put together.. without any redaction.

b. *transf.* With qualifying adj.: a period of time with a particular characteristic.

1926 WODEHOUSE *Heart of Goof* i. 32 How like life it all was!.. We strike a good patch and are beginning to think pretty well of ourselves, and along comes a George Parsloe. **1928** *Daily Express* 6 July 9/3 He dreaded to think what would happen to Kent if those players had a month's bad patch. **1958** *Daily Sketch* 2 June 12/4 A friend helps you over a sticky patch in the afternoon. **1974** I. MURDOCH *Sacred & Profane Love Machine* 213 If there were bad patches I've simply forgotten them. **1976** J. M. BROWNJOHN tr. *Kirst's Time for Payment* v. 114 All new businesses go through a sticky patch, but it's only temporary.

6. Applied to various things suggesting a patch (sense 1) in the way they are fastened, or in shape or size, or otherwise: **a.** The operculum of a periwinkle; **b.** A greased piece of cloth, leather, or other material used as the wadding for a rifle-ball; **c.** 'A projection on the top of the muzzle in some guns, doing away with the effect of dispart in laying' (Smyth *Sailor's Word-bk.* 1867); **d.** *Printing*: A piece of thin paper used to fill up low places in the impression; = OVERLAY *sb.* 2; **e.** 'A small square of thick leather sometimes used in the grinding of small tools to press the work on the stone, in order to protect the fingers from abrasion' (*Cent. Dict.* 1890); **f.** A temporary electrical connection. Usu. *attrib.* (see *patch bay*, etc., in sense 8).

1835 KIRBY *Hab. & Inst. Anim.* I. ix. 279 We find the mouth of its [periwinkle's] shell closed by a horny organ called the *patch*. **1835–40** HALIBURTON *Clockm.* (1862) 439 Something that will go down the throat like a greased patch down a smooth rifle. **1846** GREENER *Sci. Gunnery* 375 The use of patches..on the score of protecting the ball, and also cleansing the tube. **1850** R. G. CUMMING *Hunter's Life S. Afr.* (1902) 93/2 [These] contained balls and patches, two sharp clasp-knives, a compass, flint and steel. **1923** *Bell Syst. Techn. Jrnl.* II. 123 A temporary [telephone] connection made in this manner..is called a 'patch'. **1937** *Printers' Ink Monthly* May 40/1 *Patch*, a temporary and removable connection on studio equipment. **1977** R. L. DUNCAN *Temple Dogs* (1978) II. 259 He just called computer, requested a patch on the Metro interface. He wants to know what the Tokyo police have picked up.

7. patch-up [f. the phrase *to patch up*: see PATCH *v.*] An act of patching up, or repairing in an imperfect fashion. Also as *adj.*

1819 *Metropolis* III. 178 He is returned from a patch up abroad. **1898** *Westm. Gaz.* 14 Dec. 1/3 We must avoid any speedy patch-up which would bring us to another letter of resignation twelve months hence. **1901** MISS E. HOBHOUSE *ibid.* 19 June 9/1 It is all only a miserable patch-up on a great ill. **1904** *Westm. Gaz.* 30 Sept. 2/1 The kind of patch-up policy which he would accept for the next election. **1971** 'H. CALVIN' *Poison Chasers* v. 74 There may be some value in a patch-up operation. **1974** P. FLOWER *Odd Job* ii. 16 His patch-up jobs on furniture.

8. *attrib.* and *Comb.*: **patch bay**, an area in an analogue computer that receives one or more removable patch-boards; **patch-board**, a plug-board, esp. one in an analogue computer or similar device; †**patch-coat**, a patched coat; **patch cord**, an insulated lead with a plug at each end, used for making connections between the sockets of a patch-board or different pieces of electronic apparatus; **patch fox**, a North American red fox, *Vulpes Fulva*, in its yellowish colour phase, or the skin of such an animal; = CROSS-FOX; †**patch-grease**: see quot.; **patch-ice**, pieces of ice overlapping so as to form a patch (Webster 1864); **patch lead** = *patch cord* above; **patch-leather**, leather used in patching; **patch-ornament**, an ornament resembling a patch in shape or otherwise; **patch panel** *sb.*[2] = *patch-board* above; (cf. PATCH-PANEL *sb.* and *a.*); **patch-plug** = *patch cord* above; **patch pocket**, a pocket consisting of a piece of cloth sewn on like a patch; **patch-polled** *a.*, having a patch of colour on the head, esp. in *patch-polled coot* = PATCH-HEAD. Also PATCH-BOX, etc.

1948 *Patch bay [see *patch cord* below]. **1962** HUSKEY & KORN *Computer Handbk.* iv. 26 Most multipurpose electronic analog computers are programmed by means of a patchboard system which comprises (1) a patchbay with spring-contact terminations for the computing elements and (2) interchangeable removable problem boards which carry the actual interconnecting patchcords. **1949** *Math. Tables & Other Aids to Computation* III. 512 Receptacle *patch-board for 500 element connections and 25 main busses. **1961** G. MILLERSON *Technique Television Production* i. 17 Tape recorders, racks of audio amplifiers, patchboards and an electronic reverberation unit, complete the general set-up. **1971** J. H. SMITH *Digital Logic* ii. 28 The inputs and outputs of the logic elements, and the connections to the switched inputs, external terminals and indicator lamps are brought out to a programming device consisting of a patchboard and detachable panel. **1902** *Daily Chron.* 7 Jan. 6/3 The jacket.. with two *patch breast pockets with pleats. **1630** LENNARD tr. *Charron's Wisd.* I. Pref. (1670) 111 See then how strange and monstrous a *patch-coat man is. **1938** G. E. STERLING *Radio Manual* (ed. 3) vii. 442 The input may be connected to a terminal board in rear or to normal-through standard double *patch-cord jacks at front of panel. **1948** *Electronics* July 119/3 To set up the computer the elements are connected..by means of patch cords joining the proper inputs and outputs through the patch bay. **1967** [see *patch panel* below]. **1971** J. H. SMITH *Digital Logic* ii. 28 Switching problems are set up by using patch cords on the front panel. **1835** *Patch fox [see LORD *sb.* 16]. **1930** *Economist* 4 Jan. 10/2 The highest priced fur in 1927–8 was silver fox..; cross or patch fox was second. **1942** M. BOSANQUET *Saddlebags for Suitcases* 48 The most common of these [variations] is the 'cross' or 'patch' fox, which is yellow with a dark cross or patch across the shoulders. **1614** MARKHAM *Cheap Husb.* I. (1668) Table Hard Wds., **Patch-grease*..is that tallow which is gotten from the boyling of Shoo-makers shreads. **1964** C. P. GILBERT *Design & Use Electronic Analogue Computers* vi. 364 The dotted line in Fig. 6.7(*d*) encloses all the sockets within reach of amplifier 3 using short *patch leads. **1971** J. H. SMITH *Digital Logic* ii. 18 The reader is advised to have at least 50 patch leads to connect the circuits together. **1807** P. GASS *Jrnl.* 188 Each man has also a sufficient quantity of *patch-leather. **1878** JEWITT *Ceramic Art* I. ii. 27 These dots are arranged so as to form bands; and in others simply '*patch' ornaments. **1952** G. A. & T. M. KORN *Electronic Analog Computers* viii. 339 It should..be possible to provide so-called removable *patch panels of the type used in the IBM punched-card machines. **1967** *N.Y. Times* 9 Jan. 140 Basically, an analog computer consists of an assembly of individual electronic computing elements that can be interconnected by means of a 'patch panel' outside the machine. This panel is a terminal board with holes, each hole facing an internal contact. The computer operator uses 'patch cords' (wire connectors) to interconnect specific holes for the kind of operation he wants the machine to perform. **1973** *Physics Bull.* Aug. 500/2 The new system, PB100, is a large, sophisticated unit..for rapidly simulating complex digital, analogue or hybrid systems. It features removable patch panels each of which will accommodate up to 44 dual-in-line integrated circuits. **1962** *Gloss. Terms Automatic Data Processing* (*B.S.I.*) 82 *Patchcord*, [deprecated synonym] **patchplug*, in a.d.p. a connector used to interconnect the sockets of a plugboard. **1964** G. A. & T. M. KORN *Electronic Analog & Hybrid Computers* xi. 443 With a separate copper-bar signal ground behind the patchbay.., we can use the patchbay shielding as a relay ground and return each relay-coil connection through a single patchplug grounded to its shield. **1895** *Montgomery Ward Catal.* 556/1 Coat, three-button sack, four *patch pockets. **1908** *Times* (Weekly ed.) 14 Aug. p. iii/3 There are two deep patch pockets..for carrying fly-book and sandwich-case. **1928** *Daily Express* 22 May 5/2 A plain, collarless coat..with two large patch pockets. **1973** 'D. RUTHERFORD' *Kick Start* iv. 86 He wore an expensive tropical suit with patch pockets and a waist belt. **1976** *Horse & Hound* 3 Dec. 24/1 (Advt.), Two large patch pockets,..and adjustable rear belt make this a smart comfortable coat.

Hence **'patchwise** *adv.*, in the manner of a patch.

1832 AUSTIN *Jurispr.* (1879) II. xxxix. 684 Statute law stuck patchwise on a body of judiciary.

patch (pætʃ), *sb.*[2] [According to T. Wilson 1553, and Heywood 1562, orig. the name or rather nickname of Cardinal Wolsey's domestic 'fool' or jester, his real surname being *Sexton*.

Supposed by some to have been so called from his patched garb, or patched face; but perh. rather an anglicized form of It. *pazzo* fool. It seems however to have been later associated or taken as identical with PATCH *sb.*[1], as in Shakspere's 'patch'd foole'. The following quots., bear on the history of the word:

1553 T. WILSON *Rhet.* (1580) 176 As to call one Patche or Coulson, whom we see to doe a thing foolishly, because these twoo in their tyme were notable fooles. **1562** J. HEYWOOD *Epigr.* I. xliv. (1867) 106 A saiyng of Patche my lord cardinal's foole. Master Sexten, a parson of knowne wit, As he at my lord Cardinals boord did sit [etc.]. **1590** SHAKS. *Mids. N.* IV. i. 215 But man is but a patch'd foole, if he will offer to say, what me-thought I had. (See also WARTON *Hist. Poet.* (1840) III. 87; DOUCE *Illust. Shaks.* I. 258.)]

A domestic fool; a fool or foolish person generally; a clown, dolt, booby. Now only *dial.* or *colloq.* applied to an ill-natured or ill-tempered person, esp. a child. See also CROSS-PATCH.

1549 CHALONER *Erasm. on Folly* G ij, This kynde of men whom commenly ye call fooles, doltes, ideotes, and paches. **1561** PRESTON *Cambyses* E j, Hob and Lob, a ye Cuntry patches. **1588** *Marprel. Epist.* (Arb.) 3 M. Bridges was a verie patch and a duns, when he was in Cambridge. **1590** SHAKS. *Mids. N.* III. ii. 9 A crew of patches, rude mechanicals. **1598** FLORIO, *Pazzo*, a foole; a patch, a madman. **1655** FULLER *Ch. Hist.* IV. i. §19 (tr. *Gower*) But Jack the mad patch men and houses does snatch. **1830** SCOTT *Doom of Devorgoil* II. i, Thou art a foolish patch. **1900** O'NEILL *Glens* 50 (E.D.D.) As ugly as need be, the dark little patch.

patch (pætʃ), *v.* [f. PATCH *sb.*[1]]

1. a. *trans.* To put a patch or patches on; of a thing, to serve as a patch to. Also *absol.* ***to patch up***, to mend or repair in some sort by putting patches on.

1516 [see PATCHED 1]. **1523** SKELTON *Garl. Laurel* 1209 With pitche she patchid her pitcher shuld not crase. **1548** UDALL *Erasm. Par. Luke* v. 60 b, He renteth a newe vesture to patche vp an olde. **1602** SHAKS. *Ham.* v. i. 239 Oh, that that earth, which kept the world in awe, Should patch a Wall, t'expell the winters flaw. **1774** GOLDSM. *Nat. Hist.* (1776) VII. 256 It either makes a new web, or patches up the old one. *c* **1817** HOGG *Tales & Sk.* III. 77 Why patch up that tawdry gown? **1840** DICKENS *Old C. Shop* xv, Windows patched with rags and paper. **1870** J. P. SMITH *Widow Goldsmith's Daughter* xviii. 287, I could patch and darn for you. **1888** F. HUME *Mme. Midas* I. Prol., It had one mast, and a small sail all torn and patched.

b. In pa. pple., said of a person in reference to his clothing, etc.

c **1500** *How Plowm. lerned Patern.* 147 in Hazl. *E.P.P.* I. 214 He was patched, torne, and all to rente. **1597–8** BP. HALL *Sat.* IV. ii. 9 Himself goes patched like some bare cottyer. **1611** MIDDLETON & DEKKER *Roaring Girle* D.'s Plays 1873 III. 214 Zounds I am so patcht vp, she cannot discouer me.

c. To fit (a bullet) with a patch (PATCH *sb.*[1] 6 b).

1877 C. HALLOCK *Sportsman's Gazetteer* 545 If the bullet is the right size and properly patched, the patch will not be torn in putting the cartridge into the chamber.

d. 'To overlay or bring up an impression sheet with pieces of thin paper' (Jacobi *Printers' Vocab.*).

1884 SOUTHWARD *Pract. Printing* 470 *Patching the Sheet.* **1890** JACOBI *Printing* 175 Where the type stands..low it should be patched up with the very thin set-off paper.

2. To mend, repair, or make whole, in various *fig.* applications. (Usually with *up*, and implying a hasty, clumsy, imperfect, or temporary manner.)

1573–80 BARET *Alv.* P 184 To Patch, or make whole againe:..to botch: to make amends for that is done amisse. **1597** SHAKS. *2 Hen. IV*, II. iv. 252 When wilt thou leaue fighting..and begin to patch vp thine old Body for Heauen? **1601** —— *Twel. N.* I. v. 52 Any thing that's mended, is but patch'd:..sin that amends, is but patcht with vertue. **1706** E. WARD *Wooden World Diss.* (1708) 34 The Surgeon.. takes care to patch him up with Speed. **1875** W. S. HAYWARD *Love agst. World* 40 You'll have to..patch up your quarrel.

3. To make up by joining pieces together as in patchwork; hence, to make up, put together, or frame hastily or insecurely; to botch *up*.

a **1529** SKELTON *Poems agst. Garnesche* Wks. 1843 I. 125 The nexte halter ther xall be I bequeth yt hole to the: Soche pelfry thou hast pachchyd. **1563** MAN *Musculus' Commonpl.* 40 b, An aparne patched together of figge leaves. **1579** LODGE *Def. Poetry* in G. G. Smith *Eliz. Crit. Ess.* I. 84 Out of what booke patched you out Cicero's Oration? **1650** FULLER *Pisgah* I. xi. 34 The Samaritans quitted their.. Idols, and patched up a religion amongst themselves. **1726** LEONI *Alberti's Archit.* I. 23/2 Houses, which they patch'd up of Reeds and Bullrushes. **1848** KINGSLEY *Saint's Trag.* III. i. 146 Any formal, heartless matrimony Patched up by Court intrigues. **1879** BLACK *Macleod of D.* xxxii, To patch together a pair of homespun trousers.

4. a. To put on or in as a patch; to fit (a thing) into something so as to diversify it, as in patchwork. Also *fig.*; often depreciatory.

1549 COVERDALE, etc. *Erasm. Par. Gal.* v. 16 b, To haue newe clothe sowed or patched to an olde garmente. **1593** NASHE *Christs T.* Wks. (Grosart) IV. 186 It is so vgly daubed, plaistred, and patcht on. **1662** GERBIER *Princ.* 4 Things Patcht or glewed against a Wall. *a* **1825** FORBY *Voc. E. Anglia* s.v., He patched it upon me, who knew nothing of the matter. **1886** WILLIS & CLARK *Cambridge* I. 19 The present windows have been patched into the wall in such a manner as to make it impossible to trace accurately the original state of it.

b. To join as one patch to another; to piece together.

1630 J. TAYLOR (Water P.) *Laugh & be fat* Wks. II. 71/2 Thy person's odd, vnparallel'd, vnmatchd, And yet thy action's to the person patch'd. **1867** FREEMAN *Norm. Conq.* I. iv. 239 It is just possible to patch the two narratives together.

5. a. To mark (a surface) as patches of different colour or material do; to diversify or variegate with patches. (Chiefly in passive.)

1595 SHAKS. *John* III. i. 47 If thou..wert grim..Patch'd with foule Moles, and eye-offending markes. **1711** ADDISON *Spect.* No. 115 ¶6 His Stable-doors are patched with Noses that belonged to Foxes of the Knight's own hunting down. **1774** PENNANT *Tour in Scot. in 1772.* 32 Grey rocks patched with moss. **1853** KANE *Grinnell Exp.* xlvi. (1856) 423 The slopes of the hills were heavily patched with snow. **1881** MISS BRADDON *Asph.* xxvi. 290 Yellow lamps..patching with faint light an isolated statue, or a pulpit.

b. *intr.* for *refl.* To become coloured in patches.

1896 G. L. BECKE *Pacific Tales, Hollis' Debt* (1897) 120 The red, bloated face of the skipper patched and mottled, and his breath came in quick, short gasps.

6. a. To adorn (a person, the face) with patches.

1674 R. NEWCOURT in *T. Flatman's Poems* 7 Which like their Misses Patch't and Painted are. **1704** STEELE *Lying Lover* III. (1747) 46 But alas, Madam, who patch'd you today? **1766** GOLDSM. *Vic. W.* iv, Their hair plastered with pomatum, their faces patched to taste. **1881** BESANT & RICE *Chapl. of Fleet* II. i. (1883) 123 We now went..with faces patched, to the new church in Queen Square.

b. *intr.* for *refl.*

1702 FARQUHAR *Inconstant* II. i, Your ladyship has patched and painted violently. **1729** LAW *Serious C.* ii. (1732) 18 She will find it as impossible to patch or paint, as to curse or swear.

7. *intr.* ***to patch off***, to come off in patches. *rare.*

1848 THACKERAY *Bk. Snobs* vi, The plaster is patching off the..walls.

8. *Electronics.* **a.** *trans.* To connect temporarily; also with *in*, *into*; similarly to *patch out* (see quot. 1940[2]). **b.** *intr.* To be temporarily connected. **c.** *trans.* To represent or simulate by means of temporary connections.

[**1923**: implied in PATCHING *vbl. sb.*[1] 1.] **1937** *Printers' Ink Monthly* May 40/1 *Patch it in*, to tie together various pieces of apparatus to form a circuit. **1940** *Chambers's Techn. Dict.* 619/2 *Patch*, to join together units of apparatus..by flexible cords terminated on plugs, which are inserted into break-jacks bridged across the terminations of each unit. *Ibid.*, *Patch in* and *patch out*, the temporary connexion (*patching in*) of spare apparatus in a circuit with patch cords, defective apparatus being thereby *patched out*. **1948** *Electronics* July 120/2 Two inverting or summing amplifiers in the computer unit..are patched to the servo as illustrated. **1962** HUSKEY & KORN *Computer Handbk.* iv. 36 The small extra cost of duplicate resistors for a few plug-in patchboards is negligible compared with the almost incredible nuisance of patching, say, a summing integrator with patchcord connections alone. **1964** C. P. GILBERT *Design & Use Electronic Analogue Computers* vi. 363 In Fig. 6.7(*d*) unit 2 can patch directly into units 1 and 3, unit 3 can patch directly into units 2 and 4, and so on. **1966** *Times* 21 Sept. (Ascension Island Suppl.) p. iv/3, I recently picked up this telephone and asked the communications centre..to patch me in on the network. **1971** J. H. SMITH *Digital Logic* v. 79 Electronic control systems can be quickly developed by patching the required design on a simulator. **1975** J. GRADY *Shadow of Condor* (1976) xii. 190 Kevin used the powerful radio in his car to call CIA headquarters in Langley, Virginia. The technicians there patched his radio call into the old man's office phone.

patchable ('pætʃəb(ə)l), *a. rare.* [f. PATCH *v.* + -ABLE.] That can be patched.

1849 CARLYLE *Irish Journ.* (1882) Pref. 6 Like a ragged coat;..not patched or patchable any longer.

patchaw, obs. variant of PADISHAH.

'patch-box. [f. PATCH *sb.*[1] 2 + BOX *sb.*[2]] A box for holding patches for the face.

1674 *Lond. Gaz.* No. 859/4 Lost.., two silver powder Boxes, and a patch Box. **1712–14** POPE *Rape Lock* IV. 162 Thrice from my trembling hand the patch-box fell. **1758** H. WALPOLE *Let. to H. S. Conway* 16 June, If they send a patch-box to Lord George Sackville, it will hold all his laurels. **1876** MISS BRADDON *J. Haggard's Dau.* xi. 157 The poets of a patch box and powder period.

† **'patchcock, 'patchock.** *Obs. rare*−1. [Known only in the passage cited; in which also the reading is uncertain. The first element is app. PATCH *sb.*[1] (or ?[2]); the second may be COCK, or the dim. suffix -OCK. See note below.]

A term used by Spenser of the degenerate English in Ireland, either in reference to their character and habits, their mongrel breed, or their costume: ? a base or mean fellow, ? a ragamuffin.

1596 SPENSER *State Irel.* (Wks. Grosart IX. 104; Globe 636/2), The rest which dwell aboue in Connagh(t) and Munster,..and some in Leinster and Ulster, ar degenerate and growen to be as very Patchcockes [*v.r.* Patchock(e)s] as the wild Irishe.

[The Lambeth MS. 510, which was the copy submitted to the Abp. of Canterbury for licence, dated by Spenser and initialled E. S., from which Grosart prints his text, reads, lf. 39, *Patchcockes*; but three other MSS., B.M. Add. 22022 (printed in the Globe text), Harl. 7388, Camb. Dd. 10. 60 have *Patchockes, -ocks.* Camb. Dd. 14. 28 has *Rakehells.* If the word was *patchockes*, it was perhaps the same as Shakspere's 'very PAIOCKE', if this is read *pajocke.* Cf. same play III. iv. 102 'a King of shreds and patches'.]

patched (pætʃt, 'pætʃɪd), *ppl. a.* [f. PATCH *v.* + -ED[1].] **a.** In senses corresponding to those of the verb: Mended with patches; made up of pieces as in patchwork; mended, made up, or put together hastily, clumsily, or insecurely. Also ***patched-together, patched-up.***

1516 in *Myrr. our Ladye* (1873) p. l, In dede for very voluntary pouerte..she had broken patchyd sleuys. *a* **1591** H. SMITH *Wks.* (1867) II. 405 Mahomet's religion is a patched religion, mixed partly with Judaism, partly with Gentilism, partly with Papism, partly with Christianism. **1599** NASHE *Lenten Stuffe* (1871) 42 With it..the patchedest leather pilche *laboratho* may dine like a Spanish Duke. **1764** *Mem. G. Psalmanazar* 152 When he..heard my patched up story. **1792** *Anecd. W. Pitt* III. xxxix. 38 Let us have peace, ..but let it be honourable, let it be secure. A patched up peace will not do. **1840** R. H. DANA *Bef. Mast* xxxvi, The patched woolen trousers. **1905** *Daily Chron.* 13 Feb. 5/1 Japan will tolerate no patched-up peace. **1916** H. G. WELLS *Mr. Britling* III. i. 385 It was the queer halting telling of a patched-together tale. **1935** T. S. ELIOT *Murder in Cath.* i. 16 Peace, but not the kiss of peace. A patched up affair, if you ask my opinion. **1954** KOESTLER *Invis. Writing* xxii. 249 To emerge in the end with a more or less successfully patched-up personality. **1972** *Listener* 21 Dec. 872/1 A young man who deals in patched-up cars.

b. Adorned or marked with patches.

1667 PEPYS *Diary* 1 May, Peggy Pen..with only her husband's pretty sister with her..both patched and very fine, and in much the finest coach in the park. **1855** KINGSLEY *Westw. Ho!* ix, A painted, patched, fucused, periwigged, bolstered,..Lamia!

† **c.** ***patched work*** = PATCHWORK. *Obs.*

1716 M. DAVIES *Athen. Brit.* III. 51 Such Bitts and Scraps of patcht Work-Citations.

Hence † **'patchedly** *adv.*, in manner of a patch.

1549 COVERDALE, etc. *Erasm. Par. Gal.* v. 16 b, Nor can he beare with to haue..olde clothe be patchedlye sowed into a newe.

patcher ('pætʃə(r)). [f. PATCH *v.* + -ER[1].] One who patches: see the verb. Also ***patcher-up.***

1528 TINDALE *Wks.* (Parker Soc.) I. 135 He is no patcher; he cannot build on another man's foundation. **1552** HULOET, Bodger, botcher, mender, or patcher of olde garmentes. **1611** COTGR., *Renoüeur de vieilles causes*,..a peecer or patcher vp of ruinous causes. **1694** MOTTEUX *Rabelais* v. (1737) 214 Patchers, Clowters, and Botchers of old trumpery Stuff. **1841** EMERSON *Misc., Conservative* (1884) 259 A timid cobbler and patcher. **1875** JOWETT *Plato* (ed. 2) I. 295 A mender of old shoes, or patcher up of clothes.

patchery[1] ('pætʃərɪ). [f. PATCH *sb.*[1] or *v.* + -ERY.] The action of patching or mending clumsily or hastily; anything made up of pieces or fragments put together; a patchwork (usually *fig.*).

1579 FULKE *Heskins's Parl.* 239 The Greeke Article is so placed, as it can abide no such patcherie. **1623** R. BERNARD *Looke beyond Luther* Ep. Ded. 2 A new vpstart Religion, a patcherie of Iudaisme, Paganisme and Heresie. **1702** C. MATHER *Magn. Chr.* III. II. xxiii. (1852) 467 Vile human inventions..and patcheries sticht into the service of the Lord. **1834** GEN. P. THOMPSON *Exerc.* (1842) III. 31 Designating such performances as jargon and patchery. **1880** SWINBURNE *Stud. Shaks.* (ed. 2) App. 232 A thin sample of poetic patchery cobbled up and stitched together.

† **'patchery**[2]. *Obs.* [f. PATCH *sb.*[2] + -ERY.] The conduct of a 'patch'; roguery, knavery.

1582 STANYHURST *Æneis* II. (Arb.) 64 From the fathers sermons shal such fond patcherye flicker? *Ibid., Conceits* (Arb.) 140 Cleaue toe the sound *Castè*, flee from thee patcherye *Cautè*. **1607** SHAKS. *Timon* v. i. 99 You heare him cogge, See him dissemble, Know his grosse patchery.

¶ In the following the sense is uncertain.

1553 *Respublica* (Brandl) v. ix. 79 Tis a bagg of Rye in dede: vsiree, periuree, pitcheree, patcherie, pilferie, briberee, snatcherie, catcherie.

'patch-head. A local name in Maine, U.S., for the surf-scoter (*Œdemia perspicillata*), a kind of duck, from the white patches on its head.

1890 in *Cent. Dict.*

patchiness ('pætʃɪnɪs). [f. PATCHY *a.* + -NESS.] Patchy quality or condition.

a **1828** D. WORDSWORTH *Jrnl.* (1941) II. 93 The character of the Lake..is of free cheerfulness...it is not *disturbed* by buildings. *I* complained not of *patchiness* or *spottiness.* **1862** H. SPENCER *First Princ.* II. xix. §150 (1875) 407 Irregularities of distribution..would produce that patchiness which distinguishes the heavens. **1887** R. GARNETT *Carlyle* vii. 128 Nothing seems to have struck him so much as the general patchiness of the country.

'patching, *vbl. sb.*[1] [f. PATCH *v.* + -ING[1].]

1. The action of the verb PATCH, in various senses; also, the condition of being patched, or an instance of this. Also ***patching-up.***

1526 SKELTON *Magnyf.* 452 It is evyll patchynge of that is torne. **1546** J. HEYWOOD *Prov.* (1867) 47 An olde sacke axeth much patchyng. **1691** T. H[ALE] *Acc. New Invent.* 98 That patching and botching with Solder that appears upon all the Cast-lead Coverings. **1791** MRS. RADCLIFFE *Rom. Forest* ii, A little patching up would make it comfortable enough. **1832** JAMES H. *Masterton* xxiii, The eye detected some rather anomalous patchings and darnings. **1893** *British Printer* 157 Underlay wherever possible, as the less patching there is on the cylinder the less chance is there of wrinkling. **1923** *Bell Syst. Techn. Jrnl.* II. 123 In open-wire installations it has been the practice to equip each line circuit ..with a full complement of jacks suited to provide the maximum degree of flexibility in 'patching'. *Ibid.* 132 With this arrangement of apparatus, any 'ringer'..may be connected temporarily to the system by means of 'patching' cords. **1948** J. ATKINSON *Herbert & Proctor's Telephony* (new ed.) I. xvii. 346 (*caption*) Patching jack at incoming end of order wire. *Ibid.* xxi. 473 The junctions are routed through break jacks on the test jack frame and a small cord shelf accommodates a number of patching-out cords to facilitate temporary changes. **1964** C. P. GILBERT *Design & Use Electronic Analogue Computers* vi. 361 To interconnect the amplifiers, leads with a plug at each end would be inserted into the appropriate sockets giving what is known as simple direct 'patching'. *Ibid.*, The patching is carried out on the plug board before it is inserted into the 'patch' panel. **1964** G. A. & T. M. KORN *Electronic Analog & Hybrid Computers* xi. 443 Iterative differential analyzers..require frequent patching of integrator and memory control circuits.

2. The putting of patches on the face by way of adornment.

1656 *Artif. Handsom.* 78 They forbid all painting, patching, and powdering. **1765** GOLDSM. *Double Transform.* 40 Skill'd in no other arts was she, But dressing, patching, repartee. **1885** *Trans. Lanc. & Chesh. Antiq. Soc.* III. 35 The custom of patching amongst ladies.

3. The wadding for a bullet (cf. PATCH *sb.*[1] 6 b).

1835 A. B. LONGSTREET *Georgia Scenes* 286 He..drew out his patching, found the most even part of it, [etc.]. **1887** E. EGGLESTON *Graysons* xiii. (1888) 144 Taking a bullet from his pouch, he felt in his pocket for the patching.

4. *Comb.*, as ***patching-cloth, -rubber, -work.***

c **1680** *Roxb. Ball.* VII. 468 The Taylor..had patching-work for a whole season. **1896** *Godey's Mag.* (U.S.) Apr. 374/2 A circle of patching-cloth pushed through to the bottom of the tire. **1898** *Sun* 23 Mar. 4/1 Always carry in your tool-bag a fairly large piece of patching rubber.

† **'patching,** *vbl. sb.*[2] *Obs.* [f. PATCH *sb.*[2] + -ING[1].] The behaviour of a 'patch'; = PATCHERY[2].

a **1550** *Image Ipocr.* in *Skelton's Wks.* (1843) II. 446 With peltinge and patchinge, With findinge and fatchinge. **1562** J. HEYWOOD *Prov. & Epigr.* (1867) 171 After catching and snatchyng, Pyllyng and pollyng, we fall..to patchyng.

† **'patching,** *ppl. a.*[1] *Obs.* [f. PATCH *sb.*[2] + -ING[2].] Acting like a 'patch'; deceiving, knavish. Hence † **'patchingly** *adv.*, deceitfully.

1570 FOXE *A. & M.* (ed. 2) 1491/2 Others..dyd.. dissemblingly and patchingly vse some part of them. **1591** GREENE *Disc. Coosnage* Wks. (Grosart) X. 33 These cony-catchers..geuing to diuers vile patching shiftes, an honest and godly title. **1641** J. TRAPPE *Theol. Theol.* iii. 127 Some slippery persons or patching companions. **1647** WARD *Simp. Cobler* (1843) 37, I am not without some contrivalls in my patching braines.

patching, *ppl. a.*[2] [f. PATCH *v.* + -ING[2].] That patches or covers with patches.

1855 BROWNING *Love among Ruins* iv, The patching houseleek's head of blossom winks Through the chinks.

'patch-leaf. Also putch-, putcha-leaf. [A part-transl. of Bengālī *pacha-pāt*, f. Bengālī *pāt* leaf.] = PATCHOULI.

1698 FRYER *Acc. E. India & P.* 209 Goods from Acheen ..Patch Leaf, 1 Bahar Maunds 7 20 *Sear.* **1886** YULE & BURNELL *Anglo-Ind. Gloss.* 517 Patchouli, Patch-leaf, also Putch- and Putcha-leaf.

patchless ('pætʃlɪs), *a.* [f. PATCH *sb.*[1] + -LESS.] Not having or exhibiting patches. (In quot. fig.)

1927 *Observer* 1 May 6 Hundreds of different..things are mentioned; but the mentionings are all woven into a seamless, patchless, and nowhere ragged history of the subject.

† **'patchment.** *Obs. rare*−1. [f. PATCH *v.* + -MENT.] A patchwork.

a **1603** T. CARTWRIGHT *Confut. Rhem. N.T.* (1618) 205 A patchment of untruthes.

patchock: see PATCHCOCK.

patchouli ('pætʃu:lɪ, pə'tʃu:lɪ). Also 9 **pach-, pāch-, patschouli, patchouly, paccioli.** [a. *patchouli*, 'the vernacular name over the greater part of the Madras Presidency' (Sir G. Birdwood in *Athenæum* 22 Oct. 1898), the elements of which are referred by some to Tamil *pach, pachai-* green and *ilai* leaf: cf. the Bengālī *pacha-pāt* (*pāt* leaf), and Eng. *putcha-leaf*, or PATCH-LEAF.

The spelling *patchouli* appears to be French, and may have arisen in the French possessions on the Coromandel coast. If there is anything in the conjecture in Hatz.-Darm. that it is a phonetically-spelt adaptation of Eng. *patch-leaf*, this would necessarily carry back the name in Fr. to a period anterior to the earliest Eng. examples. But in French dictionaries it was entered as a neologism by Littré in 1875, and was admitted by the Académie in 1878, long after it was known in English.]

1. An odoriferous plant (*Pogostemon Patchouli*, N.O. *Labiatæ*), native to Silhat, Penang, and the Malay peninsula, the dried leaves of which are used for various purposes in the East; it yields an essential oil, from which the scent (see 2) is derived.

1851 FORBES in *Art Jrnl. Illustr. Catal.* II. p. vii/1 The.. aromatic herbs, the lavenders and rosemarys, hyssop and peppermints, patchouli and thyme, all yielding volatile oils. **1858** SIMMONDS *Dict. Trade, Patchouly*, an Indian herb. **1866** WATTS *Dict. Chem.* IV. 357 Patchouli, Pachupat or Patscha pat. **1872** *Ibid.* VI. 902 Volatile oil of patschouli gradually deposits a camphor.

2. A penetrating and lasting perfume prepared from this plant.

1845 ALB. SMITH *Scattergood Fam.* I. vii, Evening-party odours..pachouli, white-wine vapours, and cut oranges. **1856** C. HERING *Homœop. Dom. Phys.* p. xi, Perfumery, particularly musk, hartshorn, camphor, paccioli. **1866** *Treas. Bot.* 910/2 Ill effects, such as loss of appetite and sleep, nervous attacks, etc., have been ascribed to the excessive employment of Patchouli as a perfume.

3. *attrib.*, as ***patchouli camphor, oil.***

1881 WATTS *Dict. Chem.* VIII. 1497 *Patchouli camphor*, $C_{15}H_{26}O$..forms regular hexagonal crystals. **1893** *Syd. Soc. Lex.*, *Patchouli oil*,..is a viscid oil, boils at 282°–294° F., and separates out on standing as *Patchouly camphor.*

patchouli'd (pə'tʃu:lɪd), *a. poet.* Also **patchoulied.** [f. PATCHOULI + -ED[2].] Perfumed with patchouli.

1925 H. ACTON in *Oxf. Poetry* 7 The pulsing cafés and patchouli'd vamps. **1929** W. DE LA MARE in H. Granville-Barker *Eighteen-Seventies* iii. 51 The patchoulied nosegay of artifice. **1943** D. GASCOYNE *Poems 1937–42* 42 Tenebrous lanes Down which at times patchouli'd ghosts flit by.

† **'patch-,panel,** *sb.* and *a. Obs.* [f. PATCH *v.* + PANEL *sb.*[1]]

A. *sb.* One who patches panels; ? a jobbing or botching carpenter: an abusive appellation.

1593 G. HARVEY *Pierce's Super.* Wks. (Grosart) II. 280 The starkest Patch-pannell of them all, or the grossest hammer-drudge in a county. **1602** DEKKER *Satirom.* Wks. 1873 I. 219 [Woman to retired Captain] Hang thee patch-pannell, I am none a thy Charing-Crosse.

B. *adj.* Fit for patching panels or putting into patchwork; of little value as material.

1606 *Wily Beguiled* Prol., Why, noble Cerberus, nothing but patch-pannel stuff, old gallimawfries, and cotten candle eloquence.

patch panel: see s.v. PATCH *sb.*[1] 6.

'patch test. *Med.* [f. PATCH *sb.*[1] + TEST *sb.*[1]] A test for determining a patient's sensitivity to a substance, by applying to his skin a patch made of or containing it, and noting whether erythema is produced. Hence (with hyphen) as *vb. trans.*, to subject to such a test; also **'patch-testing** *vbl. sb.*

1933 R. W. & R. M. B. MACKENNA *Dis. Skin* (ed. 3) xv. 320 Recently the 'patch' or 'contact eczema' test has been much used to determine whether or not a patient is susceptible to an external irritant. **1956** *Brit. Med. Jrn.* 21 Jan. 148/1 She was patch-tested to nylon stockings of three shades and gave positive reactions to all of them. **1963** *Lancet* 5 Jan. 61/2 The patient was patch-tested with the sample that he had provided, and whereas the control patch remained unaffected, the test patch became reddened in three days, and redder and scaly in a week. **1963** V. J. FONTANA in F. Speer *Allergic Child* xv. 223 Patch testing is a helpful procedure in eliciting the specific cause in many types of contact dermatitis. **1967** *Oceanogr. & Marine Biol.* V. 366 Patch testing with pieces of the polyzoon..have confirmed that the *Alcyonidium* is the causative agent. **1968** A. ROOK et al. *Textbk. Dermatol.* I. xiv. 301/1 The patch-test was first devised by Jadassolm 1896 and later brought into general use by Bloch. *Ibid.* 310/1 Any patch-test involves a risk of sensitization.

patchwork ('pætʃwɜ:k). [f. PATCH *v.* or *sb.*[1] + WORK *sb.*]

1. a. Work composed of pieces or fragments put together, esp. in a makeshift or incongruous manner; a thing patched up; a medley, jumble. Now often viewed as *fig.* from 2.

a **1692** POLLEXFEN *Disc. Trade* (1697) A iv, It cannot be expected they should have any effect for common Good, at best, but Patch-work. **1739** *Wks. of Learned* I. 103 He that thinks the Iliad and Odysses the Patchwork of a Beggar's Rhapsodies. **1872** GEO. ELIOT *Middlem.* lxxiv, This imperfectly-taught woman, whose phrases and habits were an odd patchwork. **1887** W. S. PRATT in W. Gladden *Parish Probl.* 457 Latin and German hymns—clever patch-work often resembling real poetic creations.

b. Work of patching up: see PATCH *v.* 2. *nonce use.*

1712 SWIFT *Jrnl. to Stella* 12 Dec., I should ruin myself with endeavouring to mend them,..and I have been too much engaged in patchwork already.

2. *spec.* Work consisting of small pieces of various kinds of cloth, differing in colour and pattern, and sometimes in size and shape, sewed together by the edges, generally with ornamental effect, so as to form one article, as a counterpane, cushion, tea-cosy, etc. ***crazy patchwork***, that in which the pieces are quite irregular in shape and size: cf. CRAZY 5.

1726 SWIFT *Gulliver* I. vi, My clothes..looked like the patch-work made by the ladies in England, only that mine were all of a colour. **1809** W. IRVING *Knickerb.* III. iv, Every woman..wore pockets..fashioned with patch-work into many curious devices. **1872** G. MACDONALD *Wilf. Cumb.* I. iii. 17 The bed was covered with an equally charming counterpane of silk patchwork. **1892** MRS. ALEXANDER *Mammon* xix. 268, I wish, Claude, you would do a little of my crazy patchwork, you work so beautifully.

b. Any surface divided into many small compartments of various shapes and kinds.

1865 E. BURRITT *Walk Land's End* 243 A glorious little world of Devonshire scenery, carpeted to the rim with the picturesque patchwork of Devonshire verdure. **1880** MRS. PARR *Adam & Eve* xii, A patchwork of fields spread out and ran down to the cliffs.

3. *Mining.* (*local.*) See quot.

1897 *Jrnl. R. Agric. Soc.* Mar. 177 The ironstones were formerly dug out in extensive open-air workings [in S. Wales] known as 'patchworks'.

4. *attrib.* **a.** Made up of miscellaneous pieces or fragments; composed of a combination of odds and ends. Also *fig.* (In some cases indistinguishable from 4 b.)

1713 GAY *Guard.* No. 149 ¶17 What Horace [*Ars Poet.* ll. 15–16] says of his patch-work poets: 'Purpureus late qui splendeat unus et alter, Assuitur pannus—'. **1814** W. TAYLOR in *Monthly Rev.* LXXIII. 463 Those second-hand minds and patchwork intellects. **1876** *N. Amer. Rev.* CXXIII. 420 The patchwork rubric of the English church. **1905** *Daily Chron.* 30 Aug. 5/6 A rupture is preferable to a patch-work peace. **1956** H. J. PATON in H. D. Lewis *Contemp. Brit. Philos.* (ser. 3) 348, I never had any use for the patchwork theory popular at that time, which supposed his [*sc.* Kant's] work to be a mass of contradictions. **1977** P. SCUPHAM *Hinterland* 3 Now, the celebrated Ride stiffly through a patchwork multitude.

b. Made of, or of the nature of patchwork: see 2. Also *fig.*

1840 HOOD *Kilmansegg. Dream* vi, No patchwork quilt, all seams and scars. **1865** DICKENS *Mut. Fr.* I. xv, There was the old patch-work counterpane. **1880** MRS. PARR *Adam & Eve* i, A low chair with..a patch-work cushion. **1933** CHESTERTON *All I Survey* ix. 45, I am afraid of the Patchwork Peril, which is all colours and none. **1951** M. MCLUHAN *Mech. Bride* (1967) 144/2 Everyone is intellectually and emotionally a patch-work quilt of occupied and unoccupied territory.

5. *Comb.*

1897 MARY KINGSLEY *W. Africa* 234 Spread with clean calico and adorned with patchwork-covered pillows.

Hence '**patchworker**, a maker of patchwork; also *fig.*; '**patchworky** *a.* [-Y[1]], resembling or suggestive of patchwork.

1844 *Ainsworth's Mag.* VI. 112 A patchworker of the piquant anecdotes of the newest French memoirs. **1884** E. W. HAMILTON *Diary* 29 Mar. (1972) II. 585 The exterior [of the house, Coombe Warren] is picturesque, but almost *too* unsymmetrical and 'patch-work-y'. **1888** *Advance* (Chicago) 3 May 275/1 It would quicken the zeal of the little patchworkers also, if they could see how pretty their gay quilts look upon the beds. **1906** *Speaker* 20 Oct. 71/2 To a foreign student London presents..a patchworky spectacle. **1972** *New Yorker* 26 Aug. 50/1 (*caption*) Tie on this patchworky, wrap-around skirt. **1977** R. RICHARDSON *Discovering Patchwork* (rear cover), This book..should..have much to offer the experienced patch-worker.

patchy ('pætʃɪ), *a.*[1] [f. PATCH *sb.*[1] + -Y.] Abounding in or diversified with patches; consisting of patches or small separate areas or tracts; resembling patchwork in appearance or structure. Also, occurring only in patches, or at separate points; irregular, spasmodic.

1798 *Trans. Soc. Arts* XVI. 185 [A crop] in many places patchy, with intervals of four or five feet without any plants at all. **1845** *Jrnl. R. Agric. Soc.* VI. I. 84 The land is patchy and of different qualities. **1872** HUXLEY *Phys.* iii. 65 The layer appears patchy or spotted. **1882** *Gardener's Chron.* 4 Mar. 295 A stone or tile edging is certainly preferable to a patchy Box one. **1895** KEGAN PAUL in *Month* Aug. 458 Such a Life is often patchy and scrappy. **1905** *Sat. Westm. Gaz.* 16 Dec. 15/1 That evening I noticed a peculiarity in the pit's applause. It was 'patchy'. **1921** *Ampleforth Jrnl.* Jan. 139 Scent was patchy and a good deal of lifting was necessary to maintain the line. **1957** [see CONTAGIOUS *a.* 8]. **1967** W. CARR *Daily Tel. Beauty Bk.* 23 Those who freckle have only groups of pigment-producing cells, providing patchy, inefficient protection. **1971** *Nature* 30 July 352/2 The survey is patchy and by no means as up to date as one expects. **1976** *Shooting Times & Country Mag.* 16–22 Dec. 38/1 Many countries report varied and patchy scent.

Hence '**patchily** *adv.*, in a patchy manner.

1903 *Daily Mail* 7 Sept. 5/4 Shops,..started with some dim idea of being beautiful, have finished by becoming patchily tin. **1972** *Daily Tel.* 24 Apr. 14/8 Anyone who bites or licks her lips to concentrate will soon look patchily fungoid rather than trendy. **1974** I. MURDOCH *Sacred & Profane Love Machine* 144 His face patchily pink. **1975** G. LYALL *Judas Country* xxx. 220 I stepped cautiously out into the patchily-lit alley.

'**patchy**, *a.*[2] *colloq.* or *dial.* [f. PATCH *sb.*[2] + -Y.] Of the nature of a 'patch'; cross, ill-tempered, fractious.

1862 TROLLOPE *Orley F.* II. iii. 20 He'll be a bit patchy.. just for a while... To-morrow morning maybe he'll be just as sweet as sweet.

pate[1] (peɪt). (Also 7, 9 **pat.**) [In common use from *c* 1300: origin unknown.

Some have conjectured it to be a by-form of *plate*, comparing med.L. *platta* the clerical tonsure, and Du. and Ger. *platte* a shaven or bald head. But evidence is wanting.]

1. The head, the skull: more particularly applied to that part which is usually covered with hair. (In modern use, more or less ludicrous or humorous; not in serious or dignified use.)

c **1305** *Judas* 83 in *E.E.P.* (1862) 109 He smot him wiþ a ston behynde in þe pate þat al þe sculle to-daschte þe brayn ful out þerate. *c* **1394** *P. Pl. Crede* 839 He miȝte no maistre ben kald (for Crist þat defended), Ne puten no pylion on his pild pate. *c* **1430** LYDG. *Jack Hare* Min. Poems (Percy Soc.) 54 Now wesseil N. unto thi jousy pate, Unthrift and thou together be mett. **1535** COVERDALE *Ps.* vii. 16 His vnhappynes shall come vpon his owne heade, and his wickednes shall fall vpon his owne pate. **1593** SHAKS. *2 Hen. VI*, v. i. 135 He is a Traitor, let him to the Tower, And chop away that factious pate of his. *a* **1604** HANMER *Chron. Irel.* (1809) 325 A foole ..gave him such a blow upon the pat, that the blood ran downe his eares. **1616** R. C. *Times' Whistle* III. 969 Some curle their pates to make their lookes more faire. **1632** LITHGOW *Trav.* IX. 396 An Eagle taking his bald pate for a white rocke, let a shell-fish fall on it. **1810** COCK *Strains* I. 136 (E.D.D.) Wi' powdered pats; The auld blue Bonnet's laid aside, They maun ha'e Hats. **1883** *19th Cent.* Dec. 1092 The stubbles are close shaven as a monk's pate.

2. The head as the seat of the intellect; hence put for skill, cleverness, 'brains', and formerly sometimes for a person possessed of such.

1610 SHAKS. *Temp.* IV. i. 244 Steale by line and leuell, is an excellent passe of pate. **1614** SYLVESTER *Bethulia's Rescue* I. 109 The Able-most For Pate, Prowess, Purse. **1627–77** FELTHAM *Resolves* I. xliii. 70 To lay the plot at first, well; is matter of more pate. **1630** *R. Johnson's Kingd. & Commw.* 39 The greatest Sages of the kingdome,..and the best pates of Spaine. **1717** PRIOR *Alma* III. 355 An odd conceit, As ever enter'd Frenchman's pate. *c* **1730** YOUNG *Ep. to Pope* 65 Each shallow pate, that cannot read your name, Can read your life, and will be proud to blame. **1899** E. J. CHAPMAN *Drama Two Lives, Amph. & Ascid.* 88 Made manifest to meanest pates.

3. The skin of a calf's head.

1687 *Lond. Gaz.* No. 2225/4 Prohibiting the Exportation of all sorts of Linen Rags, Glovers Clippings, Parchment Shreads, Calves Pates. **1881** *Sci. Amer.* XLIV. 408 [The hide] is sold to the salters with the pates and tails on.

b. In the fur trade, The fur from a black patch on the head of a rabbit or hare.

1878 *Ure's Dict. Arts* IV. 381 At present hare wool is not sorted, but formerly it was divided into *black back*, *brown back*, *sides*, *pate* (useless), *cheeks* and *tail*, as in the case of rabbit wool.

pate[2] (peɪt). *north. dial.* Also 7 **payte, paite,** 8 **pait.** [Of obscure origin.

Perhaps from prec., in reference to the white top of its head, suggesting a bald pate.]

A badger. Also in *Comb.*, ***pate-head.***

1628 *Vestry Bks.* (Surtees) 91 Whosoever shall take any fox, or pate, or badger, in this parish and bring the heade to the church, shall have twelve pence paid by the churchwardens. **1653** *Ibid.* 194 To George Burne for a pate head, 6*d.* **1718** *Finghall Church-w. Acc.* (MS.), For 3e Pait Head, 1*s.* **1788** W. MARSHALL *Yorksh.* II. Gloss. (E.D.S.), *Pait*, a badger. **1883** T. & K. MACQUOID *About Yorksh.* 126 The last pate is said to have been killed hereabouts some twenty-eight years ago.

‖**pâté**[3] (pate, 'pæteɪ, 'pɑː-). Also 8 **patee.** [F. *pâté*:—OF. *pasté*: see PASTY *sb.*, PATTY.]

1. a. A pie, pasty, or patty. ***pâté de foie gras***, formerly, pie or pasty of fatted goose liver, Strasburg pie; now chiefly the goose-liver filling itself: cf. 1 b.

1706 PHILLIPS, *Petty Patees*.., a sort of small Pyes made of March-pane, and fill'd with Sweet-meats. **1768** STERNE *Sent. Journ.*, *Le Patissier*, A chevalier de St. Louis selling *patés*. **1813** *Sk. Character* (ed. 2) I. 117, I..sent off the woman with an oyster pâté. **1813** MOORE *Post-bag* iii. 4 His pâtés superb—and his cutlets sublime! **1827** LYTTON *Pelham* viii, To help myself to the *pâté de foie gras*. **1863** G. MEREDITH *Let.* 19 July (1970) I. 217 Did you have salmon at Strasbourg—and pâté de foie gras—it's not a good place for the latter. **1876** GEO. ELIOT *Dan. Der.* III. VI. xlviii. 343, I can't eat *pâté de foie gras*. **1892** A. B. MARSHALL *Larger Cookery Bk.* vi. 253 Cut up the contents of a small tin of *pâté de foie gras*. **1960** E. DAVID *French Provincial Cooking* 35 His *pâté de foie gras* and *mousse de foies de volaille*, smooth, pink, and marbled with green pistachio nuts and black truffles,.. were as good and delicate as they looked.

b. A paste made from liver or other meats. So ***pâté de campagne***, a coarse pork and liver pâté; ***pâté en croûte***, a pâté baked in a pastry surround; ***pâté maison***, a pâté cooked according to the recipe of a particular restaurant.

1901 C. H. SENN *New Cent. Cookery Bk.* xxii. 399 Fleurettes de Foie Gras (Foie Gras with Mayonnaise).—1 medium-sized tin or terrine of foie gras pâté, 1 truffle [etc.]. **1931** X. M. BOULESTIN *What shall we have To-day?* 84 Let the *pâté* get cold in the larder with a weight over it. Serve in the *terrine* in which it has cooked. **1948** *Good Housek. Cookery Bk.* II. 74 Liver and other savoury pâtés..may be served as an hors d'oeuvre. **1931** J. BERJANE *French Dishes for Eng. Tables* x. 152 Pâté de Campagne (*foie de porc*) Gascon... Chop up the liver and the fat [etc.]. **1966** P. V. PRICE *France: Food & Wine Guide* 101 A *pâté de campagne* will be a rather rough-cut *pâté*. **1967** V. CANNING *Python Project* ii. 31 He was not English. The French accent was as thick and meaty as *pâté de campagne*. *c* **1938** *Fortnum & Mason Price List* 29/2 Pâté en croutes (October to March). **1961** S. BECK et al. *Mastering Art of French Cooking* ix. 569 The recipe we have chosen to illustrate *pâté en croûte* is boned duck stuffed, reformed, surrounded with decorated pastry, and baked. **1967** A. CHRISTIE *Endless Night* xiii. 113 We had brought *pâté en croûte* with us and French bread. **1947** M. MCCARTHY *On Contrary* (1962) 6 *Open City*,.. Oscar Wilde, a reprint of Henry James were *paté de maison* to this lady who wanted the definitive flapjack. **1956** M. LASKI in *Observer* 14 Oct. 17/4 It is..misleading to say that ..*pâté de foie gras* is known under the names *pâté de foie*, *pâté de campagne*, *pâté maison*. **1963** R. CARRIER *Great Dishes of World* 40 Every French restaurant boasts its *pâté maison*. **1967** *Listener* 20 Apr. 533/3 The standardization and mass-production of food extends beyond the same tinned '*pâté maison*'..wherever one goes.

2. *Fortif.* See quot. (Erroneously written *pate.*)

1704 J. HARRIS *Lex. Techn.* I, *Pate*, in Fortification, is a kind of Platform like what they call an Horseshoe,.. generally oval, encompassed only with a Parapet... It is usually erected in Marshy Grounds to cover a Gate of a Town. **1802** JAMES *Milit. Dict.*, *Pate*, Fr.

‖**pâte**[4] (pat). [Fr., = PASTE *sb.*] **a. pâte** (erron. **pâté) brisée** (pɑt brize), short pastry.

1845 E. ACTON *Mod. Cookery* xvi. 405 Pate brisee, or French crust for hot or cold meat-pies. **1960** E. DAVID *French Provincial Cooking* 205 This is one version of the *pâte brisée*..used for most open tarts in French cookery. **1978** *N.Y. Times* 29 Mar. c. 6/6 A pâté brisée is one of the best sweet pastry doughs.

b. The clay from which porcelain is made. So **pâte dure** (pɑt dyr), hard clay; **pâte-sur-pâte** (pɑtsyrpɑt), clay applied in layers to form relief decoration; **pâte tendre** (pɑt tɑ̃dr), soft clay.

1863 W. CHAFFERS *Marks Pott. & Porc.* 163 Porcelain of the *pâte tendre* has the appearance of an unctuous white enamel, like cream;..the *pâte tendre* is also soft in another sense, being unable to bear so great a degree of furnace heat as the hard porcelain. *Ibid.*, The *pâte dure*, or true porcelain, is of the whiteness of milk, and feels to the touch of a hard and cold nature. **1870** C. SCHREIBER *Jrnl.* (1911) I. 71 We found an exquisite pâte tendre St. Cloud group. **1881** C. C. HARRISON *Woman's Handiwork* II. 104 To Minton's unmatched artist, Solon, the world is indebted for an exquisite style of ceramic ornamentation, low relief carving in clay, known as pâte-sur-pâte. **1890** [see KUTANI]. **1899** R. GLAZIER *Man. Hist. Ornament* 83 Porcelain is technically known under the terms 'hard paste' ('pâte dure') and 'soft' ('pâte tendre'). **1904** H. JAMES *Golden Bowl* I. viii. 149 He had handled nothing so precious as the Principino..whom he could manipulate..as he couldn't a correspondingly rare morsel of an earlier *pâte tendre*. **1932** R. FRY *Characteristics of French Art* III. 66 He loved to feel the *pâte tendre* of a piece of fine pottery. **1947** J. C. RICH *Materials & Methods of Sculpture* ii. 44 *Pâte sur pâte* is the phrase applied to a method of modeling very low reliefs with slip. **1959** *Times* 3 Oct. 9/5 Her sister Florence, who specialized in birds..and also painted in *pâte sur pâte*. **1964** H. HODGES *Artifacts* i. 33 In a process known as pâte-sur-pâte, clay made to the consistency of a thin paste may be painted on, layer by layer, to produce low relief modelling. **1972** *Country Life* 20 Jan. 152/2 They are early Minton pâte-sur-pâte, their maker the technically gifted Marc Louis Solon. **1974** SAVAGE & NEWMAN *Illustr. Dict. Ceramics* 215 *Pâte dure*, the French term for hard-paste porcelain. **1976** *Times Lit. Suppl.* 3 Sept. 1074/4 A display of Minton *pâte-sur-pâte* wares.

c. pâte de verre (pɑt də vɛr), powdered glass that has been refired.

1907 E. DILLON *Glass* xxii. 359 Of quite another nature is the *pâte de verre*, a substance somewhat of the nature of a glass frit, which has been made use of by the French sculptor, M. Henri Cros, in the modelling of polychrome reliefs and friezes. **1961** E. M. ELVILLE *Collector's Dict. Glass* 178/2 [James] Tassie's medium was a finely powdered potash-lead glass, or pâte-de-verre. **1978** *Guardian Weekly* 9 Apr. 14/4 Sofas are covered in bright prints, lamps are pink or blue *pate de verre*.

paté, patee, -ée, var. PATTÉE (in Heraldry).

pated ('peɪtɪd). *a.* [f. PATE[1] + -ED[2].] Having a pate (of a specified kind).

1580 LYLY *Euphues* (Arb.) 439 Grose and dull pated. *a* **1613** OVERBURY *A Wife*, etc. (1638) 210 Let him be found never so idle pated. **1756** TOLDERVY *Hist. 2 Orphans* III. 173 So jealous pated a fellow. **1834** H. BULWER *France* II. III. 144 The emptiest-pated of the male creatures that she meets.

patedelion: see PEDELION.

† **pate'faction.** *Obs.* [ad. L. *patefactiōn-em*, n. of action from *patefacĕre* to PATEFY.] The action of making open, visible, or known; a disclosing, manifestation, revelation, declaration.

1553 BALE *Vocacyon* in *Harl. Misc.* (Malh.) I. 364 The patefaction of Christe in the gospel. **1633** T. ADAMS *Exp. 2 Peter* i. 11 The like patefaction was to Peter; he 'saw heaven opened'. **1659** PEARSON *Creed* I. ii. 44 God hath also made frequent patefactions of his Deity. *a* **1703** BURKITT *On N.T., Acts* xiii. 26 By way of patefaction and discovery. **1872** F. HALL *Recent Exempl. False Philol.* 27 And now for—not to shock a clergyman by profanely applying the term revelation,—the new *patefaction*.

† **'patefy**, *v. Obs.* Also 6–7 -ify. [ad. L. *patefacĕre* to make open, to open, f. *patē-re* to be open + *facĕre* to make: cf. *liquefy*, and see -FY.] *trans.* To make open; to disclose, manifest, reveal to the eye or mind.

1533 CRANMER *Let. to Bp. of Hereford* in *Misc. Writ.* (Parker Soc.) II. 263 When the verity and truth of them shall be patified and made open unto you. **1591** R. BRUCE *Serm.* (1843) 282 He hath patefied himself to us by an heavenly light. **1667** WATERHOUSE *Fire Lond.* 63 Thus God patefies the way to his displeasure. **1788** *Trifler* No. 25. 323 It dimoves every discruciating pain from the stomach, adjuvates digestion, and patefies obstructions.

† **patel**[1], **-ell(e**. *Obs.* Also 5 -yl, 6 pattle. [ad. L. *patella* pan, knee-pan, F. *patelle* knee-pan.]

1. A pan, a frying-pan. **b.** The paten or shallow dish used with the chalice in the Eucharist.

1481 *Durham Acc. Rolls* (Surtees) 97, ij friyng patyls ferr. **1546** *Confut. N. Shaxton* F viij b, Three crosses..one wyth your thombe in your forheade, an other vpon your crowne wyth the patell of the chalice.

2. The patella or knee-pan; also *patel-bone*.

1578 BANISTER *Hist. Man* I. 35 This Patell was ordained to couer the ioynt betwene the thighe and legge. **1598** FLORIO, *Rotola del ginocchio*, the whirle bone ordained to cover the ioint of the knee, the eie-bone,..the pattle-bone.

‖ **patel**[2] ('pʌtəl). *East Ind.* Also 9 patell, -eil, -ail, pattel, potail. [a. Marāthī *patil*, Hindūstānī *patel*, app. f. Marāthī *pat* 'roll or register' (Yule).] The head-man of a village in India: the title used in the Central and Western Provinces, and frequently in S. India, but not in the Gangetic Provinces.

1802 *Chron.* App. in *Ann. Reg.* 526/2 The potail or killedar of Tirnakull has been hanged. **1816** 'QUIZ' *Grand Master* VII. 12 All his attempts could not compel The village rascally patel To get him a few fowls and rice. **1885** G. S. FORBES *Wild Life in Canara* 16 Village constables under the potails, or heads of villages. **1894** *Daily News* 4 Sept. 5/2 The patel decoyed him out of his house at night, and hacked him to pieces with a hatchet.

patelet, variant of PATLET, a ruff.

‖ **patella** (pə'tɛlə). [L. *patella* pan, knee-pan, dim. of *patina* pan, PATEN.]

1. *Anat.* A small movable bone, flattened and convex in shape, covering the front of the knee-joint; the knee-pan or knee-cap.

1693 tr. *Blancard's Phys. Dict.* (ed. 2), *Mola, Patella,* or *Rotula*, a round and broad Bone, at the joynting of the Thigh and Leg. **1706** PHILLIPS, *Patella*,..Among Anatomists, the round, broad Bone, at the joynting of the Thigh and Leg; the Whirl-bone of the Knee. **1840** G. V. ELLIS *Anat.* 622 On each side of the patella is the condyle of the femur. **1854** OWEN *Skel. & Teeth* in *Circ. Sc., Organ. Nat.* I. 252 The patella [of the lion] is well ossified. **1881** MIVART *Cat* 109 The knee-pan, or Patella, is a small bone of an elongated oval shape.

b. *transf.* In insects, the first joint of the coxa.

2. *Archæol.* A small pan or shallow vessel; the vessel so called by the Romans.

[**1398** TREVISA *Barth. De P.R.* XIX. cxxviii. (1495) nnj/2 *Patella* is a panne as it were an open crocke.] **1851** D. WILSON *Preh. Ann.* (1863) I. iii. 80 Two brass vessels which ..appear to have been Roman Patellae. **1857** BIRCH *Anc. Pottery* (1858) II. 331 One is a dish, patera, or patella.

3. A natural formation of the form of a shallow pan. **a.** In animals: A cup-like formation; a cotyle. **b.** In plants: see quot.

1671 *Phil. Trans.* VI. 2165, I have often observed on Plumb trees and Cherry trees; also on the Vine and Cherry-Laurel certain patellae or flat Husks containing worms.

4. *Zool.* A genus of Mollusca, containing the common limpet.

1753 in CHAMBERS *Cycl. Supp.*

pate'llaceous, *a. Zool.* Allied to the limpet.

1857 in MAYNE *Expos. Lex.*

patellar ('pætəlɑː(r), pə'tɛlə(r)), *a.* [f. PATELLA + -AR[1]. Cf. F. *patellaire* (Littré).] Of or pertaining to the patella or knee-pan.

1886 in *Cassell's Encycl. Dict.* **1893** A. S. ECCLES *Sciatica* 25 Some writers on sciatica have mentioned the absence of the patellar reflex as occurring in this malady. **1897** *Allbutt's Syst. Med.* II. 367 The physiological deep reflex called the 'knee-jerk' or 'patellar reflex' is sometimes exaggerated. **1899** *Ibid.* VI. 707 The patellar tendon reactions were lost.

patellaric (pætə'lærɪk), *a. Chem.* [f. mod.Bot. L. *Patellāria* a genus of lichens, deriv. of *patella*: see above.] In *patellaric acid*, an acid ($C_{17}H_{20}O_{10}$) obtained by Weigelt from the lichen *Patellaria scruposa*.

1872 WATTS *Dict. Chem.* VI. 902 Patellaric acid..yields with cold baryta-water a salt having a transient blue colour.

patellate ('pætələt), *a.* [f. PATELL-A + -ATE[2] 2.] Furnished with, or formed into or like, a patella.

1826 KIRBY & SP. *Entomol.* IV. 325 *Patellate*..when the whole joint is dilated and shaped something like a patella or platter. **1887** W. PHILLIPS *Brit. Discomycetes* 370 *Patellaria melazantha*. Fries. Sessile, waxy, dry, patellate.

patellectomy (pætə'lɛktəmɪ). *Surg.* [f. PATELL(A + -ECTOMY.] Surgical removal of the patella.

1940 *Q. Cumulative Index Medicus* XXVIII. 706/1 Patellectomy in therapy of recidivating dislocations. **1944** *Surg., Gynecol., & Obstetr.* LXXIX. 536/1 These observations..suggest that routine total patellectomy for fracture of the patella in the human may be folly. **1977** *Proc. R. Soc. Med.* LXX. 258/2 All had been considered for surgical treatment, including patellectomy.

pa'tellidan. *Zool.* [f. mod.L. *Patellidæ* the limpet family (f. *Patella* limpet) + -AN.] A member of the limpet family; in pl. = *Patellidæ*.

1835 KIRBY *Hab. & Inst. Anim.* I. ix. 272 Lamarck proceeds immediately from the Chitonidans to the Patellidans or Limpets. [**1855** W. S. DALLAS *Zool.* in *Orr's Circ. Sc., Syst. Nat. Hist.* I. 443 The *Patellidæ*, or Limpets ..are inclosed in a conical shell.]

patelliform (pə'tɛlɪfɔːm), *a.* [ad. mod.L. *patelliformis*, f. *patella*: see above and -FORM.] Having the form of a patella; shaped like a shallow pan, knee-pan, or limpet-shell.

1819 G. SAMOUELLE *Entomol. Compend.* 158 Patelliform tarsi. **1835** LINDLEY *Introd. Bot.* (1848) II. 352 The embryo of *Flagellaria indica* is patelliform. **1841** JOHNSTON in *Proc. Berw. Nat. Club* I. No. 9. 263 The shell spiral, some-times patelliform. **1887** W. PHILLIPS *Brit. Discomycetes* 80 Cups scattered or gregarious, patelliform, fleshy, pale buff.

patelline ('pætəlaɪn), *a. Zool.* [f. L. *Patella*, in Zool. 'limpet' + -INE[1].] Of or pertaining to the *Patellidæ* or limpets. So **'patellite** [-ITE[1]], a fossil limpet; **'patelloid** [-OID], *Conch.*, *a.* of the form of a patella, limpet-shaped; *sb.* a patelloid shell.

1828 WEBSTER, *Patellite*, fossil remains of the patella, a shell. **1851** RICHARDSON *Geol.* viii. (1855) 243 Some shells have a patelloid form. **1890** *Cent. Dict.*, *Patelline*.

patellofemoral (pə,tɛləʊ'fɛmərəl), *a. Anat.* [f. PATELL(A + -O + FEMORAL *a.* and *sb.*] Of or pertaining to the patella and the femur.

1934 in WEBSTER. **1964** J. McM. MENNELL *Joint Pain* xii. 126 (*heading*) The patellofemoral joint. **1978** *Sci. Amer.* Jan. 44/3 The [knee] joint includes two articulations, or movable parts, that transmit force and relative motion. One is the patellofemoral bearing surface between the patella (the kneecap) and the femur (the thighbone).

‖ **pa'tellula.** [mod.L. dim. of *patella.*] A small patella; one of the sucking disks or cups on the tarsus of water-beetles (*Cent. Dict.* 1890). So **pa'tellulate** *a.*, furnished with or formed into a patellula (*ibid.*); **pa'tellule**, a sessile receptacle in some lichens (Mayne *Expos. Lex.* 1857).

paten ('pætən). Forms: 4 **pateyn(e**, 4, 7–9 **patin**, 5 **payten**, 5–6 **patyn**, 5–7 **patent**, 5–8 **patten**, 5–9 **patene**, 7–9 **-ine**, 5– **paten**. [ME. *patene*, *-eyn(e*, a. OF. *patène* (1380 in Hatz.-Darm.), ad. L. *patena*, *patina* wide shallow vessel, pan, basin; cf. Gr. πατάνη a kind of flat dish. Cf. It. '*patena* 'any kind of dish, platter, or charger, a treene dish or wooden tray', '*patina* 'a dish or platter, a great charger' (Florio).]

1. The plate or shallow dish, usually circular and of silver, on which the bread is laid at the celebration of the Eucharist.

c **1300** *Havelok* 187 A wol fair cloth bringen he dede, And þer-on leyde þe messebok, þe caliz, and þe pateyn ok. *c* **1315** SHOREHAM *Poems* (E.E.T.S.) 52/1444 He takþ þe chalys wyþ þe wyne, And brede of þe pateyne. *c* **1425** *Voc.* in Wr.-Wülcker 648/8 *Hec patena*, patent. **1480** CAXTON *Chron. Eng.* ccxxx. 245 Charlys leyde his right hond on the paten with goddes body, and his lift hond on the missale and said we..sweren on goddes body and the holy gospels. **1548–9** (Mar.) *Bk. Com. Prayer, Commun.* Rubric, Laiyng the breade upon the corporas, or els in the paten, or in some other comely thyng, prepared for that purpose. **1649** JER. TAYLOR *Gt. Exemp.* II. Ad §12. 96 The bread of the Paten, and the wine of the Chalice. **1662** *Bk. Com. Prayer, Commun.* Rubric, Here the Priest is to take the Paten into his hands. **1718** HICKES & NELSON *J. Kettlewell* II. xxxii. 136 The Vessels..(being a Patten, two Chalices, a Flagon and a Bason). **1852** MISS YONGE *Cameos* (1877) II. xxii. 238 In full canonical attire, with the chalice and paten in his hands.

b. Used as a cover for the chalice.

c **1430** LYDG. *Min. Poems* (Percy Soc.) 99 For to make a declaracioune, On the chalice patyn. *c* **1440** *Promp. Parv.* 385/2 Patene, or pateyne of a chalys [*v. rr.* patent, paten, payten], *patena*. **1509** *Invent.* in Hearne *Collect.* (O.H.S.) V. 366 A Gret chales wt the patent gilt. **1526** *Pilgr. Perf.* (W. de W. 1531) 259 The chalice [betokeneth] the sepulcre, the paten the stone that couered the sepulcre. **1611** COTGR., *Patine*, the Patine, or couer of a Chalice. **1658** PHILLIPS, *Paten*,..a little flat saucer used by the Priests with the chalice at Masse. **1801** A. RANKEN *Hist. France* I. I. v. 468 Sixty chalices and fifteen patens or covers of pure gold.

2. *gen.* A shallow dish or plate. *arch.* or *Hist.*

[*c* **1340** *Durham Acc. Rolls* (Surtees) 203 In coquina..2 patene bone.] **1398** TREVISA *Barth. De P.R.* XVI. vii. (B.M. MS.), Ydo in concaues of yre and a paten or a shelle ydo þer vnder. **1656** BLOUNT *Glossogr.*, *Patin*,..a great Platter, a Charger, a Bason to wash in. **1678** PHILLIPS (ed. 4), *Patin*, ..a sort of Vessel wherein the Priests used to bring their sodden Meat to Table. *a* **1704** T. BROWN *Praise of Poverty* Wks. 1730 I. 103 A little silver patin, peculiarly dedicated to the Gods. **1865** SWINBURNE *Poems & Ball.*, *Masque Q. Bersabe* 13 Fed from the gilt patens fine. **1883** SOLON *O.E. Potter* i. 8 [Articles found in mounds] are jugs, pipkins, piggins, patens or bowls,..all articles made for the poor.

3. A thin circular plate of metal; anything resembling or suggesting this.

(In later writers after the Shaks. quot., in which the Qq. and Fol. 1 have *pattens*, the later Folios *patterns*. Levins 1570 has both *patten* and *pattern* as = L. *prototypon*. But cf. OF. *patenne* = *lame* plate, 'un bras de bois couvert de patennes d'argent', Godef.)

1596 SHAKS. *Merch. V.* V. i. 59 Sit Iessica, looke how the floore of heauen Is thicke inlayed with pattens of bright gold. **1870** KINGSLEY *At Last* vii, The Ipomœa Bona-nox, whose snow-white patines, as broad as the hand, open at night-fall on every hedge. **1888** *Archæol. Rev.* Mar. 72 Patins of gold on both sides of the back of his head to confine his hair.

4. *attrib.* † **paten-bred** (see BRED *sb.*); **paten-cover**, a paten forming the cover of a chalice.

1501 *Acc. Ld. High Treas. Scot.* II. 73 Item..for ij patene-breddis of iwory bane to the Gray Freris of Strivelin..iiijs. **1880** *Archæol. Cantiana* XIII. 417 The silver Communion cup, of date 1693–4, has a paten-cover.

paten, obs. form of PATENT, PATTEN

patency ('peɪtənsɪ). [f. PATENT: see -ENCY.]

1. The state or condition of being open or exposed to view; openness; manifestness, obviousness.

1656 BLOUNT *Glossogr.*, *Patency*, a lying open, or uncovered. **1658** OSBORN *Adv. Son* Wks. (1673) 202 From this patency, his Policy was not only enervated, but rendred more destructive. **1843** *Blackw. Mag.* LIV. 525 The patency of error is ever a sure prelude to its extirpation. **1886** J. E. C. WELLDON *Aristotle's Rhet.* 142 The patency and notoriety of the facts.

2. The condition of being open, expanded, or unobstructed, as a passage. (In scientific use.)

1845 G. MOORE *Power of Soul* (1846) 149 The patency of his bowels. **1861** BUMSTEAD *Ven. Dis.* (1879) 302 Unless the patency of the canal be kept up. **1898** *Allbutt's Syst. Med.* V. 700 Complete patency of the foramen ovale.

patener ('pætənə(r)). [ad. L. *patenārius*, f. *patena* PATEN: see -ER[2].] In the mediæval Church, An acolyte who held up the empty paten during a part of High Mass.

[**1439** *Mem. Ripon* (Surtees) III. 232 Uni subdiacono, uni thuribulario, uni patenario.] **1853** ROCK *Ch. of Fathers* IV. xii. 194 This offertory-cloth was not as now cast about the shoulders of the 'patener'..but folded round the paten itself. **1897** MICKLETHWAITE *Ornam. of Rubric* 35 The patener or third minister when he brought in the chalice and when he held up the paten.

patent ('peɪtənt, 'pætənt), *a.* Also 5 **patant**, 5–8 **pattent**, 6 **patentt**, **paytent**, **paten**, 6–7 **patten**. [In branch I, a. F. *patent*, *-ente*, ad. L. *patĕnt-em* open, lying open, pr. pple. of *patēre* to lie open, esp. in *lettres patentes* (1292 in Britton), med.L. *litteræ patentes*; in II, directly from L. (For the analogy of pronunciation, cf. *lātent*, *pārent*; ('pætənt) prevails in U.S. So in the derivatives. In official use in England, branches I and II are sometimes differentiated as ('pætənt) and ('peɪtənt).]

I. 1. In ***letters patent*** (Lat. *litteræ patentes*, Fr. *lettres patentes*, whence, 15–18th c., ***letters patents***); also, in 14th c., ***lettre patent***: An open letter or document (see quot. 1891), usually from a sovereign or person in authority, issued for various purposes, e.g. to put on record some agreement or contract, to authorize or command something to be done, to confer some right, privilege, title, property, or office; now, especially, to grant for a statutory term to a person or persons the sole right to make, use, or sell some invention.

[**1292** BRITTON I. i. §10 Nous les maunderoms par nos lettres patentes.] **1387** TREVISA *Higden* (Rolls) VIII. 55 Kyng William seiþ in his own lettre patent [L. *litteris suis patentibus*, **1432–50** letters patent] þat he and his successoures and men of Scotlond schulde doo homage legeaunce and feaute to the kynges of Engelond. **1398** —— *Barth. De P.R.* XIX. lxi. (1495) 898 Letters ben sealyd wyth wexe closyd and patent. **1486** *Naval Acc. Hen. VII* (1896) 3 Thomas Roger to whome it pleased the Kyng..by his letters patentes vnder his grete seall to graunte thoffice of keper and clerk of his Shipps. **1530** PALSGR. 252/2 Patent letters, *lettres patentes*. **1598** HAKLUYT *Voy.* I. 153 In testimony whereof we haue caused these our letters to be made patents. **1612** DAVIES *Why Ireland*, etc. (1787) 6 He gave license by his letters patent. **1707** CHAMBERLAYNE *Pres. St. Eng.* II. ii. 79 The King..By his Letters Patent may erect new Universities, Boroughs, Colleges, Hospitals [etc.]. *Ibid.* xiv. 189 Here [High Court of Chancery] are sealed and enrolled Letters Patents. **1863** H. COX *Instit.* I. vii. 65 Richard II was the first to confer the peerage by letters-patent. **1891** SCARGILL-BIRD *Guide to P.R.O.* 32 The Letters Patent were ..written upon open sheets of parchment, with the Great Seal pendent at the bottom..[while] the 'Litteræ Clausæ', or Letters Close,..being of a more private nature, and addressed to one or two individuals only, were closed or folded up and sealed on the outside.

fig. *a* **1592** GREENE *Jas. IV*, II. i. Wks. 198 Living by your wit as you do, shifting is your letters-patents. *a* **1625** BOYS in Spurgeon *Treas. Dav.* Ps. xix. Introd., It is a letter patent, or open epistle for all. **1660** GAUDEN *God's Gt. Demonstr.* 56 By the Letters pattents of the holy Scriptures, whereof no man..can without sin be ignorant. **1711** SHAFTESB. *Charac.* (1737) III. 338 What party by..virtue of any immediate testimonial from heaven are thus intitled? Where are the letters-patent? the credentials?

2. a. Conferred by letters patent; endowed with a patent. Of a person: Appointed by letters patent. ***patent house, theatre***, a theatre established by Royal Patent; *spec.* in London, the theatres of Covent Garden and Drury Lane, whose Patents were granted by Charles II in 1662.

1597-8 *Act 39 Eliz.* c. 4 §2 All..Proctors, Procurors Patent Gatherers or Collectors for Gaoles Prisons or Hospitalles. **1660** PEPYS *Diary* 4 May, In case the King do restore every man to his places that ever had been patent. **1707** CHAMBERLAYNE *Pres. St. Eng.* III. 501 Patent-Officers [of the Customs] in the Out-Ports. **1835** DICKENS *Sk. Boz* (1837) 2nd Ser. 166 Why were they not engaged at one of the patent theatres? *c* **1844** C. GORE in M. R. Booth *Eng. Plays of 19th Cent.* (1973) III. 16 The disproportion and caricature *established into the custom of the stage* by the exigencies of our colossal patent theatres. **1845** DISRAELI *Sybil* IV. ii, Lord Deloraine..held a good patent place which had been conferred on his descendants by the old chancellor. **1891** *Daily News* 23 Feb. 3/2 The three great patent houses—Her Majesty's, Drury Lane, and Covent Garden—which enjoy the proud privilege of opening their doors without seeking the permission of the Lord Chamberlain. **1897** L. EDMUNDS *Law Letters patent* 18 The subject of a patent privilege. **1932** *Times Lit. Suppl.* 24 Nov. 888/3 In 1832, however, the fashion [of stalls] spread at last to the patent houses. **1973** M. R. BOOTH *Eng. Plays of 19th Cent.* III. 1 Social and political change, the enlarging of the patent theatres, the broadening and inevitable coarsening of audience tastes—all this brought with it a demand for a new kind of comedy. **1973** *Times Lit. Suppl.* 19 Oct. 1272/2 During the period 1740–80 there were only two patent theatres in London: Drury Lane and Covent Garden. Unlicensed theatres were confined to musical performances, and dubiously legal public 'rehearsals' of plays.

†**b.** ***joint*** or ***joined patent***: sharing by letters patent in some privilege or office: cf. PATENT *sb.* 1, quot. 1450. Also *fig. Obs.*

1552 HULOET, Ioynt patent with another, as where, ii. men haue one office ioyntly, *duumuir.* *a* **1586** SIDNEY *Arcadia* II. (1622) 207 So incredibly blinded..that hee could thinke such a Queene [Artaxia] would be content to be ioyned-patent with another [Erona] to haue such an husband. **1608** D. T[UVIL] *Ess. Pol. & Mor.* 37 Where Prayse and Honour haue been ioyn'd patent with Exercise.

3. a. Of an invention: Protected or covered by letters patent; appropriated by letters patent to one or more persons for manufacture, use, or sale. Freq. in collocations (in some cases, of inventions formerly patented, for which the patent has expired): ***patent food***, a proprietary food preparation; ***patent fuel*** (quot. 1894); ***patent insides, outsides*** (see quot. 1970); ***patent leather*** (see LEATHER *sb.* 1); also *ellipt.*, a patent leather boot or shoe; also *fig.*; ***patent log***, a mechanical device for measuring the speed of a ship; ***patent medicine***, a proprietary medicine manufactured under patent; ***patent sail***, an automatically controlled windmill sail (see quots.); ***patent still*** [patented by Aeneas Coffey in 1830], a type of still for the continuous production of alcohol of greater strength and purity than is obtainable in a pot still, steam being used to heat the wash directly and carry off the alcoholic vapour; freq. *attrib.*

1824 BYRON *Juan* XVI. xxvi, He read an article the king attacking, And a long eulogy of 'Patent Blacking'. **1707** MORTIMER *Husb.* I. ix. 124 Madder..in King Charles the First's time..was made a Patent Commodity. **1871** *London Jrnl.* Apr. (Advt.), Dr. Ridge's patent food. **1903** 'A. MCNEILL' *Egregious English* 56 Mammas..who suckle their children out of patent-food tins. **1925** *Scribner's Mag.* Sept. 274/2 Even the 'quick lunch' takes time, so a widely advertised patent food is put up in tablet form, to be eaten at the business desk itself. **1929** GALSWORTHY *Exiled* II. 66, I have recently had to make a series of pictures for a patent food called Vital. **1964** M. LASKI in S. Nowell-Smith *Edwardian England* iv. 205 The richer parents..were more likely to feed the infant on one of the many patent foods. **1894** *Patent Specification* No. 13299. 1 By patent fuel we mean..any kind of small coals, or any mixture of various kinds thereof..moulded or compressed into blocks or briquettes of various shapes and sizes. **1900** *Daily News* 5 Nov. 7/1 Thousands of country weekly papers fill up their pages by what are known as 'patent insides'. **1882** I. M. RITTENHOUSE *Jrnl.* 8 June in *Maud* (1939) 103 The funny places in all the old patent-insides of newspapers talk about the sweet girl graduate. **1931** *Sat. Even. Post* 28 Feb. 129/2 Some publishers bought patent insides, which were the interior pages of the newspaper ready printed for use. **1968** E. RUSSENHOLT *Heart of Continent* IV. xiii. 243 The 'St. James Leader'..is an 8-page weekly (including 'patent insides'). **1970** R. K. KENT *Lang. Journalism* 98 *Patent insides* (or *outsides*), features or other syndicated material that come to a newspaper already printed on inside (or first and last) pages; readyprint pages. **1829** *Poulson's Amer. Daily Advertiser* (Philad.) 25 Apr. 3/5 Just received, an extensive assortment of Japanned Patent Leather, of superior quality. **1846** A. J. H. DUGANNE *Daguerreotype Miniature* 7 A pair of patent-leather boots and a Polka hat were the extremes of his apparel. **1849** G. G. FOSTER *New York in Slices* 64 Our young gentlemen..thus preserve their patent-leathers. **1852** MORFIT *Tanning & Currying* (1853) 453 Glazed or Varnished Leather..known in commerce as *patent leather*, is very largely used for dress boots and shoes. **1882** *Encycl. Brit.* XIV. 387/2 *Patent or Enamelled Leather.*—Leather finished with a brilliant, smooth, and glossy surface, used for dress boots and shoes,..is known under a variety of names, as lacquered, varnished, japanned, and enamelled leather, &c. **1890** O. WILDE *Pict. Dorian Gray* i, in *Lippincott's Monthly Mag.* July 8 Lord Henry..tapped the toe of his patent-leather boot. **1905** H. A. VACHELL *Hill* ii. 29 He had to varnish Grieve's patent-leathers for Sunday. **1910** J. W. TOMPKINS *Mothers & Fathers* 356 [He was] humbly removing the overshoes that covered Mr. Hammond's patent leathers. **1955** [see LAIR *sb.*[4]]. **1976** BOTHAM & DONNELLY *Valentino* iv. 35 Rodolpho reached up a hand to pat his patent leather hair into place. **1876** Patent log [see LOG *sb.*[1] 6]. **1940** *Chambers's Techn. Dict.* 509/1 The modern *patent* (or *taffrail*) *log* mechanically indicates the rate of travel by means of a submerged fly or rotator, whose revolutions are conveyed to a register on the rail of the vessel by a braided hemp line secured to the rotator. **1961** F. H. BURGESS *Dict. Sailing* 157 *Patent log*, a mechanical device with which a rotator is used, to work a dial indicating the distance run through the water. **1770** *Essex Gaz.* (Salem, Mass.) 17 Apr. 4/4 To be sold by Benjamin Eaton..in Marblehead..a collection of genuine patent medicines. **1799** *Europ. Mag.* XXXVI. 179 The venders of patent or quack medicines. **1830** SCOTT *Lett. Demonology* v. 144 The proprietor of a patent medicine, who should in those days have attested his having wrought such miracles as we see sometimes advertised. **1866** 'MARK TWAIN' *Speeches* (1923) 7 It is said by some..that Kanakas won't lie, but I know they *will* lie..lie like patent-medicine advertisements. **1887** *Spectator* 24 Sept. 1283 No greater proof of credulity than the belief in patent medicines. **1888** G. B. SHAW *Let.* 20 Sept. (1965) I. 198 Nearly all the citizens ..buy immense quantities of charms called patent medicines. **1901** *Chambers's Jrnl.* Jan. 63/1 Soaps, patent medicines, chocolates..are the things most advertised. **1914** *Rep. Sel. Comm. Patent Medicines* p. xii, in *Parl. Papers* IX, Patent and proprietary medicines differ very widely in character. At one end of the scale is the valuable scientific preparation; at the other end is the mere vulgar swindle. **1961** *Today's Health* Feb. 30/2 The medical device pirate of today, of course, is a far more sophisticated operator than his predecessor of yesteryear—the gallus-snapping hawker of snake oil and other patent medicines. **1978** P. BAILEY *Leisure & Class in Victorian Eng.* i. 15 Street preachers, stump orators and patent medicine salesmen. **1871** *Lancaster Intelligencer* 3 Apr., The editor who surrenders control of one-half of his paper to some manufacturer of patent-outsides, may make a slight reduction in his current expenses, but in the end he will lose both money and influence. **1890** *Boston Jrnl.* 7 Mar. 4/5 He was running his patent outsides for country newspapers. **1970** Patent outsides [see *patent insides* above]. **1945** *Archit. Rev.* XCVIII. 72/2 In 1807 Sir William Cubitt invented what has ever since been called 'patent sail'. **1968** J. ARNOLD *Shell Bk. Country Crafts* 170 This was the patent sail and enabled adjustment to the wind to be made without interrupting the milling. **1973** J. VINCE *Discovering Windmills* (ed. 3) 21 The most significant improvement in sail design came about in 1807 when William Cubbit [*sic*] invented his patent sail. This retained Meikle's shutters, but they were controlled automatically by a weight suspended outside the mill. **1887** A. BARNARD *Whisky Distilleries of U.K.* 12 Blenders without number can be found who will strenuously affirm that to give the public a moderate priced article with sufficient age, there is no way but to use good old Patent Still Grain Spirit as a basis. *Ibid.* (Advt.), Flemming, Bennet & McLaren... Makers of Fire Stills, Steam Stills, Coffey's Patent Stills, ..&c. **1906** *Daily Chron.* 27 Feb. 1/7 The North London magistrate held that patent-still spirit was not whisky. **1934** J. I. DAVIS *Beginner's Guide Wines & Spirits* viii. 85 Irish Whisky is always 'pot-stilled'... Some Scotch Whisky is so made, but most of it is manufactured in a patent still, which completes the distillation in one operation. **1937** *Thorpe's Dict. Appl. Chem.* (ed. 4) I. 178/1 The spirit produced in these 'patent stills'..has been used only to a limited extent for the production of spirit for whisky blending... The great bulk goes into industry for use as a raw material or as a technical solvent. **1968** I. C. TAYLOR *Highland Whisky* (An Comunn Gaidhealach) 3 The practice of blending pot-still and patent-still whiskies began about 1860. **1787** 'G. GAMBADO' *Acad. Horsemen* (1809) 34 Provide yourself with a pair of patent stirrups.

b. *fig.* and *transf.* To which one has a proprietary claim; also, special for its purpose; sovereign, superlative.

1797 NELSON in Nicolas *Lett.* II. 346 There is a saying in the fleet too flattering for me to omit telling—viz. 'Nelson's Patent Bridge for boarding First Rates', alluding to my passing over an enemy's 80-gun ship. **1807-8** SYD. SMITH *Plymley's Lett.* II. 80 That patent Christianity which has been for some time manufacturing at Clapham. **1819** CRABBE *T. of Hall* III. 94 He claims a right on all things to decide; A kind of patent-wisdom. **1838** DICKENS *Pickw.* xxxviii, Put your hand into the cupboard, and bring out the patent digester [a black bottle half full of brandy].

II. 4. Open as a door, gate, or aperture, so as to allow free passage.

1563 *Reg. Privy Council Scot.* I. 240 Sall mak the house of the Armytage patent at all tymes to hir Hienes. *a* **1578** LINDESAY (Pitscottie) *Chron. Scot.* (S.T.S.) I. 16 [He] gave command how oft scho pleissit to haue entres to the castell that it sould be patent. **1584** *Aberdeen Regr.* (1848) II. 52 At the quhilk patent portis thair sall be ane daylie wache. **1639** in Spalding *Troub. Chas. I* (Spald. Cl.) II. 36 How muche he is obliged to respect and give a patent eir heirefter to there farder grievances. **1733** CHEYNE *Eng. Malady* II. xi. §3. 231 Throwing them [the fluids] off by the safest and most patent Outlets. **1898** *Westm. Gaz.* 5 Oct. 4/2 One extremity of the tube is sealed, the other end is patent.

5. Open as to situation; not shut in; unenclosed; of unobstructed access; freely accessible. Now *rare.*

1432-50 tr. *Higden* (Rolls) I. 61 And also for the patente magnitude felethe by more efficacite the strenȝhte of þe moone then a see coartate. *Ibid.* 179 [Constantinople] Whiche is patente on euery syde to men saylenge from Asia and Europa, compassede alle moste with the grete see. **1566** *Acts & Constit. Scot.* To Rdr. ✠iij, The Romanis..had thair statutis..writtin in Tabillis, and fixit in the maist publique and patent placis. **1839** BAILEY *Festus* xix. (1852) 285 A circular temple, patent to the sun. **1867** CARLYLE *Remin.* II. 137 Nith valley lay patent to the S.

6. Spreading, expanded; *spec.* †**a.** *Her.* Applied (in early works) to a cross having expanded extremities; = PATTÉE. *Obs.*

1486 *Bk. St. Albans, Her.* C ij b, An oder cros..straythyr in the myddis then in thendys with opyn corneris..hit is calde a cros patent. And ye shall say..He berith Sable a cros paty of Siluer. *Ibid.* C iv, Hit is calde a cros flurri patent for he hath his endis opyn. **1610** GUILLIM *Heraldry* II. vii. 68 This is called a Crosse Patee..because the ends are broad and patent.

b. *Bot.* Spreading, opening wide, as petals; diverging widely from the axis, as branches or leaves; = OPEN *a.* 6. *Zool.* Patulous; having a wide aperture, or a shallow cavity.

1753 CHAMBERS *Cycl. Supp.* s.v. *Leaf*, *Patent Leaf*, one which stands almost strait out from the stalk, or nearly at right angles with it. **1819** CRABBE *T. of Hall* IX. 288 Long were the learned words, and urged with force, Panduriform, pinnatifid, premorse, Latent, and patent, papulous and plane. **1870** HOOKER *Stud. Flora* 178 Branches of cyme patent or reflexed after flowering.

7. Open to view, exposed to sight; hence, exposed to the mental view; clear, plain, evident, manifest, obvious; = OPEN *a.* 5, 12.

1508 in *Ripon Ch. Acts* (Surtees) 330 Stone, with a scriptor to be paytent uppon the same. **1528** *St. Papers Hen. VIII*, IV. 538 Yat ye King oure broyeris gude mynd may be maid patent to oure derrest son. **1639** N. N. tr. *Du Bosq's Compl. Woman* I. C iij, That which is patent even to our senses, cannot be proved but very hardly with the force of our reason. **1857** H. MILLER *Test. Rocks* iii. 136 The geologic evidence is so complete as to be patent to all. **1874** BLACKIE *Self-Cult.* 39 A patent fact, as certain as anything in mathematics. **1888** BRYCE *Amer. Commw.* I. v. 56 The disadvantages of the American plan are patent.

8. Open to general knowledge or use; generally accessible or available for use; public.

1566 *Acts & Constit. Scot.* To Rdr. ✠iij, To cause publis and make patent the Lawis. **1602** WARNER *Alb. Eng.* XII. lxx. (1612) 294 For Guinie, in her highnesse raigne acquir'd and patent made. **1834** SIR W. HAMILTON *Discuss.* (1852) 474 The Colleges would be equally patent to such dissenters as were not averse from their observances. **1838** —— in *Reid's Wks.* II. 683 *note*, The greater number of those [works] now extant were preserved and patent during the two centuries and a half intervening between the death of Aristotle and their pretended publication by Tyrannion.

9. *Comb.*, as **patent-winged** (cf. 6 b), having wings spreading widely apart.

1752 J. HILL *Hist. Anim.* 79 The patent-winged Phalaena.

ˈpatent (see prec.), *sb.* Forms: see prec. [orig. short for *letter(s) patent*: see prec. So F. *patente* (for *lettre patente*), med. (Anglo-)L. *patens* (1367 in Du Cange), It., Sp. *patente.*]

1. a. A document conferring some privilege, right, office, etc.; = *letters patent*: see PATENT *a.* 1.

[**1347** *Rolls of Parlt.* II. 169/2 Que les poveres.. approchent au Tresorer, & monstrent lour Patentes & Obligations.] *c* **1375** *Sc. Leg. Saints* xxv. (*Julian*) 160 þare-one gaf þame his patent [L. *scripsit*] þat quha-euir ware traweland by þat sted..þai suld helpe þame. **1399** *Rolls of Parlt.* III. 452 That all the Patentes and Charters that they, & any of hem hath..be ȝolden uppe into the Chauncellerie. **1423** *Ibid.* IV. 256/1 The Officers made by his patentes roialx. **1429** in Heath *Grocers' Comp.* (1869) 60 Alsoe for ye seale of owre greate patente £8 5 0. **1450** *Paston Lett.* I. 129 As for the Duche on this side Trent, Sir Thomas Tudenham had a joynte patent with the Duke of Suffolk. **1451** *Rolls of Parlt.* V. 221/1 The annuell xx marcs graunted..in theire Patentes of their creation. **1577-87** HOLINSHED *Chron.* III. 1245/1 The kings patent, or open writ, or commandement, vnder the seale of Edward the kings eldest son. **1589** *Pasquil's Ret.* D iij, I meane to be Clarke of their Audit.., my Paten is already sealed. **1695** SIBBALD *Autobiog.* (1834) 132, I..was examined..and gott my patent of Doctor ther. *a* **1715** BURNET *Own Time* (1766) I. 270 They thought fit to take out a patent, which constituted them a body, by the name of the Royal Society. **1821** J. MARSHALL *Const. Opin.* (1839) 243 The grant by a state of a patent of nobility. **1896** *Law Times* C. 357/1 An outgoing Irish Attorney-General received a patent of precedence entitling him to take work at the bar immediately after the Law Officers of the Crown.

†**b.** A papal licence or indulgence: = INDULGENCE 3. *Obs.*

1377 LANGL. *P. Pl.* B. VII. 194, I sette ȝowre patentes and ȝowre pardounz at one pies hele! *Ibid.* XIV. 191 Ac þe perchemyn of þis patent of pouerte be moste. *c* **1386** CHAUCER *Pard. Prol.* 9 Thanne my bulles shewe I alle and some Oure lige lordes seel on my patente.

†**c.** An official certificate or licence generally; *esp.* a health certificate. *Obs.*

1615 G. SANDYS *Trav.* 226 Euery ship had a neat Patent to shew that those places from whence they came were free from the infection. **1632** LITHGOW *Trav.* VII. 336, I am.. newly come from Ierusalem.., and loe there is my Patent. **1632** J. HAYWARD tr. *Biondi's Eromena* 37 It being not lawfull for them, to commerce or trafficke without their patent of health, from the place whence they parted. **1666** *Lond. Gaz.* No. 48/1 But he..immediately departed..without Patent..and is gone Westwards.

2. A licence to manufacture, sell, or deal in an article or commodity, to the exclusion of other persons; in modern times, a grant from a government to a person or persons conferring for a certain definite time the exclusive privilege of making, using, or selling some new invention.

c **1588** G. LONGE in Ellis *Orig. Lett.* Ser. II. III. 157 Dollyne and Carye obtained the Patent for making of Glass in England in September the ix[th] yeare [1566-7] of the Queene's Majesties raigne for xxj. years ensueinge..which Patent was fully expired a yeare ago. **1597** in D'Ewes *Jrnls.* 573 Abuses practised by Monopolies and Patents of priviledge. **1656** W. D. tr. *Comenius' Gate Lat. Unl.* § 799 The community..is never well provided for, if monopolies or patents bee permitted. **1701** J. PETER *Truth* 23 This Invention being limited by the Patent, to the Patentee, or his

Assigns. **1791** 'G. Gambado' *Ann. Horsem.* i. (1809) 69, I shall be able to get a patent for it, which cannot but prove very lucrative. **1800** Mar. Edgeworth *Will* v, He advises me to take out a patent for the dye. **1825** J. Nicholson *Operat. Mechanic* 618 The term of the patent being now expired, many other manufactories of this cement have been established. **1876** Rogers *Pol. Econ.* xvii. (ed. 3) 226 The law protects inventors and authors by patents and copyright. **1897** L. Edmunds *Law of Letters patent* 2 In consequence of the very numerous grants of patents for inventions, the word 'patent' has, in common parlance, come to suggest a patent for an invention only.

3. a. A process or invention which has been patented, or for which a patent has been taken out.

1862 *Illustr. Catal. Exhib.* I. Class viii. 8 The great distinctive feature of this Company's patent. **1867** J. Hatton *Tallants of B.* i, He secured shares in several important patents. **1879** *Cassell's Techn. Educ.* IV. 90/2 The word *patent* is taken to signify either the letters patent by which the monopoly is granted, or the subject-matter of the grant.

b. Elliptically for some patent commodity the name of which is understood from the context.

1888 J. Inglis *Tent Life in Tigerland* 26 A handsome ivory-handled Thomas's patent lying on the table... It carries a heavy bullet. **1898** *Daily News* 5 Apr. 9/5 An improved demand prevailed for flour... In American brands, patents ruled at 31*s.* to 31*s.* 6*d.* **1904** *Daily Chron.* 10 Mar. 4/5, I say.. it's rather rash to do gardening in patents, isn't it?

4. A territory, district, or piece of land conferred by letters patent. *U.S.*

1632 In Winthrop *Hist. New Eng.* (1853) I. 93 *note*, [Stephen Batchelor was, at a court, 3 October, 1632] required to for-bear exercising his gifts as a pastor or teacher publicly in our patent. **1634** W. Wood *New Eng. Prosp.* I. i, It is not my intent to wander far from our Patent. **1823** F. Cooper *Pioneers* viii, This term, Patent.. meant the district of country that had been originally granted to old Major Effingham, by the 'King's letters patent'.

5. *fig.* A sign or token that one is entitled to something; authority or commission to do something; leave or title to possess something.

1590 Shaks. *Mids. N.* I. i. 80 So will I grow, so liue, so die my lord, Ere I will yeeld my virgin Patent vp Vnto his Lordship. **1604** —— *Oth.* IV. i. 209 Giue her patent to offend, for if it touch not you, it comes neere no body. **1645** G. Daniel *Poems* (Grosart) II. 34 Nature's Patent, Stampt with Heaven's Great Seale. **1836** H. Rogers *J. Howe* x. (1863) 273 Dr. Crisp had a patent for nonsense and vulgarity, which defied successful imitation. **1874** Mrs. Oliphant *Rose in June* i, That hand was in itself a patent of gentility.

6. *attrib.* and *Comb.*, as ***patent age, agent, -infringer, law, -monger, solicitor***; **patent office**, an office from which patents are issued and where the claims to patents are examined; **patent-right**, the exclusive right conferred by letters patent; **patent-roll**, a parchment roll containing the letters patent issued in Great Britain (or formerly in England) in any one year: see quot. 1888.

1819 Byron *Juan* I. cxxxii, This is the *patent-age of new inventions For killing bodies, and for saving souls. **1860** Bartlett *Dict. Amer.* (ed. 3) 310 **Patent Agent*, one who procures patents for inventors. **1884** *List of Subscribers* (London & Globe Telephone Co.), Haseltine, Lake & Co... Patent Agents. **1957** *Encycl. Brit.* XVII. 371/1 Patents are usually, although not necessarily, obtained through the intervention of 'patent agents'. **1959** *Digest of Patent & Other Cases* (Patent Office) II. 778 A person who lodges and signs a complete specification as Agent for Applicant does not thereby describe himself as a Patent Agent. **1901** *Westm. Gaz.* 28 June 11/1 To prevent cutting by wicked *patent infringers and others. **1832** Babbage *Econ. Manuf.* Introd. (ed. 3) 8 The important subject of the *Patent-laws. **1803** *Poet. Petit. agst. Tractorising Trumpery* 49 While a spruce young *patent-monger Contrives to wheedle simple ninnies. **1882** W. H. Preece in *Standard* 29 Aug. 2/4 It had checked the rapacity of Company promoters and patent-mongers. **1696** *Lond. Gaz.* No. 3248/4 The *Patent Office is removed from Symond's Inn to Sir Richard Pigott's House. **1870** Emerson *Soc. & Solit.* vii. 129 The patent-office, where are the models from which every hint is taken. **1825** J. Nicholson *Operat. Mechanic* 651 The principle upon which his *patent-right is founded. **1860** Bartlett *Dict. Amer.* (ed. 3) s.v., In the United States an inventor takes out a 'patent right'; in England, 'letters patent'. **1700** Tyrrell *Hist. Eng.* II. 802 The *Patent-Rolls of this Year. **1888** W. Rye *Rec. & Rec.-searching* xiii. 98 The Patent Rolls extend from 3 John (1201), and contain innumerable grants of offices and lands, fairs and markets, confirmations, licenses to crenellate or fortify, licenses for the election of bishops, abbots, &c., creations of peers, pensions, &c., and of later years the patents for inventions.

patent ('peɪtənt, 'pæt-), *v.* [f. PATENT *sb.* and *a.*]

1. *trans.* To grant a patent to; to admit to some privilege or rank by letters patent. Now *rare*.

1789 J. Morse *Amer. Geogr.* 261 They.. patented away to their particular favorites, a very great proportion of the whole province. **1828–32** Webster, *Patent*, to grant by patent. To secure the exclusive right of a thing to a person; as, to patent an invention.. to the author. **1831** J. Holland *Manuf. Metal* I. 186 An oval link with a stay in it.. had.. been before patented to captain Brown. **1831** J. M. Peck *Guide for Emigrants* III. 319 The Military Bounty Tract.. was set apart by Congress and patented for soldiers who served in the last war. **1881** G. W. Cable *Mme. Delphine* ii. 10 They would have been patented as the dukes of Little Manchac and Barrataria.

2. a. To take out or obtain a patent for; to obtain by letters patent the sole right to produce and sell.

1822 *Technical Repository* II. 214 He patented many different modes of carrying his invention into effect. **1876** Routledge *Discov.* 14, 20 years before, Watt had patented —but had not constructed—a locomotive engine.

b. *fig.* To originate and be proprietor of. (*familiar*.)

1900 *Academy* 21 July 49/1 A tendency.. to fall into a style patented by Ouida.

3. To obtain a patent right to land. *Amer.*

1675 *Calendar Virginia State Papers* (1875) I. 8 Major Lawrence Smith.. did patent foure thousand six hundred acres of land. **1815** D. Drake *Nat. View Cincinnati* i. 51 The following is the course pursued in locating and patenting these lands. **1874** Raymond *Statist. Mines & Mining* 519 Several lodes are held in common, and are so situated that they may be patented in common or worked in common. **1883** *American* VI. 19 Another very large quantity [of public land] has been voted to the railroads, and, although much of it is not yet patented, it is open to their claims as fast as they construct their roads.

4. [from PATENT *a.* 7.] To make patent or open to sight or notice. *rare*[−1].

1889 *Chamb. Jrnl.* 2 Feb. 66/1 The charming fair one has unwillingly patented upon the snow the hideous fact that she wears high-heeled boots.

5. *Metallurgy.* To subject to the process of 'patenting' (see PATENTING *vbl. sb.* b).

1922 J. W. Urquhart *Steel Thermal Treatment* xi. 271 The process known as 'patenting' wire is of recent origin. **1932** Barr & Honeyman *Steel* xix. 102 The rods require to be patented once only.

Hence **'patented** *ppl. a.*

1837 *Penny Cycl.* VIII. 98 The patented invention of Arkwright. **1868** *Daily News* 2 Nov., His excessive anxiety to anticipate the free decision of the colonies by occupying them with a staff of patented bishops. **1891** J. B. Smith *Wire* i. 60 'Patented or improved steel wire' implies that which has been treated by a patented or special 'improving process' of annealing, hardening, and tempering. **1916** D. K. Bullens *Steel & its Heat Treatment* xvii. 402 The high strength and toughness of patented wire are due to its carbon condition and its peculiar structure. **1956** A. K. Osborne *Encycl. Iron & Steel Industry* 307/2 Best patented steel wire is wire intended for the production of steel cables which has been drawn to a maximum stress of between 80 to 90 tons per sq. in.

patent, obs. f. PATEN, PATTEN; erron. form of POTENT, staff.

patentability (ˌpeɪtəntə'bɪlɪtɪ, ˌpæt-). [f. next: see -BILITY.] Capability of being patented.

1883 H. C. Mervin (*title*) The Patentability of Inventions. **1946** *Nature* 23 Nov. 726/1 In these circumstances the requirements for patentability as a selection from the general disclosure or claim are discovery of a previously unrecognized advantage.., and limitation to a manufacture based on that discovery. **1972** *N. Y. Law Jrnl.* 10 Oct. 5/2 The general level of innovation necessary to sustain patentability remains the same. **1972** *Sci. Amer.* Oct. 45/3 Novelty, though essential for patentability, does not guarantee utility. **1978** *Nature* 22 June 584/1 Patent law has not yet got to grips with the problem of genetically-engineered bacteria, both in terms of their patentability and of the particular difficulties there might be in storing bacteria whose claim to originality lies in the properties possessed by a plasmid.

patentable ('peɪtəntəb(ə)l, 'pæt-), *a.* [f. PATENT *v.* + -ABLE.] That may be patented, capable of being patented.

1817 *Niles' Reg.* XII. 283/2 The improvement relied on by Witness was not useful, and consequently not a patentable improvement under the patent law. **1852** *Fraser's Mag.* XLVI. 499 The sense in which patentable inventions can be adopted. **1879** *Cassell's Techn. Educ.* IV. 90/2 The kinds of inventions that are patentable. **1977** *New Scientist* 7 Apr. 24/2 Although computer programs are not as such patentable, computer hardware can be protected.

patentably ('peɪtəntəblɪ), *adv.* [f. PATENTABLE *a.* + -LY[2].] In a way that satisfies the conditions for patenting anything.

1903 *Sci. Amer.* 28 Feb. 159/1 Patents have been granted in Great Britain.. without any enquiry to learn whether the inventions were patentably new.

†**'patentary**, *a. Obs. rare*[−1]. [f. PATENT *sb.* + -ARY.] Of or pertaining to a patent.

1734 Falle *Jersey* iii. (ed. 2) 192 Here then lay the Point in dispute, whether the Ordinance of Henry VII,.. or the Patentary Clause, should stand.

patentee (ˌpæt-, ˌpeɪtən'tiː). Also 7 **patenty, pattentie**. [f. PATENT *sb.* + -EE[1]: cf. *mortgagee*; perh. first in an AngloFr. form *patenté*. (Mod.F. *patenté* in same sense is only of 19th c.)] One to whom letters patent have been granted; **b.** now *esp.* one who has taken out a patent for some new invention, or the like: cf. PATENT *sb.* 2.

1442 *Rolls of Parlt.* V. 62/2 Delivered by the Fermours, Patentees, Tenaunts and Occupiours. **1495** *Act 11 Hen. VII*, c. 16 The Kinges Committees or his patentees for the kepyng of the seid Toun as afore is seid. **1583** in Hakluyt *Voy.* (1600) III. 189 With expresse prohibition.. against all others, which shall go thither without the licence of the patentee or his assignes first obteined. **1622** E. Misselden *Free Trade* (ed. 2) 72 The question is, who is then the Monopolian, whether the Patentees, or their Assignes? **1647** Clarendon *Hist. Reb.* v. §330 In all Publick Acts.. they were desired to be admitted joynt Patentees with his Majesty in the Regality. **1724** Swift *Prometheus* Wks. 1755 III. II. 150 Wood the patentee's Irish half-pence. **1765** T. Hutchinson *Hist. Mass.* I. i. 2 The patentees of the Northern colony. **1791** Boswell *Johnson* an. 1747, David Garrick, having become joint patentee and manager of Drury-lane theatre. **1818** Cruise *Digest* (ed. 2) II. 492 John Hawkins, the heir of the said Joan,.. upon a *scire facias* against the patentee, had judgement to recover the lands.

b. 1691 T. H[ale] *Acc. New Invent.* p. l, The Patentees of these New Lights. **1701** [see PATENT *sb.* 2]. **1731** *Gentl. Mag.* I. 452 Patentees of a new invented Plough. **1879** *Cassell's Techn. Educ.* IV. 91/1 Provided the patentee is the first person who has produced the substance in a sufficient quantity to make it a marketable article.

c. *fig.* †One to whom something has been granted (*obs.*); an inventor and proprietor of something.

1616 B. Parsons *Mag. Charter* 15 So God.. joyneth them patentees heere together. **1900** *Westm. Gaz.* 27 Aug. 2/2 Mr. Plunkett is the patentee of the policy of killing Home Rule by kindness. **1903** *Daily Chron.* 9 Dec. 4/3 Mr. Spencer.. may indeed be called the inventor and patentee of evolution.

Hence **paten'teed** *ppl. a.*, made a patentee, provided with letters patent.

1775 Adair *Amer. Ind.* 144 *note*, Since the patenteed race of Daublers set foot in their land.

†**'patenter**. *rare.* [f. PATENT *sb.* + -ER[1].] A patentee.

1641 *Sc. Acts Chas. I* (1817) V. 585/1 Þe saidis patenters be þe forsaid act obleist them thair aires,.. not to.. seik any greater dewetie. **1883** E. W. Hamilton *Diary* 25 Mar. (1972) II. 413 The only other person at dinner was Lane Fox, the inventor and patenter of an electric lighting system.

'patenting, *vbl. sb.* [f. PATENT *v.* + -ING[1].]

a. The process of obtaining by letters patent the sole right to purchase and sell.

1883 *Daily News* 25 Sept. 3/1 Patenting was unnecessarily and unwisely expensive, and the poor patentee was left almost without any aid or guidance.

b. *Metallurgy.* In the manufacture of wire, a process for improving ductility similar to normalizing, but involving cooling in either air or molten lead or salt.

The subject of *Brit. Patent 1104* (granted to J. Horsfall in 1854).

1891 J. B. Smith *Wire* i. 60 'The patenting or improving' of steel wire is.. an occult process.. for each manufacturer has his own.. special methods. **1916** D. K. Bullens *Steel & its Heat Treatment* xvii. 405 The structure obtained by patenting permits much further cold drawing than does the structure obtained by annealing. **1921** L. Aitchison *Engin. Steels* viii. 275 The patenting furnace is a long, open-ended chamber. **1945** *Engineers' Digest* VI. 169 (*heading*) Direct resistance heating of salt baths for the patenting of steel wire. **1961** *Engineering* 14 Apr. 516/2 A batch of 24 wires is fed through the 60 ft patenting furnace at a time, being heated to 950°C.

'patentizing, *vbl. sb. nonce-wd.* [f. PATENT *sb.* + -IZE + -ING[1].] The granting and taking out of patents.

1829 *Westm. Rev.* Apr. 417 It is a strange disease in England, the said patentizing.

patently ('peɪtəntlɪ, 'pæt-), *adv.* [f. PATENT *a.* + -LY[2].] In a patent manner; openly, obviously, manifestly, plainly, evidently, clearly.

1863 D. G. Mitchell *Farm of Edgewood* 245 So patently and egregiously wrong. **1879** Stevenson *Trav. Cevennes* 171, I saw with regret my revolver lying patently disclosed.

'patentor. [f. PATENT + -OR.]

1. One who grants a patent: correlative to *patentee*.

2. One who takes out a patent, a patentee.

1890 in *Cent. Dict.* (no quotation).

pa,tento'ternate, *a. rare.* [f. *patento-*, irreg. combining form of L. *patent-em* PATENT *a.* + TERNATE.] Patently or widely ternate.

1867 J. Hogg *Microsc.* 390 The large patentoternate spicula.

patenty, obs. form of PATENTEE.

pateque, var. PASTEQUE *Obs.*, water-melon.

‖**pater**. [L. *pater* father.]

1. ('pætə(r)) = PATERNOSTER 1 (being the first word of the Lord's Prayer in Latin).

c **1330** R. Brunne *Chron.* (1810) 341 Þat for him with deuocioun said *pater & aue*. **13..** *E.E. Allit. P.* A. 484 Neuer nauþer pater ne crede. **1632** Lithgow *Trav.* IX. 411 Pattering an abridged Pater. **1842** Barham *Ingol. Leg.* Ser. II. *Ingol. Penance*, Let a mass be sung, and a *pater* be said. **1896** *Dublin Rev.* Apr. 278 Saying a *pater* perhaps in silence for St. Edythe's intercession.

†**2.** A priest, a monk: = FATHER 6 b. Also in *Comb.* **pater-guardian** (see quot.). *Obs.*

c **1630** *Scot. Pasquil* 7 A sprincle.. held in hand of vested Pater. **1656** Blount *Glossogr.*, *Pater-guardian*, a Father-guardian; a title given to the chief of the Franciscan Friers in their Monasteries.

3. ('peɪtə(r)) **a.** Familiarly used for *father*; chiefly in schoolboys' slang.

1728 Ramsay *Monk & Miller's Wife* 25 A youth sprung frae a gentle pater. **1880** Miss Braddon *Just as I am* xiv, You are not afraid of your *pater* being caught by her elderly wiles. **1893** F. F. Moore *Gray Eye or So* II. 202 Don't let us get into a sentimental strain, pater. **1900** G. Swift *Somerley* 126 The pater will say I'm a fool, the mater'll say the girl isn't good enough for me.

b. spec. *Anthropol.* The legal father.

1949, etc. [see GENITOR[2] b]. **1951** E. E. Evans-Pritchard *Kinship & Marriage among Nuer* 113 The children clearly regard themselves as members of a legal family to which the brother of their pater does not belong, although he is their foster-father, and may also be their genitor. **1955** M. GLUCKMAN *Custom & Conflict in Afr.* iii. 71 In these institutions physiological paternity is distinguished from social fatherhood—as anthropologists put it, the *pater* need not be the *genitor*.

‖**patera** (ˈpætərə). Pl. -æ. Also 9 pattera. [L. *patera*, f. *patēre* to be open. Cf. *patina*, *patella*.]

1. *Rom. Antiq.* A broad flat saucer or dish, used esp. in pouring out libations at sacrifices.

1658 SIR T. BROWNE *Hydriot.* iii. 39 Sacrificing patera's, and vessels of libation. **1759** B. MARTIN *Nat. Hist. Eng.* II. *Herts.* 5 Many Urns, and Pateras of fine red Earth. **1842** PRICHARD *Nat. Hist. Man* (ed. 2) 190 Some hold in their right hand a drinking-cup, and in their left a patera.

2. *Arch.* An ornament resembling a shallow dish; any flat round ornament in bas-relief.

1776 H. WALPOLE *Let. to W. Mason* 29 Feb., A sphinx, masks, a patera, and a running foliage of leaves. **1784** J. BARRY in *Lect. Paint* v. (Bohn 1848) 198 The triglyphs and pateras ordinarily used. **1837** *Civil Eng. & Arch. Jrnl.* I. 59/2 The ceiling is divided into compartments, and ornamented with enriched mouldings and *pateræ*.

pateraro, -ero, var. PEDRERO, a small gun.

pateras, var. PATTRESS.

patercove, paterer: see PATRICO, PATTERER.

Pateresque (ˌpeɪtəˈrɛsk), *a.* [f. the name of Walter Horatio *Pater* (1839–94), English writer and critic.] Resembling the style of Pater's writing or his method of criticism. So **Paterian** (peɪˈtɪərɪən), *a.*

1903 BEERBOHM *Around Theatres* (1953) 274 One reason why this book is so fresh and welcome is that we see for the first time the Pateresque manner and method of criticism applied to current dramatic art. 'Pateresque' is no slight. **1905** *Westm. Gaz.* 24 July 14/1 The definition of the priest's 'triumph' as that of 'achieving as much faith as possible in an age of negation' recalls a passage from Bishop Blougram, but is truly Pateresque in its expression. **1938** L. P. SMITH *Unforgotten Years* viii. 207 The record of an attempt to see things elegantly and nobly in the Paterian spirit. **1939** *Scrutiny* VII. iv. 442 For years he cultivated a Paterian manner in his own writing. **1944** W. STEVENS *Let.* 27 Mar. (1967) 463 He considers my poems to be expressions of Paterian hedonism. **1965** K. GRAHAM *Eng. Crit. of Novel* iii. 93 An interesting Pateresque attempt to explain the flaws.. in terms of form alone. **1977** R. L. WOLFF *Gains & Losses* ii. 188 This Paterian Christianity is astonishingly like Paterian paganism.

†ˌ**paterfaˈmiliar**, *a. Obs. rare.* [f. next, after *familiar*.] Of or pertaining to a paterfamilias; paternal, patriarchal. Hence †**paterfaˈmiliarly** *adv.*

c **1650** NEEDHAM *Case of Commw. Stated* 6 The Paterfamiliar way of Government being insufficient to correct those grand enormities, there was need of some one more potent than the rest. **1654** GAYTON *Pleas. Notes* III. viii. 117 They.. send for their friends of both sexes, and very paterfamiliarly, advice them [etc.].

‖**paterfamilias** (ˌpeɪtə-, ˈpætəfəˈmɪlɪæs). [L. *paterfamiliās* the father or head of a household (*familiās*, archaic genitive of *familia*).]

1. *Rom. Law.* The head of a family or household having the authority belonging to that position over the persons composing it; also, a person of either sex and any age who is *sui juris* and free from parental control.

1850 MERIVALE *Rom. Emp.* (1865) I. i. 20 The colonies of Roman citizens planted in the provinces.. held the position of the son towards the paterfamilias. **1859** T. SANDERS *Justinian* (ed. 2) 99 The head was the *paterfamilias*, a term not expressive of paternity.., but merely signifying a person who was not under the power of another, and who, consequently, might have others under his power. **1875** MAINE *Hist. Inst.* xiii. 379 The authority of the Patriarch or Paterfamilias over his family is.. the element.. out of which all permanent power of man over man has been gradually developed.

2. The (male) head of a family or household.

c **1430** LYDG. *Min. Poems* (Percy Soc.) 170 Paterfamulias, wise and expert of olde. **1609** DEKKER *Gvlls Horne-bk.* (1812) 163 It would make the vintners believe you were *pater familias*, and kept a house. **1688** SIR E. HERBERT *Hales' Case* 21 In this Notion the Estate of every Paterfamilias may be said to be *pro bono communi* of his Family. **1754** A. MURPHY *Gray's Inn Jrnl.* (1756) II. 188, I am here a Kind of *Pater-familias* with all my little Brood of Hens and Chickens around me. **1860** THACKERAY *Round. Papers, Letts's Diary* (1862) 186 The habit of running up bills with the milliners, and swindling paterfamilias on the house bills. **1891** MRS. RIDDELL *Mad Tour* 69 The inevitable English party.., paterfamilias, materfamilias, and many daughters.

fig. **1628** VENNER *Baths of Bathe* (1650) 356 The stomach which is, as I may so say, the *Paterfamilias* of the body. *a* **1677** BARROW *Serm.* (1687) I. xxiv. 326 The.. bounty and munificence with which this great *paterfamilias* hath provided for the necessary sustenance.. of his creatures.

pateriform (ˈpætərɪfɔːm), *a.* [f. PATERA + -FORM.] Of the shape of a patera.

1826 KIRBY & SP. *Entomol.* IV. 325 *Pateriform*,.. when the joints are somewhat dilated and very short, shaped somewhat like a shallow bowl.

Paterin, -e: see PATARIN.

paterish (ˈpeɪtərɪʃ), *a. local.* [Origin obscure; the word appears in some districts as *patherish* or *potherish*.] Of a sheep: Affected with water on the brain, causing giddiness and stupidity.

1794 YOUNG *Ann. Agric.* XXII. 225 The disorders that attack [ewes] are the red-water, and being paterish, which last disease is never cured. **1805** R. W. DICKSON *Pract. Agric.* (1807) II. 706 Sheep in this situation among South Down sheep-farmers are said to be *paterish*. **1808** A. YOUNG jr. *Agric. Surv. Sussex* 335 A paterish sheep appears to be deprived entirely of its senses, and is continually turning round instead of going forward.

patern, -ize, obs. forms of PATTERN, -IZE.

paternal (pəˈtɜːnəl), *a.* [f. late L. or Com. Rom. type *paternāl-is* (med.L. 1438 in Du Cange), It. *paternale*, Sp., Pr. *paternal*, F. *paternel* (12th c. in Hatz.-Darm.), f. L. *patern-us* fatherly (f. *pater* father): see -AL[1].]

1. a. Of or belonging to a father or to fathers; characteristic of a father; fatherly.

paternal government, government as by a father, paternalism.

1605 SHAKS. *Lear* I. i. 115 Heere I disclaime all my Paternall care, Propinquity and property of blood. **1614** RALEIGH *Hist. World* II. (1634) 350 The government which this Nation underwent was first paternall. **1667** MILTON *P.L.* XI. 353 God.. still compassing thee round With goodness and paternal Love. **1788** GIBBON *Decl. & F.* xliv. IV. 203 The Roman legislators had reposed an unbounded confidence in the sentiments of paternal love. **1843** MIALL in *Nonconf.* III. 744 Report.. that our government, grown suddenly paternal, were about to abandon their prosecutions in Ireland. **1885** R. BUCHANAN *Annan Water* xix, He kissed her on the forehead with almost paternal gentleness.

b. Of or belonging to one's father; (one's) father's.

paternal roof, the home of one's father.

1667 MILTON *P.L.* VII. 219 Th' Omnific Word.. on the Wings of Cherubim Uplifted, in Paternal Glorie rode Farr into Chaos. **1828** CARLYLE in *Edin. Rev.* Dec. 293 But now, at this early age, he quits the paternal roof. **1845** J. PORTER *Thaddeus of Warsaw* (new ed.) xliii. 475 Longing earnestly for a temporary sanctuary under his friend's paternal roof. **1861** J. W. CARLYLE *Let.* 22 Sept. (1883) III. 91 If you are returned to 'the paternal roof', no need almost of this letter. *a* **1901** BESANT *Five Years' Tryst* (1902) 46 Throwing himself at the paternal feet.

c. That is a father.

1667 MILTON *P.L.* VI. 750 The Chariot of Paternal Deitie. **1697** POTTER *Antiq. Greece* II. ii. (1715) 185 Cyrus.. sacrificeth to Paternal Jupiter. *a* **1711** KEN *Christophil* Poet. Wks. 1721 I. 432 Paternal God in Filial shines, And in our Bliss with Filial joyns.

2. Inherited or derived from a father; related through a father or on the father's side.

1611 MUNDAY *Brief Chron.* 240 He affecting his paternall Kingdome forsooke Poland. *a* **1700** DRYDEN *Horace Ep.* ii. 9 Who plow'd with oxen of their own, Their small paternal field of corn. **1710** STEELE *Tatler* No. 176 ¶8, I have a good Fortune, partly paternal, and partly acquired. **1886** RUSKIN *Præterita* I. iii. 94 My paternal grandmother.. ran away with my paternal grandfather when she was not quite sixteen.

Hence **paˈternally** *adv.*

1603 OWEN *Pembrokeshire* ii. (1892) 28 Paternallye descended.. of that Ancient Brittishe line. **1817** G. ROSE *Diaries* (1860) I. 17, I am descended paternally from the family of Rose of Kilravoe. **1892** A. E. LEE *Hist. Columbus* (Ohio) I. 67 The Lenapes.. paternally styled the other Algonquins.. children or grandchildren.

paternalism (pəˈtɜːnəlɪz(ə)m). [See -ISM.]

1. The principle and practice of paternal administration; government as by a father; the claim or attempt to supply the needs or to regulate the life of a nation or community in the same way as a father does those of his children.

1881 *Chicago Times* 11 June, There is nothing in the proposal that looks in the direction of paternalism, or the ownership and administration of industrial enterprises by the government. **1888** *Co-operative News* 7 Apr. 324 Kindly paternalism has resulted in a perfect understanding between employer and workers. **1898** *Atlantic Monthly* LXXXII. 563/2 Luther.. was in questions of government the most pronounced advocate of paternalism.

2. The principle of acting in a way like that of a father towards his children.

1893 *Standard* 13 Apr., The old spirit of paternalism which induced the British lender to place the Australian States on a higher footing than foreign borrowers.

paternalist (pəˈtɜːnəlɪst), *a.* [see -IST.] = PATERNALISTIC *a.*

1928 *Britain's Industr. Future* (Liberal Industr. Inquiry) III. xviii. 237 'Welfare work' has an unpleasantly paternalist and patronising sound.

paternalistic (pətɜːnəˈlɪstɪk), *a.* [f. as PATERNALISM: see -ISTIC.] Of, pertaining to, or of the nature of paternalism. Hence **paternaˈlistically** *adv.*

1890 *Cent. Dict.*, Paternalistic. **1893** *Voice* (N.Y.) 23 Mar., There is a 'paternalistic' law on the statute books of Minnesota to which the coal combination has made itself liable. **1918** *Nation* (N.Y.) 7 Feb. p. xii/2 It is perhaps as well that a paternalistic Government, with unlimited power of taxation to make good the deficit, is behind it. **1918** E. H. GRIGGS *Soul of Democracy* xviii. 125 The breakdown of paternalistically achieved efficiency has been evident in Germany's utter failure to understand, [etc.]. **1961** *Daily Tel.* 24 Apr. 12 They are humble people, Europeans, half-castes and Africans, whose only crime is to have pursued their livelihoods unprotestingly under a paternalisitc Government which is now challenged by the spread of black nationalism. **1966** *Listener* 16 June 889/1 I felt the face of Britain was reasonably presented in this paternalistic atmosphere. **1976** *Daily Mirror* 16 July 5/7 That puts him on the side of the Labour unions, who are ununeasy about Carter, a paternalistic employer.

paternality (pætəˈnælɪtɪ). *rare.* [f. PATERNAL + -ITY.] Paternal quality or condition; a paternal personality.

1854 *Tait's Mag.* XXI. 269 Worth all the accidental paternalities and passing patriarchs, whom.. absolutism has contributed to the 'stream of time'. **1877** T. SINCLAIR *Mount* (1878) 20 Absolute human paternalities.

paternalized (pəˈtɜːnəlaɪzd), *ppl. a.* [f. as PATERNALISM + -IZE + -ED[1].] Characterized by or subjected to paternalism.

1903 *Electr. World & Engin.* 11 Apr. 597 The socialistic spirit.. that would have every man on the pay roll of the State or the municipality in a vast series of paternalised institutions.

paterne, obs. form of PATRON, PATTERN.

Paˈternian. *Ch. Hist.* [ad. L. *Paterniāni*: see Du Cange.] A member of a Manichæan sect (condemned in a council held at Rome in 367), who held that God made the upper and Satan the lower parts of the body.

c **1449** PECOCK *Repr.* (Rolls) II. 500 The sect of Paternyanys, which helden that the louȝer parties of a mannys bodi weren maad of the feend. **1659** HOWELL *Vocab.* Sect. x, Paternians. **1882** in OGILVIE (Annandale).

paternity (pəˈtɜːnɪtɪ). [a. F. *paternité* (12th c. in Hatz.-Darm.), ad. L. *paternitātem*, f. *paternus*: see PATERNAL and -ITY.]

1. a. The quality or condition of being a father; the relation of a father; fatherhood.

1582 BENTLEY *Mon. Matrones* II. 6 This truth maketh hir to feele that there is in thee true paternitie. **1582** N.T. (Rhem.) *Eph.* iii. 15 The Father of our Lord Iesus Christ, of whom al paternitie in the heauens and in earth is named. *a* **1667** JER. TAYLOR *Serm.* III. iv. (R.), Where a spiritual paternity is evident: we need look no further for spiritual government. **1786** tr. *Beckford's Vathek* 23 Having been spared the cares as well as the honour of paternity. **1869** GOULBURN *Purs. Holiness* vii. 57 That most comfortable truth, the Paternity of God.

†**b.** The rule or government of the father; patriarchal rule. *Obs.*

1614 RALEIGH *Hist. World* I. (1634) 159 That he [Nimrod] first brake the rule of Eldership and Paternity. **1711** HICKES *Two Treat. Christ. Priesth.* (1847) II. 287 It is not only an empire but a paternity.

2. The quality or personality of an ecclesiastical father: used as a title, ***Your, His Paternity***; also, †an ecclesiastical father, a monk or priest (*obs.*).

1432–43 *Petit. to Bp. of Bath* in *Cal. Proc. Chanc. Q. Eliz.* (1827) I. Introd. 24 Plese on to you gracyous lord of your reverent paternyte, and of youre hye gracyous lordschip to considere [etc.]. **1629** WADSWORTH *Sp. Pilgr.* iii. 11 Thay tooke their leaue of them and the rest of the paternities, and returned into their owne Couents. *Ibid.* 16 Whether their paternities had better eate flesh or fish. **1855** R. BOYLE *Boyle versus Wiseman* 47 His Paternity coincides with the opinion which I had entertained.

3. The paternal relation viewed from the standpoint of the child; paternal origin or descent.

1868 GLADSTONE *Juv. Mundi* v. (1870) 137 The foreign paternity of a group of distinguished men who had cast their lot in that country. **1882** 'OUIDA' *Maremma* I. iii. 69 She resolved.. to keep the secret of the baby's paternity from all.

4. *fig.* Authorship, source, origin (of a work).

1827 SCOTT *Introd. Chron. Canongate*, These Novels of Waverley, the paternity of which was likely at one time to have formed a controversy of some celebrity. **1854** EMERSON *Lett. & Soc. Aims, Quot. & Orig.* Wks. (Bohn) III. 215 Many of the historical proverbs have a doubtful paternity.

5. *attrib.* and *Comb.*, as ***paternity case, leave, suit***; **paternity test**, a blood test used to assess or discount the likelihood of paternity in a particular case; hence **paternity-testing** *vbl. sb.*

1940 D. MACCARTHY *Drama* 104 In the opening scene we have seen him confronted, as a soldier in authority, with a paternity case he cannot solve. **1973** *Guardian* 4 June 9/1 Imagine the day when firms allow their male employees paternity leave to be with their wives during the last part of their pregnancies and the first days in the life of their children. **1975** *Times* 12 Mar. 3/1 The Greater London Council.. agreed tonight that fathers on their staff should normally be allowed up to five days paternity leave. **1977** *Spare Rib* June 18/3 We're also now pressing for paternity leave, realising it's a joint thing. **1975** J. MCCLURE *Snake* viii. 108 See a doctor, get some pills... Paternity suits I don't contest, madam. **1977** D. ANTHONY *Stud Game* iii. 21, I can imagine the damage a paternity suit would do. But I'm broke, and the baby's due in less than five months. **1926** R. J. E. SCOTT *Gould's Med. Dict.* 773/2 Mayoral and Jiminez paternity test. **1943** D. HARLEY *Medico-Legal Blood Group Determination* vi. 44 (*heading*) Paternity tests. **1960** I. A. STANTON *Dict. for Med. Secretaries* 113/1 *Paternity test*, blood comparison tests to rule out the possibility of paternity. **1968** F. E. CAMPS *Grandwohl's Legal Med.* (ed. 2) xiii. 171/1 Anti-S [antibody] has been found sufficiently often for it to be used economically for paternity testing. **1972** B. KNIGHT *Legal Aspects Med. Practice* xxiii. 196 Certain haemoglobin-binding proteins in human serum, called haptoglobins, can be detected by electrophoresis... Their inheritance is.. determined on fixed genetic principles, thus making them of use in paternity testing.

paternoster ('pætə'nɒstə(r)), *sb.* Also 6 **-nostre.** [a. L. *pater noster* 'our Father', the first two words of the Lord's Prayer in Latin; in OF. *paternostre* (11th c.), *patrenostre* (12th c.), later *patenostre*, mod.F. *patenôtre* in same uses.]

1. a. The Lord's Prayer, esp. in the Latin version.

a **1000** *Sal. & Sat.* 39 (Gr.) Ðæt ȝe-palmtwiȝede Pater Noster heofonas ontyneð. *c* **1200** *Trin. Coll. Hom.* 25 þu singest þe salm þat is cleped paternoster. **1389** in *Eng. Gilds* (1870) 20 Euery brother & sister shul seyn..xx. sythes ye pater noster. *c* **1450** *Bk. Curtasye* 145 in *Babees Bk.* 303 þy pater noster he wille þe teche. **1531** TINDALE *Exp. 1 John* (1537) 16 Christ teacheth us to praye in oure Pater noster. **1642** FULLER *Holy & Prof. St.* IV. xiv. 309 Queen Marie, who got the crown by *Our Father*, and held it by *Pater noster*. **1712** ARBUTHNOT *John Bull* III. ii, Peg had taken a fancy not to say her Paternoster. **1803** SOUTHEY *Alderman's Funeral*, The multiplication-table was his Creed, His Paternoster, and his Decalogue. **1876** BANCROFT *Hist. U.S.* II. xxx. 248 She could repeat the paternoster fluently enough, but not quite correctly.

fig. **1858** O. W. HOLMES *Aut. Breakf.-t.* x. (1891) 228 Look at Nature. She never wearies of saying over her floral paternoster.

b. A repetition or recital of this as an act of worship. †*the space of a paternoster* (*obs.*): = *paternoster-while*: see 6.

c **1300** *Havelok* 2997 Seye a pater-noster stille, For him þat haueth þe rym[e] maked. **1362** LANGL. *P. Pl.* A. XI. 302 Souteris & seweris suche lewide iottis Percen wiþ a pater noster þe paleis of heuene. *c* **1450** *Mirour Saluacioun* 4275 And o pater noster more weygh in swete devocyonne Than a savtrere with sleuth. **1561** HOLLYBUSH *Hom. Apoth.* 3 Let it so abyde the space of halfe a Pater-noster. **1590** SPENSER *F.Q.* I. iii. 13 Nine hundred Pater nosters every day, And thrise nine hundred Aves she was wont to say. **1681** GREW *Musæum* I. 175 The Worm will die within the space of a Pater Noster. **1756–7** tr. *Keysler's Trav.* (1760) I. 471 They do not play here for money, but for *ave-maria's*, *pater-noster's*, and other prayers. **1856** J. H. NEWMAN *Callista* (1885) 330 He said out his seven pater nosters as he walked.

2. *transf.* **a.** Any form of words repeated or muttered by way of a prayer, imprecation, or charm. ***black p.***, ***white p.***, names given to specific charms. ***devil's p.***, a murmured or muttered imprecation; a low murmuring or grumbling to oneself. ***ape's p.***, a 'dithering' or chattering with the teeth: see APE *sb.* 6.

c **1386** CHAUCER *Miller's T.* 299 Ihesu Crist and seint Benedight Blesse this hous from euery wikked wight Ffor nyghtes uerye, the white pater noster. —— *Pars. T.* ¶434 Yet wol they seyn harm and grucche and murmure priuely for verray despit, whiche wordes men clepen the deueles Pater noster. **1530** PALSGR. 642/1, I murmure, I make a noyse, I bydde the dyuels Pater noster. **1546** J. HEYWOOD *Prov.* (1867) 32 Pattryng the diuels Pater noster to hir selfe. **1610** J. WHITE *Way True Church* To Rdr. §13. cij, White Pater noster, Saint Peters brother..Open heauen yates, and steike hell yates: And let euery crysom child creepe to it owne mother: White Pater noster, Amen. **1687** CONGREVE *Old Bach.* IV. vi, A prayer-book! Ay, this is the devil's pater-noster. **1851** LONGF. *Gold. Leg.* II. ii, This is the Black Pater-noster... Open, open, hell's gates! Shut, shut, heaven's gates! All the devils in the air The stronger be, that hear the Black Prayer. **1880** 'OUIDA' *Moths* v, *Noblesse oblige*,..that paternoster of princes.

b. A long nonsensical or tedious recital or utterance; a 'homily' or 'preachment'; a prating.

1663 DRYDEN *Wild Gallant* I. ii, Hold your prating, Frances; or I'll put you out of your Pater Nosters, with a sorrow to you. **1822** GALT *Provost* xxxi. (1868) 94 When the bailie had made an end of his paternoster.

3. a. A special bead in a rosary indicating that a paternoster is to be said, usually occurring every eleventh bead and of different size or material from the rest. **b.** Also applied to the whole rosary.

c **1250** *Lutel Soth. Serm.* 67 in *O.E. Misc.* 190 Atom [= at home] his hire pater noster biloken in hire teye. *c* **1400** MAUNDEV. (1839) xviii. 197 The Kyng..hathe abouten his Nekke 300 Perles oryent, gode and grete, and knotted, as Pater Nostres here of Amber. **1463** *Bury Wills* (Camden) 36 A peyre of bedys with pater nostris of gold, and on eche syde of the pater nostris a bede of coral, and the Aue Marys of colour aftir marbil. **1615** tr. *De Monfart's Surv. E. Ind.* 28 A certaine kind of wood called Calamba: for which the Portugalls pay 100. crownes a pound, to make Pater-Nosters with. **1714** *Fr. Bk. of Rates* 59 Pater-Nosters woodden. **1870** FROUDE *Hist. Eng.* xxxiv. XII. 334 In her hand she held a crucifix of ivory, and a number of jewelled pater-nosters was attached to her girdle.

4. Applied to things resembling a rosary: **a.** in *Fishing*, = *paternoster-line*: see 6.

1851 KINGSLEY *Yeast* iii, Here's your gudgeons and minnows, sir,..and here's that paternoster as you gave me to rig up. **1861** H. KINGSLEY *Ravenshoe* lxiv, He..saw, through the osiers, the hoary old profligate with his paternoster pulling the perch out as fast as he could put his line in. **1894** *Blackw. Mag.* Sept. 427/1 Fishing with an ordinary two-hook paternoster will catch many more fish.

b. *Arch.* A row of bead-like ornaments.

In Chambers' *Cycl.* from Fr., and repeated in some later works, but app. never in Eng. use.

1727–41 CHAMBERS *Cycl.* s.v., Pater-nosters, in architecture; a sort of ornaments cut in form of beads, either round, or oval; used on baguettes, astragals, etc. **1823** P. NICHOLSON *Pract. Build.* 589. **1842–76** in GWILT *Archit.* (ed. 7) Gloss.

c. A lift consisting of a succession of doorless compartments on an endless chain in continuous slow motion that allows entry at any time. Also *paternoster lift*.

1912 *Engineering Index* XXXI. 72/2 The 'Paternoster' continuous elevator (Ascensori a movimento continuo, o ascensori 'Paternoster'). U. Quintavalle. An endless chain elevator with several compartments... *L'Industria*—Mar. 10 1912. **1937** *Discovery* Dec. 388/2 Lifts and conveyors of the 'Paternoster' type have been installed. **1971** R. LEWIS *Error of Judgment* vi. 205 He and the victim of his attack were on a small square landing at the end of the corridor and directly in front of the paternosters. **1973** *Times* 24 Dec. 4/3 Instead of orthodox lifts, the architects..use 'paternosters', continually moving, doorless two-person lifts which reduce waiting. **1977** *Times* 19 Feb. 2/3 Passenger-carrying 'paternoster' lifts consisting of continuous chains of small cars.

†**5.** ***paternoster of flax***: see quots. *Obs.*

1658 *N. Riding Rec.* VI. 14 [A woman presented for stealing three pounds of] paternoster flacks. **1688** R. HOLME *Armoury* III. 106/2 *Pater Noster*, ten handfulls [of flax] in a strick, is 2 pounds.

6. *attrib.* and *Comb.*, *as* ***paternoster-maker***, ***-man***, ***-monger***, ***-ring***; **paternoster lake** *Physical Geogr.*, each of a line of lakes in a glaciated valley; **paternoster-line**, a line used in fishing, to which hooks or groups of hooks are attached at intervals, and also weights to sink it; **paternoster-pea**, the seed of jequirity (*Abrus precatorius*), often used as beads; **paternoster-pump**, a chain-pump: see quot.; **paternoster-tackle**, the tackle appertaining to a paternoster-line; **paternoster-wheel**, 'a water-raising device having a number of buckets on a chain' (Knight *Dict. Mech.* 1875); **paternoster-while**, the time it takes to say a paternoster.

1942 C. A. COTTON *Climatic Accidents in Landscape-Making* xix. 256 If the step-tread basins are occupied by lakes..these may follow one another like beads upon a string—'*paternoster lakes'. **1968** R. W. FAIRBRIDGE *Encycl. Geomorphol.* 468/2 Since the floor of a glaciated valley is often undulating..or with a step-like rock floor.., it is sometimes marked by a succession of lakes..rather fancifully named paternoster lakes. **1676** COTTON *Walton's Angler* xvi. (Cassell) 153 [Bleak] may be caught with a *Paternoster line: that is, six or eight very small hooks tied along the line, one half a foot above the other. **1718** JACOB *Compl. Sportsman* 148. **1869** *Routledge's Ev. Boy's Ann.* 388 A paternoster line, with a good-sized bullet above the highest hook. **1598** STOW *Surv.* 274 (*Pater Noster Rowe*) There dwelled also, turners of Beades, and they were called *Pater Noster makers. **1681** T. FLATMAN *Heraclitus Ridens* No. 26 (1713) I. 172, I believe e'er long plotting..will be no Treason in a *Pater-noster Man. **1654** WHITLOCK *Zootomia* 349 Praiers..far more prevalent, than those Verball *Pater-noster-Mongers utter over a Bead-roule. **1874** KNIGHT *Dict. Mech.* 520/1 (*Chain-pump*) When packed pistons are used, they are termed **paternoster pumps*, from the resemblance of the chain and buttons to the rosary. **1502** *Will of Bradmere* (Somerset Ho.), A *Pater noster ryng with a diamonde. **1894** *Blackw. Mag.* Sept. 427/2 Two rods, on both of which was light *paternoster tackle. **1362** LANGL. *P. Pl.* A. v. 192 He pissede a potel In a *pater-noster while. **1448** *Paston Lett.* I. 74 Al thys was don, as men say, in a Pater Noster wyle. **1600** J. PARTRIDGE *Treas. Hid. Secrets* xxvii, Let them seeth three or four Pater noster whiles. *a* **1658** FARINDON *Serm.* (1849) IV. 241 We may do it in a *Pater-noster*-while. **1888** STEVENSON *Black Arrow* 84 As though the bearer had run for a pater-noster-while.

paternoster (ˌpætə'nɒstə(r)), *v.* [f. prec. 4a.] *intr.* To fish with a paternoster-line. So **paternostering** *vbl. sb.*

1859 F. FRANCIS *Newton Dograne* (1888) 19 An adept in trolling, paternostering, fly-fishing. **1867** —— *Angling* iii. (1880) 96 Paternostering..is a very skilful..branch of angling. **1891** *Field* 21 Nov. 774/2 He paternostered while I spun.

paternosterer (ˌpætə'nɒstərə(r)). [In 1, a. OF. *patenostrier* (13th c. in Littré), in mod.F. *patenôtrier*; in 2, f. PATERNOSTER *v.* + -ER[1].]

†**1.** A maker of paternosters or rosaries. *Obs.*

1277–8 in Riley *Mem. London* (1868) 20 [Roger de Bury] paternostrer. **1311** in *Cal. Let. Bk. D Lond.* (1902) 154 [Sewel, late apprentice of Richard de Godesname] paternostrer [admitted].

2. One who fishes with a paternoster-line.

1891 *Field* 28 Nov. 824/3 To be a good paternosterer much practice is required.

pateroon, paterroon, obs. forms of PATROON.

paterophobia (pætərəʊ'fəʊbɪə). *nonce-wd.* [f. L. *pater* or Gr. πατήρ father + *-phobia*. (The proper form would be *patro-*.)] Dread or fear of the Fathers (of the early Church).

1840 G. S. FABER *Christ's Disc. Capernaum* Ded. 20 In despite of the judgment of the Anglican Church, his distressing Paterophobia so confuses his discriminating powers, as to make him fancy, that [etc.].

paterro, obs. form of PEDRERO.

Paterson ('pætəsən). *Austral.* The surname of an Australian family, used in ***Paterson's curse***, a blue-flowered weed, *Echium plantagineum*, of the family Boraginaceæ which is said to have spread from their garden near Albury, New South Wales, in the 1890s.

1905 *Agric. Gaz. New South Wales* XVI. 268 That 'Paterson's Curse' produces some feed is undoubted, but it is a smothering, rough, coarse plant, whose room is far better than its company. **1922** G. M. THOMSON *Naturalisation of Animals & Plants in N.Z.* III. 445 It [sc. *Echium plantagineum*] is a serious pest in some parts of Australia, where it is known as 'Paterson's Curse'. **1926** F. W. HILGENDORF *Weeds N.Z.* vi. 144 Paterson's Curse..is the local name of this weed where it is commonest in New Zealand, viz. in the Thames and neighbouring districts. **1930** A. J. EWART *Flora of Victoria* 971 Paterson's Curse... A weed proclaimed for the whole state. **1970** R. M. MOORE *Austral. Grasslands* xii. 189/2 Paterson's curse..has a wide distribution in South Australia, Victoria, and southern New South Wales.

patesi (pə'teɪsiː). [erron. transliteration of Sumerian *ensi*.] The ruler of a Sumerian city-state; a petty sovereign or priest-king. Hence **pa'tesiship**, the office or position of a patesi.

1894 A. H. SAYCE *Primer of Assyriol.* iii. 45 At a later date Tello lost its independence, and its rulers became merely patesis or high-priests. **1910** L. W. KING *Hist. Sumer & Akkad* iv. 101 The human kings and patesis were nothing more than ministers, or agents, appointed to carry out their will. **1927** PEAKE & FLEURE *Priests & Kings* 178 The Sumerian patesi was a magistrate who performed sacred or priestly functions. **1928** C. L. WOOLLEY *Sumerians* v. 138 Only in Nippur did the patesiship continue to descend from father to son.

patesing, var. PATISING *Obs.*, bargaining.

pateyn, -e, obs. forms of PATEN, PATTEN.

path (pɑːθ, pæθ), *sb.*[1] Pl. **paths** (pɑːθs, pæθs, pɑːðz). Forms: 1 (**paat**), **pæþ**, (*pl.* **paþas**), 1–4 **paþ**, 3 *pl.* **pæðes, peðes**; 4– **path** (4–5 **paþþe**, 4–6 *Sc.* **peth**, (5 **pethth**, 6 **paith**), 4–7 **pathe**, 5 **payth**, 6 **patth, -e**). [A Com. WGer. word: OE. *pæþ* corresponds to OFris. *path, pad* (WFris. *paed*, EFris. *pad, path, pat*, Satl. *pad*, Wang. *path*), OLG. *pad*, MDu., MLG. *pat* (*pad-*), Du., LG. *pad*, OHG. *phad, phath, pfad, fad*, MHG. *phad, phat, pfat*, Ger. *pfad*:—WGer. *paþ*; not in ON. nor Goth. The forms show that the word must have been in WGer. before the Christian era. Ulterior origin uncertain.

WGer. *paþ* has naturally been compared with Gr. πάτος 'trodden or beaten way', and with Zend *paþ* (*paþan, panþan*) 'way'; but to these it could be related only as a borrowed term, which with a word of such a sense is most unlikely. On the other hand, the occurrence of original initial *p* in Teutonic is uncertain; if this is an example, *paþ* would correspond to pre-Teut. *bat-*, which has suggested the root of L. *batuĕre* to beat.]

1. a. A way beaten or trodden by the feet of men or beasts; a track formed incidentally by passage between places, rather than expressly planned and constructed to accomodate traffic; a narrow unmade and (usually) unenclosed way across the open country, through woods or fields, over a mountain, etc.; a footway or footpath, as opposed to a road for vehicles; hence applied also to a walk made for foot-passengers, in a garden, park, wood, or the like. Sometimes said more vaguely of any way or road: cf. sense 3.

c **700** *Kentish Charter of Wihtred* in *O.E.T.* 428 Terminos, id est, bereueȝ et meȝuuines paeð et stretleȝ. *c* **725** *Corpus Gloss.* 429 (O.E.T.) *Callis* paat. *c* **1000** ÆLFRIC *Gloss.* in Wr.-Wülcker 146/35, 36 *Semita*, manna pæð. *Callis*, deora pæð. **1045** *Charter of Eadweard* in Kemble *Cod. Dipl.* IV. 98 Andlang ðaes wuduweȝes on ðone grene pæð; of ðam pæðe on ðane greatan þorn. *c* **1205** LAY. 1120 Leode nere þar nane ne wepmen ne wifmen bute westiȝe pæðes [*c* **1275** bote weste paþes]. *c* **1330** R. BRUNNE *Chron. Wace* (Rolls) 8432 Of þe Walsche, he tok to companies, Paþes to waite, & stretes, & styes. *c* **1391** CHAUCER *Astrol.* Prol., As diuerse pathes leden diuerse folke the rihte wey to Roome. *c* **1430** LYDG. *Min. Poems* (Percy Soc.) 114 He thought yt was a longe waye to the pathes end. **1513** DOUGLAS *Æneis* IX. vii. 26 The horsemen..fast forth sprentis to weil beknawin pethis. **1590** SPENSER *F.Q.* I. i. 11 That path they take that beaten seemd most bare. **1634** MILTON *Comus* 37 Their way Lies through the perplex't paths of this drear Wood. **1750** GRAY *Elegy* xxix, Slow through the church-way path we saw him borne. **1791** MRS. RADCLIFFE *Rom. Forest* ii, Paths can't be made without feet. **1837** LYTTON *E. Maltrav.* I. i, There is no path across it that I can discern.

b. A track specially laid for foot or cycle racing.

c. A track constructed for some part of machinery to run upon.

1883 [see *cinder-path*, CINDER *sb.* 7]. **1887** *Times* 31 Oct. 9 H. has achieved many excellent performances on the cinder-path. **1888** *Daily News* 16 July 3/1 The turret paths of the Inflexible... These paths—that is, the circular planes on which the rollers for the revolving of the turrets travel—are of cast iron. **1901** *Oxford Mag.* 24 Apr. 291/1 The path [for foot-racing]..after the recent frosts was loose and crumbling.

d. *Physiol.* = PATHWAY 2a.

1881 A. L. RANNEY *Appl. Anat. Nervous Syst.* III. 299 It is as certainly proved that the motor impulses travel along the anterior half of the spinal cord, while the path of sensory impressions is intimately associated with the posterior half. **1902** H. E. SANTEE *Anat. Brain & Spinal Cord* (ed. 2) x. 190 The sensory paths conduct two varieties of impulse. *Ibid.* 195 There are two auditory paths, the Cochlear and the Vestibular. **1942** F. A. METTLER *Neuroanat.* x. 201 There are thus two paths for delicate tactile sensations: a long, crossed path and an uncrossed one. **1950** *Physiol. Rev.* XXX. 461 An extrapyramidal path..appears to diverge from the cortico-spinal tract in the pons.

e. *Biochem.* A metabolic pathway (PATHWAY 2b).

1909 A. E. GARROD *Inborn Errors Metabolism* i. 7 This conception of the permanency of the metabolic paths is no new one. **1927** M. BODANSKY *Introd. Physiol. Chem.* xi. 270 The possible paths of metabolism of this amino acid are the following. **1935** C. F. & G. T. CORI in Harrow & Sherwin *Textbk. Biochem.* xx. 553 With the enzyme systems existing in muscle it seems more probable..that cleavage products of glycogen are led into the lactic acid path.

f. A schedule which is allotted to or is available to an individual train over a given route.

1961 *Guardian* 28 Apr. 30/4 The code..will indicate the class of train..and the number of its 'path' on operational timing. **1971** D. J. SMITH *Discovering Railwayana* x. 60 *Train path*, vacant line in the timetable which may be used by an extra train. **1977** *Modern Railways* Dec. 463/3 Through freight traffic can be a problem too, some of these trains have paths at the busiest times.

2. a. In Old Northumbrian used to render L. *vallis* vale, dene, and *chaos* abyss, gap; hence, *north. dial.*, A hollow or deep cutting in a road. Locally pronounced, and often written, *peth.*

*c***950** *Lindisf. Gosp.* Luke iii. 5 Ezhuelc pæð *vel* dene [*vallis*] ȝefylled bið. *Ibid.* xvi. 26 Bituih iuih & usih dene *vel* pæð [*chaos*] micel ȝefæstnad is. **1548** PATTEN *Exped. Scotl.* B ij, We marched an viii. mile til we came to a place called yᵉ Peaths [i.e. Cockburnspath]. It is a valey..a xx. skore [yards] brode from banke to banke aboue... So stepe be these bankes on eyther syde and depe to the bottom [etc.]. **1855** *N. & Q.* 1st ser. XII. 74, I was told that a fatal accident had occurred to a person 'going down the peth', a hollow wooded part of the road [near Durham]. **1904** J. T. FOWLER in *Let.*, Two of the main roads leading into and out of Durham are in cuttings through hills and are called respectively 'Crossgate Peth,' or 'The Peth',..and 'Shincliffe Peth'.

b. In Sc. and north. Eng., A steep road or path; a steep ascent or hill on a road.

(Common name of a steep ascent in a road, and hence occurring in many names of places and of steep streets or lanes in towns, in Scotland, Northumberland, Durham, etc.)

1375 BARBOUR *Bruce* XVIII. 366 Ane craggy bra..And a gret peth wp for to gang. **1496** *Acc. Ld. High Treas. Scot.* I. 297 To draw the gunnis in peththis and myris. **1513** DOUGLAS *Æneis* XI. x. 68 Him self ascendis the hie band of the hyll..Tharfor a prattik of weir devys will I, And ly at wait in quyet embuschment At athir pethis hed or secrete went. [**1590** SPENSER *F.Q.* I. x. 55 A little path, that was both steepe and long.] **1808** JAMIESON s.v. *Peth*, A peth is a road up a steep brae, but is not necessarily to be understood to be a narrow or foot-path. On the contrary..the most of *peths* are on public roads, as *Kirkliston peth* on the high-way between Edinburgh and Linlithgow; [the *Peth* and *Peth-head* near Kirkcaldy, etc.]

3. a. The way, course, or line along which a person or thing moves, passes, or travels (not necessarily a made or marked way, but more usually the imaginary line described or indicated by the moving body).

*a***1000** *Cædmon's Exod.* 487 Ne mihton forhabban helpendra pað, merestreames mod. **1388** WYCLIF *Ps.* viii. 9 The..fischis of the see that passen bi the paþis of the see. **1535** COVERDALE *Ps.* lxxvi[i]. 19 Thy waye was in the see, and thy pathes in the greate waters. **1680** FLAMSTEED *Doctr. Sphere* I. iii. 6 Every..Point on the Globe..describes a Circle about its Axis, which I call the Path of the Vertex. **1805** SOUTHEY *Madoc in Azt.* xiv, The populace..follow to the palace in his path. **1879** SIR R. BALL *Mechanics* 138 The curved path in which the ball will move.

b. *Math.* A continuous mapping of a real interval into a space.

1939 M. H. A. NEWMAN *Elem. Topology of Plane Sets of Points* vi. 143 Paths and loops are not merely sets of points. **1956** E. M. PATTERSON *Topology* iv. 76 A path in a topological space *T* is a continuous mapping $\alpha: C \to T$ of the space *C*, that is the set of real numbers *u* satisfying $0 \leqslant u \leqslant 1$ with the usual topology, into *T*. **1974** L. LOOMIS *Calculus* xi. 437 A parametric representation of a curve is often called a path. Sometimes we call the curve itself a path.

4. *fig.* A course of action or procedure, line of conduct, way of behaviour; less commonly, a course or line of thought, argument, or the like.

*a***900** *Ags. Ps.* (Th.) xxiv. 3 [xxv. 4] ȝedo me þine weȝas cuðe, and lær me þine paðas. *c* **1070** *O.E. Chron.* an. 1067 (MS. D) Forþan þe heo sceolde..þone kyng ȝerihtan of þam dweliandan pæðe. *c* **1200** *Trin. Coll. Hom.* 131 Godes paðes ben ure gode dedes..þe us shule leden to eche liue. *c* **1430** LYDG. *Reas. & Sens.* 2213, I shal folwen and pursywe Your pathis pleynly and doctryne. **1539** BIBLE (Great) *Ps.* xvi. 11 Thou shalt shewe me yᵉ path of lyfe. **1567** *Gude & Godlie B.* (S.T.S.) 97 The paithis of the Iust, God dois direct. **1642** FULLER *Holy & Prof. St.* IV. xix. 340 Seldome two successive Kings tread in the same path. **1750** GRAY *Elegy* ix, The paths of glory lead but to the grave. **1881** JOWETT *Thucyd.* I. 29 The true path of expediency is the path of right.

5. *Comb.*, as *path-deep* adj. (DEEP *a.* 2), *-side*, *-walker*; **path-breaker**, [tr. G. *bahnbrecher*], one who or something which breaks open a path; a pioneer; so *path-breaking* adj. [G. *bahnbrechend*]; **path-cleaver**, one who cleaves or cuts a path, e.g. through a forest; *fig.* one who strikes out a new track, a pioneer; **path difference** *Physics*, difference in path length; **pathfarer** [after *wayfarer*], a traveller along a path; **path-finder**, (*a*) one who discovers a path or way, an explorer; also *fig.*; (*b*) an aircraft or its pilot sent ahead of bombing aircraft to locate and mark out the target for attack; **path-finding**, the state of being a path-finder; also *attrib.*; †**path-fly**: see quots.; **path-hewer** = *path-cleaver*; **path length** *Physics*, the length of the path followed by a light ray, sound wave, or the like (in the case of light usu. after allowing for the retarding effect of the medium: cf. *optical path* s.v. OPTICAL *a.* 6); **path-master** *N. Amer.* (see quot. 1869); **path-racer**, a bicycle made for racing upon a prepared path or track; so **path-racing**.

1905 *Daily Chron.* 15 Nov. 4/3 A gentle *path-breaker in her chosen..field of the delineation of child life and child millinery. **1913** *Q. Rev.* Oct. 407 The late Frederic Seebohm's 'English Village Community' was literally a path-breaker. **1914** R. M. JONES *Spiritual Reformers 16th & 17th Cent.* iv. 46 A man of heroic spirit and a *path-breaking genius. **1973** *Times Lit. Suppl.* 27 Apr. 466/3 Not an epoch-making or path-breaking book. **1978** *Sci. Amer.* Feb. 131/3 His words apply equally well to other path-breaking discoveries in physics. **1896** *Godey's Mag.* (U.S.) Apr. 360/1 The indefatigable *path-cleaver [Fremont] who crossed mountains even the Indians believed impassable. **1929** J. K. ROBERTSON *Introd. Physical Optics* ix. 186 If the thickness of the film gradually increases, the *path difference between.. pairs of interfering rays will do so also and consequently the face of the film will be alternately light and dark. **1962** A. NISBETT *Technique Sound Studio* i. 28 (*caption*) The effective path difference (i.e. the extra distance travelled by the [sound] wave to reach the back of the ribbon 1) is equivalent to the distance D round the magnet pole-piece 2. **1880** G. MEREDITH *Tragic Com.* vi. (1892) 88 One who knew how to outstrip *path-farers. **1840** J. F. COOPER (*title*) The *Pathfinder. **1866** *Harper's Mag.* June 28/1 The great Path-finder, unfortunately for himself, took the wrong path. **1876** BANCROFT *Hist. U.S.* I. ii. 32 A great forerunner among the pathfinders across the continent. **1898** W. JAMES *Coll. Ess. & Rev.* (1920) 408 Philosophers are after all like poets. They are path-finders. **1932** C. FULLER *Louis Trigardt's Trek* 18 These were the 'pathfinders' of the greater movement that followed in their wake. **1943** *Times* 25 Nov. 4/4 Red tracer bullets were continually fired from the ground at the pathfinders' flares. **1944** [see MARKER 3 c]. **1946** *R.A.F. Jrnl.* May 168 For the crews of Bomber Command's Pathfinder Force it was all a question of time. **1959** R. COLLIER *City that wouldn't Die* i. 22 As pathfinders their function was to spotlight the target..with thousands of chandelier flares and incendiary bombs. **1973** *Nature* 2 Mar. 67/1 He was an inventor and an innovator, a path-finder and prognosticator. **1977** 10 June 16/3 A former wartime Path-finder with DFC and Bar. **1888** *Pall Mall G.* 30 Aug. 14/1 The higher capacities of the mountaineer, the instinct of *path-finding. **1943** *Jane's All World's Aircraft 1942* p. iv/2 The success.. was contributed to by the introduction of the system of path-finding. **1944** *Living off Land* iv. 85 Accurate path-finding in the bush..tests your common sense. **1948** H. BRIGHOUSE in J. Marriott *Best One-Act Plays 1946–47* 145 Well, pathfinding for Bomber Command..so a bit of marine navigation wasn't beyond me. **1961** *Listener* 30 Nov. 908/1 The development of radio aids and path-finding techniques was proceeding. **1978** R. V. JONES *Most Secret War* xviii. 148 KGr 100's pathfinding role. **1634** MOUFET *Insect. Theat.* I. xii. 75 In semitis..invenitur..unde ab Anglis vocatur *The gray *path flye.* **1753** CHAMBERS *Cycl. Supp.*, *Path-fly*, the name given by us to the fly called in Latin *humisuga*; it is found in foot-paths, and supposed to live by sucking the ground. **1877** TYNDALL *Fragm. Sc.*, *Sc. & Man*, Two great *Path-hewers, as the Germans call them. **1949** S. SILVER *Microwave Antenna* iv. 123 Fermat's principle: The optical ray or rays from a source at a point P_1 to a point of observation P_2 is the curve along which the optical *path length is stationary with respect to infinitesimal variations of path. **1956** *Nature* 10 Mar. 469/1 The summary of section A contains a useful review..of resonance and pulse velocity tests... An important omission ..is mention of the practical difficulty of measuring path-lengths sufficiently accurately in testing insitu concrete structures by the pulse velocity method. **1971** *New Scientist* 3 June 566/1 Long path-length spectroscopy is made plausible by the combination of high intensity and directionality. **1799** *Upper Canada Gaz.* (York, Ontario) 29 June 3/2 The public are much indebted to Mr. John McDougal, who was appointed one of the *path-masters at the last town meeting, for his great assiduity and care in getting the streets cleared of the many and dangerous (especially at night) constructions therein. **1869** *Rep. Comm. Agric. 1868* (U.S. Dept. Agric.) 348 The immediate supervision of construction and repairs is generally under the direction of local 'road supervisors', or 'path masters', as they are termed in some districts. **1959** *Maclean's Mag.* 20 June 83/2 The name was changed about 40 years ago because Gottlieb Watts, town path-master, could not spell it. **1968** E. S. RUSSENHOLT *Heart of Continent* IV. xi. 206 The Department of Agriculture orders that pathmasters cut weedy grain, and have the work charged to landowners. **1896** *Westm. Gaz.* 21 Nov. 7/2 His prettiest machine being a fine *path-racer. *a* **1862** THOREAU *Yankee in Canada* iii. (1866) 42 A little one-story chapel-like building..close to the *path-side. **1887** *Century Mag.* Sept. 704/1 The *path-walker is..plugging the smallest holes with sod... In ordinary times each walker has a stretch of fourteen miles to watch.

path. (pæθ), *sb.*² Also written without full stop. Abbrev. of PATHOLOGY. Freq. *attrib.*

1937 'J. BELL' *Murder in Hospital* xii. 233 He does not appear to have had any path. tests done. **1944** H. ASHTON *Yeoman's Hospital* xi. 239, I always hoped he'd land that job he wanted..in the Path. Lab. there. **1965** K. GILES *Some Beasts no More* v. 137 Sir Shelly diagnosed leukemia and it was confirmed by path. Prognosis was twelve months. **1968** C. WATSON *Charity ends at Home* vii. 90 He's like a kid in the bath when he gets into that path lab. **1972** *Guardian* 20 June 16/4 People rather miss out on their psychi, because it happens to coincide with path finals. **1978** N. FREELING *Night Lords* xiv. 61 You find a suicide which..is a phony. We wait for the path. report.

†**path,** *v. Obs.* [OE. *pæþþan*, *peþþan*, f. *pæþ*, PATH *sb.*¹: cf. MLG. *pedden* to tread. But the vb. may have been formed anew in ME. and 16th c.: cf. MHG. *pfaden* to make a path.]

1. *trans.* To go upon or along, to 'tread' (a way, etc.). *lit.* or *fig.*

a **1000** *Riddles* lxxi. 10 Ic..mearcpaðas Walas træd, moras pæðde. *a* **1000** *Boeth. Metr.* xxxi. 10 Sume fotum twam foldan peðþaþ, sume fierfete. **1577** WHETSTONE *Life Gascoigne* xiv, I left this vaine to path the vertuous waies. **1598** DRAYTON *Heroic. Ep.* xiv. 91 Pathing young Henries unadvised wayes. **1612** —— *Poly-olb.* ii. 24 Where, from the neighbouring hills her passage Wey doth path. **1728** RAMSAY *Robt., Richy, & Sandy* 32 My tup that bears the bell And paths the snaw. **1807** J. BARLOW *Columb.* v. 48 The dales disclose Their meadows path'd with files of savage foes.

2. To tread, beat down by treading, as a path; usually *fig.*

1642 ROGERS *Naaman* 423 [They] become more pathed in their sinnes by much beating upon. *a* **1653** BINNING *Serm.* (1845) 138 They choose the way that is best pathed and trodden. **1765** J. BROWN *Chr. Jrnl.* (1814) 287 What a mercy for weak and halt me that the way is here pathed.

3. *intr.* To go in or as in a path; to pursue one's course. Also *refl.* in same sense.

1598 DRAYTON *Heroic. Ep.*, *Rosamond to Hen. II* Notes, Poems (1605) 5 This Riuer did so strangely path it selfe, that the foote seemed to touch the head. **1601** SHAKS. *Jul. C.* II. i. 83 For if thou path thy natiue semblance on, Not Erebus it selfe were dimme enough, To hide thee from preuention.

4. *trans.* To pave. (Perh. prop. *pathe.*)

[App. either a simple phonetic substitution of *ð* for *v*; or from the association of a *path* with *paving*; or due to the two causes combined. Cf. PATHING, PATHMENT.]

c **1400** MAUNDEV. (1839) xxxi. 307 The stretes also ben pathed of the same stones [*Roxb.* xxxiv. 152 þe stretez er paued, *Fr.* les rues sount bien paues de tiels pierres]. *c* **1440** CAPGRAVE *Life St. Kath.* v. 285 A strete whiche was pathed with stoon. *c* **1475** *Crabhouse Reg.* (1889) 60 The Prioresse.. set vp the ymagis and pathed the chirche and the quere. **1507** *Acc. Ld. High Treas. Scot.* III. 411 To the masons of Linlithqw that pathit the chapell. **1513** DOUGLAS *Æneis* I. vii. 9 The large stretes pathit by and by.

†**pa'thaire.** *Obs. rare*⁻¹. [Origin uncertain: Mr. Gollancz conjectures a variant of *patar*, *petar*, PETARD (*Lamb's Specimens* (1893) I. 1. 297).] ? A passionate outburst.

1592 *Arden of Feversham* III. v. E iv, Such depe pathaires lyke to a cannons burst, Dischargde against a ruinated wall, Breakes my relenting hart in thousand pieces.

Pathan (pə'tɑːn), *sb.* (*a.*) Also 7 **Pattan**, **Puttan**, 8 **Patan**, 9 **Puthan**. [Hind., f. Pashto *Pakhtun.*] The name of a Pashto-speaking people inhabiting parts of south-east Afghanistan and north-west Pakistan, also called PAKHTUN. Also *attrib.* or as *adj.*

1638 T. HERBERT *Trav.* (ed. 2) 64 Most of her Pattans were slaine. **1787** C. HAMILTON *Hist. Relation Rohilla Afgans N. Provinces Hindostan* 53 The tribe of Afgans denominated Rohees, or Rohillas, (so termed from Roh, which in the Pâtan dialect signifies a mountainous country.) **1792** *Asiatick Researches* III. 6 The principal inhabitants of the mountains, called Pársici,..seem to have been destroyed or expelled by the numerous tribes of Afghâns or Patans. **1851** H. B. EDWARDES *Year on Punjab Frontier* I. 78, The people whom we geographically call Afghans, style themselves nationally Puthâns. **1864** *Athenæum* 5 Nov. 598/3 Pathans and Sikhs inspired them with feelings very little removed from panic. **1901** KIPLING *Kim* vii. 173 Except for Mahbub Ali, and he is a Pathan, I have no friend save thee, Holy One. **1903** *Strand Mag.* May 530/1 A swarthy Pathan face grinned wickedly over a rubble heap. *Ibid.* 530/2 To compete with the..Pathan in his own hills. **1915** R. W. CAMPBELL *Private Spud Tamson* iii. 23 Once on the Frontier of India he had slaughtered ten bloodthirsty Pathans in the space of an hour. **1930** *N.Y. Times* 6 Feb. 22/6 His [*sc.* Kipling's] commissioners, syces, Pathans, and budmashes continue to be as well known as the fascinating denizens of the animal kingdom celebrated in 'The Jungle Books'. **1958** A. TOYNBEE *East to West* 128 That British century had already brought the modern world to the threshold of the Pathan highlander's hovel. **1968** *Economist* 16 Nov. 31/1 Extremists..argue that the Pathans, like the Nagas, were never part of pre-partition India and should therefore be allowed to determine their own future. **1971** R. DENTRY *Encounter at Kharmel* iii. 58 Your Pathan tribesman is a realist. He enjoys cutting throats. **1973** *Times* 27 July 16/3 The Pathans are estimated to account for half the present population of Afghanistan. **1976** *Spare Rib* Nov. 12/1 It was the case of a Pathan family. The Pathans are often very orthodox Muslims—sometimes religious fanatics.

pathed (pɑːθt, pæ-), *ppl. a. rare.* [f. PATH *v.* or *sb.* + -ED.] †**a.** Beaten or trodden down as a path. *Obs.* **b.** Having or furnished with a path.

1597–8 BP. HALL *Sat.*, *Defiance Envie* 22 Nor suttle Snake doth lurke in pathed wayes. *c* **1614** SIR W. MURE *Dido & Æneas* I. 5 Path'd wayes I trace, as Theseus in his neid. **1900** *Daily News* 21 July 3/1 A huge hayfield, not fenced-in, geometrically bisected, pathed hayfield, but a hayfield run wild.

pathematic (pæθɪ'mætɪk), *a. rare.* [ad. Gr. παθηματικ-ός liable to passions or emotions, f. πάθημα what one suffers, suffering emotion, f. stem παθ-: see PATHETIC.] Pertaining to the passions or emotions; caused or characterized by emotion.

1822 GOOD *Study Med.* IV. 203 In the Pathematic variety [of complicated labour], the joint emotions..operative upon the patient's mind,..are bashfulness..and apprehension for her own safety. **1830** MACKINTOSH *Eth. Philos.* Wks. 1846 I. 161 We find no trace..of any distinction between the percipient, and what perhaps we may venture to call the emotive, or pathematic part of human nature. **1895** *Pop. Sci. Monthly* Jan. 384 Which..accounts for the loss of hair as a pathematic symptom.

So **pathe'matically** *adv.*; **pa,thema'tology**, the doctrine of passions or affections of the mind.

1811–31 BENTHAM *Logic* Wks. 1843 VIII. 230/1 Pathematically passive, corresponding to those corporeal impressions which are accompanied either with pleasure or pain. *Ibid.* App. 288/1 Pathematology: by this name may be designated the science of psychology, in so far as pleasure or pain are taken for the subject of it. **1857** MAYNE *Expos. Lex.*, *Pathematologia*, term for the doctrine of passion or affection of the mind: pathematology.

pathetic (pəˈθɛtɪk), *a.* (*sb.*) Also 6–7 **pathetique**. [ad. late L. *pathētic-us*, a. Gr. παθητικός sensitive, f. παθητός liable to suffer, f. παθ-, root of πάσχειν to suffer and πάθος suffering. Cf. F. *pathétique* (16th c. in Hatz.-Darm.), It. *patetico*.]

A. *adj.* **1.** Producing an effect upon the emotions; exciting the passions or affections; moving, stirring, affecting. †**a.** In general sense. *Obs.*

1598 MARSTON *Sco. Villanie* x. Hiij b, Some new pathetique Tragedy. **1665** BOYLE *Occas. Refl.* IV. ix. (1848) 224 The more Instructive and Pathetick passages. **1762** SYMMER in Ellis *Orig. Lett.* Ser. II. IV. 450 A very proper speech, delivered in a noble and pathetic manner.

b. In modern use: Affecting the tender emotions; exciting a feeling of pity, sympathy, or sadness; full of pathos.

1737 POPE *Hor. Epist.* II. i. 232 The Boys and Girls whom charity maintains, Implore your help in these pathetic strains. **1749** FIELDING *Tom Jones* XIV. vi, Mrs. Miller.. saying, in the most pathetic voice, 'Good Heaven! let me preserve one of my children at least.' **1798** FERRIAR *Illustr. Sterne* vi. 174 There is one passage..which the circumstances of Sterne's death render pathetic. **1829** LYTTON *Devereux* I. ii. Our parting with our uncle was quite pathetic. **1885** CLODD *Myths & Dr.* II. x. 212 Indian mothers in pathetic custom drop their milk on the lips of the dead child.

c. Used *adverbially*.

1725 POPE *Odyss.* IV. 149 Thus pathetic to the Prince he spoke. **1792** *Munchausen's Trav.* xxvi. 119, I spoke as pathetic as possible.

†**2.** Expressing or arising from passion or strong emotion; passionate, earnest. *Obs.*

1648 J. BEAUMONT *Psyche* II. cxc, Her cordial Thanks and her pathetick Vows. **1681** D'URFEY *Progr. Honesty* viii, She out of patience grows, And quells the little Rebel with pathetick blows. **1755** YOUNG *Centaur* v. Wks. 1757 IV. 241 Heaven..joins my pathetic wish.

†**3.** ? Causing a physical sensation or affection; affecting the bodily senses. *Obs. rare.*

1653 R. MASON *Let. to Auth.* in *Bulwer's Anthropomet.*, The stem, bark, leaves, and fruit are of such various.. pathetique qualities.

4. Pertaining or relating to the passions or emotions of the mind. (In early use applied to bodily movements expressive of emotion.)

1649 BULWER *Pathomyot.* I. iv. 16 That species of motion which they call Pathetique. **1681** tr. *Willis' Rem. Med. Wks.*, *Five Treat.* xvii. 117 This Nerve..serves also for the producing some pathetick motions of the Eye. **1719** SWIFT *To Yng. Clergym.* Wks. 1755 II. II. 7 Tully considered the dispositions of a..less mercurial nation, by dwelling almost entirely on the pathetick part.

b. Phr. ***pathetic fallacy***, the attribution of human response or emotion to inanimate nature. (First used by John Ruskin.)

1856 RUSKIN *Mod. Paint.* III. IV. xii. §5. 160 All violent feelings..produce..a falseness in..impressions of external things, which I would generally characterize as the 'Pathetic fallacy'. **1856** GEO. ELIOT in *Westm. Rev.* Apr. 631 Mr. Ruskin..enters on his special subject, namely landscape painting. With that intense interest in landscape which is a peculiar characteristic of modern times, is associated the 'Pathetic Fallacy'—the transference to external objects of the spectator's own emotions. **1895** C. H. HERFORD *Spenser's Shepheards Calender* p. xlviii, Pastoral nature is founded upon the 'pathetic fallacy'. **1906** W. W. GREG *Pastoral Poetry & Pastoral Drama* 93 We have here a specific inversion of the 'pathetic fallacy'. **1930** H. S. V. JONES *Spenser Handbk.* III. 64 Each elegy opens with an apostrophe to the poet's verse, and each illustrates what Ruskin called the 'pathetic fallacy'. **1930** L. POWYS (*title*) The pathetic fallacy: a study of Christianity. **1959** *Listener* 6 Aug. 223/2 Many awaited death..while the pathetic fallacy laboured away with ill winds and rain. **1968** *Ibid.* 18 Jan. 68/3 To believe that a television station should be part of its audience could seem like the Pathetic Fallacy (Communications Division), a piece of electronic anthropomorphism. **1975** M. C. DAVIS *Near Woods* v. 83 The next morning I fell under the spell of literature's pathetic fallacy at nearly every step. **1977** D WATKIN *Morality & Archit.* II. ii. 38 Le Corbusier's argument.. combines succinctly the pathetic fallacies we are investigating: that particular types of architectural form are morally regenerative and physically health-giving.

5. *Anat.* A name for the fourth pair of cranial nerves, also called *trochlear*. So ***pathetic muscle***, the superior oblique muscle of the eyeball, connected with the trochlear nerve.

1681 tr. *Willis' Rem. Med. Wks.* Vocab., *Pathetic*, to passion belonging, nerves so called by Dr. Willis. [Cf. quot. 1681 in 4, and PATHETICAL 4.] **1704** J. HARRIS *Lex. Techn.* I, *Pathetick Nerves*, are the Fourth pair arising from the Top of the Medulla Oblongata. **1842** DUNGLISON *Dict. Med. Sc.*, *Pathetic*, a name given to the superior oblique muscle of the eye, and, also, to a nerve. **1881** MIVART *Cat* 271 The fourth pair of nerves, called also the Trochlear or Pathetic. **1893** *Syd. Soc. Lex.*, *Pathetic muscle*, the *Obliquus superior* muscle of the eyeball, ..fancifully supposed to express, by its action, the passions and affections.

6. Miserably inadequate; so poor as to be ridiculous. *colloq.*

1937 PARTRIDGE *Dict. Slang* 609/2 *Pathetic*, ludicrous. **1969** *Listener* 10 July 41/1 The military government clearly thinks it is established for good. The alleged plots against it are either mythical or, when genuine, pathetic. **1974** *Liverpool Echo* (Football ed.) 26 Oct. 3/2 The standard of refereeing in English soccer is pathetic. There is no consistency.

B. *absol.* or as *sb.*

1. *absol.* ***the pathetic***: that which is pathetic; pathetic quality, expression, or feeling.

1712 ADDISON *Spect.* No. 339 ¶1 The Pathetick..may animate and inflame the Sublime, but is not essential to it. **1858** DICKENS *Lett.* (1880) II. 59, I very much doubt the Irish capacity of receiving the pathetic.

2. †**a.** *sing.* Pathetic language, feeling, etc.; pathos, or the expression of pathos. *Obs.*

1667 WATERHOUSE *Fire Lond.* 84 Holy Job's pathetique is upon a like dismal accident. *a* **1849** H. COLERIDGE *Ess.* (1851) II. 218 What a contrast to the drunken pathetic of his weeping client!

b. *pl.* Pathetic expressions or sentiments: cf. *heroics*.

1748 RICHARDSON *Clarissa* (1810) I. xxxiii. 248 Miss Pert, none of your pathetics, except in the right place. **1838** DICKENS *Nich. Nick.* ii, [He] went at once into such deep pathetics, that he knocked the first speaker clean out of the course. **1894** D. C. MURRAY *Making of Novelist* 212, I find pathetics among them, and quaint humours.

3. *pl.* The study of the passions or emotions.

1896 *Id'er* Mar. 263/2 Pathological Pathetics..had.. almost monopolised the conversation. **1899** *Westm. Gaz.* 12 Jan. 1/3 Pathetics is, or should be, the name of a study of the effects on a personality caused by an artistic appeal to the emotions.

4. *Anat.* Short for *pathetic nerve*: see A. 5.

pathetical (pəˈθɛtɪkəl), *a.* Now *rare.* [f. as prec. + -AL[1].]

1. = PATHETIC A. 1.

1573 G. HARVEY *Letter-bk.* (Camden) 32 Certain loud pathetical exclamations, and broad hyperboles. **1588** SHAKS. *L.L.L.* I. ii. 103 Sweet inuocation of a childe, most pretty and pathetical. **1660** F. BROOKE tr. *Le Blanc's Trav.* 129 They..play on flutes doleful and pathetical straines, to excite devotion. **1712** HUGHES *Spect.* No. 541 ¶7 That pathetical Soliloquy of Cardinal Wolsey on his Fall. **1859** KINGSLEY *Misc.* (1860) I. 64 In one page.., Elizabeth is a fool for listening to these pathetical 'love letters'; in the next she is hard-hearted for not listening to them.

†**2.** = PATHETIC A. 2. *Obs.*

1604 R. CAWDREY *Table Alph.*, *Patheticall*, vehement, full of passions, or mouing affections. **1648** MILTON *Tenure Kings* (1650) 13 The pathetical words of a Psalme can be no certaine decision to a poynt. **1662** GURNALL *Chr. in Arm.* verse 18. I. viii. (1669) 347/2 Thou may'st pray much in these pathetical Sallies of thy Soul to Heaven.

†**3.** = PATHETIC A. 4. *Obs.*

1603 HOLLAND *Plutarch's Mor.* 67 Prudence and wisedome..reduceth the power of this sensuall and patheticall part, unto a civill and honest habitude.

†**4.** = PATHETIC A. 5. *Obs.*

1681 tr. *Willis' Rem. Med. Wks.*, *Five Treat.* xiv. 110 Wherefore from this..conjecture..concerning the use of these Nerves, we have called them Pathetical.

pathetically (pəˈθɛtɪkəlɪ), *adv.* [f. prec. + -LY[2].] In a pathetic manner.

1. So as to excite passion or emotion; movingly, affectingly. †**a.** In general sense. *Obs.*

1592 G. HARVEY *Four Lett.* iii. Wks. (Grosart) I. 195 Patheticallie intermixt with sundry dolefull pageantes. **1661** BOYLE *Style of Script.* (1675) 247 Some devout composures are so pathetically penned, that [etc.]. *a* **1797** H. WALPOLE *Mem. Geo. II* (1847) I. viii. 243 This Mr. Pelham answered finely, seriously, and pathetically.

b. So as to excite pity or other tender emotion; in a way full of pathos.

1739 CIBBER *Apol.* (1756) II. 99 Wilks..seem'd more pathetically to feel, look, and express his calamity. **1824** GALT *Rothelan* I. II. x. 232 Pathetically ruminating on the vanity of human wishes. **1896** MRS. CAFFYN *Quaker Grandmother* 269 Her lips drooped pathetically;..her eyes filled with real tears.

†**2.** With passion or strong emotion; passionately, vehemently; feelingly, earnestly. *Obs.*

1602 MARSTON *Antonio's Rev.* IV. ii, I do hate a foole most most pathetically. **1663** BLAIR *Autobiog.* viii. (1848) 105 A gracious woman pathetically pouring out her heart to God. **1712** PARNELL *Spect.* No. 460 ¶11 The Duty of the Place [Church]..being..pathetically performed.

†**3.** So as to express emotion. *Obs.*

1681 tr. *Willis' Rem. Med. Wks.*, *Five Treat.* xvii. 120 The parts of the Face, usually moved pathetically and unthought of. [Cf. PATHETIC A. 4, 5, PATHETICAL 4.]

paˈtheticalness. Now *rare* or *Obs.* [f. as prec. + -NESS.] = PATHETICNESS.

a **1607** BRIGHTMAN *Bright Rediv.* ii. (1647) 26 He doth with great Patheticalnesse of affection breake forthe to the prosecuting of the Doctrine of Scandall in generall. **1725** BLACKWALL *Sacred Classics* (1727) I. 339 The patheticalness, grace and dignity of the sentence.

paˈtheticate, *v.* *nonce-wd.* [f. PATHETIC + -ATE[3]: cf. *authenticate*.] *trans.* To make pathetic.

1885 *Academy* 3 Oct. 221/1 To see how Bishop Percy sentimentalized and patheticated the old ballad.

†**paˈtheticly,** *adv. Obs. rare.* [f. as prec. + -LY[2].] = PATHETICALLY.

1616 J. LANE *Cont. Sqr.'s T.* v. 596 The motives weare vrgd so patheticklie. **1669** GALE *Crt. Gentiles* I. III. x. 105 His Orator that speaks patheticly.

paˈtheticness. *rare.* [f. as prec. + -NESS.] Pathetic quality or character.

1874 'OUIDA' *Two Wooden Shoes* v. 98 The familiar history had a new patheticness for her.

pathetism (ˈpæθɪtɪz(ə)m). ? *Obs.* [f. Gr. παθητός passive + -ISM.] A name for mesmerism or animal magnetism. So **ˈpathetist**, a mesmerist.

1852 A. BALLOU *Spir. Manifestations* ix. 131 Placing the phenomena [of spiritualism] on the same footing with those of Pathetism, Biology [etc.]. **1890** *Cent. Dict.*, *Pathetist*.

Pathet Lao (pəˈtɛt laʊ). [Laotian Thai, lit. 'land of the Lao'.] A communist guerrilla movement and political party (after December 1975 the ruling party) in Laos. Also *attrib.*

1954 *Times* 10 May 6/3 Earlier in the day statements by the two leaders—Mr. Son Ngoc Minh for the Khmer and Mr. Souvannouvong for the Pathet Lao—had been distributed to the Press... The Pathet Lao claim was to control half the territory. **1966** 'A. HALL' *9th Directive* xxvi. 236 The territory..is in the hands of the Pathet Lao, which takes orders from Peking. **1968** H. TOYE *Laos* v. 136 It was not long before they reached an area where the local Pathet Lao organization could protect them. **1970** LANGER & ZASLOFF *N. Vietnam & Pathet Lao* vi. 100 Prior to the Geneva Conference of 1962, the Soviet advisory role to the Pathet Lao had been very brief. **1970** *Peace News* 8 May 3/2 A Cambodian Communist Party has existed since the end of the second world war, when it fought shoulder-to-shoulder with the Pathet Lao, and the Vietminh. **1977** *Bangladesh Times* 20 Jan. 7/4 The Laotian authorities have set up a committee to censor every thing written, sung, recited or danced, the Pathet Lao news agency Khao San reported today.

pathic (ˈpæθɪk), *sb.* and *a.* [ad. L. *pathic-us*, a. Gr. παθικός suffering, remaining passive, f. stem παθ- suffer.]

A. *sb.* **1.** A man or boy upon whom sodomy is practised; a catamite. Now *rare.*

1603 B. JONSON *Sejanus* I. i, He..was the noted Pathick of the time. **1718** PRIDEAUX *Connection O. & N. Test.* II. II. 101 The first was his pathic, the second his concubine. **1795** MACKNIGHT *Apost. Epist.* (1820) I. 495 The persons who suffered this abuse were called pathics, and affected the dress and behaviour of women. **1972** STEDMAN *Med. Dict.* (ed. 22) 930/1 *Pathic*, a person who assumes the passive role in any abnormal sexual act.

2. One who suffers or undergoes something. Now *rare* or *Obs.*

1636 MASSINGER *Bashf. Lover* v. i, A mere pathic to Thy devilish art. **1649** JER. TAYLOR *Gt. Exemp.* I. Disc. iii. 92 Pathicks in Devotion, suffering ravishments of Senses. **1860** *Illustr. Lond. News* 26 May 506/2 The pathic looks like an especial goose during the operation.

B. *adj.* **1.** That is the subject of sodomy; being, or pertaining to, a catamite. Now *rare.*

1657 THORNLEY tr. *Longus' Daphnis & Chloe* 196 To become Gnatho's Pathic-boy. **1693** TATE in *Dryden's Juvenal* ii. (1697) 26 Thy Form seems for the Pathick Trade design'd. **1802** GIFFORD tr. *Juvenal* ii. 144 A mirror—pathic Otho's boast. **1959** *N. & Q.* Dec. 435/2 The Pardoner's pathic role in the perverted relationship thus suggested is clearly indicated in A 691.

2. Undergoing something, passive. Also, that suffers from disease or disorder.

1857 MAYNE, *Pathicus*, remaining passive: pathic. **1902** W. A. HAMMOND *Aristotle's Psychol.* p. lxviii, Desire, as Aristotle employs it, is not a purely pathic or affective element. **1940** HINSIE & SHATZKY *Psychiatric Dict.* 404/1 *Pathic*,..pertaining to or affected by disease or disorder. **1951** S. F. NADEL *Found. Social Anthropol.* xi. 291 Vague states of feeling ('pathic states', as they have been called). **1973** M. AMIS *Rachel Papers* 148 Rachel received this idiot outpouring with a pathic nod.

3. Pertaining to suffering or disease; morbid. *rare.*

1853 in DUNGLISON *Med. Lex.* **1893** in *Syd. Soc. Lex.*

Hence **ˈpathically** *adv.*, in a passive manner; **pathicism** (ˈpæθɪsɪz(ə)m), the practice of a pathic.

1879 LEWIS & SHORT *Lat. Dict.*, *Patientia*..B. In partic[ular], submission to unnatural lust, pathicism. **1934** *Mind* XLIII. 300 The root notion..seems to be that the given must be passively, or (should I say?) pathically received.

†**ˈpathing,** *vbl. sb. Obs.* [f. PATH *v.* 4 + -ING[1].] = PAVING *vbl. sb.*

1428–9 *Norwich Sacr. Roll* (MS.), Duobus Masons pro pathyng juxta Sanctum Willelmum. **1491–2** *Ibid.*, Roberto Blome pro le pathyng in parte boriali summi altaris. **1504–5** *Ibid.*, Pro petalis, [gloss] an[ce] pathyng stones. **1541** in Kirkpatrick *Relig. Ord. Norwich* (1845) 52 [Seventeen loads of small] Pathyng tyle [or pavements as we now call them].

pathless (ˈpɑːθlɪs, ˈpæ-), *a.* [f. PATH *sb.*[1] + -LESS.] Having no path through or across it; destitute of paths; untrodden, trackless. Also *fig.*

1591 SYLVESTER *Du Bartas* I. v. 199 What Guide conducteth..your Legions Through path-less paths in unacquainted Regions? **1631** CHAPMAN *Cæsar & Pompey* Plays 1873 III. 170 Striving to entangle men In pathlesse error. **1697** DAMPIER *Voy.* (1729) I. 14 Having travelled 7 miles in those wild pathless Woods. **1734** THOMSON *Liberty* III. 42 Orbs, Myriads on Myriads, thro' the pathless Sky, Unerring roll. **1873** J. GEIKIE *Gt. Ice Age* v. 52 In the silent and pathless desolations of central Greenland.

Hence **ˈpathlessness**.

1851 HAWTHORNE *Snow Image*, etc. (1879) 92 The street ..resolved into a drearier pathlessness than when the forest covered it. **1889** *Spectator* 13 Apr., An African forest..may stretch, like the forest of Aruwhimi, in unbroken gloom and pathlessness over an area equal to five Englands.

pathlet ('pɑːθlɪt, 'pæ-). *rare.* [f. as prec. + -LET.] A little or diminutive path.

1796 W. MARSHALL *W. England* II. 325 This pathlet was formed with the frame level in hand. **1896** A. J. C. HARE *Story of my Life* (1900) VI. xxv. 175 An old man..guided me up a steep pathlet in the rocks.

† **'pathment.** *Sc. Obs.* Also 4 **payth-**, 4–5 **paith-**, 5 **pathe-**, 6 **paithe-**, **paithtment.** [app. an alteration of *pavement* (*pament*, *payment*) after *path*, due to similarity of sound and association of meaning: cf. PATH *v.* 4.] = PAVEMENT. (In quot. *c* 1470, the ground.)

c **1375** *Sc. Leg. Saints* xviii. (*Egipciane*) 719 þan done I fel one þe paythment. *c* **1425** WYNTOUN *Cron.* v. xi. 3704 To stampe on halowyd pathement. *c* **1470** HENRY *Wallace* VIII. 936 The paithment was cled in tendyr greyn. **1538** *Aberdeen Regr.* XVII. (Jam.), The paithtment of the kirk. **1644** in W. Ross *Pastoral Wk. in Covenant. Times* ii. 27 Sums of money ..for pathment-stones.

patho- ('pæθəʊ, pə'θɒ), repr. Gr. παθο-, comb. form of πάθος suffering, disease, etc. (see PATHOS), used in scientific and technical terms, for the more important of which see their alphabetical places.

,patho-ana'tomical *a.*, pertaining to morbid anatomy. **,pathobio'logical** *a.*, relating to living organisms (e.g. bacteria) which cause disease; so **,pathobi'ologist**, one who studies these. **pathobi'ology**, the study of the biological processes associated with diseased or injured tissue. **'pathogerm**, a germ that causes disease; hence **patho'germic** *a.*, pertaining to or of the nature of a pathogerm. ‖**patho'mania**: see quot. **pa'thometer**, a (hypothetical) instrument for measuring the passions or emotions. **pa'thometry**, (*a*) the measuring, estimation, or diagnosis of different diseases; (*b*) measurement of the passions or emotions. **,pathomy'otomist** *nonce-wd.* [f. *Pathomyotomia*: see quot. 1649], one who studies the muscles concerned in the expression of emotions. ‖**patho'phobia**, (*a*) morbid dread of disease, hypochondria; (*b*) morbid fear of any kind. **patho'phoric**, **pa'thophorous** *adjs.* [Gr. -φόρος bearing], conveying or causing disease. ‖**patho'pœia** [Gr. -ποιία a making], (*a*) *Rhet.* a speech or figure of speech designed to arouse passion or emotion; (*b*) *Path.* production of disease; so **patho'pœous** *a.* [Gr. -ποιός making], producing disease.

1888 *Amer. Nat.* Feb. 113 Frank P. Billings, Director of the *Patho-Biological Laboratory of the State University of Nebraska. *Ibid.* 117 It is far more practical for *pathobiologists to stick to the name cocci for all round objects (not spores). **1971** LAVIA & HILL *Princ. Pathobiol.* i. 4 This is the subject of *pathobiology—the alterations in normal biological mechanisms that occur in response to injury. **1972** *Lancet* 20 May 1104/1 Pathobiology (a trendy name for general pathology) seems to be a fashionable subject in the United States. **1975** *Amer. Jrnl. Path.* LXXIX. 183 Pathobiology of an endocrine disease. **1897** *Daily News* 9 Dec. 8/5 It was the *patho-germ which was deadly,..the microbe was inimical to the pathogerm. **1887** A. M. BROWN *Anim. Alkal.* 158 Dr. Koch..thought he had found the *pathogermic entity. **1853** DUNGLISON *Med. Lex.*, **Pathomania*, a morbid perversion of the natural feelings, affections, inclinations..and natural impulses, without any remarkable disorder..of the intellect. **1899** *Westm. Gaz.* 12 Jan. 1/3 We believe that machines (which should naturally be called *pathometers) for registering the physical effect of music on hearers..have been planned. **18..** MOXON in *Lancet* (O.), The poor little thing..who, only seven years old and having tubercle in the brain, said it wasn't headache he suffered from, it was pain in the head. Pitifully accurate *pathometry for such a time of life. **1899** *Westm. Gaz.* 12 Jan. 1/3 A..rough-and-ready observation in pathometry. [**1649** BULWER (*title*) Pathomyotomia: or a Dissection Of the significative Muscles of the Affections of the Minde.] **1657–83** EVELYN *Hist. Relig.* (1850) I. 234 Passions..with the *Pathomyotomists are, as it were, the muscles of the soul. **1866** A. FLINT *Princ. Med.* (1880) 854 The name hypochondriasis..has very little significance as indicating the character..of the affection. The name *pathophobia is much more expressive. **1897** *Allbutt's Syst. Med.* VIII. 750 *Pathophoric bacilli. **1678** PHILLIPS, **Pathopœa*, an Expression of a Passion, in Rhetorick it is a figure by which the mind is moved to hatred, anger, or pity. **1857** MAYNE *Expos. Lex.*, *Pathopœia*, term for the induction, production, or formation of affections or diseases. *Pathopœus*, inducing or creating..diseases; *pathopeous.

pathogen ('pæθəʊdʒɛn). Also **-gene.** [f. PATHO- + -GEN.] Any agent that causes disease, esp. a micro-organism.

1880 *Libr. Univ. Knowl.* (N.Y.) VI. 647 Pathogen [the micrococcus of] contagion. **1942** E. C. STAKMAN in *Aerobiology* (Amer. Assoc. Adv. Sci. Publ. No. 17) 2/1 The possible aerial dissemination of pathogens of domestic animals by air currents is a relatively unexplored field. **1970** M. TRESHOW *Environment & Plant Response* ii. 17 Contrary to common belief, a pathogen technically does not have to be an organism or virus. A pathogen can be any component of the physical environment, including adverse climate, soil, or air relations. **1972** *Daily Colonist* (Victoria, B.C.) 8 Feb. 6/2 Diener said the new agent, which he described as a 'novel type of pathogen' or disease-causing agent, is about 80 times smaller than the smallest known virus.

pathogenesis (pæθəʊ'dʒɛnɪsɪs). *Med.* and *Path.* [f. PATHO- + GENESIS.] Production or development of disease; the process or manner of origination of a disease or bodily affection. Also **pathogenesy** (-'dʒɛnɪsɪ), **pathogeny** (pə'θɒdʒɪnɪ), in same sense. So **pathogenetic** (-dʒɪ'nɛtɪk), **pathogenic** (-'dʒɛnɪk), **pathogenous** (pə'θɒdʒɪnəs) *adjs.*, producing, or relating to the production of, disease or bodily affection; **pathogenicity** (-dʒɪ'nɪsɪtɪ), the quality or capacity of producing disease; **pathoge'netically**, **patho'genically** *advs.*, as regards pathogenesis.

1876 tr. *Wagner's Gen. Pathol.* (ed. 6) 235 Not more certainly known is the *pathogenesis of the..acute dropsies ..in tropical countries. **1897** *Trans. Amer. Pediatric Soc.* IX. 168*j*, Heredity is a most potent factor in all pathogenesis. **1898** *Allbutt's Syst. Med.* V. 1015 A contracted mitral orifice, evidently of slow pathogenesis. **1882** A. C. POPE *Homœopathy* 41 A medicine, the *pathogenesy of which may bear a likeness to several forms of disease. **1887** *Homeop. World* 1 Nov. 490 The medicine has in its pathogenesy many symptoms of a neuralgic character. **1838** H. DUNSFORD (*title*) The *Pathogenetic Effect of some of the Principal Homœopathic Remedies, translated from the German. **1899** *Allbutt's Syst. Med.* VI. 249 Infective emboli containing pathogenetic bacteria. **1928** *Amer. Jrnl. Path.* IV. 632 Primary and secondary contracted kidneys in this respect are *pathogenetically identical. **1972** ARONSON & ELLIOTT *Ocular Inflammation* xi. 258/2 Pathogenetically, the diffuse fundus lesion presents as a disseminated metastatic choroiditis,..relatively early in life. **1852** TH. ROSS *Humboldt's Trav.* II. xx. 246 In the torrid zone..the people multiply *pathogenic causes at will. **1896** *Allbutt's Syst. Med.* I. 70 Under ordinary pathogenic conditions suppuration is induced by the growth of micro-organisms within the tissues. **1904** *Brit. Med. Jrnl.* 10 Sept. 559 The cells *pathogenically affected by a toxin may not be the cells of origin or antitoxin. **1899** A. C. HOUSTON in *Nature* 7 Sept. 434/2 Allowing..virulent bacilli..to develop and display their full power of *pathogenicity. **1886** *Sci. Amer.* 4 Dec. 354/3 The distinction of the bacteria into *pathogenous and non-pathogenous is here unimportant. **1842** DUNGLISON *Med. Lex.*, **Pathogeny*, the branch of pathology, which relates to the generation, production, and development of disease. **1898** J. HUTCHINSON in *Arch. Surg.* IX. No. 36. 351 It would be unwise to assume that in that fact its whole pathogeny is included.

pathogerm, -germic: see PATHO-.

pathognomic (pæθəg'nɒmɪk), *a.* [f. PATHOGNOMY + -IC (παθογνωμικός in Gr. is said to be 'a false form').]

1. Of or pertaining to pathognomy, or to the signs and expression of the passions or feelings.

1681 tr. *Willis' Rem. Med. Wks.* Vocab., *Pathognomic*, that moveth the affections. *c* **1714** POPE, etc. *Mem. M. Scriblerus* I. xi, He has the true pathognomic sign of love. **1827** CARLYLE *Germ. Rom.* I. 178 Count Ernst had a fine pathognomic eye. **1837–9** HALLAM *Hist. Lit.* (1847) III. 403 The possession of speech, the pathognomic countenance, the efficiency of the hand, a longevity beyond the lower animals.

2. = PATHOGNOMONIC.

1684 tr. *Bonet's Merc. Compit.* VI. 185 The Pathognomick Symptome of this Disease, and that which first invaded the Patient. **1766** *Nat. Hist.* in *Ann. Reg.* 100/1 Its most pathognomic symptoms. **1872** DARWIN *Emotions* viii. 205 Constant tremulous agitation..pathognomic of the earlier stages of general paralysis.

So **patho'gnomical** *a.* = prec. 1 and 2.

1643 T. GOODWIN *Trial Christian's Growth* 128 Such symptomes as are Pathognomicall, and proper and peculiar to them. **1874** *Edin. Rev.* July 198 With the advance of power of pathognomical expression, coincides a certain loss of grandeur.

pathognomonic (pəθɒgnəʊ'mɒnɪk), *a.* and *sb.* *Med.* and *Path.* [ad. Gr. παθογνωμονικ-ός (Galen) skilled in judging of symptoms or diseases, f. παθο-, PATHO- + γνωμονικός able to give an opinion, f. γνώμων judge, knowing person.]

A. *adj.* Applied to a sign or symptom by which a disease may be known or distinguished; specifically characteristic or indicative of a particular disease.

1625 HART *Anat. Ur.* I. ii. 19 The..absolute knowledge of the disease, by meanes of the signes Pathognomonicke, proper and peculiar to euery disease. **1693** *Phil. Trans.* XVII. 720 This..hath no Pathognomonic Sign by which it is distinguish'd from other Fevers besides its Duration. **1758** MUNCKLEY in *Phil. Trans.* L. 613 It hath been thought, that a quick pulse is so essential..as to be a pathognomonic symptom of it. **1898** P. MANSON *Trop. Diseases* iii. 77 The black pigment [in malaria] is a pathognomonic..feature.

B. *sb.* A pathognomonic sign or symptom.

[**1625** HART *Anat. Ur.* I. ii. 14 Ioyne..as most pregnant.. testimonies of the disease, these inseparable accidents of the same, commonly called *pathognomonica*.] **1704** J. HARRIS *Lex. Techn.* I, *Pathognomonick*, a Term in the Art of Medicine, is a proper inseparate Sign [etc.]. **1725** N. ROBINSON *Th. Physick* 87 Those inseparable Symptoms we call its Pathognomonics or distinguishing Characters. **1822–34** *Good's Study Med.* (ed. 4) I. 674 It is not a sympton to be depended on as a pathognomonic.

So **pathogno'monical** *a. rare.*

1638 A. READ *Chirurg.* x. 70 The only pathognomonicall signe of a true convulsion.

pathognomy (pə'θɒgnəmɪ). [f. as prec., after *physiognomy*, from Gr. φυσιογνωμονία.]

1. The knowledge or study of the passions or emotions, or of the signs or expressions of them.

1793 HOLCROFT *Lavater's Physiog.* ii. 24 Pathognomy is the knowledge of the signs of the passions. **1820** *Blackw. Mag.* VI. 651 Physiognomy takes cognizance of the shapes, and pathognomy of the motions of the features. **1874** *Edin. Rev.* July 172.

2. The knowledge of the signs or symptoms by which diseases may be distinguished. *rare.*

1822–34 *Good's Study Med.* (ed. 4) I. 546 A voluminous.. classification of pulses..This branch of pathognomy.

pa'thogony. *rare*$^{-0}$. = PATHOGENY.

1882 in OGILVIE (Annandale).

pathography. [f. PATHO- + -GRAPHY.]

a. The, or a, description of disease (Dunglison *Med. Lex.* 1853). **b.** The, or a, study of the life and character of an individual or community as influenced by a disease.

1917 C. R. PAYNE tr. *Pfister's Phychoanal. Method* xxvii. 573 The history of the Catholic sainthood affords the analytic pathography an inexhaustible material. **1959** *New Statesman* 28 Nov. 760/2 The founder of Protestantism with his fits of melancholia, his anxiety attacks, night sweats, and anguish about concupiscence, is an obvious subject for historical pathography. **1972** Q. BELL *Virginia Woolf* II. i. 20 The Japanese psychiatrist Mme Miyeko Kamiya is, I believe, preparing a pathography of Virginia Woolf.

Hence **patho'graphical** *a.*, pertaining to pathography (Mayne *Expos. Lex.* 1857); **pa'thographer**, one who writes a pathography.

1974 *Times Lit. Suppl.* 15 Mar. 256/4 The pathographer must allow for the language and limitations of the theory.

pathologic (pæθəʊ'lɒdʒɪk), *a.* [ad. Gr. παθολογικ-ός, f. παθο-, PATHO-: see -LOGIC: cf. F. *pathologique* (Cotgr. 1611).] Of or belonging to pathology.

1656 BLOUNT *Glossogr.*, *Pathologick*, pertaining to Pathologie. **1852** TH. ROSS *Humboldt's Trav.* II. xxiv. 500 That vague feeling of debility..produced by want of nutrition, and by other pathologic causes.

patho'logical, *a.* [f. as prec. + -AL[1].]

1. a. Pertaining to or dealing with pathology; relating to or treating of diseases or bodily affections.

1688 BOYLE *Final Causes Nat. Things* iv. 159 The Physiological and Pathological parts of Physick. **1809** *Med. Jrnl.* XXI. 297 He..has given up all hopes of any thing important being discovered..from pathological anatomy. **1834** J. FORBES *Laennec's Dis. Chest* x. (ed. 4) 347 Noticed by almost every pathological anatomist. **1879** CALDERWOOD *Mind & Br.* iv. 80 The interest in it was stimulated and guided by pathological observations.

b. That is or may be the subject of pathology; involving or of the nature of disease; morbid. Also in more general use.

1845–6 G. E. DAY tr. *Simon's Anim. Chem.* I. 166 In certain pathological states of the system. **1858** BUCKLE *Civiliz.* (1869) II. vii. 381 The laws of their normal and pathological development. **1894** H. DRUMMOND *Ascent of Man* 122 Conditions which are pathological in one animal are natural in others. **1921** R. S. WOODWORTH *Psychol.* (1922) i. 16 The pathological method..traces the decay or demoralization of mental life instead of its growth. **1933** E. GLOVER in S. Lorand *Psycho-Anal. Today* 192 (*title*) Pathological character formation. **1949** *Sat. Rev. Lit.* (U.S.) 25 June 11/1 For Ford, you see, was what those who were not charmed by him insisted upon describing as a pathological liar. **1951** V. NABOKOV *Speak, Memory* ii. 32 Age had developed in her a pathological stinginess. **1951** M. LOWRY *Let.* 25 Aug. (1967) 256 A himself is an almost pathological liar. **1971** *Jrnl. Gen. Psychol.* LXXXV. 64 In fact..pathological anxiety might..represent a heightened susceptibility to over-arousal.

2. Pertaining to the passions or emotions. *rare.*

1796 F. A. NITSCH *Gen. View Kant's Princ. concerning Man* 195 The pathological interest aims at the agreeable and pleasing consequences of an action. **1798** A. F. M. WILLICH *Elem. Critical Philos.* 101 A rational observance of pathological laws. **1800** COGAN *Passions* ii. §2 Its pathological effect [*i.e.* of surprise] is that of a simple stimulus whose sole object is to arouse the attention. **1894** ILLINGWORTH *Personality* iv. 105 It is not the physical effect of the desire, the mere pathological feeling, but the metaphysical action of the mental image that ultimately determines my action.

3. *Math.* Grossly abnormal in properties or behaviour, as compared with the well-behaved functions normally encountered in classical applications (see quots. 1946, 1960).

1939 I. S. SOKOLNIKOFF *Advanced Calculus* iv. 105 Such pathological behavior of continuous functions led to a careful inquiry into the meaning of such geometrical concepts as the area under a curve. **1946** H. & B. S. JEFFREYS *Methods Math. Physics* i. 17 We can speak of a function of *x* that is equal to 1 if *x* is rational but to 0 if *x* is irrational. Such a function would be fairly regarded by a physicist as pathological, and he is interested in a much narrower class of functions, roughly speaking such as can be represented by graphs. **1960** *New Scientist* 25 Aug. 537/2 The term 'pathological functions' does not name any specific functions... It is applied rather informally to functions whose behaviour appears delinquent to those who expect mathematical functions to correspond only with physical events or, conversely, to possess only properties that can be represented by a graph or in a computer. Often the 'pathological' features concern continuity and smoothness. **1968** FOX & MAYERS *Computing Methods for Scientists & Engineers* ix. 179 Examples could be constructed of pathological repeated inaccurate consistency. **1971** D. W.

SCIAMA *Mod. Cosmol.* viii. 113 In this case the geometry of space is said to be hyperbolic... The volume of the space is infinite except in pathological cases that need not concern us.

patho'logically, *adv.* [f. prec. + -LY².]

1. a. In relation to pathology, or to its subject-matter, disease.

1828–32 in WEBSTER. **1868** D. COOK *Dr. Muspratt's Patients*, etc. 228 His book..on the Heart—physiologically and pathologically considered. **1879** TYNDALL *Fragm. Sc.* (ed. 6) II. xiii. 335 The bacterium of splenic fever ..[Pasteur's] investigations regarding the part it plays pathologically.

b. Corresponding to sense 1 b of the adj.: morbidly; abnormally.

1933 *Mind* XLII. 138 In the expression of his feelings and appreciations he was almost pathologically reticent. **1978** P. G. WINSLOW *Coppergold* 75 She was pathologically jealous.

2. In relation to the passions or emotions. *rare.*

1824 DE QUINCEY tr. *Kant's Idea Univ. Hist.* Wks. XIII. 133 A social concert that had been pathologically extorted from the mere necessities of situation. **1833** CHALMERS *Const. Man* (1834) II. II. iii. 237 The objects which he chooses to entertain, and..the emotions which pathologically result from them.

patho'logico-, combining form of Gr. παθολογικός PATHOLOGICAL, used in the sense 'relating to pathology and...'; as *pathologico-anatomical* (relating to pathology and anatomy), *-clinical*, *-histological*, *-psychological* adjs.

1802–12 BENTHAM *Ration. Judic. Evid.* (1827) V. 167 The branch of the pathologico-psychological system here in question. **1855** tr. *Wedl's Rudim. Pathol. Histol.* (Syd. Soc.) Pref. 5 The pathologico-histological course pursued in this work. **1876** tr. *H. von Ziemssen's Cycl. Med.* XI. 28 Pathologico-anatomical changes in the nerves. **1899** *Allbutt's Syst. Med.* VIII. 408 Pathologico-clinical groups.

pathologist (pə'θɒlədʒɪst). [f. PATHOLOGY + -IST.] One versed in pathology (see also quots. 1971, 1977); a student of or writer upon diseases.

1650 CHARLETON tr. *van Helmont's Incongruities Deflux.* Translator to Rdr., No one..among the numerous swarm of Pathologists, has discoursed of the nature and causes of such Diseases. *a* **1862** BUCKLE *Civiliz.* (1869) III. v. 417 The philosophic pathologist is as different from the physician, as a jurist is different from an advocate. **1971** *Lancet* 29 May 1124/1 A pathologist (O.E.D., probably about 1905) is 'One versed in pathology: a student of or writer upon diseases' and pathology 'treats of the causes and nature of diseases'. Even at that time, when departments of pathology were beginning to be usual in medical schools and several specialised journals included the word in their titles, that was a little out of date... The word was already used chiefly for practitioners of laboratory medicine. By the thirties it had differentiated further: non-specialised laboratory doctors called themselves 'clinical pathologists', but used alone the word was increasingly limited to practitioners of the oldest branch of the trade, morbid-anatomy-histopathology. The N.H.S. has partly reversed this trend, advertising posts, for instance, as 'pathologist with a special interest in bacteriology'. The Royal College of Pathologists goes even further, being anxious to include the non-medical biochemists, though there is..a backwoods faction which challenges the propriety of calling anyone non-medical a pathologist. **1977** *Role & Membership of College* (R. College of Pathologists) 5 The pathologist can be defined as a medical (or dental) graduate who has ultimate responsibility for the diagnostic tests performed in the pathology laboratory and for the advice given to clinicians on the selection and interpretation of tests.

pa'thologize, *v. rare.* [See -IZE.] *trans.* To treat pathologically; to treat the pathology of.

1649 BULWER *Pathomyot.* Pref. 7 Neither the great Parents of Physick, nor their Learned Off-spring had pathologized the Muscles.

pathology (pə'θɒlədʒɪ). [ad. mod. or med.L. *pathologia*, f. Gr. παθο-, PATHO- + -λογία, -LOGY: cf. F. *pathologie* (*c* 1600).]

1. a. The science or study of disease; that department of medical science, or of physiology, which treats of the causes and nature of diseases, or abnormal bodily affections or conditions.

[**1597** A. M. tr. *Guillemeau's Fr. Chirurg.* 1 b/1 *Pathologia* treatethe of the cause and occasione of the sicknesses.] **1611** COTGR., *Pathologique*, of, or belonging to, Pathologie. *a* **1682** SIR T. BROWNE *Tracts* (1684) 76 This, in the Pathology of Plants, may be the Disease of φυλλομανία. **1783** W. CULLEN *First Lines* Pref., Wks. 1827 I. 470 The many hypothetical doctrines of the Humoral Pathology. **1845** TODD & BOWMAN *Phys. Anat.* I. 28 Pathology is the physiology of disease. **1874** MAHAFFY *Soc. Life Greece* ix. 274 Greek medicine rather started from hygiene than from pathology.

b. *transf.* The sum of pathological processes or conditions.

1672 SIR T. BROWNE *Lett. Friend* §14 If Asia, Africa, and America should bring in their List [of diseases], Pandoras Box would swell, and there must be a strange Pathology. **1797** M. BAILLIE *Morb. Anat.* (1807) p. v, We shall add to our knowledge of the pathology of the body. **1807** *Med. Jrnl.* XVII. 211 Among the variety of diseases..few are involved in more obscurity as to their pathology,..than..tetanus. **1881** *Med. Temp. Jrnl.* Oct. 17 The pathology as indicated in the changes which took place in the body. **1977** D. M. SMITH *Human Geogr.* x. 278 The major metropolitan states with their high general *average* affluence levels clearly experience high levels of social pathology.

c. The study of morbid or abnormal mental or moral conditions. Also in extended use.

1842 KINGSLEY *Lett.* (1878) I. 114 Understand the pathology of the human soul, and be able to cure its diseases. *a* **1878** LEWES *Study Psychol.* i. (1879) 35 Mental Pathology ..has run a course parallel to that of Mental Physiology. **1972** W. LABOV *Language in Inner City* iv. 134 There is evidence from linguistic pathology that a deep-seated knowledge of this fact may be present in native speakers. **1972** T. KOCHMAN *Rappin' & Stylin' Out* p. xi, This book is an attempt to get beyond what Albert Murray has called the 'fakelore of black pathology' and its corollary, the 'folklore of white supremacy'.

2. The study of the passions or emotions. *rare.*

1681 tr. *Willis' Rem. Med. Wks.* Vocab., *Pathologie*, the doctrine of the passions. **18..** BENTHAM *Princ. Civil Code* I. vi. Wks. 1843 I. 304/2 Pathology is a term..not hitherto ..employed in morals, but..equally necessary here... Moral pathology would consist in the knowledge of the feelings, affections, and passions. **1817** —— *Table Springs of Action* ibid. 205 Psychological dynamics..has for its basis psychological pathology. **1833** CHALMERS *Const. Man* (1834) II. II. ii. 180.

patholopolis (pæθə'lɒpəlɪs). [f. Gr. παθολογικός, f. πάθος suffering, disease + πόλις city; see PATHOLOGIC *a.*, -POLIS.] A diseased or morally degenerate city.

1927, **1961** [see PARASITOPOLIS].

pathomania to **pathopœous**: see PATHO-.

pathophysiology (,pæθəʊfɪzɪ'ɒlədʒɪ). *Med.* [f. PATHO- + PHYSIOLOGY.] The physiological processes associated with disease or injury; the study of such processes.

1952 *Adv. Internal Med.* V. 428 Abnormalities in protein metabolism form the central problem in the pathophysiology of multiple myeloma. **1962** *Lancet* 2 June 1172/2 An analysis of the pathophysiology of these disturbances may further our understanding of cerebral function. **1972** *Ibid.* 20 May 1104/1 It is impossible to keep up with all trends in pathophysiology. **1974** M. C. GERALD *Pharmacol.* xvi. 296 We may anticipate that the etiology of these disorders will be better understood with future advances in the pathophysiology and biochemistry of mental disease. **1975** *Nature* 3 Jan. 77/2 A symposium on the pathophysiology and clinical aspects of pain.

Hence **,pathophysio'logic, -physio'logical** *adjs.*, of or involving abnormal physiological processes; pertaining to pathophysiology, **,pathophysio'logically** *adv.*, as regards pathophysiology.

1952 *Adv. Internal Med.* V. 398 From the pathophysiologic point of view, the most interesting part of the myeloma problem is the disturbance of protein metabolism. **1960** (*title*) Works of the Institute of Higher Nervous Activity. Pathophysiological series. (Academy of Sciences of the U.S.S.R.) **1962** H. G. KEITEL *Pathophysiol. & Treatment of Body Fluid Disturbances* i. 12 In many illnesses the anatomical, biochemical, and pathophysiological characteristics of the associated fluid derangement and their successful treatment have been fairly clearly defined. **1973** WASSERMAN & BROWN in Holland & Frei *Cancer Med.* xix. 1367/1 The patho-physiologic mechanisms responsible for these symptoms. **1973** *Sci. Amer.* Sept. 121/3 Selective errors in the metabolism of the monamines in specific areas of the brain may be the pathophysiological basis for psychotic disorders. **1976** *Nature* 29 July 397/2 This..results in a chronic murine hepatosplenic disease which closely resembles, pathophysiologically, human chronic schistosomiasis.

pathos ('peɪθɒs). [mod. a. Gr. πάθος suffering, feeling: so F. *pathos* (Molière 1672).]

1. That quality in speech, writing, music, or artistic representation (or *transf.* in events, circumstances, persons, etc.) which excites a feeling of pity or sadness; power of stirring tender or melancholy emotion; pathetic or affecting character or influence.

1668 DRYDEN *Dram. Poesy* Ess. (Ker) I. 81 There is a certain gaiety in their comedies, and pathos in their more serious plays. **1742** YOUNG *Nt. Th.* IX. 1632 There dwells a noble pathos in the skies, Which warms our passions. **1855** PRESCOTT *Philip II*, I. II. xi. 263 He descanted on the woes of the land with a pathos which drew tears from every eye. **1874** GREEN *Short Hist.* vii. §6. 399 The tale of Protestant sufferings was told with a wonderful pathos..by John Foxe.

b. A pathetic expression or utterance. *rare.*

1579 E. K. *Gloss Spenser's Sheph. Cal.* May 189 *And with*) A very Poeticall παθός [*ed.* **1591** pathos]. *a* **1644** WESTFIELD *Eng. Face* (1646) 127 'Lord..If thou wilt pardon this people!' It was a vehement pathos. **1853–8** HAWTHORNE *Eng. Note-Bks.* (1879) II. 294 Little pathoses..are abundant enough.

2. Suffering (bodily or mental). *rare.*

1693 tr. *Blancard's Phys. Dict.* (ed. 2), *Pathos*, vid. *Pathema* [*Pathema*, all preternatural Conturbation wherewith our Body is molested]. **1842** TENNYSON *Love & Duty* 82 Shall sharpest pathos blight us, knowing all Life needs for life is possible to will? **1853** DUNGLISON *Med. Lex.*, *Pathos*, Affection, Disease.

3. In reference to art, esp. ancient Greek art: The quality of the transient or emotional, as opposed to the permanent or ideal: see ETHOS 2.

1881 *Q. Rev.* Oct. 542 The real is preferred to the ideal, transient emotion to permanent lineaments, pathos to ethos.

pathosticate (pə'θɒstɪkeɪt), *v. nonce-wd.* [joc. f. PATHOS + PATHE)TICATE *v.*] *intr.* To induce pathos by melodramatic writing.

1901 G. B. SHAW *Cashel Byron's Profession* (rev. ed.) Pref. p. xii, In novel-writing there are two trustworthy dodges for capturing the public. One is to slaughter a child and pathosticate over its deathbed for a whole chapter.

pathway ('pɑːθweɪ, 'pæθ-). 1. A way that constitutes or serves as a path; a way by or along which one may walk or go; a path, track, way. (Often *fig.*)

a **1536** TINDALE *Pathway* Wks. (1573) 377, I supposed it very necessary to prepare this Pathway into the Scripture for you, that ye might walke surely and euer know the true from the false. **1546** BALE *Eng. Votaries* I. I viij b, Iohan Baptyst ..prepared a playne pathwaye to Christ and hys kyngedome. **1555** EDEN *Decades* 87 A pathway in the myddest of a fyeld. **1748** *Anson's Voy.* II. xiii. 270 There was but one path-way which led through the woods. **1810** SCOTT *Lady of L.* I. iv, High in his pathway hung the Sun. **1897** MARY KINGSLEY *W. Africa* 388 The great, black, winding river with a pathway in its midst of frosted silver where the moonlight struck it. **1899** *Allbutt's Syst. Med.* VII. 250 If its channels be constricted the blood takes the pathway through the locomotor organs.

2. *Physiol.* a. A chain of nerve cells forming a continuous route along which impulses of a particular kind habitually travel.

1924 R. M. OGDEN tr. *Koffka's Growth of Mind* iv. 235 Von Kries pointed out that the arousal of associations can not be explained on the basis of a mere 'pathway'-hypothesis which assumes that nervous excitations travel along fixed paths. **1934** J. H. GLOBUS *Neuroanat.* (ed. 6) 63 There will now be no difficulty in linking up the chain of nuclei and tracts, which form the optic pathways. **1952** W. F. T. TATLOW et al. *Synopsis Neurol.* ix. 162 Hyperalgesia.—Occurs when visceral and somatic (deep or superficial) afferents share pain pathway, so that on simultaneous stimulation, summation of subliminal stimuli can occur. **1971** *Sci. Amer.* July 48/2 The path-ways extending from the brain to the lower spinal cord are some two feet long. **1972** *Science* 5 May 536/2 The descending cortical and brainstem pathways to the spinal cord represent the main instrument by which the brain controls movements.

b. The sequence of reactions undergone by a compound or class of compounds in a natural environment, esp. a living organism.

1927 M. BODANSKY *Introd. Physiol. Chem.* xi. 271 Another pathway of metabolism has been suggested, namely one involving the conversion of arginine into guanidine-butyric acid,..which by β-oxidation would yield guanidine acetic acid. **1947** *Growth* XI. 232 The pathway of galactose fermentation [in yeast]. **1961** *Proc. Nat. Acad. Sci.* XLVII. 378 (*heading*) Transformation studies on the linkage of markers in the tryptophen pathway in *Bacillus subtilis*. **1967** M. E. HALE *Biol. Lichens* viii. 106 The biosynthetic pathways by which they appear to be synthesized. **1971** *Sci. Amer.* Sept. 45/2 The carbon dioxide pathways in our biosphere. **1971** *Nature* 17 Sept. 163/2 His latest experiments are an attempt to identify the pathway of incorporation of ^{3}H-thymine into DNA. **1973** *Ibid.* 13 Apr. 453/1 This information will be required..to elucidate the pathways and interactions of mercury in the estuarine and marine environment.

Hence **pathwayed** ('pɑːθweɪd, 'pæθ-) *a.*, furnished with a pathway.

1839 CLOUGH *Early Poems* iii. 4 Again in vision clear thy pathwayed side I tread.

-pathy, repr. Gr. -πάθεια, lit. 'suffering, feeling', the second element of the word HOMŒOPATHY (Gr. ὁμοιοπάθεια the quality of suffering or feeling alike, the having of like affections, sympathy), extended to ALLOPATHY, and applied, with the sense 'method of cure, curative treatment', to other compounds, as *hydropathy*, *kinesipathy*, *electropathy*, etc.

1863 KINGSLEY *Water-Bab.* iv, [They tried] Hydropathy ..Pyropathy, as successfully employed by the old inquisitors to cure the malady of thought... Geopathy, or burying him. Atmopathy, or steaming him... With all other ipathies and opathies which Noodle has invented, and Foodle tried. **1888** *St. James's Gaz.* 20 Sept., Pelopathy, or treatment by means of mud baths... Raxopathy, or the grape-cure, is more favoured in vine-producing countries than it is in England. Glossopathy is now added to the list ..[to express] the good effects which dogs can produce upon suffering humanity by applying their tongues to wounds and sores. This gentleman is now collecting a staff of suitable dogs, with a view to opening a glossopathic establishment in the neighbourhood of Zurich. **1900** *Westm. Gaz.* 6 June 10/1 Never before..has light treatment taken definite shape as it is undoubtedly doing now in a distinct 'pathy', which our contemporary christens 'photopathy'.

2. Forming the names of bodily disorders of a specified part (as MYOPATHY) or kind (IDIOPATHY).

†**'patiate**, *v. Obs. rare*⁻¹. [irreg. f. L. *pat-ī* to suffer + -ATE³.] *trans.* To suffer.

1653 R. SANDERS *Physiogn.*, *Moles* 7 Though he patiate infirmities, yet he shall recover.

†**'patible**, *sb. Obs.* [ad. L. *patibulum* a fork-shaped yoke placed on the necks of criminals, a fork-shaped gibbet, etc., f. *patē-re* to lie open + *-bulum*, forming names of instruments or utensils.] A gibbet, a cross; the horizontal bar of a cross.

1428–9 *Rec. St. Mary at Hill* (E.E.T.S.) 70 Also payd for a patyble to serle..Also payd for iiij Ewangelistes, makyng & keruyng. *c* **1450** *Mirour Saluacioun* 4127 The patible of the crosse for sheald and targe hadde hee. *a* **1548** HALL *Chron., Hen. VIII* 74 On the aultare was a deske or halpace, whereon stoode a patible of the Crucifix of fine golde. **1745** BLOMEFIELD *Norfolk* II. 638 The Patible over the Perke [Rood-loft].

attrib. **1610** GUILLIM *Heraldry* II. vii. (1660) 79 This manner of bearing of the patible Cross is warranted by Rolls of greatest Antiquity.

† **patible** (ˈpætıb(ə)l), *a. Obs.* [ad. L. *patibil-is*, f. *pat-ī* to suffer: see -IBLE.]

1. Capable of suffering or undergoing something; liable to undergo something; subject to something.

1603 HARSNET *Pop. Impost.* 115 The deuil looked like a patible old Coridon, with a payre of hornes on his heade and a cowes tayle at his breech. **1656** R. ROBINSON *Christ All* 134 [Light] is an accidental form or a patible quality. *a* **1834** COLERIDGE in *Lit. Rem.* (1839) IV. 211 [Man] is a passive as well as active being: he is a patible agent.

b. Capable of or liable to suffering; passible.

1600 W. WATSON *Decacordon* (1602) 48 The patible and withall impatible body of our Sauiour Christ. **1678** CUDWORTH *Intell. Syst.* I. v. 813 The Demoniack Bodies.. have.. Gross Matter in them, and are Patible. **1691** BAXTER *Repl. Beverley* 6 The raised wicked have not bodies less sensible, patible, or that need less food.

2. 'Capable of being suffered, endurable, tolerable'. (In Dictionaries.)

1623 COCKERAM, *Patible*, to be suffered. **1658** PHILLIPS, *Patible*, to be suffered or indured. **1731** BAILEY, *Patible*,.. sufferable. **1755** JOHNSON, *Patible*, sufferable; tolerable.

patibulary (pəˈtıbjʊlərı), *a. rare.* [f. L. *patibulum* PATIBLE *sb.* + -ARY[1]. Cf. F. *patibulaire* (15th c. in Hatz.-Darm.).] Of or pertaining to the gallows; resembling the gallows; suggesting the gallows or hanging. Chiefly *humorous.*

1646 SIR T. BROWNE *Pseud. Ep.* v. xxi. (1686) 216 Some patibulary affixion after he was slain. **1697** DENNIS *Plot & no Plot* v, I never saw a more patibulary phyz. **1801** *Sporting Mag.* XVII. 155 A certain Corn-Buyer, which had.. undergone the discipline of a patibulary suspension on a gallows. **1837** CARLYLE *Diam. Neckl.* xvi. Ess. 1888 V. 193 Yes, infinitely terrible is the Gallows; it bestrides with its patibulary fork the Pit of bottomless Terror! **1838** *Fraser's Mag.* XVII. 767 The 'I ad Grecum Pi!' of the German students (in allusion to the patibulary form of that letter).

So **paˈtibulate** *v. trans.* [cf. L. *patibulāt-us* gibbeted], to hang. *humorous nonce-wd.*

1656 BLOUNT *Glossogr.*, *Patibulated*, hanged on a Gibbet, Gallows or Cross. **1881** *Society* 11 June 3/1 That distinguished burglar after he had been duly patibulated. **1882** OGILVIE, *Patibulated.*

patience (ˈpeıʃəns), *sb.* Forms: 3-6 paci-, 4-6 pacy-, -ence, -ens(e, 6- patience. [ME. a. OF. *patience, pacience* (12th c.), ad. L. *patientia*, f. *patient-em* suffering, PATIENT: see -ENCE.]

I. The practice or quality of being patient.

1. a. The suffering or enduring (of pain, trouble, or evil) with calmness and composure; the quality or capacity of so suffering or enduring.

a **1225** *Ancr. R.* 180 To þe uttre temptaciun is neod pacience, þet is þolemodnesse. **1340** *Ayenb.* 33 Ase he ne may no þing bere be boȝsamnesse, he ne may þolye be paciense. *c* **1374** CHAUCER *Boeth.* II. pr. vii. 93 (Camb. MS.), Yif þat he wolde han suffred lyhtly in pacience the wronges þat weeren don vn to hym. *c* **1440** LOVE *Bonavent. Mirr.* v. (Sherard MS.), ȝif we cowde wel kepe pacience in tyme of aduersite. **1553** DK. NORTHUMBLD. in *Four C. Eng. Lett.* (1880) 22 God grant me pacyence to endure. **1594** SHAKS. *Rich. III*, I. i. 126 Rich... How hath your Lordship brook'd imprisonment? *Hast.* With patience (Noble Lord) as prisoners must. **1658** *Whole Duty Man* ii. §5 Patience.. is nothing else, but a willing and quiet yielding to whatever afflictions it pleases God to lay upon us. **1784** COWPER *Task* IV. 339 That thus We may with patience bear our moderate ills. **1849** M. ARNOLD *To Gypsy Child by Sea Shore* 13 Drugging pain by patience. **1868** SWINBURNE *Blake* 63 He endured all the secret slights and wants.. with a most high patience.

b. Forbearance, longsuffering, longanimity under provocation of any kind; *esp.* forbearance or bearing with others, their faults, limitations, etc.

1377 LANGL. *P. Pl.* B. XIV. 99 Þere parfit treuthe and pouere herte is, and pacience of tonge; þere is charitee. **1481** CAXTON *Reynard* xxix. (Arb.) 73 He shold the better haue pacience and pyte on Reynarte. **1591** SHAKS. *Two Gent.* IV. iv. 116, I doe intreat your patience To heare me speake. **1598** —— *Merry W.* I. iv. 5 Here will be an old abusing of Gods patience, and Kings English. **1662** STILLINGFL. *Orig. Sacr.* II. vi. §13 The patience and long-suffering of God, leading men to repentance. **1764** FOOTE *Patron* II. Wks. 1799 I. 348 *Bev.* I am happy, Sir Thomas, if—. *Sir Tho.* Your patience. There is in you, Mr. Bever, a fire of imagination [etc.]. **1873** MORLEY *Rousseau* II. 93 His discipular patience when Rousseau told him that his verses were poor,.. is a little uncommon in a prince.

c. The calm abiding of the issue of time, processes, etc.; quiet and self-possessed waiting for something; 'the quality of expecting long without rage or discontent' (J.).

c **1375** *Sc. Leg. Saints* iii. (*Andreas*) 405 Ȝet wil I with paciens a quhil here þe. **1382** WYCLIF *Luke* xxi. 19 In ȝoure pacience ȝe schulen welde ȝoure soulis [**1526** TINDALE, With your pacience possesse your soules]. **1475** SIR J. PASTON in *P. Lett.* III. 130, I beseche yow off pacyence tyll the begynnyng of the next yeer. **1526** TINDALE *Jas.* v. 7 The husbande man wayteþ for the precious frute offe the erth, and hath long pacience there vppon, vntill he receave the yerly and the latter rayne. **1615** G. SANDYS *Trav.* 153 He had not the patience to expect a present, but demanded one. **1654** WHITELOCKE *Jrnl. Swed. Emb.* (1772) II. 401 Their ambassador.. was put to the patience of staying an hower and a halfe.. before he was called in to his highnes. **1796** H. HUNTER tr. *St.-Pierre's Stud. Nat.* (1799) III. 87 Behold the fruits of eleven years patience. **1866** RUSKIN *Eth. Dust* iv. 61 Patience is the finest and worthiest part of fortitude,—and the rarest, too.

d. Constancy in labour, exertion, or effort.

1517 TORKINGTON *Pilgr.* (1884) 55 The same nyght, with grett Diffyculty and moche paciens, we war Delivered a borde into ower Shippe. *a* **1774** W. HARTE *Eulogius* Poems (1810) 382/2 He learnt with patience, and with meekness taught. **1795** SOUTHEY *Joan of Arc* II. 190 We.. in the fight opposed.. to the exasperate patience of the foe, Desperate endurance. **1871** DARWIN *Desc. Man* III. xix. (1874) 565 Genius has been declared by a great authority to be patience; and patience, in this sense, means unflinching, undaunted perseverance.

e. Personified, or represented in a figure.

1377 LANGL. *P. Pl.* B. XIII. 29 Pacience in þe paleis stode in pilgrymes clothes, And preyde mete for charite. **1509** HAWES *Past. Pleas.* xx. (Percy Soc.) 96 To wofull creatures she is goodly leche, Wyth her good syster called Pacyence. **1601** SHAKS. *Twel. N.* II. iv. 117 She sate, like Patience on a Monument, Smiling at greefe. **1884** HENLEY & STEVENSON *Three Plays, Beau Austin* I. ii, I cannot away with your pale cheeks and that Patience-on-a-Monument kind of look.

f. Phrases and locutions:

† ***patience perforce***, patience upon compulsion, i.e. when there is no other course (*obs.*). ***my patience!*** an ejaculation of surprise (*colloq.*). ***patience! have patience!*** be patient; wait a little; give or allow sufficient time. ***to have patience with*** (†*in, toward*), to show forbearance toward; so, ***to have no patience with*** (*colloq.*), to be unable to bear patiently, to be irritated by. ***out of patience***, advb. phr. (sometimes adj.), provoked so as no longer to have patience (*with*). † ***to take in patience***, to receive or accept with resignation (*obs.*).

1575 GASCOIGNE *Weedes* (*title*) *Patience Perforce. Content thy selfe with patience perforce. **1607** HEYWOOD *Wom. Killed w. Kindn.* Plays 1874 II. 138 Here's patience perforce, He needs must trot afoot that tires his horse. **1670** RAY *Proverbs* 130 Patience perforce is a medicine for a mad dog. **1873** MURDOCH *Doric Lyre* 33 *Ma patience, that beats a'! *c* **1489** CAXTON *Sonnes of Aymon* i. 58 My dere moder *haue a lytyll pacyence. **1705** VANBRUGH *Confed.* III. ii, *Flip.* Have patience, and it shall be done. **1765** GRAY *Shakespeare* 1 A moment's patience, gentle Mistress Anne. **1847** TENNYSON *Princ.* Concl. 72 'Have patience', I replied, 'ourselves are full Of social wrong'. *Ibid.* 78 This.. world of ours is but a child Yet in the go-cart. Patience! Give it time To learn its limbs. **1382** WYCLIF *Matt.* xviii. 26 *Haue pacience in me, and alle thingis I shal ȝeelde to thee. **1526** TINDALE *1 Thess.* v. 14 Forbeare the weake, have continuall pacience towarde alle men. **1855** THACKERAY *Newcomes* lxiv, I have no patience with the Colonel. **1542** UDALL *Erasm. Apoph.* 341 Archias beeyng throughly *out of pacience thretened to pull hym parforce out of the temple. **1686** tr. *Chardin's Trav. Persia* 34 Which put the Vizier so out of Patience. **1804** M. G. LEWIS *Bravo of Venice* (1856) II. iv. 316 [He] was out of all patience with himself. *c* **1386** CHAUCER *Knt.'s T.* 226 *Taak al in pacience Oure prisoun, for it may noon oother be.

g. ***muscle of patience, patience muscle***: the levator muscle of the shoulder.

1730-6 BAILEY (folio), *Patientiæ musculus* (with Anatomists), the muscle of patience, so called from the great service of it in labour. It is the same as *Levator Scapulæ.*

2. With *of*: The fact or capacity of enduring; patient endurance *of*. Cf. IMPATIENCE 1 b. *rare.*

1530 TINDALE *Answ. More* III. xiii. C iij b, Why setteth he not his eyes on the thankes geuynge for that pleasure and on the pacience of other displeasures? **1718** PRIOR *Solomon* II. 890 Patience of toil, and love of virtue fails. **1741** MIDDLETON *Cicero* II. x. 366 Patience of injuries. **1772** *Ann. Reg.* 44/1 That patience of hunger, and every kind of hardship.

† **3.** Sufferance; indulgence; leave, permission; chiefly in ***by*** or ***with your patience***. *Obs.*

1558 FRAUNCE *Lawiers Log.* Ded. ¶ ij b, By your patience be it spoken. **1583** STUBBES *Anat. Abus.* II. (1882) 66 And thus much with their patience be it spoken briefly hereof. **1591** SHAKS. *1 Hen. VI*, II. iii. 78 Nor other satisfaction do I craue, But onely with your patience, that we may Taste of your Wine. **1610** —— *Tempest* III. iii. 3, I can goe no further, Sir,.. by your patience, I needes must rest me.

II. Special senses.

4. Name for a species of Dock, called by the old herbalists *Patientia* (*Rumex Patientia* Linn.), formerly used in Britain instead of spinach, in salads, etc. Sometimes extended to other species of Dock: ***wild patience***, *Rumex obtusifolius*. See also PATIENCE-DOCK, PASSIONS, DOCK *sb.*[1] 1 b.

[The origin of this name has not been traced.]

c **1440** *Promp. Parv.* 376/1 Pacyence, herbe, *paciencia*. *c* **1450** *Two Cookery-bks.* II. 69 Take Colys,.. Betus and Borage, auens, Violette, Malvis, parsle, betayn, pacience, þe white of the lekes, and þe croppe of þe netle. **1538** TURNER *Libellus* B ij, *Hippolapathon*, officine *patientiam* uocant, vulgus *Patience*. **1546** J. HEYWOOD *Prov.* (1867) 37 Let pacience growe in your gardein alwaie. **1597** GERARDE *Herbal* II. lxxviii. §7. 314 The Monkes Rubarbe is called in Latine *Rumex satium*, and *Patientia*, or Patience, which worde is borrowed of the French, who call this herbe *Pacience*. **1611** FLORIO, *Lapato*, the wild Dock or Patience. **1629** PARKINSON *Parad. in Sole* II. xiv. 483 Garden Patience is a kinde of Docke. **1712** tr. *Pomet's Hist. Drugs* I. 44 The Leaves are like enough those of Wild Patience. **1882** J. SMITH *Dict. Econ. Plants*, Herb of Patience (*Rumex Patientia*). **1886** G. NICHOLSON *Dict. Gard.*, *Patience* or *Herb Patience*,.. a hardy perennial.. the leaves of which were formerly much used in the place of Spinach.

5. A game of cards (either ordinary playing cards, or small cards marked with numbers), in which the cards are taken as they come from the pack or set, and the object is to arrange them in some systematic order; usually for one person alone (in which case also called *solitaire*).

1816 W. WARDEN *Lett. Conduct Napoleon* (ed. 4) 198 He is sent to the sideboard to play at Patience until the new pack would deal with more facility. **1822** LADY GRANVILLE *Lett.* (1894) I. 220 We were occupied all yesterday evening with conjuring tricks and patiences of every kind. **1861** DICKENS *Gt. Expect.* xl, Playing a complicated kind of Patience with a ragged pack of cards. **1874** LADY CADOGAN (*title*) Illustrated Games of Patience. **1901** *Munsey's Mag.* (U.S.) XXIV. 873/1 This is a difficult Patience to get; its solution depends on watchfulness and luck.

6. *attrib.* and *Comb.*, as ***patience-trying*** adj.; (sense 5) ***patience board, card, case, pack, player.***

1890 *Anthony's Photogr. Bull.* III. 119 It was tiresome, patience-trying work and reminded me of the old dissected puzzles of my boyhood. **1898** *Westm. Gaz.* 11 Jan. 2/1 Always, like a skilful patience player, leave vacancies for last chances. **1901** *Munsey's Mag.* (U.S.) XXIV. 872/1 It is much more satisfactory to use a regular Patience pack than to play with ordinary cards. The Patience cards are only two and a half by one and three fourths inches. **1907** *Yesterday's Shopping* (1969) 379/2 Patience and 'Pigmy' Cards. Rounded corners, printed backs, two packs in a box. *Ibid.* 380/1 Patience Board With Cards. **1916** J. BUCHAN *Greenmantle* ii. 24 From his pocket he had taken a pack of Patience cards and had begun to play the game called the Double Napoleon. **1926-7** *Army & Navy Stores Catal.* 392 Patience Board. For playing the game of Patience off the table.

ˈ**patience**, *v. rare.* [f. prec.]

† **1.** *trans.* To endow with patience, make patient; *refl.* to be patient, have patience. Cf. PATIENT *v.* 1.

1605 *Play Stucley* in Simpson *Sch. Shaks.* (1878) I. 159 Patience but yourself awhile.

2. *intr.* To have or exercise patience.

1596 NASHE *Saffron Walden* D ij, To warne the blue-coate Corrector when he should patience and surcease. **1835** *New Monthly Mag.* XLIV. 337, I had 'swam on a gondola ' at Venice, and 'patienced' in a punt at Putney.

patience-dock. *Herb.* Also 9 **patient-dock.** [f. PATIENCE *sb.* 4 + DOCK *sb.*[1]]

1. Properly, The dock called PATIENCE, *Rumex Patientia*.

[**1640** J. PARKINSON *Theatrum Botanicum* II. iii. 154 Garden Patience is a Docke bearing the name of Rhubarbe, for some small purging quality therein.] **1820** T. GREEN *Universal Herbal* II. 498 *Rumex Patientia*; Patience Dock, or Rhubarb. **1822** J. C. LOUDON *Encycl. Gardening* 715 Herb Patience, or Patience Dock.. is a hardy perennial plant, a native of Italy, introduced in 1573. **1859** *Trans. Illinois Agric. Soc.* III. 513 Patience dock comes early, and makes good greens. **1884** MILLER *Plant-n.*, Patience-Dock, *Rumex Patientia*. *Ibid.*, *Rumex Patientia*, Monk's Rhubarb, Patience, or Patient Dock. **1972** Y. LOVELOCK *Vegetable Bk.* I. 218 The spinach dock.. is used in the early spring.. and goes by such names as patience and patient dock. **1973** C. A. WILSON *Food & Drink in Britain* vi. 204 Many other large-leaved green plants were employed in this pottage, including orache, clary, mallows, patience dock, borage and bugloss.

2. In the north of England, applied to the Bistort (*Polygonum Bistorta*), there also called PASSIONS, PASSION-DOCK, of which 'the leaves are by some boiled in the Spring, and eaten as greens' (Lightfoot *Flora Scot.* 206).

1776-96 WITHERING *Brit. Plants* (ed. 3) II. 383 *note*, The young shoots are eaten in herb pudding in the North of England, and about Manchester, they are substituted for greens under the name of *Patience Dock*. **1865** *Science Gossip* 36 (E.D.D.) In Cheshire the edible qualities of the plant are well known, but it is there called 'patient dock'. **1872** *Routledge's Ev. Boy's Ann.* Sept. 631/1 The young shoots are eaten under the name of Patience Dock.

patiency (ˈpeıʃənsı). *rare.* [f. PATIENT (after *agency*): see -ENCY.] The quality or condition of being patient or passive: see PATIENT *a.* 3, *sb.* 4.

1697 J. SERGEANT *Solid Philos.* 217 Which.. has the truest Notion of Agency in it, without any Mixture of Patiency; because the Body moved cannot re-act upon it. **1813-21** BENTHAM *Ontology* Wks. 1843 VIII. 207/1 They are each one of them agent and patient at the same time. No one exhibits more of agency, no one more of patiency, than any other. *a* **1832** —— *Logic* ibid. 228/2.

patient (ˈpeıʃənt), *a.* and *sb.* Forms: 4-6 pacy-, 4-7 paci-, 6- patient, (6 paty-). [a. OF. *pacient, passient* (13-14th c.), later *patient*, ad. L. *patient-em*, pr. pple. of *patī* to suffer.]

A. *adj.*

1. a. Bearing or enduring (pain, affliction, trouble, or evil of any kind) with composure, without discontent or complaint; having the quality or capacity of so bearing; exercising or possessing patience.

c **1320-40** [implied in PATIENTLY]. *c* **1370** *Hymns Virgin* 106 In peyne be meke and pacient. **1382** WYCLIF *Rom.* xii. 12 Ioyinge in hope, pacient in tribulacioun. *c* **1450** tr. *De Imitatione* I. xvi. 18 Studie to be pacient in suffring. **1596** SHAKS. *Merch. V.* I. iii. 110 Many a time.. you haue rated me.. Still haue I borne it with a patient shrug. **1643** MILTON *Divorce* I. viii. Wks. (1851) 39 Job the patientest of men. **1784** COWPER *Task* IV. 407, I praise you much, ye meek and patient pair, For ye are worthy. **1842** TENNYSON *St. Sim. Styl.* 15 Patient on this tall pillar I have borne Rain, wind, frost, heat, hail, damp, and sleet, and snow.

b. Longsuffering, forbearing; with *to, towards*, lenient towards, bearing with (others, their infirmities, etc.).

1377 LANGL. *P. Pl.* B. XV. 195 Paciente of tonge, And boxome as of berynge to burgeys and to lordes. **1382** WYCLIF *1 Thess.* v. 14 Resceyue ȝe syke men, be ȝe pacient to alle men. **1598** B. JONSON *Ev. Man in Hum.* III. iv, You'ld mad the patient'st body in the world, to heare you talke so, without any sense or reason. **1606** CHAPMAN *Gentlem. Usher* Plays 1873 I. 325 Thou weariest not thy husbands patient eares. **1797** MRS. RADCLIFFE *Italian* i, Ellena was the sole support of her aunt's declining years;..patient to her infirmities. **1852** BRIGHT *Hymn, 'And now, O Father'*, Most patient Saviour, who dost love us still.

c. Calmly expectant; not hasty or impetuous; quietly awaiting the course or issue of events, etc.

1382 WYCLIF *Eccl.* vii. 8 Betere is a pacient man than the enhauncende hymself. **1526** *Pilgr. Perf.* (W. de W. 1531) 41 b, Better it is to haue a pacyent soule, than to do myracles. *a* **1550** in *Dunbar's Poems* (S.T.S.) 312 Gif ȝe wald lufe and luvit be, In mynd keip weill thir thingis thre,..Be secreit, trew, and pacient. **1598** CHAPMAN *Blind Beggar* Plays 1873 I. 33 Be patient my wench and Ile tell thee. **1791** MRS. RADCLIFFE *Rom. Forest* i, The ruffian..bid him be patient awhile. **1866** RUSKIN *Eth. Dust* iv. 61, I know twenty persevering girls for one patient one; but it is only that twenty-first who can do her work, out and out, or enjoy it. **1883** R. M. BENSON *Spir. Read.* Advent 115 We must form a habit of patient expectation.

d. Continuing or able to continue a course of action without being daunted by difficulties or hindrances; persistent, constant, diligent, unwearied.

1590 SPENSER *F.Q.* I. viii. 45 Take to you wonted strength, And maister these mishaps with patient might. **1611** BIBLE *Rom.* ii. 7 Who by patient continuance in well doing seeke for glory, and honour, and immortalitie. *a* **1727** NEWTON (J.), Whatever I have done is due to patient thought. **1764** GOLDSM. *Trav.* 283 Methinks her [Holland's] patient sons before me stand. **1886** SHORTHOUSE *Sir Percival* ii. 55 So many years of patient labour.

e. *fig.* of things.

1820 KEATS *Hyperion* I. 353 And still they were the same bright, patient stars. *Ibid.* III. 98 The most patient brilliance of the moon! *a* **1861** MRS. BROWNING *Little Mattie* iii, Smooth Down her patient locks.

2. a. With *of*: Enduring or able to endure (evil, suffering, etc.); endurant of. (Cf. *impatient of*.)

c **1440** *Promp. Parv.* 376/1 Pacyent of sufferynge. **1600** J. PORY tr. *Leo's Africa* IX. 338 Neither are they so patient of hunger as of thirst. *c* **1611** CHAPMAN *Iliad* x. 145 Old man, that never tak'st repose, Thou art too patient of our toil. *a* **1706** EVELYN *Kal. Hort.* (1729) 227 Plants least patient of Cold. **1742** YOUNG *Nt. Th.* IV. 3 Thine Ear is patient of a serious Song. **1780** COWPER *Table Talk* 224 Patient of constitutional control, He bears it with meek manliness of soul. **1826–34** WORDSW. *To May* x, Streams that April could not check Are patient of thy rule.

b. Of words, writings, etc.: Capable of bearing or admitting of (a particular interpretation).

1638 CHILLINGW. *Relig. Prot.* I. Pref. to E. Knott §20 That their xxxix Articles are patient, nay ambitious of some sence wherein they may seem Catholique. **1651** JER. TAYLOR *Serm. for Year* II. xxiii. 297 A way open for them to despise the law which was made patient of such a weak evasion. **1879** LD. COLERIDGE in *Law Rep.* Com. Pleas Div. IV. 304 His language is at least patient of such an interpretation. **1894** ILLINGWORTH *Personality Hum. & Div.* vii. (1895) 169 The picture is patient of various interpretations.

3. Undergoing the action of another; passive. (Correlative to *agent*.) *rare.*

c **1611** CHAPMAN *Iliad* To Rdr. (1865) 78 [Translators] apply Their pains and cunnings word for word to render Their patient authors. *c* **1645** HOWELL *Lett.* (1650) I. 293 This motion betwixt the agent spirit, and patient matter, produceth an actual heat.

4. *spec.* in *Grammar* (see quot.).

1939 L. H. GRAY *Foundations of Lang.* xii. 374 A distinction is drawn between the ergative case as the logical subject of a transitive verb and the patient case as the subject of an intransitive verb.

5. patient Lucy orig. *U.S.* = *busy Lizzie* s.v. BUSY *a.* 11.

1946 M. FREE *All about House Plants* xvii. 161 The names Patience Plant and Patient Lucy are interesting examples of how the original meaning of a plant name can be reversed. The vernacular names are derived from the botanical name *Impatiens*,..referring to the sudden bursting of the seed pods. **1956** [see BUSY *a.* 11]. **1977** K. & G. BECKETT *Illustr. Encycl. Indoor Plants* 110/2 Busy Lizzie; Patient Lucy; Sultana. A familiar house plant, native to tropical Africa.

B. *sb.*

1. a. A sufferer; one who suffers patiently. Now *rare.*

1393 LANGL. *P. Pl.* C. XIV. 99 So þat poure pacient is parfitest lif of alle, And alle parfite preestes to pouerte sholde drawe. **1559** *Mirr. Mag., Dk. Clarence* xxi, The pacientes grief and Scholers payne. **1621** LADY M. WROTH *Urania* 547 No payne was in her that hee was not a patient of. **1654** GAYTON *Pleas. Notes* IV. xxii. 275 Nor would the Jewes, who did all in disgrace of the blessed Patient. **1712** ADDISON *Spect.* No. 486 ¶2 Let them not pretend to be free..and laugh at us poor married Patients. **1795** SOUTHEY *Vis. Maid Orleans* II. 217 A scoffing fiend,..Mock'd at his patients, and did often strew Ashes upon them, and then bid them say Their prayers aloud.

†**b.** *esp.* One who suffers from bodily disease; a sick person. *Obs.* (exc. as involved in 2).

1484 CAXTON *Fables of Alfonce* i, Whan the pacyent or seke man sawe her. **1530** PALSGR. 250/2 Pacyent a sicke body, *pacient*. **1631** JORDEN *Nat. Bathes* xvi. (1669) 150 Those patients which think to cure themselves,..are oftentimes dangerously deceived.

2. One who is under medical treatment for the cure of some disease or wound; one of the sick persons whom a medical man attends; an inmate of an infirmary or hospital.

c **1374** CHAUCER *Troylus* I. 1034 (1090) And, as an esy pacient, þe lore Abit of hym þat goþ aboute his cure. *c* **1386** —— *Melib.* ¶46 To vs Surgiens aperteneth..to oure pacientz that we do no damage. **1477** EARL RIVERS (Caxton) *Dictes* 39 The physicien Is not sure, for amongis his pacientis he may take sekenesse. **1547** BOORDE *Brev. Health* Pref. 3 b, Chierurgions ought..not to be boystiouse about his pacientes, but lovyngly to comforte theym. **1613** SHAKS. *Hen. VIII*, III. ii. 41 He brings his Physicke After his Patients death. **1799** *Med. Jrnl.* II. 345 As house-surgeon, he must have attended the patient. **1879** *Cassell's Techn. Educ.* IV. 96/1 He endeavoured..to practise medicine, but could nowhere find patients.

†**3.** A person subjected to the supervision, care, treatment, or correction of some one. *Obs.* (exc. as *transf.* from 2).

1432–50 tr. *Higden* (Rolls) VII. 341 Scharpe correccion and hasty movethe the paciente raþer to vice þen to vertu. **1526** SKELTON *Magnyf.* 2415 *Red.* Syr, is your pacyent any thynge amendyd? *Good.* Ye, syr, he is sory for that he hath offendyd. **1657** *Penit. Conf.* ix. 287 The Priests may rather justly complaine..of the scarcity of their Patients.

4. a. A person or thing that undergoes some action, or to whom or which something is done; 'that which receives impressions from external agents' (J.), as correlative to *agent*, and distinguished from *instrument*; a recipient.

1580 LYLY *Euphues* (Arb.) 404 The eye of the man is the arrow, the bewtie of the woman the white, which shooteth not, but receiueth, being the patient, not the agent. **1620** T. GRANGER *Div. Logike* 72 The mutuall touching of the agent, and patient, *id est*, of the fire heating, and thing heated by it. **1725** WATTS *Logic* I. ii. §4 When a smith with a hammer strikes a piece of iron..the iron is the patient, or the subject of passion, in a philosophical sense. *a* **1791** WESLEY *Serm.* lxvii. I. 4 Wks. 1811 IX. 224 He that is not free is not an Agent, but a Patient. **1870** SWINBURNE *Ess. & Stud.* (1875) 54 To you he [Shakespeare] leaves it..to love or hate, applaud or condemn, the agents and the patients of his mundane scheme.

b. *spec.* in *Grammar.*

1968 J. LYONS *Introd. Theoret. Linguistics* viii. 342 But this conflicts with the notion of the subject as the 'actor', rather than the 'goal' (or 'patient'). **1971** J. ANDERSON *Grammar of Case* ix. 140 Accounts of transitivity conducted in terms of 'actor-action-patient'. [*Ibid.* iv. 52 The lables 'ergative' and 'nominative' are usually used with respect to ..an inflectional..system; alternative terms are 'actif'/'nominatif' (Lafitte, 1962) 'agens'/'patiens' (Troubetzkoy, 1929).] **1975** *Language* LI. 806 It is significant that the suffix has come to designate the agent or instrument of the verbal activity in certain daughters—but not the patient, product, or location of the verbal activity.

†**'patient,** *v. Obs.* [f. PATIENT *a.*: cf. F. *patienter* intr. (16th c. in Littré).]

1. *trans.* To make patient; esp. *refl.* to calm or quiet oneself, be patient.

1551 ROBINSON tr. *More's Utop.* I. (1895) 76 'Patient iourself, good maister Freare' (quod he), 'and be not angry'. **1588** SHAKS. *Tit. A.* I. i. 121 Patient your selfe, Madam, and pardon me. **1619** W. SCLATER *Exp. 1 Thess.* (1630) 185 It should patient vs a while. **1647** TRAPP *Comm. 2 Thess.* i. 4 Faith patienteth the heart.

2. *intr.* To be patient, to show patience.

1561 NORTON & SACKV. *Gorboduc* IV. ii. F iij b, Pacient your grace, perhappes he liueth yet. **1644** DIGBY *Immort. Souls* (1645) 128 An overflowing reward for thy enduring and patienting in this thy darksome prison.

'patienthood. [f. PATIENT *sb.* 2 + -HOOD.] The state or condition of being a patient.

1970 *New Yorker* 14 Nov. 108 Millions of boys..live, as Captain Ahab says, with half of their heart and with only one of their lungs, and the world is the worse for it. Now and again, however, an individual is called upon..to lift his individual patienthood to the level of a universal one and to try to solve for all what he could not solve for himself alone. **1971** *Harper's Mag.* May 111/2 Hers [*sc.* R. Mackenzie's] is the best account of the psychology of patienthood in a modern hospital I've ever read.

patientless ('peɪʃəntlɪs), *a.* [f. PATIENT *sb.* + -LESS.] Having no patients, without patients.

1825 *New Monthly Mag.* XIII. 310 Any young aspiring surgeon, or patientless physician. **1850** B. TAYLOR *Eldorado* xxiv. (1862) 257 Patientless physicians,..and half-starved editors.

patiently ('peɪʃəntlɪ), *adv.* [f. PATIENT *a.* + -LY².] In a patient manner; with patience. (See the adj.)

c **1320** *Cast. Love* 1157 He suffred hit alle pacyently. *c* **1340** HAMPOLE *Prose Tr.* 38 How oure Lorde sufferde vs pacyently in oure syne and tuke na vengeance of vs. **1382** WYCLIF *Acts* xxvi. 3 For which thing, I biseche, heere me paciently. **1481** CAXTON *Reynard* xi. (Arb.) 25, I can not bettre it, I shal take it paciently. **1548** UDALL, etc. *Erasm. Par. Matt.* (1551) 74 The other besought his lord.., saying; deale paciently with me. **1611** SHAKS. *Cymb.* III. v. 118 Since patiently and constantly thou hast stucke to the bare Fortune of that Begger Posthumus. **1682** NORRIS *Hierocles, Gold. Verses* 20 Bear patiently what Ill by Heaven is sent. **1781** GIBBON *Decl. & F.* xlii. (1869) II. 580 He patiently endured the hardships of a savage life. **1874** GREEN *Short Hist.* iii. §7. 149 He listens patiently to the advice of his friends.

b. Hyphened to adj. (before its sb.).

1892 PATER *Wks.* (1901) VIII. 209 Wave upon wave, of patiently-wrought stone. **1900** *Daily News* 21 May 3/3 The steps of the patiently-pursued policy.

'patientness. Now *rare.* [f. as prec. + -NESS.] The quality of being patient; patience.

c **1470** G. ASHBY *Active Policy* 326 Do it with pite & pacientnesse, With no vengeance. **1587** GOLDING *De Mornay* xxviii. 492 Who hath not cause here to honour the patientnes of God? **1609** TOURNEUR *Fun. Poem on Sir F. Vere* 301 Hee..with a most un-weari'd patientness Would labour to..impresse His demonstrations. **1892** LD. LYTTON *King Poppy* vii. 279 Suffer it with queenly patientness.

†**'patientry.** *Obs. rare.* [f. PATIENT *sb.* + -RY: cf. *tenantry*.] The body of patients or persons under medical treatment.

1631 T. POWELL *Tom All Trades* (1876) 161 To see how pretily these young gamesters, Male and Female, lay about them, and engrosse the greater part of Patientrie in all places wheresoeuer.

†**patif, -yf(e,** *a. Obs. rare*⁻¹. Of uncertain origin and sense; possibly a scribal error; perh., in *cross patif*, = (cross) of (Christ's) suffering or passion.

c **1470** HARDING *Chron.* CIV. ix, For there he [Egbert] had the felde and victorye,..By vertue of the crosse patyfe [*v.rr.* patife, patyff, *MS. Harl.* 661 patife and] precyous; For whiche alwaye [after] in hys banner, Of azuer whole the crosse of golde he bear..in mynde of Christes lore, His crosse, his death, and his holy passyon.

‖**patiki** ('pɑːtiki). *N.Z.* [Maori.] A local name for a flat-fish belonging to one of several species of *Rhombosolea* found in New Zealand waters; cf. FLOUNDER *sb.*¹ 1.

[**1820** *Gram. & Vocab. Lang. N.Z.* (Church Missionary Soc.) 190 Patiki, *s.* a fish so called.] **1838** J. S. POLACK *New Zealand* I. ix. 322 The *pátiki*, between the large flounder and the sole, is equally excellent with the European fish. **1843** *N.Z. Jrnl.* No. 92 177/2 The natives..brought in an abundant supply of fine fish; mullet,..patiki, (the flounder of Europe) and other delicious species. **1855** R. TAYLOR *Te Ika a Maui* xxv. 412 *Patiki*, common name for the sole and flat-fish. **1879** *Trans. N.Z. Inst.* XII. 316 Large *Patiki*, flat fish, are occasionally speared up the river. **1949** P. H. BUCK *Coming of Maori* (1950) II. xiii. 321 One [rafter-painting] design, in which the field was roughly divided into lozenge-shaped areas, was named *patiki* (flounder) from its outline.

patin, obs. form of PATEN, PATTEN.

patina ('pætɪnə). [In sense 1, a. L. *patina, -ena*, a broad shallow dish or pan, in med.L. the plate used in the Eucharist. In sense 2, ad. F. *patine* (18th c.), of uncertain origin, but prob. from the L. word.]

†**1. a.** *Archæol.* The ancient Roman vessel so called (see above). **b.** *Eccl.* = PATEN 1.

1857 BIRCH *Anc. Pottery* (1858) II. 317 The *patina* was flat, and held soup; and was the generic name for a dish. **1868** MILMAN *St. Paul's* 85 The patina and chalice were taken from his hands.

2. a. A film or incrustation produced by oxidation on the surface of old bronze, usually of a green colour and esteemed as an ornament. Hence extended to a similar alteration of the surface of marble, flint, or other substances.

1748 H. WALPOLE *Let. to H. S. Conway* 6 Oct., Squibs.. bronzed over with a patina of gunpowder. **1797** *Monthly Mag.* III. 509 The vase is of bronze, covered by a *patina* of very fine green. **1876** MATHEWS *Coinage* Introd. 5 The thin green coating..called the *patina*, which occurs on coins which have been long buried. **1892** PATER *Wks.* (1901) VIII. 227 The old black front, with its inestimable *patina* of ancient smoke and weather and natural decay.

b. *fig.*

1933 H. NICOLSON *Diary* 24 Feb. (1966) 140 He says what the Americans lack is *patina*. **1955** KOESTLER *Trail of Dinosaur* 79 This tendency prompts people to have their wall-brackets and picture-frames artificially dirtied to lend them the patina of age; so let us call it the 'patina-snobbery'. **1957** R. HOGGART *Uses of Literary* ix. 227 He develops a strong patina of resistance, a thick and solid skin for not taking notice. **1967** N. MAILER *Cannibals & Christians* I. 13 It gives them all a high instant patina, their skin responding to the call of the wild. **1977** *Time* 18 July 28/2 Defending the rights of homosexuals.., she mingled with and took on some of the patina of the loony left. **1978** J. THOMSON *Question of Identity* x. 97 The disorder was not a mere evening's untidiness. It had taken time to build up that rich patina of squalor.

Hence **'patinaed, 'patinous,** *adjs.*, covered with a patina, patinated; also *fig.*; **pati'nation,** formation of or incrustment with a patina; a patina.

1848 DE QUINCEY *Sortilege & Astrol.* Wks. 1862 VIII. 274 Rather more patinous, if numismatists will lend me that word. **1888** J. D. BUTLER in *N. & Q.* 7th Ser. V. 364 A *virtuoso*, valuing a coin at ten times its intrinsic worth for time-blackened patination. **1898** *Nat. Science* Feb. 106 The origin of the patination of flints has been frequently discussed. **1936** *Bull. Raffles Museum, Singapore* Ser. B. No. I. 53 The neolithic implements of Puming and Pajitan.. have practically no patination at all. **1947** J. C. RICH *Materials & Methods Sculpture* vii. 199 The patination of metals is a highly specialized art. **1948** W. FAULKNER *Intruder in Dust* (1949) xi. 244 Took from the inside coat pocket a leather snap-purse patina-ed like old silver and almost as big as Miss Habersham's handbag. **1960** H. HAYWARD *Antique Coll.* 212/2 Patination and colour pose problems to a faker. **1968** D. MURPHY tr. *Gelin's Concept of Man in Bible* vii. 117 This is what I call a 'patinaed' reading. **1970** *Cabinet Maker & Retail Furnisher* 30 Oct. 301/2 The optional antique patination is hand-dyed. **1973** *Country Life* 27 Sept. (Suppl.) 91 Jacobean oak court cupboard of excellent colour and patination. **1975** *Nature* 7 Aug. 469/1 The bifaces from that site do not, on the whole, have a dark-brown polish but have a grey to white, calcareous patination or no patination at all.

patinate ('pætɪneɪt), *v.* [f. PATINA 2 + -ATE³.] *trans.* To cause to develop a patina; to cover with a patina. Also *fig.* So **'patinated** *ppl. a.*, **'patinating** *vbl. sb.*

1880 *Times* 29 Nov. 10 The little bronze head of Zeus.. finely patinated. **1920** WEBSTER, Patinate. **1934** J. & C.

GORDON *Portuguese Somersault* x. 237 Roofs of rich red-tile, patinated with lichens of varied tints. **1957** *Encycl. Brit.* IX. 382/2 When patinated flint occurs in gravels containing iron salts a yellow staining, producing the well-known ochreous patina, results. *Ibid.* XX. 231/2 The slower the patinating the more artistic the results is a good general rule to follow. **1957** *New Yorker* 6 Apr. 31 The riches Ian had inherited were so blindingly brand-new that it had taken time and pains to patinate them with good manners and good taste. **1969** L. R. ROGERS *Sculpture* vi. 210 Most sculptors today prefer a patina to a clean bronze surface and use acids..to patinate their work. **1970** G. SAVAGE *Dict. Antiques* 312/2 Handsomely patinated bronzes are much sought. **1974** K. CLARK *Another Part of Wood* iii. 103, I learnt a great deal from some lectures on the fascinating subject of Aristotle's *Poetics* by a richly patinated character named Farquharson.

‖**patine** (pəˈtiːn), *sb.* [F. *patine.*] = PATINA 2.
1883 G. H. BOUGHTON in *Harper's Mag.* Feb. 388/2 Like an old bronze with a most valuable 'patine' on the surface. **1910** G. B. SHAW *Let* 18 Sept. (1972) II. 942 Back in the dark [in a rowing-boat], without compass,..49 strokes to the minute striking patines of white fire from the Atlantic. **1940** *Harper's Mag.* Nov. 566 Her [*sc.* a pilgrim hawk's] back was an indefinable hue of iron; only a slight patine of the ruddiness of youth still shone on it. **1966** M. M. PEGLER *Dict. Interior Design* (1967) 326 *Patina or Patine*, a greenish coating on the surface of old bronze.

patine (pæˈtiːn), *v.* [f. PATINE *sb.*] *trans.* To coat or cover with a patina (sense 2). Also *fig.* Hence **paˈtining** *vbl. sb.*
1896 A. H. KEANE *Ethnol.* v. 84 Many [flints] have been deeply patined and rusted sometimes even right through. **1936** L. P. SMITH *Reperusals & Re-Collections* i. 2 Time and history adds to their significance; it patines and mellows them. **1947** J. C. RICH *Materials & Methods Sculpture* vii. 200 Brass can be patined in several colors. *Ibid.* 209 Iron and steel can be patined a blue-black by the application of a hot solution composed of 10 grains of sodium thiosulphate to each ounce of water. *Ibid.* 403/2 (Index), Chemical methods of patining bronze.

patine, var. of PATEN; obs. form of PATTEN.

patined, *ppl. a. rare*⁻¹. [f. *patin*, var. of PATEN, after the Shaks. passage in sense 3.] Set like inlaid 'patens'.
1894 *Persian Pict.* 89 Night, revealing the great depths of heaven and the patined stars.

patinize (ˈpætɪnaɪz), *v.* [f. as PATINE *v.* + -IZE.] *trans.* To coat with or as with a patina. Hence **ˈpatinizing** *vbl. sb.*
1904 *Sci. Amer. Suppl.* 27 Feb. 23548/1 The patinizing of zinc articles has become a very important question in the art industry.

patio (ˈpætɪəʊ, ˈpɑːtɪəʊ). [Sp., = court of a house.]
1. *orig.* An inner court, open to the sky, in a Spanish or Spanish-American house. Hence, in extended uses (not in Spanish or Spanish-American contexts), a courtyard or enclosure; a paved area belonging to a house and usu. adjoining it.
1828 W. IRVING in *Life & Lett.* (1864) II. 287 The patios planted with orange and citron trees and refreshed by fountains. **1887** J. BALL *Nat. in S. Amer.* 161 The building included three small courts, or patios. **1891** KIPLING *City of Dreadful Night* vi. 36 The central square, the *patio* or whatever it must be called, reeks. **1895** *Outing* (U.S.) XXVII. 38/2 The typical Mexican house is built in the form of a hollow square... In the unroofed quadrangle, or *patio*, as it is called, is spent the greater portion of what open air life the women..enjoy. **1900** ST. BARBE *Mod. Spain* 48 Crowding round the *patio* door each morning. **1941** B. SCHULBERG *What makes Sammy Run?* xi. 271 He was.. dancing with her out on the patio to the rhumba orchestra. **1947** *Chicago Maroon* 25 July 2/1 Tables will be set up in the patio with free cokes, and a faculty member or new student from each state will be on hand to welcome new students. **1949** *Here & Now* (N.Z.) Oct. 22/2 The patio is really an extra room without a roof. It is protected on three sides by the house itself and on the north by the bank. **1955** J. CANNAN *Long Shadows* i. 16 The addition of two bathrooms built over a sun-room, which reduced the sooty little triangular garden to a size convenient to the construction of a *patio.* **1957** C. BROOKE-ROSE *Languages of Love* 23 Bernard sat now in an imitation *patio* under an imitation palm-tree. **1959** *Observer* 22 Mar. 1/1 But behind is a small golf course and a patio where a naval commander could be seen arranging the cushions. Filipino mess boys have polished up the interior. **1959** N. MAILER *Advts. for Myself* (1961) 378 Eitel is smoking a cigarette on the patio. **1968** *Globe & Mail* (Toronto) 17 Feb. 45 (Advt.), Detached 4-bedroom home on large fenced lot, beautiful patio. **1969** *Daily Tel.* 11 Nov. 17 Shops, dotted about among tree-strewn patios, fountains and open-air cafés [in Paris]. **1972** [see LIMBO³]. **1973** *Irish Times* 2 Mar. 22/8 (Advt.), Bungalow: Dundrum—Scandinavian style, central heating, living room.. looking onto secluded patio. **1976** E. SCARROW *N.Z. Vegetable Gardening Guide* 5 A number of vegetables can be grown.. in tubs or pots on a patio. **1977** *Austral. House & Garden* Jan. 39/2 This sunny family room has one wall of glass looking out to the plant-hung pergola and patio and the lush small garden.
2. *Mining.* (See quot. 1881.) So *patio process.*
1845 *Chem. Gaz.* 1 Sept. 373 The preparation of magistral, an indispensable agent in the amalgamation by *patio.* **1856** *Hutching's Mag.* Sept. 104/1 The ore deposited on the *patio*, another set of laborers engage in separating the large lumps and reducing them to the size of common paving stones. **1863** *Proc. Calif. Acad. Nat. Sci.* II. 133 No experiments have been made in working this ore by the *patio* or Spanish-American amalgamation process. **1867** J. A. PHILIPS *Mining & Metall. Gold & Silver* xvi. 334 At the hacienda of Regla..the patio, comprising an area an acre and a half in extent, is carefully covered with a wooden floor. **1877** RAYMOND *Statist. Mines & Mining* 343 Amalgamating-ore, which has been worked by the old Mexican process on the patio. **1881** —— *Mining Gloss.*, *Patio*, the yard where the ores are cleaned and assorted; also, the amalgamation floor, or the Spanish process itself of amalgamating silver ores on an open floor. **1882** *Rep. to Ho. Repr. Prec. Met. U.S.* 588 Our Spanish-American neighbors, by the patio produced a very slow and incomplete contact. **1896** C. H. SHINN *Story of Mine* 82 He treated them [*sc.* silver sulphurets] with the chemicals of the *patio* process. **1913** *Trans. Inst. Mining & Metallurgy* XXII. 661 The ore is received in the 'patio' or yard adjoining the mill, where it is weighed. **1974** *Encycl. Brit. Micropædia* VII. 664/1 The patio, or Mexican, process of separating silver from the ore by amalgamation with quicksilver was perfected in Pachuca by Bartolomé de Medina in the 16th century.
3. *attrib.* and *Comb.*, as ***patio block, furniture, garden, model, stand***; **patio door**, a large, glass, sliding door leading to a garden or balcony.
1973 *Houston* (Texas) *Chron. Mag. People, Places, Pleasures* 14 Oct. 3 (Advt.), 7½" × 16" concrete patio blocks. **1979** *Sci. Amer.* Apr. 110/2 The concrete slabs were 'patio blocks' that weigh 6·5 kilograms and were 40 centimeters long, 19 centimeters wide and four centimeters thick. **1973** *Daily Tel.* 10 July 15/1 Usually the patio door is a replacement for the rather clumsy French doors which were put in by the thousand between the wars... The new sliding patio doors are vastly superior. A complete wall of glass, they can be five feet wide or even extend, with several panels, up to 24ft wide. Usually they are around 7ft high. *Ibid.* 21 July 3 (Advt.), We are Patio Door specialists. **1975** *Oxford Jrnl.* 31 Jan. 9 (Advt.), Add a new dimension to your living. With patio doors that slide open at a touch on warm summer days and close snugly to seal out the rain and draughts of winter. Their slim aluminium frames won't warp or need painting. **1976** *Homes & Gardens* July 116/2 Although patio doors are becoming an increasingly popular feature in houses, as yet there is no safety legislation governing their manufacture. **1969** *Sears Catal.* Spring/Summer 9 Moderately priced all-wood patio furniture. **1973** C. WILLIAMS *Man on Leash* (1974) i. 5 The standard small swimming pool and sundeck with patio furniture and umbrellas. **1912** J. LONDON *Let.* 18 Jan. (1966) 360, I should like to see a novel of mine come out from the presses back of the patio garden. **1976** *Outdoor Living* (N.Z.) I. 11. 44 For the patio garden in the ideal location on the sunny side of the house the list of plants is unending. **1969** *Sears Catal.* Spring/Summer 13 Patio model [gas-fired grill] with its own 18-inch diameter mounting base. *Ibid.* Barbecue on patio stand.

†**ˈpatis, patise**, *sb.*¹ *Obs.* In 5–6 patiz, patyse. [a. OF. *patiz, -is*, later *pactis*:—L. *pactītium, īcium*, sb. use of *pactīcius* agreed upon, stipulated, f. *pactum* PACT.] Terms (of peace); a bargain or treaty; tribute.
c **1500** *Melusine* 301 The patiz or trybut, that thou takest thrugh thy grete pryde, of my lord, my faders peple. *Ibid.* 324 To treate with hym for som patyse or for som peas.

†**patise**, *sb.*² *Obs.* A kind of red pigment: see quots. Also *patise-red.*
1598 FLORIO, *Saudice*, patisered or arsenike, a kinde of stone, or colour made of ceruse and red okre burned together. **1603** I. H. *Mirr. Worldly Fame* in *Harl. Misc.* (1811) VIII. 42 The patise, and arsenick red, must be ground for colours. **1622** PEACHAM *Compl. Gent.* (1661) 156 Patise, or a kinde of red or Arsenick colour.

†**patise, patish**, *v. Obs.* Also 5–6 -yse, 6 -es, -yshe, pattish. [a. OF. type **patiser*, in mod.F. *pactiser* to make a pact, f. *pactis* PATIS *sb.*¹ or *pacte* PACT. Cf. It. *patteggiare, -iggiare*, to covenant, bargain, f. *patto*:—L. *pactum.*]
1. *intr.* To make a covenant or agreement, make terms, treat, bargain, covenant, agree.
1475 *Bk. Noblesse* (Roxb.) 73 Many of theym duelling upon the marches patised to youre adverse partie also to dwelle in rest. **1530** PALSGR. 655/1, I patyse, as one frontyer towne dothe with an other in tyme of warre to save them bothe harmlesse. **1548** UDALL *Erasm. Par.* Pref. 5 She would readely patyshe and couenant with God. **1570** LEVINS *Manip.* 144/33 To Pattish, *pacisci. Ibid.* 148/21 To Patise, *pacisci, conspirare.*
b. *trans.* To covenant or stipulate for.
1542 UDALL *Erasm. Apoph.* 263 Upon the bryngyng of the money whiche the pirates patyshed for his raunsome.
2. *trans.* To exact tribute from, to tax.
c **1500** *Melusine* 304 This fals traytour geaunt shal neuer more patyse you, For he as now..hath neyther lust nor talent to aske ony tribut of you.
Hence †**ˈpatising (patesing)** *vbl. sb.*, making of terms, bargaining, treating; †**patisement**, a private or underhand pact.
1529 *St. Papers Hen. VIII*, II. 150 Imposicions,..that at an entre or exployte shalbe imponed or had, by way of patysment or agrement, upon thenemyse. **1530** PALSGR. 252/2 Patisyng a treatie of peace, as frontier townes take one of another, *patisaige.* **1560** ABP. PARKER *Corr.* (Parker Soc.) 124 To hurt the state of our churches by exercising any extraordinary patesing for packing and purchasing.

†**ˈpatisser, ˈpastisar.** *Sc. Obs.* Also 6 patesar, patticear, pottisear. [a. F. *pâtissier*, in OF. *pasticier, pastisser*, = It. *pasticciaro, pasticciere*:—L. type **pasticiārius* (in med.L. *pasticerius*), f. med.L. *pastīcium* pasty, f. *pasta* PASTE.] A seller of pastry, a pastry-cook.
1567 in Chalmers *Mary Q. Scots* (1818) I. 177 Ane Pastisar, callit Patrick Rannald. *c* **1575** in *Balfour's Practicks* (1754) 72 It is not leasum to any Fleshour to be ane Patticear. *Ibid.* 585 Ony Cuikis or Pottisearis, quha bakis pyis. **1588** *Exch. Rolls Scotl.* XXI. 368 Jhon Rannald, aid to the baxter and patesar.

‖**patisserie** (pɑtisri, pəˈtiːsərɪ). Also 8 patiscery, 9 pâtisserie. [F. *pâtisserie*, f. as prec. + *-erie*, -ERY.] **a.** Articles of food made by a pastry-cook; pastry.
[**1768** STERNE *Sent. Journ., Le Patisser*, He had a little wife, he said, whom he loved, who did the *patisserie.*] **1784** in Warrender *Marchmont* (1894) 160 [She] became the best Confectioner and Pastrycook, by making patiscery for him which he liked. **1802** [see CONFITURE]. **1828** *Harrovian* 44 (Stanf.), The young gourmands appeared to be luxuriating in a vision of 'patisserie'. **1899** MALLOCK *Individualist* xix. 187 Confiding to Lady Cornelia that 'she never touched *pâtisserie*'. **1912** R. K. WOOD *Tourist's Russia* ii. 34 All the larger cities have good patisserie shops where afternoon tea is served à la Russe. **1960** E. DAVID *French Provincial Cooking* 434 Elaborate *pâtisserie* and confectionery require practical experience and knowledge of an art quite distinct from that of normal household cookery. **1974** *Times* 25 Feb. 8/7 She gives a Viennese tea concert, at which the audience ..claps with fingers sticky from the patisserie. **1976** *Times* 1 June 6/2 For patisseries we can recommend Toutaubeurre.
b. A shop which sells *patisserie*; a pastry-cook's.
[**1884** F. E. A. GASC *Dict. French & Eng. Lang.* (ed. 3) 410/2 *Pâtisserie*,..pastry; pastry-work *or* making *or* business; biscuit-baking *or* bakery.] **1903** F. B. SMITH *How Paris amuses Itself* ii. 48 One of the most doleful sights I have seen in Paris was a sad-looking gentleman in black sitting at a cold marble-topped table of an expensive *patisserie* lunching on a weak cup of tea and a plate of cream-puffs. **1927** E. BOWEN *Hotel* xv. 181 Will you come to tea with me and Victor at the Pâtisserie? **1930** *Chambers's Jrnl.* 15 Nov. 800/1 'Let's go and get tea at a café.' The idea found instant acceptance; three or four hundred yards from the hotel we found a good *pâtisserie* and we were soon..drinking excellent tea. **1949** A. WILSON *Wrong Set* 161 It was so cool inside the patisserie that Jeremy would gladly have stayed on there for ever. **1966** A. CHRISTIE *Third Girl* i. 5 A brioche ..from the fourth shop he had tried. It was a Danish *patisserie* but infinitely superior to the so-called French one near by. **1975** N. LUARD *Robespierre Serial* ii. 6 The patisserie at the corner of the Rue Vaumar.

‖**pâtissier, patissier** (pɑtisje). [Fr.] One who makes *pâtisserie*; a pastry-cook.
1924 A. D. SEDGWICK *Little French Girl* IV. vi. 346 She had to buy a *baba-au-rhum*..and asked André to drive them across to the *pâtissier's.* **1960** E. DAVID *French Provincial Cooking* 434 A French housewife..is able to order what she requires..from that local *pâtissier* whom she knows to be most skilful and to use only the finest ingredients. **1961** A. WESKER *Kitchen* 59 *Paul.* But then I think: I should stop making pastries?..*Kevin.* Hush pâtissier! Hush! **1972** *Times* 29 July 9/3 Try the specialities of Catalan pâtissiers. **1975** *Sat. Rev.* (U.S.) 15 Nov. 50/1 Michel, the *chef de cuisine*, and André, the *pâtissier.*

Patjitanian (pædʒɪˈtɑːnɪən), *a. Archæol.* Also Pajitanian. [f. *Pajitan*, a town on the south coast of central Java + -IAN.] Of or pertaining to Pajitan or the Early Palaeolithic chopper culture discovered near there in 1935. Also *absol.*, the Patjitanian chopper industry.
[**1936** G. H. R. VON KOENIGSWALD in *Bull. Raffles Museum, Singapore* Ser. B No. 1. 52 In October, 1935, the author was travelling with Mr. M. W. F. Tweedie, Curator of the Raffles Museum, in Central Java. During this trip we discovered on the 4th of October, a new site with big stone implements of various types, including, for the first time in Java, hand-axes... The site is near Pajitan, a town on the south coast of Central Java.] **1943** H. DE TERRA in *Trans. Amer. Philos. Soc.* XXXII. 458/2 It was from the basal stratum of the 10-m. terrace that we extracted a few rolled implements of 'Patjitanian' type. *Ibid.* 459/1 My impression is that the question of the absolute age of the Patjitanian industry can be determined only when the terrace geology of the region is known. **1944** H. L. MOVIUS *Early Man & Pleistocene Stratigr. S. & E. Asia* 90/2 The Patjitanian should be placed probably in the second half of the Second Interglacial. *Ibid.* 91/1 The Patjitanian implements include many large, massive forms which have been crudely worked. **1949** K. P. OAKLEY *Man the Tool-Maker* viii. 70 No implements were found with the remains of the Java Man, *Pithecanthropus erectus*, but beds of slightly later age in Java have yielded the Patjitanian industry.., which recalls some of the artifacts of the related Pekin Man. **1964** M. W. THOMPSON tr. *Semenov's Prehist. Technol.* II. ii. 36/2 The rough hand-axes of Java (Pajitanian)..are very inexpressive stone objects. **1969** COLES & HIGGS *Archaeol. Early Man* xx. 390 A small number of Patjitanian artefacts might well be described as handaxes in African contexts. *Ibid.* 391 The stratigraphical position of the Patjitanian is not well-established, because much of this material is in a derived state in recent gravels of the Basoka River. **1974** *Encycl. Brit. Micropædia* II. 887/1 These traditions [of stone tools] include..the Patjitanian industry, Java (associated with Java man at Sangiran and Trinil).

ˈpatlander. *slang.* [f. *Patland*, slang for Ireland, f. PAT *sb.*²] An Irishman.
1820 *Sporting Mag.* VI. 271 The game of the Patlander claimed the praise of all present. **1834** M. SCOTT *Cruise 'Midge'* i. (1836) 4 There spoke your mother, you Patlander, you—there shone out Kilkenny. **1878** *N. Amer. Rev.* CXXVI. 259 Their success against brother Patlanders seemed doubly welcome.

†**patlet.** *Obs.* Also 5 patelet, 6 patlett, -led, *Sc.* paitlet(t, -lat, 8 -lich. [app. a. OF. *patelette* 'band of stuff' (Godef.), *patelette de la testiere* 'the head-dag, the broad peece of leather that runnes ouer-crosse, or through, the top of a headstall' (Cotgr.); dim. of *patte* paw, flap. The sense-history is obscure.] An article of attire; the same as PARTLET² (of which it was the original form).
a **1500** HENRYSON *Garment gude Ladeis* 27 Hir patelet of gude pansing. **1500–20** DUNBAR *Poems* xiv. 64 Sic skaith and

scorne, so mony paitlattis worne Within this land was nevir hard nor sene. **1522** *Test. Ebor.* (Surtees) V. 153 A patlett of velvett. *Ibid.* 154 My velvett jacket, to make his childer patlettes and cuyffes. **1526** SKELTON *Magnyf.* 2100, I plucked her by the patlet. **1585** *Burgh Rec. Edin.* (Rec. Soc.) IV. 445 Cumand to ony nichtbouris howssis to offer to thair seruands any clayth, paytlets, slevis, gownis. **1786** *Har'st Rig* lxxxvi. (1801) 28 They sair bemane some paitlich gown.

patly ('pætlɪ), *adv.* [f. PAT *a.* + -LY^2.] = PAT *adv.*

1632 J. HAYWARD tr. *Biondi's Eromena* 133 This businesse, so patly proposed. *a* **1713** ELLWOOD *Autobiog.* (1765) 317 Herein Demetrius and they most patly agree. **1869** BLACKMORE *Lorna D.* xxvi, The mere idea.. which he talked about as patly as if it were a settled thing.

Pat Malone (pæt mə'ləʊn). *Rhyming slang* (orig. and chiefly *Austral.*). = OWN *a.* 3. Also *ellipt.* **pat.**

1908 MRS. A. GUNN *We of Never-Never* xii. 146 He travels day after day and month after month, practically alone—'on me Pat Malone', he calls it. **1908** *Austral. Mag.* 1 Nov. 1251 'On my own' (by myself) became 'on my Pat Malone' and subsequently 'on my Pat' a very general expression nowadays. **1916** C. J. DENNIS *Moods of Ginger Mick* 110 But, torkin' straight, the Janes 'as done their bit. I'd like to 'ug the lot, orl on me pat! **1930** *Bulletin* (Sydney) 12 Mar. 47/1 On your pat now, aren't you? When did the old man go away? **1937** E. HILL *Great Austral. Loneliness* i. 22 If I was out there on me Pat Malone for too long—. **1943** N. MARSH *Colour Scheme* ix. 156 We're dopey if we let that bloke go off on his pat. **1948** V. PALMER *Golconda* xv. 120 Perhaps if I start off [singing this duet] on my pat there's some of you will take pity and not see me left. **1952** J. CLEARY *Sundowners* 276 First the missus died, then a coupla months later he went, and I was left on me pat malone. **1959** C. MACINNES *Absolute Beginners* 58 Standing there all on his Pat Malone. **1966** 'L. LANE' *ABZ of Scouse* 110 *On me tod*, by myself. An alternative phrase is *on me pat.* **1966** G. W. TURNER *Eng. Lang. Austral. & N.Z.* vi. 119 *On one's pat* 'alone'.. has reached New Zealand. **1971** *Private Eye* 2 July 16 Pat malone again! Cripes I am cheesed.

Patna ('pætnə). The name of a district in north central Bihar, India, used *attrib.* in **Patna rice**, a small-grained rice, used principally in curries and other savoury dishes. Also *ellipt.*

1845 [see CAROLINA]. **1861** MRS. BEETON *Bk. Househ. Managem.* 473 Well wash 1 lb. of the best Patna rice. **1868** *M. Jewry Warne's Model Cookery* 75/2 One and a half pound of whole Carolina or Patna rice. **1888** KIPLING *Story of Gadsbys* 48 A spattering gale of Best Patna... Throws half-a-pound of rice at G. **1902** 'KETAB' *Indian Dishes for Eng. Tables* 3 Patna rice is the best for boiling and should increase in boiling to about three times its bulk when raw. Good Patna rice has fine, rather long grains, and should be of a pale straw colour when rubbed to remove the dust. **1948** *Good Housek. Cookery Bk.* 400 For plain boiled rice, curries, risotto, and such dishes, in which the aim is to keep the grains separate, the Indian varieties of rice, such as Patna and Burma, are best. **1952** F. WHITE *Good Eng. Food* II. vi. 145 Wash ¼ lb. of Patna rice. **1960** E. DAVID *French Provincial Cooking* 97 The long-grained rice which we call Patna is usually known in France as *riz caroline.* **1965** *Guardian* 6 Aug. 6/1 Long thin Patna for its dry separate grains to accompany curries. **1970** SIMON & HOWE *Dict. Gastron.* 327/1 What we call Patna rice is Patna seed type. Very little of so-called Patna rice comes from Bihar, but the name is reserved for good quality long grain rice.

patness ('pætnɪs). [f. PAT *a.* + -NESS.] The quality or condition of being pat or to the point; suitability to a purpose or occasion; aptness.

1653 WATERHOUSE *Apol. Learn.* 116 Till the patnesse of the Conviction assured them [etc.]. **1710** *Life Bp. Stillingfleet* 86 A closeness of reference, and patness of similitudes. **1888** CLARK RUSSELL *Death Ship* I. 245, I could not but admire the patness of the mechanism to the condition of the ship.

‖**patois** (patwa), *sb.* (*a.*) [F.; 'origin unknown' (Hatz.-Darm.), see conjectures in Diez and Littré.]

a. *Properly*, a dialect (esp. in France or French Switzerland) spoken by the common people in a particular district, and differing materially from the literary language. In England, sometimes used *loosely* as a contemptuous designation for a provincial dialect or form of speech.

French scholars distinguish *dialects* as the particular forms presented by a language in different regions, so long as there does not exist a common written language. When a common language has become established as the medium of general literature, the dialects lose their literary standing and become *patois.*

1643 SIR T. BROWNE *Relig. Med.* II. §8 The *Jargon* and *Patois* of severall Provinces. **1789** MRS. PIOZZI *Journ. France*, etc. I. 314 At Venice, the sweetness of the patois is irresistible. **1832** tr. *Sismondi's Ital. Rep.* iii. 65 The Italian language, spoken at his court, first rose above the *patois* in common use throughout Italy. **1851** MAYNE REID *Scalp Hunt.* xx. 142 Their language was a Spanish *patois.* **1893** SELOUS *Trav. S.E. Africa* 7 The Dutch patois spoken in South Africa.

b. *transf.*

1790 BURKE *Fr. Rev.* Wks. V. 197 Their language is in the *patois* of fraud. **1880** *Standard* 10 Dec., A fashion.. of introducing children in novels who talk an impossible gibberish utterly unlike real baby *patois.*

c. The folk or Creole speech of the English-speaking Caribbean (esp. Jamaica).

1934 J. RHYS *Voy. in Dark* I. vi. 83 She said something in patois and went on washing up. **1953** *Caribbean Q.* III. I. 24 The hybrid dialects of French origin which in philology come under the heading *Creole.* In Trinidad the word used to denote these dialects is *Patois.* **1970** *Caribbean Stud.* July 108 *Patois*, used by many Jamaicans in reference to Jamaican Creole. **1971** *Caribbean Q.* XVII. II. 13 Same name, different referent.. patois.

d. *attrib.* or as *adj.* Of, pertaining to, or of the nature of a patois or illiterate dialect.

1789 CHARLOTTE SMITH *Ethelinde* (1814) III. 138 'Alas' cried she, in a *patois* dialect, between French and Spanish. **1799** HAN. MORE *Fem. Educ.* (ed. 4) I. 103 To ascertain that she has nothing *patois* in her dialect. **1809–12** MAR. EDGEWORTH *Mme. de Fleury* x, She.. remembered his *patois* accent. *a* **1894** MRS. DYAN *All in a Man's K.* (1899) 90 His powers of conversation in patois Pushtoo.

paton, obs. Sc. form of PATTEN.

patonce (pə'tɒns), *a. Her.* [Of uncertain origin: app. first in Leigh, wrongly attributed to Harding (who has *crosse patife*); perh. a mistaken use of F. *croix potencée*: see POTENCE.] In ***cross patonce***, a cross with its arms usually expanding in a curved form from the centre, having ends somewhat like those of the cross fleury.

1562 LEIGH *Armorie* 59 He bereth Geules, a crosse patonce [*so edd.* 1568–97; *ed.* 1612 crois patee] Or. Harding writeth, y^t kynge Egberte bare this crosse in his left hand, in battayle, and in his banner like wise. *Ibid.* 63 b, Crosses floures,.. and Crosses Patonces [*edd.* 1591, 1597, 1612 Potonces]. **1638** *Guillim's Heraldry* II. vii. (ed. 3) 92 The Field is Iupiter, a crosse Patonce Sol. **1658** PHILLIPS s.v., A crosse *Patonce*, i.e. whose ends are both broad and as it were three wayes hooked. **1821** SCOTT *Kenilw.* xii, Whose [Abbot of Abingdon's] arms.. I have seen over a stone chimney in the hall,—a cross patonce [*pr.* patonee, *ed.* 1893 patoncée] betwixt four martlets. **1868–82** CUSSANS *Her.* iv. 62 The Cross Patonce resembles a Cross Fleurie with the extremities expanded.

patootie (pə'tuːtɪ). *U.S. slang.* [Perh. a corruption of *potato* (see quot. 1921).] A sweetheart, girl-friend; a pretty girl.

1921 *Dialect Notes* V. 110 *Patootie*,.. Sweetheart. Reported from four different localities [in California]. Etymology unknown. Suggested, by sweetheart and sweet potato. **1923** G. MCKNIGHT *Eng. Words* iv. 61 In the vocabulary of modern youth, chivalry is dead... A girl.. if she is popular.. is a *darb*, a *peach*,.. a *sweet patootie.* **1935** *Nation* (N.Y.) 15 May 562/2 He calls the object of his affection a 'hot patootie'. **1948** LAIT & MORTIMER *New York: Confidential!* I. vi. 61 New Yorkers.. tell their patooties how pretty they are. **1950** *Times-Herald* (Washington) 27 Jan. I. 14/3 A batch of pretty-panned patooties. **1958** P. DE VRIES *Mackerel Plaza* 149 You like to shake a leg with a hot patootie now and then, do you? **1977** *New Yorker* 26 Sept. 32/1 She was, successively,.. the wife and/or sweet patootie of the quartet.

patorne, obs. form of PATRON, PATTERN.

†**patoun.** *Obs. rare.* [Origin and meaning uncertain. Possibly = F. *pâton* lump or bolus of dough, pellet of paste to feed chickens, f. *pâte* paste.

In the Ben Jonson passage some compare PETUN, obs. name of tobacco. Gifford suggests 'moulding of the tobacco, which was then always cut small, into some fantastic or fashionable form for the pipe'. The word in quot. 1495 may be different.]

[**1495** *Aberdeen Regr.* (1844) I. 57 Thare salbe gevin to our souerane In xxiii in wyne, xix of patoune iiii lib. 10*s.*, xii lib. skorcheatis, xxxvi *s.*] **1599** B. JONSON *Ev. Man out of Hum.* IV. iv, His villainous Ganymede and he have been droning a tobacco-pipe there ever since yesterday noon... They have hired a chamber and all, private, to practise in, for the making of the patoun,.. and a number of other mysteries not yet extant.

patrass, var. PATTRESS.

†'**patrate**, *a. Obs. rare.* [ad. L. *patrāt-us*, pa. pple. (in active sense) of *patrāre* to effect, conclude.] In ***father-patrate***, tr. L. *pater patrātus*, 'the fetial priest who ratified a treaty with religious rites' (Lewis & Short).

1533 BELLENDEN *Livy* I. ix. (S.T.S.) 55 The fader patrat was ordanit to strenth & corroborat bandis and contractis with maist solempne faith.

†**pa'tration.** *Obs. rare*$^{-0}$. [ad. L. *patrātiōn-em*, n. of action from *patrāre* to accomplish, effect.]

1656 BLOUNT *Glossogr.*, *Patration* (*patratio*), the finishing and perfecting a thing; a doing or making a thing.

patre, patrel, patremoyne, patriak, obs. ff. PATTER, PEITREL, PATRIMONY, PATRIARCH.

patri- ('pætrɪ, 'peɪtrɪ), used as the combining form of L. *pater* (*patr-is*) father, in words used in connection with the prominence of males and the importance of relationship on the male side in social organization. Some examples are given below as main words. Cf. also PATRIARCH *sb.*, PATRIARCHAL *a.*, etc.,

‖**patria** ('pætrɪə, 'peɪtrɪə). [ad. L. *patria*, fatherland.] Native country; homeland; also, heaven, as the region from which the soul is exiled while on earth and to which it longs to return.

a **1914** JOYCE *Stephen Hero* (1944) xix. 64 He refused therefore to set out for any task if he had first to prejudice his success by oaths to his patria. **1919** G. B. SHAW *What I really wrote about War* (1931) 352 As all the delegations have a different patria, and every patria has moral pretensions intolerable to and incompatible with the moral pretensions of all the other patrias, patriotism has to be dropped before any discussion is possible. **1936** H. G. WELLS *Anat. Frustration* iv. 46 The causes and devotions, the churches and organizations, the patrias and gangs, the family honour and the caste duty, to which the imagination of man.. has clung. **1957** G. V. SMITHERS in *Medium Ævum* XXVI. 151 The use elsewhere of *ælpeodig*(*-nes*) to render *peregrinus*, *peregrinatio*.. shows that *elpodigra eard* here means the heavenly home (*patria*) of good Christians (*peregrini*). **1959** C. S. LEWIS *Let.* 5 Nov. (1966) 289 It is just when there seems to be most of Heaven already here that I come nearest to longing for a *patria.* **1965** J. C. POPE in *Franciplegius* 182 The word *elpeodig* here is used with reference to the idea that good Christians are exiles and aliens on earth, destined to travel as *peregrini* toward their *patria* in heaven. **1977** *N.Y. Rev. Bks.* 26 May 30/3 The attachment of the creoles to what they had come to regard as their *patria*—a land of eternal spring as eulogized by local poets in baroque extravaganzas—required spiritual patrons which they could genuinely call their own.

patrial ('peɪtrɪəl), *a.* (*sb.*) [f. L. type **patriāl-is*, in obs. F. *patrial*, *-el* (16th c. in Godef.), It. *patriale*, f. L. *patria* fatherland.]

1. a. Of or belonging to one's native country. *rare.*

1629 MAXWELL tr. *Herodian* (1635) 296 The Image of his patriall god, whose Priest he was. **1755** J. SHEBBEARE *Lydia* (1769) II. 332 Honour, the contempt of riches, and patrial love, were strenuously inculcated. **1806** W. TAYLOR in *Ann. Rev.* IV. 237 Bequeathing the language and customs of their patrial mountains to another transatlantic country.

b. *spec.* Having the right of abode in the U.K. Also as *sb.*, one who has this right.

1971 *Sunday Times* 24 Jan. 11/1 The draft Bill.. lays down that a patrial basically is: 1. A person born in the UK or one of whose parents or grandparents were; 2. A naturalised citizen; 3. A former citizen of the Commonwealth already resident in Britain. **1971** *Times* 25 Feb. 4/4 Anyone who is patrial will be exempt from deportation. *Ibid.* 15/1 A new distinction is being drawn between patrials, who will be free of immigration control, and non-patrials who will require work permits. **1971** *Sunday Times* 28 Feb. 12/1 Conferring full patrial status on grandchildren of people born here has some strange implications. **1973** C. MULLARD *Black Brit.* v. 62 [The 1971 Immigration Bill] created a new 'right of abode' for a certain category of Commonwealth immigrant, 'patrials'. **1973** LD. BOYLE in N. Fisher *Iain Macleod* 20 Secondly, Macleod's compassion, and his strongly felt concern for the fair treatment of individuals, extended beyond those fellow-citizens who have come to be defined as 'patrials'. **1976** *Equals* Dec. 7/5 Foreign nations and people from the old Commonwealth (excluding 'patrials' and those on working holidays) made up the remainder.

2. *Gram.* Applied to a word denoting a native or inhabitant of the country or place from the name of which it is derived; also to a suffix forming such words. Also as *sb.*, a word of this class. *rare.*

1854 ANDREWS & STODDARD *Gram. Lat. Lang.* §100 A *patrial* or *gentile* noun is derived from the name of a country, and denotes an inhabitant of that country... Most patrials are properly adjectives, relating to a noun understood. **1870** MARCH *Comp. Gram. Ags. Lang.* (1883) 125 Patrial *isc*.. connotes origin from a place or stock: *Lunden-isc*, Londonish; *Engl-isc*, English.

So '**patrialism, patriali'zation.**

1971 *Sunday Times* 24 Jan. 11/2 At the end of the probationary period, the work permit holder will be able to apply for 'patrialisation'. *Ibid.*, 'Patrialism' is intended to clear it all up once and for all. **1971** *Times* 25 Feb. 4/4 Patrialism is a thin disguise for whites, albeit from the Commonwealth.

patriality (peɪtrɪ'ælɪtɪ). [f. prec. + -ITY.] Eligibility for or right to patrial status (PATRIAL *a.* (*sb.*) 1 b).

1971 *Guardian Weekly* 6 Mar. 8 In some cases, where patriality depends on ancestral connection, a certificate issued through the British High Commissioner will be needed as proof of that right. **1971** *Guardian* 9 Mar. 12/4 Mr Maudling denied that the 'patriality' concept was racialist. **1971** *Times* 19 Mar. 3 The jurists were also concerned that people arriving without work permits or certificates of patriality would be sent back to their countries of origin. **1973** *Daily Tel.* 22 Sept. 18 A woman cannot transmit United Kingdom citizenship or patriality to a man by marriage. **1974** *Ibid.* 31 Oct. 7/3 Although a passport was not essential legally to leave or re-enter the country, it had strong evidentiary value of 'patriality'. **1978** R. MAUDLING *Mem.* xi. 159 The solution we found was the introduction of the new concept of patriality.

patriarch ('peɪtrɪɑːk), *sb.* Also 3–4 **-arc**, 3–7 **-ark**, (4 **-ak**, **-eke**), 4–6 **-arche**, 4–7 **-arke**, **-arck(e**; 4–6 **patry-**. [ME. a. OF. *patriarche* (11th c. in Littré), ad. L. *patriarcha* (Tertull.), ad. Gr. *πατριάρχης* chief or head of a family, f. *πατριά* family, clan + *-αρχης* in comb. 'ruler'.]

1. The father and ruler of a family or tribe; *spec.* (*pl.*) in N.T., and uses thence derived, the twelve sons of Jacob, from whom the tribes of Israel were descended; also, the fathers of the race, Abraham, Isaac, and Jacob, and their forefathers. ***antediluvian patriarchs***, the line extending from Adam to Noah.

In the Septuagint *πατριάρχης* is applied to a head of a family or division of a tribe of Israel (2 Chron. xix. 8, xxvi. 12; cf. 1 Chron. ix. 9 *ἄρχοντες πατριῶν*, v.r. *πατριάρχαι*), also to the heads of the tribes themselves (*πατριάρχαι τῶν φυλῶν Ισραηλ*, 1 Chron. xxvii. 22); in the Jewish Book 'The Testaments of the Twelve Patriarchs', of 2nd c. B.C., as by St. Stephen in Acts vii. 9, to the twelve sons of Jacob; in 4 Macc. vii. 19 (cf.

xvi. 25), to Abraham, Isaac, and Jacob. In Acts ii. 29, applied to King David; but rarely to any one later than the 'Twelve Patriarchs'.

c **1175** *Lamb. Hom.* 81 þes patriarches, alse abel and noe and abraham. *Ibid.* 153 He sende his patriarken & propheten for to bodien his tokume. *c* **1200** ORMIN 7680, & Asær wass, þatt witt tu wel, An off þe Patriarrkess. *c* **1290** *Becket* 2301 in *S. Eng. Leg.* I. 172 Of Aungles and of patriarks [*v.r.* -arcs] and of apostles al-so. *a* **1300** *Cursor M.* 9047 (Cott.) þe patriarches [*v. rr.* patriarkes, -is] þai com wit-al Be-for þair fete he let him fal. **1382** WYCLIF *Acts* ii. 29 To seye to 3ou of the patriark Dauith. *Ibid.* vii. 9, 10 Ysaac gendride Iacob, and Iacob the twelue patriarkis. And the patriarkis hauynge enuye to Ioseph, solden hym into Egipt. **1387** TREVISA *Higden* (Rolls) II. 221 Adam deide and was i-buried in Ebron, þat is i-cleped also Cariatharbe, .. þe cite of foure, þat beþ patriarkes þat beeþ i-buried þere, þat beþ Adam, Abraham, Ysaac, and Iacob. *a* **1529** SKELTON *Ph. Sparowe* 256 Noe the patryarke, That made that great arke. **1667** MILTON *P.L.* IX. 376 So spake the Patriarch of Mankinde, but Eve .. though last, repli'd. **1727** DE FOE *Syst. Magic* I. i. (1840) 8 Such a degree as was ordinary to the patriarchs of the antediluvian age. **1852** LONGF. *Jew. Cemetery at Newport* 50 In the background figures vague and vast Of patriarchs and of prophets rose sublime.

b. By extension, One occupying a similar position in the history of any race.

1796 MORSE *Amer. Geog.* I. 78 That God created other men to be the patriarchs of the Europeans, Africans, and Americans.

2. In later Jewish history, applied (as repr. Heb. *nāsī* prince, chief) to the Chief or President of the Sanhedrim in Palestine, established under Syrian rule *c* 180 B.C., and ending with the death of the last of the Gamaliels A.D. 429. Sometimes incorrectly applied to the Exilarch or Head of the Jewish college in Babylon.

Both the Patriarch or Prince in Palestine and the Head of the college in Babylon had to be of Davidic descent. (H. Gollancz.)

1795 *Encycl. Brit.* (ed. 3) XIV. 37/1 Jewish Patriarch, a dignity. [The article is erroneous.] **1880** *Smith's Dict. Chr. Antiq.* II. 1573/2. **1885** *Encycl. Brit.* (ed. 9) XVIII. 410/2 The head of the synagogue at Babylon appears also to have been known as patriarch until 1038.

3. *Eccl.* **a.** In reference to the primitive Church, before the rupture of East and West: In earliest use, a rhetorical or honorific designation of bishops generally, which became at length the official title of the bishops of the great sees of Antioch, Alexandria, and Rome, also (from the 4th c.) of Constantinople, and (from 5th c.) of Jerusalem. **b.** Hence, in the *Orthodox Eastern Ch.*, The title of the bishops of the four patriarchates of Constantinople, Alexandria, Antioch, and Jerusalem, the Patriarch of Constantinople being the Head of the Church or ***Ecumenical Patriarch***. Also the title of the heads of the other Eastern Churches, as the Abyssinian, Armenian, Jacobite, and Coptic. **c.** In the *R.C. Ch.*, A bishop second only to the Pope in episcopal, and to the Pope and Cardinals in hierarchical rank, and next above primates and metropolitans. The title of the Latin bishops of Constantinople, Alexandria, Antioch, and Jerusalem; also, of those of the three minor patriarchates, the Indies, Lisbon, and Venice.

For various other ancient or mediæval uses of the term (in its Greek or Latin form, whence occasionally in historical use in Eng.) see *Dict. Chr. Antiq.* II. s.v. 'It was sometimes given to any metropolitan who had other metropolitans under him' (cf. b. below). 'It was adopted as the designation of their chief bishop by the Vandals'; also under the Lombard kings of Italy as the title of the bishop of Aquileia, whose patriarchate was subsequently transferred to Grado, and is now represented by that of Venice.

1297 R. GLOUC. *Chron.* (Rolls) 9869 þe king of ierusalem sir guy was þ er inome, & þe patriarc aslawe, & þe cristine ouercome. *c* **1300** *Havelok* 428 Haue he þe malisun to-day Of alle þat eure speken may! Of patriark, and of pope! *c* **1386** CHAUCER *Pard. Prol.* 15 Bulles of popes and of Cardynales Of Patriarkes & bishoppes I shewe. *c* **1400** MAUNDEV. (1839) iii. 18 Here Patriark hath as meche power ouer the See, as the Pope hath on this Syde the See. *c* **1449** PECOCK *Repr.* (Rolls) II. 416 Aboue alle patriarkis is oon pope for to reule and amende the gouernauncis of patriarkis. **1517** TORKINGTON *Pilgr.* (1884) 12 The Duke .. with all the Senyorye .. rowed in to the see, with the assistens of ther Patriarche, And ther Spoused the see with a ryng. **1547** BOORDE *Introd. Knowl.* i. (1870) 119 There was a patriarke of Ierusalem, ther is a patryarke at Constantinople, & there is a patryarke at Venis. **1698** A. BRAND *Emb. Muscovy to China* 5 Russia has its own Patriarch, who exercises the same Authority.., as the Pope does in .. Roman Catholick Countries. **1710** WHITWORTH *Acc. Russia* (1758) 47 The present Czar, on the death of the late Patriarch, sequestered the office. **1847** MRS. A. KERR tr. *Ranke's Hist. Servia* 36 These events determined the Porte not to suffer the election of another Servian Patriarch. **1850** NEALE *East. Ch.* I. 126 In correctness of speech, we are assured by Theodore Balsamon, the Patriarch of Antioch is the only Prelate who has a claim to that title: the proper appellation of the Bishops of Rome and Alexandria being *Pope*, of Constantinople and Jerusalem, *Archbishop*. **1885** *Catholic Dict.* (ed. 3) s.v., The Sixth Canon of the first Nicene Council recognises an ancient, customary, and legitimate authority in the Bishops of the three sees of Alexandria, Rome, and Antioch (named in this order) over their respective provinces. The title of 'Patriarch', however, is not given; the thing is recognised, but not the word. The title came into use in the fifth century. *Ibid.*, Since the .. Greek schism, &c. severed all these four sees from Catholic unity, the Popes have continued to nominate bishops to the lost Patriarchates; but these bishops have resided at Rome, except lately in the case of Jerusalem, the Patriarch of which .. commenced to reside at his see in 1847. Besides the Latin Patriarch of Antioch, the Holy See admits a Maronite, a Melchite, and a Syrian Patriarch of the same see, a Patriarch of Cilicia of the Armenian, and a Patriarch of Babylon of the Chaldaic, rite.

d. *transf.* Applied unofficially to the chief dignitaries of other Churches; †formerly also to the heads of other religious systems (*obs.*).

1477 EARL RIVERS (Caxton) *Dictes* 99 The patryarkes & prelates that were for that tyme cam and sayd to hym God hath yeue to the [Alexander] lordship upon many royames. **1563** WIN3ET *Four Scoir Thre Quest.* To Chr. Rdr., Wks. 1888 I. 56 Deliuerit thame .. to Iohne Knox, as to him, quha wes haldin in tha partis principal Patriark of the Caluiniane Court. **1600** J. PORY tr. *Leo's Africa* VIII. 301 A certaine craftie Mahumetan patriarke made the rude people beleeve, that [etc.]. **1637** HEYLIN *Brief Answ.* 64 The learned workes .. of Dr. Adrian Saravia against your Patriarke Theodore Beza. *a* **1670** HACKET *Abp. Williams* I. 187 The Lord Keeper's Letter sent to that Worthy Patriarch of the North [Abp. Toby Matthew]. **1733** NEAL *Hist. Purit.* II. 156 He [Laud] was ambitious of being the Sovereign Patriarch of three Kingdoms.

4. One who is regarded as the father or founder of an order, institution, or tradition, or (by extension) of a science, school of thought, or the like.

1566 *Pasquine in Traunce* 56 b, Among these Patriarches are accompted .. Saint Dominicke, who instituted the order of preaching... Why are they called Patriarches? .. Bycause they are the chiefe of the Fathers, .. that is to say of the Friers who call themselues Fathers. **1622** W. M. (*title*) The Life of the Holy Patriarch S. Ignatius of Loyola. *a* **1680** BUTLER *Rem.* (1759) I. 135 The Turk's Patriarch Mahomet Was the first great Reformer. **1756–7** tr. *Keysler's Trav.* (1760) III. 2 St. Benedict, the patriarch of the monks among the western Christians. **1758** H. WALPOLE *Catal. Roy. Authors* (1759) I. 162 He was the Patriarch of a race of genius and wit. **1855** KINGSLEY *Westw. Ho!* xxx, For John Hawkins, Admiral of the port, is the Patriarch of Plymouth seamen, if Drake be their hero. **1866** CRUMP *Banking* viii. 158 The patriarch of political economy, Adam Smith. **1871** R. ELLIS *Catullus* xxi. 1 Sire and prince-patriarch of hungry starvelings.

5. A venerable old man; *esp.* the oldest man, the 'father' of a village or neighbourhood; the veteran or oldest living representative of a class, profession, art, or the like.

c **1817** HOGG *Tales & Sk.* (1837) I. 310, I was rather viewed as their chief, next at least to the patriarch. **1820** W. IRVING *Sketch Bk., Rip Van Winkle*, He .. was reverenced as one of the patriarchs of the village. **1868** FREEMAN *Norm. Conq.* II. viii. 291 The patriarch of that great house was now a knight so poor that he craved leave of his lord to leave his service. **1888** BRYCE *Amer. Commw.* I. iii. 28 Mr. George Bancroft, now the patriarch of American literature.

b. *transf.* The head of a flock or herd; of trees, etc., the oldest and greatest; *gen.* the most venerable object of a group.

1700 DRYDEN *Palamon & Arc.* III. 1058 The monarch oak, the patriarch of the trees. **1810** SCOTT *Lady of L.* III. viii, A goat, the patriarch of the flock. **1850** R. G. CUMMING *Hunter's Life S. Afr.* (ed. 2) I. 243, I shot the patriarch of the herd, which as usual brought up the rear.

6. *attrib.* and *Comb.*, as ***patriarch-age***, ***-pupil***, ***-throne***, ***-wit***; **patriarch's age**, the lifetime of a patriarch (sense 1), a very long time.

1693 *Humours Town* 107 Some old, nonsensical Translations .. which have serv'd a Patriarch's Age to the Library of Moore-fields. **1709** POPE *Ess. Crit.* 479 That golden age .. When Patriarch-wits surviv'd a thousand years. **1868** J. H. NEWMAN *Verses on Var. Occas.* 129 Till thou didst quit Thy patriarch-throne at length. **1889** R. B. ANDERSON tr. *Rydberg's Teut. Mythol.* 95 Then the second mythic patriarch-age begins.

Hence **'patriarch** *v. nonce-wd.*, in ***to patriarch it***, to play the patriarch; **'patriarched** *a.*, having or containing a patriarch.

1632 LITHGOW *Trav.* VI. 237 Hebrons Patriarch'd Tombe. **1639** FULLER *Holy War* II. xliv. 103 Whilest Heraclius did Patriarch it in Jerusalem, one Haymericus had the same honour at Antioch. **1766** STERNE *Lett.* 25 May (1775) II. 160 A delicious Chateau .. where I have been patriarching it these seven days with her ladyship.

† **patri'archacy.** *Obs. rare*⁻¹. [f. prec. + -ACY, after *papacy*.] The see of a patriarch; a patriarchate.

1681 H. MORE *Exp. Dan.* vi. Notes 222 Urum Papai .. may indigitate .. the Patriarchacy of Constantinople.

patriarchal (peɪtrɪ'ɑːkəl), *a.* Also 6–7 -chall, 7 -call. [ad. late L. *patriarchāl-is* (Alcimus *c* 500), f. *patriarcha* PATRIARCH: see -AL¹. Cf. F. *patriarcal* (14–15th c. in Godef. *Compl.*).]

1. Of or belonging to a patriarch; of or characteristic of the patriarchs or their times.

1656 BLOUNT *Glossogr.*, *Patriarchal*, of or belonging to a Patriarch. **1687** NORRIS *Coll. Misc.*, *To Dr. Plot* ii, Who could to Patriarchal years live on. **1699** EVELYN *Acetaria* (1729) 160 Here might we attest the Patriarchal World. **1727** DE FOE *Hist. Appar.* iii. (1840) 24 Some are of the opinion, by the sons of God, there is meant the patriarchal heads of families. *a* **1763** BYROM *Disinterested Love of God* iv, This Love the patriarchal Eye, And that of Moses could descry. **1884** J. HALL *Chr. Home* 110 Servants, indeed, do not now stand to their masters as they did in patriarchal times.

2. *Eccl.* Of or belonging to a hierarchical patriarch; ruled by a patriarch; of the nature or rank of a patriarch.

Patriarchal church, a title of the five great Roman basilicas: viz. St. John Lateran, St. Peter's, St. Paul's, St. Mary the greater, and St. Lawrence extra muros.

1570 FOXE *A. & M.* (ed. 2) 11/2 The cause why the sea of Rome, emong all other patriarchall seas, is numbred for the first sea by the auncient fathers. **1579** FULKE *Confut. Sanders* 545 The Pope did erect patriarchal Seas at Aquileia, and at Senis. **1670** LASSELS *Voy. Italy* II. 162 [St. Lawrence] is one of the five Patriarchal churches, and therefore is not titular of any Cardinal. **1870–4** ANDERSON *Missions Amer. Bd.* III. iii. 42 Letters were addressed from Rome to the Patriarchal Vicar of Mount Lebanon.

b. *Her.* ***patriarchal cross***, one with two transverse pieces, the upper being the shorter: an emblem of the patriarchs of the Greek Church.

1682 GIBBON *Introd. ad Latin. Blason.* 78 *Cross Patriarchal*... As the Staves of the Popes are thrice crossed, so those of Patriarchs and Cardinals are but twice. **1882** CUSSANS *Her.* iv. (ed. 3) 60 The Patriarchal Cross is a Greek Cross, the upper limb of which is traversed by a shorter.

3. Of, pertaining to, or of the nature of a patriarchy.

1828 SCOTT *F.M. Perth* xxviii, To testify their acceptance of the patriarchal chief who claimed their allegiance. **1844** EMERSON *Lect., Yng. Amer.* Wks. (Bohn) II. 298 The patriarchal form of government readily becomes despotic. **1883** MAINE *Early Law* vii. 196 The Patriarchal theory of society is .. the theory of its origin in separate families, held together by the authority and protection of the eldest valid male ascendant. **1902** A. MACBAIN in *Skene's Highlanders Scot.* 402 The succession among the Scots was Patriarchal.

4. Resembling a patriarch, venerable, aged; like that of a patriarch.

1837 HAWTHORNE *Twice-told T.* (1851) II. ii. 34 The Select-men of Boston, plain, patriarchal fathers of the people. **1862** BURTON *Bk. Hunter* I. 43 The patriarchal head of an agreeable and elegant household. **1898** *Voice* (N.Y.) 21 Apr. 3/2 Abraham .. is a splendid figure with his long, white, patriarchal beard.

b. *transf.* Of an animal, tree, etc.: Oldest of a flock or group, aged, ancestral; of things generally: Ancient, primitive.

1837 SIR F. PALGRAVE *Merch. & Friar* i. (1844) 15 To limp .. through primitive ruts and patriarchal bridle-paths. **1839** LONGF. *Voices Nt.* Prel. iii, Beneath some patriarchal tree. **1850** R. G. CUMMING *Hunter's Life S. Afr.* (1902) 141/1 Along the spoor of the patriarchal old black buck.

Hence **patri'archally** *adv.*, in a patriarchal way.

1835 *Fraser's Mag.* XI. 482 Why might not [they] have continued to flourish patriarchally in the woods of Virginia?

patri'archalism. [See -ISM.] A patriarchal system of society or government.

1847 BARMBY in *Tait's Mag.* XIV. 267 Small farms would also be a return to Patriarchalism. **1854** *Fraser's Mag.* XLIX. 649 A sort of midway state between the heaven-derived patriarchalism of Russian theory, and the anarchy of democracy. **1887** *Athenæum* 1 Jan. 27/2 His own hypothesis as to the devolution of mother-right into patriarchalism.

patri'archalist. [f. PATRIARCHAL *a.* + -IST.] One who advocates or approves of a patriarchal system of society or government.

1923 *Contemp. Rev.* Oct. 450 The mutual contempt of the patriarchalist and the feminist is identical in its sources .. with the mutual contempt of the 'tough' and the 'tender' races.

patriarchate ('peɪtrɪɑːkət). [ad. med.L. *patriarchātus*, in F. *patriarcat* (*c* 1500 in Hatz.-Darm.), It. *patriarcato*: see -ATE¹.]

1. The office, dignity, or jurisdiction of an ecclesiastical patriarch.

1617 MORYSON *Itin.* I. 76 After that the Patriarchate of Aquilegia in Histria, was by the Popes authority translated thither. **1640** R. BAILLIE *Canterb. Self-Convict.* (1641) 41 His ancient right to the patriarchat of the whole Isle of Britaine. **1709** J. JOHNSON *Clergym. Vade M.* II. p. lxxxv, 'Tis the prevailing opinion that at the time of the Synod of Nice Patriarchates were not set up. **1885** [see PATRIARCH 3]. **1895** *Daily News* 11 Feb. 6/3 Mardin (the modern seat of the Syrian Patriarchate).

b. The province or see of a patriarch.

1640 R. BAILLIE *Canterb. Self-Convict.* 36 They will have us to believe .. that within the bounds of his owne Patriarchat he [the pope] is a prince. **1681** BAXTER *Answ. Dodwell* 140 [He] forbad the Orthodox to Preach in his Patriarchate. **1875** MERIVALE *Gen. Hist. Rome* lxxiv. (1877) 610 The great Eastern patriarchates of Antioch, Alexandria, and Jerusalem had all held themselves equal or superior to Rome.

c. The residence of a patriarch; the administrative office or official staff of a patriarch.

1860 *All Year Round* No. 73. 537 Leaving the Armenian patriarchate, you perceive, in a narrow lane to the right, the remnant of an old wall. **1897** *Daily News* 13 July 5/4 It appears the Patriarchate was unwilling to make any representations to the Porte.

2. The rank or authority of a patriarch of a tribe; a patriarchal system; = PATRIARCHY 2.

1651–3 JER. TAYLOR *Serm. of Year* I. xvii. 220 To have great families, that their own relations might swell up to a Patriarchat, and their children be enough to possesse all the regions that they saw. **1727** DE FOE *Syst. Magic* I. iv. (1840) 98 An ark for every family, or patriarchate, or tribe. **1856** OLMSTED *Slave States* 87 Never two dwellings of mankind within sight of each other; only, at long distances, often several miles asunder, these isolated plantation patriarchates. **1896** F. B. JEVONS *Introd. Hist. Relig.* xiv. 180 The patriarchate with monogamy prevailed.

patriarchdom ('peɪtrɪɑːkdəm). *rare.* [See -DOM.] The state or office of patriarch; patriarchate, patriarchship.

1572 R. T. *Discourse* 21 The Pope in his supremacie, is Abell,..in Patriarchdome Abraham. **1641** MILTON *Reform.* I. Wks. (1851) 7 The Bishops..fall to scrambling, catch who may, hee a Patriarch-dome, and another what comes next to hand.

patriarchess ('peɪtrɪɑːkɪs). *rare.* [ad. med.L. *patriarchissa* (Du Cange), OF. *patriarchece, -esce, -esse* (Godef.).] The wife of a patriarch; a female patriarch; a woman of patriarchal age; the oldest woman of a community.

1639 FULLER *Holy War* II. xxxix. (1840) 102 She was generally saluted the patriarchess. **1645** J. BOND *Occasus Occid.* 19 Sarah (if I may so call her) the Patriarchesse. **1732** *Hist. Litteraria* III. 199 The History of the Patriarchess of Constantinople is not so improbable. **1882** *Echo* 14 Apr. 4/2 Yesterday..the patriarchess of the district, attain[ed] her 100th year, being born on the 12th April, 1782.

patriarchic (peɪtrɪ'ɑːkɪk), *a. rare*$^{-1}$. [ad. late L. *patriarchic-us*, a. late Gr. πατριαρχικ-ός, f. πατριάρχης PATRIARCH: see -IC.] = next, 2.

1776 J. BRYANT *Mythol.* III. 47 The term of Nimrod's life, extend it to the utmost of Patriarchic age.., could not have sufficed for this.

patriarchical (peɪtrɪ'ɑːkɪkəl), *a.* ? *Obs.* [f. as prec. + -AL[1].]

†**1.** Of, belonging to, of the nature of, an ecclesiastical patriarch or patriarchate: = PATRIARCHAL 2.

1606 J. DOVE *Def. Ch. Govt.* 23 In that Councel, were prouincial, Diocesan, and patriarchicall Bishops. **1670** G. H. *Hist. Cardinals* I. III. 84 It was establish'd, that in every Patriarchical Church in Rome, there should be two Priests.

2. Of, pertaining to, or of the nature of the ancient patriarchs, or of the patriarchal system of government; like a patriarch, venerable. ? *Obs.*

1643 PRYNNE *Sov. Power Parl.* III. 116 Whose government was at first Paternall and Patriarchicall. **1659** GAUDEN *Tears of Ch.* IV. xvii. 519 The Patriarchicall Tradition and Practise before the Law of Moses. **1698** FRYER *Acc. E. India & P.* 56 His Meen was Patriarchical.

Hence **patri'archically** *adv.* = PATRIARCHALLY.

1887 *Spectator* 20 Aug. 1112 It is no use to take a little bit from despotically or patriarchically ruled countries and apply it to ours.

patriarchism ('peɪtrɪɑːkɪz(ə)m). [See -ISM.] The patriarchal system of social or ecclesiastical organization, government, etc.

a **1666** A. BROME *To his Rev. Friend Dr. S.* 18 Who split the Church into so many Schismes, The zeals of these eats tothers Patriarchismes. **1839** YEOWELL *Anc. Brit. Ch.* i. (1847) 6 Their form of government was pure patriarchism; that is, they were all subject to the heads of their respective families. *a* **1867** J. HAMILTON *Moses* (1870) xxi. 332 We call Paganism a corruption of Patriarchism.

Patriarchist ('peɪtrɪɑːkɪst). [f. PATRIARCH *sb.* + -IST.] A supporter of the Patriarch of Constantinople against the Exarch of Bulgaria during the schism of 1872–1945. Also *attrib.*

1903, etc. [see EXARCHIST]. **1903** *Daily Chron.* 23 Sept. 3/5 They [*sc.* the Vlachs] are attached to the Greek or Patriarchist party. **1907** A. FORTESCUE *Orthod. Eastern Ch.* IV. x. 320 The Patriarchists..stand by the Patriarch of Constantinople. **1921** *Contemp. Rev.* May 587 Bulgarian Patriarchists—*i.e.* Bulgarians who affect the Greek religion ..are numbered with the Greek inhabitants. **1972** D. DAKIN *Unification of Greece* ix. 129 Vatikiotis..reported that Greek intervention would be welcomed by the Slav-speaking patriarchists. *Ibid.* xii. 160 It was precisely in those regions where the exarchist and patriarchist school populations were evenly matched that the struggle between the two Churches was fiercest.

'patriarchize, *v. rare.* [See -IZE.] *intr.* To follow or practise a patriarchal system.

1818 G. S. FABER *Horæ Mosaicæ* II. 222 To convince the patriarchizing children of Israel that they might safely and piously receive a new legislator.

'patriarchship. *rare.* [See -SHIP.]

1. The office or dignity of an ecclesiastical patriarch; a patriarchal see, a patriarchate.

1566 STAPLETON *Ret. Untr. Jewel* IV. 188 His owne dyocese, or patriarkeship of Rome. **1691** *Lond. Gaz.* No. 2654/1 The King [of Spain] has given the Patriarchship of the Indies to Don Pedro de Porto Carrero. **1726** AYLIFFE *Parergon* 113 Prelacies, may be termed the greater Benefices; as that of the Pontificate, Patriarchship,..and the like.

2. The position or authority of an ancient patriarch.

1619 SIR J. SEMPILL *Sacrilege Handl.* App. 10 Shall we diuide Abrahams Patriarchship from his Promises?

patriarchy ('peɪtrɪɑːkɪ). [ad. Gr. πατριαρχία office of a patriarch (cf. *monarchy, tetrarchy*). Cf. also med.L. *patriarchia*, F. *patriarchie* a patriarchal church, *patriarchium* patriarchal residence or dignity (Du Cange).]

†**1.** The dignity, see, or jurisdiction of an ecclesiastical patriarch; = PATRIARCHATE 1. *Obs.*

b. The government of the Church by a patriarch or patriarchs.

1561 T. NORTON *Calvin's Inst.* IV. vii. (1634) 551 All the old Synodes command bishops to be consecrate by their owne Metropolitanes; and they never bid the bishop of Rome to be called unto it, but in his owne Patriarchie. **1641** 'SMECTYMNUUS' *Answ.* (1653) Post. 86 Whence perhaps it is that the Sea of Canterbury hath affected a Patriarchy in our dayes. **1657** J. SERGEANT *Schism Dispach't* 148 To limit the Pope's Patriarchy to a particular Province of Italy.

2. A patriarchal system of society or government; government by the father or the eldest male of the family; a family, tribe, or community so organized.

1632 LITHGOW *Trav.* v. 215 The posterity of which Patriarchy continued in bondage two hundred and fifteene yeares. **1855** J. HARRIS (*title*) Patriarchy; or, the Family: its Constitution and Probation. **1894** *Daily News* 14 Nov. 6/4 'Hierarchy and patriarchy'..summed up Alexander III.'s Slavonic policy.

patriate ('peɪtrɪeɪt), *v. Canad.* [f. RE)PATRIATE *v.*] *trans.* To bring (legislation) under the constitutional authority of an autonomous country, used with reference to laws passed on behalf of that country by its former mother-country.

1966 *Deb. Commons Canada* 28 Jan. 373/2 *Mr. T. C. Douglas* (*Burnaby-Coquitlam*):..would the Prime Minister care to indicate to the house what action the government now proposes to take with a view to having a constitution in Canada amendable by Canadians? *Right Hon. L. B. Pearson* (*Prime Minister*):..we intend to do everything we can to have the constitution of Canada repatriated, or patriated. **1976** *Daily Gleaner* (Fredericton, New Brunswick) 12 Apr. 3 (*heading*) Trudeau wants serious bid to patriate constitution. *Ibid.*, He set out three possible ways of patriating the constitution, the British North America Act. **1978** *Globe & Mail* (Toronto) 2 Jan. 10/3 These things 10 years ago were..almost academic exercises and when Victoria failed nobody saw it as a..tragedy—so Trudeau didn't succeed in patriating the constitution.

Hence **patri'ation**, the act or process of patriating; also *attrib.*

1976 *Globe & Mail* (Toronto) 20 Apr. 6/2 Haven't there been hundreds of spontaneous demonstrations across the country in support of unilateral patriation of the constitution? *Ibid.* 16 Aug. 5/6 The talks will be the most extensive on patriation of the BNA Act since the inconclusive Victoria conference in 1971. **1976** *Daily Colonist* (Victoria, B.C.) 3 Oct. 1/7 (*heading*) Patriation formula. **1978** *Globe & Mail* (Toronto) 13 Feb. 7/5 Mr. Ryan urged Premier Robert Bourassa to take a firm stand, and to refuse any patriation of Canada's constitution.

†**pa'trice.** *Obs. rare*$^{-1}$. [a. F. *patrice* (12–13th c. in Hatz.-Darm.) = It. *patrice*, ad. L. *patrīcius* belonging to the rank of the *patres*, 'fathers' or senators of Rome; as sb., a member of the ancient Roman nobility: see PATRICIAN *sb.*[1] 1.] = PATRICIAN *sb.*[1] 1.

1529 RASTELL *Pastyme, Rome* (1811) 27 Made him a patrice, and Consull of Rome.

patrice, patrich, var. PATRIX, PARTRIDGE.

patricentric (pætrɪ'sɛntrɪk), *a.* [f. PATRI- + CENTRIC *a.*] Emphasizing, organized around, or dominated by the father or male line.

1949 R. K. MERTON *Social Theory* viii. 244 Freud himself was in his patricentric character, a typical representative of a society which demands obedience. **1957** V. W. TURNER *Schism & Continuity in Afr. Society* vii. 222 The patricentric family..is attached to a locality.

patrician (pə'trɪʃən), *sb.*[1] and *a.*[1] Also 7 -tian. [f. L. *patrĭci-us* (see PATRICE) + -AN; cf. F. *patricien* (14th c.), which was perh. the model.]

A. *sb.*

1. A person belonging, or reputed to belong, to one of the original citizen families or *gentes* of which the ancient Roman *populus* consisted, and out of whom, in the first ages of the republic, the senators, consuls, and pontifices were exclusively chosen; a Roman noble. Opp. to PLEBEIAN *sb.*

1533 BELLENDEN *Livy* IV. (1822) 317 No plebeane will tak the dochter of ane patriciane but hir consent. **1607** SHAKS. *Cor.* IV. iii. 15 There hath beene in Rome straunge Insurrections: The people, against the Senatours, Patricians, and Nobles. **1695** LD. PRESTON *Boeth.* Life 25 He also design'd upon the Lives of several others of the Patritians. **1781** GIBBON *Decl. & F.* xvii. (1846) II. 24 The proudest and most perfect separation..between the nobles and the people, is perhaps that of the Patricians and the Plebeians,..in the first age of the Roman republic. **1879** FROUDE *Cæsar* vi. 54 He [Sulla] was a patrician of the purest blood.

b. In the later Roman Empire, A member of a new noble order nominated by the Emperor at Byzantium; also, an officer, orig. a member of this order, sent or appointed as representative of the Emperor to administer the western provinces of Italy and Africa. The title was afterwards assumed by Charlemagne and his successors.

1432–50 tr. *Higden* (Rolls) VI. 271 Nichoforus the patricion, honorede and luffede moche of the seide Yrene. **1653** HOLCROFT *Procopius* I. 13 The Emperour Justine.. sent Probus, Sisters son to the late Emperour Anastasius, a Patritian, with money to raise an army of Hunnes for his ayd. **1781** GIBBON *Decl. & F.* xvii. (1846) II. 25 He [Constantine] revived..the title of Patricians, but he revived it as a personal, not as an hereditary distinction. **1788** *Ibid.* xlix. IV. 486 The importance and danger of those remote provinces [Italy and Africa] required the presence of a supreme magistrate; he was indifferently styled the exarch or the patrician. **1861** J. G. SHEPPARD *Fall Rome* vi. 287 Theoderic set forth to take possession of his new inheritance, in the character of 'Patrician by the emperor's appointment'. **1872** [see EXARCH 1]. **1885** *Encycl. Brit.* XVIII. 411/1 It was as patrician of Rome that the emperor Henry IV. claimed the right to depose Pope Gregory VII. The title was abolished by Pope Eugenius III. in 1145.

c. Applied to the hereditary noble citizens of some of the mediæval Italian republics, as Venice, Genoa, etc. (= Ital. *patrizio*, †*patricio*), and to the higher order or 'gentlemen' of the Free Cities of the German Empire (= Ger. *patricier*).

1611 CORYAT *Crudities* 125 Some worthy Duke or Patritian of Venice. **1617** MORYSON *Itin.* I. 93 [tr. Latin Inscr.] To Lodwick Ariosto Poet, a Patrician of Ferraria. *Ibid.* III. 239 The Patritians [of the Imperiall Free Cities] liue vpon their reuenues, as Gentlemen. *Ibid.* 240 (*Nurnberg*) The Senate consists of forty persons, whereof thirty foure are Patricians or Gentlemen. **1820** BYRON *Mar. Fal.* I. ii. 50 The sentence pass'd on Michel Steno, born Patrician. **1840** *Penny Cycl.* XVII. 318/1 At Venice, the name of patrician was given to the members of the great council..and their descendants. *Patrizio Veneto* was a title of nobility, considered equal to that of any feudal noble not of a sovereign house. **1841** W. SPALDING *Italy & It. Isl.* II. 169.

d. *gen.* A person of noble birth or rank; a nobleman, aristocrat. Opp. to *plebeian.*

1631 T. POWELL *Tom All Trades* (1876) 148 If you sue to a [City] Company consisting of many persons Tradesmen, you must enquire who bee the most potent Patritians.. amongst them. **1841** EMERSON *Lect., Conservative* Wks. (Bohn) II. 264 The battle of patrician and plebeian.. reappears in all countries and times. **1861** THACKERAY *Four Georges* iii. (1862) 126 At the accession of George III. the patricians were yet at the height of their good fortune.

2. One versed in the writings of the Fathers; a patristic scholar. *rare.*

c **1810** COLERIDGE in *Lit. Rem.* (1838) III. 279 So great a scholar, so profound a Patrician, as Jeremy Taylor was. *a* **1834** *Ibid.* (1839) IV. 47 Luther was no great Patrician.

B. *adj.* Of, belonging to, or composed of the patricians of ancient Rome: see A. 1. Opp. to PLEBEIAN *a.*

1620 BARRET *Ded. Southwell's Poems* 70 Sulpitius, a Gentleman of Patrician blood. **1713** ADDISON *Cato* I. i, His horse's hoofs wet with Patrician blood. **1841** W. SPALDING *Italy & It. Isl.* I. 59 The power thus vested in the senate truly belonged to the patrician order; because the senate was originally composed entirely of that class. **1879** FROUDE *Cæsar* viii. 85 He had a patrician disdain of mobs and suffrages and the cant of popular liberty.

b. *gen.* Of or belonging to the Patricians in Italian or German cities, etc.; of noble or high birth or rank; noble, aristocratic. Opp. to *plebeian.*

1615 CHAPMAN *Odyss.* Ep. Ded., Let Death then reave My life now lost in our patrician loves. **1617** MORYSON *Itin.* III. 193 In free Cities, here the Patritian Order, there the common people, and otherwhere both with mixed power gouerne the City. **1820** BYRON *Mar. Fal.* II. i. 75 You have strange thoughts for a patrician dame. **1830** J. G. STRUTT *Sylva Brit.* 143 The dignity of ages afforded by the Oak, that truly patrician tree. **1853** LYTTON *My Novel* XII. xxxiii, His handsome countenance, his patrician air.

c. Applied to various aristocratic or non-popular parties in later times.

1812 *Gen. Hist.* in *Ann. Reg.* 205/2 The patrician body of troops..turned out the whole of their officers from the barracks. **1860** MOTLEY *Netherl.* (1868) II. ix. 3 The Earl in his quarrels..with the patrician party rapidly forming against him in the States.

Hence **pa'tricianate**, bad form for PATRICIATE; **pa'tricianhood**, the condition or rank of a patrician; also, patricians collectively; **pa'tricianism**, patrician quality, style, or spirit; also, patricians collectively; **pa'tricianly** *adv.*, in a patrician manner, aristocratically; **pa'tricianship** = *patricianhood.*

1859 HOBHOUSE *Italy* II. 225 It was the endeavour of the people and nobles to deprive Leo III. of all temporal power, that made him apply to Charlemagne, and merge both the republic and the *patricianate in the imperial title of the Frank. **1885** A. FORBES *Souvenirs Continents, Amer. Society* 226 In Virginia,..there was a good deal of ancestral *patricianhood. **1826** *Blackw. Mag.* XIX. 123 To claim it at the feet of *Patricianism. **1864** LOWELL *Among my Bks.* Ser. I. (1873) 230 Honest dice, uncogged by those three hoary sharpers, Prerogative, Patricianism and Priestcraft. **1893** GUNTER *Miss Dividends* 117 Trying to take her *patricianly gloved hand in his. **1824** *Blackw. Mag.* XVI. 266 Estimating the *patriziato*, or *patricianship—an aristocracy of a different kind..from that of feudal nobles—as the most powerful and enlightened party. **1867** FREEMAN in Stephens *Life & Lett.* (1895) I. 376 Burghership and patricianship being hereditary.

pa'trician, *sb.*[2] *Ch. Hist.* [ad. L. (pl.) *Patrīciānī*, f. the name of their founder, Patricius, preceptor of Symmachus the Marcionite.] A member of a heretical sect which arose in the fourth century, and held that the substance of the flesh was the work of the devil, not of God.

1659 HOWELL *Vocab.* x, The Patricians, Heronians, Proclianits. **1727–41** in CHAMBERS *Cycl.*

Pa'trician, *a.*[2] [f. L. *Patrici-us*, proper name (see PATRICK) + -AN.] Pertaining to, or founded by, St. Patrick.

1872 A. T. DE VERE *Legends St. Patrick* p. x, In the legends of the Patrician Cycle the chief-loving old Bard is ever mournful. **1882–3** in Schaff *Encycl. Relig. Knowl.* II. 1113 The Patrician Church was independent of Rome. **1890** J. HEALEY *Irel. Anc. Sch.* 67 The history of the Patrician Church in Ireland. **1932** *Universe* 26 Feb. 3/2 The Patrician sites in Co. Down. **1933** *Clergy Rev.* May 382 A normal development of the Patrician system of organization. **1950** *Month* May 379 Five chapters..with an introduction on Patrician scholarship past and present. **1963** *Times Lit. Suppl.* 19 Apr. 264/2 The Patrician controversy.

patriciate (pə'trɪʃɪət). [ad. med.L. *patriciāt-us*, f. *patrīcius*: see PATRICIAN *sb.*[1] and -ATE[1]. So F. *patriciat* (1690 in Furetière).]

1. The position, dignity, or rank of a patrician; nobility of rank.

1656 BLOUNT *Glossogr.*, *Patriciate*, the dignity and estate of them that descend of Senators. **1727–41** CHAMBERS *Cycl.* s.v. *Patrician*, This new patriciate..was erected by Constantine, who conferred the quality on his counsellours. **1854** MILMAN *Lat. Chr.* VIII. ii. III. 292 The Patriciate and Defensorship of the city of Rome. *Ibid.* VIII. ix. 544 The republic..recognised the sovereignty of the Pope; the patriciate was abolished, a prefect named with more limited powers.

b. The term or period of holding the dignity of a patrician (see PATRICIAN A. 1 b).

1875 FREEMAN *Sk. Venice, Spalato* (1881) 145 The villa near Salona where the deposed Emperor Nepos was slain, during the patriciate of Odoacer.

2. A patrician order or class; the aristocracy.

1795 tr. *Mercier's Fragm. Pol. & Hist.* I. 331 The patriciate was the gangrene of the republic, and had attacked the Senate itself. **1850** MERIVALE *Rom. Emp.* (1865) II. xi. 32 No aristocracy was ever more shortsighted at the crisis of its fate than the once glorious patriciate of Rome. **1867** FREEMAN *Norm. Conq.* I. v. 338 The English inhabitants formed a dominant class or patriciate.

patricidal (pætrɪ'saɪdəl), *a.* [f. next + -AL[1].] Of, pertaining to, or resembling a patricide; parricidal; in quots. *fig.* involving treason or faithlessness to one's country or fatherland.

1821 JEFFERSON *Autobiog.* Wks. 1859 I. 73 The States General, indignant at this patricidal conduct, applied to France for aid. **1827** *Blackw. Mag.* XXII. 613 They acted in the most wild, unconstitutional, and patricidal manner.

patricide[1] ('pætrɪsaɪd). *rare.* [f. L. type **patricīda*, f. L. *patr-em* father + *-cīda* killer, in most cases a later alteration or MS. variant of *pāri-*, *parricīda* PARRICIDE, associating the word more explicitly with *pater*, *patrem* father (or, sometimes, with *patria*).

In one place, Cicero *De Domo* 10 §28, where the word is conjoined with *frātricīda*, *sorōricīda*, Müller's text keeps *patricīda*, which occurs in 1 MS., while 3 have *parricīda*.]

A murderer of a father (or of some one so regarded); = PARRICIDE[1].

1593 R. HARVEY *Philad.* 2 We cannot thinke that Brute was a patricide. **1624** HEYWOOD *Gunaik.* IX. 436 Touching Patricides, Solon..made no law to punish such, as thinking it not to be possible in nature to produce such a monster. **1649** ORMOND *Let. to Col. Jones* in *Milton's Wks.* (1851) II. 543 They have..murthered Gods Anointed, and our King, not as heretofore some Patricides have done, to make room for some Usurper. **1694** MOTTEUX *Rabelais* IV. liii. (1737) 219 Worse than Patricides.

'patricide[2]. *rare.* [ad. L. type **patricīdium*, after prec.: see -CIDE 2.] The action of killing one's father; = PARRICIDE[2].

1625 K. LONG tr. *Barclay's Argenis* III. iii. 156 My Father ..should die by my patricide. **1665** J. WEBB *Stone-Heng* (1725) 217 Patricide, Matricide and Regicide. **1707** LD. BELHAVEN *Sp. Union w. Engl.*, Patricide is worse than parricide. **1902** B. KIDD *West. Civiliz.* vii. 236 Their patricides, fratricides, and murders.

b. *attrib.* (In quot. associated with *patria* fatherland: cf. PATRICIDAL.)

1901 *N. Amer. Rev.* Feb. 212 That..they should have.. covered their country with insults, while her sons were exposed to the enemy's bullets. This patricide policy will appear unpardonable in the eyes of future generations.

†**patrick.** *Obs.* [From the Christian name *Patrick* = L. *Patrīcius*, name of the patron saint of Ireland. Cf. *Paddy*, *Pat*.] An Irish coin of the value of a halfpenny, current in the 17th century.

1673–4 *Cal. St. Papers Dom.* 160 The priest says Mass, for which he demands and receives from all the communicants 4 patricks which makes 2*d.* English. **1688** R. HOLME *Armoury* III. 30/2 A Patrick of Ireland..worth an half penny,..was Coined in the time of King Charles the Second Excile.

patrick, Sc. and dial. variant of PARTRIDGE.

patri-clan ('pætrɪklæn). [f. PATRI- + CLAN *sb.*] A patrilineal kin group or clan; also, *occas.*, the clan of the father.

1937 W. E. LAWRENCE in G. P. Murdock *Stud. Sci. of Society* 319 'Patri-clan' and ' matri-clan', denoting small exogamous kin-groups with patrilineal and matrilineal descent respectively, are suggested to eliminate monotonous repetition of adjectives. **1957** *Contrib. Indian Sociol.* I. 52 Incidentally, 'patri-clan' is not taken here in the sense of 'patrilineal clan', but of the father's clan. **1959** G. D. MITCHELL *Sociol.* iv. 69 The Tallensi seem to make a distinction between offences committed by a man with a member of the same patri-clan, such as with a paternal aunt, daughter, or sister,..and offences committed by a man with the wife of a member of the same patri-clan, such as the wife of a father, brother, or son. **1975** G. A. COLLIER *Fields in Tzotzil* iii. 61 The second, not so widely accepted by scholars, is that Mayah social structure was and is characterized by patrilocal extended families, patrilineages, and, in some cases, fully developed patri-clans. **1978** *Language* LIV. 214 It seems likely that vocabulary replacement and differentiation relate to the development of the lexical encoding or indexing of other sociolinguistic variables, e.g. patri-clan affiliation.

patrico ('pætrɪkəʊ). *Vagabonds' Cant.* Also 6 (patriarch-co), pater-, patter-, patring cove. [First element uncertain: ? *pater* or *patter* + CO[2], lad.] A priest or parson; *esp.* a hedge-priest.

a **1550** *Hye Way to Spyttel Hous* 1047 in Hazl. *E.P.P.* IV. 69 The patryng coue in the darkman cace. **1561** AWDELAY *Frat. Vacab.* 6 A Patriarke Co doth make mariages [etc.]. **1567** HARMAN *Caveat* xv. 60 For as much as these two names, a Iarkeman and a Patrico, bee in the old briefe of vacabonds... There is a Patrico, and not a Patriarcho. **1614** B. JONSON *Barth. Fair* II. vi, You are the Patrico, are you? the patriarch of the cut-purses? **1641** BROME *Joviall Crew* IV. ii, Where's the old Patrico, our Priest, my Ghostly Father? **1782** *Gentl. Mag.* LII. 16 Patrico, or patercove,..stroling priests that marry under a hedge. **1827** LYTTON *Pelham* lxxx, My idea at the moment was to disguise myself in the dress of the pater cove. *a* **1875** in *C. Kingsley's Life & Lett.* xxviii. (1879) II. 347 The gipsies of Eversley Common.. used to call him [Kingsley] their 'Patrico-rai' (their Priest King).

patridge, dial. form of PARTRIDGE.

†**'patrie.** *Obs.* *rare*$^{-1}$. [a. F. *patrie*, ad. L. *patria* fatherland, prop. fem. of *patrius* adj., of one's father, paternal (sc. *terra*), f. *patr-em* father.] Fatherland, native country.

1589 JAS. I in *Reg. Privy Council Scot.* IV. 427, I could have abstenit langair nor the weill of my patrie could have permitted.

patrilateral (pætrɪ'lætərəl), *a.* [f. PATRI- + LATERAL *a.*] (See quot. 1964.)

1949 N. FORTES *Social Struct.* 70 Ashanti say..that a person can claim house-room in the house of a patrilateral kinsman. **1957** V. W. TURNER *Schism & Continuity in Afr. Society* vii. 222 Kafumbu's..followers were a group of uterine siblings and their children, related to him by ties of marriage and patrilateral cross-cousinship. **1964** GOULD & KOLB *Dict. Social Sci.* 486/2 *Patrilateral* is sometimes used as a synonym for *patrilineal*... It is more usual nowadays to use the term for relationships traced through the father in a matrilineal system..or for relatives on the father's side in a non-unilineal kinship system. **1969** M. FORTES *Kinship & Social Order* (1970) II. xi. 201 Patrilateral connections are, as a rule, recognized among the offspring of men whose own fathers were the sons of one man, that is, among the children of parallel cousins, but rarely beyond that stage. **1973** *Times Lit. Suppl.* 6 July 787/2 That ideal marriage partner, the father's brother's daughter... It looks well, in Kabyl society, for a man to marry his patrilateral parallel cousin.

patriline ('pætrɪlaɪn). [f. PATRI- + LINE *sb.*[2] 24.] A patrilineal line of descent.

1957, etc. [see MATRILINE]. **1972** P. LASLETT *Household & Family in Past Time* i. 18 A patriline, that is a succession of male heads of household directly descended from each other.

patrilineage (pætrɪ'lɪnɪɪdʒ). [f. PATRI- + LINEAGE 2 c.] Patrilineal lineage.

1949 J. F. HOLLEMAN *Pattern of Hera Kinship* i. 1 The relationships and their respective terminology have to be seen in the framework of patrilineages. **1955** [see LINEARITY]. **1957** V. W. TURNER *Schism & Continuity in Afr. Society* vii. 222 A system of patrilineages..requires virilocal marriage. **1969** *Tanzania Notes & Rec.* July 10 All minor local government posts, with the exception of the necessarily localised village headmen, had been consistently awarded not only to men resident in the chief's settlement, but also only to men from his own immediate patrilineage.

patrilineal (pætrɪ'lɪnɪəl), *a.* [f. PATRI- + LINEAL *a.*] Of, pertaining to, or recognizing kinship with and descent through the father or the male line.

1904, **1906** [see MATRILINEAL *a.*]. **1923** A. L. KROEBER *Anthropol.* xiii. 356 Within each area or type of culture the matrilineal tribes manifest superiority over the patrilineal tribes in a preponderance of cultural aspects. **1936** R. FIRTH *We, the Tikopia* vi. 226 In this, such aggregations differ from the ordinary *paito*..which are patrilineal kinship groups of exclusive membership. **1951** [see MATRILINEAL *a.*]. **1957** V. W. TURNER *Schism & Continuity in Afr. Society* viii. 236 This virtual equality between family and lineage as principles of local organization is at least partially responsible for the merging of patrilineal and matrilineal kin as joint members of a single genealogical generation. **1966** *Punch* 17 Aug. 262/2 There is much good sense in a matrilineal society. One suddenly finds oneself asking if it isn't perhaps the patrilineal one which is out of date? **1974** *Encycl. Brit. Micropædia* III. 484/3 Patrilineal (or agnatic) systems, in which the relationships through the father are emphasized.

Hence **patri'lineally** *adv.*

1934 in WEBSTER. **1954** J. LAYARD in E. E. Evans-Pritchard et al. *Inst. Primitive Society* v. 55 Even in England, which is predominantly patrilineal, we now have a Queen, and though she succeeds to the throne patrilineally, her son will succeed matrilineally, through her. **1955** HOMANS & SCHNEIDER *Marriage, Authority & Final Causes* 13 The only difference is that the men of B lineage, defined either patrilineally or matrilineally [etc.].

patrilinear (pætrɪ'lɪnɪə(r)). [f. PATRI- + LINEAR *a.*] = PATRILINEAL *a.*

1913 [see MATRILINEAR *a.*]. **1926** *Contemp. Rev.* Apr. 528 Among the Bakitara, a patrilinear people, Canon Roscoe shows that on a man's death the sister of the heir entered [etc.]. **1939** JOYCE *Finnegans Wake* 279 Pot price pon patrilinear plop. **1943** *Nature* 18 Sept. 317/2 The historic change from matrilinear to patrilinear inheritance has also led to important conflicts. **1950** [see MATRILINEAR *a.*].

patriliny ('pætrɪlɪnɪ). [f. PATRI- + LIN(E *sb.*[2] + -Y[3].] The observance of patrilineal descent and kinship.

1906 N. W. THOMAS *Kinship Organisations & Group Marriage Austral.* ii. 21 It is unnecessary to go into the complicated question of the relation of brother-inheritance to matriliny and patriliny. **1949** M. FORTES *Social Struct.* 76 Patriliny is not legally recognized. **1957** *Jrnl. R. Anthrop. Inst.* Jan. 40 If it were the only rule determining the rights of descendants we should be inclined to describe Norwegian kinship as based strongly on patriliny and primogeniture. **1965** [see MATRILINY]. **1974** *Encycl. Brit. Micropædia* III. 484/3 Under a patriliny, a man (or woman) is linked to his (or her) sons and daughters, his sons' children, his sons' sons' children, and so on.

patrilocal (pætrɪ'ləʊkəl). [f. PATRI- + LOCAL *a.*] Applied to the custom in certain social groups for a married couple to settle in the husband's home or community.

1906 N. W. THOMAS *Kinship Organisations & Group Marriage Austral.* iii. 30 When the husband removes and lives in his wife's group the marriage is *matrilocal*; if the wife removes it is *patrilocal*. **1920** *Q. Rev.* July 168 How could it be otherwise wherever..patrilocal marriage occurs in conjunction with matrilineal descent? **1949** M. FORTES *Social Struct.* 70 Households with male heads can be ..'patrilocal', that is, made up of a man and his dependants by marriage and paternity. **1965** L. STONE *Crisis of Aristocracy* XI. iii. 634 To use the terminology of the sociologists, temporary patrilocal residence was the norm. **1971** *Sci. Amer.* Dec. 93/3 Marriage is patrilocal among the peoples of the Upper Congo.

Hence **patrilo'cality**, the custom of patrilocal residence; **patri'locally** *adv.*, in a patrilocal manner.

1949 M. GLUCKMAN in M. Fortes *Social Struct.* 146 Members of these tribes, who..usually marry patrilocally, have been migrating into central Barotseland. **1951** E. E. EVANS-PRITCHARD *Social Anthropol.* ii. 34 He [*sc.* McLENNAN] suggested how patriliny might have developed out of matriliny through a combination of the customs of polyandry and patrilocality. **1952** M. N. SRINIVAS *Relig. & Society among Coorgs of S. India* v. 125 Men, thanks to patrilocality, are assured of continuous residence. **1969** *Language* XLV. 468 In this large household, inheritance by males followed their right to reside patrilocally.

patrimonial (pætrɪ'məʊnɪəl), *a.* [ad. L. *patrimōniāl-is*, f. *patrimōnium*: see next and -AL[1]. Cf. F. *patrimonial* (in Palsgr. 1530).]

1. a. Pertaining to or constituting a patrimony; inherited from ancestors; hereditary.

1530 PALSGR. 320/1 Patrymonyall, belongyng to a mannes enherytaunce or patrymony, *patrimonial*. **1640** *Consid. touching Ch. of Eng.* 17 Their Office is elective and for life, and not patrimoniall or hereditary. **1788** GIBBON *Decl. & F.* lxi. (1869) III. 550 Their patrimonial estates were mortgaged or sold. **1863** J. G. MURPHY *Comm. Gen.* xlvii. 22 The surrender of their patrimonial rights.

b. *patrimonial seas, waters*, etc., an area extending beyond territorial waters, the natural resources of which are the property of the coastal nation though ships and aircraft of other countries have freedom of passage through it.

1973 *Caribbean Contact* Jan. 12/3 One such [new] concept is that of 'patrimonial' waters which Foreign Minister Calvani [of Venezuela] defined thus: 'A coastal nation exercises rights of sovereignty over its natural resources, both renewable and non-renewable, that are found in the waters, the ocean floor and the subfloor of a zone adjacent to territorial waters'. **1973** *Nature* 14 Sept. 63/1 In essence next year's conference is intended to sort out the whole of the law of the sea, a brief that not only includes fishing and mineral and hydrocarbon rights in territorial waters, the so-called patrimonial waters, on the high seas and on the deep ocean floor, but also [etc.]. *Ibid.* 63/2 A number of developing nations took the stance..that patrimonial seas should be established that extend for 200 miles or to the outer edge of the continental shelf, whichever is the greater. **1973** *Internat. & Compar. Law Q.* XXII. IV. 668 The patrimonial sea can be briefly defined as an economic zone not more than 200 miles in breadth from the base line of the territorial sea (the limit of which shall not exceed 12 miles), where there will be freedom of navigation and overflight for the ships and aircraft of all nations, but in that zone the coastal state will have an exclusive right to all resources.

2. *Sociol.* A term used by Max Weber to designate a traditional type of social structure in which the chief or ruler maintains authority through his officials, army, etc., who are retained by him and whose loyalty is to him personally.

1946 GERTH & MILLS tr. M. Weber in *From Max Weber* (1947) xi. 297 As a rule, this meant that princely prerogatives became *patrimonial* in nature. Patrimonialism can also develop from pure patriarchism through the disintegration of the patriarchical master's strict authority. **1947** HENDERSON & PARSONS tr. *Weber's Theory Social & Econ. Organization* iii. 318 The primary external support of patrimonial authority is a staff of slaves, coloni, or conscripted subjects, or, in order to enlist its members' self-interest.., of mercenary bodyguards and armies. **1968** E. FISCHOFF et al. tr. *Weber's Econ. & Society* I. iii. 232 Where domination is primarily traditional, even though it is exercised by virtue of the ruler's personal autonomy, it will be called *patrimonial authority*. *Ibid.*, Patrimonial authority under which the administrative staff appropriates particular powers and the corresponding economic assets. *Ibid.* III. xvi. 1366 The patrimonial structure of the Roman ruling stratum. **1968** M. Ilford tr. *Freund's Sociol. of Max Weber* iv. 236 The old bureaucracies were essentially patrimonial in character. **1968** *World Politics* XX. 195 Patrimonial rulers ..endeavour to maximize their personal control. **1970** H. Bienen in Huntington & Moore *Authoritarian Politics in Mod. Society* 119 His [*sc.* Zolberg's] party-state emerges as a system where bureaucratic and patrimonial features coexist. **1974** tr. *Wertheim's Evolution & Revolution* i. 27 Weber's 'patrimonial bureaucracy', as a sub-type of a feudal political structure, comes much nearer to historical reality.

Hence **patri'monialism**, a system of patrimonial authority (sense 2 above); **patri'monially** *adv.*, in the way of patrimony, hereditarily, by inheritance from a father.

1641 Earl Monm. tr. *Biondi's Civil Warres* v. 125 All.. which did patrimonially belong to him in Aniou and Maine. **1700** C. Davenant *Disc. Grants* Introd., A distinction between what was their own patrimonially,..and what the state had an interest in. **1946** Patrimonialism [see sense 2]. **1968** *World Politics* XX. 195 Lately, some attempts, primarily in the field of African studies, have been made to remember the meaning of patrimonialism.

patrimony ('pætrɪmənɪ). Forms: 4 patre-, patrymoyne, patrimoigne, 4-5 -moygne, 4-7 patrimonie, -ye, 5- patrimony, (5-7 patrymonie, -y). [a. F. *patri-*, *patremoine* (12-13th c. in Hatz.-Darm.), ad. L. *patrimōnium* paternal estate, patrimony, f. *patr-em* father: see -mony.]

1. Property, or an estate, inherited from one's father or ancestors; heritage, inheritance.

1377 Langl. *P. Pl.* B. xx. 233 For þei arn poure,.. For patrimoigne hem faileth. *c* **1412** Hoccleve *De Reg. Princ.* 3760 Plato, his patrimoygne and his contree Lefte and forsook, and dwelte in wildernesse. **1513-14** *Act 5 Hen. VIII*, c. 1. *Preamble*, To recover the Royalme of Fraunce his very true patrimonye and enheritaunce. **1593** Shaks. *2 Hen. VI*, v. i. 187 To reaue the Orphan of his Patrimonie. **1697** Dryden *Virg. Georg.* iii. 534 The Shepherd..with him all his Patrimony bears: His House and Houshold Gods. **1751** Johnson *Rambler* No. 153 ⁋3 The second son of a gentleman, whose patrimony had been wasted. *a* **1854** H. Reed *Lect. Brit. Poets* vii. (1857) 260 He spent his whole patrimony in the hapless cause of his king.

b. *transf.* The estate or property belonging by ancient right to an institution, corporation, or class; *esp.* the ancient estate or endowment of a church or religious body. ***patrimony of St. Peter***, a name for the Papal States, or territory formerly held by the Pope in Italy.

1340 *Ayenb.* 41 Þo þet þe guodes of holy cherche, þe patremoyne of Iesu crist despendeþ ine kueade us. **1456** Sir G. Haye *Law Arms* (S.T.S.) 24 [He] held a grete part of the patrymonye of haly kirk on force. **1582** *Reg. Privy Council Scot.* III. 496 The patrimony of the said bischoprik. **1601** R. Johnson *Kingd. & Commw.* (1603) 112 The patrimony of S. Peter, bequeathed to the church by the countesse Matilda. **1682** Burnet *Rights Princes* v. 192 That the Goods of the Church were the Patrimonies of the Poor. **1756-7** tr. *Keysler's Trav.* (1760) II. 432 Viterbo, Perugia, and the mountainous parts of St. Peter's patrimony. *a* **1862** Buckle *Civiliz.* (1869) III. ii. 89 In a really Christian land, the patrimony of the Church would be left untouched.

c. *fig.* Applied to things (usually immaterial) received or 'inherited' from ancestors or predecessors; 'heritage'.

1581 Mulcaster *Positions* xxxvii. (1887) 155 Learning.. is the patrimonie to wittie pouertie. **1612** Brinsley *Lud. Lit.* ii. (1627) 10 To see their children to have the best education, ..which is the chiefe patrimonie. **1776** Adam Smith *W.N.* i. x. ii. (1869) I. 128 The patrimony of a poor man lies in the strength and dexterity of his hands. **1865** Livingstone *Zambesi* xxix. 601 The Gospel, the especial patrimony of the poor and the illiterate.

†**2.** The fact of inheriting from an ancestor, inheritance. *Obs.*

1484 Caxton *Fables of Alfonce* iii, It was come to hym by inherytaunce and by patrymony. *c* **1489** —— *Sonnes of Aymon* xiv. 327, I was crowned Kynge accordynge to the right of my patrymonye. *a* **1533** Ld. Berners *Gold. Bk. M. Aurel.* (1546) D v, The Emperour to inherite the empyre by Patrimonie. **1580-1** *Reg. Privy Council Scot.* III. 364 The lands.., pertening to his Majestie in proper patrimony.

‖**patrin** ('pætrɪn). *Gipsy Cant.* Also *erron.* **patteran.** [Romany *'patrin*, in Turkish Gipsy *pa'trin*, orig. 'leaf' (cf. Skr. *patra*), but now known to Eng. Gipsies only in the sense explained.] An indication which gipsies leave of the way they have travelled, by throwing down handfuls of grass or leaves pointing in the direction taken.

1873 *Slang Dict.*, *Patteran*, a gipsy trail, made by throwing down a handful of grass occasionally. **1876** Whyte-Melville *Katerfelto* xi, 'Your *patrin*? What is that?' asked my lord. 'The sign that none of our people will pass unnoticed.' **1877** Besant & Rice *Son of Vulc.* i. xi, Maybe it's the gipsy's patteran they mean. **1879** *Encycl. Brit.* X. 617 A handful of grass or leaves,..or some such mark (*patrin*, 'leaf') to guide the stragglers of the band. **1898** Watts-Dunton *Aylwin* 71/2 I've bin there the last three weeks on the patrin-chase, and not a patrin could I find.

†**patrinite** ('pætrɪnaɪt). *Min. Obs.* [Named after E. L. M. Patrin: see -ite.] An obsolete synonym of **a.** laminar felsite, **b.** Aikinite.

1811 Pinkerton *Petralogy* I. 161 *note*, It is probably of the same nature with patrinite, or laminar felsite. **1896** Chester *Dict. Names Min.*

patriot ('peɪtrɪət, 'pæt-), *sb.* (*a.*) Also 6-7 -ote. [a. F. *patriote* (15th c. in Hatz.-Darm.), ad. late L. *patriōta* fellow-countryman (in St. Greg. *Epist.* 6th c.), ad. Gr. πατριώτης, f. πάτριος of one's fathers, πατρίς one's fatherland: see -ot².]

A. *sb.* †**1.** A fellow-countryman, compatriot. *Obs. rare.*

1596 Lambarde *Peramb. Kent* (ed. 2) 246 Tenham.. where our honest patriote Richard Harrys..planted..the sweete Cherry. **1611** Cotgr., *Patriote*, a patriote, ones countrey-man. **1629** H. Burton *Truth's Triumph* 285 If hee ..finde..kinde vsage of the natiues and patriots of the country.

2. a. One who disinterestedly or self-sacrificingly exerts himself to promote the wellbeing of his country; 'one whose ruling passion is the love of his country' (J.); one who maintains and defends his country's freedom or rights.

In this use, at first, as in French (see Littré), with 'good', 'true', 'worthy', or other commendatory adjective: cf. 'good citizen'. 'Patriot' for 'good patriot' is rare before 1680. At that time often applied to one who supported the rights of the country against the King and court.

1605 B. Jonson *Volpone* iv. i, Such as were known patriots, Sound lovers of their country. **1611** Bible *Transl. Pref.* 8 Was Catiline therefore an honest man, or a good Patriot? *a* **1641** Bp. Mountagu *Acts & Mon.* ii. (1642) 147 Nehemias, a true and faithfull Patriot. *a* **1643** Ld. Falkland, etc. *Infallibility* (1646) 176 The Catholiques were knowne good Patriots under our former Kings. **1699** Dryden *To J. Driden* 171 A patriot both the King and Country serves, Prerogative and privilege preserves. **1706** Phillips, *Patriot*, a Father of his Country, a great Benefactor to the Publick. **1716** Pope *Epit. on Trumbal* 5 An honest Courtier, yet a Patriot too, Just to his Prince, and to his Country true. **1738** Glover *Leonidas* i. 262 So spake the patriot, and his heart o'erflow'd. **1750** Berkeley *Patriotism* §24 A patriot is one who heartily wisheth the public prosperity, and doth..also study and endeavour to promote it. **1814** Scott *Ld. of Isles* iii. xxvii, His was the patriot's burning thought, Of Freedom's battle bravely fought. **1855** Prescott *Philip II*, I. ii. x. 255 A band of patriots ready to do battle for the liberties of their country.

b. The name has been at various times borne or assumed by persons or parties whose claim to it has been disputed, denied, or ridiculed by others. Hence the name itself fell into discredit in the earlier half of the 18th c., being used, according to Dr. Johnson, 'ironically for a factious disturber of the government'. So sometimes, at a later date, 'Irish Patriot'.

1644 Maxwell *Prerog. Chr. Kings* 117 The specious and spurious pretences of our glorious Reformers, and zealous Patriots today. **1677** G. Hickes in Ellis *Orig. Lett.* Ser. ii. IV. 42 Encouraged..by their foresaid patriots, whereof some wish the ruin of the Church, and all of them the ruin of my Lord Duke. **1681** Dryden *Abs. & Achit.* 965 Gull'd with a Patriots name, whose Modern sense Is one that wou'd by Law supplant his Prince: The Peoples Brave, the Politicians Tool; Never was Patriot yet, but was a Fool. **1771** Earl Malmesbury *Lett.* (1870) I. 218 [This country] does not wish a war, whatever wicked patriots may endeavour, or lying newspapers print. **1780** Cowper *Table-t.* 143 A band, called patriots for no cause But that they catch at popular applause. **1798** Canning & Frere *New Morality* 113 in *Anti-Jacobin*, A steady patriot of the world alone, The friend of every country—but his own. **1827** Hallam *Const. Hist.* (1842) II. 405. **1833** Macaulay *Ess.*, *H. Walpole* (1865) I. 284/1 The name of patriot had become [*c* 1744] a by-word of derision. Horace Walpole scarcely exaggerated when he said that..the most popular declaration which a candidate could make on the hustings was that he had never been and never would be a patriot. **1888** *Times* 17 Aug. 7/2 Much to his credit, he refused to interfere in favour of the Irish patriots.

¶**c.** Erron. (with *of* or possessive) as if = lover, devotee, upholder (? confused with *patron*). ? *Obs.*

1631 Weever *Anc. Fun. Mon.* 440 A carefull Patriot of the State. **1633** Prynne *Histriomastix* 389 Adulterers, Whoremasters, Whores, &c. are the greatest Patriots,.. frequenters, upholders of these lascivious Stage-playes. *Ibid.* 826 Advancers and chiefest patriots and propugners of Monarchy. **1641** H. L'Estrange *God's Sabbath* Ep. Ded. A iij b, The Truth which it professeth will gain it some measure of acceptance with so profest a Patriot of Truth.

d. In the war of 1939-45, *spec.* a loyal inhabitant of a country overrun by the enemy, esp. a member of a resistance movement. Also *attrib.*

1945 *News Chron.* 7 May 1/5 The formal liberation of Denmark had begun. Actually the patriots had started it much earlier... When we landed the Danish patriots..had the situation under complete control. In patriot cars,..we drove down streets lined with cheering Danes. **1959** *Listener* 23 Apr. 727/2 Wingate's leadership of the ill-found 'Patriot' forces [in Ethiopia] was audacious.

3. *U.S.* **Patriots' Day**, anniversary of the Battle of Lexington and Concord in the American Revolution, 19 April 1775, observed since 1894 as a legal holiday in Maine and Massachusetts.

1897 *Boston Even. Transcript* 18 Apr. 8/4 Lowell mill agents, having heard the indignant protest against the running of machinery in the mills Patriots' Day, have decided to reconsider their action. **1909** *Springfield* (Mass.) *Weekly Republ.* 22 Apr. 11 The celebration of Patriots' day, the 134th anniversary of the battles at Lexington and Concord. The day is a legal holiday in Massachusetts and Maine. **1925** *Boston Even. Transcript* 21 Apr. 10/1 Sesquicentennial of Patriots' Day passes into history. **1948** *Daily Ardmoreite* (Ardmore, Okla.) 18 Apr. 14/7 They are down to play a second game in the afternoon, since it's Patriots' day in Boston.

B. *attrib.* or as *adj.* That is, or has the character of, a patriot; belonging to or characteristic of a patriot; patriotic.

1732 J. Hammond *Love Elegies* xiv, My Patriot Breast a nobler Warmth shall feel. **1738-49** Bolingbroke (*title*) Letters, On the Spirit of Patriotism: on the Idea of a Patriot King. **1759** Dilworth *Pope* 95 So truly patriot an attachment to the manufactures of Old England. **1813** Eustace *Class. Tour* (1821) I. iv. 163 The same patriot passion..that characterized..the ancient Romans. **1896** *Harper's Mag.* XCII. 761/2 The growing activity of the German patriot guerilla.

patrioteer (peɪtrɪə'tɪə(r)). [f. patriot *sb.* + -eer.] One who makes a public display of patriotism; one whose patriotism is spurious and insincere. Also *attrib.*

1928 *Amer. Speech* III. 262 The second camp is made up of nationalists, or, if you will, of patrioteers. **1935** *Evening Sun* (Baltimore) 11 Apr. 27/2 Some British patrioteer has grown terribly excited over the possibility that Soviet arguments broadcast from Moscow may be so strong..as to sweep the masses of Englishmen from their political moorings. **1939** *Time* 27 Feb. 9/1 By patrioteer *Time* means to describe the professional patriot, the kind of refuge-seeking scoundrel who waves a red-white-&-blue handkerchief when he should be wiping his own nose. **1941** 'Fanfarlo' in *Penguin New Writing* X. 112 A patrioteer is very simply a man who will cut his country's throat to an old tune. **1954** *Manch. Guardian Weekly* 18 Feb. 9 Talking in 'patrioteer' terms. **1954** *Birmingham* (Alabama) *News* 14 Apr. 10 They are quick to detect the phony and they can distinguish a patriot from a patrioteer. **1954** D. Riesman *Individualism Reconsidered* iii. vii. 137 Mr. MacLeish has suffered greatly from patrioteers. **1956** C. W. Mills *Power Elite* xii. 271 The American elite have not remained as patrioteer essayists have described them to us.

'patriotess. *rare.* [See -ess.] A female patriot.

1837 Carlyle *Fr. Rev.* II. iv. ix, A Patriot (or some say, it was a Patriotess, and indeed the truth is undiscoverable). **1894** *Daily News* 12 June 5/4 The inevitable 'patriotesses'.. were present.

patriotic (peɪtrɪ'ɒtɪk, pæt-), *a.* [ad. late L. *patriōtic-us* (Cassiodorus), a. Gr. πατριωτικ-ός, f. πατριώτης patriot: see -ic. Cf. F. *patriotique* (Rabelais, 16th c.).]

†**1.** Of or belonging to one's country. *Obs.*

1653 Urquhart *Rabelais* ii. vi. 31 Whilest we prestolate the coming of the Tabellaries from the Penates and patriotick Lares [F. *lares patriotiques*].

2. Having the character of a patriot; worthy or characteristic of a patriot; marked by devotion to the wellbeing or interests of one's country.

1757 *Herald* No. 6 (1758) I. 82 Dastardy! in not daring to hazard..a patriotic service to their king and country. **1771** Johnson *Falkland's Isl.* Wks. X. 64 During the protectorship of Cromwell, a time of which the patriotick tribes still more ardently desire the return. **1774** —— *Patriot* ibid. 88 By the howling of patriotick rage, the nation was for a time exasperated to such madness, that [etc.]. **1833** Ht. Martineau *Charmed Sea* i. 3 The exiles uplifted one of the patriotic chaunts. **1867** Smiles *Huguenots Eng.* v. (1880) 85 The threatened invasion of England..roused the patriotic feeling of all classes. **1868** Freeman *Norm. Conq.* II. vii. 79 The predominance of the patriotic party.

b. quasi-*sb.* in *pl.* Patriotic songs or utterances. *nonce-use.* (Cf. *heroics.*)

1899 F. Harrison *Tennyson*, etc. I. 48 A real lover of high poetry..can take delight in..the patriotics of Burns, the war-songs of Campbell.

So **patri'otical** *a.* (*rare*) = prec.; hence **patri'otically** *adv.*, in a patriotic manner.

1691 Wood *Ath. Oxon.* II. 179 Speeches..against the Bishops were much applauded among the patriotical Party. **1797** Burke *Regic. Peace* iii. Wks. VIII. 277 The opposition, whether patriotically or factiously, contending that the ministers had been oblivious of the national glory. **1821** *Blackw. Mag.* IX. 63 Like patriotical folks, all for the good of their country. **1884** Sir H. James in *Law Times* 122/1 This sacrifice, which had been so patriotically made. **1898** *19th Cent.* Apr. 523 The so-called patriotical assumption, that France can never be in the wrong.

patriotism ('peɪtrɪətɪz(ə)m, 'pæt-). [f. patriot + -ism: cf. F. *patriotisme* (1750 in Hatz.-Darm.).] The character or passion of a patriot; love of or zealous devotion to one's country. Sometimes ironically: see patriot 2 b.

local patriotism, devotion to the wellbeing of one's own locality, as distinct from that of the country or nation.

1726 Bailey (ed. 3), *Patriotism*, the acting like a Father to his Country, public Spiritedness. **1738** Bolingbroke *Patriot.* ii. (1749) 100 Patriotism must be founded in great principles, and supported by great virtues. **1750** Berkeley (*title*) Maxims concerning Patriotism. *Ibid.* §2 Being loud and vehement either against a court, or for a court, is no proof of patriotism. **1775** Johnson in *Boswell* 7 Apr., Patriotism is the last refuge of a scoundrel. **1815** Elphinstone *Acc. Caubul* (1842) I. 255 He..continued his exertions with the courage and patriotism of a Wallace. **1836** Hor. Smith *Tin Trump.* (1876) 270 Patriotism—too often the hatred of other countries disguised as the love of our own. **1871** Freeman *Norm. Conq.* IV. xviii. 146 It shows the strength of local, as distinguished from national, patriotism;..the ideas of municipal freedom which were growing up.

† '**patriotly**, *a. Obs. rare.* [f. PATRIOT + -LY[1].] Of the nature of, or characteristic of, a patriot; patriotic.

1691 T. H[ALE] *Acc. New Invent.* p. liii, Some such Patriotly Hero. *Ibid.* p. lix, To account it a Patriotly thing to promote its preservation.

† '**patriotship**. *Obs. rare*−0. [See -SHIP.]

1727 BAILEY vol. II, *Patriotship*, Office, Dignity, or Quality of a Patriot.

patripassian (pætrɪ'pæsɪən), *sb.* and *a. Ch. Hist.* Also 8 *erron.* patro-. [ad. late L. (4th c.) *patripassiān-us*, f. *pater*, *patri-* father + *passus* having suffered: so mod.F. *Patripassien*.]

A. *sb.* One who held, as certain early heretics, that God the Father suffered with or in the person of the Son for the redemption of man.

1579 FULKE *Heskins's Parl.* 61 Vnlesse M. Heskins will be a Sabellian and a Patripassian, to confound the persons of the Godhead, and say, that God the father, yea, the whole Trinitie is likewise transubstantiated in the Sacrament. **1701** tr. *Le Clerc's Prim. Fathers* (1702) 318 The Patripassians, or Disciples of Noëtus,..distinguished no Hypostases in the Deity, and..maintained that the Father had suffered as well as the Son. **1831-3** E. BURTON *Eccl. Hist.* xxi. (1845) 454 The doctrine of Praxeas..must lead us to believe that the Father himself was born of the Virgin Mary, that he suffered on the Cross... The name of Patripassians was given to persons who held this belief.

B. *adj.* Belonging to, or involving the doctrine of, the Patripassians.

1727-41 CHAMBERS *Cycl.* s.v., The Patripassian heresy was first broached by Praxeas..at the beginning of the third century. **1882** CAVE & BANKS tr. *Dorner's Chr. Doctr.* 209 Even the Patripassian mode of thought had something attractive, because it, at any rate, comprehended the presence of God himself in Christ.

Hence **patri'passianism**, the doctrine of the Patripassians; **patri'passianly** *adv.*, in the way of Patripassianism.

1847 BUCH tr. *Hagenbach's Hist. Doctr.* I. 49 Praxeas..being charged by Tertullian with Patripassianism. **1876** A. PLUMMER tr. *Döllinger's Hippolytus & Call.* IV. 268 A little while ago she [the Church] was in general Patripassianly disposed.

patripotestal (pætrɪpə'tɛstəl), *a.* [f. PATRI- + POTESTAL *a.*] Characterized by the exercise of authority by the father or his relatives in a family or household.

1906 N. W. THOMAS *Kinship Organisations & Group Marriage Austral.* i. 8 Three main types of family may be distinguished: (1) patripotestal, (2) matripotestal, (*a*) direct, and (*b*) indirect, in which the authority is wielded by the father, mother, and mother's relatives, in particular her brothers, respectively. **1944** H. P. FAIRCHILD *Dict. Sociol.* 215/2 *Patripotestal*, characterized by the exercise of authority, especially in the family or household, by the father or paternal grandfather. **1952** A. R. RADCLIFFE-BROWN *Struct. & Function Primitive Society* i. 22 A society may be called patriarchal when descent is patrilineal.., marriage is patrilocal.., and the family is patripotestal (i.e. the authority is in the hands of the father or his relatives). **1964** GOULD & KOLB *Dict. Social Sci.* 486/2 *Patripotestal* modes of social organization. **1972** D. DAVIES *Dict. Anthropol.* 144/1 *Patripotestal*, the holding of authority over a family by the father or his relative.

patrist ('peɪtrɪst, 'pæt-), *sb.*[1] *rare*−0. [prob. a back-formation from PATRISTIC *a.*, as if f. Gr. πατρ- father + -IST.] One versed in the lives or writings of the Fathers of the Christian Church.

1882 in OGILVIE (Annandale).

patrist ('pætrɪst), *sb.*[2] *Psychol.* [f. PATR(I- + -IST.] A term applied to someone whose behaviour or attitude is influenced or dominated by the father. Also *attrib.*

1953 G. R. TAYLOR *Sex in Hist.* iv. 77 Though I am no great lover of jargon, it would be tedious to refer continually to persons who have modelled themselves on their fathers. I shall therefore speak of them as patrists. **1958** —— *Angel-Makers* xiii. 272 The patrist accepts learning in the sense of mere erudition..but deeply distrusts all original inquiry. **1958** *Sunday Times* 27 Apr. 6/3 The 'Patrists', in the shape of the commercial middle class. **1977** E. J. TRIMMER et al. *Visual Dict. Sex* (1978) xxii. 248 Male-dominated or patrist societies..tend to a certain stern prudishness.

patristic (pə'trɪstɪk), *a.* and *sb.* [mod. f., as if from *patrist*, *patrism* (f. L. *patr-*, Gr. πατρ- father) + -IC: cf. mod.F. *patristique* (neologism in Littré, 1875), Ger. *patristisch* (Engelhardt 1822).]

A. *adj.* **a.** Of or pertaining to the study of the writings of the Fathers of the Church, as in ***patristic learning*** or ***scholarship***; **b.** hence, loosely, of or pertaining to the Fathers themselves, or their writings, as in ***patristic works, writings, doctrines.***

a. 1837-9 HALLAM *Hist. Lit.* II. III. ii. §9. 404 Theological controversy..became..more patristic, that is, appealing to the testimonies of the fathers. **1844** GLADSTONE *Glean.* V. xxiv. 99 A diligent student and a master of patristic learning. **b. 1874** GREEN *Short Hist.* iii. §1. 113 The chief works of Latin Literature, patristic or classical. **1875** SCRIVENER *Lect. Text N. Test.* 10 Since each primitive version was first made, or each Patristic work first published. **1885** CLODD *Myths & Dr.* II. ix. 202 A doctrine..due to Patristic theories of incorporeal souls.

B. *sb.* **1.** A student or adherent of the doctrines or opinions of the Fathers.

1842 G. S. FABER *Prov. Lett.* (1844) II. 149 The..system of the schoolmen..was..opposed by the old-fashioned Biblicists and Patricists.

2. *pl.* The study of the lives, writings, or doctrines of the Fathers. [Ger. *patristik* (1846 in Brockhaus *Convers. Lex.*), F. *patristique*.]

1847 [see PATROLOGY]. **1882-3** SCHAFF *Encycl. Relig. Knowl.* III. 1765 Patristics and Patrology are the names of that department of theology..concerning the lives, writings, and theological doctrines of the Church Fathers.

Hence **pa'tristical** *a.* = PATRISTIC *a.* (hence **pa'tristically** *adv.*, **pa'tristicalness**); **pa'tristicism** (-sɪz(ə)m), properly, a system founded upon the study of the Fathers; loosely, the doctrine or mode of thought of the Fathers themselves.

1831 J. H. NEWMAN *Lett.* (1891) I. 251, I have..received a..present of books..consisting of thirty-six volumes of the Fathers;..I am now set up in the *patristical line. **1837-9** HALLAM *Hist. Lit.* III. ii. §27 Chillingworth was..a man versed in patristical learning. **1849** CURETON *Corpus Ignat.* 291 *O λόγος Θεός*, so frequently occurring in the earliest Patristical writings. *a* **1855** J. J. BLUNT *Right Use Early Fathers* Ser. I. i. (1857) 6 Consistent with ancient patristical precedent. **1882** OGILVIE, **Patristically*, in a patristic manner. **1836** PUSEY *Let. to Newman* in Liddon *Life* (1893) I. xviii. 421 There is a good deal of close argument from the text of Scripture: no imaginativeness, or *patristicalness. **1864** DRAPER *Intell. Devel. Europe* x. I. 305 *Patristicism, or the science of the Fathers, was thus essentially founded on the principle that the Scriptures contain all knowledge permitted to man. **1899** *Speaker* 30 Dec. 338/2 High-pitched devotional patristicism.

patrix ('peɪtrɪks). Also **patrice.** Pl. **patrices.** [mod. f. L. *pater*, *patr-* father, as a correlative term to *matrix*: in Ger. *patrize* (Brockhaus *Convers. Lex.* 1846).] A die, punch, or pattern used to form matrices in type-founding, etc.

1883 *Times* 24 Mar. 12 First making a model in wax or clay, and then cutting a similar model in relief in steel, which is hardened and tempered, and is known as the hub or patrice... If an article has to be reproduced, it furnishes itself the model from which a patrice is made in cast iron. **1885** *Manch. Exam.* 22 June 5/7 The edges are filed off, and the patrix removed from the matrix.

† '**patrizate**, *v. Obs. rare.* Also 7 **-issate.** [f. L. *patrizāt*, ppl. stem of *patrizāre*, in cl. L. *patrissāre* to act like or take after one's father, as if from a Gr. type *πατρίζειν (the actual Gr. being πατριάζειν).] *intr.* To take after, imitate, or follow the example of, one's father (or ancestors).

1623 COCKERAM, *Patrissate*, to resemble ones father. *a* **1661** FULLER *Worthies, Hartford.* (1662) 22 In testimony of his true affection to the dead Father in his living Son..[he] presented it to the young Earl, conjuring him, by the cogent arguments of example and rule, to patrizate. [**1696** M. HENRY *Life P. Henry* Wks. 1853 II. 619/2 Some of the branches of the family, who did not *patrizare*, were uneasy at his being there.]

So † **patri'zation**, imitation of one's father or ancestors; † **patrize** *v.* = PATRIZATE.

a **1626** W. SCLATER *Exp. 4th ch. Rom.* (1650) Ep. Ded., The Son..moulded..into the like forme of piety, by a zealous *patrization. **1660** WATERHOUSE *Arms & Arm.* 32 So did they preserve this Memory of their Ancestors, to excite them to a patrization. **1624** GEE *Foot out of Snare* xii. 78 His worthy (truly *patrizing) Sonne. *a* **1642** SIR W. MONSON *Naval Tracts* IV. (1704) 446/1 They do Patrizize [*sic*] and follow the steps of their Predecessors.

† **pa'trocinate**, *v. Obs.* [f. L. *patrōcināt-*, ppl. stem of *patrōcinārī* to patronize, defend, related to *patrōn-em* PATRON. Cf. F. *patrociner* (1367 in Hatz.-Darm.), It. *patrocinare*, Pr., Sp., Pg. *patrocinar*.] *trans.* To defend, champion, maintain, patronize (a cause, etc.).

1611 COTGR., *Patrociner*, to patrocinate, maintaine, defend, protect, support, vphold. **1647** JER. TAYLOR *Lib. Proph.* Ep. Ded. 29 Not cald out to patrocinate euery lesse necessary opinion. *a* **1693** *Urquhart's Rabelais* III. v. **1822** MRS. E. NATHAN *Langreath* III. 290 Oh! that I had the eloquence of a Cicero..to patrocinate that glorious freedom.

† **patroci'nation**. *Obs. rare.* [n. of action from L. *patrōcinārī*: see prec. and -ATION.] The action of supporting, maintaining, or patronizing.

1640 BP. HALL *Episc.* I. xi. 42 To maintaine our owne Truths, without all feare of the patrocination of Popery. **1647** M. HUDSON *Div. Right Govt.* Ep. Ded. 10 This trifling Treatise, for the Patrocination whereof I have presumed to make my addresses to Your most Sacred Majesty.

† '**patrocine**, *sb. Obs. rare.* [a. F. *patrocine* (1409 in Godef.), ad. L. *patrōcinium* patronage, protection: see PATROCINY.] Protection, patronage, = PATROCINY.

1596 R. BRUCE *Let.* in Maitland *Hist. Edin.* I. iii. 49 The godly Barons had taken on them the Patrocine of the Church. **1644** MAXWELL *Prerog. Chr. Kings* Ep. Ded. 12 The love and zeale which have necessited me to take recourse to Your Honours patrocine.

† '**patrocine**, *v. Obs. rare*−1. [a. F. *patrocin-er*, or ad. L. *patrōcinā-rī*.] = PATROCINATE *v.*

1680 E. F. *Hist. Edw. II* (Octavo ed.) 75 When it is..not only vicious and ill affected, but doth patrocine [*Folio ed.* patronize] and maintain it in others.

† **patrociny** (pə'trɒsɪnɪ). *Obs.* [ad. L. *patrōcinium* patronage, defence, f. *patrōcinārī*: see PATROCINATE *v.*] Patronage, protection, defence, countenance, support (of a person or cause).

a **1450** *Mankind* (Brandl) 891 Mankynd ys deliueryd by my suuerall patrocynye. **1529** WOLSEY *Let. to Gardener* in Strype *Eccl. Mem.* I. App. xxxiii. 92 To take hym and his pore causis into your patrocynye and protection. **1589** R. ROBINSON *Gold. Mirr.* Ep. Ded., That your honour will vouchsafe to take on you the Patrosinie of this Treatise. **1629** *Reg. Privy Council Scot.* Ser. II. III. 23 Sir Johne..takes upoun him the patrocinie and defence of the said James. **1675** BURNET *Serm. Roy. Martyr* (1710) 47 It gave a Patrociny to those Practises.

patroclinous (pætrəʊ'klaɪnəs), *a. Biol.* [f. Gr. πατήρ, πατρ- father + κλίν-ειν to lean + -OUS.] Resembling the male rather than the female parent in inherited characters; involving or possessing a tendency to inherit a character or characters from the male parent only. So '**patrocliny**, patroclinous inheritance.

1913 *Jrnl. Exper. Zool.* XV. 590 For comparison I give the F_2 from normal males by sisters such as those to which I mated the patroclinous males. **1917** *Genetics* II. 247 The hybrids in these reciprocal crosses resemble the pollen parent strongly, i.e., they are strongly patroclinous. *Ibid.*, So far as the vegetative characters are concerned patrocliny can not be ascribed to either of the hybrids. **1936** *Ibid.* XXI. 592 It has also been shown that X chromosome inversion heterozygotes give rise to patroclinous males among their progeny. **1973** *Nature* 26 Oct. 439/2 Stimulated by Richard Goldschmidt's erroneous explanation of patroclinous inheritance in *Oenothera*.

patrogony (pə'trɒgənɪ). *nonce-wd.* [f. Gr. πατήρ, πατρ- father, after *theogony*.] A genealogy of the Fathers (of the Christian Church).

1857 J. W. DONALDSON *Christian Orthod.* 231 The 'Book of Generations of the Fathers', a sort of Patrogony.

‖ **patroillart**. *Obs.* [OF., also *patroul(l)-*, *patrullart*, f. *patrouil* puddle, mud: see PATROL *v.*] Corrupt or 'muddled' language.

1340 *Ayenb.* 211 Huo þet bit god wyþ-oute deuocion of herte: he spekþ to god patroyllart [F. *il priedieu patroullart*], ase þe ilke þet spekþ half englis and half urenss.

patrol (pə'trəʊl), *sb.* Also 7-9 **patrole**, (7 **petrol(l)**, 8 **patrouille, petrouille, -oville, padrole, patroll, patroul.** [a. F. *patrouille* (1539 in R. Estienne, 1611 in Cotgr. 'a still night-watch in warre: *faire la patrouille*, to be driuen to linger, and spend his time idly, as one thats forced to watch'), vbl. sb. from *patrouiller*: see next. Hence, also It. *pattuglia*, Sp. *patrulla*, Pg. *patrulha*; Du. *patrouille*, Ger. *patrolle*, Da. *patrol*, Sw. *patrull*, Russ. *patrúlʲ*. In Eng., as app. in some of the other langs., the sb. appears before the vb.]

1. a. The action of going the rounds of a garrison, camp, etc. for the purpose of watching, guarding, and checking irregularity or disorder; the perambulation of a city, town, or district by a police constable or detachment of police for the protection of life and property.

1664 BUTLER *Hud.* II. iii. 801 These consecrated Geese in Orders,..being then upon Petroll, With noise alone beat off the Gaul. **1693** LUTTRELL *Brief Rel.* (1857) III. 245 His majestie has ordered a nightly patrole. **1708** *Lond. Gaz.* No. 4419/5 The Dragoons..kept Patroles all Night. *a* **1734** NORTH *Exam.* III. vii. §98 (1740) 580 The Sherriffs..rode the Petroville about the City almost all Night, and no one attempted to make a Bonefire. **1833** HT. MARTINEAU *Loom & Lugger* I. v. 91 You are dreading your patrol to-night because it is beginning to snow. **1849** JAMES *Woodman* xv, The same vigilant patrol was kept up.

b. *fig.* and *transf.*

1727-46 THOMSON *Summer* 1605 Send forth the saving virtues round the land In bright patrol. **1821** CLARE *Vill. Minstr.* II. 23 The fox is loth to 'gin a long patrole. **1883** B. HARTE *Carquinez Woods* iii. 61 Mr. Brace had begun his fruitless patrol of the main street.

c. A reconnaissance flight by military aircraft.

1917 *Flying* 19 Dec. 347/3 A low patrol over the Fleet was carried out by three Flight-Lieutenants in Sopwith machines, during which they encountered and attacked a number of hostile craft. **1957** *Economist* 7 Dec. 836/2 To guard against surprise attack, bombers flying on patrol from Britain carry hydrogen bombs.

2. 'Those that go the rounds' (J.); a detachment of the guard told off for the purposes above mentioned; also, a police constable, or a detachment of such, told off to the beat of a particular district for its protection, the prevention of disorder, etc.

1670 G. H. tr. *Hist. Cardinals* III. II. 289 He sends Petrols of Soldiers constantly about. **1704** J. HARRIS *Lex. Techn.* I, *Patrouille*, or *Patroul* as we generally pronounce it, is a Round of Soldiers, to the Number of Five or Six, with a Serjeant to command them. **1800** *Asiat. Ann. Reg., Misc. Tr.* 229/2 The patrole of the city consists of 12,000 men, who receive a daily allowance of one fanam each. **1826** *Times* 5 Jan., 'This here man' (pointing to the patrol),..'has told a false affidavit'. **1868** *Regul. & Ord. Army* ¶903 Regiments encamped near villages are to send frequent patrols into them, to apprehend any Soldiers who may be there.

3. a. A detachment of troops sent out in advance of a column, regiment, etc., to reconnoitre the country and to gain information of the presence and movements of the enemy.

1702 *Lond. Gaz.* No. 3825/1 One of our Parties met with their Patrole near Pradella. **1710** *Ibid.* No. 4719/2 Our Patrouilles met with two of the Enemy's Parties. **1799** *Instr. & Reg. Cavalry* (1813) 273 Patroles must examine all villages, hollow ways and woods, that lie in the direction of their march, taking care to reconnoitre from the heights, the country below. **1827** SOUTHEY *Hist. Penins. War* II. 513 The French pushed their patroles of cavalry near the town. **1853** STOCQUELER *Mil. Encycl.* s.v., Patrols are also sent out to gain intelligence of the position and force of an enemy.

b. A unit of scouts or guides consisting of from six to eight members.

1908 R. S. S. BADEN-POWELL *Scouting for Boys* 22 A troop consists of not less than three patrols... A patrol consists of six scouts. **1908** *Scout* 18 Apr. 20/2 Several patrols together can form a 'Troop' under an officer called a Scout-master. **1917** R. E. PHILIPPS *Patrol System* ii. 13 Here is the Patrol, consisting of six, seven, or eight boys. **1946** C. CHRISTIAN *Seventh Magpie* xix. 216 Her bulging haversack bumping against her, to the extreme peril of the patrol milk supply she was carrying. **1974** *Policy, Organisation & Rules of Scout Assoc.* (ed. 3) 124 The Troop is composed of Patrols, each consisting of six to eight Scouts, including the Patrol Leader and Assistant Patrol Leader. **1977** *Guider* July 315/2 Estimated publication date is 1st September 1977, so you need to tell your Patrols about it *now* and encourage them to have a money-raising effort during the school holidays.

4. *attrib.* and *Comb.*, as ***patrol boat, box, -craft, duty, flotilla, jacket, system, tent, vessel, watch***; **patrol car**, a motor car employed by the police on patrol; **patrol leader**, (*a*) the boy scout in charge of a patrol (sense 3 b); (*b*) the leader of a military patrol; **patrol officer**, a representative of the Australian government in Papua New Guinea; **patrol-wagon**, *N. Amer.* (*a*) a wagon in which the police convey prisoners, a prison-van; (*b*) 'a light open wagon used by the underwriters' patrol in hastening to fires to protect insured goods' (Funk 1895). Also PATROLMAN.

1892 *Welsh Rev.* I. 724 A solution.. would be for certain ranges to be kept clear by official patrol boats. **1931** *Chicago Police Problems* v. 88 Each district normally has two small patrol cars. **1951** A. MARTIENSSEN *Crime & Police* iv. 49 In the Aberdeen system, the patrol cars and the beat constables have been formed into teams. **1967** N. LUCAS *C.I.D.* vi. 70 The Information Room put out an all car call for any disengaged patrols to join in the pursuit of the stolen Rover. Five patrol cars responded to the call. **1977** 'E. MCBAIN' *Long Time no See* i. 9 A radio motor patrol car was angle-parked into the curb. **1930** *Times Lit. Suppl.* 9 May 379/2 Officers who served in the French mine-sweepers and patrol-craft during the War. **1900** *Westm. Gaz.* 29 Nov. 11/2 Some gendarmes on patrol duty. **1908** *Scout* 18 Apr. 20/2 One boy is then chosen as Patrol Leader to command the patrol. **1918** E. S. FARROW *Dict. Mil. Terms* 438 Patrol leaders. **1929** E. K. WADE *Twenty-One Years of Scouting* vi. 193 Patrol leaders have taken closer command of their Patrols. **1973** *Guardian* 11 Apr. 11/4 One of my best friends used to be a patrol leader. **1977** M. JANCATH *Seatag* II. i. 63 He rifled through the files... 'Dishonourable discharge.. Patrol leader Aden.' **1924** 'R. DALY' *Outpost* i. ii. ' In my district,' put in Jessel amiably, 'there's a regulation that no patrol-officer shall be a married man.' **1935** *Discovery* Nov. 346/1 Local conditions fully justify the title of knights errant to the patrol officers and other members of the administration of Papua. **1964** *Mod. Encycl. Austral. & N.Z.* 790/1 Districts are divided into sub-districts in charge of an Assistant District Officer (A.D.O.), who has assistance from Patrol Officers (P.O.). **1880** A. W. TOURGÉE *Fool's Errand* II. xii. 507 The old 'patrol' system of the ante-bellum days.. was also one of the active causes of the rapid spread of the Klan. **1966** *Listener* 20 Oct. 571/1 Baden-Powell.. dreamed up the patrol system: autonomous groups of boys, whose leaders plan the troop programme together with the scoutmaster. **1849** E. E. NAPIER *Excurs. S. Africa* II. 67 These patrole tents.. made of light canvas,.. weighed about twenty five pounds. **1898** *Westm. Gaz.* 28 May 1/3 For the protection of her coasts.., America will depend mainly upon her monitors and emergency patrol vessels. **1887** *Courier-Jrnl.* (Louisville, Kentucky) 22 Jan. 3/5 The patrol wagon, filled with officers, was driven to the place at a breakneck speed. **1899** *Atlantic Monthly* LXXXIII. 770/1 With clamor of urgent gong, the patrol wagon rounds the corner, carrying two policemen. **1921** *Daily Colonist* (Victoria, B.C.) 5 Apr. 7/1 Dr. Tomalin was called and attended to the unfortunate man and Sergeant Blackstock and Constable Walton attended with the patrol wagon and removed him to the Jubilee Hospital. **1974** *Amer. Speech 1971* XLVI. 78 Large police van: paddy wagon, van, Black Maria, patrol wagon, patrol. **1810** *Boston* (Registry Dept.) *Records* (1904) 33rd Rep. 426 Return of the patrole watch read. **1821** *Ibid.* (1909) 39th Rep. 227 Granting permission for private patrole watches.

patrol (pəˈtrəʊl), *v.* Infl. patrolled, -olling. Forms: 7–8 **patroll**, 7– **patrol**, (8 **-rouille, roul**, 8–9 **-role**). [a. F. *patrouill-er*, in same sense, orig. to paddle or puddle in the mud, altered from earlier *patouiller* 'to padle, or dable in with the feet, to stirre vp and downe, and trouble, or make foule, by stirring' (Cotgr.): cf. OF. *patoueil* pool, puddle, mire (1473 in Godef.), mod.F. dial. *patrouil* mire; also *patouillas* 'a plash or puddle' (Cotgr.), mod.F. dial. *patouillat* a puddle or pool in the road. The military use (already in Cotgr. in *patrouille* sb.) was prob. at first a piece of French camp slang, patrolling consisting often of tramping through mire and wet. After its recognition, it passed into most of the western langs., Sp. *patrullar*, Pg. *patrulhar*, It. *pattugliare*; Du. *patrouilleeren*, Ger. *patrouill-*, *patrolliren*, Da. *patrollere*, Sw. *patrullera*.]

1. a. *intr.* 'To go the rounds in a camp or garrison' (J.); to go on patrol, to act as patrol; to reconnoitre as a patrol. **b.** To traverse on duty a particular beat or district as constable or patrolman.

1691 *Lond. Gaz.* No. 2702/2 They lay there undiscovered till.. a Trooper that was Patrolling first saw them. **1701** *Ibid.* No. 3722/1 Several Boats with Soldiers were ordered to Patroul on the River. **1709** E. WARD tr. *Cervantes* 219 They .. left him to take his rest with Martinez and twelve Men to Patrouille about. **1777** ROBERTSON *Hist. Amer.* II. VII. 284 The appointment of a considerable number of persons.. to patrole as watchmen during the night. **1832** W. IRVING *Alhambra* II. 57 Numbers of armed guards patrolled around them. **1855** CARLYLE *Misc.*, *Prinzenraub* (1857) IV. 360 Patrolled-over by mere irrational monsters. **1867** LADY HERBERT *Cradle L.* viii. 215 Finding the Europeans on the alert, and the native guard valiantly patrolling and shouting out their national war-cries. **1940** [see *dive-bomb* vb. s.v. DIVE *v.*].

c. *transf.* and *fig.*

1791 WOLCOTT (P. Pindar) *Magpie & Robin* 17 Leaving behind their bodies for rich mould, That pliable from form to form patroles, Making fresh houses for new souls. **1821** CLARE *Vill. Minstr.* I. 94 The labouring mice To sheltering hedge and wood patrole.

2. *trans.* To go over or round (a camp, garrison, town, harbour, etc.) for the purpose of watching, guarding, or protecting; to perambulate or traverse (a beat or district) as constable or patrolman; to traverse leisurely in all directions.

1765 R. ROGERS *Jrnls.* (1883) 80 We were continually employed in patrolling the woods between this fort and Ticonderoga. **1798** FERRIAR *Illustr. Sterne*, etc., *Eng. Hist.* 241 A strong body of horse patroled the streets. **1822** W. IRVING *Braceb. Hall* xx. 171 Christy often patrols the park with his dogs. **1885** *Manch. Exam.* 12 May 5/1 Armed boats will be provided for patrolling the Nile.

Hence **paˈtrolled** *ppl. a.*, **paˈtrolling** *vbl. sb.* and *ppl. a.*

1758 LD. SACKVILLE *Let. to Ld. Egremont* 12 Oct. (in *Pearson's Catal.* (1900) 68), We have detached Posts all along the Lippe,.. and even Patroling Parties as far to our right as Bentheim. **1847** *Infantry Man.* (1854) 105 Silence [is] indispensable in patrolling. **1887** *Pall Mall G.* 26 Jan. 9/1 A patrolling policeman heard cries for help. **1903** *Daily Chron.* 11 Feb. 3/5 A few yards away was the busy and patrolled Strand.

patrolatry (pəˈtrɒlətrɪ). *nonce-wd.* [f. Gr. πατήρ, πατρ- father + -LATRY.] Worship of, or excessive reverence for, the Fathers (of the Church).

1846 HARE *Mission Comf.* (1850) 237 Now that our church is threatened with a revival of patrolatry,.. notice should be drawn to the defects, as well as to the excellences of the Fathers.

patrolette (pætrəʊˈlɛt). [f. PATROL(MAN + -ETTE.] A woman or girl on patrolling duty.

1960 *Oxford Times* 1 Jan. 1/7 The Oxford office of the Royal Automobile Club invites applications from Young Ladies for the duties of patrolette. **1973** *Daily Tel.* 3 Jan. 10/3 Patrolettes and radio rescue mechanics also have new gear.

paˈtroller. [f. PATROL *v.* + -ER[1].] One on patrolling duty.

1744 *Bristol* (Va.) *Vestry Bk.* (1898) 118 To Burwell Green for his Levy, Being a patroler, 50. **1879** TOURGEE *Fool's Err.* xxxviii. 281 He ordered.. some patrollers to ride up and down the streets and prevent any interruption. **1901** B. T. WASHINGTON *Up from Slavery* 77 The 'patrollers' were bands of white men.. organized largely for the purposes of regulating the conduct of the slaves at night. **1938** W. FAULKNER *Unvanquished* 18 Into this room they would be fetched to face the Patroller. **1968** [see KETCH *v.*[2]]. **1972** R. ADAMS *Watership Down* xlix. 401 Without Campion, probably not one rabbit would have got back to Efrafa. As it was, all his skill as a patroller could not bring home half of those who had come to Watership.

patrollotism (pəˈtrəʊləʊtɪz(ə)m). *nonce-wd.* [repr. F. nonce-wd. *patrouillotisme*, f. *patrouille*, after *patriotisme*.] The system of patrols.

1837 CARLYLE *Fr. Rev.* I. VII. i, The Caricaturist promulgates his emblematic Tablature: *Le Patrouillotisme chassant le Patriotisme*, Patriotism driven out by Patrollotism. *Ibid.* iii, Sullen is the male heart, repressed by Patrollotism; vehement is the female, irrepressible.

patrolman (pəˈtrəʊlmən). orig. *U.S.* Also **patrolsman**. A man who is on patrol. *spec.* **a.** A police constable attached to a particular beat or district of a city or town.

1879 in WEBSTER *Suppl.* **1880** *Scribner's Mag.* Jan. 323 At the beginning of each watch two men set out from the station on patrol duty and follow their beats to the right and left respectively until they meet the patrol-men from the adjacent stations. **1893** STEAD *If Christ came to Chicago* (1894) 266 The nearest patrolman who sees it [a fire] hastens to his patrol-box and sends in a fire alarm. **1902** *Chambers's Jrnl.* Oct. 673/2 Nor is this all. He is well off, even if he never rises beyond the grade of patrol-man. **1955** W. GADDIS *Recognitions* II. vii. 644 The patrolman turned his attention to his charge. **1970** P. LAURIE *Scotland Yard* iii. 70 Very occasionally a patrolman meets crime in progress. **1974** *Anderson* (S. Carolina) *Independent* 20 Apr. 1B/4 Participating in the investigation and arrests were.. Patrolmen Jerry Gambrell and Jimmy McKinney of the Anderson police. **1977** 'J. FRASER' *Hearts Ease* ii. 12 The two police patrolmen were.. directing traffic.

b. A man told off to watch and inspect a line of electric wires, etc., to insure their continuing in good order.

18.. *Electric Rev.* (U.S.) XVI. 16 (Cent.) The chief lineman should.. also have charge of the carbon-setters and arc-patrolmen.

c. In general senses.

1867 J. M. CRAWFORD *Mosby* 330 [They] captured five patrolmen, from whom.. they succeeded in obtaining the countersign. **1878** *Harper's Mag.* Feb. 331/2 Each patrolman will carry a beach lantern. **1900** J. LONDON *Let.* 31 Jan. (1966) 86, I was.. a fish patrolman, a longshoreman, and a general sort of bay-faring adventurer. **1945** *Seafarers' Log* 22 June 6/1 The SS Prospector of the Alcoa SS Company, paid off here in an Army Base, and two Patrol-men managed to get aboard her. **1959** *Times* 14 Aug. 15/2 A beach patrolman said, [etc.]. **1965** M. SPARK *Mandelbaum Gate* iii. 69 The hill road to the Potter's Field bordered on disputed territory, and wanderers in the area were likely to be shot at by the patrolmen of either country. **1966** R. & D. MORRIS *Men & Pandas* v. 90 An exhausted zoo patrolman. **1974** *Country Life* 5 Dec. 1772/3 All AA patrolmen carry a copy.

patrology (pəˈtrɒlədʒɪ). [mod. f. Gr. πατήρ, πατρ- father + -λογία -LOGY. Cf. mod.L. *patrologia* (16th c.), F. *patrologie* (1878 in *Dict. Acad.*).] The study of the writings of the Fathers (of the Church), patristics; a treatise on these writings.

1600 NORTHBROOKE *Poor Man's Gard.* Ep. Ded. 3 May rather therefore be called Patrology, then Theology. **1716** M. DAVIES *Athen. Brit.* III. 49 To lay open.. the least Deformity.. they could discover or search out in the earliest Patrology. **1847** BUCH tr. *Hagenbach's Hist. Doctr.* I. 7 *note*, The distinction made by some writers,.. between Patristics and Patrology, appears to us.. unfounded.

Hence **patrologic** (pætrəʊˈlɒdʒɪk), **-ical** *adjs.*, belonging to patrology (whence **patrologico-apostolical** *a.*, pertaining to the Apostolic Fathers); **paˈtrologist**, one versed in patrology.

1715 M. DAVIES *Athen. Brit.* I. Pref. 12 The last mention'd geniuner kind of Patrologico-Apostolical Epistles. **1716** *Ibid.* II. 278 The Patrological Memoirs.. of those earliest.. Post-Nicen Centuries. *Ibid.* III. 39 Printed .. by the erudite Protestant Patrologists. *Ibid.* 49 Well read in all the Patrological Prints. **1890** E. JOHNSON *Rise Christendom* 359 The Basilian and Benedictine patrologic mythology.

patron (ˈpeɪtrən), *sb.* Forms: 3–6 **patroun**, 4–7 **patrone**, 5 **patorne**, 3– **patron**. [ME. *patroun*, a. OF. *patrun* (12th c.), *patron* (13th c.), = Pr. *padron*, *padro*, Cat. *padró*, Sp. *patron* (*padron*), Pg. *patrono*, It. *padrone* (†*patrone*), ad. L. *patrōn-us* protector, defender, patron, deriv. of *pater*, *patr-em* father.

L. *patronus* had the senses of protector and defender of his clients (viz. of individuals, of cities, or provinces); also, the former master of a freedman or freedwoman; an advocate or defender before a court of justice, or, generally, of any person or cause. In med.L. and Romanic it acquired the senses of patron saint, patron or advowee (*advocatus*) of a church, and that of lord or master, in many specific connexions; also that of exemplar, pattern. Most of these senses are represented in Eng. *patron*, but the order in which they were taken into Eng. does not correspond to that of their appearance in Latin and Romanic, sense 4, 'patron of a church', being the earliest to be adopted. The order here followed is one of convenience; the chronological order may be seen from the quotations. The sense PATTERN is now differentiated in spelling, and is treated as a distinct word.]

I. Senses connected with ancient L. *patrōnus*.

1. One who stands to another or others in relations analogous to those of a father; a lord or master; a protector; †a lord superior; †a founder of a religious order.

13.. *Gaw. & Gr. Knt.* 6 Hit watz Ennias þe athel, & his highe kynde, þat siþen depreced prouinces, & patrounes bicome Welneȝe of al þe wele in þe west iles. *c* **1380** WYCLIF *Wks.* (1880) 285 Also crist & his apostlis techen vs to lyue beter þanne þes patrouns of þes newe ordris. **1402** *Jack Upland* (Skeat) I. 33. *c* **1430** LYDG. *Min. Poems* (Percy Soc.) 110 'Syr', she sayd, 'ye be ower lord, ower patron, and ower precedent'. **1590** SPENSER *F.Q.* I. xii. 6 Unto that doughtie Conquerour they came, And.. Their Lorde and Patrone loud did him proclame. **1632** LITHGOW *Trav.* x. 444 The Patrone of so great a Monarchy. **1652** NEEDHAM tr. *Selden's Mare Cl.* 25 The Dominion for all that remaining to another Patron. **1737** POPE *Hor. Epist.* II. i. 1 While you, great Patron of Mankind! sustain The balanc'd World, and open all the Main. **1809** BAWDWEN *Domesday Bk.* 415 In these wards there are 77 mansions belonging to sokemen who have their own lands in demesne, and who may choose a patron where they will. **1838** THIRLWALL *Greece* V. 321 Sparta.. could not easily bring herself to think of the son of Amyntas, as a patron, or a master.

2. *Rom. Antiq.* One who had manumitted his slave, and who retained legal claims, of a paternal nature, upon him as freedman. Also, **b.** A person of distinction who gave his protection and aid to a client (see CLIENT 1) in return for certain services. Hence used allusively.

1560 DAUS tr. *Sleidane's Comm.* 72, I shoulde gyve an occasion unto Clientes to offende against their patrones. **1623–34** FLETCHER & MASSINGER *Lover's Progr.* v. i, It is the client's duty To wait upon his patron. **1727–41** CHAMBERS *Cycl.* s.v., The principal right which patrons had, was that of being the legal heirs of their freed-men, if they died without lawful issue born after their enfranchisement, and intestate. **1837** *Penny Cycl.* VII. 260/1 Patron and client were not permitted to sue at law, or give evidence against one another. Originally patricians only could be patrons. **1843** MACAULAY *Lays Anc. Rome, Virginia* 78, I wait on Appius Claudius, I waited on his sire: Let him who works the client wrong beware the patron's ire!

c. *Rom. Antiq.* A defender before a court of justice; an advocate, a pleader; hence *fig.* In reference to ancient Greece, used to render *προστάτης*, as applied to a citizen under whose protection a resident alien (*μέτοικος*) placed himself, and who transacted legal business for him and was responsible to the state for his conduct.

1387 TREVISA *Higden* (Rolls) IV. 219 Iulius Cesar, þat was his patroun and his vorie,..pleted for hym. **1485** CAXTON *St. Wenefr.* 14 He shold to them be a patrone in heuen. **1613** PURCHAS *Pilgrimage* I. vi. 25 Conscience as a Witnesse, Patron, or Judge within us, accuseth, excuseth, condemneth, or absolveth. **1667** MILTON *P.L.* III. 219 On mans behalf Patron or Intercessor none appeerd. **1875** WOOLSEY *Introd. Internat. Law* (1879) §67 At Athens.. domiciled strangers—*metœci*,—..needed a patron for the transaction of legal business.

3. a. 'One who countenances, supports, or protects' (J.); one who takes under his favour and protection, or lends his influential support to advance the interests of, some person, cause, institution, art, or undertaking; *spec.* in 17th and 18th c. the person who accepted the dedication of a book. (Always implying something of the superior relation of the wealthy or powerful Roman patron to his client.) Now a chief sense.

1377 LANGL. *P. Pl.* B. XII. 227 Ac kynde..is þe pyes patroun and putteth it in hire ere. *c* **1380** WYCLIF *Sel. Wks.* II. 254 þe world is his patroun, and þe fadir of pryde also. **14..** *Tundale's Vis.* (Wagner) 2159, I was some tyme thy patroun fre, To whom thou shuldest buxsum be. **1500–20** DUNBAR *Poems* lviii. 13 Off sic hie feistis of saintis in glorie, ..Quhair lordis war patrones, oft I sang thame *Caritas pro Dei armore.* **1568** GRAFTON *Chron.* II. 770 As though God and Saint Peter were the Patrones of vngracious liuyng. **1605** BACON *Adv. Learn.* I. iii. §9 Books (such as are worthy the name of books) ought to have no patrons but truth and reason. **1735** POPE *Prol. Sat.* 249 May some choice patron bless each grey-goose quill! **1749** JOHNSON *Van. Hum. Wishes* 160 There mark what ills the scholar's life assail, Toil, envy, want, the patron, and the jail. **1847** TENNYSON *Princ.* Concl. 88 A great broad-shoulder'd genial English-man,..A patron of some thirty charities. **1853** J. H. NEWMAN *Hist. Sk.* (1873) II. I. iv. 213 Kings..at various periods have been most effective patrons of art and science. *fig. c* **1760** SMOLLETT *Ode to Sleep* 2 Soft Sleep..Sweet patron of the peaceful hour.

b. A supporter, upholder, advocate, or champion of a theory or doctrine. Now *rare.*

1573 G. HARVEY *Letter-bk.* (Camden) 10, I was a great and continual patron of paradoxis. **1668** CULPEPPER & COLE *Barthol. Anat.* II. vi. 103 Patrons and favourers of the circular motion of the blood, as Harvey. **1705** STANHOPE *Paraphr.* III. 424 Those very Epistles, where the main Strength of the Patrons for a naked and unfruitful Faith is supposed to lye. **1796** BP. WATSON *Apol. Bible* 42 This fancy has had some patrons before you.

c. One who countenances or supports a practice, a form of sport, an institution, or the like. Also (in tradesmen's language), One who supports with his custom a commercial undertaking, a shop, store, etc.; a regular customer; one who uses or frequents any institution or place of resort.

1605 B. JONSON *Volpone* II. i, [Volpone, disguised as a mountebank Doctor addressing the crowd gathered before him] Most noble gentlemen, and my worthy patrons! **1891** *Falkirk Herald* 18 July 1/5 The Proprietor..thanks his Patrons for the support they have extended to him for the past 11 years. *Mod.* A great patron of the turf and the prize-ring. The patrons of the public-house, the gin-shop, etc.

II. Senses arising in mediæval Latin.

4. One who holds the right of presentation to an ecclesiastical benefice; the holder of the advowson: so called from his original function of advocate and defender: see ADVOCATE 2, ADVOWEE 2. (The earliest sense in Eng. use.)

[**1278** *Rolls of Parlt.* I. 5/1 Les eyres Wauter Ledet sunt verres patrons de la dite Eglise.] *c* **1300** *Beket* (Percy Soc.) 570 And that he, other the patroun, furst the ȝift ȝeve. *c* **1325** *Poem Times Edw. II* 56 in *Pol. Songs* (Camden) 326 Sone so a parsoun is ded and in eorthe i-don, Thanne shal the patroun have ȝiftes anon. **1393** LANGL. *P. Pl.* C. VI. 78 Popes and patrones poure gentil blod refuseþ. *a* **1450** *Knt. de la Tour* (1868) 42 The knight was lorde and patron of the chirche. **1583** BABINGTON *Commandm.* To Gentlem. Eng. (1590) **iv b, They should defend and tender the estate of the Churches whereof they bee patrons. **1616** R. C. *Times' Whistle* IV. 1357 Lawes danger to prevent, The patron with the parson will indent That he shall have the living. **1766** BLACKSTONE *Comm.* II. xviii. 276 The right of presentation to a church accrues to the ordinary by neglect of the patron to present. **1861** W. BELL *Dict. Law Scotl.* s.v. *Patronage*, It would appear that patrons were originally merely the guardians of the temporal property of particular churches. **1878** STUBBS *Const. Hist.* xix. III. 311 In 1253..he [Innocent IV] recognized in the fullest way the rights of patrons, and undertook to abstain from all usurped provisions.

5. a. 'A guardian saint' (J.); the special tutelary saint of a person, place, country, craft, or institution. (Now usually *patron saint*: see 13 c.)

c **1380** WYCLIF *Serm.* Sel. Wks. I. 73 Neiþ er þei make Baptist ne Jesus Crist þer patroun. **1511** GUYLFORDE *Pilgr.* (Camden) 11 Many relyques, as the hed and the arme of seynt Blase, which is there patron. **1560** DAUS tr. *Sleidane's Comm.* 437 b, S. James the Patrone of Spain. **1646** CRASHAW *Deo Nostro* (1652) 196 Ah, then, poor soul! what wilt thou say? And to what patron choose to pray? **1718** *Free-thinker* No. 16 ¶4 Saint Nicholas is the great Patron of Mariners. **1828** K. DIGBY *Broadst. Hon.* (1846) II. *Tancredus* 89 [St. George] was the patron of England as early as the time of Richard I. He is also patron of Malta, of Genoa, of Valentia and Arragon.

†**b.** A tutelary (pagan) divinity. *Obs.*

c **1374** CHAUCER *Anel. & Arc.* 4 You fiers god of armes Mars the rede That..Honured art as patron of that place. **1697** DRYDEN *Æneid* XII. 596 Then to the patron of his art he [the physician Iäpis] pray'd.

†**c.** *ellipt.* for *patron day* (see 12): = PATTERN *sb.* 12. *Obs.*

1890 J. HEALEY *Insula Sanct. et Doctor.* 82 A holy well where a 'patron' was formerly held on the last Sunday of July.

III. Senses repr. modern Romanic uses.

(= It. *padrone, patrone*, Sp. *patron, padron*, F. *patron.*) Cf. PADRONE, PATROON 2–3.

6. a. The captain or master of a galley, or of a coasting vessel in the Mediterranean or in N. American waters; also, the steersman of a longboat. Now *rare.*

[**1392–3** *Earl Derby's Exp.* (Camden) 232 Item pro vino.. empto per manus Johannis Payn in galeia de Gilberto famulo patroni.] **14..** in *Hist. Coll. Citizen London* (Camden) 115 Certayne lordys faughtyn whithe carykys of Gene,..and toke iiij of..them and hyr patronys. **1484** CAXTON *Fables of Poge* ix, Ther was a carryk of Jene..of the whiche carrick the patrone bare in his sheld painted an oxe hede. **1568** GRAFTON *Chron.* II. 464 Three of the greatest Caricks with their patrones, and Monsire Iaques de Burbon their Admirall were taken. **1676** *Lond. Gaz.* No. 1066/3 These particulars,..come from Naples, brought thither by the Patron of a Felucca. **1727–41** CHAMBERS *Cycl.* s.v., *Patron*..is a name given in the Mediterranean, to the person who commands the vessel and seamen; sometimes to the person who steers it. **1777** P. THICKNESSE *Year's Journey* I. viii. 59 The *Patron* of the barge..affected to shew how much skill was necessary to guide it through the main arch. **1817** J. BRADBURY *Trav. Interior Amer.* 192 Her crew consisted of five French Creoles, four of whom were oarsmen, and the fifth steered the boat, he is called the *patron.* **1820** BYRON *Mar. Fal.* I. ii. 294 How! did you say the patron of a galley? **1849** T. T. JOHNSON *Sights in Gold Region* 12 The Creoles ..were generally the patrones or captains, and the owners of the boats. **1906** [see BOSMAN]. **1968** R. F. ADAMS *Western Words* (rev. ed.) 222/1 *Patron*, a trader's name for the head of a barge engaged in the Missouri River fur trade. In river boating, a rudder man on a mackinaw.

†**b.** Extended to the captain of an ancient ship.

1490 CAXTON *Eneydos* xxvii. 95 Eneas..called to hym all the patrons & all the maystres of the shipes. **1513** DOUGLAS *Æneis* V. iv. 5 That the patrone Gyas, amyd the flude,.. Callis on his steris man, hait Meneit by name.

†**7.** A master or owner of slaves or captives (in the Levant and Barbary states). *Obs.*

1628 DIGBY *Voy. Medit.* (1868) 19 [They] gaue me leaue to carrie away all the English captiues that remained here (which were near 50), paying onely the money they cost vnto their patrones. **1697** tr. *C'tess D'Aunoy's Trav.* (1706) 227 Heretofore..a Patron might have killed his Slave as he might have killed his Dog. **1719** DE FOE *Crusoe* I. ii, My new patron or master had taken me home to his house.

‖**8.** The host or landlord of an inn (in Spain): cf. PADRONE d. Also with reference to countries other than Spain.

1878 LADY BRASSEY *Voy. Sunbeam* x. 170 [They] carried it to the inn, where I had to explain to the *patron*, in my best Spanish, that we wanted a carriage to go to the baths. **1973** *Times* 25 Aug. 12/4 To them a good restaurant without the patron's presence is a paradox. **1978** T. ALLBEURY *Lantern Network* iii. 46 They..sat..in the warmth of a small restaurant... The *patron* moved among his customers.

9. *U.S.* and *Canad.* (with capital initial). A member of a political association, in full ***Patrons of Husbandry*** (or ***Industry***), founded in the U.S.A. in 1867, or of a similar association founded in Canada in 1891, for the promotion of farming interests. Now chiefly *Hist.*

1873 *N.Y. Times* 3 July 1/2 The organization known as the Patrons of Husbandry originated in Washington in 1867, and the National Grange was organized in December of that year in this city. **1880** [see GRANGE *sb.* 5]. **1894** *Weekly Globe* (Toronto) 23 May 1 Mr John A. Leitch, the Conservative candidate for West Middlesex..said:—'The Patron Order was originated in the Western States, and was imported into Canada by dissatisfied politicians.' **1903** J. S. WILLISON *Sir Wilfrid Laurier & Liberal Party* II. xxvi. 281 The position of the Liberals was also measurably affected by their practical alliance for the campaign of 1896 with Mr. D'Alton McCarthy and the Patrons of Industry... The Patrons were an off-shoot from the farmers' organizations of the United States, and their demands embraced simplification of the laws and machinery of government, limitation of public subsidies, protection against industrial combinations, and a tariff for revenue. **1914** W. S. WALLACE in Shortt & Doughty *Canada & its Provinces* XVII. 173 Patrons, as they were called *tout court*, were representatives of the farming class. **1932** A. BRADY *Canada* iii. 104 The new organization, known as the Patrons of Industry, succeeded in 1894 in electing sixteen of its nominees to the legislature of Ontario. **1962** *New Democrat* Oct. 3/2 In 1894 the Patrons of Industry elected 14 members to the Ontario legislature. **1963** A. S. MORTON *Kingdom of Canada* 382 The Patrons did everything the Grangers did, but they added a special emphasis on co-operation. **1977** *Canad. Hist. Rev.* LVIII. 401 McCarthy gravitated further from the Conservatives, emerging as an Independent in 1893 and an ally in all but name of the Liberals and Patrons in 1896.

IV. Applied to things.

†**10.** The earlier form of the word PATTERN, q.v. for illustrations of this form. *Obs.* (in this spelling).

†**11.** A case for holding pistol-cartridges: see quot. 1834. (F. *patron, patronne.*) Also, A cartridge (Ger. *patrone*). *Obs.* exc. *Hist.*

1683 SIR J. TURNER *Pallas Armata* 173 All Horse-men should always have the charges of their Pistols ready in Patrons, the Powder made up compactly in Paper, and the Ball tyed to it with a piece of Packthred. *Ibid.* 176 He hath no more to do but to bite of a little of the Paper of his Patron. **1834** *Penny Cycl.* II. 375/2 The *Patron* was an upright semi-cylindrical box of steel, with a cover moving on a hinge, filled with a block of wood with five perforations to hold as many pistol-cartridges. **1860** FAIRHOLT *Cost. Eng.* (ed. 2) Gloss. **1862** *Cat. Spec. Exh. S. Kens.* No. 4731–2 Steel patron for holding cartridges, with embossed figures in front. Sixteenth century. Leather patron, with steel mountings and cover, and ball bag attached. Seventeenth century.

V. *attrib.* and *Comb.*

12. *attrib.*, as ***patron business, -worship***; **patron call** (*Sc.*), see quot.; **patron day**, the day of a patron saint, esp. in Ireland: see PATTERN *sb.* 12; †**patrontashe** *Mil.* [Du. *patroontasch*, Ger. *patronentasche*], a cartridge-case or ammunition-pouch.

1825–80 JAMIESON, **Patron-call*, the patronage of a church, the right of presentation. **1710** LUTTRELL *Brief Rel.* (1857) VI. 599 In the act..is a clause against papists frequenting their saints wells on particular *patron days. **1841** S. C. HALL *Ireland* I. 280 The patron-day..attracts crowds of visitors. **1689** *Acts Parl. Scot.* (1822) IX. 30/2 Money was given..for buying baggenots and *patrontashes to ther Captaines of every Company. **1818** BENTHAM *Ch. Eng.* 280 Not only in the line of public service, but in every other line, even in the line of *Patron-worship, will exertions cease.

13. In appositive construction or combination: often equivalent to an adj. **a.** That is a patron.

1781 COWPER *Hope* 414 Just made fifth chaplain of his patron lord.

b. Tutelary, as ***patron deity, god, martyr***, etc.

1700 DRYDEN *Pal. & Arc.* III. 561 The bloody colours of his patron god. **1726** POPE *Odyss.* XIX. 468 Hermes, his Patron-god, those gifts bestow'd. **1869** LECKY *Europ. Mor.* (1877) I. iii. 464 Almost every hamlet soon required a patron martyr and a local legend. **1895** SAYCE *Egypt of Hebr. & Herodotos* 122 Its [Thebes] patron-deity was Amon.

c. patron saint: = sense 5.

1717 FENTON *Ep. T. Lambard* Poems 213 By France the Genius of the Fight confest, For which our Patron-Saint adorns his Breast. **1832** G. DOWNES *Lett. Cont. Countries* I. 176 The festival of Justus, the patron saint, had attracted crowds to the village.

transf. **1856** EMERSON *Eng. Traits, Manners* Wks. (Bohn) II. 50 Sir Philip Sidney is one of the patron saints of England.

ˈpatron, *v. rare.* [cf. mod.F. *patronner*, med.L. and It. *patronare*, f. L. *patrōnus* PATRON.] *trans.* To act as patron to, to champion or favour as a patron; to patronize.

c **1624** CHAPMAN *Batrachom.* xxii, This Dedication calls no greatness, then, To patron this greatness-creating pen. **1643** SIR T. BROWNE *Relig. Med.* II. §3 Wiser Princes Patron the Arts. **1661** GLANVILL *Van. Dogm.* 186, I..am not likely to Patron them. **1865** DICKENS *Mut. Fr.* II. xiv, Why am I to be patroned and patronessed as if the patrons and patronesses treated me?

patronage (ˈpætrənɪdʒ), *sb.* [a. F. *patronage* (14th c. in Hatz.-Darm.) = It. *patronaggio*, in med.L. *patrōnāticum, -āgium*, f. L. *patrōn-us* PATRON: see -AGE.] The office or action of a PATRON: in various senses of the word.

1. *Eccl.* The right of presenting a qualified person to an ecclesiastical benefice; advowson. Originally, the protection and defence of the rights of a church, which carried with it the right of presentation.

1412 in *Laing Charters* (1899) 24 He..sal noth iniure na disese the place throuch na titil of patronage bot as it is granttit..in this indenture. **1513–14** *Act 5 Hen. VIII*, c. 11 §2 The said Erle..[shall] have and enjoye all and singler Advousons and Patronages of Churches. **1578–9** *Reg. Privy Council Scot.* III. 99 The patronage of the said bischoprik of Glasgow. **1730–6** BAILEY (folio) s.v., *Lay Patronage*..is a right attach'd to the person either as founder, or heir of the founder; or as possessor of the see to which the patronage is annexed, and is either *real* or *personal.* **1782** PRIESTLEY *Corrupt. Chr.* II. x. 246 Patronage was introduced in the fourth century. **1876** FREEMAN *Norm. Conq.* V. xxiv. 501 In either case, patronage involved, what in later times has come to be its whole substance, a right of nomination. **1883** *Chambers' Encycl.* VII. 328/2 By an act of parliament in 1874, patronage was abolished [in the Church of Scotland].

2. Guardianship, tutelary care, as of a divinity or a saint. *arch.* or *Obs.*

1582 STANYHURST *Æneis* II. (Arb.) 49 And so to bee shielded yet agayn with patronage anticque. **1609** BIBLE (Douay) *Gen.* xlviii. *Comm.*, The ancient Fathers teach the patronage and Invocation of Angels. **1702** ADDISON *Dial. Medals* ii. Wks. (Bohn) I. 295 Among the Roman Catholics every vessel is recommended to the patronage of some particular saint. **1805** SOUTHEY *Madoc in Azt.* x. 139 His the other pile, By whose peculiar power and patronage Aztlan was blest, Mexitli, woman-born.

3. a. The action of a patron in giving influential support, favour, encouragement, or countenance, to a person, institution, work, art, etc. Originally implying the action of a superior.

1553 T. WILSON *Rhet.* Ep. (1567) A j b, I therfore commende to youre Lordeschyppes tuition and patronage this traictise of Rhethorique. **1567** DRANT *Horace* Ded. *ij b, Nor any thing doth add more estimation to true nobilitye, then patronage of learning. **1752** JOHNSON *Rambler* No. 194 ¶ 4 My fears of losing the patronage of the family. **1813** MAR. EDGEWORTH *Patron.* xiv, Obtain for your girls what I call the patronage of fashion. **1839** KEIGHTLEY *Hist. Eng.* II. 75 Henry's patronage of letters was highly commendable. **1860** C. KNIGHT *Pop. Hist. Eng.* VI. vi. 91 Thanks to the example of the 'poor author' who threw the tardy patronage of lord Chesterfield in his face. **1866** GEO. ELIOT *F. Holt* i, Harold had gone with the Embassy to Constantinople, under the patronage of a high relative, his mother's cousin.

b. *spec.* Protection, defence; protectorship. ? *Obs.*

1590 SPENSER *F.Q.* II. viii. 26 Leave unto me thy knights last patronage [*i.e.* of his dead body]. *c* **1611** CHAPMAN *Iliad* VI. 469 Lest, of a father's patronage, the bulwark of all Troy, Thou leav'st him a poor widow's charge. **1706** PHILLIPS, *Patronage*, Protection, Defence. **1844** THIRLWALL *Greece* VIII. 369 Without having been able to effect anything..for ..the newly expelled Spartan exiles, who had likewise reckoned on his patronage.

†**c.** Advocacy, countenance, support. *Obs.*

1610 A. WILLET *Hexapla Dan.* 114 The multitude of those that erre, is no patronage for error. **1612** T. TAYLOR *Comm. Titus* ii. 11 This place..rightly interpreted, yeeldeth no patronage to that deuise of Vniuersall election. **1674** OWEN *Holy Spirit* (1693) 10 He doth therein undertake our Patronage, as our Advocate.

d. Countenance or favour shown with an air or assumption of superiority; patronizing.

1829 CARLYLE *Misc.* (1857) I. 279 A distinct patronage both of Providence and the Devil. **1870** DICKENS *E. Drood* ii, With a pleasant air of patronage, the Dean as nearly cocks his quaint hat as [etc.]. **1883** JOS. QUINCY *Figures of Past* 61 If there was a little savor of patronage in the generous hospitality she exercised among her simple neighbors, it was never regarded as more than a natural emphasis of her undoubted claims to precedence.

e. In commercial or colloquial use: The financial support given by customers in making use of anything established, opened, or offered for the use of the public, as a line of conveyances or steamers, a hotel, store, shop, or the like.

1804 *Ann. Rev.* II. 187/1 That the institution has all that claim to general patronage..we are disposed to deny. **1856** OLMSTED *Slave States* 76 The appearance of the other public-house indicated that it expected a less select patronage. *Mod.* 'Messrs. A. and B. have opened a new establishment for the supply of.., and hope for a share of public patronage'.

f. *Rom. Antiq.* The rights and duties or position of a patron (sense 2 b).

1697 [see CLIENTSHIP]. **1885** *Encycl. Brit.* XVIII. 413/1 The patronage and the clientage were alike hereditary.

4. The right or control of appointments to offices, privileges, etc., in the public service.

1769 *Junius Lett.* iii. 18 Is the command of the army, with all the patronage annexed to it, nothing? **1792** GOUV. MORRIS in Sparks *Life & Writ.* (1832) II. 259 The ministers possess more patronage than any monarch since Louis the Fourteenth. **1800** *Asiat. Ann. Reg., Proc. E. Ind. Ho.* 116/1 Why had they confined their inquiry to one individual charge of the abuse of patronage—that of the sale of writers appointments? **1886** *N. Amer. Rev.* CXLII. 577 The senators of each State divided their patronage to suit themselves, fulfilling the pledges of the last election and bribing voters for the next.

5. *Arms of Patronage* (*Her.*): see quots.

1727–41 CHAMBERS *Cycl.* s.v., *Arms of Patronage*, in heraldry, are those, a top whereof are some marks of subjection and dependance... The cardinals on the top of their arms bear those of the pope, who gave them the hat, to shew that they are his creatures. **1823** CRABB *Technol. Dict.*, *Patronage, Arms of* (*Her.*), those arms which governors of provinces, lords of manors, patrons of benefices, add to their family arms to betoken their right and jurisdiction.

6. *attrib.* (chiefly in senses 1 and 4), as *patronage curse, -monger, polity, reform, system*, etc.; **Patronage Secretary** (in Great Britain), the Secretary of the Treasury through whom the patronage of that department of the government is administered and appointments to departments under its control made; so *Patronage Secretaryship*.

1907 *Daily Chron.* 18 July 3/6 The patronage curse..has received the benediction of a Liberal Government. **1968** *Economist* 28 Dec. 21/2 It seemed unquestionably right to establish the teaching profession as a separate civil service beyond the reach of politicians and patronage-mongers. **1971** P. A. ALLUM *Politics & Society Post-War Naples* (1973) iv. 98 The patronage polity has been absorbed within the parliamentary system despite the contradictions between them. **1897** *Daily News* 21 Oct. 8/7 Archbishop Benson..was..greatly disappointed at his failure to get his patronage reforms, as embodied in the Benefices Bill, through. **1852** DISRAELI *Lord George Bentinck* xvii. 314 Sir Robert appointed the man of the world financial secretary of the treasury..and entrusted to the student, under the usual title of patronage secretary of the treasury, the management of the house of commons. **1873** TROLLOPE *Phineas Redux* (1874) I. xvi. 127 Roby..was at this moment Mr. Daubeny's head whip and patronage secretary. **1875** LE FANU *Will. die* xxix, That judicious rewarder of public virtue, and instructor of the conscience of the hustings, the patronage Secretary of the Treasury. **1881** *Daily Tel.* 4 Mar. 2 Whether it was with the Sanction of the Government that certain draft Editorials..have been forwarded to organs of the press by the noble lord the Patronage Secretary. **1909** *Westm. Gaz.* 16 Sept. 9/2 When he laid down the Patronage Secretaryship he assumed the offices of Lord Privy Seal and Chancellor of the Duchy of Lancaster. **1802** *Deb. Congress U.S.* 18 Feb. (1851) 580 A variety of circumstances..gave the patronage system the preponderancy, during the first three Presidential terms of election. **1976** *National Observer* (U.S.) 24 Apr. 16/4 The patronage system in the nation's fourth-largest city remains intact, and it is expected that the power it wields will be utilized with considerable impact.

†**'patronage**, *v. Obs.* [f. prec. sb.; perh. influenced by It. *patroneggiare* to patronize.] *trans.* To give patronage to; to countenance, uphold, protect, defend; to PATRONIZE.

1587 GREENE *Euphues' Censure* Ep. Ded., For that the goddesse [Pallas] did most patronage learning and souldiers. **1591** SHAKS. *1 Hen. VI*, III. i. 48 Yes, as an Out-law in a Castle keepes, And vseth it, to patronage his Theft. **1596** *Edward III*, III. iii, To patronage the fatherless and poor. **1598** R. HAYDOCKE tr. *Lomazzo* To Rdr., To patronage them from the insolent incroaching of men of no desert. **1669** STURMY *Mariner's Mag.* Aaaa ij, That I may charge you to Patronage no more than you had.

Hence †**'patronaged** *ppl. a.*; †**'patronaging** *vbl. sb.* and *ppl. a. Obs.*

1597 J. KING *On Jonas* (1618) 124 That it should be rackt to the patronaging of Temo's cosenage. ? **1650** *Don Bellianis* 254 The quiet shore of your most gentle and patronaging favours. **1726** AYLIFFE *Parergon* 411 The Patron ought..to have Honours done him in such patronag'd Church, as the best seat therein and the like.

patronal ('pætrənəl, 'peɪt-), *a.* [a. F. *patronal* (1611 in Cotgr.), ad. L. *patrōnāl-is*, f. *patrōn-us* PATRON: see -AL[1]. For the pronunciation cf. *personal*; but some say (pə'trəʊnəl); cf. DOCTRINAL.] Of or pertaining to a patron or patron saint; of the nature of a patron.

1611 COTGR., *Patronal*, patronall; of, or belonging to, a Patron; done in remembrance, or solemnized in honour, of a Patron. **1646** SIR T. BROWNE *Pseud. Ep.* 12 Their Penates and Patronall gods. **1755** JOHNSON, *Patronal*, Protecting; supporting; guarding; defending; doing the office of a patron. **1834** L. RITCHIE *Wand. by Seine* (1835) 229 One might have thought..that it was the patronal fête of the town. **1868** SMITH *Smaller Dict. Gr. & Rom. Antiq.* (ed. 7) s.v. *Patronus*, It was the duty of the patron to support his freedman in case of necessity, and if he did not, he lost his patronal rights.

‖**patronat** (patrɔna). [Fr.] An organization of industrial employers in France; French employers collectively.

1958 *Economist* 15 Nov. 616/1 There are certainly two distinct attitudes in France. One group, which includes the *patronat* or employers' federation, seems opposed to any sort of free trade area on terms possible for Britain. **1963** *Times* 13 Feb. 9/1 Against this it is argued that in 1958 the Common Market seemed to the French *patronat* a dangerous experiment, whereas now it is an established international entity. **1971** *Guardian* 15 July 16/4 We still have to decide whether the enlarged EEC will..take the place of the UK in EFTA..or whether it will insist on rules leading to tighter harmonisation... The Patronat has declared itself firmly in favour of the second solution. **1972** LD. GLADWYN *Mem.* xvii. 306, I dwelt at length on the very considerable opposition in France to the entry of the UK into the Common Market... For their part, the Patronat, having accepted the Common Market, still maintained an uncompromising opposition..to any reduction of the Common External Tariff.

patronate ('pætrənət, 'peɪt-). *rare.* [ad. L. *patrōnāt-us*, f. *patrōn-us* PATRON: see -ATE[1].] The position, right, or duty of a patron; the jurisdiction or possession of a patron.

1694 FOUNTAINHALL in M. P. Brown *Suppl. Decis. Crt. Session* (1826) IV. 143 The Lords found the Bishop's presenting, as patron, made it a patronate, but not a patrimonial mensal kirk. **1865** M. PATTISON *Ess.* (1889) I. 75 That was the idea which the master of Rosso and Cellini formed of his patronate of letters. **1880** MUIRHEAD *Gaius* 563 *Patronate* was the relationship that existed between a freedman,..and his *patronus*.

attrib. **1879** P. LORIMER *Lechler's Wiclif* I. 46 The Curia.. encourages all who have patronate rights to make pastoral appointments of a like kind.

'patrondom. *nonce-wd.* [See -DOM.] The estate or order of patrons.

1878 P. LORIMER *Lechler's Wiclif* I. 36 To that end.. behoved to be subservient both priestdom and patrondom, bishopdom and popedom.

†**pa'trone.** *Obs.* Also patronne. [a. F. *patronne* (= *galère patronne*), fem. of *patron*.] The galley which carried the lieutenant-general (= vice-admiral) of a squadron of galleys, and was usually the second galley of the squadron (the first being the *capitana* or CAPTAINESS, in the French squadron the *réale*).

1585 T. WASHINGTON tr. *Nicholay's Voy.* I. xx. 25 b, About the euening were brought intoo our Patrone..the Gouernour Vallier and the Spanish Argosin. *Ibid.* I. xxii. 28 There died also two gallie slaues and foure in the patrone. *Ibid.* II. iii. 33 b, We began to way out the bisket..in the Patronne there was scarce lefte for foure days.

patrone, obs. form of PATRON, PATROON.

patro'nee. *nonce-wd.* [See -EE.] A recipient of patronage, a presentee to a benefice.

c **1807** SYD. SMITH in Lady Holland *Mem.* (1855) II. 32 My request to him..was, if any patronee of his preferred the North to the South, that I might be allowed to gratify so singular a wish by exchanging with him.

patroness ('peɪtrənɪs, 'pæt-), *sb.* Also 5 -nyse, 5–7 -nesse, -onnesse. [ad. med.L. *patrōnissa*, fem. of *patrōnus* (after *basilissa*: see -ESS); cf. mod.F. *patronnesse* (1878 in *Dict. Acad.*), Du. *patrones*.]

1. A female patron (in senses 1–3 of PATRON); in modern usage, *esp.* one who promotes and takes a lead in social functions, as balls, bazaars, etc.

c **1440** *Promp. Parv.* 386/2 Patronesse, *patronissa* (P. *patrona*). **1509** FISHER *Fun. Serm. C'tess Richmond* Wks. (1876) 301 All the lerned men of Englonde to whome she was a veray patronesse. **1592** G. HARVEY *Pierce's Super.* (in *Archaica* (1815) II. 10), The excellent gentlewoman my patroness, or rather championess in this quarrel. **1625** BP. MOUNTAGU *App. Cæsar* 56 The Church of England no Patroness of Novell opinions. **1798** FERRIAR *Illustr. Sterne* i. 12 Margaret Queen of Navarre..patroness of literary men. *c* **1820** BYRON *Charity Ball* note, Lady Byron had been patroness of a ball. **1861** WHYTE MELVILLE *Mkt. Harb.* xxiv. 192 After much discussion by stewards and lady patronesses. **1875** POSTE tr. *Gaius* III. §49 Patronesses..had only the same rights as patrons under the statute of the Twelve Tables.

2. A female patron saint.

1526 *Pilgr. Perf.* (W. de W. 1531) 57 b, Take her for thy chefe patronesse & advocatryce. **1555** EDEN *Decades* 73 To take vnto hym the holy virgin..to bee his patronesse. **1694** *Lond. Gaz.* No. 2979/2 That the Relicts of St. Genevieve, Patroness of this City [Paris], should be carried in.. Procession. **1828** SCOTT *Chron. Canongate* Ser. II. Introd., The venerable guardian of St. Bridget probably expected the interference of her patroness.

b. A female tutelary deity; said also *fig.* of personified principles, etc.

c **1420** LYDG. *Assembly of Gods* 376 Dame Venus.. Patronesse of pleasaunce, be namyd well she myght. **1542** UDALL *Erasm. Apoph.* 342 b, Minerva was thought the patronesse of al witte. *c* **1630** MILTON *Passion* v, Befriend me Night best Patroness of grief. **1784** COWPER *Task* IV. 780 Hail, therefore, patroness of health and ease And contemplation,..Hail, rural life!

3. A female holder of an advowson.

1538 CRANMER *Let. to Cromwell* in *Misc. Writ.* (Parker Soc.) II. 362 The bishop of London..gave the institution unto the said sir Heugh Payne, leaving the patroness in suit at the common law for the same. **1818** in TODD; and in later Dicts.

†**4.** A woman who is a pattern or model to her sex: see PATTERN. *Obs.*

c **1430** LYDG. *Reas. & Sens.* 6833 Which ys Merour and patronesse, To yive example of stedfastenesse To women throgh hir noble fame.

5. *Comb.*, as *patroness saint* = sense 2.

1901 *Westm. Gaz.* 18 Sept. 2/1 The image of Ste. Anne, the patroness-saint of Brittany.

Hence **'patroness** *v.*, to play the patroness to; **'patroness-ship**, the position or office of patroness.

1834 *New Monthly Mag.* XLI. 8 The intrigues of Almack's—the petty partisanship of patronessing. **1840** MRS. GORE *ibid.* LX. 51 In London life, patronesship is a matter of election. **1846** —— *Eng. Char.* (1852) 79 Her ladyship refused the patroness-ship last season. **1865** Patronessed [see PATRON *v.*].

patronite (pæ'trəʊnaɪt). *Min.* [f. the name *Patron* (see quot. 1906) + -ITE[1].] A black, lustrous, fine-grained mixture of vanadium sulphides that occurs in Peru and is exploited as a source of vanadium.

1906 F. HEWETT in *Engin. & Mining Jrnl.* LXXXII. 385 There was discovered, on Nov. 20, 1905, in the neighborhood of Cerro de Pasco, Peru, a new material containing vanadium... The material..was taken to Señor Antenor Riza Patron, metallurgist of the Huaraucacar smelter, nine miles from Cerro de Pasco... It is suggested, in appreciation of the work of the discoverer of the material, Señor Antenor Riza Patron, that it be given the name 'patronite'. **1922** *Amer. Jrnl. Sci.* CCIII. 200 The real patronite is a black mineral of fine grain and metallic luster. In polished section it is shown to consist of a very fine-grained mixture of three minerals. **1946** J. R. PARTINGTON *Gen. & Inorg. Chem.* xxi. 644 Vanadium is widely distributed, the principal ores being carnotite.., vanadinite .., and especially the impure sulphide patronite found at 17,000 ft. in the Peruvian Andes and in North Rhodesia. **1968** I. KOSTOV *Mineral.* 146 Patronite is found as graphite-like masses associated with bravoite, native sulphur, bituminous substances, quartz and other minerals in Minas Ragra in Peru.

patronization (pætrənaɪ'zeɪʃən). [f. next: see -IZATION.] The action or fact of patronizing.

1794 *Char.* in *Ann. Reg.* 295/1 He received his first patronization under lord chief justice Singleton. **1892** HAKE *Mem. Eighty Years* 77 Pope was made a fashion through patronization.

patronize ('pætrənaɪz), *v.* [f. PATRON *sb.* + -IZE: cf. OF. *patroniser* (1456 in Godef.), med.L. *patronizāre* (1382 in Du Cange) to lead a galley as patron.]

1. *trans.* To act as a patron towards, to extend patronage to; to protect, support, favour, countenance, encourage: orig. as the act of one in a superior or influential position.

1589 G. HARVEY *Pierce's Super.* Wks. (Grosart) II. 166 Lordes on both sides, that Patronise good causes. *a* **1610** PARSONS *Leicester's Ghost* (1641) 4 Some others tooke mee for a zealous man, Because good Preachers I did patronize. **1621** T. WILLIAMSON tr. *Goulart's Wise Vieillard* A ij b, A good Booke in these dayes had need of a good man to

Patronize it. 1712 Addison *Spect.* No. 469 ¶2 He patronizes the Orphan and Widow, assists the Friendless, and guides the Ignorant. 1801 Strutt *Sports & Past.* Introd. 12 Henry the Seventh patronized the gentlemen and officers of his court in the practice of military Exercises. 1859 Geo. Eliot *A. Bede* v, It will hardly do for me to patronise a Methodist preacher, even if she would consent to be patronized by an idle shepherd.

absol. 1742 Pope *Dunc.* iv. 102 There march'd the bard and blockhead, side by side, Who rhym'd for hire, and patroniz'd for pride. 1878 E. Yates *Wrecked in Port* x. 98 Silly heads are apt to take airs at the mere idea of being in a position to patronise.

†**b.** Said of a patron saint or tutelary deity. *Obs.*

1595 Spenser *Epithal.* 391 And thou, great Iuno! which.. The lawes of wedlock still dost patronize. *a* 1604 Hanmer *Chron. Irel.* (1809) 117 At Gemblacum in Flanders, where the Church (say they) is patronized by Saint Machutus, alias Maclovius. 1632 Lithgow *Trav.* i. 28 Vnto this falsely patronized Chappell, they offer yearely many rich gifts.

†**c.** To defend, support, stand by; to advocate; to justify; to countenance. *Obs.*

1595 W. W. tr. *Plautus' Menechmus* in Nichols *Plays* (1779) 133 Facing out bad causes for the oppressors, and patronizing some just actions for the wronged. 1613 Purchas *Pilgrimage* i. iv. 18 Christ patronizeth his Disciples, plucking the eares of Corne. 1670 Marvell *Corr.* Wks. 1872–5 II. 327 Elect such an High Steward.. as may always be ready.. to.. patronize the justice of your actions. 1705 Stanhope *Paraphr.* III. 348 Nor.. may we patronize our Sloth or our Sullenness, by a pretence of incapacity to do the publick Service. 1785 Jefferson *Writ.* (1859) I. 485 Appointed by their country to patronize their rights.

†**d.** Said of things. *Obs.*

1633 T. Adams *Exp. 2 Peter* i. 4 That which is patronized by usualness, slips into the opinion of lawfulness. 1695 J. Edwards *Perfect. Script.* 40 It is so corruptly translated that it is made to patronize several of their superstitious follies. *a* 1710 Bp. Bull *Serm.* xviii. Wks. 1827 I. 436 There is no action so foolishly done, but that the examples of wise men may be alleged to patronise the folly of it.

†**2.** With *upon*: To lay the responsibility for (a thing) *upon* some one; to make or declare a person responsible for; to father *upon* any one. *Obs.*

1626 J. Pory in Ellis *Orig. Lett.* Ser. i. III. 246 For all the Kinges Royall bounty amongst them,.. they patronized upon the Queen debtes to the value of above £19000. 1633 T. Adams *Exp. 2 Peter* i. 1 Let this teach.. You of the laity, not to patronize your sins upon the example of others. 1643 Howell *Twelve Treat.* (1661) 205 That warre (which some by a most monstrous impudence would patronize upon their Majesties).

3. To assume the air of a patron towards; to treat with a manner or air of condescending notice.

1797 Mrs. Radcliffe *Italian* i, The musical genius whom she patronised. 1820 Hazlitt *Lect. Dram. Lit.* 10 Feeling much the same awkward condescending disposition to patronise these first crude attempts at poetry and lispings of the Muse. 1845 Disraeli *Sybil* i. ii, Spruce.. had a weakness for the aristocracy, who.. patronized him with condescending dexterity. 1865 Dickens *Mut. Fr.* ii. xiv, I don't want to be patronized.

4. In commercial or colloquial use: To favour or support with one's expenditure or custom; to frequent as a customer or visitor; to favour with one's presence, resort to, frequent.

1801 Mar. Edgeworth *Out of Debt* iii, 'Positively, ma'am, you must patronize my spring hat', said the milliner. 1850 R. G. Cumming *Hunter's Life S. Afr.* (1902) 24/1 One side of it was.. patronized by several flocks of Egyptian wild geese. 1885 *Daily Tel.* 17 Sept. (Cassell), Chop-houses, patronized by the clerk and the apprentice.

Hence **'patronized** *ppl. a.*, **'patronizing** *vbl. sb.*; also **'patronizable** *a.*, capable of being patronized or treated patronizingly.

1664 H. More *Myst. Iniq.* Apol. 547 Rather the taking of it away then the Patronizing of it. 1837 Arnold *Lett.* in Stanley *Life* (1845) II. 72 A.. friend.. made the same objection to Victor Cousin's tone: 'It was', he said, 'a patronizing of Christianity'. 1884 'Basil' *Wearing of the Green* II. xviii. 23 Norah's modest dress made her seem more patronisable than ever. 1897 D. Smeaton *Smollett* v. 62.

patronizer ('pætrənaɪzə(r)). [f. prec. vb. + -er¹.] One who patronizes.

1596 J. Trussell in Southwell *Tri. Death* Ep. Ded., I.. haue darde, To make you Patronizer of this warde. 1649 Blithe *Eng. Improv. Impr.* (1653) To Husb. etc., Though some esteem it matter of greatest moment, yet you will not all be found patronizers hereof. 1709 Sacheverell *Serm.* 5 *Nov.* 20 The Author, and Patronizer of Lyes. 1844 *Blackw. Mag.* LVI. 574 His youthful protégés were glad to.. become patronizers in their turn.

'patronizing, *ppl. a.* [f. as prec. + -ing².] That patronizes, esp. with an air of superiority; ostentatiously condescending or superior.

1727 Bailey vol. II, *Patronizing*.. acting the Part of a Patron. 1827 Lytton *Pelham* ii, No patronising condescension to little people. 1828 Scott *F.M. Perth* viii, The knight.. received them with a mixture of courtesy and patronising condescension. 1875 Jowett *Plato* (ed. 2) I. p. xviii, The patronizing style of Protagoras.

Hence **'patronizingly** *adv.*, with the condescension or air of a patron.

1837 Mrs. Carlyle *Lett.* I. 64 'A man of sense' (as Mrs. Buller.. said patronisingly of the Apostle Paul). 1883 A. Dobson *Fielding* vi. 165 The hitherto unfriendly *Gentleman's* patronisingly styles [it] an 'excellent piece'.

'patronless, *a.* [f. patron *sb.* + -less.] Without a patron.

1647 Fuller *Good Th. in Worse T.* Pref. (1841) 74 If any wonder that this treatise comes patronless into the world. 1710 Shaftesb. *Adv. to Author* ii. i, The Arts and Sciences must not be left Patron-less. 1867 J. Macfarlane *Mem. T. Archer* iv. 71 He was penniless and patronless.

patronly (peɪtrənlɪ), *a.* [f. as prec. + -ly¹.] Of, pertaining to, or befitting a patron.

1832 *Examiner* 433/2 The ermine is surely not more liable to patronly impression than the epaulette! 1879 A. Reed *Alice Bridge* 193 He protected little boys from bullies with patronly kindness.

‖**patronne** (patrɔn). [Fr.] A woman who is the owner or the wife of the owner of a business, esp. a café, hotel, or restaurant (in quot. 1777, a barge).

1777 P. Thicknesse *Year's Journey* I. vii. 51 Your female *Patronne*.. for they are all conducted by females. 1898 W. J. Locke *Idols* xxiii. 324 The little inn came in sight... The buxom *patronne*.. was grinding coffee. 1921 *Spectator* 9 Apr. 465/1 The *patronne* came in, and gave me a liqueur glass of rum. 1942 E. Paul *Narrow St.* v. 40 He had found that Madame Sara, as he called his *patronne*, was one of the gentlest and most patient women alive. 1955 *Times* 8 Aug. 8/7 Madame Ribard, the patronne, had surpassed herself; an omelette aux champignons that melted in the mouth, [etc.]. 1973 P. O'Donnell *Silver Mistress* i. 15 'What about your reputation with the patron?' 'Patronne. What will really shock Mme. Martine is giving us separate rooms.'

patronomate (pæ'trɒnəmeɪt). [f. Gr. πατρονόμ(ος (f. πατήρ father + νέμειν to rule), the title of certain magistrates at Sparta + -ate¹.] The office of a *patronomos* in Hellenistic Sparta.

1910 *Year's Work Class. Stud.* 68 The election of 'Divine Lycurgus' to the eponymous patronomate at Sparta for a series of years.

patronoma'tology. *rare*⁻⁰. [f. Gr. πατήρ, πατρ- father + ὄνομα(τ-) name + -λογια -logy.] The study of the origin of personal names.

1847 in Webster; and in later Dicts.

†**patro'nour.** *Sc. Obs. rare.* [Answers to an OF. type *patroneor, *-eur*, f. *patroner*, L. *patrōnāre*: see patron *v.*] = patron *sb.* 5.

c 1375 *Sc. Leg. Saints* xl. (*Ninian*) 934 Sa byrd al galouya hym honoure, þat to þame is sic patronoure.

patronship ('peɪtrənʃɪp). [f. patron *sb.* + -ship.] The office of a patron (in various senses of the word); †patronage.

1549 Latimer *5th Serm. bef. Edw. VI* (Arb.) 148 Patrons be charged.. not to seke a lucre and a gaine by his patronship. 1561 T. Norton *Calvin's Inst.* iii. xx. (1634) 431 For whereas the Scripture is full of many formes of praier, there is no example found of this patroneship [of saints]. 1688 *Emperor's Answ. to Fr. King's Manifesto* 12 His Imperial Office, and the Patronship of all Churches, thereunto annexed. 1875 Merivale *Gen. Hist. Rome* ii. (1877) 13 The patriciate and patronship belonged more or less to all the nations which surrounded Rome.

patronym ('pætrənɪm). *rare.* [f. Gr. πατρώνυμος named from the father, f. πατήρ, πατρ- father + ὄνομα, Doric ὄνυμα name: cf. πατρωνυμία a patronymic.] = next, B.

1834 *New Monthly Mag.* XL. 506 Not over-enamoured of my monosyllabic patronyme.

patronymic (pætrəʊ'nɪmɪk), *a.* and *sb.* [ad. L. *patrōnymic-us*, a. Gr. πατρωνυμικ-ός derived from or like a father's name, f. πατρώνυμ-ος: see prec. and -ic. Cf. F. *patronymique* (Cotgr. 1611), It. *patronimico* (Florio 1598).]

A. *adj.* Of a personal or family name: Derived from the name of a father or ancestor, esp. by addition of a suffix or prefix indicating descent. Also said of such a suffix or prefix.

1669 Gale *Crt. Gentiles* i. i. xi. 59 Abraham.. was called an Hebrew; by which Patronymic name, he and his Posteritie were distinguished. 1880 Earle *Philol. Eng. Tongue* (ed. 3) §318 It is sometimes patronymic, that is to say, it was the name of a family from a common ancestor. 1894 O. F. Emerson *Hist. Eng. Lang.* ix. 157 The English patronymic suffix corresponding to the Danish *-son* is *-ing*.

B. *sb.* A patronymic name; a name derived from that of a father or ancestor; a family name.

1612 Selden *Illustr. Drayton's Poly-olb.* viii. 132 To some of these, other Patronymiques are giuen. *a* 1637 B. Jonson *Eng. Gram.* ii. iii, When the proper name is used to note one's parentage; which kind of nouns the grammarians call patronymics. 1658 Phillips, *Patronymicks*, those names which men derive from their fathers or ancestours with some little addition, as *Aeneades* from *Aeneas*. 1832 Scott *Rob Roy* Introd., Their original patronymic is MacAlpine. 1870 Freeman *Norm. Conq.* I. App. 563 Glæstingabyrig, a genuine patronymic, has been corrupted into Glastonbury.

So **patro'nymical** *a.* = prec. A; hence **patro'nymically** *adv.*, by, or in relation to, a patronymic.

1656 Blount *Glossogr.*, *Patronymical*. 1751 Macfarlane *Genealog. Collect.* (1900) II. 306 He Assumed.. the Designation of Dominus De Strowan, And Patronimicallie in the Irish way, Robertus filius Duncani Dominus de Strowan. 1759 Robertson *Hist. Scot.* i. Wks. 1813 I. 21 Distinguished by some common appellation, either patronymical or local. 1856 Emerson *Eng. Traits, Race* Wks. (Bohn) II. 25 Every one of whom is named, and personally and patronymically described.

patroon (pə'truːn). Also 7–8 pateroon, (8–9 -tt-, -rr-), 8 patrone. [A variant form of *patron*, chiefly in some foreign applications of the word. In senses 1–3, ad. F. *patron*, Sp. *patron*, etc.; in sense 4, a. Du. *patroon* (pa'troːn), as used in the former Dutch colony of New Amsterdam. In the former case, of phonetic origin, *-oon* being an Eng. imitation of the Fr. or Romanic sound, as in *baboon*, *dragoon*, *harpoon*, *maroon*, *saloon*; in the later case a retention of the Du. spelling with the Eng. pronunciation of *oo*.]

†**1.** = patron *sb.* 3. *Obs.*

1662 J. Wilson *Cheats* iv. i, And do you now forget your Patroon, sirrah? Do you forget your Patroon? 1697 *C'tess D'Aunoy's Trav.* (1706) 28, I could never have imagin'd that you could have been Patroon of so foul a cause.

†**2.** A master (esp. of a slave); = patron 7. *Obs.*

1677 W. Hubbard *Narrative* (1865) II. 195 He was forced to travel with his Pateroon four or five Miles overland to Damaniscottee, where he was compelled to row, or paddle in a Canoo about fifty five Miles farther to Penobscot. 1704 J. Pitts *Acc. Mohammetans* i. (1738) 10 In this Town I lived many Years with my second Patroon.

3. The captain, master, or officer in charge of a ship, barge, or boat; the coxswain of a longboat; = patron 6. Now *rare.*

1743 Bulkeley & Cummins *Voy. S. Seas* 111 Mr. C—l the Patroon prevail'd on 'em to return to Captain C—p. *Ibid.* 166. 1769 Falconer *Dict. Marine* (1789), *Maître de chaloupe*, the coxswain, or patroon of the long-boat. 1775 Romans *Florida* 186 The vessel draws one third, the patroon or master, two shares of the remaining two thirds. 1893 Stevenson *Catriona* xxii. 261 Both our master and the patroon of the boat scrupled at the risk.

4. In *U.S.* A possessor of a landed estate and certain manorial privileges, granted under the old Dutch governments of New York and New Jersey, to members of the (Dutch) West India Company.

The New Netherlands Co., in 1629, issued a charter providing that whoever brought 50 permanent settlers should be invested with an estate of 16 miles frontage on the Hudson, extending back indefinitely. The patroons held manorial courts. Their privileges were finally abolished about 1850.

1758 L. Lyon in *Mil. Jrnls.* (1855) 13 Marched into the Pateroon Lands to Landlord Lovejoys. 1776 C. Carroll *Jrnl.* (1845) 42 Vast tracts of land on each side of Hudson's river are held by the proprietaries, or, as they are here styled, the Patrones of the manors. 1790 R. Tyler *Contrast* i. i. (1887) 5 To see the world and rub off a little of the patroon rust. 1797 Jefferson *Writ.* (1859) IV. 186 What with the English influence.. and the Patroon influence.. little is to be hoped. 1826 J. F. Cooper *Mohicans* (1829) I. xiii. 183 Tracts of country wider than that which belongs to the Albany Patteroon. 1839 Marryat *Diary Amer.* Ser. i. I. 113 Mr. Van Ransalaer still retains the old title of Patroon. 1870 Burrill *Law Dict.*, *Manor*, in American Law.. is a tract held of a proprietor by a fee-farm rent in money or in kind, and descending to oldest son, who in New York is called a patroon. 1883 J. Fiske in *Harper's Mag.* 921/1 The patroons brought many colonists with them.

Hence **pa'trooness**, 'a woman with the rights or privileges of a patroon; a female patroon' (*Funk's Stand. Dict.* 1895). So **pa'troonry**, the system of patroons; **pa'troonship**, the position, or estate, of a patroon.

1809 W. Irving *Knickerb.* ii. ix, Magnificent dreams of foreign conquest and great patroonships in the wilderness. *Ibid.* iii. v, The patroon Killian Van Rensellaer, who had come out from Holland to found a colony or patroonship. 1858 *N. York Tribune* 30 Jan. 5/3 Another Blow at Patroonry.—The land-holders of Rensselaer county.. had a meeting at West Sandlake on the 27th. 1884 *Mag. Amer. Hist.* (N.Y.) Jan. 11 His estate would be constituted a manor, or in Dutch parlance a patroonship, with privileges similar to those of a baron in England.

†**pa'troona.** *Obs.* [ad. Sp. or obs. It. *patrona*, fem. of *patron*, *patrone*, with Eng. *oo* for Romanic *ō*: cf. prec.] A mistress of slaves, in the Levant.

1704 J. Pitts *Acc. Mohammetans* 47 By the sollicitations of the Patroonas, or Mistresses themselves. *Ibid.* ix. (1738) 217, I was in hopes that my Patroona.., would now have given me my Freedom.

patrosinate, -sinie, patrouille, -roul, patroun, obs. ff. patrocin-, patrol, patron.

†**patruel.** *Obs. rare*⁻⁰. [ad. L. *patruēlis* a father's brother's (or sister's) child, a cousin-german, f. *patru-us* father's brother, paternal uncle; cf. med.L. *patruolus* brother's son, nephew (Du Cange).]

1623 Cockeram, *Patruels*, Brothers Children.

patruity (pə'truːɪtɪ). *rare.* [f. L. *patru-us* father's brother, paternal uncle, f. *patr-em* father.] The position or relationship of an uncle.

1844 J. T. Hewlett *Parsons & W.* xxxvi, Visible signs of paternity, or patruity.

patryarch, -ark, obs. forms of patriarch.

patsy ('pætsɪ), *sb. slang* (orig. *U.S.*). [Origin unknown.] A person who is ridiculed, deceived, blamed, or victimized.

1903 'H. McHugh' *Back to Woods* 68 I'm the Patsy, oh, maybe! **1920** Ade *Hand-Made Fables* 76 Sometimes they ask him to come back and be the Village Patsy once more. **1927** [see build-up a]. **1953** Wodehouse *Performing Flea* 205 That gentle pity which the kind-hearted always feel when they regard the fellow whom Fate has called upon to be the Patsy, the Squidge or, putting it another way, the man who has been left holding the baby. **1954** J. Steinbeck *Sweet Thursday* vii. 45 She's making a patsy of you. **1960** *Analog Science Fact/Fiction* Oct. 151/1 We had to have a patsy—some one to put the blame on. **1967** *Punch* 8 Feb. 211/3 Blamey blunders about, the perfect patsy, while we watch the real sex-maniac at work. **1970** J. H. Gray *Boy from Winnipeg* 57, I had grown somewhat more able to take care of myself and hence had ceased to be the school patsy. **1971** *Times Lit. Suppl.* 26 Nov. 1467/3 The police are what they would call 'the patsies', the focus for popular discontent. **1974** *Daily Tel.* 17 Apr. 1/8 [He] said yesterday he was not going to be turned into a scapegoat. 'Whatever happens I am not going to be the patsy in this business.' **1977** *Rolling Stone* 13 Jan. 32/2 He felt Silkwood had possibly been a pawn or a patsy. **1977** *Time* 9 May 24/1 Or would the politically inexperienced Frost prove a patsy and let Nixon filibuster with those same skillful diversions that always seemed to be the answers but never were?

patsy ('pætsɪ), *a.* *U.S. slang.* [Origin unknown.] Satisfactory, all right.

1930 *Amer. Mercury* Dec. 457/1 *Patsy*, all right. 'The mutt offices patsy and we walk into a collar.' **1935** A. J. Pollock *Underworld Speaks* 86/1 *Patsy*, satisfactory; O.K.; when high pressure salesmen guarantee stock purchaser not to lose and get back money invested with profit in (90) days. **1941** J. Smiley *Hash House Lingo* 42 *Patsy*, all right. **1950** H. E. Goldin *Dict. Amer. Underworld Lingo* 153/1 *Patsy*, a. (Rare) All right; okay; trustworthy.

†**patt**, *sb.* (*a.*) *Chess. Obs.* [= Du. and Ger. *patt*, F. *pat* (in *Jeu des eschets de Greco*, 1669), all in same sense, ad. It. *patto* 'covenant, agreement, pact'; hence, in Chess, 'a draw by consent', and, by extension, 'a drawn game' generally.

So used already in 1511 in Chachi's MS. collection of Chess Problems (MS., Casanetense Lib., Rome, 791, lf. 28 a) 'li andati ad fronte et sera pacta'. Specialized in F., Ger., Du., and Eng. to denote a particular kind of draw.]

The position of stalemate. **b.** as *adj.* In this position.

1735 Bertin *Chess* 67 Situation of the Game named Patt. *Ibid.* 68 And the white loses the game, the black king being Patt. *Ibid.* 71 And if the white queen takes the black queen, it loses the game by Patt. [**1904** H. J. R. Murray in *Let.*, In England from 1612 to *c* 1750, and in out-of-the-way places till *c* 1805, the player who put his opponent into 'patt' lost the game. Why, no one knows: but as the same rule held in certain continental varieties of chess which appear to have a Tatar rather than an Arabic origin, I suspect it was an innovation brought from Russia by some Elizabethan traveller. The rule, so far as book evidence goes, was never followed in France or Southern Europe, where 'patt' was always = a draw.]

pattable ('pætəb(ə)l), *a.* *rare.* [f. pat *v.* + -able.] That may be patted.

1892 *Spare Moments* 2 Jan. 7/3 It was a plump, pretty and pattable hand.

pattacoon(e, obs. forms of patacoon.

‖**pattamar, patamar** ('pætəmɑː(r)). *E. Ind.* Also 7 patte-, 8–9 patti-, pattymar, -maur, 9 petamare. [a. Pg. *patamar*, a. Konkani *pātamār* courier, *pātamāri*, Malayāl. *pattamāri*, Marāthī *patēmāri*, Gujarātī *phatēmāri* dispatch-boat, f. Marāthī *patta* tidings + *-māri*, in Marāthī, carrier.]

†**1.** An express foot-messenger, a courier. *Obs.*

1598 W. Phillip *Linschoten* 73/2 There are others that are called Patamares, which serue onlie for Messengers or Posts, to carie letters from place to place by land. **1698** Fryer *Acc. E. India & P.* 111 The Pattamars, the only Foot-posts of this Country, who Run so many Courses every Morning. **1757** J. H. Grose *Voy. E. Ind.* x. 192 Betwixt Surat and Bombay there is a constant intercourse preserved..by Pattamars, or foot-messengers, over land. **1782** *Char.* in *Ann. Reg.* 50/1 This mendicant order of religious often supply our patty-maurs with provisions on their journeys.

2. An Indian advice-boat or dispatch-boat; *spec.* a lateen-rigged sailing-vessel, with one, two, or three masts, used on the west coast of India.

1704 *Collect. Voy.* (Churchill) III. 740/2 *Patamars* are Indian Advice-boats cover'd all over for the Carriage of Letters. **1800** Wellington *Suppl. Desp.* (1858) II. 341, I take the opportunity of the dispatch of a Pattamar boat from hence. **1845** Stocqueler *Handbk. Brit. India* (1854) 101 To engage a pattamar, or large sea-going boat. **1859** Tennent *Ceylon* II. 103 Among the vessels at anchor lie the dows of the Arab, the petamares of Malabar, the dhoneys of Coromandel.

pattane, pattararo, obs. ff. patten, pedrero.

pattawalla ('pætəwɒlə). Also **pattawala, puttiwala**, etc. [ad. Hind. *patta-wālā* one wearing a belt: see puttee, wallah.] In India, a messenger or servant.

1878 Monier Williams *Mod. India* 34 Here and there a belted Government servant (called a Patti-wālā, or Patta-wālā, because distinguished by a belt)—all within call—all ready to answer..to the Sahib's summons, and eager to execute his behests. **1881** E. M. Guthrie *Life in Western India* I. vi. 12 Behind M—— stood the tall and handsome Jew, G——'s writer, and the putthawaller, with his badge of office. **1949** R. Lawrence *Indian Embers* 23 Pattawallas in stiff white, with scarlet belts and turbans, were salaaming deeply. **1971** A. D. Gorwala *Queen of Beauty* 79 Give me a cup of coffee too and tell your pattawalla not to come in and not to let anyone else in.

‖**patte** (pat, pæt). Also 8 pat. [F. *patte* paw, familiarly hand, also as in sense 2.]

†**1.** A paw; *humorously*, a hand. *Obs. rare.*

1797 Wolcott (P. Pindar) *Ode to Livery of London* 11 And on his honest earnings lay his pats [*Wks.* **1812**, pattes].

2. A short band or strap of cloth or stuff, attached by one end, and buttoning at the other, used to 'button' a coat, etc., whose edges do not overlap; also a similar band or strap attached at both ends for holding a belt or sash in place; or sewn on as a decoration or trimming of a dress.

1835 *Court Mag.* VI. p. xvii/2 There are some also closed, and these latter are trimmed with *pattes* of a very novel kind. **1869** *Latest News* 5 Sept. 7 Two long pattes, rounded and trimmed with lace, fall on each side.

3. ***patte de velours*** (də vəlur), the velvet paw (of a cat; i.e. a paw with the claws held in): used *fig.* indicative of resolution or inflexibility combined with apparent softness or gentleness. Cf. iron *a.* 3 c.

1853 C. Brontë *Villette* III. xxxiii. 84 She played before me the amiable; offered me patte de velours; caressed, flattered, fawned on me. *a* **1855** —— *Professor* (1857) I. xi. 185 The soft touch of a patte de velours. **1859** Lytton *What will he do with It?* III. vii. xviii. 150, I always felt that she had the claws of a tigress under her *patte de velours*! **1881** *Atlantic Monthly* Jan. 137/2 An innocent-looking creature, with feline manners, *pattes de velours*, and such claws! **1904** P. Pennington *Diary* 1 Jan. in *Woman Rice Planter* (1913) ii. 59 One is so apt to forget that the 'patte de velours' which every one uses in polite society is even more of a help in dealing with the most ignorant.

pattée, patée (pate, 'pætɪ), *a. Her.* Forms: 5–7 paty, 5–8 patee, 7–9 patée, 8 pattee, 9 pattée, paté. [a. F. *patté, pattée* 'pawed', in *croix pattée* 'a cross of which the extremities are widened in form of an open paw' (Littré).

But in *Bk. St. Albans*, *cros patee* or *paty* is taken as repr. L. *crux patens* 'cros patent': see patent. And in ed. 1612 of Leigh's *Armorie*, *crois patee* is substituted for the *cross patonce* of edd. 1562–97.]

Applied to a cross the arms of which are nearly triangular, being very narrow where they meet and widening out towards the extremities, so that the whole composes nearly a square.

pattée-fitchée: applied to a cross having three arms as above, but the lowest sharpened to a point (see fitché).

1486 *Bk. St. Albans, Her.* C ij b, Crucem argentatam patentem..vng cros patee dargent. Anglice sic. He berith Sable a cros paty of Siluer. *Ibid.*, This cros patent is made dyuerse in the foote of the same as hit apperith here. And then hit is calde a cros patee fixible. *c* **1500** *Sc. Poem Heraldry* 137 in *Q. Eliz. Acad.* 99, xv maner of crocis armis bere:..the iiij, paty in feir... x fovrmie. **1572** Bossewell *Armorie* 120 The fielde is Gules, a Cheuron betweene three crosses pattie [*printed* partie] dargent. **1616** Middleton *Civitatis Amor* Wks. (Bullen) VII. 285 The pectoral of black leather, with a cross paty of silver thereon. **1766** Porny *Heraldry* (1787) Dict., *Patee*, or *Pattee*,..This is said of a cross which is small in the center, and so goes on widening to the end. **1868** Cussans *Her.* iv. 59 The Maltese Cross.. differs from the Cross Paté in having the extremities of each of its limbs indented or notched. **1891** 'Phil' *Penny Postage Jubilee* 74 The next issue [of penny stamps] was in 1864... Instead of the upper angles having crosses pattée, letters were inserted.

pattel, variant of patel[2].

patten ('pæt(ə)n), *sb.* Forms: 4 patayn, 4–7 -en, 5 -eyne, 5–6 -yn, -an, 6 -in, -ent, 6–9 -ine, 9 *Sc.* paton, 6– patten (also 6 pattyn, 6–8 -in, 7 -ent, -ane). [ME. a. F. *patin* (13th c. in Littré), in med.L. *patinus* (14th c. in Du Cange), It. *pattino* 'wooden pattin or choppin' (Florio 1611); origin uncertain; perh. a derivative of *patte* paw.]

1. a. A name applied at different periods to various kinds of foot-gear, either to such as the feet were slipped into without fastening, to wooden shoes or clogs, or to the thick-soled shoes, 'chopins', or 'corks', formerly worn by women to heighten their stature. Still sometimes applied to the thick-soled or wooden shoes of the Chinese or other foreign peoples; but now, in Great Britain and America, only in sense b.

1390 in *Fabric Rolls York Minster* (Surtees) 243 Omnes ministri Ecclesiæ..utuntur in Ecclesia et in processione patens et clogges contra honestatem Ecclesiæ. **1397** in Rogers *Agric. & Prices* II. 575/4, 2 pr: patayns @ /4. **1440** *Promp. Parv.* 385/2 Pateyne, fote vp berynge (pateyne of tymbyre, k. or yron, to walke with, p.), *calopodium, ferripodium.* **1473** *Acc. Ld. High Treas. Scot.* I. 29 To Caldwele of hire chalmire, to pay for patynis and corkis..xij s. **1480** *Wardr. Acc. Edw. IV* (1830) 119, ij pair patyns of leder, price the pair xij d. **1522** More *De Quat. Noviss.* Wks. 94/1 Wretches y^t scant can crepe for age..walk pit pat vpon a paire of patens. **1530** Palsgr. 252/2 Paten for a fote, *galoche.* *c* **1530** *Crt. Love* 1087 See, so she goth on patens faire and fete. **1553** Becon *Reliques of Rome* (1563) 69 b, Some go on treen shoes or Pattyns. **1565–73** Cooper *Thesaurus* s.v. *Crepida*, Patents or shoes hauing little or no vpper leather, but a latchet. **1585** T. Washington tr. *Nicholay's Voy.* ii. vii. 37 b, Their hosen and pattins [of Sciote ladies] are of colour white. **1611** Cotgr., *Galoche*, a woodden Shooe, or Patten, made all of a peece, without any latchet, or ty of leather, and worne by the poore clowne in Winter. **1623** tr. *Favine's Theat. Hon.* ii. xiii. 224 The Romane Ladies doe yet weare their high Patines and Pantofles. **1654** tr. *Martini's Conq. China* 35 They [Chinese ladies] seldom were Shoes..; but they often use fair Pattins, which they make three Fingers high. **1698** J. Crull *Muscovy* 80 A Kind of Shooes or Pattins, made of Bark of Trees. **1796** Morse *Amer. Geog.* II. 621 Without doors they use a kind of wooden patten, neatly ornamented with shells. **1872** G. W. Curtis *Howadji in Syria* iii. iv. 308 (Funk) They all walk upon pattens four or five inches high, of ebony inlaid with pearl.

b. *spec.* A kind of overshoe or sandal worn to raise the ordinary shoes out of mud or wet; consisting, since 17th c., of a wooden sole secured to the foot by a leather loop passing over the instep, and mounted on an iron oval ring, or similar device, by which the wearer is raised an inch or two from the ground.

1575 G. Harvey *Letter-bk.* (Camden) 153 He was fajnt to cum on pattins, bycause of ye great wett. **1594** Greene & Lodge *Looking Glasse* G.'s Wks. (Rtldg.) 133 A womans eyes are like a pair of pattens, fit to save shoe-leather in summer, and to keep away the cold in winter. **1651** Cleveland *Poems* 55 When night-wandring Witches put on their pattins. **1659–60** Pepys *Diary* 24 Jan., My wife..in the way being exceedingly troubled with a pair of new pattens, and I vexed to go so slow. **1688** R. Holme *Armoury* iii. 14/2 Pattanes are Irons to be tied under shoes, to keep out of the Dirt. **1714** Gay *Trivia* i. 212 Good housewives..Safe thro' the Wet on clinking Pattens tread. *a* **1839** Praed *Poems* (1864) I. 84 She tramps it in her pattens. **1894** Hall Caine *Manxman* iii. v. 137 She heard the clatter of pattens in the room below.

c. ***to run on pattens*** (said *fig.* of the tongue): to make a great clatter.

a **1553** Udall *Royster D.* i. iii. (Arb.) 20 Yet your tongue can renne on patins as well as mine. **1553** T. Wilson *Rhet.* 118 Some talkes as thoughe their tongue went of patyns. **1575** *Gamm. Gurton* ii. iv. in Hazl. *Dodsley* III. 209 The tongue it went on patins, by him that Judas sold! **16..** *Taming of Shrew*, But still her tongue on pattens ran.

2. A round plate of wood fastened under the hoof of a horse to prevent it from sinking in boggy ground. Cf. *patten-shoe*.

1815 Dickson *Agric. Lancash.* 183 Horse-Pattens..are used for the hind feet of horses in first breaking up and cultivating the more soft moss lands in this country. **1834** *Brit. Husb.* I. 165 Pattens are not necessary for the fore feet of horses, but are often required for the hind feet, more especially when the moss is first ploughed.

3. Applied to snow-shoes, used by northern races in winter. [So F. *patin.*]

1555 Eden *Decades* 298 In the wynter they [of Permia] iorney in Artach as they doo in many places of Russia. Artach are certeyne longe patentes of woodde of almost syxe handfuls in length, whiche they make faste to theyr fiete with latchettes. **1875** *Wonders Phys. World* ii. iii. 267 Furnished with wooden pattens such as the Lapps use.

4. A skate. (*local* or *alien.*) [= F. *patin.*]

1617 Moryson *Itin.* iii. 94 They [waters frozen over] will beare some hundreths of young men and women, sliding vpon them with pattins, according to their custome. **1726** Leoni *Alberti's Archit.* II. 12/2 A sort of wooden pattens with a very fine thin bottom of steel, in which..they slip over the ice with so much swiftness. **1754–5** tr. *Negotiations Comte d'Avaux* III. 132 With iron pattins on her feet. **1887** Fenn *Dick o' the Fenns* (1888) 17 We shall get no ice for our pattens. **1893** Baring-Gould *Cheap Jack. Z.* I. xii. 184 Skates are termed *patines* in the Fens.

5. In various architectural uses = base or foot: the base of a column; the sole for the foundation of a wall: a bottom plate or sill. [So F. *patin.*]

[**1449** in Blore *Monum. Rem.* xxiii. (1826) 17 (*Contract Monumt. R. Beauchamp*) Reredoses of timber, with patands of timber, and a crest of fine entail.] **1643** *Boston Rec.* (1877) II. 74 To give notice to all men that have set up pattens, and shores against their fences in the common streets to the annoyance of the wayes. **1706** Phillips, *Patten* or *Pattin*,.. also that part of a Pillar, on which the Base is set. [**1845** Parker *Gloss. Archit.*, *Patand*, the bottom plate or sill of a partition or screen. (See quot. 1449.)]

6. *attrib.* and *Comb.*, as ***patten-nail, -ring, -sandal, -string***; **patten-shoe**, a shoe designed for a lame horse: see quot. 1819. Also patten-maker.

1545 *Rates of Customs* c iij, *Patten nayles the some iis. **1681** *Lond. Gaz.* No. 1638/4 Stolen.., a dark Brown Nag,.. marked on the near Shoulder with a *Paten-Ring. **1725** *Ibid.* No. 6388/7 Samuel Gower, late of Birmingham, Pattin-Ring-maker. **1763** *Brit. Mag.* IV. 547 Of patten-rings I mark the track along. **1639** T. de Grey *Compl. Horsem.* 306 Putting a *patten-shooe upon the contrary foot. **1754** Bartlet *Farriery* 224 The..setting on a patten shoe, to bring the lame shoulder on a stretch, is a most preposterous practice. **1819** *Pantologia*, *Patten-shoe*,..a horse-shoe so called, under which is soldered a sort of half-ball of iron, hollow within..a patten-shoe being only necessary in old lamenesses, where the muscles have been a long while contracted. **1957** R. Lister *Decorative Wrought Ironwork* 231 *Patten shoe*, in farriery, a shoe used for a hip-shot horse. Its underside is forged into a hollow hemisphere. **1963** *Times* 25 Feb. 1/7 Sometimes it was necessary to rest a leg that was strained, so a Patten shoe was obtained which had a raised heel to relax the back tendon of the leg while the horse was resting after muscular injury. **1849** C. Brontë *Shirley* II. iii. 89 Hardly worthy to tie her *patten-strings.

patten ('pæt(ə)n), *v.* [f. prec. sb. Cf. F. *patiner* to skate (1732 in Hatz.-Darm.).]

1. *intr.* To walk or go about on pattens.

1852 Dickens *Bleak Ho.* xxvii, These household cares involve much pattening and counter-pattening in the back yard.

2. To skate. *local.*

1850 KINGSLEY *Alt. Locke* xii, He..questioned me about the way 'Lunnon folks' lived, and whether they got any shooting or 'pattening'—whereby I found he meant skating.

patten, obs. f. PATEN, PATENT, PATTERN.

pattened ('pæt(ə)nd), *a.* [f. PATTEN *sb.* + -ED^2.] Wearing pattens.

1798 JANE AUSTEN *Northanger Abbey* xxiii, Wherever they went some pattened girl stopped to courtesy. **1823** in Joanna Baillie *Collect. Poems* 295 By sloven footboy, paces slow, With patten'd feet and hooded brow. **1889** A. MARY F. ROBINSON *Middle Ages, Ladies Milan* 313 The long train of brocade..so carefully arranged not to encumber nor hide those little pattened feet, that were so fain of dancing and seem so ready to awake and dance again.

'pattener. [In sense 1, a. AF. *patiner*, OF. *patinier* (1416 in Godef.), f. *patin* PATTEN: see -ER^2. In sense 2, f. PATTEN *v.* + -ER^1.]

†**1.** A patten-maker. *Obs.*

1466–7 *Mann. & Househ. Exp.* (Roxb.) 390 My mastyr paid to the patyner fore patyns, xv. d. **1664** in Holmes *Pontefract Bk. Entries* (1882) 372 Ordinances..for the good governance..of the..cowpers, patenners, turners, sawers.

2. A skater. *local.*

1893 BARING-GOULD *Cheap Jack Z.* I. xii. 185 They passed many 'patiners', men and boys.

'patten-,maker. A maker of pattens: now esp. as the name of one of the London City Companies.

[**1406** *Close Roll 7 Hen. IV* (dorso), Johannes Child, patymaker.] **1416** [see CLOG *sb.* 6]. **1464** *Rolls of Parlt.* V. 567/2 The Crafte of Patynmakers of the Cite of London. **1552** HULOET, Patten maker, *solearius.* **1794** G. ADAMS *Nat. & Exp. Philos.* III. xxxi. 235 The cutting knife, used by druggists and pattenmakers, to cut..the woods they use. *a* **1845** HOOD *Turtles* i, Two London Aldermen, no matter which, Cordwainer, Girdler, Patten-maker, Skinner.

pattent, pattentie, patte-pan, obs. ff. PATENT, PATTEN, PATENTEE, PATTYPAN.

patter ('pætə(r)), *sb.*^{1} [f. PATTER *v.*^{1}, sense 3.]

1. a. The cant or secret language of thieves or beggars, 'pedlars' French'; the peculiar lingo of any profession or class; any language not generally understood.

1758 *Jon. Wild's Adv. to Successor* (Hotten's Slang Dict.), The master who teaches them [young thieves] should be..well versed in the cant language commonly called the slang patter. **178.** PARKER *Life's Painter* 136 Gammon and Patter is the language of cant. **1796** *Grose's Dict. Vulg. Tongue, Gamon and Patter*, common-place talk of any profession; as the gamon and patter of a horse-dealer, sailor, etc. **1875** WHYTE MELVILLE *Katerfelto* x. (1876) 110 'That's my name in your patter', said the gipsy. **1884** MAY CROMMELIN *Brown-Eyes* vi. 57 It was so delightful to walk demurely..and talk a patter not understood of the other children.

b. The slang or cant name for the oratory of a cheapjack in disposing of his wares, a mountebank, conjurer, or the like; also, for talk, 'jaw', 'speechifying' of any kind.

178. PARKER *Life's Painter* 163 *Gammon and Patter*, Jaw talk, etc. **1800** *Sporting Mag.* XVI. 26 [He] was obligated to tip them a little patter. **1812** J. H. VAUX *Flash Dict.*, *Patter'd*, tried in a court of justice; a man who has undergone this ordeal, is said to have *stood the patter.* **1851** MAYHEW *Lond. Labour* I. 222, I heard, also,..of boys having of late 'taken to the running patter' when anything attractive was before the public. **1873** BESANT & RICE *Little Girl* II. xiii. 139 'He ain't no good, that teacher', said the boy. 'You go on with your patter. We're a listenin' to you'. **1880** J. A. FULLER-MAITLAND in Grove *Dict. Mus.* II. 673/2 'Patter' is the..slang name for the kind of gabbling speech with which a cheap-jack extols his wares or a conjurer distracts the attention of the audience while performing his tricks.

c. *colloq.* A contemptuous designation of 'talk'; mere talk; chatter, gabble.

1858 GEN. P. THOMPSON *Audi Alt.* I. xlix. 191 There had been a patter too, about religion, which had strengthened the belief that justice was the glory of a nation. **1865** *Cornh. Mag.* Dec. 664, I think you might have saved her from the chatter and patter of Mr. Watson; I can only stand it when I am in the strongest health. **1887** *North Star* 2 May 3/3 All this, of course, was mere platform patter.

2. Rapid speech introduced into a song; also, *familiarly*, the words of a song, comedy, etc. Now *spec.*, the speech of a comedian or a stage magician.

1876 *Athenæum* 4 Nov. 603/2 He speaks admirably what is called 'patter', and he delivers a jargon in ridicule of scientific terminology. **1880** J. A. FULLER-MAITLAND in Grove *Dict. Mus.* II. 673/2 Mozart and many other composers often introduce bits of 'patter' into buffo solos, as for instance the middle of 'Madamina' in 'Don Juan', etc. **1885** J. K. JEROME *On the Stage* 53 In the provinces, I have known a three-act comedy put on without any rehearsal at all, and with half the people not even knowing the patter. **1949** *Amer. Speech* XXIV. 40 Anything he says while performing is *patter*, and he almost never says silk handkerchief, but simply calls it a *silk*. **1952** GRANVILLE *Dict. Theatr. Terms* 134 *Patter*, quick speeches uttered between their songs by music-hall comedians. **1965** G. MELLY *Owning-Up* vi. 59, I can still remember some of the abysmal patter which he delivered. **1976** *Liverpool Echo* 6 Dec. 10/5 Songs and patter formed the mainstay of his senior citizens' act which has already won awards and will doubtless claim more.

3. *attrib.* and *Comb.*, as *patter-act*, *-allusion*, *-speech*; **patter-song**, a humorous song in which a large number of words are fitted to a few notes and sung rapidly.

1823 C. MATHEWS *Let.* 23 Feb. in A. Mathews *Mem. Charles Mathews* (1839) III. xvii. 385 The only striking subject for a patter-song is the inordinate love of title. **1839** J. ADOLPHUS *Mem. John Bannister* I. xii. 234 It formed the precedent for what are now, in the technical slang, called 'patter songs'. **1852** DICKENS *Bleak Ho.* xxxix, Little Swills, in what are professionally known as 'patter' allusions to the subject, is received with loud applause. **1880** J. A. FULLER-MAITLAND in Grove *Dict. Mus.* II. 673/2 The operettas of Messrs. Burnand, Gilbert, and Sullivan, in all of which patter-songs fill an important place. **1891** *Pall Mall G.* 6 Nov. 3/2 Foote's patter-speech beginning 'So she went into the garden to cut a cabbage leaf to make an apple-pie'. **1965** *Listener* 23 Dec. 1050/2 The Barber himself a buffo bass,..has a famous Gilbertian patter song, with compound rhyming. **1972** *Times* 24 June 11/3 A patter act is usually written so that the lines sometimes don't finish. **1975** *Ibid.* 13 Mar. 328/3 His characters, his funny voices, his patter song.

patter ('pætə(r)), *sb.*^{2} [f. PATTER *v.*^{2}] The action or fact of pattering; a quick succession of pats, taps, or similar slight sounds.

1844 J. T. HEWLETT *Parsons & W.* lv, The patter-patter of horses' feet. **1863** LD. LYTTON *Ring Amasis* II. II. III. ii. 192 The dead leaves..kept up a continual patter on the window panes, like the tapping of elfin fingers.

b. Phr. *the patter of little* (or *tiny*) *feet*: used to suggest the presence of young children or the expectation of the birth of a child. See PATTERING *vbl. sb.*^{2} and *ppl. a.*^{2}

1863 LONGFELLOW *Tales of Wayside Inn* 209, I hear in the chamber above me The patter of little feet, The sound of a door that is opened, And voices soft and sweet. **1883** LD. R. GOWER *My Remin.* II. xxi. 28 The patter of little feet, and the unconscious joyousness of children. **1924** N. COWARD *Rat Trap* III. 68 And we're to expect little clinging fingers and the patter of tiny feet. **1945** E. BOWEN *Demon Lover* 66 They knew there was going to be the patter of little feet. I wasn't actually *born*..till 1918. **1966** *Guardian* 29 Dec. 14/1 At any time now, the patter of little feet is expected to indicate that Helga's dream has at last come true... Helga is a polar bear. **1972** *Daily Tel.* 8 May 12 Amen Court..resounds with the patter of tiny feet... The Rev. Patrick Tuft, the Succentor, has become the father of triplet boys. **1977** *Times* 29 Oct. 20/1 Expectant motherhood these days is marked less by the patter of tiny feet than the tinkling of cash registers.

patter ('pætə(r)), *v.*^{1} Forms: 4–5 **patre(n**, 6 **pattur**, (*Sc.* **-ir**), 6– **-er**. [f. PATER 1 = Paternoster: from the rapid and mechanical way in which the Latin prayers were often repeated.]

†**1.** *intr.* To repeat the Paternoster or other prayer, esp. in a rapid, mechanical, or indistinct fashion; to mumble or mutter one's prayers. *Obs.*

c **1400** *Rom. Rose* 6794 For labour might me neuer please I..haue well leuer, sooth to say Before the people patter and pray. *Ibid.* 7241 Vs that stynten neuer mo To patren while that folk may vs see. *c* **1450** *St. Cuthbert* (Surtees) 1672 He saw him wende into the water Nakyd and thar in stande and pater In his prayers. **1500–20** DUNBAR *Poems* xiii. 18 Sum patteris with his mowth on beidis, That hes his mynd all on oppressioun. **1530** PALSGR. 655/1, I patter with the lyppes, as one dothe that maketh as though he prayed and dothe nat, *je papelarde.* **1612** *Trav. four Englishm.* Pref. 12 Others pattering on beades, and making large vowes. **1642** ROGERS *Naaman* 333 How shall we speake to the purpose but patter?

2. *trans.* To say over, repeat, or recite (prayers, charms, etc.) in a rapid mechanical manner.

c **1394** *P. Pl. Crede* 6 A and all myn A. b. c. after haue y lerned, And patred in my pater-noster iche poynt after oper. **1530** TINDALE *Answ. More* Wks. (1573) 271/2 While the Priest pattereth S. Iohns Gospell in Latine ouer their headès. **1538** STARKEY *England* I. iv. 132 They can no thyng dow but pattur vp theyr matyns and mas. **1546** J. HEYWOOD *Prov.* (1867) 32 Pattryng the diuels Pater noster to hir selfe. **1632** LITHGOW *Trav.* IX. 411 For want of pattering an abridged Pater. **1681** W. ROBERTSON *Phraseol. Gen.* (1693) 980 To patter out prayers, *recitare.* **1710** RUDDIMAN *Gloss. Douglas' Æneis* s.v. *Patteraris*, In some places..they yet say..to patter out Prayers, i.e. mutter or mumble them. **1805** SCOTT *Last Minstr.* II. vi, For mass or prayer can I rarely tarry, Save to patter an Ave Mary. **1856** BRYANT *Ages* xx, The well-fed inmates pattered prayer, and slept.

3. a. *intr.* To talk rapidly, fluently, or glibly, without much regard to sense or matter; to chatter, jabber; to prattle. **b.** In *Pedlars' slang*, To talk, to speak; to 'speechify' as a cheapjack does in extolling his wares, or a conjurer while performing his tricks. **c.** To talk the slang or 'patter' of thieves, beggars, etc.

c **1420** LYDG. *Story Thebes* Prol. 163 Shet your portoos a twenty deuelweye! Is no disport so to patere and seie. *c* **1440** *York Myst.* xxxv. 266 Me thynke he patris like a py. **1589** NASHE *Month's Mind* Wks. (Grosart) I. 173 See how like the old Ape this young Monkey pattereth. **1642** ROGERS *Naaman* 344 You were as good hold your tongues as patter about them. *a* **1814** C. DIBDIN *Poor Jack* i, Go patter to lubbers and swabs, d'ye see. **1829** *Blackw. Mag.* XXVI. 131, I pattered in flash, like a covey knowing. **1851** MAYHEW *Lond. Labour* I. 309/2 Those who sell something, and patter to help off their goods; those who exhibit something, and patter to help off the show. **1897** *Sporting Times* 13 Mar. 1/3 She did it in a sort of 'it's of no consequence' way that fairly amazed the learned counsel who was pattering on her behalf.

4. *trans.* (*slang.*) To speak or talk (some language); *to patter flash*, to speak slang. Also *transf.*

1812 J. H. VAUX *Flash Dict.*, *Patter*, to talk, as He patters good flash. **1857** HUGHES *Tom Brown* I. i, You all patter French more or less. **1872** *Punch* 6 July 2/1 A gentry cove of the ken does not patter family lingo. **1905** B. TARKINGTON *In Arena* 259 Between the acts the orchestra pattered ragtime and inanities from the new comic operas.

Hence **'pattering** *vbl. sb.*^{1} and *ppl. a.*^{1}

a **1536** TINDALE *Exp. Matt.* vi. Wks. (1573) 232/1 How blinde are they which thinke prayer to be the pattering of many wordes. **1557–8** PHAER *Æneid* VI. P iij, Whan furst her [the Sibyl's] pattring mouth and raging limmes wer left at rest, Eneas prinse began. **1665** BRATHWAIT *Comment Two Tales* 16 What a pattering with their Lips, as if they would cry out! **1850** W. R. WILLIAMS *Relig. Progr.* i. (1854) 22 Leaving the nursery and its pattering by rote of elementary truths.

patter ('pætə(r)), *v.*^{2} [Dim. and frequent. of PAT *v.*^{1}: see -ER^5.]

1. *intr.* To make a rapid succession of pats, taps, or slight sounding strokes, such as those of rain-drops against a window-pane; often referring mainly to the sound produced.

1611 COTGR., *Petiller*, to paddle; or, as *Petiller*; or to patter; to beat thicke and short. **1681** W. ROBERTSON *Phraseol. Gen.* (1693) 980 They come pattering down as thick as hail. **1728–46** THOMSON *Spring* 176 The stealing shower is scarce to patter heard. **1818** MRS. SHELLEY *Frankenst.* v. (1865) 65 The rain pattered dismally against the panes. **1820** W. IRVING *Sketch Bk.* II. 79, I heard the sound of little feet pattering outside of the door. **1884** *Harper's Mag.* Dec. 82/1 The acorns patter at their feet.

2. *intr.* To run with a rapid succession of short quick sounding steps.

1806–7 J. BERESFORD *Miseries Hum. Life* (1826) xx. xiii. 269 Hearing a large party pattering up stairs, and all talking at once. **1824** MISS FERRIER *Inher.* viii, Away she pattered full speed. **1864** TENNYSON *Grandmother* xx, Pattering over the boards, she comes and goes at her will. **1895** F. E. TROLLOPE *F. Trollope* II. ix. 162 She pattered downstairs and bestowed a silver sixpence on the..old pauper.

3. *trans.* (*causal.*) To cause to come or fall with a rapid succession of short slight sounding strokes.

1819 KEATS *St. Agnes* xxxvi, The frost-wind..pattering the sharp sleet Against the window-panes. **1821** CLARE *Vill. Minstr.* I. 29 Tempest, beetling loud,..Pattering the acorns from the cups adown. **1884** J. R. DRAKE *Culprit Fay* in *Harper's Mag.* Dec. 156/1 And the fluttering scallop behind would float, And patter the water about the boat.

b. To pelt or bespatter as with a shower.

1879 STEVENSON *Trav. Cevennes* 62 The trees would patter me all over with big drops from the rain of the afternoon.

Hence **'pattering** *vbl. sb.*^{2} and *ppl. a.*^{2} (freq. with allusion to PATTER *sb.*^{2} b).

1697 DRYDEN *Æneid* IX. 910 Patt'ring Hail comes pouring on the Main. **1792** MME. D'ARBLAY *Lett.* 2 Oct., In the midst of pattering showers and cloudy skies. **1801** SOUTHEY *Thalaba* I. xlviii, The pattering of the shower. **1849** LONGFELLOW *Kavanagh* xi. 40 With these day-dreams mingled confusedly the pattering of little feet. **1884** MAY CROMMELIN *Brown-Eyes* ii. 14 Eager to hear the little pattering feet. **1886** RUSKIN *Præterita* I. 288 Cliffs, with a pretty pattering stream at the bottom. **1891** T. HARDY *Tess* (1900) 116/2 A pattering of hoofs on the soil of the field. **1903** BEERBOHM *Around Theatres* (1953) 257 Napoleon may..drill a squad of small children. But..his motive..was not a delight in pattering feet and chubby cheeks. **1955** M. EWER *No Abiding Place* vii. 112 No pattering feet on the way? **1962** A. LEJEUNE *Duel in Shadows* vi. 81 All was sweetness and light,..and the pattering of tiny feet round the Christmas tree.

patter ('pætə(r)), *v.*^{3} *Austral.* '*pigeon-Eng.*' [App. from a native lang. In Collins *Vocab. Port Jackson Dialect.*] *trans.* To eat.

1833 STURT *S. Australia* II. vii. 223 He himself did not patter (eat) any of it. **1881** A. C. GRANT *Bush Life* xvii. 172 'You patter (eat) potchum?' 'Yohi' (yes), said John,..not sure how his stomach will agree with the strange meat.

pattera, patteran, var. PATERA, PATRIN.

patteraro(e, var. PEDRERO, a small gun.

patterer ('pætərə(r)). [f. PATTER *v.*^{1} + -ER^1.] One who patters. **a.** One who says paternosters, or mechanically repeats prayers, formulæ, etc.

1513 DOUGLAS *Æneis* VIII. Prol. 105 Preistis [quha] suld be patereris and for the peple pray. **1835** *Court Mag.* VI. 108/1 This pale-faced patterer of prayers and retailer of grave sayings. **1889** J. S. NICHOLSON *Dreamer of Dreams* I. i. 4 Enthusiasts for freedom and patterers of creeds.

b. One who speaks rapidly or glibly with little regard to sense or matter; one who 'speechifies' like a cheapjack; one who speaks the 'patter' or cant of a set of people.

1552 HULOET, Superfluouse patterer of wordes, *battologus.* **1849** H. AINSWORTH *Rookwood* Pref. (1878) 30 Its meaning must be perfectly clear and perspicuous to the practised patterer of Romany, or Pedlar's French. **1851** MAYHEW *Lond. Labour* I. 213/1 The class of street-orators, known in these days as 'patterers' and formerly termed 'mountebanks',—who..strive to 'help off their wares by pompous speeches in which little regard is paid either to truth or propriety'. **1870** F. JACOX *Rec. of a Recluse* I. i. 17 The street patterers of London, and those who buy their wares.

pattern ('pætən), *sb.* Forms: α. 4–8 **patron**, (5 **patroun**, 4–6 **patrone**). β. 6 **patarne**, 6–7 **-erne**, **-ern**, **patterne**, 6– **pattern**. γ. 6 **patten**. [ME. *patron*, a. F. *patron*, which still means both 'patron' and 'pattern'. In 16th c. '*patron*, with shifted accent, evidently began to be pronounced ('patrn, 'patərn) as in *apron* ('eɪpərn), and spelt *patarne*, *paterne*, *pattern*. By

1700 the original form ceased to be used of things, and *patron* and *pattern* became differentiated in form and sense.]

1. a. 'The original proposed to imitation; the archetype; that which is to be copied; an exemplar' (J.); an example or model deserving imitation; an example or model of a particular excellence.

α. *c* **1369** CHAUCER *Dethe Blaunche* 910 Truely she Was her chefe patron of beaute, And chefe ensample of al her werke. **1500–20** DUNBAR *Poems* lxxxviii. 31 O! towne of townes, patrone and not compare: London, thou art the floure of Cities all. **1581** J. MELVILL *Diary* (1842) 114 An exemple and patron of guid and godlie order to uther Nationnes.

β. **1548** UDALL, etc. *Erasm. Par. Mark* x. 64 These haue in them an ensample of innocencie and simplicitie, after the patarne wherof, proude malicious persones must be forged a newe. **1587** FLEMING *Contn. Holinshed* III. 1344/1 His gouernement, which he would fashion out after the paterne of his predecessors and great vncles. **1613** SHAKS. *Hen. VIII*, v. v. 23 She shall be .. A Patterne to all Princes liuing with her, And all that shall succeed. *a* **1745** SWIFT *Portr. fr. Life* Wks. 1841 I. 768/1 A housewife in bed, at table a slattern; For all an example, for no one a pattern. **1870** E. PEACOCK *Ralf Skirl.* III. 183 A pattern of the domestic virtues.

γ. **1570** LEVINS *Manip.* 61/10 Látten, *aurichalcum*. A Pátten, *prototypon*. [Cf. *Ibid.* 82/6 A Pasterne .. A Paterne, *prototypon*, .. A Tauerne.]

†**b.** *transf.* An image. *Obs. rare.*

1582 STANYHURST *Æneis* II. (Arb.) 49 Vlisses Attempted lewdly fro the church to imbeazel an holy Patterne of Pallas.

2. a. Anything fashioned, shaped, or designed to serve as a model from which something is to be made; a model, design, plan, or outline.

α. [**1352** in Brayley & Britton *Westminster* (1836) 183 To John Lambard, for two quatern' of royal paper for the painter's patrons 1*s*. 8*d*. *Ibid.* 185.] **1387** *Contract* in *Registr. Cart. Ecclesie S. Egidii de Edinb.* (Bann. Cl.) 25 Voutyt on the maner and the masounry as the voute abovyn Sant Stevinys auter .. the qwhylk patronne thay haf sene. Alsua .. a wyndow with thre lychtys in fourme masonnelyke the qwhilk patrone thai haf sene. ? **1421** *Lett. Marg. Anjou & Bp. Beckington* (Camden) 20 The fundament of youre chappell .. wherof I send yow the patrone. *c* **1440** *Promp. Parv.* 386/1 Patrone, forme to werk by. **1481** in *Eng. Gilds* (1870) 321 As hit apereth by patrons of blacke paper in our Comen Kofer of record. **1526** TINDALE *Heb.* viii. 5 For take hede .. that thou make all thynges accordynge to the patrone [1611 paterne] shewed to the in the mount. **1551** RECORDE *Pathw. Knowl.* I. Def., Thereof doe masons, and other worke menne call that patron, a centre, whereby thei drawe the lines [etc.].

β. **1577** B. GOOGE *Heresbach's Husb.* (1586) R ij, Those that you haue taken vp wilde, and be well framed, and proporcioned, according to my paterne. **1594** HOOKER *Eccl. Pol.* I. ii. §5 That Law which hath been the Pattern to make, and is the Card to guide the World by. **1606** CHAPMAN *Gentleman Usher* Plays 1873 I. 316 He was a patterne for a Potter, Fit t' have his picture stampt on a stone Jugge. **1644** *Direct. Publ. Worship* 19 A Patern of Prayer. **1838** LYTTON *Alice* II. ii, That proper orders should be .. transmitted .. with one of Evelyn's dresses, as a pattern for .. length and breadth. **1878** JEVONS *Prim. Pol. Econ.* iv. 37 Almost all the common things we use now .. are made by machinery, and are copies of an original pattern.

fig. **1611** SHAKS. *Wint. T.* IV. iv. 393 By th'patterne of mine owne thoughts, I cut out The puritie of his. **1655** tr. *Com. Hist. Francion* I. 8, I promise to shape my assistance by the Patterne of your commands.

b. A model or design in dressmaking, *spec.* a paper pattern from which material for a garment can be cut out and sewn together.

1792 JANE AUSTEN *Catharine* in *Wks.* (1954) VI. 207, I expect a new Cap from Town... Every Body will be longing for the pattern. **1811** —— *Sense & Sens.* I. xxi. 281 Taking patterns of some elegant new dress. **1890–1** *T. Eaton & Co. Catal.* Fall & Winter 52/1 Ours is the only store in Toronto where you can get Butterick's dress patterns. *Ibid.* 52/2 By means of a system invented .. by the Buttericks, each pattern is graded to suit every size in which it is furnished. **1911** O. ONIONS *Widdershins* 183 A mass of tissue-paper patterns and buckram linings. **1964** *McCall's Sewing* ii. 15 Without patterns, home-sewing would probably be a lost art... Not every pattern style will look equally well on everyone. **1974** D. KYLE *Raft of Swords* vi. 60 The women sew mini-dresses from McCall patterns.

3. *Founding.* †**a.** A matrix, a mould. *Obs.* **b.** A figure in wood or metal from which a mould is made for a casting.

1508 *Acc. Ld. High Treas. Scot.* IV. 109 Item, for making of ane patroun to cast gun pellokis in, iij *s.* **1821** TREDGOLD *Ess. Cast Iron* (1824) 10 In making patterns for cast iron, an allowance of about one-eighth of an inch per foot, must be made for the contraction of the metal in cooling. **1875** *Ure's Dict. Arts* (ed. 7) II. 471 Before metals can be cast .. patterns must be prepared of wood or metal, and then moulds constructed of some sufficiently infusible material capable of receiving the fluid metal. **1884** C. G. W. LOCK *Workshop Receipts* Ser. III. 18/1 The workman places the plaster statuette, which is now his 'pattern', on a bed of soft moulding-sand.

†**4.** Something formed after a model or prototype, a copy; a likeness, similitude. *Obs. rare.*

α. **1557** N. T. (Genev.) *Heb.* viii. 5 Priestes serve unto the patrone and shadowe of heauenly thynges. **1709** BERKELEY *Th. Vision* §141 Visible figures are patrons of, or of the same species with, the respective tangible figures represented by them.

β. **1570** *Homilies* II. *Wilful Reb.* III. F j b, The rebels them selues are the very figures of feends and deuyls, and their captayne the vngratious paterne of Lucifer & Satan, the prince of darknesse. **1611** BIBLE *Heb.* ix. 23 It was there-fore necessary that the patternes [WYCLIF saumpleris, TINDALE —*Genev.* similitudes, *Rheims* examplers] of things in the heauens should bee purified with these, but the heauenly things themselues with better sacrifices then these. **1714** STEELE *Lover* 15 Feb. (1723) 4 Mr. Severn has at this time Patterns sent him of all the young Women in Town.

5. 'A specimen; a part shown as a sample of the rest' (J.); a sample. Also *fig.*

1644 G. PLATTES in *Hartlib's Legacy* (1655) 252 If .. I could have his knowledge of that seed, a pattern of it, and .. ten or fifteen pound weight of it by, or before April. **1648–60** HEXHAM *Dutch Dict.*, *Een Stael ofte Monster*, a Patron or a Proofe of any marchandize or wares. *a* **1745** SWIFT (J.), A gentleman sends to my shop for a pattern of stuff; if he likes it, he compares the pattern with the whole piece, and probably we bargain. **1752** YOUNG *Brothers* III. i, For thee, Demetrius, did I go to Rome, And bring thee patterns thence of brothers love. **1829** LYTTON *Devereux* II. i, A tailor, with his books of patterns just imported from Paris.

6. An example, an instance; *esp.* a typical, model, or representative instance, a signal example.

1555 W. WATREMAN *Fardle Facions* Pref. 12 The first paternes of mankind (Adam and Eue). **1612** BP. HALL *Contempl.*, *O.T.* II. iii, What a liuely patterne doe I see in Abraham .. of a strong faith. **1704** SWIFT *T. Tub* Apol., It is another pattern of this answerer's fair dealing. **1774** GOLDSM. *Nat. Hist.* (1776) V. 249 Instead .. of descending into a minute discrimination of every species, let us take one for a pattern, to which all the rest will be found to bear the strongest affinity. **1822** LAMB *Elia* Ser. I. *Mod. Gallantry*, The only pattern of consistent gallantry I have met with.

†**7.** A precedent, an instance appealed to. *Obs.*

1588 SHAKS. *Tit. A.* v. iii. 44 A patterne, president, and liuely warrant, For me .. to performe the like. **1595** —— *John* III. iv. 16 Well could I beare that England had this praise, So we [the French] could finde some patterne of our shame. **1630** EARL MANCHESTER in *Buccleuch MSS.* (Hist. MSS. Comm.) I. 272 It would be a good pattern for other places. **1672** MARVELL *Reh. Transp.* I. 167 There is not a scold at Billins-gate but may defend herself by the patern of King James and Archbishop Whitgift.

8. a. A decorative or artistic design, as for china, carpets, wall-papers, etc.; hence, this design carried out in the manufactured article, fabric, etc.; style, type, or class of decoration, elaboration of form, or composition of parts.

1582 STANYHURST *Æneis* I. (Arb.) 38 Of plate great cup-boords, thee gould embossed in anticque Patterns. **1758** JOHNSON *Idler* No. 13 ¶7 To direct their operations and to draw patterns. **1783** JUSTAMOND tr. *Raynal's Hist. Indies* VIII. 235 Paris surpassed Persia in her carpets, .. in the elegance of her patterns, and the beauty of her dyes. **1827** LYTTON *Pelham* xl, 'Ah!' cried I, .. 'what a pretty Manchester pattern this is'. **1851** D. WILSON *Preh. Ann.* (1863) I. II. ii. 359 The forms and patterns of the various weapons. **1876** BESANT & RICE *Gold. Butterfly* Prol. i, The pattern of his check-shirt being larger.

b. *transf.* Applied to a style of figuring or marking of natural or fortuitous origin.

1849 JAMES *Woodman* vii, Forming a sort of pattern or figure inside and out. **1870** DICKENS *E. Drood* xii, The broken frames .. cast patterns on the ground. **1899** *Allbutt's Syst. Med.* VIII. 937 In other cases, the lesions display a 'pattern'. *Mod.* The patterns made by the frost on the window-panes. Butterflies of the same general type, but the markings showing different patterns.

c. *fig.* An arrangement or order of things or activity in abstract senses; order or form discernible in things, actions, ideas, situations, etc. Freq. with *of*, as ***pattern of behaviour*** = ***behaviour pattern*** (see BEHAVIOUR 6), and as second element with defining word.

1901 G. B. SHAW *Admirable Bashville* II. i. 309 Fates That weave my thread of life in ruder patterns Than these. **1906** C. S. SHERRINGTON *Integrative Action Nervous Syst.* v. 176 (*caption*) The cutaneous fields of the 'scratch-reflex', the 'flexion-reflex', the 'extensor-thrust', are areas which in nowise fit in with the pattern of the cutaneous fields of the afferent spinal roots. **1915** V. WOOLF *Voyage Out* xxii. 366 According to him, too, there was an order, a pattern which made life reasonable, or, if that word was foolish, made it of deep interest anyhow, for sometimes it seemed possible to understand why things happened as they did. *Ibid.* xxiv. 385 Perhaps, then, everyone really knew as she knew now where they were going; and things formed themselves into a pattern not only for her, but for them, and in that pattern lay satisfaction and meaning. **1922** JOYCE *Ulysses* 562 Arabesquing wearily, they weave a pattern on the floor. **1927** E. O'NEILL *Marco Millions* III. 152 The young boys and girls take up their censers and dance their pattern out backward, preceded by the musicians. **1933** H. G. WELLS *Shape of Things to Come* III. §6. 301 Old habits of thought, old values, old patterns of conduct. **1933** T. S. ELIOT *Use of Poetry* 88 There is something integral about such greatness, and something significant in his place in the pattern of history. **1936** *Nature* 18 Jan. 87/2 In these sections .. there are interesting analyses .. of the technological and economic patterns observable in material culture. **1936** A. HUXLEY *Olive Tree* 290 Our habits are not those of the Romans, Greeks and Hebrews... Patterns of behaviour change. **1937** —— *Ends & Means* iii. 22 Every culture is full of arbitrary and fortuitous associations of behaviour-patterns, thought-patterns, feeling-patterns. *Ibid.* 23 Thought-patterns, feeling-patterns and action-patterns .. have seemed in their time inevitable and natural. **1945** T. S. ELIOT *What is a Classic?* 32 Each literature has its greatness, not in isolation, but because of its place in a larger pattern, a pattern set in Rome. **1951** J. M. FRASER *Psychol.* III. xx. 236 Different patterns of relationships will develop according to what kind of task the group happens to be engaged in. **1956** A. C. GUYTON *Textbk. Med. Physiol.* xlvii. 591 Sensory impulses from the eyes, the ears, the proprioceptors, etc., .. assess whether or not the nail is being hammered and, if not, change the pattern of movement so that it will be hammered. **1956** *B.B.C. Handbk.* 1957 115 Reference has already been made .. to the pattern of viewing by those having sets equipped for both BBC and ITA programmes. **1958** *Spectator* 30 May 692/1 A study .. of the patterns of marriage. **1958** *Listener* 12 June 964/1 How the railways ought to behave in fixing the pattern of their charges. **1958** *Spectator* 8 Aug. 204/1 The pattern of supply is constantly changing. **1959** H. GARDNER *Business of Crit.* II. iii. 148 Both a study of the patterns of images, and their part in the structure of a poem, and the knowledge of ideas, theories, and beliefs current in a period are of great value as tools in an interpreter's hands. **1968** P. B. WEIZ *Elem. Zool.* viii. 123/2 A given external stimulus usually leads to the completion of several or many simultaneous reflex responses, all occurring as a single, integrated pattern of activity. **1976** *Sci. Amer.* Jan. 96/2 The limited evidence on other mammals suggests a different pattern of evolution.

d. *Linguistics.* A discernible order or arrangement in some branch of language, esp. in phonology.

1921 E. SAPIR *Language* iii. 56 Every language, then, is characterized as much by its ideal system of sounds and by the underlying phonetic pattern (system, one might term it, of symbolic atoms) as by a definite grammatical structure. **1926** *Germanic Rev.* I. I. 49 The Indo-European consonant pattern differed radically from that of Sanskrit. **1933** L. BLOOMFIELD *Language* 136 The structural pattern leads us to recognize also compound phonemes. **1935** G. K. ZIPF *Psycho-Biol. of Lang.* v. 195 The only difference between a *pattern* and a *configuration* is that the former is the more generic and collective term. One infers the nature of speech-patterns from the exemplifications of the patterns, i.e. the configurations of speech-elements. **1951** *Language* XXVII. 295 This explicit talk about the fact of patterning makes possible the distinction between the grammar (specific pattern) and grammaticalness (degree of patterning) of language. **1960** *Language Learning* X. I. 59 No two languages have the same set of patterns of pronunciation, words, and syntax. **1963** C. FRIES *Linguistics & Reading* ii. 67 The habits of pronunciation that the child develops in learning his native language are not habits of producing and hearing the separate sounds as isolatable items in individual words but rather habits of patterns of functioning contrasts in the unique structured system of a particular language. **1968** CHOMSKY & HALLE (*title*) The sound pattern of English. **1972** M. L. SAMUELS *Linguistic Evol.* xiii. 160 Noticeable in the Middle and Early Modern periods is the start of a new pattern of quantitative gradation in the verb.

e. *Physiol.* A particular sequence or arrangement of nerve impulses, in time and space, that is correlated with a particular sensation.

1947 W. E. LE GROS CLARK *Anat. Pattern* 7 The multiple nerve fibres approach the spot from different directions through the cutaneous nerve plexus, so that stimulation of a sensory spot gives rise to nerve impulses which reach the central nervous system by different routes, and thus lead to some specific pattern of excitation there. **1955** *Brain* LXXVIII. 586 There has been a revulsion from the .. idea of the nervous system as a telephone exchange, and this has found one expression in the suggestion that a specific cutaneous sensation results when the brain receives from the skin impulses which make up a characteristic pattern. **1961** T. L. PEELE *Neuroanat. Basis Clin. Neurol.* (ed. 2) xix. 448 A 'touch' pattern requires more large fibers than a 'pain' pattern. **1969** MELZACK & WALL in K. H. Pribram *Brain & Behav.* II. 145 The pattern theory proposed by Weddell and Sinclair, then, fails as a satisfactory theory of pain. **1975** —— in M. Weisenberg *Pain* i. 12/1 There can no longer be any doubt that temporal and spatial patterns of nerve impulses provide the basis of our sensory perceptions.

9. A specimen model of a proposed coin, struck by a mint, but not subsequently adopted for the currency. Distinguished from a *proof*.

1837 *Penny Cycl.* VII. 330/1 Henry VIII struck some patterns for a silver crown; but the first crown for currency was struck by Edward VI. **1879** H. PHILLIPS *Notes Coins* 12 A fine Gothic pattern crown of Queen Victoria never adopted for the national coinage. **1903** *Westm. Gaz.* 15 June 8/2 A pattern farthing of 1661 was sold at Sotheby's on Saturday for £78.

10. A sufficient quantity of material for making a garment, esp. a dress; a dress-length. *U.S.*

1847 in WEBSTER.

11. *Gunmaking.* The marks made by the shot from a gun on a target, in respect of their closeness together and evenness of distribution within a certain radius from the central point.

declared pattern: a statement by the maker of the number of pellets a shot-gun will deliver and distribute within a given radius under specified conditions, as in quot. 1892.

1859 'STONEHENGE' *Shot-Gun and Sporting-Rifle* I. ii. 14 So much depends on the pattern made at thirty and forty yards by the gun intended to be used. *Ibid.* III. i. 175 A gun can only be made to combine a certain amount of strength with regularity of pattern. *Ibid.* 176 They shall give such a pattern on the target as will prevent the escape of a partridge or grouse. **1881** GREENER *Gun* 303 Sportsmen cannot attach too much importance to regular and uniform patterns, especially in pigeon shooting, where one thin pattern will probably cause a shooter to lose a match. **1892** —— *Breech-Loader* 124 When a gun is said to make a pattern of 200, it means that 200 is the average number put within a circle 30 in. in diameter on the target, the butt of the gun being forty yards .. from the target, the load being 3 drams of black powder, or the equivalent in nitro powder, and $1\frac{1}{8}$ ounces of No. 6 shot, 270 to the ounce (304 pellets to $1\frac{1}{8}$ ounces), which is called the standard load, and originated at the Field Gun Trials of 1875, when the charge of shot was first counted. *Ibid.* 140 Sportsmen seem slow to grasp the fact that pattern is the all-important factor in the killing range of the gun. **1886** *Badminton Libr.*, *Shooting* I. 98 The coarse grain burns evenly all along the barrel, and hence gives a better pattern in regard to the shot. **1961** C. WILLOCK *Death in Covert* ii. 34 Pattern .. is the spread of the shot. **1972** *Shooting Times & Country Mag.* 1 July 14/2 The more the manufacture of shotgun ammunition is influenced by the needs of competitive clay pigeon shooting, the more it will repay game and pigeon shooters to check that they are not getting unduly close patterns. **1976** *Shooting Mag.* Dec. 52/2 A new game cartridge, .. features the exclusive Monowad, claimed by the manufacturers to deliver up to 10 per cent more pellets inside the pattern.

12. In Ireland, A patron saint's day; the festival of a patron saint; hence *transf.* the festivities with which it is celebrated: cf. PATRON *sb.* 5 c.

1745 *Season. Adv. Protest.* 19 The Papists will squander their Substance at Fairs and Patterns. **1827** HONE *Every-day Bk.* II. 383 The usual fair day or '*patron*', or, as it is usually pronounced, *pattern* or *patten*, is a festive meeting to commemorate the virtues of a patron saint. **1892** *Spectator* 22 Oct. 560 'Patterne'..primarily meant the day of the patron saint. Then it came to mean the dance on the festival day, and now is used of a dance on any holiday. **1893** W. C. BORLASE *Age Saints Cornwall* 44 Observances practised in the names of Patrick, or Bridget, or Delcan..on their pattern or festival days.

13. a. *attrib.*, passing into *adj.* Serving as a pattern or model; typical, archetypal; 'ideal', 'model'. Sometimes hyphened to following sb.

1809–12 MAR. EDGEWORTH *Vivian* iii, I..never set myself up for a pattern man. **1828** P. CUNNINGHAM *N.S. Wales* (ed. 3) II. 272 This pattern-convict is now in the service of a dissenting clergyman in the colony. **1840** J. BUEL *Farmer's Companion* 24 The average annual profit of the pattern-farm. **1849** C. BRONTE *Shirley* xxii, Two pattern young ladies, in pattern attire, with pattern deportment. **1880** MISS BRADDON *Barbara* xvi, He felt himself a pattern father.

b. *attrib.* and *Comb.*, as ***pattern-cutter, discrimination, -engraver, girl, paper, -quality, recognition, ring, store, suit, tile, trade, -work***, etc.; ***pattern-like, -phrased*** adjs.; ***pattern-wise*** adv.; **pattern baldness**, baldness in which there is a gradual loss of hair in accordance with a characteristic pattern, as in the receding hair-line that commonly occurs in men as they grow older; **pattern body** *rare*, a dress pattern taken from an existing dress; **pattern-bomb** *v.*, to bomb a target from aircraft according to a prescribed pattern in order to obtain maximum effect; so **pattern-bombing** *vbl. sb.*; **pattern book**, (*a*) a book of (industrial) patterns or designs, as of fabrics, lace, wall-papers, etc.; also *transf.* and *fig.*; (*b*) a blank book of cardboards to hold patterns; **pattern-box** *Weaving*, (*a*) a box containing several shuttles, any one of which may be sent along the 'shed' as required by the pattern in colour-pattern weaving, a shuttle-box; (*b*) 'the box perforated for the harness-cards in the Jacquard loom' (Knight *Dict. Mech.* 1875); **pattern card**, (*a*) a sample-card (of cloth, etc.); also, a book of such cards, a pattern-book; (*b*) *Weaving*, in a Jacquard attachment = CARD *sb.*[2] 10; also *fig.* and *attrib.*, as ***pattern-card cutter, maker, mounting***, etc.; **pattern-chain** *Weaving*, a device for bringing the shuttles automatically from the pattern-box to the picker in the required sequence; **pattern congruity** *Linguistics*, conformity to the structure of a language, esp. the phonological structure; **pattern-cylinder**, 'a means of operating the harness of a loom by means of a cylinder with projections which come in contact in due order of time with the respective levers which work the shed' (Knight); **pattern darning**, a type of embroidery in which darning stitches are used to form a design, freq. as a geometric background; also ***pattern darn***; **pattern-designer, -drawer**, a workman who designs or draws patterns; so ***pattern-designing, -drawing***; †**pattern-line**, in earthworks, a narrow bank of earth whose height serves as a guide for raising a piece of ground: cf. LINE *sb.*[2] 20; **pattern-maker**, one who makes patterns; *spec.* (*a*) 'one who arranges textile patterns for weaving' (Simmonds *Dict. Trade* 1858); (*b*) *Founding*, one who makes patterns for iron castings; so ***pattern-making***; **pattern-moulder**, 'a designer and maker of patterns for cast-iron foundries' (Simmonds); **pattern-paper**, the paper from which a pattern (sense 2 b) is made; **pattern practice**, in learning a foreign language, intensive repetition of its distinctive constructions and patterns; **pattern-reader** = *pattern-maker* (*a*); **pattern-room** = *pattern-shop*; **pattern setter**, (*a*) a workman or workwoman who decides upon the manner of filling up a lace or other pattern already designed and stamped; (*b*) anyone or anything that establishes a pattern or precedent; so ***pattern-setting*** adj.; **pattern shop**, that part of a factory or foundry in which patterns are prepared; **pattern variable** *Sociol.*, a term used by Talcott Parsons in his attempt to define social action as the choice between five main dichotomous patterns of behaviour; also *attrib.*; **pattern-welding**, a technique used by the Anglo-Saxons for forging sword blades; also, a piece of pattern-welded metal; so **pattern-welded** *a.*; **pattern-wheel**, (*a*) a count-wheel (see COUNT *sb.*[1] 9) or locking-plate, whose notches determine the striking of a clock (Knight); (*b*) = *pattern-cylinder*; (*c*) 'a pricking-wheel for marking out a pattern' (*Funk's Stand. Dict.* 1895).

1916 *Jrnl. Heredity* VII. 349/2 Congenital baldness must not be confused with *pattern baldness. **1956** C. AUERBACH *Genetics in Atomic Age* 16 The so-called pattern-baldness of men is due to a mutated gene which acts most effectively on the background of a male constitution. **1974** *Jrnl. Clin. Endocrinol. & Metabolism* XXXIX. 1012/1 Androgens may paradoxically cause male pattern baldness in individuals with a genetic predisposition. **1819** M. EDGEWORTH *Let.* 28 Jan. (1971) 165 The gown..is made by the very best dressmaker in Paris by a *pattern body which I got my dear Fan to take from a gown of yours. **1943** *Jane's All World's Aircraft* 23a/1 The air targets could be *pattern-bombed so that a bomb fell in every area of 50 square yards. **1944** *Britannica Bk. of Year* 770/1 *Pattern-bomb*,..to bomb, from a number of aircraft, in such a way that the relative position of the craft determines the 'pattern' of the bombs when they strike, so as to cover the target in a desired manner. **1947** *Sun* (Baltimore) 29 Mar. 2/2 Sending a fleet of jetpropelled planes from the Kurile islands (north of Japan) to pattern-bomb all of America. **1940** *War Illustr.* 5 Jan. 555 (*caption*) Wellingtons preparing for '*pattern bombing'. **1941** E. C. SHEPHERD *Mil. Aeroplane* 4 Anti-aircraft fire can..break up the formations so that mass bombing or pattern bombing becomes impossible. **1948** E. WAUGH *Loved One* 78 You couldn't really get away from the war even there. The ladies didn't seem to have a mind for anything higher than pattern-bombing. **1973** *Times* 6 June 19/5 It was subjected to air bombardment..by a process of deliberate and sustained 'pattern bombing' which wiped out the little town. **1774** N. CRESSWELL *Jrnl.* 7 Apr. (1925) 9 Spent the evening with Mr. Longsdon, who gave me a *pattern Book and desires me to do some business for him. **1821** P. EGAN *Real Life in London* I. vi. 91 And was followed by a servant with pattern-books, the other apparatus of his trade. **1846** [see EAST-END]. **1858** SIMMONDS *Dict. Trade, Pattern-book*, a book with designs for selection. **1876** J. HASLEM (*title*) Old Derby China Factory..facsimiles copied from old Derby pattern books. **1950** E. H. GOMBRICH *Story of Art* x. 141 It was in the thirteenth century that artists did occasionally abandon their pattern book altogether. **1959** *Times* 5 Nov. 15/2 Mr. Busch knows his job..but his people are pattern-book and never suprise. **1978** CADOGAN & CRAIG *Women & Children First* viii. 165 Lorna moves in a world of Women's Institute whist-drives..and Weldon's pattern books. **1773** J. WEDGWOOD *Let.* 21 Nov. (1965) 155 Voyer's Seals are sad trash, but Boden & Smiths were mounting half a Groce of them..to be sent..as *Pattern Cards. **1821** P. EGAN *Life in London* II. i. 136 Mr. Primefit, of Regent-street, was..ordered to attend upon Mr. Hawthorn, with his pattern-card, to take orders. **1822** W. IRVING *Braceb. Hall* (1823) I. 98 [Commercial travellers] changing the lance for a driving-whip, the buckler for a pattern card. **1847** MRS. SHERWOOD in *Life* vi. (1854) 95 Pictet Pere was the very pattern-card of an old French courtier. **1851** in *Illustr. Lond. News* (1854) 5 Aug. 119/2 Occupations of People..Pattern-card maker. *a* **1904** *Mod. Advt.*, Pattern Card Mounters, Cutters, and Gummers wanted. **1881** [see BEVELLER]. **1970** G. HEYER *Charity Girl* i. 17, I shall attend Hetta's wedding... I daresay Hetta will be better off with her pattern-card. **1875** KNIGHT *Dict. Mech.* 1637/2 The *pattern-chain..has links of varying hight, which, as they pass beneath the roller on lever *l*, raise it to a greater or lesser hight..and so bring the required shuttle in position to be struck by the picker. **1934** *Language* X. 124 The criterion of *pattern congruity. Particular formulations must be congruous with the general phonemic pattern of the given language. **1941** *Ibid.* XVII. 229 That /č, ǰ, š, ž/ are unit phonemes appears partly from their distribution.., partly from their behavior in clusters. .. There may be some dialects in which they can be analyzed as /tj, dj, sj, zj/ respectively, but considerations of pattern congruity make this unlikely. **1964** E. BACH *Introd. Transformational Gram.* viii. 178 It seems natural to identify simplicity with the number of symbol tokens..in the grammar. We would exclude from our count symbols of metatheory..and count as single symbols..the primes of the various parts of the grammar. This consideration seems to underlie many statements about 'pattern congruity' and the like. **1906** MRS. A. H. CHRISTIE *Embroidery & Tapestry Weaving* ix. 197 The second kind is called *pattern darning; in it the stitches are picked up in some regular order, so that they form various geometrical patterns over the surface. *Ibid.* 199 Samplers..may be seen entirely filled with these pattern darns. **1915** M. SYMONDS *Elem. Embroidery* xii. 138 Pattern darning is also used for backgrounds, in which cases the linen..should be strong but not woven too closely. **1932** D. C. MINTER *Mod. Needlecraft* 14/1 Pattern darning..consists of the regular picking up of threads in such a way as to cover a background of a design with a pattern. **1967** E. SHORT *Embroidery & Fabric Collage* i. 34 Bead embroidery must give a raised texture, shadow work or pattern darning a relatively smooth surface. **1851** in *Illustr. Lond. News* (1854) 5 Aug. 119/2 *Pattern-designer, -cutter. **1899** MACKAIL *Life W. Morris* I. 78 Morris was a pattern-designer and decorator. **1881** W. MORRIS (*title*) Some Hints on *Pattern-Designing. *Ibid.* 1 By..pattern-design,..I mean the ornamentation of a surface by work that is not imitative or historical; at any rate, not principally or essentially so. **1951** S. S. STEVENS *Handbk. Exper. Psychol.* xx. 764/2 So far we have dealt only with *pattern discriminations: the capacity to tell the difference between a triangle and a circle or between an upright triangle and an inverted triangle, and so on. **1756** ROLT *Dict. Trade*, **Pattern-Drawer*, is a person employed in drawing patterns for silk weavers, callico-printers, embroiderers, lace-workers, quilters [etc.]. **1823** J. BADCOCK *Dom. Amusem.* 48 The Kaleidoscope..an assistant to pattern-drawers of every description. **1864** A. MCKAY *Hist. Kilmarnock* 249 He has become skilled in *pattern-drawing. **1890** W. J. GORDON *Foundry* 171 There is a wide gap between an ordinary mill-hand and a *pattern-engraver. **1838** SYD. SMITH *Let. to Ld. J. Russell* Wks. 1859 II. 299/1 They preserve a childish and *pattern-like uniformity in Cathedrals. **1712** J. JAMES tr. *Le Blond's Gardening* 106 These *Pattern-Lines may be from twelve Inches to two Foot broad. **1851** C. CIST *Sk. Cincinnati in 1851* xv. 297 He engaged in the foundry..as *pattern-maker. **1858** SIMMONDS *Dict. Trade, Pattern-maker, Pattern-reader.* **1881** YOUNG *Every Man his own Mechanic* §37 [Alder] works very smoothly, and is much used by turners and pattern-makers. **1881** YOUNG *Every Man his own Mechanic* §623 *Pattern-making..is rather an important branch of the wood-working art. **1895** *Model Steam Engine* 95 Beeswax, melted and mixed with brick-dust, is very useful in pattern-making, to stop up holes, cracks, &c. **1934** C. LAMBERT *Music Ho!* III. 143 We must not think, however, that the modified internationalism of the eighteenth century is any more a permanent and integral part of musical tradition than the objective pattern-making of the period. **1937** H. READ *Art & Society* i. 23 But from the normal point of view we have to explain..the almost complete atrophy of the artistic impulse in man—at least the disappearance of the individual work of art in an undifferentiated mass of pattern-making as monotonous as the standardized products of our own machine age. **1926** J. MASEFIELD *Odtaa* iii. 59 She picked up some *pattern-paper ..snipped it with scissors..and then shook it out as a sort of cape or shawl of lace. **1879** GEO. ELIOT *Theo. Such* xv. 264 The safe and *pattern-phrased style [of literary criticism]. **1944** C. FRIES *Intensive Course in Eng. for Latin-Amer. Students* VI. 1 A..class hour is given to the '*pattern practice' and drill. *Ibid.* 2 (*heading*) Pattern practice in conversation. **1948** *Language Learning* I. I. 27 This type of completely oral pattern practice approximates the language activity involved in free conversation while..it provides the concentrated practice of simple imitation. **1960** N. BROOKS *Language & Lang. Learning* iv. 49 Pattern practice, which opens the door to analogy, may be called the antithesis of paraphrasing. **1932** H. H. PRICE *Perception* viii. 243 AB..is a *sensible* complex... It means also that the complex AB has a certain characteristic which we may call *sensible *pattern-quality.* **1938** R. G. COLLINGWOOD *Princ. Art* x. 233 A new pattern-quality emerging from a particular way of combining psychical experiences. **1976** *Shooting Times & Country Mag.* 16–22 Dec. 14/2 It is not a high-velocity cartridge: a type which, in certain guns, so often gives hostages to fortune in the shape of pattern quality, so vital for satisfactory full-range work. **1959** *Proc. Eastern Joint Computer Conf.* 225/1 These appoaches prove..to center upon analysis of the specific characteristics of patterns into parts, followed by a synthesis of the whole from the parts. In these studies, *pattern recognition of the whole, that is, Gestalt recognition, was chosen as a more fruitful avenue of approach. **1964** J. Z. YOUNG *Model of Brain* xix. 312 There is every reason to think that similar arrangements are an essential part of the pattern-recognition systems of the brain. **1970** O. DOPPING *Computers & Data Processing* xi. 173 Automatic recognition of characters is a special case of a more general problem, called pattern recognition. **1974** W. R. ADEY et al. *Brain Mechanisms & Control of Behav.* xi. 474 There has been a very earnest search for computer methods of pattern recognition. **1976** *Gloss. Documentation Terms (B.S.I.)* 47 *Pattern recognition*, machine-sensing or identification of visible patterns. **1867** *Criminal Chronol. York Castle* 111 Thomas Stearman..a *pattern-ring maker. **1844** G. DODD *Textile Manuf.* vii. 224 When the stamper has imprinted on the net the outlines of the device, a '*pattern-setter' decides on the manner in which the pattern shall be filled up. **1899** W. JAMES *Talks to Teachers* 213 We, here in America, through following a succession of *pattern-setters whom it is now impossible to trace,..have at last settled down collectively into what, for better or worse, is our own characteristic national type. **1902** —— *Var. Relig. Exper.* i. 6 It would profit us little to study this second-hand religious life. We must make search rather for the original experiences which were the pattern-setters to all this mass of suggested feeling and imitated conduct. **1973** *Tucson* (Arizona) *Daily Citizen* 22 Aug. 2 The UAW has made good use of the 'strike target' strategy it dreamed up in 1955 to put added pressure on one auto company to agree to a *pattern-setting contract. **1878** *Harper's Mag.* Apr. 648/1 Here is the great hall of the *pattern shop fragrant with new wood. **1916** 'TAFFRAIL' *Pincher Martin* xiv. 256 Before joining the destroyer he had been at the College at Dartmouth, teaching the naval cadets their business in the pattern-shop. **1964** S. CRAWFORD *Basic Engin. Processes* (1969) x. 234 A finished component drawing is sent to the pattern shop providing all essential information. **1900** *Electr. Rev.* (U.S.) 17 Aug., Our *pattern stores, which were built next the wall, were completely demolished. **1704** *Lond. Gaz.* No. 4062/8 A *Pattern-Suit, to contain Five Yards of Cloth, dark-grey..; ..a Pattern-Shirt..; a Pattern Hat. **1899** MACKAIL *Life W. Morris* II. 43 *Pattern tiles, chiefly meant for use in fireplaces, went on being produced. **1951** PARSONS & SHILS *Toward Gen. Theory Action* II. 48 The *pattern-variable scheme defines a set of five dichotomies. Any course by any actor involves (according to theory) a pattern of choices with respect to these five sets of alternatives. **1959** D. MARTINDALE in L. Gross *Symposium Sociol. Theory* II. ii. 76 In explaining this surprise, Parsons is led to assign importance to all sorts of factors not even mentioned in his set of pattern variables. **1964** I. L. HOROWITZ *New Sociol.* 15 The long trek from an action context to a paradigm for describing all types of action in a four-part pattern variable is no better..than Hegel..ending with..the perfect equation of Reason equating itself. **1948** H. MARYON in *Proc. Cambr. Antiquarian Soc.* XLI. 76 The welding of these swords represents an excessively difficult operation. I do not know of finer smith's work... I have named the technique '*pattern welding'... Examples of pattern-welding range in date from the third century to the Viking Age. **1956** *Nature* 29 Dec. 1432/2 (*caption*) Modern pattern-welded sword: experiment No. 7. *Ibid.*, Welding also came to be used successfully..in delicate work, involving the 'piling' of many sheets into a composite laminate, and developing into pattern-welding. *Ibid.* 1433/1 Most pattern-welded swords are so corroded that ..[metallographic study] is not possible. **1962** H. R. E. DAVIDSON *Sword in Anglo-Saxon England* i. 25 The ninth-century sword from the Palace of Westminster..had a pattern-welded blade. *Ibid.* 29 A means of re-using old strips of pattern-welding from worn swords to make a new blade. *Ibid.* 30 Short swords made by the pattern-welded technique. *Ibid.* 32 By the ninth century the art of pattern-welding was on the decline. **1964** H. HODGES *Artifacts* v. 88 In this process, known as pattern welding, case-hardened bars of iron were piled or faggotted white hot and forged. **1975** *Anglo-Saxon England* IV. 179 The technique of pattern-welding died out during the tenth and eleventh centuries. **1878** GEO. ELIOT *Coll. Breakf. P.* 93 Not any letters of the alphabet Wrought syllogistically *pattern-wise. **1902** *Westm. Gaz.* 29 Nov. 3/1 He had designed some of the best *pattern-work of our time.

ˈpattern, *v.* Also 6–7 patern, patterne. [f. prec. Cf. F. *patronner* (1437 in Hatz.-Darm.).]

I. †1. *trans.* **a.** To make a pattern for; to design, sketch, plan. *Obs.*

1581 SIDNEY *Apol. Poetrie* (Arb.) 34 That way of patterning a Common-wealth was most absolute, though hee [Sir T. More] perchaunce hath not so absolutely perfourmed it.

†b. To be a pattern for; to give an example or precedent for; to prefigure. *Obs.*

1588 SHAKS. *Tit. A.* IV. i. 57 See, see, I such a place there is,.. Patern'd by that the Poet heere describes, By nature made for murthers and for rapes. **1593** —— *Lucr.* 629 When patternd by thy fault fowle sin may say, He learnd to sin, and thou didst teach the way. **1603** —— *Meas. for M.* II. i. 30 When I, that censure him, do so offend, Let mine owne Iudgement patterne out my death, And nothing come in partiall. **1654** R. BOREMAN *Panegyr. Dr. Combar* 2 A duty, which is patterned to us by the practice of Heathens, Jewes, and Christians in all ages.

2. a. To make (something) after a pattern or model, or according to some fashion; to model, fashion. Const. *after, on, upon*; †also *by, from, to*.

1608 HIERON *Defence* II. 151 The Lord doth teach us to patterne our obedience to the holy Angels. **1665** SIR T. HERBERT *Trav.* (1677) 163 [A temple] patterned from that which Adam reared in Paradise. **1875** WHITNEY *Life Lang.* xii. 249 All the rest of the language should come to be patterned after that model. **1890** *Cassell's Fam. Mag.* Apr. 301/1 He has patterned his conduct on the example of his father.

†b. to *pattern out*: to work out or construct according to some pattern. *Obs.*

1599 B. JONSON *Cynthia's Rev.* v. iii, For men, by their example, pattern out Their imitations. **1641** MILTON *Reform.* I. Wks. (1851) 10 Judge whether that Kings Reigne be a fit time from whence to patterne out the Constitution of a Church Discipline.

3. To match, to parallel, to equal; to compare (a person or thing *to, with* another). *Obs.* or *arch.*

a **1586** SIDNEY *Arcadia* II. (1590) 109 The likenesse of our mishaps makes me presume to patterne my selfe vnto him. **1589** NASHE *Almond for Parrat* 19 Such a packet of male and female professors, as the world might not patterne. **1611** SHAKS. *Wint. T.* III. ii. 37. **1622** WITHER *Mistr. Philar.* Juvenilia (1633) 609 By her self must therefore she, Or by nothing pattern'd be. **1843** SYD. SMITH *Let. Amer. Debts* Wks. 1859 II. 327/2 History cannot pattern it.

4. To take as a pattern; to imitate, copy. *rare.*

1601 DOLMAN *La Primaud. Fr. Acad.* (1618) III. 735 The fire here beneath doth aptly patterne him. **1641** MILTON *Ch. Govt.* I. iii. Wks. (1851) 110 This very word of patterning or imitating excludes Episcopacy from the solid and grave Ethicall law. **1827** HOOD *Mids. Fairies* lvi, So the spider spins, And eke the silk-worm, pattern'd by ourselves. **1901** *Dundee Advertiser* 23 Apr. 4 The Highland Board has 'patterned' the Irish method in buying and allocating pure-bred animals.

†5. To exemplify, afford an example of. *Obs.*

1606 G. W[OODCOCKE] *Hist. Ivstine* XXIII. 86 To patterne and manifestly shew in him, the frailties that man's life is subiect vnto. **1620** FORD *Linea V.* in *Ined. Tracts* (Shaks. Soc.) 48 Whatsoeuer.. in those.. collections is inserted to patterne and personate an excellent man.

6. *intr.* To take example (*by* something). Also (*U.S.*), const. *after*, to take (someone or something) as a model or example (*absol.* use of sense 2). Now *rare.*

18.. MRS. DODGE *Tale of Thanks* 14 (Funk) Not a charm of earth or sky But comes for my girl to pattern by. **1878** J. H. BEADLE *Western Wilds* xxii. 356 That was a nice family for us Americans to pattern after, wasn't it? **1884** 'C. E. CRADDOCK' *In Tennessee Mts.* I. 4 They dunno what he patterned arter.

II. 7. a. *trans.* To work or decorate with a pattern, to work over with artistic designs; also *transf.* to adorn with light and shade, or with variegated marking or colouring. *to pattern out*: to lay out in a pattern.

1857 RUSKIN *Pol. Econ. Art* ii. (1868) 120 But we let the walls fall that Giotto patterned. **1862** W. W. STORY *Roba di R.* vii. (1863) I. 155 One of the Roman kitchen-gardens, patterned out in even rows and squares of green. **1877** A. B. EDWARDS *Up Nile* xxi. 659 The same kind of cartonnage, patterned in many colours on a white ground. **1880** BLACKMORE *Mary Anerley* II. v. 94 Patterned with the same zigzag. **1898** MRS. H. WARD *Helbeck of Bannisdale* 397 The damson trees were all out patterning the valleys.

b. To order or arrange (a number of things) into a pattern; to design or organize (something) for a specific purpose. Also *intr.*, to form or cast a pattern (*rare*).

1931 W. STEVENS *Harmonium* 133 A pale silver patterned on the deck And made one think of porcelain chocolate And pied umbrellas. **1967** *Boston Sunday Herald* 14 May II. 13/2 (Advt.), The s.s. Rotterdam.. patterned for epicures,.. art connoisseurs, and other bon vivants. **1967** *Times Rev. Industry* July 89/1 Organisations tend to be patterned for a variety of reasons. **1971** J. Z. YOUNG *Introd. Study Man* iii. 47 The essence of the operation that we call coding is that events patterned in one medium are made to correspond to events patterned in another. **1972** *Where* Feb. 40/1 The borders of the new jigsaw are becoming clear, even if we haven't found and patterned all the pieces yet. **1977** *Sci. Amer.* Sept. 124/3 The uppermost layers of integrated circuits are formed by depositing and patterning thin films.

c. *intr. Linguistics.* To make, fall into, or form part of a pattern (PATTERN *sb.* 8 d).

1942 *Amer. Speech* XVII. 147 They pattern congruently with the similarly distributed varieties of /p/ and /k/. **1951** TRAGER & SMITH *Outl. Eng. Struct.* ii. 53 The distributional gaps are often found to pattern as if they were themselves partials with phonemic content. **1963** *Amer. Speech* XXXVIII. 53 Most natural languages, including English, do not pattern on the finite-state model, which cannot handle certain regular processes of sentence formation. **1965** *Word Study* Feb. 7/2 We should distinguish between prepositions (which always have an object, occasionally elliptical) and verbal particles (which pattern with transitive and intransitive verbs alike). **1971** D. CRYSTAL *Linguistics* 89 The way words pattern in sequences to form sentences.

8. *intr.* Of a gun: To distribute the shot in a pattern: see PATTERN *sb.* 11.

Hence **ˈpatterner**, one who draws or composes patterns.

1889 *Standard* 13 May 3/1 Human emotion—the force which a mere patterner of spaces, a mere contemner of 'subjects', would banish from pictorial art—plays a great part in the piece.

†ˈpatternable, *a. Obs.* [f. PATTERN *v.* + -ABLE.] Capable of being matched or paralleled.

1648 J. BEAUMONT *Psyche* XX. cclvii, Our Souls it would not torture to be ty'd In patternable slavery.

patternation (pætəˈneɪʃən). [f. PATTERN *sb.* + -ATION.] The fact or action of forming, or conforming to, a pattern; *spec.* non-uniformity in the distribution of spray from a jet.

1946 M. PEAKE *Titus Groan* 399 Her hips.. swayed when she talked.., they did all but chime as her sharp, unpleasant voice.. dictated their figure-of-eight (bird's-eye view, cross-section) patternations. **1947** *Shell Aviation News* No. 110 21/3 Atomizers may, in some cases, be subjected to radical distribution tests, a specialized species of patternation with the main object of measuring the variation of spray density at different radial distances from the spray axis. **1949** *Jrnl. R. Aeronaut. Soc.* LIII. 161/1 The use of specialised atomising jets with their accompanying troubles of penetration and patternation is avoided. **1955** *Jrnl. Brit. Interplanetary Soc.* XIV. 218 By this time patternation tests were carried out [on a combustion chamber injector] as well as calibrations.

ˈpatterned, *ppl. a.* [f. PATTERN *sb.* and *v.* + -ED.] **a.** Having a pattern or patterns; decorated or worked with a pattern or design; conforming with, or forming, an arrangement or pattern. Often with defining word, as ***large-***, ***small-***, ***fancy-patterned.***

1797–1805 S. & HT. LEE *Canterb. T.* V. 24 Neat window curtains, pretty-patterned sopha, and unsoiled carpet. **1876** J. MARTINEAU *Hours Th.* 292 The horizontal sun.. piercing the forest with a patterned glory. **1882** *Archæol. Cant.* XIV. 104 A pavement.. of coloured and patterned tiles. **1930** E. POUND *XXX Cantos* v. 19 Ecbatan, City of patterned streets. **1961** *Lancet* 29 July 259/2 The release from patterned behaviour forced the choice between good and evil. **1964** GOULD & KOLB *Dict. Social Sci.* 480/2 These.. represent potentialities for the most varied outcomes, yet outcomes extremely patterned culturally. **1967** E. SHORT *Embroidery & Fabric Collage* iii. 64 When wall papers, patterned fabrics and carpets are used any embroidery must be more carefully considered to avoid a 'messy' effect. **1970** G. A. & A. G. THEODORSON *Mod. Dict. Sociol.* 293 *Patterned evasion*, a regularised way of deviating from an established social norm. **1973** *Technical Translation Bull.* XIX. 103 *Patterned glass* is the name used where the patterns are distinctive and fancy, e.g. Arctic, Hammered, Moroccan (traditional patterns still going strong) or modern types such as 'Mersey' or 'Manhattan'. **1973** J. M. WHITE *Garden Game* 64 A bright flower-patterned cretonne. **1977** *Jersey Even. Post* 26 July 10/1 Her bridesmaid.. wore a long, tiered empireline voile dress, made of a yellow and red floral patterned material.

b. ***patterned ground*** (Physical Geogr.): ground showing a definite pattern of stones, fissures, vegetation, etc. (commonly polygons, rings, or stripes), such as is typical of periglacial regions.

1950 A. L. WASHBURN in *Revue Canad. de Géogr.* IV. 8 The terms *Rutmark, Strukturboden.. stone polygons, mud circles, soil circles, mud polygons, soil polygons, fissure polygons, tundra polygons, stone stripes, soil stripes, solifluction stripes* and others have all been used to describe features here collectively named *patterned ground* for want of a satisfactory collective term in English... The writer would restrict the use of *patterned ground* to more or less symmetrical features. **1956** *Bull. Geol. Soc. Amer.* LXVII. 846/1 Frost wedging in bedrock is capable of developing several varieties of patterned ground, all intimately associated with bedrock structure. **1973** *Nature Physical Sci.* 4 June 85/2 This mechanism creates the *gilgai* of clay-rich and commonly alluvial soils in many hot sub-humid to semi-arid regions of the world. These structures are forms of patterned ground, having a surface expression as roughly polygonal to rectilinear-parallel systems of low ridges between hollows.

ˈpatterning, *vbl. sb.* **a.** The production or arrangement of patterns; *concr.* work done according to a pattern, design, or fashion.

1862 RAWLINSON *Anc. Mon.* I. vi. 388 The patterning of the pillars with chevrons is.. remarkable. **1882** F. WEDMORE in *Academy* 14 Jan. 32/3 The upholders of beautiful patterning, who.. say that exquisite painting is the first and last business of a painter. **1889** RAWLINSON *Phœnicia* 203 This sarcophagus, the edges of which are most richly adorned with patterning.

b. The fact or process of forming (part of) an abstract pattern, as of behaviour, speech, etc.

1921 E. SAPIR *Language* iv. 61 It also has a definite feeling for patterning on the level of grammatical formation. **1937** B. L. WHORF in *Language* (1945) XXI. 1 This view loses sight of various word-classes that are marked not by morphemic tags but by types of patterning. **1939** J. DOLLARD et al. *Frustration & Aggression* vii. 152 Traditional patterning identifies another group of circumstances in which the aggression may be expressed. **1952** *Internat. Jrnl. Psycho-Anal.* XXXIII. 411/2 Certain fundamental relationships, resulting in characteristic pregenital patterning.. are offered here. **1961** R. B. LONG *Sentence & its Parts* i. 22 In *he's sort of nice* the relationship if similarly upside down: *he's rather nice* shows the syntactically more ordinary patterning. **1963** *Lancet* 12 Jan. 67/1 The inseparability of genetic and environmental influences should not deter us from the study of isolated aspects of growth and patterning. **1964** *Amer. Speech* XXXIX. 140 Nineteenth- and twentieth-century works that discover and elucidate structural patterning in one or more languages. *Ibid.*, It is.. in the gradually developed concept of patterning that the structural teachings of our own day are rooted. **1964** M. CRITCHLEY *Developmental Dyslexia* xiii. 79 The evolution of behaviour can be 'conceptualised' as the process of development of intersensory patterning. **1973** *Word 1970* XXVI. 122 A deep sense of the presence of patterning in the phenomena of man. *Ibid.*, To extend the scope of linguistic inquiry.. to include.. verbal art, cultural symbolism and patterning, and so on.

patternism (ˈpætənɪz(ə)m). [f. PATTERN *sb.* + -ISM.] A name given (chiefly by its critics) to a way of describing religions (esp. those of the ancient Near East) not on the basis of historical development but on the basis of common and recurrent patterns; also, a mode of literary appreciation based on recurrent patterns. Hence **ˈpatternist**, a proponent of this theory (also *attrib.* or as *adj.*).

1951 H. FRANKFORT *Problem of Similarity in Anc. Near Eastern Religions* 10 One may admit the close relationship between the myths and rites of a religion.. without falling into the error of those 'functionalist' and 'patternist' authors who declare that a myth is merely the spoken accompaniment of ritual. **1956** *Jrnl. Theol. Stud.* VII. 276 The absurdity of labelling scholars holding such divergent views on the subject of 'patternism'.. as the 'Scandinavian' school of patternists. *Ibid.* 277 It must be admitted that some of the Scandinavian patternists have carried their interpretation of the Old Testament to lengths which invite criticism. **1957** *Scottish Jrnl. Theol.* X. 95 This volume is all the more welcome because since Professor Hooke edited *Myth and Ritual*, he has often been unjustly held responsible for all the vagaries of the wildest of the patternists. *Ibid.*, Not all will agree with Dr Hooke's patternist explanation of Elijah on Carmel and away to Horeb. **1961** *Times Lit. Suppl.* 17 Feb. p. xiii/3 Another interesting feature of Dr. Carrington's 'patternism' is his suggestion that Mark has divided his narrative into five divisions.

patternization (ˌpætənaɪˈzeɪʃən). [f. PATTERNIZE *v.* + -ATION.] Arrangement in a pattern. Cf. PATTERNATION.

1938 *Mind* XLVII. 379 When he discusses the patternisation of a square of dots he makes a series of remarks which are so significant that we must quote them at length. **1960** R. CARPENTER *Greek Sculpture* vii. 217 The patternization of the.. underlying muscular structure.

ˈpatternize, *v. rare.* [See -IZE.]

†1. *trans.* To conform to a pattern. *Obs.*

1615 JACKSON *Creed* IV. viii. §6 In our works paternized to His image, renewed in our minds, as towardly children express their noble ancestors' worth, by lively resemblance of their personages, and real imitation of their virtues.

2. To reduce to or arrange in a pattern.

1836 *Blackw. Mag.* XL. 551 When human eyes shall be happily gifted with a Kaleidoscope power to patternize all confusion,.. then will Turner be a greater painter than ever the world yet saw.

ˈpatternless, *a.* [f. PATTERN *sb.* + -LESS.] **†a.** Unmatched, peerless. *Obs.*

1613 HEYWOOD *Silver Age* III. i. Wks. 1874 III. 128 Thy curtesie equals thy actiue power: And thou in both art chiefe and patternelesse.

b. Void of pattern or design; plain, undecorated.

1861 DUTTON COOK *P. Foster's D.* v, Turkey carpets.. trodden patternless and threadbare with the use of years. **1878** H. S. WILSON *Alp. Ascents* iv. 133 A room with blank patternless walls.

c. Formless; conforming to, or possessing, no discernible arrangement or pattern.

1960 R. CARPENTER *Greek Sculpture* ix. 243 The patternless tangle of shadow in hair and beard. **1963** *Times* 20 May 4/7 Tambling was the man for the quick break and almost stole two more goals near the end to make nonsense of all Sunderland's patternless hammering. **1975** *Sci. Amer.* May 47/2 Clearly a more sensible definition of randomness is required, one that does not contradict the intuitive concept of a 'patternless' number.

ˈpatterny, *a. rare.* [f. PATTERN *sb.* + -Y.] Characterized by the (obtrusive) presence of pattern; having too much pattern.

1885 MRS. CADDY *Footsteps Jeanne d'Arc* (1886) 130 An enchanting church outside, but.. within, how coloured and patterny. **1901** *Westm. Gaz.* 18 Apr. 3/1 A patterny element like lace.

patteroller (ˈpætərəʊlə(r)). Also pateroller, patter(-)roller. Southern U.S. varr. PATROLLER; *spec.* a person who watched and restricted the movements of Blacks by night. *Obs.* except *hist.*

c **1862** J. C. HARRIS *Uncle Remus & Friends* (1892) 196 He sing en he play—oh, gals, go 'way! Whar de patter-roller never kin see. **1893** *Nation* (N.Y.) 7 Sept. 173/1 Ability to write meant ability to counterfeit passes which would outwit the ignorant midnight 'patterrollers'. **1899** B. W. GREEN *Word-bk. Virginia Folk-speech* 268 *Patteroller*, a patroller. **1917** *Dialect Notes* IV. 385 *Pateroller.* Night-guard over negro slaves on an ante-bellum plantation. Ky. **1928** S. V. BENÉT *John Brown's Body* 40 He's friends with de ha'nts and steel won't touch him But the paterollers is sure to cotch him. **1936** M. MITCHELL *Gone with Wind* xvii. 307 What are you boys doing so far from Tara? You've run away, I'll be bound. Don't you know the patterollers will get you sure? **1964** R. HAYDEN in *Negro Digest* June 47 Moon so bright and no place to hide, The cry up and the patterollers riding.

patteroon, obs. form of PATROON.

patters ('pætəz). *University slang.* [f. first syllable of PAT-BALL + -ER[6].] A university students' name for tennis.

1900 *Captain* IV. 26/1 In the Summer, a great form of 'eccer' is 'patters', a corruption of 'patball', *i.e.* tennis. **1912** A. F. WILDING *On Court & Off* v. 103 A tremendous amount of 'patters', as tennis is popularly called, is played at the University.

pattimar, pattin, obs. ff. PATAMAR, PATTEN.

Pattinson ('pætɪnsən). *Metallurgy.* [Name of Hugh Lee *Pattinson* (1796–1858), English metallurgical chemist, who patented the process in 1833 (*Brit. Pat.* 6497).] ***Pattinson('s) process***: a process formerly used for desilverizing and purifying lead (see quot. 1881).

1856 W. A. MILLER *Elem. Chem.* II. xvi. 994 (*heading*) Concentration of silver in lead by Pattinson's process. **1881** RAYMOND *Mining Gloss.*, *Pattinson process*, a process in which lead containing silver is passed through a series of melting-kettles, in each of which crystals of a poorer alloy are deposited, while the fluid bath, ladled from one kettle to the next, is proportionately richer in silver. **1912** [see PARKES]. **1946** *Thorpe's Dict. Appl. Chem.* (ed. 4) VII. 224/1 The value of the Pattinson process as a means of purifying lead is shown by the fact that lead to be used for white-lead making was frequently Pattinsonized, although the amount of silver present was too small to repay the cost of its recovery. **1964** H. HODGES *Artifacts* vi. 93 This method of enriching a lead alloy is now known as Pattinson's process.

pattinsonize ('pætɪnsənaɪz), *v.* [f. prec. + -IZE.] *trans.* To extract silver from (argentiferous lead-ore) by the Pattinson process. Hence **pattinsoni'zation** or **pattinso'nation**.

1881 RAYMOND *Mining Gloss.* s.v. *Pattinson process*, In *mechanical pattinsonation* the operation is performed in a cylindrical vessel, in which the bath is stirred mechanically, and from which, as the richer alloy crystallizes, the poorer liquid is repeatedly drained out. **1882** OGILVIE, *Pattinsonize.* **1895** *Funk's Stand. Dict.*, *Pattinsonization.*

pattipan, pattish, var. PATTYPAN, PATISE.

pattle, pettle ('pæt(ə)l, 'pɛt(ə)l), *sb. Sc.* and *north. dial.* Also 4–5 **pat(t)yl**, 5 **patil(l**, 6 **patle**. [Origin obscure; app. another form of PADDLE *sb.*[1], with which it partly coincides in meaning.]

1. A tool like a small spade with a long handle, used chiefly to remove the earth adhering to a plough; a plough-staff.

α. *c* **1375** *Sc. Leg. Saints* xxv. (*Julian*) 130 A housband a-gane oure lay Telyt his land one sownday;..þe patyl his hand clewyt to, þe muldebred quhen he suld mvk [*rime* tuk]. **1404** *Durham Acc. Rolls* (Surtees) 399, ij plogh pattyl. *c* **1470** HENRYSON *Mor. Fab.* x. (*Fox & Wolf*) ii, The husband.. cryit, and caist his patill and grit stanis. **1570** *Satir. Poems Reform.* xii. 72 Hirdmen sall hunt ȝow vpthrow Garranis gyll, Castand thair Patlis, and lat the pleuch stand still. **1785** BURNS *To Mouse* i, I wad be laith to rin an' chase thee Wi' murd'ring pattle. **1820** SCOTT *Monast.* xi, If he liked a book ill, he liked a plough or a pattle worse.

β. **1786** BURNS *Earnest Cry & Prayer* xv, Or faith! I'll wad my new pleugh-pettle, Ye'll see't or lang. **1824** SCOTT *Redgauntlet* Let. x, A hand that never held pleugh-stilt or pettle. **1858** M. PORTEOUS *Souter Johnny* 24 Pettle or plough staff, with which he cleaned the ploughshare.

†**2.** = PADLE *sb. Obs.* (See PATTLE *v.*)

3. *Comb.*, as **pattle-shaft, -tree**, the shaft or handle of a pattle.

1868 D. GORRIE *Summers & Winters in Orkneys* viii. (1871) 298 Using a pattle-tree to clear away clods. **1871** W. ALEXANDER *Johnny Gibb* xv. (1873) 92 Nae the vera pattle shafts but was broken.

†'**pattle**, *v. Sc. Obs. rare.* [f. prec. 2.] *trans.* To scrape with a hoe (*Sc.* padle) or mud-scraper.

1553–4 *Burgh Rec. Edin.* (Rec. Soc.) II. 351 Item..for ane patill to patil the kirk with. **1554–5** *Ibid.* 296 To Thomas Hallis servand for paittelling and deichting of all the steppis of the turngryss of the tolbuith, viij *d.*

†'**pattle-bone**, *Obs.*, the knee-pan: see PATEL *sb.*

'**pattock**. *local.* Also **puttock**. [? Altered from *mattock*.] A grubbing mattock: see quots.

1728 JAS. DOUGLAS in *Phil. Trans.* XXXV. 572 To take up the Saffron Heads, or break up the Ground,..they sometimes plough it, sometimes use a forked Kind of Hough called a Pattock. [So 1766 *Complete Farmer* s.v. *Saffron.*] **1903** WRIGHT *Eng. Dial. Dict.*, *Puttock*..Manufacturers of tools, whose works are in Birmingham, have frequently had the grubbing or stocking mattock asked for under this name.

pattoon, obs. var. PATTEN *sb.*

1715 *Boston News-Let.* 17 Oct. 2/2 All Persons may have Boots, Shoes, Pattoons, or anything belonging to that Trade mended. **1743** *Ibid.* 3 Feb., To be Sold..Women's & Children's Shoes & Pattoons.

pattrell, obs. form of PEITREL.

pattress ('pætrɪs). Also **pat(t)rass, pateras.** [(Corruption of) *pateras*, pl. of PATERA.] A wooden or plastic block attached to a surface to carry a gas bracket, electric light switch, ceiling rose, or the like; the base of a wall socket. Also ***pattress block, box.***

1886 J. BLACK *Gas Fitting* v. 35 Screw on the pattress blocks, pendants and brackets. **1900** P. N. HASLUCK *Pract. Gas-Fitting* iv. 80 The wooden block or pattress is now placed over the tube-bit, the screwed end being passed through the hole in the centre. **1905** C. C. METCALFE *Prac. Electr. Wiring* ii. 33 Casing brought from skirting board to pateras..will hardly be noticeable. **1928** MAYCOCK & KEMP *Electr. Wiring* (ed. 6) iii. 292 Single- and two-circuit fixture blocks,..are virtually ceiling-rose blocks embedded in hard-wood pattrasses, and without covers. **1934** *Pract. Electr. Engineer* II. 310/2 The patrasses are marked off and drilled, for the fixing and cable holes on their faces, and the conduit entry holes at their sides. **1969** A. J. COKER *Electr. Wiring* (ed. 7) v. 81 Pattress boxes are also available to convert flush-type to surface mounting. *Ibid.* 83 For fixing and wiring a surface socket-outlet, the circuit cables are first passed through a suitable knockout in the pattress block. **1973** G. A. T. BURDETT *Householder's Electr. Guide* xi. 85 These switches are mounted on moulded plastic surface pattress boxes or metal boxes which are sunk into the wall flush with the plaster. **1976** *Pract. Householder* Nov. 66/3 The ceiling roses will, or should be, mounted on pattress blocks but there is unlikely to be an earth.

patty ('pætɪ). Also 9 **pattee**. [Alteration of F. *pâté*, OF. *pasté* PASTY.] A little pie or pasty.

1710 P. LAMB *Cookery* 75 Your Mushroom Patty..is proper for second Course. *a* **1756** MRS. HAYWOOD *New Present* (1771) 171 To make Veal Patties. **1769** MRS. RAFFALD *Eng. Housekpr.* (1778) 25 Lay over it fried oysters, or oyster patties. **1848** DICKENS *Dombey* v, I see cold fowls —ham—patties—salad—lobster. **1870** RAMSAY *Remin.* iv. (ed. 18) 72 His mistress..dabbed her fork into the pattee.

'**patty-cake**. [f. PATTY + CAKE.]

1. A patty.

1865 HOLLAND *Plain T.* viii. 293, I will make patty-cakes and pastry.

2. *U.S.* var. of PAT-A-CAKE. Also *fig.*

1889 C. F. WOOLSON in *Harper's Mag.* June 119 He played patty-cake steadily with Porley, looking at the others out of the corner of his eye. **1950** O. NASH *Family Reunion* (1951) 11 All of Granny's muscles ache From half an hour of patty-cake. **1972** *Bankers' Mag.* (Boston, Mass.) Winter 93/2 The crushing price increases that are putting the older fixed incomers on welfare don't emanate from the big firms that are assumed to be playing patty cake with the unions. **1976** *Word 1971* XXVII. 34 Laura loves to play patty-cake. She laughs and flaps her hands together. She will respond to the words alone, but she does not respond to the motions alone. **1976** M. MACHLIN *Pipeline* xxxviii. 412 Ever since we started this damn pipeline, Golconda has been playing patty-cake with Friends of the Earth and all the rest.

pattymar, -maur, obs. forms of PATTAMAR.

pattypan ('pætɪpæn). Also 7 **pateepan, patti-**, 8–9 **patte-, pattipan.** [f. PATTY + PAN *sb.*]

†**1.** A pasty baked in a small pan; = PATTY. *Obs.*

1694 MOTTEUX *Rabelais* IV. xxxvi. 142 Lin'd with a great number of Forrest-Puddings, heavy Patti-pans [*Goudiveaulx massifs*], and Horse Sawsages. *a* **1700** B. E. *Dict. Cant. Crew*, *Pateepan*, a little Pye, or small Pasty.

2. A small tin pan or shape in which patties are baked.

1710 P. LAMB *Cookery* 67 It is proper you bake your Oysters on a Mazarine you serve it in, or a little Patty-pan. **1741** *Compl. Fam.-Piece* I. ii. 109 First lay a thin Crust into your Pattipan. **1769** MRS. RAFFALD *Eng. Housekpr.* (1778) 259 To make Bread Cheese-Cakes..bake them in raised crusts, or patte-pans. **1837** HOWITT *Rur. Life* II. i. (1862) 93 The iron tray of nicely laden patty-pans goes into the oven.

attrib. **1870** EMERSON *Soc. & Sol.*, *Eloquence* Wks. (Bohn) III. 24 One man is brought to the boiling-point by the excitement of conversation in the parlour... He has a two-inch enthusiasm, a patty-pan ebullition.

‖**patu** ('patʊ). *N.Z.* Also 8–9 **pat(t)oo.** Also in redupl. form. [Maori.] A short club-like weapon with sharpened edges made of stone, whalebone, or nephrite, used for striking rather than thrusting.

1769 J. COOK *Jrnl.* 12 Nov. (1955) I. 200 They have short Truncheons about a foot long, which they call Pattoo Pattoos, some made of wood some of bone and others of stone. **1770** J. BANKS *Endeavour Jrnl.* (1962) II. 26 *Patoo patoos* as they calld them, a kind of small hand bludgeon of stone, bone or hard wood most admirably calculated for the cracking of skulls. **1817** J. L. NICHOLAS *Narr. Voyage to N.Z.* I. iii. 89 The men in the canoe..exhibited..mats, spears, hooks, fishing-lines, thread, *pattoo pattoos* (war implements). **1882** T. H. POTTS *Out in Open* 82 It [*sc.* fern-root] was soaked, roasted, and repeatedly beaten with a small club (patu) on a large smooth stone, till it was supple. **1921** H. GUTHRIE-SMITH *Tutira* x. 77 Tua Kiaki pulled out a *patu* concealed beneath his mat, and with it there and then slew Te Mautaranui. **1949** P. H. BUCK *Coming of Maori* (1950) II. xi. 277 The short clubs (*patu poto*)..are made in three types: the *mere*, *kotiate*, and *wahaika*..the whalebone clubs carrying the descriptive name of *patu paraoa* (*patu*, club; *paraoa* whalebone). **1974** *Nat. Geographic* Dec. 760 (*caption*) This Tahitian war club is older than the similar patu of the New Zealand Maori.

'**patulent**, *a. rare.* [app. f. L. *patul-us* spreading, PATULOUS, with ending as in *patent*.] Open, expanded, gaping.

1709 P. BLAIR in *Phil. Trans.* XXVII. 72 The Hairs are more loose and the Pores more patulent and obvious. **1803** *Medical Jrnl.* X. 435 Pressure would approximate the sides of the uterus, and close these patulent vessels.

†'**patulicate**, *v. Obs. rare*[−0]. [f. ppl. stem of med. or mod.L. *patulicāre* to open, spread out, f. *patul-us* PATULOUS.] Hence †**patuli'cation**.

1656 BLOUNT *Glos.*, *Patulicate*, to be opened, or made wide. **1658** PHILLIPS, *Patulication*, a being opened, or made wide.

patulin ('pætjʊlɪn). *Biochem.* [f. L. *patul-um*, specific epithet of the mould, neut. of *patulus* (see PATULOUS *a.*): see -IN[1].] A colourless crystalline antibiotic compound, C_7H_6O, that was obtained from the mould *Penicillium patulum* and afterwards found to be identical with CLAVACIN and CLAVIFORMIN.

1943 H. RAISTRICK in *Lancet* 20 Nov. 625/1 Some time ago a metabolic product of *Penicillium patulum* Bainier which had not been previously encountered here was isolated and shown to have antibacterial properties; it has now been identified as anhydro-3-hydroxymethylene-tetrahydro-γ-pyrone-2-carboxylic acid, and has been given the shorter name of 'patulin'. **1947** *Sci. News* V. 98 In 1943 there was a report that a substance..called patulin had proved powerful in treating colds. Further tests on more people showed no significant improvement, however. **1953** [see CLAVATIN]. **1965** *New Scientist* 28 Oct. 253/2 He also worked out the structure of the remarkable mould product patulin, which, because of its unusual properties, was at that period a substance of considerable interest.

,**patuli'pallate**, *a. Zool.* [f. mod.L. *Patulipalla* (f. *patulus* open + *palla* mantle), Latreille's name for an order of Conchifera having an open mantle deficient in siphons: see -ATE.] Having the characters of the *Patulipalla*.

1857 in MAYNE *Expos. Lex.*

patulous ('pætjʊləs), *a.* [f. L. *patul-us* standing open, spread out, spreading, f. root of *patēre* to be open: cf. *bibulus*, *crēdulus*, etc.]

1. Open; expanded; opening rather widely.

1616 T. ADAMS *Taming of Tongue* Wks. 1862 III. 15 The ear yet hears more than ever the eye saw, and by reason of its patulous admission, derives that to the understanding whereof the sight never had a glance. **1697** *Phil. Trans.* XIX. 407 The Mouth was a very large patulous opening. **1778** DA COSTA *Brit. Conch.* 16 On the under side it is quite patulous, or wide open. **1836–9** TODD *Cycl. Anat.* II. 60/2 By elasticity the proper patulous condition of certain canals and outlets is secured.

2. Spreading: said esp. of the boughs of a tree, after Virg. *Ecl.* I. 1.

1682 GIBBON *Introd. ad Latinam Blasoniam* 84 This Cross ..is always made patulous at its ends. **1790** *Bystander* 72 Reclining..under the umbrage of a patulous beech. **1875** R. F. BURTON *Gorilla L.* (1876) I. 39 His hands and feet are large and patulous. **1881** BLACKMORE *Christowell* xv. (1882) I. 227 The boughs of the patulous tree..afford a noble amplitude.

3. a. *Bot.* (See quots.)

1756 WATSON in *Phil. Trans.* XLIX. 815 The rigid leaved Bell-flowers, with a diffusive panicle and patulous flowers. **1806** GALPINE *Brit. Bot.* 11 Calyx setaceous, patulous, longer than the spikelets. **1861** BENTLEY *Man. Bot.* 223 The sepals are..spreading outwards..divergent or patulous.

b. *Entom.* (See quot.)

1826 KIRBY & SP. *Entomol.* IV. 337 *Patulous*..when wings at rest partly cover each other.

Hence '**patulously** *adv.*, '**patulousness**.

1881 WATSON in *Jrnl. Linn. Soc.* XV. 274 Inner lip spreads patulously. **1872** COHEN *Dis. Throat* 4 Exposed to atmospheric influences..in consequence of its permanent patulousness. **1876** tr. *von Ziemssen's Cycl. Med.* V. 329 Patulousness of the fetal openings is a not infrequent consequence of extensive congenital atelectasis.

Patum Peperium ('pɑːtəm pɛ'pɪərɪʌm). [Invented name based loosely on L. *piper* pepper: *patum* is fanciful.] A proprietary name for a savoury paste; = *Gentleman's Relish* s.v. GENTLEMAN 7 c.

1884 M. L. ALLEN *Breakfast Dishes* 82 That made by C. Osborne of London, 'Patum Piperium, or Anchovy Paste,' recommended by author as the very best made. **1907** [see *Gentleman's Relish*]. **1935** *Discovery* Dec. 364/1 There used to be in Victorian times—perhaps it still exists—a breakfast compound known as 'Patum Peperium, the Gentleman's Relish'—salted anchovy with a dash of pepper. **1976** *Times* 26 Mar. 14/4 Patum Peperium, the anchovy paste known as gentleman's relish.

paturon ('pætjʊərɒn). [a. Fr. (P. Lyonet *Recherches sur l'anatomie et les métamorphoses de différentes espèces d'Insectes* (*a* 1789, published 1832) 76, f. Gk. πατ-εῖν to tread + οὐρ-ά tail + *-on*.] = FALX 2.

1926 T. H. SAVORY *Brit. Spiders* v. 44 The poison fangs or chelicerae..are two-jointed and unchelate. Various names have been given to these joints; we prefer Lyonnet's terms, unguis and paturon. **1951** LOCKET & MILLIDGE *Brit. Spiders* I. iii. 25 The chelicerae consist of two segments, the basal, called the paturon, and an apical one called the fang. **1970** K. R. SNOW *Arachnids* iv. 38 The appendages of the first segment, the chelicerae, are composed of two podomeres: a basal podomere or paturon and a distal unguis or fang.

patwari, var. PUTWARY.

paty, obs. form of PATTÉE.

patyent, patyl, obs. ff. PATIENT, PATEL[1].

patyn, patyse, var. PATEN, PATTEN, PATISE.

patzer ('pɑːtsə(r), 'pætsə(r)). *slang*. Also **potzer**. [Origin uncertain: cf. G. *patzen* to bungle.] In chess: a poor player, a 'rabbit'.

1948 *Chess Rev.* Apr. 5/2 Immediately, spectators inquired, 'Didn't you see that win?' 'Yes,' was the impudent reply. 'But, with such a potzer, I draw when I will, not when he wills.' **1959** *S. Afr. Chess-Player* VII. 11 That patzer Grivainis got Evans with an opening trap, but now the difference in strength begins to show. **1960** WENTWORTH & FLEXNER *Dict. Amer. Slang* 378/1 *Patzer*, an inferior chess player. Although said to be from the Yiddish, there is no Yiddish, German, or Hebrew word or word combination to suggest it. Prob. from 'patsy' with the familiar '-er' ending added. **1962** *Chess* 12 Mar. 190/1 When I meet these Russian potzers I'll put them in their place. **1965** tr. *A. D. de Groot's Thought & Choice in Chess* p. v, Why do masters find the good moves that patzers overlook? **1966** *New Yorker* 12 Nov. 70/1 He was at work on what in the language of the park is called a 'potzer'—a relatively weak player with an inflated ego. **1970** J. HANSEN *Fadeout* (1972) v. 41 'Do you..play chess, Mr...Brand..stetter?' 'I'm what's called a potzer.' **1972** *Daily Tel.* 28 July 15/4 So Fischer after beating off a ferocious attack..'played like a patzer', said one American Grandmaster, 'went to sleep on the job', said another. **1978** *New Statesman* 27 Oct. 556/2 He appears (or perhaps pretends) to be as tempted as the average patzer, by any old poisoned pawn, and has to have his folly explained to him.

paua ('pɑːwə). *N.Z.* Also **pawa**. [Maori.] A large gastropod mollusc of the genus *Haliotis*, esp. *H. iris*, which attaches itself to rocks by suction and is sometimes collected and used for food. Also *attrib.* Cf. ABALONE, ORMER.

[**1820** *Gram. & Vocab. Lang. N.Z.* (Church Missionary Soc.) 191 Paua, *s.* a shell-fish so called.] **1846** C. HEAPHY *Jrnl.* 6 Apr. in N. M. Taylor *Early Travellers N.Z.* (1959) 211 The mutton fish, or *pawa*, although resembling india rubber in toughness and colour, is very excellent and substantial food for explorers. *Ibid.* July 244 At Tunupoho we obtained twenty *paua* or 'mutton fish'. **1949** P. H. BUCK *Coming of Maori* (1950) I. ii. 13 The shores [of the Chatham Islands] yielded quantities of shell fish which included the *paua*. **1959** M. SHADBOLT *New Zealanders* 120 He would feel underwater, knife in hand, for the pauas. *Ibid.* 125 He heard them talking quietly in the kitchen as they prepared the meal, hammering soft the paua-steaks. **1963** *Times* 12 Jan. 1/5 This exotic New Zealand delicacy prepared from Paua (Par-War) Clams delicately flavoured with Asparagus is now obtainable from leading delicatessen and high-class food stores throughout the United Kingdom. **1966** J. K. BAXTER *Pig Island Lett.* 13 A corrugated shack With fried pauas in the pan.

2. In full, ***paua shell***. The oval shell of this mollusc, which may be as much as six inches long and two deep, distinguished by the row of holes along the back and the blue, green, and pink nacreous lining, which is used to make jewellery or other ornaments.

1873 J. H. H. ST. JOHN *Pakeha Rambles through Maori Lands* vii. 131 The eyes [of a carving] are formed of the inner coating of the 'pawa' shell, a kind of blueish mother of pearl. **1882** T. H. POTTS *Out in Open* 162 Immense heaps of paua shells..show how largely these substantial mollusks were consumed. **1920** 'K. MANSFIELD' *Bliss* 43 Chocolate custard which she had decided to serve in the pawa shell. **1931** *Times Educ. Suppl.* 11 July p. ii, (*caption*) Elaborate carving on a gateway of a Maori village... The white spots are pieces of pawa shell let into the wood. **1936** 'R. HYDE' *Check to your King* xvii. 203 The women cut their flesh with thin paua shell. **1936** N. MARSH *Death in Ecstasy* ii. 22 A figure carved in wood with protruding tongue and eyes made of pawa shell. **1949** E. DE MAUNY *Huntsman in Career* ii. 104 On top of the bookcase were pawa shell ashtrays. **1958** S. ASHTON-WARNER *Spinster* 162 The released mind revolves, flashing different colours like a paua. **1959** M. SHADBOLT *New Zealanders* 157 The large clean paua-shell ashtray gleaming copper and purple colours.

pauash, obs. form of PAVIS.

paucal ('pɔːkəl), *a. Gram.* [f. L. *paucus* few: see -AL.] Applied to a 'number' or inflected form denoting more than two but fewer than the number denoted by the plural. Hence **pau'cality**.

1964 R. H. ROBINS *Gen. Linguistics* vi. 247 A few [languages] have four [numbers], singular, dual, trial or 'paucal'..and plural. **1966** J. E. BUSE in C. E. Bazell *In Memory of J. R. Firth* 52 These systems relate ultimately.. to the activity of counting and the resultant concepts of singularity, duality, plurality, paucality and multiplicity. *Ibid.* 58 Filling Place 1 in the structure is a commutation of *t-* and absence, the latter marking the possessed as paucal. **1973** *Archivum Linguisticum* IV. 39 The..'little plural' or 'paucal' form xoxaat 'a few peaches'. **1977** *Canad. Jrnl. Linguistics 1976* XXI. II. 217 Faced with a system like that of Fijian, where there is a further distinction between trial (or paucal) and multiple within plural (Milner 1956), the reapplication of non-minimal membership would have to operate within two branches of the resulting tree diagram.

† **paucht**, *v. Sc. Obs.* [f. the stem of *pauchty*, PAUGHTY; or a back-formation from that word.] *trans.* To fill with pride, elate, uplift.

c **1602** JAMES VI *Let. Q. Eliz.* (Camden) 145, I ressaued your letter, quhiche hath so pauchtid my hairte with contentment, as nather my tongue nor my penne is able to expresse.

pauchty: see PAUGHTY.

pauci- ('pɔːsɪ-), comb. form of L. *paucus* few, little, used in *Zool.*, *Bot.*, and *Min.* to form adjs., as **pauciar'ticulate, -ated**, having few joints, in *Bot.*, slightly or loosely jointed; **pauci'dentate**, having few teeth, slightly dentated (Mayne *Expos. Lex.* 1857); **pauci'florous**, having few flowers (ibid.); **pauci'foliate**, having few leaves or folioles; so **pauci'folious**; **pauci'lithionite** [LITHIONITE], a hypothetical end-member of the lepidolite system (see quot. 1942); **pauci'locular**, having few loculi; **pauci'nervate**, slightly veined, said of a leaf, etc. (Mayne); so **pauci'nervious**; **pauci'pinnate**, pinnate with few leaflets; **pauci'radiate, -ated**, having few rays, as the fin of a fish, or the umbel of a plant (Mayne); **pauci'spiral**, having few whorls, as a shell; so **pauci'spirated**.

1852 DANA *Crust.* II. 1312 A *pauci-articulate flagellum. **1857** MAYNE *Expos. Lex.*, *Pauciarticulated. **1895** *Cambridge Nat. Hist.* III. 433 Holohepatica—Cerata mediodorsal, retractile or not, usually *paucifoliate, liver never ramified. **1942** A. N. WINCHELL in *Amer. Mineralogist* XXVII. 117 The second end-member [of the lepidolite system] ($K_2Li_3Al_5Si_6O_{20}F_4$) has no name and no varietal name in the literature seems to be appropriate. In these circumstances the writer would suggest that it be called *paucilithionite. **1963** *Mineral. Abstr.* XVI. 189/2, 142 Chemical analyses of lithium micas from the literature have been transformed to the molecules polylithionite, paucilithionite, muscovite, and siderophyllite. **1872** PEASLEE *Ovar. Tumors* 31 *Paucilocular, in opposition to polycystic. **1843** *Penny Cycl.* XXV. 386/1 Operculum..*paucispiral on the left border. **1851–6** WOODWARD *Mollusca* 102 The operculum is described as Paucispiral, or few-whirled, as in Litorina.

† **'paucify**, *v. Obs. rare.* [f. L. *paucus*, *pauci-* few, little: see -FY.] *trans.* To make few, diminish.

1648 *Brit. Bellman* in *Harl. Misc.* (ed. Park) VII. 626 To paucify the number of those you conceived would counter-vote you. **1792** COWPER *Let. to W. Hayley* 26 Dec., My opportunities of writing are *paucified*, as perhaps, Dr. Johnson would have dared to say.

pauciloquent (pɔː'sɪləkwənt), *a. rare*$^{-0}$. [f. PAUCI- + L. *loquent-em* speaking, pr. pple. of *loquī*: cf. next.] Uttering few words; speaking briefly. Hence **pau'ciloquently** *adv.*, with few words.

1656 BLOUNT *Glossogr.*, *Pauciloquent*.., that speaketh little. **1882** WALLACE *Reporters* (ed. 4) 340 The pauciloquently praising Eldon.

pau'ciloquy. *rare.* [ad. L. *pauciloqui-um* a speaking but little (Plautus), f. PAUCI- + *-loquium*, f. *loquī* to speak.] The utterance of few words; sparingness of speech.

1623 COCKERAM, *Pauciloquie*, few words. **1648** J. BEAUMONT *Psyche* XX. ccii, Fear no Discredit by Pauciloquie. **1658** PHILLIPS, *Pauciloquy*, a speaking few words, little talk. **1721** in BAILEY. **1755** in JOHNSON.

paucity ('pɔːsɪtɪ). Also 5 **paucyte**. [a. F. *paucité* (14th c. in Godef. *Compl.*), or ad. L. *paucitās*, f. *paucus* few: see -ITY.]

1. Smallness of number; fewness; a small number.

c **1425** *Found. St. Bartholomew's* (E.E.T.S.) 35 Whom the grace of God from the forsayid paucyte encresid yn-to .xxxv.^{to}. **1566** *Form Com. Prayer* in *Liturg. Serv. Q. Eliz.* (Parker Soc.) 534 That they, neither respecting their own weakness and paucity..may by thy power obtain victory. **1709** BERKELEY *Th. Vision* §70 The greater paucity of rays arriving at the eye. **1881** JOWETT *Thucyd.* I. 235 In danger of having to capitulate owing to..the paucity of its defenders.

2. Smallness of quantity; scantiness.

1650 BULWER *Anthropomet.* 230 Smal Feet argue paucity of matter. **1680** BOYLE *Produc. Chem. Princ.* II. 64 It afforded..so little oil, that the paucity seemed strange. **1858** BUCKLE *Civiliz.* (1873) II. viii. 434 From paucity of evidence, we are unable to measure them with precision.

paueillon, -elo(u)n, -eylon, obs. ff. PAVILION.

paueiss, -es(se, -ews, -eys, obs. ff. PAVIS.

paughie: see PAUGIE.

paughty, pauchty ('pɔːtɪ, *Sc.* pɑxtɪ), *a. Sc.* and *north. dial.* Also Yorksh. **pafty**. [Origin unknown.] Haughty, proud; saucy, insolent, impertinent.

1572 A. ARBUTHNOT *Mis. pure Scolar* in Pinkerton *Anc. Sc. Poems* (1786) 153 Pauchtie pryd richt sair do I detest. **1637–50** ROW *Hist. Ch. Sc.* (Wodrow Soc.) 395 Maxuell, Bishop of Rosse, (that proud and paughtie peece). **1720** RAMSAY *Wealth* 99 Even handycraftsmen..strut fou paughty in the alley. **1828** SCOTT *F.M. Perth* xxvi, The disgust which the paughty Hieland varlet had always shown for my honest trade. **1876** *Whitby Gloss.*, *Pafty*, impertinent. **1890** EDWARDS *Mod. Scot. Poets* 169, I never fleetch the paughty fair.

paugie ('pɔːgɪ). *local U.S.* Also **paughie, porgy**. [From the ending of the Narragansett Indian name *mishcuppâuog*, pl. of *mishcup*, literally 'thick-scaled', from *mishe* large, and *cuppi* scale.] Local name of a North American fish, of the bream kind, *Pagrus argyrops*, also called *scuppaug*.

1860 BARTLETT *Dict. Amer.*, *Porgy* or *Paugie*.., a fish of the *sparus* family, common in the waters of New England and New York... It is singular that one half the original name, *scup*, should be retained for this fish in Rhode Island, and the other half, *paug*, changed into *paugie* or *porgy*, in New York. **1864** WEBSTER, *Paugie*... A kind of fish; the porgy. **1870** *Putnam's Mag.* VI. 525 Porgy, Scup, and Scuppaug, names..in different sections of the Northern States. **1890** *Cent. Dict.*, *Paughie*, same as *porgy*.

† **pauh**, *int. Obs. rare.* Variant of PAH *int.*

1693 CONGREVE *Old Bach.* II. i, Egad he's a brave Fellow —Pauh, I am quite another thing, when I am with him.

pauhaugen (pɒ'hɔːgən). *local U.S.* Also **pauhagen, poghaden, pohagan, pookagan**, etc. [Abnaki (dial. of Algonkin) *pukangané* (Rasles).] Local name of the menhaden, a N. American fish.

1860 BARTLETT *Dict. Amer.* s.v. *Menhaden*, Also known by the names Bony-fish, White-fish, Hardhead, Mossbonker, and Pauhagen. *Ibid.*, *Pohagen*, or *Pauhagen*. **1864** WEBSTER, *Pauhaugen*. **1890** *Century Dict.*, *Poghaden*..the menhaden. Also *pauhagen*.

pauice, pauish, obs. forms of PAVIS.

pauilion, -il(l)on, -ilun, etc., obs. ff. PAVILION.

Pauillac (poija). [Fr., f. the name of a commune in the department of Gironde, France.] Claret produced in Pauillac. Also *attrib.* passing into *adj.*

1858 [see MARGAUX]. **1897** A. BEARDSLEY *Let.* *c* 27 Apr. (1971) 310 The Pauillac at Lapérouse is *excellent*! only 2 fr. a bottle. **1920** G. SAINTSBURY *Notes Cellar-Bk.* iv. 66 Margaux..and Pauillac..have very much fewer tricks played on them. **1966** H. YOXALL *Fashion of Life* xxv. 246, I..could separate, among the Médocs, the red Graves, Pauillacs, Margaux, St Juliens and St Estèphes. **1968** *Guardian* 29 Mar. 9/4 Ch. Ponter Canet, the best so far, with a fine Pauillac bouquet and taste. **1977** B. ROUECHÉ *Fago* I. ii. 19, I slipped the wine out of its paper bag. It was a good Bordeaux, a Pauillac of the Haute-Médoc.

pauk, pauky, etc.: see PAWK, PAWKY, etc.

Paul (pɔːl). Also 4 **Poul, Poule**; *genitive* 4 **Powlys**, 4–6 **Poules**, 5–7 **Paules**, 6 **Pawles, Powlles**, 6–7 **Powles**, 6–8 **Pauls**, 7– **Paul's**. [a. OF. *Pol*, mod.F. *Paul* = It. *Paolo*, Sp. *Pablo*:—L. *Paulum*, in nom. *Paulus*.]

1. The English form of the Latin personal name *Paulus*, well known as that of the 'Apostle of the Gentiles' (Acts xiii. 9). Used in proverbial phrases in conjunction with PETER, q.v.

2. [tr. It. *Paolo*, Paul.] The PAOLO, an obsolete Italian silver coin, worth about fivepence sterling.

1767 STERNE *Tr. Shandy* IX. xxiv, I paid five Pauls for two hard eggs. **1854** LOWELL *Jrnl. in Italy* Pr. Wks. 1890 I. 191 You give the *custode* a paul for showing you the wolf that suckled Romulus and Remus.

3. a. Paul Pry: name of a very inquisitive character in a U.S. song of 1820; often used allusively (also *attrib.*).

1829 MACAULAY *Southey's Colloq. Soc.* Ess. (1887) 118 The magistrate..ought to be a perfect jack-of-all-trades..a Paul Pry in every house, spying, eaves-dropping, relieving, admonishing [etc.]. *a* **1845** HOOD *Tale of Trumpet* xi, She had much of the spirit that lies Perdu in a notable set of Paul Prys. **1870** MISS BRIDGMAN *Rob. Lynne* II. i. 4 It will cure her of her Paul-Pry tricks. **1882** *Encycl. Brit.* XIV. 695/2 Paul Pry,..always his [Liston's] most popular part, soon became to many a real personage. **1897** *Pall Mall Mag.* Nov. 311 Some of the Paul Prys of the parish had intercepted the flyman. **1928** E. WALLACE *Double* xiii. 208 There are lots of quiet little nooks and places where a fellow can sit without a lot of Paul Prys seeing him. **1934** *Sun* (Baltimore) 27 Apr. 12/2 The Senate's theory that the way to enforce the tax laws is to give the Paul Prys of every community access to the private details of every man's gross and net income. **1956** H. G. DE LISSER *Cup & Lip* ix. 109 It would be ruinous to a doctor to be known as a paul pry. **1978** H. C. RAE *Sullivan* I. ii. 24 Twenty-five thousand dollars?.. It's the going rate for a quiet investigation, a straight Paul Pry?

b. Hence **Paul-Pry** *v. intr.*, to behave like Paul Pry; to be impertinently inquisitive or prying; also **Paul-Prying** *vbl. sb.*; **Paul Pryism**, the conduct of a Paul Pry.

1839 MARRYAT *Diary Amer.* Ser. I. I. 110 Others mounting..and Paul Prying into the bed-room windows. **1865** H. KINGSLEY *Hillyars & Burtons* xxx, Who the deuce are you, cross-questioning and Paul-Prying? **1927** *Daily Express* 6 Oct. 8/2 These restrictions were imposed during the war... Their maintenance to-day is simply part of that fussy Paul Pryism which covers the State with ridicule. **1960** *Times* 4 Mar. 13/7 The straitest champion of marital fidelity would, surely, not defend such monstrous Paul Prying.

†**4. Paul's**: popular name of St. Paul's Cathedral in London; in 16–17th c. a favourite resort of loungers, gossips, etc. *Obs.* (Now always *St. Paul's*.) Hence *attrib.* in ***Paul's Alley***, ***Paul's Chain***, now London lanes, ***Paul's Cross***, etc.

1377 LANGL. *P. Pl.* B. XIII. 65 þis freke bifor þe den of poules Preched of penaunces. [**1393** *Ibid.* C. XVI. 70 At seint paules by-for þe peuple what penaunce þei suffreden.] *a* **1460** *Gregory's Chron.* (Camden) 98 Powlys Crosse. The whiche was pronounsyd at Powlys Crosse. **1573** BARET *Alv.*

To Rdr., The right Worshipfull M. Nowell, Deane of Pawles. **1579** W. WILKINSON *Confut. Familye of Loue* 29 b, Protesting the truth of HN. his bookes openly at Paules crosse. **1596** SHAKS. *1 Hen. IV*, II. iv. 576 This oyly Rascall is knowne as well as Poules. **1597** —— *2 Hen. IV*, I. ii. 58, I bought him in Paules. **1613** —— *Hen. VIII*, v. iv. 16 We may as well push against Powles as stirre 'em. **1613** MIDDLETON *Triumphs of Truth* B ij, The Angell and Zeale.. conduct him to Pauls-chaine. *c* **1645** HOWELL *Lett.* (1655) IV. 83 While you adorn your Churches there, we destroy them here: Among other, poor Pouls looks like a great Skeleton... Truly I think nor Turk or Tartar.. would have us'd Pauls in that manner.

5. Paul Jones [the name of John *Paul Jones* (1747–92), Scottish-born naval officer noted for his victories for the Americans during the War of Independence]: a ballroom dance during which the dancers change partners after circling in concentric rings of men and women. Also *attrib.* and *fig.*

1920 *Atlantic Monthly* July 89/1 The whole sprightly, smiling, hand-clapping population seems engaged in one vast 'Paul Jones'.. with no one.. refusing to join the dance. **1934** *Punch* 14 Feb. 174/1 There was nothing doing in the matter of Paul Joneses, from which even the most emphatic protestations could not give us release. **1938** *Times* 10 Jan. 10/4 The 'party' began with 'I've been to Harlem', a change-partner dance of the 'Paul Jones' type sung to the pure English harvest-home tune, 'I've been to France and I've been to Dover'. **1942** M. DICKENS *One Pair of Feet* vii. 147 A blond A.C.2 whom I had picked up in the Paul Jones. **1958** L. DURRELL *Balthazar* xiii. 233 But now the band had begun to play a Paul Jones (perhaps the very dance in which Arnauti first met Justine?). **1967** *Times Rev. Industry* May 58/3 Driving a private car is often a death-defying Paul Jones with an endless succession of lorries. **1972** V. CANNING *Rainbird Pattern* iv. 66 Harriet.. was seduced in the back of the officer's car while Grace was dancing a Paul Jones.

6. Phrases and Combinations with *Paul's*: **Paul's betony** (erron. *St. Paul's betony*), name for a species of *Veronica*, the Wood Speedwell (*V. officinalis*), described by Paulus Ægineta as a betony; improperly applied to *V. serpyllifolia*; † **Paul's foot**, a lineal foot, the standard of which was the foot of Algar carved on the base of a column of old St. Paul's, London (*Gent. Mag.* July 1852, 57); † **Paul's man** (see quot.); **Paul's pigeon** (see quot. *a* 1661); † **St. Paul's tide**, the season about the festival of the Conversion of St. Paul (Jan. 25); † **Paul's walk**, the nave of St. Paul's Cathedral as a resort of loungers, newsmongers, etc. in 16th and 17th c.; so † **Paul's-walker**, one who frequented St. Paul's as a lounger or gossip; † **Paul's-walking** *a.*; † **Paul's work**, (?) botched work, a 'mess'.

1548 TURNER *Names of Herbes* 19 *Betonica Pauli aeginete* .. maye be called in englishe *Paules betony or wodde Peny ryal. **1551** —— *Herbal* I. F iv b, Paulis betony is myche dyfferyng from Dioscorides betony, as Paulus witnesseth hys selfe. **1646** SIR T. BROWNE *Pseud. Ep.* II. vi. 101 Betonica Pauli, or Pauls Betony, hereof the people have some conceit in reference to S. Paul, whereas indeed that name is derived from Paulus Ægineta, an ancient Physitian of Ægina. **1879** PRIOR *Plant-n.* (ed. 3) 178 Paul's Betony, .. *Veronica serpyllifolia*. **1886** BRITTEN & HOLLAND *Plant-n.*, Paul's Betony, *Veronica officinalis*. [**1419** *Liber Albus* (Rolls) I. 279 Paiement.. vii pees et demy en longur, et de le pee de Seint Poul.] **1442** *Rolls of Parliament* V. 44/1 The seide newe brigge so to be made with a draght lef contenyng the space of iiii fete called *Paules fete in brede. **1447** *Will of Sharyngton* (Somerset Ho.), Height of two poules fete. **1616** B. JONSON *Ev. Man in Hum.* Dram. Pers., Cap. Bobadill, a *Paules-man. **1816** GIFFORD *B. Jonson's Wks.* I. 6 *note*, A Paul's man, i.e. a frequenter of the middle aisle of St. Paul's cathedral, the common resort of cast captains, sharpers, gulls, and gossipers. *a* **1661** FULLER *Worthies, London* (1811) II. 65 One of St. Anthonies Pigs therein (so were the Scholars of that School commonly called, as those of St. Paul's, *Paul's Pigeons) [cf. STOW *Surv.* (1603) 75]. **1701** *Lond. Gaz.* No. 3718/4 The Fairs held at the City of Bristol at St. James-Tide, and at St. *Pauls-Tide. **1628** EARLE *Microcosm.* (Arb.) 73 *Pauls Walke is the Lands Epitome. **1658** OSBORN *Jas. I* Wks. (1673) 477 Edward Wimark the *Pauls-walker. *Ibid.* Index 20 The *Pauls-walking News-mongers—report Northumberland too.. intimate with P. Henry. **1602** DEKKER *Satiromast.* Wks. 1873 I. 212 And when he had done, made *Poules worke of it. **1620** in *Court & T. Jas. I* (1848) II. 203 But I doubt, when all is done, it will prove, as they say Paul's work. **1673** *S'too him Bayes* 15 But I must dispatch, for I see He's making Paul's work on't already.

paul, -e, paulle, obs. forms of PALL, PAWL.

Paul-Bunnell (pɔːl bʌˈnɛl). *Path.* The names of J. R. *Paul* (1893–1936) and W. W. *Bunnell* (1902–1965), U.S. physicians, used *attrib.* and *absol.* with reference to a test first described by them in 1932, in which the presence of an antibody reaction to the red blood cells of sheep confirms a diagnosis of infectious mononucleosis (glandular fever).

1938 *Amer. Jrnl. Med. Sci.* CXCVI. 79 The diagnosis was established by the clinical course, confirmed by a characteristic blood smear and a positive Paul-Bunnell test. **1952** *Brit. Med. Jrnl.* 22 Mar. 637/1 The Paul-Bunnell reaction was positive in a dilution of 1 in 28. **1958** *Woman* 27 Sept. 70/3 A special blood test, a Paul-Bunnell test, proved that it could only be glandular fever. **1970** PASSMORE & ROBSON *Compan. Med. Stud.* II. xviii. 116/2 In some cases [of glandular fever], a heterophile antibody capable of agglutinating sheep erythrocytes appears (Paul-Bunnell antibody). **1976** *Lancet* 11 Dec. 1297/1 Paul Bunnell, blood cultures, electrocardiogram, and chest X-ray were all normal.

pauldron, another form of POULDRON, a piece of armour covering the shoulder, a shoulder-plate.

1594, 1834, etc. [see POULDRON].

paulfrey, obs. form of PALFREY.

Pauli (ˈpaʊlɪ). *Physics.* The name of Wolfgang *Pauli* (1900–58), Austrian-born physicist, used *attrib.* and in the possessive to designate the *exclusion principle*, which he enunciated in 1925 (*Zeitschr. f. Physik* XXXI. 765–83).

1926 *Jrnl. Optical Soc. Amer.* XIII. 10 By means of schemes (7) and (8) we easily can write down the $\overline{m}_r$ and $\overline{m}_k$ values observing Pauli's principle. *Ibid.*, the period is closed with the *N*th electron where the Pauli principle gives only a $^1S_0$ term. **1926** *Physical Rev.* XXVIII. 339 Whether the impossibility of obtaining coordination for equivalent electrons is directly connected with Pauli's exclusion principle is difficult to say. **1928, 1930** [see *exclusion principle*]. **1946** J. R. PARTINGTON *Gen. & Inorg. Chem.* x. 257 For an atom containing more than one electron, the maximum number of electrons in each shell is fixed by Pauli's exclusion principle. **1968** C. G. KUPER *Introd. Theory Superconductivity* ix. 157 The wave function (9.51) is antisymmetric against interchange of particles, and therefore automatically satisfies the Pauli exclusion principle. **1974** G. REECE tr. *Hund's Hist. Quantum Theory* xiii. 181 The spin of the electron had hitherto been taken into account only in so far as it had no consequence beyond the Pauli principle.

Paulian (ˈpɔːlɪən), *sb.* and *a.* [f. L. *Paul-us* Paul: cf. *Christ-ian.*] **A.** *sb.*

1. *Ch. Hist.* One of a sect who rejected the personality of the Logos and the Holy Spirit, and denied the pre-existence of Christ as 'the eternal Son of God'; founded by Paul of Samosata in the 3rd century.

c **1449** PECOCK *Repr.* (Rolls) II. 498 The sect of Paulianys, which helden that Crist was not bifore Marie, but took his bigynnyng of Marie. **1764** MACLAINE tr. *Mosheim's Eccl. Hist.* (1844) I. 83/2 Paul of Samosata.. left behind him a sect, that assumed the title of Paulians, or Paulianists. **1877** MCCLINTOCK & STRONG *Cycl. Bibl. Lit.* VII. 835 One of the canons of Nice required the Paulians to be rebaptized.

2. A follower or disciple of St. Paul. *nonce-use.*

1609 BIBLE (Douay) *Deut.* xxv. *comm.*, They are called Christians, not Paulians, whom S. Paul converted.

B. *adj.* That is a follower of St. Paul. *nonce-use.*

1638 FEATLY *Strict. Lyndom.* I. 213 The Iesuit should have said, a Paulian heretique, for Clemanges and Wickliffe professe with Paul, Act 24. 14.

So **ˈPaulianist, ˈPaulianite** = A. 1.

1696 tr. *Dupin's Eccl. Hist.* I. II. 6 The errors of the Ebionites, Paulianites, Sabellians and Arians. *Ibid.* 44 The Paulianists, who distinguish'd the Word from the Son of God, and the Paraclete from the Holy Spirit. **1764** [see PAULIAN A. 1]. **1831–3** E. BURTON *Eccl. Hist.* xxviii. (1845) 591 His [Paul's] followers, who were known by the name of Paulianists, continued.. till the beginning of the fifth century.

Paulician (pɔːˈlɪʃ(ɪ)ən), *sb.* and *a.* *Ch. Hist.* [ad. L. *Pauliciānī*, a. Gr. *Παυλικιανοί*, of obscure origin, thought by some to be from *Paulus* PAUL.]

A. *sb.* A member of a sect which arose in Armenia in the 7th century, holding modified Manichæan opinions. **B.** *adj.* Of or belonging to this sect.

1727–41 CHAMBERS *Cycl.*, *Paulicians*,.. so called from their chieftain, one Paulus, an Armenian, in the seventh century. **1764** MACLAINE tr. *Mosheim's Eccl. Hist.* (1844) I. 211/2. **1840** MACAULAY *Ranke* Ess. (1887) 575 The Paulician theology.. spread rapidly through Provence and Languedoc. **1883** SCHAFF *Encycl. Relig. Knowl.* III. 2407/1 The Bulgarians.. finally united with the Eastern Church; and only a small body of Paulicians are now Catholics.

Hence **Pauˈlicianism**, the doctrine of the sect.

1839 *Penny Cycl.* XIV. 385/1 The Manichæan doctrines .. continued to have supporters, under their new name of Paulicianism, till a very late period. **1874** J. H. BLUNT *Dict. Sects* 414/2 From the close of the eleventh century Paulicianism as such ceases to be significant. **1941** [see BOGOMIL, -MILE]. **1967** N. G. GARSOIAN (*title*) The Paulician heresy. A study of the origin and development of Paulicianism in Armenia and the eastern provinces of the Byzantine empire.

paulie, pallie (ˈpɔlɪ, ˈpɑlɪ), *a.* (*sb.*) *Sc.* Also **pawlie, palie, paley.** [Origin not ascertained.] **a.** *adj.* Undersized, weakly, impotent: applied esp. to the smallest or poorest lambs of a flock, also to a poor weakly child. **b.** *sb.* An undersized lamb, one of the smallest lambs of a flock.

1818 HOGG *Brownie of B.* I. ix. 158 There was Geordie.. the flesher,.. that took away the crocks and the paulies, and my brockit-lamb. **1822** W. J. NAPIER *Pract. Store-farming* 251 The gimmer-lambs throughout, bear a proportion to the 'second' lambs and palies as two to one. *a* **1835** HOGG *Tales* (1866) 360 As for your paulie toop lamb, what care I for it? **1886** C. SCOTT *Sheep Farming* 19 Deformed and crippled specimens in Scotland are termed 'pallie lambs'.

paulin. [app. second element of TARPAULIN.] A trade name for waterproof coverings of the nature of tarpaulin, whether tarred, oiled, or painted.

[**1847–78** HALLIWELL, *Pauling*, a covering for a cart or waggon. *Linc.*] **1882** *Englishman* 2 Dec. 4/5 These Paulins are prepared from the best English Tarpaulin Canvas. *Ibid.*, Tarred, Oiled and Painted Paulins.

Pauline (ˈpɔːlaɪn), *a.* and *sb.* Also 8 **-in.** [ad. L. *Paulīn-us* adj., f. *Paulus* Paul: see -INE[1].]

A. *adj.* Of, pertaining to, or characteristic of St. Paul, his writings, or his doctrines.

1817 COLERIDGE *Biog. Lit.* II. xxiii. 307 Passages.. thoroughly Pauline. **1860** WESTCOTT *Introd. Study Gosp.* iv. (ed. 5) 243 For him [Marcion] the Pauline narrative was the truest picture of the life of Christ. **1876** C. M. DAVIES *Unorth. Lond.* (ed. 2) 36 Selections.. from the Pauline Epistles.

B. *sb.*

1. A member of certain religious orders so named.

1362 LANGL. *P. Pl.* A. II. 76 In witnesse of whuche þing, wrong was þe furste, Pers þe pardoner, Paulynes doctor. **1393** *Ibid.* C. III. 110 Of paulynes queste. *c* **1483** *Chron. London* (1827) 43 In the same yere [1310] began the ordre of Paulyns, that is to say Crowched Freres. *a* **1550** *Image Ypocrisie* III. in *Skelton's Wks.* (1843) II. 441 Some be Paulines, Some be Antonynes, Some be Bernardines, Some be Celestines.

2. A follower of St. Paul. *nonce-use.*

1740 J. DUPRÉ *Conform. Anc. & Mod. Cerem.* 32 The Primitive Christians.. never called themselves Johnians, Paulins, nor Barnabites.

3. A scholar of St. Paul's School, London.

1867 *Athenæum* 30 Nov. 715/1 [Sir Philip] Francis was a London boy by education, and a Pauline... The Paulines were especially famous for caligraphy. **1897** ABBOTT & CAMPBELL *Life Jowett* I. ii. 41 He returned to London, bringing with him the 'blue ribbon' of Oxford, an honour which at that time no Pauline had won.

Hence **Paulinian** (-ˈɪnɪən), *a.* = PAULINE *a.*; *sb.* = PAULINIST; **ˈPaulinism** (-ɪnɪz(ə)m), (*a*) the doctrine of St. Paul, Pauline theology; (*b*) an expression or feature characteristic of St. Paul; **ˈPaulinist,** an adherent of St. Paul or his doctrine; **Pauliˈnistic** *a.*, of or pertaining to a Paulinist or Paulinism; **ˈPaulinize** *v. intr.*, to follow the doctrine of St. Paul; *trans.*, to make Pauline, imbue with Paulinism (in quot., to represent as Pauline).

1874 *Supernat. Relig.* II. II. v. 5 The rapid growth.. of *Paulinian doctrine. **1883** LOOS & BEHRINGER tr. *J. Grob's Life Zwingli* xvi. 136, I preach.. as Paul writes; why do you not rather call me a Paulinian? **1857** M. PATTISON *Ess.* (1889) II. 234 The antithesis of Petrinism and *Paulinism. **1910** J. MOFFATT *Paul & Paulinism* II. 33 Paulinism.. was the outcome of the apostle's attempt to hunt out for himself the relations of the Lord Jesus Christ to God, the Law, the universe, and the church. **1916** G. B. SHAW *Androcles & Lion* Pref. p. xci, The Christianity of Jesus failed completely to establish itself politically and socially,.. whilst Paulinism overran the whole western civilized world. **1927** A. H. MCNEILE *Introd. New Testament* iv. 65 The presence in *Mark* of 'Paulinisms' or other features thought to be secondary on subjective grounds. **1882** FARRAR *Early Chr.* I. 92 Christians who wished to stand aloof alike from *Paulinists and Judaists. **1860** *Lit. Churchm.* 16 Nov. 427/1 Too much inclined to see.. sharp distinctions between the Jewish-Christians and the heathen converts.., attributing a *Paulinistic tendency to the latter. **1898** W. M. RAMSAY *Was Christ born at Bethlehem?* 51 Luke's view has.. a strong Paulinistic character. **1865** tr. *Strauss' New Life Jesus* I. 178 The account.. given in Luke with its *Paulinizing sections. **1885** *Athenæum* 3 Oct. 429/1 St. Luke's Gospel.. is Paulinized too much.

Paulism (ˈpɔːlɪz(ə)m). *nonce-wd.* [f. PAUL + -ISM.] The doctrine of St. Paul; Paulinism.

1823 BENTHAM *Not Paul* 367 Whatever is in Paul, and is not.. in any one of the four Gospels, is not Christianity, but Paulism.

Paulist[1] (ˈpɔːlɪst). [f. as prec. + -IST.]

1. (See quots.)

1678 J. PHILLIPS tr. *Tavernier's Voy.* II. I. xiii. 77 The Jesuites at Goa, are known by the name of Paulists. **1757** J. H. GROSE *Voy. E. Ind.* 79 The Jesuits, who are better known in India by the appellation of Paulists, from their head church and convent of St. Paul's in Goa.

2. A member of a Roman Catholic association, the Congregation of the Missionary Priests of St. Paul the Apostle, founded at New York in 1858.

1883 SCHAFF *Encycl. Relig. Knowl.* III. 1778.

Paulist[2] (ˈpaʊlɪst), anglicized f. PAULISTA. Hence **Pauˈlistic** *a.*

1900 Paulist [see MAMELUCO]. **1942** A. ST. JAMES tr. *Zweig's Brazil* 214 Anyone still desirous of seeing something of the Paulistic type of the nineteenth century habitation had better hurry.

Paulista (paʊˈliːstə). Also with lower-case initial. [Pg., f. *São Paulo* (see below) + *-ista* -IST.] **a.** A person of mixed Portuguese and Brazilian Indian descent; *spec.* one of the explorers and settlers of the hinterlands of southern Brazil. (*Obs.* exc. *hist.*). **b.** A native or inhabitant of the city of São Paulo in southern Brazil.

1817 SOUTHEY *Hist. Brazil* II. xxiii. 300 The Paulistas have acted so memorable a part in Brazil and Paraguay that it becomes of importance to trace their history distinctly, and clear it from fables and misrepresentations. **1884** R. G.

WATSON *Span. & Portug. S. Amer.* II. xi. 169 The search for the precious metals had long shared with slave-hunting the efforts of the *Paulistas* and others. *Ibid.* 174 *Minas Geraes* soon acquired the unenviable notoriety..of being the most turbulent settlement in *Brazil*. Its people were divided into two classes, called..*Paulistas* and *Florasteiros* or strangers. **1896** A. H. KEANE *Ethnol.* vii. 152 In Brazil the famous '*Paulistas*' (so called from the province of São Paulo), a cross between the first Portuguese immigrants and the aborigines, have always been the most vigorous and enterprising section of the community. **1910** *Encycl. Brit.* VII. 677/2 Cuyabá was founded in 1719 by Paulista gold hunters. **1932** W. S. ROBERTSON *Hist. Lat.-Amer. Nations* (ed. 2) vi. 123 'Paulistas', as the half-breed adventurers from São Paulo were called, gradually penetrated farther and farther into the interior. **1942** A. ST. JAMES tr. *Zweig's Brazil* 211 During the seventeenth and eighteenth centuries on the banks of the little river Ticté there lies a small unimportant town, more headquarters and camp than a permanent settlement of those roaming gangs, the Paulistas, who roved through the whole country..in search of loot. *Ibid.* 218 The Paulistas have a most competitive attitude toward Rio de Janeiro, and the desire not to appear inferior or less artistic. **1944** S. PUTNAM tr. *E. de Cunha's Rebellion in Backlands* ii. 63 The Paulista—and this name, in its historic signification, takes in the sons of Rio de Janeiro, Minas, São Paulo, and regions south—now arose as an autonomous type, adventurous, rebellious, freedom-loving. **1966** *Economist* 3 Sept. 902 Pleasure-loving *cariocas* (those who live in Rio), economically eager *paulistas* (those who live in São Paulo). **1976** R. PERRY *One Good Death* v. 75 The daily nightmare that many Paulistas called travelling home from work.

†**Paulistine.** *Obs.* = PAULIST 1.
1698 FRYER *Acc. E. India & P.* 70 A College..belonging to the Jesuits here, more commonly called Paulistines. *Ibid.* 150 St. Paul's was the first Monastery of the Jesuits in Goa, from whence they receive the Name of Paulistins.

Paulite[1] (ˈpɔːlaɪt). *Ch. Hist.* [f. name of *Paul*, L. *Paul-us* + -ITE[1] 1.]

1. One of an order of monks, also called Hermits of St. Paul, founded in 1215, at Budapest. Also *attrib.* or as *adj.*, of or belonging to this order.
1884 G. B. MALLESON *Battle-Fields of Germ.* vii. 221 Priests and monks of all denominations, the Benedictines, the Jesuits, the Carmelites, the Paulites. **1888** H. C. LEA *Hist. Inquisition* I. 418 He..retired to a Paulite monastery.

2. *nonce-wd.* One who is 'of Paul': see 1 Cor. i. 12.
1839 WHATELY *Dangers Chr. Faith* III. iv. (1857) 74 The Sects of Paulites, and Apollonians and the rest, would have gradually diverged more and more in doctrine.

ˈ**paulite**[2]. *Min.* [ad. Ger. *Paulit*, name given by Werner, 1812, from St. Paul Island, Labrador: see -ITE[1] 2.] A synonym of HYPERSTHENE.
1814 T. ALLAN *Min. Nomencl.* 24 Hyperstene, Labrador hornblende..Paulite. **1852** C. U. SHEPARD *Min.* (ed. 3) 199.

paulle, obs. form of PALL.

‖**Paullinia** (pɔːˈlɪnɪə). *Bot.* [mod.L. (Linnæus, 1737), from the name of C. F. Paullini, a German botanist.] A genus of tropical American and West African climbing shrubs (N.O. *Sapindaceæ*); a plant of this genus.
1753 CHAMBERS *Cycl. Supp.*, *Paulinia.* **1833** WHITTIER *Toussaint l'Ouverture* 16 The lithe paullinia's verdant fold.

paulmer, obs. form of PALMER.

paulo-post-future (ˌpɔːləupəustˈfjuːtjuə(r)), *a.* and *sb.* [ad. mod.L. *paulo post futurum*, the current rendering, from the time of Lascaris 1494, of the Greek name ὁ μετ' ὀλίγον μέλλων, the future after a little, in Sp. *el futuro de aquí a poco.* In 16th c. called also *mox futurum* 'immediate future'; and in 19th c. Grammars, 'third future', 'futurum exactum', 'futurum perfectum', 'future perfect'.]

1. A name of a tense of the passive voice of Greek verbs, the chief use of which was to state that an event will take place immediately.
[A good example of the Greek use is in Aristoph. *Plut.* 1027 φράζε, καὶ πεπράξεται, Speak and it shall be done at once, or as soon as said.]
1824 L. MURRAY *Eng. Gram.* (ed. 5) I. II. vi. 161 Some grammarians have alleged, that..we should also admit the dual number, the paulo-post future tense, the middle voice ..found in Greek.

2. *allusively.* A future which is a little after the present; a by-and-by; belonging to an immediate or proximate future.
[**1822** SHELLEY *Lett.* Pr. Wks. 1880 IV. 260 My post.. must be transformed by your delay into a *paulo post futurum.*] **1848** LOWELL *Fable for Critics* 936 Here comes Dana, abstractedly loitering along, Involved in a paulo-post-future of song, Who'll be going to write what'll never be written Till the Muse..gives him the mitten. **1887** DOWDEN *Life Shelley* I. vi. 246 Shelley's..anticipated profits were in the paulo-post-future. **1901** *Scotsman* 9 Sept. 7/4 An accumulation like this of time-expired men has a paulo-post-future effect on the working of the short-service system.

Hence ˌ**paulo-post-fuˈturatively** *adv.*, as belonging to the near future. So ˌ**paulo-ˈpost** *a.* [L. *paulo post* a little after], a little subsequent; also ˌ**paulo-ˈpast** *a.*, a little past, relating to something lately finished. (All *nonce-wds.*)
a **1843** SOUTHEY *Doctor* Interch. xx. (1848) 494 While I am treating of it paulo-post-futuratively, as of a possible case. **1849** THOREAU *Week Concord Riv.* Wed. 265 Our to-morrow's future should be at least paulo-post to theirs. **1876** C. M. DAVIES *Unorth. Lond.* 289 Conversing with little knots of his paulopost congregation. **1892** STEVENSON *Across Plains* 106 All that I say in this paper is in a paulo-past tense.

paulownia (pɔːˈlɒvnɪə, pɔːˈləunɪə). *Bot.* Also (erron.) **pawlonia.** [mod.L. (P. F. von Siebold & J. G. Zuccarini *Flora Japonica* (1835) I. 25), f. the patronymic of Anna *Paulowna* (1795–1865), daughter of Tsar Paul I and wife of William II of the Netherlands.] A deciduous tree of the genus so called, esp. *P. tomentosa*, belonging to the family Scrophulariaceæ, native to China or Japan, and bearing panicles of bell-shaped blue or lilac flowers. Also *attrib.*
1843 *Paxton's Mag. Bot.* X. 7 *Paulownia imperialis* (Imperial Paulownia)... A considerable quantity of this noble tree has lately been introduced to Britain. **1847** J. MITFORD *Lett. & Rem.* (1891) 206, I prefer them [myrtles] to Victoria Reginas or Pauloneas, or other things with hard names and gigantic leaves. **1883** *Harper's Mag.* Apr. 730/1 This golden Catalpa I purpose cutting down every year.., as is done with the paulownia. **1901** L. H. BAILEY *Cycl. Amer. Hort.* III. 1224/1 The Paulownia is one of the most conspicuous flowering trees in spring. **1971** *Country Life* 1 Apr. 741/1 A potentially large shrub or tree,..like the..tree of heaven (*Ailanthus*) or pawlonia. **1973** C. LLOYD *Foliage Plants* x. 189 A group of paulownia seedlings, grown and pruned for their enormous, furry, heart-shaped leaves. **1976** P. QUENNELL *Marble Foot* v. 182 The local carpenter made me a large knee-desk of silvery pawlonia wood.

Paulsgrave, obs. form of PALSGRAVE.

pault, paulter, etc.: see PALT, PALTER, etc.

paum(e, paumer(e, obs. ff. PALM, PALMER.

paument, obs. form of PAVEMENT.

paun, variant form of PAGNE, a loin-cloth.
1897 MARY KINGSLEY *W. Africa* 223 The native dress for men and women alike is the cloth or paun.

paun, var. PAN *sb.*[5], obs. f. PAWN *sb.* and *v.*

paunage, obs. form of PANNAGE.

†**paunce.** *Obs.* Also 4 **paunz**, 6 **pans, pawnce.** [var. of *panche*, PAUNCH *sb.*[1]: cf. PAUNCER; also, obs. F. *pance* 'the paunch..; also the fashion of a great bellied doublet, or the great bellie of a doublet' (Cotgr.).]

1. = PAUNCER 1.
c **1330** R. BRUNNE *Chron. Wace* (Rolls) 10028 Breche of maille, wyþ paunz non liche. [**1369** *Test. Karleol.* (1893) 92 Item lego..Johanni fratri meo unum par de paunce et de braces et j jac.] **1384–5** *Durham Acc. Rolls* (Surtees) 594 In j pauncs, *vs.* **1411** *E.E. Wills* (1882) 19 An holle brest-plate, a paunce of stele. **1495** *Acc. Ld. High Treas. Scot.* I. 226 Item, iij quarteris of satyne to lyne his pans. **1541** *Ibid.* in Pitcairn *Crim. Trials* I. *317 Twa Pansis of mailȝe.

2. = PAUNCER 2.
a **1500** *Medulla* in *Cath. Angl.* 42 *note*, *Renale*, a breke gyrdyl or a paunce.

3. *Comb.*, as *paunce-cloth.*
1552 in *Surrey Ch. Goods* 16 Item a pawnce cloth of blewe.

paunce, obs. form of PANSY *sb.*

†ˈ**pauncer, ˈpauncher.** *Obs.* In 5 **pancere, panchere, pawnchere, (pawun-), pauntcher, pa(w)ncherde.** [a. OF. *panciere, panchiere* fem. (also *pancier* masc.) = It. *panziera, panciera*, med.L. *pancerea, -eria*; thence also MHG. *panzier* (Ger. *panzer*), MLG. *pantzer, panscher, panser*, MDu. *pantsier*, Du. *pantser*; f. OF. *pance, panche*, now *panse*, It. *pancia* PAUNCH *sb.*[1]]

1. Part of the armour of the 14th and 15th centuries, which covered the lower part of the body.
a **1400–50** *Alexander* 4960 Nymes of ȝour nethirgloue & nakens ȝoure leggis, Pesan, pancere, & platis, all to ȝoure preue clathis. **14..** *Metr. Voc.* in Wr.-Wülcker 629/17 Panchere, *epifemur.*

2. A belt or girdle for the breeches, a breech-belt.
c **1440** *Promp. Parv.* 387/2 Pawnchere,..*lumbare, renale.* *c* **1483** CAXTON *Dialogues* 8/38 Upon the keuerchief Chertes, briches, With the pauntcher. **1483** *Cath. Angl.* 272/1 A Pawncherde (*A.* Pancherde), *renale*, etc.; *vbi* a brekebelt.

paunch (pɔːn(t)ʃ, pɑːn(t)ʃ), *sb.*[1] Forms: 4–6 **panche, paunche**, 4–8 **panch**, (5 **pawnche, pownche**), 6– **paunch.** Also *Sc.* and *north. dial.* 6 **penche, painche**, 8–9 **pench**, 9 **pensch, painch.** [ME. a. ONF. *panche* = OF. *pance*, now *panse* = Pr. *pansa*, Cat. *panxa*, Sp. *panza*, Pg. *pança*, It. *pancia*:—Com. Rom. type **pantica*, f. L. *pantex, pantic-em* paunch, bowels.]

1. The belly, abdomen; the stomach, as the receptacle of food (= BELLY *sb.* 5).
Now, as said of the human subject, usually dyslogistic, and implying prominence, gluttony, etc.
1375 BARBOUR *Bruce* IX. 398 Our lordis of france, that ay With gud morsellis farsis thair panch. **1377** LANGL. *P. Pl.* B. XIII. 87 He shal haue a penaunce in his paunche. **1486** *Bk. St. Albans* E iij b, All thyng with in the wombe saue onli the gall The paunche also. **1548** LATIMER *Ploughers* (Arb.) 26 So troubeled wyth Lordelye lyuynge..pamperynge of theyr panches. **1583** *Leg. Bp. St. Androis* Pref. 124 Packand thair penche lyk Epicurians. **1668** CULPEPPER & COLE *Barthol. Anat.* Introd., The lowest belly, commonly called Abdomen or the Paunch. **1777** G. FORSTER *Voy. round World* II. 68 He ..had a most portly paunch. **1871** R. ELLIS *Catullus* xxxix. 11 A frugal Umbrian body, Tuscan huge of paunch. **1871** B. TAYLOR *Faust* (1875) I. xxii. 196 Spider's foot and paunch of toad.
fig. **1582** STANYHURST *Æneis* III. (Arb.) 84 Deadlye Charybdis..In to gut vpsouping three tymes thee flash water angrye, From paunch alsoe spuing toe the sky the plash hastlye receaued. **1596** NASHE *Saffron-Walden* Wks. (Grosart) III. 163 Throughout the whole pawnch of his booke, hee is as infinite in commending her. **1602** MARSTON *Ant. & Mel.* I. Wks. 1856 I. 17 Straight chops a wave, and in his sliftred panch Downe fals our ship.

2. The first and largest stomach of a ruminant; the rumen.
c **1420** *Pallad. on Husb.* I. 955 A rammes paunche. **1596** DALRYMPLE tr. *Leslie's Hist. Scot.* I. 94 In place of potis and sik seithing vesselis, the painches of ane ox or ane kow thay vset. **1715** CHEYNE *Philos. Princ. Relig.* I. (1716) 360 As in Beasts, the Panch, the Read, and the Feck. **1836–9** TODD *Cycl. Anat.* II. 11/1 The..food..is received into the first stomach..which is termed the..paunch.

b. *pl.* Entrails, viscera. (Now *Sc.* and *north.*)
a **1548** HALL *Chron., Hen. VIII* 172 b, The kyng in huntyng tyme hath slain iii. C. dere, and the garbage and paunches bee cast round about in euery quarter of the Parke. **1789** DAVIDSON *Seasons, Spring* 3 Himself wi' penches staw'd, he [an eagle] dights his neb.

c. esp. as used for food; tripe.
c **1430** *Two Cookery-bks.* 7 Trype de Motoun.—Take þe pownche of a chepe. **1500–20** DUNBAR *Poems* lxxxii. 25 Panches, pudingis of Jok and Jame. **1665** LD. FOUNTAINHALL *Jrnl.* (1900) 79 We have eaten panches heir. **1724** RAMSAY *Tea-t. Misc.* (1733) I. 91 Well scraped paunches. **1825** BROCKETT *N.C. Gloss.*, *Painches*, tripe. **1827** LYTTON *Pelham* lxiii, I would sooner feed my poodle on paunch and liver.

3. *Comb.*: †**paunch-bellied** *a.*, big-bellied, pot-bellied; †**paunch-clout**, the membrane enveloping the bowels, the omentum; †**paunch-gut** *sb.*, a big belly, a pot-belly; *a.* = *paunch-bellied* (also †**paunch-gutted** *a.*); **paunch-kettle**, the paunch of an animal used like a kettle to boil flesh in; †**paunch-porer** (tr. L. *extispex*), an augur who divined by inspecting the entrails of animals; so †**paunch-poring**; †**paunch-pot**, ? a pot of a bulging shape; **paunch-swollen** *a.*, having a swollen paunch; **paunch-wrapt** *a.*, wrapped in the paunch (in quot., *in utero*).
c **1672** *Roxb. Ball.* (1888) VI. 500 A *paunch-belly'd Hostiss. **1733** MORTIMER in *Phil. Trans.* XXXVIII. 179 She [female beaver] was very thick, paunch-bellied. *c* **1440** *Promp. Parv.* 387/1 *Pawncheclowt, or trype. **14..** *Voc.* in Wr.-Wülcker 599/2 *Omentum*, *an*[ce] a pauncheclout. **1683** KENNETT tr. *Erasm. on Folly* 17 O swinish *paunch-gut God (say they). **1742** JARVIS *Quix.* II. III. xi. (1749) 247 All that paunch-gut and little carcase of thine. **1726** ARBUTHNOT *Diss. Dumpling* (ed. 5) 6 These *Paunch-gutted Fellows. **1865** TYLOR *Early Hist. Man.* ix. 268 The Asiatic *paunch-kettles. **1656** W. D. tr. *Comenius' Gate Lat. Unl.* §599. 183 Their *Extispicium*, or *panch-poring, where the extispex, or *panch-porer, did it by viewing the entrails of the sacrifices. **1600** *Will of Sir R. Bedingfield* (Somerset Ho.), [The] parcell guilt *paunche pot given at her Christening. **1638–48** G. DANIEL *Eclog* iii. 156 Till *panch-swolne Bromius sleeps. *a* **1592** MARLOWE *Ovid's Eleg.* II. xiv, She that her *paunch-wrapt child hath slain.

Hence ˈ**paunchful**, bellyful.
1824 *New Monthly Mag.* X. 507 Four times can an active fellow Eat his paunchful in a day.

paunch, panch (pɔːn(t)ʃ, pɑːn(t)ʃ), *sb.*[2] *Naut.* Also 8 **pantch.** [app. the same word as prec., and PAUNCE *sb.*; in sense prob. derived from the latter.] **a.** A thick strong mat, made of interlaced spun yarn or strands of rope, employed in various places on a ship to prevent chafing. **b.** A wooden covering or shield on the fore side of a mast (*rubbing paunch*), to preserve it from chafing when the masts or spars are lowered or raised.
1626 CAPT. SMITH *Accid. Yng. Seamen* 15 Paunches, and such like. **1627** —— *Seaman's Gram.* v. 25 That which we call a Panch, are broad clouts, wouen of Thrums and Sinnet together, to saue things from galling about the maine and fore yards at the ties, and also from the masts [etc.]. **1794** *Rigging & Seamanship* I. 13 The front-fish, or paunch, is a long plank of fir, hollowed to the convexity of the mast, and fastened on the foreside of the mast over the iron hoops. **1848** G. BIDDLECOMBE *Art Rigging* 23 *Panch*, a covering of wood, or thick texture made of plaited ropeyarn, larger than a mat, to preserve the masts, &c., from chafing. **1882** NARES *Seamanship* (ed. 6) 9 *Rubbing paunch*, a batten up and down the forepart of a lower mast, to keep the lower yards clear of the hoops when going up or down.

c. *Comb.*, as *paunch-mat, paunch-piece* (= b).
c **1860** H. STUART *Seaman's Catech.* 16 Bowsprit, paunch piece, or gammoning fish. *Ibid.* 31 Describe a paunch mat and its use. **1867** SMYTH *Sailor's Word-bk.*, *Paunch-mat*, a thick and strong mat formed by interweaving sinnet or strands of rope as close as possible; it is fastened on the outside of the yards or rigging, to prevent their chafing.

paunch (pɔːn(t)ʃ, pɑːn(t)ʃ), *v.*[1] Now *rare* or *dial.*, exc. in 2. Also 6–7 **panch(e.** [app. f. PAUNCH *sb.*[1] Palsgr. translates the English verb by a F. *pancer* which is not otherwise known;

but Florio has It. *panciare* 'to paunch or vnbowell'.]

1. *trans.* To stab or wound in the paunch; also *loosely*, to stab.

1530 PALSGR. 652/1, I panche a man or a beest, I perysshe his guttes with a weapen, *je pance.* *a* **1548** HALL *Chron., Hen. V* 50b, Other had..their bellies paunched. **1610** SHAKS. *Temp.* III. ii. 98 Batter his skull, or paunch him with a stake. **1699** GARTH *Dispens.* v. (1706) 91 One Pass had paunch'd the huge hydropick Knight. **1819** KEATS *K. Stephen* I. ii. 42 He flung The heft away..It paunch'd the Earl of Chester's horse. **1848** [see PAUNCHING below].

2. To cut open the paunch of (an animal) and take out the viscera; to disembowel, eviscerate.

1570 LEVINS *Manip.* 22/35 To Panche, *euiscerare.* **1598** FLORIO, *Viscerare*, to panche, or pull out the bowels. **1677** N. COX *Gentl. Recreat.* 80 Then he is to pounch [*ed.* 1721 paunch] him, rewarding the Hounds therewith. **1769** MRS. RAFFALD *Eng. Housekpr.* (1778) 135 When you have paunched and cased your hare. **1884** R. JEFFERIES *Red Deer* v. 99 When a stag is killed and paunched. **1906** *Chambers's Jrnl.* Sept. 681/2 The animals [*sc.* rabbits] have to be killed, bled, and paunched. **1952** F. WHITE *Good Eng. Food* II. 111 One of the things I had to do before I was twenty was to paunch and skin a hare.

†**3.** To stuff the stomach with food; to fill the belly, to glut. (Also *intr.* for *refl.*) *Obs.*

1542 UDALL *Erasm. Apoph.* II. 344b, Now ye see hym ful paunched, as lyons are... And in deede the lyons are more gentle when their bealyes are well filled. **1597–8** BP. HALL *Sat.* II. ii. 62 Rather..pale with learned cares, Than paunched with thy choyce of changed fares. **1612** tr. *Benvenuto's Passenger* I. 139 If you did but see him..in what sort he vseth to glut and panch himselfe. **1635** QUARLES *Embl.* I. ii. (1718) 10 Now glutt'ny paunches.

4. To swallow hastily or greedily. *rare.*

1599 NASHE *Lenten Stuffe* Wks. (Grosart) V. 279 The Fisherman..pauncht him vp at a mouthfull. **1892** *San Francisco Examiner* 28 Aug., Paunching blobs and dollops of fat.

Hence **'paunching** *vbl. sb.*

1591 PERCIVALL *Sp. Dict.*, *Desolladura*, paunching, *Euisceratio.* **1848** CHAMBERS *Inform. for People* I. 599/1 When..the [cow's] stomach [is] so much distended with the air, that there is danger of immediate suffocation or bursting—in these instances the puncture of the maw must be instantly performed, which is called paunching. **1892** *Pall Mall G.* 24 Mar. 2/1 The least pleasant part of the luncheon hour is the paunching of the birds..which is often a disgusting evidence of the slaughter.

†**paunch**, *v.*[2] *Obs. rare.* [a. F. *pancher*, obs. form (16–17th c. in Littré and Cotgr.) of *pencher* to incline.] *intr.* To incline, lean, have a *penchant*, physically or mentally.

1577 *F. de L'isle's Leg.* G iv, They determined a while to let her paunch some times one way, and some times another, curiously watching to what ende her behauiours would come. **1595** HUBBOCKE *Apol. Infants Unbapt.* 14 The ground and foundation is weeake: their building also vpon it, pauncheth.

paunched (pɔːn(t)ʃt, pɑːn(t)ʃt), *a.* [f. PAUNCH *sb.* + -ED[2].] Having a large paunch; big-bellied, paunchy. Also in *comb.*, as ***full-paunched***.

1649 G. DANIEL *Trinarch., Hen. V*, lix, These..full-paunch't Boetians, Contemne all Bodies bred in purer Ayre, As Atticke leanness. **1805** *Spirit Pub. Jrnls.* IX. 251 The band of paunch'd Helluos.

pauncher, variant of PAUNCER *Obs.*

paunchway, variant of PANCHWAY.

paunchy ('pɔːn(t)ʃɪ, 'pɑːn(t)ʃɪ), *a.* [f. PAUNCH *sb.* + -Y.] Having a large paunch; big-bellied.

1598 FLORIO, *Ventroso*, panchie, that hath a great belly. **1821** *Blackw. Mag.* X. 99 The mayors and sheriffs, in paunchy order,..will go down. **1861** *Jrnl. Roy. Agric. Soc.* XXII. I. 141 Calves which are in the habit of drinking too fast are..detected by a glance at their 'paunchy' condition.

Hence **'paunchiness**.

1879 *Scribner's Mag.* Dec. 178 All had grown..rivals in pious paunchiness.

paund, obs. f. PAWN *sb.*[2]; obs. pa. pple. PAWN *v.*

paune, obs. form of PAWN.

†**pauned**, obs. form of PANED.

a **1548** HALL *Chron., Hen. VIII* 69 Long and large garmentes of Blewe satten pauned with Sipres.

paunflet, obs. f. PAMPHLET.

paunse, -sie, paunt, obs. ff. PANSY *sb.*, PANT.

pauoise, -oyse, obs. forms of PAVIS.

pauper ('pɔːpə(r)), *sb.* [a. L. *pauper* poor: its English use originated in the legal phrase *in formâ pauperis*, in the form or character of a poor man or woman: see sense 1.]

1. A poor person.

a. In *Law*: One allowed, on account of poverty, to sue or defend in a court of law without paying costs (*in formâ pauperis*: see ‖IN 4): cf. also DISPAUPER.

[**1495** *Act 11 Hen. VII*, c. 12 (*heading*) An Acte to admytt such persons as are poore to sue in formâ pauperis.] **1631** *Star Chamb. Cases* (Camden) 73 My Lord Keeper pronounced this order, that the plaintiff should continue pauper. **1641** *Spiritual Courts Epit.* in *Harl. Misc.* (Malh.) IV. 420 *Busy-body.* Many of them were *in formâ pauperis.* *Scrapeall*... I had rather the judge would have given sentence against my client, than bestowed a *pauper* on me. *a* **1680** BUTLER *Rem.* (1759) I. 252 No Court allows..two single Paupers, T'encounter Hand to Hand at Bars, and trounce Each other Gratis in a Suit at once. **1768** BLACKSTONE *Comm.* III. xxiv. 400 Paupers, that is, such as will swear themselves not worth five pounds, are by statute 11 Henry VII. c. 12. to have original writs and subpœnas gratis, and counsel and attorney assigned them without fee. *Ibid.*, It seems how-ever agreed, that a pauper may recover costs, though he pays none; for the counsel and clerks are bound to give their labour to him, but not to his antagonist.

b. In general sense: A person destitute of property or means of livelihood; one who has no means, or who is dependent on the charity of others; a beggar. (Now associated with c.)

[**1493** H. PARKER (*title*) Diues and Pauper.] **1516** in *10th Rep. Hist. MSS. Comm.* App. v. 396 No lazer nor infecte paupers or poore shall come..within the town. **1812** CRABBE *Tales in Verse* xvii. *Resentment* 274 And he, a wand'ring pauper, wanting bread. **1822** SCOTT *Nigel* iv, He classes me with the paupers and mendicants from Scotland, who disgrace his court in the eyes of the proud English—that is all. **1880** MISS BRADDON *Barbara* xlvi. 315 You would have found me a disgraced man,..a pauper without a chance of fortune. **1893** in *Daily Paper* (Stead) 4 Oct. 11 We [the British Aristocracy] are, many of us little better than splendid paupers. **1894** W. T. STEAD (*title*) The Splendid Paupers: a Tale of the coming Plutocracy.

c. *spec.* A person in receipt of poor-law relief.

1775 T. MENDHAM (*title*) A Dialogue, in two Conversations, between a Gentleman, a Pauper, and his Friend; intended as an Answer to a Pamphlet published by the Rev. Mr. Potter, entitled, Observations on the Poor Laws. **1788** W. MASON (*title*) Animadversions on the present Government of the York Lunatic Asylum; in which the case of Parish Paupers is distinctly considered. **1800** SOUTHEY *Eng. Ecl.*, *Wedding* 110 A parish shell at last, and the little bell Toll'd hastily for a pauper's funeral! **1841** T. NOEL *Rymes & Roundelayes*, *Pauper's Drive*, Rattle his bones over the stones; He's only a Pauper, whom nobody owns! **1856** EMERSON *Eng. Traits*, *Ability*, The pauper lives better than the free labourer; the thief better than the pauper.

2. *attrib.* and *Comb.* **a.** *attrib.* (in apposition) or as *adj.* That is a pauper: destitute.

1809 *Med. Jrnl.* XXI. 185 To have pauper patients committed to him. **1833** HT. MARTINEAU *Berkeley the Banker* I. i. 10 Our pauper-labourers have taken his work from him. **1846** J. BAXTER *Libr. Pract. Agric.* (ed. 4) I. 11 The favourers of emigration ought to begin by educating pauper children for that purpose. **1869** LD. LYTTON *Orval* 34 A pauper prince Paid from the plunder of a pauper people.

b. *attrib.* Of, belonging or relating to, or intended for a pauper or paupers, as ***pauper-asylum***, ***-coffin***, ***-grave***, ***-list***, ***-palace***, ***-rate***, ***-system***; also in objective and instrumental comb., as ***pauper-breeding***, ***-making***, ***pauper-fed*** adjs.

1823 COBBETT *Rur. Rides* (1885) I. 305 Here has been the pauper-making work! **1834** HT. MARTINEAU in *Tait's Mag.* I. 209/1 The result of introducing a legal pauper-system into Ireland. **1837** —— *Soc. Amer.* III. 190, I was grieved to see the magnificent pauper asylum near Philadelphia, made to accommodate luxuriously 1200 persons. **1845** J. E. CARPENTER *Poems & Lyrics* 97 Poor-law minions, pauper-fed. **1854** WHYTE MELVILLE *Gen. Bounce* xix, Her child is in that pauper-coffin which she is following to the grave.

Hence **'pauper** *v. trans.* = PAUPERIZE; **'pauperage** = *pauperdom*; **'pauperate** *v. trans.* = PAUPERIZE; **'pauperdom**, (*a*) the condition of a pauper, destitution; (*b*) the realm of paupers, paupers collectively; **'pauperess**, a female pauper.

1879 TENNYSON *Falcon* I. i, Why then, my lord, we are *pauper'd out and out. *a* **1847** in Medwin *Shelley* I. 301 Those who had just risen above *pauperage. **1850** LD. OSBORNE *Gleanings* 76 This seething mass of female pauperage. **1866** LOWELL *Lett.* (1894) I. 404 We would not rob you [England] of a single one of your valuable institutions—state-church, peerage, and pauperage. **1839** J. ROGERS *Antipopopr.* XIV. ii. 306 It has *pauperated many a lawful heir. **1870** *Contemp. Rev.* XIV. 491 Its duties towards *pauperdom and those on the verge of pauperdom. **1882** *Leisure Hour* July 424/2 The rules under which their pauperdom places them. **1860** DICKENS *Uncomm. Trav.* iii, The wards-woman; an elderly, able-bodied *pauperess.

pauperism ('pɔːpərɪz(ə)m). [f. PAUPER *sb.* + -ISM. Hence mod.F. *paupérisme* (Dict. Acad. 1878), mod.Ger. *pauperismus.*] The condition of paupers; the existence of a pauper class; poverty, with dependence on public relief, as an established condition or fact among a people. Hence *concr.* the pauper class, paupers collectively.

1815 W. CLARKSON (*title*) An Inquiry into the Cause of the Increase of Pauperism and Poor's Rates. **1818** in TODD. **1825** COBBETT *Rur. Rides* 273 Be astonished, if you can, at the pauperism and the crimes that disgrace this once happy and moral England. **1827** WHATELY *Logic* (1837) 229 An increase of pauperism, i.e. of the habit of depending on parish-pay. **1857** TOULMIN SMITH *Parish* 145 Thenceforth 'pauperism' became a caste in England. **1876** FAWCETT *Pol. Econ.* II. viii. 232 Pauperism is still one of the most formidable social and economic difficulties.

pauperization (ˌpɔːpəraɪ'zeɪʃən). [f. next + -ATION.] The action of pauperizing or condition of being pauperized.

1838 W. HOWITT *Rural Life Eng.* II. III. ii. 149 The working classes..what distress, what pauperization..they have gone through. **1849** BRIGHT *Sp., Ireland* 2 Apr. (1876) 174 Demoralisation and pauperisation will go on in an extending circle. **1874** GREEN *Short Hist.* x. §4. 805 The pauperization of families who relied on them for support. **1955** *Times* 6 July 10/3 The recent C.G.T. congress..insisted that revolutionary action was the only remedy to the 'progressive pauperization' of the working class under capitalism. **1971** J. J. SHAPIRO tr. *Habermas's Toward Rational Society* vi. 110 Underprivileged groups are not social classes... Their *disfranchisement* and pauperization no longer coincide with *exploitation.* **1974** J. WHITE tr. *Poulantzas's Fascism & Dictatorship* v. iii. 259 In this process of pauperization, artisans and traders lost almost half their income.

pauperize ('pɔːpəraɪz), *v.* [f. PAUPER + -IZE.] *trans.* To make a pauper of; to reduce to the condition of a pauper, or to poverty or destitution; *esp.* to make dependent on public relief.

1834 HT. MARTINEAU *Moral* II. 47 The indigent who have been pauperized by the undue depression of wages. **1867** SMILES *Huguenots Eng.* vi. (1880) 99 Though they were poor, they were not pauperised, but thrifty and self-helping. **1902** A. M. FAIRBAIRN *Philos. Chr. Relig.* I. iv. 141 There is nothing so fatal to the manhood of a people as the charity that pauperizes.

Hence **'pauperized**, **'pauperizing** *ppl. adjs.*; also **'pauperizer**, one who pauperizes.

1834 HT. MARTINEAU *Moral* II. 75 The dreary haunts of our pauperized classes. **1844** TUPPER *Heart* i. 9 When did heart ever gain money?—bah! heart indeed—pauperizing bit of muscle! **1883** V. STUART *Egypt* 60 Arabi drove out these pauperizers of the people. **1886** in J. F. Maurice *Lett. Donegal* 4 Pauperising charity..produces the ordinary fruits which all the best friends of the poor have..preached that it does... The people become regular acting beggars.

†**'pauperous**, *a. Obs. rare*[−1]. [f. PAUPER + -OUS.] Relating to or connected with the poor.

1621 S. WARD *Happ. of Practice* (1627) 47 Haue a stocke imployed in Gods Bankes, to pauperous and pious vses.

‖**paupiettes** (popjɛt), *sb. pl.* Also in *sing.* [Fr.] The current form of POUPIETS. (See quots.)

1889 A. FILIPPINI *Table* 241 Panpiette [*sic*] of Veal à la Faubonne. **1892** A. B. MARSHALL *Larger Cookery Bk.* iv. 86 Eel paupiettes à la Française. **1906** *Mrs. Beeton's Bk. Househ. Managem.* lxii. 1666 *Paupiettes* (Fr.), slices of meat or fish rolled with forcemeat. **1936** LUCAS & HUME *Au Petit Cordon Bleu* 174 *Paupiette*, a thin slice of meat or..fish, sometimes spread with a farce, then rolled up and tied with white cotton. **1948** *Good Housek. Cookery Bk.* II. 141 Glazed paupiettes of sole. **1970** SIMON & HOWE *Dict. Gastron.* 291/2 *Paupiettes*, thinly sliced pieces of meat used as wrappers for various meat or forcemeat fillings. Also, in Escoffier's usage, fillets of sole and cabbage leaves used in the same way. The meat slices are spread with a well-spiced forcemeat and rolled up. Wrapped up in thin slices of fat bacon, they are tied up with cotton thread to be braised, baked or casseroled. Bacon and thread are removed before serving. **1975** J. SYMONS *Three Pipe Problem* xvi. 159 The soup was followed by what Sue called paupiettes de porc, pancakes with some sort of minced pork filling. **1976** *Evening Advertiser* (Swindon) 31 Dec. 13/1 (Advt.), Scottish restaurant menu at £7.00 inclusive with..Paupiette of Plaice 'Auchen-shuggle'.

paupire, obs. form of PAPER.

paurometabolous (ˌpɔːrəʊmɪ'tæbələs), *a. Entom.* [f. Gr. παῦρο-ς little, small + METABOLOUS.] Having, or of the nature of, slight or imperfect metamorphosis, as in orthopterous insects.

1895 *Cambr. Nat. Hist.* V. 199 The changes of form [in the *Orthoptera*] are much less abrupt and conspicuous than they are in most other Insects. The metamorphosis is therefore called Paurometabolous.

pauropod ('pɔːrəpɒd). *Zool.* [Anglicized sing. of mod.L. *Pauropoda*, f. Gr. παῦρο-ς little, small + -ποδος footed, f. πούς, ποδ- foot.] A myriapod of the order *Pauropoda*, resembling centipedes, but of very minute size.

1897 *Amer. Nat.* XXXI. 71 It may be added that the pauropods can climb, though scarcely as well as *Polyxenus.*

†**'pausably**, *adv. Obs. rare*[−1]. [f. **pausable* (f. PAUSE *v.* + -ABLE in a vague use) + -LY[2].] In the way of pausing or dwelling upon something; deliberately, without haste; pausefully.

a **1632** G. HERBERT *Country Parson* vi. (1830) 13 Answers [in church]..are to be done not in a hudling or slubbering fashion,..but gently and pausably, thinking what they say.

pausal ('pɔːzəl), *a.* (*sb.*) [f. L. *pausa* PAUSE *sb.* + -AL[1]: cf. *causal.*] Of or pertaining to a pause or the pause in a sentence; in *Heb. Gram.* applied to the form which a word receives in the pause, in which, in certain cases, a vowel is changed (usually lengthened), or a weakened vowel reappears in full.

1877 C. T. BALL *Merch. Taylors' Heb. Gram.* 76 In the pausal forms an original vowel, shortened to *shᵉwa* out of pause, is preserved. **1882–3** SCHAFF *Encycl. Relig. Knowl.* II. 928/1 [*ḥadrāḵ*], probably the Pausal of [*ḥadrāḵ*].

†**pau'sation**. *Obs.* [ad. late L. *pausātiōn-em* (St. Jerome, in sense 'death'), n. of action from *pausāre* to PAUSE.] The action of pausing; a pause, intermission.

14.. LYDG. *Ball. commend. Our Lady* 61 To wery wandred tent and pavilioun, The feynte to fresshe, and the pausacioun. *c* **1460** *Play Sacram.* 603 Haue do faste and mak no pausacyon. *c* **1485** *Digby Myst.* v. 463 Ther make a pawsacion.

pause (pɔːz), *sb.* Also 5–7 **pawse**, 6 **paws.** [a. F. *pause* (14th c. in Hatz.-Darm.), ad. L. *pausa* halt, stop, f. Gr. παῦσις, f. παύ-ειν to cease, stop; in the musical sense, immed. ad. It. *pausa.*]

1. a. An act of stopping or ceasing for a short time in a course of action, esp. in speaking; a short interval of inaction or silence; an intermission; sometimes *spec.* an intermission arising from doubt or uncertainty, a hesitation.

c **1440** *Promp. Parv.* 387/2 Pawse, of stynty(n)ge, or à-bydy(n)ge, *pausacio, pausa.* **1513** Douglas *Æneis* I. xi. 57 Eftir the first paws, and that cours neir gane, .. The goblettis greit with mychty wynis .. Thai fillit. **1528** Gardiner in Pocock *Rec. Ref.* I. l. 96 At this point, His holiness making a pause, I .. said [etc.]. **1595** Shaks. *John* IV. ii. 231 Had'st thou but shooke thy head, or made a pause When I spake darkely. **1697** Dryden *Æneid* IV. 627 A Pause in Grief; an interval from Woe. **1709** Steele *Tatler* No. 94 ⁋5 It cures or supplies all Pauses and Hesitations in Speech. **1847** Tennyson *Princ.* Prol. 238 Like linnets in the pauses of the wind. **1863** Geo. Eliot *Romola* xxiv, There was a pause before the preacher spoke again.

b. (Without article.) Intermission, delay, waiting, hesitation, suspense.

1593 Shaks. *Lucr.* 277 Sad pause and deep regard beseem the sage. **1606** —— *Tr. & Cr.* IV. iv. 37 Iniurie of chance Puts backe leaue-taking, iustles roughly by All time of pause. **1683–4** Wood *Life* 14 Feb. (O.H.S.) III. 89 He told me after a great deal of paus and shifting, that [etc.]. **1899** *Westm. Gaz.* 3 Aug. 2/1 Here speech is the one thing needful—pause the one thing damned.

c. Phr. ***to give pause to, to put to a pause***: to cause to stop or hesitate; to check the progress or course of; to 'pull up'. ***in*** or ***at pause*** († ***under a pause***): pausing, not proceeding, temporarily inactive or motionless; hesitating, in suspense.

1602 Shaks. *Ham.* III. i. 68 For in that sleepe of death, what dreames may come, .. Must giue vs pawse. *Ibid.* iii. 42, I stand in pause where I shall first begin. **1709** Steele *Tatler* No. 8 ⁋7 The Air was hushed, the Multitude attentive, and all Nature in a Pause. **1715** Jane Barker *Exilius* II. 84, I was under a little Pause, not knowing readily what to reply. **1719** De Foe *Crusoe* I. xii, These considerations .. put me to a pause. **1792** S. Rogers *Pleas. Mem.* I. 102 When the slow dial gave a pause to care. **1863** Cowden Clarke *Shaks. Char.* x. 271 One of those profound reflections that give one pause in studying these fine pictures of human nature. **1866** Ruskin *Crown Wild Olive* (1873) 154 You stand there at pause, and silent.

d. (See quot. 1966.) Also *fig.*

1962 *Listener* 29 Mar. 549/2 The point is clearly made by General Norstad, who says .. that what he needs in order to impose what he calls the pause, in order to identify a threat, in order to relieve himself of the intolerable choice between retreating and using nuclear weapons, is thirty divisions. *Ibid.* 19 Apr. 674/1 The time has come to declare a 'pause' on the culture-front. **1966** Schwarz & Hadik *Strategic Terminol.* 85 *Pause*, in the defense of Western Europe, a moment of reflection imposed on any aggressor before the defense resorts to nuclear weapons.

2. a. *spec.* One of the intermissions, stops, or breaks made, according to the sense, in speaking or reading; in *Prosody*, such a break occurring according to rule at a particular point in a verse, a cæsura; also, a break of definite length in a verse, occupying the time of a syllable or number of syllables. Also *transf.* in a piece of music.

c **1440** *Promp. Parv.* 387/2 Pawse, yn redynge of bokys, *periodus.* **1589** Puttenham *Eng. Poesie* II. v. (Arb.) 87–8 Three maner of pauses... The shortest pause or intermission they called *comma*... The second they called *colon*... The third they called *periodus*, for a complement or full pause. *Ibid.* 88 In a verse of seauen [sillables the Cesure ought to fall] either vpon the fourth or none at all, the meeter very ill brooking any pause. *a* **1704** Locke (J.), Those partitions and pauses which men, educated in the schools, observe. **1751** Johnson *Rambler* No. 90 ⁋2 The variety .. of the pauses with which he has diversified his numbers. **1795** Mason *Ch. Mus.* i. 16 Where Rhythm, Pause, and Accent are peculiarly attended to by the Composer. **1819** Shelley *Prometh. Unb.* II. i. 143 As you speak, your words Fill, pause by pause, my own forgotten sleep With shapes. **1824** L. Murray *Eng. Gram.* (ed. 5) I. IV. i. 364 Pauses or rests, in speaking and reading, are a total cessation of the voice during a perceptible .. space of time. **1957** B. Deutsch *Poetry Handbk.* (1958) 35 The pause in the last foot of the second line is made more emphatic because the words conclude the line and the poem as well.

b. *spec.* in *Linguistics.* The break marking juncture, sometimes regarded as having phonemic status.

1933 L. Bloomfield *Language* xii. 185 Since the constituents of phrases are free forms, the speaker may separate them by means of *pauses.* Pauses are mostly non-distinctive; they occur chiefly when the constituents are long phrases; in English they are usually preceded by a pause-pitch. **1948** *Language* XXIV. 19 Some utterances contain a perceptible time-interval during which none of the vocal organs perceptibly articulates... Such a time-interval is an *internal pause*... The absence of speech before or after an utterance is an *external pause.* **1950** *Ibid.* XXVI. 97 Pause may be regarded as a kind of zero phone, characterized by a complete lack of qualities. **1951** *Ibid.* XXVII. 520 An interrupted sequence is considered to include the phoneme of *pause.* **1952** W. P. Lehmann *Proto-Indo-European Phonol.* ii. 10 Choice of positional variant in PIE was determined by preceding and following phoneme, group of phonemes, or pause. **1968** J. Lyons *Introd. Theoret. Linguistics* v. 200 The native speaker is able to actualize the 'potential pauses' in his utterances when he wishes to, even though he does not do this normally. **1972** M. L. Samuels *Linguistic Evol.* ii. 13 Unvoicing of final consonants (i.e. voicing is not maintained till the end of the word, especially before a pause).

3. *Mus.* †**a.** A character denoting an interval of silence; a rest. *Obs.*

1597 Morley *Introd. Mus.* 9 *Phi.* What strokes be these? *Ma.* These be called rests or pauses. **1674** Playford *Skill Mus.* I. viii. 26 Pauses or Rests are silent Characters, or an artificial omission of the Voyce or Sound, proportioned to a certain Measure of Time.

b. The character 𝄐 or 𝄑 placed over or under a note or rest to indicate that its duration is to be lengthened indefinitely. (Also placed over a double bar at the conclusion of a piece, and rarely over a single bar in the course of it to indicate a short but indefinite interval of silence.)

1806 Callcott *Mus. Gram.* vi. 73 The Pause is placed over a Note to signify that the regular time of the Movement is to be delayed. **1880** in Grove *Dict. Mus.* II. 676/1 Pauses at the end of a movement, over a rest, or even over a silent bar, are intended to give a short breathing-space before going on to the next movement.

4. *Heb. Gram.* In the expressions ***in pause*** (orig. in sense 2), ***into pause***: the form that a word or vowel takes before one of the chief stops: cf. pausal.

1874 A. B. Davidson *Introd. Heb. Gram.* (1880) 27 In general only the two greatest Prose accents (viz. *Silluq*, marking the end, and *'Athnak*, marking the middle of the verse) .. throw vowels into pause. **1877** [see pausal].

5. *Comb.* ***pause-filler, -linking, -marker, -making, -pattern, rhythm, -substitute; pause-marking*** vbl. sb.; ***pause-giving*** ppl. adj.; **pause-pitch**, the pitch pattern which characteristically precedes a pause in utterance.

1967 A. Laski *Seven Other Years* i. 13 It sounded like the kind of remark which is made as a pause-filler. **1887** A. Seth *Hegelianism* ii. 74 [T. H.] Green .. constantly assumes a stream of sensations as the material upon which the pause-giving and rationally constitutive activity of thought is exercised. **1963** *Economist* 9 Nov. 577/1 Papers with .. pause-giving titles. **1970** *Canad. Jrnl. Linguistics* XV. 112 Thus, if the pause-linking rule was solely phonological we would have no way of determining whether or not it applies to these phrases. **1956** *Kenyon Rev.* XVIII. 433 The lesser pause-markers: comma, colon and semi-colon. **1880** Masson *Life Milton* VI. 517 The pointing is a mere empirical compromise, for the reader's convenience, between pause-marking and clause-marking. **1965** *Times Lit. Suppl.* 25 Nov. 1070/3 New sentence-shapes, new pause-patterns. **1933** L. Bloomfield *Language* vii. 115 We must recognize *pause-pitch* or *suspension-pitch* [,], which consists of a rise of pitch before a pause within a sentence. It is used .. to show that the sentence is not ending at a point where otherwise the phrasal form would make the end of a sentence possible: *I was waiting there* [,] *when in came the man.* **1902** E. W. Scripture *Elem. Exper. Phonetics* xxxvi. 517 A tone may be sounded for a definite time at definite intervals. The result is a 'rhythm of sound and pause,' or .. a 'pause rhythm'. **1964** J. L. M. Trim in D. Abercrombie et al. *Daniel Jones* 375 Major tone-groups .. are followed by a pause, or pause-substitute.

pause (pɔːz), *v.*[1] Also 6–7 **pawse.** [f. pause *sb.*, or ad. L. *pausāre* to halt, cease, or F. *pauser* (15th c. in Hatz.-Darm.), both derived from the sb.

L. *pausāre*, as a living word, became in It. *posare*, F. *poser*, whence pose, q.v.]

1. a. *intr.* To make a pause; to cease or intermit action (esp. movement or speech) for a short interval; to stop (temporarily), to wait; to stop for the purpose of deliberation, or on account of doubt or uncertainty; to hesitate, hold back.

1526 *Pilgr. Perf.* (W. de W. 1531) 158 b, In the psalmody .. Begin al at ones, & ende all at ones, pause all togyder. **1560** Daus tr. *Sleidane's Comm.* 289 b, After he had paused and taken deliberation. **1596** Shaks. *Merch. V.* IV. i. 335 Why doth the Iew pause? take thy forfeiture. **1601** —— *Jul. C.* III. ii. 36 If any, speake .. I pause for a Reply. *c* **1655** Milton *Sonn. to Cyriack Skinner*, Let Euclid rest and Archimedes pause. **1667** —— *P.L.* v. 64 This said he paus'd not, but with ventrous Arme He pluckt, he tasted. **1781** Cowper *Expostulation* 605 If Business .. Can pause one hour to read a serious rhyme. **1815** Shelley *Alastor* 347 The little boat .. Now pausing on the edge of the riven wave. **1847** Tennyson *Princ.* III. 140 Decide not ere you pause. **1860** Tyndall *Glac.* I. xviii. 124 We paused upon the summit to look upon the scene.

†**b.** *refl.* in same sense. *Obs. rare*⁻¹.

[Cf. F. *il se pausoit* (15th c. in Hatz.-Darm.).]

1597 Shaks. *2 Hen. IV*, IV. iv. 9 Wee .. pawse vs, till these Rebels .. Come vnderneath the yoake of Gouernment.

2. a. To stop for a time over some particular word or thing; to dwell, rest, linger *upon.*

1530 Palsgr. Introd. 21 There is no worde of one syllable .. that they use to pause upon. **1596** Shaks. *1 Hen. IV*, v. v. 15 Other Offenders we will pause vpon. **1646** Crashaw *Delights of Muses* 88 Trips From this to that, then .. pauses there. **1863** Mrs. Oliphant *Salem Ch.* xvii. 304 The eyes .. paused at him for a moment. *Mod.* He paused upon the word. The singer paused upon the closing note.

†**b.** To stay, remain, or continue temporarily in some place or state; to stop; to rest. *Obs.*

1568 Grafton *Chron.* II. 881 There they commoned and paused that night. **1571** Campion *Hist. Irel.* xv. (1633) 52 While the Princes and Potentates pawsed in this good mood.

3. *trans.* To cause to stop temporarily.

a **1542** Wyatt *Coll. Poems* (1969) 104 Sorowfull david .. y[t] .. pausid his plaint and layd adown his harp. **1908** A. S. M. Hutchinson *Once aboard Lugger* II. ii. 101 The strain on his invention paused him.

pause (pɔːz), *v.*[2] *dial.* [Derivation uncertain; connexion with F. *pousser* has been suggested, but neither the vowel nor sound of the *s* agrees.] *trans.* To kick, repulse with a kick.

1673 O. Heywood (of Bolton, Lancash.) *Diaries*, etc. (1883) III. 204 He .. paused her with his feet. **1828** *Craven Gloss.* (ed. 2), *Pause*, to kick with the foot. [In Eng. Dial. Dict. from Yorksh. and Notts.]

pauseful ('pɔːzfʊl), *a. rare.* [f. pause *sb.* + -ful.] **a.** Full of or abounding in pauses.

1877 Furnivall *Introd. Leopold Shaks.* p. xcviii, Professor Spalding contrasts the broken and pauseful versification of Shakspere with Fletcher's smoother end-stopt and double-ending lines. **1892** *Gd. Words* Oct. 658/2 Pauseful harmonies.

b. That causes a pause. (Cf. pausefully *adv.*)

1958 *Times* 5 May 12/5 A pauseful finger was being laid upon his life.

Hence **'pausefully** *adv.* (in quot., so as to cause a pause).

1866 M. Arnold *Thyrsis* xiv, I feel her finger light Laid pausefully upon life's headlong train.

pauseless ('pɔːzlɪs), *a. rare.* [f. as prec. + -less.] Having no pause, uninterrupted, ceaseless.

1849 *Fraser's Mag.* XL. 684 Richard's course had been busy, hurrying, pauseless. **1890** *Pall Mall G.* 13 Feb. 2/1 The dusky giants .. sweltering naked or half naked at their pauseless task.

Hence **'pauselessly** *adv.*, without stopping.

1839 Bailey *Festus* xi. (1852) 142 This heart let cease from prayer, these lips from praise, Save that which life shall offer pauselessly. **1883** Stevenson *Silverado Sq.* ii. 24 A broad cool wind streamed pauselessly down the valley.

†**'pausement.** *Obs. rare*⁻¹. [f. pause *v.*[1] + -ment.] The act of pausing; pause. ***to take pausement***, to pause.

1599 Porter *Angry Wom. Abingd.* (Percy Soc.) 58 Go too, take pausment, be aduisde.

pauser ('pɔːzə(r)). *rare.* [f. as prec. + -er[1].] One who pauses.

1605 Shaks. *Macb.* II. iii. 117 Th' expedition of my violent Loue Out-run the pawser, Reason.

‖**pausi'menia.** *Physiol.* [mod.L. f. Gr. παῦσι-ς cessation + μήν month: cf. catamenia.] Cessation of menstruation; menopause.

1857 in Dunglison *Med. Dict.* 687

pausing ('pɔːzɪŋ), *vbl. sb.* [f. pause *v.*[1] + -ing[1].] The action of the verb pause; stopping, intermission, hesitation.

1530 Palsgr. 252/2 Pausyng, *interpos.* **1582** Stanyhurst *Æneis* III. (Arb.) 80 After long pausing thus she sayd elflyke. **1624** Wotton *Archit.* in *Reliq.* (1651) 214 Such pausings are well reproved by Palladio. **1748** Richardson *Clarissa* (1811) IV. xxi. 118 Thy tearful pausings shall not be helped out by me.

attrib. **1807** Crabbe *Par. Reg.* III. 796 Thrice they sound, with pausing strain.

'pausing, *ppl. a.* [f. as prec. + -ing[2].] That pauses: see the verb.

1719 Tickell *On Death Addison* 16 The slow solemn knell .. The pealing organ, and the pausing choir. **1844** Browning *Boy & Angel*, With that weak voice of our disdain, Take up creation's pausing strain. **1885** Ruskin *Præterita* I. iii. 97 Lawn and lake enough .. I had, in the North Inch of Perth, and pools of pausing Tay.

Hence **'pausingly** *adv.*, with pausing.

1613 Shaks. *Hen. VIII*, I. ii. 168 With demure Confidence, This pausingly ensu'de.

pauste, -ti, -ty, var. poustie *Obs.*, power.

paut (pɔːt), *v.*[1] *Sc.* and *north. dial.* [Origin obscure.] *intr.* Of a horse: To paw the ground, stamp with the foot. Also said of a person.

1697 Cleland *Poems* 66 [He] did not cease to cave and paut, While clyred back was prickt and gald. ? *a* **1800** *Lord John* ix. in Child *Ballads* I. 397 O whare was ye, my gude grey steed .. That ye didna waken your master? I pautit wi' my foot, master, Garrd a' my bridles ring. **1828** *Craven Gloss.* (ed. 2), *Paut*, to paw... 'To paut off' t' happin', to kick off the bed clothes. [In *Eng. Dial. Dict.* from Scotl. to Lincolnsh.; also in various more or less allied senses.]

†**paut,** *v.*[2] *Obs. rare*⁻¹. App. a var. of palt *v.*, to pelt.

1611 Cotgr., *Espautrer*, to paut, pelt, thrash [etc.].

paut, variant of pát *sb.*

†**pautener,** *sb.*[1] (*a.*) *Obs.* Also 4 **-ere**, *Sc.* **paytener, -tynere,** 5 **pawtener, pautonere.** [a. AF. *pautener* = OF. *pautonier* (so in Gower), earlier *paltunier* (12th c., Godef.), 'a lewd, stubborne, or saucie knaue' (Cotgr.); in med.L. *paltōnārius*, in It. *paltoniere* 'a paltrie, cheating, loitring companion, also a carier or drouer' (Florio); deriv. of It. *paltone* 'varlet, knaue, rascall' (Florio), Pr. *paltom* (Diez). Referred by Diez to a L. type **palito, -ōnem* vagabond, vagrant, f. *pālitārī* (Plautus), iterative of *pālārī* to wander up and down. A possible source has also been sought in LG. *palt* bit, piece, e.g. of bread, whence 'beggar', *Sc.* 'gie's-a-piece'.] A vagabond, rascal.

In numerous places modern editors have misread and misprinted *pantener*. This is here corrected.

13.. *Cursor M.* 5143 (Cott.) Þou lighes now, eber pautener! *Ibid.* 16075 Vp þar stert tua pauteners. *c* **1380** *Sir Ferumb.* 859 Þou ne askapest noȝt ous, pautener, bot her riȝt þou schalt dye. **1426** AUDELAY *Poems* 16 Apon his parté pautener ys apayd. *c* **1450** *Merlin* 268 A full fell pawtener is he that twies this day thus hath yow smyten to grounde. [**1843** CARLYLE *Past & Pr.* II. xii, The Norfolk barrator and paltener.]

B. *adj.* [So in OF.] Rascally, wicked.

c **1330** R. BRUNNE *Chron.* (1810) 320 A boye fulle pautenere he had a suerd that bote, He stirte vnto þe Cofrere, his handes first of smote. **1375** BARBOUR *Bruce* II. 194 Thar wes nane off lyff sa fell, Sa pautener, na sa cruell. *c* **1375** *Sc. Leg. Saints* xl. (*Ninian*) 1111 Ȝet was he þe mast fellone man þat mycht be, & cruel and paytynere.

†**pautener,** *sb.*[2] *Obs.* Also 4–5 **pawtener,** 5 **-ere, -yner, pawtnere, pauteneere,** 6 **pawtenar, pautner.** [a. OF. *pautonniere* (1419 in Godef.), a purse, 'a shepheard's scrip' (Cotgr.).] A small bag, a wallet, scrip, purse.

c **1325** *Poem Times Edw. II* 86 in *Pol. Songs* (Camden) 327 He put in his pautener an honne and a komb. **1395** *Will of Leyghton* (Somerset Ho.), My pawtener wt Rynge of siluer & gylde pawtener. *c* **1430** *Pilgr. Lyf Manhode* III. xxii. (1869) 148 Cloutes and pauteneeres and bagges. **1463–4** *Rolls of Parlt.* V. 505/2 For weryng eny Purces, Pawteners, or Crounes of Cappes for Children. *c* **1483** CAXTON *Dialogues* 41/5 Lyon the pursser hath purses and pauteners. **1530** PALSGR. 252/2 Pautner, *malette*.

†**'pautre.** *Obs.* [app. a. F. *poutre* (OF. *poultre, poustre,* 1332–85 in Godef. *Compl.*).] A beam.

c **1425** *Voc.* in Wr.-Wülcker 667/20 Nomina pertinencia domorum... *Hec fania,* pautre. *Hec trabes,* balk. **1538** *Nottingham Rec.* III. 376 Tymbar for groynseles and pautres.

pauvilon, pauylion, obs. forms of PAVILION.

pauw, var. POU(W).

pauwau, obs. form of POW-WOW.

‖**pauxi** ('pɔːksɪ). *Ornith.* [a. Sp. *pauxi,* now *pauji* ('pauʃi), a. Mexican *pauxi* ('pauʃi); in Pg. *pawxi* ('pauʃi), F. *pauxi,* mod.L. *Pauxis.* See also altered forms under POWESE.] The Galeated Curassow (*Pauxis galeata*): see CURASSOW.

[**1651** HERNANDEZ *Animal. Mexican. Hist.* ccxxii, De Pauxi vocata ave.] **1753** CHAMBERS *Cycl. Supp., Pauxi,*.. the name of an American bird. **1827** GRIFFITH *Cuvier's Anim. K.* VIII. 119 It possesses all the characters of a genuine Pauxi. **1852** TH. ROSS *Humboldt's Trav.* II. xviii. 151 The *pauxi* and the *guacharaca,* which may be called the turkeys and pheasants of those countries.

pauyce, -yse, pavache, obs. forms of PAVIS.

pav[1]**.** (pæv). Abbreviation of PAVILION *sb.* (sense 6): *spec.* (*a*) the London Pavilion (a music-hall and theatre, later a cinema); (*b*) a cricket pavilion.

1864 HOTTEN *Slang Dict.* 197 *Pav.,* the Pavilion Theatre,—sometimes called the P.V., *i.e.,* pe-ve. **1892** *Idler* Mar. 127 One Saturday night, I wended my way to the 'Pav.'. **1901** *To-Day* 26 Sept. 266/1 The retiring victim [*sc.* a stumped batsman] came back to the Pav. **1903** [see CART *v.* 1 d]. **1934** *Observer* 1 Apr. 18/1 That long-established landmark, the London Pavilion (better known to its habitues as 'the Pav.') is following the example already set it by the Empire and the Alhambra and 'going over to the pictures'. **1978** *Guardian* 20 Mar. 9/1 St. B's always had them, especially behind the cricket pavs. **1978** L. MEYNELL *Papersnake* i. 10, I had gone over to the sports pavilion, 'the Pav'.. to make sure the gear was all right for the match.

pav[2]**.** Abbreviation of PAVLOVA. *Austral.* and *N.Z.*

1966 G. W. TURNER *Eng. Lang. Austral. & N.Z.* viii. 173 *Pavlova cake,* a meringue sweet, sometimes shortened to *pav.* **1974** *Herald* (Melbourne) 5 Apr. 23/1 The pavlova (now fondly abbreviated to the 'pav').

[**pavade, pauade,** misprint by Thynne of PANADE[1] in Chaucer's *Reeve's T.* 9 and 40, followed by Levins, Camden, Tyrwhitt, etc.; also an erroneous reading for *pauys,* PAVIS in Lydg. *Troybk.* III. xxii. (1555).

1570 LEVINS *Manip.* 8/40 A Pauade, *pagio.* **1605** CAMDEN *Rem.* (1657) 209 Lesser weapons, both defensive and offensive of our nation, as their pauad, baselard, launcegay.]

pavage ('peɪvɪdʒ). Also 5 **pavag, pawage,** 6 **pavadge,** 7–8 **-iage,** 9 **-eage.** [a. F. *pavage* (1331 in Hatz.-Darm.), in med.L. *pavagium,* f. F. *paver* to PAVE: see -AGE.]

1. A tax or toll towards the paving of highways or streets; also, the right to levy such a tax or toll.

[**1305** *Rolls of Parlt.* I. 163/1 Quod velit ei concedere muragium & pavagium in villa Warr[ewic]. **1324–5** *Ibid.* 423/1 Par quai il prient pavage & murage a dorer par VII aunz.] *a* **1500** tr. *Charter Rich. II* in Arnolde *Chron.* (1811) 22 Quyt for euer of pauage pontage and murage. *c* **1500** *Robin Hood & Potter* xiii. in Child *Ballads* III. 110/2 Wed well y non leffe, seyde þe potter, Nor pavag well y non pay. **1628** COKE *On Litt.* 58 b, Consuetudo.. signifieth also tolls .. paviage, and such like. **1707** J. CHAMBERLAYNE *St. Gt. Brit.* III. i. 240 The goods of Clergymen are discharged.. from Tolls and Customs of Average, Pontage, Murage, Pavage. **1883** PICTON *L'pool Munic. Rec.* I. 10 Paveage conceded to the town of Liverpool. **1902** SHARPE *Cal. Let. Bk. D.* 279 Allow citizens of York to pass free from payment of murage, pavage,.. and other customs.

2. The action of paving, the laying of a pavement. Also *attrib.*

1553 in *10th Rep. Hist. MSS. Comm.* App. v. 414 Massons workinge.. uppon the workes of muradge and pavadge. **1853** *Turner's Dom. Archit.* II. iii. 110 The Roadway.. was kept in repair.. by pavage rates. **1860** *Biog. & Crit. fr. 'The Times'* 272 Street regulations as to pavage.

pavais, -e, variants of PAVIS.

pavan ('pævən). Forms: (6 pavion, -yon), 6–9 **pavane, -in, -en,** 7 **-ian, -ine,** 9 **-aun,** 6– **pavan.** [a. F. *pavane* (1524–30 in Godef. *Comp.*), ad. It. *pavana* (Florio), or Sp. *pavana, pabana* (Minsheu): of disputed origin. See note below.]

A grave and stately dance, in which the dancers were elaborately dressed; introduced into England in the sixteenth century.

[**1530** ELYOT *Gov.* I. xx, We haue nowe base daunsis,.. pauions, turgions, and roundes.] **1535** LYNDESAY *Satyre* 3652 We sall leir ȝow to dance.. Ane new pavin of France. **1589** PUTTENHAM *Eng. Poesie* I. xxiii. (Arb.) 61 Daunced by measures as the Italian Pauan and galliard are at these daies in Princes Courts. **1602** MIDDLETON *Blurt, Master-Const.* IV. ii, He dances the Spanish pavin. **1652** *News fr. Lowe-Countr.* 7 Can any dance The Spanish Pavin, tricks of France. **1776** HAWKINS *Hist. Music* IV. IV. i. 387 The Pavan .. derived from the Latin Pavo.. a kind of dance, performed .. with such circumstances of dignity and stateliness as shew the propriety of the appellation. **1820** SCOTT *Monast.* xxi, Your leg would make an indifferent good show in a pavin or a galliard. **1893** MCCARTHY *Red Diamonds* I. 254 Those beautiful old-fashioned dances, pavanes, and minuets, and gavottes.

b. Music for this dance or in its rhythm, which is duple and very slow.

1545 ASCHAM *Toxoph.* (Arb.) 39 Whether these galiardes, pauanes and daunces.. be lyker the Musike of the Lydians or the Dorians. *a* **1619** FLETCHER *Mad Lover* II. i, Ile pipe him such a Paven. **1789** BURNEY *Hist. Mus.* III. v. 293 Dance-tunes such as the pavan and passamezzo. **1887** W. B. SQUIRE in *Dict. Nat. Biog.* IX. 96/2 The only extant compositions of his.. are some instrumental pavans.

c. *attrib.* and *Comb.*

1611 COTGR., *Pavanier,* a pauine-maker; a dauncer of Pauines. **1636** BUTLER *Princ. Mus.* 8 The triple is oft called Galliard-time, and the duple, Pavin-time.

[*Note.* According to the Spanish Academy, *pavana* (found in D. Pisada 1552) is a derivative of Sp. *pavo* peacock, 'in allusion to the movements and ostentation of that bird'; so Chambers 1727, from *Dict. Trévoux* 1721, 'a grave kind of dance, borrowed from the Spaniards, wherein the performers make a kind of wheel or tail before each other, like that of a peacock: whence the name'; so in M. Compan, *Dict. de la Danse* 1787, Littré, etc. See also Elyot's *Governor,* ed. Croft, I. 231, 241 notes, *Gloss.* II. 580; and cf. the German name *Pfauentanz* 'peacock-dance'. Others have attributed to the dance an Italian origin, and viewed *pavana* as reduced from *Padovana* 'Paduan' (which occurs in A. Rotta 1546); a 17th c. MS. collection of airs and dances by Dowland, Holborne, and others, in Camb. Univ. Lib., Dd. 4. 23 contains (near the end) a piece entitled *Padouana de la Milanessa.* But the phonetic difficulties in identifying the two words are serious; and they are prob. distinct terms, which may afterwards have sometimes been confused by those who knew the history of one of them only: cf. e.g. J. B. Besardus *Thesaur. Harmon.* (Cologne 1604) Pref.]

pavas, pavashe, obs. forms of PAVIS.

pave (peɪv), *v.* [a. OF. *paver* (12th c. in Littré and Hatz.-Darm.), either from L. *pavīre* to beat, strike, ram, with changed formative suffix and sense, or (as Darmesteter thinks more likely) a back formation from F. *pavement* PAVEMENT.]

1. a. *trans.* To lay or cover with a pavement (a street, road, court, yard, floor; hence, a town, house, etc.): see PAVEMENT 1.

c **1310** *Flemish Insurr.* in *Pol. Songs* (Camden) 190 The barouns of Fraunce thider conne gon, Into the paleis that paved is with ston. **1340** HAMPOLE *Pr. Consc.* 8910 Alle þe stretes of þe cete and þe lanes War even paved with precyouse stanes. *c* **1400** *Destr. Troy* 1661 A flore þat was fret all of fyne stones, Pauyt prudly all with proude colours. **1585** T. WASHINGTON tr. *Nicholay's Voy.* I. xvi. 17 b, The court is pavid with Mosaique stone. **1600–1** in Willis & Clark *Cambridge* (1886) II. 483 Flaunders tyles to paue the chimney in the.. great chamber. **1686** tr. *Chardin's Trav. Persia* 399 The Tomb is pav'd with Tiles of Cheney. **1707** MORTIMER *Husb.* (1721) II. 104 Some pave their Walks all over with large Pibbles or Flint-stones, and lay their Gravel on the Top of them. **1840** DICKENS *Barn. Rudge* ii, The roads even within twelve miles of London were,.. ill paved. **1902** *Daily Chron.* 23 Aug. 6/1 The area—one and a quarter acres—is tar-paved.

b. To overlie or cover as a pavement.

1600 ROWLANDS *Lett. Humours Blood* i. 47 They had more Rubies than wold paue Cheapside. **1818** BYRON *Ch. Har.* IV. lx, The slab which paves the princely head.

c. To form a pavement for; to be a pavement under.

1821 SHELLEY *Epipsych.* 15 The air-like waves Of wonder-level dream, whose tremulous floor Paved her light steps.

2. *fig.* **a.** To cover or overlay as with a pavement.

c **1400** *Laud Troy Bk.* 7214 Priamus wolde, that Troye hadde be paued With hethen hond and euery a membre. **1599** SHAKS. *Hen. V,* III. vii. 87, I will trot to morrow a mile, and my way shall be paued with English Faces. **1611** BIBLE *Song Sol.* iii. 10. **1647** TRAPP *Comm. 1 Cor.* i. 26 Hence it grew to a Proverb.., That Hell was paved with Priests shaven crowns, and great mens head-pieces. **17..**, **1771** Hell is paved with good intentions [see INTENTION *sb.* 5]. **1810** SOUTHEY *Curse of K.* XIV. v, Their self-devoted bodies there they lay To pave his chariot-way. **1887** I. R. *Lady's Ranche Life Montana* 154 Van grumbles,.. and says 'the ground is *paved* with pigs'.

†**b.** To render (a surface) hard or callous as if paved. *Obs. rare.*

1635 QUARLES *Embl.* I. viii. (1718) 34 But when the frequent soul-departing bell Has pav'd their ears with her familiar knell. **1738** SWIFT *Pol. Conversat.* 9 How can you drink your Tea so hot? Sure your Mouth's pav'd.

c. To write interlinear or marginal translations in (a Latin or Greek text-book). *School slang.*

1888 [implied in PAVING *vbl. sb.*]. **1897** A. SIDGWICK in P. A. Barnett *Teaching & Organisation* 308 Cases of dishonesty are pretty certain to turn up.. to 'pave' the text, *i.e.* write the English down at the side. **1940** M. MARPLES *Public School Slang* 52 A common word of special meaning is pave, which denotes the practice of writing the English meaning above words in a Greek or Latin text.

3. Phrase. *to pave the way*: to prepare the way (*for, to* something to come); to facilitate or lead on to a result or an object in view.

a **1585** CARTWRIGHT in R. Browne *Answ. Cartwright* 86 The way will bee paued and plained for mutuall entercourse. **1658** OSBORN *Adv. Son* IV. xxvi. (1896) 99 More able.. to have paved a Way to future Felicity. **1747** BERKELEY *Let. to Hales on Tar-water* Wks. III. 490 This may pave the way for its general use in all fevers. *c* **1817** HOGG *Tales & Sk.* V. 92 One lie always paved the way for another. **1883** S. C. HALL *Retrospect* I. 250 Addressing audiences to pave the way to the great work they ultimately accomplished.

pave (peɪv), *sb.*[1] Chiefly *U.S.* [app. f. PAVE *v.*, or ? short for *pavement.*] = PAVEMENT.

1835 *Southern Lit. Messenger* I. 357, I met a friend on the *pave* last week. **1859** [see NYMPH 2 b]. **1880** J. BOWICK *Montrose Characters* 138 Gaun pauchlin' alang the pave. **1889** *Harper's Mag.* Jan. 192/1, I fancy them on every pave in Rome Toward the palace faced. **1901** H. MCHUGH *John Henry* 45 Pounding the pave in front of Booze Bazaar.

fig. **1881** W. WILKINS *Songs of Study* 42 The Pit and the horseshoes o'er it Had smiles for their happy pave.

‖**pavé** (pave), *sb.*[2] Also 9 **pavée.** [F. *pavé,* sb. use of pa. pple. *pavé* paved.]

1. A paved street, road, or path: = PAVEMENT 1, 1 b.

on the pavé: see *on the* PAVEMENT.

1764 in J. H. Jesse *G. Selwyn & Contemp.* (1843) I. 272, I am in no danger of being on the *pavé!* **1768** STERNE *Sent. Journ., Nampont,* The postillion.. set off upon the *pavé* in full gallop. **1815** SCOTT *Paul's Lett.* (1839) 287 The old dame of Babylon.. is in some measure reduced to the *pavé.* **1849** THACKERAY *Pendennis* lxix, He has walked the Pall Mall *pavé* long enough. **1888** PENNELL *Sent. Journ.* 29 We went up *pavé,* and down *pavé,* and over long stretches of *pavé*.. its vileness went beyond our expectation.

2. A setting of diamonds or other jewels placed close together like the stones of a pavement, so that no metal is visible. Hence *attrib.,* as *pavé-design, -effect, -setting.*

1871 *Daily News* 25 Aug., The stones surmounted with the legend, 'Ni obliviscaris' on a pavé of diamonds. **1903** *Westm. Gaz.* 10 Dec. 4/2 The *pavé* setting makes a mosaic of the stones.

paveage, obs. form of PAVAGE.

paved (peɪvd), *ppl. a.* [f. PAVE *v.* + -ED[1].]

1. Laid with a pavement; having a pavement; †set or laid together as a pavement (*obs.*).

c **1374** CHAUCER *Troilus* II. 33 (82) And fond two oþere ladyes sette and she Wiþ-Inne a paued parlour. **1422** *Surtees Misc.* (1888) 16 The glasse wyndows, the bynkes, the paved flore. **1590** SPENSER *F.Q.* I. xii. 13 The joyous people.. with their garments strowes the paved street. **1611** BIBLE *Exod.* xxiv. 10 There was vnder his feet, as it were a paued worke of a Saphire stone. **1756** C. LUCAS *Ess. Waters* II. 125 Surrounded with a paved area. **1840** DICKENS *Old C. Shop* x, He.. arrived in a square paved court.

2. Compactly set so as to form a structure resembling a pavement: said of the teeth of some fishes.

1890 in *Cent. Dict.*

†**'pavefy,** *v. Obs. rare*[−0]. [ad. L. *pavefacĕre* to frighten, f. *pavēre* to be afraid + *facĕre* to make: see -FY.] Hence †**pave'faction.** *rare*[−0].

1656 BLOUNT *Glossogr., Pavefie,* to make afraid, to fright. **1658** PHILLIPS, *Pavefaction,* a terrifying or making afraid.

paveice, -eise, obs. forms of PAVIS.

paveleon, pavelon, obs. forms of PAVILION.

pavement ('peɪvmənt), *sb.* Forms: α. 3– **pavement,** (3–5 **paui-,** 3–6 **pauy-**). β. 4–5 **paw-,** (5–6 **pau-**), 4–6 **pa-,** 5 **pay-,** 8–9 (*dial.*) **pamment.** [a. OF. *pavement* (12th c. in Littré) = Pr. *pavamen,* Sp. *pavimiento,* It. *pavimento,* ad. L. *pavimentum* a beaten or rammed floor, f. *pavire* to beat, ram, tread down.]

1. a. A piece of paved work, a paved surface; the superficial covering or layer of a floor, yard, street, road, or area, formed of stones, bricks, tiles, or, in later times, blocks of wood, fitted closely together, so as to give a compact and more or less uniform and smooth surface; also, an undivided hard surface of cement, concrete, asphalt, or other material, used for the same purpose. ***mosaic*** or ***tessellated pavement***: see these words. Also (without *a*), paving.

(The original sense of 'hard floor formed by beating or ramming, had become obs. before the word became English.)

α. *c* **1290** *Beket* 2122 in *S. Eng. Leg.* I. 167 With þulke stroke..þut brain ful on þe pauement. *c* **1320** *Sir Beues* (MS. A) 4384 þourȝ is bodi wente þe dent, Ded a fel on þe pauiment. **1490** Caxton *Eneydos* xxvii. 101 Som.. he shal doo cast out of ye windowes doun to ye pauement. **1539** Cromwell *Let.* 18 Oct. in Merriman *Life & Lett.* (1902) II. 237 That you shuld cause the stretes and Lanes there to be vieued for the pavementes. **1585** T. Washington tr. *Nicholay's Voy.* I. vi. 4b, The pauement..was of Marber stone. **1615** Chapman *Odyss.* x. 307 The pavement rings With imitation of the tunes she sings. **1726** Pope *Odyss.* xxi. 44 With polish'd oak the level pavements shine. **1788** Gibbon *Decl. & F.* xliv. (1790) VIII. 36 The works of Justinian represent a tesselated pavement of antique and costly, but too often of incoherent fragments. *a* **1817** [see knowing *ppl. a.* 3]. **1823** P. Nicholson *Pract. Build.* 435 Floors constructed of stone are more particularly denominated pavements. **1841** *Penny Cycl.* XX. 35/2 The wooden pavement, properly so called, seems to have been first used in Russia. **1843** A. B. Blackie *Wood Pavement* 13 The efficient labour of a horse on Wooden Pavement, compared with that of the same horse on a perfectly consolidated Macadamized road, being as 42 to 17. **1900** T. Aitken *Road Making* ix. 300 Streets of many English towns are still paved with cobbles, but these are being gradually replaced by better descriptions of pavement. **1947** *Engineering News-Record* 16 Oct. 534/3 The surface of the runways, which it is hoped will be adequate for the pavement base, will be finally solidified by a 'super-compactor' unit. **1952** *Jrnl. R. Aeronaut. Soc.* LVI. 879/1 The pavement must be capable of carrying with safety the heaviest aircraft. **1977** *Bitumen* (Shell Internat. Petroleum Co.) 7 Shell companies' main interest in bitumen technology has been the engineering properties of bitumen and the structural design of roads and airfield pavements.

β. **1340** Hampole *Pr. Consc.* 9180 Þe pament of heven may lykened be, Tille a pament of precyouse stanes and perré. **1382** Wyclif *Ps.* cxviii[i]. 25 Myn soule cleuede to the pament [**1388** pawment]. *c* **1400** Maundev. (1839) xviii. 188 The paumentes of halles and chambres ben all square, on of gold and another of syluer. *c* **1440** *Alph. Tales* (E.E.T.S.) 64 [She] putt assh opon hur head, & laid hur down on þe payment & wepid bitterlie vij dayes. **1530** Palsgr. 251/2 Pamente of a strete, *paviment, pavee. Ibid.* 252/2 Paument.., *pavé.* **1895** Patterson *Man & Nat.* 73 (E.D.D.) Red handkerchiefs dot the hard cold pamments.

b. The paved part of a public thoroughfare; the roadway as distinct from the adjacent footway (now *obs.* exc. *techn.* and *U.S.*); *spec.* the paved footway by the side of a street, as distinct from the roadway. ***on the pavement*** (after F. *sur le pavé* 'on the street'), walking the streets, without lodging, abandoned.

c **1330** R. Brunne *Chron.* (1810) 270 Þe Turbeuile.. Drawen is a while on London pauiment, & siþen was he hanged as thef for treson. *c* **1400** *Sege Jerus.* 1244 (E.E.T.S.) Myȝt no man stonde in þe stret for stynke of ded corses; þe peple in þe pauyment was pite to byholde. **1602** *2nd Pt. Return fr. Parnass.* I. i. 119 In a sinne-guilty coach not closely pent, Iogging along the harder pauement. **1725** B. Higgons *Rem. on Burnet* Hist. Wks. 1736 II. II. 104 They, who had lavish'd their own in his [the King's] Defence, were suffered to starve on the Pavement. **1793** Gouv. Morris in Sparks *Life & Writ.* (1832) II. 296 His retreat must be slow till he gets to the pavement within about a league of Antwerp. *a* **1818** G. Rose *Diaries* (1860) I. 28, I was left completely on the pavement. **1874** *Graphic* 5 Sept. 226/1 The humble 'artist on stone' has found a convenient 'pitch' ..and with his stubby bits of various coloured chalk he is rapidly making sketches on the pavement. **1877** D. K. Clark in Law & Clark *Construction of Roads* 12 The surface of the pavement soon became very uneven, and not unfrequently sunk so much as to form hollows, which rendered it..dangerous to horses and carriages. **1879** Black *Macleod of D.* v, The crowd of footmen who stood in two lines across the pavement in front of Beauregard House. **1900** Shaw *Plays for Purit.* p. xii, They insisted..as pitifully as a poor girl of the pavement will pretend to be a clergyman's daughter. **1918** E. Poole *Dark People* i. 5 You could see the sidewalks on either hand, but the dark wooden pavement of the street was almost lost in shadows. **1935** H. W. Horwill *Dict. Mod. Amer. Usage* 226/1 When preparations were being made in Washington for a procession.., the newspapers of the city complained that in Pennsylvania Avenue the grandstands filled the sidewalk and compelled pedestrians to walk on the pavement. **1939** *Liverpool Daily Post* 9 Nov. 3/2 When any road works are about to be undertaken, a notice headed 'Reconstruction of Pavement' is exhibited near the scene of operations, stating that the 'pavement of this thoroughfare' is shortly to be reconstructed. It is invariably the roadway, and not the sidewalk, which in these cases receives attention. **1958** *Engineering* 4 Apr. 441/3 It will also be a double carriageway, ..comprising 7 in of granular fill on which will be laid 11 in of reinforced concrete, placed in a single pass for the full 24 ft width of each pavement. **1966** R. Ashworth *Highway Engin.* x. 171 The modern road pavement is usually composed of several layers of material of differing quality; the strongest material being placed uppermost and forming the actual running surface. **1971** D. Hamilton *Poisoners* x. 78 She was barreling out on..the road that'll take you clear down Baja California to La Paz, if you and your vehicle are tough enough to make it... The pavement ends about ninety miles south of Ensenada at present. After that, things get pretty rough. **1976** *Billings* (Montana) *Gaz.* 17 June 1-A/4 A southern Indiana woman died when her car skidded out of control on wet pavement.

c. *transf.* and *fig.*

a **1592** Greene *Selimus* 498 Were his light steeds as swift as Pegasus, And trode the ayrie pauement with their heeles. **1606** Shaks. *Tr. & Cr.* III. iii. 162 Or like a gallant Horse falne in first ranke, Lye there for pauement to the abiect reere. **1647** H. More *Cupid's Conflict* lxxx, Gathering my limbs from off the green pavement. **1827** Pollok *Course T.* VI. 58 Stars, walking on the pavement of the sky. **1887** Hall Caine *Deemster* x. 65 Large white patches came moving out of the surrounding pavement of deep black,..where the vanishing ripples left the dark sea smooth.

d. The floor of a mine (Raymond *Mining Gloss.* 1881).

e. A seam of fire-clay underlying a seam of coal.

f. (See quot. 1965.)

1899 P. Dearmer *Parson's Handbk.* v. 128 The thurifer and boat-bearer..go to the right of the priest, as he stands on the pavement. **1908** *Ritual Notes* (ed. 5) II. 59/3 When the Deacon descends to the pavement, the Thurifer will stand at his right. **1922** C. Mackenzie *Altar Steps* xix. 212 The baldacchino was given by one rich old lady, the pavement of the church by another. **1936** *Server's Manual* 6 Go and stand in some convenient place on the 'pavement' of the sanctuary. **1965** C. E. Pocknee *Parson's Handbk.* (ed. 13) ii. 23 The pavement, i.e. the level of the sanctuary between the lowest step before the altar and the communicants' rail, should extend to six feet at the very least. *Ibid.* ix. 98 He remains standing on the pavement swinging the censer until the hymn or psalm is finished. **1978** *Church Times* 20 Jan. 3/4 An application was made for a faculty to remove the sanctuary pavement and transfer from a columbarium underneath 177 caskets containing..cremated remains.

2. a. *Anat.* and *Zool.* A structure or formation resembling a pavement; a level hard surface formed by close-set teeth, bony plates, or the like.

1847 Ansted *Anc. World* xii. 279 The flat pavement of palatal bones with which these animals were provided. **1857** H. Miller *Test. Rocks* i. 62 A palate covered with a dense pavement of crushing teeth. **1871** Darwin *Desc. Man* II. xii. 6 [The] teeth..are broad and flat, forming a pavement. **1931** J. R. Norman *Hist. Fishes* vii. 126 They [*sc.* the teeth of Nurse Sharks and Hounds] are arranged in pavement fashion, and all or most of the rows are in use at the same time. **1971** P. J. P. Whitehead tr. *Budker's Life of Sharks* iii. 41 The only sharks having teeth in a 'pavement' are those belonging to the genera *Mustelus, Hexanchus* and *Heterodontus*.

b. *Geol.* A horizontal or gently sloping expanse of bare rock.

1827 G. P. Scrope *Mem. Geol. Central France* vii. 154 The lower portion of this bed is very beautifully columnar, the upper obscurely so; this latter has been in parts destroyed, and a pavement or causeway left, formed by an assemblage of upright and almost geometrically regular columns fitted together with the utmost symmetry. **1932** C. R. Longwell et al. *Physical Geol.* vii. 157 Many gentle slopes above the levels of the playas are floored with 'desert pavements' consisting of pebbles fitted so closely together and with their top surfaces so even that the general effect suggests a mosaic. **1937** Wooldridge & Morgan *Physical Basis Geogr.* xix. 288 Bare limestone surfaces commonly show a widening of joints by solution, or in extreme cases, a complex fretting or fluting of the surface... Limestone pavements tending to this type are called 'clints' or 'grykes' in the North of England. **1954** J. F. Kirkaldy *Gen. Princ. Geol.* vi. 69 The direction of ice movement can also be proved if glaciated pavements can be found. These are surfaces of rock, hard enough to be smoothed and polished by the ice and showing striations caused by the harder rocks dragged across them by the ice. **1965** *Proc. Geologists' Assoc.* LXXVI. 421 Carboniferous limestone in Great Britain and Ireland is frequently exposed in broad, curiously sculptured plateaux termed pavements. **1977** *Oxf. Diocesan Mag.* Nov. 10/1 We have botanized over a limestone 'pavement' in Westmoreland, several bogs in Scotland, [etc.].

3. A stone, brick, or tile suitable or made for paving. *local.*

1787 W. Marshall *Norfolk* (1795) II. Gloss. (E.D.S.), *Pavements*, square paving-bricks; flooring-bricks; paving-tiles. *a* **1800** *Thomas Stukely* in Child *Ballads* (1857–9) VII. 309 At last he sold the pavements of his yard, Which covered were with blocks of tin. *a* **1825** Forby *Voc. E. Anglia*, *Pamment*, a square paving brick.

4. *attrib.* and *Comb.*, as ***pavement-café***, ***-dealer***, ***-floor***, ***-side***, ***-stone***, ***-tile***, etc.; **pavement-artist**, one who draws figures or scenes on the flagged pavement in coloured chalks or pastils in order to get money from passers-by: cf. quot. 1874 in 1 b; †**pavement-beater** (see quot.); **pavement-epithelium**, epithelium in which the cells are flattened and arranged in layers like the tiles of a mosaic pavement; lamellar, squamous, or tessellated epithelium; **pavement-pounder** *slang*, a policeman; **pavement princess** *Citizens Band Radio slang* (see quots.); **pavement-rammer**, a power machine used to ram down the blocks with which a road is paved; **pavement-tooth**, a broad flat tooth forming with others a pavement in sense 2 a, as in the Port Jackson shark; **pavement-toothed** *a.*, having teeth arranged in a pavement (see sense 2 a).

1899 *Daily News* 1 Aug. 6/4 No one but the *pavement-artist can have any notion of how great the amount of dust is in London's streets. **1611** Cotgr. s.v. *Pavé, Bateur de pavez*, a *pauement-beater; a rakehell, vnthrift, loose youth, dissolute or deboched fellow. **1953** *Observer* 10 May 5/4 It isn't worth..doing much about *pavement cafés or open-air dancing. **1972** J. Aitken *Butterfly Picnic* i. 12 Several pavement cafés were thronged with elderly men. **1870** Rolleston *Anim. Life* 129 An internal layer of *pavement epithelium. **1813** Scott *Rokeby* VI. xxxiii, But flounder'd on the *pavement-floor The steed, and down the rider bore. **1942** Berrey & Van den Bark *Amer. Thes. Slang* §460/17 *Policeman*..ossifer, *pavement pounder, P.D. **1947** K. Jaediker *Tall, Dark & Dead* vii. 102 Neal had put out a teletype for my car, and some Brooklyn pavement-pounder had spotted it. **1959** I. & P. Opie *Lore & Lang. Schoolch.* xvii. 369 There are, in the London area, at least thirty nicknames... Nobby, Pavement Pounder, Peeler, Robert, [etc.]. **1976** L. Dills *CB Slanguage Dict.* (rev. ed.) 53 *Pavement princess, roadside or truckstop prostitute. **1976** *Time* 10 May 79/2 Prostitutes ('pavement princesses') who plug their charms on CB have become so common that there is even a song about them. **1976** *Daily Tel.* (Colour Suppl.) 16 July 10/2 Car-borne prostitutes..describe themselves as 'a dream for sale' in the West..a 'pavement princess' and a 'snuff-dipper' in the East. **1608** Machin & Markham *Dumb Knight* III. i. in Hazl. *Dodsley* X. 159 Thus are the *pavement-stones before the doors..worn smooth With clients dancing 'fore them. **1845** *Gentl. Mag.* XXIV. 43/1 The ancient *pavement tiles found in this neighbourhood. **1904** *Nature* 5 May 13/1 He discusses the affinities of the *pavement-toothed genus Endothiodon.

pavement ('peɪvmənt), *v.* [f. prec. sb.; cf. L. *pavīmentāre* to cover with a pavement, to pave, OF. **pavementer*, in pa. pple. *pavementé*, It. *pavimentare* to pave, all from the sb.] *trans.* To lay with a pavement; to pave. Also *transf.* Chiefly in *pa. pple.* Hence **'pavementing** *vbl. sb.*

1634 Bp. Hall *Contempl.*, *N.T.* IV. vi, The pavemented waves yielded a firm causey to thy sacred feet to walk on. **1648** —— *Select Th.* I. vii. 23 What an house hath he put him [man] into! how gorgiously arched, how richly pavemented! **1839** *Hist. Reveries* 33 All pavemented with stone and shell. **1930** R. Clements *Grey Seas* 126 The blown, empty sky, pavemented by the tossing sea. **1977** *Lancet* 20 Aug. 402/2 At 30 and 60 min, these showed an inflammatory reaction to both solutions with pavementing of polymorphs and a perivascular infiltrate.

pavemental (peɪv'mɛntəl), *a.* [f. pavement *sb.* + -al[1].] Of the nature of a pavement; consisting of pavement-teeth.

1880 Macdonald in *Jrnl. Linn. Soc.* XV. 166 The dentition is typically pavemental in the Monoecious and ribbonlike in the Dioecious Gasteropoda.

paven ('peɪvən), *ppl. a.* Chiefly *poetic.* [irreg. f. pave *v.*, after *shaven*, etc.] = paved *ppl. a.*

1634 Milton *Comus* 886 Rise,..From thy coral-pav'n bed. **1762** *St. James's Mag.* I. 60 Beating the panic-paven ground. *a* **1822** Shelley *Sp. Plato* 2 To what sublime and star-y-paven home Floatest thou? **1869** Stevenson *Let. to Mother* 18 June in *Scribner's Mag.* (1899) XXV. 42/1 One catches a cool glimpse of a paven entrance-court.

paven, variant of pavan.

paver ('peɪvə(r)). Also 6 pavore. [f. pave *v.* + -er[1]. (The 16th c. example of *pavore* seems to be imitative of words of Fr. origin; = F. *paveur*.)]

1. a. One who paves, a paviour.

1477 in *York Myst.* Introd. 21 *note*, Kidberers, Garthyners, erthe wallers, pavers, dykers. **1483** *Cath. Angl.* 271/2 A Pavere, *pavimentor*. **1597** in Ferguson & Nanson *Munic. Rec. Carlisle* (1887) 276 We desyere yor worshipe and yor brethren to let us haue an able suffycient man for or hurd,..and so lykwysse for or pavore. **1688** R. Holme *Armoury* III. 342/1 A Pavers Pick..hath a long head and back part, that it may strike deep into the ground. **1706** *Churchw. Acc. Holy Cross, Canterb.* (MS.), Pd for Lowances for the pauir..00. 02. 07. **1807** Hutton *Course Math.* II. 89 Pavers' work is done by the square yard.

b. A machine for depositing and spreading material for a road, etc., as it travels.

1947 *Engineering News-Record* 16 Oct. 535/3 A paver was used to mix the soil-cement and to deposit it along the pipe line as required. **1955** *Concrete Roads* (Road Research Lab.) xv. 279 For large works, pavers which consist of a non-tilting mixer mounted on crawler tracks are sometimes convenient. **1972** *Travelling* Autumn 33/2 The concrete slab will be laid with a very high accuracy using a purpose built slip form paver. **1977** *Bitumen* (Shell Internat. Petroleum Co.) 5 The mixes are laid by various types of mechanical paver.

2. A paving-stone or -tile.

1696 A. de la Pryme *Diary* (Surtees) 79 The pavement.. consisting of larg four square pavers all leaded. **1802** W. Fowler *Lettering of an Engraving*, A representation of Norman Pavers on the floor..at Harrington. **1894** *Athenæum* 29 Sept. 427/2 The altar face [at Walton Priory] was still tiled with yellow and black pavers arranged diamond fashion.

3. The bed-stone of a porcelain mill.

1881 *Guide Worcester Porcel. Wks.* 12 The particles are abraded..between the runners and pavers.

Hence **'pavership**, the office of paver.

1597 in Ferguson & Nanson *Munic. Rec. Carlisle* (1887) 274 Dissiring yor worshipe to concider of me..concerning the pavershipe of the citie.

paves, pavesade, -ado: see pavis, etc.

pave-stone. [f. stem of pave *v.* + stone *sb.*] = paving-stone.

1852 *Ecclesiologist* XIII. 312 The pavement is full of pave-stones with the merchants' marks of the old burghers of the town. **1894** H. Speight *Nidderdale* 380 Remains of this old thoroughfare..in the shape of large pave-stones.

‖**Pavia** ('peɪvɪə). *Bot.* [mod.L.: named by Boerhaave 1720, in honour of Peter Paaw (Pavius), Professor of Botany at Leiden 1589–1617.] A genus of trees and shrubs (N.O. *Sapindaceæ*) closely allied to the Horse-chestnut, from which they are distinguished by having a smooth, not prickly, capsule; hence called Buck-eye, or Smooth-fruited Horse-chestnut. *Pavia rubra*, the Red Horse-chestnut, a slender tree, twenty or thirty feet high, a native of the mountains of Virginia and Carolina, is a well-known ornamental tree.

1753 CHAMBERS *Cycl. Supp.*, *Pavia*, in botany, the name of a genus of plants described by Boerhaave and Linnæus. 1766 J. BARTRAM *Jrnl.* 27 Jan. in W. Stork *Acc. E. Florida* 54 Now the ash, maple, elm, and pavia, are all green. 1882 *Garden* 24 June 447/2 The Pavias constitute a group of trees allied to the Horse Chestnuts.

paviage, obs. form of PAVAGE.

Pavian ('pɑːvɪən), *sb.* and *a.* [f. *Pavia* name of a city of northern Italy (L. *Ticinum*) + -AN.]

A. *adj.* Of, pertaining to, or characteristic of Pavia or its people. B. *sb.* A native or inhabitant of Pavia.

1856 O. JONES *Gram. Ornament* xvii. 5 Our woodcuts, selected from the Piscina of the High Altar, furnish some idea of the general style of the Pavian arabesques. 1888 W. BENHAM tr. *Platina's Lives of Popes* I. 260 John the Fourteenth, a Roman, or, as some will have it, a Pavian. 1936 A. W. CLAPHAM *Romanesque Archit.* iii. 62 In some of the Pavian churches an acanthus decoration is to be met with, consisting of a regular diaper or brocade pattern of palmette leaves. 1940 G. F.-H. & J. BERKELEY *Italy in Making* III. viii. 202 The Pavian student volunteers had occupied Colà.

pavian, pavice, obs. forms of PAVAN, PAVIS.

pavid ('pævɪd), *a. rare.* [ad. L. *pavid-us* fearful, trembling, f. stem of *pavēre* to quake with fear.] Fearful, timid.

1656 BLOUNT *Glossogr.*, *Pavid*, fearful, timerous, quaking, starting. 1667 WATERHOUSE *Fire Lond.* 92 That Dread and pavid manlessness, that seised the Inhabitants. 1847 THACKERAY *Contrib. to Punch* Wks. 1902 VI. 468 The pavid matron within the one vehicle..shrieked and trembled. *a* 1863 —— *Round. Papers, Medal Geo. IV* 355 Eagles go forth and bring home to their eaglets the lamb or the pavid kid.

Hence **pa'vidity**, fearfulness, timidity. *rare*⁻⁰.

1656 BLOUNT *Glossogr.*, *Pavidity*, dread, fear, timerousness.

pavie ('peɪvɪ). *Sc.* [Origin unascertained.] A clever or nimble movement of the body, as of a juggler in performing a trick; hence, a trick.

1598 BIRRELL *Diary* in Dalyell *Fragm. Sc. Hist.* (1798) 47 A juglar playit sic sowple tricks upon ane tow..the lyk wes nevir sene in this countrie, as he raid doune the tow and playit sa maney pavies on it. 1681 COLVIL *Whig's Supplic.* I. 72 For some of such had play'd a pavie. 1697 CLELAND *Poems* 47 Well versed in Court Modes, In French Pavies, and new Com'd Nods. 1801 LEYDEN in *Compl. Scot.* Gloss., *To play sic a pavie*, or *paw*, is a common expression in the south of Scotland. 1808–18 JAMIESON, *Pavie, Paw*, 1., Lively motion of whatever kind.

pavie, erron. f. PAVIS.

pavier, obs. f. PAVIOUR.

paviin ('peɪvɪɪn). *Chem.* [f. PAVIA + -IN[1].] A fluorescent substance, $C_{16}H_{18}O_{10}$, existing in the bark of *Pavia* and other trees; also called *fraxin*.

1864–72 WATTS *Dict. Chem.* II. 708 Stokes in 1858..gave the name *paviin* from the genus *Pavia*, in all species of which it appears to exist in greater abundance than in the genus *Æsculus*. 1873 *Fownes' Chemistry* (ed. 11) 639.

pavilion (pə'vɪljən), *sb.* Forms: 3–5 **pauilon, -un,** (**pauy-, paue-, pauey-, -lon, -loun, -lun, -lown(e),** 4–5 **pauilioun,** 5–7 **-ion,** (5–6 **pauy-, paue-, -lio(u)n, -lyo(u)n, -lyun, -leon(e, -llion, -llyon, -lleon),** 5–6 **pauillon, (-yllo(u)n, -eillon, pafelioun, pauvilon),** 6–8 **pavillion,** 7 **pavilloun,** 7– **pavilion.** *β. Sc.* 4–5 **pailȝeoun, -yeoun,** 5–6 **pailȝo(u)n, -ȝown, palȝon,** 6 **pailȝeon; paill-, pallie-ȝ(e)oun; palȝoun(e, -ȝeo(u)n, -youn, -ione; palloun, -ion(e; pallieȝieoun, paylion.** [ME. a. F. *pavillon*, OF. *paveillun* (12th c.), 'tent, pavilion, canopy', also 'standard':—L. *papiliōn-em* ' butterfly, moth', transf. 'tent, pavilion' (Lampridius *a* 1300), 'a similitudine parvi animalis', Papias; in Pr. *papallo, pabalho, pav-*, Cat. *pabello, pav-*, Sp. *pabellon*, It. *padiglione*. The Sc. forms arose from vocalization and loss of the *v*.]

I. 1. a. A tent: chiefly applied to one of a large or stately kind, rising to a peak above.

1297 R. GLOUC. (Rolls) 1116 Þe emperour adde ipiȝt his pauilons [*v.rr.* pauelon, -ylon]. *a* 1300 *Cursor M.* 8195 (Cott.) Ilkan to sett þair pauilun [*v.rr.* pauelyun, -ylion, -yloun]. 1387 TREVISA *Higden* (Rolls) III. 169 Cirus sette his pauilouns wiþ ynne þe lond. *c* 1400 MAUNDEV. (Roxb.) xxvi. 121 Þai cary þaire housez with þam apon cartes, as men in oþer cuntreez duse tentes and pafeliouns [*MS. Cott.* pavyllouns]. 1422 tr. *Secreta Secret., Priv. Priv.* 129 Al the campany of the londe wolde not Suffice har tentes and Paueillons to Piche. 1481 CAXTON *Reynard* xxvi. (Arb.) 59 He hath gunnes, bombardes, tentes and pauyllyons. 1535 COVERDALE *1 Kings* xx. 12 Whan Benadab herde yt (euen as he was drynkinge with the kynges in yᵉ pauylion). 1600 J. PORY tr. *Leo's Africa* III. 165 His owne great tent is pitched in a fower square forme like vnto a castle... This royal pauilion hath fower gates. 1604 E. G[RIMSTONE] *D'Acosta's Hist. Indies* IV. vi. 220 This mountaine..resembling perfectly the fashion of a pavilion, or of a sugar loafe. 1634 SIR T. HERBERT *Trav.* 54 A mile from this Towne we see threescore blacke Pauillions... These are a people, who live wholly in Tents, and obserue the customes of the Tartars. 1774 WARTON *Hist. Eng. Poetry* (1840) I. Diss. iii. p. cxc, The royal pavilion, or booth, which stood in the fair about 1280. 1851 LAYARD *Pop. Acc. Discov. Nineveh* iv. 65 Amongst them rose the white pavilions of the Turkish irregular cavalry. 1870 BRYANT *Iliad* I. IX. 269 Atrides brought the assembled elder chiefs To his pavilion.

β. 1375 BARBOUR *Bruce* XI. 139 Sum lugit without the townys In tentis and in palȝeownys. *Ibid.* XIX. 542 That thai the pailȝownys mycht ma To fall on thaim that in thaim war. *c* 1470 *Gol. & Gaw.* 312 Thai plantit doun ane pailyeoun, vpone ane plane lee. 1501 DOUGLAS *Pal. Hon.* II. xliv, Law in the meid ane Palȝeoun picht I se, Maist gudliest, and richest that micht be. *a* 1590 MONTGOMERIE *Mindes Melodie* Ps. xix. 18 There he a throne Set for the sunne, And paylion pight, his mansion to abide. 1596 DALRYMPLE tr. *Leslie's Hist. Scot.* VII. 4 Edward..cumis in Scotl. with ane armie, and stentis his palliounis att Renfrow. ? *a* 1700 *Battle of Otterburn* xv, They lighted high on Otter-bourne, And threw their pallions down.

b. *Her.* A tent as a heraldic bearing.

1725 COATS *Dict. Her.* s.v., The Pavillions as we generally represent them are round at the Top,..as we see in the Company of Merchant Taylors of London. 1727–41 CHAMBERS *Cycl.* s.v., The pavillion consists of two parts: the top, which is the chapeau, or coronet; and the curtain which makes the mantle.

†c. A canopied litter. *Obs.*

1656 W. D. tr. *Comenius' Gate Lat. Unl.* §439. 127 Closely covered a litter; borne up above ground, a sedan; having a delicate cover besides, a pavillion. 1703 MAUNDRELL *Journ. Jerus.* (1732) 127 A large Pavilion of black Silk, pitch'd upon the back of a very great Camel, and spreading its Curtains all round about the Beast.

2. *fig.* Anything likened to a tent.

1535 COVERDALE *2 Sam.* xxii. 12 He made darknes his pauylion rounde aboute him, thicke water in the cloudes of yᵉ ayre. *a* 1586 SIDNEY *Arcadia* I. (1590) 9 b, Flowers, which being vnder the trees, the trees were to them a Pauilion, and they to the trees a mosaical floore. 1726 POPE *Odyss.* XIX. 516 The warm pavilion of a dreadful boar. 1751 JOHNSON *Rambler* No. 134 ¶8 The call..of conscience will pierce the closest pavilion of the sluggard. 1822–56 DE QUINCEY *Confess.* (1862) 269 The blue pavilion stretched over our heads.

II. In transferred or technical uses, chiefly from French.

†3. a. A covering or canopy. *Obs.*

1381 in *Eng. Gilds* (1870) 233 [A] palyoun [of cloth of gold]. *c* 1468 [see PAVILION *v.* 1 b]. 1585 T. WASHINGTON tr. *Nicholay's Voy.* II. xxii. 60 b, This vessel thus garnished is..couered with a rich pauillion of veluet or crimson satten set with gold and siluer.

†b. The velarium or awning of an amphitheatre.

1730 A. GORDON *Maffei's Amphith.* 320 Workmen, who..went to the top of the Building, to manage the Curtain or Pavilion. *Ibid.* 347 This Pavilion was called *Vela*, or *Velarium* by the Latins.

4. A French gold coin struck by Philip VI of Valois in 1329, the obverse of which represented the king seated under a canopy or *pavillon*. Also applied by collectors to the *royal d'or*, struck by the Black Prince for use in Guienne, etc.

1755 DUCAREL *Anglo-Gallic Coins* v. (1757) 25 A Royal or Pavillion..the prince appears bare-headed under a magnificent pavilion. 1837 *Penny Cycl.* VII. 331/1 Edward the Black Prince added the hardi of gold and the pavilion. 1894 C. F. KEARY in S. Lane Poole *Coins & Medals* v. 111.

†5. An article of apparel worn by lawyers; ? a gown or cloak. *Obs.*

1393 LANGL. *P. Pl.* C. IV. 452 Shal no seriaunte for þat seruyse were a selk houe, Ne pelour in hus paueylon [*v.r.* pauilon; B. III. 294 no pelure in his cloke] for pledyng at þe barre.

6. A light ornamental building or pleasure-house, such as those common in parks and public gardens, used generally for purposes of temporary shelter; also, a building attached to a cricket, football, or other ground, for the convenience of spectators and players.

The name is also sometimes given to a building appropriated to purposes of amusement. The *Marine Pavilion* at Brighton was begun in 1784 as a summer seaside residence for the Prince of Wales, afterwards George IV; it is now used as a museum and place of entertainment.

1687 A. LOVELL tr. *Thevenot's Trav.* I. 23 On the side of the Port, over against Galata, there is a Kiousk or Pavillion upon the Key. 1695 MOTTEUX *St. Olon's Morocco* 72 That Palace..consists of a great number of Pavillions, or small distinct Buildings. *Ibid.* 76 Some little Pavillions or Summer-Houses,..in each of which is a Fountain and a Watering-place for Horses. 1748 LADY LUXBOROUGH *Lett. to Shenstone* (1775) 38 My pavilion, when almost finished, was pulled down again in part, to add to it a shrine for Venus. 1753 RICHARDSON *Grandison* (1781) III. xxviii. 295 The Marchioness came to them..from one of the pavillions in the garden. 1766 ENTICK *London* IV. 449 [Description of rotunda in Vauxhall-gardens.].. The pavillions or alcoves are ornamented with paintings... Each pavillion has a table in it, that will hold six or eight persons. 1799 *Times* 1 June 3/4 The colours..were presented..to the corps in Lord's cricket ground... After the military ceremony was over, the Earl and Countess..partook of a cold collation provided for them in the pavillion. 1823 BYRON *Juan* XIV. lxxxiii, Shut up—no, not the King, but the Pavilion, Or else 'twill cost us all another million. 1853 F. GALE *Public School Matches* 10 All of a sudden the bell from the Pavilion strikes up, and the ground is gradually cleared. 1856 EMERSON *Eng. Traits, Stonehenge* Wks. (Bohn) II. 127 We..came down into the Italian garden and into a French pavilion, garnished with French busts, and so, again to the house. 1872 *Builder* 1 June 424/3 The proposed new pavilion at the Trent Bridge cricket-ground, Nottingham. *a* 1873 LYTTON *Pausanias* I. i. (1876) 30 In the centre of the deck was a wooden edifice or pavilion having a gilded roof and shaded by purple awnings. 1891 W. G. GRACE *Cricket* 207 The handsome pavilion which was recently built [at Lord's]... It is capable of accommodating 3,000 people.

7. a. A projecting subdivision of a building or façade, distinguished by more elaborate decoration, or by greater height and distinction of sky-line, forming a connecting part, an angle, or the central feature of a large pile.

c 1676 WREN in Willis & Clark *Cambridge* (1886) II. 534 The building next the court with the pavillions for the staircases. 1721 *New Gen. Atlas* 207 Each Corner of this main Building has a fair Pavillion, one for the Governor's Lodging and Council-Chamber. 1727–41 CHAMBERS *Cycl.* s.v., Pavillions are sometimes also projecting pieces, in the front of a building, marking the middle thereof.—Sometimes the pavillion flanks a corner, in which case it is called an angular pavillion. 1901 RUSSELL STURGIS *Dict. Archit.* II. Pl. 27 (s.v. *Louvre*) The whole front including the end pavilions, is nearly 600 feet long.

b. One of the several detached or semi-detached blocks or buildings into which a hospital is sometimes divided. (See 14, quots. 1885, 1903.)

1858 FLOR. NIGHTINGALE *Notes on Hospitals* (1859) 8 The example which France and Belgium have lately set us of separating their hospitals into a number of distinct pavilions. 1863 *Ibid.* (ed. 3) iii. 56 By a hospital pavilion is meant a detached block of building, capable of containing the largest number of beds that can be placed safely in it, together with suitable nurses' rooms [etc.]. 1864 E. A. PARKES *Pract. Hygiene* 298 The hospitals are to be formed by detached buildings, or pavilions arranged in line, or side by side. 1938 *Amer. Speech* XIII. 228/1 A *ward* is a unit or division in the hospital, often called a *floor, pavilion*, or by the number or letter under which it is listed. 1973 *Lancet* 7 July 33/1 Princess Alexandra Eye Pavilion, Royal Infirmary of Edinburgh.

c. *Bee-keeping.* 'The middle hive in a collateral system' (*Cent. Dict.* 1890).

†8. A flag or ensign, *esp.* the flag carried by a ship to indicate her nationality. *Obs.*

1661 CHAS. II in Julia Cartwright *Henrietta of Orleans* (1894) 111 Certainly never any ships refused to strike their pavilion when they met any ships belonging to the Crowne of England. 1696 PHILLIPS (ed. 5), *Pavilion*,..the Flag of a General Officer in a Fleet. 1778 J. ADAMS *Diary* 29 Mar., Wks. 1851 III. 113 The pilot says war is declared, last Wednesday, and that the pavilions were hoisted yesterday at every port and lighthouse.

†9. *Bot.* The spreading part of the corolla of a flower; the *vexillum* or standard in a papilionaceous flower. *Obs.*

1730 MARTYN in *Phil. Trans.* XXXVI. 386 The *Musa* is a Liliaceous Plant, with a monopetalous, irregular Flower,..composed of a Tube, which is filled with the Ovary, and a Pavilion divided into several Lobes, and forming a kind of Mouth. 1796 H. HUNTER tr. *St.-Pierre's Stud. Nat.* (1799) II. 108 You distinguish in them [papilionaceous flowers] a pavilion, two wings, and a ridge.

10. The part of a brilliant-cut diamond between the girdle and the collet.

1751 D. JEFFERIES *Treat. Diamonds* (ed. 2) Explan. Techn. Terms, Pavilions are the under sides and corners of the Brilliants and lie between the girdle and the collet. 1875 *Ure's Dict. Arts* II. 25. 1889 *Century Dict.* s.v. *Brilliant*, The girdle..forms the junction-line between the upper part, called the crown, and the lower part, called the pavilion.

11. *Anat.* a. The pinna or auricle of the ear.

1842 DUNGLISON *Med. Lex.* s.v., The Pavilion of the Ear is seated behind the cheeks, beneath the temple and anterior to the mastoid process. 1854–67 C. A. HARRIS *Dict. Med. Terminol.*, *Pavilion of the ear*, the expanding portion of the ear.

b. The fimbriated extremity of a Fallopian tube.

1857 BULLOCK *Cazeaux' Midwif.* 66 The existence of supernumerary pavilions, or fimbriated extremities, upon the same tube. 1893 in *Syd. Soc. Lex.*

12. = PAVILLON.

1875 KNIGHT *Dict. Mech.* 1642/1 The insertion of the hand into the pavilion of the French horn regulates the inflection of the sounds.

13. ***Chinese pavilion***, a musical instrument consisting of little bells attached to a frame which are rung by striking the staff of the frame on the ground.

1837 *Encycl. Brit.* (ed. 7) XIV. 617 The Chinese pavilion, the triangle [etc.] are almost entirely confined to military music, though..sometimes used in theatrical orchestras.

14. *attrib.* and *Comb.*, as ***pavilion place, principle, room, system; pavilion-maker; pavilion-like*** adj., ***-wise*** adv.; **pavilion-bed**, a bed with a pavilion-roof or canopy, a tent-bed; **pavilion-facet**, any one of the four largest facets in the pavilion of a brilliant-cut diamond; **pavilion-roof**, 'a roof sloping or hipped equally on all sides' (*Gwilt's Archit.* 1876); †**pavilion-tow**, *Sc.*, a tent-rope.

1704 *Lond. Gaz.* No. 4033/4 A *Pavilion Bed of strip'd Worsted Stuff. 1632 LITHGOW *Trav.* x. 429 There Fabrickes are aduanced three or foure yardes high, *Pauillion-like incircling. 1900 COLQUHOUN *'Overland' to China* viii. 173 In the red lacquered pillars, curved roofs, and pavilion-like character of the buildings. 1624 WEBSTER *Monuments Hon.* Wks. (Rtldg.) 366/2 John of Yeacksley, King Edward the Third's *pavilion-maker. 1594 *Battell of Balrinness* in *Scot. Poems 16th C.* (1801) II. 350 He said, ere he should ceass The standing stonnes of Strathbolgie Schould be his *palione place. 1885 *Manch. Exam.* 6 July 5/4 The new hospital is built on the *pavilion principle. 1903 *Daily Chron.* 15 Oct. 5/1 The *pavilion system—of which St. Thomas's is the only example in London—is..the ideal. *a* 1578 LINDESAY (Pitscottie) *Chron. Scot.* (S.T.S.) I.

175 [He] desyrit thame to tak ane of his awin *pallieȝoun towis..and bind his handis. **1725** De Foe *Voy. rd. World* (1840) 237 Beds, made *pavilion-wise, after the Spanish custom.

pavilion (pəˈvɪljən), *v.* [f. prec. sb.]

1. *trans.* To set or place in or as in a pavilion; to enclose in or as in a pavilion; to canopy.

13.. *K. Alis.* 2038 Daries folk is all ordeynt, And y-pavylounded in a pleyn. **1715–20** Pope *Odyss.* xx. 9 Thus pavilion'd in the porch he lay. **1804** J. Grahame *Sabbath* (1808) 105 The moon Pavilioned in dark clouds. **1818** Keats *Endym.* II. 56 A wild rose tree Pavilions him in bloom. **1839** Sir R. Grant *Hymn, 'O worship the King'* i, Our Shield and Defender, The Ancient of Days, Pavilioned in splendor And girded with praise.

†**b.** To cover (a dish): cf. pavilion *sb.* 3. *Obs.*

c **1468** in *Archæol.* (1846) XXXI. 335 Apone the saide table xvi dishes, every dishe pavilioned, one every pavillion a penon of armes. And whan the Duke was sett, the tentes and pavilions were takine from the messes.

2. To furnish or set (a field, etc.) with pavilions.

1667 Milton *P.L.* xi. 215 The field Pavilion'd with his Guardians bright. **1824** *New Monthly Mag.* X. 494 The pavilioned shores of the Thames.

Hence **paˈvilioned** *ppl. a.*

1795 J. Fawcett *Art of War* 5 See yon pavilion'd Council sitting round. **1824** [see 2].

†**paˈvilioner.** *Obs.* [See -er¹, -er².] A maker or constructor of pavilions; a tent-maker.

c **1600** in *Househ. Ord.* (1790) 4 Coupers, Smythes, Ingyners, Pavillioners, Marynors, Armorers. **1601** F. Tate *Househ. Ord. Edw. II* (1876) 11 The tailour, armorer, pavilioner.

‖**pavillon** (pavijɔ̃). [F. *pavillon* pavilion; in mod.F. also as below.] **1.** The bell-shaped mouth of a trumpet or similar musical instrument.

1879 Stainer *Music of Bible* 79 This last instrument [the English horn] does not terminate in a direct bell or *pavillon*.

2. ***pavillon chinois*** (ʃinwa) = *Chinese pavilion, jingling Johnny* (*a*).

1876 Stainer & Barrett *Dict. Mus. Terms* 347/1 *Pavillon chinois*, an instrument consisting of little bells attached to a staff. **1920, 1970** [see jingling *ppl. a.*²].

pavilyeas, obs. Sc. form of paillasse.

paviment, obs. form of pavement.

†**pavimented,** *ppl. a. Obs.* [ad. It. *pavimentato*, pa. pple. of *pavimentare* to pave.] Pavemented.

1717 Tabor in *Phil. Trans.* XXX. 560 The Pavimented Piazza was Magnificent.

pavin, -ine, variants of pavan.

paving (ˈpeɪvɪŋ), *vbl. sb.* [See -ing¹.] **a.** The action of the vb. pave; *concr.* the product of this action, a pavement; the material of which a pavement is composed.

1426–7 *Rec. St. Mary at Hill* (E.E.T.S.) 67 Payd for certeyne pavynge & mevynge of pewes in the cherche. **1448** Hen. VI *Will* in Willis & Clark *Cambridge* (1886) I. 355 The cloistre to..be sette but .ij. fete lower than the pavyng of the chirch. **1497** *Naval Acc. Hen. VII* (1896) 230 Makyng of ij overmes & payvyng the Kychyn. **1608** Willet *Hexapla Exod.* 554 A stone worke, such as they use in pauings. **1807** tr. *Three Germans* III. 59 The clattering hoofs..were heard upon the paving of the outer courts. **1863** H. Cox *Instit.* III. ix. 731 Local Acts for paving, lighting, &c. of boroughs. **1888** H. Logeman *Rule of S. Benet* p. xxxvi, Dr. Thompson ..said that the Rugby boys' slang term for this process was *paving*—paving smooth (I suppose) the rough road of learning Latin. **1914** 'I. Hay' *Lighter Side School Life* v. 138 He is greatly addicted to a more venial crime known as 'paving'. The paver prepares his translation in the orthodox manner, but whenever he has occasion to look up a word in a lexicon he scribbles its meaning in the margin of the text, or, more frequently, just over the word itself, to guard against loss of memory on the morrow. **1958** L. Foster in *Aspects of Translation* 10 The 'paving' of books by schoolboys and the old-fashioned classical 'literal crib' are rather different cases of translations intended to facilitate comprehension of the original text, not to supplant it.

b. *attrib.* and *Comb.*, as ***paving-beetle, -block, -brick, -flag, -hammer, -machine, -ram, -rammer, -rate, -roller, -sand, -slab, -wood***, etc.

1497 *Naval Acc. Hen. VII* (1896) 89 Paving rammers of tymbre. *Ibid.* 94 Paving rammes of tre. **1538** Elyot, *Pauicula*, a pauyng bytell. **1703** T. N. *City & C. Purchaser* 40 Paving-bricks..are by some call'd Paving-Tiles. **1756–7** tr. *Keysler's Trav.* (1760) III. 314 Paving-sand, upon which, as good a foundation, most of the houses in Amsterdam are built, piles being first driven into it. **1776** G. Semple *Building in Water* 41 With paving Hammers we chipped off so much more of the Bank. **1825** J. Nicholson *Operat. Mechanic* 544 Paving-slabs and chimney-pieces are found by superficial measure. **1862** H. Marryat *Year in Sweden* II. 319 These paving-flags form a staple of Öland commerce. **1869** E. Yates *Wrecked in Port* vii. 66 Men who pay for the paving-rate. **1911** *Daily Colonist* (Victoria, B.C.) 1 Apr. 7/3 The city will purchase from the Michigan Puget Sound Lumber Company a quantity of wood paving blocks sufficient to complete the pavement on View Street. **1934** *Ledger-Dispatch* (Norfolk, Va.) 11 June 7/8 There is glass sand, moulding sand, building, paving, grinding and polishing sand. **1968** J. Arnold *Shell Bk. Country Crafts* xxxi. 332 The Scots pine is planted cultivated and felled.. for the primary purpose of providing pit-props and telephone poles, railway sleepers and at one time for paving-blocks.

ˈpaving-stone. A stone prepared for paving.

c **1440** *Promp. Parv.* 386/2 Pavynge stone, or pathynge stone, *petalum*. **1520** in Gross *Gild Merch.* II. 122 Morters of Marbill et Pavyngstonys of marbyll. **1563** Shute *Archit.* Bj b, Couered the basket with a square pauing stone. **1802** Mar. Edgeworth *Irish Bulls* viii. 190 One of the combatants threw a small paving-stone at his opponent. **1884** J. Tait *Mind in Matter* (1892) 34 In tearing up the foundations of human belief, idealists have prepared paving-stones as missiles of anarchy and bloodshed.

paving-tile. A tile used for paving floors, yards, courts, foot-pavements, etc., often glazed, and sometimes bearing an ornamental design on its surface.

1426–7 *Rec. St. Mary at Hill* (E.E.T.S.) 64 Payd for xjˣˣ pavyng tyle..iijs. iiijd. **1573–80** Baret *Alv.* P 194 Pauing tiles of diuers colours, finelie set with figures of birds, or other things, or hauing like pictures wrought vpon them. **1703** T. N. *City & C. Purchaser* 40 Paving-Tiles..are of several Sizes, viz. 6. 8, 10. and 12 in. square. **1771** Woulfe in *Phil. Trans.* LXI. 126 The composition, which is used for making paving-tiles, answers very well.

pavion, obs. form of pavan.

paviour, -ior (ˈpeɪvɪə(r)). Forms: 5–9 **pavier**, (6 **pavyer**), 7– **-ior, -iour.** [f. pave *v.*; the later form *paviour, -ior*, was an alteration (perh. after *saviour*) of earlier *pavier, -yer*, which again appears to have been altered from paver, after other sbs. in -ier 1, q.v.]

1. One who paves or lays pavements.

1426–7 *Rec. St. Mary at Hill* (E.E.T.S.) 66 A pavier and his man to paue in loue lane. *c* **1515** *Cocke Lorell's B.* 9 Pauyers, bell makers, and brasyers. **1579** Fulke *Confut. Sanders* 671 The pauier hath made the lyke woorke of historie vppon the pauemente. *a* **1649** *Poem attrib. to Chas. I* (L.), The corner-stone's misplaced by every paviour; With such a bloody method and behaviour Their ancestors did crucify our Saviour. **1662** Gerbier *Princ.* 33 The Paviors (after the Bricks are laid) throw sharp Sand over them. **1743** H. Walpole *Corr.* (ed. 3) I. lxxxviii. 307 He may be reduced to turn pavior. *a* **1845** Hood *To M'Adam* ii, Thou stood'st thy trial, Mac! and shaved the road..So well, that paviours threw their rammers by.

fig. **1853** Miss De Quincey in *Friendships of Miss Mitford* (1882) II. vii. 107 A great pavior in the way of good intentions.

b. A rammer for driving paving-stones.

1875 in Knight *Dict. Mech.* **1882** in Ogilvie.

2. A paving-stone: = paver 2. In quot. 1611 *collectively* (or ? ad. OF. *paveure* pavement).

1611 Coryat *Crudities* 185 The walke a little without paued with Diamond pauier Contriued partly with free stone, and partly with red marble. **1829** *Glover's Hist. Derby* I. 88 Flags or paviers, and slate or tile stones. **1843** *Mech. Mag.* XXXIX. 192 The difference between malm paviors and stocks was fifteen..shillings per thousand.

pavis, pavise (ˈpævɪs), *sb.* Now *Hist.* Forms: 4–6 **paueys**, (4 *erron.* **-ews**), 5–6 **pauis**, (**pauys, -es, -yes**, 5–6 **-eis**, 6 **-iss, -yss, -eiss, -ois, -oys, -ash**, *Sc.* **pawes**, 6–7 **pauish, palueise**), 5–7 **pauise, -ice**, (5 **-yce, -yse, -ysse, payuese**, 5–6 **pauisse, -esse, -eice**), 7 **pavyse, -ese**, 7–8 **pavice**, 7– **pavis, -ise**, (8 **pavois, -ache, -ashe**, 8–9 **-ais**, 9 **-isse, -esse, -oise, -as**). *Pl.* orig. (*a* 1500) same as sing. paveys, -is, etc. (hence new sing. 6 pavie); but in 5 pauys(s)es, 5–6 -esses, 6 -oises, 6–7 pavishes, 8 pauashes; 7– pavises, etc. [ME. *paveys, -eis*, a. OF. *pavais* (1337 in Hatz.-Darm.), now *pavois*, ad. It. *pavese*, in Sp. *paves*, med.L. *pavensis* or *pavense* (1299 in Du Cange), also (from It., etc.) *pavēsis, pavēsius, pavēsium, pavēsus, -um, pavexius, pavissis*; app. f. the name of *Pavia* in Italy, where these bucklers were originally made (Hatz.-Darm.). Obs. in actual use since 17th c., and without any fixed current spelling. A final *e* is not etymological, but taken over from the pl. *pavises*, or the obs. *pavice* for *pavis* (cf. *mice, twice*).]

1. A convex shield, large enough to cover the whole body, used in mediæval times as a defence against archery, and esp. in sieges; the term has also been extended to denote any large shield.

The pavis of a knight or archer was usually carried by his valet, page, or attendant, and was deep enough to shelter him in front of his master.

1390 [see β]. ? *c* **1400** Trevisa *Vegecius* II. xxiv. (Roy. MS. 18. A. XII) lf. 47 Foot man with paves and shelde. ? *c* **1400** Lydg. *Æsop's Fab.* iii. 141 Agayne sharpe quarels helpith a pavice. **1412–20** —— *Chr. Troy* III. xxii. (1513) N ij b, Some wyll haue a target or a spere And some a pauys his body for to were. *c* **1475** *Pict. Voc.* in Wr.-Wülcker 784/10 *Hec sestus*, a pavis. **1483** *Cath. Angl.* 271/2 A Pavysse, *castrum*. *c* **1500** *Melusine* 362 Thenne they retourned to Lusynen where geffray dide doo hang the paueys, that he had wonne. **1513** Douglas *Æneis* VII. xiii. 67 A ballen pavis coueris thair left sydis, Maid of hart skynnis and thik oxin hydis. **1530** Palsgr. 252/2 Paves to defend one with, *pauais*. **1598** Florio, *Pauese, Pauesce*, a kinde of target or shield called a palueise. *a* **1600** *Floddan F.* ix. (1664) 83 No shield nor pavish could prevaile. **1658** Phillips, *A Pavese*, or *Pavice*, a large shield which covereth the whole body. **1786** Grose *Anc. Armour* 27 The Pavais, Pavache, or Tallevas, was a large shield, or rather a portable mantlet, capable of covering a man from head to foot. **1795** Southey *Joan of Arc* VIII. 345 The knights below, Each by his pavais bulwark'd. **1860** R. F. Burton *Centr. Afr.* I. 312 In battle they carry the Pavoise, or large hide shield, affected by the Kafirs of the Cape. **1874** Boutell *Arms & Arm.* viii. 137 The knight had his pavise carried before him by a page or valet. Square in outline, and convex in form, this pavise was sufficiently large to shelter both the page and his master.

β. *Plural.* **1390** *Earl Derby's Exp.* (Camden) 23 Johanni Peyntour pro pictura lxviij paueys domini de Willeby. ? *c* **1400** Trevisa *Vegecius* IV. vi. (Roy. MS. 18. A. XII) lf. 101 Good plentie of targes, pauysses, and sheldes. **1426** Lydg. *De Guil. Pilgr.* 7264 Pavys also that wer stronge. **1497** *Naval Acc. Hen. VII* (1896) 95 Trestelles for hakbusses.. iiijˣˣ, Pavesses for the same..iiijˣˣ. *a* **1548** Hall *Chron., Hen. VIII* 42 The shotte..they defended with Pauishes. **1617** in Heath *Grocers' Comp.* (1869) 432 Payde for the paynting and guylding of three pavyses colloured in oyle. **1808** Southey *Chron. Cid* 15 King Don Ferrando..ordered mantles to be made, and also pavaises to protect his people. **1828** Scott *F.M. Perth* xxix, Preparing to cover themselves by large shields, called pavesses.

γ. Curtailed sing. *pavie.* *c* **1575** *Balfour's Practicks, Sea Lawis* c. 91 (1754) 631 The Admiral..may alswa put pulderis, paveis, and speiris.., to wit..ane pavie and a fyre speir for three tunnis.

†**b.** As used on board a ship (being ranged along the sides as a defence against archery). Cf. sense 2 and pavisade. *Obs.*

? *a* **1400** *Morte Arth.* 3626 Ledys one leburde, lordys & oþer, Pyghte payvese one porte, payntede scheldes. **14..** Lydg. *Siege Harfleur* in Arb. *Garner* VIII. 16 These goodly ships lay there at road..On every pavis a cross red. **1512–13** *Acc. Ld. High Treas. Scot.* IV. 473 Item, for vj dusan of slottis and bandis for the pavesis of the James. **1549** *Compl. Scot.* vi. 41 Paueis veil the top vitht pauesis and mantillis. **1562** Leigh *Armorie* 35.

†**c.** A soldier bearing a pavis. *Obs. rare.*

c **1500** *Melusine* 142 Thanne had the sawdan..ordeyned his batayIles, and his Crosbowes & paueys [F. *pavilliers*].

2. A screen of pavises; a pavisade; any screen or shelter used in fighting.

1495 *Trevisa's Barth. De P.R.* XVII. cxlix. T vj/2 Of thornes men makith hegges and pauyses [*Bodl. MS.* frippes]: wyth whyche men defende and socoure themselfe and theyr owne. **1582** N. Lichefield tr. *Castanheda's Conq. E. Ind.* I. lxiv. 130 b, Carrieng his boats with him well armed and fenced, with certeine paueises made of Boordes, and sette with Flagges. *Ibid.* 135 b, With the paueices of our boates, the which were made of boards of two fingers thicke ..we did..defend them of[f].

†**3.** *fig.* A defence, protection. *Obs.*

c **1430** Lydg. *Min. Poems* (Percy Soc.) 233 Jhesus..Ageyn al enmyes sheeld, pavys, and diffence. **1500–20** Dunbar *Poems* xxxvii. 36 He wes our mychte paviss, and our scheild. *a* **1529** Skelton *Death Earl Northumb.* 48 He was their bulwark, their paues, and their wall. **1534** More *Comf. agst. Trib.* Wks. 1180 Clipped in on euery syde wyth the shielde or pauice of God.

4. *attrib.* and *Comb.*, as ***pavis-shield.***

? *a* **1400** *Morte Arth.* 3460 And one he henttis a hode of scharlette fulle riche, A pauys pillione hatt. **1894** C. N. Robinson *Brit. Fleet* 210 Sheltering behind their leather-covered wooden pavis shields.

pavis, pavise (ˈpævɪs), *v. Obs.* or *Hist.* [f. prec. sb.]

1. *trans.* To cover, shelter, or defend with a pavis. Hence **ˈpavised** *ppl. a.*

1489 Caxton *Faytes of A.* I. xxiv. 76 One syde of them shelded or paueysed with hylles. *c* **1500** *Melusine* 167 There was the Captaynne of the place & his peple wel paueysed. **1582** N. Lichefield tr. *Castanheda's Conq. E. Ind.* I. lxi. 125 If so be yᵗ our boates had not ben paueiced or fenced with their shields. **1589** Warner *Alb. Eng.* II. Prose Add. 156 The Troians laboured in trimming, pauashing [**1612** -ishing] and furnishing theyr Nauie. **1805** Southey *Madoc in Azt.* xxv. 90 And shower'd, like rain, upon the pavaised barks, The rattling shafts.

†**2.** To act as a shelter against. *Obs. rare*⁻¹.

1567 G. Fenton *Trag. Disc.* 134 b, The shade and shadowe of the trees pauisinge the vyolence of the sun.

pavisade, pavesade (pævɪˈseɪd). Now *Hist.* Also 6–8 **pavoisade.** [a. F. *pavesade, pavezade* (1550 in Hatz.-Darm.), *pavoisade* (Cotgr.), ad. It. *pavesata* (Florio), in Sp. *pavesada* (Minsheu), f. It. *pavese*: see pavis and -ade 1.] A defence or screen made of pavises or other shields joined in a continuous line, used both in land warfare and on board ship; hence, a screen of canvas run round the sides of a ship in order to defend the crew from missiles, and hide the operations on board from the view of the enemy.

1600 Holland *Livy* x. 373 The pavoisade or tortuse-fense. **1656** Blount *Glossogr.* (from Cotgr.), *Pavoisade*, any Target-fence, that of Galleys, whereby the slaves are defended from the smal shot of the Enemy. **1685** Cotton tr. *Montaigne* III. vi. (1711) III. 159 A Number of Harquebusiers, drawn up ready, and charg'd, and all cover'd with a Pavisade like a Galliot. **1708** Kersey, *Pavoisade* or *Pavezado*. **1823** Crabb *Technol. Dict.*, *Pavesade* (Mil.), *pavoisade*, or *pavisade*, French for a sail cloth hung round a galley during action to cover the slaves that row on the benches.

†**paviˈsado, paveˈsado.** *Obs.* Forms: 7 **pavoisado, -ezado**, 7–8 **-esado**, 8 **-isado.** [Altered form of prec., after Sp. *pavesada*.] = prec.

[**1599** Minsheu *Sp. Dict.*, *Pavesada*, a battell of targettiers, or a battell at sea with some defence, that they be not seene of their enemy.] **1609** Holland *Amm. Marcell.* 178 Aquileia was compassed about with a double pavoisado of shields. **1611** Florio, *Pauesáta*, a pauesado..or arming of a ship with cloth and canuase to hide the Mariners from sight of the enemie. **1775** Ash, *Pavisado*.

pavisand (ˈpævɪsænd), *v.* [f. pavisade.] *intr.* To display a formidable array of clothing and ornament; to flaunt one's appearance. Hence **'pavisander**.

1910 KIPLING *Rewards & Fairies* 297 Forth she come pavisanding like a peacock—stuff, ruff, stomacher and all. **1950** I. BROWN *Having Last Word* 90, I can picture Queen Elizabeth pavisanding at times. *Ibid.*, Among great pavisanders also was Milton's Delilah.

paviser, -or ('pævisə(r)). Forms: see quots. [Altered from OF. *paves(s)ier, -vissier, -vaisier, -voisier*, etc. (14th c. in Godef.), also *paviseur* (15–16th c., also *-vaiseur, -voiseur, -vesceur*, Godef.), f. *paveis, pavois* PAVIS *sb.*: see -ER[2].] A man armed with or bearing a pavis.

?*a* **1400** *Morte Arth.* 2831 His pelours and pauysers passede alle nombyre. *Ibid.* 3005. **1749** in MORES *Nomina* 90–101 (transl. Accts. of Edw. III) Pauisors..pauizors.. pavesours. **1826** W. C. STAFFORD *Sir Everhard* 188 These pavisers bore a large shield, somewhat resembling a boat with the stern cut off, which they raised as a bulwark before the archers when in battle. **1846–60** FAIRHOLT *Hist. Costume Eng.* Gloss., *Pavise*, a large shield..managed by a pavisor or soldier, who attended to it, and who was placed in front of an archer.

Pavlov ('pævlɒf, 'pævlɒv). Also **Pavloff**, etc. The name of the Russian physiologist Ivan Petrovich *Pavlov* (1849–1936), used *attrib.* or in the possessive to designate aspects of his work, esp. those connected with conditioning the salivary reflexes of a dog to the mental stimulus of the sound of a bell.

1911 STEDMAN *Med. Dict.* 644/2 *Pavloff method*,..a quantitative study of the modifications of the salivary reflexes caused by psychic reactions. **1922** K. DUNLAP *Elements Sci. Psychol.* xiv. 303 The development of the auditory-salivary reaction in Pavloff's dog. **1933** J. C. FLÜGEL *Hundred Years Psychol.* xi. 208 He became much concerned with Pavlov's conditioned reflex and the psychology of food. **1949** KOESTLER *Insight & Outlook* xxviii. 379 The Pavlov-trained dog, when faced with an ambiguous stimulus,..becomes deranged in all his reflexes. **1967** *Listener* 3 Aug. 138/2, I had a kind of Pavlov-dog reaction, shaking with nerves, because I'd been very nervous when I'd done that first film nine years before. **1974** *Sunday Times* (Colour Suppl.) 27 Oct. 30/4 Such de- or re-conditioning is quick, cheap, and, like Pavlov's bells, it gets results. **1976** A. WHITE *Long Silence* ii. 19 You're not a Pavlov dog, trained to bark when I ring a bell. You have a mind of your own.

pavlova (pæv'ləʊvə). *Austral.* and *N.Z.* [f. the name of Anna *Pavlova* (1885–1931), Russian ballerina.] A dessert or cake, now usually one made with meringue, whipped cream, and fruit. Also *attrib.*

1927 *Davis Dainty Dishes* (ed. 6) (Davis Gelatine, N.Z., Ltd.) 11 Pavlova... Dissolve all but a teaspoonful of Gelatine in the hot water, and all the sugar except a dessertspoonful [etc.]. **1929** K. MCKAY *Pract. Home Cookery* 155/1 *Pavlova cakes*... Cook like meringues... They are delightful and simple to make besides being a novelty. **1952** *Weekly News* (Auckland) 30 July 14/4 (*heading*) Soft-centred Pavlova Cake. *Ibid.*, R. J. S. (Nelson) writes:—Could you give me a recipe for making a pavlova with a soft centre? *Ibid.*, Most good pavlova recipes are soft inside. **1952** B. NILSON *Penguin Cookery Bk.* xviii. 396 Pavlova Cake (to use as a cake or cold sweet). **1957** *Daily Mail* 7 Oct. 11/4 Pavlova. *Ingredients*: 3 egg whites 6 oz. castor sugar 1 teaspoonful vanilla 1 teaspoonful vinegar 1 teaspoonful cornflour ½ pint double cream (whipped and flavoured) 16 oz can Australian pineapple or apricots cherries angelica. **1958** *N.Z. News* 2 Dec. 10/2 Supper included some renowned New Zealand dishes such as pavlova, whitebait, and oysters. **1960** I. CROSS *Backward Sex* 85 I'll give you some of Mum's pavlova cake for supper. **1964** *Guardian* 18 Apr. 5/4 A Pavlova..is a meringue basket so called because it spreads out like the skirts of a ballerina. **1968** *N.Z. News* 11 Dec. 11/5 Pavlova cake—the New Zealand and Australian sweet—is believed to have been created as a compliment to the famous dancer when she visited those countries. **1972** V. C. CLINTON-BADDELEY *To study Long Silence* v. 191 A *Pavlova*—a New Zealand speciality of choice fresh fruit and whipped cream wrapped in meringue-like base. **1975** *Times* 16 Dec. 12/4 A Pavlova, an Australian dessert..a meringue with cream, passion fruit, ice cream and strawberries.

Pavlovian (pæv'ləʊviən), *a.* [f. PAVLOV + -IAN.] Of, pertaining to, or connected with Pavlov, his theories, experiments, or methods. Also in extended and weakened senses.

1931 A. HUXLEY *Let.* 24 Aug. (1969) 351 The effects of such sociological reforms as Pavlovian conditioning of all children. **1951** H. HUMPHREY *Thinking* 6 In the Pavlovian system,..we have an attempt to account objectively for all psychological facts in terms of the primary interaction of organism and environment. **1952** V. NABOKOV *Nabokov's Dozen* (1959) 206 A mad Pavlovian world where..variations in simple visual values influence and gradually replace flavour. **1963** A. HERON *Towards Quaker View of Sex* 67 Some recoveries with 'deconditioning' treatment along Pavlovian lines. **1974** *Daily Tel.* 8 Feb. 8/2 The report does not hesitate to name names, a procedure that will inevitably touch off a Pavlovian response from Leftist circles to deride it as a 'Reds under the Beds' scare. **1976** *Survey* Winter 24 The Soviet Union..managed to exploit the South African issue in order to create the well-known Pavlovian reflex all through Black Africa. **1977** *Meanjin* XXXVI. 1. 108 The adroit orchestration of comedy..that is, the patrons were not treated as a collection of complete Pavlovian half-wits.

pavois, -e, variants of PAVIS.

[pavon, a spurious word, originating in a misreading by Meyrick, *Ancient Armour* III. Gloss., of OF. *panon*, PENNON.

Hence accepted by Fairholt *Costume Eng.* (1860) 97, new ed. (1885) (where a supposed figure is given), by Cussans *Handbk. of Heraldry* (1882) 275, Preble *Hist. Flag* (1880), in Ogilvie's *Imperial*, Cassell's *Encyclopædic*, Webster's, *Century*, and Funk's *Standard* Dictionaries.]

†**pavo'naceous**, *a. Obs. rare.* [Cf. PAVONAZZO.]

1688 R. HOLME *Armoury* II. 313/1 *Pavonaceous*, Pea-cock colour, a shining bluish green.

pavonated ('pævəneɪtɪd), *ppl. a. rare.* [f. L. *pāvo, pāvōn-em* peacock + -ATE[3] + -ED[1].] Coloured like a peacock's feather, as peacock copper-ore.

1798 G. MITCHELL tr. *Karsten's Min. in Leskean Mus.* 243 Very beautifully pavonated copper pyrites. *Ibid.* 291 Hæmatites pavonated in the most lively manner.

‖**pavonazzo** (pavo'nattso), *a.* and *sb.* Also 9 **-azza**. [It. *pavonazzo*, also *pavonaccio* 'of the colour of a peacock' (Florio), 'of a violet or purple colour' (Baretti):—L. *pāvōnāceum*, f. *pāvōn-em* peacock: see -ACEOUS.] Peacock-coloured: applied to a kind of red or purplish marble or breccia, often veined with a fine variety of colouring. So ‖**pavona'zzetto** [It. dim.], a similar stone.

1816 J. DALLAWAY *Stat. & Sculp.* vi. 346 A Sarcophagus ..of pavonazzo marble. **1890** *Century Dict.* s.v. *Marble*, *Pavonazzo* and *pavonazetto* are various red and purplish marbles and breccias... The most beautiful pavonazetto is that called..Phrygian marble. **1891** *Daily News* 27 Jan. 6/1 Pavonazza marble lines the walls of this saloon—a fine dado of rouge jaspe running beneath it. **1901** J. M. M. CHARLESON *Eain Macarthon* Introd. 3 A golden cross, flanked with white roses and lilies in vases of pavonazzetto.

†**pavone** (pə'vəʊn). *Obs. rare*$^{-1}$. [ad. It. *pavone*:—L. *pāvo, pāvōnem*.] A peacock.

1590 SPENSER *F.Q.* III. xi. 47 More sondry colours then the proud Pavone [*rimes* stone, alone, shone] Beares in his boasted fan.

pavonian (pə'vəʊniən), *a.* [f. L. *pāvo, pāvōn-em* peacock + -IAN: cf. F. *pavonien* (Littré).] Of or pertaining to a peacock; pavonine.

1793 YOUNG in *Phil. Trans.* LXXXIII. 179 [He] has described this phantom as of pavonian colours. **1839** BAILEY *Festus* xxxi. (1852) 506 O'er her head attendants..Pavonian canopy of azure held. **1870** E. PEACOCK *Ralf Skirl.* III. 97 The pavonian shriek of the Justice's voice.

pavonine ('pævənaɪn), *a.* and *sb.* [ad. L. *pāvōnīn-us*, f. *pāvōn-em* peacock: see -INE[1].]

A. *adj.* **1.** Of or pertaining to, resembling or characteristic of a peacock.

1656 BLOUNT *Glossogr.*, *Pavonine*, of or belonging to a Peacock or a Peahen. **1848** THACKERAY *Bk. Snobs* xx, The lanky, pavonine strut, and shrill genteel scream. **1851** RUSKIN *Stones Ven.* (1874) II. ii. 20 Groups of peacocks and lions..not expressive of very accurate knowledge either of leonine or pavonine forms.

b. *Zool.* Of or pertaining to the genus *Pavo* or sub-family *Pavoninæ*, including the peafowl.

1895 in *Funk's Stand. Dict.*

2. Resembling the neck or the tail of the peacock in colouring.

1688 R. HOLME *Armoury* II. 313/1 *Pavonine*, Peacock colour, or Peacock like. **1813** J. FORSYTH *Italy* 162 Plain marbles were stained or inlaid..: hence their pavonine beds. **1851** S. JUDD *Margaret* xvi. (1871) 135 Everything became a sort of pavonine transparency. **1857** MAYNE *Expos. Lex.*, *Pavoninus, Bot.*, having the eye-like spots resembling those seen on the peacock's tail, as the *Acherus pavoninus*: pavonine.

B. *sb.* **1.** An iridescent lustre found on some ores and metals; peacock-tail tarnish.

1805–17 R. JAMESON *Char. Min.* (ed. 3) 80 *Pavonine*, or *Peacock-tail tarnish*. This is an assemblage of yellow, green, blue, red, and brown colours, on a yellow ground... Example, Copper-pyrites. **1825** W. HAMILTON *Dict. Terms Arts & Sc.*, *Pavonine*..In *Painting*, peacock tail tarnish.

2. *Zool.* A bird of the sub-family *Pavoninæ*.

1895 in *Funk's Stand. Dict.*

pa'vonious, *a. rare.* [f. L. *pāvōn-em* peacock + -IOUS.] 'Ocellated, like a peacock's tail' (*Cent. Dict.* 1890).

'pavonize, *v. rare.* [f. L. *pāvōn-em* peacock + -IZE: cf. It. *pavoneggiare* 'to peacockize it' (Florio).] *intr.* To comport oneself as a peacock; to strut.

1882 in OGILVIE.

‖**pavor.** [L. *pavor* quaking fear.]

†**a.** (See quot.) *Obs. rare*$^{-0}$.

1656 BLOUNT *Glossogr.*, *Pavor*, great fear and dread.

b. pavor nocturnus [L. *nocturnus* nocturnal], a sudden and inexplicable terror which may afflict a sleeping person, esp. a child, in the night; = *night-terror* s.v. NIGHT *sb.* 14; similarly **pavor diurnus** [L. *diurnus* belonging to the day] (see quot. 1940).

[**1848** DUNGLISON *Dict. Med. Sci.* (ed. 7) 634/1 *Pavores nocturni seu dormientium*, fear during sleep.] **1889** *Albany Med. Ann.* June 200 The victim of night terrors, or *pavor nocturnus*, experiences an awful, unpleasant, terror stricken disturbance of the mind. **1889** J. THOMSON tr. *Henoch's Lect. Children's Dis.* I. 241 One of the rare cases of pavor diurnus which I have seen affected the son of an actor (7 years old), a nervous, anaemic, delicate child. **1900** *Lancet* 3 Feb. 292/1 Two cases of pavor diurnus..have recently been under my care. **1915** J. N. HALL *Borderline Dis.* I. iii. 96 Nightmare in adults and pavor nocturnus in young children are vivid dreams with sensations of oppression in the chest, of horror, and inability to escape some impending catastrophe. **1927** W. P. LUCAS *Mod. Pract. Pediatr.* II. xii. 698 Pavor diurnus is more rarely seen than night terrors but is more significant of a disorder of the nervous system. **1940** HINSIE & SHATZKY *Psychiatric Dict.* 406/1 *Pavor diurnus*, fear reactions which occur in the young child during the afternoon nap, similar to night terrors but not so frequently taking place as the latter. **1950** J. STRACHEY tr. *Freud's Totem & Taboo* iv. 128 Phobias of this type..are, in my opinion, at least as common in childhood as *pavor nocturnus*. **1966** *Sci. & Psychoanal.* IX. 176 The purposiveness of the rumination is seen in the fact that..the event does ultimately become commonplace... The suggestion is strong that the *pavor nocturnus* of the child may have a similar accustomizing function.

pavore, obs. form of PAVER.

pavvy ('pævi). Also **pavy**. Abbreviation of PAVILION *sb.* Cf. PAV[1].

1899 KIPLING *Stalky & Co.* 159 Forty shillin's or a month for hackin' the chucker-out of the Pavvy on the shins. **1900** FARMER *Public School Word-Bk.* 146 *Pavvy, The* (Harrow). —The pavilion on the cricket-ground. **1905** H. A. VACHELL *Hill* v. 117, I say, there's going to be a ruction in front of the Pavvy. Come on! **1961** PARTRIDGE *Dict. Slang* Suppl. 1215/1 *Pavy, the*,..The pavilion: Harrovian:..Hence, at certain other Public Schools': c. 20.

pavy ('peɪvi). [a. F. *pavie*, from *Pavie* Pavia.] A hard clingstone peach or nectarine.

1675 *Phil. Trans.* X. 373 Plums, Peaches, Pavyes, Apples and Pears. **1685** TEMPLE *Gardening* Wks. 1720 I. 183 Of the Pavies or Hard Peaches, I know none good here but the Newington. **1766** *Complete Farmer* s.v. *Peach-tree*, The French distinguish those we call peaches into two sorts, viz. pavies, and peaches. **1892** *Chambers' Encycl.* VII. 824.

pavyer, pavyon, pavyse, obs. forms of PAVIOUR, PAVAN, PAVIS.

paw (pɔː), *sb.*[1] Forms: 4–5 **powe**, 4–6 **pawe**, 5–6 *Sc.* **pow**, (**poll**), 6– **paw**. [ME. a. OF. *powe, poue*, var. of *poe* (*pooe*) = Pr. *pauta*; app. of Frankish origin, pointing to an Old Low Ger. (Niederrhein.) **pauta*, whence MDu. *pôte*, Du. *poot*, 14th c. Niederrhein. *pôte*, whence HG. *pfote* paw. F. *patte* is generally supposed to be related.

The ulterior history and relationship of OLG. **pauta* is unknown. Franck has suggested the existence of a Germanic ablaut series *peut-, paut-, put-* (*pot-*) in the sense 'poke, stir', to which he would refer the frequentatives, Du. *peuteren* to finger, pick, LG. *pöteren*, and Eng. *potter*.]

1. a. The foot of a beast having claws or nails. (Distinguished from *hoof*.)

13.. *Coer de L.* 1082 Fast aboute on the wowes, Abrod he [the lion] spredde alle hys powes. *a* **1400** *Isumbras* 181 So come a lyoun..And in hir pawes scho hent the childe. *c* **1470** HENRY *Wallace* XI. 249 The wod lyoun..With his rude pollis in the mantill rocht sa. **1513** DOUGLAS *Æneis* XI. xiii. 70 Ane hyduus wolfis..With chaftis braid, quhyte teith, and bustuus powis. *a* **1529** SKELTON *P. Sparowe* 288 The lyons in theyr rage, Myght catche the in theyr pawes, And gnawe the in theyr iawes! **1530** PALSGR. 252/2 Pawe of a beest, *patte*. **1611** BIBLE *Lev.* xi. 27 Whatsoeuer goeth vpon his pawes, among all maner of beasts. **1698** FROGER *Voy.* 159 An old Monkey..with a great piece of Bacon in his Paws. **1774** GOLDSM. *Nat. Hist.* (1776) IV. 28 The squirrel..sits up on its hinder legs, and uses the fore paws as hands. **1871** L. CARROLL *Through Looking-Glass* i, Kitty sat..on her knee,..now and then putting out one paw and gently touching the ball [of worsted].

b. The foot of any animal; *esp.* the claw of a bird. *rare.* Cf. F. *patte* (not however said of birds of prey).

c **1384** CHAUCER *H. Fame* II. 33 And with hys grym pawes stronge..Me..he [the eagle] hente. **1573** L. LLOYD *Marrow of Hist.* (1653) 95 The griping paws of a hungry Sparhawk. **1607** HEYWOOD *Wom. killed w. Kindn.* Wks. 1874 II. 99 Mine..seisd a Fowle Within her talents; and you saw her pawes Full of the Feathers. **1814** MME. D'ARBLAY *Wanderer* V. 138 Where not even a bird could find a twig for the sole of his paw. **1843** MARRYAT *M. Violet* xliv, The mud vampire, a kind of spider leech, with sixteen short paws.

c. ? Short for CAT'S-PAW.

1824 GALT *Rothelan* III. 225 His money became as paws to my vices.

2. a. Contemptuously or jocularly applied to the hand, esp. when clumsy, or awkwardly used. *colloq.*

1605 CHAPMAN *All Fooles* Plays 1873 I. 141, I made no more adoe, but layd these pawes Close on his shoulders. **1711** SWIFT *Midas* 70 Midas' dirty paws. **1742** RICHARDSON *Pamela* III. 323 He held both Hands out, and a fine pair of Paws shew'd he. **1826** COBBETT *Rur. Rides* (1885) II. 219 He ..laid his hand upon my knee! 'Take away your paw', said I. **1887** MISS E. MONEY *Dutch Maiden* (1888) 331 He stuck out his paw, and said Good-bye.

b. *transf.* 'Hand' in the sense of handiwork; handwriting, 'fist'; signature.

1628 PRYNNE *Cens. Cozens* 3 You may discouer the Authors qualities and conditions, by this his Paw, and Handyworke. **1702** C. MATHER *Magn. Chr.* VII. (1852) App. 610 To this instrument were set the paws of Edgeremet and five more of their sagamores. **1784** MME. D'ARBLAY *Diary*

17 Apr., The sight of your paw..would be well worth all the pence I have.

3. [f. PAW *v.*] The action, or an act, of pawing.

1611 COTGR., *Onglade*, a scratch, or paw with, or the print, or marke of, nayles; a nayle-marke. **1847** WHITTIER *Drovers* vi, With toss of horn and tail, And paw of hoof,.. They leap some farmer's broken pale.

4. *attrib.* and *Comb.*, as ***paw-mark***, ***print*** (also *fig.*), ***-stroke***, ***-tread***; ***paw-like*** adj. Also ***pawful***.

1925 F. M. FORD *No More Parades* ii. 73 She resembled a white Persian cat luxuriating, sticking out a tentative pawful of expanding claws. **1964** D. VARADAY *Gara-Yaka* xix. 173 The invaders replied very effectively to the warnings, and the Prodigal and his family [of lions] had a pawful of trouble. **1849** ROCK *Ch. of Fathers* II. 256 The artist's beautiful handiwork..upon its paw-like feet. **1894** 'MARK TWAIN' in *Century Mag.* June 234/2 Are you going to ornament the royal palaces with nigger paw-marks? **1929** D. H. LAWRENCE *Lett.* (1932) 833 Such dark paw-marks of the wind on the sea! **1975** *Sunday Times* 16 Nov. 44/4 Every pawmark shows up on those virgin white surfaces. **1925** *Scribner's Mag.* July 33/1, I saw..the curious paw print of a porcupine, with its little pebbled markings. **1938** M. K. RAWLINGS *Yearling* iv. 35 All about were the paw-prints of the small things. **1963** *Times* 25 Jan. 12/7 The badger, whose paw-prints are square-fronted and easily recognizable, is better off. **1968** C. NICOLE *Self Lovers* vii. 88 The whole thing has his pawprints all over it. His speciality is taking his victims swimming at dawn. **1977** D. HARSENT *Dreams of Dead* 55 Dark ooze by the apple tree stippled with massive paw-prints. **1902** J. CONRAD *Heart of Darkness* 119 Playful paw-strokes. **1892** *Pall Mall G.* 19 Dec. 6/2, I examine the powder round the doors for footmarks or paw-treads.

paw (pɔː, pɑː), *sb.*[2] *Sc.* [Origin unknown: identity with F. *pas* 'step', and PAW *sb.*[1], has been suggested; but there are difficulties with both.] In the phrases, ***to play a paw***, to play a trick; ***to play one's paws***, to play one's part in acting or in life; ***(not) to play paw***, (not) to make the slightest movement with hand or foot.

c **1560** A. SCOTT *Poems* (S.T.S.) xxv. 14 Remane with me and tary still And se quha playis best thair pawis. **1690** *Killiecrankie* in *Jacob. Songs* (1887) 39 They thought the devil had been there, That played them sic a paw then. ? *a* **1700** *Jock o' the Side* xiv. in Child *Ballads* (1889) III. 480/1 His neck in twa I wat they hae wrung, Wi hand or foot he neer playd paw. **1823** HOGG in *Blackw. Mag.* Mar. 313/2 Some day when ye couldna play paw to help yoursels.

†**paw**, *sb.*[3] *Obs.* An anglicized representation of F. *pas* 'step'. ***grand paw***, F. *grand pas*.

1660 WATERHOUSE *Arms & Arm.* 30 They indeed allowed to merits rewards and admissions to honour by grand paw's and deliberate steps of ascent. **1698** FRYER *Acc. E. India & P.* 139 They are taught little more than the Grand Paw, and to make a Salam.

paw (pɔː), *sb.*[4] *U.S.* = PA[1].

1903 *Dialect Notes* II. 324 *Paw, maw*, nouns. Father; mother. (In the North *pa; ma.*) **1919** E. O'NEILL *Rope* in *Moon of Caribees* 183 Come on back to the house, Paw. It's gittin' near supper time. **1929** W. FAULKNER *Sound & Fury* 46 Your paw told you to stay out that tree. **1933** J. V. ALLEN *Cowboy Lore* IV. 67 He said he had to leave his home, his paw had married twice. **1935** Z. N. HURSTON *Mules & Men* I. vii. 163 His paw said, 'Son, Ah don't see how you gointer do dat.' **1939** in *Jrnl. Amer. Folklore* LII. 108 I am Peetie Wheet Straw, the devil's son-in-law, The woman I married, old Satan was her paw. **1942** ADE *Let.* 1 Feb. (1973) 228 The little red school-house is a thing of the past but don't forget that it turned out some of our best people, including possibly your paw and maw and, certainly, your grandparents. **1968** E. J. GAINES *Bloodline* 247 He follow his mom and paw out the house. **1975** J. GORES *Hammett* (1976) xiv. 102 'What's the brother's name?' 'Don't rightly know. May be my paw—.'

†**paw** (pɔː), *a. slang* or *colloq. Obs.* [app. a variant of *pah* 'nasty, improper, unbecoming', adj. use of PAH *int.*, q.v. Cf. PAW *int.*] Improper, naughty, obscene. See also PAW-PAW.

1668 DAVENANT *Man's the Master* IV. i. Wks. 1874 V. 72 This Tarquin-steward would have kist me by force. *Steph.* Kiss you! fye, that's a paw-word. **1695** CONGREVE *Love for L.* V. iv, O fie, marrying is a paw Thing. **1706** E. WELLS *Answ. Dowley* 46 A paw word which is not fit to be written. **1730** T. CIBBER *Lover* II. 23 *Læt.* So you hold it politick to be a Rogue? *Gran.* Oh, that's a paw Word.

paw (pɔː), *v.* [f. PAW *sb.*[1] Cf. *to claw*.]

1. To touch or strike with the paw.

a. *trans.* Also with adv. expressing the resulting condition (quot. 1891).

1611 MIDDLETON & DEKKER *Roaring Girle* III. iii, I ha sent for a couple of beares shall paw him. **1695** BLACKMORE *Pr. Arth.* II. 161 The sporting Lyon Paws the wanton Bear. **1791** COWPER *Odyss.* x. 264 [Circe's lions and wolves] Paw'd them in blandishment. **1891** MISS DOWIE *Girl in Karp.* xiii. 177 One of his eyes was pawed out by a bear.

b. *intr.*

1667 MILTON *P.L.* VII. 464 The Tawnie Lion, pawing to get free His hinder parts. **1707** HEARNE *Collect.* 1 Nov. (O.H.S.) II. 67 A Lyoness, pawing upon yͤ arms of France. **1713** STEELE *Guard.* No. 146 ¶5 He [a young lion] did some mischief by pawing and playing with people.

2. To strike or scrape the ground with the hoofs: said of a horse, etc. **a.** *intr.*

1611 BIBLE *Job* xxxix. 21 He paweth in the valley, and reioyceth in his strength. **1690** *Newsletter* 30 Aug. in Wood *Life* (O.H.S.) III. 339 The two horses..pawed over the iron spikes with their forefeet. **1704** POPE *Windsor For.* 152 Th' impatient courser..pawing, seems to beat the distant plain. **1877** TALMAGE 50 *Serm.* 8 The horses paw and neigh to get into the stream.

b. *trans.* (the ground, etc.). Also *transf.* of a man (quot. 1887). Also with adv. (quot. 1891).

1697 DRYDEN *Virg. Georg.* III. 749 He paws the Ground. **1735** SOMERVILLE *Chase* II. 92 With Ears And Tail erect, neighing he paws the Ground. **1877** J. A. ALLEN *Amer. Bison* 468 The bulls are..fond of pawing the ground. **1887** HALL CAINE *Deemster* xii. 78 He listened with..his foot pawing the mat. **1891** MRS. L. ADAMS *Bonnie Kate* II. iii. 77 No more roans would paw up the roadway.

3. a. *trans.* To pass the hand over, touch with the hand, handle; esp. awkwardly, coarsely, indelicately, or rudely. Now esp. to fondle (usu. a woman) lasciviously. Also const. *about*, *over*. *colloq.*

1604 T. M. *Black Bk.* in *Middleton's Wks.* (Bullen) VIII. 27 His palm shall be pawed with pence. **1641** MILTON *Reform.* I. Wks. 1851 III. 17 The obscene, and surfeted Priest scruples not to paw, and mammock the sacramentall bread, as familiarly as his Tavern Biskit. **1701** FARQUHAR *Sir Harry Wildair* II. i, Have you been pawing me all this morning with them dirty fists of yours? **1847** TENNYSON *Princess* I. 20 Our great court-Galen..paw'd his beard, and mutter'd 'catalepsy'. **1889** A. R. HOPE in *Boy's Own Paper* 3 Aug. 699/3, I wish she would not *paw* me so. **1902** ADE *Girl Proposition* 58 He told himself that he was a Chump for continuing to worship one who could be pawed over and man-handled by anything that wore a Derby Hat. **1918** H. G. WELLS *Joan & Peter* xi. 387 A fellow had to..watch.. Joan being ordered about and..*pawed* about. **1928** A. HUXLEY *Point Counter Point* xi. 176 Other men were liable to pounce on you and try to paw you about and kiss you. **1934** E. O'NEILL *Days without End* II. 70 Walter was drunk, pawing over his latest female. **1942** A. CHRISTIE *Body in Library* ii. 24, I hate to see a girl..who..lets a disgusting Central European paw her about. **1955** G. FREEMAN *Liberty Man* I. iii. 51 Maureen had been mad for him to go on pawing her for hours last night. **1959** 'C. CARNAC' *Death of Lady Killer* xii. 136 A real dirty tyke he was, always trying to paw any woman within reach. **1975** J. I. M. STEWART *Young Pattullo* vii. 153 Fish, who had decent feelings, would have preferred to be pawed in privacy. **1978** D. BLOODWORTH *Crosstalk* xxxi. 240 The outraged shopper said..that when he saw her looking at him he had winked and pawed her.

b. *intr.* To pass the hand clumsily, awkwardly, or rudely. ***to paw on*** or ***over***, to handle, feel, or finger awkwardly.

1848 KINGSLEY *Saint's Trag.* IV. iv. 134 You will not let the mob..paw over all my limbs. **1876** T. HARDY *Madding Crowd* viii, A hand pawing about the door for the bobbin. **1886** *Boston* (Mass.) *Jrnl.* 22 Dec. 2/4 Those young ladies who paw upon the pianoforte.

Hence ˈ**pawing** *vbl. sb.* and *ppl. a.*

1726 LEONI *Alberti's Archit.* I. 96/2 Under Horses, make ..planks of Holm or Oke, that..by their pawing they may not spoyl both their hoofs and the pavement. **1749** J. CLELAND *Mem. Woman Pleasure* II. 134 The tiresome pawing and toying. **1798** COLERIDGE *Anc. Mar.* v. xxii, Like a pawing horse let go, She made a sudden bound. **1880** M. ARNOLD *Ess. Crit.* Ser. II. *Keats* (1888) 104 Admirers whose pawing and fondness does..harm to the fame of Keats. **1906** E. NESBIT *Railway Children* xii. 256 Like most boys ..[he] hated..kissing and holding of hands. He called all such things 'pawing'. **1931** W. FAULKNER *Sanctuary* xix. 205 Impassable, swinging hands with their escorts, objects of casual and puppyish pawings, they dawdled up the hill toward the college. **1935** *Scrutiny* IV. 128 Revolutionary feeling is for her bound up with an incessant kissing and pawing between and among the sexes. **1951** J. C. FENNESSY *Sonnet in Bottle* III. v. 82 Their pawing hands stretched out ..to feel and finger their prisoners. **1977** H. OSBORNE *White Poppy* xxix. 194 A certain amount of kissing and pawing, but absolutely no more. **1978** *Times* 7 Sept. 13/3 Ladies never touch their gentlemen in public... Pawing and clinging, with its nasty carnal implications, is reserved for..foreign adventuresses.

paw, *int.* variant of PAH.

1678 DRYDEN *Limberham* IV. i, Paw, paw! that word honour has almost turned my stomach.

pawa, var. PAUA.

pawage, pawaw, obs. f. PAVAGE, POWWOW.

‖**pawang** (ˈpaːwaŋ). Also (*rare*) **puwang**. [Malay.] A Malay sorcerer or medicine-man; a wizard or witch; a wise man, expert.

1821 J. LEYDEN tr. *Malay Annals* 51 He immediately ordered an artificer to be sent for, named Pawang Bentan. **1839** T. J. NEWBOLD *Pol. & Statistical Acct. Straits of Malacca* II. viii. 98 They have 'wise men', or Puwangs, who pretend to be able to ascertain the most favourable spots for sinking a mine. **1893** F. A. SWETTENHAM *About Perak* 33 A Malay Pâwang (medicine-man) has the same sort of nose for tin that a truffle dog has for truffles. **1906** *Macm. Mag.* Aug. 778 An old *pawang*, or sorcerer, stepped forward with a bunch of twigs of a tree for which a tiger is thought to have a peculiar dread. **1907** F. A. SWETTENHAM *Brit. Malaya* vii. 156 When a patient becomes dangerously ill..it is common ..to call in a *pâwang*, a kind of wizard or witch, who tries by incantations and other forms of the black art to lure the evil spirit from his prey. **1933** L. AINSWORTH *Confessions Planter in Malaya* 128 A 'Pawang' or witch doctor was called, and for the sum of twenty dollars he agreed to perform the complete ceremony. **1965** C. SHUTTLEWORTH *Malayan Safari* ii. 34 Contact with the spirit world is only made through the medium of the tribal *pawangs* or medicine-men. **1972** M. SHEPPARD *Taman Indera* 94 *Pawang*, an expert in any art believed to involve the use of magic.

pawed (pɔːd), *a. rare.* [-ED[2].] Having paws.

1611 COTGR., *Empieté*, pawed, pounced, clawed, talented. *Ibid.*, *Paté*, pawed, broad-footed.

pawen, variant of PAWN *sb.*[4] *Obs.*

pawes, obs. Sc. form of PAVIS.

pawk[1], **pauk** (pɔːk). *Sc.* and *north. dial.* Also 6 **palk**, (? **paik**). [Derivation unknown.] Trick, artifice, cunning device.

1513 DOUGLAS *Æneis* VIII. Prol. 81 Prattis ar reput policy and perellus paukis [*rimes* walkis, talk is, baulkis]. **1535** STEWART *Cron. Scot.* III. 274 Greit wounder had quha playit had that palk. **1583** *Leg. Bp. St. Androis* 255 Maid to be punissit for his palk [*printed* paik]; But he was stubburne in his talk. *Ibid.* 838 Ane vther Lunden paik he playit. *a* **1600** MONTGOMERIE *Misc. Poems* xviii. 68 Throu pearking of a pyet Besyde thame, vhilk thair palks espyde. **1768** W. WILKIE *Fables* 118 Pawks and wiles whar pith is wantin. **1811** MACNEILL *Bygane Times* 18 (E.D.D.) Wi' saftening sound, And pawks, to bring ilk project round.

b. In north. Eng. dial. (Yorkshire): Impertinence, forwardness, sauciness; also, an impertinent or saucy person. See *Eng. Dial. Dict.*

Hence ˈ**pawkery**, trickery, cunning.

1820 HOGG *Wint. Even. T.* II. 41 Onye sikkan wylld sneckdrawinge and pawkerye. **1830** GALT *Lawrie T.* I. viii. (1849) 29 Pawkrie is no' an ill nest-egg to begin with!

pawk[2]. *local.* A small lobster.

1768 TRAVIS in Pennant *Zool.* (1777) IV. 10 If they be under four inches, they are called [at Scarborough] *pawks*, and are not saleable to the carriers.

pawky (ˈpɔːkɪ), *a.* orig. *Sc.* and *north. dial.* Also 8 **paukie**, 9 **pauky**. [f. PAWK[1] + -Y.] **a.** Tricky, artful, sly, cunning, crafty, shrewd; esp. humorously tricky or sly, 'arch'.

1676 W. ROW *Contn. Blair's Autobiog.* xii. (1848) 407 [Leighton] carrying like a pawky prelate, refused the title of Lord. **1711** RAMSAY *Maggy Johnstoun* viii, The pawky knack Of brewing ale amaist like wine. **1785** BURNS *To James Smith*, Dear Smith, the sleeest, paukie thief That e'er attempted stealth or rief. **1867** F. FRANCIS *Angling* ix. (1880) 310 A story told of a pawky old Scot. **1870** RAMSAY *Remin.* (ed. 18) p. xvii, This quiet pawky style. **1884** *Athenæum* 28 June 819 A new school,..marked..by the same pawky humour. **1935** K. A. PORTER *Flowering Judas* 112 He went on in his pawky way trying to make clear to her his mystical faith in these men who went ragged and hungry. **1966** *Listener* 3 Feb. 171/2 With these advantages, and his convivial, pawky wit, which was enjoyed as much over the port wine as it was over tea in the withdrawing room, Radcliffe's progress was remarkable. **1970** *Daily Tel.* 10 Nov. 12/3 Beethoven's Trio in B flat, Opus 11, on the other hand, was given a rather pawky performance, and the first movement, especially, was robbed of weight by the over detached articulation. **1973** *Daily Record* (Glasgow) 6 Aug. 6/3 Her other pawky comments include: T is for *Training*: This is entered into with particular vigour by the Reserve Team, so that they may escape relegation to the First Eleven. **1976** W. GÉRIN *E. Gaskell* xiv. 146 Mr. Brontë could..be witty and pawky as his later letters to Mrs. Gaskell show.

b. In north. Eng. dial.: see quots.

1825 BROCKETT *N.C. Gloss.*, *Pauky*, saucy, squeamish, scrupulously nice—also proud, insolent, artful. **1828** *Craven Gloss.* (ed. 2), *Pauky*, proud: it does not signify here, arch or cunning, as asserted by Grose, or, sly and artful, as Dr. Jamieson explains it.

Hence ˈ**pawkily** *adv.*, cunningly, artfully, slyly; ˈ**pawkiness**, artful character, slyness.

1714 RAMSAY *Elegy on J. Cowper* vii, He pawkily on them could steal, And spoil their sport. **1823** GALT *Entail* III. xxxii. 299 'Indeed!' said Walkinshaw pawkily; 'that's a very important circumstance'. **1883** A. FORBES in *19th Cent.* Oct. 724 For the pawkiness of this proposal, the man should have been a Scotsman. **1886** *Athenæum* 6 Feb. 193 Pawkiness and poetry seem to meet and mingle in most of these Highland stories. **1963** *Times* 21 May 4/5 The Essex batsmen, only partially inhibited by the cold, pushed the score pawkily along, sending up the 50 in just over the hour. **1971** *Guardian* 8 Sept. 8/3 His pawkily British sense of humour.

pawl (pɔːl), *sb.*[1] Also 7 **pawle**, 7–9 **paul**, 8–9 **pall**. [Derivation uncertain: perh. = F. *pal* stake, L. *pālus* stake, prop, stay; cf. Du. *pal*; also Welsh *pawl* pole, stake, bar. But the early history of the word in Eng. is unknown.]

1. *Naut.* Each of the short stout bars made to engage with the whelps, and prevent a capstan, windlass, or winch from recoiling.

In a capstan the pawls are now usually attached to a part of the barrel called the *pawl-head*, and engage with the whelps in a *pawl-rim* attached to the floor or platform on which the capstan works; in a windlass, etc. (formerly also in capstans) the *pawl-rim* forms part of the barrel, and the pawls are attached to the separate *pawl-bitt* or *-post*.

1626 CAPT. SMITH *Accid. Yng. Seamen* 13 The Capsterne, the pawle, the whelps. **1627** —— *Seaman's Gram.* ii. 8 The Paul is a short piece of iron made fast to the Deck, resting upon the whelps to keepe the Capstaine from recoiling. **1704** J. HARRIS *Lex. Techn.* I. s.v., They say, *Heave a Pawle!* That is, Heave a little more for the Pawle to get hold of the Whelps: And this they call *Pawling the Capstan*. **1776** *Phil. Trans.* LX. 88 The palls or stops..of the windlass. **1840** R. H. DANA *Bef. Mast* xxiv, By the force of twenty strong arms, the windlass came slowly round, pawl after pawl. **1853** KANE *Grinnell Exp.* xi. (1856) 83 'All hands' walking round with the capstan-bars to the click of its iron pauls. **1886** J. M. CAULFEILD *Seamanship Notes* 3 *Parts of the Capstan.* Drum head,..pauls, paul rim, paul stops, paul beds, whelps.

2. A bar pivoted at one end to a support, and engaging at the other with the teeth of a ratchet-wheel or ratchet-bar, so as to hold it in a required position; a lever with a catch for the teeth of a wheel or bar.

1729 DESAGULIERS in *Phil. Trans.* XXXVI. 197 Such a Contrivance, that the Pall or Lever..does so communicate with the Catch, that..the Catch always takes. **1792** *Trans.*

Soc. Arts (ed. 2) III. 159 A pall or stop, which prevents the crane running back. *c* **1865** LETHEBY in *Circ. Sc.* I. 137/1 The latter carries a double paul, which locks into the cogs. **1884** C. G. W. LOCK *Workshop Receipts* Ser. III. 80/2 A ratchet and pawl keeps the plates in position.

3. *Comb.*, as **pawl-bitt, -post** (*Naut.*), a strong vertical post in which the pawls of a windlass are fixed; **pawl-head** (*Naut.*), the part of the capstan to which the pawls are attached: see sense 1; **pawl-press**, a press used in bookbinding, having ratchet-wheels and pawls (Knight *Dict. Mech.* 1875); **pawl-rim** (*Naut.*), a notched cast-iron ring for the pawls to catch in: see sense 1; **pawl-stone**, a stone placed at the base of a pillar, wall, or fence, to protect it from damage by wheels.

1867 SMYTH *Sailor's Word-bk.*, *Paul bitt..Paul rim. **1874** THEARLE *Naval Archit.* 109 Mast and pall bitt beams, and beams under the heel of bowsprit,..must not be less in size than the midship beam. **1897** KIPLING *Captains Courageous* 80 Under the yellow glare of the lamp on the *pawl-post. *c* **1860** H. STUART *Seaman's Catech.* 54 Parts of a Capstan. The bed, *paul rim,..drum-head, palls and bars. **1844** H. STEPHENS *Bk. Farm* I. 151 A *pawl-stone should be placed on each side of every pillar.

pawl, pál, *sb.*[2] *East Ind.* Also **pāl, pal.** [Hindī *pāl.*] A small tent with two poles and steep sloping sides.

1811 KIRKPATRICK tr. *Tippoo's Lett.* 49 Where is the great quantity of baggage belonging to you, seeing that you have nothing besides tents, *pawls*, and other such necessary articles? **1872** E. BRADDON *Life in India* v. 185 Public and private tents, shamianahs, and servants' pāls or canvas wigwams.

Comb. **1884** F. BOYLE *Borderland* 403 A pal-shaped tent, bellying on its ropes.

pawl, *v.* Chiefly *Naut.* Also **pall.** [f. PAWL *sb.*[1]]

1. a. *trans.* To stop or secure (a capstan, ratchet-wheel, etc.) by means of a pawl or pawls.

1704 [see PAWL *sb.* 1]. **1706** PHILLIPS, *To Pawl the Capstan*, to stop it with the Pawl. **1840** R. H. DANA *Bef. Mast* xv. 41 We manned the windlass..he..ordering us when to heave and when to pawl. **1890** CLARK RUSSELL *Shipmate Louise* III. xli. 286 We could 'heave and pawl' no further.

fig. **1706** E. WARD *Wooden World Diss.* (1708) 91 He e'en paul'd Capston, and turn'd a sociable Sot.

b. *intr.* for *passive.*

1819 *Pantologia* s.v. *Windlass*, If, in heaving the windlass about, any of the handspikes should happen to break, the windlass would pall of itself.

2. *fig.* (*colloq.* or *slang.*) **a.** *trans.* To bring to a standstill, stop, check, 'bring up short', 'pull up'. Also, to detect. **b.** *intr.* To stop, cease; *esp.* to stop talking.

c **1825** CHOYCE *Log Jack Tar* (1891) 55 This pawled us. **1859** HOTTEN *Dict. Slang* 71 *Pall* to detect. **1867** SMYTH *Sailor's Word-bk., Paul there, my hearty.* Tell us no more of that. **1975** H. R. F. KEATING *Remarkable Case* viii. 92 She's been palled once..a-trying ter get a look at that door.

[**pawl** in *cross-pawl*, error for SPALL, SPAWL.]

pawle, pawlfre, pawltre, obs. ff. PALL, PAWL, PALFREY, PALTRY.

pawlonia, var. PAULOWNIA.

pawm(e, obs. f. PALM *sb.*[2] and *v.*

pawment, obs. f. PAVEMENT.

pawmer(e, pawmpelion, -pilyon, obs. ff. PALMER, PAMPILION.

pawn (pɔːn), *sb.*[1] Forms: 4 poun, 4–5 poune, 5 pown(e, pon, 5–7 pawne, 6 paune, 5– pawn. [ME. a. AF. *poun*, OF. *poon, paon*, var. of *peon*, earlier *pehon, pedon* foot-soldier, pawn at chess (Godef.), = Pr. *pezo*, Sp. *peon* footman, pawn, It. *pedone* footman, *pedona, pedina* fem. a pawn:—L. *pedo, pedōn-em*, in med.L. a foot-soldier, f. *pēs, ped-* foot. The chess sense was in OF. in 13th c.] **a.** One of the pieces of smallest size and value in the game of chess.

There are eight pawns on each side, set at the beginning of the game in the rank or line immediately in front of the other pieces, and named each from the piece in front of which it stands (*king's p., queen's p., king's bishop's p.*, etc.). *three pawns gambit*, an opening at chess, now generally called from its supposed inventor *Cunningham's gambit.*

c **1369** CHAUCER *Dethe Blaunche* 661 (Fairf.) Mate in the myd poynt of the chekkere With a poune errante. **1413** *Pilgr. Sowle* (Caxton) I. xxii. (1859) 27 Whan that a pown seyith to the kyng chekmate! **1474** CAXTON *Chesse* III. i, The fyrst pawne, that is in the playe of the chesse. **1562** ROWBOTHUM *Play Cheasts* A vij b, The marchynge forthe of the Paune, for the fyrst tyme, is to make two assaultes or leapes, yf he wyll. **1656** F. B[EALE] tr. *Biochimo's Roy. Game Chesse-Play* 4 If any Pawne can arriue unto any house of the uppermost ranke of the adversary, you may..make him a Queen. **1735** BERTIN *Chess* v, The king's pawn, the bishop's pawn, and the queen's pawn must move before the knights. *Ibid.* 5 Another defence of the three Pawns gambet. **1859** GEO. ELIOT *A. Bede* v, To show you..what a foolish move you made with that pawn.

b. *fig.* (usually of a person).

1589 *Pappe w. Hatchet* 3 For a scaddle pawne, to crosse a Bishop in his owne walke. **1831** CARLYLE *Sart. Res.* I. iii, Councillors of State..playing their high chess-game, whereof the pawns are Men. **1874** MRS. WHITNEY *We Girls* xi. 245 She had put forward a little pawn of compliment toward us. **1884** LABOUCHERE in *Fortn. Rev.* Feb. 210 The constituencies had been but pawns in the game of rival politicians.

c. *attrib.* and *Comb.* ***pawn end-game, mate***, etc.; **pawn chain**, an unbroken diagonal line of pawns extending across several adjacent files; **pawn skeleton**, the structure of the pawns at the end of a chess opening; **pawn storm**, an attacking advance of pawns against a castled king.

1883 G. A. MACDONNELL *Chess Life-Pict.* 51 A strong pawn-and-two-move player. [**1818** W. S. KENNY *Pract. Chess Exercises* 45 This is better than breaking his chain of pawns.] **1937** M. EUWE *Strategy & Tactics in Chess* iii. 50 An immobile sequence of Pawns is called a pawn-chain. **1957** L. BARDEN *Guide to Chess Openings* v. 105/2 White is hoping to safeguard the base of his pawn-chain. **1973** *Sci. Amer.* June 104/2 The program now is sophisticated enough to execute very simple positional ideas such as creating pawn chains, striving for control of the center and so forth. **1939** A. ALEKHINE *My Best Games of Chess* 86/2 K-K4, P-QKt4! ..with a won Pawn end-game. **1672** BARBIER *Saul's Fam. Game Chesse play* iv, The..King..must eyther remoue himselfe out of the saide Pawnes checke, or if he cannot, it is Pawne-mate. **1914** J. DU MONT tr. *Lasker's Chess Strategy* (1915) iv. 26 Each opening is characterised by a well-defined pawn formation... Naturally the formation of a pawn skeleton is not an independent factor. **1927** *Brit. Chess Mag.* XLVII. 170 First you must learn the normal Pawn skeleton of the opening very thoroughly. **1950** R. N. COLES *Chess-Player's Week-End Bk.* 11 If the pawn skeleton remained sound, the game could be continued from one phase to another. **1926** *Brit. Chess Mag.* XLVI. 134 Herr Bachmann makes it plain that such 'modern' tactics as..the Pawn-storm against the opponent's Castled position..are not 'modern' at all. **1957** L. BARDEN *Guide to Chess Openings* iv. 69/2 If White can carry through a pawn storm and advance his KBP to KB6 then Black will be completely throttled. *a* **1500** *MS. Ashmole* 344 (Bodl.) lf. 3 b, Chek wt thy Roke in thy Pon Ward.

pawn (pɔːn), *sb.*[2] Forms: 5–6 (8) paun, 6 paune, 6– *Sc.* and *Ir.* **paund, pand,** 6–7 **pawne,** 7– **pawn.** [a. OF. *pan* (rarely *pand, pant*) 'pledge, security, surety'; also 'booty, plunder, spoil taken from the enemy', app. the same word as OFris. *pand*, MDu. *pant* (*pand-*), Du. *pand*, OLG. **pand*, OHG., MHG. *pfant*, Ger. *pfand* pledge, pawn, security, surety. The Sc. form *pand* may have come from LG., Du., or Flemish.

The ulterior history of the word is uncertain: F. *pan* pledge, was in form identical with *pan* cloth, piece, portion, pane, etc.:—L. *pannus* a cloth, a rag: some take it as the same word, and as the source of the WGer. forms (in which however the final *-d*, already in OHG., *-t*, makes a difficulty); others think the WGer. **pand* to be the source of F. *pan* pledge, and see in it also the primitive of *panding, pending*, PENNY. See Diez II. c. (in favour of Romanic source), Kluge (doubtful), Franck (inclined to Teutonic; so Skeat *Concise D.* 1901).]

1. A thing (or person) given, deposited, or left in another's keeping, as security for a debt or for the performance of some action; a pledge, surety, gage. (Now *rare*, the ordinary word being *pledge*.) **a.** *lit.*

[*c* **1145** *Charter David I* in *Charters of Edinb.* (1871) 8 Prohibeo ne aliquis capiat pandum super terram Sancte Crucis.] **1496** *Galway Arch.* in *10th Rep. Hist. MSS. Comm.* App. v. 386 Who so ever takith anny manys pledge or paun with his own proper hande. **1513** DOUGLAS *Æneis* XI. vii. 164 Livinia, the schene may, Quhilk is the pand or plege,..Of peax to be kepit inviolate. **1598** B. JONSON *Ev. Man in Hum.* IV. vii, We haue no store of monie..but you shall haue good pawnes,..this Iewell, and this gentlemans silke stockins. **1692** DRYDEN *Cleomenes* III. i, He must leave behind, for pawns, His mother, wife, and son. **1736** BERKELEY *Querist* II. §62 Wks. 1871 III. 521 Whether this bank doth not lend money upon pawns at low interest? **1875** POSTE *Gaius* III. Comm. (ed. 2) 369 If the pawnee buy in the pawn by means of a collusive bidder, the sale is void.

b. *fig.* = 'pledge.'

1573 *Epitaph* in Wood *Oxford* (O.H.S.) III. 152 Ten tender babes on me he gate, the pawnes of mariage bed. *a* **1586** in Pinkerton *Anc. Sc. Poems* (1786) 265 My hairt..Quhilk is the gadge and pand Maist suir that I can geif. **1642** FULLER *Holy & Prof. St.* v. iv. 370 The pretious ashes of the Saints (the pawn for the return of their souls). *a* **1677** MANTON *Exp. Isa.* liii. 8 Wks. 1871 III. 352 By Christ's resurrection God giveth us a pawn and earnest, as it were, that we may expect the raising of our own bodies. **1845** R. W. HAMILTON *Pop. Educ.* vii. 174 As the schoolhouse rises ..at the very base of the Rocky Mountains,—there is the emphatic pawn, which that great Republic gives,..of enlightened freedom, extending civilization, and pure religion.

†**c.** A pledge or gage of battle; = GAGE *sb.*[1] 2.

1593 SHAKS. *Rich. II*, I. i. 74 If guilty dread hath left thee so much strength, As to take vp mine Honors pawne, then stoope.

d. A person held as a pledge or security for debt, and used as a slave.

1837 J. J. H. BURGOYNE in R. R. Madden *Life Lady Blessington* (1855) III. 519 Every English merchant on that coast [Cape Coast Castle] was possessed of a retinue of 'pawns' or slaves. **1887** A. B. ELLIS *Tshi-speaking Peoples* xvii. 237 Careful to recount the names of his pawns and slaves, the amounts for which he holds the former.

2. a. The condition of being deposited or held as a pledge; state of being pledged (*lit.* and *fig.*). Almost always in phrases ***in pawn, at pawn, to pawn.*** (The usual current sense.)

1554 *Galway Arch.* in *10th Rep. Hist. MSS. Comm.* App. v. 415 Whatsoever platte or silver is lefte or put in paund. **1593** SHAKS. *Rich. II*, II. i. 293 Redeeme from broaking pawne the blemish'd Crowne. **1597** —— *2 Hen. IV*, II. iii. 7 My Honor is at pawne, And but my going, nothing can redeeme it. **1642** MILTON *Apol. Smect.* vii. Wks. 1851 III. 294 To lay the integrity of his Logick to pawn. **1667** PEPYS *Diary* 3 Oct., Her plate and jewels are at pawne for money. **1698** SOUTH *Serm.* III. x. 381 He gives his veracity in pawn to see it fully performed. **1711** PUCKLE *Club* (1817) 69 My poor wedding-ring and best petticoat in pawn for forty shillings. **1814** CARY *Dante's Inf.* XI. 62 All who..set their honesty at pawn.

b. The action of pawning or pledging.

1824 GALT *Rothelan* I. I. vi. 57 Certain trinkets which I have here for sale, or pawn. **1883** F. TURNER (*title*) The Contract of Pawn as it exists at Common Law.

3. Short for *pawnbroker.* (*vulgar colloq.* or *slang.*)

1851 MAYHEW *Lond. Labour* (1861) II. 109 Perhaps they comes to sell to me what the pawns won't take in.

4. *Comb.*, as †*pawn-keeper, -slave* (cf. 1 d), †*-taker*; †**pawn-laid** *a.*, 'laid to pawn', deposited as a pledge, pledged; †**pawn party** (now only *Hist.*), app. a game resembling blindman's buff; **pawn-ticket**, a ticket issued by a pawnbroker in exchange for a pledge deposited with him, and bearing particulars of the loan. Also PAWNBROKER, PAWNSHOP.

1552 HULOET, *Pawne keper, *depositarius.* **1597–8** BP. HALL *Sat.* IV. ii. 15 Bearing his *pawn-laid lands upon his backe As snailes their shells. **1831** H. SMITH *Festivals Games, & Amusem.* (N.Y.) 330 The village and country lasses enjoy their *spinning* and *quilting* bevies, singing-schools, and **pawn* parties, with at least an equal zest. **1952** *Amer. Speech* XXVII. 47 A pawn party must have been something like blindman's buff. **1899** MARY KINGSLEY *W. African Stud.* xviii. 435, I have known of several men who, in order to save their family from ruin..have given themselves up as *pawn-slaves to their accusers. **1697** *View Penal Laws* 31 Goods..sold to such Brokers, Frippers or *Pawn-takers. **1858** CARLYLE *Fredk. Gt.* IV. v. I. 431 Holding such a *pawn-ticket. **1875** JEVONS *Money* xvii. 201 The..kind of promissory document..represented by bills of lading, pawn-tickets, dock-warrants [etc.]. *a* **1652** BROME *Eng. Moor* III. i, Take my keys of all; In my *pawn Wardrobe you shall find to fit you.

†**pawn** (paʊn), *sb.*[3] Chiefly *Sc. Obs.* Forms: 5–6 povne, 6 powin, pown, -e, paun, 6–7 (9) pawn, -e. [a. OF. *poun, poon* (Godef.), F. *paon* (= Pr. *pao, paho, paon*, Sp. *pavo, pavon*, Pg. *pavão*, It. *pavone*):—L. *pāvo, pāvōn-em* peacock.] A peacock.

c **1450** HOLLAND *Howlat* 614 The plesand Povne. **1530** LYNDESAY *Test. Papyngo* 728 The plesand Pown, moste angellyke of hew. *a* **1578** LINDESAY (Pitscottie) *Chron. Scot.* (S.T.S.) I. 337 Thair was of meittis..pertrick and plever, duke, Brissill cok and powins. *a* **1605** MONTGOMERIE *Cherrie & Slae* (revision) ii, The paynted pawn with Argos eyis. **1627** DRAYTON *Mooncalf* in *Agincourt* etc. 158 As pyde and garish as the Pawne. [**1864** BOUTELL *Her. Hist. & Pop.* x. 64 A Peacock or Pawne, having its tail displayed, is 'in its pride'.]

†**pawn,** *sb.*[4] *Obs.* Forms: 6–7 pawne, (6 pawen), 7 (9) pawn. [= Du. *pand*, in Plantijn 1573 '*pandt* vn pan de muraille, ou vne gallerie ou cloistre, lieu où on vend quelque marchandise, ou où on se pourmeine, *xystus, peristylium, ambulacrum*'; so Kilian 1599; Hexham 1678 *pandt*, 'covert-walking-place, or gallery where things are sould; place or court environed with pillars, as in cloisters'; in mod.Du. Dict. 'a storehouse, magazine'; a Du. development of F. *pan*: see PANE *sb.*[1] senses 3, 4.]

A gallery or colonnade, a covered walk or passage, especially one in a bazaar, exchange, or arcade, alongside of which wares are exposed for sale.

1575 SIR T. GRESHAM in *Wills Doctors' Comm.* (Camden) 59 The bildings called the Royall Exchange, and all pawnes and shopes adjoyninge. *Ibid.* 60 The saide bildinges.. pawens, shopes. **1579** TWYNE *Phisicke agst. Fort.* II. iv. 166 Martes and pawnes stored with outlandish marchandize. **1598** DRAYTON *Heroic. Ep.* xvii. 95 If thou but please to walke into the Pawne, To buy thee Cambricke, Callico, or Lawne. **1599** HAKLUYT *Voy.* II. 261 (*Pegu*) This house is fiue and fifty paces in length, and hath three pawnes or walks in it, and forty great pillars gilded, which stand betweene the walks. **1609** HOLLAND *Amm. Marcell.* 342 To crie out along the Burses, Lombards and Pawnes, That the Commonwealth and all were lost. **1688** *Lond. Gaz.* No. 2404/4 The West-Pawn of the Royal Exchange, being the Place now prepared for the purpose aforesaid. **1888** BESANT *50 Yrs. Ago* 35 Jerman's Exchange..had an inner cloister and a 'pawn', or gallery..for the sale of fancy goods.

†**pawn,** *sb.*[5] *Obs. rare.* [Erroneous back-formation from PANNAGE; perh. an error of Spelman.] Mast of trees.

1664 *Spelman's Gloss., Pannagium.* Quasi *Paunagium*, silvestrium enim arborum fructus & glandes quidam *pawns* vocant. [Hence **1672** COWELL *Interpr.*, *Pannage* or *Pawnage*, *Pannagium*, Which is that Food that the Swine feed on in the Woods, as Mast of Beech, Acorns, etc. which some have called Pawnes.]

pawn (pɔːn), *v.* Forms: 6 *Sc.* **pand,** 6–7 **pawne, paune,** (*pa. pple.* **paund**), 7– **pawn.** [f. PAWN *sb.*[2]: cf. Du. *panden* to pawn, Ger. *pfänden* to distrain upon, pawn.] *trans.* To give or deposit as security for the payment of a sum of money or for the performance of some action (something to be forfeited in case of non-payment or non-performance); to pledge; to stake, wager; to risk. **a.** *lit.*: *esp.* to deposit with or hand over to some one (usually a pawnbroker) as security for the repayment of a loan.

1570 LEVINS *Manip.* 44/26 To Paune, *pignorare.* *a* **1578** LINDESAY (Pitscottie) *Chron. Scot.* (S.T.S.) I. 340 The king ..gart her pand ane hunder crouns and ane tune of wyne wpoun the Inglischemenis handis. **1592** GREENE *Groat's W. Wit* (1617) 28 His lands solde, his Iewels pawnde. **1639** FULLER *Holy War* III. vii. (1840) 128 The island he pawned to the Templars for ready money. **1711** SWIFT *Lett.* (1767) III. 253 He is over head and ears in debt, and has pawned several things. **1847** EMERSON *Poems, To Rhea*, These presents be the hostages Which I pawn for my release. **1850** W. IRVING *Goldsmith* ii. 36 Obliged to raise funds..by pawning his books.

b. *fig.* (e.g. one's life, honour, word, etc.).

1567 EDWARDS *Damon & Pithias* in Hazl. *Dodsley* IV. 55 My life I pawn for his. **1606** CHAPMAN *Monsieur D'Olive* Plays 1873 I. 218 If I knew where I might pawne mine honor, For some odd thousand Crownes, it shalbe layd. **1650** BULWER *Anthropomet.* i. (1653) 17 He will not Pawne his credit for many things that he therein delivers. **1741** RICHARDSON *Pamela* (1824) I. xvi. 28, I will pawn my life for her, she will never be pert to your honour. **1860** MOTLEY *Netherl.* (1868) I. vii. 385, I dare pawn my soul.

†**c.** *slang.* (See quot. *a* 1700.) *Obs.*

1673 R. HEAD *Canting Acad.* 72 This poor man finding himself pawn'd, and not having..money to discharge the reckoning. *a* **1700** B. E. *Dict. Cant. Crew* s.v., *To Pawn any Body*, to steal away and leave him..to Pay the Reckoning. **1725** in *New Cant. Dict.*

d. *Stock Exchange.* To deposit (stock) with a bank as security.

1902 *Encycl. Brit.* XXXII. 866/1 So much stock is 'pawned' with banks that the conclusions arrived at by the jobbers from examining only what they are carrying over themselves are liable to be falsified.

¶ *Erron.* (Confused with PALM *v.* 4.)

1787 *Minor* I. xi. 40 Those qualities which we desire to pawn upon the credulous world. **1832** MARRYAT *N. Forster* xxxviii, He has sent out his..daughters to me—pawned them off upon me.

Hence **pawned** *ppl. a.*, **'pawning** *vbl. sb.*

1607 MIDDLETON *Michaelm. Term* II. iii. 314 The pawning of thy horse. **1723** *Lond. Gaz.* No. 6153/2 That the Borrowers do make full Payments..in Money upon the pawned Stock. **1886** *Athenæum* 6 Mar. 333/3 The business-like air which belongs to continental pawning. **1903** *Times* 29 Sept., The fact that the account..was then light did not prevent the flood of pawned stock—especially 'gilt-edged' securities—that has been poured on the market since then.

pawn, obs. f. PAN *sb.*⁵, betel-leaf; var. PAND.

pawnable ('pɔːnəb(ə)l), *a.* [f. PAWN *v.* + -ABLE.] That can be pawned.

1742 JARVIS *Quix.* I. III. xxiii. (1885) 131 A thing neither pawnable nor saleable. **1886** G. R. SIMS in *Daily News* 9 Dec. 5/7 They have nothing pawnable to fall back upon. Pawning is the first thing to which the poor resort when the wolf comes to the door.

pawnage ('pɔːnɪdʒ). *rare.* [f. PAWN *v.* + -AGE.] The action or object of pawning.

1624 BP. MOUNTAGU *Immed. Addr.* 20 No Man so dearely payed the pawnage of folly. **1858** CARLYLE *Fredk. Gt.* II. xiv. (1872) I. 129 Sigismund..pawned the Newmark too,—the second Pawnage of Brandenburg.

pawnage, obs. form of PANNAGE.

pawnbroker ('pɔːn,brəʊkə(r)). [f. PAWN *sb.*² + BROKER 2.] One engaged in the business of lending money upon interest on the security of articles of personal property pawned or pledged.

1687 *Lond. Gaz.* No. 2305/3 Encouragement and Connivence..from Petty-Tradesmen, Pawn-Brokers, and others. **1730** FIELDING *Author's Farce* I. iv, Fetch my other hat hither. Carry it to the pawn-broker's. **1786** *Ir. Act 26 Geo. III*, c. 43 *title*, An Act to establish the Business of a Pawnbroker. **1833** HT. MARTINEAU *Loom & Lugger* II. v. 86 All the knives and scissors were at the pawnbroker's.

Hence (*nonce-wds.*) **'pawn,brokerage**, **'pawn,brokering**, the business of a pawnbroker, pawnbroking; **'pawn,brokeress**, a female pawnbroker; **'pawn,brokery**, (*a*) a pawnbroking establishment, (*b*) pawnbroking.

1896 *Century Mag.* Feb. 540 Every Jew..must have..a notarial authorization for *pawnbrokerage. **1833** LAMB *Let. Moxon* Lett. 1888 II. 292, I..wrote for the *Pawn-brokeress's album. **1893** *N. & Q.* 8th Ser. III. 4/1 Employed in various *pawnbrokering establishments. **1821** W. TAYLOR in *Monthly Rev.* XCIV. 493 Madame Necker.. founded a charitable *pawnbrokery at Paris. **1833** *New Monthly Mag.* XXXVIII. 84 Pawnbrokery is..a rational proceeding, for the pledge always retains the value for which it is engaged.

'pawn,broking, *vbl. sb.* [f. prec.: see -ING¹. Cf. *broaking pawne* in Shaks. *Rich. II*, II. i. 293, BROKING *vbl. sb.* 3.] The action or business of a pawnbroker; the occupation of lending money on the security of articles pawned.

1811 W. TAYLOR in *Monthly Mag.* XXXI. 6 Pawnbroking is regulated by law. **1875** T. A. TROLLOPE *Diamond cut Diamond* (1876) 338 There is always an especial run on the Government pawn-broking establishment. **1884** HORNER *Florence* (ed. 2) I. App. 566 The Monti di Pietà..were rather pawnbroking carried on by the Municipality.

So **'pawn,broking** *ppl. a.*, that carries on the business of a pawnbroker.

1765 FOOTE *Commissary* I. Wks. 1799 II. 7 That canting, couzening, money-lending, match-making, pawnbroking—.

†**pawnde**, obs. form of PANED: cf. PAUNED.

1552 in Dillon *Calais & Pale* (1892) 97 One of Clothe of golde and blewe velvet pawnde with flowers of golde.

pawne, obs. form of PAN *sb.*⁵, PAWN.

pawnee (pɔː'niː), *sb.*¹ [f. PAWN *v.* + -EE.] The person with whom something is deposited as a pawn or pledge. (Correlative to *pawner*.)

1683–5 tr. *Croke's Rep., Jac.* 245 *marg.*, Tender of the money to the executrix of a pawnee, and her refusal to restore the goods, revests them in the owner. **1745–1875** [see PAWNER]. **1875** POSTE *Gaius* III. (ed. 2) 369 The pawnee could not become the purchaser.

Pawnee (pɔː'niː), *sb.*² (and *a.*) Also 8–9 Pane. [ad. Canad. F. *Pani*, f. Ioway-Oto *panyi*.]

†**a.** The Wichita Indians, *spec.* the Wichita and Tawehash bands of the Red River of Oklahoma and Texas. *Obs.*

1770 P. PITTMAN *Present State Europ. Settlem. on Mississippi* 40 The Arcansas or Quapas Indians..bring in very frequently young prisoners and horses from the Cadodaquias, Paneise, Podoquias, &c. of which they dispose to the best advantage. **1803** in C. E. Carter *Territorial Papers U.S.* (1940) IX. 74 The length of Red River is not known, it is Six or seven hundred Miles to the Pawnie or Towiash Indians. **1830** in *Ibid.* (1954) XXI. 215 The settlers are in continual alarm from the Pawnee Indians.

b. A confederacy of Caddoan Indians, formerly inhabiting the Loup, Platte, and Republican River valleys in Nebraska; a member of this group of tribes. Also *attrib.* or as *adj.*

1778 J. CARVER *Trav. N.-Amer.* 118 This is the road they [*sc.* Indians] take when their war parties make their excursions upon the Pawnees. **1794** [see MANDAN *a.* and *sb.*]. **1806** Z. M. PIKE *Jrnl.* 22 Sept. in *Acct. Expeditions Sources Mississippi* (1810) II. 140 [I] met a Pawnee hunter. **1810** [see KIOWA *sb.*]. **1827** J. F. COOPER *Prairie* II. xi. 177 He will never see a Pawnee become a Sioux. **1841** J. WILLIAMS *Narr. Tour Indiana to Oregon* (1921) 31 The Caws..told me that the Pawnees were a bad nation, and that they had a battle with them. **1868** *N.Y. Herald* 31 July 5/3 A large band of the Sioux and Cheyennes had attacked a small party of the Pawnee scouts. **1890** J. G. FRAZER *Golden Bough* I. iii. 381 The Pawnees annually sacrificed a human victim in spring when they sowed their fields. **1901** 'MARK TWAIN' in *N. Amer. Rev.* Feb. 163 The oldest Americans are the Pawnees. **1925** Z. A. TILGHMAN *Dugout* 13 The Pawnees were late going south that year. **1946** G. FOREMAN *Last Trek of Indians* 242 The Sioux made two more raids, killing a Pawnee each time. **1959** E. TUNIS *Indians* 84/1 Many tribes had broken off from them in that time and some had moved northward up the river valleys—the Pawnee to Nebraska, the Arikara to North Dakota, for instance. **1969** *Observer* (Colour Suppl.) 18 May 32/2 Mrs Hines was brought up in a Pawnee Indian school where bull-hide boots were compulsory. **1972** *N.Y. Times* 3 Nov. 78/4 Earlier, Mrs. Martha Gras, a 71-year-old Pawnee Indian, appeared to sum up the sentiment of the Indian gathering.

c. The Caddoan language of these people.

1806 Z. M. PIKE *Let.* 2 Oct. in *Acct. Expeditions Sources Mississippi* (1810) App. II. 48, I asked..[for] a Tetau prisoner who spoke Pawnee, to serve as an interpreter. **1821** J. FOWLER *Jrnl.* (1898) 55 Mr. Roy—He Spoke Some Pane and (in) that language our Councils Ware Held. **1877** L. H. MORGAN *Anc. Society* III. iii. 440 In Mandan my brother's wife is my wife, and in Pawnee..the same. **1965** *Canad. Jrnl. Linguistics* X. 105 The structure of Pawnee as compared with Oneida. **1968** R. W. LANGACKER *Language & its Struct.* viii. 231 Other families found in this area [*sc.* the Great Plains] are Caddoan (Wichita, Caddo, Arikara, Pawnee), [etc.].

d. Special combs.: (in sense a) **Pawnee pic, pique** (see also quot. 1916); (in sense b) **Pawnee lands**, reservations of Pawnee Indians; **Pawnee Loups, Mohas, Republics, Republicans**, sub-tribes of the larger Pawnee confederacy.

1931 *Amer. Speech* VII. 4 The 'Indian reserves' were frequently referred to as the 'Pawnee lands', 'Otoe Lands', or 'Indian territory'. **1806** in *Deb. Congress U.S.* (1852) 9th Congress 2 Sess., App. 1046 Pānias Loups (or Wolves)... These are also a branch of the Panias proper. **1823** E. JAMES *Acct. Expedition Rocky Mts.* II. 165 The camp had been occupied by a war party of Skeeree or Pawnee Loup Indians. **1847** D. COYNER *Lost Trappers* (1859) 62 As Doranto proved to be a son of a grand chief of the Pawnee Loups, he was greatly prized as a captive. **1843** N. BOONE *Let.* 11 Aug. in L. Pelzer *Marches of Dragoons in Mississippi Valley* (1917) 187 Whether this was caused by a fear that we'd frighten off the buffalo, or not, they kept up a continual alarm of Pawnee Mohas. **1806** in *Deb. Congress U.S.* (1852) 9th Congress 2 Sess., App. 1075 Pania Piqûe... [Also called] Paunee Piqûe. **1856** J. P. BECKWOURTH *Life* ii. 26 The Pawnee Pics or Tattoed Pawnees. **1916** THOBURN *Hist. Oklahoma* I. 124 The confusion of the two tribes was doubtless due to the French traders and trappers, who called the Wichitas 'Pawnee Piques', i.e. 'Tattooed Pawnees', hence the corrupted American term, Pawnee Pict. **1836** L. FORD in *Army & Navy Chron.* 19 May 312/1 The Pawnee Loups, Pawnee Republics, [etc.]..lie upon the Loup fork of the Platte, twenty or thirty miles distant from the Grand Pawnee village. **1917** WILL & HYDE *Corn among Indians of Upper Missouri* 145 The Pawnee Republics had only enough corn to thicken their soup. **1806** in *Deb. Congress U.S.* (1852) 9th Congress 2 Sess., App. 1045 Pānias proper and Pānias Republican live in the same village. **1810** Z. M. PIKE *Acct. Expeditions Sources Mississippi* App. II. 14 On the La Platte, reside the grand Pawnee village, and the Pawnee loups on one of its branches, with whom the Pawnee Republicans are at war. **1823** E. JAMES *Acct. Expedition Rocky Mts.* I. 159 They arrived about noon, seventy in number, consisting of individuals of each of the three tribes called *Grand Pawnees, Pawnee Republicans*, and *Pawnee Loups*.

pawner ('pɔːnə(r)). Also (in legal works) -or. [f. PAWN *v.* + -ER¹, -OR.] One who pawns; one who deposits something as a pledge, esp. with a pawnbroker.

1745 *Gentl. Mag.* 412 The pawner, or his assignee, have no other security for the return of their goods but the honour of the pawnee. **1853** WHARTON *Pennsylv. Digest* 211 A pawnee has no better title than the pawnor. **1875** POSTE *Gaius* III. §204 The owner or pawnor who steals a pawn is suable for theft by the pawnee. **1902** *Times* 22 Mar. 4/5 Not recording the full name and address of the pawner upon the tickets.

pawn-haus, var. PONHAUS.

pawnshop ('pɔːnʃɒp). [f. PAWN *sb.*² + SHOP.] A pawnbroker's shop or place of business.

1849 J. P. ROBSON in *Bards of Tyne, The Pawnshop in a Bleeze*, The world was better far an sure When pawnshops had ne neym [= no name]. **1855** MRS. GASKELL *North & S.* I. xx. 246 For these..there seems no other resource now that their weekly wages are stopped, but the pawn-shop. **1891** E. KINGLAKE *Australian at H.* ii. 10 Pawnshops, with their three golden balls dangling in front.

pawpaw ('pɔːpɔː, pɔː'pɔː), **papaw** (pə'pɔː). Forms: α. 6–7 papaio, 7–9 papaye, 8 pappaya, papay, papey, 8– papaya (pə'paɪə), papaia, (9 popeya). β. 7 pappa, pappaw, papawe, 7–9 papa, 8 papah, paupaw, 8– pawpaw, 8–9 poupau, 7– papaw. [Originally *papaya, papay*, a. Sp. and Pg. *papaya, papayo* (the tree), adopted from a Carib dialect.

Oviedo, 1535, gives *papaya* as the name in Hispaniola; Breton, *Dictionnaire Caraibe*, 1665, has *ababai* papaye-tree; Gilij, 1782, says that some form of *papaia* is the name among all the peoples of the Orinoco, but that in Ottomac (Venezuelan Carib) it is *pappai*. From America the name was taken with the plant in the 16th c. to the East Indian archipelago, where *papaya* now occurs in Malay. The immediate source of the Eng. forms *papa, papaw, pawpaw*, etc., does not appear. F. *papaye* is from Sp.]

1. a. The fruit of *Carica Papaya* (see b), usually oblong and about 10 inches long, of a dull orange colour, with a thick fleshy rind, and containing numerous black seeds embedded in pulp; used in tropical countries as food, either raw, preserved in sugar, made into sauce, or (in an unripe state) boiled or pickled.

α. **1598** PHILLIPS tr. *Linschoten* I. (1885) II. 35 There is also a fruite that came out of the Spanish Indies, brought.. to Malacca, and from thence to India, it is called Papaios, and is very like a Mellon, as bigge as a man's fist. **1698** FROGER *Voy.* 128 As for the Papaye it's a thick fruit, and tastes somewhat like a Cucumber. **1769** *Ann. Reg.* 190/1 Their other fruits, as..Papayas, Mammeas, etc. can no ways be equivalent to our fruits. **1878** P. ROBINSON *In My Indian Garden, Fruits* 50 The rank *popeyas* clustering beneath their coronals of shapely leaves. **1914** R. BROOKE *Let.* Feb. in E. Marsh *Rupert Brooke* (1918) 108 Great squelchy tropical fruits, custard-apples, papaia, pomegranate,..and the rest. **1921** *Outward Bound* Feb. 69/1 The natives..kept bringing fresh fruit to our view—mangoes and custard apples and papia. **1932** W. S. MAUGHAM *Narrow Corner* xix. 143 Breakfast in the little hotels in the Dutch East Indies is served at a very early hour. It never varies. Papaia, *œufs sur le plat*, cold meat, and Edam cheese. **1933** H. ALLEN *Anthony Adverse* VI. xxxix. 571 The papayas were already prodigious and there were shiploads of bananas. **1937** M. COVARRUBIAS *Island of Bali* (1972) iii. 39 Dark green island of tall palms, breadfruit, mango, papaya, and banana trees. **1965** *Austral. Women's Weekly* 20 Jan. 25/1 This same cook ..concocted mango and papaya soufflés of a texture I'd never before encountered. **1972** *Kent Life* July 82/2 Fresh juicy pineapple or papayas put out the fires in your mouth. **1977** *New Yorker* 25 July 20/3 He bought papaya and melon for dinner every day.

β. **1624** CAPT. SMITH *Virginia* v. 171 (Bermudas) The most delicate Pine-apples, Plantans, and Papawes. **1634** SIR T. HERBERT *Trav.* 183 Amongst other fruits..are Lemmons, Pappaes, Cocos. **1726** SHELVOCKE *Voy. round World* 356 Those..brought us Papas, Guayavas, Cassia, Limes. **1748** *Anson's Voy.* II. xii. 267 Another fruit called a Papah. **1825** *Gentl. Mag.* XCV. I. 318 The papa is a fruit about the same size [as the grenadilla]. **1869** A. R. WALLACE *Malay Archipelago* II. 33 The only fruits seen here were papaws and pine-apples. **1902** *Westm. Gaz.* 24 Dec. 1/3 The little mustard and cress seeds out of the paw-paws. **1908** E. J. BANFIELD *Confessions of Beachcomber* I. i. 43 Until we grew fruit, the papaw, the quickest and amongst the best, vegetables were more necessary. **1918** *Chambers's Jrnl.* Oct. 669/2 The great golden paw-paw..brought in showers to the earth by a shake of the tree. **1936** *Geogr. Jrnl.* LXXXVIII. 330 Such sub-tropical fruits as bananas, pineapples, paw-paws. **1953** G. DURRELL *Overloaded Ark* vi. 106 The cook..overbalanced into a basket containing eggs and some very ripe and soft pawpaw. **1972** Y. LOVELOCK *Veg. Bk.* I. 109 The melon tree.., of Central American origin, bears fruit known as pawpaw or papaya.

b. The tree *Carica papāya* (family Caricaceæ), a native of South America, commonly cultivated throughout the tropics.

Somewhat resembling a palm, with an unbranched stem of soft spongy wood, a crown of large seven-lobed cut-edged leaves on long stalks, and male and female flowers usually on different plants. The stem, leaves, and fruit contain an acrid milky juice which has the property of rendering meat tender by means of a ferment which it contains (see PAPAIN, PAPAYOTIN).

α. **1613** PURCHAS *Pilgrimage* (1614) 505 The Papaios will not grow, but male and female together. **1796** STEDMAN *Surinam* II. xxvi. 243 Amongst the preserves were the female pappayas, the male bearing no fruit. **1796** HUNTER tr.

St.-Pierre's Stud. Nat. (1799) III. 167 Paul was as much surprized, and as sorrowful, at the sight of this large papaya loaded with fruit. **1832** W. C. BRYANT *Poems* (N.Y.) 82 For thee the wild grape glistens, On sunny knoll and tree, And stoops the slim papaya With yellow fruit for thee. **1874** E. LEAR *Indian Jrnl.* (1953) 57 Bits of palmyra-palm, papaya, and dark clumps of oak-like trees around. **1875** MISS BIRD *Sandwich Isl.* (1880) 46 There were bananas..bamboos, papayas. **1920** W. POPENOE *Man. Tropical & Subtropical Fruits* vii. 229 The fruit of the papaya, as well as all other parts of the plant, contains a milky juice. **1962** A. HUXLEY *Island* xi. 177 Gardens shaded by palms and papayas and bread-fruit trees. **1966** D. FORBES *Heart of Malaya* i. 16 There were..groves of papaya and clumps of coco-nut palms beside them. **1969** *Oxf. Bk. Food Plants* 114/1 Papaya (*Carica papaya*) is also commonly known as 'pawpaw' (sometimes spelt papaw). A native of tropical America, it is now widely planted all over the tropics. **1974** T. HEYERDAHL *Fatu-Hiva* ix. 318 The papaya was another strictly tropical American plant, and two varieties grew in the Marquesas.

β. *c* **1645** WALLER *Battle of Summer-Isl.* I. 52 The palma-christi, and the fair papà, Now but a seed (preventing Nature's law), In half the circle of the hasty year Project a shade, and lovely fruits do wear. **1657** R. LIGON *Barbadoes* (1673) 70 The Papa is but a small tree,..the top handsomely form'd to the branches. **1764** GRAINGER *Sugar Cane* IV. 6 Thy temples shaded by the trem'lous palm, Or quick papaw. **1871** KINGSLEY *At Last* i, In the midst of the yard grew, side by side..the magic trees, whose leaves rubbed on the toughest meat make it tender..a male and female Papaw. **1920** *Nature* 2 Sept. 36/1 A fungus..causes powdery mildew on the leaves of the pawpaw plant. **1948** *Archit. Rev.* CIV. 94 In a forest of bamboo, palm, bread-fruit and paw-paw trees the white temples rear their phenomenal towers. **1958** J. CAREW *Black Midas* iv. 64 We walked past banana, paw-paw, and cocoa trees. **1964** D. VARADAY *Gara-Yaka* xi. 96, I intended placing thorn fences around the paw-paw trees. **1966** B. KIMENYE *Kalasanda Revisited* 23 Anna remained as alien to Kalasanda as an orange in a pawpaw tree.

2. (Only in forms *pawpaw, papaw.*) Name in U.S. for a small N. American tree, *Asimina triloba* (N.O. *Anonaceæ*), with dull purple flowers and ovate leaves (*pa(w)paw-tree*); or for its oblong edible fruit, about 3 or 4 inches long, with beanlike seeds embedded in a sweet pulp.

1760 J. LEE *Introd. Bot.* App. 321 Papaw-tree of North America, *Annona.* *a* **1796** in Morse *Amer. Geog.* I. 577 (Ohio) Crab apple tree, paupaw or custard apple. *Ibid.* 636 (Kentucky) The coffee, the papaw, the hackberry. **1807** P. GASS *Jrnl.* 261 We got a great many papaws..a kind of fruit in great abundance on the Missouri from the river Platte to its mouth. **1832** MRS. F. TROLLOPE *Dom. Manners Americans* iv. (1839) 32 Near New Orleans the undergrowth of palmetto and pawpaw is highly beautiful. **1851** MAYNE REID *Scalp Hunt.* i. 13 The red-bird flutters down in the coppice of green pawpaws. **1866** *Treas. Bot.* 843 Papaw. **1882** *Cornhill Mag.* May 580 Often we pass by groves of young paw-paws. **1925** C. E. MULFORD *Cottonwood Gulch* xi. 148 You let me catch you foolin' 'round this ranch an' I'll turn you into pulp as soft as a paw-paws! **1969** *Northwest (Sunday Oregonian Mag.)* 14 Dec. 19/1 The fragrant aroma and rich flavor of the Pawpaw is remindful of many tropical favorites. **1970** B. MILES *Bluebells & Bittersweet* iv. 47/3 *Asimina triloba* (paw-paw)... Large drooping leaves give this a tropical look, and solitary dark-purple, bell-shaped flowers about 2 inches across in May are followed by strange cylindrical fruits 3 to 7 inches long... Paw-paws are difficult to move.

3. *attrib.*, as ***pawpaw-bush*** (= 2), ***pawpaw-thicket*** (sense 2), ***pawpaw-tree*** (= 1 b or 2).

1704 *Collect. Voy.* (Churchill) III. 769/1 A Fig-Tree or a Papey-Tree was..sold. **1705** BOSMAN *Guinea* 290 Some Papay-trees run up to the heighth of thirty foot. **1773** *Capt. Wallis's Voy.* in *Gentl. Mag.* XLIII. 542 Here [Tinian, Ladrones Is.] they got beef, pork, poultry, papaw-apples. **1894** *Outing* (U.S.) XXIV. 337/2 Our camping-place was a paw-paw thicket. **1896** *Cosmopolitan* XX. 396/1 She kept herself screened behind the ironweed and pawpaw bushes.

4. (Usu. with initial capital.) In Jamaica, a slave brought from the region of West Africa so called, in Dahomey, near the town of Ouidah. *Obs.* exc. *Hist.*

1707 H. SLOANE *Voy. Jamaica* I. p. liv, The Negros called Papas have most of these scarifications. **1725** *Ibid.* II. 376 Its [*sc.* belly-ach-weed's] use was first made known in Jamaica, by Papau-Negros, and thence call'd Papau-weed. **1740** C. LESLIE *New Hist. Jamaica* xi. 307 They generally believe there are Two Gods..; the first they call Naskew in the Papaw language. **1774** E. LONG *Hist. Jamaica* II. III. iii. 425 In 1769, several new masks appeared; the Ebos, the Papaws, &c. having their respective Connús, male and female, who were dressed in a very laughable style. **1793** B. EDWARDS *Hist. Brit. Colonies W. Indies* II. III. 73, I now proceed to the people of Whidah, or Fida. The Negroes of this country are called generally in the West Indies Papaws. **1949** *Caribbean Q.* I. I. 11, 33 were Nagoes and 24 Pawpaws from the Slave Coast.

paw-paw ('pɔːˌpɔː), *a. slang* or *colloq.* ? *Obs.* [Reduplication of PAW *a.*] A nursery expression for 'nasty, improper, naughty', used euphemistically for 'indecent, obscene, immoral'.

1796 *Grose's Dict. Vulgar T.* (ed. 3), *Paw paw Tricks*, naughty tricks: an expression used by nurses, &c. to children. **1802–12** BENTHAM *Ration. Judic. Evid.* (1827) IV. 338 Administering a little fatherly or motherly correction.. for paw-paw tricks. **1812** G. COLMAN *Br. Grins, Two Parsons* vii, All proprietors of paw-paw houses. **1825** T. H. LISTER *Granby* ix. (1836) 55 Then went to say paw-paw things of Lady Mary Wortley Montague. **1830** SCOTT *Jrnl.* 9 July, Touching the songs, an old *roué* must own an improvement in the times, when all paw-paw words are omitted.

Hence **'paw-ˌpawness.**

1828 *Examiner* 434/1 Churches will cover a multitude of actresses. Our paw-pawness hedgeth with sacred stone, and abundantly excuseth itself with Glebe Houses. **1829** *Ibid.* 49/2 Proposals for the better rewarding of paw-pawness.

paws, pawse, obs. ff. PAUSE.

pawsey, obs. f. PALSY *sb.*[1]

† **'pawson.** *Obs.* Shortened form of DIAPASON.

1606 J. RAYNOLDS *Dolarney's Prim.* (1880) 71 His nimble hand, guided by supple veynes, With heauenly pawsons, clos'd his doleful streynes.

pawtenar, -er, pawtnere, var. PAUTENER *sb.*[2]

paw-waw, variant of POWWOW.

pax[1] (pæks). Also 6 pex. [a. L. *pax* peace, in Christian L. also the kiss of peace.]

‖ **1. a.** The Latin word meaning 'peace'. *Obs.*

Cf. Pliny, *Nat. Hist.* XXVII. 3 immensa Romanae pacis maiestate.

The Latin word is familiar in certain legal phrases, as *Pax Dei, Ecclesiæ, Regis*, the peace of God, the Church, the king's peace; so ***pax Romana***, the peace which reigned between nationalities within the Roman empire (cf. also sense e).

a **1485** FORTESCUE *Wks.* 1869 476 We shulde firste have unite and pax within our land. **1535** STEWART *Cron. Scot.* III. 72 Ane man he wes of policie and pax. **1664** *Spelman's Gloss., Pax Dei, Pax Ecclesiæ, Pax Regis.* **1872** WHARTON *Law Lex.* (ed. 5), *Pax regis*, the king's peace—verge of the court. **1884** W. J. CLARKE tr. *Duruy & Mahaffy's Hist. Rome* II. I. xxxiv. 201 Later, another form expressed the advantage, which was the compensation for this imperious sway, *pax romana*, that 'Roman peace' destined to draw the nations together and blend all languages,..whose boundless majesty, *immensa romanæ pacis majestas*, the nations will honour with sincere homage. **1888** *Encycl. Brit.* XXIII. 591/1 The *pax Romana* died with the empire. **1934** G. B. SHAW *On Rocks* Pref. 183 We Romans have purchased the *pax Romana* with our blood. **1956** A. TOYNBEE *Historian's Approach to Relig.* II. xvi. 212 The final collapse of the *Pax Romana* in the third century. **1974** *Encycl. Brit. Macropædia* II. 371/2 This Pax Romana..ensured the survival and eventual transmission of the classical heritage.

b. Also combined freely with Latinized adjs. to form phrases on the model of *pax Romana*, as ***pax aeronautica, Americana, atomica, Britannica, Communistica, Egyptiana, hispanica, Sovietica***, etc.

1933 M. ARLEN *Man's Mortality* ix. 180 These privately-owned stations..were of immense service to intercommunication throughout the world... They were the visible symbols of the pax aeronautica. **1967** 'R. RAINE' *Wreath for Amer.* xxv. 182 The whole Western world..is living under..a Pax Americana, just as the world once lived in peace under a Pax Britannica. **1971** *Newsweek* 18 Oct. 17 In the opinion of many European experts, the Kremlin has a more ambitious objective: to alter the staus quo by exchanging the *Pax Americana* for a *Pax Sovietica*. **1976** *Times Lit. Suppl.* 26 Nov. 1488/5 The 'Pax Americana', a phrase which several contributors toss about carelessly, is and was a myth, if meant to take in the world as a whole. There has not been so much peace since the Second World War for the right term to be either Pax or Americana. **1966** R. ARDREY *Territorial Imperative* (1967) viii. 283 Pessimism, under the rule of a *Pax Britannica*, was a dirty little luxury which any could afford; under a *pax atomica* it carries small selective value. **1969** W. GARNER *Us or Them War* xxv. 203 I'll give you a toast, girl. The *pax atomica*! Long may it last! **1886** *Jrnl. R. United Service Inst.* May 865 We should see Pax Britannica far transcend what Pliny called the 'immensa Romanæ Pacis Majestas'. **1899** *Westm. Gaz.* 9 Dec. 2/2 The wonderful lion which figured in the Poet Laureate's 'Pax Britannica' poem. **1939** E. H. CARR *Twenty Years' Crisis* v. 104 In the past, Roman and British imperialism were commended to the world in the guise of the *pax Romana* and the *pax Britannica*. **1960** *Times* 29 Sept. (Nigeria Suppl.) p. x/3 As a result of the *Pax Britannica*..the population has increased steadily. **1967** J. CLEARY *Long Pursuit* v. 113 We brought peace to this part of the world, Pax Britannica is more than just a phrase. **1969** J. MANDER *Static Society* ii. 83 It brought greater stability..than did the *pax britannica*. **1973** *Listener* 1 Feb. 146/2 In the 19th century, the British Navy dictated the Pax Britannica and more or less guaranteed a century of peace. **1946** H. NICOLSON *Diary* 22 Aug. (1968) 75 They [*sc.* the Russians] believe that..people will say in the end, 'Anything for peace', and will accept the Pax Scythica or Communistica. **1961** L. MUMFORD *City in Hist.* iii. 88 There may well have been [in ancient Egypt] a long period, a Pax Egyptiana, that relaxed both the internal tensions and the need for external protection. **1969** J. MANDER *Static Society* ii. 83 The centuries of peace under the *pax hispanica* that shielded Latin Americans. **1945** A. HUXLEY *Let.* 7 May (1969) 522 One can only hope that the Pax Sovietica may last as long as the Pax Romana. **1969** *Sunday Times* 19 Oct. 49 There won't be a Pax Sovietica or anything like it, because the world is too big to be governed by anybody. **1977** *Time* 29 Aug. 19/3 Bell-bottom denims, miniskirts and platform shoes have turned Ulan Bator's girls into the prettiest within the Pax Sovietica.

c. *Eccl.* In Latin salutations and blessings, as ***pax vobis*** peace be with you! (see quot. 1885).

1593 PEELE *Edw. I*, Wks. (Rtldg.) 381/2 *Pax vobis, Pax vobis!* good fellows, fair fall ye. **1840** BARHAM *Ingol. Leg.* Ser. I. *Grey Dolphin*, 'Of course I shall', said St. Austin. '*Pax vobiscum*!'—and Abbot Anselm was left alone. **1885** *Cath. Dict.* (ed. 3), *Pax vobis* is said by bishops after the 'Gloria in Excelsis'. If the 'Gloria' be not said, then the bishop's salutation is the same as the priest's—viz. 'Dominus vobiscum'. The fact that 'Pax vobis' was our Lord's Easter greeting to the Apostles made it unsuitable for penitential days.

d. quasi-*int.* (in schoolboy slang). 'Keep quiet!' 'Truce!'

1852–82 ROGET *Thesaurus* §403 *Silence... Int.* hush! silence! soft! whist! tush! chut! tut! pax! **1872** *Routledge's Ev. Boy's Ann.* 615/1 There's been a sort of 'pax' called all round. **1899** KIPLING *Stalky, In Ambush* 4 '*Pax*, Turkey. I'm an ass.'

e. ***Pax Romana***, the name of an international organization of Roman Catholic students. (See also sense a.)

1957 M. P. FOGARTY *Christian Democracy in W. Europe* xvii. 263 Catholic graduates of all faculties are linked up through *Pax Romana* which also includes students. **1967** D. T. KAUFFMAN *Dict. Relig. Terms* 349/1 *Pax Romana*, world organization of Catholic students. In Europe it is called the International Movement of Catholic Students.

2. *Eccl.* The kiss of peace: see PEACE *sb.* 4; the ceremony of kissing the pax: see sense 3. *rare.*

c **1440** *Promp. Parv.* 388/1 Pax, of kyssynge (*v.r.* or kyssynge), *osculum, vel osculum pacis.* *a* **1548** HALL *Chron., Rich. III.* 26 The Cardinall song the masse, and after paxe, the kynge and the quene discended. **1568** GRAFTON *Chron.* II. 802 The sate still vntill the Paxe was geuen. **1853** ROCK *Ch. of Fathers* IV. xii. 160 The Salisbury rubric was to send, just before the communion, the 'Pax' all about the church. This..was conveyed from one to another by a kiss upon the cheek.

3. *Eccl.* A tablet of gold, silver, ivory, glass, or other material, round or quadrangular, with a projecting handle behind, bearing a representation of the Crucifixion or other sacred subject, which was kissed by the celebrating priest at Mass, and passed to the other officiating clergy and then to the congregation to be kissed; an osculatory.

It came into use during the 13th c. as a symbolic substitute for the kiss of peace: see PEACE *sb.* 2. In England its use died out after the Reformation; in the Roman Church it is now used in certain monastic communities on special occasions.

c **1375** *Lay Folks Mass Bk.* (MS. B.) 514 þere when þo prest [þo] pax wil kis, knele þou & praye þen þis. *c* **1386** CHAUCER *Pars. T.* ¶ 333 And eek he waiteth or desireth to sitte or elles to goon aboue hym in the wey or kisse pax, or been encensed or goon to offryng biforn his neighebore. *a* **1450** LYDG. *Vertue of Masse* (*c* 1505) c j b, The people of loue and hyghe degre Kysse the pax a token of vnyte. **1528** TINDALE *Doctr. Treat.* (Parker Soc.) 279 Yea to kiss the pax, they think it a meritorious deed. **1545** *Rates of Customs* c iij, Paxes the groce xiis. **1588** CROWLEY *Delib. Answ.* 40 b, Innocent the first..inuented the kissing of the Paxe at Masse. **1621** BURTON *Anat. Mel.* Democr. to Rdr. (1676) 17/1 Had he been present at a Masse, and seen such kissing of Paxes, Crucifixes, Cringes, Duckings [etc.]. **1670** LASSELS *Voy. Italy* II. 389 A rich *Pax* of Mother of Pearle. **1826** MRS. BRAY *De Foix* x. (1884) 107 He was next presented with the Pax, which he also solemnly kissed. **1840** *Penny Cycl.* XVII. 343.

fig. **1589** WARNER *Alb. Eng.* VI. xxxi. 136 Her lippes meane while my Pex: Ply Sir (quoth she) your busie trade, you are besides the Tex.

4. *transf.* (Public School slang.) A friend; good friends. ***to be good pax***, to be good friends.

1781 BENTHAM *Mem. & Corr.* Wks. 1843 X. 100 If anything should happen to jumble us together, we may perhaps be good pax. **1900** C. B. MOUNT *Let. to Editor*, At Winchester (*c* 1840) we used to talk of 'making *pax*' with some one, in sense of establishing a friendship: we even used 'Pax' in sense of 'friend':—'a great pax of mine'.

† **pax**[2]. *Obs.* A corrupt form of POX. In phr. ***pax on*** (*him, it*, etc.)!

1641 BROME *Jov. Crew* IV. i. Wks. 1873 III. 422 Pax o' your fine Thing. **1663** DRYDEN *Wild Gallant* II. i, Pax on't! **1716** ADDISON *Drummer* III. i, Pax on him, what do I give him the hearing for!

Paxarete (paxa'rete). Also **Pajarete, Pascarete, Paxarette.** [f. *Paxarete*, a small town in the Jerez district of Spain.] A mixture of fortified wine and boiled-down grape juice, formerly drunk as a sherry, now used primarily for colouring or sweetening sherry or whisky.

1827 SCOTT *Chron. Canongate* 1st Ser. II. vi. 151 When they were comfortably seated over a bottle of Paxarete. **1846** R. FORD *Gatherings from Spain* xiv. 152 It is of this grape that the rich and luscious sweet wine called *Pajarete* is made. **1891** in C. Ray *Compleat Imbiber* (1967) IX. 122 Sherry... Paxerette. **1920** G. SAINTSBURY *Notes on Cellar-Bk.* ii. 18 Light Spanish wines..for instance, the lighter Paxarettes.. which most literary people to-day associate only with Sir Telegraph in 'Melincourt'. **1958** A. L. SIMON *Dict. Wines* 122/1 The *Pajarete* or *Paxarete* liqueur wine..is mostly used for sweetening high-class sweet sherries. **1965** O. A. MENDELSOHN *Dict. Drink* 254 *Paxarete*, Spanish compound wine, also known as Pedro Ximénez, made by fortifying *arrope* (concentrated grape juice)... Also known as *pascarete* and *pajarete*.

† **'paxboard,** obs. var. of next, after BOARD *sb.*

1481 LITTLETON *Will* in *Test. Vetusta* (1826) I. 364 A paxe-borde, two cruetts, and a sakering-bell. **1500** *Inv. St. Dunstan's, Canterb.* ibid., A pax borde off latin, a crucyfyx for a pax borde off coper & gyltt.

† **paxbred.** *Obs.* Forms: 4 paxbreyd, 4–5 -brede, -bred, 6 -bredd. [f. PAX[1] + BRED *sb.* board.] = PAX[1] 3.

1350 in Riley *Mem. Lond.* (1868) 263 Paxbred. **1395** in *E.E. Wills* (1882) 5, I bequethe a chales and a paxbred. *c* **1440** *Promp. Parv.* 388/1 Pax brede, *osculatorium.* **1472** in *Wilts. Archæol. etc. Mag.* (1868) XI. 337 A pakisbrede of yvere wᵗʰ a ymage of our lorde as he swette blode. **1509** in *Suss. Archæol. Coll.* XLI. 27, iij paxbredds. [**1881** *Academy* 16 Apr. 284 A 'paxbrede' representing the crucifix with Mary and John.]

‖ **paxilla** (pæk'sɪlə). *Zool.* Pl. **-æ.** [mod.L., from classical L. *paxillus* small stake, peg.] A pillarlike pedicel in echinoderms, surmounted by a tuft of minute calcified spinelets attached to the integument.

1870 ROLLESTON *Anim. Life* 142 The spines..may carry a coronet of numerous calcified setae on their apices when they are called 'paxillae'. **1878** BELL tr. *Gegenbaur's Comp. Anat.* 206 The incompletely calcified stalk of the pedicellaria corresponds to the stalk of the paxilla of the Asterida.

Hence **pa'xillar** *a.*, of or pertaining to paxillæ; **pa'xillate** *a.*, having paxillæ; **paxi'lliferous** *a.*, bearing paxillæ; **pa'xilliform** *a.*, having the shape of a paxilla.

1857 MAYNE *Expos. Lex.* 892/1 Having the body furnished with appendices,..paxilliferous. **1889** SLADEN in *Challenger Rep., Zool.* XXX. 286 Plates of the abactinal area more or less truly paxilliform. **1890** *Cent. Dict.*, Paxillate. **1900** *Proc. Zool. Soc.* 292 Paxillar crowns are very large and oval.

†**paxillary**, *a. Obs.* Erroneous form of BASILARY, applied to the sphenoid bone.

Med.L. *basilus* appears to have been written *passillus*, and associated with *paxillus*, giving *passillare, paxillarie*.

[*c* **1400** *Lanfranc's Cirurg.* 110 (Ashm.) Þe. vij. boon is clepid passillare, þe which is not of þe boones of þe heed, but he susteyneþ alle þe oþere boonys of þe heed. [*Add. MS.* 10440 lf. 2, adds] & he is vnterberynge in þe hynder partie al þe bones of þe heued, & þerfore he is clepid þe..paxillus.] **1548–77** VICARY *Anat.* iii. (1888) 28 The seuenth and last [bone]..of the head is called Paxillarie, or Bazillarie; the whiche bone is, as it were, the wedge vnto all the other seuen bones of the head, and doth fasten them togeather. And thus be all numbred: the first is the Coronal bone,..the seuenth is Paxillari, or Bazillari.

'paxi,llose, *a.* [f. L. *paxillus* or mod.L. *paxilla* (see above) + -OSE.] **a.** *Geol.* Resembling a small stake (Ogilvie, Annandale, 1882). **b.** Of or pertaining to the *Paxillosæ*, a group of echinoderms bearing paxillæ (Funk 1895). **c.** Provided with paxillæ; paxillate.

1900 *Proc. Zool. Soc.* 290 The abactinal surface is paxillose, each paxillus having a circular crown of about eight papillæ, the centre being usually smooth.

‖**pa'xillus.** *Zool.* [L. *paxillus* small stake, peg.] = PAXILLA (Webster 1890).

Paxolin ('pæksəlɪn). Also **paxolin**. A proprietary name for a type of laminated plastic widely used as an electrical insulating material.

1918 *Trade Marks Jrnl.* 23 Jan. 86 Paxolin... Electrical insulating preparations... The Micanite & Insulators Company, Limited,..London,..manufacturers. **1924** *Harmsworth's Wireless Encycl.* III. 1529/1 Paxolin is an insulating material made of paper impregnated with a varnish consisting of phenol and formaldehyde. **1944** *Electronic Engin.* XVI. 385/3 The objective lens was mounted inside a piece of paxolin tubing. **1958** *Official Gaz.* (U.S. Patent Office) 28 Oct. TM 135/2 The Micanite & Insulators Company Limited, London, England, Filed Feb. 14, 1958. Paxolin... For electrical insulating materials. **1960** *Practical Wireless* XXXVI. 413/1 To make such a screen, a piece of thin insulating material such as paxolin is wound with 26 s.w.g. wire. **1962** N. H. CODLING in G. A. T. Burdett *Automatic Control Handbk.* viii. 16 Characteristics of grade S5 silicone glass Paxolin are given in Table 9. **1965** *Wireless World* Aug. 377/1 Each unit has been assembled on a paxolin board using connecting pins.

paxwax ('pækswæks). Now *dial.* and *colloq.* Also 5 **paxwex, paswax**, 6 **pixwex**, 7 **pax-waxe**, 7–9 **packwax**, 9 **paxywaxy**. [A word used in many dialect forms, e.g. FIX-FAX, *fic-fac, fig-fag*, etc., the earliest known being *fax-wax* or *fex-wex* (W. de Bibbesworth 13..), which appears to contain OE. *feax*, ME. *fex, fax* (see FAX *sb.*[1]), the hair of the head, and OE. **weax* growth, from *weaxan* to grow, wax; cf. the parallel Ger. synonym *haarwachs* sinew, f. *haar* hair + *wachs*, *wax-*, growth; cf. also MDu. *geel haar* 'yellow hair' = tendon.

In German, Grimm instances the second element in various forms, e.g. in OHG. *uualto-uuahso, uuinuuahs*, nerve, etc.]

A name for the stout elastic tendon extending from the dorsal vertebræ to the occiput, and serving as a support for the head, in various mammals, as the horse, ox, sheep, etc.; in others, as in man, existing in less developed form; the nuchal ligament, fixfax, whitleather.

[**13..** *Gloss W. de Bibbesw.* (MS. Camb. Gg. I. 1 lf. 280 b/2), E si ad derere le wen au col (*gloss* fax wax [*v.r.* fex wex]).] *c* **1440** *Promp. Parv.* 388/1 Paxwax, synewe (*Pynson* pax-wex). **14..** *Arund. MS.* 42 lf. 44 b, Delle..helpeþ for brussures of þe paxwax and of þe brawn. *Ibid.* 90 b, It [*Galbanum*] is gode for..þe shote in þe lacertys, i. in þe paswaxis. **1548–77** VICARY *Anat.* vi. (1888) 46 There be three maner of fleshes in the necke: the first is called Pixwex or Seruisis. **1610** MARKHAM *Masterp.* II. iii. 219 This [sinew] of the common Farriers is called pax-waxe. *a* **1682** SIR T. BROWNE *Tracts* viii. Wks. 1836 IV. 205 Words of no general reception in England, but of common use in Norfolk, or peculiar to the East Angle countries; as *bawnd, bunny, thurck,..paxwax*. **1691** RAY *Coll. Words* Pref., Paxwax..is a word not confined to Norfolk or Suffolk, but far spread over England; used, to my knowledge, in Oxfordshire. **1691** —— *Creation* I. (1692) 150 Which Aponeurosis..is taken notice of by the Vulgar by the name of Fixfax, or Packwax, or Whit-leather. **1713** DERHAM *Phys.-Theol.* (1723) 323 That strong..ligament..called the Whiteleather, Packwax,..and Fixfax. **1848** CARPENTER *Anim. Phys.* 33 The ligament of the neck of many quadrupeds, commonly known as the paxy-waxy. **1865** BANKS *Wakefield Wds.*, As tough as pax-wax.

pay (peɪ), *sb.* Also 4 **pai, payȝ**, 4–7 **paie, paye**, 5 **pey**. [a. OF. *paie* = Pr. *paia, paga*, Sp., Pg., It. *paga* f. the vb. *pagare, payer* to PAY.]

†**1.** Satisfaction, contentment, pleasure, liking. *to pay*: to a person's satisfaction, acceptably. Chiefly with possessive: *to, at* (a person's) *pay*, as he likes, so as to please him. *Obs.*

c **1300** *Body & Soul* in *Maps' Poems* (Camden) 334 A body ..That havde ben a mody knyȝt, and lutel served God to payȝ. **13..** *K. Alis.* 3796 Yut ye schole, of myn paye, Or Y go hennes, more assay! **13..** *E.E. Allit. P.* A. 1164 Hit watz not at my pryncez paye, Hit payed hym not þat I so flonc. **1362** LANGL. *P. Pl.* A. VI. 39 For þauh I Sigge hit myself, I serue him to paye, I haue myn hure of him wel, and oþer-while more. *c* **1375** *Cursor M.* 22939 (Fairf.) A potter.. quen he his new vessel for-dos & hit be noȝt vn-to his pay. *a* **1425** *Ibid.* 3655 (Trin.) Venisoun þou hast him nomen Deyntily diȝte to his pay [*earlier MSS.* behoue]. *c* **1430** *Syr Gener.* (Roxb.) 5665 Of hors and armes at his pay The Soudon yave in the same day. *a* **1529** SKELTON *E. Rummyng* 395, I dranke not this sennet A draught to my pay. **1602** *Archpriest Controv.* (Camden) II. 4 He answered him not to his pay.

2. a. The action of paying, payment (esp. of wages or hire); with *pl.*, one of the periodical payments of wages to workmen or others.

c **1440** *Promp. Parv.* 377/1 Pay, or payment, *solucio*. *c* **1570** R. TURPYN in *Chron. Calais* (Camden) Introd. 19 Payenge to the said victuallers from paie to paie that was made ther by the quenes majestie their saide sommes of money. **1602** MARSTON *Antonio's Rev.* IV. v, At the fixed day of pay. **1647** N. BACON *Disc. Govt. Eng.* I. lxiv. (1739) 133 Rather to score it up against the future, than require present pay. **1865** KINGSLEY *Herew.* iii, 'No pay no play' is as good a rule for priest as for layman. **1872** *Daily News* 2 Oct. 5 The 'pays' are the markers in the chronological table of the miner. He refers to a past event as having occurred so many pays back.

b. The condition of being paid, or receiving wages or hire: chiefly in phr. *in pay*, in receipt of wages; *in the pay of*, in the paid employment of.

1596 SHAKS. *1 Hen. IV*, III. ii. 126 Like enough,..To fight against me vnder Percies pay. **1601** R. JOHNSON *Kingd. & Commw.* (1603) 168 Armed troopes which he keepeth in continuall pay and action. **1671** R. MONTAGU in *Buccleuch MSS.* (Hist. MSS. Comm.) I. 509 His provisions for sea were already made, his men raised and in pay. **1743** BULKELEY & CUMMINS *Voy. S. Seas* Pref. 13 When they were out of Pay, they look'd upon themselves as their own Masters. **1838** THIRLWALL *Greece* IV. 197 Unless we should suppose that the murderers were in the pay of Sparta. **1865** DICKENS *Mut. Fr.* I. xv, People in your pay or employment.

3. *concr.* **a.** Money paid for labour or service; wages, hire, salary, stipend.

c **1330** R. BRUNNE *Chron.* (1810) 262 The kyng þis pay has nomen, and in cofres has. *c* **1430** *Freemasonry* (Halliw.) 23 Whenne the mason taketh hys pay of the mayster. **1590** SIR J. SMYTH *Disc. Weapons* Ded. 7 To terrifie their soldiers from demanding of their paies due. **1657** EARL MONM. tr. *Paruta's Pol. Disc.* 172 They take their lands and possessions ..making *Timari* thereof..which are Pays or Revenues assigned over to the Soldiers. **1757** JOS. HARRIS *Coins* 41 Is not their pay..scanty enough already? **1852** THACKERAY *Esmond* II. iii, I take the Queen's Pay in Quin's Regiment.

†**b.** *dead pay*: see DEAD PAY. *Obs.*

†**c.** (?) A soldier in receipt of pay. *Obs.*

1523 WOLSEY in *St. Papers Hen. VIII*, VI. 189 That the lanceknygtes being not past with the Countie Felix 7000 pays, wer at Porte Sus la Sone.

4. *fig.* **a.** Payment, or that which is paid, in any metaphorical sense; retaliation, punishment or blows inflicted; penalty or retribution suffered; recompense, etc. bestowed. Now *rare* or *Obs.*

c **1300** *Body & Soul* in *Maps' Poems* (Camden) 335 ȝeot schaltouȝ come..and I the with, for to kepen oure harde pay. *c* **1400** *Ywaine & Gaw.* 2476 The geant gaf he ful gude pay, He smate oway al his left cheke. **1590** SPENSER *F.Q.* III. x. 31 Fame is my meed, and glory vertues pay. **1592** SHAKS. *Ven. & Ad.* 89 But when her lips were ready for his pay, He winks, and turns his lips another way. **1602** —— *Ham.* I. iii. 106 That you haue tane his tenders for true pay.

†**b.** In early N. Amer. colonial use, any article used as a medium of payment. *Obs.*

1663 *Early Rec. Portsmouth, Rhode Island* (1901) 118 To sell the tounes cow..for wompom or other pay. **1681** *Town Rec. Topsfield, Mass.* (1917) I. 34/2 Twente pownd of it in siluer forti five pownd in other pay as namli in Corne porke and beefe. **1704** S. KNIGHT *Jrnl.* (1825) 42 Pay is Grain, Pork, Beef, &c. at the prices sett by the General Court that year. **1767** in *Essex Inst. Hist. Coll.* (1912) XLVIII. 75 And if you should purchase light pay, then proceed for Turks island.

5. a. *to be good* (etc.) *pay*: to be sure to pay one's debts (colloq.); *fig.* to be profitable, afford profit.

1727 GAY *Fables* I. x. 64 If you'd employ your pen, Against the senseless sons of men,..No man is better pay than I am. **1809** MALKIN *Gil Blas* III. iii. ¶ 3 Great men are good pay in the long run, they often marry rich heiresses, and then old scores are wiped off. **1842** POE *Murders Rue Morgue* Wks. 1864 I. 187 They were excellent pay. **1873** *Trans. Illinois Dept. Agric.* X. 249 Many farmers were very slow pay. **1926** J. BLACK *You can't Win* iv. 28 They were good pay, but he could not get away from his work at the right hour to find them. **1973** R. THOMAS *If you can't be Good* (1974) xii. 103 Everybody in town is falling over each other to give him credit—even though he's a slow pay.

†**b.** *better pay*, something more profitable or advantageous; an advantage. *Obs.*

13.. *Coer de L.* 364 [He] came agayn by another way, And thought to make a better pay. *a* **1330** *Roland & V.* 840 Mine worþ þe raþer pay. **14..** *Sir Beues* (MS. M) 501 He sye, it was no better paye, But shifte hym in the beste way.

6. *Mining.* A remunerative yield of metal in a bed of ore: cf. PAY- 2. Also, one of oil or natural gas. *concr.*, the bed itself.

1857 J. C. BORTHWICK *Three Yrs. in Calif.* vii. 140 After prospecting a little, we soon found a spot on the bank of the stream which we judged would yield us pretty fair pay for our labor. **1868** *Rep. J. Ross Browne Mineral Resources West of Rocky Mts.* (U.S. Treasury Dept.) 101 In 1866 they struck into pay and erected a 10-stamp mill, which is driven by a hurdy-gurdy wheel. **1877** RAYMOND *Statist. Mines & Mining* 91 It is in this stratum of 40 feet where the rich pay will be found. **1882** *Rep. to Ho. Repr. Prec. Met. U.S.* 105 Brown & Co. work a sluicing claim with good results. William George, just below, has lately got good pay. **1933** E. CALDWELL *God's Little Acre* i. 2 I've been digging in this land close on fifteen years now, and..I figure we're going to strike pay pretty soon. **1975** [see *pay zone* s.v. PAY- 2]. **1977** R. E. MEGILL *Introd. Risk Analysis* ix. 107 Every oil or gas field has a certain areal size, a thickness of the producing formation and a recovery per foot of pay.

Comb.: see PAY- in combination, 2.

7. Short for PAYMASTER. *slang.*

1878 F. DAVENPORT *On Man-of-War* 114 While the boy went forward after the steward, Pay regarded the omelet gloomily. **1914** 'BARTIMEUS' *Naval Occasions* xxiii. 216 Give it a shake, Pay, and put it on like a man! **1916** 'TAFFRAIL' *Pincher Martin* x. 173 Cashley, the fleet pay-master, was vainly endeavouring to get up a four at auction bridge... 'Going to take a hand?'..'Bridge,..not to-night, Pay; thanks, all the same.' **1942** [see BOFFIN 1]. **1944** K. D. MCCRACKEN *Baby Flat-Top* 57 The Head of the Supply Department is known universally as 'Pay'.

pay (peɪ), *v.*[1] Pa. t. and pple. **paid** (peɪd). Forms: 3–5 **paie(n, paye(n**, (3 **paiȝe**, 4 **pai**, 5 **payȝe**, 5–6 **pey**), 4–7 **paie, paye**, 4– **pay**. *Pa. t.* **paid**, in senses 13, 14 **payed**; 3–6 **payde, paide**, 4–6 *Sc.* **payit**. *Pa. pple.* **paid**, in senses 13, 14, **payed**; 4 **paȝed**, 4–6 **payde**, 5 **-id**, 5–6 *Sc.* **-it**; also 3–4 with prefixed **i-**, 3–6 **y-**, (5 **ypayt**). [ME. a. F. *payer* (12th c. in Littré) to pay, in OF. also to appease, satisfy, please (so in Cotgr. 1611) = Pr., Sp., Pg. *pagar*, It. *pagare*:—L. *pācāre* to appease, pacify, reduce to peace, in med.L. also 'to pay', f. *pāx, pāc-em* peace. The sense 'pacify', applied specifically to that of 'pacify or satisfy a creditor', came in Com. Romanic to mean 'to pay a creditor', and so 'to pay' generally. In some of the Romanic langs. the vb. has still both senses; but in Fr. as in Eng. the sense 'satisfy, please' is now obs.]

†**1. a.** *trans.* To appease, pacify, satisfy, content, please, gratify; to be acceptable to, gain or meet with the approval of: = APAY 1. Most freq. in *pa. pple.* Satisfied, content, pleased; also strengthened by *well*; so *ill paid*, displeased, dissatisfied. *Obs.*

c **1200** *Trin. Coll. Hom.* 179 And ȝiet ne wile þe louerd ben paid mid his rihcte mol. *a* **1225** *Ancr. R.* 318 Þus I souhte delit: hwu I mest muhte paien mine lustes brune. *c* **1275** LAY. 10535 Þis ihorde þe kaiser And him paide swiþe wel. *a* **1300** *Cursor M.* 7814 Wel he wend wit þis tiþing For to pai dauid þe king. **13..** *Gaw. & Gr. Knt.* 1379 How payez yow þis play? *c* **1430** *Syr Gener.* (Roxb.) 7558 The long terme did hir not pay To abide so long the mariage. *c* **1440** *Promp. Parv.* 377/2 Payyd, and qvemyd, or plesyd, *placatus*. *c* **1460** *Towneley Myst.* ii. 244 Luke well..that thou negh not the tree of life; ffor if thou do, he bese ill paide. **1496** *Dives & Paup.* (W. de W.) VII. iv. 280/2 Poore folke be not payed with suffycyent lyuynge but couete more than theym nedeth. **1501** DOUGLAS *Pal. Hon.* II. vii, I held me payit of thair estait.

†**b.** *intr.* To be satisfactory or pleasing (*to*). *Obs.*

c **1380** WYCLIF *Sel. Wks.* III. 49 Þat spirit..þe which is verrili kyndelid wiþ þe fier of þe Holy Goost, to þe which.. no passing þing paieþ, but al fleshli lust..loþiþ and is viile to it. *c* **1460** *Towneley Myst.* xx. 198 My profer may both pleas and pay To all the lordys.

2. a. *trans.* To give to (a person) what is due in discharge of a debt, or as a return for services done, or goods received, or in compensation for injury done; to remunerate, recompense.

c **1250** *O. Kent. Serm.* in *O.E. Misc.* 33 Se sergant..so paide þo werkmen and yaf euerich ane peny. **1362** LANGL. *P. Pl.* A. IV. 61 Him for his handidandi Rediliche he payede. **1456** SIR G. HAYE *Law Arms* (S.T.S.) 135 The marchand salbe payit of his hors. **1590** SHAKS. *Com. Err.* I. ii. 56 Sixe pence that I had..To pay the Sadler for my Mistris crupper. **1625** MASSINGER *New Way* IV. ii, I will pay you in private. **1710** SWIFT *Lett.* (1767) III. 69 Tell me how accounts stand between us, that you may be paid. **1813** MAR. EDGEWORTH *Patron.* iii, He had been..paid by the job. **1833** HT. MARTINEAU *Brooke Farm* v. 62, I expect they will pay me..for the outlay.

b. *to pay off* (rarely *up*): to pay in full and discharge; to give all that is owing to and thus settle accounts with; *spec.* to pay and discharge the crew of (a ship) upon completion of a commission. *to pay out*: to get rid of by paying.

1710 STEELE *Tatler* No. 143 ¶ 1, I..desired her to pay off her Coach, for I had a great deal to talk to her. **1758** J. BLAKE *Plan Mar. Syst.* 23 They shall..be paid off, and discharged. **1809** MALKIN *Gil Blas* III. ix. ¶ 1 The establishment was paid up and discharged. **1836** MARRYAT *Midsh. Easy* xi, The ship to which he had been appointed was paid off. **1836–9** DICKENS *Sk. Boz, Broker's Man*, The money was raised, and the execution was paid out. **1887** D. C. MURRAY *Old Blazer's Hero* ix, The Man in Possession had been paid out.

c. ***to pay off*** (intr. for passive, of a ship: see b).

1891 *Daily News* 27 July 5/4 The Thrush..will then go to Cowes and afterwards to Chatham, where she will pay off. **1896** *Ibid.* 21 Aug. 2/5 The Meteor..is to pay off immediately and proceed to lay up.

d. ***not if you paid me, him,*** etc.: under no circumstances; not at all.

1896 KIPLING *Seven Seas* 153 He couldn't lie if you paid him, and he'd starve before he stole! **1910** E. M. FORSTER *Howards End* xxiv. 201, I couldn't live near her if you paid me. **1952** M. ALLINGHAM *Tiger in Smoke* iv. 67, I shan't sleep, you know, I couldn't if you paid me. **1959** M. SUMMERTON *Small Wilderness* i. 8 Six months ago I was all set to read law, now I wouldn't go back to swotting if you paid me. **1979** R. JEFFRIES *Murder begets Murder* iii. 19, I wouldn't stay on here if you paid me to. The moment I've sorted everything out I'm off.

3. *fig.* or *gen.* To reward, recompense, requite, give what is due or deserved to (a person). **a.** in good or neutral sense.

a **1425** *Cursor M.* 5789 (Trin.) Say I shal hem soone pay. **1484** CAXTON *Fables of Æsop* I. xix, Thenne is the tyme come that he must be payed of his Werkes and dedes. **1610** SHAKS. *Temp.* II. i. 37 So: you'r paid. *a* **1774** GOLDSM. tr. *Scarron's Com. Romance* (1775) II. 232 He was sure to be paid on the double in treats for his condescension. **1898** H. PAUL *Men & Lett.* (1901) 170 Mr. Place and his associates, to adopt a French phrase, payed themselves with words.

b. *in malam partem*: to give (one) his deserts, visit with retribution, chastise, punish. Formerly often ***pay home*** (HOME *adv.* 5); later also ***pay off***, and in mod. colloq. use ***pay out***. ***to pay any one in his own coin***: see COIN *sb.* 7 b.

a **1450** *Knt. de la Tour* (1868) 90, Y canne not telle you the halff of her cruelte..But she was paied..atte the last. **1567** MAPLET *Gr. Forest* 101 b, If any man come neare hir behinde she payeth him home. **1582** N. LICHEFIELD tr. *Castanheda's Conq. E. Ind.* I. xlvi. 102 b, He would paye him for all his faigned lyes. **1707** *Curios. in Husb. & Gard.* 242 He pays off Aristotle and his Followers with too violent a Zeal. **1863** [see BACK *adv.* 8]. **1863** COWDEN CLARKE *Shaks. Char.* viii. 198 They, in return, (as the vulgar phrase has it,) 'pay him out'. **1888** J. HAWTHORNE *Trag. Myst.* iii, They would bear Hanier a grudge..and would plot together to pay him off. **1893** EARL DUNMORE *Pamirs* II. 252 The only way..was to pay them back in their own coin. **1914** D. H. LAWRENCE *Widowing of Mrs. Holroyd* III. 66 He'd say to himself he'd pay me out. That's what he always does say, 'I'll pay thee out for that bit—I'll ma'e thee regret it.' **1940** G. D. H. & M. COLE *Counterpoint Murder* v. 51 He told Best to do it just in order to annoy him, to pay him out. **1951** M. KENNEDY *Lucy Carmichael* I. v. 36 I'm paid out for saying I wouldn't have a wreath. I thought a sort of vague cloud round my head would look nice. **1978** J. THOMSON *Question of Identity* xiii. 140 It was his way of paying out Maguire for giving him the push.

c. *spec.* To inflict bodily chastisement upon, beat, flog. Now *dial.* or *slang*.

1581 W. FLEETWOOD in Ellis *Orig. Lett.* Ser. I. II. 285 Yet were they all sowndly payed, and sent home to there masters. **1667** PEPYS *Diary* 22 Apr., Thence home, and find the boy out of the house and office..I did pay his coat for him. *a* **1806** in R. Jamieson *Pop. Ball.* I. 329 There I paid her baith back and side, Till a' her banes play'd clatter. **1825** BROCKETT *N.C. Gloss.*, *Pay*, to beat, to drub. 'The rascal pays his wife'. **1899** F. T. BULLEN *Log Sea-waif* 312 He had been paying somebody with the 'fore-topsail sheet'.

4. To give a recompense for, to recompense, reward, requite (a service, work, or action of any kind): in a good or bad sense. Also, of a thing, To yield a recompense for, to reward.

14.. *Sir Beues* 158/3381 + 2 (MS. M) Youre service I wyll well payn! *c* **1586** C'TESS PEMBROKE *Ps.* LXII. v, Lord,..each mans work is paid by thee. **1603** SHAKS. *Meas. for M.* v. i. 415 Haste still paies haste. **1610** —— *Temp.* v. i. 70, I will pay thy graces Home both in word, and deede. **1642** J. SHUTE *Sarah & Hagar* (1649) 178 The Sin of Oppression, sure enough, will be payed home, either here, or in hell, or in both. **1748** CHESTERF. *Lett.* (1774) I. 347 It will more than pay the trouble I have taken to write it. **1865** DICKENS *Mut. Fr.* II. i, 'I hope it's a good business?'..'No. Poorly paid'. **1868** G. MACDONALD *Gospel Women* IX. i, Enough he labours for his hire; Yea, nought can pay his pain.

5. a. To give, deliver, or hand over (money, or some other thing) in return for goods or services, or in discharge of an obligation; to render (a sum or amount owed). Also with double obj. or dat. of person ('I paid him the money'), and hence in indirect passive ('he was paid the money' = 'the money was paid to him'). Also *transf.*: cf. 6 b.

a **1225** *Ancr. R.* 290 Hire wurð þet he paide uor hire. **1297** R. GLOUC. (Rolls) 10244 Sixe & sixti þousend marc hii paiden him atten ende. *a* **1300** *Cursor M.* 6745 Qua stelis scep, or ox, or cu,..Oxen fiue for an he pai. **1377** LANGL. *P. Pl.* B. XIII. 381 He profred to paye A peny or tweyne More þan it was worth. *c* **1410** LOVE *Bonavent. Mirr.* ix. (Sherard MS.), Whan Joseph hadde payed þe money for hym. **1526** TINDALE *Matt.* xviii. 29 Have pacience with me, and I will paye the all. **1596** SHAKS. *1 Hen. IV*, III. iii. 201 The Monie is paid backe againe. *a* **1692** POLLEXFEN *Disc. Trade* (1697) 12 He will pay but Sixteen Shillings of the Pound. **1771** *Junius Lett.* xlix. 256 Every shilling of it was scrupulously paid. **1848** THACKERAY *Gt. Hoggarty Diamond* xii, That in which poor Mr. Tidd invested his money did not pay 2*d.* in the pound. **1885** *Times* (weekly ed.) 11 Sept. 9/2 Irish wool that had never 'paid the King a farthing'.

b. With advbs. ***to pay away, in, over, out,*** etc. ***pay down***: to lay down (money) in payment; to pay immediately or on the spot (also *fig.*: see 7).

1557 in W. H. Turner *Select. Rec. Oxford* (1880) 265 Payeng vij^li^ done. **1623** *Nottingham Rec.* IV. 383 Alexander Staples shalbe made burgesse paying x.^li.^ downe in hand. **1668** in *10th Rep. Hist. MSS. Comm.* App. v. 61 Paying over the third part of the profits. **1722** DE FOE *Col. Jack* (1840) 60 He had paid in all the money. **1809** R. LANGFORD *Introd. Trade* 95, I was to have paid away your note tomorrow. **1878** JEVONS *Prim. Pol. Econ.* vi. §41. 50 He has already paid out a large sum as wages. **1885** *Manch. Exam.* 21 July 5/2 They had to pay down one-fourth of the price in ready cash. *a* **1901** BESANT *Five Years' Tryst* (1902) 38 Now, sir,..I pay over to you..the sum of £178. 4*s.* 10*d.*—here it is. **1951** R. W. JONES *Thomson's Dict. Banking* (ed. 10) 468/2 Paying-in slips may also contain a notice requesting customers to cross all cheques before paying them in. **1961** NEW ENG. BIBLE *Matt.* xvii. 27 Take the first fish that comes to the hook, open its mouth, and you will find a silver coin; take that and pay it in; it will meet the tax for us both. **1978** N. J. CRISP *London Deal* v. 93, I didn't pay that money in, and no one else paid it in..and handed me the slip.

c. ***to pay with the fore-topsail***: to leave port without paying one's debts or creditors. *Naut. slang.*

1843 J. F. COOPER *Ned Myers* 149 We sailed next morning, and I paid for the poor 'nigger' with the foretopsail. **1850** H. MELVILLE *White Jacket* I. ii. 5 The *middies* were busy raising loans to liquidate the demands of their laundress, or else—in the navy phrase—preparing to pay their creditors *with a flying fore-topsail*. **1910** D. W. BONE *Brassbounder* 262 Paid 'ee wi' tawps'l sheets, didn't 'e? **1929** F. C. BOWEN *Sea Slang* 101 *Pay debts with the fore topsail*, to slip away to sea in debt.

6. a. To give or hand over the amount of, give money in discharge of (a debt, dues, tribute, tithes, ransom, fees, hire, wages, etc.).

c **1380**, etc. [see DEBT *sb.* 1]. **1382** WYCLIF *Matt.* xvii. 23 Ȝoure maister payeth nat tribute? *c* **1386** CHAUCER *Prol.* 539 Hise tithes payde he ful faire & wel. **1413** *Pilgr. Sowle* (Caxton 1483) IV. xiii. 63 It passeth his power to payen his raunson. **1448** *Paston Lett.* I. 69 He hath payd hys feys. **1522** SKELTON *Why not to Court* 245 They were not payd their hyre. *Ibid.* 250 Theyr wages were nat payde. **1611** BIBLE *Ezra* iv. 13 Then will they not pay tolle, tribute, and custome. **1748** SMOLLETT *Rod. Rand.* xxxv, I have..paid scot and lot and the King's taxes. **1883** FROUDE *Short Stud.* IV. II. ii. 180 The prices which we paid for everything were preposterous. **1889** *Harper's Weekly* XXXIII. 984/2 The..Company..was able to pay dividends.

b. *transf.* Of a thing: To furnish or yield (money, etc.) for the discharge of (a debt or other obligation); also said of goods on which duty, toll, or the like is paid.

1656 B. HARRIS *Parival's Iron Age* (1659) 204 Parliament..gave him but two subsidies; which would hardly pay Advance money to the Officers and soldiers. **1818** CRUISE *Digest* (ed. 2) II. 468 That this estate should be liable to pay these debts. **1840** MARRYAT *Olla Podr.* (Rtldg.) 325 Everything must pay toll. **1868** MORRIS *Earthly Par.* I. 555 Cups that had paid the Cæsar's debt Could he have laid his hands on them.

c. With advbs. ***to pay off***: to pay in full, and thus discharge the obligation; to clear off (a debt or claim) by payment (also *fig.*, see 7). ***to pay up***: to pay the full amount of (what is) owing up to the time; to make up arrears of payment; also *absol.*

1434 *Rolls of Parlt.* V. 437/2 The residue to be paied up to the Kyng. **1711** BUDGELL *Spect.* No. 150 ¶9 I'll pay off your extravagant Bills once more. **1766** W. GORDON *Gen. Counting-ho.* 27 If..he should voluntarily pay up the abatement. **1855** MACAULAY *Hist. Eng.* xvii. IV. 71 Arrears were paid up. **1885** *Law Rep.* 29 Chanc. Div. 459 To enable the directors to pay off pressing liabilities. **1941** J. D. CARR *Case of Constant Suicides* xiv. 190 The insurance companies would have been compelled to pay up. **1972** *Daily Tel.* 13 Jan. 13/3 More than 100,000 TV licence bilkers have paid up since an anti-evasion campaign was launched last October. **1978** N. MARSH *Grave Mistake* ii. 43 I'm always having to yank him out of trouble... I'll go on paying up, I suppose.

7. *fig.* (or in figurative expressions): To give or render (anything owed, due, or deserved); to discharge (an obligation). (Also, with double obj. or dat. of person, and hence in indirect passive: cf. 5.)

a. To give, render (something that is due, or that the other person has a right to); to discharge, perform (a vow); to give up, surrender (something figured as owed, *e.g.* one's life). ***to pay one's debt to nature***, or ***nature's debt***: (*spec.*) to die: see DEBT *sb.* 4 b.

1340–70 *Alex. & Dind.* 716 A fair pokok of pris men paien to iuno. *c* **1386** CHAUCER *Merch. T.* 804 Whan he wolde paye his wyf hir dette. *c* **1435** *Torr. Portugal* 162 A-mendes the be-hovythe to pay. **1611** SHAKS. *Wint. T.* v. i. 3 You haue..indeed pay'd downe More penitence, then done trespas. *c* **1611** CHAPMAN *Iliad* II. 247 Nor would [they] pay Their own vows to thee. **1657** R. LIGON *Barbadoes* (1673) 10 Our stomachs told us, it was full high time to pay Nature her due. **1697** DRYDEN *Virg. Past.* VI. 40 To you the promis'd Poem I will pay. **1707** WATTS *Hymn*, Praise, everlasting praise, be paid To him that earth's foundation laid. **1878** BROWNING *La Saisiaz* 117 Paying piteous duty, what seemed you have we consigned [to the grave].

b. To inflict, bestow, give (punishment, a blow, etc.) as being deserved, or in return for the like; to render in retribution or retaliation.

13.. *Coer de L.* 4028 Kyng Richard hys ax in hond he hente, And payde Sarezynys her rente. *a* **1533** LD. BERNERS *Huon* lxxxiv. 265 Y^e^ traytours were payed ther desertes. **1627** CAPT. SMITH *Seaman's Gram.* xiii. 60 Hee payes vs shot for shot. *a* **1716** SOUTH *Serm.* (1727) V. xii. 482 If Popery ever comes in by English Hands..it will fully pay the Scores of those who brought it in. **1888** J. HAWTHORNE *Trag. Myst.* iii, To pay off some grudge.

c. To suffer, undergo (a punishment, penalty, etc., figured as a price paid to the person or authority that inflicts it; also, pain or trouble, as a price paid for some advantage); to suffer in retribution or requital, or as the price of anything gained.

1387 TREVISA *Higden* (Rolls) VII. 77 But he hadde i-leide doun his knyf,..boþe schul have i-payde þe payne. **1587** *Mirr. Mag.*, *Rimar* vi, Made mee pay the price of pillage with my bloud. **1615** CHAPMAN *Odyss.* v. Argt., Ulysses builds A ship;..Pays Neptune pains. **1674** BREVINT *Saul at Endor* 214 Christ..took and paied fully all the punishment due for our sins. *a* **1716** SOUTH *Serm.* (1727) V. i. 5 Inflaming themselves with Wine, till they come to pay the Reckoning with their Blood. **1890** *Spectator* 15 Feb., To forget the pain he paid for his discoveries.

d. *Arith.* In Subtraction, To compensate for 'borrowing' (see BORROW *v.*[1] 1 c) by mentally adding a unit to the subtrahend of the next higher denomination (an easier practical equivalent for the more logical process of subtracting the unit which has been 'borrowed' from the minuend). Usually ***to pay back***.

1897 *Daily News* 3 June 5/4 When some of us were boys at school we knew no other way of doing a sum in subtraction but the way of borrowing and paying back.

8. (With the notion of debt weakened to that of duty or fitness, or lost.) To render, bestow (something considered as due, deserved or befitting, *e.g.* attention, heed, respect, court, a compliment, a visit, etc.). Usually with *to* or simple dat.

1590 SHAKS. *Mids. N.* v. i. 99 Not paying me a welcome. **1654–66** EARL ORRERY *Parthen.* (1676) 381, I went..to pay her a visit. **1711** ADDISON *Spect.* No. 122 ¶5 After having paid their Respects to Sir Roger. **1766** GOLDSM. *Vic. W.* xvi, Farmer Williams..had paid her his addresses. **1796** MRS. E. PARSONS *Myst. Warning* II. 222 The Gentlemen paid her many compliments. **1866** DK. ARGYLL *Reign Law* vii. (1871) 386 Too little attention being paid to the progress of opinion. **1882** BESANT *Revolt of Man* vi. (1883) 152 They paid little heed to the sermon.

9. *absol.* or *intr.* To give money or other equivalent in return for something or in discharge of an obligation; also *fig.* : see prec. senses.

a **1300** *Cursor M.* 14040 Þai had noght quar-of for to pai. *c* **1386** CHAUCER *Reeve's T.* 213 Get vs som mete and drynke, ..And we wil payen trewely atte fulle. **1535** COVERDALE *Ps.* xxxvi[i]. 21 The vngodly borroweth and paieth not agayne. **1650** N. WALLINGTON *Hist. Notices* (1869) I. Introd. 49 Serve honesty ever,..she will pay, if slow. **1657** HEYLIN *Undeceiv. People* 4 If any..desired not to pay in kinde. *a* **1786** COWPER *Yearly Distress* 19 He that takes, and he that pays. **1855** DICKENS *Dorrit* II. xiii, 'Now, then!..Pay up!' **1875** JOWETT *Plato* (ed. 2) III. 205, I will pay when I have the money.

b. ***to pay in***: to make (regular) contributions *to* a fund.

1911 *Rep. Labour & Social Conditions in Germany* (Tariff Reform League) III. 71 Men must pay in to the trade society to which they transfer their labour. *Ibid.* 82 Employees..commence to pay into State fund when 16 years old.

10. *absol.* or *intr.* Of a thing or action: To recompense one's expense or trouble; to yield an adequate return; to be profitable or advantageous. Also ***to pay out***.

1812 H. & J. SMITH *Rej. Addr.*, *Rebuilding*, The workmen..thought it would not pay To dig him out. **1830** GEN. P. THOMPSON *Exerc.* (1842) I. 200 If land is uncultivated, it is because it will not pay. **1885** ANSTEY *Tinted Venus* iv. 44 You won't find it pay in the long run. **1909** 'O. HENRY' *Roads of Destiny* xii. 193 Nobody in the bank knows those notes as I do. Some of 'em are a little wobbly on their legs, and some are mavericks without extra many brands on their backs, but they'll most all pay out at the round-up.

b. *trans.* To be profitable to, profit (a person).

1883 *Manch. Exam.* 19 Dec. 5/2 A practice of insuring with a view to wreck would not pay the shipowning community.

c. ***to pay off***: to succeed; to be profitable or advantageous; to show results.

1951 R. MALKIN *Boxcars in Sky* 118 It was the Big Briefing which, eventually, would pay off in plenty of free space outside the advertising columns. **1953** J. WAIN *Hurry on Down* iv. 73 Like a good many insane actions, it paid off. **1957** *Listener* 7 Nov. 757/1 Still, the cool piece of blackmail and bluff paid off. **1959** *Ibid.* 4 June 969/2 There are signs, already, that this policy of patience is paying off. **1962** A. SHEPARD in *Into Orbit* 104, I could feel that all the training we had gone through with the blockhouse crew and booster crew was really paying off down there. **1967** *Technology Week* 23 Jan. 61/1 (Advt.), Our aim is to make current space hardware and experience pay off for the national space program. **1971** R. DENTRY *Encounter at Kharmel* ix. 150 Your hunch had better pay off. The Tal's the last possibility. **1978** T. ALLBEURY *Lantern Network* viii. 93 By mid-May the training had begun to pay off.

11. ***to pay for***: **a.** To give money or other equivalent value for; to hand over the price of (a thing); to bear the cost of; to recompense (labour or service) in money or otherwise. Also *transf.* Of a thing, sum of money, or other thing of value: To furnish or constitute an equivalent for; to be sufficient to buy or defray the cost of.

1362 LANGL. *P. Pl.* A. III. 132 Heo..leteþ passe prisons, and payeþ for hem ofte. Heo ȝeueþ þe Iayler Gold and grotes.., To vn-fetere þe False. *c* **1386** CHAUCER *Prol.* 834 [He] shal paye for al þat by the wey is spent. **1534** MORE *Comf. agst. Trib.* II. vi. (1847) 105 To take no thought, but make merry..and then let Christ's passion pay for all the shot.

a **1616** BEAUMONT *To J. Fletcher*, It was thy hap to throw away Much wit, for which the people did not pay. **1804** MAR. EDGEWORTH *Pop. T.*, *Will* ii, The bonnet's all I want, which I'll pay for on the nail. *Mod.* Half a crown will pay for a front seat. The fowls will soon pay for themselves in eggs.

b. *fig.* To make amends for, atone for; more usually, To suffer or be punished for (cf. 7 c).

1393 LANGL. *P. Pl.* C. XVII. 31 *Operis satisfactio* þat for synnes payeth. **1533** GAU *Richt Vay* 69 God..laid al our sinnis apone hime and he payit for thayme. **1612** BP. HALL *Contempl., O.T.* II. v, Lot payes deare for his rashnesse. **1706** E. WARD *Wooden World Diss.* (1708) 94 He's resolv'd never to be a Rogue, when he's sure to pay for it. **1900** *London Letter* 23 Feb. 286/2 An attendant.., who wantonly prodded it with a fork..paid for his cruelty, as he was knocked down, trampled upon, and ripped open by the elephant.

12. a. *trans.* = pay for: see 11.

1656 EARL MONM. tr. *Boccalini's Advts. fr. Parnass.* II. lxi. (1674) 213 Their Liberty..cannot be paid by Mountains of Gold. **1744** SARAH FIELDING *David Simple* II. v. 79 She immediately paid her Lodging. **1842** *Jrnl. R. Agric. Soc.* III. II. 185 Chalking land..costs little more than 2*l.* per acre; pays itself often in the second year.

b. *fig.* To compensate, make up for. ? *Obs.*

1596 DALRYMPLE tr. *Leslie's Hist. Scot.* I. 5 The beimes of the Sone..the hail nychte ar sein, the space of twa monethis. .. Contrare in winter,..the lenth is payed with the schortnes. **1625** USSHER *Answ. Jesuit* 171 If Montanus comes short in his testimonie, Origen..payes it home with full measure. **1738** SWIFT *Pol. Conversat.* 31 Miss says nothing; but I warrant she pays it off with Thinking. **1790** *Bystander* 246 Hermocrates was..silent, but..he paid it off with thinking.

13. *Naut.* **a.** (*trans.*) To let out (a rope or chain) by slackening it, to allow or cause to run out. (Also in reference to something let out by the rope.) Now always with *out* or *away*. Also *transf.*

1627 CAPT. SMITH *Seaman's Gram.* vii. 30 Pay more Cable, is when you carry an Anchor out in the boat to turne ouer. Pay cheap, is when you ouer set it, or turne it ouer boord faster. **1710** J. HARRIS *Lex. Techn.* II. s.v., Seamen say *Pay more Cable*, that is, let out more Cable. **1769** FALCONER *Dict. Marine* (1789), *Pay away the Cable!* slacken it, that it may run out of the ship. **1793** SMEATON *Edystone L.* §143 We paid out the Hawser by which we were riding; at the same time paying out the hawser of the catch-anchor. **1840** R. H. DANA *Bef. Mast* xv. 41 'Pay out chain', shouted the Captain, and we gave it to her. **1871** L. STEPHEN *Playgr. Eur.* (1894) iii. 84 By..throwing all my weight on to the rope, I gradually got myself paid slowly out. **1962** H. HOOD in R. Weaver *Canad. Short Stories* (1968) 2nd Ser. 211 He paid out a little string and began to run across the parking lot towards the main building. **1976** D. CLARK *Dread & Water* ii. 52 'Roped together?' 'Just like the book says... He went first and I payed out... I hadn't enough hands to cling tightly and pay out the rope'.

b. *intr.* for *passive.*

1840 R. H. DANA *Bef. Mast* xxiii. 68 We paid out on the chain by which we swung.

14. *Naut.* **a.** (*trans.*) To cause (a ship) to fall to leeward, or fall away from the wind. Now always with *off*.

1627 CAPT. SMITH *Seaman's Gram.* ix. 42 As she turnes wee say shee is payed. **1830** MARRYAT *King's Own* xiii, The commander..payed his vessel off before the wind. **1884** SIR J. HANNEN in *Law Times Rep.* L. 127/2 Her master was vainly trying to pay her head off to the eastward.

b. *intr.* for *passive.* To fall to leeward.

1669 STURMY *Mariner's Mag.* I. ii. 19 The Chase pays away more room. [Cf. *infra*, The Chase goes away room.. she is right before the Wind.] **1825** H. B. GASCOIGNE *Nav. Fame* 51 By slow degrees her head to Port Pays round. **1836** MARRYAT *Midsh. Easy* xxvi, The frigate flew round, describing a circle, as she payed off before the wind. **1899** F. T. BULLEN *Log Sea-waif* 213 There was a great bustle to get sail off her, but unfortunately she paid off rather smartly.

15. In various phrases, as *the* DEVIL *to pay*, GOD *pays* or *to pay*, *to pay through the* NOSE, *to pay the* PIPER, *to pay one's* WAY: see these sbs.

pay (peɪ), *v.*[2] Chiefly *Naut.* Pa. t. and pple. **payed** (paid). [a. ONF. *peier* (= Central F. *poier*, *poyer*) = Pr., Sp. *pegar*:—L. *picāre*, f. *pix*, *pic-em* pitch; cf. It. *peciare.*] *trans.* To smear or cover with pitch, tar, resin, tallow, or the like, as a defence against wet, etc.

1627 CAPT. SMITH *Seaman's Gram.* ii. 13 Okum..being well payed ouer with hot pitch, doth make her more tight. **1720** DE FOE *Capt. Singleton* ii. (1840) 30 Hemp, pitch and tar, to calk and pay her seams. **1831** W. IRVING *Columbus* (abr. ed.) 307 Drawing his canoe on shore..he then payed it with a coat of tar. **1853** SIR H. DOUGLAS *Milit. Bridges* 180 Above these were laid stalks of the cotton-plant and loose grass; the whole being payed over with clay.

b. With the covering substance as object.

1894 C. N. ROBINSON *Brit. Fleet* 231 Broad-headed nails hammered in close together, on which was paid a compost of tallow and resin.

pay- in combination. [PAY *sb.*, or, in some cases, the stem of PAY *v.*[1]]

1. In sbs. denoting persons or things connected with the payment of money, esp. as wages. **a.** Charged with the payment of workmen, employees, or subordinates; as ***pay-agent***, ***-clerk***, ***-commander***, ***-corps***, ***-director***, ***-inspector***, ***-sergeant***; PAYMASTER, PAYMISTRESS. **b.** Indicating, or containing a statement of amounts to be paid or the persons to whom they are to be paid; as ***pay-bill***, ***-book***, ***code***, ***-list***, ***-scale***, ***-sheet***, ***-ticket***; containing pay or wages, as ***pay-check***, ***-cheque***, ***-envelope***, ***packet***. **c.** At, from, or on which payment is made, esp. of wages to employees; as ***pay-box*** (esp. = BOX OFFICE 1), ***-desk***, ***-car***, ***-gate***, ***-office***, ***-place***, ***-room***, ***-shed***, ***-table***, ***-train***, ***-wicket***, ***-window***; PAY-DAY, ***-night***, ***-week***. **d.** For which payment is charged (opp. to *free*); as ***pay-bed***, ***-bridge***, ***-hospital***, ***-meal***, ***-school***, ***-toilet***, ***ward***; that pays for something (*e.g.* education) instead of getting it free; as ***pay-boarder***, ***-boy***.

1879 E. J. CASTLE *Law Rating* 98 Payments were made by the *pay-agent of the troop. **1895** *Brit. Med. Jrnl.* 2 Mar. 501/2 In opening..certain *pay beds the Committee of Management had simply felt that they were carrying out what they were bound to do under the constitution of the hospital. **1928** *Daily Express* 19 July 9/4 The special committee appointed..to consider the needs of the professional and middle classes recommend that additional 'pay-beds' should be provided for them by the hospitals. **1934** *Lancet* 23 June 1371/2 To establish pay-beds for patients of moderate means. **1969** 'W. HAGGARD' *Doubtful Disciple* v. 52 In his pay-bed in the hospital Jacky D was depressed. **1974** *Times* 6 Nov. 2/8 The Owen working party ..is discussing the new consultant contract and the pay-bed issue. **1976** H. WILSON *Governance of Britain* iv. 86 Fresh concern arose about government legislation and action in connection with pay-beds and private practice, in October and December 1975. **1828** WEBSTER, **Pay-bill*, a bill of money to be paid to the soldiers of a company. **1897** *Rep. Comm. Welsh Education*, Howell schools... Amongst the *pay boarders,..numbering in all thirty, there were six Nonconformists. **1669** W. PENN in *St. Papers, Dom.* 286, I send the muster and *pay books for the 'Harp'. **1896** *Idler* Mar. 251/2 We checked my figures in the pay-book with the money. **1851** DICKENS in *Househ. Words* 30 Aug. 531/2 He darts upon my luggage..pays certain francs for it, to a certain functionary behind a Pigeon Hole, like a *pay-box at a Theatre. **1889** J. K. JEROME *Three Men in Boat* xix. 313 We attracted a good deal of attention at the Alhambra. On our presenting ourselves at the pay-box we..were informed that we were half-an-hour behind our time. **1952** V. GOLLANCZ *My Dear Timothy* 20 The practice was to open this door, and let people up the long staircase to a point a little short of the pay-box. **1975** N. LUARD *Travelling Horseman* iii. 71 The butler who'd..contact[ed] them from a street pay-box. **1904** 'O. HENRY' in *Everybody's Mag.* Aug. 240/1 Joe Wheeler signs the voucher for his *pay-check. **1964** MRS. L. B. JOHNSON *White House Diary* 24 Apr. (1970) 122 How sensible these girls are to be starting on a skill that they can exchange for a paycheck almost anywhere. **1977** *Time* 10 Oct. 56/2 Chicagoans tell of a local executive who has supposedly never spent a paycheck in 30 years but lives entirely off the expense account. **1930** J. COLLIER *His Monkey Wife* xvii. 243 You take your *pay cheque at the end of the week without making a lot of fuss about the size of it. **1973** J. WAINWRIGHT *Touch of Malice* 71 The inconvenience went with the rank and the pay-cheque. **1771** in J. Phillips *Hist. Inland Navig.* (1792) 334 That..the *pay-clerk..do attend on the canal..to receive the returns..of the number of labourers..and to pay them..the amount of their several returns. **1976** *Sunday Mail* (Glasgow) 21 Nov., And that wouldn't come into line with the Government's *pay code which..limited everyone to £6 a week. **1890** *Cent. Dict.*, **Pay-corps*, in the United States navy, the corps of pay-masters. **1898** A. BENNETT *Man from North* vii. 50 Jenkins eagerly drew Richard's attention to the girl at the *pay-desk. **1919** W. DEEPING *Second Youth* vii. 64 Nearly always she sat at the same table near the pay-desk. **1932** D. L. SAYERS *Have his Carcase* xxx. 395 Bunter was four behind him in the queue at the pay-desk. **1890** *Cent. Dict.*, **Pay-director*, in the United States navy, an officer of the pay-corps, ranking with a captain. **1909** *Sat. Even. Post* 5 June 17/1 (*heading*), The *pay envelopes of the stars. **1911** E. FERBER *Dawn O'Hara* iv. 46 My bank account has always been an all too small pay envelope at the end of each week. **1973** E. TAYLOR *Serpent under It* (1974) xi. 172 Mr. Ramsay finally rrremembered that the rrrest of us like to eat, and left the pay envelopes. **1892** *Daily News* 25 Apr. 2/7 The Hampstead Home Hospital,..although a *pay hospital, has a free accident ward. **1890** *Cent. Dict.*, **Pay-inspector*, in the United States navy, an officer of the pay-corps, ranking with a commander. **1892** *Labour Commission Gloss.*, **Pay-lines*,.. tickets..issued a day before pay day to each workman stating the particulars of his pay, thus allowing him time to make any complaints as to amounts, etc., before being paid. **1757** *Act 31 Geo. II.* c. 10 Abstract §3 Every inferior Officer or Seaman..shall be paid by Proper *Pay Lists, all the Wages due to him. **1900** *Westm. Gaz.* 15 Mar. 5/2 Very few officers or non-commissioned officers could keep a pay list or a pay and mess sheet. **1820** C. MATHEWS *Let.* 25 July in A. Mathews *Mem. Charles Mathews* (1839) III. vii. 148 The common outcry was against Saturday for a second performance, as it is *pay-night, and the worst night in the week. **1891** T. HARDY *Tess* xlii, 'This is pay-night', she said. **1970** G. GREER *Female Eunuch* 288 They have taken the pay packet out of the old man's pocket when he has finally arrived home on pay-night. **1707** CHAMBERLAYNE *Pres. St. Eng.* III. xi. 385 The Navy-Office, Excise-Office, *Pay-Office [etc.] are of lesser note. **1941** 'N. BLAKE' *Case of Abominable Snowman* ix. 101 A stoppage of work and less money in the *pay-packet on Fridays. **1973** *Times* 1 Jan. 3/2 Miners' institute libraries..were financed by pennies from miners' pay packets. **1976** *Norwich Mercury* 19 Nov. 1/4 Many firms find that a hamper is much appreciated by the workforce rather than '£10 in the pay packet', particularly as payment is subject to tax but a hamper is not. **1816** *Sporting Mag.* XLVIII. 173 The plaintiff expected..to receive his money..at the usual *pay-place. **1831** *Lincoln Herald* 23 Sept. 4/4 An attempt was made to break into the *pay-room of the workhouse. **1961** *Lancet* 9 Sept. 595/1 Our results make it possible to establish a *pay-scale, based on production. **1976** F. MUIR *Frank Muir Bk.* 95 Teaching.. became a respectable profession..with its own union to keep an eye on pay scales. **1856** X. D. MACLEOD *Biogr. F. Wood* 191 The cost to us in taxation is not one fifth the usual expense for an ordinary *pay-school education. **1936** M. MITCHELL *Gone with Wind* v. lii. 905 There were no free schools. Few had money to send their children to pay schools. **1830** SCOTT *Demonol.* x. 365 Jarvis Matcham was *pay-sergeant in a regiment. **1900** *Westm. Gaz.* 14 Aug. 3/2, I have before me a *pay-sheet of a Trinidad cocoa estate for the month of May. **1850** T. MCCRIE *Mem. Sir A. Agnew* vi. (1852) 134 Saturday-night *pay-tables established in public-houses to tempt the tradesman. **1915** KIPLING *New Army* 29 The men..saluted emphatically at the pay-table, and fell back with their emoluments. **1965** 'LAUCHMONEN' *Old Thom's Harvest* xvi. 181 Every Saturday..the men were at the paytable in the ball-field. **1977** *Times Lit. Suppl.* 25 Mar. 334/5 His now receptive mind drifts back into the past where he is, once again, leader and paymaster of a racially mixed crew... The ghosts of the men again come forward to the paytable. **1721** *Lond. Gaz.* No. 5931/3 Several Blank Seamens *Pay-Tickets. **1946** E. HODGINS *Mr. Blandings builds his Dream House* ix. 132, I wouldn't come back here if you had a *pay toilet. **1947** AUDEN *Age of Anxiety* (1948) iii. 72 The scene has all the signs of a facetious culture, Publishing houses, pawnshops, and pay-toilets. **1968** *Listener* 7 Nov. 610/1 There's a song about not having a dime for a pay toilet, and another one about the sexual relevance of Kleenex. **1976** *New Yorker* 15 Nov. 66/2 There was a character named Exotica A La Carte, who lived on the proceeds of a string of pay toilets. **1895** *Brit. Med. Jrnl.* 2 Mar. 502/1 It is desirable that the system of *pay wards now in operation be so modified that the patients in those wards may..be attended in the hospital by outside practitioners of their own selection. **1766** W. GORDON *Gen. Counting-ho.* 364 The acceptation of bills..in the second or third *pay-week. **1895** *Westm. Gaz.* 11 June 5/1 The manager..was at the *pay-wicket. **1934** *Archit. Rev.* LXXV. 92/1 The first doorway has a glass window which serves as a *pay-window. **1977** A. C. H. SMITH *Jericho Gun* i. 16 It's a winning ticket. .. If you present it at the Tote pay window, even you might get some money back.

2. *Mining.* Containing precious metal or other mineral in sufficient quantity to be profitably worked; as ***pay-channel***, ***-chimney***, ***-chute***, ***-dirt*** (also contemptuous, for 'money', and *fig.*), ***-dust***, ***-gravel***, ***-ground***, ***-lead***, ***-ore***, ***-rock***, ***-shoot***, ***-streak***, ***-vein***, ***-zone***.

1877 RAYMOND *Statist. Mines & Mining* 107 The gold is ..evenly distributed through the pay chimneys. **1857** Pay dirt [see DIRT *sb.* 3 c]. **1866** *Dublin Rev.* Jan. 10 Even officers of men-of-war were seized by the gold mania, and 'ran' to soil their white hands in the precious 'pay-dirt'. **1872** RAYMOND *Statist. Mines & Mining* 87 An exception to the general rule of the 'pay' dirt lying nearest the bed-rock. In this claim the pay-lead is many feet above the bed-rock. **1884** *Century Mag.* Nov. 60/2 He lives..in a style that proves that he has lots of pay dirt somewhere. **1930** E. RICE *Voy. to Purilia* xvii. 249 As one elderly prospector expressed it: 'Thar's pay dirt in them thar hills.' **1935** *Motion Picture* Nov. 46/2 Frances Langford, the cutie whose 'pay dirt' reaches $1,000 per week. **1948** A. HUXLEY *Ape & Essence* (1949) 132 We see Loola standing in a three-foot hole wearily digging... 'When you hit the pay dirt..come and report to us.' **1953** *Economist* 24 Oct. 248 Senator McCarthy may have struck pay-dirt at last. **1967** *Ibid.* 26 Aug. 721/3 Senator Dirksen..applauds the President for permitting the bombers to attack targets within ten miles of the Chinese frontier: 'We seem to be getting close to paydirt.' **1972** *Lebende Sprachen* XVII. 34/1 US pay dirt—BE/US workable ore-bearing soil. **1973** C. CALLOW *Power from Sea* ii. 60 The thickness of the 'pay dirt'—that is the width of the sand in which the gas was contained. **1977** *Rolling Stone* 21 Apr. 88/3 Bowie hits celestial pay dirt on one of the pieces. *a* **1872** B. HARTE *Her Let.* ix, O, why did papa strike pay gravel In drifting on Poverty Flat? **1927** *Daily Tel.* 25 Oct. 2/7 The results, taken in conjunction with the pay ground passed through the haulage, gives promise of..an important shoot. **1880** *Ibid.* 3 Dec., Towns which depend upon 'bonanzas' and lodes of pay ore. **1862** 'MARK TWAIN' *Let.* 8 Feb. (1920) 51 We'll have a mill-site, water power, and pay-rock, all handy. **1947** W. A. CHALFANT *Gold, Guns, & Ghost Towns* 141 Thompson and Ramsay prospected over the same ground..and struck some pay rock that was almost the pure stuff. **1856** *Daily Even. Bulletin* (San Francisco) 11 Oct. 1/1 These lucky miners worked one, two, and even three years, to reach the pay streak. **1910** R. W. SERVICE *Ballads of Cheechako* 68 Late in the year he struck it rich, the real pay-streak at last. **1965** G. J. WILLIAMS *Econ. Geol. N.Z.* vii. 80/1 The gold is distributed over the schist bottom in more or less orientated paystreaks trending north-westerly. **1977** *New Yorker* 20 June 85/1 A pay streak appeared to be there, and what was needed now was a means of moving gravel in a major way. **1874** RAYMOND *Statist. Mines & Mining* 327 The pay-vein is narrow, and the lode probably only a spur. **1877** *Ibid.* 40 Golden Gate mine.. length pay-zone, 100 feet. **1973** C. CALLOW *Power from Sea* ii. 61 The yield was 3.6 million cubic feet a day and the 'pay zone' was 64 feet thick. **1975** *Offshore* Sept. 75/2 It encountered three pay zones between 8,468 ft and 9,595 ft, with about 130 ft of net oil pay and a smaller zone of about eight ft of gas pay.

3. a. The verb-stem in combination with object; as **pay-all**, he who or that which pays all, or bears the whole charge; **pay-rent** *a.*, serving, or furnishing money, to pay the rent; † **pay-way** *a.* (*Sc.*), 'valedictory; given when one is leaving, or for the purpose of bearing one's expenses on the road' (Jam.). Also, with advb., as **pay-back**, the fact or action of paying back; reward or return, *spec.* the net return in profits from an investment project equal to the initial capital outlay; also *attrib.*; also as *adj.*, retaliatory.

a **1652** BROME *Damoiselle* IV. i. Wks. 1873 I. 436 You were not wont To be a Boordsend-King; a *pay-all in a Tavern. **1796** COLERIDGE *Watchman* No. 1. 29 The sum of Five Thousand Pounds, to be paid on the first day of April next, at the office of John Bull, Esq. Pay-all and Fight-all to the several High contracting Powers. **1959** *Wall St. Jrnl.* (Eastern ed.) 31 Mar. 13/1 The *pay-back order affects only the Star-Bulletin and not the union. **1965** H. I. ANSOFF *Corporate Strategy* ii. 14 Three common methods for evaluation are the payback period, the internal rate of discount, and the net present worth. **1970** M. KELLY *Spinifex* iii. 63 'I can remember him taking part in a big pay-back raid a few years later.' 'Pay-back?' 'Pidgin for vendetta——.' **1971** C. R. W. WYSOCK WRIGHT in B. de

Ferranti *Living with Computer* iii. 22 This necessary investment in good education is essential although the payback may only be in the long term. **1972** *Accountant* 28 Sept. 391/2 You simply cannot say that..discounted cash flow is superior to payback. **1973** *Sunday Times* (Colour Suppl.) 10 June 46/2 Such 'payback', or revenge killings, are common in the Highlands. **1977** *Irish Times* 8 June 10/7 It would, he said, depress cash flow and would lengthen the payback period for the mine's capital cost. **1744–50** W. Ellis *Mod. Husbandm.* IV. i. 39 A *pay-rent crop of turnips. **1764** *Mus. Rust.* III. xxxii. 144 Horse-beans..will..yield a pay-rent crop. **1823** Galt *R. Gilhaize* II. xiii. 131 After partaking of Captain Hepburn's *pay-way supper.

b. pay-as-you-earn, applied to a system of collecting income tax where the tax payable is deducted by employers from current earnings; **pay-as-you-enter**, applied to a system of collecting fares in public transport where passengers pay the driver on entering the vehicle; **pay-as-you-go**, applied to a system of paying or discharging obligations as they are incurred; **pay-as-you-see**, applied to a system of supplying an extra television channel to viewers paying either by subscription or by inserting coins into a box attached to the television receiver; **pay-as-you-use**, applied to a system of paying for an article while it is being used; **pay-as-you-view** = *pay-as-you-see*.

1943 *Daily Tel.* 22 Apr. 3 As to deduction of income-tax from wages he warned the House of the experiences of other countries which had attempted the 'pay-as-you-earn' idea. **1972** *Accountant* 6 Apr. 445/2 Pay-as-you-earn rates for 1972 are so much higher than last year that they could raise the tax take by the equivalent of some £1,500 million. **1908** *Sci. Amer.* 1 Feb. 76/2 (*heading*) A new type of fare register to be used on the New York pay-as-you-enter cars. *Ibid.*, The pay-as-you-enter cars which it is proposed to install on the New York city lines will be equipped with a device for collecting and automatically registering fares. **1913** *Chambers's Jrnl.* Aug. 623/1 This [system of tram-car operation] is the 'pay as you enter', or as it is termed briefly the 'paye' system. **1966** *Daily Tel.* 12 Sept. 20/3 A bus driver in Brighton collecting a fare from a passenger yesterday when the country's first pay-as-you-enter, one-man operated double deck bus service began for an experimental period. **1840** *Farmers' Cabinet* 15 May 319/1 Pay as you go ..is the truest economy. **1888** J. Bryce *Amer. Commonwealth* II. lxvi. 507 'Pay as You Go' Convention! **1936** M. W. Childs *Sweden* xii. 214 The central government has consistently followed a pay-as-you-go tax policy. **1969** *Times* 30 Apr. 26/2 The rate of contribution needed from employees and employers jointly to finance the proposed State pensions on a 'pay-as-you-go' basis would increase from 7.7 per cent of earnings in 1972–73 to 11.4 per cent in 2002–03. *a* **1974** R. Crossman *Diaries* (1977) III. 176 We must therefore really accept pay-as-you-go. **1978** *Dumfries & Galloway Standard* 21 Oct. 5/7 (Advt.), It's pay-as-you-go; no big quarterly shocks. **1955** *Times* 6 Apr. 6/6 Sir Alexander Korda intends to seek permission of the United Kingdom authorities to operate 'pay as you see' television. **1962** *Variety* 22 Aug. 3 It's perhaps significant that all, or just about all, film distributors are leasing pictures to the Paramount-owned International Telemeter pay-as-you-see video in Etobicoke, Toronto suburb. **1929** *Radio Times* 8 Nov. 453/1 Place your order..immediately, 'Pay as you use' terms can be arranged. **1961** *Engineering* 1 Sept. 257/1 Pay-as-you-use techniques covering the leasing of vehicles, machinery and equipment of all kinds are to be introduced into Britain. **1958** *Spectator* 11 July 61/3 The vital issue of whether a Pay-As-You-View television service is allowed to operate in this country. **1963** *Ann. Reg. 1962* 443 Other recommendations of the [Pilkington] Committee were that pay-as-you-view television..should be rejected.

c. *pay-on-* ——: denoting a system of paying for a service when the action expressed has been performed or fulfilled.

1899 J. London *Let.* 29 July (1966) 46 And with these pay-on-acceptance fellows, did you ever get your check at the same time you were notified of acceptance? **1960** *Guardian* 11 Apr. 8/3 London's new..bus which..has the pay-on-entry system. **1961** *Daily Tel.* 23 May 17/6 (*heading*) 'Pay-on-reply' telephoning. *Ibid.*, Post Office engineers yesterday demonstrated the new 'pay-on-answer' coin boxes in seven telephone kiosks in the centre of Dartford, Kent.

4. Special combs. of pay *sb.*, as **paybob** *slang*, = paymaster; **pay freeze** = *pay pause*; **pay pause**, a period during which no wage or salary increases should occur, esp. as proposed in 1961 in the U.K.; **pay phone** orig. *U.S.*, a telephone that operates, or connects the caller, when coins are inserted; **pay-rise**, a wage or salary increase; **pay station** *U.S.*, (*a*) a public call-office; (*b*) a public telephone-booth; **pay-telephone** = *pay phone*; **pay television** = *pay-TV*; **pay-tone** (see quot. 1962); **pay-train** (see quot. 1969); **pay-TV**, a system of television based on the pay-as-you-see principle (see sense 3 b).

1916 'Taffrail' *Pincher Martin* viii. 125 Carn't yer get a hadvance o' money from th' paybob? **1962** Granville *Dict. Sailors' Slang* 87/1 *Paybob*, senior accountant officer. **1978** *Navy News* Dec. 6/1 The paybob and his chum never batted an eyelid as I signed my chit and I often wonder if they paid the difference. **1961** *New Scientist* 7 Sept. 568 The Chancellor of the Exchequer's pay-freeze. **1972** *Listener* 23 Nov. 690/3 The pay and wage freeze is a shoddy compilation. Over two million workers demanding pay rises are trapped in the freeze. **1975** *Guardian* 21 Jan. 26/3 The Chancellor..said there was no question of a pay freeze in the foreseeable future. **1961** *Daily Tel.* 19 Sept. 1/8 The increases for primary and secondary schools will cost £42 million a year, £5½ million less than the Burnham recommendation rejected by the Government on account of the 'pay pause'. **1969** C. Booker *Neophiliacs* vi. 158 On 25 July [1961], the Government mustered all the paraphernalia to meet a major crisis, from a 7 per cent Bank Rate to Selwyn Lloyd's celebrated 'Pay Pause', the first recent peacetime attempt by a Government to impose an overall regulation of wage increases. **1977** *Evening Post* (Nottingham) 27 Jan. 5/1 When the pay pause was relaxed for doctors earning over £8,000, it was decided not to pay the increment for another year. **1936** L. Duncan *Over Wall* ii. 31 He would then go to one of the pay phones. **1952** W. R. Burnett *Vanity Row* (1953) xiii. 90 'Where you calling from?' 'A pay-phone.' **1973** W. McCarthy *Detail* iii. 215 He gave the agent the number of a pay-phone in Burbank. **1975** *New Yorker* 27 Oct. 32/1 There are six pay phones downstairs and only five of them work. **1976** *Daily Express* 1 July 14/2 In April 1976 I asked the Post Office to change my business phone to a pay phone. **1936** J. Steinbeck *In Dubious Battle* iii. 26 Hell, we don't want only temporary pay-rises. **1957** P. Worsley *Trumpet shall Sound* x. 197 The soldiers of the Pacific Islands Regiment had achieved pay-rises. **1923** M. Watts *L. Nichols* 209 [He] rushed off to the nearest telephone pay station to call up the Grace house. **1948** *Time* 21 June 2 When you drop a nickel in a pay station and dial a call..as many as 1000 telephone relays go into action. **1973** W. McCarthy *Detail* iii. 215 He would like you to call this number...it is a pay station. **1974** *Spartanburg* (S. Carolina) *Herald* 24 Apr. A3/4 Police said Norton had answered a call from two men using a pay station, asking that a cab pick them up at a motel. **1963** A. Orlov *Handbk. Intelligence* xiii. 153 The agent avails himself of the forthcoming 'pay telephone' conversation with his superior. **1964** *Punch* 13 May 702/2 A man known to have installed a pay-telephone. **1971** A. Hunter *Gently at Gallop* viii. 89 There was a pay-telephone for customers. He fed in a coin and dialled the police-station. **1976** *Billings* (Montana) *Gaz.* 28 June 6-A/3 The chairman of the American Telephone and Telegraph Co. said Sunday a pay telephone call probably will cost a quarter in most places. **1957** *Economist* 28 Sept. 1028/2 The Federal Communications Commission has tentatively opened the airwaves to 'pay television'. **1962** *Rep. Comm. Broadcasting 1960* 262 in *Parl. Papers 1961–2* (Cmnd. 1753) IX. 259 'Subscription television' (or 'toll' or 'pay' television, as it is variously called) involves a third method of paying. **1973** *Listener* 31 May 706/1 'The big news in cable now is Pay.' He meant pay television. **1962** *Sunday Express* 4 Feb. 12 The pips are the pay-tone signal, which tells the caller that you have picked up the receiver and it is time for him to put in the coins. **1972** J. Wainwright *Night is Time to Die* (1974) 167 On S.T.D., a call-box is a dead give-away by the pay tone! **1968** D. I. Gordon in *Regional Hist. Railway Gt. Brit.* V. xii. 232 The Eastern Region is making a gallant fight. Conductor guards and the whole concept of the 'basic' railway with its Pay Trains, fast and well-integrated services, [etc.]..are all features of the current scene. **1969** *Railway Mag.* CXV. 169/2 Conductor/Guard workings ('pay trains') began on January 19 between Newcastle and Carlisle. *Ibid.* 473/2 From June 15, 'paytrains'—on which tickets are issued by the guard—were introduced by the Eastern Region. **1972** *Times* 15 June 3/1 Public transport, even in an age of one-man buses, 'pay-trains', and automatic fare collection, is much more labour intensive than other industries. **1976** P. R. White *Planning for Public Transport* ii. 53 Little detail is recorded of trip patterns on 'paytrain' services. **1956** *Britannica Bk. of Year* 492/2 Also introduced from the United States—though not yet fully accepted into British English—were such expressions as Pay TV, [etc.]. **1960** *News Chron.* 29 June 4/6 'Pay-TV', a system whereby you put some coins in a slot at the top of the set and are rewarded by several hours uninterrupted viewing. **1972** *Listener* 8 June 773/2 Pay-TV was expensive and offered very little that was new. **1976** J. Lund *Ultimate* vi. 57 He looked at the pay TV programme—'Jaws' showing on odd days it said.

payability (peɪəˈbɪlɪtɪ). [f. payable + -ity.] **a.** Ability or willingness to pay or to be profitable. **b.** Capability of being profitably worked, as a mine: see next, 3.

1826 *Blackw. Mag.* XIX. 351 Let me say one word for.. his payability. He [Sheridan] is..written down as little better than a very pleasant swindler, whose purpose was to pay no man a shilling, whom he could put off with a joke. **1894** *N.B. Daily Mail* 21 Aug. 5 The payability of the Denny-Dalton field has been proved. **1933** *Flight* 30 Mar. 296/1 We have on occasion discussed with Mr. C. C. Walker the subject of 'payability' of aircraft. **1955** *Times* 3 May 17/5 The 170 feet sampled assayed 182.32 dwts. over 5.12 inches or 933 inch-dwts. at a payability of 100 per cent. **1971** *Daily Tel.* 11 Oct. 17 The payability is low as advance development is now confined largely to the flanks of the mine where values are inclined to be more scattered.

payable (ˈpeɪəb(ə)l), *a.* [f. pay *v.*[1] + -able. Cf. F. *payable* (13th c. in Godef.), It. *pagabile.*]

1. *Comm.* Of a sum of money, a bill, etc.: That is to be paid; due, owing; falling due (usu. *at* or *on* a specified date or *to* a specified person).

1447–8 in Willis & Clark *Cambridge* (1886) I. 400 Item paiable of the seid assignement at the festes of the Anunc' of oure lady..and saint michell [etc.]. **1590** Sir F. Walsingham in *Wills Doctors' Com.* (Camden) 70 After the satisfyinge of all things paieable by her as executor. **1688** *Col. Rec. Pennsylv.* I. 233 Drew a bill payable to yᵉ Chief Proprietor. **1725** Berkeley *Let. to T. Prior* 3 June, Wks. 1871 IV. 111 A bill of forty pounds, payable here at the shortest sight. **1887** R. Buchanan *Heir of Linne* iv, To whom can I make the cheque payable?

b. Of a person: That is to be paid; whose services or salary is to be paid. *rare.*

1617 Moryson *Itin.* II. 52 Diuers Officers payable out of the reuenues.

2. That can be paid; capable of being paid. *rare.*

a **1716** South *Serm.* (J.), Thanks are a tribute payable by the poorest.

3. *Mining.* (In active sense.) Of a mine, a bed of ore, a vein of metal, etc.: That can be made to pay, or yield an adequate return for the cost of working; capable of being profitably worked. Hence *transf.* in general sense: Capable of yielding profit, commercially profitable; paying.

1859 Cornwallis *New World* I. 361 Positive individuals there are, who still assert that gold will one day be discovered in this region, in payable abundance. **1879** Atcherley *Boërland* 117 Never again did we hit upon payable gold, although we burrowed..like rabbits. **1887** Mrs. D. Daly *Digging & Squatting S. Austr.* 266 The Northern Territory only requires capital..to become a fine and payable country. **1901** *Scotsman* 5 Mar. 7/1 An opportunity..to put the Tay ferries on a more payable basis.

Hence **ˈpayably** *adv.* (cf. sense 3).

1878 *Ure's Dict. Arts* IV. 427 Their lower beds have been found to be payably auriferous.

payables (ˈpeɪəb(ə)lz), *sb. pl. Comm.* [f. the adj.] Debts that one owes; liabilities. Cf. receivable *sb.* 3.

1972 *Accountant* 12 Oct. 445/2 Money and receivables and payables. **1977** *Sci. Amer.* Apr. 95/1 (Advt.), You also get a complete package of programs for general ledger, payables, receivables, payroll, and inventory. **1977** *Detroit Free Press* 11 Dec. 18-D/7 (Advt.), Bookkeeper part-time. Full charge, receivable, payables, invoicing, and payroll.

payage, obs. var. of peage, toll.

payane, variant of payen *Obs.*, pagan.

payce, variant of peise *Obs.*, weight.

pay-day. [pay- 1.] **a.** The day on which payment is, or is to be, made; *esp.* a periodically recurring day (e.g. weekly or monthly) on which wages are, or are arranged to be, paid; on the *Stock Exchange*, the day on which a transfer of stock has to be paid for.

1529 J. Whalley in Ellis *Orig. Lett.* Ser. iii. II. 162 The next pay day the whiche shalbe apon Satterdaye come senyght. *a* **1634** Chapman *Rev. for Hon.* Plays 1873 III. 289 Where in the Sutlers palace on pay-day We may the precious liquor quaff. **1742** Young *Nt. Th.* iii. 502 Our Day of Dissolution!—Name it right; 'Tis our great Pay-day. **1867** Trollope *Chron. Barset* I. xv. 122 He had..been known to be without a shilling for the last week before pay-day. **1897** [see *account day*]. **1895** [see name-day 3]. **1899** *Daily News* 27 Feb. 6/4 On the Saturday following a Stock Exchange pay-day. **1916** 'Taffrail' *Pincher Martin* viii. 147 'Our ship's company made a bit of a pay-day over it.' 'Pay-day! 'Ow d' yer mean?'.. 'Bettin'!' **1930** R. Campbell *Adamastor* 33 We attend the Great Inspection, The Roll-call of the Resurrection, The pay-day of Eternity. **1944** Dylan Thomas *Lett.* (1966) 262 I'll be up in London.. always on payday Fridays. **1972** *Daily Tel.* 4 July 32/6 She laughed and replied 'They will have to do. It's the only pair I've got till pay day.'

b. Wages; the amount paid to a person on pay-day. *Naut.*

1915 D. W. Bone *Broken Stowage* 239 We had fondly hoped to be strutting on Liverpool streets with our women folk, a twelve-months' 'pay day' in our pockets. **1922** E. O'Neill *Anna Christie* (1923) ii. 60 'Tis no more drinking and roving about I'd be doing then, but giving my pay-day into her hand and staying at home with her as meek as a lamb. **1932** J. W. Harris *Days of Endeavour* 20 The Bos'n, his fat pay-day having dwindled away..had sailed.

payee (peɪˈiː) [f. pay *v.*[1] + -ee: cf. F. *payé* paid.] The person to whom a sum of money is, or is to be, paid; *esp.* the person to whom a bill or cheque is made payable.

1758 Ld. Mansfield in *Burrow's Rep.* II. 676 As soon as a note is indorsed by the payee, the indorser is the drawer. **1766** Blackstone *Comm.* II. xxx. 467 The third person, or negotiator, to whom it is payable..is called the *payee.* **1866** Crump *Banking* iii. 83 It is always advisable to cross cheques ..if the name of the payee's banker be known.

payelle, obs. form of pail *sb.*

†**ˈpayeme.** *Obs.* Erron. form of payen, or paynim. So †**payemy** for payeny.

c **1330** R. Brunne *Chron.* (1810) 103 Ageyn þe paemy þe Cristendam to saue. *c* **1375** *Sc. Leg. Saints* xxvii. (*Machor*) 877 A man þat..was payeme and richt crafty. *c* **1400** *Destr. Troy* 2162 Fro the parties of payeme present at home.

†**ˈpayen**, *sb.* and *a. Obs.* Forms: 3–4 **paen(e, paeyn, payene, payn, pain,** 3–5 **paien,** 3, ? 6 **payne, 4 paian, paiene,** 4–5 **payen,** 4–6 **payane.** [a. OF. *paien* (11th c.), *paian, payen*, mod.F. *païen* = Pr. *paian, pagan*, Sp., It. *pagano*, Pg. *pagão*:—L. *pāgānus*: see pagan.] = pagan (*including* Muslim).

A. *sb.* = pagan A. 1.

c **1290** *S. Eng. Leg.* I. 84/20 Among þe paeyns euerechone. **1297** R. Glouc. (Rolls) 2536 He was cristine, & 30 [*v. rr.* heo, sche] payene [*v.r. c* 1390 a paynen] was. *a* **1300** *K. Horn* 59 þe pains come to londe. *Ibid.* 85 Payns him wolde slen. *a* **1300** *Cursor M.* 7440 To-quils come in philistiens, þair felun faas þat war paens [*v.r.* payens]. *c* **1375** *Sc. Leg. Saints* xiii. (*Marcus*) 175 þe paianis vald haf brynt His cors. **1390** Gower *Conf.* III. 193, I am paien, that other seith. *a* **1450** *Knt. de la Tour* (1868) 115 This childe, that mightly maintened Goddes lawe ayenst the payent. *a* **1550** in *Skelton's Wks. Epit. Dk. Jaspar* (1843) II. 393 Katyffes vnkind thou leuest behind, paynis, Turkes, & Iewis.

B. *adj.* = pagan B. 1.

a **1300** *K. Horn* 147 Seie þe paene kyng..þat ich am hol and fer On þis lond arived her. *c* **1330** R. Brunne *Chron. Wace* (Rolls) 7365 þis ar Godes of oure paen lay. *c* **1386** Chaucer *Knt.'s T.* 1512 To doon his sacrifise With alle the rytes of his payen wyse. **1513** Douglas *Æneis* i. Prol. 466 Calliope nor payane goddis wyld May do to me no thing bot harme, I wene.

Hence †'**payenhode, pai-** *Obs.*, paganism.
c **1470** [see PAYNIMHOOD].

†'**payeny, -ie.** *Obs.* In 4 paeni, -y, paygne, paynye, -ie, peyni, pani, 4–6 pany. [ME. a. OF. *paenie, paienie, painie, payenie* (in It. *paga'nia* (Florio)), f. *paien* PAYEN + -IE = -Y. Cf. *German-y.*] The lands of pagans; the heathen (in the Middle Ages including the Saracen) part of the world; heathendom.

a **1300** *Cursor M.* 19992 (Edin. MS.) þe first passage þat þapostlis in partie made to suilc folc as of pani [*v. rr.* paeni, paeny]. **1303** R. BRUNNE *Handl. Synne* 5243 A noþer sarasyn of paynye. **13..** *Guy Warw.* (A.) 3746 Þe soudan haþ his folk y-sent: Into al peyni his sond is sent. *c* **1380** *Sir Ferumb.* 122 In al paynye nys pryncȝ ne kyng, þat berþ so gret a name. *a* **1530** *Sir Beues* (Pynson) 2409, I wolde not for al pany Se the deuyl, that made that crye!

payer ('peɪə(r)). Also 4 paiere, 4–5 payere, 5 payare, paier, 9 payor. [f. PAY *v.*[1] + -ER[1]: cf. F. *payeur* (in 13th c. in regimen *paiere*), perh. the origin.] One who pays (in senses of the verb); *esp.* one who pays a sum of money. (As correlative to *payee* occas. spelt *payor*: see -OR 2 d.)

1362 LANGL. *P. Pl.* A. VI. 41 He is þe presteste payere þat pore men habbeþ; He with-halt non hyne his huire. *c* **1440** *Promp. Parv.* 377/1 Payare, *solutor.* **1472–3** *Rolls of Parlt.* VI. 39/2 The same sommes.. to the paiers of the same shuld be restored. **1540** *Act 32 Hen. VIII*, c. 25 In the handes of the payers of the sayd pencion. **1619** FLETCHER, etc. *Knt. Malta* v. i, Ingrateful payer of my industries. **1752** E. ERSKINE *Wks.* (1871) III. 486 Fear not: though drowned in debt Thy husband is the payer. **1880** S. D. HORTON *Gold & Silver* 172 Can payees demand, or can payors give in payment, whatever merchandise they prefer?

payer, payes, obs. ff. PAIR *sb.*[1] and *v.*[2], PEACE.

paygane, -end, obs. ff. PAGAN, PAGEANT.

paying ('peɪɪŋ), *vbl. sb.*[1] [f. PAY *v.*[1] + -ING[1].] The action of PAY *v.*[1]

†**1.** Pleasing, indulgence. *Obs.*

c **1440** HYLTON *Scala Perf.* (W. de W. 1494) I. lxiii, Vayne gladnes & well payeng of thiselfe.

2. a. The action of recompensing (a person) with money, or giving (money) for something; payment; also *fig.*: see senses of PAY *v.*[1]

1456 SIR G. HAYE *Law Arms* (S.T.S.) 174 He is nocht.. to put him self in povertee.. for his fynaunce paying. *c* **1530** L. COX *Rhet.* (1899) 58 While this summe was in payenge. **1663** GERBIER *Counsel* 60 They are to mannage the paying of their own workmen. **1759** HUME *Hist. Eng.* (1812) XIV. xxviii. 13 The paying of court.. to the haughty cardinal. *Mod.* Can't we go in without paying?

b. With adverbs: see PAY *v.*[1] Also *attrib.*

1890 *Pall Mall G.* 4 Oct. 7/1 Keeping a watchful eye on.. the indicator on the paying-out drum;.. he knew.. the amount of cable paid out. **1896** *Strand Mag.* XII. 349/1 The life-line and pipe are attached,.. and the diver is ready to step over the side... There is a great splash,.. a rapid paying out of life and pipe lines. *a* **1901** BESANT *Five Years' Tryst* (1902) 89 Market day is also the one busy day at the Bank. All day long there is paying-in; all day long there is paying-out.

c. *spec.* in *paying-in slip*: in *Banking*, a form listing cash, cheques, etc. which are paid in to the credit of an account; *paying-off pennant* (or *pendant*): a pennant flown by a homeward-bound naval ship or by a merchant vessel that will shortly discharge all hands.

1898 H. T. EASTON *Work of Bank* iv. 26 The 'paying-in' slip can be utilised for pasting in the cash-book and ledger. **1968** 'C. AIRD' *Henrietta Who?* x. 91 According to the paying-in slips, she always handed it over herself. **1974** 'S. WOODS' *Done to Death* 50 When she makes up her paying-in slip for the Bank whatever cash there is has been taken over the counter. **1977** *Grimsby Even. Tel.* 14 May 5/8 Mrs. —— said she had signed other names 'on bank paying-in slips and things like that'. **1914** 'BARTIMEUS' *Naval Occasions* xxiii. 212 The paying-off pendant looks as if it were impatient. **1927** B. M. CHAMBERS *Salt Junk* 50 At last the great day came: the hoisting of the paying-off pendant, a yard for every day of the commission. It was so long that the gilded bladder on the end fouled the houses which bordered the creek. **1954** BRADFORD & QUILL *Gloss. Sea Terms* 142/2 *Paying-off pennant*, flown by a naval vessel when homeward bound from a foreign station. **1961** F. H. BURGESS *Dict. Sailing* 158 *Paying off pennant*, an extremely long pennant hoisted as a sign that a ship is shortly 'paying off'. **1977** *Navy News* Aug. 40 H.M.S. Matapan enters Portsmouth Harbour for the last time, paying off pennant suspended from a large balloon.

paying, *vbl. sb.*[2] [f. PAY *v.*[2] + -ING[1].] The action of PAY *v.*[2], q.v.

1691 T. H[ALE] *Acc. New Invent.* 36 The only.. Defence of Ships against the Worm.. was the paying the Hulls from the Waters edge downwards with Stuff. **1704** J. HARRIS *Lex. Techn.* I. s.v., A new Coat of Tallow and Soap, or one of Train-Oil, Rosin and Brimestone,.. is put upon her, that is called *Paying of a Ship.* **1882** MORRIS *Hopes & Fears for Art* iv. 137 A mere paying it over with four coats of tinted lead-pigment.

paying, *ppl. a.* [f. PAY *v.*[1] + -ING[2].] That pays; remunerative: see the verb. *paying guest*: a lodger.

1853 E. CLACY *Lady's Visit Gold Diggings Austral.* 111 The two holes were 'bottomed' before noon with no paying result. **1871** *Trans. Illinois Agric. Soc.* VIII. 238 We need not expect to get a paying crop from stiff clays. **1872** GEO. ELIOT *Middlem.* IV. VIII. 363 His skill was relied on by many paying patients. **1879** TROLLOPE *John Caldigate* I. x. 135 'It's a paying concern, I suppose,' said Caldigate. 'It has paid;.. Whether it's played out or not, I'm not so sure...' **1882** DE WINDT *Equator* 123 The latter is the most paying [crop] of all. **1893** SELOUS *Trav. S.E. Africa* I It was a very paying business. **1895** G. GISSING *Paying Guest* i. 7 It's a very common arrangement nowadays, you know; they are called 'paying guests'. **1900** *Lancet* 15 Sept. 790/1 Some few of her young men 'paying-guests'.. appeared to recognise the drug. **1929** E. F. BENSON *Paying Guests* i. 9 Never had Wentworth and Balmoral and.. Belvoir entertained so continuous a complement of paying guests. **1957** J. BRAINE *Room at Top* i. 16 Her voice paused perceptibly at the word *lodger* as if considering.. the euphemisms—paying guest.. and so on. **1958** J. CANNAN *And be a Villain* vii. 148 Next pew—paying patients.. then the doctors, the colleagues 'showing up'.

payir, obs. f. PAIR *sb.*[1]

pay-jacket, obs. f. PEA-JACKET.

payl(e, paylays, -eysse, obs. ff. PALE, PAIL, PALACE.

paylet, payllet, obs. ff. PALLET *sb.*[2]

paylion, obs. Sc. f. PAVILION.

payllard, -art, obs. ff. PALLIARD.

pay-load ('peɪləʊd). [f. PAY- + LOAD *sb.*]

a. The part of an aircraft's load from which revenue is derived; the passengers, mail, or cargo carried by an aircraft.

1930 *Times* 12 Nov. 11/4 Her [*sc.* a flying-boat's] range is determined by the amount of 'pay' load she has to carry. **1933** *Discovery* Dec. 367/2 There is no reason why the pay load should not be decreased to give an increased range but it could not carry a paying load for 2,000 miles. **1936** *Economist* 25 Apr. 190/1 From the operational aspect, the key factor of seasonal pay-loads is still present, and this must necessarily limit the prospects of large profits. **1946** R. A. MCFARLAND *Human Factors Air Transport Design* x. 406 It is often contended that extra crew members replace passengers and payload. **1951** 'N. SHUTE' *Round Bend* 145 They pulled out a revised crew accommodation.. and added a hundred and ten pounds to the payload. **1955** *Sci. Amer.* Jan. 38/2 Helicopter designers are now busily engaged in harnessing jet engines to helicopters to raise their speed, range and payload. **1970** H. A. TAYLOR *Airspeed Aircraft since 1931* 170 It is practicable to use short, lightweight loading ramps which can be carried in the aircraft with a minimum loss of space and payload. **1978** *Jrnl. R. Soc. Arts* CXXVI. 685/1 The benefits of such scaling will be greatest on aircraft having the lowest percentages by weight of payload.

b. The bombs, warhead, etc., carried by an aircraft or rocket; the instruments, equipment, manned capsule, etc., carried by a rocket.

1936 *Sky* Nov. 7/3 Let the littlest and middlesize rocket serve as the 'payload' of the biggest rocket. **1941** D. GARNET *War in Air* ii. 12 The British Bomber.. could carry less petrol and more bombs, that is to say a higher 'pay-load' of bombs than the German Bomber. **1946** J. P. BAXTER *Scientists Against Time* ii. 35 Allied scientists and intelligence officers racked their brains to determine what would be the pay load in these long-range missiles. **1955** *Times* 6 Aug. 6/1 The payload would be instruments capable of recording conditions outside the atmosphere and a telemetering apparatus to transmit findings to base. **1962** F. I. ORDWAY et al. *Basic Astronautics* iv. 121 Sounding rockets.. with 50-lb payloads designed to analyze the results of these atomic explosions. **1970** *New Scientist* 8 Oct. 77/3 The proposed payload of the US space shuttle has come down some 50 per cent in the last three months. **1974** *Globe & Mail* (Toronto) 22 Oct. 7/1 In 1972, former President Richard Nixon.. promised that NASA would launch all foreign payloads intended for peaceful purposes under basically the same conditions that apply in the United States.

c. Goods, etc., carried on a road vehicle. Also *transf.* and *fig.*

1938 *Nation* (N.Y.) 13 Aug. 144/1 The trucks have to carry all their own gas, oil, and water.. which does not leave much room for pay load. **1960** E. L. CORNWELL *Commercial Road Vehicles* ix. 250 The articulated vehicle, weight for weight, generally has a rather lower payload capacity than a rigid vehicle. **1967** G. F. FIENNES *I tried to run a Railway* vii. 84 We have the pay load of some 500 tons transferred between road and rail by some six men. **1968** D. BRAITHWAITE *Fairground Archit.* 88 But the electric 'Scenic'.. constituted the heaviest pay load ever and often required the attendance of two traction engines. **1971** M. TAK *Truck Talk* 115 *Pay load*, the cargo or freight that a trucker hauls. **1971** C. BONINGTON *Annapurna South Face* vii. 85 Another factor one had to reckon with was that people moving back up the mountain, as opposed to ferrying, could carry only a very limited pay-load of supplies, if any, since they would be carrying their own personal equipment. **1976** P. R. WHITE *Planning for Public Transport* x. 215 Although offering similar weight: payload characteristics as does an internal combustion engine and its fuel tank, such a 'fuel' would require large amounts of energy for its creation. **1978** J. B. HILTON *Some run Crooked* xiii. 132 Once the water-table overflows, there are gullies adding their pay-load from both sides.

So **Payloader, pay-**, the proprietary name of a type of heavy mobile machine used for lifting and loading.

1953 *Sun* (Baltimore) 12 Oct. 14/5 The Coast Guard informed Rukert Terminals Corporation that pay loaders could not be used in the bottom of the holds to remove the fertilizer because of possible fire hazard. The loaders are scoops operated by gasoline. **1957** *Muck Shifter* June 340/1 (*heading*) 'Four-in-one' attachment. The entire line of four-wheel-drive Hough 'Payloader' tractor-shovels will now offer Drott '4-in-1' buckets as optional equipment. **1959** *Trade Marks Jrnl.* 27 May 548/1 Payloader... Lifting, loading and mechanical handling machines and mechanisms and parts of all these goods.. The Frank G. Hough Co. Libertyville, State of Illinois, United States of America; manufacturers. **1963** T. PYNCHON *V.* xii. 347 Someday there would be cranes, dump trucks, payloaders, bulldozers to come and level the neighbourhood. **1965** *Courier-Mail* (Brisbane) 10 Nov. 1/6 A man was killed at Mica Creek power station yesterday when a payloader he was driving overturned. **1969** *Jane's Freight Containers 1968–69* 267/1 The ancillary equipment is composed of.. two 1.8 cu m payloaders, one 25 ton side-loader and several heavy-duty fork-lifts. **1977** G. A. BROWNE *Slide* xxii. 180 A heavy-duty ditch digger.. called a payloader because of its combination digging-conveying system.

payman, var. PAIN-DEMAINE *Obs.*, fine bread.

paymaster ('peɪ,mɑːstə(r), -æ-). [f. PAY- 1 + MASTER.] An official (*esp.* an officer in the army or navy) whose duty it is to pay troops, workmen, or other persons. Also *fig.*

a **1550** *Vox Pop. Vox Dei* 719 in Hazl. *E.P.P.* III. 293 Payemasters suche as bythe With Trappes your golden smythe. **1591** *Garrard's Art Warre* 71 The captaine and the other officers, as the treasurers, paymasters, comissaries. **1615** BP. HALL *Contempl.*, *O.T.* x. iv, Both good and euill are sure paymasters at the last. **1643** *Plain English* 24 Let the Parliament.. appoint pay-masters to every Regiment. **1745** *De Foe's Eng. Tradesman* vi. (1841) I. 37 If he comes to deal with the same tradesman again, he is treated like one that is but an indifferent paymaster. **1855** MACAULAY *Hist. Eng.* xvi. III. 618 All the paymasters of regiments were directed to send in their accounts without delay. **1874** GREEN *Short Hist.* v. § I. 218 Edward [III] became the pay-master of the poorer princes of Germany.

b. *paymaster-general*: the officer at the head of the department of the Treasury through which payments are made: see quot. 1863.

1702 *Lond. Gaz.* No. 3825/3 Receiver and Paymaster-General of Her Majesty's Forces. **1703** MARLBOROUGH *Lett. & Disp.* (1845) I. 92 The paymaster-general of the States. **1710** WALPOLE *Off. Not.* 25 July in *Lond. Gaz.* No. 4724/3 Which is to be paid.. by the Pay-Master-General. **1846** S. SHARPE *Hist. Egypt* ix. 307 Auletes.. at first gave Rabirius.. the office of royal *diœcetes*, or paymaster-general. **1863** H. COX *Instit.* III. vii. 697 All payments for civil salaries, allowances, and incidental charges payable in England, and all payments for the army, navy, and ordnance, are made upon the special authority of the Treasury by the Paymaster-General.

Hence '**pay,mastership,** the office of a paymaster; so '**paymaster-'generalship.**

1809 G. ROSE *Diaries* (1860) II. 398 One Paymastership of the Forces is vacant. **1898** *Daily News* 9 Dec. 5/1 Through the transference of the Earl of Hopetoun from the Paymaster-Generalship to the office of Lord Chamberlain.

payment[1] ('peɪmənt). Also 4–5 **paiement,** 5 **pament,** 5–6 **paymente, payement(e,** 6–7 **paiment,** (6 -e). [a. F. *paiement* (12–13th c. in Hatz.-Darm.), f. *payer* to PAY: see -MENT. Cf. Pr. *pagamen*, Sp., It. *pagamento.*]

1. The action, or an act, of paying; the remuneration of a person with money or its equivalent; the giving of money, etc. in return for something or in discharge of a debt.

† *bills of payment*: vouchers or receipts for moneys paid, receipted bills. *equation of payments*: see EQUATION 4.

13.. *E.E. Allit. P.* A. 597 And þou to payment com hym byfore. **1390** GOWER *Conf.* II. 297 The jueler anon forth fette The gold and made his paiement. **1422** tr. *Secreta Secret., Priv. Priv.* 133 Good pament to al men he makyd. **1465** J. PASTON in *P. Lett.* II. 219 He must inquere.. what mony he hath payd to all men.. and see his billes of payment, and take therof a titelyng. **1559** *Mirr. Mag.*, *Warwick* xv, Their paimentes wer delayd. **1686** tr. *Chardin's Trav. Persia* 9 The Sellers would take their Pieces of Five Sous in payment. *a* **1732** GAY *Fables* II. iii. 98 'Twas agreed.. His payments should in corn be made. **1892** *Pall Mall G.* 28 July 2/1 It was Mr. Lowe who first introduced the great principle of payment by results. **1893** BITHELL *Counting-ho. Dict.* s.v., When goods are offered in exchange for goods, it is popularly distinguished as 'payment in kind'.

b. Const. *of* the thing given or discharged (money, a debt, etc.).

c **1430** LYDG. *Min. Poems* (Percy Soc.) 43 If payment of dette be so renewed. **1503** *Priv. Purse Exp. Eliz. York* (1830) 92 Payement of a bill. **1588** SHAKS. *L.L.L.* II. i. 130 The paiment of a hundred thousand Crownes. **1818** CRUISE *Digest* (ed. 2) III. 325 Before the day of payment of the half year's rent.

c. Const. *of* the person who is paid.

1838 *People's Charter* (in *Chartist Circular* 5 Oct. 1839, 7/2), Payment of Members. 1. Be it enacted that every Member of the House of Commons.. shall be paid £500 per annum.

†**d.** Const. *of* the thing bought (cf. PAY *v.*[1] 12).

1526 SKELTON *Magnyf.* 2168 They.. pynche at the payment of a poddynge prycke.

2. A sum of money (or other thing) paid; pay, wages; price.

c **1449** PECOCK *Repr.* (Rolls) II. 392 Tithis and offringis and other like paymentis. **1484** CAXTON *Fables of Æsop* v. iv, He demaunded his sallary and payment. **1660** F. BROOKE tr. *Le Blanc's Trav.* 44 Most of those payments fall to the Officers and receivers shares. **1722** DE FOE *Col. Jack* (1840) 45 Two or three small payments of money, which.. lay by themselves. **1878** JEVONS *Prim. Pol. Econ.* vi. § 43. 53 Wages.. are the payments received by a labourer in return for his labour.

†**b.** *to run for good payment* (fig.): to 'pass current', be generally accepted or believed. *Obs.*

1579–80 NORTH *Plutarch* (1656) 851 Every man thought he had beene slaine, and it ran for good payment among all the Grecians.

3. *fig.* The action, or an act, of rendering to a person anything due, deserved, or befitting, or of discharging an obligation; the infliction of punishment or retribution, the giving of reward or satisfaction, a yield in return for labour, etc.; the thing so rendered or given.

13.. *Coer de L.* 6097 Whenne the Sarezynes hadden syghte, Hou plente was hys payment, Non ther durst abyde hys dent. **1375** BARBOUR *Bruce* VI. 148 [Bruce] sa gud payment can thaim ma, That fiff-sum in the furd he slew. **1470–85** MALORY *Arthur* VI. x, Syre launcelot..clafe his hede and neck vnto the throte. Now hast thou thy payement that long thou hast deserued. **1581** W. FLEETWOOD in Ellis *Orig. Lett.* Ser. I. II. 284 We examined all the seyd roogs and gave theym substanciall payment. **1613** PURCHAS *Pilgrimage* V. iii. 466 The Countrey is so fertile, that at what time soeuer corne be put into the ground, the paiment is good with increase. **1738** C. WESLEY *Hymn, 'Father of Lights, from Whom proceeds'* ii, Blessings, the Payment of the Poor, Our Lips and Hearts return. **1884** PAE *Eustace* 76, I never forget payment for a blow.

4. *attrib.* and *Comb.*

1581 *Reg. Privy Council Scot.* III. 386 To stay all payment-making. **1800** *Asiat. Ann. Reg., Proc. Parl.* 23/2 On the payment side, the customs and freight are calculated ..on the quantity of goods expected. **1892** *Daily News* 26 Mar. 3/1 A House of Commons elected under a payment system.

payment[2]. *rare.* [f. PAY *v.*[2] + -MENT.] The action of paying a ship's bottom, etc. (see PAY *v.*[2]); *concr.* the composition used for this.

1778 PRYCE *Min. Cornub.* Contents I. iii, No payment, however poisonous, will prevent the Teredo-worm from boring ships bottoms.

payment, obs. form of PAVEMENT.

paymistress ('peɪˌmɪstrɪs). [f. PAY- + MISTRESS, after *paymaster*.] A woman who superintends or manages the payment of persons or services; also *fig.* something, personified as female, that pays or remunerates a person.

1583 T. WATSON *Centurie of Loue* fin., The Labour is light, where Loue is the Paiemistres. **1590** GREENE *Never too late* (1600) 115 Thow shalt finde..folly the paymistris that rewards all amorous trauels. **1651** *Relat. Poysoning Sir T. Overbury* 20 He charged..Mrs. Turner to be..the paymistresse of the Poysoners rewards. **1886** *Sat. Rev.* 6 Mar. 329/1 Hissing the Attorney-General's Sovereign and paymistress.

payn, -e, obs. ff. PAIN, PANE; var. PAYEN *Obs.*

paynct, obs. form of PAINT *v.*

†**paynen**, obs. variant of PAYEN, PAYNIM.

13.. *Cursor M.* 7440 (Gött.) þair feloun fas, þat were painens [*v. rr.* paens, payens, paynymes]. *c* **1390** [see PAYEN A. quot. 1297].

Payne's grey (peɪnz greɪ). [f. the name of William *Payne* (fl. 1800), English artist, + GREY *sb.*] A composite pigment composed of blue, red, black, and white permanent pigments, used esp. for watercolours.

1835 [see NEUTRAL *a.* 3 c]. **1886** H. C. STANDAGE *Artists' Man. Pigments* vi. 68 Payne's grey resembles neutral tint in being a compound colour. **1888** [see GREY *sb.* 4 e]. **1924** [see NEUTRAL *a.* 3 c]. **1934** H. HILER *Notes Technique Painting* ii. 133 As to the prepared greys,..Payne's Grey, etc., they are usually mixed by the manufacturers. **1959** *Listener* 13 Aug. 254/3 The embellishment of the same green, sometimes with a touch of Payne's grey, fields. **1979** *Dryad Crafts* 49/4 Oil Colours... Payne's Grey.

payngnier, obs. form of PANNIER.

paynim ('peɪnɪm), *sb.* (*a.*) *arch.* Forms: 3–6 painime, 3–7 pay-; 4 peynim, -yme, 4–5 paynyme, (-en, -yn, painen), 4–7 paynym, 4–8 painim, 5 paynem(e, -eyme, painem, -ym, 5–6 panym, 6 -im, 6–7 -yme; 3– paynim. [ME. a. OF. *paienime, pain-, paenimme*, from earlier *paien-, paenisme*:—late L. *pāgānism-us* (Augustine), 'the religious system of the pagans, heathenism', later 'the lands or countries in which this prevailed, heathen lands': see PAYEN, PAGAN, and -ISM.]

†**1.** Pagan or non-Christian lands collectively; pagandom, heathendom. *Obs.*

c **1250** *O. Kent. Serm.* in *O.E. Misc.* 28 Ihesu crist.. anured of þo þrie kinges of painime. **13..** *Coer de L.* 612 They were redy for to wende,..As palmers were in Paynym. **1387–8** T. USK *Test. Love* II. i. (Skeat) l. 49 These thinges were figured..by the sterre to painims kinges. **14..** *Sir Beues* 3887 (MS. M) In payneme ne in Surry, I-wys, Ys none the lyke of lose ne of price.

2. A pagan, a heathen; a non-Christian; *esp.* a Muslim, a Saracen. *arch.* and *poetic.*

1382 WYCLIF *Matt.* v. 48 Whether and paynymmys don nat this thing? *c* **1400** MAUNDEV. (1839) xxix. 295 Job, that was a Paynem. **1489** CAXTON *Faytes of A.* III. xxiv. 225 They that were paynemys & of euyl byleue. **1531** ELYOT *Gov.* III. iii, Apollo, whome the paynimes honoured for god of wisedome. **1637** R. HUMPHREY tr. *St. Ambrose* Pref., The Goths..burnt as many books of the ancient Paynims as they could find. **1713** TICKELL *Prospect of Peace* Poems (1790) 159 Where..one champion's arms..Slay paynims vile, that force the fair. **1848** LYTTON *Harold* VII. iii, The godless paynims! muttered the Norman.

B. *adj.* (orig. *attrib.* use of A.) Of pagans; pagan, heathen; non-Christian; chiefly = Muslim or Saracen. In modern writers *poet.* or *Hist.*

c **1320** *Sir Beues* 496 (MS. A) ȝif ȝe seþ schipes of painim londe. *c* **1380** WYCLIF *Serm.* Sel. Wks. I. 28 To dwelle amonge Sarazynes or oþir paynym sectis. **1475** *Bk. Noblesse* (Roxb.) 75 Pompeus..that was so chevalrous a paynym knighte amongis the Romains. **1561** T. NORTON *Calvin's Inst.* I. xi. (1634) 34 It is much shame, that the panime writers are better expounders of the law of God than the Papists are. **1667** MILTON *P.L.* I. 765 Champions bold Defi'd the best of Panim chivalry To mortal combat, or carreer with Lance. **1742** YOUNG *Nt. Th.* II. 615 By Genius unawak'd, Painim or Christian. **1812** BYRON *Ch. Har.* I. xxxiv, The Paynim turban and the Christian crest. **1899** E. J. CHAPMAN *Drama Two Lives, Snake-Witch* 41 When he returned..From Paynim lands beyond the sea.

Hence †**'paynimhood** *Obs.*, the condition of being a paynim, paganism (incl. Islamism). **'paynimry**, paynims collectively, pagandom, heathenry. †**'paynimy (panemye)** *Obs.*, pagandom.

c **1470** HARDING *Chron.* XCIII. iii, Wher thei the kyng Kynygill of *paynymhode [*v.r.* paienhode], Baptized, and made a Christen manne full fyne. **1382** WYCLIF *Rom.* Prol. 300 The vices of her *paynymrie rathere myndende. **1483** *Cath. Angl.* 266/1 Paynymery, *gentilitas, paganismus.* **1835** A. FLEMING in *Harp Renfrewshire* Ser. II. (1873) 184 Paynimry's bravest and best are arrayed. **1886** FREEMAN *Methods Hist. Study* vi. 249 Robert son of Godwine, who cut a path..through the ranks of opposing paynimrie. **1481** CAXTON *Godeffroy* xcix. 150 It was anon knowen in the *panemye.

paynize ('peɪnaɪz), *v.* [f. *Payne*, name of the inventor of the process. Cf. KYANIZE.] *trans.* To impregnate (wood) with a solution of calcium (or barium) sulphide followed by one of calcium sulphate, so as to harden and preserve it.

1844 *Mirror* 7 Sept. 158/1 Wooden Rail. 5280 cubic feet, 2*s.* per foot..Paynizing..Wedges, labour, and carriage. **1850** G. GODWIN in Cunningham *Handbk. London* 240/2 All the wood employed in the construction is Paynized.

paynman, -mayn(e, var. PAIN-DEMAINE *Obs.*

paynt, etc., obs. ff. PAINT, etc.

paynye, paynym(e, -yn: see PAYENY, PAYNIM.

'pay-off. Also payoff. [f. vbl. phr. *to pay off* (in various senses): see PAY *v.*[1]] **1. a.** Winnings from gambling or the paying of these. Also *attrib.*

1905 F. HUTCHISON *Johnnie the Gent* 63 An' then there's the know-it-all-bloke that has just beat a couple of races, wit' about an ounce each way or maybe a deuce to peek. Oh, he's the wisest guy that ever give the pay-off gazebo the lofty leer when he reached for his dough. **1938** G. GREENE *Brighton Rock* IV. i. 149 'I've won, Pinkie. A tenner.'.. A young man with oiled hair stood on a wooden step paying out money... Spicer called out to him..: 'Well, Sammy, now the pay-off.' **1943** *Sun* (Baltimore) 22 Apr. 18/1 This crowd backed New Moon confidently, the final payoff being $3.90 for $2. **1964** A. WYKES *Gambling* vi. 142 If he throws a natural or crap,.. the payoff odds will be considerably smaller. **1967** *Listener* 10 Aug. 168/2 A zero-sum game is one in which the pay-offs cancel out to zero—I've won sixpence, you're sixpence down. **1970** *Globe & Mail* (Toronto) 28 Sept. 20/2 How about the $800 daily double payoff the track made one day on a bet that never was made. Is that not bookmaking?

b. *Criminals' slang.* A confidence trick in which the victim is encouraged to venture a large sum of money by the success of a bet, investment, etc., involving a small sum or one furnished by the confidence tricksters. Also, one who employs this confidence trick (= *pay-off man (a)* (sense 5 below)).

1915 G. BRONSON-HOWARD *God's Man* III. iii. 197 Specialists in check-raising, wireless wire-tapping, 'the match', 'the pay-off', and cards. **1928** [see CREEP *sb.* 1 d]. **1935** *Evening News* 29 June 3/2 The sucker is induced to put a small sum into one venture. His winnings are promptly paid and he has visions. This is the *'pay-off'*. **1938** P. J. SMITH *Con Man* ix. 192 It is to his genius that the successful swindle known as the 'Pay Off' was attributed. **1943** *Police Jrnl.* Mar. 69 *Pay off*, a confidence trick—Stock Exchange fraud.

c. The return on an investment; profit. Also, the point at which an investment begins to yield profit.

1955 *Times* 5 Aug. 9/7 Countries which entered on the first stage would be relying on the second stage for their 'pay off'. **1969** *Daily Tel.* 11 Mar. 6/1 Profits in the past two years have been held back by the Woolco development and the pay-off here still could be a long way away. **1974** *Nature* 1 Feb. 248/1 The spending proposals entail vast concentration of resources in areas which are likely to have a quick payoff. **1974** *Information Handbk. 1974–5* (Shell Internat. Petroleum Co.) 64 A major oilfield can represent an investment as high as £400 million and it may take several years to reach pay-off. **1977** *Jrnl. R. Soc. Arts* CXXV. 58/2 The second problem..was to ensure that a fairly early pay off was secured from the new investment—and this in an industry where long lead times seemed inevitable. **1978** *N.Y. Times* 30 Mar. D. 5/3 The payoff in high-technology fields is extraordinarily great.

2. The payment of bribes; graft. Also, a sum of money given as a bribe. Also *attrib.*

1930 (*film title*) The Big Payoff. **1935** D. LAMSON *We who are about to Die* xi. 193 Witnesses, juries, pay-off, fixin's—don't matter what it is... There ain't nothin' he won't do, long as you got the potatoes. **1938** R. CHANDLER in *Dime Detective Mag.* Jan. 62/1 He took my gun and his payoff money. **1950** *Sat. Even. Post* 27 May 20/1, I saw that in the Navy there's a lot of pay-off [graft]. **1958** S. ELLIN *Eighth Circle* (1959) II. iii. 44, I never took a penny of pay-off money since I got into the Department. **1971** R. DENTRY *Encounter at Kharmel* xii. 219 *Money* for everything you've been through—a piddling wee payoff to close our mouths? **1976** *National Observer* (U.S.) 4 Dec. 2/2 Tanaka is one of several Japanese officials accused of receiving $12 million in payoffs from Lockheed for promotion of the company's sales in Japan. **1977** *New Yorker* 22 Aug. 70/1 The scandal involving alleged political payoffs by agents of the South Korean government..first broke last year.

3. *Criminals' slang.* The division of the proceeds after a robbery.

1931 G. IRWIN *Amer. Tramp & Underworld Slang* 141 *Pay off*, the division of spoils after a robbery. **1935** N. ERSINE *Underworld & Prison Slang* 56 *Payoff*,..the end of a job and the splitting of the loot. **1935** A. J. POLLOCK *Underworld Speaks* 86/2 *Pay off joint*, place where the plunder (loot) is divided.

4. *transf.* and *fig.* Result, outcome, conclusion; return, recompense; punishment; the settling of accounts (in criminal contexts, esp. by murder). Also, a decisive or crucial factor; 'the ultimate'; 'the limit'. Also *attrib.*

It proved unrealistic to attempt to separate the examples that follow into clearly distinct sections. Many of them stand contextually at the border of at least two senses or embrace more than one sense.

1927 *Vanity Fair* Nov. 67/2 Conway's 'That's the pay off!' is swiftly making the rounds. It is employed when one enthusiastically describes anything that is first-rate: the acme, the last word! **1928** J. P MCEVOY *Show Girl* xiii. 195, I thought show business was all laughter and applause... It's a headache. It's a pain anywhere you sit. And then imagine falling in love on top of it. That's the pay-off. **1930** P. ANNIXTER in *Flynn's* 11 Oct. 690 (*title*) The pay-off. **1932** *News* (San Francisco) 6 Aug. 12/3, I wanted to take one of those pictures which show how the greatest pitchers of the game hold their pay-off deliveries. **1937** N. COWARD *Present Indicative* VII. 295, I had..lived far too strenuously. This [*sc.* a nervous breakdown] was the pay-off. **1937** *Sun* (Baltimore) 4 Aug. 14/1 The white-hulled defender isn't as impressive out of the water as the polished blue challenger but that isn't the payoff in this million-dollar sport. **1940** J. G. BRANDON *Gang War!* ix. 93 It's a gang 'knock-off', or 'pay-off', whichever you like. **1944** *Sun* (Baltimore) 1 Nov. 1/5 The payoff is that there is no such thing as an effective Japanese fleet today. **1952** C. DAY LEWIS tr. *Virgil's Aeneid* IX. 189 The Fates and Venus have had their pay-off, in that the Trojans Have reached our fertile land of Ausonia. **1953** R. LEHMANN *Echoing Grove* 42 The final pay-off, the practical one that always has to be gone through when there has been a death. **1957** *Times* 1 Oct. 11 It may be true, as Mr. Wilson said, that this economic crisis is 'the pay-off for the Government's policy on the past six years'. **1958** K. AMIS *I like it Here* 200 He'd carried on in the same sort of way before, explaining he was part of the history of the English novel and all the rest of it, but this was really the pay-off. **1958** *Times* 8 May 11/6 To these crews, their terrible bomb loads are the devastating pay-off element of a daring formula: at war—to prevent war. **1970** G. GREER *Female Eunuch* 156 All that they have offered in the name of generosity and altruism has been part of an assumed transaction, in which they were entitled to a certain payoff. **1970** G. F. NEWMAN *Sir, You Bastard* v. 149 All the inconvenience and suffering, and this was the pay-off. **1971** R. DENTRY *Encounter at Kharmel* xii. 199 There was nothing to be gained from beating the hell out of this foul-mouthed creep... The pay off could wait. **1976** *Survey* Summer-Autumn 45 Among the less apparent payoffs, one might well ponder the changes in regard to superficially non-political facets of Soviet life. **1977** *Time* 28 Feb. 8/2 Danish Premier Anker Jørgensen wagered his political future in January and last week collected the payoff.

b. The climax or dénouement of a story, play, etc.; the point or crux of a story, etc. Cf. *pay-off line* (sense 5 below).

1947 WODEHOUSE *Full Moon* vii. 141 A raconteur of established reputation expects something better than silence when he comes to the pay-off of one of his best stories. **1962** W. NOWOTTNY *Lang. Poets Use* iv. 96 Marvell's poem has its 'pay-off' in the ambiguity of the *da capo* with which the poem comes to a conclusion. **1969** *Listener* 15 May 698/1 Some failed even to detect the snook being cocked at them in Mary's climactic confession that she'd 'always worry about Jim'—a pay-off one could take nostalgically or ironically.

5. Special combs.: **pay-off line**, the point of a story; the 'punch-line' of a story, limerick, etc.; **pay-off man** *Criminals' slang*, (*a*) a confidence trickster; (*b*) the cashier of a gang of criminals; **pay-off matrix, table** *Game Theory*, an array specifying the utilities to the players of all the possible outcomes of a game.

1934 J. O'HARA *Appointment in Samarra* (1935) i. 16 And they always knew when to laugh, even when it was a Catholic joke, because Reilly signalled the pay-off line by slapping his leg just before it was delivered. **1944** [see *bar-fly* s.v. BAR *sb.*[1] 30]. **1965** N. COGHILL in J. Gibb *Light on C. S. Lewis* 61 We all laughed at this pay-off line. **1927** *Fresno* (Calif.) *Bee* 9 June 1/3 The complaint asserts that Justice of the Peace Murphy was introduced to Frank E. Howell, former deputy sheriff, who was alleged to have been the 'pay-off' man of the contractors. **1928** M. C. SHARPE *Chicago May* 286 *Pay-off men*,..confidence men (or women). **1932** *Sun* (Baltimore) 27 Apr. 15/7 There were frequent references to checks made payable by Plummer to an unidentified 'pay-off man'. **1934** [see NUMBER *sb.* 3 e]. **1935** A. SQUIRE *Sing Sing Doctor* v. 59 They surrounded themselves with bodyguards, flunkies, killers, fixers, pay-off men. **1938** D. CASTLE *Do Your Own Time* 287 *Pay-off Man*, cashier of a mob. **1952** J. C. C. MCKINSEY *Introd. Theory of Games* i. 7 We shall henceforth describe such a game as this by giving merely the payoff matrix. **1971** D. C. HAGUE *Managerial Econ.* vii. 138 The columns show the result of each act... The rows show the events leading to these possible results. Table 11 is therefore known as a payoff matrix (or table). **1974** ANTON & KOLMAN *Appl. Finite Math.* viii. 361 Games of the type described in this example are called matrix games and the matrix is called the payoff matrix. **1976** *Nature* 8 Apr. 481/1 He..assigned payoffs for winning, losing, getting injured in an escalated fight and so on, and used these values to construct a payoff matrix for each strategy against all others.

payola (peɪˈəʊlə). *colloq.* (orig. *U.S.*). [f. PAY *sb.* or *v.*[1] + -OLA.] A secret or indirect payment or bribe to a person to use his position, influence, etc., to promote a commercial product, service, etc.; *spec.* such a payment to a disc-jockey for 'plugging' a record or song.

1938 *Variety* 19 Oct. 41 (*heading*) Plug payolas perplexed. *Ibid.*, The payola element had made their deals with bandleaders on the expectation that they continue to get 19c, thereby making it profitable to do business with the plug at a rate of around 10c a point. **1953** *Time* 23 Feb. 56/3 A world where *cut-ins* (giving a performer a share of a song's profits), *hot stoves* (open bribes) and other forms of *payola* were standing operating procedure. **1958** S. ELLIN *Eighth Circle* (1959) II. vii. 84 The unerring way he gravitated toward the graft, the payola, the swindle. **1966** T. PYNCHON *Crying of Lot 49* iii. 61 They got the contracts. All drawn up in most kosher fashion, Manfred. If there was payola in there, I doubt it got written down. **1969** N. COHN *AWopBopaLooBop* (1970) v. 51 There was a huge scandal about in 1959, the payola fuss, and a lot of people came crashing down. **1969** [see DROPSY *sb.* 4]. **1972** P. BLACK *Biggest Aspidistra* I. iii. 30 Gramophone records began to take over from sheet music and presented fresh temptations.. Plugging re-emerged under the name of payola. **1974** *Guardian* 5 Nov. 7/2 Miss Squires and Mr Dabbs appeared in the dock together accused of 'payola' corruption. **1974** *Daily Tel.* 18 Nov. 6/1 There is growing talk of abuse of power by leading figures within the country's political establishment..at the expense of both Western businessmen and of the Kenyan people, involving payola for 'services rendered'. **1976** *Observer* 7 Nov. 1/6 (*heading*) Lockheed payola. A Spanish air force general and a colonel secretly managed the Lockheed Aircraft Corporation's sales in Spain and earned commissions worth £170,000 each. **1977** *Time* 31 Jan. 13/1 In the process of popularizing their products, the competing firms created a payola monster. They began slipping money as well as footwear to the stars of their choice.

payor, occas. var. PAYER.

ˈ**payout.** [f. vbl. phr. *to pay out* (see PAY *v.*[1] 5 b, 13).] The fact or action of paying out; the amount paid out (see also quot. 1904). Also, a place (in a shop, etc.) where payment is made.

1904 *Dialect Notes* II. 386 *Pay out*, n. Said of a well which more than returns the expense of drilling and pumping, or the capital invested in it. **1959** W. S. EVANS *Petroleum in E. Hemisphere* 19 As a result of the relatively low 'going' price for crude, his payout may be considerably longer than will be satisfactory, particularly if the price weakens further. **1960** *Guardian* 18 Dec. 5/1 The payout of stage artists by manufacturers for an advertising plug slipped into the artist's act. **1968** *Nature* 23 Nov. 752/1 Ross identified the bottom by a decrease in the rate of pay out of line from the free-spooling reel... An abrupt decrease in the rate of pay-out was indicative of bottom contact. **1970** *Globe & Mail* (Toronto) 25 Sept. B10/6 Profit..will not increase above last year's $1.05 a share because of payouts on long-range marketing programs. **1977** J. WAINWRIGHT *Day of Peppercorn Kill* 70 At the payout, she wrote a cheque. **1977** A. MORICE *Scared to Death* iv. 25 She had set off towards the pay-out windows to collect her winnings.

payr(e, obs. ff. PAIR, PEAR.

ˈ**pay-roll, payroll.** [PAY- I.] The total amount to be paid to employees in a specified period; also, (a list of) employees receiving regular pay. Freq. in phr. ***on the payroll***: employed by a particular company or person. Also *fig.*

1740 C. CIBBER *Apol. for Life* xiii. 257 The Rate of their respective Sallaries were only enter'd in our daily Pay-Roll. **1775** *Rec. New Hampsh. Comm. Safety* in *New Hampsh. Hist. Soc. Coll.* (1863) VII. 26 Examined and allowed Capt. Crafford's pay Roll of his men engaged for fourteen days. **1780** *Calendar Virginia State Papers* (1875) I. 387 Enclose pay roll & account for purchase of kettles and dutch-ovens. **1840** R. H. DANA *Bef. Mast* xxix. 103 When the crew were paid off..the owners..generously refused to deduct the amount from the pay-roll. **1898** *Westm. Gaz.* 9 July 6/1 An employer with a total pay-roll of £30,000. **1921** C. E. MULFORD *Bar-20 Three* viii. 96 Looks like some Greaser had a grudge agin' him—somebody he's mebby fired off his payroll, or suspected of cattle-liftin'. *Ibid.* ix. 113, I ain't on Kane's payroll—yet. **1958** *Punch* 23 July 98/1 Skilled British agents are showing cause why they should be retained on the pay-roll. **1964** MRS. L. B. JOHNSON *White House Diary* 11 Jan. (1970) 39 On to Goldsmith Mill where a payroll of about a hundred had been saved by the joint work of the Community and the ARA. **1968** *Time* 17 May 66 Despite all the fuss at Columbia over IDA, none of its professors are actually on the IDA payroll. **1973** 'H. HOWARD' *Highway to Murder* viii. 98 Nobody on my payroll had anything to do with Vince Portelli's killing. **1977** *New Yorker* 29 Aug. 87/1 The Italian anarchists who were convicted of murdering two men while stealing a payroll in South Braintree, Massachusetts, in 1920 were executed on August 23, 1927.

2. *attrib.*, as ***pay-roll index***; **pay-roll tax**, a tax levied on businesses according to the number of persons employed or on the wages-bill of the business.

1934 *Planning* II. xxxi. 7 The United Kingdom possesses nothing comparable to the payroll index, which is one of the major instruments of economic measurement in the United States. **1935** *N.Y. Times* 16 Jan. 2/6 The plans sent to the President by his Cabinet Committee included: unemployment insurance, financed, in part, at least by a payroll tax. **1937** M. NEWCOMER in *Stud. in Current Tax Probl.* 39 The new payroll taxes for unemployment insurance and old-age benefits will eventually become an important factor in the tax burden. **1971** *Sunday Australian* 8 Aug. 5/4 Australia's State schools paid about $15 million in payroll tax in the last financial year. **1976** in R. Crossman *Diaries* II. 58 Selective Employment Tax. A payroll tax paid by employers with some rebate for industrial enterprises.

pays, obs. f. PEACE; var. PEISE *Obs.*

‖**paysage.** *Obs.* exc. as Fr. (peizaʒ). Also 7–8 **paisage**, 7 **piesage**. [F. *paysage*, f. *pays* country: see -AGE.] **a.** A representation of rural scenery. **b.** A rural scene, landscape.

1611 COTGR., *Païsage*, Paisage, Landskip, Countrey-worke; a representation of fields, or of the countrey, in painting, &c. **1653** *Gloria & Narcissus* I. 248 A delightfull piesage, where many flockes of sheep seemingly, pastured by a goodly river side. **1661** EVELYN *Diary* 9 Aug., Some incomparable *paisages* done in distemper. **1720** POPE *Iliad* XVIII. V. 1454 (*Observ. Shield Achilles*) Between the Siege in the fourth Picture, and the Battel in the sixth, a piece of Paisage is introduced. [**1823** SCOTT *Quentin D.* Introd., The *paysage* was rather like Fontainebleau than the wilds of Callander. **1883** H. JAMES *Portr. Places* xviii. 344 A *paysage* which is two-thirds ocean.]

Hence **paysagist** (ˈpeɪzədʒɪst) [F. *paysagiste*], a landscape-painter.

1816 *Sporting Mag.* XLVIII. 78 Few Paysagists of the present school handle the brush..with less quackery. **1886** *Art Age* IV. 42 (Cent.) The lists are now open to some clever paysagist to prove that his art is the supreme flower of all.

paysan, obs. or alien form of PEASANT.

paysand, variant of PEISANT *Obs.*, weighty.

‖**paysanne** (peizan). Also 8 **paisanne**. [F. *paysanne*, fem. of *paysan*: see PEASANT.] A peasant-woman; a countrywoman. (Properly, in reference to France, or a French-speaking country.)

1748 SMOLLETT *Rod. Random* xlii, The young *paysanne* had no reason to complain of my remembrance. **1791** CHARLOTTE SMITH *Celestina* (ed. 2) I. 190 Their only servant is a mere West country paisanne. **1816** BYRON *Let.* Wks. 1899 III. 352 On the steps of a cottage I saw a young paysanne, beautiful as Julie herself. **1823** SCOTT *Quentin D.* Introd., A lively French *paysanne*, with eyes as black as jet.

paysant, -yne, obs. forms of PEASANT.

‖**Pays du Tendre** (pei dy tɑ̃dr). Also with lower-case initials. [ad. Fr. *pays de Tendre*, with ref. to *Tendre*, an imaginary country whose topography symbolized aspects of love, devised by Madeleine de Scudéry (1607–1701) in her novel *Clélie* (1654–60).] Matters concerning love; the 'region' of the affections.

1910 W. J. LOCKE *Simon* viii. 113 A crock..with one foot in the grave has no business to put the other into the *Pays du Tendre*. **1913** —— *Stella Maris* xv. 200 Herold..adventured with her into the Land of Tenderness—the *Pays du Tendre* of the old French romanticists. **1938** *Times Lit. Suppl.* 15 Jan. 43/3 The heroine's first excursion into the *pays du tendre* ends abruptly with the young man's betrothal to another girl. **1939** *Ibid.* 1 July 387/2 Mastery of this familiar type in the *pays du tendre*..is a handsome equipment for story-telling. *a* **1976** A. CHRISTIE *Autobiogr.* (1977) IV. i. 168 The art of flirtation..was an approximation, I think, to what the old troubadours called '*le pays du tendre*'.

payse, paysible, obs. ff. PEACE, PEACEABLE,

payse, paysse, variant of PEISE *Obs.*

paysen, obs. form of *peasen*, pl. of PEASE.

paytamine (ˈpeɪtəmaɪn). *Chem.* [f. *Payta* + AMINE.] An amorphous alkaloid, obtained from *Payta-bark*, a pale variety of cinchona bark, shipped from Payta in Peru. So **paytine** (ˈpeɪtaɪn), a crystallizable alkaloid obtained with paytamine.

1875 WATTS *Dict. Chem.* 2nd Suppl. 347 Paytine, $C^{21}H^{24}N^{2}O$...has a bitter taste... From alcohol it crystallises in beautiful colourless rhombic crystals. **1879** *Ibid.* 3rd Suppl. 497 *Paytine*, $C_{21}H_{20}N_2O.H_2O$... *Paytamine* is an amorphous alkaloid accompanying paytine.

payte, payten, paytener, paytent: see PATE[2], PATEN, PAUTENER *sb.*[1], PATENT.

paytrel, -ell(e, etc., var. PEITREL, POITREL.

†**payttrure.** *Obs.* Altered form of PEITREL, q.v.

13.. *Gaw. & Gr. Knt.* 168 Þe pendauntes of his payttrure, þe proude cropure,..& alle þe metail anamayld was þenne. *Ibid.* 601 Þe apparayl of þe payttrure, & of þe proude skyrtez.

payuese, payze, obs. var. PAVIS, PEISE.

pazan, variant of PASAN, the bezoar goat.

Pazand (ˈpɑːzænd). Also **Pazend.** [f. Pers. *pā-zand* interpretation of the Zend: see ZEND-AVESTA.] A transcription of, or the method of transcribing Persian sacred texts from Pahlavi (see PAHLAVI *a.* and *sb.*) into the script of the Avesta. Freq. *attrib.*, designating this mode of transcription.

[**1700** T. HYDE *Hist. Relig. Vet. Pers.* xxvi. 338 Literæ.. quæ..apud incolas vulgò audiunt..Character Zundicus, vel si Anglicè loquimur, the Zund Character; à quo aliquantulum differt Character Pazendicus.] **1772** J. SWINTON in *Phil. Trans. R. Soc.* LXI. 354 It not a little resembles that endued with the power of the short A, deduced from the Zend and Pazend, by Dr. Hyde. **1871** E. W. WEST (*title*) The book of the Mainyo-i-Khard. The Pazand and Sanskrit text... With an English translation, a glossary of the Pazand text.., a sketch of Pazand grammar, and an introduction. **1928** E. G. BROWNE *Lit. Hist. Persia* I. ii. 77 Hence the so-called Pâzend and Pârsí books, which are merely transcriptions of Pahlawí books into the unambiguous Avestic and Arabic characters respectively, all the Huzvárish, or Aramaic, words being replaced by their Persian equivalents, or supposed equivalents. *Ibid.* 81 Just as *Zend* is the 'explanation' of an Avestic text in Pahlawí, so is *Pázend* (= *paiti-zainti*) a 're-explanation' of a Pahlawí text by transcribing it into a character less ambiguous than the Pahlawí script, and substituting the proper Persian words for their respective Huzvárish equivalents. When the Avesta character is used for this transcription, the result is called 'Pázend'; when the Persian (*i.e.*, the Arabic) character is adopted, the term 'Pársí' is often substituted. In either case the product is simply an archaic or archaistic...form of 'modern' (*i.e.* post-Muhammadan) Persian, from which the whole Aramaic element has disappeared. **1934** *Trans. Philol. Soc. 1933* 56 There are reasons for believing that these Pāzand writers were active in the Central region from Kāšān to Yazd and Kirmān. **1939** L. H. GRAY *Foundations of Lang.* 319 This 'Book-Pāhlavī'..falls into two types: *Huzvarišn*, in which Semitic (Syriac) words are written, but with Iranian inflexions..; and *Pāzand*, which uses only Iranian. **1948** D. DIRINGER *Alphabet* 308 The most famous of the Persian indigenous scripts is the Pazand or Avesta alphabet, the script of the sacred Persian literature. **1968** M. BOYCE in *Handbuch der Orientalistik* IV. i. 47 It survives only in a mediaeval Sanskrit version, and in Pazand i.e. Middle Persian transcribed in mediaeval times out of Pahlavi into Avestan script. **1968** P. VAN POPTA-HOPE tr. *Rypka's Hist. Iranian Lit.* 34 In the Arab period Iranian Zoroastrian writers turned to new alphabets and attempted to use them for writing down Middle Persian texts phonetically. The writings in the Avestan alphabet are called *Pāzand*, those in the Arabic consonantal writing are called Pārsī. **1972** W. B. LOCKWOOD *Panorama Indo-European Lang.* xii. 235 Sometimes Pahlavi texts are found transcribed into vocalised Avestan script.., such texts being called Pazend.

†**pazar**, obs. form of BEZOAR [Pers. *pād-zahr*] q.v. **a.** = BEZOAR 2. **b.** = BEZOAR 3. (In the latter use app. confounded with *pazan*, PASAN.)

1563 WARDE tr. *Alexis' Secr.* II. 7 b, Two graines of Pazar, whiche is a stone that commeth out of Portugal, and is grene & tawnie. **1613** PURCHAS *Pilgrimage* (1614) 508 The Bezar-stones are likewise taken out of the maw of a Persian or Indian Goat, which the Persians call *Pazar*. **1774** GOLDSM. *Nat. Hist.* (1776) III. 75 The word bezoar is supposed to take its name either from the pazan or pazar, which is the animal that produces it; or from a word in the Arabic language, which signifies antidote, or counter-poison.

pazaree, variant of PASSAREE.

pazazz, pazzazz, varr. PIZZAZZ.

pazil, dial., etc. var. PARCEL.

pe, variant of PEE *Obs.*, coarse coat, pea-coat.

pea[1] (piː). [A new singular evolved from the earlier sing. and pl. *pease*, by writing this *peas* and treating the final -*s* as a plural inflexion. For earlier history see PEASE.]

I. The seed or plant.

1. a. The round seed of *Pisum sativum* (see 2), a well-known article of food.

Also occasionally applied to the similar seeds of other leguminous plants (see 3), esp. when used for food.

1611 BEAUM. & FL. *King & No K.* II. ii. (1619) 30 Did not his Maiestie say, he had brought vs home Peaes for our money? **1666** BOYLE *Orig. Formes & Qual.* VII. iii. (1667) 170 A little vegetable bud..not so big..as a Pea. **1677** PLOT *Oxfordsh.* v. §85 Much smaller, not exceeding the Rouncival pea..in bigness. **1711** GREENWOOD *Eng. Gram.* 49 Some words are used in both numbers, as Sheep..Pease..but it is better to say in the Singular *Pea*, in the Plural *Peas*. **1727** BAILEY vol. II, *Peas-cod*, the shell or husk of a pea. **1851** BORROW *Lavengro* lviii, To find the pea, which I put under one of my thimbles. **1866** *Treas. Bot.* 282 The peculiar form of these peas [seeds of the chick-pea] has given rise to the specific name of the plant *arietinum*.

b. ***green peas***: peas gathered for food while still green, soft, and unripe.

[*c* **1440–1833**: see PEASE *sb.* B 2 b.] **1789** *Bath Jrnl.* 8 June, Green peas begin now to come to market. **1883** LADY GREGORY in *Fortn. Rev.* 1 Oct. 575 A liberal dish of green peas.

c. Proverbial phr. ***as like as two peas***, etc.

[**1580, 1681**: see PEASE *sb.* B 2.] **1778** MISS BURNEY *Evelina* xxi, As like..as two peas are to one another. *a* **1845** BARHAM *Ingol. Leg.* Ser. III. *Bros. Birchington* xiii, A Brother, As like him in form as one pea's like another. **1864–8** BROWNING *Jas. Lee's Wife* IX. iii, We both should be like as pea and pea. **1889** MISS TYTLER *Buried Diamonds* xix, As like papa as two peas.

d. In the West Indies and southern U.S.A., a name for the seeds of various other legumes, including the red pea, *Vigna unguiculata*, and the Gungo pea, *Cajanus cajan*; esp. in phrase ***pea(s) and rice***, the name of a local dish.

1928 FREEMAN & WILLIAMS *Useful & Ornamental Plants Trinidad & Tobago* (ed. 2) 166 Vigna sesquipedalis... Yard Bean. Bodi... The young pods are edible as French beans and also the ripe dry beans. V[igna] sinensis. Cow Pea. Black Eye Pea. **1930** B. S. RHETT *200 Yrs. Charleston Cooking* 59 (*heading*) Peas and rice pilau. **1969** *Daily Tel.* 11 Jan. 14/1 [In Jamaica] 'peas' are not peas at all but kidney beans. **1970** M. SLATER *Caribbean Cooking* 32 'Peas and Rice'..is cooked on every island. **1971** *Bahamas* XXIII. III. 33/1 Being a true native son [of the Bahamas], Sidney Poitier sometimes has irresistible urges to devour such disastrous delicacies as pea 'n' rice or pea soup. **1972** C. D. ADAMS *Flowering Plants of Jamaica* 364 Vigna..cultivated in many varieties; native of tropical Asia; Black Eye Pea, Cow Pea, etc. **1973** *Advocate-News* (Barbados) 22 Jan. 13/3 (Advt.), Today's menu: Fried and boiled chicken, . . dry peas or split peas and rice.

e. [In allusion to the pea used by a thimble-rigger.] A favourite; a horse likely to win. *Sporting slang* (*obs.* exc. *Austral.*). Also *transf.* someone in a favoured or favourable position, a person with authority (*Austral. colloq.*).

1888 *Sporting Life* 11 Dec. 4/4 Sweeny. . forced the fighting, and was still the pea when 'Time!' was called. **1891** *Licensed Victuallers' Gaz.* 20 Mar. 187/3 Well, Albert, now what is the pea? we asked, hurrying towards the paddock. **1900** E. WELLS *Chestnuts* xxiii. 227 Informed me that the right pea for the race was 'L'Abbesse de Jouarre'. **1911** E. DYSON *Benno* xvi. 206 Mr. Dickson. . ran his eye down the card and chanced it. 'Dandy's the P,' he said. 'Put yer whole week's wash on Dandy, 'n hold me responsible if the goods ain't delivered.' **1953** BAKER *Australia Speaks* v. 118 Other expressions used by racing fans include: *pea*, a horse that is being ridden to win, especially when there is a doubt about the genuineness of other runners. **1958** F. HARDY *Four-Legged Lottery* xxv. 190 I've got the tip about it. Old Dapper Dan earwigged at the track. Swordsman is the pea. **1969** M. CALTHORPE *Defectors* iii. 17 'For the time being, I'm satisfied.' 'You're the pea,' Mick said. **1973** A. BUZO *Rooted* III. iii. 92 He's had his eye on her for some time, you know, but I'm the pea, she said. **1974** *Sun-Herald* (Sydney) 1 Sept. 15 The usual assumption has been that the Social Security Minister, Mr Hayden, 41, would move into the Treasury. . . Recent events have cast some doubts on that. The Deputy Prime Minister and Overseas Trade Minister, Dr Cairns, now seems the 'pea' for any change at the Treasury.

2. a. The plant *Pisum sativum*, a hardy climbing leguminous annual, which has long been cultivated in many varieties; it has large papilionaceous flowers succeeded by long pods each containing a row of round seeds (see 1). Usually distinguished as *pea-plant*.

1699 EVELYN *Acetaria* 136 Another Process for the raising early Peas and Beans. **1731-3** MILLER *Gard. Dict.* s.v. *Pisum*, 1. *Pisum hortense majus*. . the greater Garden Pea with white Flowers and Fruit. *a* **1770** M. BRUCE or LOGAN *Cuckoo* v, What time the pea puts on the bloom. **1871** BLACKMORE *Maid of Sker* xliii, To go away from my home and garden. . with no one to. . sow a row of peas.

b. With defining words distinguishing species and varieties. (In quot. *a* 1812 = SWEET PEA.)

1707 MORTIMER *Husb.* 106 The common sort of white Pea doth best in a light Land that is somewhat rich. **1731-3** MILLER *Gard. Dict.* s.v. *Pisum*, The Species are [sixteen]. . 2. . Hot-spur Pea. . . 3. . Dwarf Pea. . . 6. . Sickle Pea. . . 8. . Green Rouncival Pea. 9. . Grey Pea. . . 11. . Rose Pea. . . 14. . Union Pea. 15. . English Sea Pea. 16. . Pig Peas. **1765** *Mus. Rust.* III. Index, Grey Peas not to be harrowed in on a chalky soil. *a* **1812** WOLCOT (P. Pindar) *Ode on Crim. Con.*, The fragrant pea with blooms so thick, That curls her tendrils round a rotten stick. **1858** HOMANS *Cycl. Comm.* s.v. *Peas*, The common garden pea (*Pisum sativum*), and the common gray or field pea (*Pisum arvense*), are the most generally cultivated. **1882** *Garden* 15 July 38/2 From the Isle of Wight comes the pretty Blue Pea. **1884** MILLER *Plant-n.*, *French-Peas*, an old name for garden Peas.

3. Applied with defining words to leguminous plants more or less akin to the common pea: as **Angola pea** = *Congo pea*; **beach-pea** = *sea-pea*; **butterfly-pea**, (*a*) *Clitoria mariana* of S. America and India; (*b*) *spurred butterfly-pea*, the genus *Centrosema* (chiefly American), having a short spur on the standard of the corolla; **Congo pea**, a variety (*bicolor*) of *Cajanus indicus* (see CAJAN), with yellow flowers marked with crimson; **desert-pea**, *Clianthus dampieri*, a native of the desert parts of Australia, with bright scarlet flowers (Miller *Plant-n.* 1884); **earth-pea**, *Lathyrus amphicarpus* of Syria, which bears its pods under ground (*Treas. Bot.* 1866); **earth-nut pea**, *Lathyrus macrorhizus* (J. Lee *Introd. Bot.* (1768) App. 322); **Egyptian pea**, the CHICK-PEA, *Cicer arietinum*; **everlasting pea** (see EVERLASTING A. 4 b), *Lathyrus latifolius*, a variety of *L. sylvestris*, cultivated for the beauty of its variously-coloured flowers; also extended to other species resembling this; **flat pea**, the Australian genus *Platylobium*, from its flat pods (*Treas. Bot.*); **hoary pea**, the genus *Tephrosia*, which has leaves covered with a grey down (Miller 1884); **meadow-pea**, the Meadow Vetchling, *Lathyrus pratensis* (ibid.); **milk-pea**, the N. American genus *Galactia* (*Treas. Bot.*); **no-eye pea**, a variety (*flavus*) of *Cajanus indicus* (see CAJAN), with pure yellow flowers; **painted lady pea** (see PAINTED 4); **poison-pea** = *Swainson pea*; **sea-pea, sea-side pea**, *Lathyrus maritimus* (*Pisum maritimum*), a sea-coast species rare in England; **sensitive pea**, *Cassia nictitans* of N. America, with sensitive leaves; also *C. chamæcrista*, partridge-pea (PARTRIDGE 5 c); **Swainson pea**, the Australian genus *Swainsona* (Miller 1884); **sweet-scented pea** = SWEET PEA; **Tangier pea**, *Lathyrus tingitanus*; **tuberous(-rooted) pea** = HEATH-PEA (Miller 1884); **winged pea**, the genus *Tetragonolobus*, having quadrangular winged pods; **wood-pea**, (*a*) *Lathyrus sylvestris*, a British wild plant, the original of the everlasting pea; (*b*) = HEATH-PEA. See also CHICH, CHICK-PEA, CHICKLING[2], COW-*pea*, GLORY-*pea*, HEART-*pea*, HEATH-PEA, MOUSE-*pea*, PARTRIDGE-*pea*, PIGEON-*pea*, SWEET PEA.

1783 JUSTAMOND tr. *Raynal's Hist. Indies* V. 319 This shrub is called the *Angola pea. **1866** *Treas. Bot.* 300 The *Butterfly Pea, *C[litoria] Mariana*, . . is a slender twining plant with. . flowers of a light blue colour. *Ibid.* 189 *C[ajanus] indicus*. . is now naturalised and cultivated in the West Indies, [etc.]. . . The variety *bicolor*. . is called the *Congo pea in Jamaica. The variety *flavus*. . is called the No-eye pea. *Ibid.* 282 *C[icer] arietinum* is the Chick-pea, or *Egyptian Pea of the English. **1597** GERARDE *Herbal* 1054 The first is called *Lathyrus*, . . in English *Pease euerlasting, great wilde Tare, and Cichling. **1705** Everlasting pease [see EVERLASTING A. 4 b]. **1741** *Compl. Fam.-Piece* II. iii. 379 Tangier Pea, Everlasting Pea, and sweet-scented Pea. **1866** *No-eye Pea [see *Congo pea*]. **1633** JOHNSON *Gerarde's Herbal* Table Eng. Names, Norfolke *sea Pease. **1731-3** MILLER *Gard. Dict.* s.v. *Pisum*, English Sea Pea. . is found wild upon the Shoar in Sussex, and several other Counties. **1832** *Veg. Subst. Food* 180 The Sea-Pea is a native of this country. . . During a famine in. . 1555, the application of the seeds. . as an article of food was extensively. . practised. **1731** MILLER *Gard. Dict.*, *Lathyrus distoplatyphyllos*. . commonly called *Sweet-scented Peas. **1741** *Compl. Fam.-Piece* II. iii. 362 Hardy annual Flowers, as. . *Tangier Peas, sweet-scented Peas. **1785** MARTYN *Rousseau's Bot.* xxv. (1794) 357 Tangier Pea, another of the biflorus section. **1753** CHAMBERS *Cycl. Supp.* App. s.v., **Winged-Pea*, a name by which some call the Lotus. **1866** *Treas. Bot.* 1135 *T[etragonolobus] edulis* or *purpureus*, the Winged Pea, a native of Sicily. **1633** JOHNSON *Gerarde's Herbal* 1237 *Astragalus syluaticus*, *Wood Pease, or Heath Pease. **1711** PETIVER in *Phil. Trans.* XXVII. 386 Its Flowers and Pods resemble our Wood-Pea. **1861** MISS PRATT *Flower. Pl.* II. 129 *Vicia Orobus*. . . This Wood-vetch or Wood-pea.

II. Something small and round like the seed.

4. The eggs, roe, or spawn of certain fishes.

1758 *Descr. Thames* 172 The Female [Salmon] discharges her Pea or Spawne. **1773** *Phil. Trans.* LXIV. 120 A roe, which is here called a pea. **1802** SAMPSON *Statist. Surv. Londonderry* 330 The ova, or pea [of salmon], continue in the sand or gravel for three months.

5. a. Applied to a small point of flame. Cf. PEAK *sb.*[4]

1890 BARING-GOULD *Pennycomequicks* 43 There was gas in the room, turned down to a pea when not required for light.

b. = *pea-coal* (see sense 7); *pl.*, coals of a very small size.

1880 [see EGG *sb.* 3 b]. **1886** J. BARROWMAN *Gloss. Scotch Mining Terms* 50 *Peas*, coal a grade smaller than nuts. **1905** A. S. CUNNINGHAM *Rambles in Scoonie & Wemyss* 260 Most of the trebles, nuts, beans and peas produced at Wemyss colliery are treated by the washer. **1930** *Engineering* 5 Dec. 708/1 The employment of anthracite duffs in place of washed grains and peas. **1949** *Black Diamond* 26 Feb. 54/3 Prices range as follows: . . nut and pea, $3.50-$4.50.

6. See ISSUE-*pea*, ORANGE-*pea*.

III. 7. *attrib.* and *Comb.*, as ***pea-bloom*** (also *attrib.* in reference to form or colour), ***-blossom***, ***-crop***, ***-field***, ***-flour***, ***-hull*** (HULL *sb.*[1] 1), ***patch***, ***-picker***, ***-picking***, ***-plant***, ***-pudding***, ***-rick***, ***-root***, ***-seed***; also ***pea-like***, ***-picking***, ***-sized*** adjs.; **pea-bean** (see BEAN *sb.* 3); **pea-beetle** = *pea-bug*; **pea-blower** = *pea-shooter*; **pea-bone**, the pisiform bone of the wrist, resembling a pea in shape and size; **pea-bough**, the same as *pea-stick*; **pea-bug**, a small coleopterous insect (*Bruchus pisi*), a native of North America, now found also in Southern Europe and Britain, which infests peas, to which its larva is very destructive; also called ***pea-beetle***, ***-chafer***, ***-weevil***; **pea-bush**, an Australian heath-like leguminous shrub, *Burtonia scabra*, with purple papilionaceous flowers; **pea-chafer** = *pea-bug*; **pea-coal** (*U.S.*), coal in very small pieces like peas (Raymond *Mining Gloss.* 1881); **pea-cod** = PEASECOD (*obs.* exc. *dial.*); **pea coffee** *U.S. obs.*, a beverage made by boiling roasted peas; **pea-comb**, a triple comb occurring in some varieties of the domestic fowl (from its fancied resemblance to a pea-blossom); **pea-combed** *a.*, of poultry, having a pea-comb; **pea-crab**, a small crab of the genus *Pinnotheres*, commensally inhabiting the shell of a bivalve mollusc, as a mussel or oyster; **pea-dodger** *Austral.* = BOWLER[3]; **pea-dove**, a species of pigeon, *Zenaida amabilis*, found in W. Indies and Florida; **pea-dropper**, a contrivance for sowing peas singly (Knight *Dict. Mech.* 1875); **pea-finch**, local (midland) name of the chaffinch; **pea-flour**, flour made of peas, pease-meal; **pea gravel**, gravel consisting of particles similar in size to peas; **pea-green** *a.* and *sb.*, (of) a colour like that of fresh green peas, a nearly pure but not deep green; **pea-grit** (see quots.); **pea-gun** = *pea-shooter*; **pea-hook**, a hook for reaping peas; **pea-lamp**, a very small, round electric lamp such as is often used as an indicator light; **pea-maggot**, a caterpillar which infests peas, the larva of the *pea-moth* (Ogilvie 1882); **pea-make** (*dial.*) = *pease-make* (see PEASE *sb.* 5); **pea-meal** = *pease-meal* (ibid.); **pea-measle**, a 'measle' or hydatid which infests the rabbit and other animals, being the larva of the tapeworm of the dog; **pea-moth**, the larva of the moth *Cydia nigricana*, which feeds on peas; **pea-ore** (see quot.); **pea-rake** (see quot.); **pea-rifle**, a rifle with a thick barrel and a small round bullet like a pea; **pea-rise**, a branch of the pea-plant, esp. as a heraldic bearing; **pea-shell** = PEA-POD; **pea-sheller**, (*a*) one who 'shells' peas, i.e. takes them out of the pods; (*b*) an instrument for shelling peas; **pea-shod** *a.*, having peas in the shoes, as a pilgrim doing penance; **pea-shooter**, (*a*) a toy weapon, consisting of a long tube from which peas are shot by the force of the breath; ; (*b*) a person who shoots with this; so **pea-shooting** (whence **pea-shoot** *v.*); **pea-spawn** = sense 4; **pea-stake, pea-stick**, a stake or stick upon which a garden pea-plant is trained; **pea-straw**, the stalks and leaves of the pea-plant, used as fodder; **pea-stubble**, the stubble of pea-plants left standing after gathering the crop; **pea-urchin**, a very small species of sea-urchin of rounded form, *Echinocyamus pusillus*; **pea-viner**, a machine for picking, washing, and grading peas; **pea-weevil** = *pea-bug*. See also PEABERRY, PEA-FLOWER, PEANUT, PEA-POD, PEA-SOUP, PEASTONE, PEA-TREE, PEA-VINE.

1815 KIRBY & SP. *Entomol.* ii. (1818) I. 32 A cargo, or even a sample, of peas from North America might present us with that ravager of pulse, the *pea-beetle (*Bruchus Pisi*, L.). [**1675**: see *pease-bloom*, PEASE *sb.* 5.] **1763** MILLS *Pract. Husb.* III. 238 The flowers. . are of the *pea-bloom, or butterfly, kind. **1766** W. GORDON *Gen. Counting-ho.* 321, 1 piece peabloom [cloth]. [**1590**: see *pease-blossom*, PEASE *sb.* 5.] **1774** GOLDSM. *Nat. Hist.* I. 79 The delightful fragrance of their smell, somewhat resembling the *pea-blossom. **1821** W. IRVING in *Life & Lett.* (1864) II. 59 The three eldest boys kept the house in misery for two or three days by *pea-blowers. **1885** *St. James's Gaz.* 2 Jan. 6/1 'Branchy' pieces . . are sorted into '*pea-boughs' and fagot-wood. **1841** T. W. HARRIS *Insects Injur. Veget.* (1862) 62 This little insect. . the *Bruchus Pisi* of Linnæus. . , the. . pea-weevil, . . is better known in America by the incorrect name of *pea-bug. **1895** *Westm. Gaz.* 11 May 3/1 Another horror has supervened in the shape of a pea bug. . which attacks market gardens. **1884** MILLER *Plant-n.*, *Pea-bush, Burton's, *Burtonia scabra.* **1882** OGILVIE s.v., *Pea-beetle*. . . Called also *Pea-bug*, **Pea-chafer*, and *Pea-weevil.* **1778** H. BROOKE *Contending Bros.* II. ii, A mere niggardly good for nothing, with a heart as squeez'd and narrow as a young *peacod. **1819** SCOTT *Ivanhoe* xix, They are as like thine own, as one green pea-cod is to another. **1805** T. E. WHITE *Jrnl.* 14 July (1904) 24, I drank three or four cups of *pea coffee and then went to bed. **1818** 'A. BURTON' *Adventures J. Newcome* II. 112 Pea-coffee, Hurry-hush, and Chowder. **1851** H. MELVILLE *Moby Dick* I. ii. 14 The very spot for cheap lodgings, and the best of pea coffee. **1872-4** L. WRIGHT *Bk. Poultry* 247 This triple or *pea-comb has been found. . on the pure Malay breed. *Ibid.* 249 The comb—known as a pea-comb—is. . described as resembling three small combs joined into one, the centre one being higher than the two outside. **1868** DARWIN *Variation of Animals & Plants under Domestication* I. vii. 254 In some breeds the comb is double. . ; it is triple in the *pea-combed Brahmas. **1922** R. C. PUNNETT *Mendelism* (ed. 6) 32 The pea-combed bird contains the factor for pea but not that for rose. **1836** THOMPSON in *Entom. Mag.* III. 85 (*title*) The Metamorphoses and Natural History of the Pinotheres, or *Pea-Crabs. **1901** M. NEWBIGIN *Life by Seashore* x. 202 The tribe Catometopa. . includes the curious pea-crab, *Pinnotheres pisum*, found inside the bivalves. **1960** C. M. YONGE *Oysters* vii. 118 The hundred or so species of Pea Crabs, most of which inhabit the mantle-cavity of various species of bivalves. **1978** G. DURRELL *Garden of Gods* iv. 88 It was he. . who had got me the biggest clam shell in my collection and, moreover, with the two tiny parasitic pea-crabs still inside. **1732** W. ELLIS *Pract. Farmer* 39 This [weed] I cannot say will utterly destroy the *Pea-Crop, but will so cripple it, as not to be a quarter Value. **1805** R. W. DICKSON *Pract. Agric.* II. 583 Pea crops. **1844** H. STEPHENS *Bk. of Farm* II. 371 The produce of the pea-crop is either in abundance or a complete failure. **1933** *Bulletin* (Sydney) 5 Apr. 12/3 'Elizabeth Owen': . . the different terms applied to 'bowler' hats—I have also heard them called 'egg-boiler' and '*pea-dodgers'. **1959** BAKER *Drum* (1960) II. 133 *Peadodger*, a bowler hat. **1847** GOSSE *Birds Jamaica* 308 The *Pea-dove is frequently seen in the middle of dusty high-roads. **1860** —— *Romance Nat. Hist.* 17 The peadove from the neighbouring woods commenced her fivefold coo. [**1677** W. HUBBARD *Narr. Troubles with Indians in New-England* I. 24 If there were Indians in the Neck they should send them about a Peas-field not far off.] **1972** D. HASTON *In High Places* iii. 44 The trip was planned in the pubs of the *pea-fields of Kent, where we had been supplementing our meagre incomes. **1766** J. W. BAKER in *Compl. Farmer* s.v. *Turnip*, [The bullock] took kindly to the turnips; and on the sixteenth I began to give him, with his turnips, *pea-flower [= pea-flour]. **1881** Pea-flour [see FLADBROD, -BRÖD]. **1915** D. H. LAWRENCE *Rainbow* ii. 46 The vicar put pea-flower [*sic*] into the crocuses, for his bees to roll in. **1928** E. E. BAUER *Highway Materials* xii. 122 After the bituminous material has been applied, the entire surface must be covered with an application of *pea gravel. **1962** R. PAGE *Educ. Gardener* x. 277, I devised a very simple arrangement of areas of fine pea gravel and panels of grass. **1963** *Times* 16 Feb. 11/3 A bed of well weathered clinker ash, or small well washed pea gravel say 8 in. deep is placed on the floor of the greenhouse. **1973** C. WILLIAMS *Man on Leash* (1974) ix. 140 Bare planks. . and then another two steps down onto the grating crunch of pea gravel. **1752** FOOTE *Taste* II. Wks. 1799 I. 22 Japan of the *pea-green kind. **1861** L. L. NOBLE *Icebergs* 99 All the adjacent deep is a luminous pea-green. **1859-65** PAGE *Handbk. Geol. Terms*, **Pea-grit*, a coarse pisolitic limestone. . composed of concretionary bodies. **1885** *J. Phillips' Man. Geol.* I. 48 The Pea-grit at the base of the inferior Oolite in which the grains are as large as peas. **1823** SCOTT *Let. to Terry* 14 Feb. in *Lockhart*, The *pea gun principle. **1872** *Routledge's Ev. Boy's Ann.* July 454/2, I gave my pea-gun. [**1674–1769**: see *pease-hook*, PEASE *sb.* 5.] **1833** *Wauldby Farm Rep.* 110 in *Libr. Usef. Knowl., Husb.* III, They are cut down either with the scythe, or the *pea-hook. [**1377–1664**: see *pease-hull*, PEASE *sb.* 5.] **1717** RAMSAY *Elegy on Lucky Wood* v, Poor facers now may chew *pea-hools, Since Lucky's dead. **1855** ROBINSON *Whitby Gloss., Pea-hulls*, the shells of green peas. [**1629–1725**: see *pease-like*, PEASE *sb.* 5.] **1938** G. H. SEWELL *Amateur Film-Making* ii. 20 The glowing filament of a *pea lamp. **1950** *Electronic Engin.* XXII. 413/1 The output of this amplifier was used to light a pea-lamp mounted alongside the microphone. **1774** GOLDSM. *Nat. Hist.* VI. 163 The chrystaline humour in fishes.., being that little hard *pea-like substance which is found in their eyes after boiling. **1866** *Treas. Bot.* 248 *Centrosema*... The large and elegant pea-like flowers. **1834** *New Monthly Mag.* XLII. 421 The poachers had armed themselves with *peamakes (a long staff with a curved knife at the end, with which peas are cut). [**1820–**: see *pease-meal*, PEASE *sb.* 5.] **1830** *Kyle Farm Rep.* 45 in *Libr. Usef. Knowl., Husb.* III, Chaff or cut hay..enriched with a few potatoes, or a little *pea-meal. **1879** J. WRIGHTSON in *Cassell's Techn. Educ.* IV. 352/2 The sides and hams are powdered over with pea-meal, and are then hung in the smoke. [**1859** S. J. WILKINSON *Brit. Tortrices* 230 The larva [of *Endopisa nigricana*] feeds on the growing and unripe seeds of the Pea.] **1881** E. A. ORMEROD *Man. Injurious Insects* 131 *Pea Moth. .. The caterpillars of this Moth cause the 'worm-eaten' or 'maggoty' Peas often found in old pods. **1931** G. S. CHAPPELL *Gardener's Friend* 153 The lupines..have inherited from their lowly ancestry an appeal to..wire-worms and pea moths. **1964** F. G. W. & M. G. JONES *Pests of Field Crops* v. 93 The pea moth has become increasingly important with the intensive cultivation of peas in certain areas of Britain. **1972** *Arable Farmer* Feb. 55/2 Folithion (insecticide for pea moth control from Bayer Agrochem). **1840** W. HUMBLE *Dict. Geol., etc.*, **Pea ore*..is the pisiform iron-stone of Kirwan. **1834** *Knickerbocker* III. 35 Didn't I turn that pied heifer of yourn into my *pea patch. **1863** 'G. HAMILTON' *Gala-Days* 34 No premonition floated over from that adjoining pea-patch. **1941** J. STUART *Men of Mountains* 120 Tear off the damn Dingus silk shirts..for to make skeery-cows out'n for the pea patch! **1889** *Pall Mall G.* 17 Aug. 3/1, I came across a party of *pea-pickers. **1898** J. ARCH *Story of Life* x. 250 *Peapicking gangs were generally very large. **1901** *Daily Chron.* 7 Aug. 7/7 Instances in which children had started to work pea picking as early as two o'clock in the morning, and then had put in a full day at school. [**1758–**: see *pease-pudding*, PEASE *sb.* 5.] **1844** H. STEPHENS *Bk. of Farm* II. 239 An excellent leg of pickled pork, served with *pea-pudding. **1875** KNIGHT *Dict. Mech.*, **Pea-rake*, a rake adapted for gathering the field pea. [**1530**: see *pease-rick*, PEASE *sb.* 5.] **1766** J. W. BAKER in *Compl. Farmer* s.v. *Turnep*, I gave my sheep access to some *pea-ricks. **1862** *Catal. Internat. Exhib.* II. xi. 21 *Pea rifles for rabbit and sea-fowl shooting. **1780** EDMONDSON *Her.* II. Gloss., **Pea-rise*, a name given by Heralds to a Pea-stalk leaved and blossomed. **1744** W. ELLIS *Mod. Husbandman* Feb. v. 29 When Horse-bean and *Pea-seed are to be sown together..the stated Allowance..is..two-third Parts Beans, and one-third Part Pease. **1946** *Nature* 31 Aug. 293/1 The fungus was grown in various modifications of Czapek-Dox medium with addition of manganese sulphate, in some cases with pea-seed extract. **1960** *Farmer & Stockbreeder* 16 Feb. 97/1 It is in practice difficult to get the fertilizer below the peas without forcing the pea-seed coulters into a too-shallow position. **1755** JOHNSON, *Peascod*, **Peashell*, the husk that contains peas. **1875** KNIGHT *Dict. Mech.*, **Pea-sheller*, an implement for taking garden pease from their pods. **1899** *Westm. Gaz.* 31 May 3/2 The pea-shellers look as if they have been at work for hours. **1902** *Ibid.* 29 Sept. 3/1 At the Exhibition was a pea-sheller which will shell fourteen tons in ten hours. **1882** SOPHIA E. DE MORGAN *Mem. A. de M.* 8 The two pilgrims who went *pea-shod to Loretto. **1861** KINGSLEY *Ravenshoe* xxxvi, Dick Ferrers..carried a peashooter, and *pea-shot the noses of the leading horses of a dragful of Plungers, which followed them. **1899** A. LUBBOCK in *Daily News* 2 June 8/4 It was a favourite pastime,..for the boys, whenever the room was a bit dark, to pea-shoot at his bald, shining head. **1803** J. RUSSELL *Jrnl.* 23 Sept. in S. Walpole *Life Ld. John Russell* (1889) I. i. 6 The boys play at hoops, peg-tops, and *pea-shooters. **1833** *Boy's Week-Day Bk.* 210 When you shoot a pea through your pea-shooter, it is quite as well to know that the natives of Macouslie shoot arrows in the same manner. **1857** HUGHES *Tom Brown* I. iv, With their *pea-shooters, and long whips. **1883** 'ANNIE THOMAS' *Mod. Housewife* 100, I..became the object of the attentions of a party of young pea-shooters fresh from the excitement of a 'wake'. **1873** W. CORY *Lett. & Jrnls.* (1897) 332 Two girls within *pea-shooting.. distance. **1899** *Allbutt's Syst. Med.* VIII. 773 *Pea-sized, smooth, white bald spots. **1840** *Cottager's Man.* 41 in *Libr. Usef. Knowl., Husb.* III, Onions protected..by *pea-stakes or bushes, from being injured by frosty winds in the spring. [*c* **1325–**: see *pease-straw*, PEASE *sb.* 5.] **1745** J. MACSPARRAN *Letter Bk.* (1899) 27 Harry is come home..& has bro't home *Pea Sticks. **1855** DELAMER *Kitchen Gard.* (1861) 170 Secure a supply of pea-sticks for early spring. **1971** *Country Life* 2 Sept. 580/2 Most of the cut wood has its uses with the seasonal demand for pea sticks and bean poles. **1973** *Daily Tel.* 7 July 7/8 What can we stake our herbaceous plants with ..now that you can no longer get pea sticks? **1807** VANCOUVER *Agric. Devon* (1813) 184 The small *pea-straw or haulm, is commonly used as rack-meat for horses. **1886** C. SCOTT *Sheep-Farming* 171 Give them..as much clover and green pea straw as they will eat up. [**1523**: see *pease-stubble*, PEASE *sb.* 5.] **1807** VANCOUVER *Agric. Devon* (1813) 184 The *pea-stubbles are dressed with six or eight hogsheads of lime per acre, and sown with wheat. **1843** EMBLETON in *Proc. Berw. Nat. Club* II. No. 11. 51 Green *Pea Urchin. **1862** ANSTED *Channel Isl.* II. ix. (ed. 2) 237 The pea-urchin is particularly common in Herm. **1841** *Pea-weevil [see *pea-bug*]. **1882** *Garden* 8 Apr. 231/2 The common Pea weevil.. is very injurious to young Pea and Bean plants. **1943** C. CROW *Great Amer. Customer* 179 The *pea viner is perhaps the most marvelous of them all. Vines fresh from the field are fed into the robot which hulls the peas, grades them as to size, and sends them on their way to the cooker. **1952** J. W. DAY *New Yeomen of Eng.* ii. 32 This giant pea-viner.. deals with a ton of peas an hour. It picks them from the vines, washes, and grades them.

†**pea**[2]. *Obs. rare.* [A parallel form of *paa*, PO, OE. *páwa* and *péa* peacock: in late use perhaps deduced from the compounds: see PEA-CHICK, PEACOCK, PEAFOWL, PEAHEN.] A peafowl.

a **1000** *Phœnix* 312 Se fuȝel is on hiwe..onlicost pean. **1658** tr. *Porta's Nat. Magic* II. xiv. 46 The Indian-hen, being mixt of a Cock and a Pea, though the shape be liker to a Pea than a Cock.

pea[3] (piː). Also pee. [Said to be shortened from *peak*: cf. PEAK *sb.*[2] 4 c.] The peak or bill of the fluke of an anchor.

1833 *Penny Cycl.* I. 505/1 The bill or peak. (*Note*, Seamen by custom drop the k in *peak* and *fluke*, which they pronounce *pea* and *flue*.) *c* **1860** H. STUART *Seaman's Catech.* 53 The parts of an anchor. The ring or shackle, the shank, crown, arms, palm, pee or bill, and stock. **1885** *Times* 3 Dec. 3/4 The pea of the fluke had penetrated.

pea[4]. *local.* [prob. shortened from *pease*, *peis*, PEISE, weight, mistaken for a plural: cf. history of PEA[1].] The sliding weight used on a steelyard, safety-valve, etc.

1761 *N. Jersey Archives* XX. 529 To be sold..a large quantity of old refuse cast Iron,..Sash-weights, Stove-plates, Steelyard-peas, &c. **1838** HOLLOWAY *Dict. Provincialisms*, *Pea*... The weight which is used in weighing anything with the steel-yards. *Hants.* **1847–78** in HALLIWELL. **1874** J. RICHARDS *Mech. Humour* 43 The boilers..had a single safety-valve..with a large rectangular block of cast iron as a weight, or 'pea', as it was termed.

†**pea** (piː), *int.* ? *Obs.* An exclamation of contempt; = pooh!

1608 MIDDLETON *Mad World* I. ii. B ij b, Oh fie, fie, wife! Pea, pea, pea, pea, how haue you lost your time?

peaberry (ˈpiːbɛrɪ). [f. PEA[1] + BERRY *sb.*[1]] Name for the single round seed of the coffee-plant, occurring towards the end of the branches, through abortion of one of the usual two seeds in the fruit.

The peaberries have a higher commercial value, and are sifted out from the ordinary beans.

1879 SPON *Encycl. Arts, Manuf.*, etc. I. 691 The 'beans', usually a pair of oval, plano-convex seeds, though sometimes there is but one seed, called, from its shape, 'peaberry'. **1893** SIR G. WATTS *Dict. Econ. Prod. India* s.v., There are three commercial types as to form: Mocha, small round peaberry; Bourbon, pointed and medium-sized; and Martinique, large and flattened.

pea-bird, pee-bird. A local name for the Wryneck, from its note.

1838 MARY HOWITT *Birds & Flowers, Cuckoo* i. 'Pee! pee! pee!' says the merry Pee-bird. **1885** SWAINSON *Prov. Names Brit. Birds* 103 Wryneck (*Jynx torquilla*)..Pea bird. From its sharp utterance of the word 'pea-pea'.

peable, obs. form of PEBBLE.

Peabody (ˈpiːbɒdɪ). *U.S.* The name Peabody used *absol.* or *attrib.* in **Peabody bird** to designate the white-throated sparrow, *Zonotrichia albicollis*, whose call is said to resemble 'Sam Peabody, Peabody, Peabody'.

1865 E. A. SAMUELS in *Rep. Comm. Agric. 1864* (U.S. Dept. Agric.) 422 White-throated Sparrow—Peabody Bird —Wheat Bird... This beautiful sparrow arrives in Massachusetts by the first week in April. **1903** *N. Y. Even. Post* (Sat. Suppl.) 24 Oct. 1/1 That lovely bird, the white-throated sparrow, which under the name of 'Peabody bird' is well known in the North. **1917** W. P. EATON *Green Trails* 16 All day long in this pasture the Peabodies, or White-throated sparrows, sing their flutelike call. **1939** R. T. PETERSON *Field Guide Birds East of Rockies* 159 Song, several clear, pensive whistled notes, easily imitated. The White-throat is often called the 'Peabody bird' by New Englanders who fancy these whistled notes sound like Old Sam Peabody, Peabody, Peabody. **1940** E. T. SETON *Trail of Artist-Naturalist* 224 The night singer of the Assiniboine, was neither more nor less than the white-throated sparrow, the Peabody bird of New England, the nightingale of the farther north. **1964** A. WETMORE et al. *Song & Garden Birds N. Amer.* 369/2 The Peabody bird is in best voice in his summer home.

peace (piːs), *sb.* Forms: 2–4 pais, 2–6 pes, (3–5 pays, peys, 3–6 peis, 4 payes, 4–5 payse, pese, pees, *Sc.* and *north.* pess), 4–6 pece, (5 peese), 5–6 peas, pease, (pesse, *Sc.* peice, 5–7 peax, 6 *Sc.* peiss, pace), 6– peace. [Early ME. *pais*, a. OF. *pais* (11th c. in Littré), mod.F. *paix* (= Pr. *patz*, Sp., Pg. *paz*, It. *pace*):—L. *pac-em* (nom. *pax*) peace. The vowel has passed through *ai*, *ei*, *ê*, to *ea* (aɪ, ɛː, eː, iː), final *-ce* represents earlier final *-s* as in *advice*, *mice*, etc.]

I. 1. a. Freedom from, or cessation of, war or hostilities; that condition of a nation or community in which it is not at war with another.

1297 R. GLOUC. (Rolls) 1322 Þe prinse..nis to preisi noȝt þat in time of worre as a lomb is boþe mek and milde And in time of pes as leon boþe cruel and wilde. **1375** BARBOUR *Bruce* I. 80 At that tyme was pess and rest Betwyx Scotland and Ingland. **1484** CAXTON *Fables of Æsop* II. viii, After grete werre cometh good pees. *c* **1489** —— *Blanchardyn* i. 11 The Right happy wele of peas flowrid..in alle Cristen realmes. **1535** COVERDALE *Ecclus.* xlvii. 16 Because of his peace he was beloued. **1594** SHAKS. *Rich. III*, I. i. 24 In this weake piping time of Peace. **1652** MILTON *Sonn. Cromwell*, Yet much remaines To conquer still; peace hath her victories No less renownd then warr. **1748** GRAY *Alliance Educ. & Govt.* 41 Fix and improve the polish'd Arts of Peace. **1804** MRQ. WELLESLEY in Owen *Desp.* (1877) 443 Peace is the fairest fruit of victory. **1874** GREEN *Short Hist.* ix. § 10. 713 In vain..Walpole battled..against the cry for war... He stood alone in his desire for peace.

b. (With article.) A ratification or treaty of peace between two powers previously at war. (†Also, formerly, a temporary cessation of hostilities, a truce.) In *Hist.* often defined by *of* with the name of the place at which it was ratified.

c **1400** *Laud Troy Bk.* 17536 He..bad hem mak Be-twene hem of Grece—iff thei moste—A fynal pes, what-so it coste. *c* **1400** *Destr. Troy* 10133 When paste was the pes,..stuernly þai foghtyn. *c* **1470** HENRY *Wallace* III. 333 With thair consent Wallace this pece has tayne,..till x moneth war gayne. **1560** DAUS tr. *Sleidane's Comm.* 344 b, Thambassadours of England and Fraunce..at the last conclude a peace. **1653** H. COGAN tr. *Pinto's Trav.* xiii. 42 He would not..break the peace, which his ancestors had made with the Christians of Malaca. **1713** SWIFT *Jrnl. to Stella* 10 Mar., They are not sure the peace will be signed next week. **1803** CANNING *Sp.* 24 May, Supporters and approvers of the Peace of Amiens. **1877** T. H. DYER *Mod. Europe* xl, The advisers of the Peace of Utrecht.

†**c.** With *possessive* or *of* (the peace *of* any one, *his* peace, etc.): A state or relation of peace, concord, and amity, with him; *esp.* peaceful recognition of the authority or claims, and acceptance of the protection, of a king or lord. *Obs.*

(Has affinities with senses 2, 4, 10 a.)

1297 R. GLOUC. (Rolls) 1857 And granted hym þat kinedom and þat pes of rome. **1375** BARBOUR *Bruce* VIII. 424 To the kingis pess he brocht The forest of selcryk all hale. *Ibid.* IX. 540 Sum of the men of the Cuntre Com till his pess, and maid him ath. *c* **1425** *Eng. Conq. Irel.* 86 Aftyr al þe trauayl þat þe kynge hadde,..come þe sonnes to þe fadyres pees, & maden asseth, falsly. *Ibid.* 92 Obren, the kynge of Thomon, ayeyne hys trouth & ayeyn the kynges pees, began to withdrawen hym from the kynge. *c* **1430** *Syr. Gener.* (Roxb.) 3219, I beseche you g[ra]unt nov youre pees Vnto oure felow [Generides]. **1523** LD. BERNERS *Froiss.* I. clxxx. 215 The prouost of the marchantes of Parys hadde gette hym his peace of the duke. **1570** *Satir. Poems Reform.* xxiii. 28 Thow knawis thy self gif he was diligent To get thy peax, and slaik the of that weir. **1570–6** LAMBARDE *Peramb. Kent* (1826) 183 The Bishops and Noble men (for verie feare) became petitioners to the King for his peace, and in the ende procured it.

2. Freedom from civil commotion and disorder; public order and security. (See also 10.)

c **1154** *O.E. Chron.* an. 1135 Durste nan man mis don wið oðer on his time. Pais he makede men & dær. *Ibid.* an. 1140, & hit ward sone suythe god pais. *c* **1275** LAY. 2520 Al Brutaine ȝeo wiste..In griþe and paise [*c* 1205 in friðe]. **13..** *Solom. Coronat.* 54 in *Adam Davy*, etc. (1878) 98 Good pais þere was in hil londe, þer while he kyng was. **1422** *Rolls of Parlt.* IV. 176/1 Execution of lawe, and kepyng of Pees, stant miche in Justice of Pees. *a* **1533** LD. BERNERS *Huon* lxvi. 228, I haue..maynteyned the countre in peace & rest and good iustyce. **1670** CLARENDON *Ess.* Tracts (1727) 209 Peace is that harmony in the state, that health is in the body. **1794** tr. *Brissot's 'To his Constit.'* Pref. 24 Roland and the Brissotins..endeavouring to preserve peace. **1861** M. PATTISON *Ess.* (1889) I. 47 [In the Steelyard] Peace and order were maintained by police regulations of German minuteness and strictness.

3. a. Freedom from disturbance or perturbation (esp. as a condition in which an individual person is); quiet, tranquillity, undisturbed state. Also emphasized as ***peace and quiet(ness)***. ***bill of peace***: see quot. 1848.

a **1225** *Ancr. R.* 22 Siggeð..þe oþer viue [psalmes] uor þe peis of holi churche. *c* **1290** *S. Eng. Leg.* I. 21/70 Seint Dunston cam hom a-ȝen:..And hadde his Abbeye al in pays. **1382** WYCLIF *Luke* xi. 21 Whanne a strong armed man kepith his hows, alle thingis that he weldith ben in pees. **1480** CAXTON *Chron. Eng.* clxxiii. 156 The poure comons were in pees and in rest. **1581** LAMBARDE *Eiren.* I. ii, Sometimes..the worde *Peace* is taken for *Protection*, or *defence*: as where M. Bracton calleth the Writtes of Protection, *Breuia de pace*. **1612** DAVIES *Why Ireland*, etc. 127 The king.. commanded that Sherborn shold hold his land in peace. **1758** GRAY *Child* 6 Let him sleep in peace. **1848** WHARTON *Law Lex.*, *Peace, bill of*, a bill brought by a person to establish and perpetuate a right which he claims, and which from its nature may be controverted by different persons at different times, and by different actions... The obvious design of such a bill is to secure repose from perpetual litigation. **1859** MRS. CARLYLE *Lett.* III. 6, I shall breakfast here in peace, and quietness. **1864** TENNYSON *En. Ard.* 147 And pass his days in peace among his own.

b. In and after Biblical use, in various expressions of well-wishing or salutation.

Following L. *pax* and Gr. εἰρήνη, 'peace' often represents Heb. *shālōm*, properly = safety, welfare, prosperity.

a **1300** *Cursor M.* 17648 (Cott.) Ioseph sli greting þam gaf, 'Godds peis mot yee all haf'. **13..** *Ibid.* 5333 (Gött.) Þus Iacob his tale bigan, Pes haue Pharao þe king. *c* **1325** *Metr. Hom.* 19 Ga, he said, womman in pes. **1382** WYCLIF *Luke* x. 5 In to what euere hous ȝe schulen entre, first seye ȝe, Pees to this hous. **1526** TINDALE *John* xx. 19 Cam Iesus and stode in the myddes, and sayd to them: peace be with you [WYCLIF Pees to ȝou; 1539, 1611 peace be vnto you]. **1593** SHAKS. *2 Hen. VI*, III. iii. 26 Peace to his soule, if Gods good pleasure be. **1611** BIBLE *1 Chron.* xii. 18 Peace, peace, be unto thee, and peace be to thine helpers. **1791** MRS. RADCLIFFE *Rom. Forest* vii, Farewell! and peace attend you. **1816** SCOTT *Antiq.* xxiii, Ah! rare Ben Jonson! long peace to thy ashes! **1847** TENNYSON *Princ.* IV. 118 Peace be with her. She is dead.

4. a. Freedom from quarrels or dissension between individuals; a state of friendliness; concord, amity. (See also 11 a, 15.)

kiss of peace: a kiss given in sign of friendliness; *spec.* a kiss of greeting given in token of Christian love (see PAX) at religious services in early times; now, in the Western Ch., usually only during High Mass.

a **1225** *Juliana* 74 Ha..custe ham a cos of pes. *c* **1250** *Gen. & Ex.* 8 To alle cristenei men beren pais and luue bitwene. **1382** WYCLIF *Eph.* iv. 3 Bisy for to kepe vnite of spirit in the bond of pees. *c* **1440** *Generydes* 3416 The pese shall sone be twix vs twoo. **1534** CROMWELL in Merriman *Life & Lett.* (1902) I. 396 All malice and evill will being..expulsed.., good amyte peax & quyetnes may take place. *a* **1648** LD. HERBERT *Hen. VIII* (1683) 611 But that this question.. might well be omitted for Peace sake. **1794** COLERIDGE *Domestic Peace*, Tell me, on what holy ground May Domestic Peace be found, Halcyon daughter of the skies. **1852** [KISS *sb.* 1]. **1865** DICKENS *Mut. Fr.* I. iii, We should have no peace in our place if that got touched upon.

†b. *transf.* An author or maintainer of concord.

1382 WYCLIF *Eph.* ii. 14 He is oure pees, that made both oon. *c* **1412** HOCCLEVE *De Reg. Princ.* 5386 Crist þus seid hir vnto, I am pees verray. **1503** DUNBAR *Thistle & Rose* 181 Our princes [i.e. princess] of honour,..Our peax, our play, our plane felicite. **1560** BIBLE (Genev.) *Micah* v. 5 And he shalbe our peace.

c. = *kiss of peace*, PAX[1] 2: see a above. Also, an action symbolizing the kiss of peace.

Now usu. a light embrace, a hand-shake, or a bow.

1565 JEWEL *Repl. Harding* iii. (1611) 114 The Peace giuen to the Bishop, was not a little Table of Siluer or somewhat else, as hath beene vsed in the Church of Rome, but a very Kisse indeed. **1935** D. H. HISLOP *Our Heritage in Public Worship* xi. 243 Here, either before or after the Peace, in many rites is placed the Creed. **1957** *Oxf. Dict. Chr. Ch.* 771/1 Originally an actual kiss, the form of the Peace has been modified in all rites. **1974** R. J. HALLIBURTON in R. C. D. Jasper *Eucharist Today* vii. 90 The rubric in Series 3 gives no directions as to how the Peace is to be given. **1975** C. F. BAZLEY in C. O. Buchanan *Further Anglican Liturgies* x. 183 The Peace (in Chile called the Holy Kiss or the Love Embrace) is not included as a formal part of the service itself. **1976** *Church Times* 9 July 13/1 In recent years we have been bombarded with all kinds of fanciful and eccentric changes in the liturgy, of which 'the peace', in all its constantly changing forms, is surely the most ludicrous. *Ibid.* 8 Oct. 9/2 Staid churchwardens embraced others in the congregation during the giving of the Peace with a warmth and friendliness that they would have found difficult to express in a parish church. **1977** *Theology* LXXX. 175 The representation of 'the giving of the peace' by, rather oddly, shaking hands with one's neighbour.

†d. ***with the peace of*** (repr. L. *pace*): = without offence to; begging pardon of. *rare*⁻¹.

1669 FLAMSTEED in Rigaud *Corr. Sci. Men* (1841) II. 80 With the peace of that industrious deceased astronomer,.. I dare affirm [etc.].

5. Freedom from mental or spiritual disturbance or conflict arising from passion, sense of guilt, etc.; calmness; ***peace of mind, soul,*** or ***conscience***.

c **1200** *Vices & Virtues* 59 Siec ðat tu haue pais aȝeanes gode. **1340** *Ayenb.* 162 Þet non ne may habbe pays of herte ne stedeuest inwyt. **1382** WYCLIF *Phil.* iv. 7 The pees of God, that passith al witt, kepe ȝoure hertis. **1502** ATKYNSON tr. *De Imitatione* III. xxxiii. 102 Lete not þi pes be in þe mouþes of men. **1548–9** (Mar.) *Bk. Com. Prayer* Collect 21st Sund. Trinity, Graunt..to thy faithfull people pardon and peace. **1671** MILTON *Samson* 1334 *Off.* Regard thy self... *Sam.* My self? my conscience and internal peace. **1737** POPE *Hor. Epist.* II. ii. 65 He stuck to poverty with peace of mind. **1851** ROBERTSON *Serm.* Ser. III. xi. 138 Peace then, is the opposite of passion, and of labour, toil and effort. Peace is that state in which there are no desires madly demanding an impossible gratification. **1879** B. TAYLOR *Stud. Germ. Lit.* 92 Peace of soul comes only through Faith and Obedience.

6. a. Absence of noise, movement, or activity; stillness, quiet; inertness. (See also 13.)

13.. *Coer de L.* 1341 Beth in pes, lystenes my tale! **1377** LANGL. *P. Pl.* B. XIX. 149 The iewes preyed hem pees. *c* **1400** MAUNDEV. (1839) xxvii. 273 The See..is never still ne in pes. *c* **1515** *Cocke Lorell's B.* 13 They banysshed prayer, peas, and sadnes: and toke with them myrthe, sporte, and gladnes. **1620** MELTON *Astrolog.* 68 In the peace of midnight. **1750** SHENSTONE *Rur. Elegance* 5 Oh! peace to yonder clam'rous horn! **1846** RUSKIN *Mod. Paint.* (1851) II. III. I. vi. §2 Not like the dead and cold peace of undisturbed stones and solitary mountains. **1850** TENNYSON *In Mem.* xi, Calm and deep peace on this high wold.

b. *ellipt.* as exclamation: see PEACE *v.* 1.

7. a. In generalized sense including several of the above.

c **1380** WYCLIF *Serm.* Sel. Wks. I. 321 Þer ben two peesis, verri pees and fals pees... Verry pees is groundid in God.. and to þat pees sueþ pees wiþ alle creaturis... And þis pees stondiþ in pacience, and mekenes, and oþer vertues... Fals pees is groundid in reste wiþ oure enemys, whanne we assente to hem wiþouten aȝenstonding. ? **1630** MILTON *On Time* 16 When every thing that is sincerely good..With Truth, and Peace, and Love shall ever shine. **1690** NORRIS *Beatitudes* (1694) I. 194 God is the God of Peace; and the greatest Peace, that which passes all Understanding, is called the Peace of God. **1839** BAILEY *Festus* xx. (1852) 354 Peace is the end of all things, tearless Peace. **1857–8** SEARS *Athan.* xvii. 140 Peace is not rest or repose. It is the highest ..activity,..the activity of concording elements.

b. In alliterative association with *plenty*.

1393, etc. [see PLENTY *sb.* 3]. **1596** SPENSER *Prothalamion* vi, Let endlesse Peace your steadfast hearts accord, And blessed Plentie wait vpon you[r] bord. **1703** *New Hist. Trojan Wars* III. 17 Now the Wars are done, and Peace and Plenty are pouring in upon us. **1713** POPE *Windsor-Forest* 2 And Peace and Plenty tell, a Stuart reigns. **1823** BYRON *Age of Bronze* xv. 32 How rich is Britain! not indeed in mines, Or peace, or plenty, corn or oil, or wines. **1949** W. S. MAUGHAM *Writer's Notebk.* 306 The world has always been a place of turmoil. There have been short periods of peace and plenty, but they are exceptional.

8. With initial capital. A vigorous hybrid tea rose bearing large yellow flowers shaded with pink, belonging to a variety developed by Francis Meilland, French nurseryman, in 1939, and introduced into cultivation in 1942. Also *attrib.*

1944 R. PYLE *Let.* in A. Ridge *For Love of Rose* (1965) xii. 210 We are persuaded that this greatest new rose of our time should be named for the world's greatest desire: Peace. **1945** *Los Angeles Times* 30 Apr. I. 11/1 Today's main event [at the Pacific Rose Society show] was the official christening of the newly developed Peace rose. **1945** *Horticulture* 15 Sept. 409/2 The new rose Peace, which seems to be causing a furore, is another of many good roses coming to us from France. **1950** A. S. THOMAS *Better Roses* ix. 93 Mme A. Meilland was listed and sold in France in 1942 under this, its original and therefore correct name, but in Germany it has always been called Gloria Dei, and in Italy Gioia, while it was introduced into America in 1945 and sold under the title of Peace, its fourth name. **1963** W. BLUNT *Of Flowers & Village* 89 R[*osa*] *Andersonii*. Like a phlox-pink wild rose. Peace. For Mrs. Benham, who has promised to plant it where it can't be seen from the house. **1965** L. MEYNELL *Double Fault* II. v. 174 A heaped profusion of Peace roses looked superb in a large silver bowl. **1976** E. B. LE GRICE *Rose Growing Compl.* (ed. 2) xii. 192 Abroad this [*sc.* 1946] was the year of 'Peace' (Meilland) which was to have a profound effect on all rose breeding everywhere, giving a new standard in growth, health and size of bush and flower. **1978** M. DUFFY *Housespy* i. 9 The dusk was still full of the scent of Peace roses.

II. Phrases.

9. Phrases belonging to 1. **a.** ***peace at any price***. Also *attrib.*

[**1645** LD. DIGBY 27 Aug. in *St. Papers, Dom.* (1891) 87 Demonstrations that they will purchase their own, and..the Kingdom's quiet, at any price to the King, to the Church, and to the faithfulest of his party.] **1823** ARNOLD *Hist. Rome* (1843) Suppl. III. 455 Hannibal..probably felt..that, by purchasing peace at any price..his countrymen might again find an opportunity to recover their losses. **1882** E. W. HAMILTON *Diary* 3 Sept. (1972) I. 332 Mr. G. wrote the other day a capital letter to Mr. Richard putting the war in Egypt in a light which would be likely to convince the strongest 'peace-at-any-price' person. **1887** G. W. SMALLEY *Lond. Lett.* I. 153 Palmerston sneered at him [John Bright] as a peace-at-any-price man. **1894** LUBBOCK *Use of Life* xi. 165 Though not a 'peace-at-any-price' man, I am not ashamed to say I am a peace-at-almost-any-price man. **1896** *Westm. Gaz.* 10 Jan. 2/2 Men who are neither faddists in general nor peace-at-any-pricers in particular. **1910** BEERBOHM *Around Theatres* (1953) 579, I myself am not such a peace-at-any-price man as to be frightened away.

b. ***peace with honour***.

[**1607** SHAKS. *Cor.* III. ii. 49 That it [your policy] shall hold Companionship in Peace With Honour, as in warre. *Ibid.* v. vi. 79.] **1650** WELDON *Crt. Jas. I* 185 [Jas. I] had rather spend 100,000 li. on Embassies to keep or procure peace with dishonor, then 10,000 l. on an army that would have forced peace with honour. **1770** GEO. III *Sp. open. Parlt.* 13 Nov., The hope of being able to continue to my subjects the enjoyment of peace with honour and security. **1822** [see HONOUR *sb.* 1 c]. **1878** LD. BEACONSFIELD *Speech* 16 July, Lord Salisbury and myself have brought you back peace —but a peace I hope with honour, which may satisfy our Sovereign and tend to the welfare of the country. **1887** *N. & Q.* 7th Ser. III. 96/1. **1973** *Washington Post* 13 Jan. A23/3 President Nixon stated in Kentucky that we now had in our grasp a peace with honor instead of a peace with surrender.

10. Phrases belonging to 2.

a. ***the king's peace*** [= OE. *cyninges griþ*]: *orig.* The protection secured to certain persons by the king, as those employed on his business, travelling on the king's highway, etc.; hence, the general peace of the kingdom under the king's authority.

[**12..** *Flores Historiarum* (Rolls) II. 180 Cepit..unum de justiciariis regis..in pace regis per stratam regiam itinerantem. **1292** BRITTON I. i. §4 En dreit des Justices..de terminer apeaus et autres trespas fetz encountre nostre pes. **1327** *Proclam. Edw. III* in Walsingham *Hist. Angl.* (Rolls) I. 187 Ne quis dictam pacem nostram infringere seu violare præsumat.] **1428** in *Surtees Misc.* (1888) 3 He suld bere þe kynge's pease to John Holgate merssh all. **1433** *Rolls of Parlt.* IV. 479/1 Any affray in offence of the Kynges pees. **1476** *Ord. Worcester* in *Eng. Gilds* 388 That no man go armed..in distorbynge of the kynges pease and people. **1485** *Act 1 Hen. VII*, c. 7 §2 To eny of youre Counsell or to eny of the Justices of youre peax of the Countie. **1558** Q. ELIZ. in Strype *Ann. Ref.* (1824) I. App. i. 389 We straightly charge..our said subjects of every degree, to kepe themselves in our peax. *c* **1575** *Balfour's Practicks* (1754) 106 At the peax of our soverane Lord. **1607** COWELL *Interpr.*, *Suyte of the Kings peace*..is the persiewng a man for breach of the K. peace. **1612** DAVIES *Why Ireland*, etc. (1787) 85 The Irish, which were not in the King's peace, are called enemies. **1765** BLACKSTONE *Comm.* I. ix. 350 The king's majesty is..the principal conservator of the peace within all his dominions;..hence it is usually called the king's peace. **1769** *Ibid.* IV. xix. 198 To kill an alien, a Jew, or an outlaw, who are all under the king's peace or protection, is as much murder as to kill the most regular born English-man. **1844** LD. BROUGHAM *Brit. Const.* x. (1862) 136 He [the King] could grant 'his peace', that is, a protection from the pursuit of enemies, to any one. **1883** GREEN *Conq. Eng.* v. 212 The public peace, or observance of the customary right by man towards man, has become the king's peace, the observance of which is due to the will of the lord. **1890** SIR F. POLLOCK *Oxford Lect.* 88 By the end of the thirteenth century..the king's peace had fully grown from an occasional privilege into a common right.

b. ***the peace*** = the king's peace, in its wider sense; the general peace and order of the realm, as provided for by law.

Hence many phrases, as ***to keep the peace*** (see 14), ***break the p., breach of the p., bound*** or ***holden to*** (***keep***) ***the peace***; ***to swear the peace against*** (any one), to swear that one is in bodily fear from another, so that he may be bound over to keep the peace; also, ***commission of the peace, conservator, constable, justice, officer, sergeant of the peace; precept of the peace, sessions of the peace; to be sworn of the peace***, to be made a justice of the peace or magistrate.

[**1328** *Act 2 Edw. III*, c. 3 Burghaldres, conestables, & gardeins de la pees deinz lour gardes. **1341** *Rolls of Parlt.* II. 134/1 Felonie ne Trespas fait contre la Pees.] **1386** *Ibid.* III. 225/1 In the same yere, the forsaid Nichol', withouten nede, ayein the pees, made dyverse enarmynges. *c* **1420** *Avow. Arth.* xxii, [He] Is halden to the pees. **1444** *Rolls of Parlt.* V. 110/2 Every chief Conestable of the peas of the seid Shires. **1499** *N. Riding Rec.* (1894) 180 Ther was a precept of the peax made. **1565–73** COOPER *Thesaurus* s.v. *Conventus, Minores conventus*, sessions of the peace. **1575** in W. H. Turner *Select. Rec. Oxford* 361 The peace might be broken. **1595** BACON *Max. & Uses Com. Law* (1635) 10 At this day, conservators of the peace are out of use; and in lieu of them, there are ordained justices of peace. **1598** SHAKS. *Merry W.* II. iii. 54 *Shallow.*—I am sworn of the peace. **1643** PRYNNE *Sov. Power Parl.* III. 21 They may sweare the peace against them. **1681** OTWAY *Soldiers Fort.* III. i, I'll have him bound to the Peace instantly. **1755** BURN *Justice of Peace* (1764) II. 477 *Surety for the peace* is the acknowledging a recognizance, or bond, to the king,..for the keeping the peace. **1874** STUBBS *Const. Hist.* I. vii. 180 *note*, The peace is the relation in which all stand whilst and in so far as all continue in the union and in the right on which the community rests. He who acts against this commits a breach of the peace.

c. In analogous senses: e.g. the peace of any territorial lord; ***God's peace***, God's requirement of peace and good order; the ***Roman peace*** (*pax Romana*), the ***British peace*** (*pax Britannica*), that established within the Roman empire or the British dominions. Cf. PAX[1] 1.

1303 R. BRUNNE *Handl. Synne* 6803 Swych ryche men þat are aȝens Goddys pes. **1591** SHAKS. *1 Hen. VI*, I. iii. 74 All manner of men, assembled here in Armes this day, against Gods Peace and the Kings. **1765** BLACKSTONE *Comm.* I. Introd. iv. 117 Offences were said to be done against his peace in whose court they were tried: in a court-leet, *contra pacem domini*. **1897** *Daily News* 23 Apr. 6/2 As time passed, the English peace annoyed them exceedingly. **1900** *Ibid.* 16 July 6/3 In Durham,..it was correct to speak, not of the king's peace, but of the bishop's peace.

11. ***at peace***. **a.** In a state of concord or friendliness; not at strife or at variance; † ***at*** (any one's) ***peace***, at peace with him (*obs.*). **b.** In a state of quietness, quiet, peaceful. (See AT *prep.* 20, 21.)

c **1330** R. BRUNNE *Chron.* (1810) 88 Þei obliged þam to gyue, Fourti þousand pound, at his pes to lyue. *a* **1425** *Cursor M.* 4074 (Trin.) Fro þis tyme forþ..Wiþ ioseph were þei neuer at pes. **1560** BECON *Common-pl. of Script.* Wks. III. 68 To set at peace by hym through the bloude of hys crosse both thinges in heauen and thinges in earth. **1568** BIBLE (Bishops) *Job* xxii. 21 Reconcile thee vnto God, and be at peace. **1601** SHAKS. *Jul. C.* II. ii. 2 Nor Heauen, nor Earth, Haue beene at peace to night. **1641** HINDE *J. Bruen* lii. 173 Being so at peace with God, we have peace with our selves. **1853** A. J. MORRIS *Business* i. 7 Those who are never at peace but when they are at war. **1860** WARTER *Sea-board* II. 115 He is at peace with this world and the next!

†12. ***on, o, of peace***: in peace, in quiet. *Obs. rare.*

? *a* **1400** *Arthur* 525 Þe walsch man..clepeþ vs Sayson, And seyþ: taw or Peyd, Sayson brount [*Marg.* þat ys.. Stynkyng Saxone, be on pees]. *c* **1440** *Generydes* 3920 In his harnes slepyng still opece. *c* **1470** HENRY *Wallace* VIII. 933 Ȝeit still off pees the ost lugyt all nycht.

13. ***to hold,*** (less usually ***keep***) ***one's peace***: to remain quiet or silent; to keep silence, refrain from speaking. *arch.*

a **1310** in Wright *Lyric P.* 42 Holdeth nou or pees. **13..** *Seuyn Sag.* (W.) 65 When this was said he held his pese. **1382** WYCLIF *Exod.* xiv. 14 The Lord shal fiȝt for ȝow, and ȝe shulen hoold ȝoure pees. **1413** *Pilgr. Sowle* (Caxton) II. lxv. (1859) 59, I..held my pees, and wold no more seye. *c* **1489** CAXTON *Sonnes of Aymon* vii. 157 He had grete luste to speke, for yf he had keped his peas [etc.]. **1552** *Bk. Com. Prayer, Matrimony*, Let him now speake, or els hereafter for euer holde hys peace. **1672** VILLIERS (Dk. Buckhm.) *Rehearsal* III. ii. (Arb.) 81 Pr'ythee hold thy peace. **1745** G. WASHINGTON *Rules Civility* vi, Speak not when you should hold your peace. **1818** COBBETT *Pol. Reg.* XXXIII. 346 If we hold our tongues upon this subject, let us, for decency's sake, keep our peace as to the dependence of Canning. **1890** CLARK RUSSELL *Ocean Trag.* xxvi. III. 16, I held my peace on this new..craze.

14. ***to keep the peace*** (†***keep peace***): to refrain, or prevent others, from disturbing the public peace (see 2, 10); to maintain public order; to prevent, or refrain from, strife or commotion.

1422 [see sense 2]. *a* **1425** *Cursor M.* 9689 (Trin.) Wher of serueþ any assise..But for to kepe pees [*Cott.* to yeme þe pes] in londe? **1444** *Rolls of Parlt.* V. 123/2 Thei shall well and truly kepe the pees within the seid Toun. **1568** GRAFTON *Chron.* II. 162 Caused him to be newely sworne to kepe the peace of the lande. **1605** SHAKS. *Lear* II. ii. 51 Keepe peace vpon your liues, he dies that strikes againe. **1663** BUTLER *Hud.* I. i. 710 To keep the Peace 'twixt Dog and Bear. **1765** BLACKSTONE *Comm.* I. xiii. 411 To provide a determinate quantity of such arms as were then in use, in order to keep the peace. **1849** MACAULAY *Hist. Eng.* iii. I. 294 Dragoons..stationed near Berwick, for the purpose of keeping the peace among the mosstroopers of the border. *Mod.* The defendants were bound over to keep the peace.

15. a. ***to make peace***: to bring about a state of peace, in various senses: (*a*) to effect a reconciliation between persons or parties at variance; to conclude peace with a nation at the close of a war; (*b*) to enter into friendly relations with a person, as by a league of amity, or by submission; (*c*) to enforce public order; †(*d*) to enforce silence.

c **1154** [see 2]. *c* **1175** *Lamb. Hom.* 141 Sunnedei makede ure drihten pes bitweone heouene and eorðe. **1362** Langl. *P. Pl.* A. iii. 214 Þe kyng Meedeþ his Men, to maken pees in londe. *c* **1400** Maundev. (1839) xxii. 234 Thei seyn to certeyn Officeres,..Maketh Pees. And than seyn the Officeres, Now Pees! lysteneth! **1535** Coverdale *Josh.* x. 1 They of Gibeon had made peace with Israel. **1611** Bible *Isa.* xxvii. 5 He shall make peace with me. **1654** Cromwell *Sp.* 4 Sept. in *Carlyle*, Its a Maxim not to be despised 'Though peace be made, yet it's interest that keeps peace'. **1863** [see make *v.* 9c].

b. *to make* one's, or a person's, *peace*: to effect reconciliation for oneself or for some one else; to come, or bring some one, into friendly relations (*with* another). (In quot. *c* 1400, to admit a person to friendly relations with oneself.)

c **1315** Shoreham (Percy Soc.) 39 Thos ȝe mote Make thy pes wyth alle thre, Sorwe, schryfte, and edbote. *c* **1400** *Rom. Rose* 2552 This bargeyn ende may never take, But if that she thi pees wille make. *a* **1400-50** *Alexander* 3779 Dame Calistride..comes with hire ladis, Mas hire pes with oure prince. *a* **1533** Ld. Berners *Huon* xxi. 62 By his meanes my peace was made with the kynge. **1600** Shaks. *Twel. N.* iii. iv. 295, I will make your peace with him, if I can. **1642** Fuller *Holy & Prof. St.* ii. xix. 120 Those who have made their peace with God. **1862** Trollope *Orley F.* lv, Mrs. Furnival had gone to make her peace in Red Lion Square.

16. *no peace for the wicked* [Isaiah xlviii. 22, lvii. 21]: no rest or tranquillity for (the speaker); incessant anxiety, responsibility, or work.

1944 A. Thirkell *Headmistress* iv. 86 'It's for Dr. Perry. ..' 'No peace for the wicked,' said Dr. Perry. **1953** D. Parry *Going up—Going Down* iv. 128 'No peace for the wicked,' she said. 'But I expect it will be quiet from now on.' **1967** 'F. Clifford' *All Men are Lonely Now* i. v. 89 The painters are descending on us tomorrow... Couldn't happen at a worse time, but there's no peace for the wicked is there?

III. 17. *attrib.* and *Comb.* **a.** attrib., as *peace army*, *belt*, *hero*, *party*, *principle*, *studies*; †*peace-breach*, *-cry*, *-day*, *-haven*, *-mistress*, *-pæan*, *-plant*, *-tax*, *-time*, etc.; freq. in senses: founded, held, organized, propounded, etc., to promote peace or end a specified war; advocated by pacifists; as *peace activist*, *advocate*, *aim*, *area*, *bloc*, *camp*, *campaigner*, *conference*, *congress*, *convention*, *crank*, *demonstration*, *-feeler*, *-fighter*, *formula*, *-front*, *march*, *marcher*, *-mediator*, *meeting*, *-mentality*, *mission*, *move*, *movement*, *negotiation*, *offensive*, *offer*, *petition*, *plan*, *propaganda*, *rally*, *society*, *symbol*, *terms*, *walk*. **b.** objective and obj. gen., as *peace-breathing*, *-bringing*, *-commanding*, *-conferring*, *-giving*, *-inspiring*, *-loving*, *-preaching*, *-procuring*, *-promoting*, *-restoring* adjs.; *peace-bearer*, *-bringer*, *-concluder*, *-crier*, *-looker*, *-lover*, *-prater*, *-preserver*. **c.** locative, instrumental, etc., as *peace-abiding*, *-blessed*, *-calm*, *-complacent*, *-enamoured*, *-inspired*, *-like*, *-lulled*, *-minded*, *-trained* adjs. **d.** Special Combs.: **Peace Corps**, orig. *U.S.* (see quot. 1962); **peace economy**, an economy, characteristic of peace-time, in which a large part of the labour force produces goods for export (as opposed to being engaged in arms production, etc.); **peace establishment**, the reduced amount of troops under arms and of military supplies maintained in a standing army in time of peace; **peace-game** [after *war-game* s.v. war *sb.*[1] 11], an exercise in the maintenance of international peace; hence **peace-gaming** *vbl. sb.*; **peace-guild** (*Hist.*), a guild established for the maintenance of peace (= *frith-guild*: see frith *sb.*[1] 3); **peace line**, a line of demarcation drawn to avert conflict; **peace-parted** *a.*, that has departed this life in peace; **Peace People** (see quots.); **peace-pipe**, the tobacco-pipe of the N. American Indians, used as a token of peace (see calumet); **peace pledge**, (*a*) = frank-pledge, OE. frithborh; (*b*) an undertaking to abstain from fighting, or to seek peace (in industrial relations); **peace prize**, an award (as a *Nobel prize*) presented for a contribution to the prevention of war; **peace sign**, a sign of peace made by holding up the hand with palm outturned and the first two fingers in a V-shape; **peace talk**, conversation or discussion about peace or the ending of hostilities; *spec.* in *pl.*, a conference or series of discussions aimed at achieving peace in particular circumstances; hence **peace-talker**, **peace-talking** *vbl. sb.*; **peace-warrant**, a warrant for arrest, issued by a Justice of the Peace; **peace-wright**, one who arranges a peace. Also peace-keeper, -maker, etc.

1968 *Listener* 31 Oct. 566/1 Those *peace activists who at last year's Pentagon demonstration announced that they were going to make the Defence Department levitate 300 feet in the air. **1906** *Westm. Gaz.* 24 Mar. 6/3 Master of counsel sage and fluent pen, *Peace-advocate, averse from warlike act. **1910** W. James *Mem. & Stud.* (1911) xi. 284 Our socialistic peace-advocates all believe absolutely in this world's values. **1940** *Economist* 6 Jan. 9/2 The French have not fed much fuel to the idealist fire which has raged in this country over the discussion of *peace aims. **1957** *Ibid.* 28 Sept. 1000/1 Replace alliances by security pacts—create '*peace areas' (ranging from southern Asia to the Baltic). **1897** *Westm. Gaz.* 28 July 3/3 Should not our brave and patient *peace army [the police force] be considered? *c* **1650** *Rolls of Parlt.* II. 435/2 His ship called the Portpays or *Peace Bearer. **1836-48** B. D. Walsh *Aristoph., Acharnians* i. v, Nor had this peace-bearer then skipped away. **1758** *N. Jersey Arch.* XX. 297 Peace was solemnly ratified by a large *peace belt. **1779** Clark *Campaign Illinois* (1869) 45. *c* **1620** in Farr *S.P. Jas. I* 315 Your wisdome, bountie, and *peace-bless'd raygne. **1939** W. S. Churchill *Into Battle* (1941) 94 The first [step]..is the full inclusion of Soviet Russia in our defensive *peace bloc. **1610** Holland *Camden's Brit.* i. 350 For Robbery, *peace-breach and Foristell. **1826** A. A. Watts *Bachelor's Dilemma* vii, Pensive and *peace-breathing beauty. **1625** K. Long tr. *Barclay's Argenis* i. xx. 62 This day was not to be honoured as a *peace-bringer. **1677** Gilpin *Demonol.* (1867) 466 The comfortable and *peace-bringing promises of the gospel. **1939** R. Campbell *Flowering Rifle* i. 15 And loosing these in turn to drink and graze The *peace-calm waters and the flowery ways. **1981** *Peace News* 2 Oct. 3/3 The *Peace Camp outside Greenham Common airbase in Berkshire is still there after nearly a month. **1986** *Economist* 15 Mar. 63/3 Soviet newspapers are full of praise for the anti-nuclear activities of the women's peace camps at Greenham Common in Britain and elsewhere. **1954** B. & R. North tr. *Duverger's Pol. Parties* i. ii. 109 A large number of Europeans, very far removed from Communism, are..vulnerable to the attacks of the *Peace Campaigners. **1807** J. Barlow *Columbiad* x. 359 Enlighten'd interest, moral sense at length Combine their aids to elevate her strength, Lead o'er the world her *peace-commanding sway. **1928** S. Sassoon *Heart's Journey* 31 Paid, with a pile of *peace-complacent stone. **1643** [Angier] *Lanc. Vall. Achor* 5 Had not God..moved them to be the Peace-keepers, which were not the *peace-concluders. **1889** *Cent. Dict.*, **Peace convention* or *conference*, same as *Peace congress*. **1899** *Hazell's Ann.* *1900* 462/1 A Peace Conference was held at the Hague in May, June, and July '99. **1919** G. B. Shaw *Peace Conference Hints* i. 7 Before the Peace Conference can be discussed with any profit, it must be approached in the light of the facts. **1933** *Radio Times* 14 Apr. 75/1 The war was newly over... There was a tremendous fuss of coming and going across the Channel.. politicians..busy with the Peace Conference. **1978** *Times* 26 July 13/3 A strong performance of *The Green Table*..Kurt Jooss's allegory of the sometimes fatal effects of peace conferences. **1909** W. James *Pluralistic Universe* iii. 128 It [*sc.* the absolute] might, with all its defects, be, on account of its *peace-conferring power and its formal grandeur, more rational than anything else in the field. **1852** Grote *Greece* ii. lxxix. X. 360 The *peace-congress at Delphi. **1885** W. P. & F. J. Garrison *Life W. L. Garrison* II. 230 The *Peace Convention held in Boston, September.., 1838. **1960** H. Humphrey in *Congress. Rec.* 15 June 12634/3 Mr. President, I introduce..a bill to establish a *Peace Corps of American young men to assist the peoples of the underdeveloped areas of the world to learn the basic skills necessary to combat poverty, disease, illiteracy and hunger. **1962** *Ann. Reg.* *1961* 175 The Peace Corps was officially set up on 1 March as an organization to train and send American volunteers for service in foreign countries to help meet the need for skilled manpower. **1967** *Economist* 2 Sept. 785/2 Japan's version of the peace corps is getting into its stride. **1970** *Times* 19 Mar. (Liberia Suppl.) p. i/4 Sturdy American girls in Bermuda shorts earnestly go about the business of the Peace Corps. **1974** 'G. Black' *Golden Cockatrice* iii. 48 The Peace Corps phase in Manila.. followed by free-lancing in refugee camps outside Kowloon. **1916** D. H. Lawrence *Let.* 11 Dec. (1962) I. 491 Fusty, fuzzy *peace-cranks and lovers of humanity are the devil. **1860** Longf. *Wayside Inn, K. Olaf* xxii. vi, Love against hatred, *Peace-cry for war-cry! **1902** *Westm. Gaz.* 3 June 11/1 A fall in Kaffirs is the fact which fell to be recorded in the closing hours of *Peace-Day. **1935** A. Huxley *Let.* 5 June (1969) 395 His hobby is congresses and he has already organized one *peace demonstration—at Amsterdam in 32, I think. **1910** W. James *Mem. & Stud.* (1911) xi. 283 The military party..says..that mankind cannot *afford* to adopt a *peace-economy. **1948** G. Crowther *Outl. Money* (rev. ed.) viii. 267 A peace economy..is chiefly interested in selling to foreign countries, a war economy in buying from them. **1800** Campbell *Pleas. Hope* ii. 11 Triumph not, ye *peace-enamour'd few! **1766** in *Rep. on MSS. Mrs. Stopford-Sackville* 111 in *Parl. Papers* *1904* (Cd. 1892) XLVII. i, I see no end of the load imposed upon us, as our *peace establishment is so far beyond the ordinary supplies. **1803** *Edin. Rev.* II. 6 A peace-establishment of 500,000 men. **1942** H. Nicolson *Diaries & Lett.* (1967) 225 There are all sorts of rumours... Germany is putting out *peace-feelers. **1972** J. Williams *Home Fronts* v. 94 The Allies' curt rejection of peace feelers put out by the Chancellor. **1958** *New Statesman* 23 Aug. 230/1 Until last year Paul Robeson and Howard Fast ranked with the Dean of Canterbury as the foremost '*peace-fighters' of the English-speaking world. **1974** *Times* 16 Feb. 1/4 The chances of a *peace formula emerging from the Pay Board's enquiry into the relative position of miners' pay. **1977** *Times* 17 Aug. 2/7 Postal workers..agreed on a peace formula after a five-day dispute. **1939** H. Nicolson *Dairy* 22 Aug. (1966) 411 This smashes our *peace-front. **1968** *Guardian* 2 Dec. 9/8, I..believe.. that..practical pacifism [is] a reasonable goal. I am currently engaged in talking to computers about this in an elaborate *peace game. **1968** *Economist* 23 Nov. 72/2 More attention should be paid to using these techniques for what he calls '*peace gaming'. **1833** H. Blunt *Hist. St. Paul* ii. 126 To receive in all its *peace-giving blessedness, the gospel. **1913** *Encycl. Relig. & Ethics* VI. 215/1 The *frith gild*, or **peace gild*, so called, refers to an occasional feature of town life in Northern Europe from the 6th century. **1909** *Westm. Gaz.* 1 Sept. 9/1 The reactionary Holy Alliance was also a *peace-inspired measure. **1828** Disraeli *Voy. Capt. Popanilla* x. 119 The calm and *peace-inspiring crosier. **1873** E. Brennan *Witch of Nemi*, etc. 223 Pleasure-bound and peace-inspiring days. **1957** *Economist* 19 Oct. 209/2 When Japanese fishermen are apprehended in *Peace Line violations, they are brought to Korea and given fair and open trials. **1969** *Times* 10 Sept. 1/1 (*heading*) Army 'peace line' to replace barricades across Belfast. *Ibid.* 1/2 General Sir Ian Freeland..said that troops would start building 'peace-line' barricades today. **1972** *Belfast Tel.* 12 Oct. 6/6 No doubt when the other volumes make the shops, Ulster will get its dishonourable mentions—no-go area, provo, peaceline. **1595** Daniel *Civ. Wars* i. lxxv, *Peace-lover Wealth, hating a troublous State. **1877** Tennyson *Harold* i. ii. 113 Peace-lover is our Harold. **1591** Sylvester *Du Bartas* i. iv. 719 Sea's Soveraintess,..*Peace-loving Queen. **1836** J. H. Newman in *Lyra Apost.* (1849) 122 Peace-loving man, of humble heart and true! **1930** R. A. Knox *Caliban in Grub St.* xiii. 212 Telling us to be honest and sincere and peace-loving. **1944** *Ann. Reg.* *1943* 83 A general international organisation, based on the principle of the sovereign equality of all peace-loving States. **1955** *Ann. Reg.* *1954* 191 Broadcasts to foreign audiences continued to extol the full religious freedom allegedly existing in the U.S.S.R., and to court the 'peace-loving' Catholics. **1970** V. Canning *Great Affair* xii. 207 Basically I am a simple, peace-loving, even a dull person. **1977** T. Allbeury *Man with President's Mind* xiii. 131 The peace-loving American people. **1977** *Ann. Reg.* *1976* 485 There are still certain forces who are bent on a return to cold war politics, which led to the division of the continent into opposing blocs. Communist Parties and other democratic and peace-loving forces have fought against and continue to fight against these policies. **1871** B. Taylor *Faust* (1875) II. i. v. 67 *Peace-lulled seas. **1961** A. Wesker *Kitchen* 58 Did you go on that *peace march yesterday? **1975** P. Harcourt *Fair Exchange* 46, I proposed to wait until the Peace March had gone by. **1961** *Listener* 12 Oct. 548/2 The Western *peace marchers approaching Moscow. **1972** J. Wambaugh *Blue Knight* (1973) vi. 77 Lieutenant Hilliard..was a cool old head and wouldn't get into a flap over fifteen peace marchers. **1884** *Peace-mediator [see honest *a.* 3e]. **1939** C. Day Lewis *Child of Misfortune* iii. i. 260 Sitting on the platform at *peace meetings. **1935** A. P. Herbert *What a Word!* 243 Get your angles straight on air-mindedness, class-consciousness, *peace-mentality, stomach-awareness. **1939** *War Illustr.* 14 Oct. p. ii/3 To-day an inoffensive *peace-minded majority of the German people are being unwillingly dragged by a bloody-minded minority of their race along the road of doom. **1967** *Freedomways* VII. 118 Miss Barbara Deming.. has been very active in the Peace Movement (she has taken part in a 'peace walk'..and a *peace mission to Saigon in order to protest the war). **1976** R. Moore *Dubai* i. 10 We [Americans] have a peace mission actively working to avoid war in the Middle East. **1589** R. Harvey *Pl. Perc.* (1590) 6 Our most roiall *Peace-Mistres holds the sterne. **1940** H. Nicolson *Diary* 16 July (1967) 102 We may be faced at any moment by a German *peace move, and..a purely negative attitude is not sufficient. **1977** *Listener* 18 Aug. 195/1 If.. the peace moves collapse..what will happen to the insecure régimes in Egypt and Syria? **1953** M. McCarthy in *Reporter* (N.Y.) 22 Dec. 33/3 My fiancé..had known the organizer for years, perhaps from the *peace movement. **1975** *Guardian* 2 Dec. 6/6 Defence Counsel..accused the prosecution of conducting a smear campaign against the British peace movement. **1912** *Peace negotiation [see will *v.*[1] 46]. **1918**, etc. *Peace offensive [see offensive *sb.* 2]. **1977** *Time* 3 Jan. 46/1 While Assad and Sadat have captured world headlines with talk of a peace offensive, Rabin has been attacked at home for being timid and indecisive. **1918** C. P. Scott in D. Ayerst *Guardian* (1971) xxvii. 410 The *peace offers of the Emperor Karl, so insultingly and stupidly turned down by Clemenceau. **1966** N. Nicolson in H. Nicolson *Diaries & Lett.* *1930-39* 412 Hitler opened his attack on Poland as planned, claiming that the Poles had rejected his peace-offer. **1602** Shaks. *Ham.* v. i. 261 To sing sage Requiem, and such rest..As to *peace-parted Soules. **1880** Gladstone *Sp. at Edinb.* 17 Mar., What is called the Manchester School, or sometimes the *Peace party. **1976** *Times* 19 Oct. 12/1 The *Peace People, this misleadingly trendy title now adopted by the [Ulster] women's peace movement. **1977** *Time* 22 Aug. 6/2 A year ago last week, Catholics Betty Williams and Mairead Corrigan founded the so-called Peace People's Movement, which has attracted mass support from both Catholics and Protestants. **1977** *Arab Times* 14 Dec. 2/6 Mrs. Williams added: 'I am angry, the Peace People are angry that war at home dribbles on, and around the world we see the same stupidity gathering momentum for far worse wars than the little one which the little population of Northern Ireland has had to endure.' **1940** H. Nicolson *Diary* 19 Sept. (1967) 116 Already the Communists are getting people in the shelters to sign a *peace-petition to Churchill. **1955** *Treatm. Brit. P.O.W.'s in Korea* (H.M.S.O.) 11 From lectures on 'peace'..it was but a short step..to the production of 'peace' propaganda and 'peace' petitions by prisoners. **1779** G. R. Clark *Campaign in Illinois* (1869) 45, I told them I would defer smokeing the *Peace Pipe until I heard that they had called in all their Warriors. **1876** Bancroft *Hist. U.S.* II. xxxiii. 330 Four old men advance..bearing the peace-pipe, brilliant with many colored plumes. **1968** *Listener* 3 Oct. 429/1 The process has apparently forced the Israelis to clarify their position with a '*peace plan'. **1977** A. Wilson *Strange Ride R. Kipling* vii. 306 The Pope put forward his peace plan in 1917. **1605** Sylvester *Du Bartas* ii. iii. iii. *Law* 1314 The *peace-plant Olive. **1857** Toulmin Smith *Parish* 123 All were annually thus personally bound in '*peacepledge'. **1935** H. R. L. Sheppard *We say No* p. x, To give Pacifist opinion a chance to crystallize, I launched my Peace Pledge. **1956** A. H. Compton *Atomic Quest* 296 The 'Stockholm Peace Pledge.' In this 'peace pledge' a prime point was again made of outlawing atomic weapons. **1974** W. Foley *Child in Forest* ii. 247 This group of young left-wing idealists..belonged..to the Peace Pledge Union. **1976** *Daily Mirror* 12 Nov. 2 Jack Jones yesterday declared: 'There will be *no* dock strike.' The Transport Union leader's peace pledge came amid dockland fury at the crippling of the Dock Work Regulation Bill in the Commons. **1862** Grattan *Beaten Paths* II. 306 The *peace-preaching politicians. **1715** *Peace-preservers [see peacemaker]. **1863** W. Phillips *Speeches* i. 7 What are called *Peace principles. **1902** *Idler* Nov. 244/2 The commission appointed to decide the *peace prize. **1974** *Encycl. Brit. Micropædia* IV. 875/2 [Dag Hammarskjöld] was posthumously awarded the Nobel Peace Prize for 1961. **1643** Prynne *Sov. Power Parl.* i. (ed. 2) Pref. A ij b, State-securing, *Peace-procuring verities. **1906** *Westm. Gaz.* 12 Mar. 2/2 We certainly hope and believe that the Government will act in a *peace-promoting spirit. **1929** D.

H. LAWRENCE *Pansies* 85 Loud *peace propaganda makes war seem imminent. **1955** Peace propaganda [see *peace petition*]. **1951** 'A. GARVE' *Murder in Moscow* iii. 43, I attended a great '*peace' rally at the Bolshoi Theatre. **1975** P. HARCOURT *Fair Exchange* 41 It's not a political rally. It's a peace rally. **1780** COWPER *Table-t.* 79 To touch the sword with conscientious awe,..To sheathe it, in the *peace-restoring close, With joy. **1969** *New Yorker* 30 Aug. 21/2 Just as it finished, an Army helicopter flew over. The whole crowd..looked up and waved their forefingers in the *peace sign. **1973** D. WESTHEIMER *Going Public* iv. 67 She raised her hand in a peace sign... He realized it was not the peace sign at all. To those of the old woman's generation it was V for Victory. **1976** *Scotsman* 20 Nov., (*caption*) Brian Robertson (right) gives the 'peace sign' as he leaves the High Court handcuffed to Jeremy Salmon. **1816** N. WORCESTER *Friend of Peace* I. VII. 30 (*heading*) First annual Report of the Massachusetts *Peace Society. **1952** *Hist. Church of Brethren in Indiana* vi. 287 Miss Muir came to Manchester College in 1948 to head the department of *Peace Studies, where she has awakened an interest in the problem of peace, and inspired a desire for service in many young minds. **1969** *Jrnl. Peace Res.* VI. 395 Peace Studies. Manchester College, North Manchester, Indiana. Undergraduate interdisciplinary program embracing a number of courses. A program in existence since 1948. **1972** *New Scientist* 15 June 638/3 The Quaker appeal for money to found Britain's first university chair of peace studies has passed its first objective of £75,000 in 10 weeks. **1983** *Daily Tel.* 21 Dec. 8/3 More than 30 per cent of Labour-controlled councils.. have introduced 'peace studies' to their schools' regular timetables. Pupils..are taught about the nuclear arms race, disarmament, group conflicts and the Government's defence policy. **1970** *Time* 2 Nov. 6 *American Opinion*.. compared the familiar *peace symbol to an anti-Christian 'broken cross'... The peace design was devised in Britain for the first Ban-the-Bomb Aldermaston march in 1958. **1972** *Times* 4 Aug. 1/2 He..is..said to have cut the peace symbol (the nuclear disarmament insignia) into the ice with his skates. **1789** J. STEELE *Papers* (1924) I. 51, I only mean to hold a *peace talk. **1800** B. HAWKINS in *Georgia Hist. Soc. Coll.* (1848) III. i. 72 Peace talks are always addressed to the cabin of the Mic-co. **1852** J. REYNOLDS *Pioneer Hist. Illinois* 165 All the 'peace talks' ever presented to the red men, could not have kept them in peace, under these circumstances. **1918** W. OWEN *Let.* 10 Oct. (1967) 583 Tonight I must stand before them [*sc.* my company] & promulgate this General Order: 'Peace talk in any form is to cease in Fourth Army. All ranks are warned against the disturbing influence of dangerous peace talk.' **1930** J. CANNAN *No Walls of Jasper* 63 Look at the newspapers! Nothing but peace talk. **1958** *Times Lit. Suppl.* 10 Jan. 21/4 The campaign ended, un-Napoleonically, in the feeble peace-talks of Villafranca. **1973** *Times* 9 Nov. 1/1 Israel and Egypt have accepted a ceasefire agreement that could lead to Middle East peace talks by the end of the year. **1968** *Punch* 15 May 693/1 This is no surprise to the Korean *peace talkers. **1917** D. H. LAWRENCE *Look! We have come Through!* 126 Everything was tainted with myself..nations, armies, war, *peace-talking. **1858** J. B. NORTON *Topics* 236 They have seen an income-tax take the successive forms of a *peace-tax, a war-tax, and then a peace-tax again. **1935** MRS. BELLOC LOWNDES *Diary* 19 Dec. (1971) 136 Wickham Steed.. talked with great excitement of what has happened over the offer of *peace terms to Italy and Abyssinia. **1976** *Classical Q.* XXVI. 272 Andocides does not deal explicitly with the question of the status of the Greeks of Asia in the proposed peace-terms. **1631** MASSINGER *Believe as You List* III. ii, You keepe in pay..some *peace-trayn'd troopes. **1967** *Peace walk [see *peace mission*]. **1826** *Sunday Times* 27 Aug. 3/5 [He] was..brought before M. Swabey Esq. at the instance of his wife, on a *peace-warrant. **1855** MOTLEY *Dutch Rep.* VI. iii. (1866) 814 The *peace-wrights of Cologne.

†**peace**, *a. Obs. rare.* [f. PEACE *sb.*] Peaceful, quiet, silent, unmentioned.

c **1440** *Generydes* 320 But ye must kepe this mater husht and pece. *a* **1500** *Childe of Bristowe* 11 in Hazl. *E.P.P.* I. 111, Y pray yow in this place of your talkyng that ye be pes.

peace (piːs), *v.* Forms: 4–5 pees, 5 peass(e, 5– peace, (6 *Sc.* pece, peiss). [f. PEACE *sb.* The earliest examples are in the imperative, and may have begun as interjectional uses of PEACE *sb.* (The ME. vb. was PEASE (cf. APPEASE), found in some senses after 1600. Modern editors have in various places (e.g. Parker Society's Publ.) erroneously substituted *peace* for the original *pease*.)]

1. *intr.* In the imperative as exclamation: Be silent; keep silence. (Cf. *silence!*) *arch.*

c **1386** CHAUCER *Wife's Prol.* 838 What amble or trotte or pees or go sit doun. *Ibid.* 850 Oure hoost cride pees and that anon And seyde lat the womman telle hire tale. **1393** LANGL. *P. Pl.* C. XVI. 234 'Pees!' quaþ pacience, 'ich praye þe, syre actyf!' *c* **1460** *Towneley Myst.* ii. 400 Peasse, man, for Godis payn! **1526** TINDALE *Mark* iv. 39 He..sayde vnto the see: peace and be still [σιώπα, πεφίμωσο]. **1634** MILTON *Comus* 359 Peace brother, be not over-exquisite To cast the fashion of uncertain evils. **1735** POPE *Donne Sat.* iv. 256 Peace, fools, or Gonson will for Papists seize you. **1847** TENNYSON *Princ.* III. 230 Peace, you young savage of the northern wild!

†**2.** *intr.* To be or become still or silent; to refrain from, or cease, speaking; to keep silence.

1450 *Paston Lett.* I. 180 Heruppon the people peacyd, and stilled. *c* **1460** *Towneley Myst.* xxiii. 1 Peasse I byd euereich Wight! *Ibid.* 13 Will ye not peasse when I bid you? **1563** SACKVILLE *Induct. Mirr. Mag.* lxxii, He peaste and couched while that we passed by. **1570** LEVINS *Manip.* 204/47 To Peace, *tacēre, silēre.* **1593** SHAKS. *Rich. II*, v. ii. 80 *Yorke.* Peace foolish Woman. *Dut.* I will not peace. **1605** —— *Lear* IV. vi. 104 When the Thunder would not peace at my bidding. *c* **1633** AUSTIN *Medit., Whitsunday* (1635) 154 When to speake, and when to peace.

†**3.** *trans.* To reduce to peace; to still, calm, appease; = PEASE *v.* 4. *Obs.*

(Often a later alteration of *pease.*)

1513 DOUGLAS *Æneis* X. ii. 110 Quhen he spak, all cessit: The hevynly heich hous of Goddis was pecit [*ed.* **1553** peissit]. *a* **1533** LD. BERNERS *Gold. Bk. M. Aurel.* xiv. (1535) H, This good emperour laboured to pease [*so* 1536; *edd.* 1546, 1559 peace] this furie of the people, and to sette peace among the neybours of Rome. **1548** HALL *Chron., Hen. VI* 98 For the peacyng [*other ed.* peasynge, GRAFTON peasing] of the saied quarelles and debates.

peace, var. PEISE *Obs.*; obs. form of PIECE.

†**peaceability.** *Obs.* Forms: 4 pesiblete(e, pesyblete, 5 peasabilyte, peasibylite. [ME. a. OF. *paisibleté* (12th c. in Godef.), f. *paisible* PEACEABLE: see next.] Peaceableness, tranquillity, calm.

1382 WYCLIF *2 Macc.* ii. 23 The Lord maad helpful to hem, with al pesibletee. —— *Luke* viii. 24 The tempest.. ceeside, and pesyblete was maad. *c* **1400** tr. *Secreta Secret., Gov. Lordsh.* 114 Many heres and softe bytoknys pesabilyte and coldnesse of þe brayn. *c* **1440** HYLTON *Scala Perf.* (W. de W. 1494) II. xxxviii, Vertues of pacyence & myldenes peasibylite and louered to his euencrysten.

peaceable (ˈpiːsəb(ə)l), *a.* (*sb.*, *adv.*) Forms: α. 4–5 peisible, 4–6 pais-, pesible, (also with *y* for either *i*, and *-el* or *-il* for *-le*; also 4 peyseble, -belle, payzible, 4–5 peesible, 5 peseble, pessybyl); 4 pecible, 6 *Sc.* pecibil, (peiceabil); 5–6 peasible, -yble, (5 -eble, peass-); 6 peacible, (-eble, -ebil); *Sc.* pacibil, (-ebil). β. 4–6 pesable, (4–5 -bil, -byl(le, 5 peseable, -bel); 6 peciable, -bil, (pecesable); 5–6 peasable, (6 peass-, peac-, peax-, peaciable, *Sc.* paciable); 6– peaceable. [ME. a. OF. *paisible* (12th c. in Hatz.-Darm.), *peis-, pesible* (= Pr. *pazible, paizible*), f. OF. *pais* PEACE: see -BLE. Subseq. conformed in pronunc. and spelling to *pece*, PEACE, and to words in -ABLE (cf., for sense, *comfortable, favourable, serviceable*).]

1. Disposed to, or making for, peace; avoiding, or inclined to avoid, strife; of a peaceful character, disposition, or tendency; not quarrelsome or pugnacious. (Of persons, actions, etc.)

c **1330** R. BRUNNE *Chron. Wace* (Rolls) 4040 Pesable he was. **1340** *Ayenb.* 96 Yblissed byeþ þe paysyble uor hi ssolle by ycleped godes zones. **1386** *Rolls of Parlt.* III. 225/1 Bi gode and paisible avys of the wysest and trewest. *a* **1450** *Knt. de la Tour* (1868) 117 She..made hym paisible vnto her and vnto alle other peple. **1535** COVERDALE *Zach.* vi. 13 A peaceable councell shalbe betwixte them both. **1610** GUILLIM *Heraldry* II. vi. (1611) 56 Those gallants..in times ..of warre, proue..peaceabler and calmer then they should be. **1712** STEELE *Spect.* No. 284 ¶6 She shall give Security for her peaceable Intentions. **1774** GOLDSM. *Nat. Hist.* (1776) III. 94 The Stag is one of those innocent and peaceable animals that seem made to embellish the forest. **1815** ELPHINSTONE *Acc. Caubul* (1842) 173 The inhabitants are shepherds,..simple, peaceable, and inoffensive.

†**b.** Not talkative, taciturn; not noisy, violent, or restless; calm; quiet in behaviour. *Obs.*

1477 EARL RIVERS (Caxton) *Dictes* 74 Our lorde accepteth him for noble, that doth goode werkis though he be peasible of litle wordes. **1484** CAXTON *Fables of Poge* iv, He beganne to be peasyble and gate his wytte ageyne. **1826** COBBETT *Rur. Rides* (1885) II. 49 To make the horse peaceable enough to enable me to keep on his back.

2. Characterized by peace; free from disturbance; quiet; = PEACEFUL 2 (now the usual word).

1340 HAMPOLE *Pr. Consc.* 7833, Þare es peysebelle ioy ay lastand. **1430–40** LYDG. *Bochas* IX. xxviii. (1558) 31 In full peasyble and hole possession. **1522** MORE *De quat. Noviss.* Wks. 98 Salomon saith of vertue thus: her wayes are al ful of plesure, & her pathes are pesable. **1600** E. BLOUNT tr. *Conestaggio* 4 Remaining peaceable Lord of the Realme. **1765** BLACKSTONE *Comm.* I. Introd. iii. 73 To make a particular custom good..It must have been peaceable, and acquiesced in: not subject to contention and dispute. **1845** M. PATTISON *Ess.* (1889) I. 15 To do one's duty thoroughly is not easy in the most peaceable times.

†**b.** In physical sense: Peaceful. *Obs.*

c **1400** tr. *Secreta Secret., Gov. Lordsh.* 73 Þe wyndes litel blowyn, þe see ys paisyble. *c* **1491** *Chast. Goddes Chyld.* 10 Whan there is no tempest in a pesible weder. **1555** EDEN *Decades* 220 The sayde sea cauled *Pacificum* that is peaceable. **1613** PURCHAS *Pilgrimage* (1614) 717 This Inkie Sea, through which I vndertake a Pilots office to conduct my Readers, is more peaceable then that.

3. *Comb.*

1690 NORRIS *Beatitudes* (1692) 178 This peaceable-mindedness. *a* **1716** BLACKALL *Wks.* (1723) I. 89 A peaceable-minded Man..shews his..Desire of Peace all manner of ways.

†**B.** as *sb.* (only in *pl.*, repr. L. *pacifici, pacifica* of the Vulgate). **a.** A peaceable or friendly person. **b.** A peace-offering. *Obs.*

13.. *Minor Poems fr. Vernon MS.* xxxii. 675 Blesset be þe pesybles i-tald, Godus children schul þei be cald. **1382** WYCLIF *Ezek.* xlvi. 2 Prestis shuln do his brend sacrifice and his pesibles. *a* **1533** LD. BERNERS *Gold. Bk. M. Aurel.* (1546) Z v, He hath conquered realmes, altered [= vexed, harassed] peasibles, dystroyed cities. **1609** BIBLE (Douay) *Jer.* xx. 10 The men that were my peaceables.

†**C.** as *adv.* Peaceably. *Obs.*

1478 SIR J. PASTON in *P. Lett.* III. 222 That it was peasyble my Lordys off Suffolk. **1606** G. W[OODCOCKE] *Hist. Ivstine* XXXVIII. 122 Colchos, Paphlagonia, and Bosphorus, which he now peaceable held. **1738** tr. *Guazzo's Art Conversation* 221 They cannot live peaceable together.

peaceableness (ˈpiːsəb(ə)lnɪs). Forms: see prec. [f. prec. + -NESS.] The quality, character, or condition of being peaceable: **a.** Disposition to peace; **b.** Freedom from strife or disturbance, tranquillity.

1340 HAMPOLE *Pr. Consc.* 7832 Þare es alkyn delyces and eese, And syker peysibilnes and pese. **1382** WYCLIF *Matt.* viii. 26 He rysynge comaundide to the wyndis and the see, and a grete pesiblenesse is maad. **1530** PALSGR. 253/2 Pesablenesse, *taciturnité.* **1573** G. HARVEY *Letter-bk.* (Camden) 50 Our heaven hath not floorishid so mutch heretofore thorouh peasablenes..as it is like shortly to decai thorouh contentiusnes. **1611** SPEED *Hist. Gt. Brit.* VI. xliv. (1614), Carausius..guoerned the Province with exceeding peaceablenesse. **1709** STRYPE *Ann. Ref.* I. xxxiii. 332 That City was able to govern it self in much honesty, justice, peaceableness and religion. **1834** J. H. NEWMAN *Par. Serm.* (1837) I. iii. 37 The spread of knowledge, bringing in its train..a selfish peaceableness.

peaceably (ˈpiːsəblɪ), *adv.* Forms: see PEACEABLE. [See -LY[2].] In a peaceable manner.

1. With peaceful or friendly disposition, intention, or behaviour; amicably; so as to make for or maintain peace; without making strife, opposition, or disturbance; without quarrel or dispute.

c **1330** R. BRUNNE *Chron. Wace* (Rolls) 7300 3yf swylk be comen, & peysibly þe hauene han nomen, In pes lat þem take þer rest. **1389** in *Eng. Gilds* (1870) 52 Honestliche and peysiblyche to gon to þe forseyd chirch. *c* **1449** PECOCK *Repr.* III. xiii. (Rolls) 363 Regniden in successioun euermore oon emperour after an other pesibili to gidere. **1535** COVERDALE *Zach.* viii. 16 Execute iudgment truly and peaceably. **1599** SHAKS. *Much Ado* v. ii. 72 Thou and I are too wise to wooe peaceablie. **1599** NASHE *Lenten Stuffe* Wks. (Grosart) V. 228 Not any where is..a warlike people peaceablier demeanourd. **1709** ADDISON *Tatler* No. 96 ¶2 Good Subjects, that pay their Taxes, and live peaceably in their Habitations. **1855** MACAULAY *Hist. Eng.* xii. III. 190 With assurances that the city should be peaceably surrendered.

2. Without being subject to disturbance or opposition; in peace, quietly; tranquilly, peacefully.

1375 BARBOUR *Bruce* v. 231 It anoyis me.., That the clyffurd sa pesabilly Brukis and haldis the sen3ory That suld be mine. **1471** FORTESCUE *Wks.* (1869) 527 Kynge Knoght kepte and occupied the same lande.., and died peasibly seased tharof. **1593** SHAKS. *2 Hen. VI*, III. iii. 25 Disturbe him not, let him passe peaceably. **1727** DE FOE *Syst. Magic* I. iii. (1840) 71 We come to desire your leave, that we may go peaceably, and do the duty of our worship. **1824** MACKINTOSH *Speech* 15 June, They saw the laws obeyed, justice administered,..and the revenue peaceably collected.

3. *Comb.*

1692 *Wicked Contriv. Steph. Blackhead* in *Select. fr. Harl. Misc.* (1793) 512 Some other good and peaceably-minded man. **1781** COWPER *Conversation* 90 The clash of arguments and jar of words,..Divert the champions prodigal of breath, And put the peaceably-disposed to death.

peace-breaker (ˈpiːsˌbreɪkə(r)). [f. PEACE *sb.* + BREAKER[1] 2.] One who breaks or violates peace; one who causes or stirs up strife; one who commits a breach of the peace, a violator of public order and security.

1552 LATIMER *Serm., Matt.* v. (1562) 75b, These whisperers bee peacebreakers, and not peacemakers. **1578** *Reg. Privy Council Scot.* III. 38 The saidis thevis and peace brekaris. **1642** J. SHUTE *Sarah & Hagar* (1649) 173 Are the peace-makers blessed? Then, certainly, the peace-breakers are cursed. *a* **1716** BLACKALL *Wks.* (1723) I. 90 So far from being a Peace-maker..he is a Peace-breaker. **1883** *Manchester Guard.* 15 Oct. 5/3 The police had a lively time of it in bundling out the peacebreakers.

peaceful (ˈpiːsfʊl), *a.* Forms: see PEACE *sb.* [f. PEACE *sb.* + -FUL.]

1. Disposed or inclined to peace; aiming at or making for peace; friendly, amicable, pacific. (Now *rare*, in this sense *peaceable* being usual.)

a **1300** *E.E. Psalter* cxix. [cxx.] 7 With þa þat pais hated ai, Was I paisfull. *a* **1300** *Cursor M.* 17646 Paisful bi þi cuming hider. *c* **1400** *Apol. Loll.* 107 Snyb he þe idul, solace hem of litul hert, and be pesful to all. **1526** *Pilgr. Perf.* (W. de W. 1531) 283 b, Blessed be the peacefull, for they shall be called the chyldre of god. **1593** SHAKS. *3 Hen. VI*, II. vi. 31 Good fortune bids vs pause, And smooth the frownes of War, with peacefull lookes. **1667** MILTON *P.L.* x. 946 He..thus with peaceful words uprais'd her soon. **1774** GOLDSM. *Nat. Hist.* (1776) IV. 125 The Armadillo..; a peaceful harmless creature.

2. Full of or characterized by peace; free from strife or commotion; undisturbed, untroubled, calm, tranquil, quiet. (Now the usual sense.)

a **1340** HAMPOLE *Psalter* Prol. 3 Drouyd and stormy saules it bryngis in til clere and pesful lyf. *c* **1580** SIDNEY *Ps.* IV. vii, I in peace and peacefull blisse Will lay me down and take my rest. **1632** MILTON *Penseroso* 168 And may at last my weary age Find out the peaceful hermitage. **1697** DRYDEN *Æneid* VII. 65 That rous'd the Tyrrhene realm..And peaceful Italy involv'd in arms. **1717** POPE *Eloisa* 197 Ere such a soul regains its peaceful state. **1869** MRS. H. WOOD *Roland Yorke* III. xi, His face looks as peaceful as if it were sainted.

3. Belonging to a time or state of peace.

c **1586** C'TESS PEMBROKE *Ps.* LXXII. iii, During his rule.. shall..peacefull plenty join with plenteous peace. **1606** SHAKS. *Tr. & Cr.* I. iii. 105 Peacefull Commerce from diuidable shores. **1741** MIDDLETON *Cicero* I. i. 18 Those who applied themselves to the peacefull studies, and the management of civil affairs. **1863** MARY HOWITT *F. Bremer's Greece* II. xiv. 109 An unarmed population, accustomed only to peaceful occupations.

4. a. Not violating or infringing peace; used esp. of methods for effecting purposes for which force, violence, or war, is an alternative or more obvious means.

1876 G. HOWELL *Handy-Bk. of Labour Laws* (ed. 2) ii. 29 Peaceful picketing is no longer prohibited, for, although the Government refused..to legalise 'peaceful persuasion', yet it was distinctly declared that it was legal under the Act. **1902** *Engineering* 28 Mar. 413/3 The methods of trade unions run within the line of the law, with the single exception of the form of intimidation known as 'peaceful picketing'. **1903** E. GREY in *Hansard Commons* 18 Feb. 245 Russia seems undoubtedly..to be carrying on a process of absorption in Persia, and it is being done by what, I think, a French writer has called peaceful penetration. **1906** *Act 6 Edw. VII* c. 47 §2 *marg.*, Peaceful picketing. **1909** *Westm. Gaz.* 7 Aug. 7/2 English proposals for the peaceful penetration of China from Burma have varied considerably since 1831. **1916** *Q. Rev.* Apr. 571 A regular system of 'peaceful picketing' was set up; and wounded heroes in mufti found white feathers thrust upon them by well-meaning females. **1930** *Economist* 18 Jan. 122/2 If Canada has been subjected to peaceful penetration by the economic forces of the United States it is because [etc.]. **1935** *Discovery* Nov. 320/1 It [*sc.* the spread of grasshoppers from Angará] is rather a matter of 'peaceful penetration', of infiltration, proceeding slowly and imperceptibly through the ages. **1950** *Chambers's Encycl.* XIII. 726/1 The Conspiracy and Protection of Property Act..in effect conceded the right to strike and reinstated peaceful picketing in a modified form. **1961** *U.S. Peace Corps Fact Bk.* 22 If it is decided to make a small shift which may be required from military aid or special assistance funds, in order to carry out the purposes of the Mutual Security Act through this new peaceful program, this will be a hopeful sign to the world. **1962** N. S. FALCONE *Labor Law* xi. 343 Peaceful picketing conducted at the premises of neutral employers was for the purpose of informing the public of a primary dispute and was not intended to bring about any work stoppage among the neutral employees.

b. ***peaceful coexistence***: in the foreign policy of Soviet Russia, a concept of varying emphasis referring to relations with the capitalist West. Also *transf.* and *fig.*

In recent years *peaceful coexistence* has implied avoidance of nuclear confrontation. (Quot. 1920, cited from Carew Hunt *A Guide to Communist Jargon* (1957) 27, could not be verified as no copy of the newspaper appears to have survived.)

1920 *N.Y. Even. Jrnl.* 18 Feb., [Interview with Lenin] Our plans in Asia? The same as in Europe: peaceful coexistence with the peoples, with the workers and peasants of all nations. **1952** *Times* 2 Apr. 3/3 (*heading*) The invitations are..careful to emphasize the peaceful coexistence theme... The conference is based on the assumption..that mutually advantageous economic co-operation between Socialist and capitalist countries is quite possible. **1954** *Time* 4 Oct. 32/1 Attlee's men replied with one of those ingenious compromises that make peaceful coexistence possible between the two wings of the Labor Party: a policy favoring arms and sovereignty for the Germans but also offering to 'consider' some more Big Three talks with the Russians. **1956** R. MACAULAY *Towers of Trebizond* vi. 62 Turks do not believe in peaceful co-existence with Russia, they never have, and Father Chantry-Pigg agrees with them. **1959** *Listener* 26 Mar. 539/2 Both the Communist Party and the Church [in Poland] benefit immensely from the unprecedented type of peaceful coexistence they have worked out together. **1961** *Times* 2 Jan. 8/3 Mr. Khrushchev, at a New Year banquet.. in the Kremlin,..raised his glass and bade the whole company drink to peaceful coexistence. **1973** *Time* 25 June 31/3 Articles have appeared..applauding Brezhnev's peaceful-coexistence policy. **1977** *Lancet* 29 Oct. 903/2 Many microorganisms have been accused; so far, none have fulfilled Koch's postulates and some are known to live in peaceful coexistence with the healthy gut.

peacefully ('piːsfʊlɪ), *adv.* [f. prec. + -LY².] In a peaceful manner. **a.** So as to make for peace; with friendly behaviour, amicably, peaceably. **b.** In peace, tranquilly, quietly.

a **1300** *E.E. Psalter* xxxiv. [xxxv.] 20 Summe.. Paisfulike þat spekes. **1411** *Rolls of Parlt.* III. 650/2, I am a Justice that ..scholde have had me more discretly and peesfully. **1665** DRYDEN *Ind. Emp.* II. i, Our lov'd earth, where peacefully we slept. **1864** MISS BRADDON *H. Dunbar* xix, An old man who ended a good and prosperous life peacefully. **1904** *Minutes of Evid. R. Comm. Trade Disputes* 262/1 in *Parl. Papers 1906* (Cd. 2826) LVI. 137, I have never seen picketing conducted peacefully yet. **1920** *Act 10 & 11 Geo. V* c. 55 §2 (1) No such regulation shall make it an offence for any person or persons..peacefully to persuade any other person or persons to take part in a strike. **1935** E. WEEKLEY *Something about Words* i. 25 Unfortunately, 'refined' American is also penetrating peacefully, and I confidently expect that the English undertaker will soon describe himself as a *mortician*. **1961** *Nation* (N.Y.) 11 Nov. 371/3 Khrushchev..would like, above all, the Berlin and German problems to be settled peacefully.

'peacefulness. [f. as prec. + -NESS.] The quality, character, or state of being peaceful; disposition or inclination for peace (now *rare*); quietness, tranquillity; undisturbed condition.

1651 JER. TAYLOR *Serm. for Year* II. viii. 94 Humility, Peacefulnesse and Charity. **1755** in JOHNSON. **1813** SHELLEY *Q. Mab* IV. 157 To turn The keenest pangs to peacefulness. **1846** J. BAXTER *Libr. Pract. Agric.* (ed. 4) I. 103 The quiet stillness and peacefulness of nature. **1863** KINGLAKE *Crimea* I. xxviii. 487 The steps by which England was brought from her seeming peacefulness into a temper impatiently warlike.

'peace-,keeper. One who keeps or maintains peace; one who 'keeps the peace' or refrains from strife (? *obs.*); one who prevents or averts strife; a guardian of the peace. Also, an organization that keeps or maintains the peace; one regularly employed in the maintenance of peace between nations or communities; a soldier in a force so employed. So **'peace-keeping** *vbl. sb.* (freq. *attrib.*).

1579–80 NORTH *Plutarch* (1656) 56 Those which the Grecians call *Irenophylaces*, as who would say, peace-keepers. **1643** [ANGIER] *Lanc. Vall. Achor* 5 Had not God ..moved them to be the Peace-Keepers..they had been satisfied with blood. **1883** *Times* 6 Sept., Germany, as our Berlin correspondent said yesterday, is the peacemaker and the peace-keeper of Europe. **1961** *Times* 2 Oct. 13/3 Budgetary procedures..including the cost of peace-keeping operations. **1961** *Guardian* 24 Oct. 8/3 The problems of a disarmed world, peace-keeping machinery, etc. **1963** *Times* 22 Apr. 11/3 The development of the United Nations as a peacekeeping organization will be seriously hampered before the summer is out if its present financial difficulties are not solved. **1964** *Daily Tel.* 17 Jan. 12/2 The sending of some international peacekeeping force has become a matter of extreme urgency. **1964** *Manch. Guardian Weekly* 5 Mar. 1 If an international truce force went to the island [*sc.* Cyprus], Turkey would forgo its right to intervene for three months... This is..a rare declaration of faith in the United Nations as a peace-keeper. **1965** *Spectator* 15 Jan. 76/2 Peace-keeping is the basic function of the United Nations. **1965** *Maclean's Mag.* 1 Dec. 16 Lieutenant-General Burns ..was the first of a new breed of international trouble-shooters who now try to halt the escalators of war by policing cease-fires—the Canadian peacekeepers. **1973** TIMES 17 Sept. 16/8 Peacekeeping is..a purely temporary role; a permanently-active peacekeeper must in the end become an irritant. **1977** R. HOLLAND *Self & Social Context* ix. 274 The forces of capital and labour face each other unmediated by the normal peace-keeping functions of police intermediaries. **1978** *Globe & Mail* (Toronto) 20 Oct. 10/6 Although Mr. Jamieson refused to commit Canadian forces to a peacekeeping force in the territory, he indicated he was moving in that direction.

peaceless ('piːslɪs), *a.* [f. PEACE *sb.* + -LESS.] Devoid of peace; not peaceful; unquiet.

1522 SKELTON *Why not to Court* 72 Pratyng for peace peaclesse. **1640** G. SANDYS *Christ's Passion* IV. 254 Terrours ..affright Our peacelesse souls. **1791** J. LEARMONT *Poems* 211 In peaceless paths of Sin. **1884** M. RULE *Pref. Eadmeri Hist.* (Rolls) p. cvii, The peaceless peace concluded between king and primate in..1095.

Hence **'peacelessness.**

1852 *Meanderings of Mem.* I. 20 Coins that were tinkled, ever shook In pouch of peacelessness. **1892** STOPF. BROOKE *Short Serm.* 70 Anxiety is a fruitful source of peacelessness.

peacemaker ('piːsˌmeɪkə(r)). [f. as prec. + MAKER.] One who makes or brings about peace; one who allays strife or reconciles opponents.

1436 *Libel Eng. Policy* in *Pol. Poems* (Rolls) II. 203 Pease makers, as Mathew writeth aryght, Shull be called the sonnes of God allemight. **1534** TINDALE *Matt.* v. 9 Blessed are the peacemakers [1526, 'maynteyners of peace']. **1600** SHAKS. *A.Y.L.* v. iv. 108 Your If is the onely peace-maker. **1715** *Wodrow Corr.* (1843) II. 57 If peace-makers be blessed, peace-preservers will not want their own share. **1867** FREEMAN *Norm. Conq.* I. v. 315 The Roman Bishop appears in his proper character of a common peacemaker.

†**b.** In the colony of Pennsylvania, the name for a Justice of the Peace. *Obs.*

1683 *Col. Rec. Pennsylv.* I. 66 The Question was asked in Councill whether Peace Makers should sitt once a month.

c. Humorous term for a revolver, gun, or warship, as decisively settling a dispute.

1841 LEVER *C. O'Malley* vii. 40 The small mahogany box, which contained his peace-makers. **1861** LOWELL *Biglow P.* Poems 1890 II. 226 A feller.., Lep' up an' drawed his peace-maker, an', 'Dash it, Sir', suz he. **1880** (*title*) Dr. J. H. McLean's Peace Makers. A description of the Guns, &c., manufactured by McLean and Coloney.

So **'peace,making** *sb.*, the action of making or bringing about peace; reconciliation of opponents; conclusion of peace; **'peace,making** *a.*, that makes or brings about peace.

1556 OLDE *Antichrist* 62 b, The great and peacemaking Emperour. **1560** DAUS tr. *Sleidane's Comm.* 375 Certen articles of yᵉ same peacemaking. **1571** GOLDING *Calvin on Ps.* li. 19 Christ with the true..peacemaking or atonement. **1643** MILTON *Divorce* I. vi, That the law should be made more provident of peacemaking then the Gospel! **1878** STUBBS *Const. Hist.* III. xviii. 226 The peacemaking duke who fell at Northampton. **1887** *Pall Mall G.* 24 Jan. 1/2 It may seem like fiddling while Rome is burning to talk of peacemaking at such a moment.

'peace-man.

†**1.** A man who is at peace with (the king), or under the king's peace. *Obs.*

c **1425** *Eng. Conq. Irel.* 142 To harme of pees-men, & nat of fomen. **1473** *Waterford Arch.* in *10th Rep. Hist. MSS. Comm.* App. v. 310 None of the Kyngs liegmen nor peasmen.

2. A man who favours or advocates peace. (Now usually as two words, 'piːs 'mæn.)

1848 LOWELL *Biglow P.* Poems 1890 II. 125 I'm a decided peace-man, tu, an' go agin the war. **1872** SPURGEON *Treas. Dav.* Ps. lxviii. 30 God's people were peacemen, and only desired the crushing of oppressive nations, that war might not occur again. **1899** *Daily News* 26 Jan. 5/1 Labelling some Liberals as 'peace men' and others as 'war men'.

peacemeale, obs. form of PIECEMEAL.

peacemonger ('piːsˌmʌŋgə(r)). [See MONGER.] A hostile term for a peacemaker, or for one who aims at or advocates peace in a way which the speaker reprobates. So **'peace,mongering** *sb.* and *a.*

1808 SOUTHEY *Let. to Rickman* 13 Sept., The peace-mongers were ready to have sacrificed the honour of England. —— *Let. to H. H. Southey* 14 Nov., That peace-monger squad who would lay us at the feet of France. **1871** BLACKIE *Four Phases* I. 115 Do you really mean to stand up as a universal peacemonger? **1880** *Sat. Rev.* 24 July 124/1 Elihu Burritt's chief object in life, the great enthusiasm that inspired and possessed him.., was that of the peace-monger. **1900** *Daily Tel.* 10 May 8/7 A peace-mongering sentimentalism. **1928** *Funk's Stand. Dict.* II. 1815/2 Peacemongering, *n.* **1949** *N.Y. Times* 26 June IV. 1/2 Peacemongers, apparently in the hope that East-West tension would be lessened and the West's position softened. **1967** *Economist* 1 Apr. 26/3 He need not seek the political kudos that holders of other offices may hope to gain by public peacemongering. **1969** *Guardian* 18 Sept. 3/1 Peace-mongers who prolong the Vietnam war.

peacenik ('piːsnɪk). [f. PEACE *sb.* + -NIK.] A member of a pacifist movement, esp. when regarded as a 'hippy'; freq. *spec.* an opponent of the military intervention of the United States in Vietnam. Also *attrib.*

1965 *Time* 23 Apr. 13/2 (*heading*) War & Peaceniks. **1965** *San Francisco Examiner* 6 Sept. 14/2 Dean Plapowski.. described himself as a 'peacenik'. This, he explained, 'is probably a beatnik who's got himself hung up in pacifist and non-violent activity'. **1966** *Guardian* 17 Aug. 9/2 The 60-year-old Judge is not suspected of 'peacenik' sympathies. **1971** *Ibid.* 14 July 11/5 The air base appears to treat its peaceniks with an easy tolerance. **1974** K. MILLETT *Flying* (1975) I. 117 A tenement crammed with peaceniks who have painted the word *love* across their brickfront. **1975** P. HARCOURT *Fair Exchange* I. 56 Who is this peacenik anyway?

'peace-,offering. [f. PEACE *sb.* + OFFERING.]

1. In the Eng. Bible, as a term of the Levitical law, An offering or sacrifice presented as an expression of thanksgiving to God.

In Heb. *zebaχ hashshĕlāmīm*, or simply *shelem*, pl. *shĕlāmīm*, prob. more accurately, 'thank-offering'.

1535 COVERDALE *1 Macc.* i. 45 Antiochus..forbad ether burntofferynge, meatofferynge or peaceofferynge [*R. V.* whole burnt offerings and sacrifice and drink offerings] to be made. **1539** BIBLE (Great) *Lev.* vii. 11 This is the lawe of the peaceoffringe [COVERD. healthofferinge]. *Ibid.* 15 The flesh of the thankoffrynge in hys peaceoffringes [COVERD., The flesh of the thankofferynge in his healthofferynges; *Bishops'*, the fleashe of his peace offeringes for thankesgeuing; *Geneva*, the flesh of the peace offerings for thankes-giuing; **1611**, the flesh of the sacrifice of his peace offerings for thanksgiuing]. **1611** BIBLE *Lev.* iii. 1 And if his oblation be a sacrifice of peace offering [*R.V.* (1885) peace offerings; *marg.* Or, thank offerings]. **1698** BP. PATRICK *Comm. Lev.* iii. 1 They seem to me to have given the best account of this, who..think these were called Peace-offerings, because they were principally thankful acknowledgments of Mercies received from God's Bounty. **1860** PUSEY *Min. Proph.* 198 Peace-offerings, as tokens of the willing thankfulness of souls at peace with God.

2. An offering made to make or obtain peace; a propitiatory sacrifice or gift.

a **1661** FULLER *Worthies, Staffs.* (1840) III. 133 They [Dudley and Empson] were made a peace-offering to popular anger 1510, and were executed at Tower-hill. **1776** BURNEY *Hist. Mus.* I. 275 *note*, According to Homer's account..it was given by..[Mercury] to Apollo, as a peace-offering, and indemnification for the oxen which he had stolen. **1848** THACKERAY *Bk. Snobs* xxiv, An elegant little present, which I had brought..as a peace-offering to Mrs. Ponto.

'peace-,officer. A civil officer appointed to preserve the public peace, as a constable.

1714 *Act 1 Geo. I* c. 5 §3 High or Petty-constable and other Peace-officer. **1837** DICKENS *Pickw.* ii, The assistance of several peace officers. **1959** JOWITT *Dict. Eng. Law* II. 1320/1 *Peace officer*, a constable, coroner, justice or sheriff. **1965** *Economist* 7 Aug. p. xi/3 The officers in charge of these [S. African local labour] bureaus are now being designated 'peace officers', and have powers of arrest and search of houses. **1973** *Black Panther* 16 June 12/3 The scores of uniformed 'peace officers'. **1976** *Columbus* (Montana) *News* 10 June 1/3 They had hoped more residents would attend to express their wishes about having a full-time peace officer.

peace-time, peacetime. Also peace time. [PEACE *sb.* 17.] The time when a country is not at war. Also *U.S.* (with pl.), a period during which no declaration of war is in force. Also *attrib.*

1551 R. ROBINSON tr. *More's Utopia* I. sig. C v recto, The hole realme is fylled and besieged wyth hierede soldiours in peace tyme, yf that be peace. **1917** A. G. EMPEY *Over Top* 311 *Territorial*, a peace-time soldier with the same status as the American militiaman. **1923** *Man. Seamanship* (Admiralty) II. 5 In peace time at sea. **1938** *Sun* (Baltimore) 16 Apr. 8/3 His [*sc.* Roosevelt's] savage attacks in 1932 upon Mr. Hoover's Administration as the greatest spender of all peacetimes. **1940** *Economist* 5 Oct. 426/2 Already its price is more than four times the peace-time level. **1942** *Short Guide Gt. Brit.* (U.S. War Dept.) 23 Most British food is imported even in peacetimes. **1952** R. KNOX *Hidden Stream* xii. 106 I should want to take a good look round, as we did in the days of old-fashioned, peace-time shopping. **1955** *Times* 5 July 10/1 After transfer the Royal Navy will continue to enjoy the facilities of the Simonstown base in peace-time. **1968** S. HYNES *Edwardian Turn of Mind* viii. 273 That curious last-minute plunge toward the twentieth century that marked so strikingly that last peace-time summer. **1971** S. HILL *Strange Meeting* iii. 188, I hope all the rest will not be spoilt for leave, or peace-time. **1971** W. H. MCNEILL in A. Bullock *20th Cent.* 47/1 War-born techniques of administrative mobilization were carried over into peacetime.

peach (piːtʃ), *sb.*¹ Forms: 4–6 **peche**, 5 **peshe**, **pesshe**, (**peske**, **peesk**), 6 **peache**, 6– **peach**. [ME. a. F. *pêche*, OF. *peche*, earlier *pesche*, in ONF.

peske (= Pr. *persega*, It. *persica*, *pesca*):— late L. *persica* (med.L. in Du Cange), for cl. L. *persicum*, ellipt. for *Persicum mālum* lit. Persian apple: so *Persica mālus* or *arbor*, peach-tree.

The phonetic development in Romanic was *persica*, **persca*, *pesca*, *peske*, *pesche*, *pêche*.]

1. a. The fruit of the tree *Amygdalus persica* (see 2), a large drupe, usually round, of a whitish or yellow colour, flushed with red, with downy skin, highly flavoured sweet pulp, and rough furrowed stone; cultivated in many varieties.

The varieties are classed as CLINGSTONE or FREESTONE according as the pulp adheres to or separates from the stone. The NECTARINE is a variety with smooth skin and different flavour.

? *a* **1366** CHAUCER *Rom. Rose* 1373 And many hoomly trees ther were, That peches, coynes, and apples bere. *c* **1440** *Promp. Parv.* 395/1 Peske, or peche, frute [*v.rr.* peesk, peshe], *pesca, pomum Percicum*. *c* **1483** CAXTON *Dialogues* 13/7 Cheryes, .. strawberies, .. pesshes, medliers. **1542** BOORDE *Dyetary* xxi. (1870) 283 Peches doeth mollyfy the bely, and be colde. **1591** SYLVESTER *Du Bartas* I. iii. 569 The velvet Peach, gilt Orenge, downy Quince. **1620** VENNER *Via Recta* vii. 114 Peaches and Aprecocks are of one and the same nature. **1730–46** THOMSON *Autumn* 676 The downy peach, the shining plum, The ruddy, fragrant nectarine. **1884** MISS BRADDON *Ishmael* xxxvi, A gray velvet bodice that fitted the plump, supple figure, as the rind fits the peach.

b. *slang*. Someone or something of exceptional worth or quality; someone or something particularly suitable or desirable, esp. an attractive young woman.

1754 E. TURNER *Let.* 16 Aug. in Dickins & Stanton *18th-Cent. Corresp.* (1910) 238, I had almost forgot that orange Peach, your Niece. **1863** B. HARTE in *Daily Even. Bull.* (San Francisco) 9 Dec. 5/3 Phrases such as camps may teach, .. Such as 'Bully!' 'Them's the Peach!' **1888** *Puck* (U.S.) XXII. 415/2 An' two young darters—one eighteen. A reg'ler peach. **1904** W. H. SMITH *Promoters* vii. 134 You're a brick! You're a peach! **1907** *Punch* 2 Jan. 13/2 Prof. Br——ce: H'm! Nice pleasant expression! One who was not a purist in language might almost describe him as a '*peach*'. **1917** WODEHOUSE *Man with Two Left Feet* 62 Opinions differ about girls. One man's peach .. is another man's poison. **1919** H. L. WILSON *Ma Pettengill* iv. 111, I .. landed a hard right on the side of his jaw and dropped him just like that. It was one peach I handed him and he slumped down like a sack of mush. **1924** 'J. SUTHERLAND' *Circle of Stars* xii. 126 It's a peach of a storm, and it's getting worse every moment. **1925** F. SCOTT FITZGERALD *Let.* June (1964) 484 He's a peach of a fellow and absolutely first-rate. **1930** 'R. CROMPTON' *William—the Bad* i. 19 Now would you think that a peach like her would fall for a fat-headed chump like that? **1943** E. B. WHITE *Let.* 1 Jan. (1976) 236 You were a peach to give me such a good present. **1949** *Sunday World-Herald Mag.* (Omaha, Nebraska) 1 May 2/1 The new recipe for making a peach cordial: Buy her a drink. **1974** *Times* 1 Apr. 12/4 She had, of course, a peach of a subject. **1976** *Derbyshire Times* (Peak ed.) 3 Sept. 22/6 (Advt.), 1972 Peugeot 504, white, 34,000, a real peach, £1,395. **1976** P. DICKINSON *King & Joker* iv. 46 Louise had a history essay, a real peach for which she'd only needed to look up a few dates. **1977** D. FRANCIS *Risk* xiv. 179 Dad's brought the detestable Lida... Actually I would have liked it .. if he'd fallen for a peach.

c. ***peaches and cream***: used *attrib.* and *absol.* to designate a fair complexion characterized by creamy skin and pink cheeks.

1901 ADE *Forty Mod. Fables* 188 Give me some perfumed Dope that will restore a Peaches and Cream Complexion. **1967** 'D. SHANNON' *Rain with Violence* (1969) i. 10 Carole had very blonde hair .. and a peaches-and-cream skin. **1969** 'J. ASHFORD' *Prisoner at Bar* vii. 62 She had the perfect peaches-and-cream beauty that was often called classical English. **1975** *New Yorker* 9 June 46/3 She had a real peaches-and-cream complexion and a trim figure. **1978** J. W. WAINWRIGHT *Jury People* lxii. 211 His complexion .. was pure 'peaches and cream'.

2. The tree *Amygdalus* (*Prunus*) *persica*, N.O. *Rosaceæ*, a native of Asia, introduced in ancient times into Europe; the peach-tree.

c **1400** *Lanfranc's Cirurg.* 83 (Ashm. MS.) Þe ius of þe leeues of pechis. **1530** PALSGR. 252/2 Peache, tree, *peschier*. **1663** COWLEY *Disc., Garden* x, He bids the rustick Plum to rear A noble Trunk, and be a Peach. **1796** C. MARSHALL *Garden.* xvii. (1813) 284 Peach .. succeeds better than the nectarine, as to bearing and ripening. **1898** *Johnson's Gard. Dict.* 722/2 Do not brush off the foliage of peaches in the autumn.

3. Applied to other edible fruits resembling the peach, or to the plants producing them: **a.** *Sarcocephalus esculentus*, a climbing shrub of West Africa (***Guinea, Negro,*** or ***Sierra Leone peach***), bearing a large juicy berry arising from the fused ovaries of a cluster of flowers; **b.** the QUANDONG, *Fusanus acuminatus* or *Santalum acuminatum*, of Australia (***native peach***): **c.** *Prunus caroliniana*, the Carolina cherry-laurel (***wild peach***), also called *wild orange*; †**d.** ***wolf's peach***, the tomato (*Solanum lycopersicum*).

1760 J. LEE *Introd. Bot.* App. 322 Peach, Wolf's, *Solanum*. **1866** *Treas. Bot.* 854 Peach, Guinea, .. Native, of Australia, .. of Sierra Leone. *Ibid.* 1020 *S*[*arcocephalus*] *esculentus* has pink flowers and an edible fruit, of the size of a peach, whence it has been called the Sierra Leone Peach.

4. Short for *peach-brandy*: see 6. (*U.S.*)

1809 M. L. WEEMS *Life Gen. F. Marion* viii. 74 Suppose you take a glass of Peach. **1845** J. J. HOOPER *Some Adventures Simon Suggs* v. 53 Thar's koniac, and old peach, and rectified. **1853** KANE *Grinnell Exp.* xxxiv. (1856) 302 There the air, pure and sharply cold .. braces you up like peach and honey in a Virginia fog. **1880** *Barman's Man.* 55 *Peach and Honey*, one table-spoonful of honey; one wine-glass of peach brandy. Stir with a spoon.

5. = *peach-colour*: see 6; also *attrib.* or as *adj.*

1848 DICKENS *Dombey* xxxvii, The diamonds or the peach-velvet bonnet. **1882** *Garden* 16 Sept. 260/1 Blooms of .. rosy peach. **1900** *London Letter* 26 Jan. 133/1 Outlined in varying shades of roses from palest peach to deepest puce; .. pleatings of white chiffon edged with peach ruches.

6. *attrib.* and *Comb.*, as ***peach-bud, -down, -flavour, -flower, -graft, -kernel, -orchard, -stone***; ***peach-fed, -like*** adjs.; also with names of colours: designating that shade of the colour which is shown by the peach, as ***peach-beige, -green, -pink, -red***; **peach aphid, aphis**, one of several aphides infesting peach trees, esp. the peach-potato aphis, *Myzus persicae*; **peach-bells**, a name for the peach-leaved bellflower (*Campanula persicifolia*); **peach-black**, a black pigment made from calcined peach-stones; **peach-blight, peach-blister**, diseases of peach-trees, caused by the fungi *Monilia fructigena* and *Taphrina deformans* respectively; **peach-borer**, a name of insects whose larvæ bore through the bark of the peach-tree: *spec.* a moth, *Ægeria exitiosa*, and a beetle, *Dicerca divaricata*; **peach-brake**, a dense thicket of the 'wild peach' in Texas (see 3 c); **peach-brandy**, a spirituous liquor made from the fermented juice of peaches; **peach cobbler** *U.S.*, a cobbler (sense 4) made with peaches; **peach-colour**, (*a*) the colour of a ripe peach, a soft pale red; (*b*) the colour of PEACH-BLOSSOM, a delicate rose or pink; also *attrib.* or as *adj.*; so **peach-coloured** *a.*; **peach fly** = *peach aphid*; **peach-house**, a building in which peaches are grown under glass; **peach leaf-curl** = *leaf-curl* (*b*) s.v. LEAF *sb.*[1] 18; **peach-leaved** *a.*, having leaves like the peach; **peach Melba**: see MELBA; **peach myrtle**, name for the Australian myrtaceous shrubs of the genus *Hypocalymma*, with rose-coloured flowers; **peach oak**, name given to two N. American species of oak, *Quercus densiflora* (also *chestnut oak* or *tan-bark oak*), and *Q. phellos* (*willow oak*); **peach-palm**, a species of palm (*Guilielma speciosa*) found in tropical south America, bearing a large egg-shaped red-and-orange fruit with firm flesh which becomes mealy and edible when cooked; **peach-pip, -pit**, a peach-stone; **peach-potato aphid, aphis**, an aphis, *Myzus persicæ*, which causes leaf-curl in peach trees and other plants, and also transmits many plant virus diseases; **Peach State**, a sobriquet of the State of Georgia in the U.S.; **peach-water**, a flavouring extract obtained from peach-leaves, having a flavour of bitter almonds; **peach-wood**, a dye-wood (also called *Nicaragua wood*) resembling brazil-wood, supposed to be that of some species of *Cæsalpinia*; **peach-worm**, one of various caterpillars which infest the leaves of peach-trees, chiefly in America; **peach yellows**, a virus disease affecting cultivated peach-trees, esp. in the United States, in which the leaves become dwarfed, distorted, and yellowish, and the tree dies in a few years.

1909 F. V. THEOBALD *Insect & Other Allied Pests* 324 *Peach Aphides... At least four species of aphis attack the peach in this country. **1937** A. M. MASSEE *Pests of Fruit & Hops* vii. 163 The Peach Aphis has been recorded on a very large number of host plants, including fruit trees. **1942** *Phytopathology* XXXII. 93 (*title*) A virosis-like injury of snapdragons caused by feeding of peach aphid. **1963** *Jrnl. Insect Physiol.* IX. 875 (*title*) Some amino acid requirements of the green peach aphid, *Myzus persicae*. **1927** *Peach-beige [see GRÈGE *a.* and *sb.*]. **1597** GERARDE *Herbal* II. cxi. 366 Of *Peach bels, and Steeple bels. **1611** COTGR., *Campanettes blanches*, White Peach-bels, or Steeple-bell-flowers. [**1835** G. FIELD *Chromatogr.* 265 (Index), Black .. Peach-stone 180. *Ibid.* xxi. 180 Similar blacks are prepared of vine twigs and tendrils, .. also from peach-stones, &c. whence Almond black.] **1869** T. W. SALTER *Field's Chromatogr.* (new ed.) xxi. 407 **Peach Black*, or Almond Black, made by burning the stones of fruits, the shell of the cocoa-nut, &c., is a violet-black, once much used by Parisian artists. **1948** F. A. STAPLES *Watercolour Painting* (1951) i. 3 You will want to add the following to the palette: Raw Sienna, .. New Blue and Peach Black. **1963** *Times* 6 May 16/3 Many students will remember how much 'Corfi' enjoyed laying a wash of thickly sedimented peach black and raw sienna on a drawing that had taken weeks to prepare. **1866** *Treas. Bot.* 854 **Peach-blister*, an affection to which peach-leaves are subject, the leaves becoming thick, bladdery, and curled. **1711** W. BYRD *Secret Diary* 9 Sept. (1941) 403 After drinking two drams of *peach brandy we returned to Mrs. Randolph's. *c* **1780** [see *apple-brandy*]. **1814** SCOTT *Diary* 10 Aug. in *Lockhart*, They could get from an American trader a bottle of peach-brandy or rum. **1881** E. E. FREWER tr. *Holub's Seven Years S. Afr.* I. xi. 420 The next farm .. was that belonging to Martin Zwart, whom we found engaged in distilling peach-brandy. **1965** AMERINE & SINGLETON *Wine* xvii. 268 Wines were made also from peaches and distilled into peach brandy. **1976** J. MCCLURE *Rogue Eagle* vii. 129 As peach brandy goes, this is among the best *sluks* I've ever tasted. **1666** BOYLE *Formes & Qual.* I. iii. Wks. 1772 III. 72 A *peach-bud does .. change the sap that comes to it into a fruit very differing from that which the stock naturally produceth. **1859** BARTLETT *Dict. Amer.* (ed. 2) 90 *Cobbler*... According to the fruit, it is an apple or a *peach cobbler. **1880** [see COBBLER 4]. **1947** *Reader's Digest* Apr. 130/2 You could smell a peach cobbler all through dinner. **1976** *National Observer* (U.S.) 28 Aug. 14/3 Peach cobbler (*recipe follows*). **1599** J. RIDER *Bibl. Schol.* 1709 A *peach colour, *persicus color*. **1605** *Lond. Prodigal* I. B ij b, A peach colour satten shute, Cut vpon cloath of siluer. **1735** *Dict. Polygraph.* s.v. *Glass*, To make a Peach colour in Glass. **1597** SHAKS. *2 Hen. IV*, II. ii. 19 Take note how many paire of Silk stockings thou hast? (Viz. these, and those that were thy *peach-colour'd ones.) **1852** *Beck's Florist* June 131 *Daphne Mezereum* .. pretty peach-coloured blossoms. **1894** MRS. DYAN *All in a Man's K.* (1899) 170 She smoothed one *peach-down cheek with complacency. **1796** *New Ann. Reg.* 165 Not the shade Ambrosial, waving its *peach-flowers that blow To pearly grapes, and kiss the turf below. **1796** KIRWAN *Elem. Min.* (ed. 2) I. 29 Peach-flower red—pale whitish red. **1865** *Our Young Folks* I. 715 The *peach-fly was thus kept from laying its eggs in the soft bark at the surface of the ground. **1905** *Chambers's Jrnl.* May 368/1 The peach .. is not now obtainable, through the inroads of the peach-fly. **1971** J. DRUMMOND *Farewell Party* 8 A great sunset .. a wash of *peach-green that ran across the sky. [**1887** *Bot. Gaz.* XII. 216 (*title*) The 'Curl' of Peach Leaves. *Ibid.* Pl. XIII. (*caption*) Knowles on Peach Curl. **1888** *Amer. Naturalist* XXII. 738 *T*[*aphrina*] *deformans* Tul., causing the 'peach curl' of the leaves of the peach tree.] **1899** *Bull. Cornell Univ. Agric. Exper. Station* CLXIV. 371 *Peach leaf-curl is a disease which has long been known to the orchardist as well as to the botanist; and since the seasons of 1897 and 1898 there are probably very few peach growers .. who are unfamiliar with the disease. **1904** *Westm. Gaz.* 6 Oct. 10/2 A fungus disease called peach leaf-curl .. does injury to the extent of £600,000 annually in the United States. **1920** P. J. FRYER *Insect Pests & Fungus Dis.* xxxv. 557 Peach Leaf Curl... Plants Attacked. Peaches, nectarines and almonds. **1955** H. WORMALD *Dis. Fruit & Hops* (ed. 3) vii. 172 Peach Leaf Curl .. is found not only on peaches but also on nectarines and almonds. **1976** *Country Life* 18 Mar. 685/3 Garlic is said to protect peaches from peach-leaf curl. **1597** GERARDE *Herbal* II. cxi. 366 *Campanula Persicifolia*. *Peach-leafed Bell flower .. hath a great number of small and long leaues, rising in a great bush out of the ground, like the leaues of the Peach tree. **1834** M. SCOTT *Cruise Midge* (1863) 169 His downy cheeks as *peach-like and blooming as ever. **1882** *Garden* 9 Sept. 230/3 The *Peach Myrtle .. is one of the many beautiful Australian plants. **1835** J. MARTIN *New Gazetteer Virginia* 209 *Peach oak (so called from the resemblance of its leaves to that of the peach tree). **1897** G. B SUDWORTH *Nomencl. Arborescent Flora U.S.* 177 *Quercus phellos* Linn. Willow Oak... Common Names... Peach Oak (N.J., Del., Ohio). **1676** T. GLOVER in *Phil. Trans. R. Soc.* XI. 628 Here are likewise great *Peach-Orchards, which bear .. an infinite quantity of Peaches. **1758** *Calendar Virginia State Papers* (1875) I. 257 We .. overtook them at a peach orchard. *c* **1805** D. MCCLURE *Diary* (1899) 68 Between the house & the bank of the River was a .. peach orchard. *a* **1936** KIPLING *Something of Myself* (1937) vi. 170 A bull-kudu .. would jump the seven-foot fence round our little peach orchard. **1955** W. MOORE *Bring Jubilee* xix. 185, I made my way towards a farm on which there was a wheat-field and a peach orchard. **1974** *Sat. Rev. World* (U.S.) 2 Nov. 32/3 A long valley, green and golden with peach orchards—Canada's peach heartland. **1863** BATES *Nat. Amazon* x. (1864) 325 The celebrated '*peach-palm' .. is a common tree at Ega. The name, I suppose, is in allusion to the colour of the fruit, and not to its flavour. **1926** M. LEINSTER *Dew on Leaf* I. vii. 97 Ah Dai fingered and thumbed a fragment of the *peach-pink silk he had unfurled for her inspection. **1934** A. HUXLEY *Beyond Mexique Bay* 2 The last word in cocktail bars and peach-pink sanitary fittings. **1956** R. MACAULAY *Towers of Trebizond* xiv. 171 Through the windows I saw the circle of the Circassian mountains, indigo and brown and peach-pink in the sunset. [**1931** K. M. SMITH *Textbk. Agric. Entomol.* vi. 50 (*heading*) Potato and Peach Aphis.] **1951** *New Biol.* XI. 51 The *peach-potato aphid .. is the main carrier of the known plant virus diseases throughout the world. **1959** *Times* 27 July 9/5 The aphids responsible for spreading the viruses—mainly the peach-potato aphid *Myzus persicae*—are able to multiply on the [potato] crop during the summer. **1975** D. S. HILL *Agric. Insect Pests of Tropics* v. 163/1 Peach-Potato Aphid. .. Peach (primary host)... Potato (secondary host), and polyphagous on many other crop plants and weeds. **1926** M. LEINSTER *Dew on Leaf* 114 My unborn son waits to clutch my heart-strings with *peach-red fingers, with the call of flesh to flesh. **1935** W. DE LA MARE *Poems, 1919–1934* 377 Peach-red carnelian, apple-green chrysoprase, Amber and coral and orient pearl! **1941** G. E. SHANKLE *State Names* (rev. ed.) ii. 110 Georgia was nicknamed *The *Peach State* in 1939 because 'peaches have been an important product of Georgia since the middle of the sixteenth century'. **1954** *Nat. Geogr. Mag.* Mar. 318/1 Georgia's automobile license plates carry the legend, 'Peach State'. **1970** G. PAYTON *Webster's Dict. Proper Names* 515/1 *Peach State*, a nickname for Georgia, where peaches are now a valuable crop in the center and south. **1976** *S. Wales Echo* 26 Nov. 2/5 With out-of-state tourists flocking to Jimmy Carter's home town in Plains, Georgia, officials are looking for ways to lure the visitors to the peach state's other attractions. **1580** HOLLYBAND *Treas. Fr. Tong*, *Peschenoix*, a *Peach stone. **1889** R. BRYDALL *Art in Scot.* xiv. 288 [Nasmyth] used largely a colour he called peach-stone grey, made from calcined peach-stones. **1822** IMISON *Sc. & Art* II. 186 *Peach-wood gives a colour inferior to Brazil. **1814** *Cramer's Pittsburgh Mag. Almanac 1815* 55 (*heading*) Remedy for the *Peach Worm. *a* **1817** T. DWIGHT *Trav. New-Eng.* (1821) I. 76 The Peach Worm has been known here for about fifty years; and is now become very common. **1856** *Rep. Comm. Patents: Agric. 1855* (U.S. Dept. Agric.) 299 The ravages of the peach-worm have proved more extensive than usual. [**1808** R. PETERS in *Mem. Philad. Soc. for Promoting Agric.* I. 23 Mr. H. begins to suffer by the disease, I call the 'yellows'. *Ibid.* 24 The 'yellows' are seen making destructive ravages in Mr. Heston's peach plantation.] **1888** *Bull. U.S. Dept. Agric. Bot. Div.* IX. 9 *Peach yellows appears to be confined exclusively to the Eastern United States. **1928** F. T. BROOKS *Plant Dis.* iii. 23 The only means of checking the spread of Peach Yellows is to destroy affected trees as soon as seen. **1956** H. W. ANDERSON *Dis. Fruit Crops* vii. 265 Peach yellows is undoubtedly of American origin. **1974** K. M. SMITH *Plant*

Viruses (ed. 5) i. 2 Two years later [*sc.* 1888], Erwin F. Smith proved that the disease known as 'peach yellows' was also communicable and could be transmitted by budding.

peach, *sb.*[2] *Min. local.* [f. prec.: see quot. 1811.] Cornish miners' term for chlorite slate (see CHLORITE[1] 2); also distinguished as ***green peach***, ***blue peach***: see quots. 1877, 1881.

1778 PRYCE *Min. Cornub.* 325 When a load is composed mostly of this sort of stone, it is called a peach. **1811** PINKERTON *Petral.* I. 128 Chlorite..is the green talc of Born, and the Samnterde of old German writers, perhaps from its velvety appearance. To the Cornish miners..it is also known by the name of *peach.* **1877** *Min. Mag.* I. 75 The green peach of the Cornish tin mines is undoubtedly chlorite... Blue peach..is probably a bluish-gray variety of Tourmaline. **1881** RAYMOND *Mining Gloss.*, **Blue peach*, Corn., a slate-blue, very fine-grained schorl-rock.

‖**peach**, *sb.*[3] *Obs.* Also peech. [a. Russ. *petch*[i] oven, stove.] A (Russian) stove.

1591 G. FLETCHER *Russe Commw.* xxviii. (Hakl. Soc.) 147 All the winter time..they heat their peaches, which are made lyke the Germane bathstoaves, and..so warme the house. **1778** *Phil. Trans.* LXIX. 327 A number of billets of wood are placed in the peech or stove.

peach (piːtʃ), *v.* Forms: 5–6 peche, 6– peach. [Aphetic form of *a-peche*: see APPEACH, and cf. IMPEACH.]

1. †**a.** *trans.* To accuse (a person) formally; to impeach, indict, bring to trial. *Obs.*

c **1460** *Towneley Myst.* xix. 239 At the day of dome I shall thaym peche. **1534** WRIOTHESLEY *Chron.* (Camden) I. 25 The Lord Dakers..was pechid of high treason. **1693** TATE in *Dryden's Juvenal* ii. (1697) 27 Shou'd Verres peach Thieves, Milo Murderers, Clodius tax Bawds, Cethegus Catiline. **1727** GAY *Begg. Op.* I. x, Have him peach'd the next sessions.

fig. **1638** CHILLINGW. *Relig. Prot.* I. Pref. §18 Does he not in the same place peach Tertullian also?

b. To give incriminating evidence against, inform against (an accomplice or associate); to 'round upon'. Now *rare.*

1570 FOXE *A. & M.* (ed. 2) 1401/1 The sayd Frier.. secretlye practised to peach him by letters sent vnto the Clergie here in England. **1607** MIDDLETON *Phœnix* v. i. 246 Let me have pardon, I beseech your grace, and I'll peach 'em all. **1690** MRS. BEHN *Widow Ranter* IV. ii, Wilt thou betray and peach thy friend? **1722** DE FOE *Col. Jack* (1840) 77 He has peached me and all the others, to save his life. **1903** A. LANG in *Pilot* 20 June 591/2 Godfrey could not peach Coleman without peaching himself.

†**c.** *fig.* To betray. *Obs.*

1641 EVELYN *Diary* 2 Jan., I did not amidst all this peach my liberty nor my vertue with the rest who made shipwreck of both.

d. *transf.* To blab, divulge. *colloq.*

1852 THACKERAY *Esmond* III. ix, What! the *soubrette* has peached to the *amoureux.* **1883** HASLAM *Yet Not I* 105 I'm so thankful this has all come out without my peaching a word.

2. *intr.* or *absol.* To inform against an accomplice; to turn informer. Const. *on, upon, against.* Now chiefly *slang* or *colloq.*

1596 SHAKS. *1 Hen. IV*, II. ii. 47 If I be tane, Ile peach for this. **1632** B. JONSON *Magn. Lady* IV. ii, Will you go peach, and cry yourself a fool At grannam's cross! be laugh'd at and despised! **1717** SAVAGE *Love in Veil* III. iii, Save my life, and I'll peach. **1816** *Trial Berkeley Poachers* 34 An oath not to peach upon each other. **1847** JAMES *Convict* xxxvii, He might have got off himself if he had peached against others. **1861** HUGHES *Tom Brown at Oxf.* xii. (1889) 110 I'm not going to peach if the proctor don't send again in the morning. **1881** *Punch* 26 Nov. 241/2 Eve flirted with Jerrem; Adam, enraged, 'peached' on Jerrem. **1927** KIPLING *Limits & Renewals* (1932) 170 Will and I wouldn't have peached on him. **1966** *New Statesman* 1 July 9/2 The other members of the gang..would not hesitate to peach on him if it would serve their purpose. **1976** *National Observer* (U.S.) 17 July 17/3 Middle-level bureaucrats cravenly peach on their bosses everytime one of them does something the tiniest bit illegal, like violate the Constitution. **1978** P. LOVESEY *Waxwork* 123, I shan't ask you to peach on one of your neighbours... What I want from you is the name and address of the supplier.

Hence **'peaching** *vbl. sb.* and *ppl. a.*

a **1460** *Gregory's Chron.* in *Hist. Coll. Citizen London* (Camden) 186 There was a pechyng i-made uppon the Erle of Ormounde..for certayne poyntys of treson. **1519** HORMAN *Vulg.* 216b, In Tyberis dayes many stode in ieopardy of pechyng or of theyr lyfe. *a* **1625** FLETCHER *Bloody Bro.* III. ii, You chip pantler, you peaching rogue, that provided us These necklaces! **1818** MOORE *Fudge Fam. Paris* vi. 82 Give me the useful peaching Rat. **1859** GREEN *Oxf. Stud.* ii. §7. 92 By peaching, our hero obtained a pardon.

peach, obs. form of PECH *v. Sc.*

'peach-,bloom. **a.** The delicate powdery deposit on the surface of a ripe peach (BLOOM *sb.*[1] 4); hence, in reference to complexion, a soft pink flush like that of the peach. **b.** = next, 1.

1856 EMERSON *Eng. Traits, Race* Wks. (Bohn) II. 30 A clear skin, a peach-bloom complexion, and good teeth, are found all over the island. **1884** BLACK *Jud. Shaks.* ix, The peach-bloom of health on her cheek. **1923** D. H. LAWRENCE *Birds, Beasts & Flowers* 13 Why, from silvery peach-bloom—..This rolling, dropping, heavy globule?

c. A pink colour characteristic of the monochrome glazes on some Chinese porcelain; the glaze itself; = PEACH-BLOW a, b. Also *attrib.*

1886 *Pall Mall G.* 10 Apr. 5/1 The peculiar peach-bloom colour of the vase is what gives it its value. **1898** W. G. GULLAND *Chinese Porc.* I. 139 The following are the names by which some of the colours met with are generally indicated:—..Lavender Clair de lune Peach bloom [etc.]. **1900** F. LITCHFIELD *Pott. & Porc.* vii. 109 Some charming results were obtained in many of those beautiful self colours that collectors delight in; amongst others,..coral, lilac, peach bloom, crushed strawberry [etc.]. **1902** W. G. GULLAND *Chinese Porc.* II. 360 Here we have..peach bloom employed along with other coloured glazes in the decoration of white porcelain. **1906** [see CRUSHED *ppl. a.* 3]. **1937** *Burlington Mag.* Oct. 195/1 Thus, such apparent mysteries as double crackle,..the achievement of peach bloom, the splashes in Chün glazes..are all comfortably disposed of. **1970** *Oxf. Compan. Art* 235/2 Many people consider the most admirable wares of the K'ang Hsi period to be those with monochrome glazes... The brilliant red *sang-de-bœuf* and soft pink 'peachbloom' celadon.

'peach-,blossom.

1. The blossom of the peach-tree.

1664 EVELYN *Kal. Hort.* (1729) 198 *March*..Grape Flowers, Almonds and Peach Blossoms. **1718** QUINCY *Compl. Disp.* 174 Peach-blossoms.—These are us'd only in a Syrup.

2. *attrib., esp.* Of the colour of a peach-blossom, a delicate purplish pink.

1702 *Lond. Gaz.* No. 3835/4 Lin'd with a Peach-Blossom Silk. **1836–41** BRANDE *Chem.* (ed. 5) 889 The cobalt ore, called peach-blossom cobalt, is a hydrated diarseniate of cobalt. **1901** *Daily News* 19 Jan. 6/7 A soft, pale tone of mauve, almost peach-blossom colour.

3. Name for a species of moth (*Thyatira batis*), from the colour of the spots on its wings.

1819 G. SAMOUELLE *Entomol. Compend.* 250 Peach blossom moth. **1859** W. S. COLEMAN *Woodlands* (1862) 109 On the leaf of the Bramble feeds the caterpillar of..the Peach-blossom Moth. **1860** GOSSE *Rom. Nat. Hist.* 25 What is this approaching, with its ten patches of rosy white on its olive wings? The lovely 'peach-blossom', certainly.

'peach-blow. [See BLOW *sb.*[3]] **a.** A delicate purplish-pink colour: cf. prec., 2. Freq. *attrib.*

1829 T. FLINT *George Mason* 32 The Red Bud in a thousand places was one compact tuft of peach-blow flowers. **1837** J. L. WILLIAMS *Terr. Florida* 75 This bird is of a peach-blow colour. **1861** L. L. NOBLE *Icebergs* 176 The berg is immersed in almost supernatural splendors... The blue and the purple pass up into peach-blow and pink. **1896** *Godey's Mag.* (U.S.) Feb. 212/1 The colorings are exquisite; peach-blow pink and lime green. **1922** H. SHOEMAKER *Allegheny Episodes* xxv. 344 Her skin was transparently white, and the delicate peach-blow color in her cheeks was too hectic to betoken good health.

b. A glaze of this colour on some Oriental porcelain.

1886 *Pall Mall G.* 10 Apr. 5/1 The little peachblow or crushed strawberry vase which sold for over £4,000.

c. A variety of potato of this colour (*Cent. Dict.*).

d. A type of glass of a similar colour.

[**1886** *Official Gaz.* (U.S. Patent Office) 20 July 236/2 13,523 Glass Table-Ware and Fancy Glass Articles.. Frederick S. Shirley, New Bedford, Mass... Used since July 1, 1885 'The word "peach".'] **1886** *Pottery & Glassware Reporter* 4 Nov. 21/2 In recent years four novelties have been brought out by the New England Glass Works, under Mr. Libbey's administration. We refer to the Amberina, Pomona, Peachblow, and Agata grades of goods. **1930** L. W. WATKINS *Cambridge Glass 1818–1888* 156 The peach blow glass took its name from the Chinese peach blow porcelain... The New England [Glass Co.] peach blow is one of the loveliest and most unusual things in American glass. In color it shades by imperceptible degrees from white to a deep rose. **1933** *Antiques* (U.S.) Aug. 48 (*heading*) Peachblow Glass. *Ibid.*, Among those glass collectors who are more susceptible to color than to antiquity, 'peachblow items' are highly valued. **1944** R. W. LEE *Victorian Glass* xxii. 561 None of the glass factories at which Peachblow was produced adhered either to the shapes or to the purposes of the Peachblow porcelains. **1972** K. M. WILSON *New England Glass* vii. 352 Both the Mount Washington Peachblow and the New England Wild Rose are to be found in their natural state and also with a 'plush', or satin finish. **1975** *Daily Colonist* (Victoria, B.C.) 26 Oct. 30/6 Peachblow originated with Hobbs Brockunier around 1883. It is lined with white and shades from yellow to peach.

peachen ('piːtʃən), *a. rare.* [f. PEACH *sb.*[1] + -EN[4].] Or of resembling a peach; having a surface like that of a peach; peachy.

1825 HOGG *Q. Hynde* 26 That full set eye, that peachen chin. **1883** L. WINGFIELD *A. Rowe* I. viii. 171 Wrinkles mar a peachen check.

peacher ('piːtʃə(r)). *rare.* Also 6 pecher. [f. PEACH *v.* + -ER[1], or aphetic f. *apecher*, APPEACHER.] An accuser, indicter, informer.

1570 FOXE *A. & M.* (ed. 2) 548/2 Named *Appellatores*, (accusers or peachers of others y[t] were giltes). **1675** COTTON *Burlesque on B.* i, Who, I be judge against my Father! Thy peacher and thy Hangman rather.

peacherino (piːtʃə'riːnəʊ). *slang* (chiefly *U.S.*). [Fanciful f. PEACH *sb.*[1] 1 b.] = PEACH *sb.*[1] 1 b. Also **peache'rine, peache'roo.**

1900 *Dialect Notes* II. 48 *Peacherine*,..synonym for peach. [**1900** *Polk's Kansas State Gazetteer* IX. 695 (Advt.), As a hero you'll forever Take the 'peacherino' yam.] **1905** A. M. BINSTEAD *Mop Fair* iii. 47 Archie, who had undertaken not only to give the Dragoon a merry evening, but to ring in miracles on him in the peacherino line,..repented the loss of all his addresses. **1908** G. H. LORIMER *Jack Spurlock* iv. 71, I went up in the air like an old wife happening by the office and discovering her husband dictating to a new blonde peacherino instead of old reliable. **1910** S. E. WHITE *Rules of Game* III. xv. 273 Plant has a drag with Chairman Gay; don't know what it is, but it's a good one, a peacherino. **1928** *Chambers's Jrnl.* Feb. 98/2 Though Captain Reginald saw little of her except at meals, he realised that here indeed was a 'peacherino'. **1966** M. WOODHOUSE *Tree Frog* xxiii. 171 'She [*sc.* an aeroplane] 's a peach,' he said. 'A real peacheroo.' **1967** C. ROUGVIE *When Johnny Died* iv. 88 When I was his age, they were hauling them out from under me... And all young peacherinos, too. **1970** R. GOLDMAN *Sob Story* in *This Side of Parodies* (*National Lampoon*, U.S.) (1974) 78 'What do you think?' I asked. 'Isn't she a peacheroo?'

†**'peachery**[1]. *Obs. rare.* [f. PEACH *v.* + -ERY.] The action or practice of 'peaching'.

1654 GAYTON *Pleas. Notes* III. viii. 118 The latter, (being base Peachery) brings anothers life to a Halter.

peachery[2] ('piːtʃərɪ). [f. PEACH *sb.*[1] + -ERY.] A place where peaches are grown; a collection of growing peach-trees.

1811 L. M. HAWKINS *C'tess & Gertr.* I. 47 The product of his graperies, pineries, peacheries, cherryries. **1844** J. T. HEWLETT *Parsons & W.* xxxi, Hothouses for peacheries, pineries and graperies.

'pea-chick. [f. PEA[2] + CHICK.] The young of the pea-fowl.

1542 BOORDE *Dyetary* xv. (1870) 270 Yonge peechyken [*plural*] of a halfe a yere of age be praysed. **1634** *Althorp MS.* in Simpkinson *Washingtons* (1860) App. p. xxiii, To Mr. Prestwood for 1 peacock and a pea henn 00 13 00.. To him for 3 peachickes 00 07 06. **1878** J. INGLIS *Sport & W.* xi. 120 The peachicks, about seven or eight months old, are deliciously tender and well flavoured.

b. Applied to a young and vain person.

a **1746** SOUTHERNE (J.), Does the snivelling peachick think to make a cuckold of me? **1848** KINGSLEY *Saint's Trag.* I. i. 134 How these young pea-chicks must needs ape the grown peacock's frippery!

peachify ('piːtʃɪfaɪ), *v. nonce-wd.* [f. PEACHY *a.* + -FY.] *trans.* To make 'peachy', give a 'peachy' complexion to.

1853 READE *Chr. Johnstone* 55 A race of women that the northern sun peachifies instead of rosewoodizing.

peachiness ('piːtʃɪnɪs). [f. PEACHY *a.* + -NESS.] The quality of being 'peachy'.

1820 C. R. MATURIN *Melmoth* xxvi. (1892) III. 88 The rose-leaf tint and peachiness of their delicate cheeks. **1869** *Contemp. Rev.* XI. 357 Appreciating critics who write about its [a picture's] fruitiness, and juiciness, and pulpiness, and downiness, and peachiness.

'peachlet. *nonce-wd.* [f. PEACH *sb.*[1] + -LET.] A small or undeveloped peach; a tiny peach.

1877 BESANT & RICE *Harp & Cr.* xii. 115 The cold wind has..killed every little peachlet which was beginning to swell out on its tiny stalk.

†**'peachment.** *Obs. rare.* [Aphetic f. *apechement*, APPEACHMENT.] Accusation, charge. ***peachment of waste***: see IMPEACHMENT *of waste.*

1559 *Richmond Wills* (Surtees) 131, I gyve also to my younger sone Jhone Wandisford, all my landes in Thymylbye for the terme of hys natural lyfe and after hys deitht to returne to my son Christopher Wandisford and hys hayers without any pichement of wayst.

'peach-tree. The tree *Amygdalus persica* which bears peaches.

c **1400** *Master of Game* (MS. Digby 182) xii, Ye shall put in þe wounde þe Ius of þe leves of a peche tree ymenged w[t] quyckelyme. **1562** TURNER *Herbal* II. 48b, The peche tre floureth with the almond tre. **1774** J. BRYANT *Mythol.* II. 63 Perseus..is said..to have planted the peach tree at Memphis. **1866** *Treas. Bot.* 56/1 Peach-trees ripen their fruit very well as standards in the open air.

peachwort ('piːtʃwɜːt). [f. PEACH *sb.*[1] + WORT, tr. the med.L. name *persicāria*, f. *persica* peach, from the resemblance of the leaves to those of the peach-tree.] The plant *Polygonum persicaria.*

1597 GERARDE *Herbal* II. cix. 361 Dead Arsmart is called *Persicaria* or Peachwoort, of the likenesse that the leaues haue with those of the Peach tree. **1866** *Treas. Bot.* 854.

peachy ('piːtʃɪ), *a.* [f. PEACH *sb.*[1] + -Y.] **1.** Of the nature or appearance of a peach, esp. in colour or texture; chiefly of the cheeks: Round, soft, and having a delicate pink flush like a peach; also *transf.* of a person: Having 'peachy' complexion.

1599 T. M[OUFET] *Silkwormes* 28 No peachy marke to signifie disdaine No greene to shew a wanton mind and vaine. **1775** BARRY *Obstruct. Arts Eng.* vii. 102 A delicate, peachy, bloom of complexion, very common in England. **1877** BLACKIE *Wise Men* 332 When I was a youth, Some twenty summers on my peachy cheeks. **1973** *Country Life* 15 Feb. 425/2 Their frosted bronzed peachy-pink lipstick. **1976** *Vogue* 15 Mar. 19/1 (Advt.), One (Barley Sugar) is a peachy sort of shade.

Comb. **1852** DICKENS *Bleak Ho.* lviii, One of the peachy-cheeked charmers.

2. *slang.* Attractive, outstanding, marvellous, etc.

1926 E. GLYN *Love's Blindness* ii. 25 He..whispered to the man behind him—'Peachy bit in the eighth row—Look at the pearls.' **1929** S. ANDERSON in *Mercury Story Bk.* 228 It was a peachy time for me. **1932** J. T. FARRELL *Young Lonigan* iv. 193 He told himself that Airedales were peachy dogs, they were fighters, they could swim and liked the water, and they were smart. **1942** O. NASH *Good Intentions* 27 Do you know a picture program that Mr Oglethrip would find simply peachy? **1973** D. WESTHEIMER *Going Public* xi. 166 How about it, fellows?.. Isn't it a peachy idea? **1976** 'W. TREVOR' *Children of Dynmouth* v. 115 Your mum has a touch of style, Kate. I heard that remarked in a vegetable shop. I'd call her an eyeful, Kate. Peachy. **1977** *Time* 10 Jan. 28/3 Carter vowed that his Administration would not let New York City go into bankruptcy... Asked for a reaction to the meeting, Carey beamed; 'Peachy'.

b. ***peachy-keen*** adj. *U.S. slang* (see quot. 1960).

1960 WENTWORTH & FLEXNER *Dict. Amer. Slang* 379/2 *Peachy-keen adj.* 1 Excellent; fine... 2 All right; fair; not good enough to warrant enthusiasm but adequate. **1969** N. COHN *A WopBopaLooBop* (1970) v. 50 We dig America. We think it's really peachy-keen. **1975** J. GRADY *Shadow of Condor* (1976) iii. 52 Everything in Montana is peachy keen.

'peachy, *sb. rare.* [f. PEACH *sb.*[1], after *perry*.] A fermented liquor made from peaches.

1781 S. PETERS *Hist. Conn.* 245 They make peachy and perry; grape, cherry, and currant wines.

peacible, obs. form of PEACEABLE.

peacify ('pi:sɪfaɪ), *v. rare.* [f. PEACE *sb.* + -IFY, influenced by PACIFY *v.*] To make calm, to pacify.

1845 [see *nursery language* s.v. NURSERY 8 a]. **1922** JOYCE *Ulysses* 335 Joe and little Alf round him.. trying to peacify him. **1942** BERREY & VAN DEN BARK *Amer. Thes. Slang* §269/1 *Peacify*, to pacify.

'pea-coat. [f. after *pea-jacket*.] = PEA-JACKET.

1790 *Pennsylvania Packet* 4 Jan. 2/2 There are now lodged in the said Office.. 1 pea coat;.. 1 coatee [etc.]. **1842** DICKENS *Amer. Notes* II. viii. 244 The hoarse pilot, wrapped and muffled in pea-coats and shawls. **1845** R. BROWN in *Mem.* ii. (1866) 24 Most of the pea-coats have been laid aside. **1848** CLOUGH *Bothie* v, In heavy pea-coat his trouserless trunk enwrapping. **1861** DICKENS *Gt. Expect.* liv, We had our pea-coats with us, and I took a bag. **1974** *New Yorker* 25 Feb. 80/2 Neatly dressed in a sort of modified peacoat of generally Edwardian cut. **1976** *National Observer* (U.S.) 17 July 16/6 His youth was not exactly the Andy Hardy story. He got into trouble with teen-age drinking. At one point, he lived in a car; at another he fenced hot peacoats.

peacock ('pi:kɒk), *sb.* Forms: α. 4-6 pecok, -e, (4-5 pekok, 5-6 -cock(e, 5 -cokk(e), 6-7 peacocke, (6 peocock, pyckock), 6- peacock. β. 4 poucok, 4-5 pocok, -koc, pokok(e, 5 pokokke, poocok. γ. 4-6 pacok, (4 -cokke, 4-5 -kok(e, 5 -koc). [f. ME. **pê*:—OE. *péa* + COCK; beside which ME. had *pocock*, f. *pô*, *poo*, and *pacock*, f. (northern) *paa*, *pa-*, both repr. OE. *páwa*, a. L. *pāvo*; see PO. Cf. the parallel fem. PEAHEN, formerly *pohenne*, *pehen*; PEAFOWL is modern.]

1. a. The male bird of any species of the genus *Pavo* or peafowl, especially of the common species *P. cristatus*, a native of India, now everywhere domesticated, and well known as the most imposing and magnificent of birds; from this and its strutting gait it is treated as a type of ostentatious display and vainglory.

α. **1377** LANGL. *P. Pl.* B. XII. 240 Þat is þe pekok [*v.rr.* pacok, -kok, pocok, -kok] & þe pohenne, proude riche men þei bitokneth, For þe pekok, and men pursue hym, may nouȝte fleighe heighe. *c* **1386** CHAUCER *Reeve's T.* 6 As eny pecok he was proud and gay. *c* **1440** *Promp. Parv.* 389/1 Pekokke, byrde, *pavo, pavus.* **1553** EDEN *Treat. Newe Ind.* (Arb.) 7 Gold, Siluer, Apes, Peacockes, & Elephantes teeth. **1560** DAUS tr. *Sleidane's Comm.* 119 They are as bragge and as proude as pecockes, and iette vp and downe in all places. **1592** DAVIES *Immort. Soul* XXXIV. viii, Take heed of ouer-weening, and compare Thy peacock's feet with thy gay peacock's traine. **1781** COWPER *Truth* 58 The self-applauding bird, the peacock, see—Mark what a sumptuous Pharisee is he! **1819** KEATS *Lamia* I. 50 Eyed like a pea-cock, and all crimson barr'd. **1883** STEVENSON *Silverado Sq.* 142 Happy and proud like a peacock on a rail. **1891** *Chambers' Encycl.* VII. 824/2 Peacock (Pavo).. including at least two species—the Indian and Singhalese *P. cristatus*, domesticated in Britain and other countries, and the Malayan *P. muticus*, inhabiting Java, Borneo, and similar regions.

β. *a* **1300** *Sat. People Kildare* v. in *E.E.P.* (1862) 153 F[o]ure and xx[ti] wild ges and a poucok. **1340-70** *Alex. & Dind.* 716 A fair pokok of pris men paien to iuno. *c* **1420** *Pallad. on Husb.* I. 610 The pocok me may rere vp esely. *c* **1475** *Pict. Voc.* in Wr.-Wülcker 760/38 *Hic pavo*,.. a pocokk.

γ. *c* **1374** [See b] pakoc. *c* **1400** MAUNDEV. (Roxb.) vii. 25 He has on his heued a creste as a pacok, bot it es mykill mare þan þe creste of a pacok. *c* **1450** HOLLAND *Howlat* 81 That is the plesant Pacok, precious and pure. **1500-20** DUNBAR *Poems* xlvi. 14 A nychtingall.. Quhois angell fedderis as the pacok schone.

b. *transf.* and *fig.*, esp. referring to the vainglorious habits and ostentation attributed to the bird. ***to play the peacock***, to comport oneself vaingloriously.

c **1374** CHAUCER *Troylus* I. 154 (210) And yet as proud a pekok [*v.r.* pakoc] can he pulle. **1538** BALE *Thre Lawes* 526 Thre syppes are for the hyckock, And six more for the chyckock, Thus maye my praty pyckock, Recouer by and by. **1590** SHAKS. *Com. Err.* IV. iii. 81. *a* **1592** GREENE *Alphonsus* v. 1780 Nay then, proud pecock, since thou art so stout [etc.]. **1656** EARL MONM. tr. *Boccalini's Advts. fr. Parnass.* 84 Proudly playing the Peacocks, and publikely professing severity. **1745** G. WASHINGTON *Rules of Civility* liv, Play not the Peacock, looking everywhere about you, to see if you be well deck't. **1828** *Sporting Mag.* XXII. 134 Ben Champion, a peacock of fox-hunters. **1866** GEO. ELIOT *F. Holt* v, How came he to have such a nice-stepping long-necked peacock for his daughter?

c. The bird or its flesh as an article of food.

c **1460** J. RUSSELL *Bk. Nurture* 695 For a standard, vensoun rost, kyd, favne, or cony,.. pecok in hakille ryally. ? *c* **1475** *Sqr. lowe Degre* 318 He.. serued the kynge.. With deynty meates that were dere, With Partryche, Pecoke, and Plouere. *a* **1845** BARHAM *Ingol. Leg.* Ser. III. *Blasphemer's Warn.*, There were peacocks served up in their pride (that is tails). **1872** TENNYSON *Gareth & Lynette* 828 A feast.. Held in high hall.. And there they placed a peacock in his pride Before the damsel.

2. One of the southern constellations (*Pavo*).

1674 MOXON *Tutor Astron.* I. iii. §10 (ed. 3) 19 Twelve Constellations.., posited about the South Pole,.. 3 The Indian, 4 The Peacock, 5 The Bird of Paradise. **1868** LOCKYER *Guillemin's Heavens* (ed. 3) 335 The Phœnix, below which, returning to the horizon, and to the meridian, are found Toucan, the Crane, the Indian, and the Peacock.

†**3.** ***peacock of the sea, sea p.*** = PEACOCK-FISH.

c **1520** ANDREWE *Noble Lyfe* III. lxvii, *Pauus maris* is the Pecocke of the Se, & is lyke the pecocke of the londe, bothe his backe, necke, & hede, & the nether body is fisshe.

4. Short for *peacock-butterfly*, *peacock-moth.*

1827 *Butterfly Collector's Vade M.* 112 *Vanessa Io*, Peacock. **1832** RENNIE *Consp. Butterfl. & Moths* 143 The Peacock (*Macaria notata*) appears the end of May and beginning of June. **1869** E. NEWMAN *Brit. Moths* 87 The Peacock. *Ibid.*, The Sharp-angled Peacock.

5. Short for *peacock-blue*. Also *attrib.* or as *adj.*

1873 L. TROUBRIDGE *Life amongst Troubridges* (1966) viii. 60 A peacock grosgrain and white lace bonnet. **1881** C. C. HARRISON *Woman's Handiwork* III. 165 Peacock, turquoise, celestine, drake's neck, Damascus blue and robin's-egg blue. **1897** W. B. YEATS *Tables of Law & Adoration of Magi* 35 When the peacock curtains had closed behind us. **1922** *Daily Mail* 11 Dec. 14 (Advt.), Frock... In Brown, Lemon, Peacock, Rose, Mauve. **1924** C. MACKENZIE *Heavenly Ladder* i. 11 He.. sat for awhile on the sweet short grass of Pendhu cliffs, contemplating the peacock sea below. **1963** *New Yorker* 29 June 44 Sizes 8-18. Cranberry, peacock, olive. **1971** 'D. HALLIDAY' *Dolly & Doctor Bird* xii. 166 The sea lay clear as shellac underneath us, jade and turquoise, cerulean and peacock.

6. *attrib.* and *Comb.* **a.** Of, belonging to, like, or of the nature of a peacock or peacocks; that is (*fig.*) a peacock; as ***peacock-behaviour***, ***-Christian***, ***colour***, ***-fool***, ***-green***, ***-grey***, ***-justiciary***, ***pride***, ***ritualism***, ***-slave***, ***-train***, ***-yewtree***; ***peacock-spotted***, ***-voiced***, ***-witted*** adjs.; ***peacock-pluming*** vbl. sb.

1894 MISS COBBE *Life* I. 174 Watching their victim and exploding with glee at his *peacock behaviour. **1642** J. EATON *Honey-c. Free Justif.* 454 Ape-Saints, and *Peacock-Christians (as Luther truly calleth them). **1598** R. HAYDOCKE tr. *Lomazzo's Tracte containing Artes of Curious Paintinge, Caruinge, Buildinge* III. x. 110 The shaddowes of the simple and immixt colours of the thirde degree, suppose the aggate colour, are burnt oker, darke blew, *peacocke colour [etc.]. **1611** COTGR. s.v. *Gemmé, Couleur gemmée*, a pearle, or peacocke colour. **1622** PEACHAM *Compl. Gent.* (1661) 136 Peacocke colour, *i.e.* changeable blew, or red blew. **1893** *Scribner's Mag.* June 768/1 Their exquisite pale peacock color is without equal among the eggs of our Eastern birds. **1575** GASCOIGNE *Wks.*, *Weedes* vi. 281 For thou hast caught a proper paragon A theefe, a cowarde and a *peacocke foole. **1895** *Proc. Zool. Soc.* 264 The fore wings are *peacock-green, black in the centre. **1935** DYLAN THOMAS *Sel. Lett.* (1966) 153 You write better when you've got someone.. sneering when you go purple & using a cruel pencil over your choicest *peacock-greys. **1642** J. EATON *Honey-c. Free Justif.* 206 Apish Saints, and painted *Peacock-Justiciaries. **1596** NASHE *Saffron-Walden* Wks. (Grosart) III. 179 His *peacocke-pluming her like another Pandora.. through his incredible praising of her. **1580** SIDNEY *Ps.* XL. ii, Who bendes not wand'ring eyes To greate mens *peacock pride. **1860** EMERSON *Cond. Life* vi. (1861) 122 In creeds never was such levity; witness the heathenisms in Christianity,.. the *peacock ritualism. **1609** MARKHAM *Fam. Whore* (1868) 24 Cheaters, braggarts and the *peacock slaue, whose words and cloathes are all the welth they haue. **1820** T. MITCHELL *Aristoph.* I. 22 A plague upon these envoys, I hate their *peacock trains. **1883** HELEN F. MARTIN in *Blackw. Mag.* Jan. 10 [Cymbeline's Queen's] handsome *peacock-witted son Cloten. **1864** TENNYSON *En. Ard.* 609 The *peacock-yewtree and the lonely Hall.

b. Special combs.: **Peacock Alley** *U.S.*, the name given to the main corridor of the original Waldorf-Astoria Hotel in New York, where fashionable people promenaded; hence the main corridor of other hotels; also *attrib.*; **peacock arrow**, an arrow furnished with a peacock's feather; **peacock-bittern**, a name of the South American sun-bittern, *Eurypyga helias*; **peacock-blue**, the peculiar lustrous blue of a peacock's neck; **peacock butterfly**, a European butterfly (*Inachis io*) with ocellated wings; **peacock-coal**, iridescent coal; **peacock copper**, iridescent copper ore ('peacock ore'), esp. chalcopyrite or bornite: cf. *peacock-ore*; **peacock-eye**, the ocellus on a peacock's feather: also *attrib.*; **peacock-fan**, a fan made or trimmed with peacock's feathers; **peacock-fly, -hackle**, an artificial fly dressed with a peacock's feather; **peacock-flower**, a name applied to two leguminous trees, (*a*) *Poinciana regia* (*Royal peacock-flower*), and (*b*) *Cæsalpinia* (*Poinciana*) *pulcherrima* (also *Flower-fence*) (Miller *Plant-n.* 1884); **peacock flower-fence**, a leguminous tree, *Adenanthera pavonina* (*ibid.*); †**peacock-hatter**, 'in the Middle Ages, a plumist or milliner' (*Cent. Dict.* 1890); **peacock-iris**, a bulbous plant of South Africa, *Moræa* (*Vieusseuxia*) *glaucopis*, also known as *Iris pavonia*; also applied to other species of *Vieusseuxia*; **peacock-moth**, *Macaria notata* and *M. alternata*, of family *Geometridæ*; **peacock mottle** (see quots.); **peacock ore**, iridescent copper ore; = *peacock copper*; **peacock pheasant**, a small, south-east Asian pheasant belonging to the genus *Polyplectron*, whose markings resemble those of a peacock; **peacock-stone** (see quots.); **peacock-throne**, the former throne of the Kings of Delhi, subsequently in the possession of the Shah of Persia, adorned with the representation of a peacock's tail fully expanded, composed of precious stones; **peacock treasure-flower**, a S. African composite plant, *Gazania pavonia*, with large orange-coloured flower-heads.

1906 *N.Y. Times* 2 Dec. III. 7/2 The Waldorf-Astoria is the New York headquarters of Kalamazoo, Michigan, and Brassband, Wisconsin. Its main corridor is known as *Peacock Alley. To sit there five minutes makes a man a representative American. **1925** E. HUNGERFORD *Story of Waldorf-Astoria* vii. 139 The outstanding feature of this ground floor was a huge corridor—in after years to be known, somewhat irreverently, as 'Peacock Alley'—which was to run practically the entire length of the building, parallel to Thirty-fourth Street. **1930** J. DOS PASSOS *42nd Parallel* II. 156 Seedy-respectable or Peacock Alley clothes. **1932** L. C. DOUGLAS *Forgive us our Trespasses* (1937) x. 212 The peacock-alley of the hotel, stuffily scented, was daily, gravely, tallied off for Joan. **1974** *Washington Post* 20 Dec. D8/5 The Carr project included: Total restoration of the Willard's.. public rooms and the famous Peacock Alley. *c* **1386** CHAUCER *Prol.* 104 A sheef of *pecok [*v.r.* pocok] arwes bright and kene Vnder his belt he bar ful thriftily. **1881** C. C. HARRISON *Woman's Handiwork* I. 65 The curtains made of *peacock blue, are bordered with.. bands of turquoise blue serge. **1882** H. P. GRATTAN in *Theatre* June 348 Fashion.. was carried to the verge of caricature. Crimson and peacock blue stocks, three layers of different coloured under-waistcoats, [etc.]. **1886** *Cassell's Encycl. Dict.*, Peacock-blue. **1897** MARY KINGSLEY *W. Africa* xxiv. 553 The butterflies.. show themselves off in the sunlight, in their canary-coloured, crimson, and peacock-blue liveries. **1968** R. H. R. SMITHIES *Shoplifter* (1969) vii. 151 An improbable peacock blue evening jacket. *c* **1760** B. WILKES *Eng. Moths & Butterflies* III. i. 55 The *peacock-butterfly. You must look for the Caterpillar that produces this Fly in the great Stinging-Nettle. **1802** BINGLEY *Anim. Biog.* (1813) III. 209 The Peacock Butterfly. **1826** KIRBY & SP. *Entomol.* III. xxx. 214 The black spinous caterpillars of the common peacock-butterfly (*Vanessa Io*). **1906** R. SOUTH *Butterflies Brit. Isles* 73 Usually the Peacock butterfly assumes the perfect state but once in the year. **1965** P. WAYRE *Wind in Reeds* ix. 114 Tortoiseshell and peacock butterflies feed on the nectar. **1976** *Cumberland News* 3 Dec. 8/7 Mr Jack Thirlwell showed his prize winning films on the life style of the swallow tail and peacock butterflies. **1686** PLOT *Staffordsh.* 126 The *Peacock-coal.. is much softer than the Cannel,.. most vividly representing all the colours of the most glorious feathers in a Peacocks trayne. **1858** GREG & LETTSOM *Man. Mineral. Gt. Brit. & Ireland* 340 At Great Crinnis, St. Austell, in the neighbourhood of which town the mines produce the finest iridescent massive variety [of chalcopyrite], known as *peacock copper. **1897** *Slocan* (Brit. Columbia) *Pioneer* 4 Sept. 1/6 The Michigan claim on Toad mountain is showing up well, some very fine grey copper and peacock copper having been encountered. **1937** A. F. ROGERS *Introd. Study Minerals* (ed. 3) 300 Chalcopyrite... Color brass yellow, often with an iridescent tarnish, hence the name 'peacock copper'. **1890** *Cent. Dict.* s.v. *Pecock*, **Peacock-eye marble*, an Italian marble of mingled white, blue, and red color. **1893** *Spectator* 3 June 731 Ornaments.. on the train of the peacock,.. best described as the 'peacock-eye'. *a* **1861** MRS. BROWNING *Christmas Gifts* viii, The eyes in the *peacock-fans Winked at the alien glory. **1676** COTTON *Walton's Angler* vii. 325 There is also.. the *Peacock-fly: the body made of the whirl of a peacock's feather. **1924** G. O. WHEELER *Old English Furnit.* (ed. 3) xii. 278 Another variety [of mottle in mahogany] was once termed *peacock mottle from its supposed resemblance to the tail of that bird. **1968** *Canad. Antiques Collector* Aug. 24/2 *Honeycomb or peacock mottle.* This is a variety of figure remarkable for its fine appearance; it is associated almost entirely with the mahoganies. **1860** W. A. MILLER *Elem. Chem.* (ed. 2) II. 658 The copper pyrites.. or ordinary ore of copper, consists of a double sulphide of copper and iron... The variety, called variegated or *peacock ore, contains a larger proportion of sulphide of copper. **1877** RAYMOND *Statist. Mines & Mining* 310 A large body of fine 'peacock' ore. **1890** VOGAN *Black Police* xix. 352 [Australian], The prismatic tints of a material sulphide known to miners by the name of 'peacock ore'. **1911** *State* (Cape Town) Nov. 487 The ore is principally bornite—peacock-ore as it is often called on account of its beautiful iridescent colouring. **1964** H. HODGES *Artifacts* iv. 65 This group includes.. the iron sulphide minerals chalcopyrites (copper pyrites, $Cu_2Fe_2S_4$) and bornite (peacock ore, Cu_5FeS_4). **1977** A. HALLAM *Planet Earth* 124 (*caption*) Bornite, an important ore of copper, is often called 'peacock ore' for its iridescent tarnish. **1864** *Proc. Zool. Soc.* 373 From Calcutta... 1 *Peacock Pheasant. **1906** *Macm. Mag.* Aug. 779 A peacock-pheasant.. ceased its clamour. **1922** C. W. BEEBE *Monogr. Pheasants* IV. 55 Peacock pheasants.. are birds of the lowland forests. **1964** A. L. THOMSON *New Dict. Birds* 627/2 The peacock pheasants *Polyplectron* spp. form a very distinct genus of small pheasants with long tails and a grey or brown plumage marked with metallic green and purple ocellae on the mantle, wings, and tail. **1753** CHAMBERS *Cycl. Supp.*, *Pavonius-lapis*, the *peacock-stone, a name given by Ludovicus Dulcis.. Probably it was one of the variegated agates. **1833** *Penny Cycl.* I. 467/1 The cartilages of some large shells.. are sold by the jewellers under the name of *Peacock-stone*, or *black opals.* **1813** JAS. FORBES *Oriental Mem.* xxix. III. 84 The most superb article of this imperial spoil was the Tucht-Taoos, or *peacock-throne, in which the expanded tail of the peacock, in its natural size, was imitated in jewellery. **1895** *Outing* (U.S.) XXVII. 53/1 In 1739.. Nadir Shah, the Persian ruler, then left Delhi, carrying immense treasures.. including the renowned and beautiful peacock throne.

peacock ('pi:kɒk), *v.* [f. prec. sb.]

1. *trans.* To make like a peacock; to render vain or conceited, to puff up with vanity; *esp. refl.* to strut about or pose in order to display one's beauty, elegance, or accomplishments; to make a display; to plume oneself.

a **1586** SIDNEY *Arcadia* (1622) 56 A desire onely to please, and as it were, peacock themselues. **1834** MAR. EDGEWORTH *Helen* xiv, *Pavoneggiarsi!* untranslateable. One cannot say well in English, to peacock oneself. **1872** TENNYSON *Gareth & Lynette* 702 He was tame and meek enow with me, Till peacock'd up with Lancelot's noticing. **1883** MRS. LYNN LINTON *Ione* xviii, He 'peacocked himself' not a little on the deftness of his manipulation. **1888** —— *Thro' Long Night* III. v, It is no longer a matter for vanity, for self-gratulation, for self-peacocking.

2. *intr.* **a.** To strut about ostentatiously; to make a vainglorious display, pose. Also *to peacock it.* **b.** *Anglo-Ind.*: see quot. 1888.

1818 KEATS *Lett.* Wks. 1889 III. 112 Every man has his speculations, but every man does not brood and peacock over them till he makes a false coinage and deceives himself. **1826** SCOTT in *Q. Rev.* XXXIII. 310 How a modern drawingroom would look if filled with courtiers peacocking it about in long sweeping trains. **1867** RUSKIN *Time & Tide* xvii, You working men have been crowing and peacocking at such a rate lately. **1888** SIR R. BURTON in Lady B. *Life* (1893) I. vii. 136 Some..preferred 'peacocking', which meant robing in white grass clothes and riding..to call upon regimental ladies. **1890** J. MIDDLEMASS *Two False Moves* II. vii. 89 People of various nationalities..peacock about in fine feathers.

3. *Austral.* (See quot. 1898.) *Obs.* exc. *hist.*

1898 MORRIS *Austral. Eng.* 344/2 To *peacock* a piece of country means to pick out the *eyes* of the land by selecting or buying up the choice pieces and water-frontages, so that the adjoining territory is practically useless to any one else. **1928** 'BRENT OF BIN BIN' *Up Country* xxi. 347 They had been able to 'peacock' their runs and safeguard their holdings. **1959** BAKER *Drum* (1960) i. 14 Droughts and the activities of small selectors who 'peacocked' or 'picked the eyes out of' the country..capped the pioneers' woes.

Hence **'peacocking** *vbl. sb.* and *ppl. a.*

1837 *Civil Eng. & Arch. Jrnl.* I. 17/2 This sort of peacocking in borrowed plumes is no less dangerous than despicable. **1870** *Daily News* 19 Apr., When the 'peacocking business' (to use a slang term of military art) was over, the 3rd and 4th divisions..continued their march round the curve of the horse-shoe. **1873** MISS BROUGHTON *Nancy* I. 227 Alas! never again shall I see him mount that peacocking steed. **1891** *Wheeling* 25 Feb. 409 He felt that 'peacocking' at the Military Exhibition had taken the place of real work on many Saturdays last year. **1894** W. EPPS *Land Syst. Australasia* iii. 28 When the immediate advent of selectors to a run became probable, the lessees endeavoured to circumvent them by dummying all the positions which offered the best means of blocking the selectors from getting to water. This system, commonly known as 'peacocking', was assisted by the use of Volunteer Land Orders. **1965** *Austral. Encycl.* V. 234/1 Many of the counter-tactics employed by pastoralists were equally indefensible, notably the purchase of sites to prevent selectors from getting to water ('peacocking').

'pea,cockery. [f. PEACOCK *sb.* + -ERY.] The practice of the (human) peacock; foppery.

1872 BESANT & RICE *Ready-money Mortiboy* i, Francis Melliship is the greatest Peacock in Market Basing. I—hate—Peacockery in man or woman! **1882** BESANT *All Sorts* Prol. ii, There were none of the peacockeries, whims, and fancies, ..gimcrackeries..which..proclaim the chamber of a young man. **1883** S. W. BECK *Gloves* 5.

'peacock-,fish. A European labroid fish, the blue-striped wrasse, *Crenilabrus pavo*: from its brilliant colouring, green, blue, red, and white.

1661 LOVELL *Hist. Anim. & Min.* 234 Peacock-fish... Is an insipid and ignoble fish. The flesh is fat and gentle. **1753** CHAMBERS *Cycl. Supp.* App., *Peacock-fish*, the English name of a fish of the Turdus, or wrasse-kind.

Peacockian (pi:'kɒkiən), *a.* and *sb.* [f. the name of Thomas Love *Peacock* (1785–1866), English novelist and poet + -IAN.] **A.** *adj.* Pertaining to or characteristic of Thomas Love Peacock or his works.

1886 *Macm. Mag.* Apr. 424/2 It is not necessary..to be a believer in education, or in telegraphs, or in majorities, in order to feel the repulsion which some people evidently feel for the Peacockian treatment. **1904** A. B. YOUNG *Life & Novels T. L. Peacock* 31 The squire's chief interest in the novel..seems to be mainly 'pushing' the bottle round, while that of Dr. Gaster, the first of many clergy-men who figure in the Peacockian novels, is that of emptying it. **1927** J. B. PRIESTLEY *T. L. Peacock* vi. 160 His manner and talk are all his own and have the Peacockian sparkle and salty tang. **1930** *Times Lit. Suppl.* 13 Mar. 210/2 The Peacockian Mr. Dottery easily wins our affections. **1954** R. MACAULAY *Last Lett. to Friend* (1962) 145 It is a kind of Peacockian set of imaginary discussions between a group of people. **1963** *Listener* 21 Mar. 531/1 The visitors are all rather Peacockian. **1972** *Guardian* 20 Jan. 11/4 The Open House by Michael Innes... Sir John Appleby..intrudes on Peacockian mansion, and, overnight, identifies killer and unravels inheritance tangle. **1978** P. VAN GREENAWAY *Man called Scavener* iii. 34 A Peacockian world where conversation grows more polished than the superb sideboard.

B. *sb.* An admirer or devotee of Peacock and his writings.

1886 *Macm. Mag.* Apr. 420/2 One piece of verse..the 'War-song of Dinas Vawr'..has had some vogue, but the rest is only known to Peacockians. **1911** C. VAN DOREN *Life T. L. Peacock* xi. 277 Peacockians are wont to plume themselves upon a taste denied to the vulgar. **1973** *Times* 22 Mar. 12/3 An actor and Peacockian of some wit and taste.

pea'cockically, *nonce-wd.*: see PEACOCKISHLY.

peacockish ('pi:kɒkɪʃ), *a.* [f. PEACOCK *sb.* + -ISH[1].] Of the nature or character ascribed to a peacock; like a peacock or that of a peacock. Hence **'pea,cockishly** *adv.*; **'pea,cockishness.**

1550 BALE *Eng. Votaries* II. 104 The kynge not beynge so Pecockysh as he iudged hym, dyscretely and wysely deferred the tyme. **1834** SOUTHEY *Doctor* (1848) Pref. 9 This is to write..*pavonesquement*,..in English peacockically or peacockishly, whichever the reader may like best. **1864** *Spectator* 27 Feb. 240 An ardent, almost peacockish vanity. **1892** W. W. PEYTON *Mem. Jesus* xiii. 360 An ostentatious variation,..a peacockishness of modern philosophy.

'peacockism. *rare.* [See -ISM.] = PEACOCKERY.

1861 J. HOLLINGSHEAD in *Gd. Words* 198 Peacockism in dress has increased to an alarming extent.

†**'peacockize,** *v. Obs. rare.* [See -IZE.] *intr.* To act the peacock; to peacock oneself.

1598 FLORIO, *Zazzeare*..to go ietting idly or loytring vp and downe peacockising and courting of himselfe. *Ibid.*, *Zazzeatore*..peacockising stroker vp of his owne haire.

'peacocklike, *a.* and *adv.*

A. *adj.* Like a peacock or that of a peacock; peacockish.

1576 FLEMING *Panopl. Epist.* 290 Som swelling in arrogancie and pecoklike pride. **1587** TURBERV. *Epit. & Sonn.* (1837) 366 O dames, I would not wish you peacocklike to looke. **1898** *Westm. Gaz.* 26 May 3/2 The model makers ..are now providing us with these extensive peacock-like tails to our bodices.

B. *adv.* After the manner of a peacock.

1587 TURBERV. *Trag. T., Hist.* i. *Lenuoy*, You stately Dames, that peacockelyke do pace. **1598** SYLVESTER *Du Bartas* II. i. IV. *Handie-Crafts* 179 And Peacock-like himselfe [Adam] doth often view.

†**'peacockly,** *a.* and *adv. Obs.* exc. *arch.* [See -LY[1] and [2].] **A.** *adj.* Peacocklike. **B.** *adv.* In the manner of a peacock, with vainglorious display.

1580 LUPTON *Sivqila* 20 There is..such gawdie going, and such pecockly and new fashions euery day. *Ibid.*, Why should we that are earth, ashes and dust, pricke vp ourselues so Peacockly? **1608** TARLTON *Cobler Canterb.* (1844) 113 When Gentlemen leaue of their peacockly sutes. **1941** E. R. EDDISON *Fish Dinner* (1968) viii. 132 His coming hither but yesterday, most peacockly strained to the height of your philosophy and at an undue hour of eleven o'clock in the night.., was with purpose.

peacockry. [f. PEACOCK *sb.* + -RY.] = PEACOCKERY.

1909 *Daily Chron.* 14 Aug. 2/3 At Siena you leave Pinturicchio's 'peacockry' in the Cathedral library only to meet a bevy of youths with striped legs, tight doublets, and feathered caps tossing banners down the street of St. Catherine. **1932** *Times Educ. Suppl.* 6 Aug. 305/4 A fault among boys was what was called 'peacockry', when their vanity caused them to pinch anything to adorn their person. **1967** D. BEYFUS in L. Deighton *London Dossier* 229 Traditional British lairs of masculine peacockry.

peacock's feather, peacock feather.

1. A feather of the peacock; *spec.* one of the long feathers forming the tail coverts, adorned with iridescent ocelli or 'eyes', and used for various ornamental purposes. Hence, **b.** Taken as a symbol of vainglory, or a decoration of rank or station; **c.** (in reference to the fable of the jay decked with peacock's feathers) A 'borrowed plume'; a borrowed ornament of style or passage in a literary composition.

c **1400** MAUNDEV. (Roxb.) xxiii. 106 Made of gold and precious stanes and pacok fethers. **1500–20** DUNBAR *Poems* lxviii. 8 The sasoun soft and fair, Come in als fresche as pacok feddir. **1545** ASCHAM *Toxoph.* (Arb.) 129 At a short but,..ye Pecock fether doth seldome kepe vp ye shaft eyther ryght or leuel. **1560** PILKINGTON *Exp. Aggeus* (1562) 167 It woulde make our proude peacockes feathers too fall. **1575–85** ABP. SANDYS *Serm.* vii. §37 If wee did looke upon our blacke feete, our faire Peacocke fethers would soone fall downe. **1837** *Civil Eng. & Arch. Jrnl.* I. 17/2 We meet with a peacock's feather of some length in the following passage. **1848** THACKERAY *Bk. Snobs* xx, All these people might be so happy, and easy, and friendly,..but for an unhappy passion for peacocks' feathers in England.

2. Name for a small moth, *Yponomeuta comptella.*

1832 RENNIE *Consp. Butterfl. & Moths* 198.

Hence **'peacock-,feathered** *a.*, fitted or adorned with peacock's feathers.

1429 *Test. Ebor.* (Surtees) I. 419 Pakok-federid arrows. **1896** *Westm. Gaz.* 16 Nov. 2/1 The famous peacock-feathered cap began to show above the floor of the platform.

peacock's tail.

1. The tail-coverts of the peacock collectively, which the bird is able to erect in a resplendent vertical circle behind its body.

1570 DEE *Math. Pref.* b j b, As with a Pecockes tayle. **1653** WALTON *Angler* v. 117 The Black-fly,..the body made of black wool, and lapped about with the herl of a peacock's tail. **1794** SULLIVAN *View Nat.* II. 16 The luminous and coloured circle, tinged like the peacock's tail. *Mod. Proverb* (Sc.), When March comes in with an adder's head, it goes out with a peacock's tail.

2. Hence in various transferred applications: †**a.** An old name for the eighth proposition of the third book of Euclid, in reference to the figure.

1570 BILLINGSLEY *Euclid* III. viii. 88 Thys Proposition is called commonly in old bookes amongest the barbarous,.. the Peacockes taile.

b. The beautiful seaweed *Padina pavonia*, having broadly fan-shaped fronds marked with concentric fringed lines.

1857 WOOD *Comm. Obj. Sea-shore* 50 The name of it is the Peacock's-Tail, deriving its title from its shape. **1866** *Treas. Bot.* 835/1 *Padina pavonia*, our Turkey-feather Laver or Peacock's Tail, is one of the most remarkable species.

†**c.** A colour in alchemy. *Obs.*

1610 B. JONSON *Alch.* II. ii, Your seuerall colours, sir, Of the pale citron, the greene lyon, the crow, The peacocks taile.

d. (See quot.)

1744–50 W. ELLIS *Mod. Husbandm.* VII. I. 84 [Maple] wood is of more value than ordinary woods are, for their diapered knots and curled grain, that have given it the name of the peacock's tail.

e. A kind of pyrotechnic shower.

1799 G. SMITH *Laboratory* I. 9 This shower is commonly called the peacock's tail, on account of the various colours that appear in it.

f. *peacock's tail* (*peacock-tail*) *tarnish*: the iridescent lustre found in some ores and metallic products; = PAVONINE B. 1 (see quots. s.v.).

'peacockwise, *adv. rare.* [f. as next + -WISE.] After the manner of a peacock.

1577 STANYHURST *Descr. Irel.* i. in Holinshed *Chron.* (1587) II. 12/2 He..that..peacockwise setteth himselfe foorth to the gaze.

peacocky ('pi:kɒkɪ), *a.* (*adv.*) [f. PEACOCK *sb.* + -Y.] Suggesting a peacock in walk, bearing, self-display, or showiness; assuming airs, showy: said of a person, or of a horse in reference to its bearing.

1866 RUSKIN *Crown of Wild Olive* iii. 192 You fancy, perhaps, that there is a severe sense of duty without these peacocky motives? **1871** *Daily News* 23 Sept., There was a peacocky jauntiness about the whole regiment that is in keeping with the traditions of the light dragoon. **1889** *Sat. Rev.* 16 Mar. 326/1 The handsome, if somewhat peacocky chestnut stallion, Trocadero. **1898** J. ARCH *Story of Life* ii. 31 These peacocky youngsters would cheek the lads in smock-frocks, whenever they got a chance.

B. as *adv.* In the manner of a peacock; with a showy air.

1861 G. MEREDITH *Evan Harrington* II. ix, She's grown since she's been countessed, and does it peacocky.

pea-cod to **pea-dropper**: see PEA[1].

'pea-flower. **a.** The flower or blossom of the pea, or any large papilionaceous flower resembling this. **b.** Name for several West Indian leguminous plants having such flowers, as *Vilmorinia multiflora*, and species of *Centrosema* and *Clitoria*.

1825 *Greenhouse Comp.* I. 90 Elegant orange-coloured pea-flowers, on singular Australasian evergreen shrubs. **1884** MILLER *Plant-n.*, Pea-flower, Vilmorin's Purple, *Vilmorinia multiflora*. **1946** D. C. PEATTIE *Road of Naturalist* i. 20 In the innocent phase of spring there had bloomed an astragalus, very like a lupine, but straggling, crazy, clouded, its pea flowers sickly pink. **1977** M. ALLAN *Darwin & his Flowers* iv. 78 He found six adesmias-shrubs with pea-flowers.

Hence **'pea-flowered** *a.*, having papilionaceous flowers like those of the pea.

1866 *Treas. Bot.* 299 *Clitoria*, a large genus of pea-flowered plants.

peafowl ('pi:faʊl). [f. PEA[2] + FOWL.] A bird of the genus *Pavo*; a peacock or peahen.

1804 WILLIAMSON *Oriental Field Sp.* 98 There could not be less than twelve or fifteen hundred pea-fowls,..within sight of the spot where I stood. **1888** MRS. B. M. CROKER *Diana Barrington* ix, Twilight was falling, and the cries of the jungle-cock and pea-fowl were hushed. **1896** *List Anim. in Zool. Gardens, London* 493–4 *Pavo cristatus*..Common Peafowl: *Hab.* India... *P. nigripennis*..Black-winged Peafowl: *Hab.* Cochin China(?)... *P. spicifer*..Javan Peafowl: *Hab.* Burmah and Java.

peag (pi:g), **peak** (pi:k). Also 7 **peage, peauge, peacke.** [Orig. *pê-ag*, ad. Massachusetts Indian *piak*, pl. of *pi* (= Abnaki *biak*, *bi*), a strung bead of shell-money; found in ***wampumpeag*** (in Rasles *Abnaki Dict. 1691 wanbanbi-ak*); f. Massach. Ind. *wompi* (Delaware *wapi*) white + *piak*.] Beads made from the ends of shells, rubbed down and polished, strung together into belts, necklaces, etc.; formerly used as a currency by the North American Indians; wampum.

Two qualities were distinguished, ***white peag*** (see WAMPUMPEAG) and ***black*** (or purple) ***peag***, the latter being reckoned double the value of the former.

1649 *Rhode Isl. Col. Rec.* (1856) I. 217 Noe person..shall take any black peage of the Indians but at four a penny. **1664** *Providence* (R.I.) *Records* (1894) V. 305 He saw Scattup.. receive a considerble Some of peauge of William Harris. **1676** T. GLOVER in *Phil. Trans.* XI. 633 Their mony is of two sorts, one..made of a white kind of shell.., they put them on a string after the manner of Beads; this they call Peacke. **1677** W. HUBBARD *Narrative* 108 Having fetched out of a Swamp hard by,..a large Belt of Peag. **1705** BEVERLEY *Hist. Virginia* 58 The peak is of two sorts, or rather of two colours, for both are made of one shell, though of different parts;..the wampumpeak at eighteenpence the yard, and the white peak at ninepence. *Ibid.* III. i. (1722) 141

Upon his Neck, and Wrists, hang Strings of Beads, Peak and Roenoke. **1832** J. Durfee *What Cheer* III. xxii, 'Tis not the peag, said the sagamore, Nor knives, nor guns, nor garments red as blood, That buy the lands I hold dominion o'er. **1875** Jevons *Money* iv. 27 A foot of black peag being worth two feet of white peag.

† **ˈpeage.** *Obs.* Also 5–8 **payage**, 6– **paage.** [a. F. *péage*, in OF. also *paage* (12th c.), *paege, paiage, payage*, etc.:—**pedage* = Pr. *pezatge*, It. *pedaggio*, med.L. (f. F.) *pedāgium, peāgium, paāgium* (Du Cange):—late pop.L. *pedāticum*, f. *pēs, ped-em* foot: see -AGE.] Toll paid for passing through a place or country; = PEDAGE. *Obs.* (exc. *Hist.* or only in reference to France, etc.).

1456 Sir G. Haye *Law Arms* (S.T.S.) 238 Thai suld nouthir pay.. custume, na payage, quhill thai ar on thair voyage. **1563** tr. *Emperor's Safe Conduct* in Foxe *A. & M.* 191/2 Without paying of any maner of imposition or dane mony, peage, tribute, or any other manner of tolle. **1688** R. Holme *Armoury* II. 168/1 The Bull.. fearing neither Payage or Poundage for his Trespass. **1706** in Picton *L'pool Munic. Rec.* (1886) II. 21 Quitt of all custome, toll and payage. **1714** *Fr. Bk. of Rates* 196 All Duties of Importation, Octrois, Peages, and all others, which used to be levied upon the said Grain by the Cities, Communities, and particular Lordships. **1757** Burke *Abridgm. Eng. Hist.* III. Wks. 1812 V. 609 The payment of tolls, passages, peages, pontages and innumerable other vexatious imposts. **1776** Adam Smith *W.N.* v. i. (1869) II. 403 The turnpike tolls in England, and the duties called *peages* in other countries. **1848** Wharton *Law Lex., Paage*... Obsolete.

Hence † **ˈpeager** *Obs.* [F. *péager*, OF. *peagier* (13th c. in Littré)], a collector of toll, a toll-keeper.

1474 Caxton *Chesse* III. vii, The peagers ner they that kepe passages ought not to take other peage ne passage money but suche as the prynce or the lawe have established.

peagle, peagoose: see PAIGLE, PEAK-GOOSE.

peahen (ˈpiːhɛn). Forms: α. 5–6 **pehen, -henne,** (6 **peyhen**), 7 **pea-henne,** 7– **pea-hen.** β. 4–5 **pohenne, -hen, poohenne.** [f. ME. *pê-*, OE. *péa* + *henne* HEN. Collateral form *po-hen(ne*, f. PO, *poo*:—OE. *páwa* + *henne*.] A female peafowl, the female of the peacock.

α. *c* **1400** [see 1377 in β]. *c* **1440** *Promp. Parv.* 390/1 Pehenne, *pavona*. **1523** Fitzherb. *Husb.* §146 All clouen foted foules wyll syt but thre wekes, except a peyhen. **1570** Levins *Manip.* 61/11 A Pehen, *paua*. **1646** Sir T. Browne *Pseud. Ep.* III. vii. 121 The daily Incubation of Ducks, Peahens, and many other. **1845** Disraeli *Sybil* III. viii, His daughters who tossed their heads like pea-hens—Lady Joan and Lady Maud. **1874** *Chambers's Encycl.* VII. 341/1 The Peahen is much smaller than the male bird, has no train, and is of dull plumage, mostly brownish.

β. **1377** Langl. *P. Pl.* B. XII. 240 Þe pekok & þe pohenne proude [*v.rr.* pehen, pohen]. **1398** Trevisa *Barth. De P.R.* XII. xxxii. (Bodl. MS.), Þe poohenne sitteth abrode xxx. daies and a litel what more.

‖ **peai** (piːˈaɪ), *sb.* Also 7 **peeai, peei,** 8 **piaye,** 8–9 **peii,** 9 **paye, piai.** [ad. Carib *piai* (Tamanac *piache*); in F. *piaye* (A. Biet *Voyage en Cayenne* (1664) III. 385).] A medicine-man or witch-doctor among the Indians of Guiana and other parts of South America: cf. PIACHE.

1613 R. Harcourt *Guiana* 26 Their Peeaios, Priests, or Southsayers, at some special times haue conference with the diuell. **1667** G. Warren *Surinam* 26 Their impostors, or, as they call them, Peeies. **1732** Barbot *Guiana* in *Collect. Voy.* (Churchill) V. 553 A Piaye, or Doctor among them. **1796** Stedman *Surinam* (1806) I. 414 Exorcised by the Peii or priest. **1881** W. H. Brett *Mission Work Guiana* 53 These Piai sorcerers of the aborigines.

b. Now usually **pe'ai-man** (also **pee-ay-, pe-i-, piai-, pee-ay-, pee-a-, paiman**).

1825 Waterton *Wand. S. Amer.* iii. 191 They have a kind of a priest called a pee-ay-man. **1854** H. G. Dalton *Brit. Guiana* (1855) I. 83 After application to a Pe-i-man or Piai-man or conjurer. **1883** *Academy* 8 Dec. 375/3 The peaimen, or tribal medicine men. **1899** Redway *Guiana Wilds* 119 In the opinion of his friends some enemy was at work, and the Peaiman would drive him away.

Hence **pe'ai** *v. trans.*, to practise the arts of a peai-man upon; to treat by witch-doctoring; **pe'aiing, pe'aiism,** the practice and system of a peai-man.

1876 C. B. Brown *Brit. Guiana* vi, Peai-ing. **1881** W. H. Brett *Mission Work Guiana* 53, I was warned that they were going to piai me, that is to cause sickness or death. **1882** Im Thurn in *Jrnl. Anthrop. Inst.* 366 To explain the system of peaiism. **1896** A. Lang *Cock Lane* 39 We are fortunate in finding an educated observer who submitted to be peaied.

ˈpea-ˌjacket. Also 8 **pay-,** 9 **pee-, P-jacket.** [The first element is evidently the same as PEE *sb.*¹ (*pe, pey, P*), (which however is not evidenced after the 17th c., but may have come down later in the comb. *pe-* or *py-gown*). *Pea-jacket* may have been on the analogy of the latter, or may have been formed direct from Du. *pij-jakker*. It is very common in the New Jersey Archives, 1725–40.

Marryat's notion that the original form was *P.-jacket*, for *pilot-jacket*, appears to be a mere gratuitous surmise.]

A stout short overcoat of coarse woollen cloth, now commonly worn by sailors.

1721 *Amer. Weekly Mercury* 23 Mar. 2/2 Clothed with a double-breasted Pee-Jacket. **1725** *N. Jersey Archives* (1894) XI. 97 Run away,.. a Servant Lad Named Philip Dawsitt, he.. had on a Kersey Pea-Jacket. **1727** *Ibid.* 124 Run away .. a Servant Man,.. he has on.. a dark Drugget Pea Jacket. **1757** *Mem. of Last War in N. America* 8 The Consumption .. made of their coarse Woollens by the Men employed in the Fishery, reckoning for each a Blanket, Watch Coat, Rug, Pea-Jacket, etc. **1786** *Francis the Philanthropist* I. 77 He ventured to remark, that no other coat than a pay-jacket could become a sea-boy. **1798** *Hull Advertiser* 24 Nov. 2/2 He had on a sailor's blue pea jacket. **1825** Brockett *N.C. Gloss., Pea*, or *Pee-jacket*, a loose rough jacket or short covering; much used in severe weather by mariners... It was formerly the holiday outer-dress of the keelmen. **1833** Marryat *P. Simple* x, The men.. wore pea jackets, which are very short great coats made of what they call Flushing. **1840** —— *Poor Jack* xxii, A short P-jacket (so called from the abbreviation of *pilot's* jacket) reached down to just above his knees. **1848** A. Brontë *Tenant of Wildfell Hall* III. xv. 301 A dubious, sidelong glance at my splashed, grey trousers and rough P jacket. **1898** F. H. Smith *C. West* iii. 36 He had left his pea-jacket in the cabin. **1922** W. S. Maugham *On Chinese Screen* xlvii. 186 A pea-jacket such as you see in Leech's pictures of the sea-faring man. **1968** *Wall St. Jrnl.* 19 Feb. 1/1 A long-haired Berkeley student wearing a *Kill for Peace* button in the lapel of his black pea jacket. **1976** *Time* 20 Dec. 17/1 In his Navy pea jacket and worn brown boots,.. Jordan loped down the Senate halls, looking like the country boy he tries hard to remain.

Peak (piːk), *sb.*¹ Forms: 1 **Péac** (in Anglo-L. records 1–2 **Pech,** 2 **Pec**); 3–4 **pek,** 6 **Peke,** 7 **Peake,** 7– **Peak.** [OE. *Péac* (only in comb. *Péaclond*) of unknown origin: perh. British.

The name Peak's Arse (OE. **Péaces ærs*, Domesday *Pechesers*), applied to the Peak Cavern, has suggested a conjecture that *Péac* may have been a name for a demon (cf. the later *Devil's Arse*) cognate with OE. *Púca*, PUCK. Cf. other place-names, as OE. *Péaces-del* (Kemble *Cod. Dipl.* dccxxii), *Pechesdon* (Domesday) now Pegsdon, Bedfordshire. From the 17th c. the name has naturally been associated with PEAK *sb.*²; but the history of the latter makes any etymological connexion impossible.]

1. The name of the hilly district in the north-west of Derbyshire, England; divided into the High Peak and the Low or Lower Peak, approximately corresponding to the modern Hundreds of High Peak and Wirksworth respectively.

In 12–13th c. the word seems to have been apprehended as the proper name of the Castle Hill at Castleton, under which is the Peak Cavern. The post-Conquest use of *Peak* in the sense of OE. *Péaclond* seems to have arisen through the application of the name of Peverel's castle to the district thence governed. The Ordnance Map, without any warrant in local usage, gives the name 'The Peak' to an elevated plateau or mountain mass in the High Peak Hundred (see quot. 1874), in which it is followed by geography books, etc.

924 *O.E. Chron.* (Parker MS.), Eadweard cyning.. for þa þonan on Peac lond to Badecan wiellon. *c* **1130** Hen. Hunt. *Hist. Angl.* i. §7 Quatuor autem sunt, quæ mira videntur in Anglia. Primum quidem est, quod ventus egreditus de cavernis terræ in monte vocato Pec, tanto vigore ut vestes rejectas repellat et in altum elevatas procul rejiciat. [*a* **1135** *Charter of Hen. I* in Dugdale *Mon.* VI. 1272 Ea die qua Willelmo Peverell dominium meum de Pecco dedi.] **1173–4** *Pipe Roll* (Pipe Roll Soc.) XXI. 61 In operationibus Castellorum de Pech & de Bolesoura. **1297** R. Glouc. (Rolls) 164 Þat oþer wonder is Vpe the hul of þe pek, þe wind þere iwis Vp of þe erþe ofte comþ of holes. [*c* **1350** *Rolls of Parlt.* II. 391/1 Le Roi granta.. la Franchise.. de l'haut Pek en le Counte de Derby.] **1560** Becon *Jewel of Joye* Wks. II. 6, I trauayled into Darbyshere and from thence into the Peke. **1610** Holland *Camden's Brit., Derbyshire*, The western part beyond Derwent.. riseth high and peaketh vp with hils and mountaines, whence in old time it was called in the old English tongue Peac lond, and is at this daie.. named the Peake. **1622** Drayton *Poly-olb.* xxvi. 453 Yet for her Caves and Holes, Peake only not excells, But that I can again produce those wondrous Wells, Of Buckston. **1636–66** Hobbes (*title*) De Mirabilibus Pecci. (1678 *transl.* The Wonders of the Peake.) **1667** Lacy *Sauny the Scott* v. (1698) 43 We'll put her doon intill a Scotch Coalepit, and she shall rise at the Deel's arse o' Peake. **1802** Lamb *Let. to Manning* 24 Sept., To visit the far-famed peak in Derbyshire, where the Devil sits, they say, without breeches. **1874** *Murray's Hand-bk. Derby* etc. (ed. 2) 53/2 The great block of mountain called in the Ordnance Map 'the Peak' is really an extensive plateau comprising the several summits of Kinderscout, the Edge, Fairbrook Naze, etc.

b. Also **Peakland.**

924, 1610 [see sense a above].

1891 J. Leyland *Peak of Derbyshire* I. 1 The 'Peak of Derbyshire' is a term which, to many, does not carry with it a very definite signification, for although most of the favourite resorts of tourists are known to lie within Peakland, few have inquired as to the boundaries of that district. **1909** *Westm. Gaz.* 5 Apr. 8/1 The death occurred .. on Sunday night of.. one of the best known figures among Peakland agriculturalists. *a* **1917** R. M. Gilchrist *Peakland Faggot* (1926) 97 The moon.. foresaw a tragi-comedy in Peakland. **1926** E. Phillpotts in *Ibid.* p. viii, His [*sc.* Gilchrist's] incomparable pictures of Peakland were only won from long and self-denying service.. in the courts and sanctities of the place and people. **1931** H. Walker (*title*) Peakland poems. **1974** *Country Life* 12 Dec. 1867/1 The strange disappearance of a Peakland river.

† **2.** *transf.* A cave. *Obs. rare*⁻¹. Cf. PEAKISH *a.*² quot. 1600.

So called app. from the famous Peak Cavern.

1600 Holland *Livy* x. i. 351 Into this cave or peake [*spelunca*] the Romanes entred with their ensignes displaied.

3. *attrib.* and *Comb.*, as ***Peak country, hill, lead, scenery***; also of stone from the Peak used as material for millstones, as ***Peak burr, grinding***, etc.; † **Peak's arse,** a former name for the Peak Cavern (later ***the Devil's arse in the Peak***); **Peak-castle,** the castle at Castleton in the Peak; † **peak-wheat** (*pecke-*), a poor variety of wheat mentioned in the 16th c.

1086 *Domesday Bk., Derbyscire*, Terra castelli in Pechesers Willielm Peurel tenuer. Gernebern & Hundinc. **1523** Fitzherb. *Husb.* §13 Bere-barleye.. hathe an eare thre ynches of lengthe or more, sette foure-square, lyke pecke-whete, small cornes, and lyttel floure, and that is the worste barley. *Ibid.* §34 Englysshe wheate hath a dunne eare, fewe anis or none, and is the worste wheate, saue peake-wheate. Peeke-wheete hath a red eare, ful of anis, thyn set, and ofte tymes it is flyntered. *Ibid.* §39 The poore man of the peeke countreye, and suche other places, where as they vse to mylke theyr ewes. **1622** Malynes *Anc. Law-Merch.* 265 The Lead Mines in Ireland doe containe more siluer than these Mines of Darbieshire and Somersetshire called Peake and Mendippe Leade. **1659** Howell *Vocab.* l, Cullen meal the purest, peak or French grinding. **1681** Cotton *Wond. Peak* 47 Under this Castle yawns a dreadful Cave. [*Note*] Peake's-Arse, the sixth Wonder. **1707** Mortimer *Husb.* (1721) II. 45, I never saw any of them but on the barren peak Hills. **1709** *Lond. Gaz.* No. 4540/7 To be Lett some very good Mills at Kidlington,.. one pair of Peck Stones, one pair of French Stones. **1837** *Penny Cycl.* VIII. 425/2 The Peak castle is now an 'ill-shapen ruin', situated on the verge of the rocky precipice that forms the roof of the Peak cavern at Castleton. **1933** *Times Lit. Suppl.* 14 Dec. 891/1 We are given.. a notice of the mill's character.. down to the quality of millstones—Peak or French burr. **1936** *Ibid.* 16 May 416/4 A very individual vocabulary whose words, such as.. peak or French burr-stones.. will soon be a dead if not a forgotten language.

peak (piːk), *sb.*² Forms: 6 **pek, peke,** 6–7 **peake,** 8 **peek,** 7– **peak.** [Known from 16th c. as a later equivalent of PIKE *sb.*¹; in 15th c. the deriv. *peked*, PEAKED, appears as an equivalent of PIKED. The phonetic relations are difficult to understand; but cf. MLG. *pêk, peik*, 'pick, pike, pointed iron instrument'. It is notable that in sense 1, *peak* is identical with *beak*. (Ir. *peac* is from Eng.).

The connexion between PIKE *sb.*¹ and *peak* appears in the adjs. *piked, peaked*. From *pike*, the long point of a 14th c. shoe, instanced in Wyclif *c* 1380, we have *piked schone* in Langland *P. Pl.*, 1377. These appear *c* 1450–60 as *pekyd, peked schone*, being the first appearance of the *peke-, peak-* form. *Peake* itself is exemplified in Palsgr., 1530. In the 16th c. the forms *pike* and *peak* appear to have gone apart in sense, *pike* being confined more to a sharp piercing or pricking point (perhaps under the influence of PIKE *sb.*⁵, the weapon, introduced early in that century), while *peak* is more associated with the notion of a projecting point, not specially sharp or acuminate. *Peak* as a pointed mountain-top, or conical mountain (sense 5) is a still later (17th c.) substitution for an earlier *pike*.]

I. 1. A projecting point; a pointed or tapering extremity; †a beak or bill. Now *rare* (cf. 5 c).

1578 Lyte *Dodoens* I. xxxii. 45 The floures are smal, of a pleasant light redde: after these floures followeth certayne small narrow peakes or beakes as in the others. **1616** Surfl. & Markh. *Country Farme* 405 There breed in Trees certaine small beasts almost like to Weeuils,.. certaine of them haue long and sharpe pointed peakes or bills, these doe great harme to grafts and other young Trees. **1706** Phillips, *Peak*, the sharp Point of any thing. **1818** Keats *Endym.* IV. 497 The moon put forth a little diamond peak, No bigger than an unobserved star.

† **b.** In specific applications: The projecting front of a head-dress, formerly *esp.* of a widow's hood. *Obs.*

1530 Palsgr. 253/1 Peake of a ladyes mourning heed, *biquoquet*. **1611** Cotgr., *Biquoquet*, the peake of a Ladies mourning hood. **1706** Addison *Rosamond* III. iv, Widow Trusty, why so Fine? Why dost thou thus in Colours shine? Thou should'st thy husband's death bewail In Sable vesture, Peak and Veil. **1719** D'Urfey *Pills* II. 11 The Buxom Widdow with Bandore and Peak.

† **c.** Any pointed projecting part of a garment or article of apparel. *Obs.*

1594 Nashe *Unfort. Trav.* Wks (Grosart) V. 145 A close-bellied dublet comming downe with a peake behinde as farre as the crupper. **1617** Moryson *Itin.* III. 170 The colours of their coates weare raised with a peake behind to keepe the necke warme. **1650** Fuller *Pisgah* IV. vi. 114 Frontlets were worn betwixt their eies.. hanging down on a peak from their foreheads. **1696** *Lond. Gaz.* No. 3234/4 A Childs Peak with a Scarlet Riband,.. a red Riband Stomacher. **1795** Anderson *Brit. Embassy China* 108 The women of Pekin.. wear a sharp peak of black velvet or silk, which.. descends from the forehead almost between their eyes. **1808–18** Jamieson, *Peak*, a triangular piece of linen, binding the hair below a child's cap or woman's toy.

d. The point of a beard; †a pointed beard.

1592–3 Nashe *Four Lett. Confut.* Wks. (Grosart) II. 220 A iolly long red peake, like the spire of a steeple hee cherisht continually without cutting. **1619** H. Hutton *Follie's Anat.* A viij, Hauing his beard precisely cut ith' peake. *c* **1620** Fletcher & Massinger *Double Marriage* III. i, How he has .. run your beard into a peak of twenty! **1698** Fryer *Acc. E. India & P.* 390 His Beard is Cut neatly, and the Whiskers.. in fashion of an Half-Moon on the upper Lip, with only a decent Peak on the under.

e. The projecting part of the brim of a man's cap or the like.

1660 F. Brooke tr. *Le Blanc's Trav.* 136 A Cap of Crimson Tissu, with a Chapplet of gold, that hath a peake before, not unlike the Flower-Deluces. **1866** *Routledge's Ev. Boy's Ann.* 356 A cap is best for the head, and it is not a bad plan to line the peak inside with green. **1873** Black *Pr. Thule* i, The rain that fell off the peak of his sailor's cap.

f. An advancing or retreating point formed by the hair on the forehead.

1833 Bray *Tamar & Tavy* (1836) III. xxxviii. 193 Wishing that he should have.. a pair of fine *peaks*, as they were called, one being on either side the forehead, she caused the hair to be regularly shaved off. **1849** Longf.

Kavanagh viii, She had on her forehead what is sometimes denominated a 'widow's peak',—that is to say, her hair grew down to a point in the middle. **1938** A. MORRIS *Step-by-Step Method Water Waving* 39 (*caption*) Hair line showing peak and receding part over eyes. **1951** A. SETON *Foxfire* ii. 42 She had soft hair.., and it curled all around her heart-shaped face. Really heart-shaped, because a widow's peak cleft the white forehead. **1971** W. COOPER *Hair* vii. 206 In English folklore, if a woman's hair grows to a point low on the brow, it is said to indicate that she will live to be a widow, and so it is often called a 'widow's peak'. **1978** 'M. M. KAYE' *Far Pavilions* xxiii. 339 A small muslin turban..covered her hair and showed only the deep widow's peak in the angle where its folds crossed.

2. A promontory or point of land; a headland. Now *local*.

The lofty headland at Ravenscar, forming the southern extremity of Robin Hood's Bay, is stated in the Whitby guide-book to be called 'The Peak'.

1548 UDALL, etc. *Erasm. Par. Acts* xiii. 46 Barnabas and Saul went to Seleucia, whiche is a great promontorye, or peake on the weste parte of Antioche.

†**3.** Lace; also *spec.* a lace-ruff (quot. 1591). *Obs.*

1591 LODGE *Catharos* (Hunterian Cl.) 57 Our picked yongsters hauing their peakes starched for feare of stirring. **1692** COLES, *Peak*, (old word) lace. *a* **1700** B. E. *Dict. Cant. Crew, Peak*, any kind of Lace. [Hence in Grose, Halliwell, etc.]

4. *Naut.* **a.** The narrowed extremity of a ship's hold at the bow, the FOREPEAK; also the corresponding part at the stern, the ***after-peak***.

1693 [see FOREPEAK]. **1704** J. HARRIS *Lex. Techn.* I. s.v., There is also a Room in the Hold of a Ship, that is called the Peek: 'Tis from the Bitts forward to the Stem. Here Men of War usually keep their Powder; and Merchant-men, Outward-bound, place their Victuals here. **1867** SMYTH *Sailor's Word-bk., After-peak*, the contracted part of a vessel's hold, which lies in the run, or aftermost portion of the hold, in contradistinction to *forepeak*. **1895** SUFFLING *Land of Broads* 25 Forward in the peak is a small American cooking-stove.

b. 'The upper outer corner of those sails which are extended by a gaff' (Smyth *Sailor's Word-bk.* 1867); also, the upper end of a gaff. Hence ***gaff peak, mizzen peak***.

1711 [implied in *peak-brail*: see 6]. **1762-9** FALCONER *Shipwr.* II. 387 The head..In balance near the lofty peak they bound;..The halyards throat and peak are next applied. **1806** A. DUNCAN *Nelson* 75 Nelson directed his fleet to hoist four lights..at the mizen peak. **1840** R. H. DANA *Bef. Mast* ix, A long, sharp brig,..with..English colours at her peak. **1894** *Times* 16 June 12/2 Healy had to gybe, but, though warned to lower his peak, he performed the operation with unshortened sail.

c. The point at the end of a fluke of an anchor; = PEA *sb.*³

1793 SMEATON *Edystone L.* §143 The anchor..became suspended by the bowsprit, with the Peak upwards. **1867** SMYTH *Sailor's Word-bk., Peak of an anchor*, the bill or extremity of the palm, which, as seamen by custom drop the *k*, is pronounced pea; it is tapered nearly to a point in order to penetrate the bottom.

II. Later form of PIKE, as used of a mountain.

This comes up in 17th c., and first in uses representing Sp., Pr. *pico*. (But in the names of mountain summits in the NW. of England PIKE remains unchanged.)

5. The pointed top of a mountain; a mountain or hill having a more or less pointed summit, or of conical form.

1634 SIR T. HERBERT *Trav.* 112 The top of the high Peake of Damoan..like a Sugar-loafe. **1687** A. LOVELL tr. *Thevenot's Trav.* II. 181 We were some three Leagues off of Sannas,..it makes a Peak, but the Hill is higher than the Peak [*Fr.* il fait un pico, mais la montagne est plus haute que le pico]. **1718** PRIOR *Cloe hunting*, On Meander's bank, or Latmus' peak. **1759** tr. *Adanson's Voy. Senegal* 8 The Peak of Tenerif [F. *le Pic de Ténérif*]..appeared to us in the form of a pyramid, or more properly, of a sugar-loaf. **1789** STOCKDALE *Phillip's Voy. Botany Bay* iii, Travellers have delighted to speak of the Peak of Teneriffe as the highest mountain in the ancient world. **1796** H. HUNTER tr. *St.-Pierre's Stud. Nat.* (1799) III. 92 This mountain is called the Three Paps, because it's three peaks have that form. **1856** STANLEY *Sinai & Pal.* i. II. 76 The next day we ascended the highest peak..of the Sinai range. **1856** RUSKIN *Mod. Paint.* IV. v. xiii. §6 The notable range of jagged peaks which bound the horizon to the North East of Mont Blanc. **1877** LADY BRASSEY *Voy. Sunbeam* ii, We all rose early..to catch the first glimpse of the famous Peak of Teneriffe... It was quite ten o'clock before we saw the Peak, towering above the clouds, right ahead, about fifty-nine miles off.

b. *fig.* Highest point, summit.

1784 COWPER *Task* III. 157 Some..travel Nature up To the sharp peak of her sublimest height, And tell us whence the stars. **1820** SHELLEY *Hymn Apollo* v, I stand at noon upon the peak of Heaven. **1822** —— *Triumph of Life* 222 The peak From which a thousand climbers have before Fall'n, as Napoleon fell. **1894** H. DRUMMOND *Ascent of Man* 233 Every summit in Evolution is the base of some grander peak.

c. *transf.* The pointed top of anything; *spec.* one on a graph (cf. sense 5 e).

(Appears to combine sense 1 with 5.)

1840 DICKENS *Barn. Rudge* iv, It was..a shy, blinking house, with a conical roof going up into a peak over its garret window of four small panes of glass. **1849** LYTTON *Caxtons* III. v, Roland's forehead was singularly high, and rose to a peak in the summit. **1855** TENNYSON *Maud* I. vi. i, The budded peaks of the wood are bow'd, Caught and cuff'd by the gale. **1922** *Encycl. Brit.* XXXII. 1024/1 The potential difference of the arc electrodes is an irregular curve with sharp peaks. **1926** W. R. INGE *Lay Thoughts* II. i. 89 If we look at a chart of the births and deaths in Germany for the two generations before the Great War we shall see that each war is marked by a peak in the line showing the death rate and a ravine in the line showing the birth rate. **1968** *Brit. Med. Bull.* XXIV. 212/1 The corresponding histogram of conjugated bilirubin is markedly bimodal, and also shows an artificial peak at 0·5 mg. (100 ml.).

d. 'The high sharp ridge-bone of the head of a setter-dog' (*Cent. Dict.* 1890, citing *Sportsman's Gazetteer*).

e. A highest point in a period of any varying quantity, as electric power, traffic flow, prices, etc.; the time when this occurs; a culminating point or climax. Cf. sense 5 c.

1902 *Encycl. Brit.* XXV. 35/1 Accumulators will take the peaks of the load, relieving the machinery from sudden jerks. **1923** *Daily Mail* 28 May 4 We have long since passed the peak in this unpleasant business. **1923** *Westm. Gaz.* 11 Aug. 6/4 During the morning, evening and theatre peaks, two escalators in each group can be run in either an upward or downward direction. **1943** *Sun* (Baltimore) 2 July 17/1 Steels enjoyed a last minute upswing and assorted favorites emerged..a number at three year peaks. **1962** A. NISBETT *Technique Sound Studio* iii. 63 The closer one gets to an open piano, the more the transients associated with the strike tone will be apparent; at their strongest..they may be difficult to control without..risking momentary distortion on the peaks. **1967** *Listener* 23 Mar. 386/2 The nuclear disarmament campaign was already past its peak. **1968** *Brit. Med. Bull.* XXIV. 219/2 This is a continuous-flow analyser with its output arranged so that individual results are produced as voltage peaks following one another at intervals. **1971** *Hi-Fi Sound* Feb. 68/2 It is a basic hi-fi requirement that peaks should be accommodated without serious distortion. **1976** *Daily Tel.* 20 July 1/5 At the peak of the wages rush last year, the annual rate of increase of earnings reached 30 per cent.

f. *Phonetics.* The most prominent sound in a syllable with regard to sonority.

1935 J. S. KENYON *Amer. Pronunc.* (ed. 6) 69 The phonetic center, or 'peak' of a syllable is its point of greatest sonority. **1942** BLOCH & TRAGER *Outl. Linguistic Analysis* 22 The sounds which constitute the peaks of sonority are called syllabic. **1960** E. SIVERTSEN *Cockney Phonol.* ii. 23 Stressed simple syllable peaks do not occur before juncture, and there are other limitations in the distribution of unstressed peaks in this position. **1964** E. PALMER tr. *Martinet's Elem. Gen. Linguistics* ii. 52 A consonant like [l] when placed between consonants of lesser perceptibility or audibility such as [p] and [k], may function as syllable peaks. **1965** W. S. ALLEN *Vox Latina* 2 Sounds which may function either as peaks or as valleys of prominence, whilst classified as vowels in their peak (or 'nuclear') function, are generally termed semi-vowels..in their valley (or 'marginal') function.

g. *Surfing.* The highest point of a wave.

1963 *Surfing Yearbk.* 42/2 *Peak*, the highest point of the wave. **1965** FARRELLY & MCGREGOR *This Surfing Life* iv. 44/2 On most occasions in this sort of surf you take off straight down the peak. **1965** J. M. KELLY *Surf & Sea* ii. 26 The wind blows gently into the faces of the white-crested waves. It holds up their peaks giving you time to speed away on the clear green slopes before they break. **1968** *Surfer Mag.* Jan. 48/1 The way the peak was breaking didn't offer many rights.

III. 6. *attrib.* and *Comb.*, as ***peak-cap*** (sense 1 e); ***climber*** (sense 5 a); (sense 5 e) ***peak-clipping, -limiting***; (sense 5 f) ***peak nucleus, satellite***; ***peak-bearded, -capped, -crested, -like, -nosed, -roofed*** adjs.; **peak-arch**, a pointed or Gothic arch (Knight *Dict. Mech.* 1875); **peak brail** *Naut.*, a brail attached to the peak of a sail; **peak downhaul** *Naut.*: see quot.; **peak experience**, the momentary awareness of joy or fulfilment akin to ecstasy, of a higher and different quality from ordinary life, experienced by some people; **peak factor** *Electr.*, the ratio of the maximum value (or the difference between the maximum and minimum values) of a wave to the r.m.s. value; **peak halyard** *Naut.*, a rope or tackle for hoisting the peak of a gaff; **peak listening** (see sense 7 a); **peak piece** *Naut.*, a piece of canvas used to strengthen the peak of a sail; **peak programme meter** (see quot. 1941); **peak purchase** *Naut.*: see quot.; **peak shaving**, storage of part of the gas produced when demand is low so that it can be used to increase the supply at times of peak demand; **peak-to-peak** *a.* and *adv.*, (measured or expressed as the difference) between extreme values of a periodically varying quantity; also called **peak-to-valley** (*rare*); similarly **peak-to-mean** *a.*; **peak tye** *Naut.*, a tye used for hoisting the peak of a heavy gaff (Ogilvie 1882); **peak viewing** (see sense 7 a); **peak voltmeter** *Electr.*, a voltmeter that measures the peak value of an alternating voltage.

1905 *Daily Chron.* 12 Aug. 5/2 At one carriage a little baby-girl was held up by its mother to kiss farewell to a *peak-bearded gloire bluejacket. **1711** W. SUTHERLAND *Shipbuild. Assist.* 129 *Peek-brails. **1903** *Daily Chron.* 16 Apr. 5/1 *Peak caps are coming into fashion... Every second young man, and every third man of years, was wearing a cap in the pattern of those used for motoring. *a* **1905** *Peak-capped [in N.E.D.]. **1972** *Drive* Spring 147/1 A peak-capped driver at the helm of a Rolls-Royce Corniche. **1976** *Field* 30 Dec. 1275/3 A peak-capped figure on one knee beside a folded stretcher. **1897** *Edin. Rev.* July 56 Let the *peak-climber reflect that there are between fifty and sixty heights in the chain. **1961** *Which?* July 156/1 There are two accepted methods for achieving loudness compression. One is called A.V.C. and the other *peak clipping. **1975** G. J. KING *Audio Handbk.* iii. 60 For example, if the 1 kHz input sensitivity is 2 mV and peak clipping..occurs at 20 mV, the overload margin is said to be 10:1 or 20 dB. **1879, 1881** *Peak crested [see BLONDINETTE]. **1867** SMYTH *Sailor's Word-bk.*, **Peak downhaul*, a rope rove through a block at the outer end of the gaff to haul it down by. **1962** A. H. MASLOW *Toward Psychol. of Being* III. vi. 69 An attempt to generalize in a single description some of these basic cognitive happenings... These and other moments of highest happiness and fulfilment I shall call the *peak-experiences. **1969** H. GEIGER in Sutich & Vich *Readings Humanistic Psychol.* xvii. 307 If..there should come a kind of 'social' peak experience..a new rhythm of humane historical relationships could be established in the world. **1975** *Sat. Rev.* (U.S.) 22 Feb. 20/2, I underwent a religious-like peak experience in which the presence of divinity became almost palpable. **1976** N. POSTMAN *Crazy Talk* 85 Bombing the Vietnamese back to the Stone Age was quite possibly a 'peak experience' for millions of Americans. **1914** *Peak factor [see CREST *sb.*¹ 7 e]. **1963** WILLIAMS & PRIGMORE *Electr. Engin.* vii. 185 When deciding whether a particular voltage can be safely applied to an insulator, the r.m.s. value must be multiplied by the peak factor. **1970** *IEEE Trans. Information Theory* XVI. 86/1 The perceptual quality of synthetic speech signals depends to some extent on the 'peak-factor' (defined here as the difference between the maximum and minimum amplitudes of a signal divided by its root-mean-square value). *Ibid.*, FM signals have low peak factors. **1727-41** CHAMBERS *Cycl.* s.v. *Ship*, Plate Fig. i. 8 *Peak Hallyards. **1836** [see HALYARD 1 b]. **1959** *B.S.I. News* Dec. 14 Recommendations regarding automatic gain control or *peak limiting have also been excluded. **1871** MORRIS in Mackail *Life* (1899) I. 260 Just as this little *peak-nosed parson does. **1960** E. SIVERTSEN *Cockney Phonol.* ii. 13 A simple peak consists of one of the six vowels. A complex peak consists of one of the six vowels as *peak nucleus plus one of the peak satellites [h j w]. **1794** *Rigging & Seamanship* I. 93 Mizens..have a nock-piece and a *peek-piece. **1941** *B.B.C. Gloss. Broadcasting Terms* 23 **Peak programme meter*, instrument used (especially for the purpose of facilitating control) to measure the volume of programme peaks, averaged over a period of less than one-hundredth of a second. **1962** A. NISBETT *Technique Sound Studio* v. 94 There are several types of meter that can be used to line up equipment or check for overmodulation; but a 'peak programme meter' (PPM) seems to be the most satisfactory instrument. **1867** SMYTH *Sailor's Word-bk.*, **Peak purchase*, a purchase fitted in cutters to the standing peak-halliards to sway it up taut. **1960** *Peak satellite [see *peak nucleus* above]. **1960** *Wall St. Jrnl.* 5 Oct. 10/2 Pilot plants were being planned in this country a quarter century ago..looking for economic means of '*peak shaving.' This is the practice in which standby sources of supply are used to meet demand at peak periods. **1973** *Times* 30 July 11/3 Both are designed to absorb the stresses imposed on the gas supply system by a very cold day throughout the country in the depth of winter. The remedy is termed peak shaving. **1965** *Wireless World* July 329/1 A recording level indicator should essentially be a peak registering type because music has a large *peak-to-mean ratio. **1962** SIMPSON & RICHARDS *Physical Princ. Junction Transistors* ix. 219 The shift due to the rise in ambient temperature is thus relatively small and can be tolerated for *peak-to-peak output-current swings of about 7 mA. **1967** *Electronics* 6 Mar. 80/2 (Advt.), Model 900 Nanovolt Galvanometer. Noise: Less than 2 nV or (2 pA) peak-to-peak for all source resistances. **1973** *Nature* 9 Nov. 72/2 During the eclipse itself the stability of the aircraft was excellent: pitch $\lesssim 0{\cdot}1°$, roll $\lesssim 0{\cdot}5°$ (peak-to-peak values). **1974** HARVEY & BOHLMAN *Stereo F.M. Radio Handbk.* ii. 21 The peak-to-peak amplitude of the second harmonic between the collector and the tap on the coil is limited to approximately twice the line supply voltage. **1957** *Physical Rev.* CV. 1416/2 Nuclear emulsion as a target was found to have a significantly weaker asymmetry (*peak-to-valley ratio of $1{\cdot}40 \pm 0{\cdot}07$). **1924** *Jrnl. Sci. Instrum.* I. 281 A compact *peak voltmeter, using a thermionic rectifier for measuring positive and negative peak voltages up to 600 volts, is described. **1967** *IEEE Trans. Electr. Insulation* II. 80/2 The peak voltmeter may find wide application in corona routine measurements.

7. Passing into *adj.* **a.** Characterized by or pertaining to a greatest value or largest number; ***peak-listening, -viewing***, listening to the radio, or viewing of television, by the largest audience of the day; freq. *attrib.* (from a false analysis of phrases like *peak listening-period* as *peak-listening period*).

1903 *Electr. World & Engin.* 9 May 789/1 The direct-current ends of these rotary converters are often worked in multiple with an old generating station..during the peak-hours. **1924** *Westm. Gaz.* 8 Aug. 3/4 A drop of nearly £40,000,000 in pensions expenditure since the 'peak' year of 1920-21 is mentioned. **1937** *Archit. Rev.* LXXXII. (Suppl.) 1 Traffic congestion at the 'peak hours' is deplorable. **1946** *Vogue* June 2/2 The Sunday evening peak-listening series, 'The Challenge of our Time'. **1948** E. WAUGH *Loved One* 57 It was as though..his speech came from some distant and august studio; everything he said might have been for a peak-hour listening period. **1949** *Radio Times* 15 July 31/2 Leonard Hooper, a..dining-car attendant, tells you something about his work..especially during the holiday peak periods. **1960** M. O'CONOR et al. *Children & Television Programmes* iii. 8 Pressures of different kinds and degrees exist to compel the television organizations to seek very large audiences for at least some of the programmes placed within the peak viewing period. **1962** L. DEIGHTON *Ipcress File* xxv. 158 One long fluorescent day punctuated by interrogations like TV commercials in a peak hour play. **1966** *B.B.C. Handbk.* 14 A serious endeavour to improve the range of peak-time programmes. **1966** *Listener* 5 May 643/2 The peak age [for juvenile crime] is during the last year at school. **1969** G. REES *St Michael* xv. 184 It was not until 1948 that the figures of turnover exceeded those of the previous peak year of 1941. **1974** *Times* 19 Dec. 2/7 The fare rises..will not arrest traffic growth. Peak services to holiday areas..are being increased. **1976** *Jrnl. R. Soc. Arts* June 360/2 It would have been stupid and arrogant to think that 'Nobody will want all that news at the peak hour' or 'They ought to have half an hour's news, it is good for them.' **1977** *Herald* (Melbourne) 18 Jan. 1/1 A packed peak-hour express train tore down an overhead bridge.

b. Greatest; that is a maximum.

1903 [see LOAD *sb.* 3 f]. **1930** *Daily Express* 6 Sept. 10/1 Ordinary shares..reached a peak price of 26s. 10½d. during the 'boom'. **1946** *R.A.F. Jrnl.* May 180 At peak production, the Halifax group turned out one complete aircraft every working hour. **1949** R.-M. S. HEFFNER *Gen. Phonetics* II. v. 79 Two resonators with peak resonances below 1,200 cycles per second. **1950** *Engineering* 10 Feb. 168/2 Each cylinder of a multi-cylinder engine may be fitted with one of these gauges, and the peak pressures attained..are then read at a glance. **1958** *Times Rev. Industry* May 24/3 Important for the overall economy of gas supply are the processes used to produce for peak loads. **1959** *Ann. Reg. 1958* 431 Mr. John Davis..anticipated attendance at the cinemas would have dropped during 1958 to..just over half the peak audiences achieved in the years immediately after the war. **1973** S. FISHER *Female Orgasm* vii. 202 Ideation and fantasy do not ..play a large or consistent role during the peak arousal phase.

†**peak**, *sb.*[3] *Obs.* Also 6 pek, peke. [Origin unknown: chiefly used in the combination *hody-peke*, HODDYPEAK, q.v., also *peke hoddie, noddie*.] A dolt, noodle, silly creature. Cf. PEAK-GOOSE.

a **1529** SKELTON *P. Sparowe* 409 The doterell, that folyshe pek. —— *Col. Cloute* 264 Of suche Paternoster pekes All the worlde spekes. **1549–89** [see HODDYPEAK]. **1580** HOLLYBAND *Treas. Fr. Tong, Niez*, an idiote, a peke hoddie [1593 noddie], a simple soule, a snekesbie.

peak, *sb.*[4], **peek.** *Sc.* [Of uncertain origin: in Sc. dialects distinct in pronunciation (piːk) from PEAK *sb.*[2] (pik), to which otherwise it might be referred.] A small point of flame. Hence **peekie** *dim.*

1887 DONALDSON *Suppl. Jamieson, Peak, peek*, a very small quantity, a mere pick; as, 'a peak o' licht, a peek o' fire'. *a* **1893** J. SMITH in R. Ford *Harp Perth.* 306 Richt eerie at nicht Was yon peekie o' licht. **1903** *Dundee Advertiser* 22 Dec. 7 By the feeble light of the gas jet, which was burning at a 'peak'.

peak, *sb.*[5], variant of PEAG, wampum.

peak (piːk), *v.*[1] Also 6 peeke, peke, pecke, 6–7 peake. [Found early in 16th c.; origin uncertain.

It is not even certain that all the senses here collected have the same origin. Sense 1, and esp. 1 b (which also appears as *pecke*), may be related to PECK *v.*[2] 3; sense 3 is possibly related to PEAK *sb.*[2]: cf. PEAKING *ppl. a.* 1, PEAKISH *a.*[1] 1; sense 4 is usually taken as referring to the sharp or emaciated features of a sick person; but this may be a later association with PEAK *sb.*[2]: cf. PEAKING *ppl. a.* 2, PEAKISH *a.*[1] 3, PEAKY *a.*[2]]

†**1.** *intr.* ? To fall, drop, sink. *Obs.*

1509 HAWES *Past. Pleas.* XVI. xxvii, Alas! I wretche and yet unhappy peke Into suche trouble, misery, and thought.

†**b.** ***to peak over the perch***: *lit.* to topple or tumble off the perch, *fig.* to die. *Obs.*

App. orig. a phrase of hawking. See PERCH for various parallel phrases, e.g. *to tip over the perch, hop the perch*, etc.

1575 TURBERV. *Faulconrie* 219 If it continewe three or foure dayes, moste assuredlie the hawke wyll pecke ouer the pearch, and dye. **1633** HEYWOOD & ROWLEY *Fortune by Land* III. H.'s Wks. 1874 VI. 398 If he should peak over the pearch now, and all fall to our elder Brother.

†**2.** *intr.* To shrink, to slink. *Obs.*

[**1550** J. PROCTOR *Hist. Wyat's Reb.* 70 Wyat him selfe and v.C. men..peked on styll all alonge vnder sainct Iames parke wall, vntyll he came to charinge crosse.] **1570–6** LAMBARDE *Peramb. Kent* (1826) 325 This done, our Lady shranke againe into her shrine, and the Clerke peaked home to patch up his broken sleepe. **1598** TOFTE *Alba* (1880) 70 Not like vaine pleasure, who away doth peake, When he his Bark through want perceiues to leake. **1642** ROGERS *Naaman* 42 He over-rules him in his journey, that hee might not peake aside into this corner or that.

†**3.** To move about dejectedly or silently; to mope; 'to make a mean figure, to sneak' (J.). *Obs.*

1568 *Jacob & Esau* II. ii, Fye brother Esau, what a foly is this? About vaine pastime to wander abrode and peake, Til with hunger you make your selfe thus faint and weake. **1594** CAREW *Tasso* II. xvi, And she or scornes, or seeth not, or gaue No semblance, so till then par [? poor] thrall he peakt [*il misero ha servito*]. **1602** SHAKS. *Ham.* II. ii. 594 Yet I, A dull and muddy-metled Rascall, peake Like John a-dreames,..And can say nothing. *a* **1603** T. CARTWRIGHT *Confut. Rhem. N.T.* Pref. (1618) 29 How much more would they..let him goe peaking alone after he hath been so corrupted.

4. ? To droop in health and spirits, waste away; 'to look sickly' (J.) or emaciated. Chiefly in ***peak and pine***, a Shaksperian expression repeated by many later writers, chiefly as emphasizing *pine*.

[**1573** TUSSER *Husb.* (1878) 158 Poore sillie hen, long wanting cock to guide, Soon droopes and shortly then beginnes to peake aside.] **1605** SHAKS. *Macb.* I. iii. 23 Wearie Seu'nights, nine times nine, Shall he dwindle, peake, and pine. *a* **1652** BROME *Eng. Moor* I. i, What! suffer you to pine, and peak away In your unnatural melancholy fits. **1709** *Brit. Apollo* II. No. 29. 3/1 This is no Pin-buttock'd Wench, That Peaks as if she'd took a Drench. **1789** CHARLOTTE SMITH *Ethelinde* (1814) V. 191 After pining and peaking away twelve or fourteen years of your best-looking days. **1857** KINGSLEY *Two Y. Ago* xiv, If he will but go right on about his business,..instead of peaking and pining over what people think of him. **1881** *Leicestersh. Gloss., Peak*, to waste and dwindle in flesh.

Hence **peak and pine** as *sb.*, *nonce-use*, for *peaking and pining*.

1868 BROWNING *Ring & Bk.* v. 1603 The Babe's face, premature with peak and pine, Sank into wrinkled ruinous old age.

peak (piːk), *v.*[2] Also 6 peke, ? peeke, 6–7 peake. [f. PEAK *sb.*[2]]

1. *intr.* To project or rise in a peak. Also const. *up.*

1577 STANYHURST *Descr. Irel.* iii. in *Holinshed* (1577) I. 14/2 To eschew the daunger of the craggy rockes there on euery side of the shore peaking. **1583** STUBBES *Anat. Abus.* I. (1879) 51 Another sort..are content with no kind of Hatt, without a great bunche of feathers,..peaking on the toppe of their headès. **1609** HOLLAND *Amm. Marcell.* xv. x. 47 In these Cottian Alpes,..there peaketh up a mightie high mount, that no man almost can passe over without danger. **1610** —— *Camden's Brit.* I. 556 The Western part [of Derbyshire] riseth high and peaketh up with hils and mountaines. **1865** *Cornh. Mag.* Aug. 330 The woolly hair.. peaks down over the low forehead. **1929** R. BRIDGES *Testament of Beauty* i. 23 Untill the pyramid in geometrical enormity peak'd true. **1962** T. MASTERS *Surfing made Easy* 65 *Peak up*, when a swell begins to break. **1965** J. M. KELLY *Surf & Sea* iii. 39 This is where the wave peaks up and first starts breaking. **1968** W. WARWICK *Surfriding in N.Z.* 10/3 If you find the wave you have caught is peaking up further along the beach from you, paddle towards the peak. **1976** *Woman's Day* (N.Y.) Nov. 100/2 Don't overpluck, overpencil or change the place where your brows peak.

b. *fig.* To reach the highest point; to attain maximum intensity, activity, etc.

1958 *Bird Migration* I. I. 2 Common and Black-headed Gulls were usually present, the former peaking at 32 on 14th, the latter at 27 on 30th. **1961** T. H. WHITE *Making of President 1960* xii. 299 There were now eighteen days left to the campaign, and Mr. Nixon was free to take the gloves off and 'peak' in his own manner. **1966** *Punch* 24 Aug. 238/1 Athletes are an awkward squad... Why does a young man fail to reach his potential on the day?.. His anxiety level is so high that he peaks too early. **1968** *Guardian* 21 Sept. 1/1 My campaign, according to the polls and surveys, has not peaked too soon. **1971** *Nature* 29 Jan. 304/2 Instead, the spectrum peaks around 4 keV and falls rapidly to both higher and lower photon energies. **1973** *Times Lit. Suppl.* 6 Apr. 366/5 That wild, speculative spirit peaked in 1929. **1974** *Sci. Amer.* Sept. 143/2 Only at relatively high occupational levels do the average earnings of men peak at the same time that the needs of their families are also peaking, that is, when the children are adolescent and of college age. **1975** *Listener* 8 May 615/1 Like so many of his ilk, Man Ray peaked early, and turned dilettante. **1976** *Publishers Weekly* 26 Apr. 52/3 Growth, the very life-blood of corporate capitalism, has peaked in our time and now begun a decline towards what Jones calls 'a permanent recession'. **1977** *Horse & Hound* 25 Mar. 55/1 The eight [riders] named have been asked to programme their potential horses to 'peak' at this time but without too many competitions in advance.

c. To level *out* after reaching a peak.

1958 *Washington Post* 2 June A12/5 The Commissioner of the Bureau of Labor Statistics says the cost of living index is 'peaking out'. He follows this with the even more remarkable statement that the index may creep up further this summer after peaking out now. **1967** *Technology Week* 23 Jan. 55/3 When we learn just a trifle more about the hormonal control of brain development, these phenomena will peak out in human interest. **1971** *Daily Tel.* 2 Mar. 18/6 Since margins peaked out in the latter half of 1969 returns have not been so impressive and the rate of profit growth between the two halves has slackened from 7 p.c. to 5 p.c. **1977** *Time* 29 Aug. 46/3 General Motors shares peaked out at almost 114 in 1965 and are now down to around 65.

d. To have a peak experience (see PEAK *sb.*[2] 6).

1970 J. HOWARD *Please Touch* 20 People who 'peak' can transcend the mundane and feel ecstatically fulfilled. **1972** *Village Voice* (N.Y.) 1 June 78/4 The hill with the tall fir cross, only 30 yards from where Michael and Ellen and I had peaked on the acid.

2. *trans.* To bring to a head; to bring to a peak or maximum. Also const. *up*; and *fig.* to accentuate.

1887 *Contemp. Rev.* Dec. 770 The accumulation of the national wealth..serves mostly to heighten and peak the great social inequalities as between the capitalist and the jobbing day labourer. **1957** *Practical Wireless* XXXIII. 718/2 When a station is found, the trimmers of range 5 are adjusted to peak it up. **1960** *Ibid.* XXXVI. 375/2 Trimmers can be peaked for minimum meter reading. **1961** T. H. WHITE *Making of President 1960* xii. 296 He might move his campaign into its third, or final phase, 'peaking' it for impact on the week end before election. **1962** A. NISBETT *Technique Sound Studio* ix. 158 As the scene comes to a close the speech is faded down and the effects are lifted to swamp the line. Then after the effects have been peaked for a few seconds they too can be slowly faded out. *Ibid.* 263 *Peak up*, lift the volume either of an individual component of a mix, or of the entire programme.

peak, *v.*[3] *Naut.* Also 7 pike, 7–8 peek. [f. *pike* or *peak* in the adv. *a-pike*, A-PEAK, vertically, straight up and down, or aphetic from the adv. itself; cf., in same sense, F. *apiquer* (1751) from *à pic* advb. phrase, vertically.] *trans.* To place, put, or raise a-peak or vertically.

a. To tilt up a yard vertically, or nearly so, by the mast; to top a yard; esp. ***to peak the mizen.***

[Cf. F. *apiquer*, disposer les vergues d'un bâtiment à peu près verticalement.]

1626 CAPT. SMITH *Accid. Yng. Seamen* 30 When you ride amongst many ships, pike your yards. **1627** —— *Seaman's Gram.* ix. 45 To ride apike is to pike your yards when you ride amongst many ships. **1692** *Capt. Smith's Seaman's Gram.* xvi. 79 *Peek* [printed *Speek*] *the Mizon*, that is, put the Yard right up and down by the Mast. **1729** CAPT. W. WRIGLESWORTH *MS. Log-bk. of the 'Lyell'* 18 Nov., At night it blowing hard with Rain, Peeked the Yards, and hauled up a Range of the Sheet Cable. **1769** FALCONER *Dict. Marine* (1789), *Apiquer une vergue*, to top a sail-yard, or peek it up. **1794** *Rigging & Seamanship* I. 242 They peek the yard against the mast to shift the sail. *Ibid.* II. 255 *To Peek the Mizen*, to put the mizen-yard perpendicular by the mast. **1867** SMYTH *Sailor's Word-bk.*, To *Peak*, to raise a gaff or lateen yard more obliquely to the mast.

b. ***to peak the oars***: see quots. (Cf. A-PEAK d.)

1836 N. ISAACS *Trav. E. Afr.* II. 347 They immediately hauled down their sail, peaked their oars. **1849** J. F. COOPER *Sea Lions* I. xi. 156 The men now 'peaked' their oars, as it is termed; or they placed the handles in cleets made to receive them, leaving the blades elevated in the air, so as to be quite clear of the water. **1851** H. MELVILLE *Moby Dick* II. vi. 42 The boat's five oars were seen simultaneously peaked. **1875** KNIGHT *Dict. Mech., Peak*,..to raise the oars upright amidships. **1888** CHURCHWARD *Blackbirding* 227 Sharp, man! Peak your oars, and sit down tight on the bottom. **1890** *Cent. Dict.* s.v. *Oar, To peak the oars*, to raise the blades out of the water and secure them at a common angle with the surface of the water by placing the inner end of each oar under the batten on the opposite side of the boat.

c. Of a whale: To raise (his tail or flukes) straight up in diving vertically. Also *intr.*

1839 T. BEALE *Sperm Whale* 44 The flukes are then lifted high into the air, and the animal..descends perpendicularly ..this act..is called by whalers 'peaking the flukes'. **1840** MARRYAT *Poor Jack* vi, How could he go down head-foremost without peaking his tail in the air? **1885** WOOD in *Longm. Mag.* V. 537 A whale had..dived perpendicularly —'peaked' in whaling language.

peak, *adv.* (*sb.*[1]) *Naut.* [Aphetic f. A-PEAK *adv.*, which, by separation of its elements, appears sometimes to have been treated as *a peak*, indef. article and sb.]

†**a.** In reference to the yards: (from *ride †a-pike* or *a-peak*: see A-PEAK *adv.* c), ***to ride a broad peak.*** *Obs.*

1706 PHILLIPS s.v. *Peek*, To *Ride a broad Peek*, is much after the same manner [as to *ride a-peak*], only the Yards are raised up but half so high.

b. In reference to the cable and anchor: ***to stay peak, to ride a short stay peak*** = short stay a-peak; ***a long peak*** = long stay a-peak: see A-PEAK.

1841 R. H. DANA *Seaman's Man.* 117 A *stay-peak* is when the cable and forestay form a line. A *short stay-peak* is when the cable is too much in to form this line. **1867** SMYTH *Sailor's Word-bk.* s.v., *To stay peak*, or *ride a short stay peak*, is when the cable and fore-stay form a line: *a long peak* is when the cable is in line with the main-stay.

peak, obs. or dial. var. PIQUE.

peak: see PEEK *sb.*[1], *v.*[1] and [2].

peaked (piːkt, 'piːkɪd), *a.* Forms: 5 pekyd, peked, 6–8 peeked, 7– peaked. [f. PEAK *sb.*[2] + -ED[2]. Cf. PICKED, PIKED. In sense 2, app. connected with PEAK *v.*[1] 4.]

1. a. Having a peak; pointed, acuminated; cut, trimmed, or brought to a peak or point; cf. PEAK *sb.*[2] 5 e and PICKED *ppl. a.*, PIKED.

c **1450** *Cov. Myst.* xxv. (Shaks. Soc.) 241 Off ffyne cordewan a goodly peyre of long pekyd schon. *c* **1467** *Pol. Poems* (Rolls) II. 251 With youre longe peked schone, Therfor your thrifte is almost don. **1578** LYTE *Dodoens* III. vi. 320 The clapper or pestill..is long and thicke, and sharpe poynted peeked lyke to a horne. **1617** MORYSON *Itin.* III. 177 The Gentlewomen..weare vpon their heads a black vaile of Cipers, peaked at the forehead, with a veluet hood hanging downe behind. **1640** SOMNER *Antiq. Canterb.* 171 The ocular and peeked or pointed form of the arch. **1742** FIELDING *J. Andrews* I. xiv, Her chin was peaked. **1749** W. ELLIS *Sheph. Guide* 193 (E.D.S.) [Adder's tongue has] a peeked leaf or stalk. **1787** MME. D'ARBLAY *Diary* June, Enumerating various changes in the modes, from square shoes to peaked. **1825** MACAULAY *Milton* Ess. (1887) 19 [Charles the first] his Vandyke dress,..and his peaked beard. **1952** [see KURTOSIS]. **1965** *Wireless World* July 329/1 The frequency of the peaked response is accordingly altered by switching each arm capacitance of the parallel-T network. **1968** A. J. MERRETT *Executive Remuneration in U.K.* p. xiii, The indivisible nature of many executive roles ..necessitates great personal involvement,..and the strain of an erratic and highly peaked work load.

b. *spec.* Of a mountain, hill, etc.: Having, or rising into, a peak. Also in comb., as ***two-, twin-peaked***, etc. So of a roof.

1670 NARBOROUGH *Jrnl.* in *Acc. Sev. late Voy.* I. (1694) 39, I went..to the peeked Rock. **1797** MRS. RADCLIFFE *Italian* xiii, Its peaked head towered far above every neighbouring summit. **1856** RUSKIN *Mod. Paint.* IV. v. xiv. §10 It is curious how rarely..an instance can be found of a mountain ascertainably peaked in the true sense of the word—pointed at the top, and sloping steeply on all sides. **1868** MISS BRADDON *Dead Sea Fr.* I. ii. 18 The quaint peaked roofs and grand old churches. **1872** JENKINSON *Guide Eng. Lakes* (1879) 325 The bulky mass of Helvellyn and the peaked summit of Catchedecam.

2. Sharp-featured, thin, pinched, as from illness or want; sickly-looking, 'peaky'. Chiefly *colloq.*

1835–40 HALIBURTON *Clockm.* (1862) 38, I am dreadfully sorry, says I, to see you..lookin so peecked. **1856** MRS. BROWNING *Aur. Leigh* II. 929 The dumb derision of that gray peaked face. **1860** O. W. HOLMES *Prof. Breakf.-t.* ix, He looks peakeder than ever. **1883** J. HAWTHORNE *Dust* xxxvi. 295 As pale and peaked as a charity-school-girl. **1892** *Sporting Life* 26 Mar. 7/5 He still loses weight, and the peaked look in his face is ominous.

3. *Comb.*, as ***peaked-faced, -nosed, -looking, -roofed*** adjs.

1842 MIALL in *Nonconf.* II. 865 Going about the world, like a very peaked-nosed woman. **1889** C. KING *Queen of Bedlam* xiv. 188 Randall M'Lean, very white and 'peaked' looking, was sitting propped up in bed. **1891** 'L. MALET' *Wages of Sin* I. I. iii. 56 It'ud aggravate a saint, that it would, to hear you so taken up with a little peaked-faced bit of a maid. **1894** *Outing* (U.S.) XXIV. 197/2 A peaked-roofed construction.

Hence **'peakedness,** (*a*) the quality or condition of being peaked or pointed; (*b*) (in sense 2 above).

1832 J. P. KENNEDY *Swallow B.* iii. (1860) 43 The peculiar peakedness of her nose. **1856** RUSKIN *Mod. Paint.* IV. v. xiv. §11 No mountain in the Alps produces a more vigorous impression of peakedness than the Matterhorn. **1884** J. C. HARRIS in *Century Mag.* Nov. 121 Her general aspect of peakedness.

peake-devant, variant of PICKE-DEVANT *Obs.*

†**peak-goose, pea-goose.** *Obs.* Also 6 peek-, pick-, 7 pe-goose. [app. f. PEAK *sb.*³ + GOOSE.] A dolt, simpleton, ninny, poor creature.

a **1568** ASCHAM *Scholem.* I. (Arb.) 54 To laughe, to lie, to flatter, to face: Foure waies in Court to win men grace. If thou be thrall to none of theise, Away good Peek goos, hens Iohn Cheese. **1593** G. HARVEY *Pierces Super.* Wks. (Grosart) II. 64 The Book-woorme was neuer but a pick-goose. **1606** CHAPMAN *Mons. D'Olive* III. Plays 1873 I. 223 Courtesies a verie peagoose. **1622** FLETCHER & MASSINGER *Prophetess* IV. ii, Come, march on and humour him for his mirth... Tis a fine peak-goose. **1694** CROWNE *Married Beau* III. 28 I'm a pe-goose with a Lady, but I'm the devil with a chamber-maid. *a* **1700** B. E. *Dict. Cant. Crew, Pea-goose,* a silly Creature. *a* **1825** FORBY *Voc. E. Anglia, Peagoose,* one who has an aspect both sickly and silly.

'peakiness. [f. PEAKY *a.*¹ + -NESS.] Peaked or pointed character.

1921 L. B. TURNER *Wireless Telegr.* iii. 22 The 'peakiness' of this curve measures the 'sharpness of tuning'. **1924** W. DEEPING *Three Rooms* ii. 12 That slight peakiness about the chin, the ugly lines in the throat.

peaking ('pi:kɪŋ), *ppl. a.* Now *dial.* Also 7–9 peeking. [f. PEAK *v.*¹ + -ING².]

1. Sneaking, skulking; mean-spirited; (sometimes, app. = prying: but in that sense app. belonging to PEEKING).

1598 SHAKS. *Merry W.* III. v. 71 The peaking Curnuto her husband..dwelling in a continual larum of ielousie. **1622** MASSINGER & DEKKER *Virg. Martir* II. i, I stole but a durty pudding..and the peaking chitface page hit me ith' teeth with it. **1650** T. BAYLY *Herba Parietis* 51 That peaking devill, jealousie. **1668** TEMPLE *Let. to Ld. Arlington* Wks. 1731 II. 169, I mean not Virtue, in a peaking, formal Presbyterian Sense. **1689** HICKERINGILL *Ceremony-Monger* Concl. iii. Wks. 1716 II. 470 Not every sneaking Register and peaking Surrogate could send a Soul to Satan. **1871** W. ALEXANDER *Johnny Gibb* xiv. (1873) 84 What Tam had said was..that 'Benjie was an orpiet, peeakin, little sinner'.

2. Emaciated, sickly, drooping, pining, peaky.

a **1700** B. E. *Dict. Cant. Crew, Peeking fellow;*..a thin weazel faced fellow. **1706** PHILLIPS, *Peaking,* that is of a sickly Constitution. **1771** SMOLLETT *Humph. Cl.* 8 Aug., Let. i, Poor Liddy is in a peaking way. I'm afraid this unfortunate girl is uneasy in her mind. **1823** LADY L. STUART *Lett.* (1901) 325 She looks but peeking and has had a good deal of illness. **1879** MISS JACKSON *Shropshire Word-bk., Peaking,*..sickly; drooping: said of young poultry for the most part. 'A wet May's bad for turkies; I've lost several, an' theer's more looks very peäkin'.

Hence **'peakingly** *adv.*, in a pining or poor way; **'peakingness,** sickliness, pining condition.

1611 COTGR. s.v. *Ceincture,* They thinke their wiues liue peakingly at home, and pull strawes..or blow their fingers. **1727** BAILEY, vol. II, *Peakingly,* sicklily, wearily. *Peakingness,* Sickliness, Unthrivingness.

peakish ('pi:kɪʃ), *a.*¹ [In sense 1 app. f. PEAK *sb.*³ (also in Skelton), perh. associated with PEAK *v.*¹ 3; in sense 2 f. PEAK *sb.*²; sense 3 goes with PEAK *v.*¹ 4, PEAKING *ppl. a.* 2, PEAKY *a.*²: see -ISH¹.]

†**1.** Slothful, spiritless (L. *ignavus*); stupid; ignorant, silly: an epithet of contempt, of which it is difficult to ascertain the exact meaning. *Obs.*

(In quot. *a* 1560 with play on PEAK *sb.*¹; cf. PEAKISH *a.*²)

1519 HORMAN *Vulg.* vi. 61 He is shame faste but nat pekysshe, *verecundus est sine ignauiâ.* *a* **1529** SKELTON *Ware Hauke* 225 The pekysh parsons brayne Cowde not rech nor attayne What the sentence ment. *a* **1560** BECON *Jewel of Joye* Wks. II. 6 *Philem.* I trauayled into Darbyshere and from thence into the Peke... *Theoph.* I thynke you founde there verye peakeish people. *Phi.* Not so, I confesse to you that I founde there very good wyttes and apte vnto learnynge. **1568** *Jacob & Esau* II. i, I will see, if any [meat] be ready here at home, Or whether Iacob haue any, that peakishe mome. **1570** LEVINS *Manip.* 145/40 Peakish, *mimicus, a.* *a* **1603** T. CARTWRIGHT *Confut. Rhem. N.T.* (1618) 512 These dreamers dreame night and day,—otherwise to proue a sect or peakish order of Franciscans, etc.

2. Somewhat peaked or pointed. *dial.*

1749 W. ELLIS *Sheph. Guide* 151 A peekish Head and Tail.

3. Somewhat 'peaky' (PEAKY *a.*²).

1836 SMART, *Peakish..colloq.* having features that seem thin or sharp, as from sickness. **1900** BARRIE *Tommy & Grizel* xxvii. 327 He was rather peakish but he had not complained.

Hence †**'peakishness** *Obs.*, spiritlessness.

1519 HORMAN *Vulg.* v. 55 He rebuked hym of hys dastardnes and pekishnes [*ignaviæ*]. *a* **1575** PILKINGTON *Exp. Nehemiah* iv. 11–15 Wks. (Parker Soc.) 436 God requireth not such peakishness in a man, that he suffer himself to be wounded, that by the law of nature alloweth every man to defend himself.

†**Peakish,** *a.*² *Obs.* [f. PEAK *sb.*¹ + -ISH¹.] Of, pertaining to, or resembling that of the district of the Peak in Derbyshire.

In quots. 1592 and 1646 the sense may be 'rude, outlandish, remote as in the Peak'.

1592 WARNER *Alb. Eng.* VIII. xlii. (1612) 201 Once hunted he, vntill the Chace, long fasting, and the heate Did house him in a peakish Graunge within a Forrest great. **1593** DRAYTON *Sheph. Garl.* iv, Her skin as soft as Lemster wooll, As white as snow on Peakish Hull, Or swanne that swims in Trent. **1600** HOLLAND *Livy* XXXVIII. xlix. 1015 To preuent those Thracian theeves that they should not hide themselues within their peakish holes [*notis sibi latebris*] and ordinarie couert musets. *Ibid.* XLV. xxvii. 1219 After hee had seene the mouth of that peakish caue [*os specus*] into which they use to descend that would haue the benefit of the Oracle. **1612** DRAYTON *Poly-olb.* xi, From thence he [Mersey] getteth Goyt down from her Peakish spring. **1646** BP. HALL *Balm Gil.* XIV. iii, A plain villager in the rude Peak..returns him this answer in his peakish dialect, Nay even put fro thee, my son.

Hence †**'peakishly** *adv.*, ? obscurely, ? remotely.

1567 GOLDING *Ovid's Met.* VI. (1593) 144 [He] led her to a pelting grange that peakishly did stand In woods forgrowne [*silvis obscura vetustis*].

Peakland: see PEAK *sb.*¹

peakless ('pi:klɪs), *a. rare.* [f. PEAK *sb.*² + -LESS.] Without a peak.

1859 *Chamb. Jrnl.* XI. 296 Turning his peakless cap hind before.

Peakrel ('pi:krəl). Also 7–8 -rill, 8 -ril. [f. PEAK *sb.*¹: cf. *cockerel, mongrel.*] An inhabitant of the Peak district in Derbyshire; also applied to horses, sheep, etc.

1681 COTTON *Wond. Peak* (1682) 18 Two hob-nail Peakrills, one on either side, Your arms supporting, like a bashful bride,..And thus, from Rock to Rock they slide you down. **1769** *De Foe's Tour Gt. Brit.* III. 78 The Peakrills, as they are called, are a rude boorish Kind of People; but bold, daring, and even desperate in their Search into the Bowels of the Earth. **1808** W. MARSHALL *Review* I. 523 The stock of the more southerly heathlands are native mountain sheep, of a light frame..and bear the name of 'Peakrils'. **1899** *Daily News* 31 July 8/7 The credulous tourist..fails to perceive at a glance the purport of the Peakrels humour.

b. *attrib.* Of or belonging to the Peak district.

1779 *Archæol.* V. 375 The weight of this pig [of lead]..is ..a proper load for a small peakril horse to travel with.

'peakward, *adv.* [See -WARD.] Towards the peak (of a mountain).

1881 W. WILKINS *Songs of Study* 65 Look on the eagle wheeling up peakward.

peaky ('pi:kɪ), *a.*¹ [f. PEAK *sb.*² + -Y.]

1. Abounding in, or characterized by having, peaks.

1832 TENNYSON *Palace of Art* xxix, Hills with peaky tops engrail'd. **1855** J. D. FORBES *Tour Mont Blanc* viii. 182 The peaky ridge just described. **1858** *Chamb. Jrnl.* X. 227 The sun approached the edge of the peaky horizon.

2. Peaked, pointed; peak-like.

1869 MACDONALD *Settlement* (1877) 47 (E.D.D.) A..face, with a peaky little bit of a nose. **1878** LADY BURTON *Arabia,* etc. xii. 270 The Konkanis [wear] peaky slippers. **1887** HALL CAINE *Deemster* xxxviii. 251 A poor mongrel dog,..with ragged ears, a peaky nose. **1889** DOYLE *Micah Clarke* 209 The peaky thoughtful countenance.

3. Special collocations, as **peaky blinder,** formerly, a hooligan active in the Birmingham area and distinguished by his hat, worn pulled into a peak over the eyes.

1896 *Birmingham Daily Argus* 17 Nov. 2/3 Is there..any Volunteer officer who will come down and captain a company of budding 'peaky blinders'? **1898** *Daily News* 22 Oct. 2/5 The woman..saw the two 'peaky blinders' leaving on Thursday morning. **1901** *N. & Q.* Feb. 94/2 *Peakyblinder*..., the 'larrikins', 'rufflers', or 'hoodlums' of the Midlands are thus known from a custom they adopted of wearing the peak of their cap drawn down over their eyes when at their nefarious practices. **1971** B. SLEIGH *Smell of Privet* x. 82 A mission in..Birmingham which took in some of the notorious Peaky Blinders.

'peaky, peeky, *a.*² *colloq.* and *dial.* [Connected with PEAK *v.*¹ 4, and with PEAKED *a.* 2, PEAKING *ppl. a.* 2, PEAKISH *a.*¹ 3.] **a.** Sickly, feeble, wasted, puny; = PEAKING *ppl. a.* 2.

1821 M. EDGEWORTH *Let.* 23 Oct. (1971) 240 Poor young Worthington himself is rather peeky-weakee. He has a sore throat. **1853** [implied in PEAKYISH]. **1873** RUSKIN *Fors Clav.* xxvi. III. 16 A poor peeky, little sprouting crocus. **1881** E. J. WORBOISE *Sissie* ix, The second child has sickened, and the third is reported to be looking 'peeky'. **1889** BLACKMORE *Kit* viii, Peaky.

b. *Comb.*, as *peaky-faced* adj.

1906 *Westm. Gaz.* 12 May 11/2 A peaky-faced boy of about nine. **1910** *Chambers's Jrnl.* Jan. 53/1 He looked at the peaky-faced boy with the scared black eyes.

Hence **'peakyish** *a.*, somewhat 'peaky'.

1853 'C. BEDE' *Verdant Green* I. viii, Peakyish you feel, don't you?

peaky, var. form of PECKY *a.*

peal (pi:l), *sb.*¹ Forms: 4–6 pele, (5 peell, peyll, 5–6 peel(e, 6 peeyle, pelle), 6–7 peale, (7 pale), 6– peal. [ME. *pele*; in sense 1, aphetic f. *apele,* APPEAL; in branch II, supposed to be the same word, but the evidence is not irrefragable; no other origin, however, has suggested itself.]

I. †**1.** = APPEAL *sb. Obs.*

1377 LANGL. *P. Pl.* B. XVII. 302 For þere þat partye pursueth, þe pele [C. xx. 284 apeel, *v.r.* peel] is so huge, þat þe kynge may do no mercy til bothe men acorde. *c* **1440** *Gesta Rom.* xxiii. 78 (Harl. MS.) þou shalt come afore my lord, and avow thi pele. **1471** *Paston Lett.* III. 19 Whech woman seyd to me that che sewyd never the pele.

II. †**2.** (?) A call or summons (e.g. to prayers, to church) made by ringing a bell; a stroke on a bell, or the ringing of a bell, as a call or summons. *Obs.*

a **1380** *St. Augustine* 1642 in Horstm. *Altengl. Leg.* (1878) 89 To euensong Men rongen þe þreo peles long. *c* **1440** *Promp. Parv.* 391/1 Pele of bellys ryngynge (or a-pele of belle ryngynge), *classicum.* **1444** *Rolls of Parlt.* V. 125/1 That the Baillifs..make ryng the comune belle III pele, to gedre the Comunes togedre. **1561** BP. PARKHURST *Injunctions,* This shal be doon immediatlye after the last peale to euening praier. **1675** KEN *Man. Scholars Winch. Coll.* 4 Go into the Chappel between first and second Peal in the morning, to say your Morning Prayer.

3. The loud ringing of a bell, or of a set of bells; *spec.* a series of changes rung on a set of bells: see BOB *sb.*⁵, CHANGE *sb.* 8 b, GRANDSIRE 6.

1511 FABYAN *Will* in *Chron.* Pref. 8 Ringyng at the said obite, soo that oon pele over nyght be rong wᵗ all the bellys, and oon pele upon the mornyng. **1512** in *Southwell Visit.* (Camden) 115 At my buriall a peeyle with all the bells. **1530** PALSGR. 253/1 Peele of belles, *son de cloches.* **1572–3** in Swayne *Sarum Churchw. Acc.* (1896) 287 Ringers yᵗ Ringed iij pelle when Mr. Hooper was buried. **1671** *Tintinnalogia* 102 This Peal of Grandsire..is the absolute foundation from whence the excellent Peal of Grandsire bob..had its beginning and method. **1671–1883** [see GRANDSIRE 6]. **1787** *Europ. Mag.* XII. 434 The bells of the churches rung their dead peals during the day. **1812** J. WILSON *Isle of Palms* IV. 444 The bells ring quick a joyous peal. **1852** MRS. STOWE *Uncle Tom's C.* xxxvii, George had the satisfaction, as the bell rang out its farewell peal, to see Marks walk..to the shore. **1879** in Grove *Dict. Mus.* I. 334/2, 12 [bells], the largest number ever rung in peal.

transf. and *fig.* *a* **1548** HALL *Chron., Edw. IV* 193 To haue her fauor and folowe her desire..rather then to haue a lowryng countenaunce, and a ringyng peale, when he should go to his rest and quietnes. **1605** SHAKS. *Macb.* III. ii. 43 Ere ..The shard-borne Beetle, with his drowsie hums, Hath rung Nights yawning Peale. **1636** MASSINGER *Gt. Dk. Flor.* III. i, My pockets ring A golden peal. **176.** WESLEY *Husb. & Wives* vii. 2 Wks. 1811 IX. 86 The husband may..ring his wife a peal concerning her duty.

4. A set of bells tuned to one another; a ring of bells.

1789 G. WHITE *Selborne* 321 The day of the arrival of this tuneable peal was observed as an high festival by the village. **1860** FROUDE *Hist. Eng.* XXX. VI. 33 First began St. Paul's, ..then, one by one, every peal which had been spared caught up the sound. **1872** ELLACOMBE *Ch. Bells Devon,* etc. i. 208 Sometimes a peal of bells is cast in harmony, in which case it is called a maiden peal, and no tuning is required.

transf. **1894** FENN *In Alpine Valley* III. 61 A tiny campanula whose lavender bells clustered in a peal about the stem.

†**5.** A discharge of guns or cannon so as to produce a loud sound; esp. as an expression of joy, a salute, etc. *Obs.* exc. *Hist.*

c **1515** *Cocke Lorell's B.* 13 A pele of gonnes gan they rynge. **1577** in *Hakluyt's Voy.* (1589) 157 The Castle discharged a peale of ordinaunce. **1587** FLEMING *Contn. Holinshed* III. 1341/1 The duke of Brabant..caused a peale of a twentie or thirtie thousand harquebusses to be shot off. *a* **1649** DRUMM. OF HAWTH. *Hist. Jas. II,* Wks. (1711) 36 The king..caused discharge a pale of ordnance together. **1833** HT. MARTINEAU *Three Ages* II. 68 The best part of this day's entertainments..was the peals of ordnance both from the vessels and the shore. **1855** MACAULAY *Hist. Eng.* xiii. III. 347 The peal of a musket..was the signal.

6. A loud outburst or volley of sound.

1535 COVERDALE *Jer.* iv. 19, I haue herde the crienge of the trompettes, and peales of warre. **1596** SHAKS. *Merch. V.* III. ii. 146 Still gazing in a doubt Whether those peales of praise be his or no. *a* **1649** DRUMM. OF HAWTH. *Urania* xii. (1656) 137 At whose command clouds peales of Thunder sound. **1670** DRYDEN *2nd Pt. Conq. Grenada* V. ii, Like the hoarse peals of vultures,..When over fighting fields they beat their wings. **1671** MILTON *Samson* 233, I my self,..vanquisht with a peal of words..Gave up my fort of silence to a Woman. **1697** DRYDEN *Alexander's F.* 126 Break his bands of sleep asunder, And rouse him, like a rattling peal of thunder. **1711** ADDISON *Spect.* No. 63 ⁋7 Which very often produced great Peals of Laughter. **1848** GALLENGA *Italy, Past & Pr.* I. 121 A peal of the organ is antiphonal to a flourish of trumpets.

7. *attrib.* and *Comb.*, as *peal-book, -ringer, -ringing.*

1872 ELLACOMBE *Ch. Bells Devon,* etc. iii. 236 The peal book contains a record of peals.

peal, peel (pi:l), *sb.*² Forms: 6 pele, peall, *Sc.* peill, 6–8 peale, 7– peal, 8– peel. [In 1533 *salmon pele*: origin unascertained.] A name given to, **a.** A grilse or young salmon (now esp. one under two pounds in weight); **b.** A smaller species of salmon, *Salmo cambricus* (or *S. trutta*). (Cf. Günther *Introd. Study of Fishes* (1880) 644 Note 2.)

α. salmon peal.

1533–4 *Act 25 Hen. VIII,* c. 7 The yonge frye,..called lakspynkes smowtis or salmon pele. **1661** LOVELL *Hist. Anim. & Min.* 220 The Salmon peales or Sea Trouts, are a more light, wholesome, and well tasted meat. **1741** *Compl. Fam.-Piece* II. ii. 341 Salmon Peel are taken by dropping your Line, baited with a Brandling, gradually into the Hole. **1758** *Descr. Thames* 171 Salmon Peale..seems to be a Species of the Salmon.

β. peal, peel.

1577 *Reg. Privy Council Scot.* II. 657 Ten thowsand peill fischeis, killing and ling. **1587** HOLINSHED *Chron.* III. 1009 Plentifull of salmon, trout, peale, dace, pike, and other like freshwater fishes. **1623** R. CARPENTER *Conscionable Christian* 89 The line sometimes breaketh too, when a Peale or great fish is to be drawne vp. **1758** JAGO in Borlase *Nat.*

Hist. Cornwall 271 The Black-fish..head and nose like a peal or trout. **1851** NEWLAND *Erne* 33 *note*, Graul, called in the north a grilse and on the Shannon a peel. **1861** *Act 24 & 25 Vict.* c. 109 §4 Migratory fish of the genus salmon,..known by the names..forktail, mort, peal, herring peal, may peal, pugg peal, harvest cock.

Comb. **1903** *Longm. Mag.* May 41 When a man goes peel-fishing all day.

peal, *v.*[1] *Obs.* exc. *dial.* Forms: (1 *pīlian* (?)); 5 **pele**, *pa. t.* **pelyde, -id,** 6 **peil,** 7–8 **peal,** 9 *dial.* **peyl, peighl.** [Origin uncertain.

Cotgr. uses *peale* to render F. *piler* to pound or bruise as in a mortar:—L. *pīlāre*, already in OE. as *pīlian*; but *peal* could not answer phonetically to *piler*, esp. as it seems to be the same word that is often written in mod. dial. *pail* or *pale* (peɪl). The inclusion here of sense 1 is therefore provisional. (See also PELL *v.*, PAIL *v.*[2], PALE *v.*[3])]

†**1.** *trans.* To pound or bruise as in a mortar.

[*c* **1000** ÆLFRIC *Gloss.* in Wr.-Wülcker 114/25 *Pilurus*, uel *pistor*, se þe pilaþ, *uel* tribulaþ.] **1611** COTGR., *Pilé*, pealed, beaten, bruised, crushed, pounded, stamped. *Ibid.*, *Pilement*, a pealing, pounding, stamping, braying, beating; a crushing, or bruising. *Ibid.*, *Piler*, to peale, pound, stampe, to bray, beat, or breake, in a morter.

2. To strike or beat with repeated blows, to batter, to pelt.

?*a* **1400** *Morte Arth.* 3042 Paysede and pelid downe playsterede walles. **1583** STOCKER *Civ. Warres Low C.* III. 86 Fiftie or three score of them lustily charged then betweene the gates, and valyantly pealed them with harquebuze shot. **1592** WYRLEY *Armorie, Ld. Chandos* 54 Some one did weild A mightie stone, that head a peeces peild Of Lord Mucedent. **1686** GOAD *Celest. Bodies* II. i. 144 Is it certain then that our Aspect is able to..Peal us with a Showr? **1735** SOMERVILLE *Chase* IV. 150 [A ram] Shall..with his curl'd hard Front incessant peal The panting Wretch. **1828** *Craven Gloss.* (ed. 2), *Peyl*, to beat, to strike. [Cf. **1854** BAMFORD *Dial.* (Lancash.) (E.D.D. s.v. *Pail*), Awv pailt him weel.]

b. *intr.* To shower blows, to hammer *on*; *fig.* to 'pitch *into*'.

c **1430** *Chev. Assigne* 304 þene plukke out þy swerde, & pele on hym faste. **1874** WAUGH *Chim. Corner* (1879) 215 [Lancash.] They thunge't an' peel at one another full bat. **1884** CUDSWORTH *Dial. Sk.* 125 (E.D.D.) Just let me finish this bird cage, an I'll peyl intut an reight an' all! **1895** CLEGG *Sketches* 429 Aw've had to peighl away like a nowman.

†**3.** *intr.* Of blows: To come or fall in a shower.

c **1400** *Rowland & O.* 502 So thikke þaire dynttis to-gedir pelyde, Thaire armours hewenn laye in þe felde.

Hence †**peal** used advb. in *peale pelted*; '**pealing** *vbl. sb.* and *ppl. a.*[1], (*a*) see sense 1; (*b*) battering, beating, pelting.

1582 STANYHURST *Æneis* II. (Arb.) 56 Now be we peale pelted from top of barbican hautye. *Ibid.* II. 59 Pyrrhus..Downe beats with pealing thee doors. **1616** SURFL. & MARKH. *Country Farme* 379 Apples must be gathered..in faire weather,..and that by hand without any pole or pealing downe. **1740** SOMERVILLE *Hobbinol* II. 155 On her pale Cheeks Ghastly he gaz'd, nor felt the pealing Storm.

peal (piːl), *v.*[2] Now *dial.* Also 5 pele. [Aphetic f. *apele*, APPEAL *v.*: cf. PEAL *sb.*[1] 1.] *trans.* and *intr.* = APPEAL *v.* (in various senses).

c **1400** *Langl.'s P. Pl.* C. III. 186 On poure prouysors & on a-peles in [*v.r.* þat peleth to] þe arches. *c* **1440** *Promp. Parv.* 391/1 Pelyn or apelyn, *appello*. *c* **1450** *Bk. Curtasye* 594 in *Babees Bk.* 318 To A baron of chekker þay mun hit pele. **1648** *Chas. I's Messages for Peace* 120 What reason these men had thus to 'peale him. **1655** GURNALL *Chr. in Arm.* verse 11. I. i. 53 They peale one of another, shifting the sin rather than suing for mercy. **1894** *Northumbld. Gloss.*, *Peal*, to appeal, a shortened form. *Ibid.*, *Peel off*, to appeal off..A happy man was he who could peel off from the militia.

peal (piːl), *v.*[3] [f. PEAL *sb.*[1]]

1. *intr.* To sound forth in a peal; to resound.

1632 MILTON *Penseroso* 161 There let the pealing Organ blow, To the full voic'd Quire below. **1719** TICKELL *On Death Addison* 16 The pealing organ, and the pausing choir. **1728** POPE *Dunc.* II. 258 There, Webster! peal'd thy voice, and, Whitfield! thine. **1841** H. AINSWORTH *Old St. Paul's* II. 102 A loud clap of thunder pealed overhead. **1849** MACAULAY *Hist. Eng.* x. II. 602 Behind it rode the body guards with cymbals clashing and trumpets pealing.

†**2.** *trans.* To storm, din, or assail (the ears, or a person) *with* (loud noise, clamour, etc.). *Obs.*

Perh. with admixture of sense of PEAL *v.*[1] to batter.

1641 MILTON *Ch. Govt.* Concl. 62 They..never lin pealing our eares that unlesse we fat them like boores,..all learning and religion will goe underfoot. **1667** —— *P.L.* II. 920. **1717** FENTON *Homer in Milton's Style, Odyss.* XI. Poems 114 To Woman's Faith Unbosom nought momentous; tho' she peal Your Ear..Unlock not all your Secrets. **1719** J. T. PHILLIPS tr. *Thirty-four Confer.* 158 Priests and People pealed me with Maledictions and Abusive Words.

3. To give forth in a peal or peals; to utter loudly and sonorously.

1714 GARTH *Dispens.* v. (ed. 7) 64 Pestles peal a martial Symphony. **1745** T. WARTON *Pleas. Mel.* 198 The many-sounding organ peals on high The clear slow-dittied chaunt, or varied hymn. **1887** BOWEN *Virg. Æneid* I. 90 Loud thunder is pealed from the skies.

Hence '**pealing** *ppl. a.*[2]

1632, 1719 [see sense 1]. **1794** MRS. RADCLIFFE *Myst. Udolpho* xxix, The pealing thunder rolled onward. **1824** W. IRVING *T. Trav.* I. 115 The pealing notes swelled through the lofty aisles.

peal (piːl), *v.*[4] *Obs.* exc. *dial.* [Origin uncertain. ? Related to PEEL *sb.*[2]] (See quots.)

1674 RAY *N.C. Words*, *Peale* the pot; cool the pot. **1703** THORESBY *Let. to Ray* (E.D.S.), 'Peel the pot', cool it with the ladle, taking out and pouring in again. **1755** JOHNSON, *Peal*,..2. To stir with some agitation: as, to peal the pot, is when it boils to stir the liquor therein with a ladle. **1890** *Gloucestersh. Gloss.*, *Peal*, to pour out a liquid.

peal, obs. form of PALL, PEEL.

peale meale, obs. form of PELL-MELL.

'**pealer**[1]. *Obs.* exc. *dial.* [Aphetic f. *appealer*: cf. PEAL *v.*[2]] = APPEALER, in various senses.

1393 LANGL. *P. Pl.* C. XXI. 39 Thenne put hym forth a pelour by-for pilat, and seyde. *a* **1425** tr. *Higden* (Rolls) VII. 519 Gunnildas nory karf the fals pelours hamme. **1509** HAWES *Past. Pleas.* xxxii. (Percy Soc.) 159 Vyle peller, in lykewyse also, His tonge was scraped that he suffered wo. **1894** *Northumbld. Gloss.*, *Pealers*, appealers, applicants.

pealer[2] ('piːlə(r)). *U.S.* [var. PEELER[1] 3.] A person who displays exceptional aptitude or enthusiasm *for* an activity.

1834 S. SMITH *Sel. Lett. J. Downing* 142 Pennsylvany chaps are real pealers for electing folks when they take hold. **1869** [see STAVER *sb.*[2]].

pealite ('piːlaɪt). *Min.* [Named after A. C. Peale: see -ITE[1].] A variety of geyserite, containing only 6 per cent. of water.

1873 F. M. ENDLICH *Let. to A. C. Peale* in *6th Rep. U.S. Geol. Surv. of Territories* 154, I wish to distinguish it as a well-defined sub-species of opal, and propose to name it 'Pealite', as you were the first to find and collect the mineral.

peall, pealok, pealt, obs. ff. PELL *sb.*, PELLOCK[1], PELT *sb.*[1]

pean (piːn). *Her.* [Origin uncertain: identity with PANE *sb.*[2] has been suggested, but evidence is lacking.] One of the furs; represented as Sable powdered with 'spots' of Or.

1562 LEIGH *Armorie* 121 The sixth doublyng, is called Pean, whiche is the field, Sable, and the pouders Or. **1610** GUILLIM *Heraldry* I. iv. 14 This is blacke powdered with yellow; and in Blazon is termed Pean. **1864** BOUTELL *Her. Hist. & Pop.* iv. (ed. 3) 20, 4 Pean: Gold spots on a black field.

pean, peane, obs. ff. PÆAN, PAIN; var. PEIN.

peanut ('piːnʌt). [f. PEA[1] + NUT.] **1.** The fruit or seed of *Arachis hypogæa*, or the plant itself, native to South America, much cultivated in warm climates; the fruit is a pod ripening underground, containing two seeds like peas, valued as food and for their oil; = GROUND-NUT 2. Also applied to allied plants of similar character (or their fruit), as *Voandzeia subterranea* of Madagascar, Africa, and S. America, and *Amphicarpæa monoica* of N. America (*hog-peanut*: see HOG *sb.*[1] 13 d).

1807 *Salmagundi* 27 June 240 Young seniors go down to the flag-staff to buy peanuts, and beer. **1835** C. F. HOFFMAN *Winter in West* II. 206 Wrenching it from its roots as a Lilliputian would a peanut! **1886** A. H. CHURCH *Food Grains Ind.* 127 Half the weight of pea-nuts is oil. *Ibid.*, Pea-nuts..yield a cake well adapted for feeding cattle. **1937** A. F. HILL *Econ. Bot.* xvi. 358 The peanut is a native of Brazil but was early carried to the Old World tropics by the Portuguese explorers. It was brought to Virginia from Africa by the slaves and is now one of the most important crops of the south. **1967** N. FREELING *Strike Out* 96 His wife was..reading Proust and eating peanuts. **1968** J. W. PURSEGLOVE *Tropical Crops: Dicotyledons* I. 225 More than half the edible peanut stocks of the United States are used for peanut butter.

2. a. *pl.* Something small, trivial, or unimportant; *spec.* a small sum of money, esp. when regarded as inadequate payment. orig. *U.S. slang.*

1934 H. N. ROSE *Thesaurus of Slang* iii. 35/2 *Small robbery*,..peanuts; ex: The job was peanuts. **1936** *Metronome* Feb. 21/4 *Peanuts*, any pay from a nickel a night and down. **1941** B. SCHULBERG *What makes Sammy Run?* viii. 176 They got you working for peanuts. **1946** J. B. PRIESTLEY *Bright Day* x. 285 'How was the poker game?' 'Peanuts. All I got was about twenty-five dollars and a headache.' **1959** J. OSBORNE *World of Paul Slickey* II. x. 87 There's a thousand pounds a week from record sales..it ain't peanuts. **1968** *Globe & Mail* (Toronto) 13 Jan. 29/2 All this is peanuts compared to the steady core of 3,600 ministers who make up the United Church clergy. **1973** *Scotsman* 13 Feb. 8/5 A salary of £3000 a year is peanuts for a man at the top of his profession. **1975** *New Yorker* 26 May 23 (Advt.), Being in a region may be your only chance to sample the local delicacies. And the cost? Peanuts. **1977** *Time Out* 17 June 15/1 The *New Review*'s share of the budget is a much criticised 10% of the total, yet it's peanuts.

b. A small or unimportant person. Also in more specialized contexts (see quots.).

1942 BERREY & VAN DEN BARK *Amer. Thes. Slang* §389/1 *Insignificant or petty person*,..palooka, peanut, person of straw, picayune, [etc.]. *Ibid.*, Peanuts, rubbish, small fry, small potatoes *or* punkins, trash, truck, *persons of no consequence. Ibid.* §429/4 *Small person*,..peanut, peewee, picayune. **1945** BAKER *Austral. Lang.* viii. 157 *Peanut*, a simple-minded soldier. **1963** *Australasian Post* 14 Mar. 51/1 'And what,' I asked cheerfully, 'was this peanut's particular whinge?' **1968** *Daily Mail* 16 Mar. 6/4 Mods are the traditional enemies of Rockers, but there were no Mods that night... 'They're scared of us... We call them peanuts.' **1969** *Daily Mirror* 3 Sept. 12/4 The youths were peanuts, or skin-heads. **1970** *Observer* (Colour Suppl.) 12 Apr. 46/3 Once me and my mates used to go around robbing peanuts—mod girls.

3. a. *attrib.* and *Comb.* *peanut-digger, farmer* (so *-farming*), *oil, -picker, -seller, -shell, vendor*; *peanut-brained* adj.; **peanut boy** *U.S.*, a boy who sells peanuts and other wares; **peanut brittle**, a brittle toffee with roasted peanuts in it; **peanut butter**, a paste made with ground roasted peanuts; also *attrib.*; **peanut candy** *U.S.*, candy with roasted peanuts in it; **peanut gallery** *U.S. slang*, the top gallery in a theatre; **peanut-parcher** *U.S.* = *peanut-roaster* (*b*), also *attrib.*; **peanut politics** (*U.S. slang*), 'underhand and secret tactics' (Farmer *Americanisms*); hence **peanut politician** *U.S.*, one who deals in peanut politics; **peanut roaster** *U.S.*, (*a*) a machine in which peanuts are roasted; (*b*) *fig.* a piece of machinery that puffs or hisses; **peanut stand** *U.S.*, a booth, stall, or stand where peanuts, etc., are sold; **peanut valve** *Electronics*, a type of small thermionic valve (see quots.); also *ellipt.*

1857 *Porter's Spirit of Times* 5 Sept. 12/1 At length the mare reached the quarter pole, where a little pea-nut boy had stationed himself. **1873** 'MARK TWAIN' *Gilded Age* xxxvi. 333 In the cars,..the peanut-boy..always hands you out a book of murders if you are fond of theology. **1922** JOYCE *Ulysses* 421 Come on, you doggone, bullnecked, beetlebrowed, hogjowled, peanutbrained, weaseleyed fourflushers, false alarms and excess baggage! **1903** *N.Y. Even. Post* 2 Oct. 7 To prescribe that all records [of great eating] henceforth shall be measured in peanut brittle. **1947** J. BERTRAM *Shadow of War* 336 The same jasmine tea, the same peanut brittle. **1965** MRS L. B. JOHNSON *White House Diary* 14 Feb. (1970) 244 Luci came bounding in this morning, to give her daddy a box of peanut brittle for his Valentine. **1976** *Monitor* (McAllen, Texas) 30 Sept. 8C/7 Crunchy peanut brittle, chock-full of tasty, nutritious peanuts, isn't difficult to make if you remember to spread the candy thinly on the cookie sheet. **1903** *Harper's Mag.* Oct. 981 Four sandwiches... Two of wholewheat bread with peanut butter. **1926–7** *Army & Navy Stores Catal.* 2/2 Peanut Butter jars—each 1/-. **1974** 'R. B. DOMINIC' *Epitaph for Lobbyist* xiii. 113 A carnival with peanut butter fudge made by the Soroptimists. **1977** *Time* 14 Mar. 42/2, I grew up on peanut butter sandwiches. **1856** MRS. STOWE *Dred* I. iv. 51 Dancing, flirting, writing love-letters, and all other enormities down to eating pea-nut candy. **1901** B. MATTHEWS *Notes on Speech-Making* 53 Some postprandial addresses..resemble the peanut candy where you cannot see the candy for the peanuts. **1875** KNIGHT *Dict. Mech.*, Peanut-digger. **1976** *Time* 27 Dec. 23/3 He met Carter at a commission conference in 1973 and was one of the few who early took the peanut farmer's presidential aspirations seriously. **1977** *Time* 3 Jan. 13/2 As President Harry Truman was saved from haberdashing by failure, Jimmy Carter was saved from peanut farming by success. **1888** *Lippincott's Monthly Mag.* XLII. 734 Go to the lowest theatre in any of our large cities, or..mark what is called the 'Family Circle' by theatre proprietors and to the general world is more felicitously known as the 'Peanut Gallery'. **1945** *New Yorker* 5 May 15/1 We were sitting in the peanut gallery of the Opera House. **1975** *Audubon* Nov. 26/3, I can hear the laughter down in the pit and up in the peanut gallery. **1976** *National Observer* (U.S.) 21 Aug. 12/1 Sitting in the peanut gallery with her two young daughters, she admitted: 'I wouldn't miss it for the world. I grew up watching it.' **1882** H. H. KANE *Opium-Smoking* 35 A small glass lamp with a glass cover, perforated just above the flame, and in which sweet or peanut oil is burned. **1912** A. H. LEWIS *Apaches N.Y.* 132 He trimmed the peanut-oil lamp. **1973** R. THOMAS *If you can't be Good* (1974) ii. 13 The reports of mine that did surface were major scandals... The Peanut Oil King Affair comes to mind. **1929** W. FAULKNER *Sartoris* (1932) III. 261 'Narcissa'll take you..in her car.'..'In that little peanut-parcher?' **1942** —— *Go down, Moses* 228 The diminutive locomotive and its shrill peanut-parcher whistle. **1954** —— *Fable* 393 The shrill peanut-parcher whistle which did not presage the lurch [of the train]. **1887** *N. York Mail & Express* 27 May (Farmer *Amer.*), If the Governor would consent not to play peanut politics. **1875** KNIGHT *Dict. Mech.*, Peanut-picker. **1931** W. G. MCADOO *Crowded Yrs.* xii. 191 Any Democratic Cabinet, if not actually deficient mentally, consists of adolescents and small peanut politicians. **1977** *Lebende Sprachen* XXII. 10/2 A politician who is merely interested in small advantages is a *peanut politician*. **1902** *Sears, Roebuck Catal.* 589/3 The Boss Peanut and Coffee Roaster is the only successful roaster on the market. **1904** 'O. HENRY' in *N.Y. World Mag.* 22 May 4/2 The whistle of a peanut-roaster puffed a hot scream into his ear. **1939** *These are our Lives* (Federal Writers' Project, U.S.) 283 [He] drew out a gallon at a time as needed for his peanut roaster. **1942** BERREY & VAN DEN BARK *Amer. Thes. Slang* §769/2 *Peanut roaster*, an intake manifold with a leak. **1960** WENTWORTH & FLEXNER *Dict. Amer. Slang* 379/2 *Peanut-roaster*,..a small locomotive..an old or ramshackle automobile. **1971** M. TAK *Truck Talk* 116 *Peanut roaster*, an intake manifold with a leak. **1971** 'D. HALLIDAY' *Dolly & Doctor Bird* iii. 33 Peanut-sellers and newsvendors have free access to the front door. **1856** MRS. STOWE *Dred* I. i. 9 'There isn't one of the train that I would give *that* for!', said she, flirting a shower of peanut-shells into the air. **1862** 'MARK TWAIN' *Let.* 8 Feb. (1917) I. iii. 67 He hasn't business talent enough to carry on a peanut stand. **1864** T. PASTOR *'444' Combination Songster* 66 A blackguard by the name of McCarty..was book-keeper to a peanut-stand, And sold apples by the dozen. **1919** [see FRANKFURTER]. **1947** *Time* 27 Jan. 58/2 He was always dabbling shrewdly in dry cleaning stores and peanut stands. **1923** G. PARR *Princ. & Pract. Wireless Transmission* viii. 119 A valve which has proved very popular in America both on account of its size and low current consumption is that known as the Polar 'Pea-nut' valve. The bulb is tubular, its dimensions being 2 in. long by ½ in. diameter, and is fitted with a bayonet cap similar to the ordinary incandescent bulb. The valve requires only ·25 ampere at ·08 to 1 volt, and has a life double that of the ordinary tungsten valve. **1924** [see DETECTOR 3]. **1930** *B.B.C. Year-bk. 1931* 448/2 *Peanut Valve*, a type of three-electrode receiving valve requiring low filament current and anode voltage. The dimensions of the valve are very small and it is therefore of use where space and small battery consumption are a consideration. **1910** G. B. McCutcheon *Rose in Ring* 56 The lowliest peanut-vender was laughing in his sleeve at the sleuth. **1978** S. Naipaul *North of South* II. v. 209 The peanut vendor was guilty of waging capitalist war against socialist society.

b. *attrib.* passing into *adj.* Trivial, worthless.

1836 W. Dunlap *Thirty Years Ago* II. iii. 25 They were your pea-nut fellows, I suppose. **1854** *Congress. Globe* 19 May 1230/3, I know them—a set of peanut agitators and Peter Funk philanthropists. **1892** *Congress. Rec.* 18 June 5394/2 This country is not a peanut institution; it is a great country. **1910** G. B. McCutcheon *Rose in Ring* 203, I suppose that peanut aristocrat friend of yours has told you it ain't swell or proper to wear tights.

peaon, variant of PEON.

'pea-pod. [f. PEA[1] + POD.]

1. The pod or legume of the pea-plant, which contains the peas. (Earlier name PEASE-COD.)

1882 Ogilvie, *Pea-pod*, the pod or pericarp of the pea. **1884** Browning *Ferishtah, Two Camels* 7 Horse, ass, and mule consume their provender Nor leave a pea-pod.

2. Local name of 'a "double-ended" rowboat used by the lobster-fishermen of the coast of Maine' (*Cent. Dict.* 1890).

3. *attrib.* **pea-pod argus**, collector's name for the butterfly *Lampides bætica.*

1898 *Daily News* 22 Aug. 6/3 The pea-pod argus..is so very scarce in this country that its title to rank as a British butterfly at all is doubtful. **1900** *Ibid.* 6 Mar. 8/7 Monotonous shades of an unpleasant pea-pod tint.

peapon, variant of PEPON.

pear (pɛə(r)), *sb.* Forms: 1 peru, pere, 3 peore, 4–6 peere, 4–7 pere, (5 peyr(e, ? 5 pyre), 5–6 peer, 6 *Sc.* peir, 6–7 peare, pare, 6– pear. [OE. *pere, peru* = MDu., MLG. *pere*, Du. *peer*, LG. *peer, pêr*:—WGer. *pera*, a. late L. *pira, pēra* fem. sing., for L. *pira* pl. of *pirum* pear. From *pēra* come also It., Sp., Pg. *pera*, F. *poire*.

The mod. bot. L. *Pyrus*, is a med.L. corruption, connected by false etymology with Gr. πῦρ fire (Isidore) and *pyramid*.]

1. a. The fleshy fruit of the pear-tree (see 2), a pome of a characteristic shape, tapering towards the stalk; in the very numerous cultivated varieties much esteemed as a dessert fruit, or for stewing, etc.

c **1000** Ælfric *Gram.* vii. (Z.) 20 *Hoc pirum* seo peru. *c* **1290** *Beket* 1191 in *S. Eng. Leg.* I. 140 Applene, & peoren, and notes also. **1340** *Ayenb.* 208 God..nele þe yeue pere ne eppel ase me deþ ane childe. *c* **1430** Lydg. *Min. Poems* (Percy Soc.) 43 Appeles and peres that semen very gode, Ful ofte tyme are roten by the core. **1533** Elyot *Cast. Helthe* II. vii. (1541) 22 Peares are muche of the nature of appulles, but they ar heuier. **1634** *Althorp MS.* in Simpkinson *The Washingtons* (1860) App. p. xvi, A journey to Windsor for pares. **1730–46** Thomson *Autumn* 631 The juicy pear Lies, in a soft profusion, scattered round. **1859** Darwin *Orig. Spec.* i. (1873) 27 No one would expect to raise a first-rate melting pear from the seed of the wild pear.

b. In various similes and allusions; formerly as a type of something of very small value.

c **1380** *Sir Ferumb.* 5722 Of þyne ne schalt þow lese noȝt, þe worthy of a pere. **1399** Langl. *Rich. Redeles* Prol. 73 It shulde not apeire hem a peere. **1503** Hawes *Examp. Virt.* vii. lxii, Nor fortune without me auayleth not hym a pere. **1598** Shaks. *Merry W.* iv. v. 103 As crest-falne as a dride-peare. **1700** T. Brown *Amusem. Ser. & Com.* 93 His Body was as Rotten as a Pear. **1845** Disraeli *Sybil* iv. xi, 'But is the pear ripe?' said the diplomatist. 'The pear is ripe if we have courage to pluck it', said Lord Marney.

2. The tree *Pyrus communis* (N.O. *Rosaceæ*), or other species with similar fruit; found wild in Europe and Asia, and widely grown in many varieties for the fruit (sense 1), which under cultivation becomes edible and rich-flavoured. More usually PEAR-TREE, q.v.

a **1400** *Pistill of Susan* 82 þe popeiayes..On peren and pynappel þei ioyken in pees. **1495** *Trevisa's Barth. De P.R.* xvii. cxxiv. (W. de W.) 685 Pirus, pyre is a tree that beryth fruyte. **1785** Martyn *Rousseau's Bot.* vii. (1794) 73 The pear and apple are..two..species of the same..genus. **1846** J. Baxter *Libr. Pract. Agric.* (ed. 4) II. 200 In raising of standard pears for the orchard.

3. Applied, with defining words, to various other fruits or plants in some way resembling the pear: as ALLIGATOR *pear*, ANCHOVY-PEAR, AVOCADO *pear*, GARLIC *pear*, GRAPE *pear*, PRICKLY PEAR, STRAWBERRY *pear* (see these words); also **hard pear** (S. Africa), *Olinia cymosa*; **vegetable pear** = CHOCHO; **wild pear** (W. Indies), *Clethra tinifolia*; **wooden pear** (*Australia*), *Xylomelum pyriforme* (*Treas. Bot.* 1866).

1760 J. Lee *Introd. Bot.* App. 322 Batchelor's Pear, *Solanum.* **1880** *S. Africa* (ed. 3) 127 In these kloofs grow.. the Hard Pear..the White Pear. **1887** *Standard* 16 Sept. 5/2 The chocho of Jamaica,..the pipinella, chayota, or vegetable pear of Madeira. **1889** in *Boston* (Mass.) *Jrnl.* 25 May 6/6 The vegetable pears are an excellent substitute for butter.

4. *transf.* Applied to things resembling a pear in shape; *e.g.* the fruit or hip of the rose; a pear-shaped pearl used as an ornament. †***pear of confession***, a pear-shaped instrument of torture (cf. G. *folterbirne*).

1576 Baker *Jewell of Health* 4 The seedes within the peares of the Rose are..astringent. **1630** F. Constable *Pathomachia* III. iv. 29 Vnlesse thou confesse,..the Scottish Bootes, the Dutch Wheels, the Spanish Strappado, Linnen Ball, and Pear of Confession shall torment thee. **1690** Evelyn *Mundus Muliebris* 4 Diamond Pendants for the Ears,..or two Pearl Pears. **1727** A. Hamilton *New Acc. E. Ind.* II. xlv. 150 Some beautiful Pearls..among them a Pair of Pears worth 50L. Sterl. **1857** Gosse *Creation* 223 From the side of this 'pear' [*Botryllus*] another was developed by gemmation.

5. *attrib.* and *Comb.*, as ***pear-bin, -bud, -eater, -hoard, -leaf, -orchard, -pearl*** (cf. 4), ***-stock***; ***pear-growing, -like, -shaped*** adjs.; **pear-apple**, (*a*) a rough variety of apple: see quot. 1707; (*b*) the fruit of a prickly pear, a cactus belonging to the genus *Opuntia*; †**pear-bit**, a kind of bit for a horse (? shaped like a pear); **pear-blight**, (*a*) a destructive disease of pear-trees, caused by a bacterium (*Micrococcus amylovorus*) which turns the leaves rapidly brown; = *fire-blight* s.v. FIRE *sb.* B. 5; (*b*) a disease of pear-trees caused by a beetle (*Xyleborus*) which bores into the bark (***pear-blight beetle***, also called *pin-borer*); **pear-drop**, (*a*) a pear-shaped sweet-meat, usually flavoured with jargonelle-pear essence; (*b*) a pear-shaped jewel used as a pendant: see DROP *sb.* 10e, a; (*c*) used *attrib.* of parts of furniture, etc., shaped like pears; **pear-encrinite** (†**-encrinus**), an encrinite of the genus *Apiocrinus*, from its shape; **pear-gauge**, a gauge invented by Smeaton, consisting of a pear-shaped glass vessel and a hermetically closed tube, for measuring the degree of exhaustion of air in an air-pump (see quot. 1822); **pear-haw** = *pear-thorn*; †**pear-jonet, -jenet**, an early-ripening kind of pear (cf. JENNETING); **pear-louse**, a kind of plant-louse (*Psylla pyri* or *pyrisuga*) which infests the leaves and young shoots of the pear-tree; **pear midge**, a small gall midge, *Contarinia pyrivora*, whose larvae damage the fruit of pear trees; **pear oyster scale**, a scale-insect (*Aspidiotus ostreæformis*) infesting the pear-tree; **pear-plum**, name of several varieties of plum (? somewhat pear-shaped); **pear-quince**, a kind of quince with pear-shaped fruit; **pear-shell** (see quot.); **pear-slug**, the slug-like larva of a saw-fly, *Selandria cerasi* (*Eriocampa limacina*), which infests the leaves of the pear and other fruit-trees; also called *plum-slug, slug-worm*, etc.; **pear-sucker** = *pear-louse*; **pear-thorn**, an American species of hawthorn (*Cratægus tomentosa*); †**pear-warden**, a kind of pear: see WARDEN; **pear-wise** *adv.*, in the form of a pear; **pear-withe**, a West Indian and South American climbing shrub, *Tanæcium jaroba*. **pear-wood**, (*a*) the wood of the pear tree; (*b*) the wood of one of several West African trees, esp. *Guarea cedrata*. Also PEAR-MONGER, -TREE.

c **1440** *Promp. Parv.* 394/1 *Peere apple, *pirumpomum*. **1707** Mortimer *Husb.* (1721) II. 293 The Pear Apple is a curious pleasant Apple of a rough Coat. **1898** H. S. Canfield *Maid of Frontier* 205 He knew..which of the 'pear apples' were good to eat. **1607** Markham *Caval.* II. (1617) 57 That bytt which is called the *peare bytt. **1854** E. Emmons *Agric. N.Y.* V. 165 Atmospheric Blight..proves itself to be independent of the cause that sometimes produces the *pear blight. **1881** Miss Ormerod *Man. Injur. Insects* (1890) 330 In America this species of beetle,..known ..under the name of *Xyleborus pyri*, popularly as the 'Pear Blight' is..injurious both to Pear and Apple. **1924** *Phytopathology* XIV. 478 (*title*) Experiments in the control of cankers of pear blight. **1961** A. Schoenfeld tr. *Stapp's Bacterial Plant Pathogens* II. 134 This disease, variously called 'fire blight', 'blossom blight', 'fruit blight', 'twig blight', 'apple blight', or 'pear blight', according to the place affected, is one of the most dangerous and dreaded tree diseases of North America. **1978** A. Huxley *Illustr. Hist. Gardening* v. 176 Pear blight was specifically described as 'a vegetable apoplexy'. **1914** Eberlein & McClure *Pract. Bk. Period Furnit.* i. 27 It is necessary for us to know whether a chest or cupboard ought to have knobs, *pear drop or bail handles. **1925** Penderel-Brodhurst & Layton *Gloss. Eng. Furnit.* 121 *Pear-drop-handle*, a small pendent brass handle in pear-shape form, which came into use in England in the Restoration period. *Ibid.* 122 *Pear-drop ornament*, an ornament usually decorating the upper portion of a plain frieze,..consisting of a series of Gothic arches in relief with drops at the lower points suggesting capitals. **1960** H. Hayward *Antique Coll.* 213/1 *Pear-drop moulding*, a moulding, found below a plain cornice on late 18th cent. bookcases, carved in a repetitive design of inverted pear-shaped forms. **1658** J. Rowland *Moufet's Theat. Ins.* 1034 Such [caterpillars] as have sayl-yards, such as are called *Neustriæ*, *Pear-eaters. **1816** W. Smith *Strata Ident.* 30 That extraordinary fossil zoophite the *pear encrinus. **1843** Humble *Dict. Geol. & Min.* s.v., The pear encrinite is confined to the middle oolite. **1783** *Phil. Trans.* LXXIII. 436 The degree of rarefaction shewed by what is called the *pear-gage. **1822** Imison *Sc. & Art* I. 155 The pear-gage.. shows the true quantity of atmospheric air left in the receiver. **14..** *Voc.* in Wr.-Wülcker 603/10 *Piracium*, a *Perehorde. **1393** Langl. *P. Pl.* C. xiii. 221 Pees-coddes and *pere-Ionettes. *c* **1475** *Songs & Carols 15th C.* (Warton Cl.) 35 It wele non pere bern but a pere jenet. *a* **1822** Shelley *Pr. Wks.* (1888) I. 408 Her pointed and *pear-like person. **1884** E. A. Ormerod *Rep. Observations Injurious Insects 1883* 53 The *Pear Midge is a very small two-winged gnat fly. **1920** P. J. Fryer *Insect Pests & Fungus Dis.* xvi. 234 The pear midge..is a destructive pest on fruit. **1956** Peairs & Davidson *Insect Pests* (ed. 5) xvii. 442 The pear midge is an introduced insect, present in the northeastern states for over 50 years. **1973** H. Martin *Sci. Princ. Crop Protection* (ed. 6) xv. 358 He [*sc.* F. V. Theobald] observed the extermination of the pear midge..by fowls penned under the attacked trees. **1881** Miss Ormerod *Man. Injur. Insects* III. 288 *Pear Oyster Scale..of the same nature as the Mussel Scale of the Apple. **1647** R. Stapylton *Juvenal* vi. 96 Those mighty *peare-pearles that waigh-down her eares. **1600** Surflet *Countrie Farme* III. iii. 427 The stone of the *peare-plum-tree must be set in a cold place. **1707** Mortimer *Husb.* (1721) II. 265 Plumbs are..commonly cleft-grafted..one of the best sorts to graft them on is the Pear-Plumb. **1601** Holland *Pliny* I. 436 A smaller sort.. called Struthea (i. *Peare-quince) and these do cast a more odoriferous smell. **1766** *Compl. Farmer* s.v. *Quince-tree*, Several kinds, as the pear-quince, the apple-quince, and the Portugal quince. **1758** Ellis in *Phil. Trans.* L. 446 This Toxicodendron, with the *pear-shaped fruit. **1815** J. Smith *Panorama Sc. & Art* II. 7 A pear-shaped glass Vessel. **1897** *Allbutt's Syst. Med.* IV. 227 It [gall-bladder] will have a smooth pear-shaped outline. **1884** *Stand. Nat. Hist.* (1888) I. 352 The species of *Ficula* are known from their shape as fig or *pear shells. **1887** G. Nicholson *Dict. Gard.* III. 57 **Pear Slug*, the larva of *Eriocampa limacina*. **1707** Mortimer *Husb.* (1721) II. 251 *Pear-stocks may also be raised of Suckers,..but those that are raised of Seeds or Stones are esteemed much better. **1881** Miss Ormerod *Man. Injur. Insects* III. 286 Jumping Plant-louse. *Pear-sucker. **1882** *Garden* 28 Jan. 61/2 As soon as the buds begin to burst in the spring, the Pear suckers leave their winter quarters. **1884** Miller *Plant-n.*, *Cratægus tomentosa*. American Black-thorn or *Pear-thorn. *c* **1430** *Two Cookery-bks.* 12 Take *Pere Wardonys, an sethe hem in Wyne. **1620** Venner *Via Recta* vii. 111 Peare-Wardons..are of all sorts of Peares the best and wholsomest. **1866** *Treas. Bot.* 855/1 **Pear-withe*, a West Indian name for *Tanæcium Jaroba*. **1862** H. Marryat *Year in Sweden* II. 81 The pulpit of black *pear-wood. **1879** Baring-Gould *Germany* II. 359 Most of the carving was done in pearwood, which readily attracts the worm. **1915** J. H. Holland *Useful Plants Nigeria* III. 419 One of the finest timber trees in W. Africa [is *Mimusops Djave*], sold in Europe as 'African Pear Wood'. **1922** W. Schlich *Man. Forestry* (ed. 4) I. II. 320 The most prominent species [in Sierra Leone] are given as:—..red ironwood, very common. A species of Mimusops known as pearwood [etc.]. **1937** J. M. Dalziel *Useful Plants W. Trop. Afr.* 357 M[*anilkara*] *lacera*... African pearwood. *Ibid.*, M[*imusops*] *djave*... African pearwood. **1950** C. W. Bond *Colonial Timbers* 77 Guarea (Nigerian pearwood). **1961** F. R. Irvine *Woody Plants of Ghana* 519 *Guarea cedrata*... The names 'Nigerian Pearwood', 'Nigerian Cedar', and 'Cedar Mahogany', formerly given for this tree, are dropped as likely to cause confusion. **1971** F. H. Titmuss *Commerc. Timbers of World* (ed. 4) 134 Two species of *Guarea*..may be included in consignments of this timber, which has occasionally been sold as Nigerian Pearwood.

pear, *v. Obs.* exc. *dial.* Forms: 4–6 pere, 5 *Sc.* per, peir, peyr, 5–7 peere, 6 peer, 6–7 peare, 7 'pear. Aphetic form of APPEAR.

c **1375** *Sc. Leg. Saints* xxx. (*Theodera*) 440 þane god.. Gert til hyme ane angele pere. *c* **1450** *Coventry Myst.* xiv. (Shaks. Soc.) 131 Loke ȝe fayl, for no dowte, at the court to pere. *c* **1470** Henry *Wallace* xi. 438 And sternys wp peyr began in to thair sycht. *a* **1533** Ld. Berners *Huon* lix. 204 There was not so hardy a paynym that durst pere before the castell. **1568** T. Howell *Newe Sonets* (1879) 153 When Primrose gan to peare, on Medows bancke so green. **1599** Minsheu *Sp. Dict.*, *Assomar*, to peere vp, to appeere, to looke vp. **1623** *Althorp MS.* in Simpkinson *The Washingtons* (1860) App. p. xlviii, To the shepard at Elkington for moying, making, and ining all the hay..as peares by his bill 17 03 08. **1642** H. More *Song of Soul* I. II. ii, They 'pear and then are hid. [**1900** in *Eng. Dial. Dict.* from Scotl., Cumberland, s.w. of Engl., U.S.]

¶ See also PEER *v.*, which in some uses continues this.

Hence †**'pearand (perand)** *ppl. a.*, appearing, apparent; ***perand are***, heir apparent: cf. PARENT *a.*[1]; †**'pearandly (peirandlie)** *adv.*, appearingly, apparently; also †**'pearance (perans)**, appearance.

c **1375** *Sc. Leg. Saints* xlv. (*Cristine*) 7 Scho ves his perand are. **1382** Wyclif *Job* xxx. 8 In the lond not fulli perende [1388 apperynge]. *a* **1578** Lindesay (Pitscottie) *Chron. Scot.* (S.T.S.) I. 273 Ane..quhome they thocht maist peirandlie to haue bene the King. *c* **1375** *Sc. Leg. Saints* xxx. (*Theodera*) 132 For þu..in þis toun has rentis fare, And til haf mare has perans of are. *c* **1470** Henry *Wallace* v. 1004 Off mwne nor stern gret perans was thar nayne.

pearce, obs. form of PARSE *v.*, PIERCE *v.*

pearceite ('pɪəsaɪt). *Min.* [f. the name of Richard *Pearce* (1837–1927), British-born metallurgist and chemist + -ITE[1].] A black, lustrous, brittle sulphide of silver and arsenic, $Ag_{16}As_8S_{11}$, that occurs as tabular crystals and usu. contains copper in place of some of the silver.

1896 S. L. Penfield in *Amer. Jrnl. Sci.* CLII. 18 The author proposes that hereafter the name polybasite shall be restricted to the antimony compound..and to make of the corresponding arsenic compound..a distinct species. For the arsenical mineral he takes pleasure in proposing the name *pearceite* as a compliment to his friend, Dr. Richard Pearce, of Denver. **1942** *Econ. Geol.* XXXVII. 491 Pearceite, recognizable only in polished section, is almost invariably associated with pyrargyrite. **1963** *Amer. Mineralogist* XLVIII. 567 The traditional polybasite and pearceite actually are members of two separate solid solution series in which Sb and As substitute mutually. **1968** I. Kostov *Mineral.* 173 The crystals of pearceite, polybasite, and xanthoconite are pseudohexagonal platy {001}.

pearch, obs. form of PARCH, PERCH, PIERCE.

peare, obs. form of PAIR *v.*[2], PEAR, PEER.

pearie, obs. form of PERRY, pear-tree.

pearie, variant of PEERY, a peg-top.

peark, obs. form of PERCH, PERK.

pearl (pɜːl), *sb.*[1] Forms: 4–6 perle, peerle, 5 perl, (perll, perell, -ill, perril, 6 pearel, *Sc.* peirl(e, peirll), 6–7 pearle, 5– pearl. [ME. a. F. *perle* (also *pesle, pelle, peele, pele*, 13–14th c., Godef.) = Pr., It., Sp., Pg. *perla*, Pg. also *perola*, med.L. *perla* (J. de Vitry, *a* 1244), *pella, perula, perulus*. From Romanic also OHG. *perala, berla*, MHG. *perle, berle*, Ger. *perle*, MLG. *perle, parle*, MDu. *pārele*, Du. *paarl*. Ulterior etymology unsettled.

Many identify the word with med.L. *pĕrula*, in Isidore *pirula*, dim. of L. *pirum*, Com. Rom. *pĕra* PEAR, used in reference to shape. Others think *perla* altered from *perna*, the form in Neapolitan and Sicilian dial., and found in Sicilian Lat., in *Constitut.* of Frederick King of Sicily, early 13th c. (Du Cange), which they would identify with L. *perna*, ham, leg of mutton, also a leg-of-mutton-shaped marine bivalve, mentioned by Pliny. A dim. of the latter, **pernula*, conjectured in Du Cange (ed. 1762) is favoured by Gröber. Another suggested source is L. *pilula* globule, whence, by dissimilation of *l..l* to *r..l*, **pirula* (for which Littré compares Venetian and Veronese *pirola* from *pilula*). See Diez, Littré, Körting, etc.]

I. 1. a. A nacreous concretion formed within the shell of various bivalve molluscs around some foreign body (e.g. a grain of sand), composed of filmy layers of carbonate of lime interstratified with animal membrane; it is of hard smooth texture, of globular, pear-shaped, oval, or irregular form, and of various colours, usually white or bluish-grey; often having a beautiful lustre, and hence highly prized as a gem; formerly also used in medicine. See also MOTHER OF PEARL, SEED PEARL.

The chief source is the Pearl-oyster, *Meleagrina margaritifera*, of the Indian Seas, but pearls are yielded by many other marine, as well as by some freshwater shells, the pearl-mussels, *Unionidæ*.

[*a* **1259** MATT. PARIS *Chron. Maj.* (Rolls) V. 489 Erat quidam lapis preciosus, qui dicitur vulgariter Perla.] **13..** *E.E. Allit. P.* A. 1 Perle plesaunte to prynces paye, To clanly clos in golde so clere. **1362** LANGL. *P. Pl.* A. XI. 12 Draf weore hem leuere þen al þe presciouse Peerles þat in paradys waxen. *c* **1385** CHAUCER *L.G.W.* Prol. 153 (221) Of o perle fyn & oryental Hyre white coroun was I-makyd al. *c* **1400** MAUNDEV. (1839) xiv. 158 The fyn Perl congeleþ and wexeþ gret of the dew of heuene. **1447** BOKENHAM *Seyntys* (Roxb.) 2 A margerye perle aftyr the phylosophyr Growyth on a shelle of lytyl pryhs. **1526** TINDALE *Matt.* xiii. 46 When he had founde one precious pearle [WYCLIF, oo preciouse margarite]. **1568** GRAFTON *Chron.* II. 290 A Chapelet of fine Perles that he ware on his hed. *a* **1600** MONTGOMERIE *Sonn.* xlix, Thoght peirlis give pryce, and diamonds be deir. **1607** DEKKER & WEBSTER *Sir T. Wyatt* D.'s Wks. 1873 III. 129 Cheekes purer then the Maiden orient pearle. **1698** FRYER *Acc. E. India & P.* 320 The Pearl is a Jewel supposed to be the Geniture of a Shell-fish..congealed into a very fair, transparent, Diaphanous, beautiful Stone. **1774** GOLDSM. *Nat. Hist.* VII. 54 Whether pearls be a disease or an accident in the animal is scarce worth enquiry. **1883** *Fish. Exhib. Catal.* 77 Fancy Pearls, such as black, pink, yellow, grey; from Australia, South Pacific Islands, &c.

b. (without *a* or *pl.*) As name of the substance.

13.. *E.E. Allit. P.* A. 207 Hiȝe pynakled of cler quyt perle. *Ibid.* 255 Set on hyr coroun of perle orient. **1390** GOWER *Conf.* II. 45 The Sadles..With Perle and gold so wel begon. **1480** CAXTON *Chron. Eng.* ccxli. 273 A croune of gold pyght with ryche perle and precious stones. **1596** SHAKS. *Tam. Shr.* v. i. 77 Why sir, what cernes it you, if I weare Pearle and gold? **1626** BACON *Sylva* §380 There hath been a tradition, that pearl, and coral, and turquois-stone, that have lost their colours, may be recovered by burying in the earth. **1717** LADY M. W. MONTAGU *Let. to C'tess Mar* 1 Apr., A large *bouquet* of jewels, made like natural flowers: that is, the buds of pearl..the jessamines, of diamonds,.. etc. **1841–4** EMERSON *Ess., Compensation* Wks. (Bohn) I. 50 Like the wounded oyster, he mends his shell with pearl.

c. = MOTHER OF PEARL. Chiefly *attrib.*: see 17 a.

d. ***artificial pearl***, an imitation of the natural gem, made of glass, etc. ***blister pearl***, a flattish excrescence of pearl adhering to the shell. ***Roman pearl*** (see quot. 1875).

essence of pearl, an imitation of mother-of-pearl prepared from the scales of the bleak, herring, and other fish; now usu. called *pearl essence* (see sense 18).

1638 BAKER tr. *Balzac's Lett.* (vol. II.) 114 Whether my pearles be Orientall, or but of Venice. **1665** BOYLE *Occas. Refl.* IV. ii, The artificial Pearl made at Venice, consisting of Mercury and Glass. **1791** MACIE in *Phil. Trans.* LXXXI. 379 By adding the alkali to the bit of Tabasheer in exceedingly small quantities at a time, this substance was converted into a pearl of clear colourless glass. **1805** C. WILMOT *Let.* 26 Aug. in *Russ. Jrnls.* (1934) I. 170 A dress of white crape & roman pearls & white cameo ornaments. **1832** G. R. PORTER *Porcelain & Gl.* 236 He then proceeded to line the interior surface of these with the powdered fish scales, which he called essence of pearl, or *essence d'Orient*. **1875** *Ure's Dict. Arts* III. 518 Italy also manufactures pearls by a method borrowed from the Chinese: they are known under the name of Roman pearls, and are a very good imitation of natural ones.

2. *Her.* In blazoning by precious stones, the designation of the tincture *argent* or white.

1572 BOSSEWELL *Armorie* II. 56 b, The fielde is of yᵉ Diamond, a Bonaze Perle, Unguled topaze. **1688** R. HOLME *Armoury* III. i. 5/1 He beareth Pearl, a Chaplet garnished. **1725** COATS *Dict. Her.*, *Pearl*, being White, is us'd instead of Argent, by those who blazon the Arms of Great Men by Precious Stones instead of Colours and Metals. *c* **1828** BERRY *Encycl. Her.* I. Gloss.

3. *fig.* **a.** Something especially precious, noble, or choice; the finest or best member or part; a fine or noble example or type.

13.. *E.E. Allit. P.* A. 242 Art þou my perle þat I haf playned? **1387** TREVISA *Higden* (Rolls) VII. 85 Also þis ȝere kyng Egebrede wedded Emme, þe perle and þe precious stone of Normanes. **1503** DUNBAR *Thistle & Rose* 180 Welcome to be our princes of honour, Our perle, our plesans and our paramour. **1567** *Satir. Poems Reform.* vii. 71 Our prettie Prince, the peirle of all this land. **1605** SHAKS. *Macb.* v. viii. 56. **1639** SHIRLEY *Gentlem. Venice* I. 11 He is the very pearl Of curtesie. **1816** SCOTT *Old Mort.* xxxv, Ah, *benedicite*! how he will mourn over the fall of such a pearl of knighthood. **1859** TENNYSON *Elaine* 114 Guinevere, The pearl of beauty.

b. Prov. ***to cast pearls before swine***, to offer or give a good thing to one who is incapable of appreciating it, but may defile or abuse it. (From Matt. vii. 6.)

1362 LANGL. *P. Pl.* A. XI. 9 *Noli mittere* Margeri perles Among hogges. *c* **1380** WYCLIF *Wks.* (1880) 110 þus comaundeth crist þat men schullen not ȝeue holy þingis to hondis & putten precious perlis to hoggis. **1526** TINDALE *Matt.* vii. 6 Nether caste ye youre pearles [WYCLIF margaritis] before swyne. **1533** GAU *Richt Vay* 104 As the suine trampis the precious peirlis onder thair feit. **1645** MILTON *2nd Sonn. Tetrach.*, This is got by casting Pearl to Hoggs. **1848** DICKENS *Dombey* xxiii, Oh I do a thankless thing, and cast pearls before swine!

II. In transferred senses.

†4. a. The pupil of the eye; the crystalline lens.

1340 *Ayenb.* 158 Ase a-ye mi wyl me be-houeþ to zyenne and o[n]deruonge ine þe perle of þe eȝe þe sseþþe of þe þinge þet is him be-uore. **1604** WRIGHT *Passions* II. i. 48 If..some darknesse fall vpon the eyes, a dimme cloud is cast before the pearles thereof.

†b. A thin white film or opacity growing over the eye; a kind of cataract. *Obs.* or *dial.* [med.L. *perula*, Du Cange.]

[*c* **1400** *Lanfranc's Cirurg.* 251 þou schalt se þan vpon his iȝe a whit þing as it were a peerle.] **1382** WYCLIF *Lev.* xxi. 20 If crokid rigge, or bleer eyed; if whijt perle hauinge in the eye. *c* **1440** *Promp. Parv.* 394/2 Peerle, yn the eye, *glaucoma*. **1584** COGAN *Haven Health* cxxvi. (1612) 109 A certaine experiment to take away a fleame or pearle from the eye. **1599** A. M. tr. *Gabelhouer's Bk. Physicke* 55/1 For Catarractes or Pearles of the Eyes. **1666** SPURSTOWE *Spir. Chym.* 21 Physicians..who call..the white film which taketh away the delightful sight a Pearl in the Eye. **1747** WESLEY *Prim. Physic* (1762) 62 It cures Pearls, Rheums, and often Blindness itself. *c* **1820** in *Sheffield Gloss.* (1888), *Pearl*, a cataract in the eye.

5. A small and round drop or globule resembling a pearl in shape or aspect; e.g. a dewdrop, a tear.

c **1460** J. RUSSELL *Bk. Nurture* 283 Pike not youre nose, ne þat hit be droppynge with no peerlis clere. **1513** DOUGLAS *Æneis* XII. Prol. 134 The plane pulderyt with semely settis sovnd, Bedyit full of dewy peirlis rovnd. **1593** SHAKS. *Lucr.* 1213 Shee..wip't the brinish pearle from her bright eies. **1696–7** LISTER in *Phil. Trans.* XIX. 373 Small Transparent Pearls or Drops of a liquid Gum. **1704** POPE *Pastorals, Winter* 31 Now hung with pearls the dropping trees appear. **1852** R. S. SURTEES *Sponge's Sp. Tour* (1893) 339 'Don't know', replied the boy,..as he rubbed a pearl off his nose on to the back of his hand.

6. Rhetorically applied to white glistening teeth. Also collective: cf. 'ivory'.

1586 PETTIE tr. *Guazzo's Civ. Conv.* 34 Calling..her teeth Pearles, her lips Corall. **1648** HERRICK *Hesper.*, *Hymne to Venus*, Goddesse, I do love a girle, Rubie-lipt and tooth'd with pearl. **1775** SHERIDAN *St. Patr. Day* I. i, I believe I have drawn half a score of her poor dear pearls. **1824** BYRON *Juan* XVI. cxxi, A red lip, with two rows of pearl beneath.

7. One of the bony tubercles encircling the bur or base of a deer's antler.

1575 TURBERV. *Venerie* 54 That which is about the crust of the beame is termed pearles. *a* **1700** B. E. *Dict. Cant. Crew*, *Pearls*, the little Knobs on the Bur of a Stag. **1873** BLACK *Pr. Thule* xxv, You will discourse to your friends of the span, and the pearls of the antlers, and the crockets.

8. †a. ***Pearls of Spain***: the white grape-hyacinth (from the shape of its flowers). *Obs. rare.*

1597 GERARDE *Herbal*, Table Eng. Names, Pearles of Spaine. **1629** PARKINSON *Parad. in Sole* 115 Some English Gentlewomen call the white Grape-flower Pearles of Spaine.

b. An oat-like grass (*Arrhenatherum avenaceum*) with knotted or tuberous base: = PEARL-GRASS 2.

1886 S. A. STEWART in Britten & Holland *Plant-n.* 224 It [*Avena elatior*] is known in Co. Antrim as *Pearl*; the knobs at the base of the stem are the pearls. I have been informed that these 'pearls' are of great value as a cure for inflamed eyes.

9. One of several small white or silver balls set on a coronet; a similar ball as a heraldic bearing; also, a small white circle on a coloured ground.

1688 R. HOLME *Armoury* III. i. 4/1 The top of the circle set close together with Pearls or Buttons of Silver. **1707** CHAMBERLAYNE *Pres. St. Eng.* III. iii. 273 His [Marquis's] Coronet hath Pearls and Strawberry Leaves, intermixt round of equal height. **1725** COATS *Dict. Her.*, *Viscounts Coronet* has neither Flowers, nor Points rais'd above the Circle..but only Pearls plac'd on the Circle itself. **1882** CUSSANS *Hand-bk. Her.* xiv. (ed. 3) 179. **1897** W. MORLEY *Cat. Stamps Gt. Brit.* 19, 1*d.* pale lilac, 14 pearls..5*s.*; 1*d.* dark lilac, 16 pearls..6*d.*

10. *Printing.* Name of a size of type, formerly the smallest used, now intermediate between agate and diamond.

1656 BLOUNT *Glossogr.* s.v. *Character*, The Printers.. names of their several sorts of Letters are 1. Pearl, which is the least. 2. Non-Pareil [etc.]. **1660** FULLER *Mixt Contempl.* ix. (1841) 223 The pearle Bible printed at London, 1653. **1683** MOXON *Mech. Exerc.*, *Printing* ii. ¶2. **1824** J. JOHNSON *Typogr.* II. v. 83 As this was..a greater advance to perfection, it..was designated Pearl. **1887** T. B. REED *Hist. Lett. Foundries* 40 Pearl, though an English body in Moxon's day, appears to have been known both in France and Holland at an earlier date.

11. *Eastern Ch.* (rendering μαργαρίτης). A small particle of the consecrated bread: = PARTICLE 2 c.

1847 CDL. WISEMAN *Unreality Angl. Belief* Ess. 1853 II. 406 In the Coptic Liturgy..after the division of the Host, the priest shall take one pearl (or particle) of the three above named. [**1876–80** SMITH & CHEETHAM *Dict. Chr. Antiq.*, *Margarita* is a term for the particle of the bread which is broken off and placed in the cup as a symbol of the union of the Body and Blood of Christ.]

12. A small fragment or size of various substances: e.g. one of the pear-shaped granules into which molten metal cools when poured in drops into cold water; a small piece of clean coal; a name for a small pill or pilule, *esp.* a gelatinous capsule employed for administering liquid medicines in the form of pills.

1872 *Young Englishwoman* Oct. 543/1 *Ether pearls*, small round capsules about the size of a pea, are of marvellous efficacy in instantly calming attacks of Asthma. **1873** E. SPON *Workshop Receipts* Ser. I. 191/2 Small articles are brightened in a long narrow bag, where they are put with copper pearls. **1897** *Allbutt's Syst. Med.* III. 230 Phosphorus, gr. $\frac{1}{30}$ in pearls of which three to six are to be taken daily. **1901** *Scotsman* 15 Oct. 4/8 (Of small coal) After being washed, the pearls are drained and elevated by conveyers to a hopper.

13. A degree of condensation and stickiness reached by clarified syrup when boiled for confectionery: see PEARLED *ppl. a.*[1] 4.

1883 R. HALDANE *Workshop Receipts* Ser. II. 152/1 There are 7 essential degrees in boiling sugar:..They are:—(1) small thread, (2) large thread, (3) little pearl, (4) large pearl. *Ibid.* 162/2 Boil some clarified loaf sugar to large pearl.

14. Short for *pearl-moth*: see 18.

1832 J. RENNIE *Consp. Butterfl. & Moths* 151–2 *Margaritia* (Stephens). The Variegated Pearl..Very rare.. The Long-winged Pearl..The Sulphur Pearl [etc.].

15. Name of a kind of firework.

1884 *St. James's Gaz.* 13 June 10/2 The display included ..discharges of rockets and shells..and a cloud of pearls.

16. a. The colour of a pearl, a clear pale bluish-grey. Also *attrib.* or as *adj.* = *pearl-coloured*.

1688 *Lond. Gaz.* No. 2366/4, 6 pair of womens silk [hose] pearl, blew and green. **1899** *Westm. Gaz.* 2 Dec. 1/3 He watched the first streak of dawn change from a thin grey line of pearl into a broad band of pink and amethyst.

b. Applied to an electric light bulb that is frosted on the inside so as to diffuse the light.

1930 *Engineering* 21 Mar. 393/1 The panels are illuminated from behind by a standard 40-watt 'pearl' lamp backed by aluminium reflectors. **1938** *Times* 3 Feb. 17/1 The conclusion reached is that lamps of the pearl type give a 7½ per cent better light than the opal type at present in use. **1972** 'R. CRAWFORD' *Whip Hand* I. iii. 12 A single pearl bulb lit the store.

III. *attrib.* and *Comb.* **17. a.** attributive: (*a*) of pearl or pearls, adorned with pearls, as ***pearl-bead, -broker, -chain, -collar, -colour, necklace, -rope, string, stud, -sword, -wreath***; (*b*) made of mother-of-pearl, as ***pearl spoon***; (*c*) in sense 5, as ***pearl-cup, -dew, -drop***. **b.** objective and obj. genitive, as ***pearl-cutter, -driller, -worker***; ***pearl-bearing, -making, -producing, -sliding, -yielding*** adjs. **c.** instrumental, as ***pearl-besprinkled, -bordered, -crowned, -enamelled, -encrusted, -flushed, -gemmed, -handled, -headed, -hung, -lined, -lipped, -paved, -set, -studded, -wreathed*** adjs. **d.** parasynthetic, as ***pearl-coloured, -hued, -tinted*** adjs. **e.** similative, as ***pearl-blue, -bright, -grey*** (also as sb.), ***-pale, -pure, -round*** adjs.; also ***pearl-like*** adj.

a **1821** KEATS *Hyperion* II. 284 Like *pearl-beads dropping sudden from their string. **1667** H. OLDENBURG in *Phil. Trans.* II. 431 *Pearl-bearing Oysters are not good to eat. **1827** *Butterfly Collector's Vade Mecum* 100 *Melitæa Euphrosyne*, *Pearl-bordered Fritillary. **1914** G. FRANKAU *Tid'apa* (1915) v. 29 *Pearl-bright under purple eyelids the unshed dew of a tear. *c* **1610** LADY COMPTON in *Antiq. Rep.* (1808) III. 438, I would have..6000*l.* for a *Pearl Chain... I am so reasonable. **1795** COLERIDGE in Cottle *Remin.* (1847) 15 Benevolence is the silken thread that runs through the pearl-chain of all their virtues. **1611** COTGR. s.v. *Gemmé*, *Couleur gemmée*, a *pearle, or peacocke colour. **1655** MOUFET & BENNET *Health's Improv.* (1746) 209 The best Milk is of a Pearl Colour. **1604** T. M. *Black Bk.* in *Middleton's Wks.* (Bullen) VIII. 40 His *pearl-coloured silk stockings. **1855** BAILEY *Fairy Tale* in *Mystic*, etc. (ed. 2) 151 O'er the fields a *pearl-dew glistened. **1709** *Eng. Post* 21 Mar. Advt., Known to be a *Pearl-Driller by Trade. **1722** R. BEVERLEY *Hist. Virginia* III. i. 141 At his Ear is hung a fine Shell with *Pearl Drops. **1824** SIR J. BOWRING & H. S. VAN DYK *Batavian Anthol.* 143 Dews..on the Roses lie, Whose leaves beneath the pearl-drops bend. **1943** D. GASCOYNE *Poems 1937–42* 60 Like Some priceless *pearl-enamelled toy. **1952** R. CAMPBELL tr. *Baudelaire's Poems* 193 While Phoebe sheers Through *pearl-flushed hours, To rain down tears In glittering showers. **1796** H. HUNTER tr. *St.-Pierre's*

Stud. Nat. (1799) I. 520 A turtle-dove of Africa,..her *pearl-gray plumage. 1875 J. BLACKWOOD Let. 30 Nov. in Geo. Eliot Lett. (1956) VI. 195, I rather lean to the pearl grey which he has told me is the name of the colour. 1931 V. WOOLF Waves 110 Among the lustrous green, pink, pearl-grey women stand upright the bodies of men. 1969 in Halpert & Story Christmas Mumming in Newfoundland 182 Costumes used for disguise are listed:..fancy vests, beaver hats, pearl-gray spats. 1976 Eastern Even. News (Norwich) 9 Dec. 18/2 (Advt.), 1973 Capri 1600 XL, pearl grey, 44,934, £1280. 1901 Wide World Mag. VIII. 156/1 A *pearl-handled penknife. 1839 BAILEY Festus xix. (1852) 275 Violet, rose or *pearl-hued. 1965 F. SARGESON Mem. Peon vi. 181 A short distance from my Leonora's *pearl-hung ear. 1846 BROWNING Lett. 27 June (1899) II. 274 All your kindness is pure, entire, *pearl-like for roundness and completeness. 1924 J. A. THOMSON Science Old & New xx. 110 It seems highly probable that the walls of the *pearl-making sac are in a state of inflammation. 1708 J. LOVETT Let. 1 May in M. M. Verney Verney Lett. (1930) I. xii. 202 Tell Deare Bess her *Pearle Necklas is come. 1819 M. WILMOT Let. 8 Dec. (1935) 33, I can wear my pearl necklace clasped with the amathyst behind. 1972 J. WILSON Hide & Seek ii. 35 He reached for her imitation pearl necklace. 1895 W. B. YEATS Poems 6 A *pearl-pale, high-born lady. 1908 Westm. Gaz. 30 Dec. 2/3 There, in 'the Garden' roofed with glass, He flutes on the *pearl-paved ridge of dawn. 1879 DOWDEN Southey iv. 87 It is October that brings most often those days faultless, *pearl-pure, of affecting influence. 1925 E. SITWELL Troy Park 75 And there the *pearlropes fall like shawls. 1552 HULOET, *Pearle seller, margaritarius. 1609 MARKHAM Fam. Whore (1868) 45 That *pearl-set mouth. 1948 C. DAY LEWIS Poems 1943–47 15 What unseen clue Threads my *pearl-sliding hours. 1577 in Archæologia XIX. 296 Mending my *Pearle Spoons..ijs. vjd. 1939 L. M. MONTGOMERY Anne of Ingleside xxi. 142 'Aren't those *pearl strings pretty?'..'You'd almost think they were real.' 1927 E. GLYN 'It' xix. 172 His shirt with its incomparable two *pearl studs. 1975 S. LAUDER Killing Time on Corvo i. 8 Her plain grey suit and hat, pearl studs, gloves. 1896 Westm. Gaz. 4 Jan. 3/2 The City of London..contributing..the famous *pearl-sword with its splendid scabbard which Queen Elizabeth presented to the Corporation. 1642 H. MORE Song Soul II. App. xcix, Fair comely bodies,..rose-cheek'd, ruby-lip'd, *pearl-teeth'd, star-eyn'd. 1908 Daily Chron. 29 Sept. 7/5 He..entered the deserted garden where *pearl-tinted spikes of iris perfumed the air. 1858 SIMMONDS Dict. Trade, *Pearl-worker, a workman who cuts up mother-of-pearl shell, or forms it into buttons, papier mâché [etc.]. 1839 BAILEY Festus xxi. (1852) 377 Like the pure *pearl-wreath which enrings thy brow.

18. Special combs.: **pearl-berry**, the fruit (a small drupe) of an evergreen rosaceous shrub (*Margyricarpus selosus*) often cultivated on rock-work; also the shrub itself; also *fig.*; **pearl-bird**, (*a*) the guinea-fowl, so called from its white-spotted plumage; (*b*) the pearl-spotted barbet, an African bird of genus *Trachyphonus*; **pearl-bush**, a large handsome Chinese shrub (*Spiræa* or *Exochorda grandiflora*), bearing racemes of white flowers; **pearl button**, (*a*) a button made of a pearl; (*b*) a button made of mother-of-pearl or an imitation of it; **pearl-coated** *a.*, (*a*) *dial.*: see quot. 1828; (*b*) covered, as a pill, with a smooth pearly-white coating; so **pearl-coating**; †**pearl-cordial**, a cordial containing powdered pearl; **pearl-disease**, tuberculosis of the serous membranes in cattle; **pearl essence**, **pearlessence**, essence of pearl (see PEARL *sb.*[1] 1 d), or a synthetic imitation of this; **pearl-everlasting**, the common white everlasting, *Gnaphalium margaritaceum* (*Treas. Bot.* 1866); **pearl-eye**, †(*a*) cataract in the eye (*obs.*); (*b*) an eye of a pigeon or other bird, resembling a pearl; so **pearl-eyed** *a.*; **pearl-fish**, †(*a*) a shell-fish producing pearls; (*b*) a fish (*e.g.* the bleak) from the shining scales of which artificial pearl is made (*Funk's Stand. Dict.* 1895); (*c*) = FIERASFER; **pearl-fly**: see quot.; **pearl-fruit** = *pearl-berry* (*Treas. Bot.* 1866); **pearl-glimmer** = *pearl-mica*; †**pearl-gooseberry**, a variety of gooseberry; **pearl-grain**, the grain or unit of weight by which the value of pearls is estimated; a carat-grain, one fourth of a carat; **pearl-hardening**, a preparation of gypsum used to give body and substance to poor paper; **pearl-hen**, the guinea fowl; †**pearl-julep**, a sweet drink made with sugar of pearl; **pearl-lashing** *Naut.*, 'the lashing which holds the jaws of the gaff' (*Cent. Dict.* 1890); †**pearl-mica**, an obsolete synonym of Margarite; **pearl-moss**, a name for carrageen (*Chondrus crispus*); **pearl-moth**, a pyralid moth of the genus *Botys* or *Margaritia*, so called from its shining appearance; **pearl-mussel**, a species of mussel bearing pearls; **pearl-nautilus**, the pearly nautilus; **pearl-onion**: see ONION 2; **pearl-opal** = CACHOLONG; **pearl-perch**, a sea-fish of New South Wales (*Glaucosoma scapulare*, family *Percidæ*), excellent for food; †**pearl-plant**: see quots.; **pearl-pottery**: see quot.; **pearl-powder**, a cosmetic used to impart whiteness to the skin; = *pearl-white*; hence **pearl-powdered** *a.*; **pearl-sago**, sago in small hard rounded grains; **pearl-side**, the name of a fish, the Sheppey argentine (*Scapelus pennanti* or *humboldtii*), having pearly spots on the sides; **pearl-sinter**, a synonym of Fiorite; **pearl-snail**, the pearly nautilus; **pearl-spar**, 'an early name for crystallized dolomite showing a pearly lustre, including also some ankerite' (Chester *Dict. Names Minerals* 1896); †**pearl-spice**, spice in small rounded grains; **pearl-tea**, gunpowder-tea (*Cent. Dict.* 1890); **pearl-tree**: see quot.; **pearl-tumour**, (*a*) an encysted tumour, the surface of which is covered with white pearly scales; (*b*) a tumour in the brain, containing small calcified particles resembling grains of sand; (*c*) in cattle = *pearl-disease*; **pearl-weed** = PEARLWORT; **pearl-white** *a.*, pearly white; orig. used of PEARLWARE; also *ellipt.* as *sb.* = PEARLWARE, *pearl-powder*: see quots. Also PEARL-ASH, -BARLEY, -DIVER, etc.

1884 MILLER Plant-n., *Pearl-berry. 1924 E. SITWELL Sleeping Beauty xvii. 67 And the pearl-berries of the snow upon dark bushes freeze. 1882 Garden 3 June 384/2 The *Pearl Bush, one of the finest of the Spiræa tribe. 1717 LADY M. W. MONTAGU Let. to C'tess Mar 1 Apr., The..waistcoat ..should have diamond or *pearl buttons. 1851 in Illustr. Lond. News (1854) 5 Aug. 119/2 Occupations of People.. pearl-button maker. 1869 E. A. PARKES Pract. Hygiene (ed. 3) 97 The makers of pearl buttons, also suffer from chronic bronchitis. 1828 Craven Gloss. (ed. 2), *Peearl-coated, a sheep with a curled fleece... The small globules of the wool are supposed to resemble pearls. 1895 Westm. Gaz. 27 June 2/2 A pill is a pill, no matter how beautifully it is '*pearl-coated'. 1883 Daily News 18 Sept. 8/4 Pill-making.—Wanted, a Person, who understands *Pearl-coating. 1750 MRS. DELANY Life & Corr. (1861) II. 550 Your letters.. have been my castor, *pearl cordial, and sal volatile. 1877 tr. von Ziemssen's Cycl. Med. XVI. 770 The *pearl disease of cattle was recognized as a disease equivalent to tuberculosis. 1921 Sci. Amer. 12 Mar. 213/3 'Essence d'Orient' was easily manufactured, which was readily given the name of '*pearl essence' by the Bureau of Fisheries. 1946 SIMONDS & BREGMAN Finishing Metal Products (ed. 2) xxviii. 279 Pearl essence is used to substitute for metal powder finishes on everything from women's compacts and cosmetic containers to heavy industrial equipment and machinery. 1961 Soap, Perfumery & Cosmetics XXXIV. 60/3 By crushing or pulverising, natural and synthetic pearl essences lose part of their brilliance and become dull or greyish. 1972 P. G. I. LAUFFER in Balsam & Sagarin Cosmetics (ed. 2) I. xii. 370 Natural pearlessence, consisting of a castor oil suspension of guanine crystals prepared from fish scales, produces a beautiful pearly luster when added to lipsticks. 1844 HOBLYN Dict. Terms Med., *Pearl-eye,..old..name of cataract. 1891 Daily News 13 Nov. 7/1 The points were.. good profile, the cere or ring round the eye, pearl eye, compactness, and good colouring. 1755 JOHNSON, *Pearl-eyed, having a speck in the eye. 1864 WEBSTER, Pearl-eyed ..affected with the cataract. 1591 SYLVESTER Du Bartas I. v. 370 While the *Pearl-fish gaping wide doth glister, Much Fry (allurd with the bright silver lustre Of her rich Casket) flocks into the Nacre. 1797 Encycl. Brit. (ed. 3) XIV. 72/2 Very little is known of the natural history of the pearl fish. 1905 D. S. JORDAN Guide to Study of Fishes II. xxix. 522 In the little group of pearl-fishes, called Fierasferidæ Carapidæ, the body is eel-shaped with a rather large head. 1972 J. BINYON Physiol. of Echinoderms vi. 72 The famous pearl fish Carapus (= Fierasfer) bermudiensis..seems to live indefinitely in the cloaca and respiratory trees of this holothurian without ill-effect. 1847 JOHNSTON in Proc. Berw. Nat. Club II. No. 5. 226 The grub[s] or larvæ of the Hemerobiidæ or *pearl-flies. 1880 Libr. Univ. Knowl. (N.Y.) IX. 486 Margarite, or Pearl Mica, called also corundellite,..*pearl-glimmer. 1769 MRS. RAFFALD Eng. Housekpr. (1778) 321 To make Pearl Gooseberry Wine. Take as many of the best *pearl gooseberries when ripe as you please. 1858 SIMMONDS Dict. Trade 279/2 The troy ounce contains 600 *pearl grains, and hence one pearl grain is 4-5ths of a troy grain. 1871 Specif. Dann's Patent No. 2237. 2 To obtain *pearl-hardening..for the manufacture of paper or papier mâché. 1840 Penny Cycl. XVII. 340/1 Numida Meleagris..the..*Pearl Hen, Guinea Hen, [or] common Guinea Fowl..is..well known. 1710 T. FULLER Pharm. Extemp. 404 Its use is for the making up of *Pearl Juleps. 1820 F. MOHS Charact. Nat. Hist. Syst. Min. 53 *Pearl-Mica. Rhombohedral. 1880 [see pearl-glimmer]. 1832 Loudon's Gardener's Mag. VIII. 94 Sold in Covent Garden Market under the names of oak lungs, carrageen, or Irish *pearl moss. 1600–10 SYLVESTER Woodmans Bear lvii, Her knuckles dight With curled Roses, and her nailes With *pearle-muscles' shining scales. 1854 H. MILLER Sch. & Schm. x. (1858) 201 When the river was low, I used to wade into its fords in quest of its pearl muscles. 1578 LYTE Dodoens II. civ. 290 Cromel,..some name it also *Pearle plante. 1864 PRIOR Plant-n. (1879) 179 Pearl-plant, from its smooth hard pearly seed, the gromwell, Lithospermum officinale. 1825 J. NICHOLSON Operat. Mechanic 483 The *pearl pottery is a superb kind for elegant and tasteful ornaments, and is so much valued, that the workmen are usually locked up, and employed only on choice articles. The components of the clay are blue and porcelain clay, Cornish-stone, a little glass, and red-lead. 1632 SHERWOOD, *Pearl-powder, margariton. 1802 MAR. EDGEWORTH Mor. T., Gd. Fr. Governess (1832) 125 Ladies..who..wear pearl powder, and false auburn hair. 1826 MISS MITFORD Village Ser. II. (1863) 294 Plumed, and trained, and spangled, *pearl-powdered, or rouged. 1883 Truth 31 May 757/2 The face of a lady properly pearl-powdered. 1841 Penny Cycl. XX. 313/1 Of this granulated sago there are two varieties, the common or brown sago, and *pearl sago. 1859 YARRELL Brit. Fishes (ed. 3) I. 331 The designation of *Pearl-side is now substituted for that of Argentine. 1821 URE Dict. Chem., *Pearl Sinter, or Fiorite, a variety of siliceous sinter. Colours white and grey. 1868 DANA Min. (ed. 5) 199. 1731 MEDLEY Kolben's Cape G. Hope II. 211 The shells of the *Pearl-snails are frequently cast ashore by the sea. 1807 AIKIN Dict. Chem. II. 205 *Pearl-spar. 1843 PORTLOCK Geol. 208 Calcedony..disposed on pearl spar. 1854 J. SCOFFERN in Orr's Circ. Sc., Chem. 19 The primitive angle of pearl-spar is 106° 5'. 1470–1 Mem. Ripon (Surtees) III. 216 *Perle-spice, 6d. 1693 Phil. Trans. XVII. 620 *Pearl-Tree of Surinam, which is a kind of Euonymus. 1893 Syd. Soc. Lex., *Pearl tumour, a name for Cholesteatoma; also, for Psammoma; also, for Pearl disease. 1887 NICHOLSON Dict. Gard., Sagina..*Pearl Weed; Pearlwort. 1779 J. WEDGWOOD Let. 19 June (1965) 236, I thank her majesty for the honor she has done to the *Pearl White, and hope it will have due influence upon all her loyal subjects. 1822–34 Good's Study Med. (ed. 4) I. 148 The white oxide of bismuth, now more generally known as a cosmetic under the name of pearl-white. 1858 SIMMONDS Dict. Trade, Pearl-white, a colour; a powder made from nitrate of bismuth, and sometimes used by ladies as a cosmetic. 1866 E. METEYARD Life J. Wedgwood II. x. 482 An Italian order furnishes the accompanying tureen and plate in pearl-white ware. 1872 SYMONDS Introd. Study Dante 173 The pearl-white rose that opens to the rays of God's immediate glory. 1884 [see CREATION 5c]. 1914 G. FRANKAU Tid'apa (1915) vi. 34 Pearl-white 'gainst the darkling lustre at the black-pearl plinth of the capes. 1937 V. WOOLF Years 295 The road stretched pearl-white in front of them. 1956 G. DURRELL My Family xvi. 218 The curve of pearl-white sand was backed by the great lily-covered dune behind.

†**pearl**, *sb.*[2] *Obs.* [Goes with PEARL *v.*[2] q.v.] A clearing preparation for wine.

1682 Art & Myst. Vintners & Wine-Coopers 3 If your Canary hath a flying Lee, and will not find down, draw him into a fresh Butt or Pipe with fresh Lees, and give him a good pearl with the whites of 8 Eggs, and beat them with a handful of white Salt. Ibid. 16 A Pearl for Muskadine. Ibid., Then beat your Butt an hour; then put in your Pearl. Ibid. 43 The same Pearl serves for White Wine.

pearl (pɜːl), *sb.*[3] ? *Obs.* [perh. a transposed form of *prill*, *pryll*, a 15th c. var. of BRILL[1]; but prob. associated in colour or otherwise with PEARL *sb.*[1]] A local name of the fish BRILL.

a1672 WILLUGHBY Icthyogr. (1686) Tab. F. 1 Rhombus non aculeatus Squamosus, a Pearle Londinensibus. 1753 CHAMBERS Cycl. Supp., Pearl, in ichthyology, a name given by us in the parts about London, to that fish which is called in..the west of England, lug-a-leaf. 1762 Chron. in Ann. Reg. 148 Fish brought..867 Brill or Pearl. 1803 REES Cycl. s.v. Bret, The pearl..likewise obtains the name of bret in some parts of the country.

pearl (pɜːl), *sb.*[4] [app. another form of PURL, q.v.] One of a row of fine loops forming a decorative edging on pillow-lace, braid, ribbon, gold-lace, etc. Chiefly in Comb., as ***pearl-edge***, ***-loop***, ***-purl***, ***-tie***: see quots.

The oldest spelling seems to be PURL, app. connected with PURL *v.*[1], but whilst this has become established technically in the machine-made lace trade, popular etymology seems to favour the spelling *pearl*, prob. because the ornamental loops somewhat resemble an edging of pearl-drops.

1824 MISS MITFORD Village Ser. I. (1863) 214, I could not always control a certain wandering inclination for figured patterns and pearl edges. If Mossy had an aversion to any thing, it was to a pearl edge. 1831 PORTER Silk Manuf. 230 Ribands are frequently ornamented by having what is called a pearl-edge given to them. 1844 G. DODD Textile Manuf. vii. 228 A 'pearl edge', or something similar, is sewn on by hand round every edge. 1869 MRS. PALLISER Hist. Lace iii. 26 The flowers are connected by irregular threads overcast (buttonhole stitch), and sometimes worked over with pearl loops (picot). To these uniting threads, called by our lace-makers 'pearl ties'—old Randle Holme styles them 'coxcombs'—the Italians give the name of 'legs', the French that of 'brides'. 1880 JAMIESON, Pearl, a kind of ornamental lace used for edging; called also pearl-lace. 1886 Cassell's Encycl. Dict., Pearl-purl, a gold cord of twisted wire, resembling a small row of beads strung closely together. It is used for the edging of bullion embroidery.

pearl (pɜːl), *v.*[1] [f. PEARL *sb.*[1] or immed. a. F. *perler*, f. *perle*. Both in Fr. and Eng. the first part found is the pa. pple. (*perlé*, *pearled*), which may have been formed directly from the sb.]

1. *trans.* To adorn, set, or stud with or as with pearls, or with mother-of-pearl. (Only in *pa. pple.*)

c1386 CHAUCER Miller's T. 65 A purs of lether Tasseled with grene [v.r. 5 MSS. silk] and perled with latoun. 1538 ELYOT Dict., Clauus is a garment pirled [1545 pyrled] or powdred with spangles, lyke nayles heedes. 1564 Reg. Privy Council Scot. I. 308 Ane cowip..with ane cover peirlit with cristallyne within. 1593 NASHE Christ's T. (1613) 144 Women (seeing them so sumptuously pearled & bespangled). 1839 BAILEY Festus iii. (1852) 25 The pictured moon Pearled round with stars.

2. To sprinkle with pearly drops.

1595 B. BARNES Spir. Sonn. lxxx, A morning-dew perling the grasse beneath. c1595 SOUTHWELL St. Peter's Compl. 21 You..trees, With purest gummes perfume and pearle your ryne. 1632 QUARLES Div. Fancies I. xviii, The Dew that pearls the morning grass. a1821 KEATS Calidore 90 The evening dew had pearl'd their tresses.

3. To furnish (a stag's horns) with pearls. Only in *pa. pple.*

1575 TURBERV. Venerie 53 When the beame is great, burnished and well pearled.

4. To make pearly in colour or lustre; to suffuse with a pearly light or hue.

18.. MOIR Snow xi, Chain up the billows as they roll, And pearl the caves with light. 1846 RUSKIN Mod. Paint. (1851) I. II. II. ii §14 All the other whites of his picture are pearled down with grey or gold. 1874 SYMONDS Sk. Italy & Greece (1898) I. iv. 71 The peaked hills, blue and pearled with clouds.

5. a. To convert or reduce (barley, sago, etc.) into the shape of small round pearls.

1600, etc. [see PEARLED ppl. a.[1] 3]. 1839 URE Dict. Arts 1080 s.v. Sago, The starchy matter..is..pressed through a metal sieve to corn it (which is called pearling), and then dried. 1883 C. H. FARNHAM in Harper's Mag. Aug. 383/2

The barley for soup is pearled in a large wooden mortar with a pestle shaped like a pickaxe.

b. To refine (potassium carbonate) in the preparation of pearl-ash.

1850 *Rep. Comm. Patents 1849* (U.S.) I. 176 The process of first roasting or heating the ashes..and then pearling in the pearling oven.

6. To cover (comfits) with a coating of 'pearl' sugar: see PEARL *sb.*¹ 13. Also *intr.* for *refl.*

1883 R. HALDANE *Workshop Receipts* Ser. II. 162/2 They will be whiter and better, if partly pearled one day and finished the next. *Ibid.*, Put some of the prepared comfits in the pan, but not too many at a time, as it is difficult to get them to pearl alike.

7. *intr.* To form pearl-like drops or beads.

1595 SPENSER *Col. Clout* 507 With siluer deaw vpon the roses pearling. *c* **1626** *Dick of Devon.* IV. i. in Bullen *O. Pl.* II. 62 A cold sweat pearld in dropps all ore my body. **1727** BRADLEY *Fam. Dict.* s.v. *Brewing*, It flushes violently out of the Cock,..and then stops on a sudden and pearls and smiles in a glass like any bottled beer. **1891** *Cornh. Mag.* Apr. 379 The perspiration pearls down your face.

8. *intr.* **a.** To seek or fish for pearls.

1639 [see PEARLING *vbl. sb.* 1]. **1886** *Pall Mall G.* 25 Aug. 11/1 An Act specially dealing with the natives pearling. **1896** KIPLING *Seven Seas, Lost Legion* (1897) 97 We've pearled on half-shares in the Bay.

b. *Surfing.* (See quots.)

1962 [see PEARLING *vbl. sb.* 4]. **1967** J. SEVERSON *Great Surfing* Gloss., *Pearl* or *pearling*, while riding, the nose of the surfboard goes beneath the surface and continues downward, usually throwing the rider off (originally taken from pearl diving). **1970** *Studies in English* (Univ. Cape Town) I. 31 A milder form of wipe-out occurs when the surfboard *pearls*, in other words, the nose of the surfboard knifes under the water surface, usually throwing the surfer off. Variations on this expression include to *pearl-dive*, to *nose*, and to *plough*. **1971** *Ibid.* II. 27 If he is too far forward on the board the nose may dig in and the board *pearl* (shortened form of *pearl-dive*).

†**pearl**, *v.*² *Obs.* [Goes with PEARL *sb.*²; app. from PEARL *sb.*¹, in reference to clearness and pellucidness.] *trans.* ? To render clear and pellucid; to clarify (wine) with a clearing preparation.

1682 *Art & Myst. Vintners & Wine-Coopers* 10 As you pearl your Muskadine, so you must your Malmosey, but use not the Whites of Eggs.

pearl, *v.*³ [cf. PURL *v.*¹] 'To edge with lace' (Jamieson 1880). See PEARLED *ppl. a.*²

pearl, variant of PURL *v.* and *sb.* in knitting.

pearlaceous, occasional var. PERLACEOUS.

pearl-ash ('pɜːl,æʃ). The potassium carbonate of commerce, so called from its pearly hue. Orig. only in pl. *pearl ashes*.

α. **1727–41** CHAMBERS *Cycl.* s.v. *Ashes*,..divers sorts of ashes imported from abroad: as pot-ashes, pearl-ashes. **1776** J. CLEGG in T. Percival *Ess.* III. App. 335 Into one vessel I put a small quantity of pearl ashes. **1811** A. T. THOMSON *Lond. Disp.* (1818) 321 It assumes a spongy texture, with a blueish or greenish colour, and is then denominated pearl-ashes.

β. **1765** CROKER, etc. *Dict. Arts & Sc.* s.v. *Pot-ash*, The purity of pearl-ash..points out the method in which it has been prepared. **1796** KIRWAN *Elem. Min.* (ed. 2) II. 269 Take one part of the roasted Ore, 3 of Pearl Ash. **1866** ROSCOE *Elem. Chem.* 160 This is the crude potassium carbonate, called, when purified by re-crystallization, *pearl-ash*.

pearl-barley. [Cf. PEARL *v.*¹ 5.] Barley reduced by attrition to small rounded grains; used in making barley-water, broths, and soups.

1710 *Brit. Apollo* II. No. 112. 2/2 The Pearl-Barley bears the Preference. **1812** SIR J. SINCLAIR *Syst. Husb. Scot.* II. App. 50 Pot or pearl barley. **1875** *Encycl. Brit.* III. 376/2 Barley..prepared by grinding off the outer cuticle, which forms 'pot barley'. When the attrition is carried farther, so that the grain is reduced to small round pellets, it is called 'pearl barley'.

'pearl-,diver. **a.** One who dives for pearl-oysters.

1667 *Phil. Trans.* II. 863 The greatest length of time, that Pearl-Divers in these parts can hold under water, is about a quarter of an hour; and by no other means but Custome: For Pearl-diving lasteth not above Six weeks. **1748** *Anson's Voy.* II. viii. 217 The fish that is said frequently to destroy the pearl-divers. **1822–34** *Good's Study Med.* (ed. 4) I. 392 Diemerbroeck relates the case of a pearl-diver, who, under his own eye remained half-an-hour at a time under water, while pursuing his hunt for pearl muscles.

b. A person who washes crockery in a café or restaurant. *slang* (orig. *U.S.*).

1913 E. A. BROWN *Broke* iii. 29, I am in line for a pearl-diver's (dishwasher's) job tomorrow. **1956** *Amer. Speech* XXXI. 151 *Pearl diver*, a dish-washer in a logging cookhouse. **1970** *Daily Progress* (Charlottesville, Va.) 15 Jan. 3B/5 Euphemism has upgraded other jobs. In parts of the country, dishwashers have been called utensil maintenance men, though back at the sink they still may be 'pearl divers'.

So **'pearl-,diving**, *vbl. sb.*

1667 [see PEARL-DIVER a.] **1930** J. DOS PASSOS *42nd Parallel* v. 402 He got a job pearldiving in a lunch-room. **1970** C. KERSH *Aggravations M. Ashe* viii. 100 In the catering pearl diving is slang for dish washing.

pearled (pɜːld, *poet.* 'pɜːlɪd), *ppl. a.*¹ [f. PEARL *sb.*¹ and *v.*¹ + -ED.]

1. Furnished, set, or adorned with pearls; composed of or fitted with pearl or nacre. Chiefly *poet.*

1390 GOWER *Conf.* I. 126 Many a perled garnement Embroudred was ayein the dai. *a* **1568** *Wald my gud Ladye that I luif* 43 in *Bannatyne Poems* 658 With peirlit prenis of pacience, For hir wirschop to weir. **1634** MILTON *Comus* 834 The water Nymphs..Held up their pearled wrists and took her in. **1839** BAILEY *Festus* viii. (1852) 94 Within some pearled and coral cave. **1855** KINGSLEY *Heroes* III. (1868) 31 Galatea..in her car of pearled shells.

†**b.** Containing or yielding pearls. *Obs.*

1601 DOLMAN *La Primaud. Fr. Acad.* III. (1618) 853 This pearled fish maintaineth the kinde thereof by the egges which it breedeth. **1619** T. MILLES tr. *Mexia's*, etc. *Treas. Anc. & Mod. T.* II. 976/2 Taking pearled Oysters.

2. Formed into pearly drops; dew-besprinkled.

c **1586** C'TESS PEMBROKE *Ps.* CX. ii, As thickly sett..As pearled plaine with dropps is wett. **1598** SYLVESTER *Du Bartas* II. ii. III. *Colonies* 427 To pearl'd Auroras saffron colour'd bed. **1633** P. FLETCHER *Pisc. Ecl.* vii. 1 Her weeping eyes in pearled dew she steeps. **1753** WARTON *Ode Approach Summer* 161 From pearled bush The sunny-sparkling drop I brush. **1865** M. ARNOLD *Ess. Crit.* v. (1875) 219 That lay of pearled tears is the wide-famed Lament.

3. Formed into small rounded grains; granulated.

1600 FAIRFAX *Tasso* XVIII. xxiv, The Manna on each leafe did pearled lie. **1694** SALMON *Bate's Dispens.* (1713) 476/2 This pearled Nitre is good in all hot Diseases. **1885–94** R. BRIDGES *Eros & Psyche* Jan. xviii, A honey-cake Of pearlèd barley mix'd with hydromel.

4. In boiling of sugar for confectionery: Brought to the degree called 'pearl'; see quots. and PEARL *sb.*¹ 13.

1706 PHILLIPS (ed. Kersey), Pearled Boiling of Sugar (among Confectioners) is when after having dipt the tip of one's Fore-finger into the boiling Sugar and applied it to the Thumb, a small Thread or String continues sticking to both... This degree of Boiling may also be known, by a kind of round Pearls that arise on the top of the Liquor. **1725** BRADLEY *Fam. Dict.* s.v. *Sugar*. **1741** *Compl. Fam.-Piece* I. i. 92 Boil four Pounds of Sugar till it be pearled.

5. Like pearl in colour or lustre; pearly.

1719 LONDON & WISE *Compl. Gard.* 209 The red, and pearled, or white sort, called in English, Currans, produce Bunches, which are ripe in July. **1868** KINGSLEY *Christmas Day* 5 Red sun, blue sky, white snow, and pearled ice.

†**6.** Covered with a pearly scurf. *Obs.*

1627 S. WARD *Woe to Drunkards* 6 To whom are all kinds of diseases, deformities, pearled faces, if not to drunkards?

pearled, *ppl. a.*² [Cf. PEARL *sb.*⁴] 'Having a border of lace; ornamented with a worked border' (Jamieson 1825).

a **1670** SPALDING *Troub. Chas. I* (Spald. Cl.) II. 388 Haddoche prepairit him self noblie for death... He had on his heid ane white perllit mvtche. He had no cot, bot ane pair of blak breikis. **1886** *Cassell's Encycl. Dict.*, *Pearled*, having a border of or trimmed with pearl-edge.

pearler ('pɜːlə(r)), *sb.*¹ [f. PEARL *v.*¹ + -ER¹.] A trader engaged in pearl-fishing; an employer of pearl-divers; also, a small vessel employed in this trade.

1887 *Standard* 30 Apr., Unless the Colonial authorities look very sharply after the pearlers, they will soon exhaust the banks. **1902** *Blackw. Mag.* Apr. 534/1 He..had been in his time soldier, sailor, missionary, pearler, outlaw and mail-carrier.

pearler, *sb.*² Var. PURLER.

pearlescent (pɜː'lɛsənt), *a.* and *sb.* [f. PEARL *sb.*¹ + -ESCENT.] **A.** *adj.* Having or producing an appearance of mother-of-pearl.

1949 *Industr. Finishing* (Indianapolis) Oct. 115 (Advt.), Chem-Scale pearlescent finishes are very effective for artificial pearls, costume jewelry,..etc. **1966** *Vogue* Dec. 84/3 New pearlescent lipsticks. **1972** A. MARUSZEWSKI in Balsam & Sagarin *Cosmetics* (ed. 2) I. xi. 357 The pearl material is not to be roller milled or colloid milled, since this tends to destroy the pearlescent property of the material.

B. *sb.* A pearlescent material or finish.

1960 *Times* 6 Jan. 15/4 The Carinex range includes basic polymers... A wide range of colours..include such special effects as pearlescents, tinsels and fluorescents. **1972** A. MARUSZEWSKI in Balsam & Sagarin *Cosmetics* (ed. 2) I. xi. 357 There is another pearlescent available under the tradename of Bilite. Chemically it is bismuth oxychloride deposited epitaxially on thin platelets of white mica. **1975** P. BROWNE *Bodywork Maintenance* ix. 102/1 Acrylics loaded with pearlescents also give an iridescent effect.

So **pear'lescence**, a pearlescent effect or material.

1953 *Organic Finishing* July 12/1 There is now more attention being directed to the production of 'Pearlescence' than to the duplication of the natural product known..as Pearl Essence. We may tentatively define Pearlescence as that action on light which results in a pearly lustrous appearance. **1969** *New Scientist* 2 Oct. 26/2 One of M. Pariat's most appealing products is known as 'pearlescence'. Essentially it consists of including crystals of polycarbonate of bismuth or lead during the final calendering stage of cardboard production. **1973** J. B. WILKINSON et al. *Harry's Cosmeticology* xvi. 205 Attempts to counteract this tendency ..tend to decrease the pearlescence of the enamels.

'pearlet. *rare.* Also 6 perllet, 9 pearl-let. [dim. of PEARL *sb.*¹: cf. F. *perlette* (*a* 1560 in Littré), It. *perletta* seed-pearl.] A little pearl.

c **1569** in Nichols *Progr. Q. Eliz.* (1823) I. 271, 6*l.* for her half yeres wages for translating the Quenes perllets. **1841** T. J. OUSELEY *Eng. Melodies* 64 The infant dew..on every blade, Like pearl-lets shower'd. **1847** J. HALLIDAY *Rustic Bard* 38 Who circled his brow with pearlets white?

'pearl-,fisher. One who fishes for pearls.

1748 *Anson's Voy.* II. viii. 218 Great heaps of shells..left by the pearl-fishers from Panama. **1833** HT. MARTINEAU *Cinnamon & Pearls* i. 4 He had practised it as a preparation for becoming a pearl-fisher.

So **'pearl-,fishery**, (*a*) the occupation or industry of fishing for pearls; (*b*) the place where this is carried on, with all its apparatus. **'pearl-,fishing** = *pearl-fishery* a; also *attrib.*

1667 SPRAT *Hist. Roy. Soc.* 169 The Pearl-fishing is dangerous, being the Divers commonly make their Will, and take leave of their Friends, before they tread the Stone to go down. **1694** *Phil. Trans.* XVII. 659 A Letter from Sir Robert Redding..concerning Pearl-Fishing in the North of Ireland. **1748** *Anson's Voy.* II. viii. 218 Having mentioned the pearl-fishery, I must..recite a few particulars relating thereto. **1765** *Hist.* in *Ann. Reg.* 131/2 A very profitable pearl fishery..in the river Spey in Scotland. *c* **1850** *Arab. Nts.* (Rtldg.) 123, I then engaged myself, with the other merchants, in a pearl-fishery, in which I employed many divers on my own account. **1902** *Daily Chron.* 2 Oct. 6/4 The pearl fishing trade of Northern Australia.

'pearl-grass. [f. PEARL *sb.*¹ + GRASS.]

1. The large quaking-grass, *Briza maxima*. [From the shape and aspect of its spicules.]

1633 JOHNSON *Gerarde's Herbal* I. lxiv. 87 In English they call it Pearle-Grass, and Garden-Quakers. **1640** PARKINSON *Theat. Bot.* XIII. xvi. 1166 The greatest white Spanish Quakers, or Pearle grasse.

2. = PEARL *sb.*¹ 8 b. Also *pirl-grass*.

1794 *Statist. Acc. Scot.* XI. 374 Over-run with the creeping wheat-grass, known by the vulgar name of felt, or pirl-grass.

Pearl Harbour. [The name (*Pearl Harbor*) of a U.S. naval base on Oahu, one of the Hawaiian Islands: tr. Hawaiian *Wai Momi*, lit. 'pearl waters'.] Used with direct allusion to the military attack by Japanese aircraft on Pearl Harbour on 7 December 1941, which, delivered without a declaration of war, severely damaged the surprised U.S. Pacific fleet and began the Pacific phase of the war of 1939–45. Also *transf.* and *fig.* Hence as *v. trans.*, to attack suddenly and effectively.

1942 *Progressive* 31 Jan. 272/2 Compare these recently abandoned myths in Britain with the pre-Pearl Harbor folklore about the Japanese which prevailed in the United States. **1942** *Capital* (Topeka, Kansas) 20 Mar. 15/3 Delay along this line is the delay that spells Pearl Harbor to the vital industrial nerve centers of our economy. **1945** KOESTLER *Twilight Bar* II. 44 Maybe they are doing a Pearl Harbour on us. **1955** *Times* 22 Aug. 7/2 This dangerous local situation could be the result of military aggression or of political subversion. In fact, the real danger is not now so much of an 'atomic Pearl Harbour' as of a new Sarajevo murder, building up into a major atomic war. **1959** *Economist* 10 Jan. 99/2 It will put a premium on 'Pearl Harbour' tactics to knock out opposing missiles before they leave the ground. **1963** *Guardian* 8 Jan. 8/4 No aggressor would dare to Pearl-Harbour any member nation of this club. **1974** *Ibid.* 25 Mar. 15/4 Hornby was working for the Japanese Ministry of Education when Pearl Harbour came. **1975** *Listener* 14 Aug. 211/1 In 1970, Aston Villa were relegated to the third division. Eric Woodward, the commercial manager, describes that as 'our Pearl Harbour'. **1978** *Times* 20 May 14/2 Mrs Thatcher was caught with the Sunday morning Pearl Harbour attack by Mr Peregrine Worsthorne..in last week's *Sunday Telegraph*.

pearliness ('pɜːlɪnɪs). [f. PEARLY *a.* + -NESS.] Pearly quality or character.

1860 W. COLLINS *Wom. White* (1861) 121 Let me teach you to understand the heavenly pearliness of these lines. **1884** *St. James's Gaz.* 5 Dec. 6/2 That pearliness in which lies the greatest beauty of the human skin. **1893** J. PULSFORD *Loyalty to Christ* II. 145 Let..our whole spirit, soul, and flesh, be sacred to His Humanity.., that through His Pearliness in us we may become His incorruptible and eternal race.

pearling ('pɜːlɪŋ), *sb. Sc.* and *north. dial.* Also 7 -ine, 7–9 -in. [Goes with PEARL *sb.*⁴, PEARLED *ppl. a.*²: see -ING¹.] A kind of lace of thread or silk, for trimming the edges of garments: also called *pearling-lace*. In pl. *pearlings*, edgings of this lace; also *transf.* clothes trimmed with it.

1621 *Sc. Acts Jas. VI* (1816) IV. 625/2 That no persoun of whatsoeuir degrie salhave pearling or Ribbening vpoun þair Ruffes, Sarkis, Neipkines, and Sokkis, except þe persounes before priuiledged; and þe pearling and Ribbening..To be of those made within the kingdome of Scotland. **1644** *Sc. Acts Chas. I* (1819) VI. 76/2 On everie elne of imported pearline of threid or silke betuix three and six punds..00 12 00. *a* **1700** *Cock Laird* iii. in *Ramsay's Wks.* (1877) II. 222, I maun hae pinners With pearling [*ed.* 1829 purlins] set round. **1724** in Ramsay *Tea.-T. Misc.* (1733) I. 89 Sae put on your pearlins, Marion, And kyrtle of the cramasie. **1816** SCOTT *Old Mort.* ix, Let Jenny Dennison slip on her pearlings to walk before my niece and me. **1818** —— *Hrt. Midl.* xxvi, Pearlin-lace as fine as spiders' webs.

pearling ('pɜːlɪŋ), *vbl. sb.* [f. PEARL *v.*[1] + -ING[1].] The action of PEARL *v.*[1], in various senses.

1. a. Seeking or fishing for pearls. Also *attrib.*

1639 *Sc. Acts Chas. I* (1817) V. 259/1 The patent..to James Bannatyne for the peirling. *Ibid.* 261/1 The article against Mr. Mellwillis patent of pearling. **1886** *Pall Mall G.* 25 Aug. 11/1 Their rations consist of only a little flour when they are engaged in pearling. **1887** *Standard* 30 Apr. 5/2 The most important of the Australian pearling grounds.

b. ***pearling lugger*** (see quot. 1948).

1924 G. H. P. MUHLHAUSER *Cruise of Amaryllis* v. 233 A fair number of Australian 'black fellows' are to be found among the crews of the pearling 'luggers', as they are called, though really ketches. **1930** *Mariner's Mirror* XVI. 192 The pearling 'luggers' of the Torres Straits are usually ketch-rigged. **1948** R. DE KERCHOVE *Internat. Maritime Dict.* 525/1 *Pearl lugger, pearling lugger*, a local name given in northwest Australia to small ketch-rigged boats employed in pearl fisheries. **1978** O. WHITE *Silent Reach* vi. 71 It takes a different kind of knowhow to cut oyster rafts adrift or..sink pearling luggers..from the knowhow needed to dynamite windmills.

2. a. Formation into pearl-like grains or pellets; **b.** Coating of comfits with 'pearl' sugar: see PEARL *v.*[1] 5 and 6. Chiefly *attrib.*

1727 BRADLEY *Fam. Dict.* s.v. *Caramel*, The Fruits being thus dispos'd on the Bottom and Sides of the China-Dish, a Pearling-Pot is to be used. **1839** [see PEARL *v.*[1] 5]. **1875** KNIGHT *Dict. Mech.*, *Pearling-mill*, a mill for preparing hominy, pearling barley, etc. **1883** R. HALDANE *Workshop Receipts* Ser. II. 161/1 A ladle..and a 'pearling cot'... This last somewhat resembles a funnel without the tube.

c. Decoration of furniture or architecture with pearl-shaped carving.

1899 R. GLAZIER *Man. Hist. Ornament* 43 Later Norman work is very rich,..the lozenge and the beading or pearling. **1914** EBERLEIN & MCCLURE *Pract. Bk. Period Furnit.* 222 Besides these we find reeding, fluting, beading, pearling, spandrel fans, rosettes, and ribbons. **1925** PENDEREL-BRODHURST & LAYTON *Gloss. Eng. Furnit.* 122 *Pearling*, a series of rounded forms of the same size or graded, in more or less relief, used as a decoration on furniture. **1966** M. M. PEGLER *Dict. Interior Design* (1967) 328 *Pearling*, a series of rounded forms of the same size, or graduated like a string of beads. The pearling was used as a furniture embellishment, either in straight lines, arced, or swagged.

3. (See PEARLY *a.* 5 b.)

1885 *Pall Mall G.* 20 Jan. 4/1 The perfect pearling of her runs equalled the perfection of a musical box.

4. *Surfing.* (See PEARL *v.*[1] 8 b.)

1962 T. MASTERS *Surfing made Easy* 65 *Pearling*, when the nose of the surfboard goes under the water during a ride. **1965** J. POLLARD *Surfrider* ii. 18 The tendency of the nose of the board to dip into the water is 'pearling'. **1968** *Surfer Mag.* Jan. 56/1 The nose was curved to avoid pearling.

'pearling, *ppl. a.* [f. as prec. + -ING[2].]

†**1.** Forming pearls or pearl-like drops. *Obs.*

1595 SPENSER *Epithal.* 155 Her long loose yellow locks lyke golden wyre, Sprinckled with perle, and perling flowres a tweene. **1596** —— *F.Q.* v. ix. 50 But rather let..to fall Few perling drops from her fair lampes of light.

2. Fishing for pearls.

1894 G. BOOTHBY *In Strange Company* II. iv. (1896) 48/2 Numbers of white-sailed pearling craft dotted the bay.

pearlish ('pɜːlɪʃ), *a.* [f. PEARL *sb.*[1] + -ISH[1].] Slightly pearl-coloured or pearl-like.

1885 CLARK RUSSELL *Strange Voy.* I. xviii. 260 The bluish and pearlish tints you notice in oyster-shells. **1890** —— *Ocean Trag.* II. xviii. 96 The pearlish gleam of canvas.

pearlite ('pɜːlaɪt). [f. PEARL *sb.*[1] + -ITE[1].]

1. *Min.* Variant form of PERLITE, = PEARL-STONE.

2. *Metallurgy.* One of the forms in which carbon and iron are combined in cast steel: see quots.

1888 H. M. HOWE in *Engin. & Mining Jrnl.* 18 Aug. 132 Minerals which compose iron. Name suggested here... Pearlyte. A mixture of about $\frac{7}{8}$ ferrite and $\frac{1}{8}$ cementite. **1889** *Nature* 14 Nov. 37/2 Prof. Howe, of Boston,..even suggests mineralogical names, such as 'cementite', 'perlite', 'ferrite', for the various associations of carbon and iron. **1900** *Engineering Mag.* XIX. 752/1 This substance, which has received the name of pearlite, is an intimate mixture of thin lamellæ of ferrite and yet thinner lamellæ of a chemical combination of iron and carbon, Fe_3 C, which bears the name of cementite. Low-carbon irons and steels are composed of a conglomeration of ferrite and pearlite, but when the carbon reaches about 0·8 per cent. the ferrite granules disappear, and only the pearlite remains. **1966** C. R. TOTTLE *Sci. Engin. Materials* x. 228 A two-phase alloy will tend to corrode more readily because an electrochemical cell will be set up between the different areas. Mild steel, containing ferrite (pure iron) and pearlite (a eutectoid, itself two-phase), shows this. **1977** *Sci. Amer.* Oct. 127/1 The presence of pearlite in an iron artifact is a clear indication that the artifact has been carburized.

Hence **pear'litic** *a.*

1904 *Proc. Inst. Mech. Engin.* Nov. 1149 'Sorbitic' steels ..are produced by a much more rapid cooling than is necessary to produce the 'pearlitic' steels. **1947** *Nature* 11 Jan. 50/1 Ordinary cast iron has a mixed ferritic-pearlitic matrix, and the engineering irons are usually fully pearlitic. **1962** *B.S.I. News* June 12/2 Draft proposals considered by the committee related to chemical composition, mechanical properties and methods of test for blackheart, whiteheart and pearlitic malleable iron.

pearlized ('pɜːlaɪzd), *ppl. a.* [f. PEARL *sb.*[1] + -IZE + -ED[1].] Treated so as to resemble mother-of-pearl or to convey a suggestion of mother-of-pearl.

1955 *Britannica Bk. of Year* (U.S.) 681/2 Pearlized and luster leathers were extremely important in women's shoes and colours ranged all the way from pastels to black. **1955** *Wall St. Jrnl.* 21 Nov. 5/2 Retailers note that round, perforated pearlized beads are taxable, and oval ones aren't. **1957** *New Yorker* 1 June 70/1 For town as well as the seashore, there are hats the size of beach umbrellas—sailors of white pearlized straw with straight brims, and sailors of white starched straw curled up at the edges. **1958** *Observer* 17 Aug. 7/4 A coat of pearlised suede lined in cotton. **1969** *Guardian* 12 Aug. 7/2 Transparent make-up..available in three pearlised tan shades. **1972** 'J. MELVILLE' *Ironwood* vi. 89 The names slid easily between her pearlised lips. **1976** *Morecambe Guardian* 7 Dec. 5/1 For a children's party, she made a table arrangement using a soft toy toad, on an oasis shaped like a toadstool, decorated with apples, seed pods and pearlised foliage.

'pearl-,oyster. A pearl-bearing bivalve mollusc of the family *Aviculidæ*; *spec. Meleagrina margaritifera* of the Indian seas.

1693 SIR T. P. BLOUNT *Nat. Hist.* 169 The Pearl-Oysters are so very hard and tough,..that they always throw them away. **1748** *Anson's Voy.* II. viii. 219 The pearl oyster..was incapable of being eaten. **1863** C. R. MARKHAM in *Intell. Observ.* IV. 422 The pearl oyster..is not in reality an oyster at all, but is more allied to a mussel; having, like the latter animal, a byssus, or cable by which it secures itself to the rocks.

'pearl-,shell.

1. A shell having a nacreous coating; mother-of-pearl as naturally found. Also *rhetorically*, something resembling such a shell.

1614 SYLVESTER *Bethulia's Rescue* IV. 379 Her soft sleek slender hands..With purest Pearl-shell had each finger tipt. **1887** GUILLEMARD *Cruise of Marchesa* II. 321 To send schooners to the northern coast for pearl-shell and gum-dammar. **1903** *Daily Chron.* 30 Oct. 5/4 The pearl-shell from which mother-of-pearl ornaments are made.

2. Any shell producing pearls; a pearl-mussel.

1788 REES *Chambers' Cycl.*, *Pearl shell* or *gaper*. See Mya. [*Mya*..a bivalve shell gaping at one end... On being squeezed, they will eject the pearl.] **1815** JAS. ARBUTHNOT *Fishes Buchan* 32 *Mytellus Margaritifera*, Pearl Muscle, vulgarly called Pearl Shell.

3. *attrib.* Of or resembling a pearly shell.

a **1618** SYLVESTER *Ode Astræa* xvi, Those five nimble brethren small Arm'd with Pearl-shell helmets all. **1894** S. FISKE *Holiday Stories* (1900) 215 Hattie, listening with all her pearl-shell ears.

Hence **'pearl-,sheller**, one who fishes for pearl-shells; **'pearl-,shelling** *sb.*, the collecting of pearl-shells: *adj.* engaged in this.

1887 *Pall Mall G.* 28 Oct. 11/1 Its timber and pearl-shelling industries. *Ibid.* 11/2 Cossack is the great rendezvous of the pearl-shelling fleet. *Ibid.* 28 Nov. 12/1 Pearl shellers..working on the north-west coast of Australia with twelve schooners, seventy-five luggers, and 642 men. **1889** H. H. ROMILLY *Verandah in N. Guinea* 23 He has been everything—overlander, explorer, gold-digger, pearl-sheller. *Ibid.*, Reports of pearl-shelling and Bêche de Mer fishing.

'pearl-stone. The same as PERLITE.

1800 HENRY *Epit. Chem.* (1808) 364 The same skilful analyst has found potash in Hungarian pearl-stone. **1852** TH. ROSS *Humboldt's Trav.* I. ii. 102, I consider even the pearlstone as an unvitrified obsidian.

'pearlware. Also **pearl ware**. White-coloured pottery ware, orig. manufactured by Josiah Wedgwood.

1922 W. BURTON *J. Wedgwood & his Pottery* iv. 37 This 'pearl' ware, as Wedgwood made it, differed somewhat in composition from his cream ware, for it contained a larger proportion of ground flint and china-stone. **1948** W. B. HONEY *Wedgwood Ware* ii. 10 The 'pearl-ware' was chiefly used for tea-services made in rivalry with porcelain. **1953** W. MANKOWITZ *Wedgwood* ii. 44 The peak production period for pearlware is the first quarter of the nineteenth century. **1961** *Times* 8 Apr. 11/6 Cream-coloured earthenware and the harder, whiter pearlware. **1969** *Canad. Antiques Collector* Feb. 14/2 Round about the year 1800 this model must have been turned out by the dozen, sometimes, as in this instance, in pearlware, [etc.]. **1975** *Daily Tel.* 5 Feb. 12/5 A Leeds pearlware figure of a horse, 17 ins high, was bought anonymously for £1,350 at Sotheby's yesterday.

'pearlwort. A book-name for the genus *Sagina* of caryophyllaceous plants.

1660 RAY *Catal. Plantarum* 151 *Saxifraga Anglica Occidentalium*..Pearlwort, Chickweed-Breakstone. **1787** WITHERING *Brit. Plants* (1796) II. 215 *Sagina*... Chickweed-Breakstone. Trailing Pearlwort. **1854** S. THOMSON *Wild Fl.* (ed. 4) III. 186 Pearlworts, inconspicuous plants, with narrow leaves.

pearly ('pɜːlɪ), *a.* (*adv.*, *sb.*) [f. PEARL *sb.*[1] + -Y.]

A. *adj.* **1. a.** Round and lustrous like a pearl, as a dewdrop, etc.

c **1430** LYDG. *Min. Poems* (Percy Soc.) 242 Whan Aurora, ..Sent on herbys the perly dropys sheene. **1508** DUNBAR *Goldyn Targe* 14 The perly droppis schake in silvir schouris. **1646** CRASHAW *Poems* 113 The treasure of thy pearly dew. **1871** TYNDALL *Fragm. Sc.* (1879) I. xi. 342 The little pearly globe which we call a dew-drop.

b. Like pearl in appearance or lustre.

1603 DRAYTON *Bar. Wars* VI. xviii, The siluer-Trent on pearly sands dooth slide. **1651** JER. TAYLOR *Serm. for Year* II. xi. 136 Casting its pearly seeds for the young to breed, it [the silk-worm] leaveth its silk for man. **1776** GIBBON *Decl. & F.* xi. (1869) I. 232 Her teeth were of a pearly whiteness. **1811** PINKERTON *Petralogy* I. 380 Lustre, from glimmering to shining; between pearly and vitreous. **1839** G. BIRD *Nat. Philos.* 393 A tough, pearly opaque membrane, termed the sclerotic coat. **1873** *Daily Tel.* 26 May 4/1 The pearliest complexions did not shrink from exposure to the morning air.

2. a. Abounding in, having, or bearing pearls.

1619 T. MILLES tr. *Mexia's*, etc. *Treas. Anc. & Mod. T.* II. 977/2 The flesh..or body of the Pearly Oyster. **1714** GAY *Ep. to Lady* 24 Here I..call'd the Nereids from their pearly cells. *a* **1821** KEATS *Hyperion* I. 355 Like to a diver in the pearly seas.

b. Abounding in, or characterized by, mother-of-pearl; nacreous.

1667 MILTON *P.L.* VII. 407 Through Groves Of Coral stray..Or in thir Pearlie shells at ease, attend Moist nutriment. **1714** GAY *Trivia* III. 197 The man..that on the rocky shore First broke the oozy oyster's pearly coat. **1776** DA COSTA *Conchol.* 286 The Pearly Chambered Nautilus, or Sailor. **1822** OWEN (*title*) Memoir on the Pearly Nautilus.

3. a. Made of, set with, adorned with pearls or pearl.

1742 COLLINS *Ode to Liberty* 44 Deck'd with pearly pride. **1818** KEATS *Endym.* II. 117 The pearly cup Meander gave me. *Ibid.* III. 212 Beside this old man lay a pearly wand.

b. ***pearly gates***: the gates of heaven as described in Rev. xxi. 21, used allusively.

1853 C. F. ALEXANDER *Hymn, 'The roseate hues'*, Oh! for the pearly gates of heaven! Oh! for the golden floor! **1927** H. CRANE *Let.* 29 May (1965) 300 If I can avoid the pearly gates long enough I may do better. **1953** [see DODGER *a.*]. **1969** J. WAINWRIGHT *Big Tickle* 72 Dago said: 'A shiv kick—and pearly gates.' **1973** J. PORTER *It's Murder with Dover* xvi. 162, I heard somebody'd pushed that Marsh cat through dem pearly gates. **1977** *Gay News* 24 Mar. 21/4 Perfection's death to me, the pearly gates, and I do think pearl's awfully vulgar for gates.

c. ***Pearly King*** (or ***Queen***): a leading London costermonger, dressed in festive costume covered with pearl-buttons.

1933 *Times* 26 Aug. 9/5, I wrote..to 'Snowy Tabram, Pearly King, Islington,' asking him when and where the annual meeting of the Pearlies would take place. **1934** *Times* 1 June 13/3 The Rev. A. D. Belden..unveiled yesterday.. a statue of Henry Croft, the 'pearly king', who died four years ago. The statue represents Mr. Croft in his 'pearly king' clothes with top hat. **1935** F. W. TICKNER *London through Ages* xiv. 286 (*caption*) 'Pearly King and Queen' of the Costermongers. **1942** WYNDHAM LEWIS *Let.* 27 Jan. (1963) 315 They go about talking to themselves—in the purest idiom of the Pearly King. **1963** *Times* 16 May 15/5 Reminding me of one of the 'Pearly Kings' or button-covered costermongers that I had seen in London when I was a boy. **1967** E. SHORT *Embroidery & Fabric Collage* ii. 41 Most pearly kings and queens design and make their own costumes, the decoration being made up entirely of pearl buttons sewn on the fabric of the suit or dress. **1975** *Evening News* 26 Apr. 4/1 Pearly King Bill Davison raised thousands of pounds for charity. **1977** *Times* 28 Jan. 16/6 The silver-painted London double decker, decorated with Cockney slogans, pictures of buskers and an advertisement for an insurance company, is the contribution of the Pearly kings and queens of London to the Queen's silver jubilee, and will be used to raise money for a recently-formed Pearlies' charity appeal.

4. Of the clear greyish- or bluish-white colour of pearl, esp. as ***pearly grey***.

c **1790** IMISON *Sch. Art* II. 61 Beneath the eyes, the pleasing pearly tints are to be preserved, composed of verditer and white. **1832** HT. MARTINEAU *Each & All* iv. 53 The dressing room lamp shed a pearly light through the room. **1845** *Punch* VIII. 247 The following terms..may be used pretty much at random: 'Chiaroscuro', 'texture', 'pearly greys', 'foxy browns'. **1872** BLACK *Adv. Phaeton* xxix, A costume of pearly grey. **1978** I. MURDOCH *Sea* 437 A thick clammy pearly-grey mist surrounded the house.

5. *fig.* **a.** Exceedingly precious (like a precious pearl); of supreme (spiritual) purity or lustre.

1760–72 H. BROOKE *Fool of Qual.* (1809) IV. 69 You are too much, too pearly, too precious a treasure. **1893** J. PULSFORD *Loyalty to Christ* II. 148 We begin to long..that we may be pearly and Christ-like throughout.

b. Having a clear, round, sweet tone.

1890 in *Cent. Dict.*

6. Comb., as ***pearly-coated***, ***-coloured***, ***-teethed*** adjs.

1608 SYLVESTER *Du Bartas* II. iv. III. *Schism* 401 By night, the Moon denies to fading Flowrs Her silver sweat, and pearly-purled showrs. **1776** DA COSTA *Conchol.* 30 A pearly-coated Shell.

B. as *adv.* After the manner of, or in respect of, pearl or pearls.

1818 KEATS *Endym.* III. 760 Here is a shell; 'tis pearly blank to me. **1821** CLARE *Vill. Minstr.* II. 193 The little bell-flowers, pearly blue. **1883** R. HALDANE *Workshop Receipts* Ser. II. 361/1 A pearly-lustrous material. **1891** KIPLING *Light that Failed* xiii. 249 Maisie lifted up her face, and it was pearly white. 'No! No! Not blind! I won't have him blind!' **1952** A. G. L. HELLYER *Sanders' Encycl. Gardening* (ed. 22) 241 *H*[*ymenanthera*] *crassifolia*, yellow, pansy-like flowers, succeeded by pearly-white berries in autumn.

C. *sb.* **a.** in *pl.* Clothes adorned with pearl-buttons, such as are worn by costermongers. Also, the pearl-buttons themselves.

1886–96 MARSHALL *Pomes fr. 'Pink 'Un'*, *Bleary Bill* 60 (Farmer) Oh! why are your pearlies so bright, bleary Bill? **1897** *Daily News* 27 Jan. 7/5 A sharp-looking urchin, wearing a complete suit of coster 'pearlies'. **1898** J. D. BRAYSHAW *Slum Silhouettes* 142 He'd..a blue coat and weskit with the artfullest little pearlies you ever see. **1914** 'BARTIMEUS' *Naval Occasions* xviii. 156 What time the citizen ashore donned 'pearlies' or broad-cloth and shut up shop. **1935** P. COHEN-PORTHEIM *Spirit of London* viii. 99 There are still costermongers in their 'pearlies' (one of the prettiest dresses to be found anywhere). **1949** R. GRAVES *Seven Days in New Crete* 123 'But you should see my gala suit! It is in rain-grey linen, covered with little pearl-buttons.'..He went off to buy his pearlies. **1957** *Encycl. Brit.* VI. 511/1 (*caption*) London costermonger family of the Victorian age. These costumes, with their rich embroidery of pearl buttons or 'pearlies', are now used rarely, and only on festive occasions.

b. A costermonger or a pearly king (or queen).

1928 *Daily Express* 27 June 13/3 It is given to few men to be popular alike with princes and 'pearlies'. **1959** *Manch. Guardian* 4 Aug. 4/7 Hampstead Bank Holidays.. felt the loss of.. the beery men, the pearlies, and the 'Stout Parties'. **1974** *Times* 20 Aug. 12/2 There will be 'three Pearlies including the Pearly King of London'. **1977** [see sense 3 c above].

pearmain ('pɛəmeɪn). Forms: 5 **parmayn, permayn(e, parment;** 6–7 **pearemain(e,** 7– **pearmain,** (7 **per-, pear(e-, pair-, pare-, peermain(e, -mane, -mayn,** 7–9 **permain).** [ME. a. OF. *par-, permain*, app. ad. L. **parmānus* of Parma: see W. Foerster in *Zeitschr. f. Rom. Phil.* 1899, XXIII. 423. In mod.Ger. *parmäne.*]

†**1.** A variety of pear; app. the same as the WARDEN. *Obs.*

[**1285** *Ld. Treas. Roll 14 Edw. I* m. 1 Walterus de Burgo.. reddidit ad Scaccarium cc. pira parmennorum et duo modia vini pro se et Galfrido de Fontibus.. et Waltero de Billingeye.. pro manerio de Runham quod de Rege tenent.] *c* **1425** *Voc.* in Wr.-Wülcker 647/29 *Nomina fructuum.. Hoc uolemum*, permayne. **1483** *Cath. Angl.* 270/1 A Parmayn, *volemum*, Anglice a warden. **1611** [see 3].

2. Name of a variety of apple, of which there are many sub-varieties.

1597 GERARDE *Herbal* III. xcv. 1274 Of the apple tree.. The sommer Pearemaine... The winter Pearemaine. **1602** in *Lyly's Wks.* (1902) I. 492 Wee haue jenitings, paremayns, russet coates, pippines. **1612** DRAYTON *Poly-olb.* xviii. 675 The Pearemaine, which to France long ere to us was knowne. **1663–4** WOOD *Life* 2 Jan. (O.H.S.) II. 1 For a peck of peermanes, 6*d*; given to Mary to fetch them, 1*d*. **1707** MORTIMER *Husb.* (1721) II. 287 The Russet Pearmain.. partakes both of the Russeting and Pearmain in colour and taste, the one side being generally Russet, and the other streak'd like a Pearmain. **1834** *Penny Cycl.* II. 190/1 Hubbard's pearmain.. Autumn pearmain.. Adam's pearmain.. Lamb-Abbey pearmain. **1875** BLACKMORE *A. Lorraine* III. vi. 81 A tempting and beautiful apple, a scarlet permain.

3. *attrib.* and *Comb.*

c **1425** *Voc.* in Wr.-Wülcker 646/10 *Hec uolemus*, permayntre. **1483** *Cath. Angl.* 270/1 A Parmayn tre (*A.* parment tre), *volemus*.. a wardentre. **1611** COTGR., *Poire de parmain*, the Permaine Peare. **1616** SURFL. & MARKH. *Country Farme* 395 It is grafted.. vpon the Thorne or Quince-tree, and vpon the Peare-maine-tree. **1679** BLOUNT *Anc. Tenures* 69 It is worth the observing that in King Edward the firsts time Permain-cider was called wine.

pearmonger ('pɛəˌmʌŋgə(r)). [f. PEAR *sb.* + MONGER.] A dealer in pears. Usu. in alliterative phrase *as pert as a pearmonger.*

1565 J. HARDING *Confut. Jewell's Apol.* v. v. 247 Here pricketh forth this hasty Defender, as peart as a peare-monger. *a* **1732** GAY *New Song on New Similies* 9 Pert as a pear-monger I'd be, If Molly were but kind. **1738** SWIFT *Pol. Conversat.* 69 You are as pert as a Pearmonger this Morning. **1835** [see PERT *a.* 4 a].

pears(e, obs. forms of PIERCE.

Pearson ('pɪəsən). *Statistics.* The name of Karl *Pearson* (1857–1936), English mathematician, used *attrib.* and in the possessive to designate: **a.** The members of a family of curves described by him in 1895, which include many probability distribution functions.

1908 *Biometrika* VI. 4 Consequently a curve of Prof. Pearson's Type III may be expected to fit the distribution of s^2. **1927** H. L. RIETZ *Math. Statistics* iii. 58 The method of moments plays an essential rôle in the Pearson system of frequency curves. **1936** *Statistical Res. Mem.* I. 41 A better approximation to $p(L_1')$ might be obtained if a Pearson Type I curve were fitted with the correct first four moment coefficients. **1974** P. LUMB in I. K. Lee *Soil Mech.* iii. 51 Some of the most useful standard forms are members of the Pearson family of distributions defined by

$$\frac{d}{dx}\{\log g(x)\} = \frac{x - c_0}{c_1 + c_2 x + c_3 x^2}.$$

b. A measure of the skewness of statistical distributions, proposed by him in 1895.

1911 G. U. YULE *Introd. Theory Statistics* viii. 150 There is, however, only one generally recognised measure of skewness, and that is Pearson's measure..—

$$\text{skewness} = \frac{\text{mean} - \text{mode}}{\text{standard deviation}}\ldots$$

The numerator of the above fraction may.. be replaced approximately by 3 (mean − median). **1925** F. C. MILLS *Statistical Methods* v. 168 Pearson's formula for measuring skewness. **1962** *Lebende Sprachen* VII. 114/1 Pearson measure of skewness.

c. The product-moment correlation coefficient (see PRODUCT *sb.*[1] 6).

1912 *Jrnl. R. Statistical Soc.* LXXV. 609 Professor Pearson's coefficient.. was described and its use illustrated in two memoirs published in 1900. **1957** KENDALL & BUCKLAND *Dict. Statistical Terms* 215 The product-moment coefficient of correlation is sometimes referred to as the Pearson coefficient of correlation because of K. Pearson's part in introducing it into general use. **1973** L. D. PHILLIPS *Bayesian Statistics* x. 207 The correlation coefficient (or Pearson product-moment correlation coefficient, as it is sometimes called) is usually designated by r and is defined as $r = \frac{\Sigma Z_x Z_y}{N - 1}$. *Ibid.* xii. 294 Transform the ranks into normal scores, compute the Pearson-*r* between the pairs of scores and use the inference method just discussed.

d. The chi-square test.

1912 *Jrnl. Exper. Zool.* XIII. 203 Pearson's test depends upon a variable $\chi_2[sic] = S[(m_r - m_r')^2/m_r]$ where m_r is the theoretical frequency and m_r' the observed. **1969** H. O. LANCASTER *Chi-Squared Distribution* ix. 175 With several degrees of freedom, for class frequencies of 5 or more, the distributions of the Pearson χ^2 approximate satisfactorily to the asymptotic or theoretical χ^2 distributions.

e. A set of formulæ described by him in 1899, used for estimating human stature from the length of limb bones.

1925 S. SMITH *Forensic Med.* v. 53 (*heading*) Pearson's formulæ. **1947** *Sci. News* IV. 40 Pearson.. compiled tables relating the length of certain of the arm and leg bones to the total height of the body. These Pearson formulas are quite remarkable in their accuracy. **1966** R. JACKSON *Crime Doctors* 25 Simpson measured the only intact bone he had —the upper part of the left arm—and, using Pearson's formula, concluded that the bones were those of a woman who had been slightly over five feet tall.

Pearsonian (pɪə'səʊnɪən), *a. Statistics.* [f. prec. + -IAN.] Of or originated by Karl Pearson (see prec.); used esp. with ref. to senses a and b s.v. PEARSON.

1907 F. B. WYATT in W. P. Elderton *Frequency-Curves* p. v, In January, 1903, Mr. W. Palin Elderton read before the Institute of Actuaries an interesting paper dealing with the application of the Pearsonian frequency-curves to the graduation of a mortality experience. **1927** H. L. RIETZ *Math. Statistics* iv. 82 The degree of correlation is often measured by the Pearsonian coefficient of correlation represented by the letter *r*. **1969** *Computers & Humanities* III. 145 The correlation coefficient used here is the Pearsonian product-moment correlation. **1972** R. B. CAIN *Elem. Statistical Concepts* xix. 163 The Pearsonian coefficient of skewness brings out the relation between the mean and the median in a skewed distribution which has exactly one mode.

peart (pɪət), *a.* Also 6 **peirt,** 6– **piert,** 9 **peert.** A variant of PERT *a.*, with lengthened vowel, found already in 15th c., and formerly occurring in all the senses; still widely used in the dialects, and sometimes as a literary archaism or localism in senses no longer expressed by *pert*; esp. **a.** Lively, brisk, sprightly, active; **b.** Clever, intelligent, sharp of comprehension. See PERT.

pearten ('pɪətən), *v. dial.* [f. PREC. + -EN[5].] *trans.* and *intr.* To cheer up; to become more lively or sprightly; to hasten. Freq. const. *up.*

1879–81 G. F. JACKSON *Shropshire Word-bk.* 317 *Peärten, peärtle*,.. to revive; to enliven; to cheer. (1) 'Oh! yo'n soon *pearten* up, yo' beginnen to look better a' ready'. (2) "Er quoite *pyurtled* 'im ŏop w'en 'er come wŏam'. **1895** [see DRUTHER]. **1896** G. F. NORTHALL *Warwickshire Word-bk.* 169. **1909** *Dialect Notes* III. 356 *Pearten, v.i.* and *tr.* To hasten, go faster: often with *up*. 'We will have to *pearten up* if we expect to get there on time.' **1949** H. HORNSBY *Lonesome Valley* v. 70 Crit seemed to pearten up at that. **1951** H. GILES *Harbin's Ridge* xvi. 139 But when he peartened up, we all took fresh heart.

'pear-tree. Forms: see PEAR *sb.* and TREE.

1. The tree which produces pears: see PEAR *sb.* 2.

a **1300** *Cursor M.* 37 Of gode pertre coms god peres. **1469** *Bury Wills* (Camden) 46 The frute of the seid pertre and of an appultre. **1579** SPENSER *Sheph. Cal.* Mar. 111 Crowes.. That in our Peeretree haunted. **1697** DRYDEN *Virg. Georg.* IV. 214 He knew.. For Fruit the grafted Pear-tree to dispose. **1866** *Treas. Bot.* 945 The Common Pear-tree, *Pyrus communis*... The branches are thorny... Under cultivation the thorns disappear.

2. The wood of this tree; pear-wood.

1669 STURMY *Mariner's Mag.* II. xvi. 92 Smooth dry Box Wood or Pear-tree. *c* **1850** *Rudim. Navig.* (Weale) 134 Pieces of pear-tree or box.

3. *attrib.* and *Comb.*

c **1420** *Pallad. on Husb.* III. 701 The pertre plaunte is sette in places colde. **1633** T. JAMES *Voy. Q*, Old seasoned Peare-tree-wood.

peary, variant of PEERY, a peg-top.

peas, obs. form of PEACE.

peasant ('pɛzənt), *sb.* Forms: α. 5 **paissaunt,** 6 **paisaunte, peisant, peysant, -aunt, pesent, -aunt, pezzant,** 6–7 **paysant, pesant, pezant,** 6–8 **paisant,** 6– **peasant.** β. 6 **paysan, -yne, peysan,** 7 **paisan, peasan.** [a. AF. *paisant*, in OF. *païsent, païsant, paysant* (12th c. in Godef.), mod.F. *paysan* (13th c. in Littré), f. *païs, pays* country:—L. *pāgensis*, sc. *ager*, the territory of a *pāgus* or canton, the country. Cf. It. *paesano*, Sp. *païsano*. The β forms here are conformed (more or less) to later Fr.

The OF. ending, *-ant, -ent*, is difficult. It cannot represent L. *-ānus*; French etymologists incline to refer *païsent* to an earlier *païsenc*, formed with the German suffix *-inc, -ing*.]

1. a. One who lives in the country and works on the land, either as a small farmer or as a labourer; *spec.* one who relies for his subsistence mainly on the produce of his own labour and that of his household, and forms part of a larger culture and society in which he is subject to the political control of outside groups; also, loosely, a rural labourer.

In early use, properly only of foreign countries; often connoting the lowest rank, antithetical to *noble*; also to *prince*. Although modern sociologists agree that a 'peasant' works the land, the more wealthy peasants may also be land-owners, rentiers, hirers of labour, etc., and in these capacities share interests with completely different social groups. Hence in the analysis of many rural societies divisions within the class frequently have to be made.

α. [**1341–2** *Year-bks. 16 Edw. III*, Hill. No. 13 (Rolls) 65 Vostre tenant.. resceit la rente par mayne des paisanz [*v.rr.* paysayns, paysains] et villeyns.] **1475** *Bk. Noblesse* (Roxb.) 73 The pore comons, laborers, paissauntes of the saide duchie of Normandie. *a* **1548** HALL *Chron., Hen. V* 46 The comen people and peysantz of the countree assembled in greate nombre. **1576** GASCOIGNE *Steele Gl.* (Arb.) 57 The Peasant he should labor for their ease. **1577–87** HOLINSHED *Chron.* III. 1199/1 The pezzants about gathered themselues togither, and set vpon him and his souldiers. **1598** DALLINGTON *Meth. Trav.* K iv b, There is also the 'Subiect', that is, the poore paisant that laboureth and tilleth the fiefs. **1642** ROGERS *Naaman* 275 Heaven lies no more open to a Noble mans performances and merits, then a pezants. **1664** H. MORE *Myst. Iniq.* I. xxii. 85 There being a like fear of it .. in Princes and Peasants, in Gentle and simple. **1678** LOCKE in Ld. King *Life* 77 In Xantonge, and several other parts of France, the paisants are much more miserable. **1761** *Chron.* in *Ann. Reg.* 61/2 An address lately presented to the king of Sweden, by the speaker of the house of Peasants, assembled in diet. **1807** WORDSW. *Wh. Doe* VII. 313 Help did she give at need, and joined The Wharfdale peasants in their prayers. **1844** DISRAELI *Coningsby* III. iii, What can it signify .. whether a man be called a labourer or a peasant? **1850** H. MACFARLANE tr. *Marx & Engels's Manifesto of German Communist Party* in *Red Republican* 16 Nov. 171/2 The small manufacturers, shopkeepers, proprietors, peasants, &c., all fight against the Bourgeoisie, in order to defend their position as small Capitalists. They are, therefore, not revolutionary but conservative. **1869** LECKY *Europ. Mor.* (1877) I. i. 146 Had the Irish peasants been less chaste, they would have been more prosperous. **1878** SEELEY *Stein* I. 433 Famished drudges.. who, if they cannot be called serfs, can still less be called peasants, for a peasant properly so called must have a personal interest in the land. **1926** E. & C. PAUL tr. *Marx's Eighteenth Brumaire of L. Bonaparte* vii. 137 The interests of the peasants no longer coincide, as during the reign of the first Napoleon, with the interests of the bourgeoisie, with the interests of capital. There is now a conflict of interests. The peasants, therefore, find their natural allies and leaders in the urban proletariat, whose mission it is to subvert the bourgeois order of society. **1927** M. J. OLGIN tr. *Engels's Peasant War in Germany* 18 The small peasants (bigger peasants belong to the bourgeoisie) are not homogeneous. They are either in serfdom bound to their lords and masters,.. or they are tenants, whose situation is almost equal to that of the Irish. **1933** E. & C. PAUL tr. *Stalin's Leninism* II. 205 In the conditions prevailing in our country, the peasantry consists of various social groups,.. the poor peasants, the middle peasants, and the kulaks. It is obvious that our attitude to these various groups cannot be identical. The poor peasant is the *support* of the working class, the middle peasant is the *ally*, the kulak is the *class enemy*—such is our attitude to these respective social groups. **1934** *Encycl. Social Sci.* XII. 48/2 The term peasantry has undergone many changes in meaning in the past and is still subject to various interpretations. Common to all the shifting meanings, however, is a view of the peasant as a tiller of the soil to whom the land which he and his family work offers both a home and a living. **1938** tr. *Lenin's Sel. Wks.* X. 223 The big peasants (*Grossbauern*) are the capitalist *entrepreneurs* in agriculture who.. employ several wage workers and are connected with the 'peasantry' only by their low cultural level, habits of life and the manual labour they themselves perform on their farms. These constitute the largest of the bourgeois strata, and they are the.. enemies of the revolutionary proletariat. **1948** A. L. KROEBER *Anthropol.* (rev. ed.) vii. 284 Peasants are definitely rural—yet live in relation to market towns; they form a class segment of a larger population which usually contains also urban centers, sometimes metropolitan capitals. **1951** BONNER & BURNS tr. *Marx's Theories of Surplus Value* B. v. 192 In the capitalist mode of production the independent peasant or handicraftsman is sundered into two persons. As owner of the means of production he is capitalist, as worker he is his own wage worker. **1954** tr. *Mao Tse-tung's Sel. Wks.* I. 139 The rich peasant as a rule possesses land... The exploitation the rich peasant practises is chiefly that of hired labour. *Ibid.*, In many cases the middle peasant possesses land. The middle peasant relies wholly or mainly on his own labour as the source of his income. *Ibid.* 140 As a rule the poor peasant has to rent land for cultivation and, exploited by others, has to pay land rent and interest on loans and hire out a small part of his labour. **1956** R. REDFIELD *Peasant Society & Culture* i. 27 Those peoples are to be included in the cluster I shall call peasants who have.. this in common: their agriculture is a livelihood and a way of life, not a business for profit. **1966** E. WOLF *Peasants* 3 Peasants.. are rural cultivators whose surpluses are transferred to a dominant group of rulers that uses the surpluses both to underwrite its own standard of living and to distribute the remainder to groups in society that do not farm but must be fed for their specific goods and services in turn. **1969** *Internat. Social Sci. Jrnl.* XXI. 286 A peasant may be at one and the same time owner, renter, share-cropper, labourer for his neighbours and seasonal hand on a near-by plantation. Each different involvement aligns him differently with his fellows and with the outside world. **1971** tr. E. Feder in T. Shanin *Peasants & Peasant Societies* vii. 90 But while the landed elite [in Latin America] has no interest in the peasants' aspirations and keeps aloof from their world, it is still keenly aware of its obligations to keep the peasants in check and subservient. **1975** J. A. HELLMAN tr. *Stavenhagen's Social Classes in Agrarian Societies* v. 65 A useful distinction is sometimes made between tribal peoples, peasants, and modern farmers... In contrast to tribal or primitive peoples, peasant societies do form part of wider economic, social, and political units.

β. **1511** GUYLFORDE *Pilgr.* (Camden) 64 The herde of the peysans and suche as they mette that alle thre Galeys were reiecte. **1523** CROMWELL in Merriman *Life & Lett.* (1902) I. 39 Victuaylys.. that.. by the diligence of the paysans myght be convaide to the next strong holdys. **1550** J. COKE *Eng. & Fr. Heralds* §66 (1877) 79 We knowe your commons be vylaynes paysynes, not able to abyde the countenaunce of an Englysheman. **1642** HOWELL *Twelve Treat.* (1661) 5 In France you shall see the poor Asinin Peasan half weary of his life. *a* **1656** USSHER *Ann.* (1658) 91 A few miserable boors, or paisans. **1690** LD. LANSDOWNE *Brit. Enchanters* (1779) 177 A rural dance of Païsans. **1801** C. WILMOT *Let.* 5 Dec. in

Irish Peer (1920) 9 We met a young Paysan Savant. **1872** *Young Englishwoman* Oct. 542/1 The *paysan* blouse, so much in fashion now, has brought into favour the plain broad stitched hem. **1891** E. Dowson *Let.* 1 July (1967) 206 This is the queerest little auberge imaginable, quite *paysan*, but full of excellent folk. **1949** W. Stevens *Let.* 13 Oct. (1967) 650, I shall feel sorry about paysans and tepid by the time this reaches you.

†**b.** With various inferential connotations: = Serf, villein; also boor, clown. *Obs.*

1550 Latimer *Last Serm. bef. Edw. VI* ¶3 They oppressed the poore. They made them slaues, pesauntes, villains and bondmen vnto them. **1570** Levins *Manip.* 25/16 A Pesant, *verna, seruus.* **1576** Fleming *Panopl. Epist.* 344 Defaced by a companie of bussardly pezantes. **1594** Nashe *Unfort. Trav.* Wks. (Grosart) V. 19 A number of pesants and varlets. **1613** R. Cawdrey *Table Alph.* (ed. 3), *Pesant*, clowne.

c. Hence, as a term of abuse (cf. *villain*): Low fellow, rascal. Now *slang*, usu. implying ignorance, stupidity, or boorishness. Cf. farmer[2] 7 c.

c **1550** *Disc. Common Weal Eng.* (1893) 94 The subiectes of france, in reproche of whome we call them paisantes. **1591** *Troub. Raigne K. John* (1611) 28 Base heardgroom, coward, peasant, worse than a threshing slaue. **1598** Shaks. *Merry W.* ii. ii. 294, I will predominate ouer the pezant, and thou shalt lye with his wife. **1601** Yarington *Two Lament. Traj.* iii. ii, Thou weathercocke of mutabilitie, White-livered Paisant. **1943** Baker *Dict. Austral. Slang* (ed. 3) 58 *Peasant*, an ordinary rank. (R.A.A.F. slang.) **1947** S. Bellow *Victim* i. 10 She showed such a dread of hospitals that at last he exclaimed, 'Don't be such a peasant, Elena!' **1957** *Sunday Mail* (Glasgow) 10 Feb. 11 *Peasant*—an older person who does not..understand the goings-on of teenagers. **1958** *Listener* 14 Aug. 247/3 People who dress conventionally are called [by teddy-boys] 'peasants'. **1961** G. Smith *Business of Loving* v. 161 Laura took me out riding... I'm a complete peasant in this, but she's an expert. **1964** G. Lyall *Most Dangerous Game* xix. 146 Alone? Of course I'm not alone, you—you peasant. D' you think I drive myself? **1966** H. Kemelman *Saturday the Rabbi went Hungry* (1967) iii. 27 Well, let the big boys worry, I'm just one of the peasants.

2. *attrib.* **a.** Appositive, That is a peasant, as ***peasant-boy, -farmer, girl, -novelist, owner, -poet, -proprietor, -soldier, tenant, woman, -worker***; †formerly, sometimes passing into adj.: Of peasant nature, base. Also derivatives of these, as ***peasant, farming, proprietorship, peasant-proprietary*** adj.

1852 Dickens *Bleak Ho.* xxxi. 307 Mr. Skimpole..sang one [*sc.* a ballad] about a *Peasant boy. **1862** H. Marryat *Year in Sweden* II. 391 A peasant-boy loved the daughter of a rich Odalbonde. **1848** Mill *Pol. Econ.* I. i. iv. 72 When a *peasant farmer or proprietor lives on the produce of his land. **1896** *Daily Tel.* 5 Feb. 6/7 This hardy race of peasant-farmers. **1906** *Daily Chron.* 21 Mar. 6/6 Of peasant-farmer stock, the elder Bunsen..became tutor in an English family. **1978** R. Mitchison *Life in Scotland* iii. 47 If a man had failed as a peasant farmer there might well be no work for him as a farm labourer. **1936** tr. *Lenin's Sel. Wks.* III. 183 Landlord farming evolves in a capitalist way... *Peasant farming is also evolves in a capitalist way and gives rise to a rural bourgeoisie and a rural proletariat. **1952** *Oxf. Jun. Encycl.* VI. 135/2 Peasant farming is the general rule in France, Germany, the countries of northern Europe, and all through central Europe, as well as in the greater part of Asia. **1883** C. M. Yonge *Stray Pearls* I. ix. 99 She kept the cows and knitted like a *peasant girl. **1915** D. H. Lawrence *Rainbow* x. 250 Peasant-girls with wreaths of blue flowers in their hair. **1976** Scott & Koski *Walk-In* (1977) xix. 124 The second [woman] giggled like some empty-headed peasant girl. **1702** Rowe *Tamerl.* iv. i. 1621 The *Peasant-Hind, begot and born to Slavery. *c* **1550** Crowley *Way to Wealth* B iij b, The pore men (whom ye cal *paisaunte knaues) haue deserued more then you can deuise to laie vpon them. **1907** *Westm. Gaz.* 21 Nov. 12/2 A new book by Peter Rosegger, the Styrian *peasant-novelist,..will be published on November 25. **1951** D. Mitrany *Marx against Peasant* xii. 201 In both countries [*sc.* France and Italy] the Communists have made great efforts to win influence in the countryside, especially among landless labourers and peasant tenants, who themselves hope to become *peasant owners. **1974** J. White tr. *Poulantzas's Fascism & Dictatorship* vi. i. 275 The small peasant owners are the 'rural petty bourgeoisie' *par excellence.* **1857** Bagehot *Coll. Wks.* (1965) II. 24 The eager *peasant-poet was at fault in the..refinements of the..drawing-room. **1903** *Westm. Gaz.* 25 Mar. 2/1 The *peasant-proprietary clauses did not work; rackrenting continued, evictions increased. **1794** A. Young *Trav. France* (ed. 2) I. xix. 542 *Caussade.*—This country is full of *peasant proprietors of land. **1899** G. B. Shaw *Let.* c 23–24 Dec. (1972) II. 121 You have to deal with a war [*sc.* the Boer war] declared by a peasant-proprietor State. **1974** *Encycl. Brit. Macropædia* VI. 1064/2 Indispensable though his [*sc.* the local craftsman's] services may be, they do not give him equality with his peasant-proprietor neighbours. **1878** Jevons *Primer Pol. Econ.* x. 88 One of the best modes of holding land..is..*peasant proprietorship. **1960** R. K. Webb *Harriet Martineau* xi. 338 The abuses of peasant proprietorship in France. **1974** *Encycl. Brit. Macropædia* VI. 256/1 In agriculture, peasant proprietorship or large private estates—particularly for export products—remained the general rule [in developing non-Communist countries]. **1602** Shaks. *Ham.* ii. ii. 576 Oh what a Rogue and *Pesant slaue am I. **1966** *Sociol. Rev.* XIV. 21 By cultural intercourse and intermixture, if not by indoctrination, the *peasant-soldier is taught to think in wide national, and not village-limited terms. **1978** D. Bloodworth *Crosstalk* xvi. 130 Wang, a peasant soldier..cunning in detail..but devoid of broad perception. **1951** *Peasant tenant [see *peasant owner* above]. **1856** Dickens *Dorrit* (1857) ii. i. 323 The child carried in a sling by the laden *peasant woman..was quieted with picked-up grapes. **1891** Hardy *Tess* II. v. xxv. 209 You are an unapprehending peasant woman. **1977** G. Butler *Brides of Friedberg* vi. 155 In the woods..a group of peasant women were gathering wood. **1962** E. Snow *Other Side of River: Red China Today* (1963) xviii. 134 Another *peasant-worker dictatorship was proclaimed as a local soviet on November 18 in an area far removed from Tsalin. **1972** H. C. Stevens tr. *Galeski's Basic Concepts Rural Sociol.* vii. 174 The most numerous social categories in the Polish village today are (1) peasant owners of family farms, and (2) the highly diversified category of 'peasant-workers', i.e. families living in the village and..combining work on a farm with regular employment outside the village.

b. Of or pertaining to a peasant or peasants, as ***peasant art, class, community, family, group, league, mind, revolution, society, style***; **peasant economy**, an economy in which the family is the basic unit of production.

1934 A. Huxley *Beyond Mexique Bay* 197 It is a typical semi-sophisticated *peasant art. **1961** L. G. G. Ramsey *Connoisseur New Guide Antique Eng. Pott., Porc. & Glass* 72 The simple vigour and ingenuousness of a 'peasant' art. **1866** *Chambers's Encycl.* VIII. 379/1 Communal government is the fundamental principle of all the rights of the *peasant class. **1954** B. & R. North tr. *Duverger's Pol. Parties* ii. i. 265 It [*sc.* the Communist party in the Soviet Union] liquidated the 'Kulaks' and the land-owning middle class, and for a long time it gave the working class of the towns preponderance over a peasant class that was actually more numerous. **1974** *Encycl. Brit. Macropædia* VIII. 1164/2 The [European feudal] aristocrats considered both their own and the peasant class to be permanent, God-given arrangements of hereditary status. **1951** R. Firth *Elem. Social Organiz.* v. 166 In various *peasant communities in parts of Africa..new art sanctions have been provided in modern workshops. **1974** *Encycl. Brit. Macropædia* VIII. 1164/1 In Africa, scattered peasant communities occur in the upland areas of the Mediterranean shore. *c* **1820** S. Rogers *Italy, Arguà* 34 Where in his *peasant-dress he loved to sit. **1951** R. Firth *Elem. Social Organiz.* iii. 87 The term peasant has primarily an economic referent. By a *peasant economy one means a system of small-scale producers, with a simple technology and equipment, often relying primarily for their subsistence on what they themselves produce. **1966** D. Thorner et al. *A. V. Chayanov on Theory of Peasant Econ.* p. v, The most sophisticated and best documented studies of the theory and problems of peasant economy in the half-century from 1880 to 1930 were written by Russians. **1975** J. A. Hellman tr. *Stavenhagen's Social Classes in Agrarian Societies* v. 65 Peasant economy tends towards self-sufficiency and the household is the main unit for production and consumption, based on the intensive use of family labor. **1926** E. & C. Paul tr. *Marx's Eighteenth Brumaire of L. Bonaparte* vii. 133 In so far as millions of families live in economic circumstances which distinguish their mode of life, their interests, and their culture, from those of other classes, and make them hostile to other classes, these *peasant families form a class. But in so far as the tie between the peasants is merely one of propinquity, and..the identity of their interests has failed to find expression in a community..or in a political organization, these peasant families do not form a class. **1974** tr. *Sniečkus's Soviet Lithuania* 75 Inefficient, semi-natural farms, unbearable tax burdens, and constant anxiety over the future—such was the lot of many, many peasant families. **1934** *Encycl. Social Sci.* XII. 52/2 Even within a single country such as Germany local differences—physiographic, economic, historical—make for a very considerable variation among *peasant groups. **1974** *Encycl. Brit. Macropædia* III. 151/1 Through illegal *peasant leagues, founded in the late 1950s, and legitimate rural unions, which were authorized in 1962, many [Brazilian] peasants were able for the first time to make their needs known to the political leaders. **1975** *New Left Rev.* Nov.–Dec. 65 Their peasant leagues performed well in the clerical dominated countryside. **1911** J. London *Let.* 8 Jan. (1966) 330 Charmian has no *peasant-mind. **1941** Wyndham Lewis *Let.* 22 Nov. (1963) 310 The stuffy conservatism of the land-locked peasant-mind. **1878** *N. Amer. Rev.* CXXVII. 171 The Tuscan *peasant-plays still performed in various parts of the province. **1974** M. B. Brown *Econ. of Imperialism* xiii. 327 We could still see bourgeois and *peasant revolutions which fall far short of socialism. **1949** E. Coxhead *Wind in West* vii. 176 Hermia ..would frequently deplore the Fascist trend latent in *peasant societies. **1964** Gould & Kolb *Dict. Social Sci.* 490/2 The term *peasant society* has long referred to Europe, changing in meaning as the industrial revolution has brought about changes in European life. Usage of the term ..has recently been extended to native populations of much of the world, especially as former primitive societies have come to resemble the old European peasantry. **1974** *Encycl. Brit. Micropædia* VII. 823/3 In peasant society ultimate control of the means of production is usually not in the hands of the primary producers. **1952** G. Bemrose *19th Cent. Eng. Pott. & Porc.* vi. 31 A good deal of our unlettered art, especially the so-called *peasant style, appears to lie dormant in our racial consciousness. **1973** *Times* 24 Aug. 2/2 She was wearing a cream-coloured peasant-style blouse with blue smocking at the neck and cuffs. **1597** Shaks. *2 Hen. IV* Induct. 33 This haue I rumour'd through the *peasant-Townes. **1813** W. S. Walker *Poems* 84 Recent from toil, the weary *peasant-train Reclined their languid limbs along the plain.

c. In crafts, fashion, etc.: in the style of articles produced by peasants or of clothes worn by them, as ***peasant blouse, dress, skirt, sleeve, tapestry, weave.***

1953 'T. Sturgeon' *More than Human* iii. 167 Janie in a *peasant blouse, with a straight spear of morning sunlight bent and moulded to her bare shoulder. **1963** 'E. McBain' *Ten plus One* (1964) xii. 137 She wore one of these very low-cut peasant blouses. **1970** *New Yorker* 15 Sept. 1 (Advt.), The cultivated *peasant dress is news. **1960** C. W. Cunnington et al. *Dict. Eng. Costume* 158/1 **Peasant skirt.* 1885. A full round tennis skirt made with 2 or 3 wide tucks and a fall of lace. **1965** 'M. Neville' *Ladies in Dark* viii. 74 She was wearing a peasant skirt and blouse. **1911** *Daily Colonist* (Victoria, B.C.) 8 Apr. 20/2 (Advt.), The new *peasant sleeves are featured in the waist part of these garments. **1900** *Archit. Rev.* June p. xxii/2 A twin bedstead ..is covered with *peasant tapestry designed by Mr. Godfrey Blunt. **1962** L. Deighton *Ipcress File* vii. 45 The rugs..of simple dark-toned peasant weaves. **1975** I. S. Black *Man on Bridge* v. 66 A *peasant-weave curtain covered the window.

3. *Comb.*, as ***peasant-shooting, peasant-born, -minded*** adjs.; ***peasant-like*** adj., like or proper to a peasant.

1600 Heywood *2nd Pt. Edw. IV*, Wks. 1874 I. 118 Pesant-like, vnheard-of treachery. **1703** Steele *Tend. Husb.* ii. i, What a Peasant-like Amour do these course Words import? **1844** P. Harwood *Hist. Irish Reb.* 145 To check the system of torture, house-burning, and peasant-shooting. **1886** W. J. Tucker *E. Europe* 303 The room..was..partly peasant-like in its appurtenances and partly burgher-like. **1895** *Westm. Gaz.* 5 Nov. 2/1 A grind of Greek grammar by night will not eliminate the peasant in the peasant-born. **1961** J. Barlow *Term of Trial* i. iii. 53 The louts are essentially peasant-minded about sex.

Hence **'peasantess**, a female peasant; **'peasanthood**, peasant quality or condition; **'peasantship**, peasanthood; a peasant community, a commune (Ger. *bauerschaft*).

1841 H. F. Chorley *Music & Manners* (1844) III. 88 Here were *peasantesses, presiding over their homely wares in enormous winged caps. **1889** tr. *Mme. Carette's Empress Eugénie* vii. 223 A handsome and strong peasantess was selected to nurse the Prince. **1830** *Examiner* 773/1 The homely dress she wore in the days of her *peasanthood. **1762** tr. *Busching's Syst. Geog.* IV. 339 These prefectures consist of parishes, and the parishes in them of *peasantships, which are properly small villages..in which many peasants reside together.

†**'peasant,** *v. Obs. rare.* [f. prec. sb.] *trans.* To make a peasant of; to subject as a peasant, bondman, or serf.

1599 Marston *Sco. Villanie* i. ii, But now (sad change!) the kennell sincke of slaues Pesant great Lords, and seruile seruice craues. *Ibid.* iii. xi, The now poore Soule (Thus pesanted to each lewd thoughts controule).

peasantism ('pɛzəntɪz(ə)m). [f. peasant *sb.* + -ism.] **a.** The doctrine that political power should be in the hands of the peasants; also = Narodnikism. Hence **'peasantist** *sb.* and *a.*

1894 P. Milyoukov in *Athenæum* 7 July 23/3 'Peasantism' [in Russia] puts its faith exclusively in the character and 'spirit' of the people. *Ibid.*, The programme of the 'peasantists' (*Narodnuichestvo*)..was subjected to analysis and discussion. *Ibid.*, Another section of our Radical party ..contributed much to the criticism of the 'peasantist' programme. **1963** *Times* 3 May 12/6 Colonel Turkesh listed nine principles which..constituted the doctrine of his group. Many of these appeared to be vague abstractions, including such curiosities as 'peasantism', 'freedomism', and 'developmentism'. **1969** G. Ionescu in Ionescu & Gellner *Populism* 99 Peasantism, born in Eastern Europe in the twentieth century,..takes the individual peasant explicitly as its social prototype..blends its social-economic doctrines with a strong nationalistic concern..and it claims that the peasantry is entitled as a class to the leadership of the political society. **1969** A. Walicki in *Ibid.* 104 Denmark was and remained the model..for most East European peasantists. *Ibid.* 106 A dictatorial peasantry-class of some of the peasantist régimes in power after the First World War (and especially that of Stambolisky in Bulgaria).

b. = peasanthood.

1901 M. Franklin *My Brilliant Career* v. 25 My parents ..had dropped from swelldom to peasantism.

c. A proposal or movement for the diffusion of art among the peasants.

1903 L. F. Ward *Pure Sociol.* 454 There is probably something in the doctrine of 'peasantism', which seeks to rescue art from the exclusive control of the leisure class.

peasantize ('pɛzəntaɪz), *v. rare.* [-ize.] *refl.* To make (oneself) into a peasant.

1904 G. S. Hall *Adolescence* II. 513 They go West, to the colonies, the slums; devise new enterprises, sometimes almost want to peasantize themselves and fall in love with wheel-grease and the smell of the barnyard.

peasantly ('pɛzəntlɪ), *a.* Now *rare* or *Obs.* [f. peasant *sb.* + -ly[1].] Of, pertaining to, or characteristic of a peasant or peasants.

1569 Stocker tr. *Diod. Sic.* ii. ix. 52 To pray and require suche paysauntlie slaues of passage and recourse. **1598** Dallington *Meth. Trav.* S j b, Vertue makes Nobility, for, there are noble Peasants, and peasantly Nobles. **1611** Cotgr., *Coteret*,..a kind of peasantlie weapon vsed in old time. **1659** *Gentl. Calling* v. §17 An opinion that it is a mean and peasantly thing for a gentleman to give himself the trouble of looking after his fortune. **1697** Collier *Immor. Stage* v. §3 (1730) 145 This Peasantly Expression [Sack-wine] agrees neither with the Gentleman's figure, nor with the rest of his behaviour.

peasantry ('pɛzəntrɪ). [f. as prec. + -ry.]

1. Peasants collectively; a body of peasants.

See peasant *sb.* 1 and note there.

a **1553** Edw. VI in Burnet *Hist. Ref.* (1681) II. Collect. Records 70 The Gentlemen and Servingmen..ought not.. to have so much as they have in France, where the Peasantry is of no value. **1622** Bacon *Hen. VII* 74 In France, and Italie, and some other Parts abroad, where in effect all is Noblesse, or Pesantrie. **1770** Goldsm. *Des. Vill.* 55 A bold peasantry, their country's pride, When once destroy'd, can never be supplied. **1817** Cobbett *Taking Leave* 6 The Labouring classes..are called, now-a-days, by these gentlemen, 'the peasantry'. This is a new term as applied to Englishmen. **1841** James *Brigand* iii, His garb was unlike that of the peasantry of Savoy. **1903** W. Raleigh *Wordsworth* 172 The peasantry—if that word may be used without prejudice to designate all those who live on the land by their own labour. **1933** E. & C. Paul tr. *Stalin's Leninism* II. 206 Why is the peasantry described [by Lenin] as the last capitalist class? Because of the two main classes of which our society is composed, the peasantry is a class whose economy is based on private property and small commodity production. Because the peasantry, as long as it remains a peasantry, living by small commodity production, will throw up capitalists from its ranks. **1934** *Encycl. Social Sci.* XII. 51/2 In the strongholds of European peasantry—the states formed in the western provinces of the former Russian Empire, the Danube basin and the Balkans—the peasants won a leading position after the World War when the great landed proprietors were compelled to surrender both their land and their dominant political status. **1936** tr. *Lenin's Sel. Wks.* III. 183 The better the condition of the 'commune', the greater the prosperity of the peasantry in general, the more rapid is the process of differentiation among the peasantry into antagonistic classes of capitalist agriculture. **1951** R. Firth *Elem Social Organiz.* iii. 87 It is this close economic and social..attachment to the soil that is historically one of the main distinguishing features of a European peasantry. **1964** A. R. Holmberg in H. F. Dobyns et al. *Peasants, Power, & Appl. Social Change* (1971) ii. 33 More than 50 percent of the world's population is peasantry, the large majority of which lives in the so-called underdeveloped countries or newly emerging nations, under natural conditions and social structures that have denied peasants effective participation in the modernization process. **1966** *Sociol. Rev.* XIV. 6 The peasantry consist of small producers on land who, with the help of simple equipment and the labour of their families, produce mainly for their own consumption, and for the fulfilment of their duties to the holders of political and economic power. **1966** E. Wolf *Peasants* 11 It is only when a cultivator is integrated into a new society with a state—that is, when the cultivator becomes subject to the demands and sanctions of power-holders outside his social stratum—that we can appropriately speak of peasantry. **1971** I. Deutscher *Marxism in our Time* i. 28 We see all over the West the disappearance of those middle classes that were supposed to constitute the conservative foundation of capitalism; of the small-owning, small-holding peasantry. **1975** J. A. Hellman tr. *Stavenhagen's Social Classes in Agrarian Societies* v. 66 For some students, peasantries are merely holdovers from pre-capitalist times, which tend to disappear as capitalism develops. While this may be the case in Western Europe, the situation in the underdeveloped countries is quite different. Here we still have hundreds of millions of peasants..who are well integrated into the colonial or underdeveloped capitalist system and who, if present trends continue, will maintain peasant characteristics for many generations.

2. a. The condition of being a peasant; the legal position or rank of a peasant (or German *Bauer*); the conduct or quality of a peasant, rusticity.

1596 Shaks. *Merch. V.* ii. ix. 46 (Qo. 1) How much low Peasantry would then be gleaned From the true seede of honour? and how much honour Pickt from the chaft..of the times. **1622** F. Markham *Bk. War* ii. ix. §2. 74 Colours so borne, shew Bastardy, peasantry, or dishonor. *a* **1680** Butler *Rem.* (1759) I. 332 Else, as a Gentleman, you could have never descended to such Peasantry of Language. **1762** tr. *Busching's Syst. Geog.* IV. 208 Whoever would appear at the Diet, must previously become a country-man, or assume the peasantry. **1824** Lamb *Elia* Ser. ii. *Blakesmoor*, Till, every dreg of peasantry purging off, I received into myself Very Gentility. **1937** *Observer* 17 Oct. 19/2, I find it hard to believe that anybody, having read or seen 'The Power of Darkness', would not instantly swear..to remove from himself any traces of peasantry that he might possess.

†**b.** A small territorial division in Germany (= Ger. *bauerschaft*); a commune. *Obs. rare.*

1762 tr. *Busching's Syst. Geog.* IV. 348 One hundred and twenty-one villageships [= *dorfschaften*] and peasantries [= *bauerschaften*].

'peasanty, *a.* [-y[1].] = peasantly *a.*

1933 *Times Lit. Suppl.* 8 June 400/2 Dark peasanty men. **1970** *Daily Tel.* 4 May 13 The peasanty voile top we've photographed over calico trousers is in fact sold as a mini dress.

peascod: see peasecod.

pease (pi:z), *sb.* Forms: 1 pise, (piose), 1, 4–5 pyse, 4–6 peose, peese, pees, 5 pes, *Sc.* pess, 5 (6 *Sc.*) peise, 6 *Sc.* peis, 6–7 peaze, 5–8 (9 *arch.*) pease; 6 pees, peas (also 7– in comb., and as pl. of pea[1]). *Pl.* α. 1 pisan, pysan, 2–6 pesen, 4 peosen, -un, 4–5 pesyn, 5 pesone, 5–6 peson, 6 peesen, peasyn, (paysen), 6–8 (9 *dial.* and *arch.*) peasen, peason. β. 4 peses, -is, 6 peeses. γ. 5–6 pese, 6– pease (as in sing.). [OE. *pise* (*piose*, *pyse*) wk. fem., pl. *pisan*, a. L. *pisa* (pl. -*æ*), late collateral form (4th c. in Palladius) of *pisum*, pl. pisa, a. Gr. πίσον, earlier πίσος, pulse, pease. In ME. *pēse*, pl. *pēsen*; 16th c. *pease*, pl. *peasen*, *peses*, *pease*. Through this reduction of the pl. to *pēse*, *pease* (identical with the sing.), which became at length in pronunciation equivalent to *pēs*, *peas*, the final sibilant was *c* 1600 taken for the plural *s* (*z*), and a new singular pea[1] arose, q.v.]

A. Illustration of Forms. **1.** Singular.

c **725** *Corpus Gloss.* (O.E.T.) 1208 *Lenticula*, piose. *c* **1000** *Sax. Leechd.* II. 190 Sum pyse cyn hatte lenticulas. *c* **1050** *Cotton Cleop. Gloss.* in Wr.-Wülcker 432/25 *Lenticula*, pise. **13..** *K. Alis.* 5959 A pese nys worth thi riche slaunder. **1362** Langl. *P. Pl.* A. vii. 155 A wastour..countede pers at a peose [1377 B. vi. 171 pees] and his plouh boþe. *c* **1380** *Sir Ferumb.* 5847 By Mahoun y nolde ȝyue a pyse, for cryst ne al ys myȝte. **1390**, *c* **1400** Pese [see B. 2]. **1483** *Cath. Angl.* 273/1 A Peise, *pisa.* **1530** Palsgr. 158 *Vne poyx*, a pees. **1580**, etc. Pease [see B. 2]. **1614** Raleigh *Hist. World* i. iv. §2 Of the bigness of a great Peaze.

2. Plural (and collective).

α. *c* **725** *Corpus Gloss.* (O.E.T.) 1586 *Pisum*, piosan. *c* **1000** *Sax. Leechd.* II. 180 Pisan..ȝesodena on ecede and on wætre. *c* **1200** *Vices & Virt.* 43 To eten benen and pesen. **1362** Langl. *P. Pl.* A. vii. 176 A potful of peosun. *Ibid.* 285 Poretes, and Peosen. *c* **1385** Chaucer *L.G.W.* 648 *Cleopatra*, He pouryth pesyn vp on the hachis. *c* **1420** *Liber Cocorum* (1862) 45 Take boyled water..Sethe in þy pesone. **1523** in *Visit. Southwell* (Camden) 121 My tuffall of paysen. **1533** Elyot *Cast. Helthe* ii. (1541) 25 b, Peasyn are muche in the nature of beanes. **1542** Udall *Erasm. Apoph.* 90 To take up peasen out of yᵉ potte. **1545** Pesen [see B. 2]. **1553**, **1573** Peson [see B. 1]. *c* **1578** Frobisher in *Proc. Rec. Comm.* (1833) 561 But one hoggsed of rottyn pesons wᶜʰ hogges wolde not eytte. **1777** *Poor Robin* (N.), Cherries, gooseberries, and green peasen. **1829** Hone *Poor Humphrey's Cal.* May, This month Mackarel comes in season; And also reckon upon peason. **1880** Browning *Pietro of Abano* xliii, A taste..which—craving manna—kecks at peason.

β. **1377** Langl. *P. Pl.* B. vi. 189 A potful of peses. *c* **1380** Wyclif *Serm.* Sel. Wks. II. 71 Pesis ben divers from whete. *c* **1532** Du Wes *Introd. Fr.* in Palsgr. 915 Peeses, *pois.*

γ. *c* **1400** Maundev. (1839) xi. 129 Thare groweth..ne benes, ne pese. *Ibid.* (Roxb.) xxvi. 123 þai hafe nowþer peise ne wortes. *c* **1420** *Liber Cocorum* (1862) 19 Take whyte pese and wasshe hom wele. *c* **1440** *Alph. Tales* (E.E.T.S.) 241 If ye fynd þar cale & peas & benys, & no noder meatt. **1479** *Acta Dom. Concil.* (1839) 46/1, iiij bolle pess. **1508** Dunbar *Flyting w. Kennedie* 115 Thow lay full prydles in the peise. **1523** Fitzherb. *Husb.* §10 Thy beanes..wolde ranker grounde than pease. *Ibid.* §12 Two busshels of gray pees. **1596** Dalrymple tr. *Leslie's Hist. Scot.* i. 89 Sum vset breid of ry,..sum of peise or beanes. **1681** [see B. 2]. **1849** H. Stephens *Bk. Farm* I. 2456 Pease are sown by hand.

B. Signification. The earlier form of pea[1], q.v.

1. The plant, pea[1] 2. With defining word, applied also to other leguminous plants, as ***everlasting pease***, etc.: see pea[1] 3.

c **1000** [see A. 1]. *c* **1380** [see A. 2 β]. **14..** *Metr. Voc.* in Wr.-Wülcker 625/13 Ordium, faba, pisa, [*glossed*] barlyche, beene, pyse. *c* **1425** *Voc.* ibid. 664/22 *Hec pisa*, pese. *Hec faba*, bene. **1481** Caxton *Myrr.* ii. viii. 80 In this contree [Perse] groweth a pese which is so hoot that it skaldeth the handes of them that holde it. **1551** Turner *Herbal* i. P iij b, The herbe whiche groweth in woddes..with floures lyke vnto a pease. **1553** T. Wilson *Rhet.* (1580) 54 It yeldeth nothing els but Wheate, Barley, Beanes, and Peason. **1634** Sir T. Herbert *Trav.* 182 Carauances or Indian Pease. **1676** Grew *Anat. Leaves* ii. §9 The Leaves of Beans and Peasen. **1678** Phillips (ed. 4) s.v., That sort called Pease Everlasting, hath a very fine flower or blossom. **1795** Burke *Th. Scarcity* Wks. VII. 408 My ground under pease did not exceed an acre..but the crop was great.

2. a. A single seed, a pea (pea[1] 1). *Obs.* or *arch.* Often used as a standard in comparison of size.

c **1000**, *c* **1200**, **1362**, *c* **1385** [see A. 2 a]. **1390** Gower *Conf.* II. 275 He wol ayeinward take a bene, Ther he hath lent the smale pese. *c* **1400** Maundev. (1839) xiv. 158 Men fynden summe [Dyamandes] as grete as a pese. **1545** Raynold *Byrth Mankynde* 69 Make pylles of them to the byggenesse of pesen. **1580** Lyly *Euphues* Ep. Ded. (Arb.) 215 As lyke as one pease is to an other. **1632** B. Jonson *Magn. Lady* v. v, I'll cleanse him with a pill, as small as a pease. **1649** A. Ross *Alcoran* 406 A Pigeon being by him taught to come and pick a Pease out of his ear. **1678** J. Phillips *Tavernier's Trav.* ii. xv. 183 A few flat Peason, bruis'd, and steep'd half an hour in water. **1681** T. Flatman *Heraclitus Ridens* No. 37 (1713) I. 240 Rebellion and Witchcraft are as like as two Pease. **1713** Derham *Phys.-Theol.* viii. vi. (1727) 387 *note*, It grows bigger, to the size of a large white Pease. **1885–94** R. Bridges *Eros & Psyche* Sept. ix, A little bleb, no bigger than a pease.

†**b.** As a type of something of very small value or importance. *Obs.*

13.., **1362**, *c* **1380** [see A. 1]. *a* **1400–50** *Alexander* 2370 Loke quare it profet þam a peese, all þaire proud strenth. **1534** More *Comf. agst. Trib.* ii, Al our penaunce without Christes passion wer not worth a pease. *c* **1550** R. Bieston *Bayte Fortune* A iv, Not worthy two peason. **1598** T. Bastard *Chrestoleros* (1880) 52 He learned Logicke and Arithmetique. Yet neither brauls nor ciphers worth a peaze.

c. ***green pease***, †***peasen*** = *green peas*: see pea[1] 1 b. Also the name of a variety green when ripe.

c **1440** *Anc. Cookery* in *Househ. Ord.* (1790) 426 Take yonge grene pesen, and sethe hom. **1496** *Naval Acc. Hen. VII* (1896) 166 Green pesyn at viijᵈ the bussell. **1620** Venner *Via Recta* vii. 133 There are three sorts of Pease..the white-Pease, the gray-Pease, and the greene-Pease. The two first are vsually eaten greene before they be ripe. **1651–7** T. Barker *Art of Angling* (1820) 4 About the bigness of a green pease. **1789** Mrs. Piozzi *Journ. France* II. 191 Scarce have you tasted green pease or strawberries, before they are out of season. **1833** Ht. Martineau *Berkeley the Banker* i. v. 98 They were quite used to pluck green pease.

†**3.** *pl.* The eggs or spawn of fishes: see pea[1] 4.

1398 Trevisa *Barth. De P.R.* xiii. xxvi. (Bodl. MS.), þe female leyeþ egges oþer pesen. *Ibid.*, Alle þe egges oþer pesen [that] beþ itouched wiþ þe mylke of þe male schal be fisch.

†**4.** = *issue-pea*: see issue *sb.* 16. *Obs.*

1694 Salmon *Bate's Dispens.* iii. (1713) 718/2 *Pisa Rubra*, Red Pease... These are stronger than the former, and attract Humors more powerfully.

5. *attrib.* and *Comb.*, as ***pease-bannock***, ***-bloom***, ***-blossom*** (also *attrib.*), ***-cart***, ***-earth***, ***-field***, ***-haulm***, ***-hull*** (***-hole***, ***-hele***, ***-hule***, hull *sb.*[1] 1), ***-porridge***, ***-pottage*** (also *attrib.*), ***-pudding***, ***-rick***, ***-stack***, ***-swad***; ***pease-fed***, ***pease-like*** adjs.; **pease-bolt** = *pease-straw* (*obs.* or *dial.*); †**pease-bread**, bread made of pease-meal; **pease-brose**: see brose b; †**pease-earthnut**, the heath-pea; †**pease-eddish**, **pease-etch**, pea-stubble: see eddish 2, etch *sb.*[1]; **pease-hook** = *pea-hook* (pea[1] 7); †**pease-hooker** = prec. (*obs.*); †**pease-loaf**, a loaf of pease-bread (*obs.*); **pease-make, -meak** (*dial.*), an implement with a long handle and a crooked iron at the end, used to pull up peas, = meak *sb.*; **pease-meal**, meal made by grinding peas; also *fig.* a medley, 'mess' (quot. 1820); †**pease-rise, -straw, -stubble** = *pea-rise*, etc.: pea[1] 7. Also peasecod.

1824 Scott *St. Ronan's* xvii, Breaking them [long fasts] with sour milk and *pease bannock. **1675** Lister in *Phil. Trans.* X. 391 They call the second sort the **Pease-bloom Damp*, because, as they say, it smells like Pease-bloom. **1590** Shaks. *Mids. N.* iii. i. 189 *Bot.* Your name honest Gentleman? *Peas.* *Pease blossome. [**1774**: see *pea-blossom*, pea[1] 7]. **1807** W. Irving *Salmag.* (1824) 355 Airing their..pease-blossom breeches. **1573** Tusser *Husb.* (1878) 45 With strawisp and *peasebolt, with ferne and the brake, For sparing of fewel, some brewe and do bake. **1674** Ray *S. & E.C. Words* 74 *Pease-bolt*, i.e. Pease-straw, *Ess.* *c* **1425** *Voc.* in Wr.-Wülcker 657/28 *Panis pisacius*, *pesbred. **1601** Dent *Pathw. Heaven* 91 Hee [the covetous man] will eat pease bread, and drinke small drinke. **1811** W. Aiton *Gen. View Agric. Ayr* 271 A few [late peas] are thrown in among the beans when sown broad-cast. They are..made into meal for a species of pottage called '*pease-brose'. **1861** R. Leighton *Rhymes & Poems* (ed. 2) 12 'Pease Brose to dinner! brose alone! With neither boil nor stew! But say, what did you breakfast on?' They answer '*Pease Brose too.*' **1922** R. Thomas *Sandie McWhustler's Waddin'* v. 52 He was sittin' in his sark sleeves an' suppin' his pease-brose. *c* **1965** *Rebels Ceilidh Song Bk.* No. 2. 15 It'll be pease brose again. **1593** Nashe *Four Lett. Confut.* Wks. (Grosart) II. 232 They mounted into the *pease-cart in Cheape-side and preacht. **1616** Surfl. & Markh. *Country Farme* 550 Neither is it ever sown upon the fallowes, but upon the *Pease-earth. **1548** Turner *Names of Herbes* 18 Astragalus..may be called in english *peaserthnut. **1693** Robinson in *Phil. Trans.* XVII. 826 *Lathyrus tuberosus*, call'd..Pease-Earthnut, digg'd up and eaten by the poor People. **1804** Duncumb *Herefordsh.* Gloss., **Peas-eddis*, peas-stubble. **1886** Elworthy *W. Somerset Word-bk.*, *Pease-errish*. **1573** Tusser *Husb.* (1878) 47 White wheat vpon *peaseetch doth grow as he wold, But fallow is best. *Ibid.* 45 Fat *peasefed swine. **1716** B. Church *Hist. Philip's War* (1865) I. 31 They..got..unto the Fence of Capt. Almy's *Pease-field. **1432** in Gross *Gild Merch.* II. 233 *Pesehalme 1d. **1664** Evelyn *Kal. Hort.* (1729) 197 Cover with dry Straw, or Pease-hame. **1858** Glenny *Gard. Every-day Bk.* 223/2 Peas-haulm makes an excellent litter. **1674–91** Ray *S. & E.C. Words*, *Meag*, or *Meak*, a *pease-hook. **1769** *De Foe's Tour Gt. Brit.* II. 209 They are now lost, or converted to other Uses, even literally to Plough-shares and Pease-hooks. [**1833**: see *pea-hook*, pea[1] 7.] **1641** Best *Farm. Bks.* (Surtees) 57 Then doe wee seeke out our *pease-hookers, grinde them [etc.]. **1377** Langl. *P. Pl.* B. vii. 194, I sette ȝowre patentes and ȝowre pardounz at one *pies hele! [*v.rr.* pese hule, peese hole]. **1664** J. Wilson *Projectors* 111, From the Pease-Hulls in the Kennel, the Invention of Shiping. [**1717**–: see *pea-hull*, pea[1] 7.] **1629** Parkinson *Parad. in Sole* 338 Purplish *pease-like blossomes. **1725** Bradley *Fam. Dict.* s.v. *Lupin*, The Pease-like Sort of Seeds. [**1774**–: see *pea-like*, pea[1] 7.] **1362** Langl. *P. Pl.* A. vii. 166 Hongur..beot so þe boyes, he barst neih heore ribbes, Nedde Pers wiþ a *peose lof I-preyed him to leue. **1765** *Chron.* in *Ann. Reg.* 117/1 They fell upon [them] with such arms as they had, *pease-makes, hedge-stakes, etc. [**1834**: see *pea-make*, pea[1] 7.] **1820** *Blackw. Mag.* VII. 469 Nothing but a *peasemeal of clishmaclavers. [**1830**: see *pea-meal*, pea[1] 7.] **1842** J. Aiton *Domest. Econ.* (1857) 235 Give barley-meal or pease-meal, but not bean-meal. **1538** Bale *Thre Lawes* 1566 They loue no *pese porrege, nor yet reade hearynges in lent. **1587** Harrison *England* ii. vii. (1877) i. 172 Hewes..as..pease porrige tawnie. **1669** Pepys *Diary* 7 Apr., This house being famous for good meat, and particularly pease-porridge. **1605** Armin *Foole upon F.* (1880) 38 In Lent, when *pease pottage bare great sway. *Ibid.*, Thus simple Iohn..dyed the inside of his pocket, pease pottage tawny. **1670** Eachard *Cont. Clergy* 20 [He] had much better chuse to live with nothing but beans and pease-pottage. **1758** Johnson *Idler* No. 33 ⁋20 *Pease-pudding not boiled enough. **1841** J. T. Hewlett *Parish Clerk* I. 165 The roads were better, and not so much like peas-pudding. **1530** Palsgr. 252/2 *Pease reke, *pesiere.* [**1766**: see *pea-rick*, pea[1] 7.] *c* **1325** *Gloss. W. de Bibbesw.* in Wright *Voc.* 154 *Un warrok de peys*, a *pese rys. [**1780**: see *pea-rise*, pea[1] 7.] **1546–7** *Test. Ebor.* (Surtees) VI. 254 The *pese stacke that I have bought. *c* **1325** *Gloss. W. de Bibbesw.* in Wright *Voc.* 156 *De pessas*, *pese stree. **1580** Tusser *Husb.* (1878) 134 Choose skilfullie Saltfish..goe stack it vp drie, With peasestrawe betweene it, the safer to lie. **1844** H. Stephens *Bk. Farm* II. 375 An ox will eat pease-straw as greedily as he will hay. **1523** Fitzherb. *Husb.* §34 In some places they sowe theyr wheate vppon theyr *pees stubble. [**1807**: see *pea-stubble*, pea[1] 7.]

†**pease,** *v.* *Obs.* Forms: 3–5 paise(n, payse(n, 3–6 peyse(n, 4–5 pese(n, pees, 5 peese, (pesse), 5–6 pease, 6–7 peaze, (7 peece). [ME. *paise-n*, a. OF. *paise-r*, *paisie-r*, f. *pais*, peace *sb.*]

1. *trans.* To make peace between, reconcile (two persons, or one person *with* another).

c **1275** Lay. 8783 þenche of mine neode And paise [*c* 1205 sæhtne] me wiþ Romleode. **1297** R. Glouc. (Rolls) 12029 Vor þis trespas He ȝef þe king tuelf hundred marc & ipaised was. *a* **1300** *Cursor M.* 17083 Ur blisced leuedi nu be And pais us wit þi suet sun. *a* **1400–50** *Alexander* 5362, I prai þe ..pesse now my childire. *Ibid.* 5379 þus ware þai bath pesed. **1485** Caxton *Chas. Gt.* 215 He peased them & accorded. *a* **1652** Brome *Mad Couple* i. i. Wks. 1873 I. 2 He has..peec'd me with my Unkle.

b. *intr.* To make peace, be reconciled.

1297 R. Glouc. (Rolls) 3371 þo he adde diȝt al þat he wolde & ypaised [*v.r.* paysed] wiþ is fon. **1611** Speed *Hist. Gt. Brit.* ix. vii. §17 The two Kings peaced againe, and setled a new..league.

2. *trans.* To quell the wrath or hostility of, to appease (a person); to satisfy, content. Also, to calm the feelings of, quiet, pacify.

1303 R. Brunne *Handl. Synne* 12060 Shryfte..peseth God whan he ys wroþe. *c* **1440** *Promp. Parv.* 395/1 Peesyn, or styllyn of wrethe. **1480** Caxton *Chron. Eng.* vii. (1520) 157/1 For to peas the comyns the Duke of Suffolke was exyled. **1526** Tindale *Matt.* xxviii. 14 And yf this come to the rulers eares, we wyll pease him, and make you safe. **1548** Udall, etc. *Erasm. Par. John* Pref. 5 Whiche doeth so peyse the minde that it be not tossed. **1561** Norton & Sackv.

Gorboduc III. i, Their death and myne must peaze the angrie Gods.

3. To make satisfaction or amends for. *rare.*

1303 R. BRUNNE *Handl. Synne* 5570 And þey mowe peyse here dedys ylle.

4. To reduce to peace, set at rest, still, quell, appease (strife, wrath, etc.). Also, to quiet, calm, still, pacify (sorrow or violent feeling).

c **1330** R. BRUNNE *Chron.* (1810) 97 þus gate was þat werre pesed. *c* **1386** CHAUCER *Manciple's Prol.* 98 (Harl. MS.) For þat wol torne rancour and desese To accord and loue and many rancour pese [so *Corp., Lansd.; Ellesm. etc.* apese]. **1483** CAXTON *Gold. Leg.* 427 b/2 To pease alle dyscordaunce and stryf. **1541** BECON *News out of Heaven* Early Wks. (Parker Soc.) 49 Able to pease the divine wrath.

5. To reduce (a country or community) to a state of peace or tranquillity; to pacify.

c **1340** *Cursor M.* 8372 (Gött.) þe kingriche..þu had gret malese For to stabil it and to pese [*other MSS.* in þin pes]. **1497** BP. ALCOCK *Mons Perfect.* C iij b, Obedyence..peasith all yᵉ worlde. *a* **1548** HALL *Chron., Hen. V* 70 (*Art. Peace* c. 7) That realme..to be defended, peased and gouerned after right and equitie.

6. To reduce to stillness or silence; to quiet.

c **1330** R. BRUNNE *Chron. Wace* (Rolls) 11549 When þe noyse was wel pesed. **1340** HAMPOLE *Pr. Consc.* 4320 He sal trobel the se..And pees it and make it be stille. *c* **1450** *Ihesu, Mercy* 113 in *Pol. Rel. & L. Poems* (1866) 106 Ful gret clamour þan gon þou pese. **1526** TINDALE *Acts* xv. 12 The multitude was peased and gaue audience.

b. *intr.* (for *refl.*) To become still.

a **1400-50** *Alexander* 4159 Sone as þe wedire wex wele & þe wynde pesid.

Hence †'**peasing** *vbl. sb. Obs.*

c **1275** LAY. 11664 þe wise of þisse londe Makede paisinge [*c* 1205 hustinge]. **1425** *Rolls of Parlt.* IV. 268/2 For þe pesinge of diverse cleymes. *c* **1440** *Promp. Parv.* 395/1 Peesynge, or qwemynge, *pacificacio.* **1629** WOTTON *Let. to Sir E. Bacon* in *Reliq.* (1672) 445 The King of Spain, upon the peazing of his affairs in Italy..was resolved [etc.].

pease, obs. f. PEACE, PEISE *v.* and *sb.*, PIECE.

peasecod, peascod ('piːzkɒd). Now *arch.* or *dial.* Forms: 4 **pees-**, 4-6 **pese-**, 4-7 **pes-**, 5 **peys-**, 4-6 **-codde, -code**, 5-7 **-cod**, 6- **peasecod**, 7- **peascod.** [f. PEASE *sb.* + COD *sb.*¹] The pod or legume of the pea-plant; a pea-pod.

1362 LANGL. *P. Pl.* A. VII. 279 Al þe pore peple pesecoddes fetten. **1415** HOCCLEVE *To Sir J. Oldcastle* 466 The worm for to sleen in the pesecod. **1522** SKELTON *Why not to Court* 108 They may garlycke pyll..Or pescoddes they may shyll. **1600** SHAKS. *A.Y.L.* II. iv. 52, I remember the wooing of a peascod instead of her. **1755** SMOLLETT *Quix.* (1803) IV. 72 A post that will not afford victuals, is not worth a peasecod. **1794** COLERIDGE *Parl. Oscill.*, One peasecod is not liker to another. **1878** HUXLEY *Physiogr.* 220 The pea that may be extracted from a ripe peascod.

†**b.** In mock imprecations. *Obs.*

1606 DAY *Ile of Guls* V. i. (1881) 98 Not come! a pescod on him! **1652** URQUHART *Jewel* Wks. (1834) 218 Ho now! pescods on it, Crauford Lord Lindsay puts me in minde of him.

c. *attrib.* and *Comb.*, as *peasecod-cart*; †**peasecod ale**, (?); **peasecod-bellied** *a.*, epithet of a doublet fashionable about the end of the 16th century, having the lower part stiffly quilted and projecting; shotten-bellied; (also **peasecod-doublet**); **peasecod boat**, a boat resembling a peasecod (cf. PEA-POD 2); **peasecod-cuirass**, a cuirass made like the *peasecod-bellied doublet*; †**peasecod-plum**, name of some variety of plum; †**peasecod-time**, the season for peas; †**peasecod-tree**, the BEAN-TREFOIL or *Anagyris.*

1562 J. HEYWOOD *Prov. & Epigr.* (1867) 144 Thy tales taste all of ale. Not of *pescod ale, syr, my tales are not stale. **1846** FAIRHOLT *Costume* 263 The long-breasted doublets.. were carried down to a long peak in front, from whence they obtained the name of '*peascod-bellied' doublets. **1898** VISCT. DILLON in *Archæol. Jrnl.* Ser. II. V. 313 The peasecod-bellied doublet is reproduced in steel. **16..** DAVENANT, Step into one of your *peascod boats, whose tilts are not so sumptuous as the roofs of gundaloes. **1715** tr. *C'tess D'Anois' Wks.* 374 You would have thought him some Draught-Horse taken from a *Pease-cod Cart. **1597** SHAKS. *2 Hen. IV*, II. iv. 413, I haue knowne thee these twentie nine yeeres, come *Pescod-time. **1611** COTGR., *Anagyre*, the plant called Beane Trifolie, or *Pescod tree.

peasen, peason, obs. or dial. pl. of PEASE.

peaseweep: see PEESWEEP.

pea-soup. Also pease-soup. [f. PEASE *sb.*, PEA¹ + SOUP.] **a.** A soup made from peas. Also *attrib.* (chiefly in reference to its usual dull yellow colour and thick consistency), esp. as *pea-soup fog* (also *absol.*)

1711 SWIFT *Jrnl. to Stella* 21 Apr., I refused ham and pigeons, pease-soup, stewed beef. **1828** P. CUNNINGHAM *N.S. Wales* (ed. 3) II. 205 With a sort of pea-soup complexion. **1835** *Gentl. Mag.* Dec. 629/2 Mr. Effingham Wilson's pea-soup and porter dinners. **1849** H. MELVILLE *Jrnl. Visit to London & Continent* (1948) 45 Upon sallying out this morning encountered the oldfashioned pea soup London fog. **1887** *S. Austral. Advertiser* 8 Jan. 4/7 A month or two ago London experienced a succession of 'pea-soup fog' days. **1899** *Westm. Gaz.* 15 Mar. 2/3 A peasoup fog in March is going a little too far in the way of meteorological jokes. **1965** MRS. L. B. JOHNSON *White House Diary* 7 Apr. (1970) 256 We flew in pea soup and uncertainty. **1976** J. LEE *Ninth Man* 10 He couldn't see more than fifteen or twenty feet through this pea soup. **1978** 'M. M. KAYE' *Far Pavilions* xix. 283 Londoners groping through a pea-soup fog.

b. A French Canadian; the French spoken in Canada. *N. Amer. slang.*

1896 G. PARKER *Pomp of Lavilettes* 60 Yes, an' dey call us Johnny Pea-soups. **1912** B. HEENEY *Pickanock* 22 Pea-soup! I never drink with the likes of you, Pauquett! **1931** 'D. STIFF' *Milk & Honey Route* iii. 38 A Canadian Frenchman is a 'Canuck' or sometimes a 'pea soup'. **1937** PARTRIDGE *Dict. Slang* 612/1 *Talk pea-soup*, to talk French-Canadian. **1945** H. MACLENNAN *Two Solitudes* 49 Listen, you goddam peasoup, you're too fast with your mouth. **1959** J. W. GODSELL *I was no Lady* x. 170 I'm going to the Halfway right now to fix that damned Pea-soup. **1965** *Globe & Mail* (Toronto) 13 Oct. 6/3 Our childhood forays in Ottawa between pea-soup and English-speaking gangs.

Hence '**pea-,soupy** *a. colloq.*, resembling pea-soup (said esp. of a thick yellow fog).

1860 RUSSELL *Diary in India* II. i. 6 Half-an-hour or so had passed away in a sort of dreamy, pea-soupy kind of existence. **1883** W. SHARP in *Gd. Words* Nov. 723/2 The 'pea-soupy' character so distinctive of those [fogs] in cities.

pea-'souper. *colloq.* [f. PEA-SOUP + -ER¹.]

1. A pea-soupy or thick yellow fog. Also *pea-souper fog.*

1890 J. PAYN *Notes from 'News'* 8 The fogs we have had this year have been made too much of... You could see something in them if you looked long enough, which is not the case of a genuine Peasouper. **1907** *Daily Chron.* 30 Nov. 4/4 A country cousin who wishes to see and breathe and mingle in a metropolitan pea-souper. **1926** *Chambers's Jrnl.* Mar. 192/1 The fog..became dense—a real pea-souper. **1954** M. SHARP *Gipsy in Parlour* v. 62 The coal-burning London of my childhood was undoubtedly foggier than the London of to-day: the legend of the pea-souper, like all legends, has roots in fact. **1973** H. CARVIC *Miss Seeton Sings* (1974) 196 Fog had clamped down on Paris... The scene reminded Miss Seeton of the London pea-soupers of her childhood. **1975** G. HOWELL *In Vogue* 4/2 There were high prices and strikes, peasouper fogs, and precious little coal. **1978** *Jrnl. R. Soc. Arts* CXXVI. 490/2 Pea-souper fogs are no longer experienced in London or in other cities.

2. = PEA-SOUP b.

1942 BERREY & VAN DEN BARK *Amer. Thes. Slang* §385/5 Pea-souper, *a French-Canadian.* **1962** *Maclean's Mag.* 2 June 51/2 And *then* we can highstick those pea-soupers. **1966** [see JOE *sb.*² 7]. **1968** P. C. NEWMAN *Distemper of our Times* xix. 257 You're selling Canada to the pea-soupers!

peasse, variant of PEISE *Obs.*

peastone ('piːstəʊn). [f. PEA¹ + STONE *sb.*] A variety of limestone consisting of large rounded grains like peas; also called PISOLITE.

1821 URE *Dict. Chem.*, *Peastone*, a variety of Limestone. **1876** PAGE *Adv. Text-bk. Geol.* xvii. 311 Pisolite or peastone when the grains are large and pea-like.

peasy ('piːzɪ), *a.* [f. PEASE *sb.* + -Y.]

1. *Sc.* Abounding in or composed of peas, as *peasy bannock.*

2. a. Of the size of peas. **b.** Of the appearance, colour, etc. of peas or pease-meal.

1778 PRYCE *Min. Cornub.* Gloss. s.v. *Jigging*, In the Lead Mines, the Jigged Ore goes by the name of *Peasy.* **1812** SOUTER *Surv. Banffsh.* 57 A granite, called *peasywhin*, is found in large blocks near the surface of the moors.

peat¹ (piːt). Forms: 3-6 **pete**, (5-6 **pett**, 5-7 **pet**), 5-9 **peet**, 6-7 *Sc.* **peit(t**, 6- **peat.** [In 13th c. *pete*, in Anglo-L. *peta*, known from *c* 1200 in Scoto-Latin documents, where, like the associated *turba* 'turf', it was app. from the vernacular. Origin unknown: see *Note* below.]

1. a. (With *a* and *pl.*) A piece of the substance described in sense 2, cut of a convenient form and size for use as fuel, usually roughly brick-shaped. (Chiefly *Sc.* and *north. dial.*)

[*c* **1200** in *Liber de Melros* (Bann. Cl.) 76 Tantum terre mee..ubi sufficienter possint exsiccare petas suas et.. liberum transitum..ad ipsas petas abducendas. **1262** in *Charters &c. of Peebles* (1872) 5 Jurati dixerunt quod burgenses de Pebblys foderunt petas suas in petaria de Waltamshope. **1278** *Durham Acc. Rolls* (Surtees) 488 Henrico de Horneby et Emerico ad petas fodiendas et cariandas, 60s. **1299** *Ibid.* 500 In 163 carratis petarum cariandis 39s. 8d.] **1333** *Patent Roll 7 Edw. III*, I. m. 24 Redditum octo carectarum turbarum que dicuntur petes cum pert' in Skypwyth. *c* **1400** *Burgh Laws* c. 35 (*Sc. Stat.* I) Na man aw to punde..þaim at bryngis wodd or petys bot for wodd or petys. **1497** *Acc. Ld. High Treas. Scot.* I. 344 Item, for petis and colis to the schip..viijs. vjd. **1538** LELAND *Itin.* V. 91 Oftentimes in diggin in this Mosse for Petes or Turves they finde the hole Trees. **1572** *Satir. Poems Reform.* xxxii. 19 With Peittis, with Turuis, and mony turse of Hedder. **1607** NORDEN *Surv. Dial.* 182 Those that are first cut vp, are called *Turffes* of the vpper part, and such as are taken downward, are called *Peates.* **1610** HOLLAND *Camden's Brit.* I. 542 It yeeldeth Pets in the mores. **1710** in *Phil. Trans.* XXVII. 300 It does now afford good Peats. **1818** SCOTT *Hrt. Midl.* xxix, I often wish there was a het peat doun their throats. **1873** BLACK *Pr. Thule* i, He stirred up the blazing peats in the fire-place. *Ibid.* xviii, I asked you to bring one peat, and of course you brought two.

†**b.** A turf or sod in general. *Obs.*

1570 LEVINS *Manip.* 212/16 A Peate, *cespes.* **1612** HEYWOOD *Apol. for Actors* I. 22 Of turfe and heathy sods to make their seates, Framed, in degrees, of earth and mossy peates. **1638-48** G. DANIEL *Eclog.* i. 314 Their Corps are Covered with green Peats, The place full sett with flowers.

2. Vegetable matter decomposed by water and partially carbonized by chemical change, often forming bogs or 'mosses' of large extent, whence it is dug or cut out, and 'made' into peats (in sense 1).

1428 in Sir W. Fraser *Wemyss of W.* (1888) II. 56 To wyn and ger laboure..turfe pete and hathir..quharsumeuir thai may be fundin wythin the said landis. **1626** BACON *Sylva* §775 Turfe and Peat and Cow-sheards are cheape Fuel. **1652** FRENCH *Yorksh. Spa* i. 2 An unctuous bituminous earth, which the country People cut.., making Turfe, and Peate thereof. **1754** BURT *Lett. N. Scotl.* xviii, In digging of Peat, there have been found Fir-trees of a good magnitude. **1803** WALKER in *Trans. Highl. Soc. Scot.* II. 3 Peat is a word used in Scotland and the north of England, but seldom to be found, till of late years, in English authors. **1878** HUXLEY *Physiogr.* 233 Accumulations of partially decomposed vegetable matter form the substance known as peat or turf.

3. A dark brown resembling the colour of peat.

1971 *Homes & Gardens* Sept. 84 Quite a lot of dark browns (anything from donkey to peat.) **1975** *Times* 7 Oct. 11/4 Long-sleeve sweater..in colours loganberry, peat, brown, and mid-blue. **1978** *Country Life* 16 Nov. 1685/1 There is nothing brash about Biba colours. Moss, peat, [etc.].

4. *attrib.* and *Comb.* **a.** attributive, as *peat-barrow, -bed, -brick, -charcoal, -coke, -creel, -dealer, -ditch, -earth, -fire, -fuel, -gas, -ground, -knife, -land, -marsh, -moor, -mould, -mud, -pit, -pulp, -smoke, -soil, -swamp, -wain, -water*; **b.** objective and obj. genitive, as *peat-caster, -casting, -cutter, -cutting, -digger, -fitter, -making*; **c.** instrumental, as *peat-coloured, -roofed, -smoked, -stained* adjs. Also similative, as *peat-black, -brown* adjs. and sbs. For other combinations, with many illustrative examples, see *Eng. Dial. Dict.*

1886 A. WINCHELL *Walks Geol. Field* 245 Spread it over the whole vast *peat-bed. **1961** R. S. THOMAS *Tares* 35 Nerves strengthened with tea, *Peat-black. **1897** R. MUNRO *Prehist. Probl.* 254 A machine for making *peat-bricks. **1898** B. KIRKBY *Lakeland Words* 160 *Peat-broon, t' colour of a dried peat, er bit of undyed woo'. **1906** *Westm. Gaz.* 9 Aug. 10/1 A rush-grown pool of peat-brown water. **1962** D. FRANCIS *Dead Cert.* xv. 173 My suit was a filthy peat-brown. **1840** *Penny Cycl.* XVII. 353/1 Incorporating pitch or rosin melted in a cauldron with as much of the *peat-charcoal ground to powder as will form a tough doughy mass, which is then moulded into bricks. **1870** (*title*) On the Economical Production of Peat and Peat-Charcoal. **1889** DOYLE *Micah Clarke* 228 *Peat-coloured streams splashed down these valleys. **1579** *Reg. Privy Council Scot.* III. 192 Breking of thair *peit creillis and sleddis. **1756** COLLET in *Phil. Trans.* L. 114 No body happened to be there at that time but the *peat-cutters. **1963** *Times* 10 June 14/6, I followed a track that was once used by peat cutters. **1969** E. H. PINTO *Treen* 94/2 A peat cutter is a square-ended spade of normal length, with a right-angled, forward projecting blade at one side, like the breast plough. **1774** T. PENNANT *Tour in Scotl. & Voy. Hebrides 1772* I. 66 By the imprudence of the *peat-diggers, who were continually working on that side [of the moss]. **1894** A. GORDON *Northward Ho!* 202 The peat-digger was the most notorious carouser in Carglen. **1978** *Maledicta* II. 167 *Peat-digger*, any rural Irish person. **1903** G. W. HARTLEY *Wild Sport* i. 11 Jumping in and out of crumbling *peat-ditches. **1695** WOODWARD *Nat. Hist. Earth* II. (1723) 127 The said Trees are..found very seldom unless in this *Peat-Earth. **1754** BURT *Lett. N. Scotl.* xvi, My Landlady sat..by a little *peat-fire in the middle of the Hutt. **1866** KINGSLEY *Herew.* xix, Over the peat fire sat a very old man. **1807** VANCOUVER *Agric. Devon* (1813) 109 Digging and curing *peat-fuel upon Dartmoor. **1856** EMERSON *Eng. Traits* iv. 64 Oars, scythes, harpoons, ..*peat-knives, and hay-forks. **1907** *Daily Chron.* 1 Oct. 8/1 They wandered hand in hand across the *peatland and the marshes. **1973** MOORE & BELLAMY (*title*) Peatlands. **1977** *Undercurrents* June-July 40 They are tackling the problems of what to do with bull calves, a large acreage of peatland and the need to produce extremely high quality winter fodder in a high rainfall area. **1884** A. CAMPBELL *Rec. Argyll* 310 The people would be all off at *peat-making. **1695** WOODWARD *Nat. Hist. Earth* II. (1723) 82 The squamose Covers of the Germina or Buds..are found in..many *Peat Marshes. **1832** LYELL *Princ. Geol.* II. 215 In June, 1747, the body of a woman was found six feet deep, in a *peat-moor in the Isle of Axholm. **1860** TYNDALL *Glac.* II. xxvi. 372 It appeared as if *peat-mould had been strewn over it. **1908** *Chambers's Jrnl.* Jan. 122/2 The latest development in the production of *peat-pulp is being made in Sweden. **1814** SCOTT *Wav.* lxvii, Poor old Janet, bent double with age and bleared with *peat-smoke. **1922** JOYCE *Ulysses* 184 The peatsmoke is going to his head. **1971** *Country Life* 4 Nov. 1226/1, I may be prompted by something to recall the scent of peat-smoke. **1896** N. MUNRO *Lost Pibroch* 19 The step-mother..with hate in her *peat-smoked face. **1903** G. W. HARTLEY *Wild Sports* ix. 193 Its contents were for the thick-set, *peat-stained beast standing a little to the right. **1578** *Knaresborough Wills* I. 133 Thre *peate waynes.

d. Special Comb.: **peat-ash**, the ash of burnt peat; **peat-bank**, a bank from which peats are cut; **peat-bog**, a bog composed of peat; also *attrib.*; **peat-coal**, a soft earthy lignite; †**peat-cote**, = *peat-house*; **peat-flannel**, flannel with peat in its contexture; **peat-hag**, broken ground whence peats have been dug: see HAG *sb.*⁴; **peat-house**, an outhouse in which peats are stored; **peat-machine**, a machine for grinding peat and pressing it into 'bricks' for fuel; **peatman**, a man who digs, dries, or sells peats for fuel; **peat-marl**: see MARL *sb.*¹ 1 c; †**peat-mire**, a miry peat-bog; **peat-pan**: cf. PAN *sb.*¹ 8, quot. 1875; **peat-pot**, a hole out of which peats have been dug and in which water has collected; **peat-road**, a rough track on a mountainside for the hauling down of peats; **peat-spade**, a spade made of a shape for cutting and 'casting' peats;

peat-stack, a stack of peats built up to dry for fuel; **peat-wool**, wool impregnated with peat; also *attrib.* Also PEAT-MOSS, -REEK.

1669 WORLIDGE *Syst. Agric.* (1681) 70 Turf and *Peat-ashes must needs be very rich. **1887** MRS. SAXBY *Lads of Lunda* (1888) 198 A snow-wreath..filled one of the *peat-banks, a pit some six feet deep. **1775** LIGHTFOOT *Flora Scot.* 219 Andromeda..in *peat-bogs in the Lowlands not unfrequent. **1832** LYELL *Princ. Geol.* II. 213 A considerable portion of the European peat-bogs are evidently not more ancient than the age of Julius Cæsar. **1965** G. M. BROWN in *New Statesman* 9 July 52/2 Being under age And wringing peatbog whisky from a clout Into a secret kettle. **1859–65** PAGE *Geol. Terms* 282 Lignite beds..others soft and earthy, and known as '*peat-coal'. **1898** *Chamb. Jrnl.* Mar. 187/2 '*Peat flannel'—for so it is called—is a fine, delicately shaded flannel, containing a considerable portion of peat in its contexture. **1818** SCOTT *Hrt. Midl.* xii, Warstling wi' hunger and cauld..upon wet brae-sides, *peat-hags, and flow-mosses. **1842** G. TURNBULL in *Proc. Berw. Nat. Club* II. No. 10. 8 Brown barren moors, varied with peat-hags and covers of whins and of broom. **1339–40** *Durham Acc. Rolls* (Surtees) 538 Super reparacione del *Pethouse. **1580** *Reg. Privy Council Scot.* III. 320 Within the peithous of the neddir bailye. **1899** CROCKETT *Kit Kennedy* 149 Betty Landsborough..set him to chop wood, and stack it in the little peat-house. **1821** *Examiner* 1 Apr. 207/2 As James Johnstone, *peatman, was levelling moss. **1479** *Priory of Hexham* (Surtees No. 46) 51 Habent communam de *Petmyre..ad fodiendum et capiendum inde petas. **1828** *Craven Gloss.* (ed. 2), *Peeat-pan, a very hard stratum below the peeat, impregnated with iron, impervious to water. *c* **1425** WYNTOUN *Cron.* VIII. xxiv. 46 And hyd thame in a *pete-pot all. **1721** KELLY *Sc. Prov.* 268 Out of the Peat-Pot into the Mire. **1800** A. CARLYLE *Autobiog.* 28 Their eldest son..having missed the road.., fell into a peat pot, as it is called, and was drowned. **1872** JENKINSON *Guide Eng. Lakes* (1879) 121 Mount the hill by a *peat-road, which leads to Eel Tarn. **1573** *Richmond Wills* (Surtees) 242 A gavelocke, ij hacks, iij *peatspades, ij flainge spades, a garthe spade, vijs. **1802** C. FINDLATER *Agric. Surv. Peebles* 208 The peat-spade is furnished with a triangular cutting mouth, as also, with a cutting wing on the right side,..to cut the half decayed wood found mixed with the moss. **1583** *Reg. Privy Council Scot.* III. 577 Certane houssis, barnis and *peitstakis. **1802** SCOTT *Let. to Ellis* in *Lockhart*, The formidable hardships of sleeping upon peat stacks. **1898** *Chamb. Jrnl.* Mar. 187/1 *Peat-wool dressing. This surgical wool is extremely absorbent..; its deodorising power is great.

[*Note.* As *pete* has from the beginning been applied in the north, not to the substance, but to a shaped and prepared piece of it (cf. the expressions 'to make peats', 'peat-making'), the suggestion is offered that we may have in it one of several instances in which a word orig. meaning 'piece' has become at length the term for a piece of some particular substance. If this be so, there may be etymological connexion with the stem *pette-* which gave med.L. *petia*, *pecia* (:—**pettia*), It. *pezza*, F. *pièce*, 'piece', and is held to be of Celtic origin (Thurneysen *Keltoroman.* 20). The Old Celtic entries in the *Book of Deer*, have *pet*, genit. *pette*, in sense 'portion, piece', with which Stokes, *Goidelica* (ed. 2) 120, compares OIr. *pit* portion of food (in *terc-fit, leth-fit*). (This word is supposed to have passed into Goidelic from a Brythonic dialect: cf. Welsh *peth* portion.)]

peat[2] (piːt). *Obs.* or *arch.* [Common from *c* 1570 to 1640; re-introduced by Scott. Origin uncertain. (Not Sc., exc. in sense 3.)

Cf. MDu. *pēte*, in Kilian 1599, 'god-mother', also = *petken*, god-daughter, 'lustrica filiola, filia initialis, *vulgo* profilia'. (See also PET.)]

†**1.** Used as a term of endearment to a girl or woman = pet of a woman; hence with various shades of meaning = girl simply, light or merry girl, fondled or spoilt girl, etc. *Obs.*

1568 T. HOWELL *Arb. Amitie* (1879) 103 Alas good simple peate, Of dull and feeble braine. **1576** T. NEWTON *Lemnie's Complex.* (1633) 245 To invite and call into their companies some beautifull Damosels, and pleasant Peats to passe away the time more merrily. **1581** RICH *Farew. Milit. Prof.* (1846) 172 Being halfe convicted by the confession of the gentle peate, his new wife. **1593** DRAYTON *Man in Moon* IX. Giij, Here might you many a Shepherdess have seen,..Lettice and Parnell prety louely peates. **1596** SHAKS. *Tam. Shr.* I. i. 78 A pretty peate, it is best put finger in the eye, and she knew why. **1605** JONSON, etc. *Eastw. Hoe* v. i, God's me life, you are a peat indeed! **1632** MASSINGER *Maid of Hon.* II. ii, Of a little thing You are a pretty peat, indifferent fair too.

b. Applied to a pet animal.

a **1577** GASCOIGNE *Praise P. Sparrow* Wks. (1587) 285 As if you say but *fend cut* Phip, Lord, how the peat will turne and skip.

2. As a term of obloquy for a woman: esp. in ***proud peat***. *Obs.* in 17th c., but revived by Scott.

1599 B. JONSON *Ev. Man out of Hum.* Dram. Pers., Fallace. Deliro's wife and Idoll, a proud mincing Peat, and as peruerse as he is officious. *a* **1623** FLETCHER *Wife for Month* I. i, And ye proud peat, Ile make you curse your insolence. **1828** SCOTT *F.M. Perth* xvii, Ere he [Rothsay] takes back yonder proud peat to his table and his bed,..Douglas must be King of Scotland. **1895** MISS TYTLER *Macdonald Lass* xii. 164 You were always a proud, undaunted peat of a lass.

b. Applied as a term of dislike to a man.

[By Scott and his imitators.]

1818 SCOTT *Hrt. Midl.* li, 'I have angered the proud peat now', he said to himself, 'by finding out a likeness'. **1866** *Gd. Words* 2 Apr. 267/2 The presumptuous peat! the light-headed auld fule! to mint sic madness.

†**3.** 'Formerly, a lawyer, supposed to be under the peculiar patronage of any particular judge, was invidiously termed his peat or pet' (Scott *Redgauntlet* Let. xiii, note). Hence †**'peatry**, †**'peatship**, the personality or office of a peat.

c **1680** *R. Cook's Petit. agst. the Peats* in Maidment *Scot. Pasquils* (1868) 224 Now humbly doth shew to the Lords of the Seat, That he's likely to starve unlesse made a Peat. *Ibid.* 225 Old Nevoy by all is judged such a sott, That his peatship could never be thought worth a groat. Yet John Hay of Murie, his peatry, as I hear, By virtue of his daughter, makes thousands a year. Newbyth heretofore went snips with the peats, Bot haveing discovered them all to be cheats, Resolves for the future, his sone Willie Baird, Shall be Peat of his house, as well as Young Laird. *c* **1680** *Scot. Pasquils* (1827) xxii. 49 *Sat. on Fam. of Stairs*, His mother's tongue learn'd him his father's law; Lyke prentice taught the trade by ear, but book, In seaven years petship e'er he wrote or spoke. **1824** SCOTT *Redgauntlet* Let. xiii, As like being akin to a peatship and a sheriffdom, as a sieve is sib to a riddle.

peatery ('piːtərɪ). [f. PEAT[1] + -ERY; in the forms *petary, peatary* after med.(Anglo-)L. *petāria*, f. *peta* peat.] A place from which peats are dug or 'cast'; a peat-bog or -bank.

[*c* **1200** in *Liber de Melros* (Bann. Cl.) 76 Sciatis me dedisse ..quandam partem petarie mee in territorio de faringdun. **1337** *Durham Acc. Rolls* (Surtees) 536 *note*, In peteria de Beaurepaire, pro focali pro Abbathia.] **1810** C. CHALMERS *Caledonia* II. III. viii. 338 [He] granted them a peatary. **1853** G. JOHNSTON *Nat. Hist. E. Bord.* I. 175 Gathered specimens of a Callitriche in the peatery at Grant's-house. **1872** COSMO INNES *Scott. Legal. Antiq.* 227 They say upon their oath that the burgesses cut their peats in the petary of Waltamshope. **1873** J. GEIKIE *Gt. Ice Age* xxiii. 308 Petaries became frequent objects of grant to the abbots and convents during the Scoto-Saxon period. **1901** *Dundee Advertiser* 5 June 5 Here also are the peatries, where no end of that valuable commodity may yet be had.

pea-time. *U.S. colloq.* [f. PEA[1] 7.] The season in which peas ripen. So *fig.* in phr. ***the last of pea-time***: the last stage of anything, the end of one's life; ***pea-time is past***: a thing is finished.

1834 [see LAST *a.* 1 d.]. **1850** 'M. TENSAS' *Odd Leaves Life Louisiana Swamp Doctor* 174 It war the last of pea-time with me, sure, if I didn't rise 'fore bar did. **1862** J. R. LOWELL in *Atlantic Monthly* Jan. 128 Ther' 's ollers chaps a-hangin' roun thet can't see pea-time's past. **1867** —— *Biglow Papers* 2nd Ser. I. p. lviii, *Last of pea-time*, to be hard up. **1889** 'C. E. CRADDOCK' *Despot of Broomsedge Cove* x. 174 Ye oughter git some air an' light, Marcelly; ye look like the las' o' pea-time. **1893** M. A. OWEN *Voodoo Tales* 199 'Deed my gyarden am a-lookin' mighty bad. Hit look mo' lak de las' o' pea-time den de fust o' truck-time. **1904** [see LAST *a.* 1 d]. **1911** R. D. SAUNDERS *Col. Todhunter* 108 'What on earth's the matter, Bill?' he asked. 'You look like the last of pea-times.' **1923** *Dialect Notes* V. 238 Utterly worn out. 'He looks like the *last o' pea-time*.'

peat-moss. [f. PEAT[1] + MOSS.]

I. 1. A peat-bog: the regular name in the North.

c **1260** *Newminster Cartul.* (Surtees) 71 Per viam quæ vocatur Petemosway. **1543** *Richmond Wills* (Surtees) 39 My peat mosse at ye Stonyford brygge, and ye peat cote there bulded. **1765** DOUGLAS in *Phil. Trans.* LVIII. 187 In almost every peat-moss, there are the remains of oak trees. **1832** LYELL *Princ. Geol.* II. 213 Gradual conversion of a dry tract into a swamp, and lastly a peat-moss.

b. Without *a* or *pl.*: The substance peat.

1830 *Kyle Farm Rep.* 42 in *Libr. Usef. Knowl., Husb.* III, Peat moss was..regularly mixed with it in layers. **1856** KANE *Arct. Expl.* II. xx. 202 The fires were of peat-moss greased with the fat of the bird-skins.

II. 2. The bog-moss (*Sphagnum*); *pl.* the family of mosses that grow in peat-bogs. *rare.*

1880 BRAITHWAITE (*title*) The Sphagnaceæ or Peat Mosses of Europe and North America.

pea-tree. Name for several leguminous trees or shrubs with flowers resembling those of the pea. **a.** The genus *Caragana*, of Siberia, China, etc. **b.** The tropical genus *Sesbania*. **c.** *Æschynomene* (*Agati*) *grandiflora*, of the East Indies, cultivated in tropical countries. **d.** *Adenanthera pavonina* of the East Indies (Coral Pea-tree), called also Red Sandal-wood. **e.** The Common Laburnum. *Sc.*

1822 POLLOK in D. Pollok *Life* 157 The pea-tree bended its modest head, covered with locks of lovely yellow. **1866** *Treas. Bot.* 219 *Caragana*, the Siberian Pea Tree. *Ibid.* 855 Pea-tree, *Sesbania.* **1884** MILLER *Plant-n.*, Pea-tree, Chinese,..Coral,..West Indian.

peat-reek. [f. PEAT[1] + REEK *sb.*[1], smoke.]

1. The smoke of a peat-fire. Also *attrib.*

1803 SIR A. BOSWELL *Spirit of Tintoc* Poet. Wks. (1871) 120 He smelt like a peat-reek warming pan. **1860** G. H. K. in *Vac. Tour.* 164 They aver that it is the loss of the peat-reek and its creosote, which now goes up the grand stone chimney. **1872** BLACK *Adv. Phaeton* xxii. 308 There was a scent of peat-reek in the air.

2. A cant name for whisky distilled over a peat-fire and so supposed to be flavoured with peat-smoke; orig. the produce of a moorland illicit still, 'mountain dew'; also loosely, Highland whisky generally.

The 'peat-reek' flavour is really that of amyl alcohol, due to imperfect rectification.

1824 MACTAGGART *Gallovid. Encycl.* (1876) 91 A male o' sic food, washed down by a few glasses of peatreek. **1862** R. H. STORY in *Athenæum* 30 Aug. 270 We sat till twelve o'clock, paying our devotions to the peat-reek. **1870** J. K. HUNTER *Studies* 131 A shoemaker, who..had imbibed strongly of peat-reek whisky.

peaty ('piːtɪ), *a.* [f. PEAT[1] + -Y.] Of the nature of peat; abounding in peat.

1765 DOUGLAS in *Phil. Trans.* LVIII. 183 To free the blue from the peaty matter. **1776** WITHERING *Brit. Pl.* (1796) III. 813 On Hampstead Heath near London, in dry peaty places. **1875** CROLL *Climate & T.* xv. 244 A thin seam of peaty matter,..along the bottom of a bed of clay.

Peaucellier cell (pəʊ'sɛljeɪ sɛl). [From name of the inventor, Lieut. Peaucellier, 1864.] A plane linkage consisting of a jointed rhombus fixed by three bars to two distinct centres, so that when it oscillates about these, its angle opposite to the centres describes a straight line, thus developing a rectilineal out of a circular motion.

1875 CAYLEY *Coll. Math. Papers* IX. 317 The assumed transformation..can be effected immediately by a Peaucellier cell.

‖**peau de chagrin** (po də ʃagrɛ̃). [Fr., lit. 'skin of grained leather'.] The title of a novel by Balzac (1831), in which a piece of shagreen diminishes in size as wishes are granted through its magic power, used *fig.* or allusively to indicate the progressive diminution of the human life-span.

1861 GEO. ELIOT *Let.* 31 Dec. (1954) III. 475 The years of retrieval keep shrinking—the terrible *peau de chagrin* whose outline narrows..with our ebbing life. **1910** W. J. LOCKE *Simon* v. 56, I see my little allotted span of life shrinking visibly, like the *peau de chagrin.* **1946** L. P. HARTLEY *Sixth Heaven* v. 111 Money..[is] really like the Peau de Chagrin, and dwindles with every wish.

‖**peau-de-soie** (podəswa). [F. *peau de soie*, lit. 'silk skin, silk kid', introduced in the second half of the 19th c. as a trade name, referring to the somewhat leathery consistence of the silk; perh. suggested by the earlier term (for a different material) *pou-de-soie*: see PADUASOY, POULT-DE-SOIE.] A rich and somewhat thick silk with a dull satin face on both sides; also applied to various inferior imitations of this, and now (1904) chiefly used in the trade to designate those called 'Rhadzimirs'.

1866 READE *Griffith Gaunt* xvii. II. 56 Mrs. Gaunt..gave her the promised petticoat, and the old Peau de soie gown. **1902** *Civil Service Supply Ass. Price List* Nov. 340 Silks, Satins, etc.—22 in. Peau de Soie 2/4 to 2/11. **1912** C. MACKENZIE *Carnival* iv. 38 But when his grand-daughter,..all chiffon and ostrich plumes, took her upon a *peau de soie* lap..Jenny thought she had never experienced any sensation half so delicious. **1930** R. CUTHILL tr. *Schober's Silk* iv. 272 *Peau de Soie.*—A close, firm silk fabric. Weave: eight- or ten-shaft twill. **1958** *Times* 16 Oct. 14/3 The bride ..wore a gown of pearl coloured peau-de-soie with a train. **1974** *Times-Picayune* (New Orleans) 15 Aug. v. 6 The bride ..wore a peau de soie gown.

‖**Peau d'Espagne** (po dɛspaɲ). Also with lower-case initials. [Fr., lit. 'skin of Spain'.]

a. A perfumed leather. Cf. *Spanish leather* s.v. SPANISH *a.* 2 b. **b.** A scent supposedly suggestive of the aroma of this leather.

1855 G. W. S. PIESSE *Art of Perfumery* vii. 143 Peau d'Espagne, or Spanish skin, is nothing more than highly perfumed leather. *Ibid.*, Finally, each double skin, now called peau d'Espagne, is to be enveloped in some pretty silk or satin, and finished off to the taste of the vender. **1898** *Junior Army & Navy Stores Catal.* 190/1 Atkinson's Perfumes..Peau d'Espagne, in Fancy Ribbon Sachets..each 1/6. **1906** 'O. HENRY' *Four Million* (1916) 112 A 200-pound woman breathing a flavour of Camembert cheese and Peau d'Espagne. **1907** *Yesterday's Shopping* (1969) 37/2 *Soaps*..Peau d'Espagne—box of 3 tablets 4/9. **1912** *Maclean's Mag.* Jan. 262/2 When his mother swept into the dining-room at meal-times, her hair faultlessly arranged, and wafting *peau d'Espagne* as she moved, Eugene followed in her wake like a small dog. **1919** [see OTTO[1]]. **1922** JOYCE *Ulysses* 747 That cheap peau despagne that faded and left a stink on you. **1942** E. BOWEN *Seven Winters* 31 She used *Peau d'Espagne* scent. **1972** T. MCLAUGHLIN *Gilded Lily* vi. 70 The combination of perfume and leather could be obtained also in the form of *peau d'Espagne*, small perfumed pieces of leather that were used like lavender sachets or pot-pourri bags to hang in cupboards or tuck into pockets of clothes.

‖**peau d'orange** (po dɔrɑ̃ʒ). *Med.* [Fr., = 'orange-peel'.] A characteristic pitted appearance of the skin of the breast in some cases of breast cancer.

[**1875** *Nouveau Dict. de Méd. et de Chirurgie Pratiques* XXI. 569 La peau, au lieu d'être d'un blanc rosé, est..comparable, comme l'a si bien fait remarquer Nélaton, à la peau d'orange. **1882** A. NÉLATON *Éléments de Path. Chirurg.* (ed. 2) V. xxi. 148 Quelquefois la peau de la mamelle, suivant la comparaison du Dr Mauduyt, ressemble à une peau d'orange.] **1898** A. M. SHEILD *Clin. Treat. Dis. Breast* ix. 346 The skin..has that coarse pitted aspect to which the terms 'peau d'orange' and 'pigskin saddle' appearance have been well applied. **1948** C. ENGLISH *Dis. Breast* xi. 75 In the early stages the growth is entirely unattached to the overlying skin, but later dimpling of the skin occurs, and a condition known as 'peau d'orange' follows. **1974** R. M. KIRK et al. *Surgery* iv. 62 Invaded lymphatics are blocked causing overlying lymphoedema of the skin known as peau d'orange.

peauter, obs. form or PEWTER.

peavey, pevy ('piːvɪ). *U.S.* Also **pivie**. [From the surname, *Peavey*, of the inventor.] A lumberer's cant-hook having a spike at the end of the lever.

1878 *Lumberman's Gaz.* 16 Mar., The best cast steel Pevy made in the world. **1893** *Scribner's Mag.* June 714/2 The banking-ground swarms with men armed with pevies (which are cant-hooks furnished with strong pikes in the end). **1902** *Nation* (N.Y.) 9 Oct. 289/3 Our hands are hard-callused by peavies and poles. **1907** *Black Cat* June 24 Mehetabel launched the boat, and running along the logs, piloted it hither and thither hooked to a pivie.

pea-vine. *U.S.* [f. PEA¹ + VINE.] **1. a.** The 'vine', or climbing stem, with its foliage, of the pea-plant, or of any plant called 'pea'. **b.** Name for two leguminous plants: (*a*) the Hog-peanut (see HOG *sb.*¹ 13 d); (*b*) an American vetch, *Vicia americana*, a valuable fodder plant.

1675 J. FENWICK in *Pennsylvania Mag. Hist. & Biogr.* (1882) VI. 89 You have Grass as high as a Man's Knees.. interlac'd with Pea-Vines, and other Weeds that Cattel much delight in. **1766** J. BARTRAM *Jrnl.* 6 Jan. in W. Stork *Acc. E. Florida* 25 The last frost killed the..pea-vines, sun-flowers, [etc.]. **1835** W. IRVING *Tour Prairies* 47 The horses banqueted luxuriantly on the pea-vine. **1841** CATLIN *N. Amer. Ind.* (1844) II. xxxiii. 17 The grass is filled with wild pea-vines. **1880** *Harper's Mag.* June 23/1 A search was instituted—under the bed, in the bed,..behind the wood-pile and in the pea-vines. **1910** *Chambers's Jrnl.* June 364/1 A little beetle has climbed up the pea-vine and laid its eggs in the pod. **1973** R. D. SYMONS *Where Wagon Led* VI. xvii. 271 Both horses and cattle thrived on the good grass and plentiful pea vine.

2. pea-vine hay, the dried stalks and foliage of a pea-vine.

1846 V. AIMÉ *Plantation Diary* (1878) 111 Peavine hay is excellent this year, the vine being still green and juicy. **1860** *Southern Cultivator* XVIII. 211 A little corn with Pea Vine Hay will keep them fat. **1932** W. KELLEY *Inchin' Along* 55 Everybody knows there is nothing a mule likes better than pea-vine hay with the peas left on.

†**peaw**, dialectal var. of PO, peacock. *Obs.*

1719 STRACHEY in *Phil. Trans.* XXX. 970 Next under the three Coal Veins is the Peaw Vein, so denominated because the Coal is figured with Eyes resembling a Peacock's Tayl, ..which Bird in this Country [Somerset] Dialect is called a Peaw. [Cf. *peacock-coal*, s.v. PEACOCK *sb.* 6 b.]

peawe, obs. f. PEW.

pea-weevil: see PEA¹ 7.

peax, obs. f. PEACE, PIECE.

peaze, obs. f. PEASE, PEISE.

peb (pɛb), abbrev. PEBBLE *sb.* 1 c. *Austral. slang.*

1903 R. BEDFORD *True Eyes* 129 The session broke up—pebs and donahs wandered off in couples. **1916** C. J. DENNIS *Moods of Ginger Mick* 114 They wus pebs, they wus norks, they wus reel naughty boys. **1916** —— *Songs Sentimental Bloke* 127 *Peb*, a flash fellow, a 'larrikin'. *a* **1943** L. ESSON in *Penguin Bk. Austral. Ballads* (1964) 233 'E's the bloke to fite, 'E's the peb, gorblime. **1959** BAKER *Drum* (1960) 133 *Peb*, a larrikin.

‖**peba** ('pi:bə). *Zool.* [Shortened from Tupi *tatu-peba*, i.e. *tatu* armadillo, and *peba* low.] An American species of armadillo, *Tatusia* (*Dasypus*) *peba*, found from Paraguay to Texas; the Seven- or Nine-banded Armadillo.

[**1648** MARCGRAVE *Hist. Nat. Bras.* 231 Tatu peba Brasiliensibus, armidillo Hispanis.]

1834 *Penny Cycl.* II. 352 The *peba*..called by the Guaranis *tatouhou*, or *black tatu*, is extremely common in Paraguay. *Ibid.*, The length of the peba, from the snout to the origin of the tail, is about sixteen inches, that of the tail fourteen... It is commonly called in Brazil, tatu-peba. **1893** MIVART *Types Anim. Life* (1894) 259 The peba or nine-banded armadillo ranges from Paraguay to Texas. **1896** *List Anim. Zool. Soc.* 195 Peba Armadillo... South America.

pebble ('pɛb(ə)l), *sb.* Forms: α. 1 papol-, popel-stán, 6 pipple-, pypple-, pibple-stan(e; also 6 poppell, 7 pipple. β. 4 pobble; 3–6 puble-, 4 pibbil-, 6 pybble-ston; 6 pyble, 6–7 pible, 6–7 (*dial.* -9) pibble; 6- pebble, (6–7 (*dial.* -9) peable, peeble, 7–8 peble). [Existing in many forms, some going back to OE., the phonetic relations of which are obscure, and as yet undetermined.]

1. a. A stone worn and rolled to a rounded form by the action of water; usually applied to one of small or moderate size, less than a *boulder* or *cobble*. Also, a stone similarly rounded by attrition of ice or sand. (OE. examples, see PEBBLE-STONE.)

c **1290** *S. Eng. Leg., Magdalena* 469 Huy i-seiȝen bi þe stronde: a luytel child gon pleye with publes on is honde. **13..** *E.E. Allit. P.* A. 117 For vche a pobble in pole þer pyȝt Watz Emerad, saffer oþer gemme gent. **1542** BOORDE *Dyetary* x. (1870) 253 Ryuer or broke water,..ronnyng on pibles and grauayl. **1570** LEVINS *Manip.* 47/7 A Pebble, stone, *calculus*. **1624** BP. HALL *Serm. at Re-edified Chapell of Earle of Exceter* in *Var. Treat.* (1627) 531 A pibble out of the brook. **1635–56** COWLEY *Davideis* I. 677 The chaste stream that 'mong loose peebles fell. **1695** LUTTRELL *Brief Rel.* (1857) III. 515 There being two great guns, they charged them with pibbles instead of bullets. *c* **1760** SMOLLETT *Ode to Leven-Water* 10 With white, round, polish'd pebbles spread. **1774** PENNANT *Tour Scot. in 1772*, 22 June, At Feorling another stupendous cairn..formed of rounded stones or pebbles brought from the shore. **1813** BAKEWELL *Introd. Geol.* ii. 52 Rounded fragments from the magnitude of a pea to that of a melon are generally called pebbles. **1878** HUXLEY *Physiogr.* 132 [The fragment of rock] may ultimately be rubbed into the form of smooth round pebbles.

†**b.** (without *a*) Used collectively, or as a material; a bed, deposit, or heap of pebbles.

1574 W. BOURNE *Regiment for Sea* xxii. (1577) 60 You shall finde 38. fadom, and poppell as bigge as beanes. **1588** GREENE *Pandosto* (1607) 10 Precious Diamonds are cut.., when despised peable lye safe in the sand. **1592** LYLY *Gallathea* I. i. 13 A heape of small pyble. **1669** STURMY *Mariner's Mag.* v. xii. 54 The proper Stone for this purpose is Marble, Pibble, Blew hand Stone.

c. *fig. slang* (chiefly *Austral.*) A person or animal very hard to deal with. Also, a term of affection (applied to a person or animal). Phr. (*as*) ***game as a pebble*** (see quot. 1959) (*obs.*).

1829 P. EGAN *Boxiana* 2nd Ser. II. 20 Hudson, as *game* as a pebble, stuck to his man like glue. **1851** 'W. T. MONCRIEFF' *Scamps of London* III. i. 56, in *Sel. Dram. Wks.* I, Now, my pebbles, I'll give you a toast. *c* **1863** T. TAYLOR *Ticket-of-Leave Man* I. 11 Doctor? Nay; I'm as game as a pebble and as stell as a tree! **1874** M. CLARKE *His Natural Life* IV. vii. 415 'You're not such a pebble as folks seem to think,' grinned Frere. **1888** 'R. BOLDREWOOD' *Robbery under Arms* III. ix. 123 Then the Turon favourite—a real game pebble of a little horse—began to show up. **1890** —— *Col. Reformer* vi. (1890) 49 He was a regular pebble, and the old cow hadn't been in the yard since he was branded. **1893** K. MACKAY *Out Back* 188 Cabbage Tree Ned is as game as a pebble, and may try to dash through in spite of us. **1901** E. DYSON in *Bulletin Story Bk* 134 The Imp.., game as a pebble, despite his age and infirmities. **1918** C. FEATHERSTONHAUGH *After Many Days* 227 Traveller was game as a pebble, and he just passed Quadrant on the post and no more. **1945** BAKER *Austral. Lang.* iv. 88 *Game as a pebble*...(a *pebble* is a person, especially a larrikin, or an animal hard to control.). **1959** —— *Drum* (1960) 133 *Pebble*, a person (occasionally a horse) hard to control. Whence, *game as a pebble*, extremely courageous. **1974** D. STUART *Prince of My Country* 166 He was as hard as nails and as game as a pebble.

d. Colloq. phr. ***the only pebble on the beach*** and varr., the only person or thing to be considered in a particular situation; used *spec.* (usu. in negative contexts) with reference to an eligible man or woman.

1896 H. BRAISTED (*song-title*) You're not the only pebble on the beach. *Ibid.*, If you want to win her hand, Let the maiden understand That she's not the only pebble on the beach! **1906** E. DYSON *Fact'ry 'Ands* x. 128 S' elp me shicker, Twenty, you was the on'y pebble. **1924** H. DE SÉLINCOURT *Cricket Match* v. 156 There were other pebbles on the beach beside him. **1927** S. SPAETH *Weep some more, my Lady* x. 259 Another phrase that became a recognized part of the English language was 'You're not the only pebble on the beach', made into a song by Harry Braisted and Stanley Carter. **1930** M. KENNEDY *Fool of Family* vii. 66, I won't look at your damned things... You think you're the only pebble on the beach. **1933** E. O'NEILL *Ah, Wilderness!* I. 19 What do I care for him? He's not the only pebble on the beach. **1933** D. L. SAYERS *Hangman's Holiday* 193 The Birmingham–London express reached Rugby at 10.24, departing again at 10.28. But, swift and impressive as it was, it was not the only, or the most important, pebble on the station beach, for over against it upon the down line was the Irish Mail. **1936** G. B. SHAW *Simpleton* II. 73 The British Empire was not the only pebble on the beach. **1945** 'P. WENTWORTH' *Clock strikes Twelve* ii. 15 A heart-to-heart talk with someone who makes me feel I'm the only pebble on the beach. **1977** *World of Cricket Monthly* June 87/1 He was not the only pebble on the Middlesbrough beach.

2. A name for various gems or valuable stones. †**a.** Applied to a pearl (quot. 1600). **b.** A colourless transparent kind of rock-crystal, used instead of glass in spectacles; a lens made of this. **c.** An agate or other gem found as a pebble in streams, esp. in Scotland (***Scotch pebble***); also, various kinds of agate, as ***Egyptian pebble***, ***Mocha pebble***. **d.** Applied rhetorically to the magnetic 'stone' or 'loadstone' (quot. 1856).

1600 TOURNEUR *Transf. Metam.* xl, The pearly pibble which the Ocean keepes. **1688** R. HOLME *Armoury* II. 39/2 The Christal, and Bristow Stone, or Pipple. **1695** WOODWARD *Nat. Hist. Earth* IV. (1723) 200 Flints, Agates, Onyxes, Pebles, Jaspers, Cornelions. **1774** PENNANT *Tour Scotl. in 1772*, 23 June, Sardonyxes; and other beautiful stones, indiscriminately called Scotch pebbles. **1793** W. & S. JONES *Catal. Optical* etc. *Instr.* 1 Best double-jointed standard gold spectacles with pebbles. **1847–8** H. MILLER *First Impr.* xiv. (1857) 233 Like one of our Scotch pebbles, so common..in their rude state. **1856** EMERSON *Eng. Traits, Ability* Wks. (Bohn) II. 37 More than the diamond Koh-i-noor,..they prize that dull pebble..whose poles turn themselves to the poles of the world. **1878** HUXLEY *Physiogr.* 59 Those spectacle lenses which are said to be made of 'pebbles'. **1889** *Cent. Dict.* s.v. *Brazilian, Brazilian pebbles*, lenses for spectacles ground from pure, colorless rock-crystal obtained from Brazil.

e. A kind of earthenware invented by Wedgwood; see *pebble-ware* in 5 b.

1768 WEDGWOOD *Let. to Bentley* 21 Nov. in *Life* (1866) II. 97 We can make things for mounting with great facility and dispatch, and mounting will enhance their value greatly... Pebble will in this way scarcely be discover'd to be counterfeit. **1776** —— *Let.* 27 Jan. in Eliza Meteyard *Wedgwood & Wks.* (1873) 44, I observe what you say about Pebble vases... If we mean the general complexion of the pebble to be light, and they meet with a heavy fire in the biskit oven, the..tints will be made darker than intended.

3. a. Short for *pebble-leather*: see 5 b. Also, the rough irregular grain produced on leather by pebbling: see PEBBLE *v.* 3.

1875 [see PEBBLE *v.* 3]. **1885** C. T. DAVIS *Leather* xxix. 500 The waxed or colored split is stained on the flesh side, and it is strictly known as the 'colored pebble'.

b. Short for *pebble-powder*: see 5 b.

1880 *Encycl. Brit.* (ed. 9) XI. 328/1 Large cannon powder, such as 'pebble'..is..enclosed in cases.

4. A collector's name for certain Cuspidate moths (so called from the wavy markings on their wings resembling those of agate). **a.** The ***pebble*** or ***pebble prominent***, *Notodonta ziczac*. **b.** The ***pebble hook-tip***, *Platypteryx falcula*.

1832 RENNIE *Conspectus Butterfl. & M.* 33 The Pebble (*N. ziczac*). **1869** NEWMAN *Brit. Moths* 231 The Pebble Prominent. *Ibid.* 207 The Pebble Hook-tip.

5. *attrib.* and *Comb.* **a.** simple *attrib.* Of or pertaining to a pebble or pebbles; made or consisting of pebbles, or of agate or 'Scotch pebble', as ***pebble brooch***; made of thick glass, so as to appear almost opaque, as ***pebble (eye)glasses, lens, spectacles***.

1818 M. EDGEWORTH *Let.* 21 Dec. (1971) 150 This little *pebble brooch will reach you I hope just in time for you to give it..to Harriette for a Christmas box. **1848** THACKERAY *Van. Fair* lviii, Her mamma's..large pebble brooch. **1933** C. ST. J. SPRIGG *Fatality in Fleet Street* i. 14 His beady eyes regarded the Chief coldly behind his pebble *eye-glasses. **1818** KEATS *Endym.* II. 112 My veined *pebble floor. **1938** E. AMBLER *Cause for Alarm* xvi. 206 The pair of thick *pebble glasses..rendered me practically blind. **1958** P. MORTIMER *Daddy's gone a-Hunting* ii. 11 A stern little girl in thick pebble glasses. **1972** M. WOODHOUSE *Mama Doll* ii. 4 A short fat man with mad bushy hair and pebble glasses. **1977** J. AIKEN *Last Movement* i. 14 His eyes myopic behind thick pebble glasses. **1796** W. COMBE *Boydell's Thames* II. 279 Four large stones..which seem to be of the *pebble kind. **1955** H. SPRING *These Lovers fled Away* 437 The spectacles now had *pebble lenses. **1958** *Spectator* 30 May 687/3 The sadistic young slug of a lodger with dirty finger-nails and pebble-lens spectacles. **1964** R. CHURCH *Voyage Home* viii. 166 Thick, pebble lenses, flashed at me like headlamps. **1955** H. SPRING *These Lovers fled Away* 142 He was a dark, robust-looking youth, with flaring nostrils and *pebble spectacles. **1976** 'W. TREVOR' *Children of Dynmouth* v. 115 He wore thick pebble spectacles, behind which his eyes were unnaturally magnified. **1725** RAMSAY *Gent. Sheph.* III. i, Round the figur'd green and *pebble walks.

b. *Comb.*, as ***pebble-beach***, ***-bead***, ***-bed***, ***-crystal***, ***-paving***, ***-ridge***; ***pebble-covered***, ***-lensed***, ***-like***, ***-paved*** (poet. ***-paven***), ***-strewn*** adjs.; **pebble-beached** *a. slang*, (*a*) penniless, destitute; (*b*) dazed, absent-minded; **pebble-bed**, (*a*) *Geol.*, a conglomerate that contains pebbles, esp. one from which they readily work loose with weathering; (*b*) *Nuclear Sci.*, used *attrib.* to designate a nuclear reactor in which the fuel elements are in the form of pellets having an outer layer of moderator; **pebble-cast**, the casting or throwing of a pebble or pebbles, or a mass of pebbles cast up, *e.g.* by the sea; **pebble chopper** *Archæol.*, a primitive chopping tool made from a pebble (see *pebble tool* below); **pebble culture**, name given to a culture which uses pebbles as materials for tools, identified orig. in Africa but now known to have existed also in America, Asia, and Europe; **pebble-dashed** *a.*, treated with **pebble-dash** or **-dashing**, i.e. mortar with pebbles incorporated in it; **pebble grain**, a patterned grain produced by pebbling (see PEBBLE *v.* 3); **pebble-grained** *adj.*, (*a*) having a pattern produced by pebbling; (*b*) of lenses etc., having the appearance of pebble (see sense 2 b above); **pebble-hearted**, *a.*, hard-hearted, stony-hearted; **pebble-leather**, pebbled leather (see PEBBLE *v.* 3); **pebble powder**, a slow-burning gunpowder prepared in the form of cubes or prisms of the size of pebbles; **pebble tool** *Archæol.*, a primitive tool made by chipping and shaping pebbles, thought to be the earliest use of stone tools by man; **pebble-vetch**, a cultivated variety of *Vicia sativa* (Britten & Holl.); **pebble-ware**, a kind of Wedgwood ware in which clays of different colours are incorporated in the paste; **pebble weave**, a weave producing a rough surface. Also PEBBLE-STONE.

1890 in Barrère & Leland *Dict. Slang* II. 120/2 He had arrived at a crisis of impecuniosity compared to which the small circumstance of being *pebble-beached and stony-broke might be described as comparative affluence. **1897** *Sporting Times* 3 July 1/4 She was absolutely stony, pebble-beached to all the world. **1934** WODEHOUSE *Right Ho, Jeeves* xvii. 216 Gussie..switched on that pebble-beached smile again and tacked down to the edge of the platform. **1818** KEATS *Endym.* II. 149 Free from the smallest *pebble-bead of doubt. **1851** *Q. Jrnl. Geol. Soc.* VII. 77 The valley is..so encumbered with detritus of the overlying and reaggregated *pebble beds, that except at the town of Vichy it is almost impossible to make good observations. **1914** J. PARK *Text-bk. Geol.* xxviii. 377 The three main divisions of the Trias recognised in the British Isles are:—3. Rhætic... 2. Keuper... 1. Bunter... The Bunter consists of red and variously hued sandstones and conglomerates or pebble beds of fluviatile or fluvio-lacustrine origin. **1961** *New Scientist* 16 Mar. 695/1 W. Germany is to have what is probably the first operational 'pebble-bed' reactor... The fuel elements are balls of graphite with centres of uranium carbide. **1969** *Financial Times* 9 Jan. 7/6 The experimental 'pebble bed' reactor at Juelich more closely approaches the idea of a nuclear system into which fuel is simply shovelled. **1969** BENNISON & WRIGHT *Geol. Hist. Brit. Isles* xii. 274 The Bunter Pebble Beds characteristically occur in the Midlands... The name Pebble Beds is a descriptive term and the formation comprises sandstone with pebbles. **1868** FITZGERALD tr. *Omar* (ed. 2) xlvii, As the Sea's self should heed a *pebble-cast. **1959** J. D. Clark *Prehist. S. Afr.* v. 115 Some of these flakes were struck from cores and were not simply the waste flakes removed in preparing the *pebble-chopper. **1964** Jennings & Norbeck *Prehist. Man in New World* 164 At the basal level Butler places the Congdon I complex—peripherally flaked pebble choppers. **1974** *Encycl. Brit. Micropædia* VII. 825/3 *Pebble chopper*, or pebble tool, primordial cutting tool, examples of which have been dated at over 2,500 years BC. *a* **1728** Woodward *Nat. Hist. Fossils of Eng.* (1729) I. 32 A Peble, about the bigness of a Wallnut. 'Tis wholly pellucid... This kind the Lapidaries call *Peble-Crystal. **1931** J. D. Solomon in L. S. B. Leakey *Stone Age Cultures Kenya Colony* 264 Mr. C. van Riet Lowe.. has studied the terraces of the Vaal River, and finds... (i) High terrace, with coarse gravel containing what may be a *pebble-culture. **1955** *Sci. Amer.* Aug. 50/2 He has found two teeth of the man-ape in a deposit together with crudely chipped stone tools of the 'pebble culture'. **1970** J. D. Clark *Prehist. Afr.* ii. 68 It is a common misconception that the Oldowan tools were made from pebbles and the term 'Pebble Culture' has been used as synonymous with Oldowan. **1902** *Ann. Rep. Board of Regents Smithsonian Inst. 1901* 106 A cheap frame construction was used, the sides of which were treated with *pebble-dash and the roof made of asphalted felt covered with crushed slag. **1911** *Encycl. Brit.* XXI. 785/1 *Rough-cast* or *Pebble-dash* plastering is a rough form of external plastering in much use for country houses. **1960** [see God-wottery]. **1973** G. Moffat *Deviant Death* iv. 54 A dull collection of pebble dash houses and wood trim in cardinal colours. **1899** Sir E. Burne-Jones in Mackail *W. Morris* I. 51 Tumbly old buildings, gable-roofed and *pebble-dashed. **1940** *Chambers's Techn. Dict.* 621/1 **Pebble-dashing* (*Plast.*), a rough finish given to a wall by coating it with plaster, on to which, while it is still soft, small stones and liquid lime are thrown. **1978** *Lancashire Life* Sept. 3/2 (Advt.), A detached house.., built approximately 1938 of brick with pebbledashing to most elevations. **1897** *Sears, Roebuck Catal.* 194/3 Child's *pebble grain school shoe. **1931** W. Faulkner *Sanctuary* xv. 133 Disembodied voices blaring from imitation wood cabinets or pebble-grain horn-mouths above the rapt faces. **1969** R. T. Wilcox *Dict. Costume* (1970) 263/2 *Pebble grain*,..a leather, imitation leather or fabric given a grained surface by running it between rollers under pressure. **1971** 'O. Bleeck' *Thief who painted Sunlight* (1972) xiv. 123 His black, *pebble-grained loafers were burnished and gleaming. **1973** W. M. Duncan *Big Timer* i. 10 Pale blue eyes which stared myopically from behind thick pebble-grained glasses. **1816** Scott in *Q. Rev.* Oct. 198 Like Lance's *pebble-hearted cur. **1887** F. T. Marzials *Dickens* v. 64, I am afraid I must be rather pebble-hearted. **1885** C. T. Davis *Leather* xviii. 357 In the manufacture of *pebble and grain leathers. **1968** F. Mullally *Munich Involvement* iii. 21 The woman.. hesitated, blinking at Sullivan through *pebble-lensed glasses. **1975** D. Pitts *This City is Ours* xix. 65 [He] peered ..through heavy, pebble-lensed glasses. **1977** 'E. Crispin' *Glimpses of Moon* xiii. 284 Long-haired, pebble-lensed cissies in white coats. **1924** W. de la Mare *Ding Dong Bell* 56 The *pebble-like tattling of a robin. **1960** C. Day Lewis *Buried Day* 220 His stony eyes behind pebble-like glasses. **1841** Bryant *Poems* 41 The rush of the *pebble-paved river. **1821** Shelley *Epipsych.* 546 The *pebble-paven shore. **1838** *Civil Eng. & Arch. Jrnl.* I. 391/2 Constant repairs being required to the *pebble paving of the stables. **1875** Knight *Dict. Mech.*, *Pebble-paving*, pavement laid with pebbles from 3 to 4 inches deep. When larger stones are used, it is known as *bowlder*-paving. **1871** E. Cardwell in *Daily News* 3 Jan., We..set to work to adapt our machinery for the use of *pebble powder. **1880** *Times* 27 Dec. 9/4 The powder charge..consists of 425 lb. of pebble, or 450 lb. of prismatic powder. **1931** J. D. Solomon in L. S. B. Leakey *Stone Age Cultures Kenya Colony* 263 We thus seem to have the following succession of events in East Africa during the Pleistocene: (i) Wet period..which coincided with the epoch of the man who made *pebble-tools (Kafuan). **1959** J. D. Clark *Prehist. S. Afr.* iv. 74 It is an open question whether *Australopithecus* could have made pebble-tools, the earliest examples of intentionally made implements known. **1961** *Times* 5 Sept. 13/5 In fact..*Australopithecinae* had been found at four or five sites in association with pebble-tools. **1973** B. J. Williams *Evolution & Human Origins* ix. 148/2 These are often referred to as 'pebble-tools', as they usually represent river pebbles that have been fractured in such a way that a cutting edge is produced. *a* **1722** Lisle *Observ. Husb.* (1757) 125 The *pebble-vetch is a summer-vetch, different from the goar-vetch and not so big; they call it also the rath-ripe vetch. **1763** Mills *Pract. Husb.* I. 475 The small black-seeded vetch, which some call rathripe, and others pebble, or summer vetch. **1941** *Archit. Rev.* LXXXIX. 40 The floor is close-carpeted with a grey '*pebble-weave' material. **1958** *Woman's Jrnl.* Mar. 3 (Advt.), Classic casual in pebbleweave. **1969** R. T. Wilcox *Dict. Costume* (1970) 263/2 *Pebble weave*, a rough-surfaced fabric produced by weaving together shrunken, twisted yarns.

Hence **pebbleless** *a.*

1894 *Naturalist* 297 The unaltered pebbleless laminated shale below.

'pebble, *v.* [f. prec. sb.]

1. *trans.* To pelt with (or as with) pebbles.

1605 B. Jonson, etc. *Eastw. Hoe* III. i, We'd so pebble them with snowballs as they come from Church! **1816** Scott *Antiq.* xviii, The peasants..betook themselves to stones, and having pebbled the priest pretty handsomely, they drove him out of the parish. **1818** —— *Hrt. Midl.* iv, When we had..parliament men o' our ain, we could aye peeble them wi' stanes when they werena gude bairns.

2. To pave with pebbles.

1835 Beckford *Recoll.* 9 For the wise purpose of pebbling alleys in quaint Mosaic patterns.

3. *Leather Manuf.* To produce a rough or indented surface, such as might be produced by the pressure of pebbles, upon (leather), by a special kind of graining, done by means of a roller having a pattern upon it. Hence **pebbling** *vbl. sb.*; also *attrib.*, as *pebbling-machine*.

1875 Knight *Dict. Mech.* 1646/2 *Pebbling*, an operation to bring out the grain of leather and give it a roughened or ribbed appearance... In the *pebbling-machine*, the skin is subjected to the action of a roller with a surface the reverse of the grain or pebble to be produced. **1885** C. T. Davis *Leather* xxvi. 454 In currying it [Martin's Machine] will 'set out', pebble, 'stone out'..entirely without hand labour. *Ibid.* 467 Patents..for Pebbling Leather.

pebbled ('pɛb(ə)ld), *a.*

1. a. [f. pebble *sb.* + -ed².] Covered, strewn, or heaped with pebbles; pebbly. (Chiefly *poetic.*)

c **1600** Shaks. *Sonn.* lx, Like as the waues make towards the pibled shore. **1720** Gay *Dione* III. iii, Each..pebbled brook that winds along the dale. **1884** *Harper's Mag.* Nov. 852/1 The pebbled terraces of the beach.

b. Of spectacles, etc.: made with or having the appearance of pebble lenses. Also *fig.*

1939 Joyce *Finnegans Wake* 463 He is looking aged with his pebbled eyes. **1959** *Listener* 5 Mar. 406/2 Eccentric bookworms with pebbled glasses and bulging foreheads. **1969** R. Petrie *Despatch of Dove* I. 10 He watched minutely from behind thick-pebbled lenses. **1978** M. Butterworth *X marks Spot* 18 Shrewd eyes glittered behind pebbled lenses.

2. [f. pebble *v.* + -ed¹.] Of leather: Treated by the process called pebbling: see pebble *v.* 3.

'pebble-stone. Forms: see pebble *sb.* and stone *sb.* = pebble *sb.* 1.

c **1000** Ælfric *Hom.* I. 64 Gað to ðære sæ-strande, and feccað me papolstanas. *c* **1000** *Aldhelm Glosses* 1815 (Napier 1900) *Lapillulos*, i. paruos lapides, popelstanas. **1382** Wyclif *Prov.* xx. 17 And aftir shal be fulfild the mouth of hym with a litil pibbil ston. **1387** Trevisa *Higden* (Rolls) I. 353 Whan oþer wepene faillep þey [the Irish] hauep good publestones redy at hond. **1530** Palsgr. 259 Puble stone, *caillov.* **1555** Eden *Decades* 12 Two pybble stones of goulde weighinge an vnce. *Ibid.*, Pypple stones of gold. *Ibid.* marg., Pipple stones of golde. **1573** Twyne *Æneid* x. (1584) P vj b, On tother side, where as the streame of peablestones great store Togither rouled had. **1653** Walton *Angler* iv. 63 Opposed by rugged roots and pibble stones. **1838** *Civil Eng. & Arch. Jrnl.* I. 391/2 The pebble stones..firmly fixed in a matrix of concrete, are..found to answer completely.

fig. **1591** Shaks. *Two Gent.* II. iii. 11 Yet did not this cruell-hearted Curre shedde one teare: he is a stone, a very pibble stone.

b. As a material: = pebble *sb.* 1 b.

1663 Gerbier *Counsel* (1664) 90 Pavement with Pibble-stone, fifteen and eighteen pence the yard, square.

pebbly ('pɛblɪ), *a.* [f. pebble *sb.* + -y.]

1. Abounding in pebbles; covered or paved with pebbles.

1600 Surflet *Countrie Farme* II. xlii. 269 Hounds-toong groweth..in peblie and vntilled grounde. **1622** Drayton *Poly-olb.* xxvii. 4 Riuers rushing downe..Vpon their peably sholes. **1774** Pennant *Tour Scot. in 1772*, 10 July, A small bay with a pebbly beach. **1847** C. Bronte *J. Eyre* v, We went up a broad pebbly path.

2. *fig.* Resembling pebbles; uneven; *esp.* of textiles: having a rough surface.

1793 H. Fuseli in *Analytical Rev.* Jan. 2 The hoarseness of Northern language bound in pebbly monosyllables. **1923** [see armure]. **1936** Chesterton *Autobiogr.* 148 They had shiny pebbly eyes. **1955** *New Yorker* 19 Mar. 100 Done in pebbly navy wool, with deep raglan sleeves. **1964** *McCall's Sewing* i. 8/1 A pebbly crêpe will not noticeably add pounds, but a very rough, nubbly wool tweed may have a decided effect.

Pebidian (pə'bɪdɪən), *a. Geol.* [See quot. 1877 and -an.] Epithet of a thick sequence of volcanic rocks of Pre-Cambrian age exposed in Preseli, SW Wales. Also *absol.*

1877 H. Hicks in *Q. Jrnl. Geol. Soc.* XXIII. 230, I propose now to divide the Pre-Cambrian rocks [in the vicinity of St. David's] into two distinct series under the local names of Dimetian..for the lower, and Pebidian (*Pebidiauc* being the name of the division or hundred in which the rocks are chiefly exposed) for the upper series. **1880** *Ibid.* XXXVI. 538, I have long been disposed to consider the felspathic series in Shropshire, or at least the Lilleshall group, as representing the Pebidian. **1937** Pringle & George *S. Wales* ii. 15 In the neighbourhood of St. David's, the Pebidian tuffs occupy a broad anticlinal area which extends inland for several miles in an east-north-east direction. **1969** Bennison & Wright *Geol. Hist. Brit. Isles* iv. 80 The Caerfai Series commences with a reddish basal conglomerate, some of the pebbles being derived from the adjacent Precambrian volcanics, the Pebidian.

‖**pébrine** (pebrin). [mod.F. ad. Prov. *pebrino*, f. *pebre* pepper, in reference to the black spots (A. de Quatrefages 1858, in *Comptes Rendus* XLVII. 530).] A disease of silkworms, caused by the microsporidian parasite *Nosema bombycis* (cf. nosema), and characterized by the appearance of dark spots on the insect, whose growth is stunted.

1870 Tyndall in *Nature* 7 July 181/2 The name *pébrine*, first applied to the plague by M. de Quatrefages, and adopted by Pasteur. **1873** A. S. Packard *Our Common Insects* iii. 47 The still more formidable disease called pebrine is thought to be of vegetable origin. **1899** *Allbutt's Syst. Med.* VIII. 946 [The transmission] of the sporozoa of pebrine from the silkworm moth to its eggs and caterpillar. **1911** *Proc. Zool. Soc.* 625 The parasite *Nosema apis* was closely allied to that of pébrine, the silkworm disease due to *Nosema bombycis*. **1912** E. A. Minchin *Introd. Study Protozoa* xvi. 412 The Microsporidia first attained an unenviable notoriety through the ravages caused by *Nosema bombycis*, the cause of 'pébrine' or silkworm-disease. **1964** T. C. Cheng *Biol. Animal Parasites* v. 141/2 *Nosema bombycis* is parasitic in silk-worms and causes the fatal pébrine disease. **1972** Swan & Papp *Common Insects N. Amer.* 291 The microsporidian disease is called *pebrine* in France for the telltale spots on the infected silkworm. **1973** M. A. Sleigh *Biol. Protozoa* x. 245 *Nosema bombycis*, is responsible for the pebrine disease of silkworms, in which tissue cells of any type may be infected at any stage of growth.

pec (pɛk). *N. Amer. slang.* Also **peck.** [abbrev. pectoral *sb.* and *a.*] = pectoral *sb.* 3. Usu. *pl.*

1966 L. Cohen *Beautiful Losers* (1970) II. 159, I saw you with massive lower pecs and horseshoe triceps, with bulk and definition simultaneously. **1972** B. Rodgers *Queens' Vernacular* 147 *Pecks*, pectoral muscles. **1977** *Gay News* 24 Mar. 23/1 He sought only the most virile men—the brutes with watermelon-sized pecs and pea-sized heads.

pecadile, obs. form of piccadill.

pecan (pɪ'kæn, 'piːkæn, pɪ'kɑːn). Also 8 **paccan,** 8–9 **pecon,** 9 **pecanne, peccan(e, pekan.** [In 18th c. *paccan* = F. *pacane*, Sp. *pacana*, from the native name of the nut in various Algonkin dialects, e.g. Cree *pakan*, Ojibway *pagan*, Abnaki *pagann*.

'The common hickory nut was called *Pacan*, a general name for all hard-shell nuts, meaning that which is cracked with an instrument, by a stone or hammer. Strachey's Virginian vocabulary has *Paukauns* for walnuts. Baraga, for the Chippeway, *Pagan*, nuts, walnuts, hazel-nuts. At the West and South, this name, as *Pacanes* and modern *Pekan*, ..has been applied to a single species, the fruit of the Carya Olivae-formis'. Trumbull *Trans. Amer. Philol. Soc.* 1872, 25.]

a. The nut or fruit, olive-shaped and finely flavoured, of a species of hickory (*Carya illinoensis*) common in the Ohio and Mississippi valleys, often attaining a very great height; also, the tree itself, the pecan-tree.

1773 P. Kennedy *Jrnl.* in T. Hutchins *Descr. Virginia*, etc. (1778) 52 The timber, Bois Connu, or Paccan, Maple, Ash, Button Wood. **1797** A. Ellicott *Let.* 1 Apr. in C. V. Mathews *Andrew Ellicott* (1908) 152, I have a large Keg of Pecon Nuts put up for you. **1812** Brackenridge *Views Louisiana* (1814) 61 The pecanne..found on the low grounds..is a large tree resembling somewhat the hickory, but has a more delicate leaf. **1818** G. Flagg *Let.* 12 Sept. in *Trans. Illinois State Hist. Soc. 1910* (1912) 158, I have seen some [hogs] as fat upon Hickorynuts, Acorns, Pecons & Walnuts as ever I did those that were fatted upon Corn. **1876** *Forest & Stream* 13 July 376/2 Spending a few days at Congo, gathering pecans. **1969** *Oxf. Bk. Food Plants* 28/2 Nowadays, pecans can be bought in many British shops. *Ibid.*, The Pecan is a large tree up to 170 feet high, with grey, furrowed bark. **1975** *New Yorker* 3 Feb. 25/2 The cake.. was made of thin layers of yellow sponge cake and filled with a whipped cream laced with brandy, pecans, and a special coffee extract.

b. *bitter pecan*, bitter-seeded hickory (*Carya aquatica*), a smaller species native to the southern States. Also called *water-* or *swamp-hickory*.

c. *Comb.*, as *pecan-nut*, *pie*, *-tree*.

1786 Jefferson *Writ.* (1859) I. 506 To procure me two or three hundred paccan-nuts from the western country. *Ibid.* II. 74 The paccan-nut is, as you conjecture, the Illinois nut. The former is the vulgar name south of the Potomac. **1827** J. Coldstream in Balfour *Biogr.* ii. (1865) 23 Amongst them is a peccan nut-tree. **1883** *Pall Mall G.* 17 Sept. 4/2 He buried her under a big pecan tree [in California]. **1936** F. M. Farmer *Boston Cooking-School Cook Bk.* (new ed.) 633 Pecan Pie... 3 eggs... 1 cup light corn syrup... 1 cup finely chopped pecans. **1976** *Express-News* (San Antonio, Texas) 2 Oct. 3-E/4 The specialty-of-the-house dessert—which is made every day—is pecan pie. **1976** *Listener* 22 July 86/1 Ordinary Southern food..fried chicken and pecan pie.

pecari, -y, variants of peccary.

peccability (pɛkə'bɪlɪtɪ). [f. as next + -ity.] Capability of sinning, liability to sin.

a **1631** Donne *Six Serm.* i. (1634) 34 The peccabilitie, that possibilitie of sinning, which is in the nature of the angels of heaven. **1721** J. Clarke *Moral Evil* 44 Finite intelligent beings necessarily suppose peccability. **1855** Miss Cobbe *Intuit. Mor.* 98 *note*, Our imperfection and peccability.

peccable ('pɛkəb(ə)l), *a.* [a. F. *peccable* (13th c. in Littré) or ad. med.L. *peccābilis*, f. *peccāre* to sin, after L. *impeccābilis* sinless (cited from Gellius).]

1. Capable of sinning, liable to sin.

1604 T. Wright *Passions* v. §4. 210 All men by nature are sinners, are peccable, the iust offend often. **1741** Berkeley *Let. to Sir J. James* 7 June, Wks. 1871 IV. 272 We hold all mankind to be peccable and errable, even the Pope himself. **1857** H. Miller *Test. Rocks* iii. 154 Fitting and preparing peccable, imperfect man, for a perfect impeccable future state.

†**2.** Sinful, wrongful. *Obs.*

1633 Prynne *Histriom.* 563 Is not the selfe same sinne as sinfull, as peccable?

†**pecca'dilian.** *Obs.* Also **-dulian, -duliun.** Early corrupt forms of peccadillo (prob. from It. *peccadiglio*).

1529 More *Suppl. Soulys* Wks. 310/1 He calleth them al smal enormities, and as a man woulde say lytle prety pecadulians. **1532** —— *Confut. Tindale* ibid. 423/2, I founde in the tone some prety peccaduliuns. **1567** Drant *Horace, De Arte Poet.* Biij, Certayne Peccadilians which scape, yea in the beste. **1569** Crowley *Soph. Dr. Watson* ii. 145 Such as the Italians call Peccadulians, little pretie sinnes.

†**peccadill.** *Obs.* [a. F. *peccadille* (16th c., in early examples *peccadillo, peccatile*), ad. It. or Sp.: see below.] = PECCADILLO.

1621 T. WILLIAMSON tr. *Goulart's Wise Vieillard* 61 The slipps and peccadills of their youth. **1675** COTTON *Burlesque on B.* 16 For so small a Peccadill To send a man up Holborn-hill [i.e. to Tyburn]. **1736** J. SERCES *Popery an Enemy to Script.* 63 The Faults..are but peccadilles.

peccadill, -dilly, -dillo: see PICCADILL, etc.

†**pecca'dillie,** anglicized form of next.

1660 F. BROOKE tr. *Le Blanc's Trav.* 52 'Tis but a peccadillie for a Master to lye with his slave.

peccadillo (pɛkə'dɪləʊ). Also 6 **peccadilia,** 7 **-dil(l)io, -diglio,** 8 **-dilla;** 7 **peccha-, peca-, piccadillo; picadilio, pickadilla,** 8 **pecadiglio.** [a. Sp. *pecadillo* (-ðiljo), dim. of *pecado* sin, or It. *peccadiglio* (Florio, 1611).] A small or venial fault or sin; a trifling offence.

1591 HARINGTON *Apol. Poet. Orl. Fur.* ¶iv, I omit as his *peccadilia*, how he nicknameth priests. **1600** O. E. *Repl. Libel* I. viii. 205 The Spaniard is saide to account it but a *Peccadillo* or little fault. **1607** SIR J. H. in *Harington's Nugæ Ant.* (ed. Park 1804) II. 7 Some peccadilios of yours. **1637** BASTWICK *Litany* I. 19 Accounted..but peccadiglios. **1647** SIR R. STAPYLTON *Juvenal* vi. 85 Lust appeares a peccadillio. *Ibid.* xiii. 241 Yet these are peccadilio's. **1652** BROOKS *Precious Remedies* (1653) 29 When this *peccadillo*.. and a hot fiery furnace stood in competition. **1670** SIR J. BRAMSTON *Autobiog.* 143 This is but a picadilio. **1697** VANBRUGH *Relapse* v. iii, Mr. Bull said it was a Peckadilla. **1708** NELSON *Let. Hanger* in Secretan *Life* (1860) 192 Never reckon an excess in drinking a small fault, a *pecadiglio*. **1748** RICHARDSON *Clarissa* (1811) III. 206 She'll know enough of me, not to wonder at such a peccadilla. *a* **1845** HOOD *Ode R. Wilson* xiv, Schemes..That frown upon St. Giles's sins, but blink The peccadilloes of all Piccadilly.

attrib. **1600** tr. *Amyraldus' Treat. conc. Relig.* III. vi. 421 Those which they lookt upon as piccadillo sins. **1797** MRS. M. ROBINSON *Walsingham* II. 221 The..amours of him whose peccadillo follies are the subject of universal ridicule.

pe'ccaminous, *a.* *rare.* [f. late L. *peccāmen, -āmin-* (in Christian writers) + -OUS.] Full of sins, sinful.

It is the kind of word that Joyce may have picked up from the *O.E.D.*

1656 in BLOUNT *Glossogr.* **1668** H. MORE *Div. Dial.* II. vii. (1713) 109 In regard of our peccaminous terrestrial Personalities here. **1922** JOYCE *Ulysses* 720 A volume of peccaminous pornographical tendency entitled *Sweets of Sin*. **1939** —— *Finnegans Wake* 288 To put off the barcelonas from their peccaminous corpulums.

peccan(e, variants of PECAN.

peccancy ('pɛkənsɪ). [ad. L. *peccāntia* (Tertull. 3rd. c.), f. pr. pple. of *peccāre* to sin: see -ANCY.] The quality or condition of being peccant.

1. Moral faultiness, sinfulness.

1656 HEYLIN *Surv. France* 41 The peccancie of an old English Doctor. *a* **1679** T. GOODWIN *Election* IV. xii, Sins of commission have more of peccancy in them than sins of omission. **1784** COWPER *Task* II. 72 Where all deserve And stand exposed by common peccancy To what no few have felt. **1902** W. JAMES *Varieties Relig. Exp.* 267 As if our tears broke through an inveterate inner dam, and let all sorts of ancient peccancies and moral stagnancies drain away.

b. A sin, offence, transgression.

1648 W. MONTAGUE *Devout Ess.* I. xii. §2 This distorting of equivocall words, which passeth commonly for a triviall peccancy. **1671** *True Nonconf.* 39 Waving the immodest terme of impudence and other arrant peccancies against truth. **1879** G. MEREDITH *Egoist* xxxiv, Above most human peccancies, I do abhor a breach of faith.

†**2.** Faultiness, incorrectness. *Obs. rare*$^{-1}$.

c **1611** CHAPMAN *Iliad* III. Comm., But to make a fool *non peccans verbis*, will make a man nothing wonder at any peccancy or absurdity in men of mere language.

3. Corruptness or disorder of the humours, etc.

1665-6 *Phil. Trans.* I. 178 To cure the manifold peccancy of this juyce by Evacuations. **1747** tr. *Astruc's Fevers* 105 The saliva is impregnated with a general peccancy.

peccant ('pɛkənt), *a.* (*sb.*) [ad. L. *peccānt-em*, pr. pple. of *peccāre* to sin; in sense 3, a. OF. *peccant* (13-14th c. in Hatz.-Darm.).]

1. That commits or has committed a fault or moral offence; sinning, offending.

1604 R. CAWDREY *Table Alph.*, *Peccant*, offending, doing amisse. **1610** G. FLETCHER *Christ's Vict.* II. xxi, The shadows err'd Of thousand peccant ghosts, unseen, unheard. **1642-3** EARL OF NEWCASTLE *Declar.* in Rushw. *Hist. Coll.* (1721) V. 134 To prove them to be peccant against any authentick Rule. **1690** SOUTH *Serm.* (1697) II. vii. 295 That a peccant Creature should disapprove, and repent of every Violation of, and Declination from the Rules of Just and Honest. **1862** CARLYLE *Fredk. Gt.* XIII. iii. (1872) V. 39 The peccant Officials..fell on their knees.

b. Said of things.

1633 PRYNNE *1st Pt. Histrio-m.* III. vi. 123 [Our own statutes] precisely prohibit the satyricall depraving, traducing, or derogation of..the Sacrament of the Lords Supper in any Enterludes, Playes or Rimes (in which kinde Playes had beene formerly peccant). **1874** W. E. HALL *Rights & Duties Neutrals* III. iii. 127 He seizes the peccant property.

2. Offending against or violating some rule or principle; faulty, incorrect. ? *Obs.*

1624 F. WHITE *Repl. Fisher* 116 This Sillogisme is peccant in forme. **1726** AYLIFFE *Parergon* 177 If the Citation be evidently peccant in point of Form or Matter. **1841** D'ISRAELI *Amen. Lit., Hum. B. Jonson*, If true learning in the art of the drama be peccant, our poet is a very saintly sinner.

3. Causing disorder of the system; morbid, unhealthy, corrupt: used esp. in the humoral pathology; also, inducing disease.

1604 T. WRIGHT *Climact. Years* 15 Some few peccant humours. **1661** HICKERINGILL *Jamaica* 103 Adjourning Plagues they use to bring, In Peccant Autumns or the Spring. **1667** *Phil. Trans.* II. 621 It was not at all probable that his blood was peccant in the quantity. **1706** PHILLIPS, *Peccant*,..among Physicians, the Humours of the Body are said to be Peccant, when they contain some Malignity, or else abound too much. **1899** *Allbutt's Syst. Med.* VI. 742 The patient..pointing to the peccant tooth as the source of his woe. *Ibid.* VIII. 495 Purgatives and diuretics may be given to eliminate any peccant matter.

b. In figurative use.

1605 BACON *Adv. Learn.* I. iv. §12 Thus I have gone over these three diseases of learning: besides the which there are some other rather peccant humors, than fourmed diseases. **1727** POPE, etc. *Art of Sinking* iii, A discharge of the peccant humour in exceeding purulent metre. **1790** BURKE *Fr. Rev.* Wks. 1808 V. 58 The change is to be confined to the peccant part only. **1860** EMERSON *Cond. Life, Power* Wks. (Bohn) II. 333 Where is great amount of life, though gross and peccant, it has its own checks.

B. *sb.* A sinner; an offender.

1621 I. C. in T. Bedford *Sin unto Death* ¶vj b, No time nor age..hath beene more likely to bring forth plenty of peccants in this kinde. **1803** C. K. SHARPE *Let.* 3 Apr. in *Corr.* (1888) I. 165 A swinging blow on some peccant's rump from the cudgel of the serjeant!

Hence **'peccantly** *adv.*; **'peccantness.**

1847 WEBSTER, *Peccantly*. **1727** BAILEY vol. II, *Peccantness*, offensiveness, hurtfulness.

peccary ('pɛkərɪ). Forms: 7 **pakeera,** 7-8 **pecary,** 7- **peccary,** (8 **picary,** 9 **picaree, pec(c)ari).** [ad. *pakira, paquira*, the name in Carib of Guiana.

Spelt by the Spaniard Oviedo 1535 *baquira* or *vaquira*; *paquira* is used by the Frenchmen Biet (*Dict. des Galibis*) 1664, and Breton 1665, and is frequent in Fr. and Sp. writers of 18th c. In It., Claviger spells *pachira*. G. Warren in 1667 has *pakeera*, and the form is still current in the Apalai and Ouayana dialects of Guiana. An English writer in 1613 spells *pockiero*, which is also in the 18th c. Dictionarium Galibi; Dutch 18th c. voyagers have *peequiera*. *Pecary* appears in 1699. Buffon has *pakira* and *peccary*, Cuvier *pécari*. (Jas. Platt Junr. in *Athenæum* 8 June 1901, 727/3; *Bibliothèque Linguist. Amér.* XV. 1892.)]

A gregarious quadruped of South and Central America, allied to the swine, of which there are two species, the ***collared peccary*** extending north to Texas, and the ***white-lipped p.*** of South America.

1613 R. HARCOURT *Voy. to Guiana* 29 Swine in great numbers, whereof there are two kinds, the one small, by the Indians called *pockiero*, the other is called *paingo*. **1667** G. WARREN *Descr. Surinam* 11 Of the hogs there are three kinds. One lives like an otter..the other two are called the Pakeera and Pinko. **1697** DAMPIER *Voy. round World* (1699) 9 He..hunts about for Peccary. **1699** L. WAFER *Descr. America* 104 The country has of its own a kind of hog, which is called Pecary. **1769** E. BANCROFT *Ess. Nat. Hist. Guiana* 125 The Picary is considerably smaller than the ordinary European Hogs. **1774** GOLDSM. *Nat. Hist.* III. 183 That animal which of all others most resembles an hog..is called the Peccary, or Tajacu. **1807** HOME in *Phil. Trans.* XCVII. 154 The stomach of the pecari differs from that of the common hog. **1807** H. BOLINGBROKE *Voy. Demerary* 227 There are two kinds of hogs..numerous in all parts of Guyana, the picaree and the waree. **1846** G. A. MCCALL *Lett. fr. Frontiers* (1868) 440 The Mexican wild boar, the Peccary,..has no tail, and it has a musk-pouch on the after-part of the back, which exudes a strong smell of musk.

peccation (pɛ'keɪʃən). *rare.* [ad. L. *peccātiōn-em*, n. of action from *peccāre* to sin.] The action of sinning, sin.

1862 THACKERAY *Philip* vi, Though he roared out *peccavi* most frankly when charged with his sins, this criminal would fall to peccation very soon after promising amendment.

‖**peccavi** (pɛ'keɪvaɪ, pɛk'kɑːviː). Also 7 **pecavie.** [L. *peccāvi* 'I have sinned'.] 'I have sinned', in the phrase 'to cry *peccavi*'; hence an acknowledgement or confession of guilt.

So *peccavimus* 'we have sinned'; *peccavit* 'he has sinned'.

[**1509** FISHER *Fun. Serm. Hen. VII* Wks. (1876) 272 Kynge Dauid that wrote this psalme, with one worde spekynge his herte was chaunged sayenge *Peccaui*.] **1553** T. WILSON *Rhet.* (1580) 65 Much soner shall al other be subiect vnto him, and crie *Peccaui*. **1592** G. HARVEY *Four Lett.* Wks. (Grosart) I. 199 That he, which in the ruffe of his freshest iollity, was faine to cry..a mercy in printe, may be orderlie driuen to crie more peccauies, then one. **1600** W. WATSON *Decacordon* (1602) 179 Then were the seculars not onely bound to obey and surcease, but also to cry *peccauimus* and submit themselues to doe such penance as [etc.]. **1616** J. LANE *Cont. Sqr.'s T.* XI. 115 'Dread Dame' (quoth shee) 'because hee cries "peccauit", Wee bothe will sue his special supplicauit'. **1681** BAXTER *Acc. Sherlocke* i. 160 A true information and conviction, which may bring me to the most open *peccavi* or confession. **1730** SWIFT *Sheridan's Submission* Wks. 1755 IV. I. 259 Now lowly crouch'd, I cry peccavi, And prostrate, supplicate *pour ma vie*. **1814** MRS. J. WEST *Alicia de Lacy* II. 291 Her ears were alternately assailed by the peccavis of penitence, and the well-a-days of love. **1862** [see PECCATION].

pecco, variant of PEKOE.

†**pece.** *Obs.* Also 5 **pyece, pese,** 6 **peece,** *Sc.* **peis, peys.** [ad. med.L. *pecia*, 'vas, calix, cyathus' (Du Cange).

In other uses, *pecia* represents F. *pièce*, e.g. *pecia terræ* = F. *pièce de terre*; but the sense 'cup', 'vase', is not known for F. *pièce*. In Eng. however *pece* is a common early spelling of *piece*, and this may be a sense of English development. Cf. 'piece of plate'.]

A cup (*esp.* a wine-cup); a drinking-vessel.

1362 LANGL. *P. Pl.* A. III. 23 Coupes of clene Gold and peces of seluer. *c* **1400** *Ywaine & Gaw.* 760 A pot with riche wine And a pece to fil it yne. **1432-50** tr. *Higden* (Rolls) III. 433 After that he hade drunke wyne sende to hym by the kynge, he putte the pece [HIGD. *vas*, TREVISA the vessel] in his bosom. *c* **1440** *Promp. Parv.* 388/1 Pece, cuppe, *pecia, crater*. **1470-85** MALORY *Arthur* VIII. ii, He tooke the pyece with poyson and dranke frely. *c* **1485** *Digby Myst.* (1882) III. 535 Felle a pese, taverner. **1513** DOUGLAS *Æneis* VI. iv. 27 The warme new blude keppit in coup and peis. **1594** PLAT *Chem. Concl.* 20 Putting them into a little pewter peece.

b. ? A wine-cask or butt.

1608 SYLVESTER *Du Bartas* II. iv. III. *Schism* 545 As Claret wine from a pearc't Peece doth spout.

pece, obs. form of PEACE, PIECE.

pech (pɛːx, pɛːç), *sb.* *Sc.* and *north. dial.* Also 7-9 **pegh.** [Goes with PECH *v.*] A short laboured breath, a pant after exertion.

1500-20 DUNBAR *Poems* xiii. 53 ȝung monkis..thair hait flesche dantis, Full faderlyk, with pechis and pantis. **1572** *Lament. Lady Scot.* 400 He gaif ane greit pech, lyke ane weill fed stirk. *a* **1624** BP. M. SMITH *Serm.* xiv. (1632) 257 He made but a pegh at it, saying, She gaue me, that, that without cruelty she could not take from me. **1824** *Blackw. Mag.* XVI. 89 Don't conclude your draught with a pegh like a paviour. **1884** *Ibid.* Feb. 231 With a 'pech' of satisfaction.

pech (pɛːx, pɛːç), *v.* *Sc.* and *north. dial.* Also 6 **peigh,** 7 **peach,** 8-9 **pegh,** (9 **peich,** *north. Eng. dial.* **peff, peck).** [app. onomatopœic, with the *p* of *puff, pant* and other explosive words, and the imitative ending found also in *hech, stech.*] *intr.* To breathe hard from exertion, to fetch the breath short, to pant.

c **1440** *York Myst.* xl. 84 For pechyng als pilgrymes that putte are to pees. **1572** *Lament. Lady Scot.* 269 Now mon thay wirk and labour, pech and pant. **1595** DUNCAN *App. Etymol.* Gloss. (E.D.S.), *Anhelo*, to peigh or pant. *a* **1598** ROLLOCK *On the Passion* xx. (1616) 188 He will tye the burthen of them on their owne backes, whilest they grone and peach. **1721** RAMSAY *Prospect of Plenty* 73 Peching fou sair. **1780** MAYNE *Siller Gun* II. v, They wha had corns, or broken wind, Begood to pegh and limp behind. **1786** BURNS *Willie Chalmers* i, My Pegasus I'm got astride, And up Parnassus pechin [*rime* brechan]. **1828** *Craven Gloss.* (ed. 2), *Peff*,..to breathe with difficulty. **1894** CROCKETT *Raiders* (ed. 3) 199 At a pace that made me pech..like a wind-galled nag.

pechan ('pɛxən, 'pɛçən). *Sc.* [Derivation uncertain: cf. prec.] The stomach.

1786 BURNS *Twa Dogs* 62 Yet e'en the ha' folk fill their pechan [*v.r.* peghan] Wi' sauce, ragouts, and sic like trashtrie. **1862** HESLOP *Prov. Scotland* 82 He puts it in a bad purse that puts it in his pechan.

pechar, -er, obs. forms of PITCHER, PEACHER.

pechblende: see PITCHBLENDE.

peche, obs. f. PEACH.

pêche à la Melba, pêche Melba: see MELBA.

Pecht, var. PICT.

pecia ('piːsɪə). Pl. **peciæ, pecie, pecias.** [a. med.L. *pecia* PIECE *sb.*] A gathering of a manuscript, usu. a gathering of four leaves. **pecia system,** a system of copying pecia by pecia.

1908 H. HALL *Stud. in Eng. Official Hist. Documents* III. 380 A rarer term [in Palæography] occurs in the use of *peciae* to denote the component parts of a file of loose documents. **1912** E. M. THOMPSON *Introd. Gr. & Lat. Palaeogr.* 68 A survival of the ancient method of calculating [*sc.* the remuneration of scribes] has been found in the practice..in the middle ages, of paying by the *pecia* of sixteen columns, each of sixty-two lines with thirty-two letters to the line. **1930** R. STEELE in *Library* XI. 230 The pecia is a unit, devised mainly for estimating the rate of payment to the copyist, which seems to have arisen in the University of Bologna early in the thirteenth century. **1934** LITTLE & PELSTER *Oxford Theol. 1282-1302* I. v. 56 (*heading*) The pecia and some characteristics of Oxford scholastic manuscripts. *Ibid.* 57 The *pecia* is originally, according to the researches of Savigny and Destrez, a piece of parchment which when folded contains two sheets, i.e. 4 leaves on 8 pages. As copyists were frequently paid according to the number of *pecie* which they had written, the beginning of a new *pecia* in the original examples was not infrequently marked in the copies by a *p* or *pe*^{a} with the corresponding numeral. **1935** *Times Lit. Suppl.* 14 Dec. 858/3 The *pecia* was the loose quire, generally of four folios or eight pages, lent out by an approved 'stationer' to be copied. **1958** C. H. TALBOT in Wormald & Wright *Eng. Library before 1700* iv. 67 The unit of their [*sc.* the university scribes'] work was the *pecia*, a technical term (borrowed no doubt from the tanners and parchment makers) designating a sheep-skin which could be treated for writing on. *Ibid.* 68 The size of the *pecia* appears to have differed somewhat in the manuscripts we know, but the general conclusion seems to be that it was a sextern. **1963** R. A. B. MYNORS *Catal. MSS. Balliol Coll.* 43 The care with which it is written and its *peciae* are marked might suggest that it was intended to be kept.. as a standard copy. **1964** G. Pollard in *Beiträge zum Berufsbeurusstsein des Mittelalterlichen Menschen* (Miscellanea Mediaevalia III) 338 (*heading*) The pecia system. **1972** E. J. Dobson *Eng. Text of Ancrene Riwle* p. x, It must have been one of two copies made simultaneously from a single exemplar by a form of the *pecia* system. **1976** A. G. Judy *Kilwardby's De Ortu Scientiarum* p. xxi, There would have been exactly eighteen pecias in this copy.

† **pecify**, obs. Sc. form of PACIFY.
1533 Bellenden *Livy* I. viii. (S.T.S.) 46 Al nychtbouris liand þame about war mesit and pecifyit.

peck (pɛk), *sb.*[1] Forms: 4 pec, 4–6 **pek, pekke,** (5–6 **peke**), 5–7 **pecke,** (7 *Sc.* pect), 5– **peck.** [ME. *pek*, = OF. *pek* (13th c. in Godef., only one instance), frequent in AF., also latinized as *peccum* (or ? *-us*), *pekka*; ulterior history unknown.
Godefroy's OF. instance refers to oats for horses, which was also a chief use of *pek* in ME. In this respect *pek* was synonymous with F. *picotin* 'a pecke or the fourth part of a boisseau.. used only in the measuring of oats' (Cotgr.), a horse's feed of oats (Scheler); in med.L. *picotinus*. But the latter was evidently a deriv. of med.L. *picotus*, *-ta* a liquid measure, in OF. *picote* a wine-measure (14th c. in Godef.). The radical part of these words may be cognate with *pek*. The formal resemblances of *picote* to F. *picoter*, 'to prick often, to peck as a bird', and of *pek*, *peck* to *pek*, *pekke*, PECK *v.*[1], is notable; but *peck* sb. is known long before the vb., and cannot easily be derived from it.]

1. A measure of capacity used for dry goods; the fourth part of a bushel, or two gallons. The imperial peck contains 554·548 cubic inches, that of the United States 537·6.
The Scottish peck was the fourth part of the firlot and contained 4 lippies = 553·5625 cubic inches for wheat, but 807·55 for barley, rye, pulse, salt, and other commodities. In England, the peck formerly varied greatly according to locality and to the commodity measured. See *O.C. and Farm. Words* (E. Dial. Soc.) 173.
c **1300** *Battle Abbey Custumals* (1887) 14 Et debet cariare j ambram, j bussellum, et pek salis. **1338** in Dugdale *Monasticon* (1846) II. 584/1 In j. pekko salis. *Ibid.* 584/2, xiiij. [equi] quorum quilibet j. pekka. **1351–2** *Rolls of Parlt.* II. 240/1 Soient les Mesures, c'est assaver bussell, demi bussell, & pec, galon, potel, & quarte, en chescun Countee.. acordantz a l'estandard. **1352** *Mem. Ripon* (Surtees) I. 236 Cuidam leproso unum pek frumenti. *c* **1386** Chaucer *Reeve's T.* 90 The Millere shold nat stele hem half a pekke Of corn by sleighte. **1390** *Earl Derby's Exp.* (Camden) 6 Pro iij[bus] bussellis et j pecco auenarum, xixd. ob. *Ibid.* 29. **1464** *Mann. & Househ. Exp.* (Roxb.) 545 Paid for a pekke of otemelle, iij.*d.* *c* **1485** *Digby Myst.* (1882) II. 30 How, hosteler, how, a peck of otys. **1526** Tindale *Matt.* xiii. 33 Hid in 3 peckes off meele. [So Coverd., *Great B., Geneva, Rheims*; Wyclif mesuris, 1611 measures.] **1534** *Ord. Govt. Irel.* in *St. Papers Hen. VIII*, II. 210 They [Irish lords] toke a pecke of ootes of every plough in the sede tyme, called the greatte horse, or chefe horsis pecke. **1537** *Ibid.* 495 Item, that the greate peckes of otes.. and suche other nedeles extortions.. be clerly abolysheid. **1603** in *Rec. Old Aberdeen* (1899) 33 That na darer draiff be sauld.. nor four d. ilk pect. **1725** Bradley *Fam. Dict.* s.v. *Gallon*, In Liquids two Pottles ..make one Gallon.. But in dry Measure, two Gallons, which is six Pottles, make one Peck. **1789** Burns *Happy Trio* 1 O, Willie brew'd a peck o' maut. **1846** J. Baxter *Libr. Pract. Agric.* (ed. 4) I. 272 Nine imperial pecks to the statute acre, of good and clean Riga seed.

b. In various proverbial expressions.
1603 Dekker *Grissil* (Shaks. Soc.) 6, I think I shall not eat a peck of salt: I shall not live long, sure. **1710** Palmer *Proverbs* lxxix. 221 *title*, Every man must eat a Peck of ashes before he dies. *Ibid.*, Every man must eat a peck of dirt in his life! **1828** *Craven Gloss.* (ed. 2) s.v., 'To measure to another a peck out of one's own bushel', to think or treat others like himself. **1862** Hislop *Prov. Scot.* 31 Before ye choose a friend eat a peck o' saut with him. **1901** *Daily Chron.* 23 Aug. 5/2 'A dry summer never made a dear peck', says an old weather proverb.

c. A swarm of bees such as would fill a peck: cf. *peck-swarm* in 5.
1713 Warder *True Amazons* (ed. 2) 37 Put a Swarm of Bees of a Peck, in May, into a Hive of Glass. *Ibid.* vi. (ed. 2) 77 One Peck of Bees in one Hive, will get much more Honey than two half Pecks will do in two Hives.

d. A liquid measure of two gallons. *dial.*
1886 Elworthy *W. Som. Work-bk.* s.v., *Peck* is a measure of liquids = two gals. 'I do hear how Farmer Burge is zillin' o' very good cider vor a shillin' a peck'.

2. A vessel used as a peck measure.
1392–3 *Earl Derby's Exp.* (Camden) 158 Et pro j pecco ligneo pro mensura auenarum, iiij*d.* **1404** *Durham Acc. Rolls* (Surtees) 397, j pek pro præbenda. **1598** Shaks. *Merry W.* III. v. 113 Next to be compass'd like a good Bilbo in the circumference of a Pecke, hilt to point, heele to head. **1641** Best *Farm. Bks.* (Surtees) 109 Yow must take a spade and a pecke,.. and goe twice a day to the aunt-hills.. take up the moules and alltogeather, and putte into the pecke. **1705** Hickeringill *Priest-cr.* IV. Wks. 1716 III. 229 Can a Peck contain all the Water in the Sea? **1878** Mackintosh *Hist. Civiliz. Scot.* I. xi. 458 In 1492 three men were put in the pillory.. for having pecks of too small measure.

b. In the Isle of Man: see quot. 1903.
1887 Hall Caine *Deemster* iii. 12 The bread-basket known as the 'peck'. **1894** —— *Manxman* 32 The peck, the parchment oat-cake pan. **1903** *Eng. Dial. Dict.*, *Peck*,.. A wooden hoop, about 3 or 4 inches deep, and about 20 inches in diameter, covered with a sheep's skin, and resembling the head of a drum, it is used to keep oaten cakes in.

3. *loosely.* A considerable quantity or number, a great deal, a 'quantity', 'heap', 'lot'. Chiefly *fig.* in phr. *a peck of troubles.*
c **1535** in *Archæologia* XXV. 97 The said George.. told hym that M[r]. More was in a pecke of troubles. **1539** *Aberdeen Regr.* (Spald. Cl.) I. 159 Calling of hir commond vyld freris hvyr that scho wes, that hes ane pek of lyiss betuix thi shoulderis. **1664** [Scudamore] *Homer à la Mode* 2 Did bring upon the Græcians, double Foure or five hundred pecks of trouble. **1857** Hughes *Tom Brown* I. viii, A pretty peck of troubles you'll get into.

†**4.** An ancient measure of land. *Obs.*
1442 *Rolls of Parlt.* V. 59/1 A pek of Londe, Paster, Hethe and Maresse. *Ibid.*, Half a pek and a nayle of Londe, Pasture and Hethe.

5. *attrib.* and *Comb.*, as **peck loaf**, a loaf made from a peck of flour; † **peck-swarm**, a swarm of bees that fills a hive of the size of a peck: see 1 c.
1599 Massinger, etc. *Old Law* IV. ii, I never durst eat oysters, nor cut *peck-loaves. **1806** Surr *Winter in Lond.* I. 196 The lord mayor ordered the price of bread to be raised one penny in the peck-loaf. **1609** C. Butler *Fem. Mon.* v. Liv, All *pecke-swarmes, and other single swarmes after Mid-Cancer [are fitted] with the least, or halfe-bushell hiue.

peck, *sb.*[2] *Obs.* or *local.* [app. a local variant of PICK *sb.*, PEAK *sb.*[2]]
1. A local name of various tools: see quots.
1485 *Naval Acc. Hen. VII* (1896) 72 Gonne hamurs.. iij, Gonne pekkes.. viij. **1514** *Lett. & Pap. Hen. VIII*, I. 5721 (P.R.O.) xxii pekes for to hewe gounys stonys. **1544** *Knaresb. Wills* (Surtees) I. 47 One Carlille axe, one pekke. **1784** Young *Ann. Agric.* II. 50 (*Essex*) They cut their beans with a tool they call a peck, being a short handled scythe for one hand, and a hook for the other. **1813** —— *Agric. Essex* I. 163 The Flemish scythe is used in Foulness for cutting beans: it is called a bean peck. **1883** *Hampsh. Gloss.*, *Peck*, *sb.* a pick-axe. **1884** *Upton-on-Severn Gloss.*, *Pick*, or *Peck*, (1) A pick-axe;..(2) A pointed hammer for breaking coal. *Ibid.*, *Peck-shaft*, the handle of a pick-axe.

2. A peak.
1481–90 *Howard Househ. Bks.* (Roxb.) 139 For ij. coschyn clothis with peckkes xxiiij.*s.* **1884** *Upton-on-Severn Gloss.*, *Peck*, a point (peak): 'The peck of the shou'der'.

peck (pɛk), *sb.*[3] Also 6 **pekke,** 6–7 **pecke.** [f. PECK *v.*[1]]
1. An act of pecking; a stroke with the beak or bill; (humorously) a snappy kiss: cf. PECKY *a.*[2] 2.
1611 Cotgr., *Becquade*, a pecke, iob, or bob with a beake. **1824** Miss Mitford *Village* Ser. I. (1863) 17 The robin red-breast and the wren.. would stop for two pecks. **1859** M. Napier *Life Visct. Dundee* I. II. 314 Argyle's.. audacious but feeble peck at the throne in Scotland. **1893** Saltus *Madam Sapphira* 84 Bending toward his wife he received from that lady a rapid and noiseless peck.

2. The impression or mark made by pecking; a prick, hole, or dint; a dot; a slight surface injury.
1591 Percival *Sp. Dict.*, *Picado*, a pricke, a pecke, *morsus*, *punctura*. **1676** J. Beaumont in *Phil. Trans.* XI. 727 These [Trochites] have also a small peck in the middle making but very little impression in the stone, and seldom passing through it. **1740** Dyche & Pardon s.v., A little hole made in fruit as it hangs upon trees, is called a bird *peck*. **1797** *Encycl. Brit.* (ed. 3) VI. 671/1 In engraving the flesh, the effect may be produced in the lighter parts and middle tints by long pecks of the graver, rather than by light lines. **1852** Wiggins *Embanking* 15 Raising a bank of great bulk, turfing or gravelling the sea face, and mending every little 'peck' or injury as it occurs.

3. *slang*, orig. *Thieves' Cant.* Food, meat, 'grub'; provender.
peck-alley, the throat. *peck and perch*, board and lodging. *peck and tipple* (*booze*), meat and drink.
1567 Harman *Caveat* 86 She hath a Cacling chete, a grunting chete, ruff Pecke, cassan, and popplarr of yarum. **1641** Brome *Joviall Crew* II. Wks. 1873 III. 388 Here, safe in our Skipper, let's cly off our Peck. **1706** Mrs. Centlivre *Basset Table* Prol., Poor House-keeping, where Peck is under Locks. **1732** Mrs. Delany in *Life & Corr.* I. 346 We went to supper, and had a profusion of peck and booz. **1828** *Lights & Shades* II. 206 What's peck and perch, and a pound a-week? **1865** Dickens *Mut. Fr.* IV. vii, The serving of the 'peck' was the affair of a moment. **1893** *Kennel Gaz.* Aug. 221/2 He [a dog] wants a little more peck.

4. **peck-right**, in a group of birds, the way in which those of higher rank are able to attack those lower in the hierarchy, without provoking an attack in return; cf. PECK-ORDER, PECKING-ORDER.
1931 W. C. Allee *Animal Aggregations* xix. 344 Hens with this power [of pecking inferiors] are said to have the 'peck-right' over those submitting to the pecking. **1954** Fisher & Lockley *Sea-Birds* vii. 170 There is [among gulls], as in domestic hens, a definite order of precedence, or peck-right. **1962** J. C. Welty *Life of Birds* x. 184/2 The dominant bird is said to possess a peck right over the subordinate bird.

peck (pɛk), *sb.*[4] Abbrev. PECKERWOOD b. *U.S. Black slang.*
1932 *Evening Sun* (Baltimore) 9 Dec. 31/5 *Peck*, a white person. **1964** O. Harrington in J. H. Clarke *Harlem* 96 Every member loved old Snakes and every school-child knew that he'd once been caught in a Texas mob which was joyously barbecuing another Negro. And when old Snakes began laughing the pecks stared in amazement and let him walk right through. **1969** C. Brown in A. Chapman *New Black Voices* (1972) 183 A poor white peck will cuss. A poor white peck will cuss worse'n a nigger. I am talking about white men who ain't poor like them pecks. **1970** C. Major *Dict. Afro-Amer. Slang* 90 *Peck*, white person.

peck (pɛk), *v.*[1] Also 4–5 **pekke,** 4–7 **pek, pecke.** [app. a collateral form of PICK *v.*[1], with which it formerly often interchanged, as it still does dialectally. Cf. MLG. *pekken*, to peck with the beak.]
I. 1. *trans.* To strike with the beak, as a bird; to indent or pierce by thus striking. Often with advb. extension; esp. *peck out*, to put or pluck out by pecking.
1382 Wyclif *Prov.* xxx. 17 The eȝe that scorneth the fader, and that dispiseth the birthe of his moder, pecken hym out crowis of the stremes [1388 crowis of the stronde picke out thilke iȝe]. **1398** Trevisa *Barth. De P.R.* XVIII. viii. (Bodl. MS.), þe rauen.. fondeþ wiþ his bille to pecke oute his iȝen. [*Ibid.*, Smal briddes þat reseþ on hym to picke out his iȝen.] **1567** Maplet *Gr. Forest* 71 b, She flieth and flacketh about his eies and face, and pecketh and scratcheth out his eien. **1690** Dryden *Don Sebastian* I. i, These parrots peck the fairest fruit. **1795** Cowper *Pairing Time Antic.* 57 Soon every father-bird and mother Grew quarrelsome, and pecked each other. **1863** Kingsley *Water-Bab.* vii, All the other scaul-crows set upon her, and pecked her to death.

b. To make (a hole, etc.) by pecking: cf. PICK *v.*[1]
1768–74 Tucker *Lt. Nat.* (1834) I. 640 The beetle.. lies sprawling upon his back; until the little tit-mouse comes, pecks a hole in his side. **1815** *Sporting Mag.* XLVI. 160 A truce to pecking holes in the coat of this gentleman's book.

c. To kiss perfunctorily; to give a peck (PECK *sb.*[3] 1) to.
1969 *New Yorker* 11 Oct. 53/1 They pecked the hostess farewell. **1977** C. McCullough *Thorn Birds* xv. 343 Meggie leaned over to peck her brothers on their cheeks self-consciously.

2. *intr.* To strike with or use the beak, as a bird.
1398 Trevisa *Barth. De P.R.* XVIII. viii. (Bodl. MS.), ȝife þe asse haue a sore.. þe sparowes lepiþ þeron & peckeþ wiþ here billes. **1567** Maplet *Gr. Forest* 71 b, They neuer leaue off pecking til they haue made it verie sore. **1588** Greene *Pandosto* (1607) 27 He that striueth against Loue,.. with the Cockatrice pecketh against the steele. **1774** Goldsm. *Nat. Hist.* (1776) VI. 15 They peck and combat with their claws.
transf. **1901** in *Publ. Circ.* 7 Sept. 227/2 The modern printer merely pecks on a key-board.

b. *peck at*: to aim at with the beak, to try to peck; also *transf.*
1604 Shaks. *Oth.* I. i. 65 'Tis not long after But I will weare my heart vpon my sleeue For Dawes to pecke at. **1676** Hobbes *Iliad* xv. (1677) 229 Better in close fight to die.. Than.. peck in vain at a weak enemy. **1687** *Lond. Gaz.* No. 2251/4 Finding we slighted him, [he] stretched to Windward, and there lay pecking at us. **1831** Carlyle in Froude *Life* (1882) II. 175 The more the Devil pecks at me, the more vehemently do I wring his nose. **1874** L. Stephen *Hours in Library* (1892) I. i. 9 It was.. the greatest of triumphs when birds.. pecked at the grapes in a picture.

c. *peck at* (*fig*): To try to 'pick holes' in, or 'pick to pieces'; to carp, cavil, or nag at.
1641 'Smectymnuus' *Vind. Answ.* v. 70 The Scripture hee pecks at. **1768–74** Tucker *Lt. Nat.* (1834) II. 475 Without pecking at the Bible, they can find matters to joke upon elsewhere. **1872** Besant & Rice *Ready Money Mortiboy* viii, She had pecked at him so long, he could not have digested his dinner without his usual dessert.

3. *trans.* Of birds: To take (food) with the beak; esp. in small bits at a time. Often with *up.*
c **1386** Chaucer *Nun's Pr. T.* 147 Pekke [*v.rr.* pek, peke, *Camb.* pikke, *Harl.* pike] hem vp right as they growe and ete hem yn. **1623–4** Middleton & Rowley *Sp. Gipsy* II. i. 50 Grain pecked up after grain makes pullen fat. **1798** Wordsw. *Old Cumbld. Beggar* 20 The small mountain birds Not venturing yet to peck their destined meal. **1804** J. Grahame *Sabbath* 460 Where little birds.. Light on the floor, and peck the table-crumbs. **1883** S. C. Hall *Retrospect* II. 324 The fowls were left to peck up anything they might find.
fig. **1669** F. Vernon in A. Lang *Valet's Trag.* etc. (1903) 51, I fear you can peck but little satisfaction out of it.

b. *intr.*
1798 *Sporting Mag.* XI. 220 The pigeon.. is still alive, and pecks as well as usual.

4. *trans.* and *intr.* Of persons: **a.** To eat, to feed. *colloq.* (orig. *Thieves' Cant*). **b.** To bite, to eat daintily or in a nibbling fashion.
a **1550** *Hye Way to Spyttel Hous* 1050 in Hazl. *E.P.P.* IV. 69 Thou shalt pek my jere In thy gan for my watch it is nace gere. **1610** Rowlands *Martin Mark-all* (Hunter. Cl.) 39 Pecke is taken to eate or byte: as *the Buffa peckes me by the stampes*, the dogge bites me by the shinnes. **1665** Head *Eng. Rogue* I. iv. (1680) 33 Most part of the night we spent in Boozing, pecking rumly. **1703** *Levellers* in *Harl. Misc.* (ed. Park) V. 454 So they all fell heartily to pecking till they had consumed the whole provision. **1824** Byron *Juan* xv. lxx, The ladies with more moderation mingled In the feast, pecking less than I can tell. **1884** *Cheshire Gloss.* (E.D.S.), *Peck for one's self*, to gain one's own livelihood. **1893** Baring-Gould *Mrs. Curgenven* liii, Thanks, I'll peck a bit.

II. 5. *trans.* To strike (something) with a pick or other pointed tool, so as to indent, pit, pierce, or break it up; also, to mark with short strokes. Often with advb. complement, as *peck down*, *peck in*, *peck up*, etc.
a **1530** Heywood *Weather* (Brandl) 752, I haue peckt a good peckynge yron to naught. **1573–80** Baret *Alv.* P 219 A stone pecked, or dented in as a millstone. **1666** J. Smith *Old Age* 79 Because they cannot make their mills grow, as they daily decay by grinding; they are fain to supply that want by often pecking their milstones. **1702** S. Sewall *Diary* 20 Jan., The Father was pecking Ice off the Mill-wheel. **1848** *Jrnl. R. Agric. Soc.* IX. II. 537 [Soil] stony or gravelly, so as to require.. to be pecked with a mathook or pick. **1854** Bartlett *Mex. Boundary* II. xxix. 195 Boulders covered with rude figures of men, animals &c. all pecked in with a sharp instrument. **1874** Wood *Out of Doors* 213 The best way to dig for insects is to peck up a circular patch about eighteen inches in diameter, throw aside the frozen clods, and then to work carefully downwards. **1894** J. K. Fowler *Rec. O. Country Life* xvii. 204 Part of a wall was pecked down and carted away.

†**b.** *intr.* To strike with a pick or the like; to pick. Also *fig.* *Obs.* or *dial.*

1633 T. JAMES *Voy.* 78 A happy fellow,..pecking betwixt the Ice, strooke vpon it. **1691** WOOD *Ath. Oxon.* I. 379 His Genie being more prone to easier and smoother studies, than in pecking and hewing at Logick. **1883** *Folk-Lore Jrnl.* I. 317 Away they pecked at it hard and fast.

†**6.** *trans.* To dig or root up with something sharp. *Obs.* or *dial.*

1764 *Mus. Rust.* III. lxxvi. 338 When harvest is done, the stubble may be got up at one shilling per acre,..this is called pecking the haulm, from the method of performing the work. **1898** G. W. E. RUSSELL *Collect. & Recoll.* xxiii. 298 He..wandered about the lanes..pecking up primroses with a spud.

III. 7. Phrases: †*to peck mood*, to change one's tune (*obs.*). *to peck a quarrel*: see PICK *v.*[1]

13.. *Seuyn Sag.* (W.) 262 And sone sche gan to pekke mod. *c*1412 HOCCLEVE *De Reg. Princ.* 4347 But or þei twynned þens, þei pekkid moode.

¶ For other occasional obs. uses: see PICK *v.*[1]

peck, *v.*[2] Now chiefly *dial.* Also 6 peke, 7 pecke. [Variant of PICK *v.*[2] = PITCH *v.*[1]]

1. *trans.* To pitch, cast, fling, throw; to jerk, move suddenly. *Obs.* exc. *dial.*

1611 COTGR., *Vergette*,..a boyes play with rods or wands pecked at a heape of points. **1613** SHAKS. *Hen. VIII*, v. iii. 94 You i' th' Chamblet, get vp o' th' raile, Ile pecke you o're the pales else. **1667** DRYDEN *Maiden Queen* v. i, I can..walk with a courant slur, and at every step peck down my head. **1753** HOGARTH *Anal. Beauty* xvi. 217 'Pecking back' her elbows (as they call it) from the waist upwards. **1890** *Gloucs. Gloss.*, *Peck*..2 To pitch, fling.

†**2.** *intr.* To have a pitch, to incline. *Obs.*

1639 LD. DIGBY, etc. *Lett. conc. Relig.* (1651) 118 He that would reduce the Church now to the form of Government in the most primitive times..would be found pecking toward the Presbytery of Scotland. **1696** LORIMER *Goodwin's Disc.* vii. 50 Such a Man seems to be pecking towards the Socinians.

3. *intr.* To pitch forward; *esp.* of a horse: to stumble in consequence of striking the ground with his toe instead of coming down on the flat of his foot. *dial.* and *colloq.*

[When said of a horse, often associated with PECK *sb.*[2], *v.*[1] 5.]

*c*1770 *MS. Addit.* in Grose *Provinc. Gloss.* (1790) (E.D.D.). **1847-78** HALLIWELL, *Peck*..(4) To stumble. *Yorksh.* **1881** MISS JACKSON *Shropsh. Word-bk.*, *Peck, pick*..to pitch forward, to go head first; to over-balance. 'Mind the child dunna peck out on 'is cheer'. **1881** MRS. P. O'DONOGHUE *Ladies on Horseback* I. iii. 42 Your horse..might be apt to peck, and so give you an ugly fall. **1898** A. HOPE *Rupert of Hentzau* vi, The horse pecked and stumbled, and I fell forward on his neck. **1899** PREVOST *Cumbld. Gloss.* (E.D.D.) s.v., A horse that goes rather 'close to the ground' with his fore feet, will frequently touch the ground with his toe and make a stumble—such an one pecks from want of vigour.

†**4.** *peck over the perch*: see PEAK *v.*[1]

†**peckage** (ˈpɛkɪdʒ). *Obs. Cant.* Also peckidge. [f. PECK *v.*[1] + -AGE.] Food, victuals.

1610 ROWLANDS *Martin Mark-all* (Hunter. Cl.) 40 *Peckage* meat or *Scroofe* scraps. **1621** B. JONSON *Metam. Gipsies* Wks. (1692) 615 With the Convoy, Cheats, and Peckage. *a*1700 B. E. *Dict. Cant. Crew*, *Peckidge*, Meat.

peckawood: see PECKERWOOD b.

pecked, *a. Obs.* exc. *dial.* = PEAKED *a.*

1744-50 W. ELLIS *Mod. Husbandm.* IV. I. 92 This we shoot down in our fields in a round pecked heap. *Ibid.* 129 (E.D.S.) A ram that is pecked-arsed. **1884** *Upton-on-Severn Gloss.* s.v., A boat is peck-ed at both ends, and a trow is round at both ends.

pecked (pɛkt) *ppl. a.* [f. PECK *v.*[1] + -ED[1].] Affected or damaged by pecking. *spec.* in *Archæol.*: consisting of or characterized by pecked strokes or marks (see PECK *v.*[1] 5); *pecked curve, line*, a curve or line formed by short strokes thus ------.

1864 BOUTELL *Her. Hist. & Pop.* xvii. §2 (ed. 3) 270 A mill-stone arg., pecked sa. **1866** *Spectator* 26 May 567/1 An aggressive game cock..sent him in with a pecked and bleeding face. **1874** *Usef. Knowl. Soc. Atlas*, Map of World *margin*, Pecked lines are the co-tidal lines, or the series of points on the surface of the ocean where high water takes place at the same instant. **1959** J. D. CLARK *Prehist. S. Afr.* Pl. 12 (*caption*) Fine example of an eland in a pecked engraving style, Transvaal. **1963** *Field Archaeol.* (Ordnance Survey) (ed. 4) 43 The earth-fast boulder decorated with pecked marks and designs of uncertain age and significance is a common feature in many parts of Britain north of the Trent. *Ibid.*, Other pecked figures of axes are known elsewhere. **1971** *Nature* 21 May 160/1 This ungual must be rotated through an angle of 180° around its longitudinal axis (pecked line in Fig. 2*F*). **1975** J. B. HARLEY *O.S. Maps* iii. 33 Overhead features, distinguished by pecked lines, are shown when they are of a size and character to be useful features. **1976** *Nature* 29 Apr. 772/1 In Fig. 2 the pecked curve represents the 3-block running mean of February maximum temperatures for six stations surrounding the tree location.

peckedeuaunted, var. of PICKEDEVANTED *Obs.*

pecker (ˈpɛkə(r)). [f. PECK *v.*[1] + -ER[1].]

1. a. One who, or that which, pecks; a bird that pecks; the second element in various bird-names, as FIG-*pecker*, FLOWER-*pecker*, NUT-*pecker*; also short for WOODPECKER.

1697 DRYDEN *Virg. Georg.* IV. 18 The Titmouse, and the Peckers hungry Brood. **1717** GARTH tr. *Ovid's Met.* xiv, 'Twas here I spy'd a youth in Parian stone: His head a pecker bore [orig. *in vertice picum*]: the cause unknown To passengers. **1883** J. S. STALLYBRASS tr. *Grimm's Teutonic Mythol.* III. 973 The pecker was esteemed a sacred and divine bird. **1884** G. ALLEN in *Longm. Mag.* Jan. 294 By far the greater number of modern birds belong to the..orders of the perchers, the peckers, and the birds of prey.

b. An eater, feeder (with qualifying adj.). *slang.*

1861 C. C. ROBINSON *Dial. Leeds* (E.D.D.), He's a rare pecker. **1873** *Slang Dict.* s.v. *Peck*, A hearty eater is generally called 'a rare pecker'.

c. Abbrev. of PECKERWOOD b. *slang.*

1966 R. G. TOEPFER *Witness* xvi. 127 Not a chance. These peckers know that as well as me.

2. a. An implement for pecking; a kind of hoe.

1587 T. HARIOT *Virginia* in Hakluyt *Voy.* (1600) III. 271 The women with short peckers or parers,..of a foot long, and about fiue inches in breadth, doe onely breake the vpper part of the ground to raise vp the weeds, grasse, and olde stubbes of corne stalks with their roots. *Ibid.*, For their corne,..with a pecker they make a hole, wherein they put foure graines. **1848** *Jrnl. R. Agric. Soc.* IX. II. 551 A small narrow hoe or pecker... A small hand-pecker.

†**b.** *Telegraphy.* An obsolete type of relay. *Obs.*

In the old 'pecker' the end of the lever was V-shaped, and its up-and-down motion resembled the pecking of a bird. **1858** H. C. F. JENKIN *Papers*, etc. (1887) I. p. lxxxvi, Click, click, click, the pecker is at work.

c. *Weaving.* A shuttle-driver: = PICKER *sb.*

1831 G. R. PORTER *Silk Manuf.* 216 The ends of this shuttle-race are prolonged by boards, which form troughs or boxes, in each of which is placed a piece of wood or thick leather, called a pecker or driver, and these drivers are made to traverse on small guide wires fixed between the side rails and the ends of the troughs. **1878** BARLOW *Weaving* x. 136 When the shaft [of the draw-boy] rocks from side to side of the machine, it will carry the pecker..with it.

3. *slang.* **a.** Courage, resolution. (? *orig.* beak or bill.) Chiefly in phr. *to keep (one's) pecker up.*

In view of sense 3b a use commonly avoided by British travellers in the U.S.

1853 'C. BEDE' *Verdant Green* I. xii, Keep your pecker up. **1857** DICKENS *Lett.* 17 Aug., Keep your pecker up with that. **1873** *Slang Dict.*, *Pecker*, 'keep your Pecker up'..literally, keep your beak and head well up, 'never say die'. **1875** W. S. GILBERT *Trial by Jury* 4 Be firm, my moral pecker. **1901** R. C. LEHMANN *Anni Fugaces* 56 Weighed down by debt they yet keep up their pecker. **1918** GALSWORTHY *Five Tales* iv. 162 Keep your pecker up, and get off abroad. **1922** JOYCE *Ulysses* 320 Keep your pecker up, says Joe. She'd have won the money only for the other dog. **1928** A. MERRITT *Seven Footprints to Satan* xiii. 180, I was talkin' loud to keep my pecker up. **1934** F. W. CROFTS *12.30 from Croydon* xix. 263 Charles could not eat, in spite of the rough kindness of one of the warders, who adjured him to keep his pecker up. **1973** N. MOSS *What's the Difference?* 44/1 The Englishman in North America should beware of using the phrase 'keep your pecker up'.

b. The penis. *slang* (chiefly *U.S.*).

1902 FARMER & HENLEY *Slang* V. 289/2 The *penis*..pecker. **1936** H. MILLER *Black Spring* 142 Ought to stand on Times Square with my pecker in my hand and piss in the gutter. **1949** —— *Sexus* I. iii. 114 Walking towards the house I open my fly and let my pecker out. **1958** N. LEVINE *Canada made Me* ii. 57 Ground sunflower seeds... This will make your pecker stand up to no end of punishment. **1960** E. L. WALLANT *Human Season* ix. 97 You know how it is when the ol' pecker ain't what it used to be, hah, hah! **1964** *Amer. Folk Music Occasional* I. 12 There is a house down in New Orleans, They call it The Rising Sun, When you want to get your pecker spoilt, That's where you get it done. **1967** I. A. BARAKA in W. King *Black Short Story Anthol.* (1972) 125 Oh, Lucasta, find me here on the bed, with hard pecker and dirty feet. **1969** K. VONNEGUT *Slaughterhouse-Five* v. 107 Billy took his pecker out, there in the prison night, and peed and peed on the ground. **1971** F. NORMAN *Dodgem-Greaser* iii. 45, I unzipped my fly and exposed my pecker to the night air with one deft flick of my finger. **1975** R. H. RIMMER *Premar Experiments* (1976) i. 27 Tony's pecker would no sooner get inside me than he'd pop off.

4. *Comb.* **pecker-head** *U.S. slang*, an aggressive objectionable person; **pecker-mill**: see quot.

1802 J. DRAYTON *View S. Carolina* 121 Rice mills, called pecker, cog, and water mills... The first..so called, from the pestle's striking..in the manner of a wood pecker. **1955** *Time* 14 Nov. 116/2 When the girl's husband.., a got-rich peckerhead, finds out about that hotel visit, he ravishes his wife, just to even the score. **1977** E. LEONARD *Unknown Man No. 89* xxiii. 239 Them peckerheads'd never make it.

peckerwood (ˈpɛkəwʊd). *U.S.* [f. WOODPECKER with reversal of the two elements.]

a. A woodpecker. *dial.*

1859 BARTLETT *Dict. Amer.* (ed. 2) 314 *Peckerwood*, Western for Woodpecker. **1893** H. A. SHANDS *Some Peculiarities of Speech in Mississippi* 49 *Peckerwood*, woodpecker. Bartlett says that this word is Western. It is also heard very frequently in Mississippi, as in Tennessee. **1909** F. B. CALHOUN *Miss Minerva* 140 A big, red-headed peckerwood. **1926** E. M. ROBERTS *Time of Man* 153 Not had the sense of a pecker-wood. **1935** Z. N. HURSTON *Mules & Men* I. vi. 137 Ah wasn't gointer kill no ole tough peckerwood for you to eat, baby. **1940** R. WOOD *Amer. Mother Goose* 55 Peckerwood a-settin' on a swingin' limb, Blue-bird a-buildin' in the garden. **1947** J. H. BROWN *Outdoors Unlimited* 76 Sitting there watching the jays and peckerwoods and listening to the distant shrillings of a hawk, I thought Lucius looked tougher than a pine-knot. **1968** *Harper's Mag.* Sept. 61/1, I even liked what the kids at Tuskegee Institute called 'those crazy li'l ol' peckerwoods'.

b. *slang.* Also *peckawood.* A white person, esp. a poor one. Also *transf.*

1929 T. GORDON *Born to Be* 236 *Peckerwood*, a poor white man. **1929** C. MCKAY *Banjo* 217 For example, we have words like ofay..peckawood..and so on. **1941** W. C. HANDY *Father of Blues* vi. 86 Mound Bayou had no such words addressed to 'peckerwoods' or 'rednecks'. **1942** W. FAULKNER *Go Down, Moses* 255 Even a Delta peckerwood would look after even a draggle-tail better than that. **1947** *Sat. Rev. Lit.* (U.S.) 29 Mar. 13/2 There is a difference between white plantation people and the white 'peckerwoods' of the hills. **1966** R. G. TOEPFER *Witness* ii. 11 They was three peckerwoods had the boy. **1967** C. MAJOR in A. Chapman *New Black Voices* (1972) 299 How come so many Of us niggers Are dying over there In that white Man's war They say more of us Are dying Than them peckerwoods & it just Don't make sense. **1967** *Trans-Action* Apr. 27/2 There is a social distinction here between the white elite and the 'redneck' or 'peckerwood' families. **1967** *N.Y. Times* 7 Sept. 42/4 When I tried to get into the black caucus, they said, 'No peckerwoods allowed in here, Sonny.' **1974** *New Yorker* 29 Apr. 94/2 A horse can be well one day and a sick peckerwood the next. **1974** E. BRAWLEY *Rap* (1975) II. xxiv. 374 And we done, peckerwood, we finished.

ˈ**pecket,** *v.* [frequent. of PECK *v.*[1]; perh. after F. *picoter*, or *béqueter*.] *trans.* and *intr.* To peck repeatedly, to continue pecking.

1862 MISS THACKERAY *Story Eliz.* II. in *Cornh. Mag.* VI. 490 Empty stables, with chickens pecketting in the sun. **1866** *Village on Cliff* iii, The great carved cupboard, with the two wooden birds pecketting each other's beaks. *Ibid.* ix, Cocks and hens are pecketing the fallen grains. **1896** BARLOW *Martin's Company* 176 (E.D.D.) Equally fatal would have been the pecketing of poultry.

ˈ**peckful.** [See -FUL.] As much as fills a peck.

1856 KANE *Arct. Expl.* I. vi 64 One of my Karsuk brutes [dogs] has eaten up two entire birds'-nests..a peckful at least.

Peckham (ˈpɛkəm). [Name of a suburb of London.] **a.** Used in various joc. phrases, esp. with play on peck = food, to eat (PECK *sb.*[3] 3, PECK *v.*[1] 4). (See quots.)

Neither this sense nor the next seems to have much currency outside dicts.

1788 GROSE *Dict. Vulgar T.* (ed. 2) s.v. *All Holiday*. It is all holiday at Peckham, or it is all holiday with him; a saying signifying that it is all over with the business or person spoken of or alluded to. **1823** 'J. BEE' *Slang* 134 *Peckham* (going to), dinner. 'All holiday at Peckham'—no appetite. 'No Peckham for Ben, he's been to Clapham,' i.e. is indisposed, in a certain way. Peckish—hungry. **1864** HOTTEN *Slang Dict.* 198 *Peckham*, a facetious meaning of the name of this district, implying a dinner; 'all holiday at Peckham', *i.e. nothing to eat.* **1902** FARMER & HENLEY *Slang* V. 157/1 *Peckham.* To have (or spend) a holiday at Peckham, *verb phr.* (old)—To have nothing to eat. Going to Peckham = going to dinner. **1922** A. M. HYAMSON *Dict. Eng. Phr.* 267/2 *Peckham, To go to*, to go to dinner. **1970** *Brewer's Dict. Phr. & Fable* (rev. ed.) 814/2 *All holiday at Peckham*,..no appetite, not peckish.

b. *Peckham rye* [name of an open space in Peckham], tie. *Rhyming slang.*

1925 FRASER & GIBBONS *Soldier & Sailor Words* 221 *Peckham rye*, tie. (Rhyming slang). **1960** J. FRANKLYN *Dict. Rhyming Slang* 106/2 *Peckham Rye*, tie (necktie). 19 C., and by far the most usual term. **1973** B. AYLWIN *Load of Cockney Cobblers* 84 Tie. Peckham Rye.

peckhamite (ˈpɛkəmaɪt). *Min.* [Named 1880 after J. S. Peckham, an American chemist: see -ITE[1].] A greenish-yellow meteoric silicate of iron and magnesium.

1881 *Pop. Sci. Monthly* XVIII. 861 Professor J. Lawrence Smith has found a new meteoric mineral in the analysis of the great meteorite which fell in Emmett County, Iowa, in May, 1879, and has named it Peckhamite.

peckho, variant of PEKOE, a kind of tea.

peck horn (ˈpɛk hɔːn). *Jazz slang.* Also with hyphen and as one word. [Origin uncertain.] A mellophone, saxophone, or similar instrument.

1936 *Amer. Mercury* May p. x/2 *Peck horn*, mellophone. **1942** BERREY & VAN DEN BARK *Amer. Thes. Slang* §377/8 (*Alto*) *peck horn*, an alto horn or mellophone. **1948** MENCKEN *Amer. Lang.* Suppl. II. 705 It [*sc.* jive] arose in the honky-tonks and tingle-tangles of the pre-jazz era, and many of its current names for musical instruments go back to that era or even beyond, *e.g.*,..*pretzel* or *peck-horn* for a French horn. **1961** *Down Beat* 13 Apr. 37 This set contains a good sampling of his abilities on trumpet, alto, baritone, and the oddball peckhorn. **1966** *New Yorker* 25 June 44/2 The band generally had two trombones, three trumpets, a bass horn and a baritone horn, a peck horn, a clarinet. *Ibid.* 46/3 From the age of eight I played the upright alto—the peck horn—in my father's band. **1970** C. MAJOR *Dict. Afro-Amer. Slang* 90 *Peck horn*,..mellophone or saxophone. **1975** *Sunday Times* (Colour Suppl.) 12 July 47/1 Straight band singers were unknown in the Twenties—everyone, even Bing Crosby, had an instrument to hold. 'I had a peckhorn, like a flugel-horn.'

ˈ**pecking,** *vbl. sb.*[1] [f. PECK *v.*[1] + -ING[1].]

1. The action of PECK *v.*[1]; an instance of this; also *fig.* fault-finding.

1398 TREVISA *Barth. De P.R.* XVIII. viii. (Bodl. MS.), Þe asse may vnneþe defende hym selfe aȝens his [sparowes] rese peckinge and bitinge. **1589** R. HARVEY *Pl. Perc.* (1860) 10 If thy mill stones be not worne too blunt, for want of pecking. **1692** BENTLEY *Boyle Lect.* iii. 105 Superstitious Observation of the pecking of Chickens. **1757** BURKE *Abridgem. Eng. Hist.* Wks. X. 199 The Druids..attended with diligence the flight of birds, the pecking of chickens. **1885** W. CORY *Lett. & Jrnls.* (1897) 515 The gossip and the pecking of country towns.

2. *concr.* †**a.** A piece pecked or picked off, as in dressing stone. *Obs.* **b.** (See quot. 1875.)

1600 in Hakluyt *Voy.* III. 619 You shall finde it [white sand] like shauings and peckings of free stone. **1875** KNIGHT *Dict. Mech.* 1647/1 *Peckings, Place-bricks*, from the outside of the kiln and insufficiently burned.

pecking, *vbl. sb.*[2] [f. PECK *v.*[2] + -ING[1].]
1. The pitching or throwing (e.g. of stones). Hence ***pecking-bag***.
1857 HUGHES *Tom Brown* II. iv, He.. strides away in front with his climbing-irons strapped under one arm, his pecking-bag under the other. *Ibid.*, There close to them lay a heap of charming pebbles. 'Look here', shouted East, 'here's luck! I've been longing for some good honest pecking this half-hour. Let's fill the bags'.
2. A tossing or jerking (as of the head).
1890 CLARK RUSSELL *Shipmate Louise* I. xi. 241 With a pecking, so to speak, of her face at the gangs of men on the quarter-deck.

'pecking, *ppl. a.* [f. PECK *v.*[1] + -ING[2].] That pecks.
1727 BAILEY vol. II, *Pecking*, striking with the Bill as Birds do. **1827** MONTGOMERY *Pelican Isl.* IV. 200 She.. drove him from her seat With pecking bill, and cry of fond distress.
b. *fig.* (cf. *hacking*).
1865 *Jrnl. R. Agric. Soc.* Ser. II. I. II. 289 Troubled with a short 'pecking' cough.

pecking order ('pɛkɪŋ ˌɔːdə(r)). [f. PECKING *vbl. sb.*[1] + ORDER *sb.*, tr. G. *hackliste* (T. J. Schjelderup-Ebbe 1922, in *Zeitschr. für Psychologie* LXXXVIII. 227).] **1.** A pattern of behaviour first observed in hens and later recognized in other groups of social animals, in which those of high rank within the group are able to attack those of lower rank without provoking an attack in return.
1928 A. HUXLEY *Point Counter Point* xxvi. 438 Observing the habitual and almost sacred 'pecking order' which prevails among the hens in his poultry yard.. the politician will meditate on the Catholic hierarchy and Fascism. **1939** *Auk* LVI. 263 A position in the pecking order is not.. always determined at the first meeting. **1952** M. K. WILSON tr. *Lorenz's King Solomon's Ring* xi. 147 This can be convincingly demonstrated by the existence of an order of rank, known to animal psychologists as the 'pecking order'. **1965** *Listener* 10 June 861/1 Normal monkeys, like many other kinds of animals, form a sort of pecking order. **1972** *Country Life* 9 Mar. 541/1 The fat little bantam hen, who proved first in the pecking order.. quickly asserted herself. **1974** *Times Lit. Suppl.* 4 Oct. 1088/4 The term 'pecking order' has become part of common parlance... After a brief trial of strength, every animal in the flock or the herd learns to know its place.
2. *transf.* A hierarchy based on rank or status.
1955 H. NICOLSON *Good Behaviour* i. 7 In a perfect classless society.. similar pecking orders must exist. **1957** L. DURRELL *Justine* I. 64 There is a Pecking Order among diplomats as there is among poultry. **1959** G. ENDORE *Detour through Devon* 11 The pecking order obtains among cars on the road as well as among chickens in the barnyard. **1959** T. H. WHITE *Godstone & Blackymor* 172 The ghosts.. may have taken precedence in a kind of pecking-order, by virtue of the number of pipes which they could claim. **1961** *Times Lit. Suppl.* 29 Dec. 925/2 Man has animal instincts, instincts for desiring and holding territory and property, for creating a pecking order of dominance and hence status. **1962** *Observer* 25 Nov. 3/2 One of the most disastrous weaknesses of our whole educational system is its insistence on preserving formal hierarchies, a sort of academic pecking order. **1967** J. POTTER *Foul Play* xvi. 184 The inspector had a pretty low rating in the CID's pecking order... His office overlooked an unbroken expanse of sooty wall. **1967** M. ARGYLE *Psychol. Interpersonal Behaviour* iv. 70 Groups develop definite 'pecking orders' in terms of amount of speech and influence permitted. **1973** *Nature* 30 Nov. 318/1 One of the interpenetrating pecking orders that bedevil life in universities is the hard science/soft science hierarchy. **1976** H. WILSON *Governance of Britain* ii. 23 My own procedure was to rely on the order of precedence within the Cabinet, the so-called 'pecking-order', making clear that the second in the list chairs Cabinet.

peckish ('pɛkɪʃ), *a. colloq.* [f. PECK *v.*[1] + -ISH[1].] Disposed to 'peck' or eat; somewhat hungry.
1785 GROSE *Dict. Vulg. Tongue, Peck*, victuals;.. peckish, hungry. *a* **1825** FORBY *Voc. E. Anglia, Peckish*, hungry; disposed to be pecking. **1837** T. HOOK *Jack Brag* xv, I get peckish at night somehow. **1898** J. K. JEROME *Second Thoughts* 279 You're a bit peckish too, I expect.
b. Appetizing. *rare.*
1845 *P. Parley's Ann.* VI. 238 This perch has been kept in a small garden pond..; biting at everything peckish that comes in his way.
Hence **'peckishness**, hungriness, hunger.
18.. *Phases Bradford Life* 111 (E.D.D.), In a state of considerable peckishness.

peckle ('pɛk(ə)l), *sb. Obs.* exc. *dial.* [Reduced from *speckle*; but cf. PECKLED.] A spot, a speckle. Also attrib., as ***peckle-head***, a partridge.
1570 LEVINS *Manip.* 47/19 A Peckle, *macula. Ibid.* 125/29 A Peckil, *macula.* **1688** R. HOLME *Armoury* II. 311/1 A Partridge [is called], first a Peckle-Head. **1884** *Chesh. Gloss.*, *Pecka* or *Peckle*, a freckle.

peckle ('pɛk(ə)l), *v.*[1] *Obs.* exc. *dial.* [f. as prec.] *trans.* To speckle.
1570 LEVINS *Manip.* 47/23 To Peckle, *maculare.* **1580** HOLLYBAND *Treas. Fr. Tong, Picoter*, to peckle, to pricke thicke, to specke. **1611** COTGR., *Grivoler*, to peckle, or speckle; to spot with diuers colours. [Still in Cheshire and South Lancash. *Eng. Dial. Dict.*]

peckle ('pɛk(ə)l), *v.*[2] *rare.* [dim. or freq. of PECK *v.*[1]] *trans.* To peck slightly or repeatedly.
[*a* **1500** *Colkelbie Sow* 912 (Bann. MS.) Hir best brod hen callit lady Pekle pes.] *a* **1810** in Cromek *Rem. Nithsdale Song* 245 (Jam.) Come, byde wi' me, ye pair o' sweet birds,.. Ye sall peckle o' the bread an' drink o' the wine. **1827** HOOD *Mids. Fairies* v, And all [birds] were tame And peckled at my hand where'er I came.

peckled ('pɛk(ə)ld), *a.* Now *dial.* Also 6 peculd, 7 peackled, 8–9 pecklt. [f. PECKLE *sb.* or *v.*[1] + -ED: or perh. directly from SPECKLED.] Spotted, variegated, speckled; parti-coloured. Also *comb.*
1552–3 *Inv. Ch. Gds., Staffs.* in *Ann. Lichfield* (1863) IV. 20 Itm. iiij albes, on cope of saten bruges, & on of peculd silke. **1577** B. GOOGE *Heresbach's Husb.* (1586) 138 You must looke beside, that his toong bee not black, nor pecled. **1611** COTGR., *Gelinote de bois*, the pied, or peckled Pheasant, or wood Henne. **1615** W. LAWSON *Country Housew. Gard.* (1626) 2 When Summer cloathes your borders with greene and peckled colours. *c* **1746** COLLIER (Tim Bobbin) *View Lancs. Dial.* 5 The pecklt jump [coat]. **1858** *Jrnl. R. Agric. Soc.* XIX. II. 386 The 'peckled-faced' ones are rejected as breeding sheep. [Still in many English dialects.]
Hence **'peckledness**, spottedness, speckledness.
1611 COTGR., *Griveleure*, pecklednesse, or specklednesse.

'peckly, *a. rare.* [f. PECKLE *sb.* + -Y.] Characterized by speckles or spots, 'peckled'.
1859 *All Year R.* No. 29. 58 Shropshire and Staffordshire [had] the once famous peckly-faced breed. *Ibid.* 61 The 'peckly' face which once distinguished the hill sheep of Shropshire has become an uniform grey.

†'peckman. *Obs.* ? An officer of the royal stables.
1525 in *Househ. Ord.* (1790) 201 The six sumpter men and one Besage man, The Peckman, the King's Foole. **1684** E. CHAMBERLAYNE *Pres. St. Eng.* I. (ed. 15) 185 A Yeoman Peckman, a Yeoman Bitmaker.

peck-order ('pɛkɔːdə(r)). [f. PECK *sb.*[3] + ORDER *sb.*, tr. G. *hackliste* (T. J. Schjelderup-Ebbe 1922, in *Zeitschr. für Psychologie* LXXXVIII. 227).] = PECKING ORDER, sense 1.
1931 W. C. ALLEE *Animal Aggregations* xix. 344 The 'peck-order' decides which birds may peck others without being pecked in return. **1939** G. K. NOBLE in *Auk* LVI. 264 A peck order.. does not appear unless the birds [*sc.* night herons] are crowded together in a strange area. **1955** *Brit. Jrnl. Animal Behaviour* III. 94/2 It is now recognized that the peck-order forms the basis of all group behaviour in adult chickens. **1966** *New Scientist* 26 May 536/1 Wolves live in groups, in which certain individuals are dominant: that is, they have prior access to food, females and other amenities. This sort of arrangement may be called a peck order.
2. *transf.* = PECKING ORDER, sense 2.
1953 A. UPFIELD *Murder must Wait* xvi. 138 Amid the lower Australian peck order.. wines are imbibed from the bottle. **1962** A. SAMPSON *Anat. Brit.* I. x. 150 The Inns [of Court] have their own elaborate snobberies and peck-order. **1965** *Punch* 17 Mar. 389/1 Dons have always had an instinctive feeling for prestige, not to say 'peck-order'. **1971** W. J. BURLEY *Guilt Edged* ix. 149 The human peck-order is far more subtle than that of the hen-house.

†'peck-point. *Obs.* [f. PECK *v.*[2] + POINT *sb.*] 'A boyes play with rods or wands pecked at a heape of points' (Cotgrave (1611) s.v. *Vergette*).
1653 URQUHART *Rabelais* II. xviii, Panurge.. played away all the points of his breeches at *primus secundus*, and at peck point (in French called *Lavergette*).

Peck's bad boy, *phr. U.S. slang.* The name of a fictional character created by George Wilbur Peck (1840–1916) used allusively of an unruly or mischievous child. Also *attrib.* or as *adj.*
1883 *Peck's Sun* 14 July 1/6 The [cuff] buttons are.. gold.. and on the back they are engraved 'Geo. W. Peck, Milwaukee, from his newsboy friends of Chicago', and on top of the Russia leather case are the words, 'From Peck's Bad Boys'. **1933** E. O'NEILL *Ah, Wilderness!* I. 19 Sid Davis, his brother-in-law, is forty-five, short and fat, bald-headed, with the Puckish face of a Peck's Bad Boy who has never grown up. **1946** *True* Apr. 34/1 Insulting the advertisers has become Big Business with the Peck's Bad Boy of Radio. **1967** *Atlantic Monthly* Feb. 4 [Governor George] Wallace's motives—ego, a Peck's-bad-boy desire to make trouble, a yen to see just what would happen if a presidential election were thrown into the House of Representatives, or a combination of all these—do not actually matter. **1970** *Time* 22 June 78/2 The book is an earnest effort by Della Femina to buttress his reputation as the Peck's Bad Boy of Advertising. **1977** *Redbook* Mar. 226/3 'I'm going to be forty years old.' He laughs with disbelief. 'It blows my mind.' Yet he sounds curiously unchanged, still the exuberant Peck's Bad Boy of whatever revolution comes to hand, still taunting the establishment. **1977** *Time* 19 Sept. 56/1 Now, in an attempt to break the longest winning streak in modern sports history, a new challenger from Down Under named *Australia* is squaring off with the 1974 U.S. defender, *Courageous*, skippered by Turner—the Peck's Bad Boy of yachting—in the waters off Newport, R.I.

'Pecksniff. [A proper name of fiction: the *Warwickshire Wordbk.* of G. F. Northall 1896 has '*Picksniff*, paltry, despicable; an insignificant, paltry, contemptible person'.] The name of a character in Dickens' novel 'Martin Chuzzlewit' (1844), represented as an unctuous hypocrite, habitually prating of benevolence, etc. Used allusively. Also as *v. intr.* and in *Comb.*, as ***pecksniff-shark*** (nonce use). Hence **Peck'sniffery**, **'Pecksniffism**, conduct or utterance resembling that of Pecksniff; **Peck'sniffian** *a.*, resembling Pecksniff; whence **Peck'sniffianism** (*nonce-word*); **Peck'sniffianly**, **Peck'sniffingly** *advbs.*, in a manner resembling Pecksniff.
1851 J. CHAPMAN *Diary* 1 July in G. S. Haight *Geo. Eliot & J. Chapman* (1940) 188 Mr B. put on such an exquisitely saintlike Pecksniffian aspect as to seem nearly in heaven. **1874** J. HATTON *Clytie* (ed. 10) 101 It seemed to smile a Pecksniffian smile of pity upon her. **1885** *Pall Mall G.* 17 Mar. 3/1 This odious compound of Tartuffism, Pharisaism, and Pecksniffery. **1888** TALMAGE in *Voice* (N.Y.) 2 Feb. 7 Ask Thackeray to express your chagrin, or Charles Dickens to expose Pecksniffianism. **1893** *Athenæum* 8 Apr. 430/3 He lectures Pepys for winebibbing, and we feel very much disposed to take him to task for Pecksniffism. **1894** LLOYD GEORGE *Family Lett.* (1973) 73 That pecksniffian young gent will have to climb down a peg or two. **1901** *Scotsman* 4 Mar. 6/2 A fine benevolence of phraseology.. which, we fear, is not free from a Pecksniffian twang. **1903** G. B. SHAW *Let.* 26 Dec. (1972) II. 386 And that you are to come Pecksniffing at me in this fashion. **1913** WYNDHAM LEWIS *Lett.* (1963) 50 A new form of fish in the troubled waters of Art.. the Pecksniff-shark, a timid but voracious journalistic monster. **1914** KIPLING *Lett. of Travel* (1920) 232 A government which is not a government but the disconnected satrapy of a half-dead empire, controlled pecksniffingly by a Power which is not a Power but an Agency. **1915** G. B. SHAW *Pen Portraits* (1931) 116 To lie—lie impudently, snobbishly, spitefully, Pecksniffianly, Tartuffily. **1926** A. HUXLEY *Let.* 25 Dec. (1969) 278, I would have made him survive into the Pecksniffian epoch. **1945** R. HARGREAVES *Enemy at Gate* 212 The Tsar himself, temporarily assuming the mantle of Mr. Gladstone's best Pecksniffian manner, continued to give whining expression to pious hopes for some sort of accommodation. **1947** K. S. SORABJI *Mi contra Fa* x. 87 He is apparently unaware.. that he is.. submitting himself to the judgment of his own upper classes... This is surely nonconformist Pecksniffery gone mad. **1959** J. BRAINE *Vodi* ix. 131 At least it was recognisably the work of a human being, even if he were a greedy Pecksniffian old get who used to sneak around the factory in carpet slippers. **1963** *Times* 22 Apr. 11/1 Disgust at the Pecksniffian pose that the ruling party has shown in denying the blatantly obvious. **1971** M. S. HOWARD *Jonathan Cape* vii. 111 Edward Garnett poured scorn on the Pecksniffery of these British officials.

peck stone, peck-wheat: see PEAK *sb.*[1] 3.

pecky ('pɛkɪ), *a.*[1] *U.S.* Also peeky, peaky. [app. f. PECK *sb.*[3] + -Y.] (See quots.)
1848 DICKESON & BROWN *Rept. on Cypress Timber of Miss. & La.* 8 That species of decay to which it [the cypress] is most liable, shows itself in partial and detached spots at greater or less distances, but often in very close proximity to each other... Timber affected in this way is denominated by raftsmen *Pecky.* **1876** *Gwilt's Archit.* Gloss., *Pecky*, timber in which the first symptoms of decay appear. An American term.
[BARTLETT 1859–60 s.v. *Peaky*, or *Peeky*, misquotes Dickeson as using *peeky*; thence, Webster 1864, *Peeky*; Century *Peaky* (also *peeky, pecky*), Funk *peaky*; associated with PEAKY *a.*[2], PEAK *v.*[1]]

pecky ('pɛkɪ), *a.*[2] *colloq.* [f. PECK *v.*[1], [2] + -Y.]
1. [PECK *v.*[2]] Pitching; choppy; apt to stumble.
1864 BLACKMORE *Clara Vaughan* lxi, Knocking about on a pecky sea. **1893** *Wiltsh. Gloss.*, *Pecky*, inclined to stumble. 'Th' old hoss goes terr'ble pecky'.
2. [PECK *v.*[1]] Like the peck of a bird.
1886 F. C. PHILIPS *Jack & Three Jills* I. vii. 90 My sisters.. administered flabby, pecky kisses.

Peclet ('pɛkleɪ). Also Péclet. [Name of J. C. E. *Peclet* (1793–1857), French physicist; adopted in this context by H. Gröber *Die Grundgesetze der Wärmeleitung und des Wärmeüberganges* (1921) ii. 168.] ***Peclet number***: a dimensionless parameter used in calculations of heat transfer between a moving fluid and a solid body, equivalent to the product of the Reynolds number and the Prandtl number, viz. Dvc_p/k, where D is a characteristic length of the body, v is the speed of the fluid past it, c_p is the heat capacity of unit volume of the fluid at constant pressure, and k is its thermal conductivity.
1933 W. H. MCADAMS *Heat Transmission* vii. 173 Equations of this form, expressing hD/k in terms of the Peclet number DGc_p/k are used by many German writers such as Nusselt and Gröber. **1956** GLASSTONE *Princ. Nucl. Reactor Engin.* xi. 679 For the correlation of heat-transfer data it is now appropriate to use another dimensionless modulus, namely, the Peclet number, Pe. **1958** [see NUSSELT]. **1974** F. M. WHITE *Viscous Fluid Flow* ii. 89 In low-speed flows (V_0 less than 30 percent of the speed of sound), we can usually neglect both the pressure term and the dissipation term, leaving only the Peclet number ($RePr$) as the single important parameter.

peco, variant of PEKOE (tea).

pecon: see PECAN.

pecoraite (pɪ'kɔːrəaɪt). *Min.* [f. the name of William T. *Pecora* (b. 1913), U.S. geologist + -ITE[1].] A nickel silicate, $Ni_3Si_2O_5(OH)_4$, found as green monoclinic crystals in the Wolf Creek meteorite in Australia.
1969 G. T. FAUST et al. in *Science* 4 July 59/3 A green mineral of the serpentine group, rich in nickel, was described.. from the Wolf Creek meteorite in the desert of Western Australia. This mineral is the nickel analog of the well-known magnesium silicate, clinochrysotile. The new mineral is named pecoraite after Dr. William T. Pecora, Director of the U.S. Geological Survey, in recognition of his contributions.. to the mineralogy and geology of nickel silicate deposits in North America and South America. **1973** *Mineral. Mag.* XXXIX. 113 Pecoraite.. was found as

fracture fillings in the Wolf Creek meteorite of Western Australia.

‖**pecorino** (peko'rino). [It., f. *pecora* sheep.] An Italian cheese made from ewes' milk.

1931 C. L. T. BEECHING *Law's Grocer's Man.* (ed. 3) 242/1 '*Pecorino Romano*' *type*, '*Moliterno*' *type*... They must be kept in a dry and fresh room, turned every week and oiled with linseed oil when they begin to get mouldy. **1954** E. DAVID *Italian Food* 301, I always buy *pecorino* when I see it in London, for its taste evokes memories of good country food..and coarse red wine. **1958** J. LODWICK *Bid Soldiers Shoot* vi. 166, I was given a slice of..Italian *pecorino* cheese, some maps, and five gold sovereigns, two of them Victorias. **1967** T. A. LAYTON *Wine & Food Soc. Guide Cheese & Cheese Cookery* 84 When cured for only 5–8 months Pecorino is eaten as a table cheese. **1970** I. ORIGO *Images & Shadows* ix. 205 The delicious sheep's-milk cheese, *pecorino*, which is a speciality of this region. **1973** *Country Life* 8 Mar. 570/3 Women used to come..to milk the ewes, and to make ..the Roquefort..or the *pecorino*.

†'**pecorous**, *a.* *Obs. rare*$^{-0}$. [ad. L. *pecorōs-us*, f. *pecus*, *pecor-* cattle.]

1656 BLOUNT *Glossogr.*, *Pecorous* (*pecorosus*), full of Cattle, or where many Cattle are.

†**pect**, obs. form of PECKED *ppl. a.*: see quot.

1633 GERARD *Descr. Somerset* (1900) 132 Their markett is ..full of pect eles as they call them because they take them in those waters by pecking an eale speare on them.

pect, obs. Sc. f. PECK *sb.*[1]

pectase ('pɛkteɪs). *Chem.* [f. PECT-IN or PECT-OSE, after *diastase.*] A ferment supposed to exist in fruits, etc., and having the property of converting pectin into pectic and other related acids. Now usu. called PECTINESTERASE.

1866–77 WATTS *Dict. Chem.* IV. 363 According to Frémy, all vegetal tissues which contain pectose..contain also a kind of ferment called pectase, comparable in its mode of action to..diastase. **1893** [see PECTIC]. **1945** [see PECTINESTERASE]. **1972** [see PECTINASE].

pectate ('pɛktət). *Chem.* [f. PECT-IC + -ATE[1].] A salt of pectic acid.

1831 T. THOMSON *Chem. Inorg. Bodies* (ed. 7) II. 122 Braconnot is of opinion that the soluble pectates constitute a complete antidote against all metallic poisons. **1866–77** WATTS *Dict. Chem.* IV. 368 The pectates of the alkali-metals are soluble in water, the rest insoluble and gelatinous.

†'**pecteale.** *Obs. rare*$^{-1}$. ? (app. some kind of wild fowl; but cf. *pect eles* in PECT *ppl. a.*)

1579 E. HAKE *Newes out of Powles Ch.-yd.* iv. Dijb, Stonetiuets, Teale, and Pecteales good, with Busterd fat and plum.

pecten ('pɛktɛn). *Anat.* and *Zool.* Pl. **pectines** ('pɛktɪniːz), **pectens.** [a. L. *pecten*, *pectin-* a comb, a heckle or card, a rake, the pubic hair, an instrument for striking the strings of a lyre, a scallop-shell, etc.; f. *pec-t-ĕre* to comb, cognate with Gr. πέκ-ειν to comb. In earlier use generally with L. plural *pectines.*]

†**1.** The set of bones in the hand between the wrist and fingers; the metacarpus. *Obs.*

c **1400** *Lanfranc's Cirurg.* 157 þe boonys of þe hand þat ben clepid pecten. **1541** R. COPLAND *Guydon's Quest. Chirurg.* G iij, In the thyrde coniunction be foure bones... That coniunction is called the brest of the hande or pecten.

2. The pubes; also, the pubic bone or sharebone. ? *Obs.* [prop. L.]

[*c* **1400** *Lanfranc's Cirurg.* 176 þat boon þat goiþ ouerþwert vndir þe ars aboue þe ȝerde, & is clepid os pectinis.] **1661** LOVELL *Hist. Anim. & Min.* 15 Applied to the pecten and genitalls in a plaister it helpeth the Gonorrhea. **1710** J. HARRIS *Lex. Techn.* II, *Pecten*, in Anatomy, is the same with the *Regio Pubis.* **1855** RAMSBOTHAM *Obstetr. Med.* 5 The smallest of the three divisions of the os innominatum is the os Pubis, Pecten, or Share Bone, situated anteriorly.

3. Applied to various comb-like structures in animal bodies. **a.** A pigmented vascular process which projects from the choroid coat of the eye into the vitreous humour in birds, and in certain reptiles and fishes; also called *marsupium.*

1713 DERHAM *Phys.-Theol.* IV. ii. 104 In birds..the Choroeides hath..a curious pectinated work seated on the optick nerve. The structure of this Pecten is very like that of the *Ligamentum Ciliare.* **1856** TODD & BOWMAN *Phys. Anat.* II. 23 In birds, there is a remarkable plicated, comb-like process of the choroid,..termed the pecten.

b. Each of two comb-like appendages behind the posterior legs in scorpions.

1826 KIRBY & SP. *Entomol.* xxxv. III. 540 The poisers of Diptera and the pectens of scorpions. **1835** KIRBY *Hab. & Inst. Anim.* II. xvii. 126. **1888** ROLLESTON & JACKSON *Anim. Life* 523 Class Arachnida... The abdomen has appendages only in *Scorpionidæ*,..the pectines or combs, organs probably of touch.

c. A comb-like organ, usually formed of small stiff hairs, on the legs of certain insects, as bees.

1816 KIRBY & SP. *Entomol.* xviii. (1818) II. 118 [Humble-bees] the males... Their posterior tibiæ also want the corbicula and pecten that distinguish the..other sex.

d. The pectinated structure on the claws of certain birds. **e.** The CTENOPHORE or comb-row of a ctenophoran.

4. A genus of bivalve molluscs, having a rounded shell with radiating ribs suggesting the teeth of a comb; an animal of this genus, a scallop.

1682 SIR T. BROWNE *Let.* 15 Mar., Wks. 1836 I. 336 The pectines or skollops. **1778** KING in *Phil. Trans.* LXIX. 40 Pectens, cockles, limpets. **1835** KIRBY *Hab. & Inst. Anim.* I. viii. 264 Those elegant shells the Pectens or Comb Shells.

attrib. **1835–6** TODD *Cycl. Anat.* I. 711/2 In the Pecten family. **1849** H. MILLER *Footpr. Creat.* xi. (1874) 202 Layers of mussel and pecten shells.

pectic ('pɛktɪk), *a.* *Chem.* [ad. Gr. πηκτικ-ός, f. πηκτ-ός congealed, curdled, f. stem πηγ- of πηγνύειν to make firm or solid.] **a.** In *pectic acid*, a transparent gelatinous substance formed by chemical action from PECTIN, and forming an important constituent of fruit-jellies. Also, of or pertaining to pectin.

(By further transformation it is converted into *parapectic acid* (PARA- 2 a) and *metapectic acid.*) *pectic fermentation*, the fermentation supposed to be produced by PECTASE, which converts pectin into pectic and other related acids.

1831 T. THOMSON *Chem. Inorg. Bodies* (ed. 7) II. 120 Braconnot gave it the name of pectic acid, from the great tendency which it has to form a jelly with water. **1863** MITCHELL *Farm of Edgewood* 225 Pears have a modicum of pectic acid at a certain stage of their ripeness. **1866–77** WATTS *Dict. Chem.* IV. 363 Under the influence of acids or alkalis, pectin is gradually modified, and ultimately transformed into a strongly acid compound called metapectic acid, passing however through a series of intermediate modifications called by Frémy parapectin, metapectin, pectosic acid, pectic acid, and parapectic acid. **1893** *Syd. Soc. Lex.*, *Pectase*, an organic albuminoid ferment found in unripe fruits and roots, which determines the *Pectic fermentation.* **1930** [see GALACTURONIC *a.*]. **1964** D. D. DAVIES et al. *Plant Biochem.* iii. 147 Pectic acid is the simplest pectic substance and is the basis of the others. Pure pectic acid appears to be an unbranched chain of α-1,4 linked D-galacturonic acid units which are present in the C-1 chair form..of the pyranose ring. Any compound of this structure which is large enough to possess colloidal properties is classed as a pectic acid. Most pectic acids appear to contain about 100 units with a minimum of approximately 5 units. **1972** [see PECTINASE].

b. Applied to a class of substances that includes the pectins and other colloidal polymers of galacturonic acid.

1889 *Chem. News* 1 Nov. 221/2 The author [*sc.* L. Mangin] shows the presence of pectic compounds in vegetable membranes. **1913** HAAS & HILL *Introd. Chem. Plant Products* II. 126 Comparatively little is known about the chemistry of pectin or the pectic bodies, as there appear to be several of these substances. **1957** E. V. MILLER *Chem. Plants* i. 14 Pectin is perhaps the pectic compound with which the layman is most familiar. **1966** R. M. DEVLIN *Plant Physiol.* vii. 137 During the ripening of the fruit, protopectin is converted into the more soluble pectic substances—pectin and pectic acid. **1973** J. A. GOSS *Physiol. Plants* xvi. 344 In contrast to the other pectic substances, pectin is water-soluble, and is located in the protoplasm of the cell.

pectin ('pɛktɪn). *Chem.* [f. stem *pect-* of PECTIC + -IN[1].] **1. a.** A white neutral substance, soluble in water, formed from PECTOSE by heating with acids, or naturally in the ripening of fruits, and constituting the gelatinizing agent in vegetable juices; in the further process of ripening, it is converted into *parapectin* (PARA- 2 a), *metapectin*, and other related substances (see PECTIC). Now recognized as having a variable composition but being principally a high-molecular-weight polymer of partially methylated galacturonic acid in which galactose and arabinose residues are also present.

1838 T. THOMSON *Chem. Org. Bodies* 146 Vauquelin, who found pectin in the tamarind, considered it as the same with pectic acid. **1866–77** WATTS *Dict. Chem.* IV. 364 Green fruits..do not contain pectin ready formed, but only pectose... When the fruit is ripe, the juice..contains a large quantity of pectin, and still more of parapectin... Lastly, fruits in the over-ripe state no longer contain a trace of pectin, that substance having been converted into metapectic acid. **1913**, etc. [see PECTIC *a.* b]. **1917**, **1930** [see GALACTURONIC *a.*] **1964** B. NILSON *Pears Family Cookbk.* 223/2 Over-ripe fruit will not set so well because it will contain less pectin. **1972** *Materials & Technol.* V. xix. 703 Pectins, which occur only in certain plant tissues, are polymers of galacturonic acid linked by α-1,4-glycosidic units, with about two thirds of the carboxylic acid groups esterified with methanol. **1975** D. GREEN *Food & Drink from your Garden* I. vii. 65 Flowers yield very little sugar, but their musts will release no pectins (the glue-like substances holding plant tissues together) and so will clear easily.

b. Any of the pectic substances.

1896 *Jrnl. Chem. Soc.* LXX. I. 7 Pectin Substances... Many attempts have been made to establish a relationship between pectins and vegetable gums (carbohydrates). **1929** R. A. GORTNER *Outl. Biochem.* xxvii. 584 The pectin producing these jellies is the only water-soluble member of a group of related compounds known as the 'pectic substances', or sometimes called the 'pectins'. **1931** E. C. MILLER *Plant Physiol.* i. 12 It is now fairly well established that these substances are not chemically combined with cellulose, although they are closely associated with it, so that they are classified under the general name of the 'pectic compounds' or 'pectins'. **1966** NOWAKOWSKI & CLARKE tr. *Kretovich's Princ. Plant Biochem.* ii. 86 The ripening of fruits is characterized by the conversion of insoluble into soluble pectin.

†**2.** *attrib.* in the sense of PECTIC *a.* b. *Obs.*

1877 *Jrnl. Chem. Soc.* XXXII. 502 The formula of the group of pectin bodies. **1895** F. E. WEISS tr. *Sorauer's Pop. Treat. Physiol. Plants* vi. 123 Together with gums and acids we often find substances consisting also of carbon, hydrogen, and oxygen, which form gelatinous masses on boiling, and are termed pectin substances. **1900** A. J. EWART tr. *Pfeffer's Physiol. Plants* I. viii. 477 Many gums..seem to be in part allied to pectin substances.

Hence **pectinaceous** (-'neɪʃəs) *a.*, related to or containing pectin.

1844 DUNGLISON *Med. Lex.* s.v. *Pectinous*, A pectinous or pectinaceous vegetable principle. **1887** tr. *Sachs' Physiol. Plants* 328 The share in metabolism taken by some other organic compounds, such as pectinaceous substances.

pectinal ('pɛktɪnəl), *a.* (*sb.*) ? *Obs.* [ad. med.L. *pectinālis*, f. L. *pecten*, *pectin-*: see -AL[1].]

1. *Anat.* Belonging to the 'pecten' or pubes; *pectinal bone*, the pubic bone, sharebone.

1541 R. COPLAND *Guydon's Quest. Chirur.* I iv, Two great bones..that be coniuncte wt this spondyle of the holowe bone behynde and before in makynge the pectynall bone.

2. *Nat. Hist.* Of the nature of or resembling a comb; applied by Sir T. Browne to flat-fish, from the resemblance of the spine with its apophyses to a comb. Also as *sb.*, in *pl.* flat-fish.

1646 SIR T. BROWNE *Pseud. Ep.* IV. i. 181 Other fishes.. as pectinals, or such as have the Apophyses of their spine made laterally like a combe. *Ibid.* x. 203 Pectinall [fishes], whose ribs are rectilineall. **1656** BLOUNT *Glossogr.*, *Pectinals* ..their back-bone, and ribs do in some sort resemble a comb. **1705** EVELYN *Sylva* II. iii. (1729) 119 The Silver-Fir ..is distinguished from the rest by the pectinal Shape of it.

pectinase ('pɛktɪneɪz, -s). *Biochem.* [a. F. *pectinase* (E. Bourquelot 1899, in *Jrnl. de Pharm. et de Chimie* IX. 567): see PECTIN and -ASE.] An enzyme found in plants and in certain bacteria and fungi which hydrolyses pectin to its constituent monosaccharides.

1899 *Jrnl. Chem. Soc.* LXXVI. I. 652 In all probability it is a new ferment and the name pectinase is suggested for it. **1929** R. A. GORTNER *Outl. Biochem.* xxvii. 593 Pectinase hydrolyzes pectin (and possibly pectic acid) to its simple components, sugars and galacturonic acid. **1953** F. T. BROOKS *Plant Dis.* (ed. 2) x. 156 Brown..has indicated that the enzyme (pectinase) or enzyme complex of *B. cinerea* which softens the cell walls probably also kills the host protoplasm. **1972** *Materials & Technol.* V. 703 They [*sc.* the pectic enzymes] can be broadly classified,..into two sub-groups. These are the polygalacturonases, which cleave glycosidic linkages between adjoining galacturonic acid units, and the pectic methyl esterases... The two groups were formerly known, respectively, as pectinases and pectases.

pectinate ('pɛktɪnət), *a.* Chiefly *Nat. Hist.* [ad. L. *pectināt-us*, f. *pecten* comb: see -ATE[2].] = PECTINATED.

1793 MARTYN *Lang. Bot.*, *Pectinatum folium*, a pectinate leaf. **1826** KIRBY & SP. *Entomol.* IV. 321 *Pectinate*... Antennæ furnished on one side with a number of parallel stiff branches, resembling somewhat the teeth of a comb. **1833** A. EATON *Man. Bot. N. Amer.* II. (ed. 6) 129. **1846** DANA *Zooph.* 594 Margin of the pinnules pectinate. **1870** HOOKER *Stud. Flora* 189 Bracts with..pectinate tip and margins.

pectinate ('pɛktɪneɪt), *v.* [f. L. *pectināt-*, ppl. stem of *pectināre* to comb, f. *pecten* comb.]

†**1.** (See quot.) *Obs. rare*$^{-0}$.

1623 COCKERAM, *Pectinate*, to comb. **1656** in BLOUNT.

2. To fit together in alternation, like the teeth of two combs; to interlock. †**a.** *trans.* *Obs. rare.* **b.** *intr.* in reciprocal sense: = INTERDIGITATE.

1646 SIR T. BROWNE *Pseud. Ep.* V. xxii. 266 To sit crosse legg'd, or with our fingers pectinated or shut together is accounted bad. **1884** BOWER & SCOTT *De Bary's Phaner.* 234 The bundles..are separated from one another by other bundles, which pass between them, and pectinate with them.

pectinated ('pɛktɪneɪtɪd), *ppl. a.* Chiefly *Nat. Hist.* [f. as PECTINATE + -ED.] Formed like a comb; having straight narrow closely-set projections or divisions like the teeth of a comb.

1671 RAY in *Phil. Trans.* VI. 2278 The Tongue was..of an equal breadth to the very tip, which was toothed or pectinated about the edges. **1766** PENNANT *Zool.* (1768) I. 200 The edges of the toes [of Grouse] pectinated. **1861** MISS PRATT *Flower. Pl.* I. 4 A pectinated leaf is one whose narrow segments resemble the teeth of a comb.

'**pectinately**, *adv.* [f. PECTINATE *a.* + -LY[2].] In a pectinate manner; like the teeth of a comb.

1846 DANA *Zooph.* (1848) 652 Branchlets, long and pectinately arranged. **1875** C. C. BLAKE *Zool.* 333 The tentacles are set pectinately on two arms.

pectination (pɛktɪ'neɪʃən). [n. of action from *pectināre* to PECTINATE: see -ATION.]

†**1.** The action of combing (the hair). *Obs.*

1753 CHAMBERS *Cycl. Supp.* s.v., Frequent pectination is recommended by many physicians..as an exercise.

2. The action of interlocking or condition of being interlocked like the teeth of two combs. ? *Obs.*

1646 SIR T. BROWNE *Pseud. Ep.* V. xxii. 266 The complication or pectination of the fingers was an Hieroglyphick of impediment.

3. The condition or character of being pectinated; *concr.* a pectinated or comb-like structure.

1819 G. SAMOUELLE *Entomol. Compend.* 248 Antennæ.. with a double series of pectinations. **1874** COUES *Birds N.-W.* 513 Absence of pectination of the middle claw. **1876** F.

BRODIE in G. F. Chambers *Astron.* I. i. 15 The pectinations which fringe the whole of the edge of the umbra.

pectinato- (pɛktɪˌneɪtəʊ), combining adverbial form of L. *pectinātus* PECTINATE *a.*, prefixed to other adjs. in the sense 'pectinately'..., or 'pectinate and...'; as in ***pectinato-denticulate***, ***pectinato-erose***, ***pectinato-fimbricate***, ***pectinato-pinnate***.

1846 DANA *Zooph.* (1848) 210 Lamellæ..deeply pectinato-erose, or penetrated by oblong cellules. *Ibid.* 232 Lamellæ..finely and elegantly pectinato-denticulate.

pectineal (pɛkˈtɪnɪəl), *a.* *Anat.* [f. mod.L. *pectine-us*, f. *pecten* comb + -AL[1].] Pertaining to the pecten or pubic bone: applied to certain parts of this bone and connected structures: see quots.

1840 G. V. ELLIS *Anat.* 650 The *pectineus* muscle..arises from the pectineal line of the pubes between the spine and pectineal eminence. **1875** SIR W. TURNER in *Encycl. Brit.* I. 828/2 The pectineal border..forms part of the line of separation between the true and false pelvis.

pectinesterase (pɛktɪˈnɛstəreɪz, -s). *Biochem.* Also **pectin esterase**. [f. PECTIN + ESTERASE.] An enzyme found in plants and in certain bacteria and fungi, which hydrolyses pectin to pectic acid and methanol; = PECTASE, PECTINMETHYLESTERASE.

1945 LINEWEAVER & BALLOU in *Arch. Biochem.* VI. 373 The enzyme that acts on pectin and causes gelation in the presence of calcium has been known as pectase... Since the enzyme hydrolyzes the ester bonds in pectin we propose the name pectinesterase, which indicates the esterase character of the enzyme. **1956** *New Biol.* XX. 96 It was concluded that the enzyme pectinesterase was responsible, at least in part, for the development of disease symptoms [in the tomato shoots]. **1966** *McGraw-Hill Encycl. Sci. & Technol.* IX. 609/1 With the enzyme, pectin esterase, obtained from such sources as roots, leaves, and fruits of all higher plants and also from a number of microorganisms, the ester groups are quickly removed. **1975** *Biochim. & Biophys. Acta* CCCLXXVII. 408 The ability of *B. cinerea* polygalacturonase to degrade pectin N.F. was connected with the presence of pectinesterase in the preparation.

‖**pectineus** (pɛkˈtɪnɪːəs). *Anat.* erron. **-æus**. [mod.L., f. *pecten*, *pectin-* comb; cf. *flumineus*, *virgineus*, etc.] For *pectineus musculus*, name of a flat muscle arising from the pectineal eminence of the pubic bone and inserted into the thigh-bone just behind the small trochanter.

1704 J. HARRIS *Lex. Techn.* I, *Pectineus*, is a Muscle on the Thigh. **1872** MIVART *Elem. Anat.* 346 The pectineus and adductors of man.

pectini-, before a vowel **pectin-**, combining form of L. *pecten* comb, used in the formation of scientific words. **ˈpectinibranch** (-bræŋk), **-ˈbranchian**, **-ˈbranchiate** [BRANCHIA] *adjs.*, belonging to the *Pectinibranchia* (or *-branchiata*), a family of gastropod molluscs having comb-like gills, or ctenidia (also called *Ctenobranchia*); also as *sb.*, a mollusc of this family. **ˈpectinicorn** [L. *cornu* horn] *adj.*, having pectinate antennæ, as the division *Pectinicornia* of lamellicorn beetles (also **ˌpectiniˈcornate**); *sb.*, a beetle of this division. **pectiˈniferous** *a.* [L. *-ferus* bearing], bearing a pecten or comb-like structure. **ˈpectiniform** *a.*, (*a*) comb-shaped; (*b*) of the form of a scallop (PECTEN 4). **pectiniliac** (-ˈɪlɪæk) *a.* = ILIOPECTINEAL. **ˌpectiniˈrostrate** *a.* [L. *rostrum* beak], having a comb-like beak or snout (Mayne).

1835–6 TODD *Cycl. Anat.* I. 556/1 The *Pectinibranchiate Mollusks. **1857** MAYNE *Expos. Lex.*, *Pectinicornis*, applied to an insect having pectinated antennæ..*pectinicornate. *Ibid.*, *Pectiniferus*, having combs...*pectiniferous. **1831** J. DAVIES *Man. Mat. Med.* 135 This salt..crystallizes in *pectiniform needles. **1893** *Syd. Soc. Lex.*, *Pectiniform septum*, the median..connective tissue septum between the two corpora cavernosa of the penis.

pectinid (ˈpɛktɪnɪd). *Zool.* [f. mod.L. *pectinidæ*, f. PECTEN: see -ID[3].] A mollusc of the family *Pectinidæ* or Pecten family; a scallop.

pectinite (ˈpɛktɪnaɪt). *Palæont.* [f. L. *pectin-* PECTEN + -ITE[1].] A fossil pecten or scallop.

1677 PLOT *Oxfordsh.* v. §72 Stones resembling escallops.. the next following Pectinites. **1796** KIRWAN *Elem. Min.* (ed. 2) I. 81 Impressions or petrifactions of muscles, snails, corals, pectinites. **1852** TH. ROSS *Humboldt's Trav.* I. v. 184 The oysters and pectinites.

ˌpectinˌmethyˈlesterase. *Biochem.* Also **pectin methylesterase**, and with hyphen. [f. PECTIN + METHYL + ESTERASE.] = PECTINESTERASE.

1945 MCCOLLOCH & KERTESZ in *Jrnl. Biol. Chem.* CLX. 149 Two enzymes which act on soluble pectic substances are recognized at the present time; namely, pectinpolygalacturonase (PG),..and pectin-methylesterase (PM), which catalyses the hydrolysis of the methyl ester groups. **1954** *Biol. Abstr.* XXVIII. 27349 The purpose of the study was to determine the extent to which several plant pathogens produced pectinmethylesterase..and polygalacturonase. **1966** [see PECTINESTERASE]. **1975** *Phytochemistry* XIV. 109/2 No attempt was made to determine if pectin was being degraded..by the two step reaction catalyzed by pectinmethylesterase and endopolygalacturonase.

pectinoid (ˈpɛktɪnɔɪd), *a.* *Zool.* [f. as PECTINITE + -OID.] Resembling a pecten or scallop. (Mayne.)

pectinous (ˈpɛktɪnəs), *a.* *Chem.* [f. PECTIN + -OUS.] Of the nature of or related to pectin: = PECTINACEOUS, PECTOUS b.

1844 [see PECTINACEOUS]. **1892** *Chambers' Encycl.* IX. 788/1 The juice of the [beet] root contains..albuminous, pectinous, and other substances.

pectize (ˈpɛktaɪz), *v.* [f. Gr. πηκτ-ός fixed, congealed (cf. PECTIC) + -IZE.] *trans.* and *intr.* To change into a gelatinous mass; to congeal.

1882 OGILVIE, *Pectize*,..to congeal; to change into a gelatinous mass. *H. Spencer.* **1885** C. G. W. LOCK *Workshop Receipts* Ser. IV. 10/1 The zinc compound does not..sufficiently pectise cellulose. *Ibid.* 10/2 The film of pectised cellulose. *Ibid.*, Pectising is brought about by the copper solution.

pectolite (ˈpɛktəlaɪt). *Min.* (Also **pek-**.) [Named (*pectolith*) 1828 by Von Kobell, f. Gr. πηκτ-ός congealed + -LITE.] A whitish or greyish hydrous silicate of calcium and sodium, found in close aggregations of acicular crystals, usually fibrous and radiated in structure.

1828 *Edin. Jrnl. Sc.* IX. 367 Pektolite..a mineral which is found on natrolite. **1899** *Amer. Jrnl. Sc.* VIII. 275 Experiments relative to the constitution of pectolite.

pectoral (ˈpɛktərəl), *sb.* and *a.* Also 6 **pecturall**, 6–7 **pectorel(l**, **-all**. [As sb., in sense 1, a. OF. *pectoral* (1355 in Du Cange), ad. L. *pectorāle* breast-plate, sb. use of neuter of *pectorālis* adj., f. *pectus*, *pector-* breast; as adj., direct from the L. adj., or a. F. *pectoral* adj. (15th c. in Littré). Senses 2–4 of the sb. are absolute uses of the adj.]

A. *sb.* **1.** Something worn on the breast.

a. An ornamental plate, cloth, or other decoration, worn on the breast; an ornamental breast-plate; *spec.* (*a*) that worn by the Jewish High Priest (= BREAST-PLATE 2); (*b*) *R.C. Ch.* that formerly worn by a bishop in celebrating mass.

c **1440** *Promp. Parv.* 389/1 Pectoral of a vestyment, or other a-rayment, *pectorale, racionale.* **1445** *Instr. Queen's Coronat.* in Rymer *Fœdera* (1710) XI. 83 A Pectoral of Gold garnished with Rubees, Perles. **1506** GUYLFORDE *Pilgr.* (Camden) 7, xij crownes of fyne golde, and xij pectorals and a riche cappe. **1633** T. ADAMS *Exp. 2 Peter* i. 16 The twelve stones in Aaron's pectoral. **1775** ADAIR *Amer. Ind.* 84. **1894** *Times* 26 May 19/1 A Royal pectoral, on which two crowned hawks support the cartouche of Usertasen II.

b. A piece of armour for the breast: = BREAST-PLATE 1.

1590 SIR J. SMYTH *Disc. Weapons* 31 b, Lighting vppon their shafrons, cranets, or steele pectorells. **1706** PHILLIPS, A *Pectoral*, a Breast-plate, Armour, or Defence for the Breast. **1834** PLANCHÉ *Brit. Costume* 29 A border of metal to the collar, which acted as a pectoral.

c. An ornamental cloth for the breast of a horse: cf. PEITREL, POITREL. Also, a piece of armour to protect the breast of a horse: cf. sense 1 b. *Obs.* exc. *Hist.*

1602 SEGAR *Hon. Mil. & Civ.* II. xi. 71 His horse sadled with blacke leather,..the pectorel of blacke leather with a crosse paty of gold, hanging before the horse feete. **1653** GREAVES *Seraglio* 11 The Bridles, Pectorals, Cruppers, Saddle-clothes..set so thick with jewels of divers sorts, that the beholders are amazed. **1656** [see PEITREL, PEYTREL, PETREL *sb.*]. **1662** *Act 14 Chas. II*, c. 3 §23 A Bitt and Bridle with a Pectorell and Crupper. **1786** F. GROSE *Treat. Anc. Armour & Weapons* 30 The Poitrinal, Pectoral, or Breast Plate was formed of plates of metal rivetted together. **1821** in G. F. Laking *Catal. European Armour & Arms in Wallace Collection* (1900) 315 Armour of the Elector Joseph of Bavaria on horseback. This superb suit of black and gold, with the pectoral, chanfron, and other trappings for the horse, of the finest workmanship of the time of Henry VIII. **1824** S. R. MEYRICK *Crit. Inquiry Antient Armour* III. Gloss. s.v. Pectorale, Sometimes the ends of the pectoral were raised so high as to protect the abdomen of the knight.

d. A chest-protector.

1881 *Pop. Sc. Monthly* XIX. 150 The great majority..still stick to coarse linen next the skin, and use woolen pectorals only as counter-irritants.

2. A medicine, food, or drink, good for affections of the chest, i.e. the lungs and other respiratory organs (or, loosely, the internal organs generally).

1601 HOLLAND *Pliny* II. Explan. Wds. Art, *Pectorals, i.* such medicines as bee fit for the breast and lungs. **1699** EVELYN *Acetaria* 89 There are Pectorals for the Breast and Bowels. **1749** CHESTERF. *Lett.* 22 June, They recommend an attention to pectorals, such as sago, barley, turnips. **1830** LINDLEY *Nat. Syst. Bot.* 91 The roots of the liquorice contain..a sweet subacid mucilaginous juice, which is much esteemed as a pectoral.

3. *Anat.* Short for ***pectoral muscle***, ***pectoral fin***.

1758 J. S. *Le Dran's Observ. Surg.* (1771) 157 The Ball.. came out under the Pectoral. **1828** STARK *Elem. Nat. Hist.* I. 164 Dorsal fin conical, situated above the pectorals. **1855** BAIN *Senses & Int.* (1864) 203 The great pectoral bringing the arm forward, the deltoid lifting it away from the side.

†**4.** (See quot.) *Obs. nonce-use.*

1617 *Janua Ling.* Advt., To render the volume as portable ..and if not as a manuall or pocket-booke, yet a pectorall or bosome-booke, to be carried twixt ierkin and doublet.

B. *adj.*

1. Of, pertaining to, situated or occurring in or upon, the breast or chest; thoracic. Chiefly *Anat.*

pectoral arch or ***girdle***, the shoulder-girdle (see GIRDLE *sb.*[1] 4 b). ***pectoral fins***, the pair of lateral fins attached to the pectoral arch in fishes, usually thoracic in position, corresponding to the fore limbs of other vertebrates. ***pectoral muscles***, the muscles of the chest, esp. the *pectoralis major*, 'a large fan-shaped muscle forming the main fleshy mass of the chest on either side', and the *pectoralis minor*, 'a flat triangular muscle situated beneath the *p. major*' (*Syd. Soc. Lex.* 1893). ***pectoral respiration*** (see quot. 1834, and cf. COSTAL *a.* 1). ***pectoral ridge***, the outer edge of the bicipital groove of the humerus, into which the *pectoralis major* muscle is inserted.

1578 BANISTER *Hist. Man.* I. 21 The produced partes of the pectorall Spondilles. **1601** HOLLAND *Pliny* II. 352 The rheume or catarrhe that hath taken a way to the brest or pectorall parts. **1615** CROOKE *Body of Man* 776 The first is called *Pectoralis* the Petorall Muscle, so named from his situation, because it occupieth the forepart of the Chest. **1769** PENNANT *Zool.* III. 84 The pectoral fins are very large. **1782** MONRO *Anat.* 167 The eight upper ribs were formerly classed into pairs, with particular names.., the crooked, the solid, the pectoral, the twisted. **1831** R. KNOX *Cloquet's Anat.* 33 In general, the pectoral cavity is symmetrical. **1834** J. FORBES *Laennec's Dis. Chest* (ed. 4) 13 If the abdomen dilates with comparatively much greater force than the chest, the respiration is named abdominal; if the contrary obtains, it is called pectoral. **1888** ROLLESTON & JACKSON *Anim. Life* 341 All Vertebrata possess typically two pairs of limbs—the pectoral and pelvic.

2. *Med.* Of a medicine, food, or drink: Good for diseases or affections of the chest (or, loosely, the internal organs generally).

1576 BAKER *Jewell of Health* II. lxxxvi. 85 A pectorall water, or water for the breast,..that especiallie auaileth in the weakenesse of the stomacke. **1637** BRIAN *Pisse-Proph.* (1679) 23 Some pectoral physick to ease his cough. **1732** ARBUTHNOT *Rules of Diet* I. in *Aliments*, etc. 246 Peaches are cordial and pectoral. **1830** LINDLEY *Nat. Syst. Bot.* 314 The leaves [of Ferns] generally contain a thick astringent mucilage, with a little aroma, on which account many are considered pectoral and lenitive. **1857** MAYNE *Expos. Lex.*, *Pectoral Moss*, a common name for the *Lichen pulmonarius*.

3. Worn, or intended to be worn, on the breast.

1616 BULLOKAR *Eng. Expos.*, *Pectorall*, belonging to the breast, or which hangeth before the breast. **1727–35** CHAMBERS *Cycl.* s.v., In the Romish Church Bishops and regular Abbots wear a pectoral Cross. **1849** ROCK *Ch. of Fathers* II. vi. 175 We are led to believe that the formal use of the pectoral cross, as now worn over the chasuble, goes no farther back than the middle of the sixteenth century.

4. *fig.* Proceeding or derived from the 'breast' or 'heart', i.e. from one's internal feeling or consciousness.

1630 DONNE *Serm. Matt.* xxviii. 6 Let..no Angell of the Church,..proceed upon an *ipse dixit*, upon his own pectorall word and determination. **1633** EARL MANCH. *Al Mondo* (1636) 184 At this time a good mans tongue is in his breast, not in his mouth, his words are then so pithy and so pectorall. **1865** tr. *Strauss' New Life Jesus* I. I. viii. 44 The inflated language here used betrays already the pectoral colouring which Keim expressly claims for his work. **1890** J. F. SMITH tr. *Pfleiderer's Developm. Theol.* III. iii. (1891) 281 Neander's pectoral theology involved a serious lack of historical criticism. [Cf. next.]

ˈpectoralist. [f. prec. + -IST.] (See quot., and cf. prec. B. 4.)

1886 FARRAR *Hist. Interpr.* viii. 415 [Neander's] motto was, *pectus facit theologum*, and many sneered at his followers as pectoralists.

ˈpectorally, *adv. rare.* [f. as prec. + -LY[2].] In a pectoral manner or position: in quots., **a.** in relation to one's inward feeling, at heart; **b.** on a 'pectoral' diet: cf. PECTORAL B. 4, 2.

1662 M. MASON *Friendly Admon. Rom. Cath.* 4 Would you not then have been pectorally glad of that Indulgence? **1749** CHESTERF. *Lett.* 21 Aug., Be regular, and live pectorally.

pectoriloquy (pɛktəˈrɪləkwɪ). *Path.* [ad. F. *pectoriloquie*, f. L. *pectus*, *pector-* breast + *-loquium* speaking.] The transmission of the sound of the voice through the wall of the chest to the ear in auscultation; usually a sign of a cavity or some other affection in the lung.

1834 J. FORBES *Laennec's Dis. Chest.* (ed. 4) 36 This peculiar phenomenon (which I have denominated Pectoriloquy). **1853** MARKHAM tr. *Skoda's Auscult.* 290 The pectoriloquy is..much clearer and louder..in a gangrenous excavation, than in one formed by pulmonary abscess.

So **pectoriloquial** (pɛktərɪˈləʊkwɪəl), **pectoriloquous** (pɛktəˈrɪləkwəs) *adjs.*, of, or of the nature of, pectoriloquy; **pectoˈriloquism**, pectoriloquy.

1846 WORCESTER, *Pectoriloquial, relating to pectoriloquy. *Museum.* **1834** *Good's Study Med.* (ed. 4) II. 524 To this apparent transfer of the voice to the chest..[Laennec] has given the..name of *pectoriloquism, or mediate auscultation of the voice. **1834** *Cycl. Pract. Med.* III. 47/2 There was no metallic tinkling, *bourdonnement*, or pectoriloquism. **1862** H. W. FULLER *Dis. Lungs* 111 The production of *pectoriloquous resonance.

pectose (ˈpɛktəʊs). *Chem.* [f. stem *pect-* of PECTIC + -OSE.] An insoluble substance related to cellulose and occurring with it in vegetable tissues, esp. in unripe fruits and fleshy roots; by the action of acids, etc. it is converted into PECTIN.

1857 W. A. MILLER *Elem. Chem.* III. 83 The cellular tissue of many fruits, and of turnips, carrots, parsnips, &c., contains a substance which he [Frémy] terms *pectose*, and which is quite insoluble in water, alcohol, and ether. **1866–77** WATTS *Dict. Chem.* IV. 363 Pectose..gives the hardness to unripe fruits. It is probably isomeric with cellulose, or differs from it only by the elements of water.

Hence **pectosic** (pɛk'tɒsɪk) *a.*, in *pectosic acid*, an acid formed immediately from pectin by the action of pectase or alkalis, and converted by further action of the same into pectic acid.

1866–77 [see PECTOUS].

pectostracan (pɛk'tɒstrəkən), *a.* and *sb. Zool.* [f. mod. Zool. L. *Pectostraca* (f. Gr. πηκτ-ός congealed + ὄστρακον tile, potsherd, shell) + -AN.] **a.** *adj.* Belonging to the division *Pectostraca* of *Crustacea* in Huxley's classification, a synonym of *Cirripedia*. **b.** *sb.* A crustacean belonging to this division, a cirriped. So **pec'tostracous** *a.*

pectous ('pɛktəs), *a. Chem.* [f. Gr. πηκτ-ός congealed + -OUS.] **a.** Congealed, solidified: said of modified forms of substances ordinarily fluid. **b.** Related to pectin. *pectous acid*, name of a particular acid related to pectic acid (cf. -OUS c).

1861 GRAHAM in *Phil. Trans.* 184 Fluid colloids appear to have always a pectous modification. **1866–77** WATTS *Dict. Chem.* IV. 364 Pectase immersed in water for two or three days, is decomposed..and is then no longer capable of acting as a pectous ferment. *Ibid.* The conversion of the pectin into pectosic and pectous acids. **1875** B. W. RICHARDSON *Dis. Mod. Life* 104 In course of time..the vital tissues become thickened, or, to use the technical term, 'pectous'.

†**'pectron.** *Obs.* [An erroneous formation (thought by Barret to be French), app. derived in some way from L. *pectus, pector-* breast.] = PEITREL, POITREL.

1598 BARRET *Theor. Warres*, Gloss. 252 *Pectron*, a French word, is the arming of the brest of the horse. **1622** F. MARKHAM *Bk. War.* v. ii. §4. 166 The Horses head, necke, brest, and buttocke barbed with Pectron, Trappings, Crinier, and Chieffront.

†**pectuncle.** *Obs.* Anglicized form of L. *pectunculus* a small scallop (dim. of *pecten*: see PECTEN 4), a name formerly given to the cockles.

1753 CHAMBERS *Cycl. Supp.* s.v. *Pecten*, The genus of pectuncles, or cockles, has been made by all authors a very extensive one. **1797** *Encycl. Brit.* (ed. 3) XIV. 80/2 There are shells universally allowed to be pectens or scallops, which have no ears, and others as universally allowed to be pectuncles or cockles which have.

pectunculate (pɛk'tʌŋkjʊlət), *a. Entom.* [f. mod.L. type **pectunculāt-us*, f. *pectuncul-us*, dim. of *pecten*: see prec. and -ATE².] Having a row of minute spines or bristles; finely pectinate.

1826 KIRBY & SP. *Entomol.* IV. 310 Under Jaws.. Pectunculate... When the stipes below the feeler has a row of minute spines set like the teeth of a comb.

‖**pectus** ('pɛktəs). *Anat.* and *Zool.* Pl. **pectora**. [L., = the breast.] **a.** The breast or chest. **b.** *Ornith.* The thoracic region of the under surface of the body of a bird; usually, the anterior protuberant part. **c.** *Entom.* The lower surface of the thorax or prothorax of an insect.

1693 tr. *Blancard's Phys. Dict.* (ed. 2), *Pectus*, the foremost part of the Thorax reaching from the Neck-bone, down to the Midriff. **1834** MᶜMURTRIE *Cuvier's Anim. Kingd.* 450 In the other Nemocera, the proboscis is..directed perpendicularly or curved on the pectus.

†**pecu'arious,** *a. Obs. rare*⁻⁰. [f. L. *pecuāri-us* of or belonging to *pecu* cattle + -OUS.]

1656 BLOUNT *Glossogr.*, *Pecuarious*, serving for, or belonging to Beasts or Cattle. **1658** in PHILLIPS.

pecudiculture ('pɛkjuːdɪˌkʌltjʊə(r), -tʃə(r)). *rare.* [f. L. *pecud-em* a beast, in pl. cattle + CULTURE: after *horticulture*, etc.] The rearing of cattle.

1885 *Century Mag.* XXIX. 363 Agriculture and Horticulture. Pecudiculture.

pecul, variant of PICUL; obs. form of PECKLE.

peculant ('pɛkjʊlənt), *a. rare.* [ad. L. *peculant-em*, pres. pple. of *pecūlārī* to embezzle.] = PECULATIVE *a.*

1920 *Glasgow Herald* 16 Aug. 8/3 Conveying large sums of money into their own pockets without having to resort to the clumsy methods practised by peculant contractors..in the Napoleonic wars.

†**'peculate,** *sb. Obs.* Also 7 -at. [ad. L. *pecūlāt-us* embezzlement, f. *pecūlārī*: see next. In F. *peculat* (1568 in Hatz.-Darm.), It. *peculato*, Sp. *peculado*.] = PECULATION.

a **1649** DRUMM. OF HAWTH. *Hist. Jas. II*, Wks. (1711) 24 Articles being forged and urged against them, especially of peculate, as sale of crown-lands, waste of the king's treasure, ..transporting lands to themselves and their friends. **1656** J. HARRINGTON *Oceana* Wks. (1700) 159 Such as were arrain'd or try'd for Peculat, or Defraudation of the Commonwealth. **1686** BURNET *Trav.* iii. (1750) 153 One of the Nobles was accused of Peculat. **1753** CHAMBERS *Cycl. Supp.*, *Peculator*, one who is guilty of the crime called *peculate*.

peculate ('pɛkjʊleɪt), *v.* [f. L. *pecūlāt-*, ppl. stem of *pecūlārī* to embezzle, f. *pecūlium* private property, orig. in cattle, f. *pecu* cattle, money.]

†**1.** *trans.* To rob (the state or country) by peculation. *Obs.*

1749 W. DOUGLASS *Brit. Settlem. N. Amer.* II. 17 In Massachusetts..they peculated the Country by ruinous unnecessary Expence of Money.

2. To embezzle or pilfer (money).

1802 H. MARTIN *Helen of Glenross* III. 223 Two thousand pounds..what she justly charges me with having peculated from her Father. **1827** SOUTHEY *Hist. Penins. War* II. 619 The people..accused them of having peculated the public money. **1884** *Manchester Exam.* 1 Oct. 4/5 Several millions of taels, which they have..peculated from the Imperial funds.

3. *intr.* To practise peculation.

1861 LOWELL *E Pluribus Unum* Pr. Wks. 1890 V. 45 They ..have peculated in advance by a kind of official post-obit. **1876** ROGERS *Pol. Econ.* xi. 135 The honesty of a servant or manager, who does not embezzle or peculate.

Hence **'peculating** *vbl. sb.* and *ppl. a.*

1783 BURKE *Sp. Fox's E. Ind. Bill* Wks. IV. 93 An oppressive..rapacious, and peculating despotism, with a direct disavowal of obedience to any authority at home..is ..the state of your charter-government over great kingdoms. **1895** *Athenæum* 7 Sept. 328/1 [The endowments have] long since vanished, no doubt, into the pockets of peculating pashas.

peculation (pɛkjʊ'leɪʃən). [n. of action f. L. *pecūlārī* to PECULATE (put for L. *pecūlātus* PECULATE *sb.*): see -ATION.] The appropriation of public money or property by one in an official position; the embezzlement of money or goods entrusted to his care.

1658 PHILLIPS, *Peculation*, a robbing of the Prince or Common-wealth. **1784** COWPER *Task* II. 667 The family of plagues That waste our vitals;—peculation, sale Of honour, perjury, corruption, frauds. **1821** tr. *Rollin's Anc. Hist.* (ed. 15) III. VII. 181 To be tried for peculation. **1874** GREEN *Short Hist.* ix. §9. 700 Marlborough was dismissed from his command, charged with peculation, and condemned.

peculative ('pɛkjʊlətɪv), *a.* [f. PECULATE *v.* + -IVE.] That practises embezzlement or peculation.

1909 GALSWORTHY *Fraternity* xii. 102 Unlike other clubs, it..had special arrangements for the safety of umbrellas and such books as had not yet vanished from the library; not, of course, owing to any peculative tendency among its members, but because, after interchanging their ideas, those members would depart,..each grasping some material object in his hand. **1921** *Times Lit. Suppl.* 10 Feb. 84/3 The taxes so rapaciously collected by a host of peculative Turkish officials.

peculator ('pɛkjʊleɪtə(r)). [a. L. *pecūlātor* an embezzler, agent-n. f. *pecūlārī* to PECULATE.] One who peculates; an embezzler, esp. of public money or property.

1656 BLOUNT *Glossogr.*, *Peculator*, that robbeth the Prince or common treasure. **1783** BURKE *Sp. Fox's E. Ind. Bill* Wks. IV. 77 The supposed peculators and destroyers of Oude repose in all security in the bosoms of their accusers. **1855** MOTLEY *Dutch Rep.* II. v. (1866) 217 An infamous peculator ..rolling up a fortune with great rapidity by his shameless traffic in benefices, charges, offices.

peculiar (pɪ'kjuːlɪə(r)), *a.* and *sb.* Also 5 -ier, 6 -er, -yer, -eer, -yar, 6–7 -iare. [a. obs. F. *peculier* (16th c. in Godef.), or ad. L. *pecūliār-is* of or relating to private property, f. *pecūli-um* property in cattle, private property, that which is one's own, f. *pecu* cattle. Cf. also OF. *peculiaire* (15th c.) in same sense.]

A. *adj.*

1. That is one's own private property; that belongs or pertains to, or characterizes, an individual person, place, or thing, or group of persons or things, as distinct from others. Const. with preceding possessive (*my own, the king's own*), or with *to*.

peculiar to now always denotes 'belonging exclusively to'; formerly it might denote 'belonging specially to'.

†**a.** Of property, material possession, etc. *Obs.*

c **1460** FORTESCUE *Abs. & Lim. Mon.* ix. (1885) 130 How necessarie it is þat the kynge haue grete possescions, and peculier livelod ffor his owne suirte. *a* **1548** HALL *Chron.*, *Hen. VI* 151 The Duke of Gloucester had not so muche aduaunced..the common wealth and publique vtilite, as his awne priuate thinges & peculier estate. **1652** NEEDHAM tr. *Selden's Mare Cl.* 6 The Sun, Aer, Water, Nature did not frame Peculiar; A Public gift I claim. *a* **1668** DAVENANT *Man's the Master* IV. i, Now even all peculiar fields are turn'd to common roads about this populous town. **1724** DE FOE *Tour Gt. Brit.* I. 123 Sturbridge Fair... This square.. is separate and peculiar to the wholesale dealers in the woollen manufacture.

b. In general sense, esp. of qualities, features, characteristics, etc.

†*peculiar institution*, a cant phrase in U.S. for negro slavery, formerly often spoken of in the Southern states as 'the peculiar domestic institution of the South'. *Obs.*

1509 FISHER *Fun. Serm. C'tess Richmond* Wks. (1876) 294 The dayes that by the chirche were appoynted she kept them diligently and sereously, & in especyall the holy lent.. besyde her other peculer fastes of deuocion, as saint Anthony, mary Maudeleyn. **1551** ROBINSON tr. *More's Utop.* I. (1895) 51 There is an other [cause] which as I suppose is proper and peculiare to yow Englishe men alone. **1555** *Fardle of Facions* II. v. 148 It was a peculier maner of the Kynges of the Medes, to haue many wiues. **1708** POPE *Jan. & May* 52 All other goods by fortune's hand are giv'n, A Wife is the peculiar gift of heav'n. **1721** BAILEY, *Birch*, a Tree peculiar to Great Britain. **1766** FORDYCE *Serm. Yng. Wom.* (1767) II. xiii. 222 A timidity peculiar to your sex. **1826** DISRAELI *Viv. Grey* VI. ii, Imitating the peculiar sound of every animal that he met. *c* **1852** *S. Carolina Gaz.* (Farmer *Dict. Amer.*), The dangers which at present threaten the peculiar domestic institutions of the South.

c. *Astr.* Applied to the motion or velocity of a celestial object relative to a group of objects of the same kind; *spec.* that of a star in the frame of reference in which the average velocity of the stars in the neighbourhood of the sun is zero.

[**1890** A. M. CLERKE *Syst. Stars* xxii. 340 The motus peculiaris itself is only a projection upon the sphere of a line of travel which may make any angle with the line of sight.] **1927** H. N. RUSSELL et al. *Astron.* II. xix. 668 The peculair motions of the fainter stars are more rapid than those of the brighter. **1936** E. HUBBLE *Realm of Nebulæ* v. 106 It was expected that, when the solar motion was removed, the residual, peculiar motions of the nebulæ would be much smaller than the observed velocities and..that they would be distributed at random. **1967** R. KURTH *Introd. Stellar Statistics* ii. 14 The parallactic and peculiar motions of the stars close to the Sun..can be estimated if the hypothesis.. is adopted that the average of the peculiar motions vanishes. **1975** G. O. ABELL *Exploration of Universe* (ed. 3) xx. 396/1 The space velocity of a star, its motion with respect to the sun, is made up of both the star's peculiar velocity and a component due to solar motion. **1978** PASACHOFF & KUTNER *University Astron.* iii. 62 Most peculiar velocities are a few tens of km/sec; very few are above 100 km/sec. *Ibid.* 64 If we observe a large number of stars, their peculiar motions, since they are random, will average to about zero.

†**2.** Of separate or distinct constitution or existence; independent, particular, individual; single.

1507 FISHER *Fun. Serm. Hen. VII*, Wks. (1876) 272 He sente money to be dystrybuted for .x. M. masses peculeer to be sayd for hym. **1551** RECORDE *Pathw. Knowl.* II. Introd., Minding to reserue the proofes to a peculiar boke which I will..set forth. **1602** SHAKS. *Ham.* III. iii. 11 The single and peculiar life is bound..To keepe it selfe from noyance. *a* **1711** KEN *Hymns Evang.* Poet. Wks. 1721 I. 155 Ev'ry Thorn gave a peculiar Wound. **1799** W. TOOKE *View Russian Emp.* II. 50 The Khanate of Kazan subsisted as a peculiar state till the year 1552.

3. Distinguished in nature, character, or attributes from others; particular, special.

1590 SIR J. SMYTH *Disc. Weapons* 2 Detracting..the excellent effects of our peculiar and singular weapon the Long Bowe. **1628** FELTHAM *Resolves* II. xxxi, We seldome find any, without a peculiar delight in some peculiar thing. **1642** ROGERS *Naaman* To Rdr., Sermons are more peculiar for the suppressing of vicious manners. **1776** ADAM SMITH *W.N.* v. ii. (1869) II. 437 A more proper subject of peculiar taxation. **1849** GROTE *Greece* II. xlvii. VI. 66 The position of the Corinthians was peculiar. **1860** TYNDALL *Glac.* I. iv. 35 This latter point..is one of peculiar interest.

4. a. Having a character exclusively its own, *sui generis*; unlike others, singular, uncommon, unusual, out-of-the-way; strange, odd, 'queer'.

1608 TOPSELL *Serpents* (1658) 598 The tongue of a serpent is peculiar; for..it is also cloven at the tip. **1726** BUTLER *Serm. Forgiveness* Wks. 1874 II. 113 We are in such a peculiar position, with respect to injuries done to ourselves, that we can scarcely..see them as they really are. **1811** A. T. THOMSON *Lond. Disp.* III. (1818) 445 The odour is peculiar and aromatic; the taste gratefully acid. **1837** DICKENS *Pickw.* xx, Mr. Weller's knowledge of London was extensive and peculiar. **1888** MISS BRADDON *Fatal Three* I. i, She is a girl of peculiar temper. *Mod. colloq.* He was always thought a little peculiar.

b. *Astr.* Of a galaxy: not belonging to any of the types, elliptical, spiral, and irregular, which include almost all galaxies.

1936 E. HUBBLE *Realm of Nebulæ* ii. 47 The remaining irregulars might be arbitrarily placed in the regular sequence as highly peculiar objects. **1959** *Listener* 31 Dec. 1152/1 There are a few galaxies that do not fit conveniently into this classification of spirals, ellipticals, and irregulars. These are the 'peculiar' galaxies. **1972** JASTROW & THOMPSON *Astron.* 213 In all the cases that have been examined thus far, the unusual event that altered the appearance of the peculiar galaxy seems to have been either a *collision* with another galaxy, or a gigantic *explosion* within the galaxy. **1973** *Sci. Amer.* Dec. 39/1 One or 2 percent, however, do not conform. Because of their bizarre appearance or unusual spectra they are known to astronomers as 'peculiar' galaxies.

5. *peculiar jurisdiction* (*authority*, etc.), in *Canon Law*, a jurisdiction proper to itself, exempt from or not subject to the jurisdiction of the bishop of the diocese. Cf. B. 5.

c **1525** ABP. WARHAM *Let. to Wolsey* in Ellis *Orig. Lett.* Ser. III. cxxxv, The value of the benefices within the diocese of Canterburie and the iurisdiction peculiar of the same. **1555** J. PHILPOT in Foxe *A. & M.* (1583) 1799, I haue not offended in your Dioces. For that whiche I spake..was in Paules Churche..which..is a peculiar iurisdiction belonging to the Deane of Paules. **1726** AYLIFFE *Parergon* 94 The Archbishop whereof has also a peculiar Jurisdiction in thirteen Parishes within the City of London [etc.]. **1822** D. & S. LYSONS *Brit.*, *Devon*, Colyton... The Dean and Chapter of Exeter are patrons of the Vicarage... The Church is in their peculiar jurisdiction. **1840** *Penny Cycl.* XVII. 103/2 The living of Dorchester [Oxon.] is a perpetual curacy, in the jurisdiction of the peculiar court of Dorchester.

6. ***peculiar people*****: a.** a name applied to the Jews as God's own chosen people; hence *transf.* in religious sense. (Also ***p. race, nation,*** etc.)

1494 FABYAN *Chron.* VII. 550 Of his great mercy he hath visyted vs, I truste, his peculier people. **1535** COVERDALE *Deut.* xiv. 2 The Lord hath chosen the to be his awne peculier people from amonge all the nacions. —— *Titus* ii. 14 To pourge vs to be a peculiar people vnto himselfe. **1651** HOBBES *Leviath.* II. xxxi. 187 Having chosen out one peculiar Nation for his Subjects. **1738** WESLEY *Ps.* LI. xxi, The dear peculiar Race Their grateful Sacrifice shall bring.

b. A religious sect (called also the ***Plumstead Peculiars***) founded in 1838, and most numerous about London.

They have no preachers, creeds, ordinances, or church organization, and they rely wholly on prayer for the cure of disease, rejecting medical aid; this last is the feature which brings them specially under public notice.

1875 *Punch* 19 June 267/1 Of course the Peculiar People have the right to believe in miracle and also the right to disbelieve in medicine. **1892** *Spectator* 19 Mar. 391 Drugs may be dispensed with altogether, as by the Peculiar People or the Faith Healers. **1901** *Essex Weekly News* 29 Mar. 2/4 'Peculiar' parents censured at Barking.

†7. ***in peculiar***, as a peculiarity; in particular.

1607 TOPSELL *Four-f. Beasts* 315 Egipt had this in peculiar, that no other order, no not a senator, might be president or govern among them. **1690** LOCKE *Govt.* I. xi. §162 One may as well say,.. this Dominion was to belong in peculiar to one of his Issue. **1704** NORRIS *Ideal World* II. xii. 435 As for Truth he must be a great stranger to her and to himself too, that shall look upon it as a possession in peculiar.

B. *sb.* (absolute uses of the adj.)

I. In general senses.

1. a. A peculiar property or possession; a property or privilege exclusively one's own.

1650 T. B. *Worcester's Apophth.* 105 Leave was obtained ..that he might be buried in Windsor Castle (where there is a peculiar for the family). **1737** WHISTON *Josephus, Hist.* v. xi. §2 They would preserve..that temple which was their peculiar. **1846** GROTE *Greece* II. vi. II. 543 How far the peculiar of the primitive Sparta extended we have no means of determining. **1865** —— *Plato* I. xiv. 451 A peculiar appertaining to philosophers, distinct from though analogous to the peculiar of each several art.

†b. = *peculiar people* (A. 6 a): said of the Jews, and of Christian believers. *Obs.*

1609 BIBLE (Douay) *Mal.* iii. 17 And they shal be to me.. to my peculiar, and I wil spare them, as a man spareth his sonne. *a* **1617** BAYNE *On Eph.* (1658) 116 Beleevers are a peculiar to God, are set apart. *a* **1638** MEDE *Wks.* (1672) 181 We who are God's peculiars, must demean our selves peculiarly both toward God and man. **1659** HAMMOND *On Ps.* cvi. 40 He would own them for ever as his peculiar.

†c. One's own wife or mistress. *Obs.*

1615 G. SANDYS *Trav.* 66 Yet are they [Turks] to meddle with none but their owne peculiars: the offending woman they drowne, and the man they gansh. *a* **1700** B. E. *Dict. Cant. Crew, Peculiar*, a Mistress.

†2. ***one's peculiar***, one's private interest or special concern. *Obs.*

1625 in *Cosin's Corr.* (Surtees) I. 60 In respect of my peculiar I am better. **1637** R. ASHLEY tr. *Malvezzi's David Persecuted* 54 Hee is governed by that which appertaines to the King, and not by his owne peculiar. **1720–1** *Lett. fr. Mist's Jrnl.* (1722) II. 256 The Concern they will learn for the Affairs of the Universe, will naturally lead them to a close attention to their own Peculiar.

†3. A peculiar attribute or quality; a peculiarity; a special or exclusive characteristic. *Obs.*

1589 PUTTENHAM *Eng. Poesie* I. ii. (Arb.) 21 A peculiar, which our speech hath in many things differing from theirs. **1625** BP. MOUNTAGU *App. Cæsar* 231 Omnipresence is the absolute Peculiar of the Almighty. **1657** W. RAND tr. *Gassendi's Life Peiresc* I. 150 Peradventure [those Stigmata, or insensible parts] might..belong to some peculiar of that disease which is termed Elephantiasis. **1701** NORRIS *Ideal World* 206 There is this peculiar in vision that is not in our other senses, that it includes an outward objective perception. *a* **1750** A. HILL *Wks.* (1753) II. 396 Your poetry is a peculiar, that will make it impossible, you should be forgotten.

†4. An individual member of a class or part of a collective whole; a particular, item, or detail.

1610 HEALEY *St. Aug. Citie of God* VII. ii. (1620) 247 Why ..could not he..extend his generall power through each peculiar? **1713** DERHAM *Phys.-Theol.* VI. v. 365, I shall.. speak only of two peculiars more.

II. Specific and technical senses.

5. a. *Eccl.* A parish or church exempt from the jurisdiction of the ordinary or bishop in whose diocese it lies, either as a ***royal peculiar*** (*i.e.* a chapel exempt from any jurisdiction but that of the sovereign) or as subject to the jurisdiction of a bishop of another diocese, or to that of a dean, chapter, prebendary, etc.

court of peculiars, a branch of the court of arches having jurisdiction over the peculiars of the archbishop of Canterbury. (Peculiars were, for most purposes, abolished by Act 10 & 11 Vict. c. 98.)

1562 BP. W. ALLEY in Strype *Ann. Ref.* (1709) I. xxxi. 310 That Bishops may have jurisdiction to call all criminal causes before them, and to reform other disorders in all Peculiars, and places exempt, which be *speluncæ latronum*. **1631** WEEVER *Anc. Fun. Mon.* 309 Shorham is but a Peculiar to the Archbishop, who holds his prerogatiue wheresoeuer his lands do lie. **1658** PHILLIPS, *The Court of Peculiars.* **1704** J. HARRIS *Lex. Techn.* I, *Peculiar*, signifies a particular Parish or Church that hath Jurisdiction within its self, for Probat of Wills, &c. exempt from the Ordinary, and the Bishops Courts. **1768** BLACKSTONE *Comm.* III. v. 65 The court of peculiars is a branch of and annexed to the court of arches. It has a jurisdiction over all those parishes dispersed through the province of Canterbury in the midst of other dioceses, which are exempt from the ordinary's jurisdiction, and subject to the metropolitan only. **1865** *Pall Mall G.* 21 Aug. 9/1 Burian, the royal deanery, has been a peculiar since the days of Athelstan, and kept its privileges when other peculiars were abolished. **1899** *Westm. Gaz.* 29 Mar. 10/2 The Dean of the Arches took his title from the old Court of Peculiars of the Archbishop of Canterbury, who formerly exercised jurisdiction over thirteen exempt parishes in the diocese of London and fifty-seven parishes called 'peculiars' in other dioceses... These 'peculiars' were abolished about fifty years ago, and the Court of which the Dean of the Arches was Dean went with them.

b. *transf.* and *fig.* A place, district, office, etc., exempt from ordinary jurisdiction.

1591 G. FLETCHER *Russe Commw.* (Hakl. Soc.) 37 Out of the province..of Vagha, there is given him for a peculiar exempted out of the Chetfird of Posolskoy, 32,000 rubbels. **1605** CAMDEN *Rem.* 4 That Scotland was by them accounted an exempt kingdome, and a Peculiar properly appertaining to the Roman Chappell. **1651** N. BACON *Disc. Govt. Eng.* II. iv. (1739) 21 It [the Chancery] soon becomes a kind of Peculiar, exempting it self from the ordinary course in manner of Trial, and from the ordinary rules of Law.

†6. In the former colonies and provinces of New England: A district, or piece of land, not included in any 'town', nor as yet incorporated as a 'town'.

1720 *Connect. Col. Rec.* (1872–4) VI. 210 Resolved..That Mr. John Read, who dwells between Fairfield and Danbury, be likewise annually listed, as a peculiar to Danbury. **1737** *Ibid.* VIII. 133 All peculiars, or lands not as yet laid within the bounds of any town,..shall be assessed by the rates of the next town unto it. **1739** *Ibid.* 230 Being informed that a certain piece of land in the county of Windham..is not in any town but still remains a peculiar,..Be it enacted..That the said tract of land be annexed to the town of Voluntown. **1779** *Vermont State Papers* (1823) 297. **1809** KENDALL *Trav.* I. ii. 17 Precincts or peculiars are in some cases ordered to be rated at or in certain towns, and in such cases are rated and governed by the town.

7. a. A nickname in Oxford (*c* 1837–8) for members of the 'Evangelical' party. (Cf. A. 6 a.)

1837 J. H. NEWMAN *Let.* in Purcell *Manning* (1895) I. 224 The amusing thing is that the unfortunate Peculiars are attacked on so many sides. **1838** BP. WILBERFORCE *Diary* in Ashwell *Life* (1879) I. 119 [He] had all the faults of the low tone of the Peculiars strongly marked. **1895** PURCELL *Manning* I. 114 'Puseyites and Peculiars' stood shoulder to shoulder.

b. One of the Peculiar People: see A. 6 b.

1876 C. M. DAVIES *Unorth. Lond.* 175 (heading) The Plumstead 'Peculiars'. *Ibid.* 176 The risk..of having a.. contagious disease spread..by the manipulations of these 'Peculiars'. **1893** in *Daily News* 8 Apr. 7/4 All you who mean to follow in the same old way and be Peculiars follow me.

†peˈculiarism. *Obs.* [f. prec. + -ISM.] The doctrine or practices of 'Peculiars' (B. 7 a).

1836 NEWMAN *Let.* in Liddon, etc. *Life Pusey* (1893) I. xvi. 368 London is overrun with peculiarism. **1838** BP. WILBERFORCE in Ashwell *Life* (1879) I. iv. 119 A good man, but a poor creature, evidently set up by Peculiarism.

peculiarity (pɪkjuːlɪˈærɪtɪ). [f. PECULIAR + -ITY; cf. late L. *pecūliāritās* (St. Gregory).] The quality or condition of being peculiar.

†1. The condition or fact of belonging exclusively to oneself; exclusive possession; private ownership.

1610 BP. HALL *Epist.* v. ii. 24 What neede we to disclaime all peculiarity in goods?

†b. *spec.* The condition of being God's peculiar people. *Obs.*

1661 BAXTER *Mor. Prognost.* II. xlviii. 62 Some of them [Jews] Re-established in their own Land: But not to their antient peculiarity, or policy and Law. **1777** FLETCHER *Bible Calvinism* Wks. 1795 IV. 255 If God had made his covenants of peculiarity with all mankind, would they not have ceased to be peculiar?

2. The quality of being peculiar to or characteristic of a single person or thing; also, an instance of this, that which is peculiar to a single person or thing; a distinguishing or special characteristic.

1646 SIR T. BROWNE *Pseud. Ep.* II. v. 90 That a piece of opium will dead the force and blow [of a bullet]..I finde herein no such peculiarity, no more then in any gummy or viscose body. **1726** LEONI *Alberti's Archit.* I. 78/2 We shall speak first of those things wherein they agree; and of their peculiarities afterwards. **1850** MᶜCOSH *Div. Govt.* II. i. (1874) 114 The peculiarity of a miracle is, that it has not a cause in the natural powers operating in the Cosmos. **1853** J. H. NEWMAN *Hist. Sk.* (1873) II. I. ii. 61 It is a peculiarity of Asia that its regions are either very hot or very cold.

†3. A particular liking or regard; a partiality.

1687 BOYLE *Martyrd. Theodora* xi. (1703) 152 He could discern in her Breast such a resentment of his Services, as.. imply'd a peculiarity for his Person. **1847** EMERSON *Repr. Men, Shaks.* Wks. (Bohn) I. 362 Shakespeare has no peculiarity, no importunate topic; but all is duly given.

†b. Special attentiveness to a person; cf. PARTICULARITY 7. *Obs.*

1748 RICHARDSON *Clarissa* iii, I had not value enough for him to treat him with peculiarity either by smiles or frowns.

4. The quality of being *sui generis* or unlike others; singularity, uncommonness, oddity; also, an instance of this, an odd trait or characteristic.

1751 LD. ORRERY *Remarks Swift* (1752) 17 She died towards the end of January..absolutely destroyed by the peculiarity of her fate. **1777** BOSWELL *Johnson* 17 Sept., I said, in writing a life, a man's peculiarities should be mentioned, because they mark his character. **1817** MISS MITFORD in L'Estrange *Life* (1870) II. i. 18 There is another very singular peculiarity about Mr. Talfourd; he can't spell. **1865** R. W. DALE *Jew. Temp.* xvi. (1877) 179 You will have noticed the peculiarity of the expression.

†5. = PECULIARISM: cf. PECULIAR B. 7 a. *rare.*

1838 BP. WILBERFORCE in A. R. Ashwell *Life* (1879) I. iv. 114 They will disgust some well-intentioned Churchmen by a fanciful imitation of antiquity, and drive them into lower depths of 'Peculiarity'.

peculiarize (pɪˈkjuːlɪəraɪz), *v.* [f. PECULIAR *a.* + -IZE.] *trans.* To make peculiar.

†1. To appropriate exclusively *to*. *Obs.*

1624 HEYWOOD *Gunaik.* III. 140 He onely peculiarised to himselfe a fift part of the people, and the rest were imployed in agriculture and tillage. **1653** SCLATER *Fun. Serm.* 25 Sept. (1654) 15 *Χάρισμα*,.. a word not used in any Heathen Author, but peculiarized to the inspired penmen of Holy Writ. **1704** NELSON *Fasts & Fest.* xi. 112 There was to be no more Distinction betwixt the Children of Abraham and other People, and no one Land more peculiarized than another.

2. To give or impart peculiarity to.

1640 HOWELL *Dodona's Gr.* 75 Touching that Title, which doth peculiarize Druina's Monarch from all other. **1796** COLERIDGE *Lett., to J. Thelwall* (1895) 197 This, I think, peculiarises my style of writing. **1821** *Blackw. Mag.* IX. 515 Those distinguishing marks which peculiarize the Latin original. **1852** STONE *Ballou's Spir. Manifest.* i. 15.

peculiarly (pɪˈkjuːlɪəlɪ), *adv.* [f. PECULIAR *a.* + -LY².] In a peculiar manner.

1. In a way that is one's own, and not another person's; as regards oneself; individually.

1573–80 BARET *Alv.* P 220–1 Things that were his owne peculiarly. **1685** BOYLE *Effects of Mot.* vii. 89 Any Vault that were exquisitely built, would peculiarly answer to some determinate Note or other. **1726** *Nat. Hist. Irel.* 86 A certain sort of sea-coal..wonderful small, and peculiarly called comb. **1815** *Chron.* in *Ann. Reg.* 12/1 He would bring him to account for his conduct to himself peculiarly. **1871** MORLEY *Voltaire* (1886) 6 Many of his ideas were in the air, and did not belong to him peculiarly.

2. In a way distinct from others; particularly, especially; also *colloq.*, more than usually.

1561 T. NORTON *Calvin's Inst.* I. vi. §1 Wherby the faithfull haue alway been peculiarly seuered from the prophane nations. **1571** GOLDING *Calvin on Ps.* xxx. 13 The very course of the woords requireth, that hee should make mention here peculiarly of his own dewtie. **1650** FULLER *Pisgah* 391 Table of shew-bread..made of that gold, which his Father David had peculiarly prepared for that purpose. **1749** FIELDING *Tom Jones* v. vii, To render the lot of one man more peculiarly unhappy than that of others. **1820** W. IRVING *Sketch Bk.* I. 51 A little air of which her husband was peculiarly fond. **1891** HELEN B. HARRIS *Apol. Aristides* i. 5 The Arabs regard the spot as peculiarly sacred.

3. In a way unlike others; unusually, strangely, oddly, queerly.

1847 C. BRONTË *J. Eyre* xix. If you knew it, you are peculiarly situated: very near happiness; yes; within reach of it. **1901** *Daily Chron.* 16 July 5/1 [He] is one of those peculiarly-constituted Englishmen who rather enjoy the West Coast climate than otherwise.

peculiarness (pɪˈkjuːlɪənɪs). Now *rare.* [f. PECULIAR *a.* + -NESS.] The quality of being peculiar; peculiarity.

1561 DAUS tr. *Bullinger on Apoc.* (1573) 110b, Their peculiarnesse or diuersitie is, that Sathan hath sowen sundry heresies in the Church [etc.]. *a* **1638** MEDE *Wks.* (1672) 5 Things sacred..which have upon them a relation of peculiarness towards God. *a* **1658** J. DURHAM *Exp. Rev.* i. (1680) 25 Done to shew a peculiarness in that day and the meetings on it.

†peˈculiate, *v. Obs. rare*⁻⁰. [f. L. *pecūliāre* to provide with a peculium.] So **†peculiation**.

1656 BLOUNT *Glossogr.*, *Peculiate*..to punish by the purse, to take away a mans goods; also to enrich. **1658** PHILLIPS, *Peculiation*, a taking away a mans goods.

‖peculium (pɪˈkjuːlɪəm). [L. *pecūlium* private property; deriv. of *pecu* cattle.]

1. *Rom. Law.* The property which a father allowed his child, or a master allowed his slave, to hold as his own.

1706 in PHILLIPS. **1767** SIR J. D. STEUART *Pol. Econ.* I. II. vi. 193 Why was a *peculium* given to slaves, but to engage them to become dextrous? **1854** MILMAN *Lat. Chr.* III. v. (1864) II. 26 The peculium over which full power was vested in the son was extended by Augustus..to all which he might acquire in military service.

2. A private or exclusive possession, property, or appurtenance.

1681 GLANVILL *Sadducismus* II. 167 They know the Soul survives the Body, and therefore make their bargain sure for the possession of it as their Peculium after death. **1720** WATERLAND *Eight Serm.* ii. 51 They [the Jews] were his *peculium*, his chosen People, and..He was in a more eminent manner their God. **1771** BURKE *Lett., to Bp. Chester* (1844) I. 297 This is the peculium of blame, which your lordship has portioned out to me, and separated from the common stock. **1858** J. MARTINEAU *Stud. Chr.* (1873) 348 Believe not..they have snatched it [this planet] as their peculium quite out of the Supreme Hand. **1883** *Spectator* 3 Nov. 1406 The office has thus come to be regarded as a peculium for the youthful sons or personal friends of Judges.

†peˈcunial, *a. Obs.* [ad. L. *pecūniāl-is*, f. *pecūnia* 'money'; in earlier sense 'property', f.

pecu cattle; cognate with OTeut. **fehu*, Goth. *faihu*, OE. *feoh, féo*: see FEE.]

1. Consisting of or exacted in money; = PECUNIARY *a.* 1. **b.** Having to do with pecuniary penalties.

c **1386** CHAUCER *Friar's T.* 16 If any persone wolde vp-on hem pleyne Ther myghte asterte hym no pecunyal peyne. *a* **1548** HALL *Chron., Hen. VII* (1550) 57 Englishmen dyd litle passe vpon the obseruacion and kepynge of penall lawes or pecuniall statutes. **1582–8** *Hist. Jas. VI* (1804) 174 They should offer him a certane pecuniall sum in recompence. **1594** T. BEDINGFIELD tr. *Machiavelli's Florentine Hist.* (1595) 46 Condemned in pecuniall punishment. **1714–26** in *Mem. Gideon Guthrie* (1900) 54 We were all sentenced, they to penal and pecunial mulcts and I to banishment.

2. Of or pertaining to money; = PECUNIARY *a.* 2.

1508 *Kalender Sheph.* (1892) III. App. 180 Cease of your pecunyall pensement. **1530** PALSGR. 320/1 Pecunyall, belongynge to money, *pecunial.*

†**pe'cuniar**, *a.* *Obs. rare*$^{-1}$. [ad. OF. *pecuniaire.*] = PECUNIARY *a.* 1. Hence †**pe'cuniarly** *adv.*, pecuniarily.

1530–1 *Act 22 Hen. VIII*, c. 15 All and singular.. peynes of death, peynes corporall and pecunyar. **1656** EARL MONM. tr. *Boccalini's Advts. fr. Parnass.* II. vi. (1674) 145 They should make poor mens faults pecuniarly punishable.

pecuniarily (pɪ'kjuːnɪərɪlɪ), *adv.* [f. next + -LY².] In a pecuniary manner; in respect of money; †by exaction of money (*obs.*).

a **1614** DONNE *Βιαθανατος* II. iii. §2 (1644) 94 Salique law punishes a witch, which is convict to have eaten a man, pecuniarily, and at no high price. *a* **1734** NORTH *Lives* (1826) III. 196 There was no foundation.. to charge him criminally or pecuniarily, to which he had not answers incontrovertible. **1879** M. PATTISON *Milton* 9 Milton's father's circumstances were not such as to make a fellowship pecuniarily an object to his son. **1885** *Law Times* 28 Mar. 389/2 P. and N... became pecuniarily embarrassed.

pecuniary (pɪ'kjuːnɪərɪ), *a.* (*sb.*) [ad. L. *pecūniāri-us*, f. *pecūnia* money: see -ARY¹. In F. *pécuniaire* (13th c. in Hatz.-Darm.).]

1. Consisting of money; exacted in money.

1502 *Ord. Crysten Men* (W. de W. 1506) IV. xxi. 238 Or doth punycyons pecuniaries pryncypally by his auaryce. **1641** J. JACKSON *True Evang. T.* I. 46 He.. inflicted both corporall smart and pecuniary mulcts upon them. **1726** SWIFT *Gulliver* II. vi. 151 Whether they received any pecuniary reward for pleading. **1766** tr. *Beccaria's Ess. Crimes* xvii. (1793) 68 There was a time when all punishments were pecuniary. **1875** STUBBS *Const. Hist.* II. xiv. 138 The many pecuniary aids that he has been obliged to ask for.

b. Of an offence or law: Having a money penalty, entailing a fine.

1610 DONNE *Pseudo-martyr* 211 Hee cast in a dead sleepe all bloudy lawes, and in a slumber all pecuniarie lawes which might offend, & aggrieue them. **1651** N. BACON *Disc. Govt. Eng.* II. ix. (1739) 54 Having learned how to make capital offences pecuniary.

2. Of, belonging to, or having relation to money.

1623 COCKERAM, *Pecuniarie*, of or belonging to money. **1646** SIR T. BROWNE *Pseud. Ep.* I. iii. 11 Their Impostures .. deluding not onely unto pecuniary defraudations, but the irreparable deceit of death. **1792** *Anecd. W. Pitt* I. xxi. 333 The legacy of £10000.. had amply supplied his pecuniary wants. **1841–4** EMERSON *Ess., Prudence* Wks. (Bohn) I. 98 Imprudent genius, struggling for years with paltry pecuniary difficulties.

3. Having regard to money; of which money is the object. ? *Obs.*

1672 SIR T. BROWNE *Let. Friend* §20 Strong and healthful Generations, which happen but contingently in mere pecuniary Matches. **1775** FALCK *Day's Diving Vessel* 2 His disposition penurious; his views pecuniary.

†**B.** *sb.* Money; in *pl.*, resources in money; money matters. *Obs.*

1604 R. CAWDREY *Table Alph., Pecuniarie*, coyne. **1748** RICHARDSON *Clarissa* (1810) III. ix. 63 Old Antony has already given the mother a hint which will make her jealous of pecuniaries. **1767** J. PARSONS *Rem. Japhet* 36 To pecuniaries, the Earl of Hillsborough hath wisely added the means of instruction.

pecunious (pɪ'kjuːnɪəs), *a.* Now *rare*. Also 6 pecwnios. [ad. L. *pecūniōs-us* abounding in money, moneyed, f. *pecūnia* money: see -OUS. Cf. obs. F. *pécunieux* (Oresme 14th c.), perh. the immediate source. The negative *impecunious* is much more used.]

1. Well provided with money; moneyed, wealthy.

1393 LANGL. *P. Pl.* C. XIII. 11 Freres wollen þe louye, And .. praye for þe, pol by pol, yf þow be pecunyous. **1535** W. STEWART *Cron. Scot.* (Rolls) III. 523 Trowand that tyme tha war pecwnios. **1632** SHERWOOD, Pecunious (or full of money), *pecunieux, qui a beaucoup d' argent.* **1706** PHILLIPS, *Pecunious*, Moneyed, or full of Money. **1886** *Sat. Rev.* 11 Dec. 789/1 She succumbed to the blandishments of a pecunious squireling.

†**2.** Money-loving, avaricious. *Obs. rare*$^{-1}$.

a **1529** SKELTON *Bk. 3 Foles* Wks. 1843 I. 200 Pecunyous fooles, that bee auaryce,.. weddeth these olde wyddred women, whych hath sackes full of nobles.

So **pecuni'osity**, the state or fact of being supplied with money.

1883 G. A. MACDONNELL *Chess Life-Pict.* 166 A Frenchman, whose be-ringed fingers.. betokened a certain amount of pecuniosity.

†'**pecuny**. *Obs.* Also 5 -unie, -uyne. [a. NF. and AF. *pecunie* = Central OF. *pecune*, ad. L. *pecūnia* money.] Money.

1393 LANGL. *P. Pl.* C. IV. 393 Be þe pecunie y-payed þauh parties chide. *c* **1450** *Life St. Cuthbert* (Surtees) 8041 And noght for na pecuyne Mending of þair lyues proloyne. **1484** CAXTON *Fables of Alfonce* ii, The second fable is of the commyssion of pecuny or money.

ped¹. Also 4–6 pedde, 7 pedd. See also PAD *sb.*⁴ [Of unknown origin.] A wicker pannier; a hamper with a lid.

Chiefly in use in the Eastern Counties from Northants to Essex, and in Devon and Somerset.

1390–1 in W. Hudson *Leet Jurisd. Norwich* (1891) 73 Thomas Pennyng assuetus est accipere equos cum peddys, diversorum extraneorum et ducere in domum suam, unde Ballivi amittunt custumam suam; et est communis forstallator piscium. *c* **1440** *Promp. Parv.* 390/1 Pedde, idem quod *panere.* **1473** SIR J. PASTON in *P. Lett.* III. 102 Whyche I praye yow and Berney to gedre joyntly,.. to trusse in a pedde, and sende them me hyddre. **1565** T. JERMY *Let. to W. Paston* 31 Jan. (MS.), To the peadelers packe or the botom of his pedde or hamper. *a* **1661** FULLER *Worthies, Dorset.* i. (1662) 278 Dorsers are Peds or Panniers carried on the backs of Horses, on which Haglers use to ride and carry their Commodities. **1691** SHADWELL *Scourers* IV. i, I.. flung down all the peds with pippins about the Streets. *a* **1825** FORBY *Voc. E. Anglia, Ped*,.. a large wicker basket with a lid. Two are commonly used,.. one on each side of a horse, in which pork, fowls, butter, and eggs, are carried to market, and fish hawked about the country. **1881** *Standard* 29 July 5/8 The fish.. are packed in 'peds' or small boxes.

b. *Comb.*, as ***ped-belly, ped-market.***

a **1825** FORBY *Voc. E. Anglia, Ped-belly*,.. a belly round and protuberant like a ped. **1865** WAY in *Promp. Parv.* 389 *note*, The market in Norwich, where wares brought in from the country are exposed for sale, being known as the ped-market. **1886** ELWORTHY *W. Som. Word-bk.* s.v., There is a large ped-market at Taunton every Saturday.

ped². Abbreviation of PEDESTRIAN. *slang.* (now chiefly *U.S.*).

1863 *Tyneside Songs* 87 White and Rowan, champion peds, bangs a' the lot for racin'. **1881** *Sportsman* 31 Jan. 4/6. **1897** *National Police Gaz.* (U.S.) 26 May 10/4 The consensus of opinion is that the Irish-Scots ped. came to the mark in the pink of condition. **1962** *N.Y. Times* 26 Jan. 1/3 'Peds' is short for pedestrians in traffic engineers' jargon. **1973** D. BARNES *See the Woman* I. 134 A ped about three-quarters of a block away.

ped³ (pɛd). *Soil Science.* [f. Gr. πέδ-ον ground, earth.] (See quot. 1958.)

1951 *Soil Survey Manual* (U.S. Dept. Agric. Handbk. No. 18) 225 An individual natural soil aggregate is called a ped, in contrast to (1) a clod, caused by disturbance.., (2) a fragment caused by rupture.., or (3) a concretion caused by local concentrations of compounds that irreversibly cement the soil grains together. **1958** *U.S. Dept. Agric. Yearbk. 1957* 764/1 *Ped*, an individual natural soil aggregate such as a crumb, prism, or block, in contrast to a clod, which is a mass of soil brought about by digging or other disturbance. **1971** R. L. DONAHUE et al. *Soils* (ed. 3) ii. 41 There are four principal types of soil structure: 1. Platy. Peds exhibit a matted, flattened, or compressed appearance... 4. Spheroidal. Peds are imperfect spheres like marbles, but are usually smaller. **1972** J. G. CRUICKSHANK *Soil Geogr.* iii. 79 Clayey soils also tend to develop large columnar peds which on shrinking produce non-capillary pores.

ped-, form of PEDO- used before a vowel (as in PEDALFER).

pedage ('pɛdɪdʒ). *Obs.* exc. *Hist.* [ad. med. L. *pedāgium* (11th c. in Du Cange), for earlier L. *pedāticum*; see PEAGE.] Toll paid for passing through a place or country: = PEAGE.

1382 WYCLIF *Ezra* iv. 13 Tribute, and pedage [1388 tol, *Vulg.* vectigal], and ȝeris rentus thei shul not ȝiue. *c* **1425** *MS. Cott. Claud. A.* 2 lf. 124 b, Alle þat vnrythefully settyth tallages vppon men of holy chirche, as pedage [*pr.* podage], gwage, or any oþur vnskylful thraldom. **1607** COWELL *Interpr., Pedage* (*pedagium*) signifieth money giuen for the passing by foote or horse through any countrey. **18..** tr. *Charter to New Salisbury* an. 1228 in *Q. Rev.* (1826) XXXIV. 327 Its citizens should be quit, throughout the land, of toll, pontage, passage, pedage [*orig.* paagio], lastage, .. carriage, and all other customs. *a* **1843** SOUTHEY *Comm.-pl. Bk.* III. 396 The abbot was to wall the town, and receive pedage.

pedagogal (pɛdə'gəʊgəl), *a.* *rare.* [f. L. *pædagōg-us* PEDAGOGUE + -AL¹.] Of or belonging to a pedagogue.

1775 S. J. PRATT *Liberal Opin.* xlviii. (1783) II. 19 The threatening tone, the brow austere, Bespoke.. pedagogal tyranny. **1823** *New Monthly Mag.* VII. 386 He.. smirked his way to a pedagogal desk.

pedagogic (pɛdə'gɒdʒɪk), *a.* and *sb.* Also pæd-. [mod. f. L. *pædagōgic-us*, a. Gr. παιδαγωγικ-ός, f. παιδαγωγ-ός pedagogue: see -IC. So F. *pédagogique* (1702 in Hatz.-Darm.).]

A. *adj.* Of, pertaining to, or characteristic of a pedagogue or pedagogy; having the office or character of a pedagogue.

1781 WARTON *Hist. Eng. Poetry* l. III. 259 In the pedagogic character he [Higgins] also published Holcot's [Huloet's] *Dictionarie*, newly corrected.. &c. **1833** SIR W. HAMILTON *Discuss.* (1852) 558 Paedagogic and didactic theory. **1856** MASSON *Ess.* 393 The pedagogic era of the worthy and long dead Mr. Luke Fraser. **1881** *Nature* XXIII. 615/1 A Pedagogic Congress. **1885** J. PAYN *Talk of Town* I. 41 The pedagogic tone in which he had spoken.

B. *sb.* (usually *pl.* pedagogics.) The science, art, or principles of pedagogy.

1864 WEBSTER, *Pedagogic*,..(Ger. *pedagogik.*) The science or art of successful teaching;.. *Pedagogics*,.. The same as *Pedagogic.* **1888** *Jrnl. Educ.* 1 Aug. 369 Pedagogics can no more than theology be put on the shelf.

pedagogical (pɛdə'gɒdʒɪkəl), *a.* [f. as prec. + -AL¹.] = PEDAGOGIC.

1619 HALES *Lett. Synod Dort* 1 Jan. in *Gold. Rem.* (1688) 443 The putting of Interrogatories, which thing they much disdained as Pedagogical. **1797** *Monthly Mag.* XLVIII. 314 Voltaire.. was in a thousand degrees superior to the pedagogical fanatic. **1834** H. MILLER *Scenes & Leg.* xxviii. (1857) 410 He relinquished his pedagogical charge for a chapel in Kilmarnock.

Hence **peda'gogically** *adv.*, in the manner of a pedagogue; in relation to pedagogy.

1877 *Echo* 31 July 2/4 'The results have been most favourable', says one, 'spiritually, morally, and pedagogically'. **1884** *Athenæum* 26 Jan. 117/1.

pedagogism: see PEDAGOGUISM.

pedagogist ('pɛdəgɒdʒɪst). [f. PEDAGOGY + -IST.] One versed in pedagogics.

1894 *Educ. News* (U.S.) 14 Apr. 230 To profess one's self a Herbartian is not to reject any of the truths discovered by previous pedagogists. **1895** *Educ. Rev.* Sept. 164 Considering the meager attention that.. pedagogists have given to the principles.

pedagogue ('pɛdəgɒg), *sb.* Forms: 4–6 pedagoge, 6–8 pedagog, 6–8 (9 in sense 1) pædagogue, 7 pædagog, 6– pedagogue. [a. OF. *pedagoge* (Oresme 14th c.), also *pedagogue* (14th c. in Littré), ad. L. *pædagōgus*, a Gr. παιδαγωγός a trainer and teacher of boys, f. παῖς, παιδο- boy + ἀγωγός leader.]

1. A man having the oversight of a child or youth; an attendant who led a boy to school. *Obs.* exc. in reference to ancient times.

1483 CAXTON *Gold. Leg.* 191/1 He durst not for his pedagoge or his governour whyche was wyth hym. **1542** UDALL *Erasm. Apoph.* 183 Alexander.. had many paedagogues, nourturers and schoole maisters. **1637–50** ROW *Hist. Kirk* (Wodrow Soc.) 206 The careles education of the children of noble men,.. the sending them out of the countrey, under the charge of pædagogues suspect in religion. **1770** LANGHORNE *Plutarch* (1879) I. 203/1 The office of a pedagogue of old was.. to attend the children. *a* **1855** J. J. BLUNT *Right Use Early Fathers* Ser. I. ii. (1869) 29 The *Paedagogue* of Clemens Alexandrinus contains a number of precepts which the *Paedagogue* (who gives a name to the treatise) is supposed to impart to his pupil as he takes him to school.

†**b.** *fig.* (chiefly in reference to St. Paul's use of παιδαγωγός in *Gal.* iii. 24.)

1538 STARKEY *England* II. iii. 206 The law.. as Sayn Poule sayth dymely,.. ys the pedagoge of Chryst. **1582** N. T. (Rhem.) *Gal.* iii. 24 The Law was our Pedagogue in Christ. [WYCLIF vndirmaister, TINDALE scolemaster, 1611 Schoolemaster.] **1609** BIBLE (Douay) *1 Kings* Comm., S. Paul teaching that the whole law was a pedagogue guiding men to Christ. *a* **1633** AUSTIN *Medit.* (1635) 268 The Law.. is but the Pedagogue to the Gospel. **1653** BINNING *Serm.* (1845) 22.

2. A man whose occupation is the instruction of children or youths; a schoolmaster, teacher, preceptor. Now usually in a more or less contemptuous or hostile sense, with implication of pedantry, dogmatism, or severity.

1387 TREVISA *Higden* (Rolls) VI. 7 Sigebertus.. ordeyned scoles of lettrure.., and assignede pedagoges and maistres for children. **1494** FABYAN *Chron.* V. cxxxiii. 117 [He] ordeyned ouer them scole masters and pedagoges. **1596** NASHE *Saffron-Walden* Epistle Dedicat. **1613** SIR E. HOBY *Counter-snarle* 39 As if I were now to learne of such an Hipodidascalian Pedagogue to measure my phrase by his rule and line. **1660** PEPYS *Diary* 25 July, A Welsh schoolmaster, a good scholar but a very pedagogue. **1735** SOMERVILLE *Chase* II. 96 Cow'd by the ruling Rod, and haughty Frowns Of Pedagogues severe. **1875** GLADSTONE *Glean.* VI. v. 145 Without.. any assumption of the tone of the critic or the pedagogue.

†**b.** An assistant teacher; an usher. *Obs.*

1563–7 BUCHANAN *Reform. St. Andros* Wks. (1892) 11 The studentis.. salbe.. onder cure of the principal or sum regent or pedagogis lernit and of jugement, quha sal haif cure of thayr studie and diligens. **1613** R. CAWDREY *Table Alph.* (ed. 3), *Pædagogue*, vsher to a Schoole-maister.

†**3.** A schoolroom or school building. *Obs.*$^{-1}$

1745 POCOCKE *Descr. East* II. II. 231 Another part [of the university of Halle] is what they call the pedagogue, which is for noblemen and gentlemen; there are six youths in each room, with a master over them.

Hence '**pedagogue** *v. trans.*, to instruct as a pedagogue; **pedagoguery** ('pɛdəgɒgərɪ), (*a*) a pedagogic establishment; (*b*) the occupation of a pedagogue; **pedagoguing** ('pɛdəgɒgɪŋ) *vbl. sb.*, the acting as, or following the occupation of, a pedagogue (*attrib.* in quot.); **pedagoguish** ('pɛdəgɒgɪʃ) *a.*, characteristic of a pedagogue.

1689 PRIOR *Epist. F. Shepherd* 82 This may confine their younger Stiles, Whom Dryden *pedagogues at Will's. **1724** WELSTED *Wks.* (1787) 130 To pedagogue a man into this sort of knowledge. **1820** SYD. SMITH *Ess.* (ed. Beeton) 209 The children are.. to be taken from their parents, and lodged in immense *pedagogueries. **1872** F. HALL *Recent Exempl. False Philol.* 31 It is not because of any poverty of matter for remark in the headlong sciolism of the one and in the piddling pedagoguery of the other. **1883** T. C. HADDON in W. R. W. Stephens *Life Freeman* (1895) I. 8 In a long life of pedagoguery. **1803** A. WILSON in *Poems & Lit. Prose* (1876) I. 103 The same routine of *pedagoguing matters. **1830** *Blackw. Mag.* XXVII. 482 A climax of *pedagoguish vanity. *a* **1878** MOZLEY *Lect.* i. (1883) 15 Those narrow and pedagoguish tactics of law.

pedagoguette (pɛdəgɒˈgɛt). *nonce-wd.* [f. PEDAGOGUE + -ETTE.] A school-mistress.

1960 V. NABOKOV *Invitation to Beheading* viii. 87 The strident commands of the red-haired 'pedagoguette'.

pedagoguism, pedagogism (ˈpɛdəgɒˌgɪz(ə)m, -gəʊˌdʒɪz(ə)m). [f. PEDAGOGUE (or its Gr. original) + -ISM. Cf. obs. F. *paidagogisme* (16th c. on Littré).] The character, spirit, or office of a pedagogue; the system of pedagogy (quot. 1836).

1642 MILTON *Apol. Smect.* vii. 34 German rutters, of meat, and of ink, which..may prove good to heale this tetter of Pedagoguisme that bespreads him. **1656** BLOUNT *Glossogr.*, *Pedagogism*, the office of a Pedagogue. **1836** *Blackw. Mag.* XL. 594 Pedagogueism should be made so universal..that every mental study..should be included and confined within the schools. **1838** *Ibid.* XLIII. 768 Literature and pedagogism are in Germany identic in spirit.

pedagogy (ˈpɛdəgɒdʒɪ, -gəʊdʒɪ, -gɒgɪ). Also 6–7 peda-, pædagogie, 7– pedagogy. [a. F. *pédagogie* (Calvin 16th c.), ad. Gr. παιδαγωγία office of a παιδαγωγός: see PEDAGOGUE. So mod.Ger. *pädagogie.*]

1. The function, profession, or practice of a pedagogue; the work or occupation of teaching; the art or science of teaching, pedagogics.

1623 COCKERAM I I, Skoole-masters-ship, *pedagogie.* **1659** HEYLIN *Certamen Epist.* 334 Prince Charles..was committed to the Pedagogy of M. Thomas Murrey, a Scot by Nation. **1691** WOOD *Ath. Oxon.* I. 219 He continued, notwithstanding in his beloved Faculty of Pedagogy. **1858** BUSHNELL *Nat. & Supernat.* xii. (1864) 379 With disquisitions, theories, philosophies, pedagogies, schemes of reformation. **1900** G. C. BRODRICK *Mem. & Impr.* 12 An excellent old-fashioned teacher blissfully ignorant of 'pædagogy'.

2. *fig.* Instruction, discipline, training; a means or system of introductory training. (In 17th c. frequently used of the ancient Jewish dispensation, in reference to *Gal.* iii. 24: cf. PEDAGOGUE I b.)

1583 STUBBES *Anat. Abus.* I. (1879) 37 He would that this their meane and base attyre should be as a rule, or pedagogie, vnto vs. **1614** RALEIGH *Hist. World* II. iv. §5 The law of Moses..was..ordained to last untill the time of the Pædagogie of Gods people, or introduction to Christ, should be expired. *a* **1703** BURKITT *On N.T.*, *Acts* x. 2 Proselytes of the covenant, that is, such Gentiles as submitted themselves to..the whole Mosaical pædagogy.

3. A place of instruction; a school or college. (Also *fig.*) *Obs.* exc. *Hist.*

c **1625** DONNE *Serm. Ps. xxxii.* I, 2 S. Paul was in a higher Pedagogy, and another manner of University..caught up into the third Heavens,..and there he learnt much. **1783** W. F. MARTYN *Geog. Mag.* II. 151 An incredible number of colleges, gymnasia, pedagogies. **1895** H. RASHDALL *Univ. Eur. Mid. Ages* II. II. 609 The poorest students could not afford the cost of residence in a Pædagogy. *Ibid.* 611 The Proctors should go to the Colleges or Pædagogies of the offenders.

pedagrew, obs. form of PEDIGREE *sb.*

†peˈdaile. *Obs.* Forms: 4 pedaile, -aille, pytaille, pitaile, 4–5 pedale, 5 pedayle, pedel, pettaill, pitall. [a. AF. *pedaile* = OF. *pietaille*, *pitaille*, f. *pié*, *pied* foot, with collective suffix *-aille*: cf. CANAILLE.] Foot-soldiery, infantry.

c **1330** R. BRUNNE *Chron.* (1810) 191 Þe duke at þat bataile lost sex and þritty knyghtes, þre hundreth of pedaile. —— *Chron. Wace* (Rolls) 895 Wyþoute seriauntz & oþer pytaille [*v.r.* pedale]. *a* **1352** MINOT *Poems* vii. 56 Of pitaile was þare mekill more. *c* **1400** *Laud Troy Bk.* 4867 A thousand knyghtes..With alle the pedel better and werre. *Ibid.* 17025 Thousandes ten Off men of Armes & doghti men, With-oute comune & other pedale.

pedal (ˈpɛdəl), *sb.* [app. a. F. *pedale*, used by Rabelais in the sense 'feet' or 'trick with the feet', by Oudinot 1642, of the pedals of the organ, ad. It. *pedale* a foot, foot-stool, footstalk, stock of a tree, etc. (Florio), *pedale a' organo* 'the low key of organs' (Baretti); f. L. *pedāl-is* adj.: see next. The English use of the word by Cotgrave in 1611 before this sense is recorded in Fr. is notable.]

1. A lever worked by the foot, in various musical instruments, and with various functions.

a. In the organ: (*a*) Each of the (wooden) keys played upon by the feet, resembling those of the manuals in form and arrangement, but much larger, together consitituting the *pedal keyboard* or *pedal-board*, and usually operating upon a separate set of pipes of bass tone (*pedal-pipes*) forming the *pedal organ* (see ORGAN *sb.*[1] 2 d). (*b*) A foot-lever for drawing a number of stops out or in at once (COMBINATION-*pedal* or COMPOSITION-*pedal*). (*c*) The foot-lever by which the swell-box is opened and shut (SWELL-*pedal*). (*d*) Any one of various foot levers occasionally used, e.g. for coupling two keyboards. (*e*) Short for *pedal organ* or *keyboard.*

1611 COTGR., *Basses marches*, pedalls; the low keyes of some Organs to be touched with the feet. **1694** MOTTEUX *Rabelais* v. xx. (1737) 88 The Pedals of Turbith, and the Clavier..of Scammony. **1776** SIR J. HAWKINS *Hist. Mus.* IV. I. 150 The German organs have also Keys for the feet called Pedals. **1829** *Specif. Organ, St. James's, Bermondsey* in Grove *Dict. Mus.* II. 599 Three Composition Pedals to Great,..Pedal to couple Swell to Great. **1863** J. R. GREEN *Lett.* (1901) 121 A. is learning the organ..and is already great in the pedals. **1880** E. J. HOPKINS in Grove *Dict. Mus.* II. 606 The 'Sforzando coupler' is a movement worked by a pedal, by the aid of which the Great Organ is suddenly attached to the Swell. It reinforces the strength of the Swell to a far greater extent than by the 'crescendo' pedal... Other subsidiary pedals are occasionally introduced.

b. In the pianoforte, etc.: (*a*) A foot-lever for raising the dampers from the strings, thus sustaining the tone and rendering it fuller (***damper pedal***, often loosely called ***loud*** or ***forte pedal***). (*b*) One for softening the tone (***soft*** or ***piano pedal***), either by shifting the hammers so as to strike only one or two strings instead of three for each note, or by diminishing their length of blow, or by interposing a strip of cloth between them and the strings (***celeste pedal***); see also SOFT PEDAL. (*c*) Any one of various others occasionally used; e.g. the ***sustaining-pedal*** for sustaining a particular group of notes after they are struck; and several in late harpsichords and early pianofortes for modifying the tone, or for special effects. (*d*) Each of the keys of a pedal-board like that of an organ, sometimes attached to a pianoforte or harpsichord.

1840 *Penny Cycl.* XVIII. 141 In foreign piano-fortes we find many pedals, but in the English we have scarcely ever more than two—one for piano effects, and the other for forte. *Ibid.*, Fig. 5...*h*, Damper pedal lifter. **1861** WYNTER *Soc. Bees* 431 There was something..so innocent in her bearing, that you instinctively put down the soft pedal in your voice when addressing her. **1880** A. J. HIPKINS in Grove *Dict. Mus.* II. 678 J. S. Bach had a harpsichord with two rows of keys and pedals.

c. In the harp: Each of a set of seven foot-levers by which the pitch of the notes may be raised either one or two semitones by stopping the strings at different points, thus enabling the performer to play in any key.

1771 BURNEY *Pres. St. Music* (1775) I. 59 *note*, This method of producing the half-tones on the harp, by pedals, was invented at Brussels, about fifteen years ago, by M. Simon. **1880** A. J. HIPKINS in Grove *Dict. Mus.* II. 683 In the Harp the pedals are not keys..but it is their province to alter the pitch in two gradations of a semitone each.

d. Sometimes applied to the treadles by which the bellows are worked in a harmonium or reed-organ.

1882 OGILVIE s.v., On the harmonium and parlour-organ, the pedal works the bellows.

2. a. A lever worked by the foot in various machines or mechanical contrivances; a treadle: *esp.* in a bicycle or tricycle.

1789 E. DARWIN *Bot Gard.* II. (1791) 56 Inventress of the woof, fair Lina flings The flying shuttle through the dancing strings:.. Quick beat the reeds, the pedals fall and rise. **1869** *Routledge's Ev. Boy's Ann.* 477 The Pedals or stirrups [of a bicycle] are made of various shapes. **1885** C. G. W. LOCK *Workshop Receipts* Ser. IV. 288/1 When the pedal is depressed, the rod is raised. **1888** J. & ELIZ. PENNELL *Sent. Journ.* 182 Every turn of the pedals I felt must be the last. **1897** *Westm. Gaz.* 20 Aug. 8/1 Von Baader first constructed a velocipede with pedals in 1820.

b. *spec.* Such a lever forming one of the controls in a motor vehicle; often *attrib.*

1902 W. W. BEAUMONT in A. C. Harmsworth et al. *Motors* x. 219 The friction of the band on the drum..pulls on the band in the same direction as the pedal. *Ibid.* 220 A good form of brake is that..in which the pull on the rod F from pedal E pulls the arm D. **1909** *Westm. Gaz.* 4 Feb. 4/2 It seems to me that to dismantle the universal joint and pedal-gear means taking them out. **1926** *Scribner's Mag.* Aug. 153/1 The girl was satiated with speed. She relaxed the pressure of her foot on the pedal, and leaned back in her seat. 'Some car!' she said. **1929** *Times* 5 Nov. 7/5 The clutch pedal-shaft bearings have grease valves. **1962** *Which? Car Suppl.* Oct. 128/2 Most drivers liked the pedal controls in the VW 1500. *Ibid.* 129/1 The pedal control layouts..were generally liked. **1974** *Country Life* 21 Mar. 659/2 Pedals are nicely positioned for heel and toe driving. **1976** 'E. MCBAIN' *Guns* (1977) vi. 139 Great day for a robbery... Your driver hit the gas pedal and off you went.

†3. A footstalk, pedicel. *Obs. rare.*

1660 SHARROCK *Vegetables* 33 The best generall token of maturity is its loosness from the pedall by which it is joined to the stock. *Ibid.* 117 To serve as a foundation to the pedal of the blossom.

4. *Mus.* **a.** A note (regularly either tonic or dominant) sustained (or reiterated) in one part, usually in the bass, through a succession of harmonies some of which are independent of it; in organ-music usually sustained by holding down a pedal. Also *transf.*

Also called *pedal-point* (see 7) or *organ-point.* ***double pedal***: two notes (regularly tonic and dominant) so sustained simultaneously. ***inverted pedal***: a note so sustained in any other part than the bass, esp. in the highest part.

1854 tr. *Cherubini's Counterpoint* 66 The pedal is a note prolonged and sustained during several bars. **1856** MRS. C. CLARKE tr. *Berlioz' Instrument.* 5 The bass string can cross an upper open string..while the open string remains as a pedal. **1869** OUSELEY *Counterp.* xxii. 177 Towards the end of a fugue it is usual to place a dominant pedal. **1892** G. B. SHAW *Let.* 21 Apr. (1965) I. 337 Her voice has become much more powerful—quite Hyde Parkian in its pedal notes. **1905** *Daily Chron.* 25 Sept. 6/4 He did all that the pedal-notes of his magnificent voice could do toward realising..a character not wholly suited to his temperament.

b. On some brass and wind instruments, = FUNDAMENTAL *sb.* 2; usu. *attrib.*, as ***pedal note, tone.***

1856 M. C. CLARKE tr. *Berlioz's Treat. Mod. Instrumentation* 153/2 All trombones..possess..three notes; which are..called pedals... Supposing that the bass trombone possesses the first only of these pedal notes..it would still be of great value for certain effects. *Ibid.* 154/1 The vibrations of the pedal notes are slow, and require much wind. **1938** *Oxf. Compan. Mus.* 953/2 The actual fundamental notes are not so easy to produce [on a trombone] as the harmonics above them; they are spoken of as *Pedal Notes*— possibly because they are considered to be useful for the holding of a 'pedal', in the sense in which the word is used in the terminology of harmony.., or else, as Berlioz suggests, from their resemblance to the low pedal notes of an organ. **1944** W. APEL *Harvard Dict. Mus.* 340/1 Owing to the narrow bore..the lowest tone of this series (pedal tone) is practically unobtainable. *Ibid.* 817/1 Another term for the fundamental tone is pedal tone... A distinction is made between whole-tube instruments.. producing the pedal tone, and half-tube instruments. **1954** *Grove's Dict. Mus.* (ed. 5) VI. 608/1 These prime notes, the lowest proper tones of the instrument,..are known as pedal notes... A pedal note always stands for the first note or No. 1 in the harmonic series. On trumpets and some other instruments the pedal notes are practically impossible. **1959** *Collins Mus. Encycl.* 491/2 *Pedal*,..the fundamental (or first note of the harmonic series) on a brass instrument. A few of these notes can be produced with a slack lip on the trombone, the tuba and the B♭ section of the double horn. **1961** C. W. MONK in A. Baines *Mus. Instruments* xi. 283 This gives *E* as the bottom note of the trombone's continuous scale, leaving a gap down to the less-used fundamental or 'pedal' notes from the first-position *B'*♭ downwards.

5. *Geom.* A curve or surface which is the locus of the feet of the perpendiculars let fall from a fixed point (the ***pedal origin*** or ***pole***) upon the tangents to a given curve or surface.

negative pedal: that curve or surface of which a given one is the pedal. ***oblique pedal***: the locus of the feet of lines drawn from a fixed point to the tangents at a constant angle with them other than a right angle. ***second pedal***: the pedal of the pedal (of a curve or surface); so ***third pedal***, etc. (the pedal itself in relation to these is the ***first pedal***).

1863 CAYLEY *Coll. Math. Papers* V. 114 If rays proceeding from the point S are reflected at the given curve, then the epicycloid (or pedal) in question is the secondary caustic. **1873** B. WILLIAMSON *Diff. Calc.* (ed. 2) §183 If perpendiculars be drawn to the tangents to the pedal, we get a new curve called the *second pedal* of the original: and so on. With respect to its pedal, the original curve is styled the *first negative* pedal, etc. **1885** A. G. GREENHILL *Diff. Calc.* (1886) 24 The locus..is called the pedal of the curve with respect to *O*, and *O* is called the pole of the pedal.

6. Humorously or affectedly used for 'foot'.

1849 H. MELVILLE *Mardi* II. xliv. 204 To cool his heated pedals, he established..stopping-places. **1894** *Outing* (U.S.) XXIII. 884/2 [At Shanghai] I did see the celebrated shrunk or dwarfed feet... The first two or three pairs of these stunted pedals that I noticed excited my pity.

7. *attrib.* and *Comb.* Of, belonging to, connected with, worked by, having, or constituting a pedal or pedals (in sense 1 or 2), as ***pedal action, -bike, clavier, coupler*** (†***copula***), ***cycle, cyclist, harp, key, keyboard, mechanism, pallet, pipe, rod, soundboard, stop, tracker, work***; ***pedal-operated*** adj.; played upon the pedals of an organ, or constituting or involving a pedal (in sense 4), as ***pedal bass, note, passage***; in *Geom.* relating to a pedal curve or surface (see sense 5 above and PEDAL *a.*[1] 3); **pedal bin**, a rubbish bin with a lid which is opened by means of a pedal; **pedal-board** (see 1 a); **pedal boat**, a boat, usu. a pleasure boat, propelled by means of pedals; also **pedal-driven boat**; **pedal car**, a car, usu. a child's toy, propelled by means of pedals; **pedal-check**, a device for preventing the pedals of an organ from being pressed down; **pedal clarinet** (or **clarionet**), a clarinet sounding an octave below the bass clarinet; **pedal-craft**, pedal boats; **pedal entry**, in organ music, a point where a theme or figure is introduced on the pedal stops; also *transf.* and *fig.*; **pedal-piano**, a pianoforte fitted with a pedal-board like that of an organ; **pedal point** = sense 4 above; also *fig.*; **pedal power** [cf. POWER *sb.*[1] 4 f], a catch-phrase for the use or advocacy of bicycling as a means of transport; **pedal pusher**, a cyclist; hence in *pl.* (orig. *U.S.*), a type of girls' or women's trousers, reaching only just below the knee, suitable for wearing when cycling; also (with hyphen) *attrib.*; **pedal steel guitar**, an electric guitar fixed on a stand and connected to pedals by which the tension of the strings can be altered to produce glissando effects; also **pedal guitar, pedal steel; pedal wireless**, a small radio transceiver, with a generator powered by a foot-pedal, providing a means of communication in the Australian outback; also **pedal radio**, **pedal set**.

1880 *Pedal bass [see *pedal passage* below]. **1974** 'A. GILBERT' *Nice Little Killing* vi. 83 I've been travelling around on a *pedal-bike. **1951** *Catal. of Exhibits, South Bank Exhib., Festival of Britain* 52/1 'Binette' *pedal bin. *Ibid.* 124/1 Pedal bin for soiled napkins. **1958** *Engineering* 7 Mar. 320/2 Polythene is used widely: for pedal bins, trug baskets,..and watering cans. **1966** N. FREELING *Dresden Green* I. 14 He..picked up his pedal bin (emptied that and every morning into one of the big dustbins). **1977** J. HEALD *Just Desserts* i. 14 An empty magnum of Château Waitrose by the pedal bin in the kitchen. **1951** *Go* Apr.–May There are little safe *pedal-boats for venturing on to the lake. **1958** *New Yorker* 13 Sept. 130/3 (Advt.), The Yacht club with pedal boats, water skiing, skin diving. **1959** *Encounter* Oct. 17/2 The animated statue who looks after the pedal-boats. **1951** *Catal. of Exhibits, South Bank Exhib., Festival of Britain* 126/2 *Pedalcar, 'Austin 40'. **1968** *Radio Times* 28 Nov. 6 A pedal car, a doll's pram, a trike or a bike. **1973** *Guardian* 11 June 6 The event for Formula One pedal cars was part of the RAC L-Driver of the Year finals. **1892** *Orchestral Times* Jan. 6/2 Messrs. F. Besson & Co.'s inventive faculty seems inexhaustible... That eminent firm has recently given us..the '*Pedal' Clarionet (contra-bass clarionet). *Ibid.* 7/2 The 'Pedal' Clarionet is the deepest-voiced instrument ever constructed for orchestral use... The fingering of the pedal clarionet is similar to the ordinary clarionet. **1911** *Encycl. Brit.* XXI. 36/2 *Pedal clarinet*, a contrabass instrument invented in 1891 by M. F. Besson to complete the quartet of clarinets..; it is constructed on practically the same principles as the clarinet, and consists of a tube 10 ft. long..doubled up twice upon itself. **1959** *Collins Mus. Encycl.* 491/2 *Pedal Clarinet*, another name for the Contrabass Clarinet. **1961** J. A. MACGILLIVRAY in A. Baines *Mus. Instruments* x. 260 Of those [*sc.* contrabass clarinets] in B♭, an octave below the bass clarinet, Fontaine-Besson's 'Pedal clarinet' was the first to arouse much interest. **1966** *Listener* 27 Oct. 632/2 He includes such rare instruments as..pedal-clarinet. **1852** SEIDEL *Organ* 70 The *pedal-copula is a contrivance by which..the manual may be joined or coupled to the pedale. **1834** in Grove *Dict. Mus.* II. 600 Manual and *Pedal couplers. Radiating Pedal-board. **1957** G. BELLAIRS *Death in High Provence* ix. 105 Families..sporting on the beaches, little *pedal-craft skimming across the water. **1937** R. F. BROAD *Motor Driving made Easy* (ed. 6) vii. 94 A moment ago we used the word 'cyclist'. By this term is generally understood the *pedal-cycle user. **1963** *Times* 5 Mar. 6/3 Motor cycle casualties fell by 7,632..and pedal-cycle casualties by 3,974. **1973** J. WAINWRIGHT *Pride of Pigs* 69 Sykes arrived in a Cortina. The postman arrived *with* a pedal cycle—pushing it. **1974** *Times* 8 Feb. 15 The local authority provides a pedal cycle speedway track. **1931** *Highway Code* 12 Certain of the rules for drivers of motor vehicles..also apply..to *pedal cyclists. **1974** L. LAMB *Man in Mist* vii. 43 The early evening shoal of pedal cyclists. **1898** *Cycling* 6 The *pedal dismount..is effected by waiting till the left pedal is at its lowest and throwing the right leg over the saddle and back wheel. **1927** *Sunday Express* 14 Aug. 1 Mr. E. P. Tierney.. collapsed yesterday when attempting to carry out a test in his 12-foot *pedal-driven boat Carrie, with which he had planned to cross the Atlantic. **1928** AUDEN in *Oxf. Poetry* 2 We sang Our descant until love one day, That *pedal-entry in the fugue Roared in, swept soul and knees away. **1932** —— *Orators* I. 30 The bowel tremors at the pedal-entry. **1970** A. BELLOW *Illustr. Hist. Guitar* vii. 154 An even more unusual guitar, known as a '*pedal guitar', was constructed by Eduard Bayer. **1784** E. JONES *Mus. Rel. Welsh Bards* (1794) 105 Sometimes the *Pedal Harp is called the German Harp. **1852** SEIDEL *Organ* 33 The *pedal-keys are generally made of oak. **1896** *Godey's Mag.* Apr. 369/2 A bicycle of peculiar *pedal-mechanism. **1880** *Pedal note [see *pedal point* below]. **1908** *Westm. Gaz.* 20 Oct. 4/3 A similar powered car..with patent *pedal-operated plate clutch. *Ibid.* 10 Dec. 4/2 *(heading)* Pedal-operated car. **1936** *Discovery* July 224/2 A pedal-operated volume-control [on an electronic piano]. **1960** *Farmer & Stockbreeder* 5 Jan. 95/2 This pedal-operated device counteracts wheel-spin. **1964** W. L. GOODMAN *Hist. Woodworking Tools* 153 Holding his work in a vertical, pedal-operated vice or 'horse'. **1829** in Grove *Dict. Mus.* II. 599 *Pedal Organ... Double Pedal Pipes. **1880** F. CORDER in Grove *Dict. Mus.* 681 The following passage..is so far a *pedal passage... Songs and short pieces have been occasionally written entirely on a Pedal bass. **1829** *Pedal pipe [see *pedal organ* above]. **1852** J. HULLAH *Gram. Musical Harmony* xxvii. 71 From a very obvious and effective mode of using these (foot) keys has arisen the term **pedal point*, by which is understood a note maintained during several successive changes of chords, or passages of melody. **1880** F. CORDER in Grove *Dict. Mus.* II. 678 *Pedal point*,..is the sustaining of a note by one part while the other parts proceed in independent harmony... The sustained, or pedal note, when first sounded or finally quitted, must form part of the harmony. **1974** *Publishers Weekly* 16 Dec. 49/1 These tales are generally of high standard... But the insistent pedal point theme, the overwhelming atmosphere of misery.., makes this one to be taken in small doses. **1977** *New Yorker* 16 May 139/1 Hindemith's Requiem opens with a slow instrumental prelude, a four-note tolling ostinato over a pedal point. **1974** *Times* 5 Mar. (Europa Suppl.) p. vi/1 In the United States the bicycle is in full boom to such an extent that humorists talk of *pedal power. **1978** WATSON & GRAY *Penguin Bk. Bicycle* i. 38 Pedal power..lends itself quite naturally to the need felt by many people for..healthy exercise. **1985** *Oxford Jrnl.* 11 July (Summer Focus) 3/2 Students..find it easier to tour the area using pedal power by hiring a cycle from one of the specialist shops. **1934** M. H. WESEEN *Dict. Amer. Slang* xvii. 262 **Pedal pusher*,—a bicycle rider, especially in a race. **1942** [see PEDALLER]. **1944** *Life* 28 Aug. 65/2 When college girls took to riding bicycles in slacks, they first rolled up one trouser leg, then rolled up both. This.. has now produced a trim variety of long shorts, called 'pedal pushers'. **1945** *Liberty* 1 Sept. 68 Miss McCardell.. borrowed little-boy pants for 'pedal-pushers', the knee length shorts. **1957** H. ROOSENBURG *Walls came tumbling Down* vii. 189 His trousers had shrunk to the size of pedal-pushers. **1959** M. STEEN *Tower* I. vii. 92 A girl in..blue pedal-pusher jeans. **1960** S. PLEYDELL *Festival for Gilbert* i. 10 Black pedal-pusher trousers. **1971** Pedal-pusher [see HAPPI-COAT]. **1959** *Manch. Guardian* 5 Aug. 5/4 All the aeroplane, the *pedal-radio..and, latterly, the road-train have done to break down the isolation of life in inland central Australia. **1944** *Living off Land* iv. 77 Cars, trucks, aircraft, and radio *pedal-sets, have put an end to the old era of isolation. **1949** H. M. MADELEY *Australia* xxxiv. 138 These pedal sets are in mining camps, in lonely houses, in police stations, in nursing homes. **1869** *Routledge's Ev. Boy's Ann.* 475 Ornamental caps to keep the *pedal-stays [of a bicycle] firmly in their places. **1976** *Gramophone* Aug. 351/3 Paul Cotton..and Rusty Young (*pedal steel, dobro, mandolin etc.) excel instrumentally. **1977** *Zigzag* Mar. 30/1 This coupled with Mike Utley's delicate piano and Al Perkins' unobtrusive pedal steel makes the track one of the standout cuts on the first side. **1969** *Listener* 20 Mar. 398/3 It features another splendid electronic invention, the *pedal steel guitar which..specialises in vertiginous slides and swoops. **1969** *Rolling Stone* 28 June 17/1 Today's added use of drums, pedal steel guitar,..even harpsichord have [*sic*] made some arrangements far more complete. **1940** BAYNE & LAZARUS *Austral. Community* II. 76 Messages are sent out and received by means of the *pedal wireless or transceiver (invented by the Australian Inland Mission and now much improved). **1944** F. CLUNE *Red Heart* 7 The combination of pedal-wireless sets, to call the doctor, and of aeroplanes, to bring him to the patient, is a triumph of modern times. **1963** A. LUBBOCK *Austral. Roundabout* 25 The hundreds of transceiver or pedal-wireless sets. **1944** R. LEHMANN *Ballad & Source* 96, I was already practising my technique for Bicyclists' Dashing Hill—a piece of frantic momentum-gathering *pedal work.

pedal ('pɛdəl, 'piːdəl), *a.*[1] [ad. L. *pedāl-is* of or pertaining to the foot, of the size or dimension of a foot, f. *pēs*, *ped-em* foot: see -AL[1]. (The pronunciation ('piːdəl) is restricted to sense 1, 1 b.)]

1. Of, pertaining to, or connected with the foot or feet. **a.** *gen. rare.*

1625 N. CARPENTER *Geog. Del.* I. vi. (1635) 150 The Nadir is directly vnder our foote, and therefore may be called the Pedall point. **1801** STRUTT *Sports & Past.* II. ii. 71 Places appropriated to pedal races. **1883** CHILDERS *Sp. Ho. Comm.* 10 May, A bicycle would be held to be propelled by..pedal power.

b. *Anat.* and *Zool.*: usually in reference to the 'foot' or *podium* of a mollusc. *pedal bone*, the lowest phalangeal bone in a horse's foot; = *coffin-bone* (COFFIN *sb.* 13).

1851–6 WOODWARD *Mollusca* 187 Mouth small, proboscidiform, retractile into the pedal notch. **1866** TATE *Brit. Mollusks* ii. 18 The pedal muscles retract the foot. **1881** *Encycl. Brit.* XII. 178/1 A powerful tendon..passes down over the..phalanges, to be inserted mainly into the upper edge of the anterior surface of the last phalanx or pedal bone. **1920** F. T. BARTON *Horse* xiii. 107 Two tendons pass down the back of the foot,..the former being attached to the lower surface of the pedal-bone. **1973** EDWARDS & GEDDES *Compl. Bk. Horse* III. iii. 113/1 The end bone of the leg is the pedal bone..which corresponds to the last bone in the second finger of man. *Ibid.*, The pedal bone is roughly the shape of the foot and is of pumice-like consistency.

†**2.** Of the length or measure of a foot. *rare.*

1656 in BLOUNT *Glossogr.* **1658** in PHILLIPS.

3. *Geom.* Relating to the feet of perpendiculars; of or pertaining to the pedal of a curve or surface.

pedal curve or *surface* = PEDAL *sb.* 5. *pedal line*, the line through the feet of the perpendiculars on the sides of a triangle from any point on the circumscribed circle. *pedal origin*, *pole*: see PEDAL *sb.* 5.

1863 CAYLEY *Coll. Math. Papers* V. 113 If the given curve be a parabola, then the locus or pedal curve is a curve of the third order. **1873** B. WILLIAMSON *Diff. Calc.* (ed. 2) §184 The tangent at any point on the pedal locus. **1877** —— *Int. Calc.* (ed. 2) §144 In this case, the pedal area is a minimum. .. The distance between the pedal origins.

4. *Mus.* That is, or relates to, a pedal or pedals: see PEDAL *sb.* 1, 4, 7.

pedal ('pɛdəl), *a.*[2] [ad. It. *pedale*: see PEDAL *sb.*] Applied to the lower and thicker part of a kind of straw grown in Italy for plaiting; *ellipt.*, a special plait made from this straw, usually having five or seven strands. (Hence ***five-*** or ***seven-ends pedal***.)

1887 *Encycl. Brit.* XXII. 593/2 The straw of Tuscany, specially grown for plaiting, is distinguished into three qualities,—..from the third quality, *Santa Fioro*, only 'Tuscan pedals' and braids are plaited. **1907** *Yesterday's Shopping* (1969) 894 Fine pedal 'Homburg'... Fine pedal straw. **1923** *Daily Mail* 7 Feb. 1 (Advt.), Italian pedal straw hats... These hats are very soft and pliable, made of seven ends pedal. **1930** *Times* 13 Mar. 11/6 Fine pedal straw has returned, and is seen in a brimmed hat.., with the new sweeping line. **1962** A. SOUTHERN *Millinery* ii. 30 The fancy band straws and pedal come into this [*sc.* real Italian straws] group, the latter being dyed into fashion shades.

pedal ('pɛdəl), *v.* [f. PEDAL *sb.*] *intr.* **a.** To play upon the pedals of an organ, a pianoforte, or similar instrument. Also *trans.*, to use the pedals in playing (a passage of music, etc.); to use the pedals of. **b.** To work the pedals of a bicycle, etc. so as to propel it; also *trans.* with the bicycle, etc. as object. Also in *refl.*, *pass.*, and *fig.* uses.

1866 [To pedal on the organ is remembered]. **1888** *Art Jrnl.* LI. 125/2 There the travellers ceased to pedal [on a bicycle]. **1888** P. FURNIVALL *Phys. Training* 7 One of the difficulties of pedalling at a high speed. **1889** *Cent. Dict.* s.v., *Pedal*..*v.i.*,..to work a pedal; use the pedals, as of a piano, organ, bicycle, etc. **1892** *Harper's Weekly Mag.* 9 July 667/3 To do what?.. Pedal a bicycle or swing a tennis racket? **1896** *Queen* 25 Jan. 169/2 If young ladies are to be allowed to pedal themselves about in..London, then it will certainly be necessary to provide..some proper escort. **1909**, etc. [see PEDALLING *vbl. sb.*]. **1922** S. GREW *Art of Player-Piano* iv. 23 We correct the first condition..by ceasing to pedal for a moment or two. *Ibid.* xviii. 112 An attempt..to 'pedal' the piece in the way it is 'fingered' for the pianist. **1922** JOYCE *Ulysses* 259 Upholding the lid he..gazed..at the oblique triple (piano!) wires. He pressed..soft pedalling a triple of keys. **1924** GALSWORTHY *White Monkey* II. xi. 208 'Well,' said Michael, '*I* think we shall pedal through yet.' **1938** F. C. RAUSER tr. *Leimer & Gieseking's Rhythmics* vii. 48 All of Beethoven's Sonatas can be properly pedalled by means of the time-tread. **1954** T. A. JOHNSON *Princ. Pianoforte Pedalling* 10 It is sometimes permissible to pedal certain staccato passages. **1955** G. GREENE *Quiet American* IV. ii. 243, I found a trishaw and was pedalled home. **1961** C. CLUTTON in A. Baines *Mus. Instruments* v. 93 John Field.. was the first person to develop the use of the sustaining pedal as part of his technique, and, like Chopin, he pedalled after the note. **1973** D. MAY *Laughter in Djakarta* viii. 132 A betjak came along the street, pedalled by a very young smooth-faced boy. **1975** H. FERGUSON *Keyboard Interpretation* ix. 66 The passage must be pedaled thus. **1977** *Daily Express* 29 Jan. 35/2 Derek Underwood pedalling slowly backwards before clutching it in his hands to send Gavaskar miserably away to an accompaniment of boos and jeers from the 40,000 crowd. **1978** *Gramophone* July 231/1 The ending of 'Ende vom Lied'..is deeply impressive—I only wish he had not pedalled.

pedalfer (pɪ'dælfə(r)). *Soil Sci.* [f. PED- + AL(UMINIUM + L. *fer-rum* iron.] A soil in which there is no layer of accumulated calcium carbonate but in which oxides of iron and aluminium have tended to accumulate (generally acidic and characteristic of humid climates). Cf. PEDOCAL.

1928 [see PEDOCAL]. **1930** L. A. WOLFANGER *Major Soil Divisions of U.S.* iv. 100 The agriculture of the pedalfers is characterized by its wealth in crop variety and its extended development of crop centers. **1965** B. T. BUNTING *Geogr. Soil* viii. 95 Accumulation of Fe and Al oxides at depth is characteristic..of pedalfers, especially of podzols. **1972** C. B. HUNT *Geol. Soils* viii. 167 The significant feature of pedalfers is that moisture is sufficient to wet the soil to its capacity..and to allow excess water to..remove the soluble constituents. **1977** A. HALLAM *Planet Earth* 179 These ideas were accepted in the USA, and the concepts of pedalfers and pedocals added: pedalfers are leached soils in humid areas where aluminium and iron accumulate in the B horizon.

Hence **pedal'feric** *a.*

1928 [see PEDOCALIC *a.*]. **1930** L. A. WOLFANGER *Major Soil Divisions of U.S.* iv. 101 Although several of these crops are also grown in noteworthy quantity in the pedalferic zone, the chief production areas..are included within the pedocalic division.

pedalian (pɪ'deɪlɪən), *a. rare.* Also 7 **-ean**. [f. L. *pedāli-s* of or pertaining to a foot, of a foot long + -AN: cf. *sesquipedalian*.]

†**1.** Of a foot long; ? lengthy, tedious. *Obs.*

1634 in *Antid. Sabbat. Err.* (1636) A iv b, His Pedalean penne delivered us a Theologicall decision.

2. = PEDAL *a.*[1]

1830 MAUNDER *Dict. Eng. Lang.*, *Pedalian*, pertaining to the feet.

pedalier (pɛdə'lɪə(r)). [a. F. *pédalier* (1881 in Littré *Supplement*), f. *pédale* PEDAL *sb.*] The pedal keyboard of an organ; a similar set of pedals attached to a pianoforte or harpsichord; 'an independent bass pianoforte to be played by pedals only' (Grove *Dict. Mus.*).

1881 *Daily Tel.* 14 Feb., The lowest key on the pedalier of a large organ. **1885** J. H. MEE in Grove *Dict. Mus.* IV. 324 While learning the organ his step-father let him have a pedalier attached to his harpsichord.

Pedaline ('pɛdəlaɪn, -iːn). Also with lower-case initial. [f. PEDAL *a.*[2] + -INE[4].] A synthetic straw (see quot. 1957). Also ***Pedaline straw***.

1927 *Daily Express* 16 Feb. 4/2 (Advt.), Women's becoming hats of Pedaline Straw, trimmed and bound with Ribbon Velvet. *Ibid.* 14 Mar. 5/3 *(heading)* Fashion's new vocabulary... The following are a few additions made to her vocabulary this spring by Dame Fashion:—..*pedaline*, a new type of plait for millinery, having a polished effect. **1942** J. G. DONY *Hist. Straw Hat Industry* v. 96 *(caption)* Pedaline, a Japanese imitation of a Swiss braid... Coburg pedaline, a Japanese braid. **1957** M. B. PICKEN *Fashion Dict.* 337 *Pedaline*,..synthetic straw made of hemp fiber covered with Cellophane and woven between cotton threads. Made chiefly in Japan.

pedalism ('pɛdəlɪz(ə)m). *nonce-wd.* [f. PEDAL *a.*[1] + -ISM.] Pedal agency, action of the feet.

1863 DE MORGAN *Pref.* in *From Matter to Spirit* 41 Mrs. Hayden was seated at some distance from the table, and her feet were watched by their believers until faith in pedalism slowly evaporated.

pedalist ('pɛdəlɪst). [f. PEDAL *sb.* + -IST.] One skilled in the use of the pedals (of an organ, or of a bicycle, etc.).

1880 A. J. HIPKINS in Grove *Dict. Mus.* II. 678 An eminent pianist and remarkable pedalist. **1896** *Columbus* (Ohio) *Disp.* 26 Sept., Instead of silk waist, like her sister pedalist, she has a belted blouse.

†**pe'dality.** *Obs. rare*[−1]. [f. PEDAL *a.*[1]: see -ITY.] The fact or quality of being pedal, going on foot, or having feet, the possession of feet.

1656 [? J. SERGEANT] tr. *T. White's Peripat. Inst.* 216 Cloven-footednesse includes pedality. **1661** BLOUNT *Glossogr.* (ed. 2), *Pedality*.., ableness of foot; a measuring by or going on foot. **1692** COLES, *Pedality*, measuring by, or able going on foot. So **1775** ASH.

pedaller, pedaler. [f. PEDAL *v.* + -ER[1].] One who pedals (in var. senses of the vb.). Also in *pl.*, a name for *pedal pushers* s.v. PEDAL *sb.* 7.

The spelling *pedaler* is predominantly *N. Amer.*

1881 *Wheeling* 11 Mar. 465/2 The peddlers of the big wheel. **1922** S. GREW *Art of Player-Piano* 17 Effects in the music which you cannot hope to create until you are an experienced pedaller. **1942** BERREY & VAN DEN BARK *Amer. Thes. Slang* §426/10 *Bicyclist*,.. pedaler, pedal pusher. **1945** *Consumers' Guide* (U.S.) July 6 Another part of the Clothes Magic show illustrated what had been done in a 'make over and make do' program... Pedalers (bicycle shorts) from G.I. pants, and a stunning beach ensemble..from a discarded evening dress were a few of the other things shown. **1953** BERREY & VAN DEN BARK *Amer. Thes. Slang* (1954) (ed. 2) §87/15 *Pedalers, pedal pushers*, bicycle shorts that end just below the knee. **1972** *Village Voice* (N.Y.) 1 June 26/2 In an era of precious pedalers, back to nature sentimentalists, and ecology moralizers, Jack La Lanne is an honest, straightforward salesman. **1974** *Times* 12 Nov. 14/7 It seems against the interests of the environment to chase away harmless pedallers with a polluting petrol-engined monster. **1976** A. HILL *Summer's End* ii. 25 I'd got a pedaller that would run alright. No brakes, no mudguards. But I could pedal it. **1977** *Times* 14 June 16/7 Readers..keep complaining about the 'tedious' routine of having to apply to the Cyclists Touring Club for tickets to take their bicycles free on trains. More than 10,000 pedallers have done it without making a fuss.

pedalling, *vbl. sb.* [f. PEDAL *v.* + -ING[1].] Also pedaling. The action of the verb in var. senses. Also *fig.*, and with reference to propelling a sled. Also as *ppl. a.*

1889 *Athenæum* 9 Feb. 188/1 [Organ-music] having the best method of pedalling indicated for all the difficult passages. **1909** J. HOFMANN *Piano Playing* 42 Harmonic clarity in pedalling is the basis, but it is only the basis; it is not all that constitutes an artistic treatment of the pedal. **1911** H. BROWER *Art of Pianist* xiv. 170 Imagine what a performance of the compositions of Chopin or Liszt would sound like, deprived of proper pedaling. **1916** JOYCE *Portrait of Artist* (1969) v. 190 'It may be uphill pedalling at first. Take Mr. Moonan. He was a long time before he got to the top.'.. 'I may not have his talent.' **1925** E. H. YOUNG *William* iv. 38 A ringing of bicycle bells was heard, and then two pedalling figures..appeared. **1936** Y. BOWEN (*title*) Pedalling the modern pianoforte. **1938** F. C. RAUSER tr. *Leimer & Gieseking's Rhythmics* vii. 57 It is possible to play a *glissando* with uninterrupted pedalling. **1948** A. FOLDES *Keys to Keyboard* (1950) viii. 50 Pedalling is one of the most complicated processes in piano playing. **1954** T. A. JOHNSON *Princ. Pianoforte Pedalling* 9 (*heading*), Pedalling of Arpeggios. **1954** *Grove's Dict. Mus.* (ed. 5) VI. 345/2 We must now consider the subject of pedalling... To look at the pedal-board is often impossible and rarely helpful. **1972** *Evening Telegram* (St. John's, Newfoundland) 24 June 14/3 Pedalling is an art and must be done smoothly, in order not to jerk the sled. **1973** *Guardian* 17 Feb. 15/2 In Britain.. pedalling for pleasure is undergoing a sort of mini-renaissance. **1973** K. A. LEIBOVITCH tr. *Neuhaus's Art of Piano Playing* 165 How sad that such a great pianist as Schnabel..showed his lack of understanding in his inappropriate pedalling.

pedalo ('pɛdələʊ). [f. PEDAL *sb.* + -O[2].] A small pedal-operated pleasure boat used on lakes and at the sea-side.

The spelling in quot. 1962 is unusual.

1959 *News Chron.* 4 Dec. 3/7 One rescue team..manned a four-seat 'Pedalo' found on an untouched part of the beach. **1962** 'O. MILLS' *Headlines make Murder* xviii. 199 A shilling-an-hour pedallo. **1969** *Daily Tel.* 21 Apr. 11/5 So many beaches today are crowded with water-skiers, canoeists, *pedaloes* and sailing boats that accidents are on the increase. **1973** W. FAIRCHILD *Swiss Arrangement* v. 61 The water was glass calm and children in pedalos glided in all directions. **1976** *Daily Tel.* 20 July 15/5 A man armed with a bottle defied an RAF helicopter and two lifeboats which tried to rescue him from a drifting pedalo four miles off Margate last night. **1977** *Navy News* Feb. 18/1 Glancing through a scuttle after reading the papers lately, a member of the Andrew might have expected to see a pedalo forging ahead of his fuel-saving warship.

pedament, obs. form of PEDIMENT.

‖**pedanda** (pɛ'dændə). Also padanda, padenda, and with capital initial. [Balinese, = 'bearer of the staff'.] In Bali, a Brahman priest. Also *attrib.*

1817 T. S. RAFFLES *Hist. Java* II. p. ccxxxix, The duties and ceremonies of religion, the conducting of which is in the hands of..learned Brahmins called *Padénda*. **1877** *Jrnl. R. Asiatic Soc.* IX. 113 The *Padandas* are Brahmans who have received a complete education from another *Padanda* (their *Guru*). They must be thoroughly acquainted with religion and with literature. In order to become a Padanda, they undergo all kinds of tests... The mark of the dignity is a staff, *danda*, which they receive from the Guru... After this staff they are called *Padanda*, that is, 'bearing a staff.' **1924** T. DE KLEEN *Mudrās* 23 Although the Balinese in general are a polite and hospitable people, the *Pedandas* showed themselves very reserved, sometimes obviously hostile. *Ibid.* 27 My *Pedanda* friends in Sidemen. **1936** R. GORIS in *Netherlands Indies* 16 Feb. 71/1 There are in Bali both Padandas 'Shiva' and Padandas 'Buda'. *Ibid.* 77/1 Every bench of magistrates in Bali must have at least one Padanda sitting on it as a judge. **1937** M. COVARRUBIAS *Island of Bali* (1972) ix. 293 The *pedandas* still exert a powerful influence on Balinese life despite the fact that their relations with the people were never intimate; they represent the law, and the judges of the high native courts..are still *pedandas* in the majority. **1953** J. BELO *Bali: Temple Festival* 4 The temple priests who are the guardians of these temples have not studied as have the Brahmana high priests, the *pedanda*, who are often scholars and learned men. **1961** P. KEMP *Alms for Oblivion* vii. 116 Priests wear white, and a high priest or *pedanda* goes bareheaded and carries a staff surmounted by a crystal ball.

†**pe'daneous,** *a. Obs. rare*[−1]. [f. L. *pedāne-us* of the dimension or size of a foot, petty (f. *pēs, ped-* foot: see -ANEOUS) + -OUS. In F. *pedané* (16th c.).] Of low standing, of small account, petty.

1617 COLLINS *Def. Bp. Ely* II. viii. 321 What pedaneous author haue not they made a father of? [**1656** BLOUNT *Glossogr.*, *Pedaneous* (*pedaneus*), that goeth on foot.]

‖**pedang** (pə'dæŋ). [Malay.] A type of sword (see quots.).

1817 T. S. RAFFLES *Hist. Java* vi. 296 The *pedáng, bandól*, [etc.]..are varieties of sword. **1911** *Encycl. Brit.* XVII. 477/1 The Malays use..long swords of ordinary pattern called *pedang*. **1936** G. B. GARDNER *Keris & Other Malay Weapons* iii. 69 Theoretically this is any type of sword of foreign origin... The *pĕdang* may be straight or curved.

pedant ('pɛdənt), *sb.* (*a.*) Also 7 pædant. [a. F. *pédant* (1566 in Hatz.-Darm.) or its source It. *pedante* teacher, schoolmaster, pedant.

The origin of the It. is uncertain. The first element is app. the same as in *peda-gogue*, etc.; and it has been suggested that *pedante* was contracted from a med.L. *pædagōgānt-em*, pr. pple. of *pædagōgāre* to act as pedagogue, to teach (Du Cange); but evidence is wanting.]

†**1.** A schoolmaster, teacher, or tutor (= PEDAGOGUE 2, but often without implication of contempt; in quot. 1662 = PEDAGOGUE 1). *Obs.*

1588 SHAKS. *L.L.L.* III. i. 179, I that haue beene..A domineering pedant ore the Boy. **1599** B. JONSON *Cynthia's Rev.* II. i, Hee loues to haue a fencer, a pedant, and a musician, seene in his lodgings a mornings. **1601** SHAKS. *Twel. N.* III. ii. 80 Like a Pedant that keepes a Schoole i'th Church. **1654** H. L'ESTRANGE *Chas. I* (1655) 145 From a Countrey Pedant, he became..a Peer of the Realm. **1662** J. BARGRAVE *Pope Alex. VII* (1867) 48 He kept a small school in Rome, which he left to serve Cardinal Maffeo Barberino, to wait upon his nephews as a pedant.., conducting them every day to school to the Roman College and bringing them back again. *a* **1704** T. BROWN *Eng. Sat.* Wks. 1730 I. 27 Oldham ow'd..nothing to his birth, but little to the precepts of pedants.

2. A person who overrates book-learning or technical knowledge, or displays it unduly or unseasonably; one who has mere learning untempered by practical judgement and knowledge of affairs; one who lays excessive stress upon trifling details of knowledge or upon strict adherence to formal rules; sometimes, one who is possessed by a theory and insists on applying it in all cases without discrimination, a doctrinaire.

1596 NASHE *Saffron Walden* 43 O, tis a precious apothegmaticall Pedant, who will finde matter inough to dilate a whole daye of the first inuention of *Fy, fa, fum.* **1663** BUTLER *Hud.* I. i. 94 A Babylonish dialect, Which learned Pedants much affect. **1711** ADDISON *Spect.* No. 105 ¶4 A Man who has been brought up among Books, and is able to talk of nothing else, is..what we call a Pedant. But, methinks, we should enlarge the Title, and give it to every one that does not know how to think out of his Profession and particular way of Life. **1812** MISS MITFORD in L'Estrange *Life* (1870) I. vi. 172, I mean your learned young ladies—pedants in petticoats. **1874** GREEN *Short Hist.* viii. §2. 465 He [Jas. I] had the temper of a pedant;..a pedant's love of theories, and a pedant's inability to bring his theories into any relation with actual facts.

3. *attrib.* or as *adj.* That is, or has the character of, a pedant; of or pertaining to a pedant; pedantic.

1616 R. C. *Times Whistle* VI. 2505 Each pedant Tutour. **1670** DRYDEN *2nd Pt. Conq. Granada* III. ii, It points to pedant colleges, and cells. **1703** ROWE *Fair Penit.* v. i, The pomp of words, and pedant dissertations. **1845** CARLYLE *Cromwell* (1871) IV. 71 Respectable Pedant persons. **1875** L. MORRIS *Evensong* cliii, The pure thought smirched and fouled, or buried in pedant lore.

4. *Comb.*

1611 COTGR., *Pedantesque*, pedanticall, inkhornizing, pedant-like. **1884** SYMONDS *Shaks. Predec.* vii. 263 The honours of that pedant-rid Parnassus.

Hence **'pedantess,** a female pedant; **'pedanthood,** the condition or character of a pedant.

1784 R. BAGE *Barham Downs* I. 75 Unfeeling pedantess, says I..thou art no wife for me. **1843** CARLYLE in *Last Words of T. C.* (1892) 217 Hard isolated Pedanthood.

†**pe'dante, -'antie, -'anty.** *Obs.* Also 6–7 pæd-, 7 -ti, -tee. [app. a. It. *pedante* PEDANT (cf. *county*[2]); the ending being afterwards assimilated to Eng. *-ie, -y*, whence app. sense 2.]

1. = PEDANT.

1593 R. HARVEY *Philad.* 9 Why should not a Moonke be as credible as a Pædanty? **1605** BACON *Adv. Learn.* I. ii. §3 So was the state of Rome..in the handes of Seneca a *Pedanti*. **1625** J. PHILLIPS *Way to Heaven* A iij b, Rated, as if it had beene a Schoole-boy, by some austere Pedantee. **1630** LENNARD tr. *Charron's Wisd.* (1658) 142 The Pedantie or houshold school master.

2. A company of pedants. *rare*[−1].

1641 MILTON *Animadv.* i. 56 You cite them to appeare.. before a capricious Pædantie of hot-liver'd Grammarians.

pedanterie, -ery, obs. forms of PEDANTRY.

pedantic (pɪ'dæntɪk), *a.* (*sb.*) [f. PEDANT or It. *pedante* + -IC. Of English formation: the corresp. It. adj. is *pedantesco*, F. *pédantesque*. So mod.G. *pedantisch*, Da. and Sw. *pedantisk*.] Having the character of, or characteristic of, a pedant; characterized by or exhibiting pedantry; exaggeratedly, unseasonably, or absurdly learned. (In first quot., pedagogic, schoolmasterly.)

?*c* **1600** DONNE *Sunne Rising* i, Busie old foole, unruly Sunne,..Sawcy pedantique wretch, goe chide Late schoole-boyes. *c* **1631** T. CAREW *On Death of Donne* 25 The Muses garden with Pedantique weeds O'rspread, was purg'd by thee. **1788** REID *Aristotle's Log.* vi. §1. 128 He was without pedantry even in that pedantic age. **1825** MACAULAY *Ess.*, *Milton* 1 He does not..sacrifice sense and spirit to pedantic refinements. **1855** MOTLEY *Dutch Rep.* III. i. (1866) 338 Rather a pedantic than a practical commander, more capable to discourse of battles than to gain them. **1871** R. ELLIS *Catullus* lvii. 7 Bookish brethren, a dainty pair pedantic.

†**B.** *sb.* A pedantic person, a pedant. *Obs.*

1607 R. C[AREW] tr. *Estienne's World of Wonders* V iij b, That proud pedanticke.., who promised immortalitie to those to whom he dedicated any of his works. **1658** FRANCK *North. Mem.* (1694) 27 This Age degenerates from Potentates to Pedanticks.

pe'dantical, *a.*[1] Now *rare.* [f. as prec. + -AL[1]: see -ICAL.] = PEDANTIC *a.* (Rare after 17th c.)

1588 SHAKS. *L.L.L.* v. ii. 406 Three pil'd hyperboles,.. Figures pedanticall. **1603** NORTH *Plutarch* (1676) 1003 This banished pedanticall companion Seneca (so did she [Agrippina] qualifie him). **1756** BURKE *Vind. Nat. Soc.* Wks. I. 29 Without a pedantical exactness. **1856** FROUDE *Hist. Eng.* I. iv. 301 Fisher..was weak, superstitious, pedantical; ..but he was a singlehearted man.

†**pe'dantical,** *a.*[2] *Obs. rare*[−1]. [f. after It. **pedante*, ppl. sb. from *pedare* 'to foot it' (Florio).] Travelling on foot, pedestrian.

1622 MALYNES *Anc. Law-Merch.* 53 A way one Road broad, is called a high-way for passengers Pedanticall.

pe'dantically, *adv.* [f. PEDANTICAL *a.*[1] + -LY[2].] In a pedantic manner; with pedantry.

1631 BRATHWAIT *Whimzies, Almanack-maker* 14 Some stolen shreads he hath raked out from the kennell of other authors which most pedantically he assumes to himselfe. **1838–9** HALLAM *Hist. Lit.* III. i. §7 A profusion of learning is scattered all round, but not pedantically or impertinently. **1860** EMERSON *Cond. Life, Fate* Wks. (Bohn) II. 314 'Tis frivolous to fix pedantically the date of particular inventions.

So **pe'danticalness.**

1668 WILKINS *Real Char.* II. viii. §2. 204 Narrowness, Pedanticalness, Littleness of Mind.

pedanticism (pɪ'dæntɪsɪz(ə)m). [f. PEDANTIC *a.* + -ISM.] A pedantic expression or notion; a piece of pedantry.

18.. *Portfolio* No. 235. 129 (Cent.) Perhaps, as Cuninghame suggests, Inigo's theory was simply an embodiment of some pedanticism of James I. **1897** *Naturalist* 270 Not so larmoyant..as the first-named pedanticism.

pe'danticly, *adv.* Now *rare.* [f. as prec. + -LY[2].] = PEDANTICALLY. So **pe'danticness.**

1647 H. MORE *Cupid's Conflict* xxxviii, What thou dost Pedanticly object Concerning my rude rugged uncouth style. **1653–4** WHITELOCKE *Jrnl. Swed. Emb.* (1772) I. 388 He spake latin fluently, butt not pedanticly. **1830** W. D. COOLEY *Marit. & Inl. Disc.* (1846) III. v. xviii. 274 He does not pedanticly shun theories.

1656 EARL MONM. tr. *Boccalini's Advts. fr. Parnass.* I. xxiii. 35 Moral Sciences..are reputed meere pædantickness.

pedantie: see PEDANTE *Obs.*

pedantism ('pɛdəntɪz(ə)m). Now *rare.* [f. PEDANT + -ISM. Perh. immediately a. F. *pédantisme* (Montaigne, 16th c., in Hatz.-Darm.).]

†**1.** The office or authority of a schoolmaster; the state of being under a schoolmaster or teacher, pupillage. Also *fig. Obs.*

1603 FLORIO *Montaigne* I. xxv. (1632) 78 The first fifteene or sixteene yeares of his life, are due unto Pedantisme, the rest unto action. **1611** COTGR., *Pedagogie*,..th' Office of a Teacher; also Pedantisme. **1651** BIGGS *New Disp.* ¶232 Nor have not since my pedantisme and junior practise in the medical profession. **1656** BLOUNT *Glossogr.*, *Pedantism*, the Office or Function of a Pedant. **1658** in PHILLIPS.

2. The character or style of a pedant; pedantic phraseology, treatment, or method; pedantry.

1593 NASHE *Four Lett. Confut.* Ep. Ded., Wks. (Grosart) II. 180 Loue poetry, hate pedantisme. **1628** FELTHAM *Resolves* II. xliv, They conversing onely among bookes, are put into affectation and pedantisme. **1879** FARRAR *St. Paul* I. 32 How unutterably frivolous this apotheosis of pedantism would appear to a serious-minded..Jew.

3. With *a* and *pl.* A piece of pedantry. †**a.** The proceeding of a pedant or dogmatic pedagogue; **b.** A pedantic expression or characteristic.

1656 J. HARRINGTON *Oceana* Wks. (1700) 59 To make a man..engage to believe no otherwise than is believ'd by my Lord Bishop, or Goodman Presbyter, is a Pedantism, that has made the Sword to be a Rod in the hands of School-masters. **1858** CARLYLE *Fredk. Gt.* VIII. i. (1872) III. 1 These confused Prussian History-Books, opulent in nugatory pedantisms and learned marine-stores.

pedantize ('pɛdəntaɪz), *v.* [f. as prec. + -IZE, or a. F. *pédantiser, -izer* (Cotgr.).]

1. *intr.* To play the pedant; to speak or write pedantically. Also *to pedantize it.*

1611 COTGR., *Pedantizer*, to pedantize it, or play the Pedant: to domineere ouer lads. **1657** J. SERGEANT *Schism*

Dispach't 8 That I..am a detestable person,..one of the ἄδικοι (as he pedantizes it). **1783** AINSWORTH *Thesaurus* (ed. Morell), To pedantize, or play the pedant, *literaturam ostentare, vel venditare*. **1862** *Sat. Rev.* 4 Jan. 22/1 To vegetate and pedantize on the classics.

2. *trans.* To turn into a pedant; to make pedants.

a **1734** NORTH *Lives* (1890) III. 89 That bare reading without practice, which pedantiseth a student but never makes him a clever lawyer. **1885** *Sat. Rev.* 18 July 88/2 The cramping and pedantizing influence of a pseudo-system.

pedantocracy (pɛdən'tɒkrəsɪ). [f. PEDANT + -OCRACY. App. first used in French form *pédantocratie* by J. S. Mill writing to Comte.] A system of government by pedants; a governing body of pedants. So **pedantocrat** (pɪ'dæntəʊkræt), a ruler who governs on pedantic principles; **pedanto'cratic** *a.*, characterized by 'pedantocracy'.

[**1842** MILL *Lett. à A. Comte* 25 Feb. (1899) 28 Il ne pourrait en résulter que ce qu'on voit dans la Chine, c'est-à-dire une *pédantocratie*. **1842** COMTE *Lett. to Mill* 4 Mar. ibid. 35 Votre heureuse expression de *pédantocratie*.] **1859** MILL *Liberty* v. 203 If we would not have our bureaucracy degenerate into a pedantocracy. **1872** FARRAR *Witn. Hist.* v. 184 A Pedantocracy of unpractical Philosophers. **1883** F. HARRISON in *Contemp. Rev.* Mar. 314 He [Gambetta] was not a corrupting pedantocrat like Guizot. **1886** MORLEY *Crit. Misc.* (1888) III. 214 The fastidious or pedantocratic school of government.

pedantry ('pɛdəntrɪ). Also 7 **pedanterie, -ery**. [ad. It. *pedanteria* (used by Sidney), f. *pedante*; or its F. repr. *pédanterie* (Pasquier, 1560 in Hatz.-Darm.): see PEDANT and -ERY, -RY.]

1. The character, habit of mind, or mode of proceeding, characteristic of a pedant; mere learning without judgement or discrimination; conceit or unseasonable display of learning or technical knowledge.

1612 DONNE *Progr. Soul* ii. 291 When wilt thou shake off this pedantery Of being taught by sense and fantasie? **1646** SIR T. BROWNE *Pseud. Ep.* I. vi. 24 A practise that savours much of Pedantery. **1710** STEELE *Tatler* No. 224 ¶7 Pedantry proceeds from much Reading and little Understanding. **1766** FORDYCE *Serm. Yng. Wom.* (1767) I. vii. 298 That men are frighted at Female pedantry is very certain. **1802–25** SYD. SMITH *Ess.* (ed. Beeton) 95 Pedantry is an ostentatious obtrusion of knowledge, in which those who hear us cannot sympathise. **1841** D'ISRAELI *Amen. Lit.* (1867) 100 The pedantry of mixing Greek and Latin terms in the vernacular language is ridiculed by Rabelais.

b. with *pl.* An instance of this: a piece of pedantry, a pedantic form, expression, etc.

1581 SIDNEY *Apol. Poetrie* (Arb.) 19 Skill of gouernment, was but a Pedanteria in comparison. **1656** BLOUNT *Glossogr.*, *Pedanteries*, pedantick humors, phrase affectings, Inkhorn terms. *Br.* **1778** WARTON *Hist. Eng. Poetry* xxv. II. 133 The narrow pedantries of monastic erudition. **1864** BURTON *Scot Abr.* I. i. 19 A series of feudal pedantries.

2. Undue insistence on forms or details; slavish adherence to rule, theory, or precedent, in connexion with a particular profession or practice.

[**1724** SWIFT *Drapier's Lett.* v, The pedantry of a drapier in the terms of his own trade.] **1845** S. AUSTIN *Ranke's Hist. Ref.* III. 124 Even Erasmus, spite of the favour he enjoyed at court, found no mercy from monkish pedantry. **1863** P. BARRY *Dockyard Econ.* 119 He who slavishly adheres to rule displays pedantry at every turn. *a* **1869** VISCT. STRANGFORD *Sel. Writ.* I. 92 Pedantry, we take it, signifies undue stress laid on insignificant detail, and over-valuation of petty accuracy. **1902** FAIRBAIRN *Philos. Chr. Relig.* II. ii. 410 To require that every element in a figurative word be found again in the reality it denotes, is not exegesis but pedantry.

† **pe'danty.** *Obs. rare*⁻¹. [ad. It. type **pedante* from *pedare* to foot it (Florio).] '? Running footman' (Latham).

1606 WARNER *Alb. Eng.* XIV. xci. 369 For most, like Iehu, hurrie with Pedanties two or three.

pedanty: see PEDANTE *Obs.*

pedarian (pɪ'dɛərɪən), *a.* and *sb. Rom. Antiq.* [f. L. *pedāri-us* of or belonging to a foot, of a foot long, also in *pedarii senatores* (see below); f. *ped-em* foot: see -ARY¹ and -AN.]

a. *adj.* Applied to Roman senators of an inferior grade, who 'had no vote of their own, but could merely signify their assent to that of another'. **b.** *sb.* A pedarian senator.

The reason of the appellation is not rightly known: see the Latin Dictionaries.

1753 CHAMBERS *Cycl. Supp.*, *Pedarian*, in antiquity, those senators who signified their votes by their feet, not their tongues; that is, such as walked over to the side of those whose opinion they approved of, in divisions of the house.

† **'pedary,** *a.* (*sb.*) *Obs. rare.* [ad. L. *pedārius*: see prec. and -ARY¹.]

1. Of or relating to a foot or to the feet; in quot. used absol. or ellipt. with pl. = A pardon or indulgence for a pilgrim (who had vowed to perform a pilgrimage on foot).

1537 tr. *Latimer's Serm. bef. Convoc.* D j b, Some brought forth Canonizations,..some pardons and these of wonderful varietie, some Stationaries, some Iubilaryes, some Pocularyes for drinkers, some manuaries for handlers of reliques, some pedaries for pilgrimes, some oscularies for kyssers.

2. *Rom. Antiq.* = PEDARIAN *a.*

1598 GRENEWEY *Tacitus, Ann.* III. xiv. (1622) 84 Also many pedary Senators rose vp & stroue, who should propound things most base and abiect.

3. *fig.* Second-class, second-rate, inferior.

1657 W. MORICE *Coena quasi Κοινή* Def. xi. 128 All the School (*omnes qui de hac re meminerunt*—saith no pedary schoolman) [Vasquez].

pedate ('pɛdət), *a. Nat. Hist.* [ad. L. *pedāt-us* having feet, f. *ped-em* foot: see -ATE².]

1. Having divisions like toes, or like the claws of a bird's foot; *spec.* in *Bot.* applied to a compound or lobed leaf having a slender midrib passing through the central leaflet or lobe, and two thicker lateral ribs which branch at successive points to form the several midribs of the lateral leaflets or lobes (instead of these all arising from a common central point as in a *palmate* leaf). Applied also to the venation of a simple leaf when thus arranged. Also † **pedated** (in same sense).

1753 CHAMBERS *Cycl. Supp.*, Botany Table 2, Distinctions of the Leaves..of Plants..Pedated. **1760** J. LEE *Introd. Bot.* II. xxxi. (1765) 152 *Arum*, with pedate Leaves. **1835** LINDLEY *Introd. Bot.* (1848) II. 359. **1857** HENFREY *Bot.* §95 *Palmate* (or *digitate*) leaves are such as have a number of distinct leaflets arising from one point... The only true modification appears to be the *pedate* leaf, analogous to the pedatisect simple leaf, but with distinct leaflets. **1895** KERNER & OLIVER *Nat. Hist. Plants* Index, Pedate venation.

2. *Zool.* Furnished with or having feet, footed.

1816 KIRBY & SP. *Entomol.* xxii. (1818) II. 272 Two classes..*Apodous* larvæ,..or those that move without legs,—and *Pedate* larvæ,..that move by means of legs. **1826** *Ibid.* xlvii. IV. 365 In proportion as pedate animals approach to the human type, their motions are accomplished by fewer organs.

3. *Anat.* Expanded (at the end) like a foot.

1870 ROLLESTON *Anim. Life* 27 (Common Fowl). The similarly-expanded, or 'pedate' extremity of the external hyposternal process overlaps the posterior sternal ribs.

Hence **'pedately** *adv.*, in a pedate manner.

1821 S. F. GRAY *Nat. Arrangem. Brit. Pl.* 71 [Leaves] pedately cut. **1870** HOOKER *Stud. Flora* 10 Helleborus... Leaves palmately, pedately or digitately lobed.

pedati-, combining form of L. *pedātus* PEDATE, in botanical terminology in adjs. relating to leaves: **pedatifid** (pɪ'dætɪfɪd) [L. *-fidus* split], pedately cleft or divided at least half-way to the base; **pedatiform** (pɪ'dætɪfɔːm), approaching a pedate form, or having the ribs pedately arranged; **pedati'lobate, pe'datilobed** (pɪdeɪtɪ-), pedately divided with rounded divisions or lobes; **pe'datinerved** (pɪ'deɪtɪ-), having the nerves or ribs pedately arranged; **pedati'partite** (pɪdeɪtɪ-) [see PARTITE], pedately divided nearly to the base; so **pe'datisect, pedati'sected** (pɪdeɪtɪ-) [L. *sectus* cut].

1793 MARTYN *Lang. Bot.*, *Pedatifidum folium*, a pedatifid leaf..the parts of the leaf not being separate; but connected, as in the feet of water fowl. **1857** HENFREY *Bot.* §93 The general prefix *pedati-* may be used in the words *pedatifid*, *pedatisect*, or *pedatipartite*. **1857** MAYNE *Expos. Lex.*, Pedatifid,..pedatilobate,..pedatipartite,..pedatisected. **1866** *Treas. Bot.* 855 *Pedate*, *Pedatifid*,..*pedatiform*,..*pedatilobed*, or *pedatilobate*,..*pedatinerved*,..*pedatipartite*, or *pedatisect*, when a pedate leaf has segments separated into so many distinct leaflets.

pe'dation. *rare.* [In sense 1, ad. L. *pedātiōn-em*, n. of action f. *pedāre* to furnish with feet or props; in sense 2, n. of condition f. *pedāt-us* PEDATE.]

† **1.** (See quot.) *Obs.*

1656 BLOUNT *Glossogr.*, *Pedation*, a staking, propping or setting up of vines. **1658** in PHILLIPS.

2. *Zool.* Condition as to feet. (Cf. *dentition.*)

1857 MAYNE *Expos. Lex.*, *Pedatio*, term employed by Fabricius to denote the manner in which the feet of insects are developed, the number of articulated pieces.., the form of the different parts [etc.]: pedation.

† **'pedature.** *Obs. rare*⁻⁰. [ad. L. *pedātūra* space or extent of a foot, f. *ped-em* foot.]

1656 BLOUNT *Glossogr.*, *Pedature* (*pedatura*), a proportion of digging, building, etc. of so many foot assigned to Souldiers or workmen. Hence in PHILLIPS.

† **,peddela'potecary.** *Obs. rare*⁻¹. [? f. PEDDLE *v.*] ? A peddling apothecary, an intinerant medicine-vendor.

1561 HOLLYBUSH *Hom. Apoth.* 17 b, I my selfe haue sene a strange peddelapotecary minister to the commun people, that two or thre dyed of it.

peddelar, obs. form of PEDLAR.

pedder ('pɛdə(r)). Now *Sc.* and *dial.* Forms: 3 **peoddare**, 4–6 (9 *dial.*) **pedder**, 5 **ped(d)are**, **peder**, 8 **peddar**, 9 *dial.* **pether**, **-ur**. [app. a derivative of PED, pannier, basket, although *ped* has not yet been found so early. Cf. also PEDLAR.] One who carried about goods for sale (? in a 'ped' or pack); a pedlar. (But in one MS. of *Promp. Parv.* app. 'a maker of panniers, a basket-maker'.)

a **1225** *Ancr. R.* 66 Þe wreche peoddare more noise he makeð to ȝeien his sope, þen a riche mercer al his deorewurðe ware. *c* **1380** WYCLIF *Wks.* (1880) 12 Pedderis berynge.. precious pellure and forrouris for wymmen. **14..** *Nom.* in Wr.-Wülcker 685/18 *Hic revelus*, a peder. *c* **1440** *Promp. Parv.* 389/2 Peddare, *calatharius* (K. *qui facit calathos*), *quaxillarius*, *quassillarius*,..(P. *piscarius*). *c* **1440** *Jacob's Well* 41 Fullerys, mercerys, grocerys, vynterys, pedderys, owyn to payin þe tythe of here getyng þe here craft. **1483** *Cath. Angl.* 272/2 A Pedder (*A.* A Pedare or A Pedlare), *revolus*, *negociator*. **1513** DOUGLAS *Æneis* VIII. Prol. 55 The pirat pressis to peyll the pedder his pak. **1597** SKENE *De Verb. Sign.* s.v. *Pede-pulverosus*, Ane pedder, is called an marchand, or creamer, quha bearis ane pack or creame vpon his back. **1764** *J. Kirby's Suffolk Trav.* (ed. 2) 53 It is no unusual thing for Peddars to attend the Tides regularly, receive and pack up the Fish, on the common Key. **1807** HOGG *Mountain Bard* 188 To guard the door, An' bark at pethers, boys, an' whips. *a* **1825** FORBY *Voc. E. Anglia*, *Pedder*, one who carries wares in a *ped*, pitches it in open market, and sells from it. **1825** BROCKETT *N.C. Gloss.*, *Pedder*, *Pether*,..a pedlar—a travelling merchant.

b. *Comb.*, as ***pedder-coffe*** (COFE *sb.* 2), **-*man*.**

c **1550** LYNDESAY (*title*) Ane Discriptioun of Peder Coffeis, having na regaird till honestie in thair vocatioun. *Ibid.* 3 This hole perfyte genologie Of pedder knavis superlatyve. **1552** HULOET, Pedderman, *institor*. **1820** SCOTT *Monast.* xxxv, The pedder-coffe who travels the land.

peddle ('pɛd(ə)l), *v.* [Of obscure history: probably I and II are historically distinct words.

Branch I (exemplified 1532 in PEDDLING *ppl. a.*) was app. a back-formation from *pedler*, PEDLAR, taken as *peddl-er* implying a verb *peddle*. Branch II (1597–8 in PEDDLING *ppl. a.*) appears to be an alteration of PIDDLE *v.* (evidenced from 1545). The two seem subsequently to have acted upon each other, esp. in the derivatives. In both branches a derivative in *-ing* is known much earlier than the finite verb; cf. the relation of *gardening*, *tailoring*, formed on the sbs., to the rare finite vbs. *to garden*, *to tailor*.]

I. 1. *intr.* To follow the occupation of a pedlar; to go about carrying small wares for sale.

1532 [see PEDDLING *ppl. a.* 1]. **1591** [see PEDDLING *vbl. sb.* 1]. **1650** TRAPP *Comm. Lev.* xix. 16 As a pedlar that first fil's his pack with reports and rumors, and then go's pedling up and down. **1651** OGILBY *Æsop* (1665) 30 To deal with those [that] bear packs and peddle. **1712** ARBUTHNOT *John Bull* II. iv, To go hawking and peddling about the streets, selling knives, scissars, and shoe-buckles. **1791–1823** D'ISRAELI *Cur. Lit.*, *The Rump*, The most innocent..those whose talents had been limited by Nature to peddle and purloin.

2. *trans.* To trade or deal in as a pedlar; to carry about and offer for sale. Chiefly *U.S.*

1837 HAWTHORNE *Twice-T. T.* (1851) I. xvi. 249 Going to peddle out a lot of huckleberries. **1856** OLMSTED *Slave States* 630 Many negroes were in town, peddling eggs, nuts, brooms, and fowls. **1866** WHITTIER *Snow-bound* 455 To peddle wares from town to town. **1880** L. OLIPHANT *Gilead* ix. 281 He had peddled sacred relics through Russia.

b. *fig.* To deal out, or offer for acceptance, in small quantities; to 'retail'.

1837 EMERSON *Amer. Scholar* Wks. (Bohn) II. 175 This original unit..has been so minutely subdivided and peddled out. **1864** BOWLES in *Century Mag.* (1889) Sept. 703/2 Going around peddling his griefs in private ears. **1892** A. BIRRELL *Res Judic.* v. 132 The usual fortune of those who peddle new ideas.

II. 3. *intr.* To busy oneself with trifles; to work at something in a trifling, paltry, or petty way; to trifle, dally. (Cf. PIDDLE.)

1597–8 [see PEDDLING *ppl. a.* 2]. **1755** JOHNSON, *To Peddle*, *v.n.* To be busy about trifles... It is commonly written *piddle*. **1812** WELLINGTON in Gurw. *Desp.* VIII. 658 The court of Directors must be prevented from meddling with or peddling in the discipline of the Army. **1865** LOWELL *Ode Harvard Commem.* ii, No science peddling with the names of things..Can lift our life with wings Far from Death's idle gulf. **1867** J. HATTON *Tallants of B.* xv, It doesn't suit me to be peddling about in the old style of farming. **1877** SYMONDS *Renaiss. It.* vi. 367 Coteries..peddling with the idlest of all literary problems.

b. *trans.* with *away*: To fritter away on trifles.

1880 JEFFERIES *Hodge & M.* I. 290 The squire's time.. was peddled away.

peddler: see PEDLAR.

peddling ('pɛdlɪŋ), *vbl. sb.* [See PEDDLE *v.* and -ING¹.] The action of the verb PEDDLE.

1. The occupation of a pedlar; the carrying about of small goods for sale. ***peddling out***, dealing out or retailing in petty quantities.

1591 PERCIVALL *Sp. Dict.*, *Regatonia*, pedling, buying of small wares. **1688** J. CLAYTON in *Phil. Trans.* XVII. 792 The best of Trade that can be driven is only a sort of Scotch Pedling. **1760** C. JOHNSTON *Chrysal* (1822) II. 109 That lower species of trade called Pedling. **1862** TROLLOPE *Orley F.* vi, I call it hawking and peddling, that going round the country with your goods on your back. It ain't trade. **1898** KIPLING *Fleet in Being* ii. 22 A slow peddling-out of Admiralty allowance for the month.

attrib. **1641** EVELYN *Diary* 8 Oct., Little wagons..full of peddling merchandises, drawne by mastive-dogs. *a* **1697** AUBREY *Nat. Hist. Surrey* (1719) III. 227 Here are two Fairs, viz. on September 12th, and Whit-Tuesday; (a Pedling Fair). **1870** MORRIS *Earthly Par.* I. II. 515 Neither on peddling voyage am I come.

b. *concr.* Pedlars' wares; small goods. *nonce-use.*

1737 JAS. MURRAY *Lett.* (1901) 37 We..send our peddling to..the neighbouring colonies, for which we have European or other goods at their price.

† **c.** ***peddling French*** = pedlar's French (PEDLAR 4 b). *Obs.*

? *a* **1550** *Hye Way to Spyttel Hous* 1054 in Hazl. *E.P.P.* IV. 69 Thus they babble,.. I wote not wheder theyr pedlyng frenche.

2. The action of dealing with trifles, or in a paltry trifling way. (Cf. PIDDLING *vbl. sb.*)

1868 FARRAR *Seekers* Concl. (1875) 332 The 'moral peddling', the pedagogic display.. we have had to point out. **1899** *Allbutt's Syst. Med.* VIII. 120 What can be done quickly and thoroughly will probably be beneficial, and prolonged peddling the reverse.

ˈpeddling, *ppl. a.* [See PEDDLE *v.* + -ING².]

1. Of persons: Plying the trade of a pedlar; going about with small goods for sale.

1532 MORE *Confut. Tindale* Wks. 639/2 Yet se we wel ynough how gredely the pedelyng knaues that here bring ouer theire bookes, grispe aboute an halfepeny. **1662** J. DAVIES tr. *Olearius's Voy. Ambass.* 24 There was a passage.. from the Castle to the Church, along which came first several pedling Merchants, who sold wax Candles. **1728** MORGAN *Algiers* Pref. 11 The peddling Traders; which the wealthy Dons deem Interlopers. **1834** JAMES *J. Marston Hall* xii, I began conversing with him as a peddling Jew.

2. a. Of persons: Busying oneself with trifles, or in a trifling way; occupied with petty details, or characterized by such occupation. **b.** Of things: Of small consequence; trifling, contemptible, petty, mean, paltry, trashy. (Cf. PIDDLING *ppl. a.*)

1597–8 BP. HALL *Sat.* II. iii. 25 Since pedling barbarismes gan be in request. **1613** PURCHAS *Pilgrimage* (1614) 274 Threescore and eight sects of name, besides other pedling factions. **1693** *Apol. Clergy Scot.* 37 Our Pedling little Reformers. **1759** FRANKLIN *Ess.* Wks. 1840 III. 500 The province was to receive it in so pedling a way, as rendered it in a manner useless. **1828** *Craven Gloss.* (ed. 2), *Peddling*, trifling, of little value. **1845** CARLYLE *Cromwell* (1871) I. 1 Poor peddling Dilettantism. **1885** CLODD *Myths & Dr.* I. i. 9 We find place given to inane peddling details.

Hence **ˈpeddlingly** *adv.*, in a peddling way.

1892 *Graphic* 22 Oct. 478/3 A Minister who..is peddlingly unambitious.

pede (piːd). [f. L. *pēs, ped-em* foot: cf. It. *piede*.] A foot or base. Only *attrib.* as in **pede-cloth**, an altar-carpet; **pede-window**, a term formerly applied to the west window of a cruciform church (being at the foot of the cross).

1842 *Ecclesiologist* I. 209 Two specimens of a *pede cloth* or Altar carpet. **1846** *Ibid.* V. 187 It struck us that lychnoscopes help to explain, and were themselves explained by, pede-windows. **1870** ROCK *Text. Fabr.* I. 66 A carpet.. for covering the top of the higher step at the altar, called by some a pede-cloth.

pedee, pedie (ˈpiːdiː). *Obs.* exc. *dial.* Also 7 paddee, pedee, pedy, 7–9 peedee (ˌpiːˈdiː), 9 P.D. [Derivation uncertain: several early writers associate the word with L. *pēs, pedem* foot, *pede* on foot.] A serving-lad, footboy, groom; in 19th c., on the River Tyne, the boy on board a keel.

1642 LD. ESSEX in *Antiq. Rep.* (1807) I. 391 No Trooper ..shall suffer his Paddee to feed his Horse in the Corne, or to steale men's hay. **1646** *Sc. Acts Chas. I*, VI. 233/2 No allowance..is to bee given..for the tenth man, or the Pediese or Boys and Horse. **1658** J. JONES tr. *Ovid's Ibis* 160 *note*, Who can blame Dolon, a poor Pedee, for adventuring his life for Gold? **1661** BLOUNT *Glossogr.* (ed. 2), *Pedee* (from *pes*), a (commanders) Foot-boy. **1676** W. ROW *Contn. Blair's Autobiog.* x. (1848) 160 About 30,000 men beside boys, pedies, lackies, &c. **1706** PHILLIPS, *Pedee*, an ordinary Foot-boy, a Drudge; as 'What must I be your Pedee upon all Occasions?' ? *a* **1800** in Gilchrist *Songs* (1824) 11 So P.D. and his marrow were e'en pawk'd ashore. **1825** BROCKETT *N.C. Gloss.*, *Pee-dee*, a young lad in a keel, who has charge of the rudder. **1863** in *Tyneside Songs* 6 Wor blagaired lad, the young Pee Dee. **1894** HESLOP *Northumbld. Gloss.* s.v., The crew of a keel consisted of the skipper, two bullies, and the pee-dee, who was generally a boy from twelve to fourteen years old.

b. *Comb.*, as *pedee-solicitor*.

1675 A. HUYBERTS *Corner-Stone* 3 A junior Doctor of the gang they employed to be their Pedee-Solicitor.

†**ˈpedegorize,** *v. Obs. rare*⁻¹. [app. rudely f. *pedegre*, PEDIGREE *sb.* + -IZE.] To make a pedigree; to derive through a pedigree.

1665 SIR T. HERBERT *Trav.* 135 Abuzvez Deilamshaw,.. the hundredth in descent from Adam as they pedegorize.

pedegre(e, -grewe, -grow, etc., obs. ff. PEDIGREE *sb.*

pedel, pedeler: see PEDAILE, PEDLAR.

†**pedelion.** *Herb. Obs.* Also 6 patedelion, 6–7 padelion, -lyon. [a. F. *pied* (or †*pié*) *de lion* 'Lions foot, Lions paw, Ladies mantle,..Padelion' (Cotgr.). Also F. *pas de lion* in same sense, and *patte de lion* 'Bastard blacke Ellebore, Beares-foot, Setterwort..also, as *Pied de lion*' (Cotgr.); Littré has *pied de lion* and *patte de lion* both as = *alchémille*, lady's mantle.] A name of certain plants: **a.** Black Hellebore; **b.** ? *Leontopodium*; **c.** Lady's Mantle: cf. *lion's foot, lion's paw*, LION *sb.* 11 b.

14.. *Stockh. Med. MS.* i. 108 in *Anglia* XVIII. 297 Late take a gres..þat men clepe pedelyoun. ? **1516** *Grete Herball* clviii. K ij b, *De elleboro nigro*, Pedelyon, or lyons fote. **1578** LYTE *Dodoens* I. xcviii. 140 The latter wryters do call this herbe in..Latin *Achimilla*,..*Pes leonis*..in English Ladies mantell,..Padelion. **1589** J. RIDER *Lat. Dict.* 1751 An hearb called patedelion or pied de lion... *Leontopodium.* **1597** GERARDE *Herbal* App., Pedelion is *Helleborus niger.* **1611** COTGR., *Pied de Lion*, Lions foot, Lions paw, Ladies mantle, ..Padelion. **1640** PARKINSON *Theat. Bot.* 538 We in English [call it] Padelyon, after the French. **1864** PRIOR *Plant-n.* (1879) 175 *Padelion*,..from the resemblance of its leaf to the impress of a lion's foot, the lady's mantle.

pedement, obs. form of PEDIMENT.

†**ˈpedera, ˈpederote.** *Obs.* [cf. obs. It. *pedero, pederitti, pederite* the opal.] Old names of the opal.

1585 T. WASHINGTON tr. *Nicholay's Voy.* IV. xi. 123 b, In this place are also found..the Pederote, which Plinie calleth Opalius. **1610** W. FOLKINGHAM *Art of Survey* I. iii. 5 The purple Amethyst, greene Emerauldes, and Opall Pederas.

pederast, etc.: see PÆDERAST, etc.

pederero, variant of PEDRERO, a small gun.

†**ˈpedescript.** *nonce-word.* [f. L. *pede* with the foot + *scriptum* written, writing; after *manuscript*.] Something written by the foot; humorously used for the imprints of kicking.

1652 SHIRLEY *Honoria & Mammon* IV. i, I tell you, sir, *verbatim*: for a need, I have it all in pedescript.

pedeshaw, obs. from of PADISHAH.

‖**pedesis** (pɪˈdiːsɪs). [a. Gr. πήδησις leaping.] A name given by Prof. Jevons to the *Brownian movement* of minute particles: see BROWNIAN *a.*

1878 JEVONS in *Q. Jrnl. Sc.* Apr. 170/1 Some writers have called it the Brownian movement... I have ventured to coin ..a new word, and call the motion *pedesis*, from Gr. πήδησις leaping or bounding. **1892** *Nature* XLV. 430/1 The fact that pedesis is stopped by the addition of an electrolyte would appear to indicate that the water complices are disintegrated in the presence of ions.

pedestal (ˈpɛdɪstəl), *sb.* Forms: α. 6– pedestal (also 6 -alle, -ale, pettestale, 6–7 pedestall, 7 -estell, -istal). β. 6–8 peidestal(l, 7 piedstal(l, -stoole, piedistal. [ad. F. *piédestal* (1547 in Hatz.-Darm.), ad. It. *piedestallo*, †*piedistallo*, i.e. *pie di stallo* foot of a stall, 'the base of any frame or engine' (Florio 1611), f. *piè, piede* foot + *stallo* stall, hovel, shed, stable. In Eng. *piéd-* became *ped-*, conformed to L. *ped-em* foot.]

1. a. The base supporting a column or pillar in construction; the base on which an obelisk, statue, vase, or the like is erected; also, each of the two supports of a knee-hole writing-table, usually containing drawers.

α. **1563** SHUTE *Archit.* C ij b, If ye will set Stylobata, or Pedestal, vnder your pillor,..you shall make a foure square, ..one ende shalbe the height of the square or body of the Pedestall. *Ibid.*, Thus endeth the Pedestale or Stylobata. **1589** PUTTENHAM *Eng. Poesie* II. xi. (Arb.) 110 The Piller.. is considered with two accessarie parts, a pedestall or base, and a chapter or head; the body is the shaft. **1599** DALLAM *Trav.* (Hakl. Soc.) 63 Tow rankes of marble pillors; the pettestales of them ar made of brass. **1663** GERBIER *Counsel* 30 It seldom happens that a Pedestal is put to the Tuscan Order. **1703** MAUNDRELL *Journ. Jerus.* (1707) 20 This serv'd for a Pedestal to a Throne erected upon it. **1718** LADY M. W. MONTAGU *Let. to C'tess Bristol* 10 Apr., An obelisk..is placed..upon a pedestal of square free-stone, full of figures in bas-relief on two sides. **1845** PARKER *Gloss. Archit.* (ed. 4), *Pedestal* or *Footstall*, a substructure frequently placed under columns in Classical architecture. **1866** CARLYLE in *Mrs. C's Lett.* III. 254, I have discovered in drawers of pedestal these mournful letters. **1879** SIR G. SCOTT *Lect. Archit.* I. 87 The singular ornamentation of the pedestal or basement of the doorways.

β. **1580** HOLLYBAND *Treas. Fr. Tong*, *Piedestal d'vne colomne*, the foote of a piller, a piedestall. **1603** HOLLAND *Plutarch's Mor.* 1277 Little statues upon great bases and large piedstals. **1792** *Resid. in France* (1797) I. 348 His bust erected on the piedestal.

b. Used *fig.* in phr. *to put* (or *place*, etc.) *on a pedestal*, to regard as highly admirable or important; to accord an important place to; to exalt or magnify.

1859 [see SEAT *v.* 1 a *fig.*]. **1882** R. L. STEVENSON *Familiar Stud. Men & Bks.* 158 This is to put friendship on a pedestal indeed. **1916** G. B. SHAW *Pygmalion* 205 She wishes she could get him alone..and just drag him off his pedestal and see him making love like any common man. **1922** JOYCE *Ulysses* 638 They discovered..that their idol had feet of clay, after placing him upon a pedestal. **1930** A. ROOSEVELT in H. Powell *Last Paradise* p. xiii, In the United States we are so used to work that we can't conceive of life without it. We have placed work on a pedestal. It is our God. **1957** D. ROBINS *Noble One* xvi. 152 He had unconsciously put her on a pedestal. **1968** *Listener* 3 Oct. 440/3 When somebody becomes prime minister they're immediately put on a pedestal... Well, Ramsay fell off his pedestal. **1975** *Ibid.* 18 Dec. 815/1 The doctor is on a pedestal? Yes, unapproachable, because his expertise sets him apart.

2. a. A base, support, foundation (material or immaterial).

1591 SYLVESTER *Du Bartas* I. iii. 1027 Heav'n's chastest Spouse, supporter of this All, This glorious Building's goodly Pedestall. **1638** DRUMM. OF HAWTH. *Irene* Wks. (1711) 165 Obedience being the strongest pedestal of concord, and concord the principal pillar of state. **1649** JER. TAYLOR *Gt. Exemp.* I. Disc. iv. 120 Self-denial and Mortification, which are the Pedestal of the Crosse. **1742** YOUNG *Nt. Th.* VIII. 492 Fain would he make the world his pedestal. **1847** EMERSON *Repr. Men, Uses* Wks. (Bohn) I. 276 The true artist has the planet for his pedestal; the adventurer..has nothing broader than his own shoes.

b. Humorously applied to the foot or leg.

1812 SIR R. WILSON *Priv. Diary* I. 13, I wish my fairer countrywomen would..adopt the exterior neatness, even if nature should not..be as gracious in moulding the shape of the pedestal. **1827** *Mirror* II. 387/1 My now knock-knee pedestals bend to the bandy.

3. In technical uses: †**a.** On a railway, the 'chair' used to support the rails, or a base to support the chair (*obs.*); **b.** an axle-guard or horn-plate; **c.** the standard or each of the standards or supports of various machines or pieces of mechanism, e.g. the upright standard of a boring-machine or similar tool, that of a pillow-block which holds the brasses in which the shaft turns, etc.

1774 M. MACKENZIE *Maritime Surv.* iv. 43 Set the Brass Pedestal on a firm Support... Then hang the Quadrant on the Pillar, and by the Spirit-level and Screws in the Feet, the Pillar may be set perpendicular. **1816** *Specif. of Losh & Stephenson's Patent* No. 4067. 2 The joinings of the rails with the pedestals or props which support them. **1825** J. NICHOLSON *Operat. Mechanic* 653 A chair is..placed on a pedestal at every three or four feet distance,..according to the length of the cast iron rails. **1835** *Mech. Mag.* XXIII. 228 The pedestal for the joint..to be fastened to the sleeper with cotter bolts. **1874** KNIGHT *Dict. Mech.* 202/1 *Axle-guard*, one of the pedestals in which the boxes of an axle play vertically as the springs yield and recoil. **1896** *Heal & Son Catal.: Bedsteads, etc.* 170 Wash-stand.., Chamber Pedestal, Towel Horse. **1959** W. S. SHARPS *Dict. Cinematogr.* 116 *Pedestal*, a simple vertical support for a film projector. **1960** O. SKILBECK *ABC of Film & TV* 95 *Pedestal*, a simple, high Dolly, used in T.V. **1961** G. MILLERSON *Technique Television Production* iii. 23 A one-man camera mounting, the pedestal has high manoeuvrability. *Ibid.* 24 The pedestal column is telescopic. **1971** *Nature* 9 July 98/1 The fines were mounted on the electron microscope pedestal with a drop of absolute methanol. **1975** J. RATHBONE *Kill Cure* I. iv. 32 The cracked W.C. pedestal did not bear looking into.

d. *Television.* The level of the video signal voltage during line blanking; also, this part of the signal.

1937 *Electronics* June 15/2 From the shading panel the signal goes to a control amplifier where the pedestal level is set. This pedestal is a voltage level corresponding to black, or slightly 'blacker than black', on which the synchronizing impulses are placed and which exists throughout the return trace of the cathode beam. **1951** R. B. DOME *Television Princ.* ix. 214 The width of the horizontal synchronizing pulse is approximately half the width of its pedestal. **1956** M. SLURZBERG et al. *Essent. Television* ii. 24 The blanking signal is often referred to as a pedestal on which the synchronizing pulses are mounted. **1972** F. H. BELT *How to interpret T.V. Waveforms* 101 Video looks okay at first glance, although actually it's compressed a bit at the black end (up near where the sync pedestals should be). Also, blanking (the sync pedestal) appears widened.

4. *attrib.* and *Comb.*, as ***pedestal base, cupboard, -dance, -dancer, dancing, desk, trunk***; **pedestal-box**, a journal-box (*Cent. Dict.* 1890); **pedestal-coil, -coiler**, an upright coil of steam pipe for use as a radiator (*Funk's Stand. Dict.* 1895); **pedestal-cover**, the cap of a pillow-block; **pedestal mat**, a mat which fits around the base of a lavatory pedestal; **pedestal-rail** (*Naut.*), see quot.; **pedestal table**, one with a massive central support or foot; also used of other types of table; also ***pedestal writing table***; **pedestal vase**, a vase with a pedestal base; **pedestal (wash) basin**, a wash basin with a single columnar support.

1948 A. LANE *Greek Pott.* ii. 9 Wide and shallow with *pedestal bases. **1978** *N.Y. Times* 30 Mar. B21/9 (Advt.), Pedestal base dining tables. **1967** J. MORRISON in *Coast to Coast 1965–66* 140 There was no *pedestal basin and no tap. **1875** KNIGHT *Dict. Mech.* 1704/2 (figure of Pillow-Block), *c.* *pedestal-cover. **1896** *Heal & Son Catal.: Bedsteads, etc.* 194 *Pedestal Cupboard. **1959** G. SAVAGE *Antique Collector's Handbk.* 122 Pedestal cupboards, surmounted by urns, appear quite frequently. **1895** *Daily News* 23 Jan. 6/7 The fancy trick and burlesque bicycle act and *pedestal dance. *Ibid.*, On the authorised printed programme..the Dunedin Troupe were duly put down for two performances as bicyclists, and Mdlle. Donegan..as a *pedestal dancer. **1906** *Daily Chron.* 12 Mar. 7/1 Mrs. Lannon said *pedestal dancing was not a speciality, but they had introduced it. **1952** J. GLOAG *Short Dict. Furnit.* 353 Small *pedestal desks were introduced early in the 18th century. **1957** V. NABOKOV *Pnin* iii. 69 It [*sc.* a room] had come with two ignoble chairs..and a humble pedestal desk of indeterminable wood. **1970** *Country Life* 1 Oct. (Suppl.) 48B/1 A very fine quality Hepplewhite mahogany Pedestal Desk with bow front and dummy drawers. **1962** *Guardian* 5 Dec. 6/3 Matching bathroom sets..bath mat, *pedestal mat, lavatory seat cover. **1972** *Ibid.* 23 Feb. 18/5 Matching bathmats..pedestal mats, and loo seat covers. *c* **1850** *Rudim. Navig.* (Weale) 136 **Pedestal-rail*, a rail about 2 inches thick, that is wrought over the foot-space rail, and in which there is a groove to steady the heels of the balusters of the galleries. **1939** *Army & Navy Stores Catal.* 1032 Bedside *pedestal table..With half door..or full door. *Ibid.*, Kidney Shape Pedestal Table, fitted with six drawers. **1952** J. GLOAG *Short Dict. Furnit.* 355 *Pedestal table*, a term sometimes used for round, oval, square, or rectangular tables that are supported by a single pillar or column which rests upon a stabilising base. **1966** M. M. PEGLER *Dict. Interior Design* (1967) 329 The pedestal table is also a popular modern design with the table surface resting on a thin support which flares outward as it reaches the floor. **1975** *Habitat Catal.* 35 Pedestal table. Spun aluminium base..melamine laminate top. **1856** OLMSTED *Slave States* 383 Cypresses, with great *pedestal trunks, and protuberant roots. **1960** K. M. Kenyon *Archaeol. in Holy Land* vii. 171 Neither *pedestal vases.. nor flaring carinated bowls.. are found. **1967** *Gloss. Sanitation Terms (B.S.I.)* 62 **Pedestal wash basin*, a wash basin supported from the floor by a column-shaped base. **1883** *Heal & Son Catal.: Bedsteads, etc.* 193 *Pedestal Writing Table,.. Leather Top.

ˈpedestal, *v.* [f. prec. sb.]

1. *trans.* To set or support upon a pedestal; to furnish with a pedestal. *lit.* and *fig.*

1648 Earl of Westmoreland *Otia Sacra* (1879) 77 All the fabrick Is pedestall'd upon those precious piles. **1715** M. Davies *Athen. Brit.* I. 185 The Theater is Grounded, Pedestal'd and Carpetted over. **1802** H. Martin *Helen of Glenross* II. 255 There is nothing I detest more than being pedestaled for a genius. **1889** *Pall Mall G.* 2 Apr. 3/3 He seems to us to miss the significance of the true Imperialism which pedestals itself on Nationalism.

2. To form a pedestal for, to support as a pedestal.

1890 Hosmer *Anglo-Sax. Freedom* 121 Every convenient stump pedestalled its orator.

ˈpedestalled, -aled (-əld), *a.* [f. prec. sb. or vb. + -ed.] Provided with, set upon, or having a pedestal.

1889 *Athenæum* 14 Dec. 825/3 The clay counterparts of the 'cordoned' or pedestalled vases. **1893** Saltus *Madam Sapphira* 38 The pedestalled lamps, the yellow shaded candles. **1901** A. J. Evans in *Oxf. Univ. Gaz.* 12 Feb. 340/1 A pedestalled cup and small bowls of marble.

peˈdestrial, *a.* [f. L. *pedester* on foot, going on foot (f. *ped-em* foot, *pedes* footman) + -al[1].]

†**1.** On foot, going on foot, pedestrian. *Obs.*

1611 Coryat *Crudities* 289 Statues of worthy personages, partly equestriall, partly pedestriall. **1632** Lithgow *Trav.* vi. 252 All.. being mounted on Mules saue onely pedestriall I. **1634** Sir T. Herbert *Trav.* 29 Not a stones cast further, sleepes Tom Coriats bones, consumed in his pedestriall, ill contrived Pilgrimage.

†**2.** Of archery: Performed with the bow drawn against the foot. *Obs.*

1792 Moseley *Ess. Archery* iv. 86 A curious expedient of this pedestrial Archery, used by the Ethiopians in hunting Elephants. *Ibid.* 93 The facts relating to pedestrial Archery.

3. Fitted for walking; as, the pedestrial legs of a crab.

1890 in *Cent. Dict.*

Hence **peˈdestrially** *adv.*, on foot.

1632 W. Lynnesay in Lithgow *Trav.* Biij, A length of no such course, by ten to one, Which thou thy selfe pedestrially hast gone. **1864** in Webster.

pedestrian (pɪˈdɛstrɪən), *a.* and *sb.* [f. L. *pedester* (see prec.) + -an.]

A. *adj.* **1. a.** On foot, going or walking on foot; performed on foot; of or pertaining to walking.

1791 Wordsw. in Chr. Wordsw. *Mem.* (1851) I. 71 Your wish to have employed your vacation in a pedestrian tour. **1829** Lytton *Disowned* i, A greater degree of respect than he was at first disposed to accord to a pedestrian traveller. **1840** Dickens *Old C. Shop* xvii, Grinder.. used his natural legs for pedestrian purposes. **1880** G. Meredith *Tragic Com.* xvi, By the aid of a common stout pedestrian stick.

b. Of a statue: Representing a person on foot, as distinguished from *equestrian*.

1822 *Gentl. Mag.* XCII. i. 268 The statue.. is to be pedestrian.

2. Applied to plain prose as opposed to verse, or to verse of prosaic character; hence, prosaic, commonplace, dull, uninspired; colloquial, vulgar. [L. *pedester* = Gr. πεζός in prose, prosaic, plain, commonplace. Sometimes contrasted with the winged flight of Pegasus.]

1716 M. Davies *Athen. Brit.* II. 139 The rest moulded upon Lucretius's Splay-footed numbers, with some pedestrian spoilings out of Horace's Epistles. **1805** Roscoe *Leo X* Pref. (1827) 28 Burcardus.. his diary is written in a pedestrian and semi-barbarian style. **1819** Byron *Juan* Ded. viii, Who wandering with pedestrian Muses, Contend not with you on the winged steed. **1888** *Dict. Nat. Biogr.* XIII. 11/2 Crane's verse is of a very pedestrian order.

B. *sb.* **a.** One who goes or travels on foot; a walker; one who walks as a physical exercise or athletic performance.

1793 (*title*) The Observant Pedestrian, or Traits of the Human Heart; in a Solitary Tour from Caernarvon to London. **1802** *Gentl. Mag.* LXXII. 338 Pedestrians (under which name the moralizing travellers of the present day are well described). **1812** *Chron.* in *Ann. Reg.* 129/1 A well-known pedestrian who had been in the habit of supplying the Counties of Devon and Cornwall, with ballads. **1813** [see pedestrianism]. **1832** Marryat *N. Forster* i, As happy as a pedestrian who had accomplished his thousand miles in a thousand hours. **1895** *Westm. Gaz.* 2 Mar. 9/2 Professor Blackie in his younger years was a great pedestrian, and he used to boast that there was not a mountain in Scotland on top of which he had not been.

b. *rare.* One who is dull, prosaic, or uninspired.

1969 D. F. Horrobin *Sci. is God* iii. 24 These.. purveyors of ideas.. irritate intensely those pedestrian men who feel that they never have enough information for the proposal of a hypothesis. Unfortunately, for the pedestrians, it is the dreamers who tend to steal most of the scientific glory.

c. *attrib.* and *Comb.* ***pedestrian-operated*** adj.; **pedestrian crossing**, a marked section of the roadway where pedestrians crossing the road are given precedence over vehicular traffic; **pedestrian deck**, a series of pavements or walkways, usu. built above ground level and often roofed, reserved for pedestrians; **pedestrian precinct**, an area reserved for pedestrians only, usu. in a town centre or shopping centre.

1935 *Punch* 3 Apr. 374 (*caption*) Sorry, old man, but my wife has just signalled that she has thought of a name for our new dog, and I'm dashing along to the next *pedestrian crossing so that I can go over and hear it. **1936** [see Belisha beacon]. **1950** *Ann Reg. 1949* 473 The plaintiff.. was crossing a street.. by means of a controlled pedestrian crossing. **1973** D. Miller *Chinese Jade Affair* xvii. 164 The light at the intersection caught us.. and my glamorous chauffeur brought the little Fiat to a halt just a yard or so the wrong side of the pedestrian crossing. **1976** *Evening Post* (Nottingham) 15 Dec. 2/5 We have suggested to the City Planners that a pedestrian crossing.. would be desirable on safety grounds. **1962** *Listener* 24 May 903/2 The *pedestrian deck planned for the now abandoned project for a new town in Hook, Hampshire. **1963** *House & Garden* Mar. 35/2 Andover will also have its pedestrian deck, 15 feet above a ground level complex of footways and underpasses. **1937** *Daily Herald* 21 Jan. 3/7 No *pedestrian operated signals for crossing places. **1938** H. A. Tripp *Road Traffic* xii. 269 (*heading*) Pedestrian-operated signals. Signals fitted with buttons to be pressed by pedestrians desiring to cross the road are employed. **1953** F. Gibberd *Town Design* v. 121 A system of *pedestrian precincts as short cuts between shopping streets can be developed in a large centre. **1960** *New Left Rev.* July-Aug. 23/1 He proposed to ring the centre with an elaborate motor road, and to turn the entire central area.. into a pedestrian precinct. **1971** P. Gresswell *Environment* 183 Pedestrian precincts include roads and other areas closed to traffic. **1977** *Belfast Tel.* 24 Jan. 5/1 The police officers chased the gunmen through a pedestrian precinct into Water Street.

pedestrianate (pɪˈdɛstrɪəneɪt), *v.* [f. prec. + -ate[3] 7.] = pedestrianize.

1864 *N. & Q.* 3rd Ser. VI. 118/2, I have been pedestrinating through a corner of Oxfordshire. **1889** *Sci. Amer.* 29 June 402/2 The trial court had held that bicycling was a form of pedestrianating. **1890** B. W. Richardson in *Asclepiad* VII. 37 The poor wretches who have to pedestrinate slowly on.

pedestrianism (pɪˈdɛstrɪənɪz(ə)m). [f. as prec. + -ism.]

1. The practice of travelling on foot, walking; walking as an exercise or athletic performance.

1809 *Sporting Mag.* XXXIV. 162, I do not intend to level the least sarcasm at pedestrianism. **1813** W. Thom (*title*) Pedestrianism; or, An Account of the Performances of celebrated Pedestrians during the last and present Century. **1843** B. Cooper *Life of Sir A. Cooper* (L.), Captain Barclay's famous feat of pedestrianism—a thousand miles in a thousand hours. **1882** Sala *Amer. Revis.* (1885) 400 Comfortable pedestrianism in the greater number of young American towns is next door to an impossibility.

2. Prosaic or commonplace quality of style.

1892 *Sat. Rev.* 21 May 602/1 An almost Wordsworthian pedestrianism of style.

pedestrianize (pɪˈdɛstrɪənaɪz), *v.* [f. as prec. + -ize.] **a.** *intr.* To act the pedestrian; to go or travel on foot; to walk. Also ***to pedestrianize it.***

1811 Shelley in Hogg *Life* (1858) I. 399, I intend to pedestrianize. **1826** *Blackw. Mag.* XX. 10 You must pedestrianize it for a few unmeasured miles over hill and dale.

b. *intr.* To produce something commonplace or unremarkable; *trans.* to make (something) commonplace or prosaic.

1838 W. Howitt *Rural Life Eng.* II. i. iii. 57 We want a designer for wood-cuts.. who would pedestrianize in simple style. **1945** W. de la Mare in *Trans. R. Soc. Lit.* XXII. 99 Genius originates what talent pedestrianizes.

c. To make accessible only to pedestrians; to make into a pedestrian precinct.

1963 *Observer* 15 Dec. 6/6 He [*sc.* Prof. Buchanan] even suggested that some of these central streets.. should be closed to traffic and, in the jargon, pedestrianised. **1969** *Daily Tel.* 15 Nov. 7 (*caption*) Chancellors Way.. which will become pedestrianised when the new building.. is completed. **1971** *Hansard Lords: Official Rep. Comm. Highways Bill, 1st Sitting* 28 Apr. 11/1 The need for this provision is particularly clear where the street pattern in historic towns is being redesigned, and where it is designed to 'pedestrianise' a street and to construct a new road to give access to shop premises. **1973** *Guardian* 12 Oct. 15/2 The great effort to pedestrianise Carnaby Street. **1977** *Listener* 17 Feb. 207/3 All the streets around here—for the first time in Paris—have been pedestrianized.

Hence **peˈdestrianized** *ppl. a.*; **peˌdestrianiˈzation**; **peˈdestrianizing** *vbl. sb.* and *ppl. a.*

1834 A. Walton *Tour Banks Thames* 141 Setting forth the advantages of pedestrianising. **1861** *Sat. Rev.* 14 Sept. 275 Englishmen are distinguishable among the nations of the earth as pedestrianising animals. **1964** *Listener* 3 Sept. 341/1 We have a maze of medieval alleys..— ideal for pedestrianization. **1966** *Economist* 2 Apr. p. xv/1 After a look at what is for sale in those urbanely pedestrianised shops, one is tempted to scream it. **1967** *Times Rev. Industry* Oct. 52/3 The medieval road pattern in the city centre.. is 'natural for pedestrians' and he has an experimental scheme for pedestrianization of the upper High Street. **1971** P. Gresswell *Environment* 182 Pedestrianisation is a clumsy word to describe a simple process: closing shopping streets to traffic. **1972** *Times* 30 Dec. 16/4 The £45,000 scheme will provide 370 yards of 'pedestrianized' roadway. **1973** *Country Life* 15 Nov. 1575/2 It is to be hoped that extensive pedestrianisation and a one-way baffle system may be considered. **1974** *Oxford Times* 18 Oct. 4 Members agreed to stick to their policy of banning all but emergency ambulances from pedestrianised streets and bus lanes. **1977** *Lancashire Life* Aug. 34/1 The proof of Blackburn's pedestrianisation is in its perambulation.

†**peˈdestrious**, *a. Obs.* [f. L. *pedester* on foot, going on foot + -ous.] Going on foot, esp. as opposed to flying or swimming.

1646 Sir T. Browne *Pseud. Ep.* iii. i. 105 Men conceive they never lie down, and enjoy not the position of rest, ordained unto all pedestrious animals. **1755** Johnson, *Pedestrious*, not winged, going on foot. **1822** T. Taylor *Apuleius* 335 The mortal genus of bodies is divided into the terrene and terrestrial (or pedestrious) [etc.].

pedetentous (pɛdɪˈtɛntəs), *a. rare.* [f. L. *pedetent-im*, *-tempt-im* step by step, cautiously (F. *pede-m* foot + *tend-ĕre*, *tent-* to stretch) + -ous.] Proceeding step by step, advancing cautiously.

1837 Syd. Smith *Let. to Archd. Singleton* Wks. 1859 II. 286 That pedetentous pace and pedetentous mind in which it behoves the wise and virtuous improver to walk. **1862** *Edin. Rev.* Jan. 65 Their admission to political privileges should be one of gradual and pedetentous elevation.

pedetic (pɪˈdɛtɪk), *a.* [ad. Gr. πηδητικ-ός, f. πηδητής leaper: cf. pedesis.] Of or pertaining to pedesis. ***pedetic movement*** = Brownian movement.

1878 Jevons in *Q. Jrnl. Sc.* Apr. 171 The pedetic movement cannot be better seen than by taking a drop of old common ink which has been exposed to the air for some weeks, and examining it under thin glass with a magnifying power of 500 or 1000 diameters. **1892** *Nature* XLV. 429/2 The pedetic or Brownian motion of small particles.

pedgill (ˈpɛdʒ(ə)l), *v. dial.* [Cf. peggle *v.*]. To work hard and painstakingly *at*; to plod or persevere.

1913 D. H. Lawrence *Let.* 12 Jan. (1962) I. 175 The thought of you pedgilling away at the novel frets me. **1915** —— *Rainbow* i. 8 But at drawing, his hand swung naturally in big, bold lines, rather lax, so that it was cruel for him to pedgill away at the lace designing, working from the tiny squares of his paper, counting and plotting and niggling.

pedi-, the usual Latin and Eng. combining form of L. *pēs*, *ped-em* foot, used in numerous compounds, as L. *pedisequus*, Eng. *pedicure*, *pediform*, *pedipalp*, etc. q.v.

pediad (ˈpɛdɪæd), *a. Cryst.* [ad. Gr. πεδιάς, -άδα adj. flat, level, f. πεδίον a plain.] Of or pertaining to pedia, consisting of pedia: see pedion.

1899 W. J. Lewis *Crystallogr.* xi. 148 The class may be called the pediad class of the anorthic system.

‖**pediˈalgia.** *Med.* Also **-algy.** [f. Gr. πεδίον the metatarsus + -αλγία ache, pain.] Neuralgia in (the sole of) the foot.

1853 Dunglison *Med. Lex.*, *Pedialgia.* **1857** Mayne *Expos. Lex.*, *Pedialgia*,.. pedialgy. **1893** *Syd. Soc. Lex.*, *Pedialgia*, pain in the sole of the foot. As a neuralgia of the foot.. this occurred on a large scale in 1762 at Savigliano in Piedmont.

pediatric, etc.: see pædiatric *a.*, etc.

ˈpediatry. *rare*⁻⁰. = pædiatrics.

1890 *Cent. Dict.*, *Pediatria*, *Pediatry*, same as *pediatrics.*

pedicab (ˈpɛdɪkæb). Also **peddicab.** [f. pedi- + cab *sb.*[3]] A small pedal-operated vehicle, usu. a tricycle, serving as a taxi in countries of the Far East. Also *attrib.*

1948 *Time* 22 Nov. 15/2 The usual crush of pedicabs surged down the street. **1951** *N.Y. Herald-Tribune* 26 Mar. 1/7 The rickishaw and peddicab boys. **1953** *Here & Now* (N.Z.) July 17/1 Trishaw, or pedicab: 'a tricycle affair for one or two passengers, pedalled by a driver. In the larger cities [in China], the trishaw has almost completely replaced the rickshaw.' **1966** D. Forbes *Heart of Malaya* x. 119 He hired his pedicab for one dollar a day. **1971** *Nat. Geographic* Jan. 21 Java's tricycle taxis—rear-driven pedicabs called *betjaks*—also haul freight through city streets. **1974** *Times* 30 Apr. 8/3 In Saigon a pedicab driver set fire to himself outside the President's palace. **1977** *Time* 14 Feb. 41/3 A pedicab parked in the lobby.

pedicel (ˈpɛdɪsəl). Also 7 pedicil(l. [f. mod.Bot. L. *pedicell-us* (Linnæus *Philos. Bot.* §82 'Pedicellus est Pedunculus partialis'), dim. of *pedĭcul-us* little foot, footstalk, dim. of *pēs*, *ped-em* foot. In mod.F. *pedicelle.*]

1. *Bot.* A small stalk or stalk-like structure in a plant; applied by Grew to the filament of a stamen; in mod. use *esp.* each of the secondary or subordinate stalks which immediately bear the flowers in a branched inflorescence (the main stalk being the *peduncle*); also, a single main flowerstalk when short or slender; a small peduncle.

1676 Grew *Anat. Flowers* iii. §2 That Sort of Attire, which may be called Seminiform; being.. a little Sheaf of Seed-like Particles; standing on so many Pedicills. *Ibid.* §4 Standing sometimes double upon each Pedicil.. Sometimes fastned to their Pedicils at their middle. **1821** S. F. Gray *Arrangem. Brit. Pl.* 105 Flowers either sessile or upon pedicels. **1854** Lindley *Sch. Bot.* 11 The stalk of the flower is its peduncle: and if the latter is divided into many small stalks, its divisions are called pedicels. **1862** Darwin *Fertil. Orchids* Introd. 7 The pedicel, or prolongation of the rostellum, to which in many exotic Orchids the pollen-masses are attached.

2. *Zool.* and *Anat.* Applied to various small stalk-like structures in animals (most of which are also called PEDUNCLE).

a. In insects, the third joint of an antenna, esp. when geniculate and forming a base for the succeeding joints; also, the basal joint of the abdomen when long and slender. b. The stalk on which the eye is supported in some Crustacea, etc.; an eye-stalk. c. The stalk by which a brachiopod, cirriped, etc. is attached. d. Each of the ambulacral feet of an echinoderm. e. The PEDICLE of a vertebra.

1826 KIRBY & SP. *Entomol.* III. 366 *Pedicellus* (the *Pedicel*). The second joint of the Antenna. **1830** R. KNOX *Cloquet's Anat.* 26 Others..have compound eyes supported upon a moveable pedicel. **1851–6** WOODWARD *Mollusca* 25 The pedicel of terebratula. *Ibid.* 104 *Strombidæ*... Animal furnished with large eyes, placed on thick pedicels. **1854** [see *eye-pedicel*, EYE *sb.*[1] 28]. **1883** G. J. ROMANES in *Athenæum* 17 Mar. 349/1 The righting movements of a sea urchin when inverted on its ab-oral pole (which are performed by means of the pedicels). **1888** ROLLESTON & JACKSON *Anim. Life* 546 The tube feet or pedicels.

3. *attrib.*, as *pedicel-cell*, a cell forming a pedicel, e.g that supporting the antheridium in *Characeæ*.

1882 VINES *Sach's Bot.* 238 Beneath the pedicel-cell of the ascus shoot out filaments which form the envelope of the fructification. **1884** *Trans. Victoria Inst.* 86 These twenty-four cells, together with the pedicel cell of the globule.

Hence **pedi'cellar** *a.*, pertaining to, or of the nature of, a pedicel; **'pedicelled, -eled** *a.*, having a pedicel, pedicellate; **pedi'celliform** *a.*, of the form of a pedicel.

1806 GALPINE *Brit. Bot.* 11* *Ruppia*... Seed 4, pedicelled. **1870** HOOKER *Stud. Flora* 154 Fertile flowers subsessile, males pedicelled. **1871** COOKE *Brit. Fungi* II. 618 Ramuli pedicelliform, ascending, septate. **1900** *Proc. Zool. Soc.* 287 *Brissus carinatus*... There are 5 pedicellar pores on each side of subanal area.

‖**pedicellaria** (ˌpɛdɪsəˈlɛərɪə). *Zool.* Pl. -æ. [mod.L., f. *pedicell-us*: see prec.] In Echinoderms, Each of a number of small pincer-like organs, with two, three, or four valves, on the outside of the body, usually among and around the spines.

1872 NICHOLSON *Palæont.* 114 The modified pincer-like spines..known by the name of 'pedicellariæ'. **1888** ROLLESTON & JACKSON *Anim. Life* 193 The stalk of the Asteroid, unlike that of the Echinoid pedicellaria, is formed entirely of soft structures. *Ibid.* 558 (*Echinoidea*).

pedicellate (ˈpɛdɪsəleɪt), *a. Bot.* and *Zool.* Also pedicillate. [f. mod.L. *pedicell-us* + -ATE[2].] Having a pedicel or pedicels; *spec.* in *Zool.* belonging to the division *Pedicellata* of Echinoderms.

1828–32 in WEBSTER. **1830** LINDLEY *Nat. Syst. Bot.* 174 Flowers usually sessile, sometimes pedicellate. **1836–9** TODD *Cycl. Anat.* II. 30/2 The true or pedicellate Echinodermata. **1862** DANA *Man. Geol.* 194 Pedicellate eyes. **1872** OLIVER *Elem. Bot.* 81 In Wallflower, the peduncle..gives off successively a number of short-stalked (pedicellate) flowers.

So **'pediceˌllated** *a.* = prec.; **pedice'llation**, the condition of having a pedicel or pedicels.

1848 JOHNSTON in *Proc. Berw. Nat. Club* II. No. 6. 302, 6th [joint]..terminated with a pedicellated vesicle. **1885** GOODALE *Physiol. Bot.* (1892) 39 In the cells of many plants ..pedicellated concretions occur.

pedicle[1] (ˈpɛdɪk(ə)l). *Nat. Hist.*, etc. [ad. L. *pedīcul-us* footstalk, dim. of *pēs*, *ped-em* foot, or ad. F. *pedicule* (1557 in Hatz.-Darm.): see -CULE.]

1. *Bot.* A small stalk, footstalk, pedicel; formerly, the stalk of a leaf (= *petiole*), or of a flower or fruit (= *peduncle*); now usually, a minute stalk-like support, as those of seeds, glands, etc.

[**1562** TURNER *Herbal* II. G v b, Yᵉ floures grow..vpon a long small pediculo, that is a footlyng or footstalcke.] **1626** BACON *Sylva* §592 The close and compact substance of their leaves and the pedicles of them. **1755** *Gentl. Mag.* XXV. 210 The flowers stand on long pedicles, affixed several together to one common peduncle. **1796** WITHERING *Brit. Plants* II. 466 Leaf-stalk..beset with minute glands on pedicles. **1872** OLIVER *Elem. Bot.* II. 158 The funicle (the pedicle by which the ovule is attached to the placenta).

2. *Zool.*, etc. A small stalk; a pedicel or peduncle.

spec. a. *Path.* A stalk by which a tumour or morbid growth is attached to a part of the body. b. *Anat.* Each of the two narrow thickened parts of a vertebra connecting the centrum with the lamina, and forming part of the neural arch. c. *Zool.* The process of bones supporting the horn of a deer or any animal of the family *Cervidæ*.

1753 N. TORRIANO *Gangr. Sore Throat* 39 A whitish Eschar..held by several little Pedicles, (or stringy Fibres, like a Cancer). **1808** BARCLAY *Muscular Motions* 249 [The cerebrum and cerebellum] may each be divided..into similar halves..; each of the halves sends forth a pedicle, pedunculus, or crus. *Ibid.* 473 We observe the eyes, on moveable pedicles,..as in crabs and lobsters. **1828** STARK *Elem. Nat. Hist.* II. 348 Tribe..Sphegides..base of the abdomen narrowed into a long pedicle. **1831** R. KNOX *Cloquet's Anat.* 23 This vertebra has..a small rib-like bone placed transversely before the pedicle, which connects the processes to the body. **1841–71** T. R. JONES *Anim. Kingd.* (ed. 4) 552 In..*Orbicula*, the pedicle is wanting, the lower valve of the shell being fixed immediately to the rock. **1876** PAGE *Adv. Text-bk. Geol.* iii. 53 Garnets..projecting from pedicles of felspar.

attrib. **1851–6** WOODWARD *Mollusca* 229 Cardinal and pedicle impressions conjoined.

Hence **'pedicled** *a.*, having a pedicle, pediculated.

1880 SIR J. PAGET in *Mem. & Let.* vi. 305 The pedicled exostoses which are common on the femur and humerus.

†**pedicle**[2]. *Obs. rare*$^{-1}$. [f. L. *pedica* shackle for the feet; cf. *manicle*, MANACLE (L. *manicæ*).] A shackle for the feet, a fetter.

1627 E. KELLET *Ret. fr. Argier* 39 What..they could not effect vpon you..by manicles and pedicles of iron.

pedicru, obs. form of PEDIGREE *sb.*

pedicular (pɪˈdɪkjʊlə(r)), *a.* [ad. L. *pedīculār-is*, f. *pedīcul-us* louse. Cf. F. *pédiculaire*.] Of or pertaining to a louse or lice; lousy.

1660 HOWELL *Parly of Beasts* 26, I am not subject to breed Lice and other Vermin; And whereas this pedicular disease [etc.] attend Mankind. **1727–41** CHAMBERS *Cycl.* s.v. *Pedicularis morbus*, Herod is said to have died of the pedicular disease. *a* **1843** SOUTHEY *Doctor* ccxii. (1848) 573 The souls of their friends who are undergoing penance in the shape of fleas, or in loathsome pedicular form. **1876** BRISTOWE *Th. & Pract. Med.* (1878) 343 Impetigo in children limited to the back of the head is often of pedicular origin.

Hence **pedicu'larity** (*nonce-wd.*), the nature or personality of a louse.

1876 RUSKIN *Fors Clav.* lxvi. 183 Is there..a Divine Pedicularity?

pediculate (pɪˈdɪkjʊlət), *a.* (*sb.*) *Nat. Hist.* [f. L. *pedīcul-us* footstalk + -ATE[2].] **1.** = next.

1857 MAYNE *Expos. Lex.*, *Pediculatus*, *Bot.* having footstalks: pediculate.

2. Belonging to the group *Pediculati* of teleost fishes, characterized by the elongated basis of the pectoral fins, resembling an arm. Also as *sb.* A member of this group.

1880 GÜNTHER *Fishes* viii. 469 Pediculates are found in all seas.

pediculated (pɪˈdɪkjʊleɪtɪd), *a.* [f. as prec. + -ED[2].] Having, or borne upon, a pedicle; stalked. (Chiefly in *Path.* of morbid growths.)

1822–34 *Good's Study Med.* (ed. 4) I. 469 We observe on the surface of the lungs single vesicles..apparently pediculated. **1846** BRITTAN tr. *Malgaigne's Man. Surg.* 359 Cancer of the tongue..sometimes..is a pediculated tumour. **1856–8** *Van der Hoevens Zool.* I. 58 Phalanx.—Body pediculated.

pedicu'lation. *Path.* [ad. late L. *pedīculātiōn-em*, f. *pedīculus* louse: see -ATION.] Infestation with lice: = PEDICULOSIS.

1719–26 QUINCY *Med. Dict.* (ed. 3), *Pediculation*..is a particular Foulness of the Skin very apt to breed Lice. **1857** MAYNE *Expos. Lex.*, *Pediculatio*,..pediculation: otherwise called *Morbus pedicularis* and *Phthiriasis*.

pedicule (ˈpɛdɪkjuːl). *Nat. Hist. rare*$^{-0}$. [a. F. *pédicule* (1557 in Hatz.-Darm.), ad. L. *pedīculus* PEDICLE.] A pedicel, pedicle, or peduncle.

In modern Dicts.

pediculine (pɪˈdɪkjʊlaɪn), *a. Entom.* [f. L. *pedīcul-us* louse + -INE[1].] Belonging to the group *Pediculina* of heteropterous insects, comprising the true lice.

1893 in *Syd. Soc. Lex.*

peˌdiculo-, comb. form from L. *pedīcul-us* footstalk; in **peˌdiculo-'frontal** *a.*, (a section) through the base of the frontal convolution; so **peˌdiculopa'rietal** *a.* **peˌdiculo'phobia**: see quot.

1893 *Syd. Soc. Lex.*, *Pediculophobia*, term for a morbid dread of *Pediculosis*, associated with the delusion of its being present when it is not so in reality. **1899** *Allbutt's Syst. Med.* VII. 328 The second section through the base of the frontal convolutions forms the pediculo-frontal section. *Ibid.*, The fifth [section] is formed by dividing the hemisphere three centimetres posterior to the fissure of Rolando and.. constitutes the pediculo-parietal section.

‖**pedicu'losis.** *Path.* [f. L. *pedīcul-us* louse + -OSIS.] Infestation with lice; a diseased condition marked by the presence and multiplication of lice upon the skin; phthiriasis.

1809 in *Cent. Dict.* **1899** *Allbutt's Syst. Med.* VIII. 701 Vagabond's disease..an extensive pigmentation of the skin due to the combined effects of pediculosis, scratching, and exposure.

pediculous (pɪˈdɪkjʊləs), *a.* [ad. L. *pedīculōs-us*, f. *pedīcul-us* louse.] Infested with lice, lousy; also, of or pertaining to a louse, or characterized by lice (= PEDICULAR).

a **1550** *Image Hypocr.* IV. 540 in *Skelton's Wks.* (1843), Proude and pestiferous Pold and pediculous. **1602** DEKKER *Satirom.* Wks. 1873 I. 200 Like a lowsie Pediculous vermin th'ast but one suite to thy backe. **1824** LANDOR *Imag. Conv.*, *Jas. I & Casaubon* Wks. 1853 I. 32/2 Your pediculous friars and parti-coloured bald-coot priests. **1892** STEVENSON *Across the Plains* 291 Seized..with a pediculous malady.

pedicure (ˈpɛdɪkjʊə(r)), *sb.* [a. F. *pédicure* (1781 in Hatz.-Darm.), f. L. *pēs*, *pedi-* foot + *cūrāre* to take care of, cure.]

1. One whose business is the surgical care and treatment of the feet; a chiropodist. Also *fig.*

1842 in DUNGLISON *Med. Lex.* **1889** *Science* XIV. 308/1 Dentists, pedicures, trained nurses, and veterinarians. **1918** A. QUILLER-COUCH *Stud. in Lit.* 1st Ser. 271 Against this positive deed of friendship and thirty years of devotion little is set by sneering at Watts as 'a pedicure of the Muses'.

2. The surgical treatment of the feet, esp. in the removal or cure of corns, bunions, and the like.

1890 in *Cent. Dict.* **1893** in *Syd. Soc. Lex.* **1900** [see *face-massage* s.v. FACE *sb.* 26]. **1907** *Yesterday's Shopping* (1969) 538/2 Pedicure Scissors—2/6. Pedicure Cases—each 7/6. **1953** J. GORDON *Beauty Bk.* xvi. 167 The instruments you use for a pedicure should not be used for a manicure. *Ibid.*, *Pedicure routine*..Remove all varnish with a pad of cotton-wool. **1974** *Times* 27 Aug. 9/2 Services..include waxing, manicure, pedicure.

So **'pedicurism**, the practice or art of a pedicure; **'pedicurist** = PEDICURE 1.

1863 SALA in *Temple Bar* VIII. 73, I am afflicted with corns defying the most recondite efforts of pedicurism. **1870** W. CHAMBERS *Winter. Mentone* v. 61 The pedicurist..takes his stand behind a table and chair.

pedicure (ˈpɛdɪkjʊə(r)), *v.* [f. prec. sb.] *trans.* To cure or treat (the feet) by the removal of corns, etc. Hence **'pedicuring** *vbl. sb.*

1894 *Mute's Chron.* (Columbus, O.) 5 May, Two hot foot-baths a week and a little pedicuring will remove the cause of much discomfort. **1896** *Columbus* (Ohio) *Disp.* 6 Mar. 4/4 One's lower extremities are pedicured without cost.

pedie, pediement, obs. ff. PEDEE, PEDIMENT.

pediferous (pɪˈdɪfərəs), *a. Bot.* and *Zool.* [f. mod.L. *pedifer* (f. *pēs*, *pedi-* foot + *-fer* bearing) + -OUS.] Having feet or foot-like parts; pedigerous.

1857 MAYNE *Expos. Lex.*, *Pediferus*,..provided with feet, ..pediferous.

†**'pedifoot.** *Obs. rare*$^{-1}$. [f. L. *ped-em* foot + FOOT.] A tendril (rendering L. *pediculus*).

c **1420** *Pallad. on Husb.* IV. 375 To kepe hem long also, Let picche her pedifeet [L. *pediculos*] & honge hem hie.

pediform (ˈpɛdɪfɔːm), *a.* [f. L. type *pediform-is, f. *pēs*, *pedi-* foot: see -FORM.] Having the form of a foot: said chiefly of the organs of insects.

1826 KIRBY & SP. *Entomol.* IV. 311 Feelers..Pediform, when they resemble the legs in structure or use. **1852** DANA *Crust.* I. 13 The jointed or pediform portion of the mandibles. **1880** BASTIAN *Brain* 100 The pediform maxillary palpi.

pedigerous (pɪˈdɪdʒərəs), *a.* [f. mod.L. type **pediger* (f. L. *pēs*, *pedi-* foot + *-ger* carrying) + -OUS.] Bearing feet or legs.

1826 KIRBY & SP. *Entomol.* III. xxxv. 581 In the hexapods ..there are usually three pedigerous segments. **1877** HUXLEY *Anat. Inv. Anim.* vi. 279 Of the twenty pedigerous segments, the first eleven have each one pair of appendages.

pedigraic (pɛdɪˈgreɪɪk), *a. rare.* [irreg. f. PEDIGREE *sb.* + -IC.] Of or pertaining to a pedigree.

1872 R. C. JENKINS in *Archæol. Cant.* VIII. 60 Pedigraic matter to be collected from the above Will and Probate. **1902** *N. & Q.* 9th Ser. IX. 430/1 A pedigraic account..of this historical family.

pedigree (ˈpɛdɪgriː), *sb.* Forms: see below. [In 15th c. *pedegru*, *pee-de-grew*, etc., app. AF. forms = F. *pié (pied) de grue* crane's foot; so called 'from a three-line mark (like the broad arrow) used in denoting succession in pedigrees' (Prof. Skeat), 'a conventional mark consisting of three curved lines, which bears a distinct resemblance to the claws of a bird' (C. Sweet in *Athenæum* 30 Mar. (1895) 409, where information is given as to the appearance of old MSS. genealogies in pedigree form).]

A. Illustration of Forms.

α. 5 **pedicru, pedegru, -greu, -grewe, -grw; pedygru; pee de grew(e, 6 pede-, pedagrew; pedigrue, 6–7 -grewe.**

α. **1410** in Madox *Formul. Anglic.* xxviii. (1702) 15 Omnibus Christi fidelibus ad quos præsens Pedicru pervenerit. **1412–20** LYDG. *Chron. Troy* Epil. (1550), Who so lyst loke and doe vnfolde The pee de Grewe of these cronicles olde. *c* **1440** *Promp. Parv.* 390/1 Pedegru, or petygru, lyne of kynrede, & awncetrye. **1548** UDALL, etc. *Erasm. Par. Mark* i. 14 Genealogies and pedegrewes. **1607** SIR J. H. in Harington *Nugæ Ant.* (ed. Park 1804) II. 224 The true memories and pedigrews of their auncestors.

β. 5 **pe de gre, pedigre (?) peedeugre; 5–6 peedegre; pedegre, 6–7 -degree; 6– pedigree.**

β. **1426** LYDG. in *Pol. Poems* (Rolls) II. 131 A remembraunce of a peedeugre how that..Henry the sext, is truly borne heir unto the corone of Fraunce. *Ibid.* 135 The peedegre doth hit specifie, The figure lo of the genealogye. **1433** —— *S. Edmund* III. 299 Doun fro the stok off kynges descendyng The pe de gre by lyneal conueyyng. **1523** FITZHERB. *Surv.* Prol., If the owner make a true peedegre or conueyaunce by discente or by purchace vnto the said landes. **1547** J. HARRISON *Exhort. Scottes* B vij b, Some fetchyng their pedegre from the Goddes, and some from the deuils. **1599** SANDYS *Europæ Spec.* (1632) 144 Seeing Pedegrees change..together with mens fortunes. **1599** SHAKS. *Hen. V*, II. iv. 90 Willing you ouer-looke this Pedigree. **1815** SCOTT *Guy M.* ii, Godfrey Bertram.. succeeded to a long pedigree and a short rent-roll.

γ. 5 **petiegrew; petygru, -grwe; pytagru, -grwe; 5–6 petegreu, petigree; 6 pete-, peti-, petie-, pety-, pette-, petti-, petty-, -greu, -gru(e, -grew(e, -gre(e, -grye; (peti degree, petit(e degree); 6–7 pete-, peti-, pettigre(e.**

γ. **14..** in *Chron. R. Glouc.* (1724) 585 A Petegreu, fro William Conquerour..vn to kyng Henry the vi. *c* **1440** *Promp. Parv.* [see a]. *c* **1486** *Surtees Misc.* (1888) 47 As he can and woll more largely show unto you by petiegrew. **1499** *Promp. Parv.* 402/1 (Pynson), Pytagrwe or lyne or kinrede. **1513** BRADSHAW *St. Werburge* I. 124, I entende to make playne descrypcyon..Also of her petygre the noble excellence. **1529** RASTELL *Pastyme, Hist. Flem.* (1811) 60 As the lyne and petegre aboue shewyth. **1530** PALSGR. 253 Petygrewe, *genealogie.* **1565** in *Hakluyt's Voy.* (1904) VI. 340 They instruct in al the petigrues of princes. **1577–87** HOLINSHED *Chron.* II. 33/2 To fetch their petit degrees from their ancestors. **1587** FLEMING *Contn. Holinshed* III. 1370/2 Twelue petidegrees of the descent of the crowne of England, ..by the bishop of Rosse. **1652** H. L'ESTRANGE *Amer. no Jewes* 58 So shall wee all at last be of one Petigre.

B. Signification.

1. A genealogical stemma or table; a genealogy drawn up or exhibited in some tabular form.

1410 in Madox *Formul. Anglic.* xxviii. (1702) 15 Nos.. sigilla nostra..huic præsenti Pedicru apposuimus. **1425** *Rolls of Parlt.* IV. 267/1 My Lordes Counseill Marchall.. had yeven in to yat high place of Record a Pedegrewe. *Ibid.* 268/2 Yeving in a Peedegree in writyng. **1465** *Paston Lett.* II. 210 Be the pedegre mad in the seyd last Dewkis fadirs daijs. *c* **1660** WOOD *Life* an. 1634 (O.H.S.) I. 45 To appeare before the said officers or heralds with his armes and pedegree. **1711** MRS. LONG in *Swift's Wks.* (1841) II. 477, I wish too at your leisure you would make a pedigree for me. **1870** FREEMAN *Norm. Conq.* (ed. 2) I. App. 703 The family of which he had just given the pedigree.

2. a. One's line of ancestors; an ancestral line; ancestry; lineage, descent.

c **1440** LYDG. *Hors, Shepe & G.* 9 in *Pol. Rel. & L. Poems* (1866) 15 Be dissent conveyed the pedegrewe Frome the patryarke Abrahame. **1465** *Paston Lett.* II. 210 As for the pedegre of the seyd Dewk, he is sone to William Pool, Dewk of Suffolk. **1548** UDALL *Erasm. Par. Luke* Prol. 15 The nativitie and petigrewe of Christe. **1549** COVERDALE, etc. *Erasm. Par. Heb.* 10 Melchisedech..had neither father, nor mother, nor pedigrew. **1591** HARINGTON *Orl. Fur.* XXVI. lxix, As one that thence deriv'd his pedegrew. *a* **1683** SIDNEY *Disc. Govt.* ii. §24 Who had no better cover for his sordid extraction than a Welch Pedegree. **1700** DRYDEN *Ajax & Ulysses* 231 From Jove like him I claim my pedigree, And am descended in the same degree. **1876** FREEMAN *Norm. Conq.* V. xxiii. 331 Men had forgotten a pedigree which had to be traced through a long line of foreign princes in Flanders.

b. Of animals.

1608 TOPSELL *Serpents* 79 The true younger bees..derive their originall and petigree from the kingly stocke. **1818** [see PEDIGREED]. **1829** LYTTON *Devereux* II. i, To vouch for the pedigree..of the three horses he intends to dispose of. **1868** DARWIN *Anim. & Pl.* I. ii. 51 The pedigree of a race-horse is of more value in judging of its probable success than its appearance. **1880** HAUGHTON *Phys. Geog.* vi. 282 The modern Horse, whose pedigree [i.e. from the Eocene *Hipparion*] has been..traced by Professor Marsh.

c. *transf.* Origin and succession, line of succession; derivation, etymological descent.

1566 BARTHELET (*title*) The Pedigrewe of Heretiques, wherein is truly and plainly set out the first roote of Heretiques begon in the Church. **1582** STANYHURST *Æneis* To Rdr. (Arb.) 14 Attempt too fetche thee petit degree of woordes, I know not from what auncetoure. **1628** PRYNNE *Loue-lockes* 3 That which had its birth, source, and pedegree from the very Deuill himselfe, must needes bee odious. **1715** M. DAVIES *Athen. Brit.* I. 1 [Of the word 'Pamphlet'] Its Pedigree can scarce be trac'd higher than the latter end of Queen Elizabeth's Reign. **1833** CHALMERS *Const. of Man* II. ix. The origin and pedigree of our moral judgments. **1839** H. ROGERS *Ess.* II. iii. 127 Both words..may very probably have had the same pedigree— perhaps the same parentage.

d. *colloq.* The 'life history' of a person or thing. Also, a person's criminal record. **pedigree-man** (see quot. 1923).

1903 *Dialect Notes* II. 324 *Pedigree,*..history. 'If he doesn't go straight I'll tell his pedigree.' Not applying to family descent, but to personal history. *a* **1911** D. G. PHILLIPS *Susan Lenox* (1917) II. xvii. 397 'I run her in myself.' 'Oh, she's got a record... Why the hell didn't you say so?' 'I thought you remembered. You took her pedigree.' **1923** J. MANCHON *Le Slang* 220 *Pedigree-man,*.. un récidiviste, un cheval de retour. **1942** BERREY & VAN DEN BARK *Amer. Thes. Slang* §477/5 *Pedigree,* a prisoner's police record. **1964** 'D. SHANNON' *Root of All Evil* (1966) ix. 123 Dorothy had a little pedigree for shoplifting. **1969** C. IRVING *Fake!* (1970) xii. 147 Another element in the 'pedigree' of the painting was a certificate from a prior owner, usually one of several well-known collectors. **1975** *Times* 22 Aug. 3/3 It has been decided to establish a national register to check the pedigrees of vehicles, particularly their milages.

3. (Without article.) Descent in the abstract; esp. distinguished or ancient descent; 'birth'.

c **1460** in *Pol. Rel. & L. Poems* (ed. 2) 292 Sewte and servise we owe..To þi hiȝnesse..As royall most by pedigre. **1579** LYLY *Euphues, Let. to Alcius* Wks. 1902 I. 317 If thou clayme gentry by petegree, practise gentlenesse by thine honestie. **1676** HOBBES *Iliad* xx. 235 Though Vertue lieth not in Pedigree. **1701** DE FOE *True-born Eng.* 351 Yet she boldly boasts of Pedigree. **1826** SCOTT *Mal. Malagr.* i, I am by pedigree a discontented person. **1896** SIR W. LAWSON in *Westm. Gaz.* 4 Sept. 8/2 He did not want them to despise pedigree, because pedigree was the pedestal of the British Constitution.

4. A race or line; a family; a line of succession; *loosely*, a long series, list, or 'string' of people.

1532 MORE *Confut. Tindale* Wks. 617/1 [To] iest and rayle vpon the whole pedegre of Popes. **1596** H. CLAPHAM *Briefe Bible* I. 26 Sheths Petygre marrieth with them. **1604–13** R. CAWDREY *Table Alph., Pettigree,* stocke, or off-spring. **1837** SIR F. PALGRAVE *Merch. & Friar* (1844) 81 They are all alike, 'the whole pedigree on 'em—Radical or Conservative, Whig or Tory'.

5. *attrib.* and *Comb.* Of, pertaining to, or having a pedigree or recorded line of descent, as ***pedigree cattle, cereal, stock, wheat; pedigree-hunting, -implying, -making, -monger, -sheet.*** **pedigree-stick**, a stick carved to record the genealogy or history of a tribe.

1863 *Gard. Chron.* 23 May, I was induced last autumn to sow a considerable breadth of land with Pedigree Wheat. **1871** FREEMAN *Hist. Ess.* 34 Just as pedigree-mongers nowadays invent pedigrees. **1893** *Jrnl. Anthrop. Inst.* XXII. 319 Had the Polynesians any means of recording degrees of descent?.. *Aufau fetii* is 'the genealogy of a family', and must have been a staff bound in some especial manner to serve the purpose of a pedigree-stick. *Ibid.* 320 An undoubted pedigree-stick..is figured..in Roth's translation of Crozet's 'Voyage to Tasmania', where it is described as 'a staff recording the history of the Ngati-Rangi Tribe' of New Zealand. **1895** A. C. HADDON *Evol. Art* II. iv. 273 These carved shafts of sacred paddles and adzes were pedigree-sticks. **1897** *Geneal. Mag.* Oct. 339 Pedigree-making is to genealogy what classification is to geology, botany or zoology. **1901** *Daily News* 22 Jan. 5/2 He may go pedigree-hunting for himself, or he may employ a pedigree-hunter. **1901** *Scotsman* 28 Feb. 6/2 The Perth sale of pedigree shorthorn cattle. **1908** *Encycl. Relig. & Ethics* I. 826/2 Colley March first suggested that the carved shafts of the sacred paddles and adzes were pedigree-sticks, the patterns being 'the multitudinous human links between the divine ancestor and the chief of the living tribe'.

pedigreed (ˈpɛdɪgriːd), *a.* [f. prec. + -ED².]

a. Having a recorded pedigree: said esp. of cattle.

1818 *Sporting Mag.* II. 215 A pedigreed horse..whose pedigree was, probably, made out only by the horse-dealer. **1893** RUSKIN *Poetry Archit.* I. i. 14 In France, there prevail two opposite feelings,..that of the old pedigreed population ..and that of the modern revolutionists. **1916** *Mem. N.Y. Bot. Garden* VI. 353 The possibility of cross-sterility between sister plants of a seed progeny was proven and the interrelations of sterility studied in a pedigreed seed progeny. **1971** *Farmer & Stockbreeder* 23 Feb. 53/3 (Advt.), Ayr Bull Sale..Pedigreed, Milk Recorded and Brucellosis Accredited Ayrshire Bull Stirks. **1976** J. VAN DE WETERING *Tumbleweed* vii. 65 He is a pedigreed cat. **1977** *New Yorker* 11 July 70/1, I saw a sled being pulled by an Irish setter, another by a mongrel collie, a third by a pedigreed scottie.

b. Having a criminal record. Cf. PEDIGREE *sb.* 2 d.

1935 *Amer. Speech* X. 13/1 To have one's record in the possession of the police;..*pedigreed.* **1942** BERREY & VAN DEN BARK *Amer. Thes. Slang* §461/3 *Pedigreed crook,* one with a police record. **1971** 'A. BLAISDELL' *Practice to Deceive* viii. 112 Rodriguez and D'Arcy were out again hunting the pedigreed sex fiends.

ˈpedigreeless *a.* Having no pedigree.

1899 *Westm. Gaz.* 12 May 2/2 A pedigreeless animal.

† **ˈpedigrist.** *Obs. rare.* [f. PEDIGR(EE + -IST.] A maker of pedigrees. (Implied in next.)

† **pediˈgristical,** *a. Obs. rare.* [f. prec. + -ICAL.] Hence † **pediˈgristically** *adv.*, after the manner of a maker of pedigrees or genealogist.

1630 T. WESTCOTE *Devon* (1845) 247 This line..might.. have been pedigristically delineated..but that of right belongs to..the heralds.

† **ˈpedilave,** *Obs. rare*⁻¹. [ad. L. *pediluvium* (see below), or F. *pédiluve*, assimilated to *lave*, L. *lavāre* to wash; or ? error.] = PEDILUVIUM.

1710 T. FULLER *Pharm. Extemp.* 281 A Pedilave that is potentially Cold..useth to bring great Relief.

‖ **pediluvium** (pɛdɪˈl(j)uːvɪəm). Pl. **-ia.** Also in anglicized form **pediluvy.** [med. or mod.L., f. *pēs, pedi-* foot + *-luvium* (in comp.) washing, f. *lu-ĕre* to wash.] A foot-bath; a washing of feet. Also *attrib.*

1693 tr. *Blanchard's Phys. Dict.* (ed. 2), *Pediluvium,* a sort of Bath for the Feet. **1782** W. HEBERDEN *Comm.* xviii. (1806) 101 Warm pediluvia. **1828** WEBSTER, *Pediluvy.* **1865** AGNES STRICKLAND *Queens Eng.* I. 90 Perhaps he [King David I] was conscious of his want of skill at a *pediluvium* party; or.. had seen too much of such scenes during the life of his pious mother Queen Margaret. **1898** P. MANSON *Trop. Diseases* xxxvii. 140 Hot mustard pediluvia..are in constant use.

Hence **pediˈluvial** *a.*, of or pertaining to the washing of feet, or to a foot-bath; in quot. *sb. pl.* ceremonies connected with the washing of feet (as a religious act).

1828 LANDOR *Imag. Conv., Leo XII & Gigi,* After which holy function, go and prepare for the pediluvials.

pedimane (ˈpɛdɪmeɪn). *Zool.* [a. F. *pédimane* (Cuvier 1797), f. L. *pēs, pedi-* foot + *manus* hand.] A pedimanous quadruped: see next.

1835 KIRBY *Hab. & Inst. Anim.* II. xxiv. 491 They [the Opossums] have been called Pedimanes.

pedimanous (pɪˈdɪmənəs), *a. Zool.* [f. as prec. + -OUS.] Having feet like hands: applied to the lemurs and opossums in reference to their hind feet.

1839–47 TODD *Cycl. Anat.* III. 290/2 None of the.. pedimanous..Placentals present this condition of the hind leg. **1857** MAYNE *Expos. Lex., Pedimanus,*..applied by Vicq d'Azyr and Blainville to a Family (*Pedimani*..) of the Mammifera,..of which the feet, having the thumb opposible, are thus converted into a kind of hand: pedimanous.

† **pediˈmechan.** *Obs.* [f. L. *pēs, pedi-* foot + Gr. μηχανή machine, engine.] A kind of velocipede in which the motive power was applied by means of a spring and ratchet.

1844 *Mech. Mag.* XLI. 369 Hankins's Pedimechan or Spring Propeller.

pediment¹ (ˈpɛdɪmənt). Forms: α. 7 **peremint, peri-, perriment.** β. 7 **peda-, pede-,** 8 **pedie-, piedment,** 8– **pediment.** [An alteration of *periment, peremint*, said to be a workmen's term, and 'corrupt English'; of obscure origin: see *note* below.]

1. a. A word applied since the 17th c. to the triangular part, resembling a low gable, crowning the front of a building in the Grecian style of architecture, especially over a portico. It consists of a flat recessed field framed by a cornice and often ornamented with sculptures in relief. Also applied to similarly-placed members in the Roman and Renaissance styles, whether triangular, semicircular, or of other form, also to those of similar shapes placed over niches, doors, or windows. Hence, in *Decorative art*, Any member of similar form and position, as one placed over the opening in an ironwork screen, etc.

α. **1592** R. D. *Hypnerotomachia* 22 b, The Coronices.. were corrospondent and agreeing with the faling out of the whol worke, the Stilliced or Perimeter [*Margin.* A periment in corrupt English], or vpper part of the vppermost Coronice [orig. *il' stillicidio della suprema cornice*] onely except. **1601–2** in Willis & Clark *Cambridge* (1886) I. 451–2 Item to John Hill Joyner for xiiij yeardes of wanscott over the high table in the Colledge hall at iiˢ viᵈ the yeard 35ˢ: .. and for a periment in the middest of the same wanscott xxˢ. *Ibid.* II. 629 A phaine for the peremint of the Coundite. **1603–4** *Ibid.* 575 A Perriment on the topp of the Organs wᵗʰ the scrowles and 7 bowles for the same.

β. **1664** EVELYN *Acc. Architects,* etc. 140 Those Roofs which exalted themselves above the Cornices had usually in face a Triangular plaine or Gabel (that when our Workmen make not so acute and pointed they call a Pedament) which the antients nam'd Tympanum. **1688** R. HOLME *Armoury* III. 400/2 He beareth Argent, a Gate or Port in a Wall, with a Pedement Imbattelled between two round Towers. **1704** J. HARRIS *Lex. Techn.* I, *Pediement,* a Term in Architecture; the same with *Fronton.* **1730–6** BAILEY (folio), *Pediment,* an ornament that crowns the ordonnances, finishes the fronts of buildings, and serves as a decoration over gates, windows, niches, etc. It is ordinarily of a triangular form, but sometimes makes an arch of a circle. **1737** CHAMBERLAYNE *St. Gt. Brit.* I. III. xi. 272 Clarendon Printing-House [Oxford]. On the Tops of the South East, and West Piedments, are the Tunnels of all the Chimneys. **1796** H. HUNTER tr. *St.-Pierre's Stud. Nat.* (1799) II. 373 On one side of the pediment which crowns it is stretched along an ancient River-god. **1866** R. CHAMBERS *Ess. Ser.* II. 110 Presenting,..on the pediments of the windows, the letters S.P.T. **1870** DISRAELI *Lothair* vi, The carved and gilded pediments over the doors.

b. *Geomorphol.* A broad, gently sloping, eroded rock surface that extends outwards from the abrupt foot of a mountain in arid and semi-arid regions and is usu. slightly concave and partly or wholly covered with a thin layer of alluvium.

This is not the sense in quots. 1882, where the word denotes steep rock slopes roughly triangular in shape, more like architectural pediments.

[**1882** C. E. DUTTON *Tertiary Hist. Grand Cañon District* v. 85 Just opposite to us the pediments seem half buried, or rather half risen out of the valley alluvium. *Ibid.*, Between the alcoves the projecting pediments present gable-ends towards the valley-plain.] **1897** W. J. MCGEE in *Bull. Geol. Soc. Amer.* VIII. 92 The tide-carved coast cuts a typical granitic butte..rising sharply from the inclined foot-slope of Sierra Seri, yet the rugged-faced knob is seen to surmount a granite pediment nearly half a mile across in the line of section. **1922** *Bull. U.S. Geol. Survey* No. 730. 52 The mountains of the Papago country rise from plains which are similar in form to the alluvial plains that commonly front mountains of an arid region, but large parts of the plains are without alluvial cover and are composed of solid rock. These plains are called 'mountain pediments', a term suggested by McGee's usage. *Ibid.* 58 A mountain pediment buried in alluvium may be called a concealed pediment. **1933** [see PANFAN]. **1935** [see PEDIPLAIN]. **1960** B. W. SPARKS *Geomorphol.* xi. 257 The sharp break of slope between the pediment and the mountain front seems to point to a change of operative process, but there is no agreement as to the nature of the processes involved. **1974** [see PEDIPLAIN]. **1977** A. HALLAM *Planet Earth* 85 The low-angle (generally less than about 8°) concave surfaces which coalesce to form the pediplains are called pediments. *Ibid.*, More recently it has been argued that pediments develop through surface and subsurface weathering.

2. Referred to L. *pēs, pedem* 'foot', and used for: A base, foundation; a pavement. (Cf. next.)

1726 DART *Canterb. Cathedr.* 14 The Pedement of St. Thomas's Altar. **1747** *Gentl. Mag.* 362 His Neapolitan majesty has paved several parlours of his new palace..with mosaic and other pediments taken up entire. **1880** W. GRANT *Christ our Hope* 1 Three pediments support the viaduct of life along which Christians pass to glory.

3. *Comb.*, as ***pediment-like*** adj., ***pedimentwise*** adv.; **pediment pass** *Geomorphol.* (see quot. 1930).

1844 LINGARD *Anglo-Sax. Ch.* (1858) II. App. C. 338 At the gable ends, the trunks [of which the walls were built] rose gradually pedimentwise to the height of fourteen feet. **1874** BOUTELL *Arms & Arm.* iii. 45 An elevated visor or frontlet of a triangular pediment-like form. **1930** C. SAUER in *Univ. Calif. Publ. Geogr.* III. 370 Under less advanced conditions of pediment development we find narrow, flat, rock-floored tongues extending back from the general pediment, but still penetrating along the mountain sufficiently to meet another pediment slope extending into the mountain front from the other side... To distinguish this less advanced feature from the broad saddle plains.. we may call it a pediment pass. **1974** C. H. CRICKMAY *Work of River* viii. 206 In a few places, the upper end of the pediment is the smoothly rounded summit of a pediment pass, or rock floored gap through a low mountain ridge.

[Note. *Pediment*, in Evelyn *pedament*, in Randle Holme *pedement*, has the appearance of a derivative in *-ment*, of L. *pēs, pedi-* 'foot'. But L. *pedāmentum* was a 'vine-stake' or 'prop', It. *pedamento* 'any foundation, groundworke, base, or footing' (Florio): senses with which the modern 'pediment' has no connexion. Evelyn's word was evidently an attempted improvement upon the workmen's *periment* or *peremint*, which the translator of *Hypnerotomachia* considered to be 'corrupt English' for *perimeter*. But the corruption of *perimeter* to *periment* is difficult to imagine, and the connexion of sense (see Willis *Archit. Nomencl. Midd. Ages* 37 *note*) is far-fetched; and it seems more likely that *peremint* was a workman's corruption of *pyramid*, which a triangular gable sometimes resembles in section, and which is actually pronounced *periment*, or *purriment* by the illiterate in some districts of England (e.g. in West Somersetsh.) at the present day (1904). This would also better explain 'the peremint of the Coundite' in 1601-2 above, since the Fountain in question had no 'pediment', but a curved roof in form of an ogee cupola. If this is the derivation, we have the series *pyramid, peremint, periment, peda-, pede-, pediment*.]

†**pediment**[2]. *Obs. rare*$^{-1}$. [irreg. ad. L. *pedāmentum*, f. *pedāre* to prop (a vine): see -MENT.] A stake or prop for vines.

1727 BRADLEY *Fam. Dict.* s.v. *Chesnut*, It makes the best Stakes and Poles for Pallisades, Pediments for Vine Props and Hops.

pedi'mental, *a.* [f. PEDIMENT[1] + -AL[1].]

1. Of or pertaining to a pediment, of the nature of a pediment.

1851 C. NEWTON in *Ruskin's Stones Ven.* I. App. xxi. 406 The necessities of pedimental composition first led the artist to place the river-god in a reclining position. **1864** *Athenæum* 27 Feb. 304/2 Externally, the ends of the naves and transepts will present eight pedimental façades flanked by supporting turrets.

b. Shaped like a pediment, rising to a vertical angle; applied esp. to the 'diamond-shaped' head-dress worn by women in the 16th century.

1890 *Cent. Dict.* s.v., Commonly called by writers on costume the pedimental head-dress. **1895** *Traill's Soc. Eng.* III. 158 The butterfly and steeple head-dresses died out with Henry VII, and a head-covering, called the kennel, pedimental, or diamond-shaped head-dress, took its place.

2. Of or pertaining to a pedestal: see PEDIMENT[1] 2.

1891 G. MEREDITH *One of our Conq.* xxxvi, She read off the honorific pedimental letters of a handsome statue, for a sign to herself that she passed it.

pedimentation (pɛdɪmɛn'teɪʃən). *Geomorphol.* [f. PEDIMENT[1] + -ATION.] The formation of a pediment.

1948 *Bull. Geol. Soc. Amer.* LIX. 372 Down the slope from the knickpoint pedimentation rapidly reaches stability. **1962** L. C. KING *Morphol. Earth* v. 146 Together, scarp retreat (by gully-head erosion and mass slipping of material) and pedimentation (by bedrock levelling and sheet-waste removal) are the most potent agents modifying epigene landscapes. **1973** *Nature* 9 Nov. 75/2 Recession of valley nickpoints inland from the coastal margin was followed by valley widening, scarp retreat and pedimentation, leading ultimately to the formation of gently undulating pediplains or erosion surfaces.

pedimented ('pɛdɪməntɪd), *a.* [f. as PEDIMENTAL *a.* + -ED[2].] **1.** Having a pediment; formed with or made like a pediment.

1845 PETRIE *Eccl. Archit. Irel.* 248 The only example of a pedimented lintel, which I have met with in Ireland. **1866** *Athenæum* No. 1999. 241/2 The pedimented windows. **1875** J. C. COX *Churches of Derbysh.* I. 245 Two female figures kneeling at desks.. wear pedimented head-dresses. *Ibid.* 340 A plain incised cross with a pedimented base.

2. *Geomorphol.* Characterized by the presence of pediments (PEDIMENT[1] 1 b).

1949 *Geol. Mag.* LXXXVI. 249 Pedimented landscapes consist essentially of hillslopes and of pediments. **1960** B. W. SPARKS *Geomorphol.* xi. 258 Landscapes resembling the pedimented areas of the arid south-western parts of the United States are found on an altogether larger scale in Africa.

pedimeter, another form of PEDOMETER. Hence **pedi'metric, pe'dimetry**.

1890 in *Cent. Dict.*

pediocratic (pɛdɪəʊ'krætɪk), *a. Geol.* [f. Gr. πεδίον a plain + κράτ-ος strength + -IC.] Characterized by an overall lessening of relief as a result of erosion predominating over crustal upheaval.

1924 W. RAMSAY in *Geol. Mag.* LXI. 155 During anorogenic periods, again, the continents become more or less peneplained. I call such a condition pediocratic. **1929** L. J. WILLS *Physiogr. Evol. Britain* ii. 7 Even in the pediocratic periods, the non-spectacular phenomena of erosion and deposition, and the ordered changes in the life of the world, given the requisite length of time, produce equally profound modifications in its physiography. **1961** [see OROCRATIC *a.*].

pedion ('pɛdɪɒn). *Cryst.* Pl. **pedia**. [a. Gr. πεδίον a plain, a flat surface.] A term introduced to denote any face of an anorthic crystal; each face being bounded by a set of faces of which no two are necessarily parallel, and which are connected only by a law of rational indices.

1899 W. J. LEWIS *Crystallogr.* xi. 148 Each form consists of a single face, and will be called a *pedion*.

pedionomite (pɛdɪ'ɒnəmaɪt). *rare.* [f. Gr. πεδιονόμ-ος plain-dweller + -ITE.] An inhabitant of a plain, a dweller in a plain.

1876 BURTON *Etruscan Bologna* 16 They would overspread the surrounding lowlands, and become pedionomites.

pedipalp ('pɛdɪpælp). *Zool.* Also in L. form **pedipalpus**, pl. -i. [f. mod.L. *Pedipalpi* sb. pl. (Latreille, 1806), f. L. *pēs, pedi-* foot + *palpus* feeler, PALP.]

1. An arachnid of the group *Pedipalpi*, distinguished by large pincer-like palps; formerly including the true scorpions, now restricted to the *Phrynidæ* and *Thelyphonidæ*, or *whip-scorpions*.

1835 KIRBY *Hab. & Inst. Anim.* II. xvi. 89 In the Pedipalps.. the first pair of legs of Octopods seem to wear the form and in some measure to discharge the functions of antennæ.

2. Each of the pair of palps or feelers attached to the head just in front of the ambulatory limbs in most Arachnids; in some cases, as in scorpions, large and pincer-like or chelate.

1826 KIRBY & SP. *Entomol.* III. xxxv. 684 The first pair of pedipalps are not chelate. **1828** STARK *Elem. Nat. Hist.* II. 184 Processes behind representing jaws and pedipalpi. **1884** A. SEDGWICK *Claus' Text-Bk. Zool.* 510 [Scorpions] seize their prey.. with their large chelate pedipalps.

Hence **pedipalpal** (pɛdɪ'pælpəl) *a.*, pertaining to a pedipalp; **pedi'palpate** *a.*, provided with pedipalps; **pedi'palpous** *a.*, belonging to the group *Pedipalpi* (see 1); having large pedipalps.

1864 WEBSTER, *Pedipalpous*, pertaining to, or resembling, the pedipalps. **1877** HUXLEY *Anat. Inv. Anim.* vii. 384 The pedipalpal portion of the proboscis.

pediplain ('pɛdɪpleɪn). *Geomorphol.* [f. PEDI(MENT[1] + PLAIN *sb.*[1]] An extensive plain formed in a desert by the coalescence of neighbouring pediments (believed to represent a late stage in the cycle of erosion in arid and semi-arid climates). Cf. PEDIPLANE.

1935 MAXSON & ANDERSON in *Jrnl. Geol.* XLIII. 94 Widely extending rock-cut and alluviated surfaces of this type formed by the coalescence of a number of pediments and occasional desert domes may be called 'pediplains'. **1968** C. R. TWIDALE *Geomorphol.* xi. 308 Pediplains, .. like peneplains, are surfaces of low relief, but generally differ from the latter in a number of respects. They are smoother, and less dissected.., they are mostly dominated by concave profiles, and meet the adjacent uplands in a piedmont angle. **1973** [see PEDIMENTATION]. **1974** C. H. CRICKMAY *Work of River* viii. 211 Where pediments are sufficiently extensive to be conjoint and broadly continuous, the whole is termed a pediplain or a panfan. **1977** A. HALLAM *Planet Earth* 190 The continents as a whole were, however, almost completely worn down to pedi-plains.

Hence **'pediplained** *a.*

1970 R. J. SMALL *Study of Landforms* ii. 28 This is one of the explanations of the development, on the pediplained surfaces of South America, Africa and Australia, of very hard weathering crusts.

pediplanation (pɛdɪplə'neɪʃən). *Geomorphol.* [f. PEDI(PLANE, PEDI(PLAIN + PLANATION.] Erosion to, or the formation of, a pediplain (or pediplane).

1942 A. D. HOWARD in *Jrnl. Geomorphol.* V. 11 *Pediplanation* may be applied as a general term to the process of formation of pediplanes. **1948** *Proc. Geol. Soc. S. Afr.* L. p. xxvii, Every one of these features is ubiquitous on the terrains of Southern and Central Africa, clear proof that the landscape of those regions has evolved through pediplanation. **1963** D. W. & E. E. HUMPHRIES tr. *Termier's Erosion & Sedimentation* ii. 40 It is on plateaus, sometimes uplifted and peneplained (often those which have undergone initial pediplanation) that desert dunes (Sahara) and ice caps (Scandinavia) have developed. **1975** *Nature* 31 July 442/1 Part 2 discusses the character and development of the tropical terrain and includes chapters.. on pediments and pediplanation.

pediplane ('pɛdɪpleɪn). *Geomorphol.* [f. PEDI(MENT[1] + PLANE *sb.*[3]] A piedmont slope in arid and semi-arid regions comprising a pediment and a peripediment (or just one of these, if the other is not present). Cf. PEDIPLAIN.

1942 A. D. HOWARD in *Jrnl. Geomorphol.* V. 11 The writer proposes the term *pediplane* as a general term for all degradational piedmont surfaces produced in arid climates which are either exposed or covered by a veneer of contemporary alluvium no thicker than that which can be moved during floods. *Ibid.* 13 In some localities the up-land rocks may be extremely resistant or the basin rocks may be extremely weak... In such regions the pediplane will truncate basin sediments almost exclusively and will consist largely of peripediment. **1948** *Bull. Geol. Soc. Amer.* LIX. 370 In regions of rising base level the pedi-plane will be made up for the most part of a peripediment, and the pediment as a near-mountain zone cut on solid rock is sometimes overlooked. **1955** *Proc. Geologists' Assoc.* LXVI. 173 The combined pediment and peripediment may then be describd as a pediplane (Howard, 1942).

pedipulate (pɪ'dɪpjʊleɪt), *v. nonce-wd.* [f. L. *pēs, pedi-* foot, after *manipulate*.] *trans.* To work with the feet. So **pedipu'lation, pe'dipulator**.

1889 *Sat. Rev.* 26 Jan. 92/2 Pedipulation, on the analogy of manipulation, clearly means doing something with the feet. **1892** *Longm. Mag.* Dec. 208 My very first attempt to manipulate, or rather pedipulate those slippery engines [snow-shoes]. **1895** *Globe* 19 Feb. 1/4 Who.. ever saw a [Football] player of any note incapable of using both 'pedipulators'. **1900** O. ONIONS *Compl. Bachelor* xi. 158 Bassishaw must have been as busy in his pedipulations as an organist.

pedireme ('pɛdɪriːm). *Zool.* [f. PEDI- + L. *rēm-us* oar.] Proposed name for a crustacean whose feet serve for swimming; a copepod.

1835 KIRBY *Hab. & Inst. Anim.* II. xvii. 133 The tribe of crabs termed swimmers, these I would call Pediremes.

pediscope, var. PEDOSCOPE.

†**pe'dissequent.** *Obs. rare*$^{-1}$. [f. L. *pedisequ-us* following on foot, a foot-follower, f. PEDI- + *-sequ-us* following, *sequī* to follow, the ending conformed to L. *sequent-em* following.] A follower, an attendant. So †**pe'dissequous** *a.*, following, attendant upon something.

1607 TOPSELL *Four-f. Beasts* (1658) 107 Untill.. he [a deer] be forced to offer up his bloud and flesh to the rage of all the observant pedissequants of the hunting Goddess Diana. **1657** TOMLINSON *Renou's Disp.* 565 The melancholical Captain-humour.. also the Bilious which is pedissequous.

pedistal, obs. form of PEDESTAL.

pediunker (pɛdɪ'ʌŋkə(r)). [Etym. unknown]. A name for the grey petrel, *Procellaria cinerea*, originally used in the island of Tristan da Cunha, where this bird is common.

1910 K. M. BARROW *Three Yrs. in Tristan da Cunha* 275 The 'Pediunker' lays in May and June; it is like a petrel. **1923** A. H. MACKLIN in F. Wild *Shackleton's Last Voy.* xii. 253 Gordon Glass had with him his dog, which occasionally discovered a 'pediunker', a species of seabird which frequents the island [*sc.* Tristan da Cunha]. **1952** J. FISHER *Fulmar* xvi. 381 Barnacles on birds are rare, though they have been found in the tail-feathers of the sub-antarctic *Adamastor cinereus*, the pediunker or grey petrel. **1967** B. ROBERTS *Wilson's Birds of Antarctic* 139/2 Grey Petrel or Pediunker, *Procellaria cinerea*. Drawings of a recently killed adult ♂.

pedlar, peddler ('pɛdlə(r)), *sb.* Forms: 4-5 **pedlere**, 5 **pedlare**, 5-6 **pedeler**, 6 **peddelar**, 7- (9- chiefly *U.S.*) **peddler**, 6- **pedler**, **pedlar**. [Origin obscure.

The 14th c. *pedlere* has the form of an agent-noun, but occurs long before there is any trace of the vb. *pedle*, PEDDLE, in any sense, from which therefore it cannot be assumed to be derived. It is app. synonymous with PEDDER, and may possibly have been a modification of that word (cf. Scotch *tinkler* for *tinker*), or formed on the same basis *ped*. But the Promptorium (*c* 1440) has both *pedder* and *pedlere* with distinct explanations, and without any reference to each other.

The spelling *peddler* is usual in the U.S., and is occas. found in the U.K., esp. in sense 1 d.]

1. One who goes about carrying small goods for sale (usually in a bundle or *pack*); a travelling chapman or vendor of small wares. (Now technically distinguished from HAWKER, q.v.)

1377 LANGL. *P. Pl.* B. v. 258, I haue as moche pité of pore men as pedlere hath of cattes, þat wolde kille hem, yf he cacche hem myȝte, for coueitise of here skynnes. *c* **1430** LYDG. *Min. Poems* (Percy Soc.) 30 Now coorbed is thi bakke; Or sone shal bene as pedeler to his pakke. **1579** SPENSER *Sheph. Cal.* May 238 All as a poore pedler he did wend, Bearing a trusse of tryfles at hys backe. **1660** MILTON *Griffith's Serm.* Wks. 1851 V. 390 Not unlike the Fox, that turning Pedlar, open'd his pack of War before the Kid. **1838**, etc. [see *essence-peddler* s.v. ESSENCE *sb.* 11]. **1860** SMILES *Self-Help* ii. 40 Articles of earthenware.. were.. hawked about by.. pedlers, who carried their stocks upon their backs.

b. *fig.* One who 'deals in' something in a small way, a 'retailer'.

1681 GLANVILL *Sadducismus* II. (1726) 454 My Zeal against those Pedlers of Wit. **1870** LOWELL *Study Wind.* 152 The pedlers of rumor in the North.

c. A female pedlar, a pedlaress.

1705 VANBRUGH *Confederacy* I. ii, The rogue had a kettle-drum to his father,.. and has a pedlar to his mother.

d. One who peddles goods in some way illicitly, as stolen goods, forged notes, illegal drugs, etc. orig. *U.S.*

1872 G. P. BURNHAM *Mem. U.S. Secret Service* p. vii, *Peddler*, an itinerant counterfeit money-seller. **1929** M. A. GILL *Underworld Slang, Peddlers*, drug bootleggers. **1930** [see *drug-peddler* s.v. DRUG *sb.*[1] 1 b]. **1935** *Jrnl. Abnormal Psychol.* XXX. 363 *Peddler*, an inmate who steals and sells state property. **1935** N. ERSINE *Underworld & Prison Slang* 57 *Pint peddler*, a petty bootlegger who carries a number of pints of liquor about his person. He usually hangs around poolrooms. **1949**, etc. [see *influence-peddler* s.v. INFLUENCE *sb.* 8]. *a* **1953** E. O'NEILL *Hughie* (1959) 27 Take my tip, pal, and don't never try to buy from a dope peddler. **1953** W. BURROUGHS *Junkie* (1972) ii. 29 In fact, a peddler should not come right out and say he is a peddler... Everyone knows that he himself is the connection, but it is bad form to say so. *Ibid.* iv. 41 A peddler.. was pushing Mexican H on 103rd and Broadway. **1978** T. WILLIAMSON *Technicians of Death*

vi. 44 They're ready to deal in junk [*sc.* drugs]... Fringe groups..will start feeding the peddlers. **1978** *Guardian* 25 Aug. 11/6 The officials even wanted me to identify the street peddler from whom I bought a copy of the English book.

2. A contemptuous designation [app. f. PEDDLE *v.*] for: One who peddles, or works in a petty, incompetent, or ineffective way.

a **1585** POLWART *Flyting w. Montgomery* 153 Pedler, I pittie thee sa pinde. **1825** COBBETT *Rur. Rides* (1885) II. 41 The poor deluded creature..who knew nothing..about such matters..was a perfect pedlar in political economy.

3. *attrib.* and *Comb.*

a **1553** EDW. VI in Burnet *Hist. Ref.* (1681) II. Collect. Rec. 71 The Farmer..will be a Pedlar-Merchant. **1592** tr. *Junius on Rev.* xiii. 16 Pedlerlike abuse of indulgences. **1598** E. GILPIN *Skial.* (1878) 4 To reade these pedler rimes. **1776** ADAM SMITH *W.N.* III. iv. (1869) I. 418 In pursuit of their own pedlar principle of turning a penny wherever a penny was to be got. **1842** THACKERAY *Sultan Stork* Wks. 1900 V. 739 An old pedlar-woman, who was displaying her wares.

4. Combinations with *pedlar's.* **a. pedlar's basket**: a local name for the Ivy-leaved Toadflax, *Linaria Cymbalaria*; also for *Saxifraga sarmentosa* (Britten & H.); **pedlar's pad**: see quot.

1828 *Craven Gloss.* (ed. 2), *Pedlar's Basket*, Ivy leaved snap-dragon... *Pedlar's-Pad*, a walking stick.

b. pedlar's French: the language used by vagabonds and thieves among themselves; rogues' or thieves' cant; hence, unintelligible jargon, gibberish. (In quot. 1610 *transf.* A rogue, vagabond.)

1530 PALSGR. 727/1 They speke a pedlars frenche amongest them selfe. **1567** HARMAN *Caveat* 23 Their languag—which they terme peddelars Frenche or Canting. **1610** *Histriomastix* IV. i, When euery Pedlers-French is term'd Monsignuer. *a* **1700** B. E. *Dict. Cant. Crew, Pedlar's-French*, a sort of Gibrish..used by Gypsies, &c. Also the Beggers Cant. **1887** HALL CAINE *Deemster* xxxii, Kidnapped? No such matter... What pedlar's French!

Hence †ˈ**pedlar** *v. trans.*, to make a pedlar of; *intr.* to act as a pedlar; ˈ**pedlaress**, a female pedlar; ˈ**pedlaring**, ˈ**pedlarism**, the occupation of a pedlar, itinerant retail trade, petty dealing; ˈ**pedlarly** *a.*, belonging to or befitting a pedlar.

1661 I. B. in *A. Brome's Songs* etc. 176 Why *pedler'st thus thy Muse? Why dost set o'pe A shop of wit, to set the fidlers up? *a* **1613** OVERBURY *A Wife* (1638) 128 Some foule sunne-burnt Queane that, since the terrible statute, recanted Gypsisme, and is turned *Pedleresse. **1862** *Athenæum* 30 Aug. 266 *Pedlaring did not continue to be a pretty thing. **1892** W. W. PEYTON *Memorab. Jesus* i. 22 This is historical pedantry and critical pedlaring. **1699** T. BROWN in *Fam. & Courtly Lett.* (1700) 182 If they are not at last reduc'd to their old ancient *Pedlarism. **1617** COLLINS *Def. Bp. Ely* I. iv. 182 You long to be vntrussing your *pedlerly fardles.

pedlary (ˈpɛdlərɪ), *sb.* (*a.*) Also 6 **-arie**, 6–7 **-erie**, 6–9 **pedlery**, 9 **peddlery**. [f. PEDLAR + -Y: cf. *beggary*.]

1. The business or practice of a pedlar. Also *fig.*

1604 HIERON *Answ. Popish Rime* Wks. 1613 I. 569 Those sacraments, which holy be, You stayn'd haue with your pedlery. **1751** JOHNSON *Rambler* No. 119 ¶6, I..might..have been doomed..to the grossness of pedlary, and the jargon of usury. **1833** J. HOLLAND *Manuf. Metal* II. 320 Those 'small wares', the sale of which constituted..the staple of ancient pedlery.

b. Small goods sold by pedlars: pedlars' wares.

1593 NASHE *Christ's T.* Wks. (Gros.) IV. 142 The third time..they shall haue baser commodities: the fourth time Lute strings and gray Paper... When thus this young Vsurer hath thrust all hys pedlary into the hands of nouice heyres,..he [etc.]. **1759** *Bk. of Fairs* 9 Mwrras, Carmarthenshire, Aug. 21, for cattle, sheep, and pedlary. **1858** MRS. OLIPHANT *Laird of Norlaw* I. 290 An unbelievable accumulation of pedlery. **1890** HALLETT *1000 Miles in Shan States* 4 You may see..parties of Shans..with ..sundry articles of peddlery.

2. Trifling or contemptible practices or things; trumpery, trash, rubbish.

1530 TINDALE *Answ. More* (Parker Soc.) 170 To confirm his preaching of ear-confession and pardons, with like pedlary. **1651** BIGGS *New Disp.* ¶252 More ridiculous pedleries then the pageantries and puppetries of Bartholmew Faire. **1816** COLERIDGE *Lay Serm.* 341 Wandering..with its pack of amulets, bead-rolls,..fetisches, and the like pedlary.

B. *attrib.* or as *adj.*

1. *lit.* Belonging to a pedlar or his occupation; pedlar's.

1550 BALE *Eng. Votaries* II. 99 Saynte Godrycke..went first abroade with pedlary wares, and afterwardes on pilgrimage. **1587** HARRISON *England* III. xv, Little else..than good drinke, pies, and some pedlerie trash. **1630** *Tinker of Turvey, Tinker's T.* (1859) 18, I would have pawn'd all the pedlary packes that ever I carried. **1748** RICHARDSON *Clarissa* III. let. 2. **1824** MISS MITFORD *Village* Ser. I. (1863) 216 Solid old-fashioned silken pincushions, such as Autolycus might have carried about amongst his pedlery-ware.

†**2.** *fig.* Fit for a pedlar; pedlar-like, peddling, trashy, 'trumpery', 'rubbishy'. *Obs.*

1555 R. TAYLOR in Foxe *A. & M.* (1570) 1705/1 Hys pedlary pelfe packe is contrarye to the playne simplicitie of Christes supper. **1563** BECON *Displ. Pop. Mass* Wks. III. 43 Your peuishe, Popish, priuate pedlary peltyng Masse. **1674** EVELYN *Navig. & Commerce* Misc. Writ. (1805) 634 Condemning the pedlary and sordid vices of retailers.

pedling: see PEDDLE, PEDDLING.

pedo- (ˈpɛdəʊ, pɛˈdɒ, pɪˈdɒ), or before a vowel **ped-**, repr. Gr. πέδον ground, earth, is used in the sense 'soil' in PEDOLOGY and other technical terms.

pedo-: see PÆDO-.

pedocal (ˈpɛdəʊkæl). *Soil Sci.* [f. PEDO- + CAL(CIUM.] A soil that contains a layer of accumulated calcium carbonate (generally characteristic of dry climates). Cf. PEDALFER.

1928 C. F. MARBUT in *Proc. & Papers 1st Internat. Congr. Soil Sci.* IV. 20 A formal definition of the two groups is as follows: I. Includes all soils in whose maturely developed profiles no higher percentage of lime carbonate is found than in the parent material beneath them and in which either a shifting or an accumulation of sesquioxide and in many cases both, has taken place. II. Includes all soils with fully developed profiles in which lime carbonate is found on some horizon in the solum in higher percentage than in the parent geological formation beneath... The name *Pedalfers* is suggested as a designation for the soils of group I, and *Pedocals* for those of group II. **1938** *Nature* 21 May 925/2 It has been generally accepted that the climate of Great Britain is too wet for pedocals to develop. **1949** F. J. PETTIJOHN *Sedimentary Rocks* xii. 384 The pedalfers and pedocals are subdivided into many soil types. **1968** [see *halomorphic* adj. s.v. HALO-]. **1972** J. G. CRUICKSHANK *Soil Geogr.* v. 158 Marbut..established a classification that became the most widely known of the schemes based on soil genesis, in which he made the two-fold primary sub-division between the leached soils (pedalfers) and the non-leached (pedocals) freely drained soils. **1977** A. HALLAM *Planet Earth* 179 These ideas were accepted in the USA, and the concepts of pedalfers and pedocals added: pedalfers are leached soils in humid areas where aluminium and iron accumulate in the B horizon, and pedocals occur in more arid regions.

Hence **pedoˈcalic** *a.*

1928 *Proc. & Papers 1st Internat. Congr. Soil Sci.* IV. 23 Most of the groups of Pedalferic soils in category V were defined by Russian pedologists, but they made no attempt to differentiate the Pedocalic soils on the same basis since the Eurasian conditions do not present an opportunity for doing it. **1938** *Nature* 21 May 925/1 (*heading*) Pedocalic tendencies in soils of southern England. **1941** H. JENNY *Factors Soil Formation* vi. 191 Not all soils that are embraced by the area labeled as pedocals contain lime horizons. Only those soils which have the required normal topography and which have attained sufficient maturity deserve the attribute pedocalic.

pedœuvre (pɪˈd(j)uːvə(r)). *nonce-wd.* [f. L. *ped-em* foot, after *manœuvre*.] A planned movement or performance with the feet.

1825 COLERIDGE *Aids Refl.* (1873) 193 The bees had recourse to the same manœuvre (or rather pedœuvre).

pedogenesis (pɛdəʊˈdʒɛnɪsɪs). [f. PEDO- + -GENESIS.] Soil formation.

1936 J. S. JOFFE *Pedology* vi. 134 From the point of view of pedogenesis, the classification of the soil-forming processes, in their broad aspects, should hinge on the elements of climate. **1943** *Proc. Soil Sci. Soc. Amer.* VII. 187/1 Most investigations on mechanical separates of the soil have dealt with the physical aspects of the subject, with no relation to pedogenesis and agropedologic implications. **1963** D. W. & E. E. HUMPHRIES tr. *Termier's Erosion & Sedimentation* vi. 135 During pedogenesis (soil formation), the nature of the alteration of the titanium minerals depends more upon chemical diagenetic environmental conditions than on the nature of the parent rock. **1972** J. G. CRUICKSHANK *Soil Geogr.* ii. 42 As part of the rolé of climate in pedogenesis, its moisture and temperature components also affect the rate of decay and incorporation into the soil of surface organic litter.

Hence **pedogeˈnetic**, **-geˈnetical** *adjs.* = PEDOGENIC *a.*; **pedogeˈnetically** *adv.*

1946 *Soil Sci.* LXI. 389 Each soil series..is thus pedogenetically connected with ten other series. **1950** *Ann. Assoc. Amer. Geographers* XL. 218 Within these pedogenetic regions no one of the weathering processes occurs exclusively. **1963** D. W. & E. E. HUMPHRIES tr. *Termier's Erosion & Sedimentation* vi. 153 Butterlin (1958) believes that these soils are formed by the pedogenetic alteration of the limestones. **1978** *Nature* 30 Mar. 477/3 Work on pedogenetical formations and Quaternary deposits in central and northern Dobrudja. *Ibid.* 28 Sept. 285/2 Deeper, pedogenetically differentiated profiles in relict areas immune from rapid denudation.

pedogenic (pɛdəʊˈdʒɛnɪk), *a.* [f. PEDO- + -GENIC.] Soil-forming

1924 *Geol. Mag.* LXI. 448 (*heading*) The pedogenic processes. [*Note*] I am indebted to my friend Dr. Edward Greenly, F.G.S., for this convenient term, which aptly describes the processes of soil formation and metamorphism. **1936** *Nature* 24 Oct. 729/2 The effect of human interference as a pedogenic factor was raised in the discussion. **1943** [see *palæopedology* s.v. PALÆO-, PALEO-]. **1975** *Nature* 20 Feb. 617/2 The carbonate nodules which occur in the Pleistocene but not in the Holocene portions of the core are regarded as pedogenic and as symptomatic of a soil climate drier than the present one.

Hence **pedoˈgenically** *adv.*

1972 J. G. CRUICKSHANK *Soil Geogr.* iii. 74 The upper boundary is obvious, but the lower one may be either the maximum plant rooting depth or the base of the pedogenically altered material.

†**peˈdography.** *Obs. rare*$^{-1}$. [f. Gr. πέδον the ground + -γραφία -GRAPHY.] (See quot.)

1625 N. CARPENTER *Geog. Del.* II. ix. (1635) 140 This description of the dry-land separated from the Waters, we haue termed Pedographie.

pedology (pɛ-, pɪˈdɒlədʒɪ). [f. PEDO- + -OLOGY. Cf. G. *pedologie* (e.g. F. A. Fallou *Pedologie* (1862) I. 9), Russ. *pedológiya* (e.g. *Entsikl. Slovar′* (1898) XXIVA s.v. *pochvovedenie*; *Pochvovedenie* (1900) II. 140, (1902) IV. 1; the Fr. title of this periodical was *La Pédologie* from its inception in 1899).

The usual Russ. word for the subject has always been *pochvovédenie*, lit. 'soil science' (cf. G. *bodenkunde*, given by Fallou as a synonym of *pedologie*). The Eng. word *pedology* occurs in the galley proofs of an unpublished dict. of *c* 1900–10, according to L. D. Stamp *Gloss. Geogr. Terms* (1961) 358, but prob. only in reference to foreign equivalents.]

The scientific study of soil, esp. its formation, nature, and classification; soil science.

[**1923** M. M. MCCOOL et al. in *Soil Sci.* XVI. 106 It places soil study on a natural basis and in fact lays the foundation of a new science which we might name, podology.] **1924** G. W. ROBINSON in *Geol. Mag.* LXI. 444 (*heading*) Pedology as a branch of geology. [*Note*] The writer ventures to hope that this convenient term (Gr. πέδον = soil or earth) will be more generally used to describe the scientific study of soils. **1926** TANSLEY & CHIPP *Study of Vegetation* vii. 114 The science of the soil (sometimes called pedology) has made very great strides within the past quarter of a century. **1938** A. B. YOLLAND tr. *A. A. J. de Sigmond's Princ. Soil Sci.* 1 The first to try to liberate soil science from this position was the German geologist Frederick Augustus Fallon, who, however, by basing his soil classification upon geological-petrographic principles unconsciously subordinated pedology to geology. **1958** I. W. CORNWALL *Soils for Archaeologist* 13 For information about the earth the archaeologist turns first to the sciences of geology, geography and pedology (soil-science). **1973** *Nature* 27 July p. ii/1 (Advt.), Scientists interested in sediments and in allied fields such as pedology, geomorphology, soils engineering and cement technology will find in this book a valuable research tool.

Hence **pedoˈlogic**, **-ˈlogical** *adjs.*, of or pertaining to pedology or soil; **pedoˈlogically** *adv.*, in pedological terms; as regards pedology; **peˈdologist**, one who studies pedology.

1924 *Geol. Mag.* LXI. 450 Among mature soils, i.e. among soils which have reached a state of pedological equilibrium. *Ibid.* 454 The remaining class in Glinka's scheme is only of limited interest for western European pedologists. **1927** C. F. MARBUT tr. *Glinka's Great Soil Groups* 5 The distribution of such soil units also would be the same as that of the rocks from which derived and would be petrographic rather than pedologic. **1932** *Proc. & Papers 2nd Internat. Congr. Soil Sci.* V. 1 If it be pedologically justifiable to grant the type status to podzols. **1945** *Antiquity* XIX. 172 The pedological characters of Anglesey by which vegetation would be affected and to a large extent controlled. **1963** D. W. & E. E. HUMPHRIES tr. *Termier's Erosion & Sedimentation* ix. 192 Sedimentation in these basins..depends to a large extent on the pedologic evolution of the continents. **1964** R. FEYS in A. E. M. Nairn *Probl. Palaeoclimatol.* iii. 68 The sandstone is derived from sand which has been pedologically altered and mechanically sorted. **1972** J. G. CRUICKSHANK *Soil Geogr.* v. 159 The Marbut classification also influenced pedologists on an international level because it was discussed at international soil congresses in 1927, 1932, and 1935. **1974** *Nature* 4 Jan. 74/1 There was no known method by which termites or pedological processes could bring about the observed accumulation of calcium carbonate in termite mounds.

ˈ**pedomancy.** *nonce-wd.* [Hybrid f. *pedo-* for PEDI- foot + Gr. -μαντεια -MANCY.] A jocular term of Gabriel Harvey's for divination by the soles of the feet: taken by some later authors seriously.

1592 G. HARVEY *Pierce's Super.* (1593) 132 Pedomancie [is] fitter for such Coniurers, then either Chiromancie, or Necromancie, or any Familiar Spirite, but contempt. **1652** GAULE *Magastrom.* 165. **1656** BLOUNT *Glossogr.*, *Pedomancy*, a kind of divination by the lines of the sole of the feet. **1709** Pedimancy [see -MANCY]. **1883** *N. Brit. Advert.* 19 May 5/5 Pedomancy, or divination by the soles of the feet, may also in these times become as interesting and useful a study [as palmistry].

pedometer (pɪˈdɒmɪtə(r)). [ad. F. *pédomètre* (Bion 1723), hybrid f. *pedo-* for L. *pedi-* foot + Gr. μέτρον measure, -METER. French had also the etymologically more correct form *podomètre* (1712 in Hatz.-Darm.). In sense 2, the first element might be πέδον ground.]

1. An instrument for recording the number of steps taken, and thus approximately measuring the distance travelled on foot: usually somewhat resembling a watch in size and appearance, having a dial-plate marked with numbers, round which a pointer or index-hand travels.

[**1712** HAUTEFEUILLE *Machine arpentante* 10 Le podomètre ou conte-pas. **1723** BION *Instr. de Mathém.* 96 Cet instrument se nomme Pedometre ou Compte-pas.] **1723** E. STONE tr. *Bion's Math. Instr.* III. ii. 88 Construction of the Pedometer or Waywiser. **1727–41** CHAMBERS *Cycl.*, *Pedometer*, or *Podometer*, way-wiser; a mechanical instrument, in form of a watch; consisting of various wheels ..which by means of a chain or string fastned to a man's foot ..advance a notch each step. **1783** J. FISCHER *Patent Specif.* No. 1377. 6 The pedometer or pace- and step-teller. **1786** JEFFERSON *Writ.* (ed. Ford) IV. 194. **1876** *Handbk. Sci. App. S. Kens.* 25. **1880** MARK TWAIN *Tramp Abr.* xi. 85 Harris carried the little watch-like machine called a 'pedometer', whose office is to keep count of a man's steps and tell how far he has walked.

2. (See quot.)

1727–41 CHAMBERS *Cycl.* s.v., Pedometer is sometimes also used for a surveying wheel, an instrument chiefly used in measuring roads; popularly called the way-wiser. *Ibid.*, *Perambulator*, in surveying,.. called also pedometer.

So **pedo'metric, pedo'metrical** *adjs.*, of, pertaining to, or of the nature of a pedometer; serving to measure a distance travelled on foot; hence **pedo'metrically** *adv.*; **pedometrician** (-'ɪʃən), a maker of pedometers; **pe'dometrist**, one who uses a pedometer.

1783 J. FISCHER *Patent Specif.* No. 1377. 6 A pedometrical watch can be made also with two dyal plates. **1885** ALEX. STEWART *'Twixt Ben Nevis & Glencoe* ix, A method of pedometrically ascertaining the maximum and minimum of spring temperatures. **1827** *Blackw. Mag.* XXII. 465 No Pedometrician will ever make a fortune in a mountainous island. *Ibid.*, One tolerable pedestrian who is also a Pedometrist.

pedomotive ('pɛdəməʊtɪv), *a.* and *sb.* [erron. f. *pedo-* for PEDI- + MOTIVE, prob. after *locomotive.*] **a.** *adj.* Actuated by the foot or feet. **b.** *sb.* A vehicle worked by the foot or feet; a velocipede.

1824 *Mechanic's Mag.* II. 81 Pedomotive Carriage. **1830** *Ibid.* XIII. 34 The pedomotive-carriage.. seems to require rather too much labour. **1843** *Ibid.* XXXIX. 389 We have two or three elegantly-formed pedomotives in Birmingham now, that work upon the simplest plan possible. **1884** *Cycl. Tour. Club Monthly Gaz.* Dec. 360/2 A sociable is the steadiest of all pedomotive machines.

pedomotor ('pɛdəʊməʊtə(r)). [erron. f. *pedo-* for PEDI- + MOTOR.] A contrivance or device for the application of the foot as the driving power in a machine, as a treadle, pedal, etc.; esp. a pedomotive vehicle, as a bicycle, etc.

1844 *Mech. Mag.* XLI. 370/1 The numerous velocipedes, pedomotors, manumotors, &c., which have been brought before the public during the last thirty years. **1884** in KNIGHT *Dict. Mech.* Suppl. 665/2.

pedon ('pɛdɒn). *Soil Sci.* [a. Gr. πέδον ground, earth.] A notional column of soil that extends vertically from the surface to the parent material and is of sufficient area (usu. at least a square metre) to be representative of the surrounding soil and its horizons.

1960 SIMONSON & GARDINER in *Trans. 7th Internat. Congr. Soil Sci.* IV. 128 Nature of the Pedon. It has recently been proposed that the term, pedon.., be used as a generic term for small basic soil entities. [*Note*] The term was proposed by Guy D. Smith. *Ibid.* 129 A pedon consists of a small volume of soil which includes the full solum and the upper part of the unconsolidated parent material.., is usually less than 2 meters in depth, and has a lateral cross section that is roughly circular or hexagonal in shape and between 1 and 10 square meters in size. **1972** J. G. CRUICKSHANK *Soil Geogr.* iii. 76 Pedons have such minimal horizontal area that often they fail to reflect important features of the larger soil body. **1973** THOMPSON & TROEH *Soils & Soil Fertility* (ed. 3) xvi. 369 Soils with large variations in their properties within short horizontal distances are allowed to have pedons as large as 10 sq m.. so that their properties may be fully represented.

pedophilia, etc., varr. PÆDOPHILIA, etc.

pedo'pleural = PLEUROPEDAL (a ganglion in mollusca).

1890 in *Cent. Dict.*

pedoscope ('pɛdəskəʊp). Also **pediscope.** [f. PEDI- (erron. *pedo-*) + -SCOPE.] An X-ray machine for showing the fitting and movement of the feet inside shoes (formerly common in shoe shops).

1923 *Chambers's Jrnl.* Aug. 560/1 The machine used is called the pedoscope. **1959** *Times* 30 Apr. 6/5 The use of pedoscopes, although frowned on by The Medical Research Council, was not diminishing. **1967** *Punch* 22 Nov. 792/3 In one of the earliest scenes Harry, given a vacuum flask to smuggle to Helsinki, finds out what is inside by putting it under the X-ray of a shoe-shop's pediscope.

pedosphere ('pɛdəʊsfɪə(r)). *Geol.* [f. PEDO- + SPHERE *sb.*] The earth's soil layer.

1938 S. MATTSON in *Lantbrukshögskolans Ann.* V. 261 Soils might be said to represent the sum of the mechanical and the products of the chemical interaction of the four spheres: the lithosphere, the hydrosphere, the atmosphere and the biosphere. They constitute a dispersed system in which the material from these four spheres alternate as dispersed phase and dispersion medium. To this sphere of spheres the name of pedosphere has been given. **1946** *Nature* 6 July 31/1 G. A. Maximovich.. has calculated the average porosities of different types of rocks and has also calculated the average porosities of the geospheres. These, in percentages, are as follows: pedosphere (soils), 55; [etc.]. **1968** R. W. FAIRBRIDGE *Encycl. Geomorphol.* 416/1 On top of this [*sc.* the lithosphere] the continents have an additional soil layer or pedosphere with a depth generally of only 1-2 meters.

pedotrophic, etc.: see PÆDO-.

Pedrail ('pɛdreɪl). *Obs.* exc. *Hist.* [f. PED(I- + RAIL *sb.*[2]] A type of traction engine, patented in 1899 and 1902 by B. J. Diplock; it moves forward by means of articulated feet, instead of wheels, which support rollers upon which run rails fixed to the vehicle itself.

1902 *Daily Chron.* 29 Dec. 6/6 A recent invention of Mr. Diplock—the 'Pedrail'—was exhibited. **1903** *Ibid.* 23 Nov. 6/4 The Pedrail was primarily designed as a traction engine for the transport of heavy goods on common roads. **1908** *Chambers's Jrnl.* Mar. 270/1 The ped-rail traction-engine—an engine equipped with a number of feet placed around the periphery of its driving-wheels, thereby imparting a walking action. **1916** *Ibid.* Feb. 83/1 This device is called the pedrail, and consists of a flat chain round the wheels.., the chain being armed with discs offering a flat surface to the ground. **1959** W. J. HUGHES *Cent. of Traction Engines* xvi. 212 At the beginning of 1902 some interesting experiments were being carried out with Diplock's 'Pedrail' engine... The particular engine under notice.. besides having the Pedrail wheels,.. had four-wheel drive. **1960** R. H. CLARK *Devel. Engl. Traction Engine* xiv. 291 In Diplock's Pedrail the rail (the bottom concave run) runs over the feet by virtue of the rollers interposed between them.

‖**pedregal** (ˌpɛdrɛ'gæl, 'pɛdrɛgəl). Also erron. **pedragal.** [Sp. *pedregal* 'a stonie place' (Minsheu), f. *piedra* stone = L. *petra.*] In Mexico and south-western U.S., A rough and rocky tract, esp. in a volcanic region; an old lava-field. Also *transf.* An ice-field resembling such a tract.

1853 KANE *Grinnell Exp.* xxxiii. (1856) 289, I am struck more and more with the evidences of gigantic force in the phases of our frozen *pedragal.* **1856** —— *Arct. Expl.* I. 197 An area more like the volcanic pedragal of the basin of Mexico than any thing else I can compare it to. **1881** BRYANT & GAY *Pop. Hist. U.S.* IV. xiv. 378 His [Santa Anna's] position was flanked on the west by a rugged field of broken lava, called the Pedregal, and on the east by marshy ground.

pedrero (pɛ'drɛərəʊ). Now *Hist.* Forms: α. 6 **pedrera,** 8 **peder-, pidr-, pedrero.** β. 6-7 **petrera,** 7 **petrara, peterera, petarrero,** 8 **peteraro,** 8-9 **pet(t)erero.** γ. 7-9 **paterero,** 8 **patar-, paderero, pattararo, (paterro),** 8-9 **pat(t)er-, patararo, patter-, patarrero.** [a. Sp. *pedrero* 'a murthering peece vsed in warres, to shoot chaineshot or stones from' (Minsheu) = Cat. *pedrer*, Pg. *pedreiro*, It. *petriere*, Pr. *peirier*, F. *pierrier*, formerly *perrier*, all repr. L. type **petrārius, -um*, in med.L. *petrāria* a stone-throwing engine (Du Cange), from *petrārius* adj., f. *petra* stone: cf. PETRARY, PERRIER. The English forms show many corruptions of the original, the later ones being app. influenced by PATTER *v.*] A piece of ordnance originally for discharging stones; formerly also used to discharge broken iron, partridge-shot, etc.; and for firing salutes.

α. **1598** BARRET *Theor. Warres* v. 124 The Cannon and double Cannon; the Pedrera, Basilisco, and such like. **1704** J. HARRIS *Lex. Techn.* I, *Pedrero*, or as it is usually called by the Seamen, *Petterero*, is a small piece of Ordnance, most used on board of Ships to fire Stones, Nails, broken Iron, or Partridge-shot. **1706** PHILLIPS, *Pederero.* **1712** E. COOKE *Voy. S. Sea* 346 A Ship.. carrying 20 Guns, and 20 Brass Pedreros. **1748** *Anson's Voy.* III. viii. 380 The galeon.. had ..twenty-eight pidreroes in her gunwale. **1769** FALCONER *Dict. Marine* (1789), *Clef de pierrier*, the forelock of a pedrero or swivel-gun.

β. **1600** J. PORY tr. *Leo's Afr.* Introd. 40 Stricken with a little gunne called Petrera. **1675** in J. Easton *Narr.* (1858) 104, [I] will gett and fitt up a Petrara for Capt. Chambers. **1675** TEONGE *Diary* (1825) 65 Our greate gunns.. and our petarreros humming. **1676** *Lond. Gaz.* No. 1130/4 Three Guns, and one Peterera. **1759** FALCONER *90-Gun Ship* 47 While peteraroes swell with infant rage. **1827** SIR J. BARRINGTON *Pers. Recoll.* (1876) 9 The hereditary petereroes scarcely ceased cracking all the evening.

γ. **1689** LUTTRELL *Brief Rel.* (1857) I. 620 A French privateer of 22 guns and 16 patereroes. **1693** R. LYDE *Retaking of Ship 'Friend's Adventure'* 2 A Privateer of St. Malloes, of twenty-two Guns, eight Pattereroes. **1726** SHELVOCK *Voy. round World* 274 This ship.. of 700 tons, 8 guns, and 10 patareroes. **1755** *Mem. Capt. P. Drake* I. xii. 86 He directed the Grenadiers.. to march with Paterro's, and some Field-pieces to follow. **1762** STERNE *Tr. Shandy* V. xix, Had it been his last crown, he would have sat down and hammered it into a paderero, to have prevented a single wish in his master. **1823** in *Spirit Publ. Jrnls.* 527 They fired a four pound patterero. **1844** TUPPER *Crock of G.* liii. 337 The patereroes on the lawn thunder a salute. **1886** V. LOVETT CAMERON *Cruise 'Black Prince'* xix. 230 The fort.. mounted twenty-two iron guns besides pateraroes.

pedro ('pɛdrəʊ). Also with capital initial. [f. Sancho *Pedro*, the name of a U.S. card game.] **a.** A variant of the card game Sancho Pedro in which the sancho, or nine of trumps, does not count. **b.** The name for the five of trumps in such games. Cf. CINCH *sb.* 3.

1874 *Reno* (Nevada) *Crescent* 8 May 2/3 The five of trumps is 'pedro'. **1876** *Avalanche* (Silver City, Idaho) 15 Mar. 2/3 Whist, pedro, pool.., etc., seem to be flourishing pastimes. **1880** W. B. DICK *Amer. Hoyle* (ed. 13) 210 Pedro may be taken with any trump higher than the Five. **1929** R. S. & H. M. LYND *Middletown* 281 The growing rigidity of the social system today is centering parties more and more upon cards, pedro among the workers and bridge among the others. **1944** A. H. MOREHEAD *Pocket Bk. Games* 199 Auction Pitch has many variants. Most of them—Pedro, Pedro Sancho, Dom Pedro, Snoozer—have been swallowed up by their own ultimate creation, Cinch. **1947** *Sat. Even. Post* 17 May 102/3 He operates a pedro game.

peduncle (pɪ'dʌŋk(ə)l). *Nat. Hist.* [ad. mod. Bot. L. *pedunculus* footstalk (Linnæus *Philos. Bot.* §82 D, *Pedunculus*, truncus partialis elevans Fructificationem nec folia), dim. of *ped-em* foot.

In L. only as a late variant of *pedīculus, pedūculus* louse. In F. *peduncule* (1765 Encycl.), *pédoncule* (Dict. Acad. 1835).]

A comparatively long and slender part forming a support or attachment for some other part or member in a plant or animal body; a footstalk.

1. *Bot.* The stalk of a flower or fruit, or of a cluster of flowers or fruits; the primary or main stalk, or one of the general stalks, of an inflorescence, which bears either a solitary flower, a number of sessile flowers, or a number of subordinate stalks (*pedicels*) directly bearing the flowers. (Distinguished from a leaf-stalk or *petiole.*) Also sometimes applied to other stalks, as those that bear the fructification in some fungi.

1753 CHAMBERS *Cycl. Supp.*, *Peduncle*, among botanists, expresses that little stalk which grows from the trunk or branches of a plant, and supports the parts of fructification, the flower and the fruit, or either. **1762** *Phil. Trans.* LIII. 83 Of equal length with the peduncle. **1830** LINDLEY *Nat. Syst. Bot.* 139 Leaves either opposite or alternate; in the latter case opposite the peduncles. **1874** COOKE *Fungi* 39 In all the Pucciniæi, the peduncles are permanent.

2. *Zool.*, etc. A stalk or stalk-like process in an animal body, either normal or morbid.

spec. **a.** The stalk by which a cirriped, brachiopod, actinozoon, etc. is attached to some foreign body: = PEDICEL 2 c. **b.** A slender part or joint by which some part or organ is attached to another, as that of the abdomen in some insects, and the eye-stalk in some crustaceans: = PEDICEL 2 a, b. **c.** *Anat.* Applied to several bundles of nerve-fibres in the brain, connecting one part of it with another (some of which are also called *crura*: see CRUS 2 b). **d.** *Path.* A stalk or slender process by which a tumour or morbid formation is attached to some part: = PEDICLE 2 a.

1797 M. BAILLIE *Morb. Anat.* (1807) 348 Attached to.. the inner surface of the tunica vaginalis testis, by very small processes or peduncles. **1828** STARK *Elem. Nat. Hist.* II. 123 Lamarck divides the class Cirripeda into.. *Pedunculata.* Body supported by a tubular moveable peduncle, of which the base is fixed upon marine bodies;.. *Sessilia.* Body destitute of peduncle, and fixed by the shell. **1840** G. V. ELLIS *Anat.* 29 The crura cerebelli, or anterior peduncles of the cerebellum. **1852** DANA *Crust.* I. 405 Peduncles of eyes slender. **1868** WOOD *Homes without H.* xxx. 573 The abdomen is.. attached to a slender footstalk or peduncle. **1886** A. WINCHELL *Walks Geol. Field* 193 Living species of Lingula.. clinging by their fleshy peduncles to the wharves.

3. *Comb.*

1849-52 TODD *Cycl. Anat.* IV. 1210/2 The peduncle-like post-abdomen forms a receptacle for the ova.

Hence **pe'duncled** *a.*, furnished with or having a peduncle or peduncles, pedunculate.

1806 GALPINE *Brit. Bot.* 1* Spikes peduncled. **1821** S. F. GRAY *Nat. Arrangem. Brit. Pl.* 247 Fruit oblong, peduncled. **1870** HOOKER *Stud. Flora* 299 Umbels peduncled.

peduncular (pɪ'dʌŋkjʊlə(r)), *a. Nat. Hist.* [ad. mod.L. *pedunculār-is*, f. *pedunculus*: see prec. and -AR[1].] Of, pertaining to, or of the nature of a peduncle (in any sense).

1806 GALPINE *Brit. Bot.* 51* Verticils peduncular, many-flowered: dichotomous. **1822-34** *Good's Study Med.* (ed. 4) I. 407 To restrain polypus, as a.. term, to peduncular excrescences in the nostrils. **1888** ROLLESTON & JACKSON *Anim. Life* 694 The body of the Brachiopod lies at the.. peduncular end of the shell. **1899** *Allbutt's Syst. Med.* VII. 325 The corpus callosum is a decussation of the peduncular fibres.

pedunculate (pɪ'dʌŋkjʊlət). *a. Nat. Hist.* [ad. mod.L. *pedunculāt-us*, f. *pedunculus*: see above and -ATE[2]. In mod.F. *pédonculé* (1798 in Hatz.-Darm.).] Furnished with or having a peduncle or peduncles; supported by a peduncle; stalked.

1760 J. LEE *Introd. Bot.* I. xx. (1765) 61 When many pedunculate Flowers are produced out of one common Calyx. **1826** KIRBY & SP. *Entomol.* xlvi. IV. 306 *Pedunculate*,.. when the head is constricted behind into a distinct neck. **1852** DANA *Crust.* I. 7 The species with pedunculate eyes. **1877** HUXLEY *Anat. Inv. Anim.* vi. 298 A typical pedunculate Cirripede.

pe'dunculated, *a.* [f. as prec. + -ED.] = prec.

1752 J. HILL *Hist. Anim.* 97 The angular-bodied Sepia, with long pedunculated tentacula. **1815** KIRBY & SP. *Entomol.* ix. (1818) I. 264 The singular pedunculated eggs from which these larvæ proceed. **1835-6** TODD *Cycl. Anat.* I. 517/2 The eyes are.. either pedunculated or sessile.

pedunculation (-'eɪʃən). *Nat. Hist.* [n. of condition f. mod.L. *pedunculāt-us*: see above and -ATION.] The formation of a peduncle; the condition of being pedunculate.

1847-9 TODD *Cycl. Anat.* IV. 129/2 Pedunculation (single or multiple) is not uncommon [in lipomata].

† **'pedware.** *Obs.* [Origin obscure.

Perh. from PED, basket, though this hardly accounts for the sense, or perh. an error in Googe for PODWARE, copied by Worlidge and Phillips; but *podware* is itself of doubtful history, since *pod* = *cod* has not been found till about a century later than *podware* and *pedware.*]

Pulse; pease or beans: cf. CODWARE[1] 1, PODWARE.

1577 B. GOOGE *Heresbach's Husb.* 24 Fruites of the earth ..that beareth Coddes, as all kinde of Pulse, or pedware. *Ibid.* 25 If after two seasons of Corne, you sowe Pulse or Pedware, the barrenner ground must rest three yeeres. *Ibid.*

26 Wheate, Barley, Pedware. **1669** WORLIDGE *Syst. Agric.* (1681) 329 *Pedware*, Pulse. **1706** PHILLIPS, *Pedware*, a Country-word for Pulse, as Pease, Beans, etc.

pedygru, obs. form of PEDIGREE *sb.*

† **pee**, *sb.*[1] *Obs.* Forms: 5–7 pee, 5–6 *Sc.* pe, (*pl.* peys), 5–7 pie, 6 P, 7 py. [In 15th c. *pee*, *pe* = late MDu. *pîe*, now *pij*, *pije* 'coat of coarse woollen stuff'; found from 14th c. in comb. *courtepy* = Du. *korte pîe* short coat of this kind. Ulterior history obscure: see Franck. Now only (in the spelling *pea*) in PEA-COAT, PEA-JACKET, q.v.] A coat of coarse cloth worn by men, esp. in the 16th century.

1483 *Acta Domin. Auditorum* (1839) 112/1 Twa pee govnis ane of franch blak ane vþir of tanny, price of þe blak pee v *li.* **1490** *Acc. Ld. High Treas. Scot.* I. 191 Item, to Dave Caldwell, .. Jame Dog and Wille Balfowre, x elne of russat to be thaim peys. **1494** *Ibid.* 233, viij ellis of chamlet, rede and quhite, to be ilkain of thame a liffray pe. **1498** *Aberdeen Regr.* (1844) I. 427 To Mabuys belman xxs. to by him ane pee for to pass ilka Mononday throucht the toune. *a* **1578** LINDESAY (Pitscottie) *Chron. Scot.* (S.T.S.) I. 174 Couchrane .. was clad in ane ryding pie of blak wellvet. **1585–6** *Will of R. Thorpe* (Somerset Ho.), One grene P or maundilion. *a* **1623** FLETCHER *Love's Cure* II. i, Your lashed shoulders [covered] with a velvet pee. **1635** D. DICKSON *Pract. Wks.* (1845) I. 127 A soldier's pie was put upon him.

b. *Comb.*, as ***py-doublet, pee-, py-gown.***

1483 Pee govnis [see above]. **1648–78** HEXHAM, *Pije*, Pygown, or Rough-gown, as Souldiers and Seamen wear. **1673** *Wedderburn's Vocab.* 23 (Jam.) *Pectorale*, a py-doublet.

pee (piː), *sb.*[2] *Mining.* [History unknown.] The portion common to two veins which intersect.

1653 MANLOVE *Lead Mines* 44 (E.D.S.) Some take me for one thing, some for other free, As New thing, Old thing, Crosse-vein, Tee or Pee. **1747** HOOSON *Miner's Dict.* O iij, If one Miner have a right to this Vein, .. and another has a Right to a Vein which crosses it, and makes the *Pee*; he that comes to the Pee first takes it. **1851** *Act 14 & 15 Vict.* c. 94 §13 If any Vein shall cross another Vein, the Miner who comes to the Pee or Intersection first shall have such Pee or Intersection.

pee, *sb.*[3] *Mining.* [Origin uncertain: ? = PEA[4].] A small piece of ore.

1747 HOOSON *Miner's Dict.* S j, The first pee or bit of Ore that the Cavers find in a Morning by Purchassing. **1824** MANDER *Miner's Gloss.* (E.D.D.), 'Pee of ore', a piece of ore gotten from the vein free from all spar, kevel.

pee, *sb.*[4] Abbreviation of CALIPEE.

1764 FOOTE *Patron* I. i, Not the meanest member of my Corporation but can distinguish the pash from the pee.

pee (piː), *sb.*[5] [f. PEE *v.*[2]] **1.** An act of urination.

1902 R. MACLAGAN *Evil Eye* 51 The milk has gone along with the pee. **1946** G. MILLAR *Horned Pigeon* xii. 156 The urinals alone would have a monument the size of London's Cenotaph... When they opened the sewer trap in the monumental pee-house great clouds of mosquitoes .. rose from the opening. **1951** S. SPENDER *World within World* 273 In Russia it's so cold that when you do a pee, you can break it off in sticks. **1958** L. DURRELL *Mountolive* xiii. 244, I must just do a pee. **1966** J. CHAMIER *Cannonball* xiii. 119 Best go and have a pee, lad. **1973** *Daily Tel.* (Colour Suppl.) 23 Feb. 54/1 If people came in just to use the lavatory, he would ask them for their address 'in case I need a pee when I'm passing your house'.

2. Urine.

1961 H. RUDD *Shores of Schizophrenia* in *My Escape from CIA* (1966) 10 That gloomy, hideous building, with its smell of cedar sawdust and stale, infantile pee. **1968** R. P. WARREN *Incarnations* 43 Jesus, Wouldn't just *being* be enough without Having to have the pee .. knocked out of You by a 1957 yellow Cadillac. **1971** J. OSBORNE *West of Suez* I. 42 Do you know what the cure for chilblains was then? Soaking your feet and hands in your own pee. **1976** P. CAVE *High Flying Birds* ii. 16 Sarcasm runs off on them like pee on a plastic bedsheet.

pee (piː), *sb.*[6] *colloq.* [f. initial letter of PENNY.] Representing the pronunciation of the initial letter of 'penny', i.e. a new penny, a unit of decimal currency introduced in Britain on 15 Feb. 1971. See also *p* s.v. *P II, PENNY I. 1.

The pronunciation of *p.* as (piː) is common in everyday speech but is avoided by many people, who prefer ('pɛnɪ) (as singular) and (pɛns) (as pl.).

1971 *Observer* 14 Feb. 9/5 Everyone at the Decimal Currency Board has taken to calling new pence 'pee'. **1972** *Daily Tel.* 9 Aug. 16 If Mr. Broca had contacted us we would have sold him one not for 'seventy-eight pees', but for 69p. **1974** *Punch* 6 Mar. 362/2 The Scandinavian revenue men .. intimating that it's either an immediate fifty pee in the £ or chuck the belongings back into the red-spotted hankie and ring up a mini cab. **1974** R. RENDELL *Face of Trespass* ii. 23 May I trouble you for forty-two pee? **1974** *Observer* (Colour Suppl.) 15 Dec. 13/4 Few could be bothered to say 'new pence' for the decimal stuff, so we used 'pee', and that is what we are lumbered with today. **1976** *Times Lit. Suppl.* 2 Apr. 388/1 A small boy on the loose in London with a million pound picture in a laundry bag and 'two pee' in his pocket. **1977** *Transatlantic Rev.* LX. 187 He was accosted by a group of rotting cider bums: 'Mister .. we just need ten pee to get ourselves another bottle.'

pee (piː), *v.*[1] *north. dial.* [Origin unascertained: cf. PEEK *v.*[1]] *intr.* To look with one eye (as in taking aim); to squint; to peer.

1674 RAY *N.C. Words* 37 He pees: He looks with one eye. **1703** THORESBY *Let. to Ray* (E.D.S.), *Pee*, .. is also to look near and narrowly. **1818** TODD, *To Pee*, .. to look with one eye. In use to this day in Cumberland. **1825** BROCKETT *N.C. Gloss.*, *Pee*, to squint, to spy with one eye—to look through contracted eye-lids. **1869** *Lonsdale Gloss.*, *Pee*, .. to look with one eye, to squint, to take aim.

Hence **pee-pee** *a.*, peering, squinting.

1804 *Europ. Mag.* XLV. 20/2 Says I, that can't be Hoga's head, for Hoga had little pee pee eyes.

pee (piː), *v.*[2] *colloq.* [f. initial letter of PISS *v.*] **1.** *intr.* To urinate. Hence **'peeing** *vbl. sb.*

1879–80 *Pearl* (1970) 216 Your private parts, or cunny, Should not be let for money, They're only meant to pee with. **1886** in F. T. ELWORTHY *West Somerset Word-Bk.* **1929** C. CONNOLLY *Let.* Nov. in *Romantic Friendship* (1975) 329 It [*sc.* a kinkajou] seemed just a machine for shitting and peeing. **1932** AUDEN *Orators* II. 78 The boys, out of control, imbibe Vimto through india-rubber tubing, openly pee into the ink-pots. **1948** M. MCCARTHY in *Partisan Rev.* Mar. 227 'My God', you yell .. 'can't a man pee in his own house?' **1960** C. DAY LEWIS *Buried Day* 74 How to leave the room during lessons—I solved .. by peeing in my trousers. **1963** M. MCCARTHY *Group* iii. 56 Anybody .. who wandered in to pee during a cocktail party. **1965** J. R. HETHERINGTON *Selina's Aunt* 50, I could laugh till I peed. **1966** A. LA BERN *Goodbye Piccadilly* xi. 109, I kept wanting to pee every few minutes. **1969** P. ROTH *Portnoy's Complaint* 132 Here is how I learnt to pee into the bowl like a big man. **1971** N. SAUNDERS *Alternative London* (ed. 2) 236 As above for ladies, not so easily cured though peeing just after sex is meant to help. **1973** M. AMIS *Rachel Papers* 74 She looked fretful, importunate, almost bouncing up and down, like a little girl wanting to pee. **1975** *Sunday Times* (Colour Suppl.) 23 Feb. 26/2 The guys were forever peeing over the side so there was piss everywhere.

2. a. *trans.* To wet by urinating.

1788 E. PICKEN *Epitaph Favourite Cat* in *Poems & Epistles* 47 He never stealt, though he was poor, Nor ever pee'd his master's floor. **1948** D. BALLANTYNE *Cunninghams* 219 She nearly pees her pants every time he kids to her.

b. *refl.* To urinate into one's clothes; esp. (hyperbolically) in phr. ***to pee oneself laughing.***

1946 G. KERSH *Clean, Bright & Slightly Oiled* i. 4 Even the Sarn-Major peed 'imself laughing. **1962** K. ORVIS *Damned & Destroyed* xv. 104 You did wrong to hit .. so much... I peed myself. **1978** R. BUSBY *Garvey's Code* xii. 168 He must've realized what was going to happen .. because he peed himself right there.

pee, pee and kew: see P, the letter.

pee, variant of PEA[3].

peeble, peece, obs. forms of PEBBLE, PIECE.

peed (piːd), *a. north. dial.* [f. PEE *v.*[1] + -ED[1].] Blind of one eye.

1674 RAY *N.C. Words* 37 *Peed*, blind of one eye. **1891** RIGBY *Midsummer* xix. 197 He had evidently .. got to the 'peed' .. side of Mr. Tinklemere.

peedegre, -eugre, -igree, obs. ff. PEDIGREE *sb.*

peek (piːk), *sb.*[1] Also **peak.** [f. PEEK *v.*[1]]

1. a. A peep, a glance, a 'keek'.

1844 'J. SLICK' *High Life N.Y.* II. 41, I jest give a peak in for a minit, and streaked it upstairs. **1869** L. M. ALCOTT *Little Women* II. xx. 300 'Ain't it a sight to see her settin' there,' .. muttered old Hannah, who could not resist frequent 'peeks' through the slide. **1884** ROE *Nat. Ser. Story* vi, Their father gave them a peek into the .. brooding-room. **1893** F. ADAMS *New Egypt* 54 Eyelid-closing indolence, varied by sudden peaks of wide-staring alertness. **1938** E. AMBLER *Cause for Alarm* vii. 116 Supposing you take an occasional peek at these other guys' hands, tell me what you see. **1969** *Daily Mail* 16 Jan. 5/1 After insertion into Earth orbit I had a lot of tests to perform on the spacecraft systems but, like all the rookies before me, I must confess to a sneak peek out of the window. **1973** P. EVANS *Bodyguard Man* 10, I poked my head out and took a peek. **1974** *Black World* Sept. 40 When you get inside cock your eyes ace-deuce and snatch a peek around. **1976** *National Observer* (U.S.) 24 Jan. 19/2 He was to proceed to Cairo, take a peek at Mecca, and head west across the bulge of Africa until he either sighted the Niger or fell into it.

b. *Comb.*, as ***peek-hole***, a peep-hole.

1910 'MARK TWAIN' *Speeches* 222, I peeked through the little peek-holes they have in theatre curtains. **1927** G. ADE et al. *Let.* 4 Mar. (1973) 117 Gibraltar .. is honeycombed with tunnels, which the visitor is not permitted to see, and from those tunnels there are peek-holes out of which guns can be pointed in any direction. **1927** *Sat. Even. Post* 24 Dec. 12/2 That's Fred's peek-hole, where he sees out of. **1930** E. POUND *XXX Cantos* xvii. 79 One eye for the sea, for that peek-hole.

2. *Computing.* (Usu. written **PEEK.**) A statement or function in BASIC allowing one to read the contents of the memory location whose address is specified. Cf. PEEK *v.*[1] 2 and POKE *sb.*[3] 1 f.

1978 WAITE & PARDEE *BASIC Primer* v. 159 PEEK and POKE (EXAM and FILL in some BASICS) allow direct control over individual memory locations. **1982** STEWART & JONES *Peek, Poke, Byte & Ram!* 77 We can find out exactly which bytes are stored in which addresses in the ROM and RAM by using PEEK. **1983** R. HASKELL *Atari BASIC* xiv. 129/2 Try printing some value of PEEK to see what you get. **1985** *Personal Computer World* Feb. 143 (Advt.), Built in Atari Basic programming language supporting peek, poke and USR plus at least 8 other languages available.

peek (piːk), *sb.*[2] [f. PEEK *v.*[2]] The shrill note or pipe of a small bird.

1834 MUDIE *Brit. Birds* (1841) I. 291 The birds [meadow-pipits] .. continue uttering their feeble and complaining peek.

peek (piːk), *v.*[1] Forms: 4–5 pike, pyke, 6–7 peke, 6 peake, peeke, 7– peak, peek, (9 *dial.* pick). [In ME. *pike*, *pyke*: origin obscure.

The verbs *keek*, *peek*, and *peep* are app. closely allied to each other. *Kike* and *pike*, as earlier forms of *keek* and *peek*, occur in Chaucer; *pepe*, *peep* is of later appearance (15th c.). *Kike*, *keek*, has Teutonic cognates (see KEEK) which are wanting for *peek* and *peep*; whether the latter have in some way arisen out of *keek*, or are distinct in origin, is unknown. Quot. 1530 gives a F. *piper* = *peke*; but this sense of *piper* has been found nowhere else, and is app. an error of Palsgrave. The phonetic relations between the forms *pike, peek, peak*, are as yet unexplained.]

1. *intr.* To look through a crevice, or out of or into a recess, etc.; to peer, peep, pry, look *in*, or *out*. Also, to glance *at*.

c **1374** CHAUCER *Troylus* III. 11 (60) And Pandarus .. Come nere, and gan yn at þe curtyn pike [*Campsall MS.* pyke], And seid God do bote on al syke! **1526** SKELTON *Magnyf.* 667 Why, can ye not put out that foule freke? No, in euery corner he wyll peke. **1530** PALSGR. 655/2, I peke or prie, *je pipe hors.* **1576** GASCOIGNE *Steele Gl.* (Arb.) 68 That one eye winks, as though it were but blynd, That other pries and peekes in euery place. **1577** STANYHURST *Descr. Irel.* vi. in *Holinshed* VI. 50 If he once but frowne at them, they dare not be so hardie as once to peake out of their cabbins. **1632** HEYWOOD *1st Pt. Iron Age* III. i. Wks. 1874 III. 312 We shall haue him .. come peaking into the Tents of the Greeks. **1681** T. FLATMAN *Heraclitus Ridens* No. 39 (1713) I. 255 As like one of your Smithfield Lions, as ever he can peke out of his Nyes. **1739** 'R. BULL' tr. *Dedekindus' Grobianus* I. iv. 36 He [Crocodile] gapes: the wing'd Inhabitant of air Does to his mouth in hopes of prey repair, In ev'ry hollow Tooth securely peak, And pick from thence th'Incumbrance with his Beak. **1848** LOWELL *Biglow P.* ii. (1859) 18 You see a feller peekin' out. **1886** MORSE *Jap. Homes* vii. 317, I was guilty of the impertinence of peeking into the cupboards. **1893** *Field* 27 May 770/3 Salmon were reported as showing, or rather 'picking', to use the local phrase. **1928** *Publishers' Weekly* 22 Sept. 1120/1 One cannot escape the temptation to peek at prices however and I found one marked six shillings and took it. **1947** AUDEN *Age of Anxiety* (1948) ii. 38 Pushing through brambles, I peeked out at Her fascination. **1953** *Manch. Guardian Weekly* 29 Jan. 4 A coloured butler peeked out of a cream-coloured door. **1968** *Globe & Mail* (Toronto) 15 Jan. 21/7 Jerry Tighe, of Whitworth College in Spokane, came close to a fall in the men's two miles when he peeked over his shoulder to check the field. **1973** 'S. HARVESTER' *Corner of Playground* III. i. 165 Are you so bored with me you must peek at other men? **1973** *Black World* June 10/2 The vain Southern belle who undresses in front of the stable boy and then tells her 'Daddy' that he peeked.

2. *Computing.* (Usu. written **PEEK.**) *intr.* and *trans.* To use PEEK to ascertain the contents of (a memory or memory location). Cf. PEEK *sb.*[1] 2. Const. as in sense 1, also *to*.

1978 WAITE & PARDEE *BASIC Primer* v. 161 The variable X is set to the value found in memory location A by PEEKing at A. *Ibid.* 163 The action of PEEKing or POKEing to the location containing the speaker causes the cone to move. **1981** D. INMAN et al. *More TRS-80 BASIC* ii. 20 Since you know the program is stored in RAM starting at memory location 17129, you can PEEK into that area of memory after you have entered your program. **1982** STEWART & JONES *Peek, Poke, Byte & Ram!* 78 There are certainly some good reasons for PEEKing the ROM—you can find out how the ZX81 tells the TV to PRINT a particular character. **1983** *Austral. Microcomputer Mag.* Sept. 62/1 The home user who wants to make use of the computer should be able to without peeking and poking.

Hence **'peeking** *ppl. a.* and *vbl. sb.*

a **1700** B. E. *Dict. Cant. Crew*, *Peeking Fellow*, a meer Sneaks, one that peeps in every Hole and Corner. **1855** *Worcester Transcript* Apr. (Bartlett), The members .. behaved in such an undignified, ludicrous, peeking, bombastical manner, that they obtained the appellation of the 'smelling committee'. **1962** K. ORVIS *Damned & Destroyed* vii. 49 When I went in [to jail] they didn't even ask for peekings. **1973** *Radio Times* 20 Dec. 100/4 What's he getting for Christmas? .. 'Absolutely no peeking before Christmas morning.' **1976** D. HEFFRON *Crusty Crossed* ix. 71 'It's time you learned the difference,' she called out after me, 'between high-class spying and low-down peeking.'

peek (piːk), *v.*[2] *dial.* Also **peak.** [? Echoic.] *intr.* To speak in a thin piping voice; to peep, squeak; to utter the slightest sound.

1808–25 JAMIESON, *To peak, peek*, to peep, to speak with a small voice resembling that of a chicken. **1810** COCK *Strains* II. 135 (E.D.D.), I winna hear my frien's misca't, Sae dinna ment to peak. **1881** *Leicestersh. Gloss.*, *Peak*, .. to cry like a young bird; squeak like a young mouse, etc.

peek, obs. form of PEAK, PIQUE.

peek-a-boo. Also peek-bo. [f. PEEK *v.*[1]: cf. *keek-bo*, KEEK *v.* 3.] **a.** = BO-PEEP, PEEP-BO. (See *N. & Q.* 10th ser. II. 85, 153.) Also *attrib.* and as *vb.*

1599 B. JONSON *Ev. Man out of Hum.* IV. ii. (fol. 1616), Nay, neuer play peeke-boe [*fol.* 1640 bopeep] with me. *c* **1880** *American Song* (in N. & Q., as above), Peek-a-boo! Peek-a-boo! I see you hiding there. **1903** C. COPELAND *School of Woods* (U.S.) 29 Like a mischievous child playing at peek-aboo. **1903** [see *high sign* s.v. HIGH *a.* 21]. **1922** JOYCE *Ulysses* 46 Peekaboo. I see you. **1940** S. O'CASEY *Let.* 19 May (1975) I. 862 I'm .. kicking football with Niall; & peek a boo with Shivaun. **1950** G. BARKER *True Confession* ii. 10 But Memory flirts with seven veils Peekabooing the accidental. **1960** *Times* 22 June 5/5 Covering up behind his high 'peek-a-boo' guard, he [*sc.* Floyd Patterson] rode out the brief crisis. **1967** S. BECKETT *Stories & Texts for Nothing* 124 But peekaboo here I come again, just when most needed.

b. Used *attrib.* and *absol.* of various garments decorated with holes (see quots.).

1895 *Montgomery Ward Catal.* 306/3 Child's Sun Bonnet, made of printed lawn, peek-a-boo front. **1906** *Daily Chron.* 16 Aug. 8/1 The dreamer is embowered in soft cushions, and being punted by a River Girl, in a peek-a-boo blouse—all grace and lissomness and tan and bare arms. **1906** *Springfield* (Mass.) *Weekly Republ.* 10 May 13 In San Francisco there is no winter suit and summer suit. The same medium-weight garment is worn the year round and the peek-a-boo waist is unknown. **1907** *Westm. Gaz.* 21 Sept. 3/2 'The Peek-a-boo blouse'..is as popular here as in America. **1910** 'MARK TWAIN' *Speeches* 87 Why not adopt some of the women's styles?.. Take the peek-a-boo waist, for instance. **1913** *Maclean's Mag.* Aug. 103/1 The wars upon cigarettes, bridge whist and peekaboo waists are passing madnesses. **1930** M. SULLIVAN *Our Times* III. 499 A shirt-waist, supposed to be an extreme of daring, in which embroidered perforations permitted sight of female epidermis upon the arms and as much as two inches below the nape of the neck, was called the 'peek-a-boo'. **1957** M. B. PICKEN *Fashion Dict.* 246/2 *Peek-a-boo waist*, shirt-waist of eyelet or sheer fabric. **1959** J. BRAINE *Vodi* xiv. 195 The peekaboo blouse..now seemed vulgar, a barmaid's uniform. *Ibid.* 196 A naughty little girl who wore peekaboo blouses. **1969** R. T. WILCOX *Dict. Costume* (1970) 263/2 *Peek-a-boo blouse*, a shirtwaist of sheer lawn, voile or eyelet embroidery, a popular fashion of the 1890's and the first decade of the twentieth century. It was worn over a lacy, frilled corset cover. **1972** 'E. MCBAIN' *Sadie when she Died* x. 107 Carella ..wondered if he should tell Teddy about the brunette in the peekaboo blouse.

c. Used *attrib.* and *absol.* of a woman's hairstyle (see quots.).

1948 M. M. MILLER *Winchester's Screen Encycl.* 117/2 Her 'peek-a-boo' style secured major part for her, under new name Veronica Lake. **1966** J. S. COX *Illustr. Dict. Hairdressing* 109/2 *Peekaboo locks*, hanging hair that partly conceals the face and eyes. **1968** J. IRONSIDE *Fashion Alphabet* 195 *Peek-a-boo*, hair style that originated..in 1941. The hair was cut so that it hung about 8 inches below the shoulders; in front it covered one eye and was softly waved to the end. **1973** *Daily Tel.* 9 July 17/3 Veronica Lake, the filmstar who was famous in the 1940s for her 'peek-a-boo' hairstyle, died in Vermont, America, on Saturday of acute hepatitis. *Ibid.*, The peek-a-boo hairstyle —long blonde tresses hanging over her right eye—disappeared in 1943 after the United States Government made an official request to Paramount to cut her hair.

peekie: see PEAK *sb.*[4]

peeky, var. PEAKY *a.*[2]

peel (piːl), *sb.*[1] Forms: 4-5 pel, (4 peyl), 4- pele, (5 pell, -e), 5-6 *Sc.* peill, -e, (peyll), 6 *Sc.* peil, (piel, paile), 6-7 peele, 4, 8- peel. [Known *a* 1300 in latinized form *pēlum* (later sometimes *pēla*), in AF. *pel*, *piel*, in 14th c. ME. *pel*, *pele*, whence 15-16th c. Sc. *peil*. In sense 1 = OF. *pel*, *piel* (mod. F. *pieu*) stake:—L. *pāl-us*, *pāl-um* stake. The development of sense 2 is parallel to that of the cognate PALE *sb.*[1]; that of senses 3 and 4 is more obscure, but cf. the synonymous PILE.

For a detailed historical examination of the word, see *Peel: its Meaning and Derivation*, by Geo. Neilson F.S.A. Scot. 1893.]

†**1.** A stake. [The usual sense in OF.] *Obs. rare.*

1303 R. BRUNNE *Handl. Synne* 2120 He ȝede and clambe vpp on a pele [*v.rr.* pel, peyl; *rime* eche dele; F. *encuntre vn pel se addrescé*], And hyng þeron by þe hond. *Ibid.* 2166 þou art a-cursed, þou woste weyl, And hange were wurþy on a peyl. *c* **1330** —— *Chron. Wace* (Rolls) 4611 Longe pyles [*MS. Petyt* peeles; Wace *peus ferrés*] & grete dide þey make; Faste yn Temese dide þey hem stake, Euerylkon wyþ iren schod. *Ibid.* 4637 Iren-schod was ilka peel [*rime* ilka del].

†**2.** A palisade or fence formed of stakes; a stockade; a stockaded or palisaded (and moated) enclosure, either as the outer court of a castle, or as an independent fort or defensible position. *Obs.*

[**1298-9** *Accts.* in Jos. Stevenson *Hist. Docum. Scotl.* II. 361 Pro vadiis xlviij operariorum venientium de Westmerland et Cumberland..usque Loghmaban..ad faciendum pelum ibidem... Et pro vadiis [iv sarratorum] euntium apud Loghmaban ad sarranda ligna pro constructione peli ibidem per ij dies... Et pro vadiis carpentariorum missorum apud Loghmaban..pro factura peli ibidem per ij dies. **1299** *Let. Pat. Edw. I*, *Ibid.* II. 404 Ad ordinandum et providendum de secura custodia clausi extra castrum de Loghmaban palitio firmati. **1300** *Indenture* 2 Jan., *Ibid.* 408 Et qe les meisons quil [Robert de Clifford] ad fait en le piel de Loghmaban lui demoergent pur luy et pur ses gentz. **1300** (Sept.) *Liber Quotidianus Contrarot. Garderobæ* 165 Carpentariis facientibus pelum in foresta de Ingelwoode assidendum circa castrum de Dumfres. **1300** (Oct.) *Letter fr. Edward I.* Stevenson II. 296 Cest a savoir, que nostre seignour le roi est ale a Dounfries pour lever son pel e efforcer le chastel. **1301** *Let. fr. R. de Tilliol gardeyn de Lougchmaban to Edw. I.* 10 Sept. in Stevenson II. 432 Sachez, sire, qe..sire Johane de Soules, sire Ingram de Humframville..nous ardyrent nostre vile et assalyrent nostre pele demyway prime dekes a houre de noune. *c* **1430** FORDUN & BOWER *Scotichr.* XII. i. (1759) 220 Hoc in anno [1301] municipium de Linlithgw, quod Anglicè *Pele* vocatur, per regem Angliæ constructum est.]

c **1330** R. BRUNNE *Chron. Wace* (Rolls) 15912 Ful baldely & stille Dide he vitaille þe toun ful wel, Defensable wyþ bretaxes & pel. —— *Chron.* (1810) 157 þe Romancer it sais, R[ichard] did mak a pele, On kastelle wise alle wais, wrouht of tre fulle welle. **1375** BARBOUR *Bruce* x. 137 And at lythkow ves than a peill, Mekill, and stark, and stuffit weill Vith ynglis men. *c* **1425** WYNTOUN *Cron.* VIII. 6141 The Pele ..off Lyddale. *c* **1470** HENRY *Wallace* IX. 1693 The peyll thai tuk, and slew that was tharin. **1528** *St. Papers Hen. VIII*, IV. 492 One strong pele of ill Will Armistraunges, buylded aftur siche maner that it couth not be brynt ne distroyed, unto it was cutt downe with axes. **1535** *Sc. Acts Jas. V* (1814) II. 346 That euery landit man duelland in þe Inland or vpon þe bordouris, havand þare ane hundreth pund land..sall big ane sufficient barmkyn apoun his.. landis..of Stane and lyme..for þe Ressett and defens of him his tennentis and þer gudis in trublous tyme wᵗ ane toure in the samin for him self gif he thinkis it expedient: And þat all vther landit men of smallar Rent..big pelis and gret strenthis as þai ples for saifing of þare selfis men tennentis and gudis: And þat all the saidis strenthis barmkynnis and pelis be biggit and completit within twa yeris vnder þe pane. **1579** *Reg. Privy Council Scot.* III. 236 For puiling doun of a peill of the said George Chaleris..and sta and awaytuke XL ky and oxin. **1589** in *Exch. Rolls Scotl.* XXII. 25 The fewmailis of the park and peil of Linlithquew. **1596** DALRYMPLE tr. *Leslie's Hist. Scot.* I. 98 Bot thay far starker do make, four nuiked, of earth only, quhilke nathir can be burnte, nor wᵗout a gret force of men of weir doune can be castne..thir ar thair pailes.

†**3.** A castle; esp. a small castle or tower; = PILE *sb.*[2] *Obs.* (app. only in English writers.)

c **1384** CHAUCER *H. Fame* III. 220, I gan to romen til I fonde The castel yate on my ryght honde... Ther mette I cryinge many oon, A larges, larges, hald vp wel, God saue the lady of thys pel. **1483** *Cath. Angl.* 273/2 A Peille..A castelle. **1573** CHURCHYARD in Nichols *Progr. Q. Eliz.* (1823) I. 399 A littell Bastillion, builded on a hil..to the which piel the soulders of the main fort did repayre. **1679** [see PILE *sb.*[2]].

4. The general name, in modern writers, for the small towers or fortified dwellings built in the 16th c. in the border countries of England and Scotland, for defence against hostile forays; consisting of a massive square edifice, the ground-floor of which was vaulted, and used as a shelter or refuge for cattle, while the upper part (the access to which was by a door on the level of the first floor, with external ladder or movable stair) was the abode of the owner and his family.

(In this sense, probably orig. short for *peel-house* (see 6), i.e. house defended by a peel (in sense 2). But the name is now applied in many cases in which it has no historical support.) It is evidently akin to sense 3.

1726 GORDON *Itin. Septent.* 54 At this Town [Kirkintilloch] there is another Fort upon the Wall, called the Peel. **1792** *Archæologia* X. 102 This kind of building was called in Scotland a *peel*, and in England, a keep or dungeon. **1805** SCOTT *Last Minstr.* I. xxv, He passed the Peel of Goldiland. *Ibid.* IV. iii, The frightened flocks and herds were pent Beneath the peel's rude battlement. **1846** BROCKETT *N.C. Gloss.* II. 69 The 'peel' was a square tower strongly fortified, where cattle were secured in the bottom story at night, and the family occupied the upper part. **1882** J. HARDY in *Proc. Berw. Nat. Club* IX. No. 3. 425 The mansion..is an adaptation..of an old fortified peel to modern requirements. **1888** W. W. TOMLINSON *Comprehensive Guide Northumberland* 156 Jutting crags.. and lofty precipices, constitute the natural defences of the pele on three sides. **1894** R. S. FERGUSON *Westmorland* xviii. 280 These peels..are small and massively built towers of stone, with high-pitched roofs of slate. **1921** P. S. ALLEN *Let.* 21 Sept. (1939) 180 It is built out of the Prior's Lodgings, and includes a regular 'pele tower' such as line the Border: low towers with immensely thick walls—this one 7 ft. thick at the bottom, but with mural chambers and staircases. **1964** *Dumfries & Galloway Standard* 8 July 7, The lost Dalswinton, Conggleton and Wigtown, the pele at Lochmaben are a story in themselves. **1973** FEDDEN & JOEKES *National Trust Guide* 656 *Pele, pele tower*, a small or moderate-sized tower or keep which is easily defended. Peculiar to houses or castles on both sides of the Scottish border. Generally built between the 13th and 15th centuries.

5. Hence, the proper name of a place in the Isle of Man. (Cf. *Castletown* in the same island.)

[**1399** *Charter of Hen. IV* in Rymer *Fœdera* VIII. 95/1 Concessimus eidem Comiti Northumbriæ Insulam, Castrum, Pelam, et Dominium de Man.] *a* **1718** in Keble *Life Bp. Wilson* vi. (1863) 199 The Ordinary hath used to send for aid unto the Constable of the Castle, or of the Peel. **1765** *Act 5 Geo. III*, c. 26 *Preamble*, All the islands, castle, pele, and lordship aforesaid.

6. *attrib.*, as **peel-dike**, the wall or rampart of a peel; **peel-house, -tower** = sense 4.

1505 *Acc. Ld. High Treas. Scot.* III. 84 To bigging of the peil dikis of Linlithqw. **1586** *Reg. Privy Council Scot.* IV. 106 Ane peill house, with byre, hall and berne. **1814** SCOTT *Wav.* xli, Had you put this gentleman into the pit of the peel-house at Balmawhapple. **1851** TURNER *Dom. Archit.* I. i. 11 In the border countries these towers, commonly called Pele towers, are very usual. **1856** J. C. BRUCE *Bayeux Tap. Elucidated* ii. 36 The ancient 'peel houses' of the North of England. **1874** HARE *Story of my Life* (1900) IV. xvii. 258 An occasional peel-tower stands like a milestone of history. **1935** *Hist. Northumberland* XIV. 79 This [*sc.* Henry VIII to Charles I] forms a continuously evolving period, at first characterised by the erection of pele towers and bastle houses. **1965** N. RIDLEY *Portrait of Northumberland* 21 Scattered over wide areas of Northumberland are the Pele towers... These Pele towers were fortified dwellings, where the cattle could be driven into the ground floor rooms, to protect them from the Reivers and Moss Troopers. **1973** FEDDEN & JOEKES *National Trust Guide* 325 Consequently a wide area is studded with massive pele towers, commonly with a vaulted chamber on the ground floor into which cattle might be driven at the first warning of raiders, and upper storeys arranged for human occupation. **1980** *Historic Houses, Castles & Gardens* 48/3 Hutton-in-the-Forest.. 14th cent. Pele Tower with later additions.

peel (piːl), *sb.*[2] Forms: 4-7 pele, 5-7 peele, 5- peel, (6 piele, 6-7 peale, 8-9 peal, 9 *dial.* pale). *β.* 5, 9 *dial.* pyle. [ME. a. OF. *pele* (mod.F. *pelle* shovel):— L. *pāla* spade, shovel, baker's peel. Cf. PALE *sb.*[3]]

1. A shovel or shovel-shaped implement: now locally or dialectally applied to a fire-shovel, and in some technical uses: see quots.

Some of the early quots may belong to 2.

14.. *Voc.* in Wr.-Wülcker 599/36 Pala—Item dicitur latum instrumentum ferreum ad opus ignis, a pele. **1572** *Wills & Inv. N.C.* (Surtees) I. 349 The Kitching. One Raking croke, one Iron por, one pele, one iron coulrake ijˢ viijᵈ. **1626** in *Naworth Househ. Bks.* (Surtees) 237 Mending a shovell and a peale, vᵈ. **1686** tr. *Chardin's Trav. Persia* 81 This Past is very white... They serve it upon little Woodden Peels made on purpose. **1687** A. LOVELL tr. *Thevenot's Trav.* II. 9 Two men set a stirring of it with wooden peels. **1743** *Lond. & Country Brew.* IV. (ed. 2) 257 [They] burn it 12 Hours into a Coak..which they break and divide into pretty large Pieces with an Iron-Peal. **1807** VANCOUVER *Agric. Devon* (1813) 214 The cream..may be removed..into an open vessel, and there moved by hand with a stick about a foot long, at the end of which is fixed a sort of peal,..with which about 12 lbs of butter may be separated from the butter-milk at a time. **1825** J. NICHOLSON *Operat. Mechanic* 360 At the top of the table is a large triangular iron peel or shovel, with its fore part bearing upon the edge of the table. **1828-32** WEBSTER, *Peel*, ..in popular use in America, any large fire-shovel.

2. *spec.* A baker's shovel, a pole with a broad flat disk at the end for thrusting loaves, pies, etc., into the oven and withdrawing them from it.

c **1400** *Lanfranc's Cirurg.* 155 þis boon is lich to a pele wiþ þe whiche men setten breed into þe ouene. *c* **1475** *Pict. Voc.* in Wr.-Wülcker 808/33, 34 *Hoc furnorium*, *Hec pila*, pyle. **1519** HORMAN *Vulg.* 154 b, Sette in the bredde with a pele. *c* **1537** *Thersites* in Hazl. *Dodsley* I. 424 The backster of Bal[d] ockbury with her baking peel. **1552** HULOET, Pile for an ouen. Loke in piele. **1596** *Unton Inv.* (1841) 2 On iron peale, ij searces, j great bread grate. **1614** B. JONSON *Bart. Fair* III. ii, A notable hot Baker 'twas when hee ply'd the peele. **1688** R. HOLME *Armoury* III. 85/2 A Baker, with a Peel in his both hands. **1750** W. ELLIS *Country Housew.* 75 Set them on a peal, and lay them to bake at the oven's mouth. **1886** T. HARDY *Mayor Casterbr.* (1895) 310 (E.D.D.) Hearing a noise, out ran his wife with the oven pyle. **1887** *S. Cheshire Gloss.* s.v., We have two varieties of peels, viz. bread-peels and pie-peels. **1890** *Glouc. Gloss.*, *Pale*, or *Peel*, a flat, spade-shaped tool used by bakers, to take dishes, etc., out of the oven.

3. *Printing.* A T-shaped instrument used to hang up damp freshly printed sheets to dry.

1683 MOXON *Mech. Exerc.*, *Printing* xxv. ¶ 1 He Loads and unloads his Peel again successively, till he have Hung up the whole Heap. **1771** LUCKOMBE *Hist. Print.* 487 He takes the Handle of the Peel in his left hand, and lays the top part flat down upon the Heap. **1858** SIMMONDS *Dict. Trade*, *Peel*, ..a printer's tool for hanging up damp printed sheets on a line to dry.

4. The blade or wash of an oar. *U.S.*

1875 KNIGHT *Dict. Mech.*, *Peel*..3. (*Nautical.*) The *wash* of an oar. **1890** WEBSTER, *Peel*..Also, the blade of an oar.

5. *attrib.*, as in ***two-peel, three-peel machine***, sizes of the cutting-machine in biscuit-making; **peel-end**, the portion of a biscuit- or cracker-machine beyond the cutter.

1884 KNIGHT *Dict. Mech.* Suppl.

peel (piːl), *sb.*[3] Also 6-7 peele, (7 peil). See also PILL *sb.*[1] [Appears first in 16th c., as a collateral form of the earlier PILL *sb.*[1] (still widely used in the dialects) after PEEL *v.*[1] (Cf. also OF. *pel*, mod.F. *peau* skin, rind, peel:—L. *pell-em* skin.]

1. a. The rind or outer coating of any fruit; esp. in ***orange-, lemon-, citron-peel***; **candied peel**, the candied rind of various species of *Citrus*, esp. the citron, used as a flavouring in cookery and confectionery.

[**1388-18..**: see PILL *sb.*[1]]

1583 in Hakluyt *Voy.* (1599) II. 269 For churned milke we gaue them bread and pomgranat peeles, wherewith they vse to tanne their goats skinnes which they churne withall. **1611** COTGR., *Follicule*,..a huske, hull, peele, or skin inclosing seed. **1615** [see ORANGE-PEEL 2]. **1672** Lemmon peil [see LEMON *sb.*[1] 5]. **1712** tr. *Pomet's Hist. Drugs* I. 143 A Nut, having a green Bark or Peel. *Ibid.* 151 Candied Orange Peel. **1861-80** MRS. BEETON *Househ. Managem.* § 1871 Ingredients ..2 oz. of sweet almonds, 1 oz. of candied peel..; cut the peel into neat slices. *Ibid.* § 1878 Add the sugar, peel, ginger, spice, and treacle. **1875** EMERSON *Lett. & Soc. Aims* viii. 192 The rich feed on fruits and game,—the poor, on a watermelon's peel.

b. *Comb.*, as **peel-maker**, one who prepares candied peel.

1851 in *Illustr. Lond. News* 5 Aug. (1854) 119/3 Occupations of People... Peel-maker.

2. *Rugby Football.* The action of peeling from a set formation (see PEEL *v.*[1] 5 g).

1973 *Scotsman* 21 Feb. 18/6 Thus, when it comes to deflecting the ball for a peel, Strachan prefers to operate from No. 8 where there is a little more scope for manoeuvre. **1978** *Sunday Express* 19 Mar. 31/4 From yet another winning line-out by Martin, Graham Price slipped him a pass on the peel and Edwards lofted over a towering drop goal.

peel, *sb.*[4] *Sc.* [Goes with PEEL *v.*[2]] A match, an equal.

1722 W. HAMILTON *Wallace* VII. ii, In time of peace, he never had a peel, So courteous he was, and so genteel. **1813** PICKEN *Poems* II. 131 (Jam.) She fuish him John Gilpin, nae sang is its peil, For a pattern to work by. **1882** 'STRATHESK' *More Bits* xiv, When time was called, the numbers on each side were equal, or *peels*, in curling phraseology. **1890** J. KERR *Hist. Curling* 240 He absolutely refused to play his stone on one occasion when the game stood peels. **1918** *Kelso Chron.* 4 Oct. 3 The players were 'peels' at 12. **1956** in *Sc. Nat. Dict.* (1968) VII. 70/2 The sides finished peels.

peel, *sb.*[5], collateral f. PILLOW, now *dial.*

peel (piːl), *sb.*[6] [see PEEL *v.*[3]] In Croquet, the action of peeling.

1907 C. D. LOCOCK *Mod. Croquet Tactics* xi. 145 The croquet term 'Peel' is derived from the eminent player of that name. *Ibid.* 146 This peeling generally..takes place in the course of a single break; but sometimes, and especially in Doubles, it is worth while to go for a peel on the captain of the other side. **1914** LD. TOLLEMACHE *Croquet* xviii. 111 In Handicap games it is frequently impossible to win without a Peel of some sort. **1932** *Times Lit. Suppl.* 18 Aug. 580/2 Like golfers its [*sc.* croquet's] devotees discuss it in mystical terms of 'tices', 'peels' and 'three-ball breaks'. **1953** *Times* 17 Feb. 3/7 Cotter used the turn to its fullest advantage and finished the match with a triple peel. **1974** *Observer* 23 June 40/3 Triple peels (three in a row) were commonplace at Cheltenham.

peel (piːl), *v.*[1] Forms: (3 peolien), 4–5 **pelen, -yn,** 5–6 (9 *Sc.*) **pele,** 6 **peele, piel,** 6–8 *Sc.* **peil, (peill, peile),** 7 **peal,** 7– **peel.** [A collateral form of PILL *v.*[1], formerly used in all the senses of the latter; in later use, in Standard English, appropriated to the sense 'decorticate' and uses thence derived. For the phonology see PILL *v.*[1] (It seems possible that the comparatively modern sense-differentiation of *pill* and *pele, peel,* may have been influenced by the example of F. *piller* to pillage, rob, and *peler* to deprive of hair, to strip of skin, to peel.)]

I. To pillage, rob.

†**1. a.** *trans.* To plunder, pillage, spoil, rifle, strip of possessions (a person or place); = PILL *v.*[1] 1.

1303 R. BRUNNE *Handl. Synne* 2357 Certys þefte ryʒt wykked ys.. Namly, pore men for to pele Or robbe or bete with-oute skyle. *Ibid.* 6790 Lorde! how shal these robbers fare That the pore pepyl pelyn ful bare. *c* **1386** CHAUCER *Pars. T.* ⁋693 What seie we than of hem that pelyn & don extorcions to holy chirche? **1450** *Rolls of Parlt.* V. 204/2 Hit [the said Isle] hath be so pelyd and oppressid. *a* **1600** *Jok Up-a-lands Compl.* in *Evergreen* (1761) I. 231 Pure Commons presentlie ar peild. **1648** SYMMONS *Vind. Chas. I* 161 All the people..who have been wronged, peeled and oppressed. **1670** MILTON *Hist. Eng.* I, Archigallo..by peeling the wealthier sort, stuff'd his Treasury. **1732** BERKELEY *Alciphr.* III. §11 Would it not be a disagreeable Sight to see an honest Man peeled by Sharpers?

†**b.** *transf.* To exhaust or impoverish (soil); = PILL *v.*[1] 1 b. *Obs.*

1610 W. FOLKINGHAM *Art of Survey* I. ix. 35 Oates doe well in a leane dry Clay, though they peele a better and prepare a moist.

†**2.** To seize or take by violence or extortion; to make a prey of; = PILL *v.*[1] 3. *Obs.*

[*c* **1350–1618**: see PILL *v.*[1] 3.]

1456 SIR G. HAYE *Law Arms* (S.T.S.) 91 A man gais to the were for covatis to pele and rub gudis. ? **1507** *Comunyc.* (W. de W.) A iij, What shall than profyte thy good in plate Or poundes that thou of the people pele? **1542** UDALL *Erasm. Apoph.* 280 b, His soudiours..pieled all that euer thei could fyngre.

II. To decorticate, strip.

3. a. To strip (anything) of its natural integument or outer layer, as an orange, potato, or the like of its skin or rind, a tree of its bark; to remove the peel of; = PILL *v.*[1] 5.

[**1225–1879**: see PILL *v.*[1] 5.]

c **1430** *Two Cookery-bks.* 8 Take oynonys and schrede hem, and pele hem. **1462** in *Finchale Priory* (Surtees) 95 To fele, pele, occupie, and carie away wod and barke. **1464** *Mann. & Househ. Exp.* (Roxb.) 280 Roste an egge hard and pele it. **1698** FROGER *Voy.* 129 An Herb that can be peeled in the same manner as Hemp with us. **1747** MRS. GLASSE *Cookery* 11 To dress Potatoes. Boil them..then peel them. **1799** G. SMITH *Laboratory* I. 263 A sweet apple, peeled and cut. **1866** GEO. ELIOT *F. Holt* Introd., The basket-maker peeling his willow-wands in the sunshine. **1877** BRYANT *Planting of Apple-tree* v, Girls..Shall peel its fruit by cottage-hearth.

b. Usually *peel off*: To strip off or pare off (skin, bark, etc.); = PILL *v.*[1] 5 b. Also, to remove or separate (a label, bank-note, etc.) by peeling. Also *fig.*

[*c* **1440–1604**: see PILL *v.*[1] 5 b.] **1573–80** BARET *Alv.* P 358 To Pill off, or rather peele, as it were to pull off the skin, rinde, or the barke of a tree. **1687** A. LOVELL tr. *Thevenot's Trav.* I. 124 They peal off the Rind of them, then cut them into quarters. **1725** DE FOE *Voy. round World* (1840) 154 They peeled it off thicker or finer as they had occasion. **1790** *Trans. Soc. Arts* VIII. 27 Earth that has been peeled and burnt. **1868** BROWNING *Ring & Bk.* I. 17 Also he peeled off that last scandal-rag Of Nepotism. **1896** 'MARK TWAIN' in *Harper's Mag.* Aug. 358/1 He peeled off one of his bulliest old-time blessings, with as many layers to it as an onion. **1897** *Allbutt's Syst. Med.* IV. 116 The thickened capsule cannot readily be peeled from the surface of the liver. **1946** E. O'NEILL *Iceman Cometh* (1947) I. 75 He pulls a big roll from his pocket and peels off a ten-dollar bill. **1971** M. MCCARTHY *Birds of America* 181 With his thumbnail, unobtrusively, he peeled off the price-tag. **1977** *Monitor* (McAllen, Texas) 31 May 1B/1 She got out of the car and peeled off her gloves. **1977** H. FAST *Immigrants* I. 35 He.. took out a wad of bills, peeling off two fives and two singles. **1978** D. MURPHY *Place Apart* xii. 259 We *must* peel off the terrorist labels and look at the individuals underneath.

c. To make or form by peeling; = PILL *v.*[1] 5 c.

1885 BIBLE (R.V.) *Gen.* xxx. 37 And Jacob took him rods of fresh poplar..and peeled [1611 *and earlier vv.* pilled] white strakes in them.

d. To bare (land) of its herbage, as by shaving off, cutting down, or eating down crops, etc. close to the ground; = PILL *v.*[1] 5 d.

[**1555–1903**: see PILL *v.*[1] 5 d.]

1789 *Trans. Soc. Arts* (ed. 2) II. 107 His pastures and clover crops were peeled to the earth.

e. *to peel one's eyes*: to keep one's eyes peeled. See PEELED 4 b.

1875 J. G. HOLLAND *Sevenoaks* xii. 161 An' peel yer eyes, Mike, for I'm goin' to show ye some thin' that'll s'prise ye. **1947** A. MILLER *All my Sons* I. 12 Now go out, and keep both eyes peeled... A policeman don't ask questions. Now peel them eyes! **1976** T. HEALD *Let Sleeping Dogs Die* v. 99 I've been peeling my eyes... There are some funny goings-on going on.

4. a. *intr.* Of trees, animal bodies, etc.: To become bare of bark, skin, etc.; to cast the epidermis (as after a fever). Of skin or bark: To become detached, scale off. Also **b.** To admit of being peeled or barked. = PILL *v.*[1] 6.

[*c* **1000–1886**: see PILL *v.* 6.]

1634 SIR T. HERBERT *Trav.* 183 The rinde or skin peeles off most easily. **1641** BEST *Farm. Bks.* (Surtees) 15 A meanes to make them peele better. **1712** SWIFT *Tale of Midas* 36 Against whose torrent while he swims, The golden scurf peels off his limbs. **1837** DICKENS *Pickw.* xix, 'This is delightful..!' said Mr. Pickwick, the skin of whose expressive countenance was rapidly peeling off with exposure to the sun. **1860** TYNDALL *Glac.* I. xx. 143 Its outer surface appeared to be peeling off like a crust. *Mod.* I have been sunburnt, and my face is peeling.

5. a. *intr.* or *absol.* To take off one's clothes or outer garments; to strip, as in preparation for some exercise. (Orig. a term of pugilism; later of athletics; now *slang* or *colloq.*) Also const. *off.*

1785 GROSE *Dict. Vulg. T., Peel,* to strip: allusion to the taking off the coat or rind of an orange or apple. **1800** HURDIS *Fav. Village* 51 The swain Who, to his fair shirt peeled, from dusky dawn To latest twilight gathers the full ear. **1818** *Sporting Mag.* II. 231 He peeled in Tothill-fields with the utmost *sang froid.* **1829** MARRYAT *F. Mildmay* xvi, He began to peel, as the boxers call it. **1858** O. W. HOLMES *Aut. Breakf.-t.* i, What resplendent beauty that must have been which could have authorized Phryne to 'peel'! **1879** *Boy's Own Paper* 18 Jan. 2/1 'Look sharp and peel!' cried our captain. So we hurried to the tent and promptly divested ourselves of our outer garments. **1892** FURNIVALL in *Hoccleve's Wks.* I. p. xlvii. *note,* He peeld to scull bow down-stream. **1922** [see DISHYBILLY]. **1922** JOYCE *Ulysses* 490 Come and I'll peel off. **1950** *Variety* 13 Dec. 1/5 The gals are peelin' in 23 clubs through Los Angeles County.

b. *trans.* To strip wholly or partly of clothing; to take *off* (clothes). *colloq.*

1820 CORCORAN *Fancy* Note 89 [Randull's] figure is remarkable, when peeled, for its statue-like beauty. **1852** R. S. SURTEES *Sponge's Sp. Tour* (1893) 147 Jack was in the act of 'peeling' himself, as he called it. **1872** C. KING *Mountain. Sierra Nev.* x. 217 Sarah Jane—arms peeled—cooking up stuff. **1888** *Detroit Free Press* 20 Oct. (Farmer), She peeled off her wedding dress and boots.

c. *to peel it,* to run at full speed. *U.S. slang.*

1860 BARTLETT *Dict. Amer.* s.v., To run at full speed. 'Come, boys; peel it now, or you'll be late.'

d. *dial.* Of a dog, etc.: To show its teeth.

1890 P. H. EMERSON *Wild Life* xxvi. 109 Lor, that peeled and showed his ivories at us.

e. *to peel off, away* (Aeronaut.): to veer from a straight course, esp. one alongside another aircraft; to break away from an airborne formation. (Said of the aircraft or of the pilot.) Also *transf.*

1941 *Christian Science Monitor* 6 Mar. 4/8 Other fanciful R.A.F. Terms include..'peeling off', for veering away from another aircraft. **1941** *N.Y. Times* 27 July 21/2 To 'peel off' is to curve away from another aircraft—the movement as one machine comes up close to another and then slants away is supposed to resemble the act of peeling off the skin of a banana. **1941** *Reader's Digest* Dec. 59/2 Our fighters seemed to be doing a good job on the Huns because only one peeled off to attack us. **1943** HUNT & PRINGLE *Service Slang* 51 *Peel off,*..to break away from a formation in order to meet an attack, or to leave a squadron to initiate an attack. **1945** *News Chron.* 7 June 3/1 The Spitfire came out of the clouds high above us, peeled off in our direction, circled around for a bit and then, apparently satisfied, made off. **1953** 'N. SHUTE' *In Wet* vii. 212 He dismissed the escort [of fighter aircraft].., and they peeled away up into the clear blue sky. **1976** A. WHITE *Long Silence* vii. 53 We had picked up our fighter escort... Every so often, one of them would peel off and sweep an observation circuit. **1976** *Shooting Times & Country Mag.* 16–22 Dec. 29/2, I shot at another goose which peeled off, flew fluttering for a hundred yards, and then windmilled down stone dead. **1977** M. BABSON *Lord Mayor of Death* xviii. 191 The police car..peeled away from the procession and sped for open ground.

f. To leave, depart; to move *off* in another direction. Also *transf.* and *fig.*

1952 S. SELVON *Brighter Sun* iii. 52 'Well, one for de road, Ah peeling off now,' and after the drink he waved his hand and departed. **1958** *Times Lit. Suppl.* 31 Oct. 621/3 The drug-peddling charlatan artist peels off with the German homosexual who has more money than he knows what to do with. **1960** *Tamarack Rev.* XIV. 25 The way he have it figure out, if he stay in the work he have now, he going to be able to peel off and spend the summer on the Continent. **1968** *Surfer Mag.* Jan. 47/3 Ten-foot waves that peel off in good right and left slides. **1968** W. WARWICK *Surfriding in N.Z.* 21/2 When waves break over a sandbar they tend to either dump or peel off along the beach depending on the level of the tide. **1970** N. ARMSTRONG et al. *First on Moon* ii. 38 Just short of the point where a main highway peels off westward.., motels and cocktail lounges..nest alongside gleaming new buildings. **1974** D. GRAY *Dead Give Away* v. 54 'What do we do between tea and dinner?' asked Tony. 'I peel off to my room and read,' said Bob. **1976** *Sounds* 11 Dec. 29/4 The rhythm picks up and Ponty and Stuermer run up and down a soaring, emotive riff together before peeling off to indulge in their own fantasies in turn.

g. *spec.* In Rugby football, to move *off* in various directions from a set formation. Also const. without *off.*

1960 *Times* 24 Oct. 14/1 It was a joy to watch the smooth way in which they peeled off from a tight scrummage. **1960** *Rugby World* Nov. 6/2 From the line-out..they aim to burst through frontally, either by the now familiar 'peeling off' method introduced by their late captain, Lucien Mias, or by extending the line and creating gaps through which a break can be made. **1963** *Times* 28 Jan. 4/6 Abetted by little Lacroix at their heels, they peeled off in all directions in concerted changes of the focal point of attack. **1970** *Times* 13 Apr. 6 Wiltshire peeled from the lineout for a try after five minutes of incessant pressure. **1977** *Western Mail* (Cardiff) 5 Mar. 18/1 They were trailing only 6–7 at the interval after No. 8 Roger Lane had peeled from a close range scrum to put Adrian Jones diving at full stretch for a try.

†**6.** Phrases. **a.** *to pack and* (*or*) *peel,* ? to pack and unpack (or unwrap); to deal in any way; to have dealings. *Sc. Obs.*

Peel prob. meant 'divest of its wrapping or covering', but its sense is uncertain, and was a matter of forensic dispute already in 1680.

1503 *Sc. Acts Jas. IV* (1814) II. 245/2 And þ[t] na man pak nor pele in leitht nor vþeris placis vtouth þe kingis burrowis vnder þe pane of eschaeting of þe gudis to þe kingis vse, þ[t] be tappit sald pakkit or pelit agane þis statute. **1506** *Burgh Rec. Edin.* (Rec. Soc.) I. 109 We ar greittumlie defraudit in our cvstomes throw pakking and peling of merchand gude in Leith to be had furth of our realme. **1540** *Sc. Acts Jas. V* (1814) II. 375/2 It Is statute and ordanit þat na persoun vse pakking nor peling of woll hidis nor skynnis lois' nor laid outw[t] fre burgh and priuilege Therof. **1680** in Fountainhall *Decisions* (1759) I. 81 By the 84th act Parl, 1503, and 24th act, 1633, the merchants must only *pack and peil* at free burghs: Now loading and unloading is the same thing with packing and peiling. This was denied by the Dukes Advocates, who called 'packing' the stowing of goods in packs, and 'peiling', they did not agree what it meant. **1824** SCOTT *Redgauntlet* ch. x, I am not a person to pack or peel with Jacobites.

b. *peel and poll*: see PILL *v.*[1] 7.

peel, *v.*[2] *Sc.* Also 8–9 **peal,** 9 **peil.** [Goes with PEEL *sb.*[4]: origin unascertained.] *trans.* To equal, to match. Also in wider use in *Curling.*

a **1700** in *Poems Comp. Archers* (1726) 62 When Ardrose was a Man, He cou'd not be peal'd. **1825** JAMIESON, To *Peel, Peal, Peil,*..to equal, to match, to produce anything exactly like another. **1921** *Glasgow Herald* 25 Aug. 4/7 The Scottish Tourists..played a two-rink game [of bowls] at Balham yesterday, 'peeling' at 19 on one and losing the other by 12. **1950** *Scotsman* 9 Aug. 7/3 The players peeled at several stages in the game and were 17–17 at the seventeenth end. **1962** *Even. Dispatch* (Edinburgh) 29 Jan. 7 The last named fought back in the closing stages to peel the game [*sc.* curling] at 11 at the 13th. **1969** R. WELSH *Beginner's Guide Curling* iv. 33 *Peels,* to be equal in shots. **1971** *Rand Daily Mail* 27 Mar. 23/3 Thomson..came back into the game and peeled 15–15 on the 20th end.

peel (piːl), *v.*[3] [f. the name of Walter H. *Peel,* founder of the All England Croquet Assoc. and a leading exponent of the practice.] In Croquet, to send a ball other than one's own through a hoop. So **'peeling** *vbl. sb.*[2], **peeled** *ppl. a.*[2]

1899 L. B. WILLIAMS *Croquet* iv. 123 Closely allied to this idea that the partners must be kept together at all hazards and, in a measure, dependent upon it, is the notion that it is a player's duty to put his partner through a hoop when the balls are both for the same point. This manœuvre is occasionally necessary, especially at the last hoop. It is called 'peeling', after its greatest exponent, the late Mr. Walter Peel... Mr. Peel practised it with great accuracy and success. **1914** LD. TOLLEMACHE *Croquet* xviii. 110 The attempt is sometimes made in the second break to 'Peel' your first ball through its remaining Hoops during the course of your second break. **1960** E. P. C. COTTER *Tackle Croquet this Way* 77 To peel is to cause a ball other than the striker's ball to run its hoop in order. *Ibid.* 78 You can peel firmly and confidently, and there is less chance of Black sticking in the hoop. **1961** *Croquet* ('Know the Game' Series) 36/1 *Peel,* to send a ball other than your own through its own hoop. **1966** MILLER & THORP *Croquet* ix. 86 The better players are capable of peeling a ball through two or three hoops during a break... A ball peeled through its hoop in order scores that hoop. **1976** *Denbighshire Free Press* 8 Dec. 12/5 (Advt.), Do you find Croquet, the Croquet of Breaks and Bisques, baffling? Or do you Peel with consummate ease?

peelable ('piːləb(ə)l), *a.* [f. PEEL *v.*[1] + -ABLE.] Suitable for peeling, capable of being peeled. Hence **peela'bility.**

1958 [see CELLULOSE *sb.* c]. **1966** G. N. LEECH *Eng. in Advertising* xx. 178 *Peelability*..is not the sort of quality one would normally have occasion to mention, in talking about oranges or anything else. **1971** D. POTTER *Brit. Eliz. Stamps* xv. 163 A good-quality hinge is almost completely peelable. **1976** *Wireless World* Nov. 11 The reverse side..is covered by a peelable, tough vinyl insulation.

peel-crow, obs. variant of PILCROW.

peele, obs. form of PEAL, PEEL, PELL *sb.*[1]

peeled (piːld), *ppl. a.*[1] [f. PEEL *v.*[1] + -ED[1]. See also PILLED.]

1. Stripped of possessions, plundered, reduced to destitution. (Now as *fig.* of 3 or 4.)

1508 Dunbar *Flyting* 241 Mauch muttoun, vyle buttoun, peilit gluttoun, air to Hilhouse. **1560** Rolland *Crt. Venus* iv. 673 For laik of pith he is sa puir and peild. **1659** Gauden *Tears of Ch.* 355 The indigent and peeled Clergy. **1847** Emerson *Poems* (1857) 136 Is thy land peeled, thy realm marauded?

2. Derived or bereft of hair, bald; tonsured; = pilled *ppl. a.* 2.

[**1386–1681**: see pilled *ppl. a.* 2.]

c **1470** Henryson *Three deid Powys* Poems (ed. Laing) 31 So sall ye ly ilk ane with peilit powys. **1513** Douglas *Æneis* xiii. Prol. 33 Vpgois the bak wyth hir pelit ledderyn flycht. **1591** Shaks. *1 Hen. VI*, i. iii. 30 Piel'd Priest, doo'st thou command me to be shut out? **1653** Urquhart *Rabelais* i. xi, He..cared as little for the peeled as for the shaven.

3. a. Worn threadbare, as a garment; bare of pasture or herbage, as ground. **b.** *transf.* Beggarly, mean, wretched. (Cf. bald *a.* 4, 6.)

a **1510** Dunbar *Petition of Gray Horse* Poems lxi. 38 Pastouris that ar plane and peild. *c* **1530** Redforde *Play Wit & Sc.* etc. (Shaks. Soc.) 63 We have so manye lasshes to lerne this peelde songe, That I wyll not lye to you now and then among. **1535** Stewart *Cron. Scot.* III. 117 Pynd and puir like ony peild tramort. **1581** Pettie *Guazzo's Civ. Conv.* ii. (1586) 88b, Some rich Gentlemen..goe with a peeld threed bare cloke on their backe. **1625** Lisle *Du Bartas, Noe* 123 The mount of Emeraudes which is very high, bare and peel'd, without any herbe or tree growing thereon.

4. a. Stripped of skin, bark, rind, etc.; decorticated, excoriated.

[**1382–1828**: see pilled *ppl. a.* 4.]

1725 Bradley *Fam. Dict.* II. 7 F ij/2 Compotes of peel'd Verjuice. **1799** J. Robertson *Agric. Perth* 353 This peeled [oak] copse-wood makes excellent fuel. **1848** Lytton *Harold* vii. v, Each had had..his 'white palace' of peeled willow wands. **1894** K. Grahame *Pagan P.* 22 Pleasures of the mind whereof..the men of muscle and peeled faces are only just beginning to taste. **1894** *Northumbld. Gloss.*, *Peeled grain*, a tree branch stripped of its bark.

b. *fig.* Of the eyes: Open, on the alert: in phr. ***to keep (one's) eyes peeled***. *colloq.* (orig. *U.S.*).

1853 *Daily Morning Herald* (St. Louis, Missouri) 6 Jan. 2/1 Young man! Keep your eye peeled when you are after the women. **1872** E. Eggleston *End of World* xxvii. 186 [It would] teach the fellow to let monte alone, and keep his eyes peeled when he traveled. **1883** F. M. Crawford *Dr. Claudius* viii, 'Keep your eye peeled there, will you?' the Duke shouted. **1886** H. Stevens *Recoll. J. Lenox* 45 In reading catalogues and reports from all parts of the world, one eye at least was always kept peeled for his desiderata. **1889** Farmer *Americanisms, To keep one's eyes peeled*,..to keep a sharp look out; to be careful. A variation of 'to keep one's eyes skinned'. **1901** *Munsey's Mag.* XXIV. 568/1, I kept my eyes peeled, but I didn't see her in the afternoon crowd. **1906** *Springfield* (Mass.) *Weekly Republ.* 20 Sept. 16 The carpenters..are keeping their 'eyes peeled' for the many coins which have..slid between the planks. **1918** E. O'Neill in *Smart Set* June 96 We'll have to keep an eye peeled from now on. I know 'em. **1923** L. J. Vance *Baroque* xvi. 95 He sent a request to the door-porter to keep an eye peeled and let him know if the cab..seemed disposed to tarry in the offing. **1945** E. Newhouse in *55 Short Stories from New Yorker* (1949) 238 Keep your eyes peeled and let me know if you come across Aladdin's lamp. **1956** B. Holiday *Lady sings Blues* (1973) xxi. 167 If you're doing something wrong, you *know* it and you've got at least one eye peeled looking for trouble. **1974** 'R. Tate' *Birds of Bloodied Feather* viii. 163 Keep your eyes peeled for a break in the mist.

5. In the following passage ***scattered and peeled*** is a doubtful translation; but the expression has become a literary commonplace, *peeled* being vaguely associated with one or more of the senses above.

1611 Bible *Isa.* xviii. 2 Goe yee swift messengers to a nation scattered and peeled [*marg.* Or, outspread and polished; *Vulg.* convulsam et dilaceratam; 1382 Wyclif al to-pullid and torn; 1388 drawun up and to-rent; 1535 Coverdale a desperate and pylled folke; 1885 *R.V.* to a nation tall and smooth (*marg.* Or, dragged away and peeled)]. *Ibid.* 7. **1732** Berkeley *Serm. to S.P.G.* Wks. III. 247 They lay under the curse of God,..peeled and scattered in a foreign land. **1744** Wesley *Addr. to King* in Overton *Evangel. Revival* ix. (1886) 162 A people scattered and peeled and trodden under foot. **1781** Cowper *Expost.* 246 If Heaven spared not us, Peeled, scattered, and exterminated thus. **1883** J. Mackenzie *Day-dawn in Dark Places* 63 The harmless vassalls..are then scattered and peeled, driven hither and thither, and mercilessly killed.

fig. **1892** *Daily News* 7 Mar. 3/5 The utter rout of the Reactionaries has made the peeled and wasted remnant that remain utterly incapable of hindering the work.

Hence '**peeledness** (also **pielde-**).

1580 Hollyband *Treas. Fr. Tong, Escorcheure du siege*, the pieldenesse of the seate. **1610** Holland *Camden's Brit.* ii. 143 From a disease, scab and peelednesse.

peeler^1 ('piːlə(r)). Forms: 4–5 peler, 5–6 -our, -owr, 6 *Sc.* pelor, pellour, peiler, pieller, pealler, 7 pieler, 6– peeler. [f. peel *v.*^{1} + -er^1. See also piller.]

†**1. a.** A plunderer, spoiler, robber, thief; = piller^1 1.

a **1352** Minot *Poems* (ed. Hall) ii. 15 Now haue þai, þe pelers, priked obout. **1436** *Libel Eng. Policy* in *Pol. Poems* (Rolls) II. 164 These false coloured pelours, Called of Seynt Malouse. **1508** Dunbar *Flyting* 70 How that thow, poysonit pelor, gat thy paikis. *a* **1510** —— *Poems* xviii. 12 Than every pelour and purspyk Sayis, Land war bettir warit on me. **1535** Lyndesay *Satyre* 2469 Put thir thrie pellours into pressoun strang. **1545** Joye *Exp. Dan.* xi. AA vij b, A vyle couetouse extortioner and pieller of the people. **1608** Topsell *Serpents* (1658) 639 Apollodorus, the Theef, Pieler, and spoiler of the Cassandrines.

b. A plant that robs or impoverishes the soil.

1573 Tusser *Husb.* (1878) 49 Graie wheat is the grosest,.. and a peeler of ground. **1707** Mortimer *Husb.* (1721) I. 152 Hemp..as 'tis esteemed a Peeler of Land, 'tis best to sow it upon Lands that are rank. **1744–50** W. Ellis *Mod. Husbandm.* II. i. 38 All the oat tribe are great peelers or robbers of the goodness of the earth.

2. a. One who peels, strips, or pares off the skin or rind of fruit, the bark of trees, etc.; also, an instrument or machine for peeling.

1597 *Sc. Acts* 5 (Heading of Act Jas. I, c. 33) Steallers of greene woodde..peallers of Trees. **1755** Johnson, *Peeler*, one who strips or flays. **1846** H. Marshall *Ceylon* 11 Peelers who failed to produce monthly above 30 lbs. of cinnamon, were liable to be flogged. **1881** *Pall Mall G.* 5 Oct. 14/1 The peelers [of peaches] earn from sixty cents. to two dollars per day. **1883** *Cassell's Fam. Mag.* Aug. 528/1 The [coffee] beans again thoroughly dried and the parchment skin removed by a 'peeler'.

b. A name given to a crab when it peels or casts its shell or 'peel'. Also *attrib.*

1866 W. Gregor *Dial. Banffshire, Peeler*, the Shore-crab when casting its shell. **1880** in *Antrim & Down Gloss.* **1883** *Century Mag.* July 378/2 Large craw-fish, which were about to shed their outer cases, or shells, and which for this reason are called 'shedders', or 'Peelers'. **1911** C. O. Minchin *Sea-Fishing* xvii. 245 When the cold outer shell has cracked and is ready to fall, and the new soft shell beneath is growing to replace it, the crab is called a 'peeler', and is then in the best condition for bait. **1934** *Sun* (Baltimore) 27 July 9/8 Hook-and-line fishermen can scarcely buy the popular peeler crab bait for fishing. **1956** M. Kennedy *Salt-Water Angling* x. 321 The crab is perhaps most useful as a bait shortly before it moults—when it has developed the new shell beneath the old one,..the angler anticipating nature by stripping the old shell off it. In this stage it is known variously as a peeler, peel, pill or shedder crab. **1971** *Angling Times* 10 June 3 Van driver Colin drifted his peeler crab bait around the rocks on float tackle. **1976** *Scottish Daily Express* 24 Dec. 12/6 For the smaller fish, rag and lugworm, soft peeler crab and strips of herring or mackerel are usually acceptable.

3. *U.S.* **a.** An exceptional or noteworthy example of anything; *spec.* a violent storm.

1823 J. F. Cooper *Pioneers* I. xv. 212 It's a peeler without, I can tell you, good woman. **1834** C. A. Davis *Lett. J. Downing* 331 The Captain was all the while boastin of [his boat] the 'Two Pollies'; and well he might, for she was a peeler. **1861** *Entertaining Things* I. 197 The gale..was a steady hard blow, what sailors call a peeler.

b. A person of exceptional or unusual qualities; a lively or energetic person.

1833 S. Smith *Life & Writings J. Downing* 218 Them are Pennsylvany chaps are real peelers for electing folks when they take hold. **1834** C. A. Davis *Lett. J. Downing* 88 If he does turn broker, you'll hear more on him; for he's a peeler I tell you. **1844** 'J. Slick' *High Life N.Y.* I. 82, I was talking with a rare peeler of a gal. **1869** Mrs. Stowe *Oldtown Folks* 117 She was spoken of with applause under such titles as 'a staver', 'a pealer', 'a roarer to work'. **1881** W. M. Thayer *From Log Cabin to White House* xiii. 207 He's a peeler for work, too; ain't afraid to dirty hisself.

4. a. One who removes his clothing: *spec.* a pugilist ready to strip for a fight.

1852 *As Good as Comedy* iv. 56 'I know you hain't got the teeth to raise the skin of that varmint.' 'Hain't I, then? Just you try it, then,..and see if I ain't a peeler.' 'Will you peel?' 'Won't I, then?' 'Jake, my boy, I've come here to-day to strip the skin off you altogether.'

b. A strip-tease artist; a stripper.

1951 *Variety* 20 June 53/2 (*heading*) Old Peelers Fade Away in St. Louis Crackdown. *Ibid.*, A steady exodus from the city of strippers in..St. Louis has been reported... It results from the crackdown of the law, with the peelers being replaced by jugglers, singers and hula dancers. **1951** Green & Laurie *Show Biz* 570/2 *Peeler*, stripteaser. **1955** *Variety* 9 Mar. 62/4 Chicago, for years a stripper's haven, is now seriously beset by a dearth of peelers. **1961** A. Berkman *Singers' Gloss. Show Business* 66 *Peeler*,..strip-teaser.

5. *U.S.* A cowboy.

1894 O. Wister *Out West: Jrnls. & Lett.* (1958) 198 *Peeler*, cowpuncher. **1902** *Out West* June 623 The 7 TX peelers is all in on this play,..and the 10 EC outfit will want a hand too. **1903** [see act *v.* 9 f]. **1914** B. M. Bower *Flying U Ranch* 7 This is Mr. Mig-u-ell Rapponi, boys—a peeler straight from the Golden Gate. **1937** *Dialect Notes* VI. 618 Used in its strictest sense, the *peeler* refers to the cowpuncher who rides into the herd and 'cuts' out the horse desired. **1943** L. V. Hamner *Short Grass* 163 The driver, or 'peeler', rode the wheel horse and guides the whole team with one line.

6. In full, ***peeler log***. The trunk of a tree, esp. a softwood one, suitable for the manufacture of veneer by the use of a rotary lathe, which peels thin sheets of wood from the log.

1935 *Timberman* Dec. 3/2 Some studies should be undertaken at once to determine the economic limits of the Douglas fir peelers... The log scarcity has brought forth the Veneer specialist, who makes a business of producing and preparing peeler logs for the plywood trade. **1942** Wood & Linn *Plywoods* vi. 179 From the [North American Pacific Coast] forests the 'peeler' logs, in lengths up to 40 feet, are conveyed by water, rail or road to the plywood mills. **1948** *Q. Jrnl. Forestry* XLII. 33 Poplar plywood could be manufactured if more peeler logs were grown. **1958** W. F. McCulloch *Woods Words* 133 Peeler... A log suitable for plywood. **1966** A. W. Lewis *Gloss. Woodworking Terms* 65 *Peeler log*, log from which veneer is cut by the rotary process of peeling. **1973** *Nature West Coast* 62 Wood [of grand fir] is used for pulp, lumber and peelers (core stock for plywood).

peeler^2 ('piːlə(r)). A nickname given to members of the Irish constabulary, founded under the secretaryship (1812–18) of Mr. (afterwards Sir) Robert Peel; hence subsequently also to policemen in England: see quot. 1858. See bobby 2.

1817 Gen. Mathew in *Parl. Deb.* 1386 The Irishman.. was liable to be carried off without a moment's warning, by a set of fellows well known in Ireland..by the name of Peelers. **1818** Sir R. Peel *Let. to Gregory* 14 Apr., We must not make the Peelers unpopular, by maintaining them against the declared and unequivocal sense of the county in which they act. **1829** *Blackw. Mag.* XXV. 569 The 'Peelers' (by which significant term the whole constabulary force appointed under Mr. Goulburn's bill, as well as those by Mr. Peel's act, are known in the vernacular). **1850** Kingsley *Alt. Locke* xxxv, He's gone for a peeler and a search warrant to break open the door. **1858** *Penny Cycl.* 2nd Suppl. 494/1 Mr. Peel, as Home Secretary, introduced..the new Metropolitan Police Act [1829] which provided London with its efficient body of 'Peelers', subject to the Home Office, in lieu of the old 'Charlies'. **1881** 'Rita' *My Lady Coquette* xvi, The peelers ain't after him.

peeler^3. *local.* [Origin unknown.] In Kent: An iron bar used for drilling holes for hop-poles or wattles.

1796 J. Boys *Agric. Kent* (1813) 56 A large iron peeler to make holes in the land for the [hop] poles, costs 6^s. or 7^s. **1805** R. W. Dickson *Pract. Agric.* (1807) I. 45 Hop-peeler.—The peeler is made use of for forming holes for the hop-poles.

peel-garlic: see pilgarlic.

peeling ('piːlɪŋ), *vbl. sb.* [f. peel *v.*^{1} + -ing^1. See also pilling *vbl. sb.*]

1. The action of peel *v.*^{1}, in its various senses.

†**a.** Plundering, spoliation, robbery. *Obs.*

[**1350–1627**: see pilling *vbl. sb.*]

1649 Howell *Pre-em. Parl.* 11 This illegal peeling of the poor Peasan.

b. The stripping or removal of bark, rind, skin, or external layer.

1564 *Reg. Privy Council Scot.* I. 279 The peling of the bark of the standand treis. **1704** *Collect. Voy.* (Churchill) III. 788/1 Workmen employ'd in peeling of the Cinnamon. **1805** Forsyth *Beauties Scotl.* (1806) III. 353 Some people..in barking trees,..peeled many of them down to the ground. This..is..called peeling below the axe.

c. The coming off of bark, skin, etc.; *esp.* the scaling off of skin after fever.

1884 Bower & Scott *De Bary's Phaner.* 554 The peeling off and decay of the outermost layers. **1897** *Allbutt's Syst. Med.* II. 130 The patient's release will be dependent on the end of peeling.

d. The putting off of clothes; stripping. *colloq.*

1834 M. Scott *Cruise Midge* xvii, The operation of *peeling* was all this while going on amongst the gingham-coated gentry. **1879** *Daily News* 7 Apr. 3/2 The process of 'peeling' had to be gone through. All outer garments were soon taken off, and..deposited on board the umpire's steamer. **1938** [see outstrip *v.*^{1}].

e. ***peeling and polling***: see pilling *vbl. sb.* 1 b.

2. *concr.* **a.** That which is peeled or peels off; a strip of bark, etc.; *esp.* the rind, skin, or outer layer of fruits or roots, which is peeled off when they are prepared for food.

1597 A. M. tr. *Guillemeau's Fr. Chirurg.* 49b/2 Conserve of Roses, Marmalade, Citron peelinges. **1688** R. Holme *Armoury* ii. 85/1 The rind, peeling, or skin of any Fruit. **1796** Mrs. Glasse *Cookery* xiv. 260 Boil the peeling of the apples and the cores in some fair water. **1832** Marryat *N. Forster* x, A kid of potato-peelings. **1880** C. R. Markham *Peruv. Bark* 461 The outer bark comes off..in thin silvery peelings.

†**b.** *spec.* A thin skin or fabric formerly used as a dress material. *Obs.*

[**1611** Cotgr., *Canepin*,..th' outward thinne, and white pilling, of a dressed sheepes skin.] **1693** *Lond. Gaz.* No. 2837/4 A white Peeling Mantua flowered, lined with Green Damask. **1693** Southerne *Maid's last Prayer* iii. iii. 31, I did but stay to chuse some white Peeling for a pair of Breeches. **1769** *Dublin Mercury* 16–19 Sept. 2/2 Cardinal silks, sarsnets, peelings, and persians.

3. The name of a variety of apple. ? *Obs.*

1676 Worlidge *Cyder* (1691) 210 The Peeling is a very good lasting apple. **1731** Bailey (ed. 5), *Peeling*, a lasting Sort of Apple that makes excellent Cyder.

4. *attrib.* and *Comb.*, as ***peeling-axe***, ***-iron***, ***-mill***.

1791 *Trans. Soc. Arts* IX. 175 They bring the Coffee to a machine called a peeling-mill, where it is divested of its outside skin and pulp. **1875** Knight *Dict. Mech., Peeling-iron*, a shovel-shaped thrusting-instrument whereby bark is loosened and pried away from the wood. **1884** *Ibid.* Suppl., *Peeling axe*, a double-bitted axe used in barking trees. **1887** *Daily News* 3 Nov. 5/3 Another member of the family..had had the fever and was in the 'peeling stage'.

peeling ('piːlɪŋ), *ppl. a.* [f. peel *v.*^{1} + -ing^2. See also pilling *ppl. a.*] That peels, in the senses of the vb.

1897 J. Hutchinson in *Arch. Surg.* VIII. No. 31. 219 Patches of a peeling and desquamating psoriasis on his left hand and arm. **1900** *Ibid.* XI. No. 41. 61 Peeling patches in the palms being coincident with papules. **1900** *Westm. Gaz.* 13 Sept. 8/1 The decorative beauty of the leaves and the peeling stems.

Peelite ('piːlaɪt). [See -ite^1.] In British politics, A name given to those Conservatives who sided with Sir Robert Peel when he introduced his measure for the repeal of the Corn-laws in 1846, and who continued for some years to form a group intermediate between the Protectionist Tories and the Liberals, to the latter of whom most of them at length united themselves. So **ˈPeelism.**

1853 *Ecclesiologist* XIV. 41 His views are moderately Conservative: in fact he is an ecclesiological Peelite. **1858** TROLLOPE *Dr. Thorne* i, There.. was a taint of Peelism in the latter [the western moiety of the County]. **1895** *Edin. Rev.* July 266 The Peelites.. were soon merged indistinguishably in the Liberal party.

peell, obs. form of PELL *sb.*[1]

peel-off (ˈpiːlɒf), *sb.* and *a.* [f. phr. *to peel off*: see PEEL *v.*[1] 3, 5.] **A.** *sb.* The action of peeling off. **B.** *adj.* Designating or pertaining to this action. Also *fig.*

1939 *Flight* 18 May 504a (*caption*) The peel-off. Westland Lysander monoplanes.. start a mock dive-bombing attack. **1962** D. WARNER *Death of Bogey* IV. vi. 168 The Lanes did the peel-off. Ran it by lorry. **1972** D. E. WESTLAKE *Cops & Robbers* (1973) xi. 149 They'd busily switched the license plates on the squad car and put the new peel-off numbers on its sides.

peely-wally (ˈpiːlɪwɒlɪ, -ˈwalɪ), *a. Sc.* Also **peelie-wallie** and as one word. [‘Orig. prob. imit. of a whining, feeble sound’ (*Sc. Nat. Dict.*). Cf. Eng. dial. *pee-wee* whining, small (E.D.D.), and WALLYDRAG.] Pale, feeble, sickly, ill-looking.

1832 A. HENDERSON *Proverbs* 208 *Peelie*, thin; meagre.— *Peelie-wallie*, thin; sickly. **1833** J. KENNEDY *Geordie Chalmers* 81 But may I ride on the win' wi' auld Nanee Logan, the witch o' Glenteerie, when I gang to siccan a peely-wally concern again! **1895** W. STEWART *Lilts* 104 The sun sen's forth its flickerin' rays, Fu' peely-wally wan. **1904** ‘H. FOULIS’ *Erchie* xii. 73, I was a kind o' eccentric peely-wally soul, because I sometimes dried the dishes. **1932** ‘L. G. GIBBON’ *Sunset Song* 278 And damn it, if before a twelvemonth was up she didn't have a bairn, a peely-wally girl. **1945** B. FERGUSSON *Lowland Soldier* 25 Ye'd say he was thin, Peelywally, bow-leggit and shilpit. **1962** A. MACLEOD *Eighth Seal* vi. 71 The wee Englishman is too peelywally to start any scrapping. **1966** K. WHITE *Lett. from Gourgounel* 96 A snail.. her long peelie-wallie neck with two horns slowly prodding the air.

peen (piːn), *v.* Also **pene**. [app. of Norse origin: cf. Ihre Sw. *pæna ut en ting* to extend or beat out in length and breadth; Sw. dial. (Rietz) *pena, päna*, e.g. *päna ut jarnet* to beat iron thin, to hammer out in length and breadth; Da. dial. (Molbech) *pene, pæne, pene ud* to beat out; Norw. dial. (Ross) *penna, pænne uut* to hammer out flat.] *trans.* To beat thin with a hammer, to hammer *out*; to strike with the pein of a hammer.

1513 DOUGLAS *Æneis* VII. xi. 72 The sickyr helmis penis and forgis out. *Ibid.* VIII. Prol. 93 Sum penis furth a pan boddum to prent fals plakkis. *Ibid.* VIII. vii. 128 The glowand irne to well and peyne anon. [In Eng. Dial. Dict. from Shetland and Orkney, Cumbld., N.E. Lanc.; in Westmld. and N. Yorksh., as a shoemaker's term, ‘to beat the edge of a sole with the peen of the hammer’.] **1888** J. ROSE *Mod. Machine-Shop Pract.* II. xxv. 162/2 The side faces of the arms would require to be pened. **1902** *Internat. Libr. Technol.* IV. §44.22 Iron may be stretched by peening it; that is, by striking it with the peen of a hammer. This method is often used to loosen a collar or a nut. **1941** A. C. DAVIES *Sci. & Pract. of Welding* ii. 118 In the arc welding of cast iron the risk of fracture is definitely reduced if the short beads of weld metal are lightly peened immediately after they have been laid. **1950** *Engineering* 31 Mar. 345/3 Each run of weld is peened before the next run is applied. **1964** S. CRAWFORD *Basic Engin. Processes* i. 16 The bench fitter frequently uses different types of hand hammers for fitting operations requiring force, e.g.. peening over the end of rivets. **1977** *Good Motoring* Mar. 32/2 A leak between two cylinders caused through a plug in the underside of the head which had been ‘very poorly peened in place’.

Hence **ˈpeening** *vbl. sb.* (see also *shot peening* s.v. SHOT *sb.*[1] 31).

1885 [see PEIN *sb.*]. **1905** W. S. LEONARD *Machine-Shop Tools & Methods* (ed. 3) ii. 33 The peening affects only the outer surface of the shaft, and the turning removes this outer surface, thereby partially neutralizing the effect of the peening. **1907** *English Mechanic* 23 Aug. 49/1 After the bottom is slipped on the paning down can be done with a paning hammer.., or.. with a sheet-metal worker's common hammer. **1960** *Times Rev. Industry* Jan. 36/2 The peening of springs for increasing the fatigue life, particularly for the motor industry, can be done in air operated plant as well as the airless type. **1964** J. G. TWEEDDALE *Mech. Properties of Metals* vii. 125 Residual stresses may be induced in several ways, such as surface rolling and peening. Peening can take the form of hammer peening or shot peening.

peen, var. PEIN *sb.*

peeng, variant of PING, sound of a bullet.

1890 *Illustr. Lond. News* Christm. No. 2/3 The high soprano ‘peeng’ of a small hail of Minié bullets.

peenge (piːndʒ), *v. Sc.* and *north. dial.* Also **pinge**. [Formed perh. on *whinge*, under the influence of *peep, peek, peevish*, or the like.] *intr.* To whine, complain in a whining voice.

?**15..** in *Evergreen* (1824) I. 51 A Bytand Ballat on warlo Wives, That gar thair Men live pinging Lives. **1791** J. LEARMONT *Poems* 377 The unhappy ne'er shall peenge to me in vain. **1815** SCOTT *Guy M.* xxxix, That useless peenging thing o' a lassie there at Ellangowan. **1825** BROCKETT *N.C. Gloss.*, *Peenging, Pinging*, uttering feeble, frequent and somewhat peevish complaints. ‘A peenging bairn’—a whining child. **1900** in *Eng. Dial. Dict.* from Scotland and Northumb.

peent (piːnt), *sb. N. Amer.* Also **peeent**. [Echoic.] A representation of the high whistling sound emitted by a woodcock. Also *attrib.*

1895 F. M. CHAPMAN *Handbk. Birds of Eastern N. Amer.* 153 [The Woodcock] begins on the ground with a formal, periodic *peent, peent*, an incongruous preparation for the wild flight that follows. **1925** E. H. FORBUSH *Birds Massachusetts* I. 386 Voice [of woodcock].—A nasal ‘peent’ something like common note of Nighthawk. **1931** *Sun* (Baltimore) 11 Apr. 4/7, I heard a woodcock, ‘peent’ sing, And I saw a hum-bird rise. **1944** L. A. HAUSMAN *Illustr. Encycl. Amer. Birds* 438/2 This song [of the woodcock] is introduced, and concluded, by a series of nasal peent notes, much like the flying calls of the Nighthawk. **1953** MURPHY & AMADON *Land Birds Amer.* iii. 83/1 Both before and after these flights, they [*sc.* Woodcocks] utter a nasal call, usually written as peent. **1965** A. WETMORE et al. *Water, Prey, & Game Birds N. Amer.* 330/1 The woodcock zigzags rapidly down to earth with chirping notes. He struts across a patch of open ground, sounds his peent notes again, then soars to repeat the aerial act.

peent (piːnt), *v. N. Amer.* [f. the sb.] **a.** *intr.* To emit a high whistling sound characteristic of a woodcock. **b.** *trans.* To utter by making such a sound. So **ˈpeenting** *vbl. sb.*

1897 F. M. CHAPMAN *Bird-Life* vii. 103 Unless disturbed, he [*sc.* the woodcock] will probably return to near the spot from which he started and at once resume his *peenting*. **1956** PETERSON & FISHER *Wild Amer.* v. 56 Over downtown roof-gardens the ‘peenting’ of cruising night-hawks can often be heard. **1973** M. CROWELL *Greener Pastures* 197, I hear a woodcock ‘peenting’ over on apple tree hill. **1976** *Kingston* (Ontario) *Whig-Standard* 22 Oct. 14/1 Often, shortly after sunset, the male [woodcock] peents a nasal sound. *Ibid.*, Once landed, the peenting resumes.

peeny-wally (ˈpiːniːwɔːlɪ). Also **peeni(e)wally, peeny(-wauly)**. [Etym. uncertain; perh. PEELY-WALLY infl. by Jamaican dial. *peeny* small (see also E.D.D.).] A Jamaican name for a firefly, esp. the largest of those found on the island, *Pyrophorus plagiophthalmus.*

1907 W. JEKYLL *Jamaican Song & Story* II. 184 ‘Peeny’ is the Candlefly, which shines like my donkey's coat. **1961** F. G. CASSIDY *Jamaica Talk* xiii. 292 The big one [*sc.* firefly] is also *peeny* or *peeny-wauly*, an unexplained word, though *wauly* may refer to its shining ‘eyes’. **1962** S. WYNTER *Hills of Hebron* i. 23 When the rains stopped, the ‘peeniwallies’, hundreds of them, fluttered transparent wings against the lamp. **1971** *Islander* (Victoria, B.C.) 17 Jan. 2/3 These fireflies are affectionately called ‘peenie-wallies’ by the islanders [*sc.* Jamaicans].

peeoy (piˈoi). *Sc.* Also **peeoye, peeoe, pioy(e, pee-o-ie, pyowe.** A child's firework, consisting of a small cone of damp gunpowder, which is lighted at the top; also called a ‘spitting devil’.

1822 GALT *Provost* xxvi, He was apt to puff and fiz, and go off with a pluff of anger like a pioye. **1825** JAMIESON, *Peeoy, pioye, peeoe, s.*, a small quantity of moistened gun-powder, formed into a pyramidal shape, and kindled at the top. **1886** A. STEWART *Remin. Dunfermline* 62 Pee-o-ies made of wet powder kneaded into a paste in the hand. **1889** STEVENSON *Master of B.* ii. 22 Chapping at the man's door, .. and puttin' poother in his fire and pee-oys in his window.

peep (piːp), *sb.*[1] Forms: 5 **pepe**, 5–6 *Sc.* **peip**, 6–7 **peepe**, 7– **peep**. [f. PEEP *v.*[1]]

I. 1. An imitation or representation of the feeble shrill sound made by young birds, mice, etc.

1423 JAS. I *Kingis Q.* lvii, Now, suetë bird, say ones to me ‘pepe’. *c* **1440** *Gesta Rom.* I. xlv. 364 (Add. MS.) The Cate come beside, and herde the mouse Crie in the barme, pepe! pepe! *c* **1470** HENRYSON *Mor. Fab.* II. (*Town & C. Mouse*) xxi, How fair ye sister? Cry peip, quhair euer ye be! **1636** PRYNNE *Unbish. Tim.* Ep. (1661) 26 As a Poppet, which springeth up and down, and cryeth peep, peep. **1822** LAMB *Elia* Ser. I. *Praise Chimneysw.*, Their little professional notes sounding like the *peep-peep* of a young sparrow. **1825** JAMIESON s.v., ‘He darna *play peep*’, he dare not let his voice be heard. **1880** JEFFERIES *Gt. Estate* 91 Then the hedge-sparrows.. cry ‘peep-peep’ mournfully.

II. *sb.* **2.** A name for this sound; a cheep or faint squeak. Now *arch.* or *local.*

c **1470** HENRYSON *Mor. Fab.* XIII. (*Frog & Mouse*) i, Scho [the mouse] ran, cryand with mony pietious peip. **1513** DOUGLAS *Æneis* VI. v. 106 The todir ansueris with a petuus peip. **1562** J. HEYWOOD *Epigr.* I. xxviii, I neuer heard.. So muche as one peepe of one mouse. **1884** ROE *Nat. Ser. Story* vi, The first faint peep that should announce the senior chick.

b. A slight sound or utterance; a single item or piece of information, chiefly in neg. contexts. Cf. PIP *sb.*[2] 1 b.

1903 in *Eng. Dial. Dict.* **1908** R. W. CHAMBERS *Firing Line* xxiv. 411 Nobody's heard a peep from you. What on earth do you mean by this? **1928** S. LEWIS *Man who knew Coolidge* I. 13 I'd never made a peep about how maybe it'd be a good stunt for him to go out and maybe earn a little money on the side. **1954** *Picture Post* 2 Jan. 34/3 ‘One more peep out of you, Mister, and I'll get the boys to push you and your b—— stall in the oggin’, which was a nearby canal. *a* **1974** R. CROSSMAN *Diaries* (1975) I. 275 Not a peep came out of any of them. **1974** T. P. WHITNEY tr. *Solzhenitsyn's Gulag Archipel.* I. I. i. 10 They take you from a military hospital with a temperature of 102, as they did with Ans Bernshtein, and the doctor will not raise a peep about your arrest. **1977** P. COSGRAVE *Cheyney's Law* v. 47, I know coppers... They're not supposed to be able to take it... But there's not been a peep out of him... Maybe.. he's tougher than you are.

†**3.** A fancy name for a company or brood of chickens. *Obs. rare.*

1486 *Bk. St. Albans* F vij, A Pepe of chykennys.

4. A popular name of certain birds.

a. A young chicken. Cf. PEE-PEE[1]. **b.** *U.S.* A name given to several species of sandpiper; also to a species of rail, *Rallus carolinus.* **c.** A local name of the Meadow-pipit.

a. **1688** R. HOLME *Armoury* II. 311/1 A Cock first [called] a Peep. **1931** *Amer. Speech* VII. 20 Peeps. Little chickens. **1935** *Ibid.* X. 171/1 Peep. A chick just hatched, or a small chicken. **1943** *Sun* (Baltimore) 10 Aug. 10/3 The Boonsboro *Times* reports the birth there of a ‘peep’ with no eyes and no sign of an eye.

b. **1794** MORSE *Amer. Geog.* 168 Peep, *Rallus Carolinus.* **1864** SALA in *Daily Tel.* 27 July, A ‘Peep’ is a very abject and idiotic little bird found in New England... He is given to staggering about in an imbecile and helpless manner... The ..New England mind.. has long since endorsed the locution ‘as tight as a peep’, to express an utter state of tipsification. **1873** LONGF. *Wayside Inn* III. Prel. 77 The plover, peep, and sanderling. **1894** NEWTON *Dict. Birds* 702.

c. **1885** SWAINSON *Prov. Names Birds* 45 Meadow Pipit (*Anthus pratensis*)... Peep (Forfar.).

peep (piːp), *sb.*[2] Also 6 **pype**, 6–7 **peepe**. [f. PEEP *v.*[2]]

1. a. An act of peeping; a look or glance as through a narrow aperture or from concealment; a surreptitious, furtive, or peering glance.

1730 SWIFT *Traulus* II. 33 Hence that wild suspicious peep, Like a rogue that steals a sheep. **1784** COWPER *Task* IV. 779 He contrives A peep at Nature, when he can no more. **1786** MME. D'ARBLAY *Let. T. Twining* 10 July, When I come to town I shall never get a peep at you. **1838** DICKENS *Nich. Nick.* iv, Snawley.. took another peep at the little boy on the trunk. **1852** MRS. STOWE *Uncle Tom's C.* xix. 172 You've only seen a peep through the curtain. **1873** TRISTRAM *Moab* vii. 124 The nearer gorge.. afforded a magnificent peep.

b. *fig.* Said esp. of the first appearance of daylight, as in *peep of dawn, of the morning*, PEEP OF DAY. Also, A tiny speck of light.

1530 PALSGR. 804/1 At daye pype, *a la pipe du jour.* **1579** FENTON *Guicciard.* XIII. (1599) 608 He came by the peepe of the morning to the top of the mountaine. **1616** LANE *Contn. Sqr.'s T.* viii. 101 From morninges peepe till high midd noone. **1750** GRAY *Elegy* 98 Oft have we seen him at the peep of dawn. **1882** STEVENSON *New Arab. Nts.* (1884) 246 There was no light.. but a little peep from a lamp.

c. = PEEP-BO. *Obs.* exc. *dial.*

1677 GILPIN *Demonol.* (1867) 423 When Satan makes nice with men.. He plays at peep with them, that he may make them more earnest to follow him. **1903** in *Eng. Dial. Dict.* (cited from N.W. Derbyshire).

d. *dial.* and *U.S.* After a negative, a short interval (of sleep), a wink.

1905 R. BEACH *Pardners* (1912) ii. 49 Most people called him crazy, 'cause he had fits of goin' for days without a peep.

2. *transf.* **a.** A small aperture. **b.** A crevice for looking through; *spec.* the slit in the leaf-sight of a rifle: see *peep-sight* in 4. **c.** *dial.* An eye.

a **1825** *Balankin* iii. in Child *Ballads* IV. xciii. (1886) 323/1 At the sma peep of a window Balankin crap in. **1847–78** HALLIWELL, *Peep*, an eye. *Somerset.*

†**3.** A mode of cheating at dice: see quot. *Obs.*

1711 PUCKLE *Club* 22 Gamesters have the top, the peep, eclipse, thumbing. *Note.* Shaking the dice so forward in the box, that by an apparent face, they know when to clap down, so as to throw the reverse.

4. *attrib.* and *Comb.* [some of these are from the verb-stem, PEEP *v.*[2]]: *peep by-play, -glass, -stone*; **peep hawk** (*dial.*), a kestrel; **peep-joint**, a place where striptease is performed; **peep-machine**, a machine through which a peep-show is seen; **peep nicking-machine**: see quot.; **peep-sight**, a backsight for rifles with a peep for bringing the foresight into line with the object aimed at: see 2 b; **peep-toe** *attrib.*, designating a kind of shoe whose tip is cut away allowing the toes to be seen; also *absol.*; also **peep-toed** *a.*

1659 R. WILDE *Poems* (1870) 10 Dark-lantern language, and his *peep by-play. **1892** LUMSDEN *Sheep-head* 196 Can ye wi' thy *peep-glass explore The all eterne? **1880** *Antrim & Down Gloss.*, **Peep hawk*, the kestrel. **1960** *News Chron.* 23 Sept. 10/1 Jayne is.. head stripper in the Pink Flamingo, a gilded *peep-joint. **1938** G. GREENE *Brighton Rock* III. ii. 117 The motor-track, the shooting booths and *peep machines. *Ibid.* III. iii. 130 Framed snapshots of King Edward VII (Prince of Wales) in a yachting cap and a background of peep machines. **1884** KNIGHT *Mech. Dict.* Suppl., **Peep Nicking-Machine*, a special gun tool which forms the peep in the leaf of a rifle sight. **1881** GREENER *Gun* 151 An elevating Vernier *peep-sight attached to the stock of the rifle. **1939** *Vogue* 3 May 5 (Advt.), Blue calf thonging and heel sets off this *peep-toe sandal in blue calf, 45/9. **1940** *Ibid.* June 14 (Advt.), Only Joyce.. would think of using duck-skin and calf in this peep-toe creation for your every leisure hour. **1957** *Observer* 25 Aug. 11/7 A young French lady named Tracy, in peeptoe shoes and ice-blue, skin-tight gown with a good deal of cleavage. **1960** *News Chron.* 6 June 5/2 A blade in a tweed coat and peep-toe sandals. **1968** J. IRONSIDE *Fashion Alphabet* 133 *Peep-toe*, a rather coy name for any shoe, usually court or sling-back, from which the toe-cap is cut away to expose part of the toes. **1969** E. WILSON *Hist. Shoe Fashions* xx. 247 The war years of 1939–45 saw.. a heavy restriction in shoe-making materials. .. Peep-toes and big chunky trimmings decorated the very popular court shoe. **1976** *Vogue* 15 Mar. 77 Pale blue and navy peep-toe sandals. **1953** K. TENNANT *Joyful Condemned* xix. 173 A really pretty pair of *peep-toed, high-heeled sandals.

peep, *sb.*³ Early form of PIP *sb.*²

peep (piːp), *sb.*⁴ *U.S.* [see quot. 1943.] = JEEP *sb.*

Sources are divided as to whether peep should designate a vehicle larger or smaller than a jeep, but are agreed in referring both terms to the same type of vehicle.

1941 *N.Y. Herald Tribune* 28 June 14/3 Peep (son of a jeep) means a bantam car. **1941** *N.Y. Times* 26 Oct. xx. 3/2 The one-half ton 'jeep' command reconnaissance car, its name taken from the model designation 'G.P.', and one-quarter ton 'peep' reconnaissance cars are combat vehicles. **1943** *Amer. N. & Q.* III. 137/1, I laid down an editorial ukase that the ½-ton truck was thereafter to be the 'jeep' and the ¼-ton the 'peep'. **1946** *Amer. Speech* XXI. 245 In the Armored Force..the ¼-ton 4 by 4 is always a *peep*, the term 'jeep' being applied to the command and reconnaissance car. **1953** M. BURY *Rolling Wheels* 242 G.I.'s called a command car a *jeep*, called what you call a jeep, a *peep*—and bicycles were called *creeps*! **1962** *Amer. Speech* XXXVII. 78 The peep proved as versatile as the jeep, and had the advantages of a lower silhouette, less gasoline consumption, cheaper production, and the occupation of less cargo space when shipped.

peep (piːp), *v.*¹ Now *arch.* or *local.* Forms: 5–6 pepe, 6 *Sc.* peip, 6–7 peepe, (6 pyep, 8–9 piep), 7– peep. [Late ME. *pēpe-n*, which began *c* 1400 to take the place of the earlier *pīpe-n, pype-n*, found in same sense *a* 1250 (see PIPE *v.*¹) = OF. *piper* (12th c. in Godef. *Compl.*): cf. L. *pīpāre*, also *pīpiāre, pīpīre*, It. *pipare* and *pipiare*, all said of birds, also F. *pipier*, '*pépier* to peepe, cheepe, or pule, as a young bird in the neast' (Cotgr.) Cf. also Du., LG., mod.Ger. *piepen*, Lith. *pýpti*, Czech *pípati*, in same sense; also Gr. πῖπος, L. *pīpio* a young 'peeping' bird, Ger. *piepvogel*; all of echoic origin. *Pepe(n, peep*, corresponds in vowel to F. *pépier*, but whether connected with it, or independently formed in Eng., is not clear: see PIPE *v.*¹]

1. a. *intr.* To utter the weak shrill sound proper to young birds, mice, and some kinds of frogs; to cheep, chirp, squeak.

c **1403** LYDG. *Temple of Glas* 180 Maydens ȝung of age, That pleined sore with peping & with rage. *a* **1530** HEYWOOD *Love* (Brandl) 108 Were it but a mouse, lo, sholde pepe in your ere. **1552** HULOET, Pyep like a chycken, crane, or fawcon, *pipio*. **1566** PAINTER *Pal. Pleas.* I. 72 The yonge larkes..peping and chirping about their mother. **1601** HOLLAND *Pliny* I. 298 By the 20 day..ye shall heare the chick to peepe within the verie shell. **1611** BIBLE *Isa.* x. 14 There was none that moved the wing, or opened the mouth, or peeped [1885 *R.V.* chirped]. **1648–78** HEXHAM, *Piepen als een muys*, to Peep like a mous. **1706** PHILLIPS, To *Piep*, to cry like a chicken. **1883** *Harper's Mag.* Aug. 378/2 A brood of chickens peeped in a coop in one corner. **1885** *Scribner's Mag.* XXX. 730/1 Sometimes a nest of young chimney-swallows..would fall upon the hearth, 'pieping' for human sympathy.

†**b.** To sound shrilly; said of music. *Obs.*

1501 DOUGLAS *Pal. Hon.* I. 361 Proportion sounding dulcest, hard I peip.

2. *transf.* **a.** Of persons etc.: To speak in a weak, querulous, shrill tone; to squeak; to 'sing small'. (Chiefly contemptuous.)

c **1550** LYNDESAY *Pedder Coffeis* 23 Peipand peurly with peteouss graniss. **1570** FOXE *A. & M.* (ed. 2) 1904/1 Frier Bucknham..was so dashed, that neuer after he durst peepe outof the Pulpit agaynst M. Latymer. **1611** BIBLE *Isa.* viii. 19 Wizards that peepe [*R.V.* chirp] and that mutter. **1625** B. JONSON *Staple of N.* II. i, O, the only oracle That ever peep'd or spake out of a doublet. **1736** *Disc. Witchcraft* 12 These Oraclers, when they pretend to receive Answers from the Dead, would piep like Chickens. **1737** RAMSAY *Sc. Prov.* xlv. (1750) 123 Ye're no sae poor as ye peep. **1802** LEYDEN *Ld. Soulis* xlvi, Young Branxholm peep'd and puirly spake, 'O sic a death is no for me!' **1863** W. PHILLIPS *Speeches* vi. 136 No one has ever peeped or muttered.

b. To betray a confidence; to inform. Also *trans.*

1911 J. LONDON *Let.* 6 Mar. (1966) 340 The convicts are few and far between who come out and dare to peep a word of what they know. *Ibid.* I have known ex-cons who became dead for peeping. **1950** H. E. GOLDIN *Dict. Amer. Underworld Lingo* 154/2 *Peep*, to betray associates; to give information to the police.

peep (piːp), *v.*² Forms: 5–6 pepe, 6–7 peepe, 7– peep. [Not known till late in 15th c.; not in Promptorium or Catholicon. The earlier synonyms were *keke* (Promp.), and *peke*, in 14th c. *kike* and *pike*, to which *pepe* had probably some phonetic analogy: see PEEK *v.*¹]

1. *intr.* To look through a narrow aperture, as through the half-shut eyelids or through a crevice, chink, or small opening into a larger space; hence, to look furtively, slyly, or pryingly.

c **1460** *Towneley Myst.* xiii. 581 *Mak.* Nay, do way: he slepys. *iijus pastor.* Me thynk he pepys. **1535** COVERDALE *Song Sol.* ii. 9 He loketh in at the wyndowe, & pepeth thorow the grate. —— *Ecclus.* xxi. 23 A foole wyll pepe in at yᵉ wyndow [**1611** peepe in at the doore] in to the house. **1570** LEVINS *Manip.* 70/15 To Péepe, *inspicere*. **1590** SHAKS. *Mids. N.* IV. i. 89 When thou wak'st, with thine owne fooles eies peepe. **1596** —— *Merch. V.* I. i. 52 Some that will euermore peepe through their eyes, And laugh like Parrats at a bag-piper. **1692** BENTLEY *Boyle Lect.* viii. 241 Those remote and vast bodies were formed, not merely upon our account to be peept at through an optick glass. **1703** MAUNDRELL *Journ. Jerus.* (1732) 126 We had an opportunity just to peep into it. **1719** DE FOE *Crusoe* I. xi, I began to take Courage, and to peep abroad again. **1768–74** TUCKER *Lt. Nat.* (1834) II. 319 The little bird that peeps in at the window. **1843** CARLYLE *Past & Pr.* II. vi, One peeps direct into the very bosom of that Twelfth Century. **1860** EMERSON *Cond. Life* v. (1861) 108 We must not peep and eavesdrop at palace doors.

fig. **1590** SPENSER *F.Q.* I. i. 39 And low, where dawning day doth neuer peepe, His dwelling is.

†**b.** *Obs. slang.* (See quot. and cf. PEEPY *a.*)

a **1700** B. E. *Dict. Cant. Crew*, *As the Cull Peeps let's Mill him*, when the Man is a Sleep, let's Kill him.

2. *fig.* To emerge or protrude a very short distance into view (as from concealment); to begin to appear or show itself: chiefly said of natural objects, as daylight, flowers, distant eminences, etc. Often more distinctly *fig.* from 1: To appear as if looking out or over something.

1535 COVERDALE *Jer.* vi. 1 A plage and a greate misery pepeth out [WYCLIF is seen, 1611 appeareth, 1885 *R.V.* looketh forth] from the North. **1595** GOODWINE *Blanchardyn* II. I ij, When the day began to peepe, they tooke their horses and rode to Tormaday. **1606** SHAKS. *Ant. & Cl.* I. iv. 53 No Vessell can peepe forth: but 'tis as soone Taken as seene. **1628** GAULE *Pract. The.* (1629) 25 So was it the same Christ that peeped in the Law, through Types and Figures. **1634** MILTON *Comus* 140 Ere..The nice Morn on th' Indian steep From her cabin'd loop hole peep. **1709** POPE *Ess. Crit.* 232 Hills peep o'er hills, and Alps on Alps arise. **1770** GOLDSM. *Des. Vill.* 330 Sweet as the primrose peeps beneath the thorn. **1821** CLARE *Vill. Minstr.* I. 6 The steeple peeping o'er the wood's dark brow. **1857** W. COLLINS *Dead Secret* VI. i, The stem of a pipe peeped out of the breast-pocket of his coat.

b. Of a plant, seed, etc.: To begin to show itself above the soil; to sprout.

1593 NASHE *Christ's T.* Wks. (Grosart) IV. 185 Those blossomes which peepe foorth in the beginning of the Spring, are frost-bitten and die. **1707** MORTIMER *Husb.* (1721) II. 9 When your Plants begin to peep, Earth them up. **1765** EARL HADDINGTON *Forest-trees* 16 It [hornbeam] lies as long in the seedbed before it peeps as the ash. **1873** BRYANT *New & Old* i, Flowers, that were buds but yesterday, Peep from the ground where'er I pass.

c. Of a mental characteristic or the like: To show itself a little unintendedly, to come slightly into view unconsciously.

1579 W. WILKINSON *Confut. Familye of Love, Brief Descr.*, The doctrine of H.N. began to pepe out. **1611** SHAKS. *Wint. T.* IV. iii. 148 Your youth And the true blood which peepes fairely through 't. **1826** LAMB *Elia* Ser. II. *Genteel Style Writ.*, The way the retired statesman peeps out in his essays. **1881** LADY HERBERT *Edith* 8 Little indications of selfishness and heartlessness would peep out now and then.

3. *trans.* To cause to appear slightly; to put forth or protrude (the head, etc.) *out* from a hiding-place. **b.** To cause or allow (the eye) to peep. *rare.*

1597 SHAKS. *2 Hen. IV*, I. ii. 238 There is not a daungerous Action can peepe out his head, but I am thrust vpon it. **1669** DRYDEN *Tyran. Love* III. i, This love..Peeps out his coward head to dare my age. **1788** *Disinterested Love* I. 115 Hiding himself in the belfry, and occasionally peeping a bit of his head out. **1818** KEATS *Endym.* I. 871 A well Whose patient level peeps its crystal eye Right upward.

4. *trans.* To spy *out* by peeping. *rare.*

1817–18 COBBETT *Resid. U.S.* (1822) 235 Telling them the story of Baker's peeping out the name, marked on the sack, which the old woman was wearing as a petticoat.

peepal: see PEEPUL.

†**peep-arm**. *Obs. rare.* [f. PEEP *v.*² + ARM: cf. next.] In *phr. to play peep-arm*, to let the arm be seen as briefly as possible.

1625 B. JONSON *Staple of N.* I. i, A broken [i.e. worn out at the elbow] sleeve keeps the arm back..And thence we say, that such a one plays at peep-arm.

peep-bo ('piːpˌbəʊ). *colloq.* = BO-PEEP. Cf. PEEK-A-BOO. Hence **'peep-boing** *vbl. sb.*

1818 'A. BURTON' *Adventures J. Newcome* II. 114 His Toes played peep-boh through his Shoes. **1828** A. ROYALL *Black Bk.* II. 137, I was not disposed to play at peep-bo with him. **1837** DICKENS *Pickw.* x, Small restless black eyes, that kept winking and twinkling on each side of his..nose, as if they were playing a perpetual game of peep-bo with that feature. **1847–78** HALLIWELL, *Peep-bo*,..the term is extended to the occasional obscuration of a debtor, or of one accused of anything rendering his visibility inconvenient. **1853** MRS. GASKELL *Ruth* I. vi. 145 After some 'peep-boing', she was about to snatch a kiss, when Harry..hit Ruth a great blow on the face. **1889** 'J. S. WINTER' *Mrs. Bob* (1891) 40 The afternoon sun playing peep-bo among his thick golden curls. **1974** P. DICKINSON *Poison Oracle* vi. 153 Dorah and Peggy were playing peep-bo round a hut.

pee-pee¹ ('piːpiː). *U.S.* [Perh. onomatopœic, f. the sound made by the birds.] A young chicken, or, esp. in Jamaica, a young turkey.

1890 *Dialect Notes* I. 74 Pee-pee..a very small chicken. Eastern Pennsylvania. **1927** ANDERSON & CUNDALL *Jamaica Negro Proverbs & Sayings* 73 Cuss John Crow 'peel-head', turkey pee-pee bex [i.e. little turkey angry]. **1950** *Publ. Amer. Dial. Soc.* XIV. 51 Pee-pee: *excl.* A call to turkeys. Imitative of the cry of the poults. **1953** *Amer. Speech* XXVIII. 252 Pee-pee... A newborn or very young chick. **1961** F. G. CASSIDY *Jamaica Talk* v. 104 Young fowl, usually turkeys, are called pee-pees.

pee-pee² ('piːpiː). [redupl. PEE *sb.*⁵] = PEE *sb.*⁵

1923 J. MANCHON *Le Slang* 220 To do peepee. **1941** E. P. O'DONNELL *Great Big Doorstep* x. 143 Commado said, 'When them twins get in the show like lass time, one's gotta make pee-pee, the udda one gotta climb on the seat [etc.].' **1962** B. J. FRIEDMAN *Stern* I. 58 Do you still make peepee in your pants? **1972** H. C. RAE *Shooting Gallery* iv. 263 Time stopped. The Pee-pee was cold and swollen in her tummy.

peeper¹ ('piːpə(r)). [f. PEEP *v.*¹ + -ER¹.]

1. One who or that which peeps or cheeps.

1611 COTGR., *Pepieur*, a peeper, cheeper; puler.

2. *spec.* **a.** A young chicken or pigeon.

1591 LYLY *Endym.* v. ii, I preferre..an ancient henne before a younge chicken peeper. **1649** G. DANIEL *Trinarch., Hen. V*, cclvii, But nobly cover with a Wing wide Spread; Feathers above 'em to Surround them All, Amated peepers. **1733** BRAMSTON *Man of Taste* 14 Snails the first course, and Peepers crown the meal. **1755** JOHNSON, *Peeper*, a young chicken just breaking the shell.

b. A small tree-frog of the genus *Hyla*, esp. *H. crucifer*, found in eastern North America. *U.S.*

1857 S. H. HAMMOND *Wild Northern Scenes* 30 All is still now, save the piping notes of the little peeper along the shore. **1884** ROE *Nat. Ser. Story* vi, He said they were peepers. **1889** G. H. ELLWANGER *Garden's Story* i. 19 The chorus of the *Hylodes*, or peepers,..that piercing treble..that nothing—even the katydid—can equal in strident intensity. **1906** M. C. DICKERSON *Frog Bk.* 139 There are few people in the eastern United States who do not know the voices of the Spring Peepers... The Peepers have spring in their hearts. **1938** J. W. LIPPINCOTT *Animal Neighbours* (1940) xx. 192 The ridiculously small spring frog or peeper, an inch and a quarter long, comes first, sometime in March. **1961** D. M. COCHRAN *Living Amphibians of World* 113/1 The spring peeper, *Hyla crucifer*, is one of the earliest of the frogs to appear in spring. **1976** *Yankee* Apr. 78/2 Nearly every Easterner..has heard the spring peeper's song.

peeper² ('piːpə(r)). [f. PEEP *v.*² + -ER¹.]

1. a. One who peeps or peers; *esp.* one who looks or pries furtively, a prier, a 'Paul Pry'.

1652 GAULE *Magastrom.* 375 He..had his eyes put out; an apt punishment for all peepers and star-gazers. **1663** KILLIGREW *Parson's Wed.* v. iii. in Hazl. *Dodsley* XIV. 519 What would not I give for a peeper's place at the meeting? **1711** STEELE *Spectator* No. 53 ¶8, I doubt not but you will think a Peeper as much more pernicious than a Starer. **1795** WOLCOTT (P. Pindar) *Convention Bill* Wks. 1812 III. 380 Then let the bullet..Dismiss the saucy Peeper to the dead.

b. A private detective or investigator; occas., a policeman.

1940 R. CHANDLER *Farewell, my Lovely* xxiii. 177 Peeper, huh, pally? From the big bad burg, huh? **1943** —— *Lady in Lake* (1944) xxxv. 185 Don't bother to call your house-peeper... I'm allergic to house-peepers. **1968** R. CLAPPERTON *No News on Monday* iii. 25 Police protection for a peeper. What kind of advertisement is that? **1968** E. MCGIRR *Lead-Lined Coffin* ii. 64 He..flipped the wallet open. 'A peeper,' he said. **1970** G. F. NEWMAN *Sir, You Bastard* ii. 54 'I have an arrangement with the peeper across the road. He's had a lean time lately.' His voice was level. Moving towards him, Angie said: 'Policemen are different.' **1975** R. L. SIMON *Wild Turkey* xxii. 160 What kind of bullshit are you throwing around, peeper? You want me to slap you in the can?

2. *slang.* An eye. Chiefly *pl.*

a **1700** B. E. *Dict. Cant. Crew, Peepers*, Eyes. **1755** J. SHEBBEARE *Lydia* (1769) II. 181 An understanding as much distorted and awry as his two peepers. **1785** GROSE *Dict. Vulg. T., Peepers*, eyes; *single peeper*, a one eyed man. **1819** *Sporting Mag.* V. 6 A slight cut on the right peeper. **1848** THACKERAY *Van. Fair* xiv, A secret..invisible..to the stupid peepers of that young whiskered prig. **1858** A. MAYHEW *Paved with Gold* II. xii. 191 They went to work slogging, Jack delivering a 'head-acher'..and Ned one not to be worked at on the 'peepers'. **1901** 'H. MCHUGH' *John Henry* 93, I hate to have a girl plant her pleading peepers on me. **1908** A. N. LYONS *Arthur's* I. ii. 10, I jerked me peeper round, an' there was a girl squattin' on a tar barrel. **1928** E. WALLACE *Double* xiii. 204 Unless your poor old peepers are going wrong you would have seen them. **1937** G. FRANKAU *More of Us* iv. 42 She winked one peeper; But Innocent's eyes, downcast, still withheld her man Glances he craved. **1968** A. DIMENT *Bang Bang Birds* vii. 108 There was a leer in his rheumy peepers as he gave Marianne a mental strip. **1978** J. SYMONS *Blackheath Poisonings* III. 153 He had lost an eye long ago in the Ashanti campaign... 'I'm lucky to be alive, but I lost one of my peepers.'

3. *Cant.* **a.** A looking-glass; also (quot. 1785) a spyglass; *pl.* a pair of spectacles. **b.** A small window (*nonce-use*).

1694 *Ladies Dict.* 380 Peeper, a Looking-glass. *a* **1700** B. E. *Dict. Cant. Crew*, *Queere-peepers*, c. old fashion'd, ord'nary, black-framed, or common Looking glasses. **1785** GROSE *Dict. Vulg. T., Peeper*, a spying glass; and also a looking glass, (cant). **1825** JAMIESON, *Peepers*,..a cant term for spectacles, *Roxb.* **1899** BARING-GOULD *Bk. of West* I. ii. 30 The windows..are small, and the brown thatch is lifted above these peepers.

4. As a local name of animals and plants: **a.** A species of Tub-fish, *Trigla cuculus* (Cornwall) (*Eng. Dial. Dict.*). **b.** A local name of the Pimpernel (Lees *Flora W. Yorksh.* (1888) 795).

peep-eye ('piːpˌaɪ). *rare.* = BO-PEEP, PEEP-BO.

1887 *Harper's Mag.* Dec. 79/1 The baby..made futile efforts to play 'peep-eye' with anybody jovially disposed in the crowd.

peep-hole ('piːphəʊl). A small hole through which one can peep. Also *transf.* and *attrib.*

1681 OTWAY *Soldiers Fort.* I. i, And then for a peep-Hole, odds fish I have a peep-Hole for thee. **1716** LADY M. W. MONTAGU *Let. to Pope* 14 Sept., The Comedy..began with Jupiter's falling in love out of a peep-hole in the clouds. **1857** J. H. NEWMAN in J. Jennings *Life* (1888) 119 We see each other as through the peep-holes of a show. **1890** F. W. ROBINSON *Very strange Family* 3 Mr. Barnett had..put up the shutters, and had glass peep-holes made in every one of them. **1952** E. F. DAVIES *Illyrian Venture* xi. 209 Every sentry looked in frequently through the peep-hole in the door. **1962** *Gloss. Terms Glass Industry* (*B.S.I.*) 17 *Peephole*, a small opening in a furnace wall through which observations are made. **1963** *New Yorker* 15 June 98/3 (Advt.), These fully washable shorties.. sport dainty floral sprays of peephole petals. **1978** W. H. JOBSON *To die a Little* ix. 148 Every now and again someone lifted the flap of the round peephole in the [cell] door.

peepie-creepie (ˌpiːpɪˈkriːpɪ). [f. PEEP *v.*² + -IE and CREEP *v.* + -IE.] A portable television camera used for close shots on location.

1952 *Time* 14 July 22/3 Most startling TV innovation was a portable camera known as the walkie-lookie, or peepie-creepie, with which the enterprising TV reporter could sneak up to Mr. Delegate and catch him yelling his head off or scratching his nose. **1952** *Newsweek* 21 July 53 NBC's walkie-lookie, or 'peepie-creepie', was not a singular success in its debut. **1953** A. K. C. OTTAWAY *Educ. & Society* 82 Here it was that the 'peepie-creepie' also called the 'walkie-lookie' began to achieve prominence. **1954** F. G. CASSIDY *Robertson's Devel. Mod. Eng.* (ed. 2) viii. 188 *Walky-talky* (a portable radio..), and its recent offspring *peepie-creepie* (a portable television camera).

ˈ**peeping**, *vbl. sb.*¹ [f. PEEP *v.*¹ + -ING¹.] The action of PEEP *v.*¹; cheeping.

c **1403** [see PEEP *v.*¹]. **1552** HULOET, Pipynge or piepynge of byrdes or fowles. **1709** W. DERHAM in *Phil. Trans.* XXVI. 491 The Peeping of Chickens in the Egg,.. I have my self divers times heard that. **1863** T. W. HIGGINSON *Army Life* (1870) 71 No sound but the peeping of the frogs in a marsh. **1868** A. K. H. BOYD *Less. Mid. Age* 353 The feeble peeping of two weak.. voices singing a long duet.

ˈ**peeping**, *vbl. sb.*² [f. PEEP *v.*² + -ING¹.] The action of PEEP *v.*²: looking through a narrow opening, peering, prying; emergence into view.

1593 NASHE *Christ's T.* Wks. (Grosart) IV. 185 If at the first peeping out of the shell, a young Student sets not a graue face on it.. he is cast of and discouraged. **1593** SHAKS. *Lucr.* 1089 Why pryst thou through my window? leave thy peeping. **1653** WALTON *Angler* xvi. 210 In a morning up we rise Ere Auroras peeping. **1826** SCOTT *Woodst.* v, No one has paid for peeping since Tom of Coventry's days.

attrib. **1692** R. L'ESTRANGE *Fables* civ. 98 The Fox spy'd him.. through a Peeping Hole. **1713** STEELE *Englishm.* No. 8. 49 A next Room, into which there were the peeping Holes frequent in Taverns. **1880** BROWNING *Mulēykeh* 65, I have found me a peeping-place.

ˈ**peeping**, *ppl. a.*¹ [f. PEEP *v.*¹ + -ING².] That peeps or cheeps; cheeping.

1568 T. HOWELL *Arb. Amitie* (1879) 76 The Robine small, and peeping Wren. **1614** SYLVESTER *Bethulia's Resc.* II. 455 The peeping chicken. **1643** HORN & ROB. *Gate Lang. Unl.* xiv. §147 Young chicks, callow and unfledged.. called peeping chicks. **1894** R. B. SHARPE *Handbk. Birds Gt. Brit.* I. 107 The Meadow-Pipit.. uttering a 'peep'-ing note.

ˈ**peeping**, *ppl. a.*² [f. PEEP *v.*² + -ING².] That peeps or peers; that peeps forth or emerges slightly into view; †(*slang*) drowsy, nodding, 'winking'. ***peeping Tom***: see quot. 1837; hence allusively. Now usu. applied to a prying person, esp. with connotations of prurience; one who obtains gratification from furtively observing women not fully clothed or the sexual activity of others; = VOYEUR. Also *transf.*, *fig.*, and *attrib.* Hence ***peeping Tommery***, the activity of a peeping Tom; also ***peeping Tom-ism***.

1592 WYRLEY *Armorie* 13 Putting foorth a little cressant, or a peeping mollet. *c* **1617** MIDDLETON *Witch* v. ii, Whilst we show reverence to yond peeping moon. *a* **1700** B. E. *Dict. Cant. Crew*, *Peeping*, Drowsy, Sleepy. **1707** MORTIMER *Husb.* (1721) II. 34 The first peeping red Buds and Leaves. **1784** COWPER *Tirocin.* 235 Ere he yet begin To show the peeping down upon his chin. **1796** GROSE *Dict. Vulg. T.*, *Peeping Tom*, a nick name for a curious prying fellow. **1837** *Penny Cycl.* VIII. 118/1 The story [of Godiva] is embellished with the incident of Peeping Tom, a prying inquisitive tailor, who was struck blind for popping out his head as the lady passed. **1884** *Sat. Rev.* 14 June 779/2 A mossy recess surrounded by peeping flowers. **1915** R. FROST *Let.* 11 Nov. (1964) 17 She executes a frightfulness. Somewhere else she brings in the Peeping-Tom idea. **1926** G. HUNTING *Vicarion* ii. 38 What sort was a man who did not instinctively respect the privacy of others?—not mere physical privacy, on which any Peeping Tom might intrude, but the infinitely more intimate thing, to spy upon which was violation. **1933** *Week-End Rev.* 8 July 34/2, I can assure you that neither reporters nor sub-editors find satisfaction in playing the rô le of Paul Pry or Nosey Parker or Peeping Tom. **1955** *Sun* (Baltimore) 7 Nov. 30/7 The House Judiciary Committee is sending its general counsel here from Washington today to attend the City Council hearing on a bill to outlaw electronic 'peeping toms'. **1958** *Times* 12 Nov. 3/4 The curiously prosaic *bizarreries* of Magritte, and the peeping-Tom eroticism of such basically crude pictures as those of Labisse and Delvaux, are of the 'photographic' kind. **1960** *Spectator* 21 Oct. 602/3 Those semi-nude gambols [in a cinema film].. break any feeling of reality second by second by giving one a sense of peeping-tommery. **1963** A. HERON *Towards Quaker View of Sex* 67 *Exhibitionism* and the associated disorder *Voyeurism* (peeping-tom) involve sexual pleasure obtained respectively from displaying the naked body.. or from observing the sexual acts or organs of other people. **1966** AUDEN *About House* 42 Peeping Toms Are never praised, like novelists or bird watchers, For their keenness of observation. **1966** *Guardian* 26 Mar. 1/6 They've had Peeping Tom cameras and now they've got eavesdropping microphones. **1972** W. P. MCGIVERN *Caprifoil* i. 9 Surveillance was a constantly expanding and proliferating industry... He did have a professional view of this constantly expanding peeping Tom-ism, and it was a sour one. **1974** M. KELLY *That Girl in Alley* vii. 120 To avoid bringing myself into suspicion of peeping-tommery I moved a few steps down the yard, out of sight of the drilling class. **1977** *Transatlantic Rev.* LX. 38 At various times during the preceding year, there had been complaints of Peeping Toms.

peeple: see PEEPUL.

†ˈ**peepling.** *Obs. rare*⁻¹. [f. PEEP *v.*¹ + -LING.] A little 'peeping' animal; a chicken.

1594 O. B. *Quest. Profit. Concern.* 29 She returnes into the house to her peepling, singing, I haue her, I haue her.

peep of day. [See PEEP *sb.*² 1 b.]

1. The first appearance of daylight, the earliest dawn.

[**1530**: see PEEP *sb.*² 1 b.] **1577–87** HOLINSHED *Chron.* III. 1138/1 The morrow.., by the peepe of daie, all the batteries began. **1882** J. PARKER *Apost. Life* I. 118 The first sacrifice was offered at the very peep of day.

fig. *a* **1836** MRS. T. MORTIMER (*title*) The Peep of Day; or a Series of the earliest religious Instruction the Infant Mind is capable of receiving.

attrib. **1852** SMEDLEY *L. Arundel* 612 Always supposing our peep-of-day amusement goes as it should do.

2. ***peep-of-day boys***, a Protestant organization in the North of Ireland (*c* 1784–95), whose members visited the houses of their Roman Catholic opponents (see DEFENDER 1 d) at daybreak in search of arms. So ***peep-of-day clergyman***, ***principle***; also **peep-o'-dayism**. Also *transf.*

1780 A. YOUNG *Tour in Ireland* II. vi. 30 In England we have heard much of whiteboys, steelboys, oakboys, peep-of-day-boys, &c... All but the whiteboys were among the manufacturing protestants in the north. **1807** VANCOUVER *Agric. Devon* (1813) 468 The insurgent banditti of Tories, Hearts of Steel, Peep-o'day Boys, White Boys, &c. **1825** C. M. WESTMACOTT *English Spy* I. 267 [He] joined the peep of day boys in full cry. **1845** SYD. SMITH *Fragm. Irish Rom. Cath. Ch.* Wks. 1859 II. 340/2 A peep-of-day clergyman will no longer preach to a peep-of-day congregation. **1890** LECKY *Eng. in 18th C.* xxvi. VII. 20 A corps of volunteers which had been originally raised on Peep of Day principles. **1922** JOYCE *Ulysses* 44 Raw facebones under his peep of day boy's hat.

3. A local name of the plant Star of Bethlehem, *Ornithogalum umbellatum* (*Shropsh. Wordbk.* 1879).

peep-show (ˈpiːpʃəʊ). [f. PEEP *v.*² or *sb.*² + SHOW *sb.*] A small exhibition of pictures, etc., viewed through a magnifying lens inserted in a small orifice. Also *fig.* and *attrib.*

1851 *Househ. Words* II. 290/1 There were tambourines, books, work-boxes.. peep-show boxes, all kinds of boxes. **1861** in Mayhew *Lond. Labour* III. 88/1 Being a cripple, I am obliged to exhibit a small peep-show. **1865** DICKENS *Mut. Fr.* IV. vi, A Peep-show which had originally started with the Battle of Waterloo, and had since made it every other battle of later date. **1869** SPURGEON *J. Ploughm. Talk* 18 As boys see sights in a peepshow at our fair. **1870** LOWELL *Study Wind.* 25 The peep-shows which Nature provides with such endless variety for her children. **1894** [see *donkey-ride* s.v. DONKEY 3 a]. **1914** G. B. SHAW *Misalliance* 67, I did a cheap trip to Folkestone. I spent sevenpence on dropping pennies into silly automatic machines and peepshows of rowdy girls having a jolly time. **1937** L. MACNEICE *Poems* 110 It's no go the merrygoround, it's no go the rickshaw, All we want is a limousine and a ticket for the peepshow. **1941** J. MASEFIELD *In Mill* 110, I had seen him box in one of the little primitive peep-show cinemas. **1951** M. MCLUHAN *Mech. Bride* (1967) 48/1 *Sexual Behavior in the Human Male* is a penny arcade peep show given the chromé treatment of scientific charts and figures. **1973** *Times* 22 Mar. 8/7 The book-shops, the peep shows, the pornographic cinemas.. are all nasty. **1976** *National Observer* (U.S.) 18 Dec. 1/3 It sits in leased quarters on the eighth floor of a commercial building in a neighborhood of numerous adult book-stores and peep-show parlors on 9th street in Washington.

‖**peepul, pípal** (ˈpiːpʌl). Also 8–9 peeple, pippal, peepal, pepal, -ul, pipul. [Hindi *pīpal*:—Skr. *pippala*.] An Indian species of fig-tree (*Ficus religiosa*), regarded as sacred: = BO-TREE. Often *attrib.*, ***peepul-***, ***pipal-tree***.

1788 *Asiatick Res.* I. 390 An excavation.. in the ground.. filled with a fire of pippal wood. **1798** W. TENNANT *Ind. Recreat.* (1803) II. 356 The seeds of the peeple tree.. as often as they fall upon an old edifice spring up into trees with great rapidity. **1831** TRELAWNEY *Adv. Younger Son* II. 162 A large pepul tree grew near. **1841** ELPHINSTONE *Hist. Ind.* I. 241 The country is often scattered with old mangoe trees and lofty tamarinds and pipals. **1887** LANG *Myth, Ritual & Relig.* II. 235 The village Gods which in India dwell in the peepul or the bo tree. **1891** KIPLING *Life's Handicap* Pref. 7 Great pipal trees overhung the well-windlass.

peepy (ˈpiːpɪ), *a. dial.* and *colloq.* [f. PEEP *v.*² or *sb.*² + -Y.] **a.** Drowsy, sleepy. (Cf. PEEP *v.*² 1 b.) **b.** Characterized by peeping.

1833 *Chambers's Edin. Jrnl.* 5 Jan. 385/1 He is then a poor, peepy wretch, with blear eyes. *Ibid.* 27 Apr. 97/3 The contrast.. between the meaning of the words, and the poor, peepy.. voice in which they are given. **1847–78** HALLIWELL, *Peepy*, sleepy, drowsy. Go to peepy-by, i.e. to sleep. *Var. dial.* **1896** SNOWDEN *Web of Weaver* 8 (E.D.D.), With long waiting we fell peepy. **1898** M. P. SHIEL *Yellow Danger* 150 Peepy little bewitching eyes. **1939** N. MARSH *Overture to Death* xii. 117 It was the pot-boy, very tousled and peepy, and accompanied by a gust of stale beer. Alleyn thought that he looked like all pot-boys at dawn throughout time and space.

peer (pɪə(r)), *sb.* (*a.*) Forms: 3–5 per, 3–6 pier, 4 peor, 4–5 pare, peyre, 4–6 pere, 4–7 peere, 4–8 peir, 5 pir, pyere, peyr, pyre, peree, 5–7 piere, 6 peare, 4– peer. [ME. a. OF. *per*, *peer* (10th c. in Littré), since 16th c. *pair*, = Pr., Sp. *par*, It. *pare*, L. *par-em* equal. In OF. *per* was both adj. and sb.; in English the adj. use is quite subordinate, and only in the expression *peer to*, where it might also be viewed as the sb.]

A. *sb.* **1.** An equal in civil standing or rank; one's equal before the law.

[**1215** *Magna Carta* xxi, Comites & barones non amercientur nisi per pares suos. *Ibid.* xxxix, Nullus liber homo capiatur, vel imprisonetur,.. nisi per legale judicium parium suorum, vel per legem terrae.] **1303** R. BRUNNE *Handl. Synne* 6076 Men.. þat mow weyl, at allē ȝers, lyue as lordes, and be here pers. **1390** GOWER *Conf.* III. 168 By his side He set him doun as pier and pier. *c* **1450** tr. *De Imitatione* III. xxi. 89 Wheþer he suffre of his prelate or of his piere, or of his lower. **1587** HARRISON *England* II. xi. (1877) I. 222 When soeuer anie of the nobilitie are conuicted of high treason by their peeres, that is to saie equals. **1660** R. COKE *Justice Vind.* 16 Nor must Strafford suffer by an ordinary way of judicature by his peers,.. he must die by Act of Parliament. **1765** BLACKSTONE *Comm.* I. xii. 403 As the lords, though different in rank, yet all of them are peers in respect of their nobility, so the Commoners.. all are in law peers, in respect of their want of nobility. **1808** SCOTT *Marm.* I. xxviii, He.. strode across the hall of state, And fronted Marmion where he sate, As he his peer had been. **1877** MRS. OLIPHANT *Makers Flor.* iii. 79 The sacred chain of friendship links together those who are unequal in rank as well as those who are each other's peers.

2. a. One who takes rank with another in point of natural gifts or other qualifications; an equal in any respect. Said also of things.

c **1290** *S. Eng. Leg.* I. 453/166 Seint Martin was apostlene pier: for þe holie gost a-liȝhte In him ase in þe Apostles. *a* **1300** *Cursor M.* 7970 Of al þe psalmes o þe sauter þis psalme o penance has na per. *c* **1386** CHAUCER *Nun's Pr. T.* 30 Chauntecleer In al the land of crowyng nas his peer. **1470–85** MALORY *Arthur* XV. vi, I knowe wel thow hast not thy pyere of ony erthely synful man. **1481** CAXTON *Godfrey* clxiv. (1893) 242 He had moche leyd doun his pryde.. he wende to haue faughten peer to peer. **1535** COVERDALE *Ecclus.* vi. 15 A faithfull frende hath no peare. **1682** SIR T. BROWNE *Chr. Mor.* I. §36 Fidelity, Bounty and generous Honesty.. wherein.. the true Heroick English Gentleman hath no Peer. **1791** COWPER *Iliad* II. 491 Ulysses.. Jove's peer in wisdom. **1863** TYNDALL *Heat* v. §158 (1870) 134 When we wish to overcome molecular forces, we must attack them by their peers. **1888** BRYCE *Amer. Commw.* lxxiv. (1890) II. 607 Some of those men were the peers of the best European statesmen of the time.

b. *Anthropol.* and *Sociol.* An equal; a contemporary; a member of the same age-group or social set. Also *attrib.* (see also sense 6 a below).

1944 C. M. TRYON in *Nat. Soc. Study Educ. Yearbk.* (U.S.) I. xii. 233 Although in meeting some adult standards girls must undergo less change than boys, in their relation to their own peer culture they must often be more adaptive in relation to changing requirements. **1953** A. K. C. OTTAWAY *Educ. & Society* 109 What is called 'peer culture', in other words the community of the same age, has a very great influence on the individual. **1958** W. J. H. SPROTT *Human Groups* 71 Wherever there is an adolescent 'peer-culture' it will have an influence which competes with that of the home. **1964** MINTURN & LAMBERT *Mothers of Six Cultures* 288 Nuclear family cultures are least punitive of peer-to-peer aggression. **1966** BEREITER & ENGELMANN *Teaching Disadvantaged Children* i. 18 In reading down the list of contrasts between the home and the nursery school environment, one finds.. the same contrast could be drawn between the upper-middle-class and the lower-class child's environment: adult versus peer contacts, [etc.]. **1966** *Listener* 14 Apr. 535/2 With their peers—that is, people of the same age, sex, and status—adolescents really experience for the first time relationships embodying equality and democracy. **1971** *New Society* 18 Nov. 975/2, I have discovered that wild-born monkeys spend more time watching a live peer, than themselves, in mirrors. **1972** *Where* Mar. 95/3 You need to consider the quality of the relationship which exists between your son and the teachers, your son and his peers, and between you and the teachers. **1972** *Jrnl. Social Psychol.* LXXXVI. 111 A subject receiving positive evaluations from a group of his peers was more active in the group. **1973** *Jrnl. Genetic Psychol.* CXXII. 263 Studies of human peer-social behavior in the preschool period. *Ibid.* 275 Retrospection and Peer-Perception scores did not differ from each other. *Ibid.* CXXIII. 124 Firstborn children have greater verbal facility, and there is evidence that they have more successful relationships with their teachers than do the later born although later born are more often successful in their peer relationships. **1977** *Sci. Amer.* Sept. 177/3 Alternatively a distributed-processing system can be organized into a peer structure. All the computers.. can communicate with one another on an equal footing.

†**3.** One who is associated or matched with another; a companion, mate; a rival. In quot. *c* 1330 = wife. *Obs.* or *arch.*

13.. *K. Alis.* 1576 Damoselis plaien with peoren alle. *c* **1330** R. BRUNNE *Chron.* (1810) 105 Malde þe quene his pere in God scho did endyng. **1382** WYCLIF *Matt.* xi. 16 Children sittynge in cheepynge.. cryinge to her peeris [etc.]. *c* **1400** *Destr. Troy* 3673 Pollux the pert kyng and his pere Castor. **1467** *Waterf. Arch.* in *10th Rep. Hist. MSS. Comm.* App. v. 300 Every Maire and Maires pare.. shal have his owne voice to thelection of the Maire. **1591** SPENSER *Vis. Worlds Van.* vi, An hideous Dragon.. Strove with a Spider his unequall peare. **1657** COWLEY *Death Will. Harvey* ii, My sweet Companion, and my gentle Peere. **1730–46** THOMSON *Autumn* 493 O, glorious he, beyond His daring peers! **1817** KEATS *Endym.* IV. 271, To stray away into these forests drear, Alone, without a peer.

4. a. A member of one of the degrees of nobility in the United Kingdom; a duke, marquis, earl, viscount, or baron. Now also a man elevated to the peerage on a non-hereditary basis; = *life peer* s.v. LIFE *sb.* 17. Also = *peeress in her own right.*

Peers are of three classes: ***peers of the United Kingdom*** or ***of the realm*** (up to 1707 called ***peers of England***, from 1707 to 1801 ***peers of Great Britain***), all of whom, when of age and not otherwise disqualified, may sit in the House of Lords; ***peers of Scotland***, of whom sixteen are elected to each Parliament as representative members to sit in the House of Lords; ***peers of Ireland***, of whom twenty-eight representatives are elected for life to the House of Lords. By a declaration of the House of Lords in 1692, Bishops are only lords of Parliament, and not peers.

[**1321–2** *Act 15 Edw. II*, Nous piers de la terre, Countes & Barouns, en la presence notre Seigneur le Roi, agardoms que Sir Hugh le Despenser le fitz et Sir Hugh le Despenser le piere soient desheriteez. **1332** *Rolls of Parlt.* II. 68/2 Le Seigneur de Wake & autres Pierres de la terre.] **1382** WYCLIF *Sel. Wks.* III. 514 By counsail of peeris of þe rewme. *c* **1470** HENRY *Wallace* VIII. 15 Thai.. Besocht him fair, as a peyr off the land, To cum and tak sum gouernaill on hand. **1559** *Mirr. Mag., Rich. II* 5 The Piers and Lordes that did his cause uphold. **1593** SHAKS. *2 Hen. VI*, IV. vii. 127 The proudest Peere in the Realme shall not weare a head on his shoulders vnlesse he pay me tribute. **1654** VILVAIN *Epit. Ess.* II. i. 26 Kings rule is good, wors the Peers optimacy. **1707** E. CHAMBERLAYNE *Pres. St. Eng.* III. iii. 276 All Peers of the Realm being look'd on as the King's Hereditary constant Counsellors. **1826** DISRAELI *Viv. Grey* II. viii, The neighbouring peer, full of grace and gravity. **1869** [see *life-peer* s.v. LIFE *sb.* 17]. **1900** *Whitaker's Alm.* 120 The House of Lords.. consists of the Spiritual Lords of England.. the Temporal Peers of England, Great Britain, and the United Kingdom, and, in addition, 16 Hereditary Peers of Scotland selected to each Parliament, and 28 Hereditary or created Peers of Ireland elected for life. **1958** *Oxford Mail* 21 July 1/7 The announcement will enable the lifepeers to take their seats in the Lords in time for the opening of the next session of Parliament in November. It will be the first time women peers have been allowed to sit in the Lords. **1958** *Times* 24 July 8/7 The main point of this interim constitutional reform [*sc.* introduction of life peerages] was to enlarge Labour representation in the Upper House with working peers. **1974** *Observer* (Colour Suppl.) 24 Mar. 30/1 'We are very passionate that we are not peeresses; peeresses are the wives of peers...' Now lavatories are discreetly marked 'Peers' and 'Women Peers'.

b. In reference to France: (*a*) One of the twelve peers of France: see DOUZEPERS; (*b*) One who possessed a territory which had been erected into a lordship, and who had a right to sit in the Parliament of Paris; (*c*) A member of the Upper Legislative Chamber, 1814–1848.

[*c* **1205**, *c* **1310**: see DOUZEPERS.] *c* **1470** HENRY *Wallace* X. 911 The peryss off France was still at thair parlement. *c* **1489** CAXTON *Sonnes of Aymon* xx. 453 Rowlande was a ferde for his vncle charlemagn.. wherfor he went anone nyghe hym and soo dyde oliver, ogyer, & all the xii peres. **1494** FABYAN *Chron.* I. clv. 143 [Charles Martel] chase xii perys, which, after some wryters, are callyd dozeperys. **1611** COTGR. s.v. *Pair, La Cour des Pairs*,.. the Parliament of Paris wherein the Peeres of France may sit as Assistants. **1630** *R. Johnson's Kingd. & Commw.* 178–9 The Twelve Peeres of France have the precedence before all the rest of the Nobility... Of these Peeres, there be six of the Clergie. **1727–41** CHAMBERS *Cycl.* s.v., The title peer, in France, is bestowed.. on every lord or person, whose fee is erected into a lordship or peership. **1808** SCOTT *Marm.* VI. xxxiii, When Rowland brave and Oliver, And every paladin and peer, On Roncesvalles died! **1848** W. H. KELLY tr. *L. Blanc's Hist. Ten Y.* I. 131 Measures.. directly opposed to the constitutional charter, to the constitutional rights of the chamber of peers, to the laws of the French.

c. Applied to the ὅμοιοι of Sparta, *i.e.* those citizens who had equal right to hold state offices.

1838 THIRLWALL *Greece* IV. 373 All who were unable to defray this expense, were.. degraded into a lower class, from the rank of Peers to that of Inferiors, or Commoners. **1852** GROTE *Greece* II. lxxiii. IX. 344 A Spartan citizen, but not one of that select number called The Equals or The Peers.

5. In generalized sense: A man of high rank, in any country, state, or organization; a noble.

c **1350** *Will. Palerne* 3976, & alle þe lordes of þat lond.. & þe best burgeys.. & þe pers of spayne þat were to prison take. *c* **1440** *Bone Flor.* 233 Go we to owre cowncell perys. **1549** COVERDALE, etc. *Erasm. Par. Heb.* xii. 25 An vnnumerable syght of angels the heade peares & inhabitauntes thereof. *c* **1586** C'TESS PEMBROKE *Ps.* LXVIII. xi, Egipts greate peeres with homage shall attend. **1665** NEEDHAM *Med. Medicinæ* 21 Summoning all the Peers of the Faculty to a solemn Assembly. **1712** ADDISON *Spect.* No. 417 ¶8 The Stature and Behaviour of Satan and his Peers. *fig.* **1701** DE FOE *True-born Eng.* 27 Pride, the first Peer, and President of Hell.

6. *attrib.* and *Comb.* **a.** *attrib.* That is a peer; (sense 2 b) **peer group**, a group of people, freq. a group of adolescents, of the same age or social status. See also PEER REVIEW.

1693 G. STEPNEY in *Dryden's Juvenal* viii. (1697) 209 A Peer Actor is no monstrous thing, Since Rome has own'd a Fidler for a King. **1889** *Daily News* 31 Jan. 3/6 Their peer critic had expressed his willingness [etc.]. **1896** *Westm. Gaz.* 11 Aug. 1/3 The fashion of Peer Mayors.. delights provincial townsfolk and their womenkind. **1901** *Daily Tel.* 8 July 11/4 Lord Cardigan was the first peer-prisoner to be defended by members of the Bar. **1943** BRECKENRIDGE & VINCENT *Child Devel.* xiii. 463 Although the adolescent declares his independence of adult standards and controls, he is actually very dependent upon conformity with his peer group. **1948** J. H. S. BOSSARD *Sociol. of Child Devel.* VI. xxi. 494 This element of antagonism between peer groups and adults has been fostered through the years in a great many ways. **1957** P. LAFITTE *Person in Psychol.* viii. 104 Their standing in their peer group at school. **1959** *Listener* 19 Feb. 324/2 Each man's situation is slightly different from those of his peer-group. **1961** [see INNER *a.* (*sb.*[2]) 1 n]. **1964** GOULD & KOLB *Dict. Social Sci.* 297/1 One of these concepts is that of *peer group* which commonly refers to a group of homogeneous age composition. There is no reason, however, why this term cannot be applied to a group whose members are equal in some respect other than age. **1964** M. ARGYLE *Psychol. & Social Probl.* xv. 187 Young people between puberty and marriage are consciously aware of belonging to this peer-group, wear distinctive clothes, meet in groups at coffee-bars, [etc.]. **1966** *Listener* 14 Apr. 535/2 The gang is a relatively authoritarian form of peer group. **1972** J. L. DILLARD *Black English* i. 34 In the ghetto culture, peer group relations govern the social activity, including language, of the child to a degree far beyond its importance among middle-class whites. **1976** *Broadcast* 29 Mar. 19/1 A desire.. to be seen to be involved with peer-group heroes.

b. *Comb.*, as ***peer-maker***, ***-making***; ***-ridden*** adj.

1884 CHAMBERLAIN *Sp. at Denbigh*, The cup is nearly full. We have been too long a peer-ridden nation. **1894** *Westm. Gaz.* 30 Mar. 6/3 Mr. Gladstone has been the greatest peer-maker of this, or perhaps of any, century. **1900** *Ibid.* 29 May 2/2 Peer making used to be considered a dearly cherished prerogative of the Crown.

B. *adj.* or quasi-*adj.* Equal (*to*).

[*a* **1300** *Cursor M.* 450 To godd self wald he be pere. **1387** TREVISA *Higden* (Rolls) I. 49 Asia is most in quantite, Europa is lasse, and pere [HIGDEN *par*, 1432–50 egalle, CAXTON lyke] in noumbre of peple. *Ibid.* 179 Þe grete Constantinus bulde and made þis citee euene and pere to Rome [*æquam Romæ*]. **1567** *Satir. Poems Reform.* vi. 36 Ȝour strength to thairis on na way mycht be peir. [**1687** A. LOVELL tr. *Thevenot's Trav.* II. 23 He is Peer to the great Lords of the Countrey. **1881** *Atlantic Monthly* XLVII. 296 More than one artist whose hand has not been peer to his feeling.]

Hence **'peerhood**, the condition of being a peer, peership. Also (*nonce-wds.*) **'peerish** *a.*, of or pertaining to a peer; **'peerling**, a peer's son, an embryo peer; **'peery** *a.*, abounding in peers (so ***peeriness***).

1888 *Sat. Rev.* 9 June 704 His flourishing period of poethood and *peerhood when Louis Philippe was king. *a* **1734** NORTH *Examen* I. ii. §141 (1740) 109 Any other Peer.. might have been taken and made a *Peerish Example of. **1793** J. WILLIAMS *Life of Ld. Barrymore* 62 The gay *Peerling, who is barely entitled to the honors and immunities of manhood. **1865** *Spectator* 25 Nov. 1302/2 A monopoly of power can no more be safely allowed to peers, peerlings, and peers' sons-in-law, than to artizans. **1895** *Westm. Gaz.* 5 July 2/2 The new Cabinet is *peery to the end.. no one less than an earl gets anything this morning.

peer (pɪə(r)), *v.*[1] Forms: 4–5 pere(n, 5 peere, peyre, *Sc.* peir, 6– peer. [a. OF. *perer*, var. of *pairier*, *parer*:—L. *pariāre* to make equal, f. *parem* equal, PEER.]

†**1.** *trans.* To make equal; to class as equal; to put in the same rank or on an equal footing *with*.

1375 BARBOUR *Bruce* IX. 666 [Bruce] To quhom, in-to gude cheuelry I dar peir nane. *c* **1375** *Sc. Leg. Saints* xviii. (*Egipciane*) 1312 To þe quhilk.. al þe warld ma nocht be peryd. *c* **1610** SYLVESTER tr. *Mathieu's Mem. Mortal.* xxxii, Man.. Presume not yet to peer thee with thy God. *a* **1662** HEYLIN *Hist. Presbyt.* x. (1670) 347 Being now Peered with the Lord Chancellor, and the Earl of Essex.

2. To equal, to rank with.

a **1440** *Sir Degrev.* 1887 Was never perus myȝth hym peyre By resone ne ryȝth. **1614** T. ADAMS in Spurgeon *Treas. Dav.* Ps. cxix. 162 Of Homer it is said that none could ever peer him for poetry. *a* **1796** BURNS '*O wha is she that lo'es me*' (Chorus), O that's the queen o' womankind, And ne'er a ane to peer her. **1826** MARY HOWITT *Surrey in Captiv.* v, Young Surrey,—that brave heart That knighthood might not peer.

3. *intr.* To be equal, to rank on an equality.

1377 LANGL. *P. Pl.* B. xv. 410 Ancres and hermytes, and monkes and freres Peren [*v.rr.* peeren, peres] to apostles þorw her parfit lyuynge. *c* **1430** *Hymns Virg.* (1867) 62 He wolde haue peerid with god of blis. **1577** B. GOOGE *Heresbach's Husb.* (1586) 147 b, Hertford may well with the best peere. *a* **1847** ELIZA COOK *Old Mill-stream* ii, The Thames of Old England.. Could not peer with the mill-streamlet close to my home.

4. [f. prec. sb.] *trans.* To make (a man) a peer; to raise to the peerage, to ennoble. *colloquial.*

1753 *Dedication on Dedication* 11 He was to be peered and pension'd. **1883** TENNYSON in *Life* (1897) II. xv. 300 Her Majesty must decide as to when I am to be peered.

peer (pɪə(r)), *v.*[2] Also 6–7 peere, (8 pier). [Known from *c* 1590: of uncertain origin and history.

Exactly the same sense as 1 below was expressed in the 14th c. by PIRE *v.* (app. = LG. *piren*); and *peer* has accordingly been assumed to be merely a later form or spelling of *pire*. But, besides that there was a clear chronological gap between the two words, *peer* is not a phonetic development of *pire*, and cannot, so far as is at present known, be formally identified with that word; whether there was any irregular or ulterior connexion does not appear. In 15–16th c., *pere*, *peere*, were also ordinary spellings of PEAR *v.* = *appear*; and, in many instances (see senses 2, 3 below) the use of *peer* comes so close to that of *pear* (*appear*), that it is difficult to believe that there was not some blending of the two words, attributable to the fact that when *peer*, to look out, is said of inanimate things, the meaning is that they *appear* as if they were looking out. In several of the Shaksperian uses of *peer* it is difficult to determine whether the things are thought of as looking out, or as just appearing.]

1. *intr.* To look narrowly, esp. in order to discern something indistinct or difficult to make out.

1591 *1st Pt. Ieronimo* I. i. 109 One peeres for day, the other gappes for night. **1596** SHAKS. *Merch. V.* I. i. 19, I should be still.. Peering in Maps for ports, and peers, and rodes. **1623** JAS. I in Ellis *Orig. Lett.* Ser. I. III. 139, I have bene trowbled with Hamilton, quho.. wold needs peere over my showlder quhen I was reading thaime. **1722** DE FOE *Moll Flanders* (1840) 275, I walked about peering and peeping into every door and window I came near. **1831** POE *Raven* v, Deep into that darkness peering, long I stood. **1838** DICKENS *Nich. Nick.* xxxi, How dare you pry, and peer, and stare at me, sirrah?

b. *trans.* To search *out*, to pry *out*.

1838 *Lett. fr. Madras* (1843) 181 We did not want him to go and peer out all the gossip concerning them.

2. *intr.* (*fig.*) Said of inanimate things figured as looking out: To 'peep out' so as just to be seen; to appear slightly or in a half-hidden manner.

1592 SHAKS. *Rom. & Jul.* I. i. 126 An houre before the worshipt Sun Peer'd forth the golden window of the East. **1596** —— *1 Hen. IV*, v. i. 1 How bloodily the Sunne begins to peere Aboue yon busky hill. **1810** SOUTHEY *Kehama* XV. viii, Domes, and pinnacles, and spires were seen Peering above the sea. **1830** TENNYSON *Dirge* vi, The frail blue-bell peereth over Rare broidry of the purple clover. **1831** CARLYLE *Sart. Res.* III. xi, Already streaks of blue peer through our clouds. **1841** W. SPALDING *Italy & It. Isl.* I. 30 Towns and villages.. peer out from amidst vineyards, or clumps of the dark flat-topped pine.

3. *intr.* (*transf.*) To show (itself); to come in sight; to be seen, to appear: nearly = PEAR *v.*

1592 SHAKS. *Ven. & Ad.* 86 Like a dive-dapper peering through a wave, Who, being look'd on, dives as quickly in. **1594** PLAT *Jewell-ho.* III. 91 One inch of the neck [of the viol] only to peer aboue yᵉ ashes. **1599** SHAKS. *Hen. V*, IV. vii. 88 For yet a many of your horsemen peere, And gallop ore the field. **1611** —— *Wint. T.* IV. iv. 3 No Shepherdesse, but Flora Peering in Aprils front. **1756** HOME *Douglas* II. (1757) 28 Darkly a project peers upon my mind. **1822** B. CORNWALL *Flood of Thessaly* II. 314 The horrid rocks peered up as black as death. **1850** BLACKIE *Æschylus* II. 124, I spy the ship; too gallantly it peers To cheat mine eye.

†**4.** *trans.* To make to appear or peep out, to show a little. *Obs. rare.*

1593 SHAKS. *Lucr.* 472 Who ore the white sheet peers her whiter chin, The reason of this rash allarme to know.

peer (pɪə(r)), *v.*[3] *Sc.* and *dial.* Also 6 peir, pere. [Origin unknown.] *trans.* To pour.

('We commonly use *pour*, when greater quantities issue forth; and *pere*, when the liquor trickles down by drops, or as it were small threeds' Ruddiman *Gloss.* to Douglas.)

1513 DOUGLAS *Æneis* VI. iv. 37 The fat olie did he ȝet and peir [*ed.* **1553** pere] Apoun the entraillis, to mak thaim birn cleir. **1863** MONCRIEFF *Dream* 37 (E.D.D.) She was hindered on peering the flick. **1881** *I. of Wight Gloss.*, *Peer*, to pour out lard.

peer, obs. f. PEAR *sb.*, PEAR *v.*, PIER.

peerage ('pɪərɪdʒ). [f. PEER *sb.* + -AGE.]

1. The body of peers. **a.** in the United Kingdom.

1454 *Rolls of Parlt.* V. 242/1 The.. obeissaunce that I owe to doo.. to you the Perage of this lande. **1647** CLARENDON *Hist. Reb.* I. §11 Having so great an Influence upon the Body of the Peerage, that [etc.]. **1765** BLACKSTONE *Comm.* I. ii. 157 A bill passed the house of lords, and was countenanced by the then ministry, for limiting the number of the peerage. **1848** THACKERAY *Bk. of Snobs* xxi, We have said Bull knows nothing: he knows the birth, arms, and pedigree of all the peerage.

b. in reference to France.

1667 MILTON *P.L.* I. 586 When Charlemain with all his Peerage fell By Fontarabbia. **1875** STUBBS *Const. Hist.* II. xv. 183 The very limited peerage which in France co-existed with an enormous mass of privileged nobility.

c. in generalized sense: Nobility, aristocracy.

1725 POPE *Odyss.* I. 355 Convoke the Peerage, and the Gods attest. **1817** J. TAYLOR in Paulding *Lett. fr. South* (1835) I. 213 The peerage of knowledge or abilities.. can no longer be collected and controlled in the shape of a noble order. *a* **1854** H. REED *Lect. Brit. Poets* vi. (1857) 229 The peerage of Pandemonium stood mute in expectation of Satan's voice.

2. The rank or dignity of a peer.

1671 F. PHILLIPS *Reg. Necess.* 434 The Viscounts, a Title no longer ago than the Reign of King Henry the sixth,.. turned into a Dignity Titular, or Peerage. **1771** *Junius Lett.* lxvii. (1772) II. 308 My humble congratulations upon the glorious success of peerages and pensions, so lavishly distributed. **1841** PEEL in *Croker Corr.* II. 410 The satisfaction of answering a letter which.. does not apply for a baronetage or a peerage. **1885** FREEMAN in *Encycl. Brit.* XVIII. 458/2 The peerage differs from nobility strictly so called, in which the hereditary privileges.. pass on to all the descendants of the person first created or.. acknowledged as noble. **1892** GLADSTONE *Let. to Lyon Playfair* 13 Aug., If it is agreeable to you I should have sincere pleasure in submitting your name to her Majesty for a peerage. *fig.* **1692** R. L'ESTRANGE *Fables* clxxxviii. (1714) 202 When a Reasonable Soul descends to Abandon the whole Man to the Sensuality of Brutal Satisfactions, he forfeits his Peerage, and the very Privilege of his Character and Creation.

†**b.** The territory or fief of a peer: = PEERDOM 2.

1759 ROBERTSON *Hist. Scot.* VII. Wks. 1813 I. 539 Many of the abbeys and priories had been erected into temporal peerages.

3. A book containing a list of the peers, with their genealogy, history, connexions, titles, etc.

[**1709** A. COLLINS (*title*) The Peerage of England.] **1766** A. JACOB (*title*) A Complete English Peerage, containing a Genealogical and Historical Account of the Peers of this Realm, together with the different branches of each family. **1856** WHYTE MELVILLE *Kate Cov.* xvii, His name was in the Peerage.

†**4.** Equality. *Obs. rare*$^{-1}$.

1681 FLAVEL *Meth. Grace* xiv. 279 He had a peerage or equality with his father in glory.

5. *attrib.* and *Comb.*, as ***peerage-book***, ***-maker***.

1727–41 CHAMBERS *Cycl.* s.v., The twelve peers created at once in the late reign, was a main argument in behalf of the peerage bill. **1736–7** SAVAGE *Volunteer Laureat* No. 6, Wks. 1775 II. 224 No—trust to honour! that you ne'er will stain From peerage-blood, which fires your filial vein. *a* **1823** J. PENNEY *Linlithgowshire* (1832) 90 *note*, This peerage-maker, is however, mistaken. **1863** THACKERAY *Round. Papers, Carp at Sans Souci*, A pedigree as authentic as many in the peerage-books.

peerch, obs. form of PERCH.

peerdom (ˈpɪədəm). [f. PEER *sb.* + -DOM.]
1. The condition or rank of a peer; = PEERAGE 2.
1603 FLORIO *Montaigne* I. xli. (1632) 138 The women that succeeded in the Peeredomes of France, had..right to assist and privilege to plead. **1895** CHAMBERLAIN *Sp. Ho. Comm.* 13 May, Wherever the suspicion of peerdom attached, a Committee must be appointed to inquire into the case.
†**2.** The territory or fief of a French peer. *Obs.*
1611 COTGR., *Perrie*, a Peeredome; the estate or dignitie of a Peere. **1670** COTTON *Espernon* I. III. 128 This Castle with the demean and territory belonging to it..was soon..advanc'd into a Dutchy, and Peerdom, under the Title of the Dutchy de la Valette. **1762** tr. *Busching's Syst. Geog.* IV. 297 Menin is one of the twelve peerdoms or *Patriatus*.
3. The condition of being peer or equal; equality.
1891 W. O. NEWNHAM *Arlesford Ess.* 102 Terms of perfect loving intimacy and equality, perhaps I may be allowed to coin a word and to add 'peerdom', with our Father. **1898** *Dublin Rev.* Apr. 405 Supremacy..could not thus efface the peerdom of those over whom it was exercised.

peere, obs. form of PEAR *sb.* and *v.*, PIER *sb.*

peeress (ˈpɪərɪs). [f. PEER *sb.* + -ESS.] The wife of a peer. ***peeress in her own right***, a woman having the rank of a peer by creation or descent.
1689 *Lond. Gaz.* No. 2441/4 Tickets for the Peers and Peeresses Servants to attend at the Coronation. **1765** BLACKSTONE *Comm.* I. xii. 402 A peer, or peeress (either in her own right or by marriage) cannot be arrested in civil cases. **1878** STUBBS *Const. Hist.* III. xx. 439 There are instances of countesses, baronesses, and abbesses being summoned..to furnish their military service, but not to attend parliament as peeresses. **1898** *Whitaker's Titled Persons* 18 The rank of a Peeress in her own right is inherited by her eldest son,..or, in default of a son, by a daughter.

peerie (ˈpiri), *a.* (*sb.*) *Sc.* (now only Orkney and Shetland). [Etym. uncertain: see S.N.D.]
A. *adj.* Small, diminutive. Also in special collocations (see quots. and S.N.D.).
1808 JAMIESON, *Peerie, adj.*, little, small. *A peerie foal*, a small bannock or cake, Orkn. Shetl. **1868** D. GORRIE *Summers & Winters in Orkneys* 12 An *Oyce* or inlet, locally termed the 'Peerie Sea'. **1871** R. COWIE *Shetland* II. iv. 149 The *peerie* steamer—as the natives call her, in contradistinction to the larger one trading to the south. **1884** *Rep. H.M. Comm. Inquiry Crofters Highlands Scotl.* 1404 in *Parl. Papers* (C. 3980) XXXIV, The possession of even four ures of land constitutes the proprietor a small, or, in the vernacular, 'peerie' laird. **1891** J. J. H. BURGESS *Rasmie's Büddie* 80 An sün her peerie winkie haands O' cockaloories bricht wis fu. **1916** G. W. HOGGAN in B. Thynne *Shetland Sheep-Dog* 14 The 'peerie' Shetland Collie... These 'peerie things' are seldom seen outside—probably for fear of being tramped on. **1921** *Glasgow Herald* 1 Jan. 6/7 The mill stood ..right on top of the sluice through which the waters of the bay rushed into the 'Peerie (little) Sea'. **1922** J. FIRTH *Reminisc. Orkney Parish* (ed. 2) 75 Sometimes as many as half-a-dozen women were called to the house..to keep away the 'peerie-folk'—those unearthly visitants who were particularly busy when a new arrival came. **1929** E. LINKLATER *White-Maa's Saga* 72 The world's nae comin' to an end for a peerie while yet. **1948** C. L. B. HUBBARD *Dogs in Brit.* xviii. 205 In its home islands it [*sc.* the Shetland sheepdog] is known as the Tounie Dog or Peerie Dog. **1956** C. M. COSTIE *Benjie's Bodle* 58 Afore he kent whar he was the Peerie Laird wad be pitten tae the horn. **1959** I. & P. OPIE *Lore & Lang. Schoolch.* x. 182 There she goes, there she goes, Peerie heels and pointed toes. **1978** *New Shetlander* Summer 22/2 Whaur is du gaun, du peerie boy, Wi dee face laek a smoored fire? *Ibid.* 28/2 Da Maister sat in a peerie hoose Wi Jordan's water rinnin near.
B. as *sb.* A Shetland sheep-dog.
1949 K. M. WELLS *Owl Pen Reader* (1969) II. 211 Shetland Sheep Dogs do possess the seeing eye,..Shetland Sheep Dogs were once called 'Peeries' or 'Fairy Dogs'. **1971** F. HAMILTON *World Encycl. Dogs* 96 Shetland Sheepdog, Shetland Collie, Miniature Collie, Shetland, Sheltie, Toonie or Peerie—at some time or other the Sheltie has answered to all these names.

peerie, var. PERRY *sb.*, peg-top.

peering (ˈpɪərɪŋ), *ppl. a.* [f. PEER *v.*[2] + -ING[2].] That peers; looking narrowly and curiously; 'peeping', just appearing.
1629 MILTON *Nativity* 140 Hell it self will pass away, And leave her dolorous mansions to the peering day. **1765** FOOTE *Commissary* I. Wks. 1799 II. 15 The ten bags of tea, and the cargo of brandy, them peering rascals took from me in Sussex, has quite broken my back. **1802** *Noble Wanderers* II. 83 A tender plant, whose peering blossoms have been blighted by some chilling blast. **1870** MORRIS *Earthly Par.* III. IV. 236 Down on the sea-farers did he gaze now With curious peering eyes.
Hence ˈ**peeringly** *adv.*
1840 *Tait's Mag.* VII. 503 Jack..squinted peeringly at his revered father. **1876** G. MEREDITH *Beauch. Career* I. viii. 115 An Austrian sentinel looked on passively, and a police inspector peeringly.

peerl(e, obs. form of PEARL.

peerless (ˈpɪəlɪs), *a.* [f. PEER *sb.* + -LESS.] Without peer; unequalled, matchless.
c **1320** R. BRUNNE *Medit.* 1141 To þat pes pereles we prey þou vs bryng. **1390** GOWER *Conf.* III. 285 His doghter, which was piereles Of beaute. **1494** FABYAN *Chron.* VII. ccxl. 281 He [Henry II] was pereles in chyualry, in warre, and in lechery. **1579** SPENSER *Sheph. Cal.* June 32 Such pierlesse pleasures haue we. **1667** MILTON *P.L.* IV. 608 The moon, Rising in clouded Majestie, at length Apparent Queen unvaild her peerless light. **1715** *Wodrow Corr.* (1843) II. 691 A person wonderful for..his peerless industry. **1871** MACDUFF *Mem. Patmos* xix. 268 It stands out by itself with peerless grandeur, in annals sacred and profane.
b. in advb. constr.
1596 DALRYMPLE tr. *Leslie's Hist. Scot.* VII. 4 Sa peirles proud, as na toung of man is able to discriue.
Hence ˈ**peerlessly** *adv.*, ˈ**peerlessness**.
1599 B. JONSON *Ev. Man out of Hum.* IV. iv, The Gentlewoman..is not so peerelessely to be doted vpon. **1611** COTGR., *Singularité*, singularitie, excellencie, peerlessnesse. **1656** TRAPP *Comm. 2 Thess.* ii. 3 That breathing devil, so portentously, so peerlessly vicious. **1865** KINGSLEY *Herew.* xviii, She is peerlessly beautiful. **1894** *Chicago Advance* 8 Feb., To exhibit the peerlessness of Christian Theism.

ˈ**peerly**, *adv. rare.* Also 5 perelich. [-LY[2].]
†**1.** In the manner of a peer or equal. *Obs.*
1398 TREVISA *Barth. De P.R.* XVIII. i. (Bodl. MS.), ȝif man is defouled wiþ luste,..þan man is made pere & vnwise perelich to vnresonable bestes.
2. In the manner of a peer. *humorous nonce-use.*
1888 W. S. GILBERT *Yeomen of Guard* I. 13 The song of a merry maid, peerly proud, Who loved a lord, and who laughed aloud.

peer review. orig. *U.S.* [f. PEER *sb.* + REVIEW *sb.*] **1.** The evaluation, by experts, in the relevant field, of a scientific research project for which a grant is sought.
1971 *Hastings Center Rep.* I. June 3 (*heading*) Priorities, peer review and public policy. **1975** *Nature* 4 Dec. 382/1 At the heart of the inquiry is the so-called peer-review system, which is used in some shape or form by virtually every government agency which supports academic research. **1977** *Listener* 7 Apr. 427/3 In the relatively public competition between rival research groups seeking financial support, there is no practical alternative to 'peer review' by committees of experts in the relevant fields. **1984** *UCL Bull.* July 5/2 Peer-review is not just a formal process when one is working at CERN. It starts long before a proposal reaches the peer-review committees which allocate time on the machines.
2. The process by which a learned journal passes a paper received for publication to outside experts for their comments on its suitability and worth; refereeing.
1975 *New England Jrnl. Med.* 25 Dec. 1372/1 In many departments of this *Journal*..the reader will find reports that have passed the muster of peer review. Usually two, but occasionally three or four, experts on the topic of an article will be asked to evaluate its validity, originality and presentation. **1977** *Nature* 20 Jan. 203/1 It has been said that the warp that holds the complex fabric of science together is peer review, and the woof is the noise made by scientists who complain about it. *Ibid.* 203/3 Publishing a book is a way of avoiding peer review.
3. *gen.* An examination or review of commercial, professional, or academic efficiency, competence, etc., by others in the same occupation.
1979 *Financial Times* 26 Feb. 4/1 Peer reviews involve a complete examination of the procedures and practices adopted by accounting firms auditing companies listed on U.S. stock exchanges. **1981** *Times Higher Educ. Suppl.* 5 June 2/4 We recommend that there should be a peer review of all the departments at Chelsea..with a view to phasing out those which do not come up to the standard of the rest of the university. **1983** *Times* 16 July 3/3 There are teachers who are perfectly capable of judging their own performance, ..but some are not able to, and then we will have to bring in some sort of peer review.
Hence ˈ**peer-review** *v. trans.*, to subject to peer review; to referee (a paper); ˈ**peer-reviewed** *ppl. a.*; ˌ**peer reˈviewing** *vbl. sb.*
1975 *Nature* 4 Dec. 382/1 Most of the rest are reviewed by a panel only, frequently with the applicant along to discuss his proposals, while a few are not peer-reviewed at all. **1982** *Behavioral & Brain Sciences* V. 218/2 (*heading*) Peer reviewing: improve or be rejected. **1983** *Brit. Med. Jrnl.* 8 Oct. 1004/1 How many of their readers realise that usually these [letters] have not been peer reviewed? **1985** *Arch. Surg.* CXX. 885/1 A good 'peer-reviewed' scientific journal.

peerse, obs. form of PIERCE.

peership (ˈpɪəʃɪp). [f. PEER *sb.* + -SHIP.]
1. The status of a peer; = PEERAGE 2.
1577 *F. de L'isle's Legendarie* C iij b, Parliament did also.. expulse the Duke of Guise..from his fore sitting, which by reason of his Peereshippe he chalenged aboue a prince of France. **1817** BENTHAM *Parl. Reform* (1818) 52 Say whether Peership is honesty.
†**b.** The fief of a (French) peer; = PEERAGE 2 b.
1594 R. ASHLEY tr. *Loys le Roy* 55 b, Dukedoms, Principalities, and Peereships patrimoniall. **1727–41** [see PEER *sb.* 4 b].
2. Parity, equality.
1641 *Lords Spiritual* 15 There is much more parity or peerships betweene the Lords Spirituall and Temporall,.. then betweene the Commons and any one of them. **1884** W. C. WILKINSON *Edw. Arnold* II. vi. 156 He claims that Buddha raised woman to peership with man.

peert, obs. or dial. form of PERT.

peery (ˈpɪərɪ), *sb. Sc.* and *north.* Also piry, peary, peerie. [perh. dim. of *pere*, PEAR, from its shape.] A peg-top, made to spin with a string.
1805 McINDOE *Moses's Compl.* Poems 40 Bowls, and ba's, and taps, and pirys. **1816** SCOTT *Antiq.* xx, Mony's the peery and the tap I worked for him langsyne. **1879** THOMSON & TAIT *Nat. Phil.* I. I. §106 It is the case of a common spinning-top (peery), spinning on a very fine point. **1882** *Life J. Clerk Maxwell* iii. 51 He..took some interest in the spinning of 'pearies'.

peery (ˈpɪərɪ), *a.*[1] [f. PEER *v.*[2] + -Y.] Inclined to peer; given to peering or looking narrowly or curiously; hence, prying, inquisitive, suspicious.
a **1700** B. E. *Dict. Cant. Crew, Peery*, fearful, shy, sly. **1748** RICHARDSON *Clarissa* (1811) V. 71 They engaged a peery servant..to watch all her motions. **1821** SCOTT *Kenilw.* ix, Two peery gray eyes, which had a droll obliquity of vision. —— *Pirate* xxxi, And here..we have been wasting our precious time, till folk are grown very peery. **1891** *Temple Bar Mag.* July 365 Eyes small, bright, 'peery', and quick glancing.
b. *Rogues' Cant.* Knowing, sly.
a **1757** CIBBER *Refusal* III. (1777) 49 Are you peery, as the cant is? In short do you know what I would be at now? **1804** COLLINS *Scripscrap* 24 An old peery Sharper, deep vers'd in the game.

peery, *a.*[2]: see under PEER *sb.*

pees(e, obs. ff. PEACE, PEASE, PEISE, PIECE.

peesk, obs. form of PEACH.

peesweep, peaseweep (ˈpiːzwiːp). *Sc.* and *dial.* Also 9 peese-weep, peeswip, peasweep. [From the cry of the bird.] The lapwing or pewit.
1796 *Statist. Acc. Scotl.* XVII. 251 *Tringa vanellus*,.. Lapwing, Teuchit, peesweep. *a* **1810** TANNAHILL *Poems* (1846) 18 The peeswip's scrighin' owre the spankie-cairn. **1820** *Blackw. Mag.* VI. 568 In pursuit of the Whaup and the Peaseweep. **1891** BARRIE *Lit. Minister* xxxv, The plaintive cry of the peesweep as it rose in the air.
b. A local name of the Greenfinch.
1885 SWAINSON *Prov. Names Brit. Birds* 59 Greenfinch.. Peasweep. Because one of its notes, sounding thus, closely resembles that of the peewit.

peet, Peeter, obs. form of PEAT, PETER.

peeta, var. PITA[2].

peetweet (ˈpiːtwiːt). *U.S.* [Echoic: cf. *peewit.*] A popular name of the spotted sandpiper or sandlark of N. America (*Tringoides macularius*).
1844 J. E. DE KAY *Zool. New York* II. 247 The Spotted Sand-Lark..known among the people by the name of Peet-weet, in allusion to its notes. **1858** THOREAU *Maine W.* ii. (1864) 135 A company of peet-weets were twittering and teetering about over the carcass of a moose. **1894** NEWTON *Dict. Birds* 811 The Common Sandpiper... In America its place is taken by a closely-kindred species,..the 'Peetweet' or Spotted Sandpiper, so called from its usual cry.

peeve (piːv), *v.* orig. *U.S.* [Back-formation f. PEEVISH *a.*] *trans.* and *intr.* To irritate, exasperate; to grumble, complain petulantly. So **peeved** (piːvd) *ppl. a.*, irritated, annoyed.
1908 G. V. HOBART *Go to It* 31 It may be interesting to some people, but it gets me peeved. **1912** ADE *Knocking Neighbors* 10 The Waiter peeved at being slipped a paltry $1.60. **1919** WODEHOUSE *Damsel in Distress* xxi. 242 About a million other people who'll be most frightfully peeved at my doing the Wedding Glide without consulting them. **1923** H. G. WELLS *Men like Gods* I. i. 5 Liberalism would never do anything more for ever than sit..grumbling and peeving. **1926** *Bulletin* (Glasgow) 17 June 5, I have a letter to-day from a peeved smoker..on the huge profits disclosed by the big tobacco combines. **1934** R. MACAULAY *Going Abroad* xvii. 139, I suppose he'd peeved me in some way. **1937** G. FRANKAU *More of Us* v. 62 'Just look at that,' peeved she, one slim hand plucking High from her ankles' grace, the limbs' frail sheath. **1945** *Sun* (Baltimore) 7 Dec. 8/1 Mighty peeved at that, Lorena outs with a derringer and marches the bachelor to the nearest J.P. **1966** I. JEFFERIES *House-Surgeon* v. 101 'They were peeved, like little school-kids.'.. 'Who peeved them, Harry?' **1975** *Daily Mail* 13 June 7/4 The agency won't talk about the work; its executives are rather peeved that the news has got out.

peeve (piːv), *sb.* orig. *U.S.* [f. the vb.] A grumble, a (cause of) complaint or irritation; a peevish humour; ***pet peeve***, a special or recurring source of irritation.
It is not certain that the sb. is intended in quot. 1911.
1911 *Dialect Notes* III. 549 Some common cases of 'back-formations', or 'back-shortenings', are..*peeve*. **1919** C. H. DARLING *Jargon Bk.* 25 *Pet peeve*, the thing that provokes you the most. **1920** S. LEWIS *Main St.* 293 You're simply hot and tired, and trying to work off your peeve on me. **1936** R. E. SHERWOOD *Idiot's Delight* III. 141 Every time you get yourself into a peeve, you take it out on us. **1945** *Southwest Rev.* Summer 330/2 Such misrepresentation of this lovable American character is my pet peeve. **1963** B. S. JOHNSON *Travelling People* i. 21 Henry thought he could afford to indulge in a Peeve... This was very quickly achieved by concentrating his mind on as many of the disasters of his past as were conveniently on short call from his memory. **1973** 'TREVANIAN' *Loo Sanction* 12 His peeve lasted only a second. **1975** *Bibliognost* Aug. 27 My pet peeve? Scouts and dealers who don't identify themselves and expect you to pull out the best books in the store. **1976** *National Observer* (U.S.) 7 Feb. 8/4 Poorly designed parking garages have riled

me for a long time, but they've become a full-fledged pet peeve in recent years.

peever ('pi:və(r)). *Sc.* Also peaver, peevor, peiver. [Origin unknown.] The stone, piece of pottery, or the like, used in hopscotch. Also (freq. pl.) the game itself.

a **1850** in *Sc. Nat. Dict.* (1968) VII. 78/1 s.v. peever. **1856** J. STRANG *Glasgow & its Clubs* 218 The young misses indulged in scoring the flagstones with their peevers, for the purpose of playing at pal-lall. **1887** D. DONALDSON Jamieson, Suppl., Add. 314/2 *Peever*, the pitcher or flat stone with which the children's game of *beds* or *pallall* is played; the game is therefore sometimes called '*peever*' or '*the peever*'. West of S. **1901** R. C. MACLAGAN *Games Argyleshire* 134 Pieces of broken pottery are by Lowlanders called *Lalies*, and the broken bottom of a bowl, a *laly*, is also called a peaver. **1921** *Edinburgh Even. News* 13 June 4 Chalking and disfiguring the street playing 'peevers'. **1931** A. J. CRONIN *Hatter's Castle* III. ix. 616 We'll be lookin' on at a game o' peever next if we're not careful, like a band o' silly lassies. **1962** *3rd Stat. Acct. Scotl.* XII. xii. 147 Peevors is still played on traditional stances. **1966** *Daily Tel.* 5 Nov. 13/8 Mr. Alex Lynch says that in Scotland hopscotch is known as 'peevers'.

peevish ('pi:vɪʃ), *a.* Forms: 4 peyuesshe, 5–6 peuysh, 6 peuis(s)h(e, -ische, -ys(s)he, -yche, -ess, piuish(e, -isshe, pyuysshe, pieuish(e, pewech, peeuish(e, -esh, 7 pevish, pievish, 7– peevish. [First evidenced in end of 14th c., but rare before 1500. Derivation unknown. The exact sense of the adj. in many of the early quots. is difficult to fix, and the following treatment is in many respects only provisional.

None of the etymological conjectures hitherto offered are compatible with the sense-history.]

†**1.** Silly, senseless, foolish. *Obs.*

1393 LANGL. *P. Pl.* C. IX. 151 And bad hym 'go pisse with hus plouh, peyuesshe shrewe!' [A. VII. 143 pillede screwe; B. VI. 157 for-pyned schrewe]. **1519** HORMAN *Vulg.* 21 b, Some make serche and dyuynacion by water, some by basyns,.. some by coniuryng of a soule, and suche other: and al be acurst or pyuysshe [*partim execrabilia, partim mera ludibria*]. **1529** MORE *Dyaloge* IV. Wks. 271/1 The piuishe pleasure of the vayne prayse puffed oute of poore mortall mens mouthes. **1542** UDALL *Erasm. Apoph.* 94 b, To laugh such a peuishe trifleyng argument to skorne. **1565** JEWEL *Def. Apol.* (1567) 669 That whole tale..is nothing els, but a peeuishe fable. *c* **1586** C'TESS PEMBROKE *Ps.* XLIX. v, These, whose race approves their peeuish waie [1611 This their way is their folly]. **1633** FORD *'Tis Pity* V. iii, This is your peevish chattering, weak old man! **1676** *Doctrine of Devils* 56 Christ did his Miracles among a peevish, foolish, sottish people, (as the World accounted them).

†**b.** Beside oneself; out of one's senses; mad.

1523 SKELTON *Garl. Laurel* 266 Some tremblid, some girnid, some gaspid, some gasid, As people halfe peuysshe, or men that were masyd. **1548** UDALL, etc. *Erasm. Par. Acts* xii. 15 [They] aunswered to the mayden, Surely thou arte peuyshe. **1578** LYTE *Dodoens* III. lxxvii. 426 Suche as by taking of poyson, are become peeuishe or without vnderstanding. **1591** LYLY *Endym.* I. i, There was neuer any so peeuish to imagin the Moone eyther capable of affection, or shape of a Mistris.

†**2.** Spiteful, malignant, mischievous, harmful.

1468 [implied in PEEVISHNESS 2]. ? *a* **1500** *Chester Pl.* viii. 317 Alas! what presumption shold move that peeuish page, or any eluish gedling to take from me my crowne? **1513** DOUGLAS *Æneis* XI. xiv. 111 This ilk Aruns..thys pewech man of weir..schuke in hand hys oneschewabill speir. **1567** HARMAN *Caveat* Ep. Ded. 2 b, Their peuish peltinge and pickinge practyses. **1568** GRAFTON *Chron.* II. 176 In derision of the king, they made certaine peeuishe and mocking rymes which I passe ouer. **1570** LEVINS *Manip.* 145/42 Peuish, *prauus*. **1601** MARSTON *Pasquil & Kath.* II. 245 This crosse, this peeuish hap, Strikes dead my spirits like a thunder-clap.

b. In *mod. dial.* Of the wind: Piercing, 'shrewd'.

1828 *Craven Gloss.* (ed. 2), *Peevish*, piercing, very cold; a peevish wind. **1863** MRS. TOOGOOD *Yorksh. Dial.*, The wind is very peevish to night.

†**3.** An epithet of dislike, hostility, disparagement, contempt, execration, etc., expressing the speaker's feeling rather than any quality of the object referred to. *Obs.* Cf. mod. *plaguy*, *wretched*, etc.

1513 DOUGLAS *Æneis* XI. viii. 78 For thou sal neuer los.. Be my wappin nor this richt hand of myne, Sik ane pevyche and cative saule as thyne [*Nunquam animam talem dextra hac ..amittes*]. **1523** LD. BERNERS *Froiss.* I. ccclxi. 587 Sirs, howe is it thus..that this peuysshe douehouse holdeth agaynst vs so longe? **1534** MORE *Comf. agst. Trib.* Wks. 1185 The wolf..spyed a fayre cowe in a close... as for yonder peeuish cowe semeth vnto me in my conscience worth not half a grot. *a* **1548** HALL *Chron., Hen. VI* 115 Such..craftie imageners, as this peuishe painted Puzel was.

†**4.** Perverse, refractory, froward; headstrong, obstinate; self-willed, skittish, capricious, coy. *Obs.*

1539 CRANMER *Great Bible* Pref., Not onely foolyshe frowarde and obstinate but also peuysshe, peruerse and indurate. *a* **1553** UDALL *Royster D.* ad fin., These women be all suche madde pieuish elues, They wyll not be woonne except it please them selues. **1589** NASHE *Anat. Absurd.* 39 Nothing is so great an enemie to a sounde iudgment, as the pride of a peeuish conceit. **1591** SHAKS. *Two Gent.* V. ii. 49 This it is to be a peeuish girle, That flies her fortune when it followes her. **1621** BP. MOUNTAGU *Diatribæ* 515 Diana, evermore a peevish angry goddesse. **1623** WEBSTER *Duchess of Malfi* III. ii, We read how Daphne, for her peevish flight, Became a fruitless bay-tree. *a* **1655** VINES *Lords Supp.* (1677) 269 It would be unnatural and pievish in a child to forsake his mother. **1671** H. FOULIS *Hist. Rom. Treas.* (1681) 23 Birds were not so shie and peevish formerly.

5. Morose, querulous, irritable, ill-tempered, childishly fretful. **a.** Of persons.

In early quots. often referred to as the result of religious austerities, fasting, and the like.

c **1530** *Hickscorner* D iij, And I sholde do after youre schole, To lerne to patter to make me peuysshe. **1596** SHAKS. *Merch. V.* I. i. 86 Why should a man whose bloud is warme within, Sit like his Grandsire, cut in Alabaster?..and creep into the laundies By being peeuish? **1653** JER. TAYLOR *Serm. for Year* xxxix, Some men fast to mortifie their lust: and their fasting makes them peevish. **1708** SWIFT *Abolit. Chr.*, Excellent materials to keep children quiet when they grow peevish. **1742** YOUNG *Nt. Th.* II. 175 Body and soul, like peevish man and wife, United jar, and yet are loth to part. **1862** SIR B. BRODIE *Psychol. Inq.* II. iii. 77 One whose state of health renders him fretful and peevish in his own family.

b. Of personal qualities, actions, etc.: Characterized by or exhibiting petty vexation.

1577 FULKE *Answ. True Christian* 89 Without any contention of peuishe enuie. **1650** FULLER *Pisgah* IV. iii. 57 Gods providence on purpose permitted Moses to fall into this peevish passion [at Kadesh]. **1711** STEELE *Spect.* No. 107 ¶ 1 Unapt to vent peevish Expressions. **1822** HAZLITT *Table-t.* II. iv. 73 With a peevish whine in his voice like a beaten school-boy.

†**c.** Const. *to*, *with*. *Obs. rare.*

1655 in *Nicholas Papers* (Camden) III. 128 He is uery peuish to Mr. Ouerton and will tell him uery litle. **1697** FLOYER *Cold Baths* I. iii. (1700) 61 The People grew peevish with all Ancient Ceremonies.

†**6.** See quot. (Perhaps some error.)

1674 RAY *N.C. Words*, *Peevish*, witty, subtill.

7. in advb. constr. = PEEVISHLY.

a **1529** SKELTON *El. Rummyng* 589 She was not halfe so wyse As she was peuysshe nyse [= foolishly particular]. [**1594** SHAKS. *Rich. III*, IV. iv. 417 (*Qo.* 1, 1597) Be not pieuish, fond in great designes. *Qo.* 2 peeuish, fond; *Qos.* 3–8 peeuish fond; *Folios* peeuish found; *Malone conjectured* peevish-fond, *the reading adopted in mod. edd.*]

peevishly ('pi:vɪʃlɪ), *adv.* [f. prec. + -LY².] In a peevish manner; †foolishly, spitefully, perversely, skittishly (*obs.*); with petty vexation or discontent; morosely, querulously, petulantly.

1530 PALSGR. 840/2 Pevysshely, *vergonneusement*. **1566** T. STAPLETON *Ret. Untr. Jewel* i. 17 You do but peuishly, to builde your untruth upon that reason. **1580–3** GREENE *Mamillia* Wks. (Grosart) II. 219 An iniurious Gentleman.. who with despightfull taunts hath abused the Gentlewomen of Sicillia, most peeuishlie describing their apparell, and presumptuouslie decyphering their nature. **1601** SHAKS. *Twel. N.* II. ii. 14 Come sir, you peeuishly threw it to her: and her will is, it should be so return'd. *a* **1638** MEDE *Wks.* (1672) I If they should unwisely disvalue and peevishly reject the whole for some passages not agreeing to their particular Sentiments. **1679** J. GOODMAN *Penit. Pardoned* III. iii. (1713) 310 Men will be always sighing and complaining and peevishly refuse consolation. *a* **1680** ROCHESTER *Song* iv. Poems (1790) 17 Then if, to make your ruin more, You'll peevishly be coy. **1762–71** H. WALPOLE *Vertue's Anecd. Paint.* (1786) III. 209 Ratcliffe replied peevishly, 'Tell him he may do any thing with it but paint it'. **1832** HT. MARTINEAU *Ireland* iii. 46 Peevishly complaining of manifold evils that it was impossible to remedy.

peevishness ('pi:vɪʃnɪs). [f. as prec. + -NESS.] The quality of being peevish.

†**1.** Silliness, foolishness, folly; madness. *Obs.*

1523 SKELTON *Garl. Laurel* 637 With a pellit of peuisshenes they had suche a stroke. **1540** HYRDE tr. *Vives' Instr. Chr. Wom.* II. ix. (1557), The more wee mocke you.. and geue vnto you aboundantly that peuishenes [*ineptias illas*], which you call honour. **1552** HULOET, Peuishnes, *insania*. **1586** A. DAY *Eng. Secretary* II. (1625) 45 Were the peeuishnesse of my conceits correspondent to those vaine-glorious humours of yours.

†**2.** Perverse, refractory, obstinate, or spiteful character or behaviour; malignity, perversity. *Obs.*

1468 *Paston Lett.* II. 326 To be depryved *de omni beneficio ecclesiastico* for symony, lechory, perjory, and doubble variable pevyshnesse. **1582** G. MARTIN *Discov. Corrupt.* To Rdr. § 11 Why do they change the title, striking out S. Paules name..? what an heretical peeuishnes is this. **1601** F. GODWIN *Bps. Eng.* 223 [A] sumptuous toombe..which by the barbarous and doltish peeuishnes of some body, is pittifully defaced. **1664** H. MORE *Myst. Iniq.* II. II. xxii. 468 Undoubtedly our Heroical Reformers did not..act out of peevishness and spight, and please their own humour and impetuosity of spirit.

3. Disposition to be vexed at trifles; moroseness, querulousness; fretfulness, petty or childish ill-temper.

1561 T. NORTON *Calvin's Inst.* IV. xx. § 29 Parents shew themselves so hard..that with their peeuishnesse [*morositate*] they doe unmeasurably wearie them. **1649** JER. TAYLOR *Gt. Exemp.* II. Disc. ix. § 33 Some dispositions we have seen..assaulted by peevishnesse through immoderate fasting. **1726** BUTLER *Serm. Resentm.*, That which in a more feeble temper is peevishness, and languidly discharges itself upon everything which comes in its way,..in a temper of greater force and stronger passions, becomes rage and fury. **1857–8** SEARS *Athan.* xiv. 122 What we call the moroseness and peevishness of age are none other than the real disposition..coming forth without disguise. **1859** GEO. ELIOT *A. Bede* iv, Timid people always wreak their peevishness on the gentle.

peewee, pee-wee ('pi:wi:). [Echoic, from the cry of the bird.]

1. *Sc.* A lapwing: = PEWIT.

1886 STEVENSON *Kidnapped* xxii. 213 The moorfowl and the peewees crying upon it. **1894** CROCKETT *Raiders* 384 The spotted eggs o' the pee-wees.

2. A name in New South Wales for the Magpie Lark, *Grallina cyanoleuca*.

1898 [see MUDLARK *sb.* 3 c]. **1911** LUCAS & LE SOUËF *Birds Austral.* 340 The familiar shrill and rather whistling cry gives it [*sc.* the magpie lark] the common name of the Pee-wee or Pee-wit. **1947** *Coast to Coast 1946* 27 He can see a black-and-white bird, a pee-wee, that runs along the path between the rushes. **1956** A. BELL *Some Common Austral. Birds* 96 The Pee-wee is vigorous and unusually widespread. **1968** K. WEATHERLY *Roo Shooter* 119 There was a peewee that visited him often through the day.

3. Applied to a small child. Also, usu. *attrib.* or as *adj.*, small, tiny, composed of children, and *transf.* of animals or things, and *fig.* (*attrib.*) (*N. Amer.* and *dial.*).

1877 F. ROSS et al. *Gloss. Words Holderness* 106/1 *Pee-wee*, adj. small; diminutive. **1894** H. GARDENER *Unoff. Patriot* 169 She can play with those two peewees of Miller's, while he and I look over the stock and drive about the place a little. **1930** *Amer. Speech* VI. 133 *Peewee soft song man*, petty confidence worker. **1935** *Ibid.* X. 271/2 *Peewees*, small, stunted pigs or lambs. **1936** *Time* 6 Apr. 45/1 Merciless, ignorant, lecherous, full of peewee patriotics, he wages senseless war against the Hill People. **1946** MEZZROW & WOLFE *Really Blues* (1957) vi. 69 A peewee jockey whose onliest riding crop was a stick of marihuana. **1952** *Daily News* (N.Y.) 13 Aug. C 16/3 The Bantams, an organization of men who are what they themselves call 'peewees and proud or it' with 5 [foot] 4 [inch]..Lenny Herman as spokesman. **1958** *Cut Knife* (Saskatchewan) *Grinder* 6 Feb. 1/5 The Cut Knife Pee Wees were hosts to the Unity team and defeated them. **1965** *Western Wonderland* (Seattle) Apr. 22/1 The nine sorting categories [of logs]..are: hemlock; sawlogs..peewees..and lastly, boomsticks. **1968** *Globe & Mail* (Toronto) 17 Feb. 44 Suburban Duberger defeated nearby Vanier 4–2..in the ninth annual international pee-wee hockey tournament. **1970** C. MAJOR *Dict. Afro-Amer. Slang* 90 *Pee wee*, small; a very narrowly rolled marijuana cigarette. **1973** *New York* 26 Mar. 52/2 Why should the Rangers concern themselves with Cub Scouts and peewee players. *Ibid.* 54/3 With the sportswriters giving better notices to the peewees. **1975** *New Yorker* 12 May 113/1 All he comes up with is a cosmetic trick—a peewee Watergate analogy—by using the blunder as evidence that the producer whom Tod works for is corrupt.

b. *spec.* A small marble.

1848 BARTLETT *Dict. Amer.* 246 *Pee-wee*, the name given by boys to a little marble. **1862** C. C. ROBINSON *Dial. Leeds* 383 *Pey-wey*, a very small marble. **1902** FARMER & HENLEY *Slang* V. 160/2 *Pee-wee*... 3. (school).—A small marble. **1941** BAKER *Dict. Austral. Slang* 53 *Peewee*, a small yellow marble. **1951** J. FRAME *Lagoon* 122, I had pee-wees and bully taws and changers that weren't made of glass.

4. See PEWEE.

peeweep, peweep ('pi:wi:p), **piewipe** ('paɪwaɪp). *local.* [Echoic, from the bird's cry.]

a. A lapwing: = PEWIT 1.

a **1825** FORBY *Voc. E. Anglia*, *Pie-wipe*, the pewit or common lapwing. **1888** FENN *Dick o' the Fens* 87 I'll show you where there's more piewipes' eggs. **1892** STEWART *Shetland Tales* vi. 65 Listening to the murmuring waves and the faint cry of the 'peeweep'.

b. *transf.* (See quot. 1966.) *rare.*

a **1902** S. BUTLER *Way of all Flesh* (1903) xl. 179 Looking for a watch and purse on Battersby piewipes was very like looking for a needle in a bundle of hay. **1966** S. H. BURTON in *Ibid.* (new ed.) 391 'Piewipes' is a dialect word for lapwings—birds that are noted for building nests so well camouflaged that they are very difficult to see. The sense seems to be that the Battersby 'piewipes' are moorlands; barren featureless land affording natural camouflage.

peewit, another form of PEWIT, the lapwing.

peeyle, peezle, obs. forms of PEAL, PIZZLE.

peff, dial. variant of PECH, PEGH *v.*

peg (pɛg), *sb.*¹ Forms: 5–7 pegge, 5 pege, 7–8 pegg, 6– peg. [First mentioned in Promp. Parv. *c* 1440; of obscure history, but app. of LG. origin; cf. dial. Du. *peg* plug, peg, small wooden pin (Franck), LG. *pigge* peg (Kluge); also MDu. *pegel* 'little knob used as a mark':—ODu. **pagil* little peg, pin, or bolt, esp. as a mark (Franck); also dial. Du. *pēgel* icicle, LG. *pēgel* stake. Some also compare Da. *pig*, Sw. *pigg* pike, point, spike.]

1. a. A pin or bolt made orig. of wood, also of metal or the like, usually of a cylindrical or slightly tapering shape, and used to hold together portions of a framework, parts of machinery, etc., or for stopping up a hole, as the vent of a cask; also, a similar pin driven into or fastened in a hole in a wall, board, etc., or into the ground, and left projecting to serve for hanging up hats, clothes, etc., for holding the ropes of a tent, etc., or for marking boundaries, the level of a surface, the score in cribbage, etc. Also short for *clothes-peg*.

c **1440** *Promp. Parv.* 390/1 Pegge, or pynne of tymbyr, *cavilla*. **1483** *Cath. Angl.* 272/2 A Pege (*A.* Pegge). **1530** PALSGR. 253/1 Pegge of woode, *cheuille*. **1570** LEVINS *Manip.* 53/23 A Pegge, *clauus*. **1575** TURBERV. *Faulconrie* 276 To take a Iunyper sticke, or suche like drye tymber, and thereof to make a small sharpe pegge. **1593** NASHE *Christs T.* 24 May it be as a pegge in a vessell, to broche blood with plucking out. **1598** FLORIO, *Cauiglia*, any ring or peg fastned in the wall to tie horses to. **1654** GATAKER *Disc. Apol.* 39 As it is with an Archer..when he hath hit the white or cloven the peg. **1660** BOYLE *New Exp. Phys. Mech.* i. (1682) 8 A tapering Peg of brass. **1664** EVELYN *Sylva* (1679) 27 Oak is excellent for..pinns and peggs for tyling. **1712** ADDISON *Spect.* No. 403 ¶ 10 His Hat that hung upon a wooden Pegg by him. **1768–74** TUCKER *Lt. Nat.* (1834) I. 593 There are pegs and pins in a building as well as beams and columns. **1854** in C. Robinson *Kansas Conflict* (1892) 76 A great many Missourians have already set their pegs in that country. **1857** *Chambers' Inform. People* II. 718/2 A cribbage-board ..possesses holes for the scoring of each party, and the scoring is effected by means of pegs. **1858** GLENNY *Gard. Every-day Bk.* 239/1 Lay a verge of turf close to these pegs, and thus permanently mark one side of the road. **1875** J. D. HEATH *Croquet Player* 19 The recognised method of naming the hoops is by threes,..first hoop, second hoop, third hoop, hoops three to peg [or *post*], two to peg, one to peg, &c. **1879** MCCARTHY *Own Times* II. xxvii. 317 The tents were torn from their pegs and blown away.

b. Phrase. ***a round peg in a square hole*** (or *vice versa*), someone placed in a station unsuited or uncongenial to his peculiar capacities or disposition.

1836 FONBLANQUE *Eng. under Seven Administr.* (1837) III. 342 Sir Robert Peel was a smooth round peg, in a sharp-cornered square hole, and Lord Lyndhurst is a rectangular square-cut peg, in a smooth round hole. **1901** *Westm. Gaz.* 24 Dec. 2/2 Was there ever a more glaring case of square peg in round hole and round peg in square?

†**c.** A broach of a deer's horn: = BROACH *sb.*[1] 7.

1611 COTGR., *Chevilleures*, the broches of a Deeres head; all the pegs aboue the two lowest.

d. Applied to something resembling or suggesting a peg: see quot.

1847–78 HALLIWELL, *Pegs*, small pieces of dough rolled up, and crammed down the throats of young ducks and geese.

e. ***off the peg*** adv. phr. and (with hyphens) adj. phr.: said of (the purchase of) ready-made clothes from the peg on which they hang in a shop; available for immediate purchase or use. Also *transf.* and *fig.*

[**1879–81** G. F. JACKSON *Shropshire Word-bk.* 44 *Bought off the pegs*, said contemptuously of second-hand or 'slop-made' clothing.] *a* **1916** R. ASQUITH in Spender & Asquith *Life H. H. Asquith* (1932) II. xlviii. 234 Love ready-made or glamour off the peg. **1922** *19th Cent.* June 1026 Before the war the average undergraduate was..garbed in a 'sports' coat obviously 'off the peg'. **1926** M. A. VON ARNIM *Introd. to Sally* vi. 74 The poor Pinners would have to buy clothes off the peg. **1954** J. BETJEMAN *Few Late Chrysanthemums* 84 An officer's lady—and more so Than those who buy off the peg. **1957** *Economist* 28 Dec. 1120/2 There simply is no such thing as suitable spectacles 'off the peg'. **1959** [see *bar-tacking* s.v. BAR *sb.*[1] 30]. **1959** *Daily Tel.* 4 May 13 (*heading*) Off-the-Peg thrills of the Law. **1963** *Times* 19 Feb. 18/2 Shipowners may before long buy vessels 'off the peg' instead of each vessel's being an individual tailor-made job. **1971** *Daily Tel.* 8 Nov. 12/3 Her clothes are mostly bought 'off the peg' in Zurich boutiques. **1974** *Country Life* 28 Mar. 732/1 Georgian sash windows..have been replaced by off-the-peg glass rectangles. **1975** *Times* 11 Mar. (Italian Industry Suppl.) p. vii/4 It was the equivalent of the passage from bespoke to off-the-peg tailoring. **1977** *Navy News* June 22 (Advt.), Every Officer and Rating may be fitted immediately 'off the peg'.

f. *West Indies.* A segment of a citrus fruit. (Perh. a different word: cf. PIG *sb.*[1] 8c.)

1909 *Cent. Dict.* Suppl. 960/2 *Peg*... One of the cells or natural divisions into which an orange may be separated after removing the skin. [West Indies.] **1956** J. HEARNE *Stranger at Gate* i. 9 He moved his hand and closed it on.. the..tangerine..stripping the soft skin from the fruit and cramming the pegs into his mouth. **1971** *Caribbean Q.* XVII. II. 14 Different name, same referent.. feg/fig/peg/plug/sprig (of orange). **1973** *N.Y. Times* 3 June L 19/1 A section of an orange..is..called..' peg'.

g. *Railways.* A semaphore signal.

1911 C. E. W. BEAN *'Dreadnought' of Darling* xxxiii. 288 Recollec' that cove with a red beard we come on camped by the railway peg near Nine Mile Tank..? **1971** D. J. SMITH *Discovering Railwayana* x. 58 *Peg*, signal.

2. In special applications.

a. In stringed musical instruments, A pin of wood or metal to which the strings are fastened at one end, and which is turned to adjust the tension in tuning; a tuning-pin. Often in fig. expressions (with some of which cf. 3).

1604 SHAKS. *Oth.* II. i. 202 Oh you are well tun'd now: But Ile set downe the peggs that make this Musicke. **1645** BP. HALL *Remedy Discontents* iv. 14 Like to a skilfull Musitian, that can let down his strings a peg lower when the tune requires it. *a* **1677** BARROW *Pope's Suprem.* Introd. x. (1687) 18 Popes of high spirit and bold face..did ever aspire to scrue Papal authority to the highest peg. **1693** SOUTHERNE *Maid's Last Pr.* IV. Wks. 1721 II. 65 He takes a Base-Viol, and while he is Tuning, one of the Bullies unwinds the Pegs over his Head. **1842** TENNYSON *Vision of Sin* 87 Let me screw thee up a peg, Let me loose thy tongue with wine. **1886** STEVENSON *Dr. Jekyll* x, My love of life screwed to the topmost peg. **1898** STAINER & BARRETT *Dict. Mus. Terms* s.v. *Tuning*, String instruments of the violin, guitar, and pianoforte class are tuned by altering the tension of the strings at the end where they are carried round a moveable peg.

b. One of a set of pins fixed at intervals in a drinking vessel as marks to measure the quantity which each drinker was to drink.

See STRUTT *Compleat View* (1775) I. 48.

1796 PEGGE *Anonym.* (1809) 183 The first person that drank was to empty the tankard to the first peg or pin; the second..to the next pin, etc. **1851** LONGF. *Gold. Leg.* IV. *Refectory*, Come, old fellow, drink down to your peg! But do not drink any farther, I beg! **1865** KINGSLEY *Herew.* iv, We ourselves drink here by the peg at midday.

c. The metal pin on which a peg-top spins.

1740, 1812 [see PEG-TOP]. **1828** *Boy's Own Bk.* 12 A top with a long peg is best at this game.

d. *Shoemaking.* A pin of wood or (latterly) of brass or condensed leather, used to fasten the uppers to the sole, or the lifts to each other.

[**1765** ? implied in *pegging-awl*: see PEGGING *vbl. sb.* 3.] **1825** JAMIESON, *Peggin-awl*, a kind of awl used by shoemakers for entering the pegs or wooden pins driven into the heels of shoes. **1872** *Japanese in Amer.* 206 Shoes..are fastened on the bottom by wooden pegs, thereby creating peg factories.

e. A wedge-shaped piece of wood projecting from a jeweller's board.

1879 *Cassell's Techn. Educ.* IV. 349/1 In the centre of the hollow is a small wedge-shaped projecting piece of wood, called the *peg*, on which he performs all his operations.

f. *Cricket.* A stump.

1865 *Bell's Life in London* 1 July 9/2 Griffith then bowling Davis's centre peg. **1901** H. BLEACKLEY *Tales of Stumps* i. 31 Little Tommy tossed a slow long-hop on the leg peg,..and Nat managed to fumble it away for two. **1909** *Westm. Gaz.* 15 July 12/1 He was beaten by another fine ball from Smith, which, after pitching well outside the off peg, broke across the wicket and hit the top of the leg stump. **1972** R. ROBINSON *Wildest Tests* xi. 120 Cunis swung one so late and so far that it hit Gandotra's leg peg.

g. *Mountaineering.* = PITON 2. Also in *Comb.*

1920 G. W. YOUNG *Mountain Craft* iv. 201 My party has taken pegs three times in all, as a precaution, and used one once (on a new descent). **1946** J. E. Q. BARFORD *Climbing in Brit.* ii. 25 Pegs or large nails with rings in one end, which are driven into rocks to provide an anchor where no natural one exists. **1957** *Times Lit. Suppl.* 1 Nov. 655/2 The 'peg-bashers' have concentrated their main attention on short ferocious overhangs. **1971** [see IRONMONGERY 1 d]. **1973** C. BONINGTON *Next Horizon* viii. 120 We fully expected our route to be high-standard peg-climbing the whole way.

3. *fig.* ? The interval between two successive pegs; a step, degree. Chiefly in phr. ***to take, bring, let*** (†***pull***) (a person) ***down a peg*** (***or two***), ***a peg lower***, etc., to lower him a degree in his own or the general estimation, to humble, snub, mortify. Also, passively, ***to come down a peg.*** Cf. 2a.

1589 *Pappe w. Hatchet* To Huffe, Ruffe, etc., Now haue at you all my gaffers of the rayling religion, tis I that must take you a peg lower. **1625** in *Crt. & Times Chas. I* (1848) I. 58 Talking of the brave times that would be shortly..when.. the Bishop of Chester, that bore himself so high, should be hoisted a peg higher to his little ease. **1664** BUTLER *Hud.* II. ii. 522 We still have worsted all your holy Tricks,..And took your Grandees down a peg. **1707** HEARNE *Collect.* 24 Feb. (O.H.S.) I. 336 You'll bring me down a peg lower in my Conceit. **1732** BERKELEY *Alciphr.* vi. § 18 He is a peg too high for me in some of his notions. **1781** C. JOHNSTON *Hist. J. Juniper* II. 247 An opportunity for letting him down a peg or two. **1809** *Naval Chron.* XXIV. 32 Chance..has..raised these gentlemen a peg higher. **1894** MRS. H. WARD *Marcella* II. 324, I must take that proud girl down a peg.

b. *Mil. slang.* A charge. Usu. in phr. ***on the peg***, on a charge, under arrest.

1890 BARRÈRE & LELAND *Dict. Slang* II. 122/2 *On the peg* (military), to be under arrest... The expression is also used when a soldier is put under stoppages. **1919** [see FOR *prep.* 13 e]. **1923** J. MANCHON *Le Slang* 220 *To whip..on the peg*, mettre..aux arrêts. **1941** *Amer. Speech* XVI. 186/2 *On the peg*, under charge for misdemeanor.

4. ***to move, start, stir a peg***, to make a move.

1810 SIR J. BARROW in *Croker Papers* 27 July, Our whole squadron in the Downs, not one of which attempted to move a peg. **1841** *Punch* I. 243/1 You'll not stir a peg. **1852** MRS. STOWE *Uncle Tom's C.* viii, You've got to fork over fifty dollars, flat down, or this child don't start a peg. **1855** SMEDLEY *H. Coverdale* iii. 18 One condition without which I don't stir a peg.

5. *fig.* ***a peg to hang*** (a discourse, opinion, etc.) ***upon***, an occasion, pretext, excuse, or theme for. Also *absol.* and const. *for*.

1812 J. NOTT *Dekker's Gull's Horn-bk.* 30 *note*, The remark of a St. James's-street chairman, that 'a crust of bread and cheese was an excellent peg to hang a pot of porter upon'. **1852** GEO. ELIOT *Let.* 24–25 July (1954) II. 50 The publishing world seems utterly stagnant—nothing coming out which would do as a peg for an article. **1858** R. S. SURTEES *Ask Mamma* i, [A] quarrelsome fellow, who merely wanted a peg to hang a grievance upon. **1891** *Lancet* 3 Oct. 750 The chief use of a fact is as a peg to hang a thought on. **1909** J. R. WARE *Passing Eng.* 194/1 *Peg* (*Theatrical*, 1884). Sensation point or effect of a piece. Something upon which the actors..can build up a scene. **1929** D. H. LAWRENCE *Phoenix II* (1968) 590 And as for his relation to his women ..they are pegs to hang clothes on, and there's an end of them. **1930** E. POUND *XXX Cantos* vii. 26 The Elysée carries a name on And the bus behind me gives me a date for peg. **1953** A. HUXLEY *Let.* 19 July (1969) 678, I have been asked..to do an article on recent developments in para-psychology, using your forthcoming book as the peg on which to hang my remarks. **1966** *Listener* 10 Feb. 221/2 The event itself seemed too slight a peg on which to hang a sixty-minute programme. **1972** *Guardian* 11 Sept. 8/6 Newspapermen..with their contempt for yesterday's story, their embarrassment when confronted with master-pieces lacking any evident 'peg'. **1976** *Times Lit. Suppl.* 13 Feb. 174/3 Dr Hacking uses this theme as a series of pegs on which to hang his discussions of particular authors' philosophies of language.

6. A drink; esp. of brandy and soda-water. Chiefly in Anglo-Indian slang. (Cf. 2b.)

1864 TREVELYAN *Compet. Wallah* (1866) 158 Brandy and belattee pawnee, a beverage which goes by the name of a 'peg' (according to the favourite derivation, because each draught is a 'peg' in your coffin). **1883** F. M. CRAWFORD *Mr. Isaacs* 7 Trial..who could absorb the most 'pegs'—those vile concoctions of spirits, ice, and sodawater. **1896** A. FORBES *Camps, Quarters, &c.* 263 [She] brewed him a mild peg with her own fair hands.

7. a. A tooth, esp. a child's tooth. Now *dial.* and *nursery prattle*.

1597–8 BP. HALL *Sat.* VI. i. 290 Her grinders..shall.. waxe as ill As old Catillaes, which wont euery night Lay vp her holly pegs till next day-light. **1828** *Craven Gloss.* (ed. 2), *Pegs*, teeth.

b. A wooden leg (*colloq.*); also, a leg (*humorous*). Cf. *peg-leg* in 11.

1833 M. SCOTT *Tom Cringle* iii. 79 It had been left three inches too long, so he had to jerk himself up to the top of his peg at every step. *a* **1845** HOOD *Faithless Nelly Gray* iii, The army-surgeons made him limbs: Said he,—'They're only pegs'. **1847–78** HALLIWELL, *Peg*..(4) a leg, or foot.

8. An implement furnished with a pin, claw, or hook, used for tearing, harpooning, etc.: **a.** a prong or tine fastened to a pole or string, used for harpooning turtles, a turtle-peg; **b.** a husking-peg.

1731–48 CATESBY *Nat. Hist. Carolina* (1754) II. 39 Turtle are most commonly taken at the Bahama Islands..by striking them with a small iron peg of two inches long; this peg is put in a socket at the end of a staff twelve feet long ..[and] fastened by a string to the pole. **1827** G. A. MCCALL *Lett. fr. Frontiers* (1868) 178 The Colonel had directed Maximo to bring with him his turtle-seine, his 'peg' and all other appliances for hunting the green turtle. **1846** [see *peg-striker* in 11]. **1872** TALMAGE *Serm.* 162 Corn-husker's peg never ripped out fuller ear.

9. a. A thrusting blow. *dial.* or *slang*.

1748 SMOLLETT *Rod. Rand.* xxvii, Many cross buttocks did I sustain, and pegs on the stomach without number. **1796** *Grose's Dict. Vulg. T.* (ed. 3) s.v., A peg is also a blow with a straight arm. **1825** BROCKETT *N.C. Gloss.*, *Peg*, a blow or thump.

b. An act or effort of 'pegging on' (PEG *v.* 10); a stiff effort to make one's way. *rare.*

1894 *Outing* (U.S.) Apr. 36/2 From there to the next mark was a dead peg to windward.

10. Short for PEG-TOP 1. *rare.* ***peg in the ring***: see quot. 1847–78

1835 MARRYAT *Jacob Faithf.* v, In playing at marbles, and peg in the ring. **1840** *P. Parley's Ann.* I. 85, I wish you would change tops with me. I'll give you my two pegs for your boxer. **1847–78** HALLIWELL, *Peg-in-the-ring*, at top, is to spin the top within a certain circle marked out, and in which the top is to exhaust itself, without once overstepping the bounds prescribed. **1885** *New Bk. Sports* 311 If the full game of peg-in-the-ring be played, [there is] a good deal of excitement and varied interest.

11. *attrib.* and *Comb.*, as ***peg-hole***, ***-maker***; ***peg-like*** adj.; **peg-bag**, a bag used as a container for clothes-pegs; **peg-basket**, a repository for clothes-pegs; **peg-board**, (*a*) a board with holes and pegs used in some games; (*b*) a board having regularly spaced holes for holding hooks on which objects can be hung; hence **peg-boarding**; **peg-box, pegbox**, a structure at the head of instruments of the lute or violin type, where the strings are attached to the tuning-pegs; **peg-cutter, peg-float**: see quots.; **peg doll**, a doll made from a clothes peg or similar piece of wood; **peg-house** *slang*, (*a*) a public-house (see sense 6); (*b*) a brothel or meeting-place for male homosexuals (U.S.); **peg-ladder**, a ladder, usually fixed, with a single standard having rungs fixed through it, or to one side (Knight *Dict. Mech.* 1875); **peg leg**, a wooden leg (see sense 7b); one who has a wooden leg; also *transf.* and as *v. intr.*, to move with a limp or a stiff gait (see also quot. 1932); **'peg-legged** *a.*, having a peg leg (also *transf.*); **peg-legger**, one having a peg leg; *slang*, a beggar; **peg-man**, (*a*) a tent-pegger; (*b*) a workman who lasts pegged boots or shoes; **peg-pole**, an upright pole pierced with peg-holes, for ascent by a gymnast having two pegs in his hands which he inserts alternately; **peg-pot** = *peg-tankard*; **peg-rent**, cloak-room charges; **peg rhizoid**, in certain liverworts of the order Marchantiales, a rhizoid distinguished by peg-like processes on the inner surface; †**peg-roots**, local name of the Green Hellebore (*Helleborus viridis*); **peg-striker**, one who catches turtles with a peg (sense 8a); **peg-strip**, a strip or ribbon of wood from which pegs are split off in the pegging-machine; **peg-tankard**, one with pegs inserted at regular intervals to mark the quantity each person is to drink (see sense 2b); **peg-tooth**, a peg-shaped tooth, a canine tooth; **peg-wattled**: see quot.; **peg-wood**, dogwood used in small splinters by jewellers for cleaning the pivot-holes of watches.

1951 J. FLEMING *Man who looked Back* xl. 145 She gathered up her arty *peg-bag. **1972** P. FLOWER *Cobweb* III. 92 Already a faithful clientele. What d'you think about tea cosies and table-mats, peg bags, teapot stands and so on? **1914** D. H. LAWRENCE *Widowing of Mrs. Holroyd* I. i. 12 Jack, can you go and take the stockings in for me?.. Minnie, you take the *peg-basket. **1899** *Allbutt's Syst. Med.* VIII. 246 We can merely mention bean-bags, *peg-boards, size and form boards, as some of the apparatus found useful for the purpose [of amusing and instructing the weak-minded]. **1951** *Catal. of Exhibits, South Bank Exhib., Festival of Britain* 152/1 Pegboard; Educational Supply Association

Ltd. **1960** *Guardian* 24 Feb. 13/5 A peg board lining to the door..for extensive hanging purposes. **1962** E. GODFREY *Retail Selling & Organization* ii. 19 It [*sc.* the counter] will be replaced by shelving, pegboard or tiered stands. **1967** R. WHITEHEAD in Wills & Yearsley *Handbk. Managem. Technol.* 69 Those wonderful pegboard systems and elaborate charts designed along foolproof lines to check the flow of work are notorious for the way they fail to work. **1971** *Femina* (Bombay) 30 Apr. 27/3 Picture puzzles, peg-board, block building..sharpen motor skills. **1975** P. G. WINSLOW *Death of Angel* iv. 96 The shed was deep... Piles of what looked like sheets of metal lay along one side. Tools hung from a pegboard in the back. **1960** *Woman's Realm* 2 Apr. 10/3 Sheets of *pegboarding..make a..useful space for hanging utensils. **1962** *Friend* 3 Aug. 946/2 The most expensive item was peg-boarding for the ceiling. **1883** GROVE *Dict. Mus.* III. 81/2 It [*sc.* the rebec] was shaped like the half of a pear, and was everywhere solid except at the two extremities, the upper of which was formed into a *peg-box identical with that still in use, and surmounted by a carved human head. **1938** *Oxf. Compan. Mus.* 524/1 The head [of the lute], containing the peg-box, is generally bent back at an angle from the neck. **1961** M. W. PRYNNE in A. Baines *Mus. Instruments* vii. 158 For balance, the bent-back pegbox has to be as light as possible with very slender pegs or 'lute-pins'. **1976** D. MUNROW *Instruments Middle Ages & Renaissance* 25/4 From the twelfth to the fourteenth century, the instrument is regularly referred to in French literature as *mandoire* or sometimes *mandola* and illustrations often reveal the instrument's most recognizable feature; its sickle-shaped pegbox. **1875** KNIGHT *Dict. Mech.* 1648/1 **Peg-cutter*, an instrument or machine for removing the ends of pegs from the insides of boots and shoes. A float. **1950** *Dryad Catal.* 96 *Peg doll. Height 11"—Each 4/6. **1951** *Notes Coll. Dolls & Figurines* (Wenham, Mass., Hist. Assoc.) 50 The popular wooden play doll commonly called 'Peg-doll', 'Penny-wood', was born in the Thuringian forest. **1969** [see *Flanders baby*]. **1972** *Times* 30 June 18/2 Nanny..is one of a series of pretty peg dolls all dressed in the fashions of 1870 servants... They are..made from genuine dolly pegs, hand painted and dressed by Somerset craftsmen. **1875** KNIGHT *Dict. Mech.* 1648/1 **Peg-float*, an implement for rasping pegs from boots and shoes. **1922** C. AIKEN *Jig of Forslin* 40 And once I murdered, by the waterfront: A drunken sailor, in a *peg-house brawl. **1931** 'D. STIFF' *Milk & Honey Route* 211 *Peg house*, a place where, if the hobo wishes, he may meet *Angelina*. **1942** BERREY & VAN DEN BARK *Amer. Thes. Slang* §507/4 *Peg house*, a male homosexual brothel or gathering place. **1972** R. A. WILSON *Playboy's Bk. Forbidden Words* 222 A 'peg-boy' is a young male who prostitutes himself to homosexuals; 'peg-house', a homosexual brothel. There is an unsubstantiated story that boys in East Indian peg-houses were required to sit on pegs between customers, giving them permanently dilated anuses. **1769** J. WEDGWOOD *Let.* 6 Dec. (1965) 88 The *peg leg is much wanted. **1872** HARTLEY *Clock Alm.* 48 (E.D.D.) Besides, he's a peg leg. **1889** *Pall Mall G.* 16 Aug. 3/1 The days of the old 'peg' legs have gone by. **1903** *N. & Q.* 9th Ser. XI. 404/2 A wooden leg, in the sense of a peg-leg, Lord Uxbridge never wore. **1932** *Amer. Speech* VII. 269 When cable-tools alternately strike bottom and miss in drilling, they are said to *peg-leg*. **1969** D. FRANCIS *Enquiry* xiv. 190, I peg-legged up the back drive. **1971** M. TAK *Truck Talk* 116 *Peg leg*, (1) the first rear axle of a tandem-axle tractor when it has only single tires... (2) a three-legged trailer... (3) a trailer with one broken dolly. **1974** *Daily Tel.* 3 Sept. 14/6 During the 1914–18 war more than 20,000 men with legs amputated were fitted with clumsy wooden 'peg-legs'. **1967** B. PATTEN *Little Johnny's Confession* 18 It should scatter woodworm into the bedrooms of all *peglegged men. **1974** H. L. FOSTER *Ribbin'* vi. 245 The current trend is..ankle-length, peg-legged jeans and platform shoes in the city. **1937** PARTRIDGE *Dict. Slang* 615/2 **Peg-legger*, a beggar... Either rhyming s[lang] or ex the preceding [*sc.* peg-leg]. **1943** *Bournemouth Daily Echo* 28 Oct. 2/3 Another 'peg-legger'—as the one-legged men call themselves—was Marine Edgar Saunders. **1723** *Lond. Gaz.* No. 6193/3 Thomas Atkines,..*Pegmaker. **1859** F. A. GRIFFITHS *Artill. Man.* (1862) 35 Pole-men, *peg-men, and unpackers of tents. **1897** S. & B. WEBB *Industr. Democracy* I. 418 'Lasters'..(in hand-sewn work these are known as 'makers', in 'pegged work'..they are called 'pegmen' or 'rivetters'). **1903** *Athenæum* 24 Jan. 122/1 In 1873 a *peg-pot similarly engraved..was offered to the city, but declined. **1911** *Chambers's Jrnl.* Feb. 115/1 The man who likes to eat a meal without worry lest somebody should exchange hats with him..must pay *peg-rent. **1911** J. M. COULTER et al. *Textbk. Bot.* II. i. 516 In the Marchantiaceae, rhizoids are of two kinds, plane rhizoids.. and *peg rhizoids, in which the cell wall grows out internally into peg-like or antler-like projections. **1958** *New Biol.* XXVII. 90 One of the peculiarities of *Marchantia* is that these rhizoids are of two kinds, smooth rhizoids..and 'peg rhizoids' which have numerous peg-like thickenings on the inner surface of the wall jutting into the cell cavity. **1969** F. E. ROUND *Introd. Lower Plants* viii. 102 (*caption*) Section through a pore region of *Conocephalum*, note photosynthetic filaments, peg and smooth rhizoids and amphigastrium. **1737** S. DALE *Pharmacologia* (ed. 3) 177 Dein fibros radicum hujus per vulnus transadigunt, unde *Peg-roots dicuntur. **1846** WORCESTER, **Peg-striker*, one who catches turtles by striking them with an iron peg having a string attached to it. *Holbrook.* **1875** KNIGHT *Dict. Mech.* 1650/1 **Peg-strip*,.. invented by Sturtevant, 1858. **1796** PEGGE *Anonym.* (1809) 183 *Peg-Tankards, of which I have seen a few still remaining in Derbyshire,..hold two quarts, so that there is a gill of ale, i.e. half a pint Winchester measure, between each pin. **1884** *Leisure Hour* May 299/2 The peg-tankard.. had pegs in it, dividing the height into eight half-pints. **1967** *Times* 7 Mar. 21/6 (Advt.), A York peg tankard, by John Plummer, circa 1695. **1681** GREW *Museum* I. 43 The Teeth are about threescore, thirty in each Jaw;..*Peg-Teeth, not much unlike the Tusks of a Mastiff. **1765** *Treat. Dom. Pigeons* 82 The wattle..ought to be broad across the beak; short from the head towards the apex, or point of the bill, and tilting forwards from the head; for if otherwise, it is said to be *peg-wattled, which is very much disesteemed. **1884** F. J. BRITTEN *Watch & Clockm.* 184 A watch maker would be quite at a loss without a stock of *peg wood. **1885** C. G. W. LOCK *Workshop Receipts* Ser. IV. 327/1.

Peg (pɛg), *sb.*² [An alteration of *Meg* = *Margaret*; cf. *Polly* = *Molly, Mary*.]

1. A pet form of the female name *Margaret*: cf. also PEGGY. Hence in proverbial nicknames: ***Peg Trantum***, a romping, hoydenish girl. **†*gone to Peg Trantum's* (*Crancum's*)**, dead (*obs. slang*).

1694 MOTTEUX *Rabelais* v. vii. (1737) 30 That will sink you down to Peg-Trantums, an hundred Fathom under Ground. *a* **1700** B. E. *Dict. Cant. Crew*, Gon to *Pegtrantums*, Dead. **1706** E. WARD *Wooden World Diss.* (1708) 8 He fulfills to a Tittle the never-failing Proverb, 'Set a Beggar on Horse-back, and he'll ride to Peg Crancums'. *a* **1825** FORBY *Voc. E. Anglia*, *Peg-trantum*, a galloping, rantipole girl; a hoydenish mauther.

2. ***Old Peg*** (*dial.*): Skim-milk cheese.

1785 GROSE *Dict. Vulg. T.*, *Old Pegg*, poor Yorkshire cheese. **1796** *Ibid.* (ed. 3) s.v. *Peg*, Old Peg; poor hard Suffolk or Yorkshire cheese. **1825** BROCKETT *N.C. Gloss.*, *Old-peg*, *Aud-peg*, an inferior sort of cheese made of skimmed milk. It is also called, not inaptly, *leather hungry*.

peg (pɛg), *v.* [f. PEG *sb.*¹]

I. Uses in which an actual peg is in question.

1. a. *trans.* To fix or make fast with a peg; to fasten with or as with a peg or pegs. Also with *down, in, out, up*, etc.

1598 FLORIO, *Cauicchiare*,..to peg or pin in. **1610** SHAKS. *Temp.* I. ii. 295, I will rend an Oake, And peg thee in his knotty entrailes. **1664** EVELYN *Sylva* (1679) 13 Peg it [branch] down with a hook or two. **1718** *Entertainer* No. 19. 127 After he has mounted his Box, and methodically pegg'd his Cloak. **1846** J. BAXTER *Libr. Pract. Agric.* (ed. 4) II. 23 The plants..must be trained close to the wall, or pegged to the bank as they grow. **1857** F. L. OLMSTED *Journ. Texas* 96 When the corners [of the tent] are pegged out by the flat iron pegs attached, our night quarters are ready. **1859** W. S. COLEMAN *Woodlands* (1866) 10 Framed of oak trunks split through the centre and roughly pegged together. **1869** E. A. PARKES *Pract. Hygiene* (ed. 3) 416 Sometimes boots are not sewn, but pegged. **1873** TRISTRAM *Moab* v. 86 They..left him a whole day under a broiling sun pegged to the ground.

b. *fig.* To confine; to tie or bind *down*, to restrict.

1824–9 LANDOR *Imag. Conv.*, *Milton & Marvel* Wks. 1846 I. 123, I will not be pegged down to any plot. **1829** SCOTT *Jrnl.* 17 Mar., Here are two pleasant and pretty women pegged up the whole day 'In the worst inn's worst room'. **1872** BAGEHOT *Physics & Pol.* (1876) 219 Before he is pegged down by ancient usage.

c. *fig.* To fix the market-price; to prevent the price from falling by buying freely at a given price, or to prevent it from rising by selling freely. *Stock Exchange slang.* Also, in extended uses, to fix (a price, wage, etc.) at a certain level; to set a value on (a currency) in relation to gold or another currency; to set a numerical or quantitative limit on (something).

1882 *Pall Mall G.* 8 Apr. 6/1 Arbitrarily raising prices against them—'pegging prices up', it is called. *Ibid.*, No doubt there will be new 'peggings up.' **1891** *New York Herald* 31 May 6/2 (Farmer) Portuguese have been well pegged, but other 'Internationals' have been featureless. **1933** *Ann. reg. 1932* 26 Shortly afterwards the Bank rate was considerably reduced, and sterling was effectively 'pegged' at a gold value of about 15*s.* **1933** *Sun* (Baltimore) 13 July 10/2 The British went off gold after a strenuous effort to maintain gold parity in 1931 and it can hardly be proved that England's trade balance has improved sufficiently to permit pegging the pound at any such figure. *Ibid.* 21 July 2/4 The market was 'pegged' once before this year... The fluctuations in wheat at that time were limited to 5 cents a bushel. **1940** *New Statesman* 13 Apr. 485 The dual system ..of rationing by amount and of pegging prices is anomalous. **1944** AUDEN *Sea & Mirror* in *For Time Being* i. 5 When he learns the price is pegged to his valuation. **1949** KOESTLER *Promise & Fulfilment* 292 It is a kind of aseptic social operation, and as wages are pegged to the cost-of-living index, there is no occasion even for local strikes. **1954** *Birmingham* (Alabama) *News* 17 Feb. 1/6 The old method pegged unemployment at 2,259,000 the first week in January. **1959** *Punch* 29 Aug. 30/1 Inflation can be licked by other means, by pegging wages and profits, increasing productivity and output,..and so on. *Ibid.* 30/2, I have already encouraged my teen-agers to peg their consumption of sweets, soft drinks, records, cosmetics and cycle accessories in the hope of bringing manufacturers to heel. **1965** *Listener* 20 May 728/1 There is room for scepticism about the machinery which is supposed to peg these rents at a 'fair' level. **1970** *Times* 18 Dec. 2/5 The orchestras have had their grants pegged for three years and are in a serious position. **1971** *Morning Star* 10 May 1/5 The mark will be allowed to float, meaning its parity will no longer be pegged against the dollar. **1977** *Evening Post* (Nottingham) 27 Jan. 5/4 Planners hope to peg the cost of the tour at £60 or less per tourist.

d. *fig.* To categorize; to form an opinion of (someone, occas. something). Freq. in phr. ***to have*** (someone or something) ***pegged***: to have a fixed opinion of (that person or thing). *N. Amer. colloq.*

1920 *Collier's* 31 July 29/2, I had him pegged from the go in for what he *is*—one of them tea-room boys which will stop at nothin' but work! **1926** J. BLACK *You can't Win* xxi. 320 The expression, 'I have him pegged', which has crept into common usage, is thieves' slang..and has nothing to do with the game of cribbage. **1940** J. O'HARA *Pal Joey* 175, I tho't I could peg a joint like that from 2 mi. away. **1949** *New Yorker* 12 Nov. 28/3 An elderly lady..who pegged him looked back, and then winked. **1959** J. LUDWIG in R. Weaver *Canad. Short Stories* (1968) 2nd. Ser. 232 Naturally Mitchell has her pegged: doesn't he know this shopping trip is a fake..? **1967** M. REYNOLDS *After Some Tomorrow* 12, I peg him as a holier than thou cloddy. **1968** H. WAUGH *Con Game* ix. 91, I always knew she was a slut. An ignorant, stupid child. I pegged her from the start. **1972** D. LEES *Zodiac* 40, I had her pegged as a bit of a nut. **1976** *Publishers Weekly* 18 Oct. 52/1 Combine the pace of a Disney film with the reassurance of characters clearly good or evil and you will quickly peg what Nicolaysen's chase adventure has going for it.

2. To insert a peg into, provide with a peg.

†a. To insert or thrust a peg in the nose of (a swine, etc.) to prevent it from routing. *Obs.*

1543 *Act 35 Hen. VIII*, c. 17 §15 Unlesse the same swyne be sufficiently ringed or pegged. **1631** R. BYFIELD *Doctr. Sabb.* 100 He intended to pegge or ring an hog. [*Ibid.*, He put the pegge into the nose of the swine.]

†b. To plug; to spike (a cannon). *Obs.*

1551 CRANMER *Answ. Gardiner* III. Wks. (Parker Soc.) I. 200 And I trust I have either broken your pieces, or pegged them, that you shall be able to shoot no more. **1583** STOCKER *Civ. Warres Lowe C.* IV. 60 b, Thei..broke one peece of Ordnaunce, and pegged or poysoned an other. **1747** MRS. GLASSE *Cookery* x. 117 Take a live lobster, boil it in salt and water, and peg it that no water gets in.

c. †(*a*) To broach (a cask, etc.) (*obs.*). (*b*) To provide with a vent and peg.

1721 AMHERST *Terræ Fil.* No. 34 (1754) 181 He peg'd several buts, and gave me a glass of each to taste. **1742** *Lond. & Country Brew.* I. (ed. 4) 69 There should be first an Examination made by pegging the Vessel to prove, if such Drink is fine, the Hop sufficiently rotted, and it be mellow and well-tasted.

d. To fasten the soles on to (boots or shoes) with wooden pegs.

1850 *Rep. Comm. Patents 1849* (U.S.) 295 Improvement in Machines for Pegging Boots and Shoes. **1858** [see PEGGED *ppl. a.*]. **1895** *Montgomery Ward Catal.* 511/1 Ladies' Heavy Pegged Shoes. **1940** *Chambers's Techn. Dict.* 622/2 *Pegged-sole shoes*, a type of footwear in which the outer sole is attached to the inner sole and the upper by two or more rows of pegs; used for sea boots.

e. To insert small wooden pegs into the stalks of (tobacco).

1850 *Rep. Comm. Patents: Agric. 1849* (U.S. Dept. Agric.) 321 'Pegging' tobacco..is done by driving little pegs, about six inches long and half an inch or less square, into the stalk about four inches from the big end of the stalk. **1968** *Publ. Amer. Dial. Soc. 1966* XLV. 19 It's hard work to peg tobacco.

f. *Cricket.* To drive pegs into (the face of a bat) (see quot. 1934).

1853 F. GALE *Public School Matches* 17 The captain is going in. An old bat, well pegged but very clean, looks like business. **1906** A. E. KNIGHT *Compl. Cricketer* ii. 48 Pegging down the bat is simple, but destructive and ineffective. **1934** W. J. LEWIS *Lang. Cricket* 186 *To peg a bat*, to drive a few small pegs into the face of a bat as a remedial measure when the grain of the wood has risen with use.

3. a. To strike or pierce with a peg; to strike with the pike of a peg-top; to transfix with a turtle-peg (PEG *sb.*¹ 8 a); to harpoon. **b.** *intr.* To aim *at* with a peg or a peg-top; to use the turtle-peg.

1740 DYCHE & PARDON, *Peg*..also to strike or hit any thing with the iron point that is fastened or put into childrens toys, called castle-tops. **1806–7** J. BERESFORD *Miseries Hum. Life* (1826) III. x, Attempting to peg it [a top] down into the ring. **1815** *Misc.* in *Ann. Reg.* 547/2 Turtle abound amongst the islands... we could neither peg any from the boat, nor yet catch them on shore. **1828** *Boy's Own Bk.* 12 The moment it [a peg-top] rolls out, he may take it up, and peg at those which still remain inside. **1865** DICKENS *Mut. Fr.* III. vi, Silas pegged at him with his wooden leg. **1884** BARING-GOULD *Mehalah* xi. 156 She turned sharply round, [and] pegged at him with the umbrella.

4. a. *Cribbage.* To mark (the score) with pegs on a cribbage-board (also *absol.*); rarely, to mark the score of (a person); hence *transf.* to score (a given number of points).

1821 [see PEGGING *vbl. sb.* 1]. **1824** MISS MITFORD *Village* Ser. I. (1863) 217 Dear Mossy could neither feel to deal and shuffle, nor see to peg. **1868** PARDON *Card Player* 22 You must be careful how you peg your opponent. **1870** HARDY & WARE *Mod. Hoyle* 76 The Cribbage-board, which contains sixty-one holes, divided into compartments of five each, in which each player pegs or marks the game as follows. *Ibid.* 77 Suppose your opponent leads off with a nine, you play a six and cry 'fifteen', and peg two holes.

b. ***peg back***, (*a*) (Racing): of a horse, to pull past, overtake (another horse); also, to gain on another horse by (a specified distance); (*b*) in a game: to pick up (a point or advantage) or to change (the score) so as to reduce or eliminate an opponent's lead.

1928 *Sunday Express* 24 June 22/3 He came..in the last furlong to peg back the flying French colt. **1932** *New Yorker* 14 May 52/2 Burgoo King pegged him back three furlongs from home. **1971** *Sunday Nation* (Nairobi) 11 Apr. 44/4 Owen de Souza pegged one back for Blues in the dying minutes when he converted a penalty-push. **1977** D. FRANCIS *Risk* ii. 18 Open ditch next; Tapestry met it just right and we pegged back a length in mid-air. **1978** *Rugby World* Apr. 4/1 The Irish side had given all Wales a fright by pegging the score back to 13–13 after the visitors had gone 13–3 in front.

5. To mark with pegs; *esp.* to mark the boundaries of (a piece of ground, a claim for mining or gold-digging, etc.) with pegs placed at the corners: usually ***peg out***.

1852 W. H. HALL *Pract. Exp. Diggings Victoria* (ed. 3) 23, I..selected an unoccupied spot..pegged out eight square feet, paid the licence-fee, and returned to my mates. **1858** GLENNY *Gard. Every-day Bk.* 239/1 Ranging its [a line's] further progress with the work already pegged in. **1861** BERESF. HOPE *Eng. Cathedr. 19th C.* vii. 256 An electrotype would be cast straight from the master's clay, while the stone or marble has been pegged and roughed out by his journeyman. **1890** *Goldfields of Victoria* 17 Several other claims have been pegged out and registered. **1894** A. ROBERTSON *Nuggets*, etc. 102 He pegged the ground, and applied for a lease.

II. Transferred and figurative senses.

†**6.** To cram, gorge, glut. *Obs. rare*—[1].

(It is uncertain whether this is the same word.)

a **1400–50** *Alexander* 4278 Surfet vs wlattis, To pegge vs as a peny hoge þat praysis noȝt oure laȝes.

†**7.** To drive *in* as a peg by repeated blows. *Obs.*

1614 D. DYKE *Myst. Selfe-Deceiuing* 354 Vnlesse wee.. doe so pegge and hammer them [holy thoughts] in. *a* **1618** —— *Two Treat.* II. *Schoole Afflict.* (1618) 340 No doctrine can enter, unless it be pegged, and hammered, and knocked into vs by the fists of this sowre and crabbed schoolemaster [affliction]. **1647** TRAPP *Comm. 2 Pet.* iii. 1 So must Ministers with one Sermon peg in another.

8. a. *intr.* To aim with, or as with, a weapon *at* (or *for*); to drive *at*. **b.** *trans.* To aim (a missile) *at*.

a **1700** B. E. *Dict. Cant. Crew*, *Peg at Cocks*, to throw at them at Shrovetide. **1830** *Boston Gaz.* 26 Oct. 4 Roe continued 'pegging' at Heardson. **1875** F. I. SCUDAMORE *Day Dreams* 155 He 'pegs' for larks but is not disdainful of sparrows. **1895** FRANCIS *Daughter of Soil* iii. 34 She pegged a stone at me.

c. *peg it*: to let drive, to 'pitch' *into*. *colloq.*

1834 DOWLING *Othello Trav.* II. v, You peg it into him, and pray don't spare him. **1889** *Lic. Vict. Gaz.* 18 Jan. (Farmer), Peg it into him, snacks.

d. *trans.* Of a pointer or setter: To point at, set (a game bird).

1892 *Field* 7 May 695/1 Then Satin found birds, and directly after pegged a single bird that Crab had passed. *Ibid.* 695/3 Directly after he pegged birds properly, making a good point.

9. *intr.* To make one's way with vigour or haste. Also with *away*, *off*, etc. *dial.* and *colloq.*

1808–18 JAMIESON, *To Peg off*, or *away*, to go off quickly. **1828** *Craven Gloss.* (ed. 2), *Peg-away*, to move hastily. **1859** *Blackw. Mag.* Mar. 305/2 Fleeing..with a 'rapidité sans égal', pegging away with a unanimity that was really delightful. **1880** MISS BRADDON *Just as I am* iii, Geoffrey Blake pegged along the hard road of industrious poverty till he came to the Temple of Fortune. **1884** LE FANU in *Temple Bar Mag.* Aug. 484 Away with me out of the hall-door..and down the street I pegged like a madman.

10. *intr.* To work on persistently, to 'hammer' away; esp. *peg away*; also *peg on*, *along*. *colloq.*

1805 STAGG *Misc. Poems* 132 I' th' meanteyme th' fiddlers changt an playt As hard as they cud peg. **1809** MALKIN *Gil Blas* IV. xi. ¶6 Slices of roast meat, at which we began pegging with all possible pertinacity. **1818** KEATS *Let.* 24 Jan. (1958) I. 216 The musicians began pegging & fagging away at an overture. **1837** DICKENS *Pickw.* xxx, The particular friends resumed their attack upon the breakfast. .. 'Peg away, Bob', said Mr. Allen to his companion, encouragingly. **1862** THACKERAY *Philip* vii. **1864** ABR. LINCOLN in Leland *Life* xi. 196 [Lincoln, when asked what we should do if the war should last for years, replied] 'We'll keep pegging away'. **1867** J. R. GREEN *Lett.* II. (1901) 172 It is no good pegging away at one little point. **18..** *Amer. Hebrew* XXXIX. 52 (C.D.) We have gradually worked and pegged along year by year. **1882** 'MARK TWAIN' *Lett. to Publishers* (1967) 158, I still lack about 30,000 words... I shall peg along, day by day. **1892** *Spectator* 16 July 83/2 Mr. Field pegged on 'till the annual value of the paper..had become £160. **1956** *People* 13 May 1/6, I have just kept pegging away year after year. **1978** L. DEIGHTON *SS-GB* xiv. 115 How I envied you doing Greats, while I pegged away at my Civil Law.

11. *trans.* (See quot.) *slang.*

1819 MOORE *Tom Crib* 80, I first was hir'd to peg a Hack. *Note*, *To drive a hackney coach.*

12. *intr.* To consume pegs (PEG *sb.*[1] 6), tipple. *slang.*

1873 in *Slang Dict.* **1901** *Blackw. Mag.* Nov. 601/1 Samuel has an Indian liver. He pegs.

III. 13. peg out: see also 1, 5.

a. *trans.* (?) To exclude entirely. *Obs.*

1672–3 MARVELL *Reh. Transp.* II. 262 You have made my Lord Summus Pontifex and Pontifex Maximus to..the pegging out of the Prince.

b. *Croquet.* To put (a ball) out by making it hit the winning-peg.

1875 J. D. HEATH *Croquet Player* 48 A rover may be pegged out by the adversary, but only if he be a rover also.

c. To pay or give out (a line, etc.). *dial.*

1895 NICHOLSON *Kilwuddie* 160 (E.D.D.) Let her gang —Grannie! peg oot the line.

d. *intr. Cribbage.* To win the game by reaching the last holes before the 'show' of hands.

1870 HARDY & WARE *Mod. Hoyle* 81 He may with a very poor hand be just able to 'show' or peg out.

e. *intr.* To peg or pitch one's tent.

1898 'R. BOLDREWOOD' *Rom. Canvass Town* 5 The bright idea of 'pegging out' struck some smart pilgrim.

f. To die; to be ruined. *slang.*

1855 *Herald of Freedom* (Lawrence, Kansas) 29 Sept. 2/5 Both parties are badly cut, and we are happy to state that the free-soiler is in a fair way to 'peg out', while the pro-slavery man is out and ready for another 'tilt'. **1870** *Echo* 10 Mar. (Farmer), Then..the heart-broken man exclaimed, 'Oh, George, George, why did you peg out?' **1882** J. HAWTHORNE *Fort. Fool* I. xxii, When old Tabanaka pegs out, you'll be chief for certain. **1899** MARY KINGSLEY *W. African Stud.* i. 7 Then follows full details of the pegging-out of J. and his funeral, &c.

g. *trans.* To hang (washing) with pegs from a clothes-line.

1922 D. H. LAWRENCE *England, my England* 102 Helped his wife to peg out the washing on the clothes line in the meadow. **1974** *Country Life* 21 Mar. 633/1 The fore-ground girls selfconsciously pegging out the washing. **1978** J. THOMSON *Question of Identity* xii. 115 Betty Lovell was pegging out sheets on a washing-line.

‖**pegall** (pɛˈgɔːl). Also **peggall**, **packall**. [a. Du. *pagaal*, ad. Carib *pagāla*.] A basket of native make used by the Indians of Guyana.

[**1796** STEDMAN *Surinam* (1806) I. xv. 404 A few baskets called pagala.] **1825** WATERTON *Wand. S. Amer.* iii. 193 Hither the Indians come with monkies, parrots, bows and arrows, and pegalls. **1858** SIMMONDS *Dict. Trade*, *Packall*, *Pagala*, a kind of basket made of the outer rind of the Ita palm (*Mauritia flexuosa*). **1899** RODWAY *Guiana Wilds* 107 They..placed these articles carefully away in their pegalls, or wicker trunks.

pegall, variant of PEGGLE.

Pegamoid (ˈpɛgəmɔɪd). Also **pegamoid**. A trade name for a kind of waterproof cloth or imitation leather used in upholstery, bookbinding, etc. Also *attrib.* and *fig.*

1895 *Current Hist.* V. 731 It is claimed for 'pegamoid', a product recently placed on the markets of Europe, that it will render materials of any kind absolutely impervious to water. **1896** *Westm. Gaz.* 10 June 5/2 By imposing it on cotton cloth or impregnating it 'Pegamoid' can be turned to many and varied purposes. **1909** *Pract. Upholstery* 12 Pegamoid Cloth. This is one of the better class imitation leathers, and is obtainable in a large variety of 'grains', colours, and qualities. **1922** *Daily Mail* 10 Nov. 15 (Advt.), Seats in red, brown, green or blue rexine, pegamoid or velvet. **1957** L. DURRELL *Justine* I. 21 He is a pegamoid sloth of a man, a vast slow fellow. **1959** B. RUCK *Romantic Afterthought* xxiv. 180 The pegamoid-covered chair.

peganite (ˈpɛgənaɪt). *Min.* [Named 1830 (in Ger. *peganit*) f. Gr. πήγανον rue (the herb), in reference to its colour: see -ITE[1] 2 b.] A hydrous phosphate of aluminium, of a greenish colour, usually occurring in incrustations on quartz.

1832 SHEPARD *Min.* 178. **1868** DANA *Min.* 582 *Peganite*... Lustre greasy to vitreous. Color deep green, greenish-gray, greenish-white.

pegasse (pəˈgæs). Also **pegass**. [Etym. unknown.] A kind of peaty soil found in the Caribbean and northern S. America.

1924 *Chambers's Jrnl.* July 475/1 Suckers should be planted..15 feet apart on pegass or peat soil. **1949** *Caribbean Q.* I. III. 42 Experiments in Surinam seem to show that the pegasse lands..can be used to grow bananas. **1959** *Listener* 17 Sept. 435/1 The north-west of Guiana is a place of countless ridges of hills islanded in a sea of pegasse swamp. **1974** *Encycl. Brit. Macropædia* VIII. 507/1 *Pegasse* soil, a type of tropical peat, occurs behind the coastal clays and along the river estuaries.

Pegasus (ˈpɛgəsəs). [L., a. Gr. Πήγασος, f. πηγή spring, fount, named from the πηγαί or springs of Ocean, near which Medusa was said to have been killed. Formerly also, as in Fr., '*Pegase*, in ME. *Pegasee*.]

1. *Gr.* and *Lat. Mythol.* The winged horse fabled to have sprung from the blood of Medusa when slain by Perseus, and with a stroke of his hoof to have caused the fountain HIPPOCRENE to well forth on Mount Helicon. Hence, by modern writers (first in Boiardo's *Orlando Innamorato c* 1490), represented as the favourite steed of the Muses, and said allusively to bear poets in the 'flights' of poetic genius.

α. **1515** BARCLAY *Egloges* iv. (1570) C vj b/2 Against the Chimer here stoutly must he fight, Here must he vanquish the fearefull Pegasus. *a* **1548** HALL *Chron.*, *Hen. VIII* 66 Then entred a person called Reaport,..sitting on a flyeng horse wᵗ wynges & fete of gold called Pegasus. **1592** DAVIES *Immort. Soul* I. vii. (1714) 21 When she, without a Pegasus, doth fly. **1602** MARSTON *Ant. & Mel.* III. Wks. 1856 I. 35 The soules swift Pegasus, the fantasie. *a* **1657** LOVELACE *Falcon* 44 The heron mounted doth appear On his own Peg'sus a lanceer. **1711** SHAFTESB. *Charact.* V. III. i. (1737) II. 382 For this purpose I will allow you the pegasus of the poets. **1809** BYRON *Bards & Rev.* ix, Each spurs his jaded Pegasus apace. **1846** LONGF. (*title*) Pegasus in Pound.

β. *c* **1386** CHAUCER *Sqr.'s T.* 199 Lyk the Pegasee The hors þat hadde wynges for to flee. *c* **1439** LYDG. *Lyfe St. Albon* (1534) A ij, With full swyfte wynges of the pegasee. *c* **1470** HENRYSON *Mor. Fab.* v. (*Parl. Beasts*) xiv, The war-wolf and the pegase perillous.

attrib. and *Comb.* **1596** FITZ-GEFFRAY *Sir F. Drake* (1881) 8 Th' amber-weeping Pegase-hoofe-made fount. **1599** MARSTON *Sco. Villanie* viii, The spirits Pegase Fantasie Should hoyse the soule from such base slauery. **1600** TOURNEUR *Transf. Metam.* i, Awake sad Mercurie And Pegase-winged pace the milkie way. **1639** SIR W. ALEXANDER *Comm. Verses* in *Drumm. of Hawth.'s Wks.* (1711) p. iv, Ne're did Apollo raise on pegase wings A muse more near himself.

b. *Her.* A winged horse as a bearing, etc.

1562 LEIGH *Armorie* 202 b, He beareth Azure, A Pegasus Argent, called the horse of honour. **1678** *Lond. Gaz.* No. 1332/4 For his crest an helmet mantled, a Pegassus holding in his mouth an oaken branch. **1761** *Brit. Mag.* II. 251 Supporters. Two Pegasusses argent, wings, crests, tails, and hoofs, or. **1864** BOUTELL *Her. Hist. & Pop.* xx. §2. 334.

c. *Astron.* One of the northern constellations, figured as a winged horse, containing three stars of the 2nd magnitude forming with one star of Andromeda a large square (the ***square of Pegasus***).

1696 PHILLIPS (ed. 5), *Pegasus*, Perseus's winged Horse, a Celestial Constellation. **1868** LOCKYER *Elem. Astron.* §355. 165 The square of Pegasus is a very marked object.

2. *Zool.* A genus of fishes, typical of the family *Pegasidæ*, of peculiar form, with body somewhat like a horse's head, and one dorsal and one anal fin, suggesting wings; also called *flying sea-horses*.

1835 *Encycl. Brit.* (ed. 7) XII. 227/2. **1847** CARPENTER *Zool.* §518 The Pegasus..the pectoral fins are large, and are spread out in a wing-like manner; whence these curious Fishes have derived their name, which signifies Flying Horses.

Hence †**Pegaˈsarian**, **Pegaˈsean** (-ˈsæan, -ˈseian), **Peˈgasean** (-ˈgasian) *adjs.* [L. *Pēgasēi-us*, *Pēgase-us*], pertaining to, connected with, or resembling Pegasus; swift; poetic; †**ˈPegase** *v. trans.* (*nonce-wd.*), to serve as a Pegasus to; **ˈPegasid** *Zool.*, a fish of the family *Pegasidæ* (see 2); **ˈPegasoid** *a.*, resembling Pegasus; belonging to the *Pegasidæ*.

1607 TOPSELL *Four-f. Beasts* (1658) 253 The *Pegasarian coursers of France, by the like change of Horses, run from Lyons to Rome in five or six days. **1614** C. BROOKE *Ghost Rich. III*, Poems (1872) 140 My wingèd horse did *pegase my desire. **1590** T. WATSON *On Death Sir F. Walsingham* Poems (Arb.) 153 Weepe yee sisters of the learned hill: That your *Pægasean springs may leap their bound. **1626** WALLER *Navy* 16 We..who can fear no Force But winged Troops, or Pegasean Horse. **1628** FELTHAM *Resolves* II. xxxii. 101 Death..with a Pegasean speede, flyes vpon vnwarie Man. **1647** H. MORE *Cupid's Conflict* iii, An unexpected Pegaseian song. **1667** MILTON *P.L.* VII. 4 Above th' Olympian Hill.., Above the flight of Pegaséan wing. **1717** *Belgrade* 6 Pardon,..that thus my Pen Should strive to raise its Pegaseian Flight. **1762–9** FALCONER *Shipwr.* III. 26 From earth upborne on Pegasean wings. **1923** 'R. CROMPTON' *William Again* iv. 59 'I feel'—his Pegasean imagination soared aloft on daring wings—'I feel 's if I might *die* if I went to church this mornin' feelin' 's ill as I do now.' **1599** MARSTON *Sco. Villanie* v, How now? What droupes the newe *Pegasian Inne? **1613–16** W. BROWNE *Brit. Past.* II. ii, Ye Sisters of the Mountaine, Who waile his loss from the Pegasian Fountaine.

†**ˈpeggage.** *Obs. rare*—[0]. [f. PEG *v.* + -AGE.] The action of fastening with pegs.

1611 COTGR., *Chevillage*, a pegging, or pinning; peggage, pinnage.

pegged (pɛgd), *ppl. a.* [f. PEG *v.* + -ED[1].] Made fast, fixed, or fastened together with pegs.

1611 COTGR., *Chevillé*,..pegged, pinned; fastened with pegs. **1858** SIMMONDS *Dict. Trade*, *Pegged Boots*, boots with wooden pegs in the soles, instead of metal nails or brads. **1893** SELOUS *Trav. S.E. Africa* 135 Judging by the length of the pegged-out skin [of a lion]. **1960** H. HAYWARD *Antique Coll.* 214/1 *Pegged construction*, furniture made by joiners constructed with mortice and tenon joints, the tenon being held in the mortice by a square peg, riven or split from green wood. **1966** A. W. LEWIS *Gloss. Woodworking Terms* 100 *Pegged or pinned tenon*, tenoned joint which is fixed by having a hole drilled through it near the shoulder and a wood pin inserted. **1967** *Wall St. Jrnl.* 9 Feb. 1/4 Mr. Glick.. wears pegged pants, boots and an Army jacket. **1968** *Globe & Mail* (Toronto) 17 Feb. 46 (Advt.), Recreation room with bar and pegged floor. **1973** *N.Y. Law Jrnl.* 19 July 16/8 (Advt.), Parquet and pegged oak floors. **1974** *Times* 7 Mar. 2/6 Growers in Holland and Germany received government help through pegged oil prices.

pegger (ˈpɛgə(r)). [f. PEG *v.* + -ER[1].]

1. One who pegs: in the senses of the verb.

1611 COTGR., *Chevilleur*, a pegger. **1818** TODD, *Pegger*, one who fastens with pegs. Not now in use. **1873** *Slang Dict.*, *Peggers*, people who constantly stimulate themselves by means of brandy and soda-water. **1901** *Scotsman* 11 Nov. 2/6 The pegger of a block of claims.

2. = PEGGING-*machine*. (*Cent. Dict.* 1890.)

pegging (ˈpɛgɪŋ), *vbl. sb.* [f. PEG *v.* + -ING[1].]

1. a. The action of the vb. PEG in various senses.

1611 COTGR., *Chevilleure*, a pegging; a fastening with pegs. **1657** W. COLES *Adam in Eden* cii. 317 Called..Bearefoot, Setterwort, and Settergrasse, because Husbandmen use to make a hole, and put it into the Eare or Dewlap of their cattle, which they call Pegging or Settering. **1821** LAMB *Elia* Ser. I. *Mrs. Battel*, The pegging [at cribbage] teased her. **1846** J. BAXTER *Libr. Pract. Agric.* (ed. 4) I. 446 The poor animal has..to undergo the painful operations of pegging, blistering, swimming, and firing. **1881** *Leicestersh. Gloss.* s.v. *Peg.* **1884** SYMONDS in *Pall Mall G.* 22 Feb. 2/2 Propelling his toboggin with the sticks—or 'pegging', as it is technically called. **1885** *New Bk. Sports* 311 A great many boys never master the true overhand fashion of pegging. **1890** 'R. BOLDREWOOD' *Miner's Right* iii. 32 The adjacent lot ..was to be had for the pegging-out first. **1926** T. E. LAWRENCE *Seven Pillars* lxvii. 352 They told me something of Davenport's work: of his continual pegging away in Abdulla's sector. **1931** *Observer* 11 Jan. 19/1 Mr. Scultin's views about the pegging of wages are unknown. **1948** G. CROWTHER *Outl. Money* (rev. ed.) viii. 248 'Pegging' has usually meant 'pegging up', but we can invent the term 'pegging down' for the practice that grew up among some governments in the nineteen-thirties of maintaining their currencies at a fixed undervaluation. **1977** *Times* 24 Dec. 9/3 Continental motoring will be given added impetus..by the pegging of most cross-Channel ferry prices.

b. *level-pegging*: see as main entry.

2. *concr.* Pegs collectively, material for pegs. †**b.** *dial.* (see quots.).

1744–50 W. ELLIS *Mod. Husbandm.* VI. III. 60 This we call Peggings, being composed of those Corals that were swept off that Heap of Wheat after Throwing. **1750** —— *Country Housew.* 2 What we in Hertfordshire call Peggings ..being what comes from the Underline or Blighted, or other Wheat Ears, most of which contain in them very thin little Kernels, that will easily part from their Chaff.

3. *attrib.* and *Comb.*: **pegging-awl**, an awl for drilling holes for the pegs of shoes; **pegging-jack**: see quot.; **pegging-machine**, a machine for driving in the pegs of shoes; **pegging-rammer**: see quot.; **pegging-top** = PEG-TOP.
1765 *Chron.* in *Ann. Reg.* 158/2, 85 pair of shoemakers nippers and pincers, 33 pegging-awls, 37 awls of other sorts. **1794** *Rigging & Seamanship* I. 88 *Pegging-awl*..has 4 sharp edges towards the point, and is smaller than a stabber. **1875** KNIGHT *Dict. Mech.* 1648/2 *Pegging-jack*, an implement for holding a boot or shoe and varying its position while being pegged. *Ibid.* 1650/1 *Pegging-rammer* (*Founding*), a pointed rammer for packing the sand in molding. **1899** *Century Mag.* Oct. 958/1 The poor boy's comin' roun' as fast as a peggin'-top.

peggle ('pɛg(ə)l), *sb. dial.* Also **pegall**, **pigall**. [Origin unknown: by some associated with *pig*.] A local name for the fruit of the hawthorn; a haw.
1827 HONE *Every-day Bk.* II. 1598 'Haws'..in the west are called *pegalls* or *pigalls*. **1879** JEFFERIES *Wild Life in S. Co.* xi. 223 Pigeons feed on the peggles which cover the great hawthorn bush so thickly as to give it a reddish tint.

'**peggle**, *v. local.* [Variant of PECKLE *v.*[2]] *intr.* To peck, continue pecking.
1868 FENN in *Aunt Judy's Mag.* 1 Aug. 241 Thrush.. comes to dig and peggle away at the plums. [General in midland counties: see *Eng. Dial. Dict.*]

peggotty ('pɛgətɪ). Also **peggitty**, **peggoty**, **pegity**, and with capital initial. [Fanciful extension of PEG *sb.*[1]] A children's board game in which four players in turn place pegs in holes, the object being to complete a row of five pegs.
Pegity is registered in the U.S. as a proprietary name.
1925 *Official Gaz.* (U.S. Patent Office) 31 Mar. 996/2 Parker Bros... *Pegity*. Game of the Type of 'Go-Bang'. Played with Pegs, for Adults and Children. **1929** *Games & Toys* July 66/1 Pegity..is one of the most interesting board games ever devised. **1950** *Oxf. Jun. Encycl.* IX. 73/1 Peggotty, a very simple modern game on the Noughts and Crosses principle, is played by four players who take it in turn to stick coloured wooden pegs into holes in the board, the winner being the first to get five pegs in a row. **1958** M. STEWART *Nine Coaches Waiting* iv. 45, I brought you a game ..called Peggitty. **1974** P. DICKINSON *Poison Oracle* ii. 60 Tribesmen..played their stone-age version of peggoty in noisy groups.

peggy ('pɛgɪ), *sb.* [Altered from *Meggy*, *Maggie* = MARGARET, of which it is a familiar equivalent (cf. PEG *sb.*[2]); hence in various local and dialectal uses.]
1. A man of feminine habits, a molly, a simpleton.
1869 *Lonsdale Gloss.*, *Peggy*, a simpleton.
2. A local name of various species of the Warblers (*Sylvia*) and allied genera of birds; also of the Pied Wagtail. See quots.
1848 *Zoologist* VI. 2137 (Leicestersh.) The whitethroat [is] a 'peggy', which term includes also the garden warbler. **1879** MISS JACKSON *Shropsh. Word-bk.* s.v., The Willow Warbler;..the Chiff-chaff; and..the Wood Warbler, are respectively and alike called *Peggy* and *Peggy-Whitethroat*. **1881** *Leicestersh. Gloss.*, *Peggy*, a name given to the garden warbler, the black-cap, both the whitethroats, the sedge-warbler, and probably others of the family. **1885** SWAINSON *Prov. Names Birds* 44 *Pied Wagtail*..Peggy dishwasher (Kent). **1887** *Kentish Gloss.*, *Peggy*.., Peggy-wash-dish.
3. = DOLLY *sb.*[1] 4 a. Hence **peggy-tub**.
1823 J. BADCOCK *Dom. Amusem.* 153 Family linen or home-made cloths may be bleached with much less..wear-and-tear, than is experienced in the use of the Yorkshire Peggy-tub. **1860** BRIERLEY *Tales Lancs. Life, Traddlepin F.* ii. 144 How well she looked at a tub—how dexterously she twisted her fat red arms about when..plying the 'peggy'. **1885** FENN *Patience Wins* (1886) 169 Clothes were washed in the peggy tub, and kept in motion by a four-legged peggy.. with a cross handle.
4. ***Peggy-with-*(*her-*)*lantern*** = JACK-A-LANTERN.
1855 *Shevvild Ann.* 9 (E.D.D.) As bad as follerin Peggy wit lantern. **1869** *N. & Q.* 4th Ser. IV. 508/2 Occasionally in the plashy meadows 'Jack or Peggy-with-lanthorn' was visible after dark. **1870** E. PEACOCK *Ralf Skirl.* II. 31 Dazed ..so as not to discern the flicker of a peggy wi' her lantern from the light of day.
5. *Naut. slang.* A ship's mess-steward or menial.
1902 A. B. LUBBOCK *Round the Horn* iii. 105 An institution on board a sailing-ship is 'peggy'. Each of us take it in turn, and peggy has to fetch the grub from the galley. **1929** F. C. BOWEN *Sea Slang* 102 *Peggy*, the man who looks after the seamen's and the firemen's messes in a modern liner. In the old sailing days it was applied to the ship's boy or to a hand who was called upon to do all the odd jobs in a watch. **1930** 'GREENHORN' *Tinker, Tailor* viii. 191 The sailors' Peggy is a kind of fo'c'sle steward, and..he has to wash up the pots and pans in the forrard galley, clean out the fo'c'sle, make the bunks, and generally keep the sailors' quarters swept and garnished. **1946** J. IRVING *Royal Navalese* 133 *Peggy*, an Ordinary Seaman detailed to act as Petty Officers' mess-man. **1967** S. WATERS *Indentures Indorsed* i. 11, I was initiated into the mysteries of acting as 'Peggy'. As the name implies this menial does all the domestic chores. **1972** *Courier-Mail* (Brisbane) 19 July 24/3 Some waterfront employers think Peggy should do other work..between tea breaks and lunch.
6. (See quots.) [Perh. a different word.]
1940 *Chambers's Techn. Dict.* 622/2 *Peggies*, slates 10–14 in. long. **1959** *Archit. Rev.* CXXV. 292 *Peggies*, small sizes of slates of random sizes which are sold by weight.
7. **peggy bag**, a style of women's hand-bag orig. having side handles and outside pockets; **peggy-work** *Naut. slang*, the work of a peggy (sense 5).
1920 *Scot at Hame an' Abroad* 1 July 5/3 Mirren had a when peppermints in her *peggy bag. **1922** *Daily Mail* 11 Dec. 13 (Advt.), Peggy bags with side handle and two outside pockets. **1939–40** *Army & Navy Stores Catal.* 874/4 Peggy Bag, in plain Calf..with divided inner compartment and mirror. **1974** *Trafford Catal.* Spring-Summer 182/2 Classic 'peggy' bag with twin easy-to-get-at compartments ..twin handle length straps. **1959** SCOTT-SHAWE & WYKES *Mariner's Tale* I. iii. 29, I was escaping my *peggy-work in the *Ashmore's* galley.

peggy ('pɛgɪ), *a.* [f. PEG *sb.*[1] + -Y.] Of the form of or resembling a peg.
1882 QUAIN *Med. Dict.* 1595/1 The lower incisors are peggy and pointed.

†'**peggy-mast.** *Sc. Obs.* Forms: 5 **pegy mast**, **pygy mast**, 6 **pege mast**, *ellipt.* (*pl.*) **piggeis**. A yard to which a pennon was attached.
1494 *Acc. Ld. High Treas. Scot.* I. 253 Ane gret mast, ane ra, ane swken, a pygy mast. **1496** *Ibid.* 300 A barel of pyk and a pegy mast to the said schip. **1505** *Ibid.* III. 86 To Robert Bertoun..for ane mozan mast and ane pege mast. **1513** DOUGLAS *Æneis* III. vi. 4 For the south wyndis blast Our piggeis and our pinsalis wavit fast.

pegh, **Peght**, variants of PECH, PICT.

'**pegless**, *a.* [See -LESS.] Not having a peg.
1896 *Daily News* 25 Nov. 6/5 [The bullet with a peg] its effect is much more deadly than the pegless one.

'**peglet.** [See -LET.] A little peg.
1890 *Temple Bar Mag.* Mar. 416 A couple of tent-pegs, which..he tightens by driving in supplementary peglets.

†'**pegma**, **pegme**. *Obs.* [a. L. *pēgma*, a. Gr. πῆγμα framework fixed together, movable stage or scaffold in a theatre, f. πηγ-νύειν to fasten.] A kind of framework or stage used in theatrical displays or pageants, sometimes bearing an inscription; hence *transf.* the inscription itself.
1603 B. JONSON *Jas. I's Coronat. Entertainm.* Wks. (Rtldg.) 529/1 In the centre..of the pegme, there was an aback or square, wherein this elogy was written. **1612** CHAPMAN *Widowes T.* II. Plays 1873 III. 34 We shall heare ..what Reuells: what presentments are towards: and who penn'd the Pegmas. **1623** MIDDLETON *Triumph Integr.* Wks. (Bullen) VII. 386 Four other triumphal pegmes, are.. planted to honour his lordship's progress through the city. **1647** WARD *Simp. Cobler* 26 The Verses are even enough for such odde pegma's.

pegmatite ('pɛgmətaɪt). *Min.* [f. Gr. πῆγμα, πηγματ- in sense of 'thing joined together or conglutinated' + -ITE[1].] A coarsely crystallized kind of granite, containing little mica. Hence **pegmatitic** (-'tɪtɪk), '**pegmatoid** *adjs.*, resembling or having the structure of pegmatite.
1832 DARWIN in *Life & Lett.* I. 238 At Bahia the pegmatite and gneiss in beds had the same direction. **1852** TH. ROSS *Humboldt's Trav.* II. xxiv. 460 The pegmatites, or graphic granites. **1864** WEBSTER, *Pegmatite*,..a variety of granite, in which the quartz, as seen over the surface, has some resemblance to Oriental writing;—called also *graphic granite*. **1896** *Natural Science* Aug. 86 The pegmatitic structure of so many igneous veins.

pego ('piːgəʊ). *slang.* [Origin unknown.] The penis.
1680 in Rochester *Poems* 36 As oft as Finger, Dildoe, Pego, Rape, The Virgin Hymen, she repaires the Gap. **1691** E. WARD *Poet's Ramble* 10 *Pego*, like an upstart Hector,.. Would fain have Rul'd as Lord Protector: Inflam'd by one so like a Goddess, I scarce could keep him in my Codpiece. *c* **1763** J. WILKES *Ess. on Woman* 19 Then shall man's pride and pego comprehend His actions and erections, use and end. **1788** GROSE *Dict. Vulgar T.* (ed. 2), *Pego*, the penis of man or beast. **1879–80** *Pearl* (1970) 250 This made Neddy's Pego, accustomed to sprout, Shrink into his belly, and turn up his snout. **1974** H. R. F. KEATING *Underside* ix. 90 There's some as likes..her dirty old fingers round their pego.

pegomancy ('piːgəʊmænsɪ, 'pɛgəʊ-). *rare.* [f. Gr. πηγή spring + -MANCY: in mod.F. *pégomancie* (Littré).] Divination by springs or fountains.
1727 in BAILEY vol. II. **1824** MCCULLOCH *Scotland* IV. 43 Omens are obtained..by the mode in which the air bubbles rise. This was the Pegomancy of the Greeks.

pe-goose, obs. form of PEAK-GOOSE.

†'**pegrall**, *a. Sc. Obs.* Also **peggrell**, **pygrall**. [Origin unascertained.] Petty, paltry, trifling.
1535 LYNDESAY *Satyre* 2653 Ane peggrell theif that steillis ane kow. **1555** *Satir. Poems Reform.* xxxvi. 126 That fals and degenerat seid Of Douglassis..That of his bluide resavit pe pygrall pryce. **1567** *Ibid.* iii. 121, I did reid,..How Acan tuik the excommunicat guid:..Gif God was wraith at ane small pegrall stouth [etc.].

'**peg-top**, **pegtop**. [f. PEG *sb.*[1] + TOP *sb.*]
1. a. A pear-shaped wooden spinning-top, with a metal pin or peg forming the point, spun by the rapid uncoiling of a string wound about it.
[**1740** DYCHE & PARDON, *Peg*..also the name of a small piece of steel or iron put into childrens toys, called castle-tops.] **1788** *Massachusetts Spy* 3 Apr. 4/3 Children's Books. .. Memoirs of a Pegtop. By the Author of, The Adventures of a Pincushion. **1801** STRUTT *Sports & Past.* IV. iv. 341 The peg-top, I believe, must be ranked among the modern inventions. **1812** H. & J. SMITH *Rej. Addr.*, *Baby's Debut* iii, Quite cross, a bit of string I beg, And tie it to his peg-top's peg. **1834** CAUNTER *Orient. Ann.* viii. 110 Here we saw several Hindoo children spinning tops, precisely like the common peg-top used by children in Europe. **1887** JESSOPP *Arcady* viii. 238 If there are two men in my parish who can spin a peg-top, I don't know the second. **1923** D. H. LAWRENCE *Birds, Beasts & Flowers* 171 Chieftains, three of them abreast, on foot Strut like peg-tops. **1978** *Country Life* 14 Dec. 2103/2 Tops: humming tops, peg tops, optical tops, gyroscopes.
b. A game of spinning peg-tops.
1803 [see *pea-shooter* s.v. PEA[1] 7]. **1828** *Boy's Own Bk.* 12 Regular games at peg-top are played... The object of each player being to split the tops of his companions. **1841** T. A. TROLLOPE *Summ. W. France* I. viii. 122 The pupils and their ecclesiastical masters began playing peg-top together. **1885** *New Bk. Sports* 313 Peg-top, like marbles, appears to have very much gone out in London. **1931** P. GUEDALLA *Duke* I. iv. 22 Nor do the martial virtues thrive upon a simple diet of peg-top and battledore.
2. *pl.* = *peg-top trousers*: see 3.
1858 *Punch* 15 May 202/2 The fashion of trowsers improves, if anything, in ridicule. Henceforth pegtops are split. **1859** FARRAR *Julian Home* xx, Cut-away coat, and mauve-coloured pegtops. **1862** H. KINGSLEY *Ravenshoe* lxvi, Better than pegtops and a black bowler hat, which strike no awe into the beholders.
3. *attrib.* Having or suggesting the shape of a peg-top, as ***peg-top form, vase, whisker***; **peg-top pants**, = *peg-top trousers*; **peg-top skirt**, a skirt that is wide at the top and narrow at the bottom; **peg-top trousers**, a form of trousers very wide in the hips and narrow at the ankles, in fashion *c* 1858–65.
1858 TREVELYAN *Cambr. Dionysia*, Nor picked a pocket; nor worn peg-top trousers. **1869** E. A. PARKES *Pract. Hygiene* (ed. 3) 415 The much-laughed-at pegtop trousers seem to be, in fact, the proper shape. **1894** *Daily News* 12 Oct. 7/3 The form of trousers inclines to change to the peg-top style. **1898** *Ibid.* 17 Jan. 8/6 'The early sixties'—or 'Crinoline and peg-top trouser period'. **1902** *Daily Chron.* 26 Apr. 8/3 The sleeve..shows a new pattern, called..'the peg-top', which is pleated above, and at the wrist..is banded with taffetas, fixed with buttons. **1917** *Times* 24 Jan. 9/5, I noticed yesterday in the leading papers the leading *couturiers* announced the 'new peg-top skirt, cut on most becoming lines'. **1923** E. B. WHITE *Let.* Feb. (1976) 63 A stunning suit—real western cut with peg top pants and everything. **1956** *Punch* 15 Aug. 190/3 This Autumn Collection..emphasizing a belted natural waist-line, short peg-top skirts, and a wrapped-up look. **1970** *Daily Tel.* 23 July 15 Pegtop pants were Patou's big contribution to yesterday's fashion scene. **1972** J. MINIFIE *Homesteader* xvii. 146 The baggy end of a drummer's blue peg-top pants. **1975** G. HOWELL *In Vogue* 222 Schiaparelli's slim silhouette with ..peg-top skirt.
Hence '**pegtopped** *ppl. a.*, having peg-top trousers; ***pegtopped skirt*** = *peg-top skirt*.
1861 *Illustr. Lond. News* 15 June 549/1 Two white-hatted and pegtopped ineffables. **1959** *News Chron.* 22 July 3/3 Gently fitted jackets over stiffened pegtopped skirts. **1973** *Country Life* 8 Mar. 632/3 If this peg-topped, tapered, pencil skirt does catch on there will be resounding cheers from the girdle manufacturers.

Peguan ('pɛgjuːən), *sb.* and *a.* Also **Pegue**, **Peguer**. [f. the place-name *Pegu* (see below) + -AN.] **A.** *sb.* **a.** A native or inhabitant of the city or district of Pegu in southern Burma, the ancient capital of the Mon (MON *sb.*[2] and *a.*) people. **b.** The language of the people of Pegu. **B.** *adj.* (Also **Pegu**, the place-name used *attrib.*) Of or pertaining to these people.
c **1591** R. FITCH in Hakluyt *Princ. Navigations* (1599) II. I. 262 The Pegues if they have a sute in the law which is so doubtfull that they cannot well determine it, put two long canes into the water..and there sit men to iudge, and they both do diue vnder the water. **1727** A. HAMILTON *New Acct. E. Indies* II. xxxvi. 36 The *Peguer* finding that he could not recover his Lands without foreign Aid and Assistance, invited the Portuguese. *Ibid.* 37 Neither the Siamers nor the Peguers..understood the use of Fire Arms. *c* **1759** [see KAREN *sb.* 1]. **1800** M. SYMES *Acct. Embassy to Ava* 12 The power of the Peguers now seemed hastening to its wane. **1828** [see MON *sb.*[2] and *a.*]. **1834** *Chinese Repository* II. 504 The most important is the *Peguan*. **1851** *Ibid.* XX. 345 Frequent wars with the northern Siamese and the Peguans, or *Mons*. **1858** C. T. WINTER *Six Months Brit. Burmah* ii. 15 The inhabitants consist principally of Burmans and Peguans. **1874** J. M. HASWELL *Gram. Notes & Vocab. Peguan Lang.* p. vi, I sent a list of over sixty Peguan words to missionaries among the Kohls. **1910** L. MILNE *Shans at Home* i. 26 A vassal of the Pegu King. *Ibid.* 27 The conquering army of the Pegu king. **1920** G. A. GRIERSON *Linguistic Survey India: Index of Lang.-Names* 164 Peguan ..According to the Burma Linguistic Survey, a form of Mōn (3) spoken in Amherst District. **1932** J. G. SCOTT *Burma & Beyond* i. 16 The Khmêr went, or were pushed, farther east,..but the Mōn remained behind, and came to be known to the early merchant adventurers as Peguans. **1942** J. L. CHRISTIAN *Mod. Burma* ii. 12 The Mons, known also as Talaings or Peguans, are an ancient race. **1955** E. MANNIN *Land of Crested Lion* xv. 190 The gift of a wealthy Pegu donor. **1956** *Introducing Burma* 38 The Mon Khmer Branch consists of the Mon Group comprising—Talaing (Mon, Peguan, Martabanèse) which are spoken in the Pegu and Tenasserim Divisions. **1973** J. M. & E. G. MARING *Hist. & Cultural Dict. Burma* 147 *Mon*, A lowland Mon-Khmer ethnolinguistic group of Mongoloid racial stock... Synonyms: *Moñ, Mun, Peguan, Talaing*.

pegyll, obs. form of PICKLE.

peh, var. P'O.

Pehlevi, Pehlvi: see PAHLAVI.

peice, obs. f. PIECE; obs. Sc. f. PACE *sb.*², PASCH, PEACE.

peich, peigh, var. PECH.

peiede, peiere, obs. ff. PAID, PAIR.

Peierls ('paɪəlz). *Physics.* The name of Sir Rudolf *Peierls* (b. 1907), German-born physicist, used *attrib.* with reference to a spatially periodic distortion of a linear chain of atoms or molecules in certain solids, adduced to explain an observed change from a conducting to a semiconducting or insulating state at low temperatures.

Described by Peierls in *Quantum Theory of Solids* (1955) 108.

1973 *Solid State Communications* XII. 1130/2 The important question is whether or not one can stabilize such a system just above the Peierls transition.., so that on lowering the temperature the superconducting state becomes truly stable. **1973** *Physical Rev.* VIII. B. 574/2 The experimental superperiod of 8 × 2·88 Å due to the platinum atoms is..in exact agreement with the expected superperiod as due to a 'Peierls distortion'. **1979** *Sci. Amer.* Oct. 54/3 The Peierls transition..comes about through a periodic distortion of the lattice.

‖**peignoir** (pɛɲwar). [F., in 16th c. *peignouoir* (in Hatz.-Darm.), f. *peigner* to comb.] A loose dressing-gown worn by women while their hair is being combed; a kind of linen or flannel gown put on on coming out of a bath; misapplied to a woman's morning-gown.

1835 *Court Mag.* VI. p. xxii/1 Pelisse robes, or peignoirs of light materials..are now universally adopted in promenade dress. **1837** THACKERAY *Ravenswing* i, I shall have on my peignoir. **1880** MISS BROUGHTON *Sec. Th.* II. x, Coolly wrapped in a white *peignoir* by her window.

Comb. **1880** 'OUIDA' *Moths* I. i. 12 The last bathers, peignoir-enwrapped, were sauntering up from the edge of the sea.

peignt, obs. f. PAINT.

peil, peill(e, peiler, obs. Sc. ff. PALE *v.*, PEEL, PEELER.

†'**peimander**. *Sc. Obs.* [app. corrupt ad. OF. *pimentier*, med.L. *pigmentārius*, f. *piment*:—L. *pigment-um* a spiced drink.] A preparer of or dealer in spices or perfumes; a perfumer.

1630–56 GORDON *Hist. Earldom Sutherland* (1813) 438 Their owne claime from Gulielmus de Sancto Claro, the king's peimander.

pein (pi:n, peɪn), *sb. dial.*, *techn.*, and *U.S.* Also 7 pen, 9 pean, pene, 9- peen. [Of uncertain origin: app. a northern and Sc. form of PANE *sb.*³, perh. influenced in form by PEEN *v.* But cf. Norw. *pen*, *pænn* 'the hinder sharpened part of a hammer' (Aasen), referred by some to Sw. dial. *pen*, *pän* (Reitz), Da. *peen* fine, neat (? orig. 'thin').] **a.** The sharp or thin end of a hammer-head, opposite to the face; = PANE *sb.*³ Hence, the other end of a hammer-head from the face, whether sharp-edged or rounded.

1683 MOXON *Mech. Exerc., Printing* xi. ⁋20 The Hammer ..hath no Claws but a Pen. **1688** R. HOLME *Armoury* III. 321/2 Smiths..Hammers have no claw or slit in the Pen, as those that are for drawing out of Nails. *Ibid.*, The Pen is the small end of [a hammer]. **1825** JAMIESON, *Peen*, the sharp point of a mason's hammer. **1881** [see PANE *sb.*³]. **1885** *Spons' Mechanics' Own Bk.* 84 This process is termed 'paning' or 'pening', from the pane or pene of the hammer being generally used to perform it. **1890** *Cent. Dict.* s.v. *Peen* vb., Striking regularly all over with the peen of a hammer. **1900** in *Eng. Dial. Dict.* from Sc. and north. Counties. **1904** W. H. VAN DERVOORT *Mod. Machine Shop Tools* (ed. 4) i. 17 The machinist hammer..is made of high-grade steel, carefully tempered on head and pene. **1939** *Specification for Hand Hammers (B.S.I.)* 7 On completion, the forgings shall be hardened on the striking faces and peins only. *Ibid.* 12 (*caption*) Engineer's ball pein hammer. **1943** D. J. SWARTZ et al. *Fund. Shopwork* (1945) i. 27 The peen hammer is widely used. The head is so shaped that one end, called the peen, can be used to produce dents or depressions or to set up tension in metal. **1947** J. C. RICH *Materials & Methods Sculpture* vi. 182 In working the heavier thicknesses of $\frac{5}{16}$ inch and the $\frac{3}{8}$ inch, larger ball pein hammers are required. **1961** *B.S.I. News* Oct. 24/1 Most of the trouble was due to ..heads too hard on either the striking face of the pein. **1964** S. CRAWFORD *Basic Engin. Processes* i. 16 The three types of hammer most generally used by the fitter are (a) Ball Pein, (b) Cross Pein, and (c) Straight Pein... All three are of a standard shape at the striking face end but can be readily identified by the shape of the opposite end known as the pein. **1971** B. SCHARF *Engin. & its Lang.* ix. 63 Ball-pein hammers have one ball-shaped end (pein, peen) for hand-riveting or burring over.

b. *Comb.*, as *pein-end* (of a hammer); *pein-ended* adj. (hammer); **pein-hammer**, a hammer having a peen or sharpened end; a shoemaker's hammer.

1885 *Harper's Mag.* Mar. 558/1 The differences between peen-hammers and bush-hammers. **1939** etc. [see sense a above].

pein, peine, obs. forms of PANE, PAIN.

peinct, peint, obs. forms of PAINT.

‖**peine** (peɪn). [F. *peine* (pɛn), PAIN.] Pain, punishment. In phrase *peine forte et dure* (†occas. partly anglicized): 'severe and hard punishment', a form of punishment, formerly inflicted on persons arraigned for felony who refused to plead, in which the prisoner's body was pressed with heavy weights until he pleaded or died; pressing to death. Also used allusively. (Cf. PENANCE *sb.* 5.)

1554 *Dial. on Laws Eng.* II. xli. 133 He shal haue paine fort and dure (that is to say) he shalbe pressed to death, and he shall there forfait his goods, and not his lands. [So **1721** *St. German's Doctor & Stud.* 277.] **1815** SCOTT *Guy M.* xxxvii, I hope she has had the conscience to make her independent, in consideration of the *peine forte et dure* to which she subjected her during her life-time. **1839** KEIGHTLEY *Hist. Eng.* I. 416 The 'peine forte et dure'..was not abolished till the middle of the 18th century. **1888** *Encycl. Brit.* (ed. 9) XXIII. 465/2 A case of *peine* occurred as lately as 1726. At times tying the thumbs with whipcord was used instead of the *peine*.

‖**peineta** (peɪ'nɛtə). [Sp.] An ornamental comb worn by Spanish women with a mantilla.

1935 *Discovery* Oct. 307/2 The *peineta*, or ornamental high shell-comb which together with the *mantilla* constitutes the national head-dress of Spanish women. **1939** SPENDER & GILI tr. *Lorca's Poems* 23 *Calañés* and tall *peinetas*.

peion, -oun, -onie, obs. ff. PIGEON, PEONY.

peip, peiple, obs. Sc. forms of PEEP, PEOPLE.

peir, obs. Sc. f. PEAR *sb.* and *v.*; obs. f. PIER.

peirameter (paɪ'ræmɪtə(r)). [mod. f. Gr. πεῖρα trial, attempt, endeavour + -METER.] (See quots.)

1842 FRANCIS *Dict. Arts*, etc., *Peirameter*, an instrument, invented by Mr. J. Macneil, which indicates the amount of resistance offered by the surfaces of roads, of different constructions, to the passing of wheel carriages, etc. **1875** KNIGHT *Dict. Mech.*, *Peirameter*,..a clumsy form of dynamometer, being dragged along on the ground. The power required to move it is indicated by a finger on a dial.

peirandlie (*Sc.*), apparently: see PEAR *v.*

peirastic (paɪ'ræstɪk), *a. rare.* Also pir-. [ad. Gr. πειραστικ-ός of the nature of trying, tentative, f. πειρᾶν to try.] Involving, or performing, an attempt or experiment; experimental, tentative. So †**pei'rastical** = *peirastic*; **pei'rastically** *adv.*, in the way of attempt or experiment, tentatively.

1656 STANLEY *Hist. Philos.* v. (1701) 175/1 Of Plato's Dialogues are Physick..Logick..Ethick..Politick ..*Pirastick. **1800** *Monthly Mag.* IX. 582 This work is wholly of the pirastic kind. **1859** KINGSLEY *Misc.*, *Tennyson* I. 215 One..belonging to a merely speculative and peirastic school. *a* **1647** SIR R. FILMER *Disc. Taking Use for Money* (1678) 4 A Father to stir up..the industry of his Son, doth lend him an hundred pound with a *peirastical Covenant for gain not intending..to take any interest at all. **1817** T. L. PEACOCK *Melincourt* xviii, Proceeding *pedetentim*, and opening the subject *peirastically.

Peirce (pɜ:s). The name of the American philosopher and logician Charles Sanders *Peirce* (1839–1914) used in the possessive to indicate his theories or methods, esp. as **Peirce's Law**, a logical formula relating to implication (see quot. 1967).

1918 C. I. LEWIS *Survey Symbolic Logic* i. 100 By a further important modification of Peirce's method, a theoretically adequate logic of mathematics may be obtained. **1934** W. V. QUINE *Syst. Logistic* vii. 64 $p \supset q. \supset p: \supset p$ This is Peirce's law... The theorem has been so named by Łukasiewicz. **1949** *Jrnl. Philos.* XLVI. 513 This paper assumes Peirce's semiotic as the basis for a discussion..of the logical paradoxes. **1954** I. M. COPI *Symbolic Logic* iii. 64 Assuming Peirce's Law false leads to a contradiction. **1955** A. N. PRIOR *Formal Logic* I. iii. 50 And so *p* is true (by 'Peirce's law'). **1967** S. C. KLEENE *Math. Logic* §3. 13 $((P \supset Q) \supset P) \supset P$. (Peirce's law, 1885). **1972** LAMBERT & VAN FRAASSEN *Derivation* 49 The following principle is known as Peirce's Law.

peirce, peire, obs. forms of PIERCE, PAIR.

Peircian ('pɜ:sɪən), *a.* [f. PEIRCE + -IAN.] Of or relating to the American philosopher, Charles Sanders Peirce, his theories or methods.

1905 *Mind* XIV. 237 The Peircian pragmatist. **1949** *Mind* LVIII. 130 Mr. Feibleman is a well-known Peircian scholar. **1952** *Mind* LXI. 205 This surely manifests a thoroughly Peircean attitude. **1965** *Amer. Philos. Q.* II. 115/2 We mobilize the Peircean idea of an inductive community. **1978** N. JARDINE in Hookway & Pettit *Action & Interpretation* 123 Such a picture of scientific progress may encourage, though it does not entail, a Peircean vision of an ultimate science, an omega of human knowledge in which the essences of all things are revealed.

peirl(e, peirrie, obs. forms of PEARL, PERRY.

peirs, var. PERSE *a. Obs.*; obs. f. PIERCE, PARSE.

peirt, obs. form of PERT.

peis, obs. f. PEACE, PEASE, PEISE, PIECE.

†'**peisage, pesage**. *Obs.* [ME. a. OF. *pesage*, f. *peser* to weigh, PEISE + -AGE.] A duty paid for the weighing of goods.

[**1321** ROLLS PARLT. II. 39 Concessimus..Ricardo de Byflet custodiam Pesagii in Portu et Villa Suthantonie.] **1455** *Rolls of Parlt.* V. 311 Profittes and Emolumentes of Waters, Fisshynges, Mylnes, Cranages, Stallages, Peisages, Passages. **1706** PHILLIPS, *Pesage*, a Custom or Duty paid for the weighing of Merchandizes or Wares. **1894** MRS. GREEN *Town Life in 15th C.* I. v. 183 'Pesage',..[a] toll..for the weighing of goods.

†'**peisant, 'pesant**, *a. Obs.* Forms: 5–6 **pesaunt**, 6–7 **peisant**, 5 **peysaunt**, 6 **peysant, pessant**, 7 **peizant**; (also 5–6 *Sc.* **paisand, paysand**). [ME. a. OF. *pesant*, pr. pple. of *peser* to weigh, PEISE; in spelling *peisant* assimilated to the Eng. form of the vb.; the Sc. *paisand* was prop. pr. pple. of *paise*, PEISE, = *peising*.]

Heavy. **a.** *lit.* Having great weight, ponderous. **b.** Forcible, as a blow given with a heavy body. **c.** *fig.* That weighs or presses heavily upon one; oppressive; toilsome. **d.** Weighed down, oppressed, as with drowsiness, etc.

α. *c* **1450** *Merlin* 119 Thei smote on his helme grete strokes and pesaunt. **1483** CAXTON *G. de la Tour* cxxxiv, His hede was ryght pesaunt and heuy. **1520** *St. Papers Hen. VIII*, VI. 55 He had seen Your Grace wellde one [sword] more pesaunt then the same. **1584** HUDSON *Du Bartas' Judith* II. in *Sylvester's Du Bartas* (1621) 700 Yet like the valiant Palme they did sustaine Their peisant weight, redressing vp againe. **1600** ROWLANDS *Knave of Clubs* (Percy Soc.) 5 Misers..Which with their moyling care and pessant paines, Had scraped thousands.

β. *c* **1470** *Golagros & Gaw.* 463 Pellokis paisand to pase, Gapand gunnys of brase. **1513** DOUGLAS *Æneis* VI. vi. 61 Vnder the paysand and the hevy charge.

Hence †'**peisantly** *adv.*, heavily.

1503 HAWES *Examp. Virt.* VII. viii, His strokes..were so peysantly on hym sette.

peisant, obs. form of PEASANT.

peiscush, variant of PESHCUSH.

peise (peɪz, pi:z), *sb. Obs.* exc. *dial.* Forms: 4–5 **peys**, 4–6 **peis**, 5 **pees**, 5–6 **peyce**; **peyse**, 5–7 **peise**; 6 **peasse, peysse, pece, pese, pease**; 6–7 **peize, peyze, peaze**. β. 4–6 **pays**, 5 **payce, paiss, paysse, pass(e**, 5–6 **pais**; **payse**, 5–7 **paise**, *Sc.* **pace**, 7 **paize**. [ME. *peis*, *peys*, in 16th c. (pe:s), a. early OF., ONF. and AF. *peis* (central Fr. *pois*, now *poids*) = Pr. *pens*, *pes*, Cat. *pes*, Sp. and It. *peso*:—L. *pensum* something weighed, weight, sb. from neut. pa. pple. of *pendĕre* to weigh. The forms in *-e*, when early, represent OF. *peise*, med.L. *pensa*, *pēsa*, fem. weight, of same derivation: see Du Cange. In 16th c. the two forms ran together as (pe:z).]

†**1.** The quality of being heavy; heaviness, weight. Also in semi-*concr.* sense, said of that which is heavy: cf. *weight, load, burden*. *Obs.*

c **1330** R. BRUNNE *Chron. Wace* (Rolls) 8792 Þo stanes.. Ar so heuy, & of swylk peys. **13..** *Coer de L.* 4095 Be pays it closes togeder agen. **1398** TREVISA *Barth. De P.R.* II. xviii. (1495) ciij/1 Angels..ben not greuyd wyth wyghte nother pees of body. *c* **1450** *Cov. Myst.* (Shaks. Soc.) 237 An holy ston Ryth sad of weyth and hevy of peys. **1534** MORE *Comf. agst. Trib.* III. xxvii. (1847) 312 Lift up and let hang with the peise of all his body, bearing down upon the..wounded places. **1582** T. WATSON *Centurie of Loue* xxvii, When Charons boate hath felt her peaze [*rime* ease]. *c* **1611** CHAPMAN *Iliad* XII. 167 A stone of such a paise, That one of this times strongest men, with both hands, could not raise. **1624** BP. MOUNTAGU *Immed. Addr.* 33 Where each part sustaineth the peise alone.

†**b.** In various fig. uses of 'weight': Gravity, importance; burden (of blame, punishment, responsibility); steadying weight, 'ballast'. *Obs.*

c **1470** HENRY *Wallace* VIII. 1441 All the haill pa[i]ss [*v.rr.* pes, pais] apon him selff he sal tak. *c* **1470** HENRYSON *Fables* XII. (*Wolf & Lamb*) viii. (Bann. MS.), Off his awin deid ilk man salbeir the paiss. *c* **1500** *Three Kings Sons* 100 He thought the matier was of grete peyce, wherfore he wolde make no sodeyn answere. **1568** GRAFTON *Chron.* II. 621, xv. thousand men, in whom consisted the waight and peyse of the whole enterprise. **1589** PUTTENHAM *Eng. Poesie* II (Arb.) 144 Full heauie is the paise of Princes ire. **1602** MARSTON *Antonio's Rev.* II. Prol., That with unused paize of stile and sense, We might waigh massy in judicious scale.

†**2.** Definite or specified weight; the amount that a thing weighs. *Obs.*

1382 WYCLIF *Jer.* lii. 20 Ther was no peis [1388 weiȝte] of the bras. **1389** in *Eng. Gilds* (1870) 38 Candils..brennyng abouten his corps, of xij. *lib.* peys. **14..** in *Hist. Coll. Citizen London* (Camden) 106 Newe nowblys..of lasse wyght thenne was the olde nobylle by the paysse of an halpeny wyght. **1540** *Rec. of Elgin* (1903) 48 That the leif baksteris obserwe and keip the peis and weych[t] giffin to tham. **1610** HOLLAND *Camden's Brit.* II. 59 He tooke the peise of some of them by hand.

fig. *c* **1412** HOCCLEVE *De Reg. Princ.* 1689 Aduoutrie and periurie, and wylful slaghtre,..lik ben, and o peys þei weye. **1555** J. PROCTOR *Hist. Wyat's Reb.* 45 And thereby outweye the iuste peize of bounden duetye.

†**b.** A definite measure of weight. *Obs.*

1419 in *Fabric Rolls York Minst.* (Surtees) 37 Et in iij sem' et in iij pais' albi vitri. **1552** *Nottingham Rec.* IV. p. xxvii, For euery peyse [of tallow] sold contrary to this [order].

†c. (*of peise*, or *attrib.*) Used to distinguish certain coins of special weight, as distinguished from others of the same name but lighter. *Obs.*

1451 *Sc. Acts Jas. II* (1814) II. 40/1 þe Inglis noble new noble callit of paise sal haif cours þan for xiijs. iiijd. **1456** *Ibid.* 46/1 þe henry Ingliss noble of paiss. **1463** in *Bury Wills* (Camden) 35, I..beqwethe to Seynt Edmond and his schryne my hevy peys noble, wich weyeth xxs. **1469** in *Somerset Medieval Wills* (1901) 215, 20s. of peise grotes.

3. *concr.* A weight; a piece or lump of some heavy substance used in some way on account of its weight; *spec.* (*a*) a standard weight by which to weigh goods; (*b*) one of the weights of a clock, by which its mechanism is moved. Now *dial.*

1303 R. BRUNNE *Handl. Synne* 5949 Fals peys and fals mesure. **13..** *K. Alis.* 1620 (Bodl. MS.) Wiþ peises [*v.r.* peys] stones and Gauelok Her fon hij gynnen fast to knok. *Ibid.* 1630 Summe wiþ peys was to ffrussht Summe wiþ gauelok to deþ lussht. **1377** LANGL. *P. Pl.* B. XIII. 246, I hadde neuer,..ȝut of þe popis ȝifte Saue a pardoun with a peys of led. *c* **1430** LYDG. *Min. Poems* (Percy Soc.) 246 Lyk an horloge whan the peys is goo. *c* **1440** *Promp. Parv.* 390/1 Peys of a welle, *telo*, in K. kyptre (*ciconia*). **1479** *Yation Churchw. Acc.* (Som. Rec. Soc.) 113 Makyng of the peysys of ledde upon the belowys. **15..** *Aberdeen Regr.* (Jam.), To wend [wind] the peassis thairof [of the clock]. **1600** R. CAWDREY *Treasurie* 60 A Clocke can neuer stand still from running, so long as the peases and plummets doo hang thereat. **1637** RUTHERFORD *Lett.* I. cxxxi. (1664) 255 The wheels, paces and motions of this poor Church. **1670–90** in Edgar *Old Ch. Life Scotl.* (1885) 35 [Getting cords for the] paizes. **1880** *W. Cornw. Gloss.*, *Paysen, peizen*, weights.

†b. *fig. Obs.*

c **1380** WYCLIF *Serm.* Sel. Wks. II. 321 þe peys of Goddis riȝt mut nedis wey after mennys werkes. *c* **1412** HOCCLEVE *De Reg. Princ.* 60 Best is I stryue nat Agayne the pays [*v.r.* peys] of fortunes balaunce. **1642** ROGERS *Naaman* 208 The peize and weight which this carnall world hangs upon a Religion of form.

†4. Forcible impact, as of a heavy body; momentum, impetus; a heavy blow or fall. *Obs.*

c **1489** CAXTON *Blanchardyn* lii. 201 Alle at one peyse cam and spored their horses nyghe vnto the ooste of Subyon. **1493** *Festivall* (W. de W. 1515) 35 With a grete peyse they let the crosse and the body fall downe togyder in to the mortesse. **1590** SPENSER *F.Q.* III. ii. 20 He [Ptolemy] with a peaze it [the glass tower] brake. **1602** MARSTON *Antonio's Rev.* v. i, That she may fal with a more waightie paise.

5. Balance, poise, equilibrium; suspense; the act of balancing or holding poised. Now *dial.*

a **1400–50** *Alexander* 3260 Houande here a hand-qwile and hingand in payse [*Dubl. MS.* on payse]. **1601** R. JOHNSON *Kingd. & Commw.* (1603) 263 Their forces may.. bee saide to be ballanced with a just and equall peyze. **1609** *Ev. Woman in Hum.* II. i. in Bullen *O. Pl.* IV, Let your faire hand be beame unto the ballance And with a stedded peyze lift up that beame. **1867** ROCK *Jim an' Nell* xxx. (E.D.D.), I've lost ma paise.

peise (peɪz, piːz), *v. Obs.* exc. *dial.* Forms: 4–7 peise, peyse, payse, 5 peysse, 5–6 pase, 5–7 paise, 6 payze, (peace), *Sc.* paisse, 6–7 peize, peyze, pease, paize, 7 peiz, peayse, peaze, pese. [ME. *peise*, repr. the stem-stressed form of OF. *peser* (3rd sing. pres. *peise*) = Pr. *pessar*, *pezar*, Sp. *pesar*, It. *pesare*:—L. *pēnsāre* to weigh, freq. of *pendĕre* to weigh. In 14th c. OF., *peise* often became *poise*, and this vocalization was sometimes extended to the inf., etc., e.g. *poiser*, *poisé*, *poisons*, *poiserois*. Cf. the mod.Eng. form POISE.]

†1. *trans.* To weigh, measure the weight of, as in a balance. Also *absol. Obs.*

1362 LANGL. *P. Pl.* A. v. 131 þe pound þ at heo peysede by. **1382** WYCLIF *Isa.* xlvi. 6 3e that..siluer with a balaunce peisen. *c* **1430** LYDG. *Min. Poems* (Percy Soc.) 190 Al my body peyssed in balaunce, Weiethe not an unce. **1571** DIGGES *Pantom.* III. xv. S iij, It mought be paised or waighed in Ballance. **1586** BRIGHT *Melanch.* xiv. 72 The ballance peaseth all kinde of waighty thinges alike. **1609** HOLLAND *Amm. Marcell.* 28 To weigh and peise the mountaines.

†b. *fig.* Of non-material things. *Obs.*

c **1430** LYDG. *Min. Poems* (Percy Soc.) 179 Graunt us.. Geyn our trespas gracious indulgence, Nat lik our meritis peised the qualitė. *a* **1557** GRIMALDE *Song, Prayse of Measurekepyng* 18 Stands largesse iust, in egall balance payzd. **1559** *Mirr. Mag., Hen. VI*, x, Our wit and willing power are paysed by his will.

c. To estimate the weight of, as by lifting or poising in the hand. In quot. 1390 with obj. cl.: to estimate or guess by doing this. Now *dial.*

1390 GOWER *Conf.* III. 314 This Maister to the Cofre is come, He peiseth ther was somwhat in. **1539** TAVERNER *Gard. Wysed.* II. 9 b, The seruaunt peysynge now this, nowe that boxe..at laste chase that whiche conteyned the lead. **1610** HOLLAND *Camden's Brit.* I. 34 Pearles, the bignesse and weight whereof he was wont to peise and trie by his hand. **1880** PEARD *Mother Molly* xi. 138 She had just 'pesed' it in her hand, and the weight was nothing.

†2. *fig.* To weigh in the mind; to deliberate upon, consider, ponder; to estimate. *Obs.*

1382 WYCLIF *Prov.* xxi. 2 The Lord forsothe peiseth the hertis. **14..** HOCCLEVE *Min. Poems* (1892) 57 þat he peise and weye What myn entente is. *a* **1548** HALL *Chron., Hen. VI* 145 Peisyng..the inconueniences, and harme that might fal. **1591** SYLVESTER *Du Bartas* I. ii. 1191 Lett's peiz and ponder Th' Almighties Works. **1633** P. FLETCHER *Purple Isl.* VIII. xvi, Those vaunts in balance peysing, Which farre their deeds outweigh'd.

†3. To place or keep in equilibrium; to hold suspended or supported; to balance, poise; also (quot. 1594), to cause to sway to and fro (like something suspended) while supported in the hand.

1388 WYCLIF *Prov.* viii. 29 Whanne he peiside the foundementis of erthe. **1513** DOUGLAS *Æneis* v. vii. 84 Eneas Pasis thair wecht als lychtlie as a fas. **1567** GOLDING *Ovid's Met.* VIII. (1593) 188 The workeman..Did peise his bodie on his wings, and in the aire on hie Hoong wauering. **1589** R. HARVEY *Pl. Perc.* (1860) 21 She peaseth the sword of Iustice with an vprighte hand. **1594** PLAT *Jewell-ho.* II. 47 Hee..caused an egge to stand alone by peyzing it to and fro betweene his handes. **1633** P. FLETCHER *Purple Isl.* II. vii, Upon this base a curious work is rais'd,..Though soft, yet lasting, with just balance pais'd.

†b. To bring into or hold in mutual equilibrium, as in the scales of a balance; to balance (two things) against each other, or (one thing) against another; to make equal in weight. Usually *fig.*

1450–80 tr. *Secreta Secret.* xx. 17 The wisdome of god peysith euenly, and ordeyneth alle thingis forto serve to his creaturis. **1601** R. JOHNSON *Kingd. & Commw.* (1603) 130 The citie of Lubecke..doth in so euen a ballance peayse the differences of these twoe nations; as it suffereth not the one to practise against the other. **1622** MALYNES *Anc. Law-Merch.* 183 The needle, being a bodie indued with two seuerall properties, the one of Grauitie, and the other of Leuitie, which being equally peized, forceth him to abide in the Horizon.

†c. To be of equal weight with, weigh as much as, balance, counterbalance. *Obs.*

1577 WHETSTONE *Remembr. Gascoigne* liv, You, in Ballance of deceit wil Lawyers payze, I feare with ouer waight. **1607** MIDDLETON *Family of Love* II. iv. 231 Whose want of stoare..could not peiz thvnequall scale of auarice.

†4. To put a weight upon, add weight to; to weight, load, burden; to weigh down; to oppress; to furnish with weights (quot. 1573). *lit.* and *fig.*

1422 tr. *Secreta Secret., Priv. Priv.* 199 He became mournynge and Sorefull and hugely hym peyset that he had god so mych y-grewid. **1525** LD. BERNERS *Froiss.* II. clxx. [clxvi.] 497 He were worthy to peyse the gybet. **1573–4** in Swayne *Sarum Churchw. Accts.* (1896) 122 For ij li. of Iron to payse the clocke iiijd. **1577–87** HOLINSHED *Chron.* III. 851/2 It would helpe to peize the ballance on his side. **1594** SHAKS. *Rich. III*, v. iii. 105 Lest leaden slumber peize me down. **1627** H. BURTON *Baiting Pope's Bull* To Rdr. 4 The wise Pilot, that can make vse of baser earth for balasse, to peize the vessell.

†b. *intr.* To press downwards by its weight.

1595 SPENSER *Col. Clout* 849 The cold began to covet heat, And water fire; the light to mount on hie, And th' heavie downe to peize.

5. *trans.* To drive, bear down, etc. by impact of a heavy body, or (generally) by force; to force. Now *dial.*

? *a* **1400** *Morte Arth.* 3038 Thane boldly þay buske, and bendes engynes, Payses in pylotes. *Ibid.* 3043 Paysede and pelid downe playsterede walles. *c* **1570** *Durham Depos.* (Surtees) 116 Thou harlott preist! peiste thou me? I will be here when I lyst, in spite of thy teithe.

b. To force (open, up, loose, etc.) by weight or pressure. *dial.*

1825 BROCKETT *N.C. Gloss.*, *Pase*,..to raise, to lift up, to open with violence. **1876** *Whitby Gloss.* s.v., 'Paze it loose, the lock is blunder'd'. **1894** *Northumbld. Gloss.*, *Paise*, to weigh up, as with a crowbar. 'Paise-up that flag-stone'.

6. *intr.* To have weight, be of a specified weight, weigh (so much). Now *dial.*

1362 LANGL. *P. Pl.* A. v. 131 þ e pound þat heo peysede by peisede a quartrun more þen myn Auncel dude. **1390** GOWER *Conf.* II. 135 Hou that it peiseth Above al other metall most. *c* **1430** LYDG. *Min. Poems* (Percy Soc.) 160 A purs that peiseth lihte. *a* **1470** TIPTOFT *Cæsar* xii. (1530) 15 Litell ryngys of yren paysing a certayn weyght. **1583** STUBBES *Anat. Abus.* II. (1882) 28 To vse sinister meanes to make it pease well in waight. **1882** *Reports Provinc.* 19 (E.D.D.) This will paze more than you think.

†b. *intr.* To press heavily, to weigh. *Obs.*

c **1450** *Merlin* 37 When thei fele that the werke peyseth hevy vpon them.

Hence **peised** *ppl. a.*; **'peising** *vbl. sb.* and *ppl. a.*

1382 WYCLIF *Eccl.* vi. 15 Peising of gold and of siluer. **1513** DOUGLAS *Æneis* VIII. v. 11 Furth of plaitis gret Wyth paissit flesche plenist the altaris large [L. *cumulantque oneratis lancibus aras*]. **1602** MARSTON *Antonio's Rev.* I. v, Whose well pais'd action ever rests upon, Not giddie humours, but discretion. *a* **1628** F. GREVIL *Mustapha* Chorus i, Wks. (1633) 95 As equall peising liberality.

peise, obs. form of PEACE, PEASE, PIECE.

†**'peiseless**, *a. Obs.* In 7 peizlesse. [f. PEISE *sb.* + -LESS.] Without weight; very light.

1606 SYLVESTER *Du Bartas* II. iv. III. *Magnificence* 978 Like peizlesse plume born vp by Boreas breath.

†**'peiser.** *Obs.* [f. PEISE *v.* + -ER[1]: cf. OF. *peseor*, *-eur*, in regimen *pesere*.]

1. One who weighs, ponders, or estimates.

1382 WYCLIF *Prov.* xvi. 2 Of spiritis the peisere is the Lord [1388 the Lord is a weiere of spiritis]. **1611** COTGR., *Peseur*, a peiser, weigher; ponderer.

2. An officer appointed to weigh goods, spec. the tin from the Cornish mines.

1485 *Rolls of Parlt.* VI. 366/1 The Office of Peyser, within oure Towne and Porte of Suthanton. *Ibid.* 383/1 The Offices of Peiser and Gaoler of oure Towne of Lestwithiell. **1602** CAREW *Cornwall* 14 The officers deputed to manage this Coynage are, Porters to beare the Tynne, Peizers to weigh it.

peishwa, -wah, variants of PESHWA.

Peisistratid, var. PISISTRATID *sb.* and *a.*

†**peisy**, *a. Obs.* In 6 peizie. [f. PEISE *sb.* + -Y.] Weighty, heavy.

1599 R. LINCHE tr. *Fount. Anc. Fiction* G, Compacted of solide and peizie lead.

peit, obs. form of PEAT.

peitrel: see PEYTRAL.

peizant, peize, variants of PEISANT, PEISE.

†**'pejerate**, *v. Obs. rare*$^{-0}$. [f. L. *pējerāt-*, ppl. stem of *pējerāre* (from *per-jūrāre*) to swear falsely.] *intr.* To forswear, commit perjury. So †**peje'ration** [ad. L. *pējerātiōn-em*], a false swearing, forswearing.

1650 BRINSLEY *Antidote* 7 When the Titles of God are abused,..by way of Pejeration..or by way of wicked swearing. **1656** BLOUNT *Glossogr.*, *Peierate*, to forswear, not to do that he hath sworn to do. **1658** PHILLIPS, *Pejeration*, a forswearing.

pejorate ('piːdʒəreɪt), *v.* [f. L. *pējōrāt-*, ppl. stem of *pējōrāre* to make worse, f. *pējōr-em* worse.] *trans.* To make worse, deteriorate, worsen.

1653 R. SANDERS *Physiogn.*, *Moles* 12 If black, it pejorateth these his good fortunes. *a* **1701** SEDLEY *Grumbler* I. i, Instead of meliorating, it pejorates. **1751** FRANKLIN *Ess.* Wks. 1840 II. 316 Slaves also pejorate the families that use them. **1893** STEVENSON *Catriona* iv. 39 You do not appear to me to recognise the gravity of your situation or you would be more careful not to pejorate the same.

pejoration (piːdʒə'reɪʃən). [ad. med.L. *pējōrātiōn-em*, n. of action from *pējōrāre*: see prec.]

a. A making or becoming worse, a worsening, deterioration; depreciation (of property).

1658 PHILLIPS, *Pejoration*, a making worse. **1659** GAUDEN *Tears of Ch.* I. xiv. 131 Which pejorations, as to the piety, peace and honour of this Nation, no man..can behold, without sad and serious deploring. *a* **1734** NORTH *Lives* (1890) III. 59 Everyone chose rather to pay for amelioration than receive for pejoration. **1831** BROUGHAM in Wilson & Shaw *Lords' Repts.* V. 295 What ameliorations and what pejorations are to be taken into the account?

b. *Linguistics.* The development of a less favourable meaning or of unpleasant connotations of a word.

1889 in *Cent. Dict.* **1939** L. H. GRAY *Foundations of Lang.* ix. 259 Their [*sc.* words'] degeneration (technically termed *pejoration*;..) is often due to a selection and specialisation of some ethically lower connotation which may be implied in them. **1956** *Archivum Linguisticum* VIII. 74 And is not pejoration a general feature of semantic development? **1966** *Word Study* Dec. 7/1 Perhaps Walt Disney would be interested in the pejoration and 'spread' of the name for his major cartoon character to a word now so loosely defined that it might some day take three dictionary columns to list. **1975** *Amer. Speech 1972* XLVII. 295 In the case of two English words, borrowing [in German] has resulted in pejoration.

pejorative ('piːdʒəreɪtɪv, pɪ'dʒɒrətɪv), *a.* and *sb.* [f. L. type **pējōrātīv-us*, f. ppl. stem of *pējōrāre*: see PEJORATE and -IVE: so mod.F. *péjoratif*.]

a. *adj.* Tending to make worse; depreciatory; applied especially to a derivative word in which the meaning of the root word is lowered by the addition of a suffix or otherwise. b. *sb.* A word of this character, as *poetaster*, *poeticule*, *poetling*.

1882 OGILVIE (Annandale) s.v., Poetaster is a pejorative of poet. *a* **1889** G. MASSON *Sel. Tales Mod. Fr. Writers* (1892) 252 This substantive has now a pejorative meaning. **1892** F. ADAMS in *N. & Q.* 8th Ser. II. 151/2 The Italian *boccaccia* is a pejorative form of *bocca*, a mouth, equivalent to the modern colloquial English 'ugly mug'. **1895** F. HALL *Two Trifles* i. *A Rejoinder* 35 Horne Tooke's pejorative *grammatist*, based on the unclassical Latin *grammatista*, was ..formerly in some vogue.

Hence **pejoratively** *adv.*, in a depreciative or deteriorated sense.

1890 in *Cent. Dict.*

pejorism ('piːdʒərɪz(ə)m). [f. L. *pējor*, *pējōrem* worse + -ISM, after *pessimism*.] The belief that the world is becoming worse.

1878 MAX MÜLLER *Hibbert Lect.* vii. 371 Man has believed in pessimism, he has hardly ever believed in pejorism. **1910** R. BROOKE *Let.* 7 Nov. (1968) 261 Pejorism is the Art of thinking things Worse than they Are in order that you may thereby be the more powerfully impelled to Better them.

pejorist ('piːdʒərɪst, 'pɛdʒərɪst). [f. as PEJORISM + -IST, after *pessimist*.] One who believes that the world is becoming worse.

1919 W. DE MORGAN *Old Madhouse* i. 3 Are we the better or the worse off by the change? The Optimist says better, the Pessimist says worse. I think the present writer must be sitting on a fence—a pejorist, suppose we say, since jargon is in vogue nowadays. **1932** *Times Lit. Suppl.* 14 July 508/4 Between optimists and pessimists there are those who style themselves..bonists, malists and pejorists. **1933** A. E. HOUSMAN *Let.* 5 Feb. (1971) 329, I am not a pessimist but a pejorist (as George Eliot said she was not an optimist but a meliorist). **1958** *Listener* 31 July 171/3 Why he [*sc.* A. E. Housman] was impelled to rape the major pejorists of five literatures for phrase and form to enable him to make poetry of his own predicament.

pejority (pɪˈdʒɒrɪtɪ). [f. as PEJORISM + -ITY.] The state or condition of being worse; worseness.

1615 T. ADAMS *Blacke Devill* 72 'The last state of that man shall be worse than the first' ... This pejority of his state may be amplified in six respects.

pek, obs. form of PECK *sb.*¹, *v.*¹, PICK *v.*¹

pekan (ˈpɛkən). [Canadian Fr. *pekan*, ad. Abnaki (Eastern Algonkin) *pékané* (Rasles).] A carnivorous beast (*Martes pennanti*) of the weasel family, a native of the northern parts of North America, valuable for its fur; called also Pennant's marten; = FISHER¹ 2 b; also, the fur of this beast.

1760 T. JEFFERYS *Nat. & Civil Hist. French Dominions* I. 37 The fur of this animal [*sc.* a kind of pole-cat], as also that of the Pekan, another creature of the wild-cat kind,..are what is called the *Menuë Peleterie*, or lesser furs. **1771** T. PENNANT *Synopsis Quadrupeds* 224 The *Pekan* and *Vison* of M. de Buffon resemble each other so nearly, that I do not separate them. **1796** MORSE *Amer. Geog.* I. 200 Fisher. In Canada he is called Pekan. **1870** J. YEATS *Nat. Hist. Commerce* II. 270 The pekan inhabits North America, and is also called Hudson's Bay Sable. **1877** COUES *Fur Anim.* iii. 65 The Pekan is much the largest of the genus, and indeed of the whole Weasel kind.., excepting only the Wolverene and Grison. **1910** E. T. SETON *Life-Hist. Northern Animals* II. 926 The name 'Pekan', first recorded by Charlevoix (1744) and popularized by Buffon 1765, is the Abenaki name, adopted without change. **1963** R. D. SYMONS *Many Trails* xvii. 177 It was one of the loveliest and rarest of fur-bearers—a pekan or fisher. **1973** R. FIENNES *Headless Valley* v. 93 Pekans are better known as Fishers which is strange since they never fish.

pekan, variant of PECAN.

Peke (piːk). Also Pek, Pekie. Abbreviation of PEKIN(G)ESE *sb.* c.

1915 *Vanity Fair* (N.Y.) Jan. 52/1 England has known the Peke for some time. **1920** *Chambers's Jrnl.* 21 Feb. 177/2 Adjoining were the kennels where the Pekies live. **1922** W. J. LOCKE *Tale of Triona* ix. 105 Instead of pulling your weight you think it's your right to sit on a cushion, a passenger—or a Pekie dog—and let other people pull you. **1924** GALSWORTHY *White Monkey* II. iv. 157 I'll see what I can do, if you'll lend me your Peke for an hour or so. **1926** *Spectator* 22 May 859/2 A young lady of fashion happens to be travelling to-day..with a couple of wardrobe trunks and a fortune in sables, satchels, vanity cases, also a 'Pek'. **1936** [see ICKLE *a.*]. **1956** E. BERCKMAN *Beckoning Dream* xiii. 95 The vacant eyes, round like a Peke's. **1973** *Listener* 9 Aug. 181/3 He gave me my first dog..a tiny Pekinese puppy... He came and broke the news to me about the death of that particular peke.

peke, obs. form of PEAK *v.*, PECK *sb.*¹, PEEK *v.*

‖**pekea** (piːˈkiːə). Also piqui, pikia. [The native name in Tupi. W. Piso *De Rebus Nat. Indiarum*, Amsterdam 1658, 141, has '*Pequea* sive *Pekia*'.] A tree (*Caryocar butyrosum*) of the tea family (*Ternstrœmiaceæ*), native to Guyana, valuable for its timber, and producing nuts resembling the souari- or butter-nuts, but more oily.

1810 SOUTHEY *Brazil* III. 758 The piqui is of more importance to a country like Piauhy where drought is the great evil. **1863** BATES *Nat. Amazon* viii, The pikia..bears a large eatable fruit. **1866** *Treas. Bot.* 229/1 C[*aryocar*] *butyrosum*..is called Pekea by the natives,..its timber..is valuable for ship-building, mill-work, etc.

pek-ex, obs. form of PICKAXE.

Peking, Pekin (ˈpiːkɪŋ, -ˈkɪn). [a. F. *Pékin*, the Jesuit Missionaries' spelling of the Chinese *Pē-king* (ˈpeːˈkiːŋ), lit. 'northern capital' (opposed to *Nānking* 'southern capital'), the name of the capital of China; hence, applied attrib. or elliptically.]

The distribution of the spellings *Peking* and *Pekin* is uneven: for convenience, in sense 3 below, the spelling *Peking* is given but in some of the *attrib.* and *Comb.* uses *Pekin* occurs with equal or greater frequency.

1. a. A kind of silk stuff.

1783 JUSTAMOND tr. *Raynal's Hist. Indies* III. 193 Valencia manufactures Pekins superior to those of China. **1835** *Court Mag.* VI. p. ii/1 Some of the most novel promenade robes are composed of pekin. **1891** *Daily News* 24 Feb. 5/3 The material was..striped brocade or pekin, having on the silken stripes flowers in old rose. **1954** 'M. COST' *Invitation from Minerva* 105 The mahogany bed was draped with Pekin.

attrib. **1848** THACKERAY *Bk. Snobs* iv, The most superb Pekin bandannas.

b. A type of Chinese rug or carpet.

1904 M. B. LANGTON *How to know Oriental Rugs* viii. 223 The Peking, Tientsin, and Samarkand are the only varieties known in this country. **1913** G. G. LEWIS *Pract. Bk. Oriental Rugs* (rev. ed.) 303 Those [rugs] which reach our own shores are generally divided into three classes according to the districts from which they came, namely, Pekin, Tientsin and Thibet. **1962** C. W. JACOBSEN *Oriental Rugs* 270 The Peking is a medium priced rug, costing much less than the Sarouk and half that of a good Kirman.

c. = *Peking duck* (a).

1885 *Encycl. Brit.* XIX. 647/1 The Pekin, a white breed with pale yellowish tint in the plumage, and a very bright orange bill. **1902** *Ibid.* XXXI. 882/2 Some duck-farmers in England have..also adopted the Peking. **1972** *Guardian* 24 May 9/1 You've got your Peking, your Aylesbury, your Muscovy.

‖**2.** Fr. *pékin, péquin* (pekɛ̃): A name originally given by the soldiers under Napoleon I to any civilian; occasional in English use.

[Referred by Littré to sense 1, trousers of pekin being much worn under the Empire. Hatzfeld and Darmesteter consider this derivation doubtful.]

1827 SCOTT *Napoleon* III. 70 These professional troops.. were quite ready to correct the insolence of the pekins (a word of contempt, used by soldiers to those who did not belong to their profession). **1870** *Spectator* 19 Nov. 1371 Study was actually discouraged as fit only for pékins, and diplomatists often knew little more than soldiers. **1870** LOWELL *Study Wind.* (1886) 81 There was hardly such a thing as a *pékin*. **1899** *Speaker* 16 Sept. 282/2 The pékin, even when he sits in the Court of Cassation, is treated with contempt.

3. *attrib.* & *Comb.*, as ***Peking carpet, crepe, rug***; **Peking duck**, (*a*) a large white duck with yellow bill and legs, belonging to a breed imported from China to Britain and the U.S.A. in 1873; (*b*) a speciality of Chinese cuisine; **Peking Labrador** (see quot.); **Peking man**, a fossil hominid, *Homo erectus pekinensis*, first described in 1926 from remains found in caves near the village of Choukoutien; **Peking opera**, a stylized form of opera which evolved in China during the nineteenth century; ***Peking point*** (see quot.); **Peking spaniel** = PEKIN(G)ESE *sb.* c; **Peking stripe** (see quots.).

1969 G. SIMS *Sand Dollar* i. 14 He slumped down further in the chair, letting his feet sink deep into the Pekin washed-silk carpet. **1971** *Nat. Geographic* Oct. 548/2 The Westerner who makes his way past the propaganda finds Shantung silk, Swatow lace, Peking carpets. **1972** P. L. PHILLIPS tr. *Formenton's Oriental Rugs & Carpets* 237 (*caption*) Typical Pekin carpet woven in the second half of the nineteenth century. **1895** *Montgomery Ward Catal.* 7/2 Pekin Crepe or Momie Cloth, 29 inches wide, used for fancy party dresses, draperies, etc. **1880** L. WRIGHT *Illustr. Bk. Poultry* (rev. ed.) xxxv. 541 The Pekin Duck is one of the most valuable of recent introductions... The Pekin Duck differs from all others in the shape and carriage of its body, which is a peculiar boat or barge shape. **1902** *Encycl. Brit.* XXXI. 882/2 In America the Peking duck is universally used, and has been made by selection both larger and a better layer. **1955** F. OLIVER *Chinese Cooking* ii. 53 Peking Duck..is one of the great Chinese dishes and was always on the banquet menu in Peking. **1973** L. HELLMAN *Pentimento* (1974) 185, I was driving back to the farm trying not to listen to the noise that came from two crates of Pekin ducks. **1964** LEE SU JAN *Fine Art of Chinese Cooking* xii. 94 The recipe for the authentic Peking Duck appears in this chapter. The incomparable flavour of the duck is a result of the vapours of the wine, soy sauce, and other condiments penetrating the meat. **1973** *Country Life* 15 Mar. 699/1 The infinite variety of Chinese food, with classic dishes such as Peking duck and shark's fin soup. **1974** *Encycl. Brit. Macropædia* VII. 943/2 The greatest of all delicacies of this region is of course the Peking duck. This elaborate, world-renowned dish requires lengthy preparation and is served in three separate courses. **1975** *Nature* 6 Mar. 12/3 The Peking duck originated in China and was first noted in the U.S.A. around 1870. **1960** C. W. CUNNINGTON et al. *Dict. Eng. Costume* 268/2 *Pekin Labrador*,..a Pekin silk flowered in wreaths. **1926** *Peking Leader* 24 Oct. in *Bull. Peking Soc. Nat. Hist.* (1928) II. IV. p. xvii (*heading*) Notable archaeologists deliver addresses at 'Peking Man' meeting. *Ibid.* p. xix, His [*sc.* J. G. Andersson's] work..culminated in the discovery of the two teeth of the 'Peking Man' (Dr. Andersson did not call the ancient inhabitant by that title, but probably this will be his popular designation). **1929** *Times* 30 Dec. 9/4 The Peking man is considered to antedate Neanderthal man, and is held to be nearer the genus *Homo* than the Piltdown and Java types. **1937** *Discovery* Jan. 27/1 'Peking Man' Skulls. A fifth skull, which may prove to be the most important of all, has been found at Choukoutien. **1946** J. S. HUXLEY *Unesco* i. 10 They [*sc.* man's innate mental powers] certainly were improved..in the earliest stages of his career, from Pekin man through the Neanderthalers to our own species. **1955** *Proc. Prehist. Soc.* XXI. 39 The oldest undoubted hearths are those recorded in the Choukoutien caves, occupied by Peking Man at the beginning of the second interglacial period. **1973** *Listener* 10 May 605/2 The classical find of *Homo erectus* was..made in China. He is Peking man, about four hundred thousand years old. **1976** *Times Lit. Suppl.* 7 May 544/5 There is an interesting, if speculative, account of the nature, habits and affinities of Peking Man. **1954** *Folk Arts of New China* 41 Peking Opera is traditionally played by men even to the female characters. Peking Opera has no sets or scenery. **1965** S. KNIGHT *Let.* 1 Oct. in *Window on Shanghai* (1967) xv. 65 Extracts from Peking opera—three modern and one ancient, the story of how the Monkey King ate the peaches of Immortality. **1968** *Guardian* 4 Nov. 7/5 Peking opera..is extremely formal, a mixture of song, dance, music, and acting. Each movement and gesture and every word sung or recited is synchronised with the music. **1970** W. APEL *Harvard Dict. Music* (ed. 2) 153/1 The Peking opera has a short history (*c.* 100 years). Although the highly stylized singing and acting demands a cultivated taste, the Peking opera remains the most popular musical art form. **1971** *Guardian* 28 Dec. 12/3 The essence..is communicated to the children through slides, films..revolutionary Peking opera, books, posters. **1973** *Listener* 19 July 84/3 After 1949, a great attempt was made to play down what had become the Court opera—Peking opera—and to encourage the local traditions. **1974** *Encycl. Brit. Macropædia* XII. 675/2 Credit for the beginning of Peking opera is given to actors from Anhwei appearing in Peking in the 1790s. But Peking opera really combines elements from many different earlier forms and, like Western grand opera, can be considered to be a 19th-century product. **1960** C. W. CUNNINGTON et al. *Dict. Eng. Costume* 268/2 *Pekin point*,..a very rich white silk painted with flowers or bouquets with foliage, with a light mixture of gold in the pattern. **1962** C. W. JACOBSEN *Oriental Rugs* 270 A Peking rug is a Chinese design rug, hand woven in Japan. **1913** A. CONAN DOYLE *Poison Belt* (ed. 2) v. 163 There were three gaily dressed women, all young and beautiful, one of them with a Peking spaniel upon her lap. **1908** *Dry Goods Economist* 13 June 81/3 Péking, or pekin stripes.—A design in stripes of alternating colors, the stripes usually being of equal widths. **1960** C. W. CUNNINGTON et al. *Dict. Eng. Costume* 268/2 *Pekin*,..a silk textile of the nature of taffeta, having fine stripes running through it; hence 'Pekin stripes'.

Pekin(g)ese (piːkɪˈniːz, piːkɪˈŋiːz), *sb.* and *a.* [f. *Pekin(g)* (see PEKING) + -ESE.] **A.** *sb.* **a.** A native or inhabitant of Peking. **b.** The form of Chinese used in Peking. **c.** A Pekingese dog. **B.** *adj.* Of or pertaining to Peking; applied esp. to a breed of dwarf pug-dogs with long, silky hair, obtained originally from the Imperial Palace at Peking; ***Pekingese stitch***, a stitch in embroidery.

1849 *Ann. Propag. Faith* Mar. 94, I have been informed that you speak..Pekinese. **1866** *Leisure Hour* XV. 45/2 (*heading*) Peking and the Pekingese. **1879** *Good Words* 745/1 It is old and stiff like Pekingese Buddhism. **1888** *Peel City Guardian* 14 Apr. 281/5 A singular Pekingese New Year custom is mentioned in the Shen Pao. **1898** *Kennel Gaz.* June 266/2 Foreign Dogs..Pekin Primula..(Pekinese Spaniel). *Ibid.* July 299/3 Foreign Dogs. Jock (Pekinese Pug). **1902** *Ibid.* Jan. 19/1 In the hurried departure of the Court from Pekin during the late war..not a single Pekinese Spaniel was left to..be annexed as loot. *Ibid.* Apr. 127/3 In future the breeds will be known as 'Japanese' and 'Pekinese' only, and neither the term spaniel nor pug added. A separate Classification on the Register of Breeds has also been given to 'Pekinese'. **1904** H. COMPTON *20th Cent. Dog.* I. 261 It is now more than forty years since the first specimens of the Pekinese dog, or lion-dog of China, were imported into England. *Ibid.* 262 Thirty years had to elapse before the Pekinese dog became—I cannot call it popularised..but rather say, in evidence. **1906** *Field* 20 Oct. 663/2 Pekingese were forward in strong numbers, the best dog weighing [etc.]. **1910** *Encycl. Brit.* VI. 216/2 Cantonese is supposed to approximate most nearly to the primitive language of antiquity, whereas Pekingese perhaps has receded farthest from it. **1914** R. B. LEE *Hist. & Descr. Mod. Dogs Gt. Brit. & Ireland* (*Non-Sporting Division*) (ed. 3) Add. p. i, Many additions to the classification..have been made... The most remarkable instance..is that of the Pekingese. *Ibid.* p. v, An ideal Pekingese must have a long coat with a thick undercoat, straight and soft, neither curled nor wavy, the feather on thighs and legs long and profuse. The tail should be carried high on the loins in a loose curl. **1919** G. B. SHAW *Heartbreak House* II. 81 She has the Ancient Mariner on a string like a Pekinese dog. **1920** *19th Cent.* Sept. 384 The Grand Duchess Tatiana carried in her arms her little Pekingese dog. **1931** A. C. DIXEY *Lion Dog of Peking* III. i. 150 The Pekingese is above all fearless and sporting. **1932** D. C. MINTER *Mod. Needlecraft* 46/1 Pekinese stitch..is.. most effective... A study of Chinese work will show this stitch worked..in fine silks to give beautiful graded effects. **1934** M. THOMAS *Dict. Embroidery Stitches* 159 Pekinese Stitch may be used as a line stitch or as a solid filling where shading is necessary, and is very pretty and braid-like in effect. **1935** [see CRISP *sb.* 7]. **1950** D. JONES *Phoneme* vi. 17 In Pekingese, too, we find that the difference between the first (high-level) and third (low-rising) tones is accompanied by a difference of vowel quality and of length. **1958** *Proc. 8th Internat. Congr. Linguists* 764 Language reform in China covers the reform of the Chinese script and the standardization of Pekingese as the national language. **1960** B. SNOOK *Eng. Hist. Embroidery* 50 The stitches used [*sc.* in Black work] include chain, back, sword, Pekinese,..and speckling. **1969** *Queen* 17–30 Sept. 14/2 The hot sour soup ..and Peking duck are authentic examples of the subtle art of Pekingese cuisine. **1970** *Language* XLVI. 675 Even though Pekingese is hardly a rugged testing-ground for methods of describing phonotactic distributions..it might offer a very real test for certain kinds of prosodic analysis. **1976** A. POWELL *Infants of Spring* iii. 51 A conspicuous member of the household was Pekoe, my mother's pekinese, so huge in size that he was once mistaken for a St Bernard puppy.

Pekin(g)ology (piːkɪˈnɒlədʒɪ, piːkɪŋ-). [f. *Pekin(g)* (see PEKING) + -OLOGY.] The study of Chinese politics and current affairs.

1962 *Economist* 21 Apr. 228/1 Pekinology is the murkiest of arts, and it takes something like extra-sensory perception to glean much about Chinese policy from the session. **1966** *N.Y. Times* 3 Apr. IV. 6 Practitioners of the recondite art of Pekinology say that if Chairman Mao died tomorrow the party leadership probably would fall. **1976** *Pacific Affairs* XLIX. 126 Inevitably, a study of China's past zone of expansion leads geographically up to and into the zone of Russia's more recent expansion, and here power-politics, geo-politics, Kremlinology and Pekinology raise their hydra heads.

So **Pekiˈn(g)ologist**, an expert on or student of Chinese politics and current affairs.

1962 *Economist* 21 Apr. 228/2 He [*sc.* Chou En-Lai] mentioned light and heavy industry in that order (which is the kind of clue that Pekinologists have to fall back on). **1966** *Guardian* 27 July 8/6 If Mao wasn't actually ailing through all these months of secluded speculation, what was he doing? Our tame Pekinologist suggests: training for his epic swim. **1968** W. SAFIRE *New Lang. Politics* 76/1 A new synonym for China watcher is 'Pekingologist', coined on the analogy of Kremlinologist. **1969** *Punch* 2 Apr. 478 Fleet Street is said to be desperate for reliable Pekinologists who can churn out a thousand weekly words on the Chinese enigma. **1972** D. BLOODWORTH *Any Number can Play* xvi. 150 They've had the pekinologists declaring Mao dead, blind, gaga.

pekk, -e, obs. forms of PECK *sb.*¹

peko, var. PIKAU *sb.*

pekoe (ˈpɛkəʊ, ˈpiːkəʊ), *sb.* Also 8 peco, pecko, peckho. [From Chinese: in Amoy dialect *pek-ho*, in Cantonese *pak-ho*; from *pek*, *pak* = Mandarin *peh*, *pai* white + *ho*, Mandarin *hao* down, hair.] A superior kind of black tea, so called from the leaves being picked young with the down still on them.

1712 ADDISON *Spect.* No. 328 Coffee, Chocolate, Green, Imperial, Peco, and Bohea-Tea seem to be Trifles. **1771** J. R. FORSTER tr. *Osbeck's Voy.* I. 250 Back-ho, or Pack-ho, is that which we call Peckho, which has leaves with dots. **1859** SALA *Tw. round Clock* (1861) 141 The huge tea ware-houses, where..the flowery Pekoe or the family Souchong, slumbers in tin-foiled chests.

Hence ˈ**pekoe** *v. trans.*, to mix with pekoe tea.

1892 WALSH *Tea* (Philad.) 182 A choice or 'pekoed' Formosa will be found the most desirable and valuable. *Ibid.* 184 If the Assam be 'pekoed' so much the better.

pekul, variant of PICUL, a weight.

‖**pel.** *Obs.* [Anglo-Fr., = OF. *pel*, mod.F. *pieu*:—L. *pālus* stake: see PEEL *sb.*[1]] A stake at which swordsmanship was practised in the 14th century.

1801 STRUTT *Sports & Past.* III. i. §3 (paraphrasing AF. MS. of 14th c.) The author..strongly recommends a constant and attentive attack of the pel..for so he calls the post-quintain... The practitioner was then to assail the pel, armed with sword and shield, in the same manner as he would an adversary.

pel, obs. form of PALL, PEEL *sb.*[1], PELL *sb.*[1]

‖**pela, pé-la** (ˈpeɪlɑː). [Chinese *pai, pe-, peh-* white + *la* wax.] The white wax obtained in China from the wax insect (*Coccus pela* or *sinensis*); Chinese or China wax.

1794 PEARSON in *Phil. Trans.* LXXXIV. 383 The Chinese collect a kind of wax, much esteemed by them, under the name of Pé-la, from a coccus deposited..on certain shrubs.

‖**pelada** (pɪˈlɑːdə). *Path.* Also in Fr. form **pelade.** [F. *pelade* a disease that causes falling off of down or hair, f. *peler* to deprive of hair.] (See quots.) Hence **peladic** (pɪˈlædɪk) *a.*, of or pertaining to pelada.

1753 CHAMBERS *Cycl. Supp.*, *Pelada*, a kind of alopecia, or distempered state of the body, occasioning the shedding of the hair, arising from a venereal cause. **1857** in MAYNE. **1899** *Allbutt's Syst. Med.* VIII. 905 Microbacillus of the 'peladic utricle'... Found in the ampulliform dilatations of the hair follicles..in enormous numbers.

†**pelaˈdor, -ore.** *Obs. rare*[−1]. [a. Sp. *pelador* 'one that pilleth, maketh bald, or bare' (Minsheu), f. *pelar*:—L. *pilāre*: see PILL *v.*] A depilatory.

1616 B. JONSON *Devil an Ass* IV. iv, To know how to make Pastillos of the dutchess of Braganza,..The peladore of Isabella.

pelage, obs. form of PILLAGE.

pelage (ˈpɛlɪdʒ). [a. F. *pelage* (16th c. in Littré), the hair, wool, or fur of an animal, in reference to its kind or colour, f. OF. *peil, pel*, F. *poil* hair, down + -AGE. (Cf. *peler* to deprive of hair.)] A general and collective term for the fur, hair, wool, or similar covering of a quadruped. (Parallel to *plumage*.)

1828–32 WEBSTER, *Pelage*, the vesture or covering of wild beasts, consisting of hair, fur or wool. *Bacon.* **1848** S. W. WILLIAMS *Middle Kingd.* I. iv. 156 Bear, wolves, tigers, deer, and numerous fur-bearing animals are hunted for their pelage. **1866** HUXLEY *Preh. Rem. Caithn.* 132 The ass and the zebra are far more strikingly differentiated by their pelage than by their skulls. **1877** J. A. ALLEN *Amer. Bison* 456 A young male in summer pelage.

pelagial (pɪˈleɪdʒ(ɪ)əl), *a.* [f. L. *pelagi-us*, a. Gr. πελάγι-ος of the sea (f. L. *pelag-us*, a. Gr. πέλαγος the sea) + -AL[1].] Of or belonging to the open sea; = PELAGIAN *a.*[2] 2, PELAGIC *a.*

1899 J. A. THOMSON *Sci. of Life* xiii. 179 The distinctive population of the littoral, pelagial, abyssal, fluvial, and terrestrial areas.

Pelagian (pɪˈleɪdʒɪən), *a.*[1] and *sb.*[1] [f. L. *Pelagiān-us* (Augustine), f. *Pelagius*, latinized form (see prec.) of the name of a British monk of the 4th and 5th centuries, whose doctrines were fiercely combated by St. Augustine, and condemned by Pope Zosimus in A.D. 418.

1645 PAGITT *Heresiogr.* (1662) 229 Pelagius..his name in Welsh was Morgan, which signifies the sea.]

A. *adj.* Of or pertaining to Pelagius or his doctrines.

Pelagius denied the Catholic doctrine of original sin, asserting that Adam's fall did not involve his posterity, and maintained that the human will is of itself capable of good without the assistance of divine grace.

1579 W. WILKINSON *Confut. Familye of Loue, Brief Descr.*, Many a simple soule hath hee shamefully..deceiued with his foule Pelagian opinion. **1651** BAXTER *Inf. Bapt.* 263 Origen..being a leader and Patron of the Pelagian error. **1697** SOUTH *Serm.* (1698) III. 45 Throughout all this Pelagian Scheme, we have not so much as one Word of Mans Natural Impotency to Spiritual Things. **1879** FARRAR *St. Paul* II. 216 *note*, The Pelagian [theory] treats Adam's sin as a mere bad example.

B. *sb.* A follower of the doctrines of Pelagius.

1532 MORE *Confut. Dr. Barnes* VIII. Wks. 798/2 Sayncte Austin wrote..those woordes against..the Pelagians and the Celestians. **1553** *Articles of Religion* ix, Originall Sinne standeth not in the following of Adam, as the Pellagianes doe vainelie talke,..but it is the fault, and corruption of the nature of euery manne, that naturallie is engendred of the offspring of Adam. **1706** J. BINGHAM *Fr. Ch. Apol.* III. x, None ever disliked the use of the Lord's Prayer but only the Pelagians. **1884** RUSKIN *Pleasures of Eng.* 16 The Pelagian's assertion that immortality could be won by man's will.

pelagian (pɪˈleɪdʒɪən), *a.*[2] and *sb.*[2] [f. L. *pelagi-us* (see PELAGIAL) + -AN.]

A. *adj.* †1. Of or pertaining to the *pelagiæ conchæ* or sea shells whence purple dye was obtained. (Cf. L. *pelagium* purple colour.) *Obs.*

1601 HOLLAND *Pliny* II. 259 The Tyrians make their deep red purple, by dipping their wool first in the liquor of the Pelagian purples.

2. Of, pertaining to, or inhabiting the open sea or ocean; pelagic.

1746 DA COSTA in *Phil. Trans.* XLIV. 400 They are no pelagian Shells, as those are; Bays and Harbours are the Places where they are fish'd. **1776** —— *Conchol.* 66 Some [shell-fish] are pelagian, or inhabit only the deeps of the sea. **1832** LYELL *Princ. Geol.* II. 126 A line of shoals may be as impassable to pelagian species, as are the Alps and the Andes to plants and animals peculiar to plains.

b. Inhabiting islands in the open sea or ocean.

1842 PRICHARD *Nat. Hist. Man* (ed. 2) 346 Pelagian Negroes have long been well known as inhabitants of the interior of the Penang Islands.

B. *sb.* An inhabitant of the open sea or ocean.

1854 BADHAM *Halieut.* 75 The Mediterranean pelagians (or open sea-fish) have neither brilliancy of colour, nor delicacy of flesh.

Pelagianism (pɪˈleɪdʒɪənɪz(ə)m). [f. PELAGIAN *a.*[1] + -ISM.] The doctrine of Pelagius and his followers: see PELAGIAN *a.*[1]

1583 FULKE *Defence* viii. (Parker Soc.) 342 While you would seem to fly from Pelagianism, you fall into flat Pharisaism. **1651** BAXTER *Inf. Bapt.* 313 This doctrine which hangs the efficacy of the Holy Ghost upon man's Will, ..is downright Pelagianism. *a* **1744** BOLINGBROKE *Let. to Pope* Wks. 1754 III. 332 To assert Antipodes might become once more as heretical as arianism, or pelagianism. **1855** MILMAN *Lat. Chr.* XIV. iii. (1864) IX. 145 The Pelagianism charged against Scotus is..purely metaphysical.

Pelagianize (pɪˈleɪdʒɪənaɪz), *v.* [f. as prec. + -IZE.] *intr.* To act the Pelagian; to hold or give expression to the views of Pelagius.

1625 BP. MOUNTAGU *App. Cæsar* 83 In the point of Freewill the Church of Rome absolutely and wholly Pelagianizeth. **1674** HICKMAN *Quinquart. Hist.* (ed. 2) 31 Doth not Arminius Pelagianize in this?

Hence **Peˈlagianizing** *ppl. a.*; **Peˈlagianizer.**

1629 H. BURTON *Truth's Triumph* 315 Those Pelagianizing enemies of the grace of God. **1674** HICKMAN *Quinquart. Hist.* (ed. 2) 215 To let the new Pelagianizers see, there was no quarter for them in Oxford. *a* **1861** W. CUNNINGHAM *Hist. Theol.* (1864) II. xxv. 376 The latter class they were accustomed to call Pelagianizing Remonstrants.

pelagic (pɪˈlædʒɪk), *a.* [ad. L. *pelagic-us*, a. Gr. *πελαγικός, f. πέλαγ-ος the sea.] **a.** Of or pertaining to the open or high sea, as distinguished from the shallow water near the coast; oceanic; now *spec.* living on or near the surface of the open sea or ocean, as distinguished from its depths. Also applied *spec.* to the environment in any part of the sea away from the littoral and benthic regions and to marine life at any depth that is independent of these regions.

1656 BLOUNT *Glossogr.*, *Pelagick*, of the Sea, or that liveth in the Sea. **1802** BINGLEY *Anim. Biog.* (1813) III. 420 The Pelagic Nereis. **1832** LYELL *Princ. Geol.* II. 280 Littoral and estuary shells are more frequently liable..to be intermixed with the exuviæ of pelagic tribes. **1843** *Rep. Brit. Assoc.* 13 Seamen are..well acquainted with the general forms of the pelagic fish. **1865** GOSSE *Land & Sea* (1874) 150 The pelagic shells, or those which during life rove freely through the sea. **1882** *Nature* XXVI. 559 Used technically by naturalists, the term *Pelagic* applied to living things, denotes those animals and plants which inhabit the surface waters of the seas and oceans. *Ibid.*, I have spoken of pelagic life as belonging to the surface waters of the ocean..; but,..it is impossible as yet to limit definitely the range of pelagic forms in depth, and we shall even have to refer to some connections of the fauna of the deep ocean bottom with that of the surface. Pelagic life then includes the inhabitants of the whole ocean waters, excluding those belonging to the bottom and shores. **1891** MURRAY & RENARD in *Rep. Sci. Results Voy. H.M.S. Challenger: Deep-Sea Deposits* iv. 251 We would suggest that the term oceanic Plankton be subdivided into pelagic Plankton for the animals living in the waters from the surface to 100 fathoms, zonary Plankton for those living in the intermediate zones between 100 fathoms from the surface and 100 fathoms from the bottom,..and abyssal Plankton for those living within 100 fathoms from the bottom over pelagic deposits. **1912** MURRAY & HJORT *Depths of Ocean* ix. 562 The conception of a 'pelagic' mode of life, originally associated with the animal-life of the ocean-surface, thus gradually proved to hold true for life in mid-water also... The main characteristic of pelagic life is its independence of the bottom. **1954** N. B. MARSHALL *Aspects Deep Sea Biol.* v. 89 Swimming and floating between the surface and the deep-sea floor are the pelagic animals. **1957** *Mem. Geol. Soc. Amer.* No. 67. I. xxii. 643 The distinction between pelagic and benthic species in these depths is difficult in many cases and depends on how far from the bottom a species must live in order to be considered pelagic. *Ibid.* 645 As yet nothing is known about pelagic animals from depths greater than 6000 meters—*i.e.*, from the trenches. *Ibid.* II. vi. 97 The subdivision of the water above the bottom, the great pelagic region, is more satisfactorily established. **1962** K. F. LAGLER et. al. *Ichthyol.* xiv. 468 Marine fishes may be classed into three main categories: (*a*) the shore or shelf fauna..; (*b*) the pelagic or open sea fishes, generally living near the surface of tropical and warm-temperature seas..; (*c*) deepsea or abyssal forms, inhabiting depths greater than 100 fathoms. **1969** [see NEKTON]. **1970** D. A. ROSS *Introd. Oceanogr.* vi. 140 The pelagic realm can be subdivided into the neritic environment (the water that overlies the continental shelf) and the oceanic environment (the water of the deep sea). **1974** [see NERITIC *a.*].

b. Of sealing or whaling: Carried on or performed on the high seas. So ***pelagic sealer, whaler.***

1891 *Blackw. Mag.* Oct. 609 'Pelagic' sealing as at present carried on, cannot long be continued. **1897** *Daily News* 27 Jan. 6/6 The Commission was sent out in consequence of the statements made by the United States and Russia that the seal herd was being wiped out by pelagic sealing. **1901** *Munsey's Mag.* (U.S.) XXV. 358/1 The pelagic sealers kill the animals with guns, spears, or any effective weapon while they are in the water. **1941** J. S. HUXLEY *Uniqueness of Man* viii. 184 With the advent of pelagic whaling it seemed certain that, unless international regulation of the industry were achieved, whales would certainly become exceedingly scarce, and some species might be wiped out. **1958** *Times* 12 Nov. 11/6 The total number of whales caught last year by pelagic or factory ship expeditions in the Antarctic in 69 catching days was 35,977. **1974** *Nature* 4 Oct. 367/2 If the 1974–75 quotas for pelagic whaling in the Southern hemisphere are reached..the catch of all species next season may reach 380 thousand tons.

c. Of sea-bed material: formed within the sea itself, rather than transported from the land.

1884 MURRAY & RENARD in *Proc. R. Soc. Edin.* XII. 515 The following table shows the nomenclature we have adopted:—Terrigenous deposits... Pelagic deposits. **1891** —— *Rep. Deep-Sea Deposits* iii. 185 From the point of view of their composition, as well as of their geographical and bathymetrical position, Marine Deposits may be separated into two great divisions, viz. (I.) Pelagic Deposits—those formed towards the centres of the great oceans, and made up chiefly of the remains of pelagic organisms along with the ultimate products arising from the decomposition of rocks and minerals; and (II.) Terrigenous Deposits. **1959** A. HARDY *Fish & Fisheries* v. 103 Pelagic deposits..cover the floor of the great oceans in the depths beyond the edge of the shelf. **1970** D. A. ROSS *Introd. Oceanogr.* viii. 297 Deep-sea sediments can be divided into two major groups: pelagic sediments and terrigenous sediments.

d. = LIMNETIC *a.*

1899 G. C. WHIPPLE *Microsc. Drinking-Water* viii. 105 The plants and animals that inhabit lakes and ponds may be classified according to their habitat... The limnetic or pelagic organisms are those that make their home in the open water. **1955** C. C. DAVIS *Marine & Fresh-Water Plankton* i. 11 Lakes may be subdivided into horizontal and vertical portions. Horizontally, the relatively shallow area close to shore..is called the littoral region, while the region of open water is known as the limnetic (or pelagic) region. **1975** G. A. COLE *Textbk. Limnol.* ii. 9/1 Beyond the pond weeds..is the open water. This is the limnetic or pelagic zone, a region in the lake where shore and bottom have lessened influence.

e. Of birds: inhabiting regions of open sea beyond the edges of a continental shelf, feeding on plankton and other marine organisms, and returning to shore only in the breeding season.

1935 V. C. WYNNE-EDWARDS in *Proc. Boston Soc. Nat. Hist.* XL. 240 The typical species of these three communities [of birds] in the temperate North Atlantic might be separated as follows: 1. Inshore... 2. Offshore... 3. Pelagic. *Ibid.* 241 Pelagic birds..feed chiefly on plankton. **1936** R. C. MURPHY *Oceanic Birds S. Amer.* I. II. 323 South America..is the longest mass of land lying in the relatively open oceans of the southern hemisphere... It is natural.. that nearly all the genera, and a large proportion of the species of southern-hemisphere pelagic birds should occur within the limits of the field. **1954** FISHER & LOCKLEY *Sea-Birds* vii. 170 Little is known of the construction of pelagic flocks. **1974** A. DILLARD *Pilgrim at Tinker Creek* x. 165 The oceanic breeding grounds of pelagic birds are as teeming and cluttered as any human Calcutta.

pelagically (pɪˈlædʒɪkəlɪ), *adv.* [f. prec.: see -LY[2].] In pelagic regions.

1966 R. M. LOCKLEY *Grey Seal, Common Seal* x. 129 Seals which breed pelagically on floating icefields are threatened by fishers who hunt them today by boat, helicopter and light aircraft. **1975** *Nature* 8 May 100/3 Introductions, the American smelt and the alewife, dominated the main trench and were also common pelagically.

†**peˈlagious,** *a. Obs.* [f. L. *pelagi-us* (see PELAGIAL) + -OUS.] = PELAGIC.

1661 LOVELL *Hist. Anim. & Min.* Introd., Fishes, which are, I. Marine, and these are either *pelagious*, living in the main sea,..or *littoral.* **1857** MAYNE *Expos. Lex.*, *Pelagius*,.. of swimming birds, comprehending those that frequent the sea, where they find their food: pelagious.

pelagite (ˈpɛlədʒaɪt). *Min.* [f. Gr. πέλαγος sea + -ITE[1] 2 b.] A name given to nodules of oxide of manganese and iron obtained in deep-sea soundings in the Pacific Ocean.

1876 A. H. CHURCH in *Min. Mag.* I. 52 The singularity of the mode of formation, of the occurrence, and of the composition of these concretions should constitute no bar to their recognition as a distinct mineral species under such a name as *Pelagite.* It would at present be impossible to assign a formula to this 'pelagite'.

pelagosaur (ˈpɛləgəʊsɔː(r)). *Palæont.* [ad. mod.L. *pelagosaurus*, f. Gr. πέλαγο-ς sea + σαύρα lizard: see SAURIAN.] A genus of fossil crocodiles with amphicœlian vertebræ, found in strata of the Jurassic age.

1882 in OGILVIE (Annandale).

pelagra, variant of PELLAGRA.

pelamyd, -mid (ˈpɛləmɪd). Also 6 **palmita**; 7– (in L. form) **pelamis, -mys**, pl. **pelamides**; 8–9 **palamede**. [ad. L. *pēlamys, -myd-, pēlamis*, a. Gr. *πηλαμύς, -μυδα*. The form *palamede* represents F. *palamide* 'a young Tunnie' (Cotgr.); *palmita* = It. *palamite* 'a fish called a tunnie before it be a yeere old, a sommer whiting' (Florio).]

1. A small Mediterranean fish; a young tunny.
1598 *Epulario* G j b, To dresse a Palmita, which is a kind of Tonny. **1601** HOLLAND *Pliny* I. 243 The old Tunies and the young, called Pelamides, enter into great flotes and skuls into the sea Pontus. **1617** MORYSON *Itin.* I. 259. **1781** GIBBON *Decl. & F.* xvii. (1788) III. 13 *note*, Among a variety of different species, the Pelamides, a sort of Thunnies, were the most celebrated. **1810** ANNE PLUMPTRE *Resid. France* II. vi. 76 The palamede..seems so much of the same nature, that some persons have supposed it only the young thunny. **1854** BADHAM *Halieut.* 188 After passing the anniversary of their first birthday, these pelamyds attained maturity, and were dubbed thunnies in consequence. **1857** BIRCH *Anc. Pottery* (1858) II. 289 A pelamys or tunny.

2. Applied to the genus *Pelamys* (Cuvier 1831) of scombroid fishes.
1863 COUCH *Brit. Fishes* II. 102 Pelamid.

pelandok (pəlænˈdɒk). Also **plandok**. [Malay.] The lesser mouse-deer, *Tragulus javanicus*, native to parts of south-east Asia.
1821 J. LEYDEN tr. *Malay Annals* 89 One of his dogs roused a white pelandok. **1836** J. LOW *Diss. Soil & Agric. Penang* iii. 188 The *plandok*, or cheurotin [*sic*] of Buffon, or hornless deer, about the size of a hare, is plentiful. **1839** T. J. NEWBOLD *Pol. & Statistical Acct. Straits of Malacca* I. vii. 436 The Plandok is a favourite animal among the Malays, and frequently alluded to both in their prose compositions and poems. **1900** W. MAXWELL in W. W. Skeat *Malay Magic* v. 113 There lived a man whose wife.. was seized with a violent longing for the meat of the *pelandok* (mouse-deer). **1905** *Outing* Jan. 469/2 It may be anything from a *plandok* (mouse deer) to a tiger. **1958** [see KIDANG]. **1962** *Listener* 22 Nov. 878/2 The spider being here [*sc.* in Africa] what the *plandok* is in Malaya, a jungle Till Eulenspiegel. **1965** C. SHUTTLEWORTH *Malayan Safari* ii. 26 The flesh of the pelandok is extremely edible, and he is hunted constantly. **1969** LD. MEDWAY *Wild Mammals Malaya* 106/1 Lesser Mouse-deer. Pelandok, Kanchil... Largely nocturnal; generally solitary.

pelare, obs. form of PILLAR.

pelargic (pɪˈlɑːdʒɪk), *a.* [ad. Gr. *πελαργικ-ός* of the stork, f. *πελαργός* stork: see -IC.] Of or pertaining to the storks.
1830 tr. *Aristophanes, Birds* 217 O thou hawk of Sunium! Hail, Pelargic King!

pelargonic (pɛlɑːˈgɒnɪk), *a. Chem.* [f. PELARGON-IUM: see -IC.] Of or derived from the genus *Pelargonium*; esp. in *pelargonic acid*, a fatty acid, $C_9H_{18}O_2$, prepared from the volatile oil of plants of this genus; nonylic acid. So **peˈlargonate**, a salt of pelargonic acid; **ˈpelargone**, a crystalline substance, soluble in ether, obtained by the dry distillation of barium pelargonate; **peˈlargoˌnene**, a hydrocarbon obtained among the products of the dry distillation of hydroleic or metoleic acid; **ˈpelargyl**, the radical of pelargonic acid ($C_9H_{17}O$).
1857 MILLER *Elem. Chem.* III. 396 Pelargonic Acid..was originally extracted from the leaves of the geranium, by distilling them with water. *Ibid.*, Pelargonic anhydride..is obtained by acting upon pelargonate of baryta with oxychloride of phosphorus. **1866–77** WATTS *Dict. Chem.* IV. 370 Pelargonic acid is a colourless oil..which solidifies in the cold, melting afterwards at 10°. *Ibid.* 371 Pelargonate of Ethyl..Pelargonic ether. *Ibid.*, Chloride of Pelargyl, $C_9H_{17}OCl$, is obtained by the action of pentachloride of phosphorus on pelargonic acid.

pelargonidin (pɛləˈgəʊnɪdɪn). *Chem.* [a. G. *pelargonidin* (R. Willstätter 1914, in *Sitzungsber. d. k. preuss. Akad. d. Wissensch.* 405), f. as next: see -IDIN.] An anthocyanidin (usu. isolated as the chloride, $C_{15}H_{11}O_5Cl$) that is the aglycone of pelargonin and many other red plant pigments.
1914 *Chem. Abstr.* VIII. 3421 The pelargonin of the scarlet pelargona flower on hydrolysis gave 2 mols. dextrose and 1 mol. of pelargonidin, $C_{15}H_{11}O_6Cl$ [*sic*]. **1934** *Jrnl. Chem. Soc.* 1612 The orange-scarlet nasturtium contains a pelargonidin 3-bioside, the red *gloxinia* flowers are coloured by a pelargonidin rhamnoglycoside, and pelargonidin 3-glycosides occur in scarlet carnations, strawberries,..and in other flowers. **1937** [see DELPHINIDIN]. **1965** [see PEONIDIN]. **1966** [see CYANIDIN]. **1974** *Phytochemistry* XIII. 2002 The major anthocyanins were identified as the 3-glucoside, 3-galactoside, 3-rutinoside and 3-robinobioside of pelargonidin.

pelargonin (pɛləˈgəʊnɪn). *Chem.* [a. G. *pelargonin* (R. Willstätter 1914, in *Sitzungsber. d. k. preuss. Akad. d. Wissensch.* 405), f. G. *pelargonie* or mod.L. PELARGONIUM: see -IN¹.] An anthocyanin (usu. isolated as the red chloride, $C_{27}H_{31}O_{15}Cl$) that is the colouring matter of zonal pelargoniums and on hydrolysis gives pelargonidin and glucose.
1914 [see PELARGONIDIN]. **1934** C. C. STEELE *Introd. Plant Biochem.* xix. 221 The different species of *Primula* contain different delphinidin derivatives, while cyanin and pelargonin predominate in different coloured varieties of *Pelargonium zonale*. **1956** I. L. FINAR *Org. Chem.* II. xv. 585 Pelargonidin chloride, $C_{15}H_{11}O_5Cl$. This is formed, together with two molecules of glucose, when pelargonin chloride is hydrolysed with hydrochloric acid.

‖**Pelargonium** (pɛləˈgəʊnɪəm). *Bot.* [mod.L. (L'Heritier 1787), f. Gr. *πελαργός* stork: app. modelled on the earlier *γεράνιον, geranium*.] An extensive genus of plants of the N.O. *Geraniaceæ*, chiefly natives of the Cape of Good Hope, having showy flowers and fragrant leaves, commonly cultivated under the name of *geranium*.
1819 *Pantologia, Pelargonium*, Crane-bill, in botany. **1835** *Encycl. Brit.* (ed. 7) XI. 686/2 Pelargoniums are of easy culture, propagating readily by cuttings. **1861** *Times* 23 May, The azaleas, pelargoniums, and other spring flowers being in particularly good condition. **1890** *Golden South* 155 Pelargoniums grow three or four feet high.

Pelasgian (pɪˈlæzdʒɪən), *a.* and *sb.* Also 6 -ien. [f. L. *Pelasgi-us*, a. Gr. *Πελάσγι-ος* of or pertaining to the *Πελασγοί* or Pelasgi: see b.]

a. *adj.* = next. **b.** *sb.* One of the *Pelasgi*, an ancient race of doubtful ethnological affinities, widely spread over the coasts and islands of the Eastern Mediterranean and Ægean, and believed to have occupied Greece before the Hellenes. Also, the Indo-European language attributed to the pre-Hellenic population of Greece and the Aegean. Also *attrib.*
a **1490** J. SKELTON tr. *Diodorus Siculus' Bibliotheca Historica* (1956) I. IV. 321 Summe call theym Pelasgians by encheson that they first proceded from theym of Pelasgye which colaterallyth vnto the Grecians. **1585** T. WASHINGTON tr. *Nicholay's Voy.* II. ix. 43 The first inhabitants of [Lesbos]..were the Pelasgiens. *Ibid.*, Priape, king of the Pelasgiens. *Ibid.*, After the palasgiens, succeeded the Eoliens. **1785** T. ASTLE in *Archæol.* VII. 348 On the radical Letters of the Pelasgians and their derivatives. **1822** MITFORD *Hist. Greece* I. i. §2. 29 Strabo assures us, that the Pelasgians were antiently established all over Greece. **1869** TOZER *Highl. Turkey* II. 23 Situated in the midst of the great Pelasgian nation. **1875** *Calcutta Rev.* LXI. 4 The Celts.. were followed by the so-called Pelasgians, who then separated into Greeks and Latins. **1939** L. H. GRAY *Foundations of Lang.* 376 N. Marr..held that Caucasian was ..cognate with Basque, Etruscan, Pelasgian, and other 'Mediterranean' tongues. **1954** PEI & GAYNOR *Dict. Linguistics* 163 *Pelasgian*, an extinct language of southern Europe, variously described as Mediterranean or Japhetic, and said to have been linked with Caucasian, Basque and Etruscan. **1966** *Lingua* XVI. 277 The discussion of Pelasgian phonology offers nothing new. **1972** W. B. LOCKWOOD *Panorama Indo-European Lang.* 12 Pelasgian was apparently a living language locally in the Aegean until the fifth century B.C.

Hence **Peˈlasgianist**, a student of the Pelasgian language.
1965 *Lingua* XIII. 349, I propose to examine..in section E those 'Pelasgian' etymologies which have been agreed by three or more Pelasgianists with no dissentient. **1967** *Ibid.* XVIII. 148 Errors made with 'Pelasgian' are characterized by the effort *to cling to the customary conceptions*..both on the side of the adversaries of 'Pelasgian' and on the side of the 'Pelasgianists' themselves. **1970** *Trans. Philol. Soc.* 1969 84 This [*sc.* reconstruction of a language from its loan-words in another language] is the desperate hazard attempted by the school of 'Pelasgianists'.

Pelasgic (pɪˈlæzdʒɪk), *a.* [ad. L. *Pelasgic-us*: see prec.] **a.** Of, pertaining to, or characteristic of the Pelasgi or Pelasgians.
Pelasgic architecture, building, the oldest form of masonry found in Greece and the neighbouring lands, constructed of rough or unhewn stones piled up without cement.
1785 T. ASTLE in *Archæol.* VII. 361 Homer was a native of Ionia, where the Pelasgic alphabet was first improved. **1815** H. MARSH *Horæ Pelasgicæ* title-p., A Description of the Pelasgic or Æolic Digamma. **1831** *Encycl. Brit.* (ed. 7) III. 413/1 *margin*, Pelasgic architecture. **1840** *Penny Cycl.* XVII. 377/2. **1860** EMERSON *Cond. Life, Power* Wks. (Bohn) II. 337 With all his hairy Pelasgic strength directed on his opening sense of beauty.

b. *sb.* The Pelasgian language; = PELASGIAN b above.
1966 E. P. HAMP in Birnbaum & Puhvel *Anc. Indo-European Dial.* 114 It is convenient here to reproduce Georgiev's subgrouping of Indo-European..: Central: Greek, Deco-Mysian.., Indo-Iranian, Phrygian-Armenian, Thracian, Pelasgic.

pelaw, pelch, variants of PILAU, PILCH.

peldon (ˈpɛldən). *Coal-mining.* [Origin unknown.] 'Hard and compact siliceous rock' (Gresley *Gloss. Terms Coal-mining* 1883).

pele, obs. form of PEAL, PEEL, PELL.

pele, var. PEEL *sb.*¹ 4.

Peléan (pɪˈleɪən), *a. Geol.* Also **Peléean, Pelean**, and with small initial letter. [f. the name of Mount *Pelée*, a volcano on the island of Martinique, W. Indies, which erupted in this way in 1902: see -AN.] Of, pertaining to, or designating a type of volcanic eruption characterized by the lateral emission of *nuées ardentes* from a point of weakness in the flank and the vertical extrusion of very viscous lava in the centre which tends to become consolidated as a solid plug.
1903 ANDERSON & FLETT in *Phil. Trans. R. Soc.* A. CC. 499 We propose to adopt the term ' A Peléan Eruption' to designate this group of phenomena. **1934** C. R. LONGWELL et al. *Outl. Physical Geol.* x. 189 The Peléean phase is the most violently explosive of all. *Ibid.* 191 The extraordinary features of a Peléean cloud are that it is emitted as a horizontal blast from beneath the lava plug in the summit of the volcano; that it carries with it an enormous amount of rock fragments, [etc.]. **1935** *Publ. Carnegie Inst. Washington* No. 458. 97 The general morphological features of the Peléan summit are those of an ancient crater wall, remaining in place on all sides but one. **1938** [see *bread-crust bomb* s.v. BREAD *sb.* 10]. **1944** C. A. COTTON *Volcanoes* xii. 183 The chief product of both Vulcanian and Pelean eruptions is ash. **1965** A. HOLMES *Princ. Physical Geol.* (ed. 2) xii. 310 There are *nuée ardente* eruptions that differ in certain fundamental ways from those described as Peléan. **1972** G. A. MACDONALD *Volcanoes* x. 226 Two of the greatest Peléean eruptions of recent years are those of Bezymianny, Kamchatka, in 1956, and Mt. Lamington, New Guinea, in 1951. **1976** P. FRANCIS *Volcanoes* iii. 116 The presence of such a dome is sometimes considered to be a characteristic feature of Peléean eruptions.

pelecan, obs. form of PELICAN *sb.*

ˈpelecaˌnine, *a. Ornith.* [f. L. *pelecān-us* PELICAN *sb.* + -INE¹.] Of or pertaining to the genus *Pelecanus* of birds.
1860 *Proc. Zool. Soc.* 330 The tongue [of Balæniceps] is extremely small, an important Pelecanine character.

pelecoid (ˈpɛlɪkɔɪd), *a.* and *sb. Geom.* Also 9 *erron.* peli-. [ad. Gr. *πελεκοειδής*, f. *πέλεκυς* ax, hatchet + *-ειδης* -form, -shaped.]

a. *adj.* Hatchet-shaped. **b.** *sb.* A figure bounded by a semicircle, and two concave quadrants meeting in a point, and so resembling the blade of a battle-axe.
[**1706** PHILLIPS, *Pelecoides*, a Name which some give to a certain Geometrical Figure, that somewhat resembles a Hatchet.] **1727–41** CHAMBERS *Cycl.* s.v. *Angle*, *Pelecoid Angle*..is that in figure of a hatchet. **1864** WEBSTER, *Pelicoid*. See *Pelecoid*.

pelecypod (pɪˈlɛsɪpɒd), *a.* and *sb. Zool.* [fr. Gr. *πέλεκυς* hatchet + *-ποδος* -footed.] **a.** *adj.* Having a hatchet-shaped foot, as a bivalve mollusc; pertaining to such a mollusc. **b.** *sb.* A pelecypod mollusc. Hence **peleˈcypodous** *a.*, in same sense.
1857 MAYNE *Expos. Lex.*, *Pelecypodus*, applied..to.. Mollusca..that have a foot in form of a club or of a tongue: pelecypodous. **1890** *Cent. Dict.*, *Pelecypod*. **1897** B. WOODWARD in *Concise Knowl. Nat. Hist.* 619 In the higher Pelecypods they are filibranch. *Ibid.*, Diagram illustrating successive development of pelecypod gills.

pelegrim, -grine, obs. ff. PILGRIM, PEREGRINE.

pêle-mêle, variant of PELL-MELL.

pelemele, obs. f. PALL-MALL, PELL-MELL.

peler, obs. form of PEELER, PILLAR.

†**ˈpelerin.** *Obs. rare.* Also 5 **pilleryn**. [a. F. *pèlerin* PILGRIM.] A pilgrim.
1456 SIR G. HAYE *Law Arms* (S.T.S.) 96 Gif pilleryns may be maid prisoneris. *c* **1614** SIR W. MURE *Dido & Æneas* I. 777 We straying Pelerins will ne'r assay't.

†**pelerinage, pelrinage.** *Obs. rare.* [ME. a. F. *pèlerinage* PILGRIMAGE.] A pilgrimage.
c **1300** *Beket* 5 Gilbert..mid on Richard..to Ierusalem com. There hi dude here pelrynage. **1390** GOWER *Conf.* I. 69 The noble wommen of the toun Most comunliche a pelrinage Gon forto preie thilke ymage. *Ibid.* II. 385 Forth comth Paris with glad visage Into the temple on pelrinage.

pelerine (ˈpɛlərɪn, -iːn). Also 8 **pelorine**, 8–9 **pelerin**. [a. F. *pèlerine*, transferred use of fem. of *pèlerin* PILGRIM = pilgrim's mantle or cape.]

a. A name applied from time to time to various fashions of mantles or capes worn by women; in nineteenth century use, a long narrow cape or tippet, with ends coming down to a point in front, usually of lace or silk, or of the material of the dress.
The name appears to have been in vogue 1740–50 (it was obsolete to Fielding in 1752); again about 1764; also 1825–35, 1855–68, 1884–1904; the shape or material being probably more or less new each time.
1744 ELIZA HEYWOOD *Female Spect.* No. 5 (1748) I. 237 Her neck suffers for it, and confesses, in scarlet blushes..: this misfortune, however, she conceals under a handkerchief or pelerine, and high tucker. **1745** *Gentl. Mag.* 272 In pelerin clad, or silk manteal. **1752** FIELDING *Covent Gard. Jrnl.* 9 May, Within my memory..this [cloak]..was succeeded by the pelorine, the pelorine by the neckatee. **1764** *Mem. G. Psalmanazar* 118 A short leathern or oil-cloth cloak, not unlike what the women call a pelerine. **1827** *Souvenir* I. 21 (Stanf.) A half high canezou..composed of their Jaconet muslin, and trimmed round the bust with a row of deep points, which form a pelerine. **1831** *Lincoln Herald* 9 Sept. 3/5 The triple lappel forms a square pelerine behind. **1855** DICKENS *Dorrit* II. ix, 'Arthur', whispered Flora, 'would you object to putting your arm round me under my pelerine?' **1868** *Express* 30 Mar., The petticoat or under-skirt being of silk, the upper one of cachemire of the same shade, and the costume completed by a short pelerine tied behind. **1884** *Girl's Own Paper* 28 June 618/1 'Pelerine'

is now the usual name for the shoulder cape. **1898** *Daily News* 2 Apr. 6/5 The pelerine is to be a favourite form of mantle, many of the new capes being finished in front with long, rounded, pelerine ends.

b. *attrib.* and *Comb.* **pelerine stitch** (see quots. 1926, 1950).

1835 *Court Mag.* VI. p. ix/2 The corsage..is trimmed with a mantilla, or else in the pelerine stile, with blond lace. **1902** *Westm. Gaz.* 6 Feb. 3/1 The deep pelerine-like collar of lace or mixed lace and chiffon. **1926** J. CHAMBERLAIN *Hosiery, Yarns & Fabrics* vi. 128 The Pelerine Stitch has a limited application as a shawl stitch, but modern variations of it are used for producing (1) cellular fabric; (2) in-turned welt... This stitch or combination of stitches is based on the transferring of a formed sinker loop to one or two needles. **1950** '*Mercury*' *Dict. Textile Terms* 392/1 *Pelerine stitches*, these stitches are produced by meshing the upper and lower components of a single loop together at the next course. Modifications of these stitches produce raised designs and places and eyelet holes. By meshing the lower components of the first row of loops to a subsequent row a hem or welt is produced on a plain fabric.

Pele's hair ('piːliːz hɛə(r)). [transl. of Hawaiian *ranoho o Pele*, hair of Pelé, the goddess of the volcano Kilauea.] Volcanic glass from the volcano Kilauea, found in fine hair-like threads.

1849 DANA *Geol. Pacif.* 200 Pele's Hair. **1861** BRISTOW *Gloss. Min.* 276 *Pele's Hair*, lava blown by the wind..into hair-like fibers.

pelestre, peletre, -tur, var. PELLETER[1] *Obs.*

pelet, -ette, obs. ff. PELLET.

peletone, erron. f. PELOTON.

pelewe, obs. f. PILLOW.

pelf (pɛlf), *sb.* Also 6 **pylfe**, 9 *dial.* **pilf**. [ME. a. ONF. **pelfe*, instanced 1370 as *peuffe*, mod. Norman *peufe*, var. of OF. *pelfre* (11th c. in Godef.), *peufre* spoil; ulterior derivation uncertain; perh. related to L. *pilāre* in sense 'to pillage', F. *piller*.]

†**1.** Property pilfered or stolen, spoil, booty. *Obs.*

a **1350** *S. Nicholas* 444 in Horstm. *Altengl. Leg.* (1881) 16 Als þe theuis..Partid þaire pelf bi a wud side. *c* **1450** *St. Cuthbert* (Surtees) 5989 þair schipp, with all þair pelf, To þe mynster þai [pirates] betake, Full amendis forto make. *c* **1470** HENRYSON *Mor. Fab.* IX. (*Wolf & Fox*) xiv, Schir.. and we get of yone pelf, Ye man tak trauell and mak ws sum supple.

†**2.** Property, possessions, goods, 'gear'. *Obs.*

c **1450** *St. Cuthbert* (Surtees) 7166 þe monkes duelt be þaim self, Sa did þe nonnes, with all þair pelf. **1573** TUSSER *Husb.* (1878) 122 Go muster thy seruants, be captaine thy selfe, Prouiding them weapon and other like pelfe. **1608** SHAKS. *Per.* II. Prol. 35 All perishen, of man, of pelfe, Ne ought escapend but himselfe. **1847** *Mischief of Muses* 17 And who, from managing his master's pelf Had now begun to manage for himself.

3. Money, wealth, riches; now depreciatory: 'filthy lucre'.

1500–20 DUNBAR *Poems* lviii. 25 Thay panss nocht off the parrochin pure, Had thai the pelfe to pairt amang thame. **1549** COVERDALE, etc. *Erasm. Par. Jas.* iv. 38 You..whiske about by sea and by lande to get pelfe for your olde age. **1581** J. BELL *Haddon's Answ. Osor.* 278 Why do they uphold their pylfe with such outrage and tirannye? **1589** PUTTENHAM *Eng. Poesie* III. xxii. (Arb.) 266 'A misers mynde thou hast, thou hast a Princes pelfe.' A lewd terme to be giuen to a Princes treasure. **1590** SPENSER *F.Q.* III. ix. 4 But all his minde is set on mucky pelfe. *a* **1656** BP. HALL *Rem. Wks.* (1660) 223 Ye rich men cannot think to carry your pelfe with you into Heaven. **1720** WELTON *Suffer. Son of God* II. xvi. 422 The Covetous Man looks upon his Pelf, and adores it as his God. **1790** BURKE *Fr. Rev.* 137. **1833** HT. MARTINEAU *Charmed Sea* ix. 130 Too busy after his pelf to bestow any thought on the first marriage celebration. **1874** L. MORRIS *Professor* iii, As blind to all that passes self As any churl that slaves for pelf.

†**4.** Trumpery, trash, rubbish: frippery. *Obs.*

1555 BRADFORD *Let. to Rawlins* in Foxe *A. & M.* (1583) 1632 Forked cappes, typettes, shauen crownes, or such other baggage and Antichristian pelfe. **1565** JEWEL *Repl. Harding* To Rdr. (1611) 3 It is not sufficient..to condemne our Books for pelfe, and trash, and fardles of lies, before he see them. **1596** GOSSON *Quip for Gentlewomen* xiv, All this new pelfe now sold in shops, in value true not worth a louse. **1632** BURTON *Anat. Mel.* II. ii. IV. (ed. 4) 286 Which to her guests she shews, with all her pelfe.

b. Refuse; now *dial.*, vegetable refuse, weeds.

1589 PUTTENHAM *Eng. Poesie* III. xxiii. (Arb.) 281 Pelfe is properly the scrappes or shreds of taylors and skinners. **1600** S. NICHOLSON *Acolastus* (1876) 7 We of all people once that were the pelfe,..Almighty Ioue hath chosen to himselfe. **1646** TRAPP *Comm. John* xv. 20 Our memories are as..nets that keep the pelf, let go the clean water. **1678** PHILLIPS (ed. 4), *Pelf*..in Faulconry, is the refuse and broken remains left after the Hawk is relieved. **1828** *Farm Jrnl.* 21 Jan. (E.D.D.), Which is the best means of clearing a wood from roots and pelf? **1880** *W. Cornwall Gloss.*, *Pilf*, light grass and roots raked together to be burnt.

c. Dust; fluff. *Obs.* exc. *dial.*

1584 COGAN *Haven Health* ccxxiv. (1636) 259 Gather it.. picke it cleane from dyrt and pelfe. **1880** *W. Cornwall Gloss.*, *Pilf, Pilm, Pillem*, light dust or fluff.

d. A worthless person, a good-for-nothing. Now *dial.*

1551 SIR J. MASON *Let.* (S.P. Foreign, Edw. VI, VI. lf. 287), The olde worne pelff [Diane of Poictiers] fearing ther by to lefe some parte of her credite. **1781** J. HUTTON *Tour to Caves* (ed. 2) Gloss., *Pelfe*, a bad, or good-for-nothing person. **1876** *Mid-Yorksh. Gloss*, *Pelf*, a term bestowed on a worthless person.

5. *Comb.*, as ***pelf-licker***; ***pelf-spurning*** adj.

1653 URQUHART *Rabelais* I. liv, Here enter not base pinching Usurers, Pelf-lickers, everlasting gatherers. **1870** J. HAMILTON *Moses* iv. 78 The high-souled, pelfspurning Abraham.

†**pelf**, *v. Obs.* [ME. a. OF. *pelf-er* (also *pelf-ir*), var. of *pelfrer* to pillage, rob, f. *pelfe, pelfre* spoil: see prec. sb., and cf. PILFER *v.*] *trans.* and *intr.* To spoil, rob.

a **1300** *Cursor M.* 6149 (Cott.) For to pelf þat folk vnlel And help his folk of israel. **1387** TREVISA *Higden* (Rolls) II. 95 Infangthef pelfynde inward. **1538** BALE *Thre Lawes* 617 If ye knewe how he coulde pelfe.

pelfer, obs. form of PILFER.

†'**pelfish**, *a. Obs.* [f. PELF *sb.* + -ISH[1].] Of the nature of pelf, rubbishy, paltry.

1577 STANYHURST *Descr. Irel.* Ep. Ded. in *Holinshed* I. 1 b/2 That I may the sooner vnbroyde ye pelfish trash, that is wrapt wythin thys Treatise. —— *Contn. Hist. Irel.* Ded. *ibid.* 76/1 Hee shall bee sure, to fynde them that wyll bee more prest to blabbe forth his pelfish faultes, than they will be ready to blaze out his good desertes.

†**pelfry**. *Obs.* Forms: α. 5 **pelfere**, 6 **-fre, -frey, -fray, -fery, -fary, -pelfry**. β. 5–6 **pil-, pylfre**. [a. ONF. **pelferie*, instanced 14–15th c. in forms *peuferie, peufferie*, mod. Norm. *peuferie, peufrie* (Godef.) frippery. See also PILFERY.]

1. Things pilfered; booty, spoil.

c **1460** *Promp. Parv.* 391/1 (MS. S) Pelfrey, *spolium*. **1565** JEWEL *Def. Apol.* (1611) 642 The gaines and pelferies that the Phariseis made of the people.

2. Trumpery, rubbish, trash; = PELF *sb.* 4.

a **1529** SKELTON *Agst. Garnesche* Wks. 1843 I. 125 Soche pelfry thou hast pachchyd, And so thysselfe houyr wachyd. **1538** BP. SHAXTON in Burnet *Hist. Ref.* (1715) III. Collect. Rec. 146 Lockes of Heere, and filthy Ragges, Gobbetts of Wodde, under the Name of Parcells of the Holy Cross, and such Pelfrie. **1545** ASCHAM *Toxoph.* (Arb.) 83 He..settes out much rifraffe, pelfery, trumpery, baggage and beggerie ware. **1551** CRANMER *Answ. Bp. Gardiner* Pref. A iij, Indulgences, Beades, Pardons, Pilgremages, and suche other pelfray.

Pelham ('pɛləm). [From the surname Pelham.] In full, ***Pelham bit***, a form of bit combining the snaffle and the curb in one. So ***Pelham bridle***.

1849 YOUATT *Horse* 190 If the curb-bit is in fault, a snaffle or Pelham-bit should be used. **1851** 'CECIL' *Stud Farm* 139 The Pelham..is a species of hybrid between a curb and a snaffle. **1875** WHYTE MELVILLE *Riding Recoll.* iii. (1879) 48 A light-mouthed horse steered by a good rider, will cross a country safely and satisfactorily in a Pelham bridle. **1894** GEO. ARMATAGE *The Horse* vi. 87 The Pelham..is a curb-bit with a joint in the middle, instead of a port. It forms a double-rein bridle.

pelican ('pɛlɪkən), *sb.* Forms: 1–7 **pellicane**, 3–8 **-ican**, (5 **-ycan(n**, 6 **-ycane, pillycane**); 5– **pelican**, 7 **pelicane, -ecane**, 7–9 **pelecan**. [(Like F. *pélican* (1210 in Hatz.-Darm.), Pr. *pelican*, Sp. *pelicano*, It. *pellicano*) ad. late L. *pelicān-us*, more correctly *pelecānus*, ad. Gr. πελεκάν, applied by Aristotle (in part at least) to the pelican (οἱ πελεκᾶνες οἱ ἐν τοῖς ποταμοῖς γινόμενοι); app. closely related to πελεκᾶς, -ᾶντα woodpecker, perh. f. πελεκᾶν to hew or shape with an ax, πέλεκυς ax, hatchet, from the appearance or action of the bill.

Πελεκάν was also used by the LXX to render the Heb. *qāāth*, in two (or three) of the places in which it occurs (in Eng. versions 'pelican'); in the two others, Isa. xxxiv. 11, Zeph. ii. 14, different Greek words were used, and there the version of 1611 has 'cormorant', but the Revisers of 1885 restore 'pelican' as in Coverdale.]

I. The bird.

1. a. The name now appropriated to a genus, *Pelecanus*, of large gregarious fish-eating waterfowls, remarkable for an enormously distensible membranous pouch which depends from the lower mandible of the long hooked bill and is used for the storing of fish when caught. Two species, *P. onocrotalus*, the Common or White Pelican, and *P. crispus*, the Crested Pelican, are found in South-eastern Europe and adjacent regions, and are the original 'pelicans'; to these the North American species *P. trachyrhynchus* is very closely allied. Other species are found in the West Indies, Africa, India, the Malay Archipelago, and Australia.

In all the quotations down to 14th c., and many later, the identification is vague, the bird being itself unknown in England, and the word merely a reflex of *pelicanus* of the Vulgate in Ps. ci(i). 7, *pelicano solitudinis* 'the pelican of the wilderness', which was app. not the pelican of naturalists. In the four other places where the same Heb. word occurs, the Vulgate has *onocrotalus*, a L. name of the modern 'pelican'. Elsewhere (*Comm. in Sophon.*, op. ed. Villarsi VI. 709) St. Jerome makes two kinds of *onocrotalus*, one the water-bird, the other that of the wilderness ('onocrotalorum, duo genera, aliud aquatile, aliud solitudinis'). So Isidore (*Orig.* XII. vii. 32). These appear in the pseudo-Jerome *Brev. in Psalt.* (Villarsi VII. Appx. 271) as two kinds of *pelicanus* (here identified with *onocrotalus*); whence, ultimately, in Trevisa, quot. 1398 below.

c **1000** *Ags. Ps.* (Th.) ci. 5 [cii. 6] Ic ȝeworden eom pellicane ȝelic, se on westene wunað. *a* **1225** *Ancr. R.* 142 Dauid, anon efter þet he heuede iefned ancre to pellican, he efnede hire to niht fuel. *a* **1300** *E.E. Psalter* ci. 7 Like am I made to pellicane of annesse. **1382** WYCLIF *ibid.*, Lic I am maad to a pellican of wildernesse. **1398** TREVISA *Barth. De P.R.* v. xxviii. (Bodl. MS.), So doþ þe pellican þat hat also porphirio. *Ibid.* XII. xxx, þere beþ twei manere of Pellicans; one woneþ in watres and eteþ fische and þe oþer woneþ in lond & loueþ wildernesse. *c* **1475** *Pict. Voc.* in Wr.-Wülcker 762/15 *Hic pelicanus*, a pelycan. **1535** COVERDALE *Isa.* xxxiv. 11 But Pellicanes, Storkes, great Oules, and Rauens shall haue it in possession, & dwell there in. **1604** DRAYTON *Owle* 135 The Pellican in Desarts farre abroad, Her deare-lov'd issue safely doth unload. **1673** RAY *Journ. Low C.* 28 A Museum..and therein..a Pelecan's Skin and Bill. **1688** R. HOLME *Armoury* II. 15/1 Diverse names ascribed to the Devil..as an Owl, a Kite, a Raven, a Pellicane, from his ravening, and unsatiable desire of Devouring, Isa. 34. 11. 15. *a* **1711** KEN *Hymnotheo* Poet. Wks. 1721 III. 74 Complaining Pelicanes themselves bemoan. **1877** A. B. EDWARDS *Up Nile* vi. 139 We see a top-heavy pelican balancing his huge yellow bill over the edge of the stream, and fishing for his dinner. **1883** *Chambers's Encycl.* VII. 362/1 They often fly in large flocks, and the sudden swoop of a flock of pelicans at a shoal of fish is a striking and beautiful sight.

b. In reference to the fable that the pelican revives or feeds her young with her own blood.

This is given by Epiphanius and St. Augustine; it appears to be of Egyptian origin, and to have referred originally to another bird.

1398 TREVISA *Barth. De P.R.* XII. xxix. (Tollem. MS.), The serpent hateþ kyndely þe pellican..and styngeþ and infecteþ þe briddes: þan sche smiteþ here selfe in þe breste, and spryngeþ blood up on hem, and rereþ hem fro deeþ to lyf. *a* **1400** *Leg. Rood* (1871) 172 þe pelicane his blod did blede þer-with his briddus for to fede. **1530** LYNDESAY *Test. Papyngo* 1100 My birneist beik I laif, with gude entent, Onto the gentyll, pieteous Pillycane, To helpe to peirs hir tender hart in twane. **1591** SYLVESTER *Du Bartas* I. v. 811–32. **1593** SHAKS. *Rich. II*, II. i. 126 That blood already (like the Pellican) Thou hast tapt out, and drunkenly carows'd. **1601** CHESTER *Love's Mart., Dial.* clxxx, The Pellican..reuiues her tender yong, And with her purest bloud-shed doth asswage Her yong ones thirst. **1695** CONGREVE *Love for L.* II. vii, What, would'st thou have me turn Pelican, and feed thee out of my own Vitals? **1848** MRS. JAMESON *Sacr. & Leg. Art* I. Introd. 36 The Pelican, tearing open her breast to feed her young with her own blood, was an early symbol of our redemption through Christ.

†**c.** Hence *fig.*, applied to Christ as reviving the dead in spirit by His blood. *Obs.*

1526 *Pilgr. Perf.* (W. de W. 1531) 107 b, Y^e^ moost piteous pellycane & heuenly phisycyon, our sauyour Iesu. *a* **1649** DRUMM. OF HAWTH. *Poems* Wks. (1711) 25/1 Ungrateful soul! that..didst not think at all, or thoughtst not right, On this thy Pelican's great love and death. **1814** CARY *Dante, Paradise* XXV. 113 [St. John] who lay Upon the bosom of our pelican.

2. A representation of the pelican in art or heraldry.

pelican in her piety (in Heraldry), a pelican represented as vulning (*i.e.* wounding) her breast in order to feed her young with her blood.

a **1400–50** *Alexander* 5129 Rekanthes of rede gold railed of gemmes, With pellicans & pape-ioyes polischt & grauen. *c* **1420** LYDG. *Assembly of Gods* 807 On hys helme on hygh a pelican he bare. **1610** GUILLIM *Heraldry* III. xvii. (1611) 162 He beareth Gules, a Pellican in her nest, with wings displaied, feeding of her young ones, Or, vulned proper. **1643–4** in G. A. Poole *Churches; their Structure*, etc. (1845) vi. 56 A glorious cover over the font,..with a pelican on the top picking its breast. **1672** J. DAVIES *Anc. Rites Durham* 17 A goodly fine Lantern, or Letteron, of Brass..with a great Pelican on the height of it, finely gilt..her wings spread abroad, whereon did lye the Book. **1885** *Times* 30 Apr. 7/6 Delicately engraved representations of the Agnus Dei and the Pelican in her piety. **1897** J. WELLS *Oxford & Coll.* 199 *note*, The Corpus tradition is that Keble..was once known to have thrown bread at the Pelican.

II. Transferred applications.

3. An alembic having a tubulated head, from opposite sides of which two curved tubes pass out and re-enter at the body of the vessel; used in distilling liquors by fermentation.

1559 MORWYNG *Evonym.* 102 Let it be put into a pellicane, that is a vessell with eares or handles on ether syde one. **1610** B. JONSON *Alch.* II. iii, The Retort brake, And what was sau'd, was put into the Pellicane. **1683** SALMON *Doron Med.* I. 307 Being permixt together in a Pellican let them remain in digestion. **1706** PHILLIPS, *Pelican* or *Blind Alembick*.

4. a. An instrument having a strong curved beak, formerly used for extracting teeth.

1597 A. M. tr. *Guillemeau's Fr. Chirurg.* 27/1 We cut them [extra teeth] of[f] with our cutting pellicane. **1688** R. HOLME *Armoury* III. 398/1 A Single Beak Pellican with a screw..is an instrument to draw out corrupt and faded teeth. **1846** BRITTAN tr. *Malgaigne's Man. Oper. Surg.* 73 Amongst the multitude of instruments invented..some are absolutely bad, and ought to be rejected; such are the 'pied de biche', and the 'pelican'.

b. 'A hook somewhat in the shape of a pelican's bill, so arranged that it can be easily slipped by taking a ring or shackle from the point of the hook' (*Cent. Dict.* 1890).

5. An ancient piece of artillery; also, the shot from it.

1727–41 CHAMBERS *Cycl.* s.v., Pellican, again, is the name of an ancient piece of ordnance, carrying a ball of six pounds. **1754** H. WALPOLE *Lett. H. Mann* 6 Oct., When your relation, General Guise, was marching up to Carthagena, and the pelicans whistled round him, he said, 'What would Chloe [the Duke of Newcastle's cook] give for some of these to make a pelican pie?' **1867** SMYTH *Sailor's Word-bk.*, *Pelican*,..the old six-pounder culverin.

6. With capital initial: the proprietary name of a series of non-fiction books published by Penguin Books; a book in this series.

1937 *Bookseller* 3 Feb. 147 (Advt.), A glance at the magnificent first list below will reveal the general nature of *Pelican Books*, a new series of popular books on science, astronomy, archæology, politics, economics, history, etc. **1942** *Scrutiny* X. iv. 385 Enough passages like the above could be found.. to yield Professor Stebbing cannon-fodder for at least a chapter, if not for a whole Pelican. **1948** G. V. Galwey *Lift & Drop* vi. 158 He.. began to study the book-shelves... There was.. a fair showing of Pelicans. **1953** E. Simon *Past Masters* I. i. 15 He published a Pelican on his work under Chrichton in the Islands, which I thought you might have seen. **1957** R. Hoggart *Uses of Literacy* viii. 210 There are the dailies and weeklies,.. the Penguins and the Pelicans. *Ibid.* xi. 261 They are in the habit today of buying copies of Pelicans. **1957** *Trade Marks Jrnl.* 22 May 532/1 Pelican... Printed books, being literary, dramatic, musical or artistic works, but not including books relating to pelicans. Penguin Books Limited,.. Harmondsworth, County of Middlesex; manufacturers and publishers. **1966** 'L. Black' *Bait* viii. 128 He was reading a paper-back... It appeared to be a Pelican. **1968** *Guardian* 26 Sept. 11/1 By the time of the first Pelicans Penguins (the mother birds) were, of course, well established... Pelicans were born in 1937, the inheritors of a half century and more of self-education.

7. In full ***pelican crossing***: a pedestrian-crossing controlled by push-buttons (see quot. 1966).

1966 *Evening Standard* 26 May 11/6 We hope the Ministry will install 'pelicans'.. in the town. Pelicans would be safer than zebras and easily understood by the public—the pedestrian just pushes a button which operates red, amber and green lights telling motorists when to stop. **1969** *Daily Tel.* 9 July 17/7 Another type of push-button pedestrian-controlled crossings—to be known as Pelicans—will come into operation on Monday. *Ibid.*, Instead of the white 'X', the Pelican (*pedestrian light controlled*) crossing will show a green signal to a driver until a pedestrian presses the button to start the signal sequence. **1974** *Country Life* 30 May 1332/2 A Minister stating that 'pelicans will be interchangeable with zebras'.. was referring to the replacement of the sturdy and familiar orange beacons at the kerbside by the flashing lights and little coloured men... A circular from the DoE elucidates some of the mysteries of the pelican crossing. **1975** *Times* 22 Sept. 12/5 Question time at council meetings is peppered with inquiries and entreaties about zebra and pelican crossings and such like. **1976** *New Scientist* 24 June 702/1 The GLC survey.. studied 40 pelicans which had been converted from zebras. **1976** *Flintshire Leader* 10 Dec. 1 Residents of Oakenholt are ready to block the main road through the village in their campaign for a pelican crossing.

III. 8. *attrib.* and *Comb.*, as ***pelican brood, daughter, oil, pie***; ***pelicanwise*** adv.; **pelican-fish**, an eel-like fish (*Eurypharynx pelecanoides*), dredged from a great depth near the Canary Islands: so called from its enormously developed jaws and large gular pouch; **Pelican flag** *U.S.*, the flag of the State of Louisiana; **pelican-flower**, a West Indian evergreen climbing plant (*Aristolochia grandiflora*); Poisonous Hogweed (*Treas. Bot.* 1866); **pelican ibis**, an Asiatic wood-ibis (*Tantalus leucocephalus*); **pelican lectern**, a lectern of the shape of a pelican; **pelican's foot**, a gastropod shell (*Aporrhais pes-pelecani*), so called from its digitate outer lip; **pelican's head**, a wooden battle-club with a rounded head and a projecting beak, used by the natives of New Caledonia; **Pelican State** *U.S.*, a sobriquet of the State of Louisiana.

1818 Keats *Endym.* I. 815 Nurtured like a *pelican brood. **1605** Shaks. *Lear* III. iv. 77 'Twas this flesh begot Those *Pelicane Daughters. **1883** *Leisure Hour* 312/2 The characters of the *Eurypharynx* (wide-throated *pelican fish) are so divided. **1860** *Charleston* (S. Carolina) *Mercury* 25 Dec. 4/5 The *Pelican flag of Louisiana was unfurled in the streets, amid tremendous cheering... The Pelican flag consists of a red star upon a white field, with the ancient Louisiana emblem of a Pelican feeding her young. **1865** A. D. Richardson *Secret Service* 40 There were Pelican flags, and Lone Star flags, and devices, unlike anything in the heavens above. **1881** *Field* 13 Aug. 262/1 Conspicuous next in order.. were numbers of *pelican ibises. **1898** J. T. Fowler *Durh. Cath.* 57 The modern.. *Pelican lectern. **1859** *Harper's Mag.* May 853/2 A well-known writer in the *Pelican State writes us a good thing from one of his little folks. **1934** G. E. Shankle *State Names* 119 The name, the *Pelican State* was given to Louisiana from the fact that this bird is so frequently seen along the streams.. which fact caused it to be chosen as the emblem in the state coat of arms. **1949** *Times-Picayune* (New Orleans) *Mag.* 27 Nov. 53/2 Now Mississippi has nosed out the Pelican State. **1959** E. A. Davis (*title*) Louisiana: the Pelican State. **1974** *Encycl. Brit. Micropædia* X. 272 (*table*) State nickname(s) or slogan. .. Louisiana.. Pelican state. **1862** H. Aïdé *Carr of Carrlyon* III. 39 Their doubts feed themselves, *pelican-wise, from their own breast.

'pelican, *v. rare*⁻¹. [f. the sb.] *trans.* To swallow or eat like a pelican.

1953 Dylan Thomas *Under Milk Wood* (1954) 65 And she bursts into tears, and, in the middle of her salty howling, nimbly spears a small flatfish and pelicans it whole.

pelicanry ('pɛlɪkənrɪ). [f. pelican *sb.* + -ry: cf. *heronry*.] A place where pelicans breed.

1864 Jerdon *Birds India* II. II. 860, I have visited one pelicanry in the Carnatic, where the Pelicans have (for ages, I was told) built their rude nests on rather low trees in the midst of a village.

pelice, obs. form of pelisse.

pelicoid, variant of pelecoid.

pelike ('pɛlɪkɪ, pɛ'liːkɪ). *Gr. Antiq.* Also pelice, pellice. Pl. pelikai. [ad. Gr. πελίκα a wooden bowl, pitcher.] A type of amphora with an ovoid body, wide mouth, and broad base used for holding wine or water.

1873 S. & J. Horner *Walks in Florence* II. 435 On a Pellice, a vase rarely found in Etruria, and belonging to the most perfect style of art.., is the figure of a man binding up the arm of a youth. **1891** Nettleship & Sandys *Seyffert's Dict. Classical Antiquities* 685 (*caption*) Various shapes of Greek vases... *pĕlīkĕ*. **1902** J. H. Huddilston *Lessons from Greek Pott.* I. 75 The largest group is found on the Louvre pelike, where, although there are no persons, in addition to those named by Homer,.. are two women, introduced.. to remind us of Briseis. **1928** J. D. Beazley *Greek Vases in Poland* iii. 64 His pictures, which are chiefly on small hydriai, small pelikai, and marriage-vases, are usually taken from the life of woman. **1936** *Burlington Mag.* May 253/1 A *pelice* with snarling lion and lioness. **1967** R. S. Folsom *Handbk. Greek Pottery* 159 The name pelike was applied by early archaeologists to the one-piece amphora with a sagging belly and broad neck. In fact the name appears to have no justification, but is retained for convenience. The form first appeared about 520 B.C. and lasted until the 4th century B.C. **1971** *Ashmolean Mus. Rep. Visitors 1970* 9 A notable addition to the collection of Athenian red-figure vases is a pelike, of the 4th century B.C.

†'peliom. *Min. Obs.* [mod. (Ger. 1818) ad. Gr. πελίωμα livid spot, in reference to its greyish blue colour.] A synonym of iolite.

1820 in Mohs *Char. Nat. Hist. Syst. Min.* 68.

Pelion ('piːlɪɒn). The name of a mountain in Thessaly, used in phr. ***to pile*** (or ***heap***) ***Pelion upon Ossa*** (or ***Ossa upon Pelion***) [tr. Virgil *Georgics* I. 281 *imponere Pelio Ossam*]: to add to what is already great; to add difficulty to difficulty. Also in similar phrases.

1589 A. Fleming tr. *Virgil's Georgiks* I. 10 Thrise did they trie and giue assay vpon mount Pelius, To lay the mountaine Ossa. **1594** Nashe *Unfortunate Traveller* sig. C_4ᵛ Whosoeuer seekes by headlong meanes to enter into Heauen .. shall with the Gyaunts.. be ouer-whelmed with Mount Ossa and Peleon. **1609** Dekker *Guls Horne-Booke* 30 By talking and laughing.. you heape Pelion vpon Ossa, glory vpon glory. **1628** T. May tr. *Virgil's Georgicks* I. 14 Thrice they indeavour'd with strong hand to place the mountain Ossa on high Pelion. *a* **1734** R. North *Examen* (1740) II. v. 336 It is a Pelion upon Ossa to set Power over Power. **1919** G. B. Shaw in *Shaw on Shakespeare* (1962) 257, I might pile Pelion on Ossa with illustrations of the passages that might very well be cut out of Shakespear's plays. **1927** C. A. & M. R. Beard *Rise Amer. Civilization* I. xii. 565 In piling Ossa on Pelion, Webster did not overlook mundane considerations —the economic and political substance of the pending issue, the sale of those annoying western lands. **1957** Partridge *English gone Wrong* i. 12 'To *categorize*' and *categorization*, and those Pelion-upon-Ossa horrifics, *recategorize* and *recategorization*. **1967** *Word Study* Mar. 3/1 We discover Mount Pelion piled on Ossa, however, when we note that our teachers are even more conservative than their conservative textbooks. **1976** *Times* 28 Apr. 14/8 Piling Pelion upon Ossa (a nasty habit that foreigners are much given to) they.. calculate the rate of inflation in Britain.

peliosis (pɛlɪ'əʊsɪs). *Path.* [mod.L. (F. Swediaur *Novum Nosologiæ Methodicæ Systema* (1812) I. p. xxiii, II. 173), f. Gr. πελίωσις extravasation of blood, f. πελιός livid.] = purpura 1; ***peliosis rheumatica*** [Gr. ῥευματικός subject to a discharge], an uncommon disease characterized by localized eruptions of the skin and mucous membranes, and associated with arthritis; (now usu. regarded as the same as *Henoch-Schönlein purpura* s.v. Henoch).

1839 Dunglison *Dict. Med. Sci.* (ed. 2) 772/1 *Peliosis*, purpura, hæmorrhagica. **1850** A. T. Thomson *Pract. Treat. Dis. affecting Skin* v. 338 Under the term Peliosis, or Purpura rheumatica, Schönlein describes a disease which has been termed by others Roseola rheumatica. In this disease local extravasations occur in the skin, and erythematous patches about the joints, which are swollen and painful. **1861** *New Sydenham Soc. Yr.-bk. 1860* 403 (*heading*) On 'peliosis rheumatica' of children. **1868** C. H. Fagge et al. tr. *Hebra's Dis. of Skin* II. xxviii. 422 Alibert.. makes unnecessary distinctions between peliosis (purpura) and petechiæ. **1911** *Brit. Med. Jrnl.* 11 Feb. 331/2 That peliosis rheumatica is never of rheumatic origin is hardly capable of proof. **1968** Champion & Wilkinson in A. J. Rook et al. *Textbk. Dermatol.* I. xvii. 428/1 The separation of Schönlein's 'peliosis rheumatica' [from the Henoch-Schönlein syndrome] is no longer justified.

pelisse (pə'liːs). Also 8 pellice, 8–9 -ise, 9 -isse, pelice. [a. F. *pelisse*, formerly *pelice* = It. *pelliccia* 'any kind of furred garment' (Florio):—med.L. *pellicia* (Papias), for L. *pellicia* (or *-icea*) *tunica* or *vestis*, a coat or garment of skins or fur, f. *pell-is* skin.]

1. †a. A garment of fur. *Obs.* **b.** A long mantle or cloak lined with fur.

1718 Lady M. W. Montagu *Let. to C'tess Mar* 10 Mar., One of her slaves immediately brought her a pellice of rich brocade lined with sables. **1789** Wesley *Will* in Coke & Moore *Life* III. iv. §2 (1792) 515 My pellise I give to the Rev. Mr. Creighton. **1804** Ct. Rumford in *Phil. Trans.* XCIV. 181 We might naturally expect, that a pellisse would be warmest when worn with the hair outwards, as I have found it to be in fact. **1806** A. Duncan *Nelson* 104 A pelice of sable fur. **1874** Boutell *Arms & Arm.* ix. 182 Prototypes of more recent hussar pelisses with their fur lining.

2. a. A long mantle of silk, velvet, cloth, or other material, worn by women, reaching to the ankles, and having arm-holes or sleeves.

1755 Mrs. Delany in *Life & Corr.* (1862) 321, I don't know what you mean by a pompadour, unless it is what we call in this part of the world a pelisse; which in plain English is a long cloak made of satin or velvet, black or any colour; lined or trimmed with silk, satin, or fur, according to the fancy. **1801** *Sporting Mag.* XIX. 115 The ladies were principally dressed in sarsnet pelisses. **1837** Dickens *Pickw.* v, A tall bony woman—straight all the way down—in a coarse blue pelisse, with the waist an inch or two below her arm-pits. **1893** Georgina Hill *Hist. Eng. Dress* II. 216 The women of the last generation all wore pelisses. **1898** Lady Mary Loyd tr. *Uzanne's Fashion in Paris* ii. 39 [*c* 1800–4] Pelisses were coming into general use. They were worn long, almost reaching the ground, with wide sleeves turned back over the wrists, and round cape collars.

b. A garment worn out of doors by young children over their other clothes.

1805 T. Fremantle in *Wynne Diaries* (1940) III. 234 Mistress Tittler with a black Velour pelisse, tell her I desire she will not spoil it until I come home. **1807** Jane Austen *Let.* 7 Jan. (1952) 173 Caroline's new pelisse depended upon her mother's being able or not to come so far in the chair. **1828** M. O'Brien *Jrnl.* 20 Oct. (1968) I. 19 Mary set to work on a pelisse for the baby. **1879** *Madame Bayard's Bouquet of Fashion* No. 32 Children's Dresses. No. 941. Infant's Pelisse. **1894** L. T. Meade *Iron Grip* II. xxxi. 159 She dressed the baby in his white hat and white pelisse. **1922** Joyce *Ulysses* 490 In babylinen and pelisse, bigheaded, with a caul of dark hair.

c. Used for the ecclesiastical cassock.

1877 J. D. Chambers *Div. Worship* 26 The Pelisse or Cassock was the ordinary clerical gown or under garment.

3. *attrib.* and *Comb.*, as ***pelisse-robe***; **pelisse-cloth**, a twilled woollen fabric, used for pelisses.

1835 *Court Mag.* VI. p. x/2 Pelisse robes, both of satin and velvet, have been during the last week very much adopted.

‖pelisson. *Obs.* In 5 pely-, pellycon. [OF. *pelisson*, in 14th c. *pelicon* (*ç*) 'a furd petticoat or frocke' (Cotgr.), AF. *pellicoun*, in med.L. *pellicion-em*, It. *pelliccione* 'a great furred gown' (Florio), med.L. *pelliciōn-em*, deriv. of *pellicia* pelisse.] A furred gown; = pelisse 1.

1491 Caxton *Vitas Patr.* (W. de W. 1495) I. xxxvii. 43 b, His clothynge was oonly of a sacke, and a mantell of pellycon. *Ibid.* 50 His Frocke, his Pelycon and his Gospellis. [**1876** Planché *Cycl. Costume* I. 391 King John orders a grey pelisson with nine bars of fur to be made for the queen.]

pelite ('piːlaɪt). *Geol.* [f. Gr. πηλ-ός clay, earth, mud + -ite¹.] A rock composed of an argillaceous sediment.

1879 Rutley *Study Rocks* xiv. 299 The psammites and pelites.. are respectively represented by the various sandstones, arkose, etc., and by the tuffs.

pelitic (pɪ'lɪtɪk), *a. Geol.* [f. prec. + -ic.] Of the nature of pelite; composed of fine sediment.

1879 Rutley *Study Rocks* xiv. 299 The clastic rocks.. he divides into the psephitic, the psammitic, and the pelitic.

pelitory, obs. form of pellitory.

pell (pɛl), *sb.*¹ *Obs.* exc. *Hist.* Forms: 4 pel, 5 peall, pele, peele, peell, pelle, 6 pyll, 6– pell. [ME. a. AF. *pell*, *peal*, OF. *pel* (13th c. in Littré), mod.F. *peau* (= Pr. *pel*, *pelh*, Cat. *pell*, Sp. *piel*, It. *pelle*):—L. *pell-em* skin, leather, parchment.]

†1. A skin or hide; *esp.* a furred skin used as or forming the lining or trimming of a cloak; a cloak so lined or trimmed, a fur. *Obs.*

13.. *K. Alis.* 6697 Y wol chargen al the bestis With pellis, and siglatouns honeste. *c* **1325** *Lai le Freine* 172 Therin she leyed the child, for cold, In the pel as it was bifold. *c* **1450** *Cov. Myst.* (Shaks. Soc.) 246, ij doctorys with him arayd with pellys aftyr the old gyse. **1596** Bp. W. Barlow *Three Serm.* ii. 88 Our flesh swelleth, and like Sathyrions pelles or skinnes.. we are of vnquiet and restlesse minds.

†b. The skin with which the deciduous horns of deer are at first covered; the 'velvet'. *Obs.*

In quot. 1575 app. associated with pill, peel *sb.*

1575 Turberv. *Venerie* 242 His heade when it commeth first out, hath a russet pyll vpon it, the whiche is called Veluet. *a* **1700** B. E. *Dict. Cant. Crew*, *To Fray*,.. when Deer rub.. their Heads against Trees to get the pells of their new Horns off.

2. A skin or roll of parchment, a parchment; *spec.* each of the two pells, of receipt (*pellis receptorum*) and disbursement (*pellis exituum*), kept at the Exchequer. **b.** In *pl.* The Office of the Exchequer in which these were kept. *Obs.* exc. *Hist.*

1454 *Rolls of Parlt.* V. 249/1 That it be entred in the pele of your receipt. *Ibid.* 272/2 Which may appere in the peele of the Resceyt of youre Eschequer of Record. **1485** *Naval Acc. Hen. VII* (1896) 7 As in the Peall of Michelmasse Terme.. playnely doth apiere. **1577–87** Holinshed *Chron.* III. 1245/1 In which Easter tearme was William bishop of Yorke also made treasuror, as is prooued by the pell of *Exitus*. **1681** Nevile *Plato Rediv.* 197 No Sanctuary to fly to, but a peice of Parchment kept in the Pells. *c* **1802** Canning *Grand Consult.* Poet. Wks. (1823) 40 But our frugal doctor .. Gives his pills to the public, the Pells to his Son.

c. ***Clerk of the Pells***, an officer formerly charged with the entry of receipts and disbursements on the parchment rolls in the

Exchequer. So ***Master of the Pells***. *Obs.* exc. *Hist.*

a **1603** in *Househ. Ord.* (1790) 244 Clark of the pell; fee—£17. 10. 0. **1657** HOWELL *Londinop.* 370 Touching.. the Clerk of the Pell; his duty is, to enter every Tellers bill into a Roll call'd *Pellis Receptorum*. **1665** PEPYS *Diary* 29 Sept., Mr. Warder, Master of the Pells. **1834** *Act 4 & 5 Will. IV*, c. 15 §1 The Offices of Auditor, and of each of the Four Tellers of the Exchequer, and of the Clerk of the Pells.. are hereby abolished. **1846** *Blackw. Mag.* LIX. 464 His party.. acknowledged his services by a retiring pension, which Mr. Pitt.. exchanged for the clerkship of the pells.

3. *attrib.* and *Comb.*, as ***pell-office*** (sense 2); †**pell-monger**, a dealer in skins and furs; †**pell-wool**, wool plucked from the skin of a dead sheep; = PELT-*wool*.

1676 NEEDHAM *Pacquet Adv.* 31 May they leave off barking when he comes into the City; and not do as dogs do at a *Pell-monger. **1697** LUTTRELL *Brief Rel.* (1857) IV. 311 Mr. Lemar, a clerk in the *pell office in the exchequer. **1429** *Rolls of Parlt.* IV. 360/2 þat no man make noon inwynde withynne þe flese,.. ne þerynne to putte lokkys, *pellewolle, terre,.. ne noon oþer filthe. **1442** *Ibid.* V. 61/1 That ther be put in noon of thoo Worstedes, eny Lambe woll, nor Pell woll.

Pell (pɛl), *sb.*[2] *Math.* [See PELLIAN *a.*] ***Pell('s) equation***: any Diophantine equation of the form $ax^2 - y^2 = 1$ (a, x, and y being integers). Also *absol.*

1910 *Encycl. Brit.* I. 617/2 Although Pell had nothing to do with the solution, posterity has termed the equation Pell's Equation. **1912** E. E. WHITFORD (*thesis title*) The Pell equation. **1966** OGILVY & ANDERSON *Excursions in Number Theory* x. 129 It turns out that the equation $y^2 - Nx^2 = 1$ known as Pell's equation, has solutions in integers whenever N is not a perfect square. **1974** *Sci. Amer.* July 116/3 Whenever the coefficient is not a square the Pell has an infinity of solutions. *Ibid.* 120/2 The general Pell equation, a key to so much of this kind of number analysis.

pell, *v.* *Obs.* exc. *dial.* [Origin uncertain: cf. PEAL *v.*[1]; also L. *pellĕre* to drive.]

1. *intr.* To hurry, rush.

c **1300** *Havelok* 809 Shal ich neuere lengere dwelle, To morwen shal ich forth pelle. **1903** *Eng. Dial. Dict.*, *Pell*.. to dash, drive or strike violently; to walk with a heavy dashing step.

2. *trans.* To beat or knock violently, esp. *down*.

a **1400–50** *Alexander* 117 How þe powere out of Persy pellid doune his knyȝtis. **1601** HOLLAND *Pliny* I. 431 Beat and pell them downe with perches and poles. **1606** —— *Sueton.* 156 The buffons and jesters about him made good sport, pelling him with olive and date-stones. ? *a* **1750** *Battle Sheriff-Muir* in Child *Ballads* (1857) VII. 260 For well I wat I saw them run, Both south and north, when they begun, To pell and mell, and kill and fell.

pell, obs. form of PALL, PEEL *sb.*[1]

pellac, pellack: see PELLOCK[1] and [2].

†**pellage.** *Obs.* [f. OF. *pel* PELL *sb.* + -AGE.] A duty or impost formerly levied on skins exported.

[**1409–10** *Rolls of Parlt.* III. 625/2 [Le] Subside & Custumes des Layns & Pealx lanutz, outre le Pondage, Tonage, Aunage, Pellage, & d'autres Marchaundises.] **1691** *Blount's Law Dict.* (ed. 2), *Pellage*.., the Custom or Duty paid for Skins, Pelts or Leather.

‖**pellagra** (pɛˈleɪgrə, -ˈægrə). *Path.* [It. and mod.L. (F. *pellagre*), said to be f. *pell-is* + ?*-agra* in *chiragra*, *podagra* (gout in the hands, the feet); but perh. orig. It. *pelle agra* 'rough skin'.] An endemic disease (frequent among the peasantry of Southern Europe, esp. Lombardy, often attributed to eating diseased maize), in which the skin reddens, dries, and cracks, and the epidermis peels off in bran-like scales; the digestive organs and central nervous system are affected, and the disease often ends in insanity.

1811 HOOPER *Dict. Med.* s.v., The disease called the pelagra does not appear to have been noticed by any of our nosologists. **1840** *Penny Cycl.* XVII. 388/1 Pellagra is a disease chiefly affecting the skin, and particularly prevalent amongst the peasantry of the north of Italy. **1854** *N. Syd. Soc. Year-bk. Med. & Surg.* 176 *m*, The endemic pellagra of Aragon.. is absolutely identical with the endemic pellagra of Asturias. **1865** *Chambers's Encycl.* VII. 363/1 Pellagra, at one time the name of a.. skin-disease.. is now employed to designate a group of phenomena, of which the most prominent and significant are mental. **1874** BUCKNILL & TUKE *Psych. Med.* (ed. 3) 364 The first descriptions of pellagra appear about the year 1770.

Hence **pellagra'genic** *a.*, engendering pellagra; **pe'llagrin**, a person affected with pellagra.

1865 *Chambers's Encycl.* VII. 363/1 Of 500 patients in the Milan Lunatic Asylum in 1827, one third were pellagrins. **1903** *Brit. Med. Jrnl.* 11 July 86 Alcoholism renders the organism more prone to suffer from pellagragenic poison.

pe'llagrous, *a.* *Path.* [ad. It. *pellagroso*, F. *pellagreux*, *-euse*, f. PELLAGRA: see -OUS.] Of the nature of or pertaining to pellagra; affected with pellagra. So (in latter sense only) **'pellagrose** *a.*

1864 *N. Syd. Soc. Year-bk. Med. & Surg.* 176 *k*, Phthisis and scrofula do not appear to be at all prevalent among the pellagrose. *Ibid.* 176 *m*, The endemic pellagrous affections of Spain are absolutely identical with those of the Landes district [of France], and those of Italy with the sporadic pellagrous diseases of France. **1874** BUCKNILL & TUKE *Psych. Med.* (ed. 3) 364 Pellagrous Insanity. *Ibid.*, The total number of pellagrose in the Milanese provinces in 1856 was ..16·3 per 1000 of the population. Of these,..9 per cent. were insane.

†**pella'mountain.** *Obs.* Also 6 puliall-, 6–7 pela-, -mountayne. [app. a popular corruption of some med.L. herbalists' name, e.g. *Pulegium montanum*, or *Serpyllum montanum*: cf. also PELLETER[1]. The OF. name was *poliol*, *poulieul*.] A name of Wild Thyme.

1575 TURBERV. *Faulconrie* 223 Sage, Mints, Pelamountaine, Cloues, Cynamon, and such other sweete comfortable deuises. **1578** LYTE *Dodoens* II. xliv. 231 This herbe is now called.. in English wilde Tyme, Puliall mountayne, Pellamountayne, and running Time. **1602** CAREW *Cornwall* 19 Natures liberall hand decketh many of the sea cliffes with wilde Hissop, Sage, Pelamountayne.., and such like well-sauouring herbes. **1677** N. COX *Gentl. Recreation* II. 248 Take Germander, Pelamountain, Basil, Grummel-seed, and Broom-flowers, of each half an ounce.

pellar, -er. *dial.* (Cornwall). [? f. PELL *v.* + -AR[3], -ER[1].] An exorcist; a wizard, conjurer.

1865 R. HUNT *Pop. Rom. W. Eng.* Ser. II. 81 She and her friends were satisfied that she had been ill wished. So she went to the 'Peller'... The spell was taken off, and the old woman grew strong. *Ibid.* 77 His wife then stated that the virtue was in her and not in him; that she was of the real 'Pellar' blood. **1893** *Longm. Mag.* Feb. 389 She was going to the 'peller' to get a 'charm' said for him.

†**pellard.** *Obs.* or *Hist.* [ad. med.L. *pellarda* (1388 in Du Cange), of uncertain origin: perh. a derivative of L. *pellis*, It. *pelle* skin.] A kind of cloak or tunic: see quots.

1846 FAIRHOLT *Costume in Eng.* Gloss., *Pellard*, a garment like a super-tunic. **1876** PLANCHÉ *Cycl. Costume* I. 391 *Pellard*, another name for the houpeland.

pellatory, pellatur: see PELLITORY, PELLETER.

pelle, obs. f. PALL, PEAL.

Pellegrini-Stieda (ˌpɛlɛgriːnɪˈʃtiːdə). *Med.* The names of Augusto *Pellegrini* (*c* 1880–*c* 1940), Italian physician, and Alfred *Stieda* (1869–1945), German physician, used *attrib.* and in the possessive to designate a condition described by them in 1905 and 1908 respectively, in which ossification of the tibial collateral ligament of the knee occurs as a result of injury. [Named by R. Petrignani 1930, in *Contributions à l'Étude de la Maladie de Pellegrini-Stieda* (Thèse, Paris) 14.]

1932 *Amer. Jrnl. Roentgenology* XXVIII. 97/2 Pellegrini-Stieda's disease is of importance from its medicolegal aspect. **1945** *Surg., Gynecol. & Obstetr.* LXXXI. 212/1 The imposing name of 'Pellegrini-Stieda disease' is misleading. It implies that the one finding of the calcification over the adductor tubercle is a disease complex. **1971** A. A. MICHELE *You don't have to Ache* v. 128 A fairly common condition in men between the ages of 24 and 40 years, is hardening and calcification of the ligament at the inner side of the knee joint (Pelligrini Steida [*sic*] disorder).

peller, obs. f. PEALER[1], PILLAR; var. PELLAR.

pellere, var. PELURE[1] *Obs.*

pellet (ˈpɛlɪt), *sb.*[1] Forms: 4–5 **pelet**, (5 **-ette**), **pelote**, (5 **-ot**), **pylote**, 6 **pellete**, **-ette**, **-ot**, **-otte**, **-it**, **-yt**, **-at**, 6– **pellet**. [a. F. *pelote* (11th c.) = Pr., Sp. *pelota*, Pg. *pellota*, It. *pillotta* 'any round bundle or bal' (Florio), med.L. *pelōta*, *pilōta*, deriv. of It. *pila*, L. *pila* ball.]

1. Any globe, ball, or spherical body, usually one of small size; a ball of some plastic or soft substance, esp. of medicine or food, a bolus, a pill.

1390 GOWER *Conf.* II. 306 Of þich sche tok him a pelote, The which he scholde into the throte Of Minotaure caste rihte. *c* **1400** *Lanfranc's Cirurg.* 183 Grinde hem & tempere hem vp wiþ ius of iouis barba, & make þerof pelottis. *c* **1430** *Two Cookery-bks.* 39 Take þan þin fleysshe.. make þer-of pelettys, as it were Applys. **1481** CAXTON *Myrr.* I. xv. 48 God fourmed the world alle rounde, lyke as is a pelette. **1591** PERCIVALL *Sp. Dict.*, *Hallulla*, pellets to cram pullen. **1607** TOPSELL *Four-f. Beasts* (1658) 419 The little berries or pellets which are within the Pomgranate. **1676** WISEMAN *Chirurg. Treat.* (J.), I dressed with little pellets of lint. **1768–74** TUCKER *Lt. Nat.* (1834) II. 589 We are citizens of the universe, inhabitants of the little corner thereof, the dirty pellet where we are now stationed. **1829** SOUTHEY *All for Love* II. xxxix, As when an electric pellet of light Comes forcibly out at a touch. **1851** D. WILSON *Preh. Ann.* (1863) II. IV. iii. 260 The most primitive of Scottish coinage is the simple gold pellet. **1853** SOYER *Pantroph.* 161 The poultry ..are made to swallow pellets..composed of two parts of barley flour, and one of maize.

2. *spec.* **a.** A ball, usually of stone, used as a missile during the 14th and 15th centuries, and shot from mangonels, mortars, etc.; a cannon-ball; in later use, a bullet; now applied to small shot.

[**1339** Peletæ de plumbo: *c* **1370** Pelottes de fer: see GUN *sb.* I.] **1362** LANGL. *P. Pl.* A. v. 61 As pale as a pelet in a palesye he seemede. *c* **1384** CHAUCER *H. Fame* III. 553 Thrugh out euery Regioun Went this foule trumpes soun As swifte as pelet out of gonne. ? *a* **1400** *Morte Arth.* 3037 Thane boldly þay buske, and bendes engynes, Payses in pylotes and proues theire castes. *c* **1440** *Promp. Parv.* 391/1 Pelot, rownde stone of erthe, or other mater (*H.*, *P.* pelet), *pileus*, *vel piliolus*, *rudus*. **1489** CAXTON *Faytes of A.* II. xx. 135 Dyuers other small gonnes castyng pyllettes of leed and comon stones. **1495** *Naval Acc. Hen. VII* (1896) 274 Pyllettes of lede & dyce of yron. **1497** *Ibid.* 95 Pellettes of leed for Serpentynes. **1555** EDEN *Decades* 180 A great and verye rounde pearle,..as bygge as a smaule pellet of a stone bowe, and of the weight of xxvi. carattes. **1577** DEE *Relat. Spir.* I. (1659) 78 An yern, like a pair of tongs; in form of a Mould to cast Pellets in. **1607** TOPSELL *Four-f. Beasts* (1658) 329 To cure a wound made with harquebush-shot... First seek with an instrument whether the pellet remain within or not. *a* **1668** DAVENANT *Siege* Wks. (1673) 68 These Cannon Pellets will bruise me shrewdly. **1719** D'URFEY *Pills* (1872) V. 137 For these Guns are such pestilent Things, To put a Pellet in one's Brow. **1841** GREENER *Sci. Gunnery* vii. 251 There are many parts about the body of a bird, wherein a pellet of No. 7 will affect its vitality equal to a pellet of No. 2. **1880** JEFFERIES *Gr. Ferne F.* 252 The pellets hissing past his ears.

fig. **1523** SKELTON *Garl. Laurel* 637 With a pellit of peuisshenes they had suche a stroke, That all the dayes of ther lyfe shall styck by ther rybbis. **1641** MILTON *Animadv.* 34 It will stand long enough against the battery of their paper pellets. *a* **1764** LLOYD *Poet* Poems (1790) 185 Around the frequent pellets whistle From Satire, Ode, and pert Epistle. **1862** TYNDALL *Mountaineer* i. 7 The heavy rain-pellets..rattle with fury against the carriage.

b. A toy bullet of clay, wood, paper, etc., used in sport or play, esp. as the charge of a pop-gun.

1553 EDEN *Treat. Newe Ind.* (Arb.) 23 To blowe them oute of a trunke as we doe pellets of claye. *c* **1626** *Dick of Devon.* II. i. in Bullen *O. Pl.* II. 26 And my Devonshire blade, honest Dick Pike, Spard not his Sugar pellets among my Spanyards. **1657** W. MORICE *Cœna quasi Κοινή* xxix. 287 Childrens gunns, to shoot the pellets which they put into them. **1856** KANE *Arct. Expl.* I. vi. 56 Our rifle-balls reverberated from their hides like cork pellets from a pop-gun target.

c. = CAST *sb.* 19.

1802 G. MONTAGU *Ornith. Dict.* I. s.v. *Owl*, White. Their food is chiefly mice, which they swallow whole, and..eject the bones and fur in large pellets, which are termed castings. **1834** R. MUDIE *Feathered Tribes Brit. Islands* I. 141 Mice are preferred to birds, the feathers being more untractable than the fur, both in swallowing, and in casting pellets or quids. **1895** *U.S. Dept. Agric. Yearbk. 1894* 217 These masses, known as 'pellets' are regurgitated before fresh food is taken. **1905** *Daily News* 5 Jan. 4/3 The brown owl's pellet very rarely contains the remains of shrews. **1948** *Brit. Birds* XLI. 290, I found a secluded coomb..which, judging by the quantity of droppings and pellets below the ledges, had been used as a roosting place by a number of Ravens. **1964** A. L. THOMSON *New Dict. Birds* 608/2 Pellets are best known in respect of birds-of-prey, but..birds of very widely differing species regularly eject pellets. **1971** S. HILL *Strange Meeting* i. 31 The small, bleached bones from the owls' pellets.

d. The droppings of various small animals, esp. the rabbit, which reingests some of them.

1919 'W. N. P. BARBELLION' *Diary* 14 Apr. (1920) 129 Those sand dunes! Their characteristic feature was rabbits' skulls..and the little round dry pellets of rabbits, more numberless than the snail shells. **1939** *Nature* 10 June 982/2 Numerous coccidial oocysts were also found in the stomach pellets of the control rabbit..which appeared to prove the fæcal origin of the pellets. **1956** THOMPSON & WORDEN *Rabbit* iii. 27 A blinded rabbit took pellets direct from its anus. **1964** R. M. LOCKLEY *Private Life Rabbit* ii. 32 At night their pellets were dropped along the boundary fence. **1972** R. ADAMS *Watership Down* I. 405 Under snow they [*sc.* rabbits] may stay underground for days at a time, feeding only by chewing pellets.

3. *Her.* A roundel sable: = GUNSTONE 2.

[**1562** LEIGH *Armorie* 150 b, He beareth Or, iii Ogresses in Fesses. These are Pellettes of gunnes, and are neuer other colour, then Sable.] **1572** BOSSEWELL *Armorie* II. 81 b, Th' Ogresse is the same that we call a Pellet of a gonne. *a* **1661** FULLER *Worthies*, *Northampton*. II. (1662) 299 This Sir John bare, for his paternal Coat, Argent on a Bend Gules, three Swans proper, between as many Pellets. **1766** PORNY *Heraldry* (1777) Dict., *Pellets*, the name given to the Black Roundlets, by English Heralds alone. **1864** BOUTELL *Her. Hist. & Pop.* xv. §15 (ed. 3) 203 Lord Latymer charges a pellet upon his silver saltire. **1971** *Country Life* 27 May 1303/2 A purely secular goblet..its date 1664, its so-far unidentified maker's mark 'P.D.' with three pellets above, a cinquefoil below.

4. A circular boss or raised part, rounded or flat, in coins or decorative work.

1842 FRANCIS *Dict. Arts* etc., *Pellet*, a Gothic architectural ornament, consisting of plain, flat, circular pieces or pellets, arranged along a fascia or band, at equal distances. **1864** J. EVANS *Coins Anc. Britons* iii. 45 When a central pellet is surrounded by a circle of smaller pellets or ovals, I have called it a 'rosette' or 'star of pellets'. **1875** FORTNUM *Maiolica* xv. 168 The shallow bowl..marked at the back with the crossed circle, having a pellet in one of the quarters.

5. *attrib.* and *Comb.*, as ***pellet ornamentation*** (see 4), ***system***; ***pellet-like*** adj.; **pellet bomb**, a type of anti-personnel bomb; **pellet bow**: see quot. 1852; **pellet mill**, an apparatus for pelleting powders; **pellet moulding** *Arch.*, a moulding consisting of a flat band on which are circular flat disks (Gwilt *Archit.* Gloss. 1876); **pellet powder**, gunpowder compressed in moulds into pellets of defined quantity and form.

1970 *Guardian* 10 Mar. 12 Anti-personnel bombs..the same *pellet bombs which figured so prominently in North Vietnamese protests. They are dropped in canisters..the bomblets, each a bit bigger than a man's fist, might go on exploding for two days. **1970** *Peace News* 3 Apr. 5/3 An unexploded pellet bomb she had touched while digging in the fields. **1816** *Sporting Mag.* XLVIII. 244 Killing fourteen pheasants with a *pellet bow or air gun. **1852** R. F. BURTON *Falconry in Valley Indus* i. 7 The pellet-bow..is made of a slip of bamboo, bent in the shape of our ancient weapon; .. it has two strings stretched parallel to each other from horn to horn. About the centre a bit of canvas or coarse cloth, an inch or an inch and a half in length, is sewn tightly to the two cords, and against it the pellet, a lump of hard clay, about the size of a 'taw', is firmly held by the thumb and forefinger, which draw the bow. **1860** TYNDALL *Glac.* I. x. 65 All the way home we were battered by this *pellet-like rain. **1950** J. H. PERRY *Chem. Engineers' Handbk.* (ed. 3) 1189/1 *Pellet mills are designed to agglomerate permeable free-flowing materials into pellet form. **1971** *Power Farming* Mar. 22/1 Demand for cubed and pelleted feed has led to the development of the Cubamix single unit mobile feed plant. .. The equipment comprises the grinding and mixing section as already used on the company's Grindamix model and a separately driven Simon Barron pellet mill. **1838** PARKER *Gloss. Archit.* (ed. 2), **Pellet Moulding*, an ornament in Norman architecture. **1870** *Engineer* 16 Sept. 184/1 *Pellet powder was recommended for .. adoption with heavy guns by the Gunpowder Committee of 1866.

† **ˈpellet**, *sb.*[2] *Obs.* Forms: 5 pilet, pylet, pellet, 6 pellot. [a. OF. *pelete, -ette, pellete, -ette*, dim. of *pel*:—L. *pell-em* skin.]

1. A pellicle, a thin or fine skin or membrane. *c* **1420** *Pallad. on Husb.* I. 590 And other while an hen wul ha the pippe, A whit pilet that wul the tonge enrounde. *Ibid.* VI. 144 Oon of hem chese, Or that pellet that closith euery half The chike and pyiouncrawe, hool either half.

2. The pelt or skin of a sheep or other animal. [**1298** *Bolton Priory Compotus* lf. 21 De lana domus .. De lokettis et pelettis.] *c* **1440** LYDG. *Hors, Shepe & G.* 358 (MS. Lansd.) Of sheepe al-so comyth pilet [*MSS. Harl. & Lamb.* pelt, CAXTON pellet] & eke fell, .. Caried ovir see where men may it sell. *c* **1440** *Promp. Parv.* 398/2 Pylet, skyn, *pellis* (P. *cutis*). *c* **1470** HENRYSON *Mor. Fab.* IX. (*Wolf & Fox*) xviii, Thair sall na pedder .. pyke your pellet fra me; I sall of it mak mittenis to my lufis. **1583** *Leg. Bp. St. Androis* 12 Plucking the pellotis or euer the scheip be slane.

ˈpellet, *v.* Pples. pelleted, -eting (occas. incorrectly -etting). [f. PELLET *sb.*[1]: cf. F. *peloter.*] *trans.* **a.** To send as a pellet (*obs.*); to form or shape into pellets; *esp.* to coat (plant seed) with soluble nutritive and protective substances to facilitate handling and promote growth. **b.** To hit with (paper) pellets, small shot, etc.

1597 SHAKS. *Lover's Compl.* 18 Laundring the silken figures in the brine That seasoned woe had pelleted in teares. **1606** —— *Ant. & Cl.* III. xiii. 165 Till by degrees the memory of my wombe, .. By the discandering of this pelleted storme, Lye grauelesse. **1870** *Pall Mall G.* 7 Nov. 7 A newspaper correspondent, who, treating himself to a battue in the Emperor's preserves, delivered an erratic charge and pelleted a beater's finger. **1891** G. MEREDITH *One of our Conq.* xxxvi, The English kick at the insolence, when they are not in the mood for pelleting themselves. **1936** L. M. T. BELL *Making & Moulding of Plastics* xi. 185 For convenience and ease in the handling of the powdered compounds .., the compounds are frequently pelleted cold prior to moulding. **1944** *Sugar Beet Jrnl.* Jan. 41 A process of 'pelleting' sugar beet seed segments .. has been developed. The new process coats the rough segments with a water-soluble layer of beneficial and inert material, making the seed pieces smooth, spherical, and about the size of small seed peas. **1949** *Chem. Abstr.* XLIII. 2154 The app[aratus] is particularly adapted to pelletting Pb alloys into uniform fine shot. **1950** J. H. PERRY *Chem. Engineers' Handbk.* (ed. 3) 1189/1 Although originally designed for pelleting animal feeds, it is now being adapted to the handling of many other products. **1958** *Times* 24 Nov. 15/3 These low seed rates can be achieved .. in the case of timothy, by using seed pelleted with basic slag. **1970** *Country Life* 17–24 Dec. 1187/1 Pelletting hay has been tried without more than local acceptance. **1973** *Daily Tel.* 30 June 8/5 (Advt.), Seed pelleter with sufficient Seedex Plant Food Compound to pellet hundreds of seeds. **1974** *Nature* 22 Nov. 327/1 After incubation for 30 min at 37°, the microsomes were pelleted by centrifugation and the DNA reisolated and purified.

Hence **ˈpelleting** *vbl. sb.* and *ppl. a.*

1936 L. M. T. BELL *Making & Moulding of Plastics* xi. 185 Figure 36 shows a crank pelleting machine .. with the powder hopper removed. **1944** *Business Week* 26 Aug. 52/2 Western companies still regard the process as experimental, one question being whether the pelleting material, which easily melts from around the seed in damp midwestern soils, and thus permits emergence of the seedling, may not have more restraint in the dry western soils. **1945** A. T. BIRKBY *Phenolic Plastics* vii. 78 In the Plas[t]ics industry the term tabletting means the compression of moulding powder into a variety of small, easily-handled blocks, each of a pre-determined weight. Two other terms often used for this process are 'preforming' and 'pelleting'. **1950** J. H. PERRY *Chem. Engineers' Handbk.* (ed. 3) 1189/1 Pelleting of dusts, fumes, .. and the like can be accomplished in a rotating-drum device known as the Dwight-Lloyd Segregating Pelletizer. **1963** P. FINN-KELCEY in A. N. Duckham *Farming* III. xi. 404 Pelleting machines introduced in recent years are already proving popular with farmers who compound their own stock rations.

pelletable (ˈpɛlɪtəb(ə)l), *a.* [f. PELLET *v.* + -ABLE.] Capable of being formed into pellets. Hence **pelletaˈbility**.

1970 *Mikroskopie* XXIV. 296 (*heading*) A simplified protocol for electron microscopy processing of 'pelletable' material. **1973** *Biol. Abstr.* LV. 2932/2 Bull sperm of 296 animals was tested for pelletability. **1976** *Nature* 29 Jan. 324/2 Unknown amounts may have been associated with organelles or plastid fragments of a lower pelletability than intact etioplasts. *Ibid.* 325/1 The pelletable phytochrome investigated by many other workers seems to bind to membranous material only in the Pfr form.

ˈpelleted, *ppl. a.* [f. PELLET *v.* or *sb.*[1] + -ED.]

1. Marked or charged with (heraldic) pellets. **1623** MIDDLETON *Triumph Integr.* Wks. (Bullen) VII. 389 This Chariot drawn by two .. pelleted lions. **1766** PORNY *Heraldry* (1787) Dict., *Pelleted, Pellited*, term used to denote any Charge or Bearing marked with Pellets.

2. Formed into or supplied as pellets.

1943 *Los Angeles Times* 25 Nov. 13/5 Tests being conducted here with newly developed 'pelleted' seed show that complete seed control can be obtained and expensive hand labor .. eliminated in favor of mechanical thinners or thinning eliminated altogether. **1951** *Sci. News Let.* 28 Apr. 269/2 One of the most valuable aids to the blind gardener .. is the recent development of pelleted seeds. **1961** *Listener* 7 Dec. 992/3 Slugs are controlled with the aid of pelleted metaldehyde. **1970** *Nature* 10 Oct. 178/2 Six lambs .. were fed daily a pelleted diet of chopped lucerne hay and oats. **1973** *Guardian* 17 Mar. 8/5 Every effort should be made to sow the seed thinly. Pelleted seeds, of course, make this much easier. **1975** *N.Z. Jrnl. Agric.* Sept. 69/1 They were all fed to three weeks of age on a pelleted starter diet.

† **pelleter**[1], **peletre**. *Herb. Obs.* Forms: 4–5 pelestre, 5 peletre, -thre, -tur, pelletre, -etur, -atur, -eter, 5–6 peletyr. [ME. *peletre, -ethre*, a. AF. *peletre, -estre*, f. (by dissimilation of *r .. r*) OF. **peretre, piretre* (Cotgr.) = Sp. *pelitre* (:—**peritre*):—L. *pyr-, pirethrum*:—Gr. πύρεθρον feverfew; cf. πυρετός fever. See also PYRETHRUM. The history of sense 2 is obscure.]

1. = PELLITORY 1, the Pyrethrum of the ancients.

a **1387** *Sinon. Barthol.* (Anecd. Oxon.) 34 *Piretrum*, pelestre idem. *c* **1400** *Lanfranc's Cirurg.* 262 Seed of rosis & peletre & zinzibere. *a* **1450** *Stockh. Med. MS.* 184 Longwourt or pelethre of Spanye (*Eleborus*). *Ibid.* 214 Pelethre: *peretrum domyticum*. *c* **1450** *Alphita* (Anecd. Oxon.) 145 *Piretrum*, herba .. satis communis, radix eius multum est acuta in sapore qua utimur. gall. et a^e. pelestre. **1530** PALSGR. 253/1 Peletyr an herbe.

2. Wild Thyme (*Thymus Serpyllum*), or Garden Thyme (*T. vulgaris*). Cf. PELLAMOUNTAIN.

a **1387** *Sinon. Barthol.* (Anecd. Oxon.) 39 *Serpillum* et *herpillum* idem sunt, s. pelestre, tamen herpillum quandoque sumitur pro poligonia. *a* **1400** *Pistill of Susan* 116 Daysye and Ditoyne, Ysope and Aueroyne, Peletre [*v. rr.* pelletre, -tur] and Plauntoyne. *c* **1420** *Pallad. on Husb.* I. 1024 Of tyme is wex and hony maad swettest; Of tymbra, peletur and origon. **14..** *Anc. Cookery* in *Househ. Ord.* (1790) 441 Take .. myntes, and peletur, and costmaryn, and sauge. **1483** *Cath. Angl.* 273/2 Pelleter .., *serpillum*, herba est.

† **pelleter**[2]. *Obs.* In 6 pellytour. [ad. OF. *peletier* (12th c. in Hatz.-Darm.), mod. F. *pelletier* (16th c. in Littré), f. OF. *pel*, L. *pell-em* skin, fur.] A fellmonger.

1575 TURBERV. *Faulconrie* 12 Thin skynnes sent to the furryers and pellytours of Fraunce.

pelleter[3]. [f. PELLET *v.* + -ER[1].] An apparatus for pelleting.

1960 *Times Rev. Industry* July 51/1 BIPEL now sells much of its production outside the plastics industry. This includes pelleters for explosives, punch presses for metal work, [etc.]. **1963** P. FINN-KELCEY in A. N. Duckham *Farming* III. xi. 405 Whether an installation is to consist of a mill only, a mill and a mixer or the full layout of mill, mixer and pelleter .., considerable thought must be given to the positioning of each. **1973** [see PELLET *v.*].

pelletierine (pɛlɛˈtɪəraɪn). *Chem.* [f. name of the French chemist Bertrand Pelletier (1761–97) + -INE[5].] A colourless alkaloid ($C_8H_{13}NO$) obtained from the bark of the pomegranate.

1881 WATTS *Dict. Chem.* 3rd Suppl. 1498 *Pelletierine*, the alkaloïd of the pomegranate. **1897** *Allbutt's Syst. Med.* II. 1021 In toxic doses the action of pelletierine resembles that of curare.

pelletization (pɛlɪtaɪˈzeɪʃən). [f. next + -ATION.] The action or process of forming into pellets.

1959 *Jrnl. Iron & Steel Inst.* CXCIII. 75/3 The article deals with determining the optimum conditions for making use of 'cold' agglomeration, i.e. pelletisation in which the fine material is transformed into small spheres by mechanical rolling. **1966** KIRK & OTHMER *Encycl. Chem. Technol.* (ed. 2) IX. 435 One of the more interesting developments which originated with fluidized calcination is the technique of pelletization. **1971** *Physics Bull.* Mar. 136/2 Major cooperative projects under consideration included an iron mine and an iron ore pelletization plant in the USSR. **1977** *Jrnl. R. Soc. Arts* CXXV. 388/1 Taconite ores .. are more amenable to pelletization than higher grade Mesabi-type, deposits.

pelletize (ˈpɛlɪtaɪz), *v.* [f. PELLET *sb.*[1] + -IZE.] *trans.* To form or shape into pellets. Cf. PELLET *v.* a

1952 KIRK & OTHMER *Encycl. Chem. Technol.* IX. 900 The peat is excavated, macerated, pelletized in a long drum, and dried. **1963** *Engineering* 1 Feb. 180 The wood pulp will be pelletized for shipment to the Australian mainland. **1964** *Economist* 23 May 855/1 In America ore preparation is mainly in the form of 'pelletising' the burden. **1973** R. D. PEHLKE *Unit Processes Extractive Metall.* ii. 19 The final temperatures during induration reach 2300–2400°F, depending upon the concentrate being pelletized.

So **ˈpelletized** *ppl. a.* = PELLETED *ppl. a.* 2; **ˈpelletizing** *vbl. sb.* and *ppl. a.*

1951 *Industr. & Engin. Chem.* June 1390/1 It is not possible to use pelletized [carbon] black directly for making aqueous carbon black slurries. **1951** *Engineering* 22 June 761/2 During a recent visit to the United States, he had been most impressed with what was being done in regard to the pelletising treatment of iron ores. **1964** *Economist* 25 July 356/1 This pelletised fuel is contained in stainless steel tubes. **1968** *Sci. Jrnl.* Oct. 23/3 Bentonite is used .. as an agent for the pelletizing of iron ore. **1969** *Times* 2 May (Mining Suppl.) p. iv/7 Savage River produces magnetite from a relatively low grade deposit, grinds and concentrates this to a high grade pellet feed and pipes it 53 miles to the pelletizing plant at the port. **1970** *Times* 24 Aug. 15/6 Kawasaki is working on a system using oxygen and crude oil or liquefied natural gas combined with pre-treated, pelletized iron ore. **1977** *Cork Examiner* 4 June 17/4 The pellets will get harder with time... At no time was it considered that metal ground .. would be included in the pelletised mix. **1977** *Jrnl. R. Soc. Arts* CXXV. 394/1 Attempts to encourage the industry to construct at least some processing plants near to its raw materials have been most successful in the case of iron ore pelletizing plants.

pelletizer (ˈpɛlɪtaɪzə(r)). [f. prec. + -ER[1].] = PELLETER[3].

1942 *Ann. Rep. Progr. Rubber Technol.* 1941 V. 120 After discharge from the internal mixer the stock passes through a 'Hale Pelletizer' and the pellets are conveyed to storage bins. **1950** [see PELLETING *vbl. sb.*]. **1961** *Engineering* 9 June 788/2 Pan pelletizers are used for granulating materials in the chemical and fertiliser industries. **1970** *Materials & Technol.* III. iii. 143 The grate-kiln pelletizer.

ˈpellety, *a. Her.* [f. PELLET *sb.*[1] 3 + -Y for F. *-é* = *-ed.*] Charged with pellets; pelleted.

1572 BOSSEWELL *Armorie* II. 110b, An head de cheual rassed de Argent, pellitie, betwene two winges Sable, brydelled golde, set on a wrethe Argent and Vert, manteled Gules, doubled Argent. **1869** W. S. ELLIS *Antiq. Her.* viii. 163 *note*, Their robes decorated with paly and pellety patterns.

Pellian (ˈpɛlɪən), *a. Math.* [f. the name of John Pell, an English mathematician (1610–85): see -IAN.] Applied to a particular kind of indeterminate equation: see quot. 1875. Also *absol.*

[**1767** EULER in *Novi Commentarii Acad. Sci. Imp. Petropolitanæ* XI. 28 (*heading*) De usu novi algorithmi in problemate Pelliano solvendo. *Ibid.* 31, $pp = lqq + 1$ ... Atque hoc est illud problema olim quidem maxime celebratum a solutionis ingeniosissimae auctore Pellianum vocatum.] **1862** *Rep. Brit. Assoc. Adv. Sci.* 1861 I. 314 There does not seem to be any ground for attributing either the problem or its solution to Pell... Nevertheless the equation $T^2 - DU^2 = 1$ is often called the Pellian equation after him, probably upon Euler's authority. **1875** CAYLEY *Coll. Math. Papers* IX. 477 The Pellian equation is $y^2 = ax^2 + 1$, a being a given integer number, which is not a square (or rather, if it be, the only solution is $y = 1$, $x = 0$), and x, y being numbers to be determined: what is required is the least values of x, y, since these, being known, all other values can be found. **1911** *Encycl. Brit.* XIX. 853/1 This is usually called the Pellian equation, though it should properly be associated with Fermat, who first perceived its importance. **1974** *Sci. Amer.* July 118/3 The Pellian for square hexes is $3x^2 + 1 = y^2$, which is solved by finding the convergents of the continued fraction for the square root of 3.

pellibranchiate (pɛlɪˈbræŋkɪət), *a.* (*sb.*) *Zool.* [ad. mod. L. *Pellibranchiāta* neut. pl., f. L. *pell-is* skin + *branchiæ* gills: see -ATE[2].] Belonging to the *Pellibranchiata*, or nudibranchiate gastropods (of J. E. Gray), which have no distinct gills but breathe by means of the skin. **b.** as *sb.* A mollusc of this group.

pellican(e, pellice, obs. ff. PELICAN *sb.*, PELISSE.

pelliceous (pɛˈlɪsiːəs, -ˈlɪʃiːəs), *a. rare*[−1]. [f. L. *pellice-us, -i-us* made of skin + -OUS.] Of the nature of a thin skin, membrane, or pellicle.

1731 GALE in *Phil. Trans.* XXXVII. 160 Made of a Plant that had many pelliceous Tunicles.

pellicle (ˈpɛlɪk(ə)l). Also 6 -ycle, pel(l)ikel. [ad. L. *pellicula* small or thin skin, dim. of *pell-is* skin.] A small or thin skin; a fine sheet or layer of some substance, either covering a surface or (less usually) enclosing a cavity; a membrane, cuticle, film. Chiefly in scientific use, and applied to natural formations, as a thin membrane in an animal or plant body, a fine scum on a liquid, etc.

1541 R. COPLAND *Guydon's Quest. Chirurg.* F ij b, It hath collygaunce with the bely by his outwarde pellycle. **1547** BOORDE *Brev. Health* x. 10b, Ioynynge to the pellicles of the kydnes. **1548–77** VICARY *Anat.* viii. (1888) 61 The Lunges is deuided into fiue Lobbes or Pellikels of fiue portions. **1601** HOLLAND *Pliny* I. 466. **1669** W. SIMPSON *Hydrol. Chym.* 276 The newly ingendred juyces, in their own pellicles or membranes. **1707** *Curios. in Husb. & Gard.* 136 We need only Evaporate the humidity .. till there appear a little Pellicle on the Water. **1815** J. SMITH *Panorama Sc. & Art* I. 17 A pellicle of iron may be taken from a surface of a 100 square inches by the Chisel. *Ibid.* II. 112 Having observed how thin the pellicle of oil poured out upon water will become, without losing its effect in depriving the wind of its influence. **1871** TYNDALL *Fragm. Sc.* (1879) II. xiii. 324 A thin pellicle of india-rubber .. surrounding a pea keeps it hard in boiling water. **1872** HUXLEY *Phys.* iv. 78 The blood in each capillary of the lung is separated from the air by only a delicate pellicle.

pellicular (pɛˈlɪkjʊlə(r)), *a.* [ad. mod.L. *pelliculāris*, f. *pellicula* PELLICLE: see -AR[1].] Of, pertaining to, or of the nature of a pellicle; having or characterized by a pellicle; membranous, filmy.

1857 in MAYNE *Expos. Lex.* **1859** SEMPLE *Diphtheria* 42 Found to have no effect against the pellicular inflammation of the gums. **1883** *Hardwich's Photogr. Chem.* (ed. Taylor) 366 Substitution of Gelatine for Collodion as the agent for presenting the sensitive Bromide of Silver in a pellicular form. **1893** *Brit. Jrnl. Photogr.* XL. 745 Having developed and washed his pellicular negatives.

pellicule (ˈpɛlɪkjuːl). *rare.* [ad. L. *pellicula*; cf. F. *pellicule* (1505 in Hatz.-Darm.).] = PELLICLE.

c **1400** *Lanfranc's Cirurg.* 32 Boonis, pelliculis, gristlis, ligamentis & skyn. **1541** R. COPLAND *Guydon's Quest. Chirurg.* F ij b, His webbe withinforth is conteyned with the sayd pellicule. **1684** T. GODDARD *Plato's Demon* 93 Over which a Pellicule, or kind of Skin, in most places was spread. **1741** HANKEWITZ in *Phil. Trans.* XLI. 829 The Water, being evaporated to a Pellicule, deposits saline Crystals. **1903** *Brit. Med. Jrnl.* 14 Mar. 617 A bacillus slightly motile producing a pellicule in bouillon.

†**pellipar, -per.** *Obs. rare.* [ad. med.L. *pelliparius, -perius*, f. L. *pellis* skin + *parāre* to prepare.] A dresser of skins or hides; a skinner.

[**1390** *Earl Derby's Exp.* (Camden) 91 Cuidam pellipario pro j pilche de beuere.] *a* **1410** *York Myst.* Introd. 24 *note*, The Pellipers and other craftsmen of this city. [**1754** STRYPE *Stow's Surv.* II. App. iii. 687/2 Richard Knight Fishmonger, John Pasnur Pellipar.]

pellise, pellit, obs. forms of PELISSE, PELLET.

pelliteri, obs. form of PELTRY *sb.*[1]

pellitory (ˈpɛlɪtərɪ). Forms: 6 peli-, pely-, pellatory, pellytorie, -ye, pille-, pillitorie, -tore, 6–7 pellitorie, 7 -tarie, 6– pellitory. [Found first in 16th c.: partly (in sense 1) an alteration of the earlier *peletre, peletyr*, PELLETER[1], with changed suffix; partly (in sense 2) an alteration of **peretarie, paretarie*, PARIETARY, L. *parietāria*, It. *paretaria*, F. *pariétaire, paretaire* (f. L. *parietem* wall), by dissimilation of *r . . r* to *l . . r*.

It is not clear whether these two changes of the earlier words were independent of each other, or whether one influenced the other; but the result was that by 1550 or thereabouts both words had become *pellitory*.]

1. A composite plant, *Anacyclus Pyrethrum*, the *Pyrethrum* of the ancients, and *peletre*, PELLETER of Middle English, called distinctively ***pellitory of Spain***, a native of Barbary, the root of which has a very pungent flavour, and is used in medicine as a local irritant and salivant and as a remedy for toothache. Also applied to the root (*radix pyrethri*) as thus used.

Called by Lyte *Bastard Pellitory*: see also b.

1533 ELYOT *Cast. Helthe* IV. ii. (1541) 84 b, Them that be vexed with toothe ache . . Take Pelytory of Spayn one ducat [etc.]. **1570** LEVINS *Manip.* 105/22 Pellitorie, *pyretrum*. **1578** LYTE *Dodoens* III. xix. 342, I thinke we may wel cal it bastard Pelitory or Bertram. **1592** LYLY *Midas* III. ii, O! what will rid me of this paine? Some Pellitory fetcht from Spaine. **1597** GERARDE *Herbal* II. ccl. 619 Pellitorie of Spaine is called in Greeke πύρεθρον . . in Spanish *Pelitre* . . in high and lowe Dutch *Bertram*. **1611** COTGR., *Piretre*, Hearbe Bartram, bastard Pellitorie, right Pellitorie of Spaine. **1705** TATE tr. *Cowley's Bks. Plants* IV, The Pellitory healing Fire contains, That from a raging Tooth the Humour drains. **1773** *Gentl. Mag.* XLIII. 439 The root of pellitory of Spain . . should be held in the mouth often. **1876** HARLEY *Mat. Med.* (ed. 6) 535 Pellitory is a native of the north of Africa, whence it has been introduced into the south of Europe.

†**b.** Applied, usually with qualifying words, to other plants in some way resembling this: *esp.* (*a*) Masterwort, *Peucedanum* (*Imperatoria*) *Ostruthium*, an umbelliferous plant with a pungent root (also ***great*** or ***false pellitory of Spain***); (*b*) Sneezewort, *Achillea Ptarmica* (also ***wild*** or ***bastard pellitory***). *Obs.*

1578 LYTE *Dodoens* II. xix. 299 Of great Pellitorie of Spayne, Imperatoria, or Masterwort. *Ibid.* III. xx. 342 Of wilde Pelitory . . the whole herbe is sharpe and biting, almost in tast like Pellitory of Spayne, and for y[t] cause men cal it also wild Pellitory. **1597** GERARDE *Herbal* II. clxxviii. 484 *Ptarmica.* Sneesewoort. . . The whole plant is sharpe, biting the toong and mouth like Pellitorie of Spaine, for which cause some haue called it wilde Pellitorie. *Ibid.* ccclxxii. 848 Imperatoria. Masterworts, or False Pellitory of Spaine. **1607** TOPSELL *Four-f. Beasts* (1658) 103 If there be put unto it wilde Pellitory, it will also distract and dissipate them [serpents] again. **1738** DEERING *Cat. Stirp.* 179 *Ptarmica* . . Sneezewort. Bastard-pellitory. **1760** J. LEE *Introd. Bot.* App. 312 Pellitory of Spain, False, *Chrysanthemum*.

2. A low bushy plant (*Parietaria officinalis*, N.O. *Urticaceæ*) with small ovate leaves and greenish flowers, growing upon or at the foot of walls. Commonly distinguished as ***pellitory of the wall***. Also extended to the whole genus *Parietaria*. (See also PARIETARY *sb.*)

1548 TURNER *Names of Herbes* 41 Helxine or pardition is called in englishe Parietorie or Pelletorie of the wal . . in frenche Du parietaire. **1562** —— *Herbal* II. 13 Parietorie or Pilletorie of y[e] wall. **1580** HOLLYBAND *Treas. Fr. Tong, De l'Apparitoire*, . . an herbe called Parietory, commonly Pellitorie. **1610** B. JONSON *Alch.* III. iv, A good old woman . . did cure me With sodden ale, and pellitorie o' the wall. **1747** WESLEY *Prim. Physic* (1762) 57 A Pint of juice of Pellitory of the Wall bruised in a Marble Mortar. **1821** CLARE *Vill. Minstr.* I. 210 Where the mouldering walls are seen Hung with pellitory green. **1884** MILLER *Plant-n.*, Pellitory, American, *Parietaria pennsylvanica*. . . New Zealand, *Parietaria debilis*.

3. *attrib.* and *Comb.*

1713 PETIVER in *Phil. Trans.* XXVIII. 187 These Leaves are green, and in their Segments resemble the *Pyrethrum Canariense* or Pellitory Dasie. **1760** J. LEE *Introd. Bot.* App. 322 Pellitory-tree, *Zanthoxylum*. **1797** DOWNING *Disorders Horned Cattle* 57 Give the beast a quart of pellitory tea two or three times a day. **1861** HULME tr. *Moquin-Tandon* II. v. ii, As if they had been chewing pellitory root.

pell-mell (ˈpɛlˈmɛl, *with shifting stress*), *adv.* (*a.*, *sb.*, *v.*) Also 6 **peale meale, peale-meale,** 6–7 **pel mell, pel mel, pel-mel,** 6–8 **pelmell, pesle mesle, pesle-mesle,** (8 **pezle mezle**), 6–9 **pell mell** (7 **pel-mell, pell-mel, pelmel,** 7–8 **pall-mall**), 7–9 **pellmell,** 8–9 **pêle mêle,** 9 **pêle-mêle.** [a. F. *pêle-mêle*, in OF. *pesle mesle* (12th c.), *pelle-melle* (14th c.), for which also *mesle-pesle, melle-pelle, mesle-mesle, brelle-mesle* (12th c.). The element *mesle, mêle* was app. the stem of the vb. *mesler, mêler* to mix, mingle; the origin of *pêle* is uncertain; Diez queried *pelle, pèle* shovel, or *paele* pan, as if mixed together with a shovel, or in a pan; but the various forms in OF. suggest merely riming combinations formed on *mesle, mêle*, as in *tire-lire*, Eng. *namby-pamby*, etc.]

1. With disorderly or confused mingling; in a confused medley; together in disorder, without any order; in mingled confusion, promiscuously.

1596 Z. I. tr. *Lavardin's Hist. Scanderbeg* 162 The men lay wallowing all along vnder their tentes, pell mell amongst their horses. *a* **1641** BP. MOUNTAGU *Acts & Mon.* viii. (1642) 540 Nor were men and women intermingled pell mell in their Synagogues. **1687** A. LOVELL tr. *Thevenot's Trav.* I. 283 Then the Guns went off Pell Mell on all hands. **1766** PENNANT *Zool.* (1768) II. 448 Assuming the shape of a wedge . . for they [wild geese] cut the air the readier in that form than if they flew pelmell. **1814** JEFFERSON *Writ.* (1830) IV. 242 We should now have been all living, men, women, and children, pell-mell together. **1840** CARLYLE *Heroes* ii. (1858) 233 Shoulder-blades of mutton, flung pellmell into a chest. **1849** GROTE *Greece* II. xxxviii. V. 34 After whom, with an interval of two furlongs, the remaining host followed pell-mell. **1867** LADY HERBERT *Cradle L.* x 267 The dead and the dying were huddled pell-mell together.

b. Said of pursuers and pursued.

1579–80 NORTH *Plutarch* (1676) 129 He entred amongst them that fled into their Camp pelmell, or hand over head. **1603** KNOLLES *Hist Turks* (1621) 91 Fearing lest the enemie in that hurly burly should pell mell enter in with the rest. **1677** *Lond. Gaz.* No. 1181/4 [They] were so closely followed, that our Soldiers entred with them pell-mell into the City. **1713** *Ibid.* No. 5106/2 The Turks and Tartars entred Pellmell among the Swedes. **1859** GREEN *Oxf. Stud.* i. (O.H.S.) 14 [They] rushed pell-mell with the fugitives into the city.

c. Of combatants: Without keeping ranks; hence, at close quarters, hand to hand, man to man; in a mêlée.

1579 DIGGES *Stratiot.* 105 If at anye time they should come to the sword, or ioyne peale meale with their Enimies. **1598** BARRET *Theor. Warres* Gloss. 251 *Pel mell*, a French word, and signifieth the mingling of men together, buckling by the bosome one with another. **1663** BUTLER *Hud.* I. iii. 506 To come pell-mell to handi-Blows. **1733** FIELDING *Don Quixote in Eng.* III. xi, There they are at it pell-mell; who will be knocked on the head I know not. **1767** STERNE *Tr. Shandy* IX. xxvi, To attack the point of the advanced counterscarp, and *pêle mêle* with the Dutch to take the counterguard of St. Roch sword in hand.

†**2.** Without discrimination, indiscriminately; in the mass. *Obs.*

1586 HOLINSHED *Chron.* (1808) IV. 912 To be an actor in a tragedie of bloudshed and slaughter universallie, pesle mesle to be perpetrated. **1600** HOLLAND *Livy* XXXIV. liv. 883 These plaies and games haue been beheld and looked upon pell mell, without any such precise difference. **1606** BP. W. BARLOW *Serm.* 21 Sept. D iv, Bishops were not made χύδην pell-mell, at all aduentures. **1657** W. MORICE *Coena quasi Κοινή* v. 50 Their way of excluding men pell-mell, and in the lump. *a* **1659** BP. BROWNRIG *Serm.* (1674) I. x. 133 God sometimes punishes a Nation pell mell.

3. In disorder and hurry; with vehement onset; with a rush; in headlong haste; headlong, recklessly: often referring to the action of a single person.

1594 KYD *Cornelia* v. 266 The murdring Enemie Pesle-mesle pursued them like a storme of hayle. **1596** NASHE *Saffron Walden* 97 One Master Heath . . set vpon it and answered it in Print pell mell. **1677** YARRANTON *Eng. Improv.* 194 Two Books which were so fitted to the Countrey-mans capacity, that he fell on Pell-Mell. *a* **1734** NORTH *Lives* (1826) III. 109 Finding his brother falling thus pell-mell into affairs of trade. *Ibid.* 372 Their university learning fell in pesle mesle with their prescriptions. **1784** MME. D'ARBLAY *Diary* 3 Nov., I have not had an unpleasant thought that I have not driven away pellmell. **1824** W. IRVING *T. Trav.* I. 223, I went to work pell-mell, blotted several sheets of paper with choice floating thoughts. **1853** KANE *Grinnell Exp.* xii. (1856) 90 We were an absurd party of zealots, rushing pell-mell upon the floes with vastly more energy than discretion. **1878** *Masque Poets* 97 'Repent yourself', the Nephew sneers, And at it goes pell mell.

B. *adj.* (ˈpɛlmɛl) Disorderly and violent, tumultuous; confused, promiscuous, indiscriminate.

1585 JAS. I *Ess. Poesie* (Arb.) 17 Syne Phifers, Drummes, and Trumpets cleir do craue The pelmell chok with larum loude alwhair. **1596** SHAKS. *1 Hen. IV*, v. i. 82 Moody Beggars, staruing for a time Of pell-mell hauocke, and confusion. **1657** TOMLINSON *Renou's Disp.* Pref., The thundring and pell-mell Granadoes of impertinent contradiction. **1817** J. SCOTT *Paris Revisited* (ed. 4) 157 The pell-mell rout of the French has been described in a variety of publications. **1898** *Allbutt's Syst. Med.* V. 935 This is a pell-mell classification.

C. *sb.* Promiscuous or indiscriminate mingling; confusion, disorder; a confused mixture or crowd, a medley; a hand-to-hand fight, a mêlée.

1598 BARRET *Theor. Warres* III. i. 36 The dagger is a weapon of great aduantage in Pell mell. **1600** E. BLOUNT *Ganzoni's Hosp. Inc. Fooles* a j b, Lord, what a pell-mell of conceit and inuention you shall discouer. **1657** W. MORICE *Coena quasi Κοινή* v. 50 The old impure way of Pell-mell tends to many evils. **1831** J. WILSON in *Blackw. Mag.* XXIX. 307 Thunderbolts pursue the pell-mell of the panic. **1849** CLOUGH *Dipsychus* II. iv. 68 High deeds Haunt not the fringy edges of the fight But the pell-mell of men. **1884** TENNYSON *Becket* Prol., The Church in the pell-mell of Stephen's time Hath climb'd the throne and almost clutch'd the crown.

D. *vb. trans.* To mingle confusedly or indiscriminately; to mix up in disorder. *rare.* Hence **pell-melling** *vbl. sb.*

1606 BIRNIE *Kirk-Buriall* (1833) 31 They pel-mell the dead with the living all in one kirk. *a* **1649** DRUMM. OF HAWTH. *Fam. Epist.* Wks. (1711) 147 The game ended, kings, queens, bishops, knights, pawns, pell-melled are confusedly thrown into the box. **1792** BRACKENRIDGE *Mod. Chivalry* (1846) 23 In times of chivalry though there was a great deal of pell-melling, yet no such disorderly work.

pell mell, obs. form of PALL-MALL.

ˈ**pellock**[1], **-ack, -och** (ˈpɛlək, -ɒx). *Sc.* Forms: 4 pelok, 6 pellok, (6 -at), 7 pealock, 7–9 pellack, 8 -uck, pallach, (9 palach), 9 pelloch, -ock. [In 14th c. *pelok*, latinized *peloca*. Origin obscure: the Gael. *peileag* appears to be from Lowland Sc.] The porpoise (*Phocæna communis*). But in quots. 1331, 1541, app. some other species.

1331 in *Exch. Rolls Scotl.* I. 397 Et eidem, per vnam petram de porpoys et tres pelokis, xvs. [*Ibid.* 363 Per vnam pelocam, missam camerario, vs.] **1511** *Acc. Ld. High Treas. Scot.* IV. 337 Item, to Robert Buttone katour for ane selcht and ane pellok and salt to thaim. **1541** BELLENDEN *Descr. Alb.* ix. in *Cron. Scot.* B vj b, This firth [of Forth] is rycht plentuus of coclis, osteris, muschellis, selch, pellok, merswyne & quhalis. **1645** *Shetland Witch Trial* in Hibbert *Descr. Shetl. Isl.* (1822) 599 Being transformed in the lyknes of an pellack quhaill. **1710** SIBBALD *Hist. Fife* 53 A Palach, a great Destroyer of Salmond. **1792** *Statist. Acc. Scotl.* IV. 22 A species of sea animals . . called buckers, pellocks, or porpoises. **1828** SCOTT *F.M. Perth* iii, Gambolling like a pellack amongst the waves. **1894** CROCKETT *Raiders* 219 Like a school of pellocks in the Firth.

fig. **1755** FORBES *Jrnl. to Portsmouth* in *Ajax* etc. 28 The second chiel was a thick, setterel, swown pallach.

†ˈ**pellock**[2]. *Sc. Obs.* [app. f. PELLET *sb.*[1], with exchange of dimin. suffix: see -OCK.] A ball thrown as a missile from a cross-bow, hackbut, cannon, etc.; a bullet; = PELLET *sb.*[1] 2.

c **1470** *Gol. & Gaw.* 463 Thai bend bowis of bras braithly within; Pellokis paisand to pase, Gapand gunnys of brase. **1496** *Acc. Ld. High Treas. Scot.* I. 320 Giffin to a man to tak mesour of muldis of diuers gunnys, to send in Frans to mak pellokis of irne, xvjd. **1513** DOUGLAS *Æneis* VII. xii. 111 Wyth leyd pellokis from engynis or staf slyng . . thair fa men doun to ding. **1540** *Sc. Acts Jas. V* (1814) II. 371/2 Euery landit man within þe samin Sall haue ane hagbute of founde . . with þare calmis bullettis and pellokis of leid . . or Irne.

b. *Comb.* †**pellock-bow** *Obs.*, an arbalest.

1538 in Pitcairn *Crim. Trials* I. *293 Ane irne of ane Pellok-bow.

pellot, -otte, obs. forms of PELLET.

pellotine (ˈpɛlətiːn). *Chem.* [ad. G. *pellotin* (A. Heffter 1894, in *Ber. d. Deut. Chem. Ges.* XXVII. 2977), f. Mexican *pellote* PEYOTE: see -INE[5].] An alkaloid, $C_{13}H_{19}NO_3$, obtained from peyote and formerly used as a hypnotic; 1,2,3,4-tetrahydro-8-hydroxy-6,7-dimethoxy-1,2-dimethylisoquinoline.

1895 *Jrnl. Chem. Soc.* LXVIII. I. 120 Pellotine, . . so called from the Mexican name 'pellote', of *Anhalonium Williamsi*, crystallises in colourless, transparent, anhydrous plates, and melts at 110°. **1900** A. R. CUSHNY *Text-bk. Pharmacol. & Therapeutics* II. iii. 220 Pellotine . . has been introduced as a hypnotic, and has been favorably commented on. **1972** *Science* 9 June 1132/3 Tetrazotized benzidine spray . . aided in the identification of the four major components [from the Mexican cactus *Pelecyphora aselliformis* Ehrenberg] as hordenine . ., pellotine . ., anhalidine . . , and an unknown alkaloid.

pellour, obs. f. PEELER[1]; var. PELURE *Obs.*

pellow, obs. variant of PILAU.

†**peˈlluce.** *Obs. rare.* [app. a. obs. F. *pelusse* (Cotgr.), collateral form of *peluche* shag. plush, cf. Sp. *pelusa* down, It. *peluzzo* fine hair, soft down: see PLUSH.] Plush.

1598 HAKLUYT *Voy.* I. 98 The rich Tartars somtimes fur their gownes with pelluce or silke shag [tr. L. *de stupa setæ*, Rubruquis, 1253], which is exceeding soft, light, & warme.

pellucent (pəˈl(j)uːsənt), *a. rare.* [ad. L. *pellūcēnt-em*, pr. pple. of *pel-, perlūcēre*, f. *per* through + *lūcēre* to shine: cf. *lucent*.] = next.

1886 BIGG *Bampton Lect.* 191 As the pellucent alabaster vase shows the fire within.

pellucid (pəˈl(j)uːsɪd), *a.* (*sb.*) [ad. L. *pellūcid-us*, f. *pel-, perlūcēre* to shine through: cf. *lūcidus*,

f. *lūcēre* to shine. Frequent in scientific and literary use, but not colloquial.]

1. Having the property of transmitting, or allowing the passage of, light; translucent, transparent; clear. ***pellucid zone***: see ZONE.

1619 BAINBRIDGE *Descr. Late Comet* 10 That the Comets taile is nothing else but an irradiation of the sunne through the pellucide head of the Comet. **1642** H. MORE *Song of Soul* II. *Psychathanasia* I. ii. 5 A lamp armed with pellucid horn. **1657** S. PURCHAS *Pol. Flying-Ins.* I. iii. 6 A Bee hath four drye pellucid skinny wings. **1690** LOCKE *Hum. Und.* II. xxiii. (1695) 161 Thus Sand, or pounded Glass, which is opaque, and white to the naked Eye, is pellucid in a Microscope. **1715** tr. *Pancirollus' Rerum Mem.* I. I. iii. 10 [It] is diaphanous or pellucid, transmitting (like Glass) all Forms and Shapes. **1810** WORDSW. *Scenery of Lakes* I. (1823) 27 The water is perfectly pellucid, through which..are seen, to a great depth, their beds of rock or of blue gravel. **1840** G. V. ELLIS *Anat.* 37 The inner wall, or septum, between the ventricles, is thin, almost pellucid. **1863** TYNDALL *Heat* iv. §127 (1870) 109, I will..send the rays..through this slab of pellucid ice.

2. *fig.* †**a.** Easy to 'see through' or detect; 'transparent'. *Obs.* **b.** Showing the sense clearly, clear in style or expression. **c.** Perceiving clearly, mentally clear.

1644 R. BAILLIE *Lett. & Jrnls.* II. 150 Their craft was pellucid. **1661** K. W. *Conf. Charact.* 23 The higher he thinks to soare..the more he unvailes his own imbecility, and renders himself pellucid. **1822** LAMB *Elia* Ser. II. *Confess. of Drunkard*, To muddle their faculties, perhaps never very pellucid. **1861** J. PYCROFT *Ways & Words* 237 Writers of the school of Addison were smooth, measured, and pellucid.

†**B.** *sb.* A pellucid body or substance. *rare.*

1669 W. SIMPSON *Hydrol. Chym.* II. vii. 73 Some are diaphanous, others opake..but in pellucids, as Helmont saith, that *evestrum vitæ* reverberates it self.

pellucidity (pɛl(j)uːˈsɪdɪtɪ). [ad. L. *pellūciditās*, f. *pellūcidus*: see prec. and -ITY.] The quality or condition of being pellucid; transparency or translucency; clearness. Also *fig.*

1642 H. MORE *Song Soul* I. III. lxv, Nor did 't take in through pellucidity The penetrating light. **1756** C. LUCAS *Ess. Waters* I. 35 Our Thames..preserves her purity and pellucidity. **1868** MILMAN *St. Paul's* xviii. 463 With an incomparable ease and pellucidity of language.

peˈllucidly, *adv.* [f. PELLUCID + -LY².] In a pellucid manner.

1824 WIFFEN *Tasso* xv. lix, The waves that played Round her, each limb beneath pellucidly arrayed. **1868** *Contemp. Rev.* IX. 76 Blake is uniformly pure, sweet, pellucidly perfect in form.

peˈllucidness. [f. as prec. + -NESS.] Pellucid quality, pellucidity.

1684 BOYLE *Porousn. Bod.* vi. 96 The Pellucidness which the Stone acquires in Water. **1771** PENNANT *Tour Scot.* (1790) 97 Its pellucidness is like that of brown crystal. **1816** J. SCOTT *Vis. Paris* (ed. 5) 89 Distances are lessened by the pellucidness of the medium through which they are seen.

peˈllucido-, used as combining adverbial form of L. *pellūcidus* PELLUCID, as in **peˌllucido-ˈpunctate** *a.*, marked with pellucid dots.

1876 HARLEY *Mat. Med.* (ed. 6) 719 The leaves are alternate,..the younger ones pellucido-punctate.

pelluck, pellure, obs. ff. PELLOCK¹, PELURE.

pellycan, -cane, obs. forms of PELICAN *sb.*

†**ˈpelly ˈmelly**, *adv. phr. Obs. rare.* Also 5 **pelley melley**. [ad. OF. *pêle-mêle*, with final *e* pronounced, or with Eng. advb. suffix -LY². Found a century earlier than the simple PELL-MELL.] = PELL-MELL *adv.*

c **1450** *Merlin* 391 Thei..smyten thourgh the peple of kynge Bohors all pelly melly. *Ibid.* 397 That oo peple smyte thourgh the tother all pelley melley full desirouse eche other to a-paire. **1601** BP. W. BARLOW *Defence* 66 We..grant this prerogatiue..not to euerie man pelly melly.

pellyson, variant of PELISSON. *Obs.*

pellyt, pellytorie, obs. ff. PELLET, PELLITORY.

Pelman (ˈpɛlmən). The name of Christopher Louis *Pelman*, founder (in 1899) of the Pelman Institute for the Scientific Development of Mind, Memory and Personality in London, used *attrib.* to designate the system of memory training taught by this Institute.

1900 *Phonetic Jrnl.* 15 Dec. 790/2, I may say that I speak of the Pelman system from intimate personal knowledge. **1939** R. CAMPBELL *Flowering Rifle* IV. 113 All his Pelman course and monkey's glands With which the Charlie intellect expands. **1972** *Listener* 17 Aug. 210/3, I did a Pelman course, which hasn't done very much good because I've got the worst memory of anybody.

So **ˈPelmanism**, the system taught by the Pelman Institute; also *transf.*; a card game in which the cards lie face down and pairs must be selected from memory as successive cards are turned up; **ˈPelmanist, ˈPelmanite**, a student or advocate of Pelmanism; **ˈPelmanize** *v. intr.* and *trans.*, to practise Pelmanism; to teach (someone) Pelmanism.

1919 *Honey Pot* I. 4 (Advt.), Lots of our fellows are Pelmanising out here. **1920** *Pelman Pie* 25 (Advt.), A very large proportion of its readers are 'Pelmanists'. **1920** *Blackw. Mag.* Nov. 561/2, I fear I must be suffering from what the Pelmanites call 'mind-wandering'. **1921** *Chambers's Jrnl.* Mar. 176/1 In some Oriental way he had Pelmanised his memory. **1922** E. WALLACE *Flying Fifty-Five* xxvi. 154 Bill had begun, as he described it, to Pelmanize his horses. He was super-imposing upon the memory of one evil whistle another which had a more kindly association. **1923** *Hoyle's Games Modernized* 230 Pelmanism is..a splendid exercise for the memory, besides a source of amusement to the players—of whom there may be any number. **1931** R. CAMPBELL *Georgiad* II. 17 Broadcast your love and Pelmanise your Passion. **1934** 'E. M. DELAFIELD' *Provincial Lady in Amer.* 90 Short exercise in Pelmanism enables me to connect wave in her hair with first name, which is Marcella. **1934** *Brit. Weekly* 11 Jan. 319/3 (Advt.), Pelmanise for promotion, for progress, for success. *Ibid.*, There are in the world to-day more than half a million men and women who have become Pelmanists. **1950** *Oxf. Jun. Encycl.* IX. 114/1 In Pelmanism, a memory game, the cards are spread face downwards on the table. The players turn up two at a time, trying to find pairs. Cards which do not make pairs are turned down again, and the players must remember where they are. **1958** R. GODDEN *Greengage Summer* vii. 80 We stayed on at our table, playing cards with old packs from the bar, Racing Demon or Pelmanism or Snap. **1963** R. M. HARE *Freedom & Reason* iv. 60 Ought I not rather to take a course in Pelmanism to correct my absentmindedness? **1972** *Guardian* 15 Nov. 10/6 There is a kind of common ground here between pulp fiction, science fiction pop mysticism, and a new sort of Pelmanism that goes beyond mere self-improvement and proposes the ways and means of self-transcendence. **1975** *Daily Tel.* 11 July 11/3 Between games of ping-pong or pelmanism they spend the night reminiscing about old times over a continuous supply of drinks.

ˈpelmatogram. *rare*⁻⁰. [f. Gr. πελματο- sole of the foot + -GRAM.] A foot-print.

1890 in *Cent. Dict.* **1893** in *Syd. Soc. Lex.*

pelmatozoan (ˌpɛlmətəʊˈzəʊən), *a.* and *sb. Zool.* [f. mod. L. *Pelmatozōa*, neut. pl. (f. Gr. πελματο- (see prec.) + ζῷον animal) + -AN.]

a. *adj.* Belonging to the division *Pelmatozoa* of Echinoderms, characterized by a stalk by which they are fixed, and comprising the Crinoids and the extinct *Blastoidea* and *Cystoidea*. **b.** *sb.* An echinoderm of this division. So **ˌpelmatoˈzoic** *a.*, belonging to or characteristic of the *Pelmatozoa*.

1891 *Athenæum* 24 Jan. 125/2 Gross errors, such as putting..the pelmatozoic crinoids among the 'Stellerida'. **1900** *Lankester's Treat. Zool.* III. 19 Assumed..to be homologous with the original three radii of the primitive Pelmatozoan. *Ibid.*, The Holothurians..are primitive as regards Pelmatozoic structure.

pelmel, obs. form of PALL-MALL, PELL-MELL.

‖**pelmeny** (pɛlˈmɛnɪ), *sb. pl.* Also **-ni**. [a. Russ. *pel'méni.*] In Russian cookery, small pastry cases stuffed with meat, etc.

1943 E. M. ALMEDINGEN *Frossia* x. 376 A whole mound of *pelmeny*, little lumps of specially made pastry stuffed with meat and onions and boiled in water. **1958** N. & G. J. FROUD *Home Bk. Russian Cookery* 23 Left-over pel'meni are delicious fried in a little butter. **1962** K. PETROVSKAYA *Secrets of Russian Cooking* 163 The best, real way of preparing Siberian pelmeny is to use two kinds of meat for stuffing—beef and pork or veal and pork—and plenty of seasoning. **1972** *Times* 12 Apr. 9/2 Such Russian specialities as *Pelmeny* (a kind of ravioli).

pelmet (ˈpɛlmɪt). [Prob. ad. F. *palmette* (see PALMETTE), formerly a conventional ornament on window cornices.] A valance or horizontal strip of curtain, wood or other material, fitted across the top of a door or window, usu. to conceal curtain fittings. Hence **ˈpelmeted** *a.*, fitted with a pelmet.

1904 P. N. HASLUCK *Upholstery* 149 This pelmet is fixed to a wood lath screwed underneath the door casing. **1908** *Ladies' Field* 24 Oct. 318/2 (*caption*) Window Treatment: Pelmet and Curtains in Shadow Damask. **1922** *Daily Mail* 21 Nov. 14 If a pelmet is used it should be straight-edged. **1925** PENDEREL-BRODHURST & LAYTON *Gloss. Eng. Furnit.* 123 *Pelmet*, a word used by upholsterers and sometimes by art dealers, who prefer the word 'palmette', to denote the horizontal stiff curtains or valance hiding the rod, rings and headings of the hanging curtain decorating a door, window, bed, etc. **1932** G. B. STERN *Little Red Horses* IV. xxxix. 540 [He] had tried to picture a long-ago scene of Uncle Arthur plucking his bride back from the pelmet. **1940** C. G. TORMLEY *Furnishing your Home* xvi. 109 Pelmets well done are an improvement to most windows. **1964** *McCall's Sewing* xvi. 286 The depth of the pelmet depends on the height of the window, usually one-sixth to one-ninth the length of the curtain. **1970** *Kay & Co.* (Worcester) *Catal.* 1970–71 Autumn/Winter 544 Plywood pelmet. Available in seven lengths. Easily painted. **1974** M. CECIL *Heroines in Love* viii. 189 These magazines..gave them [*sc.* readers] the latest way with pelmets, and casseroles for winter evenings. **1974** D. FRANCIS *Knock Down* v. 59 Padded and pelmeted curtains and silk lampshades..spoke of enough money.

pelo-, combining form of Gr. πηλός clay, mud, occurring in a few rarely used scientific words, chiefly zoological. **pelobatid** (piːləʊˈbætɪd), an amphibian of the family *Pelobatidæ*, typified by the genus *Pelobates* [βάτης walker]; so **pelobatoid** (piːˈlɒbətɔɪd) *a.*, belonging to or resembling this genus or family; **pelobiid** (-ˈbaɪɪd), a beetle of the family *Pelobiidæ*, typified by the genus *Pelobius* [-βιος living]; so **pelobioid** (piːˈlɒbɪɔɪd) *a.*; **pelodytid** (-ˈdɪtɪd), an amphibian of the family *Pelodytidæ*, typified by the genus *Pelodytes* [δύτης diver]; so **pelodytoid** (piːˈlɒdɪtɔɪd) *a.*; **pelolithic** (-ˈlɪθɪk) *a. Geol.* [λίθος stone], applied to rock-strata consisting of clay; **pelomedusid** (-mɪˈdjuːsɪd), a tortoise of the family *Pelomedusidæ*, typified by the genus *Pelomedusa*; so **pelomeˈdusoid** *a.*; **ˈpelophile** *Ecol.* [a. F. *pélophile* (J. Thurmann *Essai de Phytostatique* (1849) I. xiii. 268): see -PHIL], a plant growing on mud or clay; **pelophilous** (piːˈlɒfɪləs) *a.* [-PHILOUS], clay-loving.

1956 *Nature* 18 Feb. 342/2 I have examined tadpoles of the *pelobatid *Megophrys major*. **1888** *Athenæum* 3 Mar. 279/2 He [Prof. G. B. Howes] regarded their total absence in Pelobates and Pelodytes as fresh evidence of the *pelobatoid, rather than the discoglossid affinities of the last-named genus. **1884** *Geol. Mag.* 526 The Coral Rag is only an episode in the *pelolithic series; it is absent throughout a distance of nearly 120 miles, and over this tract there is a complete passage from the Oxford into the Kimmeridge Clay. **1905** B. D. JACKSON *Gloss. Bot. Terms* (ed. 2) 345/1 *Pelophile.., a clay-loving plant. **1960** N. POLUNIN *Introd. Plant Geogr.* xvi. 528 It is also possible..to categorize marine Algae according to..the nature of their substratum (such as epiliths attached to rocks, or pelophiles growing on mud.) **1888** F. A. LEES *Flora W. Yorks.* 80 The chief *pelophilous species in the [West] Riding. **1909** E. WARMING *Oecol. Plants* lviii. 230 (*heading*) Pelophilous halophytes.

pelo(e, peloer, obs. var. PILAU, PELURE.

peloid (ˈpiːlɔɪd). [f. Gr. πηλ-ός clay, mud + -OID.] **1.** (See quots.)

1933 S. J. LEWIS in *Arch. Med. Hydrol.* XI. 181 (*heading*) Semi-solid bath media or 'peloids'. *Ibid.* 265/1 The word Peloid (Greek, πηλος) should be used as a generic name for all forms of muds, moors, etc... Artificial preparations might be described as artificial peloids. **1953** W. KOSMATH *Brit. Pat.* 695,916 This invention relates to a method for the manufacture of therapeutically effective agents for peloids, which term is here intended to mean bog peat, organic slimes, muds, clays formed by weathering, marl and the like.

2. *Geol.* A particle of microcrystalline or cryptocrystalline carbonate.

1963 E. MCKEE *Prof. Papers U.S. Geol. Survey* No. 475-C. 21/2 Grains within the limestone range in size from fine to very coarse and consist of both bioclasts and peloids (intraformational clastic particles), commonly in an aphanitic calcite matrix. **1969** —— & GUTSCHICK in *Mem. Geol. Soc. Amer.* CXIV. 24 Peloids are defined as ovoid particles of microcrystalline or cryptocrystalline material. *Ibid.* 555 Beds of peloids that seem to be the result of lime-mud deposits having been disturbed and broken up into particles are common. **1972** *Nature* 25 Feb. p. ix/1 (Advt.), Petrography of carbonate grains: oöids, pisolites, peloids and other micritic fabrics. **1976** R. C. SELLEY *Introd. Sedimentology* v. 117 Studies of modern carbonate sediments show that peloids form by a variety of processes. *Ibid.*, In..lagoons and sheltered embayments, peloids are sufficiently abundant to be a dominant rock builder.

Hence **peˈloidal** *a.*

1933 S. J. LEWIS in *Arch. Med. Hydrol.* XI. 182/1 Peloid ..is applicable in all languages in the same way as colloid or alkaloid, giving plurals and adjectives (e.g. 'peloidal') to the same models. **1969** MCKEE & GUTSCHICK in *Mem. Geol. Soc. Amer.* CXIV. 555 Peloidal limestone is defined as rock composed dominantly of particles of cryptocrystalline or microcrystalline material, commonly ovoid in shape. **1976** *Nature* 20 May 221/2 A thin oncolitic iron formation is interbedded with peloidal and oolitic ferruginous chert.

‖**peˈlon**, *a.* (*sb.*) [Sp. *pelon*, pl. *pelones*, bald, hairless.] Bald, hairless: said in Spanish America of nearly hairless races of animals there developed. **b.** *sb.* An animal of such a race.

1879 tr. *De Quatrefages' Hum. Species* 51 In America, where the oxen have a European origin, the hair commences with becoming very fine and few in number with the pelones, and disappears entirely with the calongos. **1882** A. E. SWEET *Sketches fr. Texas Siftings* 61 The pelon dog is a great favorite with the Mexicans in Texas.

pelong (piːˈlɒŋ). [Derivation uncertain: perh. ad. Malay *pĕlang* striped.] A kind of material used for gowns worn in southern India.

1687 *Charter to Fort St. George* (E. India Co.) f. 5ᵛ The said mayor and aldermen may always upon such solemn occasions wear scarlet serge gowns all made after one form or fashion..and that all the burgesses may upon such solemn occasions wear white pelong or other white silk gowns after one form or fashion to be agreed. **1798** *Acct. Interview Teshoo Lama & Capt. Samuel Turner* 6, I advanced, and, as is the custom, presented a white pelong handkerchief. **1922** C. ILBERT *Govt. of India* 23 The burgesses are, on these occasions, to wear white 'pelong', or other silk gowns. **1924** E. SITWELL *Sleeping Beauty* I. 11 Pelongs, bulchauls, pallampores. **1928** —— *Five Poems* 15 Panōpe..Sees Asia, Parthenope, Eunomia, Euphrosyne, Urania, Ausonia In feathered head-dresses as bright as sleep,..In pelongs, chelloes, and great palampores.

peloothered (pɛˈluːθəd). *rare*⁻¹. [Fanciful formation.] Drunk.

1914 JOYCE *Dubliners* 197 It happened that you were peloothered, Tom.

†**peˈlopium.** *Chem. Obs.* [mod. L. (H. Rose, 1846), f. *Pelops*, name of the mythical son of Tantalus: see -IUM.] Name given to a supposed new metal found in the mineral tantalite:

afterwards discovered to be identical with niobium (columbium). Hence †**pelopate** [-ATE[4]], a salt of 'pelopic' or niobic acid.

1849 D. CAMPBELL *Inorg. Chem.* 277 Pelopium is the other new metal discovered by M. Rose in the Bavarian tantalites. *Ibid.* 278 Pelopates are formed by similar processes to the tantalates.

Peloponnesian (pɛləpɒ'ni:ziən), *sb.* and *a.* Also 6–8 **Peloponesian.** [f. Gr. Πελοπόννησ-ος, L. *Peloponnes-us* Peloponnesus + -IAN.]

A. *sb.* A native or inhabitant of the Peloponnesus (or Peloponnese), a peninsula forming the southernmost part of the Greek mainland. **B.** *adj.* Of or pertaining to the Peloponnesus or its inhabitants. ***Peloponnesian war***, a war fought between Athens and Sparta from 431 to 404 B.C., in which Sparta and its Peloponnesian allies were victorious.

*a*1490 J. SKELTON tr. *Diodorus Siculus' Bibliotheca Historica* (1956) I. IV. 275 Oonly the Boecians and the Peloponnesians, and non other, be permytted and licenced to take away of this golde with theym. 1550 T. NICOLLS tr. Thucydides (*title*) The hystory..of the warre, whiche was betwene the Peloponesians and the Athenyans. 1579 NORTH tr. *Plutarch's Lives* 184 Pericles..was thought the only original cause & author of the Peloponnesian warres. 1629 HOBBES tr. *Thucydides' Eight Bks. Pelop. War* I. 14 This Warre, which began from the time that the Athenians and Peloponnesians brake the League. 1709 I. LITTLEBURY tr. *Herodotus' Hist.* II. IX. 370 When the Lacedemonians were advanc'd to the Isthmus, and encamp'd with their Army; the other Peloponesians..thought they could not stay behind without Disgrace. 1752 HUME *Polit. Discourses* x. 226 When they were all chas'd into town, by the invasion of their territory during the Peloponnesian war, the city was not able to contain them. 1808 W. MITFORD *Hist. Greece* II. xv. 95 The Athenians..a little before the beginning of the Peloponnesian war, sent Phormion with thirty triremes to their assistance. 1827 J. R. MAJOR *Questions Mitford's Hist. Greece* 277 The answer of the Pythoness was understood to import that the Peloponnesians would be victorious. 1890 C. W. C. OMAN *Hist. Greece* xxvii. 293 Great battles on shore were very rare during the Peloponnesian war. 1911 *Encycl. Brit.* XXI. 73/2 In 429 the Peloponnesians were deterred by the plague from invading Attica. 1959 N. G. L. HAMMOND *Hist. Greece* 167 Modern scholars have called it [*sc.* the Spartan Alliance], rather misleadingly, 'the Peloponnesian League'. 1960 A. R. BURN *Lyric Age Greece* ix. 176 The Peloponnesian Argives defeated Sparta on the field of Hysiai. 1969 C. M. WOODHOUSE *Philhellenes* iv. 115 Stanhope..adopted the idea of organising a grand conference of national unity... He..visited the seat of the provisional government at Nauplia, to persuade the Peloponnesian leaders to take part... But all was in vain. The Peloponnesians would not come. 1972 D. DAKIN *Unification of Greece* x. 143 Deliyannis..had become the eloquent and popular leader of the disgruntled Peloponnesian peasants. 1972 R. MEIGGS *Athenian Empire* x. 181 Peace..was to be made with the Peloponnesians. 1976 *Classical Q.* XXVI. 233 It is doubtful whether the Peloponnesian detachment was dispatched during the actual celebration of the Olympic games. *Ibid.* 247 The Peloponnesians began construction of the Isthmian wall immediately upon hearing of the outcome of Thermopylae.

pelore, variant of PELURE *Obs.*, fur.

‖**peloria** (pɪ'lɔərɪə). *Bot.* [mod.L., f. Gr. πέλωρ-ος monstrous, f. πέλωρ prodigy, monster; used first as a specific adj. in the name *Linaria Peloria*.] Regularity or symmetry of structure occurring abnormally in flowers normally irregular or unsymmetrical.

1859 DARWIN *Orig. Spec.* v. 145 In irregular flowers, those nearest to the axis are oftenest subject to peloria, and become regular. 1885 *Science Gossip* 184 Peloria, or the regular form of flowers normally irregular, seems to be most common among flowers with spurred petals.

Hence **pe'lorian, pe'loriate, peloric** (pɪ'lɒrɪk) *adjs.*, affected with or characterized by peloria; **pelorism** ('pɛlərɪz(ə)m) = peloria; **pelorize** ('pɛləraɪz) *v. trans.*, to affect with peloria (whence ˌ**pelori'zation**).

1896 HENSLOW *Wild Flowers* 164 In the *pelorian variety the complete number, five, may be restored. 1889 *Sci. Amer.* 11 May 293/2 In *Linaria cymbalaria* *peloriate flowers and other changes were found. 1857 MAYNE *Expos. Lex.*, *Peloricus*, that which is of unnatural size; monstrous: *peloric. 1860 DARWIN in *Life & Lett.* (1887) II. 290 There is, I believe, only one case on record of a peloric flower being fertile. 1868 —— *Anim. & Pl.* xiii. II. 58 *Pelorism is not due to mere chance variability, but either to an arrest of development or to reversion. 1876 BALFOUR in *Encycl. Brit.* IV. 129/2 In some instances, by *pelorization, it is found that tetradynamous plants become tetrandrous. 1868 DARWIN *Anim. & Pl.* xxvi. II. 346 The most perfectly *pelorised examples had six petals, each marked with black striæ like those on the standard-petal.

pelorus (pə'lɔərəs). Also Pelorus. [Name of the supposed pilot of Hannibal when he left Italy.] A compass rose equipped with one or two sighting arms, used for taking the relative bearings of sighted objects.

1854 FRIEND & BROWNING *Brit. Pat. 2652* This invention has for its object the construction and use of an instrument or apparatus which we denominate a pelorus, for determining the amount of magnetic aberration occasioned by local attraction in ships or vessels of every description,.. and by the use of which..the true course..may be from time to time accurately ascertained. 1881 S. T. S. LECKY *'Wrinkles' in Pract. Navig.* x. 67 Having a Pelorus, the first thing to do is to provide suitable stands for it in various parts of the ship, so that it may be moved from one to the other as may be found convenient. 1904 WILSON-BARKER & ALLINGHAM *Navigation* (ed. 2) iii. 17 For the purpose of obtaining bearings when the object is not visible from the standard compass..a Pelorus is very useful. 1934 J. IRVING *Navig. Small Yachts* 284 As the ship's head is steadied on a point by the steering compass the bearing of the distant object is noted by the 'pelorus', and this bearing angle (from right ahead) is applied to the compass direction of ship's head. 1943 REDPATH & COBURN *Air Transport Navig.* iv. 63 A pelorus (a dummy compass rose equipped with sighting vanes) is usually mounted on top of the hatch above the cockpit in the airplane. 1973 *Country Life* 27 Nov. (Suppl.) 66/2 Mid 18th century French brass Pelorus... With original travelling case.

pelosine ('pɛləsaɪn). *Chem.* Also pe'losia. [Arbitrarily f. *Cissam*)*pelos* (name of the genus of which *C. Pareira*, the Velvet Leaf, is a species) + -INE[5].] An alkaloid found in pareira root: = CISSAMPELINE.

1866–77 WATTS *Dict. Chem.* IV. 371 Pelosine or Cissampeline. 1876 HARLEY *Mat. Med.* (ed. 6) 723 An amorphous alkaloid, cissampelia or pelosia. 1880 GARROD & BAXTER *Mat. Med.* 187.

pelosity, *rare* var. PILOSITY.

1922 JOYCE *Ulysses* 687 To Bloom: the problems of irritability, tumescence, rigidity, reactivity, dimension, sanitariness, pelosity.

pelot, pelote, obs. forms of PELLET.

‖**pelota** (pe'lo:ta). [Sp. *pelota* ball, augmentative of *pella*:—L. *pila* ball: cf. PELLET.] A game of Basque origin, somewhat resembling tennis or rackets, played in a large court with a ball, which is struck with a kind of racket made of wicker-work and fastened on the hand by means of a leather glove attached to it.

1844 *Colburn's United Service Mag.* Apr. 492 To see a Spaniard at a festival, a bull-fight, or the rustic game of *pelota*, no one would conceive him given to melancholy. [1891 T. CHILD in *Harper's Mag.* Mar. 511.] 1895 *Westm. Gaz.* 9 May 8/2 A new outdoor game, played in the Basque provinces and at Buenos Ayres, will be seen in London this summer. It may be roughly described as a combination of racquets and tennis, and it goes by the name of pelota. 1902 *Daily Chron.* 26 June 4/3 We want to see the sturdy Basque at his pelota play. 1929 C. CONNOLLY *Let.* in *Romantic Friendship* (1975) 332 She wants to build a modern Corbusier house with a flat roof which can be used as a pelota court. 1934 R. MACAULAY *Going Abroad* xxix. 251 He was showing Hero how to hold a pelota racquet. 1974 *Spain* (Michelin Tyre Co.) 108 The overriding Basque passion.. is *pelota*... There is even a Pelota University.

pelotherapy (pi:ləʊ'θɛrəpɪ). *Med.* [f. PELO- + THERAPY.] The application of mud to the body as a therapeutic measure.

1933 S. J. LEWIS in *Arch. Med. Hydrol.* XI. 178/1 The Greek word *Pelos*..would combine with terms of Greek origin forming derivations such as Pelotherapy. *Ibid.* 182/1 'Pelotherapy' would be the medical treatment by Peloids. 1970 *Telegraph* (Brisbane) 12 June 5/1 The mud treatment —or pelotherapy—is claimed to heal body ailments.

‖**pelo'ton.** Also 8 peleton(e. [F. *peloton* (plɔtɔ̃), deriv. of *pelote* (11th c. in Hatz.-Darm.) ball, heap, platoon, Pr., Sp. *pelota*, It. *pillotta*:—pop. L. *pilotta*, dim. of *pila* ball.]

†**1.** A small ball or spherical mass. *Obs. rare.*

1716 M. DAVIES *Athen. Brit.* III. 93 To pelter him with Heaps and Clouds of those Historical Balls or Librarian Bullets, or Pelotes or Peletons. 1725 BRADLEY *Fam. Dict.* s.v. *Presage*, Other Presages of Rain are, the falling down of Chimney-Soot all on a sudden..; the heaping of Ashes into Peletones.

2. A small body of soldiers; = PLATOON.

1706 PHILLIPS, *Peloton*, see Plotton. 1744 TINDAL tr. *Rapin's Hist. Eng.* III. *Contin.* 209/1 Before he suffered any peloton of his battalion to discharge. 1883 A. FORBES in *Fortn. Rev.* 1 Nov. 664 A brilliant officer in command of anything from a peloton to an army corps.

pelour, obs. f. PEALER[1], PEELER, PILLAR; var. PELURE *Obs.*

‖**pelouse** (pəluz). [Fr.] An area of grass, a lawn; *spec.* a public enclosure at a French racecourse. Also *transf.*

1923 E. HEMINGWAY *Three Stories and Ten Poems* 36 The procession of them went around on the other side past the pelouse. 1928 *Observer* 11 Mar. 13/3 The Longchamp tote ..will unify the betting in all three parts of the course— paddock, pavilion and pélouse. 1953 E. E. CLARK *Indian Legends* 222 A large area of land in south-eastern Washington [State] thought to have been called *pelouse*, 'the grass lands' by French-Canadian voyageurs. 1957 *N. & Q.* June 270/1 On the *pelouse* of open race-courses in and near Paris. 1967 *Punch* 27 Sept. 464/3 A troutstream flows east to west towards the chateau through beautiful Dornford Yatesian pelouses.

pelowe, obs. f. PILLOW, PILAU.

pelrimage, early form of PILGRIMAGE.

pelrinage: see PELERINAGE.

'**pelsy**, *a.* Now *dial.* [f. dial. *pelse* (also *pelsh*) refuse, trash + -Y.] Of little value, trashy.

1631 R. H. *Arraignm. Whole Creature* iv. 28 A kind of light Pelsie corne, inclosed in certaine eares, which are long and swampe, and full of awnes. 1828 *Craven Gloss.* (ed. 2), *Pelsy*, mean, worthless.

pelt (pɛlt), *sb.*[1] Also 7 pealt. [Appears early in 15th c. Evidently related to PELL *sb.*[1], but actual formation obscure.

It may perhaps have been syncopated from PELLET *sb.*[2], with sense 2 of which it agrees, though such a syncope is very unusual. It may also have been a back-formation from PELT-RY (analogical to *paste, pastry*, etc.); *peltry* being = OF. *peleterie*, app. from *pelete*, PELLET *sb.*[2]]

1. The skin of a sheep or goat with short wool on; also, the raw or undressed skin of a fur-bearing animal; a fell.

1425 in Kennett *Par. Ant.* (1818) II. 250, xiv peltys bidentum. *c*1440 [see PELLET *sb.*[2] 2]. *c*1550 *Disc. Common Weal Eng.* (1893) 56 Haue not ye graisers raised the price of youre wolles and peltes? 1570 FOXE *A. & M.* (ed. 2) 746/2 Some others of them [Saints] went about in peltes and goates skinnes. 1579 TWYNE *Phisicke agst. Fort.* II. xciii. 284 Thou hast not the skynne of a Bucke, nor the pelt of a Lambe, nor the case of a Foxe. 1602 WARNER *Alb. Eng.* XI. lxvi. (1612) 281 Their store of Sables, Furres, and Pealts. 1661 FELTHAM *Resolves* (ed. 8) II. lii, God..out of pity to his creature,..put him into pelts. 1808 *Compl. Grazier* (ed. 3) 45 The whole [sheep's] body [should be] covered with a thin pelt. *a*1825 FORBY *Voc. E. Anglia*, *Pelt*, a sheep's skin with the wool on. 1837 WHITTOCK, etc. *Bk. Trades* (1842) 256 (*Furrier*) Preparing the skins or pelts of furred animals, and converting them into muffs and tippets.

2. *spec.* A raw skin of a sheep, goat, or other animal stripped of its wool or fur; the commercial name for a skin in this state before tanning.

1562 *Act 5 Eliz.* c. 22 §1 It shall not bee laufull..to make any Peltes, that is to saye, to pull, sheare, clippe or take away the Wooll of any Shepe-skinne or Lambe-skinne..unles suche person..doo make or cause to bee made therof.. laufully tanned leather or Parchement. 1641 BEST *Farm. Bks.* (Surtees) 29 The skinnes of fatte sheepe..put forth more woll, and alsoe the pelts are better, for that there is more substance to worke upon. 1688 R. HOLME *Armoury* III. 86/2 *Pelts*, are the skins when the Wooll is taken off. 1802 PALEY *Nat. Theol.* iii, A thin membrane like the pelt of a drum stretched across this passage. 1846 J. BAXTER *Libr. Pract. Agric.* (ed. 4) I. 335 The skin of the grey rabbit is cut —that is, the 'wool' is pared off the pelt, as a material for hats. 1858 SIMMONDS *Dict. Trade*, *Peltries*, *Pelts*, the commercial name given to the skins of animals before tanning.

fig. 1634 BP. HALL *Contempl.*, *N.T.* IV. xi, The church is fleeced, and hath nothing left but a bare pelt upon her back. 1894 CROCKETT *Raiders* 149 Folk that are aye taking their nap off other folks are the thinnest in the pelt themselves.

†**b.** The skin of a fish. *Obs. nonce-use.*

1584 HUDSON *Du Bartas' Judith* v. in *Sylvester's Wks.* (1621) 739 Ye Carmans bolde that all on fish do feede, And of their pelts do make your warlike weede.

3. Applied to the human skin. *humorous* or *dial.*

*c*1605 ROWLEY *Birth Merl.* v. ii, Flay off Her wicked skin, and stuff the pelt with straw. 1651 BIGGS *New Disp.* ¶ 144 The profuse sweat, that rills through the creeks of the Pelt, the pores. 1892 M. C. F. MORRIS *Yorks. Folk-talk* Gloss. s.v., They're thick i' t' pelt. 1903 *Public Opinion* 8 Oct. 471 How delightful the feel of the briny breeze and the boisterous wave on the bare pelt!

4. †**a.** A skin of an animal worn as a garment; a garment made of skin or fell. *Obs.*

1565 COOPER *Thesaurus*, *Diphtera*, a sheapardes pelte or garment made of sheepe skinnes. 1580 LUPTON *Sivqila* 21 Our father Adam..had but a leather Pelte to cover his nakednesse. 1585 HIGINS tr. *Junius' Nomenclator* 161/1 *Mastruca*..a pelt, or garments made of wolues and beares skins, which Nobles in old time vsed to weare in winter. 1649 C. WALKER *Hist. Independ.* II. 239 Some of them lead Dray-horses, wore Leather-pelts.

b. Untanned sheepskin used to form a printer's inking-pad; an inking-pad so formed, a pelt-ball.

1683 MOXON *Mech. Exerc.*, *Printing* 386 *Pelts*, Sheep Skins untan'd, used for Ball Leathers. 1824 J. JOHNSON *Typogr.* II. xxi. 655 *Pelts*, untanned sheep skins used for balls.

†**5.** Applied opprobriously to a person compared to a dried skin; (*a*) a miserly closefisted person; a niggard, a skinflint; (*b*) a withered or wizened person. *Obs.*

1545 ELYOT *Dict.*, *Aridus homo*, a drye felowe, of whom nothyng may be gotten, som do call hym a pelt, or a pynchebeke. 1757 MRS. GRIFFITH *Lett. Henry & Frances* (1767) I. 18 A diabolical, miserable pelt of an old maid called Melpomene.

6. The dead quarry of a hawk, esp. when mangled. See also quot. 1674–91.

1615 LATHAM *Falconry* (1633) 11 Put on her Hood: then lure her againe unto the dead pelt. *Ibid.* Gloss., *Pelt*, is the dead body of any fowle howsoeuer dismembred. 1674–91 RAY *N.C. Words* 54 *Pelt* is a word much used in Falconry for the skin of a Fowl stuft, or the Carcase it self of a dead Fowl to throw out to a Hawk. 1852 R. F. BURTON *Falconry in Valley of Indus* v. 60 If two [hawks] are flown.., the falconer is always flurried by their violent propensity to crab over the 'pelt'.

7. *attrib.* and *Comb.*, as †***pelt-skin***; **pelt-ball** = sense 4 b; **peltmonger**, one who deals in skins; **pelt-rot**, a skin-disease in sheep due to damp; **pelt-shaker**, *Hatmaking*, one of the workmen who prepare the pelts for the making of hats; so ***pelt-shaking***; **pelt-wool**: see quot. 1753.

1822 BEWICK *Mem.* 238 The common *pelt-balls then in use..daubed the cut and blurred and overlapped its edges. 1565 COOPER *Thesaurus*, *Pellio*,..a skinner: he that maketh thynges of skinnes: a *peltemunger. 1755 JOHNSON, *Peltmonger*,..a dealer in raw hides. 1523 FITZHERB. *Husb.* §54 There is an other rotte, whiche is called *pelte-rotte, and that commeth of greatte wete, specyally in woode countreyes. **1736** W. Ellis *New Exper. Husb.* 42. **1902** *Brit. Med. Jrnl.* No. 2146. 378 Muscular tremors ('hatter's shakes') are most often observed in those engaged in dusty post-carrotting processes (for example cutters, lockers, and *pelt-shakers). *Ibid.* 377 The various processes include (1) cleaning the skins..(7) locking, (8) *pelt-shaking. **1621** *Vestry Bks.* (Surtees) 80 Item for a *pelt skinn receyved from Lud[worth]: ij d. **1543** tr. *Act 8 Hen. VI*, c. 22 That no man..put in the same [fleese], lokkes, *peltwol, tarre, sand, yerth, grasse, nor no dyrt [*orig.* lokkes pelwoll tarre peers sablon terre ne herbe, ne nulle autre orde']. **1753** Chambers *Cycl. Supp.*, *Pelt-wool*, wool stripped of the skin or pelt of a dead sheep.

pelt, *sb.*[2] [f. pelt *v.*[1]: cf. pilt *sb.*]

1. An act of pelting; a vigorous blow or stroke, as with a missile; the act of pelting with missiles or (*fig.*) with obloquy.

1513 Douglas *Æneis* xiii. ii. 15 Wyth mony pelt scheddand thar purpour blude. *c* **1570** *Marr. Wit & Science* v. iv. in Hazl. *Dodsley* II. 391 Here is a pelt to make your knave's heart fret. **1632** Vicars tr. *Virgil* ix. 280 Troyes Ilioneus brave With a huge stone a deadly pelt him gave. **1771** Smollett *Humph. Cl.* 4 July Let. i, The cripple..gave him such a good pelt on the head with his crutch, that the blood followed. **1819** *Blackw. Mag.* IV. 727 Divers digs and many a ponderous pelt. *a* **1839** Galt *Demon of Destiny* iii. (1840) 26 Adversity assails with pelt and scorn The would be great. **1889** *Pall Mall G.* 28 May 6/3 Amusing pastimes, winding up with a general pelt of flowers.

b. The beating of rain or snow; a pelting storm.

1862 Shirley *Nugæ Crit.* vii. 301 Not the rain of the temperate zone, but a down-pour, a pelt, a water-spout. **1880** Blackmore *Mary Anerley* xl, For all things now were in one indiscriminate pelt and whirl of white. **1887** D. C. Murray *One Trav. Returns* vi. 92 The swish and pelt of the rain were heard in pauses.

2. An outburst of temper, a rage. Cf. pelt *v.*[1] 6. *Obs.* exc. *dial.*

1573 G. Harvey *Letter-bk.* (Camden) 28 Saiing further in a great pelt, that he mindid not in deed to deni me him self. **1655** Fuller *Ch. Hist.* iii. v. §30 The Pope being in this pelt, Ægidius a Spanish Cardinall thus interposed his gravitie. *a* **1700** B. E. *Dict. Cant. Crew*, *Pelt*, a Heat or Chafe. 'What a Pelt you are in!' **1880** Mrs. Parr *Adam & Eve* xxix. 399 Back he comes in a reg'lar pelt: and says, '..I'm not goin to foace [force] myself where I'm told I shan't be wanted'.

3. The action of pelting (pelt *v.*[1] 7); esp. in *full pelt*, (at) full speed.

1819 'R. Rabelais' *Abeillard & Heloisa* 230 To prison pelt —away we should go. *a* **1845** Hood *Tale of Trumpet* xxvii, Just fancy a horse that comes full pelt. **1862** H. Marryat *Year in Sweden* I. 148 Two postboys gallop up full pelt, without either saddles or stirrups. **1885** J. Payn *Talk of Town* II. 196 The others..ran on full pelt behind them.

pelt, *sb.*[3] Now only *dial.* [app. a parallel form to *palt*, found in mod.Eng. dial. in the same sense, and assumed as the stem of paltry *sb.*, which see for foreign cognates. To this apparently belong pelting *a.*, and peltry *sb.*[2]; but the phonetic history of the group is very obscure.] Trash or rubbish in the way of clothes, rags (*obs.*); also in *mod. dial.*, Refuse, waste or dirty matter.

1567 Harman *Caveat* xxiv. 76 [At night] many wyll plucke of their smockes, and laye the same vpon them in stede of their vpper sheete, and all her other pelte and trashe vpon her also. *a* **1585** Montgomerie *Flyting* 266 This prouerb, foule pelt, to thee is applyit. [Cf. **1851** T. Sternberg *Dial. Northamptonsh.* s.v., The refuse of corn that rises to the top of the sieve after reeing, is also termed *palt.*] **1866** W. Gregor *Dial. of Banffsh.* 124. **1880** Jamieson, *Pelt.* 1. A piece of strong, coarse cloth, or of a thick, dirty dress; a rag, *Banffsh.* 2. Anything that is waste or dirty, trash.

†**pelt,** *sb.*[4] *Obs. rare.* [ad. L. *pelta*: see pelta.]

1. A light shield of leather or hide: = pelta 1.

But in quots. 1617–33 the sense may be as in pelt *sb.*[1] 4.

1617 Moryson *Itin.* iii. 267 The poorer sort haue only helmets of iron, and thick leather pelts in stead of armor. **1633** J. Fisher *True Trojans* ii. v, Under the conduct of Demetiaes prince March twice three thousand, arm'd with Pelts and Glaues. **1658** Phillips, *Peltiferous*,..that carrieth a Pelt which is a kind of Target made of skins.

2. *Bot.* = pelta 2.

1758 *Phil. Trans.* L. 680 On the edges..the parts of fructification are placed, in the form of flattish oblong bodies, in these mosses called shields or pelts.

pelt (pɛlt), *v.*[1] [Known from end of 15th century: origin uncertain.

Thought by some to be the same word as ME. pilt, *pult* to thrust, push, which also had the spelling *pelt*. But the difference of sense, and the chronological break between the two, make this origin very doubtful.]

1. a. *trans.* To strike with many or repeated blows (now, in Standard Eng., with something thrown); to assail with missiles.

(The wider sense is still Sc. and north. Eng.)

a **1500** in *Ashm. MS.* 61 No. 16 Wherefore seyd ye belte Wt grete strokes I schall hym pelte. **1570** Foxe *A. & M.* (ed. 2) 372/2 The Christians inuadyng and entring into the munition incircumspectly, were pelted and pashed with stones by them which stode aboue. **1604** Shaks. *Oth.* ii. i. 12 The chidden Billow seemes to pelt the Clowds. **1621–3** Middleton & Rowley *Changeling* ii. i. 55 I'll stand this storm of hail, though the stones pelt me. **1687** A. Lovell tr. *Thevenot's Trav.* i. 159 A crowd..pelting one another with Cudgels. **1719** De Foe *Crusoe* ii. ix, They stood pelting us ..with darts and arrows. **1782** Miss Burney *Cecilia* vi. v, There came a violent shower of hail..Cecilia was..pelted. **1796** Morse *Amer. Geog.* I. 295 The soldiers..were.. insulted and pelted by a mob armed with clubs, sticks, etc. **1835** Sir J. Ross *Narr. 2nd Voy.* xlvi. 602 Make snowballs and pelt each other. **1884** Q. Victoria *More Leaves* 370 We were literally pelted with small nosegays, till the carriage was full of them.

b. *fig.* To assail with reproaches or obloquy.

1658 J. Harrington *Prerog. Pop. Govt.* (1700) 231 But Macchiavel..is deservedly pelted for it by Sermons. **1710** *Tatler* No. 190 ¶1, I..have had the Honour to be pelted with several Epistles. **1775** Johnson in Boswell *Life* (1831) III. 183 No, sir, if they had wit, they should have kept pelting me with pamphlets. **1864** Sir F. Palgrave *Norm. & Eng.* IV. 200 The surrounding multitude..pelted the Prelates with opprobrious epithets.

2. To drive by force of blows, missiles, etc.

1582 Stanyhurst *Æneis* i. (Arb.) 34 Too soyl vnacquaynted by tempest horriblye pelted. *Ibid.* iv. 96, I thinck, that the Godhead,..Thee Troian vessels too this youre segnorye pelted. **1886** Burton *Arab. Nts.* (Abr. ed.) I. Foreword 7 Lads and lasses, driving, or rather pelting, through the gloaming their sheep and goats.

3. a. *intr.* To go on striking vigorously; to deliver repeated strokes or blows. Also *fig.*

1535 Stewart *Cron. Scot.* II. 608 The Scottis..Than peltit on thair powis ane lang space, Quhill tha war slane ilkone in that same place. **1645** Milton *Colast.* 2, I still was waiting, when these light arm'd refuters would have don pelting at thir three lines. **1674** N. Fairfax *Bulk & Selv.* Ep. Ded., They play'd the Men only, when they had done, in pelting on't with the distaff. *c* **1817** Hogg *Tales & Sk.* II. 173 The smith..pelting away at his hot iron. **1819** W. Tennant *Papistry Storm'd* (1827) 134 Sanct Salvador's lang strappan steeple Had peltit five hours to the people.

b. Of rain, snow, the sun's rays: To continue to beat with force or violence. Also of missiles.

1821 Clare *Vill. Minstr.* II. 152 The storm pelted down with all his might. **1879** Atcherley *Boërland* 168 The rain began to pelt. **1889** *Repentance P. Wentworth* I. ix. 176 There was a big unshaded window..through which the sun still pelted freely. **1916** 'Boyd Cable' *Action Front* 210 Maxim and rifle bullets were still pelting from somewhere in half enfilade at long range.

4. *intr.* To strike *at* vigorously with missiles; to go on firing, 'fire away'. Also *fig.*

1565 Bp. Jewel *Let. to Bullinger* in Strype *Ann. Ref.* (1709) I. xlv. 457 Here I am again pelted at. **1591** Shaks. *1 Hen. VI*, iii. i. 82 The Bishop, and the Duke of Glosters men,..Haue fill'd their Pockets full of peeble stones; And.. Doe pelt so fast at one anothers Pate. **1698** Fryer *Acc. E. India & P.* 45 Besides innumerable [shot] in her Rigging, Masts and Sails, from those [ships] that pelted at a distance. **1848** Whately *Let.* in *Life* (1866) II. 133, I will not set up any proposal like a Shrove-Tuesday cock for you to pelt at.

5. *trans.* To go on throwing (missiles) with intent to strike. Also *fig.*

1683 Wood *Life* 11 Apr. (O.H.S.) III. 42 The rout followed, and pelted stones. **1745** H. Walpole *Let. to H. S. Conway* 1 July, When all the young Pitts and Lyttletons were pelting oratory at my father. **1862** Dickens *Bleak Ho.* xxxiii, Will somebody hand me anything hard..to pelt at her? **1916** 'Boyd Cable' *Action Front* 116 A heavy rifle and machine-gun fire which was pelted across from the opposite parts of the British line.

†**6.** *intr.* To throw out angry words. *Obs.* Cf. pelt *sb.*[2] 2: pelting *ppl. a.* 2.

[**1566**: see pelting *ppl. a.* 2.] **1593** Shaks. *Lucr.* 1418 Another smother'd seemes to pelt and sweare. **1631** R. H. *Arraignm. Whole Creature* xvi. 281 Like Children in their minoritie, that pelt it, and pule, and cry, for one toy they want. **1673** Milton *True Relig.* 15 If they who differ in matters not essential to belief,..shall stand jarring and pelting at one another, they will be soon routed and subdued. **1706** Phillips, To *Pelt*... Also to be in a Chafe or fit of Anger, to fret and fume.

7. *intr.* To beat the ground with rapid steps; to move at a vigorous and rapid pace.

1831 S. Warren *Diary Physic.* xvi. (1832) I. 382, I heard the report of a gun.., and pelted away. **1843** Lever *J. Hinton* xxxv, Two or three hundred cars, all going as fast as they can pelt. *a* **1845** Hood *To Mary* iii. i, I too longed much to pelt—but my small-boned legs falter'd. **1872** Baker *Nile Trib.* xix. 332, I saw the rhinoceros pelting away.

Hence '**pelted** *ppl. a.*

1697 Dryden *Virg. Past.* iii. 97 My Phyllis Me with pelted Apples plyes. **1900** *Westm. Gaz.* 23 July 2/3 A pelting bombardment of ice lumps,..the pelted district must have had an exciting time.

pelt, *v.*[2] [f. pelt *sb.*[1]] **a.** To strip or pluck off (the pelt or skin) *from*; to skin, fleece.

1596 Nashe *Saffron Walden* 87 He..presently vntrusseth and pelts the out-side from the lining. **1641** Spelman *De Sepult.* 31 These..doe so shave and pelt the people, that the cry thereof is very grievous. **1919** W. T. Grenfell *Labrador Doctor* ix. 176 Then having killed, 'sculped', and 'pelted' the seal, the exciting return to the vessel. **1936** D. McCowan *Animals Canad. Rockies* xxiv. 211 In Canada alone in the first decade of this century, ten millions of the animals [*sc.* mink] were pelted for the sake of the satiny fur. **1948** A. L. Rand *Mammals E. Rockies* 116 It [*sc.* a wolf] is a large, awkward animal to pelt on the trap-line. **1950** *N.Z. Jrnl. Agric.* Sept. 256 (*caption*) Pelting skins on the killing chain. **1972** 'M. Yorke' *Silent Witness* iii. 51 The Derringtons had a mink farm. 'We pelt them in November.'

†**b.** To pluck the feathers from. *Obs. rare.*

1692 R. L'Estrange *Fables* cvii. (1694) 101 A Man took an Eagle, Pelted her Wings, and put her among his Hens.

†**pelt,** *v.*[3] *Obs.* [Cf. palter *v.* and pelting *a.*

In form, this looks like the verb whence pelting *a.* is derived, but the connexion of sense is not obvious.]

intr. ? To parley or bargain; to haggle in bargaining; = palter.

1579 W. Wilkinson *Confut. Familye of Loue* 41 Those men which sell by whole sale haue a quicker dispatch,..than those which stand pelting out untill the end of the market. **1610** *Mirr. Mag.* 166, I found the people nothing prest to pelt, To yeeld, or hostage giue, or tributes pay.

†**pelt,** *v.*[4], a form of ME. pilt, to thrust, q.v.

1617 Collins *Def. Bp. Ely* i. i. 77 Whereas you patch, and pelt, and clowt euery thing into euery place that you can, like a beggers coate.

‖**pelta** ('pɛltə). Pl. **peltæ** (-tiː). [L. *pelta*, a. Gr. πέλτη a small light shield of leather.]

1. *Antiq.* A small light shield or buckler used by the ancient Greeks, Romans, etc.

1600 Holland *Livy* xxviii. v. 670 The *Peltæ* are certaine small bucklers or targuets, nothing unlike unto the Spanish Cetræ. **1702** Addison *Dial. Medals* Wks. 1736 III. 137 On the left arm of Smyrna, is the *Pelta* or Buckler of the Amazons. **1849** Grote *Greece* ii. xlix. VI 294 Lightly armed with javelins,..and the pelta or small shield.

2. *Bot.* Applied to various shield-like structures; *spec.* the apothecium or spore-case of a lichen when without an excipulum or rim, as in the genus *Peltigera* (*Peltidea*); also, a bract or scale attached by the middle like a peltate leaf.

1760 J. Lee *Introd. Bot.* i. iii. (1765) 9 The Peltæ are the Fructification of the Lichen. **1785** Martyn *Rousseau's Bot.* xxxii. (1794) 499 Ash-coloured Ground Liverwort [*Lichen caninus* Lin.]..is..veined underneath, and villous, with a rising *pelta* or target on the edge. **1858** Carpenter *Veg. Phys.* §756 This head consists of a central disk, termed the *pelta*, or shield, on which the spore cases are arranged in a radiating manner, like the spokes of a wheel.

3. *Archit.* An ornamental shield motif (see quots.).

1928 A. W. Clapham in *Archaeologia* XXVII. 227 The *Pelta Ornament*..consists essentially of pairs of half-circles set back to back in such a way that the combination forms a series of figures like a double-headed axe or an Amazon-shield. **1936** —— *Romanesque Archit.* iii. 61 Of much less frequent occurrence is the Carolingian pelta-ornament, used as a diaper on roll-mouldings at Piacenza, Modena, Cremona, and Ferrara Cathedrals. **1942** *Oxoniensia* VII. 70 The eye is at once attracted to the small field of decoration on the head allotted to an engraved and enamelled pelta-scroll flung haphazard on the surface. **1954** M. Rickert *Painting in Brit.: Middle Ages* 230 *Pelta*, a classical ornamental motif formed by two converging curves joined by another line. The ancestor of the trumpet pattern. **1965** R. Krautheimer *Early Christian & Byzantine Archit.* 362 *Pelta*, a shield-shaped design composed of a convex curve joined to two concave curves. **1967** *Antiquaries Jrnl.* XLVII. 167 On the extreme right is a border of black and white composed of small alternating semicircular forms producing the effect of a pelta pattern.

†'**peltage.** *Obs. rare*$^{-1}$. [f. pelt *sb.*[1] + -age.] Pelts collectively; peltry.

1698 G. Thomas *West-New-Jersey* 32, I shall begin with Burlington-County, as for Peltage, or Beaver Skins [etc.].

peltast ('pɛltæst). *Gr. Hist.* [ad. L. *peltasta*, ad. Gr. πελταστής, f. πέλτη: see pelta.] A kind of foot-soldier: see quot. 1849.

[**1600** Holland *Livy* xxxi. xxxvi. 794 Certaine targatiers, whom they call Peltastæ.] **1623** Bingham *Xenophon* 67 In the meane time Cherisophus..sent the Peltasts, and Slingers, and Archers ouer to Xenophon. **1838** Thirlwall *Greece* V. 269 It was with no more than 1000 Phocian peltasts. **1849** Grote *Greece* ii. xlix. VI. 258 Peltasts, a species of troops between heavy-armed and light-armed, furnished with a pelta (or light shield) and short spear or javelin.

peltate ('pɛlteɪt), *a. Bot.* and *Zool.* [ad. L. *peltāt-us* armed with the pelta.] Shield-shaped; usually of a leaf: Having the petiole joined to the under-surface of the blade at or near the middle (instead of at the base or end); hence, said of other stalked parts having similar attachment.

1760 J. Lee *Introd. Bot.* iii. vii. (1765) 190 *Peltate, Shield-fashioned*, when the Petiole is inserted into the Disk of the Leaf, and not into its Base or Margin. **1830** Lindley *Nat. Syst. Bot.* 10 Herbs, with peltate or cordate fleshy leaves. **1852** Dana *Crust.* ii. 865 The large peltate plates on either side of the body posteriorly. **1875** Bennett & Dyer tr. *Sachs' Bot.* 372 The pedicel of the hexagonal peltate scale.

So †'**peltated** *a. Obs.* = peltate; '**peltately** *adv.*, in the manner of a peltate leaf; **pel'tation**, peltate condition, or a peltate formation.

1753 Chambers *Cycl. Supp.* s.v. *Leaf*, *Peltated leaf*,..the petiole of which is affixed to the disk. **1828–32** Webster, *Peltately*, in the form of a target. *Eaton.* **1870** Hooker *Stud. Flora* 254 Nutlets..peltately attached to a thickened conical receptacle. **1881** *Jrnl. Bot.* X. 135 A similar peltation towards the extremity of the proximal expansion occurs in many of the leaves of *Nepenthes phyllamphora.*

pel'tati-, pel'tato-, mod. combining forms of L. *peltātus* peltate, as in **peltatifid** (-'tætɪfɪd) *a.* [after *pinnatifid*]; **pel,tato-'digitate** *a.*: see quot.

1866 *Treas. Bot.* 858 *Peltatifid* is applied to a peltate leaf cut into subdivisions; and *peltato-digitate* to a digitate leaf with the petiole much enlarged at the setting on of the leaflets.

'**pelter,** *sb.*[1] *rare.* [Agent-noun belonging to pelting *a.*] A paltry or peddling person.

a **1577** Gascoigne *Flowers* Wks. (1587) 41 Yea let suche pelters prate, saint Needam be their speede, We need no text to answer them but this, The Lord hath nede. **1577** T. Kendall *Flowers of Epigr.* 4 The veriest pelter pilde maie seme, to haue experience thus. [Cf. 'pilde peltinge prestes', pelting *a.* 1553.] **1922** Joyce *Ulysses* 130 That old pelters [*sic*], the editor said.

pelter, *sb.*[2] [f. pelt *v.*[1] + -er[1].]

1. a. One who pelts, esp. with missiles.

1828–32 Webster, *Pelter*, one that pelts. **1830** Gen. P. Thompson *Exerc.* (1842) I. 276 To ask why the pelters should not be put into the stocks. **1881** P. ROBINSON *Under Punkah* 186 The driver and guards..have no time to get down and catch the pelters, and therefore it is safe to pelt.

b. *humorously*. A gun or pistol; also, a small ship carrying guns.

1827 BARRINGTON *Personal Sk.* II. 10 Our family pistols, denominated pelters, were brass. **1890** *Daily News* 2 Dec. 5/3 The old 'donkey frigates' and 'ten-gun pelters' which were an old theme of jocularity in the service.

c. A pelting shower. *colloq.*

1791 J. BYNG *Torrington Diaries* (1935) II. 360 Tho' it rain'd all the way, so as to hurry me, yet it was not a pelter. **1816** JANE AUSTEN *Let.* 9 July (1952) 459 We were obliged to turn back..but not soon enough to avoid a Pelter all the way home. **1842** BARHAM *Ingol. Leg.* Ser. II. *Dead Drummer*, In vain sought for shelter From..'a regular pelter'. **1901** G. DOUGLAS *House w. Green Shutters* 145 The storm's at the burstin'!..we're in for a pelter. **1966** T. H. RADDALL *Hangman's Beach* I. vi. 83 Boats' crews and carpenters.. came out in the cold pelter to McNab's island.

d. One who or that which 'pelts' or goes rapidly: in quot. 1901 a swift horse. *colloq.* Phr. ***in a pelter***: in a hurry; at speed.

c **1889** 'F. LESLIE' *Let.* in W. T. Vincent *Recoll. Fred Leslie* (1894) II. xxiii. 97 Dear, dear! I have wasted time and ought to have been at work on our burlesque. Now I am determined to go in a pelter. **1901** *Munsey's Mag.* (U.S.) XXIV. 484/1 It ain't the first time the pelter's carried double.

e. An old or slow horse. *U.S. colloq.*

This may belong to PELTER *sb.*[1]: see *Dict. Amer.*

1856 *Knickerbocker* XLVIII. 314 When his earthly tenement yields his soul no shelter, May it animate the corpse of an ancient pelter. **1896** ADE *Artie* i. 4 It's like hitchin' up a four-time winner 'longside of a pelter. **1902** H. F. DAY *Pine Tree Ballads* 147 He'd..take a wheezy old pelter with a hopity gait and he'd make you believe..there were all kinds of pedigrees tied up in him. **1931** D. RUNYON in *Hearst's International* Sept. 84/1 Mahogany..is..not such a bad old pelter.

2. A rage, 'temper'. *dial.*

1861 BARR *Poems* 9 (E.D.D.), I couldna speak a single word, I was in such a pelter. **1888** 'R. BOLDREWOOD' *Robbery under Arms* iii. 19 Nobody ever seemed to be able to get into a pelter with Jim.

3. Something exceptionally large. *dial.*

c **1780** M. LONSDALE in S. Gilpin *Popular Poetry of Cumberland* (1875) 61 An' dall! but it's a pelter. **1892** E. J. MILLIKEN *'Arry Ballads* 70/1 Their ain't nothink the nobs is fair nuts on but wot these 'ere bellerers ban. Wy, they're down upon Sport, now, a pelter. Perposterous, ain't it, old man?

[**pelter**, *sb.*[3], 'a dealer in skins or hides'.

In *Cent. Dict.*, etc. without quot. The historical words are PELLETER and PELTIER; in mod. use also PELTERER. *Groome Pelter* in *Household Ordinances* (1790) 41 from *Liber Niger* of Edw. IV is a misreading of *grome pulter* of the MS.]

ˈpelter, *v.* Chiefly *dial.* [Iterative of PELT *v.*: cf. *patter*.] **1.** *trans.* To go on pelting or striking (also *fig.*); *intr.* to patter (as rain).

[In *Eng. Dial. Dict.* from Cumberl. to Notts.]

1715 M. DAVIES *Athen. Brit.* I. Pref. 2 Now Giles the Foot-man..pelters him with Sentences out of the Holy-Fathers and Scholastick Divinity. **1716** *Ibid.* III. 93 [see PELOTON 1]. **1828** *Craven Gloss.* (ed. 2), *Pelter*, to patter, or beat. **1939** DYLAN THOMAS *Map of Love* 12 Chimes cheat the prison spire, pelter In time like outlaw rains on that priest, water, Time for the swimmers' hands, music for silver lock And mouth.

2. *intr.* To run with rapid steps; = PELT *v.*[1] 7.

1906 W. S. MAUGHAM *Bishop's Apron* xix. 297 The strange spectacle of a comely young woman and an ecclesiastical dignitary..peltering towards the Achilles Statue as fast as they could go. **1923** *Chambers's Jrnl.* Apr. 240/2 Rawlins..peltered up on deck to recover his composure.

Hence (in sense 1) **ˈpeltering** *ppl. a.*

1858 LEVER *Martins of Cro' M.* xiv. 131 Now, rising to pace the room, or drawing nigh the window to curse the peltering rain without. **1927** *Glasgow Herald* 27 Aug. 8 The peltering rains (which were certainly general) made the grass so wet that the..cow ate far too much juice.

ˈpelterer. [f. PELTRY + -ER[1]: cf. *fruiterer*, *fripperer*, etc.] A dealer in peltry, a fellmonger.

1876 *Whitby Gloss.*, *Pelterer*, a dealer in skins or 'peltry'. A furrier. **1886** E. GILLIAT *Forest Outlaws* (1887) 295 The booths..of the pelterers with their smelling hides.

pelti-, combining form of PELTA, in a few rarely used scientific terms, chiefly botanical. †**pelˈtiferous** *a.* [L. *peltifer*], bearing a pelta or small shield. **peltiˈfolious** *a.* [L. *folium* leaf], having peltate leaves. **ˈpeltiform** *a.*, shield-shaped; of a peltate form. **peltigerine** (pɛlˈtɪdʒəraɪn) *a.*, belonging to, resembling, or characteristic of, the genus *Peltigera* of lichens, having large shield-shaped apothecia. **pelˈtigerous** *a.* [L. *peltiger*], shield-bearing (Mayne *Expos. Lex.*). **peltiˈnervate**, **ˈpeltinerved** *adjs.*, having the nerves or veins radiating from the centre as in a peltate leaf.

1656 BLOUNT *Glossogr.*, **Peltiferous*, that weareth or bears a Target like a half moon. **1857** MAYNE *Expos. Lex.*, *Peltifolius*..having peltate leaves: *peltifolious. *Ibid.*, *Peltiformis*..applied to *apotheciæ* in form of a shield..: *peltiform. **1893** *Syd. Soc. Lex.*, *Peltiform*, applied..in Mineralogy, to *couches* or beds that are convex, and inclined on the slope of a mountain. **1890** *Cent. Dict.*, **Peltigerine*. **1866** *Treas. Bot.* 858 **Peltinerved*, having ribs arranged as in a peltate leaf.

†**peltier**[1]. *Obs.* In 4 -yer. [a. OF. *peletier* (12th c.), in mod.F. *pelletier* (pɛltje), app. f. OF. *pelete*, *pellete*, *-ette*, PELLET *sb.*[2]] A furrier.

1389 *Gild of Peltyers, Norwich* in *Eng. Gilds* (1870) 29 Peltyers and oþere god men be-gunne þis gilde and þis bretherhod of seynt Willyam þe holy Innocent and marter in Norwyche.

Peltier[2] (ˈpɛltɪeɪ). *Physics.* The name of J. C. A. *Peltier* (1785–1845), French amateur scientist, used *attrib.* with reference to an effect he discovered in 1834, whereby heat is given out, or absorbed, when an electric current passes across a junction between two materials; ***Peltier coefficient***, (*a*) the quantity of heat liberated or absorbed at a junction between two conductors when unit charge passes between them; (*b*) of a material, the quantity of heat liberated or absorbed when unit electric charge traverses a junction between that material and a reference conductor.

1856 *Proc. R. Soc.* VII. 54, I hope also to be able to make determinations in absolute measure of the amount of the Peltier effect for a given strength of current between various pairs of metals. **1896** FOSTER & ATKINSON *Elem. Treat. Electr. & Magn.* xiv. 135 This coefficient, known as the Peltier coefficient,..represents for a junction of any two metals the amount of energy converted into or produced from heat per second when a current of unit strength traverses the junction. **1904** J. S. AMES *Text-bk. Gen. Physics* xliv. 681 These forces at the surface of contact of two substances are called 'Peltier electro-motive forces', having been first discovered by him. **1916** F. B. PIDDUCK *Treat. Electr.* vi. 210 In addition to the Peltier heat there is the usual heat developed by the mere passage of the current through the wires. **1958** CONDON & ODISHAW *Handbk. Physics* IV. vi. 84/2 The Peltier coefficient for a junction AB is representable as the difference of two intrinsic Peltier coefficients characteristic of each material separately. **1966** *McGraw-Hill Encycl. Sci. & Technol.* XIII. 581/2 If 1 coulomb of positive charge moves slowly around the circuit, there will be Peltier cooling in its passage from Bi to Cu at T and Peltier heating at T_0. **1972** R. W. URE in Willardson & Beer *Semiconductors & Semimetals* VIII. ii. 68 The Peltier effect at the junction between the liquid and solid phases has been used to remove the latent heat of crystallization in crystal growth.

ˈpelting, *vbl. sb.* [f. PELT *v.*[1] + -ING[1].] The action of PELT *v.*[1]; beating with missiles; persistent striking or beating.

1605 SHAKS. *Lear* III. iv. 29 Poore naked wretches, where so ere you are That bide the pelting of this pittilesse storme. **1830** CUNNINGHAM *Brit. Paint.* II. 120 To avoid the pelting of the storm of invective. **1840** DICKENS *Barn. Rudge* ii, The rude buffets of the wind and pelting of the rain.

ˈpelting, *a. arch.* [Known from *c* 1540, and very frequent to *c* 1688. Occasional in modern authors as a literary archaism. App. related to PELT *sb.*[3], and PELTRY *sb.*[2] A variant PALTING occurs 1579–80, and in mod. dialect: cf. also PALTRY.

Its form suggests that *pelting* is the pr. pple. of PELT *v.*[3]; the difficulty is that this vb. is very rare, is not found so early, and does not yield the required sense, unless it is held that *pelting* began with some such sense as 'haggling or shuffling', and passed through 'peddling', to that of 'petty, trashy, contemptible'; a sequence not proved.]

Paltry, petty, contemptible; mean, insignificant, trumpery, inconsiderable; worthless.

1540 R. WISDOME in Strype *Eccl. Mem.* I. App. cxv. 319 The putting away of pelting perdons and the roting out of famous idols. **1553** BALE *Vocacyou* 43 They are but pilde peltinge prestes. **1556** *Olde Antichrist* 133 So beggarly a suburbe, or so pelting a village. **1565** CALFHILL *Aunsw. Treat. Crosse* (1846) 10 Like a pelting pedlar, putting the best in your pack uppermost. **1573** G. HARVEY *Letter-bk.* (Camden) 12 Inforcid rather to bungle up a pelting histori then to write a set epistle. **1593** SHAKS. *Rich. II*, II. i. 60 This Land of such deere soules..Is now Leas'd out..like to a Tenement or pelting Farme. **1603** —— *Meas. for M.* II. ii. 112 Euery pelting petty Officer Would vse his heauen for Thunder. **1634** BP. HALL *Contempl.*, *N.T.* IV. xxvii, To tender a trade of so invaluable a commodity to these pelting petty chapmen for thirty poor silverlings. **1685** *Gracian's Courtiers Orac.* 186 Sometimes a little pelting fret costs a repentance, that lasts as long as life. **1820** SHELLEY *Philos. View Reform* in Dowden *Life* II. 293 A set of pelting wretches, in whose employment there is nothing to exercise ..the more majestic forces of the soul. **1873** TRENCH *Plutarch* ii. (1874) 37 Greece was a province:..Her flourishing cities..had dwindled into pelting villages.

Hence †**ˈpeltingly** *adv.*, in a mean or paltry manner.

c **1592** BABINGTON *Notes on Gen.* xxi. 22 Wks. (1622) 73 It is not euer by and by well spared, that pinchingly and peltingly is spared. **1602** *Contention betw. Liberality & Prodigality* II. iv. in Hazl. *Dodsley* VIII. 350 For thy pains I will not grease thy fist Peltingly with two or three crowns.

ˈpelting, *ppl. a.* [f. PELT *v.*[1] + -ING[2].]

1. That pelts; chiefly of rain, hail, etc.: driving, beating, lashing. Also *fig.*

1710 PHILIPS *Pastorals* ii. 99 The pelting show'r Destroys the tender herb and budding flow'r. **1817** COLERIDGE *Sibyl. Leaves, to Rev. G. Coleridge*, Chance-started friendships. A brief while Some have preserved me from life's pelting ills. **1851** HELPS *Comp. Solit.* x. (1874) 164 There is a pitiless, pelting rain this morning.

2. Violent, passionate, hot. Chiefly in ***pelting chafe***. *Obs.* exc. *dial.*

1570 FOXE *A. & M.* (ed. 2) 1645/1 *margin*, [Bp.] Boner in a pelting chafe. **1584** LYLY *Campaspe* v. iii, Good drinke makes good bloud, and shall pelting words spill it? **1624** HEYWOOD *Gunaik.* 309 This young man..being (as our English phrase sayth) in a pelting chafe. **1684** BUNYAN *Pilgr.* II. 66 When they were come to the Arbour they were very willing to sit down, for they were all in a pelting heat.

†**ˈpeltish**, *a. Obs. rare*[−1]. [f. PELT *sb.*[2] 2 + -ISH[1].] Irritable; angry, enraged.

1648 HERRICK *Oberon's Palace* 17 And flings Among the elves, if mov'd, the stings Of peltish wasps.

ˈpeltless, *a. rare.* [f. PELT *sb.*[1] + -LESS.] Without having a pelt or fur.

1897 *Outing* (U.S.) May 122 Every man in the hunt cannot kill a fox, and yet there will not be one to grumble because he returns peltless at night after a hard day's run.

‖**peltogaster** (pɛltəʊˈgæstə(r)). *Zool.* [mod.L., f. Gr. πέλτη shield (see PELTA) + γαστήρ stomach.] A genus of degenerate cirripeds, having simple bag-shaped bodies, parasitic upon hermit-crabs.

1876 *Beneden's Anim. Parasites* 38 The result of a retrogressive development like that of the peltogasters, which..lose all the attributes of their class.

ˈpeltoid, *a. rare.* [mod. f. Gr. πέλτη shield (see prec.) + -OID.] Shield-like.

1857 MAYNE *Expos. Lex.*, *Peltoīdēs*,..resembling a shield: peltoid. **1893** *Syd. Soc. Lex.*, *Peltoid*,..shield-like.

Pelton (ˈpɛltən). Also **pelton**. The name of L. A. *Pelton* (1829–1908), U.S. engineer, used *attrib.* to designate an undershot water-wheel he invented that has divided buckets fixed to the rim, which deflect a jet of water directed at them.

1885 *Engineering* 30 Oct. 433 The Pelton wheel is said to have used 162·98 cubic feet of water a minute, and to have given 107·49 horse-power, showing an efficiency of 90·2 per cent. **1916** J. PARK *Text.-bk. Pract. Hydraulics* xiv. 242 A Pelton water-wheel 3 feet in diameter, formed of a solid steel disc with phosphor-bronze buckets riveted to the rim, is working in California under a head of 2100 feet. **1962** *Times* 21 May (Commonwealth Chambers of Commerce Suppl.) p. xii/5 (Advt.), Cast steel runners and pelton wheels for hydro-electric plants. **1972** J. M. K. DAKE *Essent. Engin. Hydraulics* vi. 163 It is possible to have more than one jet operating on a Pelton wheel and two jets are quite common.

peltry (ˈpɛltrɪ), *sb.*[1] Also 5–6 **peltre**, 5 **-ie**, **pelliteri**. [In ME. a. AF. *pelterie* (Gower) = OF. *peleterie* (13th c. in Littré), mod.F. *pelleterie* (in prose pronounced pɛltri), deriv. of *peletier*, *pelletier*, furrier, PELTIER, deriv. of OF. *pel*, L. *pell-em* skin. So It. *pellettaría* 'the skinners or furriers trade' (Florio), f. It. *pelle* skin. In mod. use app. a new adoption, ? from the French in North America.

Not exemplified from *c* 1525 to 1700; and then first in reference to the North American fur trade. Not in Bailey, Johnson, Ash. In Todd, with quot. 1771.]

1. Undressed skins, esp. of animals valuable for their furs; fur-skins, pelts collectively.

1436 [see *peltry-ware* in 3]. *a* **1451** FORTESCUE *Wks.* (1869) 553 They brynge..all maner of..Peltry. **1474** CAXTON *Chesse* III. iii, Perchymyn velume peltrie and cordewan. **1701** *Col. Rec. Pennsylv.* II. 16 That the said Indians shall not sell or dispose of any of their Skins, Peltry or furr. **1771** SMOLLETT *Humph. Cl.* 26 Oct., A little traffic he drove in peltry during his sachemship among the Miamis. **1796** MORSE *Amer. Geog.* II. 25 Norway exports great variety of peltry, consisting of skins of bears, lynxes, wolves, ermine, grey squirrels, and several sorts of foxes. **1861** WILDE *Catal. Antiq. in R. Irish Acad.* 278 The peltry of hares, rabbits, dogs, and other small animals, being highly decorative as well as useful. **1880** LD. DUNRAVEN in *19th Cent.* Apr. 651 Formerly the Hudson's Bay Company transported all the peltry—that is, furs and skins—collected over a vast area, to Lake Winnipeg.

b. *pl.* Kinds or varieties of peltry.

1809 W. IRVING *Knickerb.* vii, Giving them gin, rum, and glass beads, in exchange for their peltries. **1838** *Penny Cycl.* XI. 23/1 Canoes..loaded with packs of beaver-skins and other valuable peltries. **1884** S. E. DAWSON *Handbk. Dom. Canada* 154 The fleets of canoes went out [from Montreal] with supplies or returned with peltries.

†**2.** A place or room for keeping fur-skins or pelts. *Obs. rare.*

1483 *Cath. Angl.* 274/1 A Peltry (*A.* A Pelliteri) or a skynnery, *pelliparium*. [**1861** *Our Eng. Home* 95 In the baronial mansion..there was also..the peltry for his furs.]

3. *attrib.* and *Comb.*, as ***peltry-man***, ***manufacture***, ***trade***, ***traffic***; †**peltry-ware** = sense 1.

1436 *Libel Eng. Policy* in *Pol. Poems* (Rolls) II. 171 Osmonde, coppre, bow-staffes, stile, and wex, Peltre-ware, and grey, pych, terre, borde, and flex. **1525** LD. BERNERS *Froiss.* II. clxx. 480 Laden with clothe of Brusselles, or peltre ware, comynge fro the fayres. **1746** W. HORSLEY *Fool* (1748) I. 129 The Peltry or Fur Trade. **1783** JUSTAMOND tr. *Raynal's Hist. Indies* VII. 8 The peltry trade was a very inconsiderable object. **1854** R. G. LATHAM *Native Races Russian Emp.* 51 They preserved..their original character of huntsmen, fishers,..and peltry-men.

†**ˈpeltry**, *sb.*[2] Chiefly *Sc. Obs.* Also 6–7 **-ie**, 6 **-ye**, **-ei**. [app. another form of PALTRY *sb.*, of about the same age, agreeing in the vowel with PELT *sb.*[3], and with PELTING *a.*] Refuse, rubbish, trash; a piece of rubbish.

1550 CROWLEY *Epigr.* 1366 Forsakinge the Pope wyth al his peltrye. **1553** BALE *Vocacyon* Pref. 6 b, Hys vayne beleue of purgatorye, and of other Popysh peltryes. **1566** in Peacock *Eng. Ch. Furniture* (1866) 48 A corporax a crwet wth diuerse other popishe peltrie. *a* **1567** *Gude & Godlie B., With Huntis up* xiii, At the last, he salbe downe cast, His peltrie, Pardonis, and all. **1619** A. DUNCAN *Admon.* in Row *Hist. Kirk* (Wodrow Soc.) 322 Better be pyned to death by hunger, nor for a little peltrie of the earth to perish for ever. **1755** FORBES *Jrnl. Portsmouth* in *Ajax*, etc. 29 You ne'er saw sik peltry i' your born days. **1808** JAMIESON, *Peltrie, peltry, paltrie*,.. vile trash; a term of contempt applied to any thing that is worthless or troublesome.

†**peltry**, *a. Obs.* By-form of PALTRY *a.*
c **1587** MONTGOMERIE *Sonn.* xxiv, A peltrie pultron poysond vp with pryde.

‖**pelu** ('pɛluː). [Native name.] A small leguminous tree (*Sophora tetraptera*), having very hard wood, growing in Southern Chili and Patagonia.
1884 MILLER *Plant-n.*, Pelu-tree, *Sophora tetraptera.*

‖**peludo** (pe'ludo). [Sp., sb. use of *peludo* hairy, f. *pelo*:—L. *pilus* hair.] The hairy armadillo (*Dasypus villosus*) of S. America.
1845 DARWIN *Voy. Nat.* v. (1873) 96 Of armadilloes three species occur, namely,.. the Dasypus villosus or peludo.

†**pe'lure**[1], **'pellure.** *Obs.* Forms: 4–5 pellure, pelure, pellour, pelour(e, pelur, (4 peolour, pelore, pellere, 5 peloer, pillour). [a. AF. *pellure* (14th c.), in OF. *peleure, pelure*, f. *pel*, in mod.F. *peau*:—L. *pell-em* skin, fur: see -URE.] Fur, esp. as used for the lining or trimming of a garment; furred garments collectively, furs.
c **1325** in *Rel. Ant.* II. 19 Hir wede, Purfiled with pellour doun to the teon. *c* **1330** R. BRUNNE *Chron. Wace* (Rolls) 11195 Oþer pelure ynowe þer were.. Lomb or boge, conyng or hare. ? **1370** *Robt. Cicyle* 267 Ther was never 3yt pellere half so fyne. *c* **1400** *Beryn* 3928 A mantell.. I-furrid with peloure. **1475** *Bk. Noblesse* (Roxb.) 80 The usaige of pellure and furres they have expresselie put away.
Hence †**pelured** *a. Obs.*, adorned with fur, furred; †**pelury** *Obs.* = *pelure.*
c **1400** *St. Alexius* (Laud 622) 398 Ciclatounes þat weren of prijs, Pelured wiþ Ermyne and wiþ grijs, Alle she cast away. **1460** *Lybeaus Disc.* 875 Her mantyll was rosyne, Pelvred wyth ermyne. *c* **1460** *Launfal* 237 Har manteles wer of grene felwet,.. I-pelvred with grys and gro. *c* **1470** HARDING *Chron.* LXXIV. xiii, All in graye of pelury preordinate, That was full riche, accordyng to their estate.

‖**pelure**[2] (pəlyr). [F. *pelure*, OF. *peleüre*, f. *peler* to peel, lit. peeling.] **1.** Paper as thin as an onion peeling. Usually ***pelure-paper.***
1887 *Postage Stamps of Australia & Oceania* 78 New Zealand.. Issue III. Upon very thin greyish paper (the pelure of catalogues). *Ibid.*, Issue IV. The paper.. is sometimes as thin as the so-called pelure-paper of Issue III. **1891** 'PHIL' *Penny Postage Jubilee* xiii. 204–5 Then we have ribbed, quadrillé, pelure, bâtonné, etc., papers... Pelure is somewhat of a thin hard and crisp texture.
2. ***pelure d'oignon*** (dɔɲɔ̃) [lit. 'onion-skin'], a tawny colour in wines; a wine of this colour; *spec.* the name of a wine produced in the Jura region of France; also *attrib.*
1935 SCHOONMAKER & MARVEL *Compl. Wine Bk.* i. 46 The red and *pelure d'oignon* wines of Arbois were among the many life-long favourites of that.. lover of charming ladies and good wines—Henri IV. *Ibid.* viii. 188 A good red wine is red, a deep crimson when young,.. a rather more delicate red when old, with that faint but unmistakable brownish tinge which the French call '*pelure d'oignon*'. **1951** H. W. ALLEN *Natural Red Wines* vii. 263 The depth and brightness of its divine reds, purples and browns, the perfect example of the *pelure d'oignon* hue. **1952** A. LICHINE *Wines of France* xiii. 175 When old, the red Hermitages are enormously rich in aroma and after-taste... Instead of having the complete red spectrum, the wines have a brownish tinge, which the French call *pelure d'oignon*, or onion skin. **1962** *Harper's Bazaar* Oct. 159/2 You will also find some unexpected Rhône wines.. and Pelure d'Oignon (onion skin colour). **1965** A. SICHEL *Penguin Bk. Wines* III. 160 The best red wine of the Jura.. is light in colour and is often referred to as '*pelure d'oignon*'—onion skin. **1965** O. A. MENDELSOHN *Dict. Drink* 255 *Pelure d'oignon*,.. used to denote the characteristic shiny brown hue that aged red wines may acquire. **1967** P. PURSER *Twentymen* xxvii. 187 The day's third bottle of Pelure d'Oignon, beaded with condensation from the refrigerator. **1971** *Guardian* 12 Nov. 9/3 The Montrichard.. is a pale pink—nearer the rosy yellow of pelure d'oignon than red. **1976** 'J. FRASER' *Who steals my Name?* xvi. 188 Aveyard examined his crystal glass appreciatively, then replenished it with the delicious Pelure d'Oignon Rosé wine.

pelurious (pɪ'l(j)uːrɪəs), *a. rare*⁻¹. [f. PELURE[1] + -IOUS.] Furred, hairy.
1922 JOYCE *Ulysses* 289 Sieves of gooseberries, pulpy and pelurious.

pelvi-, combining form (not in ancient L.) from L. *pelvis* basin, PELVIS, in scientific terms. **pel'viferous** *a.* [-FEROUS], bearing or having a pelvis. **'pelviform** *a.* [-FORM], basin-shaped. **pel'vimeter** [-METER, F. *pelvimètre*], an instrument for measuring the diameters of the pelvis; so **pel'vimetry**, measurement of the diameters of the pelvis. **pelvimyon** (-'maɪɒn), pl. *-ons* or *-a* [see MYON], a 'myon' or muscular unit of the pelvis (distinguished from *pectorimyon*). **pelvi'otomy** [irreg. after words from Gr.: see -TOMY], the operation of section of the pelvic bones, usually through the *symphysis pubis* (*symphysiotomy*), esp. in obstetric practice. **pelvi'rectal** *a.*, belonging to the pelvis and rectum. **pelvi'sacral** *a.*, belonging to the pelvis and sacrum. **pel'viscopy** [-SCOPY], examination of the pelvis (in quot., of the kidney). ‖**pelvi'sternum** *Comp. Anat.*, an element of the pelvic arch supposed to be homologous to the *omosternum* of the pectoral arch; hence **pelvi'sternal** *a.*, of the nature of or pertaining to a pelvisternum.
1839–47 TODD *Cycl. Anat.* III. 906/1 The whole chain of *pelviferous vertebrata. **1857** MAYNE *Expos. Lex.* 898/2 *Pelviform. **1866** *Treas. Bot.* 859 *Pelviform*, like Cyathiform, but flatter. **1823** CRABB *Technol. Dict.*, **Pelvimeter.* **1828–32** WEBSTER, *Pelvimeter*, an instrument to measure the dimensions of the female pelvis. *Coxe.* **1863** *N. Syd. Soc. Year-bk. Med. & Surg.* 337 The practice of internal *pelvimetry. **1888** COUES in *Auk* Jan. 105 These are, namely, five pectorimyons, five *pelvimyons... The five pelvimya discussed are the ambiens, and those other four [etc.]. **1857** MAYNE *Expos. Lex.*, **Pelviotomy.* **1880** ALLBUTT & PLAYFAIR *Syst. Gynæcology* 634. **1887** *Brit. Med. Jrnl.* 28 May 1163/2 Originating in the *pelvi-rectal space. **1900** *Ibid.* 3 Feb. 248 Renal *pelviscopy.

pelvic ('pɛlvɪk), *a.* [irreg. f. L. *pelvis* + -IC: cf. the better-formed F. *pelvien.*]
1. a. Of, pertaining to, contained in, or connected with the pelvis (PELVIS 1).
pelvic arch, pelvic girdle: the girdle formed by the bones of the pelvis, the hip-girdle. ***pelvic limbs***: the limbs supported by the pelvic arch; as the legs of a man, the hind legs of a quadruped, the ventral fins of a fish.
1830 R. KNOX *Béclard's Anat.* 44 The trunk.. presents two extremities, the one superior or cephalic, the other inferior or pelvic. **1857** H. MILLER *Test. Rocks* ii. 83 Without thoracic or pelvic arches. **1872** NICHOLSON *Palæont.* 303 The hind-limbs are.. connected with the trunk by means of the 'pelvic arch'.
b. ***pelvic thrust***: the repeated thrusting movement of the pelvis during sexual intercourse.
1953 A. C. KINSEY et al. *Sexual Behav. Human Female* xv. 618 The.. rhythmic pelvic thrusts during sexual activity are among the distinctive characteristics of the class Mammalia. **1966** MASTERS & JOHNSON *Human Sexual Response* xviii. 297 Male pelvic thrust and female pelvic accommodation initially are voluntary muscular attempts at sex tension increment. **1969** W. B. POMEROY *Girls & Sex* vii. 105 Intercourse continues with a series of pelvic thrusts. **1969** D. R. REUBEN *Everything you always wanted to know about Sex* (1970) vi. 90 A reasonable yardstick for male potency is the ability to continue intercourse for five to ten minutes. During that time a normally potent male will deliver from fifty to one hundred pelvic thrusts.
2. Of or pertaining to the pelvis of a crinoid.
1849 MURCHISON *Siluria* x. 223 In most Encrinites the arms issue immediately from the edge of the pelvic cup.

pelviferous to **pelvisternum**: see PELVI-.

†**pelvigraph** ('pɛlvɪgrɑːf, -æ-). *Obs.* [f. PELVI(S + -GRAPH.] An instrument for recording measurements of the pelvis. So †**pel'vigraphy**, the use of the pelvigraph.
1890 BILLINGS *Med. Dict.* II. 306/1 *Pelvigraphy*, obtaining a contour of the wall of the pelvis. **1892** F. P. FOSTER *Med. Dict.* IV. 2540/1 *Pelvigraph*, a device adopted by Pinard for recording automatically the measurements of dried pelves. **1903** J. C. EDGAR *Pract. Obstetr.* II. 184 The principle involved in the construction and application of the pelvigraph is that of the parellel rulers, one number representing a palpator for the localization of points within the pelvis, while the other is provided with a water-level and a dial index. **1904** *Lancet* 18 June 1728/1 A description is given of pelvigraphy or the method of taking a series of measurements of certain pelvic diameters and thus plotting out the size of the various pelvic planes. **1913** *Jrnl. Obstetr. & Gynæcol.* XXIV. 257 Martin's pelvigraph, introduced in 1827, was.. intended for use in the dry pelvis.

‖**pelvis** ('pɛlvɪs). *Anat.* and *Zool.* Pl. pelves ('pɛlviːz). [L. *pelvis* basin, laver; the anatomical sense is mod.L.]
1. The basin-shaped cavity formed (in most vertebrates) by the right and left haunch-bones or *ossa innominata* (consisting of the *ilium*, *ischium*, and *pubis*, on each side) together with the *sacrum* and other vertebræ; being the lowest or hindmost cavity of the trunk. Also applied to these bones themselves collectively, constituting the girdle which supports the hind limbs.
true pelvis, that part of the (human) pelvis below the ilio-pectineal line; ***false pelvis***, the space above this between the iliac fossæ.
1615 CROOKE *Body of Man* 118 These bones together with the holy-bone, make that *pelvis* or Dish which containeth part of the guts, the bladder and the womb. **1682** T. GIBSON *Anat.* (1685) VI. xvi. **1754–64** SMELLIE *Midwif.* I. 81 The brim of the Pelvis is wider from side to side than from the back to the fore-part. **1850** LYELL *2nd Visit U.S.* II. 196 Part of a human pelvis. **1865** *Reader* 28 Jan. 107/1 A good collection of pelves of individuals of both sexes.
2. The basin-like cavity of the kidney, into which the uriniferous tubules open.
1678 TYSON in *Phil. Trans.* XII. 1035 Anatomical Observations..; an unusual Conformation of the Emulgents and Pelvis. *Ibid.* 1038. **1682** T. GIBSON *Anat.* (1697) 127 Within the Kidney there is a membranous Cell or Sinus, called Pelvis, which is nothing but an extension or dilatation of the head of the Ureter. **1693** tr. *Blancard's Phys. Dict.* (ed. 2) s.v. *Choana*, The Pelvis of the Reins. **1857** G. BIRD *Urin. Deposits* (ed. 5) 316 A concretion in the pelvis of a kidney.
3. The basal part of the calyx of a crinoid.
1849 MURCHISON *Siluria* x. 223 In this remarkable Encrinite the upper edge of the pelvis is seen to be surmounted by at least twenty or twenty-five arm-joints. **1872** NICHOLSON *Palæont.* 125 A series of plates.. termed 'basal' from their position, and which constitute the 'pelvis' of Miller.
4. A basin. *rare.*
1727 DART *Canterb. Cathedr.* 13 Archbishop Islip.. left them.. four silver Pelves with four Lavatories of the same.

pelyco- (pɛlɪkəʊ), combining form of Gr. πέλυξ, πέλυκ- bowl, cup, taken as = PELVIS 1, in a few rare scientific words. **pelycography** (-'ɒgrəfɪ) [-GRAPHY], description of the pelvis. **pely'cology** [-LOGY], the anatomy of the pelvis. **pely'cometer** [-METER] = PELVIMETER.
1875 KNIGHT *Dict. Mech.*, *Pelycometer*, a Pelvimeter. **1893** *Syd. Soc. Lex.*, *Pelycography.. Pelycology.. Pelycometer.*

pelycon, obs. form of PELISSON.

pelycosaur ('pɛlɪkəʊsɔː(r)). Also **pelycosaurian.** [f. mod.L. name of order *Pelycosauria* (E. D. Cope 1878, in *Proc. Amer. Philos. Soc.* XVII. 511), f. Gk. πέλυξ, πέλυκ- bowl, cup + σαῦρος lizard.] A fossil reptile of the order Pelycosauria, known from Permian remains, and sometimes distinguished by bony spines developed from some of the vertebrae. Also *attrib.* or as *adj.*
1880 *Athenæum* 6 Nov. 612/1 Mr. Cope's group of Pelycosaurians in North America. **1930** H. H. SWINNERTON *Outl. Palæont.* (ed. 2) xii. 334 *Dimetrodon* was a typical Pelycosaurian. **1933** A. S. ROMER *Vertebr. Paleont.* xi. 222 The neural arches of pelycosaurs were (as in most reptiles) narrower than those of the cotylosaurs. *Ibid.*, The pelycosaur palate was constructed on a primitive pattern. **1954** W. E. SWINTON *Fossil Amphibians & Reptiles* vi. 29 A group of very important reptiles, the Therapsida, are descended from the *Dimetrodon*-like Pelycosaurs. **1968** A. S. ROMER *Procession of Life* xiv. 235 The central types among the therapsids were carnivores, continuing the flesh-eating tradition of the main pelycosaur stock. **1973** *Nature* 16 Mar. 203/2 *Dimetrodon grandis* was the end form of an evolutionary series of pelycosaurs that had tended to develop increasingly large sails. **1977** A. HALLAM *Planet Earth* 212 A bizarre characteristic of a number of the pelycosaurs was the development of a huge sail-like structure adorning the back.

pelyon, pelyr, obs. forms of PILLION, PILLAR.

pelytory, obs. form of PELLITORY.

†**'pemblico.** *Amer. Obs.* Also 7 **pembly-, pemli-, pimpli-, pimlico.** A name given to the dusky shear-water or cohoo (*Puffinus obscurus*), from its cry.
1624 CAPT. SMITH *Virginia* v. 171 Another small Bird there is, because she cries Pemblyco they call her so; she is seldome seene in the day but when she sings..; too true a Prophet she proves of huge winds and boysterous weather. *c* **1630** *Hist. Bermudaes* (Sloane MS. 750, lf. 4b: cf. Hakl. Soc. 1882, 4), Another smale Birde ther is, the which, by some Ale-banters of London sent ouer hether, hath bin tearmed pimplicoe, for so they Imagine (and a little resemblance putts them in mind of a place so dearely beloued) her note articulates. **1686** GOAD *Celest. Bodies* I. ii. 3 The Crow, Cock,.. Peacock, the Pimlico.

'Pembroke. Name of a town and shire in Wales and of an earldom in the British Peerage. Hence **Pembroke table**, or *ellipt. Pembroke*, a table supported on four fixed legs, having two hinged side portions or flaps, which can be spread out horizontally, and supported on legs connected with the central part by joints.
1778 *Seducers* 5 A pembroke table should this corner grace. **1790** MME. D'ARBLAY *Diary* Jan., Dr. Fisher says he hopes it was not a card-table, and rather believes it was only a pembroke work-table. **1792** *Elizabeth Percy* I. 58 These inlaid Pembrokes of wonderful workmanship. **1853** [see *conversation card*]. **1870** MRS. WHITNEY *We Girls* vi. 105 The little pembroke was wheeled out again. **1925** *Scribner's Mag.* July 94/1 A Pembroke table with unusual stretchers was in the wood-shed. **1973** [see HAREWOOD]. **1975** J. SYMONS *Three Pipe Problem* xviii. 181 She sold.. a damaged Pembroke table skilfully repaired by Fritz to a woman who was actually looking for a brass fender.

pemmican ('pɛmɪkən), *sb.* Also **pemican.** [a. Cree *pimecan*, *pimekan*, f. *pime* fat.] A preparation made by certain North American Indians, consisting of lean meat, dried, pounded, and mixed with melted fat, so as to form a paste, and pressed into cakes; hence, beef similarly treated, and usually flavoured with currants or the like, for the use of arctic explorers, travellers, and soldiers, as containing much nutriment in little bulk, and keeping for a long time.
1801 SIR A. MACKENZIE *Voy. St. Lawrence* Pref. 121 The provision called Pemican, on which the Chepewyans and other savages in the N. of America chiefly subsist in their journeys. **1827** *Chron.* in *Ann. Reg.* 58/1 Pannican, a concentrated essence of meat dryed by a fire of oak and elm wood, so as to reduce 6 lb. of the best beef to 1 lb. **1855** LONGF. *Hiaw.* xi. 31 Then on pemican they feasted, Pemican and buffalo marrow. **1869** E. A. PARKES *Pract.*

Hygiene (ed. 3) 245 The Pemmican of the arctic voyagers is a mixture of the best beef and fat dried together.

b. *fig.* Extremely condensed thought, or literary matter containing much information in few words.

1870 HUXLEY *Lay Serm.* xii. (1874) 257 A sort of intellectual pemmican. **1888** *Spectator* 8 Sept. 1211/2 It [Sir F. Bramwell's Address] is really a wonderful specimen of thought and knowledge, reduced to pemmican.

c. *attrib.*

1831 *Westm. Rev.* XIV. 441 Who will..give us a chance..of..getting rid of the soup and pemmican diet we have so long been doomed to. **1895** *Daily News* 16 Oct. 5/7 Their big pemmican cache, 124 miles distant. **1900** *Athenæum* 8 Dec. 749/2 A certain tendency to what may be described as the pemmican style.

Hence **'pemmican** *v. trans.*, to condense, compress, 'squeeze'. So **'pemmicanize** *v.*; whence **pemmicani'zation**.

1837 T. HOOK *Jack Brag* vi, As if he had seen all the dæmons of the Hartz Forest pemmican'd into one plump lady. **1839** —— in *New Monthly Mag.* LV. 1 So elaborated a history,..which..might be Pemmicaned into a comparatively few pages. **1892** *Pall Mall G.* 1 Sept. 3/2 The modern man is but rarely inclined to read his history in many volumes. He much prefers it pemmicanized. **1901** *Westm. Gaz.* 16 Dec. 4/2 What one may call the era of the Pemmicanisation of life is rapidly approaching.

pemoline ('pɛməʊliːn). *Pharm.* [Perh. f. P(H)E(NYL + I)M(INO(-) + OXAZ)OL(ID)INE, elements in its chemical name.] 2-Imino-4-oxo-5-phenyloxazolidine, $C_9H_8N_2O_2$, a white, crystalline, tasteless powder that is a stimulant of the central nervous system.

1961 *MIMS Monthly Index* Jan. 44 Kethamed Medo-Chemicals Pemoline: 20 MG. tablets. Fatigue, convalescence, etc. **1968** *Sunday Times* 27 Oct. 3 Pemoline has been known sometime to be a mild brain stimulant, midway between Amphetamine and coffee. **1973** *Lancet* 10 Nov. 1091/1 Six amphetamine users who have been taking large doses of pemoline..have become aggressive, excited and disorganised.

pemphigoid ('pɛmfɪgɔɪd), *a.* [f. PEMPHIG-US + -OID; cf. Gr. πεμφιγώδης (Hippoc.).] Resembling or of the nature of pemphigus.

1822–34 *Good's Study Med.* (ed. 4) II. 384 Hippocrates..as well as Galen, speaks of pemphigoid fever..as pestilential and malignant. **1899** *Allbutt's Syst. Med.* VIII. 671 Pemphigoid eruptions.

pemphigous ('pɛmfɪgəs), *a.* [f. next + -OUS.] Of the nature of, or affected with pemphigus.

1857 MAYNE *Expos. Lex.* 899/1 Pemphigous. **1864** W. T. Fox *Skin Dis.* 31 Pustular, and pemphigous dermatoses.

‖**pemphigus** ('pɛmfɪgəs). *Path.* [mod.L. (M. de Sauvages, 1763), f. Gr. πέμφιξ, πεμφῑγ-bubble.] An affection of the skin characterized by the formation of watery vesicles or eruptions (*bullæ*) on various parts of the body. Also in *Comb.*

1779 D. STEWART in *Duncan's Med. Commentaries* VI. 84. **1787** S. DICKSON in *Trans. R. Irish Acad.* I. 47 Observations on Pemphigus. **1800** *Med. Jrnl.* III. 265 Transparent vesicles of the size of a pea, similar to those which rise in *pemphigus.* **1897** *Allbutt's Syst. Med.* II. 206 A bulla like a pemphigus blister. **1898** P. MANSON *Trop. Diseases* xxxvii. 566 Large pemphigus-like blebs.

pemphis ('pɛmfɪs). [mod.L. (J. R. & J. G. A. Forster *Characteres Generum Plantarum* (1776) 67), f. Gr. πεμφίς cloud.] A small tree of the genus so called, esp. *Pemphis acidula*, belonging to the family Lythraceæ, and found in coastal, tropical areas of Africa and Southern Asia.

1911 *Trans. Linn. Soc. (Zool.)* XIV. 403 Throughout the northern section [of Aldabra] the *Pemphis* jungle continues. *Ibid.* 404 Near the sea the trees were all much stunted by the prevalent winds, even the hardy *Pemphis* trees being dwarfed into a low thick scrub. **1919** *Nature* 9 Oct. 118/2 The vegetation [of Aldabra] consists of four types:—(1) Mangrove swamp... (2) Pemphis bush, a dense growth of the hard-wooded *Pemphis acidula* (Lythraceae), a widely distributed sea-coast plant. **1958** *Times* 4 Nov. 12/6 The island [*sc.* Aldabra] rises only some 15 ft. above the sea and is for the most part clothed with a terrible tangle of pemphis bush. **1971** *Phil. Trans. R. Soc.* B. CCLX. 359 Isolated *Scaevola* and *Pemphis* trees have browse lines. *Ibid.* 476 One of them [*sc.* a Malagasy bulbul] was in a *Pemphis* bush.

‖**pemphix** ('pɛmfɪks). *Path.* = PEMPHIGUS.

1842 DUNGLISON *Med. Lex.*, *Pemphix*, Pemphigus. **1896** *Allbutt's Syst. Med.* I. 743 The faucial affections of small-pox, chicken-pox and pemphix.

pempidine ('pɛmpɪdiːn). *Pharm.* [f. PE(NTA- + M(ETHYL + PI(PERI)DINE.] An alkaline liquid, $C_{10}H_{21}N$, which has been used (usu. in the form of its hydrogen tartrate, a white, crystalline powder), as a ganglion-blocking agent in the treatment of severe hypertension; 1,2,2,6,6-pentamethylpiperidine.

1958 *Nature* 21 June 1717/2 In the simple..tertiary amine, 1:2:2:6:6-pentamethylpiperidine.., for which the common name pempidine has been suggested, we have a potent ganglion-blocking drug. **1960** *Lancet* 21 Jan. 143/2 In 1958 a new ganglion-blocking agent, pempidine tartrate, was made available under the trade names of 'Perolysen' and 'Tenormal'. **1961** *Ibid.* 12 Aug. 334/2 A Jamaican..was admitted to hospital and stabilised on pempidine and chlorothiazide. **1974** *Prescribers Jrnl.* XIV. 47 Ganglion blocking drugs, such as pentolinium..and pempidine.., have been omitted from this short review because in the drug treatment of hypertension they have now been largely superseded.

pemptarchie, obs. erron. f. PENTARCHY.

pen (pɛn), *sb.*[1] Forms: 1 penn, 4 *pl.* penez, 4–7 penne, 7–9 penn, 7– pen. [OE. *penn* of uncertain origin: cf. PEN *v.*[1]]

1. a. A small enclosure for domestic animals, as cows, sheep, swine, or poultry; a fold, sty, coop, etc.

(The OE. instances are of uncertain meaning.)

[**957** in Birch *Cart. Sax.* No. 1009 III. 212 Of þam penne on hean æsc. **968** *Ibid.* No. 1217. 498 And lang þæra heafda on etta penn.] **13..** *E.E. Allit. P.* B. 322 Boþe boskez & bourez & wel bounden penez. **1523** FITZHERB. *Husb.* §38 Bynde her heed with a heye rope, or a corde, to the syde of the penne. **1570** LEVINS *Manip.* 60/33 A Penne, or coup, *caula.* **1598** SHAKS. *Merry W.* III. iv. 41 Tel..how my Father stole two Geese out of a Pen. **1697** DAMPIER *Voy.* I. 369 Making of a large pen to drive the Cattle into. **1726–46** THOMSON *Winter* 266 Now, shepherds..fill their pens With food at will. **1833** HT. MARTINEAU *Loom & Lugger* I. vi. 93 They will wake up all the sheep in the pens for a mile round. **1903** *Westm. Gaz.* 2 Oct. 2/1 On some French estates the partridges are confined in large pens.

b. *transf.* A number of animals in a pen, or sufficient to fill a pen.

1873 C. ROBINSON *N.S. Wales* 31 Pens of oxen, fattened on the natural grasses. **1888** 'R. BOLDREWOOD' *Robbery under Arms* xii, Father opened his eyes at the price the first pen brought. **1904** *Daily News* 2 July 6 Her fowls were a pen of pure Minorcas and a pen of Plymouth Rocks.

c. *spec.* A division in a sheep-shearing shed. Also, the work associated with a sheep-shearing pen. *Austral.* and *N.Z.*

1891 R. WALLACE *Rural Econ. Austral. & N.Z.* xxix. 381 On the outside of the smaller pens, and near to the outer side-walls the shearers are placed. **1900** H. LAWSON *Verses, Pop. & Humorous* 168 The shearers squint along the pens, they squint along the 'shoots'. **1905** —— *When I was King* 38 The shed was cooled by electric fans that was over every shoot; The pens was of polished ma-ho-gany. **1933** L. G. D. ACLAND in *Press* (Christchurch, N.Z.) 11 Nov. 15/7 *Pen.* (1) A small yard; a division in the sheep-holding part of a wool-shed. (2) Shearers catch out of a p[en], and when they apply for work they ask for a p[en]. 'Will you keep me a p[en] for next year, boss?' is often their farewell. **1945** BAKER *Austral. Lang.* iii. 65 A shearer gets a *cut* (it is also called a *stand* or *pen*) when he is employed. **1965** *Austral. Encycl.* VIII. 86/2 Shearing became the work of a nomadic band of men who travelled..from shearing shed to shearing shed... The fortunate ones 'got their pen' at the commencement of a shearing whilst the others moved on in the hope of getting work at some other station. **1966** G. W. TURNER *Eng. Lang. Austral. & N.Z.* iii. 48 An Australian instance of this [*sc.* metonymy] is the shearer's request for a *pen*, i.e. work, some sheep to shear.

2. a. Applied to various enclosures resembling these: see quotations.

c **1620** FLETCHER & MASSINGER *Double Marriage* v. i, He's taken to the tower's strength... We have him in a pen, he cannot 'scape us. **1769** FALCONER *Dict. Marine* (1789), *Bouchots*, crawls, pens, or places inclosed by hurdles, for fishing on the sea-coast. **1829** HALIBURTON *Nova-Scotia* II. ix. 392 In winter they [the moose-deer]..describe a circle, and press the snow with their feet, until it becomes hard, which is called by hunters a yard, or pen. **1873** G. C. DAVIES *Mount. & Mere* v. 38 Put them into the penns made within the bow of a net. **18..** T. C. CRAWFORD *Eng. Life* 57 (Cent.) The place [in the House of Lords] where visitors were allowed to go was a little pen at the left of the entrance. **1888** E. EGGLESTON *The Graysons* xxx. 326 Building some rail pens to hold the corn when it should be gathered, and shucked. **1890** *Cent. Dict.*, *Pen*[1], *n.*..3. In the fisheries, a movable receptacle on board ship where fish are put to be iced, etc.

b. *spec.* in the West Indies: A farm, plantation, country house, or park. (Often spelt *penn.*)

1740 [implied in *pen-keeper*: see 4]. **1792** *Gentl. Mag.* LXII. 515 A pen in Jamaica is a farm or plantation. **1796** MORSE *Amer. Geog.* I. 763 (Jamaica), 400 breeding farms or pens, of 700 acres each. **1844** MRS. HOUSTON *Yacht Voy. Texas* I. 92 The pens, or villas of the rich inhabitants, who go there occasionally to enjoy health or coolness. **1885** LADY BRASSEY *The Trades* 222 The garden..is surrounded by a park, or 'pen', as it is called here.

c. A prison; a cell in a prison. orig. *U.S.* (cf. BULL-PEN 1 a).

Often indistinguishable from PEN *sb.*[5]

1845 W. G. SIMMS *Wigwam & Cabin* (1846) 2nd Ser. 93 Laughter..ceased on my part, as I got in sight of the 'pen' in which I was to be kept secure. **1853** F. W. THOMAS *John Randolph* 286 If I had not caught him in Baltimore..and put him in the pen there for debt, I never should have got the money. **1867** W. L. GOSS *Soldier's Story* 144 Every batch of prisoners sent into the 'pen' were accompanied by a spy in U.S. blue. **1904** *N.Y. Even. Jrnl.* 10 May 2 A panic was caused among the prisoners in the pen of the Ewen Street Police Court jail. **1948** PARTRIDGE *Dict. Forces' Slang* 139 *Pen*, a prisoner-of-war cage. (Mostly Army.)

d. A covered dock forming a berth for a naval vessel, esp. for a submarine.

1917 W. S. CHURCHILL *Second World War* (1949) II. I. xii. 216 A..harbour..with regular pens for the destroyers and submarines. **1932** A. R. BRADSHAW *Eng.-French Naval Terms* v. 76 *Destroyer pens*, les appontements. **1942** *R.A.F. Jrnl.* 16 May 19 (*caption*) These..photographs illustrate the constructional development of a possible new Naval Base and set of Submarine Pens. **1944** *Hutchinson's Pict. Hist. War* 12 Apr.–26 Sept. 229 Aircraft of Bomber Command launched a heavy attack on the 8-ft. thick E-boat pens at Le Havre. **1946** *War Report* (B.B.C.) 111 When the famous submarine pens of Cherbourg were inspected they revealed a twenty-foot thickness of reinforced concrete, designed to be absolutely impregnable to air bombardment. **1959** *Economist* 30 May 816/1 Russia does possess a foothold (complete with submarine pens) on the Mediterranean shore. **1961** F. H. BURGESS *Dict. Sailing* 158 *Pen, penns*, the spaces between a series of piers, so built that vessels may berth four to six deep between them. **1974** *Sci. Amer.* Mar. 117/1 The waste and the sorrow glow too hot to be concealed yet, even under the 5.5-meter reinforced-concrete slab over the submarine pens at Doenitz' headquarters port of Brest. **1975** *Ibid.* Oct. 6/1 There are a number of hard military targets other than missile silos, such as buried command posts, nuclear-weapons storage facilities and submarine pens that nuclear weapons may not be effective against unless they are accurate.

3. A contrivance for 'penning' or confining the water in a river or canal, so as to form a head of water; a weir, dam, or the like. ? *Obs.*

1585 *Act 27 Eliz.* c. 19 Such old and former Bayes or Pens whereupon hath lately beene..standing some iron milles. **1607** COWELL *Interpr.* s.v. *Bay, Bay* or *penn*, is a Pond-head made up of a great heighth, to keep in store of Water. **1721** PERRY *Daggenh. Breach* 58 Any Sluice, Dock-Gates, Dam, or Penn of Water. **1805** Z. ALLNUTT *Navig. Thames* 43 The Banks are sufficiently high to admit of Four Feet pen without overflowing Lands. **1840** *Evid. Hull Docks Com.* 140 There is a pen at the mouth of the Hull.

4. *Comb.*: **pen-branded** *a.*, (of an animal) branded with a mark denoting the particular pen to which it belongs; **pen-fed** *a.*, fed in a pen, or in confinement; **pen-head**, the dam or weir at the head of a mill-lead; **pen-keeper** (*W. Indies*), the overseer of a plantation or farm; **pen-mate** *Austral.* and *N.Z. slang*, a shearer who catches sheep out of the same pen (as another shearer); **pen-pond**, a pond formed by a 'pen' or dam; **pen-pot**, a cage or 'pot' for keeping crabs or lobsters in confinement; **pen-wet** (see quot.).

1890 'R. BOLDREWOOD' *Col. Reformer* (1891) 232 Cows, unbranded calves, and *pen-branded bullocks. **13..** *E.E. Allit. P.* B. 57 My polyle þat is *penne-fed & partrykes boþe. **1805** *State, Fraser of Fraserfield*, etc. 229 (Jam.) They take in water from the river Don, at the intake or *penhead of the meal-mill. **1740** *Hist. Jamaica* vii. 237 If any Person..refuse, either by himself, Overseer, or *Penn-keeper, to discover..the true Number of their Slaves, Horses, &c. **1933** L. G. D. ACLAND in *Press* (Christchurch, N.Z.) 11 Nov. 15/7 Two shearers usually catch out of one p[en] and are called *p[en]-mates. **1965** J. S. GUNN *Terminol. Shearing Industry* II. 3 'Pen mates' catch their sheep out of the same pen. **1904** *Daily Chron.* 31 Mar. 6/2 Herons..bringing their young little fishes captured from the *pen-ponds close by. **1750** COLLINSON in *Phil. Trans.* XLVII. 41 That the crab will subsist..in the fishermens *pen-pots, for the space of some months. **1851** STEPHENS *Bk. Farm* (ed. 2) II. 365/1 Rain..would easily find its way, were the sheaves inclined downwards to the centre of the stack... The sheaves that are so spoiled are said to have taken in **pen-wet.*

pen (pɛn), *sb.*[2] Also 4–7 penne, (6 pene), 7 penn, (*Sc.* pend). [ME. a. OF. *penne* (*pene, pan(n)e*), 12th c. in Godef.; = It. *penna* feather, plume, quill, pen:—L. *penna* feather (pl. pinions, wings), in late L. pen for writing (Isidore).

In OF. *penne* had senses 1, 1 b (from Vulgate), and 4 below; in mod.F. it has only those of 'long feather of the wing or tail (*remex* and *rectrix*), large feather of a bird of prey (in Falconry), feather of an arrow, plume on a heraldic crest'. Fr. and Eng. usage have thus gone widely apart, Fr. having substituted *plume*, where Eng. has retained *pen*, while *vice versa* Eng. uses *plume* in Heraldry for Fr. *penne.*]

I. A feather, a quill, and connected senses.

1. a. A feather of a bird, a plume. *Obs.* or *dial.*

1377 LANGL. *P. Pl.* B. XII. 247 Riȝt as þe pennes of þe pecok peyneth hym in his fliȝte. **1393** *Ibid.* C. XV. 180 Ac for hus peyntede pennes þe pocok is honoured. **1398** TREVISA *Barth. De P.R.* XI. iii. (Tollem. MS.), Also þe souþerne wynde..changeþ in foules and briddes olde pennes and feþeris [orig. *pennarum veterum et plumarum*]. *a* **1400–50** *Alexander* 4988 All þe body & þe brest..Was finely florischt & faire with frekild pennys. **1526** *Pilgr. Perf.* (W. de W. 1531) 63 The rauen wyll not gyue her blacke pennes for the pecockes paynted fethers. **1585** JAS. I *Ess. Poesie* (Arb.) 43 In Arabie called Fælix was she bredd This foule..Whose taill of coulour was celestiall blew, With skarlat pennis that through it mixed grew. **1625** B. JONSON *Staple of N.* v. vi, The proud Peacocke, ouer-charg'd with pennes, Is faine to sweepe the ground, with his growne traine, And load of feathers. **1828** *Craven Gloss.* (ed. 2), *Pen*, feather. **1831** *Blackw. Mag.* XXIX. 860 Hector is here chicken-hearted—crowed-down—cool in the pens—*fugy*, as the cockers say.

b. In *pl.* The flight-feathers (*remiges*) or pinions of birds regarded as the organs of flight; hence, like 'pinions', put for 'wings'. Orig. a literalism of translation after L. *pennæ* of the Vulgate: so in OF. *pennes* (Godef.). Now a poetic archaism.

1382 WYCLIF *Ps.* ciii. 3 [Thou] that gost vp on the pennys of windis [1388 on the fetheris of wyndis, Vulg. *super pennas ventorum*]. **1382** —— *Ezek.* i. 5 And four faces to oon, and four pennys to oon [1388 foure wyngis weren to oon, Vulg. *quatuor pennæ uni*]. **1513** DOUGLAS *Æneis* XII. v. 79 The lycht thai [fowlis] dirkin with thar pennys thik. **1611** SIR W. MURE *Misc. Poems* iv. 5 The tragic end of Icarus..Lyk as he did presume, too hie wt borrowed pends [*rime* endis]. **1667** MILTON *P.L.* VII. 421 Featherd soon and fledge They summ'd thir Penns..soaring th' air sublime. **1800** tr. *Haydn's Creation*, On mighty pens uplifted soars the eagle aloft. **1885–94** R. BRIDGES *Eros & Psyche* Sept. xvi, He flasht his pens, and sweeping widely round Tower'd to air.

c. A short rudimentary feather or quill just breaking through the skin of a bird; = PEN-FEATHER 2, PIN-FEATHER. Chiefly *dial.*

1828 *Craven Gloss.* (ed. 2) s.v., This chicken's full o' pens. **1880** MISS JACKSON *Shropsh. Word-bk.*, *Pens, sb. pl.* the rudimentary quills of feathers, as of fowls, ducks, &c. *a* 1900 *Eng. Dial. Dict.*, In W. Yorksh. a young bird is first 'nakt', then in 'blue pen', then 'fleggd'.

2. *spec.* The quill or barrel of a feather; the quill of a porcupine. *Obs.* or *dial.*

c 1400 *Lanfranc's Cirurg.* 89 A calose hardnesse..as it were a goos penne or ellis a kane. *c* 1400 Maundev. (1839) xxvi. 269 Griffounes..of hire ribbes and of the pennes of hire wenges men maken bowes. 1578 Lyte *Dodoens* iv. liv. 514 With the fourth men did write..as they do now vse to do with pennes and quilles of certayne birdes. 1607 Topsell *Four-f. Beasts* (1658) 117 The Porcupine, who casteth her sharp pens into the mouth of all Dogs. 1871 Cowie *Shetl. Isl.* xv. 89 Having no catheter, he relieved the patient with a 'haigrie's pen' (*i.e.* a heron's quill).

3. Transferred senses.

†**a.** A quill-like pipe or tube. *Obs. rare.*

c 1420 *Pallad. on Husb.* ix. 186 The water that gooth thorgh the leden penne [L. *condite*]. 1582 Batman *Trevisa's Barth. De P.R.* v. xxxv, By gendring of humours in the wosen and pennis of the lunges [L. *in pennis pulmonis*].

b. A quill shaped like a spoon, for taking snuff; hence, a snuff-spoon of any sort. *Sc.* and *dial.*

1790 Shirrefs *Poems* 29 Now, o' the snish he's for a dose; Wi' pen just rising to his nose. 1890 Haliburton *In Scottish Fields* 98 The pinch was conveyed to the nose by means of a bone snuff spoon or *pen*, as it was called.

c. The internal, somewhat feather-shaped shell of certain cuttle-fishes, as the squids.

[1635 Swan *Spec. M.* (1670) 342 The Calamary is sometimes called the Sea-clerke, having as it were a knife and a pen.] 1872 Nicholson *Palæont.* 295 *Teuthidæ.*—Shell consisting of an internal horny 'pen' or 'gladius', composed of a central shaft and two lateral wings. 1877 Huxley *Anat. Inv. Anim.* viii. 540 There is always an internal shell, which is either a pen, a sepiostaire, a phragmocone, or a combination of the latter with a pen.

d. The rigid petiole or midrib of a leaf. *dial.*

1818 *Edin. Mag.* Oct. 330 (Jam.) A beggar received nothing but a kail-castock, or pen, that is, the thick rib up the middle of the colewort stalk. 1886 Rea *Beckside Boggle* 290 Her hands get cut with sharp stones and bracken pens.

II. A writing tool, and derived senses.

4. a. (*a*) A quill-feather or part of one, with the quill or barrel pointed and split into two nibs at its lower end, so as to form an instrument for writing with ink; a quill-pen. Hence, (*b*) in modern use, a small instrument made of steel, gold, or other metal, pointed and split like the lower end of a quill-pen (or formed from a quill itself, a 'quill-nib'), and used, when fitted into a pen-holder, for writing with ink or other fluid; the whole contrivance, pen and pen-holder, is also collectively called a pen, the writing-part being often distinguished as a 'nib' or 'pen-nib'. Also (*c*) by extension, any instrument adapted for writing with fluid ink. (The chief current sense.)

With words expressing special purpose, as drawing-*pen*; ***geometric pen*** (for tracing curves); ***lithographic pen***; ***music pen***; ***right-line*** or ***straight-line pen*** = drawing-pen; or special construction, as fountain-*pen*, stylographic *pen*, q.v.

a 1300 *Cursor M.* 24075 (Edin.) Es na tung mai spek wit word, Ne writer write wit pennis orde. 1377 Langl. *P. Pl.* B. ix. 39 þough he couth write neuere so wel, ȝif he had no penne, þe lettre..I leue were neuere ymaked. *Ibid.* xvii. 13 þe glose was gloriousely writen with a gilte penne. 1382 Wyclif *3 John* 13, Y wolde not wrijte to thee bi ynke and penne. 1474 Caxton *Chesse* 77 On his eere a penne to wryte with. *c* 1530 L. Cox *Rhet.* (1899) 88, I wolde that they wolde set the penne to the paper. 1600 Rowlands *Lett. Humours Blood* 5 Gracing his credite with a golden Pen. 1611 Bible *Ps.* xlv. 1 The penne of a ready writer. 1611 Middleton & Dekker *Roaring Girl* iii. ii. 225 Lawyers' pens; they have sharp nibs. 1657 Austen *Fruit Trees* i. 52 With a Quill the one halfe cut away, or a Pen of steele (made thin for the purpose). 1672 *Lond. Gaz.* No. 735/4 One Pocket book covered with Vellum, with Silver Claspes and Silver Pen, and several Writings in it. *c* 1678 Mary Hatton in *H. Corr.* (Camden) I. 169 It comes in my mind to aske you if you have, in England, stel penns; because, if you have not, I will indevour to gett you some [in France]. 1710 M. Henry *Exp. Bible, Zech.* iv. 2 So that without any further Care they received Oil as fast as they wasted it, (as in those which we call Fountain-Inkhorns, or Fountain Pens). 1748 Lady Luxborough *Lett. to Shenstone* 18 Dec., A curse against crow-pens! 1750 *Fount. Knowl. Brit. Legacy* 29 The expeditious or Fountain pen..is so contrived as to contain a great quantity of ink and let it flow by slow degrees. 1786 S. Taylor *Shorthand Writing* 98 [For Short-hand] a common pen must be made with the nib much finer than for other writing..with a small cleft... But I would recommend a steel or a silver one that will write fine without blotting the curves of the letters. 1789 Mme. D'Arblay *Diary & Lett.* (1854) V. 39 And then I took a fountain pen, and wrote my rough journal for copying to my dear Sorelle. 1810 Byron *Let. to H. Drury* 3 May, I am..writing with the gold pen he gave me. 1837 Dickens *Pickw.* xxxiii, A hard-nibbed pen, which could be warranted not to splutter. 1894 J. C. Jeaffreson *Bk. Recoll.* I. i. 20 Marvellously skilful in cutting quills and nibbing pens. 1899 *N. & Q.* 9th Ser. III. 365/2 Quills as pens remained in use in some houses as the only writing tool up to a dozen to twenty years ago... Nowadays..the word 'pen' has almost dropped out of usage, except to express the pen and holder.

b. Viewed as the instrument of authorship; hence, the practice of writing or literature; †literary ability; manner, style, or quality of writing.

1447 Bokenham *Seyntys* (Roxb.) 10 Vouchesaf..My wyt and my penne so to enlumyne With kunnyng and eloquence. 1583 Earl Northampton (*title*) A Defensatiue against the Poyson of supposed Prophecies; not hitherto confuted by the penne of any man. 1605 Bacon *Adv. Learn.* ii. vii. §2. 25 To me..that do desire as much as lyeth in my penne, to ground a social intercourse between Antiquitie and proficience. 1702 Echard *Eccl. Hist.* (1710) 401 The writings of this author..shewing a very fine and polite pen. 1775 Johnson *Tax. no Tyr.* 84 Men of the pen..have strong inclination to give advice. 1820 Cobbett *Gram. Eng. Lang.* i. (1847) 12 Tyranny has no enemy so formidable as the pen. 1839 Lytton *Richelieu* ii. ii. 308 The pen is mightier than the sword. 1849 Macaulay *Hist. Eng.* iii. I. 403 The drama was the department..in which a poet had the best chance of obtaining a subsistence by his pen.

c. Including, and hence put for, the person who uses the pen, a writer or author. Now *rare.*

1563 *Mirr. Mag., Rivers* vii, What harme may hap by helpe of lying pennes. 1605 B. Jonson *Sejanus* Pref., [A book] wherein a second Pen had a good share. 1693-4 Gibson in *Lett. Lit. Men* (Camden) 217 An inequalitie of stile and composition..the necessary consequence of different pens. 1792 A. Young *Trav. France* 113 You hear of the count de Mirabeau's talents; that he is one of the first pens of France, and the first orator. 1821 *Trav. Cosmo III* 1 The translation has been faithfully made..by a distinguished pen. 1922 Joyce *Ulysses* 134 Gallaher, that was pressman for you. That was a pen.

5. Applied to other things having the function of a writing pen. †**a.** An instrument for cutting or pricking designs or letters; a stylus; a graver. *Obs.*

13.. *E.E. Allit. P.* B. 1724 þe fiste wiþ þe fyngeres..þat rasped renyschly þe woȝe with þe roȝ penne. 1560 Bible (Genev.) *Job* xix. 24 Oh that my wordes were..grauen with an yron pen in lead. 1640 Glapthorne *Hollander* iii. Wks. 1874 I. 119 Rare Paracelsian, thy Annals shall be cut in Brasse by Pen of steele. 1650 Bulwer *Anthropomet.* 236 Both men and women paint and embroider their skins with iron Pens.

b. A black-lead or other pencil. Now *dial.*

1644 Evelyn *Diary* 2 Nov., I with my black lead pen tooke the prospect. 1684 T. Goddard *Plato's Demon* 22 To read those places, which are marked with the red lead Pen. 1755 Johnson, *Pencil*..2. A black lead pen, with which cut to a point they write without ink. 1818 Scott *Hrt. Midl.* xxxix, The Duke of Argile..wrote your name down with a keelyvine pen in a leathern book.

c. ***electric pen***, ***pneumatic pen***, modern inventions which perforate the lines of writing in fine dots, whence copies are made in ink by stencilling.

1876 *Jrnl. Soc. Telegr. Engin.* V. 180 Mr. Sivewright in describing the Electric Pen said:..The object of this pen is to pierce fine holes in sheets of paper, forming stencils, from which impressions are taken.

6. Phrases. ***pen-and-pencil*** (*attrib.*), using both pen and drawing-pencil or brush; ***pen-and-wash***, using both pen and brush; also pen-and-ink.

[1658 W. Sanderson *Graphice* 1 The most excellent use of the Penn, and Pensil, is illustrated..By Mathematicall..Charts, Mapps, etc.] 1896 *Idler* Mar. 242/1 There are many well known pen and pencil men of to-day who can scarcely obtain sufficient commissions. 1893 W. G. Collingwood *Ruskin* I. 122 We have no pen-and-wash work of his before 1845. 1900 *Westm. Gaz.* 12 Nov. 2/1 The interesting pen-and-wash revivalist experiments of Mr. Roger Fry.

III. 7. *attrib.* and *Comb.* **a.** simple attrib., as ***pen-box***, ***-draughtsman***, ***-drawing***, ***-line***, ***-painting***, ***-powder***, ***-rack***, ***-sac*** (from 3 c), ***-scratch***, ***set***, ***-sketch***, ***-slip***, ***-spray***, ***-stalk***, ***-stand***, ***-steel***, ***-stroke***, ***-wright***, ***-writing***. **b.** in reference to the pen as an instrument of authorship (cf. 4 b), as ***pen-agility***, ***-combat***, ***-cuff***, ***-errantry*** (after *knight-errantry*), ***-fellow***, ***-fencer***, ***-fighting***, ***-gossip*** vb., ***-life***, ***-pains***, ***-prattle***, ***-scolding***, ***-slave***. **c.** objective and obj. gen., as ***pen-cleaner***, ***-cutter***, ***-driver***, ***-nibber***, ***-pusher***; ***pen-bearing***, ***-holding***, ***-nibbing*** adjs. **d.** instrumental, etc., as ***pen-worker***; ***pen-persecuted***, ***-written*** adjs.; also ***penlike***, ***-painted*** adjs.

1887 Heilprin *Distrib. Anim.* iii. i. 268 *Pen-bearing cuttle-fishes or calamaries. 1642 Hales *Schism* 3 As long as the disagreeing parties went no further than Disputes and *Pen-combats. 1893 *Bookworm* 316 Prynne and he came to *pen-cuffs. 1723 *Lond. Gaz.* No. 6222/10 David Shepard, ..*Pen-Cutter. 1889 J. Pennell (*title*) *Pen Drawing and *Pen Draughtsmen, their work and their methods. 1878 Browning *Poets Croisic* cii, Our middle-aged *Pen-driver drudging at his weary work. 1825 Waterton *Wand. S. Amer.* iv. i. 295 If..thou wouldst allow me to indulge a little longer in this harmless *pen-errantry, I would tell thee [etc.]. 1582 N. T. (Rhem.) Pref. 8-9 Of which sort Calvin himselfe and his *penfellows so much complaine. 1654 Baker tr. *Balzac's Lett.* IV. To Chancellor 3 These *Pen-fencers onely begge the Seal of your Authority. 1818 Southey *Lett.* (1856) III. 85 If I were not rather disposed at this time to *pen-gossip with your worship. 1871 Ruskin *Fors Clav.* vi. 5 My hand is weary of *pen-holding. 1602 Warner *Alb. Eng.* x. lxii, Infuse ye *Penn-life..into ore taken Fames by death. 1581 Mulcaster *Positions* v. (1887) 32 The pen or some other *penlike instrument. 1895 E. M. Thompson *Eng. Illum. MSS.* ii. 38 The features of the human face are indicated by very light *pen-lines alone without any attempt at modelling. 1978 *Times* 2 June 13/4 White [wall]papers with a thin pen line stripe of bright green or pink or blue. 1823 *Trans. Soc. Arts* XL. 252 This operation..may be performed still more accurately by the *Pen-nibber here represented. 1902 *Chambers's Jrnl.* Nov. 692/2 He had in everyday use: (1) wash-hand tray..(13) pen-nibber, (14) ruler. 1844 J. T. Hewlett *Parsons & W.* liv, A pent-up, emasculated, *pen-nibbing menial. *a* 1661 Fuller *Worthies* (1840) III. 262 Practical policy..beating *pen-pains out of distance in the race of preferment. 1929 E. Bowen *Last Sept.* ii. ix. 104 Cushions with *pen-painted sprays. 1862 Trollope *Let.* 28 June (1951) 115 The character of Romola..is the perfection of *pen painting. 1934 M. Allingham *Death of Ghost* xi. 130 The shop..which sold her pen paintings 'phoned her..and she spent a busy hour..getting off a consignment of table centres. *a* 1661 Fuller *Worthies* (1840) I. v. 21 Much *pen-persecuted, and pelted at with libellous pamphlets. 1593 G. Harvey *Pierce's Super.* Wks. (Grosart) II. 17 Such a Bombard-goblin..With drad *Pen-powder, and the conquerous pott. 1754 Richardson *Grandison* V. xxi. 121 The design of my *pen-prattle. 1858 Simmonds *Dict. Trade*, **Pen-rack*, a support for pens. 1883 Hyatt in *Proc. Amer. Assoc. Adv. Sci.* (1884) 338 A flap or hood-like prolongation of the mantle, forming a *pen-sac. 1884 *Chicago Advance* 6 Mar., We have not a *pen-scratch in our statute founded in such reason. 1963 L. Deighton *Horse under Water* xvii. 69 On da Cunha's simple mahogany desk was a porcelain-and-gold *pen set. 1977 R. Ludlum *Chancellor Manuscript*. ix. 105 Quinn..sat down behind his desk... His eyes fell on..his pen set. 1887 *Athenæum* 29 Jan. 166/3 Some *pen-sketches with tinted shadows. 1597 J. Payne *Royal Exch.* 32 The devill hathe his seducing secretaries or *pennslaves. 1659 Fuller *App. Inj. Innoc.* (1840) 290, I hope that memory-mistakes and *pen-slips in my book will not be found so frequent. 1905 J. W. Bradley *Illum. MSS.* ii. iii. 142 The greater part of this volume is in the..'Berry' style, *i.e.* the fine *pen-sprays of ivy leaf of burnished gold. But the first grand border is..transitional, consisting of the pen-sprays of golden ivy leaf alternating with sprays of natural flowers. 1907 K. D. Wiggin *New Chron. Rebecca* iii. 78 Last night I dreamed that the river was ink and I kept dipping into it and writing with a *penstalk made of a young pine tree. 1933 D. Gascoyne *Opening Day* i. 12 On the flap of the desk were bottles of inks, a *pen-stand in red and white mottled marble..and a profuse litter of papers. 1969 E. H. Pinto *Treen* 260/2 Horizontal tiered pen stands, as opposed to vertical pen holders, only became practical when the straight steel-nibbed pen replaced the curved feathered quill. 1898 *Cycling* 44 Covered with a *pen-steel shell or bush. 1843 Ruskin *Mod. Paint.* I. i. i. ii. §7 Three *penstrokes of Raffaelle are a greater..picture than the most finished work that ever Carlo Dolci polished into inanity. 1928 O. E. Saunders *Eng. Illumination* I. 66 The shading on the draperies is executed by penstrokes, one thick line being regularly bordered by two thin ones. 1977 *Times Lit. Suppl.* 25 Mar. 365/1 In the animation process, where the energy-charge of single penstrokes is naturally sacrificed to the blur of movement. 1712 Pope *Let.* Wks. 1751 VII. 245, I will not encroach upon Bay's province and *pen-whispers. 1901 *Daily News* 14 Feb. 9/3 *Penworkers were only being paid six to twelve shillings per week. 1870 H. Campkin in *Trans. Lond. & Middlesex Archæol. Soc.* III. 232 The Grub Street *penwrights.

8. Special Combs.: **pen-form**, the shape of hand-written letters, esp. those influenced by the writing instrument or the way it is used; so **pen-formed** *a.* ; **pen-master** , a master of the pen, a skilful writer, a calligraphist; **pen-name** [tr. pseudo-F. nom-de-plume, q.v.], a fictitious name assumed by an author, a literary pseudonym; **pen-picture**, a picture drawn with the pen; usually *fig.* a picturesque description; **pen-plume** = pen-feather; **pen-point**, (*a*) the point of a pen; (*b*) *dial.* a steel pen or nib; (*c*) literary 'point' or effectiveness; **pen-portrait** (cf. *pen-picture*); **pen recorder**, an instrument for producing a continuous graphical record of a variable measured quantity by means of a pen; so **pen-recorded** *a.*, **pen recording**; **pen-tray**, a long narrow tray for pens (often forming part of an ink-stand); **pen-trial**, something written by a scribe on a manuscript to test his pen. Also pen-case, pen-clerk, pencraft, etc.

1906 E. Johnston *Writing & Illuminating* iii. 63 For the practical study of *pen-forms use a cane or a reed pen. *Ibid.* xiv. 238 The Pen-formed letters are more easily practised. 1955 J. R. R. Tolkien *Return of King* 397 They [*sc.* dwarfs] adhered to the Cirth, and developed written pen-forms from them. *a* 1661 Fuller *Worthies, Hereford* (1662) 40 Two such Transcendent *Pen-masters..may even serve fairly to engross the will and testament of the expiring Universe. 18.. B. Taylor cited in *Webster* (1864), **Pen-name.* 1882 J. A. Noble *Sonnet in Eng. &c.* ii. (1893) 69 Christina Rossetti ..contributing, under the pen-name of Ellen Alleyne, a number of tenderly beautiful poems. 1853 *Zoologist* II. 4054 The desultory manner in which Mr. —— has arranged his *pen-pictures. 1973 *Times* 15 Dec. 4/2 Later the pupils were asked to rate the instructor on such things as intelligence, likableness, popularity and honesty, and give a short *pen picture of him. 1899 *Daily News* 16 Sept. 7/2 Ostrich feathers or painted *pen-plumes are the principal trimming. 1884 *Chamb. Jrnl.* 25 Oct. 686/1 Hitherto, iridium has been used solely for *pen-points. 1902 *Daily Chron.* 27 Mar. 3/3 If one [plot]..were reclaimed, liquefied into words and given pen-point. 1884 E. Yates *Recoll. & Exp.* II. 227 To visit and make a *pen-portrait of him. 1973 *Nature* 27 Apr. 601/1 The *pen-recorded chart appears in Fig. 1. 1947 *Canad. Jrnl. Res.* B. XXV. 397 In conjunction with a linear direct current amplifier and a Leeds and Northrup Speedomax *pen recorder, this unit allows rapid and accurate recording of a given mass spectrum. 1964 *Listener* 27 Feb. 344/2 The radiations from Jupiter..may also be recorded as a trace, using a pen-recorder, though great care has to be taken with identification. 1972 *Physics Bull.* Jan. 24/3 A permanent record of any defects can be obtained on a chart, the motion of which is synchronized with the position of the transducer.., if the output signal is fed to a pen recorder. 1942 *Rev. Sci. Instruments* XIII. 218 (*heading*) Direct *pen recording of galvanometer deflections. 1945 *Ibid.* XVI. 70/2 It was felt to be desirable to employ a pen recording system. 1858 Simmonds *Dict. Trade*, **Pen tray*, a small wooden tray for holding pens. 1882 *Catal. Dk. Hamilton's Collect.* 231 A Persian lacquer pen-tray. 1953 K. Sisam *Stud. Hist. Old Eng. Lit.* vii. 109 At the extreme top of folios 119*a*, 121*a*, 123*a*, 126*a*..is a prayer at the beginning of the sitting..; but it is also, I think, an inconspicuous *pen-trial to make sure that pen and ink will go smoothly.

1978 *N. & Q.* Oct. 405/1 Additions to..the manuscript include the clarification of texts, pen-trials, [etc.].

pen, *sb.*[3] Also 7 **penne.** [Origin unascertained.] A female swan.

(In Order of 1524 (*Archæol.* XVI. 156) the male and female are distinguished as 'sire and dam'.)

c **1550** *Order for Swannes* §27 in *Archæol. Inst. Lincoln* (1850) 309 The cignettes shalbe seazed to the King, till due proof be had whos they are, and whos was the swan that is away, be it cobb, or penne. **1641** H. Best *Farm. Bks.* (Surtees) 122 The hee swanne is called the cobbe, and the shee-swanne the penne;..the owner of the cobbe is to have the one halfe, and the owner of the penne the other halfe. **1882** P. Robinson *Noah's Ark* x. 340 The female bird—technically called 'the pen'—has equal claims to notice both for personal bravery and parental solicitude.

pen, *sb.*[4] *local.* [a. Brythonic (Welsh, Cornish) *pen* head.] A word originally meaning 'head', frequent in place names in Cornwall, Wales, and other parts of Britain, as Penzance, Penmaenmawr, Penrith, Pencaitland; in some localities, esp. in the south of Scotland, used as a separate word in names of hills, e.g. Eskdalemuir Pen, Ettrick Pen, Lee Pen, Penchrise Pen, Skelfhill Pen, etc.; rarely as common noun, 'the pen'.

[**1602** Carew *Cornwall* 55 Most of them begin with Tre, Pol, or Pen, which signifie a Towne, a Top, and a head: whence grew the common by-word By Tre, Pol, and Pen, You shall know the Cornishmen. **1628** Coke *On Litt.* 5 b, *Pen* signifieth a hill.] **1715** Pennecuik *Descr. Tweeddale* Wks. (1815) 49 Lee Pen is a high and pointed hill of a pyramidical shape... Cairn Hill..is a stupendous mountain like Lee Pen. **1775** Armstrong *Comp. to Map of Peebles* (Jam.), Hills are variously named..as Law, Pen, Kipp, Coom, Dod, Craig, Fell, etc. **1805** Scott *Last Minstr.* I. xv, From Craik-cross to Skelf-hill pen. **1890** *Gloucester Gloss.* (E.D.S.) s.v., I live just under the Pen to which Pen lane leads.

pen (pɛn), *sb.*[5] *U.S.* Abbrev. of PENITENTIARY *sb.* 7, with allusion to PEN *sb.*[1] 2 c (from which some early uses are indistinguishable).

1884 'C. E. Craddock' *In Tennessee Mts.* 68 He b'lieved the Pen could claim it ez convict labor. **1889** *Provo* (Utah) *Amer.* 28 Mar. 1/4 What John got was eighteen months in the pen. **1908** [see COLD *a.* 1 e]. **1910** 'O. Henry' *Whirligigs* xvii. 202 One year after I got to the pen, my daughter died. **1924** W. M. Raine *Troubled Waters* xxvii. 273 He escaped from the pen four days ago. **1939** J. Steinbeck *Grapes of Wrath* x. 123 I'm a-gonna tell you somepin about bein' in the pen. **1940** R. Chandler *Farewell, my Lovely* vi. 43 We got a wire from Oregon State Pen on him. **1956** B. Holiday *Lady sings Blues* (1973) xix. 159 This was the first time I met anybody from the federal pen. **1960** *Times Lit. Suppl.* 16 Sept. 589/4 A junkie..who was..busted by the nailers and after a stretch in the pen cold turkeyed. **1967** *Punch* 22 Nov. 796/2 Semple makes a pass at Carole, is rebuffed, strangles her in a demented fit, and does eighteen years in the pen for it. **1972** 'H. Howard' *Nice Day for Funeral* iii. 40 He was her meal-ticket. Why should she want him sent to the pen? **1973** M. Campbell *Halfbreed* xviii. 123, I had only been in Vancouver a few days when I met a guy just out of the Pen. **1975** *High Times* Dec. 9/1 Right now I'm in east Tennessee facing a five-to-15 year term in the state pen for something I haven't done—mainly for selling a schedule-one drug to a narc. **1977** *Time* 20 June 33/1 Another escape try from Missouri state pen, on March 10, 1966.

pen, *v.*[1] Forms: 1 ***pennian**; 3–7 **penne,** (7 **penn**), 6– **pen.** Pa. t. **penned** (pɛnd); also 7 **pend.** Pa. pple. **penned** (pɛnd); also 6–7 **pend,** (6 *arch.* **ypend**). See also PEND *v.*[2], PENT *ppl. a.* [ME. *pennen*, repr. OE. **pennian* (evidenced only in *onpennad* unpenned, opened), app. f. *penn*, PEN *sb.*[1] Connexion with LG. *pennen, pannen* to bolt (a door) and *penn* pin, peg, is not clear, as these words seem to be related to OE. *pinn* PIN, peg.]

†**1.** *trans.* To fasten, make fast (? as with a bolt or the like; to bolt). *Obs.* (See PIN *v.*)

c **1200** *Trin. Coll. Hom.* 181 Hie tuneð to hire ȝif gaten, and penneð wel faste. **1377** Langl. *P. Pl.* B. xx. 296 Conscience ..made pees porter to pynne [*MS. B* penne] þe ȝates.

2. To enclose so as to prevent from escaping; to shut in, shut up, confine. Often with *up*; also *in.* (See also PENT *ppl. a.*)

c **1200** *Trin. Coll. Hom.* 43 Ȝif ure ani is þus forswolȝen, and þus penned, clupe we to ure louerd. [*a* **1225** *Ancr. R.* 94 þet heo beoð her so bipenned.] **1393** Langl. *P. Pl.* C. vii. 219 Ich putte hem in pressours and pynned [*MS. M* pennede] hem þerynne. **1579** Spenser *Sheph. Cal.* Oct. 72 Sonne-bright honour pend in shamefull coupe [*gloss* Pent, shut vp in slouth, as in a coope or cage]. **1593** Shaks. *Lucr.* 681 For with the nightlie linnen..He pens her piteous clamors in her head. **1602** *2nd Pt. Return fr. Parnass.* III. ii. (Arb.) 40 Weede pen the prating parats in a cage. **1650** Bulwer *Anthropomet.* 185 It is a custom..to Pen them up in too streight Swathing-bands. **1687** B. Randolph *Archipelago* 34 The Venetian armada..have a custom never to be in any haven or port where they may be penn'd in. **1692** Dryden *St. Euremont's Ess.* 8 This constraint of Humours so long pen'd up. **1706** A. Boyer *Ann. Q. Anne* IV. 3, I narrowly missed being penn'd up in the bay of Gibraltar. **1899** S. R. Gardiner *Cromwell* 95 Fairfax after a magnificently rapid march penned them into Colchester.

3. *spec.* **a.** To confine (the water) in a river or canal by means of a weir, dam, or the like, so as to form a head of water; to dam up. Also *absol.* (quot. 1791). Now *rare.*

1576 in W. H. Turner *Select. Rec. Oxford* (1880) 384 They ..do..penne away the water in sommer. **1791** R. Mylne *Rep. Thames & Isis* 51 This weir may be taken away if Godstow lock pens sufficiently high. **1840** *Evid. Hull Docks Com.* 41 This mode of penning up the river so as to convert it into a dock. **1859** Lewin *Invas. Brit.* 90 At Wye is a mill-dam by which the water is penned back.

b. To confine or shut up (cattle, poultry, etc.) in a pen; to put into or keep in a pen.

c **1610** *Women Saints* 60 He pend them [the wild geese] all fast in a house. **1667** Milton *P.L.* iv. 185 Where Shepherds pen thir Flocks at eeve In hurdl'd Cotes. **1792** S. Rogers *Pleas. Mem.* II. 245 And on the moor the shepherd penned his fold. **1807** Crabbe *Par. Reg.* III. 846 Drive that stout pig and pen him in thy yard. **1891** *Times* 6 Oct. 9/6 The number of sheep penned showed an increase of 540 British and 830 foreign.

†**pen,** *v.*[2] *Obs. rare.* [f. PEN *sb.*[2] 1.] *intr.* To develop feathers, to become fledged.

1486 *Bk. St. Albans* B vij b, When she [an hawk] begynnyth to penne, and plumyth, and spalchith and pikith her selfe.

pen, *v.*[3] Forms: 5–7 **penne,** (6 **penn**), 6– **pen.** Pa. t. and pple. **penned** (pɛnd); also (*pa. pple.*) 6 **pende,** 7 **pend.** [f. PEN *sb.*[2] 4.] **a.** *trans.* To write *down* with a pen; to put into writing, set down in writing, write down, write out, write; to put into proper written form, draw up (a document); to compose and write, to indite.

1490 *Plumpton Corr.* (Camden) 100, I have bene with Thomas Horton..& pennyt ij inquisicions of dyverse wayes. **1530** Palsgr. 523/2, I can devyse a thing wel, but I can nat penne it. **1563** *Mirr. Mag., Rivers* x, The playntes alredy by the pende are brief enough. **1683** (*title*) Panegyrick upon Folly, penn'd in Latin by Erasmus, rendered into English by White Kennett. **1709** Hearne *Collect.* (O.H.S.) II. 209 They..penn'd down the words they were to speak. **1808** Scott *Marm.* vi. xv, Thanks to St. Bothan, son of mine, Save Gawain, ne'er could pen a line. **1880** Miss Braddon *Just as I am* xii, I thought of penning a letter to the *Times.*

†**b.** To write of or about, to set forth or describe in writing. *Obs.*

c **1555** Harpsfield *Div. Hen. VIII* (Camden) 283 These ..calamities, if they should be penned and set forth as the matter craveth. **1579** Gosson *Sch. Abuse* (Arb.) 25 Philammones penned the birth of Latona..in verse. **1659** Pearson *Creed* i. (1839) 95 Moses, who first penned the original of humanity.

c. *intr.* To use a pen; to write.

1904 Hardy *Dynasts* I. II. ii. 64 He pens in fits, with pallid restlessness. **1939** Joyce *Finnegans Wake* 301 He would pen for her, he would pine for her.

pen, variant of PEND *sb.*[2] and *v.*[4]

penache, obs. form of PANACHE.

penacute (piːnəˈkjuːt), *a.* (*sb.*) *Heb.* and *Gr. Gram.* [f. L. *pēne* (more correctly *pæne*) 'almost, nearly', before a vowel *pēn* + ACUTE. In this instance formed directly after *penultimate.*] Having an acute accent on the penultimate syllable; paroxytone. **b.** *sb.* A word so accented. Hence **peˈnaˈcute** *v. trans.*, to accent acutely on the penultimate syllable.

1751 Wesley *Wks.* (1872) XIV. 80 If [a word has an acute] on the last [syllable] but one, [it is termed] a penacute. **1764** W. Primatt *Accentus redivivi* 111 The Dorians penacuted verbs ending ων, ..that is, provided they were third persons plural. **1874** A. B. Davidson *Heb. Gram.* vii. 15 *note*, In continuous discourse small words or words penacute are often attracted to the end of preceding ones.

penadjacent, pæn- (piːnəˈdʒeɪsənt), *a. nonce-wd.* [f. L. *pēne, pēn-* (see prec.) + ADJACENT.] Next to adjacent.

1888 Sollas in *Challenger Rep.* LXIII. 157 The cladi of adjacent or pænadjacent fibres are given off at about the same levels.

penæid (pɪˈniːɪd), *sb.* and *a. Zool.* Also **peneid.** [ad. mod.L. *Penæidæ* pl., f. *Penæus*, name of the typical genus: see -ID[3].] **a.** *sb.* A member of the family *Penæidæ* of decapod crustaceans, allied to shrimps. **b.** *adj.* Belonging to this family. So **penæidean** (pɛniːˈɪdiːən), **peˈnæoid, penæˈoidean** *adjs.* and *sbs.*

1852 Dana *Crust.* II. 1594 The animal is probably the larve of some Penæidean. **1877** W. Thomson *Voy. Challenger* II. iii. 193 Some scarlet caridid and peneid shrimps.

penal (ˈpiːnəl), *a.*[1] Forms: 5 **penale, -alle,** 5–7 **penall,** 6–7 **pœnal, -all,** 6– **penal.** [a. F. *pénal* (12–13th c. in Hatz.-Darm.), ad. L. *pēnāl-is*, prop. *pœnālis* of or belonging to punishment, f. *pœna* penalty, ad. Gr. ποινή quit-money, fine.]

1. Of, pertaining to, or relating to punishment.

a. Having as its object the infliction of punishment, punitive; prescribing or enacting the punishment to be inflicted for an offence or transgression.

penal laws: 'those laws which prohibit an act and impose a penalty for the commission of it' (Wharton); esp. in Engl. and Irish history, 'penal laws in matters ecclesiastical' (quot. 1687); *spec.* the laws inflicting penalties upon Nonconformists and Papists. *penal code* (in Ireland), a name applied to the successive penal statutes passed in 17th and 18th centuries against Papists. (See *Dict. Eng. Hist.* 1884 s.v.)

1439 *Rolls of Parlt.* V. 8/2 Notwithstondyng full noble Ordinances penales, that have ben mad therof. **1467** in *Eng. Gilds* (1870) 403 Alle the articles penalle, ordeyned and affermed by the same. **1533** More *Debell. Salem* Wks. 1033/2 Neuer can al the wittes..make any one penal law, such that none innocent may take harme therby. **1687** Jas. II *Declar. Lib. Conscience* 4 That..the Execution of all.. Penal Laws in Matters Ecclesiastical..be immediately Suspended. *a* **1720** *Song, Vicar of Bray*, When royal James obtained the crown..The penal laws I hooted down And read the Declaration. **1764** Goldsm. *Trav.* 385 When I behold..Each wanton judge new penal statutes draw. **1782** Burke (*title*) Letter to a Peer of Ireland on the Penal Laws against Irish Catholics. **1845** Stephen *Comm. Laws Eng.* (1874) II. 20 Penal provisions intended for the better preservation of game. **1874** Froude *Eng. in Irel.* ix. iii. (1881) 350 The House of Commons was indignant..and clamoured for the reimposition of the Penal Laws. **1884** *Dict. Eng. Hist.* 809/2 The Penal Code, in Ireland, was first felt under James I. *Ibid.*, [The Irish Parliament] set to work [1695] upon the legislation known to infamy as the Irish penal code. *Ibid.* 810/2 The great Roman Catholic Emancipation Act of 1829, by which the last relics of the abominable Penal Code were swept away.

b. Of an act or offence: Liable to punishment; causing a person to incur punishment; punishable, esp. by law.

1472–3 *Rolls of Parlt.* VI. 60/1 Which eschaunge [of foreign for English money] shuld be unto theym, by dyvers other Statutes, to excessivly grevous and penall. **1568** Grafton *Chron.* II. 745 He..began..to serch out the penall offences, as well of the chiefe of his Nobilitie, as of other Gentlemen. **1673** Marvell *Reh. Transp.* II. 291 Here is a Law, that not to kneel at the Lords Supper shall be more Penall than Murther. **1769** Blackstone *Comm.* IV. xv. 217 There is..one species of battery, more atrocious and penal than the rest. **1872** Yeats *Growth Comm.* 276 A second edict made it penal to pay more.

c. Having the nature or character of punishment; constituting punishment; inflicted as, or in the way of, punishment. Also *ellipt.* as *sb.*, (*a*) (a sentence or period of) imprisonment; (*b*) a school punishment.

penal servitude, a term introduced into British criminal law in 1853, to designate imprisonment with hard labour at any penal establishment in Great Britain or its dominions; then substituted for transportation.

1600 J. Hamilton *Facile Traictise* 276 This chaingement suld be maid with..a penal satisfaction for sinnes committit. **1646** Sir T. Browne *Pseud. Ep.* vi. v. 300 Wee ..might conceave the Deluge not simply penall, but in some way also necessary. **1667** Milton *P.L.* i. 48 In Adamantine Chains and penal Fire. *a* **1826** Heber tr. *Pindar* ii. 106 In chambers dark and dread Of nether earth abide, and penal flame. **1858** Lytton *What will he do?* vii. ix, His father's misfortune (he gave that gentle appellation to the incident of penal transportation). **1858** Ld. St. Leonards *Handy-Bk. Prop. Law* xxii. 171 The punishment of a guilty person is.. penal servitude for three years. **1867** [see CAPER *sb.*[2] 1 c]. **1892** *Daily News* 17 Nov. 6/6, I was speaking to a youth who had undergone two penals..for picking pockets. **1906** D. Coke *Bending of Twig* xii. 200 He can write lines, or 'penals' instead of going to detentions. **1908** *Outlook* 26 Dec. 901/2 The very interesting article on the Milton tercentenary.. reminds me of a public school where some years ago boys had 'penals' selected from 'Paradise Lost'. **1927** W. E. Collinson *Contemp. Eng.* 77 A convict doing penal or doing time i.e. sentenced to penal servitude, is sometimes called a lag. **1937** J. M. West *Shrewsbury* vi. 71 It was at this time that 'penals' came to be written from Milton's *Paradise Lost.* **1938** F. D. Sharpe *Sharpe of Flying Squad* xvii. 191 Nick-name got four years' penal and his companion eighteen months' hard.

d. That is payable or forfeitable as a penalty.

1623 in *N. Shaks. Soc. Trans.* (1885) 505 The said Christopher Hutchinson..and the Compl[t] John Comber entred into one bond or obligacion vnto the said William Jorden in the penall somme of sixty three poundes. **1671** Milton *Samson* 508 Let another hand, not thine, exact Thy penal forfeit from thy self. **1725** Pope *Odyss.* viii. 384 Free from shame Thy captives; I ensure the penal claim. **1882** Ogilvie s.v., *Penal sum*, a sum declared by bond to be forfeited if the condition of the bond be not fulfilled. If the bond be for payment of money, the penal sum is generally fixed at twice the amount.

e. Used or appointed as a place of punishment.

1843 *Penny Cycl.* XXV. 141/1 Penal settlements are designed for the punishment of criminals convicted of very grave offences in the penal colonies. **1851** Whittier *Chapel of Hermits* 167 Lord, what is man?..chance-swung between The foulness of the penal pit And Truth's clear sky. **1876** Mathews *Coinage* xxii. 229 Cayenne is..that whole district of French Guiana within which is the penal colony of France. **1908** A. de Horsey in *Times* 15 Aug. 14/3 It is bad enough that the Isle of Wight at Parkhurst should have been selected as a penal station for the convicts of other parts of England. **1963** T. & P. Morris *Pentonville* xi. 225 Their reference group remains very firmly their 'own' prison, which some of the older men still refer to as their 'penal station'.

f. Involving, connected with, or characterized by, a penalty or legal punishment. **g.** Of, pertaining to, or subject to the penal laws, penal servitude, etc.

1647 in *10th Rep. Hist. MSS. Comm.* App. v. 495 They.. have ingadged themselves by their pennall boundes..for the payment of the forsaid summes. **1691** *Lond. Gaz.* No. 2662/4 Lost.., a last Year's Almanack, having in the Cover some Penal Bills for Money. **1861** W. Bell *Dict. Law Scot.* 626/2 An action is said to be penal when the conclusions of the summons are of a penal nature; that is, when not merely restitution and real damages, but extraordinary damages and reparation, by way of penalty, are concluded for. **1886** J. C. Monahan *Rec. Ardagh & Clonmacnoise* 37 In those penal times, Dr. O'Flynn was compelled to administer the Sacrament of Confirmation under very distressing circumstances. **1899** *Westm. Gaz.* 31 Oct. 8/3 The prisoners are divided into three classes,.. Those of the first-class, known as the penal class [etc.].

2. Painful; severe, esp. in the way of punishment. (Cf. PENALLY 1, PENALITY 2, PENALTY 1.) Now usu. of taxation and other financial burdens.

1490 *Act 4 Hen. VII*, c. 20 Whiche accions be verry penall to alle mysdoers and offenders in suche accions condempned, and moche profitable aswell to the Kyng as to euery of his Subgettes. *a* **1656** BP. HALL *Breathings Devout Soul* xlix. (1851) 205 Either he [Elijah] knew that chariot.. was only glorious, and not penal. **1709** STRYPE *Ann. Ref.* I. xxvi. 279 A law was passed for sharpening laws against Papists: wherein some difficulty had been, because they were made very penal. **1953** 'M. INNES' *Christmas at Candleshoe* i. 14 His father.. declares that penal taxation is ephemeral, and that of the really big English properties the ownership has not changed. **1957** *Sunday Times* 14 July 13/6 The motor and aeroplane, cinema, radio and television, penal taxation of large incomes and compulsory social services have transformed life. **1958** *Spectator* 15 Aug. 234/1 We have had to struggle with.. a penal Bank rate.

Hence †**penal-law** *v.* (*Obs. nonce-wd.*) *trans.*, to execute a penal law against.

1689 HICKERINGILL *Ceremony-Monger* v. Wks. 1716 II. 439 No man more zealously cries up the.. Acts of Uniformity, when he gets a Nonconformist thereby upon the Hip, and to Penal-Law him.

'penal, *a.*[2] *Anat. rare.* [f. PEN-IS + -AL[1].] Pertaining to the penis: = PENIAL *a.*

1867 *Jrnl. R. Agric. Soc.* Ser. II. III. II. 499 The penal portion of the urethra.

penality (pɪ'nælɪtɪ). Now *rare.* [a. F. *pénalité* (15th c. in Hatz.-Darm.) or ad. med.L. *pœnālitās* penalty, mulct (Du Cange), f. L. *pœnāl-is*: see PENAL *a.*[1] and -ITY. Cf. It. *penalità* 'penaltie, forfeiture' (Florio).]

†**1.** Painfulness; pain, suffering: = PENALTY 1.

c **1495** *Epitaffe*, etc. in *Skelton's Wks.* (1843) II. 391 Your plesures been past vnto penalyte. **1502** ATKYNSON tr. *De Imitatione* II. xii. 194 In greuouse temptacions & tribulacions, & penalite of lyfe. **1513** BRADSHAW *St. Werburge* II. 1060 Counnyng surgeans.. To cure this gentylman from penalite.

†**2.** = PENALTY 2. *Obs.*

1531 in W. H. Turner *Select. Rec. Oxford* 101 Suche penalytes as hathe.. ben.. accustomyd to be payed. *a* **1548** HALL *Chron., Hen. VII* 34 b, [They] banyshed oute of their landes and seigniories all Englishe.. commodities vpon great forfeytures and penalities.

3. The character or fact of being penal.

1650 SIR T. BROWNE *Pseud. Ep.* I. vi. (ed. 2) 18 Many of the Ancients denied the Antipodes, and some unto the penality [*so ed.* 1658; *edd.* 1646, 1676 penalty] of contrary affirmations. **1802–12** BENTHAM *Ration. Judic. Evid.* (1827) II. 415 Respect.. to the general nature, to the penality or non-penality, of the suit. *Ibid.* III. 253 Offences occupying a high rank in the scale of criminality or penality.

penalize ('piːnəlaɪz), *v.* [f. PENAL *a.*[1] + -IZE.]

1. *trans.* To make or declare (an action) penal or legally punishable.

1879 ESCOTT *England* I. 260 The law.. prohibits and penalises the employment of all children under ten years of age. **1890** *Tablet* 17 May 765 The Ecclesiastical Titles Act.. penalising the assumption of territorial titles by Catholic Bishops. **1892** *Law Times* XCII. 141/1 It was not the intention of the Act to penalise such 'mere blunders'.

2. *Sport.* To subject to a penalty (see PENALTY 2 c); hence *generally*, to subject to some comparative disadvantage, to handicap.

1868 *Morn. Star* 8 June, The best two-year-old field.. the winner is pretty sure to spring from the penalised lot. **1888** *Times* 31 Aug. 7/1 The principle of 'penalizing' bounty-fed sugar has been adopted by all the Powers. **1893** *Ibid.* 12 June 7/2 The Duke of Portland's Schoolbook (penalized 10 lb.) and Lord Cadogan's Stowmarket are the best of the public performers. **1896** *Cape Argus* 7 Nov., We have no income tax, and in order to raise revenue.. the poor man is penalized at almost every point of the Customs compass.

Hence **penali'zation**, the action of penalizing. (In quots. *attrib.*)

1888 *Times* 31 Aug. 7/2 The penalization policy is supported strongly by Germany, Russia, Italy and Spain. **1895** BERRY in *E. London Dispatch* (S. Afr.) 24 Apr., Inserting in the Agreement.. a penalization clause.

penally ('piːnəlɪ), *adv.* [f. as prec. + -LY[2].] In a penal manner.

†**1.** Painfully, severely. *Obs.*

c **1450** tr. *De Imitatione* III. xxx. 99 þese miseries þat penaly greueþ þe soule of þy seruant.

2. In the way of punishment or penalty. (In quot. 1651, ? Under a penalty.)

1647 TRAPP *Comm. Rev.* xviii. 2 They have fallen culpably, and shall fall penally. **1651** BIGGS *New Disp.* ¶ 26 Though charity towards our neighbour be pœnally commanded. **1690** SOUTH *Serm.* (1697) II. vii. 283 The State, and Condition penally consequent upon these Sinners. **1827** G. S. FABER *Sacr. Calend. Prophecy* (1844) I. 119 Penally given up to this second Little Horn by reason of the Apostasy in question. **1885** *Law Times Rep.* LII. 359/1 The respondent ought not to be affected penally by the omission of the board to take the prescribed steps.

So **'penalness**, 'liableness to a penalty'.

1727 BAILEY, vol. II.

penalty ('pɛnəltɪ). [Not found till after 1500; ultimately ad. med.L. *pœnālitās*, f. *pœnālis* PENAL; cf. the doublet PENALITY. The reduction of *-ity* to *-ty* suggests an AF. origin.]

†**1.** Pain, suffering. *Obs. rare.*

1513 BRADSHAW *St. Werburge* I. 3080 To dyssolve her wo and great penalte. **1642** H. MORE *Song of Soul* II. ii. II. xiv, It breaks and tears and puts to penalty This sory corse.

2. a. A punishment imposed for breach of law, rule, or contract; a loss, disability, or disadvantage of some kind, either ordained by law to be inflicted for some offence, or agreed upon to be undergone in case of violation of a contract; sometimes *spec.* the payment of a sum of money imposed in such a case, or the sum of money itself; a fine, mulct.

1512 *Act 4 Hen. VIII*, c. 6 §2 The one moitie of every of the said penalties to be to the Kyng. **1560** DAUS tr. *Sleidane's Comm.* 193 b, A penaltie was set for suche as obeyed not the decree of Spier. **1596** SHAKS. *Merch. V.* IV. i. 248 The intent and purpose of the Law Hath full relation to the penaltie, Which heere appeareth due vpon the bond. **1664** H. MORE *Myst. Iniq., Apol.* viii. 541 He would submit himself to any equitable Mulcts or Penalties. **1667** MILTON *P.L.* VII. 545 In the day thou eat'st, thou di'st; Death is the penaltie impos'd. **1758** BLACKSTONE *Comm.* I. Introd. ii. 59 These prohibitory laws do not make the transgression a moral offence, or sin: the only obligation in conscience is to submit to the penalty, if levied. **1789** *Bath Jrnl.* 27 July Advt., The Act inflicts a penalty of Ten Pounds on persons letting out News-papers to read for hire. **1865** KINGSLEY *Herew.* ii, The pains and penalties of exile did not press very hardly upon him.

b. *fig.* Suffering, disadvantage, or loss, resulting directly from some course of action, esp. from an error or fault, or incident to some position or state.

1664 H. MORE *Myst. Iniq.* xix. 72 With them Marriage cannot be omitted without very high penalties inflicted by that Nemesis interwoven with the law of Nature. **1790** BURKE *Fr. Rev.* 135 You.. in doing it have incurred the penalties you well deserve to suffer. **1837** THIRLWALL *Greece* lii. VI. 273 It was the heavy price which he had to pay for his conquests: the penalty, perhaps we may add, of suspicions too lightly indulged. **1875** BRYCE *Holy Rom. Emp.* xix. (ed. 5) 356 It is the penalty of greatness that its form should outlive its substance. **1972** *Lebende Sprachen* XVII. 134/2 Increases in strength or stiffness have always brought a weight penalty. *Ibid.* 135/1 The aircraft will accept bulky cargo with little penalty in payload.

c. *Sport.* A disadvantage imposed upon a competitor or a side (usually in the form of an advantage given to the opposite side) as punishment for a breach of rules; also, a disadvantage imposed on a competitor who has been a winner in some previous contest in order to equalize the chances; a handicap. *spec.* in *Football*, (the award of) a free kick at goal. (See also 5.)

1885 *Daily Tel.* 28 Sept. (Cassell), The conditions of the race include neither penalties nor allowances. **1897** *Encycl. Sport* I. 434/2 Within the twelve yards line, a referee must enforce law 13, and has no power to mitigate the penalty. **1898** A. E. T. WATSON *Turf* 249 When any race is in dispute, both the horse that came in first and any horse claiming the race shall be liable to all the penalties attaching to the winner of that race till the matter be decided. **1899** A. BUDD *Football* (*Rugby*) 53 Free-kicks by way of penalties shall be awarded on claims by the opposite side. **1951** E. RICKMAN *Come racing with Me* ii. 12 The weights are varied in individual cases by 'penalties' (extra weight) for previous wins. **1969** B. JAMES *England v Scotland* x. 229 Mr Skranko awarded no fewer than 55 free kicks and three penalties. **1972** G. GREEN *Great Moments in Sport: Soccer* v. 66 Dorsett shot the penalty home like a thunderbolt. **1974** *Rules of Game* 260/4 Condition (or allowance) races, in which a basic weight allowance for age and sex of horse is varied by added weight penalties for past successes (measured in prize money terms). **1977** *Horse & Hound* 14 Jan. 7/4 Early Spring.. was making an 8 lb penalty look very ordinary indeed.

d. Phr. *on, upon, under* (†*in*) *penalty*: with the liability of incurring penalty in case of not fulfilling the command or condition stated. †*upon his penalty*: at his peril (quot. 1653).

1560 DAUS tr. *Sleidane's Comm.* 23 b, Commaunding al men to eschew his.. company, under the lyke penaltie. **1600** *Child-Marriages* 176 Patrick Foord is also bounden for him as his surety, in the like penalty vnto her maiestie for his apperaunce. **1653** *Clarke Papers* (Camden) III. 8 That [he] upon his penalty forbeare to sit or act there longer. **1783** WATSON *Philip III* (1839) 209 To quit the Spanish dominions, under the penalty of perpetual servitude. **1858** O. W. HOLMES *Aut. Breakf.-t.* viii. 71 Many minds must change their key now and then, on penalty of getting out of tune or losing their voices.

e. *Bridge.* A number of points added to the opponents' score when the declarer fails to make his contract, or to the declarer's score when his call is doubled and he makes his contract.

1908 R. F. FOSTER *Auction Bridge* 37, 50 points penalty for each of the two tricks by which the bidder failed. **1935** *Encycl. Sports* 174/1 Penalties reasonably incurred may be cheaper than allowing your opponents to make game. **1964** *Official Encycl. Bridge* 417/2 *Penalty.* (1) An obligation or restriction imposed upon a side for violation of the Laws of Bridge... (2) An amount scored above the line by the declarer's opponents when the declarer fails to make a contract. **1976** *Field* 30 Dec. 1293/2 He again doubled, but, of course, this time for a penalty.

†**3.** A condition imposed; a liability, obligation.

1601 R. JOHNSON *Kingd. & Commw.* (1603) 172 Hee.. deuided his dominion amongst them,.. only with this penalty, to find alwaies in readiness a certaine number of footmen and horsemen.

†**4.** An act liable to punishment, a penal offence.

1596 *Edw. III*, II. i, It is a penalty to break your statutes.

5. (esp. in sporting phraseology, as in *penalty goal, kick*: see 2 c) *penalty bully, corner, flick, goal, kick, point, stroke, trick, try*; **penalty area**, the area in front of the goal on football and other pitches within which offences can incur the award of a penalty; **penalty bench**, in ice-hockey, seating for match officials and penalized players; also **penalty box**, (*a*) the area taken up by a penalty bench; (*b*) = *penalty area*; **penalty card** *Bridge* (see quot. 1964); **penalty carrier** *Golf*, a player who has a number of strokes added to his total as a handicap; **penalty clause**, a clause in a contract stipulating a penalty for failure to fulfil any of its obligations; **penalty double** *Bridge*, a double made to increase a score if an opponent's contract is defeated; **penalty envelope** *U.S.*, an official envelope which may only be used for its designated purpose, under penalty of a fine stated on it; **penalty killer**, in ice-hockey, a player responsible for preventing the opposing side from scoring while his own team's strength is reduced through penalties; hence **penalty killing** *ppl. a.* and *vbl. sb.*; **penalty line**, a line marking a penalty area on a football pitch; **penalty pass** *Bridge* (see quot. 1964); **penalty rate** *Austral.*, an increased rate of pay for overtime; **penalty spot**, the spot from which penalty shots or kicks are taken.

1905 P. WALKER *How to Play Assoc. Football* 12 Lines shall be marked 18 yards from each goal-post at right angles to the goal-lines for a distance of 18 yards, and these shall be connected with each other by a line parallel to the goal-lines; the space within these lines shall be the penalty area. **1910** *Encycl. Brit.* X. 621/2 If such infringement take place within the penalty area on the part of a player on the side then defending the goal,.. a 'penalty kick' is awarded to the attacking side. **1929** *Daily Express* 7 Nov. 19/1 The full-backs were often guilty of dribbling the ball in their own penalty area. **1970** A. WADE *Coach Yourself Assoc. Football* 14 When he reaches the penalty area attacker A can only shoot or pass to B. **1972** G. GREEN *Great Moments in Sport: Soccer* i. 25 Again Mortensen reached a spot right of the penalty area. **1934** WEBSTER, Penalty bench. **1962** *Amer. Speech* XXXVII. 126 Stammbach goes to the penalty bench for two minutes on account of a check. **1974** *Rules of Game* 188/1 Penalty bench with space for eight players and extra seating for timekeepers, scorer, and announcer. **1931** *Vancouver Province* 17 Jan. 7/1 Two Vancouver players [were] in the penalty box. **1954** F. C. AVIS *Soccer Reference Dict.* 90 *Penalty Box*: see Penalty Area. **1963** *Calgary Herald* 11 Nov. 9/2 Alex Faulkner was in the penalty box serving a major penalty for high-sticking Montreal's Ralph Backstrom and drawing blood. **1972** 'E. LATHEN' *Murder without Icing* vi. 62 Paul Imrie fought for the sheer joy of it. He was a constant occupant of the penalty box, he was always being thrown out of games. **1976** E. DUNPHY *Only a Game?* ii. 39 Both goals were breakaways, starting from their own penalty box. **1897** *Encycl. Sport* I. 516/2 A penalty bully is given for deliberately unfair play by the defending side in their own circle. **1909** *Westm. Gaz.* 12 Oct. 12/2 It is rarely that a penalty-bully is given in first-class hockey. **1935** *Encycl. Sports* 347/2 If necessary, time of play shall be extended to admit of a penalty bully being played, or completed. **1974** *Rules of Game* 183/5 Extra time is allowed to take a penalty bully if half or full time is already completed. **1958** *Listener* 25 Dec. 1094/2 The card would have been a penalty card as well. **1959** *Ibid.* 30 Apr. 765/3 Declarer can, in fact, treat the remaining cards of *either* defender as penalty cards. **1963** *Ibid.* 24 Jan. 186/2 Declarer could have.. treated the card led as a penalty card. **1964** *Official Encycl. Bridge* 418/1 *Penalty card*, a card that has been prematurely exposed by a defender, and must be left face up on the table until legally played or permitted to be picked up. **1908** *Westm. Gaz.* 12 June 9/3 Mr. Hunter is the only surviving 'penalty-carrier'. His handicap is plus 2, while Mr. Scrutton has an allowance of fourteen strokes. **1935** WODEHOUSE *Luck of Bodkins* xv. 170 The first thing she would do, if she was a sensible kid, would be to go to her lawyer and have a contract drawn up and signed, with penalty clauses. **1967** S. WOODGATE in Wills & Yearsley *Handbk. Managem. Technol.* 74 Some costs increase as the project duration increases, e.g. overheads, penalty clauses, lost revenue, etc. **1969** K. GILES *Death cracks Bottle* i. 13 The new part was accomplished in one cyclonic burst—five months from a standing start with penalty clauses. **1976** E. WARD *Hanged Man* xxviii. 179 The main contractors had a big penalty clause on me and hired Dieter to frighten off skilled labour so they could collect. **1935** *Encycl. Sports* 347/1 Rule 16 shall also apply to a penalty corner. **1967** J. POTTER *Foul Play* xiii. 152 The defence conceded one goal, after the opposition had been awarded a much deserved penalty corner. **1974** *Rules of Game* 183/5 Penalty corners are awarded against defenders for deliberately playing the ball over the goal line [etc.]. **1897** *Daily News* 31 May 2/6 All their resources will be taxed to the utmost to get their orders completed before 'penalty-day'. **1959** *Listener* 30 July 190/1 The theory of the responsive double is that the hand on which one would want to make a penalty double.. is of much lower frequency than the hand.. when one might prefer to give a picture of general values. **1964** *Official Encycl. Bridge* 135/2 The two main categories [of doubles] are penalty doubles and take-out doubles. **1879** *Postal Laws U.S.* §147 Requisitions for postage-stamps, stamped-envelopes,.. and official penalty-envelopes are required to be made upon printed forms. **1903** *N.Y. Times* 29 Aug. 5/1 The officials of the District Government were not entitled to the use of the mails like other Federal officials who use penalty envelopes. **1917** J. A. MOSS *Officers' Manual* (ed. 6) xxv. 272 Official letters are mailed in penalty envelopes. **1967** J. POTTER *Foul Play* ii. 25 One of the umpires..: the one, in fact, who had awarded a short corner instead of a penalty flick. **1977** *Cleethorpes News* 6 May 32/2 Skegness.. lost.. on penalty flicks to Scunthorpe last year. **1891** *Daily News* 30 Nov. 4/7

Yorkshire beat Lancashire..by the narrow margin of a penalty goal to nothing. **1951** *Sport* 27 Apr.–3 May 4/1 The Oakwell Reds would have welcomed the compensation of a penalty-goal in their 6–0 setback at Maine Road. **1979** *Times* 12 Dec. 9/6 Penalty goals rather than tries continue to decide most matches. **1895** *Pall Mall G.* 15 Oct. 9/1 It is.. impossible that they could have done anything with their penalty handicaps against such a return as this. **1889** *Daily News* 28 Nov. 6/6 Each side had a penalty kick. **1897** *Encycl. Sport* I. 434/1 The referee shall award the opposing side a penalty kick. **1925** [see EQUALIZE *v.* 4 b]. **1960** E. S. & W. J. HIGHAM *High Speed Rugby* 180 There may come a stage in a game when taking a penalty kick at goal is waste of time. **1971** *Referee's Chart* (Football Assoc.) 30 When a penalty-kick is being taken the Referee must not give the signal for the restart until the players have taken up the position ordered by the Law. **1974** *Rules of Game* 159/4 The penalty kick is taken from or behind where the offense occurred. **1962** *Kingston* (Ontario) *Whig-Standard* 14 Dec. 10/1 Not only was Westfall one of the best defencemen in the league, a good point man on the power play and a penalty killer of the first order, but he took over a left wing position just before his departure. **1966** *Hockey News* 1 Jan. 13/2 He is an accomplished man on the power play and is among the top penalty killers in the league. **1968** *Globe & Mail* (Toronto) 15 Jan. 21/1 Three seasons I spent in the National Hockey League exclusively as a penalty killer. **1963** *Kingston* (Ontario) *Whig-Standard* 6 May 11/4 Winger Bill Glashan stepped up from his penalty-killing role to score twice for Flyers. **1963** *Hockey Illustr.* Dec. 38/2 If I took him off penalty killing and put him on the power play he'd score 40 goals a year. **1970** *Globe & Mail* (Toronto) 26 Sept. 35/1 He is the centre on a checking line, a headliner on the penalty-killing unit. **1975** *Cleveland* (Ohio) *Plain Dealer* 6 Apr. 10-C/1 Their power play, keyed by Gordie, is one of the best in the league and the penalty killing, once again led by Howe, is one of the best in the league. **1929** *Evening News* 18 Nov. 13/3 The penalty lines and the touch lines were not visible. **1959** *Listener* 2 Apr. 613/3 He would not consider a penalty pass as his trick-taking capacity was far too slender. **1964** *Official Encycl. Bridge* 420/1 *Penalty pass*, a pass by a player after a take-out double from his partner and a pass by right-hand opponent. **1974** *Rules of Game* 49/2 The competition is won by the finalist with the least penalty points. **1977** *New Yorker* 10 Oct. 150/2 The umpire could have assessed him a penalty point for unsportsmanlike conduct. **1956** S. HOPE *Diggers' Paradise* 98 All workers when they 'work back'—do overtime—come on to 'penalty rates' as they are called. **1973** *Bulletin* (Sydney) 25 Aug. 3/3 We will expect to be dealt with on exactly the same basis as any other Commonwealth public servant, i.e. a 36½-hour-week, penalty rates for overtime, annual leave, sick leave, [etc.]. **1937** F. N. S. CREEK *Assoc. Football* vi. 166 Penalty Spot. **1948** B. STEEL *How to play Football* xvii. 144 As he strode back to take up position for the kick, the wind blew the ball from the penalty spot. **1960** G. GREEN in Fabian & Green *Assoc. Football* III. VIII. 55 Goalkeepers now have to remain stationary on their line until the ball is actually struck from the penalty spot. **1974** *Rules of Game* 183/3 It [*sc.* a penalty stroke in hockey] is taken from the penalty spot by an attacker. **1975** *Evening News* (Edinburgh) (Sports Final ed.) 15 Mar. 10/1 Fairley netted from the penalty spot. **1977** *Daily Mirror* 12 Apr. 28/5 Masson had scored from the penalty spot after Coventry's Brian Roberts and Alan Dugdale combined to push Peter Eastoe to the ground. **1895** W. T. LINSKILL *Golf* (ed. 3) 45 A penalty stroke shall not be counted the stroke of a player, and shall not affect the rotation of play. **1970** H. TAYLOR *Golf Dict.* 153 *Penalty stroke*, an additional stroke debited to a player (e.g. for unauthorized touching of the ball). **1974** *Rules of Game* 183/4 If the ball halts outside the circle or passes out of it, the penalty stroke is ended. **1977** *Sunday Times* 9 Jan. 30/6 England..gave away two silly goals, and were then denied an obvious penalty stroke. **1977** *Guardian* 10 Mar. 27/5 Manchester will consider themselves unlucky to have been denied a penalty stroke when the score stood at 1–1. **1909** *Westm. Gaz.* 20 Mar. 14/2 Penalty trick scores incurred during the play of a rubber are not irretrievably gone. **1923** P. TREVOR *Rugby Union Football* xi. 149 The awarding of a penalty try is an occasional happening. **1936** H. B. T. WAKELAM *Rugby Football* i. 4 The only other means by which the score can be increased is the very rare penalty try, awarded only under very exceptional circumstances by the referee, upon his deciding that a proper try would have been put on had it not been for some exceptionally flagrant breach of the laws by the opposition. **1959** in V. JENKINS *Lions Down Under* (1960) xiv. 206 A penalty-try,..the first (as far as is known) ever awarded to a touring team visiting New Zealand. **1960** Penalty-try [see IN-GOAL]. **1976** W. REYBURN *All about Rugby Football* vii. 109 *Penalty try*, awarded when, in the opinion of the referee, a player would have scored had he not been obstructed by a defender; most commonly when both are chasing a ball kicked over the goal line. Conversion of a penalty try is taken from in front of the posts, no matter where it is awarded.

penance (ˈpɛnəns), *sb.* Forms: 3–7 **penaunce**, (4 **penaunse, -ans, -aunz, -anx, -once, panance**), 4–6 **pennaunce, (-ans)**, 4–8 **pennance**, (5 **penawnce, -awunse, panans**, 6 **panence, pennence, -ens, pænance**), 3– **penance**. [a. OF. *peneance, -aance, -ance, pennance* (12th c. in Godef.):—L. *pænitentia*, f. *pænitent-em* PENITENT: see -ANCE. This popular OF. form was gradually ousted from French by the ecclesiastical form *pénitence*, a new adaptation of the L.]

†**1.** Repentance, penitence. *to do penance* [L. *agere pænitentiam*, OF. *faire penance*], to repent.

a **1300** *Cursor M.* 18489 Bot loues nu vr lauerd dright,.. and dos yur penans quils yee mai. *Ibid.* 26771 To crist þou hald þi penance fast. *c* **1375** *Sc. Leg. Saints* xviii. (*Egipciane*) 549 Ihesu cryste..þus lang in me has pennans socht. **1382** WYCLIF *Matt.* iii. 8 Therfore do ȝee worthi fruytis of penaunce. *Ibid.* xxi. 29 Afterward he stirid by penaunce [*gloss* or forthenkynge], wente. **1483** CAXTON *Gold. Leg.* 20/1, I cam not for to calle rightful men but synners to penance. **1535** COVERDALE *Bible* Prol., That his people be not blynded in theyr understondyng, lest they beleue pennaunce to be ought saue a very repentaunce, amendment, or conuersyon vnto God. **1548–9** (Mar.) *Bk. Com. Prayer, Collect St. John Baptist's Day*, To prepare the way of thy sonne our sauiour by preaching of penaunce [1662 repentance]. **1632** SANDERSON *Serm.* 518 It is but an hypocriticall semblance of Pennance..where is no care, either endeavour of reformation. **1699** BURNET 39 *Art.* xxv. (1700) 273 Penance, or Penitence, is formed from the Latin Translation of a Greek word that signifies a change, or renovation of mind.

b. In the Roman and Greek Churches, reckoned as one of the seven sacraments, and as including contrition, confession, satisfaction, and absolution.

c **1315** SHOREMAN *Poems* (E.E.T.S) i. 843–6 Penaunce hyt hys a sacrement þat men scholde fonge And mote. Penaunce heþ maneres þre, þorȝ sorȝe, schryfte, and edbote. **1553** *Articles of Religion* xxv, Those fiue commonly called Sacraments, that is to say Confirmation, Penance, Orders, Matrimonie, and extreme Unction, are not to be compted for Sacraments of the Gospell. **1657** *Penit. Conf.* iv. 49 That the Sacraments of Penance will supply all other defects. **1884** *Catholic Dict.* s.v., Lastly, penance is a sacrament of the new law instituted by Christ for the remission of sin committed after baptism.

2. The performance of some act of self-mortification or undergoing of some penalty, as an expression of penitence; any kind of religious discipline, whether imposed by ecclesiastical authority, or voluntarily undertaken, in token of repentance and by way of satisfaction for sin; penitential discipline or observance; *spec.* in *Eccl.* use, such discipline or observance, officially imposed by a priest upon a penitent after confession, as an integral part of the sacrament of penance: see 1 b. *to do penance*, to perform such acts or undergo such discipline. (The main current sense.)

c **1290** *Beket* 8 in *S. Eng. Leg.* I. 106 Gilebert him bi-þouȝte þe Croiz for-to fo In-to þe holie lond his penaunce þe bet to do. *c* **1330** R. BRUNNE *Chron.* (1810) 303 Þer penance was, þei suld go in pilgrimage. **13..** *Cursor M.* 26617 (Cott.) O sin þat opin es and kid Tak open penance and vn-hid. *c* **1375** *Sc. Leg. Saints* iii. (*Andreas*) 155 Sa suld þat ald his penance mak In prayer, almus, and in wakk. *c* **1386** CHAUCER *Pars. T.* ¶30 Hooly chirche by Iuggement destreyneth hym for to do open penaunce:—as for to goon perauenture naked in pilgrimages or bare-foot. *c* **1400** MAUNDEV. (Roxb.) viii. 30 Þai [monks] liffez in grete abstinence and in grete penaunce. **1470–85** MALORY *Arthur* XXI. vii, Grete penaunce she toke as euer dyd synful lady in thys londe. **1483** CAXTON *G. de la Tour* I ij b, She was thyrtty yere and more in a deserte makyng there her penaunce. **1556** *Chron. Gr. Friars* (Camden) 92 There was v. men..dyd opyn pennans..this was their pennans: furst to come owte of the vestre with shettes apone ther backes, and eche of them a rodde in their honddes wyth a taper lych [etc.]. **1653** H. COGAN tr. *Pinto's Trav.* vii. 21 He shut himself up for fourteen days, by way of pennance, in a Pagod of an Idol. **1727–41** CHAMBERS *Cycl.*, *Penance*, in our canon-law, is an ecclesiastical punishment, chiefly adjudged to the sin of fornication. **1752** HUME *Ess. & Treat.* (1777) II. 463 Not to mention the excessive pennances of the Brachmans. **1797** *London Courier* 29 Nov., On Sunday last the Parish Church of St. Mary, Lambeth, was..unusually crowded..to see Mr. John Oliver..do penance in a White Sheet, for calling Miss Stephenson, the domestic female of a neighbouring Baker, by an improper name. **1884** *Catholic Dict.* s.v., Penance came to mean the outward acts by which sorrow for sin is shown, and the word was supposed by St. Augustine to come from *pœna*.

b. Sufferings after death as a punishment for sins; the sufferings of purgatory, or the like. ? *Obs.*

1362 LANGL. *P. Pl.* A. XI. 301 Lewide iottis Percen wiþ a pater noster þe palais of heuene Wiþoute penaunce, at here partynge in-to heiȝe blisse. *c* **1386** CHAUCER *Sompn. T.* 16 Trentals seyde he delieuren fro penaunce Hir freendes soules. **1656** COWLEY *Pindar. Odes* Notes (1669) 9 The opinion..that souls past still from one body to another, till by length of time, and many penances, they had purged away all their imperfections. **1664** JER. TAYLOR *Dissuas. Popery* I. ii. §4 According to the old penitentiary rate, you have deserved the penance of forty thousand years. **1697** DRYDEN *Eneid* VI. 452 A hundred years they wander on the shore, At length, their penance done, are wafted o'er.

3. *transf.* in various allusions to sense 2; in later use often coinciding with sense 4.

c **1305** *Land Cokayne* 178 Whose wl com þat lond to, Ful grete penance he mot do. *c* **1374** CHAUCER *Anel. & Arc.* 347 But as þe swane..Ageynist his dethe shall synge his penavnse. *c* **1430** LYDG. *Min. Poems* (Percy Soc.) 146 Thu must of rihte yeve hym is penaunce, With this flagelle of equité and resoun. **1588** SHAKS. *L.L.L.* I. i. 115 Ile keepe what I haue sworne, And bide the pennance of each three yeares day. **1724** DE FOE *Mem. Cavalier* (1840) 240 We.. made our horses do penance for that little rest they had. **1825** B'NESS BUNSEN in Hare *Life* (1879) I. vii. 248 A person used to Dutch neatness must, I fear, be in hourly penance when waited upon by Italians. **1865** PARKMAN *Champlain* ii. (1875) 215 But rest was penance to him.

†**b.** Poor fare, sorry cheer (as of one fasting or doing penance); *to take penance*, 'to take pot-luck'. *Obs. rare.*

[So F. *faire pénitence*, Sp. *hacer penitencia*, to make sorry cheer, dine or fare poorly. Used, by way of modesty, in inviting any one to join at a meal at which no special preparation is supposed to have been made for him.]

c **1460** *Towneley Myst.* xxvii. 246 Sir, we you pray,..This nyght penance with vs to take, With sich chere as we can make. *Ibid.* 289 It is bot penance, as we saide, That we haue here. **1579** SPENSER *Sheph. Cal.* Feb. 89 For Youngth is a bubble blown vp with breath,..Whose way is wildernesse, whose ynne Penaunce.

†**4.** Pain, suffering, distress, sorrow, vexation. (In quot. 1390, the outward expression of sorrow, mourning.) *Obs.* (exc. as involved in 3).

c **1330** R. BRUNNE *Chron.* (1810) 113 Þo þat þe casteles kept, in penance þei soiorned. *c* **1386** CHAUCER *Pars. T.* ¶269 Seint poul after his penaunce in watir and in lond. **1390** GOWER *Conf.* III. 291 Thei toke upon hem such penaunce, Ther was no song, ther was no daunce. *c* **1450** *St. Cuthbert* (Surtees) 6355 He moght noght opyn his mouth.. he suffird slyke penaunce. **1525** LD. BERNERS *Froiss.* II. xciii. [lxxxix.] 278 Therby the penaunce of Sir Wylliam Helmon was greatly asswaged.

†**5.** Punishment. *Obs.*

Specifically applied by 17–18th c. legal writers to *peine forte et dure*, prob. after Britton; but his use seems quite general = 'their punishment'.

[**1292** BRITTON I. v. §2 Et si il ne se veulent aquiter, si soint mis a lour penaunce jekes autaunt qe il le prient.] **13..** *Seuyn Sag.* (W.) 1520 Gelteles he suffred this pennaunce. **1375** BARBOUR *Bruce* XIX. 51 Soyne eftir he wes sent Till his penans till dumbertane, And deit in that tour of stane. **1489** CAXTON *Faytes of A.* III. xxi. 220 So were it thenne wel a harde thynge that they shulde bere penaunce of that that they ought to be Innocent of. **1587** TURBERV. *Trag. T.* 127 That fire might be fet Wherein the wench to frie, To feele the penance of her fact. *c* **1630** in Rushw. *Hist. Coll.* (1659) I. App. 32 Upon his arraignment he stood mute, therefore the Roll is, that he was put, to pennance, that is, to strong and hard pain. **1667** MILTON *P.L.* x. 550 To aggravate Thir penance. **1769** BLACKSTONE *Comm.* IV. xxv. 320 He..shall, for his obstinacy, receive the terrible sentence of *penance*, or *peine forte et dure*.

6. *attrib.* and *Comb.*, as ***penance-doing*** sb. and adj., ***-fire, -gold, -pain, -sheet, -time***.

c **1425** *Orolog. Sapient* iii. in *Anglia* X. 349/5 Confessours & virgyns, þat suffred heer in penaunce-doynge. **1668** R. WILD *Poems* (1870) 85 And turn this surplice to a penance-sheet. **1808** SCOTT *Marm.* III. xv, Some slight mulct of penance-gold. **1848** G. B. CHEEVER *Wand. Pilgrim* lix. 310 Multitudes of penance-doing people. **1866** J. H. NEWMAN *Gerontius* v. 41 The chill of death is past, and now The penance-fire begins.

ˈpenance, *v.* [f. prec. sb.: cf. *to sentence*.] *trans.* To subject to penance; to impose or inflict penance on; to discipline, chastise.

a **1600** HOOKER *Eccl. Pol.* VI. iv. §6 He speaketh of them which sought voluntarily to be penanced, and yet withdrew themselves from open confession. **1602** WARNER *Alb. Eng.* IX. li. (1612) 230 They pennance thee and take thy goods away. **1661** FELTHAM *Resolves* II. lii. (1677) 263 Design'd.. as a Hair-shirt to pennance him for his folly in offending. **1713** *Gentleman Instr.* III. iii. (ed. 5) 397, I might bring you upon your Knees, and penance your Indiscretion. **1871** R. B. VAUGHAN *St. Thomas Aquinas* I. 195 The little cell in which Abelard prayed and penanced himself. **1888** H. C. LEA *Hist. Inquisition* II. 10 They penanced a dozen citizens by ordering them to Palestine.

Hence **ˈpenanced** *ppl. a.*; **ˈpenancing** *vbl. sb.*

1795 SOUTHEY *Joan of Arc* III. 422, I saw The pictured flames writhe round a penanced soul. **1869** *Life M. M. Hallahan* (1870) 229 His facetious threats of scolding, and penancing.

ˈpenanceless, *a. rare.* [f. PENANCE *sb.* + -LESS.] Without doing or undergoing penance.

1377 LANGL. *P. Pl.* B. x. 462 Suche lewed iottes..passen purgatorie penaunceles at her hennes partynge, In-to þe blisse of paradys.

†**ˈpenancer.** *Obs.* [a. OF. *penean-, penancier*, in both senses (13th c. in Godef.), ad. med.L. *pœnitēntiāri-us* (Du Cange): see PENITENTIARY.]

1. One who imposes penance; *spec.* a priest specially appointed to hear confession and impose penance in extraordinary cases, a penitentiary. (See also PENITENCER.)

13.. *Cursor M.* 26165 Nan mai al asoil bot pape allan.. and vnder him his penancer. *Ibid.* 26341 Oþer cases..þat biscop til him-seluen sere Haldes or til his penancer. **1377** LANGL. *P. Pl.* B. xx. 317 Persoun or parissh prest, penytancere [*v.r.* penauncer] or bisshop. [**1865** *Test. Ebor.* (Surtees) III. 314, 1397. 23rd May. Letter..authorising a marriage..by the authority of the papal penancer.]

2. One undergoing penance. *rare*—⁰.

c **1490** *Promp. Parv.* 391/2 Penawnte (*H.* penaunscer..*P.* penauncer'), *penitenciatus*.

†**ˈpenancy.** *Obs. rare.* [f. PENANCE, with altered suffix, after L. *-entia*: see -ANCY.] **a.** Penitency, repentance. **b.** Punishment; suffering (after death); = PENANCE *sb.* 5.

1611 SPEED *Hist. Gt. Brit.* IX. xxi. §93 Her penancy was seene, in her sorrowes conceiued. **1682** H. MORE *Annot. Glanvill's Lux O.* 73 That the Penancies of Reprobates are endless, I shall ever thus persuade myself.

pen and ink, pen-and-ink, *phr.*

A. as *sb.*

1. *lit.* The instruments of writing: see PEN *sb.*² 4 and INK *sb.* (Hyphened when this helps the sense.)

1463 G. ASHBY *Poems* i. 68 Hauyng pen and Inke euyr at my syde. **1517** TORKINGTON *Pilgr.* (1884) 51 He askyd pene and ynke, and wrotte hys sonne. **1762** GRAY *Let. to J. Brown* 19 July, There is but one pen and ink in the house. **1809** BYRON *Eng. Bards & Sc. Rev.* 402 Oh, Amos Cottle! for a moment think What meagre profits spring from pen and ink! **1869** *Daily News* 14 Dec., Here..we meet with a man of pen-and-ink.

2. Short for ***pen-and-ink drawing***: see B.

1860 D. G. ROSSETTI *Let.* 28 Sept. (1965) I. 375 Now one of his commissions is for a £50 pen-and-ink. **1890** *Pall Mall G.* 19 Mar. 3/1 Three pen-and-inks by Sir John Millais. **1900** *Westm. Gaz.* 20 Oct. 3/2 Some good drawings..

especially a pen-and-ink, 'Les Halles, Malines'. **1976** *National Observer* (U.S.) 10 Apr. 16/2 Mrs. Fisher had once done us a pen and ink of the Poplar Branch landing.

3. A stink. *Rhyming slang.*

1859 HOTTEN *Dict. Slang* 145 *Pen and ink*, a stink. **1935** A. J. POLLOCK *Underworld Speaks* 86/2 *Pen and ink*,..a stink. **1972** G. F. NEWMAN *You Nice Bastard* 347 *Pen* (*and ink*), stink.

B. as *adj.* (properly hyphened).

1. Using pen and ink; occupied in writing; clerkly.

1676 WYCHERLEY *Pl. Dealer* v. i, What, and the Pen and Ink Gentlemen taken too! **1745** H. WALPOLE *Lett.* (1846) II. 80 The Duke of Bedford..says he is tired of being a pen and ink man. **1819** *Edin. Rev.* XXXII. 112 One of these mercantile pen and ink emperors. **1967** A. L. LLOYD *Folk Song in England* 14 When [Cecil] Sharp was..in search of song..a wide gulf separated the pen-and-ink man from the man with bowyangs of binder twine. **1972** [see *lensman* s.v. LENS *sb.* 4].

2. Done, made, or executed with pen and ink: usually of a drawing or sketch; also, done or described in writing. (Hyphened.)

1842 DICKENS *Amer. Notes* ix. (1850) 99/1 A crooked pen-and-ink outline of a great turtle. **1861** CRAIK *Hist. Eng. Lit.* II. 193 The last blow struck in the pen-and-ink war. **1888** BURGON *Lives 12 Gd. Men* I. ii. 137 His pen-and-ink drawing from memory of that object is surprisingly accurate. **1897** *Academy* 3 Apr. 381/2 It [Cowper's correspondence] is the best pen-and-ink conversation that we have.

C. as *vb. intr.* **1.** (*nonce-use.*) To use a pen and ink, to write. (Hyphened.)

1801 SOUTHEY *Let. to G. C. Bedford* 19 Aug. in *Life* (1850) II. 159, I am..pen-and-inking for supplies, not from pure inclination.

2. To stink. *Rhyming slang.* Also *ellipt.*, as *pen.*

1892 *Sporting Times* 29 Oct. 1/2 The air began With his language to pen and ink. **1972** G. F. NEWMAN *You Nice Bastard* iv. 137 'I don't mind, provided he takes a bath.' 'Yeah, he does pen a bit.'

Hence (*nonce-wds.*) **pen-and-inkage, pen-and-inkmanship**, the use of pen and ink, the occupation of writing.

1804 SOUTHEY *Let. to J. Rickman* 20 Jan. in *Life* (1850) II. 250 If I regarded pen-and-inkmanship solely as a trade, I might soon give in an income of double the amount. **1894** *Temple Bar Mag.* Mar. 339 The sunk rock of pen-and-inkage so often the outcome of a plethora of leisure.

So †**pen and inkhorn**, as writing instruments, carried by clerks, etc.; usually *attrib.* or as *adj.* (with hyphens): Using or carrying a pen and inkhorn, engaged in writing, clerkly; learned, pedantic (cf. INKHORN 2 b).

1593 SHAKS. *2 Hen. VI*, IV. ii. 117 Hang him [the Clerk of Chatham] with his Pen and Inke-horne about his necke. **1599** JAS. I *Βασιλ. Δωρον* (1682) 86 Booke language and penne and inke-horne tearmes. **1601** CHETTLE & MUNDAY *Downf. Earl Huntington* I. iii. in Hazl. *Dodsley* VIII. 118 A paltry pen-and-inkhorn clerk. **1628** WITHER *Brit. Rememb.* II. 38 Let no man thinke, Ile racke my memory For pen-and-inkehorne termes, to finifie My blunt invention. **1655** FULLER *Ch. Hist.* IV. i. §18 They..projected the general destruction of all that wore a pen-and-ink-horn about them.

pen and inkery, *phr. nonce-use.* [f. prec. + -ERY.] The use of pen and ink; an author's business.

c **1909** W. DE MORGAN in A. M. W. Stirling *W. De Morgan & his Wife* (1922) xiv. 328, I do wish I had paid more attention to them [*sc.* birds, flowers, and trees] in my time—they would come in so useful in these later days of pen-and-inkery.

penang, var. PINANG, areca-nut or -tree.

‖**penanggalan** (pəˈnæŋgələn). Also **penangalan**. [Malay.] A female vampire (see quots.). Cf. LANGSUIR.

1839 T. J. NEWBOLD *Pol. & Statistical Acct. Straits of Malacca* II. xii. 191 The Penangalan takes up its abode in the forms of females, and afflicts them with an unnatural craving for human blood. **1900** W. W. SKEAT *Malay Magic* vi. 320 The Pĕnanggalan..is believed to resemble a trunkless human head with the sac of the stomach attached to it, and which flies about seeking for an opportunity of sucking the blood of infants. **1972** *Daily Tel.* (Colour Suppl.) 12 May 58/3 The Malayan vampire family includes ..the flamboyant Penanggalan, a monstrous vampire which also sucks at children's blood.

Penang lawyer: see LAWYER 4.

penannular (piːˈnænjʊlə(r)), *a.* [f. L. *pæne*, PENE-, nearly, almost + ANNULAR.] Nearly annular; of the form of an almost complete ring; circular with a small part of the circumference wanting.

1851 D. WILSON *Preh. Ann.* II. vi. 313 The Dilated Penannular Rings (as I would propose..to call this class of relics). **1885** J. R. ALLEN in *Mag. Art* Sept. 458/1 Armlets ..of penannular form, with expanded circular ends.

†**penant.** *Obs.* Also aunt(e. [ME. a. OF. *penant*, earlier *peneant*, *-aant*:—L. *pænitēnt-em*, PENITENT (by which *penant* was superseded *a* 1500).] A penitent; one doing penance; in last quot., one suffering in purgatory.

a **1300** *St. Gregory* 944 in Herrig's *Archiv* LVII. 69 Penaunt he semeþ wel of siȝt. **13..** *Cursor M.* 26857 (Cott.) For fals penantes men sal þam tak. *c* **1400** *26 Polit. Poems* (E.E.T.S.) xxv. 476 Thys maketh me to drowpe and dare That I am lyke a pore penaunte. *c* **1430** *Pilgr. Lyf Manhode* I. xxix. (1869) 20 Vnshette þe doore, and make your penauntes [Fr. *penans*] entre in.

penant, variant of PENNANT², kind of stone.

†**peˈnarious**, *a. Obs. rare*⁻⁰. [f. L. *penāri-us* of or pertaining to victuals, f. *pen-us* provision.]

1656 BLOUNT *Glossogr.*, *Penarious*, of or belonging to provision for victuals. **1658** in PHILLIPS.

†**ˈpenary**, *a. Obs. rare.* Also **pœnary**. [ad. L. *pœnāri-us* (Quint.), f. *pœna* penalty, punishment: see -ARY.] Pertaining to punishment, penal.

1651 HOBBES *Govt. & Soc.* xiv. §7. 217 The second [part of the Law] which is styled vindicative, or pœnary, is mandatory. **1659** GAUDEN *Tears of Ch.* I. ix. 76 Not alwayes for penary chastisments, but oft for triall of graces.

penashe, obs. form of PANACHE.

‖**penates** (pɪˈneɪtiːz), *sb. pl.* [L. *Penātēs* pl., perh. f. *penus* innermost part of a temple of Vesta, sanctuary.] In ancient Roman mythology, The guardian deities of the household and of the state, who were worshipped in the interior of every dwelling-house; often coupled with *Lares* (see LAR); household gods. Also *transf.* and *fig.*

1513 DOUGLAS *Æneis* XIII. x. 81 Penates, or the Goddis domesticall. **1549** THOMAS *Hist. Italie* 8 b. **1616** B. JONSON *Forest* ii, They saw thy fires Shine bright on every hearth, as the desires Of thy Penates had been set on flame, To entertain them. **1662** EVELYN *Chalcogr.* (1769) 27 The Penates of Laban. **1775** [see LAR 1]. **1792** W. ROBERTS *Looker-on* No. 1 (1794) I. 9 My mother had a pious regard for this relick, which was always one of her little *penates*, or pocket-gods. **1824** BYRON *Def. Transf.* II. i. 103 Yet once more, ye old Penates! Let not your quench'd hearths be Até's! **1882** PEBODY *Eng. Journalism* xv. 109 John Walter broke up his household..in Printing House Square, set up his penates at Bearwood.

penatin (ˈpɛnətɪn). *Biochem.* [f. the L. generic name PEN(ICILLIUM + the L. specific epithet *not-at-um* (see NOTATIN) + -IN¹.] = NOTATIN, (PENICILLIN 2).

1942 W. KOCHOLATY in *Jrnl. Bacteriol.* XLIV. 143/1 'Penatin' (a newly discovered antibacterial substance produced by *Penicillium notatum*). *Ibid.*, While penicillin.. has only very weak antibacterial properties against *Brucella abortus*, and practically none against *Escherichia coli*, penatin is highly bacteriostatic and bactericidal against those two organisms. **1949, 1963** [see NOTATIN].

‖**ˈpenbard.** [mod. Welsh *penbardd*, f. *pen* head + *bardd* BARD *sb.*¹ (The older W. form was *pennbeirdd*, 'chief of the bards', applied to Taliesin in *Kulhwch and Olwen*, *Mabinogion* (Rhys and Evans) 107.)] A head or chief bard.

1779 *Ann. Reg.* II. 144 He becomes a Penbardd or Pencerdd, chief of the faculty he was candidate in. **1848** LYTTON *Harold* VII. v, Still the penbard bent over his bruised harp.

Penbritin (pɛnˈbrɪtɪn, ˈpɛnbrɪtɪn). *Pharm.* A proprietary name for ampicillin, $C_{16}H_{19}O_4S$, a semi-synthetic penicillin that resembles penicillin G (benzylpenicillin) in its action against Gram-positive organisms but is more effective against Gram-negative ones, and is used esp. in treating infections of the urinary and the respiratory tracts.

1959 *Trade Marks Jrnl.* 18 Nov. 1197/1 Penbritin... Antibiotic preparations and substances... Beecham Research Laboratories Limited,..Brentford, Middlesex; manufacturers. **1960** *Official Gaz.* (U.S. Patent Office) 26 July TM131/1 Beecham Research Laboratories Limited, Brentford, England. Filed Mar. 25, 1960. Penbritin. For antibiotic preparations and substances. **1961** *Daily Tel.* 21 July 24/5 A new synthetic penicillin, Penbritin, promises to be more active against some strains of bacteria so far immune to previous penicillins and to be of increased potency against others. **1968** J. H. BURN *Lect. Notes Pharmacol.* (ed. 9) 108 Broad spectrum penicillins; one of these is ampicillin (Penbritin). **1968** *Economist* 6 July 66 The product responsible more than any other for more than doubling profits over the last four years is Beecham's penicillin mutant, Penbritin, which took a decade to develop. **1975** D. FISHLOCK *Business of Sci.* viii. 112 The scheme..set Beecham firmly on the path to its big semi-synthetic penicillins of the 1960s: Celbenin.., Orbenin and Penbritin.

ˈpen-case. [f. PEN *sb.*² + CASE *sb.*²] A case or receptacle for a pen or pens. (Cf. PENNER¹.)

1599 MINSHEU II, A penner or pencase, *vide Caxa de escrivanias*. *a* **1805** A. CARLYLE *Autobiog.* 96 He made me a present of a pen-case of his own turning.

†**b.** By extension, A case or receptacle generally. *Obs. rare*⁻¹.

1662 J. CHANDLER *Van Helmont's Oriat.* 110 But exhalations, which in the account of the Schooles, are the daily matter of Windes, Mists, Comets, Minerall*s*, Rockie Stones, saltness of the Sea, Earth-quakes, and of all Meteors, seeing they have no pen-case or receptacle in nature [*orig.* cum pennarium in natura non habeant], nor matter sufficient for so great daily things,..are wondrous dreams.

pence (pɛns), **a.** collective plural of PENNY, q.v. for forms and simple senses. Used also in a few compounds, as ***pence-collection, -dealing***, etc.; ***pence-encumbered, -paying*** adjs.; †**pence-lack**, lack of pence, want of money; **pence-table**, an arithmetical table indicating the number of shillings or pounds equivalent to given numbers of pence.

1393 LANGL. *P. Pl.* C. XXII. 378 Somme þorw pans-delynge [B. XIX. 374 penyes delynge]. **1399** —— *Rich. Redeles* III. 142 For þey..makeþ þe peple ffor pens lac in pointe ffor to wepe. **1834** *Tait's Mag.* I. 43/1 Entertainments got up for the relief of pence-encumbered pockets. **1861** DICKENS *Gt. Expect.* ix, [He] put me through my pence-table from 'twelve pence make one shilling'. **1894** *Westm. Gaz.* 11 Sept. 2/1 Their painful pence-collection likened itself in my mind to O'Connell's repeal-rent. **1899** *Athenæum* 21 Oct. 548/1 Two insular and pence-paying realms.

b. Applied *colloq.* as *sing.*, orig. to a 'new penny' of the decimal currency introduced in 1971 (see PENNY 1), and hence *gen.*

1971 *Record* (Oxf. Univ. Press) Dec. 10/2 The computer was found to be rounding up to the nearest pence the Bank Code Numbers on the Wages Slips. **1973** *Daily Tel.* 24 Oct. 16 In our village shop a customer asked for some small change but the shopkeeper was unable to oblige as she was very short or 'two pences and one pences'. **1974** *Ibid.* 19 Dec. 12 In shops and elsewhere I often hear the ungrammatical term 'one pence'. I presume this is because the occurrence of a single penny is becoming a thing of the past. **1975** M. BRADBURY *History Man* i. 3 She leads her daily deputation to the manager with comparative, up-to-the-minute lists showing how Fine Fare, on lard, is one pence up on Sainsbury's, or vice versa. **1977** *Times Lit. Suppl.* 29 Apr. 528/3 The new and the supplemented lexical entries equally reflect the times, with..*p* (but not the singular use of *pence*) for *new penny*. **1979** *Daily Tel.* 11 Apr. 2/1 A taxi passenger who refused to pay an extra charge of one pence on his fare..was killed by the driver, police said in Manila.

penceful, obs. form of PENSIFUL.

pencel, pensel, -il (ˈpɛnsəl). Now only *Hist.* or *arch.* Forms: 3 (7, 9 *arch.*) **pensile**, 4 **pensal, -cele, -cell**, 4–6 **pencel, -celle, -selle**, 4–7 **-sell**, 5 **-salle**, 6 **-syll**; *Sc.* **pin-, pynsal**; 6 (9 *Hist.*) **pensall**, 6–7 (9 *arch.*) **pencil, pensel, -sil**, 7 **-cill**, *Sc.* **pinsell**. [a. AF. *pencel* (Du Cange), reduced from *penoncel*, PENNONCEL, dim. of *penon*, PENNON. Intermediate forms are seen in the OF. dial. *pannecel, pannechel, paignichel, pengneceal, penecheal, pencheal* (Godef.), also in med.L. *pennucellus, penicelius, pencellus* (Du Cange), indicating a phonetic series *penoncel, penocel, pene-* or *penicel, pencel*. The spelling *pensil* found in some writers suggests a fancied connexion with *pensile* from L. *pendēre, pensum* to hang.]

A small pennon or streamer.

c **1275** LAY. 27183 þe king heom sette vp on an hulle mid mony pensiles [*c* 1205 mid feole here-marken]. **13..** *K. Alis.* 2688 Armed alle in gyse of Fraunce, With fair pencel and styf launce. *c* **1330** R. BRUNNE *Chron.* (1810) 169 In Philip nauie of France a pencelle þei put oute, His armes on a lance ouer alle þe schip aboute. **1375** BARBOUR *Bruce* XI. 193 Pensalis to the vynd vaffand. *c* **1400** *Laud Troy Bk.* 14391 With many a louely fair pensel Off gold, of Inde, of fair sandel. **1513** DOUGLAS *Æneis* III. vi. 4 The south wyndis blast Our piggeis and our pinsalis wavit fast. *a* **1548** HALL *Chron.*, *Hen. VIII* 1 b, The chariot was garnished with banners and Pencelles of tharmes of his dominions. *a* **1575** *Diurn. Occurr.* (Bann. Cl.) 158 Ane pensall quhairin wes contenit ane reid lyoun. **1592** WYRLEY *Armorie, Ld. Chandos* 33 Banners, pensils, stremers, wauing bright. **1688** R. HOLME *Armoury* III. xviii. (Roxb.) 122/2 Six speares or pikes, garnished with penoncells or pencills disvelopped. **1805** SCOTT *Last Minstr.* XIV. xxvii, Pensils and pennons wide were flung. **1830** *Fraser's Mag.* I. 38 With pensiles fluttering in the breeze. **1864** GREENSHIELDS *Ann. Lesmahagow* 80 Agreeing to serve under his pensall or banner.

†**b.** *transf.* A knight carrying a pennon. *Obs.*

1523 LD. BERNERS *Froiss.* I. CCXXXVII. 339 All the Companyons, to the nombre of xii. hundred pensels, And they were right hardy and valyant knightes. *Ibid.* ccclxi. 586 The names of the baners and pensels that were with the erle.

†**c.** A lady's token worn or carried by a knight.

c **1374** CHAUCER *Troylus* V. 1043 She made hym were a pencel of here sleue. *c* **1400** *Rowland & O.* 1073 For þe lufe of his leman fayre of face A glofe to his pensalle he hase. **1470–85** MALORY *Arthur* X. xlvii. 488 This damoysel..sent to hym a pensel, and prayd hym to fyghte with sire Corsabryn for her loue.

pencel, -ell, obs. forms of PENCIL.

penceless (ˈpɛnslɪs), *a.* [f. PENCE + -LESS.] Destitute of pence, or of money.

1638 BRATHWAIT *Barnabees Jrnl.* III. Gij, Ancient Stamford..Where are pencelesse purses many. **1848** LYTTON *Harold* IV. vii, My father's son stands landless and penceless.

pencey, variant of PENSY *a.*, pensive.

pench(e, Sc. form of PAUNCH; obs. f. PINCH.

‖**penchant** (pɑ̃ʃɑ̃). [F. *penchant*, sb. use of pr. pple. of *pencher* to slope, incline = Pr. *pengar*, *penjar*:—L. type **pendicāre* from *pendēre* to hang.] A (strong or habitual) inclination; a favourable bias, bent, liking.

1672 DRYDEN *Marr. à la Mode* V. i, I have so great a tendre for your person, and such a penchant to do you service. **1698**

VANBRUGH *Prov. Wife* II. ii, He has a strange *penchant* to grow fond of me. **1752** FRANKLIN *Let.* Wks. 1887 II. 259, I own I have too strong a *penchant* to the building of hypotheses. **1824** MISS MITFORD *Village* Ser. I. (1863) 215 She had a *penchant* for brown, and to brown I had a repugnance. **1839** LONGF. *Hyperion* IV. iv, The others showed a most decided *penchant* for the ancient Greek music.

penched, obs. form of PINCHED.

penchute ('pɛnʃuːt). *rare*$^{-0}$. [f. PEN *sb.*[1] 3 + CHUTE *sb.*[1]] = PENTROUGH.
1875 KNIGHT *Dict. Mech.* 1657/1 *Penchute*, a trough conducting the water from the race to the water-wheel.

pencif, penciful: see PENSIVE, PENSIFUL.

pencil ('pɛnsɪl), *sb.* Forms: 4-7 **pensel**, 5-6 **pencel**, **pinselle**, 6 **pencille**, **-ile**, **pensyle**, **pincel**, **pynsil**, **-ell**, **pinicill**, 6-7 **pensil**, **-ill**, **-ell**, **pencill**, **-ell**, 7 **pensal**, **-ile**, 7- **pencil**, *Sc.* **pincel**. [ME. a. OF. *pincel* (13th c. in Littré), mod.F. *pinceau* = Pr. *pinzel*, Sp. *pincel*:—pop.L. **pēnicellum*, for cl. L. *pēnicillum* paint-brush, pencil, dim. of *pēniculus* brush, dim. of *pēnis* tail.]

I. 1. a. An artist's paint-brush of camel's hair, fitch, sable, or other fine hair, gathered into a quill; esp. one of small and fine make, suitable for delicate work. Now *arch.* †Formerly also applied to a large brush, e.g. for spreading varnish, etc. over a surface (*obs.*).

c **1420** *Pallad. on Husb.* v. 157 Taak rubryk poured in sum litel shelle, And therwithal the baak of euery bee A pensel touche as they drynke at the welle, And note hem after whiderward they fle. *c* **1440** *Promp. Parv.* 391/2 Pencel, for portrayynge, *peniculus*. **1483** *Cath. Angl.* 280/2 A Pinselle, *pinsella*. **1534** MORE *Treat. Passion* Wks. 1297/2 We shoulde with a bundel of humility, as it were with a paynters pensell, dypped in the redde bloude of Christe, marke oure selfe on euerye syde. **1562** TURNER *Herbal* II. 88 The leues [of the Pine tree] grow in tuftes together, not vnlyke vnto..soft great pinselles that paynters vse. **1591** R. FITCH in *Hakluyt's Voy.* (1599) II. I. 263 All the Chineans, Iaponians, and Cauchin Chineans do write right downwards, and they do write with a fine pensill made of dogs or cats haire. **1605** PLAT *Delightes for Ladies* xxxviii, Laye..some gumme..with a pensill upon your past[e]. **1607** TOPSELL *Four-f. Beasts* (1658) 535 Plaisterers Pencils, wherewithal they rub wals. **1672** SALMON *Polygraph.* III. i. 165 Pensils are of all bignesses, from a pin to the bigness of a finger, called by several names, as Ducks quill fitched and pointed..Jewelling pensils and bristle Pensils. **1717** LADY M. W. MONTAGU *Let. to Abbé Conti* 29 May, The walls almost covered with little distiches of Turkish verse, written with pencils. **1826** KIRBY & SP. *Entomol.* I. (1828) IV. 542 With a camel's hair pencil take them out of the water. **1842** TENNYSON *Gardener's Dau.* 26. **1859** GULLICK & TIMBS *Paint.* 295 The smaller kinds of brushes are still sometimes termed 'pencils'; but the use of the word 'pencil' instead of 'brush' as distinctive of and peculiar to water-colour painting, has become obsolete.

b. As the instrument of art in painting, put for the painter's art, skill, or style; and transferred to word-painting or descriptive skill. Cf. BRUSH *sb.*[2] 2b.

c **1386** CHAUCER *Knt.'s T.* 1190 With soutil pencel [*v. rr.* pensel, -ell] was depeynted this storie. *c* **1600** SHAKS. *Sonn.* ci, Truth needs no colour, with his colour fix'd; Beauty no pencil. **1601** HOLLAND *Pliny* XXXV. ix. 534 He and none before him brought the pencill into a glorious name and especiall credit. *a* **1649** DRUMM. OF HAWTH. *Poems* Wks. (1711) 1 Of my rude pensil look not for such art. **1752** GRAY *Bentley* 4 Bentley..bids the pencil answer to the lyre. **1797** GODWIN *Enquirer* I. vi. 41 The rich and solemn pencil of Tacitus. **1837** W. IRVING *Capt. Bonneville* II. xvi. 274 The grandeur..of the views..beggar[s] both the pencil and the pen. **1837-9** HALLAM *Hist. Lit.* III. vii. §31 His descriptions are vivid..; his characters are drawn with a strong pencil.

c. *fig.*

1581 PETTIE tr. *Guazzo's Civ. Conv.* III. (1586) 156b, By the pensill of your iudgement to draw foorth those parts out of euerie of those customes. **1595** SHAKS. *John* III. i. 237 They were besmear'd and ouer-staind With slaughters pencill. **1655** tr. *Com. Hist. Francion* IV. 6 Apelles did never paint a Man better than I did set forth my Master by the pensil of my Eloquence. **1755** GRAY *Progr. Poesy* III. i, This pencil take..whose colours clear Richly paint the vernal year. **1837** DISRAELI *Venetia* III. iv, Tinted by the golden pencil of autumn.

2. a. An instrument for marking, drawing, or writing, formed of some solid substance which leaves a coloured mark upon a surface over which it is drawn; formed of such materials as black-lead, white or coloured chalk, charcoal, soft slate, aniline, etc., and having a tapering point for its application to the surface; *spec.* a thin cylinder or strip of such substance enclosed in a cylinder of soft wood, or in a metal case with a tapering end; usually, when not otherwise expressed, applied to one of black-lead (plumbago or graphite) so prepared. (Now the prevailing sense.)

in pencil, in pencilled writing (cf. *in ink*). ***knight of the pencil***, one whose business is done with a pencil; in racing slang, a bookmaker.

1612 BRINSLEY *Lud. Lit.* v. 47 Note them with a pensil of black lead. **1683** PETTUS *Fleta Min., Ess. Words Met.* s.v., Black Lead..of late..is curiously formed into cases of Deal or Cedar, and so sold as dry Pencils. **1708** *Lond. Gaz.* No. 4404/3 Lost.., a Pocket-Book.., with a Silver Clasp, and Wooden Pencil, tip'd with Silver at both ends. **1799** *Hull Advertiser* 23 Mar. 2/3 Velvet Writing Paper, and Metallic Pencils. **1842** ABDY *Water Cure* (1843) 52 He gave me his card, with a few words in pencil, for Priessnitz. **1880** *Print. Trades Jrnl.* XXXI. 24 Conrade Gesner..in 1565, says that people had pencils for writing consisting of a wooden handle with a piece of lead. **1885** *Punch* 7 Mar. 109/1 The Knights of the Pencil, Sir, hold that backers, like pike, are more ravenous in keen weather. **1890** *Cent. Dict., Metallic pencil*, a pencil made of an alloy of tin, lead, and bismuth. The paper to be written on with it is prepared with bone-ash.

b. In Scotl. and north of Engl. *spec.* = Slate-pencil. Hence, a fine clay-slate or other laminated shale, of which slate-pencils are made.

1878 *Borings* I. 264 (E.D.D.). **1894** *Northumbld. Gloss., Pencil*, shale, or 'plate' of a somewhat compact nature, used for coarse slate pencils.

c. A kind of crayon or pencil-like stick of colouring matter, for tinting the eye-brows, eyelashes, or lips, for theatrical or cosmetic purposes (*eyebrow-pencil*, *lip pencil*, etc.).

d. ***to have the pencil put on one*** (Criminals' slang), to be reported to the prison authorities.

1929 *Sat. Even. Post* 13 Apr. 50/3 A prisoner who is reported for some violation is written up or had the pencil put on him. **1934** H. N. ROSE *Thes. Slang* 34/2 Reported for Violation of Rules..*to be written up*; *have the pencil put on*; *have the number taken.*

II. 3. A small tuft of hairs, bristles, feathers, or the like, springing from or close to a point on a surface. Now only in *Nat. Hist.*

1599 B. JONSON *Cynthia's Rev.* IV. i, Sir, you with the pencil on your chin. **1776** WITHERING *Brit. Plants* (1796) IV. 267 Pileus bright bay, set with dark triangular pencils of hair. **1870** HOOKER *Stud. Flora* 224 Campanulaceæ... Anthers naked or tipped with a pencil of hairs.

4. a. A beam of radiation converging to or diverging from a single point, or such number of them as may fall upon any surface or be considered collectively.

1673 GREGORY in Rigaud *Corr. Sci. Men* (1841) II. 253 Pencils of the same angles are more truly reflected by a concave than refracted by a lens. **1705** C. PURSHALL *Mech. Macrocosm* 255 'Tis possible for any..Pencil of Rays to be so Refracted by a Concave Glass, that..they shall proceed from it in Parallel Lines. *c* **1790** IMISON *Sch. Art* I. 95 *Pencil*, the appearance of electric light issuing from the point of a body electrified positively. **1837** GORING & PRITCHARD *Microgr.* 180 The extreme or marginal rays of the pencil will undergo greater refraction than those..nearly coinciding with the axis of the pencil. **1879** RUTLEY *Study Rocks* ix. 80 A convergent pencil of polarised light. **1913** *Phil. Mag.* XXV. 604 A narrow pencil of α particles fell on a zinc sulphide screen. **1938** R. W. LAWSON tr. *Hevesy & Paneth's Man. Radioactivity* (ed. 2) 291 With this apparatus pencils of many micro-amperes of deuterons..have been obtained. **1967** *Listener* 30 Mar. 429/3 The picture is positioned, and a tiny pencil of X-rays is emitted at the spot where we want to analyse a pigment.

b. ***optic pencil***, the rays that pass from any point through the crystalline lens, and are again brought to a focus on the retina, thus forming a double cone with the crystalline as common base.

1704 J. NORRIS *Ideal World* II. vii. 360 Called the optick pencil, as being the instrument whereby the pictures or images of things are delineated to the eye. **1727-41** in CHAMBERS *Cycl.* s.v. *Optic.* **1786** W. HERSCHEL in *Phil. Trans.* LXXVI. 500 That Indistinctness of Vision which has been ascribed to the smallness of the Optic Pencil. **1819** in *Pantologia.*

5. *Geom.* The figure formed by a set of straight lines meeting in a point. Also extended to a set of curves of a given order, passing through a number of points corresponding to such order; and to a set of planes or curved surfaces passing through one line or curve.

1840 *Penny Cycl.* XVII. 402/1 A pencil of lines is a number of lines which meet in one point. **1859** CAYLEY *Coll. Math. Papers* II. 577 A system of points in a line is said to be a range, and a system of lines through a point is said to be a pencil. **1865** *Ibid.* V. 484 (*title*) On the intersections of a pencil of four lines by a pencil of two lines. **1890** *Cent. Dict.* s.v., *Axial pencil*,..the figure formed by a number of planes passing through a given line, which is called the basis or axis of the axial pencil.

6. Applied to objects resembling a pencil in shape. **a.** (More fully ***pencil diamond.***) A glazier's diamond; = DIAMOND *sb.* 4. *rare.*

1837 *Penny Cycl.* VIII. 475/1 The pencil diamond used by glaziers to cut glass with is a small fractured piece of diamond..of a trapezoidal shape, weighing about the 60th part of a carat, and set in a wooden handle... Two pencil diamonds are now in use, the old and the new or patent pencil.

b. A belemnite. *rare.*

1843 HUMBLE *Dict. Geol. & Min., Pencil*, a name given to the belemnite.

c. A small medicated bougie.

1890 in WEBSTER.

d. The penis. *slang.*

1937 PARTRIDGE *Dict. Slang* 616/2 *Pencil*, the male member. **1942** BERREY & VAN DEN BARK *Amer. Thes. Slang* §121/39 Male pudendum..pencil, pencil and tassel. **1967** D. FRANCIS *Blood Sport* v. 58 That Purple Emperor strain is as soft as an old man's pencil.

e. Phr. ***lead in one's pencil***: see LEAD *sb.*[1] 3.

III. 7. a. *attrib.* and *Comb.*, as ***pencil-brush***, ***-clasp***, †***-daubing***; 'made or written with a pencil', as ***pencil-drawing***, ***-line***, ***-mark***, ***-note***, ***-sketch***; objective and obj. gen., as ***pencil-maker***, ***-scrubber***, ***-seller***, ***-sharpening***; ***pencil-selling*** adj.; instrumental, as ***pencil-mark*** sb. and vb. (see also sense 7 b below), ***pencil-written*** adj.; similative, etc., as ***pencil formed***, ***-like***, ***-shaped***, ***-slim***, ***-thin*** adjs. Also with sense 'resembling a pencil in shape', as ***pencil flash(light)***, ***microphone***, ***pants***, ***skirt***, ***stripe***, ***torch***.

1822-34 *Good's Study Med.* (ed. 4) I. 67 To apply it with a *pencil-brush to the gums. **1875** KNIGHT *Dict. Mech.*, **Pencil-clasp*, a device to hold a pencil to the lappel or breast of the coat. **1873** E. SPON *Workshop Receipts* Ser. I. 4/1 The whole of the *pencil-construction should be most accurately made in the finest faint lines with a hard pencil. **1654** WHITLOCK *Zootomia* 491 No such harsh Noise, as hobling Musick, or such an offensive Sight as *Pencill-dawbing. **1929** 'E. QUEEN' *Roman Hat Mystery* IV. xxii. 307 Barry examined them..by the same *pencil flashlight—a tiny streak of illumination. **1935** R. CHANDLER in *Black Mask* Jan. 15/1, I tried throwing the beam of my pencil flash along the floor. **1830** LINDLEY *Nat. Syst. Bot.* 57 Stigmata..papulose or *pencil-formed. **1842** DUNGLISON *Med. Lex.*, **Pencil-like* [or] styloid processes. **1875** HUXLEY & MARTIN *Elem. Biol.* (1877) 33 The outgrowth of pencil-like bunches of branches. **1875** KNIGHT *Dict. Mech.* 1658/2 The Florida cedar is used by all of the principal *pencil-makers in the world. **1824** J. S. MILL in *Westm. Rev.* II. 399 Hume was not..without authority, for Mr. Brodie saw his *pencil marks opposite to this story, in the copy of Perinchief belonging to the Advocate's library. **1835** JANE MARCET *Mary's Gram.* 1 The pencil-marks on the page. **1855** D. G. ROSSETTI *Let.* 25 June (1965) I. 257 Ruskin has been reading those translations since you, and says he could wish no better than to ink your pencil-marks as his criticisms. **1858** W. CORY *Lett. & Jrnls.* (1897) 71 Such books as he must buy to pencil-mark for future reference. **1962** A. NISBETT *Technique Sound Studio* ii. 36 A '*pencil' microphone just peeping out of a well in the centre of the table. **1973** P. EVANS *Bodyguard Man* xix. 120 Her right hand was..holding a pencil-microphone. **1897** MARY KINGSLEY *W. Africa* 305, I got a *pencil note, with my letter of introduction..delivered. **1960** *News Chron.* 26 Sept. 9 This one is equally good with *pencil pants. **1774** FOOTE *Cozeners* I. Wks. 1799 II. 152 That *pencil-selling, mongrel Manasses! **1776** WITHERING *Brit. Plants* (1796) I. 310 Appendages to the keel (generally) 2 *pencil-shaped substances, with 3 divisions, fixed towards the end of the keel. **1901** *Harper's Mag.* CII. 798/1, I think he considered my *pencil-sharpening a greater accomplishment. **1851** HAWTHORNE *Ho. Sev. Gables* viii. (1852) 91 The *pencil-sketches that pass from hand to hand, behind the original's back. **1952** C. W. CUNNINGTON *Eng. Women's Clothing* ii. 245 Coatees... Worn with plain *pencil skirt. **1960** [see *kick-pleat* s.v. KICK *sb.*[1] 8]. **1974** P. HAINES *Tea at Gunter's* ix. 96 She was wearing a pencil skirt so tight she could barely walk. **1949** *Women's Wear Daily* 24 Jan. 6/5 Jacqueline Vienne features..long double-breasted jacket over *pencil slim skirts. **1976** 'J. ROSS' *I know what it's like to Die* xxii. 144 A pencil-slim ochre-coloured cigar. **1897** *Sears, Roebuck Catal.* 181/2 Boys' two-piece wash goods suit, made of heavy navy blue with *pencil stripe. **1960** *House & Garden* June 21/1 (Advt.), Alternating bands of closely spaced pencil stripes. **1970** *New Yorker* 17 Oct. 170 (Advt.), Pencil stripes, yes. Bankers pencil stripes, no. **1962** K. ORVIS *Damned & Destroyed* i. 12 A..*pencil-thin Frenchman. **1963** *Times* 25 Feb. (Canada Suppl.) p. vii/4 The huge, pencil-thin Great Lakes ships. **1978** T. GIFFORD *Glendower Legacy* (1979) 298 He came down the stairs, Dapper and pencil-thin. **1937** M. ALLINGHAM *Dancers in Mourning* iv. 59 He had a *pencil-torch in his pocket. **1948** M. GILBERT *They never looked Inside* i. 7 A glow-worm came and went ten feet away, and Rod guessed that 'Gunner' was using his pencil-torch with discretion. **1964** 'E. PETERS' *Flight of Witch* x. 166 One of those thin pencil-torches that clip in a breast pocket. **1976** 'Z. STONE' *Modigliani Scandal* IV. iv. 182 He..shone a pencil torch inside.

b. Special Comb.: **pencil-arm**, the arm of a pair of compasses that carries the pencil; **pencil beam**, a narrow, nearly parallel beam; *spec.* in *Radar*, one which in addition has an approximately circular cross-section; **pencil beard** (see quot.); **pencil-blue**, a particular shade of blue obtained from indigo, formerly used in calico-printing, for painting in parts of a design; **pencil box**, a box for holding pencils; **pencil cedar**, a name given to several species of juniper, esp. *Juniperus virginiana*, the wood of which is used for the casing of lead-pencils; also, any of several Australian trees resembling these kinds of juniper or yielding wood suitable for making pencils; **pencil-compass**, a pair of compasses, one leg of which bears a pencil; **pencil diamond**: see sense 6 a; **pencil fever**: see quot. 1873; **pencil flower**, a name for the genus *Stylosanthes* of leguminous plants (*Treas. Bot.* 1866); **pencil knife**, a knife for sharpening pencils; **pencil-lead** (see LEAD *sb.*[1] 3), black-lead or graphite as used for making pencils; a slender stick of this for fitting into a metallic pencil-case or an ever-pointed pencil; **pencil-line**, a line drawn with a pencil or resembling one so drawn; also *attrib.*, esp. in **pencil-line moustache** (see quot. 1966); † **pencil man**, a man of the 'pencil' or brush, an artist; **pencil mark** = PENCILLING *vbl. sb.* 1; **pencil moustache** = *pencil-line moustache* above; **pencil-piece**, a piece of pencil-lead of proper length for making a pencil; **pencil pusher** *U.S.*, a derogatory term for one whose occupation involves much writing with a pencil; **pencil-sharpener**, an instrument for sharpening a black-lead or slate pencil by pushing or rotating it against a cutting edge; **pencil-stone**, the mineral PYROPHYLLITE; **pencil tablet**, a notebook of rough paper suitable for writing in pencil but not in pen; **pencil-tree**, the groundsel-tree (*Baccharis halimifolia*); **pencil-vase**, a vase in which the pencils or brushes, used by the Chinese and Japanese for writing, stand upright; **pencil-wood**, the wood of the pencil cedar.

1892 E. ROWE *Hints on Chip-Carving* i. 9 Do not use the left hand to move the *pencil-arm of the compasses. **1946** *Jrnl. Inst. Electr. Engin.* XCIII. IIIA. 25/2 A Yagi aerial.. presents the possibility of obtaining a '*pencil' beam of radiation, narrow in two perpendicular planes, from an end-fire array of comparatively small dimensions. **1955** *Sci. Amer.* Mar. 38/1 This antenna has a pencil beam which at a wavelength of 65 centimeters is five degrees wide. **1965** A. NICOL *Truly Married Woman* 98 Bradshaw.. turned quickly down the road, his headlights two pencil beams in the darkness. **1966** J. S. COX *Illustr. Dict. Hairdressing* 110/1 **Pencil beard*, a narrow strip of beard from the lower lip to the chin. **1860** O'NEILL *Calico Printing* 337 *Pencil Blue.. receives its name from the manner in which it was applied to the cloth, viz., by means of a fibrous matter like an artist's pencil... Pencil blue consists of indigo in the deoxidised and dissolved state. **1907** *Yesterday's Shopping* (1969) 132/2 *Pencil Box..9 by 2½ in., 1/0. **1912** 'C. F. BENTON' *Fairs & Fetes* 118 School-supplies also may find a place here—slates and pencils..pencil-boxes and rulers. **1935** 'R. CROMPTON' *William—the Detective* xi. 235 Ties an' books an' pencil boxes. **1969** E. H. PINTO *Treen* 422 The Bavarian manufacturers of children's pencil boxes certainly knew how to bring joy to the hearts of late-Victorian and Edwardian school boys and girls. **1977** D. CLARK *Gimmel Flask* vii. 134 Remember the old pencil-boxes with sliding lids and sections inside? **1825** *Gentl. Mag.* XCV. I. 318 The **pencil*, a juniper cedar, is scarce here; it grows much like the fir-tree in every respect. **1866** *Treas. Bot.* 642/1 *Juniperus bermudiana*, Pencil Cedar; *J. virginiana*, Red Cedar. **1882** *Encycl. Brit.* XIV. 197/2 The trees [of Ladak] are the pencil cedar (*Juniperus excelsa*), the poplar and willow [etc.]. **1884** A. NILSON *Timber Trees New South Wales* 53 *D[ysoxylon] Muelleri.*—Pencil Cedar... *D. rufum.*—Bastard Pencil Cedar. *Ibid.* 110 *P[odocarpus] elata.*—Colonial Deal; White Pine; Pencil Cedar. **1908** E. J. BANFIELD *Confessions of Beachcomber* I. v. 184 A huge log of pencil cedar had been cast among the boulders. **1932** R. H. ANDERSON *Trees New South Wales* 89 Bermuda Pencil Cedar..often makes a fine tree. *Ibid.* 143 Red Bean (*Dysoxylum Muelleri*)..is also sometimes known as 'Pencil Cedar'. **1965** *Austral. Encycl.* I. 222/1 *Tieghemopanax elegans* (syn. *Panax elegans*), the black pencil cedar, is an ornamental tree with large, divided leaves, and a soft, light wood. *Ibid.* VII. 106/1 *Glochidion Ferdinandii* (variously known as white beech, pencil cedar, rain tree and 'towwar')..is a medium-sized, rain-forest tree. **1968** W. E. WILLIS *Timber* i. 6 Virginian Pencil Cedar is a species of Juniper and a favourite wood for the manufacture of pencils. **1875** KNIGHT *Dict. Mech.* 1659/2 **Pencil-compass*, one having a pencil-end at one leg; or a compass to which an ordinary pencil may be attached. **1873** *Slang Dict.*, **Pencil-fever*, a suppositious disease among racehorses.. sets in when, despite the efforts of the 'marketeers', a horse can no longer be kept at a short price in the lists, through his actual condition being discovered, and when every layer of odds is anxious to write his name down. **1883** *B'ham Weekly Post* 18 Aug. 8/5 Among the latest victims of 'pencil' fever is Elzevir, who has been doing so badly of late that the horse-watchers advise their clients to have nothing to do with him. **1817** A. EATON *Man. Bot.* 85 *Stylosanthes... elatior* (*pencil-flower). **1901** C. T. MOHR *Plant Life Alabama* 570 Stylosanthes... Pencil flower. **1926** E. O'NEILL *Great God Brown* III. iii. 81 Waving his *pencil knife with grotesque flourishes. **1875** KNIGHT *Dict. Mech.* 1658/2 The *pencil-leads as sold by stationers and jewelers for pencil-cases and ever-point pencils are little cylinders made of graphite and clay kneaded with water until it assumes the consistency of putty. **1905** *Pencil-line [listed in N.E.D., sense 7 a]. **1957** R. HOGGART *Uses of Literacy* ix. 235 A neat moustache in dark thin pencil line. **1966** J. S. COX *Illustr. Dict. Hairdressing* 110/1 *Pencil Line Moustache.* (1) A moustache consisting of a very thin line of hairs... (2) A thin line moustache drawn on the upper lip with a coloured cosmetic. **1968** R. C. GALWAY *Assignment Gaolbreak* ix. 88 He had.. a vicious-looking pencil-line moustache. **1971** B. MALAMUD *Tenants* 98 Jacob..had uneasy eyes and a pencil-line mustache. **1976** *New Yorker* 15 Nov. 23/2 Greta Garbo, with pencil-line eyebrows above sex-drugged lids, plays a bored, sensual, wicked woman. **1589** LODGE *Scillaes Metam.* etc. (Hunter. Cl.) 33. The *pencile man that with a careles hand Hath shaddowed Venus. **1710** SHAFTESB. *Charact., Adv. to Author* i. §3 As in our real portraitures, particularly those at full length, where the poor pencil-man is put to a thousand shifts, whilst he strives to dress us in affected habits, such as we never wore. **1880** H. DALZIEL *Brit. Dogs* II. 332 Feet tanned, but the knuckles with a clear black line, called the '*pencil mark', up the ridge. **1931** A. C. SMITH *About our Dogs* xvi. 245 The standard of the Black-and-Tan Terrier Club:..the forelegs tanned up to the knees, with black lines (pencil marks) up each toe. **1961** W. BROWN *Bedeviled* 77 He was a tall, thin youth with slicked-down, black hair, a *pencil moustache and shaggy sideburns. **1965** P. ROBINSON *Pakistani Agent* ii. 8 Parulekar was..in his late twenties, with a pencil moustache. **1973** H. GILBERT *Hotels with Empty Rooms* xv. 128 A cinematographical convention, like crooks with pencil-moustaches. **1839** URE *Dict. Arts* 947 The ends of the *pencil-pieces become dry first, and by their contraction in volume get loose in the grooves. **1881** *Harvard Lampoon* 20 Apr. 42/2 After various chilling repulses, our *pencil-pusher discovered a man smaller than himself. **1917** F. D. O'SULLIVAN *Enemies of Underworld* xcvi. 666/1 *Pencil pusher*, clerk. **1926** MAINES & GRANT *Wise-Crack Dict.* 12/2 *Pencil-pusher*, office employe. **1952** in Wentworth & Flexner *Dict. Amer. Slang* (1960) 382/1 The number of pencil pushers and typists has increased in the past 25 years out of proportion to the increase in factory workers. **1959** *Amer. Speech* XXXIV. 79 *Pencil pusher*, a camp book-keeper. **1961** B. JAMES *Night of Kill* ix. 120 He'd be damned if he was going to be a mid-watch pencil-pusher just to please his ulcerated pro-tem captain. **1875** KNIGHT *Dict. Mech.* 1659/2 **Pencil-sharpener*, a device against which a lead or a slate pencil is drawn or rotated in order to sharpen the point. **1886** *Cassell's Encyl. Dict.*, **Pencil-stone.* **1896** CHESTER *Dict. Names Min.*, *Pencil-stone*, a popular name for pyrophyllite, because slate pencils are made from it. **1895** *Montgomery Ward Catal.* Spring & Summer (Index), *Pencil Tablets. **1944** T. D. CLARK *Pills, Petticoats & Plows* 45 Across the way there was an assortment of school-books, pencil tablets,..and epsom salts. **1884** MILLER *Plant-n.*, **Pencil-tree.* **1890** *Cent. Dict.*, *Pencil-tree*,..so named from the long brush of pappus borne by the fruiting head. **1859** DICKINSON *Song Sol.* i. 17 (E.D.D.) T' main timmers of our house is *pencil wood.

Hence (*nonce-wds.*) **'pencillous** *a.*, of the form of a pencil; **'pencilly** *a.*, like or of the nature of a pencil or pencilling; † **'pencilry**, pencil-work.

1620 MIDDLETON & ROWLEY *World Tost at Tennis* 345, I [Time] cannot set impression on their [women's] cheeks.. But 'tis wip'd off with gloss and pencilry. **1839** BAILEY *Festus* xviii. (1848) 174 Oh! gaze on her ringlets of raven-black hair, And her delicate eyebrow's soft pencilly line. **1857** BULLOCK *Cazeaux' Midwif.* 70 The little vessels.. subdivide into very delicate ramuscules, assuming a pencillous arrangement.

pencil ('pɛnsɪl), *v.* [f. prec. sb.]

1. a. *trans.* To paint with a 'pencil' or brush (*obs.* or *arch.*); now, usually, to colour, tint, or mark with or as with a black-lead pencil. Also *fig.*

c **1532** in E. Law *Hampton Crt. Pal.* I. 364 Redd ocker for pensellyng of the new tennys play. **1641** MILTON *Ch. Govt.* II. Pref., Time enough to pencill it over with all the curious touches of art. **1854** J. S. C. ABBOTT *Napoleon* (1855) I. xxxviii. 586 The sun..pencils with beauty the violet and the rose. **1863** SIR J. B. BURKE *Viciss. Fam.* Ser. III. 290 Trial and hardship had pencilled their features with the lines of care. **1902** ELIZ. L. BANKS *Newspaper Girl* 242 The editor continued blue-pencilling other pages.

b. To depict or represent with the pencil or brush; †*transf.* to depict or paint in words (*obs.*); also (in later use), to outline, sketch, or delineate, in pencil. Also *fig.*

1610 HOLLAND *Camden's Brit.* I. 631 Lanthony..the situation of which Abbay Giraldus Cambrensis..shall pensile it out unto you for mee. **1621** T. WILLIAMSON tr. *Goulart's Wise Vieillard* 98 Horace in his art of Poetrie doth pensill and picture out an old man in this manner. **1631** WEEVER *Anc. Fun. Mon.* 372 These words thereupon being most artificially pensild. **1644** [H. PARKER] *Jus Pop.* 49 The Scripture pensils the great Monarchies under the lineaments of Lions. **1768–74** TUCKER *Lt. Nat.* (1834) I. 78 Some..very learnedly insist that the image penciled on the backside of our eye..is the object we behold. **1774** M. MACKENZIE *Marit. Surv.* 74 Then sketch the Curvature between C and B, and pencil it. **1853** KANE *Grinnell Exp.* xv, Shaded towers and sunlit pyramids of ice penciled their fantastic outlines against the sky. **1873** E. SPON *Workshop Receipts* Ser. I. 3/2 Drawings are first pencilled and then inked.

2. a. To write or jot down with a pencil.

1760–72 H. BROOKE *Fool of Qual.* (1809) III. 25, I have.. pencilled, for your use, an abstract. **1825** COLERIDGE *Aids Refl.* (1848) I. 124 The first marginal note I had pencilled on Leighton's pages. **1861** WILSON & GEIKIE *Mem. E. Forbes* xii. 427 He would..pencil down in verse the ideas as they rose in his mind.

b. To enter (a horse's name) in a betting book.

1871 'M. LEGRAND' *Cambr. Freshm.* 35 'Well, then, I've been told of an outsider', mentioning an animal whose name he had not had the pleasure of pencilling.

c. *to pencil in* (fig.), to note, register, or arrange provisionally or tentatively.

1942 BERREY & VAN DEN BARK *Amer. Thes. Slang* §628/5 Be pencilled in, to be tentatively, but not finally hired. **1959** *Times* 22 June 4/2 He is a name to pencil in for the future. **1967** *Punch* 31 May 783/1 We may have pencilled in an arrangement to throw open our houses to one another, I'm not sure. **1971** WODEHOUSE *Much Obliged, Jeeves* xii. 128 You and I, regarding Florence coolly, pencil her in as too bossy for human consumption. **1977** *Daily Mirror* 10 May 31/1 The MCC team to play Australia at Lord's from May 25–27, due to be announced later this week and traditionally a Test trial, might still be very different to the one originally pencilled in.

3. *intr.* To form into pencils (of light).

a **1774** GOLDSM. *Surv. Exp. Philos.* (1776) II. 293 Every visible point..may be considered as a candle sending forth its ray, which splits and pencils out into several other rays before it arrives at the eye.

4. *trans.* To treat or 'paint' (a wound, etc.) *with* something applied with a fine brush.

1822–34 *Good's Study Med.* (ed. 4) III. 268 Penciling the wound with lunar caustic. **1843** R. J. GRAVES *Syst. Clin. Med.* xxvi. 331 Pencilled over with Plenk's liniment. **1876** tr. *H. von Ziemssen's Cycl. Med.* IV. 80 The Application of Fluids [to the Larynx] (a) Pencilling.

pencil, variant of PENCEL.

pencil and paper, pencil-and-paper, *phr.* Usu. *attrib.* or as *adj.* Requiring (only) pencil and paper.

1930 J. B. PRIESTLEY *Angel Pavement* viii. 385 You had to pretend you were having a marvellous time because you were wearing hats from crackers and playing pencil and paper games ('Let me see, a river beginning with "V"?'). **1952** J. B. PICK *Phoenix Dict. Games* 295 (*heading*) Pencil and paper games. **1957** L. FOX *Numerical Solution Two-Point Boundary Probl.* p. v, I have included most of the worthwhile methods known to me which are suitable for pencil-and-paper and desk-machine computation. **1973** *Nature* 27 Apr. 594/2 Table 4.1 only lists some values of a simple function..which is perfectly amenable to pencil-and-paper arithmetic.

pencil-case ('pɛnsɪl'keɪs). **a.** A holder for the reception of a pencil or pencil-lead (or of a similar slender stick of prepared aniline, etc.), usually of metal, and sometimes highly ornamented; also, a case of wood, leather, etc., for keeping pencils of any kind in.

1552 HULOET, Pensyle case, *graphiarium.* **1712** J. JAMES tr. *Le Blond's Gardening* 84 This Tracing-Staff,..'tis the very Pencil-Case of him that traces Things upon the Ground. **1727–41** CHAMBERS *Cycl.*, *Port-craion*, a *pencil-case*, an instrument serving to inclose a pencil, and occasionally also used as a handle for holding it. It is usually four or five inches long, and contrived so as the pencil may be slid up and down it by means of a spring and button. **1869** WINSOR & NEWTON *List of Water Colours*, etc. 58 Round Pencil Cases. Flat leather Pencil Cases, etc. **1879** *Print. Trades Jrnl.* XXIX. 35 A large and massive gold pencil-case, a masterpiece of mechanical ingenuity.

b. *Bookbinding.* (See quot.)

1885 W. J. E. CRANE *Bookbinding* xvi. 132 This [pressing in at the joint] is very necessary, or the [end] paper may not properly 'go home' and adhere here, and..an unsightly protuberance of loose paper at the joint will be the result, which is generally termed a 'pencil case', and is a clear mark of bad bookbinding.

pencilled, -iled ('pɛnsɪld), *ppl. a.* [f. PENCIL *sb.* and *v.* + -ED.]

I. 1. Having or furnished with a pencil.

1593 NASHE *Christ's T.* (1613) 163 In a third place is there a grosse-pencild Painter.

II. 2. Painted with a 'pencil' or fine brush; depicted with or as with a 'pencil'; now, usually, drawn or sketched 'in pencil'.

1593 SHAKS. *Lucr.* 1497 So Lvcrece set a worke, sad tales doth tell To penceld pensiuenes, & colour'd sorrow. **1604** DEKKER *King's Entertainm.* Wks. 1873 I. 318 Crownes on their heads, and scepters with pensild scutchions in their hands. **1784** COWPER *Task* I. 417 Satisfied with only pencill'd scenes. **1807** CRABBE *Par. Reg.* III. 349 Her china closet..For woman's wonder held her pencilled ware.

3. Marked with or as with a pencil; delicately marked or streaked with thin concentric lines (instead of masses) of colour or shading.

1592 KYD *Sol. & Pers.* IV. i. 79 Small pensild eye browes, like two glorious rainbowes. **1829** LYTTON *Disowned* ii, His brows finely and lightly penciled. **1875** W. HOUGHTON *Sk. Brit. Insects* 89 The wings [of the insect] are often delicately pencilled. **1890** *Century Mag.* 51/2 The remainder of the plumage being penciled, or marked transversely, with narrow black lines at right angles to the shaft of the feather.

4. Written with a pencil.

1794 MRS. RADCLIFFE *Myst. Udolpho* i, The pencilled lines on the wainscot met her eye. **1875** HUXLEY in *Life* (1900) I. xxx. 448 A pencilled request that I would call on him.

5. Having or formed into pencils of rays; radiate.

1853 KANE *Grinnell Exp.* xxxiii. (1856) 287 Its penciled rays could be seen reaching nearly to the horizon.

6. *Zool.* and *Bot.* Tufted; brushy; penicillate.

1846 J. BAXTER *Libr. Pract. Agric.* (ed. 4) I. 304 The various rich-coloured stripes..of a fine tulip, should.. terminate in fine broken points, elegantly feathered or pencilled.

'penciller, -iler. [f. PENCIL *v.* + -ER[1].]

1. One who pencils; a draughtsman, a writer; *spec.* in *Calico-printing*, an artist who painted in part of the design, before the introduction of blocks.

1780 A. YOUNG *Tour Irel.* II. 36 Eighteen bleachmen.. Six pencillers. **1836** LANDOR *Peric. & Asp.* Epil., No penciller of similar compositions. **1883** Ross *Busby & its Neighbourhood* iv. 104 A good deal of the colouring was done by the hands of 'pencillers', as they were called.

2. a. *Racing slang.* A bookmaker's clerk.

1879 *Daily News* 24 Oct. 2/1 Ten races were set for decision,..business was brisk among the pencillers. **1887** *St. James' Gaz.* 2 June, When the favourite won, the accused and his clerk, or 'penciller', promptly changed their clothes and decamped.

b. A reporter. *rare.*

1897 *Chicago Advance* 22 July 111/1 Your penciller..has tarried a day to gather these scattered hints of a meeting.

'pencilling, -iling, *vbl. sb.* [See -ING[1].]

1. The action of the vb. PENCIL in various senses; *esp.* fine colouring or drawing; also *transf.* the fine tinting or marking of natural objects resembling that executed by a pencil; natural marking on animals.

1706 *Art of Painting* (1744) 389 A harsh way of penciling. **1753** HOGARTH *Anal. Beauty* xii. 96 Whether they are.. made by the pencilings of art or nature. **1831** N. P. WILLIS *Poem at Brown University* 178 Beneath The spreading trees, fine pencillings of light Stay. **1861** BERESF. HOPE *Eng. Cathedr. 19th C.* 54 Delicate pencilling replaced strong horizontal lines. **1878** LAWRENCE tr. *Cotta's Rocks* 83 The linear foldings or pencilling of frequent occurrence in gneiss. **1909** W. BATESON *Mendel's Princ. Heredity* ii. 42 Pencilling [in fowls] is a dominant to its absence. **1936** C. L. MORGAN *Sparkenbroke* VI. vii. 551 He saw a pencilling of light shine under her door. **1948** C. L. B. HUBBARD *Dogs in Brit.* xx. 309 Colour [of the Manchester terrier] is jet black, with rich mahogany tan markings..('pencillings' on the toes to be black). **1971** F. HAMILTON *World Encycl. Dogs* 659/1 Pencilling: Dark lines divided by strips of tan on feet of Manchester Terrier.

2. *concr.* A drawing or sketch with a pencil; a jotting or note, made in pencil; *fig.* a literary sketch or portrait.

1803 *Lett. Miss Riversdale* I. 325 The friction of his pocket had so completely defaced the pencilling. **1830** CUNNINGHAM *Brit. Paint.* I. 331 He used to sit and fill his copybook with pencillings of flowers. **1835** N. P. WILLIS (*title*) Pencillings by the way. **1845** GEO. ELIOT *Lett.* (1954) I. 187 Thank you for the pencillings... I see that many are obvious and important emendations. **1886** RUSKIN *Præterita* I. iv. 124 Two little pencillings from Canterbury south porch and central tower. **1886** SYMONDS *Renaiss. It.* (1898) VII. viii. 24 Ariosto's bright and many-coloured pencillings, were .. distinguished by .. firmness of drawing. **1923** J. M. MURRY (*title*) Pencillings: little essays on literature.

3. (See quot.)

1875 KNIGHT *Dict. Mech.* 1659/1 To draw a line of white paint along a mortar-joint in a brick wall, to render the joint more conspicuous and contrast with the colour of the bricks. This is termed *pencilling*.

'pencilling, *ppl. a.* [f. PENCIL *v.* + -ING².] That pencils, or uses a pencil.

1887 *Daily Tel.* 12 Mar. 5/2 A registration fee .. is extracted from every member of the pencilling fraternity [= bookmakers].

pencion, -cyon, obs. forms of PENSION.

†**'pen-clerk.** *Obs.* [f. PEN *sb.*² + CLERK.] A 'clerk' whose scholarship extended merely to the use of the pen (as distinguished from *clerk* = clergyman or scholar); a clerk, a secretary; also *fig.* In quot. 1575, a user of the pen, writer.

c **1380** WYCLIF *Wks.* (1880) 246 þei wolen not presente a clerk able of kunnynge .. but a kechen clerk as a penne clerk. **1560** PILKINGTON *Expos. Aggeus* (1562) 181 If he be but a pen-clarke. **1575** LANEHAM *Let.* (1871) 56 Az bad a penclark az I am. **1602** R. T. 5 *Godlie Serm.* 175 The holy prophets and Apostles, the pencléarkes and secretaries of the spirit of God. **1634** W. TIRWHYT tr. *Balzac's Lett.* (vol. 1) 239 None could therein any way compare with our Practitioners and Pen-clarkes.

pencraft ('pɛnkrɑːft, -æ-). *rare.* [f. PEN *sb.*² + CRAFT *sb.*] The craft or art of the pen; the occupation of, or skill in, writing; the business of a writer, writing, penmanship, authorship.

1600 HOLLAND *Livy* IX. xlvi. 349 The same yeare, C. Flavius .. sware an oth, that he would no longer be a notarie and use pencraft. **1759** STERNE *Tr. Shandy* II. iv, I would not give a groat for that man's knowledge in pen-craft. **1831** SCOTT *Ct. Robt.* Introd., To think that I merit not the empty fame alone, but also the more substantial rewards of successful pencraft. **1894** F. S. ELLIS *Reynard Fox* 255 But by good pencraft was the story Told.

pencyfe, pencyfull, obs. ff. PENSIVE, PENSIFUL.

†**pend,** *sb.*¹ *Sc. Obs.* [Derived, in some way, from F. *pendre* or L. *pendēre* to hang: cf. PAND.]

1. = PENDANT *sb.* 2.

1488 *Acc. Ld. High Treas. Scot.* I. 82 Item, a brasselat of gold with hede and pendes of gold. **1507** *Ibid.* III. 263 Item, for j pair of silver bukkilles with pendes gilt for the Kingis schone. **1513** DOUGLAS *Æneis* XII. xiv. 132 On Turnus schuldir, lo! The fey gyrdill hie set dyd appeyr, With stuthis knaw and pendeis schynand cleyr. *a* **1568** '*Wald my gud Ladye that I luif*' 47 in *Bannatyne Poems* (Hunter. Cl.) 658 Hir belt suld be of bowsumnes, .. Baith heid and pendes with hartlines, Inemmellit weill with all.

2. A hanging; a valance of a bed; = PAND.

1578 in Hunter *Biggar & Ho. Fleming* xxvi. (1862) 332 Ane pend of purpour weluot pasmentit wᵗ siluer.

pend, *sb.*² *Sc.* Also 9 pen(n. [f. F. *pendre* or L. *pendēre* to hang.] An arch; an arched or vaulted roof or canopy; the vaulted ground-floor of a 'peel' or bastel-house; an archway; an arched or covered-in passage or entry.

1533 BELLENDEN *Livy* I. viii. (S.T.S.) 50 He ordanit twa preistis to be caryit in ane chariot, maid in maner of ane pend abone þare hede [*curru arcuato*]. **1535** STEWART *Cron. Scot.* (Rolls) II. 441 On Forth thair wes ane brig of tre, But pend or piller, vpone trestis hie. *a* **1568** *Lichtoun's Dreme* 18 in *Bannatyne Poems* (Hunter. Cl.) 289, I tuke .. and kest my self rycht with ane mychtie bend Outthruch the volt and percit nocht the pend. **1616** *Aberdeen Regr.* (1848) II. 338 Twa pilleris and thrie bowis, fynelie wrocht with chapture heidis at the beginning of the symmeris of the pendis. **1635** PERSON *Varieties* I. 33 Mahomet his Chest of Iron .. doth hang miraculously unsupported of any thing, because either the pend or some verticall stone of the Vault .. is of Loadstone. *a* **1670** SPALDING *Troub. Chas. I* (Spalding Cl.) I. 313 At the wastend of the pend, quhairon the gryte stepill stands. **1770** BP. FORBES *Jrnl.* (1886) 307 Join'd to the north wall stood the building now called the College, .. the Pend still entire. **1893** STEVENSON *Catriona* i, We took shelter under a pend at the head of a close or alley. **1893** CROCKETT *Stickit Minister* 199 A low 'pend' or vaulted passage.

b. The vault of heaven.

1663 SIR G. MACKENZIE *Religious Stoic* i. (1685) 2 The stately fabrick of Heavens arched Pend. **1819** W. TENNANT *Papistry Storm'd* (1827) 43 Throu' Aurora's gildet gate, .. And up the pend, at furious rate.

c. An arched conduit; 'a covered sewer, small conduit; also, the entrance to, or the grating over, a conduit or sewer' (Jamieson 1880).

1824 MACTAGGART *Gallovid. Encycl.*, *Penn*, a sewer. **1834** MRS. MAXWELL *Let.* 5 Apr. in *Life J. C. Maxwell* ii. 27 The water gets from the pond through the wall and a pend or small bridge.

d. *attrib.* **pend-close**, an arched passage.

1535 *Aberdeen Regr.* XV. (Jam.), Fyw scoir of pendstanis & vj scoir xv. laidis of wall stanis. **1880** JAMIESON, *Penmouth*, the entrance of a pend or covered gateway.

†**pend,** *sb.*³ *Obs. rare.* [app. f. PEND *v.*³ 3.] Leaning, inclination, tendency, impetus.

1674 N. FAIRFAX *Bulk & Selv.* 65 But we are at no such pend, as we should be fain to fly to either the one or the other. *Ibid.* 119 A pend or earnest strift fromwards, which we call springsomness.

pend, *sb.*⁴ *Obs.* or *dial.* [Variant of PEN *sb.*¹: cf. PEND *v.*²] †**1.** = PEN *sb.*¹ 1. *Obs.*

1542 UDALL *Erasm. Apoph.* 120 b, The facion or lykenesse .. of a pende, wherein to kepe other beastes.

2. *dial.* Pressure; pinch, straits.

1823 E. MOOR *Suffolk Words* 272 'There's the pend': the point of pressure. **1879** in *Arch.* VIII. 172 (E.D.D.) He helps me in a pend.

†**pend,** *sb.*⁵ *Sc.* obs. variant of PEN *sb.*²

†**pend,** *v.*¹ *Obs.* Also 4 **pent.** Pa. t. **pended;** also 5 **pent.** [Aphetic f. *apend*, APPEND *v.*¹, OF. *apendre.*] *intr.* To belong, pertain *to*.

c **1320** *Sir Tristr.* 1090 A word þat pended to pride Tristrem þo spac he. *Ibid.* 1383 Alle þing .. þat pende to marchandis. **13..** *E.E. Allit. P.* B. 1270 [Thai] pyled Alle þe apparement þat pented to þe kyrke. ? *a* **1400** *Morte Arth.* 1612 O payne and o perelle that pendes there-too. *c* **1460** *Towneley Myst.* xxii. 100 Herode .. coud fynd with nokyns gyn Nothyng herapon that pent to any syn.

pend, *v.*² *Obs.* exc. *dial.* [An extended form of PEN *v.*¹: cf. PEND *sb.*⁴ and PENT *ppl. a.*] To pen or shut in; to confine, to limit. Often ***pend up***.

c **1400** *Plowman's T.* 650 Wel worse they woll him tere, And in prison woll hem [1561 him] pend. *c* **1450** *Castle Persev.* 1247 My prowd pouer schal I not pende, tyl I be putte in peynys pyt. **1542** UDALL *Erasm. Apoph.* 120 Suche frowarde creatures as many women are ought rather to bee pended up in a caige of iron. *Ibid.* 297 b, Antipater [was] .. chaced into Lamia .. & there pended up. **1571** GOLDING *Calvin on Ps.* xxi. 12 God wil pend them up in some corner.

b. *dial.* (See quot.) Cf. PEND *sb.*⁴ 2.

a **1825** FORBY *Voc. E. Anglia*, *Pend*, *v.* I. To press or pinch. Commonly said of apparel which does not fit.

pend, *v.*³ [app. a. F. *pend-re*:—late L. *pend-ĕre* for *pendēre* to hang. But in some cases aphetic f. *apend*, APPEND *v.*², or short for *depend.*]

†**1.** *trans.* To hang; to append. *Obs.*

1500–20 DUNBAR *Poems* xliii. 40 Thair seilis ar to pendit. **1600** BONDE *Scut. Reg.* 112 The Cynical Puritan would hang him .. the Independent would pende him if he did not solely depend on him as on God almighty.

2. *intr.* To hang; to depend. **a.** *fig.* (now *dial.*)

1556 J. HEYWOOD *Spider & F.* xxxix. 19 So that woorshipfulnes: and honestnes, Do pende ech on other. **1642** H. MORE *Song Soul* III. I. xv, But if we grant, .. that the souls energie 'Pends not on this base corse. **1839** BAILEY *Festus* xx. (1848) 256 Principles and doctrines pending not Upon the action of the poem here. **1859** HUGHES *Scour. White Horse* viii, 'Pend upon it, a good-bred girl like Lu wouldn't stand it.

b. *literal.* (literary affectation.)

1802 MRS. RADCLIFFE *Gaston de Blondeville* Posth. Wks. 1826 II. 149 To that great tower, still called of Cæsar, which was the keep; on it pended the prison-turret of the merchant. **1857** B'NESS TAUTPHOEUS *Quits* I. vii. 100 A bunch of ponderous seals pending over his portly paunch.

3. To hang over, impend, incline, lean. *Obs.* exc. *dial.* Cf. PEND *sb.*³

1674 N. FAIRFAX *Bulk & Selv.* 121 It asks some time to heave or pend in, before it actually starts. *a* **1825** FORBY *Voc. E. Anglia*, *Pend*, *v.*.. To incline or lean. 'The wall pends this way.'

pend, *v.*⁴ *Sc.* Also 7 **pen.** [prob. f. PEND *sb.*² (though evidenced somewhat earlier).] *trans.* To arch, arch over, vault. Hence **'pended** *ppl. a.*, arched; **'pending** *vbl. sb.*, an arching.

1491 *Acc. Ld. High Treas. Scot.* I. 181 Item, to the massonis of the Palis .. for the pendin of thre voutis. **1497** *Ibid.* I. 342 Item, .. giffin to Wat Merlioune, for his task of Dunbar, that is the pending of the hall, bigging of Hannis toure [etc.]. **1499–1500** *Durham Acc. Rolls* (Surtees) 656 Pro le pendyng ad stagnum molendini. *a* **1684** LAW *Mem.* (1818) 216 Major Learmont .. was taken .. in a vault which he diged under ground, and penned for his hiding. **1823** HOGG *Tales* (1866) 299 Ane could hae gaen oure it like a pendit brigg. **1823** W. TENNANT *Cdl. Beaton* IV. iii. 113 A gousty lump o' black pended stanewark.

pend, obs. pa. t. and pple. of PEN *v.*

†**pendace.** *Sc. Obs.* Also 6 **-ase, -ass.** [A deriv. of F. *pend-re* or L. *pend-ĕre* to hang: cf. OF. *pendace* hanging pap.] = PENDANT 2.

1502 *Acc. Ld. High Treas. Scot.* II. 348 In pairt of payment for hedis and pendases for harnessingis, .. xxviij *s.* **1511** *Ibid.* IV. 196 For the haill harnesing ungilt [of the king's mule] in bukkillis, pendasis, juncturis, naillis and utheris necessaris thairto, .. iij *li.* xij *d.* **1539** *Aberdeen Regr.* (1844) I. 159 Quhar thou tynt the pendace of thi belt in the hie publict gett.

pendale, obs. form of PENDLE *sb.*²

pendall, in *Her.*: see SPINDLE-CROSS.

pendant, -ent ('pɛndənt), *sb.* Forms: 4–6 **pendaunte,** (4–5 **-aunt,** 5 **-awnt**), 4–5 **pendande,** (4 **-aunde,** 5–6 **-and,** 6 **-on**), 5 **pennaunt,** 7 **-ant,** 5– **pendant, -ent.** [a. F. *pendant* (13th c. in Littré), sb. use of pr. pple. of *pendre* to hang.]

I. = F. *pendant* = *pente*, slope.

†**1.** Slope, declivity, inclination (of a hill, etc.). *Obs.* (So in OF.) Cf. HANGING, HANG *sb.*

1387 TREVISA *Higden* (Rolls) I. 109 þe water, þat falleþ dounward and souþward wiþ þe pendaunt toward Ierusalem, takeþ no defoul. *c* **1430** *Pilgr. Lyf Manhode* II. xcviii. (1869) 111 Up on þe pendaunt of an hidous valey, foul and deep and derk. **1578** LYTE *Dodoens* I. lxxxiii. 123 Lowe moyst wooddes, standing in the pendant or hanging of hilles. *c* **1600** NORDEN *Spec. Brit., Cornw.* (1728) 98 The towne seateth nere the nauigable Tamar, on the bendinge or pendent of a hill. **1641** HEYLIN *Help to Hist.* (1671) 358.

II. Something that hangs or is suspended.

2. A loose hanging part of anything, usually of an ornamental character, as a knob, bead, tassel, etc.; now, chiefly, an ornament of some precious metal or stone, attached to a bracelet, necklace, etc.; rarely, an ornamental fringe.

13.. *Gaw. & Gr. Knt.* 168 þe pendauntes of his payttrure. **1377** LANGL. *P. Pl.* B. xv. 7 As persones in pellure with pendauntes of syluer. *c* **1400** *Melayne* 994 He tuke þᵉ pendande in his hande. **14..** *Nom.* in Wr.-Wülcker 735/10 (*Nomina Vestimentorum*) *Hoc pendulum*, a pendand. **1555** EDEN *Decades* 79 Hanginges made of gossampine silke .. hauing golden belles and suche other spangles and pendauntes as the Italians caule *Sonaglios*. **1604** E. G[RIMSTONE] *D'Acosta's Hist. Indies* v. xxix. 419 A litter well furnished with curtins and pendants of diverse fashions. **1621** BURTON *Anat. Mel.* III. ii. III. iii. (1651) 473 Why do they .. deck themselves with pendants, bracelets, ear-rings, chains [etc.]? **1695** J. EDWARDS *Perfect. Script.* 242 Rebekah was presented .. with this forehead-pendant as a pledg. **1876** PLANCHÉ *Cycl. Costume*, *Pendants*, .. the ornaments appended to necklaces. **1877** J. D. CHAMBERS *Div. Worship* 52 Stoles and Maniples, all with pendants of gold and gems.

†**b.** *spec.* The end of a knight's belt or lady's girdle which remained hanging down after passing through the buckle, and was usually fashioned as an ornament. *Obs.*

13.. *Gaw. & Gr. Knt.* 2038 Bot wered not þis ilk wyȝe for wele þis gordel, For pryde of þe pendauntez, þaȝ polyst þay were. **1420** *E.E. Wills* (1882) 45 A gurdill of blake sylke .., with a gode bokyll & a pendaunt, & in þe same pendaunt an ymage of seynt Christofre. **1463** in *Bury Wills* (Camden) 16 To John Hert my gyrdyll with a bokyll and pendaunth of siluir, *Grace me gouerne* wretyn ther in. *a* **1548** HALL *Chron.*, *Hen. VIII* 239 The buckles and pendentes were all of fyne golde. **1577** DEE *Relat. Spir.* II. (1659) 24 She hath a girdle of beaten gold slackly buckled unto her with a pendant of gold down to the ground.

c. *spec.* The pendant part of an ear-ring, an ear-drop. (Common in 17th c.)

1555 EDEN *Decades* 161 The men and the women haue pendauntes of gold and precious stones hanginge at their eares. **1564** A. JENKINSON in *Hakluyt's Voy.* (1598) I. 346 His earerings had pendants of golde, a handfull long. **1589** NASHE *Returne of Pasquill* Wks. (Grosart) I. 138 By Gods helpe, I will hang such a payre of pendents at both your eares. *a* **1657** LOVELACE *Poems* (1864) 232 Hang a poetick pendant in her ear. **1688** *Lond. Gaz.* No. 2340/2 His Eldest Daughter not delivering her Pendants quickly they cut off her Ears with them. **1738** GLOVER *Leonidas* III. 284 Their ears grac'd with pendants. **1824** W. IRVING *T. Trav.* I. 56 A plump Flanders lass, with long gold pendants in her ears. **1882–3** SCHAFF *Encycl. Relig. Knowl.* I. 501 So-called ear-pendants .. were also attached to the ear-rings.

d. Transferred applications.

c **1586** M. ROYDON *Elegie Astrophel* i, The garnisht tree no pendant stird. **1631** BRATHWAIT *Eng. Gentlew.* (1641) 295 The poynt or pendent of her feather wags out of a due posture. **1746–7** HERVEY *Medit.* (1767) I. 128 Not a Blade of Grass, not a single Leaf, but wears the watery Pendants. **1841–4** EMERSON *Ess.* Ser. II. iii. (1876) 78 Man, ordinarily a pendant to events, only half attached.

†**3.** A natural hanging part. *Obs.*

†**a.** *pl.* = TESTES. *Obs.* (So in OF.)

c **1325** *Metr. Hom.* 55 He schar al awai ful rathe His members and his penndanz bathe. **1634** SIR T. HERBERT *Trav.* 15 They gird themselues with a piece of raw leather, and fasten a square peece like the backe of a Gloue, to it, which almost hangs so low as their pendants. **1638** FORD *Fancies* I. ii, Twit me with the decrements of my pendants? Though I am made a gelding [etc.].

†**b.** *Bot.* An anther. *Obs.*

1664 POWER *Exp. Philos.* I. 51 The chives which grow out of red Pinks, and which are tipped with red Pendents, besmeared over with a small Mealy Powder. **1727–41** CHAMBERS *Cycl.*, *Pendants*, among florists, a kind of seeds, growing on stamina, or chives. **1790** BAILEY, *Pendants* (in *Botany*) are the male Part of a Flower called *Apices*, placed on the Top of those Threads which are termed by Botanists *Stamina*.

4. Applied to mechanical constructions.

†**a.** A plumb-line. *Obs. rare.*

c **1440** *Promp. Parv.* 392/1 Pendawnt, of wrytys crafte, or masunry, *pendicula*. **1530** PALSGR. 253/1 Pendant for carpenters, *niueau*.

†**b.** A pendulum. *Obs.*

1644 DIGBY *Nat. Bodies* ix. 74 Galileo .. sayth that to make the same pendant goe twice as fast as it did, .. you must [etc.]. **1653** GAUDEN *Hierasp.* 253 Like weighty Pendants once violently swayed beyond the perpendicular line and poyse, they are a long time before they recover the point of fixation and consistency.

c. A hanging chandelier or gaselier.

1858 SIMMONDS *Dict. Trade*, *Pendant*, a hanging burner for gas. **1903** *Daily Chron.* 20 Jan. 8/1 An escape of gas from a sliding pendant in the room.

†**d.** A pendent escutcheon, a hanging shield.

1629 DEKKER *Londons Tempe* Wks. 1873 IV. 125 On the four angles, or corners over the termes, are placed four pendants with armes in them. *Ibid.* 127 At the four angles of it, four pendants play with the wind. **1727** BAILEY vol. II, *Pendants* (with *Heralds*), pendant escutcheons.

5. *Arch.* **a.** In the Decorated and Perpendicular styles: A knop or other terminal (often richly carved) together with the stem suspending it, hanging from a vault or from the framing of an open timber roof. **b.** In *Carpentry*, A similar object, usually less ornate, on the lower end of the newel at the angle of a staircase when this projects below the string. **c.** A carved (chiefly in bas-relief) or pictorial representation of fruit, flowers, etc., in a hanging position, as an ornamental or decorative feature.

1322 *Ely Sacrist Roll* in Willis *Archit. Nomencl.* (1844) 45 In cariagio et excisione petr' empt'.apud Swaffham quæ vocatur pendaunt. **1427–8** *Ibid.*, Un arche d'alabastre..avec pendants et knottes. **1587** FLEMING *Contn. Holinshed* III. 1315/2 In the top of this house was wrought..upon Canuas, works of iuie and hollie with pendents made of wicker rods. **1620** in Swayne *Sarum Churchw. Acc.* (1896) 171 Turninge of Banisters and pendantes, 8*s*. **1662** GERBIER *Princ.* 6 Pendants, Garlands,..and an infinite number of Ornaments, which are put on the Frize. **1838** PARKER *Gloss. Archit.* (ed. 2), *Pendant, Pendent*, a sculptured ornament hanging from a Gothic roof, either of stone or wood; chiefly used in the latest, or Perpendicular style. **1842–76** GWILT *Archit.* Gloss. s.v., The pendent was also used very frequently to timber-framed roofs, as in that of Crosby Hall, which has a series of pendents along the centre of it. **1859** PARKER *Dom. Archit.* III. iii. 59 Pendants are more commonly used in the roofs of halls than in those of churches. **1868** *Chambers's Encycl.* IX. 76/2 Staircases..had usually massive oak balusters..and were ornamented with carved panels, pendants, &c.

6. *Arch.* In open timber roofs: **a.** A wooden post placed against the wall, usually resting on a corbel, its upper end secured to the hammer-beam or to the lower end of the principal rafter; also called ***pendant-post***. **b.** A spandrel formed by the side-post, the curved brace, and the tie-beam or the hammer-beam. **c.** In stone-work: A shaft worked on the masonry of the wall, supporting the ribs of a vault or an arch or the pendant-post of an open timber roof, and resting on a corbel or terminating in a decorated boss.

[**1359**: see *pendant-post* in 14.] **1452** in Willis & Clark *Cambridge* (1886) I. 282 Principal Bemys with braces and pendaunttes... Item, atte euery end of the pendaunt shalbe a angell. **1579** *Ibid.* 310 Pendons to the principals, eche of vj foote longe. **1596** SPENSER *F.Q.* IV. x. 6 It was a bridge ybuilt in goodly wize With curious Corbes and pendants graven faire. **1706** PHILLIPS, *Pendent*, a Supporter of Stone in Building. **1875** PARKER *Gloss. Archit.* (ed. 4), *Pendant* This name was also formerly used for the spandrels very frequently found in Gothic roofs under the ends of the tie-beams, which are sustained at the bottom by corbels or other supports projecting from the walls. In this position it is usually called a *Pendant-post*. **1879** SIR G. SCOTT *Lect. Archit.* II. 226 These columns being converted into pendants, the structural arches supply the support demanded.

7. *Naut.* (***rigging pendant.***) A short rope hanging from the head of a (main or fore) mast, yard-arm, or clew of a sail, and having at its lower end a block or a thimble spliced to an eye for receiving the hooks of the fore and main tackles. Also a similar device used in other parts of a ship. Also called PENNANT.

Often with qualification, defining position or purpose, as *brace-, fish-, reef-tackle-, stay-tackle-, yard-tackle-, rudder-pendant.*

1485 *Naval Acc. Hen. VII* (1896) 36 Double pendaunts.. viij, Single pendaunts..viij. *Ibid.* 37 Pendaunts with double poleis [= pullies]..ij. *Ibid.*, Brasse pendaunts for the mayne yerdes.. ij. **1495** *Ibid.* 255–6. **1497** *Ibid.* 327 Pendantes for Bower takles. **1627** CAPT. SMITH *Seaman's Gram.* v. 20 A Pendant is a short rope made fast at one end to the head of the Mast or the Yards arme, hauing at the other end a blocke with a shiuer to reeue some running rope in. **1723** *Lond. Gaz.* No. 6129/3 Eleven Inch Cable laid Pendant. **1776** FALCONER *Dict. Marine, Pendent, pantoire*, is also a short piece of rope, fixed under the shrouds, upon the head of the main-mast and fore-mast, from which it depends as low as the cat-harpings, having an eye in the lower end which is armed with an iron thimble... There are..many other pendents..which are generally single or double ropes, to whose lower extremities is attached a block, or tackle. *c* **1825** CHOYCE *Log Jack Tar* (1891) 4 We..secured it [the rudder] to the stern post by means of pendants and tackles. **1862** *Catal. Internat. Exhib.* II. XII. 5 The pendants..are unwound evenly as the boat descends into the water.

b. ***Irish pendant*** (jocular), any rope yarn, reef-point, gasket, etc., hanging loose.

1840 R. H. DANA *Bef. Mast* xxii. (1854) 124 There was no rust, no dirt, no rigging hanging slack, no fag ends of ropes and 'Irish pendants' aloft.

†**8.** Used by confusion for PENNON. *Obs.*

1552 HULOET, Banners, pendauntes, or Standers, splayed in battayle, *signa infesta*. **1632** SHERWOOD, A Penon (or Pendant) in a ship, or on the top of a horsemans staffe. **1644** EVELYN *Diary* 20 Oct., Over which hang divers banners and pendants, with other trophies taken by them from the Turkes.

b. A pennon-shaped wind-vane. [mod.F. *penon*.]

1860 *Merc. Marine Mag.* VII. 25 A..roof..surmounted by an iron weather pendant.

9. *Naut.* A tapering flag, very long in the fly and short in the hoist; *spec.* that flown at the mast-head of a vessel in commission, unless distinguished by a flag or broad pendant (see b).

The flying of the pendant at half-mast denotes the death of the captain, its absence that the vessel is out of commission.

[In this sense presumably a corruption of PENNON (q.v.); perhaps by assimilation to sense 7 above; but *pendant* has been in official use from the earliest date to which the name has as yet been traced, though the accepted pronunciation is *pennant*, which has also been the most common non-official spelling since *c* 1690.]

1485 *Nav. Acc. Hen. VII* (1896) 40 Gittons of Say; Standerdes of Say;..Stremers of Say; Pendauntes of Say for the Crane lyne. **1495** *Ibid.* 260 Baners of say..Gyttornes of say..Pendantes of say with Rede Crosses and Roses. *Ibid.* 273. **1588** *Survey of the 'Ark Royal'* in *Defeat of Armada* II. 246 Streamers xiiii; Pendants xvi;..Flaggs of St. George iii. **1599** MINSHEU *Sp. Dict.*, *Gallardétes*, streamers or pendents in ships. **1688** R. HOLME *Armoury* III. xv. (Roxb.) 48/2 Pendant or Streamers, are those colours, which are hung out on the yard Armes, or from the head of the masts..to beautifie the ship. **1712** *Lond. Gaz.* No. 5051/3 The Contractors for furnishing Her Majesty's Navy with Colours (as Ensigns, Jacks, Pendants and Fanes). **1712** E. COOKE *Voy. S. Sea* 4, I will hoist a Pendant at my Mizen-Peak. **1797** NELSON in Nicolas *Disp.* (1845) II. 346, I hoisted my Pendant on the Irresistible. **1825** H. B. GASCOIGNE *Nav. Fame* 59 Our warlike Pendant, master of the seas. **1854** *Tait's Mag.* XXI. 268 With vigorous stroke of oar and pendant flying fair.

fig. **1687** *Advise to Testholders* ix. in *Third Coll. Poems* (1689) 21/2 Herbert, whose fall a greater blow did feel, From topmast pendant to the lower Keel. **1711** SHAFTESB. *Charact.*, *Moralists* II. iv, Consider where we are, and in what a universe!..when instead of seeing to the highest pendants, we see only some lower deck, and are..confin'd even to the hold and meanest station of the vessel.

b. ***broad pendant***: a short swallow-tailed pendant flown as the distinctive mark of a commodore's ship in a squadron.

1716 *Lond. Gaz.* No. 5485/3 The Swedish Fleet with two Flags and seven broad Pendants. **1743** BULKELEY & CUMMINS *Voy. S. Seas* 2 The Commodore hoisted his broad Pendant, and was saluted by every Ship in the Squadron. **1813** WELLINGTON in Gurw. *Desp.* XI. 244, I beg leave to congratulate you upon your hoisting a broad pendant. **1882** *Navy List* July 451 Table Money is..payable only while Flag or Broad Pendant is flying within the limits of Station.

c. A ship-of-war with pendant flying.

1802 G. ROSE *Diaries* (1860) I. 480 There were..101 sail of pendants.

†**10.** *Her.* = LAMBEAU. *Obs. rare.*

1634 PEACHAM *Gentl. Exerc.* III. 151 It [a label] is a kind of fillet,..it is the difference of the elder brother, the father being alive, it is drawne of two, three, four, or five pendants, not commonly above. **1727–41** CHAMBERS *Cycl.*, *Pendant*.. a term applied to the parts hanging down from the label.

III. 11. That by which something is hung or suspended: in quot. 1580, a ring or the like for a bunch of keys; now *spec.* that part of a watch by which it is suspended, consisting of the pendant-shank or stem and the pendant-ring or bow.

1580 HOLLYBAND *Treas. Fr. Tong*, *Pendant de clefs*, a pendant or thing that hangeth. **1611** COTGR., *Pendant*, a pendant; a hanger; any thing that hangeth, or whereat another thing hangs. **1678** *Lond. Gaz.* No. 1363/4 Lost..a gold Chain Watch,..the Christal and Pendant Ring broken off. **1721** *Ibid.* No. 6002/3 Lost.., a Gold repeating Watch, Name..engraved on the inner Case under the Pendant. **1824** in *Spirit Pub. Jrnls.* (1825) 50 John Sheen made such a desperate tug at his watch, that the pendant broke. **1884** F. J. BRITTEN *Watch & Clockm.* 24 In the rack with pendant up for twelve hours it [a watch] is found to have lost 8 s... With pendant down for twelve hours it is found to have lost 2 s.

b. Anything suspended or hung up: in quot. a votive offering. *rare.*

1621 BURTON *Anat. Mel.* II. i. III. i. (1651) 225 Æsculapius ..his temple was daily full of patients, and as many severall tables, inscriptions, pendants, donaries, &c...as at this day at our Lady of Loretta's.

12. A thing, esp. a picture, forming a parallel, match, or companion to another; a match, companion-piece. Also said of a person. Often pronounced as French (pɑ̃dɑ̃).

['Il se dit de deux objets d'art à peu près pareils, et destinés à figurer ensemble en se correspondant' (Littré).]

1788 W. EDEN in *G. Rose's Diaries* (1860) I. 78 It [a mere red ribbon] certainly would be considered as a *pendant* or companion to the Duke of Dorset's blue ribbon. **1809** WELLINGTON in Gurw. *Desp.* IV. 565, I think the chace out of Portugal is a *pendant* for the retreat to Corunna. **1848** MRS. JAMESON *Sacr. & Leg. Art* (1850) 287 When St. Catharine is grouped with other saints, her usual pendant is St. Barbara. **1876** GEO. ELIOT *Dan. Der.* lxii, The figure of Mirah..made a strange pendant to this shabby, foreign-looking, eager, and gesticulating man.

b. An additional statement, consideration, etc. which completes or complements another; a complement, counterpart.

1841 MISS SEDGWICK *Lett. Abr.* I. 93 Mr. B. told a pendant to this pretty story. **1862** MERIVALE *Rom. Emp.* lxii. (1865) VII. 401 The narrative of the historian forms a fitting pendant to that of the satirist. **1884** *Standard* 4 Mar. 5/2 The article called 'Rich Men's Dwellings' was avowedly a pendant to the paper..of Lord Salisbury on 'Labourers and Artisans' Dwellings'.

†**13.** *pl.* Pending or unsettled matters; 'unpaid claims' (Jam.). *Obs.*

1492 *Acc. Ld. High Treas. Scot.* I. 206 Sowme of thir pendentis .vᶜxv *li.* vjs. viijd. Of the quhilkis the comptare sais he has obligacionis and in his bukis.

IV. 14. *attrib.* and *Comb.*, as ***pendant-ring***, ***-shank*** (see sense 11); ***pendant-like***, ***-shaped*** adjs.; ***pendant-wise*** adv.; †**pendant-bearer**, pennon-bearer, ensign; **pendant-bow**, the ring or 'bow' of a watch-stem (BOW *sb.*[1] 11); **pendant-fittings**, hanging fittings for electric light; **pendant-post** *Arch.* = sense 6 a; **pendant-tackle**: see quot.; **pendant-winding** *a.*, said of a keyless watch which is wound by rotating the pendant-shank or stem; called also *stem-winding*.

1552 HULOET, *Pendant bearer, *signifer*. **1901** WATERHOUSE *Conduit Wiring* 39 Using *pendant-fittings in place of ceiling roses. *a* **1711** KEN *Hymns Evang.* Poet. Wks. 1721 I. 183 In Stars..by the Seraphs in Mosaick wrought, Jesus of Nazareth, King of the Jews, Wav'd *pendent-like. **1359** *Ely Sacrist Roll* in Parker *Gloss. Archit.* (1850) 346 In xii lapidibus pro *pendaunt postes portandis... In viii magnis arboribus quercinis pro postes pendaunts. **1850** PARKER *Gloss. Archit.*, *Pendent post*, in a mediæval principal roof truss, is a short post placed against the wall, the lower end rests upon a corbel or capital, the upper end is fixed to the tie-beam. **1875** [see sense 6]. **1843** *Penny Cycl.* XXVII. 108/1 The *pendant-shank or push-piece. **1895** *Westm. Gaz.* 29 July 8/1 Four large *pendant-shaped pearls set in diamond cups. **1884** KNIGHT *Dict. Mech.* Suppl. 666/1 **Pendant Tackle*,..a tackle rigged from the masthead pendant. **1875** *Ibid.* 1660/1 **Pendant-winding Watch*. **1545** RAYNOLD *Byrth Mankynde* 14 How be it the myddle parte ..onely heldith *pendant wise or lokith downwarde.

Hence **'pendanted** *a.*, having or furnished with pendants; **'pendanting** *sb.*, pendants collectively, or as a kind of work.

1664 EVELYN *Acc. Archit.* in *Freart's Archit.* etc. 131 The Masonry at the front of these [Arches] being cut by a peculiar slope of the Stone is call'd Pennanted, till it come to joyn with the *mensula*. **1815** J. SMITH *Panorama Sc. & Art* I. 163 A regular and valuable series, from the plain Norman round arched roof, to the elaborate pendanted roof of Henry the VII's chapel. **1851** RUSKIN *Stones Ven.* I. xxix. §4, I would rather..have a plain ridged Gothic vault, with all its rough stones visible..than all the fanning and pendanting and foliation that ever bewildered Tudor wight.

pendant, *a.* (*prep.*), the earlier but now less usual spelling of PENDENT *a.*

A. *adj.* = PENDENT *a.*, q.v.

†**B.** quasi-*prep.* = PENDING *prep.* [= F. *pendant*.] *Obs. rare.*

1642 tr. *Perkins' Prof. Bk.* ix. §598. 259 Issue in taile bringeth a Formedon against the discontinuee, and pendant the suit sheweth the deed of entail [= 'the suit being pendant'].

pendase, -ass, variants of PENDACE *Obs.*

‖**pendaul**, variant of PANDAL.

pendaunde, -aunt(e, -awnt, obs. ff. PENDANT.

pendecagon (pɛnˈdɛkəgən). *rare.* [Short for **pentedecagon*, f. Gr. πέντε five + δέκα ten + -γωνος -angled.] A plane figure having fifteen angles and fifteen sides: = QUINDECAGON.

1695 ALINGHAM *Geom. Epit.* 95 It is also necessary to inscribe a pentagone in a Circle, as also a pendecagone.

pendecule, -ekle, obs. forms of PENDICLE.

pendele, obs. form of PENDLE *sb.*[2]

‖**pendeloque.** [F. *pendeloque* (pɑ̃dəlɔk), also *pendeloche*, f. *pendeler* to dangle.] A pendant, of jewellery or the like, used as an ornament. *spec.* a gemstone esp. a diamond cut in the shape of a drop and used as a pendant. Also *attrib.*

[**1656** BLOUNT *Glossogr.*, *Pendiloches* (Fr.) jags, danglings, or things that hang danglingly; with Jewellers they are the lowest part of Jewels, which hang in that manner.] **1864** CARLYLE *Fredk. Gt.* XVI. vii. (1872) VI. 214 Seven pieces of jewelry, pendeloques, &c., with price affixed. **1945, 1949** [see NAVETTE]. **1955** M. GILBERT *Sky High* ii. 25 A pair of pendeloque-cut diamond earrings set in platinum filigree. **1959** *Times* 24 Feb. 18/7 A large fancy golden pendeloque diamond. **1960** H. HAYWARD *Antique Coll.* 214/2 *Pendeloque*, a gemstone of drop-shape, faceted and used as a pendant. **1973** *Times* 25 Aug. 17/2 There are nine well-recognized styles of lapidary work upon the diamond: brilliant-cut, step-cut, emerald-cut, rose-cut, marquise, briolette, baguette, cabochon and pendeloque. **1974** *Encycl. Brit. Macropædia* VII. 979/2 Noteworthy among the gemstones are an 86-carat pendeloque diamond, as well as large emeralds and red spinels.

†**'pendence.** *Obs. rare*$^{-1}$. [Cf. OF. *pendance* slope, inclination (Godef.), It. *pendenza* 'a downehanging' (Florio): see PENDENT and -ENCE.] Slant, inclination; pitch (as of a roof).

1624 WOTTON *Archit.* in *Reliq.* (1651) 269 The Italians are very precise in giving the Cover a gracefull pendence of sloapnesse.

pendency (ˈpɛndənsɪ). Also 7 **-ancie.** [f. PENDENT: see -ENCY.]

1. The state or condition of being pending or continuing undecided, or awaiting settlement.

1637 J. WILLIAMS *Holy Table* 43 They would not serve his turn even in that pendancie. **1726** AYLIFFE *Parergon* 79 Nor can the Appellant alledge Pendency of Suit before the Judge *a Quo*. **1848** ARNOULD *Mar. Insur.* I. iii. (1866) I. 102 At any time during the pendency of the risk. **1850** E. S. SEYMOUR *Sk. Minnesota* xii. 208 Out of this arose one or two unsuccessful arbitrations. During their pendency the mills came into the possession of the Boston Company. **1972** *N.Y. Law Jrnl.* 22 Aug. 6/1 Section 1830.12 Petitions; content; pendency of prior proceeding. **1979** 'A. HAILEY' *Overload* II. iii. 119 During the pendency of the case, surely there were backstage discussions with commission staff?

2. Pendent position; droopingness, droop. *rare.*

1770 T. WHATELY *Mod. Gardening* 142 Two or three groupes of large trees, feathering down to the bottom, and by the pendency of their branches favouring the declivity. **1831** S. WARREN *Diary Physic.* vii, Her head covered with a velvet cap, over which drooped in snowy pendency, an ostrich feather.

pendent, -ant ('pɛndənt), *a.* (*prep.*) [orig. *penda(u)nt*, a. F. *pendant*: see PENDANT *sb.* About 1600, this began to be written *pendent*, after L. *pendens, -entem*, and this has now become the more frequent spelling, though *pendant* is often used, esp. in senses associated with those of the sb.]

1. Hanging; suspended from or as from the point of attachment, with the point or end hanging downwards; dependent. Of a tree: having downhanging branches. Formerly often following its sb., esp. in Heraldic use.

† *letters pendants* (so OF.): letters having seals attached. *c* **1412** HOCCLEVE *De Reg. Princ.* 423 Gownes of scarlet, .. with pendant sleues downe On þe grounde. **1481** CAXTON *Godeffroy* cxiii. 171 He sente lettres pendantes oueral his londes. **1486** *Bk. St. Albans* B j, The pendaunte federis. **1593** NASHE *Four Lett. Confut.* Wks. (Grosart) II. 220 A iolly long red peake .. whereat a man might hang a Iewell, it was so sharpe and pendant. **1598** SHAKS. *Merry W.* IV. vi. 42 Loose en-roab'd, With Ribonds-pendant, flaring 'bout her head. **1602** —— *Ham.* IV. vii. 173 There on the pendant boughes, her Coronet weeds Clambring to hang. **1625** in Rymer *Foedera* (1726) XVIII. 237 One emrauld Pendent, one blewe Saphire, and three Pearls Pendent. **1727–41** CHAMBERS *Cycl.* s.v. *Barometer, Pendant Barometer* is a machine rather pretty, and curious, than useful. **1807** WORDSW. *Wh. Doe* IV. 91 The pendent woodbine. **1858** LYTTON *What will he do* I. v, The boat gently brushed aside their pendant boughs.

b. *pendent with*, hanging with, hung with.

1853 KANE *Grinnell Exp.* viii. (1856) 60 Their tunnel-like roofs were often pendant with icicles.

2. Overhanging; jutting or leaning over; also, descending in a steep slope; slanting; placed or hanging on a steep slope.

c **1400** *Laud Troy Bk.* 9244 With swerdes gode that were trenchaunt Fauȝt thei to-gedur by that hil pendaunt. **1515** BARCLAY *Egloges* iv. (1570) C vj b/1 A mountayne .. With pendant cliffes of stones harde as flent. **1587** FLEMING *Contn. Holinshed* III. 1008/2 The whole countrie .. is pendent towards the south and west parts. **1613–39** I. JONES in Leoni tr. *Palladio's Archit.* (1742) II. 51 The top .. is pendent, to throw the Rain-water off. **1644** EVELYN *Diary* 22 Oct., Another pendant towre like that at Pisa. **1708** J. PHILIPS *Cyder* I. 109 On .. that cloud-piercing hill Plinlimmon, from afar the traveller kens Astonish'd, how the goats their shrubby browze Gnaw pendant. **1847** EMERSON *Poems* (1857) 40 By the pendent mountain's shade.

b. *fig.* Overhanging; impending. *rare.*

1805 EUGENIA DI ACTON *Nuns of Desert* I. 28 The clouds blackened, the tempest was pendant. **1877** TENNYSON *Harold* II. ii, Having .. lied like a lad That dreads the pendent scourge.

3. Hanging or floating unsupported in the air or in space; supported above the ground on arches, columns, etc. Now *rare* or *Obs.*

c **1600** *Timon* IV. iii. (Shaks. Soc.) 67, I hearde from Pseudocheus .. that the moone was an ilande pendante in the air. **1601** HOLLAND *Pliny* XXXVI. xii. II. 578 The pendant gallery and walking place at Gnidos. **1603** SHAKS. *Meas. for M.* III. i. 126 To be imprison'd in the viewlesse windes And blowne with restlesse violence round about The pendant world. *c* **1790** IMISON *Sch. Art* I. 247 An inverted image of the object will .. seem to hang pendant in the air. **1813** EUSTACE *Tour Italy* (1815) II. 15 Strabo .. represents it as a pendent garden raised on lofty arches of white stone, planted with evergreen shrubs.

4. Hanging in the balance, remaining undecided or unsettled, pending.

1633 G. HERBERT *Temple, Lent* v, Those same pendant profits, which the spring And Easter intimate. **1829** SOUTHEY in *Q. Rev.* XLI. 412 Our then pendant disputes in America. **1832** —— *Hist. Penins. War* III. 204 To wait the effect of a treaty then pendent with Spain. **1880** MUIRHEAD *Ulpian* ii. §2 So long as the condition is pendent he remains a slave of the heir's.

5. *Gram.* Of which the grammatical construction is left incomplete.

1849 W. FITZGERALD tr. *Whitaker's Disput.* 150 Though there be in the holy scriptures some pendent sentences, and inversions. **1859** tr. *Bengel's Gnomon* I. 526 The construction of the language is pendent. **1884** FARRAR *Camb. Grk. Test., Luke* xxi. 6 Ταῦτα ἃ θεωρεῖτε. It is what is called the 'pendent nominative'.

‖ **pen'dente 'lite.** *Law.* [L. *pendente*, ablative of *pendens* hanging, pendent, *līte*, abl. of *līs* lawsuit; lit. 'with the lawsuit pending'.] While a suit is pending; during litigation: a Latin phrase of the Roman Law, often used in English context.

1726 J. AYLIFFE *Parergon Juris Canonici Anglicani* 235 Because he came in *Pendente lite*. *a* **1736** W. P. WILLIAMS *Rep.* II. 580 The ordinary should have power to grant administration during absence, as well as .. *pendente lite*. **1833** *Penny Cycl.* I. 340/1 The court will, generally speaking, allot alimony to the wife *pendente lite*, or during the continuance of the litigation. **1872** *Wharton's Law Lex.* (ed. 5) 719/1 Administration *pendente lite* is sometimes granted when an action is commenced in the Probate Court touching the validity of a will. **1964** R. W. HANSEN in A. E. Wilkerson *Rights of Children* (1973) 240 This conflict may be revealed at the pre-trial hearing before the Family Court commissioner on *pendente lite* support orders, or at the time of trial before the court. **1972** *N.Y. Law Jrnl.* 10 Oct. 1/7 Judge Motley also refused to enjoin the defendant .. pendente lite from distributing its similarly designed loudspeakers. **1973** *Ibid.* 31 Aug. 18/3 The cross motion for an order for renewal of plaintiff's motion for alimony pendente lite is denied, no sufficiently persuasive ground in support of same having been demonstrated.

pendentive (pɛn'dɛntɪv), *sb.* (*a.*) [ad. F. *pendentif, -ive* (1567 in Hatz.-Darm.), f. L. *pendent-em* hanging: see -IVE.]

1. *Arch.* Each of the spherical triangles (or triangular segments) formed by the intersection of a hemispherical dome (or in extended use, a conical surface) by two pairs of opposite arches springing from the four supporting columns; *orig.* (as in the Byzantine and derived architectures) supporting an independent dome, cupola, or the like. Also (as in Gothic architecture) extended to each of the similar segments constituting that part of a groined vault resting on a single impost.

1727–41 CHAMBERS *Cycl.* s.v., The pendentives are usually of brick, or soft stone. **1823** P. NICHOLSON *Pract. Build.* 148 Pendentives are either spherical, spheroidal, or conical. **1840** *Penny Cycl.* XVII. 402/2. **1842–76** GWILT *Archit.* §2091 To cover the ceiling of a square room with conical pendentives. **1849** FREEMAN *Archit.* 168 Four columns .. served to support the cupola. .. Being raised on a square ground plan, the angles were connected by pendentives, whose ingenious and varied combinations are especially remarkable.

¶ 2. Incorrect uses: = PENDANT 5, 6.

1845 FORD *Handbk. Spain* I. III. 374 The honeycomb stalactical pendentives .. are all constructed on mathematical principles; they are composed of numerous prisms, united by their contiguous lateral surfaces. **1861** MISS E. A. BEAUFORT *Egypt. Sepulchres* I. ii. 16 The high flat walls are unrelieved by .. any architectural ornament, save one invariable line of cornice along the top of the wall, formed of simple pendentives of three bricks in the upper row, two bricks in the second, and one brick below these. **1893** H. G. KEENE *Hist. India* I. ii. §1. 60 It is now in five storeys, the two lower divided from the rest by balconies, supported on rich pendentives going all round the circumference.

B. *adj.* Of or belonging to pendentives; of the form of or having pendentives.

1790 W. WRIGHTE *Grotesque Archit.* 8 The dome was .. ornamented with pendentive shell and frosted work. **1825** J. NICHOLSON *Operat. Mechanic* 578 *Pendentive cradling*, is a cove bracketing, springing from the rectangular walls of an apartment upwards to the ceiling, so as to form the horizontal part of the ceiling into a complete circle or ellipsis. **1840** *Penny Cycl.* XVII. 402/2 The dome of the hall or principal office of the London and Westminster Bank is a pendentive one. **1879** SCOTT *Lect. Archit.* xvi. II. 242.

'pendently, *adv. rare.* Also **-antly.** [f. PENDENT *a.* + -LY[2].] In a pendent manner; in quot. 1662, in dependence.

1662 GURNALL *Chr. in Arm.* verse 19. iii. §4 (1669) 491/2 If any in the World need walk pendantly upon God, more than others, the Minister is he. **1847** WEBSTER, *Pendently*, in a pendent manner.

pendice, obs. var. *pentise*, PENTHOUSE.

pendicle ('pɛndɪk(ə)l). Chiefly *Sc.* Also 6 -ikle, -ikill, -ekle, -ecule. [f. L. type *pendicul-um, f. *pendēre* to hang + *-culum*, suffix forming names of instruments, also often diminutive. Cf. L. *pendicul-us* (in med.L. *pendiclum*) a cord or rope to hang with.]

1. A hanging ornament, a pendant. Now *rare.*

1488 *Acc. Ld. High Treas. Scot.* I. 85 Item, a ruf and pendiclis of the same. **1560** in *Registr. Cart. Ecclesie S. Egidii* (Bann. Cl.) p. xlvii, Sanct Gelis coitt, and the litill pendekle of reid veluett that hang at his feit. **1641** R. BAILLIE *Lett. & Jrnls.* (1775) I. 251 All casts him out of their thoughts, as a pendicle at the Lieutenant's ear. **1878** H. M. STANLEY *Dark Cont.* 59 The natives dress their hair in long ringlets, .. adorned with pendicles of copper.

2. Something dependent on or pertaining to something else, as a subordinate part or adjunct; an appurtenance, appendage, dependency.

1533 BELLENDEN *Livy* I. ii. (S.T.S.) 16 Fra þe begynnyng of lavyne to þe begynnyng of Alba þe colony and pendikillis þareof war xxx ȝeris. **1577–95** *Descr. Isles Scotl.* in Skene *Celtic Scotl.* III. App. 428 The remanent .. Iles were reknit but as pertinents and pendicles of the said four Iles. **1609** *Sc. Acts Jas. VI* (1816) IV. 448 The keiping of the saidis signettis shall be .. a particular pendicle of the said office of secretarie. **1792** *Statist. Acc. Scot.* III. 330 The Parsonage of Stobo .. having four churches belonging to it, which were called the Pendicles of Stobo. **1883** STEVENSON *Silverado Sq.* 107 A pendicle of Silverado mine.

b. *spec.* A small piece of ground, a cottage, etc. forming a dependent part of an estate; in later use *esp.* such a part separately sublet.

1546 *Reg. Privy Council Scot.* I. 43 The said castell, .. parkis, medowis, pairtis and pendeculis thairof and thair pertinentis. *a* **1649** in *Drumm. of Hawth.'s Wks.* (1711) 157 That none of them trouble or molest Mr. William Drummond of Hawthornden his said lands, with houses, biggings, yards, parts, pendicles, and pertinents thereof. **1791** NEWTE *Tour Eng. & Scot.* 129 These feudal vassals let smaller lots .. to the husbandmen; and these again sub-let pendicles to the great body of the labouring people. **1814** SCOTT *Wav.* xlii. **1881** in *Edin. Rev.* July 279 To roll into one conveniently-sized farm, several of the small, often scattered, parts, pendicles, and pertinents.

pendicler ('pɛndɪklə(r)). *Sc.* [f. prec. + -ER[1].] The holder of a pendicle; an inferior tenant.

1791 NEWTE *Tour Eng. & Scot.* 130 Neither the grant of the extensive domain to the immediate tenant of the Crown, .. nor that of the husbandman to the pendicler and cotter, was .. absolute and perpetual. **1794** *Statist. Acc. Scot.* XI. 357 The parish also abounded with pendiclers, or inferior tenants. **1893** J. SKINNER *Autobiog. Metaphysician* xxxviii. 202 The antipathy of the large farmers to the pendicler class.

pendicu'lation, obs. form of PANDICULATION.

† **pen'dilatory,** *a. Obs. rare*[−1]. [f. F. *pendiller* (13th c. in Hatz.-Darm.), corresp. to a L. type *pendillāre, dim. or freq. of *pendēre* to hang: the Eng. formation is Urquhart's, after the frequent ending *-atory*: see -ORY[2].] Pendulous.

1653 URQUHART *Rabelais* I. xlii, In his dangling and pendilatory swagging [F. *en pendillant*].

pending ('pɛndɪŋ), *ppl. a.* and *prep.* [Formed after F. *pend-ant*, L. *pend-ens* hanging, in suspense, suspended, not decided, with Eng. ppl. ending -ING[2]. Cf. PEND *v.*[3]] A. *ppl. a.*

1. Remaining undecided, awaiting decision or settlement. Orig. of a lawsuit; cf. L. *pendente lite*. So ***pending basket, tray***: a basket or tray for correspondence or other papers awaiting attention or decision.

1797 NELSON in Nicolas *Disp.* (1845) II. 371, I have to thank you for your account of Prizes pending in the Admiralty Court. **1818** JAS. MILL *Brit. India* I. I. i. 13 A treaty was then pending with Spain. **1838** PRESCOTT *Ferd. & Is.* (1846) I. iii. 185 To abide the issue of the pending negotiations. **1859** LANG *Wand. India* 381 While this little, but interesting, debate was pending between the prosecutor and the prisoners. **1946** R. GRAVES *Poems 1938–45* 30 World patents pending; tested in the shops. **1955** E. WAUGH *Officers & Gentlemen* I. viii. 102 Guy turned over the papers in the 'pending' tray. **1957** M. SUMMERTON *Sunset Hour* i. 18, I threw the folder into my pending basket. **1961** 'T. HINDE' *For Good of Company* i. 18 Out-tray to his right, in- and pending-trays to his left. **1973** J. WAINWRIGHT *Pride of Pigs* 50 The day clerks .. booked it in—this avalanche of paper—and .. tossed it into a series of 'pending' trays. The night clerks *dealt* with it. **1975** *Times* 5 Dec. 2/1 An extradition warrant .. was in a tray marked 'pending'.

2. a. Hanging, overhanging. *rare.*

1756 AMORY *Buncle* (1770) I. 221 The pending rocks in view inclosed a space of four acres.

b. Impending, imminent. *rare.*

1806 *Glencore Tower* I. 181 A dreadful blow pending over thee. **1833** MRS. BROWNING *Prom. Bound* 52 Innocent of all These pending ills.

B. *prep.* or quasi-*prep.* a. The pres. pple., in Fr. *pendant*, Eng. *pending*, was used in a construction corresp. to the L. ablative absolute; thus L. *pendente lite*, F. *pendant le procès* (= *le procès étant pendant*), *pendant* or *pending the suit* (while the suit is pending): see PENDANT *a.* B. When the pple. stood before the sb., having the same function as a prep., it came gradually to be viewed as such, = During, throughout the continuance of, in the process of. Cf. DURING, NOTWITHSTANDING.

1642 J. M. *Argt. conc. Militia* 18 The King may dissolve a Parliament when he pleaseth, but, pending Parliament unadjourned, the King can not retarde their proceedings. **1726** AYLIFFE *Parergon* (J.), A person, pending suit with the diocesan, shall be defended in the possession. **1818** CRUISE *Digest* (ed. 2) V. 194 The daughter .. brought a formedon for the recovery of the estate tail; pending which all the proclamations were made. **1855** MOTLEY *Dutch Rep.* I. iii. (1866) 106 Pending the peace negotiations, Philip had been called upon to mourn for his wife and father.

b. While awaiting, until the occurrence of, until.

1838 DICKENS *Nich. Nick.* xxi, Pending his return, Kate and her mother were shown into a dining-room. **1884** *Times* (weekly ed.) 5 Sept. 15/1 Pending further emigration or clearances. **1894** C. N. ROBINSON *Brit. Fleet* 149 Pending the completion of the new building.

pendis, -ise, -ize, obs. var. *pentise*, PENTHOUSE.

pendle[1] ('pɛnd(ə)l). *Obs.* or *dial.* Also 7 pendill, -all, -el, 9 -il. [From L. *pendēre* or F. *pendre* to hang: for sense 1 cf. F. *pendille* 'a thing that hangs danglingly' (Cotgr.), and mod.F. *pendeloque* hanging ornament; cf. also PENDULE *sb.*]

† 1. A hanging ornament, a pendant. *Obs.*

1663 GERBIER *Counsel* 69 Heads and Pendills four inches Diameter, at four pence a head, six inches Diameter, six pence a head. **1667** PRIMATT *City & C. Build.* 66 Posts, Rails, Bannisters, Pendalls, and Balls for conveniency and ornament. ? *a* **1670** in W. Hunter *Biggar & Ho. Fleming* xxvii. (1862) 342 The lady gaed up the Parliament Stairs, Wi' pendles in her lug sae bonnie. **1710** RUDDIMAN *Douglas' Æneis* Gloss. s.v. *Pendes*, Pendants .. we call them pendles.

† 2. A screen hanging from the front of an altar; an altarcloth. *Obs.*

1501 *Acc. Ld. High Treas. Scot.* II. 65 For xij elne iij quarteris wellus to be offreis and crucis to the redestand and to the pendale and antependale of the altair. **1512** *Ibid.* IV. 358 For ane chessable with orphis, ane albe amyt, altar towellis, ane pendele to the altar, .. v *li.* viij *s.* ix *d.*

† 3. An overhanging part, natural or artificial: cf. JETTY *sb.* 2. *Obs.*

1581 STYWARD *Mart. Discipl.* II. 125 Some large riuer, or some deepe dale, hauing high pendles ouer it, either cast there by Art, or fortified by nature. **1663** *Boston Rec.* (1881) VII. 17 Ordered that noe Jettie nor pendill yt shall be erected but shall be full 8 foot in height from the ground.

4. A pendulum. *Obs.* or *dial.*

1742 *MS. Church Acc. Glaston* in *Rutland Gloss.* (E.D.S.) s.v., Allowed fox [the carpenter] for cutting way for the pendle. **1828** *Craven Gloss.* (ed. 2), *Pendil*, the pendulum of a clock.

'pendle[2]. *local.* Also **pendal.** [Derivation obscure.] A local term for various kinds or beds of stone as occurring in quarries. Also ***pendle-rock, -stone.***

a **1808** in Batchelor *Agric. Bedford* iv. 8 Under which is a small stone, short, thick, and hard, called the pendle rock. **1839** MURCHISON *Silur. Syst.* I. ii. 18 '*Pendle*'. Brownish hard calc grit, jointed and fissured. **1847–78** HALLIWELL, *Pendle-rock*, the top stratum in the stone-quarry at Islip, co. Oxon, is called the *pendle-rock*. **1854** MISS BAKER *Northamp. Glossary*, s.v., *Pendle*, a name given by quarry-men to the upper course in a stone-pit, whether of the upper or lower Oolite or Fuller's earth. **1900** *Stone Trade Jrnl.* Aug. (E.D.D.), The upper eight or ten feet of loose stuff [are] cleared away, thus 'ridding' the ground for the 'pendal', as the slates are called... The frost swells the bed of natural moisture in the 'pendal', and in a thaw the layers may be separated by a few blows with a hammer.

Pendleton ('pɛnd(ə)ltən). Orig. and chiefly *U.S.* The name of the *Pendleton* Woolen Mills (named after Pendleton, a town in Oregon) used to denote garments made by them, esp. a brightly coloured checked sports shirt. Also *attrib.*

1940 *Esquire* Dec. 204/1 (Advt.), Wear a Pendleton—then you'll know why Pendleton shirts have been a religion with sportsmen. **1947** E. S. GARDNER in *Amer. Mag.* Aug. 152/2 Our party is a man thirty-eight years old, bronzed, wears cowboy boots, a five-gallon hat, leather jacket, Pendleton trousers, rather chunky, and has a wide firm mouth. **1948** *Official Gaz.* (U.S. Patent Office) 28 Dec. 966/2 Pendleton [Trade Mark]. For outer shirts, lounge robes, trousers and slacks, Jackets and blazers, and men's coats. No. 535,993. **1960** *Sports Illustr.* 5 Sept. 22 (Advt.), On campus, a man worth watching will have at least one Pendleton. **1961** 'A. A. FAIR' *Shills can't cash Chips* iii. 71 The guy looked like a tall Texan. He was wearing Pendletons and cowboy boots. **1963** *Pix* 28 Sept. 62/3 *Pendletons*, bright plaid wool shirts one size too big. One point. **1977** *Guardian Weekly* 9 Oct. 16/2 She had a long, red Pendleton, a wool lumberjack shirt still smoke-musty from camping trips in the North Woods.

‖**pendopo** (pɛn'dəʊpəʊ). Also **mendopo, pendapa.** [ad. Javanese *pendâpâ.*] In Java: a large, covered porch or veranda in front of a house.

1927 H. S. BANNER *Romantic Java* iv. 56 Its [*sc.* the residence's] most arresting feature is the *Mendopo*, a huge, open-sided verandah in the front. **1958** H. FORSTER *Flowering Lotus* iii. 41 We entered the *pendopo*, skirted the piled desks and reached the 'common room'. **1961** H. GEERTZ *Javanese Family* i. 7 The greater portion of this building is the *pendapa*, a kind of oversized summer-house about a hundred feet square and always cool, dark, and dignified looking. **1971** *Nat. Geographic* Jan. 27/1 Within its gates are large, low, and lovely buildings, perfectly adapted to the hot and humid climate. The best of these are the *pendopos*, huge open-sided structures covered by four-sided roofs, supported above gleaming marble floors by columns of carved teak.

Pendragon[1] (pɛn'drægən). [Welsh = chief leader in war, *dux bellorum*, f. *pen* head + *dragon* dragon, the dragon symbol or standard, a leader in war, f. L. *draco, dracōnem* dragon, the standard of a cohort. Cf. the appellation *Insularis Draco*, with which Gildas addressed Maglocunus or Maelgwn.] A title given to an ancient British or Welsh prince holding or claiming supreme power; chief leader or ruler.

In English, chiefly known as the title of Uther Pendragon, in the *Morte Arthur*.

1470–85 MALORY *Arthur* I. i, Hit befel in the dayes of Vther pendragon when he was kynge of all Englond. **1591** SHAKS. *1 Hen. VI*, III. ii. 95 Once I read, That stout Pendragon, in his Litter sick Came to the field, and vanquished his foes. **1834** *Penny Cycl.* II. 415/2 After he [Arthur] became Pendragon. **1859** TENNYSON *Lancelot & Elaine* 423 The dread Pendragon, Britain's King of kings.

Hence **Pen'dragonish** *a.*, characteristic of a Pendragon, tyrannical; **Pen'dragonship**, the rank or position of Pendragon.

1650 B. *Discolliminium* 34 It is past my skill how to get money..till these Pen-dragonish Assessments be over. **1834** *Penny Cycl.* II. 415/2 Ambrosius, his [Arthur's] predecessor in the Pendragonship. **1859** TENNYSON *Guinevere* 395 Till yet once more ere set of sun they saw The Dragon of the great Pendragonship.

†**pen-dragon**[2]. *Obs.* [f. PEN *sb.*[2] + DRAGON[1].] A winged dragon.

1601 HOLLAND *Pliny* XII. xix. I. 372 Certaine marishes, guarded and kept with a kind of cruell Bats..and with certain flying Pen-dragons [*aligerisque serpentibus*].

Pendred ('pɛndrɛd). *Path.* [The name of Vaughan *Pendred* (1869–1946), English physician who described the condition in 1896 (*Lancet* 22 Aug. 532).] ***Pendred('s) syndrome***: a recessively inherited condition in which an enzyme deficiency leads to goitre and usu. to deafness.

1960 G. R. FRASER *Deafness with Goitre* (*Syndrome of Pendred*) (Ph.D. thesis, Univ. of London) 3 The name Pendred is suggested as a suitable eponym for this syndrome... A..study of sixty-two cases of Pendred's syndrome in forty-one sibships is described. **1966** J. B. STANBURY et al. *Metabolic Basis of Inherited Dis.* (ed. 2) x. 234/2 The patients with the Pendred syndrome do not have large goiters. **1970** J. F. SOTOS in R. M. Goodman *Genetic Disorders Man* xvi. 666/1 In a few reports thyroid disease without deafness has occurred in relatives of patients with the Pendred syndrome. **1974** J. D. MAYNARD in R. M. Kirk et al. *Surgery* xii. 250 Affected children are goitrous, hypothyroid, and sometimes deaf (Pendred's syndrome after the general practitioner who reported the first family in County Durham).

†**'pendugum.** *Obs. rare*$^{-1}$. Meaning unknown. (Some have conjectured = PENGUIN.)

a **1529** SKELTON *Sp. Parrot* 210 For Parot is no churlish chowgh, nor no flekyd pye, Parot is no pendugum, that men call a carlyng.

pendulant ('pɛndjʊlənt), *a.* Also 7– -ent. [f. L. type **pendulānt-em*, pr. pple. of **pendulāre*: see PENDULATE. Cf. It. *pendolante* 'downe-hanging or dangling' (Florio).] Pendulous, pendent.

1650 BULWER *Anthropomet.* xxi. 232 [He] brought his.. legs..to be very big..the humours descending upon their pendulent instability. **1804–5** *Miniature* (1806) I. 59 To snatch the pendulant chemise From gossamery lines. **1868** DILKE *Greater Brit.* I. I. x. 120 Its leaf is thin and spare..; and its buds pink and pendulent.

pendular ('pɛndjʊlə(r)), *a.* [f. PENDUL-UM + -AR[1].] Of or pertaining to a pendulum; resembling that of a pendulum, as a simple vibration.

1878 MAYER *Sound* 152 A simple sound is only given by a pendular vibration. **1881** BROADHOUSE *Mus. Acoustics* 157 The form of vibration known as 'pendular'.

pendulate ('pɛndjʊleɪt), *v.* [f. L. type **pendulā-re* = It. *pendolare* 'to hang sloping, to dangle downe' (Florio), f. *pendulus* PENDULOUS: see -ATE[3].] *intr.* **a.** To dangle, sway to and fro, swing like a pendulum, oscillate, undulate. **b.** *fig.* To fluctuate or oscillate between two opposite conditions; to be in suspense or undecided.

1698 *Christ Exalted* cv. 85 He had a good steddy pair of Ballances that did not pendulate an Hairs breadth. **1828** *Westm. Rev.* Apr. 442 As his [an auctioneer's] hammer pendulates. **1837** CARLYLE *Diam. Neckl.* xvi. Ess. 1872 V. 193 The ill-starred Scoundrel pendulates between Heaven and Earth. **1847** GILFILLAN in *Tait's Mag.* XIV. 69 Some pendulate perpetually between the grave and the gay. **1865** *Spectator* 14 Jan. 49 Here we have a surrounding envelope of photogenic matter, which pendulates with mighty energies, and..produces heat and light in far distant worlds.

†**pendulation** (pɛndjuː'leɪʃən). *Obs.* [f. L. *pendul-us* PENDULOUS *a.* + -ATION.] An oscillatory motion formerly ascribed to the poles of the earth.

1909 *Westm. Gaz.* 1 May 12/3 According to Professor Simroth, pendulation, which is the periodical oscillation of the earth's axes,..explains nearly every observed fact in the development and distribution of all animals. **1924** J. G. A. SKERL tr. *Wegener's Orig. Continents & Oceans* vi. 95 Unfortunately, Reibisch clothed his ideas..in the singular straight-jacket of a strict 'pendulation' of the poles in an 'orbit of swings', which is probably false.

'pendule, *sb.* Now *rare.* Also 7 **pendul.** [In sense 1, app. ad. L. *pendul-us* PENDULOUS; cf. It. *pendulo* 'downe-hanging or dangling' (Florio); in senses 2, 3, a. F. *pendule* (1664 *pendulle*).]

1. Something pendulous or suspended.

†**a.** *gen.*

1578 BANISTER *Hist. Man* VII. 90 A round, long, and litle thicke pendule, called..Vuula.

b. A hanging ornament, a pendant; an ear-pendant. *rare.* (Cf. obs. F. *pendille.*)

1683 in A. Shields *Faithful Contendings* (1780) 108 Yea, one pendule of his crown should not be yielded. **1853** KANE *Grinnell Exp.* xxviii. (1856) 230 [He] rejoiced in a couple of barbaric pendules, doubtless of bad gold, but good conducting power.

2. †**a.** A pendulum. [F. *pendule* masc.] *Obs.*

1665–6 *Phil. Trans.* I. 114 The use of Pendules for knowing by their means the State of one's Health from the different beatings of the Pulse. *a* **1683** EVELYN *Hist. Relig.* (1850) I. 12 Moved by a spring, pendule, or poise, which first gives motion to the first wheel. **1798** FRERE & CANNING *Loves of Triangles* 13 in *Anti-Jacobin* No. 23 Let playful Pendules quick vibration feel.

b. *Mountaineering.* = PENDULUM *sb.* 1 d.

1957 E. A. WRANGHAM *Sel. Climbs Range Mont Blanc* 170 Rappel down from the summit on the Verte side, go over a gendarme by a small *pendule* on the Charpoua side. **1967** COLLOMB & CREW *Sel. Climbs Mont Blanc Range* I. 180 Traverse L across a very steep ice couloir to a thin and high rock island and continue the traverse by a pendule from a peg high on this island. **1973** C. BONINGTON *Next Horizon* xvi. 232 We had a spectacular pendule by Tom Patey, as he swung out from the base of the over-hanging rock. **1973** J. BUNTING *Climbing* 90 *Pendule*, a horizontal *abseil* effected by a sideways swing.

3. a. A time-piece having a pendulum; a clock, usually small and ornamental. Now only as Fr. *pendule* (pɑ̃dyl) fem. †**b.** Short for *pendulum-watch*: see PENDULUM *sb.* 4 b (*obs.*).

1661 EVELYN *Diary* 3 May, I return'd by Fromantil's the famous clock-maker to see some pendules. **1664–5** *Phil. Trans.* I. 14 The difference..will not be at all perceived in the Penduls. **1670** *Ibid.* V. 1149 Directions how to find the Longitudes by the Pendul. **1865** *Cornh. Mag.* July 10 The little pendule on the chimney piece struck the half-hour. **1884** F. J. BRITTEN *Watch & Clockm.* 264 Escape wheels of French pendules make two revolutions a minute.

4. *attrib.*

1661 EVELYN *Diary* 1 Apr., That great mathematician and virtuoso [Huyghens], inventor of the pendule clock. **1677** PLOT *Oxfordsh.* 152 They sow also a Wheat about Weston on the Green, which from the hanging of its ear they call Pendule Wheat. [Cf. *pendulum-wheat* s.v. PENDULUM 4 b.]

pendule ('pɛndjʊl), *v.* *Mountaineering.* [f. the sb.] *intr.* To swing to and fro like a pendulum. Also *refl.*

1883 G. MACDONALD *Princess & Curdie* xvi. 128 He dropped himself a little below its level, gave the rope a swing by pushing his feet against the side of the cleft, and so penduled himself into it. **1973** C. BONINGTON *Next Horizon* x. 148 He was now sixty feet up. He paused,..let out some rope and penduled back and forth across the face, trying to work out the best line.

penduline ('pɛndjʊlaɪn), *a.* (*sb.*) [a. F. *penduline* (Buffon) = It. *pendolina* 'a kind of birde' (Florio), mod.L. *pendulīn-us*, f. *pendul-us*: see PENDULOUS and -INE[1].]

1. Applied to a bird that builds a pendulous nest, esp. the ***penduline titmouse*** of Southern and Eastern Europe (*Ægithalus pendulinus*).

1802 BINGLEY *Anim. Biog.* (1813) II. 196 The Penduline Titmouse. **1843** *Penny Cycl.* XXV. 6/1 Penduline Titmouse and nest. **1868** WOOD *Homes without H.* xi. 212.

2. Pendulous, as a bird's nest.

1885 SWAINSON *Prov. Names Brit. Birds* 31 Long-tailed Titmouse... The penduline form of the nest, and the feathers which compose the lining, have obtained for the bird the names of Jack in a bottle..Bottle tit..Feather poke.

B. *sb.* A titmouse of the genus *Pendulinus* (a synonym of *Ægithalus*), or allied to this.

1890 in *Cent. Dict.* **1902** *Speaker* 19 Apr. 76/1 The Gold Crest should surely be ranked as a Penduline.

pendulize ('pɛndjʊlaɪz), *v.* [f. as PENDULOUS *a.* + -IZE.] *intr.* To poise oneself or hover in the air; to be pendant.

1869 E. NEWMAN *Illustr. Nat. Hist. Brit. Moths* 12 He who has not seen this fairy creature pendulizing over a purple patch of the common bugle..has a delight yet to come.

'pendulograph. [f. PENDUL-UM + -GRAPH.] A curve representing a combination of musical sounds, traced by an instrument which combines the vibrations of two or more pendulums, as in the HARMONOGRAPH.

1881 J. ANDREW *Pendulograph* 18 These Pendulographs are pictures or portraits of the intervals, concords, and discords of the Musical System. They are produced by a pen placed under the control of two pendulums, which are tuned to swing..the ratios of the musical intervals. **1894** *New Sci. Rev.* Oct. 169 A pen..writes..a portrait of the chord which two corresponding strings of a sounding harp would utter to the ear. This spiral writing is a pendulograph.

pendulosity (pɛndjʊ'lɒsɪtɪ). *rare.* [f. type **pendulose* for PENDULOUS + -ITY.] The quality or condition of being pendulous; pendulousness; hanging position.

1646 SIR T. BROWNE *Pseud. Ep.* v. xiii. 254 He had slender legs, but encreased them by riding after meals; that is, the humours descending upon their pendulosity, they having no support or suppedaneous stability. **1859** G. MEREDITH *R. Feverel* xxxiii, 'I'm sure I beg pardon', Benson murmured, arresting his head in a melancholy pendulosity.

pendulous ('pɛndjʊləs), *a.* [f. L. *pendul-us* hanging down, pendent (f. *pendēre* to hang) + -OUS. For element *-ul-* cf. *crēdul-us, garrul-us*, etc.]

1. Supported or attached above so as to hang downwards; suspended; hanging down, pendent, drooping. Freq. in *Nat. Hist.*, e.g. of the nests of certain birds, the ovules, flowers, etc. of plants.

1656 RIDGLEY *Pract. Physick* 218 Gorgareon is a pendulous kernel. **1695** J. EDWARDS *Perfect. Script.* 242 This..was no ear-ring, but a pendulous jewel upon her face. **1782–3** W. F. MARTYN *Geog. Mag.* I. 232 Ears long, broad and pendulous. **1834** PRINGLE *Afr. Sk.* vi. 204 On the few straggling trees..appeared the pendulous nests of the loxia and weaver-bird. **1859** W. S. COLEMAN *Woodlands* (1866) 40 Some varieties have the branches quite pendulous like the weeping willow. **1880** GRAY *Struct. Bot.* vi. §8 (ed. 6) 277 Ovules are..pendulous, when more or less hanging or declining from the side of the cell.

†**b.** Supported or poised so as to project or overhang; suspended overhead; overhanging. (Cf. HANGING *ppl. a.* 2.) Also *fig.* Impending. *Obs.*

c **1605** ROWLEY *Birth Merl.* v. i. (1662) G iij, I will erect a Monument upon the verdant Plains of Salisbury..with pendulous stones that I will hang by art. **1605** SHAKS. *Lear* III. iv. 69 All the plagues that in the pendulous ayre Hang fated o're mens faults. **1684** T. BURNET *Th. Earth* I. 266 The pendulous gardens of Alcinous. *c* **1705** BERKELEY *Descr. Cave of Dunmore* Wks. 1871 IV. 510 A third [cave].. stopped up by the fall of such pendulous rocks as are above mentioned.

c. Hanging or floating in the air or in space. (In quot. 1638 with *fig.* allusion.) Now *rare* or *Obs.*

1638 FEATLY *Transub.* 9 And you..he hath placed in a pendulous Bishopricke adjoyning to Mausolus his sepulcher in the ayre. **1646** SIR T. BROWNE *Pseud. Ep.* II. iii. 72 The like doth Beda report of Bellerophons horse which framed of iron and placed betweene two Loadstones with winges expansed, hung pendulous in the ayre. **1667** MILTON *P.L.* IV. 1000 Wherein all things created first he weighd, The pendulous round Earth with balanc't Aire In counterpoise. **1696** WHISTON *Th. Earth* (1722) 19 Globes of Fire and Light pendulous in our Air. *a* **1849** POE *City in Sea* 27 So blend the turrets and shadows there That all seem pendulous in air.

2. *spec.* Suspended so as to swing, oscillating; hence, of movement: Of, or resembling that of, a pendulum; oscillatory, undulatory; consisting of simple vibrations.

1706 W. JONES *Syn. Palmar. Matheseos* 288 The Velocities of a Pendulous Body..describing different Arcs. **1728** PEMBERTON *Newton's Philos.* 87 The greater the arch the pendulous body moves through, the greater time it takes up. **1855** BAIN *Senses & Int.* II. iv. §7 (1864) 270 In walking there is a pendulous swing of the leg. **1879** G. PRESCOTT *Sp. Telephone* 99 [If] the plate has a simple pendulous motion.

3. *fig.* Hanging in suspense or wavering between two opinions, purposes, or tendencies; vacillating, undecided, unsettled, uncertain, doubtful. Now *rare*.

1624 F. WHITE *Repl. Fisher* 572 The third [opinion] is pendulous, with shew of Limitation, and Mitigation. **1644** PRYNNE *Rome's Master-P.* (ed. 2) 16 The Kings mind was wholy pendulous (or doubtfull). **1677** R. CARY *Chronol.* II. ii. III. xi. 245 He farther shews how Various and Pendulous Eusebius is, in making forth his Reckonings. **1779** JOHNSON *Let. to Mrs. Thrale* 4 Oct., In this doubtful pendulous state of the distemper, advice may do much. **1850** MRS. BROWNING *Sonn. fr. Portuguese* xxxvi, A love set pendulous between Sorrow and sorrow.

†**b.** Dependent, contingent, conditional (*on* or *upon* something else). *Obs.*

1654 H. L'ESTRANGE *Chas. I* (1655) 60 They are not souldered by any magnetique of Love, but..pendulous upon the variety and mutation of affaires. **1692** *Covt. Grace Conditional* 2 Arminians maintain Conditions, so as if the Efficacy of Christ's Death were pendulous thereon.

ˈpendulously, *adv.* [f. prec. + -LY².] In a pendulous manner; so as to hang or swing; with a swaying movement. Also *fig.* Waveringly, undecidedly.

1633 PRYNNE *Histriomastix* 152 Mans corrupt nature is farre more pendulously propense to vitious, than to good examples. **1697** DERHAM in *Phil. Trans.* XX. 2, I left an Eye in the Wire, to suspend the whole Barometer..that it might hang pendulously. **1873** L. WALLACE *Fair God* VII. vii. 474 Between the work of yesterday and that to come his mind played pendulously. **1882** O'DONOVAN *Merv Oasis* I. x. 175 The fruit hanging pendulously above the heads of the passers-by.

ˈpendulousness. [f. as prec. + -NESS.] The quality or condition of being pendulous; in quot. *fig.* Undecidedness, wavering.

1641 SYMONDS *Serm. bef. Ho. Comm.* B ij b, There is either reluctance,..or pendulousness of heart. **1727** BAILEY vol. II, *Pendulousness*, pendentness. **1755** in JOHNSON.

pendulum (ˈpɛndjʊləm), *sb.* Pl. -ums, formerly (rarely) -a. [a. mod.L. *pendulum* (1643 in Watt *Biblioth.*), sb. use of neut. of L. *pendul-us* PENDULOUS, lit. a pendulous or free-hanging body; in It. *pendolo* (Galileo *Operazioni Astronomiche*, 1637).]

1. a. A body suspended so as to be free to swing or oscillate; usually, an instrument consisting of a rod, with a weight or *bob* at the end, so suspended as to swing to and fro by the action of gravity, and used for various mechanical and scientific purposes; esp. as an essential part of a clock, serving (by the isochronism of its vibrations) to regulate and control the movement of the works, so as to maintain a constant rate of going, and enable it to keep regular time.

1660 BOYLE *New Exp. Phys. Mech.* xxvi. 202 We thought it not amiss to try if a Pendulum would swing faster, or continue swinging longer in our Receiver. *Ibid.* xxxvii. 316 We conveyd into our Receiver..the Pendula formerly mention'd. *a* **1677** HALE *Prim. Orig. Man.* II. iv. 152 The late discovery of the Motion of the Pendulum. **1685** BOYLE *Effects of Mot.* vi. 69 The great swing that may be given to Pendulums by a very languid force, if it successively strike the swinging body. **1785** SARAH FIELDING *Ophelia* II. i, She was as regular as a pendulum. **1844** HERSCHEL *Ess.* (1857) 583 Two pendula, a copper and an iron one,..were furnished by the Society. **1879** A. M. CLERKE in *Encycl. Brit.* X. 31/1 The experimental verification of this fact led him [Galileo] to the important discovery of the isochronism of the pendulum.

b. With qualifying word. **compound pendulum**, (*a*) a pendulum consisting of a number of weights at fixed distances; an actual material pendulum regarded theoretically, as opposed to a *simple pendulum* (see below); (*b*) a compensation pendulum whose rod consists of bars of different metals. **conical pendulum**, a pendulum so contrived that the bob revolves in a circle, the rod thus describing a cone. **mercurial** (or †**quicksilver**) **pendulum**, a compensation pendulum with a cylindrical bob containing mercury, whose upward expansion by heat counteracts the lengthening of the rod. **seconds pendulum**, a pendulum of such a length as to oscillate once every second; a pendulum 'beating seconds'. **simple pendulum**, (*a*) a theoretical or ideal pendulum consisting of a particle having weight but no magnitude, suspended by a weightless inextensible rod, and moving without friction; (*b*) a pendulum consisting simply of a bob suspended by a cord or wire, without any special contrivance, as for compensation of the effects of heat; (*c*) a pendulum unconnected with any mechanism. **spherical pendulum**, a pendulum so contrived that the bob can move in any circle on a given spherical surface (the same as *conical pendulum*). See also BALLISTIC *p.*, COMPENSATION *p.*, CYCLOIDAL *p.*, GRIDIRON *p.*, HYDROMETRIC *p.*

1726 GRAHAM in *Phil. Trans.* XXXIV. 42 The Irregularity of the Clock, with the Quicksilver Pendulum..exceeded not..a sixth Part of that..with the common Pendulum. **1727–41** CHAMBERS *Cycl.* s.v., *Simple Pendulum*..*Compound Pendulum*. **1795** HUTTON *Math. Dict.* II. 207 The length of a Pendulum, so measured..that it will perform each vibration in a second of time, thence called the second's Pendulum. *Ibid.* 210 Simple Pendulum, and Detached Pendulum, are terms sometimes used to denote such Pendulums as are not connected with any clock, or clock-work. *Ibid.*, The Mercurial Pendulum was the invention of the ingenious Mr. Graham..in 1715. **1819** *Pantologia* s.v., The conical or circular pendulum, is so called from the figure described by the string or ball of the pendulum. **1862** CAYLEY *Coll. Math. Papers* IV. 525 That the motion of the spherical pendulum is sensibly affected by the rotation of the Earth is the well-known discovery of Foucault. **1871** TAIT & STEELE *Dynamics of Particle* (ed. 3) §208 The Conical Pendulum, as it is called, when the particle moves in a horizontal plane and therefore in a circular path, the string describing a right circular cone whose axis is vertical.

c. Used of similar bodies that oscillate but are not similarly suspended: **horizontal pendulum**, an approximately horizontal rod having a heavy weight at one end and pivoted at the other so that it can swing freely in an approximately horizontal plane, supported by a thread or wire passing from the weighted end to a fixed point almost vertically above the pivot; **inverted pendulum**, a vertical rod having a heavy weight at its upper end and resting on a bearing at the other, and held in position by springs which allow it to oscillate in a vertical plane.

1844 *Trans. R. Soc. Edin.* XV. 219 The elegant inverted Pendulum or Noddy contrived by the late Mr Hardy. **1872** F. ZÖLLNER in *Phil. Mag.* XLIII. 491, I explained the principles of such a method and its practicability in an apparatus for which I proposed the name of 'Horizontal Pendulum', in order to distinguish it from other pendulum-like instruments, also suspended by two threads. **1908** C. G. KNOTT *Physics Earthquake Phenomena* iv. 61 The nearer the point of attachment to a truly vertical position above the pivot the more delicate and the less stable will the horizontal pendulum be, and the better fitted for recording small motions. **1937** D. KENNEDY tr. *Imamura's Theoret. & Appl. Seismol.* xi. 254 The form most extensively used is one that weighs a ton. It is shown in Fig. 119. The heavy bob is an inverted pendulum. Its lower point, the end of the supporting rod, rests in a socket, but as it is unstable in this condition, an arm..extends laterally from the upper end of the pendulum, and connects with a steel spring. **1972** R. B. GORDON *Physics of Earth* vi. 124 An instrument suitable for recording horizontal ground motion is the horizontal pendulum.

d. *Mountaineering.* A swinging movement like that of a pendulum, often used as a deliberate move by a climber using his momentum to swing to a new position. Also *attrib.*

1945 G. W. YOUNG *Mountain Craft* (ed. 4) v. 179 The second [artificial aid] is the *pendulum*. Like most modern technical devices, it is a perfecting of an old alpine fashion. .. By attaching a rope to the highest point convenient upon our first line, we..can swing across upon it, and reach the new set of holds. **1949** A. ROCH *Climbs of my Youth* xiv. 115 The pendulum was definitely unpleasant, and a few stones fell loose. **1965** A. BLACKSHAW *Mountaineering* ix. 268 If there is no suitable transverse crack it will be necessary to do a pendulum or a horizontal rappel. The former involves abseiling..from a piton and swinging over to the desired new position. **1971** C. BONINGTON *Annapurna South Face* x. 120 He therefore had to climb without any protection from pitons, though if he had fallen off he would have had a punishing pendulum back into the gully. **1972** D. HASTON *In High Places* x. 110 There are some devious pendulums to reach the start of the main crack system. A pendulum is an exciting move, very common to Yosemite climbing. When one line of cracks runs out and there is blank wall before another can be reached, often this gap can be filled in by fixing a piton as high as possible, going down for some way hanging on the rope, then running back and forth to get up enough momentum to make a swing into the next crack system.

2. a. *fig.* In reference to oscillation (of a person, or of opinion, etc.) between two opposites.

1769 *Junius Lett.* xv. (1771) 72 Is this the wisdom of a great minister? or is it the vibration of a pendulum? **1818** BYRON *Ch. Har.* IV. cix, Man! Thou pendulum betwixt a smile and tear. **1836** *Penny Cycl.* V. 300/1 The pendulum of opinion swings to the side opposite to that on which it has been unduly brought out of its position of equilibrium. **1900** *Westm. Gaz.* 8 Nov. 4/2 The moral of the Canada elections is that there is no swing left in the Pendulum anywhere.

b. *to play pendulum*: to swing or oscillate like a pendulum (*lit.* or *fig.*).

1893 SALTUS *Madam Sapphira* 171 Beyond asking him to play pendulum I see nothing. **1897** MARY KINGSLEY *W. Africa* iv. 77 Great rollers..make the vessels lying broadside on to them play pendulum to an extent that precludes the discharging or taking on of heavy cargo.

†**3.** A clock that goes by means of a pendulum, a pendulum-clock; also, a pendulum-watch (4 b).

1664–5 *Phil. Trans.* I. 14 The same Objection..against the exactness of these Pendulums, hath also been made here. .. This difference..will not be at all perceived in the Penduls. **1696** DERHAM *Artif. Clockm.* 62 For the use of such as would convert old Ballance Clocks into Pendulums. **1706** PHILLIPS, *Royal Pendulums*, are those Clocks whose Pendulum swings Seconds, and goes eight Days, shewing the Hour, Minutes and Seconds.

4. *attrib.* and *Comb.* **a.** simple attrib., Characterized by oscillation, or by regular movement from side to side.

1820 *Sporting Mag.* VII. 108 The pendulum shake [of the hand] may be mentioned next. **1865** *Englishm. Mag.* Jan. 13 The popular mind in England has..swayed from side to side in a somewhat pendulum-fashion.

b. *Comb.*, as ***pendulum-rod***; ***pendulum-like*** adj., ***pendulum-wise*** adv.; †**pendulum-balance**, the balance-wheel of a watch, acting as a pendulum; **pendulum-ball, -bob**, the heavy ball or bob forming the lower end of a pendulum; **pendulum-clock**, a clock that goes by means of a pendulum; **pendulum-cock** [COCK *sb.*¹ 16] (see quot.); **pendulum governor** [GOVERNOR 8], a governor consisting of two equal pendulums attached to and revolving with a spindle driven by the engine or machine to be controlled, and operating by 'centrifugal force'; **pendulum-hausse**, a hausse or breech-sight for a gun, so contrived as to remain vertical when the wheels of the gun-carriage are not on a level; **pendulum-level**, a plumb-level: see quot.; †**pendulum-piece**, a time-piece having a pendulum, a pendulum-clock; **pendulum position** *Billiards*, a position of the two object balls beside the cushions on either side of a corner pocket which makes a large number of cannons possible; **pendulum-press**, a punching-press in which the punch is driven by a swinging treadle; **pendulum-pump**, (*a*) 'a pump in which a pendulum is employed to govern the reciprocating motion of the piston'; (*b*) 'a direct-acting donkey-pump in which the fly-wheels have an oscillatory motion in a vertical plane'; (*c*) 'a pump the handle of which swings each side of its center of suspension' (Knight *Dict. Mech.*); **pendulum saw** (see quot. 1958); **pendulum-spindle**, a spindle having a pendulum attached, which it causes to revolve; **pendulum-spring**, †(*a*) the coiled hair-spring connected with the balance-wheel (*pendulum-balance*) of a watch (*obs.*); (*b*) the spring to which the pendulum of a clock is attached; **pendulum swing**, a swing or swinging movement like that of a pendulum; also *fig.*; †**pendulum-watch**, a watch of the modern type, with a balance-wheel provided with a spring and oscillating regularly, thus having the function of the pendulum of a clock (*obs.*); †**pendulum wheat** (see quot.); **pendulum-wheel**, (*a*) the escapement-wheel of a clock; (*b*) the balance-wheel of a watch (?*obs.*); **pendulum-wire**, flat steel wire used for the pendulum-springs of clocks.

1878 ABNEY *Photogr.* (1881) 255 The *pendulum apparatus, which in general outline consists of a pendulum swinging in front of sensitised paper in such a manner as to give a gradation of exposure to it, and a consequent variation in tint. **1680** *Lond. Gaz.* No. 1538/4 Lost.., a Silver Watch ..with the Hours and Minutes, a *Pendulum Ballance, without String or Chain. *a* **1688** VILLIERS (Dk. Buckhm.) *Militant Couple* Wks. (1775) 128 Sir John pushes my lady against a fine new *pendulum-clock. **1898** P. MANSON *Trop. Diseases* xiv. 226 The sounds of the heart are, like the beats of a well-hung pendulum-clock, evenly spaced. **1884** F. J. BRITTEN *Watch & Clockm.* 62 In clocks, the *pendulum cock is the bracket supporting the pendulum. *a* **1859**, **1887** *Pendulum hausse [see HAUSSE]. **1727–41** CHAMBERS *Cycl.*, *Plumb*, or *Pendulum Level*, that which shews the horizontal line, by means of another line perpendicular to that described by its plummet, or pendulum. *a* **1721** KEILL *Maupertuis' Diss.* (1734) 2 In the year 1672, Mr. Richer going to Cayenne..observed that the *Pendulum-piece he had carried with him, retarded considerably in respect of the Sun's mean Motion. **1927** *Daily Express* 26 Apr. 9/4 Reece ..made a record break of 1,151, including 568 cannons by what is known as the '*pendulum position'. **1752** ELLICOTT in *Phil. Trans.* XLVII. 480 Holes drilled in the broad part of the *pendulum-rod. **1822** IMISON *Sc. & Art* I. 82 A pendulum-rod is longer in warm than in cold weather. **1957** *Pendulum saw [see *goose saw* s.v. GOOSE *sb.* 8]. **1958** *N.Z. Timber Jrnl.* Jan. 46/1 *Pendulum saw*, a machine cross-cut saw that is drawn across the stationary wood in the process of cutting by swinging from the point of suspension like a pendulum. **1727** *Phil. Trans.* XXXV. 304 A very irregular Motion..like the *Pendulum-Spring of a Watch. **1884** F. J. BRITTEN *Watch & Clockm.* 192 In small clocks the pendulum spring is often too stout. **1926** *Amer. Speech* I. 632/2 **Pendulum swing*, applied to a type of putting stroke. **1947** C. DAY LEWIS *Colloq. Element Eng. Poetry* 9 The verse of the Romance poets, of the early Elizabethan lyricists,..

and of the Pre-Raphaelite poets represents a series of pendulum-swings towards the formal, esoteric ideal of poetic diction. **1968** J. Winearls *Mod. Dance* (ed. 2) ii. 57 The principle of the outside fall and pick up of a Pendulum Swing can be used in isolated leg and trunk movements. **1664** *Phil. Trans.* I. 13 Concerning the success of the *Pendulum-Watches at Sea for the Longitudes. **1678** Phillips (ed. 4), *Pendulum Watch*,..newly invented by Monsieur Christian Hugens of Zulichem,..in which by a Pendulum or Regulator, the time is more exactly proportioned than ever hitherto. **1707** Mortimer *Husb.* (1721) I. 127 In Berkshire is a Wheat called *Pendulum Wheat, from its hanging of its Ear much like the Cone-wheat [cf. quot. 1677 in pendule 4]. **1825** J. Nicholson *Operat. Mechanic* 492 Affected by any unequal impulse of the *pendulum-wheel upon the pallets. **1892** *Pall Mall G.* 12 Feb. 4/2 One of the electric lights that swung *pendulum-wise from the ceiling arrested the attention of the House.

'pendulum, *v.* [f. the sb.] *intr.* To hang or swing like a pendulum. Also *fig.*

1885 W. F. Crafts *Sabbath for Man* vi. 458 The Sabbath of our fathers..was far better than the extreme of laxity to which we have pendulumed. **1949** A. Roch *Climbs of my Youth* xiv. 115 We had to drive a piton into a slab and then pendulum across over the ice of the couloir. **1969** J. Elliot *Duel* I. iv. 79 A stop-watch on a long black string pendulummed from her neck. **1971** C. Bonington *Annapurna South Face* xii. 145 My progress had dropped to a single push of my jumar clamps at a time; my feet slipped on the snow steps, and I pendulumed clumsily across the arête into the gully. **1973** —— *Next Horizon* x. 146 But what if..you miss the other side and go penduluming back against the sheer ice wall, to be left hanging in the void? **1974** H. MacInnes *Climb to Lost World* xii. 212 'I'll belay you from here,' said Don. 'Then, if the stone comes away, at least you'll pendulum over to this side and shouldn't hurt yourself too much.'

pene, obs. form of pain, pen[2]; variant of pein.

pene- (piːniː), *prefix*, repr. L. *pæne* 'nearly, almost, all but', before a vowel *pæn-*, *pen-*, in a few words of rare occurrence or nonce-words, as **,pene-fe'lonious**, **,pene-'infinite** (also peninfinite), **,pene-om'nipotent** *adjs.*; in some cases formed after *peninsula*, as †**,pene-'isle** = peninsula: see penile *sb.*; †**,pene-'lake**, a piece of water almost surrounded by land (*obs.*); **pene'seismic** *a.* [ad. F. *pénéséismique* (De Montessus de Ballore *La Geogr. Séismologique* (ed. 2, 1906) 11)] (see quot.).

1890 'R. Boldrewood' *Col. Reformer* (1891) 82 'Lots', said the *pene-felonious traveller—'good place to camp'. **1647** Ward *Simp. Cobler* 47 These *pene-infinite [*later edd.* pen-infinite] insolencies, which are the most finite Infinites of misery to men. **1668** Wilkins *Real Char.* 54 *Pene-lake, Haven, Harbour, Port, Key. **1894** *Blackw. Mag.* June 822 That *peneomnipotent thing, public opinion. **1921** C. Davison *Man. Seismol.* x. 161 Peneseismic countries, in which earthquakes are severe, but fall short of destructive power.

,penecontempo'raneous, *a. Geol.* [f. pene- + contemporaneous *a.*] (See quot. 1972.)

1901 S. Buckman in *Q. Jrnl. Geol. Soc.* LVII. 144 Brought about by what may be called penecontemporaneous denudation. **1939** W. H. Twenhofel *Princ. Sedimentation* x. 375 The present trend of opinion considers that much chert and flint were deposited contemporaneously with the enclosing rocks. The views of origin may be placed in three classes of contemporaneous (syngenetic), penecontemporaneous, and subsequent (epigenetic). **1963** *Jrnl. Sedimentary Petrology* XXXIII. 64 Geologic data allow an assignment of possible penecontemporaneous (early diagenetic) origin to the dolomites of this group. **1969** *Nature* 22 Nov. 821/2 There is evidence of post-depositional weathering penecontemporaneous with deposition. **1972** *Gloss. Geol.* (Amer. Geol. Inst.) 525/2 *Penecontemporaneous*, said of a geologic process, or resultant structure or mineral, occurring immediately after deposition but before consolidation of the enclosing rock.

Hence **,penecontempora'neity**, the fact of being penecontemporaneous; **,penecontempo'raneously** *adv.*

1933 P. G. H. Boswell *On Mineral. Sedimentary Rocks* i. 1 The mode of formation of matrices and minerals that have developed penecontemporaneously or subsequently in the rocks. **1958** *Q. Jrnl. Geol. Soc.* CXIV. 45 The speaker had been unable to detect any sign of overprinting between these two fold systems..; this was interpreted as proof of penecontemporaneity of the folding. **1964** *Sedimentology* III. 136 The observations of uniform directions in certain penecontemporaneously slumped beds. **1979** *Nature* 7 June 485/1 The Entrance and the Exit Quarries, where sedimentation occurred penecontemporaneously in two separate depositories.

penede, var. penide.

penegrysse, obs. f. penny-grass.

peneid, var penæid.

penele, penelle: see panele, panel.

peneles, obs. f. penniless.

‖**Penelope** (pɪ'nɛləpiː). [a. Gr. Πηνελόπη (Herodotus), in Homer's *Odyssey* Πηνελόπεια.]

1. Name of the wife of Ulysses in ancient Greek legend, who, during her husband's long absence, unravelled every night the web she had woven during the day, and thus put off the suitors whose offers she had promised to entertain when the web should be finished; hence (after Latin), allusively for 'chaste wife'.

1581 J. Bell *Haddon's Answ. Osor.* 374b, A Strumpet doth behave her selfe more modestly amongest us Osorius, then Penelope doth amongest you. **1581** Pettie tr. *Guazzo's Civ. Conv.* III. (1586) 136b, My concubine is a great deale more modest, than thy Penelope. **1835** J. Batman in Cornwallis *New World* (1859) I. App. 378 Our absent Penelopes were, doubtless, dreaming.

2. *Zool.* A genus of gallinaceous birds of Central and South America, typical of the subfamily *Penelopinæ* or Guans: so named 1786 by Merrem.

[Cf. **1678** Ray *Willughby's Ornith.* 375 The common Wigeon or Whewer: *Penelope* Aldrovandi, tom. 3. p. 218, lin. 30.] **1836** Macgillivray tr. *Humboldt's Trav.* xxiv. 388 There is a great variety of gallinaceous birds..such as the turkey, the hocco or curassow, penelopes and pheasants.

3. *attrib.* **Penelope canvas**, a double-thread canvas used for needle tapestry work. Also *absol.*

1882 Caulfeild & Saward *Dict. Needlework* 387/2 *Penelope canvas*, a description of cotton canvas made for Berlin woolwork, in which the strands run in couples, vertically and horizontally, thus forming squares containing four threads each. **1895** *Montgomery Ward Catal.* 124/3 Java Canvas... Penelope Canvas. **1926–7** *Army & Navy Stores Catal.* 663/3 Canvas for wool work and embroidery. .. White 'Penelope'. **1975** *Islander* (Victoria, B.C.) 9 Mar. 7/2 The other type of needlepoint canvas is known as Penelope which is made up of two pairs of vertical and horizontal threads.

Hence **Penelopean** (pɪnɛləʊ'piːən) *a.*, of or pertaining to, or resembling the web or weaving, or time-gaining policy of Penelope; **Penelopine** (pɪ'nɛləpaɪn) *a. Zool.*, belonging to the subfamily *Penelopinæ* of gallinaceous birds; **Pe'nelopize** *v. intr.* to do like Penelope.

1837 Beddoes *Let.* May, Poems (1851) p. ciii, And so I weave my *Penelopean web, and rip it up again. **1903** *Contemp. Rev.* Apr. 590 The deliberate and Penelopean acts of many of his advisers. **1853** Motley in O. W. Holmes *Life* x. (1878) 72 There is nothing for it but to *penelopize, pull to pieces and stitch away again. **1841** *Congress. Globe* 27th Congress 1 Sess. App. 43/2 Diplomacy was still drawing out its lengthened thread—still weaving its long and dilatory web—still Penelopizing. **1956** 'H. MacDiarmid' *Stony Limits* 39 Nor twissel-tongued can we penelopise.

peneplain ('piːnɪpleɪn), *sb. Geomorphol.* Also **-plane**. [f. pene- + plain *sb.*[1]] A low, nearly featureless tract of land of undulating relief, esp. one held to be the product of long-continued subaerial erosion of land undisturbed by crustal movement and to represent the penultimate stage in the cycle of erosion in a humid climate; also, a former surface of this kind as it exists today (e.g. after uplift and dissection, or buried as an unconformity).

1889 W. M. Davis in *Amer. Jrnl. Sci.* XXXVII. 430 Given time enough, and the faulted ridges of Connecticut must be reduced to a low base-level plain. I believe that time enough has already been allowed, and that the strong Jurassic topography was really worn out somewhere in Cretaceous time, when all this part of the country was reduced to a nearly featureless plain, a 'peneplain', as I would call it, at a low level. **1893** *Bull. Dept. Geol. Univ. Calif.* I. iv. 158 The tilting of the Sierra Nevada peneplane was also a post-Pliocene event. **1894** *Nation* (N.Y.) 9 Aug. 99/2 A lowland of moderate relief close to sea level—a peneplain, as I should term it. **1933** *Geogr. Jrnl.* LXXXI. 331 These 'residual mountains' rise from a peneplain, that is, a plain of erosion produced during a stable period interrupting an upward movement. **1934** C. R. Longwell et al. *Outl. Physical Geol.* xv. 309 The highest ridges of the present Appalachians are remnants of a former peneplane. **1946** L. D. Stamp *Britain's Struct.* xiii. 150 The magnificent modern sea-cliffs are where the peneplanes of the past meet the seas of to-day. **1954** W. D. Thornbury *Princ. Geomorphol.* viii. 178 Although the peneplain still remains an important concept with most geomorphologists, it is now recognised that many topographic surfaces have been erroneously called peneplains. **1960** B. W. Sparks *Geomorphol.* xv. 335 Good examples of peneplains are extremely rare and some would say that they do not exist. **1968** J. Arnold *Shell Bk. Country Crafts* xxi. 255 The greater part of the many miles of walls [in Pembrokeshire] is composed of small boulders from the peneplain, which is mainly Cambrian. **1970** R. J. Small *Study of Landforms* v. 164 Most peneplains in the British Isles take the form of 'hill-top surfaces', and are so fragmented that they are by no means easy to identify. **1977** A. Hallam *Planet Earth* 301 He assumed a standard life-cycle for a river valley, marked by youth (steep-sided valleys), maturity (flood-plain floors), and old age as the river valley was worn lower and lower into a 'peneplain'.

fig. **1964** *Listener* 27 Feb. 353/2 In the eyes of a stray bitch Ribbed with hunger, heavy with young, I saw the peneplain of all imagined Misery.

peneplain ('piːniːpleɪn), *v. Geomorphol.* Also **-plane**. [f. prec. (after plane *v.*[1]), or a back-formation from next.] *trans.* To erode to a peneplain.

1923 [see kratogen]. **1931** N. M. Fenneman *Physiogr. Western U.S.* iv. 172 The original folds of all these mountains were approximately peneplaned. **1969** Bennison & Wright *Geol. Hist. Brit. Isles* viii. 181 The Old Red Sandstone of south-western Ireland rests on an irregular erosion surface which had not been peneplaned so that the beds are of variable thickness. **1970** R. J. Small *Study of Landforms* v. 164 The English Chalk country..may well have been effectively peneplained during the Pliocene period.

peneplained ('piːniːpleɪnd), *a. Geomorphol.* Also **-planed**. [f. peneplain *sb.* + -ed[2].] Made into a peneplain.

1904 Chamberlin & Salisbury *Geol.* (1905) I. iii. 85 (*caption*) A peneplaned surface where the elevations are small but steep-sided. **1922** *Bull. U.S. Geol. Survey* No. 730. 2 The older peneplaned surface was elevated, tilted, and dissected. **1963** D. W. & E. E. Humphries tr. *Termier's Erosion & Sedimentation* ii. 34 (*caption*) Both figures show the Natal monocline, where most of the peneplaned surfaces are dated by marine beds which they cut across near the coast. **1965** G. J. Williams *Econ. Geol. N.Z.* i. 2/2 The peneplained basement was deeply weathered under podozolising influences. **1978** *Nature* 13 July 131/2 Middle Jurassic sandstones were here laid down directly on the peneplaned Caledonian basement.

peneplanation (,piːniːplə'neɪʃən). *Geomorphol.* [f. pene- + planation.] Erosion to a peneplain.

1899 W. M. Davis in *Amer. Geologist* XXIII. 210 The unevenness of the uplands of to-day is a natural result of imperfect peneplanation followed by submature dissection. **1912** *Proc. Amer. Philos. Soc.* LI. 513 Peneplanation of the bituminous region had become far advanced. **1936** *Geogr. Jrnl.* LXXXVII. 22 A complicated history of peneplanation, uparching, faulting, and erosion. **1970** R. J. Small *Study of Landforms* v. 163 In an area such as the British Isles, perfectly preserved surfaces of peneplanation do not exist at or near present sea-level.

pener, penerial, -all, obs. ff. penner[1], penny-royal.

penerth, obs. f. *penn'orth*, pennyworth.

penes, pl. of penis.

Penest (pɪ'nɛst). *Greek Hist.* [ad. Gr. πενέστης.] A Thessalian serf; a bondsman; a labourer.

1835 Thirlwall *Greece* I. x. 437 The vast estates of these nobles were cultivated..by their serfs, the Penests. **1846** Grote *Greece* II. iii. (1862) II. 60 The Free Agora could not be trodden by any Penest.

penestone, obs. form of penistone.

penetauncer, variant of penitencer *Obs.*

penetrability (,pɛnɪtrə'bɪlɪtɪ). [f. penetrable: see -ity. Prob. ad. mod.L. **penetrābilitās*; cf. F. *pénétrabilité* (Huygens 1690, in Hatz.-Darm.).] The quality of being penetrable.

†**1.** Capacity of penetrating; penetrativeness.

1609 Bible (Douay) *1 Kings* Comm., The foure dowries of glorified bodies .. Impassibilitie .. Agilitie and Penetrabilitie. **1659** H. More *Immort. Soul* I. ii. §11 The Immediate Properties of a Spirit or Immateriall Substance are Penetrability and Indiscerpibility. **1687** —— *Answ. Psychop.* (1689) 122 Now for the Penetrability of Spirits, it is evident..that they can wholly penetrate one another.

2. Capability of being penetrated; *spec.* in *Nat. Philos.* The (conceived) capacity of simultaneously occupying the same space as something else (cf. penetration 1 b, impenetrability 2).

a **1648** Digby *Closet Open.* (1677) 161 According to the thickness and firmness of the piece [of meat] and penetrability of it. **1777** Priestley *Matt. & Spir.* (1782) I. iii. 33 Impenetrability being as much a property as penetrability. **1875** Lewes *Probl. Life & Mind* II. iv. §46. 282 All the facts which seem to prove penetrability only prove that the particles are mobile and separable, not that the particles themselves are penetrable.

penetrable ('pɛnɪtrəb(ə)l), *a.* (*sb.*) [ad. L. *penetrābilis*, f. *penetrāre* (see penetrate and -ble), perh. through F. *pénétrable* (Oresme *a* 1400).]

†**1.** Having the quality or capacity of penetrating; penetrative, penetrating (*lit.* and *fig.*). *Obs.*

1412–20 Lydg. *Chron. Troy* III. xxviii. (MS. Digby 230) lf. 134/1 Bawme natural That ran..Thoruȝ necke & hede in to many place, Penitrable by veynes of the face. **1430–40** —— *Bochas* III. (MS. Bodl. 263) lf. 193/2 Ther poynant poison is so penetrable. *a* **1548** Hall *Chron., Hen. VIII* 187b, His graces sight was so quike and penetrable that he saw him, ye and saw through him. **1597** A. M. tr. *Guillemeau's Fr. Chirurg.* 51b/2 The penetrable coulde is allsoe a sore enimye to all woundes in the Heade. **1668** H. More *Div. Dial., Schol.* (1713) 536 A Substance..most perfectly penetrable, which entirely passeth through every thing.

2. Capable of being penetrated or pierced; into or through which access may be gained.

a. *lit.* (also in reference to sight).

1538 Elyot, *Peruius*..that maye be gone in, penetrable. **1607** Topsell *Four-f. Beasts* (1658) 86 It is not penetrable by the eye of man. **1745** P. Thomas *Jrnl. Anson's Voy.* 12 Thick Woods so entangled with Undergrowth that..they are scarce penetrable. **1856** Kane *Arct. Expl.* II. 300 Our destination was to the highest penetrable point of Baffin's Bay.

b. *fig.* Capable of being penetrated by something immaterial, as reasoning, feeling, or thought; capable of being affected, susceptible; capable of being mentally seen into or through, discoverable.

1593 Shaks. *Lucr.* 559 His heart granteth No penetrable entrance to her playning. **1594** —— *Rich. III*, III. vii. 225, I am not made of Stones, But penetrable to your kinde entreaties. **1602** —— *Ham.* III. iv. 36. **1755** Young *Centaur* iii. Wks. 1757 IV. 186 Such a groan. It would eccho for ever in a penetrable ear. **1840** *Tait's Mag.* VII. 275 The heads of the peasantry may be thick, but they are penetrable. **1869** Ruskin *Q. of Air* §5 Involved in great, though attractive and penetrable, mystery.

B. *sb.* (*pl.*) Penetrable bodies or substances.

1658 Bromhall *Treat. Specters* IV. 277 The water..doth purge and water all penetrables.

Hence ˈ**penetrableness**, penetrability; ˈ**penetrably** *adv.* † (*a*) penetratingly (*obs.*); (*b*) so as to be penetrable.

1594 Nashe *Terrors of Nt.* Wks. (Grosart) III. 274 To make their prayers more penetrably enforcing. **1678** Cudworth *Intell. Syst.* I. v. 769 That which is Extended also, but Penetrably and Intangibly. **1684** Boyle *Porousn. Solid Bod.* v. 41 The penetrableness of Membranes to Fumes.

penetral (ˈpɛnɪtrəl). Now *rare*. Also 6 **-traile**, 7–9 **-trale**. [a. L. *penetral*, *-trāle* (usually in pl. *penetrālia*: see next), from *penetrāl-is* interior, innermost, f. stem of *penetrā-re* to PENETRATE.] The innermost part; of a temple, the sanctuary: usually in *pl.*: = next.

1589 A. M[unday] tr. *Palmendos* xxi. (1653) 125 The penetrails..of the stomack. **1657** W. Morice *Coena quasi Κοινὴ* vi. 64 Like Ægyptian Temples, specious in the Frontispiece, and a Calf or an Ape in the Penetral. **1660** H. More *Myst. Godl.* v. xi. 163 Piercing to the inmost penetrals of the heart. **1875** G. Macdonald *Malcolm* III. x. 151 It was now impossible to leave the cavern... He returned into its penetral.

β. with final *-e* (Lat. or Eng.).

a **1661** Fuller *Worthies, Cheshire* I. (1662) 180 To pierce into the Penetrales of Learning. **1787** Maty tr. *Riesbeck's Trav. Germ.* lvii. III. 102 After waiting the.efore some time the penetrale was opened, and I beheld my hero. **1827** G. S. Faber *Sacr. Calend. Prophecy* (1844) III. 72 Seated upon his throne, the mercy-seat, in the penetralē of the Temple. **1871** G. Macdonald *Sonn. concerning Jesus* iii, When from the penetrale she filled the fane.

‖**penetralia** (pɛnɪˈtreɪlɪə), *sb. pl.* [L., pl. of *penetral* or *penetrāle*: see prec.] The innermost parts or recesses of a building; *esp.* of a temple, the sanctuary or inmost shrine; hence *gen.* and *fig.* Innermost parts, recesses.

1668 Howe *Bless. Righteous* (1823) 92 From the penetralia—the secret chambers of the soul. **1710** T. Fuller *Pharm. Extemp.* 274 Admitted into the inmost *Penetralia* of the Lungs. **1779** W. Alexander *Hist. Women* iv. (1782) I. 118 So little do..[they] know what passes in all the penetralia of the harams of the East. **1849** Miss Mulock *Ogilvies* xi. (1875) 86 But the *sanctum sanctorum*, the *penetralia* of the city, is a small region surrounding the cathedral, entitled the Close. **1876** Holland *Sev. Oaks* xxiii. 323 They followed the boy into the penetralia of the great office.

Hence **peneˈtralian** *a. rare*, of or pertaining to the penetralia.

1892 Ld. Lytton *King Poppy* xi. 254 Within thy spirit's penetralian shrine.

penetralium (pɛnɪˈtreɪlɪəm). [erron. back-formation from PENETRALIA *sb. pl.*] The interior of a building. Also *fig.*

1817 Keats *Lett.* (1958) I. 194 Coleridge..would let go by a fine isolated verisimilitude caught from the Penetralium of mystery, from being incapable of remaining content with half knowledge. **1847** E. Brontë *Wuthering Heights* I. i. 5, I had no desire to aggravate his impatience, previous to inspecting the penetralium.

penetrameter (pɛnɪˈtræmɪtə(r)). *Radiography.* Formerly also **penetrometer**. [f. PENETRA-(TION + -METER.] An instrument for determining the wavelength, intensity, or total received dose of X-rays by measuring photographically their transmission through layers of metal of known thickness.

1907 M. K. Kassabian *Röntgen Rays & Electro-Therapeutics* III. iv. 431 (*heading*) Skiameters and penetrometers. **1912** J. M. Martin *Pract. Electro-Therapeutics* xiv. 242 Holzknecht's chromoradiometer, Walter's or Benoist's skiameter or penetrameter will be of service in determining the amount of radiance given off from the tube. **1923** Glazebrook *Dict. Appl. Physics* IV. 607/2 Among medical men Benoist's radiochromometer or penetrometer enjoys extensive use as a measurer of hardness. **1950** *Engineering* 7 Apr. 373/2 A penetrameter in steps of 0·010 in., with holes in each step, to calibrate the X-ray film. **1966** *McGraw-Hill Encycl. Sci. & Technol.* XI. 304*b*/2 When the smallest hole in this penetrameter can be seen in the radiograph, the penetrameter sensitivity is 2%. **1975** *Physics Bull.* Feb. 80/2 (Advt.), This issue also reports on..theoretical aspects of measuring kilovoltage by penetrameter.

ˈ**penetrance.** [f. L. *penetrānt-em* PENETRANT: see -ANCE.] † **1.** The action of penetrating; penetration. *Obs. rare*$^{-1}$.

1642 H. More *Song Soul* I. II. xii, Sith that this withouten penetrance Of bodies may be done.

2. *Genetics.* [ad. G. *penetranz* (O. Vogt 1926, in *Zeitschr. f. ges. Neurol. und Psychiatrie* CI. 809).] The extent to which a particular gene or set of genes is represented in the phenotypes of individuals possessing it, measured by the proportion of carriers having the phenotype characteristic of the gene.

1934 [see EXPRESSIVITY b]. **1946** R. R. Gates *Human Genetics* I. ii. 15 Lack of penetrance..has become a very important principle in human genetics... The gene is present in the germplasm, as shown by its transmission to the next generation, but for some reason it has completely failed to express itself in the soma. **1965** *Punch* 10 Nov. 689/2 The second complication is known as penetrance. When a gene affects every individual who carries it equally it is said to have 100 per cent penetrance. **1973** *Nature* 2 Mar. 64/2 An hereditary disease controlled by an autosomal Mendelian recessive gene with full penetrance. **1973** B. J. Williams *Evolution & Human Origins* ii. 30/1 Environmental differences may cause one carrier of a gene to pass this threshold and show the trait whereas another carrier of the same gene does not. This is referred to as incomplete penetrance.

†ˈ**penetrancy.** *Obs.* [f. as prec.: see -ANCY.] Penetrating quality; penetrativeness. (*lit.* and *fig.*)

1663 Boyle *Usef. Exp. Nat. Philos.* II. ii. 163 Powerful Menstruums, which by their activeness and penetrancy, are to unlock other Bodies. **1692** Ray *Disc.* 251 Considering the Penetrancy of such Vapours.

penetrant (ˈpɛnɪtrənt), *a.* (*sb.*) [ad. L. *penetrānt-em*, pr. pple. of *penetrāre* to penetrate, or F. *pénétrant* ppl. a. (13–14th c. in Hatz.-Darm.).] **A.** *adj.* That penetrates; penetrating.

1. *lit.* Having the property of penetrating, piercing, or making its way into anything.

1543 Traheron *Vigo's Chirurg.* II. iv. i. 68 Thys Aposteme is penetrant or persynge. **1601** Holland *Pliny* II. 87 Their sent is piercing and penetrant. **1713** Derham *Phys.-Theol.* 29 It's Rays would be less penetrant. **1887** R. Garnett *Carlyle* vii. 126 The hit was fair and penetrant.

2. *fig.* in reference to the mind, intellect, etc.: Having or showing mental penetration or insight; acute; subtle: = PENETRATING *ppl. a.* 3.

1599 Sandys *Europæ Spec.* (1632) 41 So searching and penetrant is the cunning of that Sea [= See]. **1661** Boyle *Style of Script.* (1675) 188 Whose penetrant and powerful arguments defeat not God's enemies. *a* **1734** North *Lives* (1826) II. 145 His skill was more pedantic than penetrant. **1836** W. A. Butler in *Blackw. Mag.* XXXIX. 455 He who hath The vision penetrant of Poesie.

3. *Genetics.* Producing in the phenotype the characteristic effect of the gene or combination of genes.

1955 R. B. Goldschmidt *Theoret. Genetics* III. v. 379 An incompletely penetrant effect is often based upon a system of multiple factors. **1973** B. J. Williams *Evolution & Human Origins* ii. 30/1 Genes are spoken of as fully penetrant or incompletely penetrant, but this is, in fact, as much a property of the environment as of the gene. **1978** *Nature* 27 Apr. 755/1 Gajdusek originally suggested that transmission was due to an autosomal dominant gene, fully penetrant in heterozygous females, but rarely penetrant in males unless they were homozygous.

† **B.** *sb.* **1.** A person of penetration or insight. *Obs. rare.*

a **1734** North *Exam.* I. ii. §173 (1740) 121 Our Penetrants have fancied all the Riddles..which in the Reign of King Charles II. were many, came N.N.E.

2. A penetrating coloured or fluorescent liquid used in a technique for detecting surface defects, in which the liquid is applied to the surface, excess removed, and developer applied to bring out the liquid left in the cracks and pores. Freq. *attrib.*, as ***penetrant inspection, testing***.

1951 *Materials & Methods* Feb. 92/2 Fluorescent penetrant inspection makes use of a water-washable penetrant of high fluorescence and unusual wetting or penetrating properties. **1958** H. Etherington *Nucl. Engin. Handbk.* x. 152 Penetrant-inspection methods are applicable to all metals as well as glazed ceramics, plastics, and other non-porous materials. *Ibid.*, The penetrant is drawn into surface discontinuities by capillary action. **1959** J. F. Hinsley *Non-Destructive Testing* xiv. 323 (*caption*) Crack in casting flange revealed by fluorescent penetrant. **1973** A. Parrish *Mech. Engineer's Ref. Bk.* viii. 13 Penetrant testing is the modern version of the old oil and whiting technique and is applicable to all metals and many non-metallic materials. **1975** Bram & Downs *Manuf. Technol.* ii. 67 Inspection with penetrant is probably the oldest of the major non-destructive testing methods in use today. *Ibid.*, The surface of the component is examined in order to locate the penetrant indications which have been formed in the developer coating. **1977** *Hot Car* Oct. 58/2 One wheel per batch is pressure tested and a percentage of the batch is checked by a penetrant dye for porosity.

penetrate (ˈpɛnɪtreɪt), *v.* Pa. pple. **penetrated**, †rarely **penetrate** = L. *penetratus*. [f. L. *penetrāt-*, ppl. stem of *penetrāre* to place within, enter within, pierce, etc.; related to *penitus* interior, inmost, to the inmost recesses. Cf. F. *pénétrer* (13–14th c. in Hatz.-Darm.), and see -ATE^3 7.

1589 Puttenham *Eng. Poesie* III. iv. (Arb.) 159 Also ye finde these words, *penetrate, penetrable, indignitie*, which I cannot see how we may spare them, whatsoeuer fault wee finde with Ink-horne termes: for our speach wanteth wordes to such sence so well to be vsed.]

1. *a. trans.* To make or find its (or one's) way into the interior of, or right through (something): usually implying force or effort; to pass into or through; to gain entrance or access within; to pierce. (Said also of the sight.)

In quot. 1541 to cause (a thing) to enter, insert (as in L.).

1530 Palsgr. 655/2, I penetrate, I perce or thrill thorowe a thyng, *je penetre*,..and *je tresperce*. **1541** Copland *Guydon's Quest. Chirurg.* Civb, The synewes be nat penetrate but in yᵉ teth [L. *ad dentes vero implantari videntur*]. **1547** Boorde *Brev. Health* cclxxix. 93 Coleryke humours..penytractyng the fleshe a lytel. *a* **1548** Hall *Chron., Rich. III* 56 With out resistence [we] haue penetrate the ample region..of Wales. **1610** Willet *Hexapla Dan.* 282 One bodie doth not penetrate or pierce another. **1697** Dryden *Virg. Past.* viii. 97 Verse breaks the Ground, and penetrates the Brake. **1791** Mrs. Radcliffe *Rom. Forest* v, Be more cautious how you penetrate the depths of this forest. **1849** Murchison *Siluria* iv. 76 Those strata..were also penetrated by powerful eruptions. **1860** Tyndall *Glac.* I. iii. 245 A cloud which it was almost impossible to penetrate. **1878** Huxley *Physiogr.* 64 The light instead of penetrating the snow, is thrown back from the ice-walls of each little air-cell or cavity. *Mod.* The darkness was so dense that the eye (or sight) could not penetrate it.

b. To enter and diffuse itself through; to permeate. Also with personal subj.: To cause to be permeated; to imbue (*with* something).

1680 H. More *Apocal. Apoc.* 43 The fixed purity thereof being ever penetrated by the presence of the seven Lamps of Fire. **1762–71** H. Walpole *Vertue's Anecd. Paint.* (1786) III. 151 Gibbons, whose art penetrated all materials, carved that beautiful pedestal. **1813** Bakewell *Introd. Geol.* (1815) 227 Organic remains..of large vegetables, completely penetrated with silex. **1815** Wordsw. *Sonn., 'The Shepherd, looking eastward'* 4 That little cloud..penetrated all with tender light. **1856** Froude *Hist. Eng.* (1858) I. i. 49 A vast organization which once penetrated the entire trading life of England. **1887** *Spectator* 5 Nov. 1512 The reader..should have penetrated himself—so to speak—with the atmosphere of the times.

c. To insert the penis into the vagina of (a woman). Also *absol.*

1953 H. M. Parshley tr. *S. de Beauvoir's Second Sex* IV. iii. 377 Woman, once penetrated, has no such sense of danger; but in return she feels trespassed upon in her flesh. **1960** J. Rodney *Handbk. Sex Knowledge* iv. 55 Deep penetration must not be aimed at for a number of sessions, and when the woman is ready for it she will move her body in such a way that the penis will penetrate deeply. **1963** M. McCarthy *Group* i. 24 Kay had had an awful time with Harald; five times, she insisted, before she was penetrated. *Ibid.* vi. 123 My mother..told me that a gentleman never penetrated his bride on the first night. **1975** *Times Lit. Suppl.* 21 Mar. 293/1 A character..endeavours in the course of one week to penetrate the female offspring of the entire Cabinet.

d. To infiltrate (an organization, esp. an enemy espionage network) as a spy.

1962 L. Deighton *Ipcress File* 221 He organized a train-wrecking group until it was penetrated and the survivors fled. **1967** L. James *Chameleon File* (1968) xvi. 201 We have penetrated the Cuban g-2, Mr. Wilson. We shall know if you do not do as we have asked. **1972** H. MacInnes *Message from Malaga* xix. 261 Are you forgetting my job? It is to penetrate the Lucas set up. **1977** C. McCarry *Secret Lovers* xix. 270 Did you arrange for him to double her, give him the illusion that he was penetrating your network?

2. *intr.* To make its (or one's) way *into* or *through* something, or *to* some point or place (with implication of remoteness or difficulty of access); to get in or through; to gain entrance or access.

1530 Palsgr. 655/2 A dangerouse weapen that is able to penetrate thorowe so stronge a harnesse. **1664** H. More *Myst. Iniq.* I. xii. 40 Through which distance neither her sight nor hearing can ever penetrate. **1732** Pope *Ep. Cobham* 142 Born where Heav'n's influence scarce can penetrate. **1798** Ferriar *Illustr. Sterne, Cert. Varieties Man* 211 After the natives of Europe began to penetrate into the east. **1841–71** T. R. Jones *Anim. Kingd.* (ed. 4) 430 A wide slit that allows the water freely to penetrate to the interior.

3. *fig.* **a.** *trans.* To pierce the ear, heart, or feelings of; to affect deeply; to 'touch'.

1591 Shaks. *Two Gent.* III. i. 231 Sad sighes, deepe grones, nor siluer-shedding teares Could penetrate her vncompassionate Sire. **1641** *Descr. Familie of Love* 3 He [Cupid] penetrateth the intrals of the most magnanimous. **1720** Ozell *Vertot's Rom. Rep.* II. x. 145 Like a Man penetrated with the utmost Grief. **1782** Miss Burney *Cecilia* x. x, Cecilia, astonished and penetrated, opposed the alteration. **1834** Southey *Doctor* cxxxix. (1862) 347 Certain philosophers..have been, to use the French-English of the day, deeply penetrated with this truth. **1878** R. W. Dale *Lect. Preach.* vii. 184 Men may still be penetrated with awe by the Divine Righteousness.

b. *intr.* To touch the heart, affect the feelings.

1611 Shaks. *Cymb.* II. iii. 14, I am aduised to giue her Musicke a mornings, they say it will penetrate.

4. *fig.* **a.** *trans.* To gain intellectual access into the inner content or meaning of; to get or have insight into; to see into or through; to attain knowledge of; to find out, discover, discern.

1560 tr. *Fisher's Treat. Prayer* To Rdr. Aivb, Who..so profoundly doth penetrate the comfort, ioy, and consolation commyng by true prayer. **1659** *Gentl. Calling* v. §19 If it be thoroughly penetrated, it will appear no less opposite to contentment than the former. **1734** tr. *Rollin's Anc. Hist.* (1827) VII. xvii. 259 Seleucus penetrated his scheme. **1818** Jas. Mill *Brit. Ind.* II. iv. v. 163 Clive penetrated and disappointed his designs. **1880** E. White *Cert. Relig.* 53 Men are left to penetrate their meaning by study and discovery.

b. *intr.* To gain intellectual or spiritual access, insight or knowledge; to 'see' *into* or *through*. Also, to be understood or fully realized.

1589 Puttenham *Eng. Poesie* I. iv. (Arb.) 25 They..yet penetrated further to know the diuine essences and substances separate. **1605** Bacon *Adv. Learn.* II. v. §2 In philosophy, the contemplations of man do either penetrate unto God, or are circumferred to nature. **1751** Harris *Hermes* Wks. (1841) 205 Thus it is that it [the mind] penetrates into the recesses of all things. **1866** R. W. Dale *Disc. Spec. Occas.* vii. 233 We have not yet penetrated into all the secrets of nature. **1955** E. Coxhead *Figure in Mist* iv. 134 'You're the most frightful woman I've ever met.' 'All right, it's penetrated.' **1973** G. Moffat *Deviant Death* vii.

109 We didn't notice that the gates were open..it wasn't till we came back hours later that it really penetrated.

Hence **'penetrated** *ppl. a.*; **'penetrating** *vbl. sb.* (also *attrib.*; often in reference to optical instruments: cf. PENETRATION 2 b).

1656 EARL MONM. tr. *Boccalini's Advts. fr. Parnass.* II. liv. (1674) 204 Mistaken in their penetrating into the hidden sense of their actions. **1661** BOYLE *Style of Script.* (1675) 87 Divers passages of Holy Scripture..afford out of their penetrated bowels, rich and precious mysteries of divinity. **1799** SIR W. HERSCHEL in *Phil. Trans.* (1800) 49 The power of penetrating into space by telescopes is very different from magnifying power. **1837** GORING & PRITCHARD *Microgr.* 111 An instrument whose light or penetrating power was superior to the other.

penetrating ('pɛnɪtreɪtɪŋ), *ppl. a.* [f. PENETRATE *v.* + -ING².] That penetrates; penetrative.

1. a. That pierces, or makes its way into or through something; *spec.* Having the quality of permeating the bodily system, or of strongly affecting the senses, esp. smell, taste, or hearing; sharp pungent; shrill or far-sounding.

1598 FLORIO, *Oxipori*, a kinde of piercing or penetrating medicine. **1646** SIR T. BROWNE *Pseud. Ep.* II. ii. 58 Effluxions, their penetrating natures. **1712** tr. *Pomet's Hist. Drugs* I. 197 A strong penetrating Smell. **1802** BINGLEY *Anim. Biog.* (1813) III. 349 The Penetrating Flea, or Chigoe. **1874** STUBBS *Const. Hist.* I. iii. §22. 47 Liberty is more penetrating and more extensive than elsewhere.

b. Passing readily through matter.

1902 *Nature* 31 July 318/1 Villard..first drew attention to the existence of some very penetrating rays from radium non-deviable by a magnetic field. **1928** [see COSMIC *a.* 3 c]. **1938** R. W. LAWSON tr. *Hevesy & Paneth's Man. Radio-activity* (ed. 2) xxv. 280 A penetrating particle had traversed both counters and the Wilson chamber. **1947** *Radiology* XLIX. 358/2 The malignant response elicited by penetrating radiations, irrespective of type, consisted of hemopoietic tissue tumors. **1968** M. S. LIVINGSTON *Particle Physics* iv. 74 Muons are the 'penetrating' component of the ionizing particles in cosmic radiation observed beneath great layers of earth in salt mines.

2. *fig.* That touches the heart or feelings intensely; deeply affecting.

1632 LITHGOW *Trav.* III. 107 Courteous penetrating lenity. **1851-5** BRIMLEY *Ess., Tennyson* 77 From the penetrating tenderness..of his love for the young girl.

3. *fig.* Having power to search with the mind into a thing; having or showing insight; acute, discerning.

a **1680** BUTLER *Rem.* (1759) I. 4 And bent his penetrating Brow, As if he meant to gaze her through. **1711** ADDISON *Spect.* No. 62 ⁋8 The most penetrating of all the French Criticks. **1718** *Free-thinker* No. 89. 237 Their Judgment grows clear and penetrating. **1795** BURKE *Lett., to Hussey* (1844) IV. 276 A wise person, of a penetrating and sagacious mind. **1828** SCOTT *F.M. Perth* ix, Acute features, and a penetrating look. **1875** WHITNEY *Life Lang.* ix 174 It takes a more penetrating and enlightened study to pick out the signs of original unity.

Hence **'penetratingly** *adv.*; **'penetratingness.**

1662 H. STUBBE *Ind. Nectar* iii. 55 The strength and penetratingness of their smell. **1670** COTTON *Espernon* II. VII. 332 Even the most penetratingly inquisitive began to grow weary of their suspicion. **1885** J. HAWTHORNE *Miss Cadogna* xvi. 206 Eyeing him penetratingly in her turn.

penetration (pɛnɪ'treɪʃən). [ad. late L. *penetrātiōn-em*, n. of action from *penetrāre* to PENETRATE; cf. F. *pénétration* (Oresme, 14th c.).]

1. a. The action, or an act, of penetrating or piercing; the passage of anything into or through a body; also, mutual permeation as of two fluids.

1623 COCKERAM, *Penetration*, a piercing. **1667** MILTON *P.L.* III. 585 His Magnetic beam,..to each inward part With gentle penetration, though unseen, Shoots invisible vertue even to the deep. **1800** WOLLASTON in *Phil. Trans.* XC. 241 Two fluids of unequal density are brought into contact, and unite by mutual penetration. **1803** *Ibid.* XCIII. 112 Mr. Brisson..has observed, that a mutual penetration takes place, when eleven parts of gold are alloyed with one of copper. **1826** R. SCOTT *Hayling Island* 95 Curiosity..has never induced the proprietor..to descend below the penetrations of the ploughshare. **1856** KANE *Arct. Expl.* II. App. 301 It became my duty..to attempt the penetration of this ice.

b. *Nat. Philos.* Used for a supposed or conceived occupation of the same space by two bodies at the same time: formerly *penetration of dimensions* (Scholastic L. *penetratio dimensionum*). Cf. IMPENETRABILITY 2.

1661 BOYLE *Spring of Air* II. iii. (1682) 44, I see not how the examiner's condensation can be performed without *penetration of dimensions*: a thing that philosophers in all ages have looked upon as by no means admitted by nature. **1704** J. HARRIS *Lex. Techn.* I, *Penetration of Dimensions*, is a Philosophical way of expressing, That two Bodies are in the same Place, so that the Parts of one do every where penetrate into, and adequately fill up the Dimensions or Places of the Parts of the other; which is manifestly impossible, and contradictory to Reason. **1830** KATER & LARDNER *Mech.* i. 5 There are many instances of apparent penetration; but in all these, the parts of the body which seem to be penetrated are displaced.

c. The insertion of the penis into the vagina in copulation.

1613 J. CHAMBERLAIN *Let.* 9 Sept. (1939) I. 475 What would you say yf you shold heare a churchman in open audience demaund of him..whether he had affection, erection, application, penetration, ejaculation. **1729** G. JACOB *New Law-Dict.* s.v. *Rape of women*, There must be Penetration and Emission, to make this Crime. **1848** WHARTON *Law Lexicon* 569/2 In Scotland..the following facts are necessary to be proved on a charge of rape: 1, penetration..; 2, actual force in the consummation. **1957** L. DURRELL *Justine* III. 185 The whole portentous scrimmage of sex itself, the act of penetration. **1960** [see PENETRATE *v.* 1 c]. **1963** A. HERON *Towards Quaker View of Sex* 65 'Frigidity'..implies more than failure to have orgasm: it is the inability to enjoy love-making and penetration.

d. The infiltration of a country, organization, etc., by political, financial, etc., means in order to gain influence, power, or information. Also used as a marketing term.

1931 F. L. ALLEN *Only Yesterday* vii. 176 In general the country extended its empire not by military conquest or political dictation, but by financial penetration. **1951** E. E. CUMMINGS *Let.* 3 Aug. (1969) 214 You should glimpse a huge map..to show the Soviet penetration of Greece—all but a little strip in the middle. **1964** L. DEIGHTON *Funeral in Berlin* 257 The detection and penetration of intelligence. **1971** I. DEUTSCHER *Marxism in our Time* 155 The fall in the ideological level of most of the militants..had facilitated to a certain extent the penetration of police agents into the Party. **1976** *National Observer* (U.S.) 21 Feb. 1/2 The relative decline in circulation of daily newspapers and their absolute decline in 'household penetration', has been accompanied by a growth of other printed media that duplicate one of the local daily's functions, but often better.

2. Power of penetrating, as a measurable quantity or quality. **a.** *Gunnery.* The depth to which a bullet or other projectile will penetrate any material, as earth or metal, against which it is fired.

1807 HUTTON *Course Math.* II. 336 Mr. Robins found this penetration, by experiment, to be only 5 inches. **1892** GREENER *Breech Loader* 125 The rack is placed about 4 ft. from the ground, and fired at from the standard distance (40 yards); the number of sheets pierced by one or more shots is the penetration. **1901** *Daily Chron.* 25 May 3/2 The more penetration shells have the better.

b. *Optics.* The power of an optical instrument to enable the observer to see into space, or into an object.

(*a*) In a telescope: Power of rendering distant objects visible or distinct, considered in relation to their distance; 'space-penetrating power'. It is measured by the number of times that the distance of an object would have to be increased in order that it should appear, when viewed through the telescope, exactly as it does to the naked eye at its actual distance. (*b*) In a microscope: Power of the object-glass to give distinct vision for some distance both beyond and within its exact focus.

1799 SIR W. HERSCHEL in *Phil. Trans.* (1800) 82 My telescope..possessed a power of penetration, which exceeded that of natural vision 61.18 times. *Ibid.* 83 We did not stop at the single stars..when the penetration of the natural eye was to be ascertained. **1867** J. HOGG *Microsc.* I. ii. 72 *Penetration*, or that power which enables the observer to see deep into the structure of objects without any alteration of focus.

3. *fig.* The action, or capacity, of penetrating something with the mind; ability to see mentally into or through a thing; keenness of perception or understanding; insight, acuteness, discernment.

1605 BACON *Adv. Learn.* I. To the King §2, I have been..possessed with an extreme woonder at..the penetration of your Iudgement. **1709** STEELE *Tatler* No. 57 ⁋2 You can pretend to be a Man of Penetration. **1769** *Junius Lett.* xv. (1771) 73 Common sense foresees consequences which have escaped your..penetration. **1865** DICKENS *Mut. Fr.* III. v, Mrs. Lammle [was] a woman of penetration and taste.

4. *attrib.*, as *penetration tariff*: see quot.; **penetration agent**, a spy sent to penetrate an enemy organization; **penetration aid**, an object released from a missile as a decoy to draw off any attacking missiles; **penetration twin** *Cryst.*, a twin crystal that presents the appearance of two interpenetrating crystals; so *penetration twinning*.

1966 'A. HALL' *9th Directive* ii. 22 This is a police job. I'm a penetration agent..they've made a mistake. **1976** P. HENISSART *Winter Quarry* III. xxvi. 270 As soon as I learned of McGuire's existence, I mistrusted him—a shiftless contract-agent for the CIA... I know your taste for penetration agents. **1966** *N.Y. Times Mag.* 20 Mar. 59 The decoys— 'penetration aids' in the missilemen's jargon—would range from dummy warheads to metalized-plastic warhead shapes. **1967** *Electronics* 6 Mar. 50/2 It is researching the key problem: how to distinguish the lethal reentry vehicle from the penetration aids. **1890** *Times* 24 Dec. 3/4 M. Noblemaire..has in this pamphlet defended ..'penetration tariffs'. By this expression is meant tariffs which diminish with the distances over which goods are conveyed. **1868** J. D. DANA *Syst. Min.* (ed. 5) 191 Penetration-twins, the forms not corresponding to a regular revolution, but to an irregular interpenetration of unlike parts of the crystal. **1971** C. S. HURLBUT *Dana's Man. Min.* (ed. 18) ii. 97 Twin crystals are usually designated as either contact twins or penetration twins... Penetration twins are made up of interpenetrating individuals having an irregular composition surface, and the twin law is usually defined by a twin axis. **1953** F. H. POUGH *Field Guide Rocks & Minerals* I. iv. 53 We also find attractive penetration twinning in phenakite.

penetrative ('pɛnɪtreɪtɪv), *a.* [ad. med.L. *penetrātīv-us*, f. ppl. stem of L. *penetrāre*: see -ATIVE. In F. *pénétratif, -ive* (13th c. in Hatz.-Darm.).] Having the quality of penetrating.

1. Having the quality of piercing, entering, or making its way into anything; *spec.* Having the property of entering through the senses, or of keenly affecting the sense organs; sharp, pungent. Also said of the eye or sight in reference to its piercing quality. Cf. PENETRATING *ppl. a.* 1.

1477 NORTON *Ord. Alch.* v. in Ashm. (1652) 69 Wherefore it [sweet smell] is in Aier more penetrative. **1528** LYNDESAY *Dreme* 73 The air was rycht penetratyve. **1578** LYTE *Dodoens* II. lxxix. 253 The whole herbe is of a strong, and penetratiue sauour. **1686** GOAD *Celest. Bodies* I. ix. 30 Cold is..Active and Biting, Penetrative through Glass it self. **1819** W. TAYLOR in *Monthly Mag.* XLVII. 401 The churches of England and Scotland so nearly agree in doctrine, that their ordinations might be rendered reciprocally penetrative. **1853** TRENCH *Proverbs* 140 'Where the devil cannot come, he will send'; a proverb..which excellently sets out the penetrative character of temptations.

2. *fig.* That penetrates to the seat of the feelings.

1606 SHAKS. *Ant. & Cl.* IV. xiv. 75 Bending downe His corrigible necke, his face subdu'de To penetratiue shame.

3. *fig.* Having the power of mental penetration; characterized by or showing insight; intellectually acute: = PENETRATING *ppl. a.* 3.

a **1727** SWIFT *Ep. to T. Snow* 9 O thou, whose penetrative Wisdom found The South-Sea Rocks and Shelves where Thousands drown'd. **1846** RUSKIN *Mod. Paint.* II. III. II. iii. §1 *margin*, Imagination penetrative is concerned not with the combining but apprehending of things. **1871** MORLEY *Voltaire* (1886) 6 So vigorous and minutely penetrative was the quality of his understanding.

Hence **'penetratively** *adv.*, in a penetrative manner, with penetration; **'penetrativeness**, penetrative quality, power of penetration.

1652 FRENCH *Yorksh. Spa* viii. 71 Because of its wonderfull penetrativenes leaving no part or places of the body unsearched. **1697** J. SERGEANT *Solid Philos.* 456 Got by looking more penetratively into those Distinct Natures in our Mind. **1873** M. ARNOLD *Lit. & Dogma* (1876) 165 By his incomparable lucidity and penetrativeness. **1878** GROSART in *H. More's Poems* Mem. Introd. 29/1 Of it Principal Tulloch writes penetratively.

penetrator ('pɛnɪtreɪtə(r)). [a. late L. *penetrātor*, agent-n. from *penetrāre*: see PENETRATE and -OR.] One who penetrates (*lit.* or *fig.*).

1824 W. IRVING *T. Trav.* I. 209 A digger of Greek roots, or a penetrator of pyramids. **1829** LYTTON *Devereux* IV. v, He is a perfect penetrator into human vices.

†**'penetre**, *v. Obs. rare*⁻⁰. [a. F. *pénétre-r.*] To penetrate.

c **1532** DU WES *Introd. Fr.* in *Palsgr.* 945 To penetre, *fausser* [= to pierce]. 952 *Penetrer*, to penetre or throwe.

†**'penetrive**, *a. Sc. Obs.* Also penitrive. [f. stem of F. *pénétr-er* + -IVE. Cf. *penser, pensive*.] = PENETRATIVE.

c **1480** HENRYSON *Prayer for Pest* 26 in *Bannatyne Poems* (Hunter. Cl.) 62 Slaik thy plaig that is so penetryve. **1533** BELLENDEN *Livy* I. x. (S.T.S.) 56 Thir sex brethir..ruschit with maist penetrive and awful wapynnys like þe bront of twa armyis togiddir. **1536** —— *Cron. Scot.* (1821) I. p. vii, For stormis cauld and frostis penitrive.

penetrometer (pɛnɪ'trɒmɪtə(r)). [f. PENETR(ATION + -OMETER.] **1.** An instrument for determining the consistency or hardness of a substance (as asphalt, soil or snow) by measuring the depth or rate of penetration of a rod or needle driven by a known force.

1905 C. RICHARDSON *Mod. Asphalt Pavement* IX. xxvi. 533 (*heading*) New York testing laboratory penetrometer. **1913** BLANCHARD & DROWNE *Text-bk. Highway Engin.* x. 293 Penetrometer to be used in accordance with standard method on materials solid at above temperatures. **1930** *Engineering* 18 July 61/3 The penetrometer is simply a ½-in. square bar fitted loosely in guides and loaded with weights giving steps of about ½ ton per square foot. **1966** C. FRASER *Avalanche Enigma* iv. 71 The first measurement taken is a penetrometer profile. **1971** B. BUCK tr. *Ludewig's Polyester Fibres* iv. 124 In order to determine the melting point, a grain of the polyester is placed into the container of the penetrometer and the needle is centred on the surface of [*printed* on] the substance under test. **1975** D. BAGLEY *Snow Tiger* iv. 49 This is a penetrometer... It measures the resistance of the snow.

2. Obs. var. PENETRAMETER.

penett(e, obs. form of PENNET.

pen-feather ('pɛn,fɛðə(r)). [f. PEN *sb.*² + FEATHER.]

1. A quill-feather of a bird's wing.

1602 *Withal's Dict.* 17/2 The great feather of a bird called a pen feather, *penna*. **1692** RAY *Disc.* II. iv. (1732) 192 How happens it that we find none of their Pen-feathers? **1825** SCOTT *Betrothed* Introd., Take care your own pen-feathers are strong enough to support you. **1899** *Daily News* 19 Aug. 7/5 Pen-feathers are seen on cycling hats.

2. A young undeveloped feather; a PIN-FEATHER.

1877 *N.W. Linc. Gloss.*, *Pen-feathers*, small, undeveloped feathers. **1900** *Eng. Dial. Dict.* (S. Nott.), 'A dont like pluckin this fowl; it's all pen-feathers'. *Ibid.* (Reported from many districts, northern and midland.)

pen-feathered ('pɛn,fɛðəd), *a.* [f. PEN *sb.*² 1 c + *feathered*, in the sense 'feathered with "pens" only'. Cf. the synonymous PIN-FEATHERED.]

1. Having the feathers undeveloped, or showing the quills or barrels only, without vanes (see PEN-FEATHER 2), as a young bird; half-fledged; not fully fledged; also *fig.* immature, 'callow'.

1628 EARLE *Microcosm., Aturney* (Arb.) 65 His hatching [was] vnder a Lawer; whence though but pen-feather'd, hee hath now nested for himselfe. **1659** R. WILD *Poems* (1870) 36 Not a pen-feathered lark who ne'er tried wing. **1708** PRIOR *Turtle & Sparrow* 263 My children then were just pen-feather'd, Some little corn for them I gather'd. **1858** GEN. P. THOMPSON *Audi Alt.* I. liii. 208 The most extraordinary argument, worthy of being set down in any pen-feathered logician's list of fallacies.

2. Said of a horse or his hair when rough and bristly.

1737 BRACKEN *Farriery Impr.* (1756) I. 346 So that the Hair stare, and is (what some term) pen-feather'd. **1828** *Craven Gloss.* (ed. 2), *Pen-feathered*, when the skin or hair of a horse is rough, he is said to be pen-feathered. His hair is so sticky that it resembles pens or feathers. **1874** W. WILLIAMS *Princ. Veterinary Med.* (1888) 389 The hair stands on end 'pen-feathered'.

penfieldite ('pɛnfiːldaɪt). *Min.* [f. the name of Samuel L. *Penfield* (1856–1906), U.S. mineralogist + -ITE[1].] A basic lead chloride, Pb_2Cl_3OH, occurring as very small, usu. prismatic crystals that are colourless and transparent when pure.

1892 F. A. GENTH in *Amer. Jrnl. Sci.* CXLIV. 260 While examining a lot of minerals, formed by the action of sea water on ancient slags which Mr. Geo. L. English collected at Laurion, Greece, I noticed a *very few* hexagonal crystals which proved to be a new species, for which I propose the name: Penfieldite, in honor to Prof. Sam'l L. Penfield the indefatigable worker in mineralogy and crystallography. **1954** *Mineral Abstr.* XII. 453 The stocks..of two Roman anchors recovered from the Mediterranean are covered with a crust of small crystals of anglesite, phosgenite, penfieldite, with less cerussite, hydrocerussite, and specks of metallic copper and copper stains. **1969** *Ibid.* XX. 144/2 Penfieldite, ..from Laurium, Greece, and from Sierra Gorda, Chile, has *a* 11·28, *c* 48·65 Å.

pen-fish. [f. PEN *sb.*[2] + FISH *sb.*[1]]

1. A squid or calamary (cf. PEN *sb.*[2] 3 c).

1835–6 TODD *Cycl. Anat.* I. 321/2 The common Calamary or Pen-fish.

2. The sparoid fish *Calamus penna* of the Caribbean Sea: called in Spanish *pez de pluma*.

1890 in *Cent. Dict.*

penfold ('pɛnfəʊld), *sb.* [f. PEN *sb.*[1] + FOLD *sb.*[2]] A fold for penning sheep or cattle; also, an enclosure for stray cattle, etc., a pound: = PINFOLD *sb.* (Also *fig.*)

1575 CHURCHYARD *Chippes* (1817) 154 Who is betrapt in penfold close is sure At neede to want both ayde and skoutes. **1656** EARL MONM. tr. *Boccalini's Advts. fr. Parnass.* I. xlvii. (1674) 62, I never had in my Penfolds above 500 Sheep. **1832** *Act 2 & 3 Will. IV*, c. 64 Sched. O. 30 Thence in a straight line to the southern extremity, close by a penfold, of the fence which divides the two fields. **1871** SWINBURNE *Songs bef. Sunrise, Halt bef. Rome* 275 The sheep of the priests, and the cattle That feed in the penfolds of Kings.

'penfold, *v.* [f. prec. sb.] *trans.* **a.** To divide into or as into penfolds. **b.** To confine in or as in a penfold: = PINFOLD *v.*

1830 I. TAYLOR *Unitar.* in *Logic in Theol.* etc. (1859) 82 The whole area is penfolded by pews. **1851** —— *Wesley* (1852) 105 Those partitionments within which soulless religionists are content to be penfolded.

pen-friend ('pɛnfrɛnd). [f. PEN *sb.*[2] + FRIEND *sb.*] A friend or contact with whom a regular correspondence is conducted. (See also PEN-PAL.) Hence **pen-friendship**, the relationship existing between pen-friends.

1933 *Boy's Mag.* XLVII. 106/1 Any reader at home or abroad who would like to correspond with a 'pen-friend' in another land is invited to send his name, address, and age to the Editor. **1943** F. THOMPSON *Candleford Green* iv. 65 The correspondence languished, then ceased, in the usual manner of such pen-friendships. **1945** 'O. MALET' *My Bird Sings* I. ii. 18 She had returned to England..but none the less they had kept up one of those rambling pen-friendships. **1957** R. MASON *World of Suzie Wong* I. ii. 15 It had caused my predecessor, a Pole, to propose through the post to a pen-friend in Glasgow whom he had never met. **1960** *Woman's Own* 19 Mar. 77/4, I cannot help you to find pen-friends, but..I will send you the name of a pen-friendship organisation. **1974** *Times* 2 Jan. 24/4 (Advt.), Elderly person desiring a pen friend please reply to Box 2901 B, The Times. **1975** *Bangladesh Times* 27 July 7/7, I am a boy of 18 and studying in the 2nd year Commerce. I am very interested in establishing Pen-friendship with boys and girls from all over the world, including Bangladesh. **1977** *Navy News* June 26/4 Readers seeking penfriends in the Royal Navy are listed here.

penful ('pɛnfʊl). [f. PEN *sb.*[2] 4 + -FUL 2.] The quantity (of ink) taken up by a pen at one dip; *transf.* as much as one can write with this.

1555 R. BRAHAM *Lydgate's Chron. Troy* To Rdr., I shulde neuer then haue dared, to haue bestowed hereof one penful of yncke. *a* **1662** HEYLIN *Laud* (1668) 479 An Act..which he had also signed with the same Penful of Ink. **1771** H. WALPOLE *Let. to C'tess Ossory* 27 June, I have not picked up a penful [of news] since I wrote to my lord.

‖**penghulu** (pəŋ'huːluː). Also **panghulu, pengulu.** [Malay.] In Malaysia, a head-man or chief.

1821 J. LEYDEN tr. *Malay Annals* 49 Under the bandahara immediately was the panghulu bandahari. **1894** N. B. DENNYS *Descr. Dict. Brit. Malaya* 285 The Penghulus are elected by the neighbours and confirmed by the Government. **1900** W. W. SKEAT *Malay Magic* v. 232 After my arrival with the *Pĕnghulu* the ceremony began. **1906** —— & BLAGDEN *Pagan Races Malay Peninsula* I. 500 When a village migrates, the Penghulu conducts the migration. **1927** H. M. TOMLINSON *Gallions Reach* xxvii. 219 Norrie addressed himself to the penghulu; the chief answered him with gentle explicitness. **1928** L. R. WHEELER *Mod. Malay* v. i. 194 The peasant class has various grades, from the 'penghulu' type, accustomed to exercise authority on a limited scale in his neighbourhood, to the backward natives. **1971** *Lady* 15 July 88/3 The Pengulu, the Headman, shook us by the hand and welcomed us to his domain. **1972** A. AMIN tr. *Ahmad's No Harvest but Thorn* viii. 85 Jeha remembered how Lahuma had asked her to go to the *Penghulu*'s house. **1977** P. THEROUX *Consul's File* 131 The *penghulu*, the headman, pointed out that..the rice was planted.

penglima, var. PANGLIMA.

pengo ('pɛŋgø:). Pl. **pengo, -oes.** [Hungarian *pengö*, lit. 'ringing'.] The basic monetary unit of Hungary from 1927 to 1946.

1926 *Glasgow Herald* 4 Jan. 12/2 To-day the new Hungarian currency, the pengo, is quoted for the first time. **1927** *Times* 28 Feb. 11/7 The Hungarian government has assigned a sum of 322,820 pengoes..for..a new Hungarian Legation building in London. **1930** *Observer* 23 Feb. 11/2 He earns twenty pengo a week. **1932** *Daily Express* 2 July 12/1 The amounts due to bondholders will be deposited in pengoes in the Hungarian National Bank. **1947** *Whitaker's Almanack* 917/1 The *Pengo* (of 100 *Filler*) was superseded in August, 1946, by a new currency, the *gulder*.

pengolin: see PANGOLIN.

penguin ('pɛngwɪn, 'pɛŋgwɪn). Also 6–7 **pengwin, -gwyn, -guyn, 7 -guine,** (8 **pin-**). [Origin obscure: see Note below. It appears that the name was first given to the Great Auk or Gare-fowl of the seas of Newfoundland, still called in F. *pingouin* or *pinguin* (1600 in Hatz.-Darm.). But it was soon applied also to the birds now called *penguins*, in F. *manchots* (found by Drake at Magellan's Straits in 1578), which have a general external resemblance to the northern bird, though, in the opinion of zoologists, widely removed in structure. In this sense, also, Du. and Ger. *pinguin*, Da. and Sw. *pingvin*, all from English.]

†**1.** A former name of the Great Auk or Gare-fowl (*Alca impennis*). *Obs.*

1578 PARKHURST *Let.* 13 Nov. in Hakluyt *Voy.* (1600) III. 133 Newfoundland is in a temperate Climate... There are ..many other kind of birdes store, too long to write, especially at one Island named Penguin, where wee may driue them on a planke into our ship as many as shall lade her. These birdes are also called Penguins, and cannot flie. **1582** *Ingram's Narrative* in Hakluyt *Voy.* (1589) 560 The Countrey men call them *Penguins* (which seemeth to be a Welsh name). *a* **1589** *M. Hore's Voy. Cape Breton* in 1536, ibid. 518 They came to part of the West Indies about Cape Breton, shaping their course thence Northeastwards, vntill they came to the Island of Penguin,..whereon they went and founde it full of great foules white and gray, as bigge as geese. **1620** J. MASON *New-found-land* 4 The sea fowles, are Gulles, white and gray Penguins. **1664** BUTLER *Hud.* I. ii. 60 And were invented first from Engins, As Indian Britans were from Penguins. **1678** RAY *Willughby's Ornith.* 322 The Bird called Penguin by our Seamen, which seems to be Hoiers *Goifugel*. **1792** G. CARTWRIGHT *Jrnl. Resid. Labrador* III. 55 (5 July 1785) A boat came in from Funk Island laden with birds, chiefly penguins. [**1863** LYELL *Antiq. Man* ii. 15 Among the bones of birds, scarcely any are more frequent.. than those of the auk or penguin (*Alca impennis*).]

2. a. Now, The general name of birds of the family *Spheniscidæ*, including several genera of sea-fowl inhabiting the southern hemisphere, as near Cape Horn, the Falkland Islands, the Cape of Good Hope, etc., distinguished by having the wings represented by scaly 'flippers' or paddles with which they swim under water.

1588 T. CANDISHE in Hakluyt *Voy.* (1589) 809 The Port of Desire... In this place we had gulles, puets, penguyns, and seales in aboundance. *Ibid.*, We put into the Streight of Magelan, and on the 8 [Jan. 1587] we came vnto the Islands named by Sir Francis Drake the one Bartholomewe Island, ..and the other Penguin Island. **1591** J. JANE *Last Voy. Candish* ibid. (1600) III. 85 This Penguin hath the shape of a bird, but hath no wings, only two stumps in the place of wings. **1638** SIR T. HERBERT *Trav.* (ed. 2) 13 Here ['Pengwin' or Robben Island, near Cape Town] are also birds cal'd Pen-gwins (white-head in Welch) like Pigmies walking upright. **1655** E. TERRY *Voy. E. India* 26 There are very many great lazy fowls upon and about this Island [Robben Island] with great cole-black bodies and very white heads, called Penguins. **1678** RAY *Willughby's Ornith.* 322 The Birds of this kind..the Hollanders from their fatness called Penguins. **1775** CLAYTON in *Phil. Trans.* LXVI. 103 There are four kinds; the yellow, or king penguin; the red; the black or holey, from their burrowing under ground; and the jumping jacks, from their motion. **1877** W. THOMSON *Voy. Challenger* II. 167 The penguin as a rule swims under water, rising now and then and resting on the surface. **1885** NEWTON in *Encycl. Brit.* XVIII. 45 Under the name *Impennes* we have a group of Birds, the Penguins... The title of an Order can scarcely be refused to them.

b. A machine like an aeroplane but incapable of flight, used in the early stages of an airman's training. Also, a non-flying member of an air force. *Air Force slang.*

1915 G. BACON *All about Flying* vi. 104 A 'penguin'—a machine with engine not powerful enough to raise it from the ground. **1917** J. R. MCCONNELL *Flying for France* 143 The student is put on..a low-powered machine with very small wings... It could not leave the ground. The apparatus is jokingly and universally known as a Penguin. **1918** *Everybody's Mag.* Jan. 113/2 An officer of flying status, but who for some reason does not fly, is called a 'penguin'. **1918** *Sphere* 4 May 76/2 The three official corps familiarly known as the Waacs, the Wrens, and the Penguins. **1919** *Athenæum* 11 July 582/2 Members of the W.R.A.F. were called 'Penguins' because they were 'flappers' who did not fly. **1925** FRASER & GIBBONS *Soldier & Sailor Words* 221 Penguin was also a name for a type of low-powered aeroplane with small planes or wings, used for instructional purposes. **1942** *Gen* 1 Sept. 14/2 No flier spares his contempt for the 'penguins', the nonflying administrative officers in the RAF. **1944** G. GIBSON *Enemy Coast Ahead* (1946) vi. 96 In the average Bomber Officers' Mess,..while penguins sing loudly in the mornings as they get up to shave, it was rather hard for the boys who had been up all night to get a good day's rest. **1950** PARTRIDGE *Here, There & Everywhere* 53 When an airman refers to himself as a *penguin*, he is resorting to the specialized slang of the Air Force; all he means is that he is a member of the ground staff and therefore does not fly.

c. (With capital initial.) The proprietary name of Longman Penguin Limited, formerly Penguin Books Limited (1936–1966) and The Penguin Publishing Company Limited (1966–1972), used *attrib.* and *absol.* to designate paper-backed books or series of books published by this company. Also (*rare*) as *v. trans.*, to publish as a Penguin book.

1935 *Times Lit. Suppl.* 1 Aug. 491/1 We shall look forward to more Penguin Books, and we wish the experiment—a bold one—all success. **1938** 'G. ORWELL' *Homage to Catalonia* x. 177, I..spent hours reading a succession of Penguin Library books. **1939** *Trade Marks Jrnl.* 13 Dec. 1630/1 Penguin... Printed publications, stationery and bookbinding, but not including publications on birds, or shaped sheets of paper for display purposes. Penguin Books Limited,..West Drayton, Middlesex; manufacturers and publishers. **1940** GRAVES & HODGE *Long Week-End* xxv. 426 Penguins were first published in 1936. **1948** J. BETJEMAN *Sel. Poems* 84 Whether we like to sit with Penguin books In sheltered alcoves farther up the cliff. **1950** D. E. STEVENSON *Music in Hills* vi. 50 Miss Douglas..appeared from behind a large book-case with two Penguins in her hand. **1950** W. STEVENS *Let.* 15 Aug. (1967) 687 At the moment I am reading a Penguin Classic. **1951** R. MACAULAY *Lett. to Friend* (1961) 209 *Mary Lavelle* is Penguin'd. **1956** J. SYMONS *Paper Chase* x. 69 Hedda Pont was at a table reading a Penguin thriller. **1959** J. BRAINE *Vodi* i. 11 You can have those Penguins in the bottom of the clothes locker. **1962** I. MURDOCH *Unofficial Rose* v. 51 There were a few Penguin novels, but they looked dull English tea-party stuff. **1974** *Times Lit. Suppl.* 11 Dec. 22/4 With the publication of *Barnaby Rudge* all but two of Dickens's novels..are now Penguined. **1976** *New Yorker* 15 Nov. 187/1 Michael Hamburger, introducing the Penguin anthology of Enzensberger in translation, writes of the poet's 'moral purpose at variance with his personal needs and perceptions'.

d. A man wearing evening dress (cf. *penguin suit* (*a*) in sense 3 below). *rare.*

1967 *Melody Maker* 1 Apr. 9 Good Music had the sort of melody and clipping beat that even Victor Sylvester didn't have to alter so that the Brylcreemed penguins and their sequined partners could jig about in the ballrooms. **1976** B. BOVA *Multiple Man* (1977) v. 56 These stuffed penguins and their bejeweled ladies.

3. *attrib.* and *Comb.*, as ***penguin kind***; **penguin duck**, a variety of the common duck having the feet placed far back so as to induce a nearly erect attitude like that of a penguin; **penguin grass**, the Tussock-grass of the Falkland Islands, *Poa flabellata*; **penguin rookery**, an assemblage of penguins, a penguinery; **penguin suit**, (*a*) evening dress; (*b*) a type of suit worn by astronauts.

18.. TEGETMEIER *Poultry* 310 (Cass. Suppl.) The colours of the *Penguin duck are varied. **1775** CLAYTON in *Phil. Trans.* LXVI. 100 Near the shore, where-ever there is a sandy soil, a species of grass grows, called *Penguin grass. **1774** GOLDSM. *Nat. Hist.* (1776) VI. 49 Those of the *Penguin kind..with round bills, legs hid in the abdomen, and short wings. **1885** NEWTON in *Encycl. Brit.* XVIII. 491/2 The habit of the helpless birds, when breeding, to congregate by hundreds and thousands in what are called '*Penguin-rookeries'. **1967** PARTRIDGE *Dict. Slang* Suppl. 1289/1 **Penguin suit*, a dinner jacket. **1968** R. JEFFRIES *Traitor's Crime* iv. 46 Some smooth bastard in a penguin suit. **1971** *N.Y. Times* 10 June 18 The astronauts donned the tight-fitting overalls, known as a penguin suit, in which tension is produced by several layers of rubberized material. **1971** *Daily Tel.* 1 July 30/5 During the Soyuz 9 and 11 flights, Russian cosmonauts..wore special suits, called 'penguin' suits. **1979** K. M. PEYTON *Marion's Angels* vi. 101 Geoff'd better go home for his penguin suit. I'll go up and get my tails.

[*Note.* Our earliest examples of the name *penguin* are due to Hakluyt. His account of Hore's Voyage to Cape Breton was taken down by him, some fifty years after the event, from the mouth of Thomas Buts, a survivor of the voyage. If we could be sure that the name 'Penguin Island' dated back to 1536, this would be the earliest occurrence of the word, as it is certainly the earliest English notice of the bird. Ingram's *Narrative*, if reliable, would be evidence for the name in 1568–9; but his tale is discredited, and is thus evidence only that he had heard of the penguin by 1582, four years later than Parkhurst's letter to Hakluyt. The southern fowl, found by Drake (as by Magalhaens before him) at Magellan's Straits, is fully described in *The World Encompassed by Sir Francis Drake*, published by his nephew in 1628, 'out of the Notes of Mr. Francis Fletcher', Drake's chaplain (ed. Hakl. Soc., 1854, p. 75), but no name is there given to it. The name occurs however in a MS of 1677, stated to be a transcript of Fletcher's original Notes of 1578:

'infinite were the number of fowles, which the Welsh men named Penguin, and Magilanus tearmed them geese' (*ibid.* 72); but the absence of the name from the printed work of 1628, and from three other 16th c. accounts of the voyage (*ibid.* Appendix 217, 237, 279), in which the bird is described, makes the occurrence of *penguin* in Fletcher's original Notes somewhat doubtful. The name certainly occurs in the narrative of Candishe or Cavendish, 1588; though his statement that Drake named one of the isles 'Penguin Island' is at variance with that of the eye-witnesses Fletcher and Winter (*ibid.* 76, 279), who both state that he named it *St. George's Island* 'in honour of England'. The attribution of the name *penguin* to 'the Welsh men', and its explanation as Welsh *pen gwyn* 'white head', appears also in Ingram, and later in Sir Thomas Herbert's *Travels*—in ed. 1634 as a surmise, in ed. 1638 as an accepted fact. But, besides that the Great Auk had not a white head (though it had white spots in front of the eyes), there are obvious historical difficulties, which some would remove in part by supposing the name to have been originally given by Breton fishermen. Other suggestions that the name is derived from L. *pinguis* 'fat', or is an alteration of 'pin-wing', referring to the rudimentary wings, are merely unsupported conjectures.]

penguin, var. PINGUIN, a West Indian plant.

penguinery ('pɛngwɪnərɪ). Also **penguinry**. [f. PENGUIN + -ERY.] An assemblage or colony of penguins; a place where penguins congregate and breed.

1839 FITZROY *Narr. 'Adventure'* I. 388 The old bird gets on a little eminence, and makes a great noise..holding its head up in the air, as if it were haranguing the penguinnery. **1921** H. G. PONTING *Gt. White South* 55 The Adélie penguinry was but a mile or two away. **1979** *Nature* 11 Jan. 88/2 The Adelie and chinstrap penguins feed mainly on krill, but they take different sized prey, either by active selection or by the Adelie feeding further from the rookery (or penguinery).

pengulu, var. PENGHULU.

pen-gun. *Sc.* [f. PEN *sb.*[2] + GUN *sb.*]

1. A toy air-gun made from a quill; a pop-gun. '*to crack like a pen-gun*: to be very loquacious' (Jamieson).

1807 T. CAMPBELL *Let.* 3 Oct. in W. Beattie *Life & Lett. T. Campbell* (1849) II. v. 121 We crack'd, as the Scotch say, like pen-guns. **1818** SCOTT *Hrt. Midl.* xvii, This mad quean, after cracking like a pen-gun, and skirling like a pea-hen for the haill night. **1821** *Blackw. Mag.* Aug. 35 (Jam.) Pen-guns are made and fired at the season when the turnip first comes to market; which turnip, cut in thin slices and bored through with the quill, forms the charge. **1835** MRS. CARLYLE *Lett.* I. 37 He sang, talked like a pen-gun.

2. A small cylindrical gas bomb (see quot. 1965[2]).

Registered in the U.S. as a proprietary name.

1962 *N.Y. Times* 26 May 27/8 Miss Dunsmore told him that the pen-gun had dropped from her pocket-book and a pellet had ruptured, releasing the tear gas. **1965** *Official Gaz.* (U.S. Patent Office) 4 May TM42/1 Penguin Associates, Inc., Malvern, Pa... *Pengun.* For Tear Gas Projectors and Distress and Highway Flare Projectors. First use January 1961. **1965** *Consumer Bull.* Sept. 18/2 The *Pengun* itself is a stainless steel cylinder encased in a gold-anodized aluminum tube about 4 inches long with an interior diameter of ⅜ inch. The 'cartridge' of gas fits into the tube and is released by a firing pin or plunger. **1973** J. DI MONA *Last Man at Arlington* viii. 73 Before he could say another word, she got him with a pen gun filled with mace. 'Ah Christ,' he yelled, bending over, rubbing his eyes. **1978** P. NIESEWAND *Underground Connection* 24 A pen gun which fired bursts of paralysing gas.

penholder ('pɛnˌhəʊldə(r)). [f. PEN *sb.*[2] + HOLDER[1].] **1.** A holder for a (steel or other) pen, consisting of a cylindrical rod of wood, ivory, metal, or other material, with a metal barrel or other device at the end into which a pen or 'nib' (see PEN *sb.*[2] 4) may be fixed; the pen and penholder together forming a writing instrument or 'pen' of which the penholder forms the handle.

1815 WELLINGTON *Let. to Sir C. Flint* 19 June (in *Westm. Gaz.* 12 Apr. (1904) 9/2), A small silver or thick glass inkstand, with one of Braham's patent penholders and one of his pens. **1859** *Handbk. Turning* 37 Any long slender piece of work, as a screen handle or a pen holder.

2. Used attrib. to denote a grip in table tennis in which the bat is held between thumb and forefinger.

1935 M. A. SYMONS *Table Tennis* ii. 14 There are still a large number of players who favour the 'Pen-holder' style of grip. *Ibid.*, Even top-class 'Pen-holder' grip players foozle such a shot. **1959** *Sunday Times* 5 Apr. 36/8 An aggressive opponent who smashed strongly with a pen-holder grip. **1973** *Advocate-News* (Barbados) 11 Dec. 13/3 The Chinese main armoury proved to be not their unorthodox 'pen-holder' style..but their service.

peni, obs. form of PENNY.

-penia ('pi:nɪə), repr. Gr. πενία poverty, need, is used in *Med.* to denote a deficiency, esp. of a constituent of the blood, as in GRANULOCYTOPENIA, *pancytopenia* s.v. PAN- 2. Also (*erron.*) -pœnia.

1971 *Lancet* 10 July 108/1 May I add *-penia* to the list of alternatives to *hypo-* suggested by Dr. Ell? In Greek it meant 'poverty' and it is currently used in such words as granulocytopenia and thrombocytopenia.

penial ('pi:nɪəl), *a. Anat.* [f. PENI-S + -AL[1].] Belonging to or connected with the penis.

1877 COUES & ALLEN *N. Amer. Rod.* 535 A dependent lobe, occupying the site of the penial sheath of the male. **1888** ROLLESTON & JACKSON *Anim. Life* 33 Mammals of the Rodent and other orders..possess a penial ossicle.

†**'penible**, *a. Obs.* Forms: 4 **peyneble**; 4–5 **peyn-, penyble**; 5 **pein-**, 7 **penible**. [a. F. *pénible* (12th c. in Hatz.-Darm.), f. *peine* pain: see -BLE.]

1. Painstaking, careful; putting forth effort, hard-working.

c **1386** CHAUCER *Clerk's T.* 658 The moore trewe if þat it were possible She was to hym in loue and moore penyble. —— *Monk's T.* 310, I seye, so worshipful a creature..So penyble in the werre, and curteis eke. **1481** CAXTON *Godeffroy* 209 The horses..were in this bataylle more stronge and more penyble than were the horses of the turkes.

2. Causing or involving pain or trouble; painful.

1426 LYDG. *De Guil. Pilgr.* 6634 With many woundys ful terryble, And rebukys ful penyble. **1430–40** —— *Bochas* I. xi. (1554) 22 b, Tell on anon, if it be possible, Which of their sorowes is fond most peinible. **1633** HART *Diet of Diseased* Introd. 21 His [Physician's] profession being in it selfe so penible and laborious.

Hence †**'penibly** (**peynybly**) *adv.*, painstakingly.

1303 R. BRUNNE *Handl. Synne* 5802 A trew man..þat wyl serue þe to pay, Peyneble, al þat he may. *Ibid.* 10339 But euery tyme was redy And seruede hym peynybly.

penicil ('pɛnɪsɪl). [ad. L. *pēnicill-us* PENCIL.]

1. *Nat. Hist.* A small bundle or tuft of slightly diverging hairs, resembling a paint-brush.

1826 KIRBY & SP. *Entomol.* IV. xlvi. 277.

2. *Med.* 'A tent or pledget for wounds or ulcers' (Webster 1828–32).

penicillamine (pɛnɪ'sɪləmi:n). *Chem.* and *Pharm.* [f. PENICILL(IN + AMINE.] An amino-acid, $(CH_3)_2C(SH)CH(NH_2)COOH$, produced by the hydrolysis of penicillins and used pharmacologically as a chelating agent; 2-amino-3-methyl-3-mercaptobutanoic acid.

1943 E. P. ABRAHAM et al. in *Nature* 23 Jan. 107/1 The properties of this substance, which we propose to term penicillamine, show that it represents a novel type of naturally occurring base. *Ibid.*, Penicillamine is obtained by hydrolysing barium penicillin..at 100°C. for one hour by means of *N*/10 sulphuric acid. **1947** *Sci. News* IV. 70 The synthesis of penicillin G starts with a benzyl oxazolone and with penicillamine, and attempts to recombine them. **1969** [see *hypogeusia* s.v. HYPO- II]. **1977** *Davidson's Princ. & Pract. Med.* (ed. 12) 733 This disorder [*sc.* Wilson's disease]..can now be arrested by giving copper-binding drugs (chelating agents)... The most valuable of these is penicillamine.

penicillanic (pɛnɪsɪ'lænɪk), *a. Chem.* [f. as prec. + *-an-* + -IC.] ***penicillanic acid***: an acid, $C_8H_{11}NO_2S$, whose molecular structure is the nucleus of the various penicillins and consists of a β-lactam ring fused to a molecule of 5,5-dimethylthiazolidine-4-carboxylic acid.

1953 J. C. SHEEHAN et al. in *Jrnl. Amer. Chem. Soc.* LXXV. 3293 By a cyclization procedure we have synthesized a β-lactamthiazolidine (VI)... We have chosen to call this compound methyl phthalimidopenicillanate. [*Note*] As a convenience in naming VI and similar analogs of the penicillins we suggest the terms 'penam' and 'penicillanic acid' for the following ring system and substituted ring system. **1959** *Times* 27 Oct. 6/7 The new penicillin, which is the potassium salt of 6-(-α-phenoxypropionamido) penicillanic acid, has the same range of antibacterial activity as previous penicillins. **1969** *Adv. Appl. Microbiol.* XI. 26 (*heading*) Antistaphylococcal activity of 6-substituted penicillanic acid derivatives.

penicillate ('pɛnɪsɪlət), *a. Nat. Hist.* [f. L. *pēnicill-us* (see PENICIL) + -ATE[2]. Cf. mod.F. *pénicillé*.] **a.** Furnished with a penicil or penicils; having a small tuft or tufts of hairs, scales, etc. **b.** Formed into or forming a small tuft or brush. **c.** Having markings like those made with a pencil or brush; streaked, pencilled.

1819 G. SAMOUELLE *Entomol. Compend.* 147 Joints [of tarsi] penicillate—dilated. **1835** KIRBY *Hab. & Inst. Anim.* II. xvi. 66 The penicillate family..is remarkable for several pencils or tufts of long and short scales, which distinguish the sides of the body. **1870** HOOKER *Stud. Flora* 310 Rumex ..stigmas penicillate.

So **'peniciˌllated** *a.* = PENICIL; **'peniciˌllately** *adv.*, in the form of a penicil; **ˌpenici'llation**, a growth of hairs, etc., in the form of a penicil.

1822–34 *Good's Study Med.* (ed. 4) II. 556 The black points sometimes present a stellated or penicillated arrangement. **1846** DANA *Zooph.* (1848) 127 The inner row [of tentacles],..furnished with a short fibrous penicillation at the ends. **1872** H. C. WOOD *Fresh-Water Algæ* 22 Filaments..in filiform fasciculi, which are often much elongate and penicillately exserted from the open common sheath.

penicilliform (pɛnɪ'sɪlɪfɔ:m), *a.* [ad. mod.L. *pēnicilliformis*, f. *pēnicill-us*: see -FORM.] Of the form of, or resembling, a hair-pencil; 'arranged in a brush or tuft' (*Syd. Soc. Lex.*).

1811 in HOOPER *Med. Dict.* **1831** R. KNOX *Cloquet's Anat.* 465 Fasciculate, penicilliform filaments, folded in the direction of their length. **1857** MAYNE *Expos. Lex.*, *Penicilliformis*,..resembling a hair-pencil..: penicilliform.

penicillin (pɛnɪ'sɪlɪn). *Pharm.* [f. PENICILL(IUM + -IN[1].] **1.** Orig., the antibiotic agent obtained from cultures of the mould *Penicillium notatum*; hence, any of a group of antibiotics that are all derivatives of 6-amino-penicillanic acid in which a radical replaces one of the amino hydrogen atoms, some being acids produced naturally by the growth of various moulds of the genera *Penicillium* and *Aspergillus*, whilst others are acids, salts, or esters prepared synthetically from these; they are active against many kinds of bacteria but virtually harmless to persons not allergic to them.

1929 A. FLEMING in *Brit. Jrnl. Exper. Path.* X. 227 In the rest of this article allusion will constantly be made to experiments with filtrates of a broth culture of this mould, so for convenience and to avoid the repetition of the rather cumbersome phrase 'Mould broth filtrate', the name 'penicillin' will be used. This will denote the filtrate of a broth culture of the particular penicillium with which we are concerned. **1941** H. W. FLOREY et al. in *Lancet* 16 Apr. 188/2 Enough evidence has now been assembled to show that penicillin is a new and effective type of chemotherapeutic agent, and possesses some properties unknown in any antibacterial substance hitherto described. **1947** *Sci. News* IV. 69 There are a number of naturally occurring penicillins, with somewhat different medical effectiveness. **1951** A. GROLLMAN *Pharmacol. & Therapeutics* xxii. 445 The amorphous preparations of penicillin are yellow powders with a characteristic odor and bitter taste. The crystalline pure preparations are white, odorless and practically tasteless. **1953** J. RAMSBOTTOM *Mushrooms & Toadstools* xxiii. 287 Soon after the chemical study was begun it was unexpectedly found that there was more than one kind of penicillin. The first two to be recognised were called Penicillin I and Penicillin II in this country, Penicillin F and Penicillin G in America... Later Penicillin III (X) and Penicillin IV (K) were recognised as being produced in greater or lesser amounts depending on cultural conditions. *Ibid.*, There are now five known 'natural' penicillins. All are dipeptides with the formula $C_9H_{11}O_4N_2S$ *R*—the difference between them being in the constitution of the side chain..represented by *R*. **1958** *Listener* 9 Oct. 552/1 For our modern accomplishments are genuine, from the early work we achieved in the realm of atomic science, to the discovery of penicillin and the modern progress on jet-propelled aircraft. **1970** PASSMORE & ROBSON *Compan. Med. Stud.* II. xx. 12/2 A method has been devised to use these natural penicillins as a source of a new range of compounds which can be made by chemical synthesis.., the new or semi-synthetic penicillins. *Ibid.* 13/1 These semi-synthetic penicillins have a range of novel properties which make them a major addition to the armoury of antibacterial agents. **1973** M. AMIS *Rachel Papers* 93 Just two jabs of penicillin up the bum and much humiliation at the local clinic. **1974** M. C. GERALD *Pharmacol.* xxvii. 465 The penicillins were the first antibiotics discovered and remain today the second most widely used class of drugs for the treatment of bacterial infections. *Ibid.*, The most important natural penicillin is benzylpenicillin, which is more commonly designated penicillin G. Although penicillin G is the most potent of all penicillin derivatives, it suffers from several major disadvantages.

2. ***penicillin A*** or ***B***: disused names for NOTATIN (PENATIN), which is chemically unrelated to the penicillins proper.

1941 C. E. COULTHARD et al. *Brit. Pat.* 552,619 A substance having bacteriostatic activity, which is hereinafter termed 'Penicillin A',..is produced by selecting a strain of Penicillium notatum which possesses the property..when grown on a suitable culture medium,..of maintaining the pH of the culture medium on the acid side for a considerable period. **1942** [see NOTATIN]. **1943** E. C. ROBERTS et al. in *Jrnl. Biol. Chem.* CXLVII. 47 We wish to report an antibacterial substance, penicillin B, produced by *Penicillium notatum*, which is insoluble in lipid solvents but readily separated from the culture medium by adsorption on benzoic acid. *Ibid.*, We shall refer to our product as penicillin B to differentiate it from the product obtained by Abraham *et al.*..which we shall call penicillin A. Although penicillin B may be similar to 'penatin'.., the absence of a discussion of its chemical properties prevents a comparison of the two products. **1949, 1963** [see NOTATIN].

3. *attrib.* and *Comb.*, as ***penicillin-insensitive***, ***-like***, ***-resistant***, ***-sensitive*** adjs.; **penicillin unit**, a unit of penicillin which since 1944 has been the amount having the same antibiotic activity as a certain quantity (very nearly, and orig. exactly, 0.6 microgramme) of a standard preparation of the sodium salt of benzylpenicillin (penicillin G), and which is approximately equivalent to the Oxford unit that it superseded.

1929 *Brit. Jrnl. Exper. Path.* X. 234 In some [cultures] there were a few diphtheroid bacilli which were always penicillin sensitive, and in others there were Gram-negative bacilli which were penicillin insensitive. **1953** J. RAMSBOTTOM *Mushrooms & Toadstools* xxiii. 284 *Penicillium notatum* grows best in nearly neutral media, which are equally favourable for penicillin-insensitive organisms.. which produce the enzyme penicillinase. **1946** *Nature* 28 Sept. 446/1 Penicillin-like antibiotics are produced by a number of moulds besides *Penicillium notatum*. **1942** *Proc. Soc. Exper. Biol. & Med.* LI. 387 (*heading*) Development of penicillin resistant strains of *Staphylococcus aureus in vitro*. **1971** *Nature* 4 June 284/1 Penicillin-resistant strains of staphylococci emerged in the 1950s. **1929** Penicillin-sensitive [see *penicillin-insensitive* above]. **1959** *Times* 6 Mar. 13/7 The proportion of penicillin-sensitive individuals is small. **1943** *Jrnl. Bacteriol.* XLVI. 189 To eliminate the day-to-day deviation, the Oxford group introduced the concept of the penicillin unit and the use of a standard penicillin preparation. **1947** *Jrnl. Biol. Chem.* CLXVII. 554 In the Casamino acid medium, maximum yields were obtained upon addition of 200 penicillin units per ml. of medium initially. **1953** Heilbron & Bunbury *Dict. Org. Compounds* (rev. ed.) IV. 51/2 Penicillin-F... Antibiotic activity: 1,490 Penicillin units per mg.

penicillinase (pɛnɪˈsɪlɪneɪz, -s). *Biochem.* [f. prec. + -ase.] Any of the enzymes (produced by certain bacteria) which cause the breaking up of the carbon-nitrogen bond in the lactam ring of some penicillins (so rendering them ineffective as antibiotics). Cf. lactamase.

1940 Abraham & Chain in *Nature* 28 Dec. 837/1 The activity of the enzyme, which we term penicillinase, is slight at pH5, but increases considerably towards the alkaline range of pH. **1958** *Ann. Rev. Biochem.* XXVII. 176 Cephalosporin-C possesses the interesting property of being resistant to the action of some penicillinases including that produced by penicillin resistant staphylococci. **1971** [see lactamase]. **1974** M. C. Gerald *Pharmacol.* iv. 72 Recent research has made available new penicillins that are resistant to acid hydrolysis and penicillinase attack. **1975** *Nature* 12 June 526/1 Penicillinases, or as they are now known, β-lactamases, are enzymes which specifically deactivate penicillin by hydrolysis of the β-lactam ring.

‖**penicillium** (pɛnɪˈsɪlɪəm). [mod. Bot.L., f. L. *pēnicill-us, -um.*]

1. *Bot.* A genus of ascetomycetous fungi, including several of the common moulds.

1867 J. Hogg *Microsc.* ii. i. 298 Portions of penicillium and aspergillus moulds. **1874** Cooke *Fungi* 3 The spores of Penicillium are capable of being transformed into yeast.

2. *Nat. Hist.* and *Anat.* = pencil 1, penicillus 1.

1893 *Syd. Soc. Lex., Penicillium*, term for a tuft-like mass of vessels or fibres spreading out from one point.

penicilloic (pɛnɪsɪˈləʊɪk), *a.* *Biochem.* [f. penicill(in + -oic.] ***penicilloic acid***: any of the acids produced when a penicillin is hydrolysed (as by a penicillinase) and the C-N bond of the lactam ring broken.

1945 *Science* 21 Dec. 628/2 The dicarboxylic acid obtained by hydrolysis of penicillin at the site of the potential carboxyl is termed penicilloic acid. This acid is produced in the form of salts by treatment of penicillin with alkalies and is presumably the product of the action of the enzyme penicillinase on penicillin. **1949** Mozingo & Folkers in H. T. Clarke et al. *Chem. of Penicillin* xviii. 542/1 Many of the penicilloic acids..were made in order to study their reactions with various reagents in the interest of their dehydration to the penicillins. **1959** *Observer* 11 Jan. 14/7 It [*sc.* penicillinase] acts by rapidly breaking down penicillin to penicilloic acid, which has no antibiotic activity. **1970** *New Eng. Jrnl. Med.* 16 July 119/1 Penicilloic acid appears to have an important role in some of the allergic reactions caused by penicillins.

Hence **peniciˈlloate** [-ate[1]], a salt or ester of a penicilloic acid.

1946 *Industr. & Engin. Chem.* (*Analytical Ed.*) Oct. 619/1, 8·97 equivalents of iodine per mole..is in reasonably good agreement with the range given..for penicilloates (8·5 to 8·9). **1969** Manhas & Bose *Synthesis of Penicillin, Cephalosporin C & Analogs* iii. 38 When this route..met with only limited success the cyclization of penicilloates that could not form oxazolones was investigated.

‖**penicillus** (pɛnɪˈsɪləs). Pl. -i. [L.: see pencil, penicil.]

1. *Anat.* Each of the tufts formed by the ramifications of the portal vein in the liver, and of the minute arteries in the spleen.

1822–34 *Good's Study Med.* (ed. 4) I. 332 Absorbed from the penicilli or pores of the liver. **1878** tr. *H. von Ziemssen's Cycl. Med.* VIII. 353 Each penicillus [in the spleen] with the corresponding veins, forms a closed and independent vascular system.

2. = penicil 2.

1727–41 Chambers *Cycl., Penicillus*, among chirurgeons is used for a tent, to be put in wounds or ulcers. **1893** in *Syd. Soc. Lex.*

ˈpenide. ? *Obs.* Forms: 4–5 penyde, 5–7 penede, 6 -idie, 6–7 -idee, 7 penid, 5–9 **penide**. See also pennet. [a. F. *pénide* (15th c. in Godef.), ad. med.L. *penidium*, usually pl. *-ia* (Constantinus Afer *a* 1100), a. med.Gr. πενίδιον, -ια = ‘spuma sacchari’ (frequent in Byzantine medical writers, e.g. Actuarius and Nicolaus Myrepsus); supposed to be ad. Pers. *pānīd* refined sugar, in Arab. *al-fānīd*: see alphenic. (Thence also *Diapenidion.*) Cf. Dozy & Engelmann *Glossaire* s.v. *Alfeñique*, and Devic (Littré *Supplt.*).] A piece or stick of barley-sugar, or of a similar preparation of sugar, used as a remedy for colds. (Usually *pl.*)

1390 *Earl Derby's Exped.* (Camden) 19 Pro ij lb. penydes, ij *s.* *c* **1400** *Lanfranc's Cirurg.* 219 Seþe it wiþ a litil salt & ȝeue it þe pacient & do þeron penidis. **1533** Elyot *Cast. Helthe* (1541) 81 If there be no feuer, penidees, malowes, orage, gourdes. *c* **1623** Lodge *Poore Mans Talentt* (Hunter. Cl.) 28 Take..of sugar penedes to the quantity of them all. **1683** Salmon *Doron Med.* i. 177 With sugar Penids make a Bolus for one dose. **1851** Mayhew *Lond. Labour* I. 204 If the boiled and yet soft sugar be rapidly..extended, and pulled over a hook, it becomes opaque and white, and then constitutes *pulled sugar*, or *penides.*

†**peˈnidiate**, *a.* *Obs. rare.* [f. med.L. *penidi-um*: see -ate[2].] In ***sugar penidiate***, app. = prec.

1656 Ridgley *Physick* 258 Sugar Penidiate, three ounces.

peniform (ˈpiːnɪfɔːm), *a.* [f. L. *pēni-s* + -(i)form.] Of the form of, or resembling, a penis.

1875 tr. *H. von Ziemssen's Cycl. Med.* X. 76.

penigrasse, -gres(se, obs. ff. penny-grass.

penil (ˈpiːnɪl). [a. F. *pénil* (12–13th c.):—L. type **pectiniculum*, dim. of *pecten* ‘comb’, in sense ‘hair of the pubes’.] The suprapubic or hypogastric region; the pubes.

1842 Dunglison *Med. Lex., Penil*, mons veneris. **1857** Bullock *Cazeaux' Midwif.* 45 Found on the penil, the labia majora, and the genito-crural folds.

†**ˈpenile, ˈpenisle**, *sb.* *Obs.* Also **pene-isle**. [f. L. *pæne-* almost (see pene-) + *ile*, isle, after *peninsula*. Cf. F. *presqu'île*.] = peninsula.

1611 Speed *Hist. Gt. Brit.* ix. xii. (1623) 703 A great Cape of Land or penile in Normandy. **1618** Bolton *Florus* (1636) 280 From thence he suddenly escaped to the penile of Pharus. **1627** Speed *England* i. §6 Britaine thereby is of a supposed Penisle made an Iland. **1668** Wilkins *Real Char.* ii. ii. §3. 53 Promontory, Cape,..Point, Pene-isle. **1716** M. Davies *Athen. Brit.* III. *Diss. Physick* 39 Podalirius..had her, endow'd with the Penisle call'd Chersonesus, for his Pains.

penile (ˈpiːnaɪl), *a.* *Anat.* [ad. mod.L. *pēnīl-is*, f. penis.] = penial.

1861 Bumstead *Ven. Dis.* (1879) 319. **1889** Treves *Man. Surg.* III. 633 If the calculus be in the penile part [of the urethra]. **1897** *Allbutt's Syst. Med.* II. 1081.

penillion: see pennill.

peninsula (pɪˈnɪnsjʊlə). Pl. **-as** (-əz), formerly **-æ**. Also 7 in anglicized form (or from Fr.) peninsul, -e. [a. L. *pæninsula*, f. *pæne-*, pene- almost + *insula* island: in F. *péninsule* (1544 in Hatz.-Darm.). *Pæninsula* in Livy and Pliny is translated by Holland *demie island*.]

A piece of land that is almost an island, being nearly surrounded by water; by extension, any piece of land projecting into the sea, so that the greater part of its boundary is coast-line; e.g. southern India, the Balkan Peninsula.

1538 Leland *Itin.* III. 21 This Peninsula to cumpace it by the Rote lakkith litle of a Mile. **1577** Harrison *England* i. viii. in *Holinshed* I. 14b/2 None Islandes at all..but one lytle Byland, Cape or Peninsula. **1612** Capt. Smith *Map Virginia* 4 Their corne-fields being girded therein in a manner as Peninsulaes. **1615** G. Sandys *Trav.* 220 A promontory in forme of a pene-insula. **1633** T. Stafford *Pac. Hib.* ii. xxiii. (1821) 434 That Pen-insula (being strong in its owne nature). **1754** Pococke *Trav. Eng.* (Camden) II. 108 Crossing over in a boat to the peninsula of Selsey. **1807** Pinkerton *Geog.* II. 203 The Malaian peninsula. **1860** Motley *Netherl.* (1868) I. i. 7 The Spanish and Italian Peninsulas have had a different history.

β. **1613** Purchas *Pilgrimage* viii. xiv. (1614) 816 Next is that necke or narrow extent of Land..knitting the two great Peninsuls of the North and South America together. **1617** Moryson *Itin.* i. 257 A Hill like a Peninsul. *Ibid.* 274 The region or Country called Fife which is a Peninsule..lying between two creekes of the Sea called Frith and Taye. **1665** Sir T. Herbert *Trav.* (1677) 351 A Pen-insule some call it and no Isle.

b. ***the Peninsula*** (*spec.*): Spain and Portugal.

1775 R. Twiss *Trav. Port. & Sp.* 8 This peninsula (as the natives call Portugal and Spain). **1812** Scott *Let. to Miss J. Baillie* 4 Apr., My thoughts are anxiously turned to the Peninsula. **1855** Motley *Dutch Rep.* (1861) II. 290 The romantic race which had once swayed the Peninsula.

peninsular (pɪˈnɪnsjʊlə(r)), *a.* (*sb.*) [f. L. type **pæninsulār-is*: cf. F. *péninsulaire* (1556 in Hatz.-Darm.): see prec. and -ar.] Of, belonging to, or of the nature of a peninsula.

1612 Brerewood *Lang. & Relig.* 82 Inclosed after a peninsular figure between Danubius and the sea. *a* **1771** R. Wood *Ess. Homer, Troade* (1775) 312 Its compact peninsular form. **1869** Freeman *Norm. Conq.* (1876) III. xii. 123 An insular or peninsular site was specially sought out.

b. *spec.* (usually with capital.) Of or pertaining to the peninsula of Spain and Portugal, or (*esp.*) the war carried on there in 1808–14 between the French under Napoleon and the English, Spanish, and Portuguese under Wellington.

1812 L. Hunt in *Examiner* 21 Sept. 594/2 The main objects of the peninsular War. *a* **1863** Thackeray *Mr. & Mrs. Berry* ii, He is an old Peninsular man. **1891** *Chambers' Encycl.* VIII. 26/2 Peninsular and Oriental Company..in 1840..had then had an existence of three years' duration as the Peninsular Company, which carried mails to Portugal and the South of Spain. **1899** Sir H. Maxwell *Wellington* I. xiv. 373 The Peninsular Campaign.

B. *sb.* **a.** An inhabitant of a peninsula. **b.** A soldier of the Peninsular war.

1888 *Q. Rev.* CLXVII. 196 He [Besant] speaks of the ruffling captain, who was no doubt ‘an old Peninsular’. **1889** *Nation* (N.Y.) 17 Oct. 319/2 The Arabs traded with the far-off peninsulars.

peninsularity (pɪˌnɪnsjʊˈlærɪtɪ). [f. prec. + -ity: cf. insularity.] **a.** The condition of being a peninsula. **b.** The character or habit of mind resulting from living in a peninsula, and thus having little contact with people of other nations.

1882 G. Allen in *Pop. Sc. Monthly* XX. 599 Amusing chat about the peninsularity of the Spaniards. **1891** J. Winsor *Columbus* xviii. 426 There is no proof that he ever suspected the peninsularity of Cuba.

peninsulate (pɪˈnɪnsjʊleɪt), *v.* [f. peninsula + -ate[3] 7; after *insulate.*] *trans.* To make into a peninsula; to surround (a piece of land) almost completely, as water; to divide into peninsulas.

1538 Leland *Itin.* II. 52 Newton Water and Avon ren so nere togither in the botom of the West Suburbe of Malmesbyri, that there within a Burbolt-shot the Toun is peninsulatid. **1774** Pennant *Tour Scot. in 1772*, 22 A detached tract peninsulated by sea, lake or river. **1796** Morse *Amer. Geog.* I. 534 There are six considerable rivers which, with their numerous branches, peninsulate the whole state. **1902** W. Crossing in *Devon N. & Q.* July 98 The tongue of land..peninsulated by the Swincombe river and the West Dart.

fig. **1809–10** Coleridge *Friend* (1866) 338 The..stream may..appear to comprehend and insile some particular department of knowledge which even then it only peninsulates.

Hence **peˈninsulated** *ppl. a.*

1781 Wyndham *Tour* (ed. 2) 36 The bold craggy shore, and the broken peninsulated knoles. **1846** McCulloch *Acc. Brit. Empire* (1854) I. 53 The coast of Caernarvonshire, southward from Menai Straits, is formed by the peninsulated hundred of Lleyn. **1870** W. Chambers *Winter. Mentone* i. 16 The picturesquely peninsulated shores of the Mediterranean.

peninsuˈlation. [f. peninsulate *v.*] The process of making into a peninsula; the condition of being peninsulated; peninsularity. (In quots. *fig.*)

1923 G. Barker in Drinkwater & Orpen *Outl. Lit. & Art* (1924) I. x. 194/1 From this peninsulation of the stage several things follow. **1959** *Times* 5 Sept. 9/6 It is the prospect..the isolation or peninsulation.

†**peˈnintime**, *a.* *Obs.* [f. L. *pæne-* almost, pene- + *intim-us* innermost.] Inmost but one.

1686 *Phil. Trans.* XVI. 81 The second or penintime Satellite of Saturn. **1718** J. Pound *ibid.* XXX. 771 The Radix of the penintime or second Satellite.

peninvariant (piːnɪnˈvɛərɪənt). *Math.* [f. pene- + invariant.] = seminvariant.

1860 Cayley *Coll. Math. Papers* IV. 606 The leading coefficient of a covariant..in any covariant of a binary quantic..has been termed a *peninvariant*, but a more appropriate term is *seminvariant.*

penirial(l, -ryal, obs. forms of pennyroyal.

penis (ˈpiːnɪs). Pl. **penes** (-iːz), **peni** (*erron.*), **penises**. [L. *pēnis* orig. = *cauda* ‘tail’, afterwards as here.] **a.** The intromittent or copulatory organ of any male animal (in Mammalia also traversed by the urethra).

In *Zool.* sometimes extended to organs which deposit spermatozoa without intromission. In *Entom.* formerly used to include in addition accessory structures, as claspers.

1676 T. Browne *Let.* 14 June in *Wks.* (1964) IV. 61 You may observe..the flattish heart, the Lungs,..the penis, the multiple stomack &c. **1693** tr. *Blancard's Phys. Dict.* (ed. 2), *Penis*, the Yard, made up of two nervous Bodies, the Channel, Nut, Skin, and Fore-skin, &c. **1789** W. Buchan *Dom. Med.* (1790) 325 An itching in the top of the penis. **1831** R. Knox *Cloquet's Anat.* 339 Becoming incorporated with the fibres of the symphysis pubis, and the suspensory ligament of the penis. **1841–71** T. R. Jones *Anim. Kingd.* (ed. 4) 169 In *Planaria tremellaris*, the penis..is a white contractile body, enclosed, when in a retracted state, in a small oval pouch. **1926** F. Z. Snoop *Reproduction & Sexual Evolution* 83 Havelock Ellis quotes other cases, even butterflies (if insects may be here included) who possess excrescences on their penes, which of necessity must cause pain, or something very like pain, during coition. **1929** D. H. Lawrence *Paintings*, What do you paint with, Maitre? —With my penis, and be damned! **1933** R. L. Dickinson *Human Sex Anatomy* vi. 74/2 The long penises are in general narrow and the short broad. **1943** *Amer. Jrnl. Dis. Children* LXV. 541 The penis is primarily an organ of copulation, so that its true physiologic size would be gaged by measurement of the erect phallus. *Ibid.*, The length of the fully stretched penis is practically identical with the length of the erect phallus. **1962** E. L. Cockrum *Introd. Mammalogy* iii. 76 According to Asdell (1946), Slijper has studied the structure of the penis in its relation to the duration of coitus and developed the following classification of morphological types of peni. **1965** E. W. Johnson *Love & Sex in Plain Lang.* ii. 8 A man's most obvious sexual organ is his penis. **1970** H. W. & L. R. Levi tr. *Kaestner's Invertebr. Zool.* III. v. 130 The paired penes are introduced deep into the posterior opening between the valves, reach the copulatory openings, and mating is accomplished in several minutes. **1972** *Times Lit. Suppl.* 29 Sept. 1156/4 Sexologists now make a clear distinction between ‘penis’ and ‘phallus’; the former being used to define the flaccid organ and the latter the erect organ. **1973** C. Pincher *Sex in our Time* viii. 92 Just as there are men with large or small penises so there are women with large or small vaginas. **1975** M. Seymour-Smith *Sex & Society* x. 282 The phallus is the *image* of the *erect* (never flaccid) penis. **1975** Fretter & Graham *Functional Anat. Invertebr.* (1976) xi. 352 In these sessile forms [*sc.* barnacles] the sperm are filiform and motile and transferred from one individual to the next by a long flexible penis.

b. *Comb.*, as ***penis-cover, -extender, holder, -sheath***; **penis-bone** an ossification occurring in the penis in certain Mammalia; **penis-envy** *Psychoanalysis*, an envy of the male's possession of a penis, postulated by Freud to occur in girls and possibly resulting in a castration-complex (see castration 1) or in the adoption of masculine behaviour; **penis gourd** (see quot.).

1836–9 Todd *Cycl. Anat.* II. 725/1 The repetition in the clitoris..of the penis-bone of the male.

1966 *New Statesman* 22 Apr. 589/2 Even more remarkable are the penis-covers made of narrow gourds a foot or more in length. [**1920** B. Low tr. *Freud's Psychogenesis of Case of Female Homosexuality in Internat. Jrnl. Psycho-Anal.* I. 146 She had.. developed a pronounced envy of the penis.] **1924** *Internat. Jrnl. Psycho-Anal.* V. 58 Its relation to the 'penis-envy' complex is twofold. **1946** *Mind* LV. 354 A girl's penis-envy might also be very much hidden. **1964** A. Borowik *How Many Miles to Babylon?* xv. 96 When I hear a guy talking to me about penis envy.. I feel an overpowering urge to laugh. **1972** F. Warner *Lying Figures* III. 20 You'd find penis-envy in a peach. **1973** K. Vonnegut *Breakfast of Champions* xv. 147 One time Dwayne Hoover got an advertisement through the mail for a penis-extender, made out of rubber. **1971** *World Archaeol.* III. 136 The traditional male dress is the penis gourd: a piece of the stem end of the gourd, varying in length from about three to more than twelve inches, into which the penis is inserted, leaving the scrotum exposed. **1976** *Times* 31 May 7/8 Went native in 1681 living with the Cuna Indians, coated in vegetable dies [*sic*] and clothed only in a conical silver penis holder suspended from the waist by a thong. **1925** C. K. Meek *Northern Tribes Nigeria* II. 116 Among those people who wear the penis-sheath, the sheath is usually removed before the body is laid in the grave. **1978** *Sunday Times* (Colour Suppl.) 18 June 40/1 Their chief Manuel, denied access to Government chambers in Brasilia for not wearing a suit, has forbidden any Brazilian deputy to set foot on Xavante land unless wearing a penis sheath, hair feathers and body paint.

penis, obs. pl. of penny.

penisle: see penile *sb.*

penistone ('pɛnɪstən). Forms: 6 pen(n)e-, pennie-, 6–8 **penny-**, 6–9 **pennistone**, 7 **penyston**, 7–8 **pen(n)iston**, 7– **penistone**. [Name of a small town in the West Riding of Yorkshire, where the cloth so named was made.]

†**1.** A kind of coarse woollen cloth formerly used for garments, linings, etc. *Obs.*

1551–2 *Act 5 & 6 Edw. VI*, c. 6 §1 Clothes commonlye called Pennystones or Forest Whites.. shall conteyne in lengthe beinge wett betwixt twelve and thirtene yardes. **1576** Baker *Jewell of Health* 21 A Bagge.. of whyte woollen cloth (whether the same be Pennystone or Karsie). *a* **1600** T. Smith *Let.* in Strype *Stow's Surv.* (1754) II. v. xix. 401/2 Coarse Cloths made in the North Parts, as Northern Cottons.. Checks, and Penistones. **1616** in *Rep. Comm. Inq. Charities* (1834) XXIX. 731, 40s. to be laid out in red peniston for four petticoats. **1778** *Eng. Gazetteer* (ed. 2) s.v. *Sturbridge*, Abundance of cloths,.. kerseys, cottons, penistons, and fustians, are brought to it from Yorkshire and Lancashire.

attrib. **1656** *New Eng. Hist. & Gen. Reg.* (1850) IV. 125 It is my will yt my cousine Elizabeth fich have my searge gowne, and my Read penniston petticote. **1834** M. Scott *Cruise Midge* (1859) 387 Poor drenched stormstaid devils in their blue pennistone great coats shivering on the opposite bank.

2. ***Penistone flags***, sandstone flags from the Coal Measures around Penistone, used for paving-stones.

1688 R. Holme *Armoury* III. 111/1 Rough Stone, or Penny Stone.. are rough cut out of the Quarry. **1878** A. H. Green, etc. *Geol. Yorksh. Coal-field* ii. §3. 77 The Penistone Flags are a group of very variable sandstones, with a few thin and poor coals. They are best developed around Penistone, and may be traced thence southwards to Sheffield.

penitauncery, obs. form of penitentiary.

penitence ('pɛnɪtəns). Also 4–5 **penytence**, (7 **pœni-**), 5 **penitaunce**. [a. OF. *pénitence* (11th c. in Littré), ad. L. *pænitēntia* (later *pœni-*, *pēni-*), n. of condition f. *pænitēns*: see penitent and -ence. OF. *pénitence*, as the learned form in ecclesiastical use, gradually displaced the popular *peneance*, penance.]

1. The undergoing of some discipline or exercise, voluntary or imposed by spiritual authority, in outward expression of repentance, and expiation of an offence; = penance *sb.* 2. Now *rare*, and usually including sense 2.

c **1200** *Trin. Coll. Hom.* 61 Swo ure louerd ihesu crist fette adam ut of helle, þo þe hedde his penitence enden, and swo he wile us ec, þanne we hauen ure penitence fulended. *a* **1225** *Ancr. R.* 348 Efter schrifte, hit falleð to speken of Penitence, þet is dedbote. *c* **1386** Chaucer *Pars. T.* ¶ 11 Penitence is the waymentynge of man that sorweth for his synne and pyneth hym self for he hath mysdoon. **1483** Caxton *Cato* I v, And whanne thow hast accomplysshed the penytence whiche the preest hath gyuen to the. *a* **1600** Hooker *Eccl. Pol.* vi. iv. §2 The course of discipline in former Ages reformed open Transgressors by putting them unto offices of open penitence: especially Confession. **1796** Burney *Mem. Metastasio* I. 206, I shall undertake this business, as a penitence for my sins. **1822** K. Digby *Broadst. Hon.* (1829) I. *Godefridus* 290 The ruins of Chantilly where the great Condé ended his days in retirement and the practice of penitence. **1882** 'Ouida' *Maremma* I. iii. 66 Its very priests were sent to Santa Tarsilla as a penitence.

2. The fact or state of being penitent; contrition or sorrow for sin committed, with desire and intention of amendment; repentance. (The prevailing sense.)

1591 Shaks. *Two Gent.* v. iv. 81 By Penitence th' Eternalls wrath's appeas'd. *a* **1600** Hooker *Eccl. Pol.* vi. iii. §4 The question why David's confession should be held for effectual penitence, and not Saul's. **1658** Bramhall *Schism* i. viii, The degree of the delinquents penitence or impenitence. **1741–2** Gray *Agrippina* 179 In lieu of penitence and vain remorse. **1848** Dickens *Dombey* xxiii, Is this the way you show your penitence? **1881** Trollope *Dr. Wortle's School* i. ii, He was one who thought that there should be a place of penitence allowed to those who had clearly repented of their errors.

3. *Comb.*, as (sense 1) ***penitence-garment.***

1882–3 Schaff *Encycl. Relig. Knowl.* III. 2471/1 [Waldenses] Travelling two and two together, clad in woollen penitence-garments.

†'**penitencer.** *Obs.* Forms: 4 **penet-**, 4–5 **pent-**, 4–6 **penyt-**, 4–8 **penit-**; 4–5 **-ancer(e**, 4–6 **-auncer**, 5 **-encere**, 5–7 **-encer**, 6 **-enser**, **-ar**, (7–8 **-entier**). [a. F. *pénitencier*, ad. med.L. *pæni-*, *pœnitēntiārius*, which took the place of the popular F. form *peneancier*, penancer.]

1. In the mediæval Church, a priest appointed to hear confession, assign penance, and give absolution in extraordinary cases; a penitentiary.

a **1350** *S. Andrew* 309 in Horstm. *Altengl. Leg.* (1881) 8 Ledes hir to mi penitancere, For of me has he playn powere. **1460** Capgrave *Chron.* (Rolls) 151 A Frere Prechoure cleped Raymund. He was Penytauncere undir the Pope. **1538** Bale *Thre Lawes* 1478 *Hypocrisis*.. I am a great penytensar, And syt at the pardon. **1546** Langley *Pol. Verg. De Invent.* vii. iv. 136 Of them sprong the bastard penitencers in the daies of Ihon the XXII. **1656** Blount *Glossogr.*, *Penitencer*,.. the Priest, &c. that enjoyns the offendor his penance. [**1840** Barham *Ingol. Leg.* Ser. i. *St. Nicholas*, There is Mess Michael, and holy Mess John, Sage Penitauncers I ween be they.]

2. One undergoing penance; = penancer 2. *rare.*

c **1380** *Antecrist* in Todd *3 Treat. Wyclif* (1851) 152 And for her wenches and for her children, hem þei wolen not prisoun, but make hem pentauncers. [So OF. *penitencier*.]

penitency ('pɛnɪtənsɪ). Now *rare*. [ad. L. *pæni-*, *pœnitēntia*: see penitence and -ency.] The quality or condition of being penitent.

1. Penitence as a state; repentance.

c **1450** *Seven Deadly Sins* 117 in *Pol. Rel. & L. Poems* (1866) 218 The rote of an erbe I sholde vp hale, Men call it chastite; and pounde it with penytencie. **1597** Hooker *Eccl. Pol.* v. lxxii. §7 Their Fastings were partly in token of penitencie. **1630** J. Taylor (Water P.) *Unnat. Father* Wks. ii. 139/1 Hee dyed with great penitency and remorce of Conscience. *a* **1708** Beveridge *Thes. Theol.* (1710) II. 275 Works of penitency. Humbling ourselves for sin, setting ourselves against it, turning ourselves from it. **1863** Keble *Bp. Wilson* xix. 641 The penitency.. of so conspicuous an adversary could not but encourage any favourable change.. taking place in men's minds towards the Bishop.

†**2.** A penitential practice or discipline; = penitence 1, penance. *Obs. rare.*

1597 Hooker *Eccl. Pol.* v. lxxii. §13 Two kinds ther wer of publike penitencie, the one belonging to notorious offenders.. the other appertaining to the whole church and vnto euery seuerall person whome the same containeth. **1670** G. H. *Hist. Cardinals* iii. i. 217 Ecclesiasticks who formerly imploy'd their whole times in heaping up Penitencies and Fastings. **1676** *Warn. for Housekeepers* 5–6 For to take our penitency, And boose the water cold.

penitent ('pɛnɪtənt), *a.* and *sb.* Also 4 **penytaunt**, 4–6 **penytent**. [a. OF. *pénitent* (14th c. in Littré), ad. L. *pænitēnt-em*, pr. pple. of *pænitēre* (*pœn-*, *pēn-*) to repent; this as a learned form, in ecclesiastical use, gradually displaced the popular OF. *peneant*, *-ant*, and ME. penant. In *pænitēre* and its derivatives, the original L. form is held to have been with *pæ-*, but in med.L. *pœ-* was usual; in Romanic *pe-*.]

A. *adj.* **1. a.** That repents, with serious purpose to amend the sin or wrongdoing; repentant, contrite.

c **1375** *Sc. Leg. Saints* xxxiv. (*Pelagia*) 190 [I pray] þat þu me penytent wald take & to Iesu reconforte me. *c* **1386** Chaucer *Pars. T.* ¶ 13 He shal be verray penitent. **1432–50** tr. *Higden* (Rolls) IV. 461 [Titus] seide that he didde never that thynge in his lyfe whereof he was soory and penitente. **1552** *Bk. Com. Prayer*, *Absolution*, To declare and pronounce to his people, beinge penitent, the absolution and remission of their synnes. **1667** Milton *P.L.* x. 1097 So spake our Father penitent, nor Eve Felt less remorse. **1725** De Foe *Voy. round World* (1840) 46, I made him take two of those penitent mutineers with him. **1840** J. H. Newman *Par. Serm.* III. viii, A penitent prodigal who has squandered God's gifts. **1902** W. E. Norris *Credit of County* ii, She was in short penitent, but scarcely to the extent of being remorseful.

b. *transf.* of things: Expressive of repentance.

1723 De Foe *Col. Jack* (1840) 224 Though she wrote me several penitent letters, acknowledging her crime, and begging me to forgive her.

†**2.** Regretful, grieved; relenting, sorry, vexed. Const. *of*, *upon*. *Obs. rare.*

1533 Bellenden *Livy* v. (1822) 439 Ye sal nocht be penitent of oure faith, nor we sal nocht be penitent of youre empire. **1609** Bible (Douay) *Manasseh*, Thou art our Lord, most high, benigne, long-suffering, and very merciful, and penitent upon the wickednes of men.

3. Undergoing penance. In quot. 1613 *transf.* Proper to penance or fasting days: cf. penance *sb.* 3 b, Lenten *a.* 2.

1590 Shaks. *Com. Err.* i. ii. 52 But we that know what 'tis to fast and pray, Are penitent for your default to day. **1613** Beaum. & Fl. *Coxcomb* ii. ii, Not a doore open now, but double bard,.. the very smithes that were halfe venturers, drink penitent single ale.

B. *sb.* **1.** One who repents; a repentant sinner.

1434 Misyn *Mending of Life* 108 Emonge þis þe penitent manly hym-self bus vse & gostely armore take. **1532** More *Confut. Tindale* Wks. 525/1 For penitentes are accompted among the good. **1680** Luttrell *Brief Rel.* (1857) I. 53 The earl of Rochester is lately dead,.. and though he lived but a debauch'd kind of life, yet he died a great penitent. *a* **1740** Waterland *Serm.*, *1 John iii.* 9 (1742) II. 23 The question was not about dying Penitents. **1849** Dickens *Dav. Copp.* lxi, The only unchallengeable way of making sincere.. penitents.

2. A person performing (ecclesiastical) penance; one under the direction of a confessor; also, in the early church, a member of one of four ranks into which those guilty of any of the mortal sins were divided (see quot. 1850).

1412–20 Lydg. *Chron. Troy* ii. xiii. (1513) H vj, As a penitaunt in contritioun Ye you disraye. *a* **1425** *Langl. P. Pl.* C. v. 130 Prouisour oþer prest oþer penaunt [*Camb. MS. Ff.* 5. 35, penytaunt] for hus synnes. **1546** Bale *Eng. Votaries* i. 42 Guenhera.. was after hys death deuoutely receyued into ambesburye nonrye, as a penitent. **1601** Shaks. *All's Well* iii. v. 97 Of inioyn'd penitents There's foure or fiue, to great S. Iaques bound, Alreadie at my house. **1662** *Jesuits Reasons* (1675) N iv, Who having been.. Scholars of the Jesuits, were actually, when they dyed, Penitents of the Jesuits. **1704** Nelson *Fest. & Fasts* ii. (1739) 437 A Penitent, who after Baptism having committed some grievous Sin, was.. excluded the Assemblies of Christians. **1850** Neale *East. Ch.* I. ii. ii. 208 The four orders of penitents were.. the *Flentes*, whose place was in the porch; the *Audientes*, in the narthex; the *Consistentes* and *Substrati*, in the lower part of the nave. **1854** Milman *Lat. Chr.* vii. ii, The King.. clad only in the thin white linen dress of the penitent.

3. *pl.* A name designating various Roman Catholic congregations or orders, associated for mutual discipline, the giving of religious aid to criminals, etc., or forming refuges for reformed prostitutes. Rarely in *sing.*, a member of such an association.

1693 tr. *Emilianne's Hist. Monast. Ord.* xix. 221 Henry the III,.. having seen.. the Procession of the White Penitents at Avignon. **1706** tr. *Dupin's Eccl. Hist. 16th C.* II. iv. xi. 449 Those of the Third Order of St. Francis, who are called *Penitents*, were at first only a Congregation of Seculars of both Sexes. **1727–41** Chambers *Cycl.*, *Penitents*,.. certain fraternities, or societies of persons who assemble together for prayers, make processions bare-footed, their faces covered with linen, and give themselves discipline, &c. There are *white penitents* in Italy, at Avignon, and at Lyons.. There are also *blue penitents*, and *black penitents*, which last assist criminals at their death, and give them burial. **1797** Mrs. Radcliffe *Italian* Prol. (1826) 3 A church belonging to a very ancient convent of the order of the Black Penitents. **1797** *Encycl. Brit.* XIV. 124. **1871** Hook *Ch. Dict.* 577.

†**4.** Puttenham's name for the rhetorical figure, by which the speaker or writer subsequently retracts or corrects a term used by him. *Obs.*

1589 Puttenham *Eng. Poesie* iii. xix. (Arb.) 224 Other-whiles we speake and be sorry for it, as if we had not wel spoken, so that we seeme to call in our word agaıne, and to put in another fitter for the purpose: for which.. the Greekes called this.. the figure of repentance... I following the Greeke originall, choose to call him the penitent, or repentant.

5. *Geogr.* [See quot. 1954[1].] A spike or pinnacle of compact snow or ice which results from differential ablation of a snow or ice field exposed to the sun, occurring esp. in high mountain ranges and freq. in large groups containing specimens of similar size and orientation. Freq. *attrib.* or as *adj.*

[**1910** *Geogr. Jrnl.* XXXV. 125 Among the variety of views that have been advanced, observers have practically agreed that one factor essential to the production of penitentes,.. is the unequal melting of *névé* under the application of heat in some form, principally that of the sun.] **1922** Wright & Priestley *Glaciology* viii. 288 Plate CXCV shows an example of penitent-ice from the Ferrar glacier. **1936** G. Seligman *Snow Struct.* vi. 131 It has been postulated.. that the ablative effect in penitent snow has been intensified by the presence of solid matter to absorb the sun's heat. **1941** *Amer. Jrnl. Sci.* CCXXXIX. 382 'Penitent' ice-forms, modelled in some degree by evaporation processes and associated with the same structures, have been described from Antarctica. **1954** *Jrnl. Glaciology* II. 331 We venture to translate the words used by Chileans and Argentinians into English: *penitentes* (noun), *campo de penitentes* (field of penitents). *Nieve penitente* is not used, and *nieve de los penitentes* means 'snow from the penitents'. Both expressions have been introduced into international literature by.. glaciologists who did not know Spanish very thoroughly. *Ibid.* 336 When the snow field lies directly upon the ground, the channels between the penitents often succeed in reaching the ground, and the penitents, detaching themselves from one another, assume the vague appearance of an Easter procession of white-cowled Spanish penitents. **1954** W. Noyce *South Col.* v. 83 The ice.. had ribbed and wrinkled into bigger honeycomb, more like the ice pinnacles called 'penitents'. **1959** R. E. Huschke *Gloss. Meteorol.* 416 Penitent ice is most developed on low-latitude mountains, especially the Chilean Andes, but has been found even in polar regions. **1972** *Cambridge Mountaineering* 38 An additional reason for travelling to Afghanistan had been to study certain snow formations, called penitents. *Ibid.* 39 Our 'penitents'.. were spread all over the place both on the snowfields and sometimes also on the rock surfaces... Their only use turned out to be on steep snow slopes where they provided useful handholds—provided one didn't put too much trust in them.

6. *attrib.* **penitent-form**, a form or bench for penitents; the 'stool of repentance'.

1865 *Wesleyan-Methodist Mag.* Nov. 484 She was the first to come to the penitent form. **1881** *Doctrines & Discipline Salvation Army* §28 Bring them out to the penitent form before the people, and so test them further, and pledge them publicly. **1887** Hall Caine *Deemster* iii. 45 The Testament falling open on to the penitent-form. **1896** ACKWORTH *Clog Shop Chron.* 305 (E.D.D.) An' yond's the penitent-form.

penitential (pɛnɪˈtɛnʃəl), *a.* and *sb.* Also 6–7 **-all**, 6 **penytencyal(l**, 7 **pœnitential**. [ad. med.L. *pœnitentiāl-is*, f. *pæni-*, *pœnitentia*: see PENITENCE and -AL[1]. Cf. F. *pénitentiel*; in 14–15th c. *penitencial*, *-tial* (in Godef.).]

A. *adj.* **1.** Of, pertaining to, or expressive of penitence or repentance.

1592 *Nobody & Someb.* 942 in Simpson *Sch. Shaks.* (1878) I. 313, I know his penitentiall words proceede From a remorcefull spirit. **1638** COWLEY *Love's Riddle* III, When you have shed some penitential tears For wronging of Palæmon. **1751** JOHNSON *Rambler* No. 139 ¶9 Samson, touched with this reproach, makes a reply equally penitential and pious. *c* **1845** FABER *Hymn*, '*My God, how wonderful Thou art*', I..worship thee with trembling hope And penitential tears. **1853** ROBERTSON *Serm.* Ser. III. xx. 263 The gloom of penitential life.

b. ***penitential psalms***: A name given to seven psalms (vi, xxxii, xxxviii, li, cii, cxxx, cxliii) which give especial expression to the feelings of penitence. (The earliest use of the adj. in Eng.)

1508 FISHER (*title*) The fruytful saynges of Dauyd the kynge & prophete in the seuen penytencyall psalmes. *Ibid.* Wks. (1876) 22 *Beati quorum.* This psalme of a good congruence..is called a penytencyal psalme bycause penaunce is so dylygently treated and spoken of in it. **1658** *Whole Duty Man, Priv. Devot.* 611 This Penitential Psalm [li.] may also fitly be used. **1710** J. BINGHAM *Chr. Antiq.* XIII. x. §13 The common Psalm of confession, or the Penitential Psalm..being no other but the fifty-first Psalm. **1885** *Cath. Dict., Penitential Psalms*, ..Possidius tells us that St. Augustine, when dying, caused the penitential psalms, which are few in number, to be fixed on the wall opposite his bed. Probably our penitential psalms are meant.

2. Pertaining to, expressive of, or constituting ecclesiastical penance; of the nature of a penance. ***penitential robe***, a robe worn by a public penitent.

a **1535** FISHER *Spir. Consolat.* Wks. (1876) 362 Doe you these suffrages for your owne soule, whether they be praiers or almes deedes, or any other penitentiall paynefulnesse. **1546** BALE *Eng. Votaries* I. 37 Theodorus..publyshed a serten boke of hys owne makynge, called A penytencyall summe. **1625** MEADE in Ellis *Orig. Lett.* Ser. I. III. 200 The Popes Legate, who came thither to impose upon her I know not what penitential Confession for sixteen..days, for consenting to marry our King without the Popes dispensation. **1781** COWPER *Truth* 95 Of all his conduct this the genuine sense—My penitential stripes, my streaming blood, Have purchas'd Heaven, and prove my title good. **1877** MRS. OLIPHANT *Makers Flor.* iii. 83 In penitential robes, with candle in his hand, and words of submission in his mouth. **1885** *Cath. Dict.* (ed. 3) 652/2 From the latter part of the tenth century flogging was added to the other penitential exercises.

fig. **1885** H. JAMES *Lit. Tour* xxx. 192 Streets..paved with villainous little sharp stones, making all exercise penitential.

B. *sb.* **1.** A person performing or undergoing penance, a penitent. Also, in humorous allusion (quot. 1664), a prisoner. *rare.*

1627 E. F. *Hist. Edw. II* (1680) 16 Such melancholy Meditations are deemed a fit food for Penitentials, rather than a necessary reflection for the stomack of Regal authority. **1664** BUTLER *Hud.* II. i. 819 Then in their Robes the Penitentials Are streight presented with Credentials. **1828** *Blackw. Mag.* XXIII. 413 A cathedral in which a hundred thousand penitentials might have prayed.

2. A book containing in codified form the canons of the Church relating to penance, its imposition, etc.; a penitentiary manual; = med.L. *pœnitentiāle*, *liber pœnitentiālis*.

1618 SELDEN *Hist. Tithes* vii. 169 A Penitential made for direction of Priests in auricular Confession. **1651** JER. TAYLOR *Holy Dying* v. v. (1719) 216 This Advice was inserted into the Penitential of England in the time of Theodore Archbishop of Canterbury. **1788** GIBBON *Decl. & F.* lviii. (1790) XI. 16 This mode of legislation was invented by the Greeks: their *penitentials* were translated, or imitated, in the Latin Church. **1874** STUBBS *Const. Hist.* I. vii. 204 The Anglo-Saxon Canons and Penitentials of the tenth century are in great part translations.

3. *pl.* Short for ***penitential psalms***: see A. 1 b.

1641 J. JACKSON *True Evang. T.* II. 143 That of David in the chiefe of his Penitentialls, Wash mee with hyssope, &c. **1672–5** COMBER *Comp. Temple* (1702) 14 The..words of the LI Psalm, or some other of the Penitentials.

4. *pl.* The signs, manners, utterances, demeanour, or behaviour of a penitent; apologetic demeanour, appearance, or behaviour. ? *Obs.* **b.** Mourning garments; black cloths (*colloq.*).

1748 RICHARDSON *Clarissa* (1810) V. iii. 19 How odious does sorrow make an ugly face!—Thine, Jack, and this old bedlam's, in penitentials, instead of moving compassion, must evermore confirm hatred. **1751** ELIZA HEYWOOD *Betsy Thoughtless* III. xviii. 222 (*heading*) Displays Miss Betsy in her penitentials. **1805** EMILY CLARK *Banks of Douro* II. 146 During this interval Lord Oswell was quite in his penitentials, intreating..his dear angel to return. **1861** DICKENS *Gt. Expect.* iv, Joe..emerged from his room..in a full suit of Sunday penitentials.

†**5.** *pl.* The members of some monastic order: = PENITENT B. 3. *Obs. rare*[−1].

1632 LITHGOW *Trav.* I. 15 At St. Peters Pallace..there meete 21. pilgrimes; 14. from the Trinity..and seuen from St. Peters Penitentialls.

Hence **peniˈtentially** *adv.*, in a penitential manner, in the manner of a penitent.

1648 JENKYN *Blind Guide* iv. 68 You..acknowledge it [the charge] true, though not penitentially, but impudently. **1828** *Blackw. Mag.* XXIII. 97 The soul may be sorrowfully and penitentially sensible of its sins.

penitentiary (pɛnɪˈtɛnʃərɪ), *a.* and *sb.* Also 5–7 **-enci-**, 7 **pœni-**, **pæni-**. [ad. med.L. *pœnitentiāri-us* adj. and sb., f. L. *pæni-*, *pœnitentia* PENITENCE: see -ARY[1]. The sb. senses represent various ellipt. or absolute uses of the L. adj., viz. med.L. *pœnitentiārius*, *pœnitentiāria*, **pœnitentiārium*; also = med.L. *pœnitentiāle* = *liber pœnitentiālis*. These are thus in their proximate derivation independent formations, though all going back to the adj. in L., Fr., or Eng. On this account the adj. is here placed first, though some of the sb. senses, taken direct from L. or Fr., were earlier in Eng. use.]

A. *adj.* **1.** Of or pertaining to penance; administering, or undergoing, penance.

1577 tr. *Bullinger's Decades* (1592) 576 He did quite take awaie the office of that penitentiarie Priesthood. **1581** J. BELL *Haddon's Answ. Osor.* 145 Standyng..in dispayred case, is enforced dayly to runne to the second table of Penitentiary Confession for relief. **1626** JACKSON *Creed* VIII. ii. 11 His entertainement..more despicable than the lodging or entertainement of Pœnitentiary Pilgrimes. **1629** in Cramond *Ann. Banff* (1893) II. 27 He would be enjoyned to satisfie in saccloth vpon the penitentiarie seat. **1678** *Lively Orac.* VII. ix, The penitentiary books and canons. **1845** J. H. NEWMAN *Ess. Develop m.* 413 The schism.. led to the appointment of a penitentiary priest in the Catholic Churches.

2. Pertaining to, or expressive of, penitence; repentant. *rare.*

1791 *Hist.* in *Ann. Reg.* 15/2 To publish what..might be considered as a penitentiary declaration. *a* **1806** C. J. FOX *Reign Jas. II* (1808) 169 After the death of his friends he..wrote a penitentiary letter to his father. **1817** CHALMERS *Astron. Disc.* vii. (1830) 285 At one with the humblest and most penitentiary feeling which Christianity can awaken.

3. Intended for or relating to the penal and reformatory treatment of criminals. ***Penitentiary House*** = PENITENTIARY B. 7. ***Penitentiary Act***, the Act 19 Geo. III, c. 74.

1776 BENTHAM *Fragm. Govt.* (ed. 2) Pref., The Penitentiary system had for its first advocates Mr. Eden.. and Sir William Blackstone. **1777** HOWARD *Prisons Eng.* iii. (1792) 42 The highwayman..the footpad..the habitual thief..should end their days in a penitentiary house, rather than on the gallows. **1779** *Act 19 Geo. III*, c. 74 §5 They.. shall erect..two plain strong, and substantial Edifices or Houses, which shall be called The Penitentiary Houses, for the purpose of confining and employing in hard Labour.. such..Convicts as..shall be ordered to Imprisonment and hard Labour. **1791** BENTHAM *Panopt.* Wks. 1843 IV. 144 *House of hard labour*, it was suggested..is a name by which no house will ever be called, and the well-imagined word *penitentiary-house* was put in its stead. **1818** SOUTHEY *Ess.* (1832) II. 176 Let the prison-fare be a penitentiary regimen. **1877** tr. *H. von Ziemssen's Cycl. Med.* VI. 770 Autenrieth drew attention to the frequency of scrofulosis in penitentiaries (so-called penitentiary scrophula).

4. Of an offence: Punishable by imprisonment in a penitentiary (*U.S.*).

1856 OLMSTED *Slave States* 440 As it is a penitentiary offense, the culprit spares no pains or expense to avoid conviction. **1896** *Daily News* 19 Dec. 8/1 Recall..the state of affairs at the end of the war..up to then it had been a penitentiary offence to teach a black to read and write.

B. *sb.* **I.** = med.L. *pœnitentiārius*.

1. A person appointed to deal with penitents or penances; *spec.* in R.C. Ch., an officer vested with power to deal with cases which the ordinary parish priest may be incompetent to determine.

1483 *Cath. Angl.* 274/2 A Penytenciary, *penitenciarius*. *a* **1548** HALL *Chron., Hen. VIII* 51 b, On the Sondaye folowynge the Chaunceller commaunded the Penytensary of Poules, too goo vp to hym and saye a Gospell. **1679** J. SMITH *Narr. Pop. Plot* 6 Two Jesuits..were..advanced to be the Popes Penitentiaries. **1797** *Encycl. Brit.* (ed. 3) XIV. 124 *Penitentiary*, in the ancient Christian church, a name given to certain presbyters or priests, appointed in every church to receive the private confessions of the people. **1885** *Cath. Dict.* (ed. 3) 647/1 This [public penance], in the case of secret sins, came to an end in the Church of Constantinople soon after the abolition of the presbyter ἐπὶ τῆς μετανοίας, or penitentiary, at the close of the fourth century.

b. ***grand***, ***high*** (***chief***, ***great***) ***penitentiary***, a cardinal who presides over the office called 'penitentiary' (see 4), and has the granting of absolution in cases reserved for the papal authority.

[**1581** MARBECK *Bk. of Notes* 803 The most high penitenciarie, Christ.] **1670** G. H. *Hist. Cardinals* I. III. 84 The office of chief Penitentiary is given by the Pope to a Cardinal alwayes. **1726** AYLIFFE *Parergon* 143 [The] Great Penitentiary,..together with his Counsellors, prescribes the measure of Pennance. **1727–41** CHAMBERS *Cycl.* s.v., In some places there is a *grand penitentiary*, and a *sub-penitentiary*. **1842** BRANDE *Dict. Sci.* etc. s.v., Briefs granted by the grand penitentiary are at the present time entirely gratuitous, and headed with the words 'pro Deo'.

†**2.** = PENITENT *sb.* 1 and 2. *Obs.*

1553 BECON *Reliques of Rome* (1563) 61 *Flagellatores*... They doe beate them selues with scourges... These be admitted by the bishop of Rome as penitentiaries. **1604** R. CAWDREY *Table Alph.*, *Penitentiarie*, one repenting, or doing pennaunce. **1627** JACKSON *Creed* XI. xlii. §2 Manasses.. died a Penitentiary. **1654** tr. *Scudery's Curia Pol.* 52 To take revenge on a foe, wounded, dying Penitentiarie, weeping, and bleeding for his crimes.

3. A member of a religious order so called: cf. PENITENT *sb.* 3.

1631 WEEVER *Anc. Fun. Mon.* 139 Many other reformations haue beene from time to time of the Franciscans, as by the Minims, Recollects, Penitentiaries, Capuchins, &c. **1683** LORRAIN *Muret's Rites Fun.* 254 In the Chappel of St. Petronilla [Rome], when they were digging a Grave for a Penitentiary then lately deceased.

II. = med.L. *pœnitentiāria*, F. *pénitencerie*.

4. *R.C. Ch.* The office or dignity of a penitentiary; an office or congregation in the Papal Court, presided over by the Grand Penitentiary (see 1 b), and forming a tribunal for deciding upon questions relating to penance, dispensations, etc.

1658 PHILLIPS, *Penitentiary*,..also a place in Rome, where Priests sit and hear the confessions of those that come unto them to that end. **1727–41** CHAMBERS *Cycl.*, *Penitentiary*,..an office, or tribunal in the court of Rome; wherein are examined and delivered out the secret bulls, graces, or dispensations relating to conscience, confession, &c. **1902** *Daily Chron.* 31 Dec. 5/5 A prelate of the Apostolic Penitentiary, the Congregation that deals with matrimonial questions.

III. = OF. *pen(e)ancerie*; in mod.F. *pénitenciaire* obs., *pénitencier*.

†**5.** A place of penitential discipline or punishment for ecclesiastical offences. *Obs.*

? **1421** BECKINGTON in *Lett. Marg. of Anjou & Bp. B.* (Camden) 27 Of which lesings one is, that he shulde have made a letter ysett upon Faukener is gate, thanne maire of London, and [he is] cast into the Penitauncery of Poules. **1644** H. VAUGHAN *Serm.* 13 There is an inestimable disproportion betwixt the afflictions of the severest Penitentiarie and celestiall Blisse.

6. An asylum or house of refuge for prostitutes resolving on amendment of life. *Hist.*

1806 *Evangelical Mag.* XIV. 616 The Friends of the intended London Female Penitentiary are respectfully informed that a General Meeting will be held on Thursday the 1st day of January 1807. **1854** MILMAN *Lat. Chr.* III. iv. (1864) I. 422 The feeling which induced the degraded and miserable victim of the lusts..of men to found, perhaps, the first penitentiaries for her sisters in that wretched class. **1873** LIDDON *Penit. Wk. in Ch. Eng.* Pref., The nearness of a House of Refuge or Penitentiary. **1891** *Daily News* 25 Sept. 5/4 The change of title..from the 'London Female Penitentiary Society' to the 'London Female Guardian Society' has been universally approved of... When the society was founded eighty-four years ago the term 'Penitentiary' was well understood to mean a voluntary asylum for the reception of those resolving on amendment of life.

7. A reformatory prison; a house of correction: see *Penitentiary House* A. 3. In *U.S.* 'The place of punishment in which convicts sentenced to confinement and hard labour are confined by the authority of the law' (Bouvier).

1816 *Ann. Reg.* 368 The General Penitentiary, Milbank, contained 52 males and 76 females..on the 22d May. **1825** JEFFERSON *Autobiog.* Wks. 1859 I. 47 Its principle..was adopted by Latrobe..by the erection of what is now called the Penitentiary. **1843** *Penny Cycl.* XXV. 152/1 The act 52 Geo. III., c. 44, was framed in conformity with the committee's recommendation, by which act the Penitentiary at Millbank was commenced in 1813. **1885** *Encycl. Brit.* XIX. 748 The great penitentiary still standing after many vicissitudes, but practically unaltered, at Millbank. [Demolished in 1891.] **1898** *Bouvier's Law Dict.* (by F. Rawle) II. 645 There are two systems of penitentiaries in the United States..the Pennsylvania system and the New York system.

IV. 8. = PENITENTIAL *sb.* 2, ***penitentiary book***: cf. A. 1, quot. 1678. *rare.*

1853 ROCK *Ch. of Fathers* IV. xi. 62 Theodore Archbishop of Canterbury and Ecgberht of York had, severally, drawn up a hand-book known as the penitentiary.

†**peniˈtentiaryship.** *Obs.* [f. prec. + -SHIP.] The office of penitentiary (see prec. B. 1).

1570 FOXE *A. & M.* (ed. 2) 2034/2 In the end the bishop [i.e. the Pope]..gratifyng D. Cranmer wyth the office of the Penitenciariship, dismissed them. **1691** WOOD *Ath. Oxon.* I. 192 Afterwards he obtained..the Penitentiaryship or the Prebend of St. Pancras in the Cathedral Church of St. Paul. **1716** M. DAVIES *Athen. Brit.* II. 213.

†**penitentionary.** *Obs.* = PENITENTIARY *sb.* 2.

1577 FULKE *Confut. Purg.* 173 There were small patience, mekenes, or loue, in some of the purgatory penitentionaries.

†**peniˈtentious,** *a.* *Obs. rare*[−0]. [ad. F. *pénitencieux*, *-euse*.]

1611 COTGR., *Penitencieux*, penitentious, verie penitent.

ˈpenitently, *adv.* [f. PENITENT *a.* + -LY[2].] In a penitent manner, repentantly, contritely.

1570 FOXE *A. & M.* (ed. 2) 1170/1 The sayd Baynham.. to submitte hym selfe penitently to the iudgement of the Church. **1603** SHAKS. *Meas. for M.* IV. ii. 147 Hath he borne himselfe penitently in prison? **1693** LUTTRELL *Brief Rel.* (1857) III. 100 Capt. Winter was yesterday executed:..He died very penitently. **1864** PUSEY *Lect. Daniel* viii–ix. 486 He, Whom they first pierced and then penitently gazed on, was God.

ˈpenitentness. *rare.* [f. as prec. + -NESS.] The quality of being penitent; penitency.

1727 in BAILEY vol. II. **1775** in ASH.

†**peˈnition.** *Sc. Obs.* Also 6 **-issione**. [ad. late L. *pœnitio* = *pūnitio*.] Punishment.

1547 *Burgh Rec. Stirling* 28 Apr. (1887) 48 Marioun Ray amerciat for trubling of Agnes Hendersoun..ordanis for penitioun that..scho be put in the creile and hyng thair during the will of the provest and baillies. **1551-2** *Burgh Rec. Prestwick* 30 Jan. (1834) 62 þe ourisman of þe gud towne accusyt Allexr. Browne balȝe for þe breken of ane ac ..and raferys þe penissione to þe inquest.

† **peni'tissim**, *a. nonce-wd.* [ad. L. **penitissimus*, superl. of *penitus* interior.] Innermost.

1652 URQUHART *Jewel* Wks. (1834) 243 Being convoyed into the penitissim corners of their souls.

† **'penitive**, *a. Obs. rare*⁻¹. [ad. med.L. type **pœnitīvus* = *pūnītīvus*.] Punitive, penal.

1502 *Ord. Crysten Men* (W. de W. 1506) v. iv. 388 The Iustyce penitiue sholde be to moche vnlawfuly dymynysshed.

penitote, erroneous f. PERIDOT, q.v.

† **'penitude**. *Obs. rare*⁻¹. In 7 pœni-. [ad. L. *pænitūdo* (early and post-cl.), f. *pænitēre* to repent. So OF. *pénitude* (Oresme, 14th c.).] Repentance.

1657 *Penit. Conf.* i. 7 *Μετάνοια*. which a learned Interpreter [Beza] alwayes translates *Resipiscence*, and *μεταμέλεια* in like manner alwayes by him rendred *Pœnitude*.

penk (pɛŋk), *v. rare.* [? var. PANK *v.*] *intr.* To palpitate; to throb or heave violently or rapidly.

1890 KIPLING *Barrack-Room Ballads* (1892) 27 Wot makes the soldier's 'eart to penk, wot makes 'im to perspire? **1898** —— *Stalky* in *Land & Sea Tales* (1923) 137 They bullocks drove like that—all heavin' an' penkin' an' hotted!

penk, orig. form of PINK *sb.*¹, a minnow.

penknife ('pɛnnaɪf). [f. PEN *sb.*² + KNIFE.] A small knife, usually carried in the pocket, used originally for making and mending quill pens. (Formerly provided with a sheath; now made with a jointed blade or blades which fit inside the handle when closed.)

14.. *Nom.* in Wr.-Wülcker 682/21 *Hic artavus*, a penknyfe. *c* **1450** *Medulla* in *Cath. Angl.* 50 *note*, *Scalprum*, a penne knyf. **1481-90** *Howard Househ. Bks.* (Roxb.) 514 Item, payd.. for a penknyff j. *d.* **1535** COVERDALE *Jer.* xxxvi. 23 He cut the boke in peces with a penne knyfe. **1549** *Compl. Scot.* iii. 26 Cesar.. gat xxii. straikis vitht pen knyuis in the capitol. **1658** W. SANDERSON *Graphice* 81 Sharpen then with a pen-knife. **1800** MAR. EDGEWORTH *Belinda* xv, She shut the penknife which lay upon the table. **1860** TYNDALL *Glac.* II. xvii, Was it [crack] sufficiently wide to permit the blade of my penknife to enter it?

b. *attrib.* and *Comb.*

1611 COTGR., *Ganivetier*, a pen-knife-maker. **1768-74** TUCKER *Lt. Nat.* (1834) II. 621 Your penknife sheath for him to pull open and shut again.

'penlight, pen-light. [f. PEN *sb.*² + LIGHT *sb.*] An electric torch shaped like a fountain-pen.

1958 *Practical Wireless* XXXIV. 58/2 (Advt.), Uses only one small 8d. penlight battery. **1962** E. AMBLER *Light of Day* x. 210 Miller had a pen-light in his hand and was looking at his watch. **1969** *New Yorker* 12 Apr. 78/2 There are pockets in unlikely places, such as at the ankles and shoulders, for things like scissors, penlights, and checklists. **1971** D. BAGLEY *Freedom Trap* ix. 206, I took out a pen-light and risked a flash. **1972** J. HURTT et al. *Compr. Rev. Orthoptics & Ocular Motility* xviii. 182 The patient is instructed to fixate a wall light at 20 feet while a penlight is held directly in front of his nose. **1977** 'E. MCBAIN' *Long Time no See* ii. 18 Carella took a small pen-light from his coat pocket and flashed it over the mail-boxes.

pen-maker ('pɛn,meɪkə(r)). [f. PEN *sb.*²]

1. A person who makes pens; formerly, one engaged in making and mending quill pens.

1779 in J. O. Payne *O. Eng. Cath. Missions* (1889) 78 Charles [Stewart], a penmaker. **1854** KNIGHT *Once upon a Time* II. 202 The steam-engine is now the pen-maker.

2. A machine for cutting pens from quills.

1875 KNIGHT *Dict. Mech.*, *Pen-maker*, a tool formed like a pair of pinchers for making quill-pens.

penman ('pɛnmən). Pl. penmen ('pɛnmən). [f. PEN *sb.*² + MAN *sb.*]

1. a. A man employed to use the pen for another; one whose business is to write or copy documents, etc.; a clerk, secretary, notary, scrivener. Now *rare*.

1612 ROWLANDS *Four Knaves* (Percy Soc.) 109 But Plutoe's pen-man you did late mistake, The Devil's errand, for your maisters sake. **1628** COKE *On Litt.* 120 Clerk.. a pen-man who getteth his living in some court or otherwise by the use of his pen. **1727** A. HAMILTON *New Acc. E. Ind.* I. xiii. 150 The Banyans.. are either Merchants, Bankers, Brokers or Pen-men. **1858** MASSON *Milton* I. 20 Scriveners, as the name implies, were originally penmen of all kinds of writings. **1885** *As it was Written* in *Cassell's Rainbow Ser. Orig. Novels* 138 A penman's palsy shakes my wrist.

b. *fig.* Applied to the writers of Scripture (*penmen of God* or *of the Holy Ghost*) regarded as writing from divine dictation or command. But in later use, with *holy*, *sacred*, *divine*, *inspired*, etc. = 'writer', prob. taken in sense 3.

1601 HAKEWILL *Van. of Eye* viii. (1615) 45 Moses, the pen-man of God. **1611** BIBLE *Transl. Pref.* 3 The authour being God, not man; the enditer, the holy spirit..; the Penmen such as were sanctified from the wombe, and endewed with a principall portion of Gods spirit. *a* **1656** HALES *Gold. Rem.* (1688) 2 St. Paul, one of the first Pen-men of the Holy Ghost. *a* **1659** BP. BROWNRIG *Serm.* (1674) II. xv. 186 Moses, the first Pen-man that God ever imployed. **1741** WARBURTON *Div. Legat.* II. 480 The inspired Pen-men. **1875** SCRIVENER *Lect. Text N. Test.* 7 In the case of the classical writings, so with those of the sacred penmen.

c. *Criminals' slang.* One who commits forgery.

1865 *Sessions Papers* 11 Apr. 519 For being concerned with, *Jemmy the Penman*, and others, now in custody, [etc.]. **1887** J. HAWTHORNE (*title*) An American penman: from the diary of Inspector Byrnes. **1938** F. D. SHARPE *Sharpe of Flying Squad* xxix. 297 As soon as they get some cheques or 'kites', as they call them, these are rushed off to the 'penman' or 'scribe', whose task is that of taking out crosses on them, enlarging the figures and preparing suitable letters to the bank asking them to cash the cheques. **1974** H. MCLEAVE *Only Gentlemen can Play* (1975) II. 97 You'll need a passport... I've got a penman who can doctor it.

2. A man skilled in penmanship; a skilful writer; one who writes a good hand; a calligraphist. (With qualifying adj., as *good*, *expert*, *swift*, etc.)

1591 SYLVESTER *Du Bartas* I. iv. 416 Smooth Orator, swift Pen-man. **1607** DEKKER *Westw. Hoe* II. i. Wks. 1873 II. 295 We lacke painfull and expert pen-men amongst vs. **1706** PHILLIPS, *Pen-man*, a Person skill'd in fair Writing. **1878** BROWNING *Poets Croisic* lxxv, Completed lay thy piece, swift penman Paul!

3. a. A writer or composer of a book or other writing; an author, a writer.

1592 GREENE *Def. Conny Catch.* (1859) 6 That palpable asse.. that would make any penman privy to our secret sciences. **1673** KIRKMAN *Wits* Pref., The most part of these Pieces were written by such Penmen as were known to be the ablest Artists that ever this Nation produced, by Name Shake-spear, Fletcher, Johnson, Shirley, and others. **1710** SHAFTESB. *Charact.* III. II. i. (1737) I. 224 Able Penmen rais'd to rehearse the Lives, and celebrate the high Actions of great Men. **1886** DOWDEN *Shelley* I. iv. 135 The grand ball.. taxing to the utmost the powers of the penman who described the event next day in the *Morning Herald*.

b. Const. *of* (that which is written). Now *rare*.

1610 *Mirr. Mag.* 604 The pen-man of my historie. **1624** GATAKER *Good Wife* 1 The penman of it was Salomon. **1641** J. JACKSON *True Evang. T.* III. 217 So doth the Penman of the Epistle to the Hebrewes. **1706** A. BEDFORD *Temple Mus.* vii. 154 The Pen Men of the Holy Scriptures. **1882** FARRAR *Early Chr.* I. 329 The inspiration of the Holy Spirit was not a mechanical dictation, which makes a man the pen rather than the penman of sacred utterance.

4. *Comb.*, as ***penman-like*** adj. (in quot., like the work of a penman).

1843 RUSKIN *Mod. Paint.* I. II. I. vii. §30 A violent, black, sharp, ruled penmanlike line.

penmanship ('pɛnmənʃɪp). [f. prec. + -SHIP.] The practice or performance of a penman.

1. The art of using a pen, *i.e.* of writing; the action of writing; skill in writing; style of writing, handwriting; calligraphy.

1695 AYRES (*title*) The Tutor to Penmanship, or The Writing Master.. Shewing all the Variety of Penmanship and Clerk-ship as now practised in England. **1727** W. MATHER *Yng. Man's Comp.* 52 Learn the Command of Hand by frequent Use, Much Practice doth to Penmanship conduce. **1838** JAS. GRANT *Sk. Lond.* 9 So closely is the handwriting imitated, that.. even the parties themselves can scarcely detect the imposture, in so far as mere penmanship is concerned. **1868** M. PATTISON *Academ. Org.* v. 291 A clever youth.. can discuss as many of the questions mooted by the paper, as three hours of rapid penmanship permit.

2. The action, or style, of penning, *i.e.* wording or composing, a document; literary composition.

1793 BENTHAM *Mem. & Corr.* Wks. 1843 X. 292 The penmanship of the statutes.. has, every now and then, become the subject of a dissatisfaction. **1818** —— *Ch. Eng.*, *Catech. Exam* 329 The men of law.. by whom a part was taken in the penmanship of this Act. **1818** BROUGHAM in *Parl. Deb.* 1029 He remembered that lord Kenyon had once called the composition of an auctioneer his 'penmanship', for he did not think that it deserved the appellation of 'style'.

penn, obs. form of PEN.

pennaceous (pɛ'neɪʃəs), *a. rare.* [f. mod.L. *pennāce-us* (f. *penna* feather, pen) + -OUS: see -ACEOUS.] **a.** *Ornith.* Having the structure of a pen-feather or quill-feather. **b.** *Entom.* and *Bot.* Applied to markings resembling feathers, or to surfaces or structures having such markings.

1857 MAYNE *Expos. Lex.*, *Pennaceus*,.. having the surface marked with lengthened stains,.. compared to feathers..: pennaceous. **1890** WEBSTER, *Pennaceous* (*Zoöl.*), like or pertaining to a normal feather. **1890** *Cent. Dict.*, *Pennaceous* .., having the structure of a penna or contour-feather; not plumulaceous... In *entom.*, resembling the web of a feather; having fine, close, parallel lines springing diagonally from a single line. **1893** *Syd. Soc. Lex.*, *Pennaceous*, in Botany, marked with longitudinal stains looking like feathers.

pennache -ed, obs. forms of PANACHE, -ED.

† **'pennage**. *Obs. rare.* [a. F. *pennage* (Amyot, 16th c.), f. *penne* plume: see -AGE.] = PLUMAGE.

1601 HOLLAND *Pliny* I. 287 This very bird.. is.. for the more part of her pennage, blew, intermingled yet among with white and purple feathers. **1752** CARTE *Hist. Eng.* III. 376 This nobleman's staff, lighting on the King's head-piece and taking away the pennage fastened to it with iron. **1857** MAYNE *Expos. Lex.*, *Pennage*,.. a term the same as plumage.

pennair, obs. form of PENNER¹.

‖ **pennal** ('pɛnəl). [Ger. *pe'nnāl* pen-case, school-boy, a. med.L. *pennāle* pen-case, f. *penna* pen.] Formerly, in German Protestant Universities, a slang name for a freshman, from their carrying about with them their pen-cases for use at lectures.

1882 in OGILVIE, and in later Dicts.

Hence **'pennalism** [Ger. and mod.L. *pennalismus*], an oppressive system of fagging practised upon freshmen in German Universities in the 17th century. (Abolished about the end of the 17th c.)

1863 DOWDING *Life G. Calixtus* iv. 24 Pennalism was a frightful system of 'bullying'. *Ibid.* v. 31 It was they who held pennalism, with its terrors, in check. *Ibid.* xx. 183.

pennance, -ans, obs. forms of PENANCE.

pennant¹ ('pɛnənt). [app. a compromise between PENDANT and PENNON, representing the usual nautical pronunciation of these words, of which it is now the most usual form.]

1. a. = PENDANT *sb.* 7; a rigging pendant.

1611 COTGR., *Palenc*, the Pennant; a rope which helpes to hoise vp the boat, and all heauie marchandise, aboord a ship. **1658** PHILLIPS, *Pendants* in a Ship, are short ropes made fast at one end either to the head of the mast or to a yard, or to the clew of a sail. **1755** JOHNSON, *Pennant*,.. a tackle for hoisting things on board. **1841** DANA *Seaman's Man.*, *Pendant*, or *Pennant*, a rope to which a purchase is hooked. A long strap.. with a hook or block at the other end, for a brace to reeve through, or to hook a tackle to.

b. (See PENDANT 7 b.)

1867 SMYTH *Sailor's Word-bk.*, *Irish pennants*, rope-yarns hanging about on the rigging. Loose reef-points or gaskets flying about, or fag-ends of ropes.

2. a. = PENDANT *sb.* 9, PENNON 3: see quot. 1867.

1698 FRYER *Acc. E. India & P.* 1 His Majesty, Charles II, was pleased to grant Letters of Mart: Which impowered them to wear the King's Jack, Ancient, and Pennant, and to act as Men of War. **1725** DE FOE *Voy. round World* (1840) 213 A small.. vessel, under Spanish colours, pennant flying. **1755** JOHNSON, *Pennant* (pennon, Fr.), a small flag, ensign or colours. **1816** 'QUIZ' *Grand Master* I. 24 A pennant at the peak appears, To shew the fleet they're at their pray'rs. **1867** SMYTH *Sailor's Word-bk.*, *Pennant*, a long narrow banner with St. George's cross in the head, and hoisted at the main. It is the badge of a ship-of-war. Signal pennants are 9 feet long, tapering from 2 feet at the mast to 1 foot... Broad pennant denotes a commodore, and is a swallow-tailed flag, the tails tapering. **1872** [see b]. **1895** *Funk's Stand. Dict.*, *Pennant*,.. a small flag.. flown during the performance on a naval vessel of some public function; as, a church-pennant, meal-pennant, etc.

b. = PENNON 1. Also *fig.*

1815 *Paris Chit-chat* (1816) I. 26 Myriads of pennants and white flags.. floated in the air. **1863** BARING-GOULD *Iceland* 105 He put up the little pennant which adorned the tent top. **1872** PREBLE *Hist. Flag* (1880) 11 A squire's mark was a long pennant similar to the coach-whip pennant of modern ships of war. **1878** H. M. STANLEY *Dark Cont.* II. xiii. 374 Quivering flaming pennants of flame.

c. *N. Amer. sport.* A flag symbolizing a league championship; hence, the championship itself. Also *attrib.*

1880 N. BROOKS *Fairport Nine* 188 Bill Hetherington.. was entrusted with the championship pennant. **1886** *Outing* Aug. 572/2 Questions by the dozen come in.. in regard to the probable issue of the pennant races in the professional arena. **1915** *Lit. Digest* 21 Aug. 360/3 The Cincinnati Reds ..have never yet won a pennant. *Ibid.*, The New York Giants.. are not often far from the pennant class. **1924** [see CINCH *v.* 2 b]. **1947** *Partisan Rev.* XIV. 258 The funeral was the most serious event of Samuel's life,.. but this did not prevent him from getting the evening paper when the family returned from the cemetery and studying the final scores in the major league pennant races. **1967** W. S. AVIS et al. *Dict. Canad. Eng., Senior Dict.* 821/2 *Pennant*... **2** any flag taken as emblem of superiority or success, especially in an athletic contest. **1971** L. KOPPETT *N.Y. Times Guide Spectator Sports* i. 35 The pennant winner in each league turned out to be the team with the best regular-season record. **1975** *New Yorker* 22 Sept. 98/2 The Los Angeles Dodgers have won five pennants and three World Series since their relocation.

3. *Mus.* A hook of a quaver, semiquaver, etc.: = HOOK *sb.*¹ 10 c. *U.S.*

1890 in *Cent. Dict.* **1895** in *Funk's Stand. Dict.*

4. *Comb.*, as ***pennant-bearer***; **pennant-ship**: see quot.

1812 BYRON *Ch. Har.* II. xx, Then must the pennant-bearer slacken sail, That lagging barks may make their lazy way. **1867** SMYTH *Sailor's Wd.-bk.*, *Pennant-ship*, generally means the commodore, and vessels in the employ of government.

pennant² ('pɛnnænt). [a. Welsh *pennant*, lit. 'dale-head', f. *pen(n)* head + *nant* valley; also a frequent place-name in Wales.] Now usually ***pennant grit***: the name applied to an unproductive series of gritty strata lying between the Upper and Lower Coal-measures in South Wales, whence extended to analogous strata in the Bristol Coalfield. Also ***pennant flag***, ***rock***, ***stone***.

1756 C. LUCAS *Ess. Waters* III. 224 This bath was paved with pennant flag.. a stone that divides into slates of about two inches thick. **1769** STRACHEY in *Phil. Trans.* XXX. 972 A Rock of Paving-Stone, call'd Penant,.. which Rock is sometime twenty Feet thick, or more. **1792** *Gentl. Mag.* LXII. I. 222 The stone of these two crosses is of a very hard and durable kind, usually called pennant, of a close gritty nature, and dug every where in the mountainous parts of Glamorgan. **1876** WOODWARD *Geol. E. Somerset & Bristol Coalfields* 31 [The Coal Measures] are divided into three series, an Upper productive Coal Series, a Middle and nearly unproductive series called the Pennant Grit, and a Lower productive series. **1886** JUKES-BROWNE *Hist. Geol.* 186 The Pennant Grits. This series.. forms the fine range of escarpments, which enclose the central table land of the county [Glamorgan]. **1888** PRESTWICH *Geol.* II. 95.

pennantite (ˈpɛnəntaɪt). *Min.* [f. the name of Thomas *Pennant* (1726–98), Welsh zoologist and mineralogist + -ITE¹.] A basic aluminosilicate of manganese, approximately $Mn_9Al_6Si_5O_{20}(OH)_{16}$, most specimens of which are pleochroic and orange in thin section.

1946 W. C. SMITH et al. in *Mineral. Mag.* XXVII. 217 (*heading*) Pennantite, a new manganese-rich chlorite from Benallt mine, Rhiw, Carnarvonshire. *Ibid.* 220 The names manganchlorite (Hamberg) and manganese-chlorite (Eckermann) have been applied to chlorites containing only a low percentage (1·02–2·28) MnO, so it is desirable to avoid the use of either of these names for a chlorite so rich in manganese as the mineral here described, and we therefore propose for it a new name, *pennantite*. **1954** *Ibid.* XXX. 280 The manganese-bearing chlorites include the remarkable species pennantite, chemically a klementite with the magnesium almost wholly replaced by manganese. **1970** *Mineral Abstr.* XXI. 249/2 (*heading*) The ferruginous and magnesium varieties of pennantite from the Atasui deposits in Central Kazakhstan. *Ibid.*, Fepennantite occurs in the Ushatan 1 deposit in veinlets with pyrosmalite and calcite. It is dark green. *Ibid.*, Magnesium pennantite in the Zhumast deposit occurs in marbles and in carbonate layers in braunite ore... Pleochroism α orange pink, γ light orange.

pennar(e, -ard(e, obs. forms of PENNER¹.

pennate (ˈpɛnət), *a. rare.* [ad. L. *pennāt-us* winged, f. *penna* feather: see -ATE².]

1. *Nat. Hist.* = PINNATE.

[**1704** J. HARRIS *Lex. Techn.* I, *Pennata folia*, winged Leaves.] **1857** MAYNE *Expos. Lex.*, *Pennate.*

2. = PENNIFORM.

1877 ROSENTHAL *Muscles & Nerves* 91 The fibres are attached at an angle to a long tendon, from which they all branch off in one direction (semi-pennate muscles), or in two directions like the plumes of a feather (pennate muscles).

3. Winged; *fig.* very swift.

1870 R. R. COVERDALE *Poems* 35 On pennate feet they tread the way.

pennated (ˈpɛneɪtɪd), *a.* Now *rare.* [f. as prec. + -ED.]

†**1.** *Bot.* = PENNATE 1, PINNATED. *Obs.*

1727 BAILEY vol. II, A *Pennated* Leaf.. or feather Leaf,.. in which the Parts of which the Leaf is compos'd, are set along the middle Rib; either alternately or by Pairs, as in.. Vetches, &c. **1755** in JOHNSON. **1802–3** tr. *Pallas' Trav.* (1812) I. 538 The stalk branches out with pennated leaves.

2. Feathered; having slender lateral ribs like the vane of a feather; also = PENNIFORM.

1819 G. SAMOUELLE *Entomol. Compend.* 267 Antennæ pennated in the males: serrated in the females. **1836–9** TODD *Cycl. Anat.* II. 593/2 Some appearance of a pennated muscle.

pennati-, combining form of L. *pennātus* PENNATE, as in **pennatifid, pennatilobate, pennatipartite, pennatisect, -sected** *adjs.* = PINNATIFID, etc., q.v.

1783 JUSTAMOND tr. *Raynal's Hist. Indies* I. 293 Large pennatified [*sic*] leaves. **1857** MAYNE *Expos. Lex.* 900/2 Pennatifid.. Pennatipartite.. Pennatisected. **1875** HUXLEY in *Encycl. Brit.* I. 130/1 The tentacles become flattened and serrated at the edges, or take on a.. pennatifid character.

pennatulacean (pɛnætjuːˈleɪʃ(ɪ)ən), *a.* and *sb. Zool.* [f. mod.L. *Pennatulacea* neut. pl., f. *Pennatula*, the typical genus.] **a.** *adj.* Belonging to the order *Pennatulacea* of alcyonarian polyps. **b.** *sb.* A polyp of this order. So **pennatuˈlaceous** (-ˈeɪʃəs) *a.*, **pennatuˈlarian** *a.* and *sb.*, **pennatuˈlarious** *a.* = prec.; **pennatulid** (pɛˈnætjuːlɪd), a polyp of the family *Pennatulidæ*, of which *Pennatula*, the sea-pen, is the typical genus; **peˈnnatuloid** *a.*, resembling or allied to this genus.

1857 MAYNE *Expos. Lex.* 900/2 A Family (*Pennatularia*) of Zoöphytes, having the *Pennatula* for their type: pennatularious. **1885** *Athenæum* 30 May 699/2 On a pennatulid obtained.. in the Japanese Sea at a depth of seventy-one fathoms.

pennaunce, pennaunt, obs. forms of PENANCE, PENDANT *sb.*

penne, obs. form of PEN.

penneard, obs. f. *penn'orth*, PENNYWORTH.

penned (pɛnd, *poet.* ˈpɛnɪd), *a.* [f. PEN *sb.*² + -ED².]

1. Having 'pens', i.e. wing-feathers, or quills; winged; feathered, fledged; quilled, as a porcupine. In *Her.* Having feathers of a specified tincture. ? *Obs.*

c **1470** HENRYSON *Mor. Fab.* v. (*Parl. Beasts*) xvi, Baith otter and aip, and pennit porcupyne. **1495** *Trevisa's Barth. De P.R.* XVIII. xciv. (W. de W.) ff vj/2 The lesarde.. is not fetheryd nother pennyd. **1552** HULOET, Penned, *pennatus, plumatus.* Penned or franked, *altilis, ut altilis cygnus.* **1572** BOSSEWELL *Armorie* II. 46 b, S. beareth Sable, a Sphinx d'argent, crined, and penned d'Or.

2. In parasynthetic comb. **a.** from PEN *sb.*² 1, as *hard-penned, tender-penned, weak-penned*; **b.** from PEN *sb.*² 4, as *angry-penned*, having or using an angry pen, *i.e.* writing angrily.

1486 *Bk. St. Albans* A viij b, As longe as an hawke stondeth vnder the nombre of vii. barris.. she is bot tender pennyd. *Ibid.*, She is not harde pennyde no more than a soore hawke. **1596** W. SMITH *Chloris* (1877) 4 My maiden verse.. Whose weake pend muse to flie too soone doth proue. **1708** *Brit. Apollo* No. 62. 3/1 Angry-pen'd Maid. **1968** B. HINES *Kestrel for Knave* 79, I started training Kes after I'd had her about a fortnight, when she was hard penned, that means her tail feathers and wing feathers had gone hard at their bases.

penned (pɛnd), *ppl. a.*¹ [f. PEN *v.*¹ + -ED¹.] Shut up in a pen; confined, as water, by a weir or lock: see the verb. Also with *in, up*, etc.

1794 W. VANDERSTEGEN *Pres. State Thames* 29 The practicability of rendering the rapid river Severn a penn'd navigation. **1840** *Evid. Hull Docks Com.* 138 The further your penned-up dock went up the river the better.

penned (pɛnd), *ppl. a.*² [f. PEN *v.*² + -ED¹.]

1. Written (with a pen); set down in writing. Also with adv., as *well-penned.*

1567 DRANT *Horace, Epist.* xix. F viij, That they shoulde for very spyte My penned poems teare. **1588** SHAKS. *L.L.L.* v. ii. 147 Nor to their pen'd speech render we no grace. **1757** FOOTE *Author* I. Wks. 1799 I. 132 A well penn'd address.

†**2.** Done or worked with a pen or quill. *Obs.*

1597 A. M. tr. *Guillemeau's Fr. Chirurg.* 15/2 Called the penned stitchinge, because it is done with little quilles or shaftes of a penne.

†**penneech.** *Obs.* Name of an old game at cards: see quots.

1680 COTTON *Compl. Gamester* xxi. 104 A Game called Penneech... If the Seven of Diamonds be turn'd up, that is Penneech. **1688** R. HOLME *Armoury* III. xvi. (Roxb.) 73/1 Penneech, this game hath 7 cards apeece, and a card turned vp which is Trump. Then play and he that wins the first trick turns vp another card and that is trump; and so euery trick produceth a new trump till all the seaven are playd. **1816** SINGER *Hist. Cards* 347.

†**pennell,** obs. Sc. form of PANEL.

1586–7 *Reg. Privy Council Scot.* IV. 150 Fra all comperance thairin upoun pennell inqueistis or assyisis.

penner¹ (ˈpɛnə(r)). *Obs.* or *dial.* Also 4–5 -ere, 5 *Sc.* -air, 5–6 pener, pennare, 5–8 -ar, 6 -or, -ard(e. [ad. med.L. *pennārium*, f. *penna* pen: see -ARIUM, -AR.] A case or sheath for pens, of metal, horn, leather, etc., formerly carried at the girdle, often together with an inkhorn; a pen-case; in later use, sometimes, a writing-case.

c **1386** CHAUCER *Merch. T.* 635 Priuely a penner gan he borwe, And in a lettre wroot he al his sorwe. **1398** TREVISA *Barth. De P.R.* II. iv. (1495) b iij/1 Aungels.. bere pennars and ynke hornes and other Instrumentes of wryttes. **14..** *Lat. Eng. Voc.* in Wr.-Wülcker 601/34 *Pennarium*, a Pennere. *c* **1470** HENRYSON *Mor. Fab.* VII. (*Lion & Mouse*) Prol. vi, Ane inkhorne, with ane prettie gilt pennair. **1520** WHITINTON *Vulg.* (1527) 27 One hath pyked out all the pennes from my pennarde. **1541** *Acc. Ld. High Treas. Scot.* in Pitcairn *Crim. Trials* I. *321 For ane Pennare of silver, to keip Pyke-teithe in, to þe Kingis grace. **1591** FLORIO *2nd Fruites* 89 S. Giue me my penknife, to make a pen. D. It is in your penner, you doe nothing but write. **1611** COTGR., *Escriptoire*, a Penner. **1659** HOOLE *Comenius' Vis. World* xci. (1672) 187 We put up our Pens into a Pennar [*calamario*]. **1688** R. HOLME *Armoury* III. 193/2 The Eagle holdeth a Writers penner and Ink-horn in her Beak, by the strings of it. **1864** BOUTELL *Her. Hist. & Pop.* ix. (ed. 3) 40 The Penner and Inkhorn. **1871** W. ALEXANDER *Johnny Gibb* xlii. (1873) 235 The lid o' the penner.

penner² (ˈpɛnə(r)). [f. PEN *v.*² + -ER¹.] One who pens or words a writing, document, statement, etc.; a writer *of* something (either the original composer, or a copier). Almost always with *of*.

1570–6 LAMBARDE *Peramb. Kent* (1826) 162 If Edmund Hadhenham, the penner of the Chronicles of Rochester, lye not shamefully. **1612** SIR G. PAULE *Abp. Whitgift* (1699) 40 The authors and penners of some of these libels were, John Penry and John Udall. *a* **1635** CORBET *Poems* (1807) 24 A Ballad late was made But God knowes who's the penner. **1758** BLACKSTONE *Comm.* I. Introd. i. 11 The penners of our modern statutes. **1817** CANNING in *Parl. Deb.* 1869 With regard to the address before the House; the numerous penners of it should not have launched into affirmations. **1825** BENTHAM *Offic. Apt. Maximized, Indic.* (1830) 49 The penner of this same Act of Lord Eldon's.

†**penner**³. *Obs. rare*⁻¹. See quot.

1624 HEYWOOD *Gunaik.* VII. 355 A bodkin or penner which she wore in her haire for an ornament.

penner⁴ (ˈpɛnə(r)). [f. PEN *v.*¹ + -ER¹.] One who pens cattle; also (*Austral.* and *N.Z.*) **penner-up**, one who pens sheep ready for the shearers in a shearing shed.

1897 D. McK. WRIGHT *Station Ballads* 101 The penner-up is cursing at the back, The boss is looking savage at a long Australian card. **1904** *Daily News* 2 Dec. 5/1 There are 42 different men in this gang—'penners', 'shacklers', 'hoisters', 'gutters', and so on. **1911** J. COLLIER *Pastoral Age in Australasia* xxix. 216 Besides the shearers, there are penners-up, wool-rollers, pickers-up. **1940** E. C. STUDHOLME *Te Waimate* (1954) xv. 130 The 'sheep-oh' (penner-up).. in addition to filling up the catching-pens.. weighed the bales and recorded them.. in the wool book. **1952** [see DAGGER *sb.*² b]. **1955** *People* (Austral.) 30 Nov. 20/1 The penner-up bustles more sheep up the race. **1965** J. S. GUNN *Terminol. Shearing Industry* II. 8 *Penner-up.* This shedhand keeps the sheep moving into the shed and is ready to fill the catching pen when a shearer calls sheep-oh'. One man would be full-time 'penner-up' in sheds of six or more shearing stands. **1972** E. HARGREAVES *Fair Green Weed* ii. 24, I had to go down to the cow-pen... One of the penners has had an accident... His mule shied.

pennerth, penn'eth, obs. ff. PENNYWORTH.

penneryall, obs. form of PENNYROYAL.

pennestone, obs. form of PENISTONE.

pennet (ˈpɛnɪt). *Obs.* exc. *local.* Forms: 5 penett(e, 6 pennutte, pennite, 6– pennet. [f. as PENIDE with change of suffix. Cf. OIt. *peneto*, It. *pennito* barley-sugar, OF. *penites* (1359 in Godef.).] A piece or stick of barley-sugar (or some similar confection); = PENIDE.

(In 19th c. a trade term for a sweetmeat of the toffee kind, flavoured with lemon, peppermint, etc.: see quot. 1883.)

1470–1 in *Mem. Ripon* (Surtees) III. 216 Penettes, 4*d.* **1576** BAKER *Jewell of Health* 93 b, Take of Dates, of Reysins, of Pennites of Sugar.. of eche six ounces. **1611** COTGR., *Penide*, a Pennet; the little wreath of sugar taken in a cold. **1616** SURFL. & MARKH. *Country Farme* 371 It serueth.. for the making of Almond milke, Potage, Pennets, Marchpanes, and other such daintie deuises. [**1883** *Huddersf. Gloss.*, *Pennett*, a kind of sweet, of the humbug species, cut in form like a double pyramid. **1887** *Label from Confectioner's Shop, Durham*, Lemon Pennets.]

penni (ˈpɛniː). Pl. **penni, penniä** (-iaː). [Finn.] **a.** A Finnish monetary unit, equal to $\frac{1}{100}$ markka. **b.** The name of the coin equal to this amount.

1893 W. C. HAZLITT *Coinage of European Continent* 222 *Penni*, pl. *pennia*, a Russian copper coin struck for Finland = a French centime. **1903** [see MARKKA]. **1957** *Whitaker's Almanack 1958* 964 Finland... *Markka* of 100 *Penni.* **1970** R. A. G. CARSON *Coins* (ed. 2) 397 In the later nineteenth century a distinctive coinage began to be issued by the czars of Russia as grand-dukes of Finland. The monetary unit was the silver mark, divided into 100 pennia... A monetary reform in 1963 introduced a new markka equivalent to 100 old markkaa. The types of the former 1 and 5 markkaa coins have been retained for the new 1 and 2 pennia pieces in bronze. **1974** *Encycl. Brit. Macropædia* VII. 306/2 The markkaa (made up of 100 pennia) was devaluated in 1949, 1957, and 1967.

pennied (ˈpɛnɪd), *a.* [f. PENNY + -ED².] Possessed of a penny. Chiefly in comb., as *one-pennied.*

1806 WORDSW. *Power of Music* vii, The one-pennied Boy has his penny to spare. **1901** *Westm. Gaz.* 4 July 2/3 While you dispensed the fragile chocolate To pennied youngsters.

pennif (ˈpɛnɪf). *slang* (*rare*). [Back-slang f. FINNIP.] = FINNIP; hence, any bank-note.

1862 [see JUG *sb.*² 2 b]. **1891** 'F. W. CAREW' *No. 747* xxxv. 416, I gets clean off with the scawfer and 'bout 'er thirty quid in single-pennifs and silver.

penniferous (pɛˈnɪfərəs), *a. Nat. Hist.* [f. L. *pennifer* (f. *penna* feather + *-fer* -bearing) + -OUS.] Bearing or producing feathers; feathered.

1828 STARK *Elem. Nat. Hist.* II. 14 Belly and tail penniferous. **1841** *Fraser's Mag.* XXV. 319 The giant Scotch firs, with the shrill sough of their penniferous branches. **1857** in MAYNE *Expos. Lex.* 900/2.

penniform (ˈpɛnɪfɔːm), *a. Nat. Hist.* [ad. mod.L. *penniform-is*, f. L. *penna* feather: see -FORM.] Having the form or appearance of a feather; having a central axis with diverging lines or fibres on each side, like the barbs of a feather; *spec.* applied to a muscle whose fibres are obliquely arranged on each side of a central tendon.

1713 CHESELDEN *Anat.* II. i. (1726) 73 The fibres of the penniform muscles. **1808** BARCLAY *Muscular Motions* 414 The carneous fibres by their lateral attachments shorten the tendons of penniform muscles. **1846** DANA *Zooph.* (1848) 594 Penniform or plume-shape. **1881** MIVART *Cat* 128 Sometimes the fasciculi radiate from a central band of dense fibrous tissue in a penniform or semi-penniform manner.

Hence ˌ**penniformi-ˈradiated** *a.*, radiated like the barbs of a feather; ˈ**penniform,wise** *adv.*, in a penniform manner.

1793 YOUNG in *Phil. Trans.* LXXXIII. 173 Three penniformi-radiated muscles. **1839–47** TODD *Cycl. Anat.* III. 287 The fibres converge penniformwise to a strong.. tendon.

pennigerous (pɛˈnɪdʒərəs), *a.* [f. L. *penniger* (f. *penna* feather + *-ger* -carrying) + -OUS.] Feather-bearing, feathered.

1656 in BLOUNT *Glossogr.* **1835** KIRBY *Hab. & Inst. Anim.* II. xvii. 151 The various piligerous, plumigerous, pennigerous and squamigerous animals.

penniless (ˈpɛnɪlɪs), *a.* Also **penny-**, † **peny-**, etc.: see PENNY. [f. PENNY + -LESS.] Not having a penny; having no money; poor, destitute.

c **1310** in *Pol. Songs* (Camden) 255 For thef is reve, the lond is penyles. **1406** HOCCLEVE *Misrule* 130, I were nakidly bystad By force of the penylees maladie. **1562** J. HEYWOOD *Prov. & Epigr.* I. xxiv. (1867) 98 Thou art penilesse. **1592** GREENE *Art Conny Catch.* II. 11 He was.. turned to walke penny-lesse in Mark-lane, as the prouerb is. **1699** GARTH *Dispens.* 12 Or where ill Poets Pennyless confer. **1727** BAILEY vol. II, *Penniless.* **1751** JOHNSON *Rambler* No. 171 ¶10 At length I became absolutely pennyless. **1824** BYRON *Def. Transf.* (1837) I. ii. 132 Though pennyless all. **1874** GREEN *Short Hist.* ix. §8. 680 Either course must end in leaving the Government penniless.

†**b.** *penniless bench*: name of a covered bench which formerly stood beside Carfax Church, Oxford; and app. of similar open-air seats elsewhere; prob. as being the resort of destitute wayfarers. Hence allusively. *Obs.*

1560–1 in W. H. Turner *Select. Rec. Oxford* (1880) 284 Item, to..Sylvester Kechyn, for mending the peneles benche..ij *s.* iiij *d.* **1580** LYLY *Euphues* (Arb.) 244 Every stoole he sate on was Penniles bench. **1596** BP. W. BARLOW *Three Serm.* i. 120 By which..they bring both their parentes and themselues vnto Peniless bench. *c* **1600** L. HUTTON *Antiq. Oxford* in *Eliz. Oxford* (O.H.S. 1886) 86 On the left hand, under the East end of St. Martins Church, yee see that Seate, which is called Pennelesse Bench, builded by the Cittie, as well for their solace and prospect every waie, as for the conveniencie of the Market Women in the tyme of Raine. **1615** SWETNAM *Arraignm. Wom.* (1880) p. xxiv, Ashamed to returne home againe..by weeping crosse and pennyles bench. **1629** *MS. Acc. St. John's Hosp., Canterb.*, For mending of pennye-less bench halfe a dayes worke. *a* **1672** WOOD *Life* (O.H.S.) I. 139. **1860** WARTER *Sea-board* II. 43 Though he have sometimes to sit on the Penniless Bench.

Hence ˈ**pennilessly** *adv.*; ˈ**pennilessness**.

1871 SALA in *Belgravia* XIV. 421 The pennilessness of their spouses. **1890** SAINTSBURY *Ess. Eng. Lit.* (1891) 308 Did he really journey pennilessly down to Eton?

‖**pennill** (ˈpɛnɪhl), usually in pl. **pennillion** (pɛˈnɪhlɪən), also (*erron.*) **pennillion**. [Welsh *pennill* verse, stanza (f. *penn* head), pl. *penn-, penillion.*] **a.** A form of improvised verse adapted to an air played on the harp, sung by the Welsh at the Eisteddfod and on other occasions; a stanza of such verse.

1784 E. JONES (*title*) Musical and Poetical Relicks of the Welsh Bards with a select collection of the Pennillion. **1829** T. L. PEACOCK *Misfort. Elphin* 125 The bards..struck up a sort of consecutive chorus in a series of pennillion or stanzas in praise of Maelgon and his heirship. **1887** J. THOMAS in Grove *Dict. Mus.* IV. 438 The singers continue to take up their Penill alternately with the harp. **1894** *Wales* Aug. 170/2 As he was so famous a poet, I thought he must be either a writer of hymns or of *penillion* to be sung with the harp. **1962** *Listener* 26 Apr. 740/3 The *englynion*, the *penillion telyn*.

b. *attrib.* and *Comb.*

1784 E. JONES *Mus. Rel. Welsh Bards* (1794) 61 There are several kinds of Pennill metres... The skill of the pennill-singers in this is admirable. **1887** *Times* (weekly ed.) 19 Aug. 15/3 Sir J. H. Puleston informed the Prince of the rules of pennillion singing. **1898** *Westm. Gaz.* 1 June 5/2 Eos Dâr, the leading penillion-singer, sang to the accompaniment of the harp the traditional penillion sung at Welsh weddings. **1938** *Oxf. Compan. Mus.* 1009/2 A certain limited group of harp tunes are habitually used for Penillion performances. **1962** *Times* 31 Jan. (Wales Suppl.) p. xi/6 Penillion Singing (lit., 'singing of verses') to harp accompaniment.

pennine (ˈpɛnaɪn). *Min.* [Named 1840 by Fröbel and Schweizer, because found in the Pennine Alps.] = PENNINITE.

1844 DANA *Min.* 318 The name Pennine is derived from its locality. **1878** LAWRENCE tr. *Cotta's Rocks Class.* 22 Pennine, Ripidolite and Chlinochlore are minerals resembling chlorite.

pennінerved (ˈpɛnɪnɜːvd), *a. Bot.* [f. L. *penni-*, comb. form of *penna* feather + NERVE + -ED².] Of a leaf: Having nerves or veins diverging on each side of a midrib; feather-veined, pinnately veined. Also **penniˈnervate** *a.*

1857 MAYNE *Expos. Lex.*, *Penninervis*, Bot... penninervate. **1880** GRAY *Struct. Bot.* iii. §4 (ed. 6) 93 Pinnately or Feather-veined (or Penninerved) leaves are.. those of which the veins and their subdivisions are side branches of a single central rib.

penning (ˈpɛnɪŋ), *vbl. sb.*¹ [f. PEN *v.*¹ + -ING¹.] The action of PEN *v.*¹; enclosing, confining, etc.

1626 BACON *Sylva* §152 The penning and enclosure of the air, in the concave of the well. **1751** *Act 24 Geo. II*, c. 8 §2 Locks, Weirs..and the Shutting, Penning, Opening, Drawing, Use..thereof. **1886** C. SCOTT *Sheep-Farming* 201 In penning, the dog works closely to the sheep.

ˈ**penning,** *vbl. sb.*² [f. PEN *v.*² + -ING¹.] The action of PEN *v.*²; writing, inditing.

a **1548** HALL *Chron., Edw. IV* 227 A letter..bothe for the stile & the pennyng excellently endited. **1687** *Royal Proclam.* 18 Nov. in *Lond. Gaz.* No. 2297/1 The Doubtful Penning of some Parts of the said Act. **1741** RICHARDSON *Pamela* II. 154, I suppose it is of my Sisters Penning, and he, poor Man, is the humble Copier. **1849** STOVEL *Introd. Canne's Necess.* 63 The treatment of words, and the penning of signatures, in that way was rather unusual.

ˈ**penning,** *ppl. a.* [f. PEN *v.*¹ + -ING².] That pens (see PEN *v.*¹); enclosing, shutting in.

1854 SYD. DOBELL *Balder* xxiii. 124 Herdsman's evening call, And bells of penning folds.

penninite (ˈpɛnɪnaɪt). *Min.* [Altered from PENNINE: see -ITE¹.] A mineral of the chlorite group; a hydrous silicate of aluminium, magnesium, and iron, occurring in rhombohedral crystals.

1868 DANA *Min.* (ed. 5) 495 Penninite... Pennine... Hydro-talc of Necker is penninite from the Binnen valley, in the Valais. **1882** *Min. Mag.* IV. 47.

pennipotent (pɛˈnɪpətənt), *a. rare*⁻¹. [ad. L. *pennipotens, -potent-em*, f. *penna* feather, plume (see PEN) + *potens* powerful.] Strong on the wing; strong-pinioned, powerful in flight.

1609 J. DAVIES *Holy Roode* (1878) 15/2 Vnplume their wings in flight pennipotent. **1656** in BLOUNT *Glossogr.*

pennirial(l, obs. form of PENNYROYAL.

pennis, obs. pl. of PEN, PENNY.

†ˈ**pennish,** *a. Obs. ? nonce-wd.* [f. PEN *sb.*² + -ISH¹.] Pertaining to a pen, or to writing.

1646 *Vox Populi* 17 Your Pulpit worke, and your pennish paines.

†ˈ**pennisome,** *a. Obs. ? nonce-wd.* [f. PENNY + -SOME.] Furnishing 'pence', i.e. money; lucrative, profitable.

1631 WEEVER *Anc. Fun. Mon.* 229, I finde little of any.. charitie this Bishop performed..with all these his pennisome preferments.

penniston(e, obs. form of PENISTONE.

pennite (ˈpɛnaɪt). *Min.* [Named by Hermann, 1849, from Pennsylvania, where found: see -ITE¹.] A greenish variety of Hydrodolomite (see HYDRO-), containing nickel.

1850 *Amer. Jrnl. Sc.* Ser. II. IX. 217 Hermann has made a new mineral which he calls Pennite. **1868** DANA *Min.* (ed. 5) 708 *Pennite* of Hermann, from Texas, Pa., is in apple-green to whitish crusts.

pennite, obs. form of PENNET.

penniveined (ˈpɛnɪveɪnd), *a. Bot.* [f. L. *penni-*, comb. form of *penna* feather, PEN + VEIN + -ED².] = PENNINERVED.

1855 *Macgillivray's Nat. Hist. Dee Side* (ed. Lankester) 179 Pale green and nearly opaque beneath, penniveined with reticular venules. **1872** OLIVER *Elem. Bot.* II. 253 [Palms] are usually either of the radiate- or penni-veined type.

pennon (ˈpɛnən). Forms: 4–8 **penon,** 4–5 **penoun,** 4 **pen(n)own(e,** 5 **pynoune, -youn,** ? **pynon,** *Sc.* **pannoun,** 5– **pennon.** [ME. a. OF. *penon* (also *penn-, pan-, pannon*) = Pr. *peno, penon*, OCat. *pano*, It. *pennone*, generally held to be a Romanic deriv. of L. and It. *penna*, F. *penne* feather, plume, wing (Diez, Littré, Darm.). It. had the sense 'plume of feathers', and OF. that of 'feather of an arrow', as well as that of 'streamer'. Sp. has *pendon*, Pg. *pendão*, mod.Cat. *pendó*, with intrusive *d*, perh. by association with *pender* to hang; cf. Eng. *pendant* for *pennon.*]

1. A long narrow flag or streamer, triangular and pointed, or swallow-tailed, usually attached to the head of a lance (or a helmet), formerly borne as a distinction by a knight under the rank of banneret, and sometimes having his cognizance upon it; now a military ensign of the lancer regiments.

1375 BARBOUR *Bruce* VIII. 227 Thair speris, thair pennowyns, and thar scheldis Of licht Illumynit all the feldis. *c* **1386** CHAUCER *Knt.'s T.* 120 By his Baner born in his penoun. **1387** TREVISA *Higden* (Rolls) V. 121 In the baners and penons of his knyghtes. **1390** GOWER *Conf.* III. 56 Of his contre the signe was Thre fisshes, whiche he scholde bere Upon the penon of a spere. **1456** SIR G. HAYE *Law Arms* (S.T.S.) 141 He tynis his pannoun and his haubergeoun. **14..** *Lansd. MS.* 225 lf. 431 in *Promp. Parv.* 392 *note*, A guydon to be in length ij. yardes and a half, or iij. A pennon of armes round att the end, and to be in length ij yardes. *c* **1500** *MS. Harl.* 838 lf. 5 Euery baronet..shal haue hys baner displeyd in ye feild yf he be chyef capteyn, euery knyght his penoun, euery squier or gentleman hys getoun or standard. **1591** *Garrard's Art Warre* 141 A litle Phane or Penon of silke upon a wyre... They must weore this either upon their burgonets, or upon their hats if they will. **1687** A. LOVELL tr. *Thevenot's Trav.* II. 104 At the end of this Carrere there are men who have several Arrows ready, with little penons hanging at them. **1700** DRYDEN *Pal. & Arcite* I. 115 High on his pointed lance his pennon bore, His Cretan fight, the conquer'd Minotaur. **1786** GROSE *Milit. Antiq.* I. 205 *note*, The pennon was the proper ensign of a bachelor or simple knight. Du Fresne shews that even the esquires might bear pennons, provided they could bring a sufficient suite of vassals into the field. **1801** *Ibid.* (ed. 2) II. 52 The pennon was..like a banner, with the addition of a triangular point.—By the cutting off of this point, on the performance of any gallant action by the knight and his followers, the pennon was converted into a banner; whereby the knight was raised to the degree of a banneret. **1865** WAY in *Promp. Parv.* 392 *note*, A pennon was a small flag attached to the lance, whereby the rank of the bearer was known. Wace appropriates it to the knight, and the gonfanon to the baron, but at a later time it seems to have designated the bachelor... In Harl. MS. 358, f. 5, may be seen sketches of all these ensigns; the getone being swallow-tailed, the penon triangular, and charged with the armorial bearing, the former being appropriated to the esquire or gentleman, the latter to the knight. **1882** CUSSANS *Her.* (ed. 3) 274 The Pennon..was usually affixed to the end of a lance, from which..it depended; and the Charges thereon were so emblazoned as to appear correctly when the lance was held in a horizontal position.

b. In wider or vaguer use: Any flag or banner.

? *a* **1400** *Morte Arth.* 2918 Thane sir Priamous þe prynce, in presens of lordes, Presez to his penowne, and pertly it hentes. **1530** PALSGR. 253/1 Penon a lytell baner in a felde, *pennon.* **1563** GOLDING *Cæsar* VII. (1565) 206 b, Cesar.. rolled up his banners, and hid the penons and antesignes of his souldiers. **1599** SHAKS. *Hen. V*, III. v. 49 Barre Harry England, that sweepes through our Land With Penons painted in the blood of Harflew. **1835** *Penny Cycl.* III. 408/2 The drapery of a trumpet was in early times, as now, the pennon-quarrée of a banner. **1880** 'OUIDA' *Moths* II. 234 The soft wind would blow brightly on the pretty pennons of the Kermesse pavilions.

c. *fig.* Applied to things of the shape of a pennon.

c **1618** MORYSON *Itin.* IV. IV. i. (1903) 332 Rowles baked like dry Fritters, and sett forth with Penons of Cutt paper, in the forme of Apes, Birdes, and like thinges. **1820** SCOTT *Monast.* xxiv, A pillar of dark smoke, which..spread its long dusky pennon through the clear ether. **1863** HAWTHORNE *Our Old Home* (1879) 158 Little factory villages..with their tall chimneys, and their pennons of black smoke.

d. *Her.*

1586 FERNE *Blaz. Gentrie* 197 The field is Gewles, a banner of three pennons or. **1688** R. HOLME *Armoury* III. xviii. (Roxb.) 122/1 He beareth a speare Or, garnished or adorned with a penon or penoncell Argent.

†**2. a.** A knight-bachelor; **b.** An ensign-bearer.

1475 *Bk. Noblesse* (Roxb.) 15 For he [Ser John Chaundos] had in his retenu M¹. ij^c. penons armed & x M¹. horsmen. **1568** GRAFTON *Chron.* II. 239 The Duke of Brabant had .xxiiij. Banners and lxxx. Pennons, and in all .vij. thousand men. *a* **1661** FULLER *Worthies, Hartford* II. (1662) 32 Surely he was a man of merit, being Penon or Ensign-bearer to one, Esquire of the body to three successive Kings, and M^r. of the Horse to one of their Queens.

3. The long pointed streamer of a ship; also called PENDANT and PENNANT.

1627 DRAYTON *Agincourt* lxvii, A ship most neatly that was lim'd, In all her Sailes with flags and Pennons trim'd. [In Chalmers's *Poets*, pennants, whence in Richardson.] **1632** SHERWOOD, A Penon (or *Pendant*) in a ship. **1658** PHILLIPS, *Penon*,..also a streamer in a ship. **1807** J. BARLOW *Columb.* II. 354 O hapless day!..That saw my wandering pennon mount the tide. **1852** LONGF. *Warden of Cinque Ports* ii, Flowing flag and rippling pennon. **1884** MRS. C. PRAED *Zéro* xiv, Yachts with pennons flying lay at anchor in the harbour.

†**4.** Erroneously put for PENDANT *sb.* 1, a hanging ornament. *Obs. rare.*

1546 *Richmond Wills* (Surtees) 63 Also I give to my dowghter..a girdle with penons and buckle of silver.

5. *poet.* Used by Milton, and others after him, for: A wing, pinion.

1667 MILTON *P.L.* II. 933 Fluttring his pennons vain plumb down he drops Ten thousand fadom deep. *Ibid.* VII. 441. **1740** SOMERVILLE *Hobbinol* II. 190 The..Wasp..in the viscous Nectar plung'd, His filmy Pennons struggling flaps in vain. **1796** COLERIDGE *Ode Departing Year* Epode ii, I hear the famish'd brood of prey Flap their lank pennons on the groaning wind. **1813** SHELLEY *Q. Mab* I. 204 Again the Coursers of the air Unfurled their azure pennons.

pennoncel (ˈpɛnənsɛl). *Obs.* exc. *Hist.* Forms: 4 **penonceal,** 5, 9 **-cell,** 5 **penoun-,** 7, 9 **-cel,** 9 **-cele,** 8– **pennoncel,** (9 **-celle**). [a. OF. *penoncel* (= It. *pennoncello*, 'a little plume or bunch of feathers, also a little streamer or banderoll' (Florio), med.L. *penuncellus, penonsellus*, Du Cange), dim. of *penon*, PENNON. See also the reduced form PENCEL, which is found earlier.] A small pennon borne upon a helmet or lance, a PENCEL; a pennon or pendant of a ship.

1390 GOWER *Conf.* III. 308 Than sen thei stonde on every side, Endlong the schipes bord to schewe, Of Penonceals a riche rewe. *c* **1489** CAXTON *Sonnes of Aymon* vi. 153 The kyng..fonde her besi aboute a penouncell of a spere that she made full fayr for the knyghte Reynawde. *c* **1489** —— *Blanchardyn* xviii. 56 Many a highe mast that bare grete saylles And many penoncelles, baners, and standardes that the wynde shok here and there. **1610** GUILLIM *Heraldry* IV. xiv. (1611) 224 These penoncels are made of certain smal peeces of Taffeta or Sarcenet, cut after the forme of a pennon, wherewith martiall men doe oftentimes adorne their speares and launces. **1688** R. HOLME *Armoury* III. xviii. (Roxb.) 122/2 He beareth a speare Or, garnished or adorned with a penon or penoncell Argent. **1727** BAILEY vol. II, *Pennoncels.* **1814** SCOTT *Chivalry* (1874) 33 Whom they were entitled to muster under a Penoncele or small triangular streamer somewhat like the naval pennant of the present day. *a* **1835** MOTHERWELL *Madman's Love*, The fluttering of each pennoncel By knightly lance upborne.

pennoncier (pɛnənˈsɪə(r)). *rare*⁻⁰. [a. OF. *penon-, pennoncier* (Froissart 14th c.), f. *penon* PENNON.] A knight bachelor (as distinguished from a knight banneret).

1890 in *Cent. Dict.*

ˈ**pennoned** (-ənd), *a.* [See -ED².] Having, bearing, or furnished with a pennon. Also *fig.*

1849 THACKERAY *Atra Cura* iii, No knight am I with pennoned spear. **1868** LOWELL *Invita Minerva* 2 The Bardling came, where by a river grew The pennoned reeds. **1882** FREEMAN *Reign Will. Rufus* II. vi. §2. 209 He..would show himself before their gates with a hundred thousand pennoned lances. **1897** *Westm. Gaz.* 2 July 3/1 Behind this line we get a glimpse of plumed helmets and pennoned lances of some of the cavalry.

pennor, obs. form of PENNER¹.

penn'orth, colloq. contraction of PENNYWORTH.

Pennsylvania (pɛnsɪlˈveɪnɪə). One of the middle Atlantic states of the United States, named after Admiral Sir William Penn (1621–70), in 1681. Used *attrib.* to denote articles, inhabitants, products, or varieties of plants characteristic of, or growing in,

Pennsylvania, as ***Pennsylvania anemone, ash, cap, corn, division, dwarf mountain maple, mountain laurel, salve, wagon, wind flower***; **Pennsylvania German** *sb.* and *a.* = PENNSYLVANIA DUTCH *sb.* and *a.*

1900 B. B. SMYTH *Plants & Flowers Kansas* ii. 54 On the low prairies may be found plenty of Pennsylvania anemone, a plant with..numerous branches, each terminated by a flower with five broad white sepals. **1810** P. WAKEFIELD *Excursions N. Amer.* (ed. 2) xxviii. 191 The black fir, the Weymouth pine, the red cedar, the common fir, the red maple, the Pennsylvania ash..are also common. **1971** M. TAK *Truck Talk* 116 *Pennsylvania caps*, recapped tires with an unbroken tread line. **1739** in *Colonial Rec. Georgia* (1905) III. 429 We all were disappointed by..planting the yellow Pensilvania Corn. **1929** *Papers Mich. Acad. Sci., Arts & Lett.* X. 314/1 *Pennsylvania Division*, the Twenty-eighth Division. **1785** H. MARSHALL *Arbustrum Amer.* 2 *Acer pennsylvanicum*,..Pennsylvania Dwarf Mountain Maple. **1869** *Nation* (N.Y.) 30 Dec. 583/2 The Pennsylvania German is a South German dialect. *Ibid.* 584/1 Divine service among the Pennsylvania Germans is held in High German. **1875** A. R. HORNE (*title*) Pennsylvania German manual. **1956** *Publ. Amer. Dial. Soc.* XXVI. 30 The Norwegian spoken among the immigrants showed the same combination of archaism and levelling as other American languages, though the relatively brief period of its life has not permitted the kind of consolidation found in Pennsylvania German or the colonial languages proper. **1970** *Globe & Mail* (Toronto) 25 Sept. T3/3 Mennonite and Pennsylvania-German societies will be in attendance [at a festival]. **1972** H. KURATH *Stud. Area Linguistics* 105 This divergence between Pennsylvania German (essentially a Rhine Frankish folk dialect of west central Germany) and Standard German..would tend to keep the two apart. **1785** H. MARSHALL *Arbustrum Amer.* 127 *Rhododendrum maximum*, Pennsylvania Mountain Laurel. **1899** 'J. FLYNT' *Tramping with Tramps* IV. 396 *Pennsylvania salve*, apple-butter. **1810** M. DWIGHT *Journey to Ohio* (1912) 39 This line is the shape of a Pennsylvania waggon. **1869** J. G. FULLER *Uncle John's Flower-Gatherers* 28 [The anemone] blooms later, in May and June, and is called the Pennsylvania Wind Flower.

Pennsylvania Dutch, *sb.* and *a.* **A.** *sb.* **a.** *pl.* [DUTCH *sb.* 3 a.] The descendants of the original German settlers in Pennsylvania. **b.** [see DUTCH *sb.* 1.] A Pennsylvanian dialect derived from the High German of a great number of the early settlers, with a considerable admixture of English elements. **B.** *adj.* [DUTCH *a.* 1.] Of or pertaining to the Pennsylvania Dutch or their dialect. So **Pennsylvania Dutchman**.

a **1824** J. GUILD in *Proc. Vermont Hist. Soc.* (1937) V. 293, I came across a Pennsylvania Dutch man, and I made a bargain with him. **1831** *Canad. Freeman* (Toronto) 19 May 2/3 Let Mackenzie stick to the Central Committee, the Saddlebags, & the Pennsylvania Dutch of the Home District. **1856** *Spirit of Times* 4 Oct. 71/1 But *revenons a mouton*, which, in plain Pennsylvania Dutch means how Fogie Antique caught..catfish. **1868** H. W. BEECHER *Norwood* 468 Them Pennsylvania Dutch think more of their horses than they do of themselves. **1882** P. H. GIBBONS *Pennsylvania Dutch* (ed. 3) 401 A 'Pennsylvania Dutch' remedy for whooping-cough. **1943** *Amer. Speech* XVIII. 112 The diphthong *oi* [oi] in the Pennsylvania Dutch dialects is interesting both phonemically and historically because of its infrequent occurrence. **1948** W. STEVENS *Let.* 1 Dec. (1967) 624 A true Pennsylvania Dutchman. **1974** E. MCGIRR *Murderous Journey* 98 He lapsed into Pennsylvania Dutch. The quaint idioms and all. **1976** *New Yorker* 16 Feb. 58/2 The sort of packaging that makes pancake-mix pancakes served in a Pennsylvania hotel 'Pennsylvania Dutch pancakes' instead of just pancakes. **1976** R. CONDON *Whisper of Axe* I. xvii. 103 He was served *schnitz un knepp*: apples, dumplings, and ham from the Pennsylvania Dutch.

Pennsyl'vanian, *sb.* and *a.* [f. PENNSYLVANIA + -AN.] **A.** *sb.* **1.** A native or inhabitant of Pennsylvania.

1685 [see QUAKERISTICAL *a.*]. **1747** G. WHITEFIELD *Let.* 6 May in *Wks.* (1771) II. 94 The Pensylvanians I am sure will soon regret the loss of you. **1755** in S. M. Hamilton *Lett. to Washington* (1898) I. 99 The Road upon which the Pennsylvaneans were Employ'd. **1782** 'J. H. ST. JOHN DE CRÈVECŒUR' *Lett. from Amer. Farmer* 58 Europeans.. become..either Pennsylvanians, Virginians, or provincials, under some other name. **1838** *Southern Lit. Messenger* IV. 165/1 Mr. Ingersoll, being a Pennsylvanian, stands impartial between the two extremes of the Union. **1862** *Evening Post* (N.Y.) 21 May 1/2 Words of warm congratulation were sent to the dashing Pennsylvanian by the Commanding General. **1910** *Harper's Mag.* Aug. 473/1 Georg Shock..is a Pennsylvanian. **1939** [see INSOMNIAC]. **1953** W. MOORE *Bring Jubilee* (1955) xx. 194 It was the Fourth of July, and a day of victory and rejoicing for all Pennsylvanians. **1967** *National Observer* (U.S.) 3 July 12/2 True to tradition, the Pennsylvanians are the best shots in the brigade. **1974** *Encycl. Brit. Macropædia* XIV. 28/2 Pennsylvanians still tend toward the Republican Party in state elections. **1976** *Billings* (Montana) *Gaz.* 1 July 3-B/2 Schapp urged all Pennsylvanians to listen to their message with an open mind.

2. *Geol.* The Pennsylvanian period or system.

1906 CHAMBERLIN & SALISBURY *Geol.* II. x. 556 In the arctic regions of America, the Mississippian and Pennsylvanian are not differentiated. **1960** J. M. WELLER *Stratigr. Princ. & Pract.* xii. 441 Fossils are rare and of little service in separating the Mississippian from the Pennsylvanian. **1969** [see MISSISSIPPIAN *sb.* and *a.* A. 2]. **1977** A. HALLAM *Planet Earth* 207 The Pennsylvanian started with a new transgression of the sea over the low land of the central North American continent.

B. *adj.* **1.** Of, pertaining to, or characteristic of Pennsylvania or its people.

1698 G. THOMAS *Hist. & Geogr. Acct. Pensilvania & W. New-Jersey* 2 They (as the Pensilvanian Indians) observe the New Moons with great Devotion. **1785** H. MARSHALL *Arbustrum Amer.* 51 Pennsylvanian Sharp-keyed Ash (*Fraxinus pennsylvanica*). **1853** A. BUNN *Old Eng. & New Eng.* I. viii. 167 Mr. Nicholas Biddle..issued the notorious Pennsylvanian bonds. **1959** *Chambers's Encycl.* X. 536/2 Pennsylvanian oil production is relatively much less important although quality is high.

2. *Geol.* Of, pertaining to, or designating a period and system of the Palæozoic Era in North America that succeeded the Mississippian and preceded the Permian, and corresponds more or less to the Upper Carboniferous in Europe.

1891 *Bull. U.S. Geol. Survey* No. 80. 5 The Coal Measures or Pennsylvanian series. **1906** CHAMBERLIN & SALISBURY *Geology: Earth History* II. x. 539 (*heading*) The Pennsylvanian (coal measures, Carboniferous proper) period. *Ibid.*, The need of a name to distinguish this system of rocks from those which have been described under the name Mississippian has long been felt, and the name Pennsylvanian, which has recently come into wide use in this country, was adopted because the system is well developed and well known in Pennsylvania. **1933** [see MISSISSIPPIAN *sb.* and *a.* B. 2]. **1945** *Bull. Amer. Assoc. Petroleum Geologists* XXIX. 128 The coal, oil, gas, ceramic clays, and other minerals found in rocks of Pennsylvanian age greatly exceed the value of the mineral resources found in any other system. **1960** J. M. WELLER *Stratigr. Princ. & Pract.* vi. 176 Pennsylvanian coal up to nearly 100 feet thick has been mined from several ancient Missouri sink holes of moderate or small size.

pennutte, obs. form of PENNET.

penny ('pɛnɪ). Pl. pennies ('pɛnɪz), pence (pɛns). Forms: see below. [OE. *pening, pending, penning*, later *penig* = OFris. *panning, penning, -ig*, OS. *penning* (MLG., LG. *pennink*; MDu. *penninc, -ing-*, also *pēni(n)c*; Du. *penning*), OHG. *pfenning* (*phantinc, phenting*), *pfenting* (MHG. *pfenninc, -ic, -ig-*, Ger. *pfennig*), ON. *penningr* (mod.Icel. *peningr*, Sw., ODa. *penning*, Da. pl. *penge* = ON. *pengar* 'money'); not recorded in Goth. (which has *skatts* for δηνάριος in N.T.). In early ME., Ormin had still *peninng*; but the usual ME. form after 1200 was *peni, peny*, from OE. *penig*. The forms with double *n* in OE. were chiefly Northumbrian; in ME. *pennie, penny*, with *nn*, was app. not used till the 15th c. OE. and early ME. had also, less usually, like OFris., forms in *pan-*. In ME. the plural *panezes, penezes*, passed through *panes, pannes, peniis, penis*, to the 14th c. *pans, pens*, the latter duly spelt in 16th c. *pence*. But, beside this, the fuller *penys, pennys, pennies*, continued in restricted use: see the forms in A. 2 *β*, and signification in B. 1 c.

The OE. and cognate forms point back to the types **paning*, **panding*, **panning*, a series which does not conform to any phonetic law, but suggests that the word was foreign and of unsettled form. But it was evidently of WGer., or even (unless the ON. was borrowed from OE.) of Common Germanic age. No foreign source however is known; and the suffix *-ing*, occurring in other names of coins, as *shilling, farthing*, OHG. *cheisuring*, etc., bespeaks at least a Teutonic formation on a radical element *pand* or *pan(n)*. This has been sought in WGer. **pand*, OHG. *pfant*, PAWN, with reference to a possible use of the *panding*; and in WGer. *panna*, Ger. *pfanne* PAN, with possible reference to shape. Of these words themselves the Germanic origin is uncertain.]

A. Illustration of Forms.

1. *Sing.* α. 1 **pending, pening, -inc, -penning**; 3 (*Orm.*) **peninng.** *β.* 1 **pænig, panig, pæni**, 1–2 **penig**, 2–4 **peni**, 4 **pane-** (in comp.), 4–8 **peny**, 5 **penye, -ey**, 5–7 **penie**, (6 **peany**); 5–8 **pennie**, (6 **-ye**), 5– **penny**.

α. **835** Pending [see B. 1]. *c* **950** *Lindisf. Gosp.* Matt. xxii. 19 zebrohtun him penning [*Ags. G.* anne peninc, *v.r.* ænne penig; *Hatton* enne panig]. *c* **1000** ÆLFRIC *Gram.* xxv. (Z.) 50 *Hic as*, þes peningc [*v.rr.* pening, penig, pæni]. *c* **1000** *Ags. Gosp.* Matt. xx. 9 þa onfengon hig ælc his pening [*Hatton* panig; *Lindisf.* suindrigo penningas]. *c* **1200** ORMIN 3281 Illc mann an peninng zæfe. *Ibid.* 3287.

β. *c* **1000** *Ags. Gosp.* Matt. xx. 2 He sealde ælcon ænne penig [*Hatton* ænne pænig]. *c* **1160** *Hatton Gosp.* Matt. xx. 9 þa onfengen hi ælch hys panig [*Ags. Gosp.* pening, penig]. *a* **1200** *Moral Ode* 67 He alse mid his penie se þe oþer mid his punde. *a* **1300** *Cursor M.* 22328 For a peni [*Fairf.* peny] hit sal be salde. *c* **1450** *Merlin* x. 142 For a penny that ye lese on this side, ye shall wynne tweyne. **1530** PALSGR. 253/1 Penny coyne, *denier*. **1584** POWEL *Lloyd's Cambria* 71 To giue them a penie for euerie man. **1590** RECORDE, etc. *Gr. Artes* (1640) 326 That a sterling peny, round without clipping, did then weigh 32 cornes of wheat dry. **1668** MARVELL *Corr.* Wks. 1872–5 II. 186 The taking of an half-peny and a peny. **1673** C. HATTON in *H. Corr.* (Camden) 118 To be shewn as a sight, peni apiece.

2. *Plural.* α. 1 **peningas, pendingas, pen(d)i(n)cas.** *β.* 1–2 **penegas, pan-**, 2–3 **penezes, panezes, -as**, 3 **panewes, pone-, -wæs; peniis, -ijs**, 3–4 **panes**, 4 **pannes, penis**, 4–5 **penyes**, 4–6 **penies**, *Sc.* **pennyse**, (5 **peyneyes, pennis**), 5–6 **penys, pennys, -is**, (*Sc.*) **-eis**, 6 (*Sc.*) **pennyis**, 6– **pennies.** *γ.* 4–5 **pans**, (4 **pons**), 4–6 **pens**, 5–6 **pense**, 6– **pence.** *δ.* 5 **penses, -ys.**

α. **835** *Will* in Thorpe *Charters* 474 Se mann se to londe foe azefe hire erfehonda xiii. pund pendingæ. *c* **890** K. ÆLFRED *Laws* c. 3 (Schmid 72) zebete..þæs borges bryce mid v pundum mærra pæninga. *c* **897** —— *Gregory's Past. C.* l. 391 We wiernað urum cildum urra peninga mid to plegianne. *c* **950** *Lindisf. Gosp.* Matt. xx. 9 Onfengon suindrigo penningas.

β. *c* **1000** *Ags. Gosp.* Matt. xx. 10 þa onfengon hig syndrige penegas [*Hatton* sindrie panezes]. *Ibid.* Luke x. 35 [He] brohte oðrum dæze twezen penegas [*Lindisf.* tuoege peñd, *Hatton* panezes]. *c* **1175** *Lamb. Hom.* 85 þa twein penezes. *c* **1200** *Vices & Virtues* 79 Befasteð here panezes ðe haðene menn. *c* **1205** LAY. 2369 Pælles and purpras And guldene ponewæs [*c* **1275** panewes]. *Ibid.* 14684 Twalf panewes. *a* **1290** *S. Eustace* 6 in Horstm. *Altengl. Leg.* (1881) 211 Of gold and ponewes [*v.r.* penyes] rounde. *c* **1290** *S. Eng. Leg.* I. 263/93 A man, þat 3af hire þreo rounde panes. *a* **1300** *Fall & Passion* 58 in *E.E.P.* (1862) 14 For xxx peniis he him sold. *a* **1300** *Cursor M.* 4835 (Cott.) Al redi penijs [*Gött.* penis] for to tell. *Ibid.* 13483 Qua had o penis thre hundreth Bred for to bi. *c* **1375** *Sc. Leg. Saints* vii. (*Jacobus*) 738 For pennyse thretty. **1387** TREVISA *Higden* (Rolls) II. 345 Also þis [Saturn] ordeyned pannes of bras. *c* **1400** *Apol. Loll.* 52 Of hem þat 3euen a peney, or peyneyes, to prestis. *a* **1425** *Cursor M.* 13483 (Trin.) Who so had penies þre hundreþe. **1426** LYDG. *De Guil. Pilgr.* 18037 The pennis that iudas toke. *c* **1450** *St. Cuthbert* (Surtees) 6346 Penys foure or fyue. **1500–20** DUNBAR *Poems* xxxiv. 63 Gif I ten dayis wan pennyis thre. **1512** *Act 4 Hen. VIII*, c. 19 § 14 All manner of pennys beyng siluer. *a* **1649** DRUMM. OF HAWTH. *Hist. Jas. I*, Wks. (1711) 3 Twelve pennies of the pound.

γ. *c* **1305** *Judas Iscariot* 133 in *E.E.P.* (1862) 110 þe teoþing þerof was þrettie pans. **1340** *Ayenb.* 23 þri manere of guodes..þet þe dyeuel wyle begge mid his pans. **1362** LANGL. *P. Pl.* A. Prol. 86 Seriauns..Pleden for pons and poundes þe lawe. **1377** *Ibid.* B. v. 243 To wey pens with a peys. **1382** WYCLIF *John* xii. 5 Whi is not this oynement seeld for thre hundrid pens? **1426** LYDG. *De Guil. Pilgr.* 17732 The pound for xx[ty] pans I selle. ? *a* **1500** in *10th Rep. Hist. MSS. Comm.* App. IV. 424, 21 pense in pense and half pense. **1526** TINDALE *Matt.* xviii. 28 Wone off his felowes which ought hym an hundred pence. **1549** *Brasenose Coll. Muniments* 18. 59, Fore pense.

δ. **1482** *Monk of Evesham* (Arb.) 52 Tho fyrye pensys y was compellyd to deuoure with an opyn mowthe. **1495** *Rolls of Parlt.* VI. 463/1 Receptes of Penses to the same Elizabeth.

B. Signification.

I. Original senses.

1. a. An English coin of the value of $\frac{1}{12}$ of a shilling, or $\frac{1}{240}$ of a pound; originally and for many centuries of silver, in later times of copper, (after 1860) of bronze. Denoted (after a numeral) by *d.* (for *denarius, denarii*); thus, *5d.*, fivepence. After 15 Feb. 1971 a smaller coin of the value of $\frac{1}{100}$ of a pound, for a while known as the *new penny* (see NEW *a.* 4). Denoted (after a numeral) by *p* (see P II, PEE *sb.*[6]).

The coining of silver pennies for general circulation ceased with the reign of Charles II; a small number have since been regularly coined as Maundy money. Copper pennies began to be coined in 1797; copper halfpence and farthings having been used from the time of Charles II.

a **725** *Laws of Ine* c. 59 (from Ælfred's compilation, earliest MS. *c* 925) Oxan horn bið x pæninga [*v. rr.* peninga, peniga, penega] weorð. **835** in Thorpe *Dipl. Ævi Sax.* (1865) 47 And him mon forgefe ðeran ðreotene hund pending[a]. *a* **1000** *Ecgbert. Pœnit.* IV. lx. (Thorpe *Laws* II. 222), Se riht scylling byþ a be xii penegum. *a* **1131** *O.E. Chron.* an. 1124 Se penig wæs swa ifel þæt se man þa hæfde..an pund he ne mihte cysten þær of for nan þing twelfe penegas. *c* **1330** R. BRUNNE *Chron.* (1810) 238 Edward did smyte rounde peny, halfpeny, ferthyng,..þe kynges side salle be þe hede & his name writen, þe croyce side what cite it was in coyned & smyten. **1485** CAXTON *Chas. Gt.* 245, iiij pens of money courant yerely. *Ibid.* 246 They shold wyth a good wylle pay the penyes. **1596** SHAKS. *Tam. Shr.* III. ii. 85 Nay by S. Iamy, I hold you a penny, A horse and a man is more then one, and yet not many. **1706** PHILLIPS, *Penny*, a small Coin..; its Weight is 32 Grains of Wheat well dried. **1710** J. HARRIS *Lex. Techn.* II, *Penny, Denarius*, was the first coined piece of Silver we have any account of; and for many Years the only one. **1727–41** CHAMBERS *Cycl.* s.v., The penny sterling is now nigh disused as a coin; and scarce subsists, but as a money of account. **1797** *Proclam.* 26 July in *Lond. Gaz.* No. 14031/1 We have thought fit to order, that certain Pieces of Copper shall be coined, which should go and pass for One Penny,..and that each of such Pieces of One Penny should weigh One Ounce Avoirdupois. **1837** *Penny Cycl.* VII. 330/1 The first English [silver] pennies weigh $22\frac{1}{2}$ grains troy. Towards the close of Edward III the penny weighs 18 grains, and in the reign of Edward IV it fell to 12, after previously sinking to 15. In..1551, the penny was reduced to 8 grains, and after the 43rd of Eliz. to $7\frac{23}{31}$ grains, at which weight it still continues. **1971** *Daily Tel.* 8 Mar. 12 He partly pre-empted his Budget last autumn..by promising six old pennies off the income tax.

b. Applied to local or other varieties of this coin, sometimes of different value.

Irish penny, Manx penny, copper pennies of the same value as the penny sterling with a different design on the reverse, formerly coined for Ireland and the Isle of Man; ***Scots penny***, a coin or monetary unit, equal in 17th c. to one-twelfth of the English penny; † ***penny deble***, † ***penny force***: see quot. 1598.

1538 *Aberdeen Regr.* (1844) I. 158 Dauid Bruce.. promittit to pay me the soume of thretty poundis in penny and penny-wortht Scottis. **1598** STOW *Surv.* 43 The penny weyght [to weigh] 24. graynes (which 24. by weight then appointed, were as much as the former 32. graynes of weight), a pennie force, 25. graynes and a halfe, the pennie deble, or feeble 22. graines and a halfe. **1617** MORYSON *Itin.* I. 283 The Scots haue of long time had..Placks, which they esteemed for 4 pence, but 3 of them make an English penny; also Hard-heads, esteemed by them at one penny halfe-penny, whereof eight make an English penny. *Ibid.* 284 They [the Irish] had little brasse pence, and pence of a second kinde, called Harpers, being as big as an English shilling. They had also brasse farthings, called smulkins, whereof foure made a penny. **1688** R. HOLME *Armoury* III. 25/1 An Irish Penny..hath the Stamp of the Harp and Crown upon it. **1786** CARDONNELL *Numism. Scot.* 24 Table I. In which is shown how many numeral pounds, shillings, and pennies Scots were coined out of one pound weight of gold. *a* **1850** JAS. GRAY *Introd. Arith.* (ed. 100) 11 (Scotch

Money), 2 Pennies = 1 Bodle = $\frac{1}{6}$d. Sterling. 2 Bodles = 1 Plack = $\frac{1}{3}$d. 3 Placks or 12 Pennies = 1 Shilling = 1d. [sterling]. **1898** G. B. RAWLINGS *Brit. Coinage* 135 The last Irish coinage took place under George IV, when pennies and halfpennies were struck.. 1823. *Ibid.* 192 George III. coined pennies and halfpennies for Man in 1786... *Rev.*, Three legs conjoined at the hip. *Ibid.*, Queen Victoria coined a Manx penny, halfpenny, and farthing, in 1839 only... This is the last coinage for the Isle of Man. *Ibid.* 210 In 1870 a series of nickel pennies, halfpennies and farthings was begun for Jamaica.

c. (Chiefly in reference to the pre-1970 coinage.) The full plural, *pennies* (A. 2 β), is now used only of the individual coins; *pence* (A. 2 γ) is usually collective, expressing the amount, however made up; but it is sometimes used of individual coins, when no stress is laid upon their being such. *Pence* is especially used after numerals, where from *twopence* to *elevenpence* (rarely *twelvepence*) and in *twentypence*, it is stressless ('tʌpəns) and now written in combination. With other numbers *pence* is written separately (or hyphened) and has a separate stress, as *'eighteen 'pence*.

When such a combination means a single coin, or even a single amount, it is treated as a single substantive, and may have a plural, e.g. 'a new sixpence', 'two sixpences'; 'the school-children's twopences', 'how many eightpences are there in ten shillings?' See TWOPENCE, THREEPENCE, etc. To such combinations, *halfpenny* and *farthing* are added without *and*, e.g. 'postage twopence-halfpenny', 'the early penny-farthing foreign post-card', 'a sixpence-halfpenny shop'. These phrases may also take a plural: see quot. 1724. Adjective or attributive uses of these combinations are formed with *-penny*, e.g. *twopenny*, etc.: see 10.

c **1000**- [see examples under A. 2 β]. *c* **1305**- [see under A. 2 γ]. *c* **1380** WYCLIF *Wks.* (1880) 36 To curse a man for sexe pans. **1436** *Libel Eng. Policy* in *Pol. Songs* (Rolls) II. 175, xij pens in the golden pounde. **1590** SHAKS. *Com. Err.* I. ii. 55 Oh sixe pence that I had a wensday last. **1590** —— *Mids. N.* IV. ii. 22 Sixpence a day for playing Piramus. **1724** SWIFT *Drapier's Lett.* iii. Wks. 1755 V. II. 50 We have many sorts of small silver coins,.. such as the French three-pences, four-pence half-pennies, and eight-pence farthings, the Scotch five-pences and ten-pences, besides their twenty-pences and three and four-pences. **1726-31** TINDAL *Rapin's Hist. Eng.* (1743) II. XVII. 157 Six-pences, Two-pences, Pence, and Half-pence. **1837** *Penny Cycl.* VII. 329/2 From Egbert's time, with very few exceptions, the series of English pennies is complete. *Ibid.*, Pence, halfpence, and farthings are extant of John, all struck in Ireland. **1865** *Reader* No. 148. 493/2 A large hoard of short-cross pennies. **1866** CRUMP *Banking* x. 226 Coinage of England: Athelstan A.D. 925 to Henry II A.D. 1189, silver pennies only.

2. a. Rendering L. *denarius* (see DENARIUS); also occasionally *argenteus* ('piece of silver'), and *nummus* (= *nummus sestertius*, SESTERCE). Chiefly, now only, in Biblical use and allusions thereto.

c **950** *Lindisf. Gosp.* Mark xii. 15 Brenges me penig [L. *denarium*] þætte ic ȝesii. *c* **975** *Rushw. Gosp.* John vi. 7 Tu hund peninga [L. *ducentorum denariorum*] to hlafum ne ȝinyhtsumað him. *c* **1000** *Ags. Gosp.* Luke x. 35 And brohte oðrum dæge twegen penegas [L. *duos denarios*, WYCLIF twey pens, *v.r.* pans]. *c* **1275** *Passion of our Lord* 119 in *O.E. Misc.* 40 If ich so ispede þat ich bitraye ihesu, hwat schal beon my mede? þrytty panewes, hi seyden. *c* **1380** WYCLIF *Serm.* Sel. Wks. I. 32 He toke two pens, and ȝaf hem to þe hosteler. **1387** TREVISA *Higden* (Rolls) I. 273 þey schulde euery ȝere offre foure pans [L. *quatuor nummos*] to þe chirche work of Seynt Denys. *c* **1400** MAUNDEV. (Roxb.) xi. 42 þai salde Criste for xxx. penys. **1535** COVERDALE *Jer.* xxxii. 9 Seuen sycles and ten syluer pens [L. *decem argenteos*]. **1638** JUNIUS *Paint. Ancients* 303 Antonius the Triumvir his pennies were mixed with iron. **1646** BP. HALL *Balm of Gil.* (1650) 134 Even the eleventh houre carried the peny as well as the first. **1720** OZELL *Vertot's Rom. Rep.* I. VII. 424 *note*, The Penny of Gold among the Romans was worth a Thousand Sesterces. **1796** H. HUNTER tr. *St.-Pierre's Stud. Nat.* (1799) III. 480, I do not speak of the penny paid to Cesar by St. Peter. **1881** N. T. (R.V.) *Luke* xx. 24 Shew me a penny. Whose image and superscription hath it? And they said, Cæsar's.

b. Sometimes applied to the French *denier* or 10 centime piece; also, to the now obsolete coin of Jersey of that value (*Jersey penny*), superseded in 1877 by a coin = $\frac{1}{12}$ shilling. Formerly also used to render the name of the Dutch *penning*, the German *pfennig*, the Low German *pennig*, and other foreign coins corresponding in name. In U.S. and Canad. *colloq.*, a cent.

1727-41 CHAMBERS *Cycl.* s.v., The French *penny*, or denier, is of two kinds; the Paris *penny*, called *denier Parisis*; and the *penny* of Tours, *denier Tournois*... The Dutch *penny*, called *pennink*, is a real money, worth about one fifth more than the French *penny Tournois*... At Hambourg, Nuremberg, &c. the *penny* or *pfennig* of account, is put equal to the French *penny Tournois*. **1831** *Constellation* 12 Mar. 133/4 He meant cents, but they call em pennies in New York. **1862** ANSTED *Channel Isl.* IV. App. A (ed. 2) 561 Thirteen Jersey pence are equivalent to an English shilling. **1889** FARMER *Dict. Amer.*, *Penny*, a cent, and thus about half the value of an English penny. **1898** G. B. RAWLINGS *Brit. Coinage* 194 No coins were struck for Jersey till 1841,.. the English shilling at that time being valued in Jersey at thirteen pence... The penny is as follows. **1902** 'R. CONNOR' *Glengarry School Days* 166 'Six pennies and two dimes', was Hughie's disconsolate reply. **1925** E. GLASGOW *Barren Ground* xi. 303 The price had seemed extravagant, for selling directly to her customer she had asked thirty cents a pound, while butter in Pedlar's store was never higher than ninepence in summer and a shilling in winter, measured in the old English terms which were still commonly used in Queen Elizabeth County. **1966** *New Statesman* 16 Dec. 896/3 Florin.. is only used, like the American 'penny', to describe the actual lump of metal. **1971** *Daily Colonist* (Victoria, B.C.) 28 Dec. 7/4 Persons posting first class letters will be nicked another penny starting Jan. 1. **1974** H. MCCLOY *Minotaur Country* (1975) xvi. 186 You recall the penny that was found..? And the dimes found.. after the fire?

II. From the fact that the (silver) penny was for many hundred years the chief or only coin in circulation, the name became to a great extent synonymous with 'coin', 'piece', or 'unit of money', whence the following uses:

3. = A coin: applied with a defining or descriptive adjunct to various coins of the British Isles, of distinct origin from the ordinary penny. Now *Hist.*

penny of twopence, a silver coin of the value of twopence, a half-groat; ***gold penny***, a gold coin of the value of 20 shillings issued in 1257.

1483 *Cath. Angl.* 274/1 A Peny of twa Pens (*A.* Pennys), *didragma*. **1523** *Act 14 & 15 Hen. VIII*, c. 12 As many halfe grotes called pens of two pens. **1523** FITZHERB. *Husb.* §54 Peny grasse.. hath a leafe as brode as a peny of two pens, and neuer beareth floure. **1565** in Keith *Hist. Scot.* (1754) App. 118 That thair be cunȝeit ane Penny of Silvir callit the Mary Ryall,.. of Weicht ane Unce Troce-weicht. **1578** *Reg. Privy Council Scot.* III. 31 Thair salbe ane penny or pece of gold prentit and cunyeit of twentie ane carret fine. **1700** TYRRELL *Hist. Eng.* II. (975) This Year [1257], according to the MS. Chronicle of the city of London, the King Coined a Penny of Pure Gold of the Weight of Two Sterlings, and commanded that it should go for Twenty Shillings. **1895** W. A. SHAW *Hist. Currency* i. 4 Five years later (1257) Henry III of England imitated the florin in his gold pennies.

4. a. Used as a general or vague word for a piece of money; hence, a sum of money, money.

Now chiefly in phr. ***a pretty penny***: see 9 e.

c **1330** R. BRUNNE *Chron.* (1810) 64, & alle þat he mot gete, he robbed & reft, Peny no penyworth, no þing he no left. **1340** *Ayenb.* 23 Ydeleblisse.. þet is þe dyeules peni, huermide he bayþ alle þe uayre pane-worþes ine þe markatte of þise wordle. *a* **1375** *Lay Folks Mass Bk.* App. iv. 514 Go vp to him with ful good-wille, And þi peny, him profre. *c* **1384** WYCLIF *Sel. Wks.* III. 377 þei done þis to wynne þo penye. *c* **1386** CHAUCER *Reeve's T.* 199 They hym bisoght Of herberwe and of ese as for hir peny. **1585** T. WASHINGTON tr. *Nicholay's Voy.* II. xx. 57 b, They may.. there be lodged.. without paying of any pennie. **1623** COCKERAM *Eng. Dict.* III. s.v. *Maximilean*, The Emperour gaue him a small penny. **1649** in J. Harrington *Def. Rights Univ. Oxford* (1690) 26 They living wholy upon the penny, buying all commodities but having nothing to sell. **1657** HEYLIN *Undeceiv. People* 20 The Minister hath neither corn nor hay, nor any provision for expence of houshould, but what he buyeth by the penny. **1764** H. WALPOLE *Let. G. Montagu* 24 Dec., I shall put your letter to Rheims into the foreign post with a proper penny. **1792** BURNS '*What can a young lassie*' i, Bad luck on the pennie that tempted my minnie To sell her poor Jenny for siller an' lan'! **1822** LOCKHART *A. Blair* 139 A braw little penny to her tocher.

b. In *pl.* = money: orig. as consisting ordinarily of (silver) pennies; in later use, often depreciative, 'small money', 'coppers', 'small earnings'.

c **1290** *S. Eng. Leg.* I. 26/8 To þe apostles he wende anon and to heore fet þe panes caste. *a* **1300** *Cursor M.* 5507 Wit þair penis boght was he. *c* **1470** HENRY *Wallace* VIII. 692 Pryce off pennys may mak ws no ramed. **1611** COTGR. s.v. *Sien*, Who looseth his pence forgoeth his sence. **1641** MILTON *Ch. Govt.* II. Wks. 1851 III. 139 Dispensers of treasure.. without price to them that have no pence. **1653** URQUHART *Rabelais* I. xlv. 203 He.. gave unto each of them a horse.. together with some pence to live by. **1883** G. B. GOODE *Fish. Indust.* 6 (Fish. Exhib. Publ.), Their descendants.. are to-day hauling pence up out of the water faster than their forefathers ever learned to do.

†**c.** (*Singular.*) With ordinal numeral, expressing an aliquot part of a sum of money, as ***the fifth penny***, *i.e.* every fifth penny in any number of pennies; = one-fifth of the whole amount.

1038 *Charter of Harold Haranfot* in Kemble *Cod. Dipl.* IV. 57 [He] bæd hine fultumes to þam hirode embe þone þriddan penig. *c* **1300** *Song Husbandm.* 8 in *Pol. Songs* (Camden) 149 Ever the furthe peni mot to the kynge. **1581** *Reg. Privy Council Scot.* III. 427 All and haill the erldome of Gowry, with the teind penny of all wardis. **1585** *Ibid.* 743 The first fructis and fyft penny of the same beneficeis. *a* **1618** RALEIGH *Prerog. Parl.* (1628) 8 In the 14. yeare he [Henry III] had the 15. penny of all goods given him vpon condition to confirme the great Charter. *c* **1645** HOWELL *Lett.* I. xli, None can hire or build a House, but he must pay the tenth penny. **1681** *Lond. Gaz.* No. 1654/2 The Nations of this City have declared their willingness to give twice the 20th penny, which.. will raise a Million and a halfe. **1776** ADAM SMITH *W.N.* I. ix. (1869) I. 95 In 1720 interest was reduced from the twentieth to the fiftieth penny, or from five to two per cent. **1844** G. DODD *Textile Manuf.* v. 168 Remunerated by what was termed 'the fourth penny', that is, each journeyman received as his wages.. the fourth part of the gross sum for which such cloth was sold.

†**d.** ***first penny*** = prime cost, cost price. In quot. 1674, perh. = first amount, amount starting a contribution, testimonial, etc.; a handsel. *Obs.*

1586 A. DAY *Eng. Secretary* II. (1625) 63 Seuen Buts of Sack, which cost the first pennie seuenteen Duckats the But. **1620** CAPT. SMITH *New Eng. Trials* (Arb.) 242 Her fraght, which she sold at the first penny for 2100 pounds. *c* **1645** HOWELL *Lett.* (1650) II. 48 Her cargazon of broad cloth was worth the first peny neer upon 30000*l.* **1674** MARVELL *Corr.* Wks. 1872-5 II. 424 E. of Pembroke marryed to Madame Qerronal's [*sic*] sister. The King gives 1000 first peny.

e. The particular sum of money or amount of some tax, impost, or customary payment. With defining adjunct, as ***borchel-penny***, ***cock-p.***, ***common penny***, ***earnest-p.***, ***fire p.***, ***gauge-p.***, ***God's-p.***, ***hanse-penny***, ***homage-p.***, ***Peter's-penny*** (***-pence***), ***Rome-p.***, ***scot-p.***, ***teind-p.***, ***tithing-p.***, ***ward-p.***, etc. See these.

c **1194** in *Reg. of Wetherhal* (1897) 30 Sint quiete de.. averpeni et de blodwita.. et de hundredpeni et de thethingepeni. **1444** *Rolls of Parlt.* V. 117/1 þat the peny which is called the Gauge peny, be not paied to the Gaugeour. **1461** *Ibid.* 476/1 A summe of money claymed at two law-dayes in the yere, called Tithyng peny, otherwise Tottyng-peny. **1479-81** *Rec. St. Mary at Hill* 102 The ernyst penys and potacions at diuerse tymes amonge the workemen. **1508**- [see EARNEST-PENNY]. **1562** *Reg. Privy Council Scot.* I. 222 Without payment of any compositioun or teind penny. **1845** S. AUSTIN *Ranke's Hist. Ref.* I. 79 At Regensburg, in the year 1471—the allied powers.. attempted to impose a sort of property tax on the whole empire, called the Common Penny. *Ibid.* 213 The scheme of a Common Penny was now resumed. **1890** GROSS *Gild Merch.* I. 31 There were dues at Andover called 'scot-pennies', 'hanse-pennies', and 'sige-pennies'. **1904** *Westm. Gaz.* 16 Mar. 12/1 The church was built in the old feudal days when the Bourchiers.. held estate in Chingford, and.. in 1220 an agreement was entered into between the Abbot of Waltham and the Dean and Chapter of St. Paul's by which the latter were exempted from the payment of 'Borchel Peny' and 'Ward Peny'.

5. As the type of a coin of small value, or of a small amount of money. Often in contrast with ***pound*** (see also 9 f, h); with a negative, as ***not a penny*** = not the least amount, no money at all; so ***never a penny***, ***not worth a penny***.

a **1200** [see A. 1 β]. ? *a* **1366** CHAUCER *Rom. Rose* 451 Povert al aloon, That not a peny hadde in wolde. **1414** BRAMPTON *Penit. Ps.* 46 There schal no man, for peny ne pounde, Have 'Ne reminiscaris, Domine?' **1457** *Paston Lett.* I. 414 A peny yn seson spent wille safe a pounde. **1530** in W. H. Turner *Select. Rec. Oxford* 74 Clare had never peny for hyt. **1568** GRAFTON *Chron.* II. 589 Hauing onely the name and style of the same, without any peny profite, or foote of possession. **1570** T. WILSON *Demosthenes* 97 *margin*, It is the well spent penny that saveth the pound. **1655** GURNALL *Chr. in Arm.* verse 12. v. §3 (1669) 85/1 Wilt thou stand with God for a day or two, huckle with him for a penny? **1782** MISS BURNEY *Cecilia* v. i, Never knew a man worth a penny with such a coat as that on. **1840** BARHAM *Ingol. Leg.* Ser. I. *Jackd. Rheims* vi, Never was heard such a terrible curse! But.. Nobody seem'd one penny the worse!

III. Transferred uses: chiefly elliptical.

†**6.** = PENNYWEIGHT. *Obs.*

c **1000** *Sax. Leechd.* II. 298 Pund eles ȝewihð .XII. peneȝum læsse þonne pund wætres. & pund ealoð ȝewihð .VI. peneȝum mare þonne pund wætres. **1398** TREVISA *Barth. De P.R.* XIX. cxxxi. (1495) nn iij/2 Dragma is the eyghte parte of Vncia and weyeth thre Pans of syluer. Scrupulus.. is acountyd for ten Pans. **1579** *Reg. Privy Council Scot.* III. 189 Tuicheing the reductioun of our Soverane Lordis cunyie to ellevin penny fyne. **1590** RECORDE, etc. *Gr. Artes* (1640) 127 Whereas.. the weight is called by the name of a penny, it is not ment a penny of silver money, but a penny of Gold-smiths weight, which containeth 24 Barly Corn.

†**7.** The amount bought for a penny, a pennyworth. *Obs.*

1564 *Child-Marriages* 208 All iij went to Richard Barkers house, and dronke, eithe[r] of them a peny. **1591** SPENSER *M. Hubberd* 523 Whereas thou maist compound a better penie.

8. = PENNYLAND, q.v.

IV. 9. Phrases and Proverbs.

a. ***a penny for your thoughts***: I would give something to know what you are thinking about (addressed to one in a 'brown study'). So ***penny for them*** (***'em***); also *ellipt.* as ***penny***. †**b.** ***a penny in the forehead***: in allusion to a playful nursery joke, in which a cold coin is pressed on the forehead so as to be felt as if still there after its removal: see *Notes and Q.* 9th s. VIII. 189. *Obs.* **c.** ***a penny saved is a penny gained*** (***got, earned***). **d.** ***a penny soul never came to twopence***. **e.** ***a pretty*** (***fine***, etc.) ***penny***: a considerable sum (in the way of gain or cost). **f.** ***in for a penny, in for a pound***: having entered upon a matter one must carry it through whatever it involves. †**g.** ***no penny, no paternoster***: a saying referring to priests insisting on being paid as a condition of performing services; hence = nothing for nothing; if you want a thing you must pay for it. So ***no paternoster, no penny*** = no work, no pay. ***penny nor paternoster*** (quot. 1566), neither pay nor prayers; neither love nor money. *Obs.* **h.** ***take care of the pence, and the pounds will take care of themselves***. †**i.** ***to think one's penny*** (***good***) ***silver***: to have a good opinion of oneself. *Obs.* **j.** † ***to make penny of***, to turn into money, to sell (*obs.*); ***to make a*** (***good***, etc.) ***penny of***, to make profit by (?*obs.*). (See also e.) †**k.** ***to turn*** (***wind***) ***the*** (***a***) ***penny***: to employ one's money profitably; or, to gain money. *Obs.* exc. in ***to turn an honest penny*** (see HONEST *a.* 4 b). **l.** ***pennies from heaven***: money acquired without effort or risk; also *sing.*, a windfall, a godsend. **m.** ***to spend a penny***: to visit a lavatory, to urinate (from the former price of admission to public lavatories). **n.** ***the penny has dropped***: a situation or statement has belatedly been comprehended; one has reacted belatedly. (With allusion to the mechanism of a penny-in-the-slot machine). **o.** ***two*** (also ***ten***) ***a penny***: commonplace, easily obtainable, occurring frequently. See also PENNY-WISE.

a. 1546 J. HEYWOOD *Prov.* II. iv. (1867) 50 Wherwith in a great musyng he was brought. Fréend (quoth the good man) a peny for your thought. **1738** SWIFT *Pol. Conversat.* 8 *Neverout.* Come: a Penny for your thoughts. *Miss.* It is not worth a farthing: for I was thinking of you. **1765** BICKERSTAFF *Maid of Mill* I. viii. 17 My lord, a penny for your thoughts. **1900** H. G. WELLS *Love & Mr. Lewisham* xxv. 242 'Penny,' she said after an interval. Lewisham started and looked up. '*Eh?*' **1914** C. MACKENZIE *Sinister St.* II. IV. iii. 895 'You're very silent, kiddie,' she said. 'I'll give you a penny for them.' **1921** N. KENT *Quest M. Harland* II. iv. 169 'Penny for 'em, old man,' said Dickie presently, after Michael had eaten in silence for nearly five minutes. 'My thoughts?' Michael started and laughed. **1959** J. BRAINE

Vodi xiv. 190 Harry's voice broke into her thoughts. 'Penny for 'em, old girl.' **1965** L. MEYNELL *Double Fault* II. v. 175 'Penny,' Lucian said. She laughed... 'Far too rich and rare for a penny to buy them.' **1973** J. THOMSON *Death Cap* x. 142 Finch was sitting looking thoughtfully at the report... 'Penny for them?' suggested the Sergeant.

b. **1658–9** *Burton's Diary* 9 Mar. (1828) IV. 106, I am not bound alwayes to look you in the face like children, to see if you have a penny in your forehead. *a* **1734** NORTH *Exam.* II. v. §15 (1740) 324 We may hope better of their Abilities than to be wheedled as Children with a Penny in the Forehead.

c. **1695** RAVENSCROFT *Canterbury Guests* II. iv, This I did to prevent expences, for.. A penny sav'd, is a penny got. **1811** BYRON *Hints fr. Horace* 516 A penny saved, my lad, 's a penny got. **1838** *Chamb. Edin. Jrnl.* 45 A penny saved is a penny gained. **1899** *Pall Mall Mag.* Sept. 107 A penny saved is a penny earned.

d. **1844** *Chamb. Jrnl.* II. 225 A penny soul never came to twopence. **1859** SMILES *Self-Help* ix. (1860) 235 Narrow-mindedness in living and in dealing.. leads to failure. The penny soul never came to twopence.

e. **1768** J. BYRON *Narr. Patagonia* (ed. 2) 209 By which the soldiers made a pretty penny. **1782** MISS BURNEY *Cecilia* IX. iv, If a man makes a fair penny.. he has as much title to enjoy his pleasure as the Chief Justice. **1796** MRS. GLASSE *Cookery* vii. 131 By that time the.. ingredients are reckoned, the partridges will come to a fine penny. **1885** B. HARTE *Maruja* i, Then the captain might still make a pretty penny on Amita. **1889** *Boston* (Mass.) *Jrnl.* 12 Jan., Uncle Sam's navy is costing him a pretty penny these days.

f. **1695** RAVENSCROFT *Canterbury Guests* v. i, Well than, O'er shooes, o'er boots. And In for a Penny, in for a Pound. **1823** BYRON *To Kinnaird* 23 Dec. **1840** DICKENS *Old C. Shop* lxvi, Being in for a penny, I am ready, as the saying is, to be in for a pound. *c* **1882** W. S. GILBERT *Iolanthe* II. 33 In for a penny, in for a pound—It's love that makes the world go round! **1906** L. STRACHEY in *Lit. Ess.* (1948) 142 The emendator is on an inclined plane which leads him inevitably from readjustments of punctuation to corrections of grammar, and from corrections of grammar to alterations of rhythm; if he is in for a penny, he is in for a pound. **1976** 'J. FRASER' *Who steals my Name?* xii. 149 He seemed to be having some kind of inner conflict which resolved it-self. 'All right,' he said, 'in for a penny in for a pound!' **1977** *Transatlantic Rev.* LX. 189 The cabbie steamed up to Notting Hill Gate with an In for a penny, In for a pound expression on his face.

g. **1546** *Suppl. Commons* (1871) 87 Theyr couetouse is growne into this prouerbe, 'No peny, no pater noster'. **1566** GASCOIGNE *Supposes* I. i, Pitie nor pencion, peny nor pater noster shoulde euer haue made Nurse once to open hir mouth in the cause. **1640** BASTWICK *Lord Bps.* vi. E iv b, No penny, no Pater noster; they looke more to their tithes, then to their taske. **1707** HICKERINGILL *Priest-cr.* II. ii. 22 Once was—No Pater Noster, No Penny; now—No Sermons, not a Penny, not a Farthing.

h. *a* **1724** LOWNDES in Chesterf. *Lett.* 5 Feb. an. 1750 [Old Mr. Lowndes, the famous Secretary of the Treasury.. used to say] 'take care of the pence, and the pounds will take care of themselves'. **1854** R. S. SURTEES *Handley Cross* xiii, 'A real out-and-out workin' chap, that will.. look sharp ater the pence, without leavin' the pounds to take care of themselves'.

i. **1579** TOMSON *Calvin's Serm. Tim.* 13/2 Suche as.. thought their penie good siluer. **1594** GREENE & LODGE *Looking Glasse* Lodge's Wks. (Hunter. Cl.) 17 Tho she say that she is fairest, I think my pennie siluer by her leaue. **1603** BRETON *Packet Mad Lett.* liv. (1879) 20/1 There are more Batchelors than Roger, and my penny is as good siluer as yours.

j. **1512** in Pitcairn *Crim. Trials* I. 76* To mak penny of þair landis and gudis. **15..** *Aberdeen Regr.* (Jam.), The prouest, &c., chargit the officiaris to mak penny of the claith prisit. **1726** BERKELEY *Let. to T. Prior* 1 Dec., Wks. 1871 IV. 139, I gave him old clothes, which he made a penny of. **1782** MISS BURNEY *Cecilia* v. viii, Warrant Master Harrel's made a good penny of you.

k. **1546** J. HEYWOOD *Prov.* II. viii. (1867) 75 Towne ware was your ware, to tourne the peny. *c* **1645** HOWELL *Lett.* (1754) 76 There is no State that winds the Penny more nimbly, and makes quicker Returns. **1712** ADDISON *Spect.* No. 452 ¶4 A Projector, who is willing to turn a Penny by this remarkable Curiosity of his Countrymen. **1887** MISS E. MONEY *Dutch Maiden* (1888) 5 Lucas had been sent across the seas to turn the 'honest penny' and pick up some gold.

l. **1936** J. BURKE (*song-title*) Pennies from heaven. **1965** J. D. MACDONALD *Bright Orange for Shroud* xvi. 191 'Sweetie,' I said, 'you are a penny from heaven.' **1971** P. DICKINSON *Sleep & his Brother* v. 117 Hard money is what your hospital pays you... Soft money is pennies from heaven, some dirty big company deciding to earn a bit of tax relief by financing medical research. **1972** 'W. HAGGARD' *Protectors* xiii. 154 He hadn't planned it that way... But when the pennies from heaven fell down he'd seize them.

m. **1945** H. LEWIS *Strange Story* iv. 27 'Us girls,' she said, 'are going to spend a penny!' **1955** J. CANNAN *Long Shadows* iii. 59, I wasn't sure that Trudy [a dog] had spent her penny. *Ibid.* vii. 127 We'll go indoors and pay for tea and spend a penny. **1960** M. CECIL *Something in Common* xxii. 239 It's tricky about the bathroom, but it's amazing how one can train oneself to spend a minimum of pennies. **1973** *People's Jrnl.* (Inverness & Northern Counties ed.) 28 July 10/1 Anyone on the Islands.. after that time who wants to 'spend a penny' must make a 10-minute walk.. to the public toilets.

n. [**1942** N. BALCHIN *Darkness falls from Air* IV. 70 The penny seems to have stuck in the machine that time. The proper answer to that is 'I'm flattered.'] **1951** —— *Way through Wood* xv. 214, I sat and thought for a moment and then the penny dropped. **1959** *Sunday Express* 13 Dec. 1/4, I had seen Vivienne before, but the penny didn't drop until I met her that night. **1961** S. CHAPLIN *Day of Sardine* viii. 174 It took a second or two for the penny to drop. I gave myself a shake and made over to the maybe Old Man. **1973** *Times* 1 Dec. 14 The penny had begun to drop even before the present fuel crisis.

o. **1960** *Times* 11 Jan. 17/1 Penalties were two a penny at Upper Park on Saturday. **1961** NEW ENG. BIBLE *Matt.* x. 29 Are not sparrows two a penny? **1967** *Listener* 27 Oct. 612/3 He found in India that subalterns were two a penny and invited nowhere. **1973** *Nature* 20 Apr. 492/2 Recommendations on the so-called energy crisis are by now two a penny. **1973** A. MANN *Tiara* iv. 34 Hunches are two a penny in this business. **1973** C. L. BARNHART et al. *Dict. New Eng.* 355/2 *Ten a penny* is also used in England.

V.

10. With prefixed numerals, forming adjectives of price or value: see FIVEPENNY, FOURPENNY, SIXPENNY, etc. Applied to nails, such adjectives denote the original price (in 15th c.) per hundred; as ***fivepenny nail***, a nail which cost 5*d*. a hundred, ***tenpenny nail***, a nail costing 10*d*. a hundred. (These names persisted after the prices fell, as they began to do in some places before 1500, and they were eventually used to designate *sizes* of nails.)

1426–7 *Rec. St. Mary at Hill* (E.E.T.S.) 67 Also for iij^c x peny nayl to þe vyse, ij s vj d. Also for iiij^c vj peny nayl, ijs. **1427–8** *Ibid.* 69 Also for ij^c x peny nayl to þe same werk, xx d. Also for iiij^c vj peny nayl.. ij s. Also for a c. of ij peny nayl, ij d. **1484** *Ibid.* 120 Item, for ij c di. iiij penye nayle, xx d. Item, for di. c v d nayle, ij d ob. Item, for di. a c iij penye nayle, j d ob. **1494–5** *Ibid.* 208, Item, iij c vj d naile, xv d. *Ibid.* 210 Item, iij c di. v. peny Naile, xiiij d. **1481** *Nottingham Rec.* II. 320 Unum centum et dimidium de *threpeny nayl'*, ad valentiam iiij d.; et de dimidio centum de *forpeny nayl'*, ad valentiam de ij d. *c* **1850** *Rudim. Navig.* (Weale) 135 Nails of sorts are, 4, 6, 8, 10, 24, 30, and 40-penny nails, all of different lengths.

11. *attrib.* or as *adj.* **a.** Of the price or value of a penny, costing a penny, as ***penny arcade, awful, bazaar, brick*** [BRICK *sb.*[1] 3], ***bun, commons*** [COMMONS 3 b], ***cord, dreadful*** [DREADFUL C] (also with hyphen, *attrib.*), ***hen, horrible*** [HORRIBLE B], ***ice*** (also *comb.*), ***knife, loaf, magazine, mass, newspaper, novel, novelette, paper, pie, press, roll, stamp, steamboat, toy, whistle***, etc.; for the use of or admission to which the charge is a penny, as ***penny boat, bus, club, concert, gaff*** (GAFF *sb.*[4]), ***gallery, lecture, lodging reading, show, steamer, tram***, etc.; (of a game) at which the stake is a penny, as ***penny-nap, -ombre***; (of a person) that sells something or does some work for a penny or at a cheap rate; hence, engaged in mean or inferior work; as ***penny-barber, foot-post, poet, wit***. Here *penny* (though sometimes hyphened) may be considered as an adj.: cf. *penny loaf* with *twopenny* or *sixpenny loaf*. **b.** Of or pertaining to a penny, as ***penny-breadth***, †***-brede*** (BREDE *sb.*[2]).

1908 C. E. GRIFFIN *Four Years in Europe* ix. 87 The numerous *penny arcades and moving picture shows.. were another new wrinkle in American showmanship. **1961** GETLEIN & GARDINER *Movies, Morals, & Art* I. iv. 48 The penny arcade.. can still be found in such urban areas as Times Square. **1889** E. DOWSON *Let.* 15 Mar. (1967) 49 It is very bad, very long, & distinctly '*penny awful' not 'shilling shocking'. *a* **1704** T. BROWN *Sat. on Fr. King* Wks. 1730 I. 61, I hope thou'lt in the Friars take a shop, Turn *penny-barber there. **1897** H. JAMES *Spoils of Poynton* xiii. 154 An assortment of pen-wipers and ash-trays, a harvest he had gathered in from *penny bazaars. **1966** *Guardian* 29 Aug. 4/4 The Shields tram.. full of early homecomers. They got off at the Penny Bazaar. **1976** *Times* 8 Nov. 14/5 If the Church wants.. the responsibility for the appointment of its chief pastors it must do much better than this. We are in danger of reducing a great institution to the level of a penny bazaar. **1855** THACKERAY *Newcomes* xxxvi, We came by the steamer, and I prefer the *péniboat. **1862** *Routledge's Pop. Guide Lond.* 44 The Penny boats go to and from London Bridge and Hungerford.. about every five minutes. *c* **1430** *Two Cookery-bks.* I. 7 Kyt it in smale pecys of the *peny brede. **1535** LYNDESAY *Satyre* 3576 The Saviour of men, In all this warld hes nocht ane penny braid Quhairon he may repois his heavinlie head. *a* **1550** *Wardr. Acc. Hen. VIII* in *Archæol.* IX. 250 Syxe pecis of Venysse reabande, pennye bredith of div'se colours. **1649** G. DANIEL *Trinarch., Hen. V*, xvi, One Day writes an Age; Though a Good hand, pussle an Eye to Read't A Pater-Noster, in a Penny Breadth. **1735** *Penny brick [see BRICK *sb.*[1] 3]. **1806** A. HUNTER *Culina* (ed. 3) 152 Then pour in beef gravy with the soft part of a penny brick. **1824** E. WEETON *Jrnl.* 21 July (1969) II. 309 Having had no dinner.. but some curds and one or two *penny buns. **1862** MRS. SEWELL *Patience Hart* xxx. 227, I went into a baker's shop and bought a penny bun. **1630** B. JONSON *New Inn* IV. i, Keep they their *penny club still? **1844** C. M. YONGE *Abbeychurch* xiii. 278 Elizabeth.. went to the school to receive the penny-club money. *a* **1613** OVERBURY *Charact., Meere Fellow* Wks. (1856) 105 At meales, he sits in as great state over his *penny-commons, as ever Vitellius did at his greatest banquet. **1599** SHAKS. *Hen. V*, III. vi. 50 Let not Bardolphs vitall thred bee cut With edge of *Penny-Cord, and vile reproach. **1873** *Slang Dict.*, **Penny dreadfuls*,.. those penny publications which depend more upon sensationalism than upon merit, artistic or literary, for success. **1884** *World* 20 Aug. 9/2 The wicked noblemen of the transpontine melodrama or of penny dreadfuls. **1906** M. CORELLI *Treasure of Heaven* 55 The proper way for him to behave at this juncture.. would be that he should take her tenderly in his arms and murmur, after the penny-dreadful style of elderly hero, 'My darling'. **1925** T. DREISER *Amer. Trag.* II. III. xix. 222 By him sold to a penny-dreadful publisher of Binghamton. **1941** V. NABOKOV *Real Life S. Knight* x. 91 He did not mind in the least 'penny dreadfuls' because he wasn't concerned with ordinary morals. **1963** *Times* 18 Feb. 5/3 He was perfectly happy with a 'penny dreadful', a warm fire, a friendly dog, and a good meal inside him. *a* **1625** FLETCHER *Chances* v. ii, A *penny foot-post Compell'd with cross and pile to run of errands. **1851** MAYHEW *Lond. Labour* I. 40/1 There are shops which have been turned into a kind of temporary theatre (admission one penny)... These places are called by the costers '*Penny Gaffs'. **1866** *Daily Tel.* 16 Oct. 2/4 She wished to go into the penny gaff a second time, and said she had no money. **1337–8** *Durham Acc. Rolls* (Surtees) 33 In v^xx. vij. *peny-hennys emp... viijs. xj d. **1899** F. H. DOOD in *Daily News* 13 June 8/5 '*Penny horribles' always have a public, though it is questionable if dime novels are now so prominent as they once were. **1872** B. JERROLD *London* xv. 127 We have found the *penny ice-man doing a brisk trade. *Ibid.*, The penny ice has proved too strong for the ancient ginger-beer bottle. **1896** G. B. SHAW *Our Theatres in Nineties* (1932) II. 133 Some appalling tenor from I know not what limbo of street-piano padrones, penny-icemen, and broken choristers. **1914** —— *Fanny's First Play* 169 You should be eating penny ices and enjoying yourself. **1852** *Eliza Cook's Jrnl.* 22 May 57/2 The power of the Penny has only been discovered of late years. The Penny Magazine, and the Penny Cyclopædia, fairly inaugurated the discovery. *Penny Lectures are the necessary corollary from it; and before long the Penny News-paper may fairly complete it. **1418** *Maldon, Essex, Court-Rolls* (Bundle 11, no. 3), Panis frumenti.. vocat. *penylof. **1594** BLUNDEVIL *Exerc.* I. x. (1636) 31 If a penny-loafe must weigh two pound, Wheat being at three shilling a bushell. **1840** DICKENS *Old C. Shop* xlv, A penny loaf was all they had had that day. **1779–81** JOHNSON *L.P., Swift* Wks. III. 373 At night he would go to a *penny lodging, where he purchased clean sheets for sixpence. **1835** DICKENS *Sk. Boz* (1837) 2nd Ser. 145 When *penny magazines shall have superseded penny yards of song. **1852** Penny magazine [see *penny lecture* s.v. PENNY 11]. **1591** SPENSER *M. Hubberd* 452 Their *penie masses and their complynes meete. **1889** J. K. JEROME *Three Men in Boat* xix. 306 We played *penny nap after supper. **1950** *Hoyle's Games Modernized* (ed. 20) I. 138 If a man calls three at 'penny Nap', he receives 3d. **1852** *Penny Newspaper [see beside *penny lecture* above]. **1862** *Sat. Rev.* 8 Feb. 154 A halfpenny or penny newspaper. **1861** *Punch* 5 Jan. 3/1 A weakness for.. reading *penny novels. **1896** G. B. SHAW *Our Theatres in Nineties* (1932) II. 213 You would never dream of asking why Morris did not read *penny novelettes, or hang his rooms with Christmas-number chromolithographs. **1710** SWIFT *Let. to Sterne* 26 Sept., Looking over while you lost a crown at *penny-ombre. **1834** *Tait's Mag.* I. 423/1 A set of idle *penny-page men. **1711** ADDISON *Spect.* No. 124 ¶2 Many a bulky Author would make his Appearance in a *Penny-Paper. **1600** KEMP *Nine Daies Wond.* D iij b, A *penny Poet; whose first making was the miserable stolne story of Macdoel, or Macdobeth, or Macsomewhat. **1804–6** SYD. SMITH *Mor. Philos.* (1850) 100 That race of penny poets who lived in the reigns of Cosmo and Lorenzo di Medici. **1840** *Picayune* (New Orleans) 15 Sept. 2/2 The six-penny journals have latterly grown wise enough to drop the naughty habit in which they used to indulge of swearing at the *penny press. **1843** *North Amer. Rev.* Jan. 227 They [*sc.* Dickens's *American Notes*] have been scattered all over the country by the penny press. **1860** GLADSTONE *Diary* 3 Oct. in Morley *Life* II. 184 Some of the penny press which has now acquired an enormous expansion go great lengths in my favour. **1932** T. S. ELIOT *Sel. Essays* VI. 341 Those sections about which readers of the penny press are most ready to excite themselves. **1858** *Brit. Q. Rev.* LVI. 341 This lecture is profusely illustrated, as the *penny publishers say, with cuts. **1859** *Suffolk Chron.* 13 Sept. (*heading*), *Penny Readings for the Working Classes. **1861** C. SULLEY (*title*) Penny Readings in Ipswich and Elsewhere. **1871** F. KILVERT *Diary* 3 Feb. (1938) I. 301 This evening we had our 4th Penny Reading. The room was fuller than ever. **1883** P. E. GIBBONS in *Harper's Mag.* Apr. 661/1 Penny readings are entertainments at which each who enters pays a penny. **1907** A. HUXLEY *Let.* 17 Nov. (1969) 26 Mr. Taylor wants to know for his *penny reading*. **1969** *Telegraph* (Brisbane) 25 Mar. 8/4 The provisional school was used for monthly 'penny readings'.. at that period. **1976** *Trans. Yorks. Dial. Soc.* LXXVI. 33 Traditions which must go back to 'Sir Gawain' and even 'Beowulf' when the 'oral literature' of 600 A.D. and Victorian 'Penny Readings' may seem to be not all that far apart. **1836–48** B. D. WALSH *Aristoph., Knights* I. iii, I will hack you like a *penny roll. **1601** CHESTER *Love's Mart.* etc. (1878) 179 The cause of all our monstrous *penny-showes. **1839** ROWLAND HILL *Memorandum* 13th June, The stamp-office would charge the nominal value.. (a penny a sheet for *penny stamps, twopence a sheet for twopenny stamps, etc). **1881** *Stamp Collector's Ann.* 38 (Postage stamp Savings Bank) Slips of paper.. with spaces below marked out for affixing twelve penny stamps. **1859** G. A. SALA *Twice round Clock* 11 The river glideth in peace, undisturbed by *penny steamboats. **1862** A. J. MUNBY *Diary* 7 May in D. Hudson *Munby* (1972) 121 His enjoyment of the Thames from the deck of a *penny steamer. **1881** H. JAMES *Portr. Lady* xv, They.. went on a penny-steamer to the Tower. **1933** *Radio Times* 14 Apr. 72/3 The 'penny-steamers', those cheerful launches that trail along behind the [Boat Race] umpires and the B.B.C. **1905** *Daily Chron.* 18 Dec. 4/5 The first gutter *penny-toy merchant. **1955** *Times* 11 May 12/4 Penny toys (how many of them could be bought for that coin today?). **1818** SCOTT *Rob Roy* x, Pipes! they look more like *penny-whistles. **1879** STAINER *Music of Bible* 94 Comparing a penny whistle with a common bandsman's fife. **1931** N. DOUGLAS *London Street Games* (ed. 2) 29, I went down the lane to buy a penny whistle, A copper came by and pinch my penny whistle. **1967** W. SOYINKA *Kongi's Harvest* 64 Penny whistles blow to the tune of the Carpenter's Song. **1978** W. HJORTSBERG *Falling Angel* (1979) vi. 71 Some-one played a pennywhistle. Shrill, piping notes. **1619** H. HUTTON *Follies Anat.* (Percy Soc.) 7 Times pury *penny-wits I loathing hate.

12. *Comb.* **a.** Objective and obj. gen. as ***penny-catching, -cautious, -conscious, -grubbing, picking, pinching*** adjs., ***-collector***. **b.** similative, etc., as ***penny-brown, -grey, -sized*** adjs. **c.** Special Combs.: †**penny-ale**, ale sold at a penny a gallon, thin ale (*obs.*); **penny ante** *U.S.*, the game of poker when the ante is fixed at one penny or a similarly insignificant stake; also *attrib.* or as *adj.*, contemptible, trivial; **penny-bank**, a savings bank at which a sum as low as a penny may be deposited; †**penny-bean**, ? a kind of bean with a flat round seed (*obs.*); **penny-bird**, local Irish name for the Little Grebe (also called *drink-a-penny*); **penny black**, (a specimen of) the first one-penny postage stamp issued in the

United Kingdom, on 6 May 1840; also *fig.*; **penny-boy** *slang* (see quot. 1902); (in quot. 1914, a term of mild contempt); †**penny-bred** (**-brede, -breyde**), ? a baker's moulding-board for penny-loaves (see BRED *sb.*); **penny bridal** = *penny wedding*; **penny-cress**, the plant *Thlaspi arvense*, or some other cruciferous plant with flat round pods; **penny-daisy**, prob. = *ox-eye daisy* (OX-EYE 3 b); †**penny-dale, -deal, -dole** [see DALE[2], DEAL *sb.*[2], DOLE *sb.*[1]], the dealing or distribution of a penny to each of a number of persons; in phr. ***by penny-d.***: hence as ***adv.*** at the rate of a penny each; **penny-dog**, (*a*) a kind of dogfish, also called ***miller's dog*** or ***tope***; (*b*) *Sc.* and *north. dial.* 'a dog that constantly follows his master' (Jam.); a dog of an inferior breed; †**penny-earth**[1] [ME. *penierþe*], a villainage service of ploughing, for which one penny was paid by the lord (*obs.*); **penny-earth**[2], local name of the Fuller's Earth of the Oolitic group of strata, which abounds with the round shells of *Ostrea*; †**penny-farm** (**-ferme**), a money rent, instead of services; **penny-fee** *Sc.*, a payment of a penny; 'wages paid in money' (Jam.); **penny-fish**, the John Dory (see quot.); †**penny-flower**, the plant 'Honesty' (*Lunaria biennis*), from its flat round pods (*obs.*); †**penny-full** *a.*, (of the moon) round like a penny, 'full' (*obs.*); †**penny-gavel** [GAVEL *sb.*[1]]: see quot. 1872; †**penny-grave**, a local manorial collector of money payments and dues; **penny-in-the-slot** *a.* [from the direction 'Put a penny in the slot'], (of machines and mechanical devices for putting weighing machines into action, for automatic supply of various commodities, etc.) actuated by the fall of a penny inserted through a slot or narrow opening; also *fig.*; also *ellipt.* as *sb.*; **penny-leaf, -leaves**, a name for navelwort or wall pennywort (*Cotyledon Umbilicus*), from its round leaves; **penny loafer, pennyloafer** *N. Amer.*, a type of casual shoe with a slot in which coins can be placed; †**penny-mail** *Sc.*, a small money payment in acknowledgement of feudal superiority; †**pennyman**, (*a*) an impersonation of money, also called Sir Penny; (*b*) see quot. 1610; †**pennymeal** *sb.* and *adv.*, by pence, a penny to each, = *penny-dole*; **penny-motion**, ? a penny puppet-show; **penny number**, (*a*) a cheap periodical; (*b*) *pl.* insignificant quantities (*colloq.*); **penny packet**, (*a*) = *penny steamer* s.v. PENNY 11; (*b*) a small number of persons or things; (*c*) (with hyphen) *attrib.*, contemptible, insignificant; **penny pawn** (see quot.); **penny-peeler**, an avaricious or niggardly person; **'penny piece**, a piece of any commodity sold for a penny; **'penny-'piece**, a piece of money of the value of a penny, a penny; **penny pies** = *penny-leaf*; **penny-pig** *Sc.*, an earthenware pot with a slot for collecting pence saved or received as gratuities; **penny-pincher**, a niggardly person; **penny-pinching** *a.* (*colloq.*), niggardly, parsimonious; also as *vbl. sb.*; hence (as a back-formation) ***penny-pinch*** vb. trans. and intr.; ***penny-pinched*** adj.; **penny plain** *a.*, plain and unpretentious; hence **penny-plainness**; †**penny-pouch**, a pocket or bag for coin; †**penny-'poundlike** *adv.*, at so much in the pound; †**penny-purse**, (*a*) a purse for pence or small coins; (*b*) *fig.* a penurious fellow, a niggard; †**penny-rife** *a.*, as rife or common as pennies, very common or prevalent; †**penny-room**, a place (*e.g.* in a theatre) to which the price of admission is a penny; **penny stock** *U.S.*, a common stock of value less than one dollar, and therefore highly speculative; †**penny-toller** (**penitollere**), ? an official who takes a toll of a penny; **penny-'trumpet**, a toy trumpet costing a penny; also *fig.* in reference to petty boasting; so **penny-'trumpeter**; **penny wedding**, a wedding at which each of the guests contributes money to the expenses of the entertainment and to the setting up of the newly-married couple; formerly customary among the poorer classes in Scotland, Wales, etc.; **penny-whip, -wheep**, *Sc.*, small beer sold at a penny a bottle; †**penny-white** *a.*, whitened or rendered fair with (silver) pennies, i.e. with wealth: said of a rich woman, esp. one who is not naturally beautiful (*obs.*). Also PENNY-A-LINE to PENNY-WEIGHT, q.v.

1362 LANGL. *P. Pl.* A. v. 134 *Peni Ale and piriwhit heo pourede to-gedere For laborers and louh folk. **1544** PHAER *Regim. Lyfe* (1560) Bij, To drynke onely pennye ale, or suche small drynke. **1855** 'Q. K. P. DOESTICKS' *Doesticks, what he Says* 259 Napoleon spends most of his time playing *penny 'ante' with the three Graces. **1935** A. J. POLLOCK *Underworld Speaks* 87/1 *Penny ante league*, small town racketeers. **1936** L. HELLMAN *Days to Come* III. 88 We always used to play penny-ante there. **1946** *Negro Digest* Aug. 48/1 Compared to the man Bilbo, 63-year-old John Rankin is strictly penny ante and colorless. **1976** M. MACHLIN *Pipe-line* v. 63 Prices were offered that made Royal American's earlier bids seem like penny ante. **1976** M. MAGUIRE *Scratchproof* ix. 140 I'm not a penny-ante hood. **1862** ANSTED *Channel Isl.* (1865) 557 A *Penny Bank, for savings of amounts too small to be received at the ordinary savings banks, was opened in Jersey on the 1st of January, 1862. *c* **1550** LLOYD *Treas. Health* B v, The Branne of Lupines or *penny beane layd on the hearye place, wyl make the heare to fall. **1885** SWAINSON *Prov. Names Brit. Birds* 216 Little Grebe..*Penny Bird (Lough Morne; Carrickfergus). [**1920** E. D. BACON *Line-Engraved Postage Stamps Gt. Brit.* I. 167 In 1864 an application was made to the Board of Inland Revenue for specimens of the One Penny black.] **1922** A. B. CREEKE in C. Nissen *Plating of Penny Black Postage Stamp* p. i, The cult of the '*Penny Black'—and no true British philatelist is so pedantic as to call the first postage stamp the 'Black Penny'!—has..spread amongst..many collectors. **1936** [see BLACK *sb.* 7 e]. **1972** *Daily Tel.* (Colour Suppl.) 12 May 62/1 These are so rare that they are referred to as the Penny Blacks of the cigarette card world. **1973** R. HILL *Ruling Passion* II. ii. 99 'What about the stamps?'.. 'No penny blacks, I'm afraid.' **1977** *Western Mail* (Cardiff) 5 Mar. (Rugby Suppl.) 7/1 Still, the days when English rugby victories were as rare as the Penny Black seem over. *c* **1375** *Sc. Leg. Saints* vi. (*Thomas*) 339 Gyfe he be nocht *penny bowne, Lat it til vs bath be commowne. **1902** FARMER & HENLEY *Slang* V. 168/1 **Penny-boy* (old), a boy who haunted the cattle markets on the chance of driving beasts to the slaughter-house. **1914** JOYCE *Dubliners* 273 He saw himself as a ludicrous figure, acting as a pennyboy for his aunts. **1390** *Nottingham Rec.* I. 244 Unum *penybreyde ad iiijd. **1411** *Ibid.* II. 84, j. penny-brede, iijd. **1624** in Cramond *Ann. Banff* (1893) II. 23 Anent the great abuses of *pennie brydells in aill houses. *a* **1829** *Sir Hugh* x. in Child *Ballads* (1889) III. 281/1 The nexten steed that he drew out, He was the *penny-brown. **1805** H. K. WHITE *Rem.* I. 154 *Penny-catching pamphlets. **1939** DYLAN THOMAS *Let.* July (1966) 233 People forced..to be so *penny-cautious. **1964** *Economist* 27 June 1481/2 The *penny-conscious President. **1713** J. PETIVER in *Phil. Trans.* XXVIII. 200 Broad-leaved yellow *Penny-Cress. *Alyssom luteum, Polygoni folio.* **1892** G. TRAVERS *Mona Maclean* (1893) I. 215, I found a plant of penny-cress in a piece of waste ground. **1581** J. BELL *Haddon's Answ. Osor.* 457 b, What shall we say of the Maunger? which is shewed at Rome in the Cathedrall Church of Mary Maior, not without *pennycrooching? **1920** D. H. LAWRENCE *Lost Girl* i. 24 Big *penny-daisies grew in tufts on the brink of the yellow clay. **1495** in *Test. Ebor.* (Surtees) IV. 26 To poore people be *penydale, iiij[l]. iij[s]. iiij[d]. **1521** *Ibid.* VI. 6, I will that my executors dispose oppon my beriall daye to poore people penny deale. **1530** in Weaver *Wells Wills* (1890) 25, xv[li] to be delte penydole. **1540** *Test. Ebor.* (Surtees) VI. 108, I will that no penny doll be delte for me. *c* **1680** [F. SEMPILL] *Banishm. Poverty* 6 in *J. Watson's Coll. Sc. Poems* (1706) I. 11 His wink to me hath been a Law, He haunts me like a *penny-dog. **1836** YARRELL *Brit. Fishes* II. 390 The Tope is a common species along the southern coast, where it is known by the names of Penny Dog and Miller's Dog. *a* **1300** *Gloucester Cart.* (Rolls) III. 134 Faciet unam aruram quæ vocatur *peni-herþe et valet tres denarios, quia recipiet de bursa domini quartum denarium. **1892** VINOGRADOFF *Villainage in Eng.* 282 When the ploughing-work is paid for, it may receive the name of *penyearth*. **1712** J. MORTON *Northampt.* i. II. 65 That here call'd **Penny-Earth*, a Stoney Earth with a great Number of Sea-shells in it. Some of those Shells being flat and roundish,..haue occasion'd it that Name of *Penny-Earth*. **1356** in *Jarrow Compoti* (Surtees) 37 Quia dimittuntur ad *penyferme per Priorem. **1781** BURNS '*My Nannie, O*' vi, My riches a's my *penny-fee. **1816** SCOTT *Old Mort.* viii, For the penny-fee and a' that I'll just leave it to the laird and you. **1857** C. BRONTE *Professor* II. xviii. 1 The others she had purchased with her own penny-fee. *a* **1682** SIR T. BROWNE *Tracts* iii. 99 The fish called..by some, a Peter or *Penny-fish: which having two remarkable round spots upon either side, these are considered to be the marks of St. Peter's fingers. **1578** LYTE *Dodoens* II. vi. 154 The Brabanders..do call it Penninckbloemen, that is to say, *Penny floure, or mony floure. **1597** GERARDE *Herbal* I. cxvii. 377 We cal this herb in English Pennie flower or money flower. *c* **1470** HENRYSON *Mor. Fab.* x. (*Fox & Wolf*) xxiii, The nicht was licht, and *penny full the mone. **1440** in Somner *Gavelkind* (1660) 26 Per redditum & servitium vocatum *Peny gavel, viz. reddendo annuatim eisdem Abbati & Coventui & eorum Successoribus de qualibet swillinga..decem & novem solidos & octo denarios. **1872** E. W. ROBERTSON *Hist. Ess.* 133 The system of penny-gavel, in accordance with which the land was measured into carucates or ploughlands, and a tenth of its estimated value paid to the overlord. **1579** in *Trans. E. Riding Yorks. Antiq. Soc.* (1901) VIII. 12 *Pennygrave [or collector of fines and tolls]. **1741** *Copy Court-Roll, Manor of Burstwick, Holderness, Yorks.*, Ralph Burnsall, deputy penny-grave to the Lord. **1942** *New Statesman* 11 July 25/1 The Jews of Poland, on the whole, I have found *penny-grubbing, cunning, and given to circumlocution. **1891** KIPLING *Light that Failed* xiv. 281 They've got one of them *penny-in-the-slot cash-machines. **1892** *Pall Mall G.* 3 Feb. 3/2 Penny-in-the-slot machine. **1895** *Westm. Gaz.* 17 Apr. 3/3 The idea occurred to a Mr. Brownhill, of Birmingham, of adapting the penny-in-the-slot system to the gas meters... The demand for these penny-in-the-slot meters has been of an extra-ordinary character. **1900** SHAW *3 Plays for Puritans* p. xxvi, That is why your penny-in-the-slot heroes, who only work when you drop a motive into them, are so oppressively automatic and uninteresting. **1922** D. H. LAWRENCE *England, my England* 255 I'll just put it aside o' the penny-in-the-slot. **1948** *Training of Doctor* (B.M.A.) xv. 74 The fault lies as frequently with the harried and harassed physician seeking a 'penny in the slot' diagnosis. **1954** L. FAIRFIELD *Epilepsy* i. 23 In spite of the brilliant contributions made by encephalographers to the study of epilepsy, it would be wholly wrong to give the impression that they can provide a 'penny in the slot' diagnosis. **1970** *Daily Tel.* 21 May 6/5 Hoisted on his brother's shoulder, he watches a striptease in a penny-in-the-slot machine at a fair. **1808** *Med. Jrnl.* XIX. 348 *Penny leaf..*Cotyledon umbilicus.* **1886** BRITTEN & HOLLAND *Eng. Plant-n.*, Penny Leaves,..from its round, flat leaves. **1970** *Globe Mag.* (Toronto) 26 Sept. 5/3 Chicks ..who aren't really hippie, wear really good jeans... Some have *penny loafers. **1973** *Maclean's Mag.* (Toronto) Feb. 28/1 They're classic: he's wearing checkered pants and brogues, she's got a skirt and pennyloafers. **1976** T. GIFFORD *Cavanaugh Quest* (1977) i. 15 Two highly polished penny loafers with virgin tan soles. **1491** *Act. Audit.* (1839) 146/2 þe said James allegiis þat he has þe said landis in tak for *penny male alanerly. *a* **1586** in Pinkerton *Anc. Scot. Poems* (1786) 321 Sum with deir ferme ar hirreit haill, That wount to pay bot penny maill. *c* **1440** *Castle Persev.* 2767 *Penyman is mekyl in mynde: my loue in hym I leye & laue. *Ibid.* 2779 Nyth & day, mydnyth & morn, in Penyman is al his trust. **1610** in *Calr. Doncaster Borough Rec.* (1902) IV. 18 That no butcher dwelling within this towne commonly called a penny-man shall take for wages of any other butcher for killing of meat above 2*d.* for every beast. **1480** CAXTON *Contn. Trevisa's Higden* (Rolls) VIII. 556 Enleven schyllynges eyght pens, to be delyd *penymele. **1542–5** BRINKLOW *Lament.* 8 Vnholpen..except it be on the Sondayes..by peany meale. **1601** SIR W. CORNWALLIS *Ess.* xii, Like the *penny motions able to stirre, and stare, and downe againe. **1901** G. B. SHAW *Capt. Brassbound's Conversion* III. 297 He got his romantic nonsense out of his *penny numbers. **1958** *Listener* 5 June 937/1 Pupils arrive from the depot in penny numbers. **1972** *Shooting Times & Country Mag.* 27 May 12/1 The beats of Spey near Grantown were either returning penny numbers of fish or blanks for hard fishing. *c* **1846** J. R. PLANCHÉ *Invisible Prince* I. ii. 14 Fierce whiskered gents, as ever in pea jackets, Smoked bad cigars, on board the *penny packets. **1943** HUNT & PRINGLE *Service Slang* 51 *Penny packets*, small parties of soldiers, less than a platoon, as seen from the air. **1961** *Daily Tel.* 21 Apr. 17 Lord Bridges, chairman of the Royal Fine Art Commission, yesterday condemned piecemeal, penny-packet planning of new towns and replanning of older ones. **1979** G. C. PEDEN *Brit. Rearmament* 119 The Treasury principle of locating the Air Force centrally instead of in penny packets around the Empire was observed. **1907** *Westm. Gaz.* 16 Dec. 10/1 What are known as '*penny pawns' abound in the district. A broker who keeps one of these can purchase an article of any value from a penny upwards. He is compelled to keep it for seven full days. **1925** J. GREGORY *Bab of Backwoods* xxi. 269 Willoughby, skinflint, *penny-peeler and nickel grabber that he was, smelled a deal and asked them five thousand dollars for ten acres! **1920** D. H. LAWRENCE *Lost Girl* vi. 99 This grubby *penny-picking England. **1601** STOW *Ann.* 957 The butchers of London sold *penny pieces of beefe for the reliefe of the poore, euery piece two pounde and a halfe. **1797** *Lond. Gaz.* No. 14031/2 Such Penny Pieces [shall be received] as of the Value of One Penny. **1899** CROCKETT *Ione March* xiv, 'Don't you give in, or take a penny-piece from one of them!' she said. **1938** M. K. RAWLINGS *Yearling* ii. 17 Why, you leetle ol' penny piece, you. You're good money, a'right, but hit jest don't come no smaller. Leetle ol' Penny Baxter. **1963** *Times* 25 Apr. 17/1 Coyle, he maintained, did not receive 'a penny piece' in the transactions and his only motive in disposing of the bicycles was to please his immediate superiors. **1975** E. PAGE *Element of Chance* vi. 66 In another three years..you can divorce her without her consent... I very much doubt that..you'd have to pay her a penny piece. **1866** *Treas. Bot.* 341 Its orbicular concave peltate exceedingly succulent leaves, called by children *Penny-pies. **1673** *Wedderburn's Vocab.* 13 (Jam.) *Capsella fictilis*, a *penny pig. **1827** SCOTT *Jrnl.* 24 Feb., Your penny-pig collections don't succeed. **1961** J. YAFFE in *Webster* s.v. **penny-pinch*, A sinister but fascinating kind of joy in.. penny-pinching his own family. **1961** S. N. BEHRMAN in *Ibid.*, Penny-pinched himself out of..millions of dollars. **1977** P. G. WINSLOW *Witch Hill Murder* II. v. 92 He penny-pinched on the candles..so the servants had to spend their few hours off in practically pitch darkness. **1979** *Jrnl. R. Soc. Arts* CXXVII. 126/1 The dismally penny-pinched equipment compared with foreign institutions. **1934** WEBSTER, **Penny pincher*, a niggardly or parsimonious person. **1956** F. CASTLE *Violent Hours* (1966) xviii. 174 If Forhaan had really been a penny-pincher, he would never have offered so quickly to pay for Hazel's care. **1967** *Guardian* 22 Feb. 4/7 A sparkling dialectic arose between the risk takers on the boards and the penny pinchers. **1973** 'D. SHANNON' *Spring of Violence* (1974) ix. 150 Typical of the penny-pincher miser. **1905** *Penny-pinching [listed in N.E.D.]. **1920** S. LEWIS *Main St.* xi. 144 The penny-pinching old land-thief. **1951** *Ann. Reg. 1950* 192 Mr Johnson had come under heavy fire as the man whose 'penny-pinching' with military expenditures had paved the way for the reverses in Korea. **1953** C. S. FORESTER *Hornblower & Atropos* xiii. 190 The penny-pinching clerks of a penurious government at home would scrutinize those expenditures in time. **1960** *Guardian* 20 July 6/6 Penny-pinching on new roads is inexcusable. **1971** *Ibid.* 7 Aug. 10/1 Mr Rowley's decision is both penny-pinching and short-sighted. **1973** E. BERCKMAN *Victorian Album* 34 The better-off the woman was, the more apt she'd be to play those penny-pinching tricks. **1977** *Time* 30 May 24/2 Under increasing criticism—from liberals, who regard him as too much of a pennypinching conservative,..Carter took to the hustings again by making a whirlwind, campaign-style tour of California. **1859** G. A. SALA *Twice round Clock* 253 The Scala..with its rabbit-hutch-like private boxes, whose doors are scrawled over with the *penny plain and twopence coloured-like coats of arms of the..Lombardian nobility. **1884** R. L. STEVENSON in *Mag. of Art* Apr. 227 (*title*) A penny plain and twopence coloured. **1920** 'O. DOUGLAS' *Penny Plain* vi. 60 Having been all her life so very 'twopence coloured' she wants the 'penny plain' for a change. **1974** 'S. WOODS' *Done to Death* 71 A track led to a penny-plain stone cottage. **1920** 'O. DOUGLAS' *Penny Plain* vi. 60 There is no mistake about our '*penny-plainness'—it jumps to the eye! **1643** TRAPP *Comm. Gen.* xli. 35 Neither was this a *penny-pouch, but a bag so big, as needed a bearer. *c* **1650** in Keble *Bp. Wilson* vi. (1863) 197 [The Lord's debt is first to be paid; secondly, orphans' goods; and afterwards the claimer's] *penny-pound like. **1473** *Paston Lett.* III. 83 Raff Blaundrehasset wer a name to styrte an hare..; ware that **jd.* perse. *c* **1645** HOWELL *Lett.* VI. xvii. (1650) 204 His heart was shrivelled like a Leather peny-purse when he was dissected. **1606** BIRNIE *Kirk-Buriall* (1833) 16 This superstition is..becomme most *penny-rife Papistry. *a* **1619** FLETCHER *Wit without M.* IV. v, Till you break in at plays like prentices,..and crack nuts with the scholars In *penny rooms. **1932** C. M. ALSAGER *Dict. Business Terms* 261 **Penny stocks*, a term applied to stocks that sell below one dollar per share and that are usually quoted in cents, not in fractions of a dollar, on an exchange or over the counter. **1935** *Sun* (Baltimore) 25 Oct. 22/1 More often than not..an increased turnover in what Wall Street calls the 'penny stocks' has been a sign that the market is heading toward a reaction. **1942** *Richmond* (Virginia) *Times-Dispatch* 29 Dec. 18/1 Turnover of 1,201,522 shares, propped by belated tax offerings in sizable blocks of 'penny' stocks, was the second largest of the year to date. **1967** *Economist* 28 Oct. 419/1 This is a peculiarly American worry...nowhere else are there so many thousands of 'penny' stocks ripe for speculation. **14..** *Voc.* in Wr.-Wülcker 598/13 *Numarius*,.. a *penitollere. **1783** Wolcott (P. Pindar) *Odes Roy. Acad.* vi, Sound their own praise from their own *penny trumpet. **1827** *Hansard's Parl. Deb.* XVI. 1249 Drums, and the abomination of penny trumpets were in request among the younger inhabitants. **1828** *Blackw. Mag.* XXIII. 367 Having acted as his own *penny-trumpeter. *c* **1730** Burt *Lett. N. Scotl.* xi. (1754) I. 261 They have a *Penny-Wedding: that is, when a Servant-Maid has served faithfully, and gained the good will of her master and mistress, they invite their Relations and Friends, and there is a Dinner or Supper on the Day the Servant is married... In the End every Body puts Money into a Dish..for the new Couple. *a* **1845** Hood *Kilmansegg, Honeymoon* vi, Love.. will fly away from an Emperor's match To dance at a Penny Wedding! **1785** Burns *Holy Fair* xix, Be 't whisky gill, or *penny wheep, Or ony stronger potion. **1821** *Blackw. Mag.* Dec. 671 (Jam.) To get desirably tipsy upon penny-whip for twopence. **1622** Mabbe tr. *Aleman's Guzman d'Alf.* II. 95 [Her] estate was now such..that..she was *penny-white (as we say), and so was married in the end. *a* **1700** B. E. *Dict. Cant. Crew, Penny-white*, said of her, to whom Fortune has been kinder than Nature.

'penny-a-'line, *a.* [The phrase (*a*) *penny a line* used attrib.] Of writing or a writer: Paid at the rate of a penny a line; of cheap and superficial literary quality. (Cf. PENNY-A-LINER.)

1833 *Westm. Rev.* XVIII. 199 The penny-a-line men are generally persons who are by no means qualified to report common proceedings. **1849** Thackeray *Lett.* Feb., [It] will afford matter to no end of penny-a-line speculation. **1930** *Argosy* Apr. 15/2 It's my last bit of freedom before I sink into eternal penny-a-line slavedom.

So **'penny-a-'line** *v. trans.* and *intr.*, to write at a penny a line; to review in the style of a penny-a-liner (see PENNY-A-LINER); **'penny-a-'lining** *vbl. sb.*, the practice or work of a penny-a-liner; *ppl. a.*, writing, or written, at a penny a line, or in the style of a penny-a-liner.

1849 Thackeray *Pendennis* lxxii, Dr. Johnson has been down the street many a time with ragged shoes, and a bundle of penny-a-lining for the *Gent's Magazine*. **1850** *Punch* 28 Sept. 140/1 (*heading*) Penny-a-lining under difficulties. **1851** Mrs. Gaskell *Lett.* (1966) 172, I swore I would penny-a-line and have nothing to do with publishers never no more. **1852** Mrs. Carlyle *Lett.* I. 172, I must positively interrupt this penny-a-lining, and go to bed. **1874** Geo. Eliot *Let.* 2 Nov. (1956) VI. 87 A penny-a-lining literary affair. **1878** Stubbs *Lect. Study Hist.* (1886) 129 The very penny-a-lining letters of inferior men. **1897** Hare *Story of my Life* (1900) VI. xxx. 467 Reviews, whose writers can scarcely even glance at the books they are penny-a-lining. *a* **1941** V. Woolf *Captain's Death Bed* (1950) 10 Penny-a-lining came into fashion. **1946** 'G. Orwell' *Crit. Ess.* 169 In France, all kinds of petty rats—police officials, penny-a-lining journalists, women who have slept with German soldiers—are hunted down.

,penny-a-'lineism. [f. PENNY-A-LINE *a.* + -ISM.] The practice of writing in the inflated style of a penny-a-liner; an instance of such writing.

1854 *Punch* 25 Nov. 208/2 That renowned traveller and Protestant champion [*sc.* the Editor of the *Morning Advertiser*] has accepted the appointment of Regius Professor of Penny-a-lineism. **1890** W. James *Princ. Psychol.* I. ix. 263 The whole genus of penny-a-line-isms and newspaper-reporter's flourishes give illustrations of this.

,penny-a-liner. [f. as PENNY-A-LINE *a.* + -ER[1].] A writer for a newspaper or journal who is paid at a penny a line, or at a low rate (usually implying one who manufactures 'paragraphs', or writes in an inflated style so as to cover as much space as possible); a poor or inferior writer for hire; a hack-writer for the press. (*contemptuous.*)

1834 H. Ainsworth *Rookwood* III. v, Penny-a-liners and fashionable novelists; so many damned dramatists, and damning critics. **1840** Thackeray *Paris Sk.-bk.* Wks. 1900 V. 44 This country is surely the paradise of painters and penny-a-liners. **1871** [see CENTURY 3 b]. **1889** E. Sampson *Tales of Fancy* 22 These effusions were usually written by 'Old Willey', printer, penny-a-liner, and pugilistic scribe. **1930** E. Weekley *Saxo Grammaticus* 12 That type of journalist who used to be rudely called a penny-a-liner. **1947** W. S. Maugham *Creatures of Circumstance* 9 He wouldn't have liked it if some damned penny-a-liner had made fun of Evie's effort in one of the papers.

Hence (*nonce-wd.*) **,penny-a-'linerism**, an expression in the style of a penny-a-liner.

1870 Jacox *Rec. of Recluse* II. iii. 52 A story..originally due to the fancy of a penny-a-liner. **1872** *Punch* 5 Oct. 143/2 The note of preparation, to use a penny-a-linerism, is now sounding for the winter theatrical campaign.

'penny-a-'week, *a.* [The phrase (*a*) *penny a week* used attrib.] That collects, receives, or subscribes a penny a week.

1895 G. B. Shaw *Let.* 15 Dec. (1965) I. 576 Penny-a-week men enrolled on the spur of the moment. **1914** Joyce *Dubliners* 206 Many a good man went to the penny-a-week school. **1943** *Times* (Weekly ed.) 19 May 3 The Red Cross and St. John Fund has exceeded £20,000,000... More than one fourth has been contributed through the penny-a-week committee. **1972** *Evening Telegram* (St. John's, Newfoundland) 5 Aug. 6/5 A school in the upstairs flat, the famed 'Penny-a-week' school.

penny farthing, *a.* and *sb.* **A.** *adj.* Ineffective; insignificant.

1887 Kipling *Plain Tales from Hills* (1888) 78 It was pleasant to watch her unhappiness, and the penny-farthing attempts she made to hide it. **1967** S. Beckett *Eh Joe* 17 You know that penny farthing hell you call your mind. *a* **1974** R. Crossman *Diaries* (1976) II. 60 Harold Wilson's penny-farthing report on the scandals of Party organization had come out long before the 1959 election. **1977** J. Wainwright *Day of Peppercorn Kill* 68, I..kicked hell out of every penny-farthing crook I could lay my hands on.

B. *sb.* An early form of bicycle having a large front wheel and a small rear one. Also *attrib.*

This kind of bicycle was introduced in the 1860s and was known by various names, including *ordinary* (see ORDINARY *sb.* 17 b), *bone-shaker* (see BONE *sb.* 17) for the wooden-wheeled machine, and BICYCLE for the wire-spoke machine. The name *penny farthing* does not seem to have been used until the 1920s, by which time this type of bicycle was obsolete.

1927 Ld. Birkenhead in *Sunday Express* 6 Nov. 11/6, I once rode more or less continuously on a high bicycle (called a 'penny farthing') from my native town of Birkenhead to Edinburgh. **1932** G. M. Boumphrey *Story of Wheel* xxiv. 89 These improvements had turned the bone-shaker into what was sometimes called the 'penny-farthing'. **1963** *Times* 20 May 11/1 To do without it would be like giving up our helicopters and going back to penny-farthings. **1976** *Country Life* 27 May 1385/1 Nostalgia for a world..of Norfolk jackets, muttonchop whiskers, penny-farthing bicycles.

† **'penny-,father.** *Obs.* [f. PENNY + FATHER.] A man who is too careful of his pence; an old miser, a niggard, skinflint, penurious fellow.

1549 Chaloner *Erasmus on Folly* K iij, That pennie-father skrapeth it togethers bothe by God and by the divell. **1551** Robinson tr. *More's Utopia* II. (1895) 183 Knowing them to be suche nigeshe penny fathers, that they be sure.. not the worthe of one farthinge of that heape of gold shall come to them. **1594** Drayton *Idea* 128 The Sonne of some rich Penny-father, Who..Leaves to his Sonne all he had heap'd together. **1694** Motteux *Rabelais, Pantagr. Prognost.* v. 234 Pinch-crusts, Hold-fasts, Michers, and Penny-fathers.

'penny-grass. [f. PENNY + GRASS.] Popular name of three different plants: **a.** Navelwort or Wall Pennywort, *Cotyledon Umbilicus*; **b.** Marsh Pennywort, *Hydrocotyle vulgaris* (in both cases from the round leaves); **c.** Yellow-rattle, *Rhinanthus Crista-galli* (from the flat roundish pods).

a **1387** *Sinon. Barthol.* (Anecd. Oxon.) 43 *Umbilicus veneris*,..penigresse. *c* **1450** *Alphita* (Anecd. Oxon.) 44 *Cotilidon* siue *simbalion*, umbilicus ueneris idem..penygres. **1523** Fitzherb. *Husb.* §54 Peny grasse..groweth lowe by the erthe in a marsshe grounde, and hath a leafe as brode as a peny of two pens, and neuer beareth floure. **1613** Markham *Eng. Husbandman* II. II. vii. (1635) 84 If..the Penigrasse be hard, dry, and withered, then..your Meddow is ripe. **1757** Dyer *Fleece* I. 690 Nor taintworm shall infect the yeaning herds, Nor pennygrass, nor spearwort's pois'nous leaf. **1886** Britten & Holland *Eng. Plant.-n.* App., Grass, Penny..(3) *Cotyledon Umbilicus.—Irel.*

'pennyland. *Obs.* exc. *dial.* Also 3 penilond. [f. PENNY + LAND; app. the vernacular form of med.L. *denariata* (*denarata, denerata*) *terræ* (see DENARIATE), and possibly also of *nummata terræ*, the rent of which was (sometimes at least) a penny.

Cf. 'duodecim tamen nummatas..singulos annos reddentes ei 12 denarios' (Madox *Exch.* I. 155).]

A portion or measure of land valued at a penny a year; a DENARIATE.

Its extent may have varied in different localities; one quotation in Du Cange refers to a tenement of half a rood and three denariates, whence it appears that there were more than three pennylands in half a rood. If there were four, the pennyland would be $\frac{1}{32}$ of an acre, or 5 sq. poles, enough for a house and small yard. In some parts of France the *denrée* (= *denariata*) is still a measure of 4·73 perches (Godef.). But the pennylands of Orkney and Shetland may have been of greater extent.

a **1300** *Gloucester Cart.* (Rolls) III. 134 Tenentes..Penilond ad vitam et ad voluntatem domini. **1774** G. Gifford in Low *Orkney* (1879) 145 The term Pennyland in Orkney signifies simply quantity..in Schetland it likewise marks the quality, and according to the value of the land every Mark contains more or fewer Pennies. **1822** Peterkin *Notes Orkney & Zetl.* 6 (E.D.D.) None of these pennylands, or other terms, indicate any definite extend of ground; and they are of different extent in different towns. But all the pennylands, marks or cowsworths in the same town are of equal extent. **1875** W. McIlwraith *Guide Wigtownshire* 39 The penny-land of the smith. **1898** *Shetland News* 30 Apr. (E.D.D.), Shetland, as part of the earldom of Orkney, must have been originally divided into ounce and pennylands.

penny post, penny-post. [See POST *sb.*] An organization for the conveyance of letters or packets at an ordinary charge of a penny each; *esp.* (in early use) that established *c* 1680 for London and its environs within a radius of 10 miles, and (in later use) that introduced on 10 Jan. 1840 (on the initiative of Rowland Hill) for the United Kingdom, and extended to nearly all British colonies and possessions in and after 1898.

1680 J. Stokes *Let. fr. London* 3 July in *Rhode Isl. Hist. Soc. Coll.* (1902) X, My note came..by the peny post, that is a post office, which for a peny wee cann have a letter carried to any part of the citty. **1682** Luttrell *Brief Rel.* (1857) I. 244 Mr. Do[ck]wray and partners, the inventers of the penny post here in London, are putt down..but..the duke hath thought fitt to sett it up again, and 'tis manadged by the cheif postmaster of the generall post office. **1685** P. Henry *Diaries & Lett.* (1882) 347 Write a line or two now and then by the Peny-post. **1706** Phillips, *Penny-Post*, a Post-Office that conveys Letters and Packets under a Pound-weight, paying one Penny for each to all Parts of the City of London, and ten Miles round about. **1712** Addison *Spect.* No. 457 ¶1 Proposals for a printed News-paper, that should take in the whole Circle of the Penny-post. **1794** *Gentl. Mag.* LXIV. II. 666 The extension of the penny-post hither [to Enfield] took place [on June 23]. **1825** Scott *Jrnl.* 28 Dec., A sly rogue..requested of me, through the penny-post, the loan of £50. **1840** *Penny Cycl.* XVIII. 455 Between 1814 and 1839..The Postmaster-general had authority to establish penny posts for letters not exceeding in weight four ounces, in, from, or to, any city, town, or place in the United Kingdom... There is a penny post for Dublin, the limits of which the Postmaster-general has authority to alter. **1858** R. S. Surtees *Ask Mamma* lxxviii. 342 The penny post was one of the few things that came without being long called for. **1904** *Daily Chron.* 9 Jan. 5/1 To-morrow is the sixty-fourth birthday of the Penny Post, inaugurated January 10, 1840.

b. *attrib.*, as ***penny-post letter, penny-postman, penny-post office.***

1686 *Lond. Gaz.* No. 2188/4 The General Penny-Post Office is removed from Crosby-House..to Star-Court..in Cornhill. **1688** Ashmole *Let.* in *Mem.* (1717) 97 Which the Civility of a Penny-Post Letter would have cleared and prevented. **1690** Luttrell *Brief Rel.* (1857) II. 118 His majestie hath granted Mr. Dockwra £500 per ann. out of the penny post office, in consideration of his being the first projector thereof. **1702** *Eng. Theophrast.* 358 [Busy bodies] have their stages about the town as regular as a penny postman. **1768–74** Tucker *Lt. Nat.* (1834) I. 101 The penny-postman finds no perplexity in his walks to any part of it [London]. **1864** Tennyson *Let. to W. C. Bennett* 22 Oct., Believe me, tho penny-post maddened, yours ever, A. Tennyson.

So **'penny-'postage**, the postage of letters, etc. at a charge of a penny each.

184. *Ocean Postage Envelope* Inscr., Britain! from thee the World expects an Ocean Penny Postage. **1863** *Chambers' Bk. Days* I. 89/2 A memorable day..on which the idea of a Penny Postage was first exemplified. **1890** *Pall Mall G.* 9 Jan. 7/1 The Jubilee of the Penny Post. Fifty years ago to-morrow, by virtue of a warrant published in the *London Gazette* on the 28th December, 1839, was inaugurated our system of penny postage.

† **'penny-prick.** *Obs.* An old game of which the nature is uncertain.

It appears to have consisted in aiming at a penny, perhaps placed originally as the PRICK or mark for shooting at; see also quots. *c* 1770, 1829.

1421 *Maldon, Essex, Court-Rolls* (Bundle 12, No. 8) Cum hominibus utentibus ludos illegitimos, viz. alias scaccarulos et penypryke ad gravitatem proximorum suorum. **1447** *Shillingford Lett.* (Camden) 101 Yong peple..within the saide Cloistre have exercised unlawfull games as the toppe, queke, penny prykke and most atte tenys, by the which the walles of the saide Cloistre have be defowled and the glas wyndowes all to brost. **1552** *Nottingham Rec.* IV. 102 Dyce, slyde grote, penypricke, caylles, tennes. **1610** T. Scott *Philomythie*, etc. (1616) Mjb, Their idle houres..They spend at shoue-boord, or at penny pricke, At dice, cards, tennis. [*c* **1770** in *Grose's Provinc. Gloss.* MS. Add. (P.) (E.D.D.) *Penny-prick*, a sport, throwing at halfpence placed upon sticks which are called Hobs. **1801** Strutt *Sports & Past.* IV. iv. 353. **1829** J. Hunter *Hallams. Gloss., Penny-prick*, a game consisting of casting oblong pieces of iron at a mark.]

Hence † **'penny-pricker** *Obs.*, one who played at penny-prick.

c **1515** *Cocke Lorell's B.* 11 Tyburne collopes, and peny pryckers; Bowlers, mas shoters, and quayters.

'penny-,rent. ? *Obs.* [See RENT.] Rent paid (or received) in money; annual (or periodical) payment in cash; income in money, revenue. **b.** A quit-rent of a penny.

1512 *Will of Westburn* (Somerset Ho.), In Penny-rent. **1611** Cotgr., *Denier de seruice*, Pennie rent: a quit or chiefe rent: or, the reseruation of a single pennie in lieu of all other rents and seruices (homage excepted). *a* **1619** Fletcher *Wit without M.* III. i, What jointure can he make you? Plutarch's Morals? Or so much penny-rent in the small poets? **1655** Fuller *Ch. Hist.* VI. v. 344 The Pensions were but bare Penny-Rent, whilst Abbey-Lands were lowly rated farre beneath their true valuation. **1673** Wycherley *Gentleman Dancing-M.* III. i, Though he..has two thousand five hundred seventy-three pounds sterling, twelve shillings and twopence a year penny-rent. **1729** *Season. Rem. Trade* 24 This drains from thence the Penny-rents of most of the great Estates of that Kingdom [Ireland]. **1754** Richardson *Grandison* 31 Mar.–1 Apr., He proposes a jointure of £1200 a year penny-rents, and 400 guineas a year for her [Miss Mansfield's] private purse.

'penny-,rot. [See ROT *sb.*] A name for Marsh Pennywort, from its round leaves, and supposed property of causing rot in sheep.

1597 Gerarde *Herbal* II. cxliii. 424 *Cotyledon palustris*: in English Sheepes killing Pennygrasse, Penny rot, and in the north countrie White rot.

pennyroyal (pɛnɪˈrɔɪəl). Forms: **penny** (in its var. forms) with *α.* 6–7 **ryal(l, rial(l**, etc. (rarely two words or hyphened; 10 varr.), *β.* 6–8 **royal(l**, etc. (as one word, two words, or hyphened; 13

varr.); 7- **pennyroyal**. [app. an alteration (? corruption) of the earlier *pulyole ryale*, in AF. *puliol real* = OF. *poliol, pouliol, poulieul* thyme (:—L. type **pulegiōl-um*, dim. of L. *pulegium* thyme) + *réal, royal* royal. Intervening stages between *poliol* and *pen(n)y* have not been found; mod. Walloon dialects have *poli, pouli*; mod.F. *pouliot*.]

1. A species of mint (*Mentha Pulegium*), with small leaves and prostrate habit; formerly much cultivated and esteemed for its supposed medicinal virtues.

α. **1530** PALSGR. 253/1 Penneryall an herbe, *poulliot*. **1538** TURNER *Libellus*, Origanum..est herba quam uulgus appellat Penyryall. *c* **1550** LLOYD *Treas. Health* Q iv, Leaves of Rue, Tyme, Organe, Pennyrial. **1573** TUSSER *Husb.* (1878) 94 Peneriall. **1657** C. BECK *Univ. Char.* I vij b, Penirial herb.

β. **1533** ELYOT *Cast. Helthe* (1541) 58 b, Maioram, Peny-royall. **1597** GERARDE *Herbal* II. ccxxi. 671 Our common Pennie Royall. **1607** TOPSELL *Four-f. Beasts* (1658) 197 One ounce of Thyme, one ounce of Penny-royal. **1671** SALMON *Syn. Med.* III. xxii. 422 Penyroyal..good against cold and affections of the Nerves and Joynts. **1736** BAILEY *Househ. Dict.* 459 Penny royal is..of a sharp bitter taste. **1853** SOYER *Pantroph.* 73 They may be seasoned with pepper, pennyroyal, honey, or sun-made wine.

2. Applied, usually with qualifying words, to other aromatic labiates, or other plants.

†**a.** ***wood pennyroyal***: a name proposed by Turner for the Wood Speedwell, *Veronica officinalis*. *Obs.* †**b.** ***wild pennyroyal***: Basil Thyme, *Calamintha Acinos*. *Obs.* **c.** In North America, applied to the fragrant labiate *Hedeoma pulegioides* (or other species). **d.** ***bastard*** or ***false pennyroyal***: names for two N. American labiates, *Trichostemma dichotomum* and *Isanthus cœruleus*. **e.** = *Pennyroyal-tree*: see 3.

1538 ELYOT *Dict.*, *Tragoriganon*, an herbe whiche I suppose, is callyd Peny royalle growyng wylde. **1548** TURNER *Names of Herbes* 19 It maye be called in englishe Paules Betony or wodde Peny ryal. **1552** HULOET, Peny royall, or puliel royall wyld, *calamintha, tragoriganon*. **1578** LYTE *Dodoens* II. lxxv. 247 There be three sortes of Calamynt... The second kinde which is called wild Penny-ryall, hath also square stalkes couered with softe Cotton, and almost creeping by the ground. **1760** J. LEE *Introd. Bot.* App. 322 Virginian Penny-royal, *Satureia*. **1857** HENFREY *Bot.* 350 *Hedeoma pulegioides* is the Penny-royal of the United States. **1858** LONGF. *M. Standish* VIII, Over the pastures..made fragrant by sweet penny-royal.

3. *attrib.* **pennyroyal-tree**, *Satureia viminea* (*Treas. Bot.*, 1866); **pennyroyal-water**, a liquor distilled from the leaves of pennyroyal, formerly used in medicine.

1761 MRS. DELANY in *Life & Corr.* (1861) III. 629 [She] took a cup with pennyroyal water in her own hand. **1855** DELAMER *Kitch. Gard.* (1861) 134 Pennyroyal water was formerly much distilled as an antidote to spasmodic, nervous, and hysterical affections.

pennys, obs. pl. of PEN, PENNY.

ˈpenny-stone. [f. PENNY + STONE.]

1. *Sc.* and *north.* A flat round stone used as a quoit; also, the game played with these.

1375 [see b]. **1483** *Cath. Angl.* 274/2 A Penystane, *discus*. **1519** *Priory of Hexham* (Surtees) II. 157 Ludi inhonesti.. viz. tuttes, et handball ac Pennyston. **1771** PENNANT *Tour Scot. in 1769*, 167 Antient sports of the Highlanders.. Throwing the penny-stone, which answers to our coits. **1807** J. STAGG *Poems* (Cumbld. Dial.) 12 Some play'd at pennice steans for brass. **1895** 'SARAH TYTLER' *Macdonald Lass* xiv. 186 Do you mind yon game of penny-stanes?

b. *attrib.* in ***penny-stone cast***, the distance to which such a stone is or can be thrown.

1375 BARBOUR *Bruce* XVI. 383 The vay Wes nocht a penny-stane cast of breid. **1752** D. KENNEDY in *Scots Mag.* (1753) July 336/2 Being..about two pennystone-cast before the said Mungo. **1886** STEVENSON *Kidnapped* 52 That's but a penny stonecast from Rankeillor's house.

2. A kind of ironstone, occurring in nodules, found in the Coalbrookdale coalfield, in Shropshire.

1803 J. PLYMLEY *Agric. Shropsh.* 54 Penny-measure; a pale-blue clod, in which lies a large quantity of small balls of ironstone, called pennystone. **1868** PARTON *Notes on Shropsh. Coal-field* in *Shropsh. Word-bk.* s.v., The Penny Stone is the most remarkable and productive iron-stone in Shropshire. It is composed of a series of nodules.

pennystone, obs. form of PENISTONE.

pennyweight (ˈpɛnɪweɪt). [f. PENNY + WEIGHT *sb.*] A measure of weight, equal to 24 grains, $\frac{1}{20}$ of an ounce Troy, or $\frac{1}{240}$ of a pound Troy. (Formerly = $\frac{1}{240}$ of a Tower pound, i.e. $22\frac{1}{2}$ grains, which was the actual weight of a silver penny.) Abbreviated *dwt.*

[*c* **1000** *Sax. Leechd.* I. 248 ȝenim of þam lichoman þysse ylcan wyrte mandragore, þreora peneȝa ȝewihte.] **1398** TREVISA *Barth. De P.R.* XVII. lxxi. (Bodl. MS.) A peny weiȝt of þe rote þerof [*sc.* of ferula] idronke in twei ciates of wyne. *c* **1400** *Lanfranc's Cirurg.* 62 Make of hem smale ballys þat weyȝen j. penye wyȝt. **1590** RECORDE, etc. *Gr. Artes* (1640) 133 As 24 Barley-corns dry, and taken out of the middest of the Ear, do make a penny weight, 20 of those penny weights make an ounce. **1621** BURTON *Anat. Mel.* II. iv. II. i. (1651) 377 To give Hellebor in powder to iid weight. **1789** W. MERREY *Coinage Eng.* 8 The silver penny was about twenty-two grains and a half of Troy-weight, but called a pennyweight Tower. **1877** BLACKMORE *Erema* li, In that letter the Major mingled a pennyweight of condolence with more congratulation than the post could carry for the largest stamp yet invented.

b. A proportional measure of one-twelfth used in stating the fineness of silver; see quots., and cf. CARAT 3.

1758 REID tr. *Macquer's Chym.* I. 74 Silver..is supposed to be divided into twelve parts only, which are called penny-weights: so that when absolutely pure it is said to be twelve penny-weights fine; when it contains $\frac{1}{12}$ of alloy, it is then called eleven penny-weights fine. **1825** J. NICHOLSON *Operat. Mechanic* 763 If the mass of silver be pure, it is called silver of 12 penny-weights.

ˈpennyweighter. *U.S. criminal slang.* Also **penny weighter**, **penny-weighter**. [f. PENNYWEIGHT + -ER[1].] One who steals jewellery or precious stones or metals.

1899 'J. FLYNT' *Tramping with Tramps* IV. 396 *Penny-weighters*, jewelry thieves. **1905** *Daily News* 26 July 9 In the American description of her she was said to be a 'penny weighter'... That is, one who goes into a jeweller's shop, inspects jewellery, and by means of some sticky substance on the fingers, manages to palm an article, and deposits it beneath the counter for a confederate to pick up. **1916** [see HEEL *sb.*[3]]. **1935** *Amer. Speech* X. 19/1 *Pennyweighter*, one who steals gold or silver plate. Still survives in mining camps to designate one who steals very small quantities of gold, as opposed to a high-grader who appropriates any big nuggets which he sees in the sluice boxes. Present usage restricts it to a jewel thief, or a jeweler who substitutes paste gems for genuine ones. **1950** H. E. GOLDIN *Dict. Amer. Underworld Lingo* 155/1 *Penny-weighter*, a thief who specializes in stealing uncut and unset diamonds.

So **ˈpenny-weighting** *vbl. sb.*

1903 H. HAPGOOD *Autobiogr. Thief* iii. 56 Penny-weighting is very 'slick' graft... A man..enters a jewelry store and looks at some diamond rings... Then he goes to a fauny shop (imitation jewelry) and buys a few diamonds which match the real ones he has noted. Then he and his pal, usually a woman, enter the jewelry store and..one of them ..substitutes the bogus diamonds for the good ones. **1924** G. S. DOUGHERTY *Criminal as Human Being* iii. 89 Such a performance is sometimes staged in 'penny-weighting', but ..only a single article can be taken by substitution.

pennywinkle, dial. var. PERIWINKLE[2].

ˈpenny-ˈwise, *adj. phr.* or *a.* [cf. PENNY 5.] Wise or prudent in regard to pence, *i.e.* careful (*esp.* over-careful) in small expenditures; usually in phr. ***penny-wise and pound-foolish***, thrifty in small matters while careless or wasteful in large ones.

1607 TOPSELL *Four-f. Beasts* 609 If by covetousnesse or negligence, one withdraw from them their ordinary foode, he shall be penny wise, and pound foolish: that is, suffer a great losse in his cattel, for saving from them a little meat. **1607–12** BACON *Ess.*, *Riches* (Arb.) 238 Be not penny-wise; Riches have winges, and sometymes they fly away of themselves. **1712** ADDISON *Spect.* No. 295 ¶6, I think a Woman who will give up her self to a Man in Marriage, where there is the least Room for such an Apprehension,.. may very properly be accused..of being Penny Wise and Pound foolish. **1842** THACKERAY *Miss Löwe* Wks. 1886 XXIII. 272 What a miserable penny-wise economist you have been!

Hence **penny-wisdom**, the quality of being 'penny-wise'; **penny-ˌwise-pound-ˈfoolishness**.

1829 BENTHAM *Justice & Cod. Petit.* 116 That humanity which has penny wisdom for its counsellor. **1850** *Athenæum* 23 Feb. 212/2 This seems to us the very quintessence of penny wisdom and pound folly in management. **1860** SALA *Lady Chesterf.* v. 8 Penny-wisdom, and pound-foolishness are now as prevalent as ever. **1895** *Westm. Gaz.* 3 Dec. 2/2 It is folly..to cripple and maim our own people by the penny-wise-pound-foolishness of 'twopenny-halfpenny' education.

pennywort (ˈpɛnɪwɜːt). [f. PENNY + WORT.] Name for several plants with rounded leaves.

1. (Distinctively ***wall pennywort***.) *Cotyledon Umbilicus* (N.O. *Crassulaceæ*), a common plant in the west of England and in Wales, having peltate leaves of a rounded concave form, and growing in the crevices of rocks and walls; Navelwort.

c **1400** *Lanfranc's Cirurg.* 55 Putte to þis medicyn þe ius of sum cold erbe: as morel, penywort, virge pastoris. *c* **1450** *Alphita* (Anecd. Oxon.) 41 *Cimbalaria*,..umbilicus ueneris idem. angl. penigres uel penywyt. **1578** LYTE *Dodoens* I. xxv. 37. **1579** LANGHAM *Gard. Health* (1633) 474 Wall Peniwort is good against all inflammations and hot tumors, S. Antonies fire, and kibed heeles being applied. **1756** WATSON in *Phil. Trans.* XLIX. 832 Wall Penny-wort, Kidney-wort; Leicestriensibus Navel-wort. **1858** LEWES *Sea-side Stud.* 189 From the crevices peep the stone-crop, the leaves of the foxglove, pennywort, and..other wall loving plants.

2. (***marsh pennywort*** or ***water pennywort***.) *Hydrocotyle vulgaris*, a small umbelliferous herb with rounded peltate leaves, growing in marshy places. Also extended to other species.

1578 LYTE *Dodoens* I. xxv. 37 Bycause of a certayne similitude..that it hath with Pennywurte of the wall, we do call [it] water Pennywurte. **1597** GERARDE *Herbal* II. cxliii. 424 Water Pennywoort is called..in English, Sheepes killing Pennygrasse, Penny rot. **1866** *Treas. Bot.* 606 *H[ydrocotyle] vulgaris*, common Pennywort, is one of the few British plants which have peltate leaves..it possesses no noxious properties, and sheep moreover refuse to eat it.

†**3.** (***mountain pennywort***.) *Saxifraga cuneifolia* (Dr. Stapf.). *Obs.*

1578 LYTE *Dodoens* I. xxv. 37–8 Thicke Pennywurte... Mountayne or Syngreene Pennywurte, is a rare plante, it groweth in some places of the Alpes and other mountaynes beyond the Sea.

4. *Obolaria virginica* (N.O. *Gentianaceæ*), a small North American herb with roundish upper leaves.

pennyworth (ˈpɛnɪwɜːθ), contr. **penn'orth** (ˈpɛnəθ). Forms: α. 1 **peniȝ weorð**, **peningcwurð**, 4 **paneworþ**, 4–5 **pene-**, 4–7 **peni-**, 4–8 **peny-**, 6–8 **penni-**, **-worþ**, **-worth**, etc., 6– **pennyworth** (also as two words, or with hyphen). β. 6 **penerth**, 6–7 **penworth**, 7 **pennerth**, **pen'worth**, **penn'worth**, (**penneard**, **penn'eth**), 7– **penn'orth**, (8 **pen'orth**, 8–9 **pennorth**). [f. PENNY + WORTH.]

1. The amount of anything which is or may be bought for a penny; as much as is worth a penny.

α. *a* **1000** *Charter of Orcy* in Kemble *Cod. Dipl.* IV. 278 An peningcwurð weaxes. *c* **1000** *Ags. Gosp.* John vi. 7 Nabbað hi ȝenoh on tweȝera hundred peneȝa wurþe hlafes. *c* **1000** *Sax. Leechd.* III. 38 An peniȝ weorð swefles. **1340** *Ayenb.* 37 Hi habbeþ þri paneworþes of worke uor ane peny. **1377** LANGL. *P. Pl.* B. III. 256 It is a permutacioun apertly, a penyworth for an othre. **1483** *Cath. Angl.* 274/2 A Peny worthe, *denariatum*. **1559** *Fabyan's Chron.* 705 The maior wente to the woode warfes, and solde to the poore people billet and faggot, by the peniworthe. **1573** *Nottingham Rec.* IV. 153, xviij. peyneworthe of appyles. **1758** JOHNSON *Idler* No. 35 ¶8 She..will never buy any thing by single pennyworths. **1851** D. JERROLD *St. Giles* vii. 69 Ordering..two pennyworth of ale, and bread and cheese.

β. **1566** *Churchw. Acc. St. Dunstan's, Canterb.*, One penerth of v d nayles. **1617** *MS. Acc. St. John's Hosp., Canterb.*, For thre penneard of wax candelles iijd. **1848** THACKERAY *Van. Fair* xxxviii, She had colloquies with the greengrocer about the pennorth of turnips.

b. Of land. (Cf. PENNYLAND.)

c **1598** *Knaresborough Wills* (Surtees) I. 215 One pennyeworthe of land lyinge at Norwood Edge.

c. *fig.* Amount, sum; *esp.* a very small, or the least, amount; often with negative = not the least bit, none at all; *ironically*, 'a deal', 'a lot'.

1362 LANGL. *P. Pl.* A. VIII. 49 Of þe pore peple no peneworþ to take. **1456** SIR G. HAYE *Law Arms* (S.T.S.) 155 All that I may..I suld tak fra him, and never geve him a penyworth tharof. **1590** NASHE *Pasquil's Apol.* I. B b, [She] had requited euery penni-woorth of duetie with many a pounde of fauour. **1616** SIR R. DUDLEY in *Fortescue Papers* (Camden) 16, I have never accepted from any Prince or Prelate one peniworth of Entertaynement. **1664** BUTLER *Hud.* II. iii. 57 This was the Pen'worth of his thought To pass time and uneasie trot. **1771** SMOLLETT *Humph. Cl.* 26 Apr., It [a dose of medicine] worked Mrs. Gwyllim a pennorth. **1894** BLACK *Highland Cousins* I. 18 There will not be a pennyworth of grudging in her welcome.

†**2.** That which is or may be bought for a given sum, in contrast to the money itself. (Often in *pl.*)

c **1330** R. BRUNNE *Chron.* (1810) 64 Alle þat he mot gete, he robbed & reft, Peny no penyworth, no þing he no left. **1465–6** *Mann. & Househ. Exp.* (Roxb.) 175 To pay me.. viij. li. in mony, or in klothe, swche peneworthes as I schal holde me plesed. **1516** *Will. R. Peke of Wakefield* 4 June, To pay..iiij markes in money or ells in such convenient pennyworth as they will taike for the said money. *a* **1591** H. SMITH *Serm. 1 Tim.* vi. 6 When he hath bought it,..he boasteth of his pennyworths, and saith, it is better than his money. **1656** H. PHILLIPS *Purch. Patt.* (1676) B iij b, No man will take a Lease of an house,..but he hath some reason ..to..provoke him thereunto, either by the worth of the penyworth, or the conveniency for his Trade and Living.

3. Money's worth, value for one's money; a (sufficient) return for one's payment or trouble; a bargain; †profit, advantage obtained. Usually with qualifying adj. (*good, great, fair, rich, cheap; bad, dear*, etc.); also *absol.* A good bargain; something obtained at a cheap rate, or fully worth what is given for it. (Often *fig.*)

α. **1340** *Ayenb.* 23 Þet [ydeleblisse] is þe dyeules peni huermide he bayþ alle þe uayre pane-worþes ine the markatte of þise wordle. *c* **1430** *Pilgr. Lyf Manhode* III. xxvii. (1869) 150 Riht ofte she sheweth good penyworthes. *a* **1553** UDALL *Royster D.* IV. vii. (Arb.) 75 Haue once more with haile shot, I will haue some penyworth, I will not leese all. **1592** SHAKS. *Rom. & Jul.* IV. v. 4 You take your peniworths now. Sleepe for a weeke. **1639** FULLER *Holy War* IV. xv. (1840) 205 To sell his life at such a rate that the buyer should little boast of his penny worth. **1659** *Gentl. Calling* V. xviii, If a witness prove a better pennyworth than the Judge, subornation shall do the business. **1661** BAXTER *Mor. Prognost.* II. xix. 49 Cheap Food and Rayment is every ones Penny-worth. **1667** PRIMATT *City & C. Build.* 55 They do sometimes buy very great pennyworths in old Rubbish. **1702** S. PARKER tr. *Cicero's De Finibus* II. 101 That he only design'd to make his own Pennyworths and Advantages. **1772** MRS. E. MONTAGU in Doran *Lady of last C.* vii. (1873) 173 If a blue tafety..should come in your way and seem a pennyworth, please to add it. **1819** SCOTT *Fam. Lett.* (1894) II. 44 The armour, which I have no doubt is a great pennyworth. **1868** HOLME LEE *B. Godfrey* xii. 62 You will not find it a dear pennyworth.

β. **1664–5** PEPYS *Diary* 3 Feb., Mrs. Turner..is vexed because I do not serve her..in helping her to some good penn'eths. **1678** DRYDEN *Œdipus* Prol. 33 You needs will have your pen'worths of the Play. **1716** M. W. MONTAGU *Bassette-table*, With fifty guineas (a great penn'orth!) bought.

†**b.** Price in proportion to value; (cheap, etc.) rate. Usually in phr. ***at a*** (***good***, etc.) ***pennyworth***.

1641 EARL MONM. tr. *Biondi's Civil Warres* V. 103 They had it at a dearer penny-worth. **1704** SWIFT *T. Tub* Wks. 1760 I. 57 This tract of land he bought at a very great pennyworth from the discoverers themselves. **1729** *N. Jersey Archives* XI. 167 Which said Plantation will be sold at extraordinary Penniworth.

†**c.** In appositive or adverbial construction: As a bargain, as good value for the money; cheap. (With or without qualifying adj.) *Obs.*

1466 *Mann. & Househ. Exp.* (Roxb.) 171 We pray ȝow that ȝe wol lete heme have them the bett[er] peneworthe fore howere sake. **1682** *Lond. Gaz.* No. 1780/4 A very well made Brewing Copper..may be had a very great Pennyworth. **1733–4** BERKELEY *Let. T. Prior* 7 Jan., Wks. 1871 IV. 210 Perhaps the house and garden..may be got a good pennyworth. **1771** FOOTE *Maid of B.* III. Wks. 1799 II. 231 Rich cloaths, which he has promis'd to sell me a pennorth.

†**d.** ***Robin Hood's pennyworth***: a thing or quantity sold at a robber's price, i.e. far below the real value. *Obs.*

1631 *Star Chamb. Cases* (Camden) 117 Walton the Bayliffe leavyed of the poore mans goods 77[1] att Robinhood's peniworths. **1677** W. HUGHES *Man of Sin* II. viii. 122 In Germany, there is a Robin-Hood's pennyworth to be had,..8000 years of Pardon both from punishment and fault.

†**e.** ***to cast*** (***one's***) ***pennyworths***: to reckon up what one gets for one's expenditure; to estimate the advantages and disadvantages of an undertaking; to count the cost. *Obs.*

1530 TINDALE *Pract. Prelates* Wks. (1573) 370 When the prelates of both parties had cast their peniworthes against all chaunces. **1548** UDALL *Erasm. Par. Luke* xiv, He wyll..cast his peniwoorthes in his minde what charges wyll be requisite for the finishyng of such a toure. **1589** GREENE *Menaphon* (Arb.) 72 Democles..began to cast ouer his bad peniworths, in whose face age had furrowed her wrinckles. **1594** CAREW *Tasso* (Grosart) 78 He casts his penworths by some queint deuice.

†**f.** ***to have*** (***get***, etc.) ***one's pennyworths of*** (***out of, on***): to have one's repayment or revenge on, be revenged on. *Obs.*

1567 EDWARDS *Damon & Pithias* in Dodsley *O.P.* XI. 263, I wyll have my penyworthes of thee therefore if I die. **1639** FULLER *Holy War* III. xiii. (1840) 137 Leopold..meaning now to get his pennyworths out of him, for the affront done unto him in Palestine. **1707** *Reflex. upon Ridicule* 207 They take out their Penny-worths in Satyr, and Slander.

Penobscot (pɛˈnɒbskɒt), *sb.* and *a.* Also Penobscote. [Native name: see F. W. Hodge *Handbk. Amer. Indians North of Mexico* II. 226.] **A.** *sb.* An Algonquian Indian people of the valley of the Penobscot River in Maine, U.S.A.; also, a member of this people.

[**1616** J. SMITH *Descr. New Eng.* 8 The principall habitation Northward we were at, was Pennobscot..though most [Indian peoples] be Lords of themselues, yet they hold the Bashabes of Pennobscot, the chiefe and greatest amongst them.] **1624** —— *Gen. Hist. Virginia* VI. 240 The Masachusets call their great God Kiehtan, and their Kings there abouts Sachems: The Penobscotes their greatest power Tantum, and their Kings Sagomos. **1713** in *Maine Hist. Soc. Coll.* (1859) VI. 253 In Witness whereof, We,..by name, Kireberuit, Iteansis, and Jackoit, for Penobscot,..have hereunto set our hands and seals. **1910** F. W. HODGE *Handbk. Amer. Indians* II. 226/2 The Penobscot took an active part in all the wars on the New England frontier up to 1749, when they made a treaty of peace, and have remained quiet ever since. **1942** *Fading Trails* (U.S. Dept. Interior Nat. Park Service) vii. 59 Many an aged Penobscot..still wistfully awaits the day when the..peculiar 'click-click' of caribou's feet will resound once more in the frosty air of the muskeg. **1959** E. TUNIS *Indians* 25/2 The Penobscots kept certain of their young men in strict training for running down deer! **1965** *Canad. Jrnl. Linguistics* Spring 135 There are some Algonquian Indians still living along the New England coast,..but except for a few older Penobscot, all speak English. **1974** *Encycl. Brit. Micropædia* VII. 855/1 The Penobscot assisted the French against the English in all the wars on the New England frontier until 1749, when they made peace with the English.

b. The language spoken by the Penobscot people.

1891 J. C. PILLING *Bibliogr. Algonquian Lang.* 110/2 A short catechism in Penobscot begins on page 47. *Ibid.* 199/1 Comparative vocabulary..in the..Penobscot. **1902** [see ANIMATE *ppl. a.* 4 b]. **1933** L. BLOOMFIELD *Language* 72 The *Algonquian* family..includes the languages..of New England (*Penobscot*..). **1972** *Regional Lang. Stud.—Newfoundland* IV. 2 Penobscot, a dialect closely related to Abenaki.

B. *adj.* Of or pertaining to the Penobscot people or their language.

1727 J. HEATH *Let.* 7 July in *Maine Hist. Soc. Coll.* (1853) III. 409 If Capt. Gyles..can steer the Penobscot Indians to Falmouth, it seems as though these may follow. **1779** S. LOVELL *Orig. Jrnl. Penobscot Exped.* (1881) 97 We are visited by some Penobscot Indians who are determined to proceed with us. **1819** *N. Amer. Rev.* IX. 185 A specimen of the Penobscot dialect (which we obtained from a friend in the District of Maine). **1831** *Boston Even. Transcript* 7 Oct. 1/2 Last week, a wretched and destitute Penobscot Indian was seen traversing our streets. **1854** THOREAU *Walden* 32, I have seen Penobscot Indians, in this town, living in tents of thin cotton cloth. **1893** *Chicago Tribune* 3 July 1/3 The Penobscot tribe of Indians is represented now by ten members from Old Town, Maine. **1973** A. H. WHITEFORD *N. Amer. Indian Arts* 91 Northeastern beadwork is lacy, as shown by the Penobscot collar. **1976** *Times* 27 Dec. 25/2 In Maine, the Passamaquoddy and Penobscot tribes have laid claim to 2.5 million acres of land—two-thirds of the state.

peno'logic, *a. rare.* [f. PENOLOGY + -IC.] = next.

1900 *Pop. Sci. Monthly* Feb. 468 The results of modern..penologic research.

penological (piːnəʊˈlɒdʒɪkəl), *a.* [f. as prec. + -ICAL.] Of, pertaining or relating to, penology.

1847 in WEBSTER. **1881** *Philad. Record* No. 3466. 4 Studies for penological students. **1888** W. TALLACK (*title*) Penological and Preventive Principles, with special Reference to Europe and America. **1892** *Daily News* 11 Nov. 5/4 The deliberations of the Penological Commission in Russia appointed last year have now been concluded.

penologist (pɪˈnɒlədʒɪst). [f. PENOLOGY + -IST.] One who studies or is versed in penology.

1838 LIEBER *Ess. Penal Law* 62 All penologists of note..are agreed..that insulation of the criminal is the only possible means: 1. To avoid contamination, etc. **1863** W. B. JERROLD *Signals Distress* I Penologists..will not be prepared to maintain that [etc.]. **1886** *American* XII. 313 [It] has now the approbation of American penologists.

penology (pɪˈnɒlədʒɪ). [f. Gr. ποινή fine, penalty, L. *pœna* penalty, punishment + -O-LOGY.] The scientific study of the punishment and prevention of crime; the science of prison and reformatory management.

1838 LIEBER *Ess. Penal Law* 77, I..know that sentimentalism in penology is, in its effects, cruel towards the offender as well as society. **1861** W. L. CLAY *Mem. J. Clay* vi. 35 Penology has become a more complex, not a more simple science. **1892** *Pall Mall G.* 21 May 2/2 A study in comparative morality or comparative penology.

penoscrotal (ˈpiːnəʊˈskrəʊtəl), *a. Anat.* and *Path.* [irreg. f. L. *pēnis* + SCROTAL.] Of or pertaining to the penis and scrotum.

1874 VAN BUREN *Dis. Genit. Org.* 33 When it gets fairly past the peno-scrotal angle. **1900** *Lancet* 23 June 1814/1 Evident cases of peno-scrotal hypospadias.

†**'penous**, *a. Obs. rare.* [ad. late L. *pœnōs-us* (pseudo-Aug.) painful, f. *pœna* penalty, pain; cf. F. *peineux*, OF. *penus*, It. *penoso* painful.] Painful; of the nature of or belonging to punishment.

1627 W. SCLATER *Exp. 2 Thess.* (1629) 173 Ourselues must ..procure discharge from temporall punishments by our owne voluntary passions, and penous good workes. *Ibid.* 291 Ἐπιτιμία or ἐπιτίμησις; a penous kinde of warning ioyned with reprehension.

pen-pal (ˈpɛnpæl). orig. *U.S.* [f. PEN *sb.*[2] + PAL *sb.*[1]] = PEN-FRIEND. Hence **penpalmanship**, **penpalship**, the relationship existing between pen-pals.

1938 *Educational Method* Nov. 83/1 Mary Jones of Portland, Maine, has just requested the Student Letter Exchange of Waseca, Minnesota, to supply her with the name of a 'pen pal' in Mexico City. *Ibid.*, Since its inception in July, 1936, the Student Letter Exchange has provided hundreds of thousands of 'pen pals' around the world. **1941** J. C. FURNAS *How Amer. Lives* 272 Pen-pals are not the only piece of news for the writer in the Kriebel boys' mail. **1960** *20th Cent.* June 517 There are some rather elaborate plans for forming relationships with individual Alphas, on the lines of the children's pen palships in the twentieth-century newspapers. *Ibid.*, You need to be young and so does your pen pal for this type of correspondence. **1962** J. KIRKUP tr. *Brunner's Trouble in Brusada* iii. 26 The girls..had written ..to a school class in Zurich with which they regularly corresponded, and..their pen-pals would help them to bear the cost. **1966** *Guardian* 9 June 8/1 The affair was carried on entirely by correspondence... Their penpalmanship had already begun. **1967** *Boston Herald* 1 Apr. 22/6 The children at the Dedham Country Day School are pen pals of children in Dedham, England. They've exchanged Christmas presents and a few have even visited families over there. **1972** M. MEAD *Blackberry Winter* vii. 81, I also had two pen pals whose names I got through *St. Nicholas Magazine*. **1972** C. SHORT *Naked Skier* xxii. 123 Maybe we could be pen-pals... I'll send you a postcard from New York. **1974** 'P. B. YUILL' *Hazell plays Solomon* ii. 25 'Why pay top money for information and a photograph of a child whose surname they don't know?' 'Perhaps they want a penpal?'

pen-pusher (ˈpɛn,pʊʃə(r)). [f. PEN *sb.*[2] + PUSHER.] One who is engaged in writing or desk work; a clerk; a writer (freq. derogatory).

1911 *Busy Man's Mag.* Jan. 65/2 That fellow was a pen-pusher in a dough joint—I mean a bank clerk. **1930** *Time & Tide* 24 May 663/2 Clerking! My God, any tuppenny ha'penny pen-pusher can be a clerk. **1940** *Manch. Guardian Weekly* 22 Mar. 228 From his point of view it is much better to be a pen-pusher in..obscurity than a corpse. **1948** 'N. SHUTE' *No Highway* vii. 173 Who the hell are you, anyway? Just a bloody penpusher. **1952** A. GRIMBLE *Pattern of Islands* 177, I do not suppose that George was particularly interested in Stevenson as a writing man—he never had much time for pen-pushers, as he called them. **1954** WODEHOUSE *Jeeves & Feudal Spirit* ix. 80 Florence tells me that La Morehead is one of the more costly of our female pen-pushers and has to have purses of gold flung to her in great profusion before she will sign on the dotted line. **1957** J. BRAINE *Room at Top* iii. 31, I saw myself, compared with him, as the Town Hall Clerk, the subordinate pen-pusher, halfway to being a zombie, and I tasted the sourness of envy. **1972** *Guardian* 23 Oct. 9/3 The more assiduous pen-pushers among London Transport's 6,000 administrative, technical, clerical and control staff.

So **'pen-pushing** *vbl. sb.*, writing by hand.

1936 'G. ORWELL' *Keep Aspidistra Flying* iii. 61 He dreaded..going to work... Pen-pushing in some filthy office—God! **1952** A. GRIMBLE *Pattern of Islands* 179, I knew that Charles Workman would have made a better job of the pen-pushing than I did. **1972** W. A. PANTIN *Oxf. Life* iv. 53 These volumes represent a great mass of praiseworthy industry.., whether pen-pushing or typewriter-bashing.

penroseite (ˈpɛnrəʊzaɪt). *Min.* [f. the name of Richard A. F. *Penrose*, Jr. (1863–1931), U.S. mining geologist + -ITE[1].] A selenide of nickel, ideally $NiSe_2$, which usu. also contains copper, lead, or silver, probably as impurities, and occurs in grey reniform masses.

1926 S. G. GORDON in *Proc. Acad. Nat. Sci. Philadelphia* LXXVII. 317 Penroseite was obtained in a small collection of minerals which the writer purchased from a local merchant at Colquechaca, Bolivia. *Ibid.* 321 It is a pleasure to name this new mineral in honor of Dr. Richard A. F. Penrose, Jr. **1937** *Amer. Mineralogist* XXII. 322 The minerals most likely to be intergrown with penroseite and blockite are cubic in symmetry, such as clausthalite,.., naumannite.., and argentiferous galena. *Ibid.*, Penroseite and blockite may therefore be regarded as identical minerals and the latter name may be discarded. **1968** I. KOSTOV *Mineral.* 124 Penroseite usually contains some copper and cobalt.

pens, obs. form of *pence*, pl. of PENNY.

pensal, variant of PENCEL; obs. f. PENCIL.

†**'pensative**, *a. Obs.* Also *erron.* **-itive**. [ad. Sp. *pensativo* 'pensive, full of thought, or of care' (Minsheu 1599), f. *pensar* to think: see PENSIVE and -ATIVE.] Full of thought, pensive, anxious.

1574 HELLOWES *Gueuara's Fam. Ep.* (1577) 317 We see no other thing, but that the idle woman goeth alwayes pensitiue. **1582** N. LICHEFIELD tr. *Castanheda's Conq. E. Ind.* I. lxiv. 130 b, After that he understoode how small a fleete there was left to defend his countrie withall, he could not bee but verye pensatiue. **1612** SHELTON *Quix.* I. Pref. 9 My friend seeing me so pensative, demanded of me the Reason of my musing. **1654** GAYTON *Pleas. Notes* IV. v. 201 Sancho rested much confounded and pensative of that which he heard they say, that Books of Chivalry only contained follies and lies.

pensch, Sc. form of PAUNCH.

†**pense**, *sb. Obs.* Also 6 **penss.** [a. OF. *pense* thought, f. *penser* to think; cf. PANSE, PANSY *sb.*]

1. *Sc.* Thought.

a **1568** *Considder, Man, all is bot Vanitie!* 9 in *Bannatyne Poems* (Hunter. Cl.) 136 Will we nocht prent in to oure mynd and penss That it is bot richt schort tyme we haif heir.

2. A PANSY *sb.*

1588 GREENE *Alcida* Wks. (Grosart) IX. 71 *Mer.* Then Madam, blame me not if I like Penses well... *Eriph.* Not Sir, as it is called a Pense, or as you descant a fancie: but as we homely Huswives call it, Heartsease.

†**pense**, *v. Obs.* exc. *dial.* Also 6 **pens(s.** [a. F. *penser* to think, be thoughtful (11th c. in Hatz.-Darm.), ad. L. *pensāre* to weigh, ponder, consider, freq. of *pendĕre* to hang, weigh. See also PANSE.

(OE. had adopted the L. vb. as *pinsian* to weigh, estimate, consider; but this app. did not come down into ME.)]

a. *trans.* To think of, call to mind. **b.** *intr.* To think. **c.** *trans.* (with compl.) To cause to be thought. **d.** (*dial.*) *intr.* To be fretful.

c **1500** *Lancelot* 1431 Than arthur..In to his wit memoratyve can seik Of euery gilt wich that he can pens, Done frome he passith the ȝeris of Innocens. *a* **1520** JOHNSTON *Thre Deid Pollis* 34 (Bann. MS.) With humill hairt vpoun our pollis penss. **1560** ROLLAND *Crt. Venus* II. 953 Thy Actis pensit the far mair precious. [*a* **1825** FORBY *Voc. E. Anglia*, *Pense*, to be fretful. *Jam.* to be thoughtful.]

pense, obs. form of *pence*, pl. of PENNY.

‖**pensée.** Also 5 **penci.** [In sense 1, a. OF. *pensee* (12th c.); in sense 2, only as Fr.]

†**1.** Thoughtfulness, anxiety, care; a thought, fancy. *Obs.*

c **1410** *Sir Cleges* 177 They..thanked God with god entent, And put away penci. **1474** CAXTON *Chesse* III. v, The pensee or thought is envoluped in obscurete. *c* **1477** —— *Jason* 28 Contynuyng in his amorouse pensees & thoughts.

‖**2.** (pãse) A thought or reflection put in literary form. (Consciously Fr.)

1886 BYNNER *A. Surriage* xxxi. 386 There's another *pensée* for you. **1895** *Daily News* 30 Nov. 3/1 The author was greatly addicted to what is called pensée writing.

pensee, obs. form of PANSY *sb.*

penseful: see PENSIFUL.

pensel, -ell(e, var. PENCEL; obs. ff. PENCIL.

†**'pensement.** *Obs. rare.* [a. F. *pensement* = It. *pensamento* thinking, thought, f. *penser*, *pensar* to think. Cf. *pansement* (PANSE *v.*).] Anxious thought, care, solicitude.

1508 *Kalender of Sheph.* (1892) III. App. 180 Cease of your pecunyall pensement, The whiche defyleth your entendement.

pense'rose, *a. rare.* Anglicized form of next.

1831 *Fraser's Mag.* III. 751 His lordship is..penserose and sentimental beyond conception. *Ibid.* IV. 325 The expression of his countenance in repose is generally penserose and meditative.

‖**penseroso** (penseˈroso), *a.* and *sb.* [From the title of Milton's poem *Il Penseroso* (1632), a. obs. It. *penseroso* (1578 in Tasso *Dialoghi* I), now *pensieroso* (Florio 1598), f. *pensiere* thought.]

a. *adj.* Meditative, brooding, melancholy. **b.** *sb.* A brooding or melancholy person, or personality.

1765 J. ADAMS *Diary* 23 Dec., The Il Penseroso, however, is discernible on the faces of all four. **1790** R. TYLER *Contrast* II. i. (1887) 24 How I should like to see that pair of Penserosos together. **1831** *Society* I. 78 But the penseroso humour lasted not long.

'penship. *rare*$^{-1}$. [f. PEN *sb.*^{2} + -SHIP.] Use of the pen; writing; = PENMANSHIP.

1806 WOLCOTT (P. Pindar) *Tristia* Wks. 1812 V. 272 Out flames a paragraph of pretty penship.

[**pensible,** *a.* Error for PENSILE.

[**1626** BACON *Sylvia* § 15 The Water being made pensile.] Misprinted 'pensible' in ed. 1651. Hence in **1837** RICHARDSON. **1890** *Cent. Dict.*]

†**pen'siculate,** *v.* *Obs.* *rare*$^{-0}$. [f. L. *pensiculāre, -āt-*, dim. deriv. of *pensāre* to weigh, ponder.] To consider, ponder. Hence †**pensicu'lation,** †**pen'siculative** *a.*

1623 COCKERAM I I, Carefully to Consider of, *pensiculate*. *Ibid.* I, *Pensiculatiue*, diligently considering of. **1658** PHILLIPS, *Pensitation* or *Pensiculation*, a diligent considering.

‖**pensiero** (pen'sjɛro). Pl. pensieri. [It.] A thought, an idea; an anxiety. *spec.* in Art, a sketch.

1909 JOYCE *Let.* 7 Sept. (1966) II. 231, I am dreadfully nervous from all the worry and *pensieri* I have had, very very nervous indeed. **1959** *Times* 2 Oct. 5/6 Most of the drawings are *pensieri*. **1961** M. LEVY *Studio Dict. Art Terms* 85 *Pensiero*, an alternative term for a Sketch. **1975** *Times Lit. Suppl.* 4 Apr. 378/5 Each artist was supplied with a design, or *pensiero*, which laid down the pose, proportions and drapery pattern of the statue.

'pensiful, 'penseful, *a.* *Obs.* exc. *Sc.* and *north. dial.* Forms: 5 **pense-, penceful(l,** 5–6 **pensi-, penci-, pencyfull, pensyful,** (*Sc.* 8–9 **pencefu',** 9 **pensefu'**). [f. PENSE *sb.* or PENSÉE + -FUL.]

1. Thoughtful, meditative, pensive; anxious, brooding; melancholy, sorrowful. *Obs.* exc. *dial.*

a **1450** [implied in next]. **1485** CAXTON *Paris & V.* 7 Seyng hys doughter ful tryste and pensyful for thys. *c* **1489** —— *Sonnes of Aymon* iv. 120 She was contynuelly pencyfull & sory by cause that she myghte not here noo tydynges of her children. *c* **1489** —— *Blanchardyn* xxiii. 74 He went homward.. all penseful of the wordes that he had herde of the pucelle. *Ibid.* l. 193 Wherof he had no grete Ioye, but became pencefull. **1587** FLEMING *Contn. Holinshed* III. 1011/2 He.. was verie carefull and pensifull how to recouer his countrie againe. **1865** YOUNG *Pictures* 165 (E.D.D.) Chairs that when pensefu' ye may rock in. **1876** *Whitby Gloss.*, *Pensiful*,.. sorrowful.

2. *Sc.* Conceited, giving oneself airs.

1788 PICKEN *Now-a-days* Poems 62 Fash't wi' three or four Sic pencefu' breed. **1825** JAMIESON, *Pensefu'*, *Pencefu'*, *adj.*, Proud, self-conceited, Ayrs[hire].

'pensifulness, 'pensefulness. Now *Sc.* and *north. dial.* [f. prec. + -NESS.]

a. Thoughtfulness, meditation; anxiety, brooding, care, melancholy. **b.** *Sc.* Self-conceit, affected haughtiness.

a **1450** *Fysshynge w. angle* (1883) 2 With owt stody pensifulnes or trauel. **1542** BOORDE *Dyetary* Pref. (1870) 228 Myrth is one of the chefest thynges of Physycke, the which doth aduertyse euery man.. to beware of pencyfulness. **1543** GRAFTON *Contn. Harding* 461 After dismissed [he] dyed shortely for thought and pensifulnes of mynde. **1825** [see PENSINESS 2].

pensil, -ile, -ill, var. PENCEL; obs. ff. PENCIL.

pensile ('pɛnsɪl, -saɪl), *a.* Also 7 pensil(l. [ad. L. *pensil-is* hanging down, pendent, f. *pendēre*, *pens-* to hang: see -ILE.]

1. Suspended from above, hanging down, pendent, pendulous.

1603 B. JONSON *Coronat. Entertainm.*, Ouer her state two crowns hanging, with pensile shields thorow them. **1626** BACON *Sylva* §364 It is report of some good credit, that in Deepe Caues, there are Pensile Crystall, and Degrees of Crystall that drop from Above. **1666** J. DAVIES *Hist. Caribby Isles* 310 Those pensile Beds which they call Amacs. **1771** H. WALPOLE *Vertue's Anecd. Paint.* IV. ii. 41 Gothic architecture, with all its airy embroidery and pensile vaults. **1854** HOOKER *Himal. Jrnls.* I. ii. 39 The pensile nests of the weaver bird were abundant.

b. Steeply overhanging; 'hanging' or situated on a steep declivity.

c **1750** SHENSTONE *Ruined Abbey* 6 His azure stream, with pensile woods enclos'd. *c* **1750** —— *Elegies* xxi. 11 Or pensile grove or airy cliff ascend. **1832** J. BREE *St. Herbert's Isle* 69 No pensile wood that on thy hills recline.

2. Hanging in the air or in space; suspended on arches, with void space beneath; vaulted.

1613 PURCHAS *Pilgrimage* (1614) 56, I might here also tell of those Pensile gardens, borne vp on arches, foure square, each square contayning foure hundred foote. **1703** *Univ. Dict.* s.v. *Babylon*, Babylon.. was then the wonder of the world for its walls and pensile gardens. **1718** PRIOR *Solomon* I. 256 How the pensile ball Should never strive to rise, nor fear to fall. **1830** W. PHILLIPS *Mt. Sinai* I. 678 Pensile upon space Hang countless planets.

3. That constructs a pensile nest.

1802 BINGLEY *Anim. Biog.* (1813) II. 187 The Pensile Warbler is nearly five inches long. **1868** WOOD *Homes without H.* x. 194 Pensile Mammalia. There are not many mammalia which make pensile nests. **1901** *Daily News* 19 Feb. 4/7 Another pensile bird, the Baya sparrow of India.

Hence **'pensileness, pen'sility,** the quality or state of being pensile. *rare.*

1605 BACON *Adv. Learn.* I. vi. §10 In that excellent Booke of Iob, wherein the pensilenesse of the earth,.. and the.. conuexitie of Heauen are manifestly touched. **1727** BAILEY vol. II, *Pensilness*, hanging Quality. **1640** G. WATTS tr. *Bacon's Adv. Learn.* IV. i. 183 The fluctuation or pensility of the Bowells.

'pensily, *adv.* *Obs.* exc. *dial.* [f. PENSY *a.* + -LY^{2}.]

1. Pensively, anxiously, sadly.

1469 MARG. PASTON in *P. Lett.* II. 365, I pray ȝow and requer ȝow that ye take yt not pensyly, for I wot wele yt gothe ryth ner ȝowr hart.

2. *Sc.* 'In a self-important manner' (Jam.).

1725 RAMSAY *Gentle Sheph.* I. ii, His blue bonnet.. Whilk pensylie he wears a thought a-jee.

'pensiness. *Obs.* exc. *dial.* [f. PENSY *a.* + -NESS.]

1. Pensiveness, anxiety.

c **1485** *Digby Myst.* (1882) III. 606 A! how pynsynesse potyt me to oppresse, that I haue synnyd on euery side.

2. *Sc.* (See quot.)

1825 JAMIESON, *Pensieness*, *Pensfuness*, self-conceitedness and affectation, S.

pension ('pɛnʃən), *sb.* Forms: 4–6 **pensioun,** (4 **-ci-, -sy-**), 4–7 **pencion,** 5 **pensone, pencyown,** 5–6 **pencyon,** (6 **-sy-**), 6–7 **pention,** 5– **pension.** [a. F. *pension, -un* (*c* 1225 in Hatz.-Darm.), ad. L. *pensiōn-em* payment, rent, f. *pens-*, ppl. stem of *pendĕre* to weigh, to pay: see -ION.

With the various senses cf. those of L. *pensio* in Du Cange.]

†**1.** A payment made by, or exacted from, a person or persons; a tribute, tax, charge, imposition; a contribution; a price paid or received; an expenditure, expense, outlay. Also *fig.* *Obs.*

1387 TREVISA *Higden* (Rolls) VII. 419 He hilde Edwardes lawe wiþ þe amendynge þerof; he forȝaf þe grevous pencions [Higden *pensiones noxias remisit*]. *c* **1440** *Promp. Parv.* 391/2 Pencyone, dette to be payed, *pensio*. *c* **1440** *Alph. Tales* 397 He made hym fre of al maner of tributt & pension. *a* **1529** SKELTON *Col. Cloute* 454 He payd a bitter pencyon For mannes redemcyon. **1572** R. T. *Discourse* 49 Paul the third pope of that name had registred fiue and forty thousand whores that payed euery moneth a pension or tribute to the pope, which did rise yerely to fortie thousand ducates. **1608** TOPSELL *Serpents* 76 Both rich and poor by their good husbandry do gather good customes and pensions by them [Bees]. **1627** SPEED *England* xxxviii. §3 Humber.. into which all the Riuers.. emptie themselues.. as into the common-storehouse of Neptune for all the watery Pensions of this Prouince. *a* **1638** MEDE *Wks.* (1672) 674 With some of them [Arabs] he is fain to be at a Pension for the safer passage of his Caravans.

2. *Eccl.* A fixed payment out of the revenues of a benefice, upon which it forms a charge.

[**1316** *Act 9 Edw. II*, Stat. I. c. 11 Pro corrodiis, pensionibus, vel prehendinationibus. Cf. **1327** *Act 1 Edw. III*, Stat. II. c. 10.] *c* **1380** WYCLIF *Last Age of Church* (1840) 31 Goodis of holy Chirche þat prelatis wiþ holdeþ to hem, as pensiouns, firste frutis [etc.]. *c* **1460** FORTESCUE *Abs. & Lim. Mon.* xviii. (1885) 153 Yff hit woll lyke the kynge to yeve no corodie nor pencion, wich he hath be ryght off his corowne, off euery abbey, priory, and oþer howses. *c* **1525** ABP. WARHAM *Let. to Wolsey* in Ellis *Orig. Lett.* Ser. III. II. 31 The value of the benefices within the diocesse of Canterburie.. with portions and pensions appropried and assigned to Monasteries and other religiouse places. **1627** W. BEDELL in *Lett. Lit. Men* (Camden) 137 Pensions upon Churches, &c., granted to Religious Houses. **1727–41** CHAMBERS *Cycl.* s.v. *Pensionary*, In the Romish countries it is frequent to have pensions on benefices... Pensions are now only creatable by the pope; and are never to exceed one third of the revenue. **1885** *Cath. Dict.* (ed. 3) 654/1 At the Council of Chalcedon, Maximus.. requested the sanction of the Fathers to his assigning a pension out of the revenues of the see sufficient for the support of Domnus.

†**3. a.** Any regular payment made to a person for present services; stipend, salary, wages; fee. *Obs.*

1362 LANGL. *P. Pl.* A. VIII. 48 Men of lawe.. Of princes and Prelatus heor pencion schulde aryse, And of þe pore peple no peneworþ to take. **1451** *Yatton Churchw. Acc.* (Somerset Rec. Soc.) 94 To Iohn Sloo for his pension. **1479** *Eng. Gilds* (1870) 423–4 The Pencions to be paide quarterly. Imprimis to the Maire... Item for his pencion, xx.*li.*.. Item to the Recorder... Item for his pencion, x.*li.*.. Item to the Towne Clerke for his pencion, iiij.*li.*.. Item to the Stewarde for his pencion, liij.*s.* iiij.*d.* **1549** LATIMER *1st Serm. bef. Edw. VI* (Arb.) 40 The vicar that serueth.. hath but .xii. or .xiiii. markes by yere, so that of thys pension he is not able to by him bokes, nor geue hys neyghboure dryncke. **1611** BIBLE *1 Esdras* iv. 56 He commanded to giue to all that kept the city, pensions and wages. **1656–7** DAVENANT *Rutland Ho.* Dram. Wks. 1873 III. 226 Your servants.. being confined within the narrow bounds of pension, are acomptable for all the orts by weight. **1776** ADAM SMITH *W.N.* II. ii. (1869) I. 288 If a guinea be the weekly pension of a particular person, he can in the course of the week purchase with it [etc.].

In uses which approach 4:

b. Such a payment made to one who is not a professed servant or employee, to retain his alliance, good will, secret service, assistance when needed, etc.; a subvention, a subsidy, a fixed allowance. **c.** A regular payment to persons of rank, royal favourites, etc., to enable them to maintain their state; also to men of learning or science, artists, etc., to enable them to carry on work which is of public interest or value.

1500–20 DUNBAR *Poems* lxxxiii. 27 Welcum, my pensioun most preclair; Welcum, my awin Lord Thesaurair! *a* **1548** HALL *Chron., Hen. V* 39 b, If the Frenche pencions be the susteiners of the Scottishe nobilitee.. then plucke away Fraunce, and the courage of the nobles of Scotland shal be sone daunted. **1576** FLEMING *Panopl. Epist.* 348, I meane, that your maiestie, of your owne accorde, giue many pensions to the maintenaunce of learning. **1585** T. WASHINGTON tr. *Nicholay's Voy.* II. xix. 53 He.., augmenting her estate and pention, accounteth her amongst the number of his wiues. **1639** FULLER *Holy War* II. xxxvi. (1647) 91 King Almerick.. proffereth him a pension of forty thousand Ducates yearly for his behooffull assistance. **1653** WALTON *Angler* i. 4 All men that keep Otter dogs ought to have a Pension from the Commonwealth to incourage them to destroy the very breed of.. Otters. **1671–2** SIR C. LYTTELTON in *Hatton Corr.* (Camden) 74, I heare my Lady Anne's pention was in ye banquiers hands. **1718** SWIFT *Abstr. Hist. Eng.* Lett. etc. 1768 IV. 259 The king of England agreed to deliver him [William the Lion, king of Scotland] up those twelve towns (or manours) in England which Malcolm had held under William the Conqueror; together with a pension of twelve thousand marks. **1755** JOHNSON, *Pension*, an allowance made to any one without an equivalent. In England it is generally understood to mean pay given to a state hireling for treason to his country. **1780** HARRIS *Philol. Enq.* Wks. (1841) 548 [Peter the Great] invited foreign professors not only to Petersburgh.. but to his ancient capital Moscow; at both which places these professors were maintained with liberal pensions. **1815** ELPHINSTONE *Acc. Caubul* (1842) II. 41 He holds some lands of the King, and receives a pension besides; in return, he is answerable for the safety of travellers in the Currapa Pass. **1845** S. AUSTIN *Ranke's Hist. Ref.* I. 399 To appear with his troops at Coblentz in the territory of Treves, immediately after the election, in order to earn the pension promised him by the king.

4. An annuity or other periodical payment made by a person or body of persons, now esp. by a government, a company, or an employer of labour, in consideration of past services or of the relinquishment of rights, claims, or emoluments.

Such pensions are provided in most civilized countries by the State or other public body, for its officers and servants on retirement from active service, and for soldiers, sailors, and others on being disabled in the public service, or for their wives and families in the case of death; they are also frequently granted, as a matter of bounty, to aged artists, authors, etc., in recognition of eminent achievements, or to their widows or orphans when left in straitened circumstances. *old age pension*, a pension or payment of so much per week or month paid to a workman or poor person (or, as in the U.K. now, to every one) on reaching a specified age: see OLD AGE PENSION as main entry.

1529 WOLSEY *Let. to Gardiner* in Ellis *Orig. Lett.* Ser. I. II. 11 That I may have summe convenyent pencion reservyd unto me, suche as the Kyngs hyhnes of hys nobyl charite shal thynke mete. **1601** SHAKS. *Twel. N.* II. v. 197. **1617** MORYSON *Itin.* III. 290 They who are maimed in the warres.. haue from them a Pension for life, or the value of the Pension in ready mony. **1701** J. JACKSON in *Pepys' Diary* (1879) VI. 232 The King has granted pensions to those poor families who suffered by this disaster. **1706** Q. ANNE *Message to Commons* 9 Jan., It would be very agreeable to her Majesty, if the Pension of 5000*l.* per ann. be continued and limited by Act of Parliament to his [the Duke of Marlborough's] Posterity, for the more honourable Support of their Dignities. **1768–74** TUCKER *Lt. Nat.* (1834) II. 348 We have Chelsea and Greenwich hospitals for the sick and maimed, pensions for the widows of such as have been slain. **1836** MARRYAT *Midsh. Easy* xxiv, Mr. Jolliffe not only obtained his promotion, but a pension for his wounds. **1844** H. H. WILSON *Brit. India* I. 15 Shamshir Bahadur was content to desist from opposition, and to accept a pension for himself and for his family, with permission to reside at Banda. **1858** RUSKIN *Pol. Econ. Art* Add. ii, It ought to be quite as natural and straight-forward a matter for a labourer to take his pension from his parish, because he has deserved well of his parish, as for a man in higher rank to take his pension from his country, because he has deserved well of his country. **1878** BLACKLEY *Ess. Prev. Pauperism* (1880) 28 The cost.. £14.. would entitle the insurer to receive 8*s.* a week, whenever sick, till the age of 70, after which time he would draw a pension of 4*s.* per week as long as he lived. **1892** *Academy* 2 Jan. 12/3 [He] retires on a pension after forty years' service. **1892** C. BOOTH *Pauperism* II. iv. 60 The father of the movement in favour of old-age pensions is Canon Blackley. With him must always remain the credit of whatever good may finally come out of any of these proposals. **1898** in *Bouvier's Law Dict.* II. 647 'Pensions are the bounties of the government, which Congress has the right to give, distribute, or recall at its discretion' (107 U.S. 68). **1902** *Encycl. Brit.* XXVIII. 468/2 (France) The State has to contribute to the old-age pensions, fixed.. at not less than 90 and not more than 200 francs per person in favour of people aged seventy and upwards.

†**5.** The annual (or other periodical) payment made by each member of a gild, college, or society, towards its general expenses; *esp.* that levied upon each member of an Inn of Court to defray the standing charges of the Inn (e.g. maintenance and repair of buildings and gardens, salaries of officers, wages of servants, etc.). *Obs.*

Appears in the *Black Book* of Lincoln's Inn from 1433.

1431 in *Eng. Gilds* (1870) 275 At ech of these ij. morowe spechis, euery brothir & sustir schall payen to ye costage, for his pensyon, ij. denar. **1446–7** *Black Bks. Lincoln's Inn* (1899) I. 17 It is ordeyned.. that no man be behynde of his pencyon ouer a ȝeer. **1569** *Pension Bk. Gray's Inn* (1901) 2 Hy hath one Chamber.. chargeable with payment of pencion. **1630** *Ibid.* 299 It is ordered.. that the steward from henceforth shall receive all pencions wch shalbe due for the persons of every gentleman in this Societie. **1680** DUGDALE *Orig. Jurid.* 212/2 *Pensions* are certain monys paid yearly by every one of the Society [Middle Temple]; viz. vi^{s}. viii^{d}. per annum. *Ibid.* 290 That no Officer compound for personal Pensions, but by authority from the Pension Councel. **1838** *Black Bks. Lincoln's Inn* IV. 198 To consider the propriety of discontinuing the words 'Preacher' and 'Pensions' as two items of the bills for dues. **1901** R. J. Fletcher in *Pension Bk. Gray's Inn* I *note* Pension, variously spelt in the MS. as Pencon, Pencion, Penc̄n or Pention, means a payment.

†**6. a.** Payment for board and lodging, or for the board and education of a child, etc. *Obs.*

[**1611** Cotgr., *Pension*,..also, money payed for the tabling, or boording of children.] **1696** Phillips (ed. 5), *Pension*,..a Summ pay'd by any Person for Dyet and Lodging. **1726** Swift *Gulliver* I. vi, The pension from each family for the education and entertainment of a child..is levied by the emperor's officers. **1796** Mrs. E. Parsons *Myst. Warning* III. 5 A sum sufficient to pay for my pension in a convent for two or three years. **1803** Mary Charlton *Wife & Mistress* II. 269 A household where she was to be tolerated for the pension she paid.

b. A boarding-house, a lodging-house at a fixed rate; occas. a boarding-school; †also formerly a tavern, an ordinary. Now only as Fr. (pɑ̃sjɔ̃), and usually in reference to France or other Continental country.

1644 Evelyn *Diary* 8 Sept., I settled them in their pension and exercises. *a* **1652** Brome *Damoiselle* iv. i, *Bump.* Ile make one w'ye at your new Ordinary... *Val.*..There's no such Pension in all this City. **1654** Flecknoe *Ten Years Trav.* 66 There being no Innes nor Pensions to lodge or eat at, as with us. **1687** A. Lovell tr. *Thevenot's Trav.* I. 18, I then went to lodge in Galata, at a Flemand's House..who kept a Pension. **1778** J. Adams *Diary* 12 May, My little son, and the other young Americans, at the *Pension*, dined with us. **1833** R. Pinkerton *Russia* 152 There is also a respectable *Pension* or Boarding-school for Young Ladies. **1837** Marryat *Olla Podr.* xxxvii, The price demanded is the same as at the pensions, viz. 200 francs..per month. **1845** Talfourd *Vac. Rambles* I. 155 Gay toy-shops, and flowering shrubs, and green-shuttered white 'Pensions'.

†**c.** *to be* or *live in pension*: to live as a boarder in lodgings, to board. So *to put in (to), place on pension*. *Obs.* (Now usually F. *en pension*.)

1598 Dallington *Meth. Trav.* B iv b, I would not haue him at his owne prouision. Let him be still in pension with others. **1665** *Verney Mem.* (1899) IV. 121 We are 16 of my uncle and aunts family, and all in pention, att 10*s.* a weeke for owerselves, and 7*s.* for owr servants with lodgens in. **1672–3** Dryden *Assignation* iv. i, My two nieces..are to be placed on pension there. **1714** Mrs. Manley *Adv. Riella* 96 She was put for sometime to Pension..at a poor Woman's House. [**1816** Shelley *Lett.* Pr. Wks. 1880 III. 353, I wish you to look out for a home for me and Mary and William, and the kitten who is now *en pension*.]

7. [from 5] A consultative assembly of the members of Gray's Inn, one of the Inns of Court in London: cf. parliament 5 b.

1570 *Pension Bk. Gray's Inn* 7 At this pencion yt is ordered that all suche persons [etc.]. **1664** *Ibid.* 449 It is ordred y^{t} Mr. Beale shall bee summoned to attend ye next pencion. **1663** in Waterhouse *Comm. Fortescue's De Laud. Leg.* 546 Every quarter,..the Readers and Benchers cause one of the Officers to summon the whole Company openly in the Hall at dinner, that such a night the Pension, or as some houses call it, the Parliament, shall be holden, which Pension, or Parliament in some houses, is nothing else but a conference and Assembly of their Benchers and Utter-Barresters onely. **1670** Blount *Law Dict.* s.v., That which in the Two Temples, is called a Parliament, in Lincolns-Inn, a Council; in Gray's-Inn, is called a Pension; that is, an Assembly of the Members of the Society, to consult of the Affairs of the House. **1897** *Daily News* 30 Jan. 8/5 At a pension held yesterday Mr. Mattinson, Q.C., Recorder of Blackburn, was elected treasurer of the Honourable Society of Gray's Inn for the ensuing year.

¶**8.** Put for pensioner. *Obs. rare.*

1544 *Suppl. to Hen. VIII* C j b, The greate burden wherewith this your realme..is ouercharged through the greate multytude of chauntery prestes, soule prestes.. muncke pencyons, morowe mas prestes.

9. *attrib.* and *Comb.*, as (sense 4) *pension act, pension age, benefit, book, fund, law, money, plan, right, scheme; pension-fee, -list, -monger, -schemer*, etc.; (senses 5–7) *pension book, house, roll, room, writ*; (sense 6) *pension-boarder, -keeper, principle, school*; *pension-dwelling, -paying, -proof* adjs.; **pension-parliament**: see parliament 8.

The pl. form *pensions* also occurs in some of the above expressions.

1839 *Southern Lit. Messenger* V. 314/1 A few tardy *pension acts..are all the tributes their worth has received. **1968** G. D. Gilling-Smith *Compl. Guide Pensions* (ed. 2) i. 16 The 1908 Old Age Pensions Act provided a small amount for those who were already old and unable to provide for themselves. **1898** *Westm. Gaz.* 26 July 3/1 The cost..is roughly estimated at £2,340,000 if the *pension age is sixty, and £1,455,000 if the pension age is sixty-five. **1945** *Release & Resettlement* (H.M. Govt.) xii. 40 *Pensions benefits comprise pensions for widows..and orphans, and old age pensions. **1898** *Westm. Gaz.* 26 Feb. 2/1 The villa folk.. meet the *pension-boarders on terms of slight superiority. **1557** *Order of Hospitalls* F v b, Yow shall also keepe a *Pencion-Booke whiche shall declare the Number of the poore in this Citie, relieud by this Hospitall. **1569** *Pension Bk. Gray's Inn* 2 That all thys graunt may be entred into the pencion booke. **1966** *Listener* 17 Mar. 391/2 One result of having this new unified social security administration will be that the pensions book and the National Assistance book.. will become one book. **1968** 'C. Aird' *Henrietta Who?* ix. 77 Did you ever see your mother's pension book? **1974** *Times* 6 Mar. 4/3 A child's printing outfit was used in a scheme to cash stolen pension books with a face value of more than £750,000. **1601** Holland *Pliny* I. 170 [Siccius Dentatus was honoured] with a stipend or *pension-fee out of the Exchequer & chamber of the city. **1869** *Bradshaw's Railway Manual* XXI. 361 Donation to the *pension fund, 18,573*l.* **1907** G. B. Shaw *Major Barbara* III. 269 Have you gone into the insurance fund, the pension fund, the building society, the various applications of co-operation!? **1965** H. I. Ansoff *Corporate Strategy* (1968) vi. 104 At the other extreme from a fully integrated firm is a company which primarily buys and sells. This may be an investment trust, a pension fund. **1973** A. Behrend *Samarai Affair* iv. 51 'Will the Company look after him?' 'I suppose so. Their pension fund's all right.' **1976** *New Yorker* 15 Nov. 176/2 In addition to making contract concessions, the union members, through their pension funds..have become the city's bankers, lending it nearly two billion dollars in the past year. **1577** *Pension Bk. Gray's Inn* 30 A good and substanciall chist..to remayne in the *pencion house..for the keping of the bookes of account and pencion Roles. **1601** *Ibid.* 153 Mr. Necton beinge warned to come to the pencion house hath refused to come. **1838** *Southern Lit. Messenger* IV. 766 When the revolutionary *pension-law was enacted, a majority of the war-worn veterans had travelled..beyond the reach of human reward. **1816** *Gentl. Mag.* LXXXVI. I. 116 The *Pension-list was full. **1663** in Waterhouse *Comm. Fortescue's De Laud. Leg.* 544 The four houses of Court... every one that is admitted fellow, after that he is called to the Masters Commons, payeth yearly 3. shillings 4. pence which they call the *pension mony. **1749** *New Hamps. Probate Rec.* (1916) III. 733, I give..all my Waidges Prize money Pention money [etc.]. **1854** B. P. Shillaber *Life & Sayings Mrs. Partington* 190 The old lady had presented a check for a quarter's pension-money. **1953** *Stroud's Judicial Dict.* (ed. 3) III. 2143 Pension money reduced into possession by the pensioner or his agent loses its character of pension. *a* **1843** Rose in *Byron's Wks.* (1846) 230/2 *note*, My trade of place and *pension-monger. **1901** *Empire Rev.* I. 427 Habitual drunkards and convicted criminals are to be rejected in Victoria as in the other *pension-paying colonies. **1957** Clark & Gottfried *Dict. Business & Finance* 262/1 **Pension plan*, in business, a plan established and maintained by an employer to provide in a systematic manner for the payment of regular pension amounts to retired or disabled employees. **1961** *Factory* Nov. 101/1 Choose carefully between contributory or non-contributory pension plans. **1973** *N.Y. Law Jrnl.* 31 Aug. 2/4 (Advt.), Metropolitan Life can help you set up a pension plan that will entitle you to the same Federal Income Tax deductions available to other corporations. **1807** E. S. Barrett *Rising Sun* I. 189 Quirk was *pension-proof against all this womanish artillery. **1956** G. A. Hosking *Pension Schemes* xli. 283 The existence of a pension scheme acts as a deterrent when withdrawal means loss of *pension rights. **1974** O. Manning *Rain Forest* I. vi. 87 Temporary and without pension rights, the appointment carried a special salary. **1508–9** *Black Bks. Lincoln's Inn* (1899) I. 159 Item, to the Botillers for wrytyng the *Pencion Roll ijs. viijd. **1651** *Ibid.* II. 392 The Butler is every term to make up a Pencion Roll. **1828** A. Sherburne *Mem.* vi. 239 This gentle-man.. forwarded to me certificates of the continuation of my name on the pension roll. **1907** *Westm. Gaz.* 5 Apr. 10/1 Miss Robb..was the posthumous child of Captain Robb,..and was put on the State pension-roll at birth. **1721** *Black Bks. Lincoln's Inn* III. 261 Over the *Pention Roome and under the Library of this Society. **1892** C. S. Loch *Old Age Pensions & Pauperism* 3 The returns of pauperism in England and Wales are frequently quoted as absolute evidence in favour of some kind of National *Pension Scheme. **1928** Robertson & Samuels *Pension & Superannuation Funds* viii. 79 Pension schemes are growing up not only in industry proper; many institutions..have their own schemes of superannuating those in their service. **1969** T. Parker *Twisting Lane* 16, I was in a good pension scheme too. **1973** L. Holcombe *Victorian Ladies at Work* iii. 39 The government in 1875 revived its original teacher's pension scheme, established in 1846 but abolished in 1861. **1977** W. McIlvanney *Laidlaw* xxx. 140 He's worried about his family... They don't have a great pension-scheme for house-breakers. **1902** *Westm. Gaz.* 28 May 2/1 The *pension-school life of Hanover, Dresden and Leipzig.. seems a harmless enough amusement for an ordinary girl of seventeen or eighteen with some money and sufficient good sense. **1537** *Cal. Inner Temple Rec.* (1896) I. 115 Yt is also agreed..at the said parliament that a *pencion-writt shalbe served, wherby the dettes of the Howse may the soner be paid. **1576** *Pension Bk. Gray's Inn* 27 It is agreed that a pencion writt be forthwyth suede. **1670** Blount *Law Dict.*, *Pension-Writ*. When a Pension-Writ is once issued, none, sued thereby in an Inns of Court, shall be discharged or permitted to come in Commons, till all duties be paid.

pension (ˈpɛnʃən), *v.* [f. pension *sb.*; in sense 2 corresp. to F. *pensionner* (1465 in Hatz.-Darm.), med.L. *pensiōnāre* (1382 in Du Cange).]

1. *intr.* To live or stay in a pension or boarding-house; to board and lodge.

1642 Howell *For. Trav.* (Arb.) 27 When they meet with any person of note..and journey or pension with him any time. **1649** *Nicholas Papers* (Camden) I. 129 For you to pension, unless there were company sutable for you, would not I conceave be agreeable. **1714** Lady M. W. Montagu *Let. to W. Montagu* 9 Aug., It is the same thing as pensioning in a nunnery. **1879** W. Cory *Lett. & Jrnls.* (1897) 450 The small country house where we pensioned.

2. *trans.* To grant a pension to, bestow a pension upon; also (contextually), to retain or buy over with a pension. *to pension off*, to dismiss with a pension, to pension on retirement. Also *fig.* So *pensioned-off* ppl. a.

1702 Addison *Dial. Medals* iii. Wks. 1736 III. 161 One might expect, methinks, to see the Medals of that nation in the highest perfection, when there is a society pensioned and set apart on purpose for the designing of them. **1737** Pope *Hor. Epist.* II. i. 387 The hero William, and the Martyr Charles, One knighted Blackmore, and one pension'd Quarles. **1800** Wellesley in Owen *Desp.* 657 The adoption of a plan for pensioning public officers incapable of service is required. **1848** Geo. Eliot *Let.* 8 Mar. (1954) I. 254 Certainly our decayed monarchs should be pensioned off. **1849** Macaulay *Hist. Eng.* ii. I. 208 He bribed and stimulated both parties in turn, pensioned at once the ministers of the crown and the chiefs of the opposition. **1865** Dickens *Mut. Fr.* I. xv, You have taken it into your head that I mean to pension you off. **1880** G. Meredith *Let.* 27 Apr. (1970) II. 595 Owing to the attack I suffered under last year, I have been pensioned off all work of any worth of late. **1898** G. B. Shaw *Let.* 1 Sept. (1972) II. 60 My mother and I had to pension off and get rid of a relative of hers—a woman who was an incorrigible drunkard. **1916** —— *Androcles & Lion* Pref. p. lxvi, Poor people are cancers in the commonwealth, costing far more than if they were handsomely pensioned off as incurables. *a* **1953** E. O'Neill *More Stately Mansions* (1965) III. i. 154 We'll pension off your mother, and give her the house to live alone in. **1965** D. Francis *Odds Against* xi. 154, I..asked him to lend me his hack, a pensioned-off old steeplechaser. **1968** *Listener* 5 Sept. 290 The convention system..is an old and cunning harridan, as irrelevant as Mayor Daley, and should be pensioned off. **1973** C. Bonington *Next Horizon* ix. 131 Gone was the crusty old pensioned-off guide, who lived in a little cubby-hole at the end of the..living room. **1973** *Times* 14 July 8/8 What the BBC publication seems to me to need is the attention of a first-class design consultant who might suggest for example that the rule which, like a rectangular noose, strangles each page, should be pensioned off. **1974** J. Cleary *Peter's Pence* v. 144 Cork had had no gangsters, just some pensioned-off IRA boys. **1977** *R.A.F. News* 11–24 May 18/5 This is my last match report before being pensioned off.

pensionable (ˈpɛnʃənəb(ə)l), *a.* [f. pension *v.* + -able.] **a.** Qualified for, or entitled to, a pension. **b.** Of service, or injuries sustained in it: Entitling to a pension.

1882 *W. Chester* (Pennsylv.) *Local News* II. No. 19. 1 Those who incurred pensionable disabilities. **1892** *Guardian* 22 June 937/3 A teacher arrives at pensionable age. **1906** *Westm. Gaz.* 25 Jan. 4/2 There is nothing radically pensionable about old age; grey hairs are not in them-selves a claim on society. **1908** *Daily Chron.* 9 Jan. 6/7 They will have the ultimate prospect..of appointment to permanent and pensionable establishments of the Protectorate. **1920** *Act 10 & 11 Geo. V* c. 67 Sched. viii. 4 This provision shall apply to the pensionable assistants of the petty sessions clerks at Cork and Belfast. **1945** *Release & Resettlement* (H.M. Govt.) xiii. 45 If..you require..treatment on account of the pensionable disablement, such treatment will be provided. **1955** *Times* 13 Aug. 6/6 The Civil Service is to offer pensionable jobs to men and women aged between 40 and 60. **1976** *Ulverston* (Cumbria) *News* 3 Dec. 9/4 (Advt.), The post is pensionable with promotion prospects to Executive Officer grades and above.

c. Related to, connected with, or affecting a person's pension.

1909 *Westm. Gaz.* 8 Feb. 8/3 Saturday's deputation asked for the recognition of colour service in the Forces for pensionable purposes when they reached the age of sixty. **1920** *Act 10 & 11 Geo. V* c. 67 Sched. ix, The allowance awarded..shall in no case exceed two-thirds of his actual pensionable salary. **1970** *Money Which?* Mar. 55/1 If, as well as being self-employed, you have an additional job in which you are employed (i.e. one providing you with some pensionable earnings) the £750 limit will be reduced.

Hence **pensionaˈbility**, entitlement to a pension; **ˈpensionably** *adv.*

1893 *Columbus* (Ohio) *Dispatch* 5 Oct., His claim had been rejected because he was not 'pensionably disabled'. **1930** *Times Educ. Suppl.* 24 May 235/4 Sick leave privileges, and pensionability. *a* **1966** 'M. na Gopaleen' *Best of Myles* (1968) 300 Pensionability of entire local populations in respect of military service, notwithstanding international convention as to non-combatancy of juveniles, children and women.

pensionary (ˈpɛnʃənərɪ), *sb.*[1] [ad. med.L. *pensiōnāri-us*: see pension *sb.* and -ary[1] B. 1; cf. F. *pensionnaire* (14th c. in Hatz.-Darm.).]

1. One who receives a pension; often with sinister implication: One who is attached by a pension to the interest of a person or persons (expressed or implied); a creature, hireling: = pensioner 1.

a **1548** Hall *Chron., Edw. IV* 236 Many other of his Counsaill, had been in fee and pencionaries, of the Frenche kyng. **1599** Sandys *Europæ Spec.* (1632) 182 A sure enemie to the Spaniards, and to all his Favorites, partizans, and pensionaries. **1613** Sherley *Trav. Persia* 33 The Tartars.. through their dependance vpon the Turke, whose religion they professe..and whose pentionaries they were. **1698** [R. Ferguson] *View Eccles.* 84, I will not discover at present whom I know Court Pensionaries among the Presbyterian Ministers. **1874** Motley *Barneveld* I. viii. 343 A traitor to his country and a pensionary to her deadliest foe. **1874** Green *Short Hist.* x. §2. 759 The Nabob sank into a pensionary.

†**b.** The recipient of an ecclesiastical pension.

1536 Cromwell in Merriman *Life & Lett.* (1902) II. 28 All persones and vicares and other beneficed men and pensionaries within this deanry not being resident upon their benefices.

†**c.** A soldier, etc., receiving pay. *Obs.*

1555 W. Watreman *Fardle Facions* I. iv. C vj (Ethiope), Ther are throughout the whole nacion certeine houses and stockes, that are pencionaries at armes. **1582** *Bps.' Transcripts of Norton in Kent* (MS.), Was buried Julij 6. John Quylter, one of y^{e} pensionaries of Deale castle.

d. One maintained by charity or in a charitable institution: cf. pensioner 1 c.

1753 N. Torriano *Gangr. Sore. Throat* 1 That Species of Squinancy, which reigned last Year..amongst the Pensionaries of the Visitation of St. Mary in the Back-Street.

2. [= Du. *pensionaris*.] Formerly, the chief municipal magistrate of a Dutch city, with the function of a legal adviser or speaker. *Hist.*

1587 Holinshed *Chron.* III. 1411/1 Iosse de Menin, councellor and pensionarie of Dordreght. **1727** Chambers *Cycl.*, *Pensio[n]ary*, is the first minister of the regency of each city, in the province of Holland... His office is to give his advice in matters relating to the government, either of the city in particular, or of the state in general; and in assemblies of the states of the province is speaker in behalf of his city. **1756** NUGENT *Gr. Tour, Netherl.* I. 287 [Dunkirk] is governed after the manner of Flanders by a burgomaster or mayor, echevins or aldermen, and a pensionary or recorder. **1864** KIRK *Chas. Bold* II. III. i. 45 A deputation, headed by Jean Sersanders, the pensionary of Ghent.

b. *esp.* (properly ***Grand Pensionary*** = Du. *Groot Pensionaris*): The first minister and magistrate of the state or province of Holland and Zealand in the Seven United Provinces of the Netherlands (1619–1794), who was by virtue of his office president of the legislature of the province, and permanent deputy to the States General.

The dignity was first created by Johan van Olden Barneveldt, under the title of Advocate of Holland and West Friesland; it attained to great distinction when held by Johan de Witt 1653–72.

1655 *Nicholas Papers* (Camden) II. 232 Shee sent to Mr. Oudart, who wes at the Hage, and commanded him to goe to the Pensionary de Witte and assure him [etc.]. **1668** *Lond. Gaz.* No. 283/3 The Heer de Wit is still to continue Pensionary, and for an acknowledgement of the good services he has done, his Salary is raised to 3000 Guilders per annum. **1761–2** HUME *Hist. Eng.* (1806) IV. lx. 539 They immediately dispatched Paw, pensionary of Holland [1631–36], as their ambassador extraordinary to London. **1796** MORSE *Amer. Geog.* II. 337 Grand Pensionary, formerly called the advocate of the republic. **1855** MACAULAY *Hist. Eng.* xi. III. 68 The office of Pensionary, always important, was peculiarly important when the Stadtholder was absent from the Hague. **1876** BANCROFT *Hist. U.S.* VI. xli. 235 The commercial treaty between France and the United States was, about the same time, delivered to the Grand Pensionary and to the Pensionary of Amsterdam.

c. *transf.* Applied as a satirical nickname to English statesmen.

1771 SMOLLETT *Humph. Cl.* 2 June, Ha! there's the other great phænomenon, the grand pensionary [Pitt], that weather-cock of patriotism, that veers about in every point of the political compass, and still feels the wind of popularity in his tail. **1836** DISRAELI *Runnymede Lett.* (1885) 206 This grand pensionary of bigotry and sedition presumes to stir up the people of England against your high estate.

3. = PENSIONER 5. (In quot., a church or chapel charged with an annual payment to a mother church.)

1891 P. G. STONE *Archit. Antiq. I. Wight* III. 5 The Parish of Brighstone..a chapel was built here... Being built after the foundation of Calbourne church, this latter claimed it as a pensionary.

ˈpensionary, *sb.*[2] [f. PENSION *sb.* + -ARY[1] B. 2; on L. type **pensiōnāria* or *-ārium*.] A dwelling or place of residence for pensioners: formerly, at Cambridge, a residence for undergraduates not on the foundation of a college.

1582–3 in Willis & Clark *Cambridge* (1886) II. 248 For thatchinge the barne and stable in Pensionary..xlvj[s]. **1621** *Ibid.* I. 186 The chambers in y[e] late pensionary. **1698** *Ibid.*, Y[e] Battlements in y[e] Pensionarie towards the Street. **1655** FULLER *Hist. Camb.* (1840) 41. **1886** WILLIS & CLARK *Cambridge* II. 248 Accommodation [for more students] was provided [*c* 1590] in some houses opposite the college [St. John's], on the site of which the New Divinity School partly stands. This was called 'The Pentionary'.

pensionary (ˈpɛnʃənərɪ), *a.* [ad. med.L. *pensiōnāri-us*: see PENSION *sb.* and -ARY[1] A.]

1. That is in receipt of a pension or bounty; in the pay of a person or persons expressed or implied; hence, mercenary, hireling, venal.

a **1548** HALL *Chron., Edw. IV* 236 To thintent to bragge another day, that the kynges Chamberlain of Englande, hath been pencionary, with the Frenche kyng. **1598** BARRET *Theor. Warres* V. iii. 136 Fraunce, and Flanders, too full of his pencionary troupes. **1679–88** *Secr. Serv. Money Chas. & Jas.* (Camden) 124 To Mary, widow of Henry Peacock, pencionary trumpeter to King Charles the Second, bounty ..20 0 0. **1790** BURKE *Fr. Rev.* Wks. V. 268. **1825** W. TAYLOR in *Monthly Rev.* CVI. 488 An extensive pensionary clergy. **1837** [see PARLIAMENT *sb.*[1] 8]. **1880** MASSON *Milton* VI. 221.

2. Consisting, or of the nature, of a pension.

1631 BRATHWAIT *Whimzies, Launderer* 59 Her age receives for her long service a pencionary recompence. **1771–2** *Ess. fr. Batchelor* (1773) II. 127 They even obtained pensionary favours for years. **1889** *Times* 19 June, The pensionary aid is insignificant.

†**3.** Characterized by an ecclesiastical pension or endowment. *Obs.*

1569 *Reg. Privy Council Scot.* I. 684 He is lauchfullie providit of auld in and to the vicarag pensionarie of the samyn.

‖**pensione** (pensiˈone). [It.] In Italy, a small hotel or boarding house.

1938 E. AMBLER *Cause for Alarm* v. 85, I must make a real effort to find a *pensione*. **1957** R. MACAULAY *Last Lett. to Friend* (1962) 252 We stayed in a small and pleasant *pensione* on the Giudecca Canal. **1967** R. SAWKINS *Snow in Paradise* ii. 23 He lived for a while at a *pensione* round the corner. **1969** R. AIRTH *Snatch!* iv. 30 We got to this *pensione* off Via Margutta. **1975** C. MOTT-RADCLYFFE *Foreign Body* ii. 27 They lived in a *pensione* nearby.

pensioned (ˈpɛnʃənd), *ppl. a.* [f. PENSION *v.* + -ED[1].] In receipt of a pension; now *esp.* retired on a pension; in earlier use often implying venality.

1611 COTGR., *Pensionné*, pensioned, stipended, hired by pension, that takes an yearelie stipend. **1733** POPE *Hor. Sat.* II. i. 111 Could pension'd Boileau lash in honest strain Flatt'rers and Bigots ev'n in Louis' reign? **1815** L. HUNT *Feast of Poets*, etc. 78 Mr. Southey, who is one of the pensioned reviewers in the Quarterly, does not blush to tell those who are acquainted with his former opinions..that a mere stickler for Reform..is little better than a 'house-breaker'. **1897** *Daily News* 26 Feb. 7/4 Among the others engaged..are twelve pensioned policemen, six army pensioners, and two pensioned firemen.

pensioneer (ˌpɛnʃəˈnɪə(r)), *v.* [f. PENSION *sb.* + -EER, after ELECTIONEER *v.*] To bid for votes in an election by promising higher pensions. Hence **ˌpensioˈneering** *vbl. sb.*

1959 *Daily Tel.* 9 June 17/4 The word 'pensioneering'.. has recently been added to the political vocabulary... 'Pensioner, you can't trust the Labour Party. They are simply pensioneering, trying to buy your votes on a promise of 10s.' **1960** *Times* 24 Oct. (Financial Rev.) p. xiii/3 That the paradox of comparative insecurity in the midst of affluence is a disturbing thing..has become apparent in the political field..in the shape of competitive 'pensioneering'. **1963** *Times* 23 Jan. 11/7 As the number of pensioners who could not recover financially from the great depression of the 1930's falls away, what *The Times* called 'pensioneering' becomes politically less productive. *a* **1974** R. CROSSMAN *Diaries* (1975) I. 276 Under cross-examination they got into a horrible mess and confirmed my fear that the whole strategy of our pensioneering, worked out for years before the election, had been jettisoned almost without noticing it by the Minister under the *diktat* of Douglas Houghton.

pensioner (ˈpɛnʃənə(r)). Also 5 pensener, 6–7 penc-, pentioner. [a. AF. *pensionner* = OF. *pensionnier* (1365 in Godef.) = med.L. *pensiōnārius*; f. *pension*, PENSION: see -ER[2].]

I. One who receives a pension or payment.

1. One who is in receipt of pension or regular pay; one who is in the pay of another; in early use, a paid or hired soldier, a mercenary; in 17–18th c. often with implication of base motives: a hireling, tool, creature.

1487 *Rolls of Parlt.* VI. 396/2 The said Wages, Fees and Rewardes, of the said Capiteyne, Lieutenaunte and Souldeours, Artificers, Pensioners and Feodaries, of the said Towne of Caleis and Castell ther. **1549** *Compl. Scot.* xx. 166 ȝe ar be cum sodiours & pensionaris to ȝour enemeis. **1673** *Essex Papers* (Camden) I. 76 All which gives me ground to suspect he is a Pensioner of France. *a* **1693** LD. DELAMER *Chas. II.'s Pensioners* Wks. (1694) 116 The Name of a Pensioner is very distastful to every English Spirit. **1732** POPE *Ep. Bathurst* 394 In Britain's Senate he a seat obtains, And one more pensioner St. Stephen gains. **1771** SMOLLETT *Humph. Cl.* 5 June, If all the clerks of the Treasury, of the Secretaries, the War-office and the Admiralty should take it in their heads to throw up their places, in imitation of the great pensioner [Pitt]. **1863** *Annals of Engl.* III. 63 (an. 1668) Charles [II.] became the pensioner of the French king. **1874** MOTLEY *Barneveld* I. ix. 365 A tool of the court and a secret pensioner of Spain.

b. *spec.* One who is in receipt of a pension or stated allowance, in consideration of past services or on account of injuries received in service; formerly applied esp. to the inmates of Chelsea and Greenwich Hospitals.

1706–1849 [see OUT-PENSIONER]. **1721** AMHERST *Terræ Fil.* No. 44 (1754) 234 If the single article of losing an arm or a leg gives a man the precedence of Æneas, many a poor pensioner of Chelsea college hath an equal right to it with his lordship. **1834** *Tait's Mag.* 196/2 The office of Comptrollers of Army Accounts is to be abolished, and the in-pensioners of Kilmainham are to be removed to Chelsea. **1855** MACAULAY *Hist. Eng.* xx. IV. 408 Greyheaded old pensioners who crept about the arcades and alleys of Chelsea Hospital.

†**c.** One maintained by public charity or in a charitable institution. *Obs.*

1557 *Order of Hospitalls* C j, The Number of children remaining and Pencioners relieved at the Cities charge.

†**d.** The recipient of an ecclesiastical pension; a beneficed clergyman: = PENSIONARY *sb.*[1] 1 b.

1578 *Reg. Privy Council Scot.* III. 22 Gif ony beneficit man or pensionare sall happin to be slayne,..the narrest qualifiit persoun of his kin sal have the presentatioun and provisioun of his benefice and gift of his pensioun. **1581** *Ibid.* 422 Parson of Eglischame and vicar pensioner of Kilmarnok.

e. *fig.*

1742 YOUNG *Nt. Th.* I. 67 And can Eternity belong to me, Poor Pensioner on the Bounties of an Hour? **1878** B. TAYLOR *Deukalion* I. i. 17 We, Earth's pensioners, Expect less bounty when her store is scant.

†**2.** *spec.* One of a body of gentlemen, instituted by Henry VIII in 1509, as a body-guard to the sovereign within the royal palace; a gentleman-at-arms: = GENTLEMAN 2 b. *Obs.*

Originally called *Spearmen*, in 1539 *Pensioners*, later *Gentlemen-Pensioners*; now *Gentlemen-at-arms*.

a **1548** HALL *Chron., Hen. VIII* 239 The kyng rode to the last ende of the ranke where the Speares or Pencyoners stoode. **1573–80** BARET *Alv.* P 253 Pensioner, a Gentleman about his Prince alwaie redie, with his speare: a spearer. **1598** SHAKS. *Merry W.* II. ii. 79. **1601** STOW *Annals* 973 (an. 1539) In the moneth of December, were appointed to wayte on the kings person 50. Gentlemen, called Pencioners or Speares, like as they were in the first yeere of the king. **1603** LD. G. HUNSDEN *Let. to Jas. I* in Chamberlayne *St. Gt. Brit.* (1737) 230 It pleased Her Majesty..to grace me with the Captain-ship of Her Band of Gentlemen-Pensioners. **1630–1706** [see GENTLEMAN 2 b]. **1737** J. CHAMBERLAYNE *St. Gt. Brit.* II. 229 His Majesty's Honourable Band of Gentlemen-Pensioners. *Ibid.* 231 The Band of Pensioners have the Honour to bear the King's Royal Banner.

†**b.** *transf.* A member of a body-guard, an attendant, a retainer. *Obs.*

1603 HOLLAND *Plutarch's Mor.* 417 When his guard and pensioners were come to this cottage where he [Antiochus] had beene lodged. **1632** —— *Cyrupædia* 173 Hereupon he draweth out of them a guard of ten thousand Pensioners, who night and day should watch..his Palace.

fig. **1590** SHAKS. *Mids. N.* II. i. 10, I serue the Fairy Queene,..The Cowslips tall, her pensioners bee. **1632** MILTON *Penseroso* 10 Hovering dreams, The fickle Pensioners of Morpheus train.

3. The officer in the Inns of Court who collected the pensions, kept the pension-book or pension-roll, and accounted for the moneys received (cf. PENSION *sb.* 5). *Obs.* exc. *Hist.*

1429–30 *Black Bks. of Lincoln's Inn* I. 4 Pensener. **1481–2** *Ibid.* 74 To maister Lovell, at y[t] tyme Pensionar. **1507** *Inner Temple Rec.* 9 On part to remayne in the seid chest and the other with the pencyoner. **1570** *Pension Bk. Gray's Inn* I There shalbe provided 3 dozen of sasers be the pencioner. **1651** *Black Bks. Lincoln's Inn* II. 393 It is ordered..that there shalbe a Pencioner yearely chosen. **1663** in Waterhouse *Comm. Fortescue's De Laud. Leg.* 544 Of these [Benchers] is one yearly chosen, which is called the Treasurer, or in some house Pensioner, who receiveth yearly the said pension money. **1903** *Staple Inn & its Story* 54 The pensioner, corresponding much to what we term the bursar of a college, was elected by the ancients.

†**4.** A PENSIONARY of a Dutch city or province; the (Grand) Pensionary of Holland. *Obs.*

1652 EARL MONM. tr. *Bentivoglio's Hist. Relat.* 5 The greatest is usually compos'd of one or two Burgomasters, some Sheriffs, one Scout Master, one Treasurer, and one or two Pensioners. **1669** *Lond. Gaz.* No. 428/4 The Heer Iohan de Witt Counsellor of Dordrecht, and a neer kinsman of the Pensioner of that name. **1673** TEMPLE *Observ. United Prov.* Wks. 1731 I. 32 The Pensioner..is a Civil-Lawyer, vers'd in the Customs, and Records, and Privileges of the Town, concerning which he informs the Magistracy upon Occasion, and vindicates them upon Disputes with other Towns. **1756** NUGENT *Gr. Tour, Netherl.* I. 19 The pensioner of Holland, who sits with the nobility, delivers their vote, and assists at all their deliberations.

II. One who makes a stated periodical payment.

†**5.** A tributary. *Obs. rare.*

1590 R. HICHCOCK *Quintess. Wit* 60 A State..her neighbours, to haue her their freende, doo make them selues her Pencionares. **1596** DALRYMPLE tr. *Leslie's Hist. Scot.* IV. 210 In the meine tyme the Britanis quha now x ȝeiris had bene pensioneris to the Scottis, quyetlie, throuch counsel of Conan..conspyre against the Scottis and Peychtes.

6. At Cambridge University: An under-graduate student who is not a Scholar on the foundation of a college, or a Sizar; one who pays for his own commons and other expenses; = *Commoner* at Oxford.

?*c* **1450** in *Cole's MS.* (B.M. Addit. 5845) lf. 179 b, Item, the Monkys pay to the Bedellys in Quinquagesima Dominica, every Monke that is a Pensyoner—xxd... except that he be a Graduatt, then he shall not pay. **1570** G. HARVEY *Letter-bk.* (Camden) 3 The Pensionars were also forthwith propoundid. **1775** MASON *Mem. Gray* Gray's Poems 3 From thence he removed to St. Peter's College, Cambridge, where he was admitted a pensioner in the year 1734. **1796** MORSE *Amer. Geog.* II. 111 The greater pensioners are sons of the nobility..dine with the fellows.. the lesser pensioners dine with the scholars that are on the foundation, but live at their own expense. **1888** A. DOBSON *Goldsmith* 20 He [Goldsmith] had hoped to go to Trinity College as a pensioner. **1900** *Camb. Univ. Cal*, 5 Orders in the several Colleges: 1. Head, 2. Fellows,..6. Scholars, 7. Pensioners, who form the great body of the Students, who pay for their commons, chambers, &c., 8. Sizars.

†**7.** One who lives in a house or institution paying for lodging and board; a boarder; *esp.* a girl or woman living *en pension* in a convent or school in France, Belgium, etc.; = F. *pensionnaire*. *Obs.*

1672 DRYDEN *Assignation* IV. iv, We are the two new pensioners, Laura and Violetta. **1691** tr. *Emilianne's Observ. Journ. Naples* 137 All of them take in Pensioners, and there is never a Religious House, that hath not at the least Three-score or Fourscore of them. **1745** ELIZA HEYWOOD *Female Spect.* No. 10 (1748) II. 187 She entered into a monastery, where she still lives a pensioner. **1827** SCOTT *Napoleon* ii. Wks. 1870 IX. 397 *note*, The..convent..where Josephine was..a pensioner or boarder.

8. *attrib.*, as ***pensioner guide, messenger***; ***pensioner parliament*** (see PARLIAMENT *sb.*[1] 8).

1678 LUTTRELL *Brief Rel.* 9 Nov. (1857) I. 3 It was a parliament that gave those vast summs of money, and therefore called the pensioner parliament. **1711–12** STEELE *Spect.* No. 326 ¶2 A Band of Pensioner-Matrons, and an old Maiden Relation. **1856** RUSKIN *Harbours Eng.* Pref., My pensioner guide..at Greenwich Hospital. **1898** *Daily News* 22 Mar. 5/2 Wherever there are park-keepers wanted, customs watchers, prison warders, inland revenue, or pensioner messengers, there the retired soldier has his chance.

Hence **ˈpensionership**, the office or position of a pensioner (in quot. in sense 3).

1569 *Pension Bk. Gray's Inn* (1901) 3 Mr. Stanhope for hys dilligence used in thoffice of the pentionershipp shalbe allowed on varlett.

pensionless (ˈpɛnʃənlɪs), *a.* [f. PENSION *sb.* + -LESS.] Without a pension, unpensioned.

1832 *Examiner* 834/2 Pensionless and placeless aristocrats. **1881** S. LANE-POOLE in *Macm. Mag.* XLIV. 221/1 The pensionless discharged soldier. **1969** *Guardian* 22 Oct. 10/6 If your husband dies before you are 50, and you have no children, you are thrown pensionless into a hard world. **1974** 'R. TATE' *Birds of Bloodied Feather* iii. 74 Pensionless, I looked round for a job.

‖**pensionnaire** (pɑ̃sjɔnɛr). [F. (14th c. in Hatz.-Darm.) = med.L. *pensiōnārius*, and Eng. PENSIONARY, PENSIONER.] **a.** One in receipt of a pension; a pensioner, a paid retainer. *rare.* **b.** One who boards in a French lodging-house, institution, or family. **c.** A junior member of the *Comédie Française*.

1598 DALLINGTON *Meth. Trav.* M iij b, Of his [King of France's] Expence, ..it is very hard to relate an exact proportion, considering .. the vncertainty of the numbers of Pensionaires, or prouisioned. *a* **1794** GIBBON *Autobiog. & Corr.* (1869) 73, I now entered myself as a *pensionaire*, or boarder, in the elegant house of Mr. De Mesery. **1833** L. RITCHIE *Wand. by Loire* 46 The pensionnaires of the nuns of Saint Ursula were next. **1897** *Daily News* 1 Jan. 2/3 The average age of the new pensionnaires is seventy. **1897** *Westm. Gaz.* 2 Sept. 5/2 Some young people who were staying in his house as pensionnaires. **1901** *Scotsman* 16 Apr. 8/7 The distribution of rôles among sociétaires and pensionnaires—full members of the company and salaried aspirants.

‖**pensionnat** (pɑ̃sjɔna). [Fr.] **a.** In France and other European countries, a boarding-school. **b.** = PENSION *sb.* 6 b.

1840 J. R. HOPE-SCOTT in R. Ornsby *Mem.* (1884) I. xiii. 247 Their pupils [in Germany] might come to their classes, but at night they go home, and in their pensionnats .. it was impossible to prevent the parents coming every fifteen days or so. **1853** C. BRONTË *Villette* I. vii. 121 As I spoke English, she concluded I was a foreign teacher come on business connected with the Pensionnat. **1867** J. A. SYMONDS *Let.* 26 Sept. (1967) I. 761 We do not see very much of other Pensionnats. They are formed chiefly of Germans, Russians & Americans. **1896** C. SHORTER *C. Brontë & her Circle* iv. 100 The girls were day boarders at the Pensionnat. **1933** *Times Lit. Suppl.* 28 Sept. 653/1 A mildly amusing story in mildly bad taste about a *pensionnat* in Switzerland. **1963** *Listener* 10 Jan. 73/1 There are increasing numbers of hotels .. called *pensionnats*. These differ from regular hotels in providing only the bare facilities of rooms and meals. **1967** R. PETRIE *Foreign Bodies* ii. 27 'Then this house is a *pension?* A boarding establishment? .. And not, definitely not, a *pensionnat?*' .. 'Ah, Monsieur .. we are a boarding-house, not a boarding-school.' **1972** A. CHRISTIE *Elephants can Remember* v. 78 They had children... A boy at school in England and a girl at a *pensionnat* in Switzerland.

†'**pensionry.** *Obs. rare*$^{-1}$. [f. PENSIONER: see -RY.] A body of pensioners or paid retainers.

1641 MILTON *Ch. Govt.* II. Wks. 1851 III. 177 He should need no other pretorian band nor pensionry then these, if they could once with their perfidious preachments aw the people.

†'**pensitate,** *v. Obs. rare.* [f. L. *pensit-āre*, iterative of *pensāre* to weigh carefully, consider, freq. or intensive of *pendĕre*, *pens-* to weigh: see -ATE³.] *trans.* To consider, ponder. So †**pensitation** [ad. L. *pensitātiōn-em*], consideration, pondering.

1623 COCKERAM, *Pensitate*, to consider, to ponder. *Pensitation*, a considering. **1647** LILLY *Chr. Astrol.* cxvi. 562 He that .. will well pensitate what precedes, may frame a considerable judgment. **1651** BIGGS *New Disp.* 152 A judicial and serious pensitation.

pensitive, erron. form of PENSATIVE *Obs.*

pensive ('pɛnsɪv), *a.* (*sb.*) Forms: 4-6 **pensyf**, (**-yfe**, **-yff**), 5-6 **pensif**, **-cyf**; 5-6 **pensyve**, (5 **pensiwe**, 6 **-seue**, 6-7 *Sc.* **pansiue**), 6- **pensive**. [a. F. *pensif*, *-ive* (11th c. in Hatz.-Darm.), f. *penser* to think: see -IVE.]

1. Full of thought; plunged in thought; thoughtful, meditative, musing; reflective: often with some tinge of seriousness or melancholy (cf. 3).

1362 LANGL. *P. Pl.* A. VIII. 133 Ful pensyf in myn herte; For [1377 of] þat I sauh slepynge, ȝif hit so be mihte. *c* **1440** *Partonope* 3853 Pensyfe thaughtfull alle day sytteth he. **1563** B. GOOGE *Eglogs* vi. (Arb.) 54 With pensyfe heart full fraight with thoughts, I fled from thence away. **1639** N. N. tr. *Du Bosq's Compl. Woman* I. 33 He had a greater feare of those who were pensive as Brutus. **1794** MRS. RADCLIFFE *Myst. Udolpho* i, The sweet expression of her pensive face. **1863** I. WILLIAMS *Baptistery* II. xxxi. (1874) 172 Lost in Bewild'rings of his pensive mind.

†**2.** Thoughtful or meditative as to plans and future events. Passing into **b.** Full of anxious thought or foreboding; anxious, apprehensive. *Obs.*

c **1375** *Sc. Leg. Saints* i. (*Petrus*) 320 Symon and Nero ay Ar full pensyve how þai may Confownd þe. **1422** tr. *Secreta Secret., Priv. Priv.* 138 He sholde be Purveyaunt and Pensyfe of thynges that may come aftyrwarde. **1477** EARL RIVERS *Dictes* 109 He abode in his hous right pensyf and ful of thoughte how he might escape fro this perille. **1549** COVERDALE, etc. *Erasm. Par. 2 Cor.* vii. 54, I .. was so pensyfe .. leste this infeccion myghte crepe among you. **1606** HOLLAND *Sueton.* 128 What pensive care he tooke, as touching his health and safetie. **1654** WHITLOCK *Zootomia* 15, I owe not Misery the service to meet it, by pensive fears.

3. 'Sorrowfully thoughtful, sorrowful; mournfully serious; melancholy' (J.); gloomy, sad.

c **1375** *Sc. Leg. Saints* xxx. (*Theodera*) 129, I pray þe, sir, þu tel me quhy þu art nov pensiwe & mad, & wont wes to be blith & glad. *c* **1430** LYDG. *Min. Poems* (Percy Soc.) 206 Suche as be pensyff make hem glad and murye. **1596** DRAYTON *Legends* II. 583 The heavie burthen of my pensive brest. **1664** H. MORE *Myst. Iniq., Apol.* viii. §12 For the cherishing and comforting the innocent, serious and pensive. **1703** MAUNDRELL *Journ. Jerus.* (1732) 64 She sat down weary and pensive at so sad a disappointment. **1838** LYTTON *Alice* I. ii, Seeing her mother's emotion, [she] kissed away the tears from the pensive eyes. **1871** R. ELLIS *Catullus* xcvi. 3 When to a love long cold some pensive pity recals us.

†**b.** Const. *of*, *for*, or *infin.*: Sorry. *Obs.*

c **1450** *Merlin* i. 6 My suster is so hevy and pensif of our mys-happes. **1577-87** HOLINSHED *Chron.* (1807) II. 137 King Henrie doubtlesse was right pensive for his [Becket's] death. **1615** BRATHWAIT *Strappado* (1878) 32 Pensiue still To doe whats good, but frolike to doe ill.

4. *transf.* Of things: Suggestive of, associated with, or implying thought, anxiety, or melancholy.

†**b.** Carefully considered (*obs.*).

1548 UDALL *Erasm. Par. Luke* xxi. 34 With the other pensife cares of this present life. *a* **1560** ROLLAND *Crt. Venus* II. 539 Sine to counsall thay passit all beliue. Considderit weill the sentence was pensiue. **1633** MAY *Hen. II*, VI. 439 They .. thither pensive sackcloth brought. **1685** LADY RUSSELL in *Buccleuch MSS.* (Hist. MSS. Comm.) I. 344, I have now left the country and the pensive quiet of it. *a* **1732** GAY *Fables* II. vii. 46 Would that avert one pensive hour? **1792** S. ROGERS *Pleas. Mem.* II. 207 Pensive Twilight in her dusky car. **1830** SCOTT *Demonol.* viii. 246 How have I sate while piped the pensive wind. **1860** HAWTHORNE *Marb. Faun* (Tauchn.) II. iv. 45 Adam .. never knew the shade of pensive beauty which Eden won from his expulsion.

5. *absol.* as *sb.* Pensive manner or mood.

1775 C. JOHNSTON *Pilgrim* 122 The Archbishop and he have parted not the best pleased with each other, which has put my friend a little in the pensives. *a* **1814** *Manœuvring* II. i. in *New Brit. Theatre* II. 89 Fold your arms as if you were musing—no, not so—more on the pensive.

Hence †'**pensived** *a.*, *nonce-wd.*, ? rendered pensive or sad, saddened.

1597 SHAKS. *Lover's Compl.* 219 These trophies of affections hot, Of pensiv'd and subdued desires the tender.

†'**pensivehead.** *Obs. rare.* [See -HEAD.] Pensiveness.

? *a* **1412** LYDG. *Two Merchants* 874 And seide, 'Freend, your pensifheed asswage!' *a* **1450** —— *Merita Missæ* in *Lay Folks Mass Bk.* 392 Now hope, now dred, now pensyffhede, now thought, Al thyse yfere palen myn chere and hewe.

'**pensively**, *adv.* [f. PENSIVE *a.* + -LY².] In a pensive manner: **a.** With meditation; meditatively, thoughtfully, musingly; **b.** With serious or melancholy thoughtfulness.

1569 SPENSER *Vis. Petrarch* in *Theat. Worldl.* B vj b, On herbes and floures she walked pensiuely. **1613** SHAKS. *Hen. VIII*, II. ii. *Stage direct.*, The King drawes the Curtaine and sits reading pensiuely. *Suff.* How sad he lookes; sure he is much afflicted. **1651** HOBBES *Govt. & Soc.* Pref., Whilest I contrive, order, pensively and slowly compose these matters. **1791** MRS. RADCLIFFE *Rom. Forest* viii, She sat for some time leaning pensively on her arm. **1879** FROUDE *Short Stud.* (1883) IV. v. 374 He had walked down the bank pensively while I was in the difficulty.

pensiveness ('pɛnsɪvnɪs). [f. as prec. + -NESS.] The quality or state of being pensive; thoughtfulness, usually tinged with melancholy; heaviness of mind or heart, sadness, melancholy; †anxious thought as to coming events, apprehensiveness (*obs.*).

1412-20 LYDG. *Chron. Troy* II. xiv. (1555), Now ye are gone, pensyfnesse me sleath. **1515** BARCLAY *Egloges* iii. in *Cyt. & Uplondyshm.* (Percy Soc.) p. lvii, The pensiveness and payne Of courtiers or they their wages can obtayne. **1582** N. LICHEFIELD tr. *Castanheda's Conq. E. Ind.* I. xxix. 73 The rest of the Fleete was so cast away before their eyes, wherewith they were stroken into a very great pensiuenesse. **1601** HOLLAND *Pliny* I. 8 He deliuered the army from all pensiuenes and feare. **1670** EACHARD *Cont. Clergy* 22 For him that rives blocks or carries packs, there is no great expence of parts, no anxiety of mind, no great intellectuall pensiveness. **1752** JOHNSON *Rambler* No. 204 ⁋7 The moments crept imperceptibly away through the gloom of pensiveness. **1827** J. W. CROKER *Diary* 17 Feb., There was not only no grief, but not even a decent pensiveness. **1858** HAWTHORNE *Fr. & It. Note-Bks.* II. 31 The divine pensiveness of a Madonna's face.

pensone, obs. form of PENSION.

penstemon, var. spelling of PENTSTEMON.

penster ('pɛnstə(r)). *rare.* [f. PEN *sb.*² or *v.*³ + -STER.] One who uses a pen in a small way; a petty writer; a literary hack.

1611 COTGR., *Plumeteur*, a Scribe, Clerke, Penne-man, Scriuener, Penster. **1871** G. MEREDITH *H. Richmond* I. 311 Oh! the poor penster! **1902** *Sat. Rev.* 22 Feb. 224/1 The enterprising penster who acted for a daily paper.

penstock¹ ('pɛnstɒk). [f. PEN *sb.*¹ + STOCK *sb.*]

1. A sluice or flood-gate for restraining or regulating the flow from a head of water formed by a 'pen' (see PEN *sb.*¹ 3), as in a water-mill.

1607 COWELL *Interpr.* s.v. *Bay*, Water comming out of them by a passage or flud-gate (called the penstocke). **1725** *Lond. Gaz.* No. 6420/3 A Penstock of a Pond. **1801** *Trans. Soc. Arts* XIX. 268 The penstock, which regulates the quantity of water running to the wheel. **1864** *Daily Tel.* 26 July, There are sixteen openings .. through which the sewage flows into the reservoirs as regulated by the penstocks—or floodgates.

attrib. **1791** R. MYLNE *Rep. Thames & Isis* 52 Two ten ft. Bridges to a Penstock ditch. **1861** *Times* 7 Oct., The penstock-chamber, tide flaps, and overflow channel at the junction of the High Level, the Middle Level, and the Outfall Sewers are works of magnitude and interest.

2. a. (orig. and chiefly *U.S.*) The channel or trough in which a penstock (in sense 1) is placed: = PENTROUGH. **b.** A tube by which water is conveyed from a head of water into a turbine. **c.** Also applied to the barrel of a pump, through which the water passes up.

1799 *Trans. Amer. Philos. Soc.* IV. 349 Let ABCD Fig. 1 represent a large cistern or penstock, and MKLN an orifice made in one of its sides. **1828** WEBSTER, *Penstock*, a narrow or confined place formed by a frame of timber planked or boarded, for holding or conducting the water of a mill-pond to a wheel, and furnished with a flood gate which may be shut or opened at pleasure. **1864** *Ibid.*, *Pen-stock*... 2. The barrel of a wooden pump. **1894** *Pop. Sci. Monthly* XLV. 613 A penstock .. is a great tube, usually, .. of boiler plate .. conveying water under head into the wheel-case in which the turbine revolves. **1933** *Discovery* Apr. 110/2 The station is several miles below Niagara Falls, the water being led to the 'pen-stocks' (the tubes which guide the water to the turbines) by means of a concrete canal from a point above the falls. **1955** *Times* 14 May 13/1 With the expected completion in 1955 of a modern wood-handling system and major repairs to its older penstocks, the company will have reached the end of the rehabilitation programme. **1963** *Weekly News* (Auckland) 21 Aug. 27 Six parallel penstocks made from prestressed concrete will carry the water from Lake Benmore. **1965** E. L. MYLES *Emperor of Peace River* I. xiii. 135 They whip-sawed lumber for the roof and the penstock flue [of a water mill].

'**penstock**². *rare*$^{-0}$. [f. PEN *sb.*² + STOCK *sb.*] A penholder.

1864 WEBSTER, *Pen-stock*... 3. The handle used with a metallic or other pen.

‖**pensum** ('pɛnsəm). *rare.* [L. *pensum* weight, charge, duty, in F. an 'imposition' at school; f. L. *pendĕre* to weight.] A charge, duty, or allotted task; a school-task or lesson to be prepared; also (*U.S.*) a lesson or piece of work imposed as a punishment, a school 'imposition'.

1705 J. HOWE *Wks.* (1834) 298/1 (Stanf.) Every one hath his *pensum*, his allotment of work and time assigned him in this world. **1880** J. W. SHERER *Conjuror's Daughter* 91 John Dowse .. worked at his daily task as a schoolboy sat down to his pensum. **1890** in *Cent. Dict.*

'**pensy**, *a.* Now *Sc.* and *dial.* [f. OF. *pensif*, in nom. sing. and pl. *pensis*; cf. *hasty*, *jolly*, *tardy*.]

1. = PENSIVE.

a **1400-50** *Alexander* 2990 With princez in hys palays all pensey [*v.r.* pense] he sittes. *c* **1440** *Alph. Tales* 80 Or he passyd any forther or made ane ende, he began to wax hevy & pensie for þis thoght. **1831** J. WILSON *Noct. Ambr.* xxix. (1856) III. 177 It's an inspirin retreat .. for the inditin o' a bit cheerfu' or pensie sang! **1876** WHITEHEAD *Daft Davie*, etc. 270 Her that was now so quiet and pensy.

2. a. Giving oneself airs, self-conceited. **b.** Spruce, neat.

1715 RAMSAY *Christ's Kirk Gr.* II. ix, Furth started neist a pensy blade. *a* **1806** in *Jamieson's Pop. Ball.* I. 292 There, couthie, and pensie, and sicker, Wonn'd honest young Hab o' the Heuch. **1830** J. MCDIARMID *Sk. Nat.*, *Jeanie Deans* 382 Many of the neighbours regarded her [Helen Walker] as 'a little pensy body'—that is, conceited or proud.

3. a. Fretful, peevish (of children). **b.** Fastidious (of appetite).

a **1825** FORBY *Voc. E. Anglia*, *Pensy*, fretful; uneasy. Chiefly applied to wayward children. **1866** *N. & Q.* 3rd Ser. X. 67/1 Another person, speaking of a little dog that has been much petted, says 'he is so pensy, he will not touch new milk'. **1893** in Cozens-Hardy *Broad Norfolk* 99 She is a poor 'pensey little thing'.

pensy, pensyful, pensyl, -syll, obs. ff. PANSY, PENSIFUL, PENCIL, PENCEL.

†**pent**, *sb.*¹ *Obs.* [app. from PENT *ppl. a.*: cf. *bent* ppl. a. and sb.²]

1. A place in which water is pent up; a reservoir or enclosed pool. (Cf. PEN *sb.*¹ 3.)

1570-6 LAMBARDE *Peramb. Kent* (1826) 134 A Pent and Sluyce hath been made, which both open the mouth, and scowre the bottome of the haven. **1587** FLEMING *Contn. Holinshed* III. 1537/2 The harborough was become a pent, out of the which nothing could passe out or in. **1674** *Lond. Gaz.* No. 940/4 The Sea has broke into the Pent against the Bench, and above it towards Moots Bulwark [at Dover]. **1721** PERRY *Daggenh. Breach* 123 At the .. place called the upper Pent.

2. ? State of being pent; pressure. Cf. PEND *sb.*³ and ⁴.

1674 N. FAIRFAX *Bulk & Selv.* 72 In the middlemost, where the pent or bear of it beneath was nothing at all.

pent (pɛnt), *sb.*² [Short for PENTHOUSE, or assumed as the first element of it.] A sloping roof or covering, a PENTHOUSE. (In quot. 1760 app. repr. F. *pente* sloping surface.)

[**1647** G. DANIEL *Trinarch.*, *Hen. V* cxxxvii, As all the Toyle of Princes had beene Spent To force a Lattice, or Subdue a Pinte.] **1754** *Remembrancer* (1778) V. 487/1 A pent over the base story, and shops, and a little slip of a window to light a closet by the side of the chimnies. **1760** H. WALPOLE *Let. to Earl of Strafford* 7 June, Four chambers practised under the pent of the roof. **1883** HOLME LEE *Loving & Serving* I. ii. 22 The pent over it to throw off the rain. **1895** *Jrnl. R. Instit. Brit. Archit.* 14 Mar. 350 It is well either to have a porch or pent.

pent (pɛnt), *pa. pple.* and *ppl. a.* Also 6 **pente**, *arch.* **ipent**, 6-8 *arch.* **ypent**. [In form, pa. pple.

of †PEND *v.*[2] var. of PEN *v.*[1], and so primarily = †*pended, penned*; but in its sense-development somewhat independent of the vb.]

1. Shut up within narrow limits; closely confined, imprisoned: = PENNED *ppl. a.*[1] Also *fig.* (in quot. 1811, Restricted in action, 'straitened'). Const. (*a*) as pple., (*b*) as adj.

(*a*) **1555** W. WATREMAN *Fardle Facions* II. ix. 190 This people..pente within narowe boundes. **1579** SPENSER *Sheph. Cal.* Jan. 4 His flock, that had bene long ypent. **1667** MILTON *P.L.* IX. 445 Long in populous City pent. **1728** POPE *Dunc.* III. 185 But who is he, in closet close y-pent? **1802** *Brookes' Gazetteer* (ed. 12) s.v. *Lidford*, The bridge is thrown over a part of the river that is pent between two high rocks. **1811** W. TAYLOR in Robberds *Mem.* (1843) II. 350 Since our American losses, we have been habitually pent to live. **1871** B. TAYLOR *Faust* (1875) I. viii. 118 What bliss within this narrow den is pent.

(*b*) **1602** MARSTON *Antonio's Rev.* v. iii, The States of Venice Like high-swoln floods drive down the muddie dammes Of pent allegeance. **1626** BACON *Sylva* §232 The mingling of Open Air with Pent Air. **1764** GOLDSM. *Trav.* 291 The pent ocean, rising o'er the pile. **1852** M. ARNOLD *Empedocles on Etna* I. ii. 182 In vain our pent wills fret.

b. With *in, up*, as pple. or adj.

a **1550** *Merie Tales* in *Skelton's Wks.* (1843) I. p. lxxii, I haue ben pent in..at Westminster in prison. **1581** MULCASTER *Positions* xxxix. (1887) 187 Content to be pent vp within priuate dores. **1622** CALLIS *Stat. Sewers* (1647) 54 A River..is a running Stream, pent in on either side with Walls and Banks. **1713** DERHAM *Phys.-Theol.* 15 A stagnating, confined, pent-up Air. **1866** J. B. ROSE tr. *Ovid's Met.* 86 The pent-in wave, Chafed by obstruction. **1879** MCCARTHY *Own Times* II. xxvii. 322 A relief to perplexed, pent-up emotion.

2. Of a place, room, etc.: Shut *up*, confined. (Const. as pple. or adj.)

1594 *1st Pt. Contention* viii. 21 Go get thee gone,..And in thy pent vp studie rue my shame. **1803** *Med. Jrnl.* IX. 187 The pent up bed-house, the clothes of infection unventilated and unwashed. **1872** LONGF. *Wayside Inn* II. *Finale* 39 All left at once the pent-up room, And rushed into the open air.

†**3.** Having something pent or closely confined within it; distended or strained by being overfull of something. (Const. as pple. or adj.) *Obs.*

1601 HOLLAND *Pliny* I. 20 All parchments and such like bladders or skinnes are so pent and stretched with spirit and wind, that they burst withall. **1667** N. FAIRFAX in *Phil. Trans.* II. 546 She..found some relief by it, but was after much pent in her wind. **1728** YOUNG *Love Fame* VI. 30 Thro' dreadful silence the pent heart might break.

pent, obs. or dial. form of PAINT.

penta- (pɛntə), before a vowel **pent-**, a. Gr. πεντα-, combining form of πέντε five, occurring in many words in Greek as a variant of the earlier πεντε-, and forming the initial element in various modern technical words adopted from Greek, or formed from Greek elements or on Greek analogies. In *Chem.* it indicates the presence of five atoms of some element, as in *pentacarbon*, *penta-compound* (see below), *pentachloride*, *pentafluoride*, *pentasulphide* (*-sulphuret*), *pentoxide*, and in many-worded descriptive names without number, as *penta-nitro-diazo-amido-monoxy-homo-fluorescein*.

pentabasic (-ˈbeɪsɪk) *a. Chem.*, having five atoms of a base, or of replaceable hydrogen; **pentacanthous** (-əˈkænθəs), *a. Nat. Hist.* [Gr. ἄκανθα thorn], having five spines; **pentaˈcapsular** *a.*, having five capsules; **pentaˈcarbon** *a. Chem.*, combining five atoms of carbon: cf. PENTANE; **pentaˈcarpellary** *a. Bot.*, consisting of five carpels; **ˌpentachlor(o)ˈethane** *Chem.*, a colourless liquid, C_2HCl_5, that is an intermediate in the industrial production of certain chlorinated hydrocarbons and is used as a solvent; **ˌpentachlor(o)ˈphenate** *Chem.*, a salt of pentachlorophenol, esp. sodium pentachlorophenate, C_6Cl_5ONa, a white crystalline solid; **ˌpentachlor(o)ˈphenol** *Chem.*, a colourless, crystalline solid with acidic properties, C_6Cl_5OH, which is widely used (often as its sodium salt) in insecticides, fungicides, weed-killers, wood preservatives, etc.; **pentachromic** (-ˈkrəʊmɪk) *a.*, of five colours, capable of distinguishing (only) five colours in the spectrum; †**pentaˈcoccous** *a. Bot.* [mod.L. *coccum* carpel, f. Gr. κόκκος grain, seed] = *pentacarpellary*; or, having five seeds, or five cells each containing a seed; **ˈpenta-ˌcompound**, a chemical compound of the pentacarbon series: see PENTANE; **pentaˈcrostic** *sb.* and *a.*: see quots; **penˈtactine, penˈtactinal, -acˈtinal** *adjs. Zool.* [Gr. ἀκτίς, ἀκτῖν- ray], having five rays, as a sponge-spicule; **pentaˈcyclic** *a.* (*a*) *Bot.* [Gr. κύκλος circle], said of a flower having the parts in five cycles or whorls, (*b*) *Chem.*, containing five rings in the molecule; **pentadelphous** (-əˈdɛlfəs) *a. Bot.* [Gr. ἀδελφός brother], (of stamens) united by the filaments in five bundles; (of a plant) having the stamens so united; **ˌpenta-dodecaˈhedron**, a dodecahedron contained by twelve pentagons, a pentagonal dodecahedron; **ˈpentadrachm** (-dræm) [DRACHM], an ancient Greek coin of the value of five drachmas; **ˈpentafid** *a. Bot.* [L. *-fidus* split], cleft into five, = QUINQUIFID; **penˈtagamist** [after BIGAMIST], a person who has been married five times; **pentaˈgastrin** *Pharm.*, a synthetic pentapeptide having the same action as the hormone gastrin; **ˈpentaglot** [Gr. γλῶττα, -σσα tongue; cf. *polyglot*]: see quot.; so †**pentaˈglottical** *a.*; **pentaˈhaloid** *a. Chem.*, containing five atoms of a halogen in the molecule; **ˌpentahexaˈhedral** *a. Cryst.* [see HEXAHEDRAL], having five ranges of six facets each; so **ˌpentahexaˈhedron**, a figure of this form; **pentaˈhydrate**, a hydrate that contains five molecules of water in each molecule; so **ˌpentahyˈdrated** *a.*; **pentaˈhydric** *a. Chem.*, containing five hydroxyl groups in a molecule; **pentaˈhydrite** *Min.*, native magnesium sulphate pentahydrate, $MgSO_4 5H_2O$; **ˌpentahydroˈborite** *Min.* [ad. Russ. *pentagidroborit* (S. V. Malinko 1961, in *Zapiski Vsesoyuz. Min. Obshchesvta* XC. 673)], a hydrated calcium borate, $CaB_2O_4{\cdot}5H_2O$, occurring as small, colourless triclinic crystals; **ˌpentahydroˈcalcite** *Min.* [ad. Russ. *pentagidrokal'tsit"* (P. N. Chirvinskiĭ 1906, in *Ezhegodnik" po Geol. i Mineral. Rossii* VIII. 241)], a pentahydrate of calcium carbonate, $CaCO_3{\cdot}5H_2O$, the natural occurrence of which is uncertain; **pentaˈlemma** *Logic* [after DILEMMA], an argument analogous to a dilemma, involving five alternatives; **ˈpentalogue** (-lɒg) [after DECALOGUE], a set of five rules or laws; **penˈtalogy** [cf. TRILOGY], a combination of five mutually connected parts; a pentad; **pentaˈlophodont** *a.* [Gr. λόφος ridge, ὀδούς, ὀδοντ- tooth], having five-ridged teeth, as a mastodon of the genus *Pentalophodon* (*Cent. Dict.*); **ˈpentamer** *Chem.* [-MER], a polymeric unit or molecule made up of five monomers; hence **pentaˈmeric** *a.*; †**penˈtameride** *Chem.* [after ISOMERIDE] = *pentamer*; **pentaˈmethylene** *Chem.*, (*a*) a cyclic hydrocarbon, C_5H_{10}, usu. called cyclopentane, which is a colourless volatile liquid found in petroleum; (*b*) the bivalent straight chain radical $-(CH_2)_5-$; **pentaˌmethyleneˈdiamine** (-daɪˈæmiːn) *Chem.*, a syrupy, fuming liquid, $H_2N(CH_2)_5NH_2$, now usu. called cadaverine, which is a product of the putrefaction of animal proteins; **pentaˈnucleotide** *Biochem.*, an oligonucleotide in which the number of nucleotides is five; **pentaˈpeptide** *Biochem.*, an oligopeptide in which there are five amino-acid residues in the molecule; **pentaˈpetalous**, †**-ˈpetalose** *adjs. Bot.*, having five petals; **pentaphonic** (-ˈfɒnɪk) *a. Mus.* [Gr. φωνή sound] = PENTATONIC; **pentaphyllous** (-ˈfɪləs) *a.* [Gr. φύλλον leaf], five-leaved; so †**pentaphyˈlloideous** *a.*; **penˈtapterous** *a. Bot.* [Gr. πτερόν wing], having five wings, as certain fruits; **ˈpentaptote** *Gram.* [ad. Gr. πεντάπτωτος adj. (Priscian)], a noun having five cases; **ˈpentaptych** (-ptɪk) [Gr. πτυχή fold, after DIPTYCH, TRIPTYCH], an altar-piece or the like consisting of five leaves, i.e. a central piece and two folding pieces on each side; **penˈtarsic** *a. Pros.* [ARSIS], having five stresses; **pentaˈsepalous** *a. Bot.*, having five sepals; †**ˈpentaspast** [Gr. -σπαστος from σπά-ειν to draw, pull]: see quot.; **pentaˈspermous** *a. Bot.* [Gr. σπέρμα seed], having five seeds.

1857 MAYNE *Expos. Lex.*, *Pentacanthus*, applied to a fish with five spinous rays to one of its fins,..*pentacanthous. **1730–6** BAILEY (folio), **Pentacapsular*, having five seed pods. **1775** in ASH. **1866** ODLING *Anim. Chem.* v. 108 *Pentacarbon molecules such as amido-valeric acid or phocine. **1872** *Jrnl. Chem. Soc.* XXV 232 (*heading*) Action of bromine on *pentachlorethane. **1930** T. H. DURRANS *Solvents* vii. 119 The following azeotropic mixture is known: Pentachlorethane 85%, glycol 15%, B.P. 154·5°. **1975** *Internat. Jrnl. Chem. Kinetics* VII. 331 The rate of the inhibited pyrolysis of pentachloroethane was studied over the temperature range of 820 to 865°K using the toluene-carrier technique in a stirred-flow reactor. **1849** D. CAMPBELL *Inorg. Chem.* 290 *Pentachloride of antimony, $SbCl_5$. **1880** CLEMINSHAW *Wurtz' Atom. The.* 227 Phosphorus and antimony can unite with five atoms of chlorine to form the pentachlorides. **1938** *Jrnl. Rubber Res. Inst. Malaya* VIII. 325 The material used in the trials.. consists of sodium *pentachlorphenate and is known by the trade names of 'Santophen 20 S' or 'Santobrite'. **1959** *Times* 24 Sept. 7/2 (Advt.), The most effective chemical for preventing sapstain is Santobrite, Monsanto's sodium pentachlorophenate. **1971** F. C. FORD-ROBERTSON *Terminol. Forest Sci.* 190/1 Its sodium salt (Na pentachlor(o)phenate) is water soluble and is used for preventing fungal stain and surface mould in unseasoned timber and in eradicating dry rot from buildings. **1879** *Jrnl. Chem. Soc.* XXXVI. 463 When heated at 230° with alcohol it [*sc.* perchlorophenol chloride, C_6Cl_7OH] yields *pentachlorophenol, C_6Cl_5OH (m.p. 183–184°). **1960** E. L. DELMAR-MORGAN *Cruising Yacht Equipment & Navigation* xxiv. 231 Rotproofing... Lauryl pentachlor phenol..is colourless, odourless, and very effective, and is available in an emulsion or solution form. **1972** *Timber Trades Jrnl.* 3 June 44/1 The formulation is based upon the independently established fungicides tributyl tin oxide and pentachlorophenol. **1977** *Time* 4 Apr. 56/3 They discovered that cattle in his herd, and those on at least seven other farms in the state, have been ingesting a wood preservative called pentachlorophenol (PCP)—probably when the animals licked the sides of their feed bins. **1900** *Lancet* 4 Aug. 323/1 Intermediate between normal and dichromic colour vision there are those whose vision is *pentachromic, tetrachromic, and trichromic. **1902** *19th Cent.* Apr. 607 Those who see five colours may be termed pentachromic. **1707** SLOANE *Jamaica* I. 209 It [the fruit] is *pentacoccous, or divided into five Cellulæ, containing each a blackish Seed. **1866** ODLING *Anim. Chem.* iv. 66 Of tri-, tetra-, and *penta-compounds, including glycerine, the lactic, butyric..and valeric acids. **1730–6** BAILEY (folio), **Pentachrostick*, a set or series of verses so disposed, that there are always found five acrosticks of the same name in five divisions of each verse. **1828** WEBSTER, *Pentacrostic, a.*, containing five acrostics of the same name in five divisions of each verse. **1887** SOLLAS in *Encycl. Brit.* XXII. 417/1 Modifications of the triaxon hexactine type. *a*, dagger;..*e*, *pentactine. **1875** BENNETT & DYER *Sachs' Bot.* 548 The flowers of Gramineæ and Orchideæ can be traced back to the trimerous *pentacyclic type. **1899** *Jrnl. Chem. Soc.* LXXVI. I. 742 It is one of the first cases observed of the conversion of a pentacyclic into a hexacyclic carbon compound. **1972** *Science* 16 June 1230/1 *Tetrahymena*..contains a pentacyclic triterpenoid which has not been found in other animals. **1830** LINDLEY *Nat. Syst. Bot.* 36 They [the Cotton Tree tribe] are also known by their *pentadelphous stamens. **1857** HENFREY *Bot.* §212 In Hypericaceæ we have triadelphous, and pentadelphous states; but these..are generally denominated polyadelphous. **1869** PHILLIPS *Vesuv.* x. 273 These five types of form, all regular,..and all parts of one equi-axed system, may be named and employed to designate crystals, ..the cube, octahedron,..*penta-dodecahedron. **1807** ROBINSON *Archæol. Græca* v. xxvi. 548 Besides the tetradrachm..were coined *pentadrachms and hexadrachms. **1882** OGILVIE, **Pentafid*. **1880** CLEMINSHAW *Wurtz' Atom. Theory* 113 This also applies to phosphorus *pentafluoride. **1656** BLOUNT *Glossogr.*, **Pentagamist*, one that hath had five wives. **1834** *Fraser's Mag.* IX. 483 Her father, the worthy Pentagamist. **1967** *Lancet* 11 Feb. 291/1 (*heading*) *Pentagastrin as a stimulant of maximal gastric acid response in man. **1970** PASSMORE & ROBSON *Compan. Med. Stud.* II. x. 3/1 For gastric function studies, pentagastrin has the important advantage over histamine in having no circulatory effects. **1974** *Nature* 15 Mar. 238/2 Because changes in fundic mucosal cGMP could result from release of the hormone gastrin from the antrum in response to vagal stimulation, the effect of pentagastrin in concentration sufficient to produce acid secretion..was tested. **1882** OGILVIE, **Pentaglot*, a work in five different languages. **1656** BLOUNT *Glossogr.*, **Pentaglottical*, that hath five Tongues, or is skilled in five several Languages. **1876** *Encycl. Brit.* V. 516/2 The compounds containing more than five atoms of halogen behave as mixtures of the *pentahaloid compounds with halogens.., they furnish the products of the decomposition by water of the pentahaloid compound, and also the free halogen. **1805–17** R. JAMESON *Char. Min.* (ed. 3) 204 *Penta-hexahedral when the crystal's surface consists of five ranges of planes, disposed six and six above each other. **1857** MAYNE *Expos. Lex.*, **Pentahexahedron*. **1916** *Amer. Jrnl. Sci.* CXCI. 493 It is claimed that crystals of hydrated carbonate have been found in wells and pumps. [*Note*] F. Pfeiffer..who considered them to be *pentahydrate. **1975** *Nature* 28 Aug. 718/2 Hydrated offretite..contains a K ion in each cancrinite cage, a pentahydrate of Mg in each gmelinite cage, and hydrated Ca ions in the main channels. **1851** H. WATTS tr. *Gmelin's Hand-bk. Chem.* V. 430 *Penta-hydrated.—The ordinary form of cupric sulphate. **1951** C. PALACHE et al. *Dana's Syst. Min.* (ed. 7) II. 487 Chalcanthite and the not well-established minerals pentahydrite and siderotil are isostructural with a number of artificial salts variously including the pentahydrated sulfates and selenates of Mn, Co, Cu, Zn. **1892** *Jrnl. Chem. Soc.* LXII. 29 Xylitol is..an open-chain *pentahydric alcohol, of which xylose is the aldehyde. **1952** J. K. N. JONES in E. H. Rodd *Chem. Carbon Compounds* IB. xix. 1197 Two pentahydric alcohols, adonitol (ribitol) and D-arabitol occur in nature. **1968** J. A. MONICK *Alcohols* v. 426 Ribitol..is a crystalline, 5-carbon pentahydric alcohol. **1951** C. PALACHE et al. *Dana's Syst. Min.* (ed. 7) II. 492 *Pentahydrite *Frondel* (priv. comm., 1948). **1972** *Acta Crystallogr.* XXVIII. B. 1448/2 Magnesium sulfate pentahydrate has even been reported.. to occur as a mineral (pentahydrite). **1962** *Amer. Mineralogist* XLVII. 1482 (*heading*) New boron minerals —uralborite and *pentahydroborite. **1971** [see NIFONTOVITE]. **1973** *Soviet Physics: Doklady* XVIII. 102/1 Pentahydroborite is the final member in the series of natural water-containing metaborates of calcium, all members of which are characterized by a constant ratio of $CaO{:}B_2O_3$ = 1:1 with the water content increasing from korzhinskite to pentahydroborite. **1910** *Mineral. Mag.* XV. 427 *Pentahydrocalcite... Hydrated calcium carbonate, $CaCO_3{\cdot}5H_2O$, occurring as a mould-like encrustation on chalk-marl near Nova-Alexandria, govt. Lublin, Russian Poland. **1928** *Ann. Rep. Progr. Chem.* XXIV. 308 The minerals hydroconite, hydrocalcite (trihydrocalcite, pentahydrocalcite), and lublinite periodically come to be regarded as doubtful minerals, because when re-examined on museum material they are found to be merely calcite. **1957** G. E. HUTCHINSON *Treat. Limnol.* I. x. 660 The deposition of hydrates, supposedly $CaCO_3{\cdot}3H_2O$, trihydrocalcite, and $CaCO_3{\cdot}5H_2O$, pentahydrocalcite, in nature has been recorded. **1968** I. KOSTOV *Mineral.* 531 Trihydrocalcite..and pentahydrocalcite..are unstable and easily change into calcite. **1797** W. TAYLOR in *Monthly Rev.* XXIV. 555 This *pentalogue is chiefly objectionable on account of the vague drift of the fifth commandment. **1853** FURNEAUX (*title*) The Poultry Pentalogue, or Five Rules for Fancy Fowls and Fowl Fanciers. **1904** *Athenæum* 18 June 788/2 It is easy to see that the desire to find a *pentalogy in everything has led to somewhat fanciful distinctions. **1929** *Chem. Abstr.* XXIII. 3213 From the MeOH ppt. were obtained another 2 g. of the *pentamer and 6, 4, and 6 g. of the hexa-, hepta- and octamers resp. **1955** *Jrnl. Polymer Sci.* XVI. 455 The ACA monomer, a considerable part of the linear oligomers up to approximately the pentamer.. and a small portion of the sparingly soluble cyclic oligomers dissolve. **1971** *Nature* 30 July 297/3 Thus electron microscopy has shown macroglobulin (immunoglobulin M) to consist of a cyclic pentamer of γG-like (7S) subunits. **1940** *Pentameric [see *hexameric* adj. s.v. HEXA-]. **1971** *Nature* 11 June 361/1 Only the monomer 'IgMs' could be detected inside the cell and only pentameric IgM outside. **1940** *Jrnl. Chem. Soc.* 1171 When the proportion of sulphuric acid in the Bertram-Walbaum reagent was 1-1·8% the yield of polymerides was: dimeride, 29·0; trimeride, 19·5; tetrameride, 18·4; *pentameride, 15; higher polymerides, 17%. **1899** CAGNEY tr. *Jaksch's Clin. Diagn.* (ed. 4) v. 188 These observers discovered cadaverin (*pentamethylendiamine) in the urine. **1887** *Jrnl. Chem. Soc.* LI. 241 This acid is the orthodicarboxylic acid of *pentamethylene, corresponding with phthalic acid of the benzene series. **1909** C. A. KEANE *Mod. Org. Chem.* v. 63 The simplest cyclic compounds containing four and five carbon atoms are the hydrocarbons tetramethylene, C_4C_8, and pentamethylene, C_5H_{10}. **1929** I. W. D. HACKH *Chem. Dict.* (1930) 538/1 *Pentamethylene*, the bivalent radical $-CH_2(CH_2)_3CH_2-$. **1946** E. G. ROCHOW *Introd. Chem. Silicones* iii. 48 Those pentamethylene groups which are joined to two different silicon atoms from organosilicon polymers resembling those obtained with phenylene groups. **1951** I. L. FINAR *Org. Chem.* I. xi. 203 Pentamethylene glycol (pentane-1:5-diol), $CH_2OH{\cdot}(CH_2)_3{\cdot}CH_2OH$,.. can be obtained from pentamethylene bromide. **1958** *Nomencl. Org. Chem.* (I.U.P.A.C.) A. 16 Pentamethylene $-CH_2-CH_2-CH_2-CH_2-CH_2-$. **1883** *Jrnl. Chem. Soc.* XLIV. 910 *Pentamethylenediamine, $C_5H_{10}(NH_2)_2$ is produced by the action of zinc and hydrochloric acid on an ethereal solution of trimethylene dicyanide. **1964** N. G. CLARK *Mod. Org. Chem.* xii. 247 Some [aliphatic diamines] occur in nature as a result of bacterial decomposition of proteins; for example,.. cadaverine (pentamethylenediamine). **1931** LEVENE & BASS *Nucleic Acids* x. 303 On warming a solution of the supposed *pentanucleotide in 2 per cent solution of sodium hydroxide .., Feulgen split the substance into the two component parts. **1975** *Nature* 6 Mar. 83/2 Statistical considerations indicate that coincidence among oligonucleotides of length six or more (pentanucleotides are marginal) provides strong evidence for primary structural homology in a sequence of 1,600 nucleotides. **1907** *Jrnl. Chem. Soc.* XCII. I. 901 Characteristic of this *pentapeptide and of the preceding tripeptide is the property of being precipitated from aqueous solution by ammonium sulphate. **1946** *Biochem. Jrnl.* XL. p. xliv, Their results are only compatible with the presence in the crystals studied either of a simple pentapeptide molecule or of a decapeptide which has crystallographic two-fold symmetry. **1960** *Ibid.* LXXVI. 16P/2 Appreciable hydrolysis.. took place yielding, as one of the products, a pentapeptide containing arginine, proline, glycine, and phenylalanine. **1975** *Nature* 2 Oct. 415/1 It probably does not permeate lysosomal membranes, as might be expected for a pentapeptide. **1693** *Phil. Trans.* XVII. 684 The Flowers grow in Clusters like those of the Vine, are *pentapetalose. **1706** PHILLIPS, *Pentapetalous Plants.* **1719** QUINCY *Lex. Physico-Med.* (ed. 2) 347 The Umbelliferous Plants, which have a pentapetalous Flower. **1845** LINDLEY *Sch. Bot.* vi. (1858) 104 c, Corolla monopetalous, or pentapetalous. **1881** MACFARREN *Counterp.* iii. 5 A scale.. is *pentaphonic when the 4th and 7th degrees from the key note are omitted. **1730–6** BAILEY (folio), *Pentaphyllous*, having 5 leaves. **1857** MAYNE *Expos. Lex.*, *Pentapterus*,.. having five expansions in form of wings, as the capsule of the *Evonymus latifolius*,.. *pentapterous. **1656** BLOUNT *Glossogr.*, *Pentaptotes*, nouns declined onely by five Cases. **1854** FAIRHOLT *Dict. Terms Art* 336 *Pentaptych, an altar-painting having many leaves. **1899** *Speaker* 16 Dec. 279/2 The *pentarsic line.. must consist of five bars, and at least two of the stresses must be strong and full upon the last syllables of a bar. **1857** MAYNE *Expos. Lex.*, *Pentasepalous. **1870** BENTLEY *Man. Bot.* (ed. 2) 216. **1702** RALPHSON *Math. Dict.*, *Pentaspast, an Engine consisting of five Pullies, viz. three above and two below. **1828–32** WEBSTER, *Pentaspermous, containing five seeds. *Encycl.* **1849** D. CAMPBELL *Inorg. Chem.* 311 Yellow precipitate, which is the *pentasulphide of arsenic (sulpharsenic acid). **1854** J. SCOFFERN in *Orr's Circ. Sc., Chem.* 473 *Pentasulphuret of antimony, otherwise called sulpho-antimonic acid.

pentace, obs. form of PENTHOUSE.

pentachord (ˈpɛntəkɔːd). *Mus.* [f. PENTA- + Gr. χορδή string, CHORD.]

1. A musical instrument with five strings.

1721 BAILEY, *Pentachord*, any musical instrument that has five strings. **1727–41** CHAMBERS *Cycl.* s.v., The invention of the pentachord is referred to the Scythians. **1759** in Grove *Dict. Mus.* I. 4 A piece composed on purpose for an instrument newly-invented in London, and called the pentachord. **1825** FOSBROKE *Encycl. Antiq.* 629 *Pentachord*, strung with ox leather, and touched by a goat's foot.

2. A system or series of five notes.

1811 BUSBY *Dict. Mus.* (ed. 3), *Pentachord*,.. among the ancients, sometimes signified.. an order, or system, of five sounds. **1880** W. S. ROCKSTRO in Grove *Dict. Mus.* II. 341 Each of these [ecclesiastical] Modes is divisible into two members, a Pentachord, and a Tetrachord.

†**3.** The interval of a fifth. *Obs. rare.*

1694 W. HOLDER *Harmony* (1731) 66 (Table of Intervals) 5th. Diapente, Pentachord.

pentacle (ˈpɛntək(ə)l). [In med.L. *pentaculum*, app. f. PENTA- five + *-culum*, dim. or instrumental suffix, but actual history obscure. It. had *pentacolo* 'any thing or table of five corners' (Florio), F. had (16th c.) *pentacle*, something used in necromancy (Godef. says 'a five-branched candlestick').

As applied to something worn round the neck as an amulet, some would connect it with F. *pentacol, pendacol* (14th c. in Godef.) a jewel or ornament hung round the neck, f. *pend-* hang, *à* to, *col, cou* neck.]

A certain figure (or a material object, e.g. something folded or interlaced, of that shape) used as a symbol, esp. in magic; app. properly the same as PENTAGRAM; but also used for various other magical symbols, esp. the *hexagram* or six-pointed star formed by two interlaced triangles. (See also PENTANGLE 1.)

The *pentacle of Solomon*, in H. More 1664, is the same as the *pentangle of Solomon* of *Sir Gawayne c* 1340, Sir Thomas Browne 1646, and others.

1594 CHAPMAN *Shadow Nt., Hymnus in Cynthiam* Wks. (1875) 16/2 Then in thy clear and icy pentacle, Now execute a magic miracle. **1607** DEKKER *Wh. of Babylon* Wks. 1873 II. 200 Take Periapts, Pentacles, and potent Charmes To coniure downe foule fiends. **1616** B. JONSON *Devil an Ass* I. ii, They haue.. Their rauens wings, their lights, and pentacles, With characters; I ha' seene all these. **1664** H. MORE *Myst. Iniq.* I. xviii. §3 Their Pentacles which they hang about their necks when they conjure (which they forsooth.. call the Pentacles of Solomon) are adorned and fortified with such transcriptions out of holy Scripture. [**1668–70** M. CASAUBON *Credulity & Incred.* (1672) 71 By certain *pentacula*, and seals and characters to fence themselves and to make themselves invisible against all kinds of arms and musquet bullets.] **1808** SCOTT *Marm.* III. xx, His shoes were marked with cross and spell; Upon his breast a pentacle. **1862** LYTTON *Str. Story* I, You observe two triangles interlaced and inserted in a circle? The Pentacle in short. **1885** *Sat. Rev.* 19 Sept. 380/2 The sacramental [charm] bore a figure that looked like a rough copy of the pentacle.

Hence **pen'tacular** *a.*, of, pertaining to, or of the nature of a pentacle.

In mod. Dicts.

pentacrinin (pɛnˈtækrɪnɪn). *Chem.* [f. mod.L. *Pentacrin-us* (see next) + -IN[1].] A colouring matter found in *Pentacrinus* and other crinoids.

1888 ROLLESTON & JACKSON *Anim. Life* 575.

pentacrinite (pɛnˈtækrɪnaɪt). *Palæont.* [f. mod.L. (Oken 1815) *Pentacrin-us* 'sea-lily' (f. Gr. πεντα- five + κρίνον lily) + -ITE[1] 2a.] An encrinite or fossil crinoid of the genus *Pentacrinus* or family *Pentacrinidæ*, having a pentagonal column.

1818 W. PHILLIPS *Outl. Min. & Geol.* (ed. 3) 141 Petrifactions of marine animals, as corallites, encrinites, pentacrinites, entrochites, and trochites. **1854** BAKEWELL *Geol.* 49 Another fossil abundant in the lias is the pentacrinite.

pentacrinoid (pɛnˈtækrɪnɔɪd), *a.* and *sb. Zool.* [f. as prec. + -OID.] **a.** *adj.* Allied to or resembling the genus *Pentacrinus* or family *Pentacrinidæ* of crinoids (chiefly extinct, and found as fossils). **b.** *sb.* = A pentacrinoid crinoid.

1877 HUXLEY *Anat. Inv. Anim.* ix. 551 A striking resemblance to the oral end of the young Pentacrinoid larva of Comatula. **1888** ROLLESTON & JACKSON *Anim. Life* 571 In the pentacrinoid, i.e. stalked *Antedon*.

pentactinal to **pentacyclic**: see PENTA-

pentad (ˈpɛntæd). [ad. Gr. πεντάς, -άδα, later forms of πεμπάς, -άδα a group of five: see -AD 1 a.]

1. The number five (in the Pythagorean System); a group of five.

1653 H. MORE *Conject. Cabbal.* (1713) 153 So manifest is it what special reason Pythagoras had to mention the Tetrad, rather than the Pentad, or any other number, in that form of swearing by Him that first imparted the Cabbala. **1660** STANLEY *Hist. Philos.* IX. (1701) 382/2 The Pentad is the first complexion of both kinds of number, even and odd, two and three. **1891** DRIVER *Introd. Lit. O. Test.* (1892) 48 The laws appear often to be arranged in Pentads, or groups of five.

2. a. A period of five years. (Cf. DECADE 2.)

1880 J. D. WHITNEY *Climatic Changes* vii. 337 The means of the last two pentads, 1866–70 and 1871–75, were almost exactly the same as the grand mean. **1978** *Nature* 26 Jan. 322/2 South of lat 45° S, however, they conclude that average annual temperatures increased between the 1960–64 and 1970–74 pentads.

b. *Meteorol.* A period of five days.

1906 W. MARRIOTT *Hints to Meteorol. Observers* (ed. 6) 67/2 *Pentad*, a period of five days. **1935** *Nature* 12 Oct. 614/1 There has been great discussion of the relative advantages of the 5-day period, or pentad, and the week, with the result that both units have received international approval. **1959** R. E. HUSCHKE *Gloss. Meteorol.* 416 *Pentad*, a group of five. In climatology, it is applied to a period of five consecutive days. It often is preferred to the week for climatological purposes since it is an exact factor of the 365-day year.

3. *Chem.* An element or radical that has the combining power of five units, i.e. of five atoms of hydrogen. Also *attrib.* or *adj.*

1877 WATTS *Fownes' Chem.* I. 460 Vanadium was, till lately, regarded as a hexad metal..; but Roscoe has shown that it is a pentad. **1880** *Athenæum* 11 Dec. 781/3 The authors.. conclude that in that substance phosphorus is a pentad.

Hence **pentadic** (-ˈædɪk) *a.*, of the nature of a pentad (sense 3), pentavalent; whence **pentadicity** (-ˈdɪsɪtɪ), the fact of being a pentad.

pentadactyl, -yle (pɛntəˈdæktɪl), *a.* and *sb.* Also 7 pente-. [ad. L. *pentadactyl-us*, a. Gr. πενταδάκτυλ-ος five-fingered or -toed; f. PENTA- + δάκτυλ-ος finger. In mod.F. *pentadactyle*.]

A. *adj.* Having five toes or fingers.

1828 STARK *Elem. Nat. Hist.* I. 111 *Phalangista*,.. feet pentadactyle..; anterior toes separate. **1854** R. OWEN in *Circ. Sc., Organ. Nat.* I. 226 The toe answering to the fifth, in lizards and other pentadactyle animals. **1887** *Athenæum* 23 Apr. 548/1 It is shown how primitive is the plantigrade pentadactyle foot of man.

B. *sb.* †**1.** tr. L. *pentadactylus* (Pliny), 'a kind of shell-fish' (Lewis & Short). *Obs.*

1661 LOVELL *Hist. Anim. & Min.* Introd., The turbines, are great,.. tuberous,.. muricate, or pentedactyls.

2. A person with five digits on each limb.

1880 PROCTOR *Rough Ways* 213 George, who was a pentadactyle, though somewhat deformed about the hands and feet. *Ibid.*, Marie, a pentadactyle with deformed thumbs, gave birth to a boy with six toes.

So ˌ**pentadac'tylic** *a.* = prec. A; **penta'dactylism**, the condition of being pentadactyl.

1879 tr. *Haeckel's Evol. Man* II. 300 The original parent-form of the entire group had anteriorly and posteriorly five digits (Pentadactylism). **1880** PROCTOR *Rough Ways* 213 A girl hexadactylic on the right side of the body, and pentadactylic on the left side. **1886** GÜNTHER in *Encycl. Brit.* XX. 454/2 The digital elements seem to indicate more than pentadactylism, as in the extinct *Ichthyosauri*.

pentadactylous (pɛntəˈdæktɪləs), *a.* [f. L. *pentadactyl-us* (see PENTADACTYL) + -OUS.] Having five digits (fingers or toes), or five processes resembling fingers, as a star-fish. *Obs.*

1683–4 ROBINSON in *Phil. Trans.* XXIX. 480 This appear'd to me a-kin to.. the *Stellæ Marinæ*, being Triangular, and sometimes Pentadactylous. **1856–8** W. CLARK *Van der Hoeven's Zool.* II. 609 Feet short, pentadactylous. **1875** SIR W. TURNER in *Encycl. Brit.* I. 830/1 The human foot, therefore, is a pentadactylous, plantigrade foot.

pentadecane (ˈpɛntədɪkeɪn). *Chem.* [f. late Gr. πενταδεκα- (in comb.) for πεντεκαίδεκα fifteen + -ANE 2 b.] The paraffin of the 15-carbon series, $C_{15}H_{32}$. So ˈ**pentadecine** (-dɪsaɪn), the corresponding hydrocarbon of the ethine series, $C_{15}H_{28}$; **penta'decyl**, the radical $C_{15}H_{31}$.

1872 WATTS *Dict. Chem.* VI. 903 *Pentadecane*,.. obtained from American petroleum... With chlorine it yields pentadecyl chloride... *Pentadecine*,.. homologous with ethine or acetylene.

pentadelphous to **pentagamist**: see PENTA-.

pentaerythritol (ˌpɛntæɛˈrɪθrɪtɒl). *Chem.* Formerly also **penta-erythritol, penterythritol**. [ad. G. *penta-erythrit* (Tollens & Wigand 1892, in *Ann. d. Chem.* CCLXV. 316): see PENTA- and ERYTHRITOL.] A white, crystalline, tetrahydric alcohol, $C(CH_2OH)_4$, that is prepared by the condensation of acetaldehyde and formaldehyde and is widely used in the manufacture of paints and varnishes.

1892 *Jrnl. Chem. Soc.* LXII. I. 127 *(heading)* Penterythritol: a tetrahydric alcohol obtained from formaldehyde and acetaldehyde. **1912** *Ibid.* CI. 2091 The condensation between pentaerythritol and aldehydes in general takes place readily in the presence of sulphuric acid of from 30 to 50 per cent. concentration. **1947** WINDING & HASCHE *Plastics* III. 78 The ester of penta-erythritol has become an important resin within the last few years. **1958** *Times Rev. Industry* Feb. 19/3 A large plant has been erected at Dumfries for the production of.. pentaerythritol, a material for which there is an increasing demand in the field of paints. **1972** *Materials & Technol.* IV. x. 364 Acrolein is also used for preparing resins such as the glass-clear polymer obtained when acrolein is condensed with pentaerythritol.

b. pentaerythritol tetranitrate, a white crystalline solid, $C(CH_2NO_3)_4$, used as an explosive and also as a vasodilator in the treatment of coronary ailments.

1923 *Jrnl. Chem. Soc.* CXXIII. 75 Pentaerythritol tetranitrate. **1958** A. GROLLMAN *Pharmacol. & Therapeutics* (ed. 3) xx. 456 Pentaerythritol tetranitrate, N.N.R.., although of no value for the immediate relief of anginal attacks, may by its more prolonged action reduce the number or severity of the attacks. **1972** *Materials & Technol.* IV. viii. 301 The most important [reaction].. is the esterification with nitric acid, which gives PETN or pentaerythritol tetranitrate, a very powerful detonating agent, exploding when shocked or exposed to heat.

pentageron: see PENTAGONON 1.

pentagle: see PENTANGLE.

pentaglot: see PENTA-.

pentagon (ˈpɛntəgən), *a.* and *sb. Geom.* Also 7 -one. [In A, ad. L. *pentagōn-us*, a. Gr. πεντάγων-ος pentagonal, five-cornered, f. πεντα- PENTA- + -γων-ος from stem of γωνία angle. In B, ad. L. *pentagōn-um*, Gr. πεντάγωνον, the neuter adj. used as sb. Cf. F. *pentagone* sb. (13th c. in Littré), whence the Eng. form in *-gone*.]

†**A.** *adj.* Having five angles; pentagonal. *Obs.* (or regarded as *attrib.* use of the *sb.*).

1570 BILLINGSLEY *Euclid* IV. xi. 118 In a circle geuen to describe a Pentagon figure equilater and equiangle. **1660** BARROW *Euclid* IV. xi, A Pentagone figure. **1669** STAYNRED *Fortification* 11 The Front A K in the Pentagon Fort.

B. *sb.* **1. a.** A figure, usually a plane rectilineal figure, having five angles and five sides. In *Fortif.* A fort with five bastions.

1571 DIGGES *Pantom., Math. Treat.* Def. ix. T ij, Euery equilater triangle, square, or Pentagonum. **1650** R. STAPYLTON *Strada's Low C. Warres* VII. 41 A Fort.. built in the forme of a Pentagon. **1660** BARROW *Euclid* IV. xii, About a circle given to describe an equilateral and an equiangular pentagone. **1760** GRAY *Notes Walpole* Wks. 1843 V. 201 A man.. holding a pair of compasses, and by his side a Polyedron, made up of twelve pentagons. **1800** *Asiatic Ann. Reg., Misc. Tracts* 214/2 The castle of Belgica; an old pentagon with round towers at the angles. **1870** *Illustr. Lond. News* 29 Oct. 446/2 The fort is built in a pentagon.

b. *Comb.* **'pentagon-dodeca'hedron,** a dodecahedron contained by twelve pentagons.

1895 STORY-MASKELYNE *Crystallogr.* §183 The pentagon-dodecahedron approximates.. to the regular dodecahedron of geometry in proportion as the dihedral angles.. approach equality... The regular dodecahedron.., impossible as a crystallographic form, is the limiting figure between the two classes of pentagon-dodecahedra.

2. (With capital initial.) The name given to a pentagonal building in Washington, D.C., the headquarters of the U.S. Department of Defense. Hence used allusively for the U.S. military leadership.

1945 *Amer. N. & Q.* July 54/1 (*heading*) Pentagon pip: an affliction common among Army officers and enlisted men stationed in Washington; brought on by an Army order proposing overseas duty for men whose war work has kept them heretofore in the United States. **1951** *Business Week* 29 Dec. 40 To help answer this recurring question the Pentagon set up its own watchdog—the Industrial Relations Division of Assistant Secretary Anna Rosenberg's office. **1952** *Brewer's Dict. Phr. & Fable* (rev. ed.) 697/2 *Pentagon*.., a vast five-sided building erected in Washington, D.C., to house government officials. It is said to be so great that newcomers who leave their offices never find them again. **1952** *Observer* 30 Nov. 5/4 The Pentagon, that immense monument to modern man's subservience to the desk. **1957** *Listener* 24 Oct. 664/3 The Pentagon hoped that Seato would produce a maximum morale-building effect with minimum demands on the American armed forces. **1959** *Ibid.* 4 June 972/2 The converting of Iran into a United States rocket ordnance depot is an integral part of the Pentagon plan. **1964** M. MCLUHAN *Understanding Media* v. 51 Life at the Pentagon has been greatly complicated by jet travel. **1972** A. PRICE *Col. Butler's Wolf* xiii. 142 The students didn't approve of the Kremlin any more than the Pentagon. **1974** *Jrnl. Politics* XXXVI. 82 In cases where appropriations had been provided to cover broad categories, the Defense Department should keep faith with the committee and with Congress by adhering to the detailed justifications presented in support of the Pentagon's budget. **1976** H. MACINNES *Agent in Place* ix. 85 The Pentagon might start investigating its own security.

pentagonal (pɛn'tægənəl), *a.* (*sb.*) [f. prec. + -AL[1]: cf. F. *pentagonal* (1533 in Hatz.-Darm.).]

1. *Geom.*, etc. Of or pertaining to a pentagon; of the form of a pentagon, having five angles and five sides, five-cornered or five-sided.

Pentagonal figure in quot. 1612 = PENTAGONON 1.

1571 DIGGES *Pantom.* II. ix. M iv b, The Area of this pentagonall superficies. **1612** SELDEN *Illustr. Drayton's Poly-olb.* ix. 154 The supposed.. Druttenfuss, *i.* a Pentagonall figure, ingrauen with 'Υγιεια or 'Υγεια,.. in Germany they reckon it for a preseruatiue against Hobgoblins. **1785** MARTYN *Rousseau's Bot.* xvi. (1794) 172 The species is distinguished by its pentagonal calyx. **1872** NICHOLSON *Palæont.* 110 Order 11. Asteroidea,.. the body is star-shaped or pentagonal, and consists of a central 'disc', surrounded by five or more lobes or 'arms'. **1879** *Cassell's Techn. Educ.* IV. 136/1 The Italian engineers.. adopted the pentagonal or bastion shape.

b. Applied to a solid figure or body of which the base or section is a pentagon; having five edges or dihedral angles.

1570 BILLINGSLEY *Euclid* XI. Def. x. 314 If the base be a Pentagon, then is it a Pentagonall or fiueangled Pyramis. **1771** PENNANT *Tour Scot. in 1769* (1790) 68 Great columns of stone.. regularly pentagonal or hexagonal. **1840** LARDNER *Geom.* 232 A regular pentagonal pyramid.

c. Contained by pentagons, as a solid figure.

1851 RICHARDSON *Geol.* v. (1855) 91 The pentagonal dodecahedron may likewise be formed on the cube. **1895** STORY-MASKELYNE *Crystallogr.* §177 The pentagonal icositetrahedron (or twenty-four-pentagonohedron).

2. *Arith.* ***pentagonal numbers***: the series of POLYGONAL numbers 1, 5, 12, 22, 35, 51, 70, 92, etc. formed by continuous summation of the arithmetical series 1, 4, 7, 10, 13, 16, etc.

1670 COLLINS in Rigaud *Corr. Sci. Men* (1841) II. 196 It is likewise a pentagonal number, or composed of two, three, four, or five pentagonal numbers. **1795** HUTTON *Math. Dict.*, *Figurate Numbers*, such as do or may represent some geometrical figure,.. as triangular, pentagonal, pyramidal, etc., numbers.

b. as *sb.* A pentagonal number.

1795 HUTTON *Math. Dict.* s.v. *Polygonal Numbers*, The Angles, or Numbers of Angles, are the same as those of the figure... So the angles.. of the pentagonals are 5, of the hexagonals 6, and so on. *Ibid.*, Formulæ for the sums of *n* terms of the several ranks of Polygonal numbers... Pentagonals, $\frac{3n^2 + 3n + 0}{6}n$.

Hence **pen'tagonally** *adv.*, in a pentagonal form; so †**pen'tagonary,** †**penta'go nian** *adjs.* = PENTAGONAL; **pentagono'hedron** [after *rhombohedron*, etc.], a solid figure contained by pentagons; **pen'tagonoid** *a.*, resembling a pentagon, somewhat pentagonal.

1658 SIR T. BROWNE *Gard. Cyrus* iii, The flowers before explication are *pentagonally wrapped up with some resemblance of the *blatta* or moth. **1658** R. WHITE tr. *Digby's Powd. Symp.* (1660) 72 The *pentagonary figure of every one of those stones. **1598** R. HAYDOCKE tr. *Lomazzo* I. 111 Their circular, *pentagonian, hexagonian, octagonian, square and crosse ones. **1895** STORY-MASKELYNE *Crystallogr.* §183 The pentagon-dodecahedron... The twelve-*pentagonohedron is a very characteristic form of certain mineral species. **1882** SLADEN in *Jrnl. Linn. Soc.* XVI. 203 Marginal contour *pentagonoid.

Pentagonese (ˌpɛntəgə'niːz). [f. PENTAGON *sb.* 3 + -ESE.] (See quot. 1961.)

1951 *Collier's* 24 Nov. 33/3 The great virtue of Pentagonese is the facility it provides in conveying meanings briefly. **1961** *Guardian* 20 Mar. 1/4 Pentagonese—the Defence Department's penchant for turning nouns into verbs by the addition of a suffix. **1977** P. HOWARD *New Worlds for Old* 58 *Low profile* is Pentagonese, or American defence jargon.

‖**pen'tagonon.** *Obs.* [a. Gr. πεντάγωνον, sb. use of neuter of πεντάγων-ος: see PENTAGON.]

1. = PENTAGRAM, PENTANGLE 1.

The forms *pentaganon, pentagoron, pentageron*, here cited, appear to be corruptions or scribal errors.

c **1590** GREENE *Fr. Bacon* ii. (1594) B ij, The great arch-ruler, potentate of hell, Trembles, when Bacon bids him, or his fiends Bow to the force of his Pentageron. *Ibid.* xiii. H ij, Coniuring and adiuring diuils and fiends, With stole and albe and strange Pentaganon. **1592** NASHE *P. Penilesse* Wks. (Grosart) II. 126 Some of old time put great superstition in characters, curiously engraued in their Pentagonon, but they are all vaine, and will do no good. *c* **1605** ROWLEY *Birth Merl.* v. i. (1662) G ij b, Ile binde you up with exorcisms so strong, that all the black pentagoron of hell, shall ne're release you.

2. = PENTAGON B.

1625 PURCHAS *Pilgrims* I. v. xiii. 698 A faire and strong Castle, a regular *Pentagonon* well fortified.

†**pen'tagonous,** *a. Obs.* [f. L. *pentagōn-us* (see PENTAGON) + -OUS.] = PENTAGONAL.

1661 LOVELL *Hist. Anim. & Min.* Introd., Amongst Fishes, The Cartilagineous, are plaine or long:.. The heart is pentagonous. **1673** *Phil. Trans.* VIII. 6188. **1761** ELLIS *ibid.* LII. 358 It is formed of pentagonous joints, or vertebræ.

pentagoron: see PENTAGONON 1.

pentagram ('pɛntəgræm). [mod. ad. Gr. πεντά-, πεντέγραμμον sb. from neuter of πεντέγραμμ-ος adj., formed or consisting of five lines, f. πέντε five + γραμμή line, mark.] **1.** A five-pointed figure formed by producing the sides of a pentagon both ways to their points of intersection, so as to form a five-pointed star; the 'five straight lines' of which the figure consists form one continuous line or 'endless knot'. Formerly used as a mystic symbol and credited with magical virtues. (Also called *pentalpha, pentacle* (*pentagle, pentangle*), †*pentagonon* (*-goron, -geron*).)

1833 *Fraser's Mag.* VII. 547 The pentagram was a pentagonal figure, supposed to possess the same kind of power which, amongst us, used popularly to be attributed to the horse-shoe. **1855** TENNYSON *Brook* 103 Sketching with her slender pointed foot Some figure like a wizard pentagram On garden gravel. **1878** A. W. WARD *Greene's Fr. Bacon* II. 51 Notes 209 The pentagramma, pentageron or pentalpha is the mystic figure 'produced by prolonging the sides of a regular pentagon till they intersect one another. It can be drawn without a break in the drawing'. **1895** MISS A. M. STODDART *J. S. Blackie* viii. 176, I found a hindrance—a pentagram—in my way, like Mephistopheles.

2. A series of five letters or characters.

1972 *Computer Jrnl.* XV. 260/2 The peak frequencies are steadily reduced, from one occurrence of the space symbol in seven characters in the case of single characters, to a maximum frequency of approximately 600 in 1,000 documents in the case of the most frequent pentagram, TION▽. **1974** *Sci. Amer.* Jan. 108/3 Rows 1, 2, 3, 4 and 5, in 32 parts, give the 32 pentagrams.

pentagraph, erron. form of PANTOGRAPH *sb.*

pentagrid ('pɛntəgrɪd). *Electronics.* [f. PENTA- + GRID.] A thermionic valve having five grids; a heptode. Freq. *attrib.* or as *adj.*

1933 *Wireless World* 12 May 347/1 The Pentagrid Converter.. has been recently developed in America. *Ibid.* 347/3 With the Pentagrid.. the necessary coupling occurs within the valve and, by virtue of the screening, is entirely electronic in nature. **1950** P. PARKER *Electronics* xiv. 549 Occasionally a frequency-changing valve.. has a suppressor grid; it is then called a heptode or pentagrid. **1953** A. H. W. BECK *Thermionic Valves* x. 308 In the pentagrid mixer, the local oscillation is generated by a separate valve. **1966** H. J. REICH et al. *Theory & Applications Active Devices* vii. 165 Another useful tube structure is the five-grid or pentagrid tube, in which the five grids of helical construction are mounted between the cathode and the plate. This tube affords considerable flexibility in design of certain electronic circuits. Perhaps the most frequent application.. has been in the mixer-oscillator section of radio receivers.

‖**pentagynia** (pɛntə'dʒɪnɪə). *Bot.* [mod.L., f. PENTA- + Gr. γυνή woman, female, taken in sense 'female organ, pistil'.] An order of plants in many classes of the Linnæan System, comprising those having five pistils. Hence **'pentagyn** (*rare*), a plant of this order; **penta'gynian, penta'gynious, pen'tagynous** *adjs.*, belonging to this order, having five pistils.

1760 J. LEE *Introd. Bot.* II. viii. (1765) 92 *Pentagynia*, comprehending such Plants as have five Styles. **1828–32** WEBSTER, *Pentagyn*,.. a plant having five pistils. *Pentagynian*, having five pistils. **1829** LOUDON, *Pentagynous*, having five styles. **1857** MAYNE *Expos. Lex.* 902 Pentagynious.

pentahedral (pɛntə'hiːdrəl, -'hɛdrəl), *a.* Also **pentaedral.** [f. PENTA- + Gr. ἕδρα seat, base + -AL[1]: cf. HEXAHEDRAL.] Of a solid figure or body: Having five faces; *esp.* having five lateral faces, five-sided (as a prism of pentagonal section). So †**penta'hedrical, penta'hedrous** *adjs.* in same sense; **penta'hedron**, a solid figure having five faces.

1804 WATT in *Phil. Trans.* XCIV. 310 *note*, Hexaedral and *pentaedral prisms are most abundant; then the tetraedral, the triedral, heptaedral, and octaedral. **1826** KIRBY & SP. *Entomol.* IV. 266 *Pentaedral*, that hath five sides. **1658** PHILLIPS, **Pentahedrical* figure,.. a figure which hath five sides. **1661** in BLOUNT *Glossogr.* **1775** ASH, **Pentahedron* (a different spelling), the pentaedron. *Ibid.*, *Pentaedron*, a pillar with five sides. *a* **1728** WOODWARD *Fossils* (1729) I. 120 The *pentaedrous Columnar Coralloid Bodies are compos'd of Plates set lengthways.

pentahexahedral, -hedron: see PENTA-.

pen-tail ('pɛnteɪl). [f. PEN *sb.*[2] + TAIL *sb.*[1]] In full, **pen-tail(ed) tree-shrew.** A species of tree-shrew, *Ptilocercus lowii*, found in Malaysia, Sumatra, and Borneo, and distinguished by rows of long, stiff hairs fringing the end part of its tail.

[**1848** J. E. GRAY in *Proc. Zool. Soc.* XVI. 23 Mr. Low brought with him from Borneo some mammalia and reptiles in spirits; amongst them.. was 'a rat-like animal with a pennated tail'.] **1883** *Encycl. Brit.* XV. 402/1 Pen-tail (Ptilocercus lowii). **1910** *Ibid.* XIV. 639/2 In the pen-tailed tree-shrew.. the fringes of long hair are confined to the terminal third of the tail. **1926** *Proc. Zool. Soc.* 1179 The Pen-tailed Tree-shrew, *Ptilocercus*, has not been hitherto described except for its general appearance. **1927** *Glasgow Herald* 14 May 4/2 The probability is that the pen-tail and tupaia represent two successive phases in the evolution of a Lemurid. **1967** *Jrnl. Zool.* CLII. 375 The Pentail tree-shrews.. are more insectivorous although meat is occasionally eaten. **1968** E. P. WALKER et al. *Mammals of World* (ed. 2) I. 400/1 Pen-tailed tree shrews probably feed mainly on insects and fruit. **1969** LD. MEDWAY *Wild Mammals Malaya* 47/2 (*heading*) Pentail Treeshrew. *Ibid.*, Unlike other treeshrews, the Pentail is nocturnal; it is also largely arboreal.

pental ('pɛntəl). [f. stem of PENT(ANE, etc. + *-al*, app. after *chloral.*] A name for trimethylethylene (C_5H_{10}) when used as an anæsthetic.

1891 *Lancet* 3 Oct. 789 A new anæsthetic called pental, which does not produce total unconsciousness, but only a kind of hypnosis. **1893** *Brit. Med. Jrnl.* 18 Mar. 44/1 Velez thinks pental may with advantage replace chloroform and ether in many operations of short duration. **1893** *Syd. Soc. Lex.*, *Pental.* C_5H_{10}. Trimethylethylene... It has been used as an anæsthetic, but is not a safe drug.

pentalemma to **pentalogy**: see PENTA-.

‖**pentalpha** (pɛn'tælfə). [a. Gr. πένταλφα, a synonym of πεντάγραμμον PENTAGRAM, f. πέντε five + ἄλφα the letter Alpha or *A*; from its presenting the form of an A in five different positions.] = PENTAGRAM, PENTANGLE 1.

1818 HOBHOUSE *Hist. Illustr.* (ed. 2) 344 We often see English shepherds cutting the pentalpha.. in the turf, although they never heard of Antiochus, or saw his coin, and although they are ignorant of its mystic power. **1820** D. TURNER *Tour Normandy* I. 179 The produced pentagon, or combination of triangles, sometimes called the pentalpha. **1855** E. SMEDLEY *Occult Sciences* 61 The salutary 'pentalpha'.. should be written on the stable doors.

pentamerous (pɛn'tæmərəs), *a.* [f. PENTA- + Gr. μέρος part + -OUS.] Having, consisting of, or characterized by, five parts or divisions.

1. *Bot.* Having the parts of the flower-whorl five in number. (Often written 5-*merous*.).

1835 LINDLEY *Introd. Bot.* (1848) I. 316 *Pentamerous*, if a flower consists of organs in fives. **1857** HENFREY *Elem. Bot.* 222 Trees or shrubs with.. an imbricated 5-merous calyx and corolla. **1879** BENNETT in *Academy* 11 Jan. 33/2 The four stamens of Scrophulariaceae and Labiatae are admitted to result from a degradation from the pentamerous type.

2. *Zool.* **a.** Consisting of five joints, as the tarsi of certain insects; also applied to such insects themselves, as the beetles of the group *Pentamera*. **b.** Having five radiating parts or organs, as a star-fish or other echinoderm.

1826 KIRBY & SP. *Entomol.* III. xxxv. 683 Pentamerous insects are those which have five joints in all their tarsi. **1828** *Ibid.* IV. xlvii. 376 *Tarsi* pentamerous. **1870** ROLLESTON *Anim. Life* Introd. 143 Echinodermata. Animals.. which.. combine with a radial and, ordinarily, pentamerous arrangement, traces of a bilateral symmetry.

So **pen'tameral** *a.* = prec.; **pen'tameran**, a pentamerous beetle (see 2 a, above); **'pentamere** (-mɪə(r)), each of the five divisions of a pentamerous animal; **pen'tamerism**, the condition or character of being pentamerous; **pen'tameroid** *a.*, allied to the extinct genus *Pentamerus*, of the family *Pentameridæ* of brachiopods, having somewhat pentagonal shells; *sb.* a brachiopod of this family.

1842 BRANDE *Dict. Sci.* etc., *Pentamerans, Pentamera*.. a section of Coleopterous insects, including those which have five joints on the tarsus of each leg. **1899** *Nature* 14 Sept.

460/1 Theories of stalked-ancestry, pentameral symmetry, and the like. **1900** LANKESTER *Treat. Zool.* III. 19 Variation from pentamerism may arise suddenly (discontinuous meristic variation). *Ibid.* 99 The whole animal can be divided into 5 corresponding and almost symmetrical sections, 'pentameres', by 5 imaginary 'perradial planes'.

pentamery (pɛnˈtæmərɪ). *Biol.* [f. PENTA- + Gr. μέρος part + -Y³.] A condition in which structures are present in groups of five.

1902 *Encycl. Brit.* XXV. 433/2 In the pentamery and dimery of Dicotyledons there is usually a posterior sepal with a pair of lateral prophylls. **1962** D. NICHOLS *Echinoderms* i. 14 The adult members [*sc.* echinoderms] show a body pattern having structures present in fives (pentamery).

pentameter (pɛnˈtæmɪtə(r)), *sb.* and *a.* *Pros.* [a. L. *pentameter* sb., ad. Gr. πεντάμετρος adj. consisting of five measures, sb. a verse or line of five measures; f. πεντα- five + μέτρον measure. Cf. F. *pentamètre* sb. (*c* 1500 in Hatz.-Darm.).]

A. *sb.* A verse or line consisting of five feet.

1. In Greek and Latin prosody: A form of dactylic verse composed of two similar halves (penthemimers), each consisting of two feet and a long syllable (thus equivalent to a dactylic hexameter with the second half of the third and of the sixth foot omitted); in the first penthemimer each of the two feet may be either dactyl or spondee, in the second they must both be dactyls. Most commonly used in alternation with hexameters, constituting *elegiac* verse: see ELEGIAC A. 1.

The name arose from a mistaken analysis of the verse as two dactyls (or spondees), a spondee, and two anapæsts.

1589 PUTTENHAM *Eng. Poesie* I. xxiv. (Arb.) 64 Elegie.. was in a pitious maner of meetre, placing a limping Pentameter, after a lusty Exameter, which made it go dolourously more then any other meeter. **1725** WATTS *Logic* III. ii. §3 Certain Latin words should be framed in the form of hexameters or pentameters; and this may be done by those who know nothing of Latin or of verses. *c* **1805** COLERIDGE *Misc. Poems, Eleg. Metre,* [Example] In the hexameter rises the fountain's silvery column, In the pentameter aye falling in melody back. **1874** SAYCE *Compar. Philol.* ix. 384 The charm of the Latin pentameter is enhanced by the rhyming of the last syllables of the two penthemimers.

2. Applied to lines of verse consisting of five feet in other languages; e.g. the English 'heroic' or iambic verse of ten syllables.

1706 A. BEDFORD *Temple Mus.* vi. 114 Odes and Hymns.. in several kinds of Verse..some were Pentameters. **1749** *Power Pros. Numbers* 30 The Cæsura falling constantly on the fourth Syllable in the English Pentameters or Heroicks, creates a dull Uniformity in the Flow of the Verse. **1886** BRIGGS *Messianic Proph.* xi. 340 The pentameters use quite frequently the divine name 'Adonay Jahveh.

B. *adj.* (Now attrib. use of sb.) Consisting of five metrical feet; having the form of a pentameter (see A), esp. of the dactylic pentameter.

1546 LANGLEY *Pol. Verg. De Invent.* I. viii. 17 Of the nomber of the fete, as Exameter and Pentameter which is also called Elegiacal. **1782** J. WARTON *Ess. Pope* x. II. 211 Like Ovid's Fasti, in hexameter and pentameter verses. **1854** EMERSON *Lett. & Soc. Aims, Poet. & Imag.* Wks. (Bohn) III. 171 Those weary pentameter tales of Dryden and others.

Hence **penˈtametered** *a.*, written in pentameters; **penˈtametrist**, a writer of pentameters; **penˈtametrize** *v. trans.*, to make into, or like, a pentameter.

1599 *Preserv. Hen. VII* I. (1866) 5 This trew kinde of hexametred and pentametred verse. **1803** TODD *Spenser's Wks.* I. p. xxii. *note,* English hexametrists and pentametrists. *a* **1843** SOUTHEY *Doctor, Fragm.* (1848) 674/2 Horace has been made to say the same thing by the insertion of an apt word which pentametrises the verse. **1898** W. E. HEITLAND in *Jrnl. Philol.* XXVI. 10 There was not the same risk of pentametrizing the hexameters.

pentamidine (pɛnˈtæmɪdiːn). *Pharm.* [f. PENT(ANE + *amidine* (f. AMID(E + -INE⁵).] A diamidine that is used, usu. in the form of its isethionate (a white, hygroscopic, crystalline solid), for the prevention and treatment of certain tropical diseases, esp. sleeping sickness; 1,5-di(4-amidinophenoxy)pentane, $(H_2N)(HN)C\cdot C_6H_4\cdot O\cdot (CH_2)_5\cdot O\cdot C_6H_4\cdot C(NH)(NH_2)$.

1941 FULTON & YORKE in *Ann. Trop. Med. & Parasitol.* XXXV. 229 The name 'stilbamidine' has been given to 4:4′-diamidino stilbene, 'propamidine' to 4:4′-diamidino diphenoxy propane, 'pentamidine' to 4:4′-diamidino diphenoxy pentane, and 'phenamidine' to 4:4′-diamidino diphenyl ether. **1951** A. GROLLMAN *Pharmacol. & Therapeutics* xx. 417 This led to the trial of other diamidine derivatives of which stilbamidine, propamidine and pentamidine are most widely used. **1974** *Jrnl. Protozool.* XXI. 324/2 Gutteridge..found that *C. fasciculata* mitochondrial respiration was inhibited 71% by 1 mM pentamidine. **1977** *Lancet* 3 Sept. 510/2 A man of 66 with non-Hodgkin's lymphoma was suspected of having *Pneumocystis carinii* infection, and pentamidine was given for 5 days.

‖**Pentandria** (pɛnˈtændrɪə). *Bot.* [mod.L. (Linnæus 1735), f. mod.L. *pentandr-us*, f. Gr. πεντ(α- five + ἀνδρ-, stem of ἀνήρ man, male, taken in sense 'male organ', stamen: see MONANDRIA.] The fifth class in the Linnæan Sexual System, comprising plants having five stamens not cohering. So **penˈtander** (*rare*) [F. *pentandre*], a pentandrous plant; **penˈtandrian, penˈtandrious,** and, (usually) **penˈtandrous** *adjs.*, belonging to the class *Pentandria*; having five free stamens.

1760 J. LEE *Introd. Bot.* II. xix. (1765) 113 *Pentandria,* comprehending such Plants as have five Stamina. **1785** MARTYN *Rousseau's Bot.* ix. (1794) 88. **1806** GALPINE *Brit. Bot.* 25 Tamarix. Flowers pentandrous. **1828–32** WEBSTER, *Pentander,..Pentandrian.* **1830** LINDLEY *Nat. Syst. Bot.* 220 The pentandrous corolla and 5 lobed calyx. **1857** MAYNE *Expos. Lex.* 902/2 Pentandrious, or pentandrous. **1875** BENNETT & DYER *Sachs' Bot.* 531 The same probably also happens in the pentandrous Hypericineæ.

pentane (ˈpɛnteɪn). *Chem.* [f. Gr. πέντε five + -ANE 2 b.] The general name of the paraffins of the pentacarbon series, C_5H_{12}; also called *quintane* and *pentyl hydride.* Three such hydrocarbons are known (see quot.), all colourless mobile fluids, occurring in petroleum, etc. Also *attrib.*, as *pentane lamp, vapour*, etc. So **pentaˈnoic** *a.*, in *pentanoic acid*, valeric acid; **ˈpentanol**, amyl (pentyl) alcohol; **pentene** (ˈpɛntiːn), an olefine of the pentacarbon series, C_5H_{10}; comprising four known forms, one of which is AMYLENE; **pentine** (ˈpɛntaɪn), also **ˈpentinine, ˈpentylene**, the hydrocarbon C_5H_8, of the same series, homologous with acetylene or ethine; of this eight forms are possible, and six known, the chief being VALERYLENE; **ˈpentinyl**, the radical C_5H_7, as in *pentinyl ethyl oxide*, $C_7H_{12}O$; **penˈtoic** *a.*, applied to fatty acids, aldehydes, etc. of the same series, as *pentoic* or valeric acid, $C_5H_{10}O_2$; **ˈpentone, ˈpentonene**, a hydrocarbon of the formula C_5H_6: **ˈpentyl**, the radical C_5H_{11}, of which one form is AMYL; hence **penˈtylic** *a.*

1877 WATTS *Fownes' Chem.* II. 48 Pentanes, C_5H_{12}. Of these hydrocarbons there are three modifications, viz.: 1. Normal Pentane $[CH_3(CH_2)_3CH_3]$. 2. Isopentane $[C_2H_5.CH(CH_3)_2]$. 3. Neopentane $[C(CH_3)_4]$. *Ibid.* 58 Pentenes, C_5H_{10}. Of the four possible modifications ..*Normal Pentene,* or Ethyl-allyl, $C_2H_5.C_3H_5$..boils at 37°. ..*Isopentene,* or Amylene, is obtained, together with isopentane, by distilling..amyl alcohol..with sulphuric acid. *Ibid.*, Tertiary pentyl iodide. *Ibid.* 63 *Valerylene* or *Pentine,* C_5H_6. Of this hydrocarbon two modifications are known. *Ibid.* 64 *Valylene* or *pentone,* C_5H_6,..is formed by the action of alcoholic potash on valerylene dibromide. *Ibid.* 148 Pentyl alcohols and ethers. The formula $C_5H_{12}O$ may include eight different alcohols... [1] Butyl Carbinol or Normal Primary Pentyl Alcohol... [2] Isobutyl Carbinol, Isopentyl Alchol, or Amyl Alcohol..the ordinary amyl alcohol produced by fermentation. *Ibid.* 292 Pentoic or Valeric Acids... These acids admit of four metameric modifications... The first and second are obtained by oxidation of normal pentylic and isopentylic or amylic alcohol respectively. **1892** ROSCOE *Elem. Chem.* 286 Pentyl alcohol, $C_5H_{12}O$, is obtained from pentylic acid by reducing first to the aldehyde and then to the alcohol. **1892** MORLEY & MUIR *Watts' Dict.* III. 807/2 *Pentonene*..occurs in oil deposited by compressed gas derived from bituminous shale. [**1899** *Jrnl. Chem. Soc.* LXXVI. I. 742, 2-Chlorocyclo-pentanol, $C_5H_8Cl\cdot OH$. *Ibid.* II. 1135/1 (Index), *cyclo*-Pentanol.] **1927** Pentanoic acid [see HEXANOIC *a.*]. **1937** F. C. WHITMORE *Org. Chem.* I. 129 Pentanol-2, made by either of these methods, always contained pentanol-3. *Ibid.* 298 *n*-Valeric acid, *n*-valerianic acid, pentanoic acid, *n*-propylacetic acid, $CH_3CH_2CH_2CH_2CO_2H$, is made by the oxidation of *n*-amyl alcohol. **1951** I. L. FINAR *Org. Chem.* I. vi. 105 Three amyl alcohols, *viz.*, *n*-pentanol, *iso*pentanol and 'active' amyl alcohol, have been isolated from fusel oil. **1964** N. G. CLARK *Mod. Org. Chem.* viii. 139 A mixture of higher-boiling alcohols ('fusel oil') is obtained as a by-product and forms a useful source of pentanols (amyl alcohols), $C_5H_{11}\cdot OH$. **1965** *Nomencl. Org. Chem.* (I.U.P.A.C.) C. 112 Saturated aliphatic monocarboxylic acids... Pentanoic. [*Note*] The trivial name is normally preferred.

attrib. **1895** *Daily News* 23 July 5/5 The pentane-air flame ..is produced by burning a mixture of air and pentane vapour from a suitable argand burner. **1896** *Ibid.* 30 Jan. 3/1 Mr. A. Vernon Harcourt's pentane standard had again been vindicated as a reliable and exact standard, while in practical use in gas testing the pentane-argand, proposed by Mr. Dibdin in 1886, had been chosen as a suitable substitute for candles in daily work.

pentangle (ˈpɛntæŋg(ə)l). Also 7–9 **pentagle.** [In form a hybrid f. Gr. πεντα- PENTA- + ANGLE; but, in sense 1, perhaps an accommodated form of *pentagle*, in origin a variant of PENTACLE.]

1. = PENTACLE, PENTAGRAM, PENTALPHA.

13.. *Gaw. & Gr. Knt.* 620 Then þay schewed hym þe schelde þat was of schyr goulez, Wyth þe pentangel de-paynt of pure golde hwez;..Hit is a syngne þat Salamon set sumquyle, In bytoknyng of trawþe, bi tytle þat hit habbez, For hit is a figure þat haldez fyue poyntez, And vche lyne vmbelappez and loukez in oþer, And ay quere hit is endelez, and Englych hit callen Ouer-al, as I here, þe endeles knot. **1646** SIR T. BROWNE *Pseud. Ep.* I. x. 42 They are afraid of the pentangle [*ed.* 1650 pentagle] of Solomon [*margin* (*ed.* 1650), 3 triangles intersected and made of five lines]. **1655** MOUFET & BENNET *Health's Impr.* (1746) 67 Diet is defined ..an exact Order in Labour, Meat, Drink, Sleep, and Venery: for they are thought to be Pythagoras his Pentangle or five squar'd Figure. **1827** W. G. S. *Excurs. Vill. Curate* 128 Had I but shown him the pentagle of Solomon, or the Chaldee Tetragrammaton,..how the fiend would have howled at me in vain.

2. = PENTAGON. *rare.*

1658 ROWLAND *Moufet's Theat. Ins.* 997 The water Gras-hopper of Rondoletius, whose head is like a pentangle, having as it were five corners. **1701** MOXON *Math. Dict.*, *Pentagon*..is a Geometrical Figure having five Angles... *Pentangle,* the same, only a Greek and Latin word joyned.

pentangular (pɛnˈtæŋgjʊlə(r)), *a.* [f. as prec. + *angular.*] Having five angles or angular points; pentagonal.

1661 MORGAN *Sph. Gentry* I. 44 The Mullet points are all strait and pentangular. **1673–4** GREW *Anat. Trunks* I. i. §10 Through a Glass, some appear Pentangular, others Sexangular, and Septangular. **1806–7** J. BERESFORD *Miseries Hum. Life* (1826) xviii. 189 Those pentangular divisions which characterize the back of the sea-tortoise. **1872** W. S. SYMONDS *Rec. Rocks* x. 381 It was of a pentangular shape with a bastion tower at each angle.

pentapetalose to **-phyllous:** see PENTA-.

pentaploid (ˈpɛntəplɔɪd), *a.* and *sb.* *Biol.* [f. PENTA- + -PLOID.] (Made up of somatic cells) containing five sets of chromosomes. Also as *sb.*, a pentaploid organism.

1921 *Ann. Bot.* XXXV. 185 Among the roses examined were diploid, tetraploid, pentaploid, and hexaploid forms. **1921** [see HEXAPLOID *a.* and *sb.*]. **1946** *Nature* 19 Oct. 536/1 The cytology of species of *Magnolia* has proved the existence of diploids.., tetraploids.., and pentaploids. **1968** *Canad. Jrnl. Genetics & Cytol.* X. 910 Of the progeny obtained by backcrossing the pentaploid hybrid (AABBD) from the synthetic wheat to its tetraploid *T*[*riticum*] *durum* parent as male 49% had 28 chromosomes and 28% had 29 or 30.

pentapody (pɛnˈtæpədɪ). *Pros.* [ad. Gr. type *πενταποδία, f. πεντάπους of five feet, f. πεντα- + πούς foot: cf. DIPODY.] A verse or line consisting of five feet, or a sequence of five feet in a verse.

1864 in WEBSTER. **1884** ALLEN *J. Hadley's Greek Gramm.* §1072 A single foot, taken by itself, is called a monopody; two feet, taken together, a dipody; three feet, a tripody; four, five, six, &c., a tetrapody, pentapody, hexapody, &c. **1891** *Harper's Mag.* Mar. 570/2 Even the pentapody exists in song and dance. *Ibid.*, Hundreds [of folk-songs] in Hungarian music consisting of dipodies, tetrapodies, tripodies, pentapodies, and hexapodies. **1900** H. W. SMYTH *Greek Melic Poets* 280 He [Pythermos] borrowed from Sappho the logaoedic pentapody (hendecasyllabus).

‖**pentapolis** (pɛnˈtæpəlɪs). [L. a. Gr. πεντάπολις a state of five towns, f. πεντα- five + πόλις city, town] A confederacy or group of five towns: applied in ancient times to several such groups.

[*c* **1425** WYNTOUN *Cron.* I. 1137 Pentapolis next is syne, For v. citeis þar ar fyne. **1608** SHAKS. *Pericles, Dram. Pers.*, Simonides, king of Pentapolis.] **1838** THIRLWALL *Greece* II. xii. 89 These six colonies formed an association,.. distinguished by the name of the Dorian *pentapolis.* **1882** SCHAFF *Encycl. Relig. Knowl.* III. 1653 Nicholas III.. compelled Rudolph of Hapsburg to cede the pentapolis and the exarchate of Ravenna to the papal see.

Hence **pentaˈpolitan** *a.*, of or pertainig to a Pentapolis, spec. to that of Cyrene in Lybia.

1727–41 CHAMBERS *Cycl.* s.v. *Patripassian,* Because Sabellius was of Pentapolis, and the [Patripassian] heresy spread much there, called the Pentapolitan doctrine. **1853** KINGSLEY *Hypatia* xxi, Did the Pentapolitan wheat-ships go to Rome?

pentaprism (ˈpɛntəprɪz(ə)m). Also **penta prism, penta-prism.** [f. PENTA(GONAL *a.* (*sb.*) + PRISM.] A prism whose cross-section is a pentagon with one right angle and three angles of 112½°, so that with silvered reflecting surfaces any ray entering it through one of the faces forming the right angle is deflected through 90°.

1937 *Magneto-theodolite* (Ordnance Survey) 5 The telescope is eccentrically mounted and the change over from theodolite generation to magnetometer operation..takes place in one second by throwing into the line of sight inside the telescope tube a penta-prism which reflects through 270° rays from the illuminated diaphragm of the eyepiece. **1943** D. H. JACOBS *Fund. Optical Engin.* xi. 160 The penta prism ..makes possible the modern high-precision rangefinder. This prism has the unique property of deviating a beam exactly 90° in the plane of the rays shown..even if the beam should not strike the end faces exactly normal. **1954** *Amat. Photographer* 19 May 628/2 The Rectaflex is..a..miniature of the eye-level reflex type, the camera having a manually raised 45-deg. mirror..and brilliant-type screen viewed via a pentaprism. **1977** J. HEDGECOE *Photographer's Handbk.* 11 During the past twenty years..the dominant design trend has been the single lens reflex. This includes both the universally popular 35 mm pentaprism types and roll-film versions.

pentapterous to **pentaptych:** see PENTA-.

pentarch (ˈpɛntɑːk), *sb.* [ad. Gr. type πένταρχος (used in Byzant. Gr.), f. πέντ(ε five + -αρχος ruler: cf. *tetrarch.* In mod.F. *pentarque* (Littré).] **a.** The ruler of one of a group of five districts or kingdoms. **b.** One of a governing body of five persons.

[**1656** BLOUNT *Glossogr.*, *Pentarck*..a Captain of five men.] **1793** HELY tr. *O'Flaherty's Ogygia* I. 62 None of the pentarchs under that title assumed the dominion of the whole island [Ireland]. **1798** W. TAYLOR in *Monthly Rev.* XXVII. 500 To substitute a monarch for the pentarchs of the present constitution.

'pentarch, *a. Bot.* [mod. f. Gr. πέντ(ε five + ἀρχή beginning.] Arising from five distinct points of origin, as the woody tissue of a root.

1884 BOWER & SCOTT *De Bary's Phaner.* 348 The xylem is triarch to pentarch and octarch.

pen'tarchical, *a. rare*$^{-1}$. [f. as next + -ICAL.] Of or belonging to a pentarch or a pentarchy: in quot. *fig.* (cf. next, 2 b, quot. 1633).

1641 J. JOHNSON *Acad. Love* 3 Thus was the sentinell of my pentarchical souldiers permitted to rest.

pentarchy ('pɛntɑːkɪ). Also 7 *erron.* **pempt-**. [ad. Gr. πενταρχία a rule of five, a quinquevirate, f. πέντε five + -αρχία rule.]

1. A government by five rulers; a group of five districts or kingdoms each under its own ruler.

In quot. 1871 applied to the European system of the 'Five Great Powers'.

1587 HOLINSHED *Chron., Hist. Eng.* I. 15/1 The monarchie or sole gouernement of the Iland became a pentarchie, that is, it was diuided betwixt fiue kings. **1611** SPEED *Hist. Gt. Brit.* IX. vi. §47 Dermot Mac Murgh (in that time of the Irish Pentarchie, or fiuefold Kingdome) hauing secretly stolne away the wife of Rothericke. **1799** S. TURNER *Anglo-Sax.* I. II. vi. 253 East Anglia made it a tetrarchy; Essex a pentarchy. **1871** *Echo* 27 Jan., Some writer lately deplored the dissolution of the great European Pentarchy.

2. The government of a country or district by a body of five persons; a governing body of five.

1661 *Sir A. Haslerig's Last Will & Test.* 3 Though I stood ever a profest enemy unto Monarchy, I appeared a constant Zealot for a Pentarchy. **1711** SWIFT *Examiner* 25 Jan., A picture..representing five persons as large as the life, sitting in council together like a pentarchy. **1827** SCOTT *Napoleon* ii, The inconvenience of this pentarchy.

b. *fig.*

1633 P. FLETCHER *Purple Isl.* v. xxxviii, *Auditus*, second of the Pemptarchie. *Ibid.* VI. xlii, Those five fair brethren [the senses] which I sung of late, For their just number called the Pemptarchie. **1651** BIGGS *New Disp.* 33 The Pentarchy of sences. **1855** MILMAN *Lat. Chr.* XIV. iii. (1864) IX. 119 What may be called the Supreme Pentarchy of Scholasticism [Aquinas, Bonaventura, Albertus Magnus, Duns Scotus, Ockham].

pentarsic to **pentaspermous**: see PENTA-.

pentastich ('pɛntəstɪk). [ad. mod.L. *pentastichus*, a. Gr. πεντάστιχ-ος adj. of five lines, f. PENTA- + στίχος row, line.]

1. A group of five lines of verse.

[**1656** BLOUNT *Glossogr.*, *Pentastick*,..that consists of five verses.] **1658** PHILLIPS, *Pentasticks*,..Stanza's, consisting of five verses. **1882-3** in *Schaff's Encycl. Relig. Knowl.* III. 1945 In the few instances of pentastichs..the last three lines usually unfold the reason of the thought of the first two. **1891** [see OCTASTICH].

†**2.** (See quot.) *Obs. rare*$^{-0}$.

1656 BLOUNT *Glossogr.*, *Pentasticks* (*pentastichæ*), porches having five rowes of Pillars.

pentastichous (pɛn'tæstɪkəs), *a. Bot.* [f. as prec. + -OUS.] Arranged in five rows, five-ranked; *esp.* of a stem: having five leaves in the spiral row, and thus five vertical rows or orthostichies in the phyllotaxis.

1857 MAYNE *Expos. Lex.*, *Pentastichus*,..disposed in five rows,..pentastichous. **1861** BENTLEY *Man. Bot.* 139 This arrangement of cycles of five..is termed the quincuncial, pentastichous or five-ranked arrangement.

pentastom, -e ('pɛntəstɒm, -əʊm). *Zool.* Also in L. form. [ad. mod.L. generic name *Pentastoma* (C. A. Rudolphi *Entozoorum Synopsis Mantissa* (1819) 123) or *Pentastomum* (F. C. H. Creplin *Novæ Observationes de Entozois* (1829) 76), f. PENTA- + Gr. -στομος adj. formative f. στόμα mouth; so called from the appearance of the mouth and the two pairs of chitinoid hooks adjacent to it. (So in mod.F.)] An animal of the genus *Pentastomum* or *Pentastoma*, comprising internal parasites infesting man and other animals; formerly classed as trematode worms.

1857 tr. *Kuchenmeister's Parasites Hum. Body* (Syd. Soc.) II. 7 People took these four feet for the same number of oral orifices, so that counting in the true mouth, five such openings were obtained and the animal received the name of *Pentastomum*. **1872** AITKEN *Sc. & Pract. Med.* (ed. 6) I. 196 Pruner..pointed out, in 1847, the existence of the pentastoma as a parasite in the human subject. **1878** BELL *Gegenbaur's Comp. Anat.* 298 This is most marked in Pentastomum, when the ovary is attached to a circular canal. **1890** *Century Dict.*, Pentastome. **1937** CRAIG & FAUST *Clin. Parasitol.* III. xxxi. 511 (*heading*) 'Tongue worms', Pentastomes (Linguatulida). **1956** T. W. M. CAMERON *Parasites* 149 Pentastomes or 'tongue-worms' were until recently regarded as aberrant arachnids.

So **pen'tastomoid** *a.*, resembling the genus *Pentastomum*; or belonging to the group *Pentastomoidea*, represented by this genus; *sb.* an animal of this group. **pen'tastomous** *a.*: see quot.

1857 MAYNE *Expos. Lex.*, *Pentastomus*, having five mouths or openings: pentastomous. **1890** *Cent. Dict.*, Pentastomoid.

pentastomid (pɛntə'stəʊmɪd), *sb.* and *a.* [f. mod.L. name of class *Pentastomida*, f. generic name *Pentastoma*: see prec. and -ID³.] A parasitic worm-like arthropod of the class Pentastomida; = *tongue-worm* (*b*) s.v. TONGUE *sb.* 16. Also as *adj.*, of or pertaining to a parasite of this kind. Cf. LINGUATULID.

1909 A. E. SHIPLEY in *Cambr. Nat. Hist.* IV. xx. 488 Pentastomids are unpleasant-looking, fluke-like or worm-like animals. **1943** *Trans. Amer. Microsc. Soc.* LXII. 194 (*title*) Observations on the pentastomid *Kiricephalus coarctatus*. **1957** *Jrnl. Parasitol.* XLIII. 195 Several pentastomids were removed from a series of mammals and reptiles. **1964** T. C. CHENG *Biol. Animal Parasites* xx. 549/1 Adult pentastomids are usually parasitic in the respiratory tract and lungs of vertebrates. *Ibid.* 552/2 When pentastomid eggs are fed to albino rats,..seven immature stages can be identified within the intermediate host. **1978** *Nature* 2 Mar. 93/1 The remaining 23 chapters deal with metazoan parasites (ten on the platyhelminthes,..and a chapter each on the..pentastomids and parasitic crustacea).

pentastyle ('pɛntəstaɪl), *a.* and *sb. Arch. rare*$^{-0}$. [f. PENTA- + Gr. στῦλ-ος pillar. (So in mod.F.)]

a. *adj.* Having five columns in front or at the end, as a building. **b.** *sb.* A building or portico having five columns.

1727-41 CHAMBERS *Cycl.*, *Pentastyle*, in architecture, a work wherein are five rows of columns. **1794** *Rudim. Anc. Archit.* (1810) 122 *Pentastyle*, an edifice having five columns in front. **1823** P. NICHOLSON *Pract. Build.* 590. **1882** OGILVIE, *Pentastyle*,..having five columns.

pentasyllabic (ˌpɛntəsɪ'læbɪk), *a.* [f. L. *pentasyllab-us*, a. Gr. πεντασύλλαβ-ος five-syllabled + -IC, after SYLLABIC.] Consisting of five syllables. So **penta'syllabism** (*nonce-wd.*), pentasyllabic condition; **penta'syllable**, a word of five syllables.

a **1771** GRAY *Observ. Eng. Metre* Wks. 1843 V. 257 Pentasyllabic and Tetrasyllabic [lines of verse]. These are rarely used alone. **1816** *Q. Rev.* XV. 369 It could not be done in less compass than a pentasyllable. **1892** F. HALL in *Nation* (N.Y.) 25 Aug. 145/1 '*Literarian*', however, if we can excuse its pentasyllabism, seems to recommend itself as supplying a desideratum.

Pentateuch ('pɛntətjuːk). [ad. L. *pentateuch-us*, *-um* (Tertullian *c* 207), sb. f. Gr. ἡ πεντάτευχ-ος the pentateuch (Let. of Ptolemæus Gnosticus *c* 160, in Epiphanius *Adv. Hæres.* xxxiii. §4), sb. use (sc. βίβλος) of πεντάτευχος adj. 'of five books', f. πεντα- five + τεῦχος 'implement, vessel', in post-Alexandrian Gr. 'book'. In F. *Pentateuque*]

1. Name for the first five books of the Old Testament (Genesis, Exodus, Leviticus, Numbers, and Deuteronomy) taken together as a connected group, traditionally ascribed to Moses (hence called 'the five books of Moses').

1530 PALSGR. 253/1 Penthatheukes, fyve bokes of Moyses lawe, *pentathevcon*. **1532** MORE *Confut. Tindale* Wks. 343/2 That after these bokes well learned, we bee mete for Tyndales pentateukes, and Tyndales testamente. **1586** J. HOOKER *Hist. Irel.* Ep. Ded., Then he and Iosua..did deliuer vnto them the whole Pentatychon of Moses to be dailie read & taught. **1614** SELDEN *Titles Hon.* 15 Long before his time was the Pentateuch turned into Greek. **1646** SIR T. BROWNE *Pseud. Ep.* VI. i. 276 Jerome professeth, in his translation he was faine sometime to relieve himselfe by the Samaritane Pentateuch. **1768-74** TUCKER *Lt. Nat.* (1834) II. 410 The Israelite had nothing more to do than open his Pentateuch. **1867** LADY HERBERT *Cradle L.* viii. 210 They were shown the oldest known copy of the Pentateuch.

2. *transf.* A volume composed of five books, etc.: see quots. *rare.*

1656 BLOUNT *Glossogr.*, *Pentateuch*, a volume of five Books. **1658** PHILLIPS, *Pentateuch*,..also any volume consisting of five books. **1842** DUNGLISON *Med. Lex.* s.v., By analogy some surgeons have given the name *Surgical Pentateuch* to the division of external diseases into five classes:—wounds, ulcers, tumours, luxations and fractures. **1891** CHEYNE *Orig. & Relig. Cont. of Psalter* I. i. 6 The Hebrew Psalter came together not as a book but as a Pentateuch. **1891** BLADES (*title*) The Pentateuch of Printing, with a Chapter on Judges.

Hence **Pentateuchal** (pɛntə'tjuːkəl) *a.*, of, pertaining to, or contained in the Pentateuch.

a **1846** WILLIAMS cited in Worcester. **1863** DARWIN in *Life* (1892) 257, I have long regretted that I..used the Pentateuchal term of 'Creation'. **1890** GLADSTONE *Impregnable Rock* (1892) 176 The spirit..of the Pentateuchal laws.

pentathionic (ˌpɛntəθaɪ'ɒnɪk), *a. Chem.* [irreg. f. PENTA- + Gr. θεῖον sulphur + -IC: see DITHIONIC.] In ***pentathionic acid***, an acid containing five atoms of sulphur in the molecule, $H_2S_5O_6$, colourless, inodorous, and of bitter taste. Hence **pentathionate** (-'θaɪənət), a salt of pentathionic acid.

In quot. 1849, applied to the anhydride or oxide (S_5O_5).

1849 D. CAMPBELL *Inorg. Chem.* 58 *Pentathionic acid*, S_5O_5..This acid is in solution when an excess of sulphide of hydrogen gas is passed into a saturated solution of sulphurous acid. **1881** *Athenæum* 29 Jan. 169/1 Obtaining beautifully crystallized barium and potassium pentathionates. **1881** *Nature* XXIII. 615/2 Mr. V. Lewes..describes..several potassium pentathionates... These experiments appear to establish beyond doubt the existence of pentathionic acid.

pentathlete (pɛn'tæθliːt). [ad. Gr. πενταθλητής, f. πένταθλον: see next.] **a.** An athlete who contended in the pentathlon.

1828 E. H. BARKER *Parriana* I. 522 *note*, Between Porson and Parr..the difference was as great as between..a pugilist and a pentathlete. **1873** SYMONDS *Grk. Poets* iii. (1877) 87 You give all kinds of honours..to runners, boxers, pentathletes, &c.

b. A competitor in a modern pentathlon (see next). Hence **pentath'letical** *a.*

1968 *Guardian* 19 Mar. 16/6 Athletes, pentathletes and weightlifters had taken advantage of grants..for altitude training. **1973** *Country Life* 10 May 1296/3 The heartening recruitment of pentathletes from the pony club. **1975** *Times Lit. Suppl.* 12 Dec. 1487/1 These figures [of Burne-Jones] are almost always pentathletical types: imposingly tall, long in the thigh, slim and gradual of hip, and very firmly fleshed. **1976** *Field* 26 Aug. 426/3 In saluting the modern pentathletes on 29 July for their Olympic victory, I remarked the difficulties of a team dividing a single solid prize.

‖**pentathlon** (pɛn'tæθlɒn). Also in Lat. form **pentathlum**. Pl. **-a**. [a. Gr. πένταθλον, f. πέντε five + ἆθλον contest.] **a.** *Gr.* and *Rom. Antiq.* An athletic contest consisting of five exercises (leaping, running, throwing the discus, throwing the spear, and wrestling), all performed on the same day and by the same athletes.

1706 PHILLIPS, *Pentathlum*. **1711** BUDGELL *Spect.* No. 161 ⁋7 The Commonwealths of Greece; from whence the Romans afterwards borrowed their *Pentathlum*, which was composed of Running, Wrestling, Leaping, Throwing, and Boxing. **1776** R. CHANDLER *Trav. Greece* iv. 15 Telamon and Peleus..challenged their half-brother Phocus to contend in the Pentathlum. **1852** GROTE *Greece* II. lxxx. X. 437 The pentathlon, or quintuple contest, wherein the running match and the wrestling match came first in order. **1868** W. SMITH *Dict. Gr. & Rom. Antiq.* s.v., The pentathlon was introduced in the Olympic games in Ol. 18.

b. In modern times, a series of five athletic or sporting events imitative of the ancient pentathlon, *spec.* (*a*) (in full ***modern pentathlon***) a competition consisting of fencing, shooting, swimming, riding, and cross-country running; (*b*) a competition for women, consisting of sprinting, hurdling, long jump, high jump, and putting the shot. Also *attrib.*

1905 *Olympic Games Athens* 3 *Pentathlum*, consisting of the five following events: 1) Flat race one Olympic Stade.. 2) Broad jump..3) Throwing the discus..4) Hurling the javelin..5) Wrestling. **1912** *Olympic Games Stockholm* 10/2 *Modern pentathlon*, duel-pistol shooting..swimming.. fencing..riding..cross-country race. **1929** F. A. M. WEBSTER *Athletics of To-day* vii. 107 Eighty events were decided..including a pentathlon contest and several of the field events. **1932** *New Yorker* 23 July 8/3 The Hungarian swimming and pentathlon teams arrived. **1948** E. A. BLAND *Olympic Story* xxii. 140 In 1912, when the Swedish Olympic Committee was deliberating upon the programme of events for the Vth Olympiad, they sought a test which would produce the best all-round sportsman in the world... The contest known as the Modern Pentathlon was the result. **1961** C. WILLOCK *Death in Covert* x. 189 An Olympic Pentathlon..[is] a kind of marathon in which the competitors run, ride, shoot and so on without a break. **1964** M. WATMAN *Encycl. Athletics* 130/1 The pentathlon is a five-event test of all-round ability... The pentathlon has long been a most popular women's event, and was introduced into the Olympic schedule in 1964. **1970** B. TULLOH *World Athletics Handbk.* vi. 99 With the pentathlon being omitted..the 1928 Games..reached much the same form for the men's events as it has today. **1976** *Gazette* (Montreal) 19 July O-8/4 Bromont—Thirteen riders of 47 scored a perfect 1,100 points on the modern pentathlon equestrian course. **1979** *Daily Tel.* 2 Oct. 19/4 Pentathlon is a comparatively new sport for women.

Pentathol, var. PENTOTHAL.

pentatomic (pɛntə'tɒmɪk), *a. Chem.* [mod. f. Gr. πέντε five + ἄτομος ATOM *sb.* + -IC: cf. *atomic.*] Containing five atoms of some substance in the molecule; *spec.* containing five replaceable hydrogen atoms; also = PENTAVALENT.

1872 WATTS *Dict. Chem.* VI. 72 Pentatomic Alcohols. Pinite and quercite, two saccharine bodies having the composition $C_6H_{12}O_5$, probably belong to this class of bodies. **1873** J. P. COOKE *New Chem.* 290 No definite pentatomic hydrate is known. **1873** WATTS *Fownes' Chem.* (ed. 11) 633 Glucoses may..be expected to act as pentatomic alcohols.

pentatomid (pɛn'tætəmɪd), *a. Entom.* [f. mod.L. *Pentatomidæ* pl., f. *Pentatoma*, name of the typical genus (Olivier, 1789), f. Gr. πεντα- PENTA- five + -τομος cut, in reference to the 5-jointed antennæ.] Belonging to the family *Pentatomidæ* of plant-feeding heteropterous insects, mostly of warm climates, and often brilliantly coloured. So **pen'tatomine** *a.* in same sense; **pen'tatomoid** *a.*, related to, or resembling, the *Pentatomidæ*.

1890 *Cent. Dict.*, *Pentatomine*..*Pentatomoid*. **1900** *Ibis* VI. 260 Tinnunculus Amurensis..Its stomach contained 18 large pentatomid bugs.

pentatone ('pɛntətəʊn). *Mus. rare*$^{-0}$. [f. PENTA- + TONE, after *tritone.*] 'An interval of five whole tones, an augmented sixth' (Stainer & Barrett).

pentatonic (pɛntəˈtɒnɪk), *a.* (*sb.*) *Mus.* [mod. (Carl Engel, 1864), f. PENTA- + Gr. τόν-ος TONE + -IC: cf. TONIC.] Consisting of five notes or sounds; *esp.* applied to a form of scale without semitones (equivalent to the ordinary major scale with the fourth and seventh omitted), used by various ancient nations, and by certain non-European nations, as well as in the popular melodies of different countries (often called the *Scotch scale*). Also as *sb.*, a scale with five different notes to the octave.

1864 ENGEL *Mus. Anc. Nat.* 124 A scale..consisting of only five tones, wherefore I have given it the name of *Pentatonic Scale.* **1887** L. SCOTT *Tusc. Stud.* II. iv. (1888) 222 The ancient scale being pentatonic, *i.e.* five notes, leaving out our fourth and seventh. **1891** *Athenæum* 12 Dec. 807/2 India..differs, as Europe differs, from the pentatonic and heptatonic scales of the Chinese and Indo-Chinese. **1909** F. R. BURTON *Amer. Primitive Mus.* ii. 41 This scale is not what is generally known as the pentatonic, although it consists of the same tones. **1921** H. A. POPLEY *Mus. India* iii. 28 The pentatonic was the more primitive scale among all peoples. **1928** *Grove's Dict. Mus.* (ed. 3) IV. 100/2 If we continue..to call them gaps, we may notice that they always occur at the interval of a fourth, (or fifth); and that is the distinguishing mark of the true pentatonic. **1936** E. BLOM et al. tr. *Einstein's Short Hist. Mus.* 5 In China the development from the non-semitonal to the seven-note scale is certainly traceable, even though the old pentatonic always remained the foundation of its music. **1962** [see HETEROPHONY].

Hence **pentaˈtonically** *adv.*, according to a pentatonic scale.

1965 *New Statesman* 17 Dec. 980/3 The almost complete disintegration of traditional controls in those pentatonically whirling winds, those parallel-third woodwinds that are sighing trees. **1967** H. PORTER in *Coast to Coast 1965–66* 174 'Good af-ter-noon, Mis-ter Pel-lot,' melodiously and pentatonically in duet chanted the Misses Wee.

pentatremite (pɛntəˈtriːmaɪt). *Palæont.* Also contracted **pentremite**. [ad. mod.L. *Pentatrēmites*, f. PENTA- + Gr. τρῆμα hole, aperture: see -ITE[1] 2.] An echinoderm of the genus *Pentatrēmites*, belonging to the extinct class *Blastoidea*, allied to the crinoids. So **pentatrematoid** (-ˈtriːmətɔɪd), *a.*, belonging to or resembling the *Pentatremitidæ*, typified by *Pentratremites*; *sb.* an echinoderm of this family.

1864 WEBSTER, *Pentremite*, a fossil crinoid. **1873** DAWSON *Earth & Man* vi. 153 One curious group, that of the *Pentremites*, a sort of larval form. **1890** *Cent. Dict.*, *Pentatrematoid*..*Pentatremite.*

pentauncer, obs. form of PENITENCER.

pentavalent (pɛnˈtævələnt), *a.* *Chem.* [f. PENTA- + L. *valēnt-em* having power or value.] Having the combining power of five atoms of hydrogen or other univalent element; quinquivalent.

1871 ROSCOE *Elem. Chem.* 174 The elements of the nitrogen group possess a peculiarity by which they frequently appear as if they were pentavalent. **1881** A. W. WILLIAMSON in *Nature* XXIV. 418/1 An atom of nitrogen or of antimony is only known to be trivalent in combination with hydrogen; but each of them occurs in form of a pentavalent compound with chlorine.

pentazocine (pɛnˈtæzəʊsiːn). *Pharm.* [f. PENT(ANE + AZ(O- + *-ocine* (f. OC(TA- + -INE[5]).] A tricyclic heterocyclic compound that is a non-addictive analgesic, given as the hydrochloride in tablet form or as the lactate by injection; 1,2,3,4,5,6-hexahydro-8-hydroxy-6,11-dimethyl-3-(3-methyl-2-butenyl)-2,6-methano-3-benzazocine, $C_{19}H_{27}NO$.

1964 *Jrnl. Pharmacol. & Exper. Therap.* CXLIII. 142/1 (*caption*) Compound II has been assigned the generic name 'pentazocine' and Compound IV, 'cyclazocine'. **1967** *Observer* 5 Mar. 13/1 Pentazocine, which in pain-killing potency falls between morphine and pethidine, becomes available in an injectable form (under the name Fortral) on 5 April. **1974** M. C. GERALD *Pharmacol.* xiii. 248 Pentazocine is an effective analgesic agent that also possesses modest narcotic antagonistic properties. **1977** *Sci. Amer.* Mar. 47/2 The prototype is pentazocine (Talwin), which is widely used in the U.S. and is the only powerful opiate analgesic that is not subject to stringent 'dangerous drug' regulations.

pente, obs. and dial. form of PAINT.

penteconta- (pɛntɪkɒntə), before a vowel **-cont-**, combining form, repr. Gr. πεντήκοντα fifty, in a few rare words. †**penteˈcontarch** [ad. Gr. πεντηκόνταρχος], a commander of fifty men. **penteˈcontadrachm** (-dræm) [ad. Gr. πεντηκοντάδραχμον], a Cyrenaic coin worth fifty drachmas. **pentecontaˈglossal** *a.* [Gr. γλῶσσα tongue], written in fifty languages. **penteˈcontaˌlitre** [ad. Gr. πεντηκοντάλιτρον], a Sicilian coin worth fifty *litræ* or ten drachmas.

1382 WYCLIF *1 Macc.* iii. 55 After these thingus Judas ordeynyde duykis of the peple, tribunys [*gloss* that oon ledde a thousand], and centoriouns [or ledinge an hundrid], and pentacontarkes [leders of fyfty]. **1656** BLOUNT *Glossogr.*, *Pentecontarck*, a Captain of fifty men. **1807** ROBINSON *Archæol. Græca* v. xxvi. 548 In some authors we find the word pentecontadrachm, or fifty drachms. **1846** J. B. LINDSAY (*title*) Pentecontaglossal Paternoster, or the Lord's Prayer in 50 Languages. **1850** LEITCH tr. *C. O. Müller's Anc. Art* § 132 The costly master-pieces of Sicilian engravers, the great Syracusan pentekontalitres at the head.

‖**penteˈconter**[1]. *Gr. Antiq.* [a. Gr. πεντηκοντήρ.] A commander of a troop of fifty men.

1623 BINGHAM *Xenophon* 54 The Coronels..framed six Companies, euery one consisting of an hundred men, and appointed Captaines ouer them, and Penteconters, and Enomotarches. **1850** GROTE *Greece* II. lvi. VII. 159 The Pentekontêr and the Lochage were responsible also each for his larger division.

penteˈconter[2]. *Gr. Antiq.* [ad. Gr. πεντηκοντήρης.] A ship of burden with fifty oars.

1838 THIRLWALL *Greece* IV. xxxiv. 346 Dexippus,..who was sent out with a penteconter.., sailed away to Byzantium. **1846** GROTE *Greece* I. iv, Danaos placed his fifty daughters on board of a penteconter (or vessel with fifty oars).

Pentecost (ˈpɛntɪkɒst). Also 5 **pentcost, pencost**, 5–6 **penthecost(e**, 6–7 **penticost(e**, 7 **pentycost**. [a. Christian L. *pentēcostē* (Tertullian), a. Gr. πεντηκοστή (sc. ἡμέρα or ἑορτή) fiftieth (day or feast), in Tobit ii. 1, 2 Maccabees xii. 32.]

1. A name of Hellenistic origin for the Jewish harvest festival (called in the Old Testament the Feast of Weeks) observed on the fiftieth day of the OMER (q.v.), i.e. at the conclusion of seven weeks from the offering of the wave-sheaf, on the second day of the Passover.

The first day of the Passover is always the 15th Nisan; the 16th Nisan is the First Day of the Omer or wave-offering; seven weeks from which, on the 6th Sivan, is the Feast of Weeks. Thus, in 1900, the 16th Nisan coincided with Sunday 15th April, and the 6th Sivan with Sunday 3rd June, which were also, that year, Easter Sunday and Whit-Sunday; but the Jewish festivals, being regulated solely by the moon, may fall on any day of the week: see 2.

c **1000** ÆLFRIC *Hom.* I. 312 On ðam eldan Pentecosten sette God æ ðam Israhela folce. *c* **1175** *Lamb. Hom.* 89. **1382** WYCLIF *2 Macc.* xii. 32 After Pentecost [Vulg. *post Pentecosten*, LXX μετὰ δὲ τὴν λεγομένην πεντηκοστήν], thei wenten aȝeins Gorgias, prepoost of Ydume. —— *Acts* ii. 1 Whanne the dayes Pentecostes, [*gloss* that is, fyfti; **1388** daies of Pentecost] weren fulfillid, alle disciplis weren to gidere in the same place. **1560** BIBLE (Genev.) *Tobit* ii. 1 In the feast of Pentecoste which is the holy (feast) of the seuen wekes [so in **1611**; LXX ἐν τῇ πεντηκοστῇ ἑορτῇ ἥ ἐστιν ἁγία ἑπτὰ ἑβδομάδων]. **1737** WHISTON *Josephus, Jewish War* II. iii. § 1 That feast which was observed after seven weeks, and which the Jews call Pentecost. **1900** G. T. PURVES in Hastings *Dict. Bible* III. 741/1 It is certain that the Jews celebrated the sheaf-waving on Nisan 16, and Pentecost on the fiftieth day after (Sivan 6), without regard in either case to the day of the week.

2. A festival of the Christian Church observed on the seventh Sunday after Easter, in commemoration of the descent of the Holy Spirit upon the disciples on the day of Pentecost (Acts ii.); the day of this festival, Whit-Sunday; also, the season of this festival, Whitsuntide.

The Resurrection of Christ is recorded to have taken place on the second day of the Passover, being that year the first day of the week. Seven weeks after that (and so again on the first day of the week) was the Feast of Weeks or Pentecost. In commemoration of this, these two Christian festivals are always held on the first day of the week (Sunday), and so in most cases do not coincide with the Jewish festivals.

c **1000** ÆLFRIC *Hom.* I. 312 Þes dæȝðerlica dæȝ is ure Pentecostes, þæt is, se fifteoȝoða dæȝ fram ðam Easterdæȝe. *c* **1050** *Byrhtferth's Handboc* in *Anglia* VIII. 311 Wel ȝelóme byð pentecosten on him ȝeendod. *a* **1100** *O.E. Chron.* an. 1086 Þriwa he bær his cynehelm ælce ȝeare..On Eastron he hine bær on Winceastre, on Pentecosten on Westmynstre. **1387** TREVISA *Higden* (Rolls) IV. 347 Þat ȝere about Pentecoste, þat is Witsontide, þe apostles ordeyned þe lasse Iames, Alpheus his sone, bisshop of Ierusalem. **1481** CAXTON *Godeffroy* clxv. 244 There helde they theyr penthecost or wytsontyde. **1592** SHAKS. *Rom. & Jul.* I. v. 38 Come Pentycost as quickely as it will. **1726** [see PENTECOSTAL *sb.*]. **1841** LONGF. *Childr. Lord's Supper* 1 Pentecost, day of rejoicing, had come. The church of the village Gleaming stood in the morning's sheen. **1889** H. M. LUCKOCK *Divine Liturgy* xlix. 394 He mentions Epiphany as one of the three days, and omits Pentecost. **1953** A. A. MCARTHUR *Evolution of Christian Year* IV. 165 What does the following of the year actually mean in practice in the periods after Epiphany and Pentecost? **1957** *Oxf. Dict. Chr. Ch.* 1483/1 In the RC Church the Sundays from Pentecost to Advent are usually numbered 'after Pentecost' but in the Anglican Church they are reckoned..'after Trinity', i.e. the Sunday after Pentecost. **1969** *Calendar & Lessons* (Church of England Liturgical Comm.) 5 Trinity Sunday is historically a late feast, exceptional as proclaiming a doctrine rather than commemorating an event. It is only in northern Europe that the Sundays of the unorganized second half of the Church's year have been dated from it, the octave of Pentecost, instead of from Pentecost itself. The calendar proposes that they should be called Sundays after Pentecost. **1976** B. BARKER *When Queen was Crowned* 4 Many of the acts, words and anthems in Westminster Abbey in 1953 were seen and heard on the feast of Pentecost in St Peter's Church at Bath in 973 when King Edgar was crowned. **1978** P. G. COBB in C. Jones et al. *Study of Liturgy* VI. i. 418 Pentecost is given a new prominence by becoming a third focus of the Christian Year.

attrib. **1568** GRAFTON *Chron.* II. 934 Vpon the Tuesday in Penticost weeke. **1664–5** in Swayne *Sarum Churchw. Acc.* (1896) 338 Mr. Kent penticost mony 6*s.* 8*d.* [Cf. PENTECOSTAL *sb.*]

3. *fig.* in allusion to the gift of the Holy Spirit, or the circumstances attending it recorded in Acts ii.

176. WESLEY *Serm.* lxviii. § 20 Wks. 1811 IX. 241 The grand pentecost shall 'fully come': and 'devout men in every nation'..shall 'all be filled with the Holy Ghost'. **1847** EMERSON *Poems, Problem*, Ever the fiery Pentecost Girds with one flame the countless host. **1901** W. SANDAY in *Expositor* May 327 Calvary without Pentecost is not yet in vital relation with ourselves.

4. The particular day that the Christian feast of Pentecost commemorates, when the Holy Spirit descended upon the apostles (Acts ii).

1882 G. SMEATON *Doctrine of Holy Spirit* II. 48 The Pentecost was the great day of the Holy Ghost, the opening of the river of the water of life. **1913** W. H. G. THOMAS *Holy Spirit of God* I. v. 42 To the disciples the gift of the Holy Spirit at Pentecost may be said to be analogous to the descent of the Holy Spirit on Christ at his baptism. **1925** CHESTERTON *Everlasting Man* II. iv. 250 This learned scholar says that Pentecost was the occasion for the first founding of an ecclesiastical, dogmatic and despotic Church utterly alien to the simple ideals of Jesus of Nazareth. **1938** *Doctrine in C. of E.* 161 They would lay stress upon the idea of the Spirit as guiding the Church into all truth, and as therein revealing more fully after Pentecost the significance of what our Lord did at the Last Supper. **1977** *Christian* IV. 33 Jesus' appointment of the twelve, and their special consecration at Pentecost, are not functional devices, otherwise irrelevant to the preaching of the Kingdom.

pentecostal (pɛntɪˈkɒstəl), *sb.* and *a.* [ad. L. *pentēcostāl-is* adj. (Tertullian), f. *pentēcostē*: see PENTECOST and -AL[1]. In A, ad. med.L. *pentēcostālia* (neuter pl. of adj.) pentecostal (payments).]

A. *sb.* **a.** (usually *pl.*) Offerings formerly made in the Church of England at Whitsuntide by the parishioners to the priest, or by an inferior church to the mother-church. *Obs.* exc. *Hist.*

1549 LATIMER *3rd Serm. bef. Edw. VI* (Arb.) 83, I should haue receyued a certayne dutye that they cal a Pentecostal. **1609** in W. Money *Hist. Newbury* (1887) 529 Pd for Pentecostalles, otherwise called smoke farthings. **1695** KENNETT *Par. Antiq.* ix. 597 This old custome gave birth and name to the Pentecostals or Whitsun-contributions. **1726** AYLIFFE *Parergon* 434 Pentecostals, otherwise called Whitsun-Farthings, were Oblations made by the Parishioners to the Parish-Priest at the Feast of Pentecost.

b. (With a capital initial.) = PENTECOSTALIST *sb.*

1904 in C. R. Paige *Alma White's Evangelism* (1939) I. 81 The Pentecostals refrain even from circulating an insinuating hat. **1946** in S. H. Frodsham *With Signs Following* xxiv. 273 The Pentecostals today are receiving the same kind of treatment that the Brethren received in those early days... I have heard as clear a presentation of the gospel in Pentecostal meetings as I ever heard among the Brethren. **1958** E. P. PAULK *Your Pentecostal Neighbor* 7 Pentecostals have spread..until today they compose a major portion of the Christian body. **1969** K. & D. RANAGHAN *Catholic Pentecostals* vii. 247 There is no discord between the charismatic movement and the liturgy... There has been no tendency on the part of Catholic pentecostals to substitute prayer meetings or any of the gifts for the sacramental life of the Church. **1971** D. GELPI *Pentecostalism* v. 132 Non-Pentecostals find it [*sc.* glossolalia] strange and exotic. **1972** S. DURASOFF *Bright Wind of Spirit* (1973) xi. 190 In the past Catholics have been looked on with favor only as a fertile field of evangelism by many Pentecostals. **1974** *Encycl. Brit. Micropædia* VII. 858/1 Pentecostals thus hold that a Spirit-baptized believer may receive one or more of the supernatural gifts that were known in the early Church. **1975** *Christian Order* XVI. 419 For the proverbial mess of pottage, the Pentecostals claim, the Church sold her soul to Caesar.

B. *adj.* **a.** Of or pertaining to Pentecost; like that of the Day of Pentecost in Acts ii.

a **1663** SANDERSON (J.), The collects adventual, quadragesimal, paschal, or pentecostal. **1836** KEBLE in *Lyra Apost.* LXXXIV. iii, The sacred Pentecostal eve. *a* **1842** A. REED *Hymn*, '*Spirit Divine, attend our prayer*' vi, Come as the wind—with rushing sound And pentecostal grace. **1850** ROBERTSON *Serm.* Ser. III. ix. 116 These are the pentecostal hours of our existence.

b. Resembling the mixture of nationalities in Jerusalem at Pentecost (Acts ii. 9–11); heterogeneous.

1896 KIPLING *Five Nations* (1903) 90, I have watched them in their tantrums, all that pentecostal crew, French, Italian, Arab, Spaniard, Dutch and Greek, and Russ and Jew.

c. Pertaining to or designating Christian sects, movements, and individuals who emphasize the gifts of the Holy Spirit as recorded in Acts ii, seek to express their religious feelings uninhibitedly (e.g. clapping, shouting, and speaking with tongues) and often are fundamentalist in outlook and maintain that a 'baptism in the Spirit' manifested by speaking with tongues is to be sought by all Christians; freq. (with capital initial) forming part of the name of a sect.

1904 *Daily Graphic* 8 Dec. 4/1 Camberwell has received this new form of worship with mingled feelings of tolerance, indifference and hostility, but the Pentecostal Dancers.. have maintained their steadfast resolution of dancing themselves into the hearts of their audiences—with but little success so far. **1906** *Apostolic Faith* Oct. 1/1 The waves of Pentecostal salvation are still rolling in at Azusa Street Mission. **1910** *Latter Rain Evangel* Oct. 12/1 A Pentecostal convention will be held..God willing, November 18 to Dec. 4 1910. **1924** *Ibid.* Oct. 10/1 As usual in a real Pentecostal camp meeting, it was harder to stop than to start. **1928** *Amer. Mercury* Oct. 184/2 The Pentecostal Nazarenes have largely duplicated the Methodist system of government by district conferences. **1932** M. MEAD *Changing Culture of*

Indian Tribe 108 Most of the poor whites go to the Pentecostal Church. **1946** S. H. FRODSHAM *With Signs Following* (rev. ed.) v. 41 This Pentecostal visitation became so universal in 'The Holiness Church' that it had to be renamed. It is now known as 'The Pentecostal Holiness Church'. **1958** [see HOLINESS 4 b]. **1966** *Listener* 26 May 754/1 Let us consider the West Indian Pentecostal sects. **1970** P. OLIVER *Savannah Syncopators* 56 The hand-clapping.. remained a familiar characteristic of the services of the 'Sanctified' and 'Pentecostal' churches. **1974** *Amer. Speech 1971* XLVI. 70 It is too soon to know.. whether or not the term [*sc.* jackleg preacher] is used in other urban areas where the storefront pentecostal-and-holiness churches abide. **1974** *Observer* (Colour Suppl.) 17 Nov. 34/1 There are the various 'pentecostal' movements which go in for fervent, excited forms of worship.

Pentecostalism (pɛntɪˈkɒstəlɪz(ə)m). [f. prec. + -ISM.] The beliefs and practices of the Pentecostal movement or Pentecostal sects.

1932 F. C. MARTIN *Holy Ghost versus Mod. Tongues* xix. 159 God forbid that modern Pentecostalism with the tongues deception be allowed to continue. **1936** H. J. STOLEE *Pentecostalism* ii. 11 Modern pentecostalism also has its type in the problems of the early Church. **1946** C. B. NERVIG *Christian Truth & Relig. Delusions* v. 75 Pentecostalism does teach the great essentials of the Christian religion. **1958** *Eternity* Apr. 9/3 In some ways, Pentecostalism.. has moderated its extremes in the past fifty years. **1961** B. R. WILSON *Sects & Society* 8 Some expressions of early Pentecostalism. **1966** *Listener* 26 May 754/2, I am thinking of a movement something like the Black Muslims, which is logically possible as an alternative, or in addition to, Pentecostalism. **1971** D. GELPI *Pentecostalism* i. 5 Catholic Pentecostalism has spread through wide segments of the American Church.

Pentecostalist (pɛntɪˈkɒstəlɪst), *sb.* and *a.* [f. as prec. + -IST.] **A.** *sb.* A member of any Pentecostal sect; an adherent of the Pentecostal movement. **B.** *adj.* Of or pertaining to Pentecostalism.

1925 *Forum* (N.Y.) Feb. 152 'Pentecostalists' brought to light our partial neglect of the Holy Ghost. **1928** *Amer. Mercury* Oct. 190/1 The epic case of Holy Roller healing is that of the Rev. David Wesley Myland of the Latter Rain Pentecostalists. **1956** *Gordon Rev.* Dec. 131 The Pentecostalists assert that deliverance from physical sickness is provided for in the Atonement. **1958** M. ARGYLE *Relig. Behaviour* iv. 34 The Baptists and other Evangelical groups were rather similar in 1850 to the Pentecostalists of today. *Ibid.* ix. 110 Boisen gives a case-study of a Pentecostalist leader who was an epileptic. **1961** B. R. WILSON *Sects & Society* I. i. 18 Pentecostalist stress on the Pauline declarations. **1965** *Guardian* 8 Sept. 4/3 The West Indian Pentecostalist sect drew most of its members from the lowest group of Jamaican working class. **1966** *Listener* 26 May 754/2 If Pentecostalists improve their position and become house owners or land-lords, will they leave to join a middle-class denomination, or will they restructure their Pentecostalist beliefs, so that a sect becomes a denomination? **1979** R. BLYTHE *View in Winter* ix. 300 I'm waiting [on God] not listening. Listening is Pentecostalist, and I find it very hard to do.

‖**pentecoster.** *Gr. Antiq.* [a. Gr. πεντηκοστήρ, false reading for πεντηκοντήρ.] = PENTECONTER¹.

1808 MITFORD *Greece* I. iv. 216 The officers of each mora of infantry.. were one Polĕmarch, four Lochages, eight Pentecosters, and sixteen Enomotarchs.

‖**pentecostys** (pɛntɪˈkɒstɪs). *Gr. Antiq.* Also irreg. anglicized as **ˈpentekosty** (-kɒstɪ). [a. Gr. πεντηκοστύς (pl. -ύες) a number or company of fifty, f. πεντηκοστ-ός fiftieth.] A body of fifty men, as a division of the Spartan army.

1808 MITFORD *Greece* I. iv. 216 Each Lochus consisted of four Pentecostyes, and each Pentecostys of four Enomoties. **1850** GROTE *Greece* II. lvi. VII. 111 Each lochus comprised four pentekosties.. each pentekosty contained four enômoties. **1869** W. SMITH *Dict. Grk. & Rom. Antiq.* (ed. 2) 483/1 An enomotia, pentecostys, &c.

pentegraph, erron. form of PANTOGRAPH *sb.*

Pentel (ˈpɛntəl). Also **pentel**. The proprietary name of a type of felt-tip pen.

1964 *Observer* 8 Nov. 40/3 What is the particular fascination of a Pentel? It's the new kind of thick-flowing pen—something between a felt marker and a ball-point. **1965** *Guardian* 4 Jan. 5/6 The Japanese 'Pentel' pen, has gained a foothold in British markets... The secret of the 'Pentel' is its tip... The 'Pentel'.. will write on anything including glass. **1966** *Trade Marks Jrnl.* 30 Mar. 418/2 Pentel.. writing instruments, drawing instruments, marking instruments, chalks,.. crayons and artists' brushes. Dainihon-Bungu Kabushiki Kaisha.., Tokyo, Japan; manufacturers and merchants. **1969** 'V. PACKER' *Don't rely on Gemini* (1970) ix. 76 Gamble was.. making notes with a Pentel. **1976** L. DEIGHTON *Twinkle, Twinkle Little Spy* vi. 51 Several of the hi-fi magazines were marked with a red pentel.

penteˈlateral, *a.* *rare*⁻¹. [f. Gr. πέντε five + LATERAL.] Five-sided, quinquelateral. So †**pentelater** *a.* (erron. penti-) in same sense.

1571 DIGGES *Pantom., Math. Treat.* Hh iv b, A pentilater Prisma, hauing for.. the syde of his pentagonall equiangle basis the first lyne. **1728** NICHOLS in *Phil. Trans.* XXXV. 483 Two equal pentelateral Pyramids.

Pentelic (pənˈtɛlɪk), *a.* Also 6 *erron.* **pentlike**. [ad. L. *Pentelic-us*, a. Gr. Πεντελικός, f. Πεντελή name of a deme of Attica.] Of or from Mount Pentelicus, near Athens: esp. applied to the famous white marble there quarried.

1579–80 NORTH *Plutarch* (1895) I. 266 The pillers.. are cut out of a quarrie of marbell, called pentlike marbell. **1697** POTTER *Antiq. Greece* I. viii. (1715) 39 If [the Stadium] was built of Pentelick Marble. **1881** *Archit. Publ. Soc. Dict.*, *Pentelic Marble*.. is still used (1878) as for the new academy at Athens.

So †**Penteˈlician**, **Penˈtelican** *adjs.*

1741 MIDDLETON *Cicero* I. ii. 135 The Mercuries.. of Pentelician marble, with brazen heads. **1847** EMERSON *Repr. Men, Plato* Wks. (Bohn) I. 294 They [the Greeks] cut the Pentelican marble as if it were snow.

pentene, *Chem.*: see under PENTANE.

penter, obs. form of PAINTER.

†**ˈpentereme**, *a.* *Obs. rare.* [f. Gr. πέντε five + L. *rēmus* oar.] See quot. 1656.

1656 BLOUNT *Glossogr.*, *Pentireme*, a Galley that has five Oares in a seat or rank, or a Galley wherein every oar hath five men to draw it. See *Quinquereme*. **1844** THIRLWALL *Greece* VIII. lxiv. 266 A fleet of sixty pentereme galleys.

pentes, -esse, obs. forms of PENTHOUSE.

†**ˈpentest.** *Obs. rare*⁻¹. Name of some kind of precious stone.

a **1400–50** *Alexander* 5268 Piȝt fulle of pentests and oþire proude stanes.

penteteric (pɛntɪˈtɛrɪk), *a.* *Gr. Antiq.* [ad. Gr. πεντετηρικός.] Occurring every fifth year (according to modern reckoning, every fourth, both of two consecutive occurrences being counted), as the greater Panathenæa at Athens.

1890 in *Cent. Dict.*

penthemimer (pɛnθɪˈmɪmə(r)). *Anc. Pros.* [ad. Gr. πενθημιμερής consisting of five halves, f. πέντε five + ἡμιμερής halved (ἡμι- half μέρος part).] A group or catalectic colon of five half-feet; esp. as constituting each half of a pentameter, or the first part of a hexameter when the cæsura occurs in the middle of the third foot. (Cf. HEPTHEMIMER.) Hence **pentheˈmimeral** *a.*, applied to a cæsura occurring in the middle of the third foot.

1586 WEBBE *Eng. Poetrie* (Arb.) 80 The shortnesse of the seconde Penthimimer will hardly be framed to fall together in good sence. **1795** PARR in E. H. Barker *Parriana* (1829) II. 623 Content to consider the shorter verse as composed of two penthemimers. **1869** BLACKMORE *Lorna D.* ii, I had replied to Robin now, with all the weight and cadence of penthemimeral cæsura. **1871** *Public Sch. Lat. Gram.* 467 The Pentameter.. consists of two Dactylic Penthemimers, which must be kept quite distinct. **1888** *Athenæum* 24 Nov. 704/3 The treatment of the weak and the strong penthemimeral cæsura of the dactylic hexameter.

penthouse (ˈpɛnthaʊs), **pentice** (ˈpɛntɪs), *sb.* Forms: see below. [ME. *pentis*, rarely *pendis*, app. aphetic from OF. *apentis, apendis, -deis*: cf. med.L. *appendicium* in Promp. Parv. and Cathol. Angl. = pentyce, pentis; also *appenditium* in Du Cange 'a small sacred building dependent upon a larger church', post-cl. L. *appendicium* an appendage, f. *appendĕre* to hang something on another, to attach in a dependent state. As a small building, erected as a 'lean-to' to another, has usually a roof with one slope only, the word was evidently from an early period (esp. in the aphetic form) associated with F. *pente* slope, declivity, 'hang', which became at length a regular element of the sense; hence the later popular etymology *pent-house* for *pentis*: cf. *work-house*, vulgarly *workis*.

The OF. *apendis* and *apentis* appear to represent L. *appendicium* and **appenditicium*. But the early history of the word offers difficulties, esp. that in OF. the short forms without *a-* are very rare, while in Eng. they are the earliest, *appentice* not being known before Caxton.]

A. Illustration of Forms.

α. 4 **pendize**, 6 **pendis**, 7–8 **pendice**.

c **1325** Pendize [see B. 1]. **1592** *Manch. Court Leet Rec.* (1885) II. 60 Settinge vpp a houell.. or slated pendis. **1656** Pendice [see B. 1 b]. **1749** *Fairfax's Tasso* XI. xxxiii, O'er their Heads an iron Pendice [*earlier edd.* pentise, -ice] vast.

β. 4 **pentiz**, 4–6 **pentis**, **pentys**, (5 **penttis**, **pentace**), 5–7 **pentise**, 5–6 **pentyse**, (**-yce**, **-es**, **-esse**, 6 **-isse**, **-ische**, **-ose**, 7 **-ese**, **pantise**), 6–8 (9 *arch.*) **pentice**.

c **1325** Pentiz [see B. 1]. **1381–2** *Durham Acc. Rolls* (Surtees) 389 Pro coopertura del pentys scaccarii. *c* **1420** *Wyclif's Bible, Neh.* vii. 4 *marg. gloss*, Hulkis and pentisis weren maad bisidis the wallis. **1435** *Nottingham Rec.* II. 359 Undder ye penttis. *c* **1440** *Promp. Parv.* 392/2 Pentyce, of an howse ende, *appendicium*. **1449–50** *Durham Acc. Rolls* (Surtees) 239 Pro factura ij pentacez. *a* **1500** Pentice, **1523** Pentesse [see B. 1]. **1530** Pentes, Pentys [see B. 2]. **1579** *Nottingham Rec.* IV. 182 Makyng of.. ij. pentyces. **1598** Q. ELIZ. *Plutarch* xiii. 29 Thogh pentische Like the windowe built. *a* **1599**, **1600** Pentise [see B. 1, 2]. **1615** *Manch. Court Leet Rec.* (1885) II. 306 Erectinge certen postes and coveringe them wth Large penteses. **1640** SOMNER *Antiq. Canterb.* 204 The long low Entry in the Division called the Pantise. **1804** R. ANDERSON *Cumbid. Ball.* 105 She sticks out her lip leyke a pentes. **1884**, **1901** Pentice [see B. 1, 5]. **1885** JULIA CARTWRIGHT in *Portfolio* 114 The poor.. were fed daily.. under a pentise, or covered way.

γ. 6– **penthouse**, **pent-house**, (6 **penthehouse**, 7 **paint-house**).

1530 PALSGR. 253/1 Penthouse of a house, *appentis*. **1568** GRAFTON *Chron.* II. 267 He caused all the Penthehouses of the Towne of Parys to be pulled downe. **1573–1883** Penthouse, Pent-house [see B. 1,2]. **1606** CHAPMAN *Mons. D'Olive* Plays 1873 I. 211 Faith Sir I had a poore roofe, or a paint-house To shade me from the Sunne.

B. Signification.

1. A subsidiary structure attached to the wall of a main building and serving as a shelter, a porch, a shed, an outhouse, etc. **a.** Such a structure having a sloping roof, formerly sometimes forming a covered way between two buildings, or a covered walk, arcade, or colonnade, in front of a row of buildings; a sloping roof or ledge placed against the wall of a building, or over a door or window, for shelter from the weather; sometimes also applied to the eaves of a roof when projecting considerably.

c **1325** *Metr. Hom.* 63 Thar was na herberie To Josep and his spouse Marie, Bot a pendize that was wawles, Als oft in borwis tounes es. *Ibid.* 66 In a pouer pentiz, I wys. *c* **1425** WYNTOUN *Cron.* IV. xxvi. 2648 Betwene howsis twa Quhare men gert a pentys ma. **1467–8** *Cal. Anc. Rec. Dublin* (1889) I. 328 Owyr that to make a pentyse and a fyttyng place undre, for the wyrship of the citte marchaundes.. to sat there-upon for their eyse. *a* **1500** in Arnolde *Chron.* (1811) 92 Yf ony other pentice [AFr. in *Liber Albus* I. 336, *appentices*] porche or gate be ouyr lowe lettynge the people coming or ryding. **1523** LD. BERNERS *Froiss.* I. cxxv. 150 Than kyng Philyppe.. or he went caused all ye pentessys in Parys [*les appentiz de Paris*] to be pulled downe. **1573–80** BARET *Alv.* P 254 Penthouse, or the house eauings. **1596** SHAKS. *Merch. V.* II. vi. 1. *a* **1599** in *Hakluyt's Voy.* II. II. 70 In ech side of the streetes are pentises or continuall porches for the marchants to walke vnder. **1624** WOTTON *Archit.* in *Reliq.* (1672) 48 Those Climes that fear the falling.. of much Snow, ought to provide more inclining Pentices. **1668** PEPYS *Diary* 15 June, [At Marlborough] Their houses on one side having their pent-houses supported with pillars, which makes it a good walk. **1719** DE FOE *Crusoe* I. ix, It cast off the Rains like a Penthouse. **1755** JOHNSON, *Penthouse*, a shed hanging out aslope from the main wall. **1816** SOUTHEY in *Q. Rev.* XVI. 372 Under the pent-house of a cottage. **1884** *Sat. Rev.* 5 July 13/2 The projecting corbels.. show that a pentice ran along that side.

†**b.** Without reference to a sloping roof: Any smaller building attached to a main one, an annex; *spec.* at Chester: see quots. 1810, 1886.

1483 *Cath. Angl.* 275/1 A Pentis (*A.* Pentesse), *appendix, appendicium, appendiculum; appendicius.* **1579–80** NORTH *Plutarch* (1895) IV. 249 He built that famous stately Theater.. and joyned unto that also another House, as a Penthouse [ὥσπερ ἐφόλκιόν τι] to his Theater. *c* **1650** in R. H. Morris *Chester* (1895) 200, 1497 the North syde of the Pentice was new buylded, and, 1573, the Pentice was enlarged, and the inner Pendice made higher, the nerer made lesser. The Sheriffs Court removed to the Comon Hall. **1656** W. WEBB *W. Smith's Vale-Roy. Eng.* 39 S. Peters [Chester].. underneath the church in the street is the Pendice, a place builded of purpose, where the Major useth to remain. **1708** *Lond. Gaz.* No. 4409/2 Chester, Febr. 7... The Mayor entertain'd several Gentlemen and Citizens in the Pent-house. **1810** LYSONS *Cheshire* 582 An ancient building called the Pentice,.. called in some old Charters the *appentice*, was formerly the place in which the Sheriffs' courts were held, and banquets given. *Note. Appentitium*,.. a smaller building annexed to a larger one. **1886** R. HOLLAND *Chester Gloss.* s.v., The Pentice at Chester was an ancient building attached to St. Peter's Church, which was taken down about the year 1806.

c. A shed having a sloping roof, as a separate structure.

1816 KIRBY & SP. *Entomol.* (1828) I. xiv. 432 Without other abodes than natural caverns or miserable penthouses of bark. **1840** DICKENS *Barn. Rudge* lx, Fleet Market.. was a long irregular row of wooden sheds and pent-houses.

d. A separate flat, apartment, etc., situated on the roof of a tall building.

1921 *Country Life* Apr. 65/1 Two of the elevators were designed to run to the roof, where a pent-house.. was being built. **1937** *Sunday Dispatch* 28 Feb. 2/7 You all know from American lyric writers that a pent-house is a thing stuck on a roof. It may comprise one or two floors. **1945** E. WAUGH *Brideshead Revisited* I. viii. 194 They're going to build a block of flats, and.. Rex wanted to take what he called a 'penthouse' at the top. **1948** *National Home Monthly* Feb. 21/2 Back in London in 1932.. they built London's first penthouse. **1955** A. HUXLEY *Let.* 18 Mar. (1969) 738 After that expect to be in NYC until mid-June, when I am to be lent a pent-house on Park Avenue. **1956** 'N. SHUTE' *Beyond Black Stump* ii. 52 They live in lovely sort of flats called penthouses on the top of skyscrapers. **1958** *Times Lit. Suppl.* 4 July 371/3 After years of travel they built in 1936 what the author calls a 'penthouse' in Park Lane. It was eighty feet above street level. **1978** *Country Life* 3 Aug. (Suppl.) 29/1 A Penthouse with magnificent Thames views.. to be sold on a 995 years lease at the rental of one Red Rose on Midsummer Day.

2. a. Applied to various structures or contrivances of the nature of or akin to a sloping roof, whether attached to something else or independent; as an awning over a stall or a window; a canopy; a shed for the protection of besiegers, or a covering formed of the soldiers' shields held over their heads (L. *pluteus, testudo*). **b.** *spec.* The corridor with sloping roof round three sides of a tennis-court.

1530 PALSGR. 253/1 Pentes or paves, *estal, soubtil. Ibid.* Pentys over a stall, *avuent*. **1600** FAIRFAX *Tasso* XVII. x, He on his Throne was set,.. Under a Pentise wrought of Silver bright. *Ibid.* XVIII. lxxiv, Their targets hard aboue their heads they threw, Which ioynd in one an iron pentise make.

1608 WILLET *Hexapla Exod.* 603 It might serue as a pentice to defend the vaile. **1611** COTGR., *Auvent*, a pent-house of cloth &c., before a shop window, &c. **1651** *Rec. Dedham, Mass.* (1892) III. 187 The shingling of the pent-house ouer ye Bell. **1688** R. HOLME *Armoury* III. 265/1 *Pent-house*, the place on which they first cast out the Ball [at Tennis]. **1847** LONGF. *Ev.* I. i, Hives overhung by a penthouse. **1863** WHYTE MELVILLE *Gladiators* I. 23 Under cover of a moveable pent-house,.. the head of the column had advanced their battering-ram to the very wall. **1883** GRESLEY *Gloss. Terms Coal Mining, Penthouse* or *Penthus*, a wooden hut or covering for the protection of sinkers in a pit bottom. **1911** *Encycl. Brit.* XXVI. 626/2 [Royal tennis] is now played in a walled and roofed court, 110 ft. by 38 ft. 8 in., the floor, however, measuring but 96 ft. by 31 ft. 8 in., the difference being the width of a roofed corridor, the 'pent-house', which runs along the two end walls and one of the side walls. **1935** *Encycl. Sports* 619/1 This sloping roof is called the 'penthouse', and is, perhaps, the most characteristic feature of a tennis court. **1963** *Times* 25 May 4/5 Those first four games had cost Aberdare and Warburg the first set, but they were now going well, with Aberdare the best of the four on the floor and Warburg, although he put too much on the penthouse, setting up a powerful attack.

3. *fig.* Applied to things, material or immaterial, likened to a penthouse, as serving for defence, or as projecting above something (*e.g.* the eyebrows).

1589 NASHE *Anat. Absurd.* B iij, A pretence of puritie, a pentisse for iniquitie. **1639** SHIRLEY *Ball* I. ii, Not above your forehead, When you have brush'd away the hairy pentehouse, And made it visible. **1704** SWIFT *Batt. Bks.* Misc. (1711) 253 Like a shrivled Beau from within the Penthouse of a modern Peruke. **1819** SCOTT *Ivanhoe* ii, There.. lurked under the pent-house of his eye that sly epicurean twinkle. **1859** TENNYSON *Vivien* 657 He dragg'd his eyebrow bushes down, and made A snowy penthouse for his hollow eyes.

4. (Properly with capital initial.) The name of a theatre at the University of Washington, used *attrib.* to denote a style of theatre production in which the audience sits in a circular formation around a central acting area. (Cf. ARENA 5.)

1940 *Nation's Schools* Nov. 19/1 The penthouse style was first employed by us in the autumn of 1932. *Ibid.* 20/3 Modern comedy and farce, preferably with a single interior setting, are the most successful plays for a pent-house theatre. *Ibid.* 21/3 Without the aid of scenic background and conventional stage atmosphere.. the ordinary amateur is not an effective instrument and in penthouse productions he must be effective. **1942** G. HUGHES *Penthouse Theatre* iii. 17 Plays which could not very well be done Penthouse style. *Ibid.* viii. 53 We designed a Penthouse Theatre because we had created a tradition of arena production. **1959** W. C. LOUNSBURY *Backstage from A to Z* 5 *Arena stage*... Also known as arena staging, circular staging, theatre in the round, central staging, Penthouse staging, etc.

5. *attrib.* and *Comb.*, as ***penthouse apartment, -cornice, flat, -roof, suite***; also *fig.* (see 3), as ***penthouse brows, eyebrow, hat, lid*** (= eyelid); ***nab, penthouse-like***, †***-steep*** adjs.

1935 A. SQUIRE *Sing Sing Doctor* v. 59 He developed a taste for lavish *penthouse apartments. **1948** *Sun* (N.Y.) 30 Dec. 8 (*caption*) Construction view of the eighteen-story and penthouse apartment building being erected by Samuel Rudin on the former Temple Beth-El site at the south corner of Fifth avenue and 76th street. **1882** MISS BRADDON *Mt.-Royal* II. viii. 163 This wordly dowager, with keen eyes glittering under *penthouse brows. **1691** DRYDEN *K. Arth.* III. ii, My *pent-house eye-brows, and my shaggy beard. **1947** AUDEN *Age of Anxiety* iii. 95 Peasants with penthouse eye-brows. **1972** K. BONFIGLIOLI *Don't point that Thing at Me* vii. 61 Fifth-floor *penthouse flats in Upper Brook Street. **1977** *Wandsworth Borough News* 16 Sept. 15/2 Planning Proposals... Star and Garter Mansions, Lower Richmond-road—erection of penthouse flat on the roof of the building situated between two existing false gables. **1823** SCOTT *Peveril* xxiv, His huge *penthouse hat. **1605** SHAKS. *Macb.* I. iii. 20 Sleepe shall neyther Night nor Day Hang vpon his *Pent-house Lid. **1588** —— *L.L.L.* III. i. 17 With your hat *penthouse-like ore the shop of your eies. **1699** B. E. *New Dict. Canting Crew*, **Pentice Nab*, a very broad-brimd Hat. **1785** GROSE *Dict. Vulgar T.*, *Penthouse nab*, a broad-brimmed hat. **1901** S. K. LEVETT-YEATS *Traitor's Way* x. 124 A thin slit of sky was visible between the *pentice roof. **1681** COTTON *Wond. Peak* (ed. 4) 43 The first steps.. Were easie,.. Scarce *pent-house-steep. **1948** *Time* 8 Nov. 6/1 The eleventh-floor *penthouse suite. **1973** *Times* 5 Dec. 18/1 Sir Lew Grade.. is occupying the penthouse suite of the plush Century Plaza hotel.

penthouse ('pɛnthaʊs), *v.* Also 8 pentise. [f. prec. sb.] (Almost always in pa. pple.)

1. *trans.* To furnish with a penthouse.

1615 G. SANDYS *Trav.* 32 The inferior [Mosques] are.. pent-housd with open galleries. **1777** W. GOSTLING *Canterb.* (ed. 2) 29 A stone wall.. pentised over head, was called by the poor people their cloisters.

2. *fig.* To cover or shelter as with a penthouse; to overhang as a penthouse.

1664 POWER *Exp. Philos.* I. 23 The Gloworm or Glass-worm. Her Eyes.. are pent-hous'd under the broad flat cap or plate which covers her head. **1833** WORDSW. *Wren's Nest* v, Others [nests] are pent-housed by a brae That over-hangs a brook. **1845** TALFOURD *Vac. Rambles* I. 91 The little old, odd, town of Cluses stands actually pent-housed by the mountain sides.

3. To make like a penthouse; to cause to project.

1655 FULLER *Ch. Hist.* IX. viii. §6 It being pen[t]-housed out beyond the foundation, and intent of the Statute. *a* **1661** —— *Worthies, Oxfordsh.* (1662) 329 With these Verdingales the Gowns of Women beneath their wastes were pent-housed out far beyond their bodies.

pentice, earlier form of PENTHOUSE.

†'**penticle.** *Obs. rare*$^{-1}$. Used by E. Fairfax, app. *metri gratiâ*, as = PENTICE, PENTHOUSE.

1600 FAIRFAX *Tasso* XVIII. lxxiv, Their targets hard above their heads they threw, Which join'd in one an iron pentise make,.. For that strong penticle protected well The knights, from all that flew and all that fell.

[**pentile**, mis-spelling of PANTILE, in Johnson, copied in subsequent Dicts. (Misquoted by J. from Moxon, who has *pan-tiles.*)]

‖**pentimento** (penti'mento). Also '**pentiment.** Pl. **penti'menti.** [It. *pentimento*, repentance.] In a painting (particularly in oils), a trace of an earlier composition or of alterations that has become visible with the passage of time. Also *transf.*

1903 R. FRY *Let.* 6 Mar. (1972) I. 204 What looks like a retouch above the man's left shoulder turns out on closer inspection to be an original *pentimento*. **1933** *Burlington Mag.* May 212/1 Holbein's portraits of the 1530's; a pentimento indicates that originally the *décolleté* was narrower. **1935** *Ibid.* June 259/2 There are signs of *pentimenti* on the heads and hands. **1939** *Ibid.* Sept. 96/1 The pentimenti confirm that we are dealing with an original work of the master. **1945** *Ibid.* Apr. 82/2 A striking *pentimento* is visible, in the form of a segment of a circle, over the red dress under the hands of the Virgin. **1951** R. MAYER *Artist's Handbk.* ii. 100 In galleries one may frequently find a picture in which, by reason of changes wrought by time, oxidation, etc., the refractive index of the oil film has changed and a thin coat of paint.. has become sufficiently transparent to allow under-painting or drawing to show through. The effect is called pentimento. **1961** L. G. G. RAMSEY *Connoisseur New Guide Antique Eng. Pott., Porc. & Glass* 26 On this some-what rough base the painter has to carry out his designs without benefit of rubbings-out or *pentimenti*. **1962** *Sunday Times* (Colour Suppl.) 8 Apr. 20 A pentiment in the muzzle of the greyhound who looks back over his shoulder shows that the design of the Cleveland picture was followed at first in Mr. Getty's by an assistant, and then changed by Rubens. **1966** *Listener* 9 June 845/1 X-rays reveal *pentimenti*—those first thoughts—in both edges of the ruff, between the right forearm and the chair and, above all, in her right hand, which was originally both higher up and further to the right. **1971** *Guardian* 23 Aug. 5 One of the things that distinguish an original from a copy is the existence of *pentimenti* alterations.. done while the work was being painted. **1973** L. HELLMAN *Pentimento* (1974) 3 Old paint on canvas, as it ages, sometimes becomes transparent. When that happens it is possible, in some pictures, to see the original lines... This is called pentimento because the painter 'repented', changed his mind. **1975** *Times Lit. Suppl.* 31 Oct. 1278/5 He [*sc.* an Italian writer] has recently announced that, after completing all six volumes, he intends to begin all over again with a revised edition to include any *pentimenti* where he has changed his mind.

pentine, etc. *Chem.*: see under PENTANE.

pention, -er, obs. ff. PENSION, PENSIONER.

'**pentionary**, erron. form of PENITENTIARY.

1560 DAUS tr. *Sleidane's Comm.* VII. 156b, Than go they to the master of the Penitonaries [*ad pænitentiæ præfectum*] and fyne with him for a pece of money.

pentis, -ise, -isse, obs. forms of PENTHOUSE.

pentitol ('pɛntɪtɒl). *Chem.* [f. PENT(OSE: see -ITOL.] A pentahydric alcohol.

1907 J. B. COHEN *Org. Chem. Adv. Students* I. viii. 310 (*table*) Pentitol. **1954** S. S. COHEN in D. M. Greenberg *Chem. Pathways of Metabolism* I. v. 211 Two naturally occurring pentitols, D-arabitol and ribitol (adonitol), are known. Both appear to be quite rare but are encountered in plant tissues. **1966** *New Phytologist* LXV. 219 Carbon fixed by *Xanthoria aureola* in photosynthesis appears at first mainly in the pentitol. **1971** J. F. STODDART *Stereochem. Carbohydrates* ii. 20 There are four pentitols.

Pentland ('pɛntlənd). The name of the Pentland Hills, in Midlothian, Scotland, used *attrib.* in **Pentland Crown, Dell**, etc., to designate varieties of potato developed at the Scottish Plant Breeding Station, which is located there.

1959 *Rep. Scottish Plant Breeding Station* 11 (*heading*) Potatoes.—The Registration Trials conducted by the Department of Agriculture for Scotland in 1958 contained thirteen of the Station's seedlings... One.. was registered as a new variety suitable for commercial cultivation. It has been named Pentland Crown. **1961** *Ibid.* 16 As a result of its performance in the Merit Trials conducted by the Department of Agriculture and Fisheries for Scotland the [potato] Seedling 2319(a)3 has received 'Commendation'. It has been named 'Pentland Dell', a name that will be registered in compliance with the provisions of the International Code of Nomenclature. *Ibid.* 18 A red variant has been selected from the cultivar 'Pentland Beauty' and as a preliminary to giving it the name 'Red Pentland Beauty' this variant has been entered for the Wart Immunity and Identity Tests. **1962** *Ibid.* 17 An early maturing [potato] seedling, Reference No. 2299 (10), has successfully completed the Merit Trials conducted by the Department of Agriculture and Fisheries for Scotland and.. has been named 'Pentland Envoy' a name that will be registered by the National Registration Authority. **1969** *Dict. Gardening* (R. Hort. Soc.) *Suppl.* 150/1 Pentland Beauty. Oval with pale lemon flesh. *Ibid.* 150/2 Pentland Crown. White oval shape. White flesh. Pentland Dell. Shapely white kidney —shows considerable resistance to Blight. **1971** *Arable Farmer* Feb. 3/1 Our variety was Pentland Crown planted in 30" rows. **1973** *Times* 16 Oct. 6/6 Britain's plant breeders.. are striving to keep their brand names in Europe. To our grain growers Maris means another winner from the Plant Breeding Institute at Cambridge, Pentland a good Scottish potato, and Malling an outstanding new fruit. **1976** *Cumberland News* 3 Dec. 34/4 (Advt.), Pentland Crown seed potatoes for sale, once grown from Scotch seed, blight free, excellent quality.

pentlandite ('pɛntləndaɪt). *Min.* [Named by Dufrénoy, 1856, after its discoverer Mr. Pentland: see -ITE[1].] A native sulphide of iron and nickel, of a bronze-yellow colour.

1858 GREGG & LETTSOM *Min.* 473. **1893** *Amer. Jrnl. Sc.* Ser. III. XLV. 494.

pentlike, obs. erron. f. PENTELIC.

pentobarbital (pɛntəʊ'bɑːbɪtəl). *Pharm.* The equivalent in the U.S. Pharmacopeia of PENTOBARBITONE. Also ***pentobarbital sodium, sodium pentobarbital.***

1931 *Jrnl. Amer. Med. Assoc.* 30 May 1871/1 Pento-barbital-sodium is a nonproprietary name given to the mono-sodium salt of ethyl-(1-methylbutyl) barbituric acid. **1935** *Proc. Mayo Clinic* X. 536 The next step forward was the use of the isomer.. of amytal, which was first called 'embutal'. The sodium salt was called 'nembutal' and finally, 'pentobarbital sodium'. **1955** *Sci. News Let.* 2 Apr. 219/2 The Boston doctors tested the effects of morphine, heroin, amphetamine, the sleeping medicine pentobarbital and as a control, sodium chloride, or salt. **1962** *Times* 20 Dec. 9/7 Pentobarbital anaesthesia in lions has been studied with special reference to preanaesthetic medication. **1965** *Pharmacopeia U.S.* (ed. 17) 633 Sodium pentobarbital. [*In ed. 16 as* pentobarbital sodium.] **1974** M. C. GERALD *Pharmacol.* xi. 204 Deep sedation is induced by the intravenous injection of amobarbital (Amytal) or pentobarbital (Nembutal).

pentobarbitone (pɛntəʊ'bɑːbɪtəʊn). *Pharm.* [f. PENT(ANE + -O + BARBITONE.] The synthetic compound 5-ethyl-5-(1-methyl-butyl)-barbituric acid, which is widely used as a sedative-hypnotic and anticonvulsant drug, usu. in the form of its sodium salt, $C_{11}H_{17}N_2O_3Na$, a white crystalline powder often known by the proprietary name NEMBUTAL; = PENTOBARBITAL. So ***pentobarbitone sodium, sodium pentobarbitone.***

1938 S. ALSTEAD *Poulsson's Text-bk. Pharmacol. & Therapeutics* (ed. 2) i. 41 Nembutal, pentobarbitone, sodium ethyl-methyl-butyl barbiturate. **1950** *Brit. Med. Jrnl.* 25 Mar. 706/1 The child is premedicated with atropine.. and pentobarbitone. **1960** *Times* 6 Jan. 9/5 Once the rhino is dazed, two more rangers will move in with syringes to pump 600 c.c. of pentobarbitone sodium into the hide. **1962** *Lancet* 29 Dec. 1379/1 Progressive fall in temperature down to cardiac arrest, seen in two rabbits subjected to surface cooling in a deep-freeze at 0°C while under pentobarbitone anæsthesia. **1971** *Nature* 21 May 182/1 The dog was anaesthetized with pentobarbitone and heparin was used as an anticoagulant. **1975** *Ibid.* 4 Sept. 62/1 Each rat was killed with an overdose of sodium pentobarbitone.

pentode ('pɛntəʊd). *Electronics.* [f. PENT(A- + -ODE.] A thermionic valve having five electrodes. Also ***pentode valve.***

1919 W. H. ECCLES in *Electrician* 18 Apr. 475/2 To be systematic I suggest 'tetrode' and 'pentode' for vacuum tubes with four or five electrodes. **1928** *Daily Express* 14 Dec. 5 One pentode valve will do the work of two ordinary valves, but it will be a heavy drain on dry batteries. **1932** E. V. APPLETON *Thermionic Vacuum Tubes* ix. 111 The five electrode tube or pentode possesses a screen grid as does the tetrode, but also has an additional grid situated between the anode and the screen grid. **1965** *IEEE Trans. Electron Devices* XII. 350/2 Conventional beam pentodes can be designed on the computer to have uniform cathode current density. **1973** WHITTLE & YARWOOD *Exper. Physics* xi. 296 The values recorded.. are for a pentode valve used for audio-frequency operation, generally as the output stage of an audio-frequency amplifier.

pentograph, erron. f. PANTOGRAPH *sb.*

pentoic *a.*, **pentone**, etc. *Chem.*: see under PENTANE.

pentolinium (pɛntəʊ'lɪnɪəm). *Pharm.* [f. *pent(amethylene* (s.v. PENTA-) + PYRR)OL(ID)IN(E + -IUM b.] A white, crystalline powder which has been used as a ganglion-blocking agent in the treatment of severe hypertension; pentamethylenebis(1-methyl-pyrrolidinium hydrogen tartrate), $C_{23}H_{42}N_2O_2$; also called ***pentolinium tartrate.***

1954 *Lancet* 27 Nov. 1097/2 The preparation used was 'Ansolysen' (M. & B. 2050A),.. termed pentolinium tartrate by the British Pharmacopœia Commission in 1954. **1958** J. H. BURN *Lect. Notes Pharmacol.* (ed. 5) 20 Pentolinium (Ansolysen) is similar in action to hexa-methonium, but it is more powerful. **1974** [see PEMPIDINE].

Pentomic, pentomic (pɛn'tɒmɪk), *a. Mil.* [f. PENTA- + ATOMIC *a.*] Divided into five battle groups armed with nuclear weapons.

1956 *Washington Post* 28 Dec. 1/8 The Army announced last night that it will begin reducing the manpower of its divisions early next year and revamp them into new-style 'Pentomic' units geared for atomic warfare. **1958** *Times* 4 Nov. 9/3 The plans are based on the American concept of 'pentomic' divisions. **1959** *New Statesman* 29 Aug. 238/1 Two and possibly more of the US divisions are now Pentomic (i.e. nuclear-armed), but the process of training the first British regiment of nuclear artillery has only just begun. **1961** *Observer* 4 June 10/2 Orders have been given to break up the so-called 'Pentomic' divisions in the United States Army in Europe, in which nuclear weapons have been integrated with conventional arms. **1963** *Times* 10 Jan. 11/7 The Australian Army had adapted for its own use the American 'pentomic' formation. **1972** [see *low-yield* adj. s.v. LOW *a.* 23]. **1972** *Sat. Rev.* (U.S.) 6 May 30/3 It was considered necessary to shrink the [US] army combat division from a force of three regiments containing three battalions of five companies each to a 'Pentomic' force of five battle groups of four companies.

pentomino (pɛn'tɒmɪnəʊ). [f. PENT(A- + D)OMINO by deliberately false analogy: see quot. 1961.] Any of the twelve distinct planar shapes that can be formed by joining five identical squares by their edges.

In the U.S. the pl. *Pentominoes* is registered as the proprietary name of a board game involving these shapes.

1954 S. W. GOLOMB in *Amer. Math. Monthly* LXI. 681 There are twelve distinct pentominoes. **1961** *New Scientist* 2 Nov. 316/2 A domino is formed from two adjacent squares: he [*sc.* Golomb] argues that practical needs and false etymology will justify our calling a square a monomino—whence we have a series monomino, domino, tromino, tetromino,..., and Maestro pieces then become pentominoes. **1964** *Listener* 11 June 975/3 The jigsaw pattern is made from a set of twelve pentominoes. **1965** S. W. GOLOMB *Polyominoes* 13, I learned of the true antiquity of pentominoes, one kind of polyomino. Although the name was coined in my lecture of 1953, the first pentomino *problem* was published in 1907. **1975** *Official Gaz.* (U.S. Patent Office) 21 Jan. TM279/2 Solomon W. Golomb, La Canada, Calif. Filed Sept. 13, 1972. *Pentominoes.* For equipment, consisting of the twelve distinct five-celled square figures and a playing board, for use in various combinatorial puzzles and in competitive board games... First used November 1953. **1975** A. C. CLARKE *Imperial Earth* xxiv. 173 He replaced the titanite cross in its setting between the F, N, U and V pentominoes.

penton ('pɛntɒn). *Biol.* [f. PENT(A- + -ON[1] 2.] A capsomere which occupies any of the twelve vertices of the icosahedral capsid of an adenovirus.

1966 H. S. GINSBERG et al. in *Virology* XXVIII. 782/2 The unit at the twelve corners of the icosahedron should then be termed a penton because each has 5 neighbouring units (hexons). The penton corresponds to the B or cell-detaching antigen; thus the soluble antigen should be called the penton antigen. **1970** *Nature* 17 Jan. 226/2 Adenovirus has a more complex capsid containing 240 hexons and twelve pentons each with a molecular weight of about 400,000. **1972** *Ibid.* 14 Apr. 348/1 The DNA-specific endonuclease associated with the penton bases of the virion may affect the host genome in an apparently random manner.

pentosan ('pɛntəʊsæn). *Biochem.* Also †**-ane**. [a. G. *pentosan* (Schulze & Tollens 1892, in *Ann. d. Chem.* CCLXIX. 55), after *glucosan*, *hexosan*, etc.: see PENTOSE.] Any of the class of polysaccharides, occurring widely in plants, of which the constituent monosaccharides are pentoses.

1892 *Jrnl. Chem. Soc.* LXII. 1420 (*heading*) The pentosans of woody vegetable fibre. **1913** HAAS & HILL *Introd. Chem. Plant Products* II. 51 Gums: (*a*) Natural gums and pentosanes ($C_5H_8O_4$)n. (*b*) Mucilages and pectic bodies. **1931** E. C. MILLER *Plant Physiol.* viii. 420 The pentosans have the general formula $(C_5H_8O_4)_n$ and occur, for the most part, in the cell walls of various plant parts. **1938** [see ARABAN]. **1963** R. R. A. HIGHAM *Handbk. Papermaking* ii. 34 The presence of pentosans in wood pulps helps to produce increased fibre bonding in paper. **1973** R. W. BAILEY in Butler & Bailey *Chem. & Biochem. Herbage* I. iv. 165 Hemicelluloses may be divided into two broad classes; pentosans, based largely on pentoses and non-cellulose hexosans which are pentose-free.

pentose ('pɛntəʊs). *Chem.* [f. Gr. πέντε five + -OSE[2]; first formed as G. *pentose* (E. Fischer 1890, in *Ber. d. Deut. Chem. Ges.* XXIII. 934).] **1.** 'A name given to compounds resembling glucose, but having only five atoms of carbon in the molecule; e.g. tetra-oxy-valeric aldehyde.' Any of the monosaccharides with the formula $C_5H_{10}O_5$, among which are ribose and several other naturally occurring sugars.

1890 [see *heptose* s.v. HEPTA-]. **1892** MORLEY & MUIR *Watts' Dict. Chem.* III. 807/2. **1899** CAGNEY *Jaksch's Clin. Diagn.* vii. 327 The quantitative determination of the pentose group of sugars. *Ibid.* 334 It appears that pentoses are frequently contained in beer. **1916** A. P. MATHEWS *Physiol. Chem.* ii. 30 The pentoses generally occur in nature in gums and..polysaccharides. **1927** *Jrnl. Biol. Chem.* LXXIII. 18 Any method of pentose estimation..must prove to be efficacious, not only for xylose and arabinose, but especially for *d*-ribose, for it is as ribose compounds that one finds pentose in the body. **1953** FRUTON & SIMMONDS *Gen. Biochem.* xvii. 381 A number of pentoses have been found in nature; perhaps the most important of these is D-ribose,..a constituent of nucleic acids and of several nucleotides (ATP, DPN, etc.). **1973** R. G. KRUEGER et al. *Introd. Microbiol.* viii. 263/2 Pentoses (five-carbon sugars) are carbon and energy sources for many microorganisms.

2. Special combs.: **pentose nucleic acid**, a nucleic acid in which the sugar is a pentose; (effectively synonymous with *ribonucleic acid*, RNA); **pentose phosphate cycle, pathway**, or **shunt**, a cyclic pathway in the body and in higher plants by which glucose phosphate is converted to a pentose phosphate with the reduction of NADP, the pentose phosphate being afterwards converted into phosphates of a hexose and a triose or else incorporated into nucleotides.

1934 *Biochem. Jrnl.* XXVIII. 2108 The pentose nucleic acid of the pancreas gland. **1947** *Thorpe's Dict. Appl. Chem.* (ed. 4) VIII. 622/1 The idea has arisen that deoxypentose nucleic acid is present in the nucleus, pentose nucleic acid in the cytoplasm. **1953** FRUTON & SIMMONDS *Gen. Biochem.* vii. 184 Although it was once thought that the pentose nucleic acids were characteristic of plant tissues whereas the deoxypentose nucleic acids were confined to animal cells, this separation has been shown to be incorrect. **1968** I. L. FINAR *Org. Chem.* (ed. 4) II. xvi. 724 The nucleic acids are classified according to the nature of the sugar present: the pentose nucleic acids or ribonucleic acids (R.N.A.), and the deoxypentose nucleic acids or deoxyribonucleic acids (D.N.A.). **1960** *McGraw-Hill Encycl. Sci. & Technol.* II. 40/1 The pentose phosphate pathway of glucose decomposition involves hexose monophosphates and pentose monophosphates. **1963** C. H. DOERING tr. *Karlson's Introd. Mod. Biochem.* xv. 269 (*heading*) Glucose oxidation through the pentose phosphate cycle. **1964** W. G. SMITH *Allergy & Tissue Metabolism* viii. 85 Supplies of $NADPH_2$ can be made available by shunting some of the available glucose-6-phosphate into reactions which form ribulose-5-phosphate. This in turn can be converted back to glucose-6-phosphate... The whole process is sometimes referred to as the pentose phosphate shunt. **1970** R. W. MCGILVERY *Biochem.* xxiii. 568 The adrenal cortex has an active pentose phosphate pathway that can provide NADPH in the cytosol by oxidizing glucose-6-phosphate.

pentoside ('pɛntəʊsaɪd). *Chem.* [f. PENTOS(E, after GLUCOSIDE.] A glycoside which yields a pentose on hydrolysis.

The pentosides of most interest are now referred to as nucleosides.

[**1909**: see GUANOSINE]. **1910** [see GLUCOSIDE]. **1916** A. P. MATHEWS *Physiol. Chem.* iv. 171 Guanosine is, therefore, a pentoside. *Ibid.* 172 From yeast another pentoside was isolated, an adenine pentoside called adenosine.

pentosuria (pɛntəʊ's(j)ʊərɪə). *Med.* [mod.L., ad. G. *pentosurie* (E. Salkowski 1895, in *Berl. klin. Wochenschr.* 29 Apr. 364): see PENTOSE and -URIA.] The presence of an excess of pentoses in the urine.

1902 *Med. Rev.* V. 94/2 (*heading*) The clinical importance of chronic pentosuria. **1936** *Nature* 7 Nov. 805/2 There are known to be at least two types of the rare chronic pentosuria, differing in the nature of the pentose sugar found, one being optically inactive *dl*-arabinose and the other *l*-xyloketose. **1970** PASSMORE & ROBSON *Compan. Med. Stud.* II. xxxi. 9/1 [Garrod] suggested that in alkaptonuria, albinism, cystinuria and pentosuria there was a block in a metabolic process due to an inherited deficiency of a specific enzyme.

Hence **pento'suric** *a.*, of, pertaining to, or having pentosuria; *sb.*, an individual with pentosuria.

1906 J. L. SALINGER tr. F. Blumenthal in R. C. Cabot *Mod. Clin. Med.* 267 The researches..have..made it appear unlikely that pentoses are formed in the pentosuric patient by an imperfect nuclein decomposition. *Ibid.* 271 Have pentosurics..a special liability to become diabetics? **1933** CAMERON & GILMOUR *Biochem. of Med.* vi. 91 Diabetic treatment is unsuitable to the pentosuric. **1964** D. Y. HSIA in G. A. Duncan *Dis. Metabolism* (ed. 5) v. 349 In the 1950's, Lasker reported that she had identified L-xylulose in all 72 pentosuric urines that she had tested. **1968** MARKS & SAMOLS in F. Dickens et al. *Carbohydrate Metabolism* II. xiii. 351 The existence of this pathway of glucose metabolism was first recognised as a result of studies on the biosynthesis of L-ascorbic acid in animals and of L-xylulose in pentosurics.

Pentothal ('pɛntəʊθæl). *Pharm.* Also (*erron.*) **Pentathol**, and with small initial. [Refash. of THIOPENTAL.] A proprietary name for thiopentone sodium; also called ***Pentothal sodium, sodium Pentothal.***

1935 *Proc. Mayo Clinic* X. 744 Sodium ethyl 1-methyl butyl thiobarbituric acid (thionembutal or pentothal sodium) and sodium allyl secondary butyl thiobarbituric acid (thiosebutal) induce a satisfactorily deep but relatively transitory anesthesia. **1936** *Official Gaz.* (U.S. Patent Office) 11 Feb. 238/2 Abbott Laboratories, North Chicago, Ill. Filed Dec. 6, 1935... Pentothal... For pharmaceutical product having hypnotic, sedative and anesthetic properties. Claims use since Nov. 15, 1935. **1936** *Trade Marks Jrnl.* 28 Oct. 1326/1 Pentothal... Chemical substances prepared for use in medicine and pharmacy. Abbott Laboratories.., City of North Chicago,..State of Illinois, United States of America; manufacturers of pharmaceutical products. **1940** *N. & Q.* 22 June 448/2, I observe in the press mention of two drugs to induce sleep with new names, Evipan and Pentothal. **1946** M. DICKENS *Happy Prisoner* viii. 153 Elizabeth..suggested Pentathol therapy. **1967** *Punch* 1 Mar. 321/3 One could only ask—.. after the mystics, the ESP experts and the computing machines, after the sodium pentathol examinations and the lie detector tests..—after all that was he to turn out to be this nondescript house-painter and handyman who killed at random? **1969** *Daily Tel.* 16 Dec. 15/1 Interviewed under the truth drug pentathol, he told doctors he did not realise he had done the baby any harm. **1973** G. GREENE *Honorary Consul* v. iii. 273 Dying is a wonderfully effective truth drug, better than pentathol. **1974** M. C. GERALD *Pharmacol.* xi. 195 Non-volatile anesthetics include the intravenously administered barbiturate thiopental (Pentothal).

pentoxide (pɛn'tɒksaɪd). *Chem.* [PENTA-.] A binary compound containing five equivalents of oxygen.

1863-72 WATTS *Dict. Chem.* I. 324 Pentoxide of Antimony, Antimonic Oxide..Sb_2O_5. **1881** *Athenæum* 24 Dec. 856/3 The author has prepared..a pentoxide of didymium.

pentremite: see PENTATREMITE.

pent-roof ('pɛntru:f). [mod. f. *pent-* in PENTHOUSE + ROOF *sb.*] A roof like that of a penthouse, sloping in one direction only; a shed-roof.

1835 *Court Mag.* VI. 66/2 Her masts struck, her rigging down, and her hull covered in with a pent-roof thatch, from stem to stern. **1894** H. SPEIGHT *Nidderdale* 373 A peculiar feature of this old homestead is an open pent-roof or arcade.

pentrough ('pɛntrɒf, -ɔ:-). [f. PEN *sb.*[1] 3 + TROUGH.] A trough, channel, or conduit, usually of planks or boards, constructed to convey the water from a head of water formed by a 'pen' (see PEN *sb.*[1] 3) to the place where its force is applied, as in a water-mill. (Cf. PENSTOCK[1].)

1793 *Trans. Soc. Arts* XI. 163 A Pentrough for equalizing the water falling on water-wheels. **1853** GLYNN *Power Water* 43 There is a sluice to regulate the supply at top, fixed in the pentrough, and another at bottom which regulates the expenditure.

pentryl ('pɛntrɪl). [f. PENTA-, after TETRYL 2 (prob. from there being five rather than four nitro groups in the molecule).] A crystalline compound similar to tetryl in chemical structure, explosive power, and sensitivity to detonation; $C_6H_2(NO_2)_3{\cdot}N(NO_2)CH_2CH_2ONO_2$.

1933 L. V. CLARK in *Industr. & Engin. Chem.* Dec. 1385/1 In this paper the writer presents the results of an investigation of *sym*-trinitrophenylnitraminoethyl nitrate, here-after termed 'pentryl'. *Ibid.* 1386/1 Pentryl detonates when struck a sharp blow. **1967** M. JURECKI tr. *Urbański's Chem. & Technol. Explosives* III. iii. 71 Pentryl is remarkable for its high explosive power which, according to various authors, is equal to or slightly higher than that of tetryl.

pentstemon, penstemon (pɛn(t)'sti:mən). *Bot.* [mod.L. *Pentstēmōn* (Mitchell, 1748), irreg. (for **pentastēmōn*) f. Gr. πέντε five + στήμων, taken as = stamen; from the rudimentary fifth stamen in addition to the four perfect ones characteristic of the order. The spelling and pronunciation *penstemon* are common in popular use.]

A genus of herbaceous plants of the N.O. *Scrophulariaceæ*, natives of America, cultivated for their showy clustered flowers, which are usually tubular and two-lipped, and of various colours.

1760 J. LEE *Introd. Bot.* App. 322 Pentstemon, *Chelone.* **1846** J. BAXTER *Libr. Pract. Agric.* (ed. 4) I. 325 Penstemons may be raised from slips struck in heat. **1881** CLARK RUSSELL *Ocean Free-L.* viii, Beds of dahlias, lilies..roses, pentstemons.

pentyce, -ys, -yse, obs. forms of PENTHOUSE.

pentyl, etc. *Chem.*: see under PENTANE.

†'**penuary.** *Obs. rare.* [f. late L. *penūarius* adj. = *penārius* of or for provisions, f. *penus* store or provision of food; cf. *penārius, -ia* sb. storehouse, granary.] A storehouse.

1607 BP. J. KING *Serm. 5 Nov.* 31 A whole penuarie and store-house of sin. **1633** T. ADAMS *Exp. 2 Peter* ii. 1 How would they..fill their barns, their granaries, penuaries. *Ibid.* 6 Their vault was a penuary and storehouse of destruction.

penuche, var. PANOCHE.

penuchle, penuckle, var. PINOCLE, card-game.

penult (pɪ'nʌlt), *a.* and *sb.* [Originally an abbreviated way of writing the word PENULTIMA.]

A. *adj.* Last but one, penultimate. (Common in *Sc.* in 16–17th c., mostly in reference to the day of the month; in later use chiefly scientific.)

1539 *Acc. Ld. High Treas. Scot.* in Pitcairn *Crim. Trials* I. 299* Newȝeris Giftis, þe penult and last dayis of December. **1589** R. BRUCE *Serm., Isa.* xxxviii. (1843) 164 The penult verse of the chapter. **1597** MORLEY *Introd. Mus.* 76 In your penult and antepenult notes, you stande still with your descant. **1636** W. SCOT *Apol. Narr.* (1846) 127 Moderator of the penult General Assembly. **1675** GREGORY in Rigaud *Corr. Sci. Men* (1841) II. 266 De Beaune hath that method of removing the penult term..without fractions. **1695** SIBBALD *Autobiog.* (1834) 132, I came over the fells to Jedburgh..the penult day of October 1662. **1762** KAMES *Elem. Crit.* xviii. (1833) 308 In the penult line, the proper place of the musical pause is at the end of the fifth syllable. **1828** STARK *Elem. Nat. Hist.* II. 160 Lateral appendages of the penult segment..fleshy. **1838** SIR W. HAMILTON in *Reid's Wks.* II. 690/1 The penult note applies to these. **1852** DANA *Crust.* I. 76 The penult joint of the eight posterior legs.

B. *sb.* †**1.** The last day but one (of a month). *Sc.*

a **1572** KNOX *Hist. Ref.* Wks. 1846 I. 144 The Cardinall.. caused all Bischoppis..to be convocat to Sanctandrose against the penult of Februare. *a* **1639** SPOTTISWOOD *Hist. Ch. Scot.* VI. (1677) 351 They came to London the penult of the moneth. *a* **1670** SPALDING *Troub. Chas. I* (Bann. Cl.) 90 Upon Thursday the penult of January.

2. *Gram.* The last syllable but one.

1828 in WEBSTER. **1871** *Public Sch. Lat. Gram.* 6 Words of more than two syllables have their Accent on the Penult when long. **1875** WHITNEY *Life Lang.* vii. 126 The penult of 'rædde' had a long vowel before a doubled consonant.

†**pe'nultim, -ime,** *a.* and *sb. Obs.* [ad. L. *pænultim-us*: see next. Cf. F. *pénultième* (13th c. in Littré).] Last but one; = PENULTIMATE.

c **1532** DU WES *Introd. Fr.* in *Palsgr.* 931 The tone hath an *a* in the penultyme syllable. **1538** SIR B. TUKE in Ellis *Orig. Lett.* Ser. III. III. 223 At London, the penultyme of August, 1538. **1655** FULLER *Ch. Hist.* VI. iii. 324 A second Race succeeded, derived from Norman Darcy the Penultim Lord in the last Pedigree. **1725** SLOANE *Jamaica* II. 196 The two first and last pairs [of legs] being two inches long, the Penultime not much more than half so much.

‖**penultima** (pɪ'nʌltɪmə). [Lat., properly *pænultima*, fem. of *pænultimus* PENULTIMATE (sc. *syllaba* or *nota*), f. *pæne* almost + *ultimus* last.] The last syllable but one (of a word or verse). In quot. 1776, the last but one of a series of notes.

1589 PUTTENHAM *Eng. Poesie* II. iv. (Arb.) 85 The sharpe accent falles vpon the penultima or last saue one sillable of the verse. **1749** *Power Pros. Numbers* 26 It is plain he read it thus εἱμᾰρμένην, without any Regard to the Accent on the Penultima (μέ). **1776** BURNEY *Hist. Mus.* I. 9 *Paranete Synemmenon*, penultima of this tetrachord.

penultimate (pɪ'nʌltɪmət), *a.* and *sb.* [f. PENE-, L. *pæne* almost + ULTIMATE, after L. *pænultim-us*: see prec.]

A. *adj.* Last but one; next before the last of a series of things. (Chiefly in scientific and technical use.) **b.** Occurring on the last syllable but one: cf. B. a.

1677 PLOT *Oxfordsh.* 15 They [sounds of an echo] next strike the ultimate secondary object, then the penultimate and antepenultimate. **1709** BARNES in Hearne *Collect.* 8 Feb. (O.H.S.) II. 167 Thanks for your penultimate rhapsody. **1727–41** CHAMBERS *Cycl.*, *Penultima*, or *Penultimate*, in grammar, denotes the syllable, or foot, immediately before the last.. Hence antepenultimate is that before the penultimate, or the last but two. **1813** BYRON *Br. Abydos* II. xx. *note*, One more revise—positively the last.. —at any rate, the *penultimate*. **1834** MCMURTRIE *Cuvier's Anim. Kingd.* 249 The penultimate whorl forms.. a depression which gives the aperture more or less of the figure of a crescent. **1881** MIVART *Cat* 99 The penultimate phalanx of each digit .. is hollowed out on its outer side.

b. 1862 MARSH *Lect. Eng. Lang.* 380 The great frequency of ultimate and penultimate accentuation.

B. *sb.* The last member but one of a series: *spec.* **a.** *Gram.* The last syllable but one of a word. **b.** *Whist.* The lowest card but one of a suit. **c.** *Math.* (see quot. 1872).

[**1727–41**: see A.] **1823** CRABB *Technol. Dict.*, *Penultimate*, the last syllable but one in a word. **1846** in WORCESTER. **1872** CAYLEY *Coll. Math. Papers* VIII. 526, I have had occasion to consider.. the form of a curve about to degenerate into a system of multiple curves; a simple instance is a trinodal quartic curve about to degenerate into the form $x^2y^2 = 0$, or say a 'penultimate' of $x^2y^2 = 0$. **1876** C. M. DAVIES *Unorth. Lond.* 313 He.. also leaned to long penultimates in Phrygia and Libya. **1876** A. CAMPBELL-WALKER *Correct Card* Gloss. (1880) 13 *Penultimate, the.*—Beginning with the lowest card but one of the suit you lead originally, if it contains more than four cards.

penultimatum (pɪnʌltɪ'meɪtəm). *nonce-wd.* [after PENULTIMATE and ULTIMATUM.] A demand amounting almost to an ultimatum, or sent immediately before an ultimatum.

1882 *Daily Tel.* 29 May 5 The Consuls-General hand in an ultimatum, or penultimatum, to a recalcitrant Ministry. **1899** *Westm. Gaz.* 6 Nov. 3/2 Nearly three weeks after the rejection of the 'penultimatum'.

‖**penumbra** (pɪ'nʌmbrə). [mod.L. (Kepler, 1604), f. PENE-, L. *pæne* almost + UMBRA shadow. Cf. F. *pénombre* (1671 in Hatz.-Darm.).]

1. The partially shaded region around the shadow of an opaque body, where only a part of the light from the luminous body is cut off; the partial shadow, as distinguished from the total shadow or *umbra*; *esp.* that surrounding the total shadow of the moon, or of the earth, in an eclipse, producing respectively a partial (or annular) eclipse of the sun, or a fainter obscuration bordering the full shadow on the disk of the moon.

[**1604** KEPLER *Ad Vitell. Paralipom.* 239 Quod est inter KL,NM penumbra dicatur, LN vero umbra. **1709** M. G. HANSCHIUS (in Kepler's Wks. ed. Frisch III. 516) Umbræ penumbræque (quam primus ipse in astronomiam introduxit).] **1666** *Phil. Trans.* I. 348 The Moon was not at all obscured by the true shadow, but entred only a little into the *Penumbra*. **1690** LEYBOURN *Curs. Math.* 745 The *Penumbra* towards the perfect Shadow, does, little by little, grow more and more obscure. **1769** HIRST in *Phil. Trans.* LIX. 231, I saw a kind of penumbra or dusky shade, which preceded the first external contact two or three seconds of time. **1812** WOODHOUSE *Astron.* xxxv. 366 The time at which the Moon first enters the Earth's penumbra. **1869** TYNDALL *Notes Lect. Light* §12 If the source of light be a *point*, the shadow is sharply defined; if the source be a luminous *surface*, the perfect shadow is fringed by an imperfect shadow called a *penumbra*.

b. The lighter outer part or border of a sun-spot, surrounding the darker central nucleus or *umbra*.

1834 MRS. SOMERVILLE *Connex. Phys. Sc.* xxxvii. (1849) 425 One of these spots.. with its penumbra, occupied an area of 3780 millions of square miles. **1868** LOCKYER *Guillemin's Heavens* (ed. 3) 48 If the spot and its penumbra are formed by a conical opening, the sloping sides of which reveal to us the thickness of the envelopes.

c. *Painting.* (See quot.)

1826 ELMES *Dict. Fine Arts*, *Penumbra*, in painting, drawing, &c., that point of a picture or drawing where the shade blends itself with the light... These gradations should be nearly imperceptible.

2. *fig.* A partial shade or shadow (in various metaphorical applications), esp. regarded as bordering upon a fuller or darker one.

1801 MAR. EDGEWORTH *Angelina* iv, I will defend him, madam,.. against every shadow, every penumbra of aristocratic insolence. **1836** J. ABBOTT *Way to do Good* vi. 187 It is but a penumbra, a twilight of virtue and happiness. **1862** MASSON in *Macm. Mag.* Aug. 319 Those who can surround a definite designation with the due penumbra.

penumbral (pɪ'nʌmbrəl), *a.* [f. prec. + -AL¹.] Of, pertaining to, of the nature of, or characterized by a penumbra or partial shadow. Also *fig.*

penumbral eclipse, a lunar eclipse in which only the penumbra falls on the moon's disk.

1768 *Phil. Trans.* LVIII. 331 It was remarkably distinct from the penumbral shade. **1822** IMISON *Sc. & Art* I. 443 Places which fall within this penumbral cone, and are out of the dense shadow. **1856** KANE *Arct. Expl.* II. i. 14 We are looking forward to this more penumbral darkness as an era. It has now been fifty-two days since we could read such type. **1884** TYNDALL *Let.* in *Times* 26 Nov., Between truth and untruth there lies a penumbral zone which belongs equally to both; and I have often admired the adroitness with which Mr. Chamberlain sails within the 'half-shadow'. *a* **1922** T. S. ELIOT *Waste Land Drafts* (1971) 37 Within this penumbral consciousness. **1965** *Mod. Law Rev.* XXVIII. 510 The American concern with the judicial process and the creative element in the common law is particularly appropriate in analysing the role of appeal courts, for appeal courts.. are primarily concerned with penumbral issues.

pe'numbrous, *a. rare.* [See -OUS.] = prec.

1887 W. HOLMAN HUNT in *Contemp. Rev.* July 24 In the penumbrous dulness I discerned a mass of white rock leading to the higher level. **1959** *Times* 16 May 8/6 To proceed to some stygian cellar,.. and from the penumbrous interior gathering them [*sc.* mushrooms] by the hundredweight, is not, of course, sport. **1964** *Listener* 19 Mar. 484/2 He's more readable than Grimm, and much more concerned to give a solid idea of those contradictory, penumbrous figures.

†**penur.** *Obs. rare*⁻¹. [For *penure, ad. L. *pēnūria* (cf. *provincia*, province).] = PENURY 1. So †**penured** *a. rare*⁻¹ [-ED²], reduced to destitution.

c **1461** *Paston Lett.* II. 74 He is a gentylman, and of is kyne, and in gret penur. **1570** FOXE *A. & M.* (ed. 2) 166/2 The people penured with famine woulde go xl. together vpon the rockes,.. and.. throw them selues down to the sea.

penurious (pɪ'njʊərɪəs), *a.* [= obs. F. *penurieux* (15th c.), It. *penurioso* (Florio), med.L. *pēnūriōs-us*, f. L. *pēnūria*: see PENURY and -OUS.]

†**1.** In want; needy, beggarly, indigent, poverty-stricken (also *fig.*); with *of*, lacking, wanting in.

1596 SPENSER *F.Q.* V. v. 46 Die rather would he in penurious paine,.. Then his foes love or liking entertaine. **1607** SHAKS. *Timon* IV. iii. 92. **1614** DYKE *Myst. Self-Deceiving* (1615) 57 Dives, rich in this world, became exceeding penurious in the other. *a* **1618** RALEIGH *Advice of Son* (1651) 5 God is not so penurious of friends, as to hold himself and his Kingdome saleable for the refuse and reversions of their lives, who have sacrificed the principal thereof to his enemies.

†**b.** Of things, circumstances, material conditions: Of, pertaining to, or associated with want; poor, scanty, exiguous; barren, unfertile. (In the effect upon persons, passing into a fig. sense of 2.)

1621 DONNE in *Fortesc. Papers* (Camden) 157 Neyther.. knowes how narrow and penurious a fortune I wrestle with in thys world. **1626** BACON *Sylva* §93 It is certain, that White is a penurious Colour, and where moisture is scant... Blew Violets.. if they be starved, turn Pale and White. **1633** PRYNNE *Histriomastix* 322 In these penurious times, who can hardly spare.. halfe so much? *a* **1639** W. WHATELEY *Prototypes* III. xxxix. (1640) 12 Seven most scant and penurious yeares of great famine. **1775** JOHNSON *West. Isl. Scot.* Wks. X. 488 But where the climate is unkind and the ground penurious. **1789** G. WHITE *Selborne* (1853) 3 Swell to a lake the scant penurious rill.

2. Niggardly, stingy, parsimonious, grudging; hence *transf.* indicative of stinginess, meagre, slight, mean, 'shabby'.

1634 MILTON *Comus* 726 As a grudging master, As a penurious niggard of his wealth. **1778** JOHNSON *Let. to J. Nichols* 26 Nov., I am very well contented that the Index is settled for. Though the price is low it is not penurious. **1796** BURKE *Let. Noble Ld.* Wks. VIII. 29, I ever held a scanty and penurious justice to partake of the nature of a wrong. **1830** D'ISRAELI *Chas. I*, III. viii. 163 The most affluent of our nobility, was penurious in his loans to the King.

fig. **1894** MARQ. SALISBURY *Address to Brit. Assoc.* 8 Aug., Lord Kelvin limited the period of organic life upon the earth to a hundred million years, and Professor Tait in a still more penurious spirit cut that hundred down to ten.

†**3.** Fastidious, dainty: see quot. *Obs. rare.*

1721 BAILEY, *Penurious*, covetous, niggardly, stingy; also nice. **1730** SWIFT *Panegyrick on Dean* 144 She's grown so nice, and so penurious, With Socrates and Epicurius. (*note*, Ignorant ladies often mistake the word *penurious* for *nice* and *dainty.*)

pe'nuriously, *adv.* [f. prec. + -LY².] In a penurious manner; †indigently, starvingly, poorly (*obs.*); grudgingly; scantily; meanly.

1599 B. JONSON *Cynthia's Rev.* II. ii, Unlesse 'twere Lent, Ember-weeks, or fasting dayes, when the place is most penuriously emptie of all other good outsides. **1633** T. ADAMS *Exp. 2 Peter* ii. 15 Nor is it enough to clear thee, that thou didst not injuriously get what thou hast penuriously kept. **1782** MISS BURNEY *Cecilia* V. ii, Her mother was determined.. to live as penuriously as ever. **1786** W. GILPIN *Lakes Cumbld.* (1808) II. xxix. 228 A river, considerable in its dimensions; tho penuriously supplied with water. **1860** MOTLEY *Netherl.* (1868) II. xviii. 447 Elizabeth.. shrank penuriously from the expenses of war.

pe'nuriousness. [f. as prec. + -NESS.]

†**a.** Poverty, want, scantness, dearth (*obs.*) **b.** Niggardliness, stinginess, meanness. Also *fig.*

c **1629** DONNE *Serm.*, *John* x. 10 (1640) 72 With what penuriousnesse.. of devotion.. of reverence do you meet him [Christ] here? **1630** *Ibid.*, *Job* xvi. 17. 132 The penuriousnesse of my fortune contracted by my sins. **1672** WILKINS *Nat. Relig.* 334 Those, that out of penuriousness can scarce afford themselves the ordinary conveniences of life out of their large possessions, have been always accounted poor. **1759** DILWORTH *Pope* 126 To shew the waste of some, and the sordid penuriousness of others. **1848** MILL *Pol. Econ.* II. vii. §3 (1876) 173 They are oftener accused of penuriousness than prodigality.

†**pe'nurity.** *Sc. Obs.* [f. L. *pēnūria* PENURY, with change of suffix: see -ITY.] = PENURY 1, 2.

c **1480** HENRYSON *Test. Cres.* 321 Greit penuritie Thow suffer sall, and as ane beggar die. **1513** DOUGLAS *Æneis* I. Prol. 386 Tuichand our tongis penurite. **1533** BELLENDEN *Livy* II. v. (S.T.S.) 144 Na penurite of vittalis suld follow. **1577** *Aberdeen Regr.* (1848) II. 30 The exorbitant darth of victuall and penurite thairoff. **1596** DALRYMPLE tr. *Leslie's Hist. Scot.* I. 35 In vthir places, for the penuritie of wodis, out of the ȝeard we cutt peates.

†**'penurous,** *a. Obs. rare*⁻¹. [f. PENUR or PENURY + -OUS.] Lacking, wanting.

1594 CAREW *Tasso* (1881) 50 Who list not peace, warre take he as his owne, For store of brawles was neuer penurous.

penury ('pɛnjʊərɪ). Also 5 pennury, penowry, (punyrie). [ad. L. *pēnūria* or *pænūria* want, need; perh. through F. *pénurie* (15th c. in Littré).]

1. The condition of being destitute of or straitened in the necessaries of life; destitution, indigence, want; poverty.

1432–50 tr. *Higden* (Rolls) V. 51 Origenes, lefte in grete pennury [*in summa penuria*], helde a scole of grammar at Alexandrye. *c* **1489** CAXTON *Sonnes of Aymon* iv. 121 Late vs goo agenst her.. and tell her our grete penurye and our nede. **1526** TINDALE *Luke* xxi. 4 But she of her penury [so **1611**; 1881 *R.V.* want] hath cast in all the substaunce that she hadde. **1600** SHAKS. *A.Y.L.* I. i. 42 Shall I keepe your hogs, and eat huskes with them? What prodigall portion haue I spent, that I should come to such penury? **1624** DONNE *Serm.*, *Isa.* vii. 14 (1640) 13 The sheaves in harvest, to fill all penuries. **1750** GRAY *Elegy* 51 Chill Penury repress'd their noble rage. *a* **1839** PRAED *Poems* (1864) II. 237 Penury with love, I will not doubt it, Is better far than palaces without it. **1874** GREEN *Short Hist.* ix. §5. 645 Shaftesbury's course rested.. on the belief that the penury of the Treasury left Charles at his mercy.

2. Lack, dearth, scarcity, scantness, insufficiency, want (*of* something material or immaterial).

1447 in *Epist. Acad. Oxon.* (O.H.S.) I. 261 Þe gret.. multitude of scolars, and the gret penury of boks þat ben amang us. **1454** *Rolls of Parlt.* V. 272/1 The greet punyrie and scarsite of money. **1615** G. SANDYS *Trav.* 97 In a maruellous penury of water. **1699** GARTH *Dispens.* v. 65 You owe.. to your stars your penury of sense. **1779** J. MOORE *View Soc. Fr.* (1789) I. viii. 50 There is an absolute penury of public news. **1839** DE QUINCEY *Recoll. Lakes* Wks. 1862 II. 127 In early youth I laboured under a peculiar embarrassment and penury of words.

3. Penuriousness, miserliness, parsimoniousness. Now *rare.*

1651 JER. TAYLOR *Serm. for Year* II. x. 130 God sometimes punishes.. idlenesse with vanity, penury with oppression. **1685** DRYDEN *Thren. August.* 500 Let them not still be obstinately blind,.. with malignant penury To starve the royal vertues of his mind. **1754** FOOTE *Knights* I. Wks. 1799 I. 62 He is a thrifty, wary, man... The very abstract of penury! **1806** METCALFE in Owen *Wellesley's Desp.* 810 When, by a cold penury, I blast the abilities of a nation, the ill I may do is beyond all calculation. **1871** R. ELLIS *Catullus* xxiii. 4 A father and a step-dame Each for penury fit to tooth a flint-stone.

Penutian (pə'nuːʃən, -tɪən), *sb.* and *a.* Also Penuti. [f. Maiduan *pen* two + Miwokan and Costanoan *uti* two + -AN.] **A.** *sb.* **a.** A North American Indian language stock comprising the Miwokan, Costanoan, Wintuan, Maiduan, and Yokutsan families of California. Also, a proposed language phylum comprising the Penutian stock (distinguished as *California Penutian*), the Oregon Penutian and Plateau Penutian stocks, the Chinookan and Tsimshian families, and (in the usage of some scholars) certain other language groupings of North and Central America. **B.** *adj.* Of or pertaining to Penutian.

1912 DIXON & KROEBER in *Amer. Anthropologist* XIV. 692 The new larger families and their components are: *Penutian*, comprising the groups formerly known as Maidu, Wintun, Miwok, Costanoan, and Yokuts. [Etc.] **1914** *Ibid.* XV. 649

There is available enough information on the structure of the five Penutian languages to prove their genetic affinity beyond a doubt. **1932** W. L. GRAFF *Lang.* 431 The most important North American branches: Eskimo..Penutian. **1959** *Chambers's Encycl.* VIII. 360/1 The 22 language-families of North American are: Algonquin,..Penuti, [etc.]. **1965** *Canad. Jrnl. Linguistics* Spring 78 Suggestions of affiliation with..Penutian. **1968** R. W. LANGACKER *Lang. & its Struct.* viii. 232 Continuing north, we find Takelman.. Chinookan, and Plateau Penutian (including Klamath, Modoc, Nez Percé, Cayuse, and Yakima). **1972** *Language* XLVIII. 378 Chinook Jargon, once the means of communication among the (as yet) unrelated Indo-European, Athapaskan, Salishan, Penutian, and Wakashan-speaking peoples of the Pacific North-west. **1973** H. LANDAR in *Current Trends in Linguistics* X. 1294 California Penutian. Rubruz for Yokuts, Maidu, Miwok-Costanoan, and Wintun. **1974** *Encycl. Brit. Micropædia* VII. 859/2 The Penutian languages are sometimes grouped into a yet larger stock, called either Penutian or Macro-Penutian, that includes several Meso-American Indian languages. **1977** C. F. & F. M. VOEGELIN *Classification & Index World's Lang.* 287 Their [*sc.* Dixon and Kroeber's] grouping did not extend Penutian beyond the so-called California Penutian. *Ibid.*, A dozen separate language families beside nine different language isolates..are said to be remotely related to each other within the Penutian phylum.

Hence **Pe'nutianist**, a student of Penutian.

1965 *Language* XLI. 173 Sapir's influence extends also to Penutianists.

penwiper ('pɛn,waɪpə(r)). [f. PEN *sb.*[2] 4 + WIPER.] **a.** A contrivance for cleaning a pen by wiping the ink from it; usually consisting of one or more pieces of cloth folded or fastened together, but also made in other forms (specified as 'brush penwiper', 'tassel penwiper', and the like); often of ornamental or fanciful design.

1826 E. BROWN *Let.* in C. Oman *Ayot Rectory* (1965) iv. 90 Brown holland pockets containing housewives,..pencils, penwipers, knives. **1838** DICKENS *Diary* 2 Jan. in *Lett.* (1965) I. 629, I wrote to Mrs. Hogarth yesterday,..sending as a New Years' token a pen-wiper of poor Mary's. **1840** —— *Sk. Young Couples* 88 All manner of presents, such as pocket-books, pencil-cases, pen-wipers. **1841** C. RIDLEY *Let.* Nov. in *Cecilia* (1958) vi. 74, I want to know whether you like penwipers with white linen inside? They are all so here and the housekeeper renews them now and then. **1848** THACKERAY *Bk. Snobs* xxiv, The penwiper..was the imitation of a..dahlia. **1865** DICKENS *Mut. Fr.* II. i, I only make pincushions and pen-wipers to use up my waste. *fig.* **1900** T. FOWLER in *N. & Q.* 9th Ser. VI. 74 The 'pen-wiper', a small piece of folded silk which is attached to the back of the proctor's gown [at Oxford].

b. A handkerchief. *slang.*

1902 FARMER & HENLEY *Slang* V. 170/1 *Penwiper*..a handkerchief. **1942** BERREY & VAN DEN BARK *Amer. Thes. Slang* §88/4 Handkerchief..penwiper.

penwoman ('pɛn,wʊmən). [f. PEN *sb.*[2] 4 + WOMAN, after *penman.*] A woman skilled in the use of the pen; a female writer. (Usually with qualifying adj.)

1748 RICHARDSON *Clarissa* (1811) I. xlii. 329 O what a ready penwoman! **1818** SCOTT *Hrt. Midl.* xxxix, I am nae great pen-woman, and it is near eleven o'clock o' the night. **1880** DISRAELI *Endym.* lix, Mrs. Neuchatel was a fine penwoman; her feelings were her facts, and her ingenious observations of art and nature were her news.

Hence **'penwomanship** [after *penmanship*], the practice or art of a penwoman; feminine writing.

1775 S. J. PRATT *Liberal Opin.* (1783) III. 144 She began again to indulge her favourite pleasures of penwomanship. **1803** SOUTHEY *Lett.* (1856) I. 211 Senhora, it is a hand-writing of the feminine gender—it is penwomanship.

'penwork. Also with hyphen and as two words. [PEN *sb.*[2]] **a.** Work done with a pen; writing. **b.** The decoration and ornamental lettering of illuminated books and manuscripts done with a pen; also, decoration drawn with a pen on the surface of furniture. Also *attrib.*

1644 SIR E. DERING *Prop. Sacr.* b ij, Can a leisure be found for pen-work? **1844** H. N. HUMPHREYS *Illum. Bks. Middle Ages* 6/1 The letters..terminating in the margin in long tails,..only, instead of being solid, they are formed of light lines slightly enriched with simple and delicate penwork. **1899** *Westm. Gaz.* 4 Sept. 3/3 The last pen-work of Charlotte Brontë. **1901** J. W. BRADLEY *Illum. Lett. & Borders* iv. 49 The execution [of Celtic illumination] chiefly consists in pen work in black or coloured inks. **1906** E. JOHNSTON *Writing & Illuminating* xiii. 218 Many of the most beautiful MSS. were made in pen-work throughout. And it is well that the penman should stick to his pen as much as is possible. **1928** O. E. SAUNDERS *Eng. Illumination* I. 110 What distinguishes these borders especially from earlier work are the feathery sprays, indicated by pen-work lightly touched with green and ending in flourishes like the tendrils of a vine. **1969** N. R. KER *Medieval MSS. in Brit. Libraries* I. p. xiii, The terms 'decoration'..and 'ornament'..have been used in describing the surrounds of initials to make the important distinction between work with a brush and penwork flourishings. **1973** *Times* 13 Apr. 18/6 The curiosity of the sale was a monumental Empire ebonized secretaire-cabinet, the top shaped as a temple supported on lightly draped female figures and the whole lavishly applied with classical ormolu motifs and penwork. **1976** *Codicologica* I. 78 Practically no research has been done on the history of decoration of the medieval manuscript and of the numerous elements included in that word: initials,..penwork flourishes on initials or paragraph signs, [etc.]. **1978** *Bodl. Libr. Rec.* IX. 326 Their simple penwork interlace is frequently enlivened by the inclusion of a bird or monster head, a flower or a peascod.

Hence **'penworker**, one who works with a pen; **'penworked** *a.* (in sense b).

1901 Penworker [s.v. PEN *sb.*[2] 7]. **1965** *Harper's Bazaar* June 76/3 A Regency working-table with an exquisite black pen-worked top..£70.

penworth, obs. f. *penn'orth*, PENNYWORTH.

peny, penyde, obs. forms of PENNY, PENIDE.

penyriall, penyston, obs. ff. PENNYROYAL, PENISTONE.

penytancer(e, -enser, etc., var. PENITENCER.

Penzance (pɛn'zæns). The title of James Plaisted Wilde, Lord *Penzance* (1816–99), English lawyer and amateur horticulturist, used *attrib.* in **Penzance briar, rose**, to designate a rose belonging to a group of hybrids developed by him from the sweet briar, *Rosa rubiginosa*, and distinguished by scented foliage and single flowers.

[**1891** *Jrnl. R. Hort. Soc.* XIII. p. cxviii, One of the most interesting features in the exhibition was a stand of seedling Sweet Briar hybrids raised by the Right Hon. Lord Penzance... In the case of Lady Penzance the perfume of the leaves was retained in conjunction with small single flowers of a rosy-salmon hue.] **1902** A. FOSTER-MELLIAR *Bk. of Rose* (ed. 2) ii. 20 It is a great mistake to plant these 'Penzance' or any other Sweet-briars in Rose-beds; for they are very strong growers. **1907** *Gardeners' Chron.* 15 June 382/3 Rambler, Wichuraiana, and Penzance Roses will all submit to gentle forcing. **1912** E. WILLMOTT *Genus Rosa* II. 455 With the introduction of the Penzance Briars a new race of roses came into being. **1935** N. MITCHISON *We have been Warned* II. 196 There were Penzance briars and species roses growing unpruned. **1956** B. PARK *Collins' Guide to Roses* xi. 195 Lord Penzance produced by hybridizing many distinct seedling varieties at the end of the XIXth century which he called Penzance Briars; they represent a distinct series. **1969** C. LLOYD *Gardening on Chalk & Lime* vi. 60, I should avoid the Penzance briars... They are victims of black spot.

peola (piː'əʊlə). *U.S. Black slang.* [Etym. unknown.] A light-complexioned Black person, esp. a girl.

1942 Z. N. HURSTON in A. Dundes *Mother Wit* (1973) 224/2 Dat broad I seen you with wasn't no pe-ola. **1944** C. CALLOWAY *Hepsters Dict.*, *Peola*, a light person, almost white. **1970** C. MAJOR *Dict. Afro-Amer. Slang* 90 *Peola*, a light-skinned Afro-American girl.

peolour, variant of PELURE[1] *Obs.*, fur.

peon ('piːən). Also (in sense 1) 7 **pion, pyone, peune, peun.** [In sense 1, ad. Pg. *peão* pedestrian, foot-soldier, day-labourer, and F. *pion*, foot-soldier, footman, servant on foot, whence in some E. Indian vernaculars *piūn*; in sense 2, a. Sp. *peon* in same senses; = OF. *peon*, It. *pedone*, med.L. *pedōn-em* foot-soldier, f. L. *pēs, ped-em* foot. A doublet of PAWN *sb.*[1], OF. *paon.*]

1. In India, Bangladesh, Sri Lanka (Ceylon), and Malaysia: **a.** A foot-soldier. **b.** A native constable. **c.** An attendant or orderly; a footman or messenger. Also, a person who does minor work in an office.

1609 W. FINCH in Purchas *Pilgrims* (1625) I. iv. §3. 421 The first of February, the Captaine [Hawkins] departed with fiftie Peons, and certaine Horsemen. **1613** *ibid.* IV. viii. §3. 484 Dispeeded one of my Pions to Lowribander with a Letter. **1632** R. CARTWRIGHT in *St. Papers, Col., E. Indies* 290 His poor man..was met with by the Governors 'pyones'..and clapt up in prison. **1638** SIR T. HERBERT *Trav.* (ed. 2) 35 With some Pe-unes (or black foot-boyes who can pratle some English) we rode to Surat. **1687** A. LOVELL tr. *Thevenot's Trav.* III. I. i. 2 These Pions of the Custom-house [in India]. **1697** DAMPIER *Voy. round World* (1699) 507 At this Moors Town they got a Peun to be their Guide to the Moguls nearest Camp. **1747** *Gentl. Mag.* July 341 The whole French garrison of Pondicherry, consisting of about 1000 regular troops, 200 trained peons, and many others. **1840** MALCOM *Trav. Hindustan* Gloss., *Peon* (pronounced Pune), a Hindu constable. **1896** CROKER *Village Tales* 2 Body-servants, peons, syces, and all the barrack dhobies. **1913** L. WOOLF *Village in Jungle* vii. 211 The peon and the interpreter told Babu to hold his tongue. **1927** R. J. H. SIDNEY *In Brit. Malaya To-Day* 136 Postmen, Government *peons* (messengers), prisoners themselves, all wear materials either made or made-up in Singapore prison. **1931** *Times* 17 Feb. 13/5 Five postal *peons* [servants] were injured while on duty, and the City Post Office was closed for three days... Instead of deliveries by *peons* people are asked to inquire at the post office for letters. **1969** [see DURZEE]. **1969** *Pioneer* (Lucknow) 13 Aug. 6/2 A peon in the office of the regional transport authority in Bombay attends office in his own car daily. **1971** *Ceylon Observer* (Mag. ed.) 19 Sept. 7/5 A peon has to come to the rescue of the official. **1972** *Straits Times* 26 Apr. 7/6 F and N workers have been picketing the factory..in support of a claim for free shoes for three peons. **1973** *Archivum Linguisticum* IV. 91 Peons, low-caste strangers, and their wives. **1975** *Bangladesh Times* 23 July 1/1 Six persons including a professor, a B.Sc examinee and a college peon, were arrested by the Lalbagh police on Tuesday on charge of adopting unfair means in the examination and abetment of the crime.

2. In Spanish America: A day-labourer; in S. America, a man or boy leading a horse or mule; in Mexico, *spec.* a debtor held in servitude by his creditor till his debts are worked off. Also in extended use.

1826 W. B. DEWEES *Lett. from Early Settler Texas* (1852) 56 The Peons, or lower class—are a sort of slaves, who are employed by the aristocracy. **1826** [see ARRIERO]. **1828** C. BRAND *Jrnl. Voy. Peru* v. 104 The mules were straying about ..and our wild, uncouth-looking peons were assembled round a fire, under the lee of a large rock. **1860** TYLOR *Anahuac* xi. (1861) 291 If a debtor owes money and cannot pay it, his creditor is allowed by law to make a slave or *peon* of him until the debt is liquidated. **1880** C. R. MARKHAM *Peruv. Bark* xxiii. 257 The mule owner brought with him a strong lad as peon, to assist in loading and unloading the beasts. **1945** J. L. MARSHALL *Santa Fe* 9 In 1850 New Mexico came into the Union as a free soil territory—and went on buying and selling slaves as of old, calling them *peons* and *peonas.* **1962** N. MAXWELL *Witch-Doctor's Apprentice* vii. 81 They weren't Cotos, only a white man named Rodriguez, his partner, Juan Gómez, and five peons. **1970** S. L. BARRACLOUGH in I. L. Horowitz *Masses in Lat. Amer.* iv. 125 On some traditional Andean haciendas, peons still kneel to kiss the corner of the 'patron's' poncho to show respect. **1972** P. DANIEL *Shadow of Slavery* ix. 177 In New Orleans a couple..took the peons in, gave them directions on how to proceed to..Chicago. Perhaps thirty persons excaped on this modern version of the underground railroad. **1977** *Time* 6 June 42/2 He [*sc.* Elvis Presley] periodically tossed a sweat-stained scarf to the peons below. *attrib.* **1847** W. S. HENRY *Campaign Sk. War with Mexico* xii. 134 This 'peone' system is fully equal to our slavery. **1851** MAYNE REID *Scalp Hunt.* x. 76 We see the clumsy hoe in the hands of the peon serf. **1874** RAYMOND *Statist. Mines & Mining* 332 Peon labor was but a trifling expense to the employer.

‖**3.** *pl.* **peones.** = BANDERILLERO.

1932 [see BANDERILLERO]. **1957** A. MACNAB *Bulls of Iberia* v. 50 Each matador's team consists of five assistants: two picadors, mounted, and three peones or capemen on foot —also called *banderilleros* because they plant the sticks called *banderillas.* **1967** MCCORMICK & MASCAREÑAS *Compl. Aficionado* ii. 52 The senior matador who knows and likes this breed, has told his peones not to show a cape until he gives the signal. **1976** E. P. BENSON *Bulls of Ronda* iv. 26 Navarro's peon played the bull for a few minutes before El Zorro gave the bull to Navarro. The boy began a series of passes with his cape.

peonage ('piːənɪdʒ). [f. prec. + -AGE.] The work or service of a peon; the system of having or using peons or enslaved debtors.

1. In S. America, attendance upon a horse or mule; in Mexico *spec.* the condition of a peon serf, servitude for debt; the system of holding peons. Also, in parts of southern U.S., an arrangement whereby convicts are leased to contractors. Also *transf.* and *attrib.*

1850 G. A. MCCALL *Lett. fr. Frontiers* (1868) 500 The greatest lever that could be used in overturning the present system of peonage. **1850** *Ex. Doc. 31st U.S. Congress 1 Sess. Senate* No. 64. 49 From this cause, and the miserable system of 'peonage' that prevails, the products of agriculture are barely sufficient to support the inhabitants [north of El Paso]. **1860** O. W. HOLMES *Elsie V.* xii. (1887) 134 The master who held her in peonage. **1870** J. ORTON *Andes & Amazons* iv. (1876) 79 Horse hire, peonage, and most mechanical work must be paid for in advance. *a* **1889** J. J. WEBB *Adventures Santa Fé Trade* (1931) 101 The system of peonage, or voluntary servitude, was a fixed institution. **1903** *Times* 25 Nov. 5/6 The peonage system in the South practically amounts to an attempt to restore slavery under another name. **1903** *Nation* (N.Y.) 3 Dec. 436/3 More peonage revelations in various portions of the South must be opening the eyes of those editors who criticised us last spring for believing that the Alabama cases were other than sporadic and unparalleled happenings. **1934** A. WOOLLCOTT *While Rome Burns* 291 The Guild must often wonder why.. it should ask..a company to enter into so benumbing a peonage. **1969** A. G. FRANK *Latin Amer.* xix. 302 After the French intervention and under the thirty-year reign of Porfirio Diaz, peonage returned in full force and concentration of landownership became worse than ever. **1972** P. DANIEL *Shadow of Slavery* ii. 33 The root of the peonage problem was anchored in the long-practiced abuse of black laborers. **1972** 'E. LATHEN' *Murder without Icing* (1973) xi. 107 The player..contended that, if he could be forced to..work for another team at the whim of his employer, he had been reduced to an unconstitutional state of peonage. **1972** *National Observer* (U.S.) 27 May 7/4 Federal Judge J. Robert Martin, Jr., had told the jury that Federal law required that proof of 'peonage' must be based on evidence of indebtedness. **1973** L. G. FORER in A. E. Wilkerson *Rights of Children* 31 Legality of the commitment would then be the issue—not the procedures by which he was committed or the quantum of care that he received or the existence of institutional peonage.

2. In India: The service or employment of peons as messengers, etc.: see prec. 1.

1900 *Indian Engineering* 24 Feb. 115 The hourly post..a far more satisfactory agency for the spread of their price-lists than the old cumbersome and unreliable peonage.

'peonick, obs. form of PÆONIC.

1706 HEARNE *Collect.* (O.H.S.) I. 171 Dr. Eaton writ a Discourse of ab[t] a sheet on Peonick verse.

peonidin (piː'ɒnɪdɪn). *Chem.* [ad. G. *päonidin* (Willstätter & Nolan 1915, in *Ann. d. Chem.* CDVIII. 136), f. *päonin* PEONIN: see -IDIN.] An anthocyanidin (usu. isolated as the reddish brown chloride, $C_{16}H_{13}O_6Cl$) that is the aglycone of peonin.

1915 *Chem. Abstr.* IX. 1307 Hydrolyzed by boiling 2·5 min. with 20% HCl, peonin gives 2 mols. glucose and peonidin chloride. **1956** I. L. FINAR *Org. Chem.* II. xv. 587 Peonidin is the monomethyl ether of cyanidin. **1965** J. B. HARBONE in Bonner & Varner *Plant Biochem.* xxiv. 624 While over a hundred different flavonoid aglycons have been isolated from plants, only eleven of these occur at all commonly... Six are anthocyanidins: the scarlet pelargonidin, the crimson cyanidin, the mauve delphinidin, and the three simply derived methyl ethers, peonidin, petunidin, and malvidin.

peonied: see PIONED.

peonin (ˈpiːənɪn). *Chem.* [ad. G. *päonin* (Willstätter & Nolan, 1915, in *Ann. d. Chem.* CDVIII. 136), f. *päonie* PEONY: see -IN[1].] An anthocyanin (usu. isolated as the reddish violet chloride, $C_{28}H_{33}O_{16}Cl$) that is the colouring matter of red peonies and on hydrolysis gives peonidin and glucose.

1915 *Chem. Abstr.* IX. 1307 The deep violet-red peony meal contains 3-3·5% peonin. **1946** *Nature* 7 Sept. 342/1 An acid aqueous extract of the yellow 'Hofmann's Glory' added to synthetic peonin or malvin makes the red solutions much bluer, and they then simulate the appropriate flower extracts. **1956** I. L. FINAR *Org. Chem.* II. xv. 687 Peonidin chloride..is produced..when peonin chloride is hydrolysed with hydrochloric acid.

peonism (ˈpiːənɪz(ə)m). [f. PEON + -ISM.] = PEONAGE 1.

1851 D. WEBSTER *Wks.* V. 351, I suppose there is no slavery of that description in California now. I understand that *peonism*, a sort of penal servitude, exists there, or rather a sort of voluntary sale of a man and his offspring for debt. **1857** W. W. H. DAVIS *El Gringo* ix. 231 Another peculiar feature of New Mexico is the system of domestic servitude called peonism, that has existed, and still exists, in all the Spanish American colonies.

peony (ˈpiːənɪ). Forms: α. 1 peonie. β. 3 pyone, (pioine), 4 piane, 4-5 pione, 5 pyon, -oun, -an, (pyione). γ. 5-6 pyonie, -ony, -onye, pionye, pyany, -ye, 6 pionee, 6-7 pionie, peionie, peonie, 6-9 piony, 7 peiony, pæonie, 8 pioney, 6- peony, 7- pæony. δ. 7, 9 *Eng.* and *U.S. dial.* piny. [In OE., *peonie* wk. fem., ad. late L. (and It.) *peōnia*, L. *pæōnia* (Pliny); in ME., *pione*, a. northern F. (Norm. and Picard) *pione* = OF. *peone, peoine, pioine*, mod.F. *pivoine*; in 15th c., *pyonie, piony, peony, pæony*, conformed to L. *pæōnia*, a. Gr. *παιωνία* the peony, f. *Παιών*, Pæon, the name of the physician of the gods, a physician; cf. *παιώνιος* healing, medicinal.]

1. A plant (or flower) of the genus *Pæonia* (N.O. *Ranunculaceæ*), comprising stout herbs, or rarely shrubs, with large handsome globular flowers of various shades of red and white, often becoming double under cultivation; *esp.* the commonly cultivated *P. officinalis*, a native of central Asia and southern Europe, with flowers usually dark red.

The root, flowers, and seeds were formerly used in medicine, and the seeds also as a spice (quots. 1299, 1362, etc.).

male and ***female peony***, old names for *P. corallina* and *P. officinalis* respectively. (These names are erroneously reversed in Miller's *Gardener's Dict.* and *New Syd. Soc. Lex.*) ***tree peony***, the shrubby species *P. Moutan*, a native of China.

α. *c* **1000** *Sax. Leechd.* I. 168 Ðeos wyrt ðe man peonian nemneð wæs funden fram peonio þam ealdre.

β. *c* **1265** *Voc.* in Wr.-Wülcker 557/28 *Pionia* i. pioine. **1299** *Durham Acc. Rolls* (Surtees) 495, iij li. de pyone, iijs. iijd. ob. **1362** LANGL. *P. Pl.* A. v. 155, I haue peper and piane [B. v. 312 piones; C. VII. 359 pionys] and a pound of garlek. *a* **1400** *Pistill of Susan* 108 þe persel, þe passenep..þe pyon, þe peere. *c* **1450** *Cov. Myst.* (Shaks. Soc.) 22 Here is peper, pyan, and swete lycorys.

γ. **14..** *Stockh. Med. MS.* II. 336 in *Anglia* XVIII. 315 Take v greynes of pionye. *c* **1440** *Promp. Parv.* 395/2 Pyany, herbe, *pionia*. *Ibid.* 401/1 Pyony, herbe, *idem quod* pyanye. **1533** ELYOT *Cast. Helthe* III. v. (1539) 60 b, Pourgers of choler..Pyonie. **1548** TURNER *Names of Herbes* 59 Peony the female groweth in euery countrey, but I neuer saw the male sauing only in Anwerp. **1591** SYLVESTER *Du Bartas* I. iii. 712 About an Infants neck hang Peonie, It cures Alcydes cruell Maladie. **1610** W. FOLKINGHAM *Art of Survey* I. ii. 38 Dry earth for Peionie, with sand for Paunces. **1706** PHILLIPS, *Pæonia*, the Peony or Piony, a Flower, the Roots of which are of great Use in Physick. **1784** COWPER *Task* I. 35 There might ye see the pioney spread wide, The full-blown rose, the shepherd and his lass. **1867** PEARSON *Hist. Eng.* I. 56 It is even possible that to Rome we owe the rose, the lily, and the pæony.

δ. **1616** W. BROWNE *Brit. Past.* II. iii, They did dispose The ruddy Piny with the lighter Rose. **1887** *Kentish Gloss.*, *Pinies* (pei·niz), *sb. pl.* Peonies. **1904** *Dialect Notes* II. 427 *Piny, n.*, peony. **1913** G. STRATTON-PORTER *Laddie* vi. 165 Her people..spent much money on the biggest tombstone in the cemetery, and planted pinies and purple phlox on her. **1976** *Columbus* (Montana) *News* (Joint Suppl.) 24 June 4/4 Even though it had medicinal value, colonial housewives did not as a rule include the peony in their herb gardens, but set it out among their flowers. They felt that the 'glory of the front yard was the old-fashioned early red "Piny"'.

2. *attrib.* and *Comb.* **a.** *attrib.* or as *adj.* Resembling a peony-flower, dark red; esp. of the cheeks, plump and rosy. **b.** *Comb.*, as ***peony-bush, -root, -seed; peony-faced, -flowered, -pink, -red*** adjs. †**peony-kernel**, a peony-seed; †**peony-water**, a drink made from the peony.

1548 TURNER *Names of Herbes* 59 Peony roote is hote in the fyrst and dry in the thyrde degree. **1694** SALMON *Bate's Dispens.* (1713) 16/2 You may give it either alone, or in Black-cherry-water, or Peony-Water. **1796** MRS. GLASSE *Cookery* xxi. 327 Stick the cream with piony kernels. **1810** *Splendid Follies* III. 48 Mopping their piony cheeks with a handkerchief. **1813** M. EDGEWORTH *Let.* 19 Apr. (1971) 21 Her color is less of the peony red than it used to be. **1892** T. HARDY *Well-Beloved* I. v, The beating of the wind and rain and spray had inflamed her cheeks to peony hues. **1895** *Daily Chron.* 28 Aug. 3/5 Rose-flowered, pæony-flowered, and Japanese asters. **1905** *Daily Chron.* 15 May 3/3 A pretty hat.., made in soft Manilla straw, in the natural colouring, and trimmed with one large pink peony, in soft satin and chiffon, and folded draperies of Louisine silk ribbon, in peony-pink shot with white. **1906** *Ibid.* 4 Oct. 6/5 A new variety of peony-flowered, or art dahlia, in crimson and pink, is shown. **1907** *Ibid.* 18 Sept. 3/5 Some very fine examples of the new peony-flowered variety of dahlia. **1927** *Eaton's News Weekly* 12 Mar. 20 This pretty..frock.. comes also in gooseberry green and palmetto green, or in peony red tones. **1957** T. R. H. LEBAR *Dahlias for Everyone* ii. 19 The peony flowered varieties..had comparatively flat petals. **1976** W. E. SHEWELL-COOPER *Basic Bk. Dahlia Growing* ii. 16 Paeony-flowered Dahlias have blooms with two or more rings of generally flattened ray florets, the centre forming a disc.

people (ˈpiːp(ə)l), *sb.* Forms: α. 3-6 peple; (3-5 pepule, 4-6 -ul, 5-6 -ull(e; 4-5 pepille, 4-6 -ill, 5-6 -il; 5 pepylle, 5-6 -yll; 6 *Sc.* peiple, 7 peeple). β. 4-5 poeple, (5 -ul), 5- people, (5 peopel, -ull). γ. 3-5 puple, (5 pupile, -ill, -yll, -ull); 4-5 peuple. δ. 4-5 pople, (4 -ille, 5-6 -il). [a. AF. *poeple* (Britton), *people* (Rolls of Parlt.) = OF. *pople, poeple, pueple, peuple, puple* = Pr. *poble, pobol*, Sp. *pueblo*, It. *popolo*:—L. *populum*, acc. of *populus* the people, the populace.]

1. A body of persons composing a community, tribe, race, or nation; = FOLK 1. Sometimes viewed as a unity, sometimes as a collective of number. **a.** In singular, as a collective of unity.

[**1292** BRITTON I. Introd., Edward..Roi de Engleterre.. Desirauntz pes entre le poeple qe est en nostre proteccioun.] **1340-70** *Alex. & Dind.* 1089 So..ȝe ben by-set in an yle, þat þer may comen in ȝour kiþ non vnkouþe peple. *c* **1375** *Sc. Leg. Saints* ii. (*Paulus*) 461 þu [Rome] art digne callit to be now haly folk and pepill chosyn. *Ibid.* iv. (*Jacobus*) 16 þis James,..þe wa can ta to spanȝe..þat puple to cristyne treutht to brynge. **1390** GOWER *Conf.* II. 180 Til so befell, ..That god a poeple for himselve Hath chose. *a* **1400-50** *Alexander* 3412 Ilk a pepill his possession in pes moȝt he broweke. **1562** WINȜET *Cert. Tractatis* i. Wks. (S.T.S.) I. 7 Setting vp ane peple heidles left of God. **1611** BEAUM. & FL. *King & no K.* I. i, I were much better be a king of beasts Than such a people. **1835** LYTTON *Rienzi* II. vi, Rienzi addressed the Populace, whom he had suddenly elevated into a People. **1852** TENNYSON *Ode Dk. Wellington* 151 A people's voice! we are a people yet. **1862** STANLEY *Jew. Ch.* (1877) I. 87 Whatever history exists is the history of a man,..but not of a people.

b. In sing. form, construed as a plural.

13.. *Cursor M.* 7323 (Cott.) Omang þir puple [*G., Tr.* þis folk, *F.* þaire folk] sal þou latt A stalworth man þat saul haitt. **1340-70** *Alex. & Dind.* 4 þere wilde contre was wist & wonderful peple, þat weren proued ful proude. **1600** J. PORY tr. *Leo's Africa* Introd. 41 Ouer against which cape.. do inhabite the people called Bramas. **1611** BIBLE *Isa.* viii. 19 Should not a people seeke vnto their God? **1653** HOLCROFT *Procopius* I. 13 This people are Christians,..and have..been subject to the King of Persia. **1857** BUCKLE *Civiliz.* I. xiii. 745 Every people worthy of being called a nation possess in their own language ample resources for expressing the highest ideas.

c. *pl.* **peoples**, nations, races (= L. *populi, gentes*). ***Peoples of the Sea***: name given in Egyptian records of the 19th and 20th Dynasties to various sea-borne migrant peoples who invaded and settled parts of Egypt, Syria, and Palestine. See also *Sea Peoples* s.v. SEA *sb.* 23.

This plural form was avoided in 16th c. Bible versions, and by many 17th and 18th c. writers: see d. It was thought to require defence or explanation even in 1817 and 1830.

c **1374** CHAUCER *Former Age* 2 A Blysful lyf,..Ledden the poeples in the former age. **1382** WYCLIF *Rev.* x. 11 It behoueth thee eftsoone to prophecie to hethen men, and to puplis [TINDALE to *Geneva* people, *Rhem.*, 1611, *R.V.* peoples], and to langagis, and to many kingis. [So xvii. 15 in the same versions.] **1430-40** LYDG. *Bochas* II. i. (1554) 33/b, Obedience..combineth the true opinions In hertes of peoples. **1551** ROBINSON tr. *More's Utop.* I. (1895) 26 So manye strange and vnknowne peoples and countreis. **1582, 1611** [see 1382 above] Before nations and peoples. **1639** FULLER *Holy War* v. xiii. (1840) 266 Saladin answered him, that he also ruled over as many peoples. **1665** BOYLE *Occas. Refl.* v. i. (1848) 298 A Throne, to which above an hundred other Peoples paid homage. **1778** BP. LOWTH *Transl. Isa.* xxxiv. 1 Draw near, O ye nations, and hearken; And attend to me, O ye peoples! **1806** W. TAYLOR in *Ann. Rev.* IV. 218 The moral habits of the several peoples of the earth. **1817** G. S. FABER *Eight Dissert.* (1845) I. III. ii. 208 Gen. xlix. 10 ..*people*. In the original Hebrew the word is plural. If therefore the delicacy of our ears be offended by the uncouth sound of *peoples*: let us at least..substitute the more euphonic word *nations*. **1830** GEN. P. THOMPSON *Exerc.* (1842) I. 261 To say 'The Representative of the *peoples*' [as trans. *Le Représentant des Peuples*] would not be under-stood at all. Such, however, is the idiom of the original. **1853** WHEWELL *Grotius* II. 2 The peoples who had been under his authority will be their own masters. **1864** H. SPENCER *Princ. Biol.* II. viii. §80 I. 241 The characters of neighbouring peoples. **1877** MORLEY *Crit. Misc.* Ser. II. 345 All our English-speaking peoples. **1906** J. H. BREASTED *Hist. Egypt* vi. xxiii. 477 The restless and turbulent peoples of the northern Mediterranean, whom the Egyptians designated the 'peoples of the sea', were showing themselves in ever increasing numbers in the south. **1950** H. L. LORIMER *Homer & Monuments* v. 150 On the monuments of Ramses III the most conspicuous of the Peoples of the Sea, the Shardana and Pulesati, are uniformly represented with round shields with single hand-grips. **1973** K. A. KITCHEN in D. J. Wiseman *Peoples Old Testament Times* iii. 57 The Lukka..appear as raiders in the Amarna letters *c.* 1370 B.C., as Hittite allies against Ramesses II at Kadesh *c.* 1286 B.C., and then in Libya with Libyans and others in the first attack by 'Peoples of the Sea' on Egypt, repulsed by Merenptah *c.* 1220 B.C.

†**d.** In the sense 'nations' the form *people* was also used unchanged: constantly so for the Gr. and Heb. pl. in Tindale and Coverdale and other 16th c. Bible versions founded on them (but not in Rhem.); nearly always so in Geneva, and in 1611 (where the Revisers of 1881-5 have uniformly substituted *peoples*). Also in many 18th c. writers.

1526 TINDALE *Luke* ii. 31 For myne eyes have sene the saveour sent from the Which thou hast prepared before the face of all people [*τῶν λαῶν*; so COVERD. to *Geneva*, and 1611; WYCLIF peplis, *v.r.* puplis; *Rhem.* and *R.V.* peoples]. **1535** COVERDALE *Ps.* lxvi[i]. 3 Let the people prayse the (O God), yee let all people prayse the. [*So other versions to* 1611; WYCLIF puplis, *R.V.* peoples.] —— *Dan.* iv. 1 Nabuchodonosor kynge, vnto all people, kynreddes and tunges [WYCLIF peplis, *v.r.* puplis, 1611 people, *R.V.* peoples]. **1567** *Gude & Godlie B.* Ps. ii. (S.T.S.) 85 All natiounis..The Kingis, and the peple, with ane consent, Resistis the, thy power and thy gloir. **1611** BIBLE *Isa.* ii. 4 Hee shall iudge among the nations and shall rebuke many people [WYCLIF puples, *R.V.* peoples]. **1625** N. CARPENTER *Geog. Del.* II. xiii. (1635) 214 Letters and discipline were first borrowed from the easterne people. **1793** JEFFERSON *Writ.* (1859) IV. 20 It will prove that the agents of the two people [the U.S. and France] are either great bunglers or great rascals.

e. *transf.* Of animals (in quot., after the Vulg. and Heb.). Cf. FOLK 1 b.

1382 WYCLIF *Prov.* xxx. 25 Amptis, a feble puple, that greithen in rep time mete to them [**1388** Amtis, a feble puple; **1535** COVERDALE, The Emmettes are but a weake people; **1560** (Genev.), The pismires a people not strong; **1611** The Ants are a people not strong].

2. a. The persons belonging to a place, or constituting a particular concourse, congregation, company, or class. Construed as *plural*.

As said of a congregation or body of worshippers, it sometimes approaches the sense of 'lay people', 'laity': see 4 b.

a **1300** *Cursor M.* 8651 (Cott.) All folud him,..O þe peple [*F.* poeple] of ilk tun. *c* **1330** *Amis & Amil.* 2101 Child Amoraunt stode the pople among. **1362** LANGL. *P. Pl.* A. Prol. 56, I font þere Freres..Preching þe peple. *c* **1400** *St. Alexius* (Laud 622) 563 Ffor liȝttynges grete, & þonder blast, Wel sore þe poeple was agast. **1480** CAXTON *Chron. Eng.* ccxlii. (1482) 282 Was ther a rumour..that kyng Richard come to westmynstre, and the peuple of london ranne thyder. **1548-9** (Mar.) *Bk. Com. Prayer, Morn. Prayer*, Then shalbe read ii. lessons distinctely with a loude voice, that the people maye heare. **1632** LITHGOW *Trav.* v. 184 Monasteries, the people whereof..liue vnder the order of Saint Basile. **1711** MRS. LONG in *Swift's Wks.* (1841) II. 477, I wish..you would make a pedigree for me; the people here want sadly to know what I am. **1739** GRAY *Lett., to Ashton* 21 Apr., The Abbés indeed and men of learning are a People of easy access enough. **1855** MACAULAY *Hist. Eng.* xii. III. 163 The people of Cavan migrated in one body to Enniskillen.

†**b.** As *collective sing.* A body or company of persons; a company, a multitude. Also with *pl.* *Obs.*

c **1386** CHAUCER *Knt.'s T.* 1655 The paleys ful of peples vp and doun, Here thre, ther ten. **1390** GOWER *Conf.* I. 82 He spilleth many a word in wast That schal with such a poeple trete. *c* **1400** *Destr. Troy* 1034 He [Hercules] Assemblid of Soudiours a full sadde pepull. *c* **1449** PECOCK *Repr.* IV. viii. 464 Whenne the Peplis weren clepid to gidere to him. **1482** WARKW. *Chron.* (Camden) 8 He..gaderyd a grete peple of menne. **1535** COVERDALE *2 Chron.* xxx. 13 There came together vnto Ierusalem a greate people, to kepe the feast of vnleuended bred. **1662** tr. *Schol.* to *H. More's Antid. Ath.* III. ix. §2 (1712) 171 Who..affirms that Witches have no more to do with the Devil than other wicked peoples.

c. ***People of the Book***: a body or community whose religion entails adherence to a book of divine revelation, *spec.* [tr. Arab. *Ahl al-Kitāb*] Jews and Christians as regarded in Muslim thought.

1834 A. BURNES *Bokhara* I. x. 313 The Vizier took a cup, and said, 'You must drink with us; for you are people of the book, better than the Russians.' **1861** J. M. RODWELL tr. *Koran* 635 O people of the Book! now hath our Apostle come to you to clear up to you The cessation of Apostles. **1885** T. P. HUGHES *Dict. Islam* 280/2 *Kitabi*, a term used for one of the *Ahlu 'l-Kitāb*, 'the people of the Book', or those in possession of the inspired word of God, as Jews or Christians. **1900** 'ODYSSEUS' *Turkey in Europe* v. 178 According to strict [Muslim] theology, Jews and Christians are called 'People of the Book' (Ehlu-'l-kitab), and enjoy a position superior to that of heathen polytheists. *a* **1936** KIPLING *Something of Myself* (1937) viii. 224 It is true the Children of Israel are 'people of the Book', and in the second Surah of the Koran Allah is made to say: 'High above mankind have I raised you.' **1959** [see KITAB]. **1967** *Guardian* 19 June 8/3 It..pains me, as it pains most Jews, when 'the people of the book' are compelled to wield the sword. **1976** Y. MENUHIN in D. Villiers *Next Year in Jerusalem* 334 A love of improvisation..has never been lost to the people of the Book. **1977** B. GASCOIGNE *Christians* v. 106 Jews, Christians, Muslims..are all, in the powerful phrase of the Koran, 'people of the book'.

3. Persons in relation to a superior, or to some one to whom they belong. Chiefly with possessive. **a.** The lieges or subjects of a king or other ruler, spiritual or temporal; the subjects or servants of God, of Christ, or of a Saint (quot. *c* 1450) considered as their personal sovereign or lord; the parishioners of a parish priest or parson, the congregation or 'flock' of a pastor, etc. Const. as *pl.*

[**1292** BRITTON I. v. §2 En despit et damage de nous et de noster poeple.] *a* **1300** *Cursor M.* 18371 þou es þe lauerd.. of hele, Til all þi peple for to bring Vte of thralhed til þi chosling. *c* **1430** LYDG. *Min. Poems* (Percy Soc.) 4 Beseching [God]..to send yow prosperite and many ȝeris, to the comfort of alle youre loving peple. **1444** *Rolls of Parlt.* V. 8/1 Yᵉ King..havyng compassion of his peoples compleynt. *c* **1450** *St. Cuthbert* (Surtees) 5231 þe pepil of þe saynt Fledd away with þair gude, And to durham all þai ȝode. **1556** *Chron. Gr. Friars* (Camden) 31 For cruelnes that he dyd unto hys perys and hys pepull. **1611** BIBLE *Dan.* ix. 26 The people of the Prince that shall come, shall destroy the citie. **1733** POPE *Ess. Man* III. 214 'Twas Virtue only..A Prince the Father of a People made. **1851** TENNYSON *To the Queen* vi, She wrought her people lasting good. *Ibid.* ix, Some august decree, Which kept her throne unshaken still, Broad-based upon her people's will. **1897** Q. VICTORIA *Message* 22 June, From my heart I thank my beloved people. May God bless them. **1902** K. EDWARD VII *Let. to his People* 7 Aug., The prayers of my People for my recovery were heard.

transf. **1577** B. GOOGE *Heresbach's Husb.* IV. (1586) 182 Who [king bee] must himselfe also bee depriued of his wings, if he bee to busie headed, and will alwaies be carriing his people abroade.

b. The body of attendants, armed followers, retainers, retinue, workpeople, servants, slaves; also (now less usual), crew (of a ship), troops, soldiers, 'men' (in relation to their officers). Const. *pl.*

13.. *Coer de L.* 1652 Also Robert Tourneham Gret peple with hym cam. **13..** *K. Alis.* 1032 (Bodl. MS.) All þe innes of þe toun Hadden litel foysoun þat day þat com Cleopatras So mychel poeple wiþ her was. *c* **1450** *Merlin* xxviii. 566 The kynge Bandemagn assembled his peple that he hadde xxᵐˡ. **1568** GRAFTON *Chron.* I. 42 And on a tyme goyng on huntyng, when he had lost his people, he was destroyed of Wolues. **1611** COTGR. s.v. *Mien, Il est des miens*, he is one of my seruants, people, followers. **1679** CLAVERHOUSE *Let. Earl of Linlithgow* 1 June, I mad the best retraite the confusion of our people would suffer. **1745** P. THOMAS *Jrnl. Anson's Voy.* 51 Commissioned the *Trial's* prize..with the same Commander, Officers and People. **1828** SCOTT *F.M. Perth* xii, The Douglas people are in motion on both sides of the river. **1847** G. R. GLEIG *Battle of Waterloo* II. xxx. 245 Throughout this magnificent advance the Duke was up with the foremost of his people. **1856** OLMSTED *Slave States* 659 Vegetables for the family, and for the supply of 'the people'.

c. Those to whom any one belongs; the members of one's tribe, clan, family, community, association, church, etc., collectively; esp. in public-school and university, and hence in general colloquial parlance. One's parents, brothers and sisters, or other relatives at home. ***people-in-law***, the relatives of one's wife or husband (*colloq.*). Const. as *pl.*

1382 WYCLIF *Gen.* xxv. 8 Abraham..was deed in a good elde..and he was gaderyd to his puple [**1611** was gathered to his people]. **1474** CAXTON *Chesse* II. ii. 27 And so a Quene ought to be chaste, wyse, of honest peple. **1822** C. LAMB *Let.* 23 Dec. (1935) II. 356, I rather grudge that S[outhe]y has taken up the History of your People. **1837** W. IRVING *Capt. Bonneville* III. 246, I have taught him the language of my people. **1851** CARLYLE *Sterling* II. vi. (1872) 139 Mrs. Sterling and the family had lived..with his Father's people through winter. **1886** *Hist. Sk. Foreign Missions Seventh-Day Adventists* 20/1 Eld. Lindermann after a time became estranged not only from our people but also from a large share of those whom he had been instrumental in leading to the observance of the Sabbath. **1890** WALFORD *Havoc of Smile* 11 Youths whose 'people' are so sure to be met with in Piccadilly. **1894** MRS. DYAN *All in a Man's K.* (1899) 262 John and I went down into Devonshire, for me to be introduced to my people-in-law, you know. **1897** MAX PEMBERTON in *Windsor Mag.* Jan. 267/2 A sense of freedom from the narrower control of home and people. **1900** F. VON HÜGEL *Let.* 7 July (1931) 86 But, as to the Preface, he says he would, on the one hand, even selfishly like to do so, to prevent the book seeming to appear without any support or knowledge of any of our people. **1902** *Eton Glossary* 25 Boys always speak of their relations as 'their people'. This of course is not by any means restricted to Eton. *a* **1905** *Mod. (Oxonian)* 'I shall have my people up at the Eights'. **1916** A. HUXLEY *Let.* 7 Aug. (1969) 109 I've arranged to be with my people in the country during August. **1971** 'M. INNES' *Awkward Lie* viii. 133 You know about my wife's people. **1977** *Belfast Tel.* 28 Feb. 3/7 She used to collect it [*sc.* silver paper] for the Multiple Sclerosis people, but they don't take it now.

4. a. The common people, the commonalty; the mass of the community as distinguished from the nobility and ruling or official classes. Const. as *pl.* Cf. *man of the people* s.v. MAN *sb.*[1] 18.

[**1306** *Rolls of Parlt.* I. 219/1 Pur eux & le Poeple aprendre de la foi Dieu, & faire oreisons.] *c* **1330** R. BRUNNE *Chron.* (1810) 127 To London þei him [Henry] brouht with grete solempnite. þe popille him bisouht þer kyng forto be. **1387** TREVISA *Higden* (Rolls) I. 35 Seuene persones whos dedes me writeþ in stories, þat beeþ, kyng in his rewme, knyȝt in bataile, iuge in plee, bisshop in clergie, lawefulman in þe peple, housbond in hous, religious man in chirche. **1390** GOWER *Conf.* II. 317 If I among the poeple duelle, Unto the poeple I schal it telle. *c* **1400** MAUNDEV. (Roxb.) Pref. 2 Assemblee of þe pople [*MS. C* peple] withouten lordes þat may gouerne þam es as a flokk of schepe þat has na schepe-hird. *c* **1489** CAXTON *Blanchardyn* xxxi. 116 Amonge the knyghtes & pepyll of Tourmaday. **1593** SHAKS. *3 Hen. VI*, III. iii. 35 Our People, and our Peeres, are both mis-led. **1650** *Nicholas Papers* (Camden) I. 198 The People in England are universally discontented with the daily new Taxes imposed on them. **1771** *Junius Lett.* lix. (1772) II. 264, I speak to the people as one of the people. *a* **1854** H. REED *Lect. Eng. Lit.* vii. (1878) 225 He caught the ear of the people by using the people's own speech. **1879** M. ARNOLD *G. Sand* Mixed Ess. 339 *The people* is what interested George Sand. And in France *the people* is, above all, the peasant. **1900** HOLLINGSHEAD *According to my Lights* 5 Thackeray..was not so well known in the streets as Charles Dickens—he was not so much of a 'people's man'. **1953** E. SIMON *Past Masters* IV. ii. 229 Which of them is the scion of the upper classes and which the son of the people? **1969** A. G. FRANK *Latin Amer.* xx. 328 The bourgeoisie develops at the cost of exploiting the people. **1973** *Freedomways* XIII. 11 In China, India, the Soviet Union, even in the pre-Nazi Germany of 1932 Robeson traveled, acted and sang and everywhere he met with the people. **1973** *Black Panther* 17 Nov. 9/3 If the people (and when I say 'the people' I mean the oppressed people) control Malcolm X University, if they control it without reservation or without having to answer for what is done there or who speaks there, then Malcolm X University is progressive. **1976** M. J. LASKY *Utopia & Revolution* (1977) xiv. 496 One of the essential preconditions of the establishment..of a revolutionary tradition and its associated components of utopian hope and militant temper is the creation of 'The People' as a political factor. **1977** *Private Eye* 13 May 14/3 It.. won't encourage the people to work any harder.

b. ***the people*** is sometimes contextually equivalent to 'the lay people', 'the laity', as distinguished from the clergy; although in most such cases it can be explained as = 'the congregation' (sense 2), or 'the parishioners' or 'flock' (sense 3), in relation to the priest, clergyman, or minister.

1362, **1548–9** [see sense 2]. **1548–9** *Bk. Com. Prayer, Communion*, Then shall the Prieste [1552 minister] firste receiue the Communion in both kindes himselfe, and next deliuer it to other Ministers,..and after to the people. *a* **1633** G. HERBERT *Countrey Parson* vi, Both Amen and all other answers which are on the clerk's and people's part to answer. **1879** SIMMONS *Lay Folks Mass Bk.* Introd. 18 The Church..having appointed simultaneous but separate devotions for the priest and people.

c. (Usu. with capital initial.) The prosecution in a law case as designated in certain States of the U.S.A., the equivalent of the Crown in a British law case.

1801 *Cases of Pract. Supreme Court New-York, 1791–1800* 34 Ludlow *ads.* The People. **1810** *Rep. Cases Supreme Court New-York* II. 301 The People *against* Olcott. **1849** *New York Superior Court Rep.* III. 193 J. McGay for the defendant, cited *The People v. Koeber*. **1898** *Misc. Rep. Courts of Record New York* XXV. 599 The People of the State of New York, Respondent *v.* Irving Mulkins, Appellant. **1926** *Michigan Rep.* CCXXX. 485 People v. Lorde. The people's testimony tends to show that..the defendant..went to the store of one John Kay. **1936** E. S. GARDNER *Case of Stuttering Bishop* xiv. 210 You may proceed..with the testimony in the preliminary hearing in the case of People versus Julia Branner. **1960** *California Reporter 1959* I. 245/1 People of the State of California, Plaintiff and Appellant, v. One 1952 Mercury 2-door Sedan ..Defendant, Gregorio H. Nunez, sole owner of the above described vehicle, Respondent. **1973** *N.Y. Law Jrnl.* 4 Sept. 4/7 The prosecutor mentioned that he had provided defense counsel with pre-trial statements made by the People's witnesses.

5. *Politics.* The whole body of enfranchised or qualified citizens, considered as the source of power; esp. in a democratic state, the electorate. Also used in the possessive (*spec.* in the terminology of Communism and Socialism) to designate institutions and concepts which are regarded as belonging to, derived from, or benefiting the people considered as the source of power or the basis of society. See also sense 9 below.

[*c* **1412** HOCCLEVE *De Reg. Princ.* 2886 Ffor peples vois is goddes voys, men seyne.] **1646** T. EDWARDS *Gangræna* III. 15 That all Power, Places, and Offices that are just in this Kingdom, ought only to arise from the choise and election of the people. **1648–9** *Jrnl. Ho. Comm.* 4 Jan., The Commons of England, in Parliament assembled, do Declare, That the People are, under God, the Original of all just Power. **1692** WASHINGTON tr. *Milton's Def. Pop.* M.'s Wks. 1738 I. 516 Under the word People, we comprehend all our Natives, of what Order and Degree soever; in that we have settled one Supreme Senate only, in which the Nobility also, as a part of the People..may give their Votes. **1792** GOUV. MORRIS in Sparks *Life & Writ.* (1832) II. 243 It is not possible to say, to the people or to the sea, so far shalt thou go and no farther. **1809** KENDALL *Trav.* I. vii. 50 An example, I believe solitary in the statutes, of the use of the word *people* as a body possessed of civil rights. **1811** *Weekly Reg.* 7 Sept. 9/2, I will attach myself, as an editor, to no party but the People's Party, whose wish is '*peace, liberty and safety*'. **1834** J. J. STRANG *Diary* 3 Mar. in M. M. Quaife *Kingdom of St. James* (1930) 218, I find myself nominated on what is called the people's ticket for constable. *a* **1849** EBEN. ELLIOTT '*God save the people*', When wilt Thou save the people, O God of mercy, when? **1854** C. FOX *Let.* 21 Nov. in *Jrnls.* (1972) 217 F. Maurice was much cheered by the good beginning of his People's College. **1859** MILL *Liberty* i. 12 The will of the people..practically means, the will of the most numerous or the most active part of the people;..the people consequently may desire to oppress a part of their number. **1884** *Spectator* 2 Aug. 998/2 He also accused the Government of not trusting the people, of shrinking from an appeal to the people. **1888** BRYCE *Amer. Commw.* (1890) I. xxiii. 328 The supreme law-making power is the People, that is, the qualified voters, acting in a prescribed way. **1896** *Rep. on Labor Movement U.S.A. to Internat. Socialist & T.U. Congr.* 2/2 The Socialist Labor party is steadily advancing, the so-called 'People's party'..is not less steadily passing out of sight. **1900** [see above, sense 4.]. **1927** H. DOBBS in *Lett. Gertrude Bell* II. 558 On the part of the Opposition, now definitely constituted under the name of the People's Party, with Yasin Pasha as leader, doubts were expressed as to the advantage to Iraq of the extension of the 1922 Treaty for 25 years. **1942** *Ann. Reg. 1941* 16 A number of pacifists, including leading Communists, announced that they were organising a 'People's Convention' to demand 'a People's Government' which should bring the war to an end. **1953** *Encounter* Nov. 69/1 Looking over into East Berlin, one could see only a group of six People's Police in their new grey uniforms. **1958** *Listener* 30 Oct. 682/2 The policy of adventure and provocation of People's China. **1958** *Ibid.* 25 Sept. 452/1 Lloyd George was forty-six when he introduced his 'People's' Budget. **1958** [see CO-OPERATIVE B. 2 b]. **1959** *Exchange* (N.Y. Stock Exchange) Aug. 2/1 Today we have 12,490,000 [shareholders] plus an estimated 1.4 million owners of private corporations. We have the most broadly owned, most dynamic people's capitalism ever seen on the face of the earth. **1961** *Sunday Bull.* (Philadelphia) 15 Jan. I. 5/1 Pianist Svyatoslav Richter..has been given the Soviet Union's top artistic award: 'People's Artist'. **1966** R. E. PICKERING *Himself Again* xxii. 162 This must be Bratislava. I had escaped from Hungary into Czechoslovakia... Already I imagined my stubborn silence in a windowless room with the People's Police. **1966** 'H. MACDIARMID' *Company I've Kept* v. 148 Gaeldom, but for the English, gave good promise many centuries ago of evolving an ideal 'people's state'. **1969** C. DAVIDSON in Cockburn & Blackburn *Student Power* 331 The classless society of America's 'people's capitalism'. **1972** *Buenos Aires Herald* 4 Feb. 9/4 In Buenos Aires, police continued the hunt for the 'People's Revolutionary Army' (ERP) extremists who staged the record robbery of over 400 million old pesos at the National Development Bank. **1973** *Black Panther* 21 July 7/1 Elaine Brown,..the first, genuine People's Artist America has produced. **1974** L. DEIGHTON *Spy Story* xviii. 197 It took a long time before the Russians would let the D.D.R. have submarines. But the People's Navy are all ten-year men. **1974** tr. *Sniečkus's Soviet Lithuania* 108 In recent years, an important form of ideological education—the people's universities—has become widespread. **1975** *New Yorker* 28 Apr. 99/1 When I asked one economist what models the Chinese revolution might provide for Vietnam, the man stared at me for a few moments.., and then said, 'Well, what would *you* suggest? The Cultural Revolution? People's Communes?' **1977** K. BENTON *Red Hen Conspiracy* xviii. 143 He'd have to set up..what we call a people's prison to hold the Sheikh safely.

6. a. Men or women indefinitely; men and women; persons, folk. Construed as *pl.* In phr. ***of all people***, an expression suggesting that no one more surprising could be involved.

13.. *Sir Beues* (A.) 2275 þre kinges and dukes fiue His cheualrie adoun ginneþ driue, And meche oþer peple ischent. **1362** LANGL. *P. Pl.* A. I. 7 þe moste parti of þe peple þat passeþ nou on eorþe. **1413** *Pilgr. Sowle* (Caxton 1483) IV. xxiii. 69 Lycence is nought easy to gete Spyrytes for to speken to dedely people. **1482** WARKW. *Chron.* (Camden) 5 Whereof the most peple were sory. **1605** SHAKS. *Macb.* I. vii. 33, I haue bought Golden Opinions from all sorts of people. *a* **1617** HIERON *Penance for Sin* XV. Wks. 1619–20 II. 233 They become on a sudden to be (as it were) other kind of persons and people then before they were. **1662** J. DAVIES tr. *Olearius' Voy. Ambass.* 293 The City was so depopulated, that there were not people enough left to fill the sixt part of it. **1705** STANHOPE *Paraphr.* I. 59 A Nature which cannot bear its own, and much less other Peoples Burden. **1709** STEELE *Tatler* No. 36 ¶3 'There are Some People who fancy, if Other People—' Autumn repartees; 'People may give themselves Airs; but Other People, perhaps, who make less ado, may be, perhaps, as agreeable as People who set themselves out more'. **1837** DICKENS *Pickw.* iv, The scene of action, towards which crowds of people were already pouring from a variety of quarters. **1851** S. SPENCER *Let.* 1 May (1912) 410 The *Times* yesterday contained some fine tho' rather enthusiastically loyal verses about the opening of the Exhibition by Thackeray of all people. **1922** CHESTERTON *Man who knew too Much*, Why should you, of all people, be so passionate about it? **1965** *Radio Times* 2 May 15/2 Stan and Ollie..cause some hilarious surprises when Stan becomes Lord Paddington with Ollie of all people as his manservant.

b. Often with defining words, where the singular has the distinctive *man* or *woman*: e.g. *alms-people*, applicable to *alms-men* or *alms-women*, or to both; so *coloured people*, *country-people*, *labouring people*, *lay-people*, *towns-people*, *working people*, *work-people*, *old people*, *young people*; *people of colour*, *people of quality*, etc. For these, when specific, see the qualifying element. ***good people***, formerly a courteous form of addressing an assemblage: cf. GOOD *a.* 2 c.

1429 *Rolls of Parlt.* IV. 336/2 An hole Disme of your lay poeple. **1514** BARCLAY *Cyt. & Uplondyshm.* (Percy Soc.) 5 We finde yonge people be moche improvydent. **1554** *Chron. Q. Jane* (Camden 1850) 56 Good people, I am come hether to die. *Ibid.* 57, I pray you all, good Christian people, to beare me witnesse that I dye a true Christian woman. **1625** PURCHAS *Pilgrims* IX. xii. §2 They hold that Monkies in times past were men and women, and call them in their language 'The old people'. **1667** PEPYS *Diary* 10 Apr., No more people of condition willing to live there. **1712** tr. *Pomet's Hist. Drugs* I. 148 Freely..eaten by People of Quality. **1766** GOLDSM. *Elegy Mad Dog* 1 Good people all of every sort, Give ear unto my song. **1879** SIMMONS *Lay Folks Mass Bk.* Introd. 18 It was a congregational service in which the lay people took their part in their own tongue. **1899** *Scribner's Mag.* XXV. 76/1 From daybreak..foot-people and carriages began to take up a position on the downs.

c. *emphatically.* = Human beings.

c **1450** *Merlin* 534 Ffor thei be no peple as other be, but it be fendes of helle,..ffor neuer mortall man myght do that these haue vs don. **1589** PUTTENHAM *Eng. Poesie* III. xvii. (Arb.) 191 *Raskall* is properly the hunters terme giuen to young deere, leane and out of season, and not to people. *Mod.* There were some sheep in the field, but no people.

d. *transf.* Living creatures. *poet.* or *rhet.*

a **1667** JER. TAYLOR *Serm.* (1678) II. xiii. 90 Joynts of a dead Man..fit for nothing but for the little people that creep in Graves. **1821** SHELLEY *Hellas* 523 We saw the dogfish hastening to their feast. Joy waked the voiceless people of the sea. **1899** GERTR. JEKYLL *Wood & Garden* vii, The flitting of butterflies, the hum of all the little winged people among the branches.

e. An individual, a person. *U.S. colloq.*

1926 J. Black *You can't Win* ix. 105 He's good people and I want to get him fixed up for a cell with the right folks. **1934** *Detective Fiction Weekly* 28 Apr. 113/1 'Stick yer four-bits in yer shoe', he snorted, 'I'm people.' **1949** 'N. R. Nash' *Young & Fair* I. ii. 14, I guess she's people of good heart. **1956** B. Holiday *Lady sings Blues* (1973) x. 98 A lot of creeps have been dogging Orson Welles ever since but they can't touch him. He's a fine cat... And a talented cat. But more than that, he's fine people.

7. Unemphatically, *people* becomes quasi-pronominal (cf. *a man*, MAN *sb.* 4 g), equivalent in the nominative to F. *on*, Ger. *man*, but having a corresponding objective and possessive; e.g. 'people say that he is extravagant', 'cabs waiting to bring people back', 'to give people what they want', 'one who can read people's thoughts'. In this sense *people* has in colloquial use taken the place of *men* ('men say', etc.); but in early ME. *the people* (= F. *l'on*) seems to have had a similar use.

c **1275** *On Serving Christ* 62 in *O.E. Misc.* 92 þer he polede pyne as þe peple me tolde. **1377** Langl. *P. Pl.* B. II. 214 Ac marchantz..apparailled hym as a prentice þe poeple to serue. **1599** Shaks. *Much Ado* II. i. 266 A man may liue as quiet in hell, as in a sanctuary, and people sinne vpon purpose, because they would go thither. **1600** —— *A. Y. L.* II. iii. 5 Why are you vertuous? why do people loue you? **1606** —— *Ant. & Cl.* I. i. 54 Wee'l..note The qualities of people. **1696** Prior *Secretary* 16 But why should I stories of Athens rehearse, Where people knew love, and were partial to verse? **17..** Swift *Misc.* (J.), People were tempted to lend by great premiums and large interest. **1843** J. H. Newman *Lett.* (1891) II. 425 People cannot understand a man being in a state of doubt. **1871** Morley *Crit. Misc.* Ser. I. *Carlyle* (1878) 163 Excess, on the other side, leads people into emotional transports.

8. *attrib.* and *Comb.*, as ***people-organ, -pleaser, -worship***; ***people-blinding, -born, -centred, -devouring, -oriented, -pestered*** adjs.; **people-king** [tr. L. *populus rex*, F. *peuple-roi*], a sovereign people; **people mover**, any of several means of conveying people from one place to another; **people power**, (*a*) physical effort exerted by people, as opp. to machines, etc.; (*b*) political or other pressure exercised (or app. exercised) by the people, esp. through the public demonstration of popular opinion; **people sniffer**, a device that can detect the presence of a person by chemical analysis of the air around him (see also quot. 1977); **people-state**, a democracy.

1822 R. Pollok in D. Pollok *Life* 151, I saw no *people-blinding farce kept up. **1968** *Guardian* 5 Aug. 6/6 The interests of Africa will be best served..by a *people-centred system, and African socialism is that system. **1970** *Ibid.* 23 Dec. 7/4 There is such a gulf between books that are system-centred and those that are people-centred. **1848** Buckley *Iliad* 9 A *people-devouring king art thou. **1796** Burke *Regic. Peace* i. Wks. VIII. 113 That Great Britain should..bid with the rest, for the mercy of the *people-king. **1813** tr. *Pouqueville* 125 In the estimation of these barbarians, the name of Romans, of the *people-king*, is equivalent to that of vassal or slave. **1822** T. Mitchell *Aristoph.* II. p. vi, A dramatic tetralogue, developing, in the author's peculiar manner, his idea of a people-king. **1866** Motley in *Corr.* (1889) II. 239 A Hapsburg is not like a People-King, which cannot, save by annihilation, die. **1971** J. P. Romualdi in *Science Year 1972* 375 A '*people mover', a vehicle smaller than a streetcar..will provide continuous service between the old campus in town and the new campus in the suburbs. **1972** *N.Y. Times* 1 June 30/1 Henry Ford 2d announced yesterday that the Ford Motor Company would build rapid-transit systems based on its driverless, rubber-tired people mover system being demonstrated at the Transpo '72 exhibition here. **1974** *Times* 22 Mar. (Buses Suppl.) p. i/2 Magnetic levitation, vacuum tubes, vertical take-off aircraft, and small-scale automatic and semi-automatic 'people-movers' of all kinds for urban situations. **1851** Mrs. Browning *Casa Guidi W.* I. 814 This..teacher will..build the golden pipes and synthesize This *people-organ for a holy strain. **1970** *New Society* 5 Mar. 392/2 They exhibited the familiar *people-oriented value-pattern detected many times among prospective teachers. **1975** *Nature* 27 Nov. 286/1 What more logical project for a rebuilt people-oriented science programme than to attempt to predict earthquakes. **1557** Grimalde *Lover to his Dear* 15 in *Tottell's Misc.* (Arb.) 97 *Peeplepesterd London lykes thee nought. **1579–80** North *Plutarch* (1657) 31 He..meaneth now no more a King or a Prince, but becometh a *People-pleaser, or a cruell tyrant. **1976** *National Observer* (U.S.) 25 Sept. 17/1 Kiceniuk figures it will take a ground speed of 19 or 20 m.p.h. to get the craft airborne with *people power. **1983** *Washington Post* 4 Sept. A31 Leaders of the People Power Party..agreed on the overriding objective of restoring free democratic process. **1984** *Times* 4 July 12/4 Dr Tony Gibson..a long-standing proponent of Quaker ideals and what he calls 'people power'. **1965** *Daily Tel.* 5 Oct. 22/8 A person being examined is placed in a '*people sniffer', a glass cylinder, and an analysis of the outgoing air discloses the chemical make-up of the subject. **1968** *N.Y. Times* 18 Aug. I. 3 United States troops refer to the gadget as the 'people sniffer'. It leads American officers here in the Mekong delta to enemy hide-outs by 'sniffing out' the kind of ammonia odors given off by the human body. **1973** *Times* 24 Jan. 8/6 There has been use of the Manpack Personnel Detector, or 'people-sniffer'—picking up the enemy by the smell of his sweat. **1977** *Time* 2 May 44/1 Their principal piece of equipment is a 'people sniffer', an electronic sensing device developed to catch the prowling Viet Cong. Despite its name, the instrument actually detects the minute seismic vibrations caused by a person walking. **1605** Sylvester *Du Bartas* II. iii. IV. *Captains* 1200 The *People-State, the Aristocracy, And sacred Kingdom, took authority A-like from Heav'n. **1881** C. Wordsw. in Overton & E. Wordsw. *Life* (1888) 332 A general fête of *people-worship, by the people themselves.

9. Special combs. with *people's* (chiefly in sense 5): **people's army**, (*a*) an army organized on egalitarian or communist principles; (*b*) an army composed of the common people; **People's Bureau**, the official name for a foreign embassy of the Libyan Arab Republic; **people's car**, an inexpensive motor car designed for popular sale; **people's choice**, a popular favourite; **People's Court**, (*a*) a court set up by the Nazi regime in Germany to deal with political offences; (*b*) a court in the Soviet and similar legal systems; also *transf.*; **people's democracy**, a political system in which power is regarded as being invested in the people, *spec.* a Communist state, esp. in Eastern Europe; **People's front** = POPULAR FRONT; **People's Palace**, a centre for the recreation and entertainment of the people, *spec.* a former East London institution with library, theatre, educational classes, etc., opened in 1887; also *fig.*; **people's park**, a park intended to be used by all members of a community; **People's Power** = *people power* (b), sense 8 above; *spec.* a name given in certain countries to a political party claiming to represent the interests of the people; **people's republic**, name assumed by a number of left-wing or Communist states, as *People's Republic of China*; also in gen. allusive use; **people's theatre**, a theatre run on socialist lines for the use of the community; **people's war**, (*a*) a war in which the people are regarded as fighting against the ruling classes or foreign aggression; (*b*) a war in which all members of the community are involved, a total war.

1937 E. Snow *Red Star over China* VI. i. 211 The Kuominchun, the '*People's Army' of General Feng Yu'hsiang. **1941** 'G. Orwell' *Coll. Ess.* (1968) II. 116 The Home Guard is..a sort of People's Army officered by Blimps. **1969** A. G. Frank *Latin Amer.* xxiv 366 Nowhere does Debray suggest how the guerrilla band is later to develop into the people's army. **1970** A. Sinclair *Guevara* iii. 37 The regular army must be disbanded and a people's army created..of peasants and workers and soldiers. [**1980** *Washington Post* 15 Jan. A16 Muammar Qaddafi has called on Americans living in his country to march on their embassy and turn it into a 'people's bureau'.] **1981** *N.Y. Times* 20 Aug. 1/5 Last May the Reagan Administration shut the so-called Libyan's *People's Bureau in Washington after accusations that the bureau was involved in finding and killing anti-Qaddafi exiles in the United States. **1986** *Ibid.* 1 May A8/4 People working for five Italian concerns had been asked to leave following Italy's decision..to cut the staff of the Libyan People's Bureau in Rome by 10. **1938** *Sun* (Baltimore) 7 Sept. 1/1 Award winners are Prof. Ferdinand Porsche, designer of the 'Volkswagen', Germany's new '*people's car'. **1939** *War Illustr.* 4 Nov. p. iii/1 A scheme by which German artisans paid in advance by weekly instalments for their long-promised 'people's car' would appear to have fallen through, for the great works at Fallersleben, the supposed factory for these cars, are now stated to be turning out munitions. **1958** [see BUBBLE *sb.* 2 c]. **1972** *Buenos Aires Herald* 2 Feb. 7/6 The rise of nationalism has brought demands for inexpensive 'people's cars' in Chile, Peru and Venezuela. **1953** Wodehouse *Performing Flea* 205 In Dormitory 309 the *People's Choice was good old George Travers. **1961** —— *Service with Smile* (1962) v. 80 'Why is he the people's choice?' 'Because she's got the goods on him.' **1934** H. Griffith *People's Court* 9 Comrade Chernov only turned up just in time yesterday not to make the *People's Court look ridiculous in the eyes of its clients. **1935** *Ann. Reg. 1934* I. 191 A law of May 3 constituted a new and extraordinary Court of Justice, the so-called People's Court, for all political offences. This tribunal as well as the old regular courts in numerous cases passed excessively severe sentences on opponents of the Government. **1938** *Ann. Reg. 1937* 181 In April the People's Court sentenced several Catholic priests to long periods of detention. **1946** *Ann. Reg. 1945* 205 Twenty-four People's Courts were established by Decree in Bohemia and Moravia. **1970** H. Trevelyan *Middle East in Revolution* 145 The notorious Colonel Medhawi, a cousin of Qasim, presided over the People's Court [in Iraq]. **1972** *N.Y. Law Jrnl.* 10 Oct. 1/5 The three-level federal system which emerged was composed of People's Courts with jurisdiction in rural areas; Regional Courts which are courts of first and second instance with appellate jurisdiction; and the Supreme Courts which are divided on a territorial basis into Supreme Courts of the autonomous republics, Union Republics and the U.S.S.R. **1977** *Listener* 15 Dec. 779/1 The Provisionals are now attempting to develop 'People's Courts'. **1947** *New Times* 3 Dec. 3 (*heading*) The *people's democracies—a fresh breach in the imperialist system. *Ibid.* 4/2 In the people's democracies, power has passed from the hands of the exploiting classes—the landlords and bourgeoisie—into the hands of the people. **1958** F. W. Neal *Titoism in Action* i. 1 The Communist leadership which came to power in Yugoslavia in 1945 organized the country along the lines prescribed by the Soviet Union for an Eastern European 'people's democracy'. **1974** *Times* 22 Jan. 14/2 Mr Jack Jones..made an unfortunate remark about his desire to see Britain become a People's Democracy, which is the title given to those Eastern European states which have nothing to do with the people and are not democratic; but it turned out that he meant, not a People's Democracy but a people's democracy, which is not at all the same thing and better hadn't be. **1977** P. Johnson *Enemies of Society* viii. 109 Social democrat means a Right-wing anti-Communist politician of the centre; a People's Democracy or a People's Democratic Republic is a form of Communist totalitarian state. **1937** 'G. Orwell' *Coll. Ess.* (1968) I. 271 The worker and the bourgeois..are fighting side by side. This uneasy alliance is known as the Popular Front (or, in the Communist press, to give it a spuriously democratic appeal, *People's Front). **1937** E. Snow *Red Star over China* III. iii. 99 If the Chinese People's Front is powerfully homogeneous ..the war will be short. **1958** *Spectator* 13 June 777/3 Mr. Grant's badly camouflaged appeal for a new People's Front. **1854** *Punch* 24 June 266/1 The *People's Palace will become a misnomer if the people are so confined in workshops [etc.] ..that none but the comparatively idle can visit what is expressly designed for the appreciation of the industrious. **1889** G. B. Shaw *London Music 1888–89* (1937) 210 Covent Garden is a people's palace compared with Bayreuth. **1890** Hardy *Let.* 13 Mar. (1978) I. 210 We cannot do better than what you propose—purchase a library of fiction for the People's Palace. **1892** Zangwill *Childr. Ghetto* I. 231 The Club was the People's Palace of the Ghetto. **1964** D. Owen *Eng. Philanthropy* (1965) III. x. 293 In the early 1930's the original People's Palace was destroyed by fire. It was rebuilt and since 1954 has formed a part of Queen Mary College of London University. **1967** *Guardian* 29 July 12/4 Sir John Wardlaw-Milne..has left £100,000 to the State of Jersey.. to build a 'people's palace' where tourists with children can shelter on wet days. **1970** E. J. Hirst *Seeing Glasgow* 41 The Old Glasgow Museum, People's Palace, Glasgow Green, provides a visual record of the development of Glasgow. The City's history is shown in pictures and prints. **1971** P. J. Keating *Working Classes in Victorian Fiction* iv. 96 The People's Palace was built in Whitechapel... In May 1887 the Queen travelled to the Mile End Road to declare the Palace officially open. **1975** *Scottish Field* Mar. 44/1 (*caption*) A bowl traditionally attributed to the old Delftfield pottery, now in the People's Palace Museum, Glasgow. *Ibid.* 45/1 It could mean more interest being taken in the People's Palace exhibit. **1863** Dickens *Uncomm. Trav.* (1866) xxiii. 163/1 The *People's Park near Birmingham.. was crowded with people from the Black Country. **1873** C. M. Yonge *Pillars of House* III. xxiv. 8 One of the brothers took her out in the street, or to the 'People's Park'. **1963** *Guardian* 19 Nov. 9/7 Rumford..suggested..in 1789 the laying-out of a great 'people's park' along the Isar. **1970** *Time* 23 Nov. 81 Last year he [*sc.* the chancellor of Berkeley] was unfairly blamed for the way police handled student demands that one of the university's empty lots be turned into a 'people's park'. **1976** *Times* 4 Sept. 10/5 In Bremen's 'people's park' the food is tasty. **1978** *Washington Post* 8 Apr. A17/2 Spokesmen for the opposition *People's Power slate, said..that they still hoped to win some of the 21 assembly seats being contested in Manila. **1980** *Summary World Broadcasts: Soviet Union* (B.B.C.) 17 June A3/2 They are clearly trying to dispatch the diehards into Kampuchea to continue their bandit raids against people's power. **1986** *Courier-Mail* (Brisbane) 23 Aug. 8/5 The 80-member commission was set up soon after President Aquino came to power after the February 'people's power' revolution. **1949** *Times* 8 Apr. 5/3 Mr. Rákosi..said..that 'the Hungarian Republic must be developed into a *People's Republic'. **1972** J. Poyer *Chinese Agenda* (1973) vi. 63 The khaki uniforms and green collar tabs of the Army of the People's Republic of China. **1974** *Encycl. Brit. Micropædia* III. 80/2 Congo (Brazzaville) *Official name*: République Populaire du Congo (People's Republic of the Congo). **1975** *Bangladesh Times* 18 July 2/6 The Magura Journalists Association in a meeting held recently at Magura hailed the Government of the People's Republic of Bangladesh for creating the new district of Magura. **1978** Ld. Hailsham *Dilemma of Democracy* xxii. 148 Probably our own monarch would not survive the institution in Britain of..a people's republic. **1920** D. H. Lawrence *Touch & Go* 5 A nice phrase: 'A People's Theatre'. But what about it? There's no such thing in existence as a *People's Theatre. **1929** S. W. Cheney *Theatre* xxii. 506 In Germany a real 'democratic' theatre was developed before the war, and today functions as a 'people's theatre' of a unique sort. It is, perhaps, historically important as a step toward a theatre for a new Socialistic time. The *Volksbühne* in Berlin is owned by its audiences. **1904** L. Hale (*title*) The '*People's War' in France 1870–1871. **1942** E. Waugh *Put out More Flags* i. 86 This is all that anyone talks about, thought Ambrose; jobs and the kind of war it is going to be..people's war, total war, indivisible war, war infinite, war incomprehensible. **1947** J. Bertram *Shadow of War* 9 'How about China's United Front?' I tried to tell them of what I had seen of this people's war. **1968** K. Martin *Editor* xv. 301 It was not until after Dunkirk that the idea of a People's War began to be understood. **1972** P. Black *Biggest Aspidistra* II. v. 133 The broadcasts did not cheat; the voices and sentiments were those of the people's war. **1976** M. Green *Children of Sun* viii. 311 Official propaganda presented this as a 'people's war', and emphasised the proletarian ordinariness of its heroes.

Hence **peopleize** (ˈpiːp(ə)laɪz) *v. nonce-wd.*, to render popular in character; † **ˈpeopleship** *Obs.*, the position of a commoner, plain citizenship; **peoplet** (ˈpiːplɪt), a small people, nation, or tribe.

1865 E. Burritt *Walk Land's End* vi. 208 The Established Church could not do a better thing to begin with, than to **peopleise* these magnificent edifices [the cathedrals] committed to its trust. I cannot say *popularise*, because a kind of flashy significance attaches to that word. **1650** B. *Discolliminium* 48 If I be an Esquire, I will sell my Esquireship to any honest man for a good *People-ship. **1872** R. Black tr. *Guizot's Hist. Fr.* I. 3 A *peoplet [Fr. *peuplade*] distinct from all its neighbours in features, costume, and especially language. **1880** *Episodes Fr. Hist.* 9 Charlemagne had still..much rigour to exercise in Saxony, including the removal of certain Saxon peoplets out of their country.

people (ˈpiːp(ə)l), *v.* Forms: see prec. [a. F. *peupler*, in OF. *popler*, *puepler*, *pupler* (12th c. in Hatz.-Darm.), f. *peuple*: see prec.]

1. *trans.* To furnish or fill with people or inhabitants; to populate.

c **1500** *Melusine* 18 And he began within her land..for to byld & make fayre tounes & strong Castels, and was the land within short tyme peupled raisonably. **1599** Shaks. *Much Ado* II. iii. 251 The world must be peopled. **1604** E. G[rimstone] *D'Acosta's Hist. Indies* IV. vi. 219 The force of Silver..hath peopled this mountaine more than any other place in all these Kingdomes. **1696** Whiston *Th. Earth* II.

(1722) 137 The nearest Regions must have been first and most fully peopled. **1766** Reid *Let.* Wks. I. 47/1 Our College is very well peopled this session. **1840** Thirlwall *Greece* VII. lix. 369 Seleucus founded his new capital.. Antiochia, peopling it with the inhabitants of Antigonia.

b. *transf.* To fill or stock (with animals, inanimate objects, etc.).

a **1533** Ld. Berners *Gold. Bk. M. Aurel.* (1546) Kk, O gybet.. thou arte peopled with innocentis. **1644** G. Plattes in *Hartlib's Legacy* (1655) 247 It lasts three or four.. years in the ground, according as the ground is good, and (at first) well peopled with it. **1837** J. W. Croker in *C. Papers* 8 Feb., Our influenza.. continues somehow to people the churchyards.

c. *fig.* To imagine, or represent, as peopled.

1817–18 Shelley *Ros. & Helen* 147 This silent spot tradition old Had peopled with the spectral dead. *a* **1854** H. Reed *Lect. Brit. Poets* (1857) II. xi. 87 That region which his genius has peopled with spiritual creations. **1879** Proctor *Pleas. Ways Sc.* x. 199 The fancies of men have peopled three of the four.. elements.. with strange forms of life.

2. To fill or occupy as inhabitants; to inhabit; to constitute the population of (a country, etc.).

c **1489** Caxton *Sonnes of Aymon* vi. 150 Ye sholde have see come there knyghtes, gentylmen, burgeys,.. yomen,.. so that this castell was pepled of all maner of folke. **1606** G. W[oodcocke] *Hist. Ivstine* xxxviii. 120 There is no difference between the Frenchmen that inhabit Asia, and the Frenchmen that people Italy. *a* **1727** Newton *Chronol. Amended* i. (1728) 106 The people of Caria.. began to frequent the Greek seas, and people some of the Islands therein. **1732** Pope *Ess. Man* i. 27 What vary'd Being peoples every star. **1854** Bright *Sp., Russia* 31 Mar. (1876) 236 The thousand millions of human beings who.. people this planet.

b. *transf.* and *fig.* of animals, inanimate objects, etc.

1593 Shaks. *Rich. II*, v. v. 9 These same Thoughts, people this Little World. **1611** Beaum. & Fl. *King and no K.* i. i, I.. have sent The pride of all his youth to people graves. **1632** Milton *Penseroso* 8 As thick and numberless As the gay motes that people the Sun Beams. **1805** W. Saunders *Min. Waters* 224 The variety of marine productions that people this element. **1865** Kingsley *Herew.* viii, The heroes of Troy, Alexander and his generals, peopled her imagination.

†**c.** *absol.* To settle down as inhabitants or colonists; to form a settlement. *Obs.*

1596 Raleigh *Discov. Gviana* 19 Ieronimo Ortal de Saragosa, with 130 soldiers.. was cast with the currant on the coast of Paria, and peopled about S. Miguell de Neueri. **1604** E. G[rimstone] *D'Acosta's Hist. Indies* vii. v. 508 Many talked of peopling there, and to passe no farther.

3. *intr.* (for *refl.*) To become filled or occupied with people; to grow populous.

1659 Heylin *Examen Hist.* i. 108 The world had peopled very slowly.. if Eve had not twinned at least at every birth. **1796** Morse *Amer. Geog.* I. 355 This state [Vermont] is rapidly peopling. **1892** *Home Missionary* (N.Y.) July 155 Not being on the line of a railroad, it has not peopled so fast as Creede.

peopled ('piːp(ə)ld), *ppl. a.* [f. prec. vb. + -ed¹.] Occupied by people; full of inhabitants; inhabited. Also *fig.*

1509 Hawes *Past. Pleas.* xliv. (Percy Soc.) 217 Octavyan.. Throughe the worlde and the peopled preace Letters had sent. **1591** Shaks. *Two Gent.* v. iv. 3 This shadowy desart.. I better brooke then flourishing peopled Townes. **1598** Hakluyt *Voy.* I. 5 The first peopled land that he had found since his departure from his owne dwelling. **1686** Dryden *Elegy Mrs. A. Killigrew* 126 When the peopled ark the whole creation bore. **1712** Addison *Spect.* No. 519 ¶ 2 Every part of Matter is peopled: Every green Leaf swarms with Inhabitants. **1844** Stanley *Arnold* (1858) I. vii. 324 To present to one's mind a peopled landscape.

b. with advbs.

1588 Parke tr. *Mendoza's Hist. China* 200 The suburbes.. was so well peopled. **1604** E. G[rimstone] tr. *D'Acosta's Hist. Indies* iii. xix. 178 At this day we see it lesse peopled. **1790** Burke *Fr. Rev.* 191 England, the best-peopled part of the united kingdom. **1841** W. Spalding *Italy & It. Isl.* III. 173 Cremona.. a large city not half peopled. **1859** Jephson *Brittany* xv. 251 The country.. was hilly.. and thickly peopled.

†'**peopledom.** *Obs.* [f. people *sb.* after *kingdom.*] A province, commune, deme (usually with reference to ancient Greece); also, the dominion of a people, a democracy.

1657 Earl Monm. tr. *Paruta's Pol. Disc.* 119 Greece.. was divided into many several Peopledoms. **1659** J. Harrington *Lawgiving* iii. iv. (1700) 460 The (δημοι) Peopledoms or Prytanys of Athens, which Theseus gather'd into one body. **1660** Bonde *Scut. Reg.* 333 It is the people now which make the King; if so, why ever had we any Kingdoms? why were they not called Peopledoms? **1711** E. Ward *Vulg. Brit.* vii. 80 And hope the Kingdom will become, In time, a glorious Peopledom.

'**peoplehood.** [f. people *sb.* + -hood.] The condition or state of being a people; the consciousness or awareness of being a people.

1909 in Webster. **1969** V. Ferdinand in A. Chapman *New Black Voices* (1972) 379 We the young birds of blk poetics throw our songs brilliant Against the beautiful black sky of an emerging peoplehood & with the love of us.. in our hearts. **1971** *Jrnl. Ecumenical Stud.* VIII. i. 53 This need not.. lead to a kind of reductionism which limits the significance of attempts to find historical embodiment for the biblical notion of peoplehood. **1973** *Black World* Mar. 71 For Gwen Brooks, peoplehood or race is not limited to continental boundaries. *Ibid.* Apr. 87 A sense of peoplehood is growing. **1977** *Guardian Weekly* 31 July 7/2 The mini-State, as the Palestinians conceive it, is not just a matter of territory. It is a recognition.. of their peoplehood.

'**peopleless,** *a.* [f. as peopledom + -less.] Having no people or population; uninhabited.

1621 Lady M. Wroth *Urania* 115 Delos.. once rich and populous, now poore and peoplelesse. **1643** T. Case *Serm.* in Kerr *Covenants & Cov.* (1895) 248 Thy sword hath made many a faithful minister peopleless. **1855** R. Chambers in *Chamb. Jrnl.* IV. 185/1 All seemed as desolate and peopleless as when Ingolf first approached the island.

peopler ('piːplə(r)). [f. people *v.* + -er¹.] One who peoples or causes the peopling of a country; a colonizer; an inhabitant.

1604 E. G[rimstone] tr. *D'Acosta's Hist. Indies* iii. ix. 149, I have knowne.. the Gennerall Jerome Costilla, the auntient peopler of Cusco. *Ibid.* vii. ii. 498 The second peoplers.. came from other farre countries. **1692** O. Walker *Grk. & Rom. Hist.* 63 *note*, Cham, the Son of Noah, and Peopler of Africa. **1841** Lane *Arab. Nts.* III. 137 Where are the kings and the peoplers of the earth? **1872** Blackie *Lays Highl.* 96 Peoplers of the peaceful glen.

fig. **1821** *Examiner* 627/1 Greek mythology is the religion of our poetry, the peopler of our starry spheres.

peopling ('piːplɪŋ), *vbl. sb.* [f. as prec. + -ing¹.] The action of the vb. people; settling with or occupation by people or inhabitants.

1572 (*title*) A Letter sent by I. B... wherin is conteined a large discourse of the peopling & inhabiting.. the Ardes, and other adiacent [countries] in the North of Ireland. **1690** Locke *Govt.* ii. v. §36 In the.. first Peopling of the World. **1881** W. G. Marshall *Thro' Amer.* iv. 94 The peopling of America is proceeding at a great rate. **1885** J. Ball in *Jrnl. Linn. Soc.* XXII. 23 The peopling of the Antarctic lands with their characteristic generic types [of plants].

b. *concr.* Population. *rare.*

1834 *New Monthly Mag.* XLI. 415 Next in degree amongst the rural peopling stands 'the bold yeoman'.

†**peoplish,** *a. Obs. rare*$^{-1}$. In 5 pepelyssh, poeplissh. [f. *poeple*, people *sb.* + -ish¹.] Plebeian, clownish, vulgar.

c **1374** Chaucer *Troylus* iv. 1677 Euery thing þat souned in-to badde, As rudenesse an pepelyssh [*v.r.* poeplissh] appetit.

†**peoplish,** *v. Obs. rare*$^{-0}$. [f. people *sb.* + -ish².] *trans.* To people.

1530 Palsgr. 655/2, I peplysshe, I fyll or store with people, *je peuple*... The towne is nat all thynge so bygge as Yorke, but it is better peoplysshed.

pease, obs form of pease.

peotomy (piː'ɒtəmɪ). *Surg.* [f. Gr. πέος penis + -τομια cutting.] Amputation of the penis.

1890 in *Cent. Dict.* **1893** in *Syd. Soc. Lex.*

peow-wow, variant of pow-wow.

pep (pɛp), *sb. colloq.* (orig. *U.S.*). [Abbrev. pepper *sb.*] Vigour, energy, spirit, forcefulness.

1912 *Collier's* 13 Apr. 19/1 'Sure, the good old pep,' interposed Callahan. **1916** *Daily Colonist* (Victoria, B.C.) 19 July 9/4 (Advt.), This newest Overland Four has more power, pep, punch, and speed than any other low priced.. car. **1923** Wodehouse *Inimitable Jeeves* xv. 187 That seems to be all the poor fish is able to do, dash it. He can chafe all right, but there he stops. He's lost his pep. He's got no dash. **1930** R. Macaulay *Staying with Relations* iv. 56 What a family!.. They don't have any *pep*. Only little Meg has pep and *she* won't be let grow up with it. **1930** E. Pound *XXX Cantos* xi. 51 And came back with no pep in him. **1931** E. F. Benson *Mapp & Lucia* ix. 234 A new hanging committee.. full of pep and pop and vim. **1972** *Jrnl. Social Psychol.* LXXXVIII. 279 Lively, active, full-of-pep, energetic, peppy, vigorous, activated.

2. *attrib.* and *comb.*, as **pep rally** *U.S.*, a meeting to inspire enthusiasm, esp. before a sporting event; **pep speech** = pep talk. See also pep pill, pep talk.

1945 *Boulder* (Colorado) *Daily Camera* 24 Nov. 4/2 Speaking at a pep rally.. Dr. Allen told his audience.. other schools are spending money for players. **1974** *State* (Columbia, S. Carolina) 15 Feb. 3-B/1 University of South Carolina cheerleaders will conduct a pre-game pep rally in Carolina Coliseum Saturday beginning 12:15 as a prelude to the USC-Notre Dame battle. **1977** *New Yorker* 27 June 35/1 Some activity at the college—a pep rally, a football game, a dance. **1946** D. Hamson *We fell among Greeks* vi. 73, I thought of all the 'pep' speeches we would have to deliver.

pep, *v. colloq.* [f. the sb.] (Const. *up.*) *trans.* To fill or inspire with energy or vigour, to enliven, invigorate, excite, cheer up. Also (*rare*) *intr.*, to improve, to find new life. So '**pepped-up** *ppl. a.*; **pepper-'up, pepper-'upper,** someone who or something which enlivens or stimulates; **pepping-'up** *vbl. sb.*

1925 H. L. Foster *Trop. Tramp with Tourists* 56 'Just leave them to me,' said the Social Manager. 'I'll get them started, and all pepped up, and the rest will be easy.' **1928** *Daily Express* 30 Nov. 19 University athletics are undergoing a strenuous process of 'pepping up', on strictly scientific lines. **1929** J. P. McEvoy *Hollywood Girl* ii. 28, I was all pepped up about going out there [*sc.* to Hollywood] until I met you the other night. **1931** W. Holtby *Poor Caroline* vi. 202 Keep it vivid. Pep it up with a bit o' farce. **1936** 'P. Quentin' *Puzzle for Fools* iv. 24 We all had our daily treatments and mine consisted of a thorough pepping up. **1936** *Scrutiny* V. iii. 270 Our ears are periodically offended by the ghastly and blasphemous harmonic monstrosities perpetrated by the popular peppers-up of Ye Olde Englysshe Folke Musicke. **1937** *N.Y. Post* 29 Jan. 24/3 (Advt.), Pepperupper. **1938** in Mencken *Amer. Lang.* Suppl. (1945) I. 259 A *cocktail* was therefore what I suppose today would be called a *pepper-upper*. **1945** [see hot rod]. **1959** *Encounter* Sept. 13/1 A kind of forced jollity of a pepped-up Government White Paper. **1965** Leitner & Lanen *Dict. French & Eng. Slang* 98/1 *Pepper-upper*, stimulant. **1967** N. Freeling *Strike Out* 71 You're looking a bit peaked, old chap... Have a drink to pep you up. **1971** *Daily Tel.* 19 Oct. 15/2 These 'insert' tiles are the newest idea to pep up a block of solid colour. **1972** W. P. McGivern *Caprifoil* (1973) iii. 62 A chemical intoxication that stemmed from pepped-up endocrines. **1976** *Time* 20 Dec. 40/1 To pep up sluggish sales, American Motors Corp. is offering a $253 rebate to customers who purchase its 1977 compact Pacer.

†**pe'pastic,** *a.* and *sb. Obs. rare*$^{-0}$. [= F. *pépastique*, mod.L. *pepasticum*, app. for *pepantic-um*, fr. Gr. πεπαντικός having the quality of ripening or softening; but cf. Gr. πεπασμός (Hippocrates) = πέπανσις concoction.] **a.** *adj.* Having the quality of ripening or digesting; digestive. **b.** *sb.* A medicine that assists digestion, a digestive. So †**pe'pastical** *a. Obs. rare*$^{-1}$.

1657 Tomlinson *Renou's Disp.* 699 The temperate Medicament is truly pepastical. **1706** Phillips, *Pepasticks*, Medicines that digest and allay Rawness in the Stomach, etc. **1842** Dunglison *Med. Lex.*, *Pepastic*, a medicine supposed to have the power of favouring the concoction of diseases; maturative.

pepe, obs. form of peep.

peperine ('pɛpərɪn), *a. rare.* Also pip-. [f. next.] Consisting or composed of peperino.

1756 Watson in *Phil. Trans.* XLIX. 500 On the floor there were.. bones, which were included in four pieces of the piperine stone. **1826** *New Monthly Mag.* XVI. 250 The beasts.. had crept into every.. peperine cave they could meet with.

‖**peperino** (pɛpə'riːnəʊ). *Geol.* Also piperno, piperino. [It. *peperino*, in Florio *piperigno*, dial. *piperno*, f. *pepere* pepper: so called from its consisting of small grains.] A light porous volcanic rock or tuff, usually of a brown colour, formed of sand, cinders, etc. cemented together: a name first given to the tufas of Monte Albano near Rome.

1777 Hamilton in *Phil. Trans.* LXVIII. 3 The stone in general use for building here, is.. a hard volcanic tuffa.. of the sort called Piperno in Italy. **1794** Sullivan *View Nat.* II. 197 Tufa, peperino, or piperno. **1796** Kirwan *Elem. Min.* (ed. 2) I. 415 *Piperino*.. seems a concretion of volcanic ashes. **1879** Rutley *Study Rocks* xii. 233 The piperno of Pianura, near Naples. **1882** Geikie *Geol. Sk.* 111 We took refuge in a little cave in the calcareous peperino.

peperite ('pɛpəraɪt). *Geol.* [ad. F. *pépérite* (P. L. A. Cordier *Mémoire sur les Substances minérales dites 'en Masse'* (1815) ix. 66), prob. f. *pépér(ine* peperino + *-ite* -ite¹.] A brecciated volcanic material consisting of fragments of lava and sedimentary rock, regarded by some as formed by the intrusion of lava into wet sediment, freq. under water, and by others as a product of the mixing of volcanic ejectamenta with such sediments. Cf. peperino.

1839 *Civil Engin. & Arch. Jrnl.* II. 195/1 The geological structure of Mr. Hamilton's line of route is simple, being composed of only schistose rocks,.. tertiary sandstones and limestones, granite, peperite, trachyte, basalt, and other igneous rocks. **1903** A. Geikie *Text-bk. Geol.* (ed. 4) II. 1254 These intercalations of tuff from the 'Peperites' of Auvergne, regarding which so much difference of opinion has been expressed. **1953** *Prof. Papers U.S. Geol. Survey* No. 454-B. 4/2 On Unalaska, pillows are separated from each other by peperite, fragmental igneous rock, argillite, or crustified chalcedony and quartz... Peperite is a mottled light-gray to pale-green breccia of mixed sedimentary and primary igneous debris. **1969** *Proc. Geologists' Assoc.* LXXX. 177 It is concluded that the peperites [of the Auvergne] are the product of explosive projection of basaltic ejectamenta into steadily accumulating lime-mud.

‖**Peperomia** (pɛpə'rəʊmɪə). *Bot.* [mod.L., f. Gr. πέπερι pepper.] A large genus of herbaceous plants of the pepper family (*Piperaceæ*), found in warm climates, bearing spikes of minute flowers, and in some species ornamental foliage.

1882 *Garden* 15 July 41/3 Very few of the Peperomias are worthy of general culture. **1896** *Westm. Gaz.* 18 Feb. 3/3 Covered with soft green moss and quantities of peperomias, begonias, and ferns of all possible different shapes.

peperoni, var. pepperoni.

pepful ('pɛpfʊl), *a. colloq.* [f. pep *sb.* + -ful.] Full of life or verve, vigorous.

1923 *Weekly Dispatch* 22 Apr. 5 The film is.. an American conception of the novel, with Richard Dix as a 'pep-ful' parson hero. **1933** *Punch* 29 Mar. 359/2 Mr. Joe Hayman's all-too-brief appearance as the hustling pepful American manager was, as usual, delightful.

pepin, obs. form of pippin.

†**pepinnier.** *Obs. rare*$^{-1}$. Also pepinnery. [ad. F. *pépinière* = *pépinerie* (Cotgr.), f. *pépin* pippin.] A place where plants are grown from seed; a nursery for seedlings.

1601 Holland *Pliny* xvii. x. I. 510 For to make a good pepinnier or nource-garden, there would be chosen a.. special peece of ground. [**1847–78** Halliwell, *Pepinnery*, that part of an orchard where fruit stones are set for growing.]

pepino (pɛ'piːnəʊ). *Physical Geogr.* [Sp., = 'cucumber'.] A small, conical hill characteristic of tropical and subtropical karstic regions, esp. one of those in Puerto Rico. Also *pepino hill.* Cf. HUM *sb.*[4], MOGOTE.

1899 *Nat. Geogr. Mag.* Mar. 100 Along their inner border these [hills] are of remarkable pointed character,..and are appropriately termed by the natives 'Pepinos' or cucumbers. **1915** *Ann. N.Y. Acad. Sci.* XXVI. 16 This type of topography is represented by the small level tract surrounded or dotted over with small hills, called 'pepino hills' locally, standing like haystacks above the plain. **1934** *Jrnl. Geol.* XLII. 545 The development of pepino topography is characteristic of limestones in humid tropical countries. **1954** [see MOGOTE]. **1968** R. W. FAIRBRIDGE *Encycl. Geomorphol.* 161/2 Also known as 'haystack hills', or 'tit hills', the Pepino hills are a characteristic feature of a mature karst landscape in tropical to subtropical latitudes.

‖**pepita** (pe'pita). Also anglicized as **pepit.** [Sp. *pepita* pip, kernel, whence F. *pépite.*] A lump, grain, or nugget of native metal.

1748 *Earthquake of Peru* Pref. 11 Lumps..of the purest gold unmix'd with any Dregs, as usually these Pepita's are. **1777** ROBERTSON *Hist. Amer.* VII. II. 342 Gold..is often found in large *Pepitas*, or grains. **1811** PINKERTON *Petralogy* I. 243 Pepits of copper are intermixed, and the miners only use picks.

†**peple**, obs. anglicized form of PEPLUM.

1658 PHILLIPS, *Peple*,..a hood, or kerchief; also a kinde of imbroidered vesture.

peple, obs. form of PEOPLE.

pepless ('pɛplɪs), *a. colloq.* [f. PEP *sb.* + -LESS.] Without energy or spirit.

1926 WOOD & GODDARD *Dict. Amer. Slang* 15 *Dud*,..a failure; a pepless person. *Ibid.* 17 *Fish, poor*, pepless creature. **1942** BERREY & VAN DEN BARK *Amer. Thes. Slang* §99/12 Nonalcoholic,..pepless. *Ibid.* 249/2 Lazy, indolent, ..pepless. *Ibid.* 276/8 Dull, spiritless,..pepless. **1967** *Observer* 30 Apr. 11/3 The 'vice' in Saigon..has a pepless *Playboy* flavour.

†**pe'plography**. *Obs. rare*$^{-0}$. [ad. Gr. πεπλογραφία description of the peplos of Athene, or the mythological subjects represented on it (see next); name of a work by Varro.]

1656 BLOUNT *Glossogr.*, *Peplography*,..the description of the vail, called *Peplum*.

‖**peplos, peplus** ('pɛplɒs, -əs). [a. Gr. πέπλος, in pl. πέπλα, whence L. *peplus, peplum.*] An outer robe or shawl worn by women in ancient Greece, usually of rich material and design, hanging in loose folds and sometimes drawn over the head; *spec.* that woven yearly for the statue of the goddess Athene at Athens, embroidered with mythological subjects, and carried in procession to her temple at the greater Panathenæa.

1776 R. CHANDLER *Trav. Greece* xx. 102 The procession of the Greater Panathenæa attended a peplus or garment, designed as an offering to Minerva Polias. **1850** LEITCH tr. *C. O. Müller's Anc. Art* §340 (ed. 2) 405 The Peplos, which was very much worn in early times..is recognised with certainty, in the statues of Pallas in the early style. **1875** BROWNING *Aristoph. Apol.* 4827 O child, put from thine eyes The peplos, throw it off, show face to sun!

Hence '**peplosed** (-ɒst) *a.* (*nonce-wd.*), clothed with the peplos.

1875 BROWNING *Aristoph. Apol.* 171 Peplosed and Kothorned let Athenai fall!

‖**peplum** ('pɛpləm). [L. *peplum*: see prec.]

1. = PEPLOS.

1678 CUDWORTH *Intell. Syst.* I. iv. §18. 342 Peplum is properly a womanish Pall or Veil, embroidered all over, and consecrated to Minerva. **1834** PLANCHÉ *Brit. Costume* 99 The *peplum* or veil, and the wimple, was frequently of gold tissue or richly embroidered silk. **1891** E. ARNOLD *Lt. World* 192 Tyrian girls danced by,..Clad in the purple peplums.

2. In modern use: Name of a kind of overskirt, in supposed imitation of the ancient peplum. Also, that part of a long jacket or tunic which hangs below the waist, covering the skirt; hence, a jacket or tunic of this design; also *attrib.* Hence **peplumed** ('pɛpləmd) *a.*

1866 *Queen* 28 Apr. 330/1 No dressy afternoon toilette is now considered complete without a peplum. **1893** *Westm. Gaz.* 17 Oct. 4/1 A handsome gown of crimson velvet, made with a very long train, and corsage with peplum front and a sable collar. **1896** *Daily News* 3 Oct. 6/5 The revival of the 'peplum' over-skirt, hanging in deep, bold points over an under-dress, is announced. *Ibid.*, The peplum in velvet over rich brocade. **1906** *Daily Chron.* 5 Apr. 8/1 A pointed tunic of peplum shape in soft white chiffon hemmed with..mirror velvet. **1930** *Morning Post* 8 Aug. 6 Some dresses have peplums or pleated basques. **1970** *Daily Tel.* 23 Feb. 13 The midi suit which doesn't have either a short cropped waist-length jacket or peplum is likely to be long..and belted. **1972** *Daily Tel.* 29 June 7/7 Or you can play it in strictly neat little Ginger Rogers suits, with flaring skirts, peplumed jackets. **1973** *Times* 15 May 20/5 Big-sleeved black seersucker blouse, the one that belts into a tight waist and then flares into a peplum over a full, long-tiered skirt. **1977** *New Yorker* 11 July 84/1 We see nothing of the longer, fuller skirt, the wasp waist, the peplum. **1977** *Time* 8 Aug. 37/1 Over these dresses or satin pants are worn gargantuan wraps —a peplum coat sewn with real gold thread cloth.

‖**pepo** ('piːpəʊ). *Bot.* [mod. Bot. use of L. *pepo, -onem* pumpkin, a. Gr. πέπων, short for πέπων σίκυος a gourd eaten when ripe, f. πέπων adj. ripened, ripe, mellow.] An inferior fleshy fruit, with numerous seeds attached to parietal placentæ, and a firm rind chiefly derived from the calyx; characteristic of the *Cucurbitaceæ*, as the gourd, melon, cucumber, etc.

[**1706** PHILLIPS, *Pepo*, the Pumpion, a large kind of Melon.] **1861** BENTLEY *Man. Bot.* 323 The Pepo is an inferior, one- or spuriously three-celled, many-seeded, fleshy or pulpy fruit. **1880** GARROD & BAXTER *Mat. Med.* 258 The fruit..consists of a globular pepo, about the size of an orange.

†'**pepon.** *Obs.* [ad. L. *pepon-em* (see prec.) or F. *pepon* (15–16th c. in Godef.) 'a Pompion or Melon' (Cotgr.).] A pumpkin, the fruit of *Cucurbita Pepo*; also, the plant itself.

1382 WYCLIF *Num.* xi. 5 The goordis, and the peponys [1388 & COVERD. melouns, *Genev.* pepons], and the leeke. **1533** ELYOT *Cast. Helthe* II. vii. (1541) 19 b, Melones and Pepones be almoste of one Kynde..the Pepon is moche greatter, and somwhat longe. **1570** LEVINS *Manip.* 164/15 A Peapon, *pepo.* **1578** LYTE *Dodoens* V. xxix. 587 The great Pepon. **1608** WILLET *Hexapla Exod.* 248 They preferred peppons, onyons, leekes and garlike before it. **1657** W. COLES *Adam in Eden* clxvi, To which may be added Melons, Pepons, Cucumbers, Artichokes.

pepper ('pɛpə(r)), *sb.* Forms: 1 pipor, piper, 4 peopur, 4–5 pepir, (5 pepyr(e, -ur, pepre), 4–6 piper, 4–8 peper, 6– pepper. [OE. *pipor* = OLG. **pipar*, MLG., MDu. *pēper* (LG. and Du. *peper*), OHG. *pfeffar*, MHG. and Ger. *pfeffer*, ON. *piparr* (Norw. *pipar*, Sw. *peppar*, ODa. *piberr*, Da. *peber*); Com. WGer. a. L. *piper* = Gr. πέπερι, of Oriental origin: cf. Skt. *pippalī* long-pepper. The condiment must have become known to the Germanic peoples with its Latin name before the 4th c. From OE. *pipor*, through **piopor*, **peopor*, came ME. *peopur, pepur, peper.*

(L. *piper* gave Pr. *pebre*, OF. and AF. *peivre*, F. *poivre*.)]

1. a. A pungent aromatic condiment, derived from species of *Piper* and allied genera (see 2), used from ancient times for flavouring, and acting as a digestive stimulant and carminative; *esp.* the dried berries of *Piper nigrum* or an allied species, either used whole (PEPPERCORNS) or ground into powder.

c **1000** ÆLFRIC *Gram.* ix. (Z.) 44 *Piper*, piper [*v.r.* pipor]. *c* **1000** *Sax. Leechd.* II. 24 Meng pipor wiþ hwit cwudu. *a* **1300** *Siriz* 279 in Mätzner *Altengl. Sprachpr.* 111/1 Pepir nou shalt thou eten, This mustart shal ben thi mete. **1362** LANGL. *P. Pl.* A. v. 155, I haue peper [C. VII. 359 piper] and piane, and a pound of garlek. **1488** *Nottingham Rec.* III. 269 For d. a quarter of pepur. **1543–4** *Act 35 Hen. VIII*, c. 10 They..shal for euer yelde beare and pay yerely..one pounde of pepper, in and for the acknowledgyng hym. **1562** TURNER *Herbal* II. 90 b, The vertue of all peppers in commun is to heat. *a* **1687** PETTY *Pol. Arith.* (1690) 46 Sugar, Tobacco, and Pepper..custom hath now made necessary to all sorts of people. **1781** GIBBON *Decl. & F.* xxxi. III. 223 *note*, Pepper was a favourite ingredient of the most expensive Roman cookery. **1856** EMERSON *Eng. Traits, Wealth*, Finding that milk will not nourish, nor sugar sweeten,..nor pepper bite the tongue.

b. ***black pepper***, the most usual form of the condiment, prepared from the berries dried when not quite ripe. ***white pepper***, a less pungent form, from the same berries dried when fully ripe, or from the black by removing the outer husk. (See also 3.) ***long pepper***, a similar condiment prepared from the immature fruit-spikes of the allied plants *Piper* (*Chavica*) *officinarum* and *P. longum* (*C. Roxburghii*), formerly supposed to be the flowers or unripe fruits of *P. nigrum*.

c **1000** *Sax. Leechd.* II. 186 ȝenim langes pipores .x. corn. *Ibid.* 234 Wyrc him sealfe..of blacum pipore. **13..** *K. Alis.* 7032 (Bodl. MS.) þe white Peper hijlibben by. *c* **1400** MAUNDEV. (1839) xv. 168 There is iij maner of pepper alle vpon o tree, Long peper, blak peper, and white peper... The long peper comethe first..and it is lyche the chattes of haselle that comethe before the lef. **1546** [see 4]. **1600** J. PORY tr. *Leo's Africa* Introd. 42 This tailed or long pepper so far excelleth the pepper of the east Indies, that an ounce thereof is of more force then halfe a pound of that other. **1796** MRS. RAFFALD *Eng. Housekpr.* (1778) 343 Half an ounce of black pepper, the same of long pepper. **1857** HENFREY *Elem. Bot.* 383 Long Pepper is the dried spikes of *Chavica Roxburghi*. **1866** *Treas. Bot.* 264 The Long Pepper which is imported by the Dutch is said to be produced by an allied species, *C. officinarum*. **1876** HARLEY *Mat. Med.* (ed. 6) 434 Long Pepper has been employed by the Hindoos in medicine from the earliest times.

c. In extended use, including the pungent condiments yielded by other plants: see 3.

1838 DON *Gard. Dict.* IV. 446 *Capsicum frutescens*... The ripe pods are dried in the sun... It is then fit for use as a pepper. **1886** HUNTER *Imp. Gaz. India* X. 277 Nepal.. Indian corn, rice, or pepper during the rains. **1904** *Army & Navy Store Catal.*, Coraline pepper, a kind of red pepper. Mignonette pepper, a whitish pepper.

2. a. The plant *Piper nigrum*, a climbing shrub indigenous to the East Indies, and cultivated also in the West Indies, having alternate stalked entire leaves, with pendulous green flower-spikes opposite the leaves, succeeded by small berries turning red when ripe. Also, any plant of the genus *Piper* (including *Chavica*) or (by extension) of the N.O. *Piperaceæ*.

1398 TREVISA *Barth. De P.R.* XVII. cxxxi. (Bodl. MS.) Whan the wodes of peper beþ ripe. *c* **1400** MAUNDEV. (Roxb.) xviii. 83 Pepre growez in maner of wilde wynes be syde þe treesse of þe forest, for to be suppoweld by þam. **1553** EDEN *Treat. Newe Ind.* (Arb.) 20 Pepper groweth in Calicut. **1693** SIR T. P. BLOUNT *Nat. Hist.* 51 Pepper grows best in shady places; that it hath a weak Stem, to be supported like Vines. **1858** HOGG *Veg. Kingd.* 686 Order CXCIV. *Piperaceæ*. The Peppers are confined entirely to the tropics.

b. Applied to other plants, usually with qualifying words (see 3, 7), or, in particular localities, absolutely; esp. the sweet pepper, *Capsicum annuum*, originally native to tropical America but now widely cultivated elsewhere, and its red, green, or yellow bell-shaped fruits; in quots. 1893, 1897 = PEPPER-TREE a.

[**1728** R. BRADLEY *Dictionarium Botanicum* I. s.v. *Capsicum siliqua olivaria propendens*, This Pepper hath small and long round Cods.] **1884** tr. *A. de Candolle's Orig. Cultivated Plants* II. iv. 289 It [sc. *Capsicum annuum*] was one of the peppers that Piso and Marcgraf saw grown in Brazil. **1893** KATE SANBORN *Truthful Woman S. California* 74 Marengo Avenue is lined on either side by splendid specimens of the pepper, the prettiest and most graceful of all trees here. **1897** *Outing* (U.S.) Mar. 582/1 Four magnolias were planted at each cross street, and the inter-spaces filled with peppers. **1923** H. C. THOMPSON *Vegetable Crops* xxv. 399 Peppers are grown in very much the same way as egg-plants and tomatoes. *Ibid.* 400 Of the large-fruited, sweet peppers, Ruby King, Bell or Bullnose,..and Golden Queen are well-known varieties. **1949** *Nat. Geogr. Mag.* Aug. 166/2 When we say 'peppers' without any qualifying word, we usually mean sweet or nonpungent kinds that are eaten as a vegetable, either cooked or raw in salads. **1963** L. PHILLIPS *Recipes from Guardian* 124 Crisp red and yellow pepper rings dressed with lemon juice and olive oil and seasoned well make a good salad. *Ibid.*, Scrambled eggs take on a new look if small pieces of different coloured peppers are added. **1972** Y. LOVELOCK *Vegetable Bk.* III. 320 Capsicums, or peppers, are the various-sized seedpods of a solanaceous plant, having nothing in common with the true peppers (Piperaceae) except the hot quality of some, but by no means all, of them. **1975** I. & A. MANCINELLI tr. *Bianchini & Corbetta's Fruits of Earth* 94 Peppers originated in South America, probably Brazil.

3. With qualifying words, applied to various plants furnishing pungent condiments or to such condiments themselves; sometimes to plants having leaves of a pungent flavour. **African pepper**, (*a*) *Habzelia* (*Xylopia*) *æthiopica* or other species (N.O. *Anonaceæ*); (*b*) *Capsicum fastigiatum*; **anise pepper**, *Xanthoxylon mantschuricum* of China (*Treas. Bot.* 1866); **Ashantee** or **West African pepper** = *African* CUBEBS; **bitter pepper**, *Xanthoxylon Daniellii* of China (*Treas. Bot.*); **Boulon pepper** = *African pepper* (*a*) (*ibid.*); **chili pepper**, (*a*) = PEPPER-TREE a; (*b*) erron. = CHILLI; **Chinese pepper** = *Japanese pepper* (*Treas. Bot.*); **clove pepper**, a local English name of All-spice; **Ethiopian pepper** = *African p.* (*a*.); **Guinea pepper**, (*a*) species of *Capsicum*; (*b*) species of *Amomum*: see GUINEA PEPPER; (*c*) = *African p.* (*a*); **Japanese pepper**, *Xanthoxylon piperitum* of Japan and China; **Java pepper** = CUBEB (*Treas. Bot.*); **Melegueta pepper** = *grains of Paradise*: see GRAIN *sb.*[1] 4 a.; **monkey pepper** = *African p.* (*a*) (*Treas. Bot.*); **mountain pepper**, the seeds of a species of caper, *Capparis sinaica* (*Treas. Bot.*); **Negro pepper** = *African p.* (*a*) (*Treas. Bot.*); **poor man's pepper**, (*a*) a name for species of cress (*Lepidium*: see PEPPERWORT 1); (*b*) common stonecrop, *Sedum acre*; **spur pepper**, shrubby Capsicum, *C. frutescens* (Miller *Plant-n.* 1884); **star pepper** = *bitter pepper* (*Treas. Bot.*); **Tasmanian** or **Victorian pepper** = PEPPER-TREE b, *Tasmannia aromatica* (Miller *Plant-n.*); † **white pepper**, an old name for salad rocket, *Eruca sativa*; see also 1 b; **wild pepper**, (*a*) *Vitex trifolia* of the East Indies (*Treas. Bot.*); (*b*) locally, common yarrow, *Achillea Millefolium* (Britten & Holl., 1886). See also BELL-*pepper*, BETEL-*pepper*, BIRD-*pepper*, BONNET-*pepper*, CAYENNE *pepper*, CHERRY *pepper*, COUNTRY *pepper*, CUBEB *pepper*, GOAT-*pepper*, INDIAN *pepper*, JAMAICA *pepper*, RED *pepper*, WALL *pepper*, WATER *pepper*.

1858 SIMMONDS *Dict. Trade*, **African Pepper*, the fruit of the *Xylopia aromatica*, which is used as pepper in Sierra Leone, and other parts of Africa. **1864** *N. & Q.* 3rd Ser. VI. 216/1 In this part of Yorkshire, what is called '*clove-pepper' and known to the southerns as 'all-spice' is still largely used to season cheesecakes. **1866** *Treas. Bot.* 1240 The fruits..of *X*[*anthoxylon*] *piperitum*, a Japanese species, are called *Japan-pepper. *Ibid.* 564 *H*[*abzelia*] *æthiopica*..is often called *Negro-pepper, Guinea pepper, or Ethiopian pepper, and by old authors *Piper æthiopicum*. **1760** J. LEE *Introd. Bot.* App. 322 *Poor Man's Pepper, *Lepidium*. **1866** *Treas. Bot.* 862 Poor Man's P., the provincial name of *Lepidium latifolium*. **1886** BRITTEN & HOLLAND *Eng. Plant-n.*, Poor Man's Pepper, (1) *Lepidium campestre*. Warw. (2) *Sedum acre*. Notts; Suss. Prior, p. 185. **1866** *Treas. Bot.* 219

The shrubby Capsicum, or *Spur Pepper (*C. frutescens*),.. a native of the East Indies,..has been in our gardens since 1656. **1884** MILLER *Plant-n.* **1538** TURNER *Libellus, Euzomon siue Eruca*... aliqui uocant *whyte pepper.

4. a. In allusive or proverbial expressions, usually referring to the pungent or biting quality of pepper.

c **1400** *Rom. Rose* 6029 Ladyes shulle hem such pepir brewe, If that they falle into hir laas. *c* **1530** R. HILLES *Common-Pl. Bk.* (1858) 140 Though peper be blek yt hath a gode smek. **1546** J. HEYWOOD *Prov.* II. iv. (1867) 51 Blacke inke is as yll meate, as blacke pepper is good. **1601** SHAKS. *Twel. N.* III. iv. 158 Heere's the Challenge, reade it: I warrant there's vinegar and pepper in 't. *a* **1732** GAY *New Song New Similies* 52 Her wit like pepper bites. **1820** *Sporting Mag.* VI. 80 Spring..gave the big one pepper at the ropes. **1863** READE *Hard Cash* xvi, Jump, you boys! or you'll catch pepper. **1869** *Routledge's Ev. Boy's Ann.* 468 By loading it with slugs..he should be able to give the 'varmint' pepper. **1893** FENN *Real Gold* (1894) 20 Feeling what a lie it was, I grew pepper. **1922** JOYCE *Ulysses* 171 And here's himself and pepper on him, Nosey Flynn said. **1960** *Encounter* Feb. 34/1 'Pepper', that characteristically American streak of free-wheeling, urban critical scepticism. **1966** C. ACHEBE *Man of People* vii. 81 If you insult me again I will show you pepper. **1973** J. WAINWRIGHT *Touch of Malice* 136 'Are you calling me a liar, constable?' Ripley sprinkled pepper on his voice.

†**b.** *to take pepper in the nose*: to take offence, become angry. So *to snuff pepper* in the same sense. *to have pepper in the nose* (quot. 1377): to behave superciliously or roughly. *Obs.*

1377 LANGL. *P. Pl.* B. xv. 197 Boxome as of berynge to burgeys And to lordes, And to pore peple han peper in þe nose. **1520** WHITINTON *Vulg.* (1527) 24 If ony man offende hym, he may not forthwith take peper in the nose, and show by rough wordes..that he is angred. **1602** *2nd Pt. Ret. fr. Parnass.* I. iii. 343, I tell thee this libel of Cambridge has much salt and pepper in the nose. **1624–61** R. DAVENPORT *City Nightcap* IV. in Hazl. *Dodsley* XIII. 166 Here are some of other cities..that might snuff pepper else. **1682** BUNYAN *Holy War* 267 The peevish old gentleman took pepper in the nose. **1694** MOTTEUX *Rabelais* IV. v. (1737) 20 Having taken Pepper in the Nose, he was lugging out his Sword.

5. Used *ellipt.* for PEPPER-POT.

1897 *Sears, Roebuck Catal.* 439/1 Silver plated Pepper or Salt. **1908** *Ibid.* 360/3 Handsome Salts and Peppers, hand decorated. **1966** J. DOUGLAS *How to Collect* ii. 9 A plain Queen Anne or early Georgian silver pepper can cost you a great deal. **1976** 'D. HALLIDAY' *Dolly & Nanny Bird* ii. 30 He turfed out my things on to the table. The sugar... A miniature pepper and salt. A pack of fruit gums.

6. In skipping, the speed at which the rope is turned as quickly as possible.

1901 R. C. MACLAGAN *Games Argyleshire* 229 The skipping may be done rapidly or slowly... In Kintyre slow skipping is called 'salt'; quick skipping, 'pepper'. **1948** *Jrnl. Amer. Folk-Lore* LXI. 65 In Pennsylvania the term 'pepper' means a very rapid, strenuous rhythm. In most other places it is called 'hot pepper' or 'hot peas'. **1972** F. B. MAYNARD *Raisins & Almonds* 56 Sometimes they skipped to the tune ..with the spinning rope. (Hazel did pepper faster than anybody I knew).

7. *attrib.* and *Comb.*, as *pepper-berry*, *-field*, *-plantation*, *-seed*, *-vend*; *pepper-coloured*, *-proof* adjs.; **Pepper Alley**, name of an alley in London, hence allusively in pugilistic slang (cf. quot. 1820 in 4 and PEPPER *v.* 5); **pepper-bird**, a name for the toucan (see quot.); **pepper-bottle** = PEPPER-BOX 1; **pepper-brand**, a disease of wheat (= BUNT *sb.*² 2); †**pepper-bread**, gingerbread; **pepper-bush**, (*a*) the common pepper, *Piper nigrum*, or any bushy plant called *pepper* (see 3); (*b*) *Clethra alnifolia* (Sweet Pepper-bush), a fragrant-flowered shrub of the heath family growing in swamps in the east of N. America, or *C. tinifolia* of the West Indies; **pepper-cake** [cf. Du. *peperkoek* (in Kilian), Ger. *pfefferkuchen*], local (Yorksh.) name for a pungent kind of gingerbread; **pepper-cress**, (*a*) *Teesdalia nudicaulis* (see CRESS); (*b*) garden cress, *Lepidium sativum* (Cent. Dict.); **pepper-crop**, stonecrop, *Sedum acre* (*Treas. Bot.* 1866); **pepper-dulse**, Scotch name for a pungent edible seaweed, *Laurencia pinnatifida*; **pepper-dust**, the sweepings of warehouses where pepper is stored, often used to adulterate black pepper; **pepper-elder**, name for plants of the genera *Peperomia*, *Enckea*, and *Artanthe*, allied to the common pepper; **pepper gas**, an anti-personnel 'gas' that produces irritation of the throat and nasal passages; also as *vb. trans.*, to attack with pepper gas; **pepper-gingerbread**, hot-spiced gingerbread (cf. *pepper-cake*); †**pepper-horn**, a vessel or box for holding pepper; **pepper-man**, (in quot.) a dealer in pepper; **pepper-mill**, a small hand-mill for grinding pepper (Simmonds 1858); **pepper-moth** = PEPPERED *moth*; †**pepper-nosed** *a. Obs.*, apt to take offence (cf. 4 b); **pepper-plant**, the plant *Piper nigrum*, or any plant producing 'pepper'; **pepper-pod**, the pod of any species of *Capsicum*; †**pepper-polk** *Sc. Obs.* [POKE *sb.*], a bag for pepper, a spice-bag; **pepper-porridge**, porridge flavoured with pepper; **pepper-posset**, posset flavoured with pepper; **pepper-rent**, rent paid in pepper: cf. PEPPERCORN *rent*; **pepper-rod**, a West Indian euphorbiaceous shrub, *Croton humilis* (*Treas. Bot.* 1866); **pepper-root**, any species of *Dentaria*, esp. *D. diphylla* (= PEPPERWORT 1 b), so called from the pungent-flavoured root (*ibid.*); **pepper-sauce**, a pungent sauce or condiment made by steeping 'red peppers' (capsicum-pods) in vinegar; **pepper saxifrage**, book-name for the umbelliferous genus *Silaus*; **pepper shaker** *N. Amer.* = PEPPER-CASTOR, -CASTER 1; **pepper-shrub**, any shrubby plant called 'pepper' (see 3: cf. PEPPER-TREE); **pepper soup**, a West African soup made with red pepper and other hot spices; **pepper steak** (see quot. 1970); **pepper-vine**, (*a*) the common pepper-plant, or any climbing plant called 'pepper' (see 2, 3); *spec.* (*b*) *Ampelopsis bipinnata*, a N. American plant allied to the Virginian Creeper; **pepper-weed**, any small wild plant allied to the common pepper, as species of *Peperomia*; **pepper-wheat**, wheat affected with *pepper-brand*; †**pepper-wine** (see quot.); †**pepper-worm**, a microscopic animalcule contained in pepper-water (see PEPPER-WATER 1). Also PEPPER-AND-SALT, PEPPER-BOX, etc.

1820 *Sporting Mag.* VII. 145 His mug, it was chaffed, had paid a visit to '*pepper alley'. **1821** *Ibid.* 274 It was Pepper alley on both sides. **1611** COTGR. s.v. *Poyvre verd*, Some report that the ordinarie *Pepper-berrie gathered while tis greene, and vnripe..is that which we call white Pepper. **1752** J. HILL *Hist. Anim.* 381 The Ramphastos, with a yellow rump. The *Pepper-bird. **1846** WORCESTER, **Pepper-brand*, a disease in grain. *Farm. Ency.* **1611** FLORIO, *Pepáto*,..Ginger or *Pepper-bread. **1832** *Veg. Subst. Food* 358 *Piper nigrum*... This *pepper-bush is..found native.. on the coast of Malabar. **1866** *Treas. Bot.* 862 *Sweet Pepper-bush*, an American name for *Clethra*. **1648–78** HEXHAM, *Peper-koeck*, *Pepper-cake or Spice-cake. **1818** TODD, *Pepper-gingerbread*, what is now called spice-gingerbread; and in the north pepper-cake. **1868** ATKINSON *Cleveland Gloss.* s.v., All comers to the house are invited to partake of the pepper-cake and cheese. **1962** I. MURDOCH *Unofficial Rose* x. 99 Mildred..patted her fluffy *pepper-coloured hair into place. **1978** H. JOBSON *To die a Little* v. 89, I picked up a pepper-coloured jacket. **1777** LIGHTFOOT *Flora Scot.* 953 *Fucus pinnatifidus*..This Fucus has a hot taste in the mouth, and is therefore called *Pepper Dulse by the people in Scotland, who frequently eat it as a salad. **1849** D. LANDSBOROUGH *Pop. Hist. Brit. Seaweeds* 254 It is called pepper-dulse, and it certainly has, especially when young, a very pungent smell and peppery taste... It was formerly eaten in Scotland. **1931** L. NEWTON *Handbk. Brit. Seaweeds* 340 This species [sc. *Laurencia pinnatifida*] often has a hot biting taste, and was formerly eaten in Scotland under the name of Pepper Dulse. **1972** Y. LOVELOCK *Vegetable Bk.* I. 209 Pepper dulse (*Laurencia pinnatifida*) was once eaten in Scotland but never gained great popularity. The name refers to the fact that it has often (though not always) a hot biting taste. **1844** J. T. HEWLETT *Parsons & W.* xxi, He.. took *pepper-dust instead of brown Scotch snuff. **1858** SIMMONDS *Dict. Trade*, **Pepper-elder*, a species of the pepper tribe,..abundant in Jamaica, the aromatic seeds of which afford a good substitute for the black pepper of the East Indies. **1970** *Times* 9 July 5 About 225 State and city policemen, armed with *pepper gas, submachine guns, rifles and shotguns, repelled the mob. **1973** R. HAYES *Hungarian Game* xlvi. 281 When Michael didn't open the door, they began filling the room with pepper gas. **1973** *Black Panther* 17 Nov. 5/4 The 38 have been beaten, peppergassed, maced, isolated, harrassed and now intimidated. **1976** *New Yorker* 26 Jan. 74/2 The police dispersed the demonstrators with tear gas and pepper gas. **1596** SHAKS. *1 Hen. IV*, III. i. 260 And leaue in sooth, And such protest of *Pepper Ginger-bread, To Veluet-Guards, and Sunday-Citizens. *a* **1100** *Gerefa* in *Anglia* (1886) IX. 264 Sticfodder, *piper-horn, cyste. **1648–78** HEXHAM, *Peper-huysjen*, Small Pepper-horn to put spices in. *a* **1661** HOLYDAY *Juvenal* xiv. 258 'Weigh, weigh!' cries This badger, this great *pepper-man. **1884** G. MEREDITH *Let.* 13 May (1970) II. 735 My table is the richer for a *pepper-mill. **1907** *Yesterday's Shopping* (1969) 210/2 Pepper Mills for Table. Walnut..1/3... Ivory—12/11. **1972** J. BURMEISTER *Running Scared* iv. 63, I feel like smoked salmon with four hefty winds on the pepper mill. **1864** WEBSTER, **Pepper-moth*, a moth of the genus *Biston*, having small spots on the wings resembling grains of pepper. **1580** H. GIFFORD *Gilloflowers* (1875) 113, I know some *pepernosed dame, Will tearme me foole and sawcie iack. **1611** COTGR., *Poyvrette*,..some also call so, the Guinnie *Pepper plant. **1866** *Treas. Bot.* 1126 *T*[*asmannia*] *aromatica*... The colonists call it the Pepper-plant, and use its little black pungent fruits as a substitute for pepper. **1844** W. H. MAXWELL *Sports & Adv. Scot.* v. (1855) 64 A senior major, hot as a *pepper-pod. *a* **1568** *Wowing of Jok & Jynny* vii. (Bann. MS.), Ane *pepper polk maid of a padill. **1803** *Poet. Petit. agst. Tractorising Trumpery* 92 All piping hot, as *pepper-porridge. **1669** STUBBE *Let.* 17 Dec. in *Boyle's Wks.* (1772) I. *Life* 91 It creates in the throat such a sense, as remains, after drinking *pepper-posset. **1738** SWIFT *Pol. Conversat.* 142, I hope you are *Pepper-proof. **1866** ROGERS *Agric. & Prices* I. xxv. 626 The general prevalence of *pepper-rents, (the term has survived to our time, but in the altered meaning of a nominal payment)..An obligation laid ..upon the tenant to supply his lord with a certain quantity (generally a pound) of pepper at a given day. **1648–78** HEXHAM, *Pepersauce*, *Pepper-sauce. **1864** WEBSTER, *Pepper-sauce.* **1899** *Scribner's Mag.* XXV. 100/1 His skin is full of oil, and whiskey,..and canvas-back ducks, and pepper-sauce. **1854** S. THOMSON *Wild Fl.* III. (ed. 4) 234 The *pepper saxifrage..is distinguishable by its yellow flowers. **1626** BACON *Sylva* §576 The seeds of Clove-Trees, and *Pepper-seeds. **1895** *Montgomery Ward Catal.* Spring & Summer 543/3 Salt and *pepper shakers, made of crystal blown glass, extra large capacity, and well adapted for kitchen as well as table use. Specify salt or pepper when ordering. **1911** *Daily Colonist* (Victoria, B.C.) 22 Apr. 2/1 (Advt.), Table Necessities..Pepper Shakers of Cut Glass, sterling silver tops. **1977** *Transatlantic Rev.* LX. 89 We divide up nine individual packets of sugar, six of ketchup, three rippled pepper shakers. **1693** *Phil. Trans.* XVII. 687 It's Trunk is loaded with Snails, and the *Pepper-Shrub often climbs up it like Ivy. **1830** *Hobart Town Almanack* 65 in Morris *Austral Eng.* s.v. *Pepper-tree*, A thick grove of the pepper-shrub, *Tasmania fragrans.* **1964** J. P. CLARK *Masquerade* in *Three Plays* 76 Why, Only this morning I opened my fishbasket To have stock for our *pepper soup. **1966** C. ACHEBE *Man of People* xii. 148 My father was.. eating pounded yams and pepper soup. **1951** E. DAVID *French Country Cooking* 114 **Pepper steaks*... Score the steaks..rub them with garlic and then with a thin coating of pounded peppercorns. **1965** K. GILES *Some Beasts no More* v. 125, I had some-thing to eat, they still do a good pepper steak. **1970** SIMON & HOWE *Dict. Gastron.* 297/1 *Pepper steak*, beef steak rubbed liberally with freshly-ground black pepper before cooking. **1976** K. THACKERAY *Crownbird* v. 91 The barbecue area where an African was cooking pepper steaks and kebabs. **1720** STRYPE *Stow's Surv.* (1754) II. v. ix. 262/2 They petitioned..that no Pepper might be brought in for three Years into any of her Dominions, the Time of the *Pepper-vend requiring no less. **1801** *Asiat. Ann. Reg.* II. *Misc. Tracts* 78/2 The *pepper-vine..grows very well there, and produces a large corn. **1862** BEVERIDGE *Hist. India* I. Introd. 11 The pepper-vine..entwines among the cocoas and other palms of the Malabar coast, and forms a considerable article of export. **1866** *Treas. Bot.* 1217 Vine, Pepper. *Ampelopsis bipinnata*. **1884** MILLER *Plant-n.*, Pepper-vine, Two-winged Virginian Creeper. **1871** KINGSLEY *At Last* v, That one happens to be..a *pepper-weed, first cousin to the great black-pepper bush. **1744–50** W. ELLIS *Mod. Husbandm.* II. II. 32 What we call *Pepper-wheat. **1764** *Museum Rust.* III. ii. 5 A good crop,..clear from smut and pepper-wheat. **1601** HOLLAND *Pliny* I. 421 We spice our wines now adaies also,..we adde pepper and hony therto: which some call Condite, others *Pepper wines. **1657–83** EVELYN *Hist. Relig.* (1850) I. 31 The..mite or *peper-worm, (that dust of a creature, whereof fifty thousand are contained in one drop).

'pepper, *v.* [f. prec. sb. (OE. had *piporian*, *piprian*, *ȝepiperian*, in same sense (so ON. *pipra*, OHG. *phefferôn*, MHG. and Ger. *pfeffer(e)n*, Du. *peperen*); but the current verb seems to have been formed anew in 16th c.]

1. a. *trans.* To sprinkle with pepper; to flavour or season with pepper; to treat with pepper. Also *absol.*

[*c* **1000** *Sax. Leechd.* II. 182 Sele þonne ȝepiporodne wyrtdrenc. *Ibid.*, ȝepipera mid xx corna. *Ibid.* III. 76 Pipra hit syþþan swa swa man wille.] **1581** and **1620** [see PEPPERED]. **1738** SWIFT *Pol. Conversat.* 142 This Venison is plaguily pepper'd. **1796** MRS. GLASSE *Cookery* x. 161 Dried salmon..when laid on the gridiron should be moderately peppered. **1865** J. MACGREGOR *Rob Roy Baltic* (1867) 205 There is the blind that won't pull down or stop up, and the pepper-box that won't pepper.

b. *Falconry.* To wash (a hawk) with water and pepper, in order to cleanse her from vermin, etc. [So F. *poivrer*.]

1618 LATHAM *Falconry* II. 34 Hauing on euening your water with pepper prouided, and when you haue, according to the order and accustomed manner, well washed and peppered her, take off her rufterhood. *Ibid.* 81 Vpon the receit of such a Hawke from the Cage, suddenly to make her gentle, by peppering, watching, and other such like accustomed vses.

2. To sprinkle (a surface) as with pepper; to cover, or fill with numerous small objects, spots, or dots, likened to grains of pepper; to besprinkle, dot, stud. Also *fig.* (Mostly in *pa. pple.*)

1612 J. DAVIES *Wit's Pilgr.* (1878) 46/1 Note the Lyning of the roialst Robe; Its powdred Ermyne, pepperd too with Stings. **1705** LADY WENTWORTH *Let.* 9 Mar. in *W. Papers* (1883) 40 Betty..affects to be afraid of the small pox, and thearfor I fear would be pepered with them should she get them. **1835** M. SCOTT *Cruise Midge* xxi, The neighbouring thickets were peppered with..small white-washed buildings. **1882** B. HARTE *Flip* ii, Her flushed face.. peppered with minute..freckles. **1896** *Moxon's Mech. Exerc., Printing* 422 Every page was peppered with italic.

3. To sprinkle like pepper; to scatter in small particles. Also *fig.* Also *intr.* in same sense.

1821 CLARE *Vill. Minstr.* I. 197 As grinning north-winds ..pepper'd round my head their hail and snow. **1857** [see GEEWHILLIKINS *int.*]. **1899** MISS E. TH. FOWLER *Double Thread* xii, People go peppering them [words] all over the place, utterly unconscious of the awful responsibility. **1945** C. MANN in Murdoch & Drake-Brockman *Austral. Short Stories* (1951) 263 They would be routed..by the driven sand and salt peppering into their eyes. **1947** W. DE LA MARE *Coll. Stories for Children* 14 A few hollow cockled-up bean seeds peppered down from out of their dry shucks.

4. a. To pelt with shot or missiles. Also *fig.*

c **1644** J. SOMERVILLE *Mem. Somervilles* (1815) II. 347 First peppering them soundly with ther shott. **1689** SHADWELL *Bury F.* I. i, There i'faith I pepper'd the Court with libels and lampoons. **1742** FIELDING *J. Andrews* I. xvi, I'll pepper you better than ever you was pepper'd by Jenny Bouncer. **1773** *Life N. Frowde* 135 She soon got into order and peppered us with her small Shot. **1866** GEO. ELIOT *F. Holt* ii, You may pepper the bishops a little. **1884** SALA *Journ. due South* I. xxiv. (1887) 327 Peppering the guide occasionally with Greek and Latin lore. **1885** *Century Mag.* XXX. 386/1 Galloping after us, and peppering us with shot-guns.

b. *intr.* To discharge shot or other small missiles (*at* something). Const. *away*.

In quot. 1767 said of rain, to pour heavily; in quot. 1894 (*colloq.*) to 'go at it' vigorously: cf. *pelt*.

1767 GRAY *Let. to Mason* 11 Sept., We came peppering and raining back through Keswick to Penrith. Next day, —raining still. **1884** 'MARK TWAIN' *Huck. Finn* xviii. 167 The Grangerfords..peppered away at him. **1890** W. A.

WALLACE *Only a Sister* 37 He could not possibly be peppering away at the pheasants in Sir James's covers. **1894** MORRIS in Mackail *Life* II. 300 The nightingales..O my wig, they were peppering into it.

5. a. *trans.* To inflict severe punishment or suffering upon; to 'give it' (a person) 'hot'; to beat severely, trounce; also †*to pepper* (one's) *box* or *pans* (obs.). Hence, †**b.** To punish effectually or decisively; to give (one) his death-blow (*lit.* or by hyperbole), to 'do for', ruin. Now *rare*.

c **1500** in *Babees Bk.* 404 My master pepered my ars with well good spede. **1589** NASHE *Pasquil's Retvrne* Wks. (Grosart) I. 97 Against the next Parliament, I wyll picke out a time to pepper them. **1592** SHAKS. *Rom. & Jul.* III. i. 102, I am pepper'd I warrant, for this world. **1596** —— *1 Hen. IV*, II. iv. 212. **1608** DAY *Hum. out of Br.* I. iii, And I were a man as I am no woman, i'de pepper your box for that ieast. **1609** ARMIN *Maids of More-Cl.* (1880) 89 Boy Ile pepper your pans. **1631** HEYWOOD *2nd Pt. Maid of West* IV. Wks. 1874 II. 393 She's peppered by this. **1693** SOUTHERNE *Maid's Last Prayer* II. i. Wks. 1721 II. 28 If he finds out my haunts he swears he'll pepper me. **1797** MRS. RADCLIFFE *Italian* xxii, Well, signor, he's peppered now. **1869** *Lonsdale Gloss.*, *Pepper*..2 To beat, to thrash.

6. To give pungency, spice, or flavour to: †**a.** a person: to 'heat', to excite to anger or other strong feeling (*obs.*); **b.** to 'season', 'spice' (speech or writing). Also *absol.*

1600 ROWLANDS *Lett. Humours Blood* vii. 84 Parboild in rage, pepperd in heate of ire. **1835** *Blackw. Mag.* XXXVII. 515 A novel..requires less intense, less fierce interest, than the acted drama, and, accordingly, the novelists do not pepper quite so high as the dramatists.

†**c.** To dose with praise or flattery. *Obs.*

1654 GAYTON *Pleas. Notes* 24 Our [mock] Emperour, having a spice of self conceit before, was soundly peppered now. **1774** GOLDSM. *Retal.* 111 'Till, his relish grown callous, almost to disease, Who pepper'd the highest, was surest to please. **1784** SIR J. REYNOLDS in Leslie & Taylor *Life* (1865) II. viii. 459 Vying with each other who should pepper highest.

†**7.** To infect with venereal disease. (F. *poivrer*.)

1607 DEKKER *Northw. Hoe* II. i. Wks. 1873 III. 21. **1615** J. STEPHENS *Ess. & Char.* iv. 28 And then you snarle against our simple French As if you had beene pepperd with your wench. **1694** MOTTEUX *Rabelais* v. xxi. (1737) 93. **1709** *Brit. Apollo* II. No. 44. 3/1. **1723** *Pres. St. Russia* I. 277 A Woman of the Town..having peppered some hundreds of the Preobrazinsky Guards.

pepperage, variant of PEPPERIDGE.

'pepper-and-'salt.

1. a. Name for a kind of cloth made of dark- and light-coloured wools woven together, showing small dots of black and white, dark grey and light grey, or the like, closely intermingled; also, a garment made of this. Usually *attrib.* or as *adj.* Hence, someone wearing pepper-and-salt clothes.

1774 LADY M. COKE *Jrnl.* 28 Oct. (1896) IV. 420 To bring me six yards of a Cloth I saw..that is called pepper and salt. *a* **1843** SOUTHEY *Comm.-pl. Bk.* IV. 408 A strange looking *settee*..covered with pepper and salt cloth. **1844** THACKERAY *Little Trav.* i, Tall men in pepper-and-salt undress jackets. **1845** *Ainsworth's Mag.* VII. 370 [The boy] is..installed *in* the usual pepper-and-salts, with the black velveteens for Sundays. **1849** MARRYAT *Valerie* vi, A suit of pepper-and-salt. **1887** *Pall Mall G.* 4 Aug. 6/1 Flourishing the striking red handkerchief which furnishes an agreeable relief to his general pepper-and-salt exterior. **1900** E. GLYN *Visits of Elizabeth* 236 At dinner I sat between Charlie and one of the pepper-and-salts... They are going to shoot partridges tomorrow. **1907** *Westm. Gaz.* 11 Oct. 3/2 Husband small, fussy,..violent-tempered, pepper-and-salt-check-trousered, and some-thing..in the City. **1915** W. S. MAUGHAM *Of Human Bondage* xxvi. 107 Very neat in his black coat and pepper-and-salt trousers. **1934** G. B. SHAW *Village Wooing* 129 At this A sits writing. He wears pepper-and-salt trousers of country cut, with an apron. **1978** N. MARSH *Grave Mistake* i. 16 The trousers were unmistakable: pepper-and-salt, shapeless, earthy.

b. *transf.* Used of greying hair, a moustache, or of objects resembling pepper-and-salt cloth in colour. Also, *pepper-salt*.

1853 MRS. GASKELL *Ruth* II. vi. 124 My hair is nearly white. The last time I looked it was only pepper-and-salt. **1909** *Dialect Notes* III. 414 *Pepper and salt*,..painted with white spatters over a darker background. **1930** [see LAW *sb.*[1] 16 a]. **1934** E. BOWEN *Cat Jumps* 83 Matthew had fluffy pepper-and-salt hair. **1951** T. CAPOTE *Grass Harp* (1952) i. 3 A whip-thin, handsome woman with shingled pepper-salt hair. **1955** J. THOMAS *No Banners* xix. 174 A scowling Militiaman with an enormous pepper-and-salt moustache walked up. **1957** E. HYAMS *Into Dream* 128 Clear grey eyes, pepper-and-salt hair worn in the kind of bob which was fashionable about 1925. **1976** A. PRICE *War Game* II. 219 Nayler's lankiness had aged into an acceptable scholarly stoop to which his thick pepper-and-salt thatch added distinction.

2. Name for the American plant called 'harbinger of spring' (*Erigenia bulbosa*); from the colour-contrast of its white petals and dark anthers. *U.S.*

3. *fig.*

1887 *Lantern* (New Orleans) 9 July 2/2 But let me commence my assault on the offending ones and give them pepper and salt. **1958** *Times* 24 Oct. 15/4 In Prokofiev's work Mr. Kroll emphasised the lyrical element rather more than the composer's characteristic pepper and salt.

4. pepper-and-salt fundus, a symptom of congenital syphilis, the fundus of the eye having a speckled appearance.

1940 S. DUKE-ELDER *Text-bk. Ophthalm.* III. iii. 2273 The finely pigmented or pepper-and-salt fundus, a picture characteristic of hereditary lues, wherein the entire fundus is dusted with innumerable small bluish pigmented spots between which lie round depigmented areas of a yellowish-red colour. **1975** MARTIN-DOYLE & KEMP *Synopsis Ophthalm.* (ed. 5) vi. 76 Syphilitic Retinitis... In congenital cases a form of peripheral pigmentation known as 'pepper and salt' fundus is common.

5. Forming various nonce-wds.: **pepper-and-salted** *a.*, wearing pepper-and-salt clothing; **pepper-and-saltiness**, pepper-and-salt colour; **pepper-and-salty** *a.*, pepper-and-salt coloured.

1846 R. FORD *Gatherings from Spain* xxiii. 331 This pepper-and-salted Amphion. **1880** R. BROUGHTON *Second Thoughts* I. I. vi. 83 Snow..speckled with blacks into an ugly pepper-and-saltiness. **1952** 'W. COOPER' *Struggles of Albert Woods* I. iii. 34 Dibdin's hair was the colour that is first called sandy and later pepper-and-salty.

'pepper-box.

1. a. A small box, usually cylindrical, with a perforated lid, used for sprinkling powdered pepper.

1546 *Inventories* (Surtees, No. 97) 86 A peper box, weying vj oz. iij quarters. **1598** SHAKS. *Merry W.* III. v. 149 Hee cannot creepe into a halfe-penny purse, nor into a Pepper-Boxe. *a* **1782** R. GRAVES *Fable* in Dodsley *Coll. Poems* (1782) V. 70 The pepper-box..upon the table. **1865** [see PEPPER *v.* 1].

b. In allusive expressions. (Cf. PEPPER *sb.* 4, *v.* 5.)

1821 *Sporting Mag.* VII. 273 Both now began to slash away, and the pepper box was handed from one to another. **1901** *Daily News* 25 Feb. 6/2 The swarm of nonentities upon whom..the pepper-box of titles is shaken.

2. *transf.* **a.** Applied contemptuously to a small cylindrical turret or cupola.

1821 SCOTT *Kenilw.* xii, The monotonous stone pepper-boxes which, in modern Gothic architecture, are employed. **1855** THACKERAY *Newcomes* xxii, There are a score [of pictures] under the old pepper-boxes in Trafalgar Square as fine as the best here.

b. The name given to an early type of revolver in which five or six barrels revolve round a central axis; freq. *attrib.*

1861 *Richmond* (Va.) *Examiner* 7 Dec. 3/2 The pistol is one of the old-fashioned pepper-box sort—self-cocking, and..is regarded as dangerous at either end. **1872** 'MARK TWAIN' *Roughing It* ii. 4 An old original 'Allen' revolver, such as irreverent people called a 'pepper-box'. **1887** [see *coffee-mill* s.v. COFFEE *sb.* 5 b]. **1901** W. CHURCHILL *Crisis* II. xviii. 280 Out of his pocket hung the curved butt of a big pepper-box revolver. **1915** W. B. YEATS *Reveries* (1916) 48 An old pepper-box revolver. **1920** C. W. SAWYER *Our Rifles* 65 The rifle was made about 1855, when pepper-box pistols were in everyday use. **1969** *Canad. Antiques Collector* Feb. 29/1 An early (1851) English 'Improved Revolver' which is part revolver and part pepperbox.

3. At the Eton game of fives: see quot. 1902.

1865 *Etoniana Anc. & Mod.* 178. **1889** SKRINE *Mem. E. Thring* 17 Then, when the loose ball came, clapping it into the pepper-box, dead. **1902** C. R. STONE *Eton Gloss.* 25 *Pepper-box.*—One of the great differences between Eton fives and Rugby fives is the pepper-box, the irregular buttress sticking into the court..imitated from the original fives court in the side of Upper Chapel... Originally pepper-box was the name applied only to the Dead Man's Hole, but now generally to the whole buttress.

4. *fig.* A hot-tempered person.

1867 H. KINGSLEY *Silcote of Silcotes* xiii. (1876) 77 Make love to Dora, if the young pepper-box will let you.

5. *attrib.*

1771 T. PENNANT *Tour in Scotl. 1769* 203 A slender square tower with a pepper-box top. **1825** in Hone *Every-day Bk.* I. 949 The pepper-box towers remind the spectator more of pigeon-houses than church steeples. **1836** MRS. SHERWOOD *Nun* i. 5 The pepper-box turret on each side of the gateway. **1948** J. R. FIRTH in E. P. Hamp et al. *Readings in Linguistics II* (1966) 178 The Romans and the English managed to dispense with those written signs called 'accents' and avoided pepperbox spelling.

'pepper-,castor, -caster. [See CASTOR[2].]

1. A small vessel with a perforated top, usually one of the castors of a cruet-stand, for sprinkling pepper at table.

1676 *Lond. Gaz.* No. 1079/4 A Sugar Castar. A Pepper Caster. A Mustard Pot. **1836** [see CASTOR[2] 1]. **1861** ALB. SMITH *Med. Student* 42 The simple act of pouring the vinegar into the pepper-castor. **1891** A. LANG *Angling Sk.* 122 The happy-go-lucky disposition to scatter my Greek accents as it were with a pepper-caster.

2. *transf.* **a.** = prec. 2: also *attrib.*

1859 JEPHSON *Brittany* x. 174 That hideous tower with the pepper-caster on the top.

b. A slang term for a revolver.

1889 J. JEFFERSON *Autobiog.* iii. 72 Badger and I would trudge to our room arm in arm, carrying our money in a shot-bag between us, and each armed with a Colt's patent 'pepper-caster'.

peppercorn ('pɛpəkɔːn). Forms: see PEPPER. [f. PEPPER *sb.* + CORN *sb.*[1] 2 b.]

1. a. The dried berry of Black Pepper.

c **1000** *Sax. Leechd.* II. 24 ȝenim eft senepes sædes dæl..& .xx. piporcorna. *a* **1400-50** *Alexander* 2025 How all þi soft grayns Sall vndire-put be all þe pake vn-to þir peper-cornes. **1596** SHAKS. *1 Hen. IV*, III. iii. 9 And I haue not forgotten what the in-side of a Church is made of, I am a Pepper-Corne, a Brewers Horse. **1652** HOWELL *Giraffi's Rev. Naples* II. (1663) 34 None might embeazle the value of a pepper corn. **1769** MRS. RAFFALD *Eng. Housekpr.* (1778) 283 Mix them with..a blade or two of mace, a few pepper corns, and a little salt. **1815** J. SMITH *Panorama Sc. & Art* I. 525 As absurd as to suppose that a grain of sand should command the motion of a mill-stone, or a pepper-corn that of a mountain.

b. Formerly often, and still sometimes, stipulated for as a quit-rent or nominal rent: see quots.

1607 HIERON *Serm. 2 Tim.* iv. 7 Wks. I. 221 Some great man, out of his bounty, giueth thee an inheritance of some pounds by the yeare; thou must pay a pepper corne for thy rent. **1616** R. C. *Times' Whistle* v. 2007 Sha't have a new lease for a hundred yeares,..and shalt yearly pay A pepper-corne, a nutt, a bunch of may, Or some such trifle. **1669** *Boston Rec.* (1881) VII. 50 He payeinge a pepper corne to the said Treasurer upon demand for ever on the said 29th September. **1818** CRUISE *Digest* (ed. 2) V. 379 The reservation of a peppercorn in the bargain and sale for a year is a sufficient consideration to raise a use in the bargainee, so as to make the release valid. **1898** *Encycl. Laws Eng.* s.v., In modern times building leases sometimes reserve a pepper-corn as rent for the first few years.

fig. **1646** EVANCE *Noble Ord.* 31 You can never have a firme possession, till you hold your Honours in this title, that God bestowes them, and untill you give a Pepper corne of honour unto God. **1780** COWPER *Table-t.* 110 True. While they live, the courtly laureat pays His quit-rent ode, his pepper-corn of praise.

2. *attrib.* **a.** Of or consisting in a peppercorn, as *peppercorn rent* (see 1 b); also *fig.* very small, insignificant, trivial.

1791 WOLCOTT (P. Pindar) *Remonstrance* 83 Not pepper-corn acknowledgment I owe 'em. **1860** EMERSON *Cond. Life, Worship* Wks. (Bohn) II. 396 After their peppercorn aims are gained, it seems as if the lime in their bones alone held them together. **1863** KEBLE *Bp. Wilson* xxi. 712 To whom and his heirs and assigns the property is granted for a thousand years at a peppercorn rent.

b. Used *attrib.* or as *adj.* to designate the tufted style in which Hottentots and Bushmen wear their hair; also *transf.*

1868 J. CHAPMAN *Trav. S. Afr.* I. i. 16 Bushmen with peppercorn heads. **1893** SELOUS *Trav. S.E. Africa* 107 High cheek-bones, oblique eyes, and peppercorn hair. **1935** L. G. GREEN *Great Afr. Mysteries* x. 121 Reconstructions of these bones suggested that the Strandloopers were never more than five feet in height. Some authorities declare they had peppercorn hair. **1948** H. V. MORTON *In Search of S. Afr.* viii. 251, I could see the road running ahead, disappearing for a while and emerging again upon the face of the greyish-brown plain, which was dotted with small peppercorn bushes like a Hottentot's hair. **1958** L. VAN DER POST *Lost World of Kalahari* i. 12 His [*sc.* the Bushman's] hair was black and grew in thick round clusters which my countrymen called, with that aptitude for scornful metaphor they unfailingly exercised on his behalf, 'pepper-corn hair'. **1959** J. D. CLARK *Prehist. S. Afr.* i. 17 The Hottentot closely resembles the Bushman except in stature. He..has black hair which grows in spirals and is known as 'pepper-corn hair'.

3. *Comb.*, as *peppercorn-sized* adj. **peppercorn shrub, tree** = PEPPER-TREE.

[**1830** *Hobart Town Almanack* 65 A thick grove of the pepper-shrub..grows in a close thicket to the height of from six to ten feet.] **1899** *Allbutt's Syst. Med.* VIII. 592 It is miliary to pepper-corn sized. **1901** M. FRANKLIN *My Brilliant Career* i. 1 The stringybark roof of the salt-shed..peeped out picturesquely from the musk and peppercorn shrubs. **1954** *Coast to Coast 1953–54* 76 Who do you think we see sittin' under a pepper-corn tree but this old sundowner. **1973** *Bulletin* (Sydney) 25 Aug. 43/3 Dejected peppercorn trees by the station. **1978** O. WHITE *Silent Reach* ix. 104 A line of scrawny peppercorn trees.

Hence **'peppercornish, 'peppercorny** *adjs.*, of the nature of or resembling a peppercorn.

1762 J. H. STEVENSON *Crazy Tales* 24 First his acknowledgment being paid, A pepper-cornish kind of due. **1861** DICKENS *Gt. Expect.* viii, Of a peppercorny and farinaceous character.

peppered ('pɛpəd), *ppl. a.* [f. PEPPER *v.* + -ED[1].]

a. Sprinkled or seasoned with pepper; sprinkled with small dots like grains of pepper; pelted with shot, etc.: see the verb.

1581 *Satir. Poems Reform.* xliv. 200 The peperit beif can tailȝe be the threid. **1620** VENNER *Via Recta* (1650) 259 Salt and peppered meats. **1694** MOTTEUX *Rabelais* v. (1737) 217. **1795** *Sporting Mag.* V. 49 The peppered tails returned as they came. **1860** O. W. HOLMES *Prof. Breakf.-t.* i, A shelf of peppered sheepskin reprints. **1873** *Spectator* 22 Feb. 237/1 A bit of 'peppered tongue', not worth an answer, and hardly worth an action.

b. *peppered moth*, the popular name of the geometrid moth, *Biston betularia*, which is usually light-coloured with darker flecks.

1832 RENNIE *Consp. Butterfl. & Moths* Index. **1903** F. E. HULME *Butterflies & Moths* vi. 225 The insect we have represented..is..called the Peppered Moth, or, in the words of some old entomologists, the Pepper and Salt. **1915**, **1970** [see MELANIC *a.* 2]. **1972** *Countryman* LXXVII. II. 131 Bernard Kettlewell's classic study of the peppered moth as an example of natural selection in action is finding its way into the text books. **1975** *Sci. Amer.* Jan. 90/1 Of more than 700 species of larger moths found throughout the British Isles, the peppered moth (*Biston betularia*) is surely the best-known to students of evolution.

c. *peppered steak* = *pepper steak*.

1960 J. DONON *Classic French Cuisine* v. 130 (*heading*) Steak au Poivre (Peppered Steak). **1973** D. MACKENZIE *Postscript to Dead Let.* 30 A Czech couple who serve the best peppered steak in town. **1978** *Times* 4 Mar. 11/5 Stars in Soho..does a good peppered steak (£3·25).

pepperer ('pɛpərə(r)). [In 1, f. PEPPER *sb.* + -ER[2]: cf. med.L. *piperārius* (Du Cange); in 2, f. PEPPER *v.* + -ER[1].]

1. A dealer in pepper and spices; a grocer. (The original name of the Grocers' Company of London: see quots.) *Obs.* exc. *Hist.*

[**1180** in Madox *Hist. Exchequer* (1711) 390 Gilda Piperariorum, unde Edwardus est Aldermannus.] **1309** *Hustings Rolls* No. 38. 102 in *Guildh. Rec.*, Ralph le Balancer, Pepperer. **1622** MALYNES *Anc. Law-Merch.* 74 At the suit of the Pepperers, now called Grocers of London. **1633** *Stow's Surv.* 278 In the reigne of Henry the sixth..the Pepperers or Grocers had seated themselves..in Bucklesbury. **1843** LYTTON *Last Bar.* I. i, It was but a scurvy Pepperer who made that joke. **1904** J. A. KINGDON *Strife of Scales* 8 One Andrew Godard, a Pepperer, was appointed [6 Edw. II, 1312] Keeper of the King's Beam.

2. One who or that which peppers; *fig.* a hot-tempered person; something pungent or biting.

1711–12 SWIFT *Jrnl. to Stella* 20 Feb., A 'Representation of the state of the nation to the queen'..I believe it will be a pepperer. **1865** DICKENS *Mut. Fr.* I. vi, But it's my way to make short cuts at things. I always was a pepperer.

pepperet (pɛpə'rɛt). Also pepperette. [f. PEPPER *sb.* + -ET.] *rare.* A pepper-pot.

1927 W. DEEPING *Kitty* i. 11 Regency salt-cellars, mustard-pots and pepperets. **1975** *Country Life* 20 Feb. 427/1 A condiment set..mustard pot with liner, a salt-cellar and two pepperettes. **1977** *Times* 26 July 9/7 (Advt.), This pug-dog pepperette..London, 1881..realised £105.

'pepper-grass. **a.** Any species of *Lepidium*, as *L. sativum*, common garden-cress; from the pungent taste. **b.** = PILLWORT, *Pilularia globulifera*, N.O. *Marsileaceæ*: cf. PEPPER-WORT 2.

c **1475** *Pict. Voc.* in Wr.-Wülcker 787/6 Nomina bladorum et arborum..*Hec salmea*, a pepyrgresse. **1760** J. LEE *Introd. Bot.* App. 322 Pepper-grass, *Pilularia*. **1828–32** WEBSTER, *Peppergrass*,..also, a plant of the genus Lepidium. **1856** in Olmsted *Slave States* 708 A widow and her children living, for three days and nights, on boiled weeds, called pepper grass.

pepperidge ('pɛpərɪdʒ). Also **-age**; see also PIPPERIDGE.

1. A variant of PIPPERIDGE, local English name of the Barberry.

1823 in MOOR *Suffolk Words*. *a* **1900** in *Eng. Dial. Dict.* from Hertford, Suffolk.

2. *U.S.* The Black Gum, Sour Gum, or Tupelo, a North American tree of the genus *Nyssa*, having very tough wood. esp. *Nyssa sylvatica* (cf. NYSSA). Also *attrib.*

1689 *Huntington* (N.Y.) *Town Rec.* (1888) II. 56 A piperage tree marked faceing eastward and southward. **1743** J. HEMPSTEAD *Diary* 22 Feb. (1901) 406 Wee Sawed of a pr Peperage wheels for my Stone Cart. [**1810** F. A. MICHAUX *Hist. Arbres Forestiers de l'Amérique Septentrionale* I. 30 *Peperidge* fréquemment usitée par les Hollandois du New Jersey.] **1821** J. F. COOPER *Spy* I. ix. 133 A lieutenant of cavalry..whose captain is as tough as a peperage log. **1826** F. COOPER *Mohicans* (1829) I. vi. 77 A trencher, neatly carved from the knot of the pepperage. **1864** WEBSTER, *Pepperidge*. **1866** *Treas. Bot.* 798 *N[yssa] villosa*, the Sour Gum, Black Gum, Pepperidge, or Tupelo tree, common from New England to the Carolinas. **1876** *Field & Forest* I. 66 This parasitic shrub [*sc.* American mistletoe] has been found growing on several Pepperidge or Sour-gum trees. **1900** J. DE F. SHELTON *Salt-Box House* ix. 67 A certain tract of land,..beginning at the highway near my present house ..to a pepperidge tree. **1969** T. H. EVERETT *Living Trees of World* 257/2 The pepperidge, black gum, or tupelo (*N. sylvatica*) of eastern North America ranges from Maine to Michigan, Florida and Texas. Up to 100 feet in height, it forms a flat-topped columnar or pyramidal head of usually somewhat pendulous branches and has blunt, obovate or elliptic, lustrous leaves that turn brilliant cellar and two pepperettes. **1977** *Times* 26 July 9/2 (Advt.), This pug-dog pepperette..London, 1881..realised £105.

pepperily, pepperiness: see PEPPERY.

pepperina (,pɛpə'ri:nə). *Austral.* [f. PEPPER(-TREE + *-ina*, as in CASUARINA.] = PEPPER-TREE. Also *attrib.*

1930 V. PALMER *Men are Human* xviii. 166 Nothing grew save the drooping pepperina that trailed its sheeny leaves over the kitchen roof. **1941** *Coast to Coast* 145 There was a pepperina-tree in the corner of the adjacent yard. **1967** *Southerly* XXVII. 204 Guinea-hens..roosting at night in the pepperina tree beside the back door.

peppering ('pɛpərɪŋ), *vbl. sb.* [See -ING[1].] The action of the verb PEPPER; sprinkling with, or as with, pepper; pelting with shot, missiles, etc.

1580 HOLLYBAND *Treas. Fr. Tong*, *Poivrade*, peppring. *a* **1814** *Gonzanga* v. i. in *New Brit. Theatre* III. 148 A British sailor..always ready to give the enemy a peppering. **1845** *P. Parley's Ann.* VI. 356 The peppering of the rain on the tiles and windows. **1861** DUTTON COOK *P. Foster's D.* iii, With a plentiful peppering of blacks about their plumage.

'peppering, *ppl. a.* [See -ING[2].] That peppers (see PEPPER *v.*); pungent, angry; falling heavily (as rain), 'pelting'.

1712 SWIFT *Jrnl. to Stella* 27 Mar., I sent him a peppering letter. **1827** SCOTT *Jrnl.* 30 July, One of the most peppering thunder-storms which I have heard for some time. **1878** MORRIS in Mackail *Life* (1899) I. 361 We have just had a peppering little snow-shower.

pepperish ('pɛpərɪʃ), *a.* [f. PEPPER *sb.* + -ISH[1].] Somewhat peppery; *fig.* somewhat testy or angry.

1808 SCOTT *Let. to Ellis* 18 Nov., Will not our editor be occasionally a little warm and pepperish? **1819** *Metropolis* I. 154, I remember your father..a little pepperish or so.

peppermint ('pɛpəmɪnt). [f. PEPPER *sb.* + MINT *sb.*[2]: app. after Bot.L.]

1. A species or subspecies of mint (*Mentha piperita*), cultivated for its essential oil (*oil of peppermint*: see 2).

Also applied with qualifying words to other species of mint or other labiates having similar properties.

1696 RAY *Synopsis* (ed. 2) 124 Mentha..sapore fervido Piperis. Pepper-Mint found by Dr. Eales in Hartfordshire. **1753** CHAMBERS *Cycl. Supp.* s.v. *Mentha*,..16. The common thick spiked pepper Mint. **1755** JOHNSON, *Peppermint*, mint eminently hot. **1838** T. THOMSON *Chem. Org. Bodies* 473 Oil of Peppermint..is extracted from the leaves of the..common Peppermint. **1866** *Treas. Bot.* 862 Australian Peppermint, *Mentha australis*. Small—, *Thymus Piperella*. **1884** MILLER *Plant-n.*, Chinese Pepper-mint, *Mentha arvensis glabrata*... Japanese—, *Mentha arvensis* var. *piperascens*.

2. a. The essential oil of peppermint, or some preparation of it.

It has a characteristic pungent aromatic flavour leaving an after-sensation of coolness, and is much used for flavouring sweetmeats, etc., and in medicine as a digestive stimulant and carminative, and to qualify the taste of nauseous drugs.

1836 BRANDE *Chem.* (ed. 4) 987 It is insupportably bitter, with an aroma like peppermint. **1866–77** WATTS *Dict. Chem.* IV. 187 (Oils, Volatile) The hydrocarbons from wormwood, anise, thyme, mint..group with ordinary turpentine; bay, myrtle, and rosemary stand alone... Peppermint is somewhat intermediate in its properties.

b. A lozenge flavoured with peppermint, a peppermint-drop. Also, any peppermint-flavoured sweetmeat.

1829 G. GRIFFIN *Collegians* I. iii. 56 'He gave me an O'Dell-cake when he was last here,' said one. 'And me a stick of peppermint.' **1835** J. TODD *Student's Man.* (ed. 2) 281 A handful of hot peppermints. **1883** *Harper's Mag.* Sept. 534/2 The windows were decorated..with..glass jars in which were sticks of striped candy, the half-moist peppermint, and the brown sugary squares. **1884** J. QUINCY *Figures of Past* 176 [He] produced just the stimulant required in the form of a package of peppermints. **1899** EARL ROSEBERY in *Daily News* 4 Nov. 3/2 You have an assortment of eloquent extracts like a box of peppermints to take away the taste of anything that fails to come up to the higher standard.

c. Used as a flavouring in drinks: hence, the name of a cordial, and of a liqueur (= *crème de menthe* s.v. CRÈME 1 b).

c **1770** in de Vries & Fryer *Venus Unmasked* (1967) 31 She allows gin and peppermint in the room. **1825** P. EGAN *Life of Actor* ii. 54 Now to avail me of the Friar's hint, He bade me take it in some peppermint. *c* **1863** T. TAYLOR *Ticket-of-Leave Man* I. 8 Four penn'orth of brandy,..and a little peppermint..(*stirring and sipping his brandy and peppermint*). **1865** E. H. GREENHOW in E. R. Pike *Human Documents Victorian Golden Age* (1967) 203 Wine, gin, peppermint, and other stimulants are..often given.., their actual effect being..to stupefy the child. **1870** D. J. KIRWAN *Palace & Hovel* xxxv. 516 Glass o' nice peppermint! this cold morning—ha'penny a glass! **1900** E. GLYN *Visits of Elizabeth* 77, I could bear most of it, if it wasn't for the peppermint glasses at the end, which the men have. **1963** A. L. SIMON *Guide Good Food & Wines* 742 The highly scented leaves of *Mint* are used in the making of liqueurs usually sold under the name of *Crème de Menthe* or *Peppermint*. **1972** C. DRUMMOND *Death at Bar* i. 32 A little drop of peppermint with a dash of lemonade. **1972** M. GILBERT *Body of Girl* xii. 107 Make it a gin and peppermint and I might join you.

d. Used as the name of various colours (esp. green) associated with peppermint-flavoured drinks or sweets.

1868 D. G. ROSSETTI *Let.* 17 Nov. (1965) II. 676, I wonder has Scotus's peppermint-and-mud tint been applied yet to the wall surrounding the Topsaic tapestries. **1934** A. HUXLEY *Beyond Mexique Bay* 23 The buttery glossiness of acetate silk shone, yellow, or peppermint green. **1963** A. CHRISTIE *Clocks* xiii. 113 The door was opened by an elderly woman with..a black skirt and a rather unexpected peppermint-striped jumper. **1965** R. GOULART in H. Waugh *Merchants of Menace* (1971) (*title*) Peppermint-striped goodbye. *Ibid.* 143 They drove around in an old ice-cream wagon they'd painted with peppermint stripes. **1973** *Observer* (Colour Suppl.) 30 Dec. 29/2 (*caption*) Peppermint washable satin nightdress.., £24. **1976** *Milton Keynes Express* 28 May 48/2 (Advt.), 1976 Moskvitch Estate, peppermint green..£475. **1976** N. THORNBURG *Cutter & Bone* i. 4 Bone slipped into his peppermint-stripe shirt.

3. (In full, *peppermint-tree*.) Name for several Australian species of *Eucalyptus* (*E. amygdalina*, *piperita*, etc.), yielding an aromatic essential oil resembling that of peppermint. Also, ***peppermint gum***.

1790 *J. White's Voy. N.S. Wales* App. 227 The name of Peppermint Tree has been given to this plant by Mr. White on account of the very great resemblance between the essential oil drawn from its leaves and that obtained from the Peppermint. **1880** SUTHERLAND *Tales Goldfields* 30 A woody gully, filled with peppermint and stringy-bark trees. **1911** E. M. CLOWES *On Wallaby* ix. 249 In the Wombat Forest..is found messmate, peppermint, and swamp-gum. **1936** F. CLUNE *Roaming round Darling* vi. 51 He found the poor thief by the sight of his boots poking out between two stones that made him a house under a peppermint tree. **1963** W. BLUNT *Of Flowers & Village* 94 The Australian peppermint tree (*Eucalyptus amygdalina*) is the tallest of all trees. **1966** *Southerly* XXVI. 107 The stringybarks and peppermint gums at the edges of the encircling scrub. **1967** T. KENEALLY *Bring Larks* xxv. 189 A half-uprooted peppermint hung over them.

4. *attrib.* and *Comb.* **peppermint cake** = *mint cake* (*b*) s.v. MINT *sb.*[2] 3; **peppermint-camphor** = MENTHOL; **peppermint cordial**, a cordial flavoured with peppermint; **peppermint cream**, a cream sweet flavoured with peppermint and often covered with chocolate; **peppermint-drop, -lozenge**, a lozenge made of sugar, flavoured with peppermint; **peppermint geranium**, a variety of *Pelargonium tomentosum*, with downy, scented leaves and white flowers; **peppermint gum**: see sense 3 above; **peppermint lump**, a type of sweet flavoured with peppermint; **peppermint oil** = *oil of peppermint* (see 1, 2); **peppermint-scented** *a.*, with a scent of peppermint; *spec.* **peppermint-scented geranium** = *peppermint geranium*; **peppermint-tea**, an infusion of the leaves of the peppermint; **peppermint-tree** (see 3); **peppermint-water**, a cordial distilled from peppermint.

1863 MRS. GASKELL *Sylvia's Lovers* II. xii. 220 Here's a bit o' *peppermint cake; he's main and fond on it. **1865–68** WATTS *Dict. Chem.* III. 881 *Peppermint-camphor is an alcohol containing the radicle $C_{10}H_{19}$ (menthyl). **1917** *Harrods Gen. Catal.* 1293 Schweppes cordials... *Peppermint cordial 1/6. **1974** *Guardian* 24 Jan. 6/8 Dr McGill later celebrated his acquittal with peppermint cordial. **1907** *Yesterday's Shopping* (1969) 49/2 *Peppermint Creams. **1940** 'R. CROMPTON' *William & Evacuees* ii. 49 'Thank you, dear,' said Mrs. Brown, selecting a peppermint cream. **1976** P. FERRIS *Detective* i. 3 His wife..asked him if he would buy a box of peppermint creams. **1799** F. BOSCAWEN *Let.* 10 Jan. in C. Aspinall-Oglander *Admiral's Widow* (1942) 177, I shall be glad..if you could send me 3 ounces of *pepper mint drops such as I am used to have. **1818** [see DROP *sb.* 10 e]. **1849** DICKENS *Dav. Copp.* (1850) vii. 68 He was so kind as to..dissolve a peppermint drop in it. **1878** W. S. GILBERT *H.M.S. Pinafore*, A. 1 I've chickens and conies and pretty polonies, And excellent peppermint drops. **1888** *Pop. Sci. Monthly* Apr. 785 Peppermint-drops are made of granulated sugar and water heated to the boiling-point. **1922** A. L. JEKYLL *Kitchen Ess.* iv. 36 Make a quart of good lemon jelly... Whilst warm add a handful of those large green *peppermint geranium leaves, thick as a fairy's blanket, soft as a vicuna robe, and to be found in most old-fashioned gardens. **1931** E. S. ROHDE *Scented Garden* vii. 177 The leaves of this kind were large and soft... I know it now for *Pelargonium tomentosum*, usually called the peppermint geranium. **1966** G. B. FOSTER *Herbs for every Garden* iv. 123 Peppermint geranium, with its velvety, grape-like leaves and small white blossoms is *P[elargonium] tomentosum*. **1846** LINDLEY *Veg. Kingd.* 660 The volatile oil ..is what gives their flavour to *Peppermint lozenges. **1926–7** *Army & Navy Stores Catal.* 55/2 Sweets... *Peppermint lumps. **1932** H. H. PRICE *Perception* viii. 230 The taste of a peppermint lump may linger on when the lump itself is no longer tactually present in our mouth. **1892** *Analyst* XVII. 14 Commercial samples of *peppermint oil differ in quality as well as composition. **1966** *McGraw-Hill Encycl. Sci. & Technol.* VIII. 227/2 *l*-Menthol, found as the main constituent..in peppermint oil. **1823** R. SWEET *Geraniaceæ* II. 168 This plant, often known by the name of *Peppermint-scented Geranium, is an old inhabitant of our greenhouses. **1907** *Westm. Gaz.* 3 Dec. 2/1 To return to the peppermint-scented schoolroom. **1946** M. FREE *All about House Plants* xvii. 165 *P[elargonium] tomentosum* has long-stalked, Peppermint-scented leaves. **1960** R. HEMPHILL *Fragrance & Flavour* 89 Pick and wash a bunch of peppermint-scented geranium leaves. **1875** tr. *H. von Ziemssen's Cycl. Med.* I 460 Aromatic drinks, chamomile tea, *peppermint tea, &c. **1757** A. COOPER *Distiller* II. v. (1760) 126 The simple Waters now commonly made, are Orange-flower-water,..*Pepper-mint-water, etc. **1820** *Pharmacopœia U.S.* 85 In the same manner are prepared peppermint water,..spearmint water,..rose water. **1907** *Yesterday's Shopping* (1969) 516/2 Peppermint Water..8 oz. bot 0/5. *a* **1976** A. CHRISTIE *Autobiogr.* (1977) v. 251, I did..give her an extra dollop of peppermint water.

†**'peppernel.** *Obs. rare*[−1]. [Origin obscure.] 'Apparently, a lump or swelling' (Nares).

1611 BEAUM. & FL. *Knt. Burn. Pestle* II. ii, A has a Peppernel in 's head, as big as a Pullets egg.

pepperoni (pɛpə'rəʊnɪ). Also **peperoni**. [ad. It. *peperone* chilli.] Beef and pork sausage seasoned with pepper.

1934 in WEBSTER. **1960** A. E. BENDER *Dict. Nutrition* 113/1 Pepperoni [etc.]..are slowly dried to a hard condition. **1967** *Boston Sunday Globe* 23 Apr. (Advt. section) 7/2 Pepperoni is another ready-to-eat of pork and beef with ground red pepper and the usual dry sausage seasonings. It is a little under 2 inches in diameter. **1969** R. & D. DE SOLA *Dict. Cooking* 172/2 *Peperoni*, highly seasoned Italian sausage. **1971** C. CLAIBORNE *N.Y. Times Internat. Cookbook* 440/2 Dot the surface of the pizza with one sliced peperoni sausage. **1974** *Time Out* 27 Sept. 33 It's still Fellini, which has become an identifiable substance like salami or pepperoni that can be sliced into at any point. **1976** *Times* 26 June 12/5 Pizza..with generous topping of good tomato sauce, Mozzarella cheese, peperoni and fresh mushrooms. **1977** *Custom Car* Nov. 67/3 The only action required is a wink, and wham! out comes his pepperoni!

'pepper-pot. **1. a.** = PEPPER-BOX 1.

1679 *Lond. Gaz.* No. 1381/4 One Mustard Pot and Pepper Pot of silver. **1860** EMERSON *Cond. Life, Beauty*, What! has my stove and pepper-pot a false bottom!

b. In various allusive and figurative uses: cf. PEPPER-BOX 1 b, 2, 4.

1838 JAMES *Robber* vi, Wiley would have been in the pepper-pot at Uppington by this time. **1886** *Cornh. Mag.* July 29 The old workhouse is gone, and a new one with golden vanes and pepper-pots has arisen in its stead. **1894** FENN *In Alpine Valley* I. 105 Apologise for saving that old pepperpot's life!

2. a. A West Indian dish composed of meat (or fish, game, etc.) and vegetables stewed down with cassareep and red pepper or other hot spices. Also *attrib.* in ***pepperpot soup***.

1698 E. WARD *Trip to Jamaica* 15 They make a rare Soop they call Pepper-Pot. *a* **1704** T. BROWN *Lett. fr. Dead* II. Wks. 1760 II. 215 That most delicate palate-scorching soop called pepper-pot, a kind of devil's broth much eat in the West Indies. **1792** WOLCOTT (P. Pindar) *Rights of Kings* Ode ii, Terrenes of flatt'ry are prepar'd so hot By courtiers—a delicious pepper-pot. **1796** STEDMAN *Surinam* (1813) II. xxvi. 292 Pepper-pot is a dish of boiled fish and capsicum, eaten with roasted plantains. **1899** RODWAY *Guiana Wilds* 122 She quickly returned with a calabash of thin pepper-pot and a cake of cassava bread. **1899** [see FOO-FOO]. **1949** *Caribbean Q.* I. I. 20 Pepper pot..is..the method devised by the aboriginal South American Indians to conserve the food they have got by hunting or fishing. **1958** R. HOWE *Cooking from Commonwealth* 387 (*heading*) Jamaica. Pepperpot soup. **1961** F. G. CASSIDY *Jamaica Talk* xvi. 336 Cassava liquor—once known as *casareep* and the basis of the traditional *pepperpot* soup—is not however favoured. **1965** 'LAUCHMONEN' *Old Thom's Harvest* vi. 81, I can smell pepper-pot and peas. **1970** SIMON & HOWE *Dict. Gastron.* 296/2 Jamaican pepperpot soup is thickened with yam or coconut. **1970** M. SLATER *Caribbean Cooking* 10 *Coalpots*.. used in the country, and for traditional stews and pepperpots requiring prolonged cooking. **1971** *Advocate-News* (Barbados) 17 Sept. (Guyana Suppl.) p. i/1 *Casareep*, syrup-like substance left after poison has been boiled out of juice of bitter cassava, used to prepare pepperpot. **1973** *Ibid.* 29 June 7/3 (Advt.), From the choicest Continental cuisine to the spicy Barbadian—from the generous cut of prime sirloin to the traditional Barbadian pepperpot soup—the food is the best.

b. In Pennsylvania, a stew of tripe and doughballs highly seasoned with pepper. (*Cent. Dict.*)

1794 *Massachusetts Spy* 13 Mar. 1 A wag in my neighbourhood, a lover of pepper pots. **1800** C. MACPHERSON *Mem.* 205 'And what have you got for dinner ..?'—'Me have got peppa pot, Massa.' **1825** J. K. PAULDING *John Bull in Amer.* xiv. 231 Whose principal trade consists in the exportation of Toughy and Pepper Pot. **1930** J. WILLIAMSON *Amer. Hotel* 217 A..list..of American culinary creations..would include such concoctions as.. Philadelphia pepper-pot. **1946** S. HIBBEN *Amer. Regional Cookery* 25 Lay in Dumplings for Pepperpot and cook as directed.

3. *attrib.* and *Comb.*

1883 G. MACDONALD *Donal Grant* I. 34 One house with the pepper-pot turrets. **1897** MARY KINGSLEY *W. Africa* 27 A hill, on whose summit stands Fort William, a pepper-pot-like structure now used as a lighthouse.

† **'pepper-,quern.** *Obs.* Forms: see PEPPER and QUERN[1]. A quern or hand-mill for grinding pepper; a pepper-mill.

1402-3 *Durham Acc. Rolls* (Surtees) 217, j par de pepir qwerns. *c* **1440** *Promp. Parv.* 393/1 Pepyr qwerne (*K., S.* pepirwherne), *fractillum.* **1564** *Wills & Inv. N.C.* (Surtees) I. 223, iiij stonepotts ij pep'quernes viijd. **1656** BLOUNT *Glossogr.*, *Quern* (Belg.) a handmill; as a Pepper Quern, a Mill to grinde Pepper. **1825** JAMIESON, *Pepper-curne*, a hand-mill used for grinding pepper.

'pepper-tree. A name given to various trees: cf. PEPPER *sb.* 3. *spec.* **a.** An evergreen tree or shrub of S. America, *Schinus Molle* (N.O. *Anacardiaceæ*), having a pungent red fruit; cultivated for ornament in California and Australia; **b.** Either of two Australasian evergreen trees, *Drimys aromatica* or *Pseudowintera axillaris* (HOROPITO), both belonging to the family Magnoliaceæ, and bearing small dark fruits once used as a substitute for pepper.

1691-2 SLOANE in *Phil. Trans.* XVII. 462 A Description of the *Pimienta* or Jamaica Pepper-Tree. **1745** P. THOMAS *Jrnl. Anson's Voy.* 36 Besides..there are..the Pepper Tree. **1797** *Monthly Mag.* III. 208 The number of nutmeg-trees transplanted from the Indies, is less than even that of the pepper-trees. **1827** HELLYER in Bischoff *Van Diemen's Land* (1832) 175, I saw several pepper trees, and procured the berries. **1839** T. L. MITCHELL *Three Exped. E. Australia* II. xii. 280 We also found the aromatic tea, *Tasmania aromatica*. .. The leaves and bark of this tree have a hot biting cinnamon-like taste, on which account it is vulgarly called the pepper-tree. **1857** B. I. HAYES *Pioneer Notes* (1929) 183 When I was at San Bernardino last, I obtained two small fir trees and two pepper trees. **1882** W. D. HAY *Brighter Britain!* II. vi. 195 The Horopito, or 'Pepper-tree' (*Drimys axillaris*) yields also an ornamental timber. **1883** *Century Mag.* Dec. 201/1 Bright green pepper-trees..give a graceful plumed draping. **1911** C. E. W. BEAN *'Dreadnought' of Darling* xv. 141 The thick shady wilga—rather like a pepper tree in the distance. **1939** W. FAULKNER *Wild Palms* 192 The pepper trees had been green all winter. **1949** W. HERTRICH *Huntington Bot. Gardens* 4 Where the widening of Huntington Drive was necessary, it was a great misfortune to have to eliminate all of these pepper trees. **1950** G. BRENAN *Face of Spain* iv. 92 The smooth-trunked rubber trees spread out their glossy leaves, the pepper trees trail their feathery tendrils. **1971** *Southerly* XXXI. 5 The impressions that will remain, transfigured, in his memory: the pepper tree breaking into light in the Duffield's yard. **1977** *Austral. House & Garden* Jan. 17/1 Check these and spray them too if necessary: Gardenia,..Chinese tallow tree, Pepper tree (schinus), [etc.]. **1978** 'M. M. KAYE' *Far Pavilions* x. 163 He..kissed her behind a kindly screen of pepper trees.

pepper-up(per): see PEP *v.*

'pepper-,water. **1.** An infusion of black pepper, formerly used for microscopical observation of infusorian organisms.

1686 PLOT *Staffordsh.* 97 Minute bubbles (that move like Animals in pepper water). **1691** RAY *Creation* I. (1692) 159 Those Animalcula, not long since discovered in Pepper-water, by Mr. Lewenhoek, of Delft in Holland. **1766** BAKER in *Phil. Trans.* LVI. 71 The seeds of mushrooms, the feathers of butterflies, pepper-water, &c.

2. ? Some kind of soup flavoured with pepper.

1798 *Sporting Mag.* XI. 308, I supped..in his house on mulagatoney or pepper-water.

'pepperwood. Name given to several trees having pungent or aromatic wood or bark.

Among these are *Xanthoxylum Clava-herculis*, of West Indies, etc. (HOUGH *American Woods*, 1894, v. 30); *Umbellularia Californica* (*Ibid.* 1897, VII. 34); also, *Dicypellium caryophyllatum* Nees, Brazil Clove Bark (*Pao cravo, Imyra Quiynha*), and *Licaria guianensis* (Carib *Licari-Kanali*), the Bois de Rose of Cayenne (*Treas. Bot.*, Suppt. 1874; MILLER *Plant-names*, 1884).

1856 *U.S. Naut. Mag. & Naval Jrnl.* V. 228 The timber used..is pepperwood, and was cut from the land close by the prison [*sc.* San Quentin, California]. **1858** C. E. DE LONE *Jrnl.* 5 Mar. in *Calif. Hist. Soc. Q.* (1930) IX. 253 Noticed the beautie's of the peper [*sic*] wood tree. **1882** *Humboldt Times* (Eureka, Calif.) 7 Jan. 1/4 The schooner Alaska, lying in the bay ready for sea, has on board 50,000 feet of pepperwood, commonly called California laurel. **1894** R. B. HOUGH *Amer. Woods* V. 30 *Xanthoxylum Clava-Herculis*, L. Prickly Ash, Sea Ash, Toothache Tree, Pepperwood. **1949** *Natural Hist.* Mar. 130/2 Under a pepperwood tree they did find a pile of glass flakings.

pepperwort ('pɛpəwɜːt). [See WORT]

1. A species of cress (*Lepidium latifolium*), formerly also called Dittander or Dittany; also applied to the genus *Lepidium* in general.

1562 TURNER *Herbal* II. 34b, Lepidium is called in Englishe Dittani, but foulishly and vnlearnedly; in Duche Pfefferkraut that is peperwurt. **1578** LYTE *Dodoens* v. lxvi. 631 Dittany whiche we may more rightly cal Pepperwurt, hath long brode leaues. **1607** TOPSELL *Four-f. Beasts* (1658) 420 The herb called Nard or Pepper-wort..will presently help any Beast which is bitten by the Shrew. **1676** T. GLOVER in *Phil. Trans.* XI. 629. **1857** MAYNE *Expos. Lex.*, *Pepperwort*, a common name for the *Lepidium iberis.* **1866** *Treas. Bot.*, Pepperwort, *Lepidium*.

b. Applied in N. America to *Dentaria diphylla*, also called *pepper-root*.

1861 MISS PRATT *Flower. Pl.* I. 112 The root of..the Two-leaved Coral-root, is used by the Americans instead of mustard, and is called Pepper-wort. **1866** *Treas. Bot.* 393 The roots of *D*[*entaria*] *diphylla*..are used..from Pennsylvania to Canada,..under the name of Pepperwort.

2. *pl.* A name for the N.O. *Marsileaceæ*, consisting of small aquatic plants allied to the ferns.

1846 LINDLEY *Veg. Kingd.* 71 *Marsileaceæ.*—Pepperworts. *Ibid.* 72 The main feature by which Pepperworts are known as an Order from Lycopodiaceæ. **1851** T. MOORE (*title*) A Popular History of the British Ferns..comprising the Club-Mosses, Pepperworts, and Horsetails.

b. Lindley's name for N.O. *Piperaceæ*.

1846 LINDLEY *Veg. Kingd.* 515 Order cxcvi. *Piperaceæ.*—Pepperworts. *Ibid.* 516 Pepperworts are related to Buckwheats, Saururads, and Nettles.

peppery ('pɛpərɪ), *a.* [f. PEPPER *sb.* + -Y.]

1. Abounding in pepper; of the nature of or resembling pepper, esp. in pungency or irritating effect; pungent, 'hot'. (In quots. 1699, 1709, Consisting of small grains like pepper; in 1860, Characterized by small dots in engraving.)

1699 DAMPIER *Voy.* II. I. 9 There you have black Oaz and dark Peppery Sand. **1709** *Ibid.* III. II. 182 Small Peppery Sand. **1830** LINDLEY *Nat. Syst. Bot.* 170 It has a very bitter peppery taste. **1860** O. W. HOLMES *Prof. Breakf.-t.* ii, Thy roses hinted by the peppery burin of Bartolozzi. **1900** *Daily News* 26 Oct. 3/2 You get a peppery feeling, a tickling, a dryness of the throat, an irritation of the mucous membrane.

2. *fig.* **a.** Of speech or writing: Sharp, stinging, pungent; 'highly spiced'. **b.** Of a person, his temper, etc.: Hot-tempered, irascible, irritable, testy.

1826 SCOTT *Diary* 28 Feb., Completed Malachi to-day. It is..in some places perhaps too peppery. **1844** DICKENS *Mart. Chuz.* xvii, Some good, strong, peppery doctrine. **1861** *Sat. Rev.* 14 Sept. 268 The opponent may be a peppery, narrow-minded man. **1897** *N. & Q.* 8th Ser. XII. 343/1 Dash [a dog] was small, young and peppery.

c. In extended uses: unpleasant, objectionable; strong, powerful.

1829 P. EGAN *Boxiana* 2nd Ser. II. 189 This was a short round, but *peppery*. **1901** M. FRANKLIN *My Brilliant Career* ix. 71 Gertie, the boys, and myself had to perform our morning ablutions in a leaky tin dish on a stool outside the kitchen door, which on cold frosty mornings was a pretty peppery performance. **1946** KOESTLER *Thieves in Night* 128 'We even have to hire the tractor of the Hebrews at two pounds and a half per dunum.' 'A peppery price, by Mohammed.' **1958** P. GAMMOND *Decca Bk. Jazz* iv. 55 What was then known as 'The Original Dixieland Jass Band —Untuneful Harmonists Playing Peppery Melodies'. **1958** *Which?* I. II. 25/1 The overhead-valve engine..is small in displacement, but peppery for its size.

d. Pepper-coloured.

1962 I. MURDOCH *Unofficial Rose* xxxvi. 343 Her soft peppery hair..was cut short in a neat yet raffish style about her beaming countenance.

Hence **'pepperily** *adv.*; **'pepperiness.**

1900 MISS BROUGHTON *Foes in Law* xxi. 305 The olive branch is..offered, accepted..or pepperily tossed back. **1890** *Cent. Dict.*, Pepperiness.

pep-pill ('pɛppɪl). *colloq.* (orig. *U.S.*). [f. PEP *sb.* + PILL *sb.*[2]] A stimulant drug dispensed in the form of a pill.

1937 *Time* 10 May 45/1 (*heading*) Pep-pill poisoning. The use by college students of a new, powerful but poisonous brain stimulant called Benzedrine last week kept college directors of health in dithers of worry. *Ibid.*, Students who, while cramming for final examinations, collapse,..are under suspicion of using the substance. They call it 'pepper-up', 'pep pills'. **1955** [see AMPHETAMINE]. **1955** *Sci. News Let.* 2 Apr. 219/2 Amphetamine, or Benzedrine, known as 'pep pills',..is most likely to produce pleasant sensations in normal persons. **1959** *Times* 29 May 14/6 The performance of athletes may be improved through 'pep pills' by as much as 4 per cent. **1959** *Guardian* 16 Nov. 1/4 They had..tomato sandwiches, with coffee and tea, but no 'pep' pills. **1960** *Times Lit. Suppl.* 20 May 323/2 The managerial class gets its kicks from pep pills instead of art. **1960** *Spectator* 22 July 120 The campaign then being waged by some newspapers against the pep-pill Preludin. **1965** *New Scientist* 29 July 261/2 Amphetamines and barbiturates, variously called stimulants and depressants, pep pills and 'goof balls'. **1967** *Spectator* 30 June 758/1 The Rolling Stone Mick Jagger, was found guilty of possessing pep pills. **1974** E. AMBLER *Dr. Frigo* II. 98 As for that movie star, how do you know he isn't on pep pills?

peppy ('pɛpɪ), *a.* orig. *U.S.* [f. PEP *sb.* + -Y[1].] Full of pep or vigour; spirited, energetic, lively, forceful.

1922 S. LEWIS *Babbitt* vi. 86 Wouldn't it be a good idea if I could go off to China or some peppy place, and study engineering or something by mail? **1922** E. E. CUMMINGS *Let.* 3 May (1969) 84 Thru being more or less true to the peppy thesis..I feel: more pep, pleasure in living. **1924** WODEHOUSE *Bill the Conqueror* xx. 303, I said it was the peppiest scheme of the age, a lallapaloosa. **1926** *Picture-Play Mag.* July 3/2 (Advt.), How I used to envy..Billy jazzing up a party with his peppy banjo! **1927** *Melody Maker* Sept. 883/1 They have a red 'hot' peppy dance rhythm and are thoroughly bright and interesting. **1930** E. WAUGH *Vile Bodies* vii. 129, I like your page. It's peppy. **1932** T. S. ELIOT *Sel. Essays* III. 197 There is nothing in the play to which could be applied the term appropriately used in the advertisements of some films; the 'peppy situation'. **1934** J. O'HARA *Appointment in Samarra* (1935) 15 Everyone from out of town thought it was the peppiest place in the country at Christmas. **1939** *Melody Maker* 10 June 5/3 This peppy, blonde, stage-and-concert-party artist. **1956** M. STEARNS *Story of Jazz* (1957) xvi. 180 Most of these bands recorded a novelty now and then that might be called 'peppy'. **1969** *New Yorker* 10 May 33/2 He did a peppy foxtrot. **1974** J. HELLER *Something Happened* 14 She was peppy and direct, always laughing and teasing. **1977** *Time* 14 Feb. 39/3 A.M.C...will give the Pacer a peppier engine. **1977** *Rolling Stone* 7 Apr. 69/3 It's an interesting combination and forces all the songs on *Blondie* to work on at least two levels: as peppy but rough pop, and as distanced, artless avant-rock.

Pepsi-Cola ('pɛpsɪ'kəʊlə). orig. *U.S.* Also in shortened form **Pepsi**. The proprietary names of a popular soft drink, and of the syrup preparations from which it is made.

1903 *New Bern* (N. Carolina) *Jrnl.* 25 Feb. (Advt.), Pepsi-Cola. At Soda Fountains... Aids Digestion. **1903** *Official Gaz.* (U.S. Patent Office) 16 June 1891/2 Flavoring-syrup for soda-water. Caleb D. Bradham, Newbern, N.C. Filed Sept. 23, 1902 Pepsi-Cola. **1906** *Ibid.* 12 June 2342/2 Tonic Beverage. Caleb D. Bradham, New Bern, N.C. Pepsi-Cola. Filed Apr. 15, 1905. **1916** *Ibid.* 9 May 676/1 The Pepsi-Cola Co., Newbern, N.C. Filed Mar. 19, 1915. Pepsi..A Flavoring-syrup for soda water. *Claims use* since Nov. 21, 1911. **1940** *Life* 7 Oct. 79/1 (*caption*) They [*sc.* A. B. Kent and A. H. C. C. Johnson]..are best known for these immortal lines which have even been translated into Yiddish. They are basically a swing version of *John Peel*: Pepsi-Cola hits the spot! Twelve full ounces, that's a lot, Twice as much for a nickel too—Pepsi-Cola is the drink for you! **1949** N. STREATFEILD *Painted Garden* xiv. 156 He gave her a pepsi-cola. **1953** *Trade Marks Jrnl.* 13 May 417/2 Pepsi-Cola... Non-alcoholic drinks and preparations for making such drinks, all containing cola extract..Pepsi-Cola Limited, Pepsi-Cola Factory,..Brentford, Middlesex; manufacturers and bottlers. **1957** C. MACINNES *City of Spades* I. 107 'Some orange juice or Coke?' 'Ta, Guv, I'll have a Pepsi.' **1959** *Encounter* Sept. 50/2 Mugs bearing Shakespeare's image and sold over the counter with root beer and pepsi cola. **1960** *Trade Marks Jrnl.* 17 Aug. 998/1 Pepsi... Non-alcoholic drinks and preparations for making such drinks, all containing cola extract..Pepsi-Cola Limited,..Feltham, Middlesex; manufacturers and bottlers. **1961** *Western Folklore* XX. 182 Pepsi Cola hits the spot Turn the rope and give her hot. **1966** P. WILLMOTT *Adolescent Boys E. London* 20 We went back to the club and had a drink of Pepsi and a game of darts. **1973** *Sat. Rev. World* (U.S.) 25 Sept. 22/1 She smokes a cigarette, sips a Pepsi. **1976** *National Observer* (U.S.) 21 Feb. 5/5 All that *detente* brings the United States, Reagan says, is 'the right to sell Pepsi-Cola in Siberia'.

pepsin ('pɛpsɪn). Also formerly **-ine**. [mod. (Schwann 1836, Poggendorff *Annalen* XXXVIII. 358), f. Gr. πέψ-ις digestion (f. stem πεπ- to cook, digest, etc.) + -IN[1].] A ferment contained in the gastric juice, having the property of converting proteids into peptones in the presence of a weak acid; also used medicinally in cases of indigestion, etc.

1844 in DUNGLISON *Med. Lex.* **1845** G. E. DAY tr. *Simon's Anim. Chem.* I. 22 *Pepsin.* This name..was given by Schwann, to a substance which constitutes the most essential portion of the gastric juice. **1873** RALFE *Phys.*

Chem. 129 Pepsin is a greyish-white powder, insoluble in water, alcohol, and ether, very soluble in dilute acids.

attrib. **1886** *St. Stephen's Rev.* 13 Mar. 12/1 As good as a pepsine pill before dinner. **1894** S. FISKE *Holiday Stories* (1900) 213 He forgot his dyspepsia and his pepsin tablets.

Hence **'pepsinate** *v. trans.*, to mix or treat with pepsin; **pepsi'niferous** *a.*, producing pepsin (*Cent. Dict.*); **pep'sinogen**: see quot. 1893.

1882 QUAIN *Med. Dict.* 378/2 *Pepsinated pills of pounded raw beef. **1899** W. JAMES in *Talks to Teachers on Psychol.* 206 With our future food..pepsinated or half-digested in advance. **1878** FOSTER *Phys.* II. i. §2. 220 We have a certain amount of..evidence of the existence of a matter of ferment, or *pepsinogen, comparable to the pancreatic zymogen. **1893** *Syd. Soc. Lex.*, *Pepsinogen*, the *zymogen* which is continually being formed by the protoplasm of the gastric glands, and is converted, during secretion, into pepsin, and discharged from the gland-cells.

†**pepst**, ? *pa. pple.* or *a. Obs.* [Origin unknown.] 'Apparently a term for intoxicated' (Nares).

1577 KENDALL *Fl. Epigr.* Lviij, Thou drunken faindst thy-self of late: Thou three daies after slept: How wilt thou slepe with drinke in deede, When thou art throughly pepst?

pep talk ('pɛp tɔːk). [f. PEP *sb.* + TALK *sb.*] A speech or address intended to revive morale or promote energy or enthusiasm in its hearers. So **pep talker**, one who delivers a pep talk.

1926 B. REYNOLDS *Cocktail Continentale* xiv. 107 Where the great Cicero propounded his philosophy to the ages and from which our 'Pep' talks of to-day are copied. **1931** K. K. ROCKNE *Coaching* (rev. ed.) xxii. 256 One coach I know has his football team, before a game, gather in a room which is painted red, for their so-called 'pep-talk'. **1934** J. O'HARA *Appointment in Samarra* (1935) iv. 92 'Let's get through these holidays without any more mess... I don't want to give you a pep talk—' 'I know you don't. I don't blame you.' **1935** WODEHOUSE *Luck of Bodkins* vi. 66 I've seen that expression on her face a hundred times when she was giving us a pep talk before a match. **1940** R. CHANDLER *Farewell, my Lovely* xxxvi. 169 'I'm afraid of dying, of being nothing, of not finding a man named Brunette.' He chuckled... 'You sure give yourself a pep talk'. **1943** J. B. PRIESTLEY *Daylight on Saturday* xxx. 243 I'm wondering if we couldn't invite him to lunch and ask him to give the workers a pep talk in the canteen. **1945** [see FLANNEL *sb.* 1 f]. **1951** in M. McLuhan *Mech. Bride* (1967) 36/1 Dr. Starch does not merely point out..essential qualities of executive leadership. He does not preach or deliver 'pep' talks! **1957** J. BRAINE *Room at Top* v. 47 Worse still, there were what he called Pep Talks which were made specially gruesome by the fact that, since he seemed to be able to speak and scarcely open his lips, his..voice seemed to come from nowhere. **1969** J. WAINWRIGHT *Take-Over Men* vii. 121 Forget the fancy trappings the politicians and pep-talkers hide it behind. **1971** S. HILL *Strange Meeting* iii. 167 Every now and again Coulter gives us his pep talk, about how we are going to 'go out there and show 'em'. **1973** J. WAINWRIGHT *Pride of Pigs* 120 Which was what he was supposed to be doing...taking chances. The reason..for Harris's pep talk. **1976** *New Yorker* 15 Nov. 137/2 The students were given pep talks to build up their confidence and strengthen their 'will'.

peptic ('pɛptɪk), *a.* and *sb.* [ad. Gr. πεπτικός able to digest, f. πεπτ-ός cooked, digested.]

A. *adj.* **1.** Having the quality of digesting; belonging or relating to digestion: = DIGESTIVE A. 1; used *spec.* in relation to the digestion in which pepsin is concerned, as in ***peptic digestion***, stomachic or gastric digestion; ***peptic glands***, the glands which secrete the gastric juice; ***peptic ulcer***, an ulcer that is situated in a part of the alimentary tract bathed by the gastric juice, or that is attributed to its digestive action; so ***peptic ulceration***.

1651 BIGGS *New Disp.* §295. 218 Not by the intense peptick quality, but by the vigour of the digestible.. ferment. **1660** GAUDEN *Sacrilegus* 13 Who have good stomachs to both, if they had but..some Peptick power. **1866** HUXLEY *Phys.* vi. (1869) 167 These peptic glands which, when food passes into the stomach, throw out a thin acid fluid, the gastric juice. **1878** FOSTER *Phys.* II. i. (1879) 233 Peptic digestion is essentially an acid digestion. **1898** *Allbutt's Syst. Med.* V. 294 A peptic asthma due to indiscretions in diet. **1900** DORLAND *Med. Dict.* 726/1 Peptic u[lcer]. **1903** tr. *Riegel's Dis. Stomach* II. 543 Round ulcer of the stomach. Syn.—Ulcus ventriculi simplex,.. peptic ulcer, perforating gastric ulcer. **1929** HURST & STEWART *Gastric & Duodenal Ulcer* x. 496 Other forms of œsophageal ulcer..must be excluded before a diagnosis of peptic ulcer can be made. *Ibid.*, Peptic ulceration of the œsophagus. **1955** *Sci. News Let.* 30 July 3 A child's peptic ulcer may be confused with abdominal migraine, food allergy or other intestinal conditions. **1974** H. J. DWORKEN *Alimentary Tract* vi. 88 Certain other elements determine the ability to withstand formation of peptic ulcers, although the mechanism for their action is not know. Susceptibility to gastric ulcer increases with age; duodenal ulcers are more common in men than in women. *Ibid.*, People who live in the north of England..or at high altitudes such as in the Peruvian Andes show increased frequencies of peptic ulceration.

2. Having the quality of promoting or assisting digestion: = DIGESTIVE A. 2.

1661 LOVELL *Hist. Anim. & Min.* 403 The *vertigo*, is helped by..peptick powders, if from the stomach. **1828** *Blackw. Mag.* XXIV. 53 Thanks to a peptic pill of Doctor Kitchiner.

3. Able to digest; having good digestion: = EUPEPTIC A. 2.

1827 CARLYLE *Germ. Rom.* I. 63 A sound peptic stomach does not yield so tamely to the precepts of the head or heart.

4. ? Pertaining to or caused by suppuration. (Cf. DIGESTIVE A. 4.)

1884 M. MACKENZIE *Dis. Throat & Nose* II. 167 Antemortem peptic softening can be the cause of the injury.

B. *sb.* **1.** (See quot.)

1842 DUNGLISON *Med. Lex.*, *Peptic*, a substance which promotes digestion, or is digestive.

2. *pl.* The digestive organs. *humorous.*

1842 TENNYSON *Will Waterproof* x, Is there some magic in the place? Or do my peptics differ? **1883** W. WALLACE in *Academy* 7 Apr. 235 To be taken, refrained from, or mixed, according to the constitution and condition of our peptics.

3. *pl.* 'The doctrine of digestion' (Webster 1864).

Hence **'peptical** *a.* = PEPTIC *a.*; **peptician** (pɛp'tɪʃən), a person who has good digestion; **pepticity** (pɛp'tɪsɪtɪ), good peptic condition.

1831 *Fraser's Mag.* III. 12 His..political, practical, and peptical Theory of the Universe. **1831** CARLYLE *Misc.* (1857) III. 1 The true Peptician was that Countryman who answered that 'for his part, he had no system'. **1838** —— *Let.* 27 July in Froude *Life in Lond.* v. I. 141 A bit of brown bread, and peace and pepticity to eat it with.

peptidase ('pɛptɪdeɪz, -s). *Biochem.* [f. PEPTID(E + -ASE.] Orig., an enzyme which hydrolyses peptides; now usu. restricted to enzymes (exopeptidases) which hydrolyse the terminal peptide bonds of peptides, liberating amino-acids.

1918 *Jrnl. Infectious Dis.* XXII. 148 Normal human serum contains peptidase and maintains a relatively uniform titer. **1923** *Jrnl. Chem. Soc.* CXXIV. I. 496 The proteases can be provisionally classified as follows. A. True proteases which break down protein to the peptide stage... B. Peptidases or ereptases which only split peptides or peptones. **1936** [see *endopeptidase* s.v. ENDO-]. **1958** DIXON & WEBB *Enzymes* v. 228 By no means all peptide links are hydrolysed by all peptidases. **1970** R. W. MCGILVERY *Biochem.* xv. 307 They [*sc.* lysosomes] are particulate structures in the cell..loaded with a battery of hydrolytic enzymes: peptidases to attack proteins, esterases to attack lipids, [etc.]. *Ibid.* xxvii. 658 Exopeptidases, sometimes simply called peptidases without a clarifying prefix,..attack terminal peptide bonds.

peptide ('pɛptaɪd). *Biochem.* [ad. G. *peptid*, back-formation from *di-*, *tripeptid*, etc. (E. Fischer 1902, in *Chemiker-Zeitung* XXVI. 940/2), *polypeptid* (E. Fischer 1903): see POLYPEPTIDE.] **1.** Any compound in which two or more amino-acids are linked together by peptide bonds (see sense 2 below); according to the number of amino-acid residues such compounds are dipeptides, tripeptides, etc., oligopeptides, or polypeptides. Also *attrib.* or as *adj.*

1906 *Jrnl. Chem. Soc.* XC. II. 293 (*heading*) The fate of certain amino-acids and peptides in the organism of the dog. **1927** HALDANE & HUXLEY *Animal Biol.* iv. 107 We can make ..a sugar or peptide (part of a protein molecule) which only differs from the natural variety in that its molecules are related to the natural molecules as a left hand to a right. **1949** ABRAHAM & FLOREY in H. W. Florey et al. *Antibiotics* I. vii. 331 The tomato-wilting agent produced by *Fusarium lycopersici* Sacc. was isolated by Plattner and Clauson-Kaas .., who later..showed that it was a peptide and named it lyco-marasmine. **1953** FRUTON & SIMMONDS *Gen. Biochem.* v. 135 Various strains of microorganisms elaborate substances of peptide nature which have antibacterial activity for other microorganisms. **1972** F. M. MENGER et al. *Org. Chem.* xiv. 359 The distinction between proteins and peptides is arbitrary. Compounds which have molecular weights greater than 10,000 are generally referred to as proteins. **1976** *Sci. Amer.* Feb. 32/1 There are two large classes of hormones, the peptides and the steroids. *Ibid.* 32/2 A typical peptide hormone is insulin.., human insulin consists of 51 amino acid units. **1977** *Time* 21 Nov. 40/3 Drs. Frank Ervin of U.C.L.A.'s Neuropsychiatric Institute and Roberta Palmour of the University of California at Berkeley described the substance as a variant of a peptide—a short chain of amino acids—that belongs to a family of newly discovered opiate-like brain hormones called endorphins.

2. Special comb.: **peptide bond**, a carbon-nitrogen bond of the type –CO·NH– in an organic molecule; *spec.* one between the carboxyl group of one amino-acid residue and the amino group of another; **peptide chain**, a linear sequence of amino-acid residues joined by peptide bonds; **peptide linkage** = *peptide bond*.

1935 *Jrnl. Biol. Chem.* CXI. 249 Aminopeptidase, carboxypeptidase, and dipeptidase need in addition to a peptide bond a free amino group or a free carboxyl group. **1960** *New Biol.* XXXI. 12 There are twenty main different kinds of amino acid involved in protein make-up, though they are basically alike enough to be all connected to each other by the same kind of chemical link (the peptide bond) to form the chain. **1964** N. G. CLARK *Mod. Org. Chem.* xiii. 252 Many important natural products contain the 'amide-linkage' or peptide bond, –CO·NH–; thus, the peptides and proteins..are long-chain polyamides. **1931** *Nature* 2 May 664/2 There is a strong probability that..many proteins will be based on a roughly constant weight of peptide chain. **1935** *Jrnl. Biol. Chem.* CXI. 245 Lysine is coupled in the long peptide chains of proteins with its α-amino and carboxyl groups. **1970** R. W. MCGILVERY *Biochem.* ii. 9 A protein may be only a single, long, peptide chain, but most proteins are made of several peptide chains associated together. **1925** *Proc. R. Soc.* B. XCVIII. 59 This procedure was adopted in order to bring about the scission of the peptide linkages as rapidly as possible. **1964** N. G. CLARK *Mod. Org. Chem.* xvii. 349 Proteins and polypeptides consist of chains of amino-acids linked via amide formation between the carbonyl group of one acid and the α-amino group of the next (the typical linkage, –CO·NH–, is often called a peptide-linkage or -bond).

peptidic (pɛp'tɪdɪk), *a. Biochem.* [f. PEPTID(E + -IC.] Of, pertaining to, or being a peptide. Hence **pep'tidically** *adv.*, by means of a peptide bond.

1949 F. LIPMANN in *Federation Proc.* VIII. 597/1 To simplify the following discussion, the term 'peptidic link' is introduced as generic name for a –NH·CO-link between any amino or carboxyl group. The term 'peptide link' is then reserved for the 1-carboxyl, 2-amino-link between two alpha amino acids as it occurs in protein. **1964** *Adv. Enzymol.* XXVI. 212 Muropeptides, depending on the murein type, are known to differ by containing either Lys or one or more of the DAP stereoisomers to provide the free NH_2 group for peptidic linking. *Ibid.*, One enzyme..found ..in *E. coli* cells..disconnects two C6 units tied together peptidically into a C3 molecule. **1973** *Nature* 12 Oct. 288/1 G. Sterba..suggested that peptidic neurohormones might be involved in the generation of emotions by effects in the limbic system.

peptidoglycan (pɛp,taɪdəʊ'glaɪkæn). *Biochem.* [f. PEPTID(E + -O + GLYC(O- + -AN.] = MUREIN; also, the mucopolysaccharide which forms the strands of this.

1966 *Biochem.* V. 82/1 The biosynthesis of peptidoglycan (mucopeptide) in cell-free extracts of Staphylococcus aureus..has been described by Chatterjee and Park. *Ibid.* 3091 The mechanical strength of the peptidoglycan polymer which forms the rigid network of all bacterial cell walls depends on a high degree of cross-linking between peptide and polysaccharide chains. **1968** A. WHITE et al. *Princ. Biochem.* (ed. 4) xli. 910 Murein synthesis..may be regarded as proceeding in three stages: synthesis of the precursor units, synthesis of the linear peptidoglycan strands, and cross-linking. **1969** *New Scientist* 10 July 64/1 A major component of the cortex layer [of a bacterial spore] is the polymer murein (or peptidoglycan). **1975** *Nature* 10 Apr. 482/2 The walls of all penicillin-sensitive organisms contain a structural component called peptidoglycan, which consists of glycan chains of alternating residues of N-acetylglucosamine and its 3-*O*-D-lactyl ether..and D-amino acids.

peptidolysis (,pɛptaɪ'dɒlɪsɪs). *Biochem.* [f. PEPTID(E + -O + -LYSIS.] The degradation of a polypeptide into smaller peptides or amino-acids. Cf. PEPTOLYSIS. So **,peptido'lytic** *a.*

1970 *Nature* 25 July 337/2 Studies on the mechanism of action of peptidolytic enzymes..have made much use of their ability to hydrolyse esters as well as amides. **1971** *Ibid.* 25 June 495/2 Both sets of workers compared these data with kinetic results from peptidolytic reactions. **1972** *Biochim. & Biophys. Acta* CCLXV. 70 Cleavage, for example, of a 50000-dalton peptide into fragments of 44000 and 6000 daltons, respectively, can clearly be detected... Such peptidolysis can be observed only after dissolution of the protein by the detergent, since separated peptide fragments otherwise tend to remain associated through hydrophobic interactions.

peptization (pɛptaɪ'zeɪʃən). *Chem.* [f. PEPT(ONE + -IZATION.] The transformation of a solid or semi-solid colloid into a fluid form by chemical means.

1864 T. GRAHAM in *Proc. R. Soc.* XIII. 340 Liquid silicic acid may be represented as the 'peptone' of gelatinous silicic acid; and the liquefaction of the latter by a trace of alkali may be spoken of as the peptization of the jelly. **1916** E. F. BURTON *Physical Prop. Colloidal Solutions* ii. 24 The large number of colloidal solutions prepared by the method known as peptization are examples of the resolution of a moist coagulum. **1934** *Industr. & Engin. Chem.* Nov. 1190/2 (*heading*) Peptization of lightly vulcanised rubber. **1948** A. LANE *Greek Pott.* i. 5 The coagulation can..be broken down by a process known as 'peptization', by the disintegrating action on the clay of certain chemicals. **1960** R. G. HAGGAR *Conc. Encycl. Cont. Pott. & Porc.* 210/2 Modern scholars have..demonstrated the understanding which they [*sc.* the Greeks] had of clay processes, of oxydising and reducing firing techniques, and what to-day are called 'protective colloids' and 'peptization'. **1963** D. W. & E. E. HUMPHRIES tr. *Termier's Erosion & Sedimentation* vi. 135 The peptization of colloidal ferric hydroxide occurs at pH 6·6, under the influence of humus and colloidal silica which is present in the soil. **1972** MOELLER & O'CONNOR *Ions in Aqueous Syst.* v. 113 Conversion of precipitate into a colloidal suspension is called 'peptization'.

peptize ('pɛptaɪz), *v. Chem.* [f. PEPT(ONE + -IZE.] *trans.* To convert into a sol; to cause to undergo peptization.

1864 T. GRAHAM in *Proc. R. Soc.* XIII. 340 The pure jellies of alumina, peroxide of iron, and titanic acid, prepared by dialysis, are assimilated more closely to albumen, being peptized by minute quantities of hydrochloric acid. **1934** H. N. HOLMES *Introd. Colloid Chem.* iii. 26 Glue, gelatin, soap, gum arabic, and dextrin are said to be soluble in water. In reality they are merely peptized by water—they are subdivided into particles far larger than molecules. **1939** [see DISPERSE *v.* 9]. **1955** R. K. ILER *Colloid Chem. Silica & Silicates* v. 92 Various processes have been described which involve making silica gel from acid and silicate, washing out the salts, and peptizing the wet gel by heating it under pressure in the presence of a small amount of alkali. **1972** MOELLER & O'CONNOR *Ions in Aqueous Syst.* v. 116 Freshly prepared and washed precipitates can be peptized in many cases by adding water and a little of the original precipitating reagent.

Hence **'peptized, 'peptizing** *ppl. adjs.* Also **,peptiza'bility, pep'tizable** *a.*

1921 W. D. BANCROFT *Appl. Colloid Chem.* v. 167 We may have peptization by a liquid, by a non-electrolyte, by an adsorbed ion, by a salt, or by a peptized colloid. *Ibid.* 170 Water-peptizable colloids like gelatine, gum arabic, dextrine, [etc.]..will peptize many precipitates. **1925** tr. J.

M. van Bemmelen in E. Hatschek *Foundations Colloid Chem.* 129 The peptizing agent may be removed from the solution and the colloid remains dissolved. **1934** *Industr. & Engin. Chem.* Nov. 1190 Rubber which has been lightly vulcanized with sulfur can be dissolved in benzene with the help of peptizing agents... The action of soluble zinc compounds on peptized rubber sulfur causes a gelling action. **1938** *Proc. Rubber Technol. Conf.* 289 Rubber 'softeners'..are commonly used to increase the plasticity of rubber, and it is often assumed that they act through some lubrication, swelling, or 'peptising' action on the rubber. **1963** *Ceylon Vet. Jrnl.* XI. 42 The solubility of the protein of groundnut meals has been determined by the salt-peptizability of its nitrogen.

peptizer ('pɛptaɪzə(r)). *Chem.* [f. PEPTIZ(E *v.* + -ER[1].] A substance which causes peptization, or which serves to prevent the coagulation of a colloid suspension; *spec.* a catalyst which facilitates the process of mastication or vulcanization of rubber, by preventing the recombination of broken polymer chains.

1931 E. S. HEDGES *Colloids* iii. 16 If the freshly precipitated ferric hydroxide is treated with..ferric chloride solution it disperses immediately to form a dark reddish-brown colloidal solution. We call..ferric chloride the peptizer or peptizing agent. **1946** *Shell Aviation News* No. 100. 15/3 These [*sc.* additives in oil]..may act as 'peptizers' which help to keep in suspension in the oil any insolubles which are formed. **1961** *New Scientist* 2 Mar. 549/1 Other substances, so called 'peptisers', can be added [to rubber] to ensure this simple form of stabilizing the reactive ends of the broken chains. **1963** H. VAN OLPHEN *Introd. Clay Colloid Chem.* viii. 109 When a small amount of peptizer is added to a pure clay gel, the yield stress decreases drastically. **1972** *Materials & Technol.* V. xiv. 474 Effective peptizers [of rubber] are hydrazine derivatives and organic sulphur compounds like thio-β-naphthol, pentachlor thiophenol, dibenzoyl disulphide.

peptogen ('pɛptədʒɛn). [f. Gr. πεπτό-ς (see PEPTONE, PEPTIC) + -GEN.] A general name for substances which stimulate the formation of pepsin in the gastric juice. So **pepto'genic**, **pep'togenous** *adjs.*, having the quality of forming, or stimulating the formation of, pepsin; also, having the quality of converting proteids into peptones.

1875 DARWIN *Insectiv. Pl.* vi. 129 The glands of the stomach of animals secrete pepsin as Schiff asserts, only after they have absorbed certain soluble substances, which he designates peptogenes. **1893** *Syd. Soc. Lex.*, *Peptogenic*, pepsin-producing. Term used for those substances which, introduced into the stomach, stimulate the secretion of the pepsin of the gastric juice. **1900** *Lancet* 4 Aug. Advt. 43 Peptogenic Milk Powder..converts the caseine into a condition corresponding..to the peptone-like albuminoids of breast milk.

peptolysis (pɛp'tɒlɪsɪs). *Biochem.* [f. PEPTO(NE + -LYSIS.] The degradation of a peptone or polypeptide into smaller peptides or amino-acids. Cf. PEPTIDOLYSIS.

1904 S. H. VINES in *Ann. Bot.* XVIII. 290 Accepting this connotation of 'proteolysis', the successive stages of the process may, I would suggest, be conveniently distinguished as—(*a*) peptonization, the conversion of the higher proteins into albumoses and peptones; and (*b*) peptolysis, the decomposition of peptones into nitrogenous but non-proteid substances. **1949** H. TAUBER *Chem. & Technol. Enzymes* vi. 130 The end products of peptolysis are mostly proteoses and peptones and small quantities of amino acids.

Hence **pepto'lytic** *a.*, **pepto'lytically** *adv.*

1904 *Ann. Bot.* XVIII. 290 Trypsin..forms tryptophane as one of the products of its peptolytic activity. *Ibid.* 299 It was ascertained that a filtered watery extract of yeast was always peptolytically active, however short the period of extraction might be. **1915** *Chem. Abstr.* IX. 2910 The formaldehyde titration for free amino groups in polypeptides and their hydrolytic products is a method practically adapted to the study of the action of peptolytic ferments on polypeptides. **1949** H. W. FLOREY et al. *Antibiotics* I. i. 47 Gram positive proteolytic bacteria such as ..staphylococci when grown with gram positive peptolytic bacteria..in a nitrogen-free medium secreted a bacteriolytic substance which dissolved the latter, thus making their nitrogen available.

peptonate ('pɛptənət). *Chem.* [f. next + -ATE[1] c.] An organic salt produced by the action of a peptone on an inorganic salt, in which the peptone-radical takes the place of the inorganic acid-radical.

1876 BARTHOLOW *Mat. Med.* (1879) 212 The salts of silver most probably enter the blood as albuminates and peptonates. **1897** *Allbutt's Syst. Med.* II. 934 Subcutaneous injection of the peptonate of mercury.

peptone ('pɛptəʊn). [ad. Ger. *pepton* (C. G. Lehmann, 1849, in *Ber. Sächs. Gesellsch. f. Wissensch., Math.-Phys., Cl.* I. 12), ad. Gr. πεπτόν, neut. of Gr. πεπτ-ός cooked, digested; spelt *-one* in Fr. and Eng.] The general name for a class of albuminoid substances into which proteids (the nitrogenous constituents of food) are converted by the action of pepsin or trypsin (the digestive ferments of the gastric and pancreatic juices); differing from proteids in not being coagulable by heat, and in being easily soluble and diffusible through membranes, and thus capable of absorption into the system.

1860 *N. Syd. Soc. Year Bk. Med.* 76 Peptone has a very much higher endosmotic equivalent than simple albumen. **1872** HUXLEY *Phys.* vi. 147. **1881** DARWIN *Veg. Mould* 43 In such plants as Drosera and Dionæa;..animal matter is digested and converted into peptone not within a stomach, but on the surface of the leaves.

attrib. **1878** KINGZETT *Anim. Chem.* 40 The peptone-substance is synthetically changed into solid albumin again. **1899** CAGNEY tr. *Jaksch's Clin. Diagn.* vii. 311 The peptone precipitate is dissolved by the addition of water [etc.].

peptonize ('pɛptənaɪz), *v.* [f. PEPTONE + -IZE.] *trans.* To convert (a proteid) into a peptone; *esp.* to subject (food) to an artificial process of partial digestion (predigestion) by means of pepsin or pancreatic extract, as an aid to weak digestion. Hence **'peptonized**, **'peptonizing** *ppl. adjs.*; also **peptoni'zation**, the action or process of peptonizing; **'peptonizer**, a peptonizing agent. Also *fig.*

1880 *Nature* XXIII. 169 Preparation of artificially-digested food, peptonised materials. **1881** *Ibid.* 235 In peptonisation of albuminoid substances. **1884** *Health Exhib. Catal.* 17/2 Preparations of the digestive ferments for peptonising..food. Peptonising apparatus. **1885** GOODALE *Physiol. Bot.* (1892) 366 It has the power of peptonizing proteids. **1893** *Nat. Observ.* 5 Aug. 303/1 A good comedy is the best of peptonisers. **1895** *Athenæum* 21 Sept. 392/1 Wholesome food to the apparently large public which likes its science peptonized.

'peptonoid. [f. PEPTONE + -OID.] Trade-name for a preparation containing peptones: see prec.

1893 *Syd. Soc. Lex.*, *Peptonoids of beef.*

‖**peptonuria** (pɛptəʊ'n(j)ʊərɪə). *Path.* [mod.L., f. PEPTONE + Gr. οὖρον urine: see -URIA.] The presence of peptones in the urine.

1891 *Lancet* 3 Jan. 63/2 Peptonuria occurred after the injection. **1897** *Allbutt's Syst. Med.* III. 560 Peptonuria may appear and towards the end a little albuminuria.

peptotoxin (pɛptəʊ'tɒksɪn). [f. Gr. πεπτό-ς (see PEPTIC) + TOXIN.] 'A poisonous alkaloid formed from peptones during digestion, and becoming decomposed later on, as putrefaction takes place' (*Syd. Soc. Lex.* 1893).

1890 in *Cent. Dict.* **1897** *Allbutt's Syst. Med.* II. 815 In the case of gastric digestion we have a ptomaine pepto-toxin. **1899** *Ibid.* VIII. 65 Certain toxic bodies of the nature of pepto-toxines have been found in the urine by Ewald.

Pepuzian (pɪ'pjuːzɪən). *Ch. Hist.* Also **Pepusian.** [ad. med.L. *Pepusiani, -ziani*, f. *Pepusia, -zia*, Πεπούζα.] A member of a sect of Montanists in the 2nd century, so called from Pepuza in Phrygia. Also †**Pepusite.**

1565 T. STAPLETON *Fortr. Faith* 62b, The Pepuzians would haue taught him that holy orders is no Sacrament. **1625** BR. HALL *No Peace w. Rome* §3 One while, we are Pepuzians that ascribe too much to women; then, wee are Origenists, for holding the Image of God to be defaced in man. **1653** R. BAILLIE *Dissuas. Vind.* (1655) 23 That Phrygian pepusite had gotten the beginning of his way from the heretick indeed. **1727–41** CHAMBERS *Cycl.* s.v., They had their name *Pepuzians* from a pretence that Jesus Christ appeared to one of their prophetesses in the city Pepuza in Phrygia, which was their holy city.

Pepysian ('piːpsɪən), *a.* [f. the name of Samuel *Pepys*, diarist (1633–1703) + -IAN.] Of, pertaining to, or characteristic of Pepys, his writings, his library, or the age in which he lived. So **Pepysi'ana** *sb. pl.*

1786 in *Wks. James I of Scotl.* 98 Dr Percy informs us, that this poem is preserved in the Pepysian Library, at Magdalen College, Cambridge. **1847** E. F. RIMBAULT *Nursery Rhymes* p. viii, The popular rhyme 'Three Children sliding on the Ice'..is part of a ballad preserved in the Pepysian collection. **1899** H. B. WHEATLEY *Diary of Samuel Pepys: Suppl. Vol.* (*title*) Pepysiana. **1920** *Glasgow Herald* 21 Sept. 8 Amid the distractions of business he cultivated his early literary bent and kept a diary wherein, with Pepysian frankness,..he chronicled his doings. **1927** W. DEEPING *Kitty* xxx. 385 He was a Pepysian soul and kept a diary. **1927** J. S. HUXLEY *Relig. without Revelation* iv. 119 The Pepysian interest in complete record of all facts centring on self. **1927** W. H. WHITEAR (*title*) More Pepysiana: being notes on the Diary of Samuel Pepys and on the genealogy of the family, with corrected pedigrees. **1934** *Punch* 19 Dec. 699/3 Builders' models of the Pepysian and later periods, rigged models of Dutch Indiamen,..reconstructed models by present-day experts, all find a place in this fascinating gallery.

Pequot ('piːkwɒt), *sb.* and *a.* Also **Pecoate, Pequod, Pequoitt.** [prob. f. native word *paquatanog* destroyers.] **A.** *sb.* **a.** An Indian of an Algonquian people of southern New England. **b.** The language spoken by the Pequots. **B.** *adj.* Of or pertaining to the Pequot Indians, or the language spoken by them.

1631 in *New Hampsh. Hist. Soc. Coll.* (1834) IV. 226 Wee heare their numbers exceed any but the Pecoates and Nawagansets. **1637** *Public Rec. Colony of Connecticut* (1850) I. 10 To parle w[i]th the bay aboute o[u]r settinge downe in the Pequoitt Countrey. **1654** E. JOHNSON *Hist. New-England* II. vi. 109 The English sought by all means to keepe these [fighting men] at least from confederating with the Pequods. **1714** S. SEWALL *Diary* (1882) III. 12 Commissioners met to give Govr. Sattonstall an Opportunity to vindicate himself relating to the Pequot and Mohegan Indians. **1849** O. W. HOLMES *Poems* 256 He heard the Pequot's ringing whoop. **1851** H. MELVILLE *Moby Dick* I. xvi. 110 Pequod..was the name of a celebrated tribe of Massachusetts Indians, now extinct as the ancient Medes. **1871** C. M. YONGE *Pioneers & Founders* i. 6 The Pequot Indians, a tall, well-proportioned, and active tribe, belonging to the great Iroquois nation. *Ibid.* 8 The Pequots were..at war with the Dutch. **1903** PRINCE & SPECK in *Amer. Anthropologist* V. 195 Their language, of course, remained Pequot, a dialect which shows a..striking kinship ..with the present speech of the Canadian Abenakis. **1945** C. M. WEBSTER *Town Meeting Country* 11 The Pequots were probably the bravest and most ferocious of all the New England tribes. **1979** *Arizona Daily Star* 1 Apr. A 2/2 Among their guests is to be John Hamilton, Chief Rolling Cloud of the Mohegan and Pequot American Indian tribes.

per (pə(r), pɜː(r)), *prep.* A Latin (Ital. and Old French) preposition, meaning 'through, by, by means of'; in med.L. and Fr. also in a distributive sense = 'for every..., for each...': used in Eng. in various Latin and OF. phrases, and ultimately becoming practically an Eng. preposition used freely before substantives of many classes.

I. In Lat. phrases (including med.L. and Italian).

1. a. per accidens (†also quasi-anglicized as *per accidence*) [= Gr. κατὰ συμβεβηκός] by accident, by virtue of some accessory or non-essential circumstance, contingently, indirectly. Opposed to *per se.*

1528 PAYNEL tr. *Salerne's Regim.* (1541) 49 b, Water that is temperately colde, doth somtyme per accidence, stere one to haue an appetite. **1572** [see *per se*]. *c* **1590** MARLOWE *Faust.* iii. 46 (1878) Did not my conjuring speeches raise thee? speak. *Meph.* That was the cause, but yet *per accidens*. **1654** WHITLOCK *Zootomia* 221 Causes *per se*, and Causes *per Accidens* working the same Effects. *a* **1680** CHARNOCK *Wks.* (1865) III. 230 This punishment is only accidental to the gospel, it becomes the savour of death *per accidens*, because of the unbelief of those that reject it.

b. In *Logic* applied to conversion in which the quantity of the proposition is changed from universal to particular: see CONVERSION 4.

Called by Boethius *Conversio per accidens*, because the particular affirmation in this case serves *indirectly* as converse for a universal affirmation with whose subaltern particular it is directly (*principaliter*) convertible. Aristotle's term was ἀντιστροφὴ κατὰ μέρος = 'conversion as to a part' because only part of the statement is converted.

[*a* **525** BOETHIUS *de Syllogismo Categorico* i. (ed. Basil. 1570, 539) *Per accidens* autem converti dicitur particularis affirmatio universali affirmationi, quia particularis affirmatio sibi ipsi principali convertitur.] **1677** T. GOOD *Brief Tract. Logic* 27 Conversion *per Accidens* is a change of the Subject into the place of the Predicate, *et contra*, keeping the same Quality, but changing of Quantity. **1840** WHATELY *Logic* 78 This might be fairly named conversion by *limitation*; but is commonly called *Conversion per accidens*. **1843** MILL *Logic* (1856) II. i. §2 This process, which converts an universal proposition into a particular, is termed conversion *per accidens*.

2. per annum, (so much) by the year, every year, yearly: almost always in reference to a sum of money paid or received.

1601 R. JOHNSON *Kingd. & Commw.* (1603) 89 The professor in divinity, hath per annum 1125 florens. **1677** YARRANTON *Eng. Improv.* 152 At present there is at least five hundred pounds *per Annum*, paid. **1886** D. C. MURRAY *Cynic Fortune* xii, An income of a hundred pounds per annum.

3. per consequens (†also *per consequent* [= F. *par conséquent*], *per consequence*), by consequence, consequently.

c **1386** CHAUCER *Sompn. T.* 484 An odious meschief This day bityd is to myn ordre and me And so per [*v.r.* par] consequens in ech degre Of hooly chirche. **1413** *Pilgr. Sowle* (Caxton 1483) IV. xxvi. 71 Than ben they al euene, and per consequens theyr wyttes shold ben euen. *c* **1532** DU WES *Introd. Fr.* in Palsgr. 959 Howe one may make dyverse.. sentences with one worde, and perconsequent come shortely to the french speche. **1621** BURTON *Anat. Mel.* I. ii. III. i, So *per consequens*, disturbing the Soul.

4. per contra [It.]. **a.** On the opposite side (of an account, etc.); on the other hand; as a set-off. See CONTRA C. 1.

1554 PRAT *Africa* Ep. A v b, Honour..doth the noble man ateyne; which..preferreth and aduanceth his pore seruauntes; *per contra* in how much displeasure with God,.. doth he incur in whose seruyce his poore seruantes do not floryshe. **1588** J. MELLIS *Briefe Instr.* D vj, And when this [Creditor] side or the Debitor side is full written, that you mynde to make it euen with the Debitor syde *per contra*. **1750** CHESTERF. *Lett.* (1774) II. 38 When I cast up your account..I rejoice to see the balance so much in your favour; and that the items *per contra* are so few. **1820** J. SCOTT in *Lond. Mag.* Jan., Refer, as *per contra*, to MacIvor's ideas. *a* **1832** BENTHAM *Deontol.* xi. (1834) I. 157 This will be the account on the side of profit. Per contra, he will be led to estimate—1. Sickness [etc.]. **1840** BARHAM *Ingol. Leg.* Ser. I. *Acc. New Play, Per contra*, he'd lately endow'd a new Chantry. **1903** R. FRY *Let.* 16 Mar. (1972) I. 206 The article won't do the magazine much good, but *per contra* it won't do anyone..any harm. **1919** J. STEPHENSON *Princ. & Pract. Commerc. Corr.* III. iii. 181 Your cash remittance of £1,000 of the 1st inst. came duly to hand and per contra we have purchased Frs. 25,000 French Gold Rente, which we send you enclosed. **1924** A. HUXLEY *Let.* 9 Aug. (1969) 231 The people who have deliberately set out to put great thoughts into verse have generally been the worst poets on record. But, per contra, the best poets have generally implied or directly expressed great thoughts. **1940** G. F.-H. & J. BERKELEY *Italy in Making* III. iii. 52 The Sicilians had only one great enthusiasm—to free their island from the hated

Neapolitans... *Per contra*, the Neapolitans' first aim was to maintain their hold on Sicily. **1976** *Listener* 12 Aug. 172/1 Writers from this centre of England.. suggest a centrality of English experience... *Per contra*, some explorers.. have found a too-muchness in this green country.

b. as *sb.* The opposite side (of an account, etc.). Also as *adj.*

1804 Mrs. E. Merry *Let.* in *Mem. Moore* (1856) VIII. 52 Matter arises every instant that you would convert into amusement, but the *per contra* makes us both bear the deprivation of your society with resignation. **1846** Mrs. Gore *Eng. Char.* (1852) 123 Without any per-contra of sums withdrawn therefrom. **1880** J. Payn *Confid. Agent* III. 119 There must be something.. to the *per contra*. **1972** *Times* 11 May (Spain Suppl.) p. iv/3 A similar list prepared by the *The Banker*, but based on deposits less *per contra* accounts, of world bank groups included two Spanish banks only.

5. per diem. a. (So much) by the day, every day, daily. (Cf. *per annum.*)

1520 *Rutland Papers* (Camden) 42 Labovrers heired, xl at vjd. per diem. **1625** Purchas *Pilgrims* II. vi. iv. 867 His entertainement was twentie fiue shillings *per diem.* **1742** Fielding *J. Andrews* I. viii, To attend twice *per diem* at the polite churches and chapels. **1835** Ure *Philos. Manuf.* 348 The work-people were paid 1000*l.* per diem in these several factories. **1906** *Arch. Roentgen Ray* XI. 18/2 When the method of treatment by fractional doses is carried out—for instance, ½X to 1X per diem—the quantimetric method alone is impossible. **1920** A. Huxley *Let.* 23 Dec. (1969) 193, I have to go to at least two and sometimes three theatres per diem and write about them afterwards. **1979** C. Dexter *Service of All Dead* xxxiii. 194 We're all ageing at the standard rate of twenty-four hours *per diem.*

b. as *sb.* An amount or allowance of so much every day. Also as *adj.* Chiefly *U.S.*

1809 *Deb. Congress U.S.* 13 Feb. (1853) 350 Officers of the United States.. have received.. the per diem allowance fixed by law. **1812** *Weekly Reg.* 18 Jan. 361/2 The *per diem* of the members has been raised to *four* dollars. **1839** *Congress. Globe* 25th Congress 3 Sess. App. 66/1 In that case, had he asked for his mileage and per diem, all would have considered it an insult. **1846** T. L. McKenney *Mem.* I. ix. 192, I referred to him the making up of my account for my per diem allowance. **1888** Bryce *Amer. Commw.* II. App. 650 Members of the Legislature shall receive.. a per diem and mileage;.. such per diem shall not exceed eight dollars. **1897** *Outing* (U.S.) June 281/2 In addition to the per diem above stated. **1946** E. Hodgins *Mr. Blandings builds his Dream House* xiii. 195 He would.. happily replace the tubs at a per diem rate. **1973** R. Hayes *Hungarian Game* xxxviii. 228 If I made the flight I could crib another twenty dollars on my per diem. **1974** R. Thomas *Porkchoppers* v. 39 He got another $10,000 a year from the union in per diem and expenses. **1977** D. James *Spy at Evening* iv. 21, I liked the job. I accepted. 'A *per diem* of fifty pounds—travel expenses in addition.'

6. per mensem, (so much) every month: cf. 2, 5.

1647 *Kingd. Weekly Intelligencer* No. 238. 758 (Stanf.) The addition of forty thousand pounds *per mensem* to the present sixty thousand pounds. **1810** T. Williamson *E. Ind. Vade-M.* I. 284 The manjy is usually paid from five to seven rupees per mensem. **1886** Kipling *Departmental Ditties* (ed. 2) 3 A nice retaining fee Supplied, of course, *per mensem*, by the Indian Treasury. **1916** 'Taffrail' *Pincher Martin* vi. 88 The sum of ten shillings *per mensem* was supposed.. to suffice for the midshipmen's needs in the way of extras. **1965** *New Statesman* 24 Sept. 466/3 (Advt.), The amounts mentioned below refer to Malayan dollars (per mensem) and their approximate sterling equivalent. **1974** *Nature* 30 Aug. p. xxvii/1 (Advt.), This scholarship carries a stipend of M$700 per mensem for the first 12 months followed by M$800 per mensem beyond that period.

7. per procurationem (commonly abbreviated *per proc., per pro., p.p.*; sometimes read as *per procuration*): by procuration, by the action of a procurator or official agent, by proxy or deputy.

1819 in Barnewall & Cresswell *Reports* (1828) VII. 280 Six months after date pay to my order 156*ol.*, for value received: *T. Burleigh*. Accepted per procuration of *G. G. H. Munnings.—S. Munnings.* **1882** Bithell *Counting-ho. Dict.* (1893) 242 In commerce it is usual to employ the well-known Latin phrase 'per procurationem', to call attention to the fact that a signature is made by proxy. *Ibid.* 224 The phrase 'per procurationem' is commonly contracted into '*p.p.*' **1895** *Daily News* 9 Apr. 3/6 Owing to ill health, she allowed him to sign 'per pro'.

8. per saltum, by a leap, at one bound, without intermediate steps, all at once. (Rarely *attrib.*)

1600 W. Watson *Decacordon* (1602) 14 Others to be but doctors of clowts, *per saltum*. **1640** Chr. Harvie *Synagogue* xii, To take degrees, *per saltum*, though of quick Dispatch, is but a truants trick. **1679** J. Goodman *Penit. Pard.* II. i. (1713) 151 In hopes to be made saints *per saltum.* **1842–3** Grove *Corr. Phys. Forces* (1874) 150 To account for the *per saltum* manner in which chemical combinations take place.

9. per se. a. By or in itself (himself, herself, themselves); intrinsically, essentially; without reference to anything (or any one) else.

1572 Whitgift *Wks.* (1852) II. 83 For they belong unto God properly and *per se*, to man *per accidens*. **1606** Shaks. *Tr. & Cr.* I. ii. 15 They say he is a very man *per se* and stands alone. **1704** J. Harris *Lex. Techn.* I. s.v., We say a Thing is considered *Per se*, when 'tis taken in the Abstract, and without Connexion with other things. **1748** Franklin *Lett.* Wks 1840 V. 211 Air is an electric *per se.* **1883** Sir J. C. Mathew in *Law Rep. 11 Q. B. Div.* 392 It was very questionable whether the words used were defamatory per se.

†**b.** Formerly used in naming a letter which by itself forms a word (*A per se, I per se, O per se*), or a symbol which by itself stands for a word (*and per se* = &, ampersand); hence allusively: see A, I, O (the letters).

c **1475** [see A (the letter) IV]. *a* **1530** J. Heywood *Weather* (Brandl) 104 Some saye I am I perse I. **1597** Morley *Introd. Mus.* 36, & per se, con per se [see Christ-cross 3].

10. In various phrases, as *per antiphrasin, per arsin et thesin, per deliquium* (see antiphrasis, arsis, deliquium[2]); **per aliud**, by or in another entity; extrinsically; with reference to anything else; **per anum**, by the anus, applied esp. to anal sexual intercourse; **per capita** (*Law*), 'by heads', (*a*) applied to succession when divided among a number of individuals in equal shares (opp. to *per stirpes*); (*b*) = *per caput*; **per caput**, per person or head (of population); also as *adj. phr.*; **per curiam** (*Law*), 'by action of the court', applied to a judgement, of concise and peremptory character, formulated by the whole bench; freq. *attrib.*; **per fas et (aut) nefas**, by right and (or) wrong, by means fair or foul; **per impossibile** (*Logic*), 'as is impossible', a qualification governing a proposition which can never be true; **per incuriam** (*Law*), 'by carelessness', applied to a judicial decision evidently contrary to the law or facts; also *transf.*; **per interim**, for the meantime, during the intervening time; **per mil, per mille**, in every thousand; **per minima**, through the minutest particles; **per pares**, by (his) peers; **per primam** *Med.*, in full **per primam intentionem**, 'by first intention' (see intention 10 b); **per quod** (*Law*), 'whereby', a phrase formerly used, in order to maintain the action, in a declaration of special damage; **per stirpes** (*Law*), 'by stocks' or 'families'; applied to succession when divided in equal shares among the branches of the family, the share of each branch being then subdivided equally among the representatives of that branch (opp. to *per capita*).

1890 W. James *Princ. Psychol.* II. xvii. 42 To say that we feel a sensation's seat to be 'in the brain' or 'against the eye' or 'under the skin' is to say as much *about* it and to deal with it in as non-primitive a way as to say that it is a mile off. These are all secondary perceptions, ways of defining the sensation's seat *per *aliud.* **1948** *Mind* LVII. 127 St. Thomas's proof [is] that the existence of finite beings, since it is *per aliud*, must be derived from something that exists *per se.* **1398** Trevisa *Barth. De P.R.* vii. lix. (1495) r vj b/1 A postume.. hyghte Herisipila, that is holy fyre per *Antifrasim, that is by contrary manere spekynge. **1670** Lassels *Voy. Italy* I. 153 An Academy of Wits, called *Gli Otiosi*, or Idle-men,.. *per antiphrasin*, because they are not idle. **1838** *Guy's Hosp. Rep.* III. 340 The constant symptom .. was the passing of blood per *anum. **1972** P. Green *Shadow of Parthenon* 160 Their liking for intercourse *per anum*, perhaps to preserve their virginity for the marriage market. **1972** *Mod. Law Rev.* XXXV. 107 Sexual intercourse *per anum.* **1597** Morley *Introd. Mus.* II. 114 If ..you make a Canon *per *arsin & thesin*, without anie discorde in binding maner in it. **1682** Warburton *Hist. Guernsey* (1822) 90 Patrimonial estates are divided per stirpes; purchased estates, per *capita. **1766** Blackstone *Comm.* II. xiv. 217 Their representatives.. became themselves principals, and shared the inheritance *per capita*, that is, share and share alike. **1926** Fowler *Mod. Eng. Usage* 428/2 *The entire production of opium in India is two grammes per capita yearly.* This use is a modern blunder, encouraged in some recent dictionaries. **1941** Wyndham Lewis *Let.* 9 Nov. (1963) 306 It [*sc.* Canada] reads less per capita than any other known civilised population. **1942** J. S. Huxley in *Harper's Mag.* Sept. 340/2 The U.S.S.R., in spite of its low per capita wealth, [etc.]. **1952** [see growth[1] 1 c]. **1955** *Times* 6 July 8/4 Saving *per capita* varies considerably from territory to territory, and in each territory from year to year, according to the study. **1965** *New Statesman* 30 Apr. 672/3 For the bulk of humanity per capita consumption remains the same. **1974** *Times* 25 Apr. 17/7 Let us have.. an electoral system that secures proper proportionate representation both *per capita* and by party. **1975** 'D. Jordan' *Black Account* 246 Geneva Airport, I always feel, is the richest airport in the world.. in terms of *per capita* elegance, tailoring, luggage, comfort. **1975** *Sci. Amer.* Nov. 56/1 Per capita incomes have declined in recent years. **1919** W. T. Grenfell *Labrador Doctor* (1920) iii. 60 By special arrangement with the railway and other friends, and by very simple living, the per *caput charges were so much reduced that many of the boys not only paid their own expenses, but even helped their friends. **1962** *Times* 21 May (Commonw. Chambers of Commerce Suppl.) p. v/5 India plans to.. raise the present *per caput* income in the country. **1970** K. J. Parker in G. G. Birch et al. *Glucose Syrups* v. 77 The current total *per caput* consumption of refined sugar is higher in Britain (112 lb) than in the USA (99·7 lb). **1976** *Lancet* 13 Nov. 1050/2 It may be argued that the per-caput cigarette consumption is not a good measure of the cigarette consumption in young women. **1978** *Jrnl. R. Soc. Arts* CXXVI. 651/2 The Harbin Transistor Plant was achieving very high *per caput* sales. **1890** *Cent. Dict.*, *Per *curiam*, in *law*, by the court: a phrase prefixed to judicial opinions indicating the sanction of the court to the statements therein, as distinguished from the individual opinions of a particular judge. **1955** *Bull. Atomic Sci.* Oct. 309/2 It was a brief per curiam decision in a case which involved no contested issue. **1959** Jowitt *Dict. Eng. Law* II. 1327/2 *Per curiam, per cur.*, by the court. **1972** *N.Y. Law Jrnl.* 24 Oct. 2/1 Per curiam: Order reversed, with.. costs and defendant's motion.. granted. **1973** *Ibid.* 20 Feb. 4/4 If a court writes a per curiam opinion like this, what justification is there for demanding better writing from attorneys? **1666** Boyle *Orig. Formes & Qual.* II. iii, As neither oil of tartar *per *deliquium*, nor spirit of salt will dissolve silver, so both the one and the other will precipitate it. **1600** W. Watson *Decacordon* (1602) 96 *margin*, To maintaine their reputation, *per *fas aut nefas* they care not how. **1771** *Junius Lett.* xliv. (1772) II. 153 Likely enough to be resisted *per fas et nefas*. **1847** A. De Morgan *Formal Logic* vii. 132 The moods *Baroko* and *Bokardo* do not admit of reduction to the first figure, by any fair use of the phrase: but the logicians were determined that they should do so, and they accordingly hit upon the following plan, which they called reduction *per *impossibile.* **1883** F. H. Bradley *Princ. Logic* I. vii. 217 If, I say, *per impossibile* this phantom could be real—.. the above chance of irregularity would vanish. **1896** L. T. Hobhouse *Theory of Knowl.* 199 It was a onesided error to suggest that the immediate object of vision is colour or rows of coloured points from which, *per impossibile*, extension was conceived as removed. **1912** A. Lang *Shakespeare, Bacon & Gt. Unknown* xii. 267 If he knew that the author was Bacon, and knew it under pledge of secrecy, and was asked (*per impossibile*) 'Who wrote these plays?' he had only to say, 'Look at the title-page.' **1923** H. W. B. Joseph *Labour Theory of Value in Karl Marx* vi. 145 And supposing the equilibrium in an equal exchange were *per impossibile* between satisfaction on one side and sacrifice on the other, such equilibrium could only be said to exist in single exchanges independently. **1935** *Mind* XLIV. 237 Butler's 'let it be allowed' that virtue could not be justified if (*per impossibile*) it were contrary to self-interest. **1963** J. Lyons *Structural Semantics* iii. 42 Suppose, *per impossibile*, that we were transported as investigating linguists to Athens of the fifth century B.C. **1972** *Times Lit. Suppl.* 22 Dec. 1550/4 Have you for the moment forgotten *per impossibile* in which opera the chorus 'Upon our sea-girt land' occurs. **1867** Wharton *Law Lexicon* (ed. 4) 709/1 *Per *incuriam*, through want of care. **1925** F. Newbolt *Out of Court* iii. 162 To attain this object you should first succeed in life, and have your portrait, or *per incuriam* that of a confusing name-sake, inserted in a good picture paper. **1963** *Times* 24 Apr. 5/2 Mr. Puntan now appealed against that order; and his Lordship was afraid that the Divisional Court had acted *per incuriam* in making the order they did. **1970** *Internat. & Compar. Law Q.* XIX. 340 Parts of the judgement must be regarded as given *per incuriam*, and cannot be relied upon. **1976** *Phipson's Law of Evidence* (ed. 12) xxix. 677 A document omitted *per incuriam* was allowed to be put in by the prosecution during the reply. **1724** *Lond. Gaz.* No. 6315/1 The Director of Mentz is charged with the Vote of the Electorate of Bohemia per *interim. **1902** *Encycl. Brit.* XXXI. 404/2 The bottom waters have almost uniformly a salinity of 34·8 per *mille, corresponding closely with the bottom waters of the south Atlantic. **1957** A. Grimble *Return to Islands* 102 Perhaps five or six per mil of his parishioners at most. **1957** L. F. R. Williams *State of Israel* 189 Infant mortality among the Arab community has fallen steadily to about 60 per mille of live births. **1972** *Nature* 25 Feb. 417/1 The seasonal amplitude is reduced to around 2 per mille. **1972** *Science* 22 Sept. 1099/3 The sulfur isotopic values on the west side averaged around 5·3 per mil. **1704** J. Harris *Lex. Techn.* I, If Silver and Lead be melted together, they will mingle and be united with one another *per *minima.* *a* **1734** North *Exam.* I. ii. §159 (1740) 120 His Lordship had stood his Trial *per *Pares.* **1907** *Practitioner* Sept. 335 The wound healed *per *primam*, except at the drain opening, and this was quite closed on the eighteenth day. *Ibid.* 336 Union *per primam* without any trouble. **1957** H. N. Harkins in J. G. Allen et al. *Surgery* ii. 9/1 Healing of wounds can be divided into 3 types: (1) Healing by first intention (per primam intensionum [*sic*]: primary union). **1768** Blackstone *Comm.* III. viii. 124 It is necessary that the plaintiff should aver some particular damage to have happened; which is called laying his action with a *per *quod.* **1682** Per *stirpes [see *per capita* above]. **1766** Blackstone *Comm.* II. xiv. 218 The law of England.. would still divide it only into three parts and distribute it *per stirpes*. **1881** H. W. Nicholson *Fr. Sword to Share* xiv. 96 Intestate property goes to lineal descendants *per stirpes*.

II. 1. a. In OF. phrases, some of which occur also with the more usual form par, q.v., e.g. *per charite, per company*, etc.; others are †**per maistrie**, 'by mastery', by conquest; **per my et per tout** (*Law*), 'by half and by all', by joint-tenancy; **per pais, per pays** (*Law*), 'by the country': see pais. See also peradventure, percase, perchance, perfay, perforce, perquer.

c **1330** R. Brunne *Chron.* (1810) 164 Bi þe se side he nam, & wan it per *maistrie. **1628** Coke tr. *Littleton* in *Inst.* 186a, Euery ioyntenant is seised of the land which hee holdeth ioyntly *Per *my & per tout.* **1704** J. Harris *Lex. Techn.* I. s.v., A Joynt-Tenant is said to be seised of the Lands that he holds jointly *Per my & per tout*; that is, he is seised by every Parcel, and by the whole. **1828** *Edin. Rev.* Sept. 97 A province of literature of which they were formerly seised *per my et per tout.* **1614** Selden *Titles Hon.* 280 Speciall Bastardie is triable *per *Pais.* **1664, 1768** [see pais]. **1828** D. le Marchant *Rep. Claims to Barony of Gardner* p. xxxvi, The tenant in possession offered issue, either in grand assize or per pays.

b. As a prefix in nonce-advbs. after *perchance, perhaps*, as **per-hazard, per-likelihood.**

1807 J. Barlow *Columb.* vi. 423 And some war minister *per-hazard* reads In what far field the tool of placemen bleeds. **1834–43** Southey *Doctor* ccxliv. (1848) 665/1 Discourses which perchance, and (I fear) per-likelihood, it may be thy fortune to hear.. at thy parish church.

2. In *Heraldry*, in phrases denoting partition of the shield in the direction of any of the principal ordinaries (per bend, per chevron, per cross, per fesse, per pale, per saltire): see these words; also parted, party *a.* Also *per long*: see quots. s.v. indentilly.

III. As an English preposition.

1. By, by means of, by the instrumentality of; esp. in phrases relating to conveyance, as *per bearer, per carrier, per express, per post, per rail, per steamer*, etc. Also = according to, as stated or indicated by, as *per invoice, per ledger, per margin*, etc.; as laid down by (a judge) (quot. 1818). So, in humorous slang use, (*as*) ***per usual*** = as usual; also with ellipsis of *usual*. Also (exceptionally) in other senses, as ***per this time*** = by this time, ***per instance*** = for instance (cf. F. *par exemple*). Also in other humorous and extended uses.

1588 J. MELLIS *Briefe Instr.* G j b, And for euery Debitor yee shall say. *Per* such one N., as appeareth in my olde booke A in such a leafe. **1599** *Child-Marriages* 179 Receiued, one pacquet of Lettres per poste dyrected to Mr. Maior. **1618** R. COCKS *Diary* (Hakl. Soc.) II. 28 Yet, per the pleasure of God, got her affe. **1675** in J. Easton *Narr.* (1858) 103, I hope my Brother, Knapton, Sharpe, &c. will bee here per first. **1710** STEELE *Tatler* No. 231 ¶4, I send you by this Bearer, and not *per* Bearer, a Dozen of that Claret. **1765** in *J. Hancock his Bk.* (1898) 80 My late Uncle (of whose sudden death you have undoubtedly per this time heard). **1770** T. DAVIES in *J. Granger's Lett.* (1805) 49 Send me, *per* return of the post, a proper acknowledgement. **1782** *Town & Country Mag.* Dec. 669/1, I stood with the squadron, as per margin, to the southward, all that night. **1798** WORDSW. *Let. to Cottle* 28 Aug. (in *Sotheran's Catal.* (1899) 57), A very pleasant journey per foot, per waggon, per coach, per post-chaise. **1804** *Some-thing Odd* I. 122 They're all ready and willing..per instance, Sir Somebody Something [etc.]. **1810** CAPT. TUCKER in *Naval Chron.* XXIV. 336 Men, selected as per margin. **1818** CRUISE *Digest* (ed. 2) II. 485 But, *per* Holt, the estate was limited by way of use to the issues female. **1874** W. S. GILBERT *Charity* IV, I shall accompany him, as per usual. **1922** JOYCE *Ulysses* 343 As per usual somebody's nose was out of joint. **1923** 'K. MANSFIELD' *Bad Idea in Doves' Nest* 146 So I took her up a cup of tea..as per usual on her headache days. **1938** J. PHELAN *Lifer* xxi. 212 That's right,..no grounds, as per. **1959** N. MARSH *False Scent* (1960) i. 12 He'll be bringing his present later on, as per usual. **1960** S. BARSTOW *Kind of Loving* II. vii. 263, I reckon after tonight we can't carry on as per. **1960** 'B. MATHER' *Pass beyond Kashmir* xviii. 240 It'll have to be per boot again—and across country at that. **1966** 'J. HACKSTON' *Father clears Out* 115 The Butler boys returned home (as per precedent) from breaking-in up north. **1966** *Rev. Mod. Physics* XXXVIII. 221/2 Look at one of the product tableaux obtained as per previous instructions with the markings 1, or 2,..or *N* in the various squares inserted. **1972** 'A. ARMSTRONG' *One Jump Ahead* i. 13, I came back as per usual about five o'clock. **1972** *Mod. Law Rev.* XXXV. 58 It cannot make a bare declaration (see *per* Lord Hailsham L.C., H.L.Deb., Vol. 318, col. 936). **1977** J. BINGHAM *Marriage Bureau Murders* i. 9 I'll stay in a pub... As per usual.

2. a. In distributive sense, following words of number or quantity in expressions denoting rate or proportion: For each..., for every...: = A *prep.*[1] 8 b, BY *prep.* 24 c. See also PER CENT, CENT[1] 2. Also with ellipsis of *cent*, *head*, *hour*, *week*, etc.

1598 BARRET *Theor. Warres* 54, 7 rankes at 2 men *per* ranke in the fore angles. **1611** SPEED *Hist. Gt. Brit.* IX. xiii. (1623) 732 Euery one of ech sexe..should pay by the head, or *per Pol* as they call it, twelue pence. **1663** GERBIER *Counsel* 69 Three shillings *per* doozen. **1689** *Apol. Walker's Acc. Siege Londonderry* 24 Twenty pounds Fine *per* Month. **1703** MAUNDRELL *Journ. Jerus.* (1721) 67 It is ordinarily fourteen Dollars *per* head. **1734** *Builder's Dict.* I. F vij b (*Bricks*), Their usual Price is from twelve to sixteen Shillings *per* Hundred. **1800** *Asiat. Ann. Reg., Hist. Ind.* 26/1 The allowance..was one thousand rupees per day. **1825** J. NICHOLSON *Operat. Mechanic* 546 To charge the work at per foot. **1887** MOLONEY *Forestry W. Afr.* 151 It was worth from 4*s.* to 4*s.* 6*d.* per pound. **1899** G. W. PECK *Uncle Ike* iii. 31 Listened to a heavenly choir that is paid a hundred dollars per. **1901** *Hide & Leather* 24 Aug. 30/2 He now sits in the Usher's box near the entrance to the jobbing house and draws $10 per. **1903** 'J. FLYNT' *Rise of R. Clowd* iii. 111 The percentage that Ruderick was to receive excited the liveliest interest... 'I wouldn't give any kid more'n twenty-five per.' *a* **1911** D. G. PHILLIPS *Susan Lenox* (1917) II. iv. 86 We'll get married as soon as he has a raise to twelve per. **1911** J. LONDON *Let.* 18 Oct. (1966) 353 To exploit the mediocre for the consumption of mediocrity at so much exultantly per. **1935** J. N. CHANCE *Wheels in Forest* viii. 153 The road is clear at eleven ten, and Lombard is here at eleven nineteen. That's nine minutes; an average of eighty miles per. **1946** [see BEEF *sb.* 4]. **1973** E. MCGIRR *Bardel's Murder* ii. 52 '[He] thinks his two daughters have been got at by the chauffeur.' .. 'I phoned up old Sir Omicron Pie, who kicks us back fifty per on the surgery.' **1976** *New Yorker* 23 Feb. 28/2 Many of the chain hotels are run by managing directors who have wives who think they are interior decorators and get on the payroll at twenty-five thousand per.

b. In nonce-vbs. formed on phrases belonging to this sense, as **per-sheet**, to charge at so much per sheet; PER-CENT *v.*, q.v.

1805 SOUTHEY *Let. to J. Rickman* 22 Mar. in *Life* (1850) II. 319 Per-sheeting was in use as early as Martin Luther's time, who mentions the price—a curious fact.

per, obs. f. PEAR *sb.*; var. PEAR *v. Obs.*

per-, *prefix*[1]. The Latin preposition *per* (see prec.) used in composition with verbs, adjectives, and their derivatives. A large number of these have come down through Fr. into Eng.; others have been adopted directly from Lat., or formed in Eng. on Latin elements, or (as was frequent in 16-17th c.) on words already in Eng. use. The following are the chief uses in Latin and English.

I. As an etymological element. In the senses:

1. Through, in space or time; throughout, all over: with verbs (and their derivatives), as *perambulāre* to walk through, PERAMBULATE, *perforāre* to bore through, PERFORATE, *pervadĕre* to go through, PERVADE, *pervigilāre* to watch through, PERVIGILATE; forming adjs., as *pervius* having a way through, PERVIOUS.

2. Through and through, thoroughly, completely, to completion, to the end: with verbs (and derivatives), as *perficĕre* to do thoroughly, complete, PERFECT, *permūtāre* to change throughout or completely, PERMUTE, *perpetrāre* to PERPETRATE, *perturbāre* to PERTURB; so PERUSE, etc.

3. Away entirely, to destruction, 'to the bad': with verbs (and derivatives), as *perdĕre* to do away with, destroy, lose (PERDITION), *perīre* to go to destruction, PERISH, *pervertĕre* to turn away evilly, PERVERT, *perimĕre* to take away entirely, destroy, annihilate (PEREMPTORY).

4. Thoroughly, perfectly, extremely, very: with adjs. and advbs., as *peracūtus* very sharp, PERACUTE, *perdīligens* very diligent, PERDILIGENT, *perfervidus*, PERFERVID. Formerly also in Eng. with derived sbs. (or their analogues), in sense 'very great', 'extreme', as *perdiligence*, *peradvertence*.

II. In *Chemical* nomenclature. (From 4 above.)

5. Forming sbs. and adjs. denoting the maximum (or supposed maximum) of some element in a chemical combination; esp.

a. With names of binary compounds in -IDE (formerly *-uret*), designating that in which the element or radical combines in the largest proportion with another element, e.g. PEROXIDE, PERCHLORIDE (†*perchloruret*), PERIODIDE, PERSULPHIDE (†*persulphuret*), q.v. Also **per'bromide** (†**per'bromuret**), a compound of bromine with another element or radical, in which the bromine is present in larger proportion than in other compounds: so ***per'cyanide*** (†-*cy'anuret*), ***perphosphide*** (†-*phosphuret*), etc. Hence in derivative verbs, etc.: as PEROXIDATE, -OXIDIZE, ***perphosphuretted***, etc.

This use of *per-* was introduced in 1804 by Dr. T. Thomson, in his *System of Chemistry*, ed. 2, for combinations of oxygen with a metal, *peroxide* being used to indicate 'that the metal is thoroughly oxidized', or 'combined with as much oxygen as possible': see PEROXIDE. It was subsequently extended to combinations of other elements, as PERCHLORIDE, etc. In strict chemical nomenclature names in *per-* have been to a great extent superseded by those with more definite numerical prefixes (e.g. *peroxide of manganese* by *manganese dioxide*), or by others in which the constitution of the substance is differently expressed (e.g. *perchloride* and *peroxide of iron*, by *ferric chloride*, *ferric oxide*). But the *per-* compounds are retained in some cases, especially in pharmacy and popular use.

b. With adjs. in -IC, naming oxides, acids, etc., designating that compound which contains the greatest proportion of oxygen (and, consequently, the least of the element named), as **per'bromic** ***acid***, hydrogen perbromate, $HBrO_4$; **per'chromic** ***acid***, $H_2Cr_2O_8$; **peri'ridic** ***oxide***, iridium trioxide, IrO_3; **per'nitric** ***acid***, HNO_4; **pe'rosmic** ***acid*** (= *oxide*), OsO_4; **perru'thenic** ***acid*** (= *oxide*), RuO_4, etc. See also PERCHLORIC, -IODIC, -MANGANIC, etc. Also in names of the salts of these acids, and analogous bodies, as PERCHLORATE, -IODATE, -MANGANATE, -SULPHATE, q.v., ***per'chromate***, ***peri'ridiate***, ***per'nitrate***, ***per'phosphate***, ***per'titanate***, etc.

Many of these also are now abandoned for names otherwise formed; e.g. *pernitrate of iron*, *of mercury*, now *ferric* and *mercuric nitrate*.

Formerly *per-* was also prefixed to adjs. in *-ous*, where *hypo-* is now used, as ***persulphurous*** = HYPOSULPHUROUS; so ***pernitrous***, ***perphosphorous***.

1804 [see PEROXIDE]. **1813** [see PERSULPHATE]. **1818** [see PERCHLORIC, PERCHLORIDE]. **1818** HENRY *Elem. Chem.* (ed. 8) I. 405 When 400 measures of nitrous gas and 100 measures of oxygen..are mixed together..we obtain 100 measures of a compound, called by Gay Lussac *per-nitrous acid*. Mr. Dalton..has lately proposed to call it *sub-nitrous acid*. *Ibid.* II. 12 Hypo-phosphorous or Per-phosphorous Acid. **1819** [see PERIODIDE]. **1826** *Henry's Chem.* II. 129 A solution is obtained, in which the metal is more highly oxidated, constituting per-nitrate of mercury. **1836** J. M. GULLY *Magendie's Formul.* (ed. 2) 124 Perbromuret of Iron..is a brick-red salt, very soluble, deliquescent. **1836** BRANDE *Chem.* (ed. 4) *Index*, Perbromide, Perfluoride. *Ibid.* 771 The chromate of the peroxide of iron (perchromate) is soluble. **1842** PARNELL *Chem. Anal.* (1845) 347 The soluble double compound of percyanide of cobalt and cyanide of potassium (cobalti-cyanide of potassium). **1849** D. CAMPBELL *Inorg. Chem.* 272 [They] leave, on washing with water, a pertitanate of the alkali. **1854** J. SCOFFERN in *Orr's Circ. Sc.*, *Chem.* 449 Solutions containing perchromic acid possess a beautiful blue tint. **1866** ROSCOE *Elem. Chem.* 102 Perbromic Acid, or Hydric Perbromate..obtained by the action of bromine upon perchloric acid. **1868** WATTS *Dict. Chem.* V. 138 Tetroxide of ruthenium, RuO_4, *Ruthenic tetroxide*, *Perruthenic acid*. **1873** *Fownes' Chem.* (ed. 11) 436 A deep indigo-coloured solution of basic potassium periridiate. *Ibid.*, The trioxide, or Periridic oxide, is not known in the free state. **1876** HARLEY *Mat. Med.* (ed. 6) 85 Adding again half as much bromine, the perbromide is formed. *Ibid.* 215 Iron combines with a portion of the nitric acid to form a soluble pernitrate. **1877** *Athenæum* 1 Dec. 702/2 Mounting for the microscope specimens of small animals which have been hardened in perosmic acid. **1880** CLEMINSHAW *Wurtz' Atom. The.* 233 In perruthenic acid and in osmic acid..ruthenium and osmium act as octovalent elements. **1882** *Athenæum* 13 May 607/1 They find that ozone prepared by the electrization of dry air is mixed with another gaseous compound, 'pernitric acid'. The formation of this acid is limited, like that of ozone, by a given temperature.

per-, *prefix*[2], representing OF. *per* or F. *par* (see PAR *prep.*, PER *prep.* II), in phrases which have coalesced into single words, as PERADVENTURE, PERCASE, PERCHANCE, etc.; so also (with second element Eng.) PERHAPS.

peracarid (pɛrəˈkærɪd), *sb.* (and *a.*) [f. mod.L. name of division *Peracarida* (W. T. Calman 1904, in *Ann. & Mag. Nat. Hist.* 7th Ser. XIII. 150), f. Gr. πήρα pouch + καρίς shrimp, prawn: see -ID[3].] A crustacean belonging to the division of the subclass Malacostraca so called, including sand-hoppers and woodlice possessing brood pouches. Also as *adj.* So **pera'caridan**, **peraca'ridean** *a.*

1931 W. SCHMITT *Crustaceans* in *Shelled Invertebr. of Past & Present* II. iii. 156 The two final orders comprising the peracarids. **1961** H. SCHÖNE in T. H. Waterman *Physiol. Crustacea* II. xiii. 486 Female peracaridans carry eggs and young in a marsupium between their legs. **1965** B. E. FREEMAN tr. *Vandel's Biospeleol.* ix. 117 *Spelaeogriphus* is most certainly the last relict of a primitive peracarid type. **1965** W. SCHMITT *Crustaceans* iii. 88 This [*sc.* Spelaeogriphacea] is one of the most recently established of the six peracaridean orders. *Ibid.* 89 The Spelaeogriphacea differ from all other peracaridans in having vesicular, oval gills. **1967** *Oceanogr. & Marine Biol.* V. 518 The first group includes the peracarids *Gnatha oxyurea*, *Eriopisia elongata*.. and also many (better known) decapods.

pe'racetate. *Chem.* [f. PER-[1] 5 b + ACETATE.]

†**1.** A compound of acetic acid with a base, containing a maximum proportion of the acid. *Obs.*

peracetate of iron, old name of ferric acetate.

1836 BRANDE *Chem.* (ed. 4) 1118 Peracetate of Iron may be obtained by digesting turnings and clippings of iron in acetic acid. **1864** H. SPENCER *Biol.* I. 20 Prof. Graham remarks of the peracetate of iron, that it may be made a source of soluble peroxide.

2. An ester or related derivative of peracetic acid.

1901 *Jrnl. Chem. Soc.* LXXX. I. 308 Acetic anhydride furnishes an oily product, probably ethyl peracetate. **1949** *Chem. Rev.* XLV. 8 Ethyl peracetate has been reported... This compound cannot be classed as a derivative of peracetic acid and ethyl alcohol, but rather as a derivative of acetic acid and ethyl hydroperoxide. **1967** L. F. & M. A. FIESER *Reagents for Org. Synthesis* I. 790. The reaction may proceed through the hemiacetal peracetate.

peracetic (pɜːrəˈsiːtɪk), *a. Chem.* [f. PER-[1] 5 b + ACETIC *a.*] ***peracetic acid***: $CH_3CO{\cdot}O{\cdot}OH$, a colourless, corrosive, pungent liquid that is explosive when hot and is widely used, usu. dissolved in acetic acid, as an oxidizing agent in synthesis, as a bleach and as a sterilizing agent, etc.

1903 *Jrnl. Chem. Soc.* LXXXIV. I. 398 The aqueous solution gradually suffers hydrolysis with formation of molecular proportions of acetic and peracetic acids. **1938** [see EPOXIDE]. **1965** *Economist* 20 Feb. 780/1 The new process for the oxidation of cyclohexanone to caprolactone with peracetic acid. **1970** *New Scientist* 15 Jan. 102/1 Peracetic acid is a powerful oxidizing agent that readily kills bacterial spores. **1972** NORMAN & WADDINGTON *Mod. Org. Chem.* xxi. 321 It [*sc.* nylon] can be bleached with a dilute solution of peracetic acid.

peracid (pɜːrˈæsɪd). *Chem.* Also **per-acid**. [f. PER-[1] + ACID *sb.*, as tr. G. *persäure* (von Baeyer & Villiger 1900, in *Ber. d. Deut. Chem. Ges.* XXXIII. 2480).] An acid which contains a peroxide group, esp. (in *Org. Chem.*) the group $-CO{\cdot}O{\cdot}OH$.

1900 *Jrnl. Chem. Soc.* LXXVIII. I. 626 The authors suggest that hydrogen peroxide, its acyl derivatives, and their peroxides should be called 'hydroperoxide', 'peracids' and 'peroxides' respectively. **1922** J. W. MELLOR *Comprehensive Treat. Inorg. & Theoret. Chem.* I. xiv. 959 The true peracids are either formed by the action of hydrogen peroxide on ordinary acids or their derivatives, or else they furnish hydrogen peroxide when hydrolyzed with dilute sulphuric acid. **1950** N. V. SIDGWICK *Chem. Elements* II. 871 Other compounds with the O–O link are numerous per-acids (or peroxy-acids), such as persul, phuric, perboric, percarbonic, pertitanic, perchromic, etc. **1972** *Materials & Technol.* IV. xiii. 477 All preparations of, and reactions with, organic peroxide and peracids should be conducted behind safety shields, because a reaction occasionally proceeds with uncontrollable violence.

peract (pɜːˈrækt), *v.* Now *rare*. [f. L. *peract-*, ppl. stem of *peragĕre* to perform, accomplish, f. *per-* (PER-[1] 2) + *agĕre* to drive, do.] *trans.* To practise, perform; to accomplish, carry out.

1621 *Summary of Du Bartas* I. iii. 149 In certaine sports called *Floralia*,..diuers insolencies..were peracted. **1642** H. MORE *Song of Soul* IV. xxxi, This faculty..Extends itself to whatsoever that The soul peracts. **1654** VILVAIN *Epit. Ess.* I. li, Sundry ages after the Flood peracted. **1685** H. MORE *Paralip. Prophet.* xii. 89 For the more contentfully peracting this Tax. **1892** STEVENSON *Vailima Lett.* xvii, Much waste of time,..and little transacted or at least peracted.

†**pe'raction.** *Obs. rare*$^{-0}$. [ad. L. *peractiōn-em*, n. of action f. *peragĕre*: see prec.] Performance, accomplishment.

1623 in COCKERAM. So in BLOUNT, PHILLIPS, and COLES.

†**pe'ractor.** [Agent-n. f. L. *peragĕre* to PERACT.] Name of an obsolete surveying instrument.

1674 LEYBOURN *Compl. Surveyor* 237 An Instrument which he calleth a Peractor, which is no other than a Theodelite, only the Box and Needle is fitted to the Center of the Instrument, that..the Index may be turned about, and yet the Box and Needle remain immoveable. **1766** *Compl. Farmer* s.v. *Surveying*, For the doing of this, there are several instruments very proper, especially Mr. Rathburn's quadrant upon the head of his peracter.

peracute (ˌpɜːrə'kjuːt), *a.* Now chiefly *Vet. Med.* [ad. L. *peracūtus* very sharp: see PER-[1] 4 and ACUTE.] Of diseases: Very acute or severe; attended with much inflammation.

1398 TREVISA *Barth. De P.R.* VII. xlix. (Bodl. MS.), Ilica passio..is icleped one of þe euels þat beþ icleped peracute..for..it sleeþ in one daye oþer tweyne. **1661** LOVELL *Hist. Anim. & Min.* 438 If simply acute they [the diseases] may be judged on the fourteenth day; if peracute on the seventh. **1870** S. GEE *Auscult. & Percuss.* 36 In per-acute oedemia of the lungs. **1897** *Allbutt's Syst. Med.* IV. 112 It has been proposed by Thierfelder to divide all cases into three groups; peracute, subacute and protracted. **1963** *Daily Tel.* 3 Dec. 23/1 A highland steer which went down with peracute pneumonia early yesterday recovered sufficiently to win a first prize in its class later in the morning. **1970** W. H. PARKER *Health & Dis. in Farm Animals* ix. 102 The word subacute is used to describe a condition between acute and chronic while a disease which kills very quickly..is called peracute.

peradis, obs. form of PARADISE.

peradventure (pɛrəd'vɛntjʊə(r)), *adv. arch.* Forms: see below. [ME. *per-*, *parauenture*, a. OF. phrase *per* or *par aventure*, by chance. On the one side this was syncopated to *per-*, *paraunture*, *peraunter*; on the other, the full form began in 15th c. to be conformed to L. spelling as *peradventure*, which in 16th c. superseded the earlier forms.]

A. Illustration of Forms.

α. 3–5 **per auenture**, 3–6 **perauenture**, (4 **-ere**, 5–6 **-ur**) 4–5 **par auenture**, 4–6 **parauenture**, (4–5 **-ur**, **-our**, 5 **peraventor**, **-tre**, **puraventure**).

c **1290** *Beket* 867 in *S. Eng. Leg.* I. 131 Oþur þov schalt leose þine bischopriche: and per Auenture þi lif. *c* **1350** *Leg. Rood* (1871) 65 Þan par auenture send sall he Sum of his angels to þat tre. **1377** LANGL. *P. Pl.* B. v. 648 Perauenture I be nouȝte knowe þere. **1400** in *Roy. & Hist. Lett. Hen. IV* (Rolls) 24, I clayme to be of kyn tyll yhow, and it peraventour nocht knawen on yhour parte. **1430** in Rymer *Fœdera* (1710) X. 456 Betwix whom puraventure such division shal falle. **1437** *Rolls of Parlt.* V. 439/1 Peraventre half ayenst half. *c* **1449** PECOCK *Repr.* I. xiii. 72 Perauentur summe of the writingis. **14..** in *Babees Bk.* 356 Peraventor aftyr A ȝere or tweyne. **1549** LATIMER *4th Serm. bef. Edw. VI* (Arb.) 106 But parauenture you wyll saye What and they preache not at all? **1560** DAUS tr. *Sleidane's Comm.* 119 b, Perauenture they wyll saye, it is the right of the churche. **1596** DALRYMPLE tr. *Leslie's Hist. Scot.* I. 25 The pray quhilke perauentur, thay brocht far off.

β. 4 **per aunter**, 4–5 (9 *dial.*) **peraunter**, (4 **-auntere**, **-ire**, **-ure**; **-antere**, **-tre**, 4–5 **-auntre**, 4–6 **-anter**, 5 **-awntyr**); 4–5 **par aunter**, 4–6 **paraunter**, (4 **-auntre**, **-tur**, 4–5 **-awntre**, **-ter**, **-antyr**, 6 **-anter**).

1297 R. GLOUC. (Rolls) 2018 Þat þou miȝt peraunter rome winne. **13..** *Propr. Sanct.* in Herrig's *Archiv* LXXXI. 302/329 Not once par auntur in þe wike. *a* **1340** HAMPOLE *Psalter* liv. 13, I had hid me perauntire fra him. **13..** *Minor Poems fr. Vernon MS.* xxxii. 312 Parauntur go to dampnaciun. *c* **1375** *Cursor M.* 26136 (Fairf.) Suche man peraunture miȝt him bring in mistrouþ. **1426** LYDG. *De Guil. Pilgr.* 1106 And thus peraunter stant the cas. **1426** *Rolls of Parlt.* V. 410/1 Thagh perauntre thei plesed hym. *c* **1440** *Promp. Parv.* 393/1 Perawntyr. **1535** LYNDESAY *Satyre* 4474 Peranter ar as gaukit fulis as I. **1589** PUTTENHAM *Eng. Poesie* III. xi. (Arb.) 173 To say paraunter for parauenture. **1828** *Craven Gloss.* (ed. 2), *Peraunter*, peradventure.

γ. 5–7 **peraduenture**, 5– **peradventure**, (5 **-our**, 6 **-ur**; 6 **paraduenture**, **-tter**, **-tuir**).

1470–85 MALORY *Arthur* x. lxxiii. 540 Peraduenture there wille be somme knyghtes ben displeased. **1526** SKELTON *Magnyf.* 50 Peraduenture I shall content your mynde. **1535** JOYE *Apol. Tindale* (Arb.) 44 And paraduenture cal them theirs. **1563** WINȜET *Wks.* (S.T.S.) II. 30 Paraduentuir he hes spokin thir thingis raschelie. **1611**– [see B. 3].

B. Signification.

†**1.** In a statement of fact: By chance, by accident; as it chanced, befell, or happened. *Obs.*

1297 R. GLOUC. (Rolls) 7710 Richard is o neueu brec þere is nekke þer to, As he rod an honteþ & par auntre is hors spurnde. *a* **1624** BP. M. SMITH *Serm.* vi. (1632) 115 God wrought so vpon ones conscience that peraduenture was priuy to the designe, but had been sworne before to keep it secret.

2. In a dependent clause expressing hypothesis or purpose (with *if*, *unless*, *that*, *lest*): By chance or accident, perchance; ***if peradventure***, if it chance that.

13.. *Cursor M.* 28911 (Cott. Galba) If a doghty man for det, Par auenture be in presun set. **1387** TREVISA *Higden* (Rolls) VII. 121 He..hastily wente awey, þat þere schulde no lettynge peradventure [L. *forsan*] come unto hym. **14..** HOCCLEVE *Compl. Virgin* 93 Lest þat somme folk par auenture No knowleche hadde of thy persone aright. **1568** GRAFTON *Chron.* II. 739 Least he peraduenture should be noted with the spot of Nigardship. **1603** SHAKS. *Meas. for M.* IV. vi. 5 He tells me, that if peraduenture He speake against me on the aduerse side, I should not thinke it strange. **1843** LYTTON *Last Bar.* II. ii, Unless, peradventure, their wives were comely and young. **1874** MONSIGNOR PATTERSON in *Ess. Relig. & Lit.* Ser. III. 132 If, then, peradventure, (or rather *per impossibile*,) a young candidate for ordination has passed unscathed through the pestilent State hotbeds of infidelity to which he has been statutably assigned.

3. In a hypothetical or contingent statement; and, hence, making a statement contingent: Perchance, haply; maybe, perhaps; not improbably, belike.

Used with the subjunctive or its equivalent (*peradventure he may be*, *would be*), the future tense (*peradventure he will be*), and the pres. or past indicative (*peradventure he is*, or *was there*); in the last = 'it may be the fact that...': cf. PERCHANCE 3.

1297 R. GLOUC. (Rolls) 7373 Parauntre [*v.rr.* perauentere, par auenture] me him tolde more þan soþ were. *c* **1330** *Assump. Virg.* (B.M. MS.) 9 Par auenture ȝe haue noȝt iherde How oure ladi went out of þis werde. *c* **1386** CHAUCER *Merch. T.* 426 Paraunter [*v.rr.* peraunter, perauentur] she may be youre purgatorie. **1470–85** MALORY *Arthur* II. iv. 81 Parauenture said Balyn it had ben better to haue hold yow at home. **1535** COVERDALE *Tobit* x. 2 Peraduenture Gabelus is dead, and no man wyl geue him the money. **1597** SHAKS. *2 Hen. IV*, III. ii. 315 Peraduenture I will with you to the Court. **1611** BIBLE *Gen.* xviii. 24 Peraduenture there be [COVERD. maye be] fifty righteous within the citie. —— *1 Kings* xviii. 27 Peraduenture he sleepeth, and must be awaked. **1651** HOBBES *Leviath.* I. xiii. 63 It may peradventure be thought, there was never such a time. **1742** FIELDING *J. Andrews* III. xii. 108 Peradventure I may be an hour later. **1859** TENNYSON *Elaine* 868 Peradventure had he seen her first She might have made this and that other world Another world for the sick man.

b. Qualifying a word or phrase, usually by ellipsis.

1297 R. GLOUC. (Rolls) 4204 He wole þe limemele To drawe & uorsuolwe par auenture at one mele. **1390** GOWER *Conf.* II. 239 Fortune stant in aventure, Per aunter wel, per aunter wo. **1483** *Rolls of Parlt.* VI. 256/1 By cause peradventour of privee and secrete Grauntes. **1575** *Gamm. Gurton* IV. ii. in Hazl. *Dodsley* III. 232 Lo, where he commeth towards, peraduenture to his paine. **1611** BIBLE *Transl. Pref.* 1 Hee was no babe, but a great clearke, that gaue foorth.., in passion peraduenture,..that hee had not seene any profit to come by any Synode. **1714** GAY *Sheph. Week* Proeme, I have chosen (paradventure not overrashly) to name mine by the Days of the Week.

perad'venture, *sb.* [sb. use of prec.

Johnson says 'It is sometimes used as a noun, but not gracefully nor properly'. But the use is well supported.]

1. The possibility of a thing being so or not; uncertainty, doubt; a contingency; a conjecture, chance, hazard.

[*a* **1450** *Knt. de la Tour* (1868) 56 Thus she putte condicion in her ansuere, but oure Lorde putte there inne no condicion, nor no perauenture.] **1627** USSHER *Lett.* (1686) 384 This general peradventure might run in St. Hierom's memory. **1636** BRATHWAIT *Rom. Emp.* 338 Upon better advice, and doubtfull peradventure of the successe. **1682** SIR T. BROWNE *Chr. Mor.* I. § 8 Covetousness..only affected with the certainty of things present, makes a peradventure of things to come. *c* **1790** COWPER *Wks.* (1837) XV. 335 Some to be saved infallibly, and others to be left to a peradventure. **1858** MRS. OLIPHANT *Laird of Norlaw* I. 251 The Bush and all its peradventures of hardship and solitude. **1871** H. B. FORMAN *Living Poets* 292 The poem..ends with shadowiness and peradventure.

2. Phrases. **a.** ***out of*, *past*, *beyond*, *without* (*all*) *peradventure***, out of the realm of uncertainty, beyond question, without doubt.

1542 UDALL *Erasm. Apoph.* 329 As soone as the matier was clere & out of parauentures. **1553** T. WILSON *Rhet.* 71 b, To whome [the devil] they will without peraduenture, if Goddes grace be not greater. **1570–6** LAMBARDE *Peramb. Kent* (1826) 96 In course of time, the matter was past all paraduenture. **1583** STUBBES *Anat. Abus.* II. (1882) 88 In his good time, without all peraduenture, the Lord will looke vpon him. **1639** T. DE GRAY *Compl. Horsem.* 155 This is an approved cure, and beyond all peradventure. **1739** MELMOTH *Fitzosb. Lett.* (1763) 177 True beyond all peradventure it is. **1855** MOTLEY *Dutch Rep.* III. ii. (1866) 375 This was now proved beyond peradventure. **1865** BUSHNELL *Vicar. Sacr.* III. v. 271 A state of natural punition that is, without a peradventure, endless.

†**b.** ***by*, *at* (*a*) *peradventure***, by haphazard, chance, or accident; at random, randomly. *Obs.*

[**1603** H. CROSSE *Vertues Commw.* (1878) 53 Such things as are done by chaunce-medley, or peraduenture without a setled minde.] **1633** BP. HALL *Hard Texts* Prov. xvi. 33 The lots are throwne at randome and at peradventure. **1683** *Exhortation & Advices* 4 [It] is to choose a Persuasion at a peradventure. **1684–5** SOUTH *Serm.* (1727) I. 322 A Man by meer peradventure lights into Company.

¶ **3.** Used for ADVENTURE *sb.*

1584 R. W. *Three Ladies Lond.* I. A iij, Faith ile goe seek paraduentures and be a seruing-creature.

†**peradvertence.** *Obs. rare*$^{-1}$. [f. PER-[1] 4 + ADVERTENCE.] Thorough carefulness or attention.

1526 SKELTON *Magnyf.* 2497 Syrs, I am agreed to abyde your ordenaunce, Faythfull assuraunce with good peraduertaunce.

peræon, another form of PEREION.

†**pe'raffable**, *a. Obs. rare*$^{-0}$. [PER-[1] 4.]

1623 COCKERAM, *Peraffable*, easie to be spoken to.

peraffetted, erron. f. *paraphed*: cf. PARAPH *v.*

peragall, **perage**, obs. ff. PAREGAL, PARAGE.

†**pe'ragitate**, *v. Obs. rare*$^{-0}$. [f. L. *peragitāre*: see PER-[1] 2.]

1623 COCKERAM, *Peragitate*, still to moue.

peragrate ('pɛrəgreɪt), *v.* Now *rare.* [f. L. *peragrāt-*, ppl. stem of *peragrāre*, f. *per* through + *agrum* field, country.] *trans.* To travel or pass through (a country, space, stage). Also *fig.*

1542 UDALL *Erasm. Apoph.* 266 b, When he had peragrated all the worlde as ferre as any lande went. **1665** HARVEY *Advice agst. Plague* 10 The Pestilence..peragrates the four ordinary times:..First, the Commencement... Secondly, The Augment... Thirdly, The State... Fourthly, The Declination. **1890** *Sat. Rev.* 11 Jan. 53/2 In such a book on such a subject, where the author is peragrating *loca avia Pieridum*, it is perhaps more difficult..to judge his handling.

peragration (pɛrə'greɪʃən). Now *rare.* [ad. L. *peragrātiōn-em*, n. of action from *peragrāre*: see prec.] The action of peragrating; a travelling through or traversing.

1611 COTGR., *Peragration*, a peragration,..wandering through, trauelling ouer. **1676** GLANVILL *Ess.* III. 49 What are Aristotle's peragrations of Asia, to all these? *a* **1677** HALE *Prim. Orig. Man.* II. vii. 188 By the successive peragration of these Waters.

†**b.** ***month of peragration*** (Astron.): the period of the moon's revolution from any point of the zodiac to the same point again; a sidereal (or tropical) month. (Cf. CONSECUTION 2 d.) *Obs.*

1561 EDEN tr. *Cortez' Arte Nauig.* II. xi. 38 This is called the moneth of peragration. **1646** SIR T. BROWNE *Pseud. Ep.* 212 A month of Peragration..containeth but 27. dayes, and about 8. howres. **1694** HOLDER *Disc. Time* vi. 69 The moon has two accounts of her circuit,..one her periodic month, or month of peragration:..the other is her synodic month.

peragua, obs. f. PIRAGUA, a W. Indian canoe.

perahera (pɛrə'hɛrə). Also **perahar**, **perahära**. [Sinhalese *perahera* protection, safety.] In Sri Lanka: a procession, orig. of a religious (Hindu, later also Buddhist) character, of praise or thanksgiving, or of intercession.

1681 R. KNOX *Hist. Relation Ceylon* III. iv. 78 That they may..honour these Gods, and procure their aid and assistance, they do yearly in the Month of June or July, at a New Moon, observe a solemn feast and general Meeting, called Perahar. **1817** in R. Pieris *Sinhalese Social Organization* (1956) III. 135 *Perhära*..is a very ancient ceremony in commemoration of the birth of the god Vishñu. *Ibid.* 136 Five days having expired, another ceremony, an important and essential part of the *perahära*, commences..which lasts five days more. *Ibid.* 137 The ceremony of *perahära* is continued up to the day of the full moon... On the night of the full moon..the shrine is carried in the procession. **1913** L. WOOLF *Village in Jungle* v. 113 Last night we took him in the perahera, and called upon the god to hear us. **1923** D. H. LAWRENCE *Birds, Beasts & Flowers* 170 But the best is the Pera-hera, at midnight, under the tropical stars..the Pera-hera procession, flambeaux aloft in the tropical night. **1971** *Ceylon Daily News* 17 Sept. 1/3 He will be taken in a perahera to the avasa where a felicitation meeting is to be held. **1974** *Oxf. Jun. Encycl.* (rev. ed.) I. 102/2 The principal occasion is the Perahera, a great annual pageant in Kandy, when a relic, reputed to be a tooth of Gautama Buddha, is carried about the town in grand procession on the back of a gorgeously caparisoned elephant.

‖**perahu**, var. PROA.

perai (pi'rai, piː'raɪ), **piraya** (pɪ'rɑːjə). Also 8–9 **peri**, 9 **pirai**. Also PIRANHA. [ad. Tupi *pi'raya*, in Brazilian Tupi *pi'ranʸa*, name of the fish, lit. 'scissors'.] A voracious fresh-water fish, *Serrasalmo piraya*, of the Orinoco and other rivers of tropical America, having a serrated belly and sharp lancet-shaped teeth.

[**1648** MARCGRAVE *Brasil.* 164 Piraya et Piranha.] **1753** CHAMBERS *Cycl. Supp.*, *Piraya*,..the name of a fish caught in the American rivers. **1769** E. BANCROFT *Nat. Hist. Guiana* 189 The fish called a peri by the Indians and white inhabitants, is about 18 inches in length. **1826** SYD. SMITH *Wks.* (1859) II. 75/2 The quivers were close by them, with the jaw-bone of the fish pirai tied by a string to their brim. **1862** WOOD *Nat. Hist.* III. 329 The peraya, or pirai has been removed from the Salmonidae and placed in another family. **1879** —— *Waterton's Wand.* Index, Perai..sometimes called the Blood-fish of the Orinoco, can make fatal attacks on human beings, its numbers compensating for its small size. **1883** C. F. HOLDER in *Harper's Mag.* Dec. 107/2 In the Orinoco is found the perai, whose nest..hangs pendent from some..branch, drifting in the tide.

peraill, **peral**, **peralous**, obs. ff. PERIL, -OUS.

peralatik, **peralytyk**, obs. ff. PARALYTIC.

peralin, **-ing**, obs. Sc. forms of PARELLING.

peralkalic (pɜːr'ælkəlɪk), *a. Petrol.* [f. PER-[1] 4 + ALKALIC *a.*] = next.

1902 W. CROSS et al. in *Jrnl. Geol.* X. 592 The divisions in classes I, II, and III are fivefold: Rang 1: $\frac{K_2O' + Na_2O'}{CaO'} > \frac{7}{1}$, peralkalic. **1976** *Nature* 10 June 482/1 The Saint Francois Mountains form a distinctive unmetamorphosed igneous complex comprising chiefly alkalic to peralkalic rhyolite and granite.

peralkaline (pɜːr'ælkəlaɪn), *a. Petrol.* [f. PER-[1] 4 + ALKALINE *a.*] Of a rock: containing a high proportion of soda and potash; now *spec.* (see quot. 1931).

1913 A. N. WINCHELL in *Jrnl. Geol.* XXI. 210 Along this co-ordinate igneous rocks are classified as normal or alkali-calcic.., alkaline, and peralkaline. *Ibid.* 211 Peralkaline rocks are characterized mineralogically by the presence of feldspathoids (or lenads)... Chemically they are distinguished by insufficient silica to combine with the abundant alkalies to form feldspars after saturation of other available bases as orthosilicates. **1927** S. J. SHAND *Eruptive Rocks* vii. 128 The following groups of rocks stand out as chemically distinct:— (a) A peraluminous group, characterised by primary muscovite, biotite, corundum, tourmaline, topaz, almandine, or spessartite. (b) A peralkaline group, characterised by soda-pyroxenes or soda-amphiboles, .. and by the virtual absence of anorthite... (c) A group characterised by common pyroxenes, amphiboles, olivine, [etc]. **1931** —— *Study of Rocks* iv. 52 Peraluminous rocks... The molecular proportion of alumina exceeds the molecular proportions of soda, potash and lime combined... Peralkaline rocks... The molecular proportion of alumina is less than that of soda and potash combined. **1950** *Rep. 18th Internat. Geol. Congr. 1948* II. 129 Peralkaline rocks.. only occur in stable parts of the earth's crust, outside active orogenic zones. **1974** *Nature* 24 May 315/1 Alkaline and peralkaline igneous rocks were intruded and extruded in distinct nodes. **1974** [see PERALUMINOUS *a.*].

Hence ˌ**peralka'linity**, the state of being peralkaline.

1969 *Amer. Jrnl. Sci.* CCLXVII. 242 A quadrilateral diagram in which molecular alumina is plotted against soda/potash ratio can then be employed to show the variation in alkali ratio in whole rocks.. with changes in silica content and peralkalinity. **1974** BOWDEN & TURNER in H. Sørensen *Alkaline Rocks* IV. viii. 334/2 The variation in the coloured mineral content is dependent on the peralkalinity of the granites.

peraluminous (pɜːrə'l(j)uːmɪnəs), *a. Petrol.* [f. PER-[1] 4 + ALUMINOUS *a.*] Of a rock: (see quots. 1974[1] (and 1931), 1972).

1927, 1931 [see PERALKALINE *a.*]. **1964** *Mineral. Abstr.* XVI. 488/2 A peraluminous granite stock and related pegmatites.. have been emplaced in pelitic and quartzo-feldspathic schists. **1972** *Gloss. Geol.* (Amer. Geol. Inst.) 527/1 *Peraluminous*, said of an igneous rock in which the molecular proportion of aluminum oxide is greater than that of sodium and potassium oxide combined. **1974** I. S. E. CARMICHAEL et al. *Igneous Petrology* ii. 31 This leads to four more classes of rocks, each independent of silica saturation: 1. Peraluminous rocks, in which the molecular proportion of Al_2O_3 exceeds ($CaO + Na_2O + K_2O$)... 4. Peralkaline rocks, in which $Al_2O_3 < (Na_2O + K_2O)$. **1974** W. C. LUTH in H. Sørensen *Alkaline Rocks* VI. vi. 506/1 Several key factors provide limiting conditions. These include.. the relatively large amounts of the peraluminous hydrates required.

† **pe'ramble**, *sb. rare.* [f. next: cf. PREAMBLE.] A place for walking in; an ambulatory, a cloister.

1546 in Strype *Eccl. Mem.* II. App. A. 7 At Windsor.. Al the church peramble, and the choir of the college hung and garnished as aforesaid.

† **pe'ramble**, *v. Obs.* Also 6 -bal, 6–7 -bule. [f. L. *perambulāre* (see PERAMBULATE), conformed to AMBLE *v.*] To walk about, to perambulate (*trans.* and *intr.*); also *fig.* to wander, ramble.

1508 KENNEDIE *Flyting w. Dunbar* 337, I perambalit [1568 *MS. Bann.* perambulat] of Pernaso the montayn. **1539–40** in *9th Rep. Hist. MSS. Comm.* 306 The same watche.. In dew order to peramble the circuyte of the saide towne. **1630** J. TAYLOR (Water P.) *Pennilesse Pilgr.* Wks. I. 127/1 Thus I perambuling poore John Taylor Was giu'n from Mayor to Shriefe, from Shriefe to Jaylor. **1632** LITHGOW *Trav.* IX. 422 Ceasing to peramble through any more particulars.

perambulant (pə'ræmbjʊlənt), *a. rare.* [ad. L. *perambulānt-em*, pr. pple. of *perambulāre* to PERAMBULATE: see -ANT[1].] Perambulating, strolling, itinerant.

1865 LECKY *Ration.* II. vi. 331–2 The poor found congenial recreation in fairs, dances, perambulant musicians. *Ibid.* 333 Simply a perambulant flute-player.

† **pe'rambulate**, *ppl. a. Obs.* In 6 -at. [ad. L. *perambulāt-us*, pa. pple. of *perambulāre*: see next.] Perambulated; walked through, along, or around; trodden by walking; ascertained by perambulation.

1509 HAWES *Past. Pleas.* VIII. v. (Percy Soc.) 30 That he walke not.. The perambulat waye. **1575–6** *Reg. Privy Council Scot.* II. 490 The perambulat landis betuix the landis of Creychtmontgorth and Nethertoun.

perambulate (pə'ræmbjʊleɪt), *v.* [f. L. *perambulāt-*, ppl. stem of *perambulāre* (f. *per* through, all over + *ambulāre* to walk): see -ATE[3] 5.]

1. a. *trans.* To walk through, over, or about (a place or space); formerly more generally, to travel or pass through, to traverse.

1568 [see PERAMBLE *v.* quot. 1508]. **1607** J. DAVIES *Summa Totalis* C iv, Ere once the Sunne his Round perambulate. **1665** MANLEY *Grotius' Low C. Warres* 414 The Sea, is, I cannot say, inhabited, but perambulated by the Samogitians. **1763** JOHNSON 25 June in Boswell, There is a great deal of Spain that has not been perambulated. **1879** *Cassell's Techn. Educ.* IV. 96/1 He was wont to perambulate the garden and the hothouses, lantern in hand.

b. *fig.* To 'go round', surround in position.

1863 HAWTHORNE *Our Old Home* (1879) 168 In the centre of the grassy quadrangle about which the cloisters perambulate.

c. *intr.* To walk about; to travel or move about (quot. 1800).

1607 HEYWOOD *Faire Maide* Wks. 1874 II. 48, I am perambulating before a female. **1611** CORYAT *Crudities* 29 Perambulating about some of the principall streets of Paris. **1800** COLQUHOUN *Comm. Thames* iii. 84 The boats perambulating [among the shipping] during the night. **1825** LYTTON *Falkland* I. (1827) 38 Persons who always perambulate with a book in their hands.

2. *spec.* **a.** *trans.* To travel through and inspect (a territory) for purposes of measurement and division; 'to survey, by passing through' (J.). **b.** To walk statedly or in procession around the boundaries of (a forest, manor, parish, etc.) for the purpose of formally determining or preserving them; to make perambulation of: see PERAMBULATION 3.

1612 DAVIES *Why Ireland*, etc. 249 Commissions.. to view and perambulate those Irish territories, and thereupon to divide and limit the same into.. counties. **1679–88** *Secr. Serv. Money Chas. & Jas.* (Camden) 179 A comic'on under the great seale, for perambulating the forest of Beare. **1757** MRS. GRIFFITH *Lett. Henry & Frances* (1767) I. 59 *note*, A certain annual festival [Ambarvalia], among the Romans, when they perambulated the bounds of their farms, and sacrificed to Ceres. **1799** S. FREEMAN *Town Off.* 35 The Selectmen appoint persons to perambulate, run and renew the dividing lines between the towns. **1883** *American* VI. 359 Boundary stones, which used to be annually perambulated by the mayor and corporation.

c. *intr.* To make perambulation; to beat the bounds.

1708 S. SEWALL *Diary* 12 Apr., Capt. Culliver and others perambulating for Braintrey and Milton, went with us.

3. a. *intr.* Of a (light) vehicle: to be in motion, to move about. *rare.* **b.** *trans.* To wheel, convey, or conduct (*about*) in or as in a perambulator (sense 3); to travel on or traverse in a perambulator.

1856 *Chambers's Jrnl.* 23 Aug. 116/2 The young brother.. can hardly reach to the bar, but nevertheless the light carriage perambulates obediently under his guidance. **1865** P. H. GOSSE *Year at Shore* iv. 87 The open gate of a villa reveals a little girl 'perambulating' a baby. **1902** *To-Day* 30 Apr. 8/1 Babies.. are not allowed to 'perambulate' the pavement two or three abreast. **1909** M. B. SAUNDERS *Litany Lane* xxii. 295 The Princess Max, having opened the affair, was being perambulated about as usual. **1922** J. A. DUNN *Man Trap* i. 9 Jovial of mouth and eyes despite the handicap that reduced him to being perambulated. **1929** P. GIBBS *Hidden City* xi. 50 Four acres of garden in which some neat nursemaids were perambulating the pink-cheeked babies of the well-to-do.

Hence **pe'rambulated** *ppl. a.*; **pe'rambulating** *vbl. sb.* and *ppl. a.* (in quot. 1862 (*humorous nonce-use*) = being wheeled in a perambulator).

1675 OGILBY *Brit.* Pref. 1 Their Perambulated Projections.. being much inferior to what might have been done. **1824** T. THOMPSON *Hist. Ch. Swine* 157 To confirm the custom of perambulating. **1829** H. HAWTHORN *Visit Babylon* 18 The perambulating bugs, that made every limb I had, a meal. **1862** CALVERLEY *Verses & Tr.*, '*Hic vir, hic est*' v, Each perambulating infant Had a magic in its squall. **1926** W. J. LOCKE *Stories Near & Far* 280 Then he walked round his perambulating property [*sc.* a caravan]. A big-boned brown horse ceased his munching as he approached. **1938** P. W. SERGEANT *Championship Chess* i. 26 There is little to be said for perambulating chess matches—except that they bring in more money. **1949** E. COXHEAD *Wind in West* vi. 165 We're.. all products of what Rory calls the book-learning. We're his perambulating text-books.

perambulation (pəˌræmbjʊ'leɪʃən). [a. AF. *perambulation*, med.L. *perambulātio* (both in early use in England in sense 3), n. of action from *perambulāre*: see PERAMBULATE *v.* and -ATION. Cf. It. *perambulazione* (Florio).]

1. The action of walking through; a walk, a journey on foot; formerly more generally, the action of travelling through or about; a tour.

c **1485** *Digby Myst.* (1882) II. 67, I shall.. make perambulacion, Thorow oute damaske. **1579–80** NORTH *Plutarch* (1895) II. 136 Then he sent out skowtes.. to viewe the way of their perambulation. **1632** LITHGOW *Trav.* VIII. 342 Whether discontent or curiosity droue me to this second perambulation. **1788** CUMBERLAND *Observer* No. 96 IV. 25 The fatigue of so ill-timed a perambulation disabled me from expressing that degree of admiration, which seemed to be expected. **1829** LYTTON *Devereux* II. xi, I.. venture to request you to seek some other spot for your nocturnal perambulations. **1877** 'H. A. PAGE' *De Quincey* II. xvi. 29 In the course of his daily perambulations at Lasswade.

b. Const. *of* (the place).

1642 HOWELL *For. Trav.* (Arb.) 43 In the perambulation of Italy young Travellers must be cautious.. to avoyd one kind of Furbery or cheat. **1779–81** JOHNSON *L.P.*, *Milton* Wks. II. 91 He seems to have intended a very quick perambulation of the country [Italy]. **1861** LEWIN *Jerusalem* 110 In their perambulation of the walls both started in opposite directions.

2. The action of travelling through and inspecting a territory or region; a survey. **b.** *transf.* A written account of a survey or tour of inspection.

1576 LAMBARDE (*title*) A Perambulation of Kent: Conteyning the Description, Hystorie, and Customes of that Shyre. **1605** BACON *Adv. Learn.* I. vii. §6 Adrian spent his whole reign.. in a perambulation or survey of the Roman empire. **1657** WOOD *Life* (O.H.S.) I. 215 Apr. 30... he began his perambulation of Oxfordshire: and the monuments in Wolvercot church were the first that he survey'd and transcrib'd. **1894** *Lancet* 3 Nov. 1069 The work will include a 'Perambulation', such as is found in the classic by Stowe and Strype.

3. The action or ceremony of walking officially round a territory (as a forest, manor, parish, or holding) for the purpose of asserting and recording its boundaries, so as to preserve the rights of possession, etc.; beating the bounds.

[*c* **1250** BRACTON IV. ix. (Rolls) III. 70 Fiat inde perambulatio et sic terminetur negotium.] **1540** *Act 32 Hen. VIII*, c. 12 Discrete persons.. to make parambulacions & to appoint.. wher the boundes.. shal extend. **1563** *Homilies* II. *Rogation Week* IV. (*title*), An Exhortation to be spoken to suche Paryshes where they vse theyr Perambulation in Rogation weke. **1590** *Reg. Privy Council Scot.* IV. 515 Ane court of perambulatioun haldin mair nor ane hundreth yeiris syne. **1654** *Boston Rec.* (1877) II. 119 Mr. James Oliver and Robtt Turner are appoynted to run the line betwixt Cambridge and Rocksbury, and the towne of Boston in perambulatyon. **1704** J. HARRIS *Lex. Techn.* I, *Perambulation of the Forest*, is the Surveying or Walking about the Forest, or the Limits of it, by Justices, or other Officers.. to set down the Metes and Bounds thereof. **1875** STUBBS *Const. Hist.* II. xiv. 149 The perambulations necessary for carrying out the forest reforms were ordered.

b. *transf.* A record of a perambulation.

[**1373** *Rolls of Parlt.* II. 320/2 Qe les Chartre, Franchises, & Perambulation dont ceste Bille fait mention soient ratifiez.] **1610** HOLLAND *Camden's Brit.* I. 497 King Henry the Second.. disforested it (as wee finde in an old Perambulation).

4. The boundary traced, or the space enclosed, by perambulating; circuit, circumference, bounds; district, precinct, extent. *lit.* and *fig.*

1601 JOHNSON *Kingd. & Commw.* (1603) 46 In that perambulation is contained the greater part of Hungarie. **1678** T. JONES *Heart & Right Sov.* 116 The one lying within the perambulation and jurisdiction of Divine soveraignty, the other of humane. **1705** HICKERINGILL *Priest-cr.* IV. (1721) 215 They were never quiet till they.. enlarged the Perambulations of what they had. **1860** FORSTER *Gr. Remonstr.* 226 Extending the boundaries of the forests in Essex, and annihilating the ancient perambulations. **1892** *Daily News* 25 Jan. 5/4 Nominally the Forest has a perambulation of ninety-three thousand acres.

†**5.** *fig.* Comprehensive relation or description; also, circumlocution, 'beating about the bush'. *Obs.*

1509 HAWES *Joyf. Medit.* viii, What sholde I shewe by perambulacyon All this grete tryumphe. **1605** BACON *Adv. Learn.* II. To King §15, I will now attempt to make a generall and faithfull perambulation of learning. *a* **1652** BROME *Mad Couple* I. Wks. 1873 I. 16 Leave these perambulations; to the point. [Cf. PREAMBULATION.]

6. *attrib.*

1670 in *Daily Chron.* 12 May (1904) 4/7 Spent on the perambulation dinner, £3 10s. **1886** WILLIS & CLARK *Cambridge* I. Introd. 12 A sort of boulevard, or perambulation-road (*circuitus*).

perambulator (pə'ræmbjʊleɪtə(r)). [Agent-noun f. L. *perambulāre* to PERAMBULATE: see -OR 2.]

1. One who perambulates. **a.** *gen.* One who walks or travels through or about a place; a traveller, pedestrian. Also *fig. rare.*

1611 SPEED *Hist. Gt. Brit.* VII. ii. 259 Their Metropolitane Citie Canterbury, which was the paterne (saith that Countries Perambulator [Lambarde]) that this Sigebert followed in the erection of his. **1630** J. TAYLOR (Water P.) *Wks.* II. 81 The Longing desire that America hath to entertaine this vnmatchable Perambulator. **1832** G. DOWNES *Lett. Cont. Countries* I. xix. 305 (Italy) Were it not for the canals.. the element, water, would be altogether absent from the perambulator's view. **1870** HAZLEWOOD & WILLIAMS *Leave it to Me* 3 Joe's a perambulator;.. a perambulating greengrocer, called by vulgar people a costermonger. **1925** J. BONE (*title*) The London perambulator. **1930** R. CAMPBELL *Adamastor* 64 Speed, motion, flight!.. Perambulator of the Bored And ambulance of broken hearts! **1971** *Daily Tel.* 18 Oct. 10 (Advt.), Dickens was a determined perambulator of London, either in search of material.. or simply wandering the streets.

†**b.** One who performs a perambulation for determining boundaries: see PERAMBULATION 3. *Obs.*

1667 *Rec. Muddy River & Brookline, Mass.* (1875) 39 Mr. John Hull,.. Peter Aspinwall are chosen perambulators for the bounds between Muddy River and Roxbury. **1699** *Boston Rec.* (1881) VII. 234 The perambulators chosen by the Selectmen to run the line between Charlestown and Boston. **1815** SIR W. GRANT in *Cooper's Rep., Chancery* 315 The Course taken by the Perambulators.. was such as to include the Whole of.. what they claimed as Common belonging to the Parish.

2. A machine for measuring distances, consisting of a large wheel trundled by a handle along the ground, with attached clockwork and dial for recording the revolutions; a hodometer.

1688 R. HOLME *Armoury* III. 374/2 A Perambulator.. by which they measure the distances between place and place. **1752** W. STUKELEY in *Mem.* (Surtees) III. 465 The machine called perambulator, or way-wiser, which measures the road. **1792** *Phil. Trans.* LXXXII. 113 From the mouth of Cuddalore river to the north end of the base I measured, with a perambulator, just four miles and one furlong. **1828** HUTTON *Course Math.* II. 57 The perambulator.. has a wheel of $8\frac{1}{4}$ feet, or half a pole, in circumference. **1855** J. BUTLER *Trav. & Adventures Assam* I. v. 56 Some idea may be formed of the impassable nature of the country we travelled over this day, when I state that we only came eight miles one furlong, by the perambulator, in eight hours. **a 1877** [see DELINEATOR 3]. **1913** CLOSE & COX *Text Bk. Topogr. & Geogr. Surveying* (ed. 2) iv. 76 A perambulator should not be used over very rough ground, and both it and the cyclometer should be checked over known measured distances. **1964** D. GREENHOOD *Mapping* ix. 262/2 For doing the same kind of measuring on the ground itself, there are various makes of distance meters, sometimes called 'perambulators', which are wheels that you push by a handle, like a roller toy. They register distances up to 10,000 ft. **1969** TOOLEY & BRICKER *Hist. Cartogr.* 42 (*caption*) Colles's map..was probably made with compass, plane table, and perambulator.

3. A hand-carriage, with three or four wheels, for one or two young children, pushed from behind. (The current sense; often colloquially abbreviated to *pram*.) Also *attrib.*, *Comb.*, and *fig.*

1856 *Chambers's Jrnl.* 23 Aug. 116/2 The *Perambulator*.. has given us children, looking on with their grave smooth faces at the business of life,..as they lean back philosophically in their carriages. **1856** *Punch* 22 Mar. 118/2 (*caption*) I shan't play no more with that Matilda Jenkins.—'Er doll ain't got no Perambylatur. **1857** MISS YONGE *Let.* 1 Oct. in C. Coleridge *Life & Lett.*, Then little Constantia Wood arrived driven up in a perambulator. **1860** *All Year Round* No. 52. 35 Small perambulators for the weakly dolls to be trundled in. **1861** *Temple Bar* I. 539 These creatures [*sc.* kangaroos]..have the power of carrying their delicate, prematurely born young about with them wherever they go. They have this condition, viz. a soft, warm, well-lined portable nursery-pocket, or 'perambulator'. **1866** *Leisure Hour* XV. 347/2 Certain ill-tempered bachelors did indeed protest against them, complaining that perambulator-drivers did occasionally drive their new-fangled machines against their shins. **1936** P. M. CLARK *Autobiogr. Old Drifter* iv. 47 Some time after this I was on my way to Rondebosch to meet a married cousin whom I had not seen since my perambulator days. **1972** *Daily Tel.* 3 June 32/4 They came with shopping bags, picnic baskets, babies in perambulators and pushchairs, babies in arms.

† **pe'rambulatory**, *sb. Obs.* [f. L. *perambulāre*, *-āt-*: see prec. and -ORY[1]. Cf. AMBULATORY.]

a. A place for walking about in; a walk. **b.** ? A record of a perambulation (PERAMBULATION 3).

1636 BRATHWAIT *Rom. Emp.* 233 Curious walkes and perambulatories befitting so great a Majesties residence. **1773** *Amherst Rec.* (1884) 61/2 That the Perambulatry of the Line between Hadley and Amherst Lately run..be accepted. **1843** *Knickerbocker* XXII. 85 Let..the temperance-halls and root-beer perambulatories make answer.

perambulatory (pəˈræmbjʊlətərɪ), *a.* [f. as prec. + -ORY[2].]

1. a. Given to perambulating; vagrant, wandering, strolling, itinerant. **b.** Pertaining to or characterized by perambulation.

1803 W. TAYLOR in *Ann. Rev.* I. 425 It is probable that a perambulatory population would originate. **1805** E. HOPKINS (*title*) An Abstract of the particulars contained in a perambulatory survey of above 200 miles of turnpike road. **1826** *Blackw. Mag.* XX. 277 Such..as you sometimes see in the scenery of a Perambulatory Theatre.

2. *nonce-use.* Relating to perambulators.

1856 *Tait's Mag.* XXIII. 306 We introduced the.. perambulatory patent, only to show the risk of dealing in patent rights.

‖**Perameles** (pɛrəˈmiːliːz). *Zool.* [mod.L. (G. St. Hilaire) f. Gr. πήρα bag, pouch + L. *mēles*, *mēlis* a marten or badger.] A genus of small marsupials of Australia and New Guinea, typical of the family *Peramelidæ*, or true Bandicoots. Hence **pera'melid**, an animal of this genus, a perameles; **pera'meline** *a.*, belonging to the sub-family containing *Perameles*; **pera'meloid** *a.*, akin to or resembling *Perameles*.

[**1879** A. R. WALLACE *Australas.* iii. 55 The Peramelidæ, or bandicoots and rabbit-rats, are small animals..allied to the kangaroos.] **1886** P. ROBINSON *Valley Teet. Trees* 98 Here, too, is that other eccentricity, the 'rabbit-eared Perameles', such a nondescript to look at that Nature herself must have been puzzled..to say what it was she had made.

† **pera'mene**, *a. Obs. rare*[−1]. [ad. L. *peramœnus*, f. *per-* (PER- 4) + *amœnus* pleasant.] Very pleasant.

1657 TOMLINSON *Renou's Disp.* 278 With a..red flower and peramene odour.

peramount, peramour: see PARAMOUNT, etc.

perand, perans, appearing, etc.: see PEAR *v.*

peranter(e, obs. variant of PERADVENTURE.

perantique (pɜːrænˈtiːk), *a. nonce-wd.* [See PER- 4.] Very antique or ancient.

1883 G. STEPHENS *S. Bugge's Stud. North. Mythol.* 66 Lines of verse..in a perantique dialect.

[**perareplum**, error for *peare-plum*: see PEAR *sb.*

1573 TUSSER *Husb.* (1878) 76 Perareplums, black and yellow.]

perau, obs. form of PARA[1], Turkish coin.

peraunter(e, -ire, etc., obs. ff. PERADVENTURE.

peravail, var. PARAVAIL *Obs.*

perawick, obs. f. PERIWIG.

perayle, obs. f. PAREL, PERIL.

perbend, variant of *perpend*, PARPEN.

1858 in SIMMONDS *Dict. Trade.* **1864** in WEBSTER.

perbenzoic (pɜːbɛnˈzəʊɪk), *a. Chem.* [f. PER-[1] 5 b + BENZOIC *a.*] ***perbenzoic acid***: a colourless crystalline solid, $C_6H_5CO{\cdot}O{\cdot}OH$, which is a widely used oxidizing agent, esp. for epoxidation reactions.

1903 *Jrnl. Chem. Soc.* LXXXIV. I. 397 Benzoic acetic peroxide undergoes hydrolysis in aqueous solution with production of perbenzoic and acetic acids, together with benzoic peroxide. **1938** *Thorpe's Dict. Appl. Chem.* (ed. 4) II. 373/1 Benzoyl peroxide is comparatively inert, but treatment with alcoholic sodium ethoxide yields the reactive perbenzoic acid,..which is used very widely for oxidising ethylenic compounds. **1967** L. F. & M. A. FIESER *Reagents for Org. Synthesis* I. 791 The reaction of perbenzoic acid with an olefin usually proceeds smoothly at a low temperature (0–25°) and affords an epoxide in high yield.

perboil(e, obs. form of PARBOIL.

† **perbole**, obs. aphetic form of HYPERBOLE.

1678 DRYDEN *Kind Keeper* IV. i, Will you leave your perboles and come then? *Ibid.* v. i, Nay an you are in your perboles again!

perborate (pɜːˈbɔəreɪt). *Chem.* [a. F. *perborate* (A. Étard 1880, in *Compt. Rend.* XCI. 932): see PER-[1] 5 and BORATE.] Any of a number of strongly oxidizing derivatives of boric acid which contain peroxo-anions, and are usu. prepared by the action of hydrogen peroxide on borates; *esp.* the sodium salt, a white crystalline solid of empirical formula $NaBO_3.4H_2O$, which is widely used as a bleach and is a constituent of washing powders.

1881 *Chem. News* 14 Jan. 25/2 He [*sc.* A. Étard] has obtained barium perborate,—$Bo_2O_7BaH_4 + H_2O$, a white amorphous insoluble salt. **1898** *Jrnl. Chem. Soc.* LXXIV. II. 427 The heat of decomposition by sulphuric acid was determined in the case of sodium perborate and ammonium perborate. **1916** *Chem. Abstr.* X. 2803 Hereto-fore bleaching with persalts, such as perborate, has been more costly than bleaching with chloride of lime. **1959** *Observer* 6 Sept. 18/4 Perborate bleach works only at high temperatures. **1959** *Guardian* 28 Sept. 3/6 The woollen cardigan..had..changed colour..due to the perborate (a stain-removing bleach) added..to a soap powder. **1967** E. L. MUETTERTIES *Chem. Boron & its Compounds* iii. 192 The X-ray crystal structure determination of 'sodium perborate'..reveals a dimeric tetrahedral configuration with dihedral angle equal to 64°:..and the anionic formula $B_2(O_2)_2(OH)_4{}^{2-}{\cdot}2Na^+{\cdot}6H_2O$. **1974** *Sci. Amer.* Jan. 125/2 Sodium perborate is the cheapest and safest of all peroxy salts and is much used in detergents, particularly for very-hot-water washing.

perboric (pɜːˈbɔərɪk), *a. Chem.* [ad. F. *perborique* (A. Étard 1880, in *Compt. Rend.* XCI. 931), f. *per-* PER-[1] 5 b + *borique* BORIC *a.*] ***perboric acid***: the supposed parent acid of perborates, which was formerly thought to have the formula HBO_3 and is only known in acidic solutions containing perborate anions.

1881 *Chem. News* 14 Jan. 25/2 Whilst an equimolar mixture of magnesium sulphate, ammonium chloride, and ammonia is not rendered turbid either by oxygenated water or by boric acid, a mixture of the two precipitate it abundantly, acting as perboric acid. **1924** J. W. MELLOR *Comprehensive Treat. Inorg. & Theoret. Chem.* V. xxxii. 116 Perboric acid itself has not been made... In ethereal soln. and an excess of hydrogen peroxide, the partition coeff. of boric acid increases a little corresponding with the formation of free perboric acid in the etheral soln. **1973** N. N. GREENWOOD *Chem. Boron* (1975) vi. 887 Reaction of orthoboric acid with hydrogen peroxide gives perboric (peroxoboric) acid solutions which probably contain the monoperborate anion [$HOOB(OH)_3{}^-$].

† **perbreak, -brake**, *v.*[1] *Obs.* Forms: 4–6 **perbrake** (4 **pere-**), 6 *Sc.* **perbraik**. Pa. pple. 6 *Sc.* **perbrekit**. [perh. f. L. *per* through + BREAK *v.*: cf. L. *perfringĕre*; but the early spelling *-brake* does not belong to the vb. *break* (cf. however BRAKE *v.*[1]), and the compounding of a native vb. with a L. prefix is unexpected in the 14th c. App. not to be identified with PARBREAK *v.*]

a. *trans.* To make a breach in, break through, shatter. **b.** *intr.* To suffer a breach, to burst or break asunder.

c 1330 R. BRUNNE *Chron. Wace* (Rolls) 7950 A strong castel..þat non wyþ force mighte hit take, Ne wyþ engyns hit perebrake [*v.r.* non engine perbrake]. **c 1420** LYDG. *Story of Thebes* III. in *Chaucer's Wks.* (1561) 370/2 As he that hurteleth ayenst harde stones Broseth him self, and unwarly perbraketh. **1497** BP. ALCOCK *Mons Perfect.* C iij, Thy door is open and the seale is not perbraked. **1513** DOUGLAS *Æneis* I. iv. 25 Perbrakit schippis bot cabillis thair mycht ryde. *Ibid.* VI. vi. 63 Gan grane or geig ful fast the jonit barge.., and with lekkis perbraik, Scho suppit huge wattir of the laik.

† **per'break, per'brake**, *v.*[2], parallel form of PARBREAK *v.*, to vomit, to spue.

1495 *Trevisa's Barth. De P.R.* XVIII. xxvii. (W. de W.) 787 A hounde..etyth..ofte careyne so gredily that he perbrakyth [*MSS.* brakeþ] and castyth it vp. **1567** GOLDING *Ovid's Met.* VI. (1593) 148 To perbreake up his meat againe. **1601** HOLLAND *Pliny* XX. iv. II. 40 For them that would perbreake or vomit, the best way to take it [radish], is at the end of a meale.

Hence † **per'breaker**; † **per'breaking** *vbl. sb.*

1495 *Trevisa's Barth. De P.R.* XVIII. xxvii. (W. de W.) 787 A hounde gadryth herbes..by whom he purgyth hymself wyth perbrakynge [*MSS.* brakynge] and castynge. **1576** NEWTON *Lemnie's Complex.* (1633) 175 In vomiting and perbraking. **1620** THOMAS *Lat. Dict.*, *Vomitor*,..a vomiter, a spewer, a perbraker.

perbromic (pɜːˈbrəʊmɪk), *a. Chem.* [f. PER-[1] 5 b + BROMIC *a.*] ***perbromic acid***: $HBrO_4$, a strong acid with oxidizing properties that was first prepared in 1968. Hence **per'bromate**, a salt of this acid.

Claims for the preparation of the acid and its salts in the 19th c. proved to be mistaken.

1864 *Chem. News* 30 Apr. 205/2 Perbromic acid has been fruitlessly investigated by many chemists, but M. Kaemmerer has obtained it in the most simple manner by treating perchloric acid with bromine. *Ibid.* Perbromate of potash is more soluble than the perchlorate, and less so than the bromate. **1866** ROSCOE *Elem. Chem.* 102 Perbromic Acid, or Hydric Perbromate..obtained by the action of bromine upon perchloric acid. **1912** *Chem. News* 2 Aug. 50/1 It seems that it must be finally concluded that perbromic acid and its salts are incapable of existence. **1968** *Jrnl. Amer. Chem. Soc.* XC. 1900/2 These results indicated the formation of a relatively unreactive perbromate ion and suggested that a determined effort might lead to the preparation of macro amounts of perbromates. *Ibid.* 1901/2 As expected, the volatility of perbromic acid is less than that of perchloric acid. **1973** DOWNS & ADAMS in J. C. Bailar et al. *Comprehensive Inorg. Chem.* II. xxvi. 1451 First obtained in studies of the β-decay of $^{83}SeO_4{}^{2-}$, perbromates are also formed in the γ-radiolysis of crystalline bromates. *Ibid.* 1452 On very rapid evaporation, crystallization of perbromic acid solutions occurs (possibly to give $HBrO_4, 2H_2O$) just before decomposition sets in.

Perbunan (pəˈbjuːnən). Also **perbunan**. [a. G. *Perbunan*, f. *per-* + *buna* BUNA + *N*, chem. symbol for nitrogen.] A proprietary name for a nitrile rubber first made in Germany and originally called Buna-N.

1938 *Trade Marks Jrnl.* 4 May 551/2 Perbunan... Compositions consisting mainly of reaction products obtained by the polymerisation of butadiene hydrocarbons, sold in the form of sheets, blocks, tubes, [etc.]... I. G. Farbenindustrie Aktiengesellschaft.., Frankfort-on-Main, Germany; manufacturers. **1938** *Chem. Abstr.* XXXII. 3663 The mech. and elec. properties of Buna-S and Perbunan (formerly Buna-N,..),..are described... The elec. properties of both are excellent, and Buna-S is less permeable to water than are Perbunan and natural rubber. **1940** *Jrnl. R. Aeronaut. Soc.* XLIV. 159 A cable consisting of rubber covered with a thin perbunan sheath and an oil varnished ozone-resisting braid would probably give the best results. **1959** *Times* 27 Apr. (Rubber Industry Suppl.) p. ii/4 These basic synthetic rubbers, buna S, neoprene and perbunan, developed in the 1930s, were the forerunners of the main synthetic rubbers we use to-day. **1959** *Official Gaz.* (U.S. Patent Office) 18 Aug. TM 82/1 Farbenfabriken Bayer Aktiengesellschaft, Leverkusen-Bayerwerk, Germany. Filed Feb. 12, 1959. Perbunan... For rubber and rubber substitute materials. **1973** *Nature* 14 Sept. 93/1, I have carried out some measurements on an alkaline perbunan latex dispersion.

perc, var. PERK *sb.*[3], PERK *v.*[3]

percale (‖pɛrkal, pəˈkeɪl). Forms: 7–8 **percalla, -callis, -caula(h**; 8– **percale**. [app. orig. from some Eastern source: origin uncertain (cf. however Pers. *pargālah* a rag). The mod. use is an adoption (with the material) of F. *percale* (1723 in Hatz.-Darm.). In Sp. *percal*, It. *percallo*.] **a.** *orig.* A fabric imported from the East Indies in the 17th and 18th centuries: ? = BOOK-MUSLIN: cf. quot. 1696. **b.** In mod. use, A closely woven cotton fabric, orig. of French manufacture, with higher finishing than muslin, and without gloss.

a. 1621 R. COCKS *Diary* (Hakl. Soc.) II. 160, 7 peeces white percallas. **1696** J. F. *Merchant's Ware-ho.* 33 A sort of fine Callico called Percallis, there being of it two sorts, the one is much like Sallampoires, and is made up much like it..; the next is made up like a Book; these sorts are indifferent fine, and are..much used for Shifts and Shirts, but the Book-Percallis is the strongest. **1757** *New Hist. E. Ind.* II. 143, 8100 pieces percales. **1813** W. MILBURN *Orient. Comm.*, II. 221 *Percaulahs*, Pieces R800.

b. 1840 THACKERAY *Paris Sk.-bk.* 6 A light bed which has a tall canopy of red *percale*. **1884** *Girl's Own Paper* Aug. 682/1 Quantities of cottons, chintzes, and percales are to be seen in the shops, in preparation for a hot summer. **1890** *Cent. Dict.* s.v., The soft-finished percale is an English manufacture, of less body than the French percale.

attrib. **1880** 'OUIDA' *Moths* I. 61 Look at our camelot and percale gowns that Worth sends us.

percaline (pɜːkəˈliːn, ˈpɜːkəlɪn). [a. F. *percaline*, dim. of *percale*: see prec.] A glossy kind of French cotton cloth, usually dyed of one colour.

1858 SIMMONDS *Dict. Trade*, *Percaline* (French), fine cotton print. **1888** *Harper's Mag.* Oct. 740/1 A gray calico skirt and coarse petticoat of percaline.

percarbide (pəˈkɑːbaɪd). *Chem.* [f. PER- 5 + CARBIDE.] A compound containing the maximum proportion of carbon with another element. Also **per'carburet**.

So **per'carburetted** *a.*, containing or charged with a maximum of carbon, as ***percarburetted iron***.

1826 HENRY *Elem. Chem.* I. viii. 424 This gas..termed by them *Olefiant gas*..has since been called *bi-carbureted* or *percarbureted hydrogen*. **1857** MAYNE *Expos. Lex.* 904/2 A percarburet. *Ibid. Percarburetus*..percarbureted.

†**per'case**, *adv. Obs.* (exc. *dial.*) Forms: see CASE *sb.*¹; also 4–6 (9 *dial.*) **par-**; 5 *Sc.* **percass, -chass**, 6 **-caiss, -kase**. [ME. a. AF. *par cas, per cas*, OF. *par cas*: see PER and CASE *sb.*¹ Cf. F. *par hasard*; for sematology, see PERCHANCE.]

1. In a statement of fact: By chance, as it chanced; = PERADVENTURE *adv.* 1, PERCHANCE 1.

1375 BARBOUR *Bruce* III. 481 Then hapnyt at that tyme percass, That the Erle of the Leuenax was Amang the hillis. *c* **1386** CHAUCER *Pard. T.* 557 And with that word, it happed hym par cas To take the botel, ther the poyson was. **1513** DOUGLAS *Æneis* V. vi. 75 Quhar as fast by The stirkis for the sacrifice, per cace, War newly brittnit.

2. *if* (*except, lest*, etc.) *percase*, if (lest, etc.) by chance, if the case or chance were that. Cf. PERADVENTURE *adv.* 2, PERCHANCE 2, PERHAPS 2.

c **1412** HOCCLEVE *De Reg. Princ.* 1471 If þat þou haddest per cas ben a prest. **1513** MORE *Rich. III*, Wks. 45/2 Yf shee bee percase so obstynate, and so preciselye sette vppon her own wyl, that [etc.]. **1571** CAMPION *Hist. Irel.* vii. (1633) 20 If percase for advancement of their Citties, they straine a point of truth. **1575** *Mirr. Mag.*, *Hastings* xi, Least thou differ, to thincke me kinde, per case.

3. In a hypothetical or contingent statement: It may (might) chance or be the case that...; maybe, perchance, peradventure, perhaps.

13.. *Cursor M.* 4002 (Gött.) If þu will þai sal pasce. And cum nohut in his hand percas. **1390** GOWER *Conf.* III. 14 The weies ben so slider, In which he mai per cas so falle, That he schal breke his wittes alle. *c* **1440** LYDG. *Hors, Shepe & Goos* 535 (Lansd. MS.) That thou canst nat, parcas a-nothir can. **1575** GASCOIGNE *Pr. Pleas. Kenilw.* A v, Percase she came this worthy Queene to serue. **1605** M. SUTCLIFFE *Brief Exam.* 91 They woulde percase say the same of Scotland but that theire conscience told them contrary. **1828** *Craven Gloss.* (ed. 2), *Parcaas.* **1876** *Whitby Gloss.*, *Perkeease*, or *Percase*, perchance.

b. Qualifying a word or phrase, usually with ellipsis: = PERADVENTURE B. 3 b, PERCHANCE 3 d.

[**1377** *Act 1 Rich. II*, c. 7 Repreignantz vers eux la value de cel livere, ou per cas la double value, per tiel covenant; 1611 *transl.* taking againe towards them the value of the same Liuerie, or percase the double value.] **1523** WOLSEY in Fiddes *Life* II. (1726) 71 Reasonable offers..more regarded than per-case the qualities of the person. **1574** tr. *Littleton's Tenures* 53 Yᵉ on plough land is lotted to the purparty of the one, as percase to the yonger sister. **1600** DARRELL *Detect. Harsnet* 99 The Bp. had seene him doe his tricks before that time, yea, percase, oftentimes.

percaula(h, obs. variant of PERCALE.

percayue, perce, obs. f. PERCEIVE, PIERCE.

perceant ('pɜːsənt), *a. poet. arch.* or *Obs.* Also 4–7 **persant**, 5 **perceaunt, persand**, 5–6 **persaunt**. [a. F. *perçant*, pr. pple. of *percer* to pierce.] Penetrative, keen, piercing. *lit.* and *fig.*

1377 LANGL. *P. Pl.* B. I. 155 And portatyf and persant as þe poynt of a nedle. *c* **1400** tr. *Secreta Secret., Gov. Lordsh.* I. i. 47 He was a man of..persand vndirstandynge. *c* **1400** *Rom. Rose* 2809 Hir laughing eyen, persaunt and clere. *c* **1530** *Crt. Love* 849 Now am I caught, and unwar sodenly With persant stremes of your yën clere. **1590** SPENSER *F.Q.* I. x. 47 All were his earthly eien both blunt and bad,.. Yet wondrous quick and persaunt was his spright. **1610** W. FOLKINGHAM *Art of Survey* I. vi. 11 Pellucid, milde, subtill, cleare, sweet, persant, soone hot and colde. **1819** KEATS *Lamia* II. 301 The sophist's eye, Like a sharp spear,.. Keen, cruel, perceant, stinging.

perceaue, -ceave, obs. forms of PERCEIVE.

perceauerance, var. PERCEIVERANCE *Obs.*

†**per'ceit.** *Obs. rare.* Also 4 **parceit**, 5 **perseyte**. [f. PERCEIVE, on the analogy of *deceit, receit*, etc.: cf. CONCEIT.] Perception.

1399 LANGL. *Rich. Redeles* Prol. 17 It passid my parceit.. How so wondirfull werkis wolde haue an ende. *c* **1400** *Beryn* 3785 Geffrey had ful perseyte of hir encombirment. **1681** W. ROBERTSON *Phraseol. Gen.* (1693) 1141 He hath very small perceit of what is past.

perceivable (pəˈsiːvəb(ə)l), *a.* Now *rare.* [In ME. a. OF. *percevable* (14th c. in Hatz.-Darm.); in later times referred directly to PERCEIVE *v.*]

1. 'Perceptible; such as falls under perception' (J.). **a.** By the senses: Sensible.

c **1450** *Macro Plays* (E.E.T.S.) 55/598 It ys ioy of ioys inestymable, To halse, to kys þe affyable; A louer ys sone perceyvable Be þe smylynge on me, wan þat doth remove. **1614** RALEIGH *Hist. World* (1634) 5 He created, and was the sole cause of this aspectable and perceivable universal. **1788** ANNA SEWARD *Lett.* (1811) II. 122 There was a perceivable smile upon the lips. **1847** *Illustr. Lond. News* 4 Sept. 146/1 Filthy sewers..perceivable by the nose.

b. By the mind: Intelligible, appreciable.

1567 DRANT *Horace* To Rdr. * v, I being in all myne other speaches so playne, and perceaueable. **1754** EDWARDS *Freed. Will* II. vi, All perceivable Time is judged and perceived by the Mind only by the..successive Changes of its own Ideas. **1832** HT. MARTINEAU *Hill & Valley* vi. 84 There were many perceivable reasons for this change.

†**2.** That may be gathered or collected (as taxes); = F. *percevable.* (Cf. PERCEIVE *v.* 8.) *Obs. rare.*

1569 *Act 11 Eliz.* in Bolton *Stat. Irel.* (1621) 300 As like forfeytures to your Majestie by the lawes of this Realme be leviable and perceivable.

Hence **perceiva'bility, per'ceivableness.**

1641 GASCOIGNE in Rigaud *Corr. Sci. Men* (1841) I. 45 The perceivableness of this ceasing by the contraction. **1883** A. BARRATT *Phys. Metempiric* 76 The condition of the co-existence of a plurality of monads in mutual relation, and the consequent perceivability of a universe.

per'ceivably, *adv.* Now *rare.* [f. prec. + -LY².] Perceptibly, appreciably.

1660 JER. TAYLOR *Duct. Dubit.* I. v. Rule vii, When the judgment of the man is discernibly and perceivably little. **1726** SWIFT *Gulliver* IV. i, I..found myself perceivably to improve every time. **1772–84** *Cook's Voy.* (1790) VI. 2023 They were now greatly surprized to find the distance scarce perceivably diminished.

per'ceivance. *Obs.* exc. *dial.* [a. OF. *percevance* (12th c. in Godef.), f. *percevant*, pr. pple. of *percevoir* to PERCEIVE: see -ANCE.] The capacity of perceiving, discernment, wisdom; the action of perceiving, perception (mental or physical).

1534 TINDALE *Eph.* i. 8 Which grace he shed on us aboundantly in all wisdome, and perceavaunce [1526 prudency, 1611 BIBLE prudence]. *a* **1562** G. CAVENDISH *Wolsey* (1893) 133 Havyng perceivaunce..that the truthe in this case is very doughtfull to be knowen. **1694** R. BURTHOGGE *Reason & Nat. Spirits* 57 The Eye has no Perceivance of things but under Colours that are not in them. *a* **1825** FORBY *Voc. E. Anglia* s.v., 'The boy is a dunce, and has no perceivance.' **1855** ROBINSON *Whitby Gloss.* s.v., 'I had no perceivance about it', knew nothing of the matter. **1893** COZENS-HARDY *Broad Norfolk* 85 If the man..is occasionally the worse for drink, and not to be depended upon, they say he has no persayvance over hisself.

So †**per'ceivancy** *Obs. rare*, perception.

1649 J. ECCLISTON tr. *Behmen's Epist.* vi. 85 By the formation, or impression it hath brought it selfe into the Perceivancy of the Essence. In which Perceivancy or Sensibility the Magneticall Desire is arisen.

†**per'ceivant**, *a. Obs. rare*⁻¹. [a. F. *percevant*, pr. pple. of *percevoir*: see prec. and -ANT.] Perceiving, observant, understanding.

c **1400** tr. *Secreta Secret., Gov. Lordship* 103 Þat he loke to, and be persayuant, whenne nede shal fall.

perceive (pəˈsiːv), *v.* Forms: 4–7 **perceyue, -ve, perceiue**, (4 **-cayue, -seiue**, 4–5 **-seyue, -sayue**, 5–6 *Sc.* **-sawe**, 6 **-saue, -saife, -saive**, 6 **-cive**, 6–7 **-ceaue, -ve**); 4– **perceive**; also 4–6 **par-**, 5 **pur-**. [a. OF. **perceiv-re*, northern form of *perçoivre*, now *percevoir* (stressed stem *perceiv-* = *perçoiv-*); = Pr. *percebre*, Sp. *percebir*, Pg. *perceber*:—L. *percipĕre* to take possession of, seize, get, obtain, receive, gather, collect; also, to apprehend with the mind or senses, understand, perceive; f. *per* through, thoroughly + *capĕre* to take, seize, lay hold of, etc. Both branches of the L. sense were used in OF.; mod.F. has chiefly that of 'receive, collect', which is less important in Eng., and now obs. (*Perceive* may in some cases have been aphetic for *aperceive*, APPERCEIVE.)]

I. To take in or apprehend with the mind or senses.

1. *trans.* To apprehend with the mind; to become aware or conscious of; to observe, understand. Const. *simple obj.*, *obj. clause*, or *obj.* and *inf.* or *compl.* Also *absol.*

a **1300** *Cursor M.* 8625 (Cott.) At þe last..sco parceuid, þat sco was of hir child deceuid. *c* **1330** R. BRUNNE *Chron. Wace* (Rolls) 16263 Þider cam nought þo Osewy;..When Penda hit perseiued, he made gret fare ffor þat Osewy was nought þare. **1393** LANGL. *P. Pl.* C. XX. 66 He perceyuede by his pous he was in peril to deye. *c* **1400** *Ywaine & Gaw.* 2034 Sir Ywayn persayved..That it was so ner the nyght That no ferrer ride he might. **1526** TINDALE *Mark* ii. 8 When Jesus perceaved in his sprete, that they so reasoned in them selves. **1591** SHAKS. *Two Gent.* II. i. 159 Doe you not perceiue the iest? **1681** P. RYCAUT tr. *Gracian's Critick* 143 He..perceived himself led another way. *a* **1733** MANDEVILLE *World Unmasked* (1736) 15, I perceive I shall soon have a very different opinion of that master than I have hitherto entertain'd. **1802** PALEY *Nat. Theol.* v. §7 (1819) 65 If we perceive a useful end and means adapted to that end, we perceive enough for our conclusion. **1849** MACAULAY *Hist. Eng.* vi. II. 75 The courtiers and foreign ministers soon perceived that the Lord Treasurer was prime minister only in name. **1862** H. SPENCER *First Princ.* I. iii. §20 If..the object perceived is self, what is the subject that perceives?

†**b.** Of an inanimate object: 'To be affected by' (J.). *Obs. rare*⁻¹.

1626 BACON *Sylva* §818 The Vpper Regions of the Aire perceiue the collection of the matter of Tempest and Winds, before the Aire here below.

†**2.** To take in fully or adequately; to grasp the meaning of, comprehend, understand. *Obs.*

a **1300** *Cursor M.* 10785 (Cott.) Þe feind suld noght perceiue þat a maiden suld consaiue. *c* **1460** *Towneley Myst.* vii. 92 Perceyf well what I shall say. **1526** *Pilgr. Perf.* (W. de W. 1531) 32 b, It is requyred that he haue..suche langage, as he may be perceyued of them to whome he precheth. **1559** *Prim. Hen. VIII* Pref. in *Priv. Prayers Q. Eliz.* (Parker Soc.) 12 That the youthe..vse the same, vntill thei bee of compitent vnderstandyng and knoweledge to perceiue it in latin. **1575** LANEHAM *Let.* (1871) 35 *Forte grande est la pouuoyr qu'auoit la tresnoble Science de Musique sur les esprites humains*: perceiue ye me? I haue told ye a great matter noow.

3. To apprehend (an external object) through one of the senses (esp. sight); to become aware of by sight, hearing, or other sense; to observe; 'to discover by some sensible effects' (J.). Const. as in 1.

c **1330** R. BRUNNE *Chron* (1810) 18 Þat [? *read* þan] perceyued Haldayn, þat bare þe croice on hie, Sex & þritty paiens enbussed priuelie. **13..** *K. Alis.* 1984 (Bodl. MS.) He haþ perceyued by his siȝth, þat he ne haþ aȝein hym miȝth. **1382** WYCLIF *Acts* ii. 14 Be this thing knowun to ȝou, and with eeris perseyue my wordis. *c* **1420** LYDG. *Assembly of Gods* 264 Next vnto hym, as I perceue mought, Sate the goddese Diana. *c* **1440** *York Myst.* xl. 164 By no poynte couthe I parceyue hym passe. *c* **1470** HENRY *Wallace* III. 250 Na Sothren that tyme was persawyt in thai wais, Bot he tholyt dede that come in thar danger. **1560** DAUS tr. *Sleidane's Comm.* 206 They went awaye by nyght so pryvely, that the enemy perceived it not. **1592** DAVIES *Immort. Soul* XV. v. (1714) 70 Ev'n the Ears of such as have no Skill, Perceive a Discord. **1601** SHAKS. *Jul. C.* v. iii. 13 Are those my Tents where I perceiue the fire? **1632** J. HAYWARD tr. *Biondi's Eromena* 98 By the cries she perceived the troopes to bee in a hot conflict. **1756** C. LUCAS *Ess. Waters* I. 132 No remarkable smell could be perceived from it. **1812** H. & J. SMITH *Rej. Addr.* xiii, [She] Protrudes her gloveless hand, perceives the shower. **1878** GEO. ELIOT *Coll. Breakf. P.* 226 Whatever sense perceives or thought divines.

†**4.** *refl.* (= F. *se percevoir, s'apercevoir*) and *pass.*, in senses 1 and 3. Const. *that, of.*

a. *refl. Obs.*

a **1300** *Cursor M.* 443 When he [Lucifer] parceued him be [*MS.* he] þis þat he was ouer all oþer in blis. **13..** *Guy Warw.* (A.) 7261 Gij him perceyued in þat stounde þat ..þurch wepen y-grounde..No slouȝ him man neuer mo. **1483** CAXTON *G. de la Tour* lv. E v, A seruaunt of her lord.. perceyued hym of it and told it to his lord. *c* **1489** —— *Blanchardyn* xxi. 71 I haue not perceyued me of this that ye telle me.

†**b.** *pass. to be perceived*: to be aware. *Obs.*

a **1300** *Cursor M.* 1893 (Cott.) Quen noe sagh and was parseueid þat þis rauen had him deceuid. *c* **1330** R. BRUNNE *Chron.* (1810) 159 R[ichard] was perceyued, þei were renged redie. *c* **1470** HENRY *Wallace* XI. 106 Or thai com ner that place, Off thaim persawyt rycht weill was gud Wallace.

†**5.** *trans.* To apprehend what is not open or present to observation; to see through, see into. *Obs.*

1375 BARBOUR *Bruce* X. 37 The King..Persauit thair subtilite. *c* **1380** WYCLIF *Wks.* (1880) 10 Lest here ypocrisie be parceyued. *c* **1440** *Generydes* 3193 Whanne the Sowdon perseivid his entent. **1532** MORE *Confut. Tindale* Wks. 666/2 Here is it ethe to spye and perceyue hys iuglyng well inoughe. **1651** HOBBES *Leviath.* II. xxvii. 154 They think their designes are too subtile to be perceived. **1660** STANLEY *Hist. Philos.* III. I. 35 For those who futures would perceave.

†**6.** To recognize. *Obs. rare.*

1553 T. WILSON *Rhet.* (1580) 216 Not onely could they not perceiue theim by their faces, but also they could not discerne theim by any other marke..in all their bodies.

†**7.** *intr.* To discern *between*. *Obs. rare.*

1495 *Trevisa's Barth. De P.R.* VI. v. (W. de W.) 192 By voys and face we perceyue [*MSS.* men knowiþ] bytwene chyldren and men of full aege.

II. To take into possession. Cf. L. *percipĕre*, F. *percevoir*, in lit. sense, from L. *capĕre* to take.

†**8.** *trans.* To receive (rents, profits, dues, etc.).

1382 WYCLIF *Tobit* xiv. 15 Al the eritage of the hous of Raguel he perceyvede [*Vulg.* percepit]. **1472–3** *Rolls of Parlt.* VI. 4/2 Every of the seid men Archers, to have and perceyve vi*d.* by the day oonly. **1512** *Knaresb. Wills* (Surtees) I. 4, I will that my forsaid doghters have and persaive all the revenieuse. **1596** BACON *Max. & Use Com. Law* I. xx. (1636) 73. **1625** *Concession to Sir F. Crane* in Rymer *Fœdera* XVIII. 60 To have, houlde, perceive, receive and take the said annuitie or yeerely pension of two thousand pounds.

†**b.** in gen. sense: To receive, get, obtain. *Obs.*

1482 *Monk of Evesham* (Arb.) 75 Gretely merueylde why he yat was so honeste of leuyng..had not yette perceiuyd fully reste and ioye. **1540–54** CROKE *Ps.* (Percy Soc.) 19 Full spedely let me obteyne Thy socoure, and perceyue the same. **1591** SHAKS. *Two Gent.* I. i. 144 *Pro.* Why? could'st thou perceiue so much from her? *Sp.* Sir, I could perceiue nothing at all from her; No, not so much as a ducket for deliuering your letter. **1748** J. NORTON *Redeemed Captive* (1870) 22 Mrs. Smeed was as wet..but through the good providence of God, she never perceived any harm by it.

perceived (pəˈsiːvd), *ppl. a.* [f. prec. + -ED¹.]

†**1.** (Cf. PERCEIVE *v.* 4 b.) Having perception; aware; wary, circumspect, wise. *Obs.*

c **1400** *Laud Troy Bk.* 14588 Thei sayde 'that Troyens were dissayued, And that thei were not persayued To graunte the trewes when thei it asked'.

2. Apprehended, seized with the mind, observed.

c **1440** *Promp. Parv.* 382/2 Parceyvyd, *perceptus.* **1573–80** BARET *Alv.* P 264 Plainly perceiued, or knowen: manifest, euident, *perspectus.* **1704** NORRIS *Ideal World* II. Pref. 11 The perceived agreement of this idea with the extreams. **1875** WHITNEY *Life Lang.* xiv. 290 Available for perceived needs. **1943** M. FARBER *Found. Phenomenology* xii. 335 If the eruption is therefore to be critically judged as a deception,.. illusion, etc., then the perceived, seen color of the object also does not exist. **1971** *Nature* 19 Feb. 518/1 Mr Stein's apparently innocent bill to limit noise at New York airports to 108 perceived noise decibels by July..could be..a serious threat to the viability of Concorde. **1973** *Jrnl. Genetic Psychol.* CXXII. 269 The study of perceived (subjective) age changes. **1976** *Times Lit. Suppl.* 3 Sept. 1080/2 In all these instances the KKE was reacting to actual or perceived efforts to destroy it.

Hence **perceivedly** (pəˈsiːvɪdlɪ) *adv.*; **perˈceivedness.** *rare.*

1625 in Rushw. *Hist. Coll.* (1659) I. 189 Our Allies in those parts will be suddenly and perceivedly strengthened and enabled. **1871** *Athenæum* 24 June 779 Prof. Fraser.. stating as Berkeley's ultimate doctrine, that the condition of sensible things during the intervals of our perception of them was one of potential perceivedness or perceivability. **1967** S. BECKETT *Film* 32 Anguish of perceivedness.

perceiver (pəˈsiːvə(r)), *sb.* [f. PERCEIVE + -ER¹.]

1. One who perceives, a percipient; an observer, understander.

a **1550** R. WYER tr. *C. de Pisan's C. Hyst. Troye* A j b, And where mysordre, in thy translacion is Unto the perceyuer. **1645** MILTON *Tetrach.* Introd., Under the appearance of a grave solidity, which estimation they have gain'd among weak perceivers. **1867** EMERSON *Lett. & Soc. Aims* vii. (1875) 177 Newton the philosopher, the perceiver, and obeyer of truth. **1893** PATMORE *Relig. Poetæ* 2 The Poet is, *par excellence*, the perceiver, nothing having any interest for him unless he can, as it were, see and touch it with the spiritual senses. **1947** G. MURPHY *Personality* xiv. 331 (*heading*) The perceiver. **1971** *Jrnl. Gen. Psychol.* LXXXIV. 158 The history of the gestalt psychology is filled with many other instances in which missing parts are ignored by the perceiver. **1972** *Sci. Amer.* Nov. 85/1 The students who were three-dimensional perceivers spent more time looking at the ambiguous trident. **1973** *Nature* 14 Dec. 434/2 He stresses that painters and sculptors, like poets, expect the perceiver to do at least half the work.

†**2.** One who obtains or receives; a recipient, participator. *Obs.*

c **1400** *Apol. Loll.* 10 Þus þe apostil did alle þings for þe gospel þat he schuld be maad perseyuer þer of. *Ibid.* 28 Bi þat we schal..be so perceyuers of cristis meritis. *c* **1440** HYLTON *Scala Perf.* (W. de W. 1494) II. viii, Of þe prysoner of helle makyth [it] a perceyuer of heuenly herytage. **1675** TRAHERNE *Chr. Ethics* xxxii. 540 A quick and lively perceiver, a tender sence, and sprightly intelligence.

†**perceiver**, *v. Obs. rare.* Also 5 perseuer, 6 perceuere, perceyver. [app. a. ONF. *perceivre*, *percevire* (13th c. in Godef.: see PERCEIVE) taken as the verb-stem: cf. *render*, *tender*.] *trans.* To perceive, make out.

1495 *Trevisa's Barth. De P.R.* III. xix. (W. de W.) 65 The witte of smellynge perseueryth [*MSS.* perseyueþ, perc-] and knowith smelles. **1503** HAWES *Examp. Virt.* x. xiii, Hard it wyll be loue so to couere [*i.e.* kever] But that som man shall it perceuere. **1509** —— *Past. Pleas.* XIX. xxii, Thoughe.. wyth a stormy pery The fyre was blowen, yet we dyd it cover, Bycause abrode it should nothyng perceyver.

†**perˈceiverance, -ˈance.** *Obs.* Forms: 5–7 perseuer-, -ver-, 6 perceyuer-, -ver-, perceuer-, -ver-, perceauer-, 6–7 perceiuer-, -ver-; 5–7 -aunce, -ance. [app. f. as prec. + *-ance*, as an equivalent of OF. *percevance* (f. *percevant*, pr. pple. of *percevoir*: see -ANCE), of which the natural Eng. repr. was *percevance*, later PERCEIVANCE. Through the insertion of the *-er*, the word was brought into confusion with *perseverance*, already in the language and also stressed *perˈseverance.*]

1. Faculty or capacity of perceiving; the act of perceiving; mental (rarely physical) perception, understanding: = PERCEIVANCE.

c **1440** *Gesta Rom.* li. 230 (Add. MS.) Foryetefull wille, or fleshly delectation,..defouleth the myrrours, that is, conscience and perseveraunce..so that the soule may not se god. **1509** HAWES *Past. Pleas.* VI. iv, So by logyke is good perceyveraunce To devyde the good and the euyll asondre. **1548** UDALL *Erasm. Par. Luke* xvii. 143 Lightenynge soodainlye flashynge foorthe..before ye haue any perceiueraunce that any suche thing is to come. *a* **1592** GREENE *George a Greene* (1599) D ij, This is wondrous, being blinde of sight His deepe perseuerance should be such to know us. **1618** LATHAM *2nd Bk. Falconry* (1633) 45 Then you shall perceiue that shee will haue perceiuerance and vnderstanding by the dogs remouing and giuing way with feare vnto her.

2. Perceived or perceptible appearance.

1546 LANGLEY *Pol. Verg. De Invent.* II. xv. 61 God wyllyng..to shewe the grosse wyttes of men some perceiueraunce of hymselfe. **1579–80** NORTH *Plutarch, Paulus Æmilius* (ad fin.), He sodainly fell into a rauing (without any perseuerance of sicknes spied in him before). **1600** SURFLET *Countrie Farme* VI. x. 744 If..there be any perceiuerance and shewe that the budde will likewise blossome and flowre.

So †**perceiverant** *Obs. rare*$^{-1}$ = PERCEIVER *sb.* 1.

1509 HAWES *Past. Pleas.* XI. xxiv. (1554), For first doctrine, in all goodly wise The perseuerant [1555 perceyveraunt] trouthe [1555 trowthe], in his booth [1555 bote] of wil.

†**perceiveˈration.** *Obs. rare*$^{-1}$. [f. as prec. + -ATION.] = prec. 1.

c **1440** *Gesta Rom.* li. 230 (Harl. MS.) A shrewde or a froward wil, or a fleshli delectacion, that makith foule the consienns and the perseueracion [*Add. MS.* perseverance], so that þe soule may not Se god, ne his owne perill.

perceiving (pəˈsiːvɪŋ), *vbl. sb.* [f. PERCEIVE *v.* + -ING¹.] The action of the vb. PERCEIVE in its various senses: **a.** A becoming aware, observing, cognizance, perception; †a being perceived.

1375 BARBOUR *Bruce* II. 15 The bruce..Gert priuely bryng Stedys twa. He and the clerk, for-owtyn ma, Lap on, forowtyn persawyng. *c* **1440** *Alph. Tales* 243 Þai durst not cry in þe cetie for purseyvyng, & þai went vnto þe wuddis. **1509** FISHER *Fun. Serm. C'tess Richmond* Wks. (1876) 292 To the vnderstondynge of latyn wherin she had a lytell perceyuynge. **1585** T. WASHINGTON tr. *Nicholay's Voy.* II. xxii. 60 Without the knowledge or perceiuing of their husbands. **1762** KAMES *Elem. Crit.* (1833) 475 Perceiving is a general term for hearing, seeing, tasting, touching, smelling.

†**b.** The receiving (of rents, etc.). *Obs.*

1485 *Rolls of Parlt.* VI. 319/2 The perceyvynge or taking of any issues or proffitts therof. **1503–4** *Act 19 Hen. VII*, c. 27 §1 Endentures to be made of all suche reteyndres receyvynges & perceyvynges.

perˈceiving, *ppl. a.* [f. as prec. + -ING².] That perceives; percipient; formerly (now rarely) also, discerning, penetrating, sagacious.

c **1410** *Master of Game* (MS. Digby 182) xi, A good mann and a perceyuande. **1525** LD. BERNERS *Froiss.* II. xxviii. 79 As sage and as parceyuing as any hyghe prince in his dayes. **1645** MILTON *Tetrach.* (1851) 235 It must needs bee both unjoyous and injurious to any perceaving person so detain'd. **1736** BUTLER *Anal.* I. i, Glasses..preparing objects for, and conveying them towards the perceiving power. **1862** H. SPENCER *First Princ.* I. iii. §20 (1875) 65 The mental act in which self is known, implies..a perceiving subject and a perceived object.

Hence **perˈceivingness,** the quality or state of perceiving; perception, discernment.

1897 F. THOMPSON *New Poems* 130 For I know, Albeit, with custom-dulled perceivingness.

percel(l, -mel, obs. forms of PARCEL, -MEAL.

percel(l, percely, etc., obs. forms of PARSLEY.

percemonie, obs. form of PARSIMONY.

per cent (pə ˈsɛnt), *phr.* (*sb.*) Orig. usually with full-stop (*per cent.*), as if an abbreviation of **per centum**, which is the form used in Acts of Parliament and most legal documents; but see CENT¹. Now freq. without full-stop, and as one word. [See PER III. 2 and CENT¹.]

A. *Phrase.* **a.** By the hundred; for, in, or to every hundred: with preceding numeral, expressing a proportion, as of a part to the whole amount, or *esp.* of interest to principal. See CENT¹ 2. Also with preceding numeral as an approximate estimate of extent in unquantifiable contexts. ***a*** or ***one hundred per cent***: see HUNDRED *sb.* and *a.* 2 c.

Sometimes definitely = in a hundred pounds (of sterling money), as 'a shilling per cent' = 1*s.* in £100.

1568–1888 [see CENT¹ 2]. **1939** F. PRATT *Secret & Urgent* 258 It will be noted that more than fifty per cent of all English words end in E, S, D or T. **1961** *Information & Control* IV. 65 The study of this particular data collection showed that over 95 percent of the vocabulary could be represented by 13 characters. **1973** *Times* 21 Dec. 14/6 This trouble's cut my social life by about 35 per cent. **1973** [see PERCENTAGE b]. **1975** *Sci. Amer.* Feb. 15/3 The two reasons most often given for emigrating are 'Better training in the U.S.' (69 percent) and 'Political factors' (8 percent). **1976** *Ibid.* May 108/3 Io is particularly red, and its colour, together with its high reflectivity (about 62 percent, roughly equivalent to white sand), make it a unique object in the solar system. **1976** *Daily Tel.* 20 July 1/5 Average earnings in May were 19·4 per cent. up on the previous year, compared with a 15·4 per cent. rise in retail prices.

b. With numeral forming a phrase used *attrib.* ('four per cent loan'), or as *sb.* in *pl.* ('three per cents'), denoting public securities bearing such and such a rate of interest: see CENT¹ 2 b.

1822–88 [see CENT¹ 2 b].

c. As quasi-*sb.* Percentage; one per cent.

1905 G. W. ROLFE *Polariscope* 96 The per cent of sucrose in the sample. **1934** *Jrnl. Sedimentary Petrology* IV. 68/2 In setting up a histogram, we are in effect setting up a series of separate 'bins', each of which contains a certain per cent of the grains. **1960** *Anatomical Rec.* CXXXVIII. 395/2 The statistical significance..was calculated by determining the median for the combined population and comparing the percent of the animals that had cataracts in each group. **1966** T. PYNCHON *Crying of Lot 49* v. 122 Always just that little percent on the wrong side of breaking even... Why don't I quit? **1970** *Nature* 7 Nov. 546/2 If the relative abundances of ¹⁵N and ¹⁷O in the sample are found to be a few tenths of a percent higher than normal, [etc.]. **1971** *Daily Tel.* 27 Oct. 1/3 The retail price index has risen by only three-quarters of a per cent. in the three months since June. **1972** *Science* 12 May 595/2 The magnitude of the effect is again a few tenths of a percent. **1977** *Daily Tel.* 23 Dec. 2/7 Those provincial journalists whose immediate settlement hopes have foundered over ·56 of a per cent.

B. *sb.* ***per cents*** (without preceding numeral) as *sb. pl.* Percentages; *spec.* in U.S. schools.

1850 MRS. BROWNING *Soul's Trav.* 23 The tread of the business-men who must Count their per-cents by the paces they take. **1883** *53rd Rep. Cincinnati* (Ohio) *Schools* 71 No committing text-books to memory—no cramming for per cents.

Hence **perˈcent** *v. colloq.* in U.S. schools.

1883 *Student* (U.S.) III. 286 When students are found obtaining help of others they are not percented at all. **1883** *53rd Rep. Cincinnati* (Ohio) *Schools* 71 As in Physics so in United States History, there is no percented written examination.

percentably (pəˈsɛntəblɪ), *adv. rare.* [f. PER CENT *phr.* (*sb.*) + -ABLY.] By an appreciable percentage.

1928 *Sunday Dispatch* 2 Sept. 10 Men..who are bent on reducing the moufflon population percentably.

percentage (pəˈsɛntɪdʒ). [f. PER CENT *phr.* (*sb.*) + -AGE.] **a.** A rate or proportion per cent; a quantity or amount reckoned as so much in the hundred, i.e. as so many hundredth parts of another, esp. of the whole of which it is a part; hence *loosely*, a part or portion considered in its quantitative relation to the whole, a proportion (*of* something). Freq. equivalent to 'per cent' qualifying the sb., as ***percentage error*** (= error per cent), ***point*** (= point per cent), etc.

1786–9 BENTHAM *Princ. Internat. Law* Wks. 1843 II. 548/2 The difference between the per centage gained in that trade and the per centage gained in the next most productive trade. **1809** MALKIN *Gil Blas* IV. ii. ¶4 Middle men in the trade..pocket a tolerable per centage. **1812** J. SMYTH *Pract. of Customs* (1821) 326 A Per Centage Duty on the true Value is also payable. **1834** MACAULAY *Pitt* Ess. (1887) 316 It had been usual for foreign Princes..to give to the Paymaster of the Forces a small per-centage on the subsidies. **1842** PARNELL *Chem. Anal.* (1845) 484 Calculating the Atomic Constitution of a Body from its Per-centage Composition. **1860** TYNDALL *Glac.* II. iii. 246 A certain per-centage of the heat will pass through the glass. **1886** F. HARRISON *Choice Bks.* i. 10 A serious per-centage of books are not worth reading at all. **1906** *Westm. Gaz.* 25 Jan. 8/1 Both first- and third-class passengers showed a percentage increase. **1920** H. CRANE *Let.* 30 July (1965) 41 A drawing account at the bank..in addition to a good percentage commission on everything I sell. **1928** *Britain's Industr. Future* (Liberal Industr. Inquiry) v. xxxi. 444 The choice in particular cases between block grants and percentage grants. **1941** J. S. HUXLEY *Uniqueness of Man* v. 144 It warns us not to be too hasty in drawing conclusions as to intelligence from *percentage* brain-weight, or as to the efficiency of circulation from *percentage* heart-weight. **1948** MENCKEN *Amer. Lang. Suppl.* II. 766 Percentage man. A news photographer who makes a large number of exposures, hoping that chance will give him a few good pictures. **1961** C. C. T. BAKER *Dict. Math.* 233 Percentage error = true error/actual error × 100. **1964** *Economist* 18 Jan. 182/2 The common American practice of 'percentage rents'—gearing rents and ground rents over the initial period to a percentage of turnover. **1969** 'R. CRAWFORD' *Cockleburr* I. vii. 71 I'm a percentage man... He's paying me ten per cent to get him clear with the money. **1971** *Gloss. Electrotechnical, Power Terms* (*B.S.I.*) I. iv. 7 *Percentage error*, the relative error multiplied by 100. **1971** *Times* 3 Sept. 13/1 Yesterday's action by the Bank of England in cutting Bank rate by a full percentage point. **1972** *Fremdsprachen* XVI. 61/2 Percentage point, full—*ein ganzes Prozent.* **1973** *Computers & Humanities* VII. 134 Q measures the percentage improvement, in terms of the function F. **1974** 'A. GARVE' *File on Lester* xxxvi. 129 The poll figures..were shattering—a big percentage lead for the Government. **1974** *News & Press* (Darlington, S. Carolina) 25 Apr. 16/2 Primary metal industries showed the greatest percentage increase (267 percent) over 1967.

b. *fig.* Advantage, gain; probability of successful outcome (*in* a situation, course of action, etc.). *colloq.* (orig. *U.S.*).

1862 B. HARTE *Notes 'by Flood & Field'* in *Golden Era* 14 Sept. 5/3 What's the per centage—workin' on shares, eh? **1911** *Chicago Daily News* 2 Mar. 6/6 Johnny Coulon is unable to see the percentage in taking on Frankie Conley for another pummelling in the adjacent future. **1925** *College Humor* Aug. 117/2 No percentage in staying on in this house. Darn thing's too big. **1938** D. RUNYON *Furthermore* xiii. 255 There is no percentage in hanging around brokers [*sc.* people who are broke]. **1940** *Woman* (U.S.) Sept. 69/1 Marge was courageous and a straight shooter but there was no more percentage in taking her out than one of the other guys. **1950** R. MOORE *Candlemas Bay* VI. 302, I don't see how you figure that what peas you can shell with one thumb makes any percentage to me. **1952** B. MALAMUD *Natural* 90 He decided there might be some percentage to all these comparisons. **1952** H. WAUGH *Last seen Wearing* (1953) 71 Well, hell, she turned down my dates and..there's no percentage in that. **1960** C. HATTON in *Pick of Today's Short Stories* XI. 151 Roxy..could be relied on to stir up trouble anywhere even if there was no percentage in it for Roxy. **1966** J. PORTER *Sour Cream* xii. 162 There was no percentage in hanging around the airport terminus. I had to get away. **1973** E. MCGIRR *Bardel's Murder* i. 27 He plays better bridge than ninety-eight per cent of the population... He doesn't cheat: he doesn't have to because he's got the percentage. **1976** A. PRICE *War Game* I. 123 There was no percentage in rushing him.

c. Slang phr. ***to play the percentages***: to play safely or methodically with regard to the odds in favour of success.

1964 A. WYKES *Gambling* i. 22 A considerable number of women gamblers take a strictly 'professional' approach. Ignoring 'intuition', they attack with expertise; if their game is horse racing, they are vastly knowledgeable about horses' and jockeys' past records. Others may 'play the percentages' in casinos. **1973** *Daily Pennsylvanian* 9 Oct. 6 Houston knows the game and its angles thoroughly and plays the percentages to perfection. **1977** *Tennis World* Sept. 17/3 To 'out-steady' someone is to play a superior defensive game, and 'playing the percentages' is the art of going for shots that are cheap and clean, rather than costly and glorious. Statistically it pays off better than 'going for broke'—risking everything on breath-taking winners.

Hence **perˈcentaged** (-ɪdʒd) *a.*, expressed or stated as a percentage.

1884 *New Eng. Jrnl. Educ.* XIX. 376 To judge the teacher through his character and methods rather than by percentaged results.

perˈcentage-wise, *adv.* Also **percentagewise.** [WISE *sb.*¹ II.] (Expressed) as a percentage; also more generally, (regarded) relatively.

1912 F. SODDY *Matter & Energy* ii. 53 Quite a large number of commonly occurring compounds had been analysed by chemists and the composition expressed percentage-wise as above. **1944** *Sun* (Baltimore) 5 Apr. 10/2 In that State the number of Negroes is, percentage-wise, even smaller than the number of Negroes in Maryland.

Here Negroes vote regularly. **1945** Nelson & Wright *Tomorrow's House* vi. 72/1 Very few families, percentagewise, have ever been able to afford hired help. **1955** J. A. Wheeler in W. Pauli *Niels Bohr* 176 Z^2/A does not have to change much percentage-wise to carry fission half lives from values too long to observe to values too short for reasonable stability. **1960** *Guardian* 8 Mar. 1/2 The number of deaths percentagewise is far less than other deaths..by other heating means. **1967** E. S. Gardner *Case of Queenly Contestant* (1973) xiii. 151 She told me..I could inherit a very substantial sum of money and asked me what it would be worth to me percentage-wise if [etc.]. **1972** *Amer. Speech 1968* XLIII. 211 On January 15, 1967, during the..telecast of the Super Bowl Game.., the announcer.. said, 'Bart Starr has had a terrific year, percentagewise, as well as touchdownwise.'

percental (pəˈsɛntəl), *a.* Also per cental. [f. PER CENT *phr.* (*sb.*) + -AL[1] I.] Reckoned by the hundred; calculated as a percentage.

1895 *Daily News* 18 Dec. 9/5 In wheat a fair extent of business was put through at ⅛d per cental decline. **1897** *Geogr. Jrnl.* IX. 319 A map showing, by means of six colours distinguishing different percental proportions, the distribution of German-speaking people in the lands of the Hungarian crown.

percenter. Also per center, per-center. [f. PER CENT *phr.* (*sb.*) + -ER[1].] Following a number (occas. with hyphen): that on (or from) which a percentage (specified by the number) is reckoned; a chance, situation, etc., the value of which is reckoned as a specified percentage. Also, one who lends or deals in money involving a certain rate of interest or commission.

c **1863** T. Taylor *Ticket-of-Leave Man* III. 52 *Moss* (*at the counter, getting out his bills*)... For two hundred at two months—drawn by Captain Crabbs—accepted the Honourable Augustus Greenway: that's a thirty per center. **1897** *Pall Mall G.* 2 June 2/2 He had been charged with lending money at 650 per cent..charged with being a 650-percenter. **1949** [see *influence pedlar*]. **1950** E. Hemingway *Across River* xxxiii. 208 The brown-nosers, the five and ten and twenty percenters and all the jerks. **1959** *Punch* 10 June 781/1 We are tempted to deduce that her age bracket..is a sure hundred percenter. **1960** *Times* 5 Feb. 16/5 One explanation was the rush by the public to buy the new five percenter Treasury bonds. **1976** 'Z. Stone' *Modigliani Scandal* IV. i. 154 Louis was 99 per cent sure the caller was a nutcase: but it was by following up the one-percenters that great exclusives were found.

So **-per-ˈcenting** *a.* (paying so much per cent).

1852 R. S. Surtees *Sponge's Sp. Tour* (1893) 192 What a succession of joyous, careless, dashing, sixty per centing youths we have had.

percentile (pəˈsɛntaɪl, -ɪl), *a.* and *sb.* [f. *per cent*(*um*, app. after *bissext-ile*, etc.]

a. *adj.* Pertaining to percentage; reckoned as a percentage. **b.** *sb.* Each of a series of values obtained by dividing a large number of quantities into a hundred equal groups in order of magnitude; that value which is not exceeded by the lowest group is the *first percentile*; that not exceeded by the lowest two, the *second percentile*; and so on.

1885 F. Galton in *Jrnl. Anthrop. Inst.* Feb. 276 The value which 50 per cent. exceeded, and 50 per cent. fell short of, is the Median Value, or the 50th per-centile, and this is practically the same as the Mean Value; its amount is 85 lbs. **1889** —— in *Nature* 24 Jan. 298/2 The data were published in the Journal of this Institute as a table of 'per-centiles'. **1890** *Cent. Dict.*, *Percentile*, adj. In percentage: as, *percentile* measurement. **1956** W. H. Whyte *Organization Man* (1957) 407 Don't strive to get yourself in the 70th or 80th percentile for extroversion. **1957** G. E. Hutchinson *Treat. Limnol.* I. vi. 384 (*caption*) Mean percentile absorption at different wave lengths. **1970** *Jrnl. Gen. Psychol.* LXXXIII. 154 The high dependency groups consisted of those 13 Ss whose autonomy minus deference scale percentile ranks score was 20 or above.

percentual (pəˈsɛntjuːəl), *a.* [irreg. f. PER CENT *phr.* (*sb.*) + *-ual*, after *accentual*, *eventual*, etc.]

1937 H. Tingsten *Political Behavior* iii. 147 The voting frequency of a group increases with the percentual strength of the group in question. **1949** Koestler *Promise & Fulfilment* I. iii. 31 The striking percentual increases in the statistics quoted.

Hence **perˈcentually** *adv.*

1942 L. B. Namier *Conflicts* 73 'Janus' in *The Spectator* of March 7, 1941, shows that percentually the losses of the last war do not justify the talk about a 'missing generation'.

†**ˈperceˌpier.** *Obs.* [a. F. *perce-pierre*, lit. 'pierce-stone', a name of *Alchemilla arvensis* (and other plants).] The plant *Alchemilla arvensis*. (Cf. PARSLEY-PIERT.)

1610 Holland *Camden's Brit.* I. 237 In the fields..is found Percepier, an herbe peculiar unto England. **1640** [see PARSLEY-PIERT]. **1658** Phillips, *Percepier*, a certain Herb, growing in some parts of Somersetshire, it hath small flowrs of a greenish hew, and is good to provoke urine. **1760** J. Lee *Introd. Bot.* App. 322 Percepier, *Aphanes*.

percept (ˈpɜːsɛpt), *sb. Philos.* and *Psychol.* [f. L. *perceptum* (a thing) perceived, neut. of pa. pple. of *percipĕre* to PERCEIVE: after *concept*.]

1. The object of PERCEPTION.

1837 Sir W. Hamilton *Logic* iii. (1866) I. 42 Whether it might not..be proper to introduce the term percept for the object of perception. **1880** Sidgwick in *19th Cent.* VII. 355 In any act of perception the matter that is percept or object is commonly outside the organism of the percipient. **1964** M. Critchley *Developmental Dyslexia* xiii. 78 Not only is it a matter of defective perception, but it is also one of inadequate association of lexical percepts. *Ibid.*, This process of linking one percept with another is where the principal fault may lie. **1973** *Nature* 6 July 54/2 The Necker cube has been viewed as an ambiguous figure whose configuration and accompanying instructions usually limit the number of percepts to two. **1974** *Sci. Amer.* Jan. 126/3 No one else smelled it [*sc.* poison gas], she was assured. Her enemy was so ingenious, she retorted, that his gas was odorless! Her experience was thus no percept at all, but a projection from internal ideas. **1976** Smythies & Corbett *Psychiatry* v. 55 This man had a normal percept but attached a special, personal meaning to it which was quite false.

2. The mental product or result of perceiving as distinguished from the action.

1876 Maudsley *Physiol. Mind* v. 273 A percept is the abstract of sensations, so a concept is the abstract of percepts. **1883** *Chamb. Jrnl.* 82 Has the mental percept been evoked without any antecedent sense-percept? **1899** *Allbutt's Syst. Med.* VII. 399 Word-images as integral components of percepts and concepts. **1949** *Mind* LVIII. 450 William James sometimes used the word 'percept' to refer to the content of consciousness during perception; it is this fact which has made the name 'Percept Theory' seem to me appropriate for the particular theory of perceptual consciousness which he himself supported. **1970** *Jrnl. Gen. Psychol.* LXXXIII. 66 Sex responses are numerous... The number of human percepts is low. **1972** *Sci. Amer.* Sept. 47/2 It is along this pathway that the visual image formed on the retina by light rays entering the eye is transformed into a visual percept, on the basis of which appropriate commands to the muscles are issued. **1976** *Word 1971* XXVII. 226 Each physical stimulus, after interpretation by the mental processes, will result in a percept.

†**perˈcept**, *v. Obs. rare*$^{-1}$. [f. L. *percept-*, ppl. stem of *percipĕre*.] *trans.* = PERCEIVE.

1652 Gaule *Magastrom.* 59 And is not the highest speculation of it percepted and perfected by manuall instruments, and those fallacious, too, as themselves complain?

perˈceptful, *a. rare*$^{-1}$. [f. PERCEPT *sb.* + -FUL.] Having a perception, perceptive.

1867 J. B. Rose tr. *Virgil's Æneid* 104 As when perceptful of the coming cold [iv. 403 *hiemis memores*] The frugal emmets pile their wintry grain.

perceptibility (pəˌsɛptɪˈbɪlɪtɪ). [f. next: see -ITY. Cf. F. *perceptibilité* (Diderot, 18th c.).]

†**1.** Capacity or faculty of perceiving; perceptivity. *Obs.*

1642 H. More *Song of Soul* II. iii. II. li, That spright hath no perceptibility Of his impressions. **1662** J. Sparrow tr. *Behme's Rem. Wks., Apol. conc. Perfect.* 31 Through which Voyce, the Will in the Impression generateth..also perceptibility and feeling, viz. the eternall Nature.

2. Capability of being perceived.

1678 Cudworth *Intell. Syst.* I. v. 718 The very essence of truth here is this clear perceptibility or intelligibility. **1768–74** Tucker *Lt. Nat.* (1834) I. 311 We must look for some other property in body rendering it perceivable, and this we may call perceptibility... Whether spirit has the like perceptibility too, we can never certainly know. **1843** Ruskin *Mod. Paint.* I. II. v. i. §6 According to the number of rays transmitted is the perceptibility of objects below the water.

perceptible (pəˈsɛptɪb(ə)l), *a.* [ad. late L. *perceptibil-is* (Cassiod., Boëth.), f. *percip-ĕre*, *percept-* to PERCEIVE: see -BLE. Cf. OF. *perceptible* (1372 in Hatz.-Darm.).]

†**1.** In active sense: Percipient, perceptive *of*.

1551–70 B. G. *Beware the Cat* (1864) 52 The cell perceptible of my brain intelligible was yet so gross. **1644** Digby *Nat. Bodies* vii. §6. 50 That..will not hinder them from being very hoat to the sense of feeling (which is most perceptible of dense things). **1734** Bp. T. Greene *Disc. Four Last Things* (1753) 7 When this separation happens, of the soul from the body..(the soul)..becomes..more perceptible of happiness or misery. **1772** *Birmingham Counterf.* I. i. 19 Too perceptible of the tender emotions of love.

2. Capable of being perceived by the senses or intellect, cognizable, apprehensible; observable.

1603 Holland *Plutarch's Mor.* 1032 The soule is not perceptible by any sense. **1699** Burnet 39 *Art.* i. (1700) 27 It is perceptible to every man that this is impossible. **1777** Johnson *Serm. for Dodd* in *Boswell*, Freed from their bonds by the perceptible agency of divine favour. **1866** Geo. Eliot *F. Holt* v, With a perceptible flashing of the eyes.

b. quasi-*adv.* Perceptibly, distinctly, clearly.

1771 Luckombe *Hist. Printing* 241 After a *P*..the *A* separates itself more perceptible than from any other letter.

Hence **perˈceptibleness** (*rare*), capability of being perceived.

1709 *Brit. Apollo* II. No. 43. 2/1 The Perceptibleness of Motion.

perceptibly (pəˈsɛptɪblɪ), *adv.* [f. prec. + -LY[2].] In a perceptible manner; (now chiefly) in or to a perceptible degree.

a **1714** Abp. Sharp *Wks.* (1754) III. xiii. 238 Whether this change be not always performed so perceptibly, as that the man himself can give a particular account both of the time when, and the manner how, it was wrought in him? **1794** Sullivan *View Nat.* II. 379 The nearest of which [stars].. is not perceptibly altered in magnitude. **1884** F. Temple *Relat. Relig. & Sc.* iii. (1885) 76 Our separate acts are perceptibly subject to our own control.

perception (pəˈsɛpʃən). Also 5 -sepcion, -ceptioune. [In earlier senses, a. OF. *perception* action of receiving (12th c. in Littré); in later, perh. directly ad. L. *perceptiōn-em*, lit. 'receiving, collecting', hence 'sensuous or mental apprehension, perception, intelligence, knowledge': n. of action from *percipĕre* to take, receive, PERCEIVE.] The action, faculty, or product of perceiving.

I. From the literal sense of L. *percipĕre*, to take, receive.

1. The collection or receiving of rents, etc. Now only in legal phraseology.

1493 *Acta Audit.* (1839) 184/1 The lordis..delieueris þat.. Alexr Inness of þt Ilk dois wrang in þe perceptioune vptaking and withalde of þe malez and gerssoumez of þe landis of menedy. **1723** *Pres. St. Russia* I. 60 Revenues.. which are the Czar's own both as to Propriety and Perception. **1769** *Aclome Inclos. Act* 7 Entry, distress, and perception of the rents and profits. **1847** Addison *Law of Contracts* II. i. §1 (1883) 240 The lessee had the benefit of.. the perception of the profits for the whole term purported to be granted. **1885** *Law Rep. 16 Q. Bench Div.* 62 There must have been something more than a mere perception of profits.

†**2.** The receiving or partaking of the Eucharist or sacred elements. *Obs.*

1483 Caxton *Gold. Leg.* 435/1 Ye masse may be comprysed in four partyes..the third parte dureth fro the pater noster vnto the persepcion & the fourth parte dureth fro the percepcion vnto thende of the masse. **1624** Gataker *Transubst.* 105 What this potion and perception is (saith he) it is our part to learne. **1674** *Ch. & Court of Rome* 7 The.. entire perception of the holy Eucharist.

II. From the secondary or metaphorical sense of L. *percipĕre*, to be or become cognizant of.

3. a. The taking cognizance or being aware of objects in general; sometimes practically = consciousness. In Locke esp. as distinct from *volition*.

1611 Cotgr., *Perception*, a perception; a perceiuing, apprehension, vnderstanding. **1632** Sherwood, A perceiuing or perception, *perception, appercevance*. **1665** Glanvill *Def. Van. Dogm.* 20 Perception of spirituals, universals and other abstracts from sense, as Mathematical lines,..self reflection, Freedom,..are not at all competible to body or matter. **1665** —— *Scepsis Sci.* xii. 64 The Best Philosophy..derives all sensitive Perception from Motion, and Corporal impress. **1690** Locke *Hum. Und.* II. i. §9 Having Ideas and Perception being the same thing. *Ibid.* vi. §2 The two great and principal Actions of the Mind..are these two: Perception, or Thinking, and Volition, or Willing. **1725** Watts *Logic* I. i, First, the Nature of Conception or Perception shall just be mentioned.. Perception is that Act of the Mind (or as some Philosophers call it, rather a Passion or Impression) whereby the Mind becomes conscious of any Thing, as when I feel Hunger, Thirst, or Cold, or Heat; when I see a Horse, a Tree, or a Man; when I hear a human Voice, or Thunder. **1751** Harris *Hermes* I. ii. (1786) 15 By the Powers of *Perception*, I mean the *Senses* and the *Intellect*.

†**b.** By Bacon used of the fact of being affected by an object without contact, though consciousness is absent. *Obs.*

1626 Bacon *Sylva* IX. Pref., It is certaine, that all Bodies whatsoeuer, though they haue no sense, yet they haue Perception:..and sometimes this Perception in some kinde of Bodies is farre more subtill than the Sense:..a Weather-Glasse will finde the least difference of the Weather in Heat or Cold, when Men finde it not. *Ibid.* §462 It is..reported that..a Cucumber..will, in 24 houres shoot so much out, as to touch the pot [of water]: which if it be true..discouereth Perception in Plants, to moue towards that which should helpe and comfort them. *Ibid.* §819 Great Mountaines haue a Perception of the Disposition of the Aire to Tempests, sooner than the Valley's or Plaines below.

4. a. The taking cognizance or being aware of a sensible or quasi-sensible object.

1704 J. Harris *Lex. Techn.* I, *Perception*, is the clear and distinct apprehension of any Object offered to us, without forming any Judgement concerning them. **1736** Butler *Anal.* I. i, The whole apparatus of vision, or of perception by any other of our senses. **1813** Sir H. Davy *Agric. Chem.* (1814) 55 Vegetables are living structures distinguished from Animals by exhibiting no signs of perception. **1836** J. Taylor *Phys. The. Another Life* 62 Now we think of five species of perception, hereafter we may become familiar with a hundred or a thousand. **1868** N. Porter *Hum. Intellect* I. iii. §102 (1872) 119 Perception, in the technical and limited sense of the term, is appropriated to the knowledge of material objects, and of the external world. This knowledge is gained or acquired by means of the senses, and hence, to be more exact, we call it sensible perception, or, more briefly, sense-perception. **1882** *Proc. Soc. Psych. Research* I. 13 Gathering evidence on the obscure but important question of what may be termed supersensuous perception.

b. *loosely*. Personal observation; esp. sight.

1817 Jas. Mill *Brit. India* v. ii. II. 358 By withdrawing the pretended mother from the perception of disinterested witnesses. *Ibid.* v. viii. 680 His agents..did state whatever they chose, matters of hearsay, as much as of perception.

5. The intuitive or direct recognition of a moral or æsthetic quality, e.g. the truth of a remark, the beautiful in objects.

1827–48 Hare *Guesses* Ser. II. (1873) 562 When our feelings are the most vivid our perceptions are the most piercing. **1830** Mackintosh *Eth. Philos.* Wks. 1846 I. 16 Other philosophers..have concluded, that the utility of actions cannot be the criterion of their morality, because a perception of that utility appears to them to form a faint and inconsiderable part of our Moral Sentiments. **1840** Whewell *Philos. Induct. Sci.* (1847) II. 569, I should propose the term..Callæsthetic, the science of the perception of beauty. **1860** Tyndall *Glac.* II. ix. 270 Such pleasure the direct perception of natural truth always imparts. **1890** 'R. Boldrewood' *Col. Reformer* (1891) 291 The ordinary prudences and severities of conscience might be calmly placed behind the perceptions. **1903** Raleigh *Wordsworth* 158 Perception..is a transaction between the outer powers that operate on the mind through the senses and the inner powers of the mind itself, which impose their own forms on the things submitted to it.

6. In strict philosophical language (first brought into prominence by Reid): The action of the mind by which it refers its sensations to an external object as their cause. Distinguished from *sensation*, *conception* or imagination, and *judgement* or inference.

1762 KAMES *Elem. Crit.* III. 379 External things and their attributes are objects of perception: relations among things are objects of conception. **1785** REID *Intell. Powers* I. i. (1803) 28 The perception of external objects by our senses, is an operation of the mind of a peculiar nature, and ought to have a name appropriated to it... I know no word more proper to express this act of the mind than perception. *Ibid.* 27 We are never said to *perceive* things, of the existence of which we have not a full conviction... Thus *perception* is distinguished from *conception* or imagination. Secondly, Perception is applied only to external objects, not to those that are in the mind itself... Thus *perception* is distinguished from *consciousness*. Thirdly, The immediate object of perception must be something present, and not what is past. We may remember what is past, but do not perceive it... And thus it is distinguished from *remembrance*. In a word, perception is most properly applied to the evidence which we have of external objects by our senses. But..the word is often applied by analogy to the evidence of reason or of testimony, when it is clear and cogent. **1840** MILL *Diss. & Disc.* (1859) II. 91 The writer who first made *Perception* a word of mark and likelihood in mental philosophy was Reid, who made use of it as a means of begging several of the questions in dispute between him and his antagonists. **1842** SIR W. HAMILTON in *Reid's Wks.* I. 160/2 According, as in different senses, the subjective or the objective element preponderates, we have sensation or perception. **1843** MILL *Logic* I. iii. §4 Besides the affection of our bodily organs from without, and the sensation thereby produced in our minds, many writers admit a third link in the chain of phenomena, which they call a Perception, and which consists in the recognition of an external object as the exciting cause of the sensation. **1855** MISS COBBE *Intuit. Mor.* I. 46 Every *perception* necessitates this double element of sensation and intuition,—the objective and subjective factor in combination. **1856** FERRIER *Inst. Metaph.* v. v. 149. *a* **1860** WHATELY *Commpl. Bk.* (1864) 83 We have a distinct view of the difference between the past and the present, because we have a perception of the latter, and only a conception of the former. **1860** MANSEL *Metaph.* I. 67–8 Perception..has been used by various writers in a wider or a narrower sense—sometimes as synonymous with consciousness in general, sometimes as limited to the apprehensions of sense alone. Under the latter limitation it has been found convenient to make a further restriction, and to distinguish between sensation proper and perception proper. **1876** MAUDSLEY *Physiol. Mind* iv. 221 *Perception* includes not only the internal feeling, but the reference of it to an external cause. **1884** J. SULLY *Outlines Psychol.* vi. 152. **1943** M. FARBER *Found. Phenomenology* xiii. 396 The perception realizes the possibility of the development of the *intending-this* with its definite relation to the object. **1962** MACQUARRIE & ROBINSON tr. *Heidegger's Being & Time* I. iii. 130 When the experience of hardness is Interpreted this way, the kind of Being which belongs to sensory perception is obliterated, and so is any possibility that the entities encountered in such perception should be grasped in their Being. **1965** *New Statesman* 3 Sept. 327/4 He [*sc.* Merleau-Ponty] held..that the higher forms of human behaviour—art, science, political life—could only be understood in their genesis from original perception.

7. The (or a) faculty of perceiving (in any of the preceding senses 3–6).

[**1678** NORRIS *Coll. Misc.* (1699) 232 That faculty of Perception whereby I apprehend Objects, whether Material or Immaterial, without any Material Species.] **1712** ADDISON *Spect.* No. 519 ¶4 Existence is a blessing to those beings only which are endowed with perception. **1841–4** EMERSON *Ess., Love* Wks. (Bohn) I. 75 He is a new man, with new perceptions. *Ibid., Manners* 212 Defect in manners is usually the defect of fine perceptions. **1856** SIR B. BRODIE *Psychol. Inq.* I. ii. 48 The organ may be so imperfect that the perception of colours may be in a great degree..wanting. **1873** M. ARNOLD *Lit. & Dogma* Pref. 25 Perhaps the quality specially needed for drawing the right conclusion from the facts..is best called perception, delicacy of perception. **1873** SYMONDS *Grk. Poets* vi. 182 Had the Greek race perceptions infinitely finer than ours? **1890** C. L. MORGAN *Anim. Life & Intell.* ix. 372, I regard the bees in their cells..as workers of keen perceptions and a high order of practical intelligence.

8. a. The result or product of perceiving; = PERCEPT 2.

1690 LOCKE *Hum. Und.* I. iv. §20 Whatever Idea is in the Mind, is either an actual Perception..or by the Memory it can be made an actual Perception again. *Ibid.* IV. xi. §4 'Tis plain, those Perceptions are produced in us by exteriour Causes affecting our Senses. **1739** HUME *Hum. Nat.* (1874) I. I. i. 311 All the perceptions of the human mind resolve themselves into two distinct kinds, which I shall call Impressions and Ideas. **1780** BENTHAM *Princ. Legisl.* v. §1 Pains and pleasures may be called by one general word interesting perceptions. **1831** BREWSTER *Nat. Magic* vi. (1833) 148 Its invisibility to surrounding friends soon stamps it with the impress of a false perception.

†**b.** *transf.* A perceptible trace or vestige. *Obs.*

1650 BULWER *Anthropomet.* 88 No tract at all nor any perception of hairs is to be seen either in the lips or chin.

9. *Psychol.* The neurophysiological processes, including memory, by which an organism becomes aware of and interprets external stimuli or sensations (closely related to PERCEPTION 4 and 6). So *attrib.* and *Comb.*, as **perception psychology**, that branch of psychology which is concerned with the study of perception.

1875 A. J. ELLIS tr. *Helmholtz's On Sensations of Tone* I. iv. 99 There are several much more complicated cases in which many sensations must concur to furnish the foundation of a very simple perception. **1913** A. A. BRILL tr. *Freud's Interpr. of Dreams* vii. 426 We assume that a first system of apparatus takes up the stimuli of perception, but retains nothing from them—that is, it has no memory. **1949** D. O. HEBB *Organization of Behavior* i. 16 According to these ideas, perception does depend on exciting specific parts of the receptor surface. **1951** LICKLIDER & MILLER in S. S. Stevens *Handbk. Exper. Psychol.* 1040/1 Although the perception of speech is a psychological problem, it remained for telephone engineers..to develop procedures for the quantitative investigation of speech perception. **1956** J. R. SMYTHIES *Anal. of Perception* p. ix, In order to construct a comprehensive theory of perception..it would be necessary to have at least a good working knowledge of epistemology and the philosophy of sense perception, neurology, neuroanatomy and neurophysiology, psychiatry and psychopathology with particular reference to the effects produced by the hallucinogenic drugs, anthropology, physics and experimental psychology. **1958** M. E. SPIRO *Children of Kibbutz* VI. xvi. 435 Assumptions derived from an adaptation of psychoanalytic, learning, and perception theories. **1964** M. A. K. HALLIDAY et al. *Linguistic Sci.* iii. 60 Psychological phonetics..has arisen out of modern developments in perception psychology. **1968** R. N. HABER *Contemp. Theory & Res. Visual Perception* (1970) p. vi, While it will be clear throughout this book that memory and what is traditionally known as perception cannot be distinguished by any but the most arbitrary of rules. **1974** *Drive* Autumn 3/1 At least one perception expert considers they could, indeed, be doing far more in teaching distance assessment in a following situation at speeds over 30mph. *Ibid.* 29/2 The university's department of perception-psychology aims to produce a lighting system that gives clearer warning of a car's presence to pedestrians and on-coming traffic.

per'ceptional, *a.* [f. prec. + -AL[1].] Of, pertaining to or of the nature of, perception.

1862 F. HALL *Hindu Philos. Syst.* 264 The mistake in question is not perceptional, but inferential. **1874** CARPENTER *Ment. Phys.* App. (1879) 721 Particular parts of the convolutions may be special centres of the classes of perceptional Ideas that [etc.].

Hence **per'ceptionalism** *Philos.*, the 'common sense' doctrine in philosophy, that what men call their perceptions are true perceptions of the very things they claim to perceive.

1891 E. J. HAMILTON *Modalist* 5 The philosophy from which the following chapters derive their force..has been named *Perceptionalism*... This philosophy prizes highly the Aristotelian doctrine of 'common sense' or 'common perception',..but differs from it in being a developed system.

per'ceptionalist, *a. rare.* [f. PERCEPTION + -AL[1] I + -IST.] Of or pertaining to philosophical theories of knowledge that are based on perception.

1847 J. D. MORELL *Hist. View Philos.* (ed. 2) I. i. 130 On this perceptionalist controversy, consult Sir W. Hamilton's admirable article.

per'ceptionism. *nonce-wd.* [See -ISM.] The theory that derives all knowledge ultimately from sense-perception.

1882 BERESF. HOPE *Brandreths* II. xxv. 124 To curb the caprices of arrogant perceptionism.

perceptive (pəˈsɛptɪv), *a.* (*sb.*) [f. L. *percept-*, ppl. stem of *percipĕre* to perceive + -IVE.]

1. Characterized by or capable of perceiving; pertaining to or having perception; instrumental to perception.

1656 *Artif. Handsom.* 145 They have more perceptive eyes than ever I had. **1678** NORRIS *Coll. Misc.* (1699) 10 A Body ..exquisitely Perceptive of the least Impressions. **1785** REID *Intell. Powers* 279 Our active and perceptive powers are improved and perfected by use and exercise. **1877** E. CAIRD *Philos. Kant* v. 91 All monads are with Leibnitz perceptive beings. **1897** WATTS-DUNTON *Aylwin* II. ii, Your mother's perceptive faculties are extraordinary.

b. Of ready perception, intelligent. Also with *of*.

1860 RUSKIN *Mod. Paint.* V. IX. xii. §14 Its great men, whose hearts were kindest, and whose spirits most perceptive of the work of God. **1868** DICKENS *Lett.* (1880) II. 396 With an audience so finely perceptive..the labour is much diminished.

†**2.** Perceptible, cognizable. *Obs.*

1754 EDWARDS *Freed. Will* IV. ix. (ed. 4) 368 Contrary to the revealed or perceptive Will of God. **1813** T. BUSBY tr. *Lucretius* I. III. 236 When rich wines their essences diffuse, —Or unguents—no perceptive weight they lose.

B. *sb.* †**1.** One who perceives, a percipient being. *Obs. rare.* Cf. INTELLIGENT B. 1.

1694 R. BURTHOGGE *Reas. & Nat. Spir.* VIII. ii. 263 The Original Perceptive is sensible of all, (and needs must, for he that made the Eye must needs see, and he that planted the Ear, must needs hear; and he that gave an heart unto man must needs understand).

2. *pl.* The perceptive faculties or organs.

1858 H. SPENCER *Ess.* I. 254 The mind..must keep its perceptives active enough to recognise the least easily caught sounds. **1879** G. MEREDITH *Egoist* III. ix. 181 By the patient exercise of his quick perceptives.

per'ceptively, *adv.* [f. prec. + -LY[2].] In a perceptive manner; in respect of perception.

1768–74 TUCKER *Lt. Nat.* (1834) II. 296 Our mental organization..can [never] produce an actual perception without a perceptive substance within to discern them; which substance cannot be a compound, nor can perceptively reside unless in an individual. **1855** DICKENS *Lett.* (1880) I. 413 Enormous effect at Sheffield. But really not a better audience perceptively than at Peterboro. **1899** E. S. HALDANE *J. F. Ferrier* iii. 46 It is not an essential that feelings should be perceptively referred to an external object.

per'ceptiveness. [f. as prec. + -NESS.] The quality of being perceptive; readiness of perception; intelligence, insight.

1852 THACKERAY *Esmond* II. xv, Looking into Esmond's heart..with that perceptiveness affection gives. **1873** HELPS *Anim. & Mast.* viii. (1875) 207 Great intellectual gifts are not required on the part of the lesser personage of the two companions, but only perceptiveness and receptiveness.

perceptivity (pɜːsɛpˈtɪvɪtɪ). [f. as prec. + -ITY.] = prec.

1690 LOCKE *Hum. Und.* II. xxi. §73 *Perceptivity*, or the Power of Perception, or Thinking; *Motivity*, or the Power of Moving;..I crave leave to make use of these two new Words. **1768–74** TUCKER *Lt. Nat.* (1834) II. 460, I may believe myself a conscient, not a consciousness;..nor a perceptivity, but a perceptive spirit. **1809** *Edin. Rev.* XV. 127 Dr. Walker adduces this fact in proof of the perceptivity of plants. **1876** MRS. WHITNEY *Sights & Ins.* xxiv. 237 She impaneled a jury of her own clear, strong perceptivities.

percepto-, combining form from L. *percept-um* (see PERCEPT), as **per,cepto-'motor** *a.*, applied to action apparently automatic, but really due to mental perception and experience: e.g. the blinking of the eye when any object comes close to it.

1878 tr. *H. von Ziemssen's Cycl. Med.* XIV. 697 These 'percepto-motor' reflex acts still exhibit a high degree of automatism.

perceptron (pəˈsɛptrɒn). [f. PERCEPT *sb.* + -TRON.] A model or machine devised to represent or simulate the ability of the brain to recognize and discriminate, orig. based on statistical concepts.

1958 F. ROSENBLATT in *Psychol. Rev.* LXV. 386 (*heading*) The perceptron: a probabilistic model for information storage and organization in the brain. *Ibid.* 387/2 The theory has been developed for a hypothetical nervous system, or machine, called a perceptron. The perceptron is designed to illustrate some of the fundamental properties of intelligent systems in general, without becoming enmeshed in the special..conditions which hold for particular biological organisms. **1962** W. S. HOLMES in G. L. Fischer et al. *Optical Character Recognition* 213 A program of pattern recognition research based on early concepts of Dr. Frank Rosenblatt..has turned toward the application of perceptrons to useful tasks such as the recognition of printed characters. **1966** Y. BAR-HILLEL in *Automatic Transl. of Lang.* (NATO Summer School, Venice 1962) 22 Though certain electronic devices (such as perceptrons) have been built which can be 'trained' to perform certain tasks..and though computers have been programmed to do certain things..it would be disastrous to extrapolate from these primitive exhibitions of artificial intelligence to something like translation. **1971** *New Scientist* 2 Sept. 525/2 There are some 50 approaches to neuron modelling and machines were constructed based on some of these models. Perhaps the most famous..was the Perceptron device built at the Cornell Aeronautical Laboratory. **1978** A. BUNDY et al. *Artificial Intelligence* v. 184 The important point about a perceptron is that it makes a global decision about a figure by weighing only local evidence.

perceptual (pəˈsɛptjuːəl), *a.* [f. L. type **perceptu-s* (cf. *conceptu-s*), from *percipĕre* to PERCEIVE + -AL[1]: cf. *conceptual*.] Of or pertaining to perception; of the nature of percepts. ***perceptual defence***, a raising of the threshold of perception when the stimulus is emotionally charged in an unfavourable way; ***perceptual-motor*** adj., involving motor behaviour as guided by or dependent on perception.

1878 S. H. HODGSON *Philos. of Reflection* I. 315 The conceptual order being the obverse aspect of the perceptual. **1889** MAX MÜLLER in *19th Cent.* Mar. 399 Our perceptual images. **1890** *Athenæum* 25 Jan. 121/2 The origin of concepts or universals was traced to acts of attending to perceptual data for the purpose of harmonizing them with their perceptual context. **1948** L. POSTMAN in *Jrnl. Abnormal Psychol.* XLIII. 152/1 Value orientation may.. raise thresholds for unacceptable stimulus objects. We shall refer to this mechanism as perceptual defense. **1950** *Jrnl. Personality* XIX. 85 These data were interpreted as indicative of a perceptual defense to emotional stimuli originating at a level which precedes full conscious awareness. **1951** *U.S. Human Resources Research Center Research Bull.* No. 51–7 (*title*) The influence of types of instructions on the performance of a perceptual-motor task. **1955** [see MECLOZINE]. **1962** J. G. TAYLOR *Behavioral Basis of Perception* vi. 130 It is no more possible for one person to make comparisons with another person's perceptual field than it is to describe the dimensions of personality in terms of centimeters, grams, and seconds. **1968** J. B. OXENDINE *Psychol. of Motor Learning* i. 14 A forehand stroke in tennis would be classified as a perceptual-motor skill, and swimming would not. **1969** FREEMAN & GIOVANNONI in Lindzey & Aronson *Handbk. Social Psychol.* (ed. 2) V. 688 Studies of schizophrenics indicate that perceptual thresholds and estimation of size are dependent on the emotional concomitants of the visual stimuli. **1970** M. J. MELDMAN *Dis. Attention & Perception* v. 95 The phenomenon of perceptual defense and the relationship of emotion to perception. **1972** *Village Voice* (N.Y.) 1 June 36/5 Dr. Krippner told me just a few of the non-drugging approaches that could and should be used with children whose classroom behavior is 'divergent'—vitamin therapy, perceptual-motor therapy, [etc.]. **1976** *Classical Q.* XXVI. 39, I shall be illustrating the perceptual case, so let me simply note here a few examples from the case of pleasure and pain. **1977** *Times Lit. Suppl.* 29 Apr. 529/2 We do not observe the seventeenth-century butcher directly vivid though the picture is; we see him through the perceptual schemata of the artist and his patron.

Hence **per'ceptualize** *v.*, to express in perceptual terms; **per,ceptuali'zation**.

1896 W. CALDWELL *Schopenhauer's Syst.* iii. 167 A highly interesting feature..is his pronounced tendency to *perceptualise intellection*, to assimilate all real knowledge to the type of perception and immediate apprehension. **1968** P. MCKELLAR *Experience & Behaviour* iv. 121 This hallucination represents an instance of a perceptualization of the man's realization of what had happened to him.

perceptually (pə'sɛptjuːəlɪ), *adv.* [f. PERCEPTUAL *a.* + -LY[2].] In a perceptual manner.

1878 S. H. HODGSON *Philos. of Reflection* I. 394 We might pick out those differents which are most strongly contrasted perceptually. **1909** W. M. URBAN *Valuation* xiv. 394 When the object is neither perceptually verifiable nor continuous with other truth judgments, a readjustment of reality-meanings takes place. **1922** A. G. HOGG *Redemption from this World* vi. 197 Thus miracles..render perceptually obvious both the personality and the infinitude of the Divine will. **1932** H. H. PRICE *Perception* vi. 164 We attribute a characteristic to some material thing which is now being perceptually accepted. **1972** *Science* 9 June 1149/2 We reported this ability to perceptually synthesize missing phonemes.

perceptum (pə'sɛptʌm). Pl. **percepta**. [L. *perceptum* (a thing) perceived, neut. of pa. pple. of *percipĕre* to PERCEIVE.] = PERCEPT 1.

1887 S. H. HODGSON *Let.* 10 Dec. in R. B. Perry *Tht. & Char. of W. James* (1935) II. 82 An immediate perception of spatial extension as part..of the visual perceptum. **1913** *Mind* XXII. 14 To instinctive action there corresponded a *perceptum* or percept which was its object. **1920** S. ALEXANDER *Space, Time & Deity* II. 92 The perceived object or thing, the perceptum, is a contemplated synthesis. **1929** A. N. WHITEHEAD *Process & Reality* 22 When science deals with emotions, the emotions in question are percepta. **1936** W. F. R. HARDIE *Study in Plato* ii. 12 Plainly its plausibility will depend on what characteristics of *percepta* are held to preclude their being known.

perceptuo- (pə'sɛptjuːəʊ), combining form of L. *perceptu-s*, pa. pple. of *percipĕre* to perceive, as ***perceptuo-motor*** adj. = *perceptual-motor* adj. s.v. PERCEPTUAL *a.*

1973 K. WEDELL (*title*) Learning and perceptuo-motor disabilities in children. **1974** *Nature* 8 Nov. 121/1 A series of experiments in perceptuo-motor adaptation that provide fairly direct evidence favouring the existence of such a mechanism. *Ibid.* 122/2 Perceptuo-motor effects were found for the voiceless stop consonants but not for their voiced counterparts.

percer, obs. f. PIERCER.

perceueraunce, -everance, variants of PERCEIVERANCE *Obs.*

percevere, perceyue, -ceyve, obs. ff. PERSEVERE, PERCEIVE.

perch (pɜːtʃ), *sb.*[1] Forms: 4–6 **perche**, 7–8 **pearch**, 7– **perch**. [a. F. *perche*:—L. *perca* (Pliny), a. Gr. πέρκη: cf. περκνός dark-coloured, περκάζειν to become dark.]

1. a. A common spiny-finned freshwater fish (*Perca fluviatilis*) of Europe and the British Isles, the flesh of which is used as food. Hence extended to the other species of *Perca*, as the common yellow perch of N. America (*P. americana* or *flavescens*), or to the family *Percidæ* in general. (Pl. now rare, the collective singular being used instead, as with other names of fishes.)

13.. *K. Alis.* 5446 Fleiȝeyng foules blake,..of perches and of savmouns, Token and eten grete foysouns. **1387** TREVISA *Higden* (Rolls) I. 423 In þe oþer [pond] is perche and trouȝtis. **1496** *Bk. St. Albans, Fishing* (1883) 28 The perche is a daynteuous fysshe & passynge holsom. *a* **1552** LELAND *Itin.* V. 70 Good Pikes, and Perches in greate Numbre. **1653** WALTON *Angler* ix. 179 The Pearch..is one of the fishes of prey, that, like the Pike and Trout, carries his teeth in his mouth. **1704** POPE *Windsor For.* 142 The bright-ey'd perch with fins of Tyrian dye. **1870** MORRIS *Earthly Par.* III. IV. 296 Within the mill-head there the perch feed fat.

b. Applied on the Pacific coast of the United States to any fish of the viviparous family *Embiotocidæ* or surf-fishes; also locally to various other fishes, usually with qualifying word (see 2).

1882 J. E. TENISON-WOODS *Fish N.S. Wales* 31 *Lates colonorum*, the perch of the colonists..really a fresh-water fish, but..often brought to the Sydney market from Broken Bay and other salt-water estuaries... The perch of the Ganges and other East Indian rivers (*L. calcarifer*).. extends to the rivers of Queensland. *Ibid.* 45 The..genus *Chilodactylus* is..largely represented in Tasmania and Victoria, one species being commonly imported from Hobart Town in a smoked and dried state under the name of 'perch'. **1890** *Cent. Dict.* s.v. *Embiotocidæ*, Nearly all are marine, abounding on the Pacific coast of the United States, where they are among the inferior food-fishes, and are called perches, porgies, shiners, etc.

2. With qualifying word, applied (chiefly locally) to various fishes of the family *Percidæ*, and to some of other families, resembling the common perch or taking its place as food.

black perch, a name for dark-coloured species of *Centropristis*, also called *black bass*; also for various other dark-coloured fishes allied to or resembling the common perch; **blue perch**, (*a*) the BURGALL or CUNNER (*Ctenolabrus adspersus*, fam. *Labridæ*); (*b*) a Californian surf-fish, *Ditrema laterale* (fam. *Embiotocidæ*); **buffalo-perch**, (*a*) the freshwater drum, *Haplodinotus grunniens*, fam. *Sciænidæ* (see DRUM *sb.*[1] 11); (*b*) a buffalo-fish, *Ictiobus bubalus*, fam. *Catostomidæ* (see BUFFALO *sb.* 2, 5); **grunting perch** = *buffalo-perch* (*a*); **pearl-perch**: see quot. 1898; **red perch**, (*a*) the rose-fish *Sebastes marinus* of the North Atlantic; (*b*) in Australia and Tasmania, species of *Anthias*; (*c*) in California, *Hypsipops rubicundus*; **sea-perch**, (*a*) a fish of the genus *Labrax*, a bass; (*b*) a fish of the genus *Serranus* or family *Serranidæ*; (*c*) = *red perch*; (*d*) = *blue perch* (*a*); **tiny perch**, a fish of the family *Elassomidæ*, very small freshwater fishes of the Southern United States; **white perch**, (*a*) *Morone americana*, family *Labracidæ*; (*b*) a local name of the *Buffalo-perch* (*a*); (*c*) various species of the *Embiotocidæ* (see 1 b); **yellow perch**, the common perch of North America (see 1). See also GOLDEN *perch*, GREY *p.*, LOG *p.*, MAGPIE *p.*, etc.

1611 COTGR., *Perche de mer*, the sea Pearch; a wholesome, rough-find, and tonguelesse, rocke-fish. **1661** LOVELL *Hist. Anim. & Min.* 214 The Sea-perch... The head with honey helps pustules, &c. **1729** in *Dampier's Voy.* (ed. 3) III. II. 415 The Red-listed Pearch. Is good to eat. **1818** RAFINESQUE *Let.* 20 July in Jordan *N. Amer. Ichthyol.* (1877) 13 Red Perch. **1836** *Penny Cycl.* VI. 423/1 *Centropristes nigricans*, one of the species known by the name of the black-perch or black-bass, is abundant in the rivers of the United States. **1855** LONGF. *Hiaw.* v. 47 He..Saw the yellow perch, the Sahwa, Like a sunbeam in the water. **1860** Blue perch [see BURGALL]. **1879** GOODE *Fisheries U.S.* 34 *Sebastes Marinus*, ..Norway Haddock; Hemdurgan; Red Perch.—Polar Seas and South to Cape Cod. **1882** J. E. TENISON-WOODS *Fish N.S. Wales* 48 *Sebastes percoides*... In Victoria it is called the Red Gurnet perch. **1883** E. P. RAMSAY *Food Fishes N.S. Wales* 35 (Fish. Exhib. Publ.) The most important of our freshwater fishes are..the two species of the Murray Cod (*Oligorus*), the Golden Perch (*Ctenolates*), 2 species, the Silver Perch and MacLeay's Perch (*Therapon*), the River Perch (*Lates*), 2 species. **1898** MORRIS *Austral. Eng.*, *Black-Perch*, a river fish of New South Wales, *Therapon niger*, family *Percidæ*. *Ibid.*, *Fresh-water Perch*, name given in Tasmania to the fish *Microperca tasmaniæ*. *Ibid.*, *Murray-Perch*, a fresh-water fish, *Oligorus mitchelli*, closely allied to ..the Murray-Cod. *Ibid.*, *Pearl-Perch*, a rare marine fish of New South Wales, excellent for food, *Glaucosoma scapulare*, family *Percidæ*. *Ibid.*, *Sea-Perch*, a name applied..in Sydney, to the Morwong [*Chilodactylus*], and Bull's-eye [*Priacanthus macracanthus*]; in New Zealand and Melbourne, to Red-Gurnard [*Sebastes percoides*].

3. *Comb.*, as ***perch-like***, ***-shaped*** adjs.; **perch-backed**, *a.*, resembling in shape a perch's back; **perch-hole**, a hole in which perch are found; **perch-pest**, a crustacean parasite of the perch; †**perch-stone**: see quot. 1658.

1658 PHILLIPS, The *Perch-stone*, a white stone found in the head of a Perch. **1835** KIRBY *Hab. & Inst. Anim.* II. Index, Perch-pest. [Cf. p. 31, Pest of the Perch..takes its station usually within the mouth, fixing itself, by means of its sucker, in the cellular membrane.] **1840** *Penny Cycl.* XVII. 432/1 Perch-like fishes whose operculum is produced behind. **1872** EVANS *Anc. Stone Implements* xxiv. 567 Lunate and perch-backed implements..are very scarce. **1883** E. P. RAMSAY *Food Fishes N.S. Wales* 9 (Fish. Exhib. Publ.) A more important fish..is a fine perch-shaped *Glaucosoma*,..named *G. scapulare*. **1906** *Macm. Mag.* June 574 Agatha by the side of the perch-hole, very erect, with a still more erect fishing-rod, surprised by the..angler.

perch (pɜːtʃ), *sb.*[2] Forms: 3–6 **perche**, 6 **pearche**, 6–8 **pearch**, 7 **peerch**, 5– **perch**. See also PERK *sb.*[1] [a. F. *perche* (13th c. in Littré) = Pr. *perja*, *perga*, Cat. *perca*, Sp. *percha*, It. *pertica*:—L. *pertica* pole, long staff, measuring-rod.]

I. 1. a. A pole, rod, stick, or stake, used for various purposes, *e.g.* for a weapon, a prop, etc. *Obs.* or *dial.* in gen. sense.

c **1290** *S. Eng. Leg.* I. 273/78 Cristofre bi-side þulke watere..In his hond a long perche he bar, is staf as þei it were. Ȝwane any man wolde ouer þat watur, opon is rug he him caste And tok is perche and bar him ouer. [**1419** *Liber Albus* III. ii. (Rolls) I. 260 Item, si ascun perche dascune taverner soit pluis large, ou soi pluis extendent que nest ordeigne.] *c* **1440** *Promp. Parv.* 393/1 Perche, or perke, *pertica*. **1578** LYTE *Dodoens* III. lix. 399 The tame Hoppe.. windeth it selfe about poles and perches. **1600** HOLLAND *Livy* I. xxxv. 26 Scaffolds born up twelue foot high from the ground with forked perches or props. **1725** BRADLEY *Fam. Dict.* s.v. *Willow*, Within two years they will be gallant Perches. **1902** *Contemp. Rev.* Dec. 839 The men knock the fruit from the trees with long poles and perches.

†**b.** A heavy staff used in fulling or walking cloth by hand. *Obs.*

[**1350–75**: see PERK *sb.*[1] 1 b.] **1387** TREVISA *Higden* (Rolls) IV. 409 þe Iewes stened þis Iames..and..smyte out his brayn wiþ a walkere his perche [L. *pertica fullonis*].

c. A pole set up in a shallow or other special place in the sea, a river, etc., to serve as a mark for navigation.

1465 [see *perch money* in 6]. **1672** in Picton *L'pool Munic. Rec.* (1883) I. 308 A Perch at the lower end of the Key. **1683** *Ibid.*, Wee order that the Perch bee..sett upp at the blacke rocke. **1702** *Lond. Gaz.* No. 3781/4 A Perch..with a white Brush upon it. **1858** *Merc. Marine Mag.* V. 175 There is a Bright Tide Light, and two perches on the western side. **1875** BEDFORD *Sailor's Pocket Bk.* v. (ed. 2) 139 Perches with balls, cages, &c. will..be at turning points.

d. The centre pole by which the hinder carriage is connected to the fore-carriage in wagons and in some kinds of coaches and other four-wheeled vehicles.

1668–9 PEPYS *Diary* 6 Feb., The bolt broke that holds the forewheels to the perch, and so the horses went away with them, and left the coachman and us. **1728** VANBR. & CIB. *Prov. Husb.* II. i, Crack! went the Perch! Down goes the Coach! **1794** W. FELTON *Carriages* (1801) I. 45 Sometimes the perch is made of a bent form, called a compass perch. **1863** *Q. Rev.* CXIV. 313 It is difficult for us to understand how a four-wheeled plaustrum, without a perch, was ever coaxed round a curve—how it turned nobody knows.

II. 2. a. A bar fixed horizontally to hang something upon; a peg.; = PERK *sb.*[1] 2. *Obs.* or *Hist.*

? *a* **1366** CHAUCER *Rom. Rose* 225 A mantyl henge hir fast by, Upon a perche, weike and smalle. *c* **1391** —— *Astrol.* II. §23 Thow most haue a plomet hanging on a lyne heyer than thin heued on a perche. *c* **1440** *Gesta Rom.* ix. 24 (Harl. MS.) [She] hongyd it vp on a perche in hire chambir. **1538** ELYOT *Dict.*, *Petiolus*, a lytle foote: also a perche whereon frutes or onyons be hanged. **1860** WEALE *Dict. Terms*, *Perch*, a small projecting beam, corbel, or bracket, near the altar of a church. **1871** KINGSLEY *At Last* xi, A 'perch' for hanging clothes..just such as would have been seen in a mediæval house in England.

†**b.** A bar to support a candle or candles, esp. as an altar-light: cf. PERCHER[2] and PERK *sb.*[1] 2 b.

[**1302** *Reg. Palat. Dunelm.* (Rolls) III. 47 Pertica, super quam ponuntur cerei et candelæ.] **1499**, **1532–3** [see *perch-candle* in 6]. **1565** CALFHILL *Answ. Treat. Crosse* 140 b, My Lord Maior hath a perch to set on hys perchers when hys gesse be at supper.

c. *Theatr.* A platform from which lights are directed on to the front of the stage; *pl.*, the lights placed on this platform.

1933 P. GODFREY *Back-Stage* i. 18 The stops controlling the amber circuits in No. 1 batten, floats, and P. and O.P. perches slide up to full. *Ibid.* vii. 90 'What's in your perches?' 'Ambers, sir.' **1934** A. P. HERBERT *Holy Deadlock* 215 From time to time he gave a quiet order to an invisible person called Joe about Batten Number One, about a border or a perch, a flat or the floats. **1957** *Oxf. Compan. Theatre* (ed. 2) 472/2 The mobility of the bridge is allied in control with the 'perches' or ladder-type boomerangs, which can be moved on or off stage according to the width of the scene. *Ibid.* 474/2 The spot batten and perches will, when a cyclorama is used, illuminate adequately the acting area to within a certain distance of the cyclorama. **1959** RAE & SOUTHERN *Internat. Vocab. Techn. Theatre Terms* 58 *Perch*, platform for tormentor spot. **1967** *Punch* 16 Aug. 242/3 For *Figaro* and Verdi's *Macbeth*.., John Christie had to bring in a lighting bridge and sixty floods and perches from Glyndebourne.

3. a. A bar fixed horizontally for a hawk or tame bird to rest upon.

c **1386** CHAUCER *Knt.'s T.* 1346 What haukes sitten on the perche aboue. —— *Nun's Pr. T.* 64 As Chauntecleer among hise wyues alle Sat on his perche that was in the halle. *c* **1400** MAUNDEV. (1839) xxii. 241 [Ther] ben sett upon a perche 4 or 5 or 6 gerfacouns. **1575** TURBERV. *Faulconrie* 115 So neare that they maye sit close togyther on the pearche. **1613** PURCHAS *Pilgrimage* (1614) 504 The pearches whereon they set their Canarie birds, which else would be killed by Pismires. **1774** GOLDSM. *Nat. Hist.* (1776) V. 340 Standing upright upon the perch like a sparrow-hawk. **1852** R. F. BURTON *Falconry Vall. Indus* vi. 64 She is placed, unhooded, on her perch. *Note*, The perch is a round rod projecting from the wall, garnished with cloth, which hangs beneath it like a towel.

b. Anything serving for a bird to alight or rest upon; also *transf.* for anything, or for a person. ***to take one's perch***: to perch, to alight. ***peck and perch***: see PECK *sb.*[3] 3.

1470–85 MALORY *Arthur* VI. xvi, A Faucon came fleynge ..and she flewe vnto the elme to take her perche. **1526** *Pilgr. Perf.* (W. de W. 1531) 156 She flyeth vp to a perche or braunche of a tree, and after her maner she syngeth full swetely. **1603** SHAKS. *Meas. for M.* II. i. 4 We must not make a scar-crow of the Law,..let it keepe one shape, till custome make it Their pearch, and not their terror. **1638** SIR T. HERBERT *Trav.* (ed. 2) 11 Some Boobyes, weary of flight, made our Ship their pearch. **1856** KANE *Arct. Expl.* II. xxvii. 269 The tides rose over it, and the waves washed against it continually, but it gave a perfectly safe perch to our little boats. **1877** BRYANT *Odyssey* v. 405 The sea-nymph took her perch On the well-banded raft.

c. *fig.* An elevated or secure position or station. (Often with direct allusion to a bird's perch.)

1526 *Pilgr. Perf.* (W. de W. 1531) 2 b, Euen so man..may ..flye vp neuer so hye..from perche to perche, from pleasure to pleasure, from honour to honour. **1654** H. L'ESTRANGE *Chas. I* (1655) 87 Never did the Prerogative descend so much from perch to popular lure, as by that concession [of the Petition of Right]. **1818** KEATS *Endym.* III. 14 They proudly mount To their spirit's perch. **1884** PAE *Eustace* 63 It gives me a lift to the perch that I'd long had an eye for.

d. *colloq.* A small seat on a vehicle, usually elevated, for the driver, or for a livery servant.

1841 LEVER *C. O'Malley* cviii, The postilion was obliged to drive from what (Hibernicè speaking) is called the perch, no ill-applied denomination to a piece of wood which about the thickness of one's arm, is hung between the two fore-springs and serves as a resting-place. **1875** KNIGHT *Dict. Mech.*, *Perch*..(Vehicle)..An elevated seat for the driver.

e. In *fig.* phrases (*colloq.* or *slang*). ***to throw, turn***, etc., ***over the perch, to knock off one's perch***, etc.: to upset, vanquish, ruin, 'do for', put an end to, be the death or destruction of; also in weakened senses: to disconcert, humiliate, snub; ***to come*** (or ***get***) ***off one's perch***: to climb down, to adopt a less arrogant or condescending manner.

So ***to tip over the perch, hop the perch***, etc.: to be ruined or vanquished; to die. ***cannot flutter above the perch*** (quot. 1649): said of a young bird, hence of an inexperienced or ignorant person. *to peak* or *peck over the perch*: see PEAK *v.*[1] 1 b.

[*a* **1529**: see PERK *sb.*[1] 3 b.] **1568** FULWELL *Like Will to Like* E iij, Charged to make privy serche, So that if we may be got, we shalbe throwen ouer the perche. **1587** HAKLUYT *Voy.* (1810) III. 400 Some drugge that should make men pitch over the perch. **1594** NASHE *Unfort. Trav.* 17 It was inough if a fat man did but trusse his points, to turne him ouer the pearch [in the sweating sicknes]. **1649** G. DANIEL *Trinarch., Hen. IV*, clx, As yet some cannot flutter 'boue the Perch. **1702** T. BROWN *Lett. fr. Dead* Wks. 1760 II. 237 For fear when I am once got into the grave, the grim tyrant should give me a turn over the perch, and keep me there. **1737** OZELL *Rabelais* III. Prol. 15 Either through Negligence, or for want of ordinary Sustenance, they both tipt over the Perch. **1791** CHARLOTTE SMITH *Celestina* (ed. 2) I. 132 The old girl must hop the perch soon. **1822** SCOTT *Pirate* xl, Such a consummate idiot as to hop the perch so sillily. **1864** *Athenæum* 22 Oct. 523/3 Lord John Russell..took the Dean off his perch. **1896** *Dialect Notes* I. 421 'Come off your perch,' stop being fresh. **1900** 'FLYNT' & 'WALTON' *Powers that Prey* 238 'It's up to you to do the talking... All I've got to do is just to sit quiet.'.. 'Sure! I'll say it fast enough. But you can come off your perch just the same.' **1915** MRS. BELLOC LOWNDES *Diary* 24 Mar. (1971) 60 The American said: 'What you've first got to do is to come off your perch—and listen to what we want...' The great man gave in and got off his perch. *a* **1916** 'SAKI' in *Coll. Short Stories* (1930) 316 Mrs. Quabari, to use a colloquial expression, was knocked off her perch. **1923** G. MCKNIGHT *Eng. Words* iv. 65 *Stop crowing* becomes *come off the perch*. **1931** M. ALLINGHAM *Look to Lady* xv. 156 For Gawd's sake come off yer perch and listen to this seriously. **1936** S. SASSOON *Sherston's Progress* III. 151 Tells Hooper to come off his perch and put the kettle on, which isn't well received by the golden-haired one. **1976** D. CLARK *Dread & Water* v. 104, I reckon..that he's been knocked off his perch by our form of investigation.

†**f.** [Obliquely derived from prec. phrases: cf. PERCH *v.* 6, to die.] Death. *Obs. slang.*

1722 W. BROMLEY *Let. to J. Grahme* 22 Apr. in J. Bagot *Col. J. Grahme* (1886) 32 My letters yesterday put me into a very great quandary, upon hearing of your friend's perch [i.e. the death of the Earl of Sunderland]. *Ibid.* 6 May, I do not believe that any of my friends rejoice at the late perch, though I am told that others have shown very indecent joy.

4. A wooden bar, or frame of two parallel bars, over which pieces of cloth are pulled, in order to examine them thoroughly; formerly also used in dressing cloth, blankets, etc., with hand-cards: cf. PERCH *v.* 5; *Obs.* or *dial.* [So in French.] Also, a horizontal bar used in softening leather.

a **1533** LD. BERNERS *Gold. Bk. M. Aurel.* (1546) Cc ij b, Ye haue strayned it on the tentours, and drawen it on the perche. **1666** W. SPURSTOWE *Spir. Chym.* 118 Cloth that is drawn over the Perch. *Ibid.* 164 The circumspect Merchant contents not himself with the seeing and feeling of his Cloth ..but he puts it upon the Perch, and setting it between the light and himself, draws it leasurely over, and so discovers, not only the rents and holes that are in it, but the inequality of the threads, etc. **1883** *Almondbury & Huddersf. Gloss.* **1898** *Hide & Leather* 24 Sept. 21/3 After drying they [*sc.* skins] are softened, dry, over a perch with a moon-knife. **1902** *Mod. Amer. Tanning* I. 201 When the pelt is about half dry, it must be worked over what is called a perch. **1903** H. R. PROCTER *Princ. Leather Manuf.* 188 'Perching' ..[consists] in fixing the skins on a horizontal pole (the 'perch'), and working them with..a tool formed somewhat like a small shovel with a semicircular blade. **1909** H. G. BENNETT *Manuf. Leather* 359 In perching the mechanical treatment is less violent, the goods being fixed on a 'perch'—a horizontal pole about 5 feet above the ground—and scraped by means of the 'moon-knife'. **1940** [see PERCHING *vbl. sb.*[1]].

III. 5. A rod of a definite length used for measuring land, etc.; hence **a.** A measure of length, esp. for land, palings, walls, etc.; in Standard Measure equal to $5\frac{1}{2}$ yards, or $16\frac{1}{2}$ feet, but varying greatly locally: see quots. Also called POLE or ROD.

1398 TREVISA *Barth. De P.R.* XIX. cxxix. (Add. MS. 27944), þe pase conteyneþ fyue feet and þe perche elleuene passe and ten feete. [Some error: L. has *passus pedes*. v. *partica pedes* .xx.] **1491** *Act 7 Hen. VII*, c. 14 Bounde to repaire ccccLxvij perches, every perche of xviij fote, of the pale of the parke. **1523** FITZHERB. *Husb.* §12 An acre of grounde by the statute, that is to say .xvi. fote and a halfe, to the perch or pole, foure perches to an acre in bredth, and fortye perches to an acre in lengthe. **1542** RECORDE *Gr. Artes* (1575) 207, 5 yardes and a halfe make a Perche. **1669** WORLIDGE *Syst. Agric.* (1681) 330 A Perch, or Lug is sixteen foot and a half Land-measure, but is usually eighteen foot to measure Coppice-woods withal. **1672** PETTY *Pol. Anat.* (1691) 52 The Perch of Ireland is 21 Foot. **1763** *Museum Rust.* I. lxxiii. 315 Besides these statute measures, there are in England what may be called customary perches, differing one from the other in length in various counties. *a* **1850** JAS. GRAY *Introd. Arith.* (ed. 100) 8, *Tables*, $5\frac{1}{2}$ Yards = 1 Pole or Perch.

b. A superficial measure of land, equal to a square of which each side is a lineal perch; a square perch or pole (normally $\frac{1}{160}$ of an acre).

1442 *Rolls of Parlt.* V. 59/1 A quarter and an half of a perche, and a pek of Londe. **1571** DIGGES *Pantom.* II. xii. N iij, There is in that parke 1188 acres, and 24 perches. **1654** WHITLOCK *Zootomia* 200 Not to lose a Pearch of my many Acres, through imperfect Survey. **1766** *Compl. Farmer* s.v. *Lucern*, A perch of transplanted lucern. **1836** LANDOR *Peric. & Asp.* Wks. 1846 II. 371/1 Pindar! you have brought a sack of corn to sow a perch of land. **1863** MORTON *Cycl. Agric.* in *O.C. & F. Words* (E.D.S.) 174 *Perch* (*Guernsey*) 7 yards squared for land measure, making $1\frac{3}{5}$ perches. (*Jersey*) $7\frac{1}{3}$ yards = 22 feet [squared], $\frac{1}{90}$ of an acre.

c. A solid measure used for stone, containing a lineal perch (see a) in length, and usually $1\frac{1}{2}$ feet in breadth and 1 foot in thickness; but varying locally, and for different materials.

1823 P. NICHOLSON *Pract. Build. Price-bk.* 90 An Irish rod or perch of stone-walling..is twenty-one feet in length, eighteen inches in breadth, and twelve inches in depth. **1849** D. G. MITCHELL *Battle Summer* (1852) 57 Will these blouse-men, who sup in Tuilleries today, hammer stone tomorrow at ten sous a perch? **1863** MORTON *Cycl. Agric.* in *O.C. & F. Words* (E.D.S.) 174 (*Devon*) Perch of stone work, $16\frac{1}{2}$ feet in length, 1 in height, and 22 inches in thickness [= $30\frac{1}{4}$ feet]; of cob work, 18 feet in length, 1 in height, and 2 in thickness.

IV. 6. *attrib.* and *Comb.*: **perch-bolt**, the bolt or pin upon which the perch of a carriage turns; †**perch-candle** = PERCHER[2] (*obs.*); **perch-carriage**, a 'carriage', or framework of a vehicle (CARRIAGE 28), having a perch; **perch-coach**, a coach having a perch; **perch-hoop**, in a vehicle, 'the hoop that unites the other timbers to the perch' (Felton); **perch-iron**, a general term for the iron parts of a carriage-perch (Knight *Dict. Mech.* 1884); **perch-loop**, an iron fastened to a carriage-perch, having loops for the straps which pass to the bed, to limit the swing of the body (ibid.); **perch money**, money paid for the maintenance of perches (sense 1 c) in a harbour, etc.; **perch-plate**, an iron plate placed above, below, or at the side of a carriage-perch; **perch-pole**, a climbing-pole used by acrobats; **perch-stay**, one of the side rods which pass from the perch of a carriage to the hind axle as braces.

1794 W. FELTON *Carriages* (1801) I. 40 The under carriage is the conductor, and turns by means of a lever, called a pole, acting on a centre pin, called a *perch-bolt. **1879** *Cassell's Techn. Educ.* IV. 174/2 The perch-bolt, or centre-point on which the wheels lock round. **1499** *Promp. Parv.* 393 (Pynson) *Perche candell, *perticalis*. **1532-3** in Swayne *Sarum Churchw. Acc.* (1896) 265 Halfe dowsen of perche Candelles vij *d.* ob. **1800** *Hull Advertiser* 11 Oct. 2/4 A neat post chaise, with *perch carriage. **1815** *Paris Chit-Chat* (1816) I. 101 [He] paces along gravely with two enormous black horses, and in a *perch-coach. **1794** W. FELTON *Carriages* (1801) I. 102 A *perch hoop, which unites the wings to the perch, by being tightly drove over them. **1465** *Cal. Anc. Rec. Dublin* (1889) I. 323 Hit is ordeynet.. that al..pay *perche mony to the water baliffes of the havvyn of the seid citte. **1794** W. FELTON *Carriages* (1801) I. 52 The side *perch-plates. [p. 45 Plating with iron the sides of perches is a great improvement.]

perch (pɜːtʃ), *v.*[1] Forms: see PERCH *sb.*[2] [a. F. *perche-r* (14th c. in Littré), f. *perche* PERCH *sb.*[2]]

I. 1. *intr.* To alight or rest as a bird upon a perch, to settle, or to stand or sit, as a bird, properly upon a bar, bough, etc. with its feet grasping the support. Hence *transf.* of persons and things: To alight or settle, or to stand, sit, or rest, upon something (usually at a height above the ground, and affording narrow standing-room).

1486 *Bk. St. Albans* C viij, She perchith when she stondyth on any maner bowe or perch. **1530** PALSGR. 656/1, I perche, as a hauke or byrde..on a boughe or perche, *je perche*. *a* **1586** SIDNEY *Arcadia* II. Poems 1873 II. 55 Her shoulders be like two white doues, Pearching within square royall rooues. **1601** SHAKS. *Jul. C.* V. i. 80. **1663** CHARLETON *Chor. Gigant.* 29 Where ever the Roman Eagle pearch'd. **1712** ARBUTHNOT *John Bull* III. ii, Thou wilt be hung up in chains, or thy quarters perching upon the most conspicuous places of the kingdom. **1804** J. GRAHAME *Sabbath* 440 Birds of dazzling plume Perch on the loaded boughs. **1862** JOHNS *Brit. Birds* (1874) 174 A long and almost straight [claw] is best adapted for perching on the ground.

2. *trans.* To set or place upon a perch, to cause to perch; to set up on a height, or as on a perch. Also *refl.*

1575 TURBERV. *Faulconrie* 115 When you see them sit close that one to that other for warmth..pearche them and lewre them both togither. *a* **1687** H. MORE (J.), If you could perch yourself as a bird on the top of some high steeple. **1853** KANE *Grinnell Exp.* xxxi. (1856) 265 The driving ice, and the groaning pressures which have perched us thus upon a lump of drift. **1883** GILMOUR *Mongols* xviii. 217 Crows perch themselves on the top of loaded camels.

3. *pa. pple.* (from 1 and 2, being the result either of having perched or being perched). Standing, seated, or settled as a bird upon a perch; set up on an eminence, esp. with little standing-room.

c **1384** CHAUCER *H. Fame* III. 901 How that myn Egle fast by Was perched hye vpon a stoon. **1627** DRAYTON *Agincourt* lxix, Bedfords an Eagle pearcht vpon a Tower. **1633** *Battle of Lutzen* in *Harl. Misc.* (Malh.) IV. 188 You shall find the heavenly benediction perched on the points of your swords. **1669** WORLIDGE *Syst. Agric.* (1681) 247 The most part of them..are shot with a Fowling-piece, either perched by a Dog, or otherwise, or flying. **1835** SIR J. ROSS *Narr. 2nd Voy.* vi. 88 A castle perched on its summit. **1860** TYNDALL *Glac.* I. ii. 19 Upon the..moraine..were perched enormous masses of rock. **1862** JOHNS *Brit. Birds* 290, I have always failed to observe it actually perched and singing. **1877** BLACK *Green Past.* xxxvii. (1878) 297 The Lieutenant, perched up beside the driver was furnished with a couple of umbrellas. **1884** *Manch. Exam.* 13 May 5/2 The heights on which the old town is perched.

II. †**4.** *trans.* To furnish with, or fasten to, a 'perch' or pole, for a prop or support. *Obs.*

1398 TREVISA *Barth. De P.R.* XVII. clxxvii. (Add. MS. 27944) It [vine] haþ vertue and might to bynde hemself togideres and beþ perched & trayled and bounde to tryen þat ben nyȝe þerto.

5. To stretch (cloth from the loom) upon a perch (PERCH *sb.*[2] 4), for the purpose of examining and burling, or detecting and removing imperfections, such as knots or holes, or (formerly) of raising the nap by hand-cards. (Later done by *gigging*; see GIG *v.*)

Hence, dial. (*a*) To examine piecework of any kind before payment, or to submit such work for examination by the employer. (*b*) To raise a nap on woollen cloth. (*Eng. Dial. Dict.*).

1552 *Act 5 & 6 Edw. VI*, c. 22 Certen Milles called Gigge Milles, for the perchinge and burlinge of Clothe, by reason whereof the true Draperie of this realme ys wonderfully empayred. **1892** *Chambers's Encycl.* X. 730/1 *Perching* consists in making a close inspection of the piece with the object of marking all defects.

6. [From the phrases *hop the perch*, etc.: PERCH *sb.*[2] 3 e.] To die. *slang.* (Cf. PERCHER[1] 6.)

1886 *Sporting Times* 3 Aug. 1/3 (Farmer) 'Well, s'pose I perched first?' 'Well', replied Pitcher, 'I should just come in where you were lying' [etc.].

†**perch**, *v.*[2] *Obs.* [Collateral form of PERK *v.*[1] The existence of *perk* as a northern form of PERCH *sb.*[2] and *v.*[1], appears to have led to some confusion between PERCH *v.*[1] and PERK *v.*[1], and given rise to this variant of the latter.]

intr. To raise or exalt oneself, to push or set oneself *up* aspiringly, self-assertingly, or presumptuously; = PERK *v.*[1] 1, 1 b.

1581 J. BELL *Haddon's Answ. Osor.* 299 b, Contemning the authoritie of the higher powers..[they] will presume so proudly to pearch through intollerable pryde, to make themselves their coequalles. **1598** DRAYTON *Heroic. Ep.* xiv. 143 Some..which proudly pearch so hie. **1599** NASHE *Lenten Stuffe* C ij, In Anno 1240, it [Yarmouth] perch vp to be gouernd by balies. **1621** HAKEWILL *David's Vow* 211 It never leaves pearching and pushing forward, till it set it selfe higher than is meet.

Hence †**perched** *ppl. a.* = PERKED; †**perching** *vbl. sb.* and *ppl. a.*, perking.

1575 LANEHAM *Let.* (1871) 51 More, fayr, eeuen, and fresh holly treez, for pearching and proining, set within. **1598** *Herrings Tayle* D j b, His pearching hornes are ream'd a yard beyond assise. **1600** *Hosp. Inc. Fooles* A iv, Those pearched Cuckoes that laugh at all the world. **1617** B. JONSON *Vision of Delight* 132 Nor purple Phesant..with a pearched pride Wave his dis-coloured necke, and purple side.

perch, obs. form of PARCH *v.*

percha (ˈpɜːtʃə). Short for GUTTA-PERCHA.

1876 PREECE & SIVEWRIGHT *Telegraphy* 236 Unless they are quite loose they will damage the percha. *Ibid.* 238 One side of the percha should be well warmed for about two inches back, and then brought forward over the joint.

perchance (pəˈtʃɑːns, -æ-), *adv.* (*sb.*, *a.*) *arch.* Forms: 4 **par chance, par chaunce, per chance,** 4–6 **parchaunce, perchaunce,** 5 **perchauns, -chawnce,** 6 **parchance, perchanse,** 4, 6– **perchance.** [ME. a. AF. *par chance* (Gower *Mirour* 14876), f. OF. *par* by, and *chance* CHANCE: cf. F. *par hasard*, also PERADVENTURE, PERCASE, and the later PERHAPS.]

†**1.** In a statement of fact: By chance; as it happens or happened: = PERADVENTURE *adv.* 1, PERCASE 1. *Obs.* exc. *arch.*

1340 HAMPOLE *Pr. Consc.* 2489 For our gude dedys er ofte done wrang,..Or parchaunce done oute of charité. **1390** GOWER *Conf.* I. 358 It fell per chance upon a day A Rovere of the See was nome. **1500-20** DUNBAR *Poems* xlii. 15, I said, 'Is this ȝour gouirnance, To tak men for thair luking heir?' Bewty sayis, 'Ȝa, schir, perchance ȝe be my ladeis presoneir'. **1601** SHAKS. *Twel. N.* I. ii. 5–6 *Vio*... Perchance he is not drown'd: What thinke you saylors? *Cap.* It is perchance that you your selfe were saued. **1815** W. H. IRELAND *Scribbleomania* 165 Descending astounded, asylum to seek, She pops, as perchance, upon kind Mistress Meeke.

2. In a conditional clause or the like (in quot. 1865, an interrogative sentence): By any chance; as may be, as is possible: = PERADVENTURE *adv.* 2, PERCASE 2, PERHAPS 2.

c **1400** *Rom. Rose* 5042 If with childe they be perchaunce. **1596** SHAKS. *Merch. V.* V. i. 75 If they but heare perchance a trumpet sound. **1676** LISTER in *Ray's Corr.* (1848) 125 If perchance anything has escaped his diligence. **1791** COWPER *Odyss.* XXI. 458 Should ye hear perchance a groan. **1865** SWINBURNE *Poems & Ball., Ilicet* 31 Sleep, is it sleep perchance that covers Each face? **1870** BRYANT *Iliad* I. III. 102 Lest perchance He smite thee with his spear.

3. Qualifying a statement so as to express possibility with uncertainty: It may be that; maybe, haply: = PERADVENTURE *adv.* 3, PERCASE 3, PERHAPS 1. Used **a.** with the subjunctive mood or its equivalent (perchance there may, might, would be); **b.** with the future indic. (perchance there shall or will be); **c.** with the pres. and past tenses indic. (perchance there is, was, has been, etc.).

In a. the statement is already contingent, and *perchance* may be taken, as in 1 and 2, in its literal sense of 'by chance', 'there may, might, would by chance be'; but in c. the statement is made contingent by *perchance*, and we cannot there substitute 'by chance', the meaning being 'it may chance to be the fact that there is, was, or has been'. This is also true of b., but there the event itself being future and so subject to contingency, the use of 'perchance' is somewhat transitional between a. and c. The loss of the subjunctive inflexions in Eng., and the levelling of this mood in form under the indicative, makes some early examples, esp. of the past tense, doubtful between a. and c.; thus 'perchance they had' might mean 'perchance they might have'; and it may have been in this way that a phrase originally = L. *forte* has come to be used as = *forsitan*. Cf. also the development in 'it may be that he is here', 'may be he is here', and (*dial.*) 'he is maybe here'.

a. **1390** GOWER *Conf.* I. 117 It mai par chance faile. *Ibid.* III. 10 Per chance in such a drunkeschipe I mai be ded. *c* **1570** *Pride & Lowl.* (1841) 18 Perchaunce an issue hereon may be ioynt. *a* **1661** FULLER *Worthies* (1840) III. 159 Some perchance would assign another reason. **1719** YOUNG *Revenge* II. i, Something perchance may happen To soften all to friendship, and to love. **1835** J. H. NEWMAN *Par. Serm.* (1837) I. xxi. 320 They thought death perchance might be a change for the better. *a* **1848** R. W. HAMILTON *Rew. & Punishm.* viii. (1853) 375 This view may perchance be discarded.

b. *a* **1400** *Evang. Nicod.* 377 in Herrig's *Archiv* LIII. 398 His blode mot on vs fall And on our childer bathe. Sir Pilate said: parchaunce so sall. *c* **1400** MAUNDEV. (Roxb.) xxxi. 139 Godd..will perchaunce take wreke on þam. **1542-5** BRINKLOW *Lament.* (1874) 87 Perchaunce ye wyll saye, ye seke no soche thynge thereby? **1610** SHAKS. *Temp.* II. ii. 17 Perchance he will not minde me. **1791** COWPER *Iliad* XVIII. 244 Panic-seized, perchance The Trojans shall from fight desist. **1822** SHELLEY *Calderon* II. 134 Many still Are mine, and many more, perchance shall be.

c. *c* **1400** *Apol. Loll.* 37 Frend, perchauns þu hawtist to wete & enquire. *c* **1420** *Pallad. on Husb.* I. 110 The lond is good, the colour nought, perchaunce. **1559** *Mirr. Mag., Warwick* xiii, Perchaunce thou thinkest. **1606** SHAKS. *Ant. & Cl.* I. i. 20, 25 Fuluia perchance is angry... Perchance? Nay, and most like. **1740** C. PITT *Virg. Æneid* I. 779 Perchance,..He roams the towns, or wanders thro' the woods. **1858** G. MACDONALD *Phantastes* (1878) II. xiv. 37 This shadow was perchance my missing demon.

d. Qualifying a word or phrase, by ellipsis: = PERADVENTURE 3 b, PERCASE 3 b, PERHAPS 1 b.

1382 *Pol. Poems* (Rolls) I. 266 Er he a childe put hir withinne, And perchaunce two at ones. **1390** GOWER *Conf.* III. 354 Noght al per chance as ye it wolden. **1522** SKELTON *Why not to Court?* 634 Parchaunce halfe a yere, And yet neuer the nere. **1602** SHAKS. *Ham.* III. i. 65 To dye to sleepe, To sleepe, perchance to Dreame: I, there's the rub. **1683** WOOD *Life* 22 May (O.H.S.) III. 55 The Laboratory, perchance one of the most beautiful and useful in the world. **1862** LONGF. *Wayside Inn* Prel. 91 Let me in outline sketch them all, Perchance uncouthly.

B. quasi-*sb.*

†1. *by perchance*: by chance. *Obs. rare.*

1495 *Trevisa's Barth. de P.R.* XVII. clxxv. (W. de W.) 717 By perchaunce it happyth that it crokyth and bendeth.

2. The word 'perchance', or a statement qualified by it; an expression of uncertain possibility.

a **1677** BARROW *Serm.* Wks. 1716 II. 178 Interposing.. now and then his may-be's and perchances.

C. quasi-*adj.* (in predicate.) Dependent on chance. *nonce-use.*

1891 J. SMITH *Fellowship* iii. 40 There is no intention to show that the life in Christ is perchance, haphazard, something which may begin today and end tomorrow.

†**perchant.** *Obs. rare*⁻⁰. [= F. *perchant* (in same sense) sb. use of pr. pple. of *percher* to perch.] (See quot.; app. never in Eng. use.)

1727-41 CHAMBERS *Cycl., Perchant*, among fowlers, or decoy-bird, which the fowler has fastened by the foot, and which flutters about the place where it is tied, to draw other birds to it. [Hence in mod. Dicts.]

perche, obs. form of PERCH, PIERCE.

perched (pɜːtʃt, *poet.* 'pɜːtʃɪd), *ppl. a.*[1] [f. PERCH *v.*[1] + -ED[1] and [2].]

1. Seated as a bird upon a perch; set up on a high point; *spec.* in *Geol.* applied [after F.] to a block or boulder left resting upon a pinnacle or other narrow support by the melting of the ice which carried it thither; also to blocks left in such a position by other causes; more generally, having an elevation that is exceptionally high in relation to the immediate locality; applied esp. to ground water separated from an underlying saturated zone by an intervening unsaturated zone.

1384- [see PERCH *v.*[1] 3]. **1859-65** PAGE *Geol. Terms, Perched Blocks.* **1863** LYELL *Antiq. Man* xv. 294 If the glacier is lowered greatly by melting, these circles of large angular fragments, which are called 'perched blocks', are left in a singular situation near the top of a steep hill or pinnacle. **1878** HUXLEY *Physiogr.* 164 Such stones [poised perhaps on the very edge of a precipice, or balanced upon a mere point] known as perched blocks or *blocs perchés*. **1883** R. W. DIXON *Mano* I. ii. 5 That blinking hood Which in the perched owl's orbs by daylight lies. **1900** H. JAMES *Little Tour in France* (ed. 2) vi. 62 In the matter of position Amboise is certainly supreme in the list of perched places. **1901** *Bull. Mus. Compar. Zoöl.* XXXVIII. 134 (*heading*) Perched boulders. **1906** A. C. VEATCH et al. in *Prof. Papers U.S. Geol. Survey* No. 44. 57 There are..a number of more or less limited areas of saturated beds above the main one. These perched ground-water tables are for the most part confined to the moraine. **1923** *Water-Supply Papers U.S. Geol. Survey*, No. 494. 42 If water poured into the well all drains out the well evidently ends in an unsaturated bed and the overlying ground water is perched. *Ibid.* 57 The term *perched* may be applied to streams in the same way as it is applied to ground water. **1956** W. EDWARDS in D. L. Linton *Sheffield* i. 8 All the igneous rocks are basaltic... Their clayey tops support 'perched' water-tables in parts of the limestone uplands. **1968** R. W. FAIRBRIDGE *Encycl. Geomorphol.* 740/1 'Cirques'..are formed at the heads of glaciers both large and small—including a great many perched, or hanging, glaciers of small dimensions. *Ibid.* 823/2 (*caption*) Perched block of Bluff Sandstone.., due to slumping, followed by slope retreat. **1972** J. G. CRUICKSHANK *Soil Geogr.* iii. 84 Any cemented or compacted horizon..can function in the same way and support a perched water table with accumulating soil water.

2. Furnished with a perch or perches: a. for birds. b. Of a carriage: cf. PERCH *sb.*[2] 1 d.

1671 MILTON *Samson* 1692 And as an ev'ning Dragon came, Assailant on the perched roosts,..Of tame villatic Fowl. **1794** W. FELTON *Carriages* (1801) I. 57 Coaches and phaetons, either perched or crane-necked.

perched, *ppl. a.*[2]: see under PERCH *v.*[2]

percher[1] ('pɜːtʃə(r)). [f. PERCH *v.*[1] and [2] + -ER[1]: cf. F. *percheur.*] A person or animal that perches.

I. From PERCH *v.*[2]

†1. One who aspires to a high position; a self-assertive person. *Obs.*

1581 MULCASTER *Positions* iv. 16 So is it worthy praise to rest in some degree which declareth a pearcher, though abilitie restraine will that it cannot aspire whervnto it would.

II. From PERCH *v.*[1]

2. A bird that perches.

1775 WHITE in *Phil. Trans.* LXV. 260 [The young swallows] then are conducted to the dead..bough of some tree, where..they are attended with great assiduity, and may then be called *perchers*.

3. *spec.* A bird having feet adapted for perching; a member of the *Insessores* or perching birds.

1835-6 TODD *Cycl. Anat.* I. 267/1 The perchers..always live in pairs. **1873** W. CORY *Lett. & Jrnls.* (1897) 304 Singers and perchers are scarce where the land is too dry for worms. **1884** *Century Mag.* XXVIII. 489 Entirely a ground bird and not a percher.

4. A person perched on a height or eminence.

1814 in C. W. Hatfield *Hist. Notices Doncaster* (1866) 86 The approach of the badger..was to be signalled by the percher [who has perched himself in a tree].

5. A workman employed in perching cloth (see PERCH *v.*[1] 5); a burler. [OF. *percheur.*]

1890 *Cent. Dict.* s.v. *Perch*[2], *v.*, The cloth is stretched in a frame, and the percher carefully examines the whole texture for imperfections, which may consist of burs and knots, which he carefully removes, or of holes, which he nicely darns.

6. *slang.* A dying person. (Cf. PERCH *v.*[1] 6.)

1714 VISCT. BOLINGBROKE *Let. to J. Grahme* 21 Jan. in J. Bagot *Col. J. Grahme* (1886) 28 The Queen is well, though the Whigs giue out that she is, what they wish her, 'a percher'.

7. See quot. (Perh. a different word.)

1891 WRENCH *Winchester Word-bk., Percher*, a Latin cross laid horizontally against the name of an absentee on any roll. [Remembered by Rev. C. B. Mount in 1839.]

8. *Cricket.* A ball that 'perches' or hangs in the air; *spec.* = BOUNCER 6.

1913 *Cricket* 14 June 305/2 Every bowler pitches short sometimes, and..the resultant 'rib-roaster', 'percher', 'flier', 'bouncer',..is no more than an ordinary risk. **1961** *Times* 23 June 4/1 As big a percher as can ever have been missed in a match between England and Australia.

†**percher**[2]. *Obs.* Also 5 -ere, -or, (pierchier), 5-6 perchour, 6 pearcher. [f. PERCH *sb.*[2] (sense 2 b), i.e. 'candle for placing on a perch'. The forms suggest an AF. **percher* = F. **perchier*, L. type **perticāri-us*, but examples are wanting.] A tall candle, of wax or tallow: see quot. 1706.

a **1331** *Mem. Multorum Hen. Prior Canterb.* in *MS. Cott. Galba E.* IV. lf. 45 Item, candele que vocantur perchers continent in longitudine xv pollices; unde xviij perchers pond. j. li. cere. *c* **1374** CHAUCER *Troylus* IV. 1245 Ffor by þe percher [*v.r.* morter] which þat I se brenne I knowe wel þat day is not fer henne. **1392-3** *Earl Derby's Exped.* (Camden) 252 Pro iiij. torches et perchers [*MS.* pchs] emptis. **1426-7** *Rec. St. Mary at Hill* 67 For a pound perchors for lyȝt to þe werke men i d ob. **1432** *Nottingham Rec.* II. 130 In torches ..priketes et pierchiers. *c* **1440** *Promp. Parv.* 393/2 Percher, candylle,..*perticalis.* **1513** *Bk. Keruynge* in *Babees Bk.* 279 Drawe the curtynes, than se there be morter or waxe of perchoures be redy. **1562** A. BROKE tr. *Rom. & Jul.* Shaks. Wks. 1803 XX. 324 In her hand a percher light The nurce beares up the stayre. **1577** tr. *Bullinger's Decades* II. i. (1592) 103 Seneca sayth, Let..no man sette pearchers or taper light before the Gods. **1613-18** DANIEL *Coll. Hist. Eng.* (1626) 104 Forty great long perchers of the Kings best candles. **1706** PHILLIPS, *Perchers*, the Paris-Candles formerly us'd in England; also the bigger sort of Candles, especially of Wax, which were commonly set upon the Altars.

‖**Percheron** (pɛrʃərɔ̃). [Fr. adj. from *le Perche*, a district of France comprising the departments of Orne, Eure-et-Loir, Sarthe, Loir-et-Cher.] A horse of a noted breed raised in le Perche, combining strength with lightness and speed, much used in France for artillery and for heavy coaches, and now largely bred in the western United States.

1875 S. SIDNEY *Bk. Horse* xi. 241 The Percheron is another breed of trotting cart-horses, which has in name a considerable reputation in England... These Percherons, in their best form, were the post-horses of France. **1901** *Scribner's Mag.* Apr. 414/2 Heavy wagons..all drawn by stocky Percherons and big Western grays or stout Canada blacks.

perchess, obs. form of PURCHASE.

'**perching,** *vbl. sb.*[1] [f. PERCH *v.*[1] + -ING[1].]

1. The action of the verb PERCH (in various senses). In quot. 1483, provision of perches in a fairway or the dues paid for this: cf. PERCH *sb.*[2] 1 c; in quot. 1818 = perching-place.

1483 *Cal. Anc. Rec. Dublin* (1889) I. 364 All manner of men that occupieth shippes..shall pay to the Watyr-bailliff, for his perchyng, ii. d of silver, as oft tymes as thei comyth yn and out. **1552** [see PERCH *v.*[1] 5]. **1818** KEATS *Endym.* I. 535 Pluck down A vulture from his towery perching. **1892** S. BARBER *Beneath Helvellyn's Shade* 46 The 'perching' of boulders by the agency of ice in the glacial period.

attrib. **1883** MARTIN & MOALE *Vertebr. Dissect.* 132 This is the perching muscle, and is so arranged that when the bird flexes the leg upon the thigh..the flexor muscles of the toes are pulled upon and the foot made to grasp the perch. **1888** E. EGGLESTON *Graysons* in *Century Mag.* June 274 He managed..to get perching-room on the window-sill. **1889** *Women's Union Jrnl.* 15 Nov. 87 Having their work carried to the perching room [to be examined: see PERCH *v.*[1] 5].

2. A process for softening skins in leather-making; cf. PERCH *sb.*[2] 4. Freq. *attrib.*

1897 C. T. DAVIS *Manuf. Leather* (ed. 2) 361 There are.. above the perching room.., two large logwood tanks. *Ibid.* 362, 12 Slocomb perching machines. These perching machines take the place of hand work. **1903, 1909** [see PERCH *sb.*[2] 4]. **1940** *Chambers's Techn. Dict.* 625/2 *Perching* (*leather*), a process for stretching and softening a skin by working over it with a crutch stake, on the flesh side, while it is fixed to a horizontal pole (*perch*).

'**perching,** *ppl. a.*[1] [See -ING[2].] That perches; *spec.* in *Ornith.* applied to the INSESSORES or birds with feet adapted for perching; insessorial.

1774 BEATTIE *Minstr.* II. viii, The perching eagle oft was heard to cry. **1823** VIGORS in *Trans. Linn. Soc.* XIV. 405, I wish..to designate this order by the title of *Insessores* or *Perching Birds.* **1880** A. R. WALLACE *Isl. Life* iii. 35 The whole series of British Passeres or perching birds.

perching, *vbl. sb.*[2] and *ppl. a.*[2]: see PERCH *v.*[2]

perchist ('pɜːtʃɪst). *poet. nonce-wd.* [f. PERCH *sb.*[2] + -IST.] A trapeze artist.

1938 L. MACNEICE *Earth Compels* 18 Perchists... They rise into the tent's Top like deep-sea divers... Hang by their teeth Beneath the cone of canvas.

perchling ('pɜːtʃlɪŋ). [f. PERCH *sb.*[1] + -LING[1] 2.] A small perch or percoid fish.

1852 *Fraser's Mag.* XLVI. 90 The small group of diminutive perchlings, of transparent bodies, called *Ambassis.*

per'chlor. Abbrev. of *perchloride* (of mercury).

1896 *Allbutt's Syst. Med.* I. 429 The thermometer placed in '$\frac{1}{20}$ carbolic' or '$\frac{1}{500}$ perchlor' for a few minutes.

perchlor-, per,chloro-. *Chem.* Combining form of *perchloric, perchloride, perchlorinated*; chiefly indicating a compound in which there is the maximum replacement of hydrogen by chlorine, as in ***perchloracetic, perchloraldehyde, -benzene, -ethane, -ethylic, perchloroquinone***, etc.

1857 MILLER *Elem. Chem.* III. 182 These perchlorinated compound ethers, such as the perchloracetic ether..and perchloroformic ether..are very unstable. *Ibid.*, Amongst these products perchloraldehyd..is always present. *Ibid.* 354 Perchlorokinone, chloranile ($C_{12}Cl_4O_4$)..forms pale yellow flakes of pearly and metallic lustre. **1862** *Ibid.* (ed. 2) III. 409 Perchloroquinone. **1866** ODLING *Anim. Chem.* 123 By treatment with chlorine, all four bodies yield..chloranil $C_6Cl_4O_2$, or perchloroquinone. **1882** *Athenæum* 11 Nov. 632/1 Perchlorethane, perchlorbenzene, and nitrogen were obtained.

perchlorate (pə'klɔərət). *Chem.* [f. PER-[1] 5 b + CHLORATE.] A salt of perchloric acid. Hence **per'chlorated** *ppl. a.* (see quot.).

1826 *Henry's Elem. Chem.* I. 537 Per-chlorate of potassa does not change vegetable colours. **1856** MILLER *Elem. Chem.* II. 536 No insoluble perchlorate is known: the perchlorate of potash is the least soluble of these compounds. **1880** CLEMINSHAW *Wurtz' Atom. The.* 140 The alkaline sulphates, selenates, permanganates, and perchlorates are isomorphous with each other. **1857** MAYNE *Expos. Lex.* 905/1 *Perchlorated ether has been employed to designate a body obtained either by combining directly chlorine with olefiant gas, or [etc.].

perchloric (pə'klɔərɪk), *a. Chem.* [f. PER-[1] 5 b + CHLORIC.] In ***perchloric acid***, hydrogen perchlorate, $HClO_4$, the oxygen acid of chlorine containing more oxygen than CHLORIC acid ($HClO_3$).

1818 W. HENRY *Elem. Chem.* (ed. 8) I. 437 The perchloric acid will then consist of one atom of chlorine = 33·5, united with seven atoms of oxygen = 52·5. **1856** MILLER *Elem. Chem.* II. 536. **1869** ROSCOE *Elem. Chem.* (1871) 115 Perchloric acid is one of the most powerful oxidizing agents known.

perchloride (pə'klɔəraɪd). *Chem.* [PER-[1] 5 a.] A compound of chlorine with another element or radical, containing the maximum proportion of chlorine. (These are now usually otherwise expressed; e.g. perchloride of carbon (perchlorinated chloride of ethylene), *carbon trichloride* C_2Cl_6, perchloride of iron (trichloride of iron), *ferric chloride* Fe_2Cl_6, as distinguished from *ferrous chloride* (proto- or dichloride of iron) $FeCl_2$.) So **per'chlorinated,** combined or charged with the maximum proportion of chlorine; hence **perchlori'nation.** †**per'chloruret** *Obs.* = *perchloride.*

1818 W. HENRY *Elem. Chem.* II. 15 In the chloride of phosphorus its elements are united atom to atom; while in the per-chloride two atoms of chlorine are combined with one of phosphorus. **1843** R. J. GRAVES *Syst. Clin. Med.* 32 Some denominate sublimate perchloride [of mercury]. **1881** J. RIDGE in *Med. Temp. Jrnl.* XLVI. 83 He was placed on full diet..and was ordered perchloride of iron. **1857** MILLER *Elem. Chem.* III. 180 An alcoholic solution of potash decomposes *perchlorinated ether. **1863–72** WATTS *Dict. Chem.* I. 766 Several perchlorinated compound ethers ..yield trichloride of carbon, when similarly treated. **1882** *Athenæum* 11 Nov. 632/1 The authors have studied the effect of exhaustive *perchlorination..on quinolin [etc.]. **1857** MAYNE *Expos. Lex.* 905/1 A *perchloruret.

perchloroethylene (pəˌklɔːrəʊ'ɛθɪliːn). *Chem.* Also **perchlorethylene.** [ad. G. *perchloräthylen*, f. *per-* PER-[1] 5 + *chlor-* CHLORO- + *äthylen* ETHYLENE.] A colourless, non-flammable, toxic liquid, C_2Cl_4, which is widely used as a solvent, esp. in dry cleaning fluid, and medicinally for the treatment of worm infestations; = TETRACHLOROETHYLENE.

1873 *Jrnl. Chem. Soc.* XXVI. 866 The action of sodium ethylate on perchloroethylene has been studied by Fischer and Geuther. **1875** *Ibid.* XXVIII. 746 The distillate which comes over slowly consists of perchlorethylene holding in solution aniline and carbon sesquichloride. **1954** A. K. DOOLITTLE *Technol. Solvents & Plasticizers* xii. 720 Perchloroethylene finds use as a dry-cleaning, metal-degreasing, and rubber solvent, and as an anthelmintic. **1963** *Economist* 12 Jan. 115/2 The customer can watch her clothes tumbling through a solvent (perchlorethylene). **1971** *Daily Tel.* 10 June 1/4 Perchloroethylene can cause drowsiness, coma and death if taken in sufficient quantities. **1976** *Sci. Amer.* May 52/2 The apparatus..basically consists of a tank of 100,000 gallons of the common dry-cleaning fluid perchloroethylene.

percid ('pɜːsɪd), *sb.* and *a.* *Ichthyol.* [f. mod.L. *Percidæ* pl., f. L. *perca* PERCH *sb.*[1]: see -ID[3].]

a. *sb.* A fish of the family *Percidæ*, typified by the genus *Perca* or perch. **b.** *adj.* Belonging to the family *Percidæ*. Also **'percidal** *a.*

1890 in *Cent. Dict.*

perciform ('pɜːsɪfɔːm), *a.* *Ichthyol.* [ad. mod.L. *perciformis*, f. L. *perca* PERCH *sb.*[1]: see -FORM.] Of the form of, or resembling, a perch; *spec.* belonging to the division *Perciformes* comprising the *Percidæ* and several allied families.

1880 DAY in *Jrnl. Linn. Soc.* XV. 52 On the Coromandel coast..I found the small perciform Therapons residing inside Medusae.

percil(e, obs. forms of PARSLEY.

percimonious, obs. form of PARSIMONIOUS.

percine ('pɜːsaɪn), *a.* and *sb.* *Ichthyol.* [f. mod.L. *Percīnæ* pl., f. L. *perca* PERCH *sb.*[1]]

a. *adj.* Belonging to the subfamily *Percinæ* of the *Percidæ*. **b.** *sb.* A fish of this subfamily.

1890 in *Cent. Dict.*

percipience (pə'sɪpɪəns). [f. L. type **percipientia*, f. *percipient-em*, pr. pple. of *percipĕre* to PERCEIVE: see -ENCE.] The action or condition of perceiving; perception, cognizance.

1768–74 TUCKER *Lt. Nat.* (1834) I. 313 Sense or percipience is the standing so circumstanced as that the impulse of objects striking upon us may be transmitted so as to raise perceptions. **1836** I. TAYLOR *Phys. The. another Life* (1858) 126 The mind's..percipience of sensitive pleasure. **1886** GURNEY *Phantasms of Living* I. 406 An example of collective telepathic percipience. **1891** HARDY *Tess* (1892) 378 She lay in a state of percipience without volition.

percipiency (pə'sɪpɪənsɪ). *rare.* [f. as prec. + -ENCY.] †**a.** = prec. (*obs.*). **b.** The quality of being percipient.

1662 H. MORE *Philos. Writ.* Pref. Gen. (1712) 13 A necessary requisite of that which is capable of the function of Common-percipiency. **1845** MRS. BROWNING *Lett.* 3 Mar. (1897) I. 243 The review amused me..by its percipiency about your remembering me during your travels in the East.

percipient (pə'sɪpɪənt), *a.* and *sb.* [ad. L. *percipient-em*, pr. pple. of *percipĕre* to PERCEIVE.]

A. *adj.* That perceives or is capable of perceiving; conscious; observing; seeing; discerning.

1692 BENTLEY *Boyle Lect.* ii. 52 A percipient and rational Creature. **1764** REID *Inquiry* vi. §4. 137 It..can only be the act of a percipient or thinking being. **1802–12** BENTHAM *Ration. Judic. Evid.* (1827) II. 497 Employed in the character of attesting (i.e. percipient and signing) witnesses. **1838–9** HALLAM *Hist. Lit.* III. III. iii. §86. 73 The eternal basis of conviction,..the consciousness of a self within, a percipient indivisible Ego. **1862** MAURICE *Mor. & Met. Philos.* IV. ix. §128. 648 The man becomes through a divine life percipient of God.

B. *sb.* **a.** One who or that which perceives.

1662 H. MORE *Philos. Writ.* Pref. Gen. (1712) 13 That vital Sympathy and Coactivity, that transforms objects in their exactest circumstances to the common Percipient. **1665** GLANVILL *Scepsis Sci.* v, The Soul is the sole Percipient, which alone hath animadversion and sense properly so called. **1744** HARRIS *Three Treat.* II. i. (1765) 56 Nature passes to the Percipient through all the Senses. **1867** LEWES *Hist. Philos.* (ed. 3) II. 301 In the very act of imagining it, you include an ideal percipient.

b. *spec.* in *Telepathy*, etc. One who perceives something outside the range of the senses, or 'on whose mind a telepathic impact falls'.

1885 *Proc. Soc. Psychical Research* III. 92 An apparition of a dead person whose death was unknown to the percipient. **1886** GURNEY *Phantasms of Living* I. 6 We call the owner of the impressing mind the *agent*, and the owner of the impressed mind the *percipient*. **1898** *Month* Jan. 52 *note*, Intimate personal relations between the writer and the percipient of the vision. **1955** *Sci. Amer.* Oct. 116/3 As a result of extensive tests, mainly involving two extraordinarily gifted 'percipients' in the business of card guessing, Soal and his co-worker Bateman were converted from doubt to ardent belief. **1966** K. R. RAO *Exper. Parapsychol.* i. 6 The hypothesis that the *percipient*, not the agent, is the likely initiator of the psi experience. **1974** *Listener* 3 Jan. 22/2 Some of the target images were lantern-slides... The guessers or 'percipients' were asked to try to draw the image.

percive, obs. form of PERCEIVE.

perclose, obs. variant of PARCLOSE *sb.*

†**perclose**, obs. var. PARCLOSE *v.*, to enclose; to close, conclude.

1535 *St. Papers Hen. VIII*, II. 260 At Chester we receyved letters from Mr. Brabazon, whiche we send you herin perclosed. **1538** *Ibid.* III. 73 Which if we may have before the perclosing of this letter, your Lordship shall have them herin inclosed. **1542** *Ibid.* 437 At the perclosing of your saide Treasorers laste accompte. **1558** *Cal. Anc. Rec. Dublin* (1889) I. 472 After the same..accompt perclosed and no surplusage fonde.

†**perco'arcted**, *ppl. a. Obs. rare*[−0]. [f. PER- 2 + COARCTED.]

1623 COCKERAM, *Percoarcted*, brought into a narrow roome.

†**per'coct**, *v.* *Obs. rare.* [f. L. *percoct-*, ppl. stem of *percoquĕre*, f. PER- 2 + *coquĕre* to boil, cook.] *trans.* To boil or heat through or thoroughly. So **per'coct** *ppl. a.* [ad. L. *percoctus* pa. pple.], *fig.* 'overdone', hackneyed.

1635 SWAN *Spec. M.* vi. (1643) 302 The heat of the sunne percocting those waters which are extreamly salt. **1657** TOMLINSON *Renou's Disp.* 715 Turpentine..may be added when the Salve is percocted. **1879** G. MEREDITH *Egoist* II. xi. 246 To abstain from any employment of the obvious, the percoct,..likewise..the overstrained.

percoid ('pɜːkɔɪd), *a.* and *sb.* *Ichthyol.* [mod. f. L. *perca* + -OID: first in F., in pl. *Percoïdes*, Cuvier's name for the perch family of acanthopterygious fishes (*Percidæ*).]

a. *adj.* Resembling or akin to a perch; belonging to the perch family of fishes. **b.** *sb.* A fish of the perch family. So **per'coidean** *a.* and *sb.*; **per'coideous** *a.*

[**1840** *Penny Cycl.* XVII. 431/2 *Percidæ*, or *Percoïdes* of Cuvier. *Ibid.*, The first division of the Percoïdes, according to Cuvier, comprises [etc.].] *Ibid.* 433/1 In the fifth division of Percoïd fishes the ventral fins are placed in advance of the pectorals. **1846** SMART Suppl. s.v., Percoids are a tribe of acanthopterygian fishes, of which the perch is the type. **1851** GOSSE *Nat. in Jamaica* 190 It was of a percoid form.. and about a foot in length. **1887** *Athenæum* 9 July 58/3.

percolate ('pɜːkələt), *sb.* [ad. L. *percōlāt-um* strained, neuter pa. pple. of *percōlāre*: see next.] A product of percolation.

1885 C. G. W. LOCK *Workshop Receipts* Ser. IV. 205/2 Each successive part of the percolate lessens the sugar in the percolator. **1898** *Rev. Brit. Pharm.* 7 The alcohol is recovered from the last two percolates, and the residual extract dissolved in the reserved percolate.

percolate ('pɜːkəleɪt), *v.* [f. L. *percōlāt-*, ppl. stem of *percōlāre*, f. *per* PER- 1 through + *cōlāre* to strain, f. *cōl-um* a strainer.]

1. a. *trans.* To cause (a liquid) to pass through the interstices of a porous body or medium; to strain or filter (naturally or artificially). Loosely, To cause (a finely divided solid) to trickle or pass through pores or minute apertures, to sift. Now *rare.*

1626 BACON *Sylva* §396 Springs on the Tops of High-Hills are the best: For..they..are more Percolated thorow a great Space of Earth. **1658** EVELYN *Fr. Gard.* (1675) 292 You shall percolat it through a sieve or course cloath. **1715** tr. *Pancirollus' Rerum Mem.* I. IV. x. 190 Strainers, through which they percolated Snow to cool their Wines. *c* **1842** LANCE *Cottage Farmer* 23 Oatmeal..undressed, percolated between the fingers into boiling water.

b. *fig.*

a **1677** HALE *Prim. Orig. Man.* II. i. 129 The Evidences of Fact are as it were percolated through a vast Period of Ages, and many very obscure to us. **1808** BENTHAM *Sc. Reform* 48 Double-refined, and treble-refined, by being percolated through the lips and pens of Commissioners and Commissioners' Clerks, and Agents, and Writers to the Signet. **1970** P. LAURIE *Scotland Yard* iv. 92 Churchill's funeral was ten years' planning, and it probably contained, percolated through a succession of intermediate heroes, elements of Nelson's. **1978** *Time* 6 Nov. 28/2 Connecticut's Ella Grasso, the first woman to win a governorship in her own right, says these victories will percolate women into office in a few years.

c. To prepare (coffee) in a percolator.

1966 *New Statesman* 3 June 819/1 First found percolating stale morning coffee in his office. **1974** 'J. Ross' *Burning of Billy Toober* xiv. 127 Rogers made the mortuary in twenty minutes, not stopping to shave or percolate coffee. **1978** N. J. CRISP *London Deal* v. 72 The man-servant was percolating coffee.

2. a. *intr.* Said of a liquid: To pass through a porous substance or medium; to filter, ooze, or trickle through.

1684 BOYLE *Porousn. Anim. & Solid Bod.* vi. 94 A tradition, that in..the West Indies they have..large Vessels, wherein they put water to percolate, as it were, through a strainer. **1687** A. LOVELL tr. *Thevenot's Trav.* II. 62 Through these Jars the Water transpires and percolates into an earthen Vessel underneath. **1726** SWIFT *Gulliver* III. v, Extracting the nitre, and letting the aqueous or fluid particles percolate. **1813** BAKEWELL *Introd. Geol.* (1815) 109 The caverns have been formed by the agency of water percolating through natural fissures. **1878** HUXLEY *Physiogr.* 24 The water which has percolated through the sandy beds.

b. *fig.* (cf. *filter*, *trickle*.)

1867 LEWES *Hist. Philos.* (ed. 3) II. 399 That influence.. has percolated down to the most ordinary intelligences. **1876** GLADSTONE *Homeric Synchr.* 251 The worship of Isis had percolated at several points into the Greek Peninsula. **1934** C. LAMBERT *Music Ho!* III. 185 Oriental influences.. have percolated naturally through these racial frontiers. **1935** B. MALINOWSKI *Coral Gardens* II. VI. 244 The magic percolates,..so that practically everybody in the village knows it. **1977** P. D. JAMES *Death of Expert Witness* III. 128 News percolated through a village community by a process of verbal osmosis.

3. *trans.* Of a liquid: To ooze or filter through (a porous body or medium); to permeate.

1794 SULLIVAN *View Nat.* I. 258 It suffers that rain to percolate the earth. **1799** KIRWAN *Geol. Ess.* 118 Water percolating the pores of the basalt. **1885** R. BUCHANAN *Master of Mine* vii, It was actually percolated with sea-water oozing through the solid granitic mass.

fig. **1865** MERIVALE *Rom. Emp.* VIII. lxvii. 306 A senate.. so freely percolated by the blood of the lower classes. **1965** *New Statesman* 7 May 737/2 One reason why this has so slowly percolated British consciousness..is British reporting.

4. *intr.* To walk, to stroll. *U.S. slang.*

1942 Z. N. HURSTON in A. Dundes *Mother Wit* (1973) 223/1 Then he would..percolate on down the Avenue. **1945** L. SHELLY *Jive Talk Dict.* 15/2 *Percolate*, to meander.

Hence **'percolated** *ppl. a.*; **'percolating** *vbl. sb.* and *ppl. a.*; ***percolating filter***, a type of filter used in the treatment of sewage, usu. after the removal of suspended solids, consisting of a bed of inert, porous material such as crushed rock through which the sewage is allowed to percolate, so that noxious organic matter is removed by aerobic micro-organisms.

1694 'S. S.' *Loyal & Impart. Satirist* 22 In you Socratick Wisdom do's survive And flow with purer percolated streams. **1864** W. K. TWEEDIE *Lakes & Rivers of Bible* i. 20 Like percolating water it [bitumen] exudes through the veins into the wells. **1872** C. KING *Mountain. Sierra Nev.* ix. 191 Under the influence of the..constant percolating of surface waters. **1880** GEIKIE *Phys. Geog.* iv. 246 Limestone is liable to be dissolved and removed by percolating rain-water. **1901** S. BARWISE *Bacterial Purification of Sewage* iv. 37 The Commissioners in their Report speak of two artificial filtration processes—Contact Beds and Continuous Filtration. In this book I have adopted the phrase 'Percolating Filters', instead of that of 'Continuous Filters', because some of the continuous filters are worked intermittently, and intermittent continuous filtration is a verbal contradiction. **1936** [see BACTERIUM 2]. **1972** *Water Research* VI. 781 In the United Kingdom conventional sewage treatment by sedimentation plus secondary treatment by percolating filters or activated sludge plants is not normally adequate to provide an effluent acceptable for re-use.

percolater, var. PERCOLATOR.

percolation (pɜːkəʊ'leɪʃən). [ad. L. *percōlātiōn-em*, n. of action from *percōlāre* to PERCOLATE.] The action or process of percolating.

a. The action of straining or filtering a liquid through some porous material; filtration; *spec.* in *Pharmacy*, the process of obtaining an extract by passing successive quantities of a dissolving liquid through a pulverized substance until all the soluble matters are extracted (= DISPLACEMENT 3 c).

1613 PURCHAS *Pilgrimage* v. xiii. 512 This freshnesse of the springes..may rather be ascribed to percolation and strayning through the narrow spongie passages of the earth. **1626** BACON *Sylva* §3 It seemeth Percolation or Transmission, (which is commonly called Straining) is a good kinde of Separation, Not onely of Thick from Thin.. But of more subtile Natures. **1799** *Med. Jrnl.* I. 402 The.. utility of Mr. Collier's new machines for percolation. **1822** T. TAYLOR *Apuleius* 207 She defecates, by percolation, the precious wine. **1885** C. G. W. LOCK *Workshop Receipts* Ser. IV. 198/1 Percolation..is a kind of filtration, commonly called 'by displacement', employed for extracting the essence from roots, herbs, seeds, barks, &c.

b. The action of passing, as a liquid, through the interstices of some porous body or substance; an oozing through.

1646 SIR T. BROWNE *Pseud. Ep.* II. i. 56 Petrifications, or Minerall indurations, like other gemmes proceeding from percolations of the earth disposed unto such concretions. **1799** KIRWAN *Geol. Ess.* 378 Dense strata of clay..alone could detain the sea water, and prevent its percolation. **1841–71** T. R. JONES *Anim. Kingd.* §838 (ed. 4) 345 The chyle or nutritive material extracted by the food exudes..by a species of percolation, through the walls of the intestine.

1862 DANA *Man. Geol.* 662 The waters..reach the ocean only by percolation through the beach.

†**c.** *Phonetics.* Used of the emission of the breath through a narrow opening between two of the organs of speech, in producing vocal sounds. *Obs.*

1668 WILKINS *Real Char.* III. x. 361 Percolation of the breath betwixt both the Lips contracted round-wise which makes the vocal whistling sound. *Ibid.*, Percolation of the breath between the top of the Tongue and the roots of the Teeth. **1711** J. GREENWOOD *Eng. Gram.* 254 Letters framed by a percolation or straining of the Breath through a kind of Chink betwixt the Tongue and upper Teeth.

d. *fig.*

1660 JER. TAYLOR *Duct. Dubit.* II. ii. rule ii, If we list to observe that..Pythagoras..and Socrates had great names amongst the leading Christians, it is no wonder if in the percolation something of the relish should remain. **1873** *Daily News* 27 Aug., People grow weary of waiting for the slow percolation of that doctrine through the official mind.

e. *attrib.*

1895 *Daily News* 8 Oct. 9/5 A paper was read..on 'The Relative Value of Percolation Gauges'. **1899** CAGNEY tr. *Jaksch's Clin. Diagn.* i. 94 The greater ease with which watery blood neutralises the acid..in the percolation tests.

percolative (ˈpɜːkəleɪtɪv), *a. rare.* [f. PERCOLATE *v.*: see -ATIVE.] Having the quality of percolating or allowing percolation.

1863 *Jrnl. R. Agric. Soc.* XXIV. II. 579 Separating the retentive soils from the percolative, water-bearing soils.

percolator (ˈpɜːkəleɪtə(r)). Also percolater. [Agent-n., in L. form, from *percōlāre* to PERCOLATE.] **a.** One who or that which percolates. **b.** An apparatus for percolating or straining a liquid; a filter or strainer: (*a*) for straining coffee; (*b*) for obtaining an extract by percolation (see PERCOLATION a). Also *attrib.*

1842 FRANCIS *Dict. Arts, Percolator,* a filtering machine. **1845** E. ACTON *Mod. Cookery* xxvii. 647 It will be stronger if slowly filtered in what is called a percolator, or coffee-biggin, than if it be boiled. **1857** HENFREY *Bot.* §653 Through these tissues the juices freely percolate..they act as percolators. **1861** MRS. BEETON *Bk. Househ. Managem.* 875 Let the coffee be freshly ground..; put it into a percolater, or filter,..and pour *slowly* over it..boiling water. **1869** *Pattern Bk. Copper, etc., Ware* (H. Loveridge & Co.) 103 Coffee Percolators. **1871** 'M. LEGRAND' *Cambr. Freshm.* xiv. 238 Taking occasional sips of black coffee—at making which, in a patent percolator, Mr. Samuel had become..quite a proficient. **1885** C. G. W. LOCK *Workshop Receipts* Ser. IV. 198/2 Gradually pour into the percolator sufficient of the..liquid to be filtered, to drive before it, or 'displace', the liquid contained in the mass. **1958** *Times* 6 Nov. 12/6 If we wanted a pint of essence of ginger, we just put 10 oz. of powdered Jamaica ginger into a percolater, and allowed sufficient rectified spirit to pass through to collect a pint. **1963** *B.S.I. News* May 35 Electric coffee percolators. **1978** L. DEIGHTON *SS-GB* xv. 126 She tipped the coffee into the percolator top, closed the lid and set it on the heat.

c. *transf.* (*a*) A carburettor; (*b*) a house-rent party (HOUSE *sb.*[1] 24); loosely, any party. *U.S. slang.*

1942 BERREY & VAN DEN BARK *Amer. Thes. Slang* §82/4 *Carburetor,* carb, jug, juicer, juice pot, mixer, percolator, pot, sifter. **1946** R. BLESH *Shining Trumpets* xiii. 303 The great South Side institution of 'rent party' (locally known as 'skiffle', 'shake', or 'percolator'). **1956** S. LONGSTREET *Real Jazz* xvi. 126 You could always..get together..and charge a few coins and have..a percolator. **1967** PARTRIDGE *Dict. Slang* Suppl. 1289/2 '*To have a shake, rave or percolator*..to have a party' (Anderson): beatniks': since ca. 1959. **1971** M. TAK *Truck Talk* 117 *Percolator,* the carburetor. **1974** H. L. FOSTER *Ribbin'* iv. 141 In Chicago, these parties were called a 'parlour social', 'gouge', 'struggle', 'percolator', 'too terrible party', or the 'skiffle'.

percollice, -collois, obs. ff. PORTCULLIS.

percomorph (ˈpɜːkəmɔːf), *a.* and *sb. Ichthyol.* [f. mod.L. *Percomorphi* pl., f. L. *perca*, Gr. πέρκη, PERCH *sb.*[1] + Gr. -μορφος, f. μορφή form.] **a.** *adj.* Belonging to the order *Percomorphi* of Cope, comprising most of the spiny-finned fishes. **b.** *sb.* A fish of this order. So **perco'morphic, perco'morphous** *adjs.*

1885 COPE *Orig. Fittest* xi. (1887) 330 The double bony floor of the skull of the Distegous percomorph fishes is a complication which places them at the summit of the line of true fishes.

percontation (ˌpɜːkɒnˈteɪʃən). *rare.* [ad. L. *percontātiōn-em*, n. of action from *percontāre*, *-ārī* to inquire, interrogate.] A questioning, inquiry. So **percontatorial** (pəkɒntəˈtɔərɪəl) *a.*, given to, or pertaining to, questioning; inquisitive.

1623 COCKERAM, *Percontation,* an enquiry. **1656** STANLEY *Hist. Philos.* VIII. (1701) 310/1 Percontation is a thing for which we cannot answer significantly, as Interrogation, *yes*: but as thus, *He dwelleth in such a place.* **1835-8** S. R. MAITLAND *Dark Ages* ii. (1844) 24 Between a percontation and interrogation, the ancients made this distinction—that the former admitted a variety of answers, while the latter must be replied to by 'yes' or 'no'. **1853** THACKERAY *In United States,* This percontatorial foible has grown with the national growth. **1861** *Sat. Rev.* 18 May 496 The forms of the house, on putting a question, do not admit the percontatorial process to be continued.

percophid (ˈpɜːkəfɪd). *Ichthyol.* [f. mod.L. *Percophidæ* pl., f. *Percophis* (f. L. *perca*, Gr. πέρκη PERCH *sb.*[1] + Gr. ὄφις serpent): see -ID[3].] A fish of the family *Percophidæ* (typical genus *Percophis*), allied to perches, but with elongated body and pointed head. So **'percophoid** *a.*, belonging to this family; *sb.* = *percophid.*

†**per'cribrate,** *v. Obs. rare.* [f. L. *percrībrāt-*, ppl. stem of *percrībrā-re* to sift thoroughly, f. PER- 2 + *crībrāre* to sift, f. *crībrum* a sieve, f. root *cer-*, *cr-*, of *cernere* to sift + instrumental suffix *-brum.*] *trans.* To pass through or as through a sieve, to sift. So †**percri'bration,** passage through or as through a sieve.

1664 POWER *Exp. Philos.* I. 59 The bloud is so divided by the minuteness of their Capillary Vessels, or percribration through the habit of the Parts. **1668** H. MORE *Div. Dial.* II. xviii. (1713) 145 Thy Brain thus blown up by the percribrated influence of thy moist Mistress, the Moon. **1681** GLANVILL *Sadducismus* II. (1726) 378 Instances of their easy percribration through porous bodies.

†**per'cruciate,** *v. Obs. rare*[−0]. [f. L. *percruciāre*, f. PER- 2 + *cruciāre* to torment: see CRUCIATE.]

1656 BLOUNT *Glossogr., Percruciate,* to torment greatly.

perculace, -cullas, -cullice, etc., obs. ff. PORTCULLIS.

perculsion (pəˈkʌlʃən). *rare.* [f. L. type **perculsiōn-em*, f. *perculs-*, ppl. stem of *percellĕre* to upset, strike with consternation, etc.]

†**a.** Consternation, shock of mind or feeling. *Obs.* **b.** A physical stroke or shock. So †**per'culsive** *a. Obs.*, characterized by giving a shock.

1609 BP. W. BARLOW *Answ. Nameless Cath.* 20 As the paines are vnsufferable to flesh and blood, so haue they a very perculsiue force euen vpon the Soule. **1657** REEVE *God's Plea* Ep. Ded. 9 They are not yet come to her dejections, trepidations, perculsions. **1822-34** *Good's Study Med.* (ed. 4) IV. 176 An ovulum, detached..by the force of the orgastic perculsion.

†**per'cunctorily,** *adv. Obs. nonce-wd.* [irreg. f. PER- + L. *cunctārī* to delay, loiter, after *perfunctorily.*] In a loitering manner, lazily.

1615 T. ADAMS *Blacke Devill* 27 This is he that makes men serue God percunctorily, perfunctorily—to go slowly to it, to sit idly at it.

percur (pəˈkɜː(r)), *v. rare.* [ad. L. *percurrĕre* to run through, f. PER- 1 + *currĕre* to run: cf. *concur*. Cf. F. *parcourir.*] *trans.* To run through, traverse (either of actual motion, or of extension).

1657 TOMLINSON *Renou's Disp.* 285 A leaf..with three strokes percurring its longitude. **1835** URE *Philos. Manuf.* 384 The fan produces its greatest effect when the points of its wings percur in revolving about eighty feet per second.

†**percu'rration.** *Obs.* [erron. f. PERCUR *v.* + -ATION, for **percursion.*] A running through.

1785 *Gentl. Mag.* LV. I. 265, I have chosen the Empire of Russia as the theatre of my percurrations.

percurrent (pəˈkʌrənt), *a. rare.* [ad. L. *percurrent-em*, pr. pple. of *percurr-ĕre*: see PERCUR.] Running through; continuing or extending throughout, or from one end to the other; *spec.* in *Bot.* said of a midrib or other nerve extending from the base to the apex of a leaf.

1578 BANISTER *Hist. Man* I. 32 All the motions.. excellently percurrent, and yet at length to cease, or end at these bones. **1882** OGILVIE (Annandale), *Percurrent,* running through from top to bottom. **1886** *Cassell's Encycl. Dict., Percurrent,* running through. Obsolete, except in botany.

percursory (pəˈkɜːsərɪ), *a. rare.* [f. L. *percursor* one who runs through: see -ORY[2].]

a. Characterized by running through something rapidly or hastily. **b.** *humorously.* Running or moving swiftly along.

1837 LOCKHART *Scott* vii. (1839) I. 289 He visited some of the finest districts of Stirlingshire and Perthshire;..not in the percursory manner of his more boyish expeditions. **1864** J. LEECH in J. Brown *Horæ Subs.* (1882) 40 Look at the tail of his descending friend's horse. Look at another's percursory 'Lincoln and Bennett' bowling along!

percuss (pəˈkʌs), *v.* [f. L. *percuss-*, ppl. stem of *percutĕre* to strike or thrust through, f. PER- 1 + *quatĕre* to shake, strike, dash, etc.]

†**1.** *trans.* To strike so as to shake or give a shock to; hence *gen.* to strike, hit, knock, give a blow to. Also *fig. Obs.* (in general sense).

1560 ROLLAND *Crt. Venus* II. 146 Percust he was into perplexitie. **1615** G. SANDYS *Trav.* 6 Earth quakes percussed, men with the affright. **1626** BACON *Sylva* §117 Solid Bodies, if they be very softly percussed, give no Sound. **1694** MOTTEUX *Rabelais* v. (1737) 229 Our Auricles, percuss'd by Fame sonorous.

2. *Med.* To tap or strike gently (some part of the body) with the finger or an instrument, for purposes of diagnosis, or of therapeutics.

1834 J. FORBES *Laennec's Dis. Chest* (ed. 4) 17 When we percuss comparatively the two sides of the chest. **1897** *Allbutt's Syst. Med.* II. 382 The joints or muscles affected, may be percussed, pressed or moved with impunity.

b. *absol.* or *intr.*

1849-52 TODD *Cycl. Anat.* IV. 1034/1 Percussing over the 5th rib at its junction with its cartilage. **1883** T. L. BRUNTON in *Nature* 8 Mar. 437/2 Thus he percusses rapidly over a nerve when the pain is dull or grinding, and percusses slowly when the pain is acute.

Hence **per'cussed** *ppl. a.* (in *Her.* = PERCUSSANT); **per'cussing** *ppl. a.*

1572 BOSSEWELL *Armorie* II. 42 [Lions] are borne... Their tayles forked,..descendante, percussed, and contercoloured. **1665** HOOKE *Microgr.* 55 Storms, or Oars, or other percussing bodies. **1897** *Allbutt's Syst. Med.* IV. 656 The sound produced by the impact of the percussing finger on the one percussed.

percussant (pəˈkʌsənt), *a. Her.* [f. as PERCUSS *v.* + -ANT, after other heraldic adjs. as *passant*, *rampant*, etc.] Said of the tail of a lion or other animal when represented as bent round as if lashing its side: cf. *percussed* in prec.

c **1828** BERRY *Encycl. Her.* I. Gloss., *Percussant,* or *Percussed,*..sometimes applied to the tail of a lion, or other animal, when lying on the back or side, as if he were beating and striking himself therewith. **1889** in ELVIN *Dict. Her.*

percussion (pəˈkʌʃən), *sb.* [ad. L. *percussiōn-em*, n. of action from *percutĕre*: see PERCUSS. Cf. F. *percussion* (14th c. in Littré), perh. the immediate model.]

1. a. The striking of one body with or against another with some degree of force, so as to give a shock; impact; a stroke, blow, knock. Usually in reference to solid bodies; more rarely to liquids, or to air (as producing sound). Chiefly in scientific use. ***centre of percussion***: see CENTRE *sb.* 16.

1544 PHAER *Regim. Lyfe* C vij, Sometyme the sayde payne [of the eye] commeth by percussion or strykynge. **1603** HOLLAND *Plutarch's Mor.* 1348 He saith: That we doe.. heare by the percussion and beating of the aire. **1654** R. CODRINGTON tr. *Iustine,* etc. 561 Antoninus Verus..did die by a percussion of blood in the head, which Disease the Greeks call the Apoplexy. **1669** *Phil. Trans.* IV. 1088 The Doctrine of Percussion on which depends that of the Cuneus or Wedge. **1794** G. ADAMS *Nat. & Exp. Philos.* III. xxxi. 259 Percussion puts all the parts of the wood into a tremulous motion. **1822** IMISON *Sc. & Art* II. 29 No heat seems to follow from the percussion of liquids in soft bodies. **1879** *Cassell's Techn. Educ.* IV. 146/2 Fulminating silver, even when moist, will explode by percussion.

b. *transf.* and *fig.*: *e.g.* the striking of sound upon the ear; the ictus or rhythmic 'beat' in verse; the stroke of an 'evil eye', etc.

1607 SHAKS. *Cor.* I. iv. 59 With thy grim lookes, and The Thunder-like percussion of thy sounds Thou mad'st thine enemies shake. **1625** BACON *Ess., Envy* (Arb.) 511 The Times, when the Stroke, or Percussion of an Enuious Eye doth most hurt, are, when the Party enuied is beheld in Glory. **1674** tr. *Rapin's Refl. Aristotle's Treat. Poesie* Pref. 13 In the Italian and Spanish..all the Rimes are dissyllable, and the percussion stronger.

2. Specific applications.

a. The striking of a fulminating powder, or *percussion-cap* (see 5), so as to produce a spark and explode the charge in a fire-arm. Also *concr.*, a percussion gun.

1810 *Sporting Mag.* XXXVI. 273 He used one of Forsyth's gun-locks, which, flintless, goes off by percussion. **1821** P. EGAN *Real Life in London* I. i. 8 My new patent double-barrelled percussion. **1829** tr. P. W. Schmidt (1824) in *Jrnl. Franklin Inst.* 100 On some kinds of fulminating powder inflammable by percussion and their use in fire-arms. **1846** GREENER *Sci. Gunnery* 90 Percussion has been for some years introduced into the service, for igniting the charge of all large guns.

b. *Med.* The action of striking or tapping with the finger, or with a small hammer (*percussion-hammer*) upon a part of the body, either to ascertain the condition of some internal organ by the sound produced, or for therapeutic purposes.

If the stroke is made directly upon the body, it is called ***immediate percussion***; if upon something placed against the body (e.g. a finger of the other hand, or a small instrument made for the purpose), ***mediate percussion***.

1834 J. FORBES *Laennec's Dis. Chest* (ed. 4) 471 Percussion of the thorax yielded a much clearer sound on the right than on the left side. **1843** R. J. GRAVES *Syst. Clin. Med.* Introd. Lect. 16 How much has the treatment of pectoral diseases been improved by the application of auscultation and percussion? **1893** *Syd. Soc. Lex.* s.v., Medical percussion was known to Hippocrates, but was only used in abdominal diseases. It was not until the time of Auenbrugger that its use was suggested for diseases of the chest.

c. ***instrument of percussion***: a musical instrument that is played by percussion or striking.

Mostly applied to those used chiefly or solely for marking rhythm, and either struck with a stick or the hand (as the drum, triangle, tambourine), or struck together in pairs (as cymbals); rarely to stringed instruments in which the strings are struck by hammers. Hence *percussion* is sometimes used collectively for the instruments of percussion in an orchestra, or their players (cf. *strings, wind, wood*).

1776 BURNEY *Hist. Mus.* (1789) I. 255 Musical instruments chiefly of percussion. **1838** *Penny Cycl.* XII. 498 *Instruments, Musical,* are, 1. *Keyed,* as the Organ, Piano-forte, etc.;..4. of *Percussion,* as the Drum, Cymbals, etc. **1889** G. B. SHAW *How to become Mus. Critic* (1960) 164 Brass and percussion [are] behind the wood wind and under the stage. **1904** *Daily News* 25 Feb. 8/5 Almost all the strings are pupils of the conductor, and the wind and percussion are prominent members of London orchestras.

d. A device in some reed-organs by which a small hammer is caused to strike the reed as the air is admitted to it, thus quickening the production of the sound.

1879 A. J. Hipkins in Grove *Dict. Mus.* I. 667 Another major invention was that of Martin, who gave the harmonium..'quicker speech', i.e. made the sound more quickly follow the descent of the key. The invention is known as 'percussion'.

e. ***bulb of percussion***: see bulb *sb.* 4 b.

3. *Mus.* The actual 'striking' or sounding of a note or chord, esp. of a discord, as distinguished from *preparation* and *resolution*.

1880 C. H. H. Parry in Grove *Dict. Mus.* II. 685 *Percussion*..is the actual sounding of the discord.

†**4.** *Chiromancy.* A name for the outer edge of the palm of the hand: see quots. *Obs.*

1644 Bulwer *Chirol.* 75 The hand thus closely shut and the fingers all turned in... The nether part..Chiromancers call the pomell or percussion. **1653** R. Sanders *Physiogn.* 14 The percussion is the outer part, which moves when we strike anything. *Ibid.* 116 Such lines in the percussion of the hand denote drowning.

5. *attrib.* and *Comb.* Of, for, pertaining to, or worked by percussion; *esp.* made or constructed so as to be ignited or exploded by percussion (cf. 2 a), as ***percussion arm, bullet, fuse, gun, match, primer, tube***; belonging to, used for, or produced by medical percussion (sense 2 b), as ***percussion blow, dullness*** (= dull sound), ***hammer, massage, note, resonance, sound, stroke, thrill, tone***; **percussion cap**, a small copper cap or cylinder containing fulminating powder, exploded by the percussion of a hammer so as to fire the charge of a fire-arm; **percussion drill**, a drill worked by percussion; **percussion figure**, a characteristic figure produced by a blow with a pointed instrument on a thin plate of certain crystals; **percussion grinder**, 'a machine for crushing quartz or other hard material by a combined rubbing and pounding process' (Knight *Dict. Mech.*); **percussion instrument** = *instrument of percussion*: see 2 c; **percussion-lock**, a form of lock for a fire-arm in which the charge is fired by means of a *percussion cap*; **percussion powder**, the powder used in percussion caps, consisting, since *c* 1823, of mercury fulminate, previously composed chiefly of perchlorate of potash; **percussion-sieve**, an apparatus for sorting ores according to size by means of two inclined sieves which are agitated by levers (Knight); **percussion-stop**, a draw-stop in a reed-organ which puts the percussion (2 d) into action; **percussion-table**, an apparatus for sorting ores according to weight, consisting of a slightly inclined table or frame which is shaken intermittently by a mechanical appliance.

1844 *Regul. & Ord. Army* 104 The *Percussion Arm does not require so much repair as the Flint Musket. **1823** *Specif. J. Day's Patent* No. 4861 Nipple or spill to receive the copper *percussion caps. **1895** Guttmann *Manuf. Explos.* II. 275 Percussion caps were first made by Joseph Egg, an English gun-maker, in 1815. **1892** Greener *Breech-Loader* 2 The percussion-cap gun was a great improvement on the flint-lock, and although its day was short, it may be regarded as the most durable gun ever made. **1890** W. J. Gordon *Foundry* 43 The hard whinstone is excavated by *percussion drills and dynamite. **1904** *Daily Chron.* 13 June 6/3 Special rules..including one prohibiting the use of percussion rock-drills in hard stone. **1875** Knight *Dict. Mech.*, **Percussion-fuse*, a fuse in a projectile set in action by concussion when the projectile strikes the object. **1879** *Cassell's Techn. Educ.* IV. 122/2. **1827** J. Shaw in *Jrnl. Franklin Inst.* 283 The slowest powder was much the safest in the *percussion gun. **1819** *Trans. Soc. Arts* XXXVI. 80 *Percussion gun-lock. Silver medal voted to Mr. Collinson Hall. **1898** *Allbutt's Syst. Med.* V. 212 Percussion..with a pleximeter and *percussion-hammer..yields a clear metallic sound. **1872** Yeats *Techn. Hist. Comm.* 53 The Egyptians had many of the wind, stringed, and *percussion instruments at present known. **1829** in *Reg. Deb. Congress U.S.* (1831) 21st Congress 2 Sess. App. p. xcii/2 I have used the *percussion locks but little, but believe them admirably well constructed for general use. **1845** Mrs. Carlyle *Lett.* I. 356 A pair of pistols with percussion-locks. **1887** D. Maguire *Art of Massage* (ed. 4) ii. 20 His *percussion massage is nothing more than that employed by the ancients. **1880** Barwell *Aneurism* 73 *Percussion notes were dull on the inner two inches of the clavicle and in a semicircle extending down to the first rib. **1819** T. B. Johnson *Shooter's Comp.* 102 *Percussion powder..ignites with a blow. **1825** Col. Hawker *Instr. Yng. Sportsmen* (ed. 4) 77 Mr. Joyce..establishing a manufactory of this anticorrosive percussion powder in which he does away entirely with the oxymuriate. **1824** *Franklin Inst. Rep.* in *Mech. Mag.* III, Joshua Shaw's improved *percussion primers. **1838** *Civil Eng. & Arch. Jrnl.* I. 358/1 When the percussion primer strikes. **1876** *Trans. Clinical Soc.* IX. 110 Over the right side the *percussion-resonance was normal. **1868** *Rep. to Govt. U.S. Munitions War* 28 Full-cock the hammer, pull the trigger, causing the hammer to strike the *percussion-slide.., forcing it against the rim of the cartridge, and exploding it. **1875** Knight *Dict. Mech.*, **Percussion-stop*, a piano-forte stop to the organ, which renders the touch like the former. **1853** Markham tr. *Skoda's Auscult.* 21 The fluid in the cavity is disturbed by the *percussion-stroke, and a sound, similar to the movement of saliva in the mouth, is then produced. **1875** Knight *Dict. Mech.*, **Percussion-table.* **1881** Raymond *Mining Gloss.*, *Percussion-table.* **1870–93** S. Gee *Auscult. & Percuss.* iii. (ed. 4) 75 *Percussion Thrill. A peculiar quivering sensation..sometimes produced by percussion. **1839** J. Marsh in *Jrnl. Franklin Inst.* XXIII. 114 *Percussion tubes for cannon.

Hence **per'cussional** *a.*, of or pertaining to percussion; **per'cussionize** *v.* = percussion *v.*

1776 Hawkins *Hist. Music* I. iii. vii. 341 His [Cassiodorus'] division of instrumental music..into three parts, namely, percussional, tensile, and inflatile. **1832** G. T. Vigne *Six Months in Amer.* II. 76 In New York..a gunmaker had put over his door, 'Flint and steel guns altered and percussionized'.

per'cussion, *v.* [f. prec. sb.] *trans.* **a.** To fit (a fire-arm) for being fired by percussion (see prec. 2 a). **b.** To treat with percussion massage. Hence **per'cussioning** *vbl. sb.* (in both senses); **per'cussioner,** (*a*) a workman employed in percussioning fire-arms; (*b*) an instrument used in percussion massage.

a. 1846 Greener *Sci. Gunnery* 176 The percussioning of a gun, (as the fitting in of nipple, boring breeches, filing cocks, &c. is termed). **1881** —— *Gun* 250 When percussioned the gun is shot at a target. *Ibid.*, In the days of muzzle-loaders the percussioner's branch was a very important one.

b. 1887 D. Maguire *Art of Massage* (ed. 4) ii. 32 They use..the properly called percussioner,..a bundle of birch branches. *Ibid.* iii. 47 That the part being percussioned should become accustomed..to the manipulation. The ways of percussioning are numerous.

percussionist (pəˈkʌʃənɪst). [f. percussion *sb.* + -ist.] †**a.** One who uses a percussion gun. *Obs.*

1817 *Sporting Mag.* L. 45 He deals in death blows as a percussionist, By his patent detonating, weather proof, water proof, fire proof guns.

b. A player of a percussion instrument.

1950 Webster Add. p. cxix, *Percussionist*, one skilled in the playing of percussion instruments. **1955** L. Feather *Encycl. Jazz* 256/1 His use of the top cymbal..was imitated by countless other percussionists. **1962** *Times* 18 Apr. 7/6 In the course of the piece everybody is a percussionist. **1969** *Daily Tel.* 15 Feb. 15/1 A truly professional percussionist rather than just another polished, expert drummer. **1977** *Listener* 18 Aug. 216/1 In the second programme they had Tristram Fry, the percussionist.

per'cussive (pəˈkʌsɪv), *a.* (*sb.*) [f. L. *percuss-*, ppl. stem of *percutĕre* (see percuss) + -ive.] Having the property of striking; of, pertaining to, characterized by, or connected with percussion.

1793 Holcroft tr. *Lavater's Physiogn.* xiii. 69 Great original and percussive power. **1800** Vince *Hydrostat.* xi. (1806) 114 The same body will always give the same tone, whether the percussive stroke be greater or less. **1857** H. Spencer *Ess.* I. 24 The first musical instruments were without doubt percussive. **1876** Bristowe *Th. & Pract. Med.* (1878) 415 The auscultatory and percussive phenomena..may differ little if at all from those which attend capillary bronchitis. **1882** *Rep. to Ho. Repr. Prec. Met. U.S.* 595 Percussive machinery that expends its force on metal.

B. *sb.* A musical instrument of percussion.

1890 in *Cent. Dict.*

Hence **per'cussively** *adv.*, **per'cussiveness.**

1863 A. M. Bell *Princ. Speech* 162 In *upbraid, upborne, upmost*, ..&c., ..the *P* is a mere stop of the voice and loses its final percussiveness. **1890** *Cent. Dict.*, *Percussively.* **1958** *Times* 9 Oct. 7/1 The tense percussiveness of Bartok's concerto. **1970** *Daily Tel.* 16 June 14/2 He lets unfold..a veritable rhapsody of percussiveness (by no means just Brahms's in E flat) and reveals the soul in staccato. **1976** *Gramophone* Sept. 424/1 Queffélec, however, never plays with the almost brutal percussiveness of Bernstein.

per'cussor (pəˈkʌsə(r), -ɛ(r)). [a. L. *percussor* a striker, etc., agent-n. from *percutĕre*: see percuss *v.* Cf. mod.F. *percusseur* (Littré).] One who or that which percusses or strikes; *spec.* a small instrument for medical percussion, a percussion-hammer.

1890 in *Cent. Dict.* **1896** *Allbutt's Syst. Med.* I. 374 Dr. Granville's percussor.

percutaneous (pɜːkjuːˈteɪniːəs), *a.* [f. L. *per cutem* through the skin + *-aneous*, after *cutaneous*: cf. *circumforaneous, subterraneous.*] Made, done, or effected through the skin. Hence **percu'taneously** *adv.*, through the skin.

1887 *Amer. Jrnl. Psychol.* Nov. 184 Percutaneous stimulation..gave results with somewhat greater irregularity. **1902** *Brit. Med. Jrnl.* 12 Apr. 929 A man, who injected something into the larynx percutaneously. **1904** *Ibid.* 17 Sept. 39 The so-called percutaneous sutures.

per'cute, *v.* [a. F. *percute-r*, ad. L. *percutĕre*: see next.] *trans.* = percuss *v.* 2; esp. in massage.

1887 D. Maguire *Art of Massage* (ed. 4) iv. 98 After having..frictioned and percuted the muscles of the neck.

percutient (pəˈkjuːʃ(ɪ)ənt), *a.* and *sb.* ? *Obs.* [ad. L. *percutient-em*, pr. pple. of *percutĕre* to strike through, etc.: see percuss.] **a.** *adj.* Striking, percussive. **b.** *sb.* Something that strikes; the striking agent or body.

1626 Bacon *Sylva* §190 Where the Aire is the Percutient, ..against a Hard Body, it never giveth an Exteriour Sound. **1656** tr. *Hobbes' Elem. Philos.* (1839) 347 The velocity of the percutient is to be compared with the magnitude of the ponderant. **1666** *Phil. Trans.* I. 306 The Vehemence of the Percussion depends as much upon the length of the percutient Body, as upon the velocity of the Motion.

Percy (ˈpɜːsɪ). The masculine Christian name used, freq. with connotations of weakness or effeminacy, as a representative name for **a.** a conscientious objector; **b.** (see quot. 1932); **c.** in the armed services, an officer or an educated man.

1916 G. B. Shaw in *Nation* 27 May 258/2 Mobbed and pilloried and photographed in the 'Daily Sketch' as 'Percy' (all Percies are now—shade of Hotspur!—supposed to be cowards). **1932** E. Weekley *Words & Names* 91 *Percy*..is still used in the United States of the typical young Englishman. **1961** Partridge *Dict. Slang* Suppl. 1217/2 *Percy*, in the Royal Navy, has, since ca. 1925, meant an effeminate man; but since ca. 1940, also and esp. a studious, quiet, educated man as opposed to an uncouth 'tough'. **1974** 'B. Mather' *White Dacoit* xxi. 216 Most of the young Percies in our mob had to take their boots off to count up to twenty. *Ibid.* xxiii. 237 There's a young Percy in charge... The Percy says to one of them, 'What's your unit, my man?'

percyl(l, -cyly, obs. forms of parsley.

percylite (ˈpɜːsɪlaɪt). *Min.* [Named by Brooke, 1850, after Dr. Percy, who analysed it: see -lite.] An oxychloride of lead and copper, found in minute sky-blue cubical crystals (but see quot. 1974).

1850 *Philos. Mag.* Ser. iii. XXXVI. 131. **1889** *Min. Mag.* VIII. 172 The crystals are..percylite. **1974** *Mineral. Rec.* V. 286 We believe that type percylite has been shown to be a mixture [of boleite and pseudoboleite] and that the same is true of percylites from other major localities.

Percynne, obs. form of Persian.

†**perd.** *Obs. rare*$^{-1}$. [app., from the rime, for *pert, perte*, a. OF. *perde, perte* = It. *perdita* 'loss':—late L. or Romanic **perdita* sb. from pa. pple. of L. *perdĕre* to lose. (OF. had also a rare masc. form *perd, pert*:—L. type *perditum*.)] Loss.

c **1330** R. Brunne *Chron. Wace* (Rolls) 3841 Non wolde helpe restore his perd [*rime* pouert].

perdao, -au, -aw, var. pardao *Obs.*, E. Indian coin.

perde, obs. form of pard, a panther.

perdicine (ˈpɜːdɪsaɪn), *a.* *Ornith.* [f. mod.L. *perdicin-us* in *Perdicinæ* (sc. *aves* birds), f. L. *perdix, -icem* partridge.] Of or related to a partridge; pertaining to the subfamily *Perdicinæ* of the family *Phasianidæ*, of which *Perdix*, the partridge, is the typical genus.

1890 in *Cent. Dict.*

†**perdicle.** *rare*$^{-0}$. In 5 -ycle. A name for some precious stone: app. aetites or eagle-stone.

c **1440** *Promp. Parv.* 394/1 Perdycle, precyous ston, *ethites*.

‖**per'dido.** *Obs. rare*$^{-1}$. [Sp. *perdido* adj. lost, used as subst.: see perdue.] A desperado.

a **1734** North *Exam.* iii. vi. §70 (1740) 475 The Duke of Monmouth, with his Party of Perdidos, had a Game to play which would not shew in quiet Times.

perdie (†**perde, -ee**), var. pardie, 'by God'.

†**'perdifoil, 'perdifol.** *Obs. rare.* [Anglicized from mod.L. *perdifolius*, f. *perd-ĕre* to lose + *folium* leaf.] A plant which annually loses its leaves; a deciduous plant. So †**perdi'folious** *a.*, deciduous; not evergreen.

1657 Tomlinson *Renou's Disp.* 269 Its leaves are perdifolious; it germinates every year [*sed perdifolia et quotannis germinans*]. **1727** Bailey vol. II, *Perdifols*, Plants that shed their leaves. **1775** Ash, *Perdifol*, a plant that drops its leaves in winter. **1803** B. S. Barton *Elem. Bot.* ii. 66 The Passion-flower of America and the Jasmine of Malabar, are evergreens in their native climates, but become perdifoils when they are transplanted into Britain.

perdigie, obs. erroneous form of prodigy.

perdigwena, variant of perdrigon *Obs.*

†**per'diligent,** *a.* *Obs. rare*$^{-1}$. [ad. L. *perdīligent-em*: see per-^{1} 4.] Very diligent. Hence †**per'diligence,** thorough diligence.

1694 Motteux *Rabelais* v. xxiii. 105 Your..Industry internected with perdiligent Sedulity, and sedulous Perdiligence.

†**perdi'sturb,** *v.* *Obs. rare*$^{-1}$. [f. per- 2 + disturb *v.*] *trans.* To disturb or hinder greatly.

1538 Fitzherb. *Just. Peas* 103 Yf any perdisturbe or let the execution of this acte [etc.].

†**'perdit, 'perdite,** *a.* *Obs. rare.* [ad. L. *perdit-us*, pa. pple. of *perdĕre* to lose: see perdition.] Lost to virtue; abandoned, wicked.

a **1632** T. Taylor *God's Judgem.* ii. vii, A young man of a most perdit and debaucht course of life. **1645** Pagitt *Heresiogr.* (1662) 286 The most perdite sort of men.

Hence †**'perditly** *adv.*, (*a*) in a wicked manner, abandonedly, (*b*) desperately [cf. L. *perdite amare* to be desperately in love].

a **1632** T. TAYLOR *God's Judgem.* II. iv. (1642) 50 Omphale..of whom he was perditly enamoured. **1637** HEYWOOD *Dialogues* ii. Wks. 1874 VI. 118 A thousand times had rather wish to die, Than perditly to affect one base and vile.

perdition (pəˈdɪʃən). Also 4 -cyun, 4–6 -cion, -cioun, etc. [ME. a. OF. *perdiciun* (11th c. in Littré), *perdicion*, F. *perdition*, ad. L. *perditiōn-em*, n. of action from *perdĕre* to make away with, destroy, lose; f. PER- 3 + *dare* to give, put.]

1. The fact or condition of being destroyed or ruined; utter destruction, complete ruin. Now *rare*.

a **1340** HAMPOLE *Psalter*, etc. 520 (Deut. xxxii. 35) Bisyde is þe day of perdicyun. **1382** WYCLIF *ibid.*, Nyȝ is the day of perdicioun [Vulg. *dies perditionis*; COVERD., the tyme of their destruccion is at honde]. —— *Prov.* vi. 15 To this anoon shal come his perdicioun, and sodeynli he shall be to-treden [Vulg. *perditio sua*; COVERD. destruccion, 1611 calamity]. **1456** SIR G. HAYE *Law Arms* (S.T.S.) 87 The parting of him and his company out of the ost, put all the lave in poynt of perdicioun. *a* **1548** HALL *Chron., Hen. VII* 27 b, What losse & perdicion of many noble Capitaynes and stronge souldiours must..ensue at the assaute. **1604** SHAKS. *Oth.* II. ii. 3 Certaine tydings..importing the meere perdition of the Turkish Fleete. **1643** tr. *Hildanus' Exper. Chyrurg.* iv. 9 A great Combustion..leaveth behinde it a..withered scarre, by reason of the perdition and contraction of the skin. **1682** SIR T. BROWNE *Chr. Mor.* II. §7 A Man may be cheaply vitious, to the perdition of himself. **1829** W. IRVING in *Life & Lett.* (1864) II. 371, I trust in a few days to finish the narrative of the invasion and perdition of Spain.

†**b.** In affected or rhetorical use: Loss, diminution, lessening. *Obs.*

1599 SHAKS. *Hen. V*, III. vi. 103 The perdition of th'athuersarie hath beene very great, reasonnable great. **1602** —— *Ham.* v. ii. 117 Sir, his definement suffers no perdition in you. **1610** —— *Temp.* I. ii. 30 There is no soule, No not so much perdition as an hayre Betid to any creature in the vessell.

†**c.** That wherein ruin or destruction lies; the 'ruin' of anything. *Obs.* or *arch.*

c **1625** MILTON *Ode Death Fair Infant* x, To turn Swift-rushing black perdition hence. **1649** JER. TAYLOR *Gt. Exemp.* II. Ad Sect. xii. 93 Free revellings, carnivals and balls, which are the perdition of precious hours. **1718** ROWE tr. *Lucan* x. 94 Thou lewd perdition of the Latian name!

2. *Theol.* The condition of final spiritual ruin or damnation, the future condition of the wicked and finally impenitent or unredeemed; the fate of those in hell, eternal death.

(A special theological application of the word, which has led to its disuse in the general sense.)

1382 WYCLIF *John* xvii. 12 No man of hem perischide, no but the sone of perdicioun [Vulg. *nisi filius perditionis*]. —— *Phil.* i. 28 The which is to hem cause of perdicioun [*gloss*, or of damnacioun, TINDALE, a token of perdicion]. **1432–50** tr. *Higden* (Rolls) III. 123 This Antecriste..is callede the son of perdicion. **1563** *Homilies* II. *Nativity* (1859) 407 Children of perdition and inheritors of hell fire. **1614** RALEIGH *Hist. World* I. vi. §3. 85 [They] daylie trauaile towards their eternall perdition. **1781** COWPER *Hope* 387 If appetite, or what divines call lust,..Be punished with perdition, who is pure? **1869** BROWNING *Ring & Bk.* XI. 2283 Would you send A soul straight to perdition, dying frank An atheist?

b. In imprecations. (Cf. *damnation*.)

1604 SHAKS. *Oth.* III. iii. 90 Excellent Wretch: Perdition catch my Soule But I do loue thee. *a* **1619** FLETCHER *Bonduca* III. v, Perdition Take me for ever, if in my fell anger, I do not out-do all example. **1841** LANE *Arab. Nts.* I. 106 'Perdition to unfaithful wives!' **1894** R. BRIDGES *Feast of Bacchus* II. 566 Perdition take me now!

†**c.** The place of destruction or damnation. *Obs.*

In Wyclif, after the Vulgate, rendering Hebr. *abaddōn* the place of perishing, Hades; in Coverdale and 1611 rendered 'destruction'.

1382 WYCLIF *Job* xxviii. 22 Perdicioun and deth seiden, With oure eris wee han herd the fame of it. —— *Prov.* xxvii. 20 Helle and perdicioun neuere ben fulfild. —— *Ps.* lxxxvii[i]. 12 [11] Whether sum man shal telle in sepulcris thi mercy; and thi treuthe in to perdicioun. **1667** MILTON *P.L.* I. 47 Flaming from th' Etherial Skie With hideous ruine and combustion down To bottomless perdition.

3. *Comb.* **perdition-money**: see quot.

1683 BARNARD *Heylin* lvi. 173 The exacting of Sconses or perdition mony, which he [as Treasurer of Westminster] divided among them that best deserved it, who diligently kept Prayers, and attended upon other Church Duties.

Hence **perˈditionable** *a.*, deserving perdition.

1827 POLLOCK *Course T.* III. 529 Wild, blasphemous, perditionable thoughts, That Satan in them moved.

†**perˈditious**, *a. Obs. rare*⁻¹. [irreg. f. prec. after *ambitious*, etc.] Given over to perdition.

1609 DEKKER *Raven's Alm.* D iij b, The faster that fire-workes are throwne amongst these perditious children the lowder will grow their rage.

‖**ˈperdix.** The Latin word for 'partridge', retained in the Douay Bible, and used in Ornithology as a generic name: see PARTRIDGE, PERDICINE.

1609 BIBLE (Douay) *1 Sam.* xxvi. 20 The king of Israel is come forth to seeke one flea, as the perdix is pursued in the mountaines. **1840** *Penny Cycl.* XVII. 435/2 The genus *Perdix*, Briss...is made to contain the subgenera *Perdix*..*Chætopus*..*Coturnix*..*Ptilopachus*..and *Ortyx*.

perdon(e, -oun, obs. forms of PARDON.

ˈperdricide. *humorous nonce-wd.* [f. F. *perdrix* partridge + -CIDE 1.] A partridge-killer: in quots. appositive = Partridge-killing.

1826 SYD. SMITH *Wks.* (1859) II. 79 The perdricide criminals are more numerous than the violators of all the branches of the Decalogue. **1837** C. LOFFT *Self-formation* II. 129 When I..heard from my perdricide comrades there the tale of their September exploits. **1864** *Q. Rev.* CXVI. 203 No 'perdricide' gentleman could..imagine that [etc.].

†**ˈperdrigon.** *Obs.* (Also 6 perdigwena, 8 padrigon.) [a. F. *perdrigon* (Littré), in 16th c. *perdigoine*, in Cotgr. *perdigonne*, in Pr. *perdigon*, *perdrigon*, properly 'young partridge', according to Littré and Hatz.-Darm. from its colour.] A variety of plum, black, violet, or white (Littré), formerly highly valued for its flavour.

1599 HAKLUYT *Voy.* II. 165 Of later time was procured out of Italy..the plumme called the Perdigwena. **1664** EVELYN *Kal. Hort.* (1729) 233/2 Plums, Perdrigon, White, Blue, Primordial, Reine Claud. **1727** BRADLEY *Fam. Dict.* s.v. *Exposition to Sun*, The White perdrigon which we esteem one of our best plums. **1733** MILLER *Gard. Dict.* s.v. *Prunus*, The Violet Perdrigon Plum. **1770** FOOTE *Lame Lover* III. 62 A damascen plum..does pretty well indeed in a tart, but..to compare it with the queen mother, the padrigons..the green-gages, or the orlines. **1884** HOGG *Fruit Manual* 730.

perdu, perdue (pəˈdjuː, ˈpɜːdjuː, ‖pɛrdy), *a.* and *sb.* (Also 7 pur-due; par-, perdieu, -dew.) [a. F. *perdu* 'lost, perished; forlorne, past hope of recouerie, cast away' etc. (Cotgr.); app. originally introduced in the Fr. military phrase *sentinelle perdue*, and so usually spelt *perdue*; in later times often (now usually) treated as an alien Fr. word, and written *perdu* or *perdue*, according to gender.]

A. *adj.* (or *pa. pple.*).

†**1.** In ***sentinel perdue, perdue sentinel*** (called by Barret 1598 *forlorne sentinell*): **a.** The post of a sentinel (see SENTINEL *sb.* 1) in a very advanced and dangerous position, where he can hardly hope to escape death. **b.** A sentinel posted in such a position. *Obs.*

(Quot. 1591 is punctuated 'breaches in espials, in sentinels, perdues'; if this is right, the quot. belongs to B. 1.)

1591 *Garrard's Art Warre* I. 1 In Trenches, where perchance hee shall stand a number of houers in the water and myre vp to the knees: and besides vp on the Bulwarkes, breaches, in espials, in Sentinels perdues, and such like, when occasion requires and necessitie constraines. [**1598** BARRET *Theor. Warres* IV. ii, The proper *forlorne Sentinell* is that which is set either on horse-backe or foote..neare vnto the enemies campe:..so neare vnto the enemie, that being discryed and seene, he shall with great difficulty retire and escape.] **1628** BURTON *Anat. Mel.* Democr. to Rdr. (ed. 3) 32 So many..desire to enter vpon breaches, lye sentinell perdue, giue the first onset [etc.]. *a* **1648** LD. HERBERT *Life* (1764) 74 Sir Edward Cecill..used often during this Siege, to go in person in the night time, to try whether he cou'd catch any Sentinells perdues. **1688** R. HOLME *Armoury* III. xix. (Roxb.) 149/2 A Perdue sentinell is..layd down in the open field, where he lyeth on his belly with his eare to the ground to heare what he can from the enemy.

2. In other connexions:

†**a.** Placed in an extremely hazardous position, such as that of a 'forlorn sentinel', or a 'forlorn hope'; hence, in a desperate case, lost. *Obs.*

1618 FLETCHER *Loyal Subj.* I. i, *Putf.* How stand you with him [the Duke], Sir? *Theod.* A perdue captain, Full of my father's danger. **1653** GAUDEN *Hierasp.* 235 Where..peevish cavils and pertinacious calumnies,..do but rally themselves, as in a case *perdue*, to see what can be done by volleys of rayling Rhetorick. **1656** BLOUNT *Glossogr.*, *Perdu*, lost, perished, forlorn, past hope of recovery, cast away.

†**b.** Lying out, passing the night out of bed. *Obs.*

1634 CAREW *Cœl. Brit.* Wks. (1824) 154 Though it be to the surprize of a perdu page or chambermaid.

c. Lying hidden; hidden, concealed; disguised. Now chiefly as Fr.

a **1734** NORTH *Exam.* I. ii. §160 (1740) 113* The Trick of a Brace of perdue Witnesses, charged and primed in order to a short Turn. **1837** H. AINSWORTH *Crichton* II. ii, A Huguenot perdue in the Louvre.

3. In phrase ***to lie perdu***. (Also, ***to set, leave, stand,*** etc. ***perdu***.) Now chiefly as Fr.

a. In military usage: Placed as an outpost, sentinel, guard, scout, etc., in an exposed, hazardous position; hidden and on the watch; (lying) in ambush, in wait, in order to surprise or attack. Often *transf.* or *fig.*

1607 B. BARNES *Divils Charter* E iv b, This very night must I stand *Perdue* for this bloudy service. **1611** BEAUM. & FLETCHER *King & No King* I. i. **1624** MASSINGER *Bond-man* II. i, There's a sport too, Named lying perdue..'tis a game Which you must learn to play at. *a* **1625** FLETCHER *Woman's Prize* I. iii, I'll stand *perdue* upon 'em. **1628** WITHER *Brit. Rememb.* IV. 761 Suggestion lay pur due by Contemplation, And sought to disadvantage Meditation. **1629** SHIRLEY *Wedding* IV. iii, Let's steal away before we be discovered. I do not like when men lie perdu. **1642** FULLER *Holy & Prof. St.* IV. ix. 278 It is unfitting he should lie Perdue, who is to walk the round. *a* **1668** DAVENANT *Siege* Wks. (1673) 82 A Weezel That lies Perdue for a Hens Nest. **1678** BUTLER *Hud.* III. iii. 34 This Hudibras..by the Furies, left Perdue. *a* **1716** SOUTH *Serm.* (1727) VI. xii. 418 If a Man is always upon his Guard, and (as it were) stands perdieu at his Heart, to spy when Sin begins to peep out in these first Inclinations. **1767** STERNE *Tr. Shandy* IX. xvi, Bridget stood perdue within, with her finger and her thumb upon the latch, benumb'd with expectation. **1837** WHITTOCK, etc. *Bk. Trades* (1842) 287 Overtaken in his solitary career, lying 'perdue' behind some tree, or bush. **1884** *Manch. Weekly Times* 11 Oct. 4/6 Probably in the village inn a skilful penny-a-liner is lying *perdu*..to get a scrap of their conversation.

b. Hidden away; concealed; out of sight, withdrawn from sight. Now usually as Fr., spelt *perdu* or *perdue* according to gender. (*a*) Of persons.

1701 J. PHILIPS *Splendid Shilling* (1715) 6 This Caitif..oft Lies perdue in a Nook or gloomy Cave. **1754** RICHARDSON *Grandison* (1781) I. xxv. 174 Mr. Greville was not gone out of town, but intended to lie perdue. **1819** SCOTT *Leg. Montrose* xiv, Hold..We must lie perdue, if possible. **1855** CARLYLE *Misc.*, *Prinzenraub* (1857) IV. 345 They seek shelter in a cavern, stay there perdue for three days. **1855** BROWNING *Instans Tyrannus* iii, All in vain! Gold and jewels I threw, Still he couched there perdue. **1870** MISS BROUGHTON *Red as Rose* xiv, She has been lying *perdue*,..deeply buried in the unwonted luxury of a French novel.

(*b*) Of things, qualities, etc.

1758 *Misc.* in *Ann. Reg.* 373/2 The ingenious author tells us..the general's intention remains *perdu*. **1809** W. IRVING *Knickerb.* III. ii. (1849) 150 A host of honest, good-fellow qualities..which had lain perdue. **1876** BESANT & RICE *Gold. Butterfly* Prol. i, Hidden in the belt of each, or carried *perdu* in the trouser's-pocket. **1893** SELOUS *Trav. S.E. Africa* 441 [It] had lain perdu in my head all that time.

†**B.** *sb. Obs.* [Partly short for *sentinel perdue* or F. *enfants perdus*, see below, 2 c; partly elliptical or contextual uses of the phrases in A. 3: cf.

c **1600** BACON *Apol. conc. Ld. Essex* 61 Madame..you haue put me like one of those that the Frenchmen call *Enfans perdus*, that serue on foote before horsmen.]

†**1.** = *sentinel perdue*, A. 1 a. *Obs. rare.*

1611 TOURNEUR *Ath. Trag.* II. vi, I would you would relieue me, for I am So heauie that I shall ha' much adoe To stand out my perdu.

†**2.** A soldier placed in a position of special danger, as an outlying sentinel, or ordered on some hazardous enterprise, as to act as scout or skirmisher, lead in an assault, etc., and hence considered as virtually lost or in a desperate case. *Obs.*

1605 SHAKS. *Lear* IV. vii. 35 (Quarto) To watch, poor Perdu With this thin helme. **1614** C. BROOKE *Trag. Rich. III* xlii, The centynels are plac't; *perdu's* are sent. **1632** B. JONSON *Magn. Lady* III. iv, Your old Perdues, who, after time, do think..that they are shot-free. **1638** *Mass. Hist. Collect.* Ser. III. VI. 6 Having..laid out our pardues, we betook ourselves to the guard. **1648** in Rushw. *Hist. Coll.* IV. II. 1173 Our Purdues lie so near the Enemy, as to hear them discourse. **1681** L. ADDISON *Disc. Tangier* 7 The Earl in person every night laid Perdues to prevent Surprisals. **1706** PHILLIPS, A *Perdue*, a Sentinel or Soldier plac'd in an advanced and dangerous Post.

fig. *a* **1641** SUCKLING *Completion Writing Shaks.* Poems (1646) 30 Out of the bed the other fair hand was On a green sattin quilt..There lay this pretty perdue, safe to keep The rest o' th' body that lay fast asleep.

b. *collectively.* The body of troops on outpost duty; the watch, guard. *Obs.*

1622 T. SCOTT *Belg. Pismire* 31 Such are the Guard, the Sentinell, the Watch, the Perdu for the Common-wealth. **1654** H. L'ESTRANGE *Chas. I* (1655) 69 During this siege, there was taken by the English perdu, a French man [etc.].

c. *pl.* = FORLORN HOPE [F. *enfants perdus*]; a body of soldiers selected for a specially hazardous military duty. *Obs.*

c **1610** SIR J. MELVIL *Mem.* (1683) 15 The King..sent a number of Infantry Perdews to his Trenches, to bring on the Skirmish. **1611** COTGR. s.v. *Perdu*, *Enfans perdus*, perdus: or the forlorne hope, of a campe (are commonly Gentlemen of Companies). **1614** SYLVESTER *Bethulia's Rescue* v. 327 Two thousand Perduz first Give bravely th' Onset. **1656** BLOUNT *Glossogr.*, *Perdues*,..the forlorn hope of a Camp,..are so called, because they are given for lost men, in respect of the danger of their service.

d. *transf.* One who acts as a watcher, scout, or spy. *Obs.* (From 3 a.)

1639 FULLER *Holy War* v. xxii. 267 Poland..lying constant perdue of Christendome against the Tartarian. **1650** —— *Pisgah* II. 57 Shepheards lying constant Perdues in defence of their flocks. *a* **1661** —— *Worthies*, *Northumbld.* II. (1662) 314 The Sheriffs..who in effect, lay constant Perdues against the neighbouring Scots. *a* **1700** B. E. *Dict. Cant. Crew* s.v. *Budge*, *Standing Budge*, c. The Thieves Scout or Perdu. *a* **1734** NORTH *Exam.* II. iv. §116 (1740) 292 Sir William Waller the Perdue, was the Discoverer..and, by his Diligence, the Man taken and sent to Newgate.

e. *transf.* A person in a lying or crouching posture. *Obs. rare.*

1681 COTTON *Wond. Peak* (ed. 4) 33 Eccho tir'd with posting, does refuse To carry to th' inquisitive Perdu's That couchant lye above, the trembling news.

†**3.** A morally abandoned person; a desperado; a profligate, a roué. *Obs.*

1612 CHAPMAN *Widdowes T.* II. i. Wks. 1873 III. 23 Profane Ruffins, Squires to Bawds & Strumpets,..Debaucht perdu's.

†**perdu, perdue**, *v. Obs. rare.* [f. prec. sb.]

1. *intr.* (with *it*). To lie *perdu*, act the part of a *sentinel perdue*, act warily.

1656 S. H. *Gold. Law* 33 Thus the Lord Fairfax did no wrong; but wisely Sentinel'd and Perdu'd it to prevent Surprisals, and the better to surprize his Surprizers.

2. *trans.* (*refl.*) To place in ambush, hide.

1658 R. FRANCK *North. Mem.* (1821) 61 An ordinary Artist may kill a trout, provided he purdue himself at a reasonable distance.

†**per'duce**, *v. Obs.* [ad. L. *perdūc-ĕre* to lead, bring through, f. PER- 1 + *dūcĕre* to lead.] *trans.* To bring on, lead on; to induce.

1570 FOXE *A. & M.* (ed. 2) 1932/1 You might easely be perduced to acknowledge one Church with vs. **1610** GUILLIM *Heraldry* III. xvii. (1660) 205 By the motion of the Feet our bodies are perduced from place to place. **1657** TOMLINSON *Renou's Disp.* 298 Exsiccating ulcers and perducing them to a skar. **1665** HARVEY *Advice agst. Plague* 26 Carbuncles..easily perduced to a laudable maturation.

So †**per'duction** [ad. L. *perductiōn-em*, n. of action from *perdūcĕre*]. *Obs. rare*$^{-0}$.

1656 BLOUNT *Glossogr., Perduction*, a bringing or leading through.

†**perduell.** *Obs. rare*$^{-0}$. [ad. L. *perduellis* a public or private enemy, f. PER through + *duellis* a warrior.]

1623 COCKERAM, *Perduell*, a strong stubborne enemie.

perduellion (pɜːdjuː'ɛlɪən). *Rom.* and *Sc. Law.* [ad. L. *perduelliōn-em*, f. *perduellis*: see prec.] Hostility against the state or government; treason. (*Obs.* in *Sc. Law.*)

1533 BELLENDEN *Livy* I. x. (S.T.S.) 60 This law of perduellioun was of maist horribil cryme. **1693** *Apol. Clergy Scot.* 61 On the 13th of October 1582, the Assembly of the Church at Edenburg, did by an Act approve of that perduellion [the Capture of the King]. **1774** BP. HALLIFAX *Anal. Rom. Law* (1795) 130 The punishment of Perduellion was 1. *Ultimum Supplicium*, or Natural Death of the Criminal. **1818** SCOTT *Hrt. Midl.* xii, I am of opinion..that this rising..to take away the life of a reprieved man, will prove little better than perduellion.

So †**per'duellism** [a. Fr. *perduellisme* 'Treason against Prince or Countrey' (Cotgr.)].

1656 BLOUNT *Glossogr., Perduellion*, or *Perduellism*, treason against the King or Country.

[**perdulous** in Johnson, copied in later Dicts.; spurious word (misprint for PENDULOUS).]

perdun(e, obs. form of PARDON.

perdurability (pədjʊərə'bɪlɪtɪ). Also 5 -blyte, -blete, -bylyte. [In ME. a. OF. *par-, perdurablete* (12th c. in Godef.). The mod. word is a new formation from *perdurable*.] The quality of being perdurable; continuous duration; everlastingness; permanence. In mod. use chiefly in *Philos.*

c **1374** CHAUCER *Boeth.* II. pr. vii. 45 (Camb. MS.) Natheles..as many yeeres as ther-to may be multyplyed ne may nat certes ben comparysoned to the perdurablyte þat is endeles. **1413** *Pilgr. Sowle* (Caxton 1483) IV. xxiii. 69 This is nought in thyn choys, nouther qualite ne quantite, ne perdurabylyte of thy peyne. **1483** CAXTON *Gold. Leg.* 345/2 That by that forme the perdurablete of theire Goddes sholde be shewed.

1865 MILL *Exam. Hamilton* 192 Something which is distinguished from our fleeting impressions by what, in Kantian language, is called Perdurability. *a* **1873** —— *Ess. Relig.* (1874) 200 Substance is but a general name for the perdurability of attributes. **1877** BOWEN *Mod. Philos.* xv. 269 What is this necessary axiom..but the perdurability of material substance?

perdurable (pə'djʊərəb(ə)l, 'pɜːdjʊərəb(ə)l), *a.* Also 5–6 par-. [a. OF. *per-, pardurable* (12th c. in Godef.) = Pr. *perdurable*, It. *perdurabile*, ad. late L. *perdūrābilis* (Boeth.), f. *perdūrāre*: see PERDURE and -BLE. Very rare from *a* 1660 to 1800, and by Johnson considered obs.; common again in 19th c.] Enduring continuously, lasting, permanent; everlasting, as measured by human life or human history.

c **1250** [implied in PERDURABLY]. *c* **1374** CHAUCER *Boeth.* II. met. iii. 27 (Camb. MS.) It is certeyn and establyssed by lawe perdurable þat nothinge þat is engendred nys stedefast ne estable. **1387–8** T. USK *Test. Love* II. viii. (Skeat) I. 87 The thank of a people..procedeth of no wyse jugement; never is it stedfast pardurable. **1430–40** LYDG. *Bochas* VIII. Prol. (1558) 1 b, For to make our names perdurable. *c* **1460** FORTESCUE *Abs. & Lim. Mon.* xiv. (1885) 142 Perdurable livelod ffor the sustentacion off his estate. *a* **1548** HALL *Chron., Hen. VI* 141 b, Gain is not alwaies perdurable, nor losse alwaies continuall. **1599** SHAKS. *Hen. V*, IV. v. 7 O perdurable shame, let's stab our selues. **1645** MILTON *Colast.* Wks. 1738 I. 305 What thing in the nature of a Covenant shall bind the other to such a perdurable mischief? **1806** H. SIDDONS *Maid, Wife, & Widow* I. 204 A friendship ..of a more perdurable nature than a thousand of those which are daily moulded out of bows, smiles, curtesies. **1814** SOUTHEY *Roderick* XVI. 287 Leaving a name perdurable on earth. **1865** MILL *Exam. Hamilton* 199 The existence of a perdurable basis of sensations. **1880** T. HODGKIN *Italy & Inv.* III. viii. II. 540 [That] so vast and perdurable a structure as the Roman Empire could utterly perish.

b. *esp.* (in theological lang.) Everlasting, eternal, as opposed to things of this world and of time.

c **1386** CHAUCER *Pars. T.* ¶1 The blissful lif that is perdurable. *c* **1450** *Merlin* 93 In soche maner that thow lese not the lif perdurable. *a* **1536** *Calisto & Melib.* in Hazl. *Dodsley* I. 64 The mighty and perdurable God be his guide. **1657–82** EVELYN *Hist. Relig.* (1850) I. iii. §5. 248 The material and perishing substance can never comprehend what is immaterial and perdurable. **1882–3** in *Schaff's Encycl. Relig. Knowl.* III. 2525/1 The separate and perdurable personality of man.

c. Of material things: Able to withstand wear or decay; imperishable; lasting indefinitely.

c **1374** CHAUCER *Boeth.* I. pr. i. 2 (Camb. MS.) Hyr clothes weeren maked of riht delye thredes and subtil craft of perdurable matere. **1586** FERNE *Blaz. Gentrie* II. 20 Black.. is the most perdurable of all other colours. **1604** SHAKS. *Oth.* I. iii. 343, I confesse me knit to thy deseruing, with Cables of perdurable toughnesse. **1624** HEYWOOD *Gunaik.* VI. 294 Having perdurable monuments raised to her as well in Babilon as in Athens. **1816** SOUTHEY *Lay of Laureate* xiv, Sculpture there had done her fitting part, Bidding the forms perdurable arise Of those great Chiefs. **1849** JAMES *Woodman* xix, I am of granite..hard and perdurable.

Hence **per'durableness** (*rare*), the quality of being perdurable; perdurability.

1628 COKE *On Litt.* I. i. §11 Our Author speaketh here of the amplenesse, and greatnesse of the estate, and not of the perdurablenesse of the same. **1727** in BAILEY vol. II. **1858** *Sat. Rev.* 13 Mar. 259/1 One more proof of the perdurableness of aristocracies.

perdurablete, obs. form of PERDURABILITY.

perdurably (see PERDURABLE), *adv.* Also 3 par-. [f. PERDURABLE *a.* + -LY², or directly after the OF. adv. *pardurablement*.] In a perdurable manner; permanently, lastingly; everlastingly, eternally.

c **1250** *O. Kent. Serm.* in *O.E. Misc.* 31 Ne for þo litle sennen, þet no man hine ne mai loki nis noon deseu[e]rd pardurableliche fram gode, ne fram holi chereche. *c* **1374** CHAUCER *Boeth.* v. pr. iv. 128 (Camb. MS.) Thilke same symple forme of man þat is perdurablely in the dyuyne thoght. *a* **1450** *Knt. de la Tour* (1868) 70 That she wolde not late hem reyne euer in that synne, to be loste perdurably. **1509** HAWES *Past. Pleas.* (Percy Soc.) 208 That after your lyfe frayle and transitory You may than live in joye perdurably. **1603** SHAKS. *Meas. for M.* III. i. 115 If it were damnable,..Why would he for the momentarie tricke Be perdurably fin'de? **1872** P. BAYNE *Days of Jezebel* I. i. 3 Promise-words..should be like to those Left perdurably graven in the rock By Sidon's cunning workmen.

perdurance (pə'djʊərəns). Now *rare.* [a. obs. F. *par-, perdurance* (15–16th c.), f. *pardurant* pr. pple.: see -ANCE.] Permanence, duration.

1508 FISHER *Penit. Ps.* cii. Wks. (1876) 194 Ferre aboue the perduraunce of heuens, or of the erth. **1592** WYRLEY *Armorie, Ld. Chandos* 30 We..high honors plant as if perdurance had promised continuall showring. *a* **1650** MAY *Satir. Puppy* (1657) 59 Or else erect new Castles in the Air, and strengthen their foundation with half an hours perdurance longer then the former. **1875** VEITCH *Lucretius* 76 Space, Time, Cause, Identity, Perdurance, and other notions.

per'durant, *a. rare*$^{-1}$. [ad. L. *perdūrānt-em*, pr. pple. of *perdūrāre* to PERDURE: see -ANT. Cf. obs. F. *perdurant* (16th c. in Godef.).] Lasting, continuous, permanent.

1872 BLACKIE *Lays Highl.* 44 Nature hates perdurant peace.

†'**perdurate**, *v. Obs. rare*$^{-1}$. [f. L. *perdūrāre* (see next) + -ATE³.] = PERDURE *v.*

15.. *Christmas Carols* (Percy Soc.) 37 Christe, Secret in forme of bread, In mydst of us shall perdurate.

perduration (pɜːdjʊ'reɪʃən). *arch.* [Noun of action f. L. *perdūrāre* to PERDURE: cf. late L. *perdūrātio* (Gloss. Cyril. in Quicherat), and obs. F. *perduration*.] The action of enduring indefinitely; continuous duration, continuance.

1508 FISHER *Penit. Ps.* cii. Wks. (1876) 197 Almyghty god ..hauynge euerlastynge perduracyon, without begynnynge, without ende. **1603** HARSNET *Pop. Impost.* 116 To multiply the torments of helfire upon any Devil, unto immensity of weight and Infinity of Perduration. **1658** PHILLIPS, *Perduration*,..a lasting very long. **1825** *Blackw. Mag.* XVIII. 286 Happily such perduration of good or ill can be inflicted only in a fairy tale.

perdure (pə'djʊə(r)), *v.* [a. obs. F. *par-, perdurer*, ad. L. *perdūrāre*, f. PER- 2 + *dūrāre* to harden, endure, f. *dūrus* hard.] *intr.* To continue, endure, last on.

c **1450** *Cov. Myst.* (Shaks. Soc.) 254 ȝe wole not redresse Be mowthe ȝour dedys mortal but therin don perdure. **1590** GREENWOOD *Answ. Def. Read Prayers* 27 Yt was the chief part of their office, to perdure in the worde and prayer. **1854** HICKOK *Mental Philos.* 76 The mind perdures while its energizing may construct a thousand lines. **1963** J. WIESENFARTH *Henry James* iv. 91 The romp of Aggie and Petherton perdures through the conversation. **1973** BOILÈS & HORCASITAS tr. *M. León-Portilla's Time & Reality in Thought of Maya* ii. 33 For longer than a millennium and a half, not a little of Maya symbolism has perdured. **1979** *Nature* 22 Mar. 348/1 Thus enough maternal gene products (mRNAs or proteins) may perdure in embryonic cells to allow normal segmentation and cuticular differentiation.

Hence **per'during** *ppl. a.*, lasting, enduring continuously.

1501 DOUGLAS *Pal. Hon.* Epil. 6 Thy Maiestie mot haue eternallie..Felicitie perdurand in this eird. *a* **1600** *Flodden F.* vii. (1664) 68 And in perduring peace remain. **1890** J. SKINNER *Dissert. Metaphysics* 109 The Soul is revealed intuitively as a perduring living agent or entity. **1951** C. KLUCKHORN et al. in Parsons & Shils *Toward Gen. Theory Action* IV. 399 A value or values restrain or canalize impulses in terms of wider and more perduring goals. **1977** *Dædalus* Summer 63 The assignment and reassignment of meaning must be investigated as processes in the domain of resilience possessed by each population recognizing itself to be culturally perduring.

perdy, -dye, obs. forms of *perdie*, PARDIE.

pere, obs. f. PAIR, PEAR, PEER, PERRIE, PERRY¹, PIER.

‖**père** (pɛr). Also pere. [Fr., = father.]

1. Applied as a prefix to the name of a French priest; = FATHER *sb.* 6 e.

1619 J. CHAMBERLAIN *Let.* 30 Oct. (1939) II. 270 The Jesuites hold a chapter of theyre order at Rome whether Pere Coton is sent out of France. **1699** M. LISTER *Journey to Paris* 96, I bought the works of Pere Pezaron, a Bernadin, now Abbot de Charmoyse near Rheims. **1777** P. THICKNESSE *Year's Journey* I. xx. 174 Nor did the whole community afford but a single member (pere tender, a Fleming) who could speak French. **1879** R. L. STEVENSON *Trav. with Donkey* 119 There was Père Apollinaire hauling his barrow. **1978** *Times* 3 Nov. 7/1 (Advt.), The Sayings of Père Patriarche... 'To buy wine with uncertainty lacks any amusement.'

2. The father, senior: appended to a name to distinguish between a father and son of the same name. Cf. FILS.

1802 M. EDGEWORTH *Let.* 8 Dec. (1979) 58 M. Delessert père at a card table with another gentleman. **1858** O. W. HOLMES *Autocrat of Breakfast-Table* 28, I have not taken the trouble to date them, as Raspail, *père*, used to date every proof he sent to the printer. **1893** E. DOWSON *Let.* *c* 28 Nov. (1967) 299, I am dining with Horne & Horne Père at the Constitutional tonight. **1907** 'ELIZABETH' *Fraulein Schmidt & Mr. Anstruther* xxxiii. 120 Collins *père* is a person who makes nails in Manchester. **1948** E. S. TURNER *Boys will be Boys* v. 80 It will be seen that there was a Harkaway *père* and a Harkaway *fils*. **1964** *Guardian* 18 June 9/3 Everything about Tabarly père gives a kind of ageless impression of the sea... All this is highly relevant in considering Tabarly fils. **1972** J. WAIN in Cox & Dyson *20th-Cent. Mind* I. xi. 364 Yeats *père* moved his household many times, and William was educated in London or Dublin by fits and starts. **1977** *N.Y. Rev. Bks.* 10 Nov. 10/2 Zola père was a Venetian of distinguished family.

3. In phrases ***père de famille*** (də famij) [see FAMILLE], father of a family, family man; ***père et fils*** (e fis) [see FILS], father and son.

1820 M. EDGEWORTH *Let.* 14 May (1979) 124, I could not see in either his figure or face any hint of the young père de famille. **1853** *Thackeray Let.* in *Lett. A. T. Ritchie* (1924) iv. 52 The quantity of acquaintances and ½ acquaintances that as père de famille I did not care to make whole acquaintances. **1862** —— *Philip* II. ii. 33, I am secretly of the disposition of the time-honoured *père de famille* in the comedies. **1871** D. G. ROSSETTI *Let.* ? Aug. (1967) III. 963 Constant calls on Urizen père et fils..in the nature of supplications. **1962** *Observer* 1 July 19/4 Through this gate came Agamemnon the victim and Orestes the avenger, prototypes of the two Hamlets, *père et fils*. **1964** *Ibid.* 27 Sept. 24/6 A rather stuffy English *père de famille*. **1964** *House & Garden* Oct. 111/1 In this dual promotion *père et fils* certainly succeeded. **1973** I. BUTLER *Eldest Brother* viii. 78 The rôle of '*père de famille*' and respectable bourgeois. **1978** N. MARSH *Grave Mistake* iv. 113 You should hear the Rattisbons, *père et fils*, on the subject.

pereago, obs. form of PIRAGUA.

Père David (pɛr david). The name of Armand *David* (1826–1900), French missionary naturalist, used *attrib.*, in the possessive, or *absol.*, in **Père David('s) deer** to designate *Elaphurus davidianus*, a large, long-tailed deer discovered by him in China in 1865, named after him by A. Milne-Edwards in 1866, and now extinct in the wild in its native land, although it survives in zoological gardens and parks, esp. in a large herd at Woburn Abbey, Bedfordshire, established by the 11th Duke of Bedford soon after 1900.

[**1871** P. L. SCLATER in *Trans. Zool. Soc.* VII. 333 This fine animal is one of the many zoological discoveries which are due to the researches of M. le Père Armand David, Missionary of the Congregation of Lazarists at Pekin.] **1898** R. LYDEKKER *Deer of all Lands* 237 The general appearance of Père David's deer, when roaming in the park at Woburn Abbey, being quite unlike that of any other member of the group. **1927** G. JENNISON *Nat. Hist.: Animals* 290 It is known to Europeans as the Père David Deer from the Naturalist Missionary who discovered it in 1865. **1955** *Times* 11 May 12/7 Chief among them [*sc.* the Woburn deer] is the herd of 300 Père David's deer—a species now extinct in its native China and existing only at Woburn and in a few small offshoots (for example, at Whipsnade) from the Woburn herd. **1973** G. DURRELL *Beasts in my Belfry* v. 96 Undoubtedly the rarest animals in our care, a pair of young Père David deer. *Ibid.* 100 An outbreak of foot-and-mouth disease..could have exterminated the Père David very successfully. **1975** *New Yorker* 24 Mar. 34/2 The Père David deer, six hundred and forty extant, twenty-seven in the Bronx.

peregal, variant of PAREGAL *Obs.*, equal.

peregrin, variant of PEREGRINE.

†'**peregrinage**. *Obs. rare.* [ad. med.L. *peregrināgium* (1236 in Du Cange = *peregrīnātio*), f. *peregrīn-us* (see PEREGRINE) + *-āgium*, ad. Romanic *-aggio, -age*: see -AGE. Godef. gives one instance of *pérégrinage* in F., but only of early 16th c.] = PEREGRINATION, PILGRIMAGE (q.v.).

1340 *Ayenb.* 187 Vele men makeþ to god sacrefices of uestinges, of peregrinages, of ssarpnesses of bodye. [*Fr. orig.* (MS. Cott. Cleop. A 5 lf. 141), sacrifices de ieuner, de pelerinages.]

†ˈ**peregrinancy.** *Obs.* *rare*⁻¹. [f. L. *peregrīnānt-em*, pr. pple. of *peregrīnārī*: see next and -ANCY.] Sojourning; pilgrimage.

1674 STAVELEY *Rom. Horseleach* (1769) 280 The Church in this world is..in a state of peregrinancy and militancy.

peregrinate (ˈpɛrɪgrɪˌneɪt), *v.* (Also 6–7 *erron.* peri-.) [f. L. *peregrīnāt-*, ppl. stem of *peregrīnārī* to sojourn or travel abroad, f. *peregrīn-us* foreign, a foreigner: see PEREGRINE. Cf. F. *pérégriner*, Sp. *peregrinar*, It. *peregrinare*, to go on pilgrimage.] *intr.* To travel, journey.

1593 NASHE *Christ's T.* 28 That Sepulcher..which you perigrinate to adore. **1632** LITHGOW *Trav.* I. 9 They haue perigrinated to know the life of States. **1793** W. ROBERTS *Looker-on* No. 39 (1794) II. 82 It is of late the custom to peregrinate by night. **1812** SCOTT *Let. to J. B. S. Morritt* 12 Oct. in *Lockhart*, We peregrinated over Stanmore, and visited the Castles of Bowes..and Brougham. **1864** *London Soc.* VI. 392 She peregrinated calmly in a pinched bonnet.

b. To sojourn in a foreign country.

1755 JOHNSON, *Peregrinate*,..to live in foreign countries.

c. *trans.* To travel along or across; to traverse.

1835 *Fraser's Mag.* XI. 33 The path I was about to peregrinate was..hackneyed beyond conception. **1878** BESANT & RICE *Celia's Arb.* II. xvii. 271, I pick up rags and tatters of information as I peregrinate the streets. **1885** G. MEREDITH *Diana of Crossways* II. ii. 55 He could have wished himself peregrinating a bridge.

Hence ˈ**peregriˌnating** *vbl. sb.* and *ppl. a.*

1611 COTGR., *Pelerinant*, peregrinating, wandering, or going on Pilgrimage. **1805** EUGENIA DE ACTON *Nuns of Desert* I. 293 Not one thought was bestowed upon the peregrinating culprits. **1862** *Westm. Rev.* Jan. 65 Peregrinating bishops produce no effect upon them.

ˈ**peregrinate,** *a. rare.* [f. L. *peregrīnāt-us* having travelled or sojourned abroad, pa. pple. of *peregrīnārī*.] Foreign-fashioned, having the air of one who has lived or travelled abroad. (A purposely pedantic term put by Shakspere into the mouth of Holofernes; thence taken by Lytton.)

1588 SHAKS. *L.L.L.* v. i. 15 *Ped*... He is too picked, too spruce, too affected, too odde, as it were, too peregrinat, as I may call it. *Curat.* A most singular and choise Epithat. **1853** LYTTON *My Novel* I. iv, Imagine this figure, grotesque, peregrinate, and to the eye of a peasant, certainly diabolical.

peregrination (ˌpɛrɪgrɪˈneɪʃən). [a. F. *pérégrination* (12th and 16th c. in Littré), or ad. L. *peregrīnātiōn-em*, n. of action from *peregrīnārī* to PEREGRINATE. Cf. It. *peregrinazione*, Sp. *peregrinacion*.]

1. The action of travelling in foreign lands, or of journeying from land to land; hence, by extension, of travelling from place to place.

a **1548** HALL *Chron., Hen. IV* 19 His daily peregrinacion in the desert, felles and craggy mountains of [Wales]. *a* **1550** in *Boorde's Introd. Knowl.* (1870) Forewords 23 The Perègrination of Doctor Boarde. **1604** E. G[RIMSTONE] *D'Acosta's Hist. Indies* VII. iv. 505 This going forth and peregrination of the Mexicaines, will happily seeme like to that of Egypt. **1650** HOWELL *For. Trav.* (Arb.) 11 Amongst those many advantages, which conduce to enrich the mind with variety of Knowledge,..Peregrination, or Forraine Travell is none of the least. **1763** JOHNSON *Life Ascham* Wks. IV. 626 The purse of Ascham was not equal to the expence of peregrination. **1818** SCOTT *Hrt. Midl.* i, Before they had advanced far on their peregrination.

b. With *a* and *pl.* A course of travel (properly abroad); a journey, esp. on foot; a perambulation; in *pl.* = travels. Also, A narrative of travels.

1548 HOOPER *Ten Commandm.* x. 167 How light so euer this vngodlie people make there gaddynges or peregrinations: they shalbe culpable and accomptable for as many faultes, as is donne by his familie throwghe his absence. **1585** T. WASHINGTON tr. *Nicholay's Voy.* I. i. 1 The nauigations and peregrinations Orientals of Nicholas. **1604** E. G[RIMSTONE] *D'Acosta's Hist. Indies* III. xxvii. 202 The Peregrination which I have written. **1711** ADDISON *Spect.* No. 130 ¶4 The vicious Habits and Practises that he had been used to in the Course of his Peregrinations. **1777** ROBERTSON *Hist. Amer.* I. 31 The wild fanaticism..first incited men to enter upon those long and dangerous peregrinations. **1820** W. IRVING *Sketch Bk.* I. 151 My peregrinations about this great metropolis. **1853–8** HAWTHORNE *Eng. Note-Bks.* (1879) II. 321 [He] recently published a book of his peregrinations.

†**c.** A going as a pilgrim; a pilgrimage. *Obs.*

1528 ROY *Rede me* (Arb.) 106 Hathe Englond soche stacions Of devoute peregrinacions As are in Fraunce and Italy? *a* **1552** LELAND *Itin.* IV. 71 [Throgmorton] his Father ..dyed in Peregrination going to Hierusalem. **1637–50** ROW *Hist. Kirk* (Wodrow Soc.) 75 Workes of supererogation, meritis, pardones, perigrinationeis, and stationeis.

†**d.** The migration or transplantation of a plant, etc. *into* another country. *Obs. rare.*

1679 EVELYN *Sylva* (ed. 3) xxv, Concerning the Peregrination of that tree [Elm] into Spain.

e. *fig.* A systematic going through a subject, writing, course of study, etc. **f.** The 'pilgrimage' or 'journey' of life: see 2 b.

1615 CROOKE *Body of Man* 197 Being ariued at this place in the tract of my Anatomicall Perigrination. **1653** R. MASON *Commend. Let.* in *Bulwer's Anthropomet.*, When first I cast up this account of your ingenious peregrination through the world. **1717** L. HOWEL *Desiderius* (ed. 3) 126 Modesty..is absolutely necessary to be retain'd thro' the whole Course of our Peregrination till we arrive at the Love of God.

†**2.** A sojourning in a foreign land; the condition of dwelling as a sojourner; sojourn. *Obs.* or *arch.*

1630 R. N. tr. *Camden's Hist. Eliz.* 125 If he [the Czar] should..be constrained..to leave his country, she promised ..to receiue..him..with all honour worthy so great a Prince,..to assigne unto him a convenient place for his perigrination. *a* **1638** MEDE *Wks.* (1672) 597 [The] 430 years of the Peregrination [in Egypt] Exod. 12. [40]. The 40 years travail in the Wilderness. **1692** BENTLEY *Boyle Lect.* vi. 191 Ἐπιδημία ἐς ἀνθρώπους Θεοῦ, a Peregrination of a God among men. **1697** BP. PATRICK *Comm. Exod.* vi. 4 He thinks the Peregrination of the Fathers is attributed here to the Children.

b. *fig.* Man's life on earth viewed as a 'sojourn in the flesh'.

Often associated with the sojourn or 'tabernacling' of the Israelites in the desert; hence in later use passing into the notion of 'pilgrimage', and so of the 'journey' through life, as a fig. sense of 1. (In quot. 1523, prob. referring to Lydgate's transl. of *le Pelerinage de Vie humaine*.)

1523 SKELTON *Garl. Laurel* 1221 Of Mannes Lyfe the Peregrynacioun, He did translate, enterprete, and disclose. **1549** *Compl. Scot.* Prol. 18 The schort tyme of this oure fragil peregrinatione. **1585** ABP. SANDYS *Serm.* ix. ¶19 The Israelites dwelt in tents, vncertaine of their abode, euer readie to shift: whereby they represent vnto vs our peregrination in this mortalitie. **1626** DONNE *Serm., Ps. xc.* 14 (1640) 808 The Saints..pray that God would powre down vpon vs graces for our Peregrination here, as He hath done vpon them in their Station there. **1702** C. MATHER *Magn. Chr.* III. II. xxviii. (1852) 506 In the eighty third year of his peregrination. **1733** P. SHAW tr. *Bacon's Philos. Wks.*, *Wisd. Ancients* I. 573 Thro' all the Journey and Peregrination [*in itinere sive peregrinatione*] of human Life.

†**c.** *transf.* A place of sojourn. *Obs.* *rare*⁻¹.

1609 BIBLE (Douay) *Wisd.* xii. 7 They might receive a peregrination [Gr. ἀποικίαν, *Vulg.* peregrinationem] worthie of the children of God, which is a land of al most deare to thee.

peregrinator (ˈpɛrɪgrɪneɪtə(r)). Now only *affected.* [a. L. *peregrīnātor*, agent-n. from *peregrīnārī* to PEREGRINATE.] One who peregrinates; a traveller in foreign lands, or (loosely) from place to place; a pilgrim; a wanderer.

1610 *Chester's Tri.* (1844) Address 10 Like a poore Peregrinator..contented to passe through the Purgatorie of the Printing-house. **1668** M. CASAUBON *Credulity* 66 He makes himself a great peregrinator, to satisfie his Curiosity. **1819** W. TAYLOR in *Monthly Rev.* LXXXVIII. 501 Careful to record facts of practical utility to future peregrinators. **1829** T. L. PEACOCK *Misfort. Elphin* xii, More materials for absorbing thought, than the most zealous peregrinator,..is likely to have at once in his mind.

Hence ˈ**peregriˌnatory** *a. rare*, characteristic of a peregrinator; moving from place to place.

1773 *Observ. Pres. St. Poor* 107 There are among them some unquestionably honest and commendably industrious ..accustomed to that peregrinatory mode of living. **1906** *Chambers's Jrnl.* Feb. 150/1 One sees in the streets.. peregrinatory makers of sugar puppets.

peregrine, peregrin (ˈpɛrɪgrɪn), *a.* and *sb.* Forms: 4–5 **peregryn(e,** (6 **pelegryne),** **perrygryne,** 7 **perigrine,** 6– **peregrine,** 7– **-grin.** [ad. L. *peregrīn-us* coming from foreign parts, foreign, a foreigner, f. *pereger* that is abroad or on a journey, *peregre* adv., abroad, to or from foreign parts, f. *per* through + *ager* field, territory, land, country; cf. F. *peregrin* adj., migratory, foreign (16th c.), sb. a pilgrim, in Oresme *a* 1400 (Godef.). In Eng. found first, and until the 16th c. only, in the name of the *faucon peregryn* or *peregrine falcon*, in OF. *faulcon pelerin* (under the influence of which Ld. Berners has *fawcon pelegryne*). The inherited form of L. *peregrīnus*, through Romanic and OF., is PILGRIM, q.v.] **A.** *adj.*

1. Foreign, belonging to another country; outlandish, strange; imported from abroad; also, †foreign, extraneous, or alien to the matter in hand (*obs.*). ***peregrine tone*** (med.L. *tonus peregrinus*), name of one of the Gregorian 'tones' or chants.

c **1530** L. COX *Rhet.* (1899) 52 Other prohemes (whiche.. are not set out of the very mater it selfe)..are called peregrine or straunge prohemes. *c* **1540** *Pilgr. T.* 188 in *Thynne's Animadv.* (1865) 82, I toke him to be a straunger; ..we ware both perrygryne. **1574** HELLOWES *Gueuara's Fam. Ep.* (1577) 165 You aske me histories so straunge and peregrine, that my wittes may not in any wise but needes go on pilgrimage. **1585** SIR J. MELVIL *Let.* in *Wodrow Soc. Misc.* (1844) I. 439 Mr. Craig to preach openly against the Peregrine ministers. **1609** DOULAND *Ornith. Microl.* 35 There is another Tone, which many call the Peregrine, or strange Tone,..it is very seldome vsed in our Harmony. **1679** EVELYN *Sylva* xxiv. (ed. 3) 119 Our Damasco-Plum, Quince, Medlar, Figue,..as well as..several other Peregrine trees. **1728** MORGAN *Algiers* I. Pref. 25 Matters of so peregrine and grotesk a Nature as this [History]. **1831** GEN. P. THOMPSON *Exerc.* (1842) I. 333 Some persons have declared the style of the author [Bentham] to be.. occasionally peregrine and difficult. **1893** *Working Mens' Coll. Jrnl.* Oct. 259 In my own small garden I have four peregrine species of grass.

2. *Astrol.* Of a planet: Situated in a part of the zodiac where it has none of its essential dignities.

1588 J. HARVEY *Disc. Probl.* 108 Jupiter..extolled, and preferred aboue Saturne, who at that instant is Peregrine, and out of all his essentiall dignities. **1663** DRYDEN *Wild Gallant* Prol. 26 Venus, the lady of that house, I find Is Peregrine. **1706** PHILLIPS s.v., Among Astrologers, a Planet is said to be peregrine, when found in a Sign or Place of Heaven, where it has none of its five Essential Dignities, viz. House, Exaltation, Triplicity, Term, or Face. **1819** J. WILSON *Compl. Dict. Astrol.* 168 The lord of the house being combust, retrograde or peregrine.

†**3.** Upon a pilgrimage; upon one's travels; travelling abroad. *Obs.*

1655 M. CARTER *Hon. Rediv.* (1660) 209 Certain peregrine Christians going to visit the Holy Sepulchre. **1658** OSBORN *Adv. Son* Wks. (1673) 55, I am not much unwilling to give way to peregrine motion for a time. **1768** STERNE *Sent. Journ.* (1778) I. 25 (*Desobligeant*) The whole army of peregrine martyrs; more especially those travellers who set out upon their travels..under the direction of governors.

4. peregrine falcon (also 4–5 **faucon peregryn(e, 6 fawcon pelegryne,** and see B. 3): a typical species of falcon (*Falco peregrinus*) of very wide distribution, and formerly held in the greatest esteem for hawking. [The name is merely an Englishing of the med.L. *falco peregrinus* (used *c* 1250 by Albertus Magnus *De Animal.* XXIII. viii, Falconum genus quod vocatur peregrinum); the Fr. is *faucon pélerin* (used *c* 1263 by Brunetto Latini); It. *falcone pellegrino* (13th c.); all meaning 'pilgrim falcon'; so called because the young were not, like the *nidaces*, *niais*, or EYAS hawks, taken from the nest (which is usually built on an inaccessible crag or precipice), but caught on their passage or 'pilgrimage' from their breeding-place: 'faucons que om apele pelerins, parce que mes ne trueve son nif, ains est pris aussi comme en pelerinage', Brunet. Lat. *Trésor* cl. (ed. Chabaille 202). Hence also the name *passage-hawk*; in Eng. transl. of Buffon, *pilgrim falcon* or *hawk*. (See also HAGGARD *sb.*)]

There are numerous local races, varieties, or sub-species, some of which, as the American peregrine or Duck-hawk (*Falco anatum*) and the Australian *F. melanogenys*, are by many ornithologists ranked as distinct species.

c **1386** CHAUCER *Sqr.'s T.* 420 A ffaucon peregryn [*v.r.* -gryne] thanne semed she Of fremde Land. **1486** *Bk. St. Albans* D iij b, Ther is a Fawken peregryne. And that is for an Erle. **1525** LD. BERNERS *Froiss.* II. xlvi. 159 Fawcons pelegrynes, that haue stande and rested longe on the perche hath grete desyre to flye abrode. **1575** TURBERV. *Falconrie* 33 Of the Haggart Falcon, and why she is called the Peregrine, or Haggart. **1774** GOLDSM. *Nat. Hist.* V. 121 The peregrine falcon does not moult till the middle of August. **1843** YARRELL *Hist. Birds* I. 32 The great docility of the Peregrine Falcon, and the comparative ease with which the birds are procured, has rendered them the most frequent objects of the falconer's care and tuition. **1875** W. MᶜILWRAITH *Guide Wigtownshire* 139 These precipices are frequented by the peregrine falcon.

5. ***peregrin prætor*** [L. *prætor peregrīnus*], a second prætor appointed at Rome B.C. 47, to administer justice between Roman citizens and peregrins, or between peregrins themselves: see B. 1.

1880 MUIRHEAD *Gaius* I. §6 The two praetors, the urban and the peregrin.

B. *sb.* **1.** A sojourner in a foreign land; a person residing in a place where he is a stranger or foreigner; now only in *Rom. Antiq.* A resident in ancient Rome not having the rights of citizenship, an alien denizen.

1593 BILSON *Govt. Christ's Ch.* 7 Isaac and Iacob soiourned as strangers and peregrines first in the land of Canaan. *a* **1656** USSHER *Ann.* VI. (1658) 430 They were peregrines and strangers in the land of the Jews. **1675** CROWNE *Country Wit* III. 47 b, The great favours and honours you were pleas'd to confer on me, who am but a peregrine. **1880** MUIRHEAD *Gaius* I. §68 If a woman who is a Roman citizen has by mistake married a peregrin as if he also were a citizen, she is permitted to prove cause of error. *Ibid.* IV. §37 In the same way a peregrin feigns citizenship when he is pursuer in the same action.

†**2.** A pilgrim; a traveller in a foreign land. *Obs.*

1570 FOXE *A. & M.* (ed. 2) 468/1 In the which yeare were numbered of peregrines goyng in, and commyng out euery day at Rome, to the estimation of fiue thousand. **1625** PURCHAS *Pilgrims* IX. vii. §1 Here [Mecka] we found a maruellous number of Strangers, and Peregrines or Pilgrims. **1654** GAYTON *Pleas. Notes* III. ii. 76 The story of an Outlandish Peregrine, or Traveller.

3. = *peregrine falcon*: see A. 4.

1555 EDEN *Decades* 283 There are also ierfalcons sakers and peregrines whiche were vnknowen to the ancient princes. **1612** SELDEN *Illustr. Drayton's Poly-olb.* v. 85 Whether these here are the Haggarts (which they call Peregrin's), or Falcon-gentles, I am no such Falconer to argue; but this I know, that the reason of the name of Peregrin's is giuen, for that they com from remote and vnknowne places. *a* **1661** FULLER *Worthies, Shropsh.* 4 The Aryes of Pembrook-shire, where Perigrines did plentifully breed. **1759** B. MARTIN *Nat. Hist. Eng.* II. *Pembroke* 359 Excellent Faulcons, called Peregrins. **1865** KINGSLEY *Herew.* xx, Out of the reeds..shot the peregrine.

4. Usu. with initial capital. A red-skinned variety of peach with white flesh, developed and introduced by the Rivers nursery in 1903.

1903 *Jrnl. R. Hort. Soc.* XXVIII. p. cxcii, Award of Merit... To Peach 'Peregrine'..from Messrs. Rivers, Sawbridgeworth. **1907** *Daily Chron.* 13 June 6/4 A specimen peregrine peach tree grown in quite a small flower-pot is seven feet high, and bears much fruit. **1929** E.

A. BUNYARD *Anat. Dessert* 89 In mid-August we have Peregrine, that finest of recent peaches, combining flavour, appearance, and good crop in a manner rarely found. **1958** *Listener* 20 Nov. 853/3 The most outstanding variety of peach is Peregrine. **1971** G. E. WHITEHEAD *Grow Fruit in your Greenhouse* viii. 94 The peach 'Peregrine' and the nectarine, 'Pine Apple', make an ideal pair.

peregrinity (pɛrɪ'grɪnɪtɪ). [ad. F. *pérégrinité* (Rabelais 16th c.), or ad. L. *peregrīnitās* the condition of a *peregrīnus* or foreigner: see -ITY.] The condition of being a foreigner or alien, esp. in *Roman Antiq.* (see quot. 1880); †the quality or fact of being foreign, foreignness, outlandishness, strangeness (*obs.*).

1591 G. FLETCHER *Russe Commw.* (Hakl. Soc.) 151 This causeth the Emperours to..be very warie for excluding of all peregrinitie that might alter their fashions. **1607** *Schol. Disc. agst. Antichr.* II. v. 33 The affected peregrinitie of his straunge attire. **1774** BOSWELL *Jrnl. Tour Hebrides* 29 Aug., He said to me..'these people, sir,..may have somewhat of a peregrinity in their dialect, which relation has augmented to a different language'. I asked him if *peregrinity* was an English word. He laughed and said, 'No'. **1807** F. WRANGHAM *Serm. Transl. Script.* 21 Stamped with idiotism or with peregrinity. **1880** MUIRHEAD *Gaius* 566 *Peregrinity*, the condition of those who, being free, were neither citizens nor colonial or Junian latins, though possibly Roman subjects. **1900** *Jrnl. Educ.* Mar. 206/2 A mere concomitant of peregrinity.

b. A sojourn or journeying abroad. *rare.*

1831 CARLYLE *Sterling* II. iv, Five health-journeys which ..he had to make in all. 'Five forced peregrinities'. *Ibid.* vi, A new removal, what we call 'his third peregrinity', had to be decided on.

‖**pereion, peræon** (pə'raɪən, pə'ri:ən). *Zool.* [A factitious term intended to represent Gr. περαιόων, περαιῶν, pr. pple. of περαιοῦν 'to carry across, transport', erron. taken as 'to walk about'. Later users of the term have more exactly transliterated the reputed Gr. source as *peræon*.] A name for the thorax in Crustacea, as bearing the ambulatory limbs. Cf. PLEON. Hence **pe'reiopod**, (also **pe'ræopod, perei'o-, peræ'opodite**), one of the ambulatory limbs attached to the pereion.

1855 C. SPENCE BATE in *Rep. Brit. Assoc.* (1856) 27 Thoracic segments, (*Pereion*, from περαιόω to walk about: *pereion*, part which supports the walking legs. This and the following [*pleon*] are suggested instead of the old and incorrect synonyms of *thorax, abdomen*, &c.). *Ibid.* 35 *The pereiopoda*, or walking feet.—This includes the five posterior thoracic feet of authors. **1877** W. THOMSON *Voy. Challenger* I. ii. 131 At the base of the first segment of the pereion. **1877** *Encycl. Brit.* VI. 635/2 In the adult *Mysis*, eight pairs of limbs (that is to say the five pairs of *pereiopodites* or 'walking-feet', and the three pairs of maxillipeds or 'jaw-feet') are all furnished with two branches. **1893** STEBBING *Crustacea* iv. 44 The trunk..is often called the peræon, intended to signify the ambulatory part. *Ibid.* 45 The possession of chelæ is not confined to the first pair of so-called peræopods. **1932** J. S. HUXLEY *Probl. Relative Growth* iii. 87 Those pereiopods which are used as walking legs..have a definite but slight growth-gradient. **1964** *Oceanogr. & Marine Biol.* II. 467 In these displays, serving a threat function, the crab stands higher on its pereiopods. **1970** *Nature* 16 May 661/2 The pereiopods of *M*[*erguia*] *rhizophorae* are more robust than in most marine shrimps.

†**pere-jonette.** In 5 pereionet(t)e, also perionet. = *pear-jonet*: see PEAR *sb.* 5.

c **1386** CHAUCER *Miller's T.* 62 She was ful moore blisful on to see Than is the newe pereionette tree. [*So* 4 *MSS.*; *Camb.* pere Ionete tre, *Lansd.* perionet tree.]

perell, obs. form of PARREL, PEARL, PERIL.

perella (pə'rɛlə), **perelle** (pə'rɛl). [ad. F. *perrelle*, var. of *parelle*, L. *parella*: see PARELLIC.] The lichen *Lecanora Parella*, or the dye obtained from it.

1783 JUSTAMOND tr. *Raynal's Hist. Indies* V. 230 The plant know'n by the name of Perella, which is made use of in dying scarlet. **1858** SIMMONDS *Dict. Trade*, *Perelle*, a name for the crab's-eye lichen,..found on rocks in mountainous countries, which yields a purple dye.

peremint, peremounte, obs. ff. PEDIMENT, PARAMOUNT.

†**pe'rempt**, *v. Civil Law. Obs. rare.* [f. L. *perempt-*, ppl. stem of *perimĕre* to destroy, cut off, kill, etc.: see PEREMPTORY.] *trans.* To do away with, extinguish, quash (a legal process or suit). So †**pe'remption** *Obs.*, quashing.

1726 AYLIFFE *Parergon* 82 Nor is it any Objection to say, That the Instance of the Cause of Appeal is perempted by the Desertion of an Appeal. *Ibid.* 151 This Peremption of Instance was introduced in Favour of the Publick, lest Suits should otherwise be rendered immortal and perpetual.

†**pe'remptor**, *a.* (*sb.*) *Sc. Obs.* Forms: 6 -oir, -oure, 6–7 -our, 7–8 -or. [a. F. *péremptoire* (13th c. in Littré), ad. L. *peremptōri-us* PEREMPTORY. Cf. F. *exception péremptoire* in Littré.]

= PEREMPTORY. (Chiefly in Sc. Law.)

c **1470** [implied in PEREMPTORLY]. **1549** *Compl. Scot.* Ep. 6 For falt of ane peremptoir conclusione. **1561** *Reg. Privy Council Scot.* I. 167 To propone all his defenssis peremptouris and dilatouris, quhilkis thai will use. **1576** *Ibid.* II. 540 In respect..that the samyn day wes peremptour. **1582** *Ibid.* III. 503 His Majestie hes ordanit and appointit his court of justiciarie to be haldin..as secund court peremptoure to all personis arreistit to this present court. **1609** SKENE *Reg. Maj.*, *Forme Proces* 111 This secund summons is peremptour. *Ibid.* 115 For ane peremptour exception proponed, and lawfully proven, causes the proponer therof, to be perpetually..absolved. **1721** RAMSAY *Content* 193 The missive letter and peremptor bill Forbade them rest.

b. *ellipt.* as *sb.* A peremptory exception, defence, or plea: see PEREMPTORY A. 1.

1571 BANNATYNE *Jrnl. Trans. Scot.* (1806) 110 So am not I bound to answir thame, nor yit there accusatione, till that they give answir to my peremptour.

peremptorily ('pɛrəm(p)tərɪlɪ, pə'rɛm-), *adv.* [f. PEREMPTORY + -LY[2].] In a peremptory manner; so as to preclude debate, discussion, or opposition.

1. So as to fix or settle the matter; so as to decide the question; decisively, conclusively; so as to leave no doubt; definitely, positively.

1513 JAS. IV *Let. to Hen. VIII* 26 July in Hall *Chron.*, *Hen. VIII* 29 b, The sayd metyng of our and your commissioners at the borders, was peremptorily appoyncted betwyxt you and vs. **1596** BACON *Max. & Use Com. Law* II. (1635) 51 A fine..barreth estates peremptorilie. **1677** GALE *Crt. Gentiles* II. IV. 500 What their sin was cannot be peremtorily determined. **1743** H. WALPOLE *Lett. to Mann* I. lxxiv. 266 Monday is fixed peremptorily. **1878** R. W. DALE *Lect. Preach.* vi. 165 The question cannot be determined peremptorily. **1882–3** *Schaff's Encycl. Relig. Knowl.* III. 2473/2 The worship of saints and the doctrine of purgatory were peremptorily rejected as opposed to Scripture.

b. In the way of a peremptory citation.

1591 GREENE *Disc. Coosnage* (1592) 18 The scitation shalbe peremptorily serued in his parish Church.

c. In the way of 'peremptory challenge' (PEREMPTORY 1); without giving a reason for the objection.

1660 *Trial Regic.* 33 You may Challenge five and thirty Peremptorily. If you go beyond; you know the Danger. **1681** *Trial S. Colledge* 21 *Mr. Just. Jones.* Do you challenge him peremptorily, or with cause? **1708** J. CHAMBERLAYNE *St. Gt. Brit.* I. III. vi. (1737) 186 A prisoner may challenge 35 of the Juries peremptorily in High-Treason. **1874** *Chambers' Encycl.* VII. 354/2 Those who, on being arraigned for felony,..peremptorily challenged more than twenty jurors.

d. As at a peremptory time or in obedience to a peremptory order: without fail.

1715 in Picton *L'pool Munic. Rec.* (1886) II. 19 Every Councill man that does not attend at two o'clock..or within half an hour after two o'clock in the afternoon peremptorily.

†**2.** Absolutely, without exception or question.

1626 BACON *Sylva* §400 Some Organs are so peremptorily necessary, that the Extinguishment of the Spirit doth speedily follow. **1683** VILLIERS (Dk. Buckhm.) *Rehearsal* III. i. (ed. 4) 25 This Song is peremptorily the very best that ever yet was Written. **1788** H. WALPOLE *Let. to Earl Strafford* 12 Sept., September..has hitherto been peremptorily fine.

†**3.** Determinedly; obstinately. *Obs.*

c **1555** HARPSFIELD *Divorce Hen. VIII* (Camden) 129 If he stood stiffly and peremptorily, he and his house lived ever after in perpetual and public ignominie. **1661** *Funerals Montrose* in *Harl. Misc.* (Park) VII. 299 One who stuck peremptorily to the present marquis.

4. In the way of positive belief or assertion; with full assurance; positively, dogmatically.

1571 GOLDING *Calvin on Ps.* li. 18 He speaketh not peremptorily, as though God rejected the sacrifyses. **1596** SHAKS. *1 Hen. IV*, II. iv. 472. **1638** BAKER tr. *Balzac's Lett.* (vol. II.) 145 It is not fit..to affirme anything too peremptorily. **1752** H. WALPOLE *Lett.* (1846) II. 457 Stone at first peremptorily denied having seen that book. **1822–34** *Good's Study Med.* (ed. 4) I. 341, I..have not yet employed it on a scale that enables me to speak peremptorily.

5. In the way, or with an air, of positive command or the like; imperatively; imperiously.

1630 PRYNNE *Anti-Armin.* 177 That which euery man is peremptorily bound to beleeue, must needs be true. **1677** HORNECK *Gt. Law Consid.* iii. (1704) 60 It is he that peremptorily commands this consideration. **1839** JAMES *Louis XIV*, I. 139 The Swedes..peremptorily insisted upon taking their departure. **1896** GEN. H. PORTER in *Century Mag.* Nov. 29, I had to order him peremptorily to leave the battery.

peremptoriness ('pɛrəm(p)tərɪnɪs, pə'rɛm-). [f. as prec. + -NESS.] The quality or character of being peremptory; positiveness, absoluteness; conclusiveness, imperativeness, assurance, dogmatism, imperiousness; †fixed determination, obstinacy, etc.

1586 A. DAY *Eng. Secretary* II. (1625) 29 Finding by such peremptorinesse my sense to bee ouercome, you..cut me yet thirtie pound shorter. **1602** WARNER *Alb. Eng.* Epit. (1612) 375 This vnexpected peremptorinesse in him amazed and misliked not a few. **1649** ROBERTS *Clavis Bibl.* 413 The Peremptorinesse of Gods purpose to ruine Babylon. **1699** BURNET *39 Art.* xiv. (1700) 134 Words..delivered in the strain and peremptoriness of a Command. **1748** RICHARDSON *Clarissa* (1810) I. xvii. 114 No peremptoriness, Clary Harlowe: once you declare yourself inflexible, I have done. **1876** GREEN *Stray Stud.* 318 Her exhortations at the sick-bed have a somewhat startling peremptoriness about them.

†**peremptorize**, *v. Obs. rare.* [a. obs. F. *peremptoriser* (16th c. in Godef.), or (in quot. 1644) f. PEREMPTORY + -IZE.] **a.** See quot. 1611. **b.** To make peremptory or absolute.

1611 COTGR., *Peremptoriser*, to peremptorize; to grant, or passe away peremptorily. **1644** J. GOODWIN *Innoc. Triumph.* (1645) 67 Authoritie..to peremptorize by fire and sword all their limitations whatsoever, as agreeable to God's Word.

†**pe'remptorly**, *adv. Sc. Obs.* [f. PEREMPTOR + -LY[2]: cf. F. *péremptoirement* (1349 in Hatz.-Darm.).] = PEREMPTORILY.

c **1470** HENRYSON *Mor. Fab.* VI. (*Parl. Beasts*) iii, Summonit the scheip before the wolf, that he Peremptourlie ..Compeir. **1564** *Reg. Privy Council Scot.* I. 292 His procuratour, quha proponit peremptourlie ane exceptioun. **1639** DRUMM. OF HAWTH. *Hist. Jas. V*, Wks. (1711) 99 [Before 1530] suits of law were peremptorly decided by baillies, sheriffs, and other judges.

peremptory (pə'rɛm(p)tərɪ, 'pɛrəm-), *a.* (*adv.*, *sb.*) Also 6–7 **peremtory, -ie**, (6 **perentory, paremptory, parantarie, peremytorie, peremmatory**, 7 **parantory, perremtory**). [ad. (through AFr. *peremptorie*, F. *péremptoire*) L. *peremptōri-us* destructive, deadly, mortal; that puts an end to, decisive; f. *peremptor* destroyer, *perempt-us*, pa. ppl. of *perimĕre* to take away entirely, cut off, destroy (f. PER- 3 + *emĕre* to buy, purchase; orig., to take): see -ORY. Introduced into French and English as a term of Roman Jurisprudence, in which use retained in Scots Law (in 16–17th c. usually as PEREMPTOR); thence, in transferred senses, also in English Law, and at length in general use. (Sense 6 was taken later from the more literal L. sense.)]

I. 1. In Roman Law, used in the sense 'that destroys, puts an end to, or precludes all debate, question, or delay', hence 'decisive, final', in ***peremptory edict, decree, ordinance*** (*peremptorium edictum*, Digest 5. I. 70), and ***peremptory exceptions, defence, plea*** (*peremptoriæ exceptiones*, Gai Inst. 4 § 120, 121), viz. such as tend to quash the action (see EXCEPTION 4); hence, also, in Eng. Law, ***peremptory challenge*** (CHALLENGE *sb.* 3) or ***exception*** (quot. 1596), an objection without showing any cause, allowed to a prisoner against a certain number of jurymen; ***peremptory mandamus***, a mandamus in which the command is absolute, usually issued after one found insufficient; ***peremptory writ***, an original writ directing the sheriff to enforce the defendant's appearance in court without option; so ***peremptory citation***, etc.

[*c* **1250** BRACTON IV. xx. (Rolls) III. 206 Sunt enim exceptiones, quæ competunt contra breve, & assisam differunt, sed non perimunt... Est etiam quædam peremptoria quantum ad personam unius & dilatoria judicii, & non peremptoria quantum ad personam alterius. **1292** BRITTON, Exceptioun peremptorie: see EXCEPTION 4.] **1530–1** *Act 22 Hen. VIII*, c. 14 No person arrained for any pety treason murder or felony be from hensforthe admitted to any peremytorie chalenge aboue the nombre of .xx. [**1561**, etc.: see PEREMPTOR.] **1581** LAMBARDE *Eiren.* IV. xiv. (1588) 557. **1592** GREENE *Upst. Courtier* (1871) 39 He hath his peremtory scitation ready to scite him to the archdeacons or officials court. **1596** SPENSER *State Irel.* Wks. (Globe) 619/2 A fellon in his tryall..may have..thirty-six exceptions peremptorye agaynst the jurours. **1596** BACON *Max. & Use Com. Law* I. ii. (1636) 8 There is no reason.. but it should be a peremptory plea to the person in a writ of error as well as in any other action. **1770** *Junius Lett.* xli. 216 By what law or custom you were authorized to make a peremptory challenge of a juryman. **1809** J. MARSHALL *Const. Opin.* v. (1839) 125 A peremptory mandamus must be awarded. **1838** W. BELL *Dict. Law Scot.* s.v. *Defences*, Peremptory defences..are positive allegations which enter into the merits of the cause itself, and have the effect either of taking away the ground of action, or of extinguishing its effects. **1880** MUIRHEAD *Gaius* IV. §120 Exceptions..are peremptory that remain available always, and cannot be excluded; such are the exceptions of constraint or dole.

b. Hence, in ordinary language, †(*a*) Of a conclusion, statement, fact, etc.: Admitting no contradiction or denial, incontrovertible; settling the matter, conclusive, decisive, definite, final. (*Obs.*, or merged in 4.) (*b*) Of a command, order, etc.: Admitting no refusal; imperative.

(*a*) **1532** MORE *Confut. Tindale* Wks. 465/1 The finall peremptorye stoppe against al contradiccion. *a* **1548** HALL *Chron.*, *Hen. VIII* 174 He in no wise woll take the defiaunce dooen by your Herault as a paremptory intimacion of warre. **1640** REYNOLDS *Passions* xxxviii, A mathematician's conclusions ought to be peremptory and grounded on principles of infallible evidence. **1718** HEARNE *Collect.* (O.H.S.) VI. 367 The chief reason..was to get a peremptory Answer from the V. Chancellor whether I should print Neubrigensis.

(*b*) **1576** FLEMING *Panopl. Epist.* 9 *margin*, Ouer the which he had peremptorie gouernment, and iudiciall authoritie. **1607** ROWLANDS *Diog. Lanth.* 11 The Theife..in the peremptory tearmes of 'Stand, deliuer your Pursse'. **1759** JOHNSON *Rasselas* xxxiii, A peremptory command would have compelled obedience. **1843** CARLYLE *Past & Pr.* IV. iii, New imperious peremptory necessities. **1878** BOSW. SMITH *Carthage* 405 The orders of the Senate were peremptory.

2. *Law.* Said of a day or time decreed or definitely fixed for the performance of some act, esp. in a court of law. Rarely in general use. ?*Obs.*

1513–14 *Act 5 Hen. VIII*, c. 1 The seid Chaunceller.. shall prefix and assign unto hym a convenyent peremptorie day to prove hys objeccion. **1579** in *Archæol. Cant.* II. 81 A parantarie daye for us to apper before the saied exchetor. **1656** EARL MONM. tr. *Boccalini's Advts. fr. Parnass.* II. xciv. (1674) 247 They..prefixt five days for the first, five for the second, and five more for the last peremptory tearm, for every one to come in. **1754** RICHARDSON *Grandison* IV. xxiv. 174, I may as well fix a peremptory day at once.

b. Hence, Positively fixed; absolutely determined or settled; absolutely requisite, essential.

1596 DRAYTON *Leg.* iv. 454 For ways there be the greatest things to hit, If Men could find the peremptorie gate. **1625** BACON *Ess., Seditions & Tr.* (Arb.) 411 [That] no Euill shall appeare so peremptory, but that it hath some Out-let of Hope. *a* **1711** KEN *Preparatives* Poet. Wks. 1721 IV. 85 Should Agony upon you seise, Pray not for peremptory Ease. **1860** EMERSON *Cond. Life, Wealth* Wks. (Bohn) II. 346 It is a peremptory point of virtue that a man's independence be secured.

†**c.** *colloq.* 'Absolute', utter, thorough. *Obs.*

1598 B. JONSON *Ev. Man in Hum.* I. i, What would you doe, you peremptory gull?

†**3.** Precluding all doubt or hesitation in regard to action; resolute; resolved, determined (*to do* something, or *that* something be done); also, in a bad sense: Obstinate, stubborn, self-willed. (Of a person, or thing personified, or of purpose, action, etc.) *Obs.*

1589 GREENE *Menaphon* (Arb.) 21 The ayre yeelding preiudiciall sauors, seemd to be peremptory in some fatall resolution. **1595** SHAKS. *John* II. i. 454 Not death himselfe In mortall furie halfe so peremptorie, As we to keepe this Citie. *a* **1641** SUCKLING *Let.* Wks. (1646) 85 Excuse me if I.. continue peremptory in the resolution I have taken. **1659** in *Burton's Diary* (1828) IV. 301 He proved a peremptory fellow, and would not confess. **1702** *Eng. Theophrast.* 183 When we are fickle and irresolute, we brag of being obstinate and peremptory. **1711** SHAFTESB. *Charac.* II. i. (1737) II. 230 There are hardly any-where at this day a sort of People more peremptory. **1759** FRANKLIN *Ess.* Wks. 1840 III. 279 The House is peremptory, and will admit of no alteration in their bill.

4. Of persons, or their words, actions, etc. (often in reference to manner): Positive in opinion or assertion; quite certain, fully assured; *esp.* in bad sense, Intolerant of debate or contradiction; over-confident, showing too much assurance, dogmatic.

1586 A. DAY *Eng. Secretary* II. (1625) 21, I am not a little grieued to think that you should in that peremptorie sort you do, attribute vnto me the name of so base and vnfit a dealing. **1588** SHAKS. *L.L.L.* v. i. 11 His humour is lofty, his discourse peremptorie. **1691** RAY *Creation* II. (1692) 94 In my denial of the Spontaneous Generation of Plants, I am not so confident and peremptory. **1706** ESTCOURT *Fair Examp.* III. i, They are able to put the peremptoriest Witness to a Nonplus. **1861** O. W. HOLMES *Bread & Newspaper* in *Old Vol. Life* (1891) 13 Say what you like,—only don't be too peremptory and dogmatic. **1862** MAURICE *Mor. & Met. Philos.* IV. vii. §1. 333 The dogmatism and peremptory propositions of Hobbes.

5. Intolerant of refusal or opposition; insisting on compliance or obedience; imperious, dictatorial. (Now the most usual sense.)

1591 SHAKS. *Two Gent.* I. iii. 71 To morrow be in readinesse, to goe, Excuse it not: for I am peremptory. **1614** B. JONSON *Barth. Fair* IV. i, Iustice Overdo is a very parantory Person. **1773** GOLDSM. *Stoops to Conq.* v. i, Ha! ha! ha! The peremptory tone in which he sent forth his sublime commands! **1837** DICKENS *Pickw.* ii, Tupman was somewhat indignant at the peremptory tone in which he was desired to pass the wine.

†**II. 6.** Deadly, destructive. *Obs.*

1567 FENTON *Trag. Disc.* 24 [She] doth threaten my yonge and tender yeares with more perentorye plages. **1605** BACON *Adv. Learn.* I. vii. §3 Those Notions of Religion, policie and moralitie; which do preserve them..from all ruinous and peremptory errours and excesses. **1614** W. B. *Philosopher's Banquet* (ed. 2) 3 There are subjectory and pertinent peremptorie infirmities..therevnto belonging.

†**B.** as *adv.* **a.** *colloq.* Absolutely, entirely. **b.** By a peremptory order; without fail. *Obs.*

1533–4 *Act 25 Hen. VIII*, c. 3 §1 Every person and persones that..chalenge peremptorie above the nomber of xx. [Cf. quot. 1530–1 in 1.] **1598** B. JONSON *Ev. Man in Hum.* I. v, The most peremptory absurd clowne of christendome, this day, he is holden. [**1709** STRYPE *Ann. Ref.* I. ii. 64 That he [Boner] should make his answer by words on Wednesday next peremptory at nine of the clock.]

†**C.** *ellipt.* as *sb.* Short for *peremptory challenge, citation, command, rule, writ*, etc. *Obs.*

1606–7 BACON *Rep. Naturalization* in *Lett. & Life* (1868) III. 327 If want of health may not excuse attendance, nor want of hearing answer for not reporting, he knew not what to say for himself. For others they have stood as peremptories, but to him they cannot serve as dilatories. **1644** PRYNNE & WALKER *Fiennes's Trial* 8 He procured sixe or seven successive adjournments of the day of triall (some of them after a perremtory)..thereby to tire out the Prosecutors. *a* **1670** HACKET *Abp. Williams* I. (1692) 174 Two or three afternoons he allotted every week to hear peremptories. **1737** *Order of Cork Water Club* 21 Apr. in *N. & Q.* 9th Ser. VII. 489 No man be allowed more than one bottle to his share, and a peremptory. **1753** RICHARDSON *Grandison* (1810) II. xvi. 172, I went up with my father's *peremptory*, as I may call it, to my sister.

perende, appearing: see PEAR *v.*

perendinate (pəˈrɛndɪneɪt), *v. rare.* [f. ppl. stem of med.L. *perendināre* (in cl. L. only in vbl. sb. *perendinātio*, Martial), f. *perendin-us* (the day) after to-morrow, f. *perendiē*; on the day after to-morrow (Gr. πέραν beyond, L. *diē* on the day).]

a. *trans.* To put off till the day after to-morrow, to defer from day to day. *rare.* **b.** *intr.* To stay from day to day, to make an indefinite stay. So **peˈrendinant** [ad. med.L. *perendinānt-em*, pr. pple.]: see quot.; **perendiˈnation**, *rare*, 'a putting off till the day after to-morrow'.

1656 BLOUNT *Glossogr., Perendinate*.., to put off for a day, or till the next day after to morrow. **1658** PHILLIPS, *Perendination*, a putting off for a day. **1886** WILLIS & CLARK *Cambridge* I. Introd. 88 The word perendinant (*perendinans*) was originally applied to persons who availed themselves of the hospitality of religious houses, by making long visits. *Ibid.* 89 The Master and Scholars are not to permit any one to perendinate within their walls for a longer period than a fortnight. *Ibid.*, The founder of Queen's College..prohibits his scholars to grant to any perendinating stranger a chamber for life.

perendure (pɜːrənˈdjʊə(r)), *v. rare.* [f. PER- 2 + ENDURE.] *intr.* To endure or last through a long time, or throughout a process or course of action. Hence **perenˈduring** *ppl. a.*

18.. *Encycl. Brit.* (O.), Perenduring Rome. **1896** *Chicago Advance* 26 Mar. 452/2 Self is not the 'I' as the perenduring subject of all its acts.

perengale, variant of PAREGAL *Obs.*

†**peˈrenmity.** *Obs. rare.* [PER- 4.] Excessive enmity.

1585 GREENE *Planetomachia* Wks. (Grosart) V. 55 There had been such a perenmitie betweene the house of the *Valdracchie* and the *Celij*, that [etc.].

†**peˈrennal,** *a. Obs.* [Cf. OF. *perennel* (14th c. in Godef.), ad. L. type **perennāl-is* = L. *perennis*.] = PERENNIAL.

c **1485** *Digby Myst.* (1882) III. 637 Good lord of lorddes, my hope perhenuall [? perhennall], With þe to stond In grace and fawour to se. **1635** PERSON *Varieties* I. 5 In respect of the Heavens perennall and incessant rotation, and the Ayres continuall revolution. **1681** RYCAUT tr. *Gracian's Critick* 37 Those perennal Streams of Fountains.

perennate (pəˈrɛneɪt), *v.* [f. ppl. stem of L. *perennāre*, f. *per* through + *annus* year, or f. *perennis*: see next.] **a.** *trans.* To make perennial or lasting. *rare.* **b.** *intr.* To last or live through a number of years, as a perennial plant. Hence **peˈrennating** *ppl. a.*, **pereˈnnation.**

1623 COCKERAM, *Perennate*, to last many yeares. **1698** *Money Masters all Things* 16 So tho' Money can't perennate your days, Yet after Death, she hath the power to raise You into Bliss. **1888** I. B. BALFOUR in *Nature* 20 Dec. 188/2 Properly to understand perennation, the perennating portions must be examined at all periods of the resting season as well as when they are starting anew into vegetative activity. **1905** I. B. BALFOUR tr. *C. E. von Goebel's Organogr. Plants* II. 689/1 Perennating, geophilous shoot. **1913** [see *chamæphyte* s.v. CHAMÆ-]. **1926** TANSLEY & CHIPP *Study of Vegetation* ii. 21 The perennating buds..continue the growth of the plant from season to season. **1927** *Forestry* I. 108 Besides overwintering in the buds, the fungus perennates on dead oak-leaves. **1969** F. E. ROUND *Introd. Lower Plants* xiii. 153 Vegetative propagation of the gametophyte from gemma-like outgrowths is common in some genera [of ferns] and in a few these even become thickened and act as perennating organs. **1971** *Country Life* 16 Dec. 1736/3, I nearly always get a casual crop of mushrooms, though where the spawn comes from is a mystery. Perhaps it perennates in the ground below the [compost] heap. **1977** J. L. HARPER *Population Biol. of Plants* iii. 62 For perennial plants the seed is an alternative means of perennation. *Ibid.* xxi. 651 In most plants the seed is a perennating organ.

perennial (pəˈrɛnɪəl), *a.* and *sb.* [f. L. *perenni-s* lasting through the year or years (f. *per* through + *ann-us* year) + -AL¹: cf. PERENNAL.]

A. *adj.* **1. a.** Lasting, continuing, or extending throughout the year; said esp. of a spring or stream which flows through all seasons of the year.

(But both in this and b, the sense is capable of being understood as 'Lasting through successive years, never-failing, perpetual', as in 2, of which continuance through all the seasons of the year is the condition.)

1703 DAMPIER *Voy.* (1729) III. I. 296 Rivers, Brooks, and Perennial Springs. **1713** DERHAM *Phys.-Theol.* II. v. (1727) 50 *note*, There is such a Thing as Subterraneous Heat..As is manifest from the smoking of perennial Fountains in frosty Weather. **1879** A. R. WALLACE *Australasia* xvi. 309 Their rapid flow and perennial supply of water are excellently adapted for irrigation.

†**b.** Remaining green or leafy throughout the year; evergreen. (Of plants or their leaves.) *Obs.*

1644 EVELYN *Diary* 8 Nov., A row..covered over with the natural shrubbs, ivy, and other perennial greenes. **1688** R. HOLME *Armoury* II. 117/1 Perenniel leaves..last all the year. **1762–9** FALCONER *Shipwr.* III. 363 Where round the scene perennial laurels bloom.

2. a. Lasting through a succession of years, or through a long, indefinite, or infinite time; enduring, lasting, permanent, never-failing, continual, perpetual; everlasting, eternal. ***perennial philosophy*** = PHILOSOPHIA PERENNIS.

1750 JOHNSON *Rambler* No. 72 ⁋3 A constant and perennial softness of manner. *c* **1750** SHENSTONE *Elegies* xiii. 19 Myriads in Time's perennial list enroll'd. **1839** CARLYLE *Chartism* iv. (1858) 17 A government and guidance of white European men which has issued in perennial hunger of potatoes to the third man extant. **1865** DICKENS *Mut. Fr.* I. x, Perennial youth is in her artificial flowers. **1933** W. R. INGE *God & Astronomers* i. 13 The perennial philosophy.. is the only system which will be found ultimately satisfying. **1945** A. HUXLEY (*title*) The perennial philosophy. *Ibid.* p. vii, Rudiments of the Perennial Philosophy may be found among the traditionary lore of primitive peoples in every region of the world, and in its fully developed forms it has a place in every one of the higher religions. **1962** E. WYNNE-TYSON *Philos. of Compassion* 3 The most fundamental difference between the teachings of the western religions and those of the perennial philosophy and of the original Creed of Christ. **1974** R. C. ZAEHNER *Our Savage God* 12 'All is One, and One is All..', seems to have been..what Aldous Huxley considered to be the kernel of.. the 'perennial philosophy'.

b. Of plants, their roots, etc.: Remaining alive through a number of years; said esp. of a herb which dies down to the root and shoots up afresh every year: opp. to *annual* and *biennial.*

1672–3 GREW *Anat. Roots* I. i. §16 In what particular way, some Roots become Perennial. Some are wholly so, as those of Trees, Shrubs, and divers other woody Plants. **1760** J. LEE *Introd. Bot.* III. xxiii. (1765) 234 In warm Regions, Plants that are annual with us will become perennial or arborescent. **1880** HAUGHTON *Phys. Geog.* vi. 299 The vegetation consists mainly of perennial herbs and shrubs. **1891** E. PEACOCK *N. Brendon* II. 433 The perennial sweet-pea which she had planted.

c. *Zool.* and *Anat.* Growing continually from persistent pulps, as the incisor teeth of a rodent.

d. *Entom.* (*a*) Living for more than one year, as an insect. (*b*) Forming colonies which are continued from year to year, as ants, bees, etc.

¶**e.** *loosely.* Recurring year after year.

1845 MᶜCULLOCH *Taxation* I. iv. (1852) 124 The difference between A's actual income of 1000*l.* and the corresponding perennial income of 660*l.*, that is, 340*l.*, will, if accumulated for twenty-seven years and a half, at 4 per cent., produce 16,500*l.*

B. *sb.* **1.** A perennial plant: see A. 2 b.

1763 MILLS *Syst. Pract. Husb.* II. 413 It may destroy annual plants, such as corn, entirely; but in perennials, like grass, it destroys only the leaves or blades. **1868** ROGERS *Pol. Econ.* xiv. (1876) 197 The cotton-plant..grows freely as a perennial in all tropical climates; it flourishes as an annual over..the warmer part of the temperate zones. **1880** GRAY *Struct. Bot.* iii. §1. 32 Perennials are plants which live and blossom or fructify year after year. They may or may not have perennial roots.

2. Something that lasts, or remains fresh, through a succession of years. (Always with conscious allusion to sense 1.)

1771 MRS. GRIFFITH *Hist. Lady Barton* III. 65 She..told me that..the most constant lovers were not to be considered more than perennials. **1827** LAMB *Let. to H. C. Robinson*, His jokes..were old trusty perennials,..always as good as new. **1889** *Pall Mall G.* 31 July 3/2 Belonging to the annuals rather than the perennials of poetry.

Hence **perenniˈality**, the quality of being perennial; something that is perennial; **peˈrennialize** *v. trans.*, to make perennial or permanent.

1841 *Blackw. Mag.* XLIX. 152 The truths to which they are so much attached have a pereniality of new aspects. **1858** CARLYLE *Fredk. Gt.* x. ii. (1872) III. 212 Mere ephemera..not related to the Perennialities at all. **1898** *Speaker* 3 Sept. 287/1 Welling springs, converging to a hollow, have perennialised a wide shallow pool. **1977** J. L. HARPER *Population Biol. of Plants* xviii. 543 It is often possible to extend the perenniality of a biennial by continually preventing seed formation.

perennially (pəˈrɛnɪəlɪ), *adv.* [f. PERENNIAL *a.* + -LY².] In a perennial way; throughout the year, or a succession of years; constantly, permanently, perpetually, eternally.

1784 *Parody* in Boswell *Johnson*, A captive in thy ambient arms, Perennially be thine. **1831** CARLYLE *Sart. Res.* II. ix, Thou findest the Altar still there, and its sacred Lamp perennially burning. **1877** E. R. CONDER *Bas. Faith* ix. 396 Duty or Obligation is submission to the authority of moral law, recognised by conscience as perennially binding.

¶**b.** *loosely.* Year after year.

1861 SMILES *Engineers* II. II. v. 154 The attacks of the ague to which they were perennially subject. **1862** ANSTED *Channel Isl.* IV. xxiii. (ed. 2) 537 The contrôle, whose office is perennially vacant.

perennibranch (pəˈrɛnɪbræŋk), *a.* and *sb. Zool.* [f. mod.L. *Perennibranchia* neut. pl., f. *perennis* PERENNIAL + BRANCHIA.] **a.** *adj.* Having permanent gills; belonging to the division *Perennibranchia* (or *Perennibranchiata*) of Amphibians, which retain their gills through life. **b.** *sb.* An amphibian of this division. Also **perenniˈbranchiate** *a.* and *sb.* (opposed to CADUCIBRANCHIATE).

[**1835** KIRBY *Hab. & Inst. Anim.* II. xxii. 412 *Perennibranchia*, or the *Proteus, Siren, Axolot.*] **1835** *Penny Cycl.* III. 186/2 Reptiles belonging to the perennibranchiate family. **1848** CRAIG, *Perennibranchiates.* **1875** HUXLEY in *Encycl. Brit.* I. 762/1 It is probable..that no known Labyrinthodonts were perennibranchiate. **1888** ROLLESTON & JACKSON *Anim. Life* 404 In the perennibranch *Urodela* [the gills] are retained. **1890** *Cent. Dict., Perennibranch, a.* and *n.*

†**peˈrennious,** *a. Obs.* [f. L. *perenni-s* + -OUS; cf. *illustrious*, etc.] = PERENNIAL.

1628 PRYNNE *Brief Survay* Epist., The perennious preseruation and propagation of that pure orthodox and sincere Religion. **1629** H. BURTON *Truth's Triumph* 328 From the perennious and pure fountaine of Gods will and pleasure, doe flow . . the waters of life.

†**pe'rennity.** *Obs.* [ad. L. *perennitās*, f. *perennis* perennial: see -ITY. Cf. OF. *per(h)ennité* (Godef.) in Dict. Acad. 1878.] The quality of being perennial; continuance for several years, or through a long or indefinite time; permanence, perpetuity.

1597 J. KING *On Jonas* (1618) 107 Cesternes that are broken and cannot holde, I say not water of life and perennity, but no water at all. **1641** J. TRAPPE *Theol. Theol.* Contents i. §6 Of the perennity and perpetuity of the Scriptures. **1713** DERHAM *Phys.-Theol.* II. v. (1727) 51 *note*, The Perennity of divers Springs, which always afford the same Quantity of Water.

perentele: see PARENTELE.

perentie (pə'rɛntɪ). *Austral.* Also **parenti, perenty.** [Aboriginal name.] A large, burrowing, monitor lizard, *Varanus giganteus*, which may be as much as eight feet long and is found in desert areas of central and northern Australia. Also *attrib.*

a **1928** E. R. WAITE *Reptiles or Amphibians S. Austral.* (1929) v. 125 Perentie or Sjonba... The discovery of the gigantic goana on the Komodo Islands illustrates the inadvisability of naming specimens by comparative measurements. The Perentie is, however, the largest Australian species. **1942** C. BARRETT *On Wallaby* iii. 43 Perenties three yards long were said to exist in the ranges. **1944** *Living off Land* ii. 24 The large Parenti lizard provides about the best food supply of the reptiles. **1963** E. WORRELL *Reptiles Austral.* 83 Perenty... Length to 8 feet. This is Australia's largest monitor. **1968** V. SERVENTY *Wildlife Austral.* v. 126 The goannas range from the short-tailed goanna, a seven-inch long sprite, to the eight-foot giant of the inland, the perentie. **1973** *Panorama* (Austral.) Oct. 5/3 (*caption*) Dick Lang with a perentie he chased and caught.

perentory: see PEREMPTORY.

†**pe'requal.** *Obs. rare.* [f. L. type **peræquāl-is*, f. PER- 4 + *æquāl-is* equal; cf. PAREGAL, PEREGAL.] An equal, peer, match.

a **1578** LINDESAY (Pitscottie) *Chron. Scot.* (S.T.S.) I. 135 No man of hollsome judgement bot will grant we had no perequall in Ewrope.

pere'quation. [a. F. *perėquation*, ad. L. *peræquatiōn-em*, n. of action from *peræquāre* to make quite equal, f. PER- 2 + *æquāre* to EQUATE.]

1611 COTGR., *Perequation*, a perequation; an equalling, or making euen. **1920** *Times* 4 Aug. 4/3 This price we pay for English coal has obliged us to force up the interior price for our own coal, by a 'perequation', so as not to handicap those . . who are obliged by geographical reasons to burn English coal only. **1954** *Economist* 19 June 983 A perequation levy is collected from coal sold by countries where the average costs of production are lower than the weighted average. **1973** H. TREVELYAN *Diplomatic Channels* ix. 132 It was egalitarianism run mad, the doctrine of the perequation of misery.

pe'requitate, *v. rare.* [ad. L. *perequitāre*: see -ATE³, f. PER- 1 + *equitāre* to ride.] *trans.* To ride through, traverse on horseback.

1780 JOHNSON *Let. to Mrs. Thrale* 15 June, Among the heroes of the Borough, who twice a-day perambulate or perequitate High Street . . rides . . Sir Richard Hotham. **1957** P. M. KENDALL *Warwick Kingmaker* III. vi. 158 A poor clerk of Evreux, leaving the royal cavalcade to take a message to his Chapter and immediately setting forth with their reply, had to ride for sixty-six days before he caught up with his perequitating sovereign [*sc.* Louis XI].

†**'perer.** *Obs.* Also 5 **peryr.** [a. AF. *perer* = OF. *perier*, F. *poirier* pear-tree, f. OF. *peire*, F. *poire* PEAR.] A pear-tree.

14.. *Pistill of Susan* 70 (MS. P.) The palme and þe popeler, þe perer [*other MSS.* perie] and the ploume [*MS.* plowine, *rime* sowme]. **14..** *Songs & Carols* xxxi. (Warton Cl.) 36 In the myddis of my gardyn is a peryr set.

†**pe'rrerrate,** *v. Obs. rare*⁻⁰. [f. L. *pererrāre.*]
1623 COCKERAM, *Pererrate*, to wander vp and downe.

†**pere'rration.** *Obs.* [n. of action from L. *pererrāre*: see prec.] A wandering through various places; a rambling; a travelling about.

1608–11 BP. HALL *Epist.* v. ii, What need wee to . . spend our daies in a perpetuall pererration? **1658** EVELYN *Let. to E. Thurland* 8 Nov., Unlesse . . noblemen make wiser provisions for their educations abroad, above . . the ordinary commerce and import of their wild pererrations.

peresche, obs. f. PARISH, PERISH, PIERCE.

peresil, obs. form of PARSLEY.

perester (pə'rɛstə(r)). *Chem.* [f. PER-¹ 5 + ESTER.] An ester of a peracid.

1933 *Jrnl. Amer. Chem. Soc.* LV. 351 The perester on standing at room temperature . . hydrolyzes to yield methyl hydroperoxide and the original monomethyl ester of camphoric acid. **1946** *Ibid.* LXVIII. 642/1 Organic peresters cannot be classified as derivatives of organic peracids and alcohols, but rather as derivatives of organic acids and hydroperoxides. **1975** *Org. Reaction Mechanisms 1973* iii. 80 Induced decompositions of peresters have been brought about by trialkyltin radicals.

‖**perestroika** (pɛrɪ'strɔɪkə). *Pol.* Also **perestroyka.** [a. Russ. *perestroĭka* restructuring.] The 'restructuring' or reform of the Soviet economic and political system, first proposed at the 26th Party Congress in 1979 and actively promoted under the leadership of Mikhail Gorbachev from 1985. Cf. GLASNOST.

[**1981** tr. *Rep. Central Comm. CPSU XXVI Congr.* III. ii. 102 The restructuring of all social relations . . is consummated in the period of developed socialism. **1981** *Summary World Broadcasts: Soviet Union* 26 Feb. C24 They are outlined in the 26th April 1979 decision of the CPSU Central Committee. This is a long-term document. Essentially it deals with restructuring (Russian: perestroyka).] **1986** *Washington Post* 23 Feb. A1/2 If words can define an era, then *perestroika* is the catchword here before Tuesday's opening of the Communist Party Congress as Soviet leader Mikhail Gorbachev enters a decisive phase of his leadership. **1986** *Sunday Tel.* 9 Nov. 2/6, I can see Mr Gorbachev on television going on about something he calls *Perestroika*, roughly translated as 'the restructuring'. **1987** tr. *Gorbachev's Perestroika* ii. 60 After the 27th CPSU Congress and several Plenary Meetings of the Central Committee, the problems and the course of perestroika are being enthusiastically discussed by all sectors of Soviet society. **1987** *Daily Tel.* 9 Feb. 18/1 This is not to say that the *perestroyka*, the renovation of Soviet society, for which we have given Mr Gorbachev ample credit, is unimportant. **1987** *Observer* (Colour Suppl.) 25 Oct. 39/1 Let conversation turn to the perestroika and mostly you hear grumbles: about higher prices, harder work —and the vodka famine.

†**'peretre.** *Obs.* Also 5 **peretyr, pertyr.** [a. OF. **peretre*, Cotgr. *piretre*, ad. L. *pir-*, *pyrethrum*: see PELLETER, PELETRE, and PYRETHRE.]
= PELLITORY 1, Pellitory of Spain.

c **1440** *Promp. Parv.* 394/1 Peretre, herbe (*P.* peretyr), *peretrum. Ibid.* 395/2 Petyr, herbe (or peretre; *P.* pertyr).

perewake, -wig, -wyke, obs. ff. PERIWIG.

†**pe'rexcellently,** *adv. Obs. rare*⁻¹. [See PER- 4.] Very excellently, very highly.

c **1450** *Mirour Saluacioun* 2659 The king his Sugits luvid so perexcellently.

pereye, obs. f. PERRIE, PERRY; var. PORREY *Obs.*

†**per'fabricate,** *v. Obs. rare*⁻⁰. [f. L. *perfabricāre* (see PER- 2 and FABRICATE).]
1623 COCKERAM, *Perfabricat*, to go through with building.

perfay (pə'feɪ), *int. arch.* Forms: α. 4–5 **parfay,** 4 **parfai, par-fai,** 5 **par-fay, -fey, parfey(e, -faie.** β. 5–6 **per fey,** 5 **perfey(e,** 4–6, 9 *arch.* **perfay.** [ME. a. OF. *par fei*, AF. also *par fai, fay*, f. *par* by (PAR *prep.* 1) + OF. *feid, feit, fei*, mod.F. *foi*:—L. *fidem* FAITH.]

By (my) faith; verily, truly: cf. FAY *sb.*¹ 6 b. (*Obs.* in ordinary use since 16th c., but revived by some modern poets.)

a **1300** *Cursor M.* 298 (Cott.) þe erth it has na sun parfai [*G.* parfay, *F.* perfay, *Tr.* perfey]. *Ibid.* 597 Parfay [*v. rr.* parfai, forsoþe] þat es bot eth to rede. **1375** BARBOUR *Bruce* I. 39 The land vj ȝer, and mayr perfay, Lay desolat eftyr hys day. *c* **1386** CHAUCER *Miller's T.* 495 Som maner confort shal I haue parfay. *c* **1450** *St. Cuthbert* (Surtees) 7838 þai Did mare harme þan gude parfay. *a* **1550** *Image Hypocr.* III. 408 And then, my lordes, perfay . . Not all your gold so gay . . Shall serve youe to delaye. **1570** LEVINS *Manip.* 196/47 Parfay, *medius fideus.* **1819** W. TENNANT *Papistry Storm'd* (1827) 15 She had task't hersel, perfay, To work before a certain day A pair o' stockins. **1865** SWINBURNE *Poems & Ball.* Ser. I. *Masque Q. Bersabe* 117 This knave hath sharp fingers perfay. **1870** MORRIS *Earthly Par.* I. I. 338 Perfay all goeth more than right.

perfect ('pɜːfɪkt), *a.* (*adv.*, *sb.*) Forms: see below. [Orig. ME. *parfīt*, *-fite*, a. OF. *parfit*, *-fite* (11th c. in Littré):—L. *perfect-um*, pa. pple. of *perficĕre* to accomplish, perform, complete, f. PER- 2 + *facĕre* to do, make. Subsequently influenced by OF. *parfet*, *-fete*, *-feit*, *-fait*, in which the radical part is *fet*, *fait* (pa. pple. of *faire*):—L. *factum.* At length gradually conformed (partly through *parfaict*, *perfaict*, *perfect*) to the L. original *perfectus.* The change of *par-* to *per-* went on from 14th to 16th c. In ME. and 16th c. the stress varied between *per'fite* and *'perfit*; in Scotch (pər'fəit) is still prevalent in some senses, and in others displaced by ('pɛrfɪt).]

A. Illustration of Forms.

1. α. 3–4 **parfijt,** 4–5 **-fiȝt,** 5 **-fyght,** 5–6 **-fight.** β. 4–5 **perfiȝt,** 5–6 **-fyght,** 6 **-fight,** 7 **-fyit.**

α. *c* **1290** *S. Eng. Leg.* I. 58/160 ȝif þou wolt parfijt beo, sul al þi guod. **1382** WYCLIF *1 John* ii. 5 Forsothe who kepith his word, verily in him is parfijt charite. **1387** TREVISA *Higden* (Rolls) III. 363 þat parfiȝt welþe þat is nouȝt in worldly richesse. **1477** EARL RIVERS (Caxton) *Dictes* 17 Withoute witte he may not be parfight in science. **1485** CAXTON *Chas. Gt.* 22 For pees and parfyght vnyon. **1556** J. HEYWOOD *Spider & F.* lxxxv. 6 Our parfight sight from blindnesse standeth . . in aduersite.

β. **1387** TREVISA *Higden* (Rolls) V. 185 He hadde perfiȝt knowleche of sevene artis. *a* **1529** SKELTON *Prayer to Father* 4 Of all perfections the essencial most perfyght! **1556** J. HEYWOOD *Spider & F.* xviii. 4 Both partes apeere of so pure perfight skill. **1650** *Presbytery Bk. Strathbogie* (1843) 137 For the making vp of a perfyit manse and gleib.

2. α. 3–5 **parfite,** 4–6 **-fyte.** β. 4– **perfite, -fyte.**

α. *a* **1300** Parfite [see B. 3]. *c* **1375** *Sc. Leg. Saints* i. (*Petrus*) 256 For thefis amang þame pece parfyte vill have. *c* **1450** tr. *De Imitatione* I. iv. 6 þe parfite bileueþ not lightly all þinges þat men telliþ. *a* **1533** LD. BERNERS *Huon* lxxxviii. 278 Suche as he had parfyte trust in.

β. *c* **1340** Perfite [see B. 3 a]. **1432–50** tr. *Higden* (Rolls) V. 185 Perfite knowlege of the vij sciences liberalle. **1500–20** DUNBAR *Poems* xlvii. 14 To wryte Quhat plesans is in lufe perfyte. *a* **1568** ASCHAM *Scholem.* I. (Arb.) 40 A separate and perfite note. **1611** SIR W. MURE *Misc. Poems* i. 34 Once taist yat nectared delyte, Of all pleasoures yᵉ most perfyte. *a* **1699** KIRKTON *Hist. Ch. Scot.* (1817) 301 Making the island happy by a perfyte union. [**1808–25** JAMIESON, *Perfit, Perfite*... The term is still used to denote one who is exact in doing any work, or who does it neatly. The accent is on the last syllable. **1851** W. ANDERSON *Rhymes* (1867) 34 (E.D.D.) There's few sae perfite as we should be.]

3. α. 3– 6 **parfit,** 4–6 **-fyt,** (6 **-fytte**). β. 4–7 (*dial.* -9) **perfit,** (6 **-fitt, -fytt**), 5–7 **perfyt.**

a **1300** *Cursor M.* 12483 (Cott.) Maister es he self parfit [*v. rr.* parfite, -fitt, perfite]. **13..** *Minor Poems fr. Vernon MS.* 573 Parfyt love is ther non. *c* **1430** LYDG. *Min. Poems* (Percy Soc.) 48 Pore in spirit, parfit in pacyence. **1450–1530** *Myrr. our Ladye* 310 God . . made them parfyt in kynde on the Saterday. **1555** HARPSFIELD in *Bonner's Homilies* 4 Her he made parfytte. **1560** WHITEHORNE *Ord. Souldiours* (1588) 45 b, If you will make it parfiter.

β. *c* **1374** CHAUCER *Boeth.* III. pr. ii. 51 (Camb. MS.) Blysfulnesse is a perfyt [*v.r.* perfit] estat. **1559** BP. SCOT in Strype *Ann. Ref.* (1824) I. App. x. 444 The fawters therof contende, that it is most perfitt. **1603–32** FLORIO *Montaigne* I. xl. (ed. 3) 132 Sound, and in perfit health. [But FLORIO 1598–1611, COTGR. 1611 spell *perfect.*] **1610** J. MELVILL *Autobiog.* (Wodrow Soc.) 259 The King efter his perfyt age of twentie and a yeirs. **1628** LE GRYS tr. *Barclay's Argenis* 222 That excellent old mans perfitest remission. **1645** J. DURYE [Scotchman] *Israel's Call* 31 Perfit holines. [**1808–25** Perfit: see A. 2 β.]

4. α. 5–7 **parfet,** (6 **-fett, -fayt(e).** β. 6 **perfait, -fayt,** 6–7 **perfet,** (6 **-fett**).

α. **1419** SIR W. BARDOLPH in Ellis *Orig. Lett.* Ser. II. I. 76 God . . ȝeve ȝow ryght goode lyf and longe parfet helthe of body. **1530** PALSGR. 780, I weare heare nexte my bodye as parfayte folkes do. ? **1668** LADY LYTTELTON in *Hatton Corr.* (Camden) 54, I am infinitely reioyced to heare . . of her parfet recovery.

β. **1526** TINDALE *2 Cor.* xii. 9 My strengthe is made perfait throu weaknes. **1536** R. BEERLEY in *Four C. Eng. Lett.* (1880) 34 An yf yt were never so perfett. **1538** STARKEY *England* I. ii. 62 Euery thyng . . more perfayt in hys nature. **1593** Q. ELIZ. tr. *Boeth.* v. pr. v. 115 With a steddyer & perfeter Judgement. **1667** MILTON P.L. VIII. 415 Supream of things Thou in thy self art perfet, and in thee Is no deficience found. [The words *perfect* and *imperfect* occur 34 times in Milton's Poems, and in 22 instances the spelling is *perfet, imperfet* (A. J. Wyatt *Note to P.R.* IV. 468).]

5. α. 6 **parfecte, -faict.** β. 6 **perfecte, perfaict(e,** 6– **perfect.**

α. **1552–3** *Inv. Ch. Goods Staffs.* in *Ann. Lichfield* IV. 46 A juste true and a parfecte survey. **1593** Q. ELIZ. *Boeth.* I. pr. i. 3 Parfaict for fine workmanship.

β. **1526** TINDALE *Matt.* v. 48 Ye shall therfore be perfecte, even as youre hevenly father is perfecte. [So **1535** COVERD.] —— *Luke* i. 3 Booth were perfect before God. —— *Acts* xi. 24 He was a perfaicte man. **1530** PALSGR. 320 Parfyte . . Perfecte (Fr.) *perfect . . parfect.* **1551** T. WILSON *Logike* (1580) 44 b, The perfect ende of all. [*Perfect* became the usual spelling *c* 1590.]

B. Signification. **I.** General senses.

†**1.** Thoroughly made, formed, done, perfomed, carried out, accomplished. *Obs.*

a. Of a legal act: Duly completed.

c **1330** R. BRUNNE *Chron.* (1810) 254 To þat ilk scrite Edward set his seale, þat his gift was perfite, & with witnes leale. **1567** *Sc. Acts Jas. VI* (1597) §1 The acceptation of the said office of Regentrie . . sall be halden, repute, and esteemed lawfull, sufficient, and perfite.

b. Of offspring: Fully formed.

Passing into sense 3: see esp. 3 c.

1387 TREVISA *Higden* (Rolls) II. 197 Somtyme a womman conceyueth twey children and is but a litel tyme bytwene; and so þe children ben afterward i-bore oon after oþer, and beeþ perfit i-now. *c* **1400** MAUNDEV. (1839) v. 48 And the first Day next after men fynden in the askes a worm; and the secunde day next after men fynden a brid quyk and perfyt. **1538** ELYOT *Dict.*, *Abortio* . . to brynge forthe a chylde, or it be perfecte [COOPER perfite].

c. Of full age; either = grown up, adult, or of an age legally competent for a specified function.

1382 WYCLIF *2 Macc.* v. 24 Comaundynge to hym for to slea alle of perfit age. **1547** J. HARRISON *Exhort. Scottes* A vj b, He shal at his perfect yeres bee restaured to the whole isle of Britayn. **1565** *Reg. Privy Council Scot.* I. 358 Thai may entir within thre termis nixt eftir thair perfyte age of xiiii yeris. **1605** SHAKS. *Lear* I. ii. 77 Sonnes at perfect age, and Fathers declin'd. **1773** MONBODDO *Lang.* (1774) I. I. i. 11 When he comes to be of perfect age.

2. a. Fully accomplished; thoroughly versed, trained, skilled, or conversant. Const. *in*, *with*, †*of* a subject. *arch.*

a **1300** *Cursor M.* 12483 þou broght me not a barn to lere Bot maister es he self parfit. **1387** TREVISA *Higden* (Rolls) III. 219 Among alle he [Plato] is i-preysed for a parfite techere of philosofie. *Ibid.* VII. 71 By craft of þe sterres, in þe whiche craft he was perfit inow. **1450–80** tr. *Secreta Secret.* 21 He that is a parfit studiaunt in that science. *c* **1510** MORE *Picus* Wks. 3/1 [He] was in dede, both a parfet philosophre, and a parfet diuine. **1578** T. N. tr. *Conq. W. India* 212 They were very perfite with theyr bowes. **1592** GREENE *Disput.* 20 The Hawke that is most perfect for the flight. **1597** SHAKS. *2 Hen. IV*, IV. i. 155 Our Men more perfect in the vse of Armes. **1606** HOLLAND *Sueton.* 48 He deemed nothing lesse beseeming a perfit and accomplished Captaine, than hast-making and rashnesse. **1669** GALE *Crt. Gentiles* I. II. ix. 137 They . . were admitted to the state of, τελείων, the perfect, and so made partakers of al Mysteries. **1831** SIR W. HAMILTON *Discuss.* (1853) 406 The Master, Doctor, or perfect graduate, was, in like manner . . obliged immediately to commence . . and to continue for a certain period publicly to teach. **1838** WHEWELL in *Life* (1881) 192 The other persons.. not being very perfect in their duties.

†**b.** Completely prepared; made ready. *Obs.*

1382 WYCLIF *1 Kings* vi. 7 Forsothe the hows.. is beeldid of stonus ouer scorchid and parfite. **1568** BIBLE (Bishops') *ibid.*, The house.. was built of stone perfite before it was brought.

c. Thoroughly learned or acquired, got by heart or by rote, 'at one's fingers' ends'. Also of a person: Having learnt one's lesson or part thoroughly. (Cf. *letter-perfect*, *word-perfect*.)

1581 MULCASTER *Positions* v, That the learning to write be not left of, vntil it be verie perfit. **1588** SHAKS. *L.L.L.* v. ii. 562, I hope I was perfect. I made a little fault in great. [Cf. lines 553-4.] **1592** —— *Ven. & Ad.* 408 The lesson is but plain, And once made perfect, never lost again. **1603** —— *Meas. for M.* v. i. 82 When you haue A businesse for your selfe: pray heauen you then Be perfect. **1665** PEPYS *Diary* 21 Sept., To refresh myself in my musique scale, which I would fain have perfecter than ever I had yet. **1844** ALB. SMITH *Adv. Mr. Ledbury* (1847) II. ii. 174 Mrs. Grimley kindly undertook to prompt, as the performers were not all very perfect. *Mod.* (School). Try to get this lesson perfect.

3. a. In the state proper to anything when completed; complete; having all the essential elements, qualities, or characteristics; not deficient in any particular.

a **1300** *Cursor M.* 11626 (Cott.) Ne haf yee for me na barnsite, For i am self man al parfite. *a* **1325** *Athanasian Creed* 30 in *Prose Psalter* 195 He is parfit God, parfit man, beand of resonable soule & of mannes flesshe. **1548-9** (Mar.) *Ibid.* in *Bk. Com. Prayer*, Perfecte God, and perfecte man. **1571** *Articles of Religion* ii, Two whole and perfect natures, that is to say, the Godhead and manhood.

b. Of actions, states, qualities, and the like.

c **1340** HAMPOLE *Prose Tr.* iii. 7, I had.. na perfite contrycyone. **1382** WYCLIF *1 John* iv. 18 Drede is not in charite, but parfijt charite sendith out drede [**1526** TINDALE, Parfet love casteth out all feare]. *c* **1386** CHAUCER *Prol.* 338 He.. heeld opinion that pleyn delit Was verray felicitee parfit. *c* **1475** *Partenay* 3994 She allwais loued me with hert parfight. **1548-9** (Mar.) *Bk. Com. Prayer, Communion*, Who made.. a full, perfect, and sufficient sacrifyce, oblacion, and satysfaccyon, for the sinnes of the whole worlde. **1748** *Anson's Voy.* III. i. 301 It had been a perfect calm for some days. **1841** MISS MITFORD in L'Estrange *Life* (1870) III. viii. 124 That Mr. Newman is a man of.. perfect sincerity, I have no doubt. **1869** TYNDALL *Notes Lect. Light* §11 There is no such thing as perfect transparency or perfect opacity.

c. Of productions material or immaterial. (1 b may belong here.)

1413 *Pilgr. Sowle* (Caxton 1483) v. xiv. 107 Ther is no body parfit withouten thre dymensions. **1526** *Pilgr. Perf.* (W. de W. 1531) 1 Lyke as the great worlde was made perfecte in vij dayes. **1593** SHAKS. *3 Hen. VI*, II. i. 26 Three glorious Sunnes, each one a perfect Sunne. **1628** T. SPENCER *Logick* 276 Aristotle is of opinion, that this onely is the forme or figure of a perfit Syllogisme. **1665** PEPYS *Diary* 22 Sept., He did twelve feet under ground find perfect trees over-covered with earth. **1697** tr. *Burgersdicius' Logic* I. xxiv. 98 Speech is either perfect or imperfect. Perfect is that that absolves the Sentence. **1872** J. F. CLARKE *Self-Culture* xvi. (1889) 349 Nature finishes everything... Every little flower is perfect and complete, from root to seed.

†**d.** Sound; of sound mind, sane. *Obs.*

1470-85 MALORY *Arthur* XVII. v. 695 Whanne he sawe the letters and vnderstood them, yet he entryd, for he was ryghte parfyte of his lyf. **1552** HULOET, Perfecte or sounde, *integer*. **1605** SHAKS. *Lear* IV. vii. 63, I feare I am not in my perfect mind. *a* **1619** FLETCHER *Mad Lover* I. ii, What postures he puts on! I do not think he's perfect.

4. a. In the state of complete excellence; free from any flaw or imperfection of quality; faultless. But often used of a near approach to such a state, and hence capable of comparison, *perfecter* (= more nearly perfect), *perfectest* (= nearest to perfection).

a **1340** HAMPOLE *Psalter* x. 2 þaim thynke þat þaire vndirstandynge and þaire conuersacioun is perfitere þan oþer. *c* **1380** WYCLIF *Sel. Wks.* III. 449 To teche a perfitere weie to hevene þan evere Crist dide himself. **1529** MORE *Dyaloge* I. Wks. 129/2 Than had our lord not made hys order and course perfite in the begynnynge. **1542** BOORDE *Dyetary* ix. (1870) 251 Abstynence for this matter is.. the parfytest medysone. **1565** *Satir. Poems Reform.* i. 80 My pen is not in perfytt plight her graces to displaie. **1590** R. PAYNE *Descr. Irel.* (1841) 3 Most of them speaking good and perfit English. **1685** TEMPLE *Ess. Gard.* Wks. 1731 I. 185 The perfectest Figure of a Garden I ever saw.. was that of Moor-Park in Hertfordshire. **1784** JOHNSON *Let. to Sastres* 20 Oct., A perfect performance of any kind is not to be expected, and certainly not a perfect dictionary. **1841** L. HUNT *Seer* II. (1864) 64 The perfectest prose-fiction in the language. **1853** J. H. NEWMAN *Hist. Sk.* (1873) II. IV. viii. 197 The barbarian, in his own estimate, is perfect already; and what is perfect cannot be improved. **1877** MORLEY *Crit. Misc.* Ser. II. 391 The only people whom men cannot pardon are the perfect.

b. *spec.* Of supreme moral excellence; righteous, holy; immaculate.

c **1290** [see A. 1]. **1340** HAMPOLE *Pr. Consc.* 3766 For sum þat semes gude here and parfite,.. after þe dede, er dampned als-tite. **1388** WYCLIF *Matt.* v. 48 Be ȝe parfit, as ȝoure heuenli fadir is parfit. **1450-1530** *Myrr. our Ladye* 76 None maye wythstonde eny temptacyon be he neuer so parfyt, wythout specyall helpe, and grace of god. **1526** [see A. 5 β]. **1611** BIBLE *Ps.* xxxvii. 37 Marke the perfect man, and behold the vpright: for the end of that man is peace. **1743** WESLEY *Serm. Chr. Perfect.*, Every one that is perfect is holy: and every one that is holy is, in the Scripture sense, perfect.

c. Of things: Marked by moral perfection.

1535 COVERDALE *Ps.* xviii. 30 The waye of God is a perfecte waye. *Ibid.* xix. 7 The lawe of the Lorde is a perfecte lawe. **1738** WESLEY *Ps.* CXXXIX. xiv, Guide me in thy perfect way.

d. *a perfect day* (*colloq.*), a day of which every part has been enjoyable; *esp.* in phr. *the end of a perfect day*.

1910 C. JACOBS-BOND *Perfect Day* (song) 6 For mem'ry has painted this perfect day With colors that never fade, And we find at the end of a perfect day The soul of a friend we've made. **1923** *Liverpool Echo* 13 Sept. 6/3 (*heading*) The boy and the balloon. The sad end of a perfect day. **1976** S. KAUFMAN *Master & Other Stories* (1977) 193 Nothing crossed her mind as she floated, a thing made of air, and dreamily listened to the carrying voices from shore, except the one thought: What a perfect day.

5. Completely corresponding to a definition, pattern, or description.

a. Of a geometrical figure, a point of space or time, and the like: Exact, precise.

c **1391** CHAUCER *Astrol.* I. §18 Som of hem semen perfit cercles, & somme semen inperfit. **1574** BOURNE *Regiment for Sea* xvii. (1577) 46 The perfit houre and minute of the chaunges of the Moone. **1701** NORRIS *Ideal World* I. ii. 53 Other figures therefore I do see, and those perfect ones. **1823** H. J. BROOKE *Introd. Crystallogr.* 62 It is capable of being reduced again to the perfect octahedron. **1860** TYNDALL *Glac.* I. x. 65 Heavy hail had fallen,.. the stones being perfect spheres.

b. Of a copy, representation, etc.: Accurately reproducing or reflecting the original; exact, correct. †Of a notion, thought, etc.: Exactly corresponding to the facts, correct (*obs.*).

1540-1 ELYOT *Image Gov.* 2 In this boke was expressed of gouernaunce so perfyte an image. **1592** T. DIGGES (*title*) A Perfit Description of the Cœlestiall Orbes. **1595** SHAKS. *John* v. vi. 6 *Hub.* Whose there? Speake hoa... *Bast.* Hubert, I thinke. *Hub.* Thou hast a perfect thought. **1611** BIBLE *Transl. Pref.* 4 That Translation was not so sound and so perfect, but that it needed in many places correction. **1790** PALEY *Horæ Paul.* i. 6 A more perfect copy procured at Aleppo. **1867** HOWELLS *Ital. Journ.* 299 The perfectest reproduction of the Greek theater in the world.

c. Fully answering to what the name implies. Also in phrases *perfect gentleman, lady*.

c **1449** PECOCK *Repr.* II. xv. 233 Samaritanys.. weren not perfite and ful Iewis neither thei were perfite and ful hethen. *a* **1548** HALL *Chron., Hen. IV* 10 b, Made hym as he surely coniectured his perfite frende, where in dede he was inwardly his dedly enemie. *a* **1613** OVERBURY *A Wife*, etc. (1638) 286 The Devil is the perfectest Courtier. **1807** WORDSWORTH *Poems* I. 15 A perfect woman; nobly plann'd, To warn, to comfort, and command. **1818** BYRON *Beppo* xxxii. 17 In short, he was a perfect cavaliero, And to his very valet seem'd a hero. **1833** KEBLE *Serm.* vi. (1848) 142 That combination of sweetness with firmness.. which constitutes the temper of a perfect public man. **1834** G. CRABBE JUN. in *Poet. Wks. G. Crabbe* I. vi. 147 Miss Waldron.. could sing a jovial song like a fox-hunter,.. and yet there was such an air of high *ton*, and such intellect mingled with these manners, that the perfect lady was not veiled for a moment. **1856** C. M. YONGE *Daisy Chain* I. xxiii. 245 Her instinct showed her that she was talking to a man of high ability. A perfect gentleman she saw him to be. **1872** GEO. ELIOT *Middlem.* I. II. xvi. 299 Rosamond.. was active.. in being from morning till night her own standard of a perfect lady. **1903** G. B. SHAW *Revolutionist's Handbk.* i, in *Man & Superman* 182 This.. is a great advance on the popular demand for a perfect gentleman and a perfect lady. **1949** E. COXHEAD *Wind in West* i. 25 You'll like the Fletchers—Hermia is a wonder, the perfect wife. **1967** A. WILSON *No Laughing Matter* III. 320 All perfect ladies.. eat messily, don't they? **1972** J. PORTER *Meddler & her Murder* iv. 49, I never knew old Adam was a womanizer! Must say, he's always behaved like a perfect gentleman with me. **1978** H. MACINNES *Prelude to Terror* iv. 34 The perfect hostess.. a woman putting a guest at ease with food and drink.

d. Entire, unqualified; pure, unmixed, unalloyed.

1590 SHAKS. *Mids. N.* I. ii. 98 Either your straw-colour beard, your orange tawnie beard,.. your perfect yellow. **1591** —— *Two Gent.* IV. iv. 194. **1595** —— *John* I. i. 90 Mine eye hath well examined his parts, And findes them perfect Richard. **1600** J. PORY tr. *Leo's Africa* II. 71 The walles, the towers, and the gates built all of perfect marble. **1648** in *Bury Wills* (Camden) 217 My damaske sword, with the handle of perfect gold. **1699** VANBRUGH *False Friend* II. i, You talk.. like a perfect stranger to that tenderness methinks every son should feel for a good father. **1878** HUXLEY *Physiogr.* 6 To a perfect stranger.. such a method of description would be unintelligible.

e. Mere, sheer; unmitigated, utter. (Qualifying something bad, repulsive, or disliked.) Chiefly *colloq.* or *dial.*

1611 SHAKS. *Temp.* I. i. 32 His complexion is perfect Gallowes. **1714** ADDISON *Lover* No. 39 ⁋2 He.. has.. reduced himself to a perfect skeleton. **1748** *Anson's Voy.* I. viii. 79 The storm.. proved a perfect hurricane. **1792** A. WILSON *Watty & Meg* in *Poems & Lit. Prose* (1876) II. 5 She's tired wi' perfect skelping. **1801** MACNEILL *Poet. Wks.* (1856) 139 (E.D.D.) Worn to perfect skin and bane. **1804-6** SYD. SMITH *Mor. Philos.* (1850) 187 A man whose chin terminated in a point.. would be a perfect horror. **1818** SCOTT *Hrt. Midl.* xxiv, The queen tore her biggonets for perfect anger. **1861** QUINN *Heather* (1863) 156 Gar a thief forget himsel', An' blush for perfect shame. *Mod. colloq.* It is perfect nonsense to say that he cannot.

f. Complete, utter (referring to a person in neutral or favourable contexts).

1903 G. B. SHAW *Man & Superman* I. 40 You seem to understand all the things I dont understand; but you are a perfect baby in the things I do understand. **1919** T. K. HOLMES *Man from Tall Timber* xxiv. 292 That Anabelle Whitman is a perfect scream. **1927** C. CONNOLLY *Let.* 27 Jan. in *Romantic Friendship* (1975) 231 Thou art heavenly he a 'perfect scream'. **1931** T. E. LAWRENCE *Lett.* (1938) 713 The Coroner was a perfect pet. **1959** *Listener* 4 June 998/2 He [*sc.* Harry Secombe] is indeed a Perfect Scream in both senses of that noun. **1961** PARKS & LEIGHTON *My Thirty Years backstairs at White House* xiii. 190 Rob Roy was a perfect angel with the First Family.

†**6.** Completely assured, fully informed, certain: of a statement or speaker. *Obs. rare.*

1568 GRAFTON *Chron.* II. 700 He had perfect worde that the Duke of Clarance came forwarde towarde him with a great armie. **1611** SHAKS. *Wint. T.* III. iii. 1 Thou art perfect then, our ship hath toucht vpon The Desarts of Bohemia. **1611** —— *Cymb.* III. i. 73, I am perfect, That the Pannonians.. for Their Liberties are now in Armes.

†**7.** In a state of complete satisfaction; satisfied, contented. *Obs. rare.*

1605 SHAKS. *Macb.* III. iv. 21 Then comes my Fit againe: I had else beene perfect. **1607** —— *Timon* I. ii. 90 Might we but haue that happinesse my Lord.. we should thinke our selues for euer perfect.

II. Technical senses.

8. *Arith.* Applied to a number which is equal to the sum of its aliquot parts. (Formerly in other senses: see quots. 1422, *c* 1440.)

1422 tr. *Secreta Secret., Priv. Priv.* 214 Do thou that they bene ten, fore tene is a perfite nombyr, and hit contenyth in hym-sylfe foure nombres, that is to witte, one and two, and thre and foure. *c* **1440** *York Myst.* xliv. 9 We are leued a-lyue, elleuyn,.. Or we begynne vs muste be even,.. For parfite noumbre it is none, Off elleuen for to lere. **1570** BILLINGSLEY *Euclid* VII. def. xxiii. 187 The partes of 6 are 1. 2. 3,.. and mo partes 6 hath not:.. wherefore 6 is a perfect number. So likewise is 28 a perfect number... This kinde of numbers is very rare. **1674** JEAKE *Arith.* (1696) 5 Perfect Numbers are almost as rare as perfect Men. **1709-29** V. MANDEY *Syst. Math., Arith.* 5 There are found but few Perfect Numbers.. to wit, from 1 to 40,000000, only these: 6, 28, 496, 8128, 130816, 2096128, 33,550336;.. all the Perfect Numbers begin by turns from 6 and 8. **1795** HUTTON *Math. Dict.* s.v. **1901** *Ann. Math.* II. 103 By a perfect number is meant a number which is equal to the sum of those of its divisors which are less than the number. Thus 6 = 1 + 2 + 3 is a perfect number. *Ibid.* 104 His [*sc.* Sylvester's] proof of the non-existence of odd perfect numbers. **1958** R. V. ANDREE *Sel. Mod. Abstr. Algebra* i. 30 The first four perfect numbers were discovered by the end of the first century. By 1870, only four more had been found. Between 1870 and 1950, four additional even perfect numbers were discovered... Since then, five more perfect numbers have been found. **1971** *Sci. Amer.* June 56/2 Whether or not there are any odd perfect numbers is still undecided.

9. *Gram.* †**a.** Of verbs: Regular. *Obs.* **b.** Applied to the tense which denotes a completed event or action viewed in relation to the present; hence (with qualification) to any tense expressing action completed at the time indicated: see PLUPERFECT, *future perfect* (FUTURE *a.* 2).

1530 PALSGR. Introd. 30 Verbes parsonall be of thre sortes, parfyte, anomales, and defectyves. *Ibid.* 84 The preterperfit tens, as *je ay parlé* I have spoken. *Ibid.* 88 The preter parfit tens. **1581** E. CAMPION in *Confer.* II. (1584) N iv b, I pray you what *tempus* is it? *Campion.* The perfect *tempus*, euen as *clausis* the Latine worde is. **1727-41** CHAMBERS *Cycl.*, *Perfect*, in grammar. Preter or preterit-perfect tense, is an inflection, marking a time perfectly past. **1879** BAIN *Higher Eng. Gram.* 166 The infinitive followed by a past participle forms a perfect infinitive active: 'to have loved', 'having loved'.

10. *Mus.* (Opp. to IMPERFECT *a.* 7.)

†**a.** In mediæval music, applied to a note when reckoned as three times the length of a note of the next lower denomination; and hence to those 'modes', etc. characterized by such relative value of the notes (answering to what is now called triple time or rhythm). *Obs.* **b.** *perfect concords* (†*cords*) or *consonances*: a name including the concords of a unison, fifth, and octave, and sometimes a fourth (as distinguished from the thirds and sixths). Hence **c.** Applied to the intervals of a fourth, fifth, and octave, in their normal form (opp. to *augmented* and *diminished*): now sometimes (like thirds, sixths, etc.) called *major*. So *perfect chord* or *triad*, a name for the common chord in its direct position (involving a perfect fifth), as opp. to the *imperfect* or *diminished triad*. **d.** *perfect cadence*: a cadence consisting of the direct chord of the tonic preceded by a dominant or subdominant chord (authentic or plagal cadence), and forming a full close: opp. to *imperfect* and *interrupted cadence*.

1597 MORLEY *Introd. Mus.* 18 The Moode perfect of the lesse prolation is, when all go by two, except the Semibreefe: as two Longes to the Large:.. three Semibreeues to the Breefe. *Ibid.*, The moode perfect of the more is, when all go by three; as three Longes to the Large: three Breeues to the Longe [etc.]. *Ibid.* 72 You must not rise nor fall with two perfect cordes togither. *Ibid.* Annot., Why some of those consonants [= consonances].. are called perfect, and othersome vnperfect, I can giue.. no reason. **1667** Perfect Concords [see IMPERFECT *a.* 7]. **1704** J. HARRIS *Lex. Techn.* I, *Perfect Fifth*, the same with *Diapente*. **1727-41** CHAMBERS *Cycl.*, *Perfect*, in music, denotes something that fills, and satisfies the mind, and the ear.—In which sense we say, perfect cadence, perfect concord, &c. **1875** OUSELEY *Harmony* xiii. 154 The perfect cadence corresponds exactly to a full stop in writing. **1880** W. S. ROCKSTRO in Grove *Dict. Mus.* I. 766 Mode, Time, and Prolation were themselves capable of assuming a Perfect or an Imperfect form... Notes, even when Perfect by virtue of the Mode, Time, or Prolation in which they were written, could be made Imperfect.

e. *perfect pitch*, the ability to judge pitch absolutely, and hence recognize the pitch of any individual note. (Cf. *absolute pitch* (b) s.v. ABSOLUTE *a.* 16.)

1949 F. TOWERS *Tea with Mr. Rochester* 19 She is very musical, and has perfect pitch. **1958** *Gramophone* Oct. 17 Listeners with perfect pitch are warned that, this being the Schnitger organ at Cappel, all the works here sound a semitone higher than usual. **1971** *Nature* 2 Apr. 337/1 Few people possess 'perfect pitch' and it is not known whether it is learned or inherited. **1975** *Sunday Times* (Colour Suppl.) 13 July 47/4 Although he does not sight read he has perfect pitch. **1976** *Gramophone* Aug. 318/3 Listeners with perfect pitch should be warned that the present issue sounds a semitone lower than normal.

11. a. *Physiol.*, *Anat.*, etc. Having its proper characteristics developed to the fullest degree; typical.

1693 tr. *Blancard's Phys. Dict.* (ed. 2) s.v. *Perfecta Crisis*, One Crisis is called perfect, another imperfect;..perfect is that which frees the Patient perfectly and entirely from the Distemper; and it is either salutary or deadly. **1805** *Med. Jrnl.* XIV. 84 Inoculated cow pock, under its most perfect form. **1830** R. Knox *Béclard's Anat.* 244 Perfect cartilages also occur under the form of incrustation or plates. **1841–71** T. R. Jones *Anim. Kingd.* (ed. 4) 721 Most of the parts enumerated as entering into the composition of a perfect or typical skeleton. **1856** Grindon *Life* xxv. (1875) 322 'Perfect' is used by the naturalist to express the degree in which those peculiarities are developed which characterize a particular group. **1863** *Chambers' Encycl.* V. 589/2 The mouths of mandibulate Insects are sometimes called *perfect*, and those which exhibit a different character, *imperfect*.

†**b.** (See quot.) *Obs.*

1727–41 Chambers *Cycl.*, *Perfect*, in physiology. A *perfect* animal is used by some writers for that which is born by univocal generation; in opposition to insects, which they pretend to be produced by equivocal generation.

12. *Bot.* Having all four whorls of the flower (calyx, corolla, stamens, and pistils).

1706 Phillips, *Perfect flowers* (among Herbalists) are those that have the finely colour'd small leaves, call'd Petala, with the Stamina, Apices, and Stylus. **1727–41** Chambers *Cycl.* s.v., *Perfect flowers* are such as have petala, pistil, stamina, and apices. **1861** Bentley *Man. Bot.* 557 *Combretaceæ*... Leaves exstipulate, entire, without dots. Flowers perfect or unisexual.

13. *Ent.* In the most completely or finally developed form or phase of existence, as ***perfect insect, state***, etc.

1834 *Encycl. Brit.* (ed. 7) IX. 86/2 Mouffet..mistook the aquatic larvæ of Libellulæ for creatures entirely distinct from the perfect insects. *Ibid.* 87/2 The imago or perfect condition. **1863** *Chambers's Encycl.* V. 591/1 The intermediate or pupa state often differs little..from the perfect state.

14. *Physics.* Conceived as existing in a state of ideal perfection, as ***perfect elasticity, gas***.

1849 Thomson in *Trans. R. Soc. Edin.* XVI. 545 A perfect thermodynamic engine..is a machine by means of which the greatest possible amount of mechanical effect can be obtained from a given thermal agency. **1850** Rankine *Ibid.* XX. 148 The elasticity of a perfect gas at a given temperature varies simply in proportion to its density. **1867** Thomson & Tait *Nat. Phil.* I. 514 That property of perfect elasticity towards which highly elastic bodies in nature approximate. *Ibid.* 592 A *perfect fluid*..is an unrealizable conception, like a rigid, or a smooth, body: it is defined as a body incapable of resisting a change of shape. **1867** Besant *Hydrodynamics* (ed. 2) 1 A perfect fluid is assumed to have no 'viscosity', no property of the nature of friction.

15. *Printing.* ***perfect ream***, a ream of 516 sheets, = ***printer's ream***: see ream *sb.*[3] Also applied to sheets that have been printed on both sides.

1841 W. Savage *Dict. Art of Printing* 701 The reader, in revising the second form, then sees the sheet perfect, which is necessary to ascertain that the matter follows. **1888** Jacobi *Printers' Vocab.* 98 Reams of paper made up to a printer's ream, i.e. 516 sheets, are said to be 'perfect'. **1960** G. A. Glaister *Gloss. Bk.* 303/2 In edition binding the printed sheets are said to be perfect as soon as some or all of the sheets (and plates) have been printed.

16. *Bot.* Applied to the stage in the life cycle of a fungus at which sexual spores are produced, and to a fungus in that state.

1891 G. Massee *Brit. Fungi* 32 The incomplete form is considered as belonging to the same genus as the perfect form. **1909** *Mycologia* I. 115 A single boll [of cotton]..was examined in the laboratory and found to be covered with the perfect stage of the *Colletotrichum*. **1945** G. R. Bisby *Introd. Taxon. & Nomencl. Fungi* xvi. 87 The perfect state is that which ends in the ascus stage in the *Ascomycetes*, in the basidium in the *Basidiomycetes*, in the teleutospore or its equivalent in the *Uredinales*, and in the spore in the *Ustilaginales*. **1950** E. A. Bessey *Morphol. & Taxon. Fungi* i. 18 In fungi with several stages of development to which different names have been given, the species epithet that is to be retained is the one applied to the 'perfect' stage of the fungus. **1967** M. E. Hale *Biol. Lichens* iii. 45 The parasymbiont *Abrothallus suecicus* is the perfect stage of the imperfect fungus *Phoma*. **1971** [see imperfect *a.* 8 b].

17. Applied to a form of bookbinding in which the single leaves of a book are attached individually to the spine by an adhesive, instead of the printed sheets being folded and sewn.

1893 *Amer. Bookbinder* July 86 (*heading*) Perfect library binding. *Ibid.*, Mr. Crawford is the inventor of what is known as the 'perfect library binding'. **1910** G. A. Stephen *Commerc. Bookbinding* 9/2 A revolution in the method of binding monthly magazines was inaugurated by the invention of the Sheridan 'Perfect Binder'. **1926** *Amazing Stories* July 359/1 We..took immediate ways and means to do away with the old-fashioned binding, and you now hold in your hand a magazine bound with the so-called 'Perfect' binding. **1956** H. Williamson *Methods Bk. Design* xix. 332 Sewing, rounding, backing, and lining can all be dispensed with in the unsewn or 'perfect' methods of binding. **1960** *Times Lit. Suppl.* 3 June 360/3 The so-called 'perfect' binding, in which, the backs of the quires having been guillotined away, the resultant single leaves are held hopefully together by adhesive. **1977** *Ibid.* 28 Jan. 104/2 The pages are now smaller, the paper thinner,..and the binding is perfect (ie, imperfect). **1977** *Special Libraries* Feb. 6A/2 Perfect bound ('newspeak' for 'unsewn') bindings on books have caused librarians grief and libraries money (for rebinding) since they fall apart so readily... I urge publishers not to utilize this type of binding until they have really perfected the process.

18. *Econ.* Designating (notional or actual) ideal market conditions in which adverse factors are removed; ***perfect competition***, competition in which all elements of monopoly are absent and the market price of a commodity is beyond the control of individual buyers and sellers.

1897 *Q. Jrnl. Econ.* XII. 125 In passing from the study of perfect monopoly to that of perfect competition, Cournot considers also the intermediate case of a few, say two, competitors. **1906** *Ibid.* XX. 211 Perfect competition is the fundamental hypothesis of economics in the sense that perfect competition is postulated in nearly every argument as to economic equilibrium. **1922** H. A. Silverman *Substance Econ.* vi. 72 Perfect competition..is not usually realized in practice. **1939** Lyness & Emmet *Introd. Econ.* iv. 38 The characteristics of a perfect market are, firstly, full information... Secondly, complete accessibility... Thirdly, full freedom of choice. **1944** A. Cairncross *Introd. Econ.* xiv. 180 The first requirement of perfect competition ..is that the market..should be perfect; a perfect market being one in which buyers have no preferences as between the different units of the commodity offered for sale, sellers are quite indifferent to whom they sell, and both buyers and sellers have full knowledge of prices in other parts of the market. **1969** D. C. Hague *Managerial Econ.* iii. 59 There is an established market where all buyers and sellers can keep in close touch with each other, and have become used to doing so. Economists sometimes say that there is then a *perfect market*. **1971** I. Deutscher *Marxism in our Time* (1972) xii. 259 Even when, for the sake of argument, he [*sc.* Marx] assumed perfect competition, he did it only in order to prove that that competition was necessarily self-destructive. **1974** M. B. Brown *Econ. of Imperialism* ii. 30 The classical vision of an economy where there is perfect competition reaches its apogee in the Theory of Free Trade. **1976** *Economist* 16 Oct. 21/2 Foreign exchange markets do not quite match up to the ideal of perfect competition described by theory.

19. *Math.* **a.** Of a set of points: closed, and such that every neighbourhood of each point of the set contains at least one other point of the set.

1906 *Q. Jrnl. Math.* XXXVII. 23 *P* is a rim point, so that the rim is closed, and, being dense in itself, is perfect. **1926** J. E. Littlewood *Elem. of Theory of Real Functions* (ed. 2) iv. 50 A perfect set is an existent set which is closed and dense-in-itself. **1957** J. R. Aumann et al. tr. *Hausdorff's Set Theory* vi. 133 The null set is everything: isolated, dense-in-itself, closed, perfect. **1970** C. A. Rogers *Hausdorff Measures* ii. 61 A set is perfect if it is closed, non-empty and dense in itself.

b. Of a group: such that the subgroup generated by the set of commutators of the group is the group itself.

1898 *Amer. Jrnl. Math.* XX. 277 Since a perfect group is identical with its derivatives, it cannot be isomorphic to any Abelian group whose order exceeds unity. **1908** H. Hilton *Introd. Theory Groups of Finite Order* x. 134 Every simple group is perfect. **1940** D. E. Littlewood *Theory of Group Characters* x. 174 A group is perfect if it is identical with its commutator subgroup. Hence the condition that a group is perfect is that it possesses no character satisfying $\chi_0 = 1$ save that character which is unity for every operation. **1959** J. S. Lomont *Applications of Finite Groups* ii. 2 Let us call a group (of order > 1) perfect if it is identical with its commutator subgroup. Every perfect group is then insolvable.

C. as *adv.* = perfectly. *Obs.* exc. *dial.* or *poet.*

c **1470** *Golagros & Gaw.* 1100 As I am cristynit perfite. *a* **1550** in *Dunbar's Poems* (S.T.S.) 317 In the cuntre he and I Can nocht dwell baith perfyte. **1567** Turberv. *Piers to T.* Epit. etc. 9 b, Men dæmen may you are not perfite wise. **1596** Dalrymple tr. *Leslie's Hist. Scot.* I. 61 Thay had the similitude of perfyte schapen foulis. **1682** Creech tr. *Lucretius* (1683) 214 No Compound's perfect solid, free from Pore. **1726–31** Tindal *Rapin's Hist. Eng.* (1743) II. xvii. 102 A perfect honest man. **1830** Tennyson *Madeline* ii, Frowns perfect-sweet along the brow.

D. quasi-*sb.*

1. That which is perfect, perfection. *rare*, *poetic*.

1842 Tennyson *Two Voices* 292 That type of Perfect in his mind In Nature can he nowhere find.

2. *Gram.* Elliptical for *perfect tense*: see B. 9 b.

1841 R. G. Latham *Eng. Lang.* §180 One of two forms, sometimes..that of the Greek Perfect, and sometimes..that of the Greek Aorist. **1848** J. W. Donaldson *Grk. Gram.* §425 The perfect expresses the state or condition consequent on an action. **1888** B. H. Kennedy *Shorter Lat. Primer* 72 The *Perfect* in the sense of *I have loved* is *Primary*: in the sense of *I loved* it is *Historic*.

¶**3.** *perfit, -fet, -fight*: an occasional copyist's error for profit (due to confounding the MS. contractions for *per-* and *pro-*).

1495 *Trevisa's Barth. De P.R.* iv. ix. (W. de W.), Bothe for nede and for perfyght [L. *utilitatem*].

4. [tr. med.L. *perfectus* in the same sense (also used).] Among the Catharist heresy of the Albigenses in the 12th and 13th centuries, one who had received the consolamentum or spiritual baptism, thereby accepting all the precepts of Albigensian doctrine.

1742 L. Brown tr. *Bossuet's Hist. Variations Protestant Churches* II. xi. cxl. 156 In regard of those four thousand *Cathari*,..none were understood by that name but the *perfect* of the Sect... When the Sect was weaken'd, tho' there were but four thousand perfect *Cathari*, yet..the multitude..of simple *Believers*, was then infinite. **1826** in J. C. L. S. de Sismondi *Hist. Crusades against Albigenses* p. xvii, They were divided into two classes, the *perfect* and the *believers*. **1832** S. R. Maitland *Albigenses & Waldenses* x. 271 Those men who assert that they alone are good christians whom the most Holy Roman Church persecuted, and condemns, and calls *perfecti*, or *consolati* (more properly *desolati*) heretics. **1888** H. C. Lea *Hist. Inquisition Middle Ages* I. ii. 84 The Perfects would die rather than violate the precept. *Ibid.* iii. 103 If the Perfect is exhorted by the God in whom he believes to tell all about his life, he will faithfully detail it without falsehood. **1926** A. L. Maycock *Inquisition* ii. 40 The 'Perfect' were forbidden to eat meat, eggs, cheese or anything that was the result of sexual procreation. **1957** N. Cohn *Pursuit of Millennium* (1970) viii. 140 The Catharist *perfecti* dominated the religious life of a large part of southern France for half a century or more. **1961** [see endura]. **1970** [see consolamentum]. **1975** *Times* 24 Feb. 15/5 Fox had resembled a Perfectus, with no sense of sin... Penn represents another type of Cathar.

perfect (pəˈfɛkt, ˈpɜːfɪkt), *v.* Forms: α. 5–6 parfyte, etc. (see prec.). β. 5 perfyght, 6–7 perfite, -fait, 6– perfect. [f. perfect *a.*, in its various late ME. and early mod.Eng. forms. Now usually pronounced *per'fect*, as if directly f. ppl. stem of L. *perficĕre* to accomplish, finish, complete.]

1. a. *trans.* To bring to completion; to complete, finish, consummate; to carry through, accomplish.

1494 Fabyan *Chron.* ii. xxviii. 20 He began the .iiii. hyghe wayes of Bretayne, the whiche were fynysshed and parfyted of Belynus his sone. *Ibid.* vi. clxiv. 158 Whiche conclusyon perfyghted, Lewys..retornyd into Germany. **1512** *Helyas* in Thoms *Prose Rom.* (1828) III. 30 After that the false olde woman had parfet and doone their treason. **1529** Cromwell in Merriman *Life & Lett.* (1902) I. 324 All which bokes be not yet..parfyted unto my mynde. **1562** Bp. Jewel *Apol. Ch. Eng.* ii. i. Wks. (Parker Soc.) III. 59 There he..shall sit, till all things be fully perfitted. **1588** A. King tr. *Canisius' Catech.* in *Cath. Tractates* (S.T.S.) 193 The boilding of the wallis of Ierusalem was perfaitit be Nehemia. **1596** Drayton *Leg.* iii. 347 To perfect my command. **1624** Quarles *Sion's Elegies* iii. 11 Labour perfected, with the evening ends. **1629** Sir W. Mure *True Crucif.* 2088 The Worke of Man's salvation to perfite [*rime* delite]. **1641** Milton *Reform.* i. (1851) 10 Exact Reformation is not perfited at the first push. **1644** —— *Areop.* (Arb.) 39 The Councell of Trent..brought forth, or perfeted those Catalogues. **1725** Pope *Odyss.* ii. 125 Then urg'd, she perfects her illustrious toils. **1875** Stubbs *Const. Hist.* II. xv. 291 This design was perfected in 1295.

b. *Printing.* To complete the printing of a sheet of a book, etc. by printing the second side.

1824 J. Johnson *Typogr.* II. 661 When one side is printed, it revolves from one cylinder to the other, and is then perfected by the second form. **1888** Jacobi *Printers' Vocab.* 98 Perfect up..the printing of the second side of the paper in half-sheet or sheet work. **1899** J. Southward *Mod. Printing* III. xii. 117 Rotary web machines also perfect the paper..before it is delivered. **1927** R. B. McKerrow *Introd. Bibliogr.* i. ii. 21 It is often evident..that the printer printed the whole number of impressions on one side before starting to perfect. *Ibid.* iii. i. 261 It is possible that a sheet may be perfected from a wrong forme. **1964** F. Bowers *Bibliogr. & Textual Criticism* iii. i. 71 The specific example of *Match Me in London* and its sheet that was perfected out of phase. **1972** P. Gaskell *New Introd. Bibliogr.* 132 The sixteenth-century account of Le Roy suggests that the heap was normally printed as white paper in the morning, turned at the midday break, and perfected in the afternoon.

†**2.** To bring to full development. *Obs.*

1398 Trevisa *Barth. De P.R.* viii. xvi. (Add. MS. 27944) þe sonne..ordeyneþ and disposiþ & parfitiþ alle þingis in þis worlde. **1607** Topsell *Four-f. Beasts* (1658) 259 The males are sooner perfited in the womb then the females.

3. To make perfect or faultless; to bring to perfection; *loosely*: To bring nearer to perfection; to improve.

c **1449** [see perfecting *vbl. sb.*]. **1567** Drant *Horace, De Arte Poet.* B ij, Those verses reprehende..Correcting, and perfyting them with ouernotynge hande. **1575–85** Abp. Sandys *Serm.* xxii. §12 Perfiting himselfe in Godlinesse. **1630** Lennard tr. *Charron's Wisd.* iii. xiv. §22 (1670) 452 Learning marreth weak wits and spirits, perfitteth the strong and natural. *a* **1703** Burkitt *On N.T.* Heb. vii. 12 To perfect sinful man, is to free him from the guilt of sin,..and to make him..capable of communion with God. **1859** Thackeray *Virgin.* vi, George especially perfected his accent so as to be able to pass for a Frenchman. **1875** Lyell *Princ. Geol.* II. iii. xxxvi. 289 When the art of the breeder has been greatly perfected.

4. To make (a person) perfect *in* some art, etc.; †to instruct or inform completely (*obs.*).

1603 Shaks. *Meas. for M.* iv. iii. 146 Her cause, and yours Ile perfect him withall. **1610** —— *Temp.* i. ii. 79 Being once perfected how to graunt suites, How to deny them. **1628** Bp. Hall *Old Relig.* 154 That which can perfit the teacher, is sufficient for the learner. **1819** A. Balfour *Campbell* I. lii. 23 It will take five or sax years to *perfyte* him in that language. **1823** Galt *Entail* I. xiii. 96 To send her for three months to Edinburgh; there, and in that time, to learn manners, 'and be perfited', as her mother said, 'wi' a boarding-school education'.

5. *intr.* To come to perfection or maturity. *rare.*

1870 Morris *Earthly Par.* iv. Epil. 437 And all those images of love and pain, Wrought as the year did wax, perfect, and wane.

perfecta (pəˈfɛktə). orig. *U.S.* [abbrev. Amer. Sp. *quiniela perfecta* perfect quinella.] A method of betting in which the bettor must pick the first and second finishers of a race in the correct order. Also *attrib.*

1971 *New Yorker* 20 Feb. 107 For horseplayers who hopefully bet on exactas, perfectas, quinellas, doubles, and such, I can report that..an exacta paid $25,257. **1971** L. Koppett *N.Y. Times Guide Spectator Sports* x. 184 In the 'perfecta'..you must pick the first two [finishers] in the correct order. **1972** *Telegraph* (Brisbane) 17 June 18/3 His target was to fix races which were the subject of 'perfecta betting'. **1974** *Cleveland* (Ohio) *Plain Dealer* 26 Oct. 8-D/4 He also had the $13.80 perfecta in the seventh. **1975** *Ibid.* 6

Apr. 13-C/1 A new ruling allows Northfield four (instead of three) perfecta races nightly, which will be raced as the third, fifth, seventh and tenth races. To pick a winning perfecta combination, you must pick the first two horses that finish a race, in order.

perfectability, var. PERFECTIBILITY.

perfectation (pɜːfɪk'teɪʃən). *rare.* [f. PERFECT *v.* + -ATION.] The action or process of making or becoming perfect.
1832 GEN. P. THOMPSON *Exerc.* (1842) II. 55 Man's perfectation is a flower that may be increased without the possibility of showing it in a state it cannot go beyond. 1874 W. R. GREG *Rocks Ahead* 8 The change is not a carrying out, a completion, a perfectation of our former system, but a reversal of it.

perfected (see the vb.), *ppl. a.* [f. PERFECT *v.* + -ED[1].] Made perfect, completed.
1552 HULOET, Perfected and ended, *integer.* 1848 MAURICE *Serm. Lord's Prayer* iii. (1861) 28 They require that which is different in kind from anything which their eyes see, not merely *that* in an improved and perfected form.
Hence **perfectedly** *adv.*, perfectly, completely.
1693 BEVERLEY *True St. Gosp. Truth* 18 When indeed with a Face perfectedly open, we shall behold as in a Mirror, .. Iesus Christ the Image of God in his own Glory. 1892 B. MATTHEWS in *Harper's Mag.* July 279/1 We might suppose that the present spelling of the English language was in a condition perfectedly satisfactory.

perfecter ('pɜːfɪktə(r), pə'fɛktə(r)). Also 5 perfiter, (-our), -fyter, parfiter, -fyȝter. [f. PERFECT *v.* + -ER[1]: cf. PERFECTOR.] One who or that which perfects, completes, or finishes; a consummator.
c 1410 EDW. DK. YORK *Master of Game* (MS. Digby 182) Prol. (cf. ed. 1904 pp. 6–7), He shal se, whiche houndes commeth in the vanchace and the myddell and whiche ben perfitours [*v.rr.* parfiters, perfyters] after that that shall come. *Ibid.*, To loke .. which houndes ben vanchasours and perfiters [*v.r.* parfyȝters]. 1611 COTGR., *Parfaiseur*, a perfecter, accomplisher, finisher. 1678 CUDWORTH *Intell. Syst.* I. iv. 485 The Ancients .. supposing this God [Saturn] to be the Giver and Perfecter of all happiness to men. 1740 WARBURTON *Div. Legat.* II. IV. v. 277 The Inventor and Perfecter of the Arts of Life. 1881 N. T. (R.V.) *Heb.* xii. 2 Looking unto Jesus the author and perfecter of our faith.

perfectibi'larian, perfecti'bilian. *nonce-wds.* = PERFECTIBILIST: see next.
1816 T. L. PEACOCK *Headlong Hall* i, These four persons were, Mr. Foster, the perfectibilian; Mr. Escot, the deteriorationist; Mr. Jenkison, the statu-quo-ite [etc.]. 1832 *Fraser's Mag.* VI. 499 Every unwashed artisan has become .. a philosopher, a perfectibilian, and so forth. 1852 *Blackw. Mag.* LXXII. 278 We should have left it to the Perfectibilarian to show what probability there is that this ignorant and disorderly class will .. be absorbed in the higher.

perfectibilism (pɜːfɪk'tɪbɪlɪz(ə)m). [f. as PERFECTIBLE + -ISM.] The doctrine of the perfectibility of human nature in this life. So **perfec'tibilist**, one who holds this doctrine.
1798 W. TAYLOR in *Monthly Rev.* XXVII. 513 He had originally intended for them the name of Perfectibilist. 1852 *Tait's Mag.* XIX. 749 Satires of socialism and perfectibilism. 1883 *Sat. Rev.* 8 Dec. 725/1 We are *in rebus snobbicis* at any rate perfectibilists. The snob of this generation .. is a much more odious reptile than he of the last.

perfectibility (pəfɛktɪ'bɪlɪtɪ). Also perfectability. [f. next: cf. F. *perfectibilité* (1771 in Hatz.-Darm.).]
1. Capability of being perfected or becoming perfect; the quality of being improvable to perfection; *spec.* the capacity of man, individual and social, to progress indefinitely towards physical, mental, and moral perfection; the doctrine of this capacity.
1794 MATHIAS *Purs. Lit.* (1798) 210 A most affectionate .. regard for the welfare of mankind, who are to exist some centuries hence, when the endless perfectibility of the human species (for such is their jargon) shall receive its completion upon earth. 1809 *European Mag.* LV. 18 A man who understood (to use an expression of the new school) the perfectibility of which our language was capable. 1882–3 *Schaff's Encycl. Relig. Knowl.* II. 1038/1 'The religion of humanity', whose fundamental dogma is the spontaneous perfectibility of the human race without any human aid. 1970 *Sci. Jrnl.* Apr. 4/1 The US places more reliance on technological solutions and has more faith in human perfectability than any other nation today. 1975 *Christian* II. 229 The potential for perfectability.
2. *loosely.* A state of perfection or improvement; *concr.* A person who has attained to this. *rare.*
1809 W. IRVING *Knickerb.* I. v. (1861) 29 Let us suppose .. that the inhabitants of the moon .. had arrived at .. such an enviable state of perfectibility, as to control the elements. 1815 W. H. IRELAND *Scribbleomania* Pref. 6, I do not .. arrogate to myself perfectibility in a literary sense. 1828 P. CUNNINGHAM *N.S. Wales* (ed. 3) II. 271 There was a 'Margaret' also in the female convict-ship .. who had attained to such religious and moral perfectibility, that [etc.]. 1872 LEVER *Ld. Kilgobbin* lxxiv, We live amidst human perfectabilities—all of Irish manufacture.
Hence **per,fectibili'tarian**, an upholder or advocate of human perfectibility, a perfectibilist.

1873 MORLEY *Rousseau* II. 118 The intense exaltation of spirit produced both by the perfectibilitarians and the followers of Rousseau.

perfectible (pə'fɛktɪb(ə)l, 'pɜːfɪktɪb(ə)l). Also 9 -able. [f. PERFECT *v.* or *a.* + -IBLE, as if from a L. type **perfectibilis*, perhaps used in med. or mod.L.: cf. It. *perfettibile* 'that may be perfected' (Florio 1611), F. *perfectible* (Diderot 1767, admitted by Acad. 1798).] Capable of being perfected or brought to perfection.
1635 PERSON *Varieties* II. 64 Every thing perfectible striveth to attaine to its own perfection. *a* 1839 GALT *Demon of Destiny* VII. (1840) 44 Superior beings shall hereafter rise, Made hence perfectable. 1898 L. STEPHEN *Stud. Biographer* I. vii. 250 Man, he [Godwin] thought, was perfectible, and a litle calm argument would make him perfect.

perfecting (see the vb.), *vbl. sb.* [f. PERFECT *v.* + -ING[1].] **a.** The action of the vb. PERFECT; carrying out, completion, consummation; also the fact of becoming complete or perfect.
[*c* 1449 PECOCK *Repr.* V. xiii, For this cause of the more perfiting lordis and ladies it is alloweable .. hem to haue mansiouns couenable for them within the monasteries.] 1494 FABYAN *Chron.* II. an. 1382 (R.) To mete for the perfyghting of this accorde. 1583 *Reg. Privy Council Scot.* III. 604 For heiring, futting, and perfyting of the compt of umqwhile Andro Buke. 1611 BIBLE *Eph.* iv. 12 He gaue some .. Pastors, and teachers: For the perfecting of the Saints. 1705 STANHOPE *Paraphr.* III. 424 In order to the perfecting of a Christian's Salvation. 1860 TYNDALL *Glac.* I. xxi. 147 The gradual perfecting of the structure. 1951 S. JENNETT *Making of Bks.* vii. 101 The printing of the second side of the sheet is known as perfecting. 1972 P. GASKELL *New Introd. Bibliogr.* 133 It appears to coincide with the practice of consecutive perfecting at different presses.
b. *attrib.*, as ***perfecting cylinder***; **perfecting machine** or (*U.S.*) **press**, a printing machine, on which the sheet, as it passes through, is printed first on one side and then on the other. (Cf. PERFECT *v.* 1 b.)
1967 V. STRAUSS *Printing Industry* vi. 298/2 A third cylinder .. is denoted as the 'perfecting cylinder' because of its paramount importance to the perfecting operation. 1847 *Mech. Mag.* Jan. 36/1 Mr. Little .. has his perfecting machine .. (as those which print a sheet of paper on both sides before leaving the machine are called). 1880 F. J. F. WILSON *Typogr. Printing Machines* xi. 61 Perfecting machines are of three kinds—1. The Web. 2. The Drop-bar. 3. The Gripper. The above terms signify the manner by which white paper is conveyed into the tapes. 1973 J. MORAN *Printing Presses* ix. 133 Between 1836–63 Napier made at least eighty-seven perfecting machines. 1858 *Printer* (N.Y.) I. 95 This wonderful achievement .. the perfecting press. 1902 R. HOE *Short Hist. Printing Press* 17 In 1814 Koenig patented a continuously revolving Cylinder Press... This press, termed a 'perfecting press', was afterwards improved by Applegath and Cowper. 1967 V. STRAUSS *Printing Industry* vi. 279/1 Perfecting presses, or perfectors .. print both sides of the sheet in one color in one pass through the press.

perfection (pə'fɛkʃən), *sb.* Forms: 3 perfectiun, 4–5 perfeccioun, 4–6 -yon(e, -ion(e, 5–7 perfectioun(e, 5– perfection. [a. OF. *perfection* (12th c.), *perfeccion* (13–14th c. in Godef. *Compl.*), ad. L. *perfectiōn-em*, n. of action f. *perficĕre, perfect-*: see PERFECT *a.*]
1. The action, process, or fact of making perfect or bringing to completion; completing, consummating, finishing, accomplishing.
1382 WYCLIF *Num.* vi. 21 Aftir that that he hath auowid in thouȝt, so he shal do, to the perfeccioun of his holynes. 1526 *Pilgr. Perf.* (W. de W. 1531) 1 b, Euery religious persone sholde intende the perfeccyon of his soule. 1585 T. WASHINGTON tr. *Nicholay's Voy.* IV. i. 114 The auncients also had their superiours, which admonished them in the perfection of their dutie. 1678 TEMPLE *Let. to Ld. Treasurer* Wks. 1731 II. 479 After all the Applauses have been given me here upon the Perfection of the last Treaty. 1732 LAW *Serious C.* v. (ed. 2) 70 To make the most of a short life, to study your own perfection. 1871 MORLEY *Voltaire* (1886) 10 For this process of perfection, we need first the meditative, doubting, critical type.
†2. The fact or condition of being perfected or completed; completion; completed state, completeness. *Obs.*
a 1225 *Ancr. R.* 372 Hundred is ful tel, & noteth perfectiun, þet is, ful dede. 1388 WYCLIF *Heb.* vii. 19 The lawe brouȝt no thing to perfeccioun. 1489 CAXTON *Faytes of A.* III. xiii. 197 The thynge shal be conducted and brought to a gode endynge and perfection. 1563 *Homilies* II. *Nativity* (1859) 402 'When the fulness of time was come', that is, the perfection and course of years appointed from the beginning. 1602 MARSTON *Antonio's Rev.* III. iv, Woman receiveth perfection by the man. 1679 G. R. tr. *Boaystuau's Theat. World* 1st Pref. 5 This work (which I thank God, I have now brought to perfection).
b. The full growth or development of anything; the maturity of a plant, animal, etc.
c 1566 J. ALDAY tr. *Boaystuau's Theat. World* Sij, Although somewhat maye be added to all other Artes .. this [printing] alone hath entred with such .. perfection into this worlde, that [etc.]. 1578–9 *Reg. Privy Council Scot.* III. 113 Seing his majestie dalie growand .. to the gretar perfectioun of aig. 1611 BIBLE *Luke* viii. 14 They .. bring no fruite to perfection. *a* 1682 SIR T. BROWNE *Tracts, Plants Script.* §30 He planted many [Cedars] though they did not come to perfection in his days. 1774 GOLDSM. *Nat. Hist.* (1776) VII. 204 They continue in the womb till they come to such perfection as to be able to burst from the shell. 1855 MILMAN *Lat. Chr.* XIV. v, The creation, growth, perfection of new languages.

†**c.** *Mus.* The condition of being 'perfect', as a note, interval, etc. (see PERFECT *a.* 10). ***prick of perfection***: a dot used to make a note 'perfect', i.e. to lengthen it by one-half. *Obs.*
1614 T. RAVENSCROFT (*title*) A Briefe Discovrse Of the true (but neglected) vse of Charact'ring the Degrees by their Perfection, Imperfection, and Diminution in Measurable Musicke. 1674 PLAYFORD *Skill Mus.* viii, This prick of perfection or addition is ever placed on the right side of all notes .., for the prolonging the sound of that note it follows to half as much more as it is. 1880 W. S. ROCKSTRO in Grove *Dict. Mus.* I. 767 Ways in which the Perfection of certain notes may be changed to Imperfection, and *vice versa*.
3. The condition, state, or quality of being perfect or free from all defect; supreme excellence; flawlessness, faultlessness. But often treated as a matter of degree: Comparative excellence.
c 1315 SHOREHAM (E.E.T.S.) I. 1396 Þe ordre of deakne, Þet hys of more perfeccioun Þane hys ordre of subdeakne. 1460 CAPGRAVE *Chron.* (Rolls) 82 In his tyme felle a grete debate betwix Iewis and hethen, vhich sect vas of most perfeccion. 1570 BILLINGSLEY *Euclid* III. Introd. 81 Of al figures the circle is of most absolute perfection. 1610 SHAKS. *Temp.* II. i. 167, I would with such perfection gouerne Sir: T' Excell the Golden Age. 1711–12 SWIFT *Improv. Eng. Tongue* ¶6 The Roman Language arrived at great Perfection before it began to decay. 1860 TYNDALL *Glac.* II. xxvii. 376 In different glaciers, .. these veins display various degrees of perfection.
b. *concr.* An embodiment of perfection; a perfect person, place, etc.
1594 SHAKS. *Rich. III*, I. ii. 75 Vouchsafe (diuine perfection of a Woman) Of these supposed Crimes, to giue me leaue .. but to acquit my selfe. 1604 —— *Oth.* I. iii. 100. 1611 BIBLE *Lam.* ii. 15 Is this the citie that men call the perfection of beauty? *c* 1830 SYD. SMITH in Lady Holland *Life* I. 351 A beautiful girl .. exclaimed, 'Oh, Mr. Sydney! this pea will never come to perfection'. 'Permit me then', said he taking her hand, .. 'to lead perfection to the pea'. 1852 MISS SEWELL *Exper. Life* xviii. (1858) 128 This would be the very perfection of a dress for you.
4. The condition or state of being morally perfect; holiness; †in ME. *spec.* The austerity of monastic life, monastic discipline (*obs.*). ***Christian perfection***, the relatively perfect holiness attainable by man, in distinction from the absolute divine perfection. ***counsel of perfection***: see COUNSEL *sb.* 2 b.
a 1340 HAMPOLE *Psalter* xiv. 5 Þis perfeccioun is Þat Þe deuel & Þe warld haf na pouste in vs. 1390 GOWER *Conf.* I. 18 For ther ben somme, .. That god .. Hath cleped to perfeccioun In the manere as Aaron was. 1470–85 MALORY *Arthur* XXI. ix. 855 Therfore lady sythen ye haue taken you to perfeccion I must nedys take me to perfection. *Ibid.* x. 856 Whan they sawe syr Launcelot had taken hym to suche perfeccion they .. toke suche an habyte as he had. 1494 FABYAN *Chron.* V. cxxxv. 121 Amonge theyse bretherne was one named Cedman, a man of great perfeccion. 1552 ABP. HAMILTON *Catech.* (1884) 19 Matrimonye was degenerat fra the first perfectioun. 1554–9 *Songs & Ball.* (1860) 3 The lantarne to lead us in the pathe of perfecttyon. 1743 WESLEY *Serm. Chr. Perfection* 8 Christian Perfection therefore does not imply .. an Exemption either from Ignorance or Mistake, or Infirmities, or Temptations. Indeed it is only another Term for Holiness. 1789 —— *Wks.* (1872) IV. 445 The doctrine of Christian Perfection, which God has peculiarly entrusted to the Methodists. 1882 A. M. FAIRBAIRN in *Contemp. Rev.* XLII. 868 The grand aim of the Buddhist is to attain a perfection like Buddha's.
5. The most perfect degree, the highest pitch (*of* a quality, condition, faculty, etc.); the extreme or height (*of* anything good or evil).
a 1340 HAMPOLE *Psalter* Prol. (1884) 4 Þis boke of all haly writ is mast oysed in halykyrke seruys, forÞi Þat in it is perfeccioun of dyuyne pagyne. *c* 1380 WYCLIF *Wks.* (1880) 366 Moyses lawe is moralle in Þis poynte Þat longeÞ to Þe perfeccyon of presthode. 1624 CAPT. SMITH *Virginia* IV. 125 The other Saluages assaulted the rest and slew them ... But fearing this murther would come to light .. would now proceed to the perfection of villanie. 1729 BUTLER *Serm.* xii. Wks. 1874 II. 154 The perfection of goodness consists in love to the whole universe. 1842 MISS MITFORD in L'Estrange *Life* (1870) III. ix. 142 The perfection of cunning is to conceal its own quality.
6. Proficiency in some accomplishment or art.
a 1568 ASCHAM *Scholem.* (Arb.) 89 Whan .. tyme shall breed skill, and vse shall bring perfection. 1677 EVELYN *Diary* 10 Sept., Having the Latin, French, and Spanish tongues in perfection. 1704 ADDISON *Italy* (1733) 37 Fence, Dance, and Ride in some tolerable Perfection. 1856 EMERSON *Eng. Traits, Ability* Wks. (Bohn) II. 40 Every man is trained to some one art or detail, and aims at perfection in that. 1879 HARLAN *Eyesight* v. 54 Such perfection has been reached in the manufacture of artificial eyes, that [etc.].
7. (With *a* and *pl.*) A quality, trait, feature, endowment, or accomplishment of a high order or great excellence.
1572 H. MIDDELMORE in Ellis *Orig. Lett.* Ser. II. III. 8 Suerly Monsieur is a goodly gentilman, and hathe many perfections in him. 1604 E. G[RIMSTONE] *D'Acosta's Hist. Indies* VI. xvi. 466 The Indians of Peru had one perfection, which was, to teach their young children all artes and occupations necessary for the life of man. 1667 DRYDEN *Sir Martin Mar-all* III. i, I am not Master of any of those Perfections; for, in fine, Sir, I am wholly ignorant of Painting, Musick, and Poetry. 1784 J. POTTER *Virtuous Villagers* II. 111, I constantly discover new graces, new perfections, and new merits, unobserved before.
8. Phrase. ***to perfection***: completely, perfectly.
1388 WYCLIF *Job* xi. 7 In hap .. thou schalt fynde Almyȝti God til to perfeccioun. 1611 BIBLE *ibid.*, Canst thou finde out the Almightie vnto perfection? 1751 R. PALTOCK *P. Wilkins* xxxiv, They were pleased with it [the fire] to perfection. 1766 GOLDSM. *Vic. W.* xvii, Olivia .. acted the

coquette to perfection. **1898** MRS. ISAB. BISHOP *Korea* xviii, Nagasaki..lighted, cleaned, and policed to perfection.

per'fection, *v. rare.* [f. prec. sb.: cf. F. *perfectionne-r* (Cotgr. 1611).] *trans.* To bring to perfection, to perfect. Hence **per'fectioned** *ppl. a.*

1548 [see PERFECTIONING]. **1651** tr. *De-las-Coveras' Don Fenise* 305 We lived there in great repose, imploying the time..in perfectioning our loves. **1799** in *Spirit Pub. Jrnls.* III. 243 All persons are interested in perfectioning these new bases of the conjugal connexion. **1841** D'ISRAELI *Amen. Lit.* (1867) 700 This perfectioned model of a government.

per'fectional, *a. rare.* [ad. med.L. *perfectiōnālis*, in OF. *perfectionnal*, f. L. *perfectiōn-em* PERFECTION + -AL[1].] Of, pertaining to, or of the nature of perfection.

1495 *Trevisa's Barth. De P.R.* I. (W. de W.) A iv/1 The names whyche betoken or sygnyfye dyuyne or godly perfeccyon been callyd names perfeccionalles [*orig.* nomina perfectionalia, *Corbichon's Fr.* les noms perfectionnaulx]. **1659** PEARSON *Creed* xii. (1839) 549 Life eternal may be looked upon under three considerations: as initial, as partial, and as perfectional... I call that perfectional, which shall be conferred..immediately after the blessing pronounced by Christ, 'Come, ye blessed children of my Father'.

†**per'fectionary.** *Obs. rare*[−1]. [f. PERFECTION + -ARY.] ? = PERFECTIONIST b.

1647 TRAPP *Comm. Matt.* xix. 17 None but a proud Luciferian would have said, as Vega, the Popish perfectionary, did.

per'fectionate, *v.* Now *rare.* [prob. f. med. or mod.L. **perfectiōnāre*: cf. OIt. *perfettionare* (Florio 1598), F. *perfectionner* (Cotgr. 1611); or (in 16th c. writers) after the Fr.: see PERFECTION *v.* and -ATE[3].] *trans.* To bring to perfection; to make perfect or complete; to perfect; †to make (a person) perfect *in* (a study, etc.) (*obs.*).

1570 FOXE *A. & M.* (ed. 2) Ooiij/1 Ye greatnes of my Priesthode:..begon in Melchisedech:.. continued in the children of Aaron: perfectionated in Christ. **1598** BARRET *Theor. Warres* I. ii. 13 Histories..sharpen and perfectionate the wits of man. **1634** W. TIRWHYT tr. *Balzac's Lett.* 71 To augment the merit of our faith, and the more to perfectionate our Piety. **1695** DRYDEN *Parall. Poetry & Paint.* Ess. (Ker) II. 122 In this manner..painters and sculptors..perfectionate the idea, and advance their art even above nature itself. **1755** JOHNSON, *Perfectionate*... This is a word proposed by Dryden, but not received nor worthy of reception. **1784** J. BARRY in *Lect. Paint.* i. (1848) 66 Laws..for perfectionating human nature. **1849** THACKERAY *Pendennis* xxiii, Every great artist..has need of solitude to perfectionate his works. **1863** COWDEN CLARKE *Shaks. Char.* iv. 102.

Hence **per'fectionated** *ppl. a.*, **per'fectionating** *vbl. sb.* and *ppl. a.*; also **per'fectionator**, one who makes perfect.

1695 DRYDEN tr. *Du Fresnoy's Art Paint.*, *Observ.* §24 He has..founded an Academy for the Progress and Perfectionating of Painting. **1795** tr. *Mercier's Fragm. Pol. & Hist.* I. 183 Nature..forms man precisely for a perfectionated Society. **1818** *Blackw. Mag.* III. 23 Poetry.. is also a selective and perfectionating art. **1839** *New Monthly Mag.* LVI. 381 Man..is but a more complicated zoophyte, a perfectionated stomach. *a* **1849** H. COLERIDGE *Ess.* (1851) II. 119 Pope was not the founder, but head scholar and perfectionator of a school. **1867** J. LEGGE *Confucius* (1877) 28 A system of social perfectionating.

perfectio'nation. *rare.* [n. of action from prec.: see -ATION.] The action of bringing to perfection, perfectioning; the fact of being made perfect.

1812 in *Spirit Pub. Jrnls.* XVI. 358 The new System of Anti-mnemonics, to the perfectionation of which the Chevalier has devoted the last fifty years of a long life. **1840** BLACKIE in Anna M. Stoddart *Life* (1895) I. viii. 194 The law of the universe is Perfectionation—that is to say, progression from bad to good..and from better to best.

per'fectioner. *rare.* [f. PERFECTION *v.* + -ER[1].] One who or that which brings to perfection.

1883 R. CUST *Mod. Lang. Afr.* Introd. 19 Language has been the handmaid of Religion, and Religion the herald, instrument, and perfectioner of Civilization.

per'fectioning, *vbl. sb.* [f. PERFECTION *v.* + -ING[1].] The action of bringing to perfection.

1548 UDALL *Erasm. Par. Luke* xxiv. 186 Christe..taught the perfeccionyng of the lawe, whan he pronounced those straunge beatitudes neuer afore heard of. **1693** EVELYN *De la Quint. Compl. Gard.* II. 95 Culture really contributes to the Perfectioning of its new Productions. **1762** FOOTE *Orators* I. i, The perfectioning of our countrymen in..the right use of their native language. **1877** HUXLEY *Anat. Inv. Anim.* i. 59 The gradual perfectioning of the respiratory machinery.

per'fectionism. [f. after PERFECTIONIST: see -ISM.] **1.** A system or doctrine of religious, moral, social, or political perfection; *esp.* the theory that moral perfection can be or has been attained by man; *spec.* (with capital P) the system of the Perfectionists of Oneida Creek, N.Y.

1846 WORCESTER cites *Ch. Ob.* **1870** *Athenæum* 5 Feb. 187 Oneida Creek Perfectionism. **1890** *Spectator* 19 July, Professor Dicey..does not arrive at his conclusions by any reference to abstract theories or appeals to political perfectionism. **1892** *Academy* 2 July 25/2 He [Tolstoy] continues to develope his cherished ideas on the subject of perfectionism and self-improvement.

2. Refusal to accept any standard short of perfection.

1937 *Nation* (N.Y.) 30 Oct. 465/2 Labor..cannot afford perfectionism. **1945** F. D. ROOSEVELT *Public Papers & Addresses 1944–5* (1950) 498 Perfectionism, no less than isolationism or imperialism or power politics, may obstruct the paths to international peace. **1957** *Listener* 24 Oct. 642/1 Sir Lewis Namier once gave up writing a book he had planned because some manuscripts in private hands were not made available to him. This was a fine example of scientific perfectionism. **1968** P. B. AUSTIN *On Being Swedish* iii. 21 Perfectionism always implies, at a deeper level, its opposite.

perfectionist (pəˈfɛkʃənɪst), *sb.* (and *a.*). [f. PERFECTION *sb.* + -IST.] **1. a.** One who holds any theory or follows any practice as to the attainment of religious, moral, social, or political perfection.

1694 S. JOHNSON *Notes Past. Let. Bp. Burnet* I. 66 Must the Wise and Free and Great Men of a Nation be Slaves for Company with such Perfectionists in Church-Doctrine? **1892** W. B. SCOTT *Autobiog. Notes* I. 128 As a perfectionist in poetry, whose thought and rhythm were one, he [Leigh Hunt] seemed to hold Coleridge above all others.

b. *esp.* One who holds that religious or moral perfection may be attained; (with capital P) a name at various times assumed by or given to sects, parties, or persons, who held this doctrine, or claimed to have attained moral or spiritual perfection.

1657–83 EVELYN *Hist. Relig.* (1850) I. p. xviii, Men of all religions..were protected and encouraged under notion of New Lights, Perfectionists, a Godly Party [etc.]. *a* **1665** J. GOODWIN *Filled w. the Spirit* (1867) 231 The apostle saying unto the Galatians, 'So that ye cannot do the things that ye would', is as a sword passing through the soul of those who are called perfectionists amongst us, casting down the crown of their conceit of perfection to the ground. **1748** RICHARDSON *Clarissa* (1811) III. xx. 124, I have read in some of our perfectionists enough to make a better man than myself either run into madness or despair. **1791** HAMPSON *Mem. J. Wesley* III. 197 Perfectionists and Anti-perfectionists were the grand divisions of methodism. **1882** FARRAR *Early Chr.* II. 408 *note*, Whether there is any special allusion to Gnostic Antinomian Perfectionists.

c. *spec.* (with capital P.) A member of the communistic community of Oneida Creek, N.Y.

1867 DIXON *New Amer.* (ed. 6) II. xx. 208 On the opposite verge of thought..stands a body of reformers who call themselves, in their dogmatic aspect, Perfectionists, in their social aspect, Bible Communists. **1874** J. H. BLUNT *Dict. Sects, Perfectionists*, a..sect of Antinomian Communists, established about the year 1845 by John Humphrey Noyes. **1875** *N. Amer. Rev.* CXX. 227 The success that he ascribes to the Shakers, the Perfectionists, and the rest.

d. *attrib.* (in various senses).

c **1847** WHITTIER *Fame & Glory* Prose Wks. 1889 III. 389 There are..perfectionist reformers..who wait to see the salvation which it is the task of humanity itself to work out. **1856** R. A. VAUGHAN *Mystics* x. i. Notes (1860) II. 307 Many were beginning to seek in this perfectionist doctrine a refuge from the exactions of the priesthood. **1867** DIXON *New Amer.* (ed. 6) I. xxii. 243 According to all the Perfectionist prophets, Holiness and Liberty are the two primary elements in the atmosphere of heaven,—that is to say of a perfect society.

2. a. One who is only satisfied with the highest standards.

1934 in WEBSTER. **1951** 'J. TEY' *Daughter of Time* ii. 28 A worrier: perhaps a perfectionist. A man..anxious over details. **1969** 'R. GORDON' *Facts of Life* ii. 14, I hated performing anything badly... Like so many women doctors, I was a perfectionist. **1978** *Vogue* 1 Mar. 114/1 Bette Davis's misfortune is to be a perfectionist in an industry run by opportunists.

b. as *adj.* Demanding perfection or perfectionism (sense 2).

1958 *Times Rev. Industry* Aug. 50/3 The extreme sensitivity of the Talysurf and its companion instrument aroused some resistance among engineers at first. They claimed that the methods were too perfectionist for everyday practical purposes. **1977** *Listener* 17 Mar. 332/2 Let us not be élitist, perfectionist... Singapore does provide its people with a decent..existence. **1978** P. BOARDMAN *Worlds of Patrick Geddes* vii. 226 P.G. certainly could be called a perfectionist parent. He urged them from early years to take notes.

Hence **perfectio'nistic** *a.*, (*a*) of or pertaining to Perfectionists; (*b*) tending towards perfectionism (sense 2).

1882–3 *Schaff's Encycl. Relig. Knowl.* III. 1841 Löscher.. rejected those chiliastic, terministic, and perfectionistic doctrines [of the pietists]. **1968** P. B. AUSTIN *On Being Swedish* xvii. 124 In its heaviness of spirit, a bleakness of insight so intense that all its perfectionistic arrangements can obviously only be oil on the stormy waters. **1977** W. J. BATE *Samuel Johnson* II. viii. 117 Johnson's fears of insanity ..[were] a fanciful delusion resulting from a perfectionistic notion of 'sanity'.

per'fectionize, *v. rare.* [See -IZE.] *trans.* To bring to perfection; to perfectionate, perfect.

1839 MRS. SHELLEY *Notes Shelley's Prometh. Unb.* S.'s Wks. 1882 I. p. lxv, That man could be so perfectionized as to be able to expel evil from his own nature..was the cardinal point of his system. **1843** *Tait's Mag.* X. 617 Steam allows us leisure to examine into old abuses, and perfectionize new reforms. **1846** H. W. TORRENS *Rem. Milit. Hist.* 374 We must..endeavour to perfectionize our military system.

Hence **per'fectio,nizing** *vbl. sb.* and *ppl. a.*; also **per'fectionizement**, **per'fectionizer**.

1821 *Tales Landlord* New Ser. III. *Witch Glas Llyn* 18 From Italy and Greece he had brought with him an unquenchable thirst for perfectionizing. **1841** *Blackw. Mag.* L. 481 Ye accomplishment perfectionizers..this is the fate that awaits your daughters at last. **1844** *Ibid.* LV. 200 The theories of the perfectionizement of the fair sex now issuing from the press. **1851** WOODWARD *Mollusca* 4 The perfectionizing of the functions of nutrition and reproduction.

per'fectionment. [f. PERFECTION *v.* + -MENT, after F. *perfectionnement* (1725 in Hatz.-Darm.).] The action of bringing to perfection; perfecting.

1827 I. TAYLOR *Transm. Anc. Bks.* xiii. (1859) 160 The general perfectionment of reason and of taste. **1831** SOUTHEY in *Q. Rev.* XLV. 420 The whole profits being to be applied to the perfectionment of civilization. **1860** FARRAR *Orig. Lang.* i. 27[Of writing] there is the clearest proof of its human origin and gradual perfectionment.

†**per'fectious,** *a. Obs. rare*[−1]. [f. PERFECTION: see -OUS.] Of the nature of perfection.

1607 COKE *Charge at Norwich Assizes* 6 The glory of her dignity shall receiue perfectious Honor.

'perfectism. [f. PERFECT *a.* + -ISM.] The doctrine or system of the Perfectists, esp. of the German Pietists.

1830 PUSEY *Hist. Enq.* II. viii. 225 These men..still continued incessantly to warn their congregations by name against Francke and Pietism and Perfectism.

Perfectist (ˈpɜːfɪktɪst). *Obs.* exc. *Hist.* [f. as prec. + -IST.] = PERFECTIONIST 1: esp. applied to those of the 17th c., and to the German Pietists of the 18th c.

1618 *Barnevelt's Apol.* D, Winberger is principall of the Perfectists, and you of the Arminians. **1630** G. WIDDOWES *Schysmatical Puritan* F ij b, A Mechanicke..is receiued amongst the Perfectists for a lawfull preacher, if their non-Ecclesiasticall spirit calls him. **1641** D. CAWDREY *Three Serm.* 68 These late upstart Perfectists. **1830** PUSEY *Hist. Enq.* II. viii. 197 In 1700 an edict was renewed forbidding the preaching against the Pietists. 'Since certain Lutheran preachers..toss about in many sermons..the false names of Pietists, Perfectists, new holy Quakers, and such like'. *Ibid.* 225 They warn incessantly against the Perfectists.

perfectivation (pəfɛktɪˈveɪʃən). [f. PERFECTIVE *a.* + -ATION.] The action of rendering a verb perfective.

1926 G. W. S. FRIEDRICHSEN *Gothic Version of Gospels* vii. 100 This is an instance of the colourlessness of verbal prefixes when used as an instrument of perfectivation. **1954** PEI & GAYNOR *Dict. Linguistics* 163 *Perfectivation*, the transformation of an imperfective verb into a perfective one by a morphological change. **1962** R. W. ZANDVOOT in F. Behre *Contrib. Eng. Syntax* 15 Mossé..believes in perfectivation in O.E. by means of the prefix *ge-*.

perfective (pəˈfɛktɪv), *a.* and *sb.* Now *rare* except in *Gram.* [ad. L. type **perfectīv-us* (perh. in mod.L.: cf. It. *perfettivo*, Sp. *perfectivo*): see PERFECT *v.* and -IVE.]

A. *adj.* **1.** Tending to make perfect or complete; conducive to the perfecting or perfection *of* anything.

1596 BACON *Max. & Use Com. Law* I. xiv. (1636) 59 This enrolment is no new act, but a perfective ceremony of the first deed of bargaine and sale. **1620** T. GRANGER *Div. Logike* 31 That which is agreeable to, and perfectiue of his kind. **1693** TYRRELL *Law Nat.* 314 Causes (whether efficient, or perfective). **1771** WESLEY *Wks.* (1872) V. 295 The far more excellent way, more perfective of the Soul. **1839** BAILEY *Festus* xi. (1852) 134 The purifying wave, perfective fire. **1865** MOZLEY *Mirac.* i. Notes 219.

2. In process of being perfected, or of attaining the perfect state.

1848 JOHNSTON in *Proc. Berw. Nat. Club* II. No. 6. 293 Dugès was..able to see..the eight legs in a perfective state. **1852** DICKENS *Lett.* (1880) I. 274 Not knowing the immense resources and the gradually perfective machinery necessary to the production of such a journal.

3. *Gram.* Expressing completion of action: applied to that kind or species of verbal action (Ger. *aktionsart*) which is considered as completed or finished, and so to forms or modifications of the verb which express completed action: opposed to IMPERFECTIVE.

Originally applied to one of the branches or 'aspects' of the verb in the Slavonic languages; more recently to verb-forms in other Indo-European languages, esp. those compounded with a preposition, expressing the completion of the action expressed by the simple verb, as L. *ēdere* to eat, *comēdere* to eat up; *suādēre*, *persuādēre*, etc.

1844 R. GARNETT in *Proc. Philol. Soc.* (1854) I. 268 In the Slavonic languages..a regular..distinction is made between perfective and imperfective verbs, that is, between those expressing an action completed at once and not repeated, and those denoting continuance or reiteration. **1887** MORFILL *Serbian Gram.* 31 The perfective aspect denotes either that the action has been quite completed or that it will definitely cease. **1889** [see DURATIVE *a.*]. **1895** P. GILES *Manual Compar. Philol.* §545 When present and aorist are found in the same verb [in Greek], the former is the durative, the latter the perfective or momentary form. **1924** [see ASPECT *sb.* 9b]. **1968** J. LYONS *Introd. Theoret. Linguistics* viii. 396 The English 'perfect with *have*'..was at first restricted to transitive verbs, and thus preserved its relationship with the perfective passive without *have* (still current in such sentences as *The work is done, The house is built*). **1975** *Language* LI. 444 The tenses were divided into an imperfective and a perfective set with three tenses in each.

B. *sb.* †**1.** A perfectionist. *Obs. rare.*

1600 W. WATSON *Decacordon* (1602) 57 Vnworthie creatures to be iustly censured of by these worthie perfectiues [the Jesuits]. *Ibid.* 132 High conceited perfectiues.

2. *Gram.* A perfective use or form of a verb.

1904 J. H. MOULTON in *Expositor* Nov. 361 Ἀγωνίζεσθαι is only used in the durative present, but καταγωνίσασθαι..is a good perfective. **1949** *Archivum Linguisticum* I. 176 Perfectives are not always easy to recognize formally. **1968** J. LYONS *Introd. Theoret. Linguistics* vii. 314 Many perfectives [in Russian] are derived by prefixation of the corresponding imperfectives. **1970** B. M. H. STRANG *Hist. English* II. i. 100 The tendency to regularise verb-forms also appears in the use of *has*, etc. to form perfectives.

Hence **per'fectively** *adv.*, in a perfective way, in a way tending to completeness; **per'fectiveness, perfec'tivity**, the quality of being perfective; **per'fectivize** *v. trans.*, to render perfective; **per'fectivizing** *ppl. a.*, rendering perfective.

1701 GREW *Cosm. Sacra* II. vii. §20. 73 As Virtue is seated Fundamentally, in the Intellect; so, Perfectively, in the Phancy. So that Virtue, is the Force of Reason. **1704** NORRIS *Ideal World* II. xii. 481 Their intrinsick excellency or essential perfectiveness of the understanding. **1774** FLETCHER *Grace & Justice* Wks. 1795 IV. 177 The..gospel is found..perfectively in the Acts of the Apostles and the Epistles. **1809–10** COLERIDGE *Friend* (1818) III. 155 Plato..philosophized legitimately and perfectively, if ever any man did in any age. **1904** J. H. MOULTON in *Expositor* Nov. 360 In οἱ ἀπολλύμενοι, strongly durative though the verb is, we see its perfectivity in the fact that the goal is ideally reached. *Ibid.* 357 The compounded adverb..perfectivises the simplex, the combination denoting action which has accomplished a result, while the simplex denoted action in progress. *Ibid.* 358 The meaning of the Present-stem of these perfectivised roots naturally demands explanation. **1908** *Expositor* July 91 The function of the perfectivising preposition is to supply a present answering to the past ἔσχον. **1949** *Archivum Linguisticum* I. 7 Let us suppose that we have a set of distinct prepositions each identical with a perfectivising prefix. **1961** *Brno. Studies in English* III. 99 The function the Czech perfectivizing verbal prefix may play. **1964** *Philos. Rev.* LXXIII. 20 Ryle..was perhaps led to this opinion partly by the perfectiveness of 'to see'.

†**'perfectless**, *a. Obs. rare.* [irreg. f. PERFECT *a.* + -LESS.] Devoid of perfection, imperfect.

1591 SYLVESTER *Du Bartas* I. vii. 133 Fond epicure, thou ..Imaginedst a God so perfect-less.

perfectly ('pɜːfɪktlɪ), *adv.* Forms: see PERFECT *a.* [f. PERFECT *a.* + -LY^2.] In a perfect manner or degree.

1. So that nothing is left undone and no part is wanting; completely, thoroughly.

1303 R. BRUNNE *Handl. Synne* 12093 He þat shryueþ hym parfytely, Asswyþe..He haþ forȝyvenes of Goddys ȝyfte. *a* **1340** HAMPOLE *Psalter* xv. 7 Perfitly may we noght be wiþouten synn. *c* **1400** MAUNDEV. (Roxb.) vii. 25 On þe secund day þat worme es turned till a fowle perfitely fourmed. **1530** PALSGR. Introd. 32 The thre generall distinctions of tyme, present, parfytly past, and to come. *a* **1656** BP. HALL *Rem. Wks.* (1660) 42 They were all perfitly reclaimed. *a* **1692** POLLEXFEN *Disc. Trade* (1697) A iv, Goods perfectly manufactured which hinder the consumption of our own..ought to be discouraged. **1776** GIBBON *Decl. & F.* xii. I. 334 The troubles..had never been perfectly appeased. **1833** LYELL *Princ. Geol.* III. 311 The large accumulations of perfectly-rolled shingle.

b. In full measure; to the fullest extent; without any shortcoming or failure.

a **1340** HAMPOLE *Psalter* cv. 24 He is maste at loue þat.. perfytliest lufis heuen. **1482** WARKW. *Chron.* (Camden) 16 There was suche a grete myste, that nether of them myght see othere perfitely. **1560** DAUS tr. *Sleidane's Comm.* 232 In lyke maner shall we also..know more perfitly our parentes, wyues, children, and what so euer is besydes. **1653** WALTON *Angler* i. 4, I hate them [otters] perfectly, because they love fish so well. **1676** tr. *Guillatiere's Voy. Athens* 80 Osman ..(who understood perfectly the humour of the Turks in those parts)..advised him to threaten. **1695** LD. PRESTON *Boeth.* v. 235 Affirming that that Universal is nothing which Reason thinks it so perfectly sees. **1866** GEO. ELIOT *F. Holt* i, I understand the difficulty perfectly, mother.

2. In a manner or way that is perfect or faultless in form, style, or nature; with perfect or complete exactness, correctness, fitness, or excellence; to perfection.

c **1375** *Sc. Leg. Saints* vi. (*Thomas*) 14 Gyfe he his varke dois parfytly. *c* **1400** *Beryn* 3300 Ffor .iij preciouse stonys been within the hafft Perfitlych I-couchid. *c* **1450** HOLLAND *Howlat* 183 Parfytlye thir Pikmawis..With thar party habitis present tham thar. *a* **1533** LD. BERNERS *Huon* xl. 132 Teche hyr to speake perfeyghtly the language of frenche. *c* **1540** HEYWOOD *Four PP.* in Hazl. *Dodsley* I. 383 By the mass, learn to make courtesy..Nay, when ye have it perfitly, Ye shall have the devil and all of courtesy. **1596** DANETT tr. *Comines* (1614) 290 Whereof he discoursed perfectlier than my selfe that came from thence. **1722** DE FOE *Plague* (1754) 25 They cannot be so perfectly call'd the Fore-runners, or Fore-tellers, much less the Procurers of such Events. **1789** JEFFERSON *Writ.* (1859) III. 9 Mr. Littlepage has returned.. to Warsaw, where he has been perfectly received by the King. **1903** *Blackw. Mag.* Dec. 772/2, I had trained it into being a perfectly mannered house pet. *Mod.* She acted the part perfectly. The dress fits perfectly.

†**b.** In a manner morally or religiously perfect; righteously. *Obs.*

1340 HAMPOLE *Pr. Consc.* 3428 Swa parfitely may nane lyf here, With-outen veniel syns sere. *c* **1386** CHAUCER *Wife's Prol.* 111 He spak to hem that wolde lyue parfitly. *c* **1491** *Chast. Goddes Chyld.* 13 Though I wyll but fayntly, my wylle is to wylle perfyghtly.

3. To the fullest possible degree or extent; entirely, quite: with an *adj.*, *adv.*, or *phr.*

[**1460–70** *Bk. Quintessence* I Restorid..and be mad hool parfiȝtly.] **1555** EDEN *Decades* 32 The earth is not perfectlye rownde. **1563** T. GALE *Antidot.* II. 25 When it is boyled enoughe, it wyll bee perfitely Redde. **1677** LADY CHAWORTH in *12th Rep. Hist. MSS. Comm.* App. v. 43 The D[uchess] is perfectly well again. **1719** DE FOE *Crusoe* II. ii, Whom I knew..perfectly well. **1722** —— *Col. Jack* (1840) 327, I was perfectly easy. **1753** EARL OF BATH in *World* No. 17 Every body is dressed so perfectly alike. **1790** MRS. INCHBALD *Wedding Day* I. ii, *Lady Contest.* Would not that do as well? *Lord Rakeland.* Perfectly as well. The very thing. **1807** T. THOMSON *Chem.* (ed. 3) II. 378 Take a quantity of fixed alkali perfectly dry. **1826** DISRAELI *Viv. Grey* v. v, But all looked perfectly *comme il faut*. **1846** RYLAND *Foster's Life & Corr.* II. 472 Unostentatious and perfectly simple address. **1896** *Law Times Rep.* LXXIII. 615/1 The railway line..was perfectly straight for a distance of over 700 yards.

b. *Physics.* See PERFECT *a.* 14.

1784 G. ATWOOD *Rectil. Motion & Rotation* 376 In the impact of perfectly elastic bodies. **1824** WHEWELL *Mechanics* (ed. 2) 248 Bodies are called perfectly elastic when the force of restitution is equal to the force of compression.

perfectness ('pɜːfɪktnɪs). Forms: see PERFECT *a.* [f. as prec. + -NESS.] The quality or condition of being perfect (in the various senses of the adj.); perfection. (In early use chiefly in the religious sense of a perfect life.)

a **1340** HAMPOLE *Psalter* Prol. (1884) 3 Þe sange of psalmes ..does away synne, it quemes god, it enformes perfytnes. **1377** LANGL. *P. Pl.* B. x. 200 Poule preched þe peple þat parfitnesse loued. *c* **1400** *Lanfranc's Cirurg.* 90 Boile alle þese to þe perfiȝtnesse of a sirup. *c* **1430** LYDG. *Min. Poems* (Percy Soc.) 59 Pristhode liuethe in perfitenesse, And can in lytel haue suffisaunce. **1464** *Rolls of Parlt.* V. 562/1 That every of the seid Clothes..be.. sealed..in witnes and record of the forseid true lengh, brede and parfitnes. **1526** TINDALE *Col.* iii. 14 Above all these thynges put on love, which is the bonde off parfectnes. [So later Eng. vv.; WYCLIF and *Rhem.* perfection.] *a* **1529** SKELTON *Col. Cloute* 978 Theyr chambres thus to dresse With suche parfetnesse And all suche holynesse. **1535** COVERDALE *Job* ii. 9 Dost thou yet contynue in thy perfectnesse? curse God, & dye. **1588** SHAKS. *L.L.L.* v. ii. 173 *Pag.* Once to behold with your Sunne beamed eyes, With your Sunne beamed eyes... *Bero.* Is this your perfectnesse? be gon you rogue. **1607** MARKHAM *Caval.* IV. (1617) 29 There is nothing..which brings a horse either to perfitnesse or imperfitnesse, but onely practise. **1795** COLERIDGE *Plot Discovered* 33 That Constitution, from whose present perfectness they derive their only possible justification. **1838–9** HALLAM *Hist. Lit.* II. v. §82 In this varied delineation of female perfectness, no earlier poet had equalled him [Spenser]. **1871** PALGRAVE *Lyr. Poems* 72 Home of the peace earth cannot give In her most perfect perfectness! [*Mod. Sc. Maxim*, Practice maks perfyteness.]

perfecto (pə'fɛktəʊ). orig. *U.S.* Also **Perfecto, Perfectos.** [Sp. *perfecto* perfect.] A type of cigar, thick in the centre and tapering at each end.

Also used in the names of various brands of cigar and cigarette.

1894 *Harper's Weekly* 5 May 429/2 A minute later two of the raggedest-looking tramps you ever saw were trudging westward through the rain, each smoking a Carolina Perfecto costing thirty-five cents apiece. **1897** *Sears, Roebuck Catal.* 24/2 La Flor de Portuondo, Perfectos. A 5 inch cigar. **1898** H. E. HAMBLEN *Gen. Manager's Story* 3 The old gentleman..blowing the smoke from his 'perfecto' out into the cool starlight. **1904** 'O. HENRY' *Four Million* (1906) 74 He always..handed out real perfectos to the delighted boys. **1931** E. S. GARDNER in *Detective Fiction Weekly* 14 Mar. 302/2 He took a box of perfectos..and selected one. **1944** S. BELLOW *Dangling Man* (1946) 149, I sucked tranquilly at my Perfecto Queen and said to myself, 'It's in the bag.' **1953** *Trade Marks Jrnl.* 5 Aug. 707/2 Perfectos Finos... Cigarettes for export. British-American Tobacco Company, Limited, Westminster House, 7, Millbank, London, S.W.1; Tobacco Manufacturers. **1960** R. K. HEIMANN *Tobacco & Americans* 248/2 Where fat perfectos and 'banker' sizes had once ruled the glassed counters, slim panetelas and palmas moved to the front row. **1961** C. WILLOCK *Death in Covert* iv. 78 Crumbe-Howard took a Perfectos Finos from a gold case. **1968** D. MACKENZIE *Three minus Two* 85 Smith chose a Perfecto and lit it. **1973** 'D. JORDAN' *Nile Green* xiii. 54, I took a Perfectos from the silver box and tried to light a match on my thumbnail.

perfector (pə'fɛktə(r)). In sense 2 also **perfecter.** [a. L. *perfector*, agent-n. from *perficĕre* to accomplish, etc.: see PERFECT.] **1.** One who perfects or completes; = PERFECTER.

1587 GOLDING *De Mornay* vi. 81 The Soule..is..after a sort the perfection (or rather the perfector) of the body. **1836** LYTTON *Athens* (1837) II. 406 Men who form the first steps in the progress between the originator and the perfector. **1883** B. W. RICHARDSON *Cycling an Intell. Pursuit*, The perfectors of geographical research.

2. *Printing.* = *perfecting machine*, *press* s.v. PERFECTING *vbl. sb.* b.

1899 J. SOUTHWARD *Mod. Printing* III. xii. 124 (*caption*) Dawsons' Patent Fast Gripper Perfecter. **1940** *Chambers's Techn. Dict.* 626/1 *Perfector*, a type of machine which prints both sides of the paper before delivery. **1951** S. JENNETT *Making of Bks.* vii. 101 These machines are in effect two presess combined in one, printing one side of the sheet first and the other side immediately afterwards. They are called perfecters. **1975** *Bookseller* 6 Dec. 2590/3 Paper of 100 per cent recycled content can now be used for printing on offset litho perfectors.

†**per'fectory**, *a. Obs. rare*$^{-1}$. [f. L. *perfect-*, ppl. stem: see -ORY.] = PERFECTIVE 1.

1693 BEVERLEY *True St. Gosp. Truth* 31 Any other Grace Preparatory, or Perfectory.

perfectu'ation. *rare.* [f. L. *perfectu-s* (*u-* stem) a perfecting or completing (Tertull.), f. *perficĕre*, *perfect-um* to complete: see PERFECT *a.*] Completion, consummation, accomplishment.

1883 *Mod. Thought* Jan. 27 A more rapid success and a readier perfectuation of desires.

†**per'fecture.** *Obs. rare*$^{-1}$. [f. L. *perfect-*, ppl. stem (see above) + -URE: cf. *confecture*, etc.] The fact of being perfected or matured; perfection.

a **1552** LELAND *Itin.* VI. 53 [When] the Corne is mervelus faire to the Yee, and ready to shew Perfecture it decayith.

per'fervent, *a. rare.* [f. PER- 4 + FERVENT.] Very fervent; of great fervour.

1888 *Harper's Mag.* Dec. 158/1 Prompting others to gifts and alms by kindly poems, by perfervent essays.

perfervid (pə'fɜːvɪd), *a.* [ad. mod.L. *perfervid-us*, f. PER- 4 + *fervidus* FERVID; chiefly in the phrase *perfervidum ingenium Scotorum*, founded on Buchanan's *Scotorum præfervida ingenia* (*Rerum Scotic. Hist.* XVI. li.).

Perfervidus, though quite regular in form, is not recorded in ancient Latin; an instance of *perfervida* formerly cited from Columella v. 5 is an erroneous reading in Gesner's ed. (1737) for *præfervida*.]

Very fervid, glowing, or ardent.

1856 MASSON *Ess., Scot. Infl. Brit. Lit.* 395 Without maintaining at present that all Scotchmen are perfervid..it will be enough to refer to the instances which prove at least that some Scotchmen have this character. **1875** HELPS *Soc. Press.* xxii. 339 The next generation has something in it of the brilliant nature of the Irish, or the perfervid nature of the Scotch. **1884** HOWELLS in *Harper's Mag.* Dec. 115/2 With perfervid gratitude.

Hence **perfer'vidity**, **per'fervidness**, also **'perfervour**, perfervid quality.

1861 J. BROWN *Horæ Subs.* Ser. II. 425 This perfervor of our Scottish love-songs. **1884** *Sat. Rev.* 1 Nov. 559/2 We are disposed to regret these manifestations and consequences of the perfervidity of Birmingham. **1890** *Spectator* 4 Oct., The characteristic of the Scotchman is perfervidness, exhibiting itself in strenuosity, in enthusiasm, and in excess.

perfervidly (pə'fɜːvɪdlɪ), *adv.* [f. PERFERVID *a.* + -LY^2.] In a perfervid manner.

1906 *Macm. Mag.* Oct. 884 The General was gripping de Pellotin's hand perfervidly. **1922** JOYCE *Ulysses* 709 Symposium of incoordinately abstract, perfervidly concrete mercantile coexreligionist excompatriots.

perficient (pə'fɪʃənt), *a.* (*sb.*) *rare.* [ad. L. *perficient-em*, pr. pple. of *perficĕre* to complete, finish, accomplish (see PERFECT *a.*).]

A. *adj.* That accomplishes or achieves something; effectual, actual.

1659 H. L'ESTRANGE *Alliance Div. Off.* 269 The essential and perficient Act of Confirmation, *viz.* Imposition of Hands. **1765** BLACKSTONE *Comm.* I. xviii. 481 The king being the sole founder of all civil corporations, and the endower the perficient founder of all eleemosynary ones, the right of visitation of the former results..to the king; and of the latter to the patron or endower. **1888** *Science* XII. 3/1 The perficient objection [to pronouncing grace] was probably the inconvenience to the service of the repast.

B. *sb.* One who perfects or completes.

1641 H. L'ESTRANGE *God's Sabbath* 11 Rest being..The perfection of the perficient and of the thing perfected. **1662** EVELYN *Chalcogr.* 106 Certain it is that practise and experience was its Nurse and perficient.

[WEBSTER 1828 (copied by later dicts.) gives the sense 'One who endows a charity'; app. founded upon quot. 1765 in A; but for this, as a sb., there appears to be no evidence.]

‖**perfide** (pɛrfid), *a.* [Fr., = treacherous.] In phr. ***perfide Albion***, with reference to the Fr. phr. *la perfide Albion*, 'perfidious Albion' (see ALBION).

1846 [see ALBION]. **1899** BEERBOHM *Around Theatres* (1924) I. 52 Had Mr. Kipling been born a Frenchman..he ..would..be known to us only as a..fulminator against '*perfide Albion*'. **1926** GALSWORTHY *Silver Spoon* II. iv. 142 *Perfide Albion!* Heh! We always wait till the last moment to declare our policy... Gives the impression that we serve time. **1947** H. NICOLSON *Diary* 2 Jan. (1968) 88 We always go through these stages of being beastly to our friends because we are frightened of our enemies. It is this that has earned us the reputation of *perfide Albion*. **1972** R. MAYNE *Europeans* v. 119 The phrase '*la perfide Angleterre*', later to become '*perfide Albion*', may have been coined by Jacques Bérigne Bossuet in a sermon on New Year's Day, 1654.

†**'perfidently**, *adv. Obs. rare*$^{-1}$. [f. **perfident* adj., ad. L. *perfīdens*, *-fīdent-em*, f. PER- 4 + L. *fīdent-em* trusting, confident, bold, pr. pple. of *fīd-ĕre* to trust: cf. *confident*, *diffident*.] With thorough trust or confidence; very confidently.

1650 B. *Discolliminium* 53 The Grand Cause of this Realme, so perfidently indeavoured, and highly applauded by some, so counter-wrought and condemned by others.

†**per'fidiate**, *a. Obs. rare.* [f. L. *perfidia* PERFIDY + -ATE^2.] Marked by perfidy; = next, b.

1632 LITHGOW *Trav.* x. 437 The notes of their abiured names, and perfidiat paines.

perfidious (pə'fɪdɪəs), *a.* [ad. L. *perfidiōs-us*, f. *perfidia* PERFIDY: see -OUS: cf. It. *perfidioso* = *perfido* (Florio 1598).] Characterized by perfidy; guilty of breaking faith or violating confidence; deliberately faithless; basely treacherous.

a. Of persons.

1598 FLORIO, *Perfido, Perfidioso*, perfidious, trecherous. **1601** SHAKS. *All's Well* v. iii. 205 He's quoted for a most perfidious slaue. **1628** SIR R. BOYLE *Diary* (Grosart) II. 277 The former conveighances the perfiddeows Lo Beaumont deceased had made. **1734** tr. *Rollin's Anc. Hist.* (1827) V. XIV. viii. 402 He thought himself skilful in proportion as he was perfidious. **1827** LYTTON *Pelham* xvii, I am the victim of a perfidious woman. **1855** MACAULAY *Hist. Eng.* xix. IV. 266 The most covetous and perfidious of mankind.

absol. **1651** tr. *De-las-Coveras' Don Fenise* 63 Don Pedro, so was this perfideous called.

b. Of actions, etc.

1603 KNOLLES *Hist. Turks* (1638) 298 The wicked author of that perfidious war. **1696** TATE & BRADY *Ps.* cxix. 163 Perfidious Practices and Lies I utterly detest. **1759** DILWORTH *Pope* 53 A knowledge of his underhand and perfidious dealing. **1848** LYTTON *Harold* III. ii, The perfidious surrender of Alfred, Edward's murdered brother.

perfidiously (pəˈfɪdɪəslɪ), *adv.* [f. prec. + -LY².] In a perfidious manner; with perfidy.

1589 RIDER *Bibl. Schol.* 1078 Perfidiously, *infideliter*. **1607** SHAKS. *Cor.* v. vi. 91 Perfidiously He ha's betray'd your businesse. **1631** GOUGE *God's Arrows* III. §57. 290 Zedekiah perfidiously and perjuriously maintained war against Nebuchadnezar. **1781** GIBBON *Decl. & F.* (1869) III. lxv. 631 He perfidiously violated the treaty. **1864** BRYCE *Holy Rom. Emp.* xx. (1875) 364 Austria at Campo Formio perfidiously exchanged the Netherlands for Venetia.

perˈfidiousness. [f. as prec. + -NESS.] The quality of being perfidious; unfaithfulness; base treachery.

1597 HOOKER *Eccl. Pol.* v. lxii. §17 The harme of other mens perfidiousnes it lay not in vs to auoide. **1651** BAXTER *Inf. Bapt.* 202 Perfidiousness lies most in breaking Covenants and Oaths. **1722** *Lond. Gaz.* No. 6114/5 Monsters of Ingratitude and Perfidiousness. **1818** HALLAM *Mid. Ages* (1872) I. iii. II. 411 Tyrants detested for their perfidiousness and cruelty. **1935** E. R. EDDISON *Mistress of Mistresses* iii. 54 Perfidiousness is a common waiter in most princes' courts. **1963** *Times* 30 Jan. 9/4 Mr. Macmillan's journey to Moscow..resurrected in Dr. Adenauer's mind all repressed fears of the perfidiousness of Albion.

perˈfidity. *rare.* [f. L. *perfid-us* (see next) + -ITY.] = next.

1607 TOPSELL *Four-f. Beasts* 530 In the male [hamster] there is this perfidity, that when they have prepared al their sustenance..hee doth shut out the female, and suffereth her not to approch nie it. **1692** R. L'ESTRANGE *Josephus, Antiq.* II. xv, The very Fatigue of the Expedition would make them repent both the Perfidity and the undertaking. **1903** J. KELMAN *Honour towards God* iii. 22 Instances are only too common in which Pagan and Mohammedan honour has shamed the perfidity of so-called Christians.

perfidy (ˈpɜːfɪdɪ). [a. F. *perfidie* (16th c. in Godef. *Compl.*) = It. *perfidia* (Florio 1598), Sp. *perfidia* (Minsheu 1599), ad. L. *perfidia* faithlessness, treachery, f. *perfid-us* that breaks faith or promise, faithless, treacherous, f. PER- 3 + *fid-ēs* faith.] The deceitful violation of faith or promise; base breach of faith or betrayal of the trust reposed in one; treachery; often, the profession of faith or friendship in order to deceive or betray.

1592 HARVEY *Four Lett.* Wks. (Grosart) I. 200 The Athenians were noted for lauish amplifieng..the Carthaginians for deceitfull perfidie. **1607** SIR E. HOBY in Ellis *Orig. Lett.* Ser. I. III. 86 Many other things he reporteth of the perfidy of the French nation. *a* **1776** HUME *On Morals* (1777) App. iv., These great virtues were balanced by great vices; inhuman cruelty; perfidy more than punic: no truth, no faith, no regard to oaths, promises or religion. **1782** PRIESTLEY *Corrupt. Chr.* II. IX. 186 It was.. a..deliberate act of perfidy. **1885** S. COX *Expositions* xxv. 331 The name of Judas has become a byword of covetousness and perfidy.

†**perˈfinish,** *v. Obs.* [f. PER- 2 + FINISH *v.*, after obs. F. *par-, perfinir* (Palsgr.), or med.L. *perfinīre.*] *trans.* To finish thoroughly, complete.

1523 CROMWELL in Merriman *Life & Lett.* (1902) I. 31 After this grete acte well and victoryously perfynysshed.

†**perˈfix,** *v. Obs.* [f. PER- 2 + FIX *v.* (L. had *perfigĕre, perfix-*, in the sense 'transfix'. OF. had *parfix* adj., fixed (as a day)).] *trans.* To fix firmly or definitely; to determine.

1509 HAWES *Past. Pleas.* (Percy Soc.) 87 My mynde.. Bothe daye and nyght upon you hole perfyxte. **1612** *Two Noble K.* III. vi, Take heed..this quarrel Sleep till the hour perfixt. **1699** BURNET *39 Art.* xix, The Jewish Religion had a Period perfixed, in which it was to come to an End. **1776** NIMMO *Stirlingshire* xi. 263 They surrendered before the day perfixed.

Hence †**perˈfixed, perfixt** *ppl. a.* ***perfixed salt*** = fixed salt (FIXED 4 b). †**perˈfixtly** *adv.*, definitely, precisely.

1605 TIMME *Quersit.* II. vi. 128 Whatsoeuer it contained of the volatile salt wil reside in the bottome with his perfixed salt. **1685** *Col. Rec. Pennsylv.* I. 139 Six days before the perfixt day for holding the Court. **1605** SYLVESTER *Du Bartas* II. iii. III. *Law* 561 Sith the holy man Foretels perfixtly what, and where, and when.

†**perˈflable,** *a. Obs.* [ad. L. *perflābil-is* that can be blown through, f. *perflāre*: see PERFLATE.] That may be blown through; open or permeable to the wind; allowing of ventilation.

c **1420** *Pallad. on Husb.* I. 1002 But make hit high, on euery half perflable. **1603** FLORIO *Montaigne* II. xii. (1632) 288 Epicurus makes the Gods, bright-shining, transparent and perflable. **1620** VENNER *Via Recta* Introd. 6 In an house, to the end it may be perflable, it is expedient to haue windowes on euery side.

†**perflant,** *a. Her. Obs. rare*⁻¹. [ad. L. *perflānt-em*, pr. pple. of *perflāre*: see next.] Blowing.

1678 JORDAN *Tri. London* 11 A shield, Argent, charged with the four Winds, Perflant.

perflate (pəˈfleɪt), *v.* Now *rare.* [f. L. *perflāt-*, ppl. stem of *perflāre*, f. PER- 1 + *flāre* to blow. Cf. *inflate.*] *trans.* To blow through, ventilate.

c **1540** BOORDE *The boke for to Lerne* B ij b, Come thou south wynde and perflat my gardyn. **1620** VENNER *Via Recta* Introd. 5 They cannot be freely perflated and purified with the windes. **1798** W. BLAIR *Soldier's Friend* 55 The canvas should be drawn up every day, the straw well shaken, and perflated by the wind. **1831** JANE PORTER *Sir E. Seaward's Narr.* II. 123 We permitted it [the air] to perflate our dwelling by night as well as by day.

Hence **perˈflating** *vbl. sb.* and *ppl. a.*

1869 E. A. PARKES *Pract. Hygiene* (ed. 3) 128 In some systems..the perflating power of the wind has been used.

†**perˈflatile,** *a. Obs.* [ad. post-cl. L. *perflātilis* that can be blown through, f. *perflāt-us* blown through, pa. pple. of *perflāre*: see prec.] Exposed to wind; subject to ventilation; airy.

1664 EVELYN *Sylva* (1679) 3 [We note] the more lofty, poor, and perflatile [places] for yew, box, and the like. **1667** C. MERRET in *Phil. Trans.* II. 465 [To] make that Story fitter for drying of Corn, and more perflatile. **1699** EVELYN *Acetaria* (1729) 157 Aery and moderately perflatile Grounds.

perflation (pəˈfleɪʃən). [ad. L. *perflātiōn-em*, n. of action from *perflāre* to PERFLATE. Cf. F. *perflation* (Paré *c* 1550).] The action of blowing through; free passage of wind or air; ventilation.

1658 SIR T. BROWNE *Gard. Cyrus* iv, They had the advantage of a fair perflation from windes. **1695** WOODWARD *Nat. Hist. Earth* IV. (1723) 228 Which the Miners effect by Perflations with large Bellows. **1775** JOHNSON *Journ. Hebrides* 182 That [barn]..was so contrived..as by perpetual perflation to prevent the mow from heating. **1816** A. C. HUTCHISON *Pract. Obs. Surg.* (1826) 206 Cleanse and thoroughly ventilate, by a perflation of air, the place from whence they came. **1901** *Brit. Med. Jrnl.* 9 Mar. 570/2 The alternative rooms must be situated..in such a manner as to secure perflation from opposite fronts.

†**ˈperfluence.** *Obs.* In 6 *Sc.* **perfluens.** [f. as next: see -ENCE.] The action of flowing through; flow (of words).

a **1520** MERSAR in *Bannatyne MS.* (Hunter. Cl.) 604/28 Be nocht of wirdis our grit [= words over great] perfluens.

ˈperfluency. *rare.* [f. PERFLUENT: see -ENCY.] Williams's rendering of *toddaid*, lit. 'a dissolving', name of a Welsh metre of 10 + 9 syllables. So **perˈfluid** *a.*, 'dissolving': applied to the 'conveyed' word or words that follow the rime-word in the first line of the *toddaid*: as in

A vynno evo a *vydd*—yn ei vro
A'r hyn a vynno na bo ni *bydd*.

1856 J. WILLIAMS *Gram. Edeyrn* §1761 The perfluency consists of nineteen syllables, having two homœorythms in the stave, with a perfluid word, like the recurrent word of a direct homœorythm systich, ending on the tenth syllable.

perfluent (pəˈfluːənt), *a.* [ad. L. *perfluent-em*, pr. pple. of *perflu-ĕre* to flow through (in 16th c. F. *perfluer*), f. PER- 1 + *flu-ĕre* to flow.] Flowing through; having the quality of flowing through.

perfluent battery, a kind of galvanic battery operated by a liquid flowing through.

1673 GREW *Veget. Roots* II. §59 The Water being more perfluent than the rest, will..strain, with a lighter Tincture of them. **1742** *Lond. & Country Brew.* I. (ed. 4) 16 Chalk.. administers nothing unwholesome to the perfluent Waters. **1809** COLERIDGE in *Sir H. Davy's Rem.* (1858) 111 Its inclosed stream or perfluent water-force. **1884** KNIGHT *Dict. Mech.* Suppl., *Perfluent Battery*, one in which the exciting liquid flows through the cells or cell to keep it constant.

perfluorinated (pəˈfluːərɪneɪtɪd), *ppl. a. Chem.* [f. PER-¹ 5 + FLUORINATED *ppl. a.*] Applied to a (usu. organic) compound, radical, etc., in which fluorine has replaced hydrogen to the maximum extent short of altering the characteristic functional groups of the species.

1947 *Chem. Rev.* XL. 52 This method cannot in general be used successfully..to prepare fluorocarbons or other perfluorinated compounds which are of much significance. **1972** *Materials & Technol.* IV. vii. 237 A number of perfluorinated aromatic and heteroaromatic compounds have been synthesized in recent years. **1974** *Physics Bull.* June 226/2 Electrolytic generation from water has made progress with the use of solid electrolytes such as perfluorinated sulphonic acid, which could allow efficiencies of up to 95% for the conversion from electrical energy to energy stored in the form of hydrogen.

perfluoro- (pəˈfluːərəʊ), *pref. Chem.* [f. PER-¹ 5 + FLUOR- + -O.] Used to designate organic compounds, radicals, etc., in which hydrogen has been replaced by fluorine to the maximum extent short of altering the characteristic functional groups of the species.

1947 *Industr. & Engin. Chem.* Mar. 236/2 Perchlorobenzene is a high melting solid, whereas perfluorobenzene is a liquid boiling at about the same temperature as benzene... Also, the boiling points of the perfluoroalkanes having more than five carbon atoms are actually lower than those of the hydrocarbons. *Ibid.* 241/1 The members of the panel..made the recommendation that the prefix 'perfluoro' be used to denote complete substitution by fluorine of all positions attached to the carbon skeleton. **1951** I. L. FINAR *Org. Chem.* I. v. 89 When catalysts other than copper..are used,..perfluoro-compounds are obtained, e.g. *n*-heptane gives perfluoro-heptane. **1962** P. J. & B. DURRANT *Introd. Adv. Inorg. Chem.* xxiii. 913 Perfluoroethylene polymerises under pressure in contact with an aqueous solution of a persulphate to yield the polymer teflon. **1971** *Nomencl. Org. Chem.* (I.U.P.A.C.) (ed. 2) C. 145 Halogen-containing compounds or radicals in which all hydrogen atoms, except those whose replacement would affect the nature of characteristic groups..present, have been replaced by halogen atoms of the same kind may be named by adding the prefixes 'perfluoro-', 'perchloro-', ..[etc.] to the name of the corresponding non-halogenated compound or radical. **1972** *Materials & Technol.* IV. vii. 252 The excellent electrical properties of perfluoropolymers, which have been known for many years, are shared by the simple fluorocarbons. **1976** *Nature* 4 Mar. 8/1 Perfluoropropane, C_3F_8, appears to be an ideal refrigerant.

Hence **per,fluoroˈcarbon**, any binary compound of carbon and fluorine, analogous to a hydrocarbon.

1947 *Industr. & Engin. Chem.* Mar. 292/1 Until October 1941 no practical general method for the synthesis of perfluorocarbons had been reported in the literature. **1961** G. H. BEAVEN et al. *Molecular Spectrosc.* I. iii. 101 Organic solvents for use down to 200 mμ are limited, in practice, to the saturated hydrocarbons and the aliphatic alcohols and ethers, although perfluorocarbons may be used more, as they become more readily available. **1972** *Materials & Technol.* IV. vii. 231 The perfluorocarbons are synthesized either by direct fluorination using elemental fluorine or by vapour phase fluorination techniques using hydrogen fluoride and a suitable catalyst. *Ibid.* 251 One of the most successful ways to coat a surface is to incorporate the fluorochemical in a polymer in which the perfluorocarbon chains consitute a series of side chains.

perfoliate (pəˈfəʊlɪət), *a. Bot.* and *Entom.* [ad. mod.L. *perfoliāt-us* (f. PER- 1 + *foli-um* leaf: see -ATE² 2), used in 16th c. in *Perfoliata*, name of the plant *Bupleurum rotundifolium.*

1548 TURNER *Names of Herbes* (1881) 85 Perfoliata is an herbe... The Germans cal it Durchwassz. It maye be called in englishe Thorowwax, because the stalke waxeth thorowe the leaues. **1611** COTGR., *Perfoliate* [Fr.], Through-wax, through-leafe (an hearbe). **1706** PHILLIPS, *Perfoliata*, (Lat.) the Herb Thorough-Wax.]

1. *Bot.* Having the stalk apparently passing through the leaf, the result of a congenital union of the edges of the basal lobes round the stem. Said orig. of a plant and its stalk; in later use *transf.* of the leaf.

1687 CLAYTON in *Phil. Trans.* (1739) XLI. 150 This Plant has several woody Stalks,..as I remember, perfoliat. **1785** MARTYN *Rousseau's Bot.* xix. (1794) 260 Known by its yellow corollas and upright smooth perfoliate stalks. **1753** CHAMBERS *Cycl. Supp.* s.v. *Leaf, Perfoliate leaf*, that whose disk is pierced by the stalk. **1845** LINDLEY *Sch. Bot.* vi. (1858) 77 Leaves..perfoliate. **1859** W. S. COLEMAN *Woodlands* (1862) 131 The Perfoliate Honeysuckle. **1880** GRAY *Struct. Bot.* (ed. 6) 107 It is the stem which is literally *perfoliate*, i.e. which seemingly passes through the leaf; but it is customary, though etymologically absurd, to call this a perfoliate leaf!

2. *Ent.* Of antennæ: Having the joints dilated or expanded laterally all round, so as to appear like a series of round plates pierced by a shaft or stem. Also **perˈfoliated.**

1752 J. HILL *Hist. Anim.* 52 The Dytiscus, with brown, perfoliated antennæ. The great Water Beetle. **1819** G. SAMOUELLE *Entomol. Compend.* 166 Perfoliate club of antennæ. **1826** KIRBY & SP. *Entomol.* IV. xlvi. 323 Perfoliate Knob. **1828** STARK *Elem. Nat. Hist.* II. 261 Antennæ..with the first three joints longer than the following, perfoliated, the last elongated and conical.

perfoliˈation. [f. prec.: see -ATION.] The condition of being perfoliate.

1880 GRAY *Struct. Bot.* iii. §4 (ed. 6) 107 Uvularia perfoliata..reveals the explanation of the perfoliation: the base of the lower leaves conspicuously surrounds and encloses the stem: that of the upper is merely cordate and clasping; the uppermost simply sessile by a rounded base.

ˈperforable, *a. rare.* [ad. L. type **perforābilis*, f. *perforā-re*: see -BLE.] That can be perforated.

1890 in *Century Dict.* **1926** J. M. ROBERTSON *Mr. Shaw & 'The Maid'* v. 46 The real question is simply whether his shield is perforable.

perforant (ˈpɜːfərənt), *a.* [ad. L. *perforānt-em*, pr. pple. of *perforāre*, or a. F. *perforant*, pr. pple. of *perforer* to PERFORATE.] Perforating.

1833 MRS. BROWNING *Prometh. Bound* 85 Heavily now Let fall the strokes upon the perforant gyves.

perforate (ˈpɜːfərət), *ppl. a.* [ad. L. *perforāt-us*, pa. pple. of *perforāre*: see PERFORATE *v.*].

= PERFORATED: construed as pple. and as adj.

1540-1 ELYOT *Image Gov.* 40 Suche abuses can not be longe hidde from princes, that haue theyr eares perforate (as is the prouerb). **1597** A. M. tr. *Guillemeau's Fr. Chirurg.* C ij b/1 Applyede cleane through the perforate tonge. **1626** BACON *Sylva* §470 An Earthen Pot perforate at the Bottom to let in the Plant. **1661** LOVELL *Hist. Anim. & Min.* Introd., The teeth are serrate and sharp, and two are.. perforate, by which they ejaculate their poyson. **1870** HOOKER *Stud. Flora* 33 Alyssum..septum entire or perforate.

perforate (ˈpɜːfəreɪt), *v.* [f. L. *perforāt-*, ppl. stem of *perforāre* to bore through, pierce through; f. PER- 1 + *forā-re* to bore, pierce.]

1. *trans.* To make a hole or holes right through; to pierce with a pointed instrument or projectile; to bore through; *spec.* to make rows or series of small holes or perforations separating coupons, stamps, etc., in a sheet.

1538 ELYOT *Dict.*, *Inforo*..to perforate or make a hole. **1597** A. M. tr. *Guillemeau's Fr. Chirurg.* 26 b/1 We should perforate or thrust them throughe. **1646** SIR T. BROWNE *Pseud. Ep.* IV. vi. 194 We tooke out the guts and bladder, and also perforated the Cranium. **1732** ARBUTHNOT *Rules of Diet* 407 Worms will perforate the Guts. **1772–84** *Cook's Voy.* (1790) V. 1799 Some of them..perforate the lower-lip into separate holes. **1875** KNIGHT *Dict. Mech.* 1668/2 The machine will perforate 250 sheets [of postage stamps] per hour, and the punches and holes are adjustable for stamps of different sizes. **1876** PREECE & SIVEWRIGHT *Telegraphy* § 120 Key *a* causes 1, 2, and 3 to perforate the paper in one vertical line. **1891** 'PHIL' *Penny Post. Jubilee* 73 The red penny was first issued imperforated... Later [1854] it was perforated with fifteen oval holes. **1896** *Times* 16 Dec. 5/2 The wounds ..showed that the destruction of bone and tissue perforated by the new bullet was tremendous.

b. To make a hole or holes into the interior of (a thing); to bore into; to make an opening into.

1712 BLACKMORE *Creation* I. 20 Tell, what could drill and perforate the Poles, And to th' attractive Rays adapt their Holes? **1856** STANLEY *Sinai & Pal.* ix. 337 Large caves.. still perforate the rocky sides of the hill. **1863** BATES *Nat. Amazon* II. 96 The ground is perforated with the entrances to their subterranean galleries.

c. To 'pass through' in position (cf. PASS *v.* 1 d); to extend or be continued through the substance of.

1820 W. IRVING *Sketch Bk.* I. 242 Dark passages, with which this old city is perforated, like an ancient cheese. **1831** R. KNOX *Cloquet's Anat.* 510 [The nerve] descends obliquely outwards, perforates the glutæus maximus muscle,..and expands upon its posterior surface. **1840** G. ELLIS *Anat.* 56 The divisions of the eighth nerve..again perforate the dura mater through smaller openings.

2. To form (a hole, etc.) by boring or punching.

1876 PREECE & SIVEWRIGHT *Telegraphy* § 120 The punches which perforate these holes in the paper.

3. *intr.* To penetrate, make its way *into* or *through* something; to make a perforation.

1775 *Sterne's Sent. Journ. Contin.* III. 179 Casting a most amorous leer through those beautiful eye-lashes, which penetrated farther than I thought it possible for a single look to perforate. **1897** *Allbutt's Syst. Med.* III. 975 The stomach ..may become adherent to the transverse colon into which the ulcer perforates.

b. In pass. sense: To suffer perforation, to become perforated.

1897 *Allbutt's Syst. Med.* III. 889 The cysts are apt to perforate and to burst.

ˈ**perforated**, *ppl. a.* [f. prec. + -ED[1].]

1. a. Pierced with one or more holes: said esp. of a thing constructed with small holes, spaces, or openings passing through (as a wall or carved panel).

perforated muscle, the short flexor of the toes, and the superficial flexor of the fingers, the tendons of which are perforated by those of the *perforating muscles* (see below). ***perforated tape***, tape in which data are recorded by means of the pattern of holes punched in it; cf. TAPE *sb.*[1] 2 b, *paper tape* s.v. PAPER *sb.* 12, *punched tape* s.v. PUNCHED *ppl. a.* 2.

1597 A. M. tr. *Guillemeau's Fr. Chirurg.* 13 b/2 The bullet-drawer with the ring, or with the perforated spoon. **1676** WORLIDGE *Cyder* (1691) 96 A grater made of perforated Latten. **1727–41** CHAMBERS *Cycl.* s.v. *Chair*, The perforated Chair, wherein the new elected pope is placed, F. Mabillon observes, is still to be seen at Rome. **1758** J. S. *Le Dran's Observ. Surg.* (1771), *Perforatus Musculus*, the Perforated Muscle. **1866** *Cornh. Mag.* Aug. 170 A series of perforated brass saucers or colanders. **1876** *Gwilt's Archit.* §2224*l*, Perforated zinc..is extensively employed in filling up squares in sashes, or panels in partitions, to assist ventilation. **1890** *Electrician* 4 July 235/1 The key-board no longer gives direct electric contacts, but produces mechanically a perforated tape on which the signs are represented by holes at their respective places. **1904** *Brit. Med. Jrnl.* 17 Dec. 1628 The occurrence of a perforated gastric ulcer. **1964** N. N. BISWAS *Princ. Telegr.* iv. 93 Transmission on the line may be made either from the keyboard or by a perforated tape on the tape transmitter. **1973** GOACHER & DENNY *Teleprinter Handbk.* ii. 35/2 The perforated tape forms a permanent record of all the code signals involved in a particular message in a form suitable for storage.

b. *Her.* Said of a charge pierced with a hole or holes. See also quot. 1704.

1486 *Bk. St. Albans, Her.* C v, Thys cros masculatit sum tyme is perforatit in the masculys as it is opyn in the persyng. **1704** J. HARRIS *Lex. Techn.* I, *Perforated*... The Armorists use it to express the passing or penetrating of one Ordinary (in part) thro' another; as thus. He beareth Or, a Bend Ermine Perforated thro' a Chevron Gules.

c. *Nat. Hist.* Full of little holes or perforations, cribrose. *Bot.* Having translucent dots which resemble holes, as in species of *Hypericum*.

1678 PHILLIPS (ed. 4), *Perforated*, a term applyed to Herbs, as when the leaf of any Herb being held against the light, seemeth full of little holes.

d. *Conch.* Applied to a spirally wound shell of which the centre is hollow instead of solid.

1851–6 WOODWARD *Mollusca* 100 The axis of the shell, around which the whorls are coiled, is sometimes open or hollow; in which case, the shell is said to be perforated, or umbilicated (e.g. Solarium).

e. *Anat.* ***perforated space*** or ***spot, anterior*** and ***posterior***, small regions within the skull perforated by numerous holes for the passage of blood-vessels.

1886 *Cassell's Encycl. Dict.* s.v., The anterior perforated space or spot constituting a depression near the entrance of the Sylvian fissure, and the posterior forming a deep fossa between the peduncles at the base. **1899** *Allbutt's Syst. Med.* VII. 608 In passing across the anterior perforated space it [the Sylvian artery] gives off a number of branches.

2. Made or outlined by perforations. *rare.*

c **1790** IMISON *Sch. Art* II. 55 Then with some fine pounded charcoal..rub over the perforated strokes, which will give an exact outline. **1891** 'PHIL' *Penny Post. Jubilee* 153 Perforated Initials on Stamps.

ˈ**perforating**, *ppl. a.* [f. as prec. + -ING[2].] That perforates; boring, passing through; *spec.* applied to certain arteries, nerves, etc., which pierce or pass through other structures; *fig.* of mind or intellect: Piercing, penetrating.

perforating machine = PERFORATOR 1 b, c. ***perforating muscle***, the long flexor of the toes, and deep flexor of the fingers, the tendons of which perforate those of the *perforated muscles*; so ***perforating arteries***. ***perforating ulcer***, an ulcer in any part which perforates the structure; *esp.* an ulcer commencing on the sole or palm and slowly extending so as sometimes to perforate the foot or hand.

1661 K. W. *Conf. Charac.* To Rdr. 1 To suppose..that your penetrating and perforating intellectualls will extract some honey from this aloes. **1704** J. HARRIS *Lex. Techn.* I, *Perforatus*, is a Muscle belonging to the Fingers,..its Tendons are Perforated to admit those of the Perforating Muscles to pass thro' them to their Insertions. **1842** DUNGLISON *Med. Lex.*, *Perforating Arteries*, in the hand,.. in the thigh,..in the foot. **1878** T. BRYANT *Pract. Surg.* I. 172 Perforating ulcer of the foot was so called by Vesigné of Abbeville in 1850. **1878** tr. *H. von Ziemssen's Cycl. Med.* VIII. 162 A perforating ulcer of the œsophagus, analogous to 'perforating ulcer of the stomach'. **1895** *Westm. Gaz.* 18 Sept. 3/2 One man had no less than three perforating wounds all in a perfectly clean condition.

perforation (pɜːfəˈreɪʃən). [ad. late L. *perforātiōn-em*, n. of action from *perforāre* to perforate; cf. OF. *perforacion*, *-ation* (14th c. in Hatz.-Darm.), perh. the immediate source.]

1. a. The action of perforating, boring through, or piercing; the fact or condition of being perforated; *spec.* the making of a row or series of small holes in a leaf or sheet of paper, so as to enable a portion to be easily torn off.

c **1440** *Gesta Rom.* iv. 10 (Harl. MS.) Sir,..some tyme is suche holiyng and perforacion goode, and not wikkide. **1626** BACON *Sylva* § 500 The likeliest way [is] the perforation of the body of the tree in several places one above the other, and the filling of the holes [etc.]. **1836–41** BRANDE *Chem.* (ed. 5) 269 The mechanical force..is shown by the perforation of paper. **1881** SPOTTISWOODE in *Nature* 6 Oct. 548/1 Gun-cotton itself..merely shows signs of perforation like the card. **1891** 'PHIL' *Penny Post. Jubilee* 147 Next follows the perforation [of the sheets of stamps], which is performed by machinery.

b. *Surg.* The formation, through accident or disease, of a hole through the thickness of any structure, as through the wall of the intestine, etc.

1666 BOYLE *Orig. Formes & Qual.* (1667) 16 Bloudy Fluxes occasion'd by the perforation of the Capillary Arteries. **1876** BRISTOWE *The. & Pract. Med.* (1878) 224 Perforation of the bowel may occur in patients of all ages. *Ibid.* 229 If signs of perforation manifest themselves, our only hope lies in keeping the patient under the influence of opium or morphia. **1882** *Med. Temp. Jrnl.* LI. 108 If perforation should take place let me have large and repeated doses of opium.

2. A hole made by boring, punching, or piercing; an aperture passing through or into anything; a passage, shaft, tunnel; each one of a row or series of small holes punched in a leaf or sheet of paper, or between postage or other stamps in a sheet, in order to facilitate their separation.

1543 TRAHERON *Vigo's Chirurg.* IX. 241 For remotion of thys aposteme, ye muste make a new and larger perforation or borynge. **1599** A. M. tr. *Gabelhouer's Bk. Physicke* 34/1 Inoculated Pearles, or Pearles without perforationes. **1665** HOOKE *Microgr.* 38 Pipes of Glass, with a very small perforation. **1783** POTT *Chirurg. Wks.* II. 18 They have no perforations or apertures. **1870** *Routledge's Ev. Boy's Ann., Suppl.* Mar. 4/1 [Stamps] with pin-pricked perforations. **1891** 'PHIL' *Penny Post. Jubilee* 150 A simple perforation is that which the perforating machine has produced by punching the paper completely out, leaving a regular series of small round holes between each row of stamps.

3. The natural orifice of an organ or part of the body.

1615 CROOKE *Body of Man* 945 The first externall perforation..is called by a proper name, *Meatus Auditorus, the hole of Hearing*. **1688** BOYLE *Final Causes Nat. Things* iv. 148 That admirable perforation of the uvea, which we call the pupil. **1797** M. BAILLIE *Morb. Anat.* (1807) 417 The hymen is sometimes found without a perforation in it, so that the vagina is completely shut up at its external extremity.

4. *attrib.* and *Comb.*, as ***perforation-sound***; **perforation-gauge**, in *Philately*, a gauge or rule for readily counting the number of stamp-perforations in a given length (conventionally, two centimetres); **perforation plate** *Bot.* (see quot. 1933).

1879 *St. George's Hosp. Rep.* IX. 788 On inflation, air passes into the tympanum without perforation sound. **1891** 'PHIL' *Penny Post. Jubilee* 152 In order to ascertain the various sizes of perforations a perforation gauge has been invented. **1933** *Tropical Woods* XXXVI. 7 *Perforation plate*, a term of convenience for the area of the wall (originally imperforate) involved in the coalescence of two members of a vessel. **1953** K. ESAU *Plant Anat.* xi. 223 The perforations of vessel members commonly occur on the end walls, but they may be present on the lateral walls too. The wall bearing the perforation is called the perforation plate. *Ibid.* 233 A pitted wall part became a scalariform perforation plate, which changed into a simple perforation plate. **1975** S. CARLQUIST *Ecol. Strategies of Xylem Evol.* i. 13 There are even dicotyledons with simple perforation plates and scalariform lateral-wall pitting.

perforative (ˈpɜːfərətɪv), *a.* (*sb.*) [a. F. *perforatif*, *-ive* (in Cotgr.), f. L. *perforāt-*, ppl. stem of *perforāre* to perforate + -IVE.] Having the character of perforating; tending to perforate.

1597 A. M. tr. *Guillemeau's Fr. Chirurg.* 12/2 Settle the perforatiue trepane verye fast on the broken bone. **1727–41** CHAMBERS *Cycl.* s.v. *Trepanum*, There are also perforative trepans, and exfoliative ones. **1878** tr. *H. von Ziemssen's Cycl. Med.* VIII. 238 According to another view, perforative peritonitis is to be regarded as a particular form of this disease. **1898** *Allbutt's Syst. Med.* V. 736 Perforative pericarditis may result from the bursting of any neighbouring abscess.

†**B.** *sb.* An instrument used to perforate; *spec.* the perforative trephine for piercing the skull. *Obs.*

1758 J. S. *Le Dran's Observ. Surg.* (1771) 304, I performed the Puncture.., and having withdrawn the Perforative, a white Pus..was discharged by the Canula.

perforator (ˈpɜːfəreɪtə(r)). [Agent-noun in L. form, from *perforāre* to PERFORATE. In mod.F. *perforateur* (Littré).]

1. An instrument or machine used for perforating.

a. *Surgery*, (*a*) a trephine; (*b*) an instrument for penetrating the fœtal skull. **b.** A power-machine for drilling rock in order to blast it, in tunnelling, etc. **c.** A machine for perforating postage-stamps, etc.; also, that used for perforating the paper-ribbons used in some forms of telegraphy.

1739 S. SHARP *Surgery* xiii. 61 Withdrawing the Perforator, leave the Waters to empty by the Canula. **1767** GOOCH *Treat. Wounds* I. 245 After making many adjacent holes, with a drill or perforator, as far as the *meditullium*. **1790** R. BLAND in *Med. Commun.* II. 454 We are under the necessity of using the perforator and crotchet. **1822–34** *Good's Study Med.* (ed. 4) IV. 152. **1871** *Daily News* 18 Sept., At the beginning of December we heard quite clearly the blows of the perforators against the rocks. **1876** PREECE & SIVEWRIGHT *Telegraphy* § 119 The [Wheatstone] apparatus consists of three parts: the *perforator*, which prepares the message by punching holes in a paper ribbon; the *transmitter*..and the *receiver*. **1900** *Daily News* 13 Oct. 6/3 When the perforators have bored a hole some three feet deep, it is filled with dynamite and fired.

2. A boring organ possessed by some insects, variously used as a sting, an ovipositor, etc.

1828 STARK *Elem. Nat. Hist.* II. 335 Tenthredo... Perforator not projecting beyond the anus. *Ibid.* 336 Some have the last half segment of the abdomen prolonged into a point, with a projecting perforator of three filaments.

perforatory (ˈpɜːfərətərɪ), *a.* [f. ppl. stem of L. *perforāre* to PERFORATE: see -ORY[2].] Of or pertaining to perforation; perforative.

1867 *Philatelist* I. 64 Desiring specimens of perforatory varieties.

perforce (pəˈfɔəs), *adv.*, *sb.* Forms: 4 **par force**, 4–6 **parforce**, 6– **perforce**, (6 **perforse**, *Sc.* **perforss**, 7 **per force**). [ME. a. OF. *par force* by force (12th c.): see FORCE *sb.* 5 b.]

A. Phrase, adverb.

1. †**a.** By the application of physical force or violence; by violence; forcibly. *Obs.*

c **1330** *Arth. & Merl.* 8040 (Kölbing), .xv. þousinde [paiens], þat hadden born hem oȝan Parfors in to Bedingham. **13..** *Seuyn Sag.* (W.) 488 Par force he hadde me forth i nome. *a* **1400** *K. Alis.* 2533 (Bodl. MS.) Antioche & Tyberye also Abouten hij gonnen goo Par force smyten in to þe þrenge And duden beastes from oþere drenge. **1494** FABYAN *Chron.* v. cxxiii. 100 They encountred the sayde people y[t] caryed the sayd treasoure and stuffe, & parforce toke it from the knyghtes. *a* **1533** LD. BERNERS *Huon* xlviii. 162. **1545** RAYNOLD *Byrth Mankynde* 73 It..draweth out the secondine parforce. **1624** CAPT. SMITH *Virginia* 62 The Salvages assayed to carry him away perforce. **1670** NARBOROUGH *Jrnl.* in *Acc. Sev. Late Voy.* I. (1694) 110 Unless such Ships of force were to go thither and Trade per force.

b. In weakened senses: By constraint of circumstances or of the prospect of physical force; by moral constraint; compulsorily, of necessity.

1542 UDALL *Erasm. Apoph.* 237 b, By this craftie meanes he constreigned Caesar in maner parforce to geue hym perdone. **1579** SPENSER *Sheph. Cal.* Nov. 127 Flouds of teares flowe in theyr stead perforse. **1675** HOBBES *Odyssey* (1677) 231 Twelve days the wind continued at north, Which kept the fleet perforce within the bay. **1748** WESLEY *Wks.* (1872) II. 109, I went, perforce, into the main street. **1813** SCOTT *Trierm.* III. x, He paused perforce, and blew his horn. **1868** E. EDWARDS *Ralegh* I. xxv. 606 The reader must perforce, on that one point, make his own inferences.

c. quasi-*adj.* Of necessity; necessitated, forced.

1580 LYLY *Euphues* (Arb.) 408 Which by so much the more is to be borne, by howe much the more it is perforce. **1895** J. SMITH *Perm. Message Exod.* ix. 123 Here we have no perforce succumbing to an irresistible decree.

d. ***patience perforce***: see PATIENCE *sb.* 1 f. So ***to be patient perforce***, etc.

c **1560** A. SCOTT *Poems* (S.T.S.) xx. 9 Perforss tak paciens, And dre thy destiny. **1568** GRAFTON *Chron.* II. 746 She being.. without comfort of defenders, by pacience perforce, was compelled to suffer and susteyne. **1575–1680** [see PATIENCE 1 f]. **1655** FULLER *Ch. Hist.* III. ix. §28 The Papal party did struggle for a time, till at last they were patient perforce.

e. ***perforce of***, properly 'per force of', 'by force of', 'by dint of'.

1809 COLERIDGE *Lett., to D. Stuart* (1895) 540 Periods.. alarmingly long, perforce of their construction. **1868** TENNYSON *Lucretius* 167 Do they.. so press in, perforce Of multitude?

B. quasi-*sb.* and *sb.*

1. quasi-*sb.* in phrases ***by perforce***, by force or compulsion; ***of perforce***, of necessity. Also *nonce-use* = necessitating cause or circumstance.

1525 LD. BERNERS *Froiss.* II. clxvi. [clxii.] 459 Nowe by perforce they cause the cardynalles to entre into conclaue, and to chuse a Pope. **1871** MRS. WHITNEY *Real Folks* iii. (1872) 89 With this backing, and the perforce of there being nobody else, young Dr. Ripwinkley had ten patients within the first week. **1897** *Westm. Gaz.* 7 Aug. 3/1 Of perforce he is an authority on the subject.

†**2.** *sb.* A military officer of inferior rank to a quarter-master, in the Scottish Army, 17th c. (Jamieson suggests A drum-major.) *Obs.*

1643 *Sc. Acts Chas. I* (1819) VI. 47/1 With power to the said Colonell To nominat and appoynt.. a perforce... The pay of the perforce to be monethlie 18 lib.

†**per'force**, *v. Obs.* Also 5–6 par-. [a. OF. *parforcier, -forcer*, f. *par* through + *forcer* to FORCE.] *lit.* To force greatly.

1. *refl.* (= obs. F. *se parforcer*). To strive or endeavour to the utmost; to do one's best.

c **1489** CAXTON *Sonnes of Aymon* vi. 138 Yf ye wyll parforce yourselfe a lityll, this paynymes shall not holde afore vs. **1490** —— *Eneydos* xix. 71 She parforseth hyr self, wyth hir grete teeth to ete the rotes vnder the grounde. **1541** R. COPLAND *Guydon's Quest. Chirurg.* R ij b, Yf God.. gyue me good fortune I shall perforce me to make it hole complete.

2. *trans.* To force, constrain, oblige.

1509 in *Mem. Hen. VII* (Rolls) 442 The kynge.. wyl not in no wyse be perforsyd forto confyrme the sayed maryaje. **1530** PALSGR. 652/2, I parforce a man, I constrayne hym to do a thyng. *a* **1541** WYATT *Poet. Wks.* (1861) 122 When other run, perforc'd I am to creep.

perforcedly (pəˈfɔəsɪdlɪ), *adv. rare*$^{-1}$. [f. *perforced*, pa. pple. of prec. + -LY^2; app. influenced by PERFORCE *adv.*] Under the constraint of force or necessity.

1855 BROWNING *An Epistle* 179 He holds on firmly to some thread of life (It is the life to lead perforcedly).

†**'perfored** (-ɪd), *a. Her. Obs.* [ad. F. *perforé* pa. pple., perforated.] = PERFORATED *ppl. a.* 1 b.

1661 MORGAN *Sph. Gentry* II. i. 15 A Cross having the four ends.. clamped.. as the Milroin it self is.. and is perfored as that is also.

perform (pəˈfɔːm), *v.* Forms: α. 4–6 **par-, perfourme(n, parforme(n,** (6 **perfurme),** 4–7 **performe,** 5– **perform.** β. 4–5 **par-, perfourne(n, perforne(n; par-, perforny, perfourny.** [ME. a. OF. *par-, perfourmer, -furmer, -former* (rare, and chiefly AF.; 1291 in Godef.). This may have been originally f. *par-* (= PER- 2) + *former* FORM *v.*, or *forme* FORM *sb.*, so that the etymological sense would be 'to carry through in due form'; on the other hand, it may have arisen as an etymologizing or a merely phonetic alteration of the much more frequent OF. *parfournir* (in AF. also rarely *parfourner*, 1st conj.) to accomplish entirely, achieve, complete, f. *par-* + *-fournir* to FURNISH: see PERFURNISH *v.* Whatever the formal etymology may have been, the AF. *parfourmer* and its Eng. representative derive their meaning entirely from *parfournir.* In the last quarter of the 14th c., some Eng. writers substituted *par-, perfo(u)rn(e*, in imitation of the form generally current in Fr., for the older *par-, perfo(u)rme.* The innovation, however, was soon abandoned: the forms with *n* occur in some 15th c. MSS. of Langland, Chaucer, and Gower, but our quotations exhibit no examples from works originally written later than 1400.]

†**1. a.** *trans.* To carry through to completion; to complete, finish, perfect (an action, process, work, etc.). *Obs.*

α. *c* **1374** CHAUCER *Troylus* III. 417 Þis grete emprise Parforme it out, for now is most nede. **1382** WYCLIF *Phil.* i. 6 He that bigan in ȝou a good work, schal performe til into the day of Jhesu Crist [**1611** will performe it (*marg.*) or will finish it; **1881** *R.V.* will perfect it]. *c* **1440** *Alph. Tales* 159 Þer chiftan.. chargid hym to perform at he had begon. **1481** CAXTON *Myrr.* I. xx. 60 The sonne.. hath performed his cours round aboute therthe. **1535** COVERDALE 1 *Chron.* xxvii. 24 Ioab.. had begonne to nombre them, and performed it not. **1620** T. GRANGER *Div. Logike* 32 Confirmed by appetite, or affection, performed by nature, and outward adiuuants.

β. *c* **1386** CHAUCER *Merch. T.* 551 (Ellesm.) Parfourned [*so Heng.*; 5 *MSS.* par-, perfo(u)rmed] hath the sonne his Ark diurne.

b. To complete or make up by addition of what is wanting. Also with *up. Obs.*

c **1391** CHAUCER *Astrol.* II. §10 Than shal the remenant þat leueth performe the howr inequal by nyght. **1494** FABYAN *Chron.* v. lxxxiv. 62 Then to furnysshe or perfourme the Story of Vortiger, nedefull it is or necessary to retourne to the matier where we before laft. **1530** *Privy Purse Exp. Hen. VIII* (1827) 26 Delivered.. to performe up A somme .xls. **1537** in Strype *Eccl. Mem.* I. App. lxxxviii. 229 That the sacrament of Confirmation is a sacrament performing the sacrament of Baptism.

β. *c* **1386** CHAUCER *Sompn. T.* 553 (Ellesm. & Heng.) The Confessour.. Shal parfourne vp the nombre of his Couent.

c. To make up or supply (what is wanting).

a **1533** LD. BERNERS *Huon* cli. 577, I pray to god to parfourme that she wantethe. **1551** ROBINSON tr. *More's Utop.* II. (1895) 170 The lacke of the one is performed and fylled vp with the aboundaunce of the other.

†**2. a.** To finish making, complete the construction of (a material object or structure). ***bed performed***, a bed fully furnished, a bed complete. *Obs.*

c **1450** LOVELICH *Grail* xliv. 191 And whanne the towr performed Is, thanne schal it be Clepid with-Owten Mys; 'the towr Of Merveilles'. *c* **1483** CAXTON *Dialogues* 33 Donaas the doblet maker Hath performed [*orig.* parfaicte] my doublet. **1494** in *Somerset Med. Wills* (1901) 323 To performe my bed abovesaid a paire of shetes owte of my cofer. **1531** in Weaver *Wells Wills* (1890) 77 To my servante Margery,.. a crocke, a flockebed performyd.

b. *esp.* To complete by addition of ornament, to 'finish off', decorate, trim. *Obs.*

1420 *E.E. Wills* (1882) 46 Also a dosen of peutre vessell performyd. **1483** in *Antiq. Rep.* (1807) I. 40 The furr of the same trappour performed with xxij ermyn bakks. **1530** in Weaver *Wells Wills* 18 Half a dossyn of pewter vessells performyd. **1612** *Wardr. Acc. P'cess Elizabeth's Marriage*, Rich white florence cloth of silver to make one goun for a bride maiden, and to performe another.

†**3. a.** To make, construct (a material object); to execute (a piece of work, literary or artistic). *Obs.*

1463 in *Bury Wills* (Camden) 43 That my executours performe [*ed.* pfoore] and do make Seynt Marie awter, Rysbygate, and ye croos beforn my gate. **1478** [see PERFORMING *vbl. sb.* 3]. **1505** in Gage *Hist. Suffolk* (1838) 145 Paid to Oliver mason for.. performing a dore. **1535** COVERDALE *Ecclus.* Prol., I laboured and dyd my best to perfourme this boke. **1610** *Map Nottinghams.*, Performed by Iohn Speede and are to be sold in Popes head Alley. **1711** W. SUTHERLAND *Shipbuild. Assist.* 6 A Ship.. may be as well performed as such large Buildings. **1766** ENTICK *London* IV. 408 The goodness of the pavement, lately performed with Scotch stone. **1774** J. BRYANT *Mythol.* II. 442 A garland.. of Mosaic, or inlaid work, and not ill performed.

b. *absol.* or *intr.* To compose a work or treatise; to write (*upon* a subject). *Obs. rare.*

1703 S. PARKER *Eusebius* VI. 107 Hyppolitus.. another of the Writers of that time,.. perform'd upon the Six Days-Creation, and upon part of the Sacred History immediately following it.

†**4.** To bring about, bring to pass, cause, effect, produce (a result). Also with obj. clause. *Obs.*

α. **13..** *E.E. Allit. P.* B. 542 Lo! suche a wrakful wo.. Parformed þe hyȝe fader on folke þat he made. **1382** WYCLIF *Prov.* xvi. 30 That.. thenketh shreude thingis,.. parformeth euel. **1393** LANGL. *P. Pl.* C. XVI. 173 Al þe witt of þis worlde.. Can nat performen a pees.. Profitable for boþe parties. **1548** GEST *Pr. Masse* in H. G. Dugdale *Life* (1840) App. I. 91 O holy Trinite performe that thys sacryfyce.. may be acceptable to the. **1610** SHAKS. *Temp.* I. ii. 194 Hast thou, Spirit, Performd to point, the Tempest that I bad thee? **1700** MAIDWELL in *Collect.* (O.H.S.) I. 313 This beneficial act.. may perform the support of this.. academy. **1715** DESAGULIERS *Fires Impr.* Title-p., Altering.. Chimneys.. already Built, so that they shall perform the same Effects.

β. *c* **1374** CHAUCER *Boeth.* III. pr. ii. 67 (Add. MS.) Certys þer nys non oþer þing þat may so weel perfourny [*v.r.* performe] blisfulnesse as an estat plenteuous of alle goodes. **1377** LANGL. *P. Pl.* B. XIII. 78 Þis goddes gloton.. he perforneth [*v.r.* performeþ; C. XVI. 87 perfourneþ] yuel. **1390** GOWER *Conf.* III. 351 Ovide ek seith that love to parforne [*rime* Satorne] Stant in the hond of Venus the goddesse.

5. To carry out in action (a command, request, promise, undertaking, etc.); to carry into effect, execute, fulfil, discharge.

α. [**1291** in R. de Avesb. *Mirab. Gesta* (1720) 18 Qil.. eit la seisine de tut la terre & des chastiels Descoce tauntqe droit soit fait & performe.] *c* **1350** *Will. Palerne* 1558 Wenestow þat i wold his wille now parfourme? *c* **1391** CHAUCER *Astrol.* Prol., There ben some conclusions þat wole nat in alle thinges performen hir byhestes. **1413** *Pilgr. Sowle* (Caxton) I. xxi. (1859) 22 Yf it so were that he had ony tyme perfourmed his promysse. **1535** COVERDALE *Ps.* lx[i]. 8 Yt I maye daylie perfourme my vowes. **1665** MANLEY *Grotius' Low C. Warres* 385 He was not onely not able to perform his threats, but also unable to defend himself. **1728** YOUNG *Odes to King* 22 Our Fleet, if war, or commerce, call, His will performs. **1875** DASENT *Vikings* I. 148 Sigvald had.. performed the first of the two conditions.

β. **1377** LANGL. *P. Pl.* B. XIV. 290 Pore men perfornen [C. XIX. 128 parfournen] þe comaundement. *Ibid.* XV. 320 Who perfourneth þis prophecye of the peple þat now lybbeth?.. If any peple perfourne þat texte, it ar þis pore freres! *c* **1380** *Sir Ferumb.* 355 Yf þou þyn auaunt perforny myȝt, a-rys vp anon and diȝt þe. *Ibid.* 1994 By Mahoun,.. parforny y wol þy red. **1390** GOWER *Conf.* III. 131 Which of his kinde mot parforne The will of Marte and of Satorne. **1395** *E.E. Wills* 10 To parfourne trewly this testament.

6. a. To carry out, achieve, accomplish, execute (that which is commanded, promised, undertaken, etc., or, in extended sense, any action, operation, or process undertaken or entered upon); to go through and finish, to work out, do, make.

α. **13..** *E.E. Allit. P.* C. 406 Þenne al.. Par-formed alle þe penaunce þat þe prynce radde. **1382** WYCLIF *John* v. 36 The workis that my fadir ȝaf to me that I performe hem, the ilke workis that I do. **1447** BOKENHAM *Seyntys* (Roxb.) 26 Than fynt he hymself.. More strong to performyn his journe. **1526** *Pilgr. Perf.* (W. de W. 1531) 16 b, Let euery persone.. go forth strongly.. performynge his pilgrymage to our lorde god. **1600** J. PORY tr. *Leo's Africa* VIII. 313 The inhabitants of Cairo.. will promise much, but performe little. **1605** SHAKS. *Macb.* III. iv. 77 Murthers haue bene perform'd Too terrible for the eare. **1617** MORYSON *Itin.* III. 271 They performe this office for three yeeres. **1652** NEEDHAM tr. *Selden's Mare Cl.* 335 That Sea-Fight perform'd between the French Fleet.. and the English Fleet. **1669** STURMY *Mariner's Mag.* I. ii. 36 To perform the foregoing Problem Arithmetically. *c* **1750** in 'Bat' *Crick. Man.* (1850) 30 It [cricket] is performed by a person who.. defends a wicket. **1797** MRS. A. M. BENNETT *Beggar Girl* (1813) V. 270 While this operation was performing [= being performed], another carriage was heard. **1799** *Hull Advertiser* 23 Mar. 1/4 The Lazaretto where the French were performing quarantine. **1849** THACKERAY *Pendennis* xxvii, I have had to go up and perform the agreeable to most of them. **1868** LOCKYER *Elem. Astron.* ix. (1879) 319 The Moon's nodes perform a complete revolution in nineteen years.

β. [**1315** *Rolls of Parlt.* I. 351/2 Qe les busoignes tochauntes li et son Roiaume ne seient faites ne perfurnies sanz assent de li.] **1377** LANGL. *P. Pl.* B. v. 405, I parfourned [*v.r.* performed] neure penaunce as þe preste me hiȝte. *c* **1386** CHAUCER *Doctor's T.* 151 (Ellesm. & Heng.) How þat his lecherie Parfourned sholde been ful subtilly.

†**b.** Loosely, in antithesis to *promise*, etc.: To grant, furnish, give, pay, that which is promised.

a **1569** [see PERFORMED *ppl. a.* below]. **1582** N. T. (Rhem.) *John* xii. 19 *note*, He [Holy Ghost] is promised and performed onely to the Church and chiefe gouernors and general councils thereof. *a* **1661** FULLER *Worthies, Sussex* (1662) 167 Performing Life to those to whom he promised it.

c. *absol.* or *intr.* To do or carry out what one has to do, or has undertaken; to discharge one's function, do one's part; to do, act (well, ill, etc.).

1382 WYCLIF 2 *Cor.* viii. 11 Now forsothe and in dede performe ȝe. **1607** SHAKS. *Cor.* I. i. 271 Though he performe To th' vtmost of a man. **1696** LUTTRELL *Brief Rel.* (1857) IV. 109 All their utensils and moulds.. which performed with great dexterity. **1737** BRACKEN *Farriery Impr.* (1757) II. 84 Horses.. that would perform better upon a Journey than such as eat twice the Quantity. **1858** BUSHNELL *Nat. & Supernat.* ii. (1862) 29 Paul found it present with him to will, but could not find how to perform. **1886** *St. Stephen's Rev.* 13 Mar. 11/2 Florin [racehorse].. performed most moderately.

7. a. *spec.* To do, go through, or execute formally or solemnly (a duty, public function, ceremony, or rite; a piece of music, a play, etc.).

[*c* **1386** CHAUCER *Prioress' T.* 4 Noght oonly thy laude precious Parfourned is by men of dignitee, But by the mouth of children thy bountee Parfourned is.] **1613** PURCHAS *Pilgrimage* (1614) 62 They abhorred the killing of Kine, but performed much worship to them. **1687** A. LOVELL tr. *Thevenot's Trav.* I. 109 Four Churches.. where Divine-Service is performed but once a year. **1709** STEELE *Tatler* No. 4 ¶4 The Opera of Pyrrhus and Demetrius was performed with great Applause. **1766** ENTICK *London* IV. 447 Several.. songs are performed. **1771** T. HULL *Sir W. Harrington* (1797) III. 102 All the time the ceremony was performing [= being performed]. **1804–6** SYD. SMITH *Mor. Philos.* (1850) 175 Any air.. performed upon such an instrument as the bagpipe. **1848** WHEWELL in Todhunter *Acc. His Writ.* (1876) II. 343 His brother.. had then just written a play which was performing at the Français. **1848** DICKENS *Dombey* iii, The funeral.. having been *performed* to the entire satisfaction of the undertaker. **1872** J. L. SANFORD *Estimates Eng. Kings, Chas. I* 334 The mass performed by the priest at the altar.

b. To act, play (a part or character).

1610 SHAKS. *Temp.* III. iii. 83 Brauely the figure of this Harpie, hast thou Perform'd (my Ariell). **1711** STEELE *Spect.* No. 141 ¶2 In Acting, barely to perform the Part is not commendable, but to be the least out is contemptible. **1802** tr. *Ducray-Duminil's Victor* III. 272 One of my people.. in the habit of an ecclesiastic performed the hypocrite to admiration. **1805** W. COOKE *Mem. S. Foote* I. 67 Foote himself performed the character of Buck at Drury-lane.

c. *absol.* or *intr.* To act in a play; to perform music, play or sing; to go through a performance.

1836 LANE *Mod. Egypt.* (1849) II. vii. 113 Players of low and ridiculous farces.. called *Mohhabbazee'n*.. frequently perform at the festivals prior to weddings and circumcisions. **1842** MACAULAY *Ess., Fredk. Gt.* (1887) 695 He.. performed skilfully on the flute. **1903** *Daily Chron.* 23 Nov. 5/1 Much better adapted.. to a soloist—whether performing on larynx, violin or piano.

†**d.** *trans.* To play upon, play (a musical instrument). *Obs. rare.*

1811 Busby *Dict. Mus.* (ed. 3) s.v. *Master of Song*, To teach the children of the chapel-royal to sing, and to perform the organ.

e. *intr.* To display extreme anger or bad temper; to swear loudly; to make a great fuss. *Austral. slang.*

1901 M. Franklin *My Brilliant Career* xix. 163 Bad-tempered is a tame name for it. You should have seen the dust he raised the other day with old Benson. He just did perform. **1911** L. Stone *Jonah* v. 45 Ow'l Chook perform, if 'e ain't at Ada's? **1959** Baker *Drum* (1960) ix. 68 We say that a man *performs* when he is indulging in a frenzy of anger or vituperation.

Hence **per'formed** *ppl. a.*

c **1440** *Promp. Parv.* 383/1 Parformyd.., *perfectus, completus.* *c* **1530** *Pol., Rel. & L. Poems* (1866) 31 A performyd towre & a baare cofyr make, ovyr late, the greate bilder wyse. **1538** Elyot *Dict., Actus*.., performed. *a* **1569** Kingesmyll *Man's Est.* ix. (1580) 51 The promise of the hoped and performed Saviour. [Cf. 6 b above.]

performability (pəˌfɔːməˈbɪlɪtɪ). [f. performable *a.* + -ility.] The capability of being performed.

1947 A. Einstein *Mus. Romantic Era* xv. 222 He [*sc.* Alkan] lost his sense of proportion, with regard to both the performability and the dimensions of his piano works. **1962** H. C. Weston *Sight, Light & Work* (ed. 2) vi. 185 Levels of illumination which are supposed to give equal visibility or 'performability' for widely differing visual tasks.

performable (pəˈfɔːməb(ə)l), *a.* [f. perform *v.* + -able.] Capable of being performed; that may be carried out, executed, effected, or done.

1548 Gest *Pr. Masse* in H. G. Dugdale *Life* (1840) App. i. 93 An issue no lesse perfourmable then resonable. **1650** Durye *Just Re-prop.* 28 Nothing is farther required of them then what they proclaime themselves to be a performable duty. **1701–2** Locke *On Miracles* Wks. 1804 III. 455 Operations performable only by Divine Power. **1903** *Hibbert Jrnl.* Mar. 599 A rite not performable without the bishop.

†**b.** (A thing) To be performed or done. *Obs.*

1577 Hellowes *Gueuara's Chron.* 35 Suche thinges as they should commaunde to be perfourmable. **1663** Boyle *Usef. Exp. Nat. Philos.* i. iii. 62 The remembering of it they hold to be an act of Religion, performable by all Man-kinde.

performance (pəˈfɔːməns). [f. perform *v.* + -ance: perh. formed in Anglo-Fr. (It occurs as French in a memorandum by Mary Stuart of 14 Feb. 1571–2, in Godef.)] The action of performing, or something performed.

1. The carrying out of a command, duty, purpose, promise, etc.; execution, discharge, fulfilment.

Often antithetical to *promise.*

1531 *Dial. on Laws Eng.* ii. vi, The sayde executours delyuer the goodes of theyr testatour in perfourmance of the sayde bequest. **1598** *Child-Marriages* 162 The maior of the said Citie.. shall Cause performans of this agrement to be had vpon either side. **1601** Shaks. *All's Well* ii. i. 205 Thy will by my performance shall be seru'd. **1611** Bible *Luke* i. 45 There shall be a performance of those things which were told her from the Lord. **1623** in *N. Shaks. Soc. Trans.* (1885) 503 Securitie.. for the performance of the said intier pencion of three shillinges. **1725** De Foe *Voy. round World* (1840) 154 Bail or security for the performance. **1785** Paley *Mor. Philos.* iii. i. v. 111 Promises are not binding, where the performance is unlawful. **1814** Cary *Dante's Inf.* xxiv. 75 To fair request Silent performance maketh best return.

2. a. The accomplishment, execution, carrying out, working out of anything ordered or undertaken; the doing of any action or work; working, action (personal or mechanical); *spec.* the capabilities of a machine or device, now esp. those of a motor vehicle or aircraft measured under test and expressed in a specification. Also used *attrib.* to designate a motor vehicle with very good performance.

1494 Fabyan *Chron.* iv. lxxv. 54 For the parfourmaunce of the rest or other dele of the same. **1578–9** in *Monthly Mag.* (1813) 1 Aug. 44 The boy offendinge, by his father or mother whipped, the constable seeinge the performance therof. **1669** Sturmy *Mariner's Mag.* i. ii. 33 In performance of the last Problem,.. the Lines A and C, must be set upon one and the same Line. **1766** A. Cumming *Clock & Watch Work* 161 Thus may the performance of watches be made.. to approximate that of clocks. **1825** J. Nicholson *Operat. Mechanic* 77 That there is a certain velocity.. which will procure to an overshot-wheel the greatest performance. **1832** *Mechanics' Mag.* 30 June 224/2 Extraordinary railway performances... On two occasions, a load amounting to 100 tons was drawn by one engine.. a distance of above 30 miles, in an hour and a half. **1840** *Min. Proc. Inst. Civil Engin.* 34 The paper is accompanied by.. tabular statements of their performances during the year 1839, showing the number of miles traversed by each engine, the weight conveyed, [etc.]. **1845** Stephen *Comm. Laws Eng.* (1874) II. 639 The performance of a *post mortem* examination. **1879** Harlan *Eyesight* iv. 46 In the performance of some experiment. **1883** W. H. Maw *Recent Pract. Marine Engin.* I. 216/1 On the first regular journey from Queensborough to Flushing, the Prinses Marie made the journey of 101½ knots in 372 minutes, giving a mean speed of 17·12 knots.. and the coal consumption.. being 1·92 lb. per indicated horse-power per hour, an excellent performance considering that the cylinders are not steam jacketted. **1907** *Proc. Incorporated Inst. Automobile Engineers* I. 235 A formula of this kind.. is most useful in comparing the performance of small engines with large. **1931** R. N. Liptrot in *Handbk. Aeronautics* (R. Aeronaut. Soc.) ii. 98 The top speeds and best rates of climb are now plotted against altitude, giving the required performance of the aircraft. **1952** W. W. Balding in *Bk. of Motor Car* 98/2 If one carefully studies the reports of technical performance.., one quickly recognises the importance attached to vehicle-acceleration. **1961** *Times* 7 Nov. 19/1 In Britain a thriving business has grown up in tuning and modifying the engines of existing models to give more performance. **1968** Miller & Sawers *Technical Devel. Mod. Aviation* vi. 173 The superior performance offered by the first bombers with swept-back wings won them the orders. **1969** *Daily Tel.* 1 Oct. 16/8 Performance: Acceleration: 0–60 mph 12·3 seconds; 50–70 mph in top gear 13 seconds. Speed in gears, 1st 30 mph, 2nd 48 mph, 3rd 75 mph... Fuel consumption: 26·3 mpg (overall); 30·6 mpg (touring). **1976** *Ibid.* 18 Feb. 10 (Advt.), Today we give you details of a high-performance FM tuner. **1976** *Daily Mail* (Hull) 30 Sept. 11/3 A performance car with a top speed in excess of 100 mph, it runs at over 30 mpg on two-star petrol. **1977** P. Harcourt *At High Risk* i. 90 If you're interested in performance cars, as I am, you're also mildly interested in the people who drive them.

b. Something performed or done; an action, act, deed, operation. Often in emphatic sense: A notable deed, achievement, exploit.

1599 Shaks. *Hen. V*, iii. *Chorus* 35 Still be kind, And eech out our performance with your mind. **1605** —— *Macb.* v. i. 13 Besides her walking, and other actuall performances, what.. haue you heard her say? **1693** *Humours Town* A v b, I cou'd never much value their Performances. **1744** Eliza Heywood *Female Spect.* No. 8 (1748) II. 62, I am not apt to be vain of my own performances. **1866** Geo. Eliot *F. Holt* xi, He.. had given especial attention to certain performances with a magnet.

c. A piece of work (literary or artistic); a work, a composition. Now *rare* or merged in b.

1665 Glanvill *Def. Van. Dogm.* 51 That great man, the excellence of whose philosophick genius and performances, the most improv'd spirits acknowledge. **1706** E. Ward *Wooden World Diss.* (1708) To Rdr. A iv b, As for the Performance itself, it is but an Essay. **1753** Hogarth *Anal. Beauty* xi. 89 In justice to so fine a performance [statue of Apollo].. we may subjoin an Observation or two on its perfections. **1818** Garrow *Hist. & Antiq. Croydon* 59 He published.. lives of.. Saints, and other performances. **1861** Craik *Hist. Eng. Lit.* II. 338 The celebrated performances of Robertson and Gibbon. **1875** Jowett *Plato* (ed. 2) I. 46 His performances in prose are bad enough.

d. *Psychol.* The observable or measurable behaviour of a person or animal in a particular, usu. experimental, situation.

1898 E. L. Thorndike in *Psychol. Rev. Monogr. Suppl.* II. iv. 39 The best interpretation of even the most extraordinary performances of animals has been that they were the result of accident and association or imitation. **1901** *Psychol. Rev. Monogr. Suppl.* III. vi. 2 All human performances, when objectified in units of space, time, etc., seem to follow certain laws of variability. **1912** *Psychol. Rev.* XIX. 73 (*title*) The influence of caffein on the speed and quality of performance in typewriting. **1938** R. S. Woodworth *Exper. Psychol.* vi. 138 Several varieties of performance preferential have been discovered. **1949** Stouffer & DeVinney in S. A. Stouffer et al. *Amer. Soldier* I. iii. 85 Morale is presumed to be an important element in performance. **1951** *Mind* LX. 2 The performance or non-performance of a certain act.. we shall call performance-values. **1959** E. Ginzberg et al. *Patterns of Performance* xiii. 272 We did not choose the concept of performance potential because of its predictive value. **1964** Cofer & Appley *Motivation* xi. 520 This distinction between learning and performance and the effects of drive on performance constitute the second problem.

e. *Linguistics.* (See quots.) Opp. *competence.*

1963 N. Chomsky in R. D. Luce et al. *Handbk. Math. Psychol.* II. 326 A generative grammar.. can be regarded as a partial theory of what the mature speaker of the language knows. It in no sense purports to be a description of his actual performance. **1964** —— in *Proc. 9th Internat. Congr. Linguists* 915 Clearly the description of linguistic competence provided by the grammar is not to be confused with an account of actual performance. **1964** *Harvard Educ. Rev.* XXXIV. 263 The distinction between competence and performance or language and speech is quite crucial for understanding at least three goals related to linguistic descriptions proper. **1966, 1969** [see competence 4 f]. **1971** B. L. Liles *Introd. Transformational Gram.* i. 8 Another way of stating this is to say that he is interested in the speaker's competence, or knowledge of the language, rather than in his performance, or actual use of it. **1976** *Word 1971* XXVII. 144 He simply recalls our linguistic habits, our performances, as Chomsky would say.

3. *spec.* **a.** The action of performing a ceremony, play, part in a play, piece of music, etc.; formal or set execution.

c **1611** Chapman *Iliad* xxiv. 707 While that work and all the funeral rites Were in performance. **1777** W. Dalrymple *Trav. Sp. & Port.* clxx, I saw.. a French play represented here with some degree of performance. **1891** Martineau in *Law Times* XC. 250/2 It was a piece of music arranged for a band, and could only be of value for the purposes of public performance.

attrib. **1894** *Daily News* 23 July 5/5 An action.. for infringement of copyright, or rather performance-right.

†**b.** A ceremony, rite, or public function performed. *Obs.*

1673 *True Worship God* 14 Enquiry.. concerning the performances in use amongst the Heathens in the worship of their gods. **1758** S. Hayward *Serm.* p. xiv, To think there is nothing in religion; by which means our public performances are despised.

c. The performing of a play, of music, of gymnastic or conjuring feats, or the like, as a definite act or series of acts done at an appointed place and time; a public exhibition or entertainment.

1709 Steele *Tatler* No. 4 ¶4 A great Part of the Performance was done in Italian. **1836–9** Dickens *Sk. Boz, Priv. Theatres*, The hour fixed for the commencement of the performances. **1875** Jowett *Plato* (ed. 2) IV. 25. **1897** *Westm. Gaz.* 12 July 5/1 According to his evidence a performance was not a performance unless paid for and money was taken at the doors.

d. A display of temperament, anger, or exaggerated behaviour; a fuss or 'scene'; a difficult or annoying action or procedure. *colloq.*

1936 G. B. Shaw *Six of Calais* 94 They tear a piece of linen from the back of his shirt, and bind his mouth with it. He barks to the last moment. John of Gaunt laughs ecstatically at this performance, and sets off some of the soldiers. *Ibid.* 100 *Peter* (growling in his face like a dog) Grrrr!!! *The King* (returning the growl chin to chin) Grrrr!!!!!! They repeat this performance, to the great scandal of the Queen, until it develops into a startling imitation of a dog fight. **1962** A. Nisbett *Technique Sound Studio* x. 176 Dialling is rather more of a performance than being on the receiving end of a phone call. **1964** J. Symons *End of Solomon Grundy* iii. iii. 180 For Christ's sake don't let's make a performance out of it. **1971** A. Price *Alamut Ambush* i. 16 He had to come here and tell you all about it and make a great performance of it.

†**4.** Trimming, or a set of (fur) trimmings. Cf. perform *v.* 2 b; performing *vbl. sb.* 2. *Obs.*

c **1525** *Skinner's Inv.* in *Codicil to Will of T. Burgh* (Somerset Ho.), Item a performaunce of fox poutes xvjd... Item a performaunce of conye wombys xijd.

5. *attrib.* and *Comb.*, as **performance art**, a form of visual art in which the activity of the artist forms a central feature, combining static elements with dramatic performance; so **performance artist**; **performance bond**, a bond issued by a bank or other financial concern, guaranteeing the fulfilment of a particular contract; **performance test**, (*a*) *Psychol.* (in sense 2 d), a non-verbal test of capability or intelligence based on the performance of certain manual tasks; (*b*) the measurement of weight gain, food conversion, and other heritable characteristics of farm animals, as a guide to selective breeding; also **performance testing**; so **performance-tested** *a.*, having had heritable qualities evaluated.

1971 *Rolling Stone* 24 June 37 *Performance art* is basically an extension of art into the theater, often involving more or less set programs at specified times and places... A.. work of performance art was staged by.. cars whose drivers all sounded their horns according to a pre-arranged score, and the noise was broadcast by a local radio station. **1976** *National Observer* (U.S.) 7 Feb. 20/2 Not quite the same as theater or dance, though it combines elements of both, performance art grew out of *avant-garde* movements, particularly in poetry and painting, that swept Europe early this century. **1978** *Times* 23 Nov. 18/1 Three fine arts graduates were discovered walking around East Anglia with a pole on their heads, supported by a council grant for a work of performance art. **1976** *Observer* 11 Apr. 2/3 Despite his outlandish name, P-Orridge.. is one of Britain's leading young 'performance' artists, a type of art in which the artist includes himself in his work. **1976** *Loughborough Monitor* 26 Nov. 7/4 Mr. Richards, who describes himself as a performance artist and lives in Nottingham, had applied for a grant for his Christmas show. **1979** *Listener* 22 Feb. 293/2 There were performances by three performance artists... Kevin Atherton stripped off all his clothes on the gallery steps. **1938** *Sun* (Baltimore) 3 June 4/3 It is.. a general practice that the solicitor writing the 'bid bonds' also writes the 'performance bond' of the same contractor if his bid is accepted. **1965** Perry & Ryder *Thomson's Dict. Banking* (ed. 11) 436/1 Perhaps the most common type of performance bond is that given on behalf of a customer who is entering upon a housing contract for a local authority. **1970** *Globe & Mail* (Toronto) 26 Sept. B1/7 A performance bond with the amount of $10-million issued by the Commercial Union Insurance Co. in favor of Prince Albert [Pulp] is in existence. **1977** *Offshore Engineer* Apr. 18/1 Venezuelan conditions included a 25% performance bond and no progress payments. **1917** Pintner & Paterson (*title*) A scale of performance tests. *Ibid.* p. v, The work grew directly out of the psychological examination of deaf children... This work was begun in 1914 with the standardization of a few performance tests. **1921** R. S. Woodworth *Psychol.* (1922) xii. 275 Language plays little part in a performance test. **1932** J. L. Lush in *Proc. Soc. Animal Production* xxiv. 52 The swine Record of Performance test is regarded as a progeny test of the sire and dam rather than as a performance test of the individual pigs which are fattened and slaughtered. **1954** *Jrnl. Animal Sci.* XIII. 215 Few sheep breeders have the necessary assistance, time and facilities to conduct a progeny and performance testing programme. **1959** *Ibid.* XVIII. 1464 Seven years' data.. were analyzed to determine the effectiveness of using final weight as a criterion in the selection of performance tested bulls. *Ibid.* 1465 Fifteen bulls and twenty-three heifers were placed on experiment to compare three systems of performance testing. **1970** Preston & Willis *Intensive Beef Production* iii. 132 Performance testing involves the measurement of traits in the live animal... The major advantage of performance testing is that it permits evaluation of the animal at a much earlier age than is possible with progeny testing. *Ibid.* 137 Bulls on performance test should not be given hormone treatment. *Ibid.*, The object of any system of performance testing must be to evaluate.. genetic differences between animals in terms of their phenotypic expression. **1971** *Farmer & Stockbreeder* 23 Feb. 13/3 Co-operative breeding schemes, designed to get the most impressive, performance-tested bulls widely used. **1972** *Encycl. Psychol.* II. 379/2 Performance tests are especially useful for subjects with some speech disability. **1977** *N.Z. Herald* 8 Jan. 2-8/7 (Advt.), Modern methods of management are being used to produce performance-tested rams and bulls for the department's other blocks throughout the province.

Hence †**per'formancer** *Obs.*, one who goes through a performance, a performer. So also

† **per'formancy** *Obs.*, performance; **per'formant** *nonce-wd.* (cf. *informant*), a performer.

1621 LADY M. WROTH *Urania* 363 Cleare force must bee found in the best performancers of them. **1608** *Merry Devil of Edmonton* in Hazl. *Dodsley* X. 263 No conjurations, nor such weighty spells As tie the soul to their performancy. **1809** COLERIDGE in *Sir H. Davy's Rem.* (1858) 110, I contemplate Dr. Stock as the performant.

† **perfor'mation.** *Obs.* [f. PERFORM *v.* or AF. *performer*: see -ATION. (It occurs in a Fr. letter of Mary Stuart, 14 Dec. 1584, in Godef.)] The action of performing; = PERFORMANCE (in its various early senses).

1504 in *Bury Wills* (Camden) 96 Item I wyll that all my londys and tenements . . shall remayn to the performacion of the prestes seruyce duryng the seid xx^ti yeerys. **1505** in *Mem. Hen. VII* (Rolls) 251 The Kynge hymselfe sitithe in cownsaile with hys lords abowte the performacion of the quynes wille. **1529** in Ellis *Orig. Lett.* Ser. II. II. 23 To be contynuall suter to your Highnes for the performacion of the saide ccccc markes. **1599** HAKLUYT *Voy.* I. 164 This Indenture made . . for the performation of ye things vnderwritten.

performative (pə'fɔːmətɪv), *a.* and *sb.* [f. PERFORM *v.* + -ATIVE, as in *imperative.*]

A. *adj.* Of or pertaining to performance; *spec.* designating or pertaining to an utterance that effects an action by being spoken or written or by means of which the speaker performs a particular act. **B.** *sb.* Such an utterance. Hence **per'formatively** *adv.*, **per'formativeness**.

1955 J. L. AUSTIN *How to do Things with Words* (1962) i. 6 What are we to call a sentence or an utterance of this type? I propose to call it a performative sentence or a performative utterance, or, for short, 'a performative'. **1955** A. J. AYER in B. I. Evans *Stud. in Communication* 27 There are very many uses of language, prescriptive, ritualistic, playful, or performative, which are not fact-stating. **1956** J. HOLLANDER in *Jrnl. Aesthetics* XV. 239 A *performative* system of scansion . . would present a series of rules governing a locutionary reading of a particular poem, before a real or implied audience. It would end up by *describing* not the poem itself, but the unstated canons of taste behind the rules. Performative systems of scansion, disguised as descriptive ones, have composed all but a few of the metrical studies of the past. **1960** *Proc. Aristotelian Soc.* LX. p. v, The most famous of his [*sc.* J. L. Austin's] discoveries in this field was of the element of performativeness that enters into many kinds of utterance ordinarily classified as statements. **1963** J. LYONS *Structural Semantics* ii. 33 The philosophers have accustomed us to the wide variety of uses which the verb *know* can have. . . Among them they distinguish what has been called a 'performative' use. **1964** R. H. ROBINS *Gen. Linguistics* 23 It is best to regard knowledge of the meaning or meanings of a word as a performative knowledge (like knowing how to ride a bicycle). **1970** *Language* XLVI. 35 It is probable that the notion of the declarative sentence can be defined in terms of performatives. *Ibid.* 100 *For* clauses . . provide important evidence for the performative analysis. **1973** *Archivum Linguisticum* IV. 82 Being an imperative construction, it would presumably require the postulation of an underlying performative. **1973** *Times Lit. Suppl.* 5 Oct. 1161/5 Illocutionary acts of *x*-ing could be made explicit . . by use of the 'performative' first-person present-indicative form 'I *x*'—e g, acts of asking by prefacing the question by the phrase 'I ask you: . .'. **1973** G. W. TURNER *Stylistics* vii. 208 A performative utterance has validity if the speaker's social position entitles him to make it; it is therefore often part of an occupational language. **1976** *Archivum Linguisticum* VII. 69 The same applies to the everyday use (as opposed to the analysis) of speech act labels, whether these are used performatively or not. **1976** P. DONOVAN *Relig. Lang.* vii. 80 Performative words are used, for instance, when we vote for a motion by saying 'Aye', bid in an auction by shouting 'Fifty pounds', or adjourn a meeting with the words 'The meeting is adjourned'. **1978** *Listener* 30 Mar. 396/3 When I say, 'I promise', or 'I bet' or 'I apologise' or 'Thanks' . . these he called 'performatives'.

performatory (pə'fɔːmətərɪ), *a.* and *sb.* [f. as prec.: see -ORY².] = prec. Hence **per'formatorily** *adv.*

1949 *Mind* LVIII. 359 To make a promise is to perform an *act* in which language is involved as an integral part. . . Mr. J. L. Austin distinguishes this as the 'performatory' use of language. I am indebted to him for this point. **1949** *Philosophy* XXIV. 90 There are . . performatory sentences like 'I name this ship Shamrock'. **1951** *Aristotelian Soc. Suppl. Vol.* XXV. 207 Group I [*sc.* the verbs 'advise', 'order', 'command', 'tell'] can be used performatorily, but Group II [*sc.* the verbs 'persuade', 'induce', 'cause', 'get'] cannot; thus I can say 'I advise you to make yourself scarce before he comes', but not 'I persuade you to make yourself scarce before he comes'. **1955** J. L. AUSTIN *How to do Things with Words* (1962) i. 6 Formerly I used 'performatory': but 'performative' is to be preferred. *Ibid.* ii. 12 A few simple utterances of the kind known as performatories or performatives. **1966** L. J. COHEN *Diversity of Meaning* (ed. 2) i. 1 Their arguments have often relied on such distinctions as those between customary and indirect meaning, logical words and object words, . . or performatory and non-performatory verb-uses. **1967** *Listener* 2 Feb. 162/1 The listener . . may have expected a more substantial work than was due to be played. . . If he perseveres with it, what sounded prefatory can come to sound performatory.

† **per'forment.** *Obs.* [For **performment*, f. PERFORM + -MENT.] Performance.

1527 in *Southwell Visit.* (1891) 130 For a performent of the same my wille. *Ibid.* 131 For a performent of my laste wille. **1624** MIDDLETON *Game at Chess* Induct. 62 Pawns argue but poor spirits and slight performents. *a* **1641** BP. MOUNTAGU *Acts & Mon.* iii. (1642) 202 [He] enableth all unto endowments and performents beyond nature.

performer (pə'fɔːmə(r)). [f. PERFORM + -ER¹.] One who (or that which) performs.

1. a. One who carries out or fulfils a promise, undertaking, etc.; one who executes or does an action or piece of work; an agent, doer, worker.

1588–9 *Reg. Privy Council Scot.* IV. 364 The partie observair and performair of the premissis. *a* **1592** GREENE *Jas. IV*, II. ii, A fit performer of our enterprise. **1604** SHAKS. *All's Well* III. vi. 65. **1655** FULLER *Hist. Camb.* (1840) 108 The 'undertakers' in our present age have happily lost their first name in a far better of 'performers'. **1866** J. G. MURPHY *Comm. Exod.* xxxiii. 19 The Keeper of covenant, the Performer of promise.

b. Said of a horse in reference to its style of performance in racing, etc.: cf. quots. s.v. PERFORM 6 c.

1884 *Illustr. Sport. & Dram. News* 16 Feb. 563/2 What a pity it is that such a good-looking horse . . should be such an uncertain performer!

2. a. One who performs a part in a play, a piece of music, athletic exercises, tricks, etc., as a public exhibition of art or skill; one who gives or takes part in a performance or public entertainment; an actor, player, singer, etc.

1711 STEELE *Spect.* No. 141 ¶2 In Theatrical Speaking, if the Performer is not exactly proper and graceful, he is utterly ridiculous. **1741** H. WALPOLE *Lett. to Mann* (1834) I. xvi. 58 We have got the famous Bettina to dance, but she is a most indifferent performer. **1776** BURNEY *Hist. Mus.* (1789) I. II. i. 280 Celebrated performers on the flute. **1836–9** DICKENS *Sk. Boz, Mrs. J. Porter*, None of the performers could walk in their tights, or move their arms in their jackets. **1845** E. HOLMES *Mozart* 5 An admirable performer on the violin.

b. One who 'performs' (see PERFORM *v.* 7 e); one who causes trouble or disturbance. *slang* (chiefly *Naut.*).

1937 PARTRIDGE *Dict. Slang* 619/1 *Performer*, . . one who is apt to make a great fuss or noise. **1946** *Seafarers' Log* 6 Dec. 10/5 You get a performer aboard a ship who makes it bad not only for himself but for the crew and the Union. **1958** E. S. LAND *Winning War with Ships* xiv. 193 In the early months of World War II unions were battling against a threat of the Navy taking over merchant marine personnel because of reported incidents of drunkenness, insubordination and trouble making by individuals whom the unions called 'performers'.

†**3.** That which brings about or produces something. *Obs.*

1616 ANTHONY (*title*) The Apologie or Defence of a verity . . called Avrvm Potabile . . especially auaileable for the . . comforting of the Heart and vitall Spirits the performers of health.

per'forming, *vbl. sb.* [f. PERFORM + -ING¹.] The action of the verb PERFORM, in various senses.

†**1.** Finishing, completion, full accomplishment.

1388 WYCLIF *Dan.* ix. 27 The desolacioun schal contynue til to the parformyng and ende. *c* **1440** *Promp. Parv.* 383/2 Parformynge, *complecio, perfectio.* **1563–7** BUCHANAN *Reform. St. Andros* Wks. (1892) 16 Thre ȝeris efter the performing of thys reformation.

†**2.** Finishing off, decoration, trimming. *Obs.*

1465 *Mann. & Househ. Exp. Eng.* (Roxb.) 491 Item, paid hym fore performynge of the valaunce, iij.*s.* iiij.*d.* **1467** *Ibid.* 411 Item, for di. a yerde of lynenge for performynge, vij.*d.* **1503** *Privy Purse Exp. Eliz. York* (1830) 89 For half a furre of shankes for the perfourmyng of the same gown vj.*s.* **1518** *Harl. MS.* 2284 lf. 14, v Mantelles of lyberdes wombes for performyng of a gowne of russet velute.

†**3.** Making, construction; composition. *Obs.*

1478 MARG. PASTON in *P. Lett.* III. 230 Chargyng yow that it be not solde to none other use than to the performyng of yowyr fadyrs toombe. **1489** CAXTON *Faytes of A.* III. i. 168 To thy helpe in the perfourmynge of this present boke.

4. a. Carrying out, execution, doing, performance.

c **1420** LYDG. *Assembly of Gods* 837 Foryeuenes of Trespas, . . Performyng of Penaunce. **1526** *Pilgr. Perf.* (W. de W. 1531) 63 b, From the performynge of his dutyes. **1575–85** ABP. SANDYS *Serm.* xxii, The performing of my office amongest you, I must confesse, hath ben much unlike. **1663** GERBIER *Counsel* cj, Men of parts endeavour the performing of their task.

b. *spec.* of a play, music, etc.: in quots. *attrib.*; **performing art**, an art (such as the dance, drama, etc.) involving public performance (chiefly *pl.*); **performing right**, the right of performing a piece of music, etc.; usu *pl.*

1889 *Daily News* 8 Feb. 2/2 If foreign authors really possess valuable performing rights, it is only just that they should be paid the moderate fees they demand. **1897** HIPKINS in *Daily News* 2 July 6/5 The London Philharmonic pitch is now A = 439 for 20 deg. Centigrade, . . practically agreeing with the performing pitch of Vienna and also of Paris. **1899** *Westm. Gaz.* 10 June 6/3 The performing rights of a lyric. **1929** J. B. PRIESTLEY *Good Companions* III. iii. 534 Performing rights, sheet music, gramophone records. . . There's bags of money in it. **1946** *N.Y. Times* 7 June 21/5 The High School of the Performing Arts will differ from other vocational or academic schools in several important details. **1961** V. KREPELA in *Webster* s.v. performing adj., Project an image of the U.S. through displays, films, publications, fine arts, and the performing arts. **1967** CHUJOY & MANCHESTER *Dance Encycl.* 719/2 The function of Performing Arts School is not to create artists, but rather to prepare competent craftsmen. **1968** *Listener* 8 Aug. 177/3 When I did my first film . . someone said: 'It may not be so much money they are paying you down, but you get an income from it for performing rights.' **1971** *Times* 22 Feb. (Canada Suppl.) p. vii/3 It is much more comfortable politically to subsidize the performing arts (where results can be seen and enjoyed by large numbers of voters) than to support the creative individuals. **1974** *Times* 9 Oct. 18/1 All that is best in our performing arts depends for its survival on money. **1976** *National Observer* (U.S.) 23 Oct. 15/2 You'll find some kind of alliance developing among performing-arts centers in cities like Washington, Denver, Los Angeles. **1977** *Rolling Stone* 7 Apr. 35/2 The performing-rights organization negotiates license fees with *commercial* users (nonprofit organizations, such as churches and schools, are exempt from paying for use of copyrighted material).

per'forming, *ppl. a.* [f. as prec. + -ING².]

1. That performs, carries out, executes, or does something; acting, doing.

1707 WATTS *Hymn 'Begin, my tongue'* ii, Sing the sweet promise of his grace, And the performing God. **1845** BROWNING *Soul's Trag.* II, But have there not been found, too, performing natures, not merely promising?

2. *spec.* Applied to animals trained to perform feats or tricks as a public exhibition; esp. designating a flea trained to perform tricks; also *fig.*

1854 DICKENS *Hard T.* I. iii. 14 Signor Jupe was that afternoon to 'elucidate the diverting accomplishments of his highly trained performing dog Merrylegs'. **1886** *Pall Mall G.* 3 June 4/1 Performing lions, performing dogs, and performing leopards are common enough in the show business. **1889** G. B. SHAW *London Music 1888–89* (1937) 205 The only artist who never gets accustomed to his part is the performing flea who fires a cannon. **1922** E. WALLACE *Flying Fifty-Five* vii. 45 Your last stable was a stable of performing fleas, for I swear you know nothing about horses. **1953** WODEHOUSE (*title*) Performing flea: a self-portrait in letters. **1966** M. WOODHOUSE *Tree Frog* xviii. 134 Driver came me a look as though I were a performing seal. **1973** 'E. PETERS' *City of Gold & Shadows* ii. 29 The secret of success with performing fleas . . is to synchronise your orders with their hops. **1978** D. BLOODWORTH *Crosstalk* xxi. 167 I'm a cop. I run a team of performing dogs—the best in the business.

perforne, -forny, -fornys, -fourne, etc.: see PERFORM, PERFURNISH.

† **per'fossion.** *Obs. rare.* [ad. late L. *perfossiōn-em*, n. of action from *perfodĕre* to dig through, f. PER- 1 + *fodĕre* to dig.] A digging or boring through; perforation.

1695 J. EDWARDS *Perfect. Script.* 249 The females underwent troublesome . . perfossions in the lappets of their ears.

† **per'fract,** *a. Obs. rare.* [ad. L. *perfract-us*, pa. pple. of *perfringĕre* to break through, f. PER- 1 + *frangĕre* to break.] (?) That has broken through or transgressed laws or rules.

1616 R. CARPENTER *Past. Charge* 42 The perfract and obstinate hath a portion, and that is reprehension.

† **perfre'tation.** *Obs.*^−0 [f. L. *perfretāre* to sail over, f. PER- 1 + *fretum* strait, channel.]

1656 BLOUNT *Glossogr.*, *Perfretation*, a passing over, or through the Sea.

† **'perficate,** *v. Obs.* [f. L. *perfricāt-*, later ppl. stem (beside *perfrict-*) of *perfricāre* to rub all over, f. PER- 2 + *fricāre* to rub.] *trans.* To rub thoroughly or all over.

1597 A. M. tr. *Guillemeau's Fr. Chirurg.* 32 b/1 We first of all perfricate and rubbe the place. **1599** —— tr. *Gabelhouer's Bk. Physicke* 15/1 That it may be perfricated to poulder. **1620** VENNER *Via Recta* (1650) 320 The belly and stomack must not be perfricated. **1755** JOHNSON s.v. *Rub*, To scour; to wipe; to perfricate.

perfrication (pɜːfrɪ'keɪʃən). [n. of action from prec. Cf. PERFRICTION¹.] Rubbing all over, thorough rubbing; vigorous friction, chafing.

1607 TOPSELL *Four-f. Beasts* (1658) 196 Rub them therewith every day, and they are cured by that perfrication. **1658** PHILLIPS, *Perfrication*, or *Perfriction*, a rubbing or chafing throughly. *c* **1817** HOGG *Tales & Sk.* II. 215 Severe perfrication was requisite. **1893** in *Syd. Soc. Lex.*

† **per'frict,** *a. Obs. rare*^−1. [ad. L. *perfrict-us*, pa. pple. of *perfricāre* to rub all over; in allusion to the phr. *perfricāre frontem* (*faciēm*, *ōs*) to rub the blushes from one's face, i.e. to cast off all shame.] Unblushing, 'brazen'.

1660 WATERHOUSE *Arms & Arm.* 153, I have not so perfrict a forehead to justifie London in all her demeanors.

† **perfriction**¹ (pə'frɪkʃən). *Obs. rare.* [f. L. *perfrictiōn-em*, n. of action (in ancient L.) from *perfricāre* (ppl. stem *perfricāt-* and *perfrict-*): see PERFRICATE.] = PERFRICATION.

1656 BLOUNT *Glossogr.*, *Perfriction* . ., a rubbing, or fretting hard or throughly. **1708** *Brit. Apollo* No. 94. 2/2 A Glass Tube . ., violently heated by Perfriction.

† **per'friction**². *Obs. rare.* [ad. L. *perfrīctiōn-em* a chilling through, n. of action f. *perfrīgēre* to be chilled through, f. PER- 2 + *frīgēre* to be cold.] A thorough chill, a violent cold.

1607 TOPSELL *Four-f. Beasts* (1658) 203 The body of the patient must be first washed or anointed with Acopus, so as all perfrictions by sweat may be avoided. **1656** BLOUNT *Glossogr.*, *Perfriction* . ., a great, through or quaking cold, a shivering for cold, which goeth before the fit.

† **per'frigerate,** *v. Obs.* [f. ppl. stem of L. *perfrīgerā-re*, f. PER- 2 + *frīgerāre* to make cool.] *trans.* To cool or chill through or thoroughly.

So † **perfrige'ration** [also in mod.F.], the action of cooling or condition of being cooled through.
1585 GREENE *Planetomachia* Wks. (Grosart) V. 104 The peculiar diseases to this starre are.. windinesse, imbecillitie of heate, perfrigerations, and such others. **1650** BULWER *Anthropomet.* x. 106 The heart-strings of these women must be very much perfrigerated, by reason of the inward defect of heat. *Ibid.*, The advenient perfrigeration of inspired aire. **1658** tr. *Porta's Nat. Magic* IV. xiv. 140 Perfrigerated Argil .. will keep corn thirty or forty years from corruption. **1661** LOVELL *Hist. Anim. & Min.* Introd., Their breathing is not acknowledged by diverse, who acknowledg only perfrigeration.

† **per'fumatory**, *a.* and *sb. Obs. rare.* [ad. F. *parfumatoire*, f. *parfumer* (cf. obs. It. *perfumare*, *-ato*): see -ORY.] **a.** *adj.* **b.** *sb.* (See quots. and cf. FUMATORY.)
1611 COTGR., *Parfumatoire*, perfumatorie, perfuming; vsed in, or for, perfumes. **1639** LEIGH *Crit. Sacra* (1642) 451 A perfumatory or incense Altar. **1755** JOHNSON, *Perfumatory* adj., that which perfumes.

perfume ('pɜːfjuːm, pə'fjuːm), *sb.* Also 6 **par-**. [a. F. *parfum* (1528 in Laborde *Gloss.*), = obs. It. *perfumo*, Sp. *perfumo*, sb. from obs. It. *perfumare*, Sp. *perfumar*, F. *perfumer*: see next.
Orig., like the vb., stressed *per'fume*: so in 18th c. dicts., and in Webster 1828; usually in 17–18th c., and frequently in 19th c. poets; but Shaks. has '*perfume* 7 times against 3, and Walker 1791 considered the stress fixed on *per-*; on the other hand Todd, 1818, held it was 'sometimes though rarely so stressed'; but during the 19th c. this became the predominating prose usage.]
1. a. *orig.* The odorous fumes or vapour given off by the burning of any substance, esp. by such as emit an agreeable odour, as incense. **b.** Hence, The volatile particles, scent, or odour emitted by any sweet-smelling substance; the fragrance diffused by liquid scent, exhaled by flowers, etc.
1533 ELYOT *Cast. Helthe* IV. ii. (1541) 74 b, I toke for a parfume the ryndes of olde rosemary and burned them. **1538** —— *Dict.*, *Suffitio*, & *suffitus*, a perfume or fumigacyon. **1555** EDEN *Decades* 43 *Animæ album*, whose perfume is of most excellent effect to heale the reumes. **1578** LYTE *Dodoens* I. xii. 20 The parfume of the dryed leaues layde vpon quicke coles.. helpeth suche as are troubled with the shortnesse of winde. *c* **1592** MARLOWE *Massacre Paris* I. iii, Methinks the gloves have a very strong perfume. *c* **1600** SHAKS. *Sonn.* civ, Three April perfumes in three hot Junes burn'd. *c* **1620** ROBINSON *Mary Magd.* 1044 Perfumes, exhaled from yʳ spicy beds. **1756–7** tr. *Keysler's Trav.* (1760) III. 383 St. Antony's remains is said continually to emit a most fragrant perfume, which is chiefly smelt at a crevice behind the altar. **1810** SCOTT *Lady of L.* I. xxxv, The wild rose, eglantine and broom, Wafted around their rich perfume. **1870** YEATS *Nat. Hist. Comm.* 208 The perfume of most flowers depends on the presence of a fragrant volatile or essential oil.
c. *fig.* Fragrance, savour; repute.
c **1586** C'TESS PEMBROKE *Ps.* L. viii, My dearest worship I In sweete perfume of offred praise doe place. **1622** BACON *Hen. VII* 140 Perkin, for a perfume before him as he went, caused to be published a proclamation. **1822** LAMB *Elia* Ser. II. *Detached Th.*, The sweetest names, and which carry a perfume in the mention, are Kit Marlowe, Drayton [etc.]. **1850** MRS. JAMESON *Leg. Monast. Ord.* (1863) 209 She.. shed over the whole district the perfume of her sanctity.
2. A substance, natural or prepared, which emits, or is capable of emitting an agreeable odour; a fluid containing the essence of flowers or other odorous substances; scent. Orig. applied to such as diffuse a sweet-smelling odour when burned.
1542 BOORDE *Dyetary* xl. (1870) 302 A lytell of some perfume to stande in the mydle of the chamber. **1555** EDEN *Decades* 250 They are these folowynge..: Cinamome,.. Spekenarde, Cassia, sweete perfumes. **1560** BIBLE (Genev.) *Exod.* xxx. 35 Thou shalt make of them perfume composed [1611 a perfume, a confection; *R.V.* incense, a perfume] after the arte of the apotecary. **1644** DIGBY *Nat. Bodies* viii. § 1. 53 Perfumes.. fill the ayre, that we can putt our nose in no part of the roome, where a perfume is burned, but we shall smell it. **1717** LADY M. W. MONTAGU *Let. to Mrs. Thistlethwayte* 1 Apr., Little arches to set pots of perfume, or baskets of flowers. **1841** LANE *Arab. Nts.* I. 69 Perfumes which are generally burnt in these performances. **1871** TYNDALL *Fragm. Sc.* (1879) I. ii. 57 Patchouli acts more feebly on radiant heat than any other perfume yet examined.
3. *attrib.* and *Comb.*, as ***perfume atomizer***, ***-burner***, ***farm***, ***-pot***, ***spray***; ***perfume-distilling***, ***-laden***, ***-sprayed*** adjs.
1897 *Sears, Roebuck Catal.* 329/1 A fine imitation cut glass perfume atomizer. **1942** E. PAUL *Narrow St.* xxviii. 254 He began to throw Jeanne's toilet articles at her, perfume atomizer, box of powder, lipstick, mirror. **1973** M. & G. GORDON *Informant* xxxvi. 142 Out spilled a wallet, lipstick, .. a perfume atomizer, nail file. **1837** H. AINSWORTH *Crichton* I. 298 By the faint light of the two perfume-distilling lamps. **1887** MOLONEY *Forestry W. Afr.* 345 *Acacia Farnesiana*,.. cultivated on the perfume farms of the South of France.. for the perfume obtained from the flowers and known as Cassie. **1874** LISLE CARR *Jud. Gwynne* I. vii. 228 Perfume-laden buds. **1836–48** B. D. WALSH *Aristoph.*, *Acharn.* IV. vi, Hold out your perfume-pot! **1898** *Illustr. London News* 22 Jan. 126 (Advt.), These concentrated perfume sprays give a delightful refreshing coolness. **1926–7** *Army & Navy Stores Catal.* 498/2 Perfume sprays. **1975** D. BEATY *Electric Train* 42 Daphne was sitting at the dressing-table, her perfume spray in her hand. **1922** JOYCE *Ulysses* 523 As they are now, so will you be, wigged, singed, perfumesprayed, ricepowdered, with smoothshaven armpits.

perfume (pə'fjuːm), *v.* Also 6 **par-**. [a. F. *parfume-r* (1418 in Caumont *Voy. en Jhérusalem* 139; *gands parfumez*, 1528 in Laborde *Gloss.*), = obs. It. *perfumare*, Sp. *perfumar*, f. PER- 1, 2 + *fumare* to smoke, lit. to perfuse with smoke.]
1. *trans.* To fill or impregnate with the smoke or vapour of some burning substance; † **a.** of some substance for disinfecting or the like: to fumigate.
1538 ELYOT *Dict.*, *Suffio*.., to perfume. **1560** DAUS tr. *Sleidane's Comm.* 209 b, They fayne that she dyed of the plage, and perfume the house with the graines of Iuniper. **1582** HESTER *Secr. Phiorav.* I. xvii. 18 Then parfume hym with Cinaber fiue or sixe mornynges. **1607** TOPSELL *Four-f. Beasts* (1658) 273 Take a wreath of Pease-straw or wet hay, and putting fire thereunto, hold it under the Horses nose, so as the smoke may ascend up into his head; then being thus perfumed [etc.]. **1722** *Lond. Gaz.* No. 6031/1 The Houses were disinfecting or perfuming.
b. of incense or other substance emitting an agreeable odour. (Now merged in 2.)
1546 BALE *Eng. Votaries* I. (1560) 92 b, They are.. Lighted, Processioned, Censed, Smoked, Perfumed and Worshypped. **1555** EDEN *Decades* 162 They perfume their temples with frankensence. *a* **1633** G. HERBERT *Country Parson* xiii, He takes order.. that the Church be.. strewed, and stuck with boughs, and perfumed with incense. **1658** A. FOX *Wurtz' Surg.* II. xviii. 126 Sometimes I perfumed these warm clothes with Frankincense.
† **c.** To cause to emit pungent or odorous vapour in burning; to use as a fumigating agent. *Obs. rare.*
1607 TOPSELL *Four-f. Beasts* (1658) 188 With the hoofs of a Goat they drive away Serpents, and also with the hairs by burning and perfuming them in the place where the Serpents lodge. *Ibid.* 200.
2. To impregnate with a sweet odour; to impart a sweet scent to. (Now the ordinary sense.)
1539 in *Lit. Rem. Edw. VI* (Roxb.) I. p. xxviii, Rayment .. brought of newe, to and for his Grace's bodye.. shalbe purely brusshed, made clene, ayred at the fyer, and perfumed throughly. **1596** SHAKS. *Tam. Shr.* I. ii. 152 Take your paper too, And let me haue them verie wel perfum'd; For she is sweeter then perfume it selfe. **1598** DRAYTON *Heroic. Ep.*, *Q. Margaret to Dk. Suffolk* 89 My Daisie-flower, which erst perfumde the ayre. **1718** LADY M. W. MONTAGU *Let. to C'tess of Mar* 10 Mar., She is perfumed and dressed in the most magnificent and becoming manner. **1856** G. WILSON *Gateways Knowl.* (1859) 67, I am not aware that it is held essential to the anointing coronation-oil that it be perfumed.
fig. **1573** TUSSER *Husb.* (1878) 8 With losses so perfumid was neuer none aliue. **1604** T. WRIGHT *Passions* V. 255 In all suiters presentes, a man of a bad scent may easily feele a smell of profit, which perfumeth those gifts. **1661** BOYLE *Style of Script.* (1675) 199 David and his princes.. perfum'd that vast offering.. with this acknowledgment to God.
† **3.** *intr.* To exhale like incense or perfume. *Obs.*
1546 LANGLEY *Pol. Verg. De Invent.* I. v. 12 Howe Iupiter and the other goddes.. repared thyther to feele the fragrant odours that perfumed from the sacrifices.
Hence **per'fuming** *ppl. a.*
1707 MORTIMER *Husb.* (1721) II. 176 Tarragon is one of the perfuming, or spicy Furnitures of our Sallets. **1719** LONDON & WISE *Compl. Gard.* 205 To contribute towards the giving a perfuming relish.

perfumed ('pɜːfjuːmd, pə'fjuːmd), *ppl. a.* [f. PERFUME *v.* or *sb.* + -ED. (Cf. F. *parfumé*, 1528.)]
1. Impregnated with sweet odour; scented.
1538 ELYOT, *Dict.*, *Suffitus*, perfumed. **1589** GREENE *Menaphon* (Arb.) 36 His Samela, whose breath was perfumed aire. **1597** SHAKS. *2 Hen. IV*, III. i. 12 In the perfum'd Chambers of the Great. *a* **1674** CLARENDON *Hist. Reb.* XIII. § 33 A present of Plate, Jewels, and perfum'd Leather. **1813** SIR H. DAVY *Agric. Chem.* (1814) 103 Perfumed distilled waters. **1876** T. HARDY *Ethelberta* (1890) 35 She has just been dancing with that perfumed piece of a man they call Mr. Ladywell.
2. Having a natural perfume; fragrant or sweet-smelling; scented.
c **1620** ROBINSON *Mary Magd.* 318 The Pinke, yᵉ Daffodill and Cheuisance, All in Perfumed sets, yʳ fragrant heads aduance. **1719** LONDON & WISE *Compl. Gard.* 73 The tail'd Pear.. by some esteem'd because it is much perfum'd. **1836** *Penny Cycl.* VI. 432/1 *C. Mahaleb*, the perfumed cherry.
† **3.** *fig.* 'Fragrant' to the mind. *Obs.*
1625 B. JONSON *Staple of N.* I. ii, Studied And perfumed flatteries. **1641** MILTON *Ch. Govt.* II. iii. (1851) 172 Perfumed bankets of Christian consolation. *a* **1661** FULLER *Worthies, Glostersh.* (1662) 362 Muriel.. left a perfumed Memory to all the Neighbourhood.

perfumeless ('pɜːfjuːm-, pə'fjuːmlɪs), *a.* [f. PERFUME *sb.* + -LESS.] Destitute of perfume or of perfumes.
1885 G. C. LORIMER in *Homilet. Rev.* (U.S.) Sept. 232 As perfumeless as the edelweiss. **1892** *Pall Mall G.* 14 July 1/3 Another perfumer with a quick eye for business, grasped the situation of perfumeless Paris in an instant.

perfumer[1] (pə'fjuːmə(r)). [f. PERFUME *v.* or *sb.* + -ER: perh. after F. *parfumeur* (1528 in Laborde *Gloss.* 431), f. *parfumer* to perfume.]
1. One employed to fumigate or perfume rooms.
1599 SHAKS. *Much Ado* I. iii. 60 Being entertain'd for a perfumer, as I was smoaking a musty roome [etc.].
2. One engaged in making or selling perfumes.
1573–80 BARET *Alv.* P 286 A perfumer or that maketh a perfume, *suffitor*. **1587** GOLDING *De Mornay* xvii. (1592) 273 He dealt with reason as perfumers doe with Oyles. **1660** F. BROOKE tr. *Le Blanc's Trav.* 22 Their kitchins may be taken for perfumers shops so sweet and odoriferous. **1724** *Lond. Gaz.* No. 6250/10 Perfumer of Gloves. **1828** T. HOOK *Punning* v, Perfumers men of *scents* must be.
Hence **per'fumeress**, a female perfumer.
1631 *Celestina* I. 15 Shee was a Laundresse, a Perfumeresse, a Former of Faces.

† **perfumer**[2]. *Obs.* Also 7 **-ier**. [ad. F. *parfumier* cabinet of perfumes, f. *parfum*, PERFUME *sb.*] A casket of perfumes; a vessel for perfuming.
1591 PERCIVALL *Spanish Dict.*, *Sahumador*, a perfuming pan, or a perfumer. **1601** HOLLAND *Pliny* VII. xxix, Hauing found among the spoils of Darius the king, his perfumier or casket of sweet ointments. **1681** *Lond. Gaz.* No. 1585/4 Stolen.., two Silver hilted Swords,.. a Silver Perfumer,.. a Drabdeberry Riding Coat.

perfumery (pə'fjuːmərɪ). [f. PERFUMER[1]: see -ERY. In mod.F. *parfumerie* (in Littré).]
a. The preparation of perfumes; the business of a perfumer. **b.** Preparations used in perfuming; perfumes as a class of substances. **c.** A perfumer's place of business.
1800 tr. *Lagrange's Chem.* II. 387 Fourcroy is of opinion that it might be employed in perfumery. **1844** DICKENS *Mart. Chuz.* v, Compromises between medicine and perfumery, in the shape of toothsome lozenges and virgin honey. **1860** EMERSON *Cond. Life, Consid.* Wks. (Bohn) II. 413 The service of a perfumery or a laundry. **1865** *Public Opinion* 7 Jan. 19 Perfume, as its name imports, was.. originally incense, the earliest use of perfumery having been to offer sweet odours to the gods. **1893** F. G. KENYON *Hyperides* Introd. 16 Midas was employed by Athenogenes as manager of a perfumery.
attrib. **1841** ELPHINSTONE *Hist. Ind.* II. IX. iii. 341 Every department, from the Mint and the Treasury down to the fruit, perfumery, and flower offices.

per'fuming, *vbl. sb.* [See -ING[1].] The action of the verb PERFUME. **a.** Burning of incense, etc.; fumigation; disinfecting. **b.** Scenting.
1548 ELYOT *Dict.*, *Suffitio*.., a perfumyng or fumigacion. **1560** DAUS tr. *Sleidane's Comm.* 342 Smoking and perfuming with sensours [*orig.* fumigationes atque suffitus thuribulis]. **1656** EARL MONM. tr. *Boccalini, Pol. Touchstone* (1674) 260 The perfuming of Gloves with Ambergreese. **1873** E. SPON *Workshop Receipts* Ser. I. 383/2 Perfuming [of soap] is generally done when the paste is in the frame.
c. *attrib.* and *Comb.*, as ***perfuming-pan***, ***-pot***, ***-room***, ***-vessel***.
1564–78 BULLEYN *Dial. agst. Pest.* (1888) 49 Forgette not sweete perfumes of Rose water, cloues, maces, vinegar in a perfuming pan. **1647** TRAPP *Comm. Acts* v. 41 The martyrs .. released for a season, seemed to come.. out of a perfuming-house rather than a prison-house. **1655** MOUFET & BENNET *Health's Improv.* (1746) 95 Boil it gently in a perfuming Pot with Spiknard and white Wine. **1772** *Ann. Reg.* 2/1 Over their graves are generally little open stone-buildings, which.. have a niche for a perfuming vessel.

† **perfumist.** *Obs.* [f. PERFUME *sb.* + -IST.] One who practises perfuming, or uses perfumes.
1603 *Mirr. Worldly Fame* in *Harl. Misc.* (Malh.) II. 529 Remember that perfumist, who being bedaubed with.. ointments,.. when he should have thanked Vespasian.. for an office received, was highly rebuked by him.

perfumy ('pɜːfjuːmɪ), *a.* [f. PERFUME *sb.* + -Y.] Having or emitting perfume; fragrant.
1853 MISS YONGE *Heir of Redclyffe* vii, They basked in the fresh breezy heat and perfumy hay. **1876** *Blackw. Mag.* Dec. 714 Rich.. perfumy wine.

† **per'function.** *Obs. rare*⁻⁰. [ad. L. *perfunctiōn-em*, n. of action from *perfung-ī*, *perfunct-* to fulfil, perform, go through, endure.] (See quot.)
1656 BLOUNT *Glossogr.*, *Perfunction*, a doing or enduring a thing to the end, an accomplishing or finishing a matter.

perfunctionary (pə'fʌŋkʃənərɪ), *a. rare.* [f. as prec. + -ARY, after FUNCTIONARY.] Perfunctory, formal; suggesting or having the air of an official or functionary.
1838 *New Monthly Mag.* LIV. 206 A female voice, in a soft but somewhat perfunctionary tone, demanded 'Est ce qu'on peut allumer le feu?' **1864** *Gd. Words* 227/2 With the air.. of a drill-sergeant, upright as a sign-post, grave and perfunctionary in guise.

perfunctorily (pə'fʌŋktərɪlɪ), *adv.* [f. PERFUNCTORY *a.* + -LY[2].] In a perfunctory manner; as a necessary duty to be got rid of; as a matter of mere form or routine.
1581 MULCASTER *Positions* xxxvii. (1887) 162 Not perfunctorilie taken knowledge of, but thoroughly examined. *c* **1616** S. WARD *Coal from Altar* (1627) 69 Why is it that some of vs pray.. in publique so briefly, so perfunctorily, and feebly? **1768–74** TUCKER *Lt. Nat.* (1834) II. 489 The office of a clergyman may be performed.. either perfunctorily, as a task necessary for entitling him to receive his tithes or his stipend,.. or carefully and conscientiously, as a trust reposed in him by God. **1885** *Law Times* 28 Feb. 311/2 Loose law carelessly and perfunctorily administered.

per'functoriness. [f. as prec. + -NESS.] The quality of being perfunctory.
1654 WHITLOCK *Zootomia* 454 The nimble Perfunctorinesse of some Commentators (that skip over hard Places). **1657** W. MORICE *Coena quasi Κοινή* Pref. 24 There will be less fear.. of negligence and perfunctoriness. **1882** *Athenæum* 11 Mar. 314 Nor can Justin Martyr's testimony to the gospel be compressed into a few sentences without perfunctoriness.

†**perfunc'torious**, *a. Obs.* [f. L. *perfunctōri-us* perfunctory + -OUS.] = PERFUNCTORY.

1609 *Hume's Admonitioun* in *Wodrow Soc. Misc.* (1844) 586 In executing your particular charges then, thair is a gryt negligence, a lothing, a perfunctorius doing. *a* **1653** BINNING *Serm.* (1845) 297 It must be a perfunctorious, superficial, and empty joy. **1819** MCCRIE *Melville* I. iii. 97 The perfunctorious performance of their official task.

†**perfunc'toriously**, *adv.* [f. prec. + -LY[2]; answ. to late L. *perfunctōrie.*] = PERFUNCTORILY.

1652 MARBURY *Comm. Habak.* i. 2 Prayers.. perfunctoriously vented in the church. **1724** *Wodrow Corr.* (1843) III. 155 As ignorantly and perfunctoriously gone about as any part of our worship. **1824** LANDOR *Imag. Conv.*, *Middleton & Magliabechi* Wks. 1853 I. 119/1 He was inclined to execute his duty too perfunctoriously.

per'functorize, *v. rare.* [f. PERFUNCTORY + -IZE.] *trans.* To perform in a perfunctory manner; to go through as a piece of routine.

1866 *Contemp. Rev.* II. 504 All heartiness.. must be absent from services where the stalls are empty, and only one canon and one minor canon perfunctorize the duties.

perfunctory (pəˈfʌŋktərɪ), *a.* [ad. late jurid. L. *perfunctōri-us* 'done in a careless or superficial manner, slight, careless, negligent', lit. 'characteristic of one whose aim is to get through or get rid of a matter', f. *perfunctor*, agent-n. from *perfungī* to perform, discharge, go through, get done with, get rid of: see -ORY.]

1. Of a thing: Done merely for the sake of getting through the duty; done as a piece of routine, or for form's sake only, and so without interest or zeal; formal, mechanical; superficial, trivial.

1581 [implied in PERFUNCTORILY]. **1593** G. HARVEY *Pierce's Super.* in *Archaica* (1815) II. 206 It is little of value ..that can be performed in such perfunctory pamphlets on either side. **1655** STANLEY *Hist. Philos.* III. (1701) 120 Alexander had not been great, if Xenophon had not said, even the perfunctory actions of valiant Persons ought to be recorded. **1690** BOYLE *Chr. Virtuoso* I. 16 Divine Artifice.. not to be discovered by the perfunctory looks of Oscitant or Unskilful Beholders. **1829** SOUTHEY *Sir T. More* II. 101 Attendance at divine service, at times when the service is merely perfunctory. **1885** J. PAYN *Talk of Town* I. 254 [He] just glanced at the two documents in a perfunctory manner.

b. Of a person: Acting merely by way of duty; official; formal; lacking personal interest or zeal.

1600 W. WATSON *Decacordon* (1602) 141 None but such as will be Iesuiticall wholly, and not perfunctory, may find any fauour there. **1644** MILTON *Areop.* (Arb.) 58 The presumptuous rashnesse of a perfunctory licencer. **1701** NORRIS *Ideal World* I. v. 323 How many perfunctory inquirers there are that carelessly interrogate this Divine oracle. **1870** LOWELL *Among my Bks.* Ser. I. (1873) 267 How little that perfunctory person dreamed of what was going on under his nose.

†**2.** Stated in formal terms, or with official formality. *Obs. rare*$^{-1}$.

1647 CLARENDON *Hist. Reb.* VI. §104 A formal, and perfunctory Message should be sent to his Majesty, whereby they thought a Treaty would be enter'd upon.

per'functurate, *v. rare.* [f. L. type **perfunctūra*, f. *perfungī* (see PERFUNCTORY) + -ATE 6.] *trans.* To perform or do in a perfunctory manner.

1860 in WORCESTER (cited from *North Brit. Rev.*).

†**per'furnish**, *v. Obs.* Chiefly *Sc.* and *north. dial.* Forms: α. 4–5 **perfornys, -yce**, 4–6 **perfurnis, -ys, -ysch, -isshe**, 5 **perfournys**, (*Caxton* **parfor-, -four-, -furny(s)she**), 6 **perfurneis(e, -eiss**, 9 *arch.* **perfurnish**. β. 5 **perfourmys**, 6 *Sc.* **perfurmis, -meis**. [f. F. *parfourniss-*, lengthened stem of *parfournir*, in OF. to achieve, complete, accomplish, furnish completely, furnish with what is wanting to completeness (in Britton, Gower, etc.), f. *par* through = PER- 2 + *fournir* to accomplish, complete, supply, FURNISH, q.v. *Perfurnish* is connected with *perform* by the intermediate ME. *parfourne*, *parfourny* (see PERFORM), and 16th c. *perfurmis*, *perfourmys*, here.]

1. *trans.* To perform, carry out, execute: = PERFORM 5, 6.

α. *c* **1375** BARBOUR *Bruce* XII. 61 This wes the first strak of the ficht, That wes perfornyst douchtely. **1442** *Aberdeen Regr.* (1844) I. 397 Thai sall fulfill and perfornyce his said werk efter the tenour of the endentour. *c* **1489** CAXTON *Blanchardyn* xliii. 169 To parfurnysshe her request. **1512** *Helyas* in Thoms *Prose Rom.* (1828) III. 63 Then Helyas perfurnisshed his purpose. *a* **1572** KNOX *Hist. Ref.* Wks. 1846 I. 445 To perfurneise hir wicked interprises.

β. **1592** *Lyndesay's Monarche* 4151 Quhen thay had done perfurmeis [*ed.* 1552 perfurneis] his intents.

b. *intr.* for *pass.* To admit of being carried out.

1393 *Test. Ebor.* (Surtees) I. 186 In kase be that this wytword will noght perfurnysche, I will it be abrydged; for I will hafe of na mans part bot of myne aune.

2. To furnish, supply (orig. what was wanted to complete): = PERFORM I b. †Also with *forth*.

α. **1533** BELLENDEN *Livy* III. ii. (S.T.S.) 247 To perfurnis þis batall,..the latynis..war commandit to gif þair maist reddy support. **1536** —— *Cron. Scot.* (1821) II. 469 Ane of thir clannis wantit ane man to perfurnis furth the nowmer. *a* **1557** *Diurn. Occurrents* (Bannatyne Cl.) 37 To perfurneiss ane thowsand horsmen for thrie monethis. *a* **1578** LINDESAY (Pitscottie) *Chron. Scot.* (S.T.S.) I. 288 Pulder and bullat sic as he might perfurneis at that tyme. **1819** W. TENNANT *Papistry Storm'd* (1827) 178 That near him did perfurnish'd stand Wi' a' his battle-gear.

β. **1420** *Searchers Verdicts* in *Surtees Misc.* (1888) 15 Thay sall hafe all the lede that ys thare nowe, and perfourmys the remenand of thayr costes.

3. To decorate, trim, 'furnish': = PERFORM 2 b.

1375–6 *Durham Acc. Rolls* (Surtees) 582 In perfurnisyng capucium domini Prioris..ex furura propria.

4. To finish, bring to completion: = PERFORM I.

α. *c* **1450** *St. Cuthbert* (Surtees) 7937 This thing to ende to perfournys. *c* **1489** CAXTON *Sonnes of Aymon* xii. 304 Goo a side & lete vs parfornysshe our batayll. **1490** —— *Eneydos* xvi. 62 To gyue hym commaundement..that he parfournyshe hys vyage.

β. **1553** *Douglas' Æneis* III. viii. 82 Fra that perfurmist [*MS.* perfurnist] was our offerand day.

perfusate (pəˈfjuːzeɪt). *Med.* [f. PERFUS(E *v.* + *-ate*, after *filtrate*, *precipitate*, etc.] Any fluid used for perfusion.

1915 *Amer. Jrnl. Physiol.* XXXVIII. 201 Winterstein perfused new-born rabbits with saline solution..and concluded that the hydrogen-ion concentration of the perfusate governed the function of the respiratory center. **1938** *Nature* 29 Oct. 800/2 The frog's liver perfused with a saline solution can secrete natural and artificial pigments in concentrations many hundred times those in the perfusate. **1961** *Jrnl. Clin. Invest.* XL. 1079/2 Solutions pumped into the oral end of the tube entered the intestine at a known site; 15 cm distally the perfusate was aspirated and collected from the anal end of the tube. **1968** *Sci. Jrnl.* Nov. 63/3 The use of balanced salt solution perfusates without red cells (solutions having a composition similar to extra-cellular fluid). *Ibid.* 64/2 Blood and a variety of other perfusates were studied.

perfuse (pəˈfjuːz), *v.* [f. L. *perfūs-*, ppl. stem of *perfundĕre*, f. PER- + *fundĕre* to pour out.]

1. *trans.* To overspread with any moisture; to besprinkle (*with* water, etc.); to bedew; to cover or suffuse with anything shed on (e.g. radiance, colour, grace, goodness).

1526 *Pilgr. Perf.* (W. de W. 1531) 182 b, In mouth and lyppes, all perfused with grace. **1625** JACKSON *Creed* V. xii, Each as it were to perfuse itself with its own goodness. **1686** GOAD *Celest. Bodies* I. ii. 3 Some Creatures..perfusing themselves with water. **1732** J. WHALEY *Poems* 175 The Cheek with red perfus'd, the down-cast Eye. **1862** THOREAU *Excursions, Wild Apples* (1863) 297 Red inside, perfused with a beautiful blush.

2. To pour (something) through; to diffuse through or over; to cause to flow through. Also *fig.*

1666 HARVEY *Morb. Angl.* xii. 144 These clouds, as they are raised out of the Sea..being perfused through the Air. **1857** *Truths Cath. Relig.* (ed. 4) 178 They have the devil infused, perfused, and transfused into them. **1904** *Brit. Med. Jrnl.* 17 Sept. 681 By perfusing Locke's fluid through the coronary system of the heart of cat or rabbit.

3. *Med.* To supply (an organ, tissue, or body) with a fluid artificially by circulating it through blood vessels or other natural channels; to pass a fluid through (a hollow organ).

1903 *Jrnl. Physiol.* XXIX. 266 The method of examining the physiological action of an organ or tissue by perfusing it by blood after its removal from the body has already proved of great value. **1920** *Amer. Jrnl. Physiol.* LII. 101 Using a mixture of red cells and whole serum or diluted serum or modified Locke's solution, the investigator should be able to perfuse satisfactorily the various organs or combinations of organs and tissues. **1962** *Lancet* 6 Jan. 13/2 Radiography will then reveal whether anastomoses exist, by showing the radio-opaque material in arteries which were not perfused. **1965** *Gut* VI. 387/2 After perfusing the intestine for 30 minutes a steady state is reached, and intraluminal contents are then aspirated through a hole. **1966** *Maclean's Mag.* 2 Apr. 18/3 The current belief is that before freezing the body should be perfused—that is, the blood should be replaced with a chemical that would prevent, or at least minimize, cellular damage during freezing. **1971** *Jrnl. Physiol.* CCXVI. 735 The lumen was perfused with a raffinose-electrolyte solution having a low sodium concentration.

Hence **per'fused** *ppl. a.*, (of an organ, etc.) kept supplied with a flow of fluid; (of a fluid) supplied as a substitute for blood; **per'fusing** *vbl. sb.*

1903 *Jrnl. Physiol.* XXIX. 271 Difficulties in the way of obtaining a sufficiently rapid rate of flow through the perfused organ. **1906** *Ibid.* XXXV. 54 The amount of oxygen in the perfused liquid and the rate of perfusion were as far as possible controlled. **1916** *Amer. Jrnl. Physiol.* XL. 516 With the perfusing fluid running..a cannula is passed into the popliteal below the nutrient artery. **1962** *Lancet* 6 Jan. 13/2 Another unreported source of error is the perfusing of hearts still affected by rigor mortis.

perfusion (pəˈfjuːʒən). [ad. L. *perfūsiōn-em*, n. of action f. *perfundĕre*: see prec.]

a. The action of pouring (a fluid) on or over; shedding on; diffusion through.

1574 NEWTON *Health Mag.* 9 There should ensue an oyntement or perfusion of temperate oyle. **1632** tr. *Bruel's Praxis Med.* 291 The perfusion of naturall heate..doth giue life to the wormes. **1666** HARVEY *Morb. Angl.* iv. 47 A perfusion of a just proportion of gall. **1700** SIR J. FLOYER *Cold Baths* I. ii. 41 A large Perfusion of Cold Water recollects the heat. **1775** SIR E. BARRY *Observ. Wines* 294 Leave to others the active parts of the perfusions, detersions, &c.

b. *spec.* The pouring over of water in baptism, as opposed to immersion.

1607 *Schol. Disc. agst. Antichr.* I. ii. 112 What, and serueth the signe of the water..for the time only of the perfusion? **1711** J. GALE *Refl. Wall's Hist. Inf. Bapt.* 134 This rite was wont to be performed by immersion, and not by perfusion. **1889** DRYSDALE *Hist. Presbyt. Eng.* 439 Perfusion (pouring or sprinkling) was not accounted unlawful.

c. *concr.* That which has been poured over. *rare.*

1848 *Ecclesiologist* VIII. 99 Wine for the ablution of the chalice of the mass, and also another chalice to receive the perfusion of the fingers.

d. *Med.* The process of passing through an organ or tissue a fluid, esp. treated blood or a substitute for blood; the treatment of a patient by a continuous transfusion of prepared blood. Freq. *attrib.*

1903 *Jrnl. Physiol.* XXIX. 266 Special arrangements were provided for quantitatively determining the changes of the blood gases in the perfusion. **1910** *Ibid.* XL. 297 Perfusion experiments with tortoise hearts were made by Gaskell in 1883, his perfusion liquid being a mixture of 1 part of sheep's blood and 2 of saline. **1940** C. S. SHERRINGTON *Man on his Nature* iii. 87 The perfusion-fluid itself is chemical nutriment for all the cells of the body, supporting their energy-needs. **1963** *Gastroenterology* XLIV. 134/2 Absorption was studied by transintestinal intubation with polyvinyl tubing..with a perfusion technique. **1969** *Jrnl. Physiol.* CCIV. 22P In order to show that it was the ionic composition of the perfusion fluid which produced the changes..rather than the experimental procedure, perfusion of both vasa deferentia with Krebs-Ringer preceded perfusion of one vas deferens with the test solution. **1972** *Brit. Med. Jrnl.* 1 Jan. 23/1 Two patients in deep hepatic coma due to fulminant viral hepatitis were treated by extracorporeal baboon liver perfusion. *Ibid.* 23/2 The liver was aseptically removed from healthy baboons..; it was immediately cooled by perfusion with a chilled electrolyte solution..and then taken to the perfusion apparatus in the patient's room. Perfusion was started after 30–40 minutes of cold ischaemia and was maintained for a period of 13–16 hours.

perfusionist (pəˈfjuːʒənɪst). *Med.* [f. prec. + -IST.] The member of a surgical team responsible for the perfusion of a patient while his circulation is interrupted.

1964 *Sunday Mail Mag.* (Brisbane) 25 Oct. 2/3 The doctor who assembles the machine is a perfusionist. He will operate the machine during the operation. **1975** *Islander* (Victoria, B.C.) 21 Sept. 3/4 Although there are five anaesthetists, Mr. Kemna is the only perfusionist and assists at every open heart operation.

perfusive (pəˈfjuːsɪv), *a.* [f. L. *perfūs-*, ppl. stem (see PERFUSE) + -IVE.] Having the character of being shed all over, or diffused all through.

1817 COLERIDGE *Biog. Lit.* 159 The perfusive and omnipresent grace which have preserved, as in a shrine of precious amber, the Sparrow of Catullus, the Swallow, the Grass-hopper, and all the other little loves of Anacreon. **1869** W. G. T. SHEDD *Homiletics* iii. 85 Unity that is thorough and perfusive, and moulds the multitudes of materials.

Pergamene (ˈpɜːgəmiːn), *sb.* and *a.* Also **Perga'menian** (6 **Pargamenian**, 9 **-onian**), **Perga'menic**. [f. L. *Pergamum*, Gr. *Πέργαμος*, *-ον* city and capital of an ancient kingdom in Asia Minor.] **A.** *sb.* An inhabitant of Pergamum. **B.** *adj.* Of or pertaining to Pergamum, the school of sculpture that flourished there in the third and second centuries B.C., or the Church founded there in the first century after Christ.

1579 NORTH tr. *Plutarch's Lives* 1056 He wrote vnto the Pargamenians in this sorte. [**1608** TOPSELL *Serpents* 122 Wee doe read that the Pergameni did buy..certaine peeces of a Cockatrice.] **1774** T. REID in Ld. Kames *Sk. Hist. Man* II. III. 168 He [*sc.* Aristotle] was the first we know, says Strabo, who composed a library. And in this the Egyptian and Pergamenian kings, copied his example. *a* **1823** R. CULBERTSON *Lect. Revelation* (1826) I. xvi. 214 Pergamos.. together with all that territory over which the Pergamonian princes bore rule, was bequeathed by Attalus..to the Romans. **1865** J. B. LIGHTFOOT *Galatians* 5 The Pergamene prince Attalus the first effectually curbed their power. **1867** C. M. YONGE *Pupils of St. John* vi. 87 The sharp piercing two-edged sword of the Word of God..was held up threateningly to warn the Pergamenes. **1896** *Pall Mall Gaz.* 19 May 3/2 A victorious king..is to be met by a troop of priests, and conducted to the Pergamenic altar. **1903** *Westm. Gaz.* 23 Sept. 3/2 Visitors..will be delighted to recognise the Pergamenian type of the so-called 'Dying Alexander'. **1904** W. M. RAMSAY in *Expositor* June 407 The honourable history and the steadfast loyalty of the Pergamenian Church ..had been tarnished by the error of a small part of the congregation. *Ibid.* 409 We shall find that both in the Thyatiran and in the Pergamenian letter St. John exalts the dignity, authority and power that shall fall to the lot of the victorious Christian. **1926** *Chambers's Jrnl.* 11 Sept. 649/1 It is this temple..which is referred to as 'Satan's throne' in St John's letter to the Pergamene Church. **1947** E. V. HANSEN *Attalids of Pergamon* vi. 157 Five envoys were sent by the Pergamenes to both cities to obtain..the evidence of the contending parties. *Ibid.* viii. 277 Another sculptor who had a long career at the court of the Attalids was a native Pergamene, Epigonus the son of Charius. **1960** R. CARPENTER *Greek Sculpture* vii. 191 The Pergamenian rulers conceived the ambition to bring that golden period to life. **1968** G. E. BEAN *Turkey's Southern Shore* vi. 81 The figure of Nike, goddess of victory, which appears on..coins of Side may commemorate a victory won by the city against the Pergamenes. **1972** P. M. FRASER *Ptolemaic Alexandria* I. iii. 98 A Pergamene inscription tells us that the supreme magistrates of the city..were appointed by the King at least on one occasion. **1972** 'M. INNES' *Open House* xiv. 138 This revolting masterpiece of the Pergamene school.

pergameneous (pɜːgəˈmiːniːəs), *a.* [f. L. *pergamēn-a* PARCHMENT + -EOUS.] Of the nature or texture of parchment; parchmenty.
1826 KIRBY & SP. *Entomol.* III. xxxv. 606 Something between coriaceous and membranous, which I shall express by the term *pergameneous*. *Ibid.* IV. xlvii. 371 *Tegmina* generally pergameneous, reticulated with nervures. **1866–8** OWEN *Anat. Vertebr.* (L.), This is closed by a pergameneous expansion. **1899** *Allbutt's Syst. Med.* VIII. 708 The consistence of the skin is..somewhat pergameneous.

†**pergamenous.** *Obs. rare*⁻⁰. = prec.
1656 BLOUNT *Glossogr.*, *Pergamenous*, of or belonging to, or full of Parchment or Velum.

pergamentaceous (pɜːgəmɛnˈteɪʃəs), *a.* [f. med.L. *pergament-um* PARCHMENT + -ACEOUS.] Parchmenty; = PERGAMENEOUS.
1847–9 TODD *Cycl. Anat.* IV. 20/1 Polypary pergamentaceous or corneous. **1875** HUXLEY in *Encycl. Brit.* I. 763/1 [They] are apt to become tough and almost pergamentaceous in spirit specimens.

pergana: see PERGUNNAH.

†**perge,** *v. Obs. rare*⁻¹. [ad. L. *perg-ĕre* to go on, proceed. Prob. founded on the use of the L. imper. *perge* (ˈpɜːdʒiː), 'go on, proceed', as in:
1588 SHAKS. *L.L.L.* IV. ii. 54 *Perge*, good M. Holofernes, *perge*.]
intr. To go on, proceed.
1607 WILKINS *Miseries Inforced Marr.* II, Thou art a good Frank, if thou pergest thus, thou art still a companion of gallants.

pergelisol (pɜːˈdʒɛlɪsɒl). *Geomorphol.* [f. PER-¹ + L. *gel-āre* to freeze + -I- + -SOL.] = PERMAFROST.
1946 K. BRYAN in *Amer. Jrnl. Sci.* CCXLIV. 635 It is impossible to make a verb or a verbal noun from 'permafrost' as 'permafrosting' and 'permafrosted' imply that a permanent surface or coating has been applied... Further, the term cannot be easily converted into other European languages. These various objections can be met by a new term... Such a word is 'pergelisol'. **1963** *Geomorphol. Abstr.* 38 Canada, in the opinion of Dr. Hamelin, can be divided into eleven periglacial 'provinces'. The first four provinces: Elizabeth, Victoria, Keewatin and Innuit are closely associated with continuous pergelisol. **1968** R. W. FAIRBRIDGE *Encycl. Geomorphol.* 1185/1 The south- to west-facing slopes thaw earlier and more deeply than the opposite ones, where the pergelisol remains near the surface. **1972** SPARKS & WEST *Ice Age in Brit.* iv. 99 With this wholly admirable intensification of study [of periglacial phenomena] has come a wholly regrettable spate of jargon, not all of which fortunately has found favour. Thus, most people still speak of frost shattering rather than congelifraction, active layer rather than mollisol, permafrost rather than pergelisol.

perget(te, pergit, obs. forms of PARGET.

‖**pergola** (ˈpɜːgələ). [a. It. *pergola* 'any arbor, boure or close walke of boughes, namely of vines' (Florio):—L. *pergula* projecting roof, shed, vine arbour; f. *pergĕre* to proceed, come forward.]
1. An arbour formed of growing plants trained over trellis-work; esp. a covered walk so formed.
1675 EVELYN *Terra* (1729) 39 Twixt East and North erect a *Pergola* or Shed, so contriv'd with a Cover, as to exclude or admit the Rain, snow and weather at pleasure. **1849** RUSKIN *Sev. Lamps* ii. 43 In the cupola of the Duomo at Parma..we might have taken the vines for a veritable pergola. **1866** SYMONDS *Sk. Italy & Greece* I. v. (1874) 95 Vines..climb the six stories, to blossom out into a pergola upon the roof. **1896** M. D. FAIRBAIRN in *Daily News* 15 Sept. 6/1 The pergola, or vine-clad arbour, is before the door.
†**2.** An elevated stand or balcony. *Obs. rare.* [Cf. It. *pergolo* covered balcony.]
1654 EVELYN *Diary* 20 July, Neere this [Wilton] is a pergola or stand, built to view the sports. **1656** FINETT *Ambassadors* 210 He was ordained his standing in the Pergola of the Banquetting House.

†**pergracil,** *a. Obs. rare*⁻⁰. [ad. L. *pergracilis* very slender.]
1623 COCKERAM, *Pergracill*, leane, slender.

†**perˈgraphical,** *a. Obs. rare*⁻⁰. [f. L. *pergraphic-us* very skilful, very artful (f. PER- 4 + *graphicus*) + -AL¹.] Hence †**perˈgraphically** *adv.*
1623 COCKERAM, *Pergraficall*, cunning. *Ibid.* II, Very Cunningly done, *Pergraffically*. **1656** BLOUNT *Glossogr.*, *Pergraphical*.., very cunningly made or done, artificial, workmanlike.

†**perˈgrateful,** *a. Obs. rare*⁻¹. [f. PER- 4 + GRATEFUL, after L. *pergrāt-us* very agreeable.] Very agreeable to the mind or senses.
1657 TOMLINSON *Renou's Disp.* 338 They mutuate a flavour pergratefull to the stomach.

‖**pergunnah, pergana** (pəˈgʌnə). Also 8 purgunnah, 9 pergunna. [a. Pers. and Urdu *parganah* district.] A division of territory in India, comprising a number of villages; a subdivision of a *zillah*.
1765 HOLWELL *Hist. Events* I. (1766) 217 The lands of the twenty-four Purgunnahs, ceded to the Company by the treaty of 1757. **1799** GRANT in R. Patton *Asiat. Monarchies* (1801) 208 *note*, The Moghul empire, in its greater divisions of soubahs, circars, pergunnahs, corresponding to our denominations of provinces, counties, hundreds, or parishes. **1844** H. H. WILSON *Brit. India* II. 536 The office of Kanungo in each Pergana, or district, was revived. **1895** MRS. B. M. CROKER *Village Tales* (1896) 117 The people of the pergunnah..do not know you.
attrib. **1844** H. H. WILSON *Brit. India* I. 464 Where the collections were regulated by pergunna or district rates.

†**perˈhap,** *adv. Obs. rare.* [A form parallel to PERHAPS, formed on the singular HAP, chance.] = PERHAPS; perchance.
1570 LEVINS *Manip.* 27/30 Perhappe, *forté, fortasse.* **1573** J. FOULER in *Sir T. More's Comf. agst. Trib.* To Rdr. *iv b, Though that perhap to other folke he seeme to liue in al worldly wealth and blisse. **1634** *Harington's Orl. Fur.* II. xxxviii, Perhap a man, or some infernall sprite.

†**perˈhappen,** *adv.* ? *dial. Obs.* [app. an alteration of *perhaps* or *perhap*, after *may-hap*, dial. *may-happen*, *mappen*; cf. the similar W.Midl. dial. *behappen*.] = PERHAPS.
1756 TOLDERVY *Hist. 2 Orphans* II. 26 If..you do these things here, perhappen you'll do the same at another place. *Ibid.* 56, I am not afraid to own my name, though perhappen you are. [So *passim*.]

perhaps (pəˈhæps), *adv.* (*sb.*) Also 5 per happous (?), 6 **perhapis, perhappes.** In vulgar or careless speech often shortened to P'RAPS, q.v. [f. PER *prep.* II. 1 + *happes*, *haps*, pl. of *happe*, HAP *sb.*, chance, accident: cf. *on*, *upon*, *in happ(es* (HAP 4 b); *perhap* and *perhappes* appeared later than *peradventure*, *percase*, and *perchance*, which *perhaps* has now in great measure superseded. This later origination explains the absence of a sense-development parallel to that of the other words.
Perhaps occurs only thrice in the Bible of 1611, all in the N.T., and all originally in the Rhemish version.]
1. A word qualifying a statement so as to express possibility with uncertainty: It may be, possibly; = PERCHANCE 3 (and with the same constructions).
(The examples *c* 1430 are uncertain. The reading of the MS. (Harl. 372 lf. 45, 51) may be *per happous*, but it may just as well be *per happons*, or, in the second instance, *per happans*. In this uncertainty the quots. are left here, as being the earliest traces of any form of the word.)
[*c* **1430** LYDG. *Min. Poems* (Percy Soc.) 34 She wol per happous (?) maken hir avowe. *Ibid.* 35 Per happous (?) one is loved that wol not fade.]
1528 ROY *Rede me* (Arb.) 98 Savynge wother whyles perhapis They gett a feawe broken scrapis. **1546** *Supplic. of Poore Commons* (E.E.T.S.) 85 Perhappes some one of vs hath hylded c. shepe. **1590** SHAKS. *Com. Err.* II. i. 4 Perhaps some Merchant hath inuited him. **1598** MERES *Palladis Tamia* 286 To thinke on this, may pleasure be prehaps another day. **1617** MORYSON *Itin.* I. 110 Perhaps I haue seene a more sumptuous monument, but a more beautifull did I neuer see. **1677** JOHNSON in *Ray's Corr.* (1848) 128 Perhaps I may give farther answer to this query. **1766** GOLDSM. *Vic. Wakef.* xix, Perhaps I shall never see him or happiness more. **1876** T. HARDY *Ethelberta* xxxiii, Mr. Julian says that perhaps he and his sister may also come for a few days before the season is over.
b. Qualifying a word or phrase, usually with ellipsis: cf. PERADVENTURE 3 b, PERCASE 3 b, PERCHANCE 3 d.
1534 MORE *Comf. agst. Trib.* III. xxiv. Uj, But as it maie be, perhappes ye: so it may be, perhappes naye. **1615** G. SANDYS *Trav.* 6 The Towne..stretcheth along..perhaps a mile in length. **1712** HEARNE *Collect.* (O.H.S.) III. 297 Perhaps abᵗ yᵉ time of Edw. I. or later. **1809** MALKIN *Gil Blas* XII. i. (Rtldg.) 423 A little too broad, perhaps. **1883** *Manch. Exam.* 29 Nov. 5/1 There are three, or perhaps four, courses open to us.
2. In a conditional clause: As may happen or be the case; as is possible; by any chance: = PERADVENTURE 2, PERCASE 2, PERCHANCE 2. Now *rare*, and chiefly in ***unless perhaps.***
1576 FLEMING *Panopl. Epist.* 405 Vnlesse (perhappes) you vse these or such lyke woords. **1582** N. T. (Rhem.) *Acts* viii. 22 Pray to God, if perhaps this cogitation of thy hart may be remitted thee. —— *2 Cor.* ii. 7 Lest perhaps [so **1611**; 1881 *R.V.* by any means] such an one be swallowed vp with ouer great sorow. **1600** J. PORY tr. *Leo's Africa* VI. 281 Not one drop of water is to be found, vnlesse perhaps some raine falleth. *Mod.* You may take this, unless, perhaps, you would prefer to wait for a better.
B. *sb.* **a.** A statement qualified by 'perhaps'; an expression of possibility combined with uncertainty, suspicion, or doubt; an avowedly doubtful statement. **b.** Something that may happen (or exist), or may not; a mere possibility.
1534 MORE *Comf. agst. Trib.* III. xxiv. Uj, All his forgeueness goeth, cosin, you se wel, but by perhappes. **1641** J. SHUTE *Sarah & Hagar* (1649) 38 Often have we known those that have cast themselves upon this perhaps, to have been taken away suddenly. *a* **1680** CHARNOCK *Delight in Prayer* Wks. (1849) 241 Little comfort can be sucked from a perhaps. **1790** COWPER *Let. to S. Rose* 3 Jan., I always feel in my heart a perhaps importing that we have possibly met for the last time. **1843** CARLYLE *Past & Pr.* III. i, We quietly believe this Universe to be intrinsically a great, unintelligible Perhaps. **1866** RUSKIN *Eth. Dust* iv. 60 We can make ourselves uncomfortable to any extent with perhapses.
Hence **perˈhaps** *v.*, (*a*) *intr.* To use the word 'perhaps'; to make expressly doubtful or conjectural statements; (*b*) *trans.* to qualify with 'perhaps' as an expression of uncertainty.
1789 J. WHITE *Earl Strongbow* II. 95 He, probably, would have continued perhapsing against Ireland. **1792** *Elvina* I. 77, I perhaps'd every thing.

perhapser (pəˈhæpsə(r)). *slang.* [f. PERHAPS *adv.* (*sb.*) + ER¹.] A risky stroke in cricket.
1954 J. FINGLETON *Ashes crown Year* xxiii. 247 Morris somewhat luckily got Bedser fine for 4... It was what cricketers know as a 'perhapser'. **1957** D. STIVENS *Scholarly Mouse* (1958) 86 Did you ever see such a p'rapser—he pushed a yorker away for four!

†**perˈhendinancer.** *Obs. rare.* [For **perendinanc-er*, f. med.L. *perendinare* (erron. *perhend-*) to stay, sojourn, lit. to defer till the day after to-morrow: see PERENDINATE.] A sojourner, a lodger.
1489 *Injunct. Prioress Appleton* in Dugdale *Monast. Angl.* (1825) V. 654/2 Item that yee take noe perhendinauncers or sojorners into your place from hensforward, but if they be children or ellis old persons. **1736** F. DRAKE *Eboracum* I. ix. 385.

perhenuall, obs. corrupt form of PERENNAL.
[Cf. med.L. *perhennis* for *perennis*.]

perhexiline (pəˈhɛksɪliːn). *Pharm.* [Arbitrary blend of PI)PERIDINE and HEXYL.] A white crystalline solid which is a vasodilator, tablets of the maleate of which are given for the relief of angina pectoris; 2-(2,2-dicyclohexylethyl)-piperidine, $C_{19}H_{35}N$.
1969 *Current Therapeutic Res.* XI. 99 A clinical study was undertaken to explore the effectiveness of perhexiline in relief of angina pectoris. **1970** *Chest* LVIII. 579/2 There was slowing of the heart rate as a result of the infusion of perhexiline. **1977** *Lancet* 30 July 260/1 The Committee on Safety of Medicines has circulated an adverse-reactions warning about perhexiline maleate ('Pexid'). *Ibid.* 12 Nov. 1028/1 During treatment with perhexiline maleate hypoglycæmia, hyperlipidæmia, and liver dysfunction have been reported.

†**perˈhibit,** *v. Obs. rare.* [f. L. *perhibit-*, ppl. stem of *perhibēre* to hold out, ascribe, etc., f. PER- 2 + *habēre* to have, hold.] *trans.* To hold (to be), to repute.
1657 TOMLINSON *Renou's Disp.* 567 Galen is perhibited its Author..because he celebrated it.

†**perˈhiemate,** *v. Obs. rare*⁻⁰. [f. ppl. stem of L. *per-hiemāre*, f. *per* through + *hiems* winter.] *intr.* To spend or pass the winter.
1623 COCKERAM, *Perhiemate*, to winter at a place.

perhorresce (pɜːhɒˈrɛs), *v.* [f. PER- 2 + L. *horrēscĕre* to begin to shake, to shudder, etc.] *trans.* To shudder at.
1895 W. WALLACE in *Fortn. Rev.* Apr. 544 The subjective idealism Mr. B. perhorresces.

peri (ˈpɪərɪ). [mod. ad. (cf. Fr. *péri*) Pers. *pārī* or *pĕrī*, in Pehlevi *parīk* evil genius, malevolent elf or sprite, Avestan (Zend) *pairikā* one of several beautiful but malevolent female demons employed by Ahriman to bring comets and eclipses, prevent rain, cause failure of crops and dearth, etc.; in mod. Persian, poetically represented as a beautiful or graceful being (cf. *fairy* in Eng.); hence such combinations as *parī-rū* 'fairy-faced', *parī-paykar* 'fairy-formed', etc. (But the word has no etymological connexion with *fairy*.)]
In Persian Mythology, one of a race of superhuman beings, originally represented as of evil or malevolent character, but subsequently as good genii, fairies, or angels, endowed with grace and beauty. Hence *transf.* 'a fair one'.
1777–80 RICHARDSON *Persian Dict.* Diss. p. xxxv, Those beings, who inhabited the globe immediately before the creation of man, they call *Peris* and *Dives*... The Peris are described as beautiful and benevolent; and though guilty of errors which had offended Omnipotence, they are supposed, in consequence of their penitence, still to enjoy distinguished marks of divine favour. *Ibid.* xxxvi, The Peris and Dives are supposed to be formed of the element of fire. ..Perfume is the only food of the Peris. **1786** tr. *Beckford's Vathek* (1868) 64 Are the Peries come down from their spheres? **1813** BYRON *Bride Abydos* I. v, My Peri! Ever welcome here! **1817** MOORE *Lalla R.*, *Paradise & Peri*, One morn a Peri at the gate Of Eden stood disconsolate. **1889** C. C. R. *Up for Season* 240 Peers, peasants, peris of opera and play, Lords, ladies, and louts.

peri, obs. form of PERAI, South American fish.

peri-, *prefix*, repr. Gr. περί prep. and adv., 'round, around, round about, about', combined in these senses with verbs and their derivatives, substantives and adjectives; (*a*) in adverbial construction, as περιβλέπειν to look around, περιστρέφειν to turn round, περίοδος a going round, περίπατος walking about, περίχρυσος gilded all over; from the sense 'all over', it was an easy extension to those of 'altogether, quite, very, exceedingly, beyond measure', as in περικαλλής right beautiful, very beautiful, and that of 'going beyond' or 'exceeding', as in περιτοξεύειν to overshoot. (*b*) In prepositional construction, forming parasynthetic adjs. and derived sbs., e.g. περικάρδιος 'situated περὶ καρδίᾳ, around or about the heart', thence τὸ περικάρδιον 'the membrane surrounding the heart, the pericardium'.

A small number of technical Greek words in περι- were adopted in ancient Latin; more were added in late and mediæval Latin; most of these are represented in the modern Romanic langs., and in English (see PERICARDIUM, PERICARP, PERIOD, PERIPATETIC, PERIPHERY, PERIPHRASE, PERIPLUS, PERISTYLE, PERITONEUM); and, on the model of these, adaptations of ancient Greek compounds in περι-, and new compounds from Greek elements (frequently also from Latin elements), have been introduced in great numbers in modern scientific Latin (esp. in biological nomenclature), and in the scientific terminology of the modern languages generally, in which *peri-* has been found to be a convenient prefix for denominating the structure or region lying round a defined organ or part. Most of these terms are (with the appropriate modification of form) of international currency, and it is often difficult to ascertain in which of several languages a particular term was first used.

The more important *peri-* words (including those of historical standing, and those in more or less general use) will be found in their alphabetical places; others of less importance or more exclusively technical use follow here.

1. In numerous scientific terms, chiefly anatomical and pathological.

In these *peri-* has a prepositional relation to the sb. implied in the succeeding element (see (*b*) above).

a. In adjs. = situated or occurring about or around, surrounding or enclosing (the part, organ, etc. denoted by the second element); sometimes also = pertaining to the part, or thing, denoted by a corresponding sb. (see b): as **,periadven'titial**, situated outside the *adventitia* or outer coat of a blood-vessel; **periam'pullary**, around an *ampulla* or dilated mouth of a duct (in quot., that of the bile-duct); **peri'anal**, around or about the anus (*Syd. Soc. Lex.*); **peri'apical**, situated or occurring around the apex of the root of a tooth; **,periaque'ductal**, situated around the aqueduct of the mid-brain; **periar'terial**, around an artery or arteries; **periar'ticular** [L. *articulus* joint], around a joint; **peri'axial**, around an axis; *spec.* around the axis-cylinder of a nerve; **peri'branchial** (-kɪəl), around the branchiæ or gills; **peri'bronchial** (-kɪəl), around the bronchial tubes; **peri'bursal**, around a *bursa mucosa* in a joint; **pericæcal** (-'si:kəl), around the cæcum; **perica'pillary**, around a capillary blood vessel; **peri'cellular**, around a cell or cells; **perice'mental**, of or pertaining to the pericementum; **perice'phalic** [Gr. κεφαλή head], round the head, as the external carotid artery; **peri'cerebral**, around the brain, or the cerebral hemispheres; **perichordal** (-'kɔ:dəl), around the notochord or spinal cord; **pericho'roidal** (-kɒr-), around the choroid coat of the eye; **peri'colic**, situated or occurring around the colon; **peri'corneal**, around the cornea of the eye (*Syd. Soc. Lex.*); **peri'cortical**, around the cortex (see CORTEX 3); **pericystic** (-'sɪstɪk) [Gr. κύστις bladder], around the bladder, or a cyst; **peri'dental** [L. *dens* tooth] = *periodontal*; **peri'dural**, around the *dura mater*; **peri'endymal**, **perie'pendymal**, around the *ependyma* or lining membrane of the cerebral ventricles and spinal canal; **perifa'scicular** [L. *fasciculus* bundle], around a bundle, e.g. of nerve-fibres; **peri'fibral**, **peri'fibrous**, around a fibre, as the *perifibrum* of a sponge (see b); **perifo'llicular**, around a follicle; **perigangli'onic**, around a ganglion; **peri'gastric** [Gr. γαστήρ belly, stomach], around the stomach or alimentary canal; **peri'genital**, situated in the area around the genitals; **peri'glandular**, around a gland; **peri'glottic** [Gr. γλῶττα tongue], around the base of the epiglottis; **perignathic** (-'gnæθɪk) [Gr. γνάθος jaw], around the jaws; **perigo'nadial**, situated around a gonad; **peri'hæmal** *Zool.* [ad. G. *perihämal* (H. Ludwig 1877, in *Zeitschr. f. Wissensch. Zool.* XXX. 123)], used to designate certain vessels and cavities in echinoderms and other invertebrates (see quots.); **perihe'patic** [Gr. ἧπαρ liver], around the liver; **peri-in'testinal**, around the intestines; **perilaryngeal** (-'rɪndʒɪəl), around the larynx; **perilen'ticular**, (the space) surrounding the crystalline lens of the eye; **peri'lobular**, around the lobes or lobules (of the liver or lungs); **perilym'phangial** [L. *lympha* lymph + Gr. ἀγγεῖον vessel], around a lymphatic vessel; **perimetrial** (-'mi:trɪəl) [Gr. μήτρα uterus], around the uterus (= PERIMETRIC *a.*[2]); **peri'nephral**, **peri'nephric** [Gr. νεφρός kidney], around the kidney (so **peri'nephrial**, pertaining to the *perinephrium*: see b); **peri'nuclear**, around the nucleus; **peri'ocular** [L. *oculus* eye] = *periophthalmic*; **perio'dontal** [Gr. ὀδούς tooth], around a tooth, pertaining to the *periodontum* (see b); hence **perio'dontally** *adv.*; **peri-œsophageal** (-i:səʊ'fædʒi:əl), around the œsophagus; **perioophoric** (-əʊəʊ'fɒrɪk) [Gr. ᾠοφόρον ovary], around the ovary; **peri-oph'thalmic** [Gr. ὀφθαλμός eye], around the eye; **peri'optic** [see OPTIC] = *periorbital*; **peri'oral** [L. *ōs*, *ōr-* mouth], around the mouth; **peri'orbital**, around the orbit of the eye; **peripancre'atic**, around the pancreas; **peripa'pillary**, around the optic papilla; **peri'penial**, (muscular fibres) surrounding the penis; **peri'petalous**, around the petals of a plant, or the petaloid ambulacra of an echinoid; **peripharyngeal** (-fə'rɪndʒɪəl), around the pharynx; **peri'portal**, around the portal vein (*Syd. Soc. Lex.*); **peripro'static**, around the prostate gland; **peripy'loric**, around the pylorus; **peri'rectal**, situated around the rectum; **peri'renal** [L. *rēn* kidney] = *perinephric*; **peri'rhinal** [Gr. ῥίς, ῥιν- nose], around the nose (*Syd. Soc. Lex.*); **peri'splenic**, around the spleen; **perisy'novial**, around the synovial membrane; **peritho'racic**, around the thorax; **peri'tonsillar**, around a tonsil or the tonsils; **peritracheal** (-'treɪkɪəl), around the trachea of an insect; **peri'ungual** [L. *unguis* nail], around the nail; **,periure'teric**, around one or both ureters; **periu'rethral**, around the urethra; **peri'uterine**, around the uterus; **peri'vascular** [L. *vasculum* vessel], around a vessel or vessels (usu. blood-vessels); **peri'venous** [L. *vēna* vein], around a vein; **periven'tricular**, around a ventricle; **peri'vesical** [L. *vēsīca* bladder], around the bladder; **peri'visceral**, around the viscera; **perivi'telline**, around the vitellus or yolk of an ovum. (See quotations after c.)

b. In sbs. (mostly in Latin form) denoting a part, organ, etc., surrounding or enclosing that denoted by the second element: as PERIANTH, -ANTHIUM, PERICARDIUM, etc.

‖**perice'mentum**, the substance surrounding the cement of a tooth; **'perichord** [see CHORD], the sheath or investment of the notochord; ‖**peri'denteum** [f. L. *dens, dent-* tooth, after PERICARDIUM] (see quot.); ‖**peri'desmium** [Gr. δεσμός band], 'the areolar tissue ensheathing a ligament' (*Syd. Soc. Lex.*); ‖**peri'didymis** [after *epididymis*], the *tunica albuginea* enveloping the testicle (*Syd. Soc. Lex.*); ‖**peri'fibrum**, a sheath surrounding a fibre and other parts in a sponge; ‖**peri'gamium** [Gr. γάμος marriage] *Bot.*, an involucre enclosing both male and female reproductive organs in mosses; ‖**peri'glottis** [a. Gr. περιγλωττίς a covering of the tongue], the epithelium or skin of the tongue; also, the epiglottidean gland; ‖**peri'nephrium** [Gr. νεφρός kidney], the connective tissue which envelops the kidney; ‖**perio'dontium**, † **-o'dontum** [Gr. ὀδούς tooth], orig., the periodontal membrane, which invests the fang of a tooth; in mod. use, all the tissues surrounding a tooth, including the alveolar process, the cementum, and the gingiva, as well as the periodontal membrane; ‖**perioph'thalmium** [Gr. ὀφθαλμός eye], the nictitating membrane of a bird's eye; ‖**peripho'ranthium** *Bot.* = PERICLINIUM; ‖**peri'stethium** [Gr. στῆθος breast], Kirby's name for a part of the thorax of an insect, now usually called *mesosternum*; ‖**periten'dineum**, the connective tissue forming the sheath of a tendon (*Syd. Soc. Lex.*); ‖**peri'thelium** [after *epithelium*], a layer of cells like epithelium, lining a vessel or cavity; vascular epithelium; ‖**peri'zonium** [Gr. ζωνή belt] *Bot.*, a name for the thin non-siliceous membrane of a young auxospore in diatoms. (See quotations after c.)

c. *Path.* In sbs. in -ITIS (-'aɪtɪs), denoting inflammation occurring in the parts around or about that denoted by the second element, or in the part denoted by a corresponding sb. (see b); with corresponding adjs. in *-itic* (-'ɪtɪk); as PERICARDITIS, PERINEURITIS, PERITYPHLITIS, etc., q.v., and many others, of which the following are examples.

periade'nitis [Gr. ἀδήν gland], inflammation of the connective tissue around a gland; **periarte'ritis** [coined in Ger. as *periarteritis nodosa* (Kussmaul & Maier 1866, in *Deutsch. Arch. f. klin. Med.* I. 484)], of the outer coat of an artery; = *polyarteritis* s.v. POLY- 1; *periarteritis nodosa* (nəʊ'dəʊzə) [L. *nōdōsus* knotty, f. *nōdus* a knot], an often fatal form of periarteritis characterized by the formation of aneurysms; hence **periarte'ritic** *a.*; **periar'thritis** [Gr. ἄρθρον joint], of the tissues round a joint (*Syd. Soc. Lex.*); **peribron'chitis**, of the peribronchial connective tissue; **,pericemen'titis**, inflammation of the pericementum of a tooth; **peri'cholecy'stitis** [CHOLECYST], of the peritoneum immediately covering the gall-bladder (*Syd. Soc. Lex.*); **perico'litis (-colo'nitis)**, of the connective tissue round the colon; **pericol'pitis** [Gr. κόλπος bosom, taken as = vagina], of the connective tissue round the vagina (*Syd. Soc. Lex.*); **pericowpe'ritis**, of the connective tissue around Cowper's glands; **pericy'stitis** [Gr. κύστις bladder], of the connective tissue around the urinary bladder; **,pericystoma'titis**, 'of the surrounding coat or membrane of an ovarian cystoma' (Billings 1890); **perides'mitis**, of the *peridesmium* (see b); **perididy'mitis**, of the *perididymis* (see b); **,periencepha'litis** [ENCEPHALON], of the membranes surrounding the brain, esp. the pia mater; **periente'ritis** [Gr. ἔντερον intestine], 'of the subperitoneal connective tissue surrounding the intestine' (*Syd. Soc. Lex.*); **periga'stritis**, 'of the peritoneal coat of the stomach' (Billings); **perihepa'titis** [Gr. ἧπαρ liver], of the serous tissue forming the capsule of the liver; **perilaryn'gitis**, of the connective tissue round the larynx (*Syd. Soc. Lex.*); **perilymphang(e)'itis** [see *perilymphangial* in a], of the connective tissue around a lymphatic vessel; **perime'tritis** [Gr. μήτρα uterus], of that part of the peritoneum about the uterus (hence **perime'tritic** *a.*); **perimye'litis** [Gr. μυελός marrow, taken as = spinal cord], of the membranes surrounding the spinal cord; **perine'phritis**, of the *perinephrium* (see b) or tissue surrounding the kidney (hence **perine'phritic** *a.*, relating to perinephritis; also erron. = *perinephric*: see a); **periodon'titis**, of the *periodontum* (see b); **periœsopha'gitis**, of the connective tissue around the œsophagus (*Syd. Soc. Lex.*); **perioophoritis** (-əʊfə'raɪtɪs) [Gr. ᾠοφόρον ovary], of that part of the peritoneum contiguous to the ovary (*Syd. Soc. Lex.*); **perior'bitis** [contr. for *periorbititis*], of the periorbital membrane (see a); **perior'chitis** (see quot.); **peripachymeningitis** (-,pækɪmenɪn'dʒaɪtɪs), of the outer layer of the dura mater; **periphacitis** (-fə'saɪtɪs) [Gr. φακός lentil, taken as = lens], of the capsule of the crystalline lens of the eye (Mayne *Expos. Lex.*); **periphle'bitis** [Gr. φλέψ, φλεβ- vein], of the connective tissue forming the sheath of a vein (hence **periphle'bitic** *a.*); **peripleu'ritis**, of the areolar tissue beneath the pleura; **peri,pylephle'bitis** [Gr. πύλη gate, φλέψ vein], of the connective tissue surrounding the portal vein (*Syd. Soc. Lex.*); **perisalpin'gitis** [Gr. σάλπιγξ trumpet, taken as = Fallopian tube], of that part of the peritoneum adjacent to the Fallopian tube (*ibid.*); **perisple'nitis**, of the peritoneal tissue forming the capsule of the spleen (hence **perisple'nitic** *a.*); **peritonsi'llitis**, of the tissue surrounding the tonsil; **periure'thritis**, of the tissue surrounding the urethra; **perivascu'litis**, of the perivascular sheath (see a) of a blood-vessel, esp. of the retinal vessels (*Syd. Soc. Lex.*); **perivisce'ritis**, of the tissues round the viscera.

1897 *Allbutt's Syst. Med.* II. 143 In very severe cases [of Scarlatina] the Adenitis is often associated with a low form of *periadenitis. *Ibid.* III. 721 Carcinoma starting in the duodenum near the biliary papilla—juxta-ampullary or *peri-ampullary carcinoma, as it has been called. **1890** BILLINGS *Med. Dict.* II. 311/1 *Perianal. **1897** *Q. Jrnl. Microsc. Sci.* XL. 291 [In the larval form of *Phoronis*] there are three prominent ciliated bands... Of the three the perianal band is the most prominent. **1971** G. H. BOURNE *Ape People* xi. 246 Goodall suggests that the function of the swollen perianal region of the sexually receptive chimpanzee ..is to signal to males..that the female is in fact in estrus. **1977** *Lancet* 20 Aug. 403/2 The perioral and perianal zones are bright and red. **1920** ENDELMAN & WAGNER *Gen. & Dental Path.* xxxi. 422 The *periapical tissues may be invaded by bacteria which from the start give rise to chronic symptoms. **1974** H. P. HITCHCOCK *Orthodontics for Undergraduates* xxviii. 480 Periapical lesion around a replanted tooth. **1950** *Physiol. Rev.* XXX. 460 Excitable foci may be followed caudal-ward..through the *periaqueductal grey. **1973** *Nature* 26 Oct. 447/2 Binding in the periaqueductal area of the midbrain was about the same as that of the posterior amygdala. **1898** *Allbutt's Syst. Med.* V. 2 In each lobule the peribronchial tissue (as well as the *peri-arterial) is continuous with the perilobular tissue. *Ibid.* 313 Both the *periarteritic and peribronchial granulations may occur as separate nodules. **1876** DUNGLISON *Dict. Med. Sci.* (rev. ed.) 773/2 **Peri-arteriitis*, inflammation of the sheath of an artery. **1880** A. FLINT *Princ. Med.* 196 To..inflammatory changes in the outer coat of the arteries the name *periarteritis* is applied. **1892** F. P. FOSTER *Med. Dict.* IV. 2547/1 *P[eriarteritis] nodosa*, a thickening of the intima and infiltration of the adventitia of an artery, producing a nodular prominence. **1933** *Practitioners Libr. Med. & Surg.* III. cxii. 1136 Periarteritis nodosa is a rare disease affecting medium-sized arteries in any portion of the body, most commonly in males between the ages of twenty and forty. **1961** R. D. BAKER *Essent. Path.* viii. 136 The interaction of antigen and antibody may produce lesions in the heart, liver and kidneys resembling those of periarteritis nodosa. **1974** R. M. KIRK et al. *Surgery* ii. 9 Generalised diseases such as infections, uraemia, diabetes, scurvy, periarteritis..nodosa..and food allergies may be associated with frailty of the capillary walls. **1897** *Allbutt's Syst. Med.* III. 80 *Periarticular bony formations may cause entire dislocation of a joint. **1881** E. R. LANKESTER in *Encycl. Brit.* XII. 548/2 The *Actinozoa*.. exhibit a differentiation of this space into an axial and a *periaxial portion. **1878** BELL *Gegenbaur's Comp. Anat.* 400 A cavity formed around the branchial chamber by the lumen of these united sacs, the *peribranchial space (perithoracic chamber of authors). **1873** T. H. GREEN *Introd. Pathol.* (ed. 2) 297 The thickening of the *peri-bronchial tissue which sometimes occurs in chronic bronchitis. **1876** tr. *Wagner's Gen. Pathol.* (ed. 6) 243 *Peri-bronchitis..is a term applied to inflammation of the outer halves of the bronchial wall. **1897** *Allbutt's Syst. Med.* III. 132 The redness, *peri-bursal swelling, and tenderness slowly disappeared. **1879** *St. George's Hosp. Rep.* IX. 353 *Pericæcal inflammation. **1928** *Anatomical Rec.* XXXIX. 45 The impression seems to be general..that there is but one type of *pericapillary cell. **1953** *Jrnl. Appl. Physics* XXIV. 1424/1 They [*sc.* the endothelial cells] possess..a large number of vesicles concentrated immediately under the cell membranes facing both the capillary lumen and the pericapillary spaces. **1977** *Lancet* 25 June 1364/2 The basal ganglia, thalamus, corpus callosum, and cerebral white-matter are peppered with innumerable pericapillary and periarteriolar microinfarcts, which sometimes coalesce into larger areas of softening. **1896** *Allbutt's Syst. Med.* I. 121 An extensive *pericellular cirrhosis in cattle. **1899** *Ibid.* VII. 537 The nerve-cells of the brain are placed within pericellular sacs. **1886** *Pericemental [see IMPLANTATION 5 b]. **1940** H. K. BOX *Twelve Periodontal Studies* v. 84 The formation, in the pericementum, of a new tissue..changes the normal arrangement of the pericemental structures, and..replaces the bone substance of the alveolar process. **1882** *Dental Rec.* II. 441 A little sensitiveness becomes noticeable.. indicating a beginning of *pericementitis. **1969** LUEBKE & MULLANEY in Morris & Bohannan *Dental Specialities in Gen. Practice* viii. 357/2 Pericementitis..sometimes follows overinstrumentation or overmedication of a noninfected canal. **1879** C. F. W. BÖDECKER in *Dental Cosmos* XXI. 593 The *pericementum (root membrane, or alveolo-dental periosteum, etc., as it has been termed by former writers) is a formation of connective tissue, identical with the periosteum which covers all bones. **1900** *Lancet* 18 Aug. 539/1 The pericementum compressed between the root of the teeth and the alveolus very quickly became necrosed. **1940** Pericementum [see *pericemental* above]. **1890** BILLINGS *Nat. Med. Dict.* II. 311 *Pericephalic artery. **1876** tr. *Wagner's Gen. Pathol.* (ed. 6) 158 The peri-vascular lymphatic spaces communicate freely with the *peri-cerebral spaces. **1878** BELL *Gegenbaur's Comp. Anat.* 447 *Perichordal tissue. **1876** tr. *Wagner's Gen. Pathol.* (ed. 6) 151 The *perichoroidal space and its efferent canals. **1907** *Allbutt's Syst. Med.* (ed. 2) III. 1015 *Pericolic inflammation may be excited by external violence. **1939** *Times* 20 Feb. 12/7 Lieutenant-Colonel Anderson I.M.S., successfully operated on Lord Brabourne, the Governor of Bengal, at Government House yesterday for pericolic inflammation. **1965** *Arch. Surg.* XCI. 407/2 The final diagnosis was pericolic abscess surrounding a solitary diverticulum of the ascending colon. **1883** *Standard* 3 Jan. 5/6 The cause of death was perityphlitis and suppurating *pericolitis. **1857** DUNGLISON *Med. Lex.* 694 **Pericolonitis*. **1889** G. A. BERRY *Dis. Eye* I. ii. 72 *Pericorneal injection. **1878** A. HAMILTON *Nerv. Dis.* 100 A *peri-cortical collection of blood. **1874** VAN BUREN *Dis. Genit. Org.* 78 The connective tissue around the gland is always largely implicated.., making the disease mainly a *peri-cowperitis. **1876** GROSS *Dis. Bladder* 31 The tumor may be a *pericystic accumulation of pus. **1874** VAN BUREN *Dis. Genit. Org.* 240 *Peri-cystitis is the formation of matter in the connective tissue around and outside of the bladder. **1889** J. M. DUNCAN *Clin. Lect. Dis. Wom.* (ed. 4) xliii. 377 Purulent *pericystomatitis..usually leading to general peritonitis and death. **1859** J. TOMES *Dental Surg.* 90 The absorption being performed by the *peridental membrane. *Ibid.* 439 Two distinct structures..the *peridenteum of the tooth and the periosteum of the bone. **1753** CHAMBERS *Cycl. Supp.* s.v. *Periosteum*, This [membrane]..when it covers..the ligaments [is called] **peridesmium*. **1853** in DUNGLISON. **1899** *Allbutt's Syst. Med.* VI. 881 Secondary inflammatory processes..occurring in the *peridural cellular tissue. **1896** *Ibid.* I. 184 Considered as primary *periencephalitis. **1846** J. E. DAY tr. *Simon's Anim. Chem.* II. 500 Analysis of the fluid found in the peritoneum of a boy..who died from *perienteritis. **1899** *Allbutt's Syst. Med.* VII. 22 Hallopeau ..uses the word *peri-ependymal..as synonymous with central. *Ibid.* VI. 704 Proliferation of the intra- and *peri-fascicular connective tissues. **1884** A. HYATT in *Proc. Boston Soc. Nat. Hist.* XXIII. 83 The threads are surrounded by a *perifibral membrane. *Ibid.*, This *perifibrum envelopes the spicules as well as the fibre. **1899** *Allbutt's Syst. Med.* VIII. 586 Confined to the immediate neighbourhood of the follicles, the sebaceous glands, and the *perifollicular papules. **1863** BERKELEY *Brit. Mosses* Gloss. 312 **Perigamium*, the portion of the fertile reduced branchlets which contains the archegonia. **1899** *Allbutt's Syst. Med.* VI. 733 Thickening of the *periganglionic tissue. **1856** ALLMAN *Fresh-Water Polyzoa* 23 That the *peri-gastric fluid consists mainly of water which has obtained entrance from without. **1962** *Science Survey* III. 261 The perianal and *perigenital glands of the *Mustelidae* like the stoat, skunk, civet, and others..play an important part in the sexual and social life of their carriers. **1971** *Nature* 7 May 50/1 These results clearly established a sex difference in the development of perigenital adipose tissue. **1842** DUNGLISON *Med. Lex.*, **Periglottis*, epiglottic gland. **1888** *Nature* 22 Mar. 498/2 The *perigonadial spaces (so-called generative glands) and the pericardial space..are, then, the cœlom of the mollusca... In Cephalopods..the pericardial and perigonadial cœlomic remnants are continuous, and form one cavity. **1942** GROVE & NEWELL *Animal Biol.* xiv. 220 Each gonad then acquires a cavity—the primary gonadial cavity—and becomes almost completely surrounded by a secondary or perigonadial cavity (gonocoel). **1881** *Q. Jrnl. Microsc. Sci.* XXI. 171 The space..between the water-vessel above and the ambulacral epithelium below, which is traversed by the perforated longitudinal septum, was named by Ludwig the '*perihæmal canal'. It had been previously called the nerve-vessel or nerve-canal, and was supposed to form an integral part of the blood-vascular system. Now, however, it is regarded by Ludwig merely as a derivate of the body-cavity. **1897** *Ibid.* XL. 321 The front dorsal part of the trunk cœlom is produced into a pair of perihæmal spaces, embracing the dorsal blood-vessel. **1962** D. NICHOLS *Echinoderms* ii. 27 Perihaemal system. As its name suggests, this system normally surrounds the haemal complex, though some recent authors prefer to call it the hyponeural sinus system, referring to its relation to one part of the nervous system. **1880** A. FLINT *Princ. Med.* 590 Inflammation of the serous investment of [the liver]..is called *perihepatitis. **1856** WOODWARD *Mollusca* III. 335 The lower part of the alimentary canal continues surrounded by..the '*peri-intestinal sinus'. **1893** *Syd. Soc. Lex.*, **Perilaryngitis*..often ends in *perilaryngeal abscess. **1889** G. A. BERRY *Dis. Eye* I. iv. 96 The intermediate free portion of the membrane fills in the *perilenticular space. **1896** *Allbutt's Syst. Med.* I. 840 Slight *perilobular cell infiltration in the portal canals. **1891** *Quain's Anat.* (ed. 10) II. I. 387 In the serous membranes, rounded nodules..are developed either around or at one side of an enlarged lymphatic (**perilymphangial nodule*). **1899** *Allbutt's Syst. Med.* VI. 439 [Lymphangitis] is practically always associated with inflammation of the tissues immediately surrounding the vessels—*peri-lymphangitis. **1859** TODD *Cycl. Anat.* V. 689/1 *Perimetrial inflammation occasionally reaches the suppuration stage. **1863** *N. Syd. Soc. Year-bk. Med.* 402 The cellular tissue between the folds of the broad ligaments of the uterus is the primary seat of *perimetritic exudations. **1875** JONES & SIEV. *Pathol. Anat.* (ed. 2) 757 *Perimetritis is..inflammation of the peritoneal covering of the uterus. **1899** *Allbutt's Syst. Med.* VI. 912 A marginal or *perimyelitis as it is called being the result. **1897** *Ibid.* IV. 342 A remarkable absence of *perinephric fat. **1877** tr. *H. von Ziemssen's Cycl. Med.* XV. 544 Inflammations of the Kidney..and of the *Perinephritic Tissues. **1880** A. FLINT *Princ. Med.* 907 Perinephritic abscess. **1842** DUNGLISON *Med. Lex.*, **Perinephritis*, inflammation of the external cellular and fibrous membranes of the kidney..*Rayer*. **1896** *Allbutt's Syst. Med.* I. 212 Shrunken nuclei lying in *peri-nuclear vacuoles. **1893** *Syd. Soc. Lex.*, **Peri-ocular space*, the space that surrounds the eyeball..between it and the wall of the orbit. **1854** *Jrnl. R. Agric. Soc.* XV. II. 308 The *periodontal covering to the tooth. **1899** *Allbutt's Syst. Med.* VI. 743 Inflammation of the periodontal membrane. **1955** J. OSBORNE *Dental Mech.* (ed. 4) ix. 148 *Periodontally diseased teeth. **1975** H. THOMSON *Occlusion* xi. 215 Periodontally disturbed abutment teeth..may have to be crowned and splinted to sound adjacent teeth. **1872** L. P. MEREDITH *Teeth* (1878) 93 More cases of root troubles, as abscesses, *periodontitis, etc., occur in teeth filled with amalgam. **1878** T. BRYANT *Pract. Surg.* I. 557 The 'alveolo-dentine membrane', or *periodontum, invests the root of the tooth and lines the bony socket. **1881** T. E. SATTERTHWAITE *Man. Histol.* viii. 108 The development of the cement takes place precisely as bone is produced, viz., from the periosteum, or..from the fibrous tissue of the tooth-sac, the periodontium. **1922** K. H. THOMA *Oral Roentgenol.* (ed. 2) iv. 196 *Periodontium*, the pericementum and all investing structures of the teeth. **1927** O. E. INGLIS *Burchard's Text-bk. Dental Path. & Therapeutics* (ed. 7) xvi. 536 All those tissues which invest the teeth including the pericementum .., the alveolar process and the gingivae, particularly the marginal and cemental gingivae are now generally understood as included in the term periodontium. **1940** H. K. BOX *Twelve Periodontal Studies* ii. 29 In 1920, the writer first used the term 'periodontium' to designate the supporting tissues of the teeth, and to embrace as the three essential tissue-components, the gingivae, the periodontal membrane, and alveolar process. As the word 'periodontium' was occasionally used to denote the periodontal membrane, it was felt that the usage of the term in this new sense would make for exactness in terminology. **1969** *Gloss. Terms Dentistry* (*B.S.I.*) 67 *Periodontium*, the collective term for the tissues immediately surrounding the teeth. **1897** *Allbutt's Syst. Med.* III. 369 *Periœsophageal abscess. **1900** *E. R. Lankester's Treat. Zool.* III. viii. 22 A perioesophageal sinus..is completely..separated from [the body cavity]. **1889** J. M. DUNCAN *Clin. Lect. Dis. Wom.* (ed. 4) 214 The abscess is *peri-oophoric. *Ibid.* 180 Liability to oophoritis and to *peri-oophoritis. **1886** TRISTRAM in *Ibis* Ser. v. IV. 42 The white *periophthalmic line reaching to the forehead. **1691** RAY *Creation* II. (1692) 36 The nictating Membrane or *Periophthalmium. **1893** *Syd. Soc. Lex.*, **Perioral*, surrounding the mouth. **1896** *Cambridge Nat. Hist.* II. 298 In the peri-oral region of *Spatangus purpureus*. **1893** *Syd. Soc. Lex.*, **Periorbital membrane*. **1875** H. WALTON *Dis. Eye* 50 *Periorbitis is meant to include inflammation of the orbital bones, and of their investing periosteum. **1890** BILLINGS *Nat. Med. Dict.* II. 314 **Periorchitis*.., inflammation of the tunica vaginalis testis. **1899** *Allbutt's Syst. Med.* VI. 881 External spinal pachymeningitis..is also designated '*peripachymeningitis'. **1897** *Ibid.* IV. 265 Inflammation, which becomes extended to the *peripancreatic tissue. **1893** *Syd. Soc. Lex.*, **Peripapillary*, situated round the optic *papilla*. **1890** BILLINGS *Nat. Med. Dict.* II. 314 *Peripenial muscle. **1856** HENSLOW *Dict. Bot. Terms*, **Peripetalous*. **1857** MAYNE *Expos. Lex.*, *Peripetalus*,..applied by Mirbel to nectaries which surround the corol or the petals..: peripetalous. **1877** HUXLEY *Anat. Inv. Anim.* ix. 574 Others surround the outer extremities of the petaloid ambulacra, and are termed peripetalous. *Ibid.* x. 602 A ciliated *peripharyngeal band. **1896** *Allbutt's Syst. Med.* I. 609 A *periphlebitic abscess. **1879** BUMSTEAD *Ven. Dis.* 765 Schüppel has described..syphilitic *periphlebitis. **1893** *Brit. Med. Jrnl.* 18 Feb. 346/1 **Peripleuritis* is applied to an affection whose chief feature is suppurative cellulitis of the thoracic wall. It is not necessarily confined to the neighbourhood of the pleuræ. **1860** SIR H. THOMPSON *Dis. Prostate* (1868) 59 Deep perineal or *periprostatic [abscesses]. **1897** *Allbutt's Syst. Med.* III. 953 The *perirectal connective tissue. *Ibid.* 674 The *perirenal fat.. normally tends somewhat in the same direction. *Ibid.* 574 *Perisplenic abscess..described in connection with malaria. **1899** *Ibid.* VI. 267 The most diagnostic value attaches..to a *perisplenitic friction rub. **1880** A. FLINT *Princ. Med.* 590 *Perisplenitis signifies a local peritonitis about the spleen. **1876** tr. *Wagner's Gen. Pathol.* (ed. 6) 150 Broad canals clothed with endothelium (or *perithelium), in the axis of which are found the blood vessels. **1878** *Perithoracic [see *peribranchial* above]. **1876** tr. *von Ziemssen's Cycl. Med.* VI. 914 *Peritonsillar, or retrotonsillar abscess. **1897** *Allbutt's Syst. Med.* IV. 752 Connection between acute lacunar tonsillitis, *peritonsillitis and acute rheumatism. **1899** *Cambridge Nat. Hist.* VI. 332 *Peritracheal spaces in which run tracheae. **1899** CHEYNE & BURGHARD *Surgical Treatment* II. x. 171 *Peri-ungual onychia. **1900** DORLAND *Med. Dict.* 496/1 **Periureteric*, about the ureter. **1962** *Lancet* 6 Jan. 31/2 The causes of hydronephrosis included prostatic hypertrophy, bladderneck obstruction, periureteric fibrosis, and aberrant renal vessels. **1874** VAN BUREN *Dis. Genit. Org.* 79 *Peri-urethral abscess. *Ibid.* 78 *Peri-urethritis. **1872** T. G. THOMAS *Dis. Women* (ed. 3) 64 *Peri-uterine cellulitis or pelvic peritonitis. **1873** A. FLINT *Nerv. Syst.* i. 56 The blood vessels here [in the cerebro-spinal centres] are surrounded by what have been called *perivascular canals. **1879** *St. George's Hosp. Rep.* IX. 149 The brain small,..the ventricles and perivascular canals increased in size. **1898** *Allbutt's Syst. Med.* V. 796 An aspiratory *periventricular effect caused by the adhesions. **1876** GROSS *Dis. Bladder* 262 Inflammation of the *perivesical and periprostatic, connective and vascular tissues. **1867** J. HOGG *Microsc.* II. ii. 370 In the *perivisceral cavity of the earth-worm. **1898** *Allbutt's Syst. Med.* V. 1036 The *perivisceritis of Huchard. **1890** *Quain's Anat.* (ed. 10) I. I. 10 Half of the germinal vesicle is extruded into the *perivitelline space. **1887** GARNSEY & BALFOUR tr. *Goebel's* (1877) *Outlines* 19 The two cells..grow..alongside of one another to the normal size of auxospores, and on their outer surface..appears a membrane of cellulose, the *perizonium.

†**2.** In *Crystallography*, used (orig. in Fr., by Haüy) to form adjs. applied to prisms derived from primary four-sided prisms, whose faces are increased to the number indicated by the names, by the development of secondary facets on their edges: as ***peridecahedral***, ***-dodecahedral***, ***-hexahedral***, ***-octahedral***; so ***peripolygonal***; also ***periorthogonous***: see quots. *Obs.*

1805–17 R. JAMESON *Char. Min.* (ed. 3) 198 *Peri-hexahedral*, *peri-octahedral*, *peri-decahedral*, and *peri-dodecahedral*, when the primitive four-sided prism is changed by means of decrements into a six, eight, ten or twelve sided prism. *Ibid.* 207 *Peri-polygonal* (*F. peri-polygone*), when the prism has a great number of lateral planes, such as the peri-polygonal tourmaline. **1857** MAYNE *Expos. Lex.*, *Peri-orthogonus*, applied by Haüy to a variety of which the primitive form, which is a rhomboidal prism, changes into a rectangular prism by the effect of decreases: periorthogonous.

periagua (also †periaga, -go(e, -guay, etc.), another form of PIRAGUA.

‖**perialgia** (pɛrɪˈældʒɪə). *Path.* Also **perialgy**. [mod.L., f. Gr. περί exceedingly + ἄλγος pain.] Excessive pain. Hence **periˈalgic** *a.*

1853 DUNGLISON *Med. Lex.*, *Perialgia*, a very violent pain. **1857** MAYNE *Expos. Lex.*, *Perialgia*,..perialgy. **1890** in BILLINGS *Med. Dict.* II. 311. **1893** *Syd. Soc. Lex.*, Perialgia, Perialgic.

perianth (ˈpɛrɪænθ). *Bot.* Formerly in L. form **perianthium**. [app. directly after F. *périanthe* (Rousseau 1771–7), ad. mod.L. *perianthium* (17th c. in Ray), f. Gr. περί about + ἄνθος flower (after Gr. περικάρπιον: see PERICARP).]

1. A structure surrounding, or forming the outer part of, a flower; a floral envelope.

†**a.** In earlier use, a synonym of CALYX; and, like it, applied also to an INVOLUCRE or whorl of bracts, as that at the base of the flower-head in the *Compositæ*. *Obs.*

α. [**1686** RAY *Hist. Plant.* I. 22 Semina..quæ nullo præter perianthium..tegmine donantur.] **1706** PHILLIPS, *Perianthium*, or *Calyx* (among Herbalists) the Flower-cup in most Plants. **1748** *Phil. Trans.* XLV. 169 The Bud or Rudiment..appears in Autumn wrapped up in a conic scaly *Perianthium*. **1762** EHRET in *Phil. Trans.* LIII. 82 At the base of this..petal is situated an irregular..triphyllous periantheum. **1806** GALPINE *Brit. Bot.* 44* Stratiotes. Spatha 2-leaved. Perianthium superior, 3-cleft.

β. **1785** MARTYN *Rousseau's Bot.* xxi, The early *Hepatica* ..has a perianth of three leaves, which being remote from the flower, is rather an involucre than a calyx. *Ibid.* xxvi, The calyx or perianth common to the whole flower.

b. Now, The outer part or envelope of a flower, which encloses the essential organs (stamens and pistils); either *double*, i.e. the calyx and corolla collectively, esp. when so much alike as to appear to constitute a single part; or *single*, when there is only one, which may be either green (*sepaloid*) like an ordinary calyx, or coloured (*petaloid*) like an ordinary corolla.

1828 STARK *Elem. Nat. Hist.* II. 477 The Dicotyledonous plants with a double perianth, but with the corolla formed of a single petal attached to the calyx. **1835** LINDLEY *Introd. Bot.* (1848) I. 326 The word Perianth signifies the calyx and corolla combined. **1857** HENFREY *Bot.* §189 A large number of the Monocotyledonous orders possess a petaloid perianth; that is, there are two circles of petaloid organs, which, from their resemblance, or their actual coherence, have the appearance of a single hexamerous whorl. **1880** GRAY *Struct. Bot.* vi. §1 (ed. 6) 164.

c. In liverworts, a leafy or membranous covering surrounding the archegonium; in mosses, the cluster of leaves surrounding the sexual organs in the 'flower'.

1857 HENFREY *Bot.* §320 (Hepaticæ) The vaginule,.. the circle of leaves, often confluent, surrounding it, form the *perigone, perianth* or *involucel*. **1866** *Treas. Bot.* 863 [In liverworts] the involucre and perianth coexist sometimes in the same plant. **1875** BENNETT & DYER tr. *Sachs' Bot.* 293 Besides the envelopes just named [perichætium, etc.], there is also often in Hepaticæ (but not in Mosses) a so-called *Perianth*, which grows as an annular wall at the base of the archegonium, and finally surrounds it as an open sac.

2. *attrib.* and *Comb.*, as ***perianth-leaf***, ***-segment***, ***-tube***, ***-whorl***.

1870 HOOKER *Stud. Flora* 356 *Herminium*.. Perianth-segments incurved. *Ibid.* 362 *Trichonema*.. spathe longer than the perianth-tube. **1875** BENNETT & DYER *Sachs' Bot.* 556 Both of the trimerous perianth-whorls petaloid.

Hence †**peri'antheous, peri'anthial** *adjs.*, having, or pertaining to, a perianth.

1857 MAYNE *Expos. Lex.*, *Perianthеus, Bot.*, applied to a flower provided with a.. perianth: perianthеous.

periapsis (pɛrɪ'æpsɪs). *Astr.* [f. PERI- + APSIS, after PERIGEE, PERIHELION, etc.] That point in the path of a natural or artificial satellite at which it is closest to a primary.

1964 J. L. NAYLER *Dict. Astronautics* 194 *Periastron* (*periapsis*), the nearest point on the orbit of a stellar satellite to the star, or in a binary star the point at which the companion is nearest to the primary. **1971** *Nature* 26 Nov. 168/3 The manoeuvre, which changed the orbit of the spacecraft so that periapsis (closest approach to Mars) is now 868 miles. **1972** *Daily Colonist* (Victoria, B.C.) 25 Feb. 5/2 Pioneer will be close to Jupiter for about four days (100 hours) and will see the planet in full sunlight 50 hours before periapsis, or the closest point of the fly-by. **1976** *Sci. Amer.* June 59/1 Those commands will.. place the spacecraft in an elliptical orbit around Mars that will vary in altitude from 33,000 kilometers at apoapsis down to 1,500 kilometers at periapsis.

periapt ('pɛrɪæpt). Also formerly in Gr. form **periapton**, pl. **-a**. [a. F. *périapte* (16th c. in Godef.), ad. Gr. περίαπτον, in same sense, f. περί about + ἅπτο-ς fastened, f. ἅπτειν to fasten.] Something worn about the person as a charm; an amulet.

1584 R. SCOT *Discov. Witchcr.* XII. vii. (1886) 180 All their charmes, periapts, characters, amulets. **1591** SHAKS. *1 Hen. VI*, II. iii. 2 Now helpe ye charming Spelles and Periapts. **1661** LOVELL *Hist. Anim. & Min.* 216 Some use it as a periapt against enchauntments. **1669** W. SIMPSON *Hydrol. Chym.* 74 Many periapta become effectual by being such polite bodies. **1727–41** CHAMBERS *Cycl.*, *Periapton*, a kind of medicine.. which being tied about the neck, is supposed to prevent, or cure diseases. **1816** COLERIDGE *Lay Serm.* 341 Superstition.. goes wandering.. with its pack of amulets, bead-rolls, periapts, fetisches, &c. **1861** LADY LLANOVER in *Mrs. Delany's Life & Corr.* II. 274 *note*, Dr. Graham.. mentions.. a spider having been sewn up in a rag and worn as a periapt about the neck to charm away the ague.

periaqua, obs. form of *periagua*: see PIRAGUA.

periarterial to **-articular**: see PERI- a, c.

periaster, periastron (pɛrɪ'æstə(r), -'æstrən). *Astron.* Also **periastre**. [mod. f. Gr. περί close around + ἄστρον star, after PERIHELION, PERIGEE.] That point in the orbit of a heavenly body revolving around a star (as a companion star in a binary system, a comet, etc.) at which it is nearest to the star. Also *attrib.* Hence **peri'astral** *a.*, of or pertaining to the periastron.

1851 NICHOL *Archit. Heav.* 223 The swiftness with which certain individuals of the Double Stars sweep past their *perihelia*,—or rather their periasters—is amazing. **1867–77** G. F. CHAMBERS *Astron.* Vocab. 918 Periastre. **1872** PROCTOR *Ess. Astron.* iii. 40 Twenty millions of years.. must have elapsed since those comets were last in periastral passage. **1876** *Athenæum* 16 Dec. 805/2 The small star is now at or near its periastron. **1887** LOCKYER in *Proc. R. Soc.* XLIII. 154 In some [variable stars].. the variation would seem to be partly due to swarms of meteorites moving around a bright or dark body, the maximum light occurring at periastron. **1890** J. THORNTON *Adv. Physiog.* xiv. §225.

periauger, var. PIRAGUA 2.

periaxial: see PERI- a.

periblast ('pɛrɪblæst). *Biol.* [f. Gr. περί around + -BLAST.] **a.** The main part of the substance of a cell, as distinct from the external cell-wall and the internal nucleus: = PERIPLAST b. **b.** The outer layer of protoplasm in the egg of a teleostean fish, surrounding the central yolk.

1857 DUNGLISON *Med. Lex.* 694 *Periblast*.., the amorphous matter, which surrounds the *endoblast*.. or cell nucleus, and undergoes segmentation. **1889** H. V. WILSON *Embryol. Sea Bass* in *Bull. U.S. Fish Comm.* (1891) IX. 216 Sections through this stage are the most important for the study of the formation of the periblast. *Ibid.* 217 The central periblast layer becomes thicker than in the earlier stages.

periblastic (pɛrɪ'blæstɪk), *a. Embryol.* [f. as prec. + -IC.] **a.** In Haeckel's nomenclature, Applied to a meroblastic ovum which germinates by segmentation of the superficial part, becoming successively a *perimonerula*, *pericytula*, *perimorula*, *periblastula*, and *perigastrula*.

1876 LANKESTER in *Q. Jrnl. Microsc. Sc.* XVI. 62 The periblastic mode of development is most common in the Arthropods, in Tracheata as well as Crustacea;.. The essential point about the periblastic type is this, that the food-material collects at an early stage of development centrally, so as to be completely enveloped by the formative protoplasm.

b. Of or pertaining to the periblast (see prec. b).

1889 H. V. WILSON (as above) 216 They [the marginal cells] are even marked off from the surrounding periblastic protoplasm.

‖**periblastula** (pɛrɪ'blæstjuːlə). *Embryol.* [mod.L., f. PERI- + BLASTULA.] The BLASTULA arising from a PERIBLASTIC ovum.

1876 LANKESTER in *Q. Jrnl. Microsc. Sc.* XVI. 63 In such cases the fertilised egg passes at once to the Periblastula stage, and cannot be said to exhibit either a *Peri*-monerula or *Peri*-cytula, or *Peri*-morula stage.

periblem ('pɛrɪblɛm). *Bot.* [mod. (Ger., Hanstein 1868) ad. Gr. περίβλημα anything thrown or put round, f. περιβάλλειν to throw round, put on (as a covering).] Term applied to the embryonic cells of the growing-point of Phanerogams from which the primary cortex is developed.

1873 MACNAB in *Q. Jrnl. Microsc. Sc.* XIII. 50 In the Periblem tissues the lateral branches and leaf-structures originate. **1884** BOWER & SCOTT *De Bary's Phaner.* 8 The separation of plerome and periblem does not appear in all cases so sharply marked. **1885** GOODALE *Physiol. Bot.* (1892) 155 In the earliest stage of its development the leaf is a mere papilla consisting of nascent cortex (periblem) and nascent epidermis (dermatogen).

‖**peribolus** (pə'rɪbələs), **-os** (-ɒs). [a. Gr. περίβολος compass, circuit, enclosure (as of a temple), whence in eccl. L. *peribolus* (Vulgate); f. περί round + βολ-, from βάλλειν to throw: cf. prec.] In *Gr. Antiq.* An enclosure or court around a temple; the wall bounding such an enclosure. Hence applied to an exterior enclosure in early Christian churches.

1706 PHILLIPS, *Peribolus* (in Archit.) the outward Wall encompassing any Place; also a Park or Warren. **1776** R. CHANDLER *Trav. Greece* iii. 12 The temple was inclosed by a peribolus or wall. **1861** LEWIN *Jerusalem* 207 The old wall, the outer peribolus of the Temple platform.

attrib. **1891** A. B. EDWARDS *Pharaohs, Fellahs & Expl.* 43 The peribolos wall twenty-four feet in thickness.

peribranchial to **-cæcal**: see PERI- a, c.

‖**pericambium** (pɛrɪ'kæmbɪəm). *Bot.* [mod.L. (Nägeli and Leitgeb 1868), f. Gr. περί around + CAMBIUM, q.v.] A term applied to the outer portion of the vascular cylinder or stele, lying between the vascular bundles internally and the innermost layer of the cortex externally. It was originally used with special reference to roots.

The term has now been generally abandoned for PERICYCLE.

1875 BENNETT & DYER *Sachs' Bot.* 144 The formation of lateral roots in a mother-root commences.. in a layer of tissue which must be considered the outer layer of the plerome, and is called Pericambium. **1899** *Nat. Science* Dec. 458 Pericambium was given up for the better term, pericycle, because the form was apt to be confused with cambium.

†**pericard**, *sb.* and *a. Obs.* [ad. F. *péricarde* (Paré, *c* 1560; in Cotgr.), ad. L. *pericardium*: see below.] **A.** *sb.* = PERICARDIUM.

1639 J. W. tr. *Guibert's Char. Physic.* III. 143 If they desire to have the heart embalmed by it selfe,.. make an Incision in the pericard. **1696** *Phil. Trans.* XIX. 331 In the Pericard was little or no Serum.

B. *adj.* [ad. Gr. περικάρδιος: see PERICARDIUM.] Surrounding or enveloping the heart.

1708 *Brit. Apollo* No. 31. 2/2 Contain'd in Membrane Pericard.

pericardiac (pɛrɪ'kɑːdɪæk), *a.* [f. PERICARDI-UM, after *cardiac*.] = PERICARDIAL. Hence **pericardiaco-phrenic** (pɛrɪkɑːˌdaɪəkəʊ'frɛnɪk) *a.* [see PHRENIC], name of certain branches of the internal mammary artery which are connected with the pericardium and the diaphragm.

1822–34 *Good's Study Med.* (ed. 4) II. 562 Beneath the pericardiac covering of the heart. **1875** HUXLEY & MARTIN *Elem. Biol.* (1877) 133 The heart is a short, thick, somewhat hexagonal symmetrical organ lodged in the pericardiac sinus. **1893** *Syd. Soc. Lex.*, Pericardiaco-phrenic arteries.

pericardial (pɛrɪ'kɑːdɪəl), *a.* [f. PERICARDI-UM + -AL[1].] Of, pertaining to, occurring in, or connected with the pericardium. (In quot. 1654 app. used for 'cordial'.)

pericardial fluid, the serous fluid or lymph secreted by the inner layer of the pericardium.

1654 GAYTON *Pleas. Notes* II. iv. 51 Her breasts.. never leaves the trepidations, till she hath got a Pericardiall Julip, which she loves at her heart. **1831** CARLYLE *Sart. Res.* III. ii, Without which Pericardial Tissue the Bones and Muscles (of Industry) were inert, or animated only by a Galvanic vitality. **1846** P. M. LATHAM *Lect. Clin. Med.* xxiii. 105 The effects of pericardial inflammation. **1880** GÜNTHER *Fishes* 151 The pericardial and peritoneal sacs.

So **peri'cardian, peri'cardic** [F. *péricardique* (Cotgr.)] *adjs.*, in same sense.

1656 BLOUNT *Glossogr.*, *Pericardian*, belonging to the *Perichard*,.. a membrane.. involving the whole heart. *Ibid.* s.v. *Vein*, *Pericardick Vein*, the second branch of one of the two main ascendant branches of the hollow vein; whence it runnes to the Pericardium. **1868** DUNCAN tr. *Figuier's Insect W.* Introd. 13 By the aid of this.. the blood can penetrate the heart from the pericardic chamber.

‖**pericarditis** (ˌpɛrɪkɑː'daɪtɪs). *Path.* [f. PERICARD-IUM + -ITIS.] Inflammation of the pericardium. Hence **pericarditic** (-'ɪtɪk) *a.*

1799 HOOPER *Med. Dict.*, *Pericarditis*, inflammation of the pericardium. **1834** J. FORBES *Laennec's Dis. Chest* (ed. 4) 571 Cases of chronic pericarditis. **1854** JONES & SIEV. *Pathol. Anat.* (1875) 35 Cases of pericarditis of renal origin. **1857** MAYNE *Expos. Lex.* 907/2 Pericarditic.

‖**pericardium** (pɛrɪ'kɑːdɪəm). *Anat.* Also 6 **-don**, 6–7 **-dion**, 7 anglicized **pericardie**; see also PERICARD. [Latinized form of Gr. (τὸ) περικάρδιον (the membrane) round the heart (Galen), neuter of περικάρδιος adj., f. περί around + καρδία heart.] The membranous sac, consisting of an outer fibrous and an inner serous layer, which encloses the heart and the commencements of the great vessels. Also applied to the sac enveloping or enclosing the heart or corresponding organ in certain invertebrates.

1576 NEWTON *Lemnie's Complex.* 105 b, The pannicle or coffyn of the heart, called *Pericardion*. **1578** BANISTER *Hist. Man* I. 24 b, *Pericardon* (whiche is the *Inuolucre* of the hart). **1615** CROOKE *Body of Man* 358 All that distance which is betweene the Basis or broad end of the heart and this *Pericardium*. **1658** PHILLIPS, *Pericardie*, (Greek) the film, or thin skin, wherein the heart is enwrapped. *a* **1711** KEN *Hymns Evang.* Poet. Wks. 1721 I. 170 One.. from his Pericardium streaming ey'd Both Blood and Water. **1860** ALFORD *Comm. N.T.* John xix. 34 The spear perhaps pierced the pericardium or envelope of the heart. **1888** ROLLESTON & JACKSON *Anim. Life* 133 Fresh-water Mussel... Next to the pericardium is the non-glandular thin-walled duct.

Hence **ˌpericard(i)'ectomy** [-ECTOMY], surgical removal of all or part of the pericardium; **periˌcardiocen'tesis** [Gr. κέντησις pricking], surgical puncturing of the pericardium; **pericardiotomy, pericardotomy** (-'ɒtəmɪ) [-TOMY], the operation of making an incision into the pericardium.

[**1900** DORLAND *Med. Dict.* 491/2 Pericardicentesis.] **1900** *Lancet* 13 Oct. 1063/2 In 1898 Podrey did a pericardotomy for a bullet wound of the heart. **1901** *Brit. Med. Jrnl.* 9 Mar. 38/2 Reichard finds that resection of a rib is absolutely necessary in pericardiotomy. **1913** STEDMAN *Med. Dict.* (ed. 2) 672/2 Pericardectomy... Pericardiectomy. **1938** M. THOREK *Mod. Surg. Technic* II. xxxi. 1206 Technic of pericardiocentesis. *Ibid.* 1212 (*heading*) Pericardiectomy in the treatment of the Pick syndrome. **1956** W. P. CLELAND in Bailey & Love *Short Pract. Surg.* (ed. 10) xliii. 892 At operation (pericardectomy) it is essential to remove the thickened pericardium from the ventricles. **1967** S. TAYLOR et al. *Short Textbk. Surg.* xvi. 223 Constrictive pericarditis... Pericardiectomy is the treatment of choice, and is best done through a vertical incision splitting the sternum, which affords excellent exposure. **1977** *Lancet* 6 Aug. 301/2, 15 underwent pericardiocenteses (with recurrent of effusion afterwards) before definitive therapy by pericardial drainage and local steroid instillation. *Ibid.* 15 Oct. 817/1, 3 of these 17 had tamponade which was successfully treated by pericardectomy.

pericarp ('pɛrɪkɑːp). *Bot.* [= F. *péricarpe* (1556 in Hatz.-Darm.), It. *pericarpio* (Florio), ad. 16th c. L. *pericarpium*, a. Gr. περικάρπιον pod, husk, shell, f. περί around + καρπός fruit. In earlier use in the L. form: see PERICARPIUM[1].] A seed-vessel; the case containing the seed or seeds, comprising the outer shell, rind, or skin, and the enclosed pulp, etc. if any; the wall of the ripened ovary or fruit of a flowering plant. (See ENDOCARP, EPICARP, MESOCARP.) Also applied to a special structure containing the spores in certain cryptogamous plants, as the cystocarp of florideous algæ.

1759 B. STILLINGFLEET *Misc. Tracts*, *Biberg's Œcon. Nat.* (1762) 63 Most of the pericarps are shut at top, that the seeds may not fall. [*Note*] Whatever surrounds the seeds is called by botanical writers a *pericarpium*, and as we want an English word to express this, I have taken the liberty to call it a pericarp. **1785** MARTYN *Rousseau's Bot.* x. (1794) 99 A bilocular pericarp, or seed-vessel of two cells. **1835** LINDLEY *Introd. Bot.* (1848) II. 3 Every fruit consists of two principal parts, the pericarp and the seed. **1875** BENNETT & DYER *Sachs' Bot.* 236 Articulated branches, which.. form the peculiar 'Pericarp' of Lejolisia [a florideous alga].

Hence †**peri'carpic** *a.* = PERICARPIAL; **pericar'poidal** *a.*, resembling a pericarp.

1819 LINDLEY tr. *Richard's Observ.* 37 The pericarpic direction of the embryo. **1890** *Cent. Dict., Pericarpoidal.*

peri'carpial, *a.* [f. next: see -AL[1].] Of or pertaining to a pericarp.

1830 LINDLEY *Nat. Syst. Bot.* Introd. 30 An ovarium.. consists of one or several connected pericarpial leaves, called carpella. **1876** HARLEY *Mat. Med.* (ed. 6) 381 The pericarpial coats being rejected.

‖**peri'carpium**[1]. *Bot.* Now *rare.* [mod. (16th c.) L., a. Gr. περικάρπιον.] = PERICARP.

1691 RAY *Creation* I. (1692) 99 Besides this use of the Pulp or Pericarpium for the guard and benefit of the Seed, it serves also..for the..Sustenance of Man and other Animals. **1748** *Phil. Trans.* XLV. 565 Its Pericarpium is a round dry Capsule, slightly four-corner'd. **1830** LINDLEY *Nat. Syst. Bot.* 124 Decandolle considers the rind of the Orange to be of a different origin and nature from the pericarpium of other fruit. **1866** *Treas. Bot., Pericarpium,* the peridium of certain fungals.

‖**peri'carpium**[2]. *Med. Obs.* [med. or mod.L., a. Gr. περικάρπιον bracelet, f. περί around + καρπός wrist.] A plaster applied to the wrist, formerly used as a cure for various affections.

1663 BOYLE *Usef. Exp. Nat. Philos.* II. v. x. 212 Turpentine and Soot,..outwardly applyed are the main Ingredients of Pericarpiums, extoll'd against Agues. **1741** *Compl. Fam.-Piece* I. i. 80 An often try'd Pericarpium or Wrist-Plaister for Defluxions and Fumes of the Eyes.

perice, obs. form of PERISH *v.*

pericellular to **-cementum:** see PERI- a, b.

pericentre (pɛrɪ'sɛntə(r)). [f. PERI- + CENTRE, after *perihelion.*] That point, in the (eccentric) orbit of a body revolving around a centre, at which it is nearest to that centre.

1902 NEWCOMB *Study Univ.* 159 The point nearest the latter is called the periastron or pericentre, and corresponds to the perihelion of a planetary orbit.

So **peri'central,** *a.* = PERICENTRIC *a.* 1.

1889 BENNETT & MURRAY *Cryptog. Bot.* 192 These pericentral tubes are often connected with one another and with the axial cell by threads of protoplasm. **1890** *Cent. Dict., Pericentral tubes,* in *bot.,* in the so-called polysiphonous seaweeds, the ring of four or more elongated cells surrounding the large central elongated cells.

pericentric (pɛrɪ'sɛntrɪk), *a.* [f. PERI- + CENTRIC *a.*] **1.** Arranged or situated around a centre or central body.

1857 MAYNE *Expos. Lex., Pericentricus, Bot.,* applied by A. Richard to the insertion of stamens when the undivided part of the calyx being plane or only concave, the stamens appear to be disposed around the centre, as in the *Polygoneæ*: pericentric. **1895** *Funk's Stand. Dict., Pericentric,* accumulated or deposited around a central point: specifically, in geology, said of lava accumulated on the sides of a cone, either in streams or as falling fragments.

2. *Cytology.* [cf. -CENTRIC 2.] Involving parts of a chromosome at both sides of the centromere. Opp. PARACENTRIC *a.*

1938 [see PARACENTRIC *a.*]. **1962** *Lancet* 6 Jan. 21/2 Chromosome analyses in a girl with mongolism and in her parents have disclosed abnormalities which we attribute to pericentric inversion of a maternal 21st chromosome. **1973** *Nature* 3 Aug. 260/2 The very fact that some X chromosomes, such as that of the mouse are acrocentrics reveals that pericentric inversions did occasionally occur. **1977** *Ibid.* 6 Jan. 65/2 The aberrant chromosome was interpreted as an aneusomic recombinant from the father who was heterozygous for a pericentric inversion of chromosome 4.

pericerebral: see PERI- a.

perichætial (pɛrɪ'kiːtɪəl), *a.* *Bot.* Also 9 **perichætal.** [f. next + -AL[1].] Belonging to or constituting the perichætium.

1821 S. F. GRAY *Nat. Arr. Brit. Pl.* I. 221 Perichætial leaves.—Imbricated leaf-like organs surrounding the reproductive organs [of Mosses]. **1835** LINDLEY *Introd. Bot.* (1848) II. 107 [The sporangium] is..surrounded by leaves of a different form from the rest, and distinguished by the name of *perichætial* leaves.

‖**perichætium** (pɛrɪ'kiːtɪəm). *Bot.* [mod.L. (in Linnæus *Gen. Plant.* (ed. 5, 1754) 487), f. Gr. περί around + χαίτη long hair, as of a mane, leaves, foliage; in modern use taken also as = 'bristle'.

Perichætium (on the analogy of *perianthium, pericarpium,* etc.) ought to mean 'that which surrounds or encircles the hair or foliage', but is employed to express the hair or foliage that surrounds.]

A whorl or cluster of modified leaves at the base of a group of reproductive organs, or of the fructification, in mosses and some liverworts.

1777 LIGHTFOOT *Flora Scot.* II. 737 Haller ranks this moss [*Bryum cæspiticium*] among the *Hypnums* on account of the vagina or *perichætium* at the base of the filament. **1796** WITHERING *Brit. Plants* (ed. 3) I. 364 An anther taken out of the Perichætium or leafy calyx. **1863** BERKELEY *Brit. Mosses* Gloss. 312 *Perichætium,* the leaves immediately surrounding the base of the fruit stalk.

perichætous (pɛrɪ'kiːtəs), *a.* *Zool.* [f. mod.L. *Perichæta,* a genus of worms having the segments surrounded by bristles (f. as prec.) + -OUS.] Surrounded by bristles; having segments surrounded by bristles, as earthworms of the genus *Perichæta.*

1870 ROLLESTON *Anim. Life* 125 The œsophageal or 'calciferous' glands, structures said to attain a great development in the Perichætous worms. **1896** *Cambridge Nat. Hist.* II. 268 The 'perichaetous' condition of some earth-worms.

periche, obs. form of PERISH.

pericholecystitis: see PERI- c.

‖**perichondrium** (pɛrɪ'kɒndrɪəm). *Anat.* [mod.L., f. Gr. περί around + χόνδρος cartilage; after PERIOSTEUM. In mod.F. *périchondre.*] A membrane, consisting of fibrous connective tissue, enveloping the cartilages except at the joints.

1741 MONRO *Anat. Bones* (ed. 3) 51 Cartilages are.. covered with a Membrane named *Perichondrium,* which is a-kin to the *Periosteum* of the Bones. **1756** *Gentl. Mag.* XXVI. 516 To take them off with a cutting instrument, destroying the periosteum and perichondrium. **1881** MIVART *Cat* 287 The mucous membrane..is inseparably united with the periosteum and perichondrium of the different parts.

Hence **peri'chondrial** *a.,* surrounding or investing a cartilage; of or pertaining to the perichondrium; ‖**perichon'dritis,** inflammation of the perichondrium (hence **perichon'dritic** *a.,* pertaining to or affected with perichondritis); ‖**perichon'droma, -ome,** a tumour growing from the perichondrium.

1839–47 TODD *Cycl. Anat.* III. 1005/2 *Perichondrial lining of the cartilaginous passages. **1878** BELL *Gegenbaur's Comp. Anat.* 451 By investing or growing around the cartilage, forming a perichondrial ossification. **1846** tr. *Hasse's Descr. Diseases Circ. & Resp.* II. v. 276 No difference is observable between this disease and *perichondritis. **1880** A. FLINT *Princ. Med.* 292 Inflammation of the tissues immediately surrounding the laryngeal cartilages is called *laryngeal perichondritis.* **1875** JONES & SIEV. *Pathol. Anat.* (ed. 2) 142 Carilaginous tumours arise..more rarely on the outside, under or from the periosteum (*perichondroma).

perichord to **-choroidal:** see PERI- a.

‖**perichoresis** (,pɛrɪkɒ'riːsɪs). *Theol.* [a. Gr. περιχώρησις going round, rotation.]

= CIRCUMINCESSION, q.v.

[**1781** GIBBON *Decl. & F.* xxi. *note,* The περιχώρησις, or *circumincessio* is perhaps the deepest and darkest corner of the whole theological abyss.] **1858** J. MARTINEAU *Stud. Chr.* (1873) 79 Are we to understand the phrase three persons, to mean three beings united by 'perichoresis'? **1895** EDWARDS in *Expositor* Oct. 243 The perichoresis within the Trinity does not touch the Logos so far as He is incarnate.

‖**pericladium** (pɛrɪ'kleɪdɪəm). *Bot.* [mod.L. (Link 1825), f. Gr. περί around + κλάδος branch.] The sheathing base of a leaf-stalk when expanded so as to surround the supporting branch.

1832 LINDLEY *Introd. Bot.* 95 When the lower part only of the petiole is sheathing, as in Umbelliferæ, that part is sometimes called the *pericladium.* **1856** in HENSLOW *Dict. Bot. Terms.*

periclase ('pɛrɪkleɪs). *Min.* [ad. mod.L. *periclasia* (Scacchi, 1840), erron. f. Gr. περι- very, exceedingly + κλάσις breaking, fracture: intended to refer to its very perfect cleavage. (But Gr. περίκλασις means twisting or wheeling round; brokenness, ruggedness.)] A mineral consisting of magnesia with a small admixture of protoxide of iron, found in greenish crystals or grains, in ejected masses of crystalline limestone at Vesuvius and elsewhere. Also called **periclasite** (pɛ'rɪkləsaɪt).

1844 DANA *Min.* 405 Periclase..occurs in the calcareous blocks of Mont Somma. **1868** *Ibid.* 134 Periclasite. **1872** *Nevill Catal. Min.* 28 Periclasite, small but perfect crystals in calcite.

Periclean (pɛrɪ'kliːən), *a.* [f. proper name *Pericle-s* + -AN.] Of or pertaining to Pericles (B.C. *c* 495–429) and his age in Athenian history, the period of the intellectual and material pre-eminence of Athens. Also *transf.*

a **1822** SHELLEY *Ess. & Lett.* (Camelot ed.) 46 The Greeks of the Periclean age. **1874** MAHAFFY *Soc. Life Greece* i. 2 If one of us were transported to Periclean Athens. **1901** *Daily Chron.* 4 Oct. 4/6 She..has striven towards the Periclean ideal of the woman least spoken of for good or evil among men. **1901** *Westm. Gaz.* 12 Dec. 4/2 Raeburn..lived during what Sir Walter Armstrong quite justly calls the Periclean age of Edinburgh.

periclinal (pɛrɪ'klaɪnəl), *a.* (*sb.*) [f. Gr. περικλιν-ής (see next) + -AL[1]: cf. *anticlinal.*]

1. *Geol.* Sloping in all directions from a central point: = QUAQUAVERSAL.

1876 PAGE *Adv. Text-bk. Geol.* iv. 84 They are found in dome-shaped positions, and sloping on every side from a common centre or apex, and then they are said to be periclinal, cycloclinal, or quaquaversal. **1881** JOHNSTON in *Pop. Sci. Monthly* XIX. 53 The subjacent rock would thus have a quaquaversal or periclinal dip away on all sides.

2. a. *Bot.* [= Ger. *perikline* (Sachs 1878).] Applied to those cell-walls at a growing-point which run in the same direction as the circumference of the shoot. More widely, occupying or occurring in a layer parallel to the surface of an organ. Also as *sb.* = periclinal wall or plane.

1882 VINES *Sachs' Bot.* 951 The planes of the walls in a growing-point are classified thus: *a. Periclinal,* those which are curved in the same direction as the surface (seen in longitudinal section). *b. Anticlinal*... *c. Radial*... *d. Transverse. Ibid.,* If the outline (in longitudinal section) of the growing-point is a parabola, the periclinals will constitute a system of confocal parabolas of different parameter. **1885** GOODALE *Physiol. Bot.* (1892) 382. **1965** BELL & COOMBE tr. *Strasburger's Textbk. Bot.* 69 (*caption*) Each segment becomes divided by a periclinal wall..into an inner and an outer (cortical) cell. **1965** K. ESAU *Plant Anat.* (ed. 2) iv. 76 The lateral meristems are particularly distinguished by divisions parallel with the nearest surface of the organ (periclinal divisions). **1975** M. E. MCCULLY in Torrey & Clarkson *Devel. & Function of Roots* vi. 111 The daughter cells of these periclinal divisions lack the intense basophilia of the parent epidermal cells.

b. Applied to a type of chimæra (see quot. 1968). Also as *sb.,* a periclinal chimæra. [ad. G. *periklinalchimäre* (E. Baur 1909, in *Zeitschr. f. induktive Abstammungs- u. Vererbungslehre* I. 344).]

1916 *Jrnl. Genetics* VI. 78 Proof that a plant is a periclinal chimaera may..be obtained from adventitious buds arising in internodes of the stem, as well as from those formed on roots. **1925** *Ibid.* XVI. 44 Simple white-over-green periclinals would presumably..give only white seedlings. **1959** *New Biol.* XXX. 39 In periclinal chimeras there is often great variation in the pigment distribution pattern. **1963** *Heredity* XVIII. 270 The striped varieties of *Commelina, Tradescantia* and *Zebrina* have also been shown to be periclinal chimeras with a rather specialised development. **1968** R. RIEGER et al. *Gloss. Genetics & Cytogenetics* 59 Chimeras..in plants may be classified.. according to their structure into a) sectorial (different tissues grow side by side and occupy distinct sectors of varying size), b) periclinal (different tissues are disposed one with the other..), c) mericlinal (actually an interrupted periclinal..).

Hence **peri'clinally** *adv.,* (*a*) with a dip on all sides from a central point; (*b*) *Bot.,* in the manner of a periclinal division or chimæra.

1890 in *Cent. Dict.* **1916** *Jrnl. Genetics* VI. 79 Plants in which the variegation affected the skin periclinally. **1963** *Heredity* XVIII. 281, LI which does not divide periclinally in the apex may do so frequently during leaf development. **1975** M. E. MCCULLY in Torrey & Clarkson *Devel. & Function of Roots* vi. 111 When the young primordium is about one-third of the way across the cortex a few epidermal cells at its tip divide periclinally and thus produce the root cap initials.

pericline ('pɛrɪklaɪn). *Min.* [mod. f. (Breithaupt 1823) Gr. περικλινής sloping all round, on all sides, f. περί around + -κλινής sloping, f. κλίνειν to bend, lean; in reference to the great inclination between the terminal and lateral faces.] A variety of ALBITE found in large opaque white crystals in the chloritic schists of the Alps. Also *attrib.,* as **pericline twin,** a twin crystal in which the macrodiagonal axis is the twinning-axis, as is frequent in crystals of pericline.

1832 C. U. SHEPARD *Min.* 186 Perikline. Heterotomous feldspar. **1868** DANA *Min.* (ed. 5) 350 Pericline is in large, opaque, white crystals. **1898** *Naturalist* 176 A zonal structure as well as twinning both on the pericline and albite plans.

‖**peri'clinium.** *Bot.* [mod.L. (Cassini 1818), f. Gr. περί around + κλίνη couch.] The involucre of *Compositæ.*

1826 G. N. LLOYD *Bot. Terminol.* 148 *Periclinium,*..a term used by Cassini to denote the common calyx of compound flowers. **1832** LINDLEY *Introd. Bot.* 102 In Compositæ, the involucrum often consists of several rows of imbricated bracteae... Linnæus called it *calyx communis,*.. Richard *periphoranthium,* Cassini *periclinium.*

†**pe'riclitancy.** *Obs. rare*[−0]. [f. L. *perīclitānt-em,* pr. pple. of *perīclitārī*: see below and -ANCY.] = PERICLITATION.

1656 BLOUNT *Glossogr., Periclitancy, Periclitation,* a proving, adventuring,..jeoparding, or putting in hazard.

†**pe'riclitate,** *ppl. a.* *Obs.* [ad. L. *perīclitāt-us* tried, tested, pa. pple. of *perīclitārī*: see next.] Exposed to peril, imperilled.

1525 *St. Papers Hen. VIII,* VI. 481 The occasion of longer division in Cristendome, wherby the hole state of the same may be periclitate and put in extreme daunger.

†**pe'riclitate,** *v.* *Obs.* [f. L. *perīclitāt-,* ppl. stem of *perīclitārī* to expose to risk, danger, or peril, f. *perīculum, perīclum* trial, risk, danger; cf. F. *périclíter* (1390 in Godef.).] *trans.* To expose to peril; to imperil, endanger, risk.

1623 COCKERAM, *Periclitate,* to hazard. **1657** TOMLINSON *Renou's Disp.* 390* They would periclitate their lives. **1765** STERNE *Tr. Shandy* VIII. iii, Such a dose of opium! periclitating, pardi! the whole family of ye.

b. *intr.* for *pass.* In *pr. pple.* (also as *ppl. a.*).

1694 MOTTEUX *Rabelais* v. (1737) 232 Our State's naufrageous and periclitating. **1853** *Tait's Mag.* XX. 262 The policy of Metternich..would appear to be the one obligatory on the statesmen of that ever periclitating monarchy.

†**pericli'tation.** *Obs.* [a. F. *périclitation* (*a* 1530 in Godef.), ad. L. *perīclitātiōn-em*, n. of action from *perīclitārī*: see prec.]

1. The action of exposing or condition of being exposed to peril; peril, danger, hazard, jeopardy.

1527 *St. Papers Hen. VIII*, VI. 585 To the danger and periclitacion of Cristes feithe. **1599** A. M. tr. *Gabelhouer's Bk. Physicke* 49/1 It may without anye periclitatione be administrede to them. **1625** CHAS. I *Sp.* Wks. 1662 I. 361 Your own Periclitation necessitates an early Resolution. **1659** H. L'ESTRANGE *Alliance Div. Off.* 316 Corporal maladies, which are accompanied with great periclitation.

2. An experiment, esp. one involving risk; a trial, a venture. [So in L.]

1658 PHILLIPS, *Periclitation*, (lat.) an adventuring, hazarding, or endangering. **1670** MAYNWARING *Physician's Repos.* 81 This Prescription..is grounded upon some former periclitations. **1897** HOWELLS *Landl. Lion's Head* 227 During his social and financial periclitations in a region wholly inconceivable to her.

†**pericli'tator.** *Obs.* [agent-n. in L. form from L. *perīclitārī*: see above.] One who makes a venture or experiment; an experimenter.

1602 F. HERING tr. *Obendörfer's Anat.* Ep. Ded. Aij, Bolde Periclitators in the Practise of Physicke. **1657** TOMLINSON *Renou's Disp.* 114, I will not relate stories..of these impious periclitatours.

pericolitis to **-colpitis**: see PERI- c.

periconch ('perɪkɒŋk). *Zool.* [f. Gr. περί around + κόγχη shell.] A shell growing around the body in the veliger or larval form of a mollusc.

1888 *Proc. Boston Soc. Nat. Hist.* XXIII. 542 Professors Hyatt and Brooks consider the protoconch in cephalous molluscs as..probably derived from the periconch of Scaphopods.

‖**pericope** (pə'rɪkəpiː). [Late L. *pericopē* (Jerome) section of a book, a. Gr. περικοπή a section, f. περί around + κοπή cutting, περικόπ-τ-ειν to cut round. In mod.F. *péricope*.] A short passage, section, or paragraph in a writing.

1658 W. BURTON *Itin. Anton.* 59 You shall have the whole pericope, as it is in the Translation of Ptolemie from the Arabick. *Ibid.* 71 A corrected reading of the whole Pericope. **1884** *Edin. Rev.* Jan. 137 The pericope of 'the woman taken in adultery' is entirely omitted from this work. **1889** LIGHTFOOT *Ess.* '*Supernat. Relig.*' 203 This pericope is an interpolation where it stands.

b. *Eccl.* A portion of Scripture appointed for reading in public worship.

1695 J. EDWARDS *Perfect. Script.* I. xiii. 566 Jerome speaks of a *Pericope* of Jeremiah. **1869** GINSBURG in *L'pool Lit. & Phil. Soc. Proc.* XXIII. 313 Next in point of antiquity is the division of the Pentateuch into 175 Pericopes. **1884** D. HUNTER tr. *Reuss's Hist. Canon* i. 3 These passages..were disconnected fragments,..simply pericopes or lessons, as they were called afterwards in the Christian Church.

c. *Anc. Pros.* 'A passage consisting of strophe and antistrophe' (Liddell & Scott s.v. περικοπή).

Hence **pericopic** (perɪ'kɒpɪk) *a.*, of, pertaining to, or connected with a pericope, esp. in relation to the lesson for the day.

1888 J. KER *Lect. Hist. Preaching* vii. 117 The passage for the day was called a Pericope or section, this gave rise to the Pericopic system of preaching, which prevails still on the Continent in many Protestant churches. *Ibid.* ix. 160 Every minister who cares to have an intelligent congregation should adopt some 'pericopic' system, reserving freedom for occasional divergence from it.

pericorneal to **-cowperitis**: see PERI- a, c.

†'**pericrane.** *Obs.* [a. F. *péricrâne* (1541 in Hatz.-Darm.), ad. med. or mod.L. *pericranium*: see next.] = PERICRANIUM (chiefly in sense 2).

1682 D'URFEY *Butler's Ghost* 159 For with all Calmness I'le maintain, Had Wisdom seiz'd your Pericrane,.. You would just Sentiments pursue, And grant my Depositions true. **1708** T. WARD *Eng. Ref.* III. (1710) 17 These issu'd out of Penrys Brain, And Vdal's fruitful Pericrane. **1764** *Museum Rust.* II. lxxxi. 280 Though no great scholar, [he] may have many things treasured up in his pericrane. **1804** HUDDESFORD *Wiccamical Chaplet* 158 Ajax a rock in's arms could take And hurl it at your pericrane.

‖**pericranium** (perɪ'kreɪnɪəm). Also 6–7 in Gr. form **pericranion.** [med. or mod.L., a. Gr. περικράνιον, neuter of περικράνιος round the skull, = ἡ περικράνιος χιτών the membrane under the skin of the skull, f. περί around + κρανίον skull.]

1. *Anat.* The membrane enveloping the skull, being the external periosteum of the cranial bones.

[**1525** tr. *Brunswick's Surg.* A iv b/2 That panicle that is named of Galienus pericraneum dothe couere all the hole panne, and is somwhat lyke to senewes.] **1541** R. COPLAND *Guydon's Quest. Chirurg.* D iv, Of what substaunce is the great pannacle that is called Pericranium, and wherof bredeth it? **1741** MONRO *Anat. Bones* (ed. 3) 66 *Periosteum* (common to all the Bones, but in the Scull distinguished by the Name of *Pericranium*). **1878** T. BRYANT *Pract. Surg.* I. 198 It is probable that the blood is effused beneath the pericranium.

2. *loosely* (usually in affected or humorous use): **a.** The skull, cranium; **b.** The brain, esp. as the seat of mind or thought. Now *rare*.

1590 MARLOWE *2nd Pt. Tamburl.* I. iii, Cleave his pericranion with thy sword. **1621** FLETCHER *Isl. Princess* II. v, The clerk and he are cooling their pericraniums. **1630** DEKKER *2nd Pt. Honest Wh.* IV. i, We whose pericranions are the very limbecks and stillatories of good wit. **1700** T. BROWN *Amusem. Ser. & Com.* 10 The Caprichio came Naturally into my Pericranium. **1816** T. L. PEACOCK *Headlong Hall* i, Arguing..various knotty points which had puzzled his pericranium. **1847** L. HUNT *Men, Women, & B.* II. iv. 52 A possessor of oaks thick as his pericranium.

Hence **peri'cranial** *a.*, of or pertaining to the pericranium (whence **peri'cranially** *adv.*, in quot. *humorously* = so as to cover the skull); **pericranics** (-'krænɪks), *humorous*, 'brains', wits; ‖**pericra'nitis**, inflammation of the pericranium.

1890 *Cent. Dict.*, *Pericranial*. **1841** *Fraser's Mag.* XXIII. 220 My wife had taken..the book, and..the wig, and, placing the latter pericranially where the former had been, she gave the volume to the countess. **1800** LAMB *Let. to Manning* 22 Aug., To speculate strangely on the state of the good man's pericranicks. **1852** J. MILLER *Pract. Surg.* iv. (ed. 2) 58 Idiopathic pericranitis is more frequently chronic than acute.

†'**pericrany.** *Obs.* In 7 -ie; pl. -ies. Anglicized form of PERICRANIUM.

1658 PHILLIPS, *Pericranie*,..the hairy scalp, or skin that covereth the skull. **1718** OZELL tr. *Tournefort's Voy.* I. 103 The smoke..began to muddle the poor Peoples Pericranies. **1735** SWIFT *Poetry* Misc. V. 171 And when they join their Pericranies, Out skips a Book of Miscellanies.

periculant (pə'rɪkjʊlənt), *a. nonce-wd.* [f. L. *perīculānt-em*, pr. pple. of rare L. *perīculārī*, f. *perīcul-um* danger + -ANT.] In danger, in peril.

1896 HOWELLS *Impressions & Exp.* 70 A Purgatory..out of which one can hopefully undertake to pray periculant spirits.

pe'riculous, *a.* [ad. L. *perīculōs-us*, f. *perīculum* danger, peril: see -OUS.] = PERILOUS.

1547 BOORDE *Brev. Health* Pref. 4 In periculus causes one Chirurgion ought to consult with an other. *a* **1552** LELAND *Itin.* III. 47 Driven toward the Mouth of this Water, wher is no Haven, but periculus Rokkes. **1646** SIR T. BROWNE *Pseud. Ep.* IV. xii. (1650) 187 Saturne..doth cause these periculous periods. **1683** E. HOOKER *Pref. Pordage's Mystic Div.* 20 Periculous tempestivities, hard Seasons. **1835** HOGG in *Fraser's Mag.* XI. 359 'Tis really ridiculous To turn into frolic a case so periculous. **1932** W. E. D. ALLEN *Hist. Georgian People* iii. 27 The land is poor and snowbound, craggy and periculous. **1959** A. A. MACGREGOR *Phantom Footsteps* iii. 70 The mountain's precipitous upper slopes at the time were treacherously encased in ice, its ravines deceptively filled with periculous snow.

Hence †**pe'riculousness** *Obs.*

1547 BOORDE *Brev. Health* cclxxxv. 94 b, Phlebothomy the whiche I dyd neuer vse in this matter, consideryngе the periculisnes of it.

pericycle ('perɪsaɪk(ə)l). *Bot.* [mod. (Van Tieghem, in Fr. 1882), ad. Gr. περίκυκλος all round, spherical, περικυκλοῦν to encircle.] A term applied (instead of the earlier PERICAMBIUM) to the outer portion of the vascular cylinder, lying between the vascular bundles internally, and the endodermis or innermost layer of the cortex externally.

1894 SCOTT *Structural Bot.* 61 Surrounding the whole ring of vascular bundles on the outside is a layer of thin-walled cells, the *pericycle*. **1896** HENSLOW *Wild Flowers* 39.

pericyclic (perɪ'saɪklɪk), *a. Chem.* [f. PERI- + CYCLIC *a.*] Of a reaction: involving a concerted rearrangement of bonding in which all the bonds broken or formed in the reaction lie on a closed ring, whether or not a cyclic molecule is involved.

1969 WOODWARD & HOFFMANN in *Angewandte Chemie* (Internat. Ed.) VIII. 848/1 In our development of the theme of orbital symmetry control of concerted chemical changes, we have laid the basis for a general consideration of all pericyclic reactions—that is, reactions in which all first-order changes in bonding relationships take place in concert on a closed curve. **1974** GILL & WILLIS *Pericyclic Reactions* iv. 99 The basic tenet of the Woodward-Hoffmann theory is that orbital symmetry is conserved in concerted pericyclic reactions. *Ibid.* vi. 162 The six-electron cyclo-addition and reversion processes are by far the most common of all pericyclic changes... Within this category falls the well-known Diels-Alder reaction. **1975** W. R. DOLBIER in Buncel & Lee *Isotopes in Org. Chem.* I. ii. 27 The class of reactions which are presently known as pericyclic or multi-centered reactions..include cyclo-additions, electrocyclic reactions and sigmatropic processes.

pericynthion (perɪ'sɪnθɪən). *Astr.* [f. PERI- + Gr. Κύνθιον, neut. of Κύνθιος, adj. designating Mt. Kynthos on Delos, the birthplace of Artemis, goddess freq. associated with the moon.] That point at which a spacecraft in lunar orbit is closest to the moon's centre: applied esp. if the spacecraft was not launched from the moon.

1959 SPITZ & GAYNOR *Dict. Astron. & Astronautics* 295 *Pericynthion*, that point in the orbit of a moon rocket which is closest to the moon. **1969** *Times* 17 May 8/6 Then the descent engines of the L.M. will be fired..to propel it into an orbit in which it will swing around the moon in an elliptical orbit. At its nearest (pericynthion) it will be eight nautical miles from the surface.

pericystic to **-cystostomatitis**: see PERI- a, c.

pericyte ('perɪsaɪt). *Histology.* [ad. G. *pericyt* (K. W. Zimmerman 1923, in *Zeitschr. f. Anat. und Entwicklungsgeschichte* LXVIII. 67): see PERI- and -CYTE.] One of many flattened branching cells found around capillary blood vessels.

1925 *Amer. Jrnl. Anat.* XXXV. 257 The 'pericytes' of mammals which Zimmerman has described. **1928** *Anatomical Rec.* XXXIX. 45 The designations Rouget cells, adventitial cells, and pericytes are used indiscriminately on the assumption that they connote the same structures. **1965** HAM & LEESON *Histol.* (ed. 5) xxii. 592 Opinion soon changed, and it was generally conceded that such cells as could be seen just outside the endothelium of the capillaries and the venules of most of the bodies of mammals were not contractile. Moreover, the noncontractile cells in this location came to be known by the terms of perivascular cells or pericytes. **1976** W. J. CLIFF *Blood Vessels* iv. 68 Pericytes are non-contractile cells which have well-developed phagocytic powers. *Ibid.* 71 Pericytes have primarily a mechanical supporting function within the walls of minute blood vessels.

‖**pericytula** (perɪ'sɪtjuːlə). *Embryol.* [mod.L., f. PERI- + CYTULA.] The CYTULA arising from a PERIBLASTIC ovum.

1876 LANKESTER in *Q. Jrnl. Microsc. Sc.* XVI. 62 Haeckel is inclined from this to assert as a general rule that the Perimonerula acquires a nucleus, becomes a Pericytula, and then cleaves into two, four, &c., cells, to form the Perimorula.

peridental to **-denteum**: see PERI- a, b.

periderm ('perɪdɜːm). [mod. f. Gr. περί around + δέρμα skin: in mod.F. *périderme*.]

1. *Zool.* A hard or tough covering investing the body in certain Hydrozoa.

1870 NICHOLSON *Man. Zool.* 77 It is invested by a strong corneous or chitinous covering, often termed the 'periderm'.

2. *Bot.* A name introduced (in Ger. *peridermis*) by von Mohl (1836), to designate the corky layers of plant-stems; subsequently extended to include the whole of the tissues formed from the cork-cambium of phellogen.

[**1839** LINDLEY *Introd. Bot.* (ed. 3) 89 The *Epiphlœum* of Link, *Phlœum* or *Peridermis* of Mohl, consisting of several layers of thin-sided tubular cells.] **1849** J. H. BALFOUR *Man. Bot.* § 85 After a certain period,..the corky portion becomes dead, and is thrown off.., leaving a layer of tabular cells or *periderm* below. **1875** BENNETT & DYER tr. *Sachs' Bot.* 81 The formation of cork is very frequently continuous, or is renewed with interruption; and when this occurs uniformly over the whole circumference, there arises a stratified cork-envelope, the Periderm, replacing the epidermis, which is in the meantime generally destroyed.

Hence **peri'dermal** *a.*, of or pertaining to the periderm.

1884 BOWER & SCOTT *De Bary's Phaner.* 545 The peridermal structures always arise in a layer of cells which has already been differentiated. *Ibid.*, The formation of bark is the immediate consequence of the internal formation of periderm, and the name is as a rule employed for the dried-up tissues and the adjacent peridermal layers conjointly.

peridesmitis, -desmium: see PERI- b, c.

‖**peridiastole** (,perɪdaɪ'æstəliː). *Physiol.* [mod. (Gendrin, in Fr.) f. Gr. περί over, beyond + DIASTOLE.] 'Term for the hardly appreciable interval of time between the diastole of the heart and the following systole' (*Syd. Soc. Lex.*). Hence **peridiastolic** (-daɪə'stɒlɪk) *a.*, belonging to the peridiastole. (Cf. PERISYSTOLE, -IC.)

1842 DUNGLISON *Med. Lex.*, *Diastole*,..the almost inappreciable time, which elapses between the diastole and systole has been called *perisystole*, and that which succeeds to the diastole, *peridiastole*. **1875** HAYDEN *Dis. Heart* 81 Peridiastolic phenomena are, complete relaxation of auricles and ventricles, and free entrance of blood from great veins into auricles, and from auricles into ventricles. **1876** tr. *H. von Ziemssen's Cycl. Med.* VI. 56 It is a matter of choice if any one likes to imitate Gendrin, and distinguish a peridiastolic as well as a presystolic murmur, and a perisystolic one.

perididymis, -didymitis: see PERI- b, c.

peridinial (perɪ'dɪnɪəl), *a. Zool.* [f. mod. Zool. L. *Peridīnium*, f. Gr. περιδῑνής whirled round, περιδῑνεῖν to whirl round.] Belonging or related to the genus *Peridinium* (wreath-animalcules), or family *Peridiniidæ* of infusorians.

peridinian (perɪ'dɪnɪən). *Biol.* Also **peridinean, peridiniean.** [f. mod.L. generic name *Peridinium* (C. G. Ehrenberg *Organisation, Systematik und geographisches Verhältniss der Infusionsthierchen* (1832) II. 74/2), f. Gr. περιδῑνής whirled round: see -AN.] A dinoflagellate, usually from a marine habitat, belonging to the order Peridinales. Also *attrib.* or as *adj.*

1912 MURRAY & HJORT *Depths of Ocean* x. 674 Among plants the peridineans..are noted for their power of emitting light. **1928** RUSSELL & YONGE *Seas* i. 25 The Peridinians..can be considered either plants or animals as they have certain characteristics of both. **1935** F. E. FRITSCH *Struct. & Reprod. Algae* I. 664 The Peridiniean flora of warmer zones..differs very markedly from that of colder seas. **1963** D. W. & E. E. HUMPHRIES tr. *Termier's Erosion & Sedimentation* xi. 236 Most of the flagellates giving rise to 'waterbloom' are Peridineans. **1976** P. BOUGIS *Marine Plankton Ecol.* i. 11 Generally, a peridinian has chlorophyll and is autotrophic. *Ibid.* 12 *Noctiluca* is now placed in the Peridiniales... Its spores are of the peridinian type.

‖**peridium** (pɪˈrɪdɪəm). *Bot.* Pl. **-ia.** [a. Gr. πηρίδιον, dim. of πήρα leathern bag, wallet.] The outer coat or envelope of certain fungi, which encloses the spores; it is variously shaped, and often partly gelatinous.

1823 in CRABB *Technol. Dict.* **1826** G. N. LLOYD *Bot. Terminol.* 148 *Peridium*, a thin membrane in some Fungi, which separates in various ways, under which lie the seeds or seed-bearing bodies. **1832** LINDLEY *Introd. Bot.* I. iii. 209 *Peridium*, is also a kind of covering of sporidia; *peridiolum* is its diminutive. **1861** BENTLEY *Man. Bot.* 387. **1874** COOKE *Fungi* 34 The peridia are seated upon this mycelium.

Hence **peˈridial** *a.*, of or pertaining to the peridium; **peˈridiiform** *a.*, of the form of a peridium; **peˈridiole** [mod.L. *peridiolum*, dim. of *peridium*], a small or secondary peridium, or the inner layer of a peridium when double.

1832 [see PERIDIUM]. **1832** LINDLEY *Introd. Bot.* 207 *Peridiole*, Fr.; the membrane by which the sporules are immediately covered. **1857** MAYNE *Expos. Lex., Peridiolum*, .. a peridiole. **1874** COOKE *Fungi* 35 Externally there is a filamentous tunic, composed of interlaced fibres, sometimes called the peridiole. **1887** GARNSEY & BALFOUR tr. *De Bary's Fungi* lxxxix. 312 A very massive peridial wall.

peridot (ˈpɛrɪdɒt). Forms: 4 peridod, (penitot), 4–5 peritot(e, (pelidod(de), 5 perydo, perydote, -tote; 8–9 peridot(e, (9 peritot). [a. F. *péridot*, in OF. *peritot* (1220 in Du Cange), *peridol*, *-don*, *peredo*, *pelido* (Godef.), in med. (Anglo-)L. *peradota* (1272 in Du Cange).

The uncertain forms and foreign appearance of the word have suggested an Oriental origin; but there appears to be no valid basis for the conjecture of its identity with Arabic *farīdat* 'pearl, precious stone'.]

†**a.** In ME., A name of the chrysolite. *Obs.* (bef. 1500). **b.** (From Fr. after 1700.) A jeweller's term for the variety of chrysolite called OLIVINE.

[**1265** *Wardrobe Acc.* on *Pipe Roll* 53 Hen. III m. 2 *dorso*, j Iaspis cum cassa et j anulus cum peridota et j saphirus. **1348** *Test. Ebor.* (Surtees) I. 51 Unum anulum cum peridod imposito. **1358** *Ibid.* 70 Annulum meum aureum cum lapide vocato pelidod.] **13..** *E.E. Allit. P.* B. 1472 Penitotes, & pynkardines, ay perles bitwene. *c* **1400** MAUNDEV. (1839) xx. 219 The grene ben of Emeraudes, of Perydos [F. *peridoz*], and of Crisolytes. *c* **1400** *Siege of Troy* 1496 in *Archiv neu. Spr.* LXXII. 47 With Charbuncles that shynes bryght And Perytotes of moche myght. *c* **1420** *Anturs of Arth.* xxxi. (Irel. MS.), His polans with his pelidoddes were poudert to pay. *c* **1460** *Emare* 155 Deamondes and koralle, Perydotes and crystall, And gode garnettes bytwene.

b. 1706 PHILLIPS, *Peridot* (Fr.), a precious Stone of a greenish Colour. **1788** tr. *Cronstedt's Min.* (ed. 2) I. 142 The oriental crysolite and peridot are the very same gem. **1811** PINKERTON *Petral.* II. 31 The common chrysolite, or peridot of the French. **1877** W. JONES *Finger-ring* 247 A gold ring with a stone called Peritot. **1885** *Encycl. Brit.* XVIII. 534/1 *Peridote*, a name applied by jewellers to the green transparent varieties of olivine. When yellow, or yellowish-green, the stone is generally known as 'chrysolite'.

attrib. **1874** DAWKINS in *Ess. Owens Coll. Maunch.* v. 136 Identity of composition may be traced between the meteorite of Chassigny and the peridot rock of New Zealand.

Hence **periˈdotic** *a.*, pertaining to, of the nature of, or containing peridot.

1880 *Mineral. Mag.* III. p. ix (*heading*) On some peridotic rocks from the island of St. Paul's. **1891** MURRAY & RENARD in *Rep. Sci. Results Voy. H.M.S. Challenger: Deep-Sea Deposits* vi. 374 Manganese is rarer in these rocks, but is found as a constituent of pyroxenic, amphibolic, and peridotic minerals.

peridotite (ˈpɛrɪdətaɪt). *Petrogr.* [As used in English ad. G. *peridotit* (H. Rosenbusch *Mikrosk. Physiogr.* (1877) II. 522; previously F. *péridotite* had been used for an olivine-basalt (Cordier & d'Orbigny *Descr. des Roches* (1868) II. 118); f. G. *peridot*, F. *péridot* PERIDOT: see -ITE¹.] Any of the group of plutonic rocks containing little or no feldspar but substantial olivine, usu. with pyroxene, amphibole, or other mafic minerals.

1878 J. D. DANA *Man. Mineral. & Lithol.* (ed. 3) 451 Doleryte... There are two series: A. Ordinary, B. Chrysolitic, and for the latter the name Peridotyte has been used. **1882** A. GEIKIE *Text-bk. Geol.* 151 A series of crystalline rocks composed essentially of olivine, with usually one or two other magnesium silicates.. has been classed by Rosenbusch under the general name of Peridotites. **1897** —— *Anc. Volcanoes Gt. Brit.* I. 31 Picrites or other varieties of Peridotites. **1931** S. J. SHAND *Study of Rocks* vii. 114 Kimberlite.., the matrix of all African diamonds.., is a highly serpentinised peridotite. **1950** E. E. WAHLSTROM *Introd. Theoret. Igneous Petrol.* xiii. 291 Dunite, a variety of peridotite, is almost 100 per cent olivine. **1963** [see *melanocratic* adj. s.v. MELANO-]. **1972** *Mineral. Mag.* XXXVIII. 437 The peridotite consists dominantly of coarse-grained (2 mm) olivine with minor interstitial clinopyroxene and amphibole of similar grain size.

Hence **peridoˈtitic** *a.*, containing, consisting of, or resembling peridotite.

1886 J. J. H. TEALL *Brit. Petrogr.* iv. 68 Peridotitic, hornblendic, and augitic rocks have been serpentinised. **1935** BRANSON & TARR *Introd. Geol.* iii. 13 Magmas occurring to depths of 10 miles are of one type, those that are 10 to 40 miles (the maximum thickness of the crust) down are of another type, and those in the layer (approximately 900 miles thick) next below the crust are of still another. These three regions of the earth's body are known as the granitic, gabbroid or basaltic, and peridotitic zones. **1971** *Nature* 22 Oct. 522/2 The general hypothesis of sea-floor spreading envisages the upwelling of peridotitic mantle material beneath mid-oceanic ridges. **1974** *Mineral. Mag.* XXXIX. 798 Peridotitic rocks in the Massif du Sud.. have suffered about 30% serpentinization.

peridrome (ˈpɛrɪdrəʊm). [ad. Gr. περίδρομ-ος running round, a surrounding rim or gallery, f. περί round + -δρομος running, δρόμος a race or course: in mod.F. *péridrome.*] (See quots.)

1623 COCKERAM, *Peridrome*, a gallery. **1876** GWILT *Archit.* Gloss., *Peridrome*, the space, in ancient architecture, between the columns of a temple and the walls enclosing the cell.

peridural: see PERI- a.

perie, var. PERRY *Obs.*, pear-tree.

perieces: see PERIŒCI.

‖**periegesis** (ˌpɛrɪiːˈdʒiːsɪs). [a. Gr. περιήγησις, lit. the action of leading about as a guide, f. περί around + ἥγησις leading; hence, a description such as that given by a guide.] A description of a place or region. (In quot. 1820, A journey or progress about, a tour.) So **periegetic** (ˌpɛrɪiːˈdʒɛtɪk) *a.* [ad. Gr. περιηγητικός befitting a περιηγητής or guide, descriptive], giving a description of a place or of objects of interest.

1627 B. JONSON *Underwoods* xvi, In thy admired Periegesis, Or universal circumduction Of all that read thy Poly-Olbion. **1820** LAMB *Elia* Ser. I. *Two Races of Men*, In his *periegesis*, or triumphant progress throughout this island. **1850** LEITCH tr. *C. O. Müller's Anc. Art* (ed. 2) §35 Periegetic authors who described remarkable objects in places famed for art. **1857** J. W. DONALDSON *Chr. Orthod.* 228 The book of Joshua.. actually mentions (xviii. 9) a periegesis of the Holy land 'described by cities into seven parts in a book'.

‖**perielesis** (ˌpɛrɪiːˈliːsɪs). *Mus.* [a. Gr. περιείλησις rolling round, convolution, f. περί round + εἴλησις whirling, f. εἰλεῖν to wind.] In mediæval music, A long ligature (LIGATURE *sb.* 4) or series of notes sung to one syllable, usually towards the end of a phrase or melody.

1880 W. S. ROCKSTRO in Grove *Dict. Mus.* II. 691 *Perielesis*,.. a long and sometimes extremely elaborate form of Ligature, sung towards the close of a Plain Chaunt Melody... Like the Cadenza in modern music, the Perielesis generally makes its appearance in connection with the penultimate or antepenultimate syllable of a final phrase.

periencephalitis, etc.: see PERI- c.

‖**perienteron** (pɛrɪˈɛntərɒn). *Embryol.* and *Zool.* [mod.L., f. PERI- + Gr. ἔντερον intestine.] A space between the outer and inner layers (ectoderm and endoderm) of a gastrula, being the remnant of the blastocœle persisting after gastrulation, and forming a primitive body-cavity or perivisceral space, as distinct from the *archenteron* or primitive intestinal cavity. Hence **perienteric** (-ɛnˈtɛrɪk) *a.*, of, pertaining to, or contained in the perienteron; perivisceral.

1877 HUXLEY *Anat. Inv. Anim.* xii. 685 The perienteron.. may give rise directly to the perivisceral space, or channels, of the adult. **1878** BELL *Gegenbaur's Comp. Anat.* 50 The body-cavity, or perienteric cavity.

perier, perierer, variants of PERRIER *Obs.*

periergy (ˈpɛrɪɜːdʒɪ). *rare.* [ad. Gr. περιεργία, f. περίεργος over-careful, f. περί + ἔργον work.] (See quots.)

1589 PUTTENHAM *Eng. Poesie* III. xxii. (Arb.) 265 Therefore the Greekes call it *Periergia*, we call it ouer-labor, iumpe with the originall: or rather (*the curious*) for his ouermuch curiositie and studie to shew himselfe fine in a light matter. **1730–6** BAILEY (folio), *Periergy*, needless caution or trouble in an operation. **1823** CRABB *Technol. Dict., Periergy* (*Rhet.*).., a bombastic or laboured style.

perifascicular to **-follicular:** see PERI- a, b.

perifoveal (pɛrɪˈfəʊvɪəl), *a. Anat.* [f. PERI- + FOVEA.] Applied to the part of the retina regarded as the periphery of its central region, surrounding the parafovea.

1926 *Brit. Jrnl. Ophthalm.* X. 229 (*heading*) The perifoveal circulation. **1941** S. L. POLYAK *Retina* xv. 196 From the axial center to the anterior retinal boundary there are.. seven regions: the central area, composed of (*I*) central fovea, (*II*) parafoveal region, and (*III*) perifoveal region or areal periphery; and the extra-areal periphery, composed of (*IV*) near periphery, (*V*) middle periphery, (*VI*) far periphery, and (*VII*) extreme periphery. *Ibid.* xvi. 213 The perifoveal region or the periphery of the central area is its most outward belt... Inwardly it begins at points where the ganglion cell layer still contains four rows of cells. Outwardly it ends where the ganglion layer becomes reduced to a single row of closely packed cells. **1966** *Jrnl. Physiol.* CLXXXVII. 456 There is considerable antagonistic interaction between rod and cone signals at the ganglion cell layer in the perifoveal retina of dark-adapted monkeys.

Hence (as a back-formation) **periˈfovea**, the perifoveal region.

1963 H. DAVSON *Physiol. of Eye* (ed. 2) II. i. 86 (*heading*) Parafovea and perifovea. **1964** J. Z. YOUNG *Model of Brain* ix. 160 The larger parasol bipolars and garland and giant ganglion cells make contact with hundreds or thousands of bipolars and thus cones (and rods) of the fovea and perifovea. **1975** *Nature* 6 Feb. 406/2 When fovea and perifovea are stimulated together (as in everyday life) foveal responses are relatively depressed suggesting that different retinal regions interact abnormally.

perifusate (pɛrɪˈfjuːzeɪt). *Med.* [f. next + *-ate*, after PERFUSATE.] The liquid that results from perifusion.

1969 *Lancet* 25 Oct. 883/1 In the perifusion system, 4–6% of the total pancreatic I.R.I. leaked into the perifusate during the initial 'washing' of the freshly cut tissue. **1978** *Nature* 19 Jan. 272/2, 6 mM L-glucose was added to a perifusate containing 3 mM D-glucose without significantly changing the rate of $^{42}K^+$ efflux as compared with controls maintained in 3 mM D-glucose alone.

perifuse (ˈpɛrɪfjuːz), *v. Med.* [f. PERI- after PERFUSE *v.* 3.] *trans.* To subject to an enveloping flow of liquid. So **ˈperifused** *ppl. a.*

1969 *Lancet* 25 Oct. 882/1 (*heading*) Dynamic aspects of proinsulin release from perifused rat pancreas. **1972** *Diabetes* XXI. 989/2 The islets were perifused with glucose (1·0 mg./ml.). **1974** [see PERIFUSION]. **1975** *Nature* 1 May 71/1 Cycloheximide (5 μM) was added to the medium used to perifuse one group of halved pituitaries whereas the other group received only the control medium. **1978** *Ibid.* 19 Jan. 272/1 (*caption*) Effect of D-glucose on potassium efflux.., and insulin release.. from perifused rat islets.

perifusion (pɛrɪˈfjuːʒən). *Med.* [f. PERI- after PERFUSION d.] The action or process of perifusing.

1969 *Lancet* 25 Oct. 882/1 We used a perifusion system in which small pieces of pancreas are washed by a continuous flow of buffer. Although, unlike perfusion systems, this method does not utilise an intact vascular bed it has the advantage of permitting simultaneous control and test experiments to be done on the same pancreas. **1974** *Jrnl. Endocrinol.* LXIII. 23P The glands were perifused with KRBGA only for a period of 1 to 2 h and then challenged by 5 min perifusion with hypothalamic extract in KRBGA. **1978** *Nature* 19 Jan. 272/2 A perifusion system was used to monitor continuously the dynamics of $^{42}K^+$ efflux from preloaded isolated rat islets.

perigale, -all, variants of PAREGAL *Obs.*

perigastric, -gastritis: see PERI- a, c.

‖**perigastrula** (pɛrɪˈgæstruːlə). *Embryol.* [mod.L. (Haeckel 18..) f. PERI- + GASTRULA.] The GASTRULA arising from a PERIBLASTIC ovum. Hence **periˈgastrular** *a.* So **perigastruˈlation**, the formation of a perigastrula.

1876 LANKESTER in *Q. Jrnl. Microsc. Sc.* XVI. 63 The invagination of the Periblastula to form the Perigastrula. **1879** tr. *Haeckel's Evol. Man* I. viii. 200 Surface cleavage results in a Bladder-gastrula (*Perigastrula*).. the usual form among Articulated Animals.

perigee (ˈpɛrɪdʒiː). *Astr.* Forms: see below. [In current form, a. F. *périgée* (1557 in Hatz.-Darm.), ad. 15–16th c. L. *perigēum*, *perigæum* (cf. *musée*:—*musæum*, etc.), ad. late Gr. περίγειον, in Ptolemy, 'perigee', neuter of περίγειος adj., 'close around the earth', f. περί around + γέα, γῆ the earth. In earlier Eng. use the word was used in its Gr. or L. form (*-geon*, *-gæon*, *-geum*, *-gæum*).]

1. That point in the orbit of a planet at which it is nearest to the earth. In the Ptolemaic astronomy, applicable to any planet; now usually restricted to the moon and artificial satellites; rarely used of the position of the sun when the earth is in *perihelion*. Opposed to APOGEE 1.

α. In form **perigeon, -gæon, -geum, -gæum**; pl. **-a**, †**-ons**, †**-ums**; phrase *in perigeo.*

1594 BLUNDEVIL *Exerc.* VII. xliv. 344 b, His [the sun's] swift motion is when he is in the opposite point to the *Auge*, called *Perigeon*. **1603** SIR C. HEYDON *Jud. Astrol.* xi. 248 Those points which we call *Apogæa*, or *Perigæa*. **1621** BURTON *Anat. Mel.* II. ii. IV. (1651) 284 The motion of the planets, their magnitudes, apogeums, perigeums, excentricities. **1682** *Phil. Trans.* XIII. 82 The Satellite was then in *Perigæo*. **1704** J. HARRIS *Lex. Techn.* I, *Perigæon*, or *Perigæum*, is a Point in the Heavens, wherein a Planet is said to be in its nearest Distance possibly from the Earth. **1715** CHEYNE *Philos. Princ. Nat. Relig.* I. 213 If the Moon is then in her *Perigeum*. **1794** SULLIVAN *View Nat.* I. 393 When both luminaries are in the equator, and the moon in perigeo. **1799** W. TOOKE *View Russian Emp.* I. 56 Four [days] before the full moon, two after its transit through the perigaeum. **1844** LINGARD *Anglo-Sax. Ch.* (1845) II. xi. 173 From Pliny ..[they] inferred, that in the perigeum their velocity must be apparently increased.

β. In form †**perigé**, †**perige, perigee.**

1594 J. DAVIS *Seaman's Secr.* I. Wks. (Hakl. Soc.) 245 Her [the moon's] swift motion is in the opposite of auge or perigee. **1598** SYLVESTER *Du Bartas* II. ii. IV. *Columnes* 605 What Epicicle meaneth, and Con-centrik, With Apogé, Perigé, and Eccentrik. **1638** WILKINS *New World* I. (1684) 53 If there were any Light proper to the Moon, then would that Plannet appear Brightest when she is Eclipsed in her Perige, being nearest to the Earth. **1642** H. MORE *Song of Soul* II. i. II. vi, As Cynthia in her stouping Perigee, That deeper wades in the earths duskish Cone. **1705** C. PURSHALL *Mech. Macrocosm* 119 The Moon is not.. always.. in Perigee, when in Opposition to the Sun. **1834** *Nat. Philos., Astron.* i. 35/1 (U. Kn. Soc.) The sun is in perigee about the 30th of December. **1834** MRS. SOMERVILLE *Connex. Phys.*

Sc. xiii. (1835) 115 The spring tides are much increased when the moon is in perigee, because she is then nearest to the earth. **1962** J. GLENN in *Into Orbit* 142 We planned for an apogee, or high point, of about 145 miles and a perigee or low point, of about 85 miles. **1966** *Electronics* 3 Oct. 179 It will orbit out to an apogee of 138,000 miles for the interplanetary readings and then dip back to a perigee of 120 miles.

†**2.** The point of the heaven at which the sun has the least altitude at noon; i.e. at the winter solstice. Opp. to APOGEE 2. *Obs.*

1640 G. WATTS tr. *Bacon's Adv. Learn.* 146 The *Apogée* or middle point; and *Perigée* or lowest point of heaven. **1646** SIR T. BROWNE *Pseud. Ep.* VI. v. 293 In the Apogeum or highest point (which happeneth in Cancer) it is not so hot under that Tropick on this side the Equator as unto the other side in the Perigeum or lowest part of the Eccentric.

3. *fig.* (Cf. APOGEE 3.)

1651 BIGGS *New Disp.* 155 Diseases in *Perigæo* or declination. **1662** GLANVILL *Lux Orient.* xiv. 119 They have had their Perigæ's as well as their Apogæ's;..their Verges towards the body and its joys as well as their aspires to nobler..objects. **1670** EACHARD *Cont. Clergy* 54 Sometimes he withdraws himself into the apogæum of doubt, sorrow, and despair; but then he comes again into the perigæum of joy, content, and assurance.

So **peri'geal, peri'gean** *adjs.* [f. L. *perigē-um* + -AL[1], -AN], of or pertaining to perigee.

1743 *Phil. Trans.* XLVIII. 166 A new method for measuring the difference between the apogeal and perigeal diameters of the sun. **1812** WOODHOUSE *Astron.* xxxiii. 313 The apogean and perigean lunar distances. **1867–77** G. F. CHAMBERS *Astron.* II. i. 172 The Moon being..in a perigean position.

‖**perigenesis** (pɛrɪ'dʒɛnɪsɪs). *Biol.* [mod.L., f. Gr. περί round, about + GENESIS.] Haeckel's term for a theory of reproduction which attributes the phenomena to rhythmical vibrations of plastidules or protoplasmic molecules; 'wave-generation'.

1879 COPE *Orig. Fittest* I. vi. 229 The Dynamic Theory of reproduction I proposed in 1871, and it has been since adopted by Haeckel under the name of perigenesis.

periglacial (pɛrɪ'gleɪsɪəl, -ʃəl, -ʃɪəl), *a.* *Geomorphol.* [ad. G. *periglazial* (W. Łoziński 1909, in *Bull. internat. de l'Acad. des Sci. de Cracovie*: *Classe des Sci. math. et nat.* I. 16): see PERI-[1] and GLACIAL *a.*] Characteristic of or being a region where the influence of an adjacent ice sheet or glacier, or of frost action, is important in forming or modifying the landscape.

1928 *Amer. Jrnl. Sci.* XVI. 163 The complete realization that continental glaciation implies that a zone of periglacial climate borders the ice should lead to interesting and fruitful studies of the zone immediately south of our extensive glacial boundary. **1936** *Proc. Prehist. Soc.* II. 61 Although the Thames Valley was not actually invaded by ice..it was subject to peri-glacial phenomena. **1954** *Sci. News* XXXIII. 67 The processes of earth sculpture operating in periglacial conditions, perhaps a considerable distance from the ice-front, produce deposits and landforms of a special type. **1967** *Jrnl. Glaciol.* VI. 551 The limited earlier work in Southern Africa suggested that the Pleistocene climate was too dry for glaciation to have occurred, but the existence of oversteepened slopes, solifluction slumps and cirques is indicative of a periglacial environment. **1973** *Boreas* II. 9 Bonafide 'periglacial' forms and deposits of late Pleistocene age are present in the Drakensberg and adjacent parts of the northeastern Cape Province.

Hence **peri'glacially** *adv.*, in or by a periglacial environment.

1941 *Trans. R. Soc. Edin.* LX. 406 The Thames lay periglacially to the ice-sheets of East Anglia. **1962** *Proc. Yorkshire Geol. Soc.* XXXIII. 336 Dartmoor..preserves the finest set of periglacially formed tors in Britain. **1972** *Trans. Norfolk & Norwich Naturalists' Soc.* XXII. 229 (*heading*) Periglacially modified chalk and chalk ridge-diapirs from Norwich, Norfolk.

,periglaci'ation. *Geomorphol.* [f. PERI- + GLACIATION, after prec.] The state of being subject to a periglacial climate; periglacial processes collectively.

1957 M. T. TE PUNGA in *Tijdschr. Koninklijk Nederlandsch. Aardijkskundig Genootschap* LXXIV. 408 Wind-worked pebbles and boulders..are well known as relics of periglaciation in many parts of the world. **1963** *Geomorphol. Abstr.* 38 (*heading*) Periglaciation of Canada. **1968** *Geogr. Abstr.* A. 30 The scarp..was formed during the Quaternary when the region underwent severe periglaciation with immense frost riving and modification of plateau valleys. **1970** R. J. SMALL *Study of Landforms* i. 2 Our knowledge of the vital role of periglaciation in shaping the landscapes of present-day temperate areas is based almost wholly on analysis by geomorphologists of the distribution and character of solifluxion gravels, 'head', 'coombe rock' and the like.

periglandular to **-gnathic**: see PERI- a, b.

†**pe'rignous,** *a.* *Obs. rare*[−1]. For *perineous = PERINEAL.

1541 R. COPLAND *Guydon's Quest. Chirurg.* I iv, Where oughte incysyon to be made for the stone in the bladder? At the necke without the seame perignous.

perigon ('pɛrɪgɒn). *Geom.* [irreg. f. PERI- + Gr. γωνία angle.] The angular magnitude traced out by a line in turning once completely around one end as centre; an angular quantity of 360 degrees, or four right angles.

1868 SANDEMAN *Pelicotetics* 304 A right angle is both one half of a hemiperigon or a hemisemiperigon, and one fourth of a perigon. **1892** G. B. HALSTED *Elem. Synth. Geom.* 6 If we turn still more, until the moving ray has made a complete rotation..the angle is called a perigon.

perigonal (pə'rɪgənəl), *a.* [irreg. f. PERIGONE + -AL[1].] = PERIGONIAL.

1881 CARPENTER *Microsc.* §339 (ed. 6) 411 The antheridia or male organs of *Sphagnaceæ*..are grouped in catkins at the tips of lateral branches, each of the imbricated perigonal leaves enclosing a single globose antheridium on a slender footstalk.

perigone ('pɛrɪgəʊn). Also in L. form peri'gonium. [a. F. *périgone*, ad. mod.L. *perigonium*, f. Gr. περί round + γόνος offspring, seed.

Perigonium was introduced by Hedwig (1787) for the floral envelopes generally, and also used by him specially of Mosses; it was applied by Ehrhart in 1788 to the floral envelopes in Phanerogams: so *périgone* by De Candolle 1813.]

1. *Bot.* **a.** = PERIANTH 1 b.

1819 LINDLEY tr. *Richard's Observ. Fruits and Seeds* 13 *note*, That part in *Carex* which Linnæus called a nectarium ..is perhaps, as Mr. Brown has observed, a true *perigonium*. **1832** —— *Introd. Bot.* 114 Some writers, among whom are Link and De Candolle, have substituted *Perigonium* for *Perianthium*... Ehrhart, with whom the name Perigonium originated, called it double when the calyx and corolla are.. distinct, and single if they are not distinguishable. **1880** GRAY *Struct. Bot.* vi. §1 (ed. 6) 164 Floral Envelopes, Perianth, or Perigone, the floral leaves or coverings. *Ibid.*, *Perigonium*, a later term [than perianthium], has the advantage of meaning something around the reproductive organs.

b. The leafy investment of the male organs of mosses; the male 'perianth' (PERIANTH 1 c).

1863 BERKELEY *Brit. Mosses* Gloss. 312 *Perigonium*, the male inflorescence. **1875** BENNETT & DYER tr. *Sachs' Bot.* 320 The male perianth (*Perigonium*) [in mosses]..is of three different forms. **1889** BENNETT & MURRAY *Cryptog. Bot.* 142 The male perianth or *perigone* is usually composed of broader, shorter, and thicker leaves..not unfrequently red.

2. *Zool.* A sac formed by the outer parts of the gonophore of a hydroid.

1871 G. J. ALLMAN *Monogr. Gymnoblastic Hydroids* I. p. xv, *Perigonium*.., the walls of a sporosac by which the generative elements are confined, and in which, when fully developed, three laminæ may be demonstrated. **1888** —— in *Challenger Rep.* XXIII. II. p. xxxv, The *perigonium* or sac formed by the more external parts of the gonophore.

Hence **perigonial** (pɛrɪ'gəʊnɪəl) *a.* [mod.L. *folia perigonialia* (Hedwig)], pertaining to a perigonium.

1870 BENTLEY *Man. Bot.* (ed. 2) 366, 3 or 6 small leaves, ..termed perigonial, and constituting collectively a perigone.

‖**Périgord** (perigɔr). Also 8 (corruptly) -gorde, -go. Name of a district in the south-west of France, famous for its truffles. Hence **Périgord pie**, a meat pie flavoured with truffles; also applied to other rich or highly-seasoned pies.

1752 MRS. DELANY in *Life & Corr.* 80 A perigord pie had been sent for on the occasion, to be directed to a merchant in Dublin. **1768** *Hist.* in *Ann. Reg.* 170/2 The bill of fare.. Perigo Pye. **1900** *Westm. Gaz.* 20 Jan. 2/1 Now, if there was one delicacy above another that Ralph prized it was a Périgord pie.

Périgordian (peɪrɪ'gɔːdɪən), *a.* *Archæol.* Also Perigordian. [tr. F. *Périgordien* (D. Peyrony 1933, in *Bull. Soc. Préhist. Française* XXX. 558), f. the place-name *Périgord* (see PÉRIGORD) + -IAN.] A name given to an Upper Palaeolithic culture represented by flint tools of the kind found at Laugerie-Haute in the Périgord region of Dordogne (see quot. 1938). Also *absol.* as *sb.*

1938 *Proc. Prehist. Soc.* IV. 4 Peyrony..has found at Laugerie Haute an industry of blunted-back blades... He concludes that in the Chatelperron-Laugerie Haute-La Gravette succession we are dealing with a culture totally different from the so-called Middle Aurignacian,..and he proposes to group all those industries characterised by the blunted-back blade under the title of Perigordian. **1941** *Ann. Reg. 1940* 342 A remarkable painted cave of Perigordian art was found at Lascaux in the Dordogne. **1949** M. C. BURKITT *Old Stone Age* (ed. 2) iv. 64 The *Audi* and *Châtelperron* knife blades form an evolving series characteristic of the Périgordian element in the early Aurignacian. **1956** H. READ *Art of Sculpture* ii. 34 There can be little doubt that the so-called *Venus* of Laussel attributed by the Abbé Breuil to the Périgordian period, is such a cult object. **1970** BRAY & TRUMP *Dict. Archaeol.* 174/1 *Périgordian*, French terminology for a series of Upper Palaeolithic flint industries which are thought to represent a continuing technological tradition. *Ibid.* 174/2 No known site has a complete and unbroken 'Périgordian' sequence. **1977** D. K. BHATTACHARYA *Palaeolithic Europe* iv. 168 In 1933, Dr. Peyrony declared that what was earlier thought to be lower and upper Aurignacian, is in reality a tradition different from Aurignacian and he named this Perigordian.

‖**Perigordine** (perigɔrdin), *sb.* and *a.* Also -gour-, -jourdine. [a. F. *périgordine*, fem. of -*in*, f. *Périgord*: see PÉRIGORD.] **A.** *sb.* A country dance of Périgord, sometimes accompanied by singing; also, the music for such a dance, in lively triple rhythm.

1880 in Grove *Dict. Mus.*, Perigourdine.

B. *adj.* Of or pertaining to Périgord, esp. to the gastronomic specialities of the region.

1931 A. DE CROZE *What to eat & drink in France* 230 Sanguète périgourdine..blood of chicken browned in goose dripping with garlic, shallots, and verjuice. **1951** E. DAVID *French Country Cooking* 192 A kind of soufflé eaten cold, a Périgordine speciality. **1959** *Times* 7 Feb. 9/1 The food.. tends to be lighter, though quite as delicious as the famed Périgourdine fare farther west. **1973** *Times* 22 Mar. 15/8 (Advt.), Lovely Perigourdine house XVIIIth century.

‖**perigraphe** (pə'rɪgrəfɪ). [a. Gr. περιγραφή line drawn round, f. περί around + γραφή writing, line.] †**a.** An inscription around something. *Obs.* **b.** (See quot. 1753.)

1674 JEAKE *Arith.* (1696) 86 This piece of Coin..shewed the Vessel in which the Manna was, inscribed with the Perigraphe *Shekel Israel*. **1753** CHAMBERS *Cycl. Supp.*, *Perigraphe*, a word usually understood to express a careless or inaccurate delineation of any thing: but in Vesalius it is used to express the white lines or impressions that appear in the musculus rectus of the abdomen. [Copied by Webster 1828 with substitution of *Perigraph* for *Perigraphe*; whence in subseq. Dictionaries, with a derivative adj. *Perigraphic*.] **1956** 'H. MACDIARMID' *Stony Limits* 38 We turn in vain This way and that and but changing perigraphs gain.

perigrine, perigua, obs. forms of PEREGRINE, PIRAGUA.

Périgueux (perigœ). *Cookery.* The name of a city in the Périgord region of south-west France used *attrib.* to designate a type of sauce made with truffles.

1846 A. SOYER *Gastronomic Regenerator* 25 *Sauce Perigeux.* Put four middling-sized truffles..into a stewpan with a glass of sherry. **1877** E. S. DALLAS *Kettner's Bk. of Table* 340 Perigueux sauce..is the best brown sauce, with a glass of sherry or Marsala added to it, and a quantity of chopped truffles. **1937** X. M. BOULESTIN *Finer Cooking* II. 84 For the Sauce Périgueux.—Chop the trimmings of the truffles finely and cook them in a small saucepan with a glass of Madeira. **1956** C. BROWN et al. *Four-in-One Bk. Continental Cookery* 337 Dish up, and serve with Périgueux Sauce. **1972** G. A. BROWNE *11 Harrowhouse St.* (1973) v. 51 Next came Tournedos Rossini. Filets of beef..covered with Périgueux sauce.

‖**perigynium** (pɛrɪ'dʒɪnɪəm). *Bot.* Rarely anglicized as **perigyne** ('pɛrɪdʒɪn). [mod.L., f. Gr. περί round + γυνή woman, wife, in Bot. 'pistil'.] Name introduced by Link for a structure surrounding the ovary. In current use: **a.** A membranous sac, investing the ovary in the Sedges (*Carex*); the utriculus. **b.** A part of the leafy investment of the female organs of mosses. **c.** The membrane investing the archegonium in some liverworts (= PERIANTH 1 c).

1821 in GRAY *Nat. Arr. Brit. Pl.* I. 163. **1863** BERKELEY *Brit. Mosses* Gloss. 312 *Perigynium*, the leaves encircling the fertile bud. **1870** HOOKER *Stud. Flora* 398 Fruit in Carex enclosed in the perigynium. **1882** VINES *Sachs' Bot.* 359 A perigynium..grows round the archegonia as a special membranous envelope.

perigynous (pə'rɪdʒɪnəs), *a.* *Bot.* [f. mod.L. *perigyn-us* (Jussieu 1789) (f. Gr. περί around + γυνή wife, female, pistil) + -OUS. In mod.F. *périgyne*.] Situated around the pistil or ovary: said of the stamens when growing upon some part surrounding the ovary (either the calyx, or the corolla, or the edge of the hollowed receptacle); also said of a flower in which the stamens are so placed. Opp. to EPIGYNOUS and HYPOGYNOUS.

1807 R. A. SALISBURY in *Trans. Linn. Soc.* VIII. 1 That insertion of the Stamina which the celebrated Jussieu has denominated Perigynous. **1830** LINDLEY *Nat. Syst. Bot.* Introd. 27 Or they [stamens] contract an adhesion..with either the calyx or corolla, when they become *perigynous*. **1875** BENNETT & DYER *Sachs' Bot.* 200 The perigynous flower of a rose.

So **pe'rigyny**, the condition of being perigynous.

1880 GRAY *Struct. Bot.* vi. §3 (ed. 6) 183 The perigyny may be..merely the adnation of petals and stamens to calyx, ..or..the adnation of the calyx. **1887** *Athenæum* 10 Dec. 787/3 The shortening of the axis within the flower, giving the transition from hypogyny through perigyny to epigyny.

‖**perihelion** (pɛrɪ'hiːlɪən). *Astr.* Also 7–8 -ium. Pl. -ia. [A Græcized form of mod.L. *perihēlium* (f. Gr. περί close about + ἥλιος sun), the latter introduced by Kepler on the analogy of *perigēum*, περίγειον (see *Prodr. Dissert. Cosmographicarum*, 1596, and *Epitome Astronom. Copernic.* 1618). Cf. F. *périhélie* (1740 in Hatz.-Darm.).]

1. That point in the orbit of a planet, comet, or other heavenly body, at which it is nearest to the sun. Opp. to APHELION.

1666 *Phil. Trans.* I. 240 Not at present in the *Perihelium* of its Orbe, but nearer its *Aphelium*. **1690** LEYBOURN *Curs. Math.* 768 The *Aphelium* is P, and the *Perihelium* X. *Ibid.* 773 In Figure XXXV..*a* is the *Aphelion*, *p* the *Perihelion*. **1698** KEILL *Exam. The. Earth* (1734) 319 Comets..after their return from the Regions beyond Saturn, before they arrive at their Perihelia again. **1714** DERHAM *Astro-Theol.* VIII. iv. (1726) 237 The Comet in 1680, in its Perihelion, was above 166 times nearer the Sun than the Earth is. **1715** tr.

Gregory's Astron. I. 147 In its ascent from the Sun, from the Perihelium to the Aphelium. **1834** MRS. SOMERVILLE *Connex. Phys. Sc.* xii. (1835) 108 The return of comets to their perihelia. *Ibid.* xxxv. 374 When the comets are in perihelio. **1880** A. R. WALLACE *Isl. Life* viii. 138 During the period we are now discussing..the south polar area, having its winter in perihelion, would have had less ice.

attrib. **1676** HALLEY in Rigaud *Corr. Sci. Men* (1841) I. 239 The perihelion distance [of a planet]. **1867–77** G. F. CHAMBERS *Astron.* IV. ii. 292, Dec. 9, 1838, was the epoch of the next perihelion passage. **1881** PROCTOR *Poetry Astron.* xi. 397 Clouds of meteoric matter..making their perihelion swoop around the sun.

2. *fig.* Highest point, 'zenith'.

1804 W. TAYLOR in *Ann. Rev.* II. 232 Mr. Pitt was now in the perihelion of his popularity. **1873** H. SPENCER *Stud. Sociol.* ix. 239 From the perihelion of patriotism he is carried to the aphelion of anti-patriotism.

Hence **peri'helial, peri'helian** *adjs.*, of or belonging to perihelion. (Now *rare* or *Obs.*)

1690 LEYBOURN *Curs. Math.* 772 As is the Aphelian Distance of the Planet to the Perihelian Distance. **1738** MACHIN in *Phil. Trans.* XL. 220 The Perihelian Distance.. is many times less than the Semi-distance of the Foci. **1784** *Phil. Trans.* LXXV. 144 To find the position of the axis and the perihelial distance.

perihepatic, -hepatitis: see PERI- a, c.

perihermenial (ˌpɛrɪhəˈmiːnɪəl), *a.* [f. Gr. περὶ ἑρμηνείας: see below. Cf. med.L. '*periermeniæ*, Interpretationes' (Du Cange).] Pertaining to or characteristic of Aristotle's treatise *Περὶ ἑρμηνείας* ('concerning interpretation'); also, Of or pertaining to interpretation. Also (erron.) **periher'miacal.**

a **1529** SKELTON *Replyc.* Wks. 1843 I. 209 Surmysed vnsurely in their perihermeniall principles. [*margin*] Perihermenias, Latine interpretatio, &c. **1716** M. DAVIES *Athen. Brit.* II. 151 [He] could never be prevail'd upon..by the Perihermeniacal Innuendo's of both Universities..to undertake..the History of the Reformation of the Church of England. **1890** *Cent. Dict.* s.v., Aristotle's doctrine in this book [*Περὶ ἑρμηνείας*] does not precisely agree with that of his 'Analytics', and is called *perihermenial doctrine.*

peri-intestinal: see PERI- a.

perijove (ˈpɛrɪdʒəʊv). *Astr.* [= F. *périjove* (1766 in Bailly *Essai* 80), in mod.L. *perijovium*, f. PERI- + L. *Jov-em* Jupiter, after *perigee, perihelion.*] That point in the orbit of any one of Jupiter's satellites at which it is nearest to Jupiter.

1837 WHEWELL *Hist. Induct. Sc.* VII. iv. II. 229 Determining the direction of the motions of the perijove and node of each satellite. **1838** *Penny Cycl.* XI. 385/2 The first satellite..will either be moving from perijove towards apojove, or from apojove towards perijove. **1881** *Nature* XXIII. 298/2.

perikaryon (pɛrɪˈkærɪɒn). *Anat.* Pl. **-karya.** [f. PERI- + Gr. κάρυον nut, kernel.] The cell-body of a neurone; that part of a nerve cell which contains the nucleus.

1897 M. FOSTER *Text Bk. Physiol.* (ed. 7) III. i. 928 It will be convenient to distinguish by a separate name between the processes whether axon or dendrite, and the part from which these processes start, namely the body of the cell surrounding the nucleus; the latter might be called the perikaryon. **1961** *New Scientist* 12 Oct. 117/3 In the invertebrates the [nerve] fibre is not so long and does not usually end on a blood vessel; the perikaryon instead provides more or less all the available storage space. **1975** *Nature* 25 Dec. 746/2 Brain tissue..after this treatment exhibits only weak nonspecific fluorescence with some bright yellow autofluorescent granules in large neuronal perikarya. **1977** P. B. & J. S. MEDAWAR *Life Sci.* xv. 122 The most obviously cell-like part of the neurone is called the cell-body or perikaryon, and this houses the nucleus.

peril (ˈpɛrɪl), *sb.* Forms: 3- peril; also 3–5 perile, -yl, 4 -ele, 4–5 -ille, -yle, -elle, 4–6 -el, 4–7 -ill, 5 -aill, -eill, -eyl(l, 5–6 -ylle, -ayle, 5–7 -ell, -yll; 4–6 paril, etc.; 6 perr-; (also 5 peral, -ol, pearl, 6 pearil, pearrell). [a. F. *péril* (10th c. in Littré) = Pr. *peril, perilh*, Cat. *peril*, It. *periglio*:—L. *perīculum, perīclum* experiment, trial, risk, danger, f. root of *ex-peri-rī* to try, make trial of + *-culum*, suffix naming instruments.]

1. a. The position or condition of being imminently exposed to the chance of injury, loss, or destruction; risk, jeopardy, danger.

a **1225** *Ancr. R.* 194 Gostlich fondunge..mei beon, uor þe peril, icleoped breoste wunde. **1297** R. GLOUC. (Rolls) 2208 Of peril a se & eke a lond. *a* **1300** *Cursor M.* 24852 (Cott.) Þe mariners..war neuer in parel [*v.r.* perel] mar. **1390** GOWER *Conf.* II. 168 Saturnus after his exil Fro Crete cam in gret peril. ? *a* **1400** LYDG. *Chorle & Byrde* 183 Who dredeth no paryll, in paryll he shall falle. *a* **1533** LD. BERNERS *Huon* lxxxiii. 257 He was neuer in his lyfe in suche perell. **1575** *Mirr. Mag., Dk. Somerset* xliv, Constant I was in my Princes quarel, To dye or liue and spared for no parel. **1595** SHAKS. *John* III. i. 295 The perill of our curses light on thee So heauy, as thou shalt not shake them off. **1749** SMOLLETT *Regicide* II. viii, Glory Is the fair child of peril. **1832** W. IRVING *Alhambra* II. 166 Having commanded at Malaga during a time of peril and confusion. **1875** JOWETT *Plato* (ed. 2) V. 128 In the hour of peril.

b. Const. (*a*) *of* that which is exposed to danger (chiefly with *life*); (*b*) *of* the evil fate that threatens, or (*obs.* or *arch.*) *of* the cause of danger; †(*c*) *to* with *inf.* (*obs.*).

1340 HAMPOLE *Pr. Consc.* 161 In grete perille of saul es þat man þat has witt and mynde and na gude can. *c* **1450** *St. Cuthbert* (Surtees) 1740 In perill of þair lyues þai stode. **1596** SHAKS. *Merch. V.* II. ii. 173 To be in perill of my life with the edge of a featherbed. **1790** PALEY *Horæ Paul.* Wks. 1825 III. 174 He acquitted himself of this commission at the peril of his life. **1840** DICKENS *Barn. Rudge* ii, You were never in such peril of your life as you have been within these few moments.

c **1375** *Cursor M.* 26193 (Fairf.) Quen men is in perel [*Cott.* wath] of dede. **1377** LANGL. *P. Pl.* B. XIV. 301 Þorw þe pas of altoun Pouerte myȝte passe with-oute peril of robbynge. **1481** CAXTON *Myrr.* II. vi. 76 Kynge Alysaundre ..eschewed the parell and daunger of thise olyfauntes. **1553** BALE *Vocacyon* in *Harl. Misc.* (Malh.) I. 330 In parell of the sea, in parell of shypwrack. **1634** SIR T. HERBERT *Trav.* 5 The..ship-boyes were in perill of those Sharkes. **1876** GEO. ELIOT *Dan. Der.* xlviii, A vessel in peril of wreck.

c **1385** CHAUCER *L.G.W.* 1277 *Dido*, There as he was in paril for to sterue. *c* **1489** CAXTON *Blanchardyn* lii. 201 He was in pereyll to lose hym selfe and all his ooste. **1596** SHAKS. *Tam. Shr.* Induct. ii. 124 In perill to incurre your former malady.

2. (with *a* and *pl.*) A case or cause of peril; *pl.* dangers, risks.

peril of the sea (Marine Insurance): see quot. 1872.

a **1300** *Cursor M.* 4051 (Cott.) O perils [*v.r.* perelis] þat he fell in Sum-quat to tell i sal bigin. **1382** WYCLIF *2 Cor.* xi. 26 In perelis of flodis, in perelis of theues, in perelis of kyn, in perels of hethen men [etc.]. **1450–80** tr. *Secreta Secret.* 21 Pereylis and disesis that are to come of werres, pestilencis [etc.]. *a* **1548** HALL *Chron., Hen. IV* 15 b, To auenture themselfes on a newe chance and a doubtfull parell. **1774** GOLDSM. *Nat. Hist.* (1776) VI. 181 Scarce one in a thousand survives the numerous perils of its youth. **1817** W. SELWYN *Law Nisi Prius* (ed. 4) II. 893 It is the province of the jury to determine, whether the cause of the loss be a peril of the sea or not. **1872** *Wharton's Law Lex.* s.v., Perils of the sea ..are strictly the natural accidents peculiar to the water, but the law has extended this phrase to comprehend events not attributable to natural causes, as captures by pirates, and losses by collision, where no blame is attachable to either ship, or at all events to the injured ship. **1875** JOWETT *Plato* (ed. 2) I. 93 Soldiers,..who are courageous in perils by sea. **1884** *Manch. Exam.* 3 May 5/1 The certain perils of such an alliance.

3. Phrases. **†a.** ***at all peril***(*s*: at whatever risk; be the consequences what they may. ***by the*** (***for, up***) ***peril of my soul, upon my peril***, etc.: used as asseverations. ***in peril of***: at the risk of, under the penalty of (see also 1 b). *Obs.*

13.. *E.E. Allit. P.* C. 85 At alle peryles, quoth þe prophete, I aproche hit no nerre. **1362** LANGL. *P. Pl.* A. VI. 47 Nai, bi þe peril of my soule, quod pers. *c* **1386** CHAUCER *Wife's Prol.* 561 My gaye scarlet gytes, Thise wormes ne thise Motthes ne thise mytes Vpon my peril frete hem neuer a deel. —— *Merch. T.* 1127 Vp peril of my soule I shal nat lyen. **1470–85** MALORY *Arthur* IV. i. 119 Ye lady, on my parel, ye shal see hit. **1607** SHAKS. *Cor.* III. iii. 102 Wee.. banish him our Citie In perill of precipitation From off the Rocke Tarpeian. [**1820** BYRON *Mar. Fal.* I. ii, That I speak the truth, My peril be the proof.]

b. ***at*** (**†*on, to***) ***your*** (***his***, etc.) ***peril***: you (etc.) taking the risk or responsibility of the consequences: esp. in commands, or warnings, referring to the risk incurred by disregard or disobedience.

1433 *Rolls of Parlt.* IV. 477/1 Such as they woll answere fore atte here perille. **1480** CAXTON *Chron. Eng.* ccxiv. 200 He sente hastely that they shold not fyght, and yf they dyd that they shold stonde to hir owne perylle. ? *a* **1550** *Freiris of Berwik* 541 in *Dunbar's Poems* (1893) 303 Gif thow dois nocht, on thy awin perrel beid [= be it]. **1590** SHAKS. *Mids. N.* III. ii. 175 Disparage not the faith thou dost not know, Lest to thy perill thou abide it deare. **1632** MASSINGER *City Madam* IV. ii, Master Shrieve and Master Marshal, On your perils, do your offices. **1664** in *Buccleuch MSS.* (Hist. MSS. Comm.) I. 541 As they will answer the contrary at their perils. **1696** PHILLIPS (ed. 5), *Peril*,..sometimes used by way of threatning. Do such a thing at your Peril. **1719** DE FOE *Crusoe* II. xi, We..bade them keep off at their peril. **1832** HT. MARTINEAU *Hill & Valley* iii. 46 Shew yourselves at your peril. **1881** R. BUCHANAN *God & Man* I. 141, 'I must do my master's bidding.' 'At your peril! I have but to give the word, and they would duck you in the horsepond.'

†c. ***without the peril of***: beyond the (dangerous) reach or power of: cf. DANGER *sb.* 1 b. *Obs. rare.*

1590 SHAKS. *Mids. N.* IV. i. 158 To be gone from Athens, where we might be Without the perill of the Athenian Law.

†4. A matter of danger; a perilous or dangerous matter. Const. ***it is peril***, it is dangerous (to do something). *Obs.*

1297 R. GLOUC. (Rolls) 6786 Þe heiemen of þe lond wolde hom al day mene þat hii nadde non eir of him & þat gret peril it was Vor þer miȝte com to al þe lond gret wo uor such cas. *c* **1386** CHAUCER *Wife's Prol.* 89 Peril is bothe fyr and tow tassemble. *c* **1400** MAUNDEV. (Roxb.) xxvi. 123 It es grete peril to pursue þe Tartarenes. *a* **1450** *Knt. de la Tour* (1868) 60 Whedir it were perelle to do her counsaile or not. *c* **1540** *Pilgr. T.* 164 in *Thynne's Animadv.* 81 You know what perrele it is togither to ley hyrdis fast vnto the fyer.

5. *attrib.* and *Comb.*, as ***peril-proof, -daring*** adjs.; **peril point** *U.S. Econ.* (see quot. 1965).

1605 SYLVESTER *Du Bartas* II. iii. II. *Fathers* 75 A broad thick breastplate..High peril-proof against affliction. **1807** MONTGOMERY *W. Indies* II. 141 The valiant seized in peril-daring fight. **1948** *Congress. Rec.* 26 May 6503/2 No foreign trade agreement could be entered into until the Tariff Commission reports to the President its findings as to the so-called peril-point below which tariffs may not be cut. **1949** *Sun* (Baltimore) 11 July 10/2 The main innovation in the Republican program is the so-called 'peril-point' report which must be made to the President by the Tariff Commission. **1949** *Economist* 17 Sept., *Peril Points.* This year's battle over American tariff policy opened just as the Administration was assuring Sir Stafford Cripps and Mr Bevin that the United States would pursue policies appropriate to a great creditor nation. **1961** *Ibid.* 9 Dec. 1025/2 The President's authority to lower tariffs being renewed grudgingly but limited by 'peril points' and 'escape clauses'. **1965** *McGraw-Hill Dict. Mod. Econ.* 376 *Peril point*, the maximum cut in a U.S. import duty which could be made for a given commodity without causing serious injury to domestic producers or to a similar commodity.

Hence **'perilless** *a.*, without or free from peril.

a **1614** SYLVESTER *Litt. Bartas* 313 In their chamber pain-lesse, peril-lesse.

peril (ˈpɛrɪl), *v.* [f. prec. sb.]

1. *trans.* To put in peril, expose to danger; to imperil, endanger, risk, hazard.

1567 MAPLET *Gr. Forest* 37 b, If..hir yong be hurt or perilled in their eiesight. **1586** JAS. VI in Ellis *Orig. Lett.* Ser. I. III. 19 It micht perrell my reputation amongst my subjectis. **1647** TRAPP *Comm. Rev.* i. 5 Jonathan perilled his life..for love of David. **1832** HT. MARTINEAU *Each & All* iii. 34 The world would be perilled by their coming together. **1856** KANE *Arct. Expl.* I. xv. 178 It threatened to encroach upon our anchorage, and peril the safety of the vessel.

2. To take the risk of, venture upon. *rare.*

1849 W. E. AYTOUN *Edin. after Flodden* x, Thou hast done a deed of daring Had been perilled but by few.

†3. *intr.* To be in danger. *Obs. rare.*

1641 MILTON *Ch. Govt.* II. iii. Wks. (1847) 50 To start back, and glob itself upward from..any soil wherewith it may peril to stain itself. **1647** TRAPP *Comm. Matt.* xiv. 23 Whilst the disciples were perilling, and well-nigh perishing, Christ was praying for them.

Hence **'perilled** *ppl. a.*, exposed to danger.

1845–6 TRENCH *Huls. Lect.* Ser. I. vii. 120 To do battle for some perilled truth. **1846** —— *Mirac.* xxxii. (1862) 449 The natural instinct of defence and love to their perilled Lord.

perilaryngeal, -laryngitis: see PERI- a, c.

†peri'leptic, *a.* *Obs. rare*[−1]. [ad. Gr. περιληπτικός, f. περιλαμβάνειν to comprehend, f. περί around + λαμβάνειν to take, seize.] Comprehensive; characterized by comprehension.

1678 CUDWORTH *Intell. Syst.* I. iii. §37. 163 The things in the world, are not administred merely by Spermatick Reasons, but by Perileptick (that is, Comprehensive Intellectual Reasons).

perill, obs. form of PEARL, PERIL.

‖perilla (pəˈrɪlə). *Bot.* [mod.L. (Linnæus, 1764); origin unknown.] A small genus of Labiates, natives of eastern Asia; esp. *P. ocimoides*, grown as a half-hardy ornamental plant on account of its deep-purple leaves.

1788 REES *Chambers's Cycl.*, *Perilla*, in Botany... There is only one species. **1887** *G. Nicholson's Dict. Garden.*, *Perilla*, a genus consisting of only two or three species,..natives of the mountains of India and China. **1900** *Echo* 12 June 1/5 Geraniums, calceolarias, perilla, and coleus were not allowed to intrude their weedy presence.

perilobular: see PERI- a.

perilous (ˈpɛrɪləs), *a.* (*adv.*) Forms: see PERIL, and cf. PARLOUS. [a. AF. *perillous* = OF. *perillos, -eus*, mod.F. *périlleux*:—L. *perīculōs-um*, f. *perīcul-um*: see PERIL and -OUS.]

1. Fraught with peril; causing or occasioning great danger; full of risk; dangerous; hazardous.

c **1290** *S. Eng. Leg.* I. 258/84 Heo come to a deop watur and perilous. *c* **1350** *Will. Palerne* 1191 Þere þe pres was perelouste, he priked in formest. *c* **1375** *Sc. Leg. Saints* xxix. (*Placidas*) 2 Lat penance is rycht perolouse. *c* **1470** *Gol. & Gaw.* 1104 Ane wounder peralous poynt. **1484** CAXTON *Fables of Æsop* III. xx, To conuerse with folke of euylle lyf is a thyng moche peryllous. **1545** RAYNOLD *Byrth Mankynde* 62 This is the parellous maner of byrth that is. **1643** PRYNNE *Sov. Power Parl.* I. (ed. 2) 21 Put to death as a perilous enemy to the Kingdome. **1789** BELSHAM *Ess.* I. viii. 165 Mr. Locke and his friends are reduced to a most perplexing and perilous dilemma. **1836** W. IRVING *Astoria* III. 165 The latter felt they were in a perilous predicament. **1849** MACAULAY *Hist. Eng.* vi. II. 32 The most arduous and perilous duties of friendship.

†2. Capable of inflicting or doing serious harm; arousing a feeling of peril; greatly to be dreaded or avoided; dreadful, terrible, awful; = PARLOUS 2. *Obs.*

c **1386** CHAUCER *Reeve's T.* 269 Alayn auyse thee The Millere is a perilous man. *c* **1430** LYDG. *Min. Poems* (Percy Soc.) 119 A perilous clymbyng whan beggers up arise To hye estate. **1525** LD. BERNERS *Froiss.* II. ccxlii. [ccxxxix.] 747 They are the peryloust people of the worlde, and most outragyoust if they be vp. **1530** PALSGR. 588/1 It is a perylous noyse, I tell you, to here a bee hosse in a boxe. *a* **1548** HALL *Chron., Rich. III* 29 b, When any blusteringe wynde perelous thunder or terrible tempest, chansed. **1579** W. WILKINSON *Confut. Familye of Loue* 26 b, Instructed how with a malitious mynde and perilous wit, he might runne descant at will. **1592** SHAKS. *Rom. & Jul.* I. iii. 53 It had vpon it brow..A perilous knock, and it cryed bitterly. **1606** HOLLAND *Sueton.* 134 With her perilous fingers..shee would not sticke to lay at the face and eyes of other small Children playing together with her.

†B. as *adv.* = PARLOUS B. *Obs.*

1598 R. BERNARD tr. *Terence, Heautont.* III. iii, This is a perilous naughtie queane. **1849** JAMES *Woodman* xii, Lovel, you look perilous grim.

perilously (ˈpɛrɪləslɪ), *adv.* [f. prec. + -LY[2].] In a manner involving peril; very dangerously.

1340 *Ayenb.* 254 Hy ulyȝþ perilousliche zuo þet hy hyre spilþ, and ualþ ofte into þe grines of þe uoȝelere of helle.

1377 LANGL. *P. Pl.* B. Prol. 151 A cat of a courte..pleyde wiþ hem perilouslych. 1481 CAXTON *Godeffroy* clxxiv. 258 Wherof cam grete stenche..wherof the ayer was corrupte ouer peryllously. 1561 T. NORTON *Calvin's Inst.* IV. xx. (1634) 740 Many herein doe perillously erre. 1624 SANDERSON *Serm.* I. 112 People, as they are suspicious, will be talking paralously. 1709 STRYPE *Ann. Ref.* I. xl. 413 The Queen fell perillously sick. 1897 MARY KINGSLEY *W. Africa* 596 Head man comes perilously near breaking his neck by frequent falls among the rocks.

perilousness. [f. as prec. + -NESS.] The quality of being perilous; dangerousness.

1571 GOLDING *Calvin on Ps.* Ep. Ded. 3 The perilousnes of this present time. 1727 in BAILEY vol. II. 1852 MISS YONGE *Cameos* (1877) IV. iv. 45 A sense of the perilousness of the post to any honest man.

†**'perilsome,** *a. Obs.* [f. PERIL *sb.* + -SOME.] Fraught with peril; perilous.

1593 NASHE *Christ's T.* Wks. (Grosart) IV. 239 They so poyson the ayre..that from them proceedeth thys perrilsome contagion. 1628 WITHER *Brit. Remem.* III. 241 No time to come Can send me to a place, so perilsome, That I shall feare it. 1650 DAVENANT *Gondibert* Pref., The people be often the greater enemy, and more perilsome, being nearest.

perilune (pɛrɪ'luːn). *Astr.* [f. PERI- + L. *lūna* moon; cf. PERIGEE, PERIHELION, etc.] That point at which a spacecraft in lunar orbit is closest to the moon's centre: applied esp. if the spacecraft was launched from the moon.

1960 *Aeroplane* XCIX. 638/2 Lunar gravity should draw the probe into an orbit which has a period of about 10 hr., an apolune (farthest distance from the Moon) of approximately 3,000 miles and a perilune (closest distance) of 1,500 miles. 1968 *Sci. Jrnl.* Oct. 5/2 The orbital velocity at perilune—altitude 100 km, 2°N latitude—was about 7200 km/hour relative to the Moon. 1969 *Nature* 12 July 129/2 Choosing the major axis of the orbit to pass through the mascon..is equally effective in nullifying the orbital instability represented by cumulatively increasing displacements of perilune and apolune.

perilymph ('pɛrɪlɪmf). *Anat.* [mod. f. PERI- + LYMPH.] The clear fluid contained within the osseous labyrinth of the internal ear, and surrounding the membranous labyrinth. (Distinguished from ENDOLYMPH.)

1836–9 TODD *Cycl. Anat.* II. 536/2 In birds the perilymph is in much less quantity than in the mammifera. 1879 CALDERWOOD *Mind & Br.* iii. 74 The vestibule..has a bony wall, and in its cavity is the fluid perilymph in which the membranous vestibule is suspended.

perilymphangial, etc.: see PERI-.

ˌ**perilym'phatic,** *a.* [In 1, f. PERILYMPH + -ATIC; in 2, f. PERI- + LYMPHATIC.]

1. Pertaining to the perilymph.

1877 BURNETT *Ear* 145 The perilymphatic cavity is inserted into the lymphatic tract of all vertebrates. 1899 *Allbutt's Syst. Med.* VII. 548 The peri-lymphatic space of the internal ear.

2. Situated around the lymphatic vessels.

1879 BUMSTEAD *Venereal Diseases* (ed. 4) 612 This perilymphatic inflammation is found in the thickness of the capsule of Glisson.

perimancie, obs. form of PYROMANCY.

‖**perimeningitis** (ˌpɛrɪmiːnɪn'dʒaɪtɪs). *Path.* [mod.L., f. *perimēninx* dura mater (f. Gr. περί around + μῆνιγξ membrane, pia mater) + -ITIS.] Inflammation of the *Perimeninx*, or dura mater of the brain and spinal cord: = PACHYMENINGITIS.

1857 in MAYNE *Expos. Lex.* 1892 GOWER *Dis. Nervous Syst.* I. 266. 1899 *Allbutt's Syst. Med.* VI. 881 External spinal pachymeningitis.—This condition is also designated 'peripachymeningitis' or simply 'perimeningitis'.

perimenopausal (ˌpɛrɪmɛnə'pɔːzəl), *a. Med.* [f. PERI- + MENOPAUSAL *a.*] Occurring at around the time of the menopause.

1961 J. K. FROST in Novak & Jones *Textbk. Gynecol.* (ed. 6) xxxvi. 774 Except postpartum, the parabasal type cell does not exfoliate normally until the later years of the reproductive period, or the perimenopausal period. 1961 *Obstetr. & Gynecol.* XVII. 331/1 Many of our colleagues use ovarian hormones, especially estrogens, for the control of the perimenopausal syndrome. 1970 TE LINDE & MATTINGLY *Oper. Gynecol.* (ed. 4) xxxvi. 795/2 With the current liberal use of estrogen and progesterones in the perimenopausal age group for pregnancy protection and menopausal symptoms, the physician must be particularly alert to the camouflaged symptoms of endometrial carcinoma in patients using steroid hormones. 1977 *Lancet* 8 Oct. 762/2 There was a 6% (P < 0·001) excess of left-sided tumours, primarily at perimenopausal and postmenopausal ages.

So **peri'menopause,** the perimenopausal period.

1962 J. K. FROST in Novak & Woodruff *Gynecol. & Obstetr. Path.* (ed. 5) xxxv. 608/2 Following the initial period of endocrine adjustment in the establishment of menses (perimenarche) and extending into the disruption of endocrine interplay (perimenopause), the hormonal pattern varies widely within each lunar cycle. 1969 *Obstetr. & Gynecol.* XXXIII. 581/2 More than 120 women..were seen initially for, and found to have problems relating to, the perimenopause or menopause.

periment, obs. form of PEDIMENT.

peri'meristem. *Bot.* [mod. (Rassow, in Ger. 1872) f. PERI- + MERISTEM.] The outermost layer of the meristem at a growing point, which develops into the outer cortex and dermatogen.

1884 BOWER & SCOTT *De Bary's Phaner.* 294 Exomeristem ..is divided into the Mesomeristem..and the Perimeristem, which is the outer zone, forming the external cortex and the Dermatogen. Endistem, Existem, Mesistem, and Peristem are abbreviated expressions for these successive layers.

perimeter (pə'rɪmɪtə(r)). [ad. L. *perimetros*, a. Gr. περίμετρος circumference, f. περί around + μέτρον measure: cf. It. *perimetro* (Florio 1611), F. *périmètre* (1541 in Hatz.-Darm.).]

1. a. The continuous line or lines forming the boundary of a closed geometrical figure (curved or rectilineal), or of any area or surface; circumference, periphery, outline; also, the measure or length of the circumference. (Cf. DIAMETER 1, 2.)

1592 R. D. *Hypnerotomachia* 22 b, The Stilliced or Perimeter, or vpper part of the vppermost Coronice. 1620 T. GRANGER *Div. Logike* 173 A perimeter, which is the circuite, or compasse of a figure. 1696 WHISTON *The. Earth* I. (1722) 21 Of all Figures, whose Perimeters are equal, the Circle is the most capacious. 1776 *Kentish Trav. Comp.* 327 In less than three months, the whole perimeter..or inclusion of the harbour, was finished. 1840 LARDNER *Geom.* 100 The perimeter of the polygon will continually approach to coincidence with the circumference of the circle in which it is inscribed. 1881 CASEY *Sequel to Euclid* 16.

fig. 1632 B. JONSON *Magn. Lady* Induct., He makes that his centre attractive to draw thither a diversity of guests, all persons of different humours to make up his perimeter.

†**b.** Applied to a space surrounding something.

1641 MILTON *Ch. Govt.* II. iii. (1851) 168 In respect of a wodden table and the perimeter of holy ground about it.. the Priest esteems their lay-ships unhallow'd and unclean.

c. *Mil.* A defended boundary of a troop position. Also *transf.*, the boundary of an airfield or civil airport.

1943 J. DUFFY *Australians in Malaya* 41 Possibly this was true of an attack from the sea, but on the northern perimeter were no adequate defences. 1958 *Spectator* 11 July 52/3 I can tell you what really happened in the fighting round the perimeter. 1967 *Boston Herald* 1 Apr. 14/6 The enemy opened up with mortar and howitzer fire, hitting American troops who had pulled back into defensive perimeters. 1974 *Guardian* 1 Aug. 1/7 Soldiers..moved on to the airport perimeter. 1977 *Times* 9 Sept. 15/7 After six hours without food in a plane on the perimeter at Heathrow the flight was cancelled.

2. An instrument for measuring the field of vision and determining the visual powers of different parts of the retina.

1875 H. WALTON *Dis. Eye* 1070 The perimeter brought out by C. C. Jeaffreson, seems to be the best. 1899 *Allbutt's Syst. Med.* VI. 846 Their precise determination and localisation require the assistance of the perimeter.

attrib. 1889 G. A. BERRY *Dis. Eye* 553 The result of a perimeter examination..recorded on a chart.

3. *attrib.* and *Comb.*, as (sense 1 c) *perimeter fence, road*; **perimeter track,** a runway round an airfield. See also sense 2.

1974 A. PRICE *Other Paths to Glory* III. i. 249 Soldiers.. patrolling the perimeter fence. 1976 *Scottish Daily Express* 27 Dec. 1/2 Two wolves were shot dead only yards from the perimeter fence by zoo director Roger Wheater. 1974 *Times* 7 Jan. 1/4 There were five road blocks of troops and police on the airport perimeter road where it passes close to runways. 1946 *Happy Landings* (Air Ministry) July 10/1 The Spitfire was taxying out for take-off, along the perimeter track. 1959 J. L. NAYLER *Dict. Aeronaut. Engin.* 187 *Perimeter track*, a taxi track round the perimeter of an airfield for the use of aircraft and motor vehicles.

Hence **pe'rimeterless** *a.*

1849 *Tait's Mag.* XVI. 380 Illimitable, perimeterless, immutable space.

perimetral (pə'rɪmɪtrəl), *a. rare.* [f. L. *perimetr-os* (see prec.) + -AL[1]: cf. *diametral.*] = PERIMETRIC *a.*[2] 1.

1685 H. MORE *Paralip. Prophet.* xxxii. 290 The words.. relating to the..inner House, intimate a Perimetral dimension thereof. 1971 J. NEEDHAM *Sci. & Civilisation in China* IV. III. xxviii. 94 (*caption*) Diagrams to elucidate Chinese and Western building construction... Comparison of the fundamental Chinese building design with that of Greek and Gothic building... Normally the Greek gable covered the perimetral colonnade.

perimetrial, -metritis: see PERI- a, c.

perimetric (pɛrɪ'miːtrɪk), *a.*[1] *Anat.* and *Path.* [f. Gr. περί around + μήτρα uterus + -IC.] Situated or occurring around the uterus.

1889 J. M. DUNCAN *Clin. Lect. Dis. Wom.* xxviii. 227 Lumps produced by perimetric inflammation and adhesions.

perimetric (pɛrɪ'mɛtrɪk), *a.*[2] [f. Gr. περίμετρ-ος PERIMETER + -IC: cf. METRIC.]

1. Pertaining to a perimeter or circumference.

1890 in *Cent. Dict.*

2. Pertaining to or obtained by a perimeter (PERIMETER 2) or perimetry.

1899 *Allbutt's Syst. Med.* VI. 761 A perimetric chart.. shows merely a small central spot of clear vision around the point of fixation. *Ibid.* VIII. 108 Perimetric observations show that frequently the fields of vision are narrowed generally for both eyes.

So **peri'metrical** *a.*; hence **peri'metrically** *adv.*

1882 OGILVIE (Annandale), *Perimetrical*, pertaining to the perimeter. 1897 *Allbutt's Syst. Med.* VI. 763 Studying perimetrically a case of homonymous hemianopsia.

perimetry (pə'rɪmɪtrɪ). [f. as PERIMETER + -Y: cf. *geometry*, etc.]

1. Measurement round; perimeter. Now *rare.*

1570 DEE *Math. Pref.* a iij b, To be certified, either of the length, perimetry, or distance lineall. 1571 DIGGES *Pantom.* II. xiv. N iij b, The one is equall to the semidiameters, the other to the perimetrie or circumference. 1903 *Westm. Gaz.* 9 Jan. 2/1 The contention..that cranial perimetry has but little relation to cerebral quality is no doubt well founded.

2. Measurement of the field of vision by means of the perimeter (PERIMETER 2).

1893 *Syd. Soc. Lex.*, *Perimetry*, the measuring the dimensions of the field of vision by means of the *perimeter.* 1899 *Allbutt's Syst. Med.* VI. 847 It is unnecessary..to convert perimetry into a solemn function.

‖**perimonerula** (ˌpɛrɪməʊ'nɛr(j)ʊlə). *Embryol.* [mod.L., f. PERI- + MONERULA.] The MONERULA arising from a PERIBLASTIC ovum.

1876 [see PERICYTULA].

perimorph ('pɛrɪmɔːf). *Min.* [mod. f. Gr. περί around + μορφή form.] (See quot. 1882.) Hence **peri'morphic, peri'morphous** *adjs.*, pertaining to or of the nature of a perimorph; **peri'morphism,** perimorphic condition.

1882 GEIKIE *Text-bk. Geol.* II. II. ii. 61 A mineral which encloses another has been called a Perimorph; one enclosed by another an Endomorph. 1888 TEALL *British Petrogr.* Gloss. 442 *Perimorphism.* Sheerer termed those crystals perimorphic which consist merely of a thin rind, the interior being filled with other minerals. 1888 A. HARKER in *Q. Jrnl. Geol. Soc.* XLIV. 453 Perimorphic hornblende..bordering augite-cores. 1893 *Syd. Soc. Lex.*, *Perimorphous crystals*, crystals which are made up of a nucleus of one mineral surrounded by an envelope of another.

‖**perimorula** (pɛrɪ'mɒr(j)ʊlə). *Embryol.* [mod.L., f. PERI- + MORULA.] The MORULA arising from a PERIBLASTIC ovum.

1876 [see PERICYTULA].

†**pe'rimplish,** *v. Obs.* Also -esh. [f. OF. *parempliss-*, lengthened stem of *paremplir* to fulfil thoroughly, f. *par-* = PER-2 + *emplir*:—L. *implēre* to fill up.] *trans.* To fulfil, accomplish, complete. Also †**perim'plenish** *v.* Hence †**pe'rimplishment,** fulfilment, completion.

1499 *Will of Benjamen* (Somerset Ho.), Perimplenisshing my said testament. 1554 T. SAMPSON in Strype *Eccl. Mem.* III. App. xviii. 48 The perimplishment of your justification. 1596 H. CLAPHAM *Briefe Bible* II. 141 The perimplishment of Daniels halfe weeke of yeares. 1621 BOLTON *Stat. Irel.* 9 (25 Hen. VI) Many times they do not perimplish the same.

perimyelitis: see PERI- c.

‖**perimysium** (pɛrɪ'mɪsɪəm). *Anat.* [irreg. f. Gr. περί around + μῦς muscle (stem μυ-): cf. *pericarpium*, etc.] The sheath of connective tissue enveloping a muscle. Hence **peri'mysial** *a.*, pertaining to the perimysium.

1842 DUNGLISON *Med. Lex.*, *Perimysium*, Fascia. 1877 ROSENTHAL *Muscles & Nerves* 198 Their covering of muscle-sheath (perimysium). 1899 *Allbutt's Syst. Med.* VII. 215 The perimysium undergoes changes.

perinatal (pɛrɪ'neɪtəl), *a. Med.* [f. PERI- + NATAL *a.*[1] and *sb.*[1]] Of or pertaining to the period comprising the latter part of fœtal life and the early postnatal period (commonly taken as ending either one week or four weeks after birth: see quots.).

1952 *Amer. Jrnl. Publ. Health* XLII. 505/2 Such conditions as birth injury, congenital malformation, cerebral palsy, and epilepsy..may possibly be traceable to perinatal causes. 1958 *Economist* 22 Feb. 654/2 The phrase perinatal mortality has been coined to describe the combined death rate of babies born dead and those who die in the first week of life. 1966 *Ann. Rev. Med.* XVII. 213 The perinatal period extends from the completion of embryonic differentiation into recognizable organ structures to the end of the first month of postnatal extra-uterine existence. 1973 *Where* Apr. 102/3 If they smoke after the third month of their pregnancy there is an excess of peri-natal deaths of about 30 per cent. 1976 *Lancet* 30 Oct. 941/1 The French Government aimed to reduce the burden of handicap caused by conditions arising in the perinatal period (defined as the period from 28th week of gestation to the end of the first week of life). In 1968 40,000 French children who had survived the first year of life were judged to have a handicap of perinatal origin. 1977 *Ibid.* 25 June 1357/2 The W.H.O. recommendation reads: 'It is recommended that national perinatal statistics should include all fetuses and infants delivered weighing at least 500 g (or, when birthweight is unavailable, the corresponding gestational age (22 weeks) or body length (25 cm crown-heel)), whether alive or dead.

†**perin'dulgent,** *a. Obs. rare*[−0]. [ad. L. *perindulgēnt-em*: see PER- 4 and INDULGENT.]

1623 COCKERAM, *Perindulgent*, very gentle, courteous.

perine ('pɛraɪn). *Bot.* [ad. mod.L. *perinium* (Strasburger 1882), f. PERI-, app. after EXTINE, INTINE.] The outermost coat of a pollen-grain or spore when there are three (*intine*, *extine* or *exine*, and *perine*).

1895 KERNER & OLIVER *Nat. Hist. Plants* (1902) II. 100 The wall of pollen-grains is, as a rule, three-layered. These three layers are:—the internal one or *intine*, the middle one or *extine*, and the external one or *perine*... The various sculpturings, prickles, and other unevennesses of the outer coat really appertain to the perine.

perineal, -æal (pɛrɪ'niːəl), *a.* [f. PERINE-UM + -AL[1].] Of, pertaining to, or situated in the perineum. ***perineal body***: see PERINEUM.

1767 A. CAMPBELL *Lexiph.* (1774) 23, I suffered a total perineal excoriation. **1835-6** TODD *Cycl. Anat.* I. 178/1 These muscles..have the effect of making tense the different perinæal aponeurosis. **1868** SIR H. THOMPSON *Dis. of Prostate* 3 The posterior layer of the deep perineal fascia.

peri'neo-, used as combining form of PERINEUM, in a few terms of anatomy, pathology, etc.:

peri'neocele (-siːl) [Gr. κήλη tumour], perineal hernia; **peri'neo,plasty**, a plastic operation on the perineum; so **peri,neo'plastic** *a.*; **perineorrhaphy** (-'ɒrəfɪ) [Gr. ῥαφή sewing, suture], suture of the perineum when ruptured; **peri,neo-va'ginal** *a.*, relating to the perineum and vagina (*Syd. Soc. Lex.*); **peri,neo-'vulvar** *a.*, relating to the perineum and vulva.

1811 HOOPER *Med. Dict.*, *Perinæocele.* **1857** MAYNE *Expos. Lex.* 911/1 A perineocele. **1893** *Syd. Soc. Lex.*, *Perineo-plastic operation*, perineorrhaphy. **1875** tr. *H. von Ziemssen's Cycl. Med.* X. 555 The operation of perineoplasty. **1872** T. G. THOMAS *Dis. Women* (ed. 3) 129 The operation which is now generally adopted..has received the name of perineorraphy. **1857** BULLOCK *Cazeaux' Midwif.* 48 The nerves are derived from the deep branch of the perineo-vulvar branch of the internal pudic.

perinephral, -ic, etc.: see PERI- a, b, c.

perinerve ('pɛrɪnɜːv). *Anat.* [f. PERI- + NERVE.] = PERINEURIUM.

1873 A. FLINT *Nerv. Syst.* i. 28 They [capillaries] never penetrate the perinerve.

‖**perineum, perinæum** (pɛrɪ'niːəm). *Anat.* [Late L. (Cæl. Aurel. *c* 440) ***perinæum, -nēum***, a. Gr. περίναιον, περίνεος, or perh. properly πηριν-: cf. in same sense πηρίνα; also πηρίς or πηρίν, acc. πηρῖνα scrotum.] The region of the body between the anus and the scrotum or vulva; denoting either the surface of this, or the mass of tissue (*perineal body*) of which this surface forms the base.

1632 SHERWOOD, The perineum, *perinée.* **1693** tr. *Blancard's Phys. Dict.* (ed. 2), *Perinæum*, the Ligamentous Seam betwixt the Cod and the Fundament. **1754-64** SMELLIE *Midwif.* I. 93 The perinaeum. **1804** ABERNETHY *Surg. Obs.* 234, I made a division in the perinæum. **1842** E. WILSON *Anat. Vade M.* 193 The muscles of the perineum are situated in the outlet of the pelvis.

perineural (pɛrɪ'njʊərəl), *a.* [f. Gr. περί around + νεῦρ-ον nerve + -AL[1]: cf. *neural.*] Surrounding or investing a nerve, or a bundle of nerve-fibres.

1899 *Allbutt's Syst. Med.* VI. 501 There is in all these cases..leucocytal infiltration of the perineural sheath.

‖**perineuritis** (,pɛrɪnjʊ'raɪtɪs). *Path.* [mod.L., f. next + -ITIS.] Inflammation of the perineurium. Hence **perineuritic** (-'ɪtɪk) *a.*, pertaining to or affected with perineuritis (in quot. misused for *perineural*).

1878 A. HAMILTON *Nerv. Dis.* 57 One a peri-neuritis, and the other an inflammation of the optic nerve itself. **1893** A. S. ECCLES *Sciatica* 13 Distension of the perineuritic lymph-spaces. **1897** *Allbutt's Syst. Med.* II. 58 Lepra-cells, which infiltrating the perineurium produce perineuritis.

‖**perineurium** (pɛrɪ'njʊərɪəm). *Anat.* [mod.L., f. Gr. περί around + νεῦρον nerve: cf. *pericarpium*, etc.] The sheath of connective tissue enveloping a bundle of nerve-fibres. Hence **peri'neurial** *a.*, of or pertaining to the perineurium.

1842 DUNGLISON *Med. Lex.*, *Perineurion*, Neurilemma. **1893** A. S. ECCLES *Sciatica* 13 In the lymphatics of the epineurium and the lymph-spaces of the perineurium. **1899** *Allbutt's Syst. Med.* VI. 637 The thickened perineurium and interstitial tissue.

perinuclear, -ocular: see PERI- a.

period ('pɪərɪəd), *sb.* Forms: 5 **peryod, paryode**, 6 **peryode, periode**, 6– **period**: see also PARODY *sb.*[2] [a. F. *période* (14th c. in Hatz-Darm.) = Sp. *período*, It. *periodo*, ad. L. *period-us*, a. Gr. περίοδος going round, way round, circuit, revolution, cycle of years, periodic recurrence, course, recurring fit of disease, orbit of a heavenly body, rounded sentence, f. περί around + ὁδός way; in ancient L. used only of the period or cycle of the four Grecian games, and of a complete sentence; in med.L. in other of the Gr. senses.]

I. A course or extent of time.

†**1.** The time during which anything runs its course; time of duration. *Obs.*

1413 *Pilgr. Sowle* (Caxton 1483) IV. xxvi. 72 For the tyme and paryode bifore ordeyned of the first maker. **1614** RALEIGH *Hist. World* V. iii. §13. 424 Unto all Dominions God hath set their periods. **1626** BACON *Sylva* §587 How by Art to make Plants more lasting than their ordinary Period. **1672** SIR T. BROWNE *Let. Friend* §11 Many Temples early gray have out-lived the Psalmist's period.

2. a. *Chronol.* A round of time or series of years, marked by the recurrence of astronomical coincidences (e.g. the changes of the moon falling on the same days of the solar year), used as a unit in chronology; e.g. the *Callippic*, *Dionysian*, *Julian*, *Metonic period.* Cf. CYCLE *sb.* 2.

1613 [see JULIAN]. **1694** HOLDER *Disc. Time* (J.), A cycle or period is an account of years that has a beginning and an end too, and then begins again as often as it ends. **1696-1876** [see CALLIPPIC]. **1704** J. HARRIS *Lex. Techn.* I, *Period*, in Chronology, signifies a Revolution of a certain Number of Years; as the *Metonick Period*, the *Julian Period*, and the *Calippick Period.* **1718** PRIDEAUX *Connect. O. & N. Test.* II. IV. 231 In the language of Chronologers a Cycle is a round of several years and a Period a round of several Cycles. **1727-1876** [see DIONYSIAN 3].

b. *Astron.* The time in which a planet or satellite performs its revolution about its primary.

1727-41 CHAMBERS *Cycl.* s.v., The periods of the comets are now many of them pretty well ascertained. **1741** WATTS *Improv. Mind* I. xvi. §2 Tell these persons..that the earth, with all the planets, roll round the sun in their several periods. **1834** *Nat. Philos.*, *Astron.* iii. 69/1 (Usef. Knowl. Soc.) Her time of being again in the same direction with the sun, is called her *synodic period*, or *synodic revolution. Ibid.* 70/2 Her return to the same position with respect to the equinox, or her *tropical period*, will be shorter. **1854** BREWSTER *More Worlds* ii. 29 Its [Uranus'] year, or annual period, is eighty-four years.

†**c.** *Physiol.* ***period of the blood***: see quot.

1727-41 CHAMBERS *Cycl.* s.v., *Period of the blood*,..the circle of the blood, or the tour it makes round the body, for the support of life.

d. *Physics.* The interval of time between the recurrence of phases in a vibration, etc.

1865 TYNDALL *Radiation* xv. 52 The rays of light differ from those of invisible heat only in point of period. **1869** —— in *Fortn. Rev.* Feb. 230 The energy transmitted to the eye from a candle-flame half a mile distant is more than sufficient to inform consciousness; while waves of a different period, possessing many times this energy have no effect whatever. **1879** THOMSON & TAIT *Nat. Phil.* I. I. §54 The Period of a simple harmonic motion is the time which elapses from any instant until the moving point again moves in the same direction through the same position.

e. Any round or portion of time occupied by a recurring process or action, or marked by the regular recurrence of a phenomenon.

1850 McCOSH *Div. Govt.* II. i. (1874) 133 The tides of the ocean..flow in periods. **1862** TYNDALL *Mountaineeer.* xi, The heart beats by periods. **1902** *Westm. Gaz.* 19 Aug. 8/1 This hypothesis is in full accord with the 'climate-period of thirty-five years' recently put forward by Professor Brückner.

3. a. *Path.* The time during which a disease runs its course; that occupied by each attack of intermittent fever from its accession to its remission; also, each of the temporal phases distinguishable in the course of a disease.

1543 TRAHERON *Vigo's Chirurg.* 50/2 Optalmia hath certaine paroxysmes or fyttes, and periodes or courses. **1726** QUINCY *Lex. Phys.-Med.* (ed. 3), *Period* is the Space in which a Distemper continues from its Beginning to its Declension; and such as return after a certain Space, with like Symptoms, are called *Periodical Distempers.* **1893** *Syd. Soc. Lex.*, *Period*,..the time during which a disease progresses from its accession to its declension; also, those marked changes that characterize the progress of a disease, of which there are said to be five,—the *invasion*, the *augment*, the *state*, or full development, the *decline*, and the *termination. Ibid.*, The term period was also applied to the time between two attacks of intermittent fever. It was divided into two parts, the accession..and the remission.

b. *sing.* and *pl.* Menses, catamenia. Also ***monthly period***(*s*) and *attrib.*

1822-34 *Good's Study Med.* (ed. 4) IV. 121 The exact day between any two periods of menstruation in which semination has taken effect. **1879** *St. George's Hosp. Rep.* IX. 777 Her habit is for the periods to recur every five weeks, rather freely. **1891** I. ELLIS *Essentials of Conception* 28 (Advt.), Ladies' 'period' towels. **1893** *Syd. Soc. Lex.*, *Periods.* **1922** JOYCE *Ulysses* 368 Some women for instance warn you off when they have their period. **1939** M. SPRING RICE *Working-Class Wives* vi. 145 She suffers from 'period pains'. **1953** H. MILLER *Plexus* (1963) iii. 112 Between times I wondered what was eating her. Maybe her period coming on. **1956** R. M. LESTER *Towards Hereafter* x. 123 In January 1952 I missed a period and with high hopes I went to see my G.P. and told him the glad news. **1970** G. GREER *Female Eunuch* 52 The genteel..'I've got my period'. **1976** W. H. CANAWAY *Willow-Pattern War* xv. 156 She'd cried off at the last minute with a period pain.

4. a. An indefinite portion of time; *spec.* of history, or of some continuous process, as life (generic or individual), distinguished and characterized by the same prevalent features or conditions.

1712 ADDISON *Hymn*, '*When all thy Mercies*' xi, Through every Period of my Life Thy Goodness I'll pursue. **1780** BURKE *Sp. at Bristol* Wks. III. 383 The Reformation, one of the greatest periods of human improvement, was a time of trouble and confusion. **1809-10** COLERIDGE *Friend* (1865) 116 We have most of us, at some period or other of our lives, been amused with dialogues of the dead. **1865-6** H. PHILLIPS *Amer. Paper Curr.* II. 148 The winter periods proved always trying to the American cause. **1870** MAX MÜLLER *Sc. Relig.* (1873) 66 Niobe was, in a former period of language, a name of snow and winter.

b. *Geol.* One of the larger divisions of geological time; usually subordinate to an *era*: see EPOCH 5 c.

1833 LYELL *Princ. Geol.* III. 54 The period next antecedent we shall call Eocene. **1853** PHILLIPS *Rivers Yorksh.* iv. 124 All Holderness was a sea-bed in the 'glacial' period. **1863** [see CRETACEOUS 2]. **1895** *Funk's Stand. Dict.* s.v., In the scheme of nomenclature proposed by the International Geological Congress *period* is the chronological term of the second order, to which *system* is the corresponding stratigraphic term; as, Silurian period or system.

c. Any specified portion or division of time. *spec.* (*a*) a portion of an artist's life characterized by a particular style; (*b*) freq. with poss. adj.: the particular historical or cultural portion of time with which one is concerned.

a **1751** BOLINGBROKE *Stud. Hist.* (1752) I. vi. 236 The particular periods into which the whole period should be divided. **1793** BURKE *Corr.* (1844) IV. 141 Twenty years would be too long a period to fix for such an event. **1818** CRUISE *Digest* (ed. 2) III. 499 Where a person acquires a second right, he is allowed a new period of twenty years to pursue his remedy. **1855** MILMAN *Lat. Chr.* XI. viii, The termination of a centenary period in the history of man. **1865** SWINBURNE *Anactoria* 302 Till time wax faint in all his periods. **1891** O. WILDE *Pict. Dorian Gray* xix. 319 What has become of that wonderful portrait he did of you?.. It belonged to Basil's best period. **1921** W. S. MAUGHAM *Circle* I. 13, I want you to look at this chair I've just got... About 1750, I should say... It's exactly my period. **1925** R. FRY *Let.* 1 May (1972) II. 568 Lady Cunard..wanted a Picasso of the blue period. **1952** 'W. COOPER' *Struggles of Albert Woods* II. iv. 100, I hardly know Picasso's rose period from his blue. **1958** M. KELLY *Christmas Egg* I. 29 He had been at a loss for the date of the battle of Agincourt, and had excused himself with the plea that it was outside his period. *a* **1966** M. ALLINGHAM *Cargo of Eagles* (1968) i. 16 I'm certain there's an early fortress..just waiting to be uncovered... That's not my period and so is not my province. **1973** M. MACKINTOSH *King & Two Queens* ii. 27 The Picasso Museum..has very good examples of his pink and blue periods? **1978** J. HANSEN *Man Everybody was Afraid Of* xii. 93 She handed Dave one of the mugs. 'From my potting period.'

d. ***the period***: the time in question or under consideration; *esp.* the present day: cf. DAY *sb.* 13 b (*b*). Also ***out of period***: anachronistic.

1859 A. J. MUNBY *Diary* 19 July in D. Hudson *Munby* (1972) 39 An Englishman of the period, smoking a cigar; his dress is 'civilized'—he wears gloves. **1868** MRS. LYNN LINTON in *Sat. Rev.* 14 Mar. 340/1 The girl of the period is a creature who dyes her hair and paints her face. **1871** M. COLLINS *Mrq. & Merch.* II. i. 2 Some of them grow 'fast', and 'loud'—mere 'girls of the period'. **1902** G. B. SHAW *Mrs. Warren's Profession* Pref. p. xv, Both plots conform to the strictest rules of the period. **1933** E. O'NEILL *Ah, Wilderness!* I. 15 Scene—Sitting room of the Miller home in a large small-town in Connecticut—about 7:30 in the morning of July 4th, 1906. The room is..furnished with the scrupulous medium-priced tastelessness of the period. **1961** C. WILLOCK *Death in Covert* iii. 66 A serving-wench..asked him: 'Sack, mulled claret, or Madeira?' Mr Goss felt that two at least of these were out of period. **1969** Y. CARTER *Mr. Campion's Farthing* ii. 15, I hate getting out of period but sometimes one has to be modern. **1976** *Listener* 20 May 647/4 Wesley..had the imaginative and technical powers to transcend the humdrum idiom of so much church music of the period without, at the same time, discarding its essential nature.

e. *Educ.* A portion of time set aside for a lesson or other activity; cf. *free period* s.v. FREE *a.* D. 2.

1876 C. M. YONGE *Womankind* xiii. 92 Most people's breakfast hour coincides with this only period permitted [in National Schools] for religious teaching. **1930** *Times Educ. Suppl.* 18 Jan. 21/2 The pupil has five periods a week..for French. **1948** 'N. SHUTE' *No Highway* vi. 167 'What about the school?' 'I've only got one period to-morrow.' **1955** E. BLISHEN *Roaring Boys* I. 30, I had an odd period of history with one of the first-year classes. **1966** J. PARTRIDGE *Middle School* i. 24 Nearly every class has a 'library period'. **1974** H. L. FOSTER *Ribbin'* i. 8 Hey, Teach, we work a period, read comics a period, and then take off the last period—OK?

f. One of the intervals into which the playing time of a sporting fixture is divided.

1898 *Encycl. Sport* II. 128/2 The duration of play in a match shall be one hour, divided into three periods of twenty minutes. **1935** *Encycl. Sports* 359/2 Two time-keepers..inform the referee..that the end of each period or rest has arrived. **1968** *Globe & Mail* (Toronto) 5 Feb. 17/2 Pit Martin also scored for a three-goal first period for Chicago and Wayne Maki tallied early in the second. **1974** *State* (Columbia, S. Carolina) 3 Mar. 1-D/1 The Paladins opened 11-point leads on three occasions in the final period.

II. Completion, end of any course.

5. a. The point of completion of any round of time or course of action or duration; consummation, termination, conclusion, end. Phrases: ***to put*** (†***give, set***) ***a period to***, † ***bring, come to a period***; † ***to set down one's*** (or ***the***) ***period*** (perh. with some allusion to 11 b). Now *arch.*

[*c* **1374**, **1430-40**: see PARODY *sb.*[2]] **1590** GREENE *Mourn. Garm.* Wks. (Grosart) IX. 150 She glaunced her lookes on all,..but at last she set downe her period on the face of Alexis, thinking he was the fairest. **1591** SHAKS. *1 Hen. VI*, IV. ii. 17 The period of thy Tyranny approacheth. **1599** B. JONSON *Cynthia's Rev.* V. iii, To end And give a timely period to our sports. **1601** R. JOHNSON *Kingd. & Commw.* Ded., I put a period to these lines. *a* **1636** LYNDE *Case for Spectacles* (1638) Ep. Ded., Death..sets a period to all suits in Courts. **1647** CLARENDON *Hist. Reb.* VII. §391 This Answer was return'd to his Majesty; which put a period to all Men's hopes. **1670** EVELYN *Let. Ld. Treasurer* 20 Jan. in *Diary*, The subiect of it being..yᵉ warr..not yet brought to a period. **1705** STANHOPE *Paraphr.* I. 140 A thing past and now come to a Period. **1734** WATTS *Relig. Juv.* (1789) 86 Let us hold the period of life ever in our view. **1750** JOHNSON *Rambler* No. 54 ¶2 A man accustomed..to trace things from their origin to their period. **1814** CARY *Dante, Paradise* XVI. 137 The just anger that hath..put a period to your gladsome days. **1882** STEVENSON *New Arab. Nts.* (1884) 96, I mean to put a period to this prodigality.

†**b.** The final stage of any process or course of action; the concluding sentence, peroration; the finish, consummation, final event, issue, outcome.

c **1530** L. COX *Rhet.* (1899) 66 The periode or conclusion standethe in the bryefe enumeracyon of thynges spoken before, and in mouynge the affectyons. **1581** J. BELL *Haddon's Answ. Osor.* 404 Mystres money made upp alwayes the peryode of the play. **1616** W. FORDE *Serm.* 64 So shall it be the period and end of my discourse. **1713** ADDISON *Cato* I. iii, O think what anxious moments pass between The birth of plots, and their last fatal periods. **1769** ROBERTSON *Chas. V*, VII. III. 28 Conducting the deliberations..to such a successful period.

†**c.** An end to part of a course; a stop. *Obs. rare.*

1590 MARLOWE *2nd Pt. Tamburl.* I. iii, Yet shall my soldiers make no period Until Natolia kneel before your feet. **1634** SIR T. HERBERT *Trav.* 101 All terrene joyes are mixt with discontent and periods.

†**d.** Death. *Obs. rare.*

a **1639** WOTTON *Parallel Essex & Buckhm.* in *Reliq.* (1651) 34 Touching the Dukes [Buckingham's] suddain period. **1682** SIR T. BROWNE *Chr. Mor.* II. §11 The Tragical Exits and unexpected periods of some eminent Persons.

†**6.** The highest point reached in any course; the acme. *Obs.*

1595 MARKHAM *Sir R. Grinvile* (Arb.) 78 Since last the sunne Lookt from the hiest period of the sky. **1604** E. G[RIMSTONE] *D'Acosta's Hist. Indies* II. vii. 98 When the sunne is in the period of his force in the burning Zone. **1606** SHAKS. *Ant. & Cl.* IV. xiv. 107. **1608** D. T[UVIL] *Ess. Pol. & Mor.* 43 b, Nor was the massacre of this his warlike sonne the period of his furie.

†**7.** A particular point in the course of anything; a point or stage of advance; a point of time, moment, occasion. *Obs.*

1600 W. WATSON *Decacordon* (1602) 341 If you aske of the Mathematician, how to passe betwixt two periods, he will tell you that [etc.]. **1664** BUTLER *Hud.* II. ii. 657 At fit Periods the whole Rout Set up their throats with Clam'rous shout. *c* **1790** IMISON *Sch. Art* II. 82 Farenheit's scale is most generally in use, and the remarkable periods of heat are as follows: 212 water boils, 175 spirits of wine boils, 112 fever-heat, 98 blood-heat [etc.]. **1793** SMEATON *Edystone L.* §281 *note*, The work being now brought to such a period that it could go on with less interruption.

†**8.** A limit in space, appointed end (of a journey or course). *Obs.*

1605 WILLET *Hexapla Gen.* 463, 50 miles beyond..which was the vtmost period of their journey. **1633** BP. HALL *Hard Texts* Ezek. i. 17 They moued all four together and went right on to the period appointed. **1789** in *Burke's Corr.* (1844) III. 87 Our best friends will not march, unless they can perceive a period to their journey.

†**9.** *fig.* The end to be attained, the goal. *Obs.*

1586 MARLOWE *1st Pt. Tamburl.* v. ii, If these had made one poem's period. **1598** SHAKS. *Merry W.* III. iii. 47 This is the period of my ambition. *Ibid.* IV. ii. 237. **1613** —— *Hen. VIII*, I. ii. 209 There's his period To sheath his knife in vs. **1618** M. BARET *Horsemanship*, *Cures* 18 When you haue gotten the period of your desire. **1643** MILTON *Divorce* Pref. (1851) 18 This therefore shall be task and period of this discourse. *a* **1674** CLARENDON *Surv. Leviath.* xxx. (1676) 184 Which without doubt must be the natural and final period of all his Prescriptions in Policy and Government.

III. In Grammar, Rhetoric, Music, etc.

10. a. A complete sentence. (Cf. Aristotle *Rhet.* III. ix.) Usually applied to a sentence consisting of several clauses, grammatically connected, and rhetorically constructed. Hence, in *pl.*, rhetorical or grammatical language.

[**1533** MORE *Apol.* xiv. 103 b, A very colde skuse to a man lerned that wyll way the hole periodus togyther.] **1579** E. K. in *Spenser's Sheph. Kal.* Ep. to Harvey, The whole Periode and compasse of speache so delightsome for the roundnesse, and so graue for the straungenesse. **1593** NASHE *Four Lett. Confut.* 82, I know two seuerall periods or full pointes in this last epistle, at least fortie lines long a piece. **1634** MILTON *Comus* 585 Not a period Shall be unsaid for me. **1675** TEMPLE *Let. to King* Wks. 1731 II. 330 He went on, and read a long Period in Cypher. **1764** GRAY *Corr. N. Nicholls* 19 Nov., If you will not take this as an excuse, accept it at least as a well-turned period, which is always my principal concern. **1782** COWPER *Table T.* 517 If sentiment were sacrificed to sound, And truth cut short to make a period round. **1869** HUXLEY in *Sci. Opin.* 21 Apr. 464 Those oddly constructed periods which seem to have prejudiced many persons against reading his works. **1875** WHITNEY *Life Lang.* x. 209 To put clauses together into periods.

b. In *Ancient Prosody*, A group of two or more cola (COLON² 1); a metrical group or series of dicolic, tricolic, etc. verses.

1837-9 HALLAM *Hist. Lit.* I. ii. §6 He was the first..who replaced the rude structure of periods by some degree of rhythm. **1882** BLADES *Caxton* 126 The Greek grammarians ..called a complete sentence a period, a limb was a colon, and a clause a comma. **1883** [see COLON² 1].

11. a. A full pause such as is properly made at the end of a sentence.

1587 GREENE *Penelopes Web* Wks. (Grosart) V. 151 She fell into consideration with her selfe that the longest Sommer hath his Autumne, the largest sentence his Period. [**1589** PUTTENHAM *Eng. Poesie* II. iv. (Arb.) 88 The third they called *periodus*, for a complement or full pause, and as a resting place and perfection of so much former speach as had bene vttered.] *Ibid.* 89 Much more might be sayd for the vse of your three pauses, comma, colon, and periode. **1590** SHAKS. *Mids. N.* v. i. 96 Make periods in the midst of sentences. **1593** —— *Lucr.* 565 She puts the period often from his place. *a* **1637** B. JONSON *Eng. Gram.* II. ix, The distinction of a perfect sentence hath a more full stay, and doth rest the spirit, which is a pause or a period.

b. The point or character that marks the end of a complete sentence; a full stop (.). Also added to a statement to emphasize a place where there is or should be a full stop, freq. (*colloq.*) with the implication 'and that is all there is to say about it', 'and it is as simple as that'.

1609 J. DAVIES *Holy Roode* (1878) 20/2 No Commaes but thy Stripes; no Periods But thy Nailes. **1612** BRINSLEY *Lud. Lit.* 95 In reading, that he [the scholar] doe it distinctly, reading to a Period or full point, and there to stay. **1748** J. MASON *Elocut.* 24 A Comma stops the Voice while we may privately tell one, a Semi-colon two; a Colon three: and a Period four. **1824** L. MURRAY *Eng. Gram.* (ed. 5) I. 405 When a sentence is complete and independent..it is marked with a Period. **1866** MASON *Eng. Gram.* (ed. 7) 121 Punctuation..4 The Full stop or Period. **1934** J. O'HARA *Appointment in Samarra* (1935) viii. 248 'An unscrupulous woman can make a man— ' 'Period.' **1946** *Sun* (Baltimore) 2 Oct. 8 (Advt.), A cigarette is supposed to give you *pleasure*. Period. **1947** *Mind* LVI. 65 The empirical evidence suggests the generalisation and supports it. If it does, it does. Period. **1948** H. LAWRENCE *Death of Doll* i. 21 'Lucky Monny to have her own pocket.' 'Stop that. Lucky Monny, period.' **1951** C. ARMSTRONG *Black-Eyed Stranger* (1952) xvii. 150, I don't want to think you are a romantic young thing, period. **1956** J. L. AUSTIN in *Proc. Brit. Acad.* XLII. 113 It does *not* follow either that 'I panted whether or not I ran' or that 'I panted' period. **1958** RICE & 'MCBAIN' *April Robin Murders* (1959) xxii. 245 But Browne doesn't care... He wants the money, period. **1960** 'M. CRONIN' *Begin with Gun* xii. 141 'You know how nosy I am about unsolved crimes.' 'Nosy. Period.' **1964** V. NABOKOV *Defence* x. 156, I can't abandon him. And I won't. Period. **1972** *Science* 12 May 638/1 Don't know, but we have exceeded it: 7. Don't know, period: 10. **1974** H. L. FOSTER *Ribbin'* vi. 285 It is wrong for any teacher to have an affair with a student, period. **1976** *Shooting Times & Country Mag.* 16–22 Dec. 18/1 So far as the Spey was concerned this year, however, the fish did not arrive—period! **1977** *Language* LIII. 409 If this is the view R got from 'On generative semantics', he is illiterate, period.

12. *Mus.* 'A complete musical sentence' (Stainer & Barrett 1898).

1866 ENGEL *Nat. Mus.* iii. 83 A period, however, does not necessarily always embrace eight bars. **1880** C. H. H. PARRY in Grove *Dict. Mus.* II. 692 A Period is one of the divisions which characterise the form of musical works..the lesser divisions are phrases.

13. *Arith.* A set of figures in a large number marked off by commas placed between or dots placed over, as in numeration, circulating decimals, and the extraction of the square or cube root.

1674 JEAKE *Arith.* (1696) 15 A Period is a comprehension of Degrees..as 123..12345, &c. *a* **1677** *Cocker's Arith.* i. §10. 6 A Period..when a Number consists of more than three figures or places, whose proper order is to prick or distinguish every third Place..so..63.452. **1690** LEYBOURN *Curs. Math.* 4 Numbers..of Three Figures, or Places..may properly be called a Period. **1704** J. HARRIS *Lex. Techn.* I. s.v., A Period in Numbers, is a Distinction made by a Point, or Comma after every sixth Place or Figure; and is used in Numeration, for the readier distinguishing and naming the several Figures or Places. **1859** BARN. SMITH *Arith. & Algebra* (ed. 6) 76 The part [of a circulating decimal] which is repeated is called the Period.

14. *Math.* The interval between any two successive equal values of a periodic function, i.e. one whose values recur in the same order while that of the variable increases or decreases continually.

1879 CAYLEY *Coll. Math. Papers* X. 468 The theta-functions have the quarter-periods (1, 1), the half-periods (2, 2), and the whole periods (4, 4). **1882** MINCHIN *Unipl. Kinemat.* 13 If $\phi\ (x + n\lambda) = \phi\ (x)$,..$n$ being any integer and λ a constant, $\phi\ (x)$ is a periodic function of x, its period being λ.

15. *Chem.* A horizontal row in the periodic table of the elements; the set of elements occupying such a row, usu. comprising an alkali metal and those elements of greater atomic number up to and including the next noble gas. Cf. GROUP *sb.* 3 c (ii).

1879 *Chem. News* 5 Dec. 268/1 In the first [table] the elements are placed in large periods, with their atomic weights. In the second they are arranged in groups and series, that is to say, in small periods, in such a manner that the differences between the odd and even series become very apparent. *Ibid.* 19 Dec. 291/1 We see..that the members at the beginning of the large periods (as well as the small periods commencing with Na and Li) are metals of a very strongly pronounced alkaline nature. **1946** [see LANTHANIDE 1]. **1965** PHILLIPS & WILLIAMS *Inorg. Chem.* I. ii. 40 (*caption*) The series of elements from Li to Ne will be referred to as the first row or the first short period, and similarly the series Rb to Xe as the fourth row or the second long period. **1974** D. M. ADAMS *Inorg. Solids* ii. 37 Across each period of the Periodic Table, ionic radii decrease with increasing charge and atomic number.

IV. 16. a. *attrib.* or as *adj.* in sense 'belonging to, characteristic, imitative, or representative of, a particular (past) period' esp. in style or design in architecture, dress, furniture, literature, etc.

Freq. in inexact or euphemistic use.

1905 (*title*) Borgia: a period play. **1906** G. KOBBÉ *How to appreciate Music* 47 A pianoforte has no business in a 'period' room. If the person is rich enough to afford 'period' rooms, he also can afford a music room. **1908** *Westm. Gaz.* 17 Dec. 4/1 Some of them..may be said to be striving to create a 'period' type of carriage for themselves. **1914** EBERLEIN & MCCLURE (*title*) The practical book of period furniture. **1920** W. R. LETHABY in *Form in Civilization* (1922) 12 That which now professes to be designed in a style, or, as the still more disgusting slang runs, to be 'period work', has not the essence of life. **1925** in F. Madan *Oxford outside Guide-Bks.* (ed. 2) 202 (Advt.), Write for new illustrated Catalogue containing fullest particulars of Minty Bookcases, including various 'period' styles at moderate prices. **1927** *Times* 28 Oct. 17/3 The bride..wore a period gown of cream chiffon velvet, trimmed with seed pearls. **1928** *Daily Sketch* 2 Aug. 15 (*caption*) 'Period' pages... The little pages were replicas of the old-time uniform of the Queen's Bays. **1931** *Times Lit. Suppl.* 26 Mar. 249/2 The contrast between these two volumes makes an interesting study. Neither is 'period-printing'; but the Chapman is properly 'spacious' for an Elizabethan work; and the Pope [etc.]. **1935** N. MITCHISON *We have been Warned* II. 154 'You'll be saying you like the "Idylls of the King" next.' 'Oh, but I do. They're so deliciously period.' **1937** D. L. SAYERS *Busman's Honeymoon* xviii. 346, I was going to.. have the spit turned by electricity. And an electric cooker for the days when we didn't feel so period. **1940** L. MACNEICE *Last Ditch* 18 Cranks, hacks, poverty-stricken scholars, In pince-nez, period hats or romantic beards. **1958** B. NICHOLS *Sweet & Twenties* 79 The word 'treasure' is charmingly period. In the upper classes it implied the perfect Jeeves or the ideal nanny. **1960** R. A. KNOX *Occasional Sermons* xl. 331 It is all quite convincing, and beautifully period. Why is it so period? **1965** *Listener* 25 Nov. 869/3 A series of Edith Wharton's novels are being reprinted..; great period interest, and well worth re-examination. **1967** E. SHORT *Embroidery & Fabric Collage* iii. 74 The heavy curtains associated with the period four-poster. **1974** *Listener* 10 Jan. 59/3 *Whose body?*..one of Dorothy Sayers's Lord Peter Wimsey stories..is period stuff, thick with now discarded or at least unfashionable snobberies. **1976** *Liverpool Echo* 24 Nov. 5/4 The undeniable pleasure of watching sport, natural history, travel, ballet, period dramas and even the news is taken for granted. **1977** *N.Y. Rev. Bks.* 29 Sept. 12/4 Baum was a handsome young man with gray eyes, straight nose, dark brown hair, and a period mustache that looked to be glued on. **1977** *Radio Times* 12 Nov. 4/3 It was great fun but it was 'period' and we wanted to get back to the present.

b. Special Combs., as **period-luminosity** *a. Astr.*, relating the period of a variable star, esp. a Cepheid, to its luminosity; **period-piece**, a work of art, furniture, literature, etc., considered from the aspect of its associations with or evocativeness of a past period of time; contemptuously, such a work possessing interest only from such associations or evocativeness.

1918 H. SHAPLEY in *Contrib. Mt. Wilson Solar Observatory* No. 153. 2 For parallaxes obtained with the period-luminosity curve the accuracy appears to surpass that of direct measures on any object for which the parallax is less than 0″·01, and is essentially independent of distance. **1950** *Sci. News* XV. 46 We can..get from the [light] curve the mean apparent magnitude and the period. From the period-luminosity relation we then find the absolute magnitude, and so, knowing both *m* and M we can find the distance. **1964** *Listener* 21 May 831/2 It was by studying the short-period variables in the Small Cloud, fifty years ago, that Miss Henrietta Leavitt, at Harvard..made the discoveries that led on to the 'period-luminosity law' of Cepheid stars. **1927** S. ERTZ *Now East, Now West* iii. 32 She saw she would have the pleasure of buying certain things —period pieces—that she could either sell at the end of their stay or take back to America. **1931** *Times Lit. Suppl.* 24 Dec. 1033/2 Spenser supported the remote splendour of his mythical heroes with deliberately archaic language, turning his poem into a period piece. **1934** C. LAMBERT *Music Ho!* III. 172 The English folk song..is nothing more than a very pretty period piece. **1943** H. PEARSON *Conan Doyle* v. 81 Nowadays we can see that the facile saga of Sherlock Holmes is far more valuable even as a 'period piece' than the diligent epic of Edward the Third. **1957** *Essays & Stud.* X. 54 But I am here concerned with Robert Elsmere not primarily as a work of art but as a symbol or symptom of a certain phase of liberal religious thought in the later nineteenth century —as a 'period piece' if you will, only that I prefer not to use a phrase which might suggest (wrongly, as I think) that the book is a mere antique. **1961** L. MUMFORD *City in Hist.* xiii. 408 Washington..might have been a miracle of the solo town planner's art: a final period-piece to close the epoch. **1972** S. HYNES *Edwardian Occasions* xv. 188 The essays.. are belles-lettres of the most inoffensive kind..period pieces even when [Maurice] Hewlett wrote them. **1975** M. DRABBLE *Realms of Gold* IV. 269 Mays Cottage was a period piece, completely unrestored, which in these days seemed to be an asset.

†**ˈperiod,** *v. Obs.* [f. prec. sb.]

1. *trans.* To bring to a termination, put a period to; to end, conclude; to dissolve.

1595 *Polimanteia* (1881) 46, I am loath to bee too long in my aduisements to you,..and therefore heere I period them. **1607** SHAKS. *Timon* I. i. 99 Your..Letter he desires To those haue shut him vp, which failing, Periods his comfort. **1668** HOWE *Bless. Righteous* (1825) 301 It will calmly period all thy troubles. **1678** GALE *Crt. Gentiles* III. 95 This ingenuous Concession..were sufficient to period our Controversie.

2. *intr.* To come to a conclusion, conclude.

1628 FELTHAM *Resolves* I. lxi, You may period upon this; that where there is the most pitty from others, there is the greatest misery in the partie pittied. **1656** S. H. *Gold. Law* 88 Here then I period. **16..** BARTON *Holiday's Acknowl.* (N.), 'Tis some poor comfort that this mortal scope Will period.

Hence †'perioding *vbl. sb.*, finishing, concluding.

1659 RUSHW. *Hist. Coll.* I. 39 This Parliament..to continue for the Enacting of Laws, and Perioding of things of Reformation, as long as the necessity of the State shall require the same.

periodate, per-iodate (pəˈraɪədeɪt). *Chem.* [See PER- 5.] A salt of periodic acid. (In Pharmacy, short for *calcium periodate*, an antiseptic.) ***periodic acid-Schiff*** (Biol.), phr. used *attrib.* and *absol.* to designate a procedure for the detection of carbohydrates by first oxidizing them to polyaldehydes with periodic acid and then staining with Schiff's reagent.

1836 BRANDE *Chem.* (ed. 4) 343 A sparingly soluble white salt is obtained, which is a periodate of soda. **1871** ROSCOE *Elem. Chem.* 122 Periodic Acid, or Hydrogen Periodate. **1890** *Pall Mall G.* 6 Jan. 2/3 A medical contemporary mentioned that one sniff of periodate crystals would cure an attack of influenza. **1892** *Times* 28 Oct. 3/5 It is claimed that in the early stage of cholera periodate is successful in 95 per cent of the cases. **1947** *Jrnl. Laboratory & Clin. Med.* XXXII. 911 McManus reported the use of a periodic acid-Schiff technique for the demonstration of mucin. **1956** *Nature* 3 Mar. 432/2 Secretory inclusions which are positive to the periodic-acid-Schiff test are conspicuous in the non-ciliated iodine-binding cells of the endostyle of *Ciona*. **1960** E. GURR *Encycl. Microsc. Stains* I. 274 The author describes ..results obtained with silver staining and periodic acid-Schiff. **1974** H. C. COOK *Man. Histol. Demonstr. Techniques* i. 16 They [*sc.* basement membranes] may be demonstrated ..by the periodic acid-Schiff (PAS) technique and a variant of this, the Allochrome method.

So **periodic, per-iodic** (pɜːraɪˈɒdɪk) *a.*, as in ***periodic acid***, H_5IO_6, an acid containing a larger proportion of oxygen than iodic acid; **pe'riodide** or † **peri'oduret**, a combination of iodine with another element or radical in a larger proportion than in a simple iodide.

1819 BRANDE *Chem.* 138 Periodide of phosphorus is a black compound, formed by heating one part of iodine with rather more than 20 of phosphorus. **1836** *Ibid.* (ed. 4) 343 An aqueous solution of pure periodic acid is formed. **1853** W. GREGORY *Inorg. Chem.* 117 Periodic Acid. IO_7 = 183·1. Analogous to perchloric acid. **1857** MAYNE *Expos. Lex.* 912/1 Perioduret. **1897** *Allbutt's Syst. Med.* II. 742 One sixteenth of a grain of periodide [i.e. of mercury] or of corrosive sublimate.

ˌperio'deutic, *a. rare*⁻⁰. [f. late Gr. περιοδευτής a traveller; a physician, f. περι-οδεύ-ειν to travel about.] Pertaining to, or of the nature of, a quack.

1857 in MAYNE *Expos. Lex.* **1893** in *Syd. Soc. Lex.*

periodic (pɪərɪˈɒdɪk), *a.*[1] [a. F. *périodique* (14th c. in Hatz.-Darm.), ad. L. *periodicus* (Pliny), a. Gr. περιοδικός coming round at certain intervals, f. περίοδος PERIOD: see -IC.]

1. Of, pertaining, or proper to the revolution of a heavenly body in its orbit, as ***periodic motion, time***.

1642 HOWELL *For. Trav.* (Arb.) 87 In as short a compas of time as the Sun finisheth his periodic annuall motion. **1715** tr. *Gregory's Astron.* I. 192 If the Sun were retained by the same Force [Gravity], propagated so far as itself, the Cubes of the Distances of the Sun and Moon..would have the same Ratio as the Squares of their Periodic Times. **1833** HERSCHEL *Astron.* viii. 248 A direct method of ascertaining the periodic time of each planet.

2. Characterized by periods; recurring at regular intervals; *spec.* in *Path.* having regularly recurring symptoms, as ***periodic fever***. Often *loosely*, Recurring or reappearing at intervals; intermittent.

periodic classification or ***system*** (*Chem.*): an arrangement or classification of the chemical elements according to the periodic law; ***periodic function*** (*Math.*): see PERIOD *sb.* 14. ***periodic inequality*** (*Astron.*): see INEQUALITY 4. ***periodic law*** (*Chem.*): the statement of the fact (first pointed out by Mendeléeff in 1869) that the properties of the chemical elements are periodic functions of their atomic weights; i.e. that when arranged in the order of these weights, the elements fall into recurring groups or series, so that those having similar chemical and physical properties recur at regular intervals; now recognized to be a function of atomic number rather than of atomic weight, thus removing certain discrepancies in the original scheme; ***periodic table*** (*Chem.*): a table of the elements arranged according to the periodic law; *spec.* one in which they are arranged in order of atomic number, usu. in rows, such that groups of elements possessing analogous electronic structures, and hence exhibiting similar properties, form vertical columns ('groups') of the table.

1661 LOVELL *Hist. Anim. & Min.* 365 The boulimos is a great periodick appetite, often ending in nauseousnesse. **1742** YOUNG *Nt. Th.* VI. 154 Periodic Potions for the Sick. **1750** H. WALPOLE *Lett. to Mann* (1834) II. 328, I have advised several who are going to keep their next earthquake in the country to take the bark for it, as it is so periodic. **1805** *Med. Jrnl.* XIV. 88 The fevers of the periodic class exhibit great variety of condition. **1822–56** DE QUINCEY *Confess.* (1862) 25 The fretting..of anxiety, which..he kept alive by this periodic exaction. **1850** J. F. W. HERSCHEL in *Phil. Trans. R. Soc.* CXL. 400 If A_x, B_x, &c. be simply constant, the function may be termed a periodic one, since it assumes in periodic and constantly recurring succession the values A, B, C..N, A, B, &c. *ad infinitum*. **1859** PARKINSON *Optics* (1866) 104 The cylindrical beams transmitted through these annular lenses sweep the horizon and produce a revolving or periodic light. **1872** *Phil. Mag.* XLIII. 251 The regular progression in physical and chemical properties observable in members of the same family..are either consequences of, or closely related to, these 'periodic laws'. **1875** *Chem. News* 24 Dec. 293/1 The periodic law indicates the gaps which still exist in the system of the known elements, and enables us to predict the properties of the unknown elements. *Ibid.* 294/1 These characters of [gallium]..have been obtained..by considering its place in the periodic system of the elements. **1879** CAYLEY *Coll. Math. Papers* XI. 529 The functions sin u, cos u, are periodic, having the period 2π, $\begin{smallmatrix}\sin\\\cos\end{smallmatrix}(u + 2\pi) = \begin{smallmatrix}\sin\\\cos\end{smallmatrix}(u)$; and the half-period π, $\begin{smallmatrix}\sin\\\cos\end{smallmatrix}(u + \pi) = -\begin{smallmatrix}\sin\\\cos\end{smallmatrix}u$; the periodicity may be verified by means of the foregoing fractional forms. **1880** CLEMINSHAW *Wurtz' Atom. The.* 154 A function of the atomic weights, which function is periodic. **1881** STOKES in *Nature* XXIV. 617/2 A system of any kind subject to periodic disturbing forces. **1881** *Chem. News* 14 Jan. 16/1 The criticism of Prof. Wurtz upon the periodic classification. **1882** MINCHIN *Unipl. Kinemat.* 13 A function of a variable, x, is said to be a periodic function..if its values repeat themselves for values of the variable differing by a constant. **1895** THOMSON & BLOXAM *Bloxam's Chem.* (ed. 8) 278 The Periodic Table has found a twofold application. **1913** Periodic system [see *atomic number* s.v. ATOMIC *a.* 1] **1919** *Jrnl. Chem. Soc.* CXV. 11 The occupant of a separate place in the periodic table of elements. **1930** *Engineering* 21 Mar. 372/2 The sequence of the elements in the old periodic table with its eight groups and seven periods. **1957** Periodic table [see LANTHANIDE 1]. **1969** J. W. VAN SPRONSEN (*title*) The periodic system of chemical elements. **1974** *Encycl. Brit. Macropædia* IV. 116/2 The periodic classification places elements with similar electron arrangements in vertical columns. **1974** GOLDBERG & DILLARD *College Chem.* ii. 38 The periodic law..states that the properties of the elements are periodic functions of their atomic numbers.

3. Of or pertaining to a rhetorical or grammatical period; characterized by or expressed in periods.

1701 tr. *Le Clerc's Prim. Fathers* (1702) 276 Those Letters are not writ in a Periodick Style, as the Orations. **1840–1** DE QUINCEY *Rhetoric* Wks. 1859 XI. 52 The splendour of his periodic diction, with his fine delivery, compensated his defect in imagery. **1860** MARSH *Eng. Lang.* xvii. 361 The Italian resembles the Latin in independence of fixed laws of periodic arrangement. **1875** JOWETT *Plato* (ed. 2) III. 527 Anaxagoras never attained to a connected or periodic style.

4. = PERIODICAL *a.* 5. *rare.*

1835 I. TAYLOR *Spir. Despot.* i. 19 The despotism of the Periodic Press. **1904** *Westm. Gaz.* 30 Apr. 5/2 There is in all these respects no better model for the journalist or periodic writer. **1930** H. G. WELLS *Autocracy of Mr. Parham* II. iv. 128 The need of a stronger and clearer guidance in our periodic literature.

5. Relating to a period or space of time. *rare.*

1884 J. TAIT *Mind in Matter* (1892) 168 A periodic conception of the [six] 'days' would at once suggest itself,.. the divine rest embracing an indefinite period.

6. as *sb. pl.* = PERIODICAL *sb.* 3.

1920 C. E. MULFORD *Johnny Nelson* xvii. 222 That's th' worst of them periodics! You can't never tell when they'll start.

periodic, *a.*[2], **per-iodic:** see under PERIODATE.

periodical (pɪərɪˈɒdɪkəl), *a.* (*sb.*) [f. as PERIODIC *a.*[1] + -AL[1].]

A. *adj.* **1.** = PERIODIC *a.* 1. † ***periodical month***: see quot. 1690.

1603 HOLLAND *Plutarch's Mor.* 1024 Nature.. determined motion with periodicall revolutions. **1690** LEYBOURN *Curs. Math.* 467 The Periodical Month is that interval of time, in which the Moon returneth to the same place in the Zodiack from whence she departed. **1704** J. HARRIS *Lex. Techn.* I. s.v., The Periodical Motion of the Moon, is that whereby she finishes her Course round about the Earth in a Month. *a* **1721** KEILL *Maupertuis' Diss.* (1734) 37 The Periodical times of the Planets. **1846** JOYCE *Sci. Dial., Astron.* xiv. 98 This is called the periodical month.

2. a. Recurring after more or less regular periods of time; characterized by periods (of occurrence, variation, etc.): = PERIODIC *a.*[1] 2.

periodical cicada, a species of N. American cicada (*C. septendecim*), the larva of which remains buried from 13 to 17 years underground. ***periodical river, stream***, etc., one that flows and dries up in successive periods.

1601 HOLLAND *Pliny* XX. iii. 38 Intermittent fevers which the Greeks call Periodicall. **1611** COTGR., *Periodic, -ique*, periodicall. **1646** SIR T. BROWNE *Pseud. Ep.* IV. xii. 215 Plato, who measured the vicissitude and mutation of States, by a periodicall fatality of number. **1661** BLOUNT *Glossogr.* (ed. 2) s.v., An Ague is called a Periodical disease, because it keeps a just time of its return. **1783** JUSTAMOND tr. *Raynal's Hist. Indies* II. 224 The rains, as in the other countries situated under the tropics, are periodical. **1800** *Hist. Ind.* in *Asiat. Ann. Reg.* 9/1 At the commencement of the northerly periodical winds. **1833** HERSCHEL *Astron.* xii. 381 Among the stars are several which..undergo a regular periodical increase and diminution of lustre... These are called periodical stars. **1850** R. G. CUMMING *Hunter's Life S. Afr.* (1902) 58/1 We encamped on..a periodical stream, in the gravelly bed of which fine spring-water could be obtained by digging. **1881** STOKES in *Nature* XXIV. 613/2 These [sun] spots as to their frequency and magnitude appear to be subject to a periodical inequality. **1890** *Cent. Dict.* s.v. *Cicadidæ*, Some species, like the seventeen-year locust or periodical cicada, are noted for their length of life underground.

b. Occurring in a regular succession.

periodical colours: a series of coloured rings or bands due to the interference of light waves, in which almost the same colours are repeated several times in similar order, e.g. Newton's rings.

1830 HERSCHEL *Stud. Nat. Phil.* II. ii. 100 Doubly refracting substances exhibit periodical colours by exposure to polarized light. **1831** BREWSTER *Optics* xiv. 125 The new series of periodical colours which cross both the ordinary and the lateral images.

3. *Arith.* Of, pertaining to, or expressed in, periods (sense 13). *rare.*

1674 JEAKE *Arith.* (1696) 15 The Periodical Division shews the thousandth place of the Number.

4. = PERIODIC 3. ? *Obs.*

1683 CAVE *Ecclesiastici* 335 Nazianzen's [style] is..more sententious and periodical. **1710** ADDISON *Whig Exam.* No. 4 ¶4 Your high nonsense..is loud and sonorous, smooth and periodical. **1780** HARRIS *Philol. Enq.* II. iv. 103 The author..would refer..to the beginnings of his Hermes and his Philosophical Arrangements, where some attempts have been made in this periodical style.

5. a. Of literary publications, magazines, etc.: Published at regular intervals longer than a day, as weekly, monthly, etc. **b.** Written in or characteristic of such publications; writing for or connected with magazines, etc.

In b, rather an attrib. use of the sb., B. 1.

1716 ADDISON *Freeholder* No. 45 ¶7 No Periodical Author ..must effect to keep in vogue for any considerable time. **1766** W. GORDON *Gen. Counting-ho.* 260 Magazines and such periodical writings. **1806** SOUTHEY *Lett., to Lieut. Southey* 5 Mar., He..knows good from bad, which is not very often the case with periodical critics. **1838–9** HALLAM *Hist. Lit.* IV. vi. §35 The Mercure Galant was a famous magazine of light periodical amusement. *a* **1854** H. REED *Lect. Eng. Lit.* vii. (1878) 231 The periodical literature, destined to acquire such unbounded influence in the news-paper press, and the leading reviews. **1882** FROUDE *Carlyle* I. 259 Some [literary men] were selling their souls to the periodical press.

6. Assuming a system of periods. (*nonce-use.*)

1825 CULBERTSON *Lect. Rev.* xiii. 184 All the periodical interpreters consider the Church of Ephesus as the hieroglyphic of the Universal or Catholic Church during the age of the Apostles.

B. *sb.* [elliptical use of the adj.]

1. A magazine or miscellany, the successive numbers of which are published at regular intervals (as weekly, monthly, etc.). Not applied to a book published in parts, nor usually to a daily, weekly, or monthly newspaper. Also *attrib.*

1798 J. ANDERSON in *Washington's Writ.* (1893) XIV. 53 *note*, It will be a monthly periodical. **1839** LOWELL *Lett.* (1894) I. 46 [To] get paid for contributions to periodicals. **1878** LECKY *Eng. in 18th C.* I. iv. 519 The 'Gentleman's Magazine'..was speedily followed by..the 'London Magazine': and in 1750 there were eight periodicals of this kind. **1878** *Harper's Mag.* Jan. 192 He used to look into the windows of the periodical stores. **1910** A. E. BOSTWICK *Amer. Publ. Library* 282 In some New York branches periodical reading rooms may be used as assembly rooms. **1938** L. M. HARROD *Librarians' Gloss.* 99 *Magazine case*, a cover for periodicals, usually having some contrivance for holding the magazine-cord, rod, etc. Also called 'Periodical case' and 'Reading case'. **1961** T. LANDAU *Encycl. Librarianship* (ed. 2) 275/2 *Periodical stack*, a stack constructed to display periodicals, with space on lower shelves for storage of back numbers.

2. *nonce-uses.* **a.** = Periodical motion; **b.** A periodical examination.

1892 *Ohio Statesman* 3 May, The superior planets.. making their regular periodicals around the sun in their regular periods. **1897** ABBOTT & CAMPBELL *Life & Lett. Jowett* II. v. 136 They were examined at their various 'periodicals' to test their progress.

3. *pl. U.S. slang.* Recurring drinking bouts or sprees.

1890 in BARRÈRE & LELAND *Dict. Slang* II. 124/1 Are you in the book business?.. Ma and pa were talking last night about your having your little periodicals. **1902** H. L. WILSON *Spenders* x. 107 They telegraphed the Butte National to wire his description, and the answer was 'tall and drunk'. Well, son, his periodicals wa'n't all.

Hence **peri'odicalness**, the quality of being periodical or recurring periodically. *rare.*

1670 *Phil. Trans.* V. 2075 The opinion of Galen and others concerning the Periodicalness or Stated returns of that Flux. **1727** in BAILEY vol. II, and in mod. Dicts.

peri'odicalist. *rare.* [See -IST.] A writer for periodicals. So **peri'odicalism, peri'odicalize** *v.*

1824 *New Monthly Mag.* X. 223 We periodicalists who live to shoot folly as it flies. **1837** *Fraser's Mag.* XVI. 530 It is a real injury to our literature when the slap-dash spirit of periodicalism comes into Cyclopædias. **1858** G. GILFILLAN *Let.* in Watson *Life* (1892) 224, I am preaching and periodicalising briskly.

periodically (pɪərɪˈɒdɪkəlɪ), *adv.* [See -LY[2].] At regularly recurring or definite intervals; also *loosely*, from time to time, every now and then.

1646 SIR T. BROWNE *Pseud. Ep.* III. xvii. 149 They commonly doe both proceed unto perfection, and have legitimate exclusions, and periodically succeed each other. *a* **1745** W. BROOME (J.), There will be a regular flux and reflux..every eight hours periodically. **1825** MCCULLOCH *Pol. Econ.* II. v. 198 It may even be doubted, whether Turkey and Egypt are upon an average much less populous for the plagues which periodically lay them waste. **1860** TYNDALL *Glac.* I. vii. 51 Over this summit the glacier is pushed, and has its back periodically broken.

b. *nonce-use.* In a magazine or 'periodical'.

1838 *Fraser's Mag.* XVII. 315 The crime is not the writing mischievously, or shamefully, but of writing periodically.

periodicity (ˌpɪərɪəˈdɪsɪtɪ). [ad. F. *périodicité* (1796 in Hatz.-Darm., *Dict. Acad.* 1835), f. L. *periodic-us*: see PERIODIC and -ITY.]

1. a. The quality or character of being periodic; the quality of regular recurrence; tendency to recur at (more or less) regular intervals. (Chiefly in scientific use.)

1833 HERSCHEL *Astron.* xii. 380 Wherever we can trace the law of periodicity—the regular recurrence of the same phænomena in the same times. 1868 LOCKYER *Guillemin's Heavens* (ed. 3) 27 We shall see..that the number of [sun] spots follow a certain periodicity. 1879 [see PERIODIC 2]. 1882 VINES *Sachs' Bot.* 755 A similar periodicity exists in the growth of leaves when day and night alternate normally.

b. *Chem.* The complex periodic variation of the properties of the chemical elements with increasing atomic number.

1879 ROSCOE & SCHORLEMMER *Treat. Chem.* II. II. 506 The law of periodicity was afterwards further developed by Meyer and Mendelejeff. 1907 *Westm. Gaz.* 4 Feb. 6/3 Gallium, scandium, and germanium, all subsequently discovered, did fit into the scale of 'periodicity'. 1969 A. J. IHDE in J. W. Van Spronsen *Periodic Syst. Chem. Elem.* p. x, The periodic table reached its final forms before atomic structure revealed the basis for periodicity.

c. The frequency of a periodic phenomenon, esp. an alternating current.

1900 *Jrnl. Soc. Arts* XLVIII. 848/2 The other carrying about 20 amperes with a periodicity of 60 cycles per second. 1913 *Chambers's Jrnl.* Jan. 102/1 The electricity used for wireless telegraphy is..used under different conditions as to pressure and periodicity. 1938 *Times* 13 Oct. 8/3 The periodicities of the front and back springs are arranged at a predetermined variance so that coincidence should not occur. 1943 *Gloss. Terms Electr. Engin.* (*B.S.I.*) 11 *Frequency* (*periodicity*, deprecated), the number of cycles per second. The reciprocal of the period.

2. *Physiol.* Recurrence of the 'monthly period'; menstruation: cf. PERIOD *sb.* 3 b.

1848 [see PERIODOSCOPE]. 1875 *N. Amer. Rev.* CXX. 187 In this harsh climate..in their case, periodicity, nervous system, intellect, and health require especial care.

periodide: see under PERIODATE.

periodi'zation. [f. PERIODIZE *v.* + -ATION.] Division into periods of time; *spec.* the grouping of historical and cultural events in chronological periods (see PERIOD *sb.* 4c) for the purposes of discussion and evaluation.

1938 [see CONCEPT *sb.* 2c]. 1952 K. R. POPPER *Open Society* (ed. 2) II. xii. 59 No doubt, his [*sc.* Hegel's] vast historicist generalizations, periodizations, and interpretations fascinated some historians. 1957 K. A. WITTFOGEL *Oriental Despotism* ix. 395 This periodization appeared again in an article in 1916. 1963 R. M. GRANT *Hist. Introd. New Testament* i. 14 The question of periodization arose in the second century... Generally speaking, historians have differentiated three periods. 1967 L. DEUEL *Conquistadors without Swords* xxi. 285 Uaxactún yielded a continuous series of pottery which made it possible to establish a complete overall Maya stratigraphy and periodization. 1970 B. BREWSTER tr. *Althusser & Balibar's Reading Capital* (1975) II. iv. 94 On this level, then, the whole problem of the science of history would consist of the division of this continuum according to a *periodization* corresponding to the succession of one dialectal totality after another. 1973 *Times Lit. Suppl.* 16 Nov. 1386/1 Accepting the traditional periodization of world history according to the days of creation. 1974 J. WHITE tr. *Poulantzas's Fascism & Dictatorship* IV. 233 The general line which was progressively dominant in the USSR and in the Comintern can allow us to make a relatively clear periodization of the Comintern, a periodization which can also be very useful for the history of the USSR. 1976 *Brit. Jrnl. Sociol.* XXVII. 301 In as far as sociology defines its object of investigation as 'society', 'the social system' or some such general unspecified synonym, it denies itself any rigorous principle of historical periodization.

'periodize, *v.* [f. PERIOD *sb.* + -IZE.]

†**1.** *trans.* To bring to a period or end; to terminate. *Obs.*

1611 SIR W. MURE *Elegie* 22 The frouning faits, alwayes my fatall foes, Nocht bot our mynds permits to meet, to periodize our woes. 1658 COKAINE *Obstinate Lady* I. ii, Stir not then thou glorious Fabrick of the heavens, And periodize the Musick of the spheres. 1683 E. HOOKER *Pref. Pordage's Mystic Div.* 98 For periodizing, or putting an end ..to the..altercations, disputations and dubitations of.. Mystic Theologie.

2. To divide (a portion of time) into periods; to assign (historical and cultural events) to specified periods. Cf. prec. So (*rare*) **'periodizer,** one who periodizes in this way; **'periodizing** *vbl. sb.*

a 1943 R. G. COLLINGWOOD *Idea of Hist.* (1946) II. 54, I will take a single example of medieval periodizing. In the twelfth century Joachim of Floris divided history into three periods. 1959 *Listener* 20 Aug. 291/2 The fifteenth century has been a favourite hunting ground for the periodizers of history. 1965 K. CHARLTON *Educ. Renaissance Eng.* ii. 40 The dangers of periodizing history and of ignoring the carry-over of medieval ideas alongside and within humanistic thought have already been mentioned. 1970 B. BREWSTER tr. *Althusser & Balibar's Reading Capital* (1975) II. iv. 103 This is antipodal to the empirically visible history in which the time of all histories is the simple time of continuity and in which the 'content' is the vacuity of events that occur in it which one later tries to determine with dividing procedures in order to 'periodize' that continuity. 1972 *Language* XLVIII. 423 Lyons' manner of 'periodizing' Chomsky's intellectual history has its justification, but a somewhat different distribution of emphasis might be fairer to the histories of both linguistics and rationalism. 1973 *Sci. Amer.* Sept. 194/2 The bulk of the text summarizes and criticizes the theories for Bode's law in the context of an overall view of the origin of the solar system, an event that Nieto broadly periodizes along the lines of Sir Fred Hoyle's nebular-plus-magnetic theory.

periodogram (pɪəri'ɒdəgræm). [f. PERIOD *sb.* + -O + -GRAM.] A diagram or method of graphical representation which is designed to detect or display any periodicity (usu. with time) in a set of measurements of a quantity; *spec.* one in which the results of harmonic analysis of the data, performed on the assumption in turn of different periods of variation, are plotted as a function of the period. Freq. *attrib.*, as **periodogram analysis**, the analysis of data by means of a periodogram.

1898 A. SCHUSTER in *Terrestr. Magn.* III. 24 It is convenient to have a word for some representation of a variable quantity which shall correspond to the 'spectrum' of a luminous radiation. I propose the word *periodogram*. *Ibid.* 25 The periodogram of the sound emitted by an organ pipe or a violin string consists of a series of equidistant 'lines'. 1906 *Proc. R. Soc.* A. LXXVII. 141 The periodigram..is the diagram representing the intensity of periodic variations as determined from the sum of the squares of the two Fourier coefficients belonging to each assumed period. 1919 *Nature* 26 June 338/1 A periodogram analysis of the Greenwich temperature records. 1939 J. A. SCHUMPETER *Business Cycles* I. iv. 165 This is the most successful application so far made of the periodogram analysis to economic data. 1957 G. E. HUTCHINSON *Treat. Limnol.* I. v. 334 Olson (1950) examined the matter by means of periodogram analysis and found no evidence of a period near 12 hours. 1974 *Nature* 8 Feb. 339/3 The apparently erratic optical fluctuations have been analysed by various investigators using power spectra and the so-called periodogram techniques.

periodograph (pɪəri'ɒdəgrɑːf, -æ-). [f. PERIOD *sb.* + -O + -GRAPH.] **1.** A periodogram; orig. *spec.* a curve drawn in a periodogram.

1899 A. SCHUSTER in *Trans. Cambr. Philos. Soc.* XVIII. 108 With T as abscissa and S^2 as ordinate, draw a curve, which may be called the 'Periodograph'... It will be seen that the 'Periodograph' corresponds exactly to the curve which represents the distribution of energy in the spectrum. 1936 *Rev. Econ. Statistics* XVIII. 63/2 Like the Fourier periodogram, this periodograph will show distinct peaks in the vicinity of real periodicities. 1950 CONRAD & POLLAK *Methods in Climatol.* (ed. 2) xi. 370 The name 'periodograph' is no longer used and Schuster's 'periodograph' is now called a 'periodogram'.

2. An instrument for automatically making a periodogram analysis or Fourier analysis of a curve by optical means.

1930 G. A. R. FOSTER in *Jrnl. Textile Inst.* XXI. T18 The grating periodograph now described is an instrument which has been..designed for the examination of the irregularities in cotton spinning products... The periodograph is simply a method of carrying out automatically the periodogram analysis..of series of observations for hidden periodicities. 1946 *Suppl. Jrnl. R. Statistical Soc.* VIII. 44 In the correlation periodograph, due to Martindale, the grating of the grating periodograph is replaced by a replica of the curve on a reduced scale. 1973 *Physics Bull.* Mar. 154/2 The 'Periodograph' was never applied to the analysis of electron micrographs until Warren (1972) had the ingenious idea of replacing the grating by a series of point sources such as flashlamp bulbs and interposing a micrograph between the bulbs and the final screen.

perio'dology. [See -OLOGY 1.]

1857 DUNGLISON *Med. Lex.* 695 *Periodology*.., the doctrine of periodicity in health and disease. 1893 in *Syd. Soc. Lex.*

periodontal, etc.: see PERI- a, b, c.

periodontia (pɛrɪə'dɒntɪə). *Dentistry.* orig. *U.S.* [f. *periodont(ium* s.v. PERI- 1 b + -IA[1].] = PERIODONTICS.

1914 *Items of Interest* July 429 We..deem it for the best interests of the public and the profession that a society should be formed, to the end that those especially interested may meet and work together..for the scientific investigation of periodontoclasia and caries, and that the practice of oral prophylaxis and periodontia as an exclusive speciality may be encouraged. 1924 *Glasgow Herald* 5 Mar. 9/4 Harold Box..holds the position of Professor of Dental Pathology and Periodontia at the Royal College of Dental Surgeons at Toronto, Canada. 1960 S. SORRIN *Pract. of Periodontia* p. vii/1 The treatment for periodontal disease is of interest not only to the specialist in periodontia but also to the general practitioner of dentistry. 1960 *Times* 27 July 3/2 (Advt.), Applications are invited for the appointment of Head of Department of Periodontia.

Hence **perio'dontic** *a.* = *periodontal* adj. s.v. PERI- 1 a.

1926 R. J. E. SCOTT *Gould's Med. Dict.* 984/1 *Periodontic*, same as periodontal. 1978 *N.Y. Times* 30 Mar. B18/2 (Advt.), Dentist. Experienced for general practice... Crown and bridge, periodontic, endodontic, pedodontic.

periodontics (pɛrɪə'dɒntɪks), *sb. pl.* (const. as sing.). *Dentistry.* [f. as prec.: see -IC 2.] The branch of dentistry concerned with periodontal tissue, disorders, etc.

1948 L. I. GROSSMAN *Handbk. Dental Pract.* v. 83/1 Periodontics is that branch of dentistry which deals with the science and treatment of periodontal disease. 1960 S. SORRIN *Pract. of Periodontia* i. 1 The practice of periodontics is based on an understanding and recognition of the healthy periodontium. 1969 BOHANNAN & SAXE in Morris & Bohannan *Dental Specialities* vii. 260/1 Time devoted to periodontics in the traditional dental educational program has been woefully inadequate. 1975 J. E. CHASTEEN *Essent. Clin. Dental Assisting* xi. 200/1 Periodontics is the branch of dentistry that deals with the diagnosis and treatment of diseases which destroy the supporting tissues of the teeth.

periodontist (pɛrɪə'dɒntɪst). *Dentistry.* [f. PERIODONT(IA + -IST.] A specialist or expert in periodontics.

1920 STEDMAN *Med. Dict.* (ed. 6) 755/2 *Periodontist*, a dentist who specializes in periodontia. 1954 *Sydney Morning Herald* 26 Oct. 1/3 The judges were an orthodontist (for straightness), a periodontist (for condition of the gums), and a children's dental specialist. 1963 E. B. WHITE *Let.* 6 May (1976) 500 A periodontist..proposes to remove a small section of my gum. 1965 J. C. MUHLER *Fifty-Two Pearls* ix. 93 In most cases the family dentist will ..refer the patient to a periodontist (a dental specialist who treats diseased gingiva or bone). 1969 BOHANNAN & SAXE in Morris & Bohannan *Dental Specialities* vii. 259/2 There are ..not enough practicing periodontists to treat all periodontal disease. 1978 *Detroit Free Press* 16 Apr. 14C/4 (Advt.), A local Don Juan periodontist is murdered.

periodontitis, -odontium: see PERI- c, b.

periodontoclasia (ˌpɛrɪədɒntəʊ'kleɪsɪə). *Dentistry.* [f. as PERIODONTIA + Gr. κλάσ-ις breaking (f. κλάειν to break) + -IA[1].] Destruction or degeneration of periodontal tissue.

1914 [see PERIODONTIA]. 1960 S. SORRIN *Pract. of Periodontia* iv. 128/2 Pulpal disease may invade the periodontal space, producing inflammation and periodontoclasia.

periodontology (ˌpɛrɪədɒn'tɒlədʒɪ). *Dentistry.* orig. *U.S.* [f. as PERIODONTIA + -OLOGY.] = PERIODONTICS.

1914 *Items of Interest* July 529 (*heading*) A statement to the profession. From the American Academy of Oral Prophylaxis and Periodontology. 1920 *Jrnl. National Dental Assoc.* Feb. 159 (*heading*) Fundamentals of periodontology. 1960 S. SORRIN *Pract. of Periodontia* p. vii, Constant ferment of research and practical application is vital to progress in the art and science of periodontology. 1962 R. BRADLAW in Blake & Trott *Periodontology* p. v, Periodontology has not had the emphasis in dental education that it should have had. 1972 *Science* 2 June 1033/1 Department of Periodontology, Harvard School of Dental Medicine, Boston, Massachusetts.

periodontosis (ˌpɛrɪəʊdɒn'təʊsɪs). *Dentistry.* [f. as PERIODONTIA + -OSIS.] A periodontal disorder; *spec.* one in which there is a loss of alveolar bone, leading to displacement or loosening of teeth, without inflammation.

1936 DUNNING & DAVENPORT *Dict. Dental Sci.* 422/2 *Periodontosis*, a diseased condition of the periodontal membrane. 1942 ORBAN & WEINMANN in *Jrnl. Periodontology* XIII. 31 (*heading*) Diffuse atrophy of the alveolar bone (periodontosis). 1962 BLAKE & TROTT *Periodontology* iii. 28 Incidence of periodontal associated with alveolar bone destruction and pocket formation. This type of disease has been divided into chronic periodontitis .., which is inflammatory, and periodontosis.., which is principally degenerative. Periodontosis is often complicated by inflammation and the condition is then called periodontitis complex. 1975 J. D. MANSON *Periodontics* (ed. 3) xviii. 222 (*heading*) Juvenile periodontitis ('periodontosis'). *Ibid.*, Orban and Weinmann (1942) coined the term 'periodontosis' believing that the condition represented a degeneration of the periodontal ligament. However, there is no evidence for that belief.

periodoscope (pɪəri'ɒdəskəʊp). [See -SCOPE.] (See quot. 1893.)

1848 W. T. SMITH (*title*) The Periodoscope, with its application to Obstetric Calculations and the Periodicities of the Sex. 1857 in MAYNE *Expos. Lex.* 1893 *Syd. Soc. Lex.*, *Periodoscope, Obstet.*, a dial, constructed to help in calculating the day on which labour will most probably occur, invented by Tyler Smith.

‖**periœci** (pɛrɪ'iːsaɪ), *sb. pl.* In 6 sometimes **perieces.** [med.L., a. Gr. περίοικοι, pl. of περίοικος, lit. dwelling round, neighbouring; also as below. In F. *périœciens*; in 16th c. *perieciens*, *perieces*: see quot. 1594.]

1. Dwellers under the same parallel of latitude, but opposite meridians. (Cf. ANTŒCI.)

1594 R. ASHLEY tr. *Loys le Roy* 123 b, In our time the Castilians haue sayled beyond the Canaries, and bearing towards the West, passed vnto our *Perieces*. 1652–62 HEYLIN *Cosmogr.* Introd. (1674) 20/1 'Periœci' are such as dwell in the same Parallel, on the same side of the Æquator, how distant soever they be East and West. 1682 SIR T. BROWNE *Chr. Mor.* I. §23 Fools, which are Antipodes unto the Wise, conceive themselves to be but their *Periœci*, and in the same parallel with them. 1704 J. HARRIS *Lex. Techn.* I. s.v., *Periœci*..have the same Seasons of the Year..at the very same time; as also the same Length of Days and Nights. 1772 J. H. MOORE *Pract. Navig.* (1828) 53.

2. *Gr. Hist.* The dwellers in the country round a city, or in the surrounding country towns and villages. Hence **peri'œcic** (-'œkɪc), **peri'œcid** (-'œkɪd) *adjs.*

1846 GROTE *Greece* II. vi. II. 483 The Periœkus was also a freeman and a citizen not of Sparta, but of some one of the hundred townships of Laconia. *Ibid.*, The island of Cythêra ..one of the Periœkic townships. *Ibid.* vii. II. 580 The dominion of Elis over her Periœkid territory. 1869 RAWLINSON *Anc. Hist.* 127 The injudicious severity with which Argos treated her perioecic cities. 1873 SYMONDS *Grk. Poets* iii. 85 The bitter hatred and contempt which the Greek nobles in a Dorian state felt for the *Perioeci*, or farmers of the neighbouring country.

periœsophageal to **-orbitis:** see PERI- a, b, c.

periogue, perioque, obs. forms of PIROGUE.

perionet: see PERE-JONETTE, PEAR *sb.* 5.

‖**perionychia** (ˌpɛrɪəʊˈnɪkɪə). *Path.* [mod.L., f. Gr. περί around + ὄνυξ, ὀνυχ- nail.] Inflammation round the nails.

1879 BUMSTEAD *Ven. Dis.* 579.

periost (ˈpɛrɪɒst). *Anat.* [f. mod.L. PERIOST(EUM.] = PERIOSTEUM.

1900 in DORLAND *Med. Dict.* **1902** *Proc. Zool. Soc.* I. 212 The perisclerium is continuous with the periost of the pedicle portion [of the horn]. **1927** HALDANE & HUXLEY *Animal Biol.* ix. 185 The basal joint.. was removed and a piece of healthy bone with its bone-forming membrane (periost) grafted in from another situation. **1959** *Jrnl. Exper. Zool.* CXLII. 631 Both the periost and hypertrophied areas show a strong black deposit of cobalt sulphide. **1973** *Biol. Abstr.* LVI. 719/1 In the periost, described were fibroblasts, precursor cells, [etc.].

periosteal (pɛrɪˈɒstɪəl), *a.* [f. PERIOSTE-UM + -AL[1].] Surrounding or occurring around a bone; of, pertaining to, or connected with the periosteum.

1830 S. COOPER *Dict. Pract. Surg.* (ed. 6) 465 These are the periosteal exostoses of Sir Astley Cooper. **1845** TODD & BOWMAN *Phys. Anat.* I. 112 A layer of tissue.. which may be called the periosteal layer. **1875** H. WALTON *Dis. Eye* 53 A periosteal swelling.

periosteo-, used as combining form of PERIOSTEUM, as in **periˌosteo-alˈveolar** *a.* [see ALVEOLAR], belonging to the periosteum (of the jaw-bone) and the sockets of the teeth; **periˈosteophyte** [Gr. φυτόν plant, growth], a bony growth from the periosteum; **periˈosteoˌtome** [Gr. -τομος cutting], 'the special knife used for periosteotomy' (*Syd. Soc. Lex.*); **periosteˈotomy** [Gr. τομή a cutting], 'the operation of cutting through the periosteum' (*ibid.*).

1897 *Allbutt's Syst. Med.* II. 932 Periosteo-alveolar swelling. **1889** TREVES *Man. Surg.* II. 96 These periosteal new growths are known pathologically as *osteophytes*, or more correctly as *periosteophytes*.

periˈosteous, *a. rare.* [f. PERIOSTE-UM + -OUS.] = PERIOSTEAL.

1822–34 *Good's Study Med.* (ed. 4) II. 58 The tendinous and periosteous variety [of whitlow].

‖**periosteum** (pɛrɪˈɒstiːəm). *Anat.* Also 6–7 -ium, 7 -ion. [mod.L., for ancient L. *periosteon* (Cælius Aurelianus *c* 420), a. Gr. περιόστεον, neuter of περιόστεος adj. 'round the bones', f. περί round + ὀστέον bone. In F. *périoste* (Paré 16th c.).] The dense fibro-vascular membrane which envelops the bones (except where they are covered by cartilage), and from the inner (vascular) layer of which bone-substance is produced.

1597 A. M. tr. *Guillemeau's Fr. Chirurg.* 2/2 That verye tender and sensible pellicle, *Periostium.* **1651** BIGGS *New Disp.* 186 *Periostion* or Coat environing the Scull. **1741** MONRO *Anat.* (ed. 3) 153 They are said to have no proper *Periosteum* within the Sockets. **1835–6** TODD *Cycl. Anat.* I. 433/2 The periosteum is a fibrous membrane of a dull white colour. **1881** MIVART *Cat* 256 The periosteum of the neural canal.

¶ **b.** = PERIOSTRACUM.

1774 GOLDSM. *Nat. Hist.* VII. 10 Shells..have an external crust, or periosteum, as Swammerdam calls it.

‖**periostitis** (ˌpɛrɪɒˈstaɪtɪs). *Path.* Also more etymologically **periosteitis** (-tiːˈaɪtɪs). [f. prec. + -ITIS. In F. *périostéite, -ostite.*] Inflammation of the periosteum. Hence **periostitic** (-ˈɪtɪk) *a.*, pertaining to or affected with periostitis.

1843 R. J. GRAVES *Syst. Clin. Med.* xxviii. 354 The others ..were labouring under ozæna and periostitic pains. *Ibid.* 361 Periostitis is one of the most common effects of mercurialization. **1854** JONES & SIEV. *Pathol. Anat.* (1875) 838 Simple periostitis is either suppuration or ossification.

‖**periostracum** (pɛrɪˈɒstrəkəm). *Zool.* [mod.L., f. Gr. περί around + ὄστρακον shell of a mussel, etc.] The outer horny covering of the shell of a mollusc or brachiopod. Hence **periˈostracal** *a.*, pertaining to the periostracum.

1840 *Penny Cycl.* XVII. 452/1. **1841** *Ibid.* XXI. 373/1 The external coat or layer, Epidermis and Periostracum of authors, is of a somewhat horny or membranaceous character. **1870** NICHOLSON *Man. Zool.* 230 All living shells have an outer layer of animal matter, which is known as the 'epidermis', or 'periostracum'.

periot, variant of PERIT *Obs.*, minute weight.

periotic (pɛrɪˈɒtɪk), *a.* (*sb.*) *Anat.* [f. Gr. περί around + οὖς, ὠτ- the ear, ὠτικ-ός of the ear.] Surrounding the ear: applied to those bones of the skull (*prootic, epiotic,* and *opisthotic*) which constitute a protective case or capsule for the internal ear; usually confluent or entirely fused, forming the petrosal or petromastoid portion of the temporal bone. *ellipt.* as *sb.* A periotic bone.

1866 BRANDE & COX *Dict. Sci.* etc., *Periotic Bones*.., the bones which surround the internal ear, or *labyrinth.* **1870** ROLLESTON *Anim. Life* 8 A conjugate foramen between the squamosal and the periotic. **1872** MIVART *Elem. Anat.* 106 These three bony barriers protecting the internal ear may be conveniently spoken of as the periotic mass.

peripachymeningitis to **peripapillary**: see PERI- a, c.

†**peripatetian** (-ˈiːʃ(ɪ)ən). *Obs.* Also 6 peripatecian, -etion, -icien, 7–8 -ician, (6 paripatecian, 7 pyripatition). [For *peripateti-cian, ad. F. *péripatéticien*, f. L. *peripatētic-us* PERIPATETIC + *-ien*, -IAN.]

A philosopher of the Peripatetic school.

a **1533** LD. BERNERS *Gold. Bk. M. Aurel.* (1546) Bij, Peripaticiens, Academiens and Epicuriens. **1559** AYLMER *Harborowe* Cjb, Stoickes, Academikes, Paripatecians. *c* **1590** GREENE *Fr. Bacon* xi. 73, I will..walk up and down, and be a peripatetian and a philosopher of Aristotle's stamp. **1631** R. H. *Arraignm. Whole Creature* xii. §1. 108 Any Axiome of Aristotle amongst his Pyripatitions. **1753** tr. *Voltaire's Micromegas* 36 An old peripatician lifting up his voice, exclaimed..'The soul is perfection and reason'.

b. One who walks or travels about (with play on prec. sense).

1598 BP. HALL *Sat.* v. iii. 33 Yet certes Mæcha is a Platonist, To all, they say, saue who so do not list; Because her husband a farre-trafiq'd man, Is a profest Peripatecian.

peripatetic (pɛrɪpəˈtɛtɪk), *a.* and *sb.* Forms: (5 perypatetik), 6 perrepateticke, peripatetycke, 6–7 -tike, -tique, 7–8 -tick, 8- peripatetic. [a. F. *péripatétique* (in 14th c. *pery-*, Hatz.-Darm.), ad. L. *peripatēticus* belonging to the peripatetic philosophy, a. Gr. περιπατητικός given to walking about, f. περιπατητ-ής one who walks about, f. περί about, around + πατεῖν to tread, to walk; in reference to the custom of Aristotle, who taught while walking in a περίπατος or place for walking in the Lyceum at Athens.]

A. *adj.* **1.** Of or belonging to the school or system of philosophy founded by Aristotle, or the Aristotelian sect; Aristotelian; held or believed by this sect of philosophers. (With capital P.)

1566 PAINTER *Pal. Pleas* I. 63 Phocion a peripatetique philosopher. **1664** POWER *Exp. Philos.* I. 57 The Controversie 'twixt the Peripatetick and Atomical Philosophers. **1751** JOHNSON *Rambler* No. 85 ⁋13 The old peripatetick principle, that Nature abhors a Vacuum. **1837** WHEWELL *Hist. Induct. Sc.* (1857) I. 193 The mixed Peripatetic and Platonic philosophy of the time.

2. Walking about or from place to place in connexion with some occupation or calling; itinerant.

Often humorous, with a glance at sense 1.

1642 HOWELL *For. Trav.* (Arb.) 13 Peregrination..may be not improperly called a moving Academy or the true Peripatetique Schoole. **1662** S. P. *Acc. Latitude Men* 15 A certain Peripatetick Artificer..came that way, who undertook to mend it. **1768** STERNE *Sent. Journ.* 13. **1812** L. HUNT in *Examiner* 11 May 301/2 A persecuted and peripatetic lady. **1831** CARLYLE *Sart. Res.* II. viii, His Peripatetic habits, favourable to Meditation. **1899** *Allbutt's Syst. Med.* VII. 258 Peripatetic mountebanks used..to include a goat among their stage properties.

†**b.** *loosely.* Used for pacing up and down in, as a gallery or cloister. *Obs.*

1631 BRATHWAIT *Whimzies, Exchange-man* 31 Entring now the long peripatetick gallery, they are encountred with volleyes of..questions.

c. *fig.* Of speech: Rambling. *rare.*

1865 DICKENS *Mut. Fr.* I. xi, [He] prolonged to the utmost stretch of possibility a peripatetic account of an archery meeting.

B. *sb.* **1.** A disciple of Aristotle; a member of the sect of philosophers who held the doctrines of Aristotle.

c **1400** tr. *Secreta Secret., Gov. Lordsh.* 47 Oon sect þat er namyd [per]ypatetiks affermes þat he steigh to þe emperien heuene yn þe semynge of fir. **1550** BALE *Eng. Vot.* II. 81 b, The peripatetyckes or naturall philosophers of Aristotle's secte. **1701** tr. *Le Clerc's Prim. Fathers* (1702) 5 The School-men, who were Peripateticks, explained Divinity by Aristotle's Principles. **1830** MACKINTOSH *Eth. Philos.* Wks. 1846 I. 24 The mediocrity in which the Peripatetics placed Virtue.

2. One who walks about; a traveller; an itinerant dealer or trader. (Mostly *humorous.*)

1617 J. MOORE *Mappe Mans Mort.* II. iv. 109 The Diuell is a Peripateticke,..alwaies walking and going about, seeking whom he may ensnare. **1712** STEELE *Spect.* No. 376 ⁋1 It seems the peripatetic who walked before her was a watchman in the neighbourhood. **1798** SOUTHEY in Robberds *Mem. W. Taylor* I. 221, I have a traveller, and I am afraid I shall want another of these peripatetics. **1864** LOWELL *Fireside Trav.* 195 John and Jonathan are always in a hurry when they turn peripatetics.

3. *pl.* Journeyings to and fro; movements hither and thither. *humorous.*

1769 MRS. GRIFFITH *Delicate Distress* I. 218 (F. Hall). **1811** L. M. HAWKINS *C'tess & Gertr.* I. 41 You can divine their 'having friends to dinner' by the white-aproned satellites of the confectioner, and the preternatural peripatetics of pots and kettles.

peripatetical (pɛrɪpəˈtɛtɪkəl), *a.* Now *rare.* [f. L. *peripatētic-us* (see prec.) + -AL[1].]

1. Of, pertaining to, or relating to the Peripatetic philosophers or their system; also = PERIPATETIC *a.* 1. Now *rare* or *Obs.*

1569 J. SANFORD tr. *Agrippa's Van. Artes* 67 b, These doth Thomas of Aquine follow fighting with a peripateticall argument. **1570** DEE *Math. Pref.* Aiv, All maner of Philosophie, Academicall, or Peripateticall. *a* **1688** CUDWORTH *Immut. Mor.* IV. i. (1731) 147 Other Opinion called Peripatetical, that asserts the Eduction of Immaterial Forms out of the Power of Matter. **1692** RAY *Disc.* ii. (1732) 70 Unless we will grant a peripatetical condensation and rarefaction.

2. = PERIPATETIC *a.* 2. (Mostly *humorous.*)

1633 T. ADAMS *Exp. 2 Peter* iii. 8 He wearies..his indefatigable solicitor, and makes his peripatetical profession tedious to him. *a* **1634** RANDOLPH *Pedlar* Poems (1652) 32 A Peripateticall Iourny-man that like another Atlas carries his heavenly shop on 's shoulders. **1854** *Fraser's Mag.* L. 345 The British Association,..the Archæological Institute, and the other peripatetical gatherings.

†**b.** ? Of the nature of a formal or strutting walk.

1589 NASHE *Pref. Greene's Menaphon* (Arb.) 10 Hauing starched their beardes most curiouslie, to make a peripateticall path into the inner parts of the Citie. **1607** DEKKER *Westw. Hoe* II. i. Wks. 1873 II. 293 A Constable new chosen kept not such a peripateticall gate.

Hence **peripaˈtetically** *adv.*, in the course of walking about or moving on.

1837 CARLYLE *French Rev.* I. VII. vii, The tall Marquis.. looks peripatetically on this scene from under his umbrella. **1871** *Daily News* 18 Sept., [He] divided his attention between a homely breakfast, consumed peripatetically, the despatch of orderlies, and the elaboration of details.

†**peripaˈtetican.** *Obs.* = PERIPATETIC *sb.* 1.

1559 AYLMER *Harborowe* Aij b, Philosophers, as Academians, Peripateticans, Stoikes, Epicures.

†**peripaˈteticate**, *v. nonce-wd.* [f. PERIPATETIC + -ATE[3]: cf. *rusticate.*] *intr.* with *it*: To 'do' the peripatetic, to walk on foot.

1793 SOUTHEY *Let. to G. C. Bedford* 31 July, I am here and there, and everywhere;..now peripateticating it to Cambridge, and now an equestrian in the land of cyder.

peripateticism (ˌpɛrɪpəˈtɛtɪsɪz(ə)m). [f. PERIPATETIC + -ISM 2.]

1. The Peripatetic system of philosophy.

1661 GLANVILL *Van. Dogm.* xvi. 152 From this stock grew School-divinity, which is but Peripateticism in a Theological Livery. **1725** WATTS *Logic* IV. ii. §5 Reading over the mere dry definitions and divisions of Scheibler's Compendium of Peripateticism. **1837–9** HALLAM *Hist. Lit.* III. iii. §4 The universities of Altdorf and Helmstadt were the chief nurseries of the genuine Peripateticism.

2. The habit or practice of walking about, or of travelling from place to place. (Mostly *humorous.*)

1820 *Blackw. Mag.* VIII. 92 Fourth-rate drudgery, doomed to dwindle..into unfeed peripateticism in the outer house. **1859** *All Year Round* No. 6. 133 That sham peripateticism that the old traveller affects on board ship.

†**peripaˈtetism.** *Obs. rare*[−1]. [a. F. *péripatétisme* (1670 in Hatz.-Darm.), f. Gr. περιπατητ-ής one who walks about + -ISM.]

= prec. 1.

1671 R. BOHUN *Wind* 48 In the more flourishing raign of Peripatetisme.

peripatize (ˈpɛrɪpəˌtaɪz), *v. rare.* [f. Gr. περιπατ-εῖν to walk about, περίπατ-ος a walk + -IZE.] *intr.* To play the peripatetic; to walk about.

1641 J. JOHNSON *Acad. Love* 4 Here I began to peripatize and philosophate upon the force and efficacie of this passion. **1843** LYTTON *Last Bar.* I. vii, The garden, in which..he was wont to peripatise.

‖**peripatus**[1], **-os** (pəˈrɪpətəs, -ɒs). [L. *peripatus* = Gr. περίπατος, f. περί about + πάτος way, path.] The walk in the Lyceum where Aristotle taught; hence *transf.* the school of Aristotle, or Peripatetic school of philosophy (cf. 'the Porch').

1682 SIR T. BROWNE *Chr. Mor.* III. §21 Sleep not in the Dogma's of the Peripatus, Academy, or Porticus. Be a moralist of the Mount. **1858** R. A. VAUGHAN *Ess. & Rem.* I. 5 He sees them walking in the *peripatus*, or sitting in the shady retirement of the exedra. **1867** LEWES *Hist. Philos.* (ed. 3) I. 280 [Aristotle] simply received permission to teach in the morning and evening at the *peripatos*,..[of which] the shady walks offered facilities to his accustomed habit of walking to and fro during the delivery of lectures.

‖**Peripatus**[2] (pəˈrɪpətəs). *Zool.* [mod.L., a. Gr. περίπατος (one) walking about: see prec.] A remarkable genus of Arthropods, constituting the family *Peripatidæ* (sometimes considered as a separate order or class, *Protracheata*, held to represent a primitive ancestral type of both myriapods and insects). The species are worm-like creatures with a pair of antennæ, a pair of jaws, and numerous legs, inhabiting damp places among decaying wood and the like, in the West Indies and Central America, South Africa, Australasia, and New Zealand. Hence **peˈripatid, peripaˈtidean, peˈripatoid** *adjs.*, of, pertaining or allied to *Peripatus.*

The animal was found at St. Vincent by Rev. L. Guilding, and described by him under this name in *Zool. Jrnl.* II. 443 (1826) as a new genus of Mollusca.

1840 tr. *Cuvier's Anim. Kingd.* 397. **1847** CARPENTER *Zool.* §839 Lastly, we may mention a very curious genus *Peripatus*, which is probably to be placed in this order [*Annelidæ*]. **1878** BELL *Gegenbaur's Comp. Anat.* 237 Peripatus has a simple form of body very similar to that of the Annulata. **1888** ROLLESTON & JACKSON *Anim. Life* 522.

peripediment ('pɛrɪpɛdɪmənt, pɛrɪ'pɛdɪmənt). *Geomorphol.* [f. PERI- + PEDIMENT[1].] A broad, gently sloping surface that is the top of a thickness of detrital alluvium and either extends outwards from a mountain-foot in an arid or semi-arid region or else smoothly continues the line of an intervening pediment.

1942 A. D. HOWARD in *Jrnl. Geomorphol.* V. 11 The term peripediment is suggested for a pediplane which levels an earlier basin fill. If both elements of the pediplane are present, the peripediment is always beyond and peripheral to the pediment. **1970** R. J. SMALL *Study of Landforms* ix. 308 The smaller and steeper bajadas tend to mask only the upper part of the rock pediment, burying the piedmont angle, but the larger and more gently sloping fans may be so extensive as to grade into the alluvial deposits of the peripediment. **1975** *Nature* 7 Aug. 468/1 This gravel.. seems to have been deposited as a series of large confluent fans derived from the escarpment, which form an extensive ..peripediment.

peripetalous: see PERI- a.

‖**peripeteia, -tia** (,pɛrɪpɪ'taɪə, -tiːə). Also anglicized as **peripety** (pə'rɪpɪtɪ), in 8 -ie. [a. Gr. περιπέτεια a turn right about, a sudden change, esp. that on which the plot of a tragedy hinges, f. περιπετής, lit. 'falling round', f. περί around + stem πετ- of πίπτειν to fall. The form *peripety* is ad. F. *péripétie* (Vauquelin, 16th c.).] A sudden change of fortune or reverse of circumstances (in a tragedy, etc., or, by extension, in the actual course of affairs). Also, according to the theory of Jung, the third stage, culmination, or turning point of a dream.

1591 HARINGTON *Orl. Fur., Apol. Poet.* ¶ vij b, They would haue an heroicall Poem (aswell as a Tragedie) to be full of *Peripetia*. **1652** URQUHART *Jewel* Wks. (1834) 230 In the peripetia of this drammatical exercitation. **1713** SWIFT *Frenzy J. Dennis* Wks. 1755 III. I. 143 Here is no *peripetia*, no change of fortune in the tragedy. **1864** KINGSLEY *Rom. & Teut.* iv. 119 A strange peripetia for the Amal. **1877** MORLEY *Crit. Misc.* Ser. II. 120 It would take a volume to follow out all the peripeteias of the drama. **1960** R. F. C. HULL tr. *Jung's On Nature of Dreams* in *Coll. Wks.* VIII. 295 The third phase brings the culmination or *peripeteia*. Here something decisive happens or something changes completely. **1976** S. HYNES *Auden Generation* vii. 193 In that pattern, 1936 is the peripeteia, the point where the action turned.

β. **1753** *Adventurer* No. 83 ¶ 2 A fable is called complex, when it contains both a discovery and a peripetie. **1886** SYMONDS *Renaiss. It., Cath. React.* (1898) VII. xiv. 256 What peripeties of empire, may we not observe and ponder. **1904** *Sat. Rev.* 23 Jan. 107 By no means..let us have a peripety caused by the casual overhearing of something in the nick of time. **1911** BEERBOHM *Zuleika D.* ix. 151 For him to fall in love was a violent peripety, bound to produce a violent upheaval. **1942** K. W. BASH tr. *Jacobi's Psychol. C. G. Jung* iii. 79 *Peripetie*, which forms the 'backbone' of every dream, the weaving of the plot. The intensification of events to a crisis or to a transformation, which may also consist in a catastrophe. **1950** *Brit. Jrnl. Psychol.* XL. 236 Jung goes on to discuss the structure of dreams... He distinguishes.. the culmination or peripety, and..the final lysis or solution. **1964** M. MCLUHAN *Understanding Media* x. 103 So sudden an upsurge of academic training into the marketplace has in it the quality of classical peripety or reversal.

periphacitis, -pharyngeal: see PERI- a, c.

peripherad (pə'rɪfəræd), *adv.* *Anat.* [f. PERIPHER-Y + *-ad*: cf. CENTRAD.] To or towards the periphery; outwards, or away from the centre.

1808 BARCLAY *Muscular Motions* 243 Cavities that have ducts or passages opening peripherad. *Ibid.* 443 Accessory ligaments peripherad of the capsules. **1845** TODD & BOWMAN *Phys. Anat.* I. 235 The mental stimulus is propagated no further peripherad than the point of section.

peripheral (pə'rɪfərəl), *a.* and *sb.* [f. Gr. περιφερ-ής (see PERIPHERY) + -AL[1].] **A.** *adj.* **1.** Of, pertaining to, or situated in, the periphery; constituting or characteristic of the circumference or external surface; esp. in *Anat.*, etc., of the surface or outward part of an organic body, esp. in ***peripheral neuritis***, inflammation of one or more nerves of both sides; and with reference to the circulation, as ***peripheral resistance***. Also *fig.*, marginal, superficial, on the fringe.

1808 BARCLAY *Muscular Motions* p. xxi, An aspect.. towards the circumference of any part, peripheral; and if towards its centre, central. **1845** G. E. DAY tr. *Simon's Anim. Chem.* I. 123 The conveyance of arterial blood to the peripheral system. **1872** DARWIN *Emotions* i. 35 Reflex actions..are due to the excitement of a peripheral nerve. **1877** M. FOSTER *Text Bk. Physiol.* I. iv. 92 It is this peripheral resistance (in the minute arteries and capillaries) ..which gives the circulation of the blood its peculiar features. **1881** *Census of Eng. & Wales, Prelim. Rep.* p. ix, The increase of population [in London] in the past..decade was entirely peripheral. **1882** VINES *Sachs' Bot.* 876 The ligulate peripheral flowers of *Bellis perennis*. **1893** ROSS & BURY *Peripheral Neuritis* 1 Peripheral neuritis has..a clinical and an anatomical aspect. **1909** *Jrnl. Physiol.* XXXVIII. 237 Peripheral reference is the earliest phenomenon of recovery. **1915** W. M. BAYLISS *Princ. Gen. Physiol.* viii. 242 The peripheral resistance of the arterial system, resulting from the division into small arterioles, is due entirely to the internal friction of the blood, not to friction against the walls of the vessels. **1949** E. A. NIDA *Morphol.* (ed. 2) 84 A peripheral morpheme never consists of a root and is always structurally 'outside' of the nuclear constituent. *Ibid.*, Note, however, that infixes and some replacives are 'peripheral' even though they are formally included within the nuclear constituent. **1956** D. L. ABRAMSON *Diagnosis & Treatm. Peripheral Vascular Disorders* p. xiii, The physiology of the peripheral circulation. **1962** *Lancet* 27 Jan. 193/2 Chromosome analysis of peripheral-blood leucocytes grown in tissue culture. **1962** *Listener* 29 Mar. 542/2 We must distinguish between the kinds of conventional forces useful in Europe and those that might be used in the peripheral areas. *Ibid.* 10 May 825/2 Dr O'Leary mentions it in his conclusion, but it is peripheral to his main interest. **1965** M. MORSE *Unattached* i. 44 He said little and was essentially peripheral, mildly amused, and always following. **1972** R. HARTENSTEIN *Princ. Physiol.* ix. 421 Peripheral resistance and the force and rate of cardiac contractions are the major overall factors that determine blood pressure, velocity of flow, and the distribution of blood. **1973** *Word 1970* XXVI. 101 Discussion of the ultimate phonetic output of /S/ (or /z/) is peripheral to the core of this paper. **1976** *Vancouver Province* 18 June 21/2 Canadian cultural expression will remain peripheral to Canadians—unless we tackle the economics.

2. *Computers.* Applied to equipment that is used in conjunction with a computer without being an integral or necessary part of it, and to operations involving such equipment.

1956 *Proc. Eastern Joint Computer Conf. 1955* 67/2 An important current trend is toward peripheral equipment with corresponding flexibility. **1962** *Gloss. Terms Automatic Data Processing (B.S.I.)* 25 *Peripheral transfer*, the process of transferring a block of data between peripheral equipment and a store or between two units of peripheral equipment. **1963** A. M. HILTON *Logic, Computing Machines, & Automation* vi. 256 Electric typewriters and machines to perforate paper tape are among the most widely used items of peripheral equipment, particularly for small computing-machine systems. **1967** *Times* 6 May 17/1 Many vital pieces of equipment that go into a computer installation are not made in Europe. These units, which come under the heading of peripheral equipment, are becoming more and more important. **1970** *Sci. Amer.* Oct. 102 East Germany will probably supply peripheral equipment; Hungary, magnetic memories and software (programs).

B. *sb.* *Computers.* A peripheral device. Usu. *pl.*

1966 *Economist* 10 Sept. 1048/1 It just has not got the sort of money needed to develop and market a complete line of data processing equipment and the associated 'peripherals'. **1970** *Physics Bull.* July 306/2 External storage is made up of a variety of bulk or file storage units of very large capacity, which are operated as peripherals to the central processor. **1971** B. DE FERRANTI *Living with Computer* 89 To prevent the CPU from slowing to the speed of a peripheral, a buffer may be used so that the peripheral transfers information to the buffer at its own speed while the CPU does other work. **1973** T. ALLBEURY *Choice of Enemies* xii. 53 Computer peripherals,..the bits and pieces you hang on and plug into computers. **1977** D. BAGLEY *Enemy* xii. 81 A small computer with a variety of input and output peripherals including an X-Y plotter.

pe'ripherally, *adv.* [f. prec. + -LY[2].] In a peripheral way or position; at or with regard to the periphery.

1855 H. SPENCER *Princ. Psychol.* (1872) I. I. vi. 125 The feelings called sensations, of which the strong forms are peripherally initiated. **1870** ROLLESTON *Anim. Life* Introd. 36 The peripherally-placed portions of the organs of special sense. **1884** BOWER & SCOTT *De Bary's Phaner.* 304 Branches..may..anastomose peripherally or internally.

† **'periphere.** *Obs. rare*[−1]. = PERIPHERY.

1642 H. MORE *Song of Soul* II. iii. III. xxxix, Sith water in a wooden bucket born Doth fit itself unto each periphere.

peripheria: see PERIPHERY.

peripherial (pɛrɪ'fɪərɪəl), *a.* *rare.* [f. L. *peripherī-a* PERIPHERY + -AL[1].] = PERIPHERAL.

1672-3 GREW *Anat. Roots* I. iii. §28 The Peripherial Lines are in some [Roots] more entire Circles, as in Dandelion; in others, made up of shorter Chords, as in Potato. **1894** *Geol. Mag.* Oct. 438 In a length of 173 mm. along the periphery [of an ammonite] there are 21 peripherial ribs, which are connected with 7 primary ribs.

peripheric (pɛrɪ'fɛrɪk), *a.* [mod. f. L. *peripheria* + -IC: cf. *astronomic, philosophic*, etc. In mod.F. *périphérique* (Littré).] Of, pertaining to, or of the nature of a periphery; = PERIPHERAL.

1809 COLERIDGE *Friend* (1866) 284 *note*, Fiendish guilt when it makes itself existential and peripheric. **1835** LINDLEY *Introd. Bot.* (1848) I. 387 The peripheric swelling ..quickly constitutes a kind of little utricle. **1870** tr. *Stricken's Man. Hum. Histol.* xv. (N. Syd. Soc.) 470 The peripheric layer of the dentine. **1880** *Times* 21 Dec. 3/4 All rapid exercise diminishes the peripheric temperature. **1888** E. R. LANKESTER *Adv. Sc.* (1890) 329 Von Baer..adopted Cuvier's divisions..as the peripheric, the longitudinal, the massive, and the vertebrate types of structure.

peri'pherical, *a.* [f. as prec. + -AL[1].] = prec.

1690 LEYBOURN *Curs. Math.* 321 The Proportion of the whole Superficies of a Sphere, to the Quadrat of the Diametre, is the same with that of the Peripherical Quadrat to the whole Superficies. **1835** LINDLEY *Introd. Bot.* (1848) I. 386 A slight peripherical and continuous swelling is seen. **1859** TODD *Cycl. Anat.* V. 441/2 Organs developed upon the nerve tubes, between their central and peripherical termination.

Hence **peri'pherically** *adv.*

1850 LEITCH tr. *C. O. Müller's Anc. Art* (ed. 2) § 194 In Ravenna there is the church of San Vitale, which is quite peripherically built, on an octagonal ground plan. **1869** C. RABACHE in *Eng. Mech.* 17 Dec. 329/2 They gravitate peripherically..round their planet.

pe,ripheri'zation. *rare.* [f. PERIPHER(Y + -IZATION.] Obscurity or indirectness of expression.

1926 E. POUND *Let.* 15 Nov. (1971) 202 Ms. arrived this A.M... I will have another go at it, but up to present I make nothing of it whatever. Nothing..short of divine vision or a new cure for the clapp can possibly be worth all the circumambient peripherization.

pe'ripherous, *a.* *rare*[−1]. [f. as PERIPHERAL + -OUS.] Of the nature of, or forming, a periphery.

1816 G. S. FABER *Orig. Pagan Idol.* III. 240 Exhibiting to the eye seven peripherous steps or stages.

periphery (pə'rɪfərɪ, 'pɛrɪfərɪ). Also 4-6 **periferie**; 7 in L. form **peri'pheria.** [= OF. *periferie, -pherie*, ad. late L. *peripherīa* circumference, etc., a. Gr. περιφέρεια circumference, line round a circle, outer surface, deriv. sb. from περιφερής moving round, revolving round; f. περί round about + φέρ-ειν to bear, carry: cf. L. *circum-ferens* bearing or moving round.]

† **1.** Each of the layers or strata (lower, middle, and upper) of the atmosphere enveloping the earth. (= med.L. *periferia* in same sense.) *Obs.*

1390 GOWER *Conf.* III. 93 This Air in Periferies thre Divided is.

2. The line that forms the boundary, esp. of any round or rounded surface. *spec.* in *Geom.* The circumference of a circle or of any closed curvilinear figure; also, the sum of the sides of a polygonal figure; a perimeter; †formerly *rarely*, an arc, a section of the circumference (*obs.*). Also *fig.*

1571 DIGGES *Pantom.* III. iii. Q ij, The side of the Cone augmented in halfe the Peripherie of his base. **1589** PUTTENHAM *Eng. Poesie* II. xi. (Arb.) 114 The figure Ouall.. keeping within one line for his periferie or compasse as the rounde. **1660** BARROW *Euclid* III. xxix, In equal circles equal right lines subtend equal peripheries. **1797** *Encycl. Brit.* (ed. 3) II. 522/2 A spectator at rest, without the periphery of the moon's orbit. **1825** J. NICHOLSON *Operat. Mechanic* 667 A locomotive steam-engine does not exert the same constant force on the peripheries of the wheels of the carriage, when it moves at different velocities. **1842** E. WILSON *Anat. Vade M.* (ed. 2) 5 In flat bones the osseous tissue radiates..from a central point towards the periphery. **1858** J. MARTINEAU *Stud. Chr.* 270 Whose vision is bounded by the periphery of a given creed.

β. **1644** EVELYN *Diary* 12 Nov., The whole oval peripheria 2888½ palmes. **1650** BULWER *Anthropomet.* 187 The Peripheria of the Breast is two Geometrical foot and two inches. **1693** tr. *Blancard's Phys. Dict.* (ed. 2), *Peripheria*, the Circumference of the Body, or any Entrail thereof.

b. More generally: The external boundary or surface of any space or body; something forming such a boundary.

1666 HARVEY *Morb. Angl.* xxvi. (1672) 61 Sufficient to exterminate noxious humours to the periphery or outward parts. **1803** SYD. SMITH *Wks.* (1859) I. 38/1 We possess the whole of the sea-coast, and enclose in a periphery the unfortunate King of Candia. **1809** W. IRVING *Knickerb.* (1861) 60 Laying his hands on each side of his capacious periphery, and rolling his half-closed eyes around. **1841** LEVER *C. O'Malley* xiii, In one instant he became the centre to a periphery of kicks: cuffs: pullings, and haulings. **1879** CALDERWOOD *Mind & Br.* ii. 10 The periphery or external extremities of the system, where there is contact with the outer world. **1898** *Allbutt's Syst. Med.* V. 1 The lobules, which may be regarded as the pulmonary periphery.

c. *loosely*, A surrounding region, space, or area.

1759 B. MARTIN *Nat. Hist. Eng.* I. *Middlesex* 261 Spacious Peripheries of Enrichment. **1822-29** *Good's Study Med.* (ed. 3) II. 593 Some seem to dissolve..and hence spread their influence through very confined peripheries. **1872** tr. *Figuier's Hum. Race* i. 49 Throughout the whole periphery of this country there exists no identity either of customs, language or religion.

periphlebitic, -itis: see PERI- c.

periphonic (pɛrɪ'fɒnɪk), *a.* [f. PERI- + PHONIC *a.*] Such as to reproduce the vertical as well as the horizontal distribution of sound that has been recorded, by means of one or more loudspeakers above the level of the listener in addition to ones around him at his own level.

Whether this is the sense in quot. 1970[1] is uncertain.

1970 *Times* 25 June 7/2 The French pieces were almost as uneventful, even with benefit of this excellent multi-channel, so-called periphonic, sound. **1970** M. GERZON in *Studio Sound* Aug. 338/1 The second part of this article is devoted to the use of these considerations in obtaining a system of Periphonic (Greek: *peri-*, around) sound reproduction, i.e. the reproduction of sound in all spatial directions. **1974** *Nature* 13 Dec. 537/1 A minimum of four loudspeakers are geometrically necessary to surround the listener in three dimensions and give periphonic reproduction. **1976** *Gramophone* Feb. 1398/1 The real potential of four channels lies in periphonic reproduction using at least six loudspeakers. *Ibid.*, Although four channels are in a sense ideal for periphonic reproduction, it can be realised using only three channels.

Hence **pe'riphony,** periphonic reproduction.

1970 M. GERZON in *Studio Sound* Sept. 380/1 While Granville Cooper has recently described a system of periphony called 'tetrahedral ambiophony', this is only one of many possible periphonic techniques. **1974** *Nature* 13 Dec. 537/1 To satisfy the psycho-acoustic criteria sufficiently well, however, the practical minimum is..six [loudspeakers] for periphony.

periphractic (pɛrɪ'fræktɪk), *a. Geom.* [mod. f. Gr. περίφρακτ-ος fenced round (f. περιφράσσειν, f. φράσσειν to fence) + -IC. (Orig. app. in Ger. by Listing.)] Said of a region having one or more internal bounding surfaces (or curves, when the region is plane) unconnected with the external boundary (e.g. a globe with an internal cavity, or a circular race-course round an enclosed space), so that a closed surface (or line, when the region is plane) may be drawn within the region, such that it cannot be contracted to a point without passing out of the region. (Cf. CYCLIC 5.) Hence *transf.* as ***periphractic number***, the number of independent internal boundaries in such a region.

1881 MAXWELL *Electr. & Magn.* I. 17 When a region encloses within itself other regions, it is called a Periphractic region. *Ibid.* 24 The most familiar example of a periphractic region within which the solenoidal condition is satisfied is the region surrounding a mass attracting or repelling inversely as the square of the distance. *Ibid.* 23 The whole number of lines to be drawn to remove the periphraxy is equal to the periphractic number or the number of internal surfaces. **1895** H. LAMB *Hydrodynamics* 43 Let us suppose that the region occupied by the irrotationally moving fluid is periphractic, i.e. that it is limited internally by one or more closed surfaces.

periphrase ('pɛrɪfreɪz), *sb.* [a. F. *périphrase* (1555 in Hatz.-Darm.), ad. L. *periphrasis*: see PERIPHRASIS.] = PERIPHRASIS.

1589 PUTTENHAM *Eng. Poesie* III. vii. (Arb.) 166 Speaking ..by periphrase or circumlocution when all might be said in a word or two. **1674** BOYLE *Excell. Theol.* I. iii. 85 The same infallible Teacher..imploys the vision of God as an emphatical periphrase of felicity. **1727** POPE, etc. *Art of Sinking* 88 Periphrase is another great aid to prolixity. **1866** GEO. ELIOT *F. Holt* ii, Mr. Jermyn had a copious supply of words, which often led him into periphrase.

periphrase ('pɛrɪfreɪz), *v.* [a. F. *périphrase-r* (Cotgr. 1611), f. *périphrase* PERIPHRASIS.]

1. *trans.* To express by periphrasis.

1624 QUARLES *Job* Pref., I commend to thee heere the Historie of Job, in part, Periphrased; in part, Abridged. **1814** W. TAYLOR in *Monthly Rev.* LXXIII. 475 Delille thus paraphrases and periphrases the passage.

2. *intr.* To use circumlocution; to speak or write periphrastically.

1652 GATAKER *Antinom.* 34 It would be over teadious..to be continually paraphrasing or periphrasing of them. **1828** WEBSTER, *Periphrase*, v. i. to use circumlocution.

periphrasis (pə'rɪfrəsɪs). Pl. -ses (-si:z). [a. L. *periphrasis*, a. Gr. περίφρασις circumlocution, periphrase, f. περιφράζειν to express periphrastically, f. περί round about, around + φράζειν to declare.]

1. That figure of speech which consists in expressing the meaning of a word, phrase, etc., by many or several words instead of by few or one; a roundabout way of speaking, circumlocution.

1533 MORE *Apol.* ix. Wks. 865/1 A fayre fygure,..that is I trowe called periphrasis. **1589** PUTTENHAM *Eng. Poesie* III. xviii. (Arb.) 203 Then haue ye the figure Periphrasis,..as when we go about the bush, and will not in one or a few words expresse that thing which we desire to haue knowen, but do chose rather to do it by many words. **1657-8** in *Burton's Diary* (1828) II. 414 You do not express it but by periphrasis and circumlocution. **1759** STERNE *Tr. Shandy* I. xi, Yorick had no impression but one..which..he would usually translate into plain English without any periphrasis. **1864** *Theol. Rev.* Mar. 16 Some name is needful if we would avoid the loose clumsiness of perpetual periphrasis. **1880** MCCARTHY *Own Times* III. xxxii. 60 The plain truth may as well be spoken out without periphrasis.

2. An example or instance of this figure; a roundabout phrase. (The pl. *periphrases* is not distinguished in writing from that of *periphrase*.)

1579 E. K. *Gloss Spenser's Sheph. Cal.* Mar. 116 *Stouping Phæbus*, is a Periphrasis of the sunne setting. **1612** T. TAYLOR *Comm. Titus* ii. 9 The Gospel, which by a periphrasis is called the doctrine of Christ. *a* **1638** MEDE *Wks.* (1672) 6 Those divine Periphrases or circumlocutions which the Lord himself more than once makes of an *Holy People*. **1690** LOCKE *Hum. Und.* II. xxii. §7 And instead of either of those Names, use a Periphrasis to make any one understand their meaning. *Ibid.* III. x. §31 He that hath complex Ideas without Names for them..is necessitated to use Periphrases. **1754** SHERLOCK *Disc.* (1759) I. xiv. 364 The exhortation..is only a Periphrasis for Faith. **1865** *Reader* 1 Apr. 365/1 The Laplanders and Tunguy only speak of the bear and the tiger by a periphrasis.

†**b.** *fig.* An amplification, a larger expression.

a **1657** LOVELACE *Poems* (1864) 205 Till he but one new blister is And swells his own periphrasis. *a* **1658** CLEVELAND *Hecatomb* 100 She, she it is that doth contain all Bliss, And makes the World but her *Periphrasis*.

periphrast ('pɛrɪfræst). *rare.* [ad. Gr. type *περιφραστής, agent-n. from περιφράζειν: see prec.] One who uses, or renders something by, periphrasis.

1879 F. HARRISON *Choice Bks.* (1886) 57 Edward Fitzgerald, the translator or periphrast of Omar Kayyam.

periphrastic (pɛrɪ'fræstɪk), *a.* [ad. Gr. περιφραστικ-ός periphrastic, f. περιφράζειν: see PERIPHRAST and -IC. Cf. F. *périphrastique* (16th c. in Littré).] Of the nature of, characterized by, or involving periphrasis; circumlocutory; roundabout.

periphrastic conjugation (in Grammar), a conjugation formed by the combination of a simple verb and an auxiliary, as distinct from a simple formation from the verb-stem. ***periphrastic genitive***, an equivalent of the genitive case, formed by aid of a preposition, as *of* in Eng., *de* in Fr.

1805 H. TOOKE *Purley* II. 495 They borrowed the whole Latin or French words..instead of using their own periphrastic idiom. **1826** SCOTT *Woodst.* viii, The tongue poured forth its periphrastic language in such profusion. **1874** SAYCE *Compar. Philol.* vii. 289 The periphrastic genitive..must be referred to a later period. **1884** H. SWEET *Addr. Philol. Soc.*, The periphrastic forms of the English verb.

†**peri'phrastical**, *a.* [See -ICAL.] = prec.

a **1638** MEDE *Wks.* (1672) 54 Periphrastical, but evident sense. **1717** *Wodrow Corr.* (1843) II. 291 The language is become too periphrastical.

peri'phrastically, *adv.* [f. prec. + -LY².] In a periphrastic manner; by periphrasis.

1668 WILKINS *Real Char.* II. iv. 67 They may as well be expressed Periphrastically here as in all other Languages. **1791** BOSWELL *Johnson* 21 Mar. an. 1776, They [rats] are thus..periphrastically exhibited in his poem..: 'Nor with less waste the whisker'd vermin race, A countless clan, despoil the lowland cane'. **1865** *Pall Mall G.* 3 Nov. 10 It is impossible to translate the sentence except periphrastically.

periphraxy ('pɛrɪfræksɪ). *Geom.* [f. late Gr. περίφραξ-ις a fencing round: see PERIPHRACTIC.] The condition of being periphractic.

1881 MAXWELL *Electr. & Magn.* I. 23 [see PERIPHRACTIC]. **1895** H. LAMB *Hydrodynamics* 70 For spaces of two dimensions, periphraxy and multiple-connectivity become the same thing.

periphyll ('pɛrɪfɪl). *Bot.* [ad. F. *périphylle*, adj. and sb., f. Gr. περί about + φύλλον leaf.]

1848 LINDLEY *Introd. Bot.* (ed. 4) II. 307 In many plants ..glands are evidently provided for [secretion]... M. Trinchinetti..names them periphylls because they chiefly occur near the periphery [of the leaf].

‖**periphysis** (pə'rɪfɪsɪs). *Bot.* Also anglicized as **'periphyse.** [mod.L., a. Gr. περίφυσις, f. περί around + φύσις growth. In mod.F. *périphyse*.] 'A sterile capilliform hyphal branch projecting from the wall of the pyrenocarp of certain Fungi, when there is no hymenium in the cavity' (B. D. Jackson *Gloss. Bot. Terms* 1900).

1887 tr. *De Bary's Morphol. Fungi* 192.

periplasm ('pɛrɪplæz(ə)m). [mod. (De Bary 1881) f. Gr. περί around + πλάσμα anything formed: see PLASM.] **1.** *Bot.* The portion of the protoplasm in the sexual organs of the *Peronosporeæ*, left over after the differentiation of the sexual cells.

1887 tr. *De Bary's Morphol. Fungi* v. 134 The space between the oosphere and the wall of the oogonium continues to be filled with a slightly granular hyaline protoplasm, the *periplasm*, which may easily be overlooked.

2. *Microbiology.* The region of a bacterial or other cell immediately within the cell wall, outside the plasma membrane. Hence **peri'plasmic** *a.*

1961 P. MITCHELL in Goodwin & Lindberg *Biol. Struct. & Function* II. 590 Observations forced us to the conclusion that the glucose-6-phosphatase of intact *Escherichia coli* is enclosed in a region between the cell wall and the surface of the osmotic barrier component which we might appropriately call the 'periplasm'. **1967** *Science* 16 June 1453/3 Some time ago Mitchell proposed that glucose-6-phosphatase activity is located in such a 'periplasmic space'. **1974** *Jrnl. Bacteriol.* CXIX. 243/2 To determine whether the Hg(II)-reducing activity is present in the cytoplasm, the periplasm, or both. *Ibid.* 244/1 Alkaline phosphatase is one of the periplasmic enzymes. **1978** *Sci. Amer.* Oct. 74/2 The rat proinsulin would then 'hitch-hike' with the bacterial penicillinase into the periplasmic space, from which it could be extracted and then assayed with an antibody technique.

periplast ('pɛrɪplæst). *Biol.* [f. Gr. περί around + πλαστ-ός formed, moulded.]

†**a.** The intercellular substance or matrix in which the organized structures of a tissue are embedded (*obs.*). **b.** The main substance or body of a cell (esp. of a highly organized cell, as an ovum), as distinct from the external coating or cell-wall and the internal nucleus. **c.** A cell-wall or cell-envelope. Hence **peri'plastic** *a.*, of or pertaining to the periplast.

1853 HUXLEY in *Med.-Chirurg. Rev.* Oct. 297 To the former..we shall throughout the present article give the name of *Periplast*, or periplastic substance,..to the latter, that of *Endoplast*... We regard it as quite certain, that that portion which corresponds with the periplast, forms a continuous whole through the entire plant. *Ibid.* 306 The periplast..which has hitherto passed under the names of cell-wall, contents, and intercellular substance. **1861** J. R. GREENE *Man. Anim. Kingd., Cœlent.* 35 Its homogeneous periplast [is] traversed in all directions by a complex mesh-work of threads, which remain quite distinct from the endoplasts about which they diverge. **1867** J. MARSHALL *Outl. Physiol.* II. 643 Animal cells..in their most complete condition, as in the ovum,..consist, like a vegetable cell, of a cell wall or envelope, the *periplast*; of fluid or semi. fluid contents, the *endoplast*; of a *nucleus*, and usually of one, two, or more *nucleoli*. **1870** BEALE *Protoplasm* 14 His [Huxley's] 'endoplast' and 'periplastic substance' of 1853 together constitute his 'protoplasm' of 1869. **1901** G. N. CALKINS *Protozoa* 113 Klebs (1892) distinguishes two types of peripheral structures, the periplasts and outer coats... The periplasts include all cuticular differentiations which are a living part of the organism.

peripleuritis: see PERI- c.

periplum ('pɛrɪplʌm). [L., neut. f. PERIPLUS.] In the poetry of E. Pound (see quot. 1940).

1940 E. POUND *Cantos* lix. 83 Periplum, not as land looks on a map But as sea bord seen by men sailing. **1948** —— *Pisan Cantos* (1949) lxxiv. 7 The great periplum brings in the stars to our shore. *Ibid.* 13 Under the grey cliff in periplum. *Ibid.* lxxxii. 118 Three solemn half notes Their white downy chests black-rimmed On the middle wire Periplum.

‖**periplus** ('pɛrɪplʌs). [L. *periplūs* (Pliny), a. Gr. περίπλους a sailing round, f. περί around + πλόος, πλοῦς voyage: in F. *périple*, It., Sp. *periplo*.]

1. The action of sailing round, circumnavigation; a voyage (or journey) round a coast-line, etc.; a circuit. **b.** *transf.* A narrative of such a voyage.

1776 R. CHANDLER *Trav. Greece* 221 The harbour of Epidaurus is long. Its periplus or circuit has fifteen stadia. **1853** DE QUINCEY *Autobiog. Sk.* xv. Wks. 1862 XIV. 455 My mother now entered upon a *periplus*, or systematic circumnavigation of all England. **1854** THOREAU *Walden* (1863) 319 It is wafted past the site of the fabulous islands of Atlantis and the Hesperides, makes the periplus of Hanno.

b. 1803 W. TAYLOR in *Ann. Rev.* I. 438 Many a periplus, many an itinerary was published. **1869** LIDDELL & SCOTT *Grk. Lex.* s.v. Περίπλοος, *Periplus* is the title of several geograph. works, still extant, by Scylax, Nearchus, Agatharchides, Hanno. **1904** W. H. STEVENSON in *Eng. Hist. Rev.* Jan. 139 *note*, This Greek original was made up from a periplus from the Pillars of Hercules to Gades.

2. A manœuvre in ancient Greek naval combats.

1850 GROTE *Greece* II. lx. VII. 448 *note*, The periplus practised by a lighter ship to avoid direct collision against a heavier. *Ibid.* lxiv. VIII. 234 This diekplus and periplus were the special manœuvres of the Athenian navy.

peripneumony (pɛrɪp'nju:mənɪ), ‖**peri-pneumonia** (-pnju:'məʊnɪə). *Path.* Now *rare* or *Obs.* [a. F. *péripneumonie* (Paré, 16th c.), in 14th c. *peripleumonie*, ad. L. *peripneu-*, *-pleumonia*, a. Gr. περιπλευμονία (Hippocr.), later περιπνευμονία, f. περί around, about + πλεύμων, later πνεύμων lungs: see PNEUMONIA.] The old name for inflammation of the lungs; = PNEUMONIA.

α. *c* **1550** LLOYD *Treas. Health* A vj, A sodeyne laxe folowing a pleurysie of a peripneumony [*mispr.* peripeunomy] is verye peryllouse. **1601** HOLLAND *Pliny* II. 167 Excellent for the pleurisie and Peripnewmony, *i.* the inflammation of the lungs. **1698** FRYER *Acc. E. India & P.* 378. **1752** SHENSTONE *Wks. & Lett.* (1777) III. 191 The peripneumony under which he laboured..had terminated in an adhesion of the lungs to the pleura. **1822-34** *Good's Study Med.* (ed. 4) I. 483 *note*, Hooping-cough complicated with bronchitis or peripneumony. **1879** *Cassell's Techn. Educ.* IV. 251/2 His body, by the King's command, was dissected by Harvey, who attributed Parr's death to peripneumony.

β. **1603** HOLLAND *Plutarch's Mor.* 745 The malady called *Peripneumonia*, that is to say, the inflammation of the lungs. **1710** T. FULLER *Pharm. Extemp.* 106 A Nitrous Draught.. is chiefly prevalent against..Peripneumonia. **1876** tr. *H. von Ziemssen's Cycl. Med.* V. 5 Among the Greek and Roman writers 'Pleuritis' and 'Peripneumonia' comprised the sum of their knowledge of this class of diseases.

Hence **peripneumonic** (-'mɒnɪk) [Gr. περιπνευμονικός] *a.*, pertaining to or affected with pneumonia; *sb.*, a person affected with pneumonia; †**peripneu'monical** *a.* = *peripneumonic* adj. (*obs.*).

1656 BLOUNT *Glossogr.*, *Peripneumonical*, sick of a Peripneumony. **1684** tr. *Bonet's Merc. Compit.* VI. 204 There arises every Year a Fever, with a great many Peripneumonick Symptoms. *Ibid.* XI. 386 Shortness of breath, and other accidents, such as use to afflict Peripneumonicks. **1793** BEDDOES *Consump.* 133 Peripneumonic fevers, or inflammations of the lungs. **1822-34** *Good's Study Med.* (ed. 4) II. 134 Dissections of peripneumonic subjects.

peripneustic (pɛrɪp'nju:stɪk), *a. Entom.* [mod. f. Gr. περί around, about + πνευστικ-ός of or fit for breathing, f. stem πνευ- of πνέ-ειν to breathe.] Of insect-larvæ: see quot. 1899.

1891 A. LANG *Comp. Anat.* I. vi. 482 The tracheal system of peripneustic larvæ may be modified in various ways by adaptation to different modes of life. **1899** *Cambridge Nat. Hist.* VI. 450 Some larvae have stigmata arranged along the sides of the body after the fashion normal in Insect-larvae; these are called 'peripneustic'.

periportal: see PERI- a.

periproct ('pɛrɪprɒkt). *Zool.* [f. Gr. περί around + πρωκτ-ός the anus.] That part of the perisome or body-wall of an echinoderm which surrounds the anus: opp. to PERISTOME.

1877 HUXLEY *Anat. Inv. Anim.* ix. 569 In Echinus, the apical extremities of the ambulacra abut upon the five smaller of the ten single plates which surround the periproct.

So **peri'proctic, peri'proctous** *adjs.*, surrounding the anus; pertaining to the periproct; **periproc'titis,** inflammation of the connective tissue about the anus; hence **periproc'titic** *a.*

1877 tr. *Ziemssen's Cycl. Med.* VII. 377 During the course of the periproctitis. *Ibid.*, The periproctitic exudation is occasionally absorbed. **1890** BILLINGS *Nat. Med. Dict.*, Periproctic.

periprostatic: see PERI- a.

pe'ripter, -ere. ? *Obs. Arch.* [a. F. *périptère* (1559 in Hatz.-Darm.), ad. med.L. *peripteron* (Vitruv.), a. Gr. περίπτερον, neuter of περίπτερος winged about, f. περί about + πτερόν wing.] A peripteral building. So ‖**peripteros, pe'riptery.**

1696 PHILLIPS (ed. 5), *Peripter*, a sort of Temple, which had Pillars on all the Four quarters [ed. 1706 *Peripteron* or *Periptere*]. **1704** J. HARRIS *Lex. Techn.* I, *Periptere*, in Architecture, is a Place encompassed round with Columns. **1760** RAPER in *Phil. Trans.* LI. 799 Temples of this form were usually peripteres..as the two temples of Vesta. **1823** P. NICHOLSON *Pract. Build.* 590. **1826** ELMES *Dict. Fine Arts, Periptery*, an edifice or temple environed..by a range of insulated columns.

peripteral (pəˈrɪptərəl), *a.* [f. as prec. + -AL¹.] Having a single peristyle or row of pillars surrounding it, as an ancient Greek temple.

1826 ELMES *Dict. Fine Arts, Peripteral*,..having columns all round. According to Vitruvius, the fourth order of temples. **1845** FORD *Handbk. Spain* VII. 529 It was peripteral, with fluted granite pillars and Corinthian capitals. **1846** ELLIS *Elgin Marb.* I. 32 A peripteral hexastyle temple.

peripylephlebitis, -pyloric, etc.: see PERI- c, a.

Perique (pɛˈriːk). Also perique. [Louisiana F. (see quot. 1931).] In full ***Perique tobacco.*** A strong, dark, Louisiana tobacco.

1882 *Congress. Rec.* 6 Apr. 2642/2 Perique tobacco may be sold by the manufacturer or producer..in the form of carottes..without the payment of tax. **1885** E. CUSTER *Boots & Saddles* 84 The officers gave this chief tobacco—Perique I think it is called. **1931** W. A. READ *Louisiana-French* 57 *Perique* is said to have been the popular pseudonym of Pierre Chenet, an Acadian who first produced this variety of tobacco. **1941** E. P. O'DONNELL *Great Big Doorstep* iv. 63 Evvie's composition dealt with Louisiana products... 'Rice, cotton, perique tobacco, and fur.' **1949** *Tobacco* 7 Apr. 15/1 Perique is the only tobacco steeped in its own juice, and has a mildly fermented smell, like wine. **1976** *National Observer* (U.S.) 12 June 17-A/5 (Advt.), It's Perique, a zesty, dark and aromatic tobacco.

perirenal, -salpingitis, etc.: see PERI- a, c.

perisarc (ˈpɛrɪsɑːk). *Zool.* [f. Gr. περί around + σάρξ, σαρκ-α flesh, as if from a Gr. *περισάρκιον (cf. *pericarp-ium*): cf. Gr. περίσαρκος surrounded by flesh.] The horny or chitinous case investing the cœnosarc in some Hydrozoa. Hence **peri'sarcal, peri'sarcous** *adjs.*, pertaining to or consisting of the perisarc.

1871 ALLMAN *Monogr. Gymnoblastic Hydroids* I. p. xiv, Perisarc... The unorganized chitinous excretion by which the soft parts are to a greater or less extent invested. **1877** HUXLEY *Anat. Inv. Anim.* iii. 133 It obviously answers to the perisarc of a Tubularian, and its presence in the embryo of the Hydra, in which no perisarc is developed by the adult, suggests [etc.]. **1888** ROLLESTON & JACKSON *Anim. Life* 245 The hydranths are lodged in perisarcal cups or *hydrothecæ* (= *calycles*). *Ibid.*, This hydrophyton consists of the cœnosarc..and its perisarcal investment.

‖**perisaturnium** (ˌpɛrɪsəˈtɜːnɪəm). *Astr.* [mod.L., f. PERI- + *Saturnus* Saturn, after *perijovium* PERIJOVE, *perihelium* PERIHELION.] That point in the orbit of any one of Saturn's satellites at which it is nearest to Saturn.

1838 *Penny Cycl.* XI. 399/2 The rate of progression of the perisaturnium of any satellite. **1867–77** G. F. CHAMBERS *Astron.* I. xiii. 152 The longitude of the peri-saturnium. **1878** NEWCOMB *Pop. Astron.* 556.

perische, obs. form of PERISH, PIERCE.

Periscian (pɛˈrɪsiən, -ʃɪən), *a.* and *sb.* [f. L. *Periscii*, a. Gr. Περίσκιοι (see next) + -AN: cf. F. *periscien* (1576 in Hatz.-Darm.).]

a. *adj.* Of or pertaining to the Periscii (in quot. *fig.*). **b.** *sb.* (in *pl.*) = PERISCII.

1594 R. ASHLEY tr. *Loys le Roy* 9 b, Periscians are they which haue their shadowes round about them in form of milstones. **1616** BULLOKAR *Eng. Expos., Periscians*, people dwelling so neere either of the two Poles, that their shadowes goe round about them like a wheele. **1682** SIR T. BROWNE *Chr. Mor.* III. § 11 In every clime we are in a periscian state, and with our Light, our Shadow and Darkness walk about us. **1715** tr. *Gregory's Astron.* I. 209 The Inhabitants of these Zones..are called Periscians, because the shadow (the Sun not setting) moves round about them.

‖**Periscii** (pəˈrɪsɪaɪ, -ˈɪʃɪaɪ), *sb. pl.* [med.L., a. Gr. περίσκιοι, pl. of περίσκιος throwing a shadow all round, f. περί around + σκιά shadow.] Those who dwell within the polar circles, whose shadows revolve around them as the sun moves around the heavens on a summer day.

1625 N. CARPENTER *Geog. Del.* I. x. (1635) 227. **1652–62** HEYLIN *Cosmogr.* Introd. (1674) 20/1 Periscii are such as dwell beyond the Polar Circles,..because their shadows are on all sides of them. **1704** J. HARRIS *Lex. Techn.* I.

periscope (ˈpɛrɪskəʊp), *sb.* [f. Gr. type *περίσκοπ-ος looking round, a looker round (cf. κατάσκοπος), f. περί around + σκοπός look, σκοπεῖν to look.]

I. 1. A 'look round'; a general or comprehensive view, a survey. *rare*⁻¹.

1822–34 *Good's Study Med.* (ed. 4) I. 643 The following passage, in which he [Dr. Ferguson] is taking a medical periscope of the island of Antigua.

II. 2. Name of a variety of photographic object-glass.

1865 *Athenæum* 4 Nov. 617/1 Steinheil's periscope, a new photographic object-glass. **1890** *Anthony's Photogr. Bull.* III. 129 Why the many styles of objectives..? 'Orthoscope, Tachyscope, Euryscope, Platyscope, Periscope.'

3. An apparatus used in a submarine boat, for obtaining a view of objects above the water by a system of mirrors. Also, a similar kind of tube-and-mirror or -prism apparatus used on land, as in trench warfare. See *trench-periscope.*

1899 *Westm. Gaz.* 17 Jan. 5/2 Various experiments are being carried out in order to provide these vessels with 'eyes', and notably with an apparatus known as the periscope, which is based on the principle of the dark room in photography, and which, by means of a tube, can be raised to the surface of the water. **1902** A. S. HURD in *19th Cent.* Feb. 226 The use of what is known as the periscope. This..by a system of mirrors carries to the officer below a reflection of what is occurring above. **1917** A. G. EMPEY *Over Top* 303 *Periscope*, a thing in the trenches which you look through. **1951** 'M. INNES' *Operation Pax* v. xiii. 251 Remnant was fiddling with a long forceps and a couple of mirror-like stainless-steel plates. 'First-rate periscope,' he said. **1976** *Sci. Amer.* Dec. 32/3 The crane operator, protected by heavy shielding and observing his tasks through a periscope, could remove and install any of the equipment by using impact wrenches to manipulate the connectors at the ends of the jumpers.

4. *attrib.* and *Comb.*, as ***periscope-wise*** adv.; **periscope depth** (see quot. 1928); **periscope level** = *periscope depth.*

1928 C. F. S. GAMBLE *Story N. Sea Air Station* xviii. 309 German submarines, when travelling awash, could reach 'periscope depth' (that is, the depth at which the fully extended periscope just reaches to the surface—normally 45 feet) in 1½ minutes. **1974** L. DEIGHTON *Spy Story* xviii. 194 'Periscope depth', said Ferdy... The Captain..took us up to periscope level. **1923** J. S. HUXLEY *Ess. Biologist* iii. 116 It [*sc.* the grebe] lifts its head and neck above the water, periscope-wise, to assure itself of its direction.

'periscope, *v. poet.* [f. the sb.] *intr.* To look as if through a periscope.

1934 DYLAN THOMAS *18 Poems* 12 Where fishes' food is fed the shades Who periscope through flowers to the sky.

periscopic (pɛrɪˈskɒpɪk), *a.* [f. as PERISCOPE *sb.* + -IC: cf. *telescopic*. In mod.F. *périscopique*.] Enabling one to see distinctly for some distance around the axis of vision: applied to a lens or eye-glass so formed as to give a wide field of view; also to concavo-convex lenses.

1804 WOLLASTON in *Nicholson's Jrnl.* VII. 241 Experiment proving the Advantage of Periscopic Spectacles. **1812** —— in *Phil. Trans.* 370 On a Periscopic Camera Obscura and Microscope. **1822** IMISON *Sc. & Art* I. 461 These glasses are called Periscopic spectacles, from their affording the opportunity of looking round. **1875** KNIGHT *Dict. Mech.* 1668/2 Dr. Wollaston's periscopic lens for microscopes had two plano-convex lenses ground to the same radius, and between their plane surfaces a thin plate of metal with a circular aperture. **1899** CAGNEY *Jaksch's Clin. Diagn.* x. (ed. 4) 434 The periscopic eye-pieces..are very excellent.

So **peri'scopical** *a.* = PERISCOPIC *a.*

a **1846** *Eclec. Rev.* cited by WORCESTER.

periscopism (ˈpɛrɪskəʊˌpɪz(ə)m). [f. as PERISCOPE *sb.* + -ISM.] The capacity of seeing all round, or over a wide field of vision, without moving the eye; the faculty of periscopic vision.

1877 *Nature* 21 June 151/1 The purpose of the structure is to give periscopism to the eye. **1881** LE CONTE *Sight* I. ii. 37 This defect of a homogeneous lens, Dr. Hermann shows, is entirely corrected by the peculiar structure of the crystalline [lens]; therefore this structure confers on the eye the capacity of seeing distinctly over a wide field, without changing the position of the point of sight. This capacity he calls periscopism. *Ibid.* iii. 76 In the lower animals..in which periscopism is so important.

perish (ˈpɛrɪʃ), *v.* Forms: α. 3–5 periss-en, (3 -i, 4 -y), 4–5 perisse, 4–6 peris, (-ys(e, 4 perijs, 5 *Sc.* perice, 5–6 perise), 6 *Sc.* periss, (-eis, perreis(s). β. 4–5 perisch-en, (4 -i, perriche-n, 4–5 periche-n), 4–6 perisch(e, -isshe, -ysshe, (-ysch(e, -issche, 4–5 -yssche, 6 -iszshe, *Sc.* perrisch), 4–6 perishe, (-ysh(e, 5 -esch(e, 6 -esh, -essh, pearishe), 4–7 perisch, 6– -perish. γ. 4–5 pers-en, -i, persh(en, persch(e, perch(yn. δ. 4 paris, 5 -ische, -ysche, 6 -ich, 9 *north. dial.* par(r)ish. [ME. a. OF. *periss-*, lengthened stem of *perir* to perish, = Pr. *perir*, It. *perire*:—L. *perīre* to pass away entirely, come to nothing, be lost or destroyed, lose one's life, etc., f. PER- 3 + *īre* to go.]

1. a. *intr.* To come to a violent, sudden, or untimely end; to suffer destruction; to lose its life, cease to exist, be cut off. (Chiefly of living beings.) Jocose phr. ***or perish in the attempt.***

c **1250** *O. Kent. Serm.* in *O.E. Misc.* 32 Hise deciples.. seiden to him, lord saue us, for we perisset[h]. **1297** R. GLOUC. (Rolls) 6936 þat ich mote þoru þis fure Brenne bi neþe & perissy [*v. rr.* persi, perischi, perisshe]. *a* **1300** *Cursor M.* 20049 Womman sal peris o na barn, Ne nan wit mischiue be forfarn. **1340–70** *Alex. & Dind.* 452 For þei þat sailen on þe see..perichen ful ofte. **1382** WYCLIF *Luke* xv. 17 Forsothe I perische here thurȝ hungir. *c* **1475** *Rauf Coilȝear* 20 In point thay war to parische. **1484** CAXTON *Fables of Æsop* v. viii, The mooste parte of the corne..perysshed that same yere by cause of the grete rayne that felle. *a* **1533** LD. BERNERS *Huon* lii. 158 The shyppe..pereshyd, and all my company. **1535** COVERDALE *2 Kings* ix. 8 That all the house of Achab maye periszshe. **1542–3** *Act 34 & 35 Hen. VIII*, c. 8 § 1 Many rotte, and perishe to deathe for lacke of helpe of surgery. **1671** MILTON *Samson* 676 The common rout, That..Grow up and perish as the summer flie. **1719** DE FOE *Crusoe* I. vi, I was ready to perish for Thirst. **1776** PAINE *Com. Sense* (1791) 7 [To] disable him from living, and reduce him to a state in which he might rather be said to perish than to die. **1793** SMEATON *Edystone L.* Contents p. vii, The Lighthouse and all therein perished. **1829** SOUTHEY *Sir T. More* II. 288 In danger of perishing with hunger. **1836** W. IRVING *Astoria* III. 252 Who..lingered in the wilderness to perish by the hands of savages. **1861** T. HUGHES *Tom Brown at Oxf.* I. ii. 23 However, he addressed himself manfully to his task; savage indeed, and longing to drive a hole in the bottom of the old tub, but as resolved as ever to get to Sandford and back before hall time, or perish in the attempt. **1865** TROLLOPE *Belton Est.* i. 1 His son Charles was now dead,—had perished by his own hand. **1870** L. M. ALCOTT *Old-Fashioned Girl* xvii. 337 He.. sternly resolved to be an honor to his family, or perish in the attempt. **1978** *Country Life* 30 Nov. 1915/4 Too often publishers are determined to illustrate or perish in the attempt.

b. (Chiefly *Theol.*) To incur spiritual death, be lost. Of a nation or community: To suffer moral or spiritual ruin.

c **1250** *O. Kent. Serm.* in *O.E. Misc.* 33 Sigge we to him, lord sauue us þet we ne perissi. *a* **1325** *Athanasian Creed* 2 in *Prose Psalter* 193 þe which [faith] bot ȝif ichon kepe hole & nouȝt de-fouled, wyþ-outen drede he shal peris wyþ-outen ende [**1548–9** *Bk. Com. Prayer* without doubt he shal perishe euerlastingly]. *c* **1380** WYCLIF *Wks.* (1880) 370 ȝif þe gospel is hid, it is hid to hem þat perschen [**1382** *2 Cor.* iv. 3 perischen]. **1562** WINȜET *Cert. Tractatis* i. Wks. (S.T.S.) I. 6 He..sall require the blude oute of ȝour handis of the smallaste ane that sall perise throw ȝour negligence. **1644** MILTON *Educ.* 1 The reforming of Education..for the want whereof this nation perishes. **1781** COWPER *Expost.* 95 When nations are to perish in their sins, 'Tis in the church the leprosy begins. **1782** PRIESTLEY *Corrupt. Chr.* I. III. 295 Jerom..thought that no christian would finally perish. **1856** RUSKIN *Mod. Paint.* IV. v. v. § 4 Knowledge is good..yet man perished in seeking knowledge.

c. Of things material: (*a*) as opposed to things spiritual or eternal; (*b*) (esp. of rubber) as the effect of decay or exposure to destructive conditions; (*c*) to be lost, wasted, or squandered.

c **1375** *Sc. Leg. Saints* xvi. (*Magdalena*) 76 Bot martha, þat was rycht wyse, Wald nocht thole þare landis perice, Bot bathe þar partis wysly steryt. **1382** WYCLIF *John* vi. 12 He seide to his disciplis, Gedare ȝe the relyfs that ben left, that thei perischen not. *Ibid.* 27 Worche ye not mete that perischith. *c* **1400** *Rule St. Benet* 1455 Al þe vessel of þe abbay Aw hir to ȝeme in right aray, So þat non perise ne be lorn. **1434** MISYN *Mending of Life* ii. 108 Qwhy ȝernis þou with grete desire þingis þat sall perys? **1533** GAU *Richt Vay* 36 The kingis of the vardil ar vntit with olie quhilk perisis. **1857** RUSKIN *Pol. Econ. Art* ii. (1868) 120 Giotto's frescos at Assisi are perishing..for want of decent care. **1884** *Queen* 29 Mar. (Advt.), A flat elastic section (which, unlike rubber elastic, will not heat the person or perish in wear). **1885** C. G. W. LOCK *Workshop Receipts* Ser. IV. 210/2 The joints are apt to 'perish' by the action of the acids. **1910** *Bradshaw's Railway Guide* Apr. facing p. xv (Advt.), Self-filling fountain pen... No rubber to perish. **1971** C. M. BLOW *Rubber Technol. Manuf.* ii. 36 Familiar to all is the liability of rubber to 'perish', to harden and crack or soften to a sticky residue.

d. Of things immaterial: To come to an end, pass away.

a **1300** *Cursor M.* 8789 Sir king..we dut vr dede Sal perijs. *a* **1325** *Prose Psalter* xl[i]. 5 He shalle dien, and his name shal peris. **1432–50** tr. *Higden* (Rolls) V. 281 Valentinianus themperour..dredenge Aecius..causede hym to be sleyne at Cartago, with whom the fortune of the Weste pereschede. **1567** *Gude & Godlie B.* (S.T.S.) 88 Saif vs, gude Lord, and succour send, For perysit is halynes. **1763** J. BROWN *Poetry & Mus.* v. 78 Bards of ancient Greece, whose Songs have perished in the Wreck of Time. **1856** STANLEY *Sinai & Pal.* vi. (1858) 271 The Phœnician power which the Prophets denounced, has entirely perished.

e. In imprecations. Now only in phr. ***perish the thought.***

1526 TINDALE *Acts* viii. 20 Perish thou and thy money togedder. **1599** SHAKS. *Hen. V*, IV. iii. 72 Perish the man, whose mind is backward now. [**1700** C. CIBBER *King Richard III* 52 Perish that thought!] **1717** POPE *Elegy Unfort. Lady* 45 So perish all, whose breast ne'er learn'd to glow For others good, or melt at others woe. **1773** GOLDSM. *Stoops to Conq.* II, Perish the baubles! Your person is all I desire. **1810** SCOTT *Lady of L.* II. xxxiv, Perish my name, if aught afford Its chieftain safety save his sword. **1893** H. JAMES *Let.* in C. Mackenzie *My Life & Times* (1963) II. 317, I don't in the least pretend that any scenario I can send you ..is..my *last word*. Perish the thought—it isn't the way I work. **1926** W. S. MAUGHAM *Constant Wife* III. 150 Perish the thought. I've worked like a dog..and last night..I downed tools. **1953** R. MACAULAY *Let.* 23 Jan. in *Last Lett.*

to Friend (1962) 75 Which disposes of your notion that I should ever write to Miss Prescott. Perish the thought! **1961** *New Left Rev.* Mar.–Apr. 59/1 Had he, perish the thought, been privately soaking? **1974** 'D. Fletcher' *Lovable Man* II. 120 Oh, one wouldn't go as far as that. Perish the thought.

2. In *pa. pple.* with the auxiliary *be*, expressing the resulting state (as with OF. *perir*). Now chiefly said of the effect of exposure to weather, cold, hunger, etc.: cf. 1 c, 3 d, f. Also in *pres. pple.* with the auxiliary *be* (now the more usual form with reference to exposure to (cold) weather).

The formal correspondence of this to the passive of a transitive verb led *c* 1400 to the transitive use of the simple tenses (sense 3), which has not been developed in French. (Some of these may be taken as passive of 3.)

1297 R. Glouc. (Rolls) 4648 Þe relikes nolde hii noȝt bileue.. Vor raþer hii wolde ymartred be þan hii yperissed were. *c* **1380** Wyclif *Sel. Wks.* II. 70 Þis sone of myn was deed, and is quykened aȝen, and he was perished [**1382** *Luke* xv. 24 he perischide], and is founden. **1389** in *Eng. Gilds* (1870) 117 If he dey, yat is for to say, if he be periched be water or be lond. **1474** Caxton *Chesse* 75 A shyppe is soon perisshed and lost by a litil tempest. **1531** Elyot *Gov.* I. xvii, Nothinge was perisshed sauue a litle bagage. **1545** Raynold *Byrth Mankynde* 79 Yf the matrice be perysshed or otherwyse viciate. **1577–87** Holinshed *Chron.* III. 1185/1 The spire of the steeple was so perished that not long after the same was taken downe. **1640–1** *Kirkcudbr. War-Comm. Min. Bk.* (1855) 76 The poore sogers are almost perisched.. for want of schoes and clothes. **1667** Wood *Life* (O.H.S.) II. 113 [Laid] in a by-place expos'd to weather, and thereby are much perish'd, and become not legible. **1795** Burke *Scarcity* Wks. VII. 410 Several farmers..cut the green haulm as fodder for the cattle, then perished for want of food in that dry and burning summer. **1845** Mrs. Carlyle *Lett.* I. 313 We were all perished with cold. **1885** A. Edwardes *Girton Girl* III. i. 11 You have given me hot coffee when I was perishing with cold. **1895** *Times* (weekly ed.) 23 Aug. 675/4 The rope was perished and should never have been used for the work. **1930** W. S. Maugham *Cakes & Ale* viii. 96 Isn't it awful, the weather? You must be perishing.

3. *trans.* **a.** To bring to destruction, destroy; to put to death, kill (a person, etc.), wreck (a ship, building, etc.). *Obs.* or *arch.* (exc. as in d).

c **1400** *26 Pol. Poems* 131 These ben myn enemyes, lord, echone, Euer aboute to perysshe me. *c* **1400** *Destr. Troy* 11360 Thies wicked men bothe Haue purpost hom plainly to perisshe our londes. **1432–50** tr. *Higden* (Rolls) I. 145 The dogges..be so greete and feerse that thei..peresche lyones. **1549** Wriothesley *Chron.* 23 Apr. (Camden) II. 10 A fire at Broken wharfe..brent and perished aboue six howses. **1622** R. Hawkins *Voy. S. Sea* lxi. (Hakl. Soc.) 294 Another [wound] through the arme, perishing the bone, and cutting the sinewes. **1632** Lithgow *Trav.* VIII. 355 Their Burser.. had almost perished his owne life. **1790** Burns *Tam o' Shanter* 168 For mony a beast to dead she shot, And perish'd mony a bonie boat. *a* **1845** Hood *The Mary* vii, Many foul blights Perish'd his hardwon gains. **1898** W. P. Ridge *Mord Em'ly* xv. 228 Chrise, I'll perish you, if you ain't careful.

†**b.** To destroy spiritually; to ruin morally.

c **1440** *Alph. Tales* 106 He had so many thoghtis of syn in his mynde þat he was like to be perisshid þerwith. **1490** Caxton *Eneydos* xxiii. 86 In my priue closet, where I was perisshed. **1555** Bonner *Homilies* ii. 11 When we were peryshed he saved vs. **1750** *Student* I. 299 Wishing God to perish his body and soul, if ever he appear'd on the scaffold to do the act or lift up his hand against him.

c. To lose (a possession); to waste, squander (property, etc.). *to perish the pack*, to spend all one has. Now only *dial.* and *Sc.*

c **1400** *Destr. Troy* 7614 To put hom in perell to perysshe þere lyues. *a* **1600** in *Hakluyt's Voy.* III. 845 This night we perished our maine tressletrees. **1638** Ford *Fancies* IV. i, If you have not perish'd all your reason. *c* **1656** Bramhall *Replic.* vi. 235 If a Merchant doe reckon only the price which his commodity cost him beyond Sea,..he will soon perish his Pack. **1691** J. Wilson *Belphegor* I. ii, One..that has perish'd his own Fortune, to save the Publick. **1822** Galt *Sir A. Wylie* xciii, Her son perished the pack, and they say has spoused his fortune and gone to Indy.

d. With material object: To destroy, cause to decay; esp. as the result of exposure to weather or injurious conditions. (See also 2.)

1547 Boorde *Introd. Knowl.* i. (1870) 121 There is no wynde nor wether that dothe hurte or peryshe them. **1613** Fletcher, etc. *Honest Man's Fort.* I. ii, His wants And miseries have perish'd his good face. **1778** [W. Marshall] *Minutes Agric.* 28 Jan. an. 1775, Will the frost perish the exposed fibres?

†**e.** With immaterial object: To destroy, do away with, put an end to. *Obs.*

a **1300** *Cursor M.* 22250 O rome Imparre þe dignite Ne mai na wai al perist be. **1470–85** Malory *Arthur* XVII. ix. 703 In suche a maner entred the sone of god in the wombe of a mayd mary whos vyrgynyte ne was perysshed ne hurte. **1509** Barclay *Shyp of Folys* (1874) II. 255 We coueyte nat to perysshe theyr fame in any wyse. **1593** Bilson *Govt. Christ's Ch.* xiii. 265 The generall rage of ignorance and oblivion, that hath..perished the best writers before our times. **1628** Feltham *Resolves* II. [I.] ii, The best way to perish discontentments. **1643** Steer tr. *Exp. Chyrurg.* xiii. 48 That they grow not..to a pin and webbe, or else cleane perish the sight.

f. Said of the effect of cold, hunger, or privation, in withering or shrivelling up, or reducing to a moribund condition. Now chiefly *dial.*

1719 De Foe *Crusoe* II. i, Rains and Cold..benumb and perish their limbs. **1867** Baker *Nile Tribut.* iii. 61 The extreme heat of the sun and simoon perishes all vegetation. *Mod. dial.* (Essex) The want of sleep perished me.

ˈperish, *sb.* [f. prec. vb.] **1.** The act of perishing: in phr. ***upon the perish***, on the point or in process of perishing. (Cf. *on the wane.*) *rare*⁻¹.

1825 Cobbett *Rur. Rides* (1830) I. 319 Everything seems upon the perish.

2. *Austral.* A state of near starvation, great thirst, or any kind of deprivation or destitution; esp. in phr. ***to do a perish***: to come to such a state. Also trivially (see quot. 1941).

1894 *Argus* (Melbourne) 28 Mar. 5/4 When a man or party has nearly died through want of water he is said to have 'done a perish'. **1903** R. Bedford *True Eyes* 312 If Xavier Quinn hadn't found this show three months ago ye'd have done a perish. **1924** *Truth* (Sydney) 27 Apr. 6 *Perish, doing a*, to shiver; to be cold. **1929** K. S. Prichard *Coonardoo* v. 60 But we near done a perish for water, You. **1935** H. H. Finlayson *Red Centre* iii. 28 The constant struggle out of one 'perish' into another. **1941** Baker *Dict. Austral. Slang* 53 *Do a perish*, suffer greatly from thirst, hunger or destitution. 'In a city, to sleep out in parks, to be homeless.' **1942** 'M. Innes' *Daffodil Affair* II. v. 64 'He didn't die,' said Hudspith. 'He perished.' 'He did a perish,' said Appleby corroboratively and idiomatically. **1944** F. Clune *Red Heart* 19, I did a thousand miles in eleven weeks on camel-back to find Lasseter's track, and follow it into the country where he did a perish. **1953** D. Stivens *Gambling Ghost* 3 You'll do a perish, mate, and no mistake. You're two hundred miles as the crow flies from anywhere. **1959** H. P. Tritton *Time means Tucker* 15/1 The train-crew who had made us do a perish on the Galathera Plain. **1969** 'A. Garve' *Boomerang* ii. 71 His intention was to enjoy this trip..not to 'do a perish' in the Never Never.

perish, -e, obs. forms of PIERCE.

perishability (pɛrɪʃəˈbɪlɪtɪ). *rare.* [f. next: see -ITY.] Perishableness.

1811 Shelley in Dowden *Life* (1886) I. iv. 133 Inquiries into our intellect, its eternity or perishability. **1847** Lewes *Hist. Philos.* (1857) 61 The mutability and perishability of all individual things.

perishable (ˈpɛrɪʃəb(ə)l), *a.* (*sb.*) [f. PERISH *v.* + -ABLE; cf. F. *périssable* (*c* 1400 in Hatz.-Darm.).] **1.** Liable to perish; subject to destruction, decay, or death; *esp.* naturally subject to speedy decay, as organic substances, minerals which rapidly weather or become decomposed, and the like.

1611 Cotgr., *Perissable*, perishable. **1648** J. Goodwin *Youngling Elder* 33 All books whatsoever are perishable. *a* **1687** Petty *Pol. Arith.* (1690) 18 Silver, Gold, and Jewels, ..are not perishable, nor so mutable as other Commodities. **1776** Adam Smith *W. N.* I. xi. (1869) I. 238 Of all the productions of land, milk is perhaps the most perishable. **1790** Cowper *Adam* IV. vii, Thou perishable flesh and form of clay. **1810** E. Weeton *Jrnl.* Apr. (1969) I. 257 He will sometimes order such quantities of perishable household articles, that one half are sometimes wasted. **1839** Murchison *Silur. Syst.* I. xxvii. 341 Non-micaceous perishable shale. **1849** Helps *Friends in C.* (1851) II. 185 Systems, constitutions, and the like are perishable things. **1862** Dickens *Lett.* (1880) II. 172 It is not made of a perishable material. **1929** F. C. Bowen *Sea Slang* 102 *Perishable Cargo.* In the 18th century, slaves or fruit. **1958** M. Roberts *Gustavus Adolphus* II. i. 43 Gustav Vasa.. discharged his debt to Lübeck in goods, and sometimes in goods of a dangerously perishable nature: at least one instalment was paid in butter.

2. a. *absol.* quasi-*sb.* ***the perishable***, that which is perishable or transitory.

1821 Byron *Heav. & Earth* i. 28 Were I the Seraph, And he the perishable. **1843** J. Martineau *Chr. Life* (1867) 10 It is the Immortal against the Perishable. *a* **1854** H. Reed *Lect. Eng. Lit.* ii. (1878) 61 In the elder literature, the perishable has passed away.

b. *sb. pl.* Things liable to decay: said chiefly of food-stuffs in transit.

1742 Richardson *Corr.* (1804) I. 83 The fall of the leaves fills the pools, the ponds, and the dikes..with particles, and animalcula, and perishables, of vegetable as well as animal nature. **1807** Moore *Mem.* (1853) I. 224 Recollections are too like the other perishables of this world. **1880** Muirhead *Gaius* II. §64 A procurator may alienate perishables belonging to his principal. **1895** *Spectator* 26 Oct. 553/2 Perishables like fish and flowers.

Hence **ˈperishably** *adv.*, in a perishable manner, by being perishable.

1891 *Gd. Words* Aug. 519 So strange it seems to me Beauty should perishably find its close.

perishableness (ˈpɛrɪʃəb(ə)lnɪs). [f. prec. + -NESS.] The quality of being perishable.

1690 Locke *Govt.* II. v. §48 Supposing..nothing in the island, either because of its commonness, or perishableness, fit to supply the place of money. **1825** *New Monthly Mag.* XVI. 479 A deep and melancholy sense of the perishableness of the noblest qualities. **1852** Lewis *Methods Observ. Politics* I. 221 They [written memorials] have a monumental character as opposed to the perishableness of mere speech.

perished (ˈpɛrɪʃt), *ppl. a.* [f. PERISH *v.* + -ED¹.] That has perished, in the senses of the vb.; decayed, wasted; dead or brought to the point of death with cold or privation.

1538 Elyot, *Perditus*.., loste, perysshed, withoute recouerie, out of hope. **1579** Langham *Gard. Health* 587 The leaues & root boyled in water and Hony, & drunke, healeth the perished lungs. **1685** *Lond. Gaz.* No. 1998/4 A brown bay Mare above 14 hands high,..a little perisht in her Wind. **1747** H. Glasse *Art of Cookery* xxi. 161 If any soft or perished Place appear on the Outside [of cheese], try how deep it goes. **1757** W. Thompson *R. N. Advoc.* 46 It is no longer a Wonder, such perished Stores should be bought up. **1823** Galt *Gilhaize* II. xxix. 282 The mourning women, and the perished child in the arms. **1883** A. Lang in *Contemp. Rev.* Dec. 842 The perished plays of Sophocles and Æschylus might any day be brought to light. **1888** 'R. Boldrewood' *Robbery under Arms* xli, 'Dining at the camp!' says Aileen, looking regularly perished. *a* **1922** T. S. Eliot *Waste Land Drafts* (1971) 75 Over perished plains, stumbling in cracked earth. **1922** H. P. Stevens in S. Morgan *Prep. Plantation Rubber* xxi. 306 After a time, vulcanised rubber tends to harden, cracks appear on the surface when the article is bent or stretched, and eventually the rubber becomes rotten and 'perished'. **1923** B. D. W. Luff *Chem. of Rubber* vii. 86 Spiller found that the unvulcanised rubber coating on a piece of fabric after six years had lost its original properties and had become hard and brittle, or 'perished', to use the term now applied to such a change. **1950** J. Cannan *Murder Included* vii. 158 A perished washer might account for the dripping. **1964** R. Petrie *Murder by Precedent* iii. 39 The half-perished suspenders and wrinkled stockings. **1965** D. Francis *Odds Against* xiii. 178 Weather forecasts are as reliable as a perished hot-water bottle. **1967** Leyland & Watts in J. A. Brydson *Devel. with Natural Rubber* v. 67 If this were so, then under the more severe running conditions.., casing compounds based conventionally on natural rubber would reach a perished condition in a relatively short time. **1978** *Country Life* 30 Nov. 1915/3 Old nylon stockings.. infinitely superior to perished rubber releasing corroded wire.

perishen, -oner, obs. ff. PARISHEN, PARISHIONER.

ˈperisher. [f. PERISH *v.* + -ER¹.] **a.** That which perishes or destroys; esp. an extreme (of any course of action); a 'plunger'; also applied to persons as a term of contempt, and more generally, with an overtone of pity. Also (*little*) ***perishers*** pl., children. *slang.*

1888 'R. Boldrewood' *Robbery under Arms* xli, He..went in an awful perisher—took a month to it, and was never sober day or night the whole time. **1896** *Idler* Mar. 282/1 Those perishers in the gallery didn't know anything about Shakespeare. **1908** A. N. Lyons *Arthur's* II. i. 106 Poor ole perisher's 'fraid to come in, 'e is. **1924** R. Keable *Recompence* i. 9 But we can't hear of a soul, or, if we do, the perisher funks this place. **1935** Wodehouse *Luck of Bodkins* xv. 181 If you ask me, they don't learn the little perishers nothing. **1942** —— *Money in Bank* (1946) xi. 85 Most modern young men are squirts and perishers. **1957** R. Park *One-a-Pecker* (1958) xi. 199 He had no name. In the thaw they buried him in the pass, and his epitaph was *Some Poor Bloody Perisher.* 1864. **1979** *Guardian* 30 Apr. 13/2, I taught the whole school..about Palm Sunday... Not one of the little perishers knew.

b. *Austral.* = PERISH *sb.* 2.

1903 R. Bedford *True Eyes* 292 Of course that country we went to on the Peak was a shicer. Just's well you didn't come—we near did a perisher there. **1903** 'T. Collins' *Such is Life* I. 7 You will understand that the bullock drivers' choice of accommodation lay between the selection, the ram-paddock, and a perisher on the plain... A perisher on the plain is seldom hard to find in a bad season, when the country is stocked for good seasons. **1936** A. Russell *Gone Nomad* vi. 44 Where one flood will leave behind a well-filled waterhole..the next, probably, will fill the hole with sand. And that is precisely what had happened here... It looked as if we were in for what the Inlander calls a 'perisher'.

c. *Naval slang.* A periscope. Hence in extended uses (see quot. 1962).

1925 Fraser & Gibbons *Soldier & Sailor Words* 221 *Perisher*, periscope. **1948** Partridge *Dict. Forces' Slang* 139 *The Perisher*, the C.O.'s course for submarine commanders. **1952** E. Young *One of our Submarines* viii. 115 At one time the course on which we were embarked had been called the Periscope School; hence the grimly humorous contraction 'Perisher'. Now it was officially the C.O.Q.C., or Commanding Officers' Qualifying Course, but, by tradition we were still known as the perishers. *Ibid.* 125 Ours happened to be the first perisher course to have Teddy Woodward for instructor. **1962** Granville *Dict. Sailors' Slang* 87/2 *Perisher, the*, periscope course for officers selected to command submarines. A 'perishing' difficult examination. 2. An officer undergoing this course, which is officially styled *the Commanding Officers Qualifying Course.* **1973** D. Reeman *Go in & Sink!* i. 16 We did our *Perisher* together, and even when I got *Tristram* he was given *Tryphon.*

ˈperishing, *vbl. sb.* [f. PERISH *v.* + -ING¹.] The action of the vb. PERISH: **a.** A going to destruction, suffering death; †**b.** A destroying, causing destruction (*obs.*).

a. *a* **1340** Hampole *Psalter* xiii. 4 Ilkan is cause of oþer perischynge. **1382** Wyclif *Ezek.* xxviii. 8 Thou shalt die in the perishynge of slayn men. **1643** Milton *Divorce* xiii. (1851) 54 Who shall answer for the perishing of all those souls? **1768–74** Tucker *Lt. Nat.* (1834) I. 640 Painful perishings by fire. **1864** Skeat *Uhland's Poems* 74 Feuds and traitorous deeds And perishing of precious seeds.

b. *c* **1400** *Destr. Troy* 11986 Haue pytie..of this pure maidon; Put hir in some place fro perisshyng of hondes. **1523** Fitzherb. *Husb.* §62 Se the knyfe go no deper than the thycknes of the bone for perysshynge of the brayne. **1690** Locke *Govt.* II. v. §46 The exceeding of the bounds of his just property..the perishing of anything uselessly.

c. *spec.* of rubber.

1913 B. D. Porritt *Chem. of Rubber* i. 12 The oxidation of rubber..is technically known as 'perishing'. **1935** Dawson & Porritt *Rubber* 602/1 *Perishing*, the final stage in the ageing of vulcanised rubber which becomes oxidised with the formation of resinous materials, losing its characteristic elastic properties. **1954** H. J. Stern *Rubber* v. 152 The 'perishing' of rubber, particularly of manufactured rubber articles, has been a source of trouble to all concerned from the time of Hancock down to the present day. **1961** D. W. Huke *Introd. Natural & Synthetic Rubbers* v. 80 One of the most important problems a rubber compounder has to face is the perishing—usually referred to as the ageing—of rubber.

perishing (ˈpɛrɪʃɪŋ), *ppl. a.* [f. as prec. + -ING².] That perishes.

1. That goes to destruction; that passes out of existence, or suffers decay, dissolution, or death.

c **1450** tr. *De Imitatione* I. i. 2 To seke perishyng ryches and to truste in hem is vanite. **1663** GERBIER *Counsel* d iv a, The perishing Buildings of Mortalls. **1710** SWIFT *Tatler* No. 230 ⁋10 All new affected Modes of Speech..are the first perishing Parts in any Language. **1844** WILLIS *Psyche* 36 The glory of the human form Is but a perishing thing.

2. That causes destruction or death; deadly: said of cold, privation, or the like. Also *Austral.*, with reference to PERISH *sb.* 2.

1422 tr. *Secreta Secret., Priv. Priv.* 246 The colde, and moistnesse, wych is perissynge and contrarie to the lyfe. **1634** RAINBOW *Labour* (1635) 22 It cannot be said to be causally perishing. **1813** T. BUSBY tr. *Lucretius* v. *Comm.* p. vi, Destroyed by..the perishing power of frost. **1893** EARL DUNMORE *Pamirs* II. 138 A night of perishing cold. **1941** I. L. IDRIESS *Great Boomerang* xvii. 124 Sixty miles to water, along a perishing track on a perishing day.

3. *colloq.* Applied disparagingly to anything: insignificant; troublesome; also as an intensive and as a filler.

1847 E. BRONTË *Wuthering Heights* II. xiii. 266 Do you imagine..that healthy, hearty girl, will tie herself to a little perishing monkey like you? **1903** KIPLING *Five Nations* 196 We were sugared about by the old men (Panicky, perishin' old men). **1916** 'TAFFRAIL' *Pincher Martin* iii. 32 A long coaling in the winter is the 'perishin' limit', as some one put it. **1918** [see BLIGHTY, BLIGHTY *sb.* c]. **1930** [see *flat spin* s.v. FLAT *a.* 15]. **1952** M. ALLINGHAM *Tiger in Smoke* iv. 75 These perishing crooks, who do they think they are all of a sudden?

4. a. as *adv.* Excessively, perishingly.

1888 E. MARSHALL *Bristol Diamonds* ix. 106 It is perishing cold to-day. **1906** *Westm. Gaz.* 26 Feb. 4/2 I'm perishing hungry. I feel as if I should drop. **1933** M. LOWRY *Ultramarine* ii. 63 You've been a perishing long time with that coffee! **1945** G. MILLAR *Maquis* i. 21 They all say it's perishing cold in the aircraft.

b. Used as a mere intensive.

1959 M. GILBERT *Blood & Judgement* v. 54 He..turns right at the top, because it's the only way he perishing well can turn.

Hence **ˈperishingly** *adv.*, so as to cause to perish; deadly.

1698 FRYER *Acc. E. India & P.* 298 Perishingly cold with frosty Winds. **1876** SMILES *Sc. Natur.* vi. (ed. 4) 97 These sleeping-places were perishingly cold.

perishless (ˈpɛrɪʃlɪs), *a.* [f. PERISH *v.* + -LESS.] That cannot perish; imperishable.

1605 SYLVESTER tr. *Du Bartas's Weekes & Workes* 628 We must, to make vs blest,..propose our selues that perfect, perish-les, That true vnfained good, that good all danger-les From th'vniust spoile of theeues. **1885** J. BEVERIDGE *Poets of Clackmannanshire* 144 Wallace of perishless renown. **1915** *Times* 31 Mar. 9/3 The perishless faith of the lover takes their spears of rebellion into its own wounds to hide them.

ˈperishment. Now *dial.* [f. PERISH *v.* + -MENT. Cf. F. *périssement* (16th c. in Littré).]

†**a.** Destruction, damage, loss. *Obs.* **b.** *dial.* 'Starvation' by cold.

1548 UDALL, etc. *Erasm. Par. John* xii. 84 To bestowe life is no perishemente but auantage. *a* **1549** LATIMER *Let.* in Foxe *A. & M.* (1583) 1755 Iustices that be to much naturall, to theyr owne perishment both Body and Soule. **1822** BEWICK *Mem.* ix. 116 Before she had waded through it, she got very wet and a *perishment* of cold. **1855** ROBINSON *Whitby Gloss., A Perishment*, a severe cold.

perisome (ˈpɛrɪsəʊm). *Zool.* Also **perisom**; also in L. form **perisoma** (pɛrɪˈsəʊmə). [= mod.F. *périsome*, and mod.L. *perisōma*, f. Gr. περί about + σῶμα body.] The integument or body-wall of an echinoderm, upon which the external calcareous skeleton is developed. Hence **periˈsomal, perisoˈmatic, periˈsomial** *adjs.*, of or pertaining to the perisome.

1872 NICHOLSON *Palæont.* 102 The class Echinodermata ..is distinguished by the fact that the external envelope of the body ('perisome') has the power of secreting calcareous matter to a greater or less extent. **1877** HUXLEY *Anat. Inv. Anim.* viii. 513 The genus Stylifer, which infests Star-fishes and Sea-urchins, sometimes imbedding itself in the perisoma. **1877** W. THOMSON *Voy. Challenger* I. iii. 172 The perisom is divided into four muscular bands. **1877** HUXLEY *Anat. Inv. Anim.* ix. 594 Portions of the perisomatic skeleton of the aboral region. **1893** *Syd. Soc. Lex., Perisomal, ..Perisomatic,..Perisomial.*

perisperm (ˈpɛrɪspɜːm). *Bot.* [ad. F. *périsperme* ad. mod.L. *perisperm-um* (Jussieu 1789), f. Gr. περί around + σπέρμα seed.] The mass of nutritive tissue or 'albumen' outside the embryo-sac in some seeds (distinguished from the *endosperm* within the embryo-sac); also, the tissue of the nucellus, which sometimes persists in the ripe seed (Brongniart 1827). Formerly used for the 'albumen' generally; also for the *testa* or integument of the seed (Richard 1808).

1819 LINDLEY tr. *Richard's Observ. Fruits & Seeds* 84 Endosperm;..Jussieu called it *Perisperm*; Gærtner *Albumen.* **1835** HENSLOW *Descr. & Phys. Bot.* §269 In many cases this nutriment, or 'amnios',..is not wholly absorbed by the ripening ovule; and it ultimately becomes the 'albumen' or 'perisperm' of the seed, and is then farinaceous, hard, or oily. **1852** TH. ROSS *Humboldt's Trav.* I. vi. 214 The horned perisperm of the coffee-tree. **1885** GOODALE *Physiol. Bot.* (1892) 437 The food within the developing embryo sac is termed endosperm; if around it, perisperm.

Hence **periˈspermal, periˈspermic,** *adjs.*, pertaining to, or having, a perisperm.

1819 LINDLEY tr. *Richard's Obs.* 23 The origin of the perispermic vessels. **1866** *Treas. Bot., Perispermic*.. furnished with albumen. **1876** HARLEY *Mat. Med.* (ed. 6) 443 The husk and perispermal membrane are inert.

perispheric (pɛrɪsˈfɛrɪk), *a. rare.* [f. PERI- + SPHERIC.] 'Globular; having the form of a ball' (Webster 1828); spherical. Also **periˈspherical** *a.*

1828 WEBSTER cites *Journ. of Science* for *Perispheric.* **1846** WORCESTER, *Perispheric, Perispherical*, spherical; round.

perisplenic to **perisplenitis**: see PERI- a, c.

perispome (ˈpɛrɪspəʊm), *a.* and *sb. Gr. Gram.* [abbrev. of *periˈspomenon* (also in use) = Gr. περισπώμενον, neuter pr. pple. passive of περισπᾶν to draw around, mark with the circumflex (any syllable).] **a.** *adj.* Having a circumflex accent on the last syllable. **b.** *sb.* A word so accented.

1818 BLOMFIELD tr. *Matthiæ Gr. Gram.* II. 958 *Perispomena*, περισπώμενα, which have the circumflex on the last syllable, as φιλῶ, τιμῶ, ποὺς. **1845** JELF *Gr. Gram.* I. iii. 36 *Perispomena*—when the circumflex is on the ultima; as, κακῶς, πας. **1867** tr. *Curtius's Grk. Gram.* (ed. 2) §21 A word having a circumflex on the last syllable is called *perispomenon. Ibid.* §93 After a perispome the accent of the enclitic is entirely lost.

Hence **ˈperispome** *v.*, to place a circumflex accent on the last syllable.

‖**perispoˈrangium.** *Bot.* [f. PERI- + SPORANGIUM.] A structure surrounding or investing the sporangium in cryptogams.

1856 in HENSLOW *Dict. Bot. Terms.* **1866** *Treas. Bot.* 865 *Perisporangium*, the indusium of ferns when it surrounds the spore-cases or sori. **1867** J. HOGG *Microsc.* II. i. 272 A number of sporidium-bearing filaments emanate from a kind of membrane at the base of a spheroidal cellular perisporangium.

perispore (ˈpɛrɪspɔə(r)). *Bot.* [a. F. *périspore*, ad. mod.L. *periˈsporium* (Richard 1808; also in Eng. use), f. Gr. περί around + σπόρος seed: see SPORE.] †**a.** Name for the hypogynous bristles of some sedges (see PERIANTH, PERIGYNIUM). *Obs.* **b.** The skin or integument of a spore.

1848 LINDLEY *Introd. Bot.* (ed. 4) I. 313 These [hypogynous setæ] are probably of the nature of the hypogynous scales of Grasses, and have been named *perispores* [earlier edd. *perisporum*] by some French writers. **1857** MAYNE *Expos. Lex., Perisporium*,..term applied by L. C. Richard and Persoon to the threads which surround the seed of the *Cyperaceæ.* Hedwig and some other botanists have substituted this term for that of *pericarp* in cryptogamious plants: a perispore. **1859** TODD *Cycl. Anat.* V. 217/1 The spores are developed each in the interior of a perispore.

perissad (pəˈrɪsæd), *sb.* (*a.*) [mod. f. Gr. περισσό-ός superfluous, redundant, in Arith. uneven, odd (f. περί in sense 'over, beyond') + -AD.]

1. *Chem.* An element or radical whose quantivalency is represented by an odd number, as a monad, triad, or pentad; opp. to ARTIAD. Also *attrib.* or as *adj.*

1870 [see ARTIAD]. **1877** WATTS *Fownes' Chem.* I. 257 Elements..of uneven equivalency,..are designated generally as perissads. *Ibid.* 258 In every saturated or normal compound..the sum of the perissad elements is always an even number. **1893** *Syd. Soc. Lex., Perissad, Chem.*, having a valency which is represented by an odd number.

2. *Zool.* = PERISSODACTYL (as *adj.*).

1893 *Syd. Soc. Lex., Perissad..Zoöl.*, belonging to the *Perissodactyla.*

perisse, perisshe, obs. ff. PERISH, PIERCE.

perissodactyl, -yle (pərɪsəʊˈdæktɪl), *a.* and *sb. Zool.* [ad. mod.L. *perissodactyl-us*, f. Gr. περισσό-ς uneven, odd + δάκτυλος digit.]

a. *adj.* Having an odd number of toes on each foot, as an angulate mammal; odd-toed; belonging to the division *Perissodactyla* of *Ungulata.* **b.** *sb.* A perrissodactyl ungulate or hoofed animal: *pl.* in *-s* or *-a.* Opposed to ARTIODACTYL.

a. 1849–52 TODD *Cycl. Anat.* IV. 922/2 The elephant.. belongs to the..perissodactyle group of Pachyderms. **1872** NICHOLSON *Palæont.* 424 The three existing genera of Perissodactyle Ungulates.

b. 1854 OWEN *Skel. & Teeth* in *Circ. Sc., Org. Nat.* I. 242 The bony palate extends further back than in the perissodactyles. **1875** C. C. BLAKE *Zool.* 33 Three great divisions of Perissodactyla exist, of which the Rhinoceros, the Tapir, and the Horse form the existing types. **1877** LE CONTE *Elem. Geol.* III. (1879) 508 He..divided all Ungulates into Perissodactyls (odd-toed) and Artiodactyls (even-toed).

So **perissoˈdactylate, perissodacˈtylic, perissoˈdactylous** *adjs.* = prec. a.

1889 *Nature* 28 Nov. 84/1 Two species of the remarkable Perissodactylate genus *Macrauchenia.*

periˈssology. *Rhet.* ?*Obs.* [ad. late L. *perissologia*, a. Gr. περισσολογία, f. περισσολόγος speaking too much, f. περισσός, redundant + λόγος speech.] Redundance or superfluity of speech; use of more words than are necessary; pleonasm.

1583 FULKE *Defence* (Parker Soc.) 136 Haue not the most elegant authors used hyperbatons, perissologies, and other figures that are counted faults of speech? [**1589** PUTTENHAM *Eng. Poesie* III. xxii. (Arb.) 264 *Macrologia*, or long language ..: it is also named by the Greeks *Perissologia.*] **1656** BLOUNT *Glossogr., Perissology*, superfluous speaking. **1776** CAMPBELL *Philos. Rhet.* (1801) I. 359 If we should say *the alcoran* we should fall into a gross perissology.

Hence **perissoˈlogical** *a.* (*rare*⁻⁰), 'redundant in words' (Webster 1828).

perissosyllabic (pəˌrɪsəʊsɪˈlæbɪk), *a.* [f. Gr. περισσοσύλλαβ-ος having a syllable over (f. περισσός) + -IC.] Having a redundant syllable or syllables.

perissosyllabic hexameter, a name for the 'greater Archilochian' measure, in which three trochees (or two trochees and a spondee) are substituted for the last two feet of the ordinary hexameter (as in Horace, Bk. I. Ode iv.).

peristalith (pəˈrɪstəlɪθ). *Archæol.* [irreg. f. Gr. περίστα(τος standing round + λίθος stone. Better *periˈstatolith.*] A ring or row of standing stones surrounding a burial-mound, or the like.

1882 C. ELTON *Orig. Eng. Hist.* 131 Buried in the earth and surrounded by a ring of stones, or 'peristalith' of an oblong form. **1898** *Edin. Rev.* Apr. 441 The rim of the stone-circle or 'peristalith'.

‖**peristalsis** (pɛrɪˈstælsɪs). *Physiol.* [mod.L., repr. a. Gr. περίσταλσις, cf. περισταλτ-ικός in next.] Peristaltic movement: see next.

1859 TODD *Cycl. Anat. & Phys.* V. 313/1 A peristalsis.. which sets out from the cardiac extremity. **1875** H. C. WOOD *Therap.* (1879) 38 Diarrhœa, due to a violently increased peristalsis. **1878** FOSTER *Phys.* I. iv. §4. 142 In a twisted tube like that of the vertebrate ventricle, ordinary peristalsis would be impotent to drive the blood onward.

peristaltic (pɛrɪˈstæltɪk), *a. Physiol.* [ad. Gr. περισταλτικ-ός (Galen), f. περιστέλλ-ειν lit. to send round, f. στέλλειν to set, place, array, make ready, dispatch, send. Cf. F. *péristaltique* (1680 in Hatz.-Darm.).] Applied to the automatic muscular (vermicular) movement which takes place in the alimentary canal and other hollow or tubular organs, consisting of rhythmic wave-like contractions in successive circles, by which the contents of the organ are propelled along it.

1655 CULPEPPER, etc. *Riverius* IX. vii. 266 This vomiting cometh by the Peristaltick motion of the Guts. **1676** COLE in *Phil. Trans.* XI. 609 Both these kinds of vessels seem to have a peristaltick contraction of their own. **1753** N. TORRIANO *Midwifry* 14 The inverting peristaltic Motion of the Fallopian Tube. **1881** DARWIN *Veg. Mould* 116 When the earth was in a very liquid state it was ejected in little spurts, and when not so liquid by a slow peristaltic movement.

b. *transf.* (*Electr.*). See quot.

1856 THOMSON *Math. & Phys. Papers* (1884) II. lxxv. 80, I..venture to introduce the term *peristaltic* to characterize that kind of induction by which currents are excited in elongated conductors through the variation of electrostatic potential in the surrounding matter.

Hence **periˈstaltically** *adv.*, in a peristaltic manner; with peristaltic action or movement.

1859 TODD *Cycl. Anat.* V. 678/1 The food is propelled onwards peristaltically. **1868** OWEN *Anat. Vertebr.* III. 501 Insulating the peristaltically winding intestines from the constant respiratory movements of the abdominal walls.

peristaphyline (pɛrɪˈstæfɪlɪn), *a. Anat.* [ad. mod.L. *peristaphylin-us*, f. Gr. περί around + σταφύλινος adj., f. σταφυλή bunch of grapes, swollen uvula. Cf. mod.F. *péristaphylin* (Littré).] Situated about the uvula: applied to two muscles, the ***external peristaphyline*** (or *tensor palati*), and the ***internal peristaphyline*** (or *levator palati*).

[**1704** J. HARRIS *Lex. Techn.* I, *Peristaphilinus, internus & externus*, are Muscles of the Uvula.] **1840** G. V. ELLIS *Anat.* 236 The *circumflexus palati*, or external peristaphyline muscle..consists of a vertical and a horizontal portion.

peristerite (pəˈrɪstəraɪt). *Min.* [f. Gr. περιστερά pigeon, dove + -ITE¹ 2 b.] A variety of ALBITE exhibiting a slight iridescence or opalescence like that of the plumage on a pigeon's neck.

1843 T. THOMSON in *Lond. & Edin. Philos. Mag.* XXII. 189 *Peristerite*..was sent me also from Perth in Upper Canada... It is light brownish red, and exhibits a play of colours, chiefly blue, on the surface. **1868** DANA *Min.* 356.

peristeroid (pəˈrɪstərɔɪd), *a. Ornith.* [mod. f. Gr. περιστερά pigeon + -OID.] Of or pertaining to the *Peristeroideæ*, a group of birds in Sundevall's classification (1873) identical with the *Columbæ* or pigeons.

peristeromorph (pəˈrɪstərəmɔːf). *Ornith.* [f. mod.L. *peristeromorphæ*, pl. fem. of *peristeromorphus*, f. Gr. περιστερά pigeon + μορφή form.] A member of the group *Peristeromorphæ* in Huxley's classification (1867), identical with the *Columbæ* or pigeons. So **peristeroˈmorphic,**

peristero'morphous *adjs.*, belonging to or having the characters of the *Peristeromorphæ*.

peristeronic (pərɪstəˈrɒnɪk), *a.* [app. f. Gr. περιστερών, -ῶνα dove-cot (f. περιστερά dove, pigeon) + -IC.] Pertaining to or concerned with pigeons; suggestive of pigeons.
1868 *Rules Peristeronic Soc.* 1 That the Society be called the National Peristeronic Society. **1876** FULTON & WRIGHT *Bk. Pigeons* 386 Of the National Peristeronic Society it may be said that it holds the position of the first pigeon society of the day. **1893** *Ibid.* (ed. Lumley) vii. 58 Who would talk of a pigeon's 'eye-lids' that has any knowledge of matters peristeronic? **1904** *Times* 6 Jan. 8/5 The National Peristeronic Society was founded by the amalgamation of the National Columbarian and the Philo-Peristeronic Societies. **1931** J. CANNAN *High Table* 21 A discourse.. which Anne and Cecilia punctuated with polite little peristeronic sounds.

peristeropod (pəˈrɪstərəpɒd), *a.* and *sb. Ornith.* [ad. assumed Gr. *περιστερόποδ-ες, pl. of *περιστερόπους pigeon-footed.] **a.** *adj.* Belonging to the *Peristeropodes*, a section of *Alectoromorphæ* or gallinaceous birds in Huxley's classification (1868), having the toes arranged on a level as in pigeons. **b.** *sb.* A member of this group. So **periste'ropodan** *a.* and *sb.*; **periste'ropodous** *a.*

peristethium: see PERI- b.

peristomatic (ˌpɛrɪstəʊˈmætɪk), *a. Bot.* [f. PERI- + STOMA (pl. *stomata*).] Surrounding a stoma of a leaf.
1876 J. H. BALFOUR in *Encycl. Brit.* IV. 90/1 In Ceratopteris thalictroides the stoma is bounded by three cells,—two of which.. are crescentic and concave inwardly, while the third surrounds them,.. and has on this account been called peristomatic.

peristome (ˈpɛrɪstəʊm). Also in L. forms pe'ristoma (pl. -ata), peri'stomium (pl. -ia). [= F. *péristome* (18..), ad. mod.L. *peristoma* (Hedwig 1782), f. Gr. περί around + στόμα mouth; altered (by Ehrhart 1787) to *peristomium*, after *pericarpium*, etc.]
1. *Bot.* The fringe of small teeth around the mouth of the capsule or sporangium in mosses.
1796 WITHERING *Brit. Plants* (ed. 3) I. 73 *Peristoma*, the fringe at the mouth of the Capsule of Mosses. **1818** HOOKER & TAYLOR *Musc. Brit.* Introd. 4 The absence or presence of the fringe of the Peristome which Hedwig employed to so much advantage. **1830** LINDLEY *Nat. Syst. Bot.* 320 One or more rows of cellular rigid processes, called collectively the peristomium, and separately teeth. **1875** BENNETT & DYER *Sachs' Bot.* 331 We must now examine somewhat more closely the origin of the Peristome.
2. *Zool.* **a.** The margin of the aperture of the shell of a mollusc. **b.** Any special structure or set of parts around the mouth or oral opening in various invertebrates, as insects, crustacea, hydrozoa, infusoria; in echinoderms, the part of the body-wall surrounding the mouth (opp. to PERIPROCT); in certain worms, as earthworms, the first true somite, situated behind the *prostomium* or *præstomium*, and bearing the mouth.
a. 1851-6 WOODWARD *Mollusca* 101 The margin of the aperture is termed the peristome. **1870** ROLLESTON *Anim. Life* 47 The columella is seen in the angle..; its umbilicus is partly.. concealed by the reflection over it of the peristome.
b. 1875 HUXLEY & MARTIN *Elem. Biol.* (1877) 93 (In *Vorticellæ*) *a.* The prominent everted rim (*peristome*). **1877** HUXLEY *Anat. Inv. Anim.* v. 232 (*Chætopoda*) The first somite, which contains the mouth, is the peristomium. *Ibid.* ix. 569 (*Echinodermata*) The ambulacral plates are continued on the peristome to the margins of the mouth. **1888** ROLLESTON & JACKSON *Anim. Life* 781 (*Hydrozoa Acraspeda*) The mouth.. is situate in the centre of a disc or peristome of great mobility. **1896** *Cambridge Nat. Hist.* II. 481.
Hence **peri'stomal**, **peri'stomial** *adjs.*, surrounding the mouth, circumoral; pertaining to, of the nature of, or having a peristome.
1888 ROLLESTON & JACKSON *Anim. Life* 547 Peristomal gills of some *Echinoidea*. **1900** *Proc. Zool. Soc.* 278 The peristomal plates.. number in adults normally 9 in one row and 8 in the other row of the pair. **1870** NICHOLSON *Man. Zool.* 99 Between the mouth and the circumference of the disc is a flat space, without appendages of any kind, termed the 'peristomial space'. **1881** SPRUCE in *Jrnl. Bot.* X. 18 Recklessly bandied about among peristomial genera. **1896** *Cambridge Nat. Hist.* II. 313 There are four long peristomial cirri on each side. *Ibid.* 185 The peristomial depression.

peristrephic (pɛrɪˈstrɛfɪk), *a.* [irreg. f. Gr. περιστρέφειν to turn round + -IC. (The etymological form would be *peristreptic*.)] Turning round, revolving, rotatory (as a panorama). Also **peri'strephical** *a.*
1827 *Blackw. Mag.* XXII. 385 The whole visible nocturnal sphere is peristrephical. **1838** *Ibid.* XLIII. 709 They accompany our ken like a peristrephic panorama. **1851** J. CAIRNS *Let.* in MacEwan *Life* (1895) 351 Opening up a peristrephic picture of the Christian world.

‖**peristrophe** (pəˈrɪstrəfɪ). *Obs. rare*⁻¹. [a. Gr. περιστροφή.] A turning round, a revolution.
1716 M. DAVIES *Athen. Brit.* III. 12 A strange Peristrophe of Policy and Religion.

peristyle (ˈpɛrɪstaɪl), *sb.* (*a.*) *Arch.* Also 7-9 in L. form **peri'stylium**, 9 in Gr. form **peri'stylon**. [a. F. *péristyle* (1554 in Hatz.-Darm.), ad. L. *peristȳlum*, *peristȳlium*, in Gr. περίστυλον sb., neuter of περίστυλ-ος having pillars all round, surrounded by a colonnade, f. περί around + στῦλος pillar.] A row of columns or colonnade surrounding a temple or other building, or a court, cloister, etc.; less properly, the court or space having round it such a row of columns.
1612 PEACHAM *Gentl. Exerc.* I. v. 17 All manner of compartments, bases, perystiles, plots, buildings, &c. **1673** RAY *Journ. Low C.* 268 A large square Court compassed about with the fairest *peristylium* or Cloyster that I ever saw. **1776** GIBBON *Decl. & F.* xiii. I. 396 A *peristylium* of granite columns. **1833** ELLIS *Elgin Marbles* (Libr. Ent. Knowl.) I. 72 When the exterior of a temple was not surrounded by a peristyle or colonnade, the temple was said to be apteral. **1878** SMITH *Dict. Gr. & Rom. Antiq.* 425/1 Round the peristyle were arranged the chambers used by the men.
¶ Erroneously applied to the columned porch of a church or other large building, to a pillared verandah, etc.
1694 MOTTEUX *Rabelais* v. vii. 24 You go through a large *Peristile, alias* a long Entry set about with Pillars. **1704** J. HARRIS *Lex. Techn.* I. s.v., *Peristyle* is sometimes taken for a row or rank of Columns, as well without as within any Edifice;.. Sometimes this was call'd *Antiprostyle*. **1863** MARY HOWITT *F. Bremer's Greece* I. vii. 239 Crowding and crushing.. about the peristyle and steps of the church. *Ibid.* II. xii. 27. **1866** MRS. RITCHIE *Village on Cliff* xiii. 195 When the wedding-party came out into the peristyle of the church, the carriages had both disappeared.
B. *adj.* Surrounded by a colonnade.
1862 *Sat. Rev.* 15 Mar. 303 That the Mausoleum was composed of an oblong peristyle building.
Hence **peri'stylar** *a.*, pertaining to, having, or of the nature of a peristyle.
1876 J. FERGUSSON *Hist. Indian Archit.* IV. ii. 335 All round the court there is a peristylar cloister with cells.

perisynovial: see PERI- a.

‖**perisystole** (pɛrɪˈsɪstəliː). *Physiol.* [mod.L. *perisystole* (Bartholine 1651), f. Gr. περί around + συστολή contraction; in F. *périsystole* (1762 in *Dict. Acad.*).] 'The short interval of time between the systole and the following diastole of the heart; inappreciable except when the heart's action is failing' (*Syd. Soc. Lex.*). Hence **perisystolic** (-sɪˈstɒlɪk) *a.*, belonging to the perisystole.
1664 POWER *Exp. Philos.* I. 60 Without any interloping perisystole at all. **1668** CULPEPPER & COLE *Barthol. Anat.* II. vi. 104 They confound the Perisystole or quiet posture of the heart. [**1651** BARTHOLINUS II. vi. 251 Confundunt perisystolen seu quietum.] **1758** J. S. tr. *Le Dran's Observ. Surg.* (1771) Dict., *Perisystole*, that Instant of rest between the Systole and Diastole of the Heart. **1853** MARKHAM *Skoda's Auscult.* 213 A murmur arising at the root of the aorta, during the ventricular systole, is more perisystolic, than a murmur arising in the ventricles. **1875** HAYDEN *Dis. Heart* 81 The perisystolic phenomena.

†**'perit.** *Obs.* Also 6 **peryott**, 6-7 **periot**, 8 **perrot**. [Origin unascertained.] A measure of weight equal to $\frac{1}{216}$ of a grain. (Cf. DROIT².)
1564 *Conference of Weightes* (MS. Rawl. D. 23 lf. 6) The mynters.. devyde a droyte into .20. peryottes, and a peryott into .24. blanckes. **1649** *Acts & Ordin. Parl.* c. 43 (Scobell) 65 Twenty Mites makes a Grain; Twenty four Droits makes a Mite; Twenty Perits makes a Droit; Twenty four Blanks makes a Perit. **1680-1725** [see BLANK sb. 10]. **1838** *Murray's Hand-bk. N. Germ.* 40 These tulip roots were never bought or sold, but.. The bulbs, and their divisions into perits, became like the different stocks in our public funds, and were bought and sold at different prices from day to day.

†**pe'rite**, *a. Obs.* Also 6 **peryt**. [a. obs. F. *perit*, *-ite* (*c* 1500), or ad. L. *perīt-us* 'experienced', properly pa. pple. of **perīrī* (in *ex-perīrī* to make trial of).] Experienced, expert, skilful, skilled.
1529 *Chart. Jas. V.* in McCrie *Life A. Melville* (1819) I. 459 Ye said Maister Hary.. has made under him gude and perite scolaris. **1594** O. B. *Quest. Profit. Concern* 10 No decree could demonstrate vnto them any thing sufficient to respect a more ciuill and perite life. **1652** ASHMOLE *Theat. Chem.* Prol. 11 Linus is said to be the most Perite of any Lyrick Poet. **1820** *Blackw. Mag.* VII. 668 Friends who are in the habit of exercising a profuse rather than a perite hospitality.
Hence †**pe'ritely** *adv.*, skilfully. *Obs.*
1657 TOMLINSON *Renou's Disp.* 158 This hath been so peritely adulterated.

peritectic (pɛrɪˈtɛktɪk), *a.* and *sb.* [ad. G. *peritektisch* (W. Guertler *Metallographie* (1912) I. vi. 278), f. Gr. περί around, about + τηκτικ-ός able to dissolve (f. τήκειν to melt): cf. EUTECTIC *a.* and *sb.*] **A.** *adj.* Of, pertaining to, or designating a reaction that occurs between the solid phase and the liquid phase during the cooling of a mixture, with the formation of a new solid phase; *peritectic point*, the state at which all three phases coexist in equilibrium, the composition being such that a fall in temperature results in the disappearance of the two phases that exist above that temperature; also, the point representing this state in a constitutional diagram.
1924 JEFFRIES & ARCHER *Sci. of Metals* ix. 323 There are different solid phases in equilibrium with the melt above and below the peritectic temperature. During the peritectic reaction there are three phases (two solid and one liquid) in equilibrium, so that the temperature must remain constant until at least one of the phases disappears. **1936** *Nature* 18 Apr. 657/2 Preliminary results from an X-ray study of the peritectic reaction α + liquid → β in the Cu-Zn system prove that the orientations assumed by the β-phase are definitely related to the orientation of the α-phase. **1965** PHILLIPS & WILLIAMS *Inorg. Chem.* I. viii. 302 The cases in which there is one or more eutectic or peritectic points.. reflect rather an unfavourable interaction between A and B which may well be caused by size differences in the atom. **1967** A. H. COTTRELL *Introd. Metall.* xv. 230 The composition at r.. is the peritectic composition and the isothermal line pq marks the peritectic temperature. Just above this temperature there is no β-phase in any alloy; just below, all alloys from p to q contain some β. The silver-platinum system has a simple peritectic diagram. **1968** B. BAYLY *Introd. Petrol.* 330 If we knew that all Hawaiian rocks were generated from one homogeneous initial magma pool, we would conclude that there was necessarily a peritectic relation. **1973** J. G. TWEEDDALE *Materials Technol.* I. vi. 163 The reverse type of change to a eutectic reaction called a peritectic reaction can occur in many materials—this cannot be used to induce supersaturation but may be a means for producing a stable solid solution structure.
B. *sb.* A peritectic point or temperature.
1929 *Jrnl. Iron & Steel Inst.* CXIX. 337 In carbon steels, between the temperature of freezing and that of the peritectic, iron containing a maximum of 0·07 per cent. of carbon is the only solid to separate. **1975** *Nature* 20 Nov. 220/2 Any model of the igneous processes which produced the eucrites must account for this preferential generation of liquids at peritectic *A* (Fig. 1).
Hence **peri'tectically** *adv.*, by a peritectic reaction.
1935 G. E. DOAN *Princ. Physical Metall.* iv. 158 At 1500° the melt and δ crystals react peritectically to form γ-iron solid-solution crystals. **1967** A. H. COTTRELL *Introd. Metall.* xv. 233 Fig. 15.12 shows an example in which the γ primary solution also forms peritectically.

peritectoid (pɛrɪˈtɛktɔɪd), *a.* [f. prec. + -OID, after EUTECTOID *a.* and *sb.*] Of, pertaining to, or designating a reaction analogous to a peritectic reaction but involving three solid phases.
1936 H. L. ALLING *Interpretative Petrol. Igneous Rocks* viii. 97 The diagram shows that hedenbergite, $CaFeSi_2O_6$ on heating dissociates before reaching the solidus, forming a solid solution. I suggest this may be called a 'peritectoid' reaction. **1967** A. H. COTTRELL *Introd. Metall.* xv. 235 Eutectoid and peritectoid changes occur in the solid state which are the exact analogues of the eutectic and peritectic forms of the liquid-solid change. **1973** J. G. TWEEDDALE *Materials Technol.* I. vi. 163 There is also a form of reaction in the solid state, called the peritectoid reaction which is similar to the peritectic reaction.

peritendineum: see PERI- b.

‖**perithecium** (pɛrɪˈθiːsɪəm). *Bot.* Pl. **-ia**. Also anglicized as **perithece** (ˈpɛrɪθiːs). [mod.L. (Persoon 1796), f. Gr. περί around + θήκη case: cf. *pericarpium*.] A cup-shaped or flask-shaped receptacle, usually with a narrow opening, inclosing the fructification in certain fungi, etc.; spec. in the *Pyrenomycetes*. Hence **peri'thecial** *a.*, pertaining to the perithecium.
1832 LINDLEY *Introd. Bot.* 209 *Perithecium*, is a term used to express the part which contains the reproductive organs of Sphæria and its coordinates. **1839** *Ibid.* (ed. 3) 271 Lichens.. Perithecium is the part in which the asci are immersed. **1857** BERKELEY *Cryptog. Bot.* §274. **1875** BENNETT & DYER *Sachs' Bot.* 256 *Pyrenomycetes*.. The asci are formed in the interior of small flask-shaped or roundish receptacles.. here termed *Perithecia*. **1889** BENNETT & MURRAY *Cryptog. Bot.* 355 The Ascomycetes may be classed in three divisions:.. the *Pyrenomycetes*, with *pyrenocarps* or *peritheces* (hymenia within flask-shaped bodies open at the neck). *Ibid.* 356 The perithece does not differ essentially from the apothece.

perithelium, -thoracic: see PERI- a, b.

†**pe'rition.** *Obs. rare*⁻¹. [n. of action from L. *perīre*, *perit-um* to PERISH.] Perishing, destruction, annihilation.
1640 BP. HALL *Chr. Moder.* I. xiv. 168 Were there an absolute perition in our dissolution.

peritomous (pəˈrɪtəməs), *a. Min.* [f. Gr. περί around + -τομός cut, cutting.] (See quot.)
1835 C. U. SHEPARD *Mineral.* I. xxiv, *Peritomous. Note*, Implying that cleavage takes place in more than one direction parallel to the axis, and that the faces are all of the same quality.

peritomy (pəˈrɪtəmɪ). *Surg.* [f. Gr. περιτομή circumcision, f. περί around + τομή cutting.] Circumcision, esp. of the cornea.
1889 G. A. BERRY *Dis. Eye* I. ii. 62 Performing the operation of peritomy or syndectomy. **1890** in BILLINGS *Nat. Med. Dict.*

peritoneal, -æal (pɛrɪtəʊˈniːəl), *a.* [f. PERITONEUM, -ÆUM + -AL¹.] Of, pertaining to, situated in, or affecting the peritoneum.
1767 GOOCH *Treat. Wounds* I. 427 Each carrying along with it a peritonæal coat. **1797** *Phil. Trans.* LXXXVII. 205 There was.. all the appearance of peritoneal inflammation. **1866** A. FLINT *Princ. Med.* (1880) 590 The peritoneal

thickening and fibrous adhesions which result from circumscribed peritonitis.

peritoneoscopy (pɛrɪtəʊˈniːəskɒpɪ, ˌpɛrɪtəʊnɪˈɒskəpɪ). *Med.* [f. PERITONEO- + -SCOPY.] Visual examination of the peritoneal contents by means of a narrow instrument passed through a small incision in the peritoneum.

1936 in STEDMAN *Med. Dict.* (ed. 13). **1959** BAILEY & LOVE *Short Pract. Surg.* (ed. 11) xxiv. 501 For many years peritoneoscopy has been advocated for inspecting intraperitoneal organs without the necessity of laparatomy, but comparatively few surgeons employ it. **1974** R. M. KIRK et al. *Surgery* vi. 108 The diagnosis may be confirmed by needle biopsy, surgical biopsy, or at peritoneoscopy using an endoscope inserted through a small abdominal incision.

‖**peritoneum, -æum** (ˌpɛrɪtəʊˈniːəm). *Anat.* [L. *peritonæum, -ēum* (in Cæl. Aurel., *c* 420), a. Gr. περιτόναιον (-ειον), sb. from neuter of περιτόναιος adj., f. περίτονος stretched around or over, f. περί around + -τονος, from ablaut stem of τείνειν to stretch: cf. TONE. Formerly also *peryto'neon* from Gr., and *'peritone* = F. *peritoine* (1541 in Hatz.-Darm.).] The double serous membrane which lines the cavity of the abdomen, of large extent and complex form, having numerous folds (as the *omenta, mesenteries*, etc.) which invest and support the various abdominal viscera.

In vertebrates below mammals, which have no diaphragm, The membrane lining the whole body-cavity, corresponding to the mammalian peritoneum and pleura combined (hence sometimes called *pleuroperitoneum*). Also applied to similar membranes lining the body-cavity and investing the alimentary canal in some invertebrates, as insects.

1541 R. COPLAND *Guydon's Quest. Chirurg.* H ij b, What is the perytoneon, and wher of is it dyryuate? **1545** RAYNOLD *Byrth Mankynde* I. xv. (1552) 46 The kell called *Peritoneum.* **1594** T. B. *La Primaud. Fr. Acad.* II. 348 There is an other coate or skinne called Peritone, because it is spread round about the lower belly. **1615** CROOKE *Body of Man* 344 The wounds of the muscles of the lower belly and of the *Peritonæum* or rim are not mortall. **1671** RAY in *Phil. Trans.* VI. 2275 The Abdomen was compassed about with a strong Peritonæum. **1753** CHAMBERS *Cycl. Suppl.* s.v., In the fish kind, the peritoneum.. is very variously coloured. **1804** ABERNETHY *Surg. Obs.* 8 The peritoneum. **1872** PEASLEE *Ovar. Tumors* 3 A peculiar epithelium, not a continuation of that of the peritonæum. **1893** *Syd. Soc. Lex., Peritoneum*... The structure in the *Brachiopoda* that holds the alimentary canal suspended in the perivisceral cavity... The outer layer of the digestive canal in the *Insecta.*

Hence **perito'neo-** in *Comb.*, as ***peritoneo-va'ginal*** *a.*, having relation to the peritoneum and vagina.

1898 G. S. HERMANN *Dis. Women* 843 The peritoneo-vaginal method.

peritonism (ˈpɛrɪtəʊnɪz(ə)m). *Path.* [f. as next + -ISM: in mod.L. *peritonismus.*] (See quots.)

1897 *Allbutt's Syst. Med.* III. 625 The hæmorrhage may produce the symptoms of acute peritoneal damage which have been described under the title of 'Peritonism'. *Ibid.* 795 The symptoms, which are mainly those of intense abdominal pain, and collapse, and usually with vomiting, have been described under the title of 'peritonism'.

‖**peritonitis** (ˌpɛrɪtəʊˈnaɪtɪs). *Path.* [mod.L., f. Gr. περίτον-ος (see PERITONEUM) + -ITIS. In mod.F. *péritonite.*] Inflammation of the peritoneum, or of some part of it.

1776 W. CULLEN *First Lines Physic* (1778) I. vii. 293 We have given a place in our Nosology to the Peritonitis; comprehending under that title not only the inflammations affecting the peritonaeum.. but also those affecting the extensions of this membrane in the omentum and mesentery. **1880** BEALE *Slight Ailm.* 90 The pain of peritonitis is one of the most terrible.. that any human being can have to bear.

Hence **peritonital** (-ˈaɪtəl), **peritonitic** (-ˈɪtɪk) *adjs.*, pertaining to or affected with peritonitis.

1879 *St. George's Hosp. Rep.* IX. 2 Peritonitic signs on admission. **1883** *Summary* 26 July 3/3 The Bishop.. is not out of danger, and.. cannot be considered so until the peritonital inflammation is subdued. **1896** *Allbutt's Syst. Med.* I. 641 Various results of the peritonitic affection.

peritonsillar to **peritracheal:** see PERI- a, c.

peritorie, -ye, var. PARIETARY, pellitory.

peritreme (ˈpɛrɪtriːm). *Zool.* Also in L. form peri'trema. [a. F. *péritrème* (Audouin 18..), f. Gr. περί round + τρῆμα perforation, hole.]

a. A small chitinous ring surrounding a breathing-hole in an insect. **b.** The margin of the aperture of a univalve shell: = PERISTOME 2 a (*Syd. Soc. Lex.*).

1843 OWEN *Comp. Anat. Invertebr.* Gloss. 383 *Peritrema* .., the raised margin which surrounds the breathing holes of scorpions. **1870** NICHOLSON *Man. Zool.* 203 Pulmonary sacs, opening upon the under surface.. by.. stigmata, each of which is surrounded by a raised margin, or 'peritrema'. **1888** HUXLEY & MARTIN *Elem. Biol.* iv. 274 The mouth or peritreme of the shell [of a snail].

So **peri'trematous** *a.*, surrounding an aperture; belonging to the peritreme.

1890 in *Cent. Dict.* **1893** in *Syd. Soc. Lex.*

peritrichan (pəˈrɪtrɪkən), *a.* and *sb. Zool.* [f. mod.L. *Peritricha*, f. Gr. περί around + τριχ-, stem of θρίξ hair.] **a.** *adj.* Belonging to the division *Peritricha* of *Infusoria*, having a band of cilia around the body. **b.** *sb.* An infusorian of the division *Peritricha.* So **pe'ritrichous** *a.*; hence **pe'ritrichously** *adv.*, with a girdle of cilia.

1875 HUXLEY in *Med. Times & Gaz.* 5 May 495/1 According to the distribution of the cilia, Stein has divided them into the *Holotricha*,.. the *Heterotricha*,.. the *Hypotricha*,.. and the *Peritricha*, in which they [the cilia] form a zone round the body. **1877** —— *Anat. Inv. Anim.* ii. 109 The process of sexual reproduction observed by Stein in the peritrichous Infusoria. **1888** ROLLESTON & JACKSON *Anim. Life* 831 The.. ring which supports the sucker of all the Peritrichan *Urceolarina* save *Licnophora. Ibid.* 832 The perioral contractile collar of the Peritrichan, *Torquatella typica.* **1900** *Nature* 13 Sept. 465/2 Both are actively motile and peritrichously ciliated.

peritroch (ˈpɛrɪtrɒk). *Zool.* [ad. mod.L. *peritroch-us*, a. Gr. περίτροχος circular, round, f. περί around + τροχός a hoop, a wheel, anything round; f. τρέχ-ειν to run.] A circlet of cilia resembling a wheel, as in a rotifer; an organism or embryo having such a circlet. Hence **pe'ritrochal** *a.*, pertaining to or of the nature of a peritroch.

1890 in *Cent. Dict.*

‖**peritrochium** (pɛrɪˈtrəʊkɪəm). *Mech.* [mod.L., a. Gr. περιτρόχιον a wheel (see prec.); ἄξων ἐν περιτροχίῳ = *axis in peritrochio*, the wheel-and-axle.] A wheel, as constituting part of the mechanical power called the wheel-and-axle.

1704 J. HARRIS *Lex. Techn.* I. s.v., The use of this *Peritrochium*, is to make the Cylinder or Axis be turned the more easily by the means of Staves or Levers, which are fix'd in its Circumference. See *Axis in Peritrochio.* **1796** [see AXIS[1] 1]. **1798** EDGEWORTH *Pract. Educ.* (1822) II. 121 This organ is usually called in mechanicks, *the axis in peritrochio*,.. the word windlass or capstan, would convey a more distinct idea to our pupils. **1866** in BRANDE & COX *Dict. Science*, etc. [See AXIS[1] 1.]

peritropal (pəˈrɪtrəpəl), *a. Bot. rare.* [f. mod.L. *peritrop-us* (Jussieu) + -AL[1]. In F. *péritrope* (Richard 1808).] Of an embryo or ovule: = AMPHITROPAL, HEMITROPOUS. Also **pe'ritropous** *a.*

1819 LINDLEY *Richard's Observ. Fruits & Seeds* 22 If it [the seed] be attached to the axis, or to an axile trophosperm, by an hilum equi-distant from the two ends or occupying the whole length of the inner edge, it is called *peritropal. Ibid.* 86 Peritropal.. directed from the axis towards the sides of the pericarp. **1835** —— *Introd. Bot.* (1848) II. 378 *Peritropal*, directed from the axis to the horizon,.. only applied to the embryo of the seed. **1880** GRAY *Struct. Bot.* viii. 313 Centrifugal (or peritropous), when [the radicle is] turned toward the sides.

¶ Erroneously explained by Worcester:

1846 WORCESTER, *Peritropal*, turning around; rotary. *Hooker.* (Hence in some later Dicts.)

‖**peritrope** (pəˈrɪtrəʊpiː). *rare.* [= Gr. περιτροπή turning round, revolution, circuit.]

a **1656** USSHER *Ann.* vi. (1658) 600 This Peritrope is worth the observation, That on the same day of the same moneth, that the Temple should happen to be taken, and that after 543 years.

peritrophic (pɛrɪˈtrɒfɪk), *a. Entom.* [ad. F. *péritrophique*, f. Gr. περί around + τροφή food, τροφικός feeding.] Surrounding the food: applied by Balbiani (died 1899) to a chitinous membrane lining the stomach in various insects.

1900 MIALL & HAMMOND *Harlequin Fly* ii. 59 The peritrophic membrane has been found in nearly every Dipterous larva examined.

‖**perityphlitis** (ˌpɛrɪtɪˈflaɪtɪs). *Path.* [mod. L., f. PERI- + Gr. τυφλόν the cæcum or blind-gut (Galen), neuter of τυφλός blind, after *typhlitis.*] Inflammation of some part (the connective tissue, the peritoneum, etc.) around or adjacent to the cæcum. (When seated in the *appendix vermiformis* of the cæcum, now distinctively called *appendicitis.*) Also loosely applied to inflammation of the cæcum itself (strictly called *typhlitis*).

1844 DUNGLISON *Med. Lex., Perityphlitis*, inflammation of the cellular substance surrounding the cæcum. **1852** J. MILLER *Pract. Surg.* (ed. 2) 333 Induced, on the right side, by irritation forming the perityphlitis of Burns and others. **1897** *Allbutt's Syst. Med.* III. 879 Fitz in 1886 placed the pathology of perityphlitis upon a sound basis. **1902** *Bulletin* 24 June, The King is suffering from perityphlitis. **1902** *Westm. Gaz.* 24 June 7/3 It is only in recent years that the word 'appendicitis' has been coined. Formerly all inflammatory affections of this part of the bowel were called perityphlitis.

Hence **perityphlitic** (-ˈɪtɪk) *a.*, pertaining to, of the nature of, or affected with perityphlitis.

1894 *Lancet* 3 Nov, 1026 A perityphlitic abscess was opened, and the wound subsequently became diphtheritic. **1897** *Allbutt's Syst. Med.* III. 887 The vermiform appendix, removed from the midst of a perityphlitic abscess.

‖**periu'ranium.** *Astron.* [mod.L., f. PERI- + *Uranus*: cf. PERISATURNIUM.] That point in the orbit of any satellite of Uranus, at which it is nearest to Uranus.

a **1900** (Noted by Assistant Secy. Royal Astronomical Society).

peri-urban (ˈpɛrɪɜːrbən), *a.* [f. PERI- + URBAN *a.* and *sb.*] Esp. in Africa: immediately adjoining a city or conurbation.

1948 *Rep. Native Laws Comm., 1946–48* (Dept. Native Affairs, S. Afr.) 5/1 Johannesburg is still grappling desperately with its problem of peri-urban squatters, of whom over 50,000 have already been collected in the controlled squatters' camps of Moroka and Jabavu. **1952** L. MARQUARD *Peoples & Policies S. Afr.* 51 In 1947 the Department of Native Affairs estimated that 154,000 urban and peri-urban houses were required for Africans. **1961** *Times* 25 July 8/3 The fashionable peri-urban district some 11 miles from Johannesburg. **1971** *E. Afr. Standard* (Nairobi) 13 Apr. 9/8 Patients from the rural and peri-urban areas. **1971** E. JONES in J. Spencer *Eng. Lang. W. Afr.* 67 These figures are for Freetown only; there were for example 1,216 persons in Regent Town, one of the several peri-urban settlements. **1974** *Times* 17 Sept. 15/5 Unified Family Courts have been set up in peri-urban areas of Vancouver. **1976** *Nature* 1–8 Jan. 40/1 Thirty-six peri-urban Kikuyu infants.. participated in the study.

periurethral to **perivitelline:** see PERI- a, c.

periwig (ˈpɛrɪwɪg), *sb.* Now only *Hist.* Forms: α. 6 perwyke, perewyke; 6–7 perwick(e, 7 peri-, perawick(e; perewake; periwike. β. 6–7 perwig, perewig(e, perywygge, perrywig, -wigge, perriwigg(e, 6–8 periwigg(e, perriwig, perrewig, perywig, periwyg, -weg, 6– periwig. γ. 6 periwinke, pere-, periwincle, 7–8 periwinkle. [In 16th c., *perwyke*, alteration of *'perruck, 'perug*, a. F. *perruque* (15th c.): see PERUKE. By corruption, or 'popular etymology', *perwyke* became *perewyke, perewig, perrywig, periwig*, whence by abbreviation, WIG.]

1. An artificial imitation of a head of hair (or part of one); worn formerly, first by women and then by men, as a fashionable head-dress; retained by judges, barristers, etc., as part of their professional costume; used by actors as a part of their make-up, and generally as a means of personal disguise, a concealment of premature grey hairs, or a covering for baldness; a WIG.

α. **1529** *Privy Purse Exp. Hen. VIII* (1827) 13 For a perwyke for Sexten the kinges fole. *c* **1532** DU WES *Introd. Fr.* in *Palsgr.* 902 The perwyke, *la perrucque.* **1568** SIR F. KNOLLYS *Let. to Cecil* in *Antiq. Rep.* (1808) II. 394 She [Mary Seaton] did set sotche a curled Heare upon the Queen [Mary Stuart], that was said to be a Perewyke, that shoed very delycately. **1648–60** HEXHAM, *Hooft-hayr*, Head-haire, or a Perwick. **1688** R. HOLME *Armoury* II. 463 The sorts of perawicks are, a short bob, a long perawick with side hair.., a grafted wig [etc.].

β. **1579** LYLY *Euphues* (Arb.) 116 Take from them their perywigges, their paintings [etc.].. and thou shalt soone perceiue that a woman is the least parte of hir selfe. **1614** RALEIGH *Hist. World* v. iii. §5 He was.. glad to vse Perwigs of haire, and false beards of diuers colours. **1641** MILTON *Animadv* i. 7 To have the Periwigs pluk't off that cover your baldnesse. **1656** WOOD *Life* 4 Sept. (O.H.S.) I. 209, I bought me a perewige of my barber, 6*s.* **1667** PEPYS *Diary* 29 Mar., To a periwigg-maker's, and there bought two periwiggs mighty fine. **1710–11** SWIFT *Jrnl. to Stella* 15 Jan., It has cost me three guineas to-day for a periwig. **1790** BURKE *Fr. Rev.* 334 They took an old huge full-bottomed perriwig out of the wardrobe of the antiquated frippery of Louis XIV. **1865** MISS BRADDON *Sir Jasper* i, It related to.. a time in which men wore fantastically frizzed periwigs upon their heads.

γ. **1580** HOLLYBAND *Treas. Fr. Tong, Perruquier*, he that maketh Perewincles. **1598** BP. HALL *Sat.* III. v. 8 Th' unruly winde blowes off his periwinke. *a* **1700** B. E. *Dict. Cant. Crew, Periwinkle*, a Perruque or Periwig. **1730–6** in BAILEY (folio).

†**b.** *transf.* and *fig. Obs.*

1589 *Pappe w. Hatchet* D, Martins conscience hath a periwig; therefore to good men he is more sower than wig. **1596** B. GRIFFIN *Fidessa* (1876) 46 So soone as peeping Lucifer Auroraes starre, The skie with golden perewigs doth spangle. *a* **1661** FULLER *Worthies* I. (1662) 77, I left a Vacuity for them. For which Bald Place, the Reader (if so pleased) may provide a Perewake. **1703** T. N. *City & C. Purchaser* 59 When a Place is bald of Wood, no Art can make it a Perriwig in hast.

†**2.** An alleged kind of marine animal: see quots.

1634 W. WOOD *New Eng. Prosp.* I. ix. 36 The luscious Lobster with the Crabfish raw, The Brinish Oister, Muscle, Periwigge. *Ibid.* 39 The Perewig is a kind of fish that lyeth in the oaze like a head of haire, which being touched conveyes itself leaving nothing to bee seene but a small round hole. **1670** S. CLARKE *Four Chiefest Plant.* 37. **1672** JOSSELYN *New Eng. Rarities* 29 Periwig,.. Perwinkle or Sea Snail or Whelk. **1674** —— *Voy. New Eng.* (1675) 110 The Perriwig is a shell-fish that lyeth in the Sands flat and round as a shovel-board piece and very little thicker; these at a little hole in the middle of the shell thrust out a cap of hair, but upon the least motion of any danger it drawes it in again.

3. *attrib.* and *Comb.*, as ***periwig-company, -maker***, etc.; ***periwig-pated*** adj.

1598 FLORIO, *Perucchiera*, a periwig [1611 perwig] or gregorian maker. **1602** SHAKS. *Ham.* III. ii. 10 To see a robustious Pery-wig pated [*Qos.* Perwig-pated] Fellow, teare a Passion to tatters. **1663** *Newes* 4 Feb., George Grey, a Barber and Perrywigge-maker [notifies] that any one having long flaxen hayr to sell may repayr to him. **1744–50** W. ELLIS *Mod. Husbandm.* II. I. 72 (E.D.S.) Thetches, when they are sown thick and grow well, commonly run into a periwig matting growth. **1813** *Examiner* 10 May 297/2 Young periwig-pated gentlemen. **1834** Macaulay *Ess.*, *Pitt* (1887) 306 The periwig-company.

'periwig, *v. arch.* [f. prec. sb.] **a.** *trans.* To put a periwig on; to dress, cover, or conceal with, or as with, a periwig. Often *fig.*

1598 Sylvester *Du Bartas* II. i. IV. *Handie-cr.* 187 To glaze the Lakes, and bridle up the floods And perriwig with wooll the balde-pate woods. **1639** Fuller *Holy War* IV. ii. 168 Map-makers, rather then they will haue their maps naked and bald, do periwig them with false hair, and fill up the vacuum with imaginary places. **1658** Bromhall *Treat. Specters* IV. 254 Phœbus's harbinger, did periwigg the horizon with his silver'd locks. **1733** Swift *Legion Club* 91 Discord periwig'd with snakes. **1825** Hone *Every-day Bk.* I. 50 The .. ginger-bread bakers periwig a few plum-buns with sugar-frost. *a* **1843** Southey *Comm.-pl. Bk.* IV. 258/2 To lard a good story with prettinesses, were like periwigging and powdering the Apollo Belvidere.

†**b.** To make (hair) into a wig. *Obs. rare*$^{-1}$.

1606 Warner *Alb. Eng.* XVI. cii. 402 The haire .. was perwigged, once Hers.

periwigged ('pɛrɪwɪgd), *ppl. a.* [f. prec. sb. and vb. + -ED.] Wearing or having on a periwig.

1606 Warner *Alb. Eng.* XVI. cii. 403 The rude perwigged Drudge Salutes the Guests. *a* **1658** Cleveland *Wks.* (1687) 383 Yield Periwig'd Impostor, yield to Fate. **1892** *Athenæum* 21 May 670/1 The appropriate rendezvous for periwigged beaux.

periwincle, periwink(e, obs. vars. PERIWIG.

periwinkle[1] ('pɛrɪwɪŋk(ə)l). Forms: α. 1 peruincæ, 2–3 pervenke, 4 parvenke, -uink, pervink(e, -vynke, 4, 5 -venke, -uenk(e, -uinke, 5 -uynke. β. 5 per-, parwynke, 6 pyrwynke, 7 periwink. γ. 6 pervinkle, -uinkle, -uincle, -winkle, -wincle, -winckle, -wyncle, -wynckle, perywinkle, periuyncle, -wyncle, -winckle, 6–7 pervincle; 6– periwinkle, (7 perewinkle, 8 periwincle). [In OE. *peruince*, a. L. *pervinca* (App. Herb. 4th c.), earlier *vinca pervinca* (Pliny), whence also It. *provenca*, *-vinca*, F. *pervenche*, Norman F. *pervenke*. In ME., *pervinke* and (after AF.) *per-*, *parvenke*, late ME. *perwynke*, in 16th c. altered to *pervinkle*, *perwyncle*, and finally to *periwinkle*, usual since 1600. (See note to PERIWINKLE[2].)

The derivation of L. *pervinca* is not clear: some connect it with L. *pervincĕre* to conquer completely, with various suggested explanations. Cf. sense 2.]

1. The common name of plants of the genus *Vinca* (N.O. *Apocynaceæ*), esp. of the two European species, *V. minor* and *V. major*, the Lesser and Greater Periwinkle, evergreen trailing sub-shrubs with light blue starry flowers, varying in *V. minor* with pure white.

In early times a garland of this flower was placed on the heads of persons on their way to execution, with which some have connected the It. name *fiore di morte*, flower of death.

α. *c* **1000** Ælfric *Gloss.* in Wr.-Wülcker 136/10 *Uinca*, peruincæ. **11..** *Voc.* ibid. 544/39 *Uinca*, pervenke. *c* **1306** *Execution Sir S. Fraser* in *Pol. Songs* (Camden) 218 Y-fetered were ys legges under his horse wombe: .. A gerland of peruenke set on ys heved. *c* **1330** *Owayn Miles* (1837) 41 Rose and lili diuers colours Primrol and paruink. ? *a* **1366** Chaucer *Rom. Rose* 1432 Ther sprang the violete al newe, And fresshe pervinke, riche of hewe. **1430–40** Lydg. *Bochas* VI. i. (1554) 144 Thou hast .. Crowned one with laurer .. Other with peruinke made for the gybet. *c* **1450** *Alphita* 144 Peruinca uel prouinca, .. gall. et a^e. peruenke.

β. *a* **1450** *Stockh. Med. MS.* II. 395 in *Anglia* XVIII. 317 Parwynke is an erbe grene of colour. *c* **1475** *Pict. Voc.* in Wr.-Wülcker 786/19 *Hec pervinca*, .. a perwynke. **1547** Salesbury *Welsh Dict.*, *Gwichiad pysc*, pyrwynke. **1608** Topsell *Serpents* (1658) 637 The Egyptian Clematis or Periwink .. is very good against the poyson of Asps.

γ. [**1501** *Will of Hylle* (Somerset Ho.), ij of my goblettes of pirwyncles.] **1538** Turner *Libellus*, *Clematis daphnoides*, latinis *uinca peruinca*, anglis Perwyncle dicitur. **1551** —— *Herbal* I. K vj b, *Vinca peruinca*, .. called in Englyshe perwyncle, or periwyncle.... It hath prety blewe floures and the herbe crepeth vpon the grounde very thyke. **1578** Lyte *Dodoens* 32 Peruincle hath many small and slender long branches. **1601** Holland *Pliny* XXI. xi. 92 The Pervincle .. continueth fresh and greene all the yeare long. **1611** Florio, *Herba topiaria*, the hearbe Perewinkle. **1741** *Compl. Fam.-Piece* II. iii. 373 Double purple and large Periwinkle. **1798** Wordsw. *Lines Early Spring* iii, Through primrose tufts, in that green bower, The periwinkle trailed its wreaths. **1866** *Cornh. Mag.* Nov. 547 White periwinkles, flinging their light of blossoms and dark glossy leaves down the cliff channels of the brawling streams.

†**2.** *fig.* **a.** One who surpasses or excels; the fairest or choicest; the 'flower': cf. the 'pink of perfection'. *Obs.* [So OF. *pervenke*: De tous vins ce est le pervenke (Godef.).]

13.. *Song, Sir Piers Birmingham* in Ritson *Anc. Songs* (1792) 40 þos kniȝtis euch-one of him mai mak mone as peruink of ham alle. *a* **1400** *Love Song* (Harl. MS. 2253, lf. 72 b/2), Heo is lilie of largesse Heo is paruenke of prouesse. *a* **1440** *Sir Degrev.* 730 Corteys lady and wyse, .. thou arte pervenke of pryse.

†**b.** Playfully applied to a girl or woman. *Obs.*

1633 Shirley *Wittie Fair One* IV. G iv, (To a chambermaid) Quicke periwincle to thy mistris now. **1640** —— *Loves Crueltie* II. C iij b, Very good, I shall love this periwinke.

3. †**a.** *Her.* In blazoning by flowers and plants, the designation of the tincture *azure* or blue. *Obs.*

1725 Coats *Dict. Her.*, *Perwinkle*, .. pitch'd upon by the Inventors of the new Way of Blazon by Flowers and Herbs .. to supply the word *Azure*. **1727** in Bailey Vol. II.

b. A blue colour like that of the periwinkle flower. Also *attrib.* and as *adj.*

1922 *Daily Mail* 20 Dec. 1 (Advt.), *Lingerie crepe*.... In a full range of charming colours, including Pink, Sky, Jade, Flesh, Shrimp, Saxe, .. Fawn, Periwinkle and Cham. **1973** L. Cooper *Tea on Sunday* i. 22 His waisted periwinkle coat. **1977** C. Storr *Tales Psychiatrist's Couch* 83 'Plenty of time to think of getting married later, that's what I say,' Liz said, fixing me with those bulging periwinkle eyes.

4. *attrib.* and *Comb.*

1902 *Westm. Gaz.* 23 Jan. 2/1 Ball frock .. of pale chiffon, periwinkle-wreathed. *Ibid.* 4 Feb. 2/1 Wherever you stand .. you see the sea—the wonderful periwinkle blue, heaving slowly between the sparkling white sands.

periwinkle[2] ('pɛrɪwɪŋk(ə)l). Forms: 6 (?) pirwyncle, purwinkle, pur-, perwynkle; periwinkil, -wyncle; 6–7 perewincle; 7 perwinkle, -winckle, perewinkle, periwinckle, -winkel, 7– periwinkle, (7–8 -wincle, 9 perri-; *dial.* pennywinkle, -wilk). Also β. 6 periwinke, -winck.

[Known in this form only from 16th c.; but OE. had in the same sense a word variously read (in pl.) *pinewinclan* and *winewinclan* (owing to confusion of the letters p and p = *w*). The MSS. favour the latter, which may however be a scribal error, as *pinewincle* would explain the 16th c. literary, and mod. dial. forms. In any case the second element is the same. It is noteworthy that the first certain appearance of *per-*, *periwyncle*, agrees so closely with that of *perwyncle*, PERIWINKLE *sb.*[1], from ME. *parvenke*, *perwynke*, as if in some way **pinewincle* and *perwinke* had coalesced in the form *perwyncle*, *periwinkle*.]

1. The English name of a gastropod mollusc of the genus *Littorina*, esp. *L. littorea* the common European coast species, much used for food, having a dark-coloured turbinate shell. Formerly, and still sometimes, used in a wider sense.

1530 Palsgr. 253/2 Perivyncle a shellfysshe, *bigorneau*, *uineau*. **1552** Huloet, Purwinkle fyshe, *coclea*. **1555** Eden *Decades* 209 Of the leaste of these welkes or perewincles they make certeyne lyttle beades of diuers sortes and colours. **1570** Levins *Manip.* 128/34 A Periwinkil. *Ibid.* 138/31 A Periwynkle, *cochlea*. **1601** Holland *Pliny* I. 218 In like manner do Perwinkles and Snailes. **1611** Speed *Theat. Gt. Brit.* xxiv. (1614) 47/2 At Alderley .. upon the hilles to this day are found cockles, periwinckles and oysters of solid stone. **1697** Dampier *Voy.* (1729) I. 173 A great many Perewincles and Muscles. **1712** E. Cooke *Voy. S. Sea* 174 On the Rocks, abundance of Periwinkles. **1837** Dickens *Pickw.* xxxviii, [Sam Weller says] I merely quote wot the nobleman said to the fractious pennywinkle ven he vould'nt come out of his shell by means of a pin. **1851–6** Woodward *Mollusca* 11 The limpet and periwinkle live between tide-marks, where they are left dry twice a-day. [**1863** *Tyneside Songs* 46 Sometimes pennywilks, crabs, an' lobsters aw bring. **18..** *Eng. Dial. Dict.*, Pennywinkle [Northumb. to Kent and Devon].]

β. **1545** Elyot *Dict.*, *Coclea*, a snayle hauing a shell, also a fishe callyd a pyrwinke [**1565** Cooper perwinke, 1573 perwinkle]. **1570** Levins *Manip.* 138/26 A Periwinke, *cochlea*. **1586** Bright *Melanch.* vi. 27 Some are of harder shels, as oysters, periwincks, etc.

b. The shell of this mollusc. *rare*$^{-1}$.

1625 Purchas *Pilgrims* IX. xii. §4 The Manamotapa and his subjects, weare a white Periwinkle in the fore-head for a Iewell.

†**2.** = COCHLEA 2 (of the ear). *Obs.*

1633 P. Fletcher *Purple Isl.* v. 58 *note*, The last passage [of the ear] is called the Cochlea, Snail or Periwincle; where the nerves of hearing plainly appear.

3. *attrib.* and *Comb.*

1612 Peacham *Gentl. Exerc.* II. iv. 124 A Ladie .. vpon her head a Coronet of Periwinckle and Escallop shelles. **1836** Col. Hawker *Diary* (1893) II. 101 An army of periwinkle pickers. **1841** *Ibid.* 203 Mobbed with periwinkle men to freight the crafts for Billingsgate.

Hence **'periwinkled** *a.*, having or abounding in periwinkles; **'periwinkler**, a gatherer or seller of periwinkles; **'periwinkling** *vbl. sb.*, the gathering of periwinkles; †**periwinkling** *ppl. a.*, winding like the cavity of a periwinkle shell: said of the cavity of the ear.

1883 A. Stewart *Nether Lochaber* xliii. 265 The 'periwinkled shore' is a thousand times better than the 'barren barren shore' of Tennyson. **1837** Col. Hawker *Diary* (1893) II. 122 All the Billingsgate periwinklers are out to-day. **1841** *Ibid.* 199 Swarming with vessels for gunning, eel picking, and periwinkling. **1607** *Lingua* IV. ii, I set and frame all words and .. make them fit For the perewinkling porch, that winding leads From my close chamber to your lordships cell.

periwinkle, obs. variant of PERIWIG *sb.*

perjink (pə'dʒɪŋk), *a. Sc.* Also 9 prejink, per-, prejinct. [Origin unknown. The word has the form of a Fr. or L. derivative; Jam. suggests a F. **parjoint* or L. **perjunctus*; but these words, even if they existed, would hardly give the sense.] Exact, precise, minutely accurate; prim, neat.

1808 Jamieson, *Perjink*, 1. Exact, precise, minutely accurate; *prejink*, Fife. 2. Trim, so as to appear finical. **1821** Galt *Ann. Parish* xxxvii. 299 All my things were kept by her in a most perjinct and excellent order. **1843** Bethune *Sc. Fireside Stor.* 121 She was a perjink body, and carried her head our heigh. **1889** Barrie *Window in Thrums* xiv, He was looking unusually perjink.

β. **1808** Prejink [see above]. **1822** Galt *Provost* xxvii. 203 The exposure that prejink Miss Peggy had made of herself. **1829** *Blackw. Mag.* XXVI. 242 A prim and prejink-looking fellow. **1839** Moir *Mansie Wauch* xxiv. 306 Mr. Batter .. looked as prejinct as a pikestaff.

Hence **per'jinks (pre-)** *sb. pl.*, in phr. *on one's perjinks*, on one's good behaviour, careful of details; **per'jinkety (pre-)** *a.* = *perjink*; **per'jinkity (pre-)** *sb.*, in *pl.*, exact details, niceties, proprieties; **per'jinkly (pre-)** *adv.*, with minute accuracy, primly.

1822 Galt *Sir A. Wylie* xl. II. 68 If we maun be on our prejincks, will you an' her baith rin awa thegither? **1822** —— *Steam-boat* ix. 180 A young genteel man, with a most methodical gravat, prejinctly tied. **1830** —— *Lawrie T.* v. iv. (1849) 205 Jointures, and tochers, and a' the other prejinkities of marriage-articles. **1887** Ruskin *Præterita* II. 390 [She] had always what my mother called 'perjinketty' ways, which made her typically an old maid in later years.

perjonet(te: see PERE-JONETTE, PEAR *sb.* 5.

†**per'journey**, *v. Obs. rare*$^{-1}$. [f. PER- 1 + JOURNEY *v.*] *intr.* To pass through.

1566 *Burgh Rec. Edinb.* (1875) III. 218 Quhilk dur salbe patent to all the nychtbouris of this burgh, to periurnie, gang, rest, and pas thair tyme, in the yeard foirsaid gratis.

†**'perjurate**, *v. Obs. rare*$^{-0}$. [f. L. *perjūrāt-*, ppl. stem of *perjūrāre*: see PERJURE *v.*] = PERJURE *v.*

1623 Cockeram, *Perjurate*, to forsweare. **1626** Minsheu *Ductor* (ed. 2), To Periurate or to Periure.

†**perju'ration**. *Obs.* [ad. med. (Anglo-) L. *perjūrātiōn-em* (12th c. in Du Cange), n. of action f. *perjūrāre*: see PERJURE *v.* Cf. obs. F. *parjuration* (15th c. in Godef.).] The action or an act of perjuring oneself; perjury.

1570 Foxe *A. & M.* (ed. 2) 1652/1 The Cardinall .. forgaue them all theyr periurations, schismes, and heresies. **1623** Cockeram, *Periuration*, a forswearing. **1706** Farquhar *Recruiting Officer* II. iii, For me .. to take such an oath, 'twou'd be downright perjuration. **1723** *Briton* No. 21 (1724) 93, 'I did shaave shaveral of our Friends from downright Parjuration, for all dey have taaken de Oatesh'.

†**'perjurator**. *Obs. nonce-wd.* [Agent-n. in L. form f. *perjūrāre*: see PERJURE *v.*] Perjurer.

1689 T. Plunket *Char. Gd. Commander* 55 False Jury-men, Perjurors, Perjurators, Have at the Court, found potent animators.

†**'perjure**, *sb.*[1] (*a.*) *Obs.* Also 6 periur. [a. AF. *perjur* (Gower), *parjur*, in F. *parjur(e* (12–13th c.), or ad. L. *perjūr-us* one who swears falsely; an oath-breaker, a perjured person; cf. PERJURE *v.*] One who commits perjury; a perjurer.

[**1341** *Rolls of Parlt.* II. 130/1 Qar trop' y ad parjurs en son Roialme.]

a **1540** Bale in Ellis *Orig. Lett.* Ser. III. III. 153 Sum of them ar knowne for common perjurs. **1546** —— *Eng. Votaries* I. (1550) 75 b, Callynge them all that nought was, As hypocrytes, dyssemblers, dodypolles, .. periures. **1588** Shaks. *L.L.L.* IV. iii. 47 He comes in like a periure, wearing papers. [See note, s.v. PERJURED 2.] **1615** Brathwait *Strappado* (1878) 151 Vow-breaking periure, that her selfe adornes, With thousand fashions, and as many formes.

b. as *adj.* Perjurious, perjured.

c **1420** Lydg. *Siege Thebes* 2049 Thow art .. deceyveable and falsly ek forsworn, And ek periur of thyn assured ooth. *a* **1600** Montgomerie *Misc. P.* xviii. 70 To tell the halk in haist sho hyde, The kyt wes palȝard and perjure.

†**per'jure**, *sb.*[2] *Obs. rare*$^{-1}$. [prob. a. F. *parjure*, ad. L. *perjūrium* false oath.] = PERJURY.

1390 Gower *Conf.* II. 389 Of Covoitise and of Perjure, Of fals brocage and of Usure.

perjure ('pɜːdʒə(r)), *v.* Also 5–6 par-. [a. OF. *parjure-r* (11th c. in Littré):—L. *perjūrāre* to swear falsely, break one's oath, f. PER- 3 + *jūrāre* to swear. In AF. in Britton; in Eng. found first in pa. pple., in 15th c.]

†**1.** *intr.* To swear falsely, to commit perjury; to bear false witness while on oath; to be false to an oath, promise, etc. *Obs.*

[**1292** Britton IV. ix. §2 Et si acun soit fet parjurer a escient par acun sovereyn. *transl.* If any one be made to perjure knowingly by any lord superior.] **1647** N. Bacon *Disc. Govt. Eng.* I. lxiv. (1739) 135 He procures a Dispensation from Rome to perjure and oppress without sin. **1731** Swift *Judas* Misc. 1735 V. 64 Some who can perjure thro' a two Inch Board; Yet keep their Bishopricks, and scape the Cord. **1788–9** Gibbon *Autobiog.* (1896) 388 Resolved to abjure and perjure, as occasion might serve.

†**b.** With obj. clause (or ? compl.). *Obs. rare.*

a **1586** Sidney *Arcadia* (1622) 249 Plentifully perjuring how extremely her her son loved her.

c. *reflexive. to perjure oneself*: to forswear oneself. [So in F. *se parjurer*, from 11th c.] Now the usual const.

1755 Johnson, *Perjure, v.a.*... It is used with the reciprocal pronoun [**1818** Todd *adds*: as, 'he perjured himself']. **1772** Priestley *Inst. Relig.* (1782) I. 114 A person who has .. perjured himself [is] the bane of society. **1797** *Encycl. Brit.* (ed. 3) XIV. 151/1 No man will perjure himself (says Aristotle) who apprehends vengeance from Heaven and disgrace among men.

d. quasi-*passive* (see PERJURED). *to be perjured*: to be forsworn, to be guilty of perjury.

1477 Earl Rivers (Caxton) *Dictes* 11 Kepe you that ye be not pariured and let trouth be alwey in your mouthe. *a* **1533** Ld. Berners *Huon* cxxxi. 487, I had rather be pariuryd then to fordo that thynge that god wyll haue done to punysshe the. **1649** JER. TAYLOR *Gt. Exemp.* I. Disc. ii. §21 To be perjur'd for the saving ten thousand pounds. **1719** YOUNG *Revenge* I. i, And are you perjur'd then for virtue's sake? How often have you sworn? **1780** *New Newgate Cal.* V. 27 It is probable, that if Birch had been perjured, he would have been prosecuted.

†**2.** *trans.* To prove false to or break (an oath, vow, promise, etc.). *Obs.*

1483 CAXTON *G. de la Tour* D j b, Than she lyeth and periured her feith and trouthe. **1555** CRANMER *Let. to Q. Mary* in Foxe *A. & M.* (1583) 1891 Which othes be so contrary y^t the one must needs be periured. **1652** GAULE *Magastrom.* 307 He could not foresee how Laomedon would perjure his promise. **1809** *Susan* I. 195 Even before the solemn vow had passsed their lips, determined to perjure it.

†**3.** To prove false to (a person) to whom one has sworn faith. *Obs. rare.* [In 15–16th c. Fr.]

1610 FLETCHER *Faithf. Sheph.* III. i, She..did pray For me that perjur'd her.

†**4.** To make perjured, cause to commit perjury. *Obs. rare.*

1606 SHAKS. *Ant. & Cl.* III. xii. 30 Women are not In their best Fortunes strong; but want will periure The ne're touch'd Vestall.

perjured (ˈpɜːdʒəd), *ppl. a.* (*sb.*) [pa. pple. of prec. vb., after AF. *perjuré*, OF. *parjuré* pa. pple. of the intrans. vb., lit. (one) that has perjured or committed perjury. (From viewing it in Eng. as passive, app. arose the quasi-passive const. of the vb.: see prec. 1 d.)]

1. That has committed perjury; guilty of perjury; forsworn; deliberately false to an oath, vow, promise, etc.

1453 in *Trevelyan Papers* (Camden) 25 If he [the chaplain] be lecherus or perjured, a theaff, or a murderar. **1495** *Act 11 Hen. VII*, c. 25 §6 To call in the supposed perjured persones afore the seid Chaunceller. **1558** PHAER *Æneid* II. D ij, By this deceit, and through the craft of Sinon false periewrd. **1594** SHAKS. *Rich. III*, I. iv. 55 Clarence is come, false, fleeting, periur'd Clarence. **1682** BURNET *Rights Princes* Pref. 37 In which Case he is in truth neither a Liar nor is he perjured. **1709** STEELE *Tatler* No. 105 ¶3, I hope you won't be such a perjured Wretch as to forswear your self. *a* **1859** MACAULAY *Hist. Eng.* xxiii. V. 87 Perjured traitors who richly deserved axes and halters.

b. *absol.* and quasi-*sb.*

1526 TINDALE *1 Tim.* i. 10 The lawe is..geven..to lyars and to periured. **1604** T. M. *Black Bk.* in *Middleton's Wks.* (Bullen) VIII. 28 How many villains were in Spain,..how many perjurds in France. **1605** SHAKS. *Lear* III. ii. 54 Thou Periur'd, and thou Simular of Vertue.

†**2.** Characterized by perjury; perjurious. *Obs.*

In quot. 1588 alluding to the former practice of attaching to a convicted perjurer a paper announcing his guilt: cf. quot. 1546 s.v. PERJURY, and PAPER *sb.* 7 b.

1588 SHAKS. *L.L.L.* IV. iii. 125 O would the King, Berowne and Longauill, Were Louers too, ill to example ill, Would from my forehead wipe a periur'd note: For none offend, where all alike doe dote. *a* **1635** CORBET *Elegie on Dr. Ravis* Poems (1647) 18 Their hired Epitaphs, and perjur'd stone, Which oft belies the soule when she is gone. **1814** SCOTT *Ld. of Isles* IV. xxvii, By her who brooks his perjured scorn, The ill-requited Maid of Lorn.

†**3.** Falsely sworn; forsworn. *Obs.*

1590 SPENSER *F.Q.* II. x. 40 The recompence of their periured oth. **1697** DRYDEN *Virg. Ecl.* viii. 25, I my Nisa's perjur'd Faith deplore; Witness ye Pow'rs by whom she falsly swore!

Hence ˈ**perjuredly** *adv.*, in the manner of one perjured; with perjury; perjuriously.

1553 BALE tr. *Gardiner's De Vera Obed.* Pref. A v, These incarnate Devilles, which coulde so advisedly saye yea than, and so impudently, so rashely, so periuredly..saye naye now. **1570** FOXE *A. & M.* (ed. 2) 258/2 King Steuen..ended hys lyfe after he had reigned xix. yeares periuredly.

†ˈ**perjurement.** *Obs.* [a. OF. *par-*, *perjurement* (14–15th c. in Godef.), f. *parjurer*: see PERJURE *v.* and -MENT.] False swearing; perjury.

c **1430** *Pilgr. Lyf Manhode* III. xxix. (1869) 151 For periurement may not be but if mensonge make him come foorth. **1490** CAXTON *Eneydos* xxv. (*heading*), How dydo made her lamentacyons repreuynge the periuremente of Laomedon.

perjurer (ˈpɜːdʒərə(r)). Also 6 -our. [app. a. AF. *par-*, *perjurour*, f. *parjurer* to PERJURE: see -OR. (Few examples from 1650 to 19th c.)] One who commits perjury, *spec.* in the legal sense; one who proves false to an oath or solemn promise; one who is forsworn or has perjured himself.

1553 BALE tr. *Gardiner's De Vera Obed.* Pref., Couetous catchers, doublefaced periurours. **1580** HOLLYBAND *Treas. Fr. Tong*, *Parjure*, a forsworne man, a Periurer. **1655** H. VAUGHAN *Silex Scint.*, *Rules & Lessons* viii, The perjurer's a devil let loose. **1755** JOHNSON, *Perjurer*, one that swears falsely. **1828** P. CUNNINGHAM *N.S. Wales* (ed. 3) II. 317 The perjurers were allowed to slip out of court without even a reprimand. **1878** STUBBS *Const. Hist.* III. xviii. 49 He was a perjurer who on a false plea had raised the nation against Richard.

So ˈ**perjuress**, a female perjurer.

1898 *Speaker* 8 Oct. 432/2 A perjuress cannot be flogged, and no one at present proposes to flog her.

perjurious (pəˈdʒʊərɪəs), *a.* Also 7 par-. [ad. L. *perjūriōs-us*, f. *perjūrium* PERJURY.]

†**1.** Of persons: Guilty of perjury; false to an oath, promise, etc.; perjured, forsworn. *Obs.*

c **1540** [implied in PERJURIOUSLY]. **1603** KNOLLES *Hist. Turks* (1621) 297 Shew thy power upon thy perjurious people, who in their deeds denie thee their God. **1699** POMFRET *Love Triumphant* 197 Trusting to perjurious woman's truth. **1829** J. DONOVAN tr. *Catechism of Trent* III. ix. Quest. 6 To the witness himself it is also most irksome to be known as false and perjurious.

2. Of actions, etc.: Characterized by, exhibiting, accompanied by, or resulting from perjury.

1602 WARNER *Alb. Eng.* Epit. 376 His [Harold's] pariurious appropriating to himselfe of the kingdome. **1695** J. SAGE *Article* Wks. 1844 I. 373 The Presbyterian preachers condemned the undertaking as unlawful and perjurious. *a* **1734** NORTH *Exam.* II. iv. §84 (1740) 272 The holy Reach, of this perjurious Scandal, was, that [etc.]. **1872** JEAFFRESON *Brides & Bridals* II. xxiii. 317 The old corrupt and perjurious suits for nullification of marriage.

perjuriously (pəˈdʒʊərɪəslɪ), *adv.* [f. prec. + -LY².] In a perjurious manner; with perjury.

c **1540** tr. *Pol. Verg. Eng. Hist.* (Camden) I. 164 Penda, whome hee, breaking perjuriuslie his vow, afterwarde murthered. **1612** DEKKER *If it be not good* Wks. 1873 III. 315 One of you two is periuriously forsworne. **1698** [R. FERGUSON] *View Eccles.* 77 If..he should perjuriously depose at the Kings Bench. **1884** A. A. PUTNAM *10 Yrs. Police Judge* xxiv. 207 [To] enforce the law and punish those who perjuriously stand in the way of the enforcement.

perˈjuriousness. *rare.* [f. as prec. + -NESS.] The quality of being perjurious.

1823 BENTHAM *Not Paul* 257 Of the perjuriousness of Paul's intent, a short proof..is thus already visible, in the indignation excited.

†ˈ**perjurous,** *a. Obs.* [f. L. *perjūr-us* (see PERJURE *sb.*¹) + -OUS.] = PERJURIOUS.

a **1584** (*title*) Orations of Arsanes agaynst Philip the Trecherous Kyng of Macedone..and of Scanderbeg prayeng ayde of Christian Princes agaynst periurous murderyng Mahumet. **1609** SIR E. HOBY *Let. to T. H[iggons]* 18 Make him a sorrowfull witnesse of your periurous vow. **1634** S. R. *Noble Soldier* II. ii. in Bullen *O. Pl.* I. 287, I am cheated by a perjurous Prince. **1849** in Lee *Hist. Columbus* II. 410 Old Ananias..with Sapphira, his perjurous wife.

perjury (ˈpɜːdʒərɪ). Also 5–6 par-. [a. AF. *perjurie* (rare OF. *parjurie*); in mod.F. *parjure*, ad. L. *perjūrium* false oath, oath-breaking, f. *perjūr-āre* to PERJURE.]

The action of swearing to a statement which is known to be false, or of taking an oath which it is not one's intention to keep; *spec.* in *Law*, The crime of wilfully uttering a false statement or testimony in reference to a matter material to the issue involved, while under an oath or affirmation to tell the truth, administered by a competent authority; the wilful utterance of false evidence while on oath.

In legal usage, perjury was first the offence of jurors in giving a wilfully false verdict, they being sworn to give a true verdict according to their knowledge; as an offence of witnesses it was apparently gradually evolved in connexion with the change in the nature of Trial by JURY (q.v.); 'there is no trace in the statutes, or in the reported proceedings of the courts, of any penal law against perjury in witnesses, as distinguished from that of jurors, earlier than the reign of Henry VIII' (*Penny Cycl.* XVII. 459/2; but see quot. 1495. In this act 'false serement' appears to be the equivalent of 'perjury' in the modern sense).

[**1292** BRITTON IV. ix. §2 Parjurie est mensonge afermé par serment.] **1387–8** T. USK *Test. Love* I. vii. l. 51 Every ooth ..muste haue these lawes, that is, trewe jugement and rightwysenesse;..if any of these lacke, the ooth is y-tourned in-to the name of perjury. **1436** *Rolls Parlt.* IV. 501/2 The grete dredeles and unshamefast Perjurie, that orriblely contynueth, and daily encresseth in the commune Jurrours of ye said Roialme. **1477** EARL RIVERS *Dictes* 11 Enforce you not to cause them swere that ye knowe wil lye, lest ye be parteners to theyr pariury. **1495** *Act 11 Hen. VII*, c. 25 §6 If perjury be commytted by proves in the Kinges Courte of the Chauncery or before the Kinges honorable Councell or els where, that..the..Chaunceller..make like proces to call in the supposed perjured persones. **1546** in W. H. Turner *Select. Rec. Oxford* (1880) 180 John Lewes..shall for hys perjury..suffer xl dayes prysonment.., and also to ware a paper for perjury wythyn the seyd Cyty thre severall markett dayes. *a* **1548** [see PAPER *sb.* 7 b]. *a* **1634** COKE *On Litt.* III. lxxiv. (1648) 164 Perjury is a crime committed, when a lawfull oath is ministred..to any person, in any judiciall proceeding, who sweareth absolutely, and falsly in a matter materiall to the issue. **1782** COWPER *Table T.* 418 When Perjury..Sells oaths by tale, and at the lowest price. **1840** *Penny Cycl.* XVII. 459/2 *Perjury*, by the common law of England, is the offence of falsely swearing to facts in a judicial proceeding. **1875** JOWETT *Plato* (ed. 2) V. 171 Where there would be a premium on perjury, oaths..should be prohibited as irrelevant.

b. Applied also to the violation of a promise made on oath, the breaking of a vow or solemn undertaking; a breach of oath.

1532 MORE *Confut. Barnes* VIII. Wks. 792/2 That.. running oute of religion in apostacy, breakynge of vowes, and freres weddinge nunnes, and periury were no synne at all. **1550** BALE *Apol.* 47 He withdrewe hys anger, putte vp hys swearde, and neuer thoughte anye synne in that periury or breakynge of hys vowe. **1568** GRAFTON *Chron.* II. 736 The Ambassadours would not haue the truce proclaimed, thinking therby, to saue the Duke from periurie, which had sworne, neuer to conclude a peace, till [etc.]. **1632** MASSINGER & FIELD *Fatal Dowry* IV. i, No pain is due to lover's perjury: If Jove himself laugh at it, so will I. **1871** R. ELLIS *Catullus* lxiv. 148 Lo they fear not promise, of oath or perjury reck not.

c. with *a* and *pl.*: An instance of the foregoing; a false oath; a wilful breach of oath.

c **1440** *York Myst.* xxvi. 75 Loo! sir, þis is a periurye. **1495** *Act 11 Hen. VII*, c. 25 §1 The haynous and detestable perjuries daily commytted within this realme in enquestes and Juries. **1592** SHAKS. *Rom. & Jul.* II. ii. 92 At Louers periuries They say Ioue laught. **1610** WILLET *Hexapla Dan.* 286 Their periuries,..profane oathes are notoriously knowne. **1719** YOUNG *Busiris* I. i, It is an oath well spent, a perjury Of good account in vengeance, and in love. **1840** MACAULAY *Ess.*, *Clive* (1851) II. 520 The perjuries which have been employed against us.

d. *Comb.*, as *perjury-begetting*, *-mongering*, etc.

1802–12 BENTHAM *Ration. Judic. Evid.* (1827) II. 397 Judges, by whom evidence in these perjury-begetting shapes has exclusively been received. **1826** HOR. SMITH *Tor Hill* (1838) III. 153 An exclusive command of the perjury-market. **1877** TENNYSON *Harold* v. i. 178 The perjury-mongering Count Hath made too good an use of Holy Church!

perk (pɜːk), *sb.*¹ *Obs.* exc. *dial.* Also 5–7 perke, 6 pyrke, 6–7 pirke, 6–9 pirk. [A parallel form of PERCH *sb.*², chiefly in northern, north midl., and East Anglian use. Cf. NFr. *perque.*]

I. †**1.** A pole, stake: = PERCH *sb.*² 1. *Obs.*

1483 *Cath. Angl.* 276/1 A Perke, *pertica*. *c* **1490** *Promp. Parv.* 394/2 (MSS. K. & H.) Perke, or perche, *pertica*. **1513** DOUGLAS *Æneis* XI. ii. 65 He bad the capitanis and the dukis all..Gret perkis bair of tymmer saplyng..To wryte and hyng tharon baith all and sum The namys of thar ennemys ourcum. **1613** PURCHAS *Pilgrimage* VIII. iv. 628 Cabans.. made with perkes, and covered with barkes of trees.

†**b.** A fuller's perch: = PERCH *sb.*² 1 b. *Obs.*

c **1350** *St. James* 255 in Horstm. *Altengl. Leg.* (1881) 56 A walker perk byside him stode..With þat perk his heued he brak. *c* **1375** *Sc. Leg. Saints* vii. (*Jacobus Minor*) 215 þane ane a walkare perk hynt And gafe sancte Iamis sic a dynte þat he þe harne-pane brak in twyn.

II. 2. A bar fixed horizontally to hang something on or support something against: see quots. Chiefly *dial.* Cf. PERCH *sb.*² 2. Also *dial.* a rope used for the same purpose, as a clothes-line, etc.

1818 W. MUIR *Poems* 56 On every pirk the clouts are clashing. *a* **1825** FORBY *Voc. E. Anglia*, *Perk*,..a wooden frame against which sawn timber is set up to dry. **1825** JAMIESON, *Perk*,..a rope extended for holding any thing in a house. *Ayrs.* **1882** OGILVIE (Annandale), *Perk*, a pole placed horizontally, on which yarns, etc. are hung to dry; also a peg (perket) for similar purposes.

b. A bar or bracket to support candles (= PERCH *sb.*² 2 b) or an image. *Obs.* or *Hist.*

1475 *Will of Rightwise* (Somerset Ho.), Lumini de le perke alias le Rodelofte. **1794** *Gentl. Mag.* LXIV. I. 16/2 A perk or pedestal for an image. **1838** PARKER *Gloss. Archit.* (ed. 2), *Perch*, *Perk*, *Pearch*, an old term for a bracket. **1887** W. H. H. ROGERS *Mem. West* x. (1888) 178 On the right..is the perk or bracket on which the image..was..once stationed.

3. A perch for a tame bird, or anything on which a bird may alight and rest. Also *transf.* a seat for a person. See PERCH *sb.*² 3–3 d. Now *dial.*

c **1400** MAUNDEV. (Roxb.) xvi. 73 A sperhawke sittand apon a perke. *a* **1440** *Sir Degrev.* 47 Haukes of nobulle eyre, Tylle his perke ganne repeyre. **1560** ROLLAND *Seven Sages* 98 This saw the Py on his Pirk quhair scho sat. **1602** F. HERING tr. *Obendörfer's Anat.* 15 Lyke a Daw vpon a Perke. **1828** *Craven Gloss.* (ed. 2), *Peeark*, a pearch for fowls. **1863** MRS. TOOGOOD *Yorks. Dial.*, The hens have all gone up to their peark.

fig. **1651** N. BACON *Disc. Govt. Eng.* II. vii. (1739) 41 Their minds once..upon the Wing, can hardly settle any where, or stoop to the Perk again.

†**b.** In *fig.* phrases: *to prick, turn over the perk*: see PERCH *sb.*² 3 e. *Obs.*

a **1529** SKELTON *Garnesche* 157 He wyl..make youer stomoke seke Ovyr the perke to pryk. **1601** DENT *Pathw. Heaven* 152 Then they will hoist a man, and turne him over the pirke.

4. A horizontal bar or frame over which cloth is drawn so as to examine it thoroughly; = PERCH *sb.*² 4. Also the act or process of perching or examining, as *to stand the perk*. *W. Yorksh. dial.*

See Eng. Dial. Dict.

III. 5. A lineal measure: = PERCH *sb.*² 5. *dial.*

1825 JAMIESON, *Perk*, a pole, a perch. *Ayrsh.* **1879** in MISS JACKSON *Shropsh. Word-bk.* **1900** in *Eng. Dial. Dict.* from Glouc., Worc., Heref., Shropsh.

IV. 6. *Comb.* **perk-tree**, a long pole; now *dial.*, a pole used to support a clothes-line.

c **1375** *Sc. Leg. Saints* xix. (*Cristofore*) 216 In-sted of staf, a ployk he had, Wele nere as a perktre mad. **1548** *Aberdeen Regr.* (1844) I. 259 Item, perkis and perktrees xxxs.

perk (pɜːk), *sb.*² *colloq.* Abbreviation of PERQUISITE. (Usually in plural, *perks.*)

1824 J. MACTAGGART *Scottish Gallovidian Encycl.* 383 *Pirkuz*, any kind of perquisite. **1869** J. GREENWOOD *Seven Curses of London* ix. 169 The species of dishonesty alluded to ..is called by the cant name of 'perks', which is a convenient abbreviation of the word 'perquisites', and in the hands of the users of it, it shows itself a word of amazing flexibility. It applies to such unconsidered trifles as wax candle ends, and may be stretched so as to cover the larcenous abstraction by our man-servant of forgotten coats and vests. **1876** *Punch's Almanack for 1877* 12/3 Christmas Carol (By a Poor Expectant of Perks)... When other Govs. for other clerks Shall 'strike upon the bell', And proffer..The 'tips' they love so well... Then, *Yule*, remember me! **1887** *Pall Mall G.* 7 Sept. 5/1 An order that free blacking is no longer to be among the 'perks' of Government office-keepers. **1891** *Daily News* 2 Mar. 2/1 In the good old days waste-paper went as the 'perks' of Government officers. **1897** A. BENNETT *Jrnl.* 16 Dec. (1932) I. 66 'My missis,' he said, 'has extraction money and toothpowder money for 'er perks.' **1939** J. MASEFIELD *Live & Kicking Ned* 147 It's the Old

Man's perk to order some damned silly thing. **1941** J. Cary *Herself Surprised* lxiv. 160 But she would do her own housekeeping. 'For I hate waste,' she said, 'and I never allow perks.' **1957** A. Grimble *Return to Islands* 7, I began bargaining for better pay and perks than she had mentioned. **1959** *News Chron.* 20 Oct. 6/1 The post [of Speaker] was in danger of becoming a Tory perk. **1961** H. S. Turner *Something Extraordinary* v. 116 The child allowance..is regarded as a perk for the parents. **1970** G. F. Newman *Sir, You Bastard* 11 Perks were part of the profession. **1976** *Daily Mirror* 16 July 9/6 British Rail are cutting back on travel perks for their top managers following last year's £500 million loss. **1977** *Times* 8 Feb. 17/1 The philistines would be foolish to regard aid for the arts merely as a perk provided by all for the esoteric pursuits of the few.

perk, *sb.*[3] Also perc. [Abbrev. of percolator.] **a.** A coffee percolator. **b.** Coffee made in a percolator.

1934 F. E. Baily *Fleet St. Girl* iii 59 Amazing coffee Charles makes in that electric perc. **1941** J. Smiley *Hash House Lingo* 42 *Perk*, coffee. **1945** Baker *Austral. Lang.* xv. 264 *Perc* from percolator. **1956** H. Gold *Man who was not with It* (1965) xxx. 277 But don't try to use the perc, you're too stupid. **1960** Wentworth & Flexner *Dict. Amer. Slang* 384/1 *Perk, perc* n., percolated coffee, as opposed to that boiled in a pan. Orig. cowboy use; later hobo use.

perk (pɜːk), *a.* Also 6 perke, 7 peark(e. [Of uncertain origin: goes with perk *v.*[1] (which is known much earlier). The Welsh *perc* compact, trim, *percus* smart, are from Eng.] Self-assertive, self-satisfied, saucy, pert, 'cocky'; brisk, lively, in good spirits; smart.

1579 Spenser *Sheph. Cal.* Feb. 8 They wont in the wind wagge their wrigle tailes, Perke as Peacock. *a***1640** W. Fenner *Cont. Christ's Alarm* (1657) 10 It makes the heart peark, and brisk. **1642** Rogers *Naaman* 52 To suffer us to wax pearke, and sawcy with him. **1821** Clare *Vill. Minstr.* I. 124 The dew-rais'd flower was perk and proud. *a***1825** Forby *Voc. E. Anglia, Perk*, adj. brisk; lively; proud. **1892** *Cosmopolitan* XII. 120/2 How perk and military the bearing of each.

perk (pɜːk), *v.*[1] Also 5 pyrk, 6 pirke, *Sc.* park, 6–7 peark(e), perke, 7 pirck, perck, peerk, pierk, 7–8 pirk. [Of uncertain origin: goes with perk *a.* It has been suggested to be the same word as perch *v.*[1] (cf. perk *v.*[2]); but there are obvious difficulties. Welsh *percu* to smarten, trim, is from Eng. (cf. sense 2). The sense-development is also uncertain.]

I. *intr.* **1. a.** To carry oneself in a smart, brisk, or jaunty manner; to assume or have a lively, self-assertive, or self-conceited attitude or air.

*c***1380** *Minor Poems fr. Vernon MS.* liii. 81 Þe popeiayes perken, and pruynen for proude. *a***1550** *Pore Helpe* 344 in Hazl. *E.P.P.* III. 264 But these babes be to yonge, Perkynge vpon theyr patins. **1632** Quarles *Div. Fancies* I. iv, O! what a revishment 't had been to see Thy little Saviour perking on thy Knee! *a***1734** North *Exam.* I. ii. §97 The Loyalists.. who sneaked, and their Enemies insulted, while he sat pirking there. **1801** Lamb *Let. to Manning* Apr., By perking up upon my haunches, and supporting my carcase with my elbows, I can see the white sails. **1957** M. Spark *Comforters* viii. 197 Her whole body seemed to perk with delight.

b. To lift one's head, raise oneself, or thrust oneself forward, briskly, boldly, or impudently. Also with *up*.

*a***1591** H. Smith *Wks.* (1866–7) I. 35 When their father and mother fall out, they [children] perk up between them like little mediators, and with many pretty sports make truce. *a***1624** Bp. M. Smith *Serm., Heb.* i. 1 (1632) 201 The snaile, when..he will be pearking and peeping abroad. **1676** Etheredge *Man of Mode* I. i, She shall..perk up i'the face of Quality. **1827** in Hone *Every-day Bk.* II. 190 Chinese figures, their round, little-eyed, meek faces perking sidewise. **1839–40** W. Irving *Wolfert's R.* iii. (1855) 15 The loquacious cat-bird flew from bush to bush with restless wing..or perked inquisitively into his face. **1842** Barham *Ingol. Leg.* Ser. II. *Old Woman in Grey*, The old woman perk'd up as brisk as a bee. **1901** G. Douglas *House w. Green Shutters* 288 She tossed her head, and perked away from him on her little high heels.

c. *fig.* To exalt oneself or thrust oneself forward ambitiously or presumptuously; to behave impudently or insolently; to play the upstart. Also with *up*.

1529 Latimer *1st Serm. Card* ¶26 These proude Phariseys which..wyll perke and presume to sitte by Christ in the Church. **1571** Golding *Calvin on Ps.* i. 4 Although yᵉ vngodly persone perke vp like a highe tree. **1620** Sanderson *Serm., 1 Cor.* xii. 7 §23 It is a very hard thing..to excell others in gifts, and not perke aboue them in self-conceipt. **1647** Trapp *Comm. Jas.* iv. 12 What dost thou then do pierking into his place? **1683** Bunyan *Case Consc. Resolved* (1861) II. 673 That they should not give heed to women that would be perking up on matters of worshipping God. **1686** F. Spence tr. *Varillas' Ho. Medicis* 33 Piero de Medici, whose father perk'd up onely out of the Order of bare Gentlemen. *a***1703** Burkitt *On N.T.* 1 Cor ix. 27 He knew that Hagar would quickly perk up, and domineer over Sarah. **1812** Southey *Omniana* I. 35 Be sure not to suffer your reason to perk up and be dictating therein.

d. Also *to perk it*.

1661 Feltham *Resolves* II. i. 176 Shall..the worm offer to perk it up at the face of Man? **1683** Bunyan *Case Consc. Resolved* (1861) II. 673 When Miriam began to perk it before Moses. **1714** Pope *Epil. Rowe's J. Shore* 46 That Edward's Miss thus perks it in your face. *a***1734** North *Exam.* II. v. §14 Better..to bogtrot in Ireland, than to pirk it in Preferment no better dressed.

e. *fig.* Of a thing: To project or stick up or out, or to rise or lift itself, in a manner suggesting briskness or self-assertion.

1583 Stubbes *Anat. Abus.* I. (1879) 50 Hattes.. Sometimes they were them sharp on the crowne, pearking up like a sphere [= spear]. **1642** Rogers *Naaman* 63 We are like to light Corke, which..(except a man hold it under by a strong hand) will pearke to the top. **1651** N. Bacon *Disc. Govt. Eng.* II. vi. (1739) 36 This Gourd..might prove no less prejudicial by creeping upon the ground, than by perking upward. **1842** Dickens *Amer. Notes* xii. (1850) 120/2 Ancient habitations, with high garret gable-windows perking into the roofs. **1866** R. Chambers *Ess.* Ser. I. 43 Her neat apron,..from the front of which perk out two smart, provoking-looking pockets.

f. With *up*: To recover from depression or sickness; to recover liveliness. *colloq.*

*a***1656** Ussher *Ann.* vi. (1658) 542 Thus Asia, which before was plagued with the Publicans..begins to pirck up again. *c***1670** O. Heywood *Diaries*, etc. (1881) II. 346 To bow down his head as a bulrush, which in a wet day stoops, but in a sun-shine day perks up again. **1706** Phillips, To *Perk up*, or *Perk up again*,..to recover after Sickness. **1892** *Gentlewoman's Bk. Sports* I. 163 You will soon perk up, quite ready to start again. **1936** Wodehouse *Laughing Gas* iii. 31 As the days went along, I found myself perking up a bit. I seemed to be making progress. **1936** M. Mitchell *Gone with Wind* vii. 132 Dr. Fontaine admitted that he was puzzled, after his tonic of sulphur, molasses and herbs failed to perk her up. **1957** M. Spark *Comforters* i. 18 Then she perked up. **1957** E. Eager *Magic by Lake* iv. 89 It seemed to do him good. For he perked up noticeably, and the flush of health began to appear on his wan cheek. **1962** *Listener* 20 Dec. 1041/1 The rate of growth dropped to 3 per cent. between 1958 and 1961. It is only in the past year or so that it has perked up. **1977** *Time* 10 Jan. 44/2 The Christmas results constituted fresh evidence that consumers are starting to spend again and the sluggish economy is perking up. **1977** *Lancet* 6 Aug. 291/2 Within days of stopping propranolol the patient perked up and became once more his old self.

II. *trans.* **2. a.** To make spruce or smart, to smarten; to prank, to trim, as a bird does its plumage. Also with *up, out*.

*c***1485** *Digby Myst.* (1882) III. 358 Now I, prynse pyrked prykkyd in pryde. **1590** Lodge *Euphues Gold. Leg.* (Cassell) 184 She looked like Flora perched in the pride of all her flowers. **1613** Shaks. *Hen. VIII*, II. iii. 21 Tis better to be lowly borne,..Then to be perk'd vp in a glistring griefe, And weare a golden sorrow. **1753** *School of Man* 4 The She-Linnet..prunes her wings, cleanses her tail, and perks herself out to enjoy a fine day. **1838** J. P. Kennedy *Rob of Bowl* xiv. 148 You are not quite a woman yourself—though you perk yourself up so daintily. **1843** Carlyle *Past & Pr.* III. iii, His poor fraction of sense has to be perked into some epigrammatic shape, that it may prick into me. **1850** Hawthorne *American Note-Bks.* (1883) 374 Poor enough to perk themselves in such false feathers as these.

b. To enliven; elevate; stimulate interest in. Usu. with *up*.

1965 *Amer. Speech* XL. 287 The plentiful examples..are often entertaining enough..to perk up the laziest student. **1968** *Globe & Mail* (Toronto) 17 Feb. 9/3 The election so perked up spirits that many people began talking of new possibilities of cooperation and solidarity among the 22 active member states of the OAS. **1973** *Publishers Weekly* 1 Jan. 53/1 His hardnosed critique of modern capitalism.. and his incisive study of the New Left's shortcomings..are sufficiently pragmatic to perk the interest of a good many readers concerned with change. **1976** *Scotsman* 15 Dec. 20/4 In the last week nearly £1 million—in theory at any rate —has changed hands down south as clubs attempt to perk up ailing sides with that most obvious of remedies. **1976** *Time* 20 Dec. 32/2 After 34 years of perking up Washington as a White House reporter..Auntie Mameish Liz Carpenter is heading home to Austin, Texas.

c. To say or comment in a brisk, lively, or self-assertive manner. *rare.*

1940 W. Empson *Gathering Storm* 15 Small lar that sunned itself in Mercury And perked one word there that made space ends meet. **1973** C. Himes *Black on Black* 135 'Maybe it's some scoff from the government's thing for the poor folks,' she perked hopefully.

3. a. To raise briskly or smartly, to prick up; to hold *up* smartly or self-assertively; to thrust or poke *out*. Also *refl. to perk oneself*.

*a***1591** H. Smith *Serm.* (ed. Tegg) I. 310 As the little birds perk up their heads when their dam comes with meat. **1602** *2nd Pt. Return fr. Parnass.* I. vi. 469 You light skirt starres, ..By glomy light perke out your doutfull heads. **1642** Rogers *Naaman* 170 The spirit of presumption, which prides and pearks up it selfe. **1652** Culpepper *Eng. Physic.* 216 A Monster called Superstition perks up his head. **1784** Cowper *Task* vi. 318 The squirrel..there whisks his brush, And perks his ears. **1821** Clare *Vill. Minstr.* II. 176 A flower..Perks up its head. **1826** Scott *Jrnl.* 26 Apr., Those [papers] you are not wanting perk themselves in your face again and again. **1874** Burnand *My Time* xii. 104 'Dear me!' ejaculated her mother, pretending to perk herself up. **1879** Jefferies *Wild Life in S. Co.* 165 [The blackbird] perks his tail up, and challenges the world with the call already mentioned.

b. *pa. pple.* Raised, erect, sitting upright.

1797–1802 G. Colman *Br. Grins, Lady of Wreck* II. xvi, Perked on its..haunches stood the..reptile. **1879** Dowden *Southey* 7 The small urchin, long perked up and broad awake.

Hence **perked** *ppl. a.*, **'perking** *vbl. sb.*

*a***1624** Bp. M. Smith *Serm., 1 Pet.* v. 6 (1632) 169 The kingdome of God is neither sitting, nor standing, nor perking, nor stouping. **1828** *Craven Gloss.* (ed. 2), *Peearked*, perched, elated, proud. **1828** P. Cunningham *N. S. Wales* (ed. 3) II. 150 It is only our native coachman with his spread-out fan-tail and perked-up crest.

perk, *v.*[2] Now *dial.* Also 6–7 pearke. [Collateral form of perch *v.*[1], chiefly northern and E. Anglian. Cf. NFr. *perquer* = F. *percher*. Its later use sometimes approaches perk *v.*[1]] *intr.* Of birds: To perch; also *transf.* of persons.

[**1513** Douglas *Æneis* xii. Prol. 237 The cowschet crowdis and pirkis on the rys.] **1588** Greene *Perimedes* Wks. (Grosart) VII. 72 The Eagle and the Doue, pearke not on one branche. *a***1600** Montgomerie *Misc. P.* xviii. 41 This girking pearkit in a place, Quharin ouer long he did delyt. **1797–1802** G. Colman *Br. Grins, Luminous Hist.* xxx, Beauties who on eminences perk. *a***1825** Forby *Voc. E. Anglia, Perk*, v., to perch.

†**b.** quasi-*passive* and *refl.* To set oneself or be set, esp. on some elevation. Chiefly in pa. pple., which prob. in origin belonged to the intr. use. *Obs.*

1513 Douglas *Æneis* III. iv. 72 Ane, on a rokkis [*printed* rolkis] pynnakle perkit hie Celeno clepit, a drery prophetes. *a***1529** Skelton *Ware the Hauk* 70 On the rode loft She perkyd her to rest. **1588** Greene *Pandosto* Ded. (1607) 3 Cæsars Crowe durst neuer crie, *Aue*, but when she was pearked on the Capitoll. **1639** Sanderson *Serm., Rom. xv.* 6 §20 One Man..hath perked himself up at length in the Temple of God. **1794** U. Price *Ess. Picturesque* I. 215 The prim squat clump is perked up exactly on the top of every eminence.

perk, *v.*[3] *colloq.* (orig. *U.S.*). Also perc. [Abbrev. of percolate *v.*] **a.** *trans.* To make (coffee) in a percolator; to boil (coffee) *up*. Also *absol.* **b.** *intr.* Of coffee: to percolate, bubble, or boil (also said of the vessel). Also *transf.* and *fig.* Hence **perked** *ppl. a.*, **'perking** *vbl. sb.*

In *fig.* uses not easily distinguished from perk *v.*[1] 1 f.

1934 in Webster. **1936** Mencken *Amer. Lang.* (ed. 4) v. 192 To *perc* (to make coffee in a *percolator*). **1939** C. Morley *Kitty Foyle* 330 We..flopped ourselves down and perked some coffee. **1940** C. McCullers *Heart is Lonely Hunter* (1943) I. iv. 46 An electric coffee-pot was perking on the table. **1943** in Simmons & Meyer *This is your Amer.* III. 33 This unit will toast the bread..perk the coffee. **1948** F. Brown *Murder can be Fun* (1951) vii. 102 I'll start some coffee perking. **1952** G. W. Brace *Spire* (1953) xx. 202, I always perked the stuff... We thought the perking was as good as magic. *Ibid.*, I decided the perked stuff was too thin. **1960** 'E. McBain' *Give Boys Great Big Hand* vi. 54, I think the coffee's perking. **1964** *Which?* Feb. 47/2 All the percolators were allowed to 'perc' for 10 minutes. **1972** *Newsweek* 10 Jan. 19 By summer, so the calculations go, the economy will be perking quite nicely, and the President will go to the people as the agent of newfound prosperity. **1972** *Daily Colonist* (Victoria, B.C.) 25 June 7/4 They are designed to boost employment and get slow-growth areas of Canada perking from a new-industry point of view. **1973** K. Giles *File on Death* iii. 78 Come in, sport, and take some coffee. I was just perking some up. **1976** D. Heffron *Crusty Crossed* ix. 72 She showed us how to perk the coffee and conquer the toaster. **1977** P. Harcourt *At High Risk* i. 37 While I waited for the coffee to perc, I made my bed.

perk, perke, obs. or dial. forms of park.

perkily ('pɜːkɪlɪ), *adv.* [f. perky *a.* + -ly[2].] In a perky manner; self-assertively, with self-assurance; 'cockily'; pertly.

1878 *Tinsley's Mag.* XXIII. 186 Daisies and buttercups.. peer perkily at one another. **1886** J. R. Rees *Pleas. Bookworm* i. 32 How perkily, on the shelf..does the little 12mo...shoulder it alongside his bigger brother in 4to. **1901** G. Douglas *House w. Green Shutters* 116 'Order, order!' cried Wilson perkily.

†**Perkin**[1] ('pɜːkɪn). *Obs.* [A dim. form of the name *Pierre, Piers*, or *Peter*: cf. *Peterkin*.] From the name *Perkin Warbeck*, alleged to be that of the personage who professed to be the younger son of Edward IV, and as such claimed the crown in 1495: A pretender to the throne, or to any exalted position.

1685 Evelyn *Diary* 15 July, Yet this Perkin [the Duke of Monmouth] had been made to believe that the King had married her [Mrs. Barlow]. **1715** Mrs. Centlivre *Gotham Election* I. Wks. 1760 III. 177 I'll undertake to prove this Fellow deep in the Interest of young Perkin. *Ibid.* 185 You'd spend every Shilling of my Portion in Defence of Liberty and Property, against Perkin and the Pope.

perkin[2] ('pɜːkɪn). [? f. purr (or ? f. perry[2]) + -kin: cf. pomperkin.] (See quots.)

If the word was derived from *perry*, it must have been applied orig. to a weak kind of perry, analogous to *ciderkin* from cider; but of this evidence has not been found.

1785 Grose *Dict. Vulg. T.*, *Perkin*, water cyder. *c***1791** *Encycl. Brit.* (ed. 3) s.v. *Husbandry* §238 The liquor, called cyderkin, purre, or perkin, is made of the murk or gross matter remaining after the cyder is pressed out. **1863** Morton *Cycl. Agric.* II. 720–7 (E.D.S.) *Perkin* (Wilts, Glouc.), the washings after the best cyder is made.

Perkin[3] ('pɜːkɪn). *Chem.* [The name of Sir William *Perkin* (1838–1907), English chemist.]

a. ***Perkin's mauve, †purple***, or ***violet***, a dye that was first prepared by Perkin in 1856 by oxidizing crude aniline with potassium dichromate, and was the first synthetic dye to be used commercially; = mauve *sb.*

1860 *Chem. News* 21 Jan. 74/2 Notices of some of the patents taken out for the preparation and use of the new purple dyes generally known as the 'mauve or Perkins' [*sic*] Purple', [etc.]. **1886** Roscoe & Schorlemmer *Treat. Chem.* III. III. 319 Other patents were soon taken out for this colour, and it came into the market under different names, such as Tyrian purple, Aniline violet, Perkin's violet, [etc.]. **1908** *Jrnl. Chem. Soc.* XCIII. 2247 Many of the products obtained by these inventors could not have been Perkin's mauve at all, and,..not one of these rival processes was enabled to compete successfully with the original 'bichromate' method. **1964** N. G. CLARK *Mod. Org. Chem.* xxii. 454 Perkin's Mauve, as the substance was called, became the first synthetic dye. **1971** E. GURR *Synthetic Dyes* 123 Mauveine (mauve; Perkin's violet) is a basic dye of the azine group... Mauveine has been obsolete for several decades past.

b. ***Perkin('s) reaction*** or ***synthesis***, any of a number of types of reaction discovered by Perkin, esp. that in which, typically, an arylacrylic acid is formed by the condensation of an aromatic aldehyde with the anhydride of an aliphatic acid, in the presence of the sodium salt of the latter.

1882 *Jrnl. Chem. Soc.* XLII. 190 (*heading*) Interpretation of syntheses by Perkin's reaction. **1908** *Ibid.* XCIII. 2226 About 1867 he [*sc.* Perkin] must have commenced these researches.. which.. culminated in that beautiful method of synthesising unsaturated acids now known as the 'Perkin synthesis'. **1960** GOWAN & WHEELER *Name Index Org. Reactions* (ed. 2) 189 Perkin synthesis of alicyclic compounds. Compounds containing active methylene groups react with polymethylene dihalides in the presence of a base.. to yield alicyclic compounds. **1972** *Materials & Technol.* IV. xiii. 462 Acetic anhydride is the most applicable reagent in the Perkin reaction. **1973** B. J. HAZZARD tr. *Organicum* 479 In the Perkin synthesis, aldehydes or ketones are treated with anhydrides of aliphatic carboxylic acids, giving rise to α, β-unsaturated carboxylic acids.

perkin, variant of PARKIN, gingerbread.

perkiness ('pɜːkɪnɪs). [f. PERKY *a.* + -NESS.] The quality of being perky; self-assertiveness; 'cockiness'; liveliness.

1883 HALL CAINE *Cobwebs Crit.* v. 149 His [poetry].. was more open to the charge of cheerful perkiness. **1885** HUXLEY in *Life* (1900) II. vii. 104 The perkiness of last week was only a spurt.

perking ('pɜːkɪŋ), *ppl. a.* [f. PERK *v.*[1] + -ING[2].] That perks: in various senses of PERK *v.*[1]

1602 W. BAS *Sword & Buckler* B iij b, The pearking Citizen and minsing Dame of any paltrie beggerd Market toune. **1824** MISS MITFORD *Village* Ser. I. (1863) 223 Mr. Beck.. was a little insignificant, perking.. man. *a* **1851** MOIR *Mayday* iii, The perking squirrel's small nose you see From the fungous nook of its own beech-tree.

Hence **'perkingly** *adv.*, in a perking manner.

1841 *Tait's Mag.* VIII. 618 He drew up his head perkingly.

Perkinism ('pɜːkɪnɪz(ə)m). *Med.* Also †**Perkinsism.** [See -ISM.] A method of treatment introduced by Elisha Perkins, an American physician (died 1799), for the cure of rheumatic diseases; it consisted in drawing two small pointed rods, one of steel and one of brass, called 'metallic tractors', over the affected region; tractoration. So **Perki'nean, Perki'nistic** *adjs.*, of or pertaining to this method; **'Perkinist**, a follower of the method of Perkins; **'Perkinize** *v.*, to practise Perkinism; **Per'kinsian** *a.*, pertaining to Elisha Perkins.

1798 C. C. LANGWORTHY (*title*) A View of the Perkinean Electricity; or, an Inquiry into the Influence of Metallic Tractors. *Ibid.* App. 41 His father's discovery, which may with propriety be termed Perkinism, or.. Perkinean Electricity. **1803** FESSENDEN (*title*) Terrible Tractoration; a Poetical Petition against Galvanizing Trumpery and the Perkinistic Institution. *Ibid.* 34 To crush the Perkinising faction. **1824** MCCULLOCH *Scotland* IV. 63 He who believes in Perkinism or Bletonism or Mesmerism. **1853** DUNGLISON *Med. Lex.*, *Perkinist*,.. *Perkinistic.* **1880** *Libr. Univ. Knowl.* (N.Y.) XI. 515 The practice was called 'Perkinsism'. *Ibid.*, A Perkinsian institution.. was established [in London] for the benefit of the poor.

†**Perkinite.** *Hist. Obs.* Also -en-. A sympathizer with Sir Wm. Perkins, executed in 1696, for his share in a plot to murder William III; applied by enemies to Jacobites generally. Also *attrib.*

1705 HICKERINGILL *Priest-cr.* II. viii. 81 Bloody Jesuites, and the Tackers, and the Perkenites. **1709** *Let. to Ld. M[ayor]* 4 The Perkinite Faction. *Ibid.* 8 Men who hold no Correspondence with the Papists or Perkinites. **1711** E. WARD *Vulg. Brit.* XIV. 165 In all their Perkinite Addresses.

perkish ('pɜːkɪʃ), *a.* [f. PERK *a.* + -ISH[1] 3.] Somewhat perk or forward; rather perky.

1889 *Univ. Rev.* Mar. 365 A perkish young woman who takes her foibles from a mother who 'went wrong'.

'perkness. *rare.* [f. PERK *a.* + -NESS.] The quality of being perk or elated; 'cockiness'.

a **1640** W. FENNER *Cont. Christ's Alarm* (1657) 10 The law hath discovered his estate unto him, and pulled down the pearkness of his spirit.

perk test ('pɜːk tɛst). *U.S.* [f. PERC(OLATION + TEST *sb.*[1]] The act of percolating water through earth as a test of suitability for a septic tank. Hence **'perk-tested** *ppl. a.*

1974 *State* (Columbia, S. Carolina) 1 Apr. 9-B/6 (Advt.), Near Hilton, 158' on water, 208' in depth, 161' on rear, water system & perk test approved (restricted). **1976** *Washington Post* 19 Apr. C20/3 (Advt.), Surveyed, staked, recorded & 'perk' tested. **1976** *Billings* (Montana) *Gaz.* 30 June 7-D/2 (Advt.), Beautiful view, live stream, good road, perk test, soil samples comp. Protective restrictions. Ready to build on.

perky ('pɜːkɪ), *a.* [f. PERK *v.*[1] or *a.* + -Y.] Self-assertive, forward, somewhat obtrusive or assuming; self-conceited, 'cocky'; jaunty; smart.

1855 TENNYSON *Maud* I. x. i, Seeing his gewgaw castle shine,.. There amid perky larches and pine. **1864** *Realm* 18 May 3 Those perky little magicians who manipulate and decipher the lightning with such autocratic unconcern. **1876** 'P. PYPER' *Mr. Gray & Neighbours* I. 53 No fortress of daily prayers, set up by a perky young cleric. **1885** E. GARRETT *At Any Cost* viii. 135 She gave a perky little cough, and opened her mission. **1887** A. JESSOPP *Trials Country Parson* (1890) 22 They give utterance to perky platitudes about the clergy.

perl, obs. form of PEARL.

perlaceous (pɜː'leɪʃəs), *a.* [f. med.L. and Rom. *perla* PEARL + -ACEOUS.] Resembling pearl in appearance; pearly, nacreous.

1777 PENNANT *Zool.* (ed. 4) IV. 93 *Anomia Ephippium*,.. color of inside perlaceous. **1841** JOHNSTON in *Proc. Berw. Nat. Club* I. 264 Aperture white, perlaceous.

perlament, obs. form of PARLIAMENT.

perlarian (pɜː'lɛərɪən), *a.* [f. mod.L. *Perlāria*, f. generic name *Perla*.] Of or pertaining to the genus *Perla* or family *Perlidæ*, or stone-flies.

1890 in *Cent. Dict.*

per'larious, *a.*[1] *rare*$^{-0}$. = PERLACEOUS.

1857 in MAYNE *Expos. Lex.* **1893** in *Syd. Soc. Lex.*

per'larious, *a.*[2] *rare*$^{-0}$. = PERLARIAN.

1857 in MAYNE *Expos. Lex.*

†**perlassent**, *adv. phr. Obs. rare*$^{-1}$. [a. OF. phr. *par l'assent*.] By mutual consent or agreement.

1548 PATTEN *Exped. Scotl.* L vj, When thei [hostile borderers secretly in league] perceiued thei had bene spied, thei haue begun to run at [one] another, but so apparauntly perlassent as yᵉ lookers on resembled their chasyng like yᵉ running at base, in an vplondish toun.

†**'perlate, per'lated**, *adjs. Chem. Obs.* [ad. mod.L. *perlāt-um*, f. *perla* PEARL: see quot. 1802.] In ***perlate*** or ***perlated acid***, Bergman's name for acid phosphate of sodium.

1789 J. KEIR *Dict. Chem.* 136/2 The substance to which Bergman has given the name of perlated acid. **1802** T. THOMSON *Chem.* (1807) II. 569 Haupt described it in 1740 under the name of *sal mirabile perlatum*, or 'wonderful perlated salt'. It was called *perlated* from the grey, opaque, pearl-like colour which it assumed when melted by the blow-pipe. **1857** MAYNE *Expos. Lex.*, *Perlate Acid.*

perlative ('pɜːlətɪv). *Linguistics.* [f. L. *perlatus*, *pa. pple.* of *perferre*, to carry through, convey + -IVE.] A grammatical case signifying movement alongside or means of transportation.

1953 *Trans. Philol. Soc.* 1952 72 The use of the perlative case.. is of some interest. *Ibid.*, The perlative would seem to indicate going 'alongside' so as to be 'at'. **1966** G. S. LANE in Birnbaum & Puhvel *Anc. Indo-European Dial.* 217 A distinguishes formally between an instrument in *-yo* and a so-called perlative in *-ā*.

perle (pɜːl). *Pharm.* [a. F. *perle* pearl: cf. PEARL *sb.* 12.] A pellet: see quot. 1893.

1887 *Medical News* L. 291 Whenever delirium is present, it is allayed with the ice-bag to the head, or by the internal use of ether (in *perles*), or of the bromides. **1893** *Syd. Soc. Lex.*, *Perle*,.. a globule coated with gelatine, and containing some liquid substance, either volatile or of unpleasant taste.

perle, obs. f. PEARL; obs. var. PURL.

perleau ('pɜːləʊ). *U.S. dial.* Also perlo. = PILAU.

1933 in *Amer. Speech* VIII. III. 40/2 A month later I went down to Uncle Rich's hunting cabin for a perleau supper. **1935** Z. N. HURSTON *Mules & Men* I. i. 31 There was plenty of chicken perleau and baked chicken. **1955** *This Week* 25 Sept. 32/1 Perlo in local parlance [north Florida] is a chicken pilau.

perlection (pə'lɛkʃən). *rare.* [ad. L. *perlectiōn-em* (*pell-*), n. of action from *perlegĕre* to read through.] The action of reading through.

1660 WATERHOUSE *Arms & Arm.* 135 Perlection of Authours, and perusal of Records and Entries. **1885** BURTON *Arab. Nts.* (1887) III. 277 Readings and perlections of the Koran.

†**'perlegate**, *v. Obs. rare.* [irreg. f. L. *perlegĕre* (see prec.) + -ATE[3].] *trans.* To read through.

1597 A. M. tr. *Guillemeau's Fr. Chirurg.* *v, To perlegate my scriptums and writinges.

perlemoen (pɜːrlə'mʊn). *S. Afr.* Also **paarlmoer.** [Afrikaans, f. Du. *parelmoer* mother of pearl.] = KLIPKOUS.

1853 L. PAPPE *Synopsis Edible Fishes Cape Good Hope* 12 Amongst the mollusca, none are more eagerly caught, and none have such a deserved reputation as *Haliotis Midae Lin.* (Klipkous; Sea-ear), and a species of *Stomatia* (Paarlmoer). **1911** J. D. F. GILCHRIST *S. Afr. Zool.* ix. 192 The transposition of the organs [of unequal-sided molluscs].. may be so complete that the visceral loop is pulled into the form of the figure 8. Forms in which this occur.. are the ordinary Limpet.., the Perlemoen or Klipkoes of South African Seas.., and the common periwinkle. **1947** [see KLIPKOUS]. **1950** *Cape Times* 5 July 14/3, I have already mentioned having enjoyed a *perlemoen* dish out at Blaauwberg. **1958** L. G. GREEN *S. Afr. Beachcomber* xi. 127 South Africans are compensated for the scarcity of scallops by an abundance of *perlemoen*. This is the abalone of America and the *ormer* of the Channel Islands. They grow up to nine inches, and one of that size makes a rich meal indeed. **1966** [see KLIPKOUS]. **1970** G. CROUDACE *Scarlet Bikini* ii. 14 Perlemoen was said to have the effect of oysters upon the human libido.

perleque, *Sc.*: see PURLICUE.

perles, perlew, obs. ff. PEERLESS, PURLIEU.

†**per'librate**, *v. Obs. rare*$^{-0}$. [f. ppl. stem of L. *perlībrāre*, f. PER- 4 + *lībrāre*, f. *lībra* balance.] To weigh exactly. So †**perli'bration.**

1623 COCKERAM, *Perlibrate*, to weigh. *Perlibration*, a weighing.

†**per'ligate**, *v. Obs. rare*$^{-0}$. [f. ppl. stem of med.L. *perligāre*, f. PER- 2 + *ligāre* to bind.] To bind hard. So †**perli'gation.**

1623 COCKERAM, *Perligate. Perligation*, a hard binding.

perligenous (pə'lɪdʒɪnəs), *a. rare.* [f. med.L. *perla* pearl + *-genous*, in sense 'producing': cf. -GEN I.] Producing or causing the formation of pearls.

1803 SYD. SMITH *Ceylon* Wks. 1859 I. 42 The secret of infecting oysters with this perligenous disease.

perline ('pɜːlaɪn), *a. Zool.* [f. mod.L. *Perla*.] Belonging to the genus *Perla*, or family *Perlidæ* or stone flies.

1893 in *Syd. Soc. Lex.*

perlite ('pɜːlaɪt). *Min.* Also **pearlite.** [= F. *perlite*, G. *perlit*, mod. f. F. and Ger. *perle* PEARL: see -ITE[2].] A peculiar form of obsidian and other vitreous rocks, in which the mass sometimes assumes the form of enamel-like globules; pearlstone; *spec.* fine or coarse grains of this mineral used, with appropriate nutrient solutions, as a medium for the growth of plants.

1833 LYELL *Princ. Geol.* III. 222 Resinous silex.., pearlite, obsidian, and pitchstone abound. **1879** RUTLEY *Study Rocks* xi. 193 Perlite must be regarded as the vitreous condition of the felsitic rhyolites. **1882** GEIKIE *Text-bk. Geol.* II. II. vi. 141 Perlite (Pearlstone) another vitreous condition of sanidine lava.. of vitreous or enamel-like globules. **1956** T. M. MORRISON in *N.Z. Jrnl. Agric.* XCIII. 503/1 The coarse grade of expanded perlite now on the market in New Zealand is ideal for plant growth. *Ibid.* 503/3 Perlite is cheap enough to be thrown out after several crops have been raised in it. **1971** 'D. HALLIDAY' *Dolly & Doctor Bird* viii. 106 We saw the trucks going by from the big netted nursery... Trucks full of potted plants, and bags of horticultural perlite, and Canadian sphagnum peat moss. **1976** A. C. BUNT *Mod. Potting Composts* ii. 38 Perlite is an alumino-silicate of volcanic origin and is widely used in the USA and New Zealand, both countries having large natural deposits of this mineral.

Hence **per'litic** *a.*, of or pertaining to perlite.

1879 RUTLEY *Study Rocks* xi. 183 Showing that the perlitic structure had no existence when the rock was in a state of fluxion. **1881** JUDD *Volcanoes* 110.

perlo, var. PERLEAU.

perlo'cution. [ad. med. or mod. L. *perlocūtiōn-em*, f. PER- I + *locūtio* speaking.]

†**a.** The action of speaking, utterance, elocution. *Obs. rare.*

1599 A. M. tr. *Gabelhouer's Bk. Physicke* 29/2 It opitulateth the perloquutione exceedingelye.

b. *Philos.* A speech act, such as persuading or convincing, that may or may not be successfully achieved by an illocutionary act such as entreating or arguing. Also *attrib.* So **perlo'cutionary** *a.*

1955 J. L. AUSTIN *How to do Things with Words* (1962) viii. 101 Act (C. *a*) or Perlocution. He persuaded me to shoot her. *Ibid.* 102 We can similarly distinguish the locutionary act 'he said that..' from the illocutionary act 'he argued that..' and the perlocutionary act 'he convinced me that..'. **1969** J. KAMINSKY *Lang. & Ontology* viii. 111 It could be said to have perlocutionary act potential in that it is clearly meant to have an effect on Jones. **1973** *Times Lit. Suppl.* 5 Oct. 1161/5 Austin called a speaker's act perlocutionary so far as, by saying something, the speaker produced some intended or unintended effect on the feelings, thoughts or actions of someone. **1976** *Archivum Linguisticum* VII. 67 Perlocutionary effects have to do with whether or not one actually succeeds in apologizing, persuading, or whatever, over and above communicating the fact that one is attempting to do this. **1977** *Language* LIII. 197 Both getting the officer to evict them and getting them to leave are perlocutionary *sequels* to the illocutionary act of asking the question.

perlocy, obs. form of PALSY.

Perlon ('pɜːlɒn). Also **perlon.** A proprietary name (first used in Germany) for nylon 6, a type of nylon produced by the polymerization of caprolactam.

1941 *Chem. Abstr.* XXXV. 7200 In Germany the polymer is known as Igamide, the fiber as Perlon. **1954** *Brit. Rayon & Synthetic Fibres Man.* i. 45 Perlon (nylon 6) is a polyamide chemically resembling nylon 66 very closely. **1958** *Official Gaz.* (U.S. Patent Office) 28 Jan. TM 110/1 Perlon-Warenzeichenverband E.V., Frankfurt (Main), Germany. Filed Nov. 21, 1955... Perlon... For nylon fibers, filaments, strands, [etc.]. **1958** *Trade Marks Jrnl.* 12 Mar. 265/2 Perlon.. synthetic textile fibres. Perlon-Warenzeichenverband Eingetragener Verin..,

Frankfurt/Main, Germany; merchants. **1960** *Vogue Pattern Bk.* Autumn 45 Girdle in lightweight Perlon elastic with a Perlon taffeta front panel. **1973** C. Bonington *Next Horizon* xii. 168 Economising on weight, we had used 7 mm perlon,..with a breaking strain of 2,000 lb. **1976** M. & G. Gordon *Ordeal* (1977) xvii. 181 They carried pitons, nuts, stoppers, braided perlon cord..and other mountain-climbing equipment.

perlous, -ouse, obs. forms of parlous.

perlowre, perloyn, obs. ff. parlour, purloin.

†**per'lucid** *a.*, obs. variant of pellucid.

1695 Tryon *Dreams & Vis.* ii. 14 More rare and perlucid Exhalations. **1713** A. Campbell *Doctr. Mid. State* (1721) 94 To make it Transparent or Perlucide.

perlustrate (pəˈlʌstreɪt), *v. Obs.* exc. in techn. use. [f. ppl. stem of L. *perlustrā-re* to wander through, traverse completely, f. per- 1, 2 + *lustrāre* to traverse, survey, review, examine. Cf. obs. f. *perlustrer* (15–16th c. in Godef.).]

trans. To travel through and view all over; to survey thoroughly. Also *absol.*

1535 Boorde in Ellis *Orig. Lett.* Ser. iii. II. 298 Sens my departyng from yow I haue perlustratyd Normandy, Frawnce, Gascony, and Leyon. **1691** T. Jackson in *Thoresby's Corr.* (1832) I. 112 At nine also at night, they perlustrate to see that all the students be within the college. **1701** *Hawick Kirk Sess. Rec.* 25 May, The elders who perlustrate yᵉ toun in time of public worship. **1891** *Oxford Mag.* 6 May 320/1 The Curators of the Bodleian are once a year to perlustrate all parts of the Library.

perlustration (pɜːlʌˈstreɪʃən). [n. of action f. prec.: cf. L. *lustrātio* lustration.] **a.** The action of perlustrating; a going round and viewing or surveying thoroughly.

1640 G. Watts tr. *Bacon's Adv. Learn.* v. ii. 220 The Art of Invention and Perlustration hetherto was unknown. **1642** Howell *For. Trav.* (Arb.) 70 By the perlustration of such famous Cities, Castles, Amphitheaters, and Palaces. **1657** —— (*title*) Londinopolis; an Historicall Discourse or Perlustration of the City of London. **1817** T. L. Peacock *Melincourt* xxxii, They rose, as usual, before daylight, that they might pursue their perlustration. **1946** L. P. Hartley *Sixth Heaven* v. 98 The interest of seeing whether he was before or behind his schedule..helped..the process of perlustration. **1967** *Times* 15 Mar. 6/5 Mr. Hugh Fraser..asked the Prime Minister whether cables and radio telegrams sent by M.P.s were privileged from perlustration by the security services. *Ibid.*, Perlustration was in common use in the secret police of the Tsarist regime. **1972** *Oxf. Univ. Gaz.* CII. Suppl. No. 8. 47 The Curators conducted a perlustration of the Library on 29 May—the first ever at Rhodes House.

b. *fig.* The action of going through and examining a document; *esp.* the inspection of correspondence while passing through the post.

1896 *Edin. Rev.* July 142 The 'perlustration' of papers he held to be quite as defensible as the bribing of office-clerks. **1902** *Ibid.* Oct. 536 The 'perlustration' of foreign correspondence in the post-office was an ordinary expedient in all countries.

So **perlu'strator** [late L.], one who perlustrates.

1807 J. Hall *Trav. Scotl.* I. 114 These morning and evening visits were called Perlustrations, and the Hebdomader, in reference to this..was called the Perlustrator.

†**per'lustre,** *v. Sc. Obs. rare.* [a. obs. F. *perlustrer*: see perlustrate.] = perlustrate.

1535 Stewart *Cron. Scot.* (1858) I. 115 As he had perlustrit all the land. *Ibid.* III. 100 This nobill king perlustrit all his land.

perlyment, obs. form of parliament.

perm (pɜːm), *sb.*[1] *colloq.* Abbrev. of *permanent wave* s.v. permanent *a.* (*sb.*) 1 d.

1927 *Home Chat* 22 Oct. 200 How long does a 'perm' last? **1929** N. Royde-Smith *Summer Holiday* 113 The old girl's had a perm. Look at the waves. **1932** *Modern Weekly* 30 Apr. 136 You can have a 'perm.', or you may find a tong wave best. **1937** G. Frankau *More of Us* xv. 162 All perfume, perm and pearls and prominent teeth. **1943** J. B. Priestley *Daylight on Saturday* vii. 43 There was a girl called Elsie, who was a fake blonde, had a terrific perm. **1954** Wodehouse *Jeeves & Feudal Spirit* xii. 109 This aunt who sat before me clutching feverishly at her perm. **1960** M. Spark *Ballad of Peckham Rye* iii. 45 She moved her hand across her perm, nipping each brown wave in turn between her third and index fingers. **1976** *National Observer* (U.S.) 31 Jan. 8/2 After carrying around a headful of perfectly straight hair, I now sport a crown of exotic, wavy, fluffy, jaunty, tousled, perky, spirally, bouncy curls. I have a perm.

perm, *sb.*[2] *colloq.* Abbrev. of permutation 5.

1956 *News Chron.* 1 Nov. 10/8 Perms and plain paper bets accepted. **1958** L. Gibbs *Gowns & Satyr's Legs* xix. 128 He studied it [*sc.* a printed paper] intently, being in the process of constructing what..he called a 'perm'. **1958** *Punch* 27 Aug. 265/3 No pools investor of quality would seek advice from hacks who write:..Middlesbrough rate high in homes perm. **1971** *E. Afr. Standard* (Nairobi) 10 Apr. 2/7 (Advt.), See our collector for coupons, plans and perms. **1973** *Weekly News* (Glasgow) (Football Suppl.) 11 Aug. 3/1 And perm fans especially welcome the chance to cover more matches that the lower stakes give. **1974** *Guardian* 26 Nov. 27/2 Littlewoods have introduced a new perm—the £½ plan—using 12 selections which gives tight cover for only 50p. One is guaranteed 24 points if any nine matches result as score draws, and there are several other combinations which would provide a first dividend with only eight.

perm, *v.*[1] *colloq.* [f. perm *sb.*[1]] *trans.* To give a permanent wave to (the hair). So **permed** *ppl. a.*, having a permanent wave.

1928 *Daily Express* 17 Mar. 9/5 These girls took their chairs at 7.30 p.m... Three hours later they rose 'permed', as one says in the profession. **1931** S. Holme in *Repertory* 6 June 10/2 Thea spent nearly all day at the hairdresser's having her hair 'permed'. **1936** A. Christie *ABC Murders* xi. 83 Her hair had evidently recently been permed, it stood out from her head in a mass of rather frizzy curls. **1952** *News Chron.* 8 July 4/1 Children's hair differs from adults in that it is finer in texture and less elastic. Meaning that what perms Mother won't necessarily perm daughter. **1956** I. Murdoch *Flight from Enchanter* 192 Her elaborately permed hair. **1959** *News Chron.* 11 Aug. 6/2 There is a growing tendency for British mothers to perm children's hair. **1960** F. Raphael *Limits of Love* iii. v. 328 Newly permed brown hair. **1970** 'D. Halliday' *Dolly & Cookie Bird* iv. 52 His golden, permed sideburns glistened. **1973** J. Thomson *Death Cap* v. 75 She had her brother's..gingerish, greying hair, although hers was permed into a lot of little waves.

perm, *v.*[2] *colloq.* [Abbrev. permute *v.* or f. perm *sb.*[2]] To make a selection of (so many) from a larger number; to make a permutation of (permutation 3 b).

1959 *Times* 9 Mar. 11/4 One trusting citizen, having duly filled in a complex formula 'perming' a number of matches, looked upon his labour as a guarantee that dividends would automatically come pouring in. **1968** *Guardian* 11 July 9/7 Perm any six of these reasons to find out why an aircraft..crashed last week. **1972** *Ibid.* 3 Apr. 9/3 He went about it..composing 50 horoscopes in a single night... Then daily he permed any 12 from 50 so that 'conflict within the home' would befall Leos one week and Scorpios another. **1973** *Milestones* Summer 21/1 There are 12 all told, if you perm the alternatives of 2- or 4-door body shells and four engine sizes (of which two are also available in hotted up 'Sport Special' form). **1976** J. Snow *Cricket Rebel* 51 At the start he would 'perm' any two from three with the new ball, each bowler taking a turn at bowling with the wind at his back. **1976** *Shooting Mag.* Dec. 18/1 Gilstone Manor—I dare not use its real name—sits on the edge of a National Park (perm any one from nine) and is a hybrid i.e. a cross between Cold Comfort Farm and 'Upstairs Downstairs'. **1976** *Sunday Mail* (Glasgow) 26 Dec. 35/3 Pools Guide... Perm any 3 from 6 in first and second columns with any 2 from 3 in third column—20 × 20 × 3—1200 lines at 1/8p per line = £1.50 staked.

permaceti, -cetty: see parmacety.

permafrost (ˈpɜːməfrɒst). [f. perma(nent *a.* (*sb.*) + frost *sb.*] Subsoil or other underground material that is at a temperature of less than 0°C throughout the year, as in Arctic regions; permanently frozen ground.

1943 S. W. Muller *Permafrost or Permanently Frozen Ground* 3 The expression 'permanently frozen ground'..is too long and cumbersome and for this reason a shorter term '*permafrost*' is proposed as an alternative. **1952** *Sci. News Let.* 2 Aug. 70/3 Currently it is studying permafrost, permanently frozen ground that creates many problems in construction work. **1955** Peterson & Fisher *Wild Amer.* (1956) xxxiii. 357 Here on the tundra the permafrost forbids any digging and the Eskimos bury their dead above the ground. **1958** *New Biol.* XXVI. 90 In the sub-arctic the peat has a permafrost layer, that is a layer, usually a foot or two below the surface, which remains frozen for the whole year round, and acts as an impermeable layer. **1968** R. W. Fairbridge *Encycl. Geomorphol.* 838/1 Many other engineering problems result from changes in the mechanical properties of permafrost caused by thawing or freezing of its moisture beneath such structures as roadways or heated buildings. **1971** *New Scientist* 8 Apr. 70/1 The heated pipeline would be laid for several hundred miles over or through a peaty soil where the permafrost may reach as much as 500 metres depth. **1974** T. P. Whitney tr. *Solzhenitsyn's Gulag Archipel.* I. i. ii. 24 This wave poured forth, sank down into the permafrost, and even our most active minds recall hardly a thing about it. **1975** *Nature* 1 May 27/1 A possible reason is that the increasing permafrost in the soil forced the late Vikings to change their burial customs. **1977** *New Yorker* 9 May 95/2 There is ice under the tundra, mixed with soil as permafrost, in some places two thousand feet deep.

†**permain, -mane,** *v. Obs. rare.* Also 5 **permayne.** [a. F. *per-*, *parmaindre*, *parmenir*, *-oir*:—L. *permanēre*: see permanent. (Cf. *remain*.)] *intr.* To remain, continue.

1456 Sir G. Haye *Law Arms* (S.T.S.) 225 Law of nature..permaynis for ever undefoulit. **1657** Tomlinson *Renou's Disp.* 386* The concreted liquor..permanes very long suaveolent.

permain, -man, obs. forms of pearmain.

permalloy (ˈpɜːmælɔɪ). [f. perm(eability + alloy *sb.*] Any of a series of alloys consisting chiefly of nickel and iron, which have very high magnetic permeability and are widely used in electrical equipment, esp. in telecommunications.

1923 Arnold & Elmen in *Jrnl. Franklin Inst.* CXCV. 621 For convenience we call these peculiarly magnetic alloys by the general name 'permalloy', which serves at the same time to recall their characteristic capability of attaining high initial permeability. **1925** *Chambers's Jrnl.* Apr. 220/1 The conductor of this distortionless cable is composed of a special alloy, known as permalloy. **1926** *Glasgow Herald* 9 Sept. 8/4 The Western Union Telegraph Company announce that the laying of the new permalloy cable between England and New York was successfully completed on Sunday last. **1932** [see Mumetal]. **1946** [see *nickel-iron* s.v. nickel *sb.* 3 b]. **1965** *Wireless World* Sept. 431/1 The auto-transformer core should be of magnetically soft material such as permalloy, mumetal, H.C.R. alloy or some similar grade. **1969** E. N. Simon *Dict. Alloys* 127 Permalloy 45 contains basically 45 nickel, 55 iron, per cent. *Ibid.*, Permalloy 4-79 contains basically 79 nickel, 4 molybdenum, the balance iron, per cent...and is used for audio coils, transformers and magnetic shields.

†**'permanable,** *a. Obs.* Also 5 **parm-.** [a. ONF. *permainable* (Ph. de Thaun), *permanable*, OF. *parmenable*, f. stem of *permanent, parmenant*: see permanent.] Enduring, permanent.

1413 *Pilgr. Sowle* (Caxton) iv. xxix. (1859) 61 [To] stablysshe a thynge to be nought remeuyd oute of his place, but for to standen stedfastly, alwey permanable. *c* **1422** Hoccleve *Learn to Die* 767 Þat blisful hy contree which nat may varie, but is permanable. **1571** *Satir. Poems Reform.* xxviii. 5, I se na plesure permanabill, Bot as the weid it widderis sone away.

permanence (ˈpɜːmənəns). [ad. med.L. *permanentia* (1319 in Du Cange), f. *permanēnt-em* permanent (see -ence); perh. through F. *permanence* (Oresme, 14th c.), OF. *parmanance*, *-menance* (12–13th c.).]

1. The fact, condition, or state of being permanent; continued existence or duration; continuance, abiding.

1432–50 tr. *Higden* (Rolls) II. 215 Assiduite of feyntenesse longethe to a man, impossibilite of permanence [Higden *impossibilitas permanendi*] lyȝhtenes to falle. **1556** Lauder *Tractate* (1864) 4 Hov kyngis hes no erthlie permanence. **1651** Hobbes *Leviath.* iii. xxxiv. 213 Which place is manifest for the permanence of Evill Angels. **1660** R. Coke *Justice Vind.* 2 Memory cannot be, without permanence of the thing perceived. **1830** Lyell *Princ. Geol.* I. 111 The permanence of the snow..is partly due to the floating ice.

2. The quality of being permanent; permanency, abidingness.

a **1677** Hale *Prim. Orig. Man.* i. iii. 73 That hath or may have such a kind of permanence or fixedness in being. **1775** Harris *Philos. Arrangem.* Wks. (1841) 299 With respect to all kinds of qualities..there is one thing to be observed, that some degree of permanence is always requisite. **1841–4** Emerson *Ess.*, *Spir. Laws* Wks. (Bohn) I. 66 The permanence of all books is fixed by..the intrinsic importance of their contents. **1874** Micklethwaite *Mod. Par. Churches* 223 The essential quality of a monument is permanence.

'permanency. [f. as prec. + -ency.]

1. The quality of being permanent; enduring nature or character; abidingness, lastingness.

1555 Eden *Decades* 338 There are..but fewe which hold not sum smaul portion therof [gold], more or lesse according to the mixtion and permanencie of theyr substances. **1682** Norris *Hierocles* 87 The solidity and permanency of vertue. **1746** Hervey *Medit.*, *Refl. Fl.-Gard.* (1767) I. 127 They want nothing but Solidity and Permanency; to equal them with the finest Treasures of the Jeweller's Casket. **1865** *Reader* 7 Oct. 392/3 Recording their beauty..in all the permanency of print. *Mod.* The position has no permanency; it may come to an end at any time.

2. A (concrete) example of something permanent; a permanent person, thing, position, etc.

1841–4 Emerson *Ess.*, *Politics* Wks. (Bohn) I. 242 A mob cannot be a permanency. **1853** Kane *Grinnell Exp.* xix. (1856) 149 A seeming permanency compared with the ephemeral ruins that beat against its side. **1884** *Truth* 13 Mar. 379/1, I only wish he might be considered a permanency. *Mod.* Only a temporary engagement, not a permanency.

permanent (ˈpɜːmənənt), *a.* (*sb.*) [ad. L. *permanēnt-em*, pr. pple. of *permanēre* to stay to the end, f. per- 1, 2 + *manēre* to stay; perh. through F. *permanent* (14th c.), OF. *perma-*, *parmenant* (13th c. in Godef.).]

1. a. Continuing or designed to continue indefinitely without change; abiding, lasting, enduring; persistent. Opposed to *temporary*.

1432–50 tr. *Higden* (Rolls) II. 255 Other thynges be permanente as thei were [Higden *cætera autem permanent*]. **1481** Caxton *Myrr.* Prol. 1 Wordes ben perisshyng vayne & forgeteful, And writynges duelle & abide permanent. **1526** *Pilgr. Perf.* (W. de W. 1531) 16 We haue no dwellyng place ne Cite here permanent. **1610** Willet *Hexapla Dan.* 80 A stable and permanent knowledge. **1780** Harris *Philol. Enq.* Wks. (1841) 467 Human institutions perish, but nature is permanent. **1832** Ht. Martineau *Demerara* ii. 25 There was a permanent population of 300 slaves on the estate at that time. **1869** E. A. Parkes *Pract. Hygiene* (ed. 3) 117 In permanent barracks a man is allowed 600 cubic feet [of air].

†**b.** That remains fixed, motionless. *Obs. rare*$^{-1}$.

1588 Greene *Perimedes* 32 Richesse is..as brittle as Glasse, standing vpon a Globe that is neuer permanent.

c. *Bot.* = persistent *a.* Opposed to *fugacious*.

1785 Martyn *Rousseau's Bot.* v. (1794) 53 These [styles] are permanent, or continue after the petals and stamens fall off. **1847** in Craig.

d. In special collocations: as *permanent alimony*, alimony granted for life to a woman who obtains legal separation from her husband: see quot. 1833; *permanent blue*, artificial ultramarine; *permanent dye*, a long-lasting dye used in hairdressing; *permanent gas*, a name formerly given to those gases which were supposed to be incapable of liquefaction, as oxygen, hydrogen; *permanent hardness*, hardness of water that is not removable by boiling; ***permanent magnet***, a magnet whose property continues after the magnetizing current has ceased to pass through it; so ***permanent magnetism***; ***permanent pasture***, land left unploughed for a long period, used for growing grass; ***permanent press***, a process designed to produce lasting creases in materials for clothing; the fabric treated in this way; ***permanent rank***: see quot. 1867; ***permanent revolution***, a concept orig. attributed to L. D. Trotsky (1879–1940) which envisaged the dependence of Russia's bourgeois and proletarian revolution on a continuing process of European revolutions; also *transf.*; ***permanent secretary***, a senior grade of the civil service, now normally denoting a permanent administrative officer of the highest grade in a Department of State; ***permanent set*** (Mech.), a deformation that remains after the removal of the stress that produced it; ***permanent tint*** = *permanent dye* above; ***permanent tooth***, one of those which last during life, as opp. to a *milk-tooth*; ***permanent under-secretary***, (*a*) a senior permanent adviser to a minister who is a Secretary of State; (*b*) a senior grade of the civil service below that of a permanent secretary and normally applied to the head of a division within a Department of State; ***permanent wave***, a special process designed to produce a lasting wave in the hair (also as *vb.*); the wave so produced; so ***permanent waver***, ***waving***; ***permanent way*** (***road***), the finished road-bed of a railway, as distinguished from a contractor's temporary way; also *attrib.*; ***permanent white***, 'sulphate of barium, used as a water-colour pigment' (Watts *Dict. Chem.* 1866–77).

1833 *Penny Cycl.* I. 340/1 It [alimony] may be either temporary or permanent:..in the second case, when a decree of divorce has been obtained,..a permanent provision may be given to her [the wife]. **1886** H. C. Standage *Artists' Man. Pigments* iii. 32 Permanent Blue is a pale ultramarine with a cobalt hue. **1895** *Montgomery Ward Catal.* Spring & Summer 252/3 Artists Tube Oil Colors... Permanent Blue. **1939–40** *Army & Navy Stores Catal.* 372/2 Moist water colours... Permanent mauve.. Permanent blue. **1881** *Syd. Soc. Lex.* s.v. *Cartilage*, Cartilage is..permanent when it remains such during life. **1966** J. S. Cox *Illustr. Dict. Hairdressing* 110/2 *Permanent dye*, a dye in which the susceptibility to lose colour under normal conditions has been reduced to a minimum. **1871** B. Stewart *Heat* §65 The three permanent gases which have never been liquified. **1888** *Encycl. Brit.* XXIV. 409/1 The remaining or permanent hardness consists of sulphate of lime and other soluble salts. **1969** H. T. Evans tr. *Hägg's Gen. & Inorg. Chem.* xxvi. 666 Carbonate precipitation on boiling causes the water to lose its carbonate hardness or temporary hardness while a permanent hardness remains. **1840** Barham *Ingol. Leg.* Ser. I. *Jackd. Rheims*, A Cardinal's Hat mark'd in 'permanent ink'. **1828** F. Watkins *Pop. Sk. Electro-Magnetism* 12 If a steel needle be inserted in a coil and removed again immediately, it will become a permanent magnet. **1879** tr. *Du Moncel's Telephone* 53 Operated by permanent magnets in place of batteries. **1827** J. Cumming *Man. Electro Dynamics* 259 If it be possible to give permanent magnetism to steel by this species of electricity. **1965** A. H. Morrish *Physical Princ. Magn.* i. 1 Permanent and induced magnetism represent two of man's earliest scientific discoveries. **1861** M. H. Sutton in *Jrnl. R. Agric. Soc.* XXII. 416 (*title*) Laying down land to permanent pasture. *Ibid.* 421 We offer the foregoing hints, on laying down permanent pastures, &c., founded on our own experience and observation during full thirty years. **1897** W. S. Everitt *Pract. Notes Grass & Grass Growing E. Anglia* iii. 44 First select the land which is suitable for a permanent pasture. **1924** W. J. Malden *Grassland Farming* viii. 101 If permanent pasture seeds are sown in the spring without a corn crop, they may or may not..make growth which will be valuable to feed during the first summer. **1968** F. W. Gould *Grass Systematics* i. 5 Geese feed extensively on rice ..and also take significant amounts of forage from temporary and permanent pastures of the Gulf Coastal Prairie. **1964** *Mod. Textiles Mag.* Dec. 55 (*heading*) Garments with permanent press finishes. *Ibid.* 55/2 The concept of *permanent press finish*... is being widely.. exploited in the men's and boys' casual and work slacks market. *Ibid.* 59/1 There are a number of competing processes now being offered..with claims of permanent creasing, permanent pressing, permanent shape retention, etc. **1965** *Observer* 10 Apr. 3/4 This new material..is generally known as 'permanent-press', a description which applies to a new process for treating cotton-and-Dacron goods so that they will never lose their shape or pleating. **1967** *Family Herald* 6 July 35/1 Permanent press involves treating the fabric chemically with a resin compound and then setting or 'curing' it by high heat in an oven. **1969** *Time* 18 Apr. 61 Foreign competition is most severe in man-made-fiber textiles, the most rapidly growing segment of the industry since advancing technology gave the world wash-'n'-wear shirts and permanent-press pants. **1978** *N.Y. Times* 30 Mar. A6/1 (Advt.), Made just for us by this top maker, a handsome selection of short sleeve shirts in solids, stripes, plaids and patterns. All in easy care permanent press polyester and cotton. **1867** Smyth *Sailor's Word.bk.*, *Permanent rank*, that given by commission, and which does not cease with any particular service. **1928** Permanent revolution [see Menshevism]. **1942** S. Neumann (*title*) Permanent revolution. **1964** I. Deutscher in *Trotsky's Age of Permanent Revolution* 18 Trotsky is deeply committed to one element in classical Marxism, its quintessential element: permanent revolution. **1972** D. Bloodworth *Any Number can Play* xx. 206 My fidelity to the Maoist theory of permanent revolution is absolute. **1975** *Guardian* 22 Jan. 10/1 Trotsky was the hero..and the notion of 'permanent revolution' was the great hope. **1825** Tredgold *Railroads* 33 For permanent roads the rails are usually fixed by spikes driven into wooden plugs in the blocks of stone. **1867** E. E. Bridges *Treasury* (1964) 233 My Lords are of opinion that the office should now be given a more substantive character than that of Assistant Secretary and they are pleased to direct that its title shall be that of 'Permanent Secretary to the Treasury'. *a* **1974** R. Crossman *Diaries* (1975) I. 25 She continued the war, capturing Fred Willey and putting him in a room by himself in our Ministry while she got hold of his new Permanent Secretary, Mr Bishop, and lectured him. **1976** H. Wilson *Governance of Britain* iv. 99 The Treasury took the lead in setting up official inter-departmental committees, some at permanent-secretary level. **1822** T. Tredgold *Pract. Ess. Strength of Cast Iron* ii. 24 The second table..is intended to show the greatest weight a beam of cast iron will bear in the middle of its length, when it is loaded with as much as it will bear, so as to recover its natural form when the load is removed. If a beam be loaded beyond that point, the equilibrium of its parts is destroyed, and it takes a permanent set. **1888** Permanent set [see set *sb.*[1] 16]. **1935** *Jrnl. R. Aeronaut. Soc.* XXXIX. 554 The highest stress in service should be below the true elastic limit of the material in order to avoid 'permanent set'. **1972** E. N. Simons *Testing of Metals* i. 21 The proof stress..is the load or stress that, applied for a minimum period of 15 min, gives a plastic extension or permanent set of 0·1% (or 0·5% with certain alloys). **1836** *Penny Cycl.* VI. 380/1 A calf has usually two front teeth when he is dropped,..these milk-teeth.. gradually wear and fall out, and are replaced by the second and permanent teeth. **1966** J. S. Cox *Illustr. Dict. Hairdressing* 110/2 *Permanent tint*, a euphemism for Permanent Dye. **1968** J. Ironside *Fashion Alphabet* 191 One very rarely hears the word 'dyeing' nowadays; it is always 'tinting'. There are permanent tints (which last through the life of the hair); semi-permanent tints [etc.]. **1904** *Rep. War Office (Reconstruction) Comm.* II. 9 in *Parl. Papers* (Cd. 1932) VIII. 101 The Council should consist of seven members—four military and three civil— with the Permanent Under-Secretary as Secretary. **1917** G. Bell *Let.* 20 July (1927) II. 420, I wish you would go and see Sir A. Hirtzel, the Permanent Under-Secretary. **1959** P. Fleming *Siege at Peking* vii. 106 The fullest account of what they did do is contained in a confidential letter written on 4 September by Sir Claude MacDonald to Mr Bertie, the Permanent Under-Secretary of State at the Foreign Office. **1974** P. Gore-Booth *With Great Truth & Respect* 324 The Permanent Under-Secretary of any department of Government is the senior official or civil servant in that department. The word 'permanent' is accurate in the sense that, if there is a change of government or of Secretary of State, you do not have to move out or even go through a formal process of resignation and reappointment. **1978** *Illustr. London News* Nov. 134/3 He certainly was an extraordinary figure—the last of the permanent under secretaries (PUS in professional jargon) to spend the whole of his effective career in Whitehall. **1909** *Hairdresser* June 6/1 Children who have undergone the X-ray treatment for ringworm are growing curly hair... Would it be possible for a lady who desires to secure a permanent wave to undergo the treatment? **1919** *Honey Pot* I. II. 1 (Advt.), Permanent waves... T. Vasco Ltd. **1922** U. Sinclair *They call me Carpenter* ix. 27 Would you like to see how we make eet—the permanent wave? **1925** *Scribner's Mag.* July 20 (Advt.), You will enjoy your permanent wave at Nestle's. **1928** *Daily Express* 23 Aug. 3/6 The curling irons and the tentacles of the permanent waver will be busier than ever in the autumn season. **1928** R. Macaulay *Keeping up Appearances* viii. 70, I want a permanent wave at twelve o'clock to-day. **1932** *Woman's Pictorial* 12 Mar. 14/2 What is a permanent wave? Answer (so far as my experience goes): a wave that is anything but permanent. **1946** *Mod. Beauty Shop* Dec. 128/2 Some hair which I permanent waved did not take the permanent. **1964** N. G. Clark *Mod. Org. Chem.* xvi. 352 If these linkages are broken (by reducing agents), the fibres bent to an artificial shape, and new disulphide linkages formed (by oxidizing agents), the fibres retain their new shape. This is the basis of 'permanent-waving' hair. **1967** O. Wynd *Walk Softly* v. 70 The Katsugis, celebrated for having dyed their long black hair bright orange, then permanent-waving it. **1968** J. Ironside *Fashion Alphabet* 196 At first permanent waving tended to give tight waves and curls, but over the past twenty years or so the tendency has been for a softer more natural looking permanent. **1975** *Times* 26 Aug. 12/8 Beauty salons..in the hectic flush of the permanent wave boom. **1838** *Mechanics' Mag.* 13 Oct. 32/2 The permanent way between Deptford High-street and the Greenwich terminus, is in a very forward state. This portion of the line is laid on longitudinal wooden sleepers, with three-feet bearing. **1842** J. Pope in *Proc. Inst. Civ. Eng.* 72 Description of the permanent way of the South-eastern railway. **1869** *Bradshaw's Railway Manual* XXI. 392 Upwards of 4,000,000 *L.* was expended in England for permanent way materials, locomotives, stores, &c., sent out from that country. **1879** E. J. Simmons *Mem. Station Master* (1974) iii. 37 The station and line were occasionally enveloped in a very thick fog. On these occasions, we were allowed to employ one of the permanent-way men to stand all night on the line beyond the signals with his hand lamp. **1888** *Times* 15 Oct. 10/2 A railway accident, causing great damage..to the permanent way. **1906** *Daily Chron.* 31 Jan. 4/5 Instructions had been issued to the permanent-way staff to adhere..to the regulations. **1926** T. E. Lawrence *Seven Pillars* vi. lxxviii. 409 It was impossible to leave them joined up to the exploder in the proper way, since the spot was evident to the permanent-way patrols as they made their rounds. **1957** J. Bledlow *Cotswolds in Colour* 47 Work was being done on the permanent way. **1967** G. F. Fiennes *I tried to run a Railway* iv. 40 They took Ticket Inspector Whipp at Liverpool Street and threw him off the platform on to the permanent way. **1973** *Railway Mag.* Mar. 129/2 Five of these engines were kept for permanent-way and shunting duties at Neasden. **1842** Francis *Dict. Arts* etc., *Permanent White*,..the sulphate of barytes, a valuable color for many purposes, as no chemical substance will decompose it or change its colours. **1854** Permanent white [see constant *a.* 4 f]. **1860** C. M. Yonge *Hopes & Fears* I. i. iv. 108 The front was all over scaffolds and cement, in all stages of colour, from rich brown to permanent white. **1934** H. Hiler *Notes Technique Painting* ii. 89 Permanent white (a special preparation of oxide of zinc prepared for oil painting).

†**2.** Of persons: Continuing steadfast *in* a course.

1432–50 tr. *Higden* (Rolls) IV. 349 The sonnes and doȝhters of the seide Nicholas were permanente [*permanserint*] in chastite alle the tyme of theire life. *a* **1548** Hall *Chron.*, *Edw. IV* 213 b, All the tounes..wer permanent and stiffe on the parte of kyng Henry.

3. *absol.* or as *sb.* **a.** ***the permanent***, that which endures or persists. **b.** A permanent person or thing. **c.** See quot. 1882.

1826 Lamb *Elia* Ser. II. *Pop. Fallacies* ii, Sharp distinctions of the fluctuating and the permanent. **1856** Dove *Logic Chr. Faith* vi. §6. 413 This spiritual life is the permanent of humanity. **1882** Caulfeild & Saward *Dict. Needlework*, *Permanents*, these are cotton cloths, of a light description, similar in texture to Turkey Cambrics; some of them have a slight glaze. They are dyed in a variety of colours, and are much employed for the trimming of dresses. **1891** H. Jones *Browning* 229 If man be..a permanent that always changes from earliest childhood to old age.

d. = *permanent wave* above.

1926 *Hairdressing* 10 Sept. 241/1 This can only be done by superior work; namely, excellent setting of the finished permanent. **1932** *New Yorker* 4 June 64/3 (Advt.), A deep-wave marcel permanent styled for you alone in the modern manner. **1939** A. Huxley *After Many a Summer* II. i. 6 Facials, Permanents, Manicures... Next door to the beauty shoppe was a Western Union office. **1941** J. C. Furnas *How Amer. Lives* 324 Twice a year she goes to a beauty shop to have a new 'permanent'. **1948** E. Waugh *Loved One* 78 Permanents, facials, wax—everything you get in a beauty parlour. **1951** E. Paul *Springtime in Paris* v. 117 Is there anything wrong with Yvette's beauty parlour..? I'm going there this afternoon—for a permanent. I hope it lasts a week. **1974** *New Yorker* 3 June 90/2 It is not uncommon for a woman to be receiving a permanent in one barber chair while a man is shaved in the other. **1976** N. Thornburg *Cutter & Bone* xii. 283 Their women were..constantly fussing with yesterday's permanents.

permanentize ('pɜːmənəntaɪz), *v.* [f. permanent *a.* (*sb.*) + -ize.] To make permanent. So **'permanentizing** *vbl. sb.*

A word of little value and rarely found in serious writing. —R.W.B.

1961 *Guardian* 20 Mar. 1/4 The latest word to be added to Pentagonese..is 'permanentise'. **1963** *Punch* 6 Nov. 665/1 The Ferrets have set about permanentising their idyll. **1966** *Ibid.* 21 Dec. 911/3 Meanwhile jeopardising our chance of permanentising the Sino-Soviet *détente*, and welding the Communist bloc more dangerously together. **1975** M. Bradbury *History Man* ii. 20 Society's technique for permanentizing the inherent contingency of relationships.. that is to say, they got married.

permanently ('pɜːmənəntlɪ), *adv.* [f. permanent *a.* (*sb.*) + -ly[2].] In a permanent manner; so as to last or continue; lastingly, enduringly; 'for good'.

1471 Ripley *Comp. Alch.* Pref. ii. in Ashm. *Theat. Chem. Brit.* (1652) 127 That Mercury teynyth permanently. **1556** J. Heywood *Spider & F.* lxxviii. 145 The feare heeld not permanentlie. **1664** H. More *Myst. Iniq.* I. I. xiv. 48 That Law which is writ in our hearts by the finger of God, durably and permanently. **1794** G. Adams *Nat. & Exp. Philos.* II. xx. 371 The changes of colour, in permanently-coloured bodies. **1880** Geikie *Phys. Geog.* iv. 196 In volcanic districts the water is often even at the boiling-point, and remains so permanently. **1885** *Geol. Mag.* Decade III. II. 516 On the depth of the permanently frozen stratum of soil in British North America. **1903** G. B. Shaw *Man & Superman* III. 103 With such a majority as mine I cannot be kept permanently out of office. **1921** *Daily Colonist* (Victoria) 18 Mar. 9/4 (Advt.), Ladies come and have your hair permanently waved... We have the latest machines and are expert in the art. **1929** A. Noyes *Return of Scare-Crow* i. 11 There were pictures of permanently waved young women, with carefully arranged flowers in their hair. **1930** J. Cannan *No Walls of Jasper* 192 She stood..with..the sun in her eyes, and the wind in her permanently-waved hair. **1959** *Housewife* June 46 Shirt and permanently-pleated skirt. **1962** *Guardian* 15 Jan. 4/4 Drip-dry, uncrushable, and permanently pleatable cottons. **1969** *Jane's Freight Containers 1968–69* 105 A new permanently-coupled articulated flat car developed by Union Pacific. **1975** G. Howell *In Vogue* 208/2 Nylon transformed the fifties wardrobe..the fake furs and the permanently pleated nightdresses.

So **'permanentness** (Bailey vol. II, 1727).

permanganate (pə'mæŋgənət). *Chem.* [f. next: see -ate[4].] A salt of permanganic acid, as ***potassium permanganate*** or ***p. of potash***, $Mn_2K_2O_8$.

1841 Brande *Chem.* (ed. 5) 725 Permanganate of Ammonia,..Permanganate of Potassa. **1856** Miller *Elem. Chem.* II. 921 Most of the permanganates are freely soluble in water. **1871** tr. *Schellen's Spectr. Anal.* xxxvi. 130 A thin layer of potassium permanganate solution. **1885** C. F. Holder *Marvels Anim. Life* 128 Permanganate of potash is the best antidote to the poison of snakes.

permanganic (pɜːmæŋ'gænɪk), *a. Chem.* [f. per- 5 b + manganic.] In ***permanganic acid***, the acid $Mn_2H_2O_8$, obtained from manganese.

1836 Brande *Chem.* (ed. 4) 635 *Permanganic Acid.* It is supposed by Mitscherlich, that the salt obtained by adding peroxide of manganese to fused chlorate of potassa,.. contains manganese in the highest state of oxidizement. **1865–72** Watts *Dict. Chem.* III. 819 Permanganate of Hydrogen, or Permanganic acid, $Mn_2H_2O_8$. **1879** *Cassell's Techn. Educ.* IV. 255/2 The ores of manganese may readily be detected by the fine red colour of permanganic acid.

†**permansible**, *a. Obs. rare*[−1]. [prob. repr. an OF. *permansible, or med.L. *permansibilis, f. L.

permans-, ppl. stem of *permanēre*: see -IBLE.] Enduring, permanent.
1500-20 DUNBAR *Poems* xxxvii 31 [He] brocht the sawlis to joy euir permansible [rimes *te'rrible*, *ho'rrible*].

†**per'mansion.** *Obs.* [ad. L. *permansiōn-em*, n. of action from *permanēre* (see PERMANENT). Cf. obs. F. *permansion* (16th c. in Godef.).] Abiding, continuance; = PERMANENCE 1.
1646 SIR T. BROWNE *Pseud. Ep.* III. xvii, From female unto male, from male to female againe, and so in a circle to both without a permansion in either. 1659 PEARSON *Creed* v. (1839) 331 This interpretation supposeth that..Hades signifieth not death itself,..but the state and condition of the dead, or their permansion in death.

permansive (pə'mænsɪv), *a.* *Gram.* [f. L. *permans-um* supine of *permanēre* to remain (see PERMANENT *a.* (*sb.*)) + -IVE.] Applied to a tense in certain languages which is used to denote a more or less permanent state.
1866 E. HINCKS in *Jrnl. R. Asiatic Soc.* Dec. 485 The verbal forms belonging to each conjugation may be divided into two great classes, which I call permansive and mutative. The former denotes continuance in the state which the verb signifies in that conjugation; the latter denotes change into that state. 1872 A. H. SAYCE *Assyrian Gram.* 52 The Assyrian verb is rich in tenses. It possesses a Permansive, or Perfect as it is generally called in Semitic grammars, of comparatively rare occurrence in the historic inscriptions, but sufficiently common in the tablets; besides four more other tenses. 1924 O. JESPERSEN *Philos. Gram.* xx. 269 It [*sc.* the perfect tense] is a present, but a permansive present: it represents the present state as the outcome of past events, and may therefore be called a retrospective variety of the present. 1939 L. H. GRAY *Foundations of Lang.* 359 In the historic period, Semitic possesses..two aspects (telic and atelic, commonly called perfect and imperfect..), to which Akkadian adds a permansive. 1972 HARTMANN & STORK *Dict. Lang. & Linguistics* 21/1 Permansive aspect expressing a permanent state as a result of a completed action etc.

permeability (ˌpɜːmiːə'bɪlɪtɪ). [f. PERMEABLE + -ITY: in F. *perméabilité* (1625 in Hatz.-Darm.).]
1. a. The quality or condition of being permeable; capability of being permeated; perviousness. Also, the degree to which a solid allows the passage of fluid through it, measured by the ***coefficient of permeability*** (or ***permeability coefficient***), the volume of fluid flowing through unit cross-section in unit time under a unit (pressure or concentration gradient).
1759 WILSON in *Phil. Trans.* LI. 328 Confirmations of the permeability of glass. 1805 W. SAUNDERS *Min Waters* 487 The permeability of the skin to heat. 1882 GEIKIE *Text-bk. Geol.* III. II. ii. §2. 351 The permeability of subterranean rocks. 1902 *Sci. Abstr.* V. 856 (*heading*) Permeability of animal membranes. *Ibid.* 857 Inactive membranes..offer but little resistance to the passage of the different ions, and the permeability does not alter by contact with the solution. 1917 *Rep. & Mem. Advisory Comm. Aeronaut.* No. 317. 4 This permeameter is readily adapted to the determination of temperature coefficients of permeability. 1920 *Ibid.* No. 360. 4 The average permeability of rubbered airship fabrics ..is not usually much less than 10 litres per sq. metre per day. 1931 *Jrnl. Gen. Physiol.* XIV. 408 This definition of permeability is seen to possess a definite physical meaning *viz.*, the number of cubic micra of water entering the cell per minute per unit area of membrane, per atmosphere of difference in osmotic pressure between interior and external medium. 1960 *Ibid.* XLIII. 523 (*heading*) Experimental study of the independence of diffusion and hydrodynamic permeability coefficients in collodion membranes. 1962 R. C. S. WALTERS *Dam Geol.* xiv. 67 The permeability [of the Oxford clay] ranged from 12×10^{-6} to $4{\cdot}1 \times 10^{-6}$ cm per sec. 1966 *McGraw-Hill Encycl. Sci. & Technol.* XII. 453/2 The permeability coefficient varies from 100 cm/sec for clean gravel to 10^{-9} cm/sec for heavy clay.
b. *magnetic* (etc.) *permeability*: see quot. 1872. (*magnetic*) *permeability*, also, one of the physical parameters of a medium, equal to the ratio of the magnetic induction B to the magnetic field strength H at any point in it; also (more fully ***relative permeability***), the ratio of the permeability of a medium to the permeability of free space; ***permeability of free space***, a constant μ_0 which in the C.G.S. electromagnetic system of units is unity and in the International System of Units is defined as a base quantity with the value $4\pi\ (12{\cdot}57) \times 10^{-7}$ henry per metre.
Of the different permeabilities mentioned in quot. 1872, the magnetic kind is the only one that has gained currency.
1872 THOMSON in *Papers Electrostatics & Magn.* 484 We have thermal permeability, a synonym for thermal conductivity; permeability for lines of electric force, a synonym for the electro-static inductive capacity of an insulator; magnetic permeability, a synonym for conducting power for lines of magnetic force. 1892 J. A. EWING *Magn. Induction* ii. 56 Prof. Knott has proposed to call this quantity the 'differential susceptibility'; similarly dB/dH may be called the differential permeability. 1896 BEDELL *Princ. of Transf.* 40 The reluctance, R, or magnetic resistance.. varies..inversely as the cross-section and permeability. 1939 L. F. BATES *Mod. Man.* ii. 67 Pure iron has an initial permeability of about 250. 1942 *Phil. Mag.* XXXIII. 488 The universal constant $1/\mathbf{a}c^2$ occurring in (12.2) has the value..$1/10^7$ ohm sec./m...and is called the permeability of empty space. Consistency practically compels us to call the constant $\mu/\mathbf{a}c^2$ in (12.3) the permeability of the medium. 1944 [see PERMITTIVITY]. 1962 CORSON & LORRAIN *Introd. Electromagn. Fields* v. 177 The constant μ_0 is called the permeability of free space and is arbitrarily taken to be exactly $4\pi \times 10^{-7}$ newton/ampere² in rationalized m.k.s. units. *Ibid.* vii. 284 Figure 7-17 shows magnetization data for several different kinds of iron, with lines of constant relative permeability indicated. The detailed shape of the magnetization curve and the maximum permeability achieved with a given sample of iron depend on the purity, the method of annealing, and on the thickness of the sheets. 1971 *Nature* 16 July 208/2 The indiscriminate use of the symbol μ..both for the permeability of free space and that of ferromagnetic materials may temporarily confuse the unwary.
2. Special Comb.: **permeability tuning** *Electronics*, tuning in which the resonant frequency of a circuit is changed by moving a magnetic core into or out of a coil forming part of it, so as to change its inductance.
1933 W. J. POLYDOROFF in *Proc. IRE* XXI. 694 The apparent inductance is increased to tune to lower frequencies by introducing a magnetic core into the field of the coil. As the core is inserted into the coil, more lines of the magnetic field are intercepted by the core, and, in effect, the average apparent permeability of the medium surrounding the coil increases from 1 (for air) to a certain maximum... For this reason, and for other reasons.., it is appropriate to describe this method as 'Permeability Tuning'. 1968 *Radio Communication Handbk.* (ed. 4) iv. 35/2 Although permeability tuning has been most successfully used for many years by one major American company, the mechanical and electrical complications involved in band-switched receivers have resulted in little progress in this field by amateur constructors.

permeabilize ('pɜːmiːəbɪlaɪz), *v.* *Biol.* [f. L. *permeābil-is* PERMEABLE *a.* + -IZE.] *trans.* To make permeable. So **'permeabilized** *ppl. a.*
1971 *Nature* 3 Dec. p. ix/2 DNA synthesis—Observation in permeabilized yeast mutants. 1973 *Developmental Biol.* XXXV. 382/2 A technique..to permeabilize eggs for cytochemical and metabolic studies. *Ibid.* 384/1 The permeabilized eggs were..very sensitive to the composition of the incubation medium. 1974 *Jrnl. Bacteriol.* CXVIII. 1186/1 Several techniques have been used to permeabilize bacterial cells.
Hence ˌ**permeabili'zation**, the action of permeabilizing.
1973 *Nature New Biol.* 2 May 18/1 The synthesis observed is due to the growth of newly initiated chains, not merely the extension of chains initiated during normal growth before permeabilization. 1973 *Developmental Biol.* XXXV. 386/2 The permeabilization of the vitelline membrane of *Drosophila* eggs with octane offers the opportunity to study the influence of different substances on development and facilitates cytochemical investigations of the egg. 1974 *Jrnl. Bacteriol.* CXVIII. 1186 A cell permeabilization procedure is described that reduces viability less than 10%.

permeable ('pɜːmiːəb(ə)l), *a.* [ad. L. *permeābilis* that can be passed through, f. *permeā-re* to PERMEATE: see -BLE. Cf. F. *perméable* (1587 in Hatz.-Darm.).]
1. Capable of being permeated or passed through; permitting the passage or diffusion of something through it; penetrable; pervious. Const. *by*, *to*. (In first quot., That can be traversed or journeyed through, passable.)
1432-50 tr. *Higden* (Rolls) I. 63 The hilles callede Caspii ..vnnethe permeable with oxen [HIGDEN *vix plaustro permeabiles*]. 1658 SIR T. BROWNE *Gard. Cyrus* iii. 56 It slides down the softer and more permeable Orifice into the Omasus or third stomack. 1773 FRANKLIN *Lett.*, etc. Wks. 1840 V. 454 Different kinds of glass, permeable or impermeable to electricity. 1858 BUSHNELL *Serm. New Life* ii. (ed. 7) 31 It is the grand distinction of humanity, that it is made permeable by the divine nature. 1893 SIR R. BALL *Story of Sun* 251 Cast steel is as permeable to ether as a grove of trees is permeable to wind.
†**2.** Capable of permeating; penetrative. *Obs.*
1661 LOVELL *Hist. Anim. & Min.* Introd., It generateth good, temperate, and permeable juyce. 1752 G. RANDOLPH *Bath Water* 53 Bath water..is withal so active and permeable as to reach the remotest parts.
Hence **'permeableness** = PERMEABILITY; **'permeably** *adv.*
1684 BOYLE *Porousn. Anim. & Solid Bod.* viii. 128 The Permeableness of ordinary Glass Vessels to Chymical Liquors. 1847 WEBSTER, *Permeably*, in a permeable manner.

permeameter (pɜːmiː'æmɪtə(r)). [f. PERMEA(BILITY + -METER.] **1.** An instrument for measuring the magnetic permeability of a substance or object.
1890 S. P. THOMPSON in *Jrnl. Soc. Arts* 12 Sept. 885/2 *Permeameter Method*, this is a method which I have myself devised for the purpose of testing specimens of iron... For carrying it out a simple instrument is needed, which I venture to denominate as a permeameter. 1931 *Bureau of Standards Jrnl. Res.* (U.S.) VI. 355 The permeameters in general use for commercial magnetic testing have an upper limit of about 300 gilberts per centimeter. 1936 C. E. WEBB in Vigoureux & Webb *Princ. Electr. & Magn. Measurements* II. xii. 309 The average magnetic properties of a non-uniform specimen may often be found more accurately in the Fahy permeameter than in permeameters dependent on the production of equality of flux or of magnetic potential at a limited number of points in the magnetic circuit. 1969 *IEEE Trans. Magnetics* V. 662/1 Straight magnetic samples are usually tested on hand compensated permeameters.
2. An instrument for measuring the permeability of a substance, esp. soil, to fluids.
1917 G. A. SHAKESPEAR in *Rep. & Mem. Advisory Comm. Aeronaut.* No. 317. 3 The following is a brief account of a permeability tester which was designed for the rapid testing of balloon and airship fabrics... The apparatus (called a 'permeameter' for short) consists of a shallow cylindrical vessel of cast iron, about 13 cm. in diameter [etc.]. 1941 D. P. KRYNINE *Soil Mech.* iii. 54 The general idea of permeameters or apparatus to determine the coefficient of permeability k in the laboratory is (*a*) to create a flow of water through a sample of a thickness L and having a definite cross section A [etc.]. 1971 B. F. CURTIS in R. E. Carver *Procedures Sedimentary Petrol.* xiv. 353 Although liquid permeameters are used when thought necessary, it is far more common to measure permeabilities using gas as the moving fluid. 1974 A. KÉZDI *Handbk. Soil Mech.* I. vi. 129/1 Constant head permeameters are particularly suited to the testing of highly pervious coarse grained soils. For soils with medium to low permeability, the falling head permeameters are used.

permeance ('pɜːmiːəns). [f. as next + -ANCE.] The fact of permeating or penetrating; in quot. 1845 *transf.* something that permeates. *spec.* in *Electr.*: see quot. 1893, and cf. PERMEABILITY b.
1845 MOZLEY *Ess.*, *Blanco White* (1878) II. 139 A First Cause, an intellectual permeance, an Anima Mundi. 1853 E. J. SHEPHERD *Lett. to Dr. Maitland* iv. 24 The permeance of his writings throughout the Churches of Christendom. 1893 O. HEAVISIDE *Electro-Magn. The.* I. ii. §31. 29 Permeability gives rise to permeance... Permeance is the reciprocal of reluctance.

permeant ('pɜːmiːənt), *a.* [ad. L. *permeānt-em*, pr. pple. of *permeāre* to pass through: see -ANT¹.] Permeating; passing or diffusing itself through something.
1646 SIR T. BROWNE *Pseud. Ep.* II. v. 85 Gold..entereth not the veynes with those electuaries, wherein it is mixed, but taketh leave of the permeant parts, at the mouthes of the miseraicks. 1839 BAILEY *Festus* xix. (1852) 297 One divine all-permeant unity. 1877 BLACKIE *Wise Men* 65 The power Of that fine flowing permeant element [water].

permease ('pɜːmɪeɪz, -s). *Biochem.* [ad. F. *perméase* (H. V. Rickenberg et al. 1956, in *Ann. de l'Inst. Pasteur* XCI. 843), f. *permé(able* PERMEABLE *a.*: see -ASE.] Any enzyme which assists the passage of a substrate into a cell through the cell wall.
1957 *Bacteriol. Rev.* XXI. 169/1 During the past few years, however, definite proof of the existence, in bacteria, of stereospecific permeation systems, functionally specialized and distinct from metabolic enzymes, has been obtained... The generic name 'permeases' has been suggested for these systems. 1970 *New Scientist* 1 Jan. 8/1 This so-called 'permease' has since been found to be a protein, located in the cell membrane, which somehow transfers lactose from the outside of the cell to the interior. 1975 D. V. PARKE *Enzyme Induction* i. 7 Maltase and maltose permease are induced together by maltose in yeast.

permeate ('pɜːmiːeɪt), *v.* [f. L. *permeāt-*, ppl. stem of *permeāre* to pass through, f. PER- 1 + *meāre* to go, pass.] *trans.* To pass, spread, or diffuse itself through; to penetrate, pervade, saturate. (Of things material or immaterial.)
1660 BOYLE *New Exp. Phys. Mech.* xvii. 120 Numbers of them [emanations] do always permeate our Air. 1695 WOODWARD *Nat. Hist. Earth* III. i. (1723) 136 This Heat.. permeating the Interstices of the Sand, Earth, or other Matter. *a* 1704 in Somers *Tracts* II. 234 All held a vital Principle that doth permeate the whole World. 1801 SOUTHEY *Thalaba* v. i, He..felt the coolness permeate every limb. 1875 *Lyell's Princ. Geol.* II. III. xli. 420 There are marvellously few species which permeate the whole of the archipelagos. 1880 T. A. SPALDING *Eliz. Demonol.* 31 This intense credulousness..permeated all classes of society.
b. *intr.* with *through*, *into*, *among*, etc.: To penetrate, diffuse itself.
1656 STANLEY *Hist. Philos.* v. (1701) 211/1 Sublunary invisible Deities, which permeate through the Elements of Matter. 1788 T. TAYLOR *Proclus* I. 64 The reasons or proportions of abundance and sterility, permeate through all the mathematical disciplines. 1863 S. WILBERFORCE *Sp. Missions* (1874) 14 Producing its own proper effect upon the heathen among whom it permeates.
Hence **'permeating** *ppl. a.*
1664 EVELYN *Sylva* xxx, [To separate] stony particles from that permeating water. 1684 BOYLE *Porousn. Anim. & Solid Bod.* iv. 37 The Penetrant, or Permeating Fumes. 1810 SOUTHEY *Kehama* VII. v, The permeating light Shed through their substance thin a varying hue.

permeation (pɜːmiː'eɪʃən). [n. of action from prec.: see -ATION.] The action of permeating or fact of being permeated; penetration; pervasion.
1623 COCKERAM, *Permeation*, a passing ouer. 1652 BP. HALL *Invis. World* I. ii, Not a meer involution only, but a spiritual permeation and inexistence. 1657 TOMLINSON *Renou's Disp.* 709 Oyl of Spike, which by its tenuity will cause better permeation for the rest. 1830 LYELL *Princ. Geol.* I. 90 The effect..of percolation by mineral waters, of permeation by elastic fluids. 1882 GEIKIE *Text-bk. Geol.* II. II. vi. 168 The permeation of water from the surface.

permeative ('pɜːmiːeɪtɪv), *a.* [f. L. *permeāt-*, ppl. stem of *permeāre* to PERMEATE + -IVE.] Having the quality of permeating; penetrative, pervasive.
1657 TOMLINSON *Renou's Disp.* 572 Camphyre..makes the Electuary more grateful and its permeative quality more efficacious. 1885 M. PATTISON *Mem.* vii. 305 [Due] to the silent permeative genius of science.

permeator ('pɜːmiːeɪtə(r)). [a. L. *permeator*, f. *permeāre* (see PERMEATE *v.*).] **1.** One who or that which permeates; in quot. 1944, ? an infiltrator.
1944 G. B. SHAW *Everybody's Pol. What's What?* xxxi. 271, I, a Fabian permeator, knew the questions and had

doctrinaire answers ready for some of them. **1969** *Ann. Rev. Plant Physiol.* XX. 602 Wartiovaara..compared the permeability constants of homologue series of permeators (e.g., alcohols..) and concluded that two parallel and alternative pathways for permeation of molecules through the protoplasm did not exist. *Ibid.*, The breaking of hydrogen bonds between permeator molecule and water during the passage of the permeator through the membrane is considered to be the important feature.

2. A vessel divided into two by a semi-permeable membrane, used in the large-scale removal of solutes from a liquid by reverse osmosis.

1975 M. J. HAMMER *Water & Waste-Water Technol.* vii. 266 In addition to the permeators, a basic reverse osmosis system consists of pretreatment pumps.., tanks and appurtenances for cleaning and flushing, and a disposal system for waste brine. *Ibid.* (*caption*) A module of 24 reverse-osmosis permeator units used to desalt a municipal ground-water supply. **1977** *Design Engin.* July 6/3 A new high-capacity permeator..can convert thousands of gallons of seawater into potable water every day.

Permian ('pɜːmɪən), *a.* (*sb.*) *Geol.* [f. *Perm*, the name of a province in Eastern Russia (now a region of the R.S.F.S.R.): see -IAN.]

1. [Named by Sir R. Murchison (1841) on account of the extensive development of these strata in the province of Perm.] Name of the uppermost division of the Palæozoic series of strata, lying below the Trias and above the Carboniferous formation, and consisting chiefly of red sandstone and magnesian limestone. Also *ellipt.* as *sb.* The Permian system, or a formation belonging to it; *pl.* = Permian strata.

1841 MURCHISON in *Lond. & Edin. Phil. Mag.* XIX. 419 The carboniferous system is surmounted, to the east of the Volga, by a vast series of beds of marls, schists, limestones, sandstones and conglomerates, to which I propose to give the name of 'Permian system'. **1847** ANSTED *Anc. World* i. 14 The periods marked by the presence of Vegetables, and the..Reptilian Animals: Permian and Carboniferous. **1854** F. C. BAKEWELL *Geol.* 40. **1866** J. JONES in *Intell. Observ.* No. 48. 437 The Permians adjoining South Staffordshire.

2. The name of the people of Perm and the language spoken by them.

1886 [see *cis-uralian* adj. s.v. CIS- 1.]. **1908** T. G. TUCKER *Introd. Nat. Hist. Lang.* 132 Permian, embracing Permian proper, Siryenian and Votiak. These are spoken by sparse populations near the Urals in the E.N.E. of European Russia. **1932** W. L. GRAFF *Lang.* 405 Permian, with its two varieties Zyrian and Votyak. **1933** L. BLOOMFIELD *Lang.* 68 Four further branches of the Finno-Ugrian stock... Permian, consisting of Votyak and Zyrian. **1961** L. F. BROSNAHAN *Sounds of Lang.* viii. 177 The languages of this family.., Permian, Votyak.

Permic ('pɜːmɪk), *a.* [f. as prec. + -IC.] = PERMIAN *a.* (*sb.*)

Permian is the more usual term.

1921 A. W. GRABAU *Textbk. Geol.* II. xxxviii. 506 (*heading*) The Permian or Permic system. **1964** *Language* XL. 96 Komi..and Udmurt..comprise the Permic group of the Uralic family. **1967** *Ural-Altaische Jahrbücher* XXXIX. 163 (*title*) Split, shift and merger in the Permic vowels.

permillage (pə'mɪlɪdʒ). [f. PER *prep.* + L. *mille*, F. *mille*, thousand + -AGE, after PERCENTAGE.] Rate per thousand; an amount reckoned as so much in the thousand.

1886 *Jrnl. Anthropol. Inst.* XV. 363 We cannot assume from this list that..where Jews have a higher 'permillage' they produce more experts per million in that branch. **1900** *Fortn. Rev.* Jan. 62 It should, perhaps, be remarked that I have reduced Dr. Galton's results to permillages. **1960** *Amer. Mineralogist* XLV. 6 (*caption*) The structure of perrierite projected on (010). The numbers give the *y*-parameters as permillage of the *b*-length. **1967** *Oceanogr. & Marine Biol.* V. 152 See Table VII, in which enrichment of ^{18}O is expressed in terms of $\delta^{18}O$, the permillage enrichment relative to Standard Mean Ocean Water.

permineralization (pə,mɪnərəlaɪ'zeɪʃən). *Geol.* [f. PER-¹ + MINERALIZATION.] The action or result of fossilization by the deposition of minerals from solution in the interstices of hard tissue. Hence **per'mineralize** *v. trans.*, **-'mineralized** *ppl. a.*

1893 C. A. WHITE in *Rep. U.S. Nat. Museum 1892* 264 There are seven different natural conditions in which fossil remains are recognizable, three of which relate to substance, three to form, and one to both. To those relating to substance I have applied the terms permineralization, histometabasis, and carbonization... The term permineralization applies to that condition of fossil remains of animals which differ least from their original condition as parts of living animals. **1915** C. SCHUCHERT *Text-bk. Geol.* II. xvii. 436 The great majority of fossil specimens preserve more or less of the original hard or mineral substance of the individual plant or animal, and to this may have been added in the organic interstices more or less of other mineral substances during the process of fossilization, forming the permineralized fossils. **1952** R. C. MOORE et al. *Invertebr. Fossils* i. 4/1 Shells and bones, which are somewhat porous, may be made more dense by deposition of mineral substances by ground water. Hard parts altered in this way are permineralized; the process of alteration is termed permineralization or petrifaction. **1958** C. L. & M. A. FENTON *Fossil Bk.* i. 5 This process [*sc.* petrification]..takes place in two related ways. The simpler, termed permineralization, takes place when fat and other organic substances decay while water containing dissolved mineral matter soaks into every cavity and pore of hard—especially limy—structures. *Ibid.* 7 (*caption*) Permineralized corals that preserve both shape and structure. **1979** *Nature* 19 Oct. 640/2 Microfossils detected in the upper Brioverian dolomitic limestones..are permineralised in carbonate rather than silica.

perminvar ('pɜːmɪnvɑː(r)). Also **Perminvar**. [f. PERM(EABILITY + INVAR(IABLE *a.* (*sb.*)] Any of a series of alloys containing nickel, iron, and cobalt which have an approximately constant magnetic permeability over a range of field strengths.

The name is proprietary in the U.S.

1928 *Official Gaz.* (U.S. Patent Office) 12 June 277/1 Western Electric Company..N.Y. Filed Nov. 8, 1927. Perminvar..For ferromagnetic alloys comprising nickel, iron, and cobalt. Claims use since Aug. 23, 1927. **1928** G. W. ELMEN in *Jrnl. Franklin Inst.* CCVI. 318 We have chosen 'perminvar' as the name for alloys in the iron-cobalt-nickel series, which are characterized, when properly heat treated, by constancy of permeability for a considerable range of the lower part of the magnetization curve. **1939** *Chem. Abstr.* XXXIII. 6775 Rapidly cooled Perminvar (45% Ni, 30% Fe, 25% Co) exhibits a clear increase in specific heat over a rather broad temp. range. **1962** N. H. CODLING in G. A. T. Burdett *Automatic Control Handbk.* viii. 21 Perminvar, comprising nickel, cobalt and iron, subjected to heat treatment, has nearly constant permeability for inductions below 1000 G. **1968** S. J. ROSENBERG *Nickel & its Alloys* 131/2 Useful alloys in the Perminvar class include the nickel-iron-alloys Conpernik (50% Ni) and Isoperm (40% Ni).

permirific (pɜːmaɪ'rɪfɪk), *a.* [ad. med.L. *permirific-us*: see PER- 4 and MIRIFIC.] Very wonderful or marvellous.

1868 KINGSLEY *Hermits* 314 By the permirific sweetness of the harmony, an exceeding operation of sacred virtue is perceived more manifestly to spring forth [transl. *Reginald's Life St. Godric* (*a* 1200) i. Permirifica harmoniæ dulcedine.]

†**per'miscible**, *a. Obs. rare*⁻¹. [f. L. *permiscēre* to mix thoroughly (see PERMISTION) + -IBLE.] Capable of being thoroughly mixed.

1477 NORTON *Ord. Alch.* v. in Ashm. *Theat. Chem. Brit.* (1652) 58 Fier..causeth matters permiscible to be. **1656** in BLOUNT *Glossogr.* Hence in PHILLIPS, BAILEY, JOHNSON, etc.

‖**permis de séjour** (pɛrmi də seʒur). [Fr.] Permission to stay in a country; a permit allowing this, a residence permit. Also *fig.*

1884 A. FORBES *Chinese Gordon* iv. 130 All persons residing in Darjour must have a *permis de séjour*. **1885** W. JAMES *Lit. Remains H. James* 14 The ordinary empirical ethics of evolutionary naturalism can find a perfect *permis de séjour* under the system's wings. **1923** *Michelin Guide Gt. Brit.* (ed. 7) 861 Passengers not of French nationality must present themselves to the local authorities to obtain a 'Permis de séjour' if staying in France over 14 days. **1951** E. AMBLER *Judgment on Deltchev* xviii. 219, I propose to have your visa and *permis de séjour* cancelled. **1960** O. MANNING *Great Fortune* xxiv. 256 Should his *permis de séjour* be cancelled, Foxy or Fitzsimon would see that it was renewed. **1972** J. AIKEN *Butterfly Picnic* iv. 65, I will see that your *permis de séjour* is extended.

†**per'mise**, *v. Obs.* In 5 -yse. [app. f. F. *permis-e*, pa. pple. of *permettre* to PERMIT: cf. COMMISE, also *premise*, *promise*.] = PERMIT *v.*

1456 SIR G. HAYE *Law Arms* (S. T. S.) 285 Quhat casis ar tholit and permysit at the plesance of princis. **1481** CAXTON *Myrr.* III. viii. 145 This consenteth and permyseth he that is almyghty. **1491** —— *Vitas Patr.* (W. de W. 1495) v. xiv. 343 b/2 He sholde be permysed to entre in to the chirche.

†**per'miss**. *Obs. rare*⁻¹. [app. ad. L. *permiss-us*, f. ppl. stem of *permittĕre* to PERMIT.] ? Leave, permission.

1643 MILTON *Divorce* II. i, Christ meant not to be taken word for word, but like a wise physician, administering one excess against another, to reduce us to a permiss.

permissible (pə'mɪsɪb(ə)l), *a.* [a. OF. *permissible* (15th c. in Godef.) = It. *permissibile*, prob. ad. med.L. *permissibilis*, f. *permiss-*, ppl. stem of *permittĕre* to PERMIT.] That can or ought to be permitted; allowable; *permissible dose* (see quot. 1954).

1426 LYDG. *De Guil. Pilgr.* 10840 Yt ys at alle tymes Permyssyble to pylgrymes To bern A skryppe & ek a staff. **1656** BLOUNT *Glossogr.*, *Permissible*, which may be permitted or suffered. **1755** in JOHNSON. **1832** AUSTIN *Jurispr.* (1879) I. xii. 365 Sanction is not of the essence of permissible law. **1848** MILL *Pol. Econ.* I. 88 They may think such conduct permissible. **1874** GREEN *Short Hist.* viii. §1. 455 A course of doctrine and discipline, from which no variation was legally permissible. **1954** *Brit. Jrnl. Radiol.* XXVII. 245/2 Permissible dose is defined as that dose of ionizing radiation that, in the light of present knowledge, is not expected to cause appreciable bodily injury to a person at any time during his lifetime. **1960** *Lebende Sprachen* V. 163/2 The pilots who fly the modern airplane are subjected to a rather heavy dose (very close to the permissible dose) from the self-illuminating control-instruments.

Hence **permissi'bility**, **per'missibleness**, the quality of being permissible, allowableness; **per'missibly** *adv.*, in a permissible way, as may be permitted, allowably.

1727 BAILEY vol. II, *Permissibleness.* **1846** WORCESTER cites DR. ALLEN for *Permissibly.* **1882** OGILVIE cites *Eclec. Rev.* for *Permissibility.* **1882–3** *Schaff's Encycl. Relig. Knowl.* I. 35 The ages of permissibility. **1892** *Times* 3 Aug. 7/3 If his rendering of the word was not quite what is understood by it.., it was permissibly near.

permission (pə'mɪʃən). [ad. L. *permissiōn-em*, n. of action from *permittĕre* to PERMIT. Cf. F. *permission* (1539 in R. Estienne), It. *permissione.*]

1. The action of permitting or giving leave; allowance; liberty or licence granted to do something; leave.

1432–50 tr. *Higden* (Rolls) II. 211 Thei may thro the permission of God [*Deo permittente*] transfigurate similitudes. *Ibid.* 427 The permission and sufferaunce of God. **1537** CROMWELL in Merriman *Life & Lett.* (1902) II. 110 The permyssyon of hym to haue suche a Scope to worke myschyffes at his pleasur. **1560** DAUS tr. *Sleidane's Comm.* 78 b, The same was done by my leave and permission. **1601** SHAKS. *Jul. C.* III. i. 247. **1671** MILTON *P.R.* I. 496 Do as thou find'st Permission from above. **1777** SHERIDAN *Sch. Scand.* III. i, Stanley has obtained permission to apply personally to his friends. **1834** L. RITCHIE *Wand. by Seine* 151 Proceeds of a sale of permissions to eat butter during Lent. **1872** GEO. ELIOT *Middlem.* I. v, I have your guardian's permission to address you.

†**2.** Giving up, abandonment. *Obs. rare*⁻¹.

1677 GALE *Crt. Gentiles* II. III. 25 By God's secret judicial dereliction and permission of them.

3. *attrib.* †**permission cap (bonnet)**, ? a cap permitted to be worn on occasions or in places where it was proper to be uncovered, ? a skull-cap; **permission ship**, a ship having permission or licence to enter a port otherwise closed.

1722 RAMSAY *Three Bonnets* I. 21 Here's three *permission bonnets for ye. **1685** *Lond. Gaz.* No. 2031/1 His Majesties High Commissioner..in his return..having the High Constable on his right hand and the Great Marshall on his left, with *Permission Caps and in their Robes. **1690** *Ibid.* No. 2564/4 A Guinea Negro Boy,..on his head a black Cloth Permission Cap,..strayed away.., on the 3d instant. **1667** *Cal. St. Papers, Dom.* 563 A French *permission ship of 300 tons came in [to Deal] with linen, and is gone up to London. **1698** LUTTRELL *Brief Rel.* (1857) IV. 360 The house of commons, in a committee on the African trade, resolved, that the company should have liberty to trade..and that all permission ships or interlopers shall pay to the company 10£. per cent. before they trade thither.

permissioned (pə'mɪʃənd), *a. rare.* [f. prec. + -ED².] Having permission granted; doing something by permission.

1770 J. CLUBBE *Misc. Tracts, Physiogn.* etc. I. 94 Permission'd dedicators I look upon in the light of private taylors, who carry home suits of virtues, as the others do suits of cloaths. **1819** WIFFEN *Aonian Hours* (1820) 140 Such two may meet no more permissioned and alone.

permissive (pə'mɪsɪv), *a.* [a. OF. *permissif*, *-ive*, f. L. *permiss-*, ppl. stem of *permittĕre* to PERMIT: see -IVE.]

1. Having the quality of permitting or giving permission; that allows something to be done or to happen; not forbidding or hindering. In modern use freq.: tolerant, liberal, allowing freedom, *spec.* in sexual matters; freq. in phr. *permissive society*. Hence as *sb.*, a permissive person.

permissive bill: *spec.* a bill, introduced into Parliament several times between 1864 and 1877, having as its object to give to each parish the right to refuse the issue of licences to sell intoxicating liquors: the 'local option' movement is a later development of the principle of the bill.

1603 SHAKS. *Meas. for M.* I. iii. 38 When euill deedes haue their permissiue passe. **1646** S. BOLTON *Arraignm. Err.* 18 God would by this permissive providence of his, have us take heed as well what we heare, as how we heare. **1664** H. MORE *Apol.* VII. Aph. v. 537 This command is not a Positive but a Permissive command. **1808** BENTHAM *Sc. Reform* 112 Was it not meant that it should be, in the first instance, imperative upon somebody, and then eventually permissive to somebody else? **1832** LEWIS *Use & Ab. Pol. Terms* 36 Permissive legislation as in the case of legal rules established by courts of justice. **1865** *Morn. Star* 6 July, An Elector asked Mr. Mill if he was in favour of the Permissive Bill. **1887** CAYLEY *Coll. Math. Papers* XII. 434 This result..may contain only integer powers of $z - c$..and we then say that the point on the curve is a 'permissive' point. Or it may contain fractional powers of $z - c$..and we then say that the point..is a 'prohibitive' point. **1934** *Sun* (Baltimore) 25 May 6/2 All he asked was that the 'permissive' features of the pay-off provisions be made 'directive'. Later he explained that this would mean simply that the FDIC be 'authorized and directed' instead of 'authorized and empowered' to appraise the assets of the closed banks. **1946** *Amer. Psychologist* I. 416/2 If the counselor creates a warm and permissive atmosphere in which the individual is free to bring out any attitudes and feelings which he may have [etc.]. **1956** C. A. TONSOR in *Clearing House* XXX. v. 289, I realize that in the face of the permissive tendencies of the age, there is not much respect for rules. **1967** *Punch* 15 Mar. 372/2 If, in the nineteenth century, sadists in mortar-boards, and often in dog-collars also, belaboured little Johnny's bottom in order to knock Latin grammar into his head, some of today's jeans-and-gimmicks permissives may go too far the other way. **1968** *Listener* 4 Jan. 18/3 This dreadful dilemma of the puritan in a permissive society. **1970** *Times* 5 Feb. 9 It [*sc.* a proposal for a world-wide cricket tour] also irritates the extreme cricket-establishment people, some of whom seem to relish the thought of the tour, barbed wire and truncheons and all, to show that they are not going to be dictated to by the long-haired permissives. **1970** G. GREER *Female Eunuch* 45 The permissive society has done much to neutralize sexual drives by containing them. **1971** *Publ. Amer. Dial. Soc. 1969* LII. 14 Americans tend to be permissive in matters of pronunciation and vocabulary. **1971** J. WAINWRIGHT *Last Buccaneer* II. 106 He was nineteen years old and there are few nineteen-year-old male virgins in the permissive age. **1972** *Guardian* 6 July

14/1 The charge against the permissive society is that the controls have slipped: things are being permitted that ought not to be permitted. **1976** U. HOLDEN *String Horses* ix. 106 My kiddies all have their Daddies. My Herb belongs to Jim. I'm not permissive. **1976** F. ZWEIG *New Acquisitive Society* I. v. 47 The prevailing ethic of today is the ethos of the permissive society. **1977** *Time* 10 Oct. 24/3 Neither a cajoling arm twister like Lyndon Johnson nor a permissive parent like mild-mannered Mike Mansfield, Byrd is distinguished by his ability to gauge correctly what a majority of the Senate wants.

2. Permitted, allowed; not forbidden or hindered; done, or acting, under permission or on sufferance; that may or may not be done, optional.

permissive waste (*Law*): waste that is allowed to happen by neglect of repairs.

c **1420** LYDG. *Assembly of Gods* 1731 The dedely enemy of mankynde, By hys power permyssyue, entryd the ymages Withyn the temples. **1586** FERNE *Blaz. Gentrie* 239 For that which is lawfull with Kings is not permissiue to subjects. **1667** MILTON *P.L.* VIII. 435 Thus I embolden'd spake, and freedom us'd Permissive, and acceptance found. **1790** BURKE *Fr. Rev.* 319 At present the officers are known at best to be only permissive, and on their good behaviour. **1818** CRUISE *Digest* (ed. 2) I. 266 Tenant for years is also punishable for permissive waste. **1971** *Mod. Law Rev.* XXXI. 698 A student who uses a conventional law textbook may be excused if he gains the impression that much of his professional career will be spent in advising about perpetuities, permissive waste and the principal mansion house.

3. Expressing permission or exhortation: applied to the verbal mood which expresses permission or an exhortation. Also as quasi-*sb.*

1845 [see ADHORTATIVE *a.*]. **1892** H. SWEET *New Eng. Gram.* I. 108 The combination of *may* and its preterite *might* with the infinitive (*may see, might see*) is called the permissive mood, as in *may you be happy!* **1898** *Ibid.* II. 116 Thus the present permissive is used in independent sentences to express wish: *may you succeed!* **1924** O. JESPERSEN *Philos. Gram.* xxiii. 320 As a tentative scheme of the purely notional ideas expressed more or less vaguely by the verbal moods and auxiliaries of various languages we might perhaps give the following list... 1. Containing an element of will... Permissive: you may go if you like. **1955** J. L. AUSTIN *How to do Things with Words* (1962) xii. 158 In the special case of permissives we might ask whether they should be classified as exercitives or as commissives. **1976** J. S. GRUBER *Lexical Struct. Syntax & Semantics* I. vi. 167 *Let* can be used as a fairly general Permissive Agent of Motion.

Hence **per'missively** *adv.*, in a permissive way, by permission; **per'missiveness**, the quality or fact of being permissive.

1622 BACON *Holy War* Misc. Wks. (1629) 108 To heare it spoken to concerning the Lawfulnesse, not only permissiuely, but whether it be not obligatory. **1835** GLADSTONE *Let. to Pusey* in Liddon, etc. *Life Pusey* (1893) I. xiii. 306 It would give me pleasure to see Dissenters avail themselves, permissively, but to the utmost practicable extent, of our Church education. **1837** SYD. SMITH *Let. to Archd. Singleton* Wks. 1859 II. 278/1 There is in the declaration a permissiveness and good humour which in public men has seldom been exceeded. **1876** GEO. ELIOT *Dan. Der.* xlviii, She threw a royal permissiveness into her way of saying [etc.]. **1946** *Amer. Psychologist* I. 420/2 When genuine acceptance and permissiveness are your tools it requires nothing less than the whole complete personality. **1958** B. SPOCK *Baby & Child Care* (new ed.) 56 *Strictness or permissiveness?*.. This looms as a big question for many new parents. **1966** *Listener* 6 Oct. 492/2 Permissiveness can rarely have gone further than it does today, and it may be.. that we shall soon be due for a reaction, and a return to stricter standards. **1969** J. MANDER *Static Society* ix. 303 The *permissiveness* of Brazilian society is an important element in her reputation for tolerance in racial and social matters. **1971** *Daily Tel.* 21 July 14 Perhaps it is time..for Parliament to have another look at the whole subject of abortion, family planning and perhaps permissiveness in general. **1973** M. AMIS *Rachel Papers* 130 The so-called new philosophy, 'permissiveness' if you like, seen from the right perspective, is only a new puritanism, whereby you're accused of being repressed or unenlightened if you happen to object to infidelity, promiscuity, and so on. **1974** F. WARNER *Meeting Ends* II. i. 35 With the new laws I suppose we've priced ourselves out of the marriage market. With 'permissiveness' a man can have it all, so why should he take on a bloodsucking estate as well?

permissivism (pə'mɪsɪvɪz(ə)m). [f. PERMISSIV(E *a.* + -ISM.] Attitudes or beliefs that are regarded as excessively tolerant or permissive.

1968 *Manch. Guardian Weekly* 17 Oct. 3 But the most impressive tributes to 'the high priest of permissivism', as he [*sc.* Benjamin Spock] once described himself, were casual. Not a single baby cried during the 90 minutes of protest. **1972** *Sat. Rev.* (U.S.) 20 May 30/2 Permissivism—i.e., the notion that all art is good art, etc.

permissivist (pə'mɪsɪvɪst). [f. PERMISSIV(E *a.* + -IST.] A person considered excessively indulgent toward generally unacceptable or unconventional behaviour or attitudes, *spec.* in sexual matters.

1966 *Times* 16 Feb. 13 Theatrical permissivists should ask themselves whether, if there must be censorship, it is not better from their point of view that it should remain with a rationally indefensible institution, which is in no position to enforce for long unpopular or unjustifiable standards. **1970** [see PABLUM]. **1972** *Daily Tel.* 13 Apr. 8/6 Since sex is a mere function away from all feeling it may be discussed, say the permissivists, in whatever detail, without anyone suffering any harm. **1973** *Church Times* 16 Nov. 9 The permissivists meanwhile demand..evidence, confident that it is.. unobtainable.

permissory (pə'mɪsərɪ), *a. rare*⁻¹. [f. L. *permiss-* (see PERMISSIVE *a.*) + -ORY.] = PERMISSIVE 2.

1862 *Lond. Rev.* 16 Aug. 137 The advantages of this permissory choice are obvious.

†**per'mistion.** *Obs.* [ad. L. *permistiōn-em* (var. of *permixtiōnem*), in F. *permistion* (Paré 1560), It. *permistione* 'a through-mixing' (Florio).] An occasional variant of PERMIXTION.

1615 CROOKE *Body of Man* 277 Seede is..made of the permistion of the surplusage of the last Aliment and of the influent or errant spirits. **1674** BOYLE *Excell. Theol.* II. iii. 148 Because of the intimate union, and, as it were, permistion..of the soul with the body.

permit (pə'mɪt), *v.* [ad. L. *permittĕre* to let go, give up, surrender, allow, suffer, permit, f. PER-1, 3 + *mittĕre* to let go, let loose, send: perh. after F. *permettre*, 13th c. *parmetre* (Godef.), 14th c. *permetre* (Littré); It. *permettere*, in same sense.]

I. To allow, suffer, give leave; not to prevent.

1. *trans.* With the action or fact as object: To admit or allow the doing or occurrence of; to give leave or opportunity for. With simple obj., obj. cl., or inf.; sometimes also with indirect obj. (dat.) of agent (with or without *to*).

1489 CAXTON *Faytes of A.* III. xii. 192 To a man in deffense is permytted to hurt another. **1538** STARKEY *England* I. iv. 113 The law doth command no such intaylyng, but permyttyth hyt only. **1539** BIBLE (Great) *1 Cor.* xiv. 34 It is not permitted vnto them to speake. **1596** DALRYMPLE tr. *Leslie's Hist. Scot.* I. 117 He permitis, that in general parleaments twa or thrie of thame be present. **1697** POTTER *Antiq. Greece* I. iv. (1715) 14 It being permitted any Man.. to make an Appeal to the People. *a* **1700** DRYDEN (J.), Age ..permits not that our mortal members..should retain the vigour of our youth. **1848** THACKERAY *Van. Fair* liv, Sir Pitt ..would by no means permit the introduction of Sunday papers into his household. **1856** FROUDE *Hist. Eng.* I. iii. 183 Appeals were permitted only from one ecclesiastical court to another. **1866** HOWELLS *Venet. Life* iii. 34, I permit myself, throughout this work, the use of [etc.].

2. a. With the agent, etc. as direct object: To allow, give leave to (a person or thing) *to do* (or undergo) something. With inf. act. or pass. (rarely without *to*); sometimes *ellipt.* with simple obj.

1514 BARCLAY *Cyt. & Uplondyshm.* (Percy Soc.) 22 No law permytteth, nor wylleth man..To commyt mordre. **1526** TINDALE *Acts* xxvi. 1 Thow arte permitted to speake for thy silfe. **1594** WILLOBIE *Avisa* L j b, When tyme permits you not to talke. **1614** JACKSON *Creed* III. xxv. §4 To permit malefactors trauerse the equitie of publique lawes. **1640** HABINGTON *Queen of Arragon* II, Will you permit The Generall kneele so long? **1748** *Anson's Voy.* II. vi. 205 They had been permitted to wait on him. **1766** GOLDSM. *Vic. W.* xii, Nothing could prevail upon her to permit me from home. **1771** *Junius Lett.* l. (1772) II. 195 Permit me to recommend him to your Grace's protection. **1881** HENTY *Cornet of Horse* x. (1888) 97 Words..which Sir William had in his anger permitted himself to use.

b. *refl.* with *in*: To allow oneself to indulge in or commit; not to refrain from. (Cf. ALLOW 9.)

1678 H. MORE *Lett.* (1694) 29 Whoever permits himself in any sin..is his own Prison and Jailour. **1849** FROUDE *Nemesis of Faith* 79 Having..never permitted themselves in extravagance. **1870** RUSKIN *Lect. Art* (1875) 96 They will permit themselves in awkwardness, they will permit themselves in ugliness.

3. a. *absol.* or *intr.* To give leave or opportunity; to allow; (usually in subord. cl. with *as* or *if*); *spec.* in phr. ***weather permitting***, if the weather permits or allows, and in similar phrases.

1553 EDEN *Treat. Newe Ind.* (Arb.) 32 As..they presupposed the roundenesse of the earth would permitte. **1612** BRINSLEY *Lud. Lit.* ix. (1627) 147 To examine over all the noted words, as time permits. **1818** CRUISE *Digest* (ed. 2) IV. 412 As far as the law would in that case allow or permit. **1840** C. BROWN in H. E. Rollins *Lett. J. Keats* (1958) I. i. 422 'Weather permitting', unless of the bad and excessive kind, was not of much force in our agreement. **1895** J. W. BUDD in *Law Times* XCIX. 544/2 A matter on which, had time permitted, I should have been glad to have said something. **1922** JOYCE *Ulysses* 611 It was not so dear, purse permitting, a few guineas at the outside, considering the fare to Mullingar where he figured on going was five and six there and back. **1957** R. W. ZANDVOORT *Handbk. Eng. Gram.* I. ii. 36 Compare also the phrase *weather permitting*, where the meaning implied is one of condition. [*Note*] Also *funds permitting*, and similar combinations. **1978** T. ALLBEURY *Lantern Network* iii. 32 Arms..will be dropped to your instructions, weather permitting.

b. *intr.* with *of*: To allow of, admit of.

1860 TYNDALL *Glac.* I. xii. 87 The crack was not wide enough to permit of the entrance of my finger nail. **1875** E. WHITE *Life in Christ* IV. xxvi. (1878) 426 It consisted with the Divine wisdom to permit..of the corruption of patriarchal theology into pantheism and world-wide idolatry.

II. †**4.** *trans.* To put, or allow to pass, out of one's own keeping or power into that of another (or of some force, influence, etc.); to commit, submit, hand over; to give up, resign, leave; to refer (to the will of). Const. *to* (*unto*). *Obs.*

1545 JOYE *Exp. Dan.* Ded. A iv b, Whiche my labours I permytte to the judgement of the godly & learned. **1614** RALEIGH *Hist. World* v. v. §7. 691 That..they should wholly permit themselves to the good pleasure of the Senate. **1667** MILTON *P.L.* XI. 554 What thou livst Live well, how long or short permit to Heav'n. **1725** POPE *Odyss.* IX. 403 He..then permits their udder to the lambs. **1802** PALEY *Nat. Theol.* xxvi. (1819) 457 There are advantages in permitting events to chance.

†**5.** To leave undone, unused, etc.; to let pass, let slip, pass by, pass over, pretermit, omit. *Obs.*

1566 PAINTER *Pal. Pleas.* (1813) II. 177 Shee, good gentlewoman, woulde permyt no duetye..unperformed. **1588** GREENE *Pandosto* (1607) 38 If they permitted this good weather, they might staye long yer they had such a faire winde. **1692** *Narr. Earl Nottingham*, Not to leave it possible to be objected to him that he had permitted any-thing that might prevent the escape of the French ships.

permit ('pɜːmɪt, *formerly* pə'mɪt), *sb.* [f. PERMIT *v.* (with later shifting of stress: Bailey, Johnson, Webster 1828 have *per'mit*).]

1. A written order giving permission to do something, a warrant, a licence; esp. one permitting the landing or removal of dutiable or excisable goods.

1714 *Fr. Bk. of Rates* 122 The Goods shall be again visited ..and the Sufferance or Permit shall be examined by the Clarks of the Office. **1745** P. THOMAS *Jrnl. Anson's Voy.* 299 Here we lay..not having a Permit from the *Chautuck*, which Permit they call a *Chop*. **1860** *Merc. Marine Mag.* VII. 157 Vessels are not allowed to leave..the..Dock until they have presented their permits to the..Dock Master. **1864** KNIGHT *Passages Work. Life* I. 72 The liquor-merchant did not dare to send out a dozen of wine or a gallon of spirits without a permit. **1884** *Times* (weekly ed.) 10 Oct. 13/1 The Serf was required to carry a written permit or passport.

attrib. and *Comb.* **1737** J. CHAMBERLAYNE *St. Gt. Brit.* II. 86 Eighteen Permit Writers in Excise, Coffee, Tea, etc. **1774** in *14th Rep. R. Comm. Hist. Manuscripts* App. x. 393 in *Parl. Papers 1895* (C. 7883) LIX. 1 Have coaxed the people to part with their money and give paper in return to keep up armies of placemen, permit men, custom house officers, pensioners and soldiers. **1901** *Daily Chron.* 4 Dec. 5/3 Permits issued by the South African Permit Office..will be necessary for all persons landing in South Africa. **1921** *Daily Colonist* (Victoria, B.C.) 11 Mar. 4/1 It will be a method of checking bootlegging, and preventing those who are not permit-holders from coming into possession of liquor. **1926** T. E. LAWRENCE *Seven Pillars* v. lvii. 300 A mixed body of Egyptian and British military police came round the train... It was proper to make war on permit-men, so I replied crisply. **1933** *Brit. Birds* XXVII. 138 Last year and again this year, this colony was wiped out,..and so permit-holders visited the colonies on the gravel bed instead. **1945** *Seafarers' Log* 13 Apr. 7/1 To members in full standing, who bring in their friends for permit cards, study the last weeks LOG on the Agents Conference pertaining to permit men. **1977** *Evening Gaz.* (Middlesbrough) 11 Jan. 14/5 But it will not affect last year's winner, Tsuru, one of two representatives for Somerset permit-holder and wholesale butcher Tony Cobden who has also declared Rio.

2. Permission, leave (esp. formally given). (In first quot. *fig.* from 1. In uses like those in quots. *a* 1816, 1885, sometimes stressed *per'mit*.)

c **1730** FIELDING *Rape upon Rape* IV. vii, He that would sin with impunity must have thy permit. **1733** *Pol. Ballads* (1860) II. 238 For sure 'tis unjust as well as unfit We should sell our own goods without their permit. *a* **1816** BENTHAM *Offic. Apt. Maximized, Introd. View* (1830) 14 If the fraternity of lawyers..could not find adequate inducement for giving it their permit. **1885** in *Law Times* LXXVIII. 393/2 The rank of Q. C. is..merely a permit to a barrister to do a certain kind of barristerial work.

†**per'mittable, -ible**, *a. Obs.* [f. PERMIT *v.* + -ABLE, -IBLE: cf. ADMITTABLE, COMMITTABLE.] = PERMISSIBLE.

1574 HELLOWES *Gueuara's Fam. Ep.* (1577) 355 It is not permittible for any man to bee iudge of himselfe. **1753** *Scots Mag.* Mar. 116/1 Neutral [ships] upon which the Prussians had laden permittable merchandize.

†**per'mittance.** *Obs.* [f. PERMIT *v.* + -ANCE: cf. ADMITTANCE.] **1.** = PERMISSION 1.

1580 H. GIFFORD *Gilloflowers* Ep. Ded. (Grosart) 27 Hauing by your Worships fauourable permittance, conuenient oportunity in your seruice. *a* **1653** GOUGE *Comm. Heb.* vi. 3 Our purposes must be submitted to Gods permittance. **1713** DERHAM *Phys. Theol.* v. v. (1727) 296 When this System of Air comes, by Divine Permittance, to be corrupted with poisonous, acrimonious Steams. **1912** *Housemaster's Lett.* 124 The wilful misuse of them or the callous permittance of them to go blunt and to rust.

2. *Physics.* = CAPACITANCE.

1887 O. HEAVISIDE in *Electrician* 3 June 79/2 A telegraph circuit, when reduced to its simplest elements,..still has no less than four electrical constants, which may be most conveniently reckoned per unit length of circuit—viz., its resistance, inductance, permittance, or electrostatic capacity, and leakage conductance. **1890** [see ELASTANCE]. **1908** *Jrnl. Inst. Electr. Engin.* XL. 58 Dr. Heaviside's permittivity..is measured in terms of the permittance of unit volume.

permitted (pə'mɪtɪd), *ppl. a.* [f. as prec. + -ED¹.] **a.** Allowed; not forbidden or hindered.

1704 H. WARING (*title*) The Access to Virtue; or, Permitted Approach of a Court Penitent to the Divine Astrea. **1790** HAN. MORE *Relig. Fash. World* 138 An habit of self-denial in permitted pleasures easily induces a victory over such as are unlawful. **1877** FROUDE *Short Stud.* (1883) IV. 114 He indulged his natural inclinations at all permitted times.

b. ***permitted hours***: the hours during which the sale of intoxicating liquor is legal.

1923 W. B. CAPPER *Licensed Houses* III. lxxii. 211 In Wales and Monmouthshire, however, there are no permitted hours for licensed premises on Sundays. **1946** H. DUGDALE *Managem. of Public-House* x. 67 Occasionally, the permitted hours applicable to a public-house do not sufficiently meet the requirements of the neighbourhood wherein the 'house' is situated. **1964** V. HEATON *Pub of your Own* xvi. 115 Though licensed premises may not sell intoxicating liquor after the permitted hours, nor may it be consumed later than ten minutes after permitted hours, there is no compulsion either to close the premises or to hide any display of liquor.

Hence **per'mittedly** *adv.*, allowedly.

1824 T. S. MULOCK in *N. & Q.* 9th Ser. VII. 501/1 The force..of the Satanic craft permittedly practised upon you.

permittee (pɜːmɪ'tiː). [f. as prec. + -EE.] A person to whom something is (formally) permitted; the recipient or holder of a permit.

1846 in WORCESTER, citing RITCHIE.

permitter (pə'mɪtə(r)). [f. as prec. + -ER[1].] One who permits or allows.

c **1643** *Maximes Unfolded* 30 [They] make men the sole efficient, and God the approver and permitter. **1754** EDWARDS *Freed. Will* IV. xi. (1762) 254 If by the Author of Sin, is meant the Permitter,..I don't deny that God is the Author of Sin. **1811** W. R. SPENCER *Poems* 45 Author of good, Permitter of distress.

permittible, variant of PERMITTABLE.

permitting (pə'mɪtɪŋ), *vbl. sb.* [f. PERMIT *v.* + -ING[1].] The action of the verb PERMIT; permission. (Now chiefly gerundial.)

1645 MILTON *Tetrach.* Deut. xxiv. 1, 2 So that the sin was not in the permission,..(for then the permitting also had bin sin) but only in the abuse. **1656** EARL MONM. tr. *Boccalini's Advts. fr. Parnass.* I. lxv. (1674) 82 The permitting of Heresie. **1748** *Anson's Voy.* II. vi. 204 The permitting the Pilot to stay with them as their guardian.

permittivity (pɜːmɪ'tɪvɪtɪ). *Physics.* [f. PERMIT *v.* + -IVITY.] One of the physical parameters of a medium, equal to the ratio of the electric displacement D to the electric field strength E at any point in it; also (more fully ***relative permittivity***), the ratio of the permittivity of a medium to the permittivity of free space: = *dielectric constant*; ***permittivity of free space***, a constant ϵ_0 which in the C.G.S. electrostatic system of units is unity and in the International System of Units is $1/\mu_0 c^2$ ($= 8{\cdot}854 \times 10^{-12}$) farad per metre, where μ_0 is the permeability of free space and c is the speed of light.

1887 O. HEAVISIDE in *Electrician* 17 June 124/1 Nomenclature Scheme... Permittance. Permittivity. **1890** [see ELASTANCE]. **1938** G. P. HARNWELL *Princ. Electr. & Electromagn.* i. 12 If the charges are measured in coulombs and if r is in meters and F in newtons, the constant κ_0 has the value $\kappa_0 = ..8{\cdot}85 \times 10^{-12}$ farads/meter... This constant.. is known as the permittivity of free space. **1944** *Phil. Mag.* XXXV. 83 Guggenheim has suggested the term *permittivity* for the fundamental quantity and *specific inductive capacity* or *dielectric constant* for the derived quantity. In conformity with the other suggestions in this paper it would be more uniform to adopt *permittivity* and *relative permittivity*... Similarly in the magnetic case we have *permeability* and *relative permeability*. **1946** *Nature* 6 July 33/2 The paper contains a description of apparatus used for measurements at frequencies of about 3,000 Mc./s...and a statement of typical experimental results obtained with a specimen of polythene, which at the above frequency had a permittivity of 2·27. **1962** CORSON & LORRAIN *Introd. Electromagn. Fields* ix. 317 The permittivity of free space ϵ_0 can..be determined directly from measurements involving electrostatic phenomena. **1971** *Engineering* Apr. 44/1 The capacitance C (microfarads) of a parallel plate capacitor..is..proportional to the relative permittivity ϵ_r of the dielectric medium. **1974** HARVEY & BOHLMAN *Stereo F.M. Radio Handbk.* vii. 148 Because of the presence of water vapour in particular, the permittivity of the air in the troposphere is greater than unity.

†**per'mix**, *v. Obs.* [Back-formation from *permixt*, PERMIXED, q.v.; cf. COMMIX, MIX.] *trans.* To mix thoroughly, intermingle. (See next.) Hence †**per'mixable** *a.*, capable of being 'permixed'.

1678 R. R[USSELL] *Geber* I. 18 And be permixed with that which in them is of a permixable Substance. *Ibid.* II. i. II. 60 Permixing Sol, or Luna, with Venus. **1683** SALMON *Doron Med.* II. 488 Permix them with burning wine.

†**per'mixed, per'mixt**, *ppl. a. Obs.* [orig. ad. L. *permixt-us*, pa. pple. of *permiscēre* to mix thoroughly, intermingle (f. PER- 2 + *miscēre* to mix); afterwards treated as pa. pple. of PERMIX: cf. COMMIXED, MIXED.] Thoroughly mixed, intermixed, intermingled. (Const. as *pple.* or *adj.*)

c **1420** *Pallad. on Husb.* IV. 812 Blacke, bay, and permyxt gray. **1432–50** tr. *Higden* (Rolls) II. 149 In Albania, where thei did abyde afterwarde..permixte with Britones. **1502** ATKYNSON tr. *De Imitatione* II. xi. 190 The pure loue of Iesu nat permixed with any inordinauns of fauour or affeccion. **1659** STANLEY *Hist. Philos.* XIII. (1701) 565/2 A leaf of Colewort, whose small Pores are pester'd with little Bodies variously permixt. **1660** tr. *Paracelsus' Archidoxis* I. II. 15 When water is permixed with vinegar.

†**permixtion**. *Obs.* Also 6–7 -mixion. [ad. L. *permixtiōn-em* (also *permistiōn-*), n. of action from *permiscēre* (see prec.). Cf. obs. F. *permixtion* (15th c. in Godef. *Compl.*).] A thorough mixture or mingling; intermingling; mixture.

1432–50 tr. *Higden* (Rolls) III. 469 The elementes..thro the permixtion of whom [*quorum permixtione*] the stature of man compacte, is made. **1447** BOKENHAM *Seyntys* (Roxb.) 45 Permixtion Of sundry kynredes. **1590** R. BRUCE *Serm.* i. Biv, Make ather a confusion or permixion of tham. **1657** TOMLINSON *Renou's Disp.* II. xiii. 408 By permixion with other Medicaments, it doth not depose its ferity. **1685** *Cooke's Mellif. Chirurg., Inst.* 376 Black [Urine] is from a permixtion of preternatural Melancholy.

So †**per'mixtive** *a.* [f. L. *permixt-* ppl. stem + -IVE], having the quality of mixing thoroughly; †**per'mixture** = PERMIXTION.

1528 PAYNEL *Salerne's Regim.* Pb, The grosser..that meate is, the bygger the drynke parmyxtiue and delatiue shulde be. **1604** PARSONS *3rd Pt. Three Convers. Eng.* 145 This permixture going on for some few yeares. **1684–5** BOYLE *Min. Waters* 88 An invisible permixture of.. Arsenical Fumes, may give the Water..an Emetic Quality.

,Permo-Carbo'niferous, *a. Geol.* [f. *Permo-*, used as comb. form of PERMIAN + CARBONIFEROUS.] Forming a transition between the Carboniferous and Permian systems; applied to certain Palæozoic formations in Bohemia and in N. America. Also, pertaining to or including the Permian and the Carboniferous systems or periods. Also *absol.*

1874 *Q. Jrnl. Geol. Soc.* XXX. 217 Taking into consideration the great thickness of the Carboniferous in Nova Scotia and the large development of this Upper Permo-Carboniferous member, it would not be surprising that in this last we may have a chronological equivalent of part at least of the European Permian. **1885** LYELL *Elem. Geol.* xxiii. (ed. 4) 352 In the basins of Pilsen and Rakowitz in Bohemia, the flora of the strata is Carboniferous, but the fauna is decidedly like that of the Permian series. These strata, which are called Permocarb[oniferous], have yielded 43 species of Amphibians. **1897** *Trans. Manchester Geol. Soc.* XXV. 207 *(heading)* On the Permo-Carboniferous boundary. **1928** C. DAWSON *Age of Gods* i. 5 The vast glaciation of Permo-Carboniferous times..marks the end of the Primary Palæozoic world. **1955** G. G. WOODFORD tr. *Gignoux's Stratigr. Geol.* v. 156 The great variety of facies of the Permo-Carboniferous in Europe and the harmonious way in which they can be grouped make of this system, seen as a whole, a magnificent illustration of stratigraphic synthesis. **1971** A. G. SMITH in I. G. Gass et al. *Understanding Earth* xv. 224/1 The distribution of Permo-Carboniferous tillites.

,Permo-Pennsyl'vanian, *a. Geol.* [f. as PERMO-CARBONIFEROUS *a.* + PENNSYLVANIAN *sb.* and *a.*] Belonging either to the lowest Permian or the uppermost Pennsylvanian. Also *absol.*

The equivalent in the U.S. of *Permo-Carboniferous*.

1937 *Bull. Amer. Assoc. Petroleum Geologists* XXI. 1252 Late Pennsylvanian and Permo-Pennsylvanian. Figure 2 represents a composite of late Pennsylvanian and early Permian time. **1965** *Ibid.* XLIX. 1572/2 An early sequence of Permo-Pennsylvanian sediments accumulated in this bay.

permoralize (pə'mɒrəlaɪz), *v. nonce-wd.* [f. PER- 2 + MORAL + -IZE, after *demoralize.*] *trans.* To permeate with moral influence: opp. to *demoralize*.

1888 G. A. SMITH *Isaiah* xx. 328 Forgiveness of such a kind cannot be either unjust or demoralising. On the contrary, we see Jerusalem permoralised by it.

†**per'motion**. *Obs. rare*[−1]. [ad. L. *permōtiōn-em* (Cicero).] Stirring; mental emotion.

1656 STANLEY *Hist. Philos.* (1687) 133/1 They [Cyrenaics] held..That nothing judgeth but by interiour permotion.

Permo-Triassic (,pɜːməʊtraɪ'æsɪk), *a. Geol.* [f. as PERMO-CARBONIFEROUS + TRIASSIC *a.*] Of or pertaining to the Permian and the Triassic systems or periods. Also *absol.*

1876 [see SILURIAN *a.* 2 a]. **1903** J. LE CONTE *Elements Geol.* (ed. 5) III. v. 619 Some indications of glaciation have been reported from other horizons than the Permo-Triassic. **1926** *Proc. Geologists' Assoc.* XXXVII. 11 By the close of Permo-Triassic times the climate would have altered considerably from that at the commencement of the period. **1956** W. EDWARDS in D. L. Linton *Sheffield* i. 3 They are being exploited, for oil as well as for coal, below the 'cover' of Permo-Triassic rocks. **1969** BENNISON & WRIGHT *Geol. Hist. Brit. Isles* xii. 272 The drawing of the Permo-Triassic boundary is fraught with difficulties. **1977** *Offshore Engineer* May 51/1 Effective basement in the Gulf of Valencia area appears to be hard Carboniferous sandstones and clays, overlain in some areas by Permo-Triassic sands and evaporites.

So **Permo-'Trias**, the Permo-Triassic system or period.

1926 *Proc. Geologists' Assoc.* XXXVII. 1, I am convinced that the divisions of the Permo-Trias, in Britain, are not time-divisions, but represent, to a considerable extent, merely different conditions of deposition. *Ibid.*, In Britain the Permo-Trias formations are always unconformable to and rest upon an uneven surface of the rocks below. **1969** BENNISON & WRIGHT *Geol. Hist. Brit. Isles* xi. 255 Strata of continental facies were laid down over wide areas in the succeeding Permian and Triassic Periods... Frequently considered together as the Permo-Trias, there are however significant palaeontological differences.

permoysaunt, obs. form of PARMESAN.

perm. s(ec)., permsec, abbrevs. of 'permanent secretary' (esp. in an African country).

1942 PARTRIDGE *Dict. Abbrev.* 78/2 *P.S...* Permanent Secretary. Also *Perm.S.* **1975** J. WYLLIE *Butterfly Flood* xxii. 95 The Perm. Sec's. house was..much pillared and porticoed. **1976** *Daily Times* (Lagos) 8 July 5/3 *(heading)* Permsec files counter-claim. *Ibid.* 16 Oct. 19/1 *(heading)* Why retired permsec's daughter stole in London.

permselective (pɜːmsɪ'lɛktɪv), *a. Chem.* [f. PERM(EABLE *a.* + SELECTIVE *a.*] Of an ion-exchange membrane: permeable to anions but not to cations, or *vice versa*; more generally, selectively permeable to certain molecules or ions. Hence **,permselec'tivity**.

1953 A. G. WINGER et al. in *Jrnl. Electrochem. Soc.* C. 178/2 For the purpose of this paper, an ideal permselective membrane will be defined to be a membrane which, when subjected to a potential gradient, permits passage of cations to the exclusion of anions, or vice versa. *Ibid.* 179/1 In any electrolytic process ion concentrations are appreciable and perfect permselectivity is an idealized situation of little practical interest. **1962** S. B. TUWINER *Diffusion & Membrane Technol.* ix. 177 The most important factor which affects permselectivity for a given membrane is the concentration of the electrolyte. **1968** *Encycl. Polymer Sci. & Technol.* VIII. 636 The ability of an ion-exchange membrane to discriminate between ions of different sign is called its permselectivity. **1969** W. R. R. PARK *Plastics Film Technol.* viii. 197 A process which may come to have the universal utility of distillation is the use of permselective membranes for the separation of mixtures of liquids or gases. **1971** A. F. STANCELL in Tobolsky & Mark *Polymer Sci. & Materials* xii. 263 The preferred permeation of one molecule through a polymer with respect to other diffusing molecules is termed membrane permselectivity.

†**per'mue**, *v. Obs. rare.* [a. OF. *per-*, *parmuer* (14th c. in Godef.):—L. *permūtāre*: see PERMUTE.] *trans.* To change completely.

a **1450** *Knt. de la Tour* (1868) 167 It was colde wynter, and gret froste, and gret wynde, and that permuueded her coloure [*que lui permua la couleur*].

permutability (pəmjuːtə'bɪlɪtɪ). [f. next + -ITY.] The quality or condition of being permutable. **a.** Changeableness, mutability. **b.** Interchangeableness.

1662 J. CHANDLER *Van Helmont's Oriat.* 151 The desire of permutability or much changeableness. **1885** *Trans. Amer. Philol. Assoc.* July App. 41 The alternation or permutability of certain sounds.

permutable (pə'mjuːtəb(ə)l), *a.* [ad. late L. *permūtābilis* (Ammianus, Boeth.), f. *permūtā-re*: see PERMUTE and -ABLE.] That may be permuted.

1. Capable of being exchanged; interchangeable.

1776 J. RICHARDSON *Arab. Gram.* 8 Some letters are permutable, being such in general as are formed by the same organs.

2. Liable to change; changeable.

1662 [implied in PERMUTABILITY]. **1846** WORCESTER cites BUCKINGHAM.

Hence **per'mutableness; per'mutably** *adv.*

1847 in WEBSTER.

permutant (pə'mjuːtənt). *Math.* [ad. L. *permūtānt-em*, pr. pple. of *permūtāre*: see PERMUTE and -ANT[1].] A function formed of the aggregate of all possible permutations of a set of characters or indices, each being positive or negative as it is obtained by an even or odd number of interchanges.

1851 CAYLEY *Coll. Math. Papers* II. 26 The term permutant is due to him [J. J. Sylvester]—intermutant and commutant are merely terms framed between us in analogy with permutant, and the names date from the present year.

permutate ('pɜːmjʊteɪt), *v.* [f. L. *permūtāt-*, ppl. stem of L. *permūtāre*: see PERMUTE.]

†**1.** *trans.* To change, alter: = PERMUTE 2. *Obs.*

1597 A. M. tr. *Guillemeau's Fr. Chirurg.* 53/1 Corrodent bones doe alter and permutate the remanent part of bone. **1599** —— tr. *Gablehouer's Bk. Physicke* 61/1 You shall as then finde the Antes permutatede into water.

2. To exchange; to change the order of, go through the permutations of: = PERMUTE 1, 3. Also *absol.*

Probably regarded by those who use it as a back-formation from *permutation*.

1898 ZANGWILL *Dreamers Ghetto* iv. 110 Lurya..who.. wore a fourfold garment to signify the four letters of the Ineffable Name,..and who, by permutating these, could draw down spirits from Heaven. **1969** *Daily Tel.* 5 May 14/3 One gets the impression that..three basic dress designs were drawn up and three basic jacket patterns, and ever since designers have been..endlessly permutating these like resigned pools punters. **1971** *Ibid.* 18 June 22 If your baldness cure is a mixture of known ingredients, however you permutate their quantities, it won't get patent protection. **1975** *Times Lit. Suppl.* 18 Apr. 416/3 The plot, involving revelations about hitherto unsuspected relationships and passions permutating with unforeseen power. **1978** *Gramophone* Jan. 1321/2 Coleman really did reject the old package of chords; but what Coltrane did was to find a new way of permutating them, running through the scales they suggested.

permutated ('pɜːmjuːteɪtɛd), *ppl. a.* [f. PERMUTAT(ION + -ED[1].] In *Football Pools*: subjected to permutation.

1947 [see BANKER[2] 5].

permutation (pɜːmjuː'teɪʃən). [a. OF. *permutacion* (14th c. in Hatz.-Darm.), ad. L. *permūtātiōn-em*, n. of action f. *permūtāre* to PERMUTE.]

†**1.** Exchange of one thing for another; interchange; commutation; barter. *Obs.*

1362 LANGL. *P. Pl.* A. III. 242 In Marchaundise nis no Meede, I may hit wel avoue; Hit is a permutacion, a peni for anoþer. **1432–50** tr. *Higden* (Rolls) IV. 43 Men of Cartago sende Marcus Regulus to Rome, desirenge the permutacion of theire men in captiuite. **1582** N. T. (Rhem.) *Matt.* xvi. 26 What permutation shal a man giue for his soule? **1622** MALYNES *Anc. Law-Merch.* 83 An exchange of commodities or rather a permutation of commodities. **1754** ERSKINE *Princ. Sc. Law* (1809) 311 Permutation differs from a sale chiefly in this, that, in permutation, one subject is to be given in barter or exchange for another.

2. a. Change from one state, position, etc. to another; alteration; transmutation. Now *rare*.

c **1374** CHAUCER *Troylus* v. 1541 Fortune whiche þat permutacion Of þinges hath. *c* **1397** —— *Lack Stedf.* 19 The worlde hath made a permutacion Fro Ryght to wrong. **1415** HOCCLEVE *To Sir J. Oldcastle* 17 A fair permutacion fro Crystes lore to feendly doctryne. **1543** TRAHERON *Vigo's Chirurg.* II. III. xvii. 62 Thyrdely, it [quinsy] is ended by permutatyon, or chaungynge to some other parte of the bodye. **1650** SIR T. BROWNE *Pseud. Ep.* v. xxii. (ed. 2) 230 They..who think that at the confusion of tongues, there was no constitution of a new speech in every family; but a variation and permutation of the old, out of one common language raising severall dialects. **1790** BURKE *Fr. Rev.* 226 The violent convulsions and permutations that have been made in property. **1856** DARWIN in *Life & Lett.* (1887) II. 75 The continents have undergone within this same period such wonderful permutations.

b. A changed form; a transmutation.

1883 *Q. Rev.* Oct. 496 The image of Buddha, here typified by a seemingly female permutation, cast also in bronze.

c. *Logic.* A form of immediate inference from a proposition by negating it and substituting a contradictory predicate; obversion.

1851 W. H. KARSLAKE *Aids Study Logic* I. 64 The third form of Immediate Inference which we have to speak of is, what may be called *Permutation.* **1906** H. W. B. JOSEPH *Introd. Logic* 214 In Permutation, or (as it has been also called) Obversion, there is no transposition of terms, but the quality of the proposition is changed. **1931** R. M. EATON *Gen. Logic* 206 Obversion, also known as permutation differs from conversion in that the subject and predicate do not change places.

3. *Math.* †**a.** Transposition of the two middle terms of a proportion. *Obs.* (now expressed by *permutando* or *alternando*). **b.** The action of changing the order of a set of things lineally arranged; each of the different arrangements of which such a set of things is capable. (Cf. COMBINATION 5 b.) Hence *gen.*, in *pl.* (usually in phr. ***permutations and combinations***): Variations of order or arrangement, various arrangements.

1570 BILLINGSLEY *Euclid* v. def. xii. 133 Proportion alternate, or proportion by permutation is, when the antecedent is compared to the antecedent, and the consequent to the consequent. **1656** tr. *Hobbes's Elem. Philos.* II. xiii. 112 If four Magnitudes be in Geometrical Proportion, they will also be Proportionals by Permutation, (that is, by transposing the Middle Terms). **1710** J. HARRIS *Lex. Techn.* II, *Variation*, or Permutation of Quantities, is the changing any number of given Quantities, with respect to their Places. **1806** HUTTON *Course Math.* I. 148 The doctrine of permutations, combinations, &c. is of very extensive use in different parts of the Mathematics; particularly in the calculation of annuities and chances. **1838** DE MORGAN *Ess. Probab.* 32 Different arrangements of the same things make different permutations. **1884** J. PARKER *Apost. Life* III. 192 The letters are but six-and-twenty in number..but..through how many permutations, may those letters be thrown or passed!

4. *Philol.* **a.** The interchange of consonants occurring regularly in cognate words belonging to related languages, as in L. and Gr. *duo*, Eng. *two*, Ger. *zwei*; L. and Gr. *tria*, Eng. *three*, Ger. *drei*.

1860 HALDEMAN *Anal. Orthogr.* xi. 63 The well-known Grimm's law, is a permutation. **1869** FARRAR *Fam. Speech* i. (1873) 22 Those regular permutations of letters in different linguistic families.

b. In the semantic theories of Nils Gustaf Stern: see quot. 1931.

1931 G. STERN *Meaning & Change of Meaning* xiii. 361 Permutations are unintentional sense-changes in which the subjective apprehension of a detail—denoted by a separate word—in a larger total changes, and the changed apprehension (the changed notion) is substituted for the previous meaning of the word. **1933** *Mod. Lang. Notes* XLVIII. 386 The linguistically conditioned changes are.. analyzed into shifts of..'permutation' and 'adequation'. **1965** *Eng. Stud.* XLVI. 405 The type of semantic change involved is that called by Gustaf Stern 'permutation'.

5. *Football Pools.* A system whereby any combination of a specified number of entries drawn from a larger, selected, number of chances may be considered for a dividend.

1952 *Times* 16 May 7/5 The whole business of forecasting, study of form, permutations, and all the rest of it is, in fact, pure nonsense. **1954** M. CROFT *Spare the Rod* III. v. 198 Football pools—that's the safest bet... Once you've worked up an interest in permutations you can sit down and leave them alone for a whole day. **1959** *Listener* 19 Feb. 347/3 The complications of this revenge put as much strain on one's attention as does the filling of a 'Pools' coupon with recommended permutations. **1960** *Comp* 20 Feb. 7/2 Find the straightforward permutation of allowing for any 3 from 8.

6. *attrib.*, as **permutation-lock**, a lock in which certain parts can be transposed or shifted, so that it is necessary to arrange them in some particular way in order to shoot or withdraw the bolt.

1847 SAXE *Rape Lock* xxix, In the locks of safes, and those safety locks They call the Permutation. **1875** KNIGHT *Dict. Mech.* 1340/2 The *letter, puzzle, permutation,* or *combination* lock has usually a series of notched rings, which must be turned until all the notches are in line in order to enter or withdraw the bolt. *Ibid.* 1669/1 The permutation principle was introduced into tumbler-locks by Dr. Andrews of New Jersey, about 1841.

Hence **permu'tational** *a.*, relating to permutation or permutations: **permu'tationist**, one who holds or advocates a theory of permutation.

1888 J. T. GULICK in *Jrnl. Linn. Soc.* XX. 250² These numerators are found in the 7th line of a table of figures which I call the Permutational Triangle. **1874** S. WILBERFORCE *Ess.* I. 79 Can any permutationist pretend that experience gives us any reason for believing that any change of food,..could ever change the one type into the other?

permutatory (pəˈmjuːtətərɪ), *a. rare.* [ad. med. or mod.L. *permūtātōri-us*, f. *permūtāre*: see next and -ORY.] Of the nature of, or involving, exchange. Also **permuta'torial** *a.*

1853 WHEWELL *Grotius* II. 55 Permutatorial acts either separate the parties or produce a community between them. **1855** LORENZ tr. *Van der Keessel's Sel. Theses* dcccxcviii, [This] should be understood..of permutatory contracts.

permute (pəˈmjuːt), *v.* [ad. L. *permūtāre* to change thoroughly, interchange, exchange (f. PER- 2 + *mūtāre* to change), or a. F. *permuter* (14th c. in Oresme) = OF. *permuer*: see PERMUE.]

†**1. a.** *trans.* To change one for another; to exchange, interchange. *Obs.*

1377 LANGL. *P. Pl.* B. XIII. 110, I wolde permute my penaunce with ȝowre for I am in poynte to dowel! *c* **1450** *St. Cuthbert* (Surtees) 6511 þat Eata and Cuthbert Permote þair bischopryks same, Cuthbert to Eland, he to Hexham. **1555** in Hakluyt *Voy.* (1599) I. 259 To buy, sel, trucke, change and permute al and euery kind..of wares. **1622** MALYNES *Anc. Law-Merch.* 91 A certaine equalitie in the value of things permuted. **1657** REEVE *God's Plea* 165 Merchandise ..by permuting for Native commodities, it gaineth the varieties of all Countries.

b. *absol.* To exchange benefices. *Obs.*

1393 LANGL. *P. Pl.* C. III. 185 Notories on persons þat permuten ofte. **1540** *Act 32 Hen. VIII*, c. 10 Euerye of the sayd benefyces..should be..vtterly voyde, as if the said offender had resygned and permuted. **1706** in PHILLIPS.

2. a. To change thoroughly; to change, alter, transmute. Now *rare* or *Obs.*

c **1440** *Promp. Parv.* 394/2 Permutyn, or holy chawngynn, *permuto.* **1623** COCKERAM, *Permute*, to change. **1683** GADBURY in *Wharton's Wks.* Pref. 7 Reduction to the very lowest Ebb of Fortune cannot permute a truly well grounded and inbred Loyalty. **1686** AGLIONBY *Painting Illustr.* 206 Giving leave to a Lady, to permute a Vow she had made. **1846** *Proc. Philos. Soc.* III. 1 In certain cases a letter may have been permuted, that is, changed to some kindred letter.

b. *Logic.* To submit to the process of permutation or obversion.

1906 H. W. B. JOSEPH *Introd. Logic* 215 The process of permuting and then converting is called Conversion by Negation.

3. *Math.* and *Linguistics.* To subject to permutation; to alter the order of; to re-arrange in a different order. (Cf. PERMUTATION 3 b.)

1878 CAYLEY in *Encycl. Brit.* VIII. 498/1 When the columns are permuted in any manner, or when the lines are permuted in any manner, the determinant retains its original value. **1887** *Longm. Mag.* Oct. 587 He will hold to the letters and permute their order to suit his own convenience. **1967** D. G. HAYS *Introd. Computational Linguistics* 153 We may be required to permute those elements. **1968** *Language* XLIV. 31 To account for the fairly flexible ordering of major constituents in a German sentence.., we must have a number of optional rules that permute the subject, object, and adverbials. **1975** N. CHOMSKY *Logical Struct. Linguistic Theory* x. 422 In actually formulating $\phi_5{}^P$ as a grammatical transformation we must be careful to indicate that the element *K*..and the following verb are not permuted when *K* belongs to the preceding noun phrase.

Hence **per'muter**, one who permutes.

1552 HULOET, Permuter, *permutator.* **1755** JOHNSON, *Permuter*, an exchanger, he who permutes. **1818** in TODD [citing Huloet]. Hence in mod. Dicts.

permuted (pəˈmjuːtɪd), *ppl. a.* [f. PERMUTE *v.* + -ED¹.] Subjected to permutation; transposed.

1846 *Proc. Philol. Soc.* III. 2 In Irish orthography, the permuted letter instead of being displaced by its substitute is merely preceded, or as the Irish grammarians express it, eclipsed by it. **1970** O. DOPPING *Computers & Data Processing* xxiii. 373 Provided that the titles of the material one wishes to register are sufficiently descriptive, the permuted title systems have many advantages. **1971** *Computers & Humanities* V. 309 Scope of present study: to produce permuted indices. **1971** D. I. SLOBIN in W. O. Dingwall *Survey Linguistic Sci.* 352 Structures requiring permutation of elements will first appear in non-permuted form. **1976** *Gloss. Documentation Terms* (*B.S.I.*) 47 *Permuted title*, a title in which the significant words have been rearranged, so that they can be used in indexing.

permutite (ˈpɜːmjʊtaɪt, pəˈmjuːtaɪt). [ad. G. *permutit*, f. L. *permūt-āre* to exchange + *-it* -ITE¹.] **a.** Any of a class of artificial zeolites which are widely employed as ion-exchangers, esp. for the softening of water. **b.** Written **Permutit** or **permutit** (-ɪt). A proprietary name for ion-exchange materials and equipment utilizing such zeolites. Also *attrib.*, as ***permutit(e) process***, the softening of water by treatment with any of these substances.

1907 *Chem. Abstr.* I. 2755 He [*sc.* A. Feldoff] reports the use of Permutite (after Gans) in the refinery at Glogau where much better yields of sugar were obtained by its use than without it. **1910** *Trade Marks Jrnl.* 12 Jan. 44 Permutit... Chemical substances..being artificially prepared compounds for the purification of water, molasses and saccharine juices. *Ibid.* 53 Permutit... Filters and engineering and building contrivances for supplying and distributing water,..J. D. Riedel Aktiengesellschaft,.. Berlin, Germany; manufacturers. **1911** *Chambers's Jrnl.* 29 Apr. 352/1 For the removal of iron and manganese and for the destruction of germ-life, manganese permutit is used in place of the sodium permutit. **1913** *Official Gaz.* (U.S. Patent Office) 4 Nov. 266/2 The Permutit Company, New York, N.Y. Filed Aug. 19, 1913. Permutit... water purifying and treating materials. **1917** A. SMITH *Introd. Inorg. Chem.* (ed. 3) xxxv. 724 In the permutite process the water is simply filtered through sodium silico-aluminate. **1925** *Glasgow Herald* 13 Feb. 6/2 Under the head of artificial silicates mention should be made of glass, Portland cement, water glass, and the permutites. **1943** *Thorpe's Dict. Appl. Chem.* (ed. 4) VI. 276/2 After partition between 70% alcohol and hexane the alcoholic layer is filtered through 'permutite' to remove adrenalin. **1963** R. R. A. HIGHAM *Handbk. Papermaking* x. 245 This process [*sc.* base exchange] relies on the exchange of sodium ions for those of calcium and magnesium and is referred to as the Zeolite or Permutit method of water softening. **1974** D. M. ADAMS *Inorg. Solids* vii. 255 This process [*sc.* cation exchange] forms the basis of the Permutit water-softening process in which Ca^{2+} is removed from 'hard' water by exchange for sodium. **1974** D. W. BRECK *Zeolite Molecular Sieves* i. 11 The accepted term for synthetic aluminosilicates which are crystallographically amorphous and are prepared for the ion exchange properties is 'permutite'... The chemical composition of most permutites is represented by an empirical formula in terms of the oxides: $Na_2O{\cdot}Al_2O_3{\cdot}xSiO_2{\cdot}yH_2O$ in which *x* often has a value of 5–6.

pern (pɜːn), *sb.* [ad. mod.L. *pernis* (Cuvier 1817), an erroneous adaptation of Gr. πτέρνις name of a kind of hawk.] A bird of the genus *Pernis*; the HONEY-BUZZARD.

1840 tr. *Cuvier's Anim. Kingd.* 171 The Perns or Honey Buzzards. The Common Pern..pursues insects, and principally Bees and Wasps. **1879** BRIGHTWELL in *B'ham Weekly Post* 21 June 5/2 The honey buzzard (*Pernis apivorus*)...The Pern, as it is sometimes called, does not feed on honey, but on the honey-makers, digging up bees' nests to get at the busy citizens.

†**Pern** (pɜːn), *v.*¹ *Obs.* Also 6 **Pearn.** *trans.* To deal with after the manner of Dr. Perne, Master of Peterhouse, Cambridge, 1554–80, who changed his opinions adroitly; to change (a profession, creed, etc.) for some ulterior end.

c **1589** *Dial. Tyran. Dealing Bps.* D ij, *Jacke.* What Doctor Pearne? Why he is the notablest turnecoate in al this land, ..it is made a prouerbe..that if one haue a coate or cloake that is turned, they saye it is Pearned. **1608** SYLVESTER *Du Bartas* II. iv. IV. *Schisme* 293 Those that, to ease their Purse, or please their Prince, Pern their Profession, their Religion mince.

pern (pɜːn), *v.*² Also **perne.** [f. *pern* var. PIRN *sb.*²] *intr.* In the poetry of W. B. Yeats: to move with a winding motion.

It has been suggested (1961 *N. & Q.* Jan. 9/1) that PERN *v.*² is the same word.

1920 W. B. YEATS *Michael Robartes* (1921) 17 Though I had long perned in the gyre, Between my hatred and desire, I saw my freedom won And all laugh in the sun. **1920** [see GYRE *v.* 3]. **1928** [see GYRE *sb.* 1]. **1938** W. B. YEATS *New Poems* 34 Those new dead That come into my soul and escape Confusion of the bed, Or those begotten or unbegotten Perning in a band.

pern, *v.*³: see PERNYNG.

pern, perne, varr. PIRN *sb.*²

†**pernable,** *a. Obs.* [a. AF. *pernable* = OF. *prenable* (12th c. in Wace), f. *pern-* = *pren-*, stem of *prendre* to take.] Proper to be taken or caught.

1390 GOWER *Conf.* III. 373 Thou miht noght make suite and chace, Wher that the game is nought pernable [*v.r.* parnable].

Pernambuco (pɜːnæmˈbuːkəʊ). Also 6 **fernandobuck,** 6–7 **fernan(d)buck,** 8 **fernambu(c)k, fernebourge.** The name of a state in Brazil, used *attrib.* and *absol.* to designate the hard, reddish timber of the tree *Cæsalpinia echinata*, of the family Leguminosæ, which is used for dyeing as well as decorative woodwork. Cf. BRAZIL¹ 1.

1595 *Drake's Voy.* (Hakluyt Soc.) 13 In this place was great store of fruite and much fernandobuck. **1598** FLORIO, *Scotano*, a red wood called brasill or fernanbucke. **1617** FYNES MORYSON *Itin.* III. 534 Fernandbuck wood. **1703** T. S. *Art's Improv.* 28 [To stain wood red] Take Fernebourge, half a Pound, and Rain Water. **1712** tr. *Pomet's Hist. Drugs* I. 68 Most in Use is the Brazil-Wood, call'd Fernambuck. **1722** *Act Encour. Silk Manuf.* in *Lond. Gaz.* No. 6040/7 Brazil or Fernambuck Wood. **1794** H. BARHAM *Hortus Americanus* 23 The true Brasil is called Pernambuca, being the place from whence they come in Brasil. **1829** C. SEALSFIELD *Tokeah* II. 124 The carriage whirled along the levee, through oyster and orange shops; mountains of Pernambuco logs and bricks. **1870** J. YEATS *Nat. Hist. Commerce* II. 219 Brazil wood is imported principally from Pernambuco, and is also known by the name of Fernambuk wood in allusion to the place of importation. **1902** G. S. BOULGER *Wood* II. 271 Peach-wood (*Cæsalpinia echinata* Lam: Order *Leguminosæ*). Central and South America. Known also as 'Lima, Nicaragua or Pernambuco-wood'. **1920** A. L. HOWARD *Man. Timbers of World* 40 Used as a dye-wood.. there is nothing that will yield the same result as the Pernambuco or brazil-wood. **1943** RECORD & HESS *Timbers of New World* 275/2 The principal foreign demand for the timber at present is.. for the manufacture of violin bows and in this trade it is known as Pernambuco, taking its name from the Brazilian state where the best grades originate. **1976** *Early Music* Oct. 521/1 (Advt.), Suppliers of wood for stringed and wind instruments: Poplar, Lime, Maple, Fruitwood, Ebony, Box, Rosewood, Walnut, Beech, Holly, Oak, Ash, Mahogany... African Blackwood and Pernambuco.

pernancy (ˈpɜːnənsɪ). *Law*. Also 7 purnancie. [f. as PERNABLE *a.* + -ANCY: cf. AF. *pernance* = OF. *prenance* the action of taking into possession.] The taking or receiving of anything; taking into possession; receipt, as of rents, tithes, etc.

1642 tr. *Perkins' Prof. Bk.* ix. §606. 262 If.. a stranger is purnor of the rent and the grauntee doth surrender his deed by which the rent was made.. the same shall extinguish the rent notwithstanding that the purnancie be made with the assent of the tenant of the land. **1670** BLOUNT *Law Dict.*, *Pernancy*.., a Taking or Receiving. Tythes in Pernancy, *i.* Tythes taken, or that be taken, in kind. **1766** BLACKSTONE *Comm.* II. xi. 163 When the actual pernancy of the profits (that is, the taking, perception, or receipt,..) begins. **1818** HALLAM *Mid. Ages* (1872) I. 254 [They] had an actual possession, or in our law-language, *pernancy* of the profits.

pernavigate (pəˈnævɪgeɪt), *v.* [orig. in pa. pple., after L. *pernavigātus* sailed through, f. PER- 1 + *navigāre* to NAVIGATE.] *trans.* To sail through; to steer one's course through. Also *fig.*

1652 H. L'ESTRANGE *Amer. no Jewes* 10 The streight of Anian (pernavigated onely in words). **1860** *Macm. Mag.* I. 228 By which it grips, understands, and pernavigates experience.

†**ˈpernegate**, *v. Obs.* [f. ppl. stem of L. *pernegāre* to deny altogether, f. PER- 2 + *negāre* to deny.] *trans.* To deny absolutely; to deny flatly or stoutly. Hence †**perneˈgation**, absolute denial.

1623 COCKERAM, *Pernegate*, to deny. *Ibid.*, *Pernegation*, a denying. **1650** B. *Discolliminium* 45 The full benefit of all the.. tergiversations, excusations, contemporations, pernegations.. that I.. can devise.

†**ˈpernel**, variant of PARNEL, wanton young woman; applied in ridicule to an effeminate man.

1533 MORE *Apol.* xxvii. Wks. 893/2 Tindall.. is as lothe, good tender pernell, to take a lyttle penaunce of the prieste, as the Ladye was to come anye more to dyspelyng. **1560** PILKINGTON *Expos. Aggeus* H ij, These tender pernels must have one gowne for the daye, another for the night. **1581** NOWELL & DAY in *Confer.* I. (1584) C j b, Master Campion being the Popes tender Pernell, accounteth a little racking of him selfe, to be.. crueltie.

ˈpernette. [ad. It. *pernetto*, pl. *-i*, dim. of *perno* hinge, pivot.] A small iron pin, one of those used to support pottery in the kiln, so as to expose the bottom of the piece to the full heat.

1884 KNIGHT *Dict. Mech.* Supp.

pernettya (pəˈnɛtɪə). Also pernettia. [mod.L. (C. Gaudichaud-Beaupré 1825, in *Ann. Sci. Nat.* V. 102), f. the name of A. J. *Pernetty* (1716–1801), French explorer.] A small evergreen shrub of the genus so called, belonging to the family Ericaceæ, native to South America, New Zealand, or Tasmania, and bearing leathery leaves and white or pink flowers, followed by white, red, or purplish berries.

1835 *Edwards's Bot. Reg.* XX. 1675 (*heading*) Pointed-leaved Pernettia. **1840** *Ibid.* XXVI. 63 (*heading*) Narrow-leaved Pernettya. **1888** *Garden* 4 Feb. 106/2 Where cut flowers are needed sprays of the Pernettyas are very useful. **1916** L. H. BAILEY *Stand. Cycl. Hort.* V. 2555/1 The pernettyas are low much-branched shrubs with dense and small evergreen leaves and small nodding flowers, followed by very decorative berries varying in color from white to purplish black. **1962** *Listener* 6 Sept. 370/3 If you.. want one of the heaviest berried shrubs I know, get some pernettya seedlings. **1973** C. D. BRICKELL in A. Gemmell *Sunday Gardener* iii. 85 *Pernettya* has already been mentioned for winter use, but the berries are well coloured by October.

†**perˈniciable**, *a. Obs. rare*$^{-0}$. [ad. L. *perniciābilis*, f. *perniciēs*: see PERNICIOUS *a.*[1], -ABLE.]

1656 BLOUNT *Glossogr.*, *Perniciable*, bringing destruction, causing death, mortal, dangerous.

†**pernicion** (pəˈnɪʃən). *Obs.* Also 6 -tioune, 7 -tion. [ad. late and med.L. *perniciōn-em* destruction (3rd c. in Gargilius) = cl. L. *perniciēs*.] Total destruction; perdition; ruin.

c **1530** L. COX *Rhet.* (1899) 56 Sore punysshement and pernicion to mysdoers. **1596** DALRYMPLE tr. *Leslie's Hist. Scot.* III. 192 A cruel battel strukne.. almaist to the pernitioune of baith the armies. **1663** BUTLER *Hud.* I. ii. 935 But Ralpho.. Looking about, beheld Pernicion Approaching Knight from fell Musician. **1691** *Andros. Tracts* II. 257. **1736** H. BROOKE *Univ. Beauty* III. 348 Ye pitied, envied wretched great, Who veil pernicion with the mask of state.

†**perniciˈosity.** *Obs. rare.* [f. L. *perniciōs-us* (see next) + -ITY. Cf. mod.F. *perniciosité* (Littré).] The quality of being pernicious, destructiveness.

a **1568** A. KID *Richt Fontane* 71 in *Bannatyne Poems* (Hunter. Cl.) 264 Drownand in vice and perniciosite.

pernicious (pəˈnɪʃəs), *a.*[1] Also 6 par-, -tyous, 6–7 -tious. [ad. F. *pernicieux* (13–14th c. in Hatz.-Darm.), ad. L. *perniciōs-us* destructive, baneful, ruinous, f. *perniciēs* destruction, ruin, death, f. PER- 2 + *nex*, *nec-em* death, destruction: cf. *pernecāre* to kill outright.]

a. Having the quality of destroying; tending to destroy, kill, or injure; destructive, ruinous; fatal.

pernicious anæmia [tr. G. *perniciöse* (now *perniziöse*) *anämie* (A. Biermer 1868: see *Correspondenzblatt für schweiz. Aerzte* (1872) 1 Jan. 15)], a form of anæmia which formerly advanced to a fatal termination without interruption, but is now susceptible to treatment. ***pernicious contrary***, in paper-making, a substance difficult to detect in the raw material, which inhibits the pulping process; cf. CONTRARY *sb.* 3 d. ***pernicious fever***, that which proves dangerous or fatal at an early stage.

1521 FISHER (*title*) Sermon.. made agayn ye pernicyous doctryn of Martin luuther. **1529** MORE *Dyaloge* I. Wks. 112/1 The confutacion of those perylouse and perniciouse opinions. **1547** J. HARRISON *Exhort. Scottes* a ij b, A thyng detestable before God,.. and pernicious to the parties. **1578** LYTE *Dodoens* 24 The decoction of Fumeterre.. driueth forth.. all.. pernicious humors. **1646** SIR T. BROWNE *Pseud. Ep.* IV. ix. 199 A Pestilence.. that proved pernitious and deadly to those that Sneezed. *a* **1704** T. BROWN *Two Oxford Schol.* Wks. 1730 I. 13 Men of pernicious principles. **1752** HUME *Pol. Disc.* x. 187 He is a pernicious citizen, said M. Curius, who cannot be contented with seven acres. **1804** ABERNETHY *Surg. Obs.* 73 The dreadful effects of this pernicious disease. **1874** *Med. Times & Gaz.* 21 Nov. 581/2 (*heading*) Pernicious anæmia: a new disease. *Ibid.* 582/1 Under the name of 'Progressive Pernicious Anæmia', Dr. Biermer, of Zürich, has described an affection which differs from ordinary simple anæmia in a marked manner, and which.. appears to be a disease *sui generis*. **1898** *Allbutt's Syst. Med.* V. 519 The first general account of pernicious anæmia is due to Dr. Thomas Addison. **1936** *Discovery* Apr. 123/1 Pernicious anaemia, a disease which was reckoned incurable until 1926, and which, since then, it has been found possible to keep under control by large and frequent doses of fresh liver. **1961** [see CONTRARY *sb.* 3 d]. **1963** R. R. A. HIGHAM *Handbk. Papermaking* ii. 50 (*heading*) Pernicious contraries in waste paper. **1968** PASSMORE & ROBSON *Compan. Med. Stud.* I. v. 15/2 The patient with pernicious anaemia formerly died, because he was unable to transport one-millionth of a gram of the vitamin [*sc.* B_{12}] daily across one or two millimetres of the gut wall. Nowadays he receives an injection of the vitamin at fortnightly or monthly intervals. With this, he is in every respect a normal healthy person. **1972** *Listener* 21 Sept. 383/2 Some 5 per cent or so of waste paper is tainted by what the industry calls 'pernicious contraries'—substances like the bitumen used to waterproof paper or board.

b. That harbours evil designs; wicked; villanous. Now *rare* or *Obs.*

1555 EDEN *Decades* 116 Consider howe pernitious a kynde of men this is. **1605** SHAKS. *Lear* III ii. 22 Seruile Ministers That will with two pernicious Daughters ioyne Your high-engender'd Battailes. **1662** J. DAVIES tr. *Mandelslo's Trav.* 95 Resolv'd that they should.. make away that pernicious Minister. **1791** COWPER *Odyss.* XI. 467 Victims of a pernicious woman's crime.

perˈnicious, *a.*[2] *rare.* [f. L. *pernix*, *pernīci-* nimble, quick, fleet (f. PER- 2 + *nīti*, *nix-us* to press forward, strive) + -OUS.] Rapid, swift.

a **1656** USSHER *Ann.* VI. (1658) 580 Young men, pernicious in respect of their agility [Quoting *Vell. Paterc.* II. xxxiv. 'velocitate pernicibus']. **1667** MILTON *P.L.* VI. 520 Part incentive reed Provide, pernicious with one touch to fire. [Cf. HORACE *Ars Poet.* 165 Amata relinquere pernix.] **1835** KIRBY *Hab. & Inst. Anim.* (1852) II. 115 Though some birds are of such pernicious wing, there are others.. that have only rudiments of wings.

perniciously (pəˈnɪʃəslɪ), *adv.* [f. PERNICIOUS *a.*[1] + -LY[2].] In a pernicious manner; destructively, ruinously; wickedly.

c **1559** R. HALL *Life Fisher* in *Fisher's Wks.* (E.E.T.S.) II. p. xxxviii, Vsing his seditious booke pernitiously penned to catch the ignorant sort. **1613** SHAKS. *Hen. VIII*, II. i. 50 All the Commons Hate him perniciously, and o' my Conscience Wish him ten faddom deepe. **1660** MILTON *Free Commw.* Wks. 1851 V. 447 They who in pursuance therof so perniciously would betray us. *a* **1797** H. WALPOLE *Mem. Geo. II* (1847) II. ii. 68 Never was a noble country so perniciously neglected. **1828** W. SEWELL *Oxf. Prize Ess.* 26 A principle essentially and perniciously erroneous.

perniciousness (pəˈnɪʃəsnɪs). [f. as prec. + -NESS.] The quality of being pernicious; destructiveness, ruinousness.

1581 J. BELL *Haddon's Answ. Osor.* 472 b, This notorious See.. doth ouerwhelme the whole state of yᵉ world with vnrecoverable perniciousnes. **1651** BIGGS *New Disp.* ¶ 115 The perniciousnesse of laxatives. **1712** BERKELEY *Pass. Obed.* §24 The absurdity and perniciousness of those notions. **1884** *Manch. Exam.* 23 Sept. 5/1 To point out its perniciousness and the temptations to which it exposes its victims.

†**perˈnicity.** *Obs.* [ad. L. *pernīcitās*, f. *pernix*: see PERNICIOUS *a.*[2]] Swiftness, celerity.

1592 NASHE *P. Penilesse* (ed. 2) 37 By the incomparable pernicitie of those ayrie bodies we [spirits].. out strip the swiftnes of men, beasts and birds. **1657** THORNLEY tr. *Longus' Daphnis & Chloe* 69 The ship, with an irrevocable pernicity and swiftnesse was carried away. **1704** NORRIS *Ideal World* II. vii. 356 Whose resistence being increased by the swiftness and pernicity of their motion.

pernickety (pəˈnɪkɪtɪ), *a.* [Of obscure origin; originally Scotch (and perh. north. Eng. dial.: see *Eng. Dial. Dict.*); but in common use in U.S., and more recently introduced in literary English by writers of Scottish nationality.

There is a shorter Sc. form *pernicky*, which may have been a childish attempt at *particular* (quasi *partickie, parteckie*): of this, *pernickety* may be an onomatopœic expansion. Association with the *knick* group of words, *knick-knack*, *knick-knacket*, *knickety-knock*, etc. may have been vaguely present. Cf. the colloquial variant *pernackity, pernackety*.]

Of persons, their attributes or actions: Precise or particular about minutiæ or trifles; fastidious, punctilious. Of things: Requiring precise or particular handling or care; ticklish.

1808–18 JAMIESON, *Pernickitie*.. precise in trifles; applied also to dress, denoting trimness, S. *perjink* synon. **1814** HILL in *Macm. Mag.* (1881) XLV. 72/2 Dear Doctor, I received yours last night, and a.. vexing, pernickety, humorous, witty, daft letter it is. **1822** GALT *Provost* xxxi. I never saw any mortal man look as that pernicketty personage, the bailie, did at this joke. **1868** G. MACDONALD *R. Falconer* II. 152 But Robert wadna like me to tak siller whaur I did nae wark for't... He's some pernickety, Robert. **1884** E. INGERSOLL in *Harper's Mag.* May 875/2 Any white man.. grows lame and impatient at such confining and pernickety work. **1885** A. BIRRELL in *Contemp. Rev.* Jan. 30 The pernickety little player [Garrick] was chary about lending his splendidly bound rarities. **1891** B. MATTHEWS *Americanisms & Brit.* (1892) 29 The grammarian, the purist, the pernicketty stickler for trifles. **1892** *Spectator* 27 Feb. 290/1 Restrictions, some of them a trifle pernickety. **1899** A. LANG in *Blackw. Mag.* Aug. 271/1 Our age is more precise, more pernickety.. as to evidence.

Hence **perˈnicketiness.**

1890 in *Century Dict.* **1900** *Spectator* 15 Dec. 877 It behoves every Minister to be careful to the point of fastidiousness, or, if you will, pernickittiness.

pernio (ˈpɜːnɪəʊ). *Med.* Pl. **perniones** (pɜːnɪˈəʊniːz). [a. L. *pernio*, *perniōn-* chilblain (f. *perna* haunch or ham).] A chilblain.

1676 R. WISEMAN *Several Chirurgicall Treat.* I. xiii. 62 Pernio is a peculiar Inflammation, and belongeth to Blood; it raiseth a thick red Swelling with itching pain in the Hands and Feet. Those affecting the Hands are generally called Chilblanes... When they affect the Feet they are called Kibes. **1822** J. M. GOOD *Study of Med.* II. 313 That the pernio or chilblain belongs to the genus erythema is perfectly obvious. **1885** in tr. *H. von Ziemssen's Handbk. Dis. Skin* 169 Such is the mode in which chilblains (perniones) make their appearance. **1941** J. MASEFIELD *Gautama* 19 Cures for all from pernio to spasms. **1959** H. L. DUVRIES *Surg. of Foot* v. 103 Repeated mild frostbite produces vasomotor instability resulting in chilblains, or perniones. **1974** *Arch. Dermatol.* CIX. 57/1 Our cases best fit into the classification of acute pernio or chilblains.

perniosis (pɜːnɪˈəʊsɪs). *Med.* [mod.L., f. prec. + -OSIS.] A chilblained condition of the skin.

1896 N. WALKER tr. *Unna's Histopath. of Dis. of Skin* I. 20 In rare cases the point of the nose.. is the seat of a perniosis. **1952** M. K. POLANO *Skin Therapeutics* iii. 97 A good cream in perniosis. **1968** R. J. CAIRNS et al. in A. J. Rook et al. *Textbk. Dermatol.* I. xv. 337/1 Papular perniosis may closely mimic erythema multiforme. **1974** PASSMORE & ROBSON *Compan. Med. Stud.* III. I. xvii. 27/1 (*heading*) Perniosis (chilblains).

pernitrous *Chem.* = hyponitrous: see PER-[1] 5 b.

†**ˈpernize**, *v. Obs. rare.* [See -IZE.] = PERN *v.*[1]

1611 COTGR., *Retourner sa robbe*,.. to Pernize, or Apostatize it; to play the turne-coat.

†**pernocˈtalian.** *Obs. rare.* [f. med.L. *pernoctālia* all-night vigils, f. *pernoctāre*: see next and -AN.] One who keeps vigil all night.

1846 HOOK *Ch. Dict.* (ed. 5), *Pernoctalians*, watching all night, long a custom with the more pious Christians, especially before the greater festivals.

perˈnoctate, *v.* [f. ppl. stem of L. *pernoctāre*, f. PER- 1 + *nox*, *noct-em* night.] To stay all night; to pass the night.

1623 COCKERAM, *Pernoctate*, to tarry all night. **1923** *Blackw. Mag.* Aug. 250/1 Families of Oriental pilgrims, pernoctating within the Church, will squat down in front of the Tomb of Christ. **1975** *Wadham Coll. Gaz.* I. I. 6 The second event that demands to be recorded is the arrival of the first women undergraduates. The first to pernoctate as a member of the college came from Kingston, Ontario, to read law. **1978** 'M. INNES' *Ampersand Papers* iii. 28 A bedroom.. and sitting-room were in permanent readiness for him should he be minded to pernoctate at Treskinnick.

pernoctation (pɜːnɒkˈteɪʃən). [ad. L. *pernoctātiōn-em* a passing the night, n. of action f. *pernoctāre*: see prec.] The action of passing or spending the night; esp. in *Eccl.* use, spending the night in prayer; an all-night vigil.

1633 PRYNNE *Histriomastix* 429 Those Diabolicall pernoctations which are this day practised. **1649** JER. TAYLOR *Gt. Exemp.* I. Disc. iv. §16. 128 Instances of sack-cloth,.. long fasts, pernoctation in prayers. **1725** H. BOURNE

Antiq. Vulg. xii. 117 Among the primitive Christians the Lord's day was always ushered in with a Pernoctation or Vigil. **1839** W. O. MANNING *Law Nations* IV. vi. (1875) 194 The rule of pernoctation and twenty-four hours possession. **1893** *Dict. Nat. Biog.* XXXV. 334/1 He [F.H.H.A. Mahomed]..used to go to Cambridge evey evening by the last train in order to perform the pernoctation essential for keeping a term.

Pernod (pɛrnɔ, 'pɜːnəʊ). Also **pernod**. The proprietary name of a drink manufactured by the firm of *Pernod* Fils and used as an aperitif; a glass of Pernod. Also *attrib.*

Before 1918 the name referred to a brand of absinthe.

[**1876** *Trade Marks Jrnl.* 11 Oct. 574 Pernod Fils... Louis Pernod, on behalf of self and partner, Fritz Pernod, trading as Pernod, Fils, Pontarlier, Doubs, France; manufacturers of absinthe.] **1908** C. E. GRIFFIN *Four Years in Europe* vi. 58 Men and women sit day and night, sipping their wine or *pernod* (absinthe). **1914** *Blast* June 13 Oh blast France... Blast aperitifs (Pernots, Amers picon) Bad change Naively seductive Houri salon-picture Cocottes. **1919** *Century Mag.* Aug. 446/2 He..poured a glass of Pernod. **1928** J. RHYS *Postures* xvi. 163 Then she would drink a couple of Pernods ..to deaden the hurt. **1931** *Daily Express* 23 Sept. 9/3 There are small cafés, with men and women drinking the yellow-greenish pernod, the near-absinthe, now that the manufacture of absinthe is forbidden, but as like absinthe as one pea is like another. **1936** BENTLEY & ALLEN *Trent's Own Case* xi. 130 Trent called for a Pernod. **1942** 'N. SHUTE' *Pied Piper* i. 19 He would take a little glass of Pernod with Madame? **1958** E. DUNDY *Dud Avocado* I. i. 9 Glancing down at my Pernod, I discovered..that I'd already finished it. **1964** *Sun-Herald* (Sydney) 21 June 11/2 Five men unconscious on the floor of the hold and five empty pernod bottles. **1967** S. BECKETT *Stories & Texts for Nothing* VII. 110 But what is this I see..at pernod time. **1975** *Times* 29 July 5/8 Fendi shapes Pernod coloured mink..into trench coats. **1976** J. VAN DE WETERING *Corpse on Dike* vi. 72 The first French I read here was on the label of the Pernod bottle.

†**pernor.** *Law. Obs.* Also 5-7 pernour(e, (5 -er), 7 parnor, purnor. [a. AF. *pernour* = OF. *preneor, -eur* taker, f. *prendre, pren-ant* to take.] A taker or receiver, esp. of rent or profits of land or other property.

[**1292** BRITTON I. xxii. §14 Nos pernours de vitayle ou de autre chose [*transl.* Our takers of victuals or other things]. **1341** *Rolls of Parlt.* II. 133/2 Et qe les Pernours puissent prendre les Leynes.] **1485** *Act 1 Hen. VII*, c. 1 That the Demaundaunt in every suche cas have his accion ayenst the ..pernours [*Roll of P.* Perner] of the profittes of the Londes or Tenementes demaunded. **1531** *Dial. on Laws Eng.* I. xxx, That wryt of annuyte lyeth neuer agaynst the pernoure: but onlye agaynst the grantour or his heyres. **1642** tr. *Perkins' Prof. Bk.* ix. §606. 262 If there be grauntee of a rent charge in fee, and a stranger is purnor of the rent.

†'**pernyng.** *Obs. rare*$^{-1}$. [?

Usually taken as vbl. sb. or pr. pple. of a conjectural vb. *pern*, metathesized variant of *prene*, PREEN. But the passage is obscure. Perh. 'bitwene' governs 'tortors and trulofez'.]

13.. *Gaw. & Gr. Knt.* 611 On brode sylkyn borde & bryddez on semez, As papiayez paynted pernyng bitwene Tortors & trulofez entayled so þyk.

peroba (pə'rəʊbə). [Pg., f. Tupi.] Any of several Brazilian hardwood trees, esp. *Aspidosperma peroba* and other members of this genus, belonging to the family Apocynaceæ, or *Paratecoma peroba*, of the family Bignoniaceæ; also, the wood of these trees.

1875 T. LASLETT *Timber & Timber Trees* xxv. 184 Peroba is stronger than teak, but not so heavy. **1920** A. L. HOWARD *Man. Timbers of World* 209 Peroba Branca... The wood is light greyish-yellow in colour, close and fine in the grain. *Ibid.* 210 Peroba Rosa... This wood is of a pale rose colour with some darker streaks. **1936** *Nature* 9 May 790/2 First Class restaurant [of the Queen Mary]: Peroba, with feature panels in selected maple burr. **1956** *Handbk. Hardwoods* (Forest Prod. Res. Lab.) 185 Red peroba (Great Britain). The name peroba rosa is applied to a group of species of *Aspidosperma*, of which the principal one is *A. peroba*. **1971** F. H. TITMUSS *Commerc. Timbers of World* (ed. 4) 236 White Peroba is essentially a timber for high-quality furniture, panelling and veneers. **1978** *Sunday Times* (Colour Suppl.) 18 June 47/1 Once lush rain forest, ablaze with jacaranda and peroba trees, settlement is rapidly turning into a wasteland.

perochial(l, obs. ff. PAROCHIAL.

perochito: see PARAKEET.

peroffer, obs. f. PROFFER.

perofskite, var. PEROVSKITE.

perogua, perogue, obs. ff. PIRAGUA, PIROGUE.

†**peroke.** *Obs. rare*$^{-1}$. [perh. a variant of PERUKE, which, as also the It. *perrucco*, orig. meant 'hair of the head', 'long locks', 'shock of hair'.] app. The floss silk of a cocoon.

1540 *Treas. Poore Men* 7 b, Rawe sylke & namely of the Peroke of the sylke worme.

perokito: see PARAKEET.

peromelous (pɪə'rɒmɪləs), *a. Zool.* [f. Gr. πηρομελής with maimed limbs (f. πηρός maimed + μέλος limb) + -OUS.] Having the limbs defective or wanting, as the group *Peromela* (Duméril 1841) or *Ophiomorpha* of Amphibians, now *Aistopoda*.

1875 HUXLEY in *Encycl. Brit.* I. 751/1 Some Labyrinthodonts were devoid of limbs, or peromelous. *Ibid.* 770/2 The peromelous modification of the Labyrinthodont type.

peron, peronall, obs. ff. PERRON, PARNEL.

peronate ('pɪərənət), *a. Bot.* [ad. L. *pērōnātus* rough-booted, f. *pēro* boot of hide.] (See quot.)

1832 LINDLEY *Introd. Bot.* 396 *Peronate*; laid thickly over with a woolly substance, ending in a sort of meal... This term is only applied to the stipes of Fungi. **1866** *Treas. Bot.* 866/2.

‖**perone** ('pɛrəniː). *Anat.* Also **perona.** [mod. L. *peronē, perona*, a. Gr. περόνη a pin, a buckle, the fibula.] The FIBULA or small bone of the leg.

1693 tr. *Blancard's Phys. Dict.* (ed. 2), *Perona*, also called *Fibula*, because it joyns the Muscles of the Leg. **1709** BLAIR in *Phil. Trans.* XXVII. 150 The *Perone* was fix'd to the *Tibia* at the upper part, by a Pin. **1758** J. S. *Le Dran's Observ. Surg.* (1771) 334 The *Peronè* was broke obliquely.

peroneal (pɛrəʊ'niːəl), *a. Anat.* [f. mod.L. *peronæ-us* (f. *peronē*: see prec.) + -AL[1].] Pertaining to or connected with the *perone* or fibula.

1831 R. KNOX *Cloquet's Anat.* 223 A branch of the peroneal artery. **1872** MIVART *Elem. Anat.* 177 Called the fibula, or peroneal bone of the leg.

peroneo- (pɛrəʊ,niːəʊ), comb. form of mod.L. *peronēus, -æus*, PERONEAL, forming adjs. applied to ligaments, muscles, etc. connected with the fibula and with some other part denoted by the second element: as **peroneo-cal'caneal, peroneo-'tarsal, peroneo-'tibial**. These may also be used ellipt. as sbs. (sc. *muscle*, etc.).

1831 R. KNOX *Cloquet's Anat.* 225 Anterior Peroneo-tarsal Ligament. **1872** HUMPHRY *Myology* 21 A part of the posterior peroneo-tarsal ligament.

‖**peroneus** (pɛrəʊ'niːəs). *Anat.* [mod.L. (prop. adj., sc. *musculus* muscle), f. PERONE.] Name given to various muscles connected with the fibula.

1704 J. HARRIS *Lex. Techn.* I, *Peroneus primus*, a Muscle of the *Tarsus*. **1872** HUMPHRY *Myology* 22 Insinuating itself between the peroneus muscle and the fibula. **1875** HUXLEY & MARTIN *Elem. Biol.* (1883) 232 The *peroneus*: the largest and most external [muscle].

Peronism ('pɛrɒnɪz(ə)m). [ad. Sp. *Peronismo* (also used), or f. the name *Perón* (see below) + ISM.] The political ideology of Juan Domingo Perón (1895–1974), president of Argentina from 1946 to 1955 and from 1973 to 1974, advocating nationalism and the organization of labour in the interests of social progress; the political movement supporting Perón or his policies.

1946 *Times* 4 June 5/6 Although the Labour Party is the left wing and the Peronista Radicals are the right wing of Peronismo, the schism is more a struggle for the fruits of office than a conflict of ideology. **1953** G. I. BLANKSTEN *Perón's Argentina* III. xii. 281 Peronism..was not naziism. It was not fascism. It was not communism... It was *justicialismo*, or the 'Third Position'. **1957** *Economist* 21 Dec. 1063/2 Peronism is near its end as an organized movement. General Perón has suffered two or three severe defeats since he was overthrown. **1962** *Listener* 28 June 1102/2 The late Frondizi government encouraged a revival of Peronism. **1964** G. GERMANI in I. L. Horowitz *New Sociol.* 408 A comparative analysis of fascism and peronism ..may be found in Gino Germani, *La integración política de las masas y el totalitarismo.* **1964** J. R. SCOBIE *Argentina* ix. 233 'Peronismo', a doctrine and a political movement which emphasized the importance of the working man. **1972** *Buenos Aires Herald* 1 Feb. 7/2 Members of the youth movement charged..that death of militant member Enrique Castro was due to groups in Peronism that followed the moderate line of former party chief Jorge Daniel Paladino. **1975** *New Yorker* 28 Apr. 18/1 (Advt.), A didactic, explosive, semi-documentary on Peronism and the necessity to create national consciousness in Argentina and other Latin-American countries. **1977** *Time* 11 Apr. 37/2 We are not ready for elections until Peronism is dismantled and forgotten.

Peronist ('pɛrɒnɪst), *a.* [ad. Sp. *Peronista* (also used), or f. as prec. + -IST.] Of, pertaining to, or advocating Peronism. Also as *sb.*, a supporter of Perón or of Peronism.

1946 [see prec.]. **1955** *Times* 7 May 7/4 A group of 10 Peronista deputies belonging to the General Confederation of Labour submitted a Bill yesterday in the Argentine Congress. **1958** *New Statesman* 8 Mar. 291/2 Though Frondizi's victory was won with the help of the Communist and Peronist parties, he would have won even without their support. **1960** *Economist* 15 Oct. 243/2 The xenophobia of the Peronist years. **1963** *Times* 26 Feb. 11/6 The Peronists, despite their internal bickerings, retained their fundamental unity. **1969** J. MANDER *Static Society* viii. 245 Borges never concealed his contempt for the *peronista* régime. **1970** G. GERMANI in I. L. Horowitz *Masses in Lat. Amer.* xvi. 595 The basis of the new political movement was provided by.. Perónist penetration of the older unions. **1971** *Guardian* 17 Apr. 10/3, I was only 12 when Peron fell in 1955, but I have always been a Peronist. **1974** *Times* 15 Oct. 9/3 Three car loads of men..shot up the headquarters of the Peronist youth organization.

‖**peronium** (pə'rəʊnɪəm). *Zool.* Pl. **-ia.** [mod.L., a. Gr. περόνιον, dim. of περόνη fibula, pin.] Each of the cartilaginous processes connecting the bases of the tentacles with the marginal ring in the *Narcomedusæ*, a section of the *Hydrozoa*. Hence **pe'ronial** *a.*, of or pertaining to a peronium.

1888 ROLLESTON & JACKSON *Anim. Life* 749 In the *Narcomedusæ*,..a nerve extends from the outer ring beneath each peronium. In the *Peganthidæ*..the peronia are very rudimentary. **1898** SEDGWICK *Textbk. Zool.* I. 136 *Otoporpae* or peronial streaks of ectoderm passing from the auditory tentacles may be present.

‖**Peronospora** (pɛrəʊ'nɒspərə). *Bot.* [mod.L., f. Gr. περόνη pin, etc. (see PERONE) + σπόρος seed, SPORE.] A genus of minute parasitic fungi (moulds or mildews), of which several species cause very destructive diseases in various plants, as *P. viticola* in the grape-vine, and *P. infestans* in the potato.

1884 S. HIBBERD in *Times* 27 Dec., Definite tracing of the resting spores of the peronospora. **1892** *Daily News* 9 July 3/5 Vines and olives are promising, and the peronospora.. has till now caused no sensible damage. **1895** *Times* 2 Jan. 13/2 Reports of the appearance of peronosporos on the growing crop [of currants].

peroperative (pə'rɒpərətɪv), *a. Surg.* [f. PER-[1] 1 + OPERATIVE *a.* and *sb.*] Given, performed, or occurring during the course of an operation. Hence **pe'roperatively** *adv.*

1976 *Lancet* 14 Aug. 325/2 (*heading*) Single-dose peroperative antibiotic prophylaxis in gastrointestinal surgery. **1977** *Ibid.* 2 July 6/1 None of the four patients with preoperative or peroperative peritoneal soiling had post-operative infection. *Ibid.* 6 Aug. 304/2 There are several papers demonstrating the efficacy of a combination of lincomycin and gentamicin (or tobramycin) given in one or two doses peroperatively.

peropod ('pɪərəpɒd), *a.* and *sb. Zool.* [f. mod. Zool. L. *Pēropoda*, f. Gr. πηρός maimed + ποδ- foot.] **a.** *adj.* Having rudimentary hind limbs, as certain serpents; belonging to the division *Peropoda* of serpents, including the pythons, boas, etc. **b.** *sb.* A serpent of this division. So **pe'ropodous** *a.*

1878 BELL *Gegenbaur's Comp. Anat.* 490 In all Ophidii, among which the Peropoda only are provided with any rudiments at all.

†**pe'ropus.** *Obs.* Also 7 **paropa, parapos, piropus,** 8 **pyropus.** [Origin unascertained.] A kind of fabric used in the early part of the seventeenth century, the same as or similar to PARAGON.

c **1605** *Alleg. Worsted Weavers* (B.M. Add. MS. 12504, art. 64) A peropus and paragon [are] all one [cloth]. *Ibid.* [see PARAGON *sb.* 5]. **1622** BONOEIL *Making Silk* 25 Be it say, Piropus, the backside of old Veluet, or such like stuffe as hath no swell on it. **1623** J. TAYLOR (Water P.) *Praise Hempseed* Wks. (1630) III. 64/2 Rash, Taffata, Paropa, and Nouato, Shagge, Fillizetta, Damaske and Mockado. **1624** in *Naworth Househ. Bks.* (Surtees) 214, 10 yards of watered peropus..to make my Lady a cassock, xxx[s]. **1625** in J. C. Jeaffreson *Middlesex County Rec.* II. 184 Stealing of a peece of imbrodered Peropus. **1706** in Watson *Coll. Scot. Poems* I. 28 No proud Pyropus, Paragon, Or Chackarally.

peroqua, peroque, obs. ff. PIRAGUA, PIROGUE.

peroral (pɜː'rɔːrəl), *a.* [f. PER-[1] + ORAL *a.* (*sb.*)] Occurring or carried out by way of the mouth.

1908 *Lancet* 18 Apr. 1183/2 Sauerbruch's low-pressure apparatus, Brauer's high-pressure apparatus, and Kühn's method of producing high pressure by per-oral tubage had now made the way for the surgeon an easy one. **1974** *Jrnl. Infectious Dis.* CXXX. 225 The susceptibility of the newborn mouse to peroral infection with a group B coxsackievirus (B_5) was compared with susceptibility to parenteral infection with this agent.

So **pe'rorally** *adv.*

1934 in WEBSTER. **1969** *Canad. Jrnl. Physiol. & Pharmacol.* XLVII. 841/2 The rats were administered water perorally. **1976** *Lancet* 18 Dec. 1320/1 Jejunal-biopsy specimens were taken perorally with the Crosby capsule.

perorate ('pɛrəreɪt), *v.* [f. ppl. stem of L. *perōrāre* to speak at length or to the close, f. PER-1 + *ōrāre* to speak.]

1. *intr.* To speak at length, deliver an oration.

1603 SIR C. HEYDON *Jud. Astrol.* xxii. 493 Now hauing perorated (as he thinkes) sufficiently, he beginnes to growe to a conclusion. **1620** BRENT tr. *Sarpi's Counc. Trent* II. 125 They should demand of the Pope, some man of worth to perorate against the accused. **1827** CARLYLE *Misc., Richter* (1869) 4 Dr. Gabler and Dr. Spazier were perorating over the grave. **1873** M. ARNOLD *Lit. & Dogma* (1876) 331 They will let the intelligent Unitarian perorate for ever about the Atonement if he likes.

b. *trans.* To utter with declamation, declaim.

1681 COLVIL *Whigs Supplic.* (1751) 119 Thus did he perorat his fliting. **1850** CARLYLE *Latter-d. Pamph.* ii. (1872) 60 A foolish stump-orator, perorating..mere benevolences.

2. *intr.* To sum up or conclude a speech or oration; to utter the peroration of a speech.

1808 DE QUINCEY *Let. to Sister* 20 June in 'H. A. Page' *Life* (1877) I. 140, I summed up or perorated by impressing on his misguided mind that [etc.]. **1818** HOBHOUSE *Hist. Illustr.* (ed. 2) 336 The following innocent conclusion with which Visconti perorates. **1855** BROWNING *Old Pict. Florence* xxxiv, How we shall prologuize, how we shall perorate.

Hence '**perorating** *ppl. a.*

1897 *Daily News* 17 Mar. 6/4 [He] has that besetting sin of perorating speakers—he drops his voice at the close of his periods.

peroration (pɛrɒ'reɪʃən). [ad. L. *perōrātion-em* the winding up of a speech, n. of action from L. *perōrāre*: see prec. So obs. F. *péroration*, F. *péroraison*.]

1. The concluding part of an oration, speech, or written discourse, in which the speaker or writer sums up and commends to his audience with force or earnestness the matter which he has placed before them; hence, any rhetorical conclusion to a speech.

c **1440** CAPGRAVE *Life St. Kath.* IV. 536 This was at þat tyme hir peroracyon. **1570** FOXE *A. & M.* (ed. 2) 1205/2 Finally in the end of hys peroration, he concludeth the whole summe of hys minde, in this effect. **1663** COWLEY *Verses & Ess.* (1669) 73 Which if I should undertake to do I should never get to the Peroration. **1790** BURKE *Fr. Rev.* Wks. V. 131 When he arrives at his peroration. **1875** HELPS *Soc. Press.* viii. 113 He should be all along preparing for his conclusion, or peroration.

2. A discourse; a rhetorical passage.

1593 SHAKS. *2 Hen. VI*, I. i. 105 Nephew, what means this passionate discourse? This peroration with such circumstance. **1607** TOPSELL *Four-f. Beasts* Ep. Ded., Leauing these perorations, I will endeauor to proue vnto you [etc.]. **1649** BULWER *Pathomyot.* Pref. A vj b, Dr. Floud being the first that in his peroration exhibited such a kind of Method. **1833–6** J. H. NEWMAN *Hist. Sk.* (1873) II. II. xi. 295 At other times, his peroration contains more.. elevated sentiments.

Hence **pero'rational** *a.*, of or pertaining to a peroration.

1868 *Spectator* 1 Feb. 120 One of those desperate snatches at a perorational metaphor which always remind one of Mr. Toots's peroration at the wedding breakfast.

perorative ('pɛrɒreɪtɪv), *a.* [f. PERORAT(ION + -IVE.] Appropriate to or suggestive of a peroration.

1921 *Glasgow Herald* 29 Oct. 4 Messrs. Hart (said Cleland in a perorative phrase..) are of that class in society who have found their way to philosophy without the aid of regular tuition.

perorator ('pɛrəreɪtə(r)). *rare.* [Agent-n. in L. form from *perōrāre* to PERORATE.] One who perorates; †the speaker of an epilogue.

1560 INGELEND *Disob. Child* (Percy Soc.) 55 Here the Ryche Man and his Sonne go out, and in commeth the Peroratour. **1827** CARLYLE *Germ. Rom.* III. 219 Six well-conditioned perorators.

So **pe'roratory** *a.*, of or pertaining to peroration; *sb.*, utterance of a peroration.

1882 *Society* 16 Dec. 8/1 A string of rounded peroratory periods. **1903** *Westm. Gaz.* 2 Dec. 2/2 There were occasional lapses into what we can only call sentimental peroratory.

peroratorical (ˌpɛrərə'tɒrɪkəl), *a.* [f. PERORATOR after ORATORICAL *a.*] Characteristic of a peroration; perorational.

1927 C. E. MONTAGUE *Right off Map* vi. 56 His voice was taking on the peroratorical note.

†**pe'rore**, *v. Obs. rare.* [a. F. *pérore-r* (1507 in Hatz.-Darm.), ad. L. *perōrāre* to PERORATE.] *intr.* To perorate, make a peroration.

1594 R. ASHLEY tr. *Loys le Roy* 76 When you perored and pleaded. *Ibid.* 95 In Athens.. it was not lawful in peroring to moue affections.

perosen, -in, variants of PERROSIN *Obs.*

perosis (pə'rəʊsɪs). *Vet. Sci.* [ad. Gr. πήρωσις maiming, f. πηροῦν to maim.] A disease of poultry (see quot. 1937).

1931 *Science* 4 Sept. 249/2 Several of the stations reported that when the 'uniform diet' was fed to chicks kept in confinement a high percentage of them became afflicted with perosis (deforming leg weakness). **1937** *Jrnl. Nutrition* XIV. 155 Perosis.. is an anatomical deformity of the leg bones of young chickens, turkeys, pheasants, grouse and quail... The symptoms generally found are gross enlargement of the tibial-metatarsal joint, twisting or bending of the distal end of the tibia and of the proximal end of the metatarsus, and slipping of the gastrocnemius tendon from its condyles. **1950** *New Biol.* VIII. 104 There is some evidence that the disease in hens known as perosis may be due to manganese deficiency. **1970** *Poultry Sci.* XLIX. 1753/1 Perosis is an extremely complex condition that can be produced experimentally by an inadequate intake of several different nutrients.

perosmate (pə'rɒzmeɪt). *Chem.* [f. PER-[1] 5 + OSMATE.] A salt of osmium containing the anion $[OsO_4(OH)_2]^{2-}$, in which osmium has an oxidation state of 8. Formerly represented as $M_2O.OsO_4$ (where M is an alkali metal) and called osmiates (see OSMIATE).

The passage in ed. 7 (1890) of *Bloxham's Chem.* corresponding to quot. 1895 occurs s.v. OSMIATE.

1895 THOMSON & BLOXAM *Bloxam's Chem.* (ed. 8) 470 By dissolving perosmic anhydride in potash, potassium perosmate is supposed to be formed, but this has not been isolated. **1949** *Thorpe's Dict. Appl. Chem.* (ed. 4) IX. 134/1 Addition of alcohol to the clear solution and washings precipitates the ruthenium.. and reduces the perosmate to violet osmate. **1973** S. E. LIVINGSTONE in J. C. Bailar et al. *Comprehensive Inorg. Chem.* III. xliii. 1232 Potassium osmate $K_2[OsO_2(OH)_4]$.. is best prepared by reduction with alcohol of potassium perosmate $K_2[OsO_4(OH)_2]$, which can be prepared by treating OsO_4 with cold KOH. *Ibid.*, The octavalent state.. occurs in the tetroxide OsO_4, the perosmate $[OsO_4(OH)_2]^{2-}$, [etc.].

perosseous (pə'rɒsɪəs), *a. Physiol.* [f. PER- + L. *os* bone, after *osseous*.] Taking place through the substance of the bone.

1899 *Allbutt's Syst. Med.* VIII. 108 We should expect.. that the perosseous hearing should be affected step by step with the meatal.

perovskia (pɛ'rɒvskɪə). Also **perowskia, perowskya.** [mod.L. (G. Karelin 1841, in *Bull. Soc. Imp. des Naturalistes de Moscou* 15), f. the name of V. A. *Perovski* (1794–1857), once governor of the Russian province of Orenburg.] A herb or sub-shrub of the genus so called, belonging to the family Labiatæ, native to temperate regions of west and central Asia, and bearing panicles of deep blue flowers.

1907 *Gardeners' Chron.* 21 Dec. 426/1 In the case of Perovskia there is added charm in the pretty inflorescences late in autumn. **1961** *Amat. Gardening* 25 Nov. 8/3 It is best not to cut down the long stems of perowskia until the spring. **1973** C. D. BRICKELL in A. Gemmell *Sunday Gardener* iii. 85 *Perovskia*, with tall upright growths with grey-green aromatic leaves, will reach four feet, with long sprays of lavender-blue in September.

perovskite (pə'rɒfskaɪt). *Min.* Also **perof-, perow-.** [Named 1839 from personal name *Perovski*: see -ITE.] Titanate of calcium, occurring in crystals varying in colour from yellow to black, and usu. containing lanthanides or alkali metals in place of much of the calcium and often niobium in place of some of the titanium; also, a particular variety or specimen of this mineral, or (more widely) any mineral having the same crystal structure. Freq. *attrib.*, with reference to its structure.

1840 *Edin. New Philos. Jrnl.* XXIX. 418 (*heading*) Perowskite, a new mineral species. *Ibid.* It is named Perowskite, in honour of M. von Perowski, an intelligent Russian mineralogist. **1844** DANA *Min.* (ed. 2) 424 Perovskite consists principally of titanic acid or oxide and lime. **1872** *Nevill Catal. Min.* 122 Perowskite. **1878** LAWRENCE tr. *Cotta's Rocks Class.* 39 Perofskite occurs as an accessory in chlorite-schist. **1906** J. P. IDDINGS *Rock Minerals* 463 Perovskite occurs in basic igneous rocks, peridotite, melilite-basalt, alnöite, and in nephelite- and leucite-bearing rocks, that is, in titaniferous rocks low or comparatively low in silica. **1939** R. C. EVANS *Introd. Crystal Chem.* viii. 204 The structure of perovskite corresponds to the composition ABO_3 and has the cubic or pseudo-cubic unit cell shown in Fig. 46. *A* ions are situated at the corners of the cell and a *B* ion at its centre, while the faces are centred by oxygen. *Ibid.* 205 The appearance of KIO_3 and $RbIO_3$ among the compounds with the perovskite structure is of particular interest. **1955** *Physical Rev.* XCVIII. 1201/2 $KNbO_3$ and $KTaO_3$ are ferroelectrics of the perovskite type. **1956** *Electronic Engin.* XXVIII. 132 The remarkable and technically important properties of $BaTiO_3$ and other perovskite-type ceramics. **1962** W. A. DEER et al. *Rock-Forming Min.* V. 50 Hevesy *et al.* (1929) reported that for a number of perovskites the ratio Ti:Nb was about 3,000:1 and Ti:Ta 7,000:1. **1970** *Mineral. Abstr.* XXI. 155/1 The composition of synthetic complex perovskites can be expressed in terms of simpler formula units... E.g. $Pb(W_{1/2}Fe_{1/4}Li_{1/4})O_3 = \frac{3}{8}[Pb(W_{1/3}Fe_{2/3})O_3] + \frac{5}{8}[Pb(W_{3/5}Li_{2/5})O_3]$.

peroxidase (pə'rɒksɪdeɪz, -s). *Biochem.* Formerly also **peroxydase.** [a. F. *peroxydase* (G. Linossier 1898, in *Compt. Rend. des Séances de la Soc. de Biol.* L. 373), f. *peroxyde* PEROXIDE: see -ASE.] Any of a large class of iron-containing enzymes found esp. in plants which catalyse the oxidation of a substrate by peroxides, usu. hydrogen peroxide.

1903 *Jrnl. Chem. Soc.* LXXXIV. I. 378 The substance is a very powerful peroxydase, and renders hydrogen peroxide.. very active towards pyrogallol, gallic acid, aniline, [etc.]. **1907** J. B. COHEN *Org. Chem. Adv. Students* I. ix. 357 Many other vegetable oxidases have been described, including the so-called 'peroxidases' which activate hydrogen peroxide and possibly other peroxides. **1925** *Jrnl. Chem. Soc.* CXXVIII. I. 615 Peroxydases are found to be present in abundance in most common dried seeds in the resting condition. **1956** *New Biol.* XXI. 46 The same haem is shared by all haemoglobins and myoglobins, as well as.. other compounds of biological importance, notably the enzymes catalase and peroxidase. **1971** *New Scientist* 25 Feb. 411/2 The presence of ethylene in a young pea cell causes an increase in the level of the enzyme peroxidase which is capable of tacking the OH group onto proline.

Hence **peroxi'datic** *a.*, characteristic of a peroxidase.

1945 *Biochem. Jrnl.* XXXIX. 300/2 It is conceivable that in addition to alcohols catalase may promote a peroxidatic oxidation of other biologically important substances. **1954** A. WHITE et al. *Princ. Biochem.* xvi. 368 The catalatic splitting of hydrogen peroxide to water becomes merely a special case of a peroxidatic reaction, where hydrogen peroxide serves both as substrate and as acceptor. *Ibid.*, Catalase also exhibits peroxidatic activity. **1972** I. YAMAZAKI et al. in Åkeson & Ehrenberg *Struct. & Function Oxidation-Reduction Enzymes* 326 Peroxidatic reactions are catalyzed in the presence of various non-specific catalysts, such as transition metal ions and their coordination complexes.

peroxide (pə'rɒksaɪd). *Chem.* [f. PER- 5 a (see note there) + OXIDE.] **1. a.** That compound of oxygen with another element which contains the greatest possible proportion of oxygen. Now usu. restricted to those oxides which have at least one pair of oxygen atoms bonded to each other in the molecule, or which contain the anion O_2^{2-}.

1804 T. THOMSON *Chem.* (ed. 2) I. 103 When a metal has combined with as much oxygen as possible, I shall denote the compound formed by the term *peroxide*; indicating by it, that the metal is thoroughly oxidized. Thus we have.. the terms *protoxide* and *peroxide* to denote the minimum and maximum of oxidizement; and the terms *deutoxide*, *tritoxide*, etc. to denote all the intermediate states which are capable of being formed. **1804** HATCHETT in *Phil. Trans.* XCIV. 324 The air,.. after the wax is burned, combines with the superficial part of the oxide, and converts a portion of it into the red or peroxide. **1812** SIR H. DAVY *Chem. Philos.* 380 There are two definite combinations of tin and oxygene: the first, which may be called the *protoxide*, is gray; the second, which may be called the *peroxide*, is white. **1854** J. SCOFFERN in *Orr's Circ. Sc.*, *Chem.* 305 Binoxide or Peroxide of Hydrogen. **1873** DAWSON *Earth & Man* vi. 110 Peroxide of iron or iron rust. **1881** BELL *Sound by Radiant Energy* 38 A test-tube containing peroxide of nitrogen.

b. Any organic compound containing two linked oxygen atoms in its molecule.

1858 B. C. BRODIE in *Proc. R. Soc.* IX. 362, I have to add a new term to this series, of which hitherto no analogue has existed. This term is the peroxide of the organic radical, —the body which in the series of acetyl corresponds to the peroxide of hydrogen or barium in the series of the metal. **1881** *Chem. News* 20 May 233/1 The peroxide of ethyl remains as a dense syrupy liquid, miscible with water. **1922** H. G. DENHAM *Inorg. Chem.* xiii. 198 True peroxides are held to possess the linking present in hydrogen peroxide, –O–O–. **1950** N. V. SIDGWICK *Chem. Elements* II. 871 From hydrogen peroxide are derived a large number of compounds containing the O–O link; not only organic derivatives such as the alkyl and acyl peroxides, the percarboxylic acids.. but also many inorganic derivatives, in which one or more oxygen atoms of a basic or inorganic oxide, or an oxy-acid, are replaced by O–O groups. The binary inorganic compounds are commonly known as peroxides: this name should be confined to O–O compounds, but is often extended to include any metallic oxides with an unusually large amount of oxygen, such as PbO_2 and MnO_2. **1971** *Nomencl. Org. Chem.* (I.U.P.A.C.) (ed. 2) C. 161 Ethyl phenyl peroxide $C_6H_5O-OC_2H_5$. **1973** E. A. V. EBSWORTH et al. in J. C. Bailar et al. *Comprehensive Inorg. Chem.* II. xxii. 783 Organic peroxides decompose readily to give free radicals. *Ibid.* 784 Many transition metal peroxides are dangerously explosive.

2. Short for *peroxide blonde*. colloq.

1918 G. FRANKAU *Poetical Wks.* (1923) II. 108 Thy merchant-princes, whose week-end peroxides Hastened, safe-screened in many a Triplex-glass car. **1919** E. JORDAN *Girl in Mirror* (1925) ii. 45 'She's probably a peroxide,' he said. 'Even if she isn't, she can't hold a candle to your sister.'

3. Special Combs., as **peroxide blonde** *colloq.*, a woman with peroxided hair; **peroxide bond**, a single bond between two oxygen atoms in a molecule; **peroxide group**, the divalent group –O–O–; **peroxide hair**, hair bleached with hydrogen peroxide; **peroxide shampoo** (see quot.).

1920 S. LEWIS *Main St.* 314 Have you heard about this awful woman that's supposed to have come here to do dressmaking—a Mrs. Swiftwaite—awful peroxide blonde? **1927** A. CHRISTIE *Big Four* xiv. 187 (*title*) The peroxide blonde. **1947** N. MARSH *Final Curtain* vi. 90 An old man.. doting on a peroxide blonde. **1974** *Times* 26 Oct. 8/8 The corny peroxide blondes with their plucked eyebrows. **1949** *Chem. Rev.* XLV. 399 Whether the decomposition of a given hydroperoxide involves radical or cationic intermediates probably depends on the amount of polarization of the peroxide bond. **1961** A. G. DAVIES *Org. Peroxides* x. 143 Familiarity with the homolysis of the peroxide bond delayed the recognition that the above reaction is often heterolytic. **1899** *Jrnl. Chem. Soc.* LXXVI. II. 659 The authors have obtained two new series of compounds which contain the peroxide group. **1939** F. A. PHILBRICK *Inorg. Chem.* xvii. 274 In structure the true peroxides are distinguished by containing in the molecule one or more peroxide groups, –O–O–, such as are present in hydrogen peroxide. **1968** *Jrnl. Chem. Soc.* A. 397/1 The great majority of transition-metal peroxide complexes involve a co-ordinated bidentate peroxide group, but a few are known in which the peroxide functions as a bridging ligand. **1937** W. S. MAUGHAM *Theatre* i. 2 Notwithstanding her cropped peroxide hair and her heavily-painted lips she had the neutral look that marks the perfect secretary. **1966** J. S. COX *Illustr. Dict. Hairdressing* 111/1 *Peroxide shampoo*, a soft soap shampoo incorporating a small quantity of 20 vol. peroxide of hydrogen and two or three drops of ·880 ammonium hydroxide.

Hence †**pe'roxidate, pe'roxidize** *vbs. trans.* and *intr.*, to convert, or become converted, into a peroxide; to combine with the largest possible proportion of oxygen; whence **peroxi'dation, pe'roxidizement**, conversion into a peroxide; **pero'xidic** *a.*, having the properties of a peroxide; containing or forming part of a peroxide group.

1827 FARADAY *Chem. Manip.* xiv. 310 Till the whole of the earth is peroxidized. **1839** URE *Dict. Arts* 39 The peroxidation of the iron renders it less soluble in the sulphuric acid. *Ibid.* 225 In order to fix the iron by its peroxidizement. **1842** PARNELL *Chem. Anal.* (1845) 334 To prevent the peroxidation, by the air, of any appreciable quantity of the protoxide of iron. **1857** MAYNE *Expos. Lex.* 918/2 Peroxidated. **1880** GARROD & BAXTER *Mat. Med* 150 The use of the chlorine and carbonate of zinc.. is to peroxidize and precipitate any iron. **1945** *Jrnl. Org. Chem.* X. 416 This liberation of iodine indicated that peroxidic compounds had been formed in these solvents during ozonization. **1949** *Chem. Rev.* XLV. 385 In the decomposition of organic peroxides, rupture of the bond between the two peroxidic oxygens is often accompanied by cleavage of an adjacent carbon-to-carbon bond. **1956** *Nature* 21 Jan. 129/2 The first product is probably the hydroperoxide.., and indeed very labile, strongly peroxidic, solids have been detected, but isolation has not been possible. **1961** A. G. DAVIES *Org. Peroxides* iii. 56 Peroxylauric acid..loses about 15 per cent of its peroxidic oxygen after 1 week at 25°.

pe'roxided, *ppl. a.* [f. PEROXIDE + -ED[1].]

a. Treated with (hydrogen) peroxide. **b.** Having bleached hair. Also *absol.*

1906 B. VON HÜTTEN *What became of Pam* x. 71 Miss Vesey had highly peroxided hair and a manner of suspicious dignity. **1910** BARONESS ORCZY *Lady Molly* ix. 234 An over-dressed, much behatted, peroxided young woman. **1930** *Observer* 18 May 15/3 Simon, and Sylvia whom he loved, and Sylvia's peroxided mamma were agreeable company. **1946** WODEHOUSE *Joy in Morning* iv. 29 What was it? Blackmail? Does he want you to pinch damaging correspondence from the peroxided? Has some quick-thinking adventuress got him in her toils? **1947** D. M. DAVIN *Gorse blooms Pale* 205 The hair, peroxided it was. **1976** *Times* 5 Mar. 9/5 Two tanned and peroxided matrons in their fifties.

peroxisome (pə'rɒksɪsəʊm). *Cytology.* [f. PEROXI(DE + -SOME[4].] An organelle present in the cytoplasm of many kinds of cell which contains the reducing enzyme catalase and usu. some oxidases that produce hydrogen peroxide.

1965 C. DE DUVE in *Jrnl. Cell Biol.* XXVII. 25A The name *peroxisome* is proposed for the microbodies of rat liver and for the particles of similar biochemical nature existing in kidney and in *Tetrahymena pyriformis.* The peroxisomes contain large amounts of catalase and several hydrogen peroxide-producing oxidases. **1970** *Sci. Amer.* Sept. 113/3 Recently the cells of higher organisms have been found to contain organelles called peroxisomes, whose major function is thought to be the protection of cells from oxygen. **1975** *Science* 21 Nov. 787/1 Peroxisomes (microbodies), cytoplasmic constituents characterized morphologically by a single limiting membrane and a finely granular or homogeneous matrix, have recently been recognized as ubiquitous structures in animal and plant cells.

Hence **peroxi'somal** *a.*

1969 *Jrnl. Protozool.* XVI. 430/2 The 6 acid hydrolases studied have almost identical distribution patterns, differing clearly from those of the mitochondrial malate dehydrogenase, peroxisomal catalase and urate oxidase. **1972** *McGraw-Hill Yearbk. Sci. & Technol.* 321/1 Although peroxisomal respiration will be considered primarily, the entire process of photorespiration involves the mitochondrion. **1975** *Science* 21 Nov. 789/1 Recent studies ..failed to demonstrate the presence of peroxisomal oxidases in these catalase-containing particles isolated from Harder's gland.

peroxo(-) (pə'rɒksəʊ), *prefix* and quasi-*adj. Chem.* [f. PER-[1] 5 + OXO(-): cf. PEROXIDE.]

A. *prefix.* Used in inorganic chemistry in the names of compounds, complexes, etc., that contain a peroxide group. **B.** Hence as quasi-*adj.*: containing or being a peroxide group. Cf. PEROXY(-).

PEROXY(-) is the usual form in organic chemistry.

1910 *Jrnl. Chem. Soc.* XCVIII. II. 858 Tetraethylenediamine-μ-ammoniumperoxocobalticobalte salts. *Ibid.* 869 On heating with concentrated sulphuric acid, it is decomposed with evolution of oxygen and nitrogen, the volumes of these gases obtained showing that the compound contains a peroxo-group and tervalent and quadrivalent cobalt. **1930** *Chem. Abstr.* XXIV. 2672 In the presence of air and light, peroxo compds. possessing unusual oxidizing powers are produced in addn. to the usual Fe^{+++} and Fe^{++} complex ions. **1943** THORNE & ROBERTS tr. *Ephraim's Inorg. Chem.* (ed. 4) xi. 321 The simplest..of the multinucleate cobaltammines are the peroxo-salts $[(NH_3)_5Co-O-O-Co(NH_3)_5]X_4$. **1959** R. S. CAHN *Introd. Chem. Nomencl.* 19 Peroxoacids, in which $-O-$ is replaced by $-O{\cdot}O-$, are similarly distinguished by the prefix peroxo- (peroxy- or simply per- have frequently been used in the past), as, for example, in HNO_4 peroxonitric acid. **1960** HESLOP & ROBINSON *Inorg. Chem.* xxxvii. 527 There are two peroxo-acids of sulphur, $H_2S_2O_8$, peroxodisulphuric acid, and H_2SO_5, peroxomonosulphuric acid. **1966** COTTON & WILKINSON *Adv. Inorg. Chem.* (ed. 2) xiii. 376 The peroxo acids are useful oxidants and sources of free radicals. **1971** *Nomencl. Inorg. Chem.* (I.U.P.A.C.) (ed. 2) 33 The prefix peroxo-, when used in conjunction with the trivial names of acids, indicates substitution of $-O-$ by $-O-O-$. **1973** [see PERBORIC *a.*].

peroxy(-) (pə'rɒksɪ), *prefix* and quasi-*adj. Chem.* [f. PER-[1] 5 + OXY-: cf. PEROXIDE.]

A. *prefix.* Orig. used in the names of compounds containing a larger proportion of oxygen than the parent compound, now in the names of compounds, radicals, etc., that contain a peroxide group. **B.** Hence as quasi-*adj.*: Containing or being a peroxide group. Cf. PEROXO(-).

PEROXO(-) is now the usual form in inorganic chemistry.

1878 *Jrnl. Chem. Soc.* XXXIV. 237 The relation between hæmatin and peroxyhæmoglobin must be sought by investigating the bearing of the albumin. **1900** *Chem. News* 16 Feb. 83/2 We thus obtain a microcrystalline compound, the peroxysulphate of silver, which is decomposed by warm water. **1912** *Jrnl. Chem. Soc.* CII. II. 156 The reaction may be considered a general one for differentiating between three peroxy-salts and hydrogen peroxide additive products. **1956** *Nature* 28 Jan. 182/1 Hydrogen in and on the metal now becomes anodic, and by reaction with oxygen doubtless goes into transient peroxy compounds. **1961** A. G. DAVIES *Org. Peroxides* iii. 55 There are three important types of acyl peroxides—the peroxyacids.., the peroxyesters.., and the diacyl peroxides. **1961** E. G. E. HAWKINS *Org. Peroxides* p. xii, Peroxy ($RO_2{\cdot}$) radicals,..give substitution products with many reactive molecules. **1964** *Economist* 25 July 356/2 A virulent family of pollutants known as peroxy-acylnitrates (PANs). **1971** *Nomencl. Inorg. Chem.* (I.U.P.A.C.) (ed. 2) 41 In conformity with the practice of organic nomenclature, the forms peroxy [etc.]..are also used but are not recommended. **1973** E. A. V. EBSWORTH et al. in J. C. Bailar et al. *Comprehensive Inorg. Chem.* II. xxii. 780 The peroxy-group may replace an oxygen atom as a bridge between two other groups, giving compounds such as $Me_3SnOOSnMe_3$. **1975** J. O. SCHRECK *Org. Chem.* iii. 60 Acyl radicals are precursors of peroxyacyl nitrates, which are lacrimators often associated with smog.

Perp, perp. (pɜːp), abbrev. PERPENDICULAR *a.* 3. Now freq. in colloq. allusive use. Also *ellipt.*

1867 *Murray's Handbk. Trav. Yorkshire* 116/1 The great features of the exterior..are the North Porch, and the West Front... Both of these are Perp... The West Front..is as fine an example of a Perp. composition. **1894** K. BAEDEKER *Gt. Brit.* (ed. 3) 407 The most striking features of the exterior [of York Minster] are the noble *W. Façade* (Dec.; towers, 201 ft. high, Perp.) [etc.]. **1933** J. E. MORRIS *Northumberland* (ed. 3) 247 Much of the other work is modern and misleading,..the 'Perp.' W. window of the S. aisle, *c.* 1832. **1937** A. CHRISTIE *Dumb Witness* vii. 68 Though an attractive specimen of what the guidebook calls Early Perp. it [*sc.* a church] had been so conscientiously restored in Victorian vandal days that little of interest remained. **1945** J. BETJEMAN *New Bats in Old Belfries* 46 Grey-blue of granite in the small arcade (Late Perp). **1951** N. PEVSNER *Middlesex* 143 The tomb in the aisle chapel is purely Perp. **1957** 'J. WYNDHAM' *Midwich Cuckoos* I. i. 10 The church is mostly perp. and dec., but with a Norman west doorway and font. **1967** 'M. HUNTER' *Cambridgeshire Disaster* ix. 60 The usual slab of village with a nice old Perp. church. **1974** SHERWOOD & PEVSNER *Oxfordshire* 118 The wall-shafts of the nave [of Christ Church Cathedral] have Perp. shafts with concave-sided capitals. **1974** *Times* 10 Jan. 16/7 His love of Gothic architecture made him befriend cathedrals, abbeys and churches, particularly the Perp and Dec so abundant in East Anglia.

†**perpacate,** *v. Obs. rare*[−0]. [f. ppl. stem of L. *perpācāre* to quiet completely, f. PER- 2 + *pācāre* to PACATE.]

1623 COCKERAM, *Perpacate,* to set all things in order.

perpen, variant of PARPEN.

perpend (pə'pɛnd), *v. arch.* [ad. L. *perpendĕre* to weigh exactly, ponder, consider, f. PER- 2 + *pendĕre* to weigh, pay, ponder.]

1. a. *trans.* To weigh mentally, ponder, consider, examine, investigate. (With simple obj. or obj. cl.)

1527-8 FOX *Let. to Gardiner* in Strype *Eccl. Mem.* (1721) I. App. xxvi. 79 My Lords grace..perpending and pondering the exoneration of his own conscience. **1599** SHAKS. *Hen. V,* IV. iv. 8 Perpend my words O Signieur Dewe, and marke. **1660** H. MORE *Myst. Godl.* x. ii. 496 They being not at leisure to perpend things to the bottom. **1762** STERNE *Tr. Shandy* VI. xvi, There are a thousand resolutions..weighed, poised, and perpended. **1821** BYRON *Juan* v. lxxii, I shall perpend if your proposal may Be such as I can properly accept. **1930** J. BUCHAN *Castle Gay* xi. 172 He retired to the inn..to write out his notes and perpend the situation. **1939** JOYCE *Finnegans Wake* I. 187 Perpending that Putterick O'Purcell pulls the coald stoane out of Winterwater's and Silder Seas sing for Harreng our Keng. **1966** 'H. MACDIARMID' *Company I've Kept* vii. 172 The chapters in Professor Hofrichter's book..should be carefully perpended by those who fail even yet to see the full significance of Ezra Pound's great slogan: 'Make it new!'

b. *absol.* or *intr.*

1601 SHAKS. *Twel. N.* v. i. 307 Therefore, perpend my Princesse, and giue eare. **1848** *Blackw. Mag.* LXIV. 107 Perpend upon this..at your leisure. **1868** W. R. GREG *Lit. & Soc. Judgm.* 152 They are..too impatient to perpend and reflect.

†**2.** To weigh in a balance. (A Latinism.) *Obs.*

1660 STANLEY *Hist. Philos.* IX. (1701) 375/2 He thinks how long Cancer the day extends, And Capricorn the night: Himself perpends In a just ballance, that no flaw there be, Nothing exuberant, but that all agree.

Hence **per'pending** *vbl. sb.*; †**per'pendment.**

1667 WATERHOUSE *Fire Lond.* 48 Great enterprises alwayes requiring grave perpendment of the method. **1681** R. FLEMING *Fulfill. Script.* (1801) I. 246 O that these would but by a serious perpending consider the work of the Lord. **1868** F. E. PAGET *Lucretia* 190, I had barely finished my perpendings and explorations, when [etc.].

perpend, obs. form of PARPEN.

†**per'pendant, -ent,** *a. Obs. rare.* [f. PER- 4 + PENDANT, -ENT.]

a. Remaining appendant. **b.** Hanging down very much.

1642 tr. *Perkins' Prof. Bk.* x. §643. 278 A man seised of a mannor unto which an advowson is appendant doth thereof enfeoffe a stranger 'Exceptis, reservatis etc. or Praeter' one acre, and name the acre, and the Advowson, this is a good exception... And the Advowson shall be perpendant unto the acre which is reserved. **1650** BULWER *Anthropomet.* xi. 108 Their perpendent Lips hang down above a Cubite low.

†**'perpender.** *Masonry. Obs.* [f. *perpend,* PARPEN + -ER[1].] = PARPEN.

1611 COTGR., *Perpins,* perpenders, or perpent stones; stones made iust as thick as a wall, and shewing their smoothed ends on either side thereof. **1755** in JOHNSON [erroneously explained as 'a coping stone'].

†**per'pendicle.** *Obs. rare.* [a. OF. *perpendicle* (14th c. in Hatz.-Darm.), ad. L. *perpendiculum* plummet, plumb-line, f. **perpendĕre,* f. PER- 2 + *pendĕre* to hang. Cf. mod.F. *perpendicule* (16th c.), It. *perpendicolo.*] A plumb-line.

14.. in Halliwell *Rara Math.* (1841) 58 Come toward and go froward til þe perpendicle, þat es to say þe threde whereon þe plumbe henges falle vpon þe mydel lyne of þe quadrant. **1656** BLOUNT *Glossogr., Perpendicle,* a plumb line, ..with lead at the end. **1755** JOHNSON, *Perpendicle,* anything hanging down by a straight line. **1867** SMYTH *Sailor's Word-bk., Perpendicle,* the plumb-line of an old quadrant.

perpendicular (pɜːpən'dɪkjʊlə(r)), *a., adv.,* and *sb.* Also 6 -pent-. [a. OF. *perpendiculer, -ier,* = Sp. *perpendicular,* It. *perpendicolare,* ad. L. *perpendiculār-is,* f. *perpendicul-um*: see prec. and -AR[1]. Mod.F. has the parallel form *perpendiculaire,* ad. L. *perpendiculārius* (both forms in Frontinus 1st c.).]

A. *adj.* **1.** Situated at right angles to the plane of the horizon, or directly up or down; vertical.

c **1391** CHAUCER *Astrol.* II. §23 Thow most haue a plomet hanging on a lyne heyer than thin heued on a perche, & thilke lyne mot hange euene perpendiculer by-twixe the pool & thin eye. **1555** EDEN *Decades* 121 It receaueth the soonne beames at noonetyde directly perpenticuler ouer their heades. **1638** SIR T. HERBERT *Trav.* (ed. 2) 193 In the Sunnes perpendicular glances, wee found it hot. **1725** DE FOE *Voy. round World* (1840) 326 The water of the lake was swelled about two feet perpendicular. **1822** IMISON *Sc. & Art* I. 74 Measure the perpendicular height of the fall of water, in feet. **1892** GREENER *Breech Loader* 211 The prettiest of shots and a difficult one to make is the perpendicular shot.

b. Of an ascent or descent: Nearly vertical; very steep, precipitous.

1596 SHAKS. *1 Hen. IV,* II. iv. 378 The sprightly Scot of Scots, Dowglas, he that runnes a Horse-backe vp a Hill perpendicular. **1822** BYRON *Heaven & Earth* I. iii, Trees that twine their roots with stone In perpendicular places. **1838** DICKENS *Nich. Nick.* iii, A female voice, proceeding from a perpendicular staircase at the end of the passage. **1880** *Fraser's Mag.* May 650 Slippery steps..connect the various stories of this perpendicular hamlet.

c. Of persons: Of erect figure or attitude when standing or riding; also, upright; (*humorous*) in a standing position.

1768 STERNE *Sent. Journ.* (1775) I. 44 (*Bidet*) He canter'd away before me as happy and as perpendicular as a prince. **1826** MISS MITFORD *Village* Ser. II. (1863) 319 A stiff perpendicular old maid. **1851** CARLYLE *Sterling* II. i. (1872) 89 A stout broad gentleman of sixty, perpendicular in attitude. **1859** *Sunday Times* 16 Oct. 5/3 Every seat..was occupied and perpendicular accommodation threatened to be at a premium. **1897** *Daily News* 24 Mar. 7/3 In the slang of the trade perpendicular drinking is the drinking that goes on at bars, the customer standing.

†**d.** *fig.* Directly leading *to,* entailing, or antecedent *to*; direct. *Obs.*

[**1579** J. STUBBES *Gaping Gulf* F iv b, Thys french mariage is..the very rightest perpendicular downfal that can be imagined from the point france to our English state.] **1632** LITHGOW *Trav.* IV. 166 To these of the first reason, there is another perpendicular cause. **1646** SIR T. BROWNE *Pseud. Ep.* I. xi. 44 Distorting the order and theorie of causes perpendicular to their effects. **1651** BIGGS *New Disp.* 149 The prime indication perpendicular to health, and conducible to perfect restauration.

†**e.** Directly dependent. *Obs.*

1555 EDEN *Decades* 48, I haue added this [book] to the tenthe as a perpendiculer lyne, and as it were a backe guyde or rerewarde to the other. *Ibid.* 50, I wyll nowe therfore soo make an ende of this perpendiculer conclusion of the hole Decade. **1632** LITHGOW *Trav.* II. 58 A perpendicular Prouince annexed to it. **1691-8** NORRIS *Pract. Disc.* (1711) III. 239 To have our Wills intirely conformable, and as it were Perpendicular to his.

2. *Geom.* Of a line or plane: Having a direction at right angles to a given line, plane, or surface. Const. *to* (†*with*).

A line is said to be perpendicular (now more usually NORMAL) to a curve when it meets the tangent at the point of intersection at right angles.

1570 BILLINGSLEY *Euclid* I. def. x. 3 The right lyne which standeth erected, is called a perpendiculer line to that vpon which it standeth. **1624** WOTTON *Archit.* in *Reliq.* (1651) 224 That the Walls be most exactly perpendicular to the Ground-Work; for the right Angle..is the true cause of all Stability, both in Artificial and Natural Positions. **1667** PRIMATT *City & C. Build.* 159 How to draw a Perpendicular Line from any Point, to any Line given. **1715** LEONI *Palladio's Archit.* (1742) I. 11 The middle of the upmost Wall ought to be perpendicular with the middle of the nethermost. **1882** MINCHIN *Unipl. Kinemat.* 37 Moving in a plane perpendicular to the axis.

3. *Arch.* Applied (first by Rickman) to the third or Florid style of English Pointed Architecture, developed out of the Decorated style in the latter part of the fourteenth century, and prevalent throughout the fifteenth, characterized by the vertical lines of its tracery.

1812-15 RICKMAN *Styles of Archit.* (1817) 44 *Perpendicular English...* The name clearly designates this style, for the mullions of the windows, and the ornamental pannellings run in perpendicular lines. **1820** D. TURNER *Tour Normandy* I. 167 Nowhere..have I been able to trace among our Gallic neighbours the existence of the simple perpendicular style. **1875** STUBBS *Const. Hist.* II. xvii. 625 The unmeaning symmetry of the Perpendicular Style. **1904** J. T. FOWLER *Durham Univ.* 10 Three good Perpendicular windows.

4. *Comb.*

c **1865** LD. BROUGHAM in *Circ. Sc.* I. Introd. Disc. 6 The third side of a perpendicular-sided triangle.

†**B.** *adv.* In a perpendicular manner; perpendicularly, vertically. *Obs.*

[*c* **1391**: see A. 1.] **1527** R. Thorne in Hakluyt *Voy.* (1589) 253 The one in the Occidentall part descendeth perpendicular vpon the 175 degree. **1699** Evelyn *Kal. Hort.* (ed. 9) 63 If the Tree be too ponderous to be lifted perpendicular by the Hand alone. **1792** *Munchausen's Trav.* Suppl. 80 To fall near two miles perpendicular.

C. *sb.* **1.** An instrument or appliance for indicating the vertical line from any point: e.g. a mason's or builder's plumb-rule or plumb-level; a gunner's level: see quots.

1603 B. Jonson *Jas. I Entertainm.* Wks. (Rtldg.) 531/2 In her lap she held a perpendicular or level, as the ensign of evenness and rest. **1664** Butler *Hud.* II. iii. 1019 I'll make them serve for perpendic'lars As true as e'er were used by Bricklayers. *a* **1727** Newton *Chronol. Amended* i. (1728) 148 Dædalus..invented the chip-ax, and saw, and wimble, and perpendicular. **1792** *Trans. Soc. Arts* (ed. 2) III. 184 An instrument..called a Perpendicular, to be used instead of a quadrant of altitude with the artificial globes. **1819** *Pantologia, Perpendicular*, in gunnery, is a small instrument, used for finding the centre line of a piece in the operation of pointing it to a given object. **1859** F. A. Griffiths *Artil. Man.* (1862) 121 One quadrant, one perpendicular, for every four or five mortars.

2. A line at right angles to the plane of the horizon, a vertical line; also, a vertical plane or face; *loosely*, a very steep or precipitous face; a steep. ***the perpendicular*** (sc. line, direction).

1632 Lithgow *Trav.* x. 432 The Perpendiculars of long-reaching Caucasus. **1656** Heylin *Surv. France* 4 Rising from the bottom to the top in a perpendicular. **1756–7** tr. *Keysler's Trav.* (1760) III. 343 The tower of this church is observed to lean a little from the perpendicular. **1772–84** *Cook's Voy.* (1790) IV. 1501 The tide rises and falls about six feet, upon a perpendicular. **1817** Byron *Manfred* II. ii. 4 O'er the crag's headlong perpendicular. **1837–9** Hallam *Hist. Lit.* I. I. iii. §29. 160 Fioravanti..is said..to have restored to the perpendicular [a tower] at Cento seventy-five feet high, which had swerved five feet. **1838** *Civil Eng. & Arch. Jrnl.* I. 394/1 The length of the *Ruby* is 155 feet between the perpendiculars.

b. Upright or erect position or attitude; also *fig.* moral uprightness, rectitude.

1859 Geo. Eliot *A. Bede* iv, For my part, I think it's better to see when your perpendicular's true, than to see a ghost. **1862** Lowell *Biglow P.* Ser. II. iii, They suit..nut your Southun gen'leman thet keeps his parpendic'lar. **1874** T. Hardy *Madding Crowd* iii, Springing to her accustomed perpendicular like a bowed sapling..she seated herself in the manner demanded by the saddle. **1884** Tennyson *Becket* II. ii, Your lordship affects the unwavering perpendicular.

c. (*slang.*) A meal taken standing; an entertainment or party at which most of the guests remain standing.

1871 'M. Legrand' *Camb. Freshm.* xxi, This was the first occasion on which he had been honoured with an invitation to a Perpendicular, as such entertainments are styled. **1873** *Slang Dict., Perpendicular*, a lunch taken standing-up at a tavern bar. **1882** Edna Lyall *Donovan* ix. I. 207, I dutifully attended my mother to three fashionable crowds—'perpendiculars' is the best name for them, for there is generally barely room for standing. **1890** Romanes in *Life* 266 Yesterday we had here [at Edinburgh] what at Cambridge used to be called a 'perpendicular'—twenty students to supper.

3. *Geom.* A straight line at right angles to a given line, plane, or surface. (Chiefly in phr. ***to draw a perpendicular to*** a line, ***to raise a p. upon*** a line, ***to let fall a p. upon*** a line from a point without it, etc.)

1571 Digges *Pantom., Math. Treat.* def. xxiii. T iij, A line falling from any solide angle of these bodyes perpendicularlye on the opposite playne or base, shall be named that solides Perpendiculare. **1704** J. Harris *Lex. Techn.* I, *Perpendicular* to a Parabola, is a Right Line cutting the Parabola in the Point in which any other Right Line touches it, and which is also its self Perpendicular to that Tangent. **1806** Hutton *Course Math.* I. 286 A Perpendicular is the Shortest Line that can be drawn from a Given Point to an Indefinite Line. **1827** *Ibid.* II. 346 A perpendicular measures the distance of any point from a plane.

perpendicularity (pɜːpəndɪkjuːˈlærɪtɪ). [f. L. type **perpendiculāritās*, f. *perpendiculār-is*: see prec. and -ity. Cf. mod.F. *perpendicularité* (1741 in *Dict. Acad.*), Sp., It. *perpendicularità*.]

1. Vertical or upright position; upright attitude or posture; verticality.

1589 Puttenham *Eng. Poesie* II. x. (Arb.) 102 In buildings of stone or bricke the mason giueth a band..to hold in the worke fast and maintaine the perpendicularitie of the wall. **1664** Power *Exp. Philos.* II. 110 Pendents..multiply their undulations before they rest in their desired Perpendicularity. **1760** Stiles in *Phil. Trans.* LII. 42 The column supported its perpendicularity near a quarter of an hour. **1874** Parker *Goth. Archit.* II. vi. 195 Perpendicularity is..the characteristic of these windows. **1874** T. Hardy *Madding Crowd* xviii, His square-framed perpendicularity showed more fully now than in the crowd and bustle of the market-house.

2. *Geom.* Position or direction at right angles *to* a given line, surface, or plane.

1725 Watts *Logic* I. ii. §3 The perpendicularity of these lines to each other, is the difference of a right angle. **1841** J. R. Young *Math. Dissert.* ii. 73 They preserve their perpendicularity to one another. **1872** Proctor *Ess. Astron.* xxv. 321 Perpendicularity of intersection.

perpendicularly (pɜːpənˈdɪkjʊləlɪ), *adv.* [f. perpendicular *a.* + -ly^2.] In a perpendicular manner. **1.** Directly up or down, vertically.

1555 Eden *Decades* 94 The soonne hauinge his course perpendicularly or directly ouer the same. **1605** Shaks. *Lear* IV. vi. 54 The altitude Which thou hast perpendicularly fell. **1725** De Foe *Voy. round World* (1840) 333 It rose about two fathoms perpendicularly. **1885** *Spectator* 8 Aug. 1045/1 The trees..grow perpendicularly for 100 feet before the branches commence.

†**b.** *fig.* Directly. *Obs.*

1658 J. Jones *Ovid's Ibis* 48 Gods presence is everywhere but more perpendicularly in his Temple. **1688** Norris *Theory Love* Pref. 4 To write nothing but what is directly and perpendicularly to the Point in hand.

2. *Geom.* At right angles to some line or plane.

1570 Billingsley *Euclid* I. Post. iv. 6 A right angle is caused of one right lyne falling perpendicularly vppon an other. **1667** Primatt *City & C. Build.* 159 A right Line drawn cuts the Line given perpendicularly. **1703** Moxon *Mech. Exerc.* 208 You must not hold the Blade of this Tool perpendicularly before the Work,..but aslant. **1879** *Cassell's Techn. Educ.* VI. 349/2 Cogs or pins placed perpendicularly to the face of the wheel.

perpenˈdicularness. *rare.* [f. as prec. + -ness.] Perpendicularity.

1606 G. W[oodcocke] *Hist. Ivstine* xxiv. 90 Munified..with the Perpendicularnes and quarry of the rocke. **1727** in Bailey vol. II.

†**perpenˈsation.** *Obs.* *rare*$^{-0}$. [ad. L. *perpensātiōn-em*, from *perpensāre* to weigh or consider carefully, freq. of *perpendĕre* to perpend.]

1623 Cockeram, *Perpensation*, a due examining. **1658** Phillips, *Perpension*, or *Perpensation*.

†**perˈpensed,** *a.* *Obs.* *rare*$^{-1}$. [f. OF. *perpensé* (13th c.), pa. pple. of *perpenser*, or f. L. *perpens-us* (see perpensity) + -ed.] Thoroughly considered, thought out, deliberate: = L. *perpensus*. Hence †**perˈpensedly** *adv.*, with deliberation, deliberately: = L. *perpense*.

c **1540** tr. *Pol. Verg. Eng. Hist.* (Camden No. 29) 102 That he might set forwarde his perpensed malitious Enterprise. **1624** Bp. Mountagu *Immed. Addr.* 156 If men doe not consider their sayings perpensedly.

perˈpension. [n. of action f. L. *perpendĕre*, *perpens-* to perpend.] Mental weighing; thorough consideration or reflection; deliberation.

1646 Sir T. Browne *Pseud. Ep.* I. vii. 25 Unto reasonable perpensions it hath no place in some Sciences, small in others. **1661** Boyle *Style of Script.* 238 The Disparity of the Influences of the Bare Belief and the Due Perpension of a Truth. **1674** R. Godfrey *Inj. & Ab. Physic* Pref., To do which, after serious perpension, I was easily inclin'd. **1890** R. L. Stevenson *Let.* 13 July (1911) III. 165 Upon these points, perpend, and give me the results of your perpensions.

†**perˈpensity.** *Obs.* *rare*$^{-1}$. [f. L. *perpensus* deliberate, pa. pple. of *perpendĕre* + -ity.] Attention.

1704 Swift *T. Tub* ix, I desire the reader to attend with the utmost perpensity.

†**perˈpensive,** *a.* *Obs.* *rare*$^{-1}$. [f. L. *perpens-us* deliberate + -ive.] Deliberative.

1647 Ward *Simp. Cobler* 38 It is rather Christian modesty than shame..to be very perpensive.

perpent, variant of parpen.

†ˌ**perperaˈcute,** *a.* *Obs.* [f. per- 4 + peracute (which already contains the same prefix).] Intensely or excessively acute.

1647 Ward *Simp. Cobler* 23 To still the sad unquietnesse and per-peracute contentions of that most comfortable and renowned island. **1661** Lovell *Hist. Anim. & Min.* 438 If simply acute they may be judged on the fourteenth day: If peracute on the seventh; if perperacute on the fourth. **1665** Harvey *Advice agst. Plague* 10 Per-per-acute malign Feaver. **1671** Blagrave *Astrol. Physic* 26 There are also some Sicknesses perperacute.

†ˈ**perperous,** *a.* *Obs.* *rare*$^{-0}$. [f. L. *perper-us* heedless, inconsiderate, faulty, erroneous + -ous.] Hence †ˈ**perperously** *adv.* *Obs.* *rare*$^{-1}$ [= L. *perpere*], foolishly, erroneously, wrongly; †ˈ**perperitude** *Obs.* *rare*$^{-0}$, inconsiderateness, foolish error.

1623 Cockeram, *Perperitude*, rudenesse. **1657** Tomlinson *Renou's Disp.* 398 Not the factitious Lacca as some perperously imagine. **1657** *Physical Dict., Perperously*, foolishly and unskilfully.

†**perˈpession.** *Obs.* *rare.* [ad. L. *perpessiōn-em*, f. per- 1, 2 + *passiōn-em* suffering, passion.]

1. Endurance of suffering.

a **1603** T. Cartwright *Confut. Rhem. N.T.* (1618) 629 Free from all perpession or painfull passion. **1628** Gaule *Pract. The.* (1629) 167 Yet was our Sauiour both..terrified in the apprehension of Wrath; and in the perpession of Death, crucified. **1659** Pearson *Creed* xii. (1741) 393 The eternity of destruction in the language of Scripture signifies a perpetual perpession and duration in misery.

2. Suffering of impact or influence. *rare*$^{-1}$.

1675 J. Smith *Chr. Relig. App.* II. 13 Ascribing all..to the Perpessions, Collisions, Mutations and Mixtures of Natural Beings among themselves.

†**perpet.** *Obs.* Abbreviation of perpetuana.

1715 in Somers *Tracts* II. 38 Flannels, Perpets, Serges and Stuffs Exported from Christmas 1708 to Christmas 1709. **1745** *De Foe's Eng. Tradesman* xlvii. (1841) II. 190 The county of Essex is chiefly taken up with the manufacture of bags and perpets.

perpetrable (ˈpɜːpɪtrəb(ə)l), *a.* [ad. late L. *perpetrābilis* (Tertull. *c* 200), f. *perpetrāre*: see below and -able.] Capable of being perpetrated.

a **1734** North *Exam.* I. iii. (1740) 128 No Wickedness perpetrable with Safety will be left undone.

†ˈ**perpetrate,** *pa. pple.* *Obs.* Also 5–6 -at. [ad. L. *perpetrāt-us*, pa. pple. of *perpetrāre*: see next. In use before introduction of the finite vb., and after that as its pa. pple., until displaced by *perpetrated*.] Perpetrated.

1472–3 *Rolls of Parlt.* VI. 19/1 Treasons and Felonyes..by any persone done or perpetrat. *a* **1548** Hall *Chron., Edw. IV* 244 The great tyrannye..that he and his people had perpetrate and committed. **1549** *Compl. Scot.* x. 82 These cruel inuasions perpetrat contrar oure realme. *c* **1614** Sir W. Mure *Dido & Æneas* I. 375 Pigmalion's cruell crime, Against her mate in privy perpetrate.

perpetrate (ˈpɜːpɪtreɪt), *v.* [f. ppl. stem of L. *perpetrāre* to carry through, execute, perform, f. per- 1 + *patrāre* to bring to pass, effect. In Latin, the thing perpetrated might be good or bad; but in Eng. the verb, having been first used in the statutes in reference to the committing of crimes, has been associated with evil deeds.]

trans. To perform, execute, or commit (a crime or evil deed).

1547 *Act 1 Edw. VI*, c. 12 §5 Yf anny parsone being ons conuicted..shall..eftsones commit or perpetrate anny of the offences before mentioned. **1581** Lambarde *Eiren.* II. vii. (1588) 264 If the offence bee perpetrated in a Barne of the house. **1634** Sir T. Herbert *Trav.* 34 To perpetrate like villany on the other Princes. **1749** Smollett *Regicide* v. ii, The auspicious hour To perpetrate the deed. **1855** Prescott *Philip II*, I. I. vi. 79 All the usual atrocities were perpetrated by the brutal soldiery.

†**b.** in neutral sense. *Obs.* *rare.*

1663 Butler *Hud.* I. i. 881 Success, the mark no mortal Wit, Or surest hand can always hit: For whatsoe'er we perpetrate, We do but row, w'are steer'd by Fate.

c. *colloq.* Used humorously of doing anything which the speaker affects to treat as execrable or shocking; as ***to perpetrate a pun, a caricature***, etc.

1849 C. Bronte *Shirley* xxxi, Sir Philip induced two of his sisters to perpetrate a duet. **1861** Craik *Hist. Eng. Lit.* II. 173 It was now that they [Tate and Brady] perpetrated in concert their version, or perversion, of the Psalms, with which we are still afflicted. *Mod.* One of the worst puns ever perpetrated.

Hence ˈ**perpetrated** *ppl. a.*, ˈ**perpetrating** *vbl. sb.*

1552 Huloet, Perpetrated, *perpetratus*. **1643** Milton *Divorce* II. iii, The perpetrating of an odious and manifold sin. **1660** R. Coke *Justice Vind.* Ep. Ded. 3 The most perpetrated villany committed in the sight of the sun. **1697** Dryden *Æneid* VIII. 452 The forests, which..Fierce Romulus for perpetrated crimes A sacred refuge made.

perpetration (pɜːpɪˈtreɪʃən). [ad. L. *perpetrātiōn-em*, n. of action from *perpetrāre* to perpetrate: so in mod.F. (Littré).] The action of perpetrating or performing (an evil deed); the committing (of a crime); also, the action perpetrated; a wicked or cruel action; an atrocity.

c **1450** *Mirour Saluacioun* 3961 Of a synne dedely..after perpetracionne. **1534** *Act 26 Hen. VIII*, c. 6 §1 The people of Wales..haue..perseuered in perpetracion and commission of diuers & manifold theftes. **1680** *Counterplots* 4 The flagitious Atchievements and most nefandous perpetrations of that Parliament. **1797** Mrs. Radcliffe *Italian* iv, A man whose passions might impel him to the perpetration of almost any crime. **1854** J. H. Newman *Lect. Hist. Turks* III. I. 136 The savage perpetrations of Zingis and Timour.

†**b.** Performance (in neutral sense). *Obs.* *rare.*

a **1631** Donne *Serm., Matt.* v. 16 (1640) 79 In the acting and perpetration of a good work.

c. *colloq.* The execution of something which the speaker humorously affects to consider very bad or 'atrocious', or as execrably performed.

1849 Rock *Ch. of Fathers* I. 215 The whimsical perpetrations of Borromini.

perpetrator (ˈpɜːpɪtreɪtə(r)). [a. L. *perpetrātor*, agent-n. from *perpetrāre* to perpetrate.] One who perpetrates or commits (an evil deed).

1570 Foxe *A. & M.* (ed. 2) 110/2 Estemed as menquellers and perpetratours of most wicked factes. **1769** Blackstone *Comm.* IV. iii. 34 The actor or absolute perpetrator of the crime. **1828** Scott *F.M. Perth* xix, The perpetrator of this foul murder. **1862** Burton *Bk. Hunter* (1863) 183 What is often said..of other crimes..if the perpetrator be sufficiently illustrious, it becomes a virtue.

Hence ˈ**perpeˈtratress, perpetratrix** (-ˈtreɪtrɪks) [see -ess, -rix], a female perpetrator.

1889 H. F. Wood *Englishman of Rue Caïn* vi. 82 Mistress Lurid, perpetratress of those naughty tales. **1894** *Westm. Gaz.* 15 June, Constance Kent..the perpetratrix of the Road murder.

†ˈ**perpetre,** *v.* *Obs.* *rare.* [a. F. *perpétre-r* (14th c.), ad. L. *perpetrāre*.] *trans.* To perpetrate.

1490 Caxton *Eneydos* vi. 26 Y^e detestable cryme, perpetred and commysed in the persone of her swete and late amyable husbonde. **1491** —— *Vitas Patr.* (W. de W. 1495) I. xxviii. 24 b/1 He beynge on a time in his cell or lytyl hous was perpetred & commysed a murdre by some homycides.

perpetuable (pə'pɛtju:əb(ə)l), *a. rare.* [f. L. *perpetu-āre* to perpetuate: see -ABLE.] Capable of being perpetuated.

1885 GOODALE *Physiol. Bot.* (1892) 444 When once originated they [sports or varieties] are perpetuable by any of the processes of bud-propagation just described.

perpetual (pə'pɛtju:əl), *a.* (*adv.* and *sb.*) Also 4 -ewel, 4-7 -uel, 5 -ueil, 6 parpetuall, (perputall). [a. F. *perpétuel* (12th c. in Hatz.-Darm.) = It. *perpetuale*, ad. L. *perpetuāl-is* (in Quint., along with *universāl-is*), deriv. of *perpetuus* continuous, unbroken, permanent, f. PER- 1 + (?) *petĕre* to aim at, seek.]

A. *adj.* 1. a. Lasting or destined to last for ever; eternal, unceasing; permanent (during life). Phr. *perpetual student* (also *perpetual scholar*): used of one who stays on as a student at a university or similar institution far beyond the normal period.

perpetual curate: see CURATE 2; so *p. curacy, cure*.

a 1340 HAMPOLE *Psalter* xxiv. 7 Kepe noght til vengeaunce perpetuel þe trespasis of my ȝouthed. 1377 LANGL. *P. Pl.* B. XVIII. 198 þat her peyne be perpetuel & no preyere hem helpe. *c* 1400 MAUNDEV. (Roxb.) xxiv. 112 He graunt his lettres of perpetuele peess till all Cristen men. 1456 SIR G. HAYE *Law Arms* (S.T.S.) 79 Men that war symple and nocht witty of perpetuale thingis. 1466 in *Archæologia* (1887) L. I. 50 Mr. william leek vicar perpetuall. 1483 CAXTON *G. de la Tour* C v b, He dyde his wyf to be..putte in pryson perpetuel. *a* 1533 FRITH *Another Bk. agst. Rastell* (1829) 227, I affirm hell & perpetual damnation. 1678 CUDWORTH *Intell. Syst.* I. iv. 571 Following Plato, we should say, That God was Eternal; but the World only Perpetual. 1742 YOUNG *Nt. Th.* I. 166 How I dreamt Of Things impossible!.. Of Joys perpetual in perpetual Change! 1810 in *Risdon's Surv. Devon* 413 Clawton is a perpetual cure. 1830 R. KNOX *Béclard's Anat.* Life 15 Béclard..was unanimously appointed to the office of perpetual secretary to that learned society. 1878 HUXLEY *Physiogr.* 64 The [mountain] top will be enveloped in perpetual snow. 1924 G. CALDERON tr. *Tchekhof's Cherry Orchard* I. 132 Yes, I expect I shall be a perpetual student. *Ibid.*, The 'Perpetual Student' has become a common type in Russia during the last fifteen or twenty years. 1960 G. BUTLER *Death lives Next Door* i. 10 The perpetual scholar; the man who is always proceeding to the next and then the next degree. 1967 E. GRIERSON *Crime of one's Own* xix. 154 He looked a little on the young side..to spend his life in lending libraries. The perpetual student? 1975 'J. BELL' *Victim* vi. 71 The real university-type fanatics and loud-mouthed perpetual students.

b. *perpetual motion*, motion that goes on for ever; *spec.* that of a hypothetical machine, which being once set in motion should go on for ever, or until stopped by some external force or the wearing out of the machine. Hence *perpetual-motionist*.

1593 HARVEY *Pierce's Super.* Wks. (Grosart) II. 287 Entelechy..shewing whence they [divine minds] came by their heauenly and perpetuall motion. 1611 B. JONSON *Char. Author* in *Coryat's Crudities* b iij, He is alwaies Tongue-Maior of the company, and if euer the perpetuall motion be to be hoped for, it is from thence. *a* 1626 BACON *New Atl.* (1900) 43 We have divers curious Clocks;..And some Perpetuall Motions. 1646 SIR T. BROWNE *Pseud. Ep.* II. ii. 65 Petrus Peregrinus..a Fenchman, who two hundred yeeres since left a Tract of the Magnet and a perpetuall motion to be made thereby. 1702 SAVERY *Miner's Friend* 80, I know the Notions of the Perpetual Motion, or Self-moving Engine. 1862 H. SPENCER *First Princ.* II. xxii. (1875) 493 It is of the same order as the belief that misleads perpetual motion schemers. 1872 DE MORGAN *Paradoxes* 342 A perpetual motionist wanted to explain his method.

c. That serves, is applicable, or remains valid for all time to come, or for an unlimited time; e.g. † *perpetual injunction, settlement*.

perpetual action, a legal action for which there is no limitation of time; *perpetual almanac* = *perpetual calendar* (*b*); † *perpetual alms* = Frank Almoign: see ALMOIGN 2; *perpetual calendar*, (*a*) a calendar which can be adjusted to show any combination of day, date, and month; (*b*) a set of tables from which the day of the week can be reckoned for any date; (*c*) (in full *perpetual calendar clock*) a clock which indicates the date and automatically takes account of the length of each month; † *perpetual caustic*, common or lunar caustic: see CAUSTIC *sb.* 1; † *perpetual pill*: see quot. 1727; *perpetual screw* = ENDLESS screw.

c 1450 *Godstow Reg.* 35 To be had and to be hold into fre and perpetuel almesse. 1503-4 *Act 19 Hen VII*, c. 29 *Preamble*, To hold..of your Highnesse and of your heyres in free & perpetuall Almes. 1641 WILKINS *Math. Magick* I. ix, Another invention, commonly styled a *perpetuall screw*, which hath the motion of a wheel and the force of a screw, being both infinite. 1651 G. W. tr. *Cowel's Inst.* 238, I call those [actions] perpetuall..which have not any set time expresly allotted for their continuance. 1683 *Lond. Gaz.* No. 1832/4 Sir S. Morland's Perpetual Almanack. 1704 J. HARRIS *Lex. Techn.* I, *Infernal-Stone*, or *Perpetual Caustick*, is a Chymical Operation, whereby Silver is rendred Caustick by the Salts of Spirit of Nitre. 1727-41 CHAMBERS *Cycl.* II. s.v. *Regulus*, Of this regulus [of antimony]..are made..the antimonial pills... These pills, having.. performed their office and been discharged the body, will serve the same purpose again, and again; whence they have obtained the name of *perpetual pills*. 1799 P. MOORE in R. Patton *Asiat. Mon.* (1801) 194 *note*, The manifest, and by no means unnatural, fruit of this last zemindarry system, called *the perpetual settlement*. 1818 CRUISE *Digest* (ed. 2) IV. 548 The Lord Chancellor decreed that a perpetual injunction should be awarded against Lord Forbes and his trustees. 1844 H. H. WILSON *Brit. India* I. 443 Regulations were passed in..1802,..announcing the principles of a perpetual settlement, which..was effected in the districts..subject to the authority of the Madras Government. 1881 *Encycl. Brit.* XII. 76 On the 17th February 1577 was signed the 'Perpetual Edict', which ratified the Pacification of Ghent. 1895 *Montgomery Ward Catal.* 254/3 Perpetual Calendar, made of celluloid and..imitation silver..silk ribbons with dates, etc. 1904 HARBOTTLE *Dict. Allusions* 193 *Perpetual League*, a league entered into in 1291 by the three Forest Cantons of Switzerland. 1960 H. HAYWARD *Antique Coll.* 215/1 *Perpetual calendar clock*, clock including a calendar, which corrects itself for the short months... The mechanism consists of a slotted wheel revolving once a year ..with slots of varying length which control the movement of a lever, allowing it to pass one or more teeth of the calendar wheel at a time. 1962 E. BRUTON *Dict. Clocks & Watches* 130 *Perpetual calendar*, calendar worked by a clock which corrects for months of different lengths (and sometimes for leap years also). 1971 L. P. DAVIES *Shadow Before* iii. 30 A perpetual calendar confirmed his earlier estimate. 1973 W. J. BURLEY *Death in Salubrious Place* v. 105 The perpetual calendar said Wednesday August 25th. Clarissa had changed it that morning.

d. = PERENNIAL *a.* 2 b.

1882 *Garden* 4 Feb. 75/3 The Beta maritima; known as the Perpetual or Beet Spinach.

e. Never ending, endless in succession in space.

1873 BLACK *Pr. Thule* xiii, This city of perpetual houses.

f. Of an investment: irredeemable. Also *ellipt.* or as *sb.* Cf. ANNUITY 3.

1869 *Bradshaw's Railway Manual* XXI. 30 Perpetual 4 per cent. stock... Present terminable 4½ per cent. stocks. 1882 R. BITHELL *Counting-House Dict.* 224 Consols—commonly called Bank Annuities—are perpetual. 1948 G. CROWTHER *Outl. Money* (rev. ed.) ii. 75 The mediums, the longs and the perpetuals are liquid at a price. 1965 PERRY & RYDER *Thomson's Dict. Banking* (ed. 11) 436/2 *Perpetual annuity*... The purchaser cannot obtain the principal back, but he can sell his right to the annual payment to someone else.

2. a. Continuing or continued without intermission; constant; continuous; unfailing; uninterrupted.

perpetual bellows, a bellows capable of giving a continuous blast of air.

c 1380 WYCLIF *Sel. Wks.* III. 431 To be bonde to perpetual kepyng of siche maner signes. 1484 CAXTON *Curiall* 3 He shal be enuoyed [*pr.* ennoyed] now here, now there as a courrour or renner perpetuell. 1552 ABP. HAMILTON *Catech.* (1884) 38 The well..and perpetuall spring of gudnes. 1594 T. B. *La Primaud. Fr. Acad.* II. 437 The humours and qualities are in perpetuall motion. 1697 DRYDEN *Virg. Georg.* IV. 540 With Waters drawn from their perpetual Spring. 1755 MRS. DELANY *Life & Corr.* (1861) III. 384 The melancholy hurry of business..for some time to come will necessarily keep her spirits in a perpetual flutter. 1758 REID tr. *Macquer's Chym.* I. 362 Excite the fire violently with a pair, or more, of perpetual bellows till the Iron melt. 1837-9 HALLAM *Hist. Lit.* I. v. §16 This produced ..perpetual barbarisms and deviations from purity of idiom.

b. Continuous or unbroken in spatial extent.

1658 EARL MONM. tr. *Paruta's Wars Cyprus* 109 An almost perpetuall shore, which extends it selfe for the space of thirty miles from the mouth of the Adice, to that of Piave. 1670-98 LASSELS *Voy. Italy* II. 20 Great Pillars of freestone ..whose *capitelli*..are joyned to one another above by arches and a perpetual cornice. 1791 COWPER *Iliad* VII. 381 [To Ajax] Agamemnon gave the chine Perpetual.

c. *perpetual check*: in Chess and related games, a situation in which one player cannot prevent the other from making an unlimited sequence of checking moves (and thus obtaining a draw). Also ellipt. as *perpetual*.

1820 J. S. BINGHAM tr. *E. Dal Rio's Incomparable Game of Chess* 44 At the end of the game..the Rook sometimes draws the game against the Queen, and is admirable in making a drawn game by perpetual check. 1856 C. TOMLINSON *Chess Player's Ann.* 120 'You might have drawn the game,' said he, 'by perpetual check.' 1960 R. C. BELL *Board & Table Games* I. ii. 60 [Shatranj.] *Perpetual check* was considered a drawn game. 1973 *Correspondence Chess* Spring 385/2 Black either has to take a perpetual or allow White to queen a P with a dangerous check.

B. Used as *adv.* = PERPETUALLY.

c 1374 CHAUCER *Boeth.* II. Pr. iv. 28 (Camb. MS.) Or ellis yt last nat perpetuel. 1439 in *Ancestor* July (1904) 15 That the said nonnes sette me in here martilage to pray for me perpetuall. 1552 LYNDESAY *Monarche* 695 Motioun continuall, Quhilk doith indure perpetuall. 1607 SHAKS. *Timon* IV. iii. 503 You perpetuall sober Gods. *c* 1742 GRAY *Ignorance* 4 Where rushy Camus' slowly-winding flood Perpetual draws his humid train of mud. 1817 JAS. MILL *Brit. India* II. IV. viii. 282 The tribute..was reduced from nine lacs perpetual, to seven lacs per annum, for the space of six years.

b. *perpetual-flowering carnation*, a variety of carnation with a long flowering season, usually grown in a cool greenhouse, as it is not hardy out of doors.

1885 T. BAINES *Greenhouse & Stove Plants* 93/2 Carnation (Perpetual Flowering)... With a sufficient number of plants they may be had in bloom all the year round. 1900 J. DOUGLAS in W. D. Drury *Bk. Gardening* iii. 55 Perpetual-Flowering Carnations are generally propagated by slips. 1926 M. C. ALLWOOD *Carnations* viii. 55 The Perpetual-flowering Carnation can be planted in May. 1960 *Times* 29 June 17/3 Perpetual-flowering carnations and pinks form a very attractive exhibit. 1971 S. BAILEY *Perpetual-Flowering Carnations* (rev. ed.) 18 The perpetual-flowering carnation owes its origin to at least two *Dianthus* species, namely *D. caryophyllus* and *D. sinensis*.

C. *sb.* (elliptical uses of the adj.)

1. a. = PERENNIAL *sb.* 1. b. One of several continuously blooming varieties of rose.

c 1710 CELIA FIENNES *Diary* (1888) 300 All sorts of Perpetualls as well as Annualls. 1859 LOUDON *Gardening* 1054 Roses... Damask perpetual. Hybrid perpetual. 1890 *Daily News* 28 Jan. 6/6 A choice selection of hybrid perpetuals, tea-scented, and moss kinds.

2. A machine used in shearing cloth: see quot.

1879 *Cassell's Techn. Educ.* IV. 342/2 The shearing is.. effected by means of a machine called a 'perpetual', consisting of a roller with cutting blades passing spirally round it.

†3. A hereditary or heritable office. *Obs.*

1568 CECIL in Robertson *Hist. Scot.* (1759) App. xxvii, Providing he shall not dispose of any offices or perpetuals to continue any longer, but to these offered of the premises.

perpetualism (pə'pɛtju:əlız(ə)m). [f. PERPETUAL *a.* + -ISM.] Lasting, perpetual, or universal quality, *spec.* as a doctrine in political science or religion.

1885 *Encycl. Brit.* XIX. 391/1 Cosmopolitanism..and what has been called perpetualism, or the assumption of a system applicable to every social stage, were alike discredited. 1905 *Westm. Gaz.* 31 July 6/7 Perpetualism abolishes both hell and heaven. 1931 *Observer* 8 Nov. 24 The hybridist who can develop even a slight measure of perpetualism in this plant will sweep the horticultural board of its best cups and medals.

perpetualist (pə'pɛtju:əlıst). [f. PERPETUAL *a.* + -IST.] One who is in favour of the perpetuity of something; *spec.* a name applied in the U.S. to those who favoured the perpetuation of Negro slavery in the States.

1850 LYELL *2nd Visit U.S.* II. 97 Those slave-owners who are called perpetualists, who maintain that slavery should be permanent. 1872 H. WILSON *Hist. Slave Power* I. 574 It was ..a most potent weapon in the hands of the apologists, perpetualists, and propagandists of slavery.

perpetuality (pəpɛtju:'ælıtı). [ad. L. type **perpetuālitās* (It. *perpetualità*, rare OF. *perpetualité*), f. L. *perpetuālis* PERPETUAL: see -ITY. Cf. the earlier form PERPETUALTY.] The quality, state, or condition of being perpetual; perpetuity.

1543 Perpetualitee [see PERPETUALTY, quot. *c* 1470]. 1802 W. TAYLOR in Robberds *Mem.* I. 431, I..found in the restlessness of curiosity a perpetuality of occupation. 1813 *Yankee* 13 Aug. 3/4 There will not be much difficulty in proving the *non* perpetuality of Mr. Redheffer's invention.

perpetually (pə'pɛtju:əlı), *adv.* [f. PERPETUAL *a.* + -LY².]

1. Everlastingly, eternally, for ever; in perpetuity; indefinitely, for the rest of one's life. *arch.*

c 1386 CHAUCER *Knt.'s T.* 1176 That thou and I be dampned to prison Perpetuelly. 1426 AUDELAY *Poems* 25 Therfore damnyd schalt thou be, Into hel perpetually. 1491 *Act 7 Hen. VII*, c. 10 The foreseid statute..shuld be in his force and virtue fro thens perpetuelly to endure. 1535 COVERDALE *Ps.* lxxvii. 69 There he buylded his temple on hye..that it might perpetually endure. 1580 SIDNEY *Ps.* IX. v, He to all his judgments shall apply Perpetually. *a* 1688 VILLIERS (Dk. Buckhm.) *Restoration* Wks. (1775) 106 Can shame remain perpetually in me, And not in others?

2. Incessantly; persistently; continually, constantly; with constant recurrence.

c 1380 WYCLIF *Sel. Wks.* III. 431 þo þat..bynden hem to kepe perpetuelly. *c* 1420 LYDG. *Assembly of Gods* 2095 Oure habitacion chaungeth Fro ioy to peyne & woo perpetuelly. 1553 *Short Catech.* in *Lit. & Doc. Edw. VI* (1844) 506 Yet is his Godhead perpetually present with us. *a* 1635 NAUNTON *Fragm. Reg.* (Arb.) 62 He lived almost perpetually in the Camp. 1711 ADDISON *Spect.* No. 105 ¶6, I might likewise mention the Law-Pedant, that is perpetually putting Cases. 1855 MACAULAY *Hist. Eng.* xviii. IV. 127 Encroachments were perpetually committed. 1870 DICKENS *E. Drood* ii, Crisparkle..perpetually pitching himself head-foremost into all the deep running water.

per'petualness. [f. as prec. + -NESS.] The quality of being perpetual: = PERPETUALITY.

1611 COTGR., *Duree*, euerlastingnesse, perpetualnesse, long lasting. 1727 in BAILEY vol. II. 1856 RUSKIN *Mod. Paint.* III. IV. x. §8 A pathetic sense of its perpetualness, and your own transientness. 1875 G. DAWSON *Every day Counsels* (1888) 106 The perpetualness of some men's stings.

†**perpetualty** (pə'pɛtju:əltı). *Obs.* [a. OF. *perpetuaulté*, *-elté*, *-auté*, repr. L. type **perpetuālitātem*: see PERPETUALITY.]

= PERPETUITY 1.

c 1380 WYCLIF *Wks.* (1880) 477 þey don harm to cristis chirge bi perpetualte in þer synne. 1387-8 T. USK *Test. Love* I. viii. (Skeat) l. 116 Yet scriptures for great elde so been defased, that no perpetualtie maie in hem been iudged. *c* 1470 HARDING *Chron.* C. i. (MS. Bodl. Arch. Seld. B. 10), Athelarde..held his tyme ay forth the souerante In heritage and perpetualte [*ed.* 1543 perpetualitee].

perpetu'ana. *Hist.* Also 7-8 perpetuano, 7 -uanno, -uno, 8 -uanee. See also PERPET. [app. a factitious trade name, f. It. or Sp. *perpetuo*, L. *perpetuus*, with Romanic ending *-ana*. Hence F. *perpétuane*.]

A durable fabric of wool manufactured in England from the 16th c. (Cf. the similar names *everlasting*, *durance*, *lasting*, etc.) Also *transf.* and *fig.*

1599 B. JONSON *Cynthia's Rev.* III. ii, Our gentleman ushers, that will suffer a piece of serge or perpetuana to come into the presence. 1611 FLORIO *Ital. Dict.*, *Duraforte*,..the stuffe Perpetuana. **1640** in Entick *London* II. 172 Drapery, Perpetuannoes. **1685** J. DUNTON *Lett. fr. New-Eng.* (1867) 14 The Cloathes of the Israelites.. in the Wildernesse, never waxed old, as if made of Perpetuano indeed. **1691** *Lond. Gaz.* No. 2703/4 Stolen.., 34 Pieces of Colchester Perpetuano's. **1714** *Fr. Bk. of Rates* 403 The Stuffs called Bays, Perpetuana's, &c. of the Manufacture, which are sent to Italy. **1727** W. MATHER *Yng. Man's Comp.* 407 Kers[ies], Cottons, Bays, Perpetuanees, Fustians, and Norwich Stuffs. **1778** *Eng. Gazetteer* (ed. 2) s.v. *Sudbury*, Sudbury.. drives a good trade in perpetuanas, says, serges, &c. **1846** J. S. BURN *For. Prot. Refugees* 5 The Flemings taught the manufacturing of our Wool into Broadcloth, Rashes, Flannel and Perpetuanas. **1972** A. PLUMMER *London Weavers' Company 1600–1970* xiv. 292 Indian wrought silks and painted and dyed calicoes became extremely fashionable, taking the place of English silks, half-silks, slight silks, worsted stuffs, says and perpetuanas.

attrib. and *Comb.* **1606** DEKKER *Sev. Sinnes* (Arb.) 27 The sober Perpetuana-suited Puritane. **1607** MARSTON *What you will* I. ii, Hee's in his old perpetuana sute. **1648** SIR E. DERING *Acc. Bk.* (N.), For a counterpayne to the yellow perpetuana bed.

perpetuance (pə'pɛtju:əns). [a. OF. *perpétuance* (13th c. in Godef.), f. *perpétuer* to perpetuate, pr. pple. *perpétuant*: see -ANCE.] The action of perpetuating; the fact or condition of being perpetuated; perpetuation.

1558 CAVENDISH *Poems*, etc. (1825) II. 154 Nothyng hathe here perpetuance. **1573** *New Custom* II. i. in Hazl. *Dodsley* III. 25 If trust to the gospel do purchase perpetuance Of life unto him. **1870** E. MULFORD *Nation* xvii. 341 To serve its end in the perpetuance of slavery. **1877** M. ARNOLD *Last Ess. on Ch.* Pref. 6 The transformation of religion which is essential for its perpetuance.

perpetuant (pə'pɛtju:ənt). *Math.* [ad. L. *perpetuānt-em*, pr. pple. of *perpetuāre*: see -ANT.]

1. A seminvariant not reducible to a sum (or sum of products) of seminvariants of lower degree.

1885 CAYLEY *Coll. Math. Papers* XII. 251 A seminvariant which is not reducible is said to be irreducible, or otherwise to be a perpetuant. This notion of a perpetuant is due to Sylvester, see his Memoir 'On Subinvariants'.

attrib. **1904** *Athenæum* 21 May 660/1 'On Perpetuant Syzygies', by Messrs. A. Young and P. W. Wood.

2. = PERPETUANA.

1753 E. BOWEN *Map of Devon*, The chief Manufactures [of Devon] are Kerseys, Serges, Druggets, Perpetuants, fine and coarse Cloths, and Lace, in all which many Families are employd.

per'petuate, *ppl. a.* [ad. L. *perpetuāt-us*, perf. pple. passive of *perpetuāre* to PERPETUATE.] Made perpetual; perpetually continued. Const. as *pple.* and as *adj.*

1503–4 *Act 19 Hen. VII*, c. 32 *Preamble*, The wele suertie and comfort perpetuat of theym ther heires and successours. **1801** SOUTHEY *Thalaba* I. xxiii, The trees and flowers remain, By Nature's care perpetuate and self-sown.

perpetuate (pə'pɛtju:eɪt), *v.* [f. ppl. stem of L. *perpetuā-re* to make perpetual, f. *perpetu-us* perpetual: see -ATE[3]. Cf. F. *perpétuer* (14th c. in Hatz.-Darm.).] **a.** *trans.* To make perpetual; to cause to endure or continue indefinitely; to preserve from extinction or oblivion. Also *absol.*

1530 PALSGR. 656/1, I perpetuate, I contynue a thing for ever. **1579** FENTON *Guicciard.* III. (1599) 117 He iudged it was a better meane to perpetuate his greatnesse. **1660** R. COKE *Justice Vind.* 5 For we see all things are.. perpetuated by generation in their species. *a* **1711** KEN *Hymnotheo* Poet. Wks. 1721 I. 306 Each courts its Mate, And in their Young themselves perpetuate. **1713** STEELE *Englishman* No. 50. 320 The Memory of a Benefactor.. may be perpetuated by erecting Statues, &c. **1768** BLACKSTONE *Comm.* III. xxvii. 450 If witnesses to a disputable fact are old and infirm, it is very usual to file a bill to perpetuate the testimony of those witnesses. **1864** BRYCE *Holy Rom. Emp.* ix. (1875) 145 It [the revived Romano-Germanic Empire] perpetuated the name, the language, the literature, such as it then was, of Rome. **1894** E. FAWCETT *New Nero* ii. 26 That soulless and mysterious will-to-live, which for ever creates, protects, and perpetuates, though blindly and dumbly, unconscious that she does either.

†**b.** To continue or extend without intermission.

a **1619** FOTHERBY *Atheom.* II. xiv. §4 (1622) 357 (tr. Ovid *Metam.* I. 4) Ye gods draw on, perpetuate my rime, From Worlds first being, to my present time. **1790** HAN. MORE *Relig. Fash. World* 147 Is it not to be regretted.. that they do not like to perpetuate the principle, by encouraging it in their servants also?

Hence **per'petuated** *ppl. a.*; **per'petuating** *vbl. sb.* and *ppl. a.*

1607 HIERON *Wks.* I. 431 They, which.. most study the perpetuating of their fortunes. **1681–6** J. SCOTT *Chr. Life* (1747) III. 191 A continued and perpetuated Intercession. *a* **1711** KEN *Christophil* Poet. Wks. 1721 I. 522 Thou leav'st me longing for a brighter Ray, And for a more perpetuated Stay. **1774** in Picton *L'pool Mun. Rec.* (1886) II. 241 For the perpetuating the testimony of ancient witnesses.

perpetuation (pəpɛtju:'eɪʃən). [ad. med.L. *perpetuātiōn-em* (Du Cange), n. of action from L. *perpetuāre* to perpetuate: cf. F. *perpétuation* (15th c.), It. *perpetuazione* (Florio).] The action of perpetuating or making perpetual; permanent continuation; preservation from extinction or oblivion.

c **1380** WYCLIF *Sel. Wks.* III. 216 Of alle evelis þat comeþ bi weiward curatis is maad a perpetuacion. **1395** PURVEY *Remonstr.* (1851) 11 Perpetuacion, or euere lastinge duringe. **1471** RIPLEY *Comp. Alch.* Pref. i. in Ashm. *Theat. Chem. Brit.* (1652) 121 O pytewouse puryfyer of Soules and puer perpetuation. **1620** BP. HALL *Hon. Mar. Clergy* I. vii. 40 Those.. may vow.. an holy perpetuation thereof to their end. **1646** SIR T. BROWNE *Pseud. Ep.* v. xxi. 267 The perpetuation of a very ancient custome. **1752** JOHNSON *Rambler* No. 203 ⁋8 Some.. provide for the perpetuation of families and honours. **1867** SMILES *Huguenots Eng.* i. (1880) 11 This invention [printing].. contained within itself a self-preserving power which ensured its perpetuation. **1874** STEPHEN *Comm.* v. viii. (ed. 7) III. 463 A court of equity.. permitting any of the parties interested to institute proceedings.. with a view to the mere perpetuation of the testimony.

perpetuative (pə'pɛtju:ətɪv), *a.* [f. PERPETUATE *v.* + -IVE.] Having a tendency or inclination to perpetuate.

1957 P. WORSLEY *Trumpet shall Sound* 273 Such movements can be either revivalistic—stressing the readoption of customs fallen into desuetude—or perpetuative—seeking to maintain the existing order. **1977** *Dædalus* Summer 61 My personal view is that anthropology is shifting from a stress on concepts such as structure, equilibrium, function, system to process, indeterminacy, reflexivity.. but with a tender perpetuative regard for the marvellous findings of those who, teachers of the present generation, committed themselves to the discoveries of 'systems' of social relations and cultural 'items' and 'complexes'.

perpetuator (pə'pɛtju:eɪtə(r)). [Agent-n. from PERPETUATE *v.*: see -OR.] One who perpetuates.

1863 J. G. MURPHY *Comm. Gen.* iii. 24 The author and perpetuator of a universe of being. **1871** SMILES *Charac.* i. (1876) 27 They are the heirs of their greatness, and ought to be the perpetuators of their glory.

perpetuity (pɜ:pɪ'tju:ɪtɪ). [ME. *perpetuite*, a. F. *perpétuité* (13th c. in Littré) = Pr. *perpetuitat*, Sp. *perpetuidad*, It. *perpetuità*; ad. L. *perpetuitātem*, f. *perpetu-us*: see PERPETUAL and -ITY.]

1. The quality or state of being perpetual; endless or indefinite duration or existence.

c **1450** *Macro Plays* (E.E.T.S.) 30/822 Thy obstinacy wyll exclude [thee] fro þe glorius perpetuite. **1494** FABYAN *Chron.* VI. clix. 149 Than the Emperour.. transmutyd the sentence of deth vnto perpetuyte of pryson, & losynge of his syght. **1497** BP. ALCOCK *Mons Perfect.* B iij, This materyal tabernacle, which myght have no perpetuyte. **1587** GOLDING *De Mornay* ix. (1592) 130 If we say that the Elementes and the liuing wights continue their perpetuities in their kinds. **1691** RAY *Creation* I. (1692) 51 For the Stability and Perpetuity of the whole Universe. **1735–8** BOLINGBROKE *On Parties* 144, I need not descend into more Particulars to shew the Perpetuity of free Government in Britain. **1765** BLACKSTONE *Comm.* I. vii. 249 A third attribute of the king's majesty is his perpetuity... The king never dies. **1858** FROUDE *Hist. Eng.* IV. xviii. 28 The final treaty.. conceived upon a basis which promised perpetuity.

b. Phrases. *in, to, for perpetuity*: to all time, for ever; for an indefinitely long or unlimited period.

1439 *Rolls of Parlt.* V. 28/2 To endure to the next Parlement, and so forth in perpetuite. **1574** tr. *Littleton's Tenures* 107 b, The chaplayne.. may charge y[e] chauntry with a rent charge in perpetuitye. **1652** J. WRIGHT tr. *Camus' Nat. Paradox* IV. 226 There to continue to perpetuity, under pain of beeing Hanged if ever they returned. **1717** BULLOCK *Wom. a Riddle* IV. 45, I cou'd contemplate on these lines to perpetuity. **1802** WELLINGTON in Gurw. *Desp.* III. 473 His Highness.. hereby assigns and cedes in perpetuity to the Honorable East India Company, all the territories detailed. **1862** DARWIN *Fertil. Orchids* ii. 69 We have here a plant which is self-fertilized for perpetuity.

2. A perpetual possession, tenure, or position.

1406 HOCCLEVE *Misrule* 374 For what thyng þat is lent,.. Thow ther-in haast no perpetuitee. **1538** *Ord. Lichfield Gild* (E.E.T.S.) 10 [They] did admytt William Wylnehale, priest, to be one of the prestes of the gild as to a perpetuyte. **1650** W. BROUGH *Sacr. Princ.* (1659) 500 What a folly is this to preferre a lease to a perpetuity. **1847** L. HUNT *Men, Women, & B.* II. ix. 164 One system of morals.. acted upon, and associated with flourishing perpetuities.

b. *Law.* Of an estate: The quality or condition of being inalienable perpetually, or for a period beyond certain limits fixed, or conceived as being fixed, by the general law; an estate so restricted or perpetuated.

1596 BACON *Max. & Use Com. Law* I. (1635) 47 Perpetuity, which is an intaile with an addition of a Proviso Conditionall, tyed to his estate, not to put away the land from his next heire. **1607** NORDEN *Surv. Dial.* III. 111 For nothing is therein to be inserted, but matter of perpetuitie, in recommending the present state of the Mannor vnto posterities. **1702** *Lond. Gaz.* No. 3839/4 The Perpetual Advouson of Staplehurst,.. is to be disposed of, either the Perpetuity, or the next Presentation. **1818** CRUISE *Digest* (ed. 2) IV. 403 The Judges have, for many centuries, established it as a rule, that real property should in no case be rendered perpetually unalienable; or, as it is usually expressed, the perpetuities should not be allowed. **1858** LD. ST. LEONARDS *Handy Bk. Prop. Law* xvii. 119 To curb the rising desire to evade the wholesome rule of law as to perpetuities.

3. A perpetual annuity. Hence, The amount or number of years' purchase required to buy a perpetual annuity; the number of years in which the simple interest or annuity on a principal sum will equal the principal.

1806 HUTTON *Course Math.* I. 266 An annuity may also be for a certain number of years; or it may be without any limit, and then it is called a Perpetuity. **1838** DE MORGAN *Ess. Probab.* 189 Each.. would have to pay for a perpetuity, if the preceding fallacy were admitted.

†**per'petuous,** *a. Obs. rare.* [f. L. *perpetu-us* PERPETUAL + -OUS. (Cf. rare ONF. *perpetuweus* in Godef.)] = PERPETUAL *a.* 1. Hence †**per'petuously** *adv.*, perpetually.

1611 SPEED *Theat. Gr. Brit.* (1614) 123 Great pitie it is that so famous a worke should not be perpetuous. *Ibid.* 23 It deserved to be perpetuously memorable. **1683** E. HOOKER *Pref. Pordage's Mystic Div.* 71 A Conjunction which I wold ever call Copulativ, and make, if I could, perpetuously Consummativ.

‖**perpetuum mobile** (pɜ:'pɛtʊəm 'məʊbɪli:, -ʊm 'məʊbɪleɪ). [f. L. *perpetu-us* continuous + *mobil-is* movable, after PRIMUM MOBILE.]

1. = *perpetual motion* s.v. PERPETUAL *a.* 1 b. Freq. in allusive use.

a **1688** CUDWORTH *Treatise Freewill* (1838) 28 This is an ever bubbling fountain in the centre of the soul, an elater or spring of motion, both a *primum* and a *perpetuum mobile* in us, the first wheel that sets all the other wheels in motion, and an everlasting and incessant mover. **1904** B. RUSSELL in *Mind* XIII. 337 'There is no *perpetuum mobile*' does not mean 'whatever exists differs from the *perpetuum mobile*'. **1933** J. N. FINDLAY *Meinong's Theory of Objects* iii. 89 That China is a Republic, that there is no *perpetuum mobile*, that dirigible airships exist, all these may indifferently be called circumstances or states of affairs. **1953** R. F. C. HULL tr. *Jung's Psychol. & Alchemy* in *Coll. Wks.* XII. II. iii. 172 This theme was already hinted at in dream g, with its pendulum clock, a *perpetuum mobile*. **1964** V. NABOKOV *Defence* x. 162 The passionate chess player is just as ridiculous as the madman inventing a *perpetuum mobile*.

2. *Mus.* = *moto perpetuo* s.v. MOTO.

1893 J. S. SHEDLOCK tr. *Riemann's Dict. Music* 588/2 *Perpetuum mobile*.. the name given to pieces written from beginning to end in notes of equal, and short value. **1938** *Oxf. Compan. Mus.* 708/2 *Perpetuum mobile*,.. a rapid instrumental composition that proceeds throughout in notes of the same value. **1969** W. S. NEWMAN *Sonata since Beethoven* xii. 508 The rondo is a virtual *perpetuum mobile*. **1972** H. TISCHLER tr. *Apel's Hist. Keyboard Music to 1700* xix. 664 One of the four pieces.. is a kind of *perpetuum mobile* in 12/8. **1978** *Times* 6 Apr. 16/8 Ravel asked Enesco if he would mind running through the whole sonata with him. They played it through, including the punishing perpetuum mobile.

perpeyn, perpin (in Masonry): see PARPEN.

perphenazine (pə'fɛnəzi:n). *Pharm.* [f. PI)PER(IDINE + PHEN(YL + AZINE, constituent parts of the systematic name.] A whitish powder that is a derivative of phenothiazine and has actions and uses similar to, but stronger than, those of chlorpromazine, being used as a sedative and anti-emetic and in the treatment of alcoholism; 2-chloro-10-{3-[4-(2-hydroxy-ethyl)piperazin-1-yl]propyl}phenothiazine, $C_{21}H_{26}N_3OClS$.

1957 *Jrnl. Pharmacol. & Exper. Therap.* CXX. 376 Sch3940 is now known by the generic name of perphenazine and is marketed under the trade name, Trilafon. **1971** P. K. BRIDGES *Psychiatric Emergencies* vi. 158 Chlorpromazine.., trifluoperazine.. and perphenazine (Fentazin, Trilafon) are commonly given to patients with neurotic illnesses. **1978** *Nature* 23 Mar. 331/2 Chlorpromazine and perphenazine were found.. to be as effective as conventional tricyclic antidepressant drugs in the treatment of certain forms of depression.

†**per'placid,** *a. Obs. rare*[−1]. [f. PER- 4 + PLACID.] Thoroughly placid or quiet.

1660 BURNEY Κέρδ. Δῶρον (1661) 32 A perplacid strain of acknowledging authority.

†**per'plant,** *v. Obs. rare*[−1]. [f. PER- 2 + PLANT *v.*] *trans.* To plant or fix firmly.

a **1548** HALL *Chron., Rich. III* 51 b, His especiall truste and confidence was perplanted in the hope of their fidelitie.

†**per'plead,** *v. Obs. rare*[−1]. [f. PER- 2 + PLEAD *v.*] *intr.* To plead strongly.

1581 J. BELL *Haddon's Answ. Osor.* 340 b, As touching Prescription of Antiquity, Osorius perpleding [orig. *contestans*] demaundeth of Haddon, in what wise he defendeth y[t] his innovation.

†**perplex,** *sb. Obs. rare.* [f. assumed L. type **perplexu-s*, after next and L. *plexu-s* plaiting, twining, braid.] = PERPLEXITY; entanglement.

1652 H. L'ESTRANGE *Amer. no Jewes* 36 Ready to perform that office with the least trouble and perplex. **1762** GOLDSM. *Cit. W.* cxiii, There, there's a perplex! I could have wished.. the author.. had added notes.

†**per'plex,** *a. Obs.* [ad. L. *perplex-us* involved, confused, intricate, f. PER- 2 + *plexus* interwoven, entangled, involved, intricate, pa. pple. of *plectĕre* to plait, interweave. (L. had no vb. *perplectĕre*.) OF. had also *perplaist, perplix* (15th c.), *perplex, -e* (16th c.) repr. the L. adj.

In this family of words, the chronological order of the senses in Eng. reverses the logical and historical development in L.]

1. Of persons: Perplexed, puzzled, bewildered.

c **1380** WYCLIF *Sel. Wks.* II. 422 Þe Popis lawe.. makiþ hem [men] perplex, and bindiþ her conscience wiþ feyned bondis. **1520** WHITINTON *Vulg.* (1527) 13, I am perplexe or doutfull in this mater. **1546** COVERDALE tr. *Calvin's Treat.*

Sacram. C ij, So dyd the sophisticall doctors..holde the myserable consciences to muche perplexe.

2. Of things: Intricate, and hence difficult to unravel or clear up; involved, tangled.

1534 More *Treat. Passion* Wks. 1309/1 An other maner of rekenynge, with which wee shall not neede to medle. This muche is perplex inough. 1563-87 Foxe *A. & M.* (1596) 1621/1 Obscure and perplexe kind of writing. 1610 J. Dove *Advt. Seminaries* 2 The matter..seemeth perplexe, and very difficult. 1684 Ray *Corr.* (1848) 139 To give some light..by ..extricating what is perplex and entangled.

perplex (pəˈplɛks), *v.* [Formed under the influence of PERPLEX *a.* and PERPLEXED *ppl. a.*, and at first used only in pa. pple., apart from which the earliest trace of the vb. is in the end of the 16th c.; it occurs once in Shaks.: see quot. 1595. As to sense-development see PERPLEX *a.*]

1. *trans.* To fill (a person) with uncertainty as to the nature or treatment of a thing by reason of its involved or intricate character; to trouble with doubt; to distract, confuse, bewilder, puzzle.

[1477: see PERPLEXED *ppl. a.* 1.] 1595 Shaks. *John* III. i. 222 *Fra.* I am perplext, and know not what to say. *Pan.* What canst thou say, but wil perplex thee more? If thou stand excommunicate, and curst? 1604 —— *Oth.* v. ii. 346. 1611 Bible *2 Cor.* iv. 8 We are perplexed, but not in despaire. 1623 Conway in Ellis *Orig. Lett.* Ser. I. III. 155 That which pinch't and perplex't most. 1670-1 Marvell *Corr.* Wks. (Grosart) II. 374, I think we shall perplex one of them against the other, so that neither shall make any promise. 1791 Cowper *Iliad* xviii. 577 Perplex not with these cares thy soul. 1855 Prescott *Philip II*, I. ii. xii. 287 Their contradictory accounts..serve only to perplex..the student.

†b. To torment, trouble, vex, plague. *Obs.*

1686 tr. *Chardin's Coronat. Solyman* 129 His Distemper still perplex'd him. 1691 Ld. Lansdowne *Adolphus* etc., Cloe's the wonder of her sex, 'Tis well her heart is tender, How might such killing Eyes perplex, With Virtue to defend her. 1703 Maundrell *Journ. Jerus.* (1732) 138 We were a little perplex'd by the Servants.

2. To render (a thing) intricate or complicated in character and hence difficult to understand or deal with; to make (a thing) doubtful or uncertain through intricacy; to complicate, confuse, muddle.

*a*1619 Fotherby *Atheom.* ii. iii. §3 (1622) 219 A very good, and a sound reason; though somewhat, perhaps, perplexed vnto the vulgar vnderstanding, through [etc.]. 1641 J. Jackson *True Evang. T.* iii. 228 Our peace both of Church and Common-wealth hath beene a little plundered and perplexed. 1658-9 *Burton's Diary* (1828) IV. 160 It is clearly out of order to perplex the question. 1701 Swift *Contests Nobles & Comm.* iii, He added three hundred commons to the senate, which perplexed the power of the whole order, and rendered it ineffectual. 1771 Wesley *Wks.* (1872) V. 135 Perplexing a subject plain in itself. *a*1871 Grote *Eth. Fragm.* iii. (1876) 61 It is possible by a cloud of unmeaning words to perplex the question. 1894 T. E. Page *Æneid* ii. 178 Notes 222 Editors perplex the passage.

3. To bring into an intricately involved physical condition; to cause to become tangled; to entangle, intertwine; to intermingle.

1620-55 I. Jones *Stone-Heng* (1725) 25 White, perplexed (as it were) with a ruddy Colour. 1642 H. More *Song of Soul* ii. iii. iii. lxviii, An heap of Orbs disorderly perplext. 1711 Addison *Spect.* No. 56 ¶3 A thick Forest made up of Bushes, Brambles, and pointed Thorns, so perplexed and interwoven with one another, that it was impossible to find a Passage through it. 1765 Goldsm. *Double Transform.* 71 Now to perplex the ravell'd noose, As each a different way pursues. 1835 T. T. Stoddart *Art Angling in Scot.* (1836) 41 Some trout..attempt to cut or perplex the tackle among stones or weeds. 1860 Hawthorne *Transform.* (Tauchn.) II. xvii. 192 The complication of narrow streets which perplex that portion of the city.

Hence **perˈplexing** *vbl. sb.*

*a*1649 Drumm. of Hawth. *Irene* Wks. (1711) 170 When ye beget..anxious entangling and perplexing of consciences.

perˈplexable, *a. rare.* [ad. L. *perplexābilis* perplexing, ambiguous, obscure, f. *perplexārī* to cause perplexity, f. *perplexus*: see PERPLEX *a.*] †a. Tending to perplex, doubtful, ambiguous. *Obs.* b. Capable of being perplexed, entangled, or confused. Hence †**perplexaˈbility** (in 6 -ibility), perplexity.

1592 R. D. *Hypnerotomachia* 73 This..was not made without..much labour, and incredible diligence, with a perplexibility of understanding to knowe the mysticall conceite. 1656 Blount *Glossogr.*, *Perplexable* (*perplexabilis*), doubtful, ambiguous; hard to conceive and understand.

perplexed (pəˈplɛkst), *ppl. a.* Also 6-8 perplext. [app. in origin an alteration of PERPLEX *a.*, assimilated to pa. pples. in accordance with its quasi-participial force as implying a resultant state. As to the sense-development see PERPLEX *a.*]

1. Of a person: Involved in doubt or anxiety on account of the intricate character of the matter under consideration; bewildered, puzzled: see PERPLEX *v.* 1. Formerly in a more general sense: Troubled: cf. PERPLEXITY 1 b.

1477 Earl Rivers (Caxton) *Dictes* Prol., In diuerse & many sondry wyses man is perplexid with worldly aduersitees. 1529 More *Dyaloge* Wks. 165 That it might please his goodnes in so great a parell not to leue me perplexed. 1578 Banister *Hist. Man* viii. 103 Glandules.. pouryng forth teares in a perplexed mynde. 1611 Bible *Joel* i. 18 The herds of cattle are perplexed, because they haue no pasture. 1706 Phillips, *Perplexed*, confounded, troubled. 1836 Mrs. Browning *Poet's Vow* i. xiii, Mad winds that howling go!..perplexed seas That stagger from their blow!

2. Of things, conditions, language, etc: Full of doubt or difficulty from its intricate or entangled condition; intricate, involved, complicated.

1529 More *Dyaloge* i. Wks. 165/1 Why shoulde not I in such perplexed case after helpe called for of God, take the one parte at aduenture by Lot? 1576 Fleming *Panopl. Epist.* 399 Ambrosius is..in some places..perplext and cumbersome to bee vnderstoode. *a*1668 Davenant *Man's the Master* iii. i, This is the most perplext encounter that I ever saw. 1785 Reid *Intell. Powers* ii. x. 287 His style is disagreeable, being full of perplexed sentences. 1832 Lewis *Use & Ab. Pol. Terms* xi. 93 On this point his language is somewhat perplexed.

3. Of material objects: Having the parts intricately intertwined or intermingled; intricate, entangled.

1605 Bacon *Adv. Learn.* ii. vii. §5 The formes of substances..(as they are nowe by compounding and transplanting multiplied) are so perplexed. 1664 Evelyn *Sylva* xii, That perplext canopy which covers the seat in his Majesties garden at Hampton-court. 1748 *Anson's Voy.* iii. x. 413 The history and inventions of past ages, recorded by these perplexed [Chinese] symbols, must frequently prove unintelligible.

perplexedly (pəˈplɛksɪdlɪ), *adv.* [f. prec. + -LY^2.] In a perplexed manner.

1. With mental perplexity or bewilderment.

1650 *Sc. Metr. Ps.* cxliii. iv, My spirit is therefore overwhelm'd in me, perplexedly. *a*1693 *Urquhart's Rabelais* iii. xxv. 210 Most perplexedly desirous to know the Name, of him who should be his Successor. 1827 G. S. Faber *Sacr. Calend. Prophecy* (1844) III. 356 All persons seem to be perplexedly looking out for a crisis of some description or other. 1870 Burton *Hist. Scot.* (1873) VII. lxxv. 33 A point on which many were perplexedly meditating and doubting.

2. In an involved, intricate, or confused manner; intricately, confusedly, ambiguously, obscurely. Now *rare* or *Obs.*

1617 Hales *Serm.* 6 Going about rather perplexedly to search the controversies, then grauely to compose them. 1625 Hart *Anat. Ur.* i. ii. 16 It is a wonder to heare how doubtfully and perplexedly..they will..prate of the patients sicknesse. 1706 J. Gardiner tr. *Rapin on Gard.* ii. 68 There Trees, confus'd and wild, perplextly stay, Observe no Order, and no Laws obey. 1796 T. Green *Diary Lover of Lit.* (1810) 12 The intermediate materials are capriciously divided and perplexedly arranged.

perplexedness (pəˈplɛksɪdnɪs). [f. as prec. + -NESS.] The state or quality of being perplexed; perplexity: of persons or things: see PERPLEXED.

1608-11 Bp. Hall *Medit. & Vows* iii. §81 They, through paine of body, and perplexedness of minde, shall be least able to resist. *a*1628 F. Grevil *Sidney* (1652) 244 To hold the attention of the Reader..in the strangeness or perplexedness of witty Fictions. 1653 Ashwell *Fides Apost.* 9 Plaine, without Perplexednesse, or Obscurity. *a*1693 *Urquhart's Rabelais* iii. xliv. 363 The Anxiety and Perplexedness of Humane Wits. *a*1714 Abp. Sharp *Wks.* (1754) I. iii. 62 The uncertainty and perplexedness of all human events.

perˈplexer. *rare.* [f. PERPLEX *v.* + -ER^1.] One who perplexes.

1694 Motteux *Rabelais* iv. xlvi. (1737) 185 Perplexers of Causes.

†**perˈplexful**, *a. Obs. rare.* [f. PERPLEX *sb.* or *v.* + -FUL 1.] Full of perplexity; perplexing.

1618 T. Adams *Heaven made sure* Wks. 1861 I. 63 There are many mysteries..which curious wits with perplexful studies strive to apprehend. 1633 —— *Exp. 2 Peter* ii. 4 Had I followed all the perplexful..questions of the school.

perˈplexing, *ppl. a.* [f. PERPLEX *v.* + -ING^2.] That perplexes; causing perplexity.

*a*1631 Donne *Serm., Ps. ii. 12* (1640) 412 A subtile, and perplexing intricacy, in the Doctrinall part. 1667 Milton *P.L.* viii. 183 With perplexing thoughts To interrupt the sweet of Life. 1714 Gay *Trivia* i. 10 Long perplexing Lanes. 1870 Freeman *Norm. Conq.* (ed. 2) I. App. 758 He is a perplexing writer to deal with.

perˈplexingly, *adv.* [f. prec. + -LY^2.] In a manner that perplexes; bewilderingly.

1830 *Blackw. Mag.* XXVII. 10 The mind or person being called, somewhat perplexingly perhaps, by logicians, the subject. 1897 *Naturalist* 247 Later they became..more perplexingly numerous still.

†**perˈplexion**. *Obs. rare.* Also 5 -plyxcyon, 6 -plection. [ad. late L. *perplexiōn-em*, n. of condition f. *perplex-us* PERPLEX *a.* (cf. *union*).] A state or condition of being perplexed; perplexity.

*c*1485 *Digby Myst.* (1882) iii. 1986, I woll ponysch swych personnes with perplyxcyon. 1585 T. Washington tr. *Nicholay's Voy.* iv. xi. 123 [His life] was mixed with a great manner of perplections. 1611 Heywood *Gold. Age* iii. i. Wks. 1874 III. 40 Amazement, warre, the threatning Oracle, All muster strange perplexions 'bout my braine.

†**perˈplexitive**, *a.* and *sb. Obs. rare.* Also 6 perplexatyue. [f. L. *perplexāt-*, ppl. stem of L. *perplexārī* + -IVE, or irreg. f. PERPLEXITY + -IVE.] a. *adj.* Tending to perplex; perplexing. b. *sb.* An occasion of perplexity or anxiety.

1542 Boorde *Dyetary* xxxix. (1870) 300 Let hym resorte to mery company to breke of his perplexatyues. 1660 Fisher *Rusticks Alarm* Wks. (1679) 428 Costly Comments..and more perplexitive Unfoldings of it [the Word], that are made by our Schoolmen. 1709 Mrs. Manley *Secret Mem.* I. 110 Vapours, a Distemper all new and perplexitive.

perplexity (pəˈplɛksɪtɪ). [ad. post-cl. L. *perplexitās* (Ammianus), f. *perplex-us* (PERPLEX *a.*), or a. F. *perplexité* (14th c. in Godef. *Compl.*).] The condition of being perplexed.

1. Inability to determine what to think, or how to act, owing to the involved, intricate, or complicated condition of circumstances, or of the matters to be dealt with, generally also involving mental perturbation and anxiety; puzzled condition, embarrassment, bewilderment, distraction.

*c*1300 in Wyntoun *Cron.* vii. 3625 Succoure Scotland and remede That stad is in perplexyte. 1375 Barbour *Bruce* xi. 619 Thai war in gret perplexite Bot with gret travale, nocht-for-thi, Thai thame defendit manfully. 1390 Gower *Conf.* III. 348 Tho was betwen mi Prest and me Debat and gret perplexite. 1480 Caxton *Chron. Eng.* i. (1520) 6/2 The chyldren of Israell were in greate perplexyte. 1573-80 Baret *Alv.* P 306 To be in so great danger and perplexitie, that he cannot tell what to do. *a*1674 Clarendon *Hist. Reb.* ix. §118 The King had stayed at Hereford..in great perplexity, and irresolution. 1748 *Anson's Voy.* iii. vi. 346 As we had no observation of our latitude at noon, we were in some perplexity. 1866 G. Macdonald *Ann. Q. Neighb.* xxxii. (1878) 550, I had been in great perplexity how to let her know that I was there.

†b. Trouble, distress. *Obs.*

1375 Barbour *Bruce* xx. 78 His maill eiss [malease = disease] of Ane fundyng Begouth; for, throu his cald lying.. Him fell that herd perplexite. *c*1420 Lydg. *Assembly of Gods* 200 Let me the mater here Why he ys brought in thys perplexyte. 1540-54 Croke *Ps.* (Percy Soc.) 19 Turne not asyde fro me thy face, When perplexitie doeth appere. 1549 *Compl. Scot.* vii. 71 Ther can nocht be ane mair vehement perplexite as quhen ane person beand in prosperite at his hartis desire, ande syne dechays in miserabil aduersite. 1574 *Reg. Privy Council Scot.* II. 383 The said Issobell and hir.. bairnis ar in grit perplexitie and povertie. 1658 Phillips, *Perplexity*,..also trouble, or anguish of minde.

2. With *a* and *pl.* a. An instance of this condition; a state of doubt or mental difficulty.

*c*1491 *Chast. Goddes Chyld.* 12 Some falle in perplexitees for a thyng that nought is to charge or lityl. 1532 More *Confut. Tindale* Wks. 486 But if the sygnificacyon bee knowen, then liued the chosen people of God in the old law in a strange perplexitie. 1671 Milton *Samson* 304 Till by thir own perplexities involv'd They ravel more, still less resolv'd. 1750 Johnson *Rambler* No. 36 ¶8 Accidents which produce perplexities, terrors, and surprises.

b. Something that causes perplexity, trouble, or disturbing doubt; a matter or cause of trouble or difficulty.

1598 Meres *Palladis Tamia* 284 To bewaile..the perplexities of Loue. 1609 Bible (Douay) *Susanna* i. 22 Susanna sighed and sayd: Perplexities are to me on everie side. 1665 *Phil. Trans.* I. 105 All is involved with perplexities. 1870 J. H. Newman *Gram. Assent* i. iv. 63 It is to me a perplexity that grave authors seem to enunciate as an intuitive truth, that everything must have a cause. 1877 Froude *Short Stud.* (1883) IV. i. ii. 24 The condition of the clergy was a pressing and practical perplexity.

3. An intricately involved, entangled, or confused state *of* anything. a. Of material objects.

1664 Evelyn *Sylva* (1679) 4 Dropp'd, and disseminated amongst the..perplexities of the mother-roots. 1779 J. Moore *View Soc. Fr.* (1789) I. xxiv. 190 The difficulty and perplexity of the road. 1800 *Asiat. Ann. Reg., Misc. Tracts* 14/1 Toilsome and intricate marches..with successive difficulties to encounter, from the perplexities of the country. 1855 J. R. Leifchild *Cornwall* 129 Upon a comparison of various classes of miners..the intelligence of any class will be found directly proportionate to the perplexity of the minerals to be mined. 1881 W. G. Palgrave in *Macm. Mag.* XLV. 34 The dense perplexity of dwarf palm, garlanded creepers, glossy undergrowth.

b. Of affairs, a subject of study, etc.

1743 Johnson *Let.* 1 Dec., With respect to the interest, which a great perplexity of affairs hindered me from thinking of. 1794 Sullivan *View Nat.* I. 127 This subject, as I before observed, with all its perplexities, was much agitated by the ancients. 1879 Calderwood *Mind & Br.* 69 Psychology has its own share of perplexity.

†**perˈplexive**, *a. Obs. rare.* [f. L. *perplex-us* PERPLEX *a.* + -IVE: cf. L. *complexīvus*.] Having the quality of perplexity, tending to perplex. Hence **perˈplexiveness**, the quality of perplexing or causing perplexity.

1620 B. Jonson *News fr. World Moon* Wks. (Rtldg.) 615/1 Tut, that's no news: your perplexive glasses are common. 1659 H. More *Immort. Soul* i. ii. (1662) 18 If the perplexiveness of imagination may hinder assent, we must not believe mathematicall demonstration.

†**perˈplexly**, *adv. Obs. rare*$^{-1}$. [f. PERPLEX *a.* + -LY^2.] In a perplexed manner; confusedly.

1670 Milton *Hist. Eng.* v. Wks. 1851 V. 211 This is the summe of what pass'd in three years against the Danes,..set down so perplexly by the Saxon Annalist.

perˈplexment. *rare.* [f. PERPLEX *v.* + -MENT.] Perplexed condition, perplexity.

1826 *Blackw. Mag.* XX. 336 The perplexment occasioned by such an extraordinary mass of materials.

perplext, -ly, obs. forms of PERPLEXED, -LY.

perpli'cation. *rare*⁻⁰. [cf. L. *perplicāt-us* interlaced, entangled.] (See quots.)

1656 BLOUNT *Glossogr.*, *Perplication*, . . a folding to and fro. **1853** DUNGLISON *Med. Lex.*, *Perplication*, a method of tying arteries.

† **per'polished**, *ppl. a. Obs. rare.* [f. PER- 4 + POLISHED. Cf. obs. F. *parpolir*, *parpoliss-* (16th c.).] Thoroughly or highly polished.

1616 J. LANE *Cont. Sqr.'s T.* IX. 7 Aspiringe pinackles, perpolishd towres. *Ibid.* x. 261 All these perpolishd I will statelie build.

† **perpo'lite**, *a. Obs.* [ad. L. *perpolīt-us*, pa. pple. of *perpolīre* to polish well or thoroughly, f. PER- 2 + *polīre* to polish: cf. F. *parpoli* (16th c.).] Highly polished or refined in style.

1596 NASHE *Saffron Walden* Ded., Not . . a more perpolite Doctor than thy selfe. **1597** A. M. tr. *Guillemeau's Fr. Chirurg.* *vj, This excellente, exquisite, and perpolite peece of worcke. **1648** HERRICK *Hesper.*, *To M. J. Harmar*, When first I find those numbers thou do'st write, To be most soft, terce, sweet, and perpolite.

† **per'ponder**, *v. Obs. rare.* [f. PER- 2 + PONDER *v.*] *intr.* To ponder or consider thoroughly.

1599 NASHE *Lenten Stuffe* 21 Then perponder of the red herringes priority. *Ibid.* 68 Nowe I perponder more sadlie vppon it, I thinke I am out indeede.

† **perpo'tation.** *Obs. rare*⁻⁰. [ad. L. *perpōtātio* continued drinking, drinking bout.]

1623 COCKERAM, *Perpotation*, ordinarie drunkennesse. **1721** BAILEY, *Perpotation*, a thorough drunkenness.

perpoynt, obs. form of PARPEN, PORCUPINE.

perprise, perprisioun: see PURPRISE, etc.

† **per'prudent**, *a. Obs. rare*⁻¹. [f. PER- 4 + PRUDENT.] Very prudent.

1535 BOORDE in Ellis *Orig. Lett.* Ser. III. II. 298 Our most armipotentt, perprudentt, circumspecte, dyscrete, and gracyose Souereyng Lord the Kyng.

† **perpu'sil**, *a. Obs. rare*⁻¹. (*erron.* -cil.) [ad. L. *perpusill-us*, f. PER- 4 + *pusillus* weak.] Very small. So † **perpu'sillity**, extreme minuteness.

1597 A. M. tr. *Guillemeau's Fr. Chirurg.* 27 b/2 The vaynes . . throughe there perpusillitye and rotunditye, they avoyde the poyncte of the lancet. *Ibid.* 31 b/2 Horseleeches are little and perpucil creatures like wormes.

† **perpyne.** *Obs.* Corrupt form of PORCUPINE, applied to a French gold coin issued *c* 1507 by Louis XII, and bearing the device of a porcupine. It weighed about 53 grains troy, the contemporary English sovereign being 240 grains.

1525 in *Lett. & Pap. Hen. VIII*, IV. I. 660.

† **perquellies, -les.** *Obs.* (?)

It is uncertain what Coverdale meant; *perquellis* resembles some 16th c. forms of *portcullis*.

1535 COVERDALE *2 Sam.* v. 8 Who so euer smyteth the Iebusites, and optayneth the perquellies [*ed.* **1537** perquelles] the lame & the blynde, which (Iebusites) Dauids soule hateth. [LXX. ἁπτέσθω ἐν παραξιφίδι; *Vulg.* tetigisset domatum fistulas; 1382 WYCLIF touchide the goters of the hows eues; 1388 hadde touchid the goteris of roouys; 1539 *Great B.*, *Cranmer*, *Bps'*., *Geneva*, getteth vp to the gutters, 1611 gutter, 1885 *R.V.* let him get up to the watercourse.]

† **per'quer, -'queir, -'quire**, *adv.* (*a.*) *Sc. Obs.* Also 4 -quere, 6 -quier. [a. F. *par cœur* (in OF. *queur* (11th c.), *cuer* (12–15th c.), *cueur* (14–15th c.), by heart, by memory, perfectly, exactly.] By heart, by memory; hence, perfectly, accurately, exactly. *to have perqueir*: to 'have by heart', to know or remember perfectly.

1375 BARBOUR *Bruce* I. 238 Than all perquer he suld it wit. *c* **1375** *Sc. Leg. Saints* xxx. (*Theodera*) 414, & leryt sa, for he was wyse, Al þat til a monk suld fere, In to schort tyme wele perquere. **1500–20** DUNBAR *Poems* xc. 32 Gif thow can nocht schaw furth thi synnes perqueir. **1577** in Balfour *Oppress. Orkn. & Shetl.* (1859) 19 He [the Lawrightman] . . pronuncit the decreitis perqueyre in default of scrybis. *a* **1586** SIR R. MAITLAND *Poems* (1830) 16 Nor of ane Princes the dewtie and the det, Quhilk I beleif thy heichnes hes per queir. *a* **1610** SIR J. SEMPLE in *Sempill Ballatis* (1872) 247 The fearefull babe quho knawes his task perqueir. **1638** BAILLIE *Lett.* (1775) I. 17 A number of othir passages I had perquire. **1722** RAMSAY *Three Bonnets* I. 102 Could newest aiths genteelly swear, And had a course o' flaws perquire.

b. *loosely.* Certainly, without doubt, forsooth, verily; rightly, uprightly.

a **1550** in *Dunbar's Poems* (1893) 312 For he that pacience can nocht leir, He sall displesance haif, perqueir. **1562** A. SCOTT *Poems* i. 46 Lat perversit prelettis leif perqueir.

B. *adj.* Thoroughly versed, 'perfect'; ready.

1572 *Satir. Poems Reform.* xxx. 72 Rype of ingyne, with iudgement perqueir. *c* **1600** MONTGOMERIE *Cherrie & Slae* 1467 Thair neirest perquierest Is always to them baith. **1742** R. FORBES *Ajax's Sp.* in *Poems Buchan Dial.* (1785) 2 At threeps I am na' sae perquire, Nor auld-farren as he.

perquest (pəˈkwɛst), *v. rare*⁻¹. [app. f. PER- 1 + QUEST, after L. *perquīrĕre*: see next.] *trans.* To search through.

1891 STEVENSON & L. OSBOURNE *Wrecker* xv, There never was a ship more ardently perquested; no stone was left unturned, and no expedient untried.

† **per'quire**, *v. Obs. rare.* [ad. L. *perquīrĕre* to make diligent search for, f. PER- 2 + *quærĕre* to seek: cf. OF. *parquerir*.] *trans.* To search through, or make diligent search into. Hence † **per'quiring** *ppl. a.*, inquiring.

1597 A. M. tr. *Guillemeau's Fr. Chirurg.* b iv b/2 Mr. Rabet, a verye inventive and perquiringe man. **1659** CLOBERY *Div. Glimpses* 73 Perquire Zoographurs, and none recite, A Romane Pope turn'd willing Anchorite.

perquisite (ˈpɜːkwɪzɪt). Also 5, 7 perquesite (7 -itt), 6–8 perquisit (7 -itt). [ad. L. *perquīsītum* that which is diligently searched for or asked after, in med.L. a thing acquired or gained, an acquisition, f. L. *perquīrĕre* (see prec.).]

† **1.** *Law.* Property acquired otherwise than by inheritance: see PURCHASER, and cf. CONQUEST *sb.* 6.

[*c* **1250** BRACTON II. xxx. §3 Ea quæ dicta sunt, secundum quosdam locum habent de perquisito in utroque casu de hæreditate vero descendente aliud erit. *c* **1290** FLETA I. xi, Tenementorum quædam . . tenentur in Capite de Corona quædam vero de Rege per escaetam vel per perquisitum.] *c* **1450** tr. *Charter c* 1255 in *Godstow Reg.* (E.E.T.S.) 257 The londis the whiche the same Alisaundir had bothe of the yifte of the said Raaf his fadir and also of his owne getyng of perquysitis in karsynton. **1596** BACON *Max. & Use Com. Law* I. xi. (1636) 50 Though the law giveth it not in point of inheritance, but onely as a perquisite to any of the bloud so hee be next in estate. **1670** BLOUNT *Law Dict.*, *Perquisite* . . , signifies any thing gained by ones own industry, or purchased with ones own Money; contradistinguished from that which descends to one, from Father, or other ancestor. **1704** J. HARRIS *Lex. Techn.* I.

† **b.** In generalized use: An acquisition. *Obs.*

1655 JER. TAYLOR *Gold. Grove* To Rdr., Not in the Purchases and Perquisites of the World.

2. *Law.* Casual profits that come to the lord of a manor, in addition to his regular annual revenue. For the sources of these see quot. 1579.

[**1379** in Madox *Formulare* (1702) 65 Manerium de Chacombe in Comitatu Northamptoniæ, cum omnibus suis pertinentiis . . redditibus, serviciis, pratis, pasturis et perquisitis Curiarum.] *a* **1552** LELAND *Itin.* II. 50 King Richard the first gave to Cirencestre the Cortes and Perquisites of 7. Hundredes therabout yn Glocestreshir. *c* **1570** *Pride & Lowl.* (1841) 36 Nowe hath a churle . . take it in leace, To wytte the lordship with the perquisite. **1579** *Expos. Termes of Lawe* 156 b, *Perquisites* are aduauntages and profittes that come to a mannor by casualty, and not yearely: as Escheates, Hariotes, Relyefes, wayfes, strayes, forfaytures, amercements in courts, wardes, maryages, goods and landes purchased by villaines of the same mannor, and diuers such like things that are not certeine but happen by chaunce, sometymes more often then at other tymes. **1622** CALLIS *Stat. Sewers* (1647) 102 If the Copyhold were overflowed by the Sea, the Lord should lose his Freehold of the soil, his Seigniory, yearly Rents and Fines for admittances, and all other perquesites. **1766** BLACKSTONE *Comm.* II. vi. 88 Marriage, or the *valor maritagii*, was not in socage tenure any perquisite or advantage to the guardian, but rather the reverse. **1818** CRUISE *Digest* (ed. 2) IV. 320 A court baron being incident to a manor of common right, the manor cannot be granted by a private person, with an exception of the court baron and its perquisites; but may be so granted by the King. **1890** GROSS *Gild Merch.* I. 6 Commutation of tolls, court perquisites, and other town dues.

3. *generally.* Any casual emolument, fee, or profit, attached to an office or position in addition to salary or wages.

1565 JEWEL *Def. Apol.* (1611) 641, I leaue out the yeerely perquisites that the Pope made of his Elections, Preuentions, Dispensations, Pluralities, Trialities, Totquots, Tolerations: for his Bulles, his Seales, his Signatures: for Eating Flesh, for Egs, for White meat, for Priests Concubines, and for other like merchandise. **1573** in Gross *Gild Merch.* II. 76 The wardens . . shall have the same perquisits that they nowe have. **1661** J. STEPHENS *Procurations* 44 *Procurationes* for his visitation, *ut supra*, which is a perquisit or profit of his Spirituall Jurisdiction. **1691** T. H[ALE] *Acc. New Invent.* p. lxvii, That part of their Office that enabled them to receive several Admiralty Perquisites and Droits. **1693** LUTTRELL *Brief Rel.* (1857) III. 96 Colonel Goddard, Governour of Bermudas . . is to be allowed £500 per annum, besides the perquisites of his government. **1759** ROBERTSON *Hist. Scot.* I. I. 13 When the officers of the Crown received scarcely any salary besides the fees and perquisites of their office. **1765** BLACKSTONE *Comm.* I. iv. 219 The queen . . is intitled to an antient perquisite called queen-gold, or *aurum reginæ*. **1825** JEFFERSON *Autobiog.* Wks. 1859 I. 66 There shall be no establishment of officers . . with either salaries or perquisites. **1869** BALDW. BROWN *Misread Passages* ix. 121 The meat offered in sacrifice was in some measure the perquisite of the priest.

b. *fig.*

1705 VANBRUGH *Confed.* I. iii, Ah, Flippanta, the perquisites of quality are of an unspeakable value! **1712** ADDISON *Spect.* No. 469 ¶1 To an honest Mind the best Perquisites of a Place are the Advantages it gives a Man of doing Good. **1897** *Westm. Gaz.* 23 Apr. 2/2 The King [Humbert] seems to have treated the matter [attempt to assassinate him] very coolly, remarking, 'It is only one of the little perquisites of my trade'.

c. Any article that has served its primary purpose, or that is supposed to be no longer in use, which is customarily left to subordinates, attendants, employees, or servants to turn to their own profit, or which they claim a customary right to take or 'pick up' for their own use.

Such are the perquisites of an executioner or hangman, of valets, ladies' maids, cooks, college 'scouts', employees or assistants in any work in which there tends to be some waste or superfluity.

c **1709** PRIOR *Widow & Cat* 39 Was it fit To make my cream a perquisite, And steal, to mend your wages? **1735** SOMERVILLE *Chase* II. 285 These claim the Pack, the bloody Perquisite For all their Toils. **1853** 'C. BEDE' *Verdant Green* I. vi, Verdant discovered the extended meaning of the word perquisites [among college servants]. **1855** PRESCOTT *Philip II*, I. I. vii. 100 The pillage of a place taken by storm was regarded as the perquisite of the soldier. **1861** SMILES *Engineers* II. 196 The lightermen claimed as their right the perquisites of 'wastage' and 'leakage', and they took care that these two items should include as much as possible.

d. A gratuity expected or claimed by some employees, waiters, servants, and the like, from those to whom they perform services in connexion with the duties for which they are employed; a customary 'tip'.

1721 AMHERST *Terræ Fil.* No. 42 (1754) 222 Most candidates get leave of the proctor, by paying his man a crown, (which is call'd his perquisite,) to chuse their own examiners. **1727** GAY *Begg. Op.* II, Your father's perquisites for the escape of prisoners must amount to a considerable sum in the year. **1803** *Censor* 1 Mar. 33, I would meet another objection, namely, that what is given to servants at inns is not to be looked upon as wages, but as perquisites. **1841** W. H. AINSWORTH *Old St. Pauls* I. 325 A party of choristers . . were demanding 'spur-money' of him—an exaction which they claimed as part of their perquisites.

e. More vaguely: The emoluments or income from any office.

Prob. so called first in cases where the income consisted solely or mainly of casual receipts or gratuities.

1712 HEARNE *Collect.* (O.H.S.) III. 413 Dr. Hudson made . . [me] second Keeper of the Bodleian Library with Liberty allow'd . . of being Keeper of the Anatomy Schoole . . on purpose to advance the perquisites of the Place which are very inconsiderable. **1784** COWPER *Task* VI. 848 Where he that fills an office, shall esteem Th' occasion it presents of doing good More than the perquisite.

† **4.** *concr.* An adjunct, appurtenance, or proper accompaniment of anything. *Obs.*

[**1494** *Will of W. Stanborough* (Somerset Ho.), Item lego dicte ecclesie . . unum craterem argenteum . . ad fabricandum exinde novam crucem argenteam cum aliis perquesitis.] **1667** PEPYS *Diary* 22 Aug., My wife very fine to-day, in her new suit of laced cuffs and perquisites. **1686** tr. *Chardin's Trav. Persia* 383 Casbin . . the City is much decay'd, . . and . . it has lost all those Perquisites that set forth the Pomp and Grandeur of a sumptuous Court.

5. *fig.* A thing to which one has the sole right.

1793 WOLCOTT (P. Pindar) *Ep. to the Pope* Prol. 8 King-making unto man is justly given, Once the great perquisite indeed of Heaven. **1838** PRESCOTT *Ferd. & Is.* (1846) II. ix. 452 The government kept a most jealous eye upon what it regarded as its own peculiar perquisites. **1877** BLACK *Green Past.* xxv. (1878) 198 Assaults on seats [in parliament] deemed even more a personal perquisite than his own.

6. *attrib.* and *Comb.*

1712 (*title*) The Perquisite Monger. **1731** *Gentl. Mag.* I. 100 The modern practice of perquisite-taking, which he says may be stiled a skreen for bribery. **1809** E. S. BARRETT *Setting Sun* I. 94 The perquisite-mongers . . blow out the candles with all expedition, to save as much as possible for themselves. **1899** *Daily News* 20 July 5/2 This method . . does away with . . the abominable perquisite system.

[**perquisite**, *a.*, error for *prerequisite*.]

'**perquisited**, *a. rare*⁻¹. [f. PERQUISITE *sb.* + -ED².] Having or receiving perquisites; 'tipped'.

a **1743** SAVAGE in Johnson *Life*, If perquisited varlets frequent stand, And each new walk must a new tax demand.

perquisition (pɜːkwɪˈzɪʃən). [a. F. *perquisition* (15th c. in Godef. *Compl.*), ad. med.L. *perquīsītiōn-em*, from L. *perquīrĕre*: see PERQUIRE.]

† **1.** The gaining or obtaining of something otherwise than by inheritance: cf. PERQUISITE *sb.* 1. *Obs. rare.*

1461 *Rolls of Parlt.* V. 490/2 Pardons made by any of the seid late pretended kynges, to any Body or persons . . for purchace, perquisicion or receyvyng of any of the premisses.

b. The exaction of perquisites. *nonce-use.*

1834 *Tait's Mag.* I. 632/1 Even criminal judicature flings its scarlet robe over the sin of perquisition; Newgate itself claims 'something above wages' for its turnkeys, something known by the name of 'garnish'.

2. A thorough or diligent search; careful investigation or inquiry; *spec.* (after French use), a domiciliary or other search ordered by law for the discovery of a person, or of incriminating documents, etc.

1611 COTGR., *Perquisition* . . , a perquisition, diligent search, or serious inquirie. **1626** T. H[AWKINS] *Caussin's Holy Crt.* 302 The second [degree of good prayer] . . is, the perquisition, to wit, the search of veritye s. **1744** BERKELEY *Siris* §126 So fugitive as to escape all the filtrations and perquisitions of the most nice observers. **1793** SIR M. EDEN in *Ld. Auckland's Corr.* (1862) III. 109 Orders were given by the Government . . to make the most exact perquisitions after him. **1839** JAMES *Louis XIV*, IV. 41 Papers . . found during the Perquisitions in Normandy. **1898** *Westm. Gaz.* 13 July 9/1 A perquisition was made at the house of Madame Esterhazy . . but with no result.

†**per'quisitive.** *Obs. rare*⁻¹. [ad. L. type **perquīsītivum*, f. *perquīsīt-um* PERQUISITE: see -IVE.] = PERQUISITE *sb.* 3.

c **1380** WYCLIF *Wks.* (1880) 393 þe clerkis han many grete & smale perquisitiuys.

perquisitor (pə'kwɪzɪtə(r)). [a. L. *perquisitor*, agent-n. from *perquīrĕre*: see PERQUIRE. Cf. F. *perquisiteur* (Oresme, 14th c. in Godef. *Compl.*) = a.] †**a.** A thorough searcher. *Obs. rare*⁻⁰. **b.** The original acquirer of an estate to which his descendants have succeeded; the first purchaser: cf. PERQUISITE *sb.* 1. *rare.*

1656 BLOUNT *Glossogr.*, *Perquisitor* (Lat.) an enquirer, or diligent searcher. *a* **1867** CHIEF JUSTICE WOODWARD in Roberts's Appeal, 39 *Penn. St. Repts.* 420 This proviso is a legislative recognition of the general common law principle of descents, that inheritable blood is only such as flows from the perquisitor of the estate.

†**perquis'quilian,** *a. Obs. nonce-wd.* [f. PER- 4 + L. *quisquili-æ* trifles, rubbish + -AN: cf. QUISQUILIAN.] Thoroughly trifling or worthless.

1647 WARD *Simp. Cobler* 26 The very pettitoes of infirmity, the gyblets of perquisquilian toyes.

perradial (pə'reɪdɪəl), *a. Zool.* [f. PERRADI-US + -AL¹; cf. *radial.*] Pertaining to the *perradii* or primary rays of a hydrozoan or other cœlenterate; primarily radial.

1880 E. R. LANKESTER in *Nature* 4 Mar. 414/1 An organ.. may be..per-radial, inter-radial, or adradial in position. **1881** —— in *Encycl. Brit.* XII. 558/2 The eight arms of the disc and their tentaculocysts are [four] perradial and [four] interradial. **1888** ROLLESTON & JACKSON *Anim. Life* 717 (Ctenophora) The funnel gives origin to two 'perradial' vessels. *Ibid.* 781 (Hydrozoa Acraspeda) Four of them, the *perradial* tentacles,..correspond to the four angles of the mouth; four others, the *interradial* tentacles, second in development, to the centres of the square sides of the mouth, and the remaining eight *adradial* tentacles occupy the intervals between the per- and interradial.

perradiate (pə'reɪdɪeɪt), *v.* [f. PER- 1 + RADIATE *v.*] *trans.* To radiate through; to penetrate or intersect with rays.

1839 BAILEY *Festus* x. (1848) 105 All dark things brightened, all contrariants blent; And truth and love, perradiating life, Be the new poles of nature. *Ibid.* xix. 218 The stars, Perradiated each like thunderbolts, Stand clustered into omniformal spheres.

‖**perradius** (pə'reɪdɪəs). *Zool.* Pl. -ii (-ɪaɪ). [mod.L., f. PER- 4 + RADIUS *sb.*] Each of the primary rays or radiating parts of certain cœlenterates.

1880 E. R. LANKESTER in *Nature* 4 Mar. 414/1 The first four radii [of a discomedusan hydrozoan] to appear in the course of the growth from a simpler phase of development are called the per-radii, the next four (between these) the inter-radii, the next eight between these the adradii.

perrafrase, obs. form of PARAPHRASE *sb.*

perraling, erron. form of PARPALLING.

perre, obs. f. PERRY²; var. PORRAY *Obs.*, pottage.

perre, perree, var. PERRIE *Obs.*, jewellery.

perregal, variant of PAREGAL *Obs.*

†**perreptation.** *Obs. rare*⁻⁰. [n. of action from L. *per-reptāre* to creep or crawl through.]

1656 BLOUNT *Glossogr.*, *Perreptation*, a creeping into every corner, a diligent searching.

perrerer, var. PERRIER *Obs.*

perrewig, obs. f. PERIWIG.

perrey, var. PERRIE, PERRY¹ and ², PORRAY *Obs.*, pottage.

perrhenic (pə'ri:nɪk), *a. Chem.* [f. PER-¹ 5 b + RHEN(IUM + -IC.] ***perrhenic acid,*** a strong acid, $HReO_4$, which is known only as a colourless aqueous solution and is an oxidizing agent.

1929 *Chem. Abstr.* XXIII. 1833 Yellow oxide, Re_2O_7,..is water sol[uble], hygroscopic, forming a strong acid, perrhenic acid. **1962** P. J. & B. DURRANT *Introd. Adv. Inorg. Chem.* xxiv. 1019 Rhenium heptoxide dissolves freely in water to form perrhenic acid. *Ibid.*, Many salts of perrhenic acid are known. **1973** R. D. PEACOCK in J. C. Bailar et al. *Comprehensive Inorg. Chem.* III. xxxix. 946 Perrhenic acid is a strong acid; this is shown by the pH of its aqueous solution, its attack upon metals, [etc.].

Hence **pe'rrhenate** [-ATE⁴], a salt of this acid; the anion ReO_4^-.

1929 *Chem. Abstr.* XXIII. 4632 Perrhenates of non-volatile bases can be ignited in O_2 without decompn. **1950** N. V. SIDGWICK *Chem. Elements* II. 1295 Perrhenates are formed with great ease by the action of oxidizing agents..on metallic rhenium or its lower oxides and their derivatives. **1962** COTTON & WILKINSON *Adv. Inorg. Chem.* xxx. 801 After concentration, the perrhenate is precipitated by addition of potassium chloride as the sparingly soluble salt, $KReO_4$. **1972** *Inorg. Syntheses* XIII. 219 This difficulty has been overcome for ReH_9^{2-} by a synthesis of the disodium salt in which an ethanol solution of sodium perrhenate is reduced with sodium metal to give the hydride in *ca.* 35% yield.

perriago, -agua, -aguer, -augre, -awger, obs. ff. PIRAGUA.

†**perri'diculous,** *a. Obs. rare*⁻¹. [f. L. *perrīdicul-us* (f. PER- 4 + *rīdiculus* laughable) + -OUS.] Thoroughly ridiculous.

c **1600** *Timon* II. v, I hate these perridiculous asses Whose braines containe, noe, not one ounce of witte.

†**'perrie, 'perry.** *Obs.* Chiefly *poet.* Forms: α. 4–5 (6) perre, 4–5 perree, -ey, -eye, (4 perey, 5 pere, pirre, 6 pyrre). β. 4–5 perrye, -ie, 5–6 perry, (5 pery). γ. 5 pierrye, 6 pierrie, (9 pierie). [a. OF. *pierrie, pierie* (Godefroy), syncopated form of *pierrerie*, OF. *perrerie*, f. *pierre* stone + *-erie*: see -ERY 1.

The syncopated form is evidenced in 14–16th c. in Godef.; app. Anglo-Fr. must have had *perrie* (from *perrerie, perr'rie, per'rie*) as the source of 14th c. ME. *perrie, perrye*, whence later *perry*. In the forms *perré* (the earliest and most frequent in ME.), *perree, perrey, -eye*, the termination is not easy to account for. (? F. *perré, -ée* pa. pple. used sbst.; cf. Pr. *peyrat*:—L. *petrātum*.) The late 15th and 16th c. forms *pierrye, pierrie* followed later French.]

Precious stones or gems collectively; jewellery.

α. *c* **1330** R. BRUNNE *Chron. Wace* (Rolls) 10042 A riche coroumal wiþ perre. *c* **1350** *Will. Palerne* 53 In gode cloþes of gold a-greþed ful riche Wiþ perrey and pellure pertelyche to þe riȝttes. **13..** *Minor Poems fr. Vernon MS.* xxviii. 66 Heie perle, of al perey þe pris. **1377** LANGL. *P. Pl.* B. x. 12 Al þe precious perre þat in paradys wexeth [*v. rr.* perree, pere, perrie, perreye]. *c* **1386** CHAUCER *Monk's T.* 315 She was al clad in perree [*v. rr.* perre, perrye, perry] and in gold. *c* **1430** LYDG. *Min. Poems* (Percy Soc.) 46 Ryche attyres of stonys and perre [*rime* be]. *c* **1450** *Erle Tolous* 327 Rychely sche was cladd, In golde and ryche perre [*rime* free]. [**1555** *Lydgate's Chron. Troy* II. xi. Gj/1 And all aboue reysed was a see, Ful curyously of stones and perre [*so MS. c* 1425]. **1558** —— *Bochas* VIII. xxii. 14 b, With royal rubies, gold, stones, nor pyrre.]

β. ? **1370** *Robt. Cicyle* 268 Alle was set with perrye [*rime* crystyanté]. **1386** *Will Sir R. Grene* (Somerset Ho.), Capucium de perry. **1390** GOWER *Conf.* I. 143 For cloth of gold and for perrie, which him was wont to magnefie. ? *a* **1400** *Morte Arth.* 2461 Appayrellde with perrye and pretious stones. ? *c* **1475** *Sqr. lowe Degre* 719 Ye ware the pery on your head. ? *a* **1500** *Chester Pl.* iv. 93 Therfore horse, harnes, and perye, As falles for my dignitie, The tythe of yt I take of thee. *c* **1560** *How a Merchande* 51 in Hazl. *E.P.P.* I. 198 He boghte hur perry to hur hedd Of saphers and of rubeys red.

γ. **1481** CAXTON *Godeffroy* xl. 78 As moche as two myghty men myght susteyne of pierrye. *a* **1541** WYATT *Faithful lover giveth his Mistress his heart* Poems (1815) 152, I can-not give broaches nor rings,..Pierrie, nor pearl, orient and clear. [**1880** *Contemp. Rev.* Mar. 421 All this fine pierie, The riches of the land and of the sea.]

perrie, obs. form of PERRY¹, ², PIRRIE, a squall.

†**perrier**¹. *Obs.* Also 5 perrerer, perierer, 7 perier. [a. OF. *perrier* (12–13th c. in Hatz.-Darm., now *pierrier*) = Sp. *pedrero*, It. *petriere*, repr. a L. type **petrārius*, and parallel to OF. *perrière*, med.L. *petrāria* (Du Cange) in same sense, deriv. of L. *petra*, F. *pierre* stone: cf. PETRARY and PEDRERO.] *orig.* A ballistic engine or cannon for discharging stones; later, a small gun with which ships were armed = PEDRERO.

c **1400** tr. *Secreta Secret., Gov. Lordsh.* 111 If þou shall assayll castels, vse Instrumentz castyng stones, as Mangoles or Perrerers. **1481** CAXTON *Godeffroy* clxxiv. 257 They.. dyde do make engyns, perierers, Magonneauls, castellys, chattes. **1524** in *Hakluyt's Voy.* (1599) II. 79 Artillerie of the Turkes..cannons perriers of brasse, that shot a stone of three foote and a halfe. **1643** *Lanc. Tracts* 174 The noise of 9 canon and 2 periers. **1696** PHILLIPS (ed. 5), *Perriers*, a small sort of Great Guns that shoot Stones, carried by Privateers. [**1885** C. W. C. OMAN *Art of War* 57 Against walls fifteen to thirty feet thick, the feeble..perrieres, catapults,..and so forth, beat without perceptible effect.]

Perrier² ('pɛrieɪ). The proprietary name of an effervescent natural mineral water from the South of France.

1907 *Trade Marks Jrnl.* 30 Oct. 1928 Perrier... Natural mineral water obtained from the spring known as 'Source Perrier' situated at Vergeze in France. St. John Harmsworth, trading as Perrier,..London,..merchant. **1907** *Yesterday's Shopping* (1969) 27 Mineral waters (natural)... Perrier..Table water. **1928** A. HUXLEY *Point Counter Point* xiii. 244 If only Grace could be bottled like Perrier water. **1957** [see ITALIAN *sb.* 6]. **1960** I. FLEMING *For your Eyes Only* 14 He always stipulated Perrier, for in his opinion expensive soda water was the cheapest way to improve a poor drink. **1973** D. MACKENZIE *Postscript to Dead Let.* 173 Tully was drinking beer. There was a bottle of Perrier in front of Misty. **1975** *New Yorker* 30 June 33/3 She measures his orange juice and Perrier water as carefully as if it were a Martini. **1977** *Rolling Stone* 30 June 73/4 At the Caffe Tartufo, while I lunch, she orders a Perrier water and tosses a carefully rolled stick of Doublemint into her mouth.

perrierie, var. PIERRERIE *Obs.*

perrierite ('pɛrɪəraɪt). *Min.* [a. It. *perrierite* (Bonatti & Gottardi 1950, in *Atti d. Accad. naz. d. Lincei*: *Rendiconti. Classe di Sci. fis.*, etc. IX. 361), f. the name of Carlo *Perrier* (1886–1948), Italian mineralogist: see -ITE¹.] A silicate of lanthanides, titanium, iron, and other elements, occurring as black or reddish brown, prismatic, monoclinic crystals.

1951 *Chem. Abstr.* XLV. 7923 (*heading*) Perrierite, a new mineral. **1962** *Mineral. Mag.* XXXIII. 45 These experiments..suggest that perrierite is probably an oxidized form of chevkinite. **1966** *Amer. Mineralogist* LI. 1394 Recent *x*-ray studies of metamict minerals which occur in Virginia have shown that some of the materials heretofore reported as allanite or chevkinite are actually perrierite. **1971** *Ibid.* LVI. 308 Chevkinite and perrierite exhibit thermal polymorphism only within certain compositional ranges.

Perrier-Jouët (ˌpɛrieɪ'ʒu:eɪ). The proprietary name of the champagne produced by the firm of Perrier-Jouët of Epernay.

1891 in C. Ray *Compleat Imbiber* (1967) IX. 122 All Brands of Champagne in stock..Pommery Greno, Perrier Jouet, Heidsieck, Giesler. **1899** O. WILDE *Importance of being Earnest* III. 136 He drank..an entire pint bottle of my Perrier-Jouet, Brut, '89. **1914** C. MACKENZIE *Sinister St.* II. III. xii. 745 Forty Good Eggs drank forty-eight bottles of Perrier Jouet '93. **1920** G. SAINTSBURY *Notes on Cellar-Bk.* v. 71 The very best [champagne] I ever had was a Perrier-Jouet. **1971** J. DOXAT *Drinks & Drinking* 165 *Perrier Jouet*, this champagne has a fine 1961 extra dry *cuvée reserve.* **1975** N. FREELING *What are Bugles blowing For?* xvi. 93 The waiter had brought a 'Belle Epoque' bottle of Perrier-Jouet.

perril, obs. f. PEARL, PERIL.

perriment, perritore, perriwig, perriwinkle, perrochioun, obs. ff. PEDIMENT, PARITOR, PERIWIG, PERIWINKLE, PAROCHIAN.

†**perrogate,** *v. Obs. rare*⁻⁰. [f. ppl. stem of L. *perrogāre* to ask one after another.]

1623 COCKERAM II, To Desire a thing heartily, *perogate.*

perron ('pɛrən, or as F. ‖pɛrɔ̃). Also 4 peroun, 5 peron. [a. F. *perron* (11th c. in Littré) = Pr. *peiro, peiron*, It. *petrone* large stone, great rock, f. L. *petra*, F. *pierre* stone.]

1. A large block or solid erection of stone, with or without steps, used as a platform, the base of a market-cross, a sepulchral monument, etc.

c **1380** *Sir Ferumb.* 4429 Out of þe tour þan cam he doun, And set hym on an heyȝ peroun, Y-mad as a chayre. **1470–85** MALORY *Arthur* x. v. 419 The Peron that Merlyn had made to fore where sire Lancyor..was slayne. *Ibid.* lxxxvii. 568 The peron and the graue besydes Camelot. *c* **1530** LD. BERNERS *Arth. Lyt. Bryt.* (1814) 133 There was pyght in the myddes of the felde a grete perron, wheron there was hanginge a riche and a goodly shelde. [**1611** COTGR., *Perron*..also, a square Base of stone, or mettall, some fiue or six foot high, whereon, in old time, Knights errant placed some discourse, challenge, or proofe, of an aduenture.]

b. *spec.* (see quot.).

1863 KIRK *Chas. Bold* I. I. vii. 297 Liège... In the centre of the Square, on a pedestal of several steps stood a pillar... The *Perron*—regarded as an emblem of the civic organization..—was an object of patriotic reverence and affection. *Ibid.* II. ii. 450.

2. *Arch.* A platform, to which one ascends by steps, in front of a church, mansion, or other large building, and upon which the door or doors open; sometimes applied to a double flight of steps ascending to such a front door.

[*c* **1475** *Partenay* 4974 And when that Gaffray was descendid tho, At the perron longe bode not in þat place, At castell finding hys fader by grace.] **1723** CHAMBERS tr. *Le Clerc's Treat. Archit.* I. 129 By Perron we mean an Ascent or Elevation given to the Entrance of a Building. The Portail ..of a Church..or any other great Building..ought to have a Perron. **1843** THACKERAY *Ir. Sk. Bk.* I. i. 39 Whiskey-and-water was ordered, which was drunk upon the *perron* before the house. **1862** LYTTON *Str. Story* xxi, An imposing pile,.. with..grand *perron* (or double flight of stairs to the entrance). **1864** SIR F. PALGRAVE *Norm. & Eng.* III. 21 Standing on the lofty Perron of the tall Ducal Palace. **1898** QUILLER-COUCH *Stevenson's St. Ives* 306 The landlord welcomed us on the perron.

perroquet, p. auk: see PARAKEET, PAROQUET.

perrore, obs. form of PARURE.

†**perrosin.** *Obs.* Forms: 5 perrosin, -yn, 6 perosin, -en, pirrosyn, 6–7 perrosen, 7 per-rosin. [app. a corruption of AF. **peis-resin* = OF. *pois-* or *poix-resin* 'the resin of turpentine' (Littré). Cf. PITCH-RESIN.] An old name for a resin of some kind, app. the dry resin obtained from pine trees; colophony.

c **1450** *M.E. Med. Bk.* (Heinrich) 173 Tak þre quarterons of clene rosyn, & a quarteron of good perrosyn, & half a pounde of good oile de olyue. *Ibid.* 174 As sone as þy rosyn & þy perrosyn beth molten & relented. **1545** *Rates of Customs* C j b, Perosen the C. pound xiiis. iiiid. **1563** T. GALE *Antidot.* II. 52 Boyle your Rosyne, Pirrosyn and Waxe, with four vnce of deare suet. **1600** SURFLET *Country Farme* I. iv. 11 The best are made of aller tree, firre tree, or pine tree, out of which distilleth perrosen [*Fr. orig.* duquel sort la poix resine]. **1601** HOLLAND *Pliny* II. 181 Taken in wine with dry per-rosin [*resina sicca*], it [*sphagnos*] causeth one most speedily to make water. *Ibid.* 182 Of the dry per-rosins [*in sicco genere*], those are in most request which be white, pure, transparent, or cleare, quite through.

perrot, variant of PERIT *Obs.*, minute weight.

perrotatory (pə'rəʊtətərɪ), *a.* [f. PER- 1 + ROTATORY.] Passing through a series of terms or objects as if arranged in a circle, so that one passes from the last immediately to the first again.

1890 in *Cent. Dict.*

perrotine (pɛrəʊ'tiːn). [a. F. *perrotine*, f. *Perrot*, name of the inventor.] A machine for printing calico in colours by means of wooden blocks.
1839 URE *Dict. Arts* 216 The Perrotine is a machine for executing block-printing by mechanical power. **1883** R. HALDANE *Workshop Receipts* Ser. II. 211/1 Print on the white and red discharges with the perrotine, or with a two-colour cylinder machine.

†**perrour**, obs. form of PARURE.
a **1400–50** *Alexander* 1536 Poudird with perry was perrour & othire. **1550** BALE *Image Both Ch.* III. Bbb iv, Theyr copes perrours, and chysibilles, whan they bee in theyr prelately pompeus sacrifices.

perruck(e, -ruke, perruque: see PERUKE.

perruquerian (pɛruː'kɪərɪən), *a. nonce-wd.* [f. next: see -AN.] Of or pertaining to a perruquier.
1836 DICKENS *Sk. Boz, Boarding House* i, The shining locks of those chef-d'œuvres of perruquerian art.

‖**perruquier** (pɛrykje). Also 8 peruquier; rarely anglicized as PERUKIER, q.v. [Fr., f. *perruque* PERUKE.] One who makes, dresses, or deals in perukes; a wig-maker.
1753 FOOTE *Eng. in Paris* I. i, All the fraternity of men makers,..taylors, perruquiers, hatters, hosiers. **1837** THACKERAY *Ravenswing* ii, The tailor..exposed his head to the..perruquier's gaze. **1882** SERJT. BALLANTINE *Exper.* viii. 85, I remember a fashionable perruquier being tried many years ago.

†**perry**[1], **pery, pirie.** *Obs.* Forms: α. 1 piriȝe, pirȝe, pyriȝe, 1–5 pirie, pyrie, 5 pire, piry(e, pyry(e, pirry, purye, 7 pyrrie. β. 4–5 perie, -y(e, 5 pere, pereye, 6 perrie, perrey (pearie). [OE. *pirȝe, piriȝe, pirie, pyrie*, wk. fem., of obscure formation, taken by Pogatscher to represent a late L. type **pirea*, **pērea* (sc. *arbor* tree), from a late L. adj. **pire-us*, **pēre-us*, f. *pirum*, Rom. *pēra* pear. (But no trace of such adj. has been found in L. or Rom.)
The historical series *piriȝe, pirie, perie, perrie*, **perry*, is exactly parallel to that of *miriȝe, mirie, merie, merrie, merry*, the *i* in both becoming *e* before *r*, which again was doubled after the short vowel.]
A pear-tree; sometimes distinctively the wild pear-tree. Also *attrib.*
937 in Birch *Cart. Sax.* II. 429 þanon..up on stream..midde weardne up on þa pyrian. **972** *Ibid.* III. 586 And-lang dic on þa pyriȝan of pære pyriȝan on þone longan apuldre. *c* **1000** ÆLFRIC *Gloss.* in Wr.-Wülcker 137/37 *Pirus*, piriȝe. —— *Gram.* vii. (Z.) 20 *Hæc pirus* þeos pyriȝe, *hoc pirum* seo peru. **13..** *Seuyn Sag.* (W.) 555 A fair gardin,..Ful of appel tres, and als of pirie; Foules songe therinne murie. **1362** LANGL. *P. Pl.* A. v. 16 Piries and Plomtres weore passchet to þe grounde. *c* **1386** CHAUCER *Merch. T.* 937 Thus I lete hym sitte vp on the pyrie [*v. rr.* purye, pyrye, Pyry, pirry, pire, pirie]. **1398** TREVISA *Barth. De P.R.* XVII. ii. (Tollem. MS.), As whan a pery is graffid on an appeltre. *a* **1425** *Cursor M.* 37 (Trin.) Of good pire com gode perus. **14..** *Voc.* in Wr.-Wülcker 603/11 *Piretum*, anglice Pereye. **1577** B. GOOGE *Heresbach's Husb.* (1586) 87b, You may graffe the Apple upon the Perrey, the Hawthorne, Plome tree, Servisse tree, ..Poplar, Willowe and Peare. **1578** LYTE *Dodoens* VI. xxxi. 697 High as a Perrie, or wilde Peare tree. **1601** HOLLAND *Pliny* I. 474 There be some Pyrries and Apple trees that bring forth fruit twice a yeare.
attrib. **14..** *Songs & Carols* xxxi. (Warton Cl.), To gryffyn here a gryf of myn pery tre. **1523** FITZHERB. *Husb.* §137 A pere or a wardeyn wold be graffed in a pyrre stock. **1586** W. WEBBE *Eng. Poetrie* (Arb.) 76 Now Melibœe ingraft pearie stocks, sette vines in an order. **1603** STOW *Surv.* 48 That he should buy certaine perie plants.

perry[2] ('pɛrɪ). Forms: 4 pereye, ? piri, 5 peirrie, pirre, 5–6 perre, pirrey, 6 perie, pirrie, 6–7 pery(e, perrie, 7 perrey, pyrrey, -ie, piry, 6– perry. [ME. *pereye*, a. OF. *peré* (13–16th c.), *perey* (14th c. in Godef.):—late L. type **pērātum*, f. late L. *pēra* = L. *pirum* pear.] A beverage resembling cider, made from the juice of pears expressed and fermented.
c **1315** SHOREHAM *Poems* i. 205 Ine wine me ne may, Inne siþere, ne inne pereye [*rime* reneye]. **1362** LANGL. *P. Pl.* A. v. 134 Peni Ale and piriwhit heo pourede to-gedere. *c* **1440** *Promp. Parv.* 394/1 Perre, drynke, *piretum*. *c* **1480** HENRYSON *Test. Cres.* 441 Tak mowlit breid, peirrie, and ceder sour. **1483** *Cath. Angl.* 281/2 Pirrey (Pirre), *piretum*. **1577** HARRISON *England* II. vi. (1877) I. 161 A kind of drinke made..of peares is named pirrie. **1577–87** HOLINSHED *Chron.* III. 1197/1 Botes laden with wine, cider, perrie. **1623** LISLE *Ælfric on O. & N. Test.* Ded. xxxiv, Syd'r in Kent,..Pyrrie in Wostersheere. **1693** EVELYN *De la Quint. Compl. Gard.* I. 117 The great Pear plantations, planted for the making of Perry in those places where Vines cannot prosper. **1765** BLACKSTONE *Comm.* I. viii. 319 Excise..at first laid upon..the makers and venders of beer, ale, cyder, and perry. **1840** *Cottager's Man.* 5 in *Libr. U. Kn., Husb.* III, Cider, perry, wines..might easily be obtained by an additional half acre.
b. *attrib.* and *Comb.* as *perry farmer, perry pear*.
1836 *Penny Cycl.* V. 250 The cider and perry farmer will feel the benefit of this. **1896** *Jrnl. R. Horticult. Soc.* Nov. 208 One of our oldest perry pears, the Longland, equals the well-known Catillac for stewing.

perry[3], variant of PERRIE *Obs.*, jewellery.

perry[4], variant of PIRRIE, gust of wind.

perryall, perrygryne, perrywig, obs. ff. PAIRROYAL, PEREGRINE, PERIWIG.

perryite ('pɛrɪaɪt). *Min.* [f. the name of Stuart H. *Perry* (1874–1957), U.S. mineralogist + -ITE[1].] A nickel-rich mineral also containing silicon and phosphorus that is reported to have been found in several meteorites.
1965 FREDRIKSSON & HENDERSON in *Trans. Amer. Geophysical Union* XLVI. 121/2 The Horse Creek, Baca County, Colorado, iron meteorite, found in 1937, is unique for four reasons:..(4) this iron contains about 3% of Perryite, nickel silicide, a new mineral... The approximate chemical composition of Perryite is Ni 81%, Si 12%, Fe 3% and P 5%. **1968** *Mineral. Mag.* XXXVI. 852 The South Oman enstatite chondrite also contains perryite, but its abundance is much less than in Kota-Kota... In this meteorite, perryite occurs as small laths, usually associated with kamacite. **1970** *Geochim. et Cosmochim. Acta* XXXIV. 169 Electron-microprobe analysis of Si, P and Ni in the metal grains and associated schreibersite and perryite of eight enstatite achondrites shows that the compositions of these phases are relatively constant within a given meteorite, but show substantial variations between meteorites.

persaife, -saive, obs. forms of PERCEIVE.

persalt, per-salt ('pɜːˌsɒlt, -ˌsɔːlt). *Chem.* [f. PER- 5 + SALT.] A salt formed by combination of an acid with the peroxide of a metal.
1820 FARADAY *Exp. Res.* x. 30 The per-salts give it [rhubarb paper] an olive-green-tint, while the proto-salts produce no change. **1836–9** TODD *Cycl. Anat.* II. 504/1 A sub-phosphate, which on reaching the lungs became a persalt. **1883** *Hardwich's Photogr. Chem.* (ed. Taylor) 61 Free Ammonia..usually throws down a red Sesquixoide from the Persalts of Iron.

Persan, -sante, obs. forms of PERSIAN.

†**persanate,** *v. Obs.* [f. L. *persānāt-*, ppl. stem of *persānāre* to cure completely, f. PER- 2 + *sānāre* to heal.] *trans.* To cure perfectly.
1623 in COCKERAM. **1657** TOMLINSON *Renou's Disp.* 431 Telephus wounded by Achilles was thereby persanated.

persand, -sant, -saunt, variants of PERCEANT *Obs.*, piercing.

persar, obs. form of PIERCER.

†**per'satanize,** *v. Obs. rare*[−1]. [f. PER- 2 + SATANIZE.] *trans.* To possess thoroughly with or by Satan.
1857 *Truths Cath. Relig.* (ed. 4) 178 His [Luther's] assertion is 'that Zuinglius, and all who adhere to his doctrine, are insatanized, supersatanized and persatanized'.

persaue, -sawe, -sayue, obs. ff. PERCEIVE.

persche, obs. f. PARISH, PERISH *v.*, PIERCE.

†**per'scribe,** *v. Obs. rare.* [ad. L. *perscrībĕre*, f. PER- 1, 2 + *scrībĕre* to write.] *trans.* To write out, write or describe at length or in full.
1538 LELAND *N.Y. Gift* in *Itin.* I. p. xxii, [Thou] that from tyme to tyme hath with greate Diligence..perscribed the Actes of yowr moste noble Prædecessors, and the Fortunes of this your Realme.

perscrutation (pɜːskruː'teɪʃən). [a. obs. F. *perscrutation* (early 16th c.), ad. L. *perscrūtātiōn-em*, noun of action f. *perscrūtāre*: see PERSCRUTE.] A thorough searching or investigation; careful scrutiny, examination.
1603 FLORIO *Montaigne* I. xxii. (1632) 51 The first and universall reasons are of a hard perscrutation. **1678** R. R[USSELL] tr. *Geber* II. i. I. iii. 27 Void of Ingenuity in every Perscrutation. **1843** CARLYLE *Past & Pr.* II. viii, Such guessing, visioning, dim perscrutation of the momentous future!
So **per'scrutate** *v. trans.*, to make a careful or thorough investigation; †**perscru'tator** [a. L. (post-cl.) *perscrūtātor*], one who investigates thoroughly (Blount *Glossogr.* 1656).
1900 A. LANG in *Contemp. Rev.* Dec. 789 We had all savage languages perscrutated by new Bopps and Kuhns.

†**per'scrute,** *v. Obs. rare.* [a. obs. F. *perscruter*, ad. L. *perscrūtāre*, f. PER- 2 + *scrūtāre* = *scrūtārī* to search closely, examine.] *trans.* To search carefully; to scrutinize thoroughly.
a **1545** BOORDE (*title*) The pryncyples of Astronamye, the whiche diligently perscrutyd is in maner a pronosticacyon to the worldes end. **1547** —— *Introd. Knowl.* vii. (1870) 144 Yf they haue reason to perscrute the mater.

†**Perse,** *sb.*[1] *Obs.* Forms: 4–6 *pl.* Perses, -is, 5–6 *sing.* Pers. Also (*pl.*) 4–5 Persees, -eis, 5 -ies, Percys, -eys: see PARSEE. [a. OF. *Perses* pl.:—L. *Persās*, in nom. *Persæ* Persians (whence, also, OE. had *Perse*, pl. *Perseas*).] A Persian; *pl.* Persians.
[*c* **893** K. ÆLFRED *Oros.* II. v. §2 þa wæron ða Perse mid þæm swiþe ȝeeȝsade. *Ibid.*, On Perseum.] **1382** WYCLIF *Dan.* v. 28 Thi kyngdam is departed, and is ȝouen to Medis and to Persis. **1398** TREVISA *Barth. De P.R.* XV. cxviii. (MS. Add. 27. 944), þider Nemroth þe geaunt went..and tauȝt þe perses [*v.r.* Persis] to worschepe þe sonne. **1552** LYNDESAY *Monarche* 3783 The ram with hornis two, Comparit tyll Pers and Mede, all so. **1568** BIBLE (Bishops') *Dan.* vi. 12 The lawe of the Medes and Perses that altereth not.

perse (pɜːs), *a.* and *sb.*[2] *arch.* Forms: 4–6 pers, 4 perce, peers, (5 perske), 6 peirs, 5, 7– perse. [ME. a. OF. *pers, -e*, = Pr. *pers*, It. *perso*:—late L. *persus* (in med.L., Du Cange): see *Note* below.]
In early writers, Blue, bluish, bluish-grey; in later writers often taken (after Italian) as a dark obscure blue or purplish black; also *sb.* as name of the colour, or of a stuff of the colour.
? *a* **1366** CHAUCER *Rom. Rose* 67 It hath hewes an hundred payr, Of gras & floures, inde and pers, And many hewes ful dyvers. *c* **1386** —— *Prol.* 439 In sangwyn and in pers he clad was al. *Ibid.* 617 A long surcote of pers vp on he hade. **1438** *Bk. Alexander Gt.* (Bann. Cl.) 107 (Flowers) Purpur, bloncat, pale & pers. *c* **1500** *Melusine* 126 The eldest..hath one eye redde, & that other ey is perske & blew. **1513** DOUGLAS *Æneis* XII. Prol. 106 Behaldand thame sa mony diuers hew, Sum pers, sum paill, sum burnet, and sum blew. **1658** PHILLIPS, *Perse*, sky colour. **1848** J. A. CARLYLE tr. *Dante's Inferno* (1849) 78 The water was darker far than perse [*buia molto piu che persa*]. **1884** VERN. LEE *Euphorion* II, Whirled incessantly in the perse, dark, stormy air.
b. *Comb.* as †*perseblewe*.
a **1490** BOTONER *Itin.* (1778) 88 Cum tribus robis de purpyre et de perseblewe.
[*Note.* The Romanic word was perh. a back-formation from *Persia*, or L. *Persæ* Persians, *Persicus* Persian. Med.L. had also, in same sense, *perseus*, and *persicus* (cf. *perske* above). Du Cange approves of the view of Acarisius that *perseus* was a deriv. of *persa*, Ital. name of marjoram, referring to the colour; others would explain *persicus* as peach-coloured, from *persica* PEACH (itself from *Persicus* Persian).
In Ælfric's Gloss. (Wr.-Wülcker 163/29) L. *perseus* is glossed *blæwen*, i.e. light blue. But Florio 1611 makes It. *perso* 'a darke or blacke mourning colour; some take it for the colour of dead Marioram. Some have also vsed it for a Peach colour.' Cf. DANTE *Convito* IV. xx. 14 Il perso è un colore misto di purpureo e di nero, ma vince il nero. See also Littré as to range of meaning in French, and P. TOYNBEE *Dante Studies* 314 The colour *perse* in Dante and other mediæval writers.]

perse, obs. form of PARSEE, PIERCE.

‖**persea** ('pɜːsiːə). [L., a. Gr. περσέα.] **a.** *Ancient Mythol.* Name of a sacred fruit-bearing tree in Egypt and Persia. **b.** In *Bot.*, a genus of trees and shrubs, N.O. *Lauraceæ*, common in tropical America and the West Indies, of which one species *P. gratissima*, produces the AVOCADO or ALLIGATOR *pear*. Also *persea-tree*.
1601 HOLLAND *Pliny* XV. xiii, The tree Persea..is far different from the Peach-tree Persica, and beareth fruit like vnto Sebesten, of colour red. **1706** PHILLIPS, *Persea*, (Gr.) a Tree that grows in Egypt like a Peach-tree, and bears a Fruit of the Bigness of a Pear or Apple. [**1846** LINDLEY *Veg. Kingd.* 537 The fruit of Persea gratissima, so much esteemed in the West Indies under the name of the Avocado pear.] **1858** C. W. GOODWIN in *Cambr. Ess.* 238 She requests to have the persea-trees cut down. **1877** A. B. EDWARDS *Up Nile* xii. 317 The sacred hawk sitting in the centre of a fan-shaped persea tree. **1895** SIR J. W. DAWSON in *Expositor* July 60 [The tree of life] represented by different species, as the palm, the banyan, the persea, the oak,..the mistletoe.

†**'persecate,** *v. Obs. rare*[−0]. [f. ppl. stem of L. *persecāre* to cut through, f. PER- 1 + *secāre* to cut.] (See quot.) Hence also †**perse'cation.**
1623 COCKERAM, *Persecate*, to cut. *Persecation*, a cutting.

persecute ('pɜːsɪkjuːt), *v.* Also 6 persequut(e, -kute, parsecute. [a. F. *persécute-r* (Oresme, 14th c.), f. L. *persecūt-*, ppl. stem of *persequī* to pursue, follow with hostility or malignity, f. PER- 1, 2 + *sequī* to follow. (Littré and Hatz.-Darm. derive F. *persécuter* immed. from *persécuteur*.)]
†**1.** To pursue, chase, hunt, drive (with missiles, or with attempts to catch, kill, or injure). *Obs.*
c **1477** CAXTON *Jason* 8b, Iason and Hercules persecuted them with their arowes as long as they dured. **1535** COVERDALE *Josh.* viii. 17 They lefte the cite stondinge open, that they mighte persecute Israel. **1551** ROBINSON tr. *More's Utop.* II. (1895) 260 Theire enemies..haue persecuted them flying, some one way and some an other. **1697** DRYDEN *Virg. Georg.* I. 416 With Balearick Slings, or Gnossian Bow, To persecute from far the flying Doe.
†**b.** To follow up, pursue, prosecute (a subject); to carry out, go through with. *Obs.*
1546 LANGLEY tr. *Pol. Verg. De Invent.* I. viii, My purpose is onely to speak of the Inventers,..not to persecute the particulars. *a* **1661** FULLER *Worthies, Linc.* (1662) 144 Such persecute the Metaphor too much.
2. To pursue with malignancy or enmity and injurious action; *esp.* to oppress with pains and penalties for the holding of a belief or opinion held to be injurious or heretical.
1482 CAXTON *Trevisa's Higden* IV. xiii. 200b, [He] refreyned hym in many thynges, and in especial that he shold not persecute ne greue cristen men. **1526** TINDALE *Matt.* v. 11 Blessed are ye when men shall revyle you, and persecute you,..ffor my sake. —— *John* v. 16 And therfore the iewes did persecute Jesus, and sought the meanes to slee hym. **1651** HOBBES *Leviath.* III. xlii. 276 In a place where the Civill Power did persecute, or not assist the Church. **1689** POPPLE tr. *Locke's 1st Let. Toleration* 12 That the Church of Christ should persecute others,..I could never yet find in any of the Books of the New Testament. **1779** BURKE *Corr.* (1844) II. 269 Though I am..a very attached son of the Church of England, I think myself bound not to wish to persecute you. **1784** COWPER *Task* III. 309 Some contagion,

kind to the poor brutes We persecute. **1832** TENNYSON *You ask me why* 17 Should banded unions persecute Opinion, and induce a time When single thought is civil crime. **1880** L. STEPHEN *Pope* ii. 58 The belief that a man is persecuted by hidden conspirators is one of the common symptoms in [insanity].

3. To harass, trouble, vex, worry; to importune.

1585 T. WASHINGTON tr. *Nicholay's Voy.* I. ii, [He] was taken with a grieuous sickenes, which persecuted him so violently, that men dispayred of his life. **1698** FRYER *Acc. E. India & P.* 310 By labouring in the Heat of the Day to get over the Mountains, we were persecuted with Diary Fevers. **1742** POPE *Dunc.* IV. 260 He may..Plague with Dispute, or persecute with Rhyme. **1879** G. MEREDITH *Egoist* xlix, 'Which is the cause of your persecuting me to become your wife!'

4. To prosecute (a person, †or suit) at law. Now only a dialectal or humorous substitution for PROSECUTE *v.*

1484 CAXTON *Curiall* 4 b, Peple whyche by fraude and franchyse studye for to drawe from one and other suche wordes by whiche they may persecute them. **1560** DAUS tr. *Sleidane's Comm.* 271 He wyll persecute his suite against the Byshop. **1655** STANLEY *Hist. Philos.* III. (1701) 124/1 Crito in pursuit of this Counsel made choice of Archidamus, an excellent Lawyer, but poor, who being obliged by his gifts and kindness, persecuted eagerly all such as molested not him only, but any of his friends. **1784** *dial.* in *N.W. Linc. Gloss.* s.v., 'Hoever is taken in the fact shall be percicuted according to law, by the parish expens'. **1866** BROGDEN *Provinc. Words Linc.* (E.D.D.), 'Trespassers will be persecuted'. Notice near the Foss-dyke, Lincoln.

Hence **'persecuted** *ppl. a.*, **'persecuting** *vbl. sb.* and *ppl. a.*

1542 BALE *Manne of Synne* 37 This cruell persecutynge, thys murtherynge of innocentes. **1552** HULOET, Persecuted, *persequutus.* **1697** DRYDEN *Æneid* XII. 1087 The deep-mouth'd hound..following still..The persecuted creature, to and fro. **1709** STANHOPE *Paraphr.* IV. 119 The blaspheming, the persecuting Saul. **1781** COWPER *Expost.* 278 Thou that hast set the persecuted free. **1855** PUSEY *Doctr. Real Presence* Note R. 267 The new-made Christian was taken to the persecuting Emperor Diocletian.

persecu'tee. [f. PERSECUTE *v.* + -EE (= F. *persécuté*).] One who is persecuted.

1882 BUCKLAND *Notes & Jot.* 339, I doubt whether the wretches [parasites of the whale] can afford much domestic pleasure and comfort to the persecutee.

persecution (pɜːsɪ'kjuːʃən). Also 4 **par-**; 5 **persecussion, -sicution,** 6 **-sequtioun, -quution.** [ME. *persecucion*, etc., a. OF. *persecution, persecucion, -qucion* (12th c.), ad. L. *persecūtiōn-em*, n. of action from *persequī* to PERSECUTE.]

1. a. The action of persecuting or pursuing with enmity and malignity; *esp.* the infliction of death, torture, or penalties for adherence to a religious belief or an opinion as such, with a view to the repression or extirpation of it; the fact of being persecuted; an instance of this.

a **1340** HAMPOLE *Psalter* xxvi. 6 If persecucyon of þe world, or temptacyons wax ageynes me. **1340** —— *Pr. Consc.* 4451 Gret parsecucion þan sal he wyrk Agayn cristen men. **1375** BARBOUR *Bruce* IV. 5 His fayis..Maid sic A persecucioune,..On thaim that till hym luffand wer. **1382** WYCLIF *Matt.* v. 10 Blessid be thei that suffren persecucioun for riȝtwisnesse [1388 persecusioun]. **1460** CAPGRAVE *Chron.* (Rolls) 64 He counceled him that he schuld sese fro the persecucion of Cristen men. **1560** DAUS tr. *Sleidane's Comm.* 115 b, At the same time chaunceth a persecution against the Lutherians. **1643** SIR T. BROWNE *Relig. Med.* I. §25 Persecution is a bad and indirect way to plant Religion. **1665** BOYLE *Occas. Reflec.* v. ii. (1848) 302 To thrive by Persecution..is not the incommunicable Prerogative of Divine Truths;..even Errors do often gain by it too. **1785** PALEY *Mor. Philos.* VI. x. 580 Persecution produces no sincere conviction, nor any real change of opinion; on the contrary, it depraves the public morals by driving men to prevarication and commonly ends in a general tho' secret infidelity. **1828** MACAULAY *Ess., Hallam* (1887) 59 To punish a man, because we infer from the nature of some doctrine which he holds..that he will commit a crime, is persecution, and is, in every case, foolish and wicked. **1880** LIDDON in *Spectator* 13 Nov. 1446 In the judgment of the early Christians, the proceedings of Decius and Diocletian were persecutions. To the Pagans of the day ..they were simply legal prosecutions.

b. A particular course or period of systematic infliction of punishment directed against the professors of a (religious) belief; as, the ten persecutions of the Christians under the Roman Empire, the Marian persecution, etc.

1387 TREVISA *Higden* (Rolls) V. 111 Þis eiȝteþe ȝere of Dioclicianus was þe firste ȝere of þe grete persecucioun þat was under Dioclicianus in þe Est and Maximianus in þe West. *c* **1400** *Three Kings Cologne* xxxvi. 134 Þer began aȝene a newe persecucioun of heresye aȝens þe cristen feiþ. **1494** FABYAN *Chron.* IV. lxvii. 46 Seynt Alboon, at Verolamy was martyred, In the .x. persecucion of the Churche, as wytnessyth Policronicon. **1776** GIBBON *Decl. & F.* xvi. (1819) II. 434 The celebrated number of ten persecutions has been determined by the ecclesiastical writers of the fifth century. **1875** SCRIVENER *Lect. Text N. Test.* 8 The last and most cruel of the persecutions to which believers were subjected throughout the Roman empire, that of Diocletian.

c. *transf.* Persistent or continued injury or annoyance from any source; sometimes humorously applied to the annoying importunity of advisers, beggars, suitors, etc.

1585 T. WASHINGTON tr. *Nicholay's Voy.* II. xiii. 48 b, Not altogether exempt of diuers persecutions, as well by warres, fire, pestilence, earthquakes, as sundry other calamities. **1605** SHAKS. *Lear* II. iii. 12 Ile..with presented nakednesse out-face The Windes, and persecutions of the skie. **1662** J. DAVIES tr. *Olearius' Voy. Ambass.* 6 There it was we met with the first persecution of Flies, Gnats, and Wasps. **1803** JANE PORTER *Thaddeus* xi. (1831) 96 While their fears rendered him safe from their well meant persecution, he gained some respite from vexation.

d. *Psychol.* The irrational sense of being victimized by malign forces which features in many forms of mental disorder and is now commonly considered paranoid.

1881 *Jrnl. Nerv. & Mental Dis.* VIII. 28 We may have delusions of persecution which are systematized and such which are unsystematized. **1883** T. S. CLOUSTON *Clin. Lect. Mental Dis.* vi. 255 The third great class of delusional cases are those of suspicion and persecution. **1926** W. MCDOUGALL *Outl. Abnormal Psychol.* xx. 337 The two forms of delusion mentioned.., delusions of persecution and of grandeur, are the fundamental and most frequent. **1970** HINSIE & CAMPBELL *Psychiatric Dict.* (ed. 4) 542/1 A form of paranoia characterized by more or less incessant quarrelsomeness due to alleged persecution.

†2. The action of pursuing, pursuit, chase; pursuance, prosecution (of an aim, etc.); quest. *Obs.*

1432-50 tr. *Higden* (Rolls) II. 331 Grete Alexander the Conqueroure,..in the persecucion of Darius [HIGDEN, in persequendo Darium; TREVISA, whan he pursewed Darius]. **1647** JER. TAYLOR *Lib. Proph.* xiii. §3 A hearty persecution of the rules of good life.

†3. (Legal) prosecution. *Obs. rare.*

1535 *Act 27 Hen. VIII*, c. 20 §3 Their lawfull accion demaunde or persecucion, appeles prohibicions and all other their lawful defences and remedies in euery suche suite.

4. *attrib.* and *Comb.*, as ***persecution-fancier***, ***mania*** (an insane delusion that one is persecuted; also *transf.* and in extended uses); (esp. in sense 1 d) ***persecution complex***, ***fantasy***; **persecution maniac**, a person of unbalanced mind suffering from delusions of persecution.

1961 J. HELLER *Catch-22* (1962) xxvii. 294 You've got a bad persecution complex. You think people are trying to harm you. **1966** 'H. MACDIARMID' *Company I've Kept* v. 139 The delusions of a man unbalanced by a persecution-complex. **1971** *Rand Daily Mail* 3 Apr. 5/8 We shall develop a persecution complex and go round moaning that we are misunderstood. **1826** SYD. SMITH *Wks.* (1859) II. 123/2 It is delicious to the persecution-fanciers to reflect that no general bill has passed in favour of the Protestant Dissenters. **1950** T. WIESENGRUND-ADORNO et al. *Authoritarian Personality* IV. xvi. 615 The persecution fantasy of what the Jews *might* do to her, is used..as a justification of the genocide committed by the Nazis. **1892** D. H. TUKE *Dict. Psychol. Med.* II. 934/2 From a medico-legal point of view, cases of persecution-mania afford matter for consideration of the greatest importance. **1899** *Allbutt's Syst. Med.* VII. 698 Even 'persecution mania' may be an early symptom of general paralysis. **1903** R. FRY *Let.* 21 Jan. (1972) I. 200 Langton Douglas..has the persecution mania ..and I need hardly say B.B. looms large. **1934** *Punch* 7 Mar. 278/1 The present [Russian] régime's..persecution-mania, misrepresentation of the outside world and progressive debasement of the arts are..set-backs to the advantage of what Miss Hamilton..calls 'the Insect State'. **1942** E. WAUGH *Put out More Flags* iii. 203 He had left his persecution mania downstairs with his hat and umbrella. **1968** C. RYCROFT *Crit. Dict. Psychoanal.* 115 Persecution mania is an obsolete term for paranoia. **1978** I. MURDOCH *Sea* 69, I have never gone in for persecution mania and do not propose to start now. **1943** J. S. HUXLEY *Evolutionary Ethics* iii. 19 Unable to bear the condemnation of his super-ego, the persecution-maniac projects this into society, thus ..being able to accuse the world of cruelty or oppression. **1955** KOESTLER *Trail of Dinosaur* I. 19 The persecution-maniacs in the West who still lived on the Red Scare had by that time become a dwindling, reactionary minority.

Hence **perse'cutional** *a.*, of or relating to persecution.

1887 *Alien. & Neurol.* VIII. 663 Dr. Robinson..finds persecutional delusions common as well as what he calls 'homicidal mania'. **1899** *Allbutt's Syst. Med.* VIII. 193 Various delusions, generally of the 'persecutional' kind.

persecutive ('pɜːsɪkjuːtɪv), *a. rare.* [f. L. *persecūt-*, ppl. stem of *persequī* + -IVE.] Of a persecuting character; tending or addicted to persecution. Hence **'persecutiveness.**

1659 GAUDEN *Tears Ch.* IV. ii. 396 Use is made of persecutive and compelling power; which is rather brutish than humane. **1664** H. MORE *Myst. Iniq.* II. II. i. 338 If the Devil be a Beast, that which makes him so is the wickedness of his nature, his persecutiveness of the Church of God. **1814** SCOTT *Wav.* xxxiv, Gilfillan..refused to permit his followers to move to this profane, and even, as he said, persecutive tune. **1864** *Realm* 22 June 2 They do more harm to real religion by their one-sided persecutive views than all the Renans and Colensos in existence.

persecutor ('pɜːsɪkjuːtə(r)). Also 5-6 **-our,** 6-7 **-er.** [orig. a. AF. *persecutour* = F. *persécuteur*, OF. *persecutur* (12th c.), ad. L. *persecūtōr-em*, agent-n. from *persequī* to PERSECUTE: see -OR, -OUR. Also with *-er* of Eng. origin: see -ER[1].] One who persecutes; 'one who harasses others with continued malignity' (J.); *esp.* one who harasses others on account of opinions or belief.

1484 CAXTON *Fables of Æsop* VI. viii, We haue a grete enemye, whiche is a grete persecutour ouer vs alle. **1526** TINDALE *1 Tim.* i. 13, I was a blasphemar, and a persecuter, and a tyraunt. **1621** BURTON *Anat. Mel.* III. iv. I. iii. (1651) 666 Lucian, that adamantine persequutor of superstition. **1642** MILTON *Apol. Smect.* Wks. 1851 III. 301 A needlesse and jolly persecuter call'd Indifference. **1776** GIBBON *Decl. & F.* xvi. (1819) II. 418 The ancient apologists of christianity have censured, with equal truth and severity, the irregular conduct of their persecutors.

persecutory ('pɜːsɪˌkjuːtərɪ), *a.* [f. as prec.: see -ORY.]

1. a. Given to persecution, persecutive. **b.** Of or relating to persecution. Now used esp. with reference to PERSECUTION 1 d.

1654 S. CLARKE *Eccl. Hist.* 173 The crafty fetches, and persecutory drifts whereby he endeavoured to allure the Catholicks to the Arian Heresie. **1701** BEVERLEY *Apoc. Quest.* 32 A City, and Empire, so Persecutory of his Servants, as Pagan Rome. **1881** *Jrnl. Nerv. & Mental Dis.* VIII. 33 We have such [*sc.* delusions] of a depressive erotic character, usually persecutory. **1899** *Allbutt's Syst. Med.* VIII. 395 In many cases persecutory and exalted delusions are inextricably mixed. **1936** W. S. SADLER *Theory & Pract. Psychiatry* xix. 334 The child can very early acquire a 'persecutory complex' built up out of his memory feelings of being many times unjustly treated. **1952** *Brit. Jrnl. Psychol.* XLIII. 81 Religion is a form of psychotherapy which promotes a belief in the existence of idealized good objects as a defence against persecutory and depressive guilt. **1962** *Lancet* 19 May 1065/1 He soon developed persecutory ideas and was admitted to hospital. **1963** *Observer* 2 June 18/6 Cameras planted all over the place like persecutory eyes.

†2. Pursuant *of. Obs. rare.*

1774 HALLIFAX *Anal. Rom. Law* (1795) 90 Actions were persecutory 1. of the Thing. 2. of the Penalty. 3. of Both.

persecutress ('pɜːsɪkjuːtrɪs). [f. PERSECUTOR + -ESS.] A female persecutor.

1647 R. STAPYLTON *Juvenal* vi. 105 *note*, Juno, the patronesse of the chast, and implacable persecutresse of immodest women. **1760** H. WALPOLE *Let. to Sir D. Dalrymple* 3 Feb., Resentment against her persecutress. **1889** *Cornh. Mag.* Mar. 322 The persecutress was relentless.

persecutrix (pɜːsɪ'kjuːtrɪks). *rare.* [a. L. *persecūtrix*, fem. of *persecūtor.*] = prec.

a **1572** KNOX *Hist. Ref.* Wks. 1846 I. 244 A cruell persecutrix of Goddis people. **1816** KIRBY & SP. *Entomol.* iv. (1818) I. 132 The venom was ejaculated into the eyes and upon the lips of its persecutrix. **1842** G. S. FABER *Prov. Lett.* (1844) I. 23 If Rome be an idolatrous persecutrix of the real people of God.

Persee, obs. form of PARSEE.

perseic (pə'siːɪk), *a. rare.* [f. *per se* (PER *prep.* 9) + -IC.] Of or pertaining to perseity.

1890 in *Century Dict.*

Perseid ('pɜːsiːɪd). *Astron.* [ad. mod.L. *Persēis*, pl. *Persēidēs*, Gr. Περσηΐς, pl. -ΐδες, daughter of Perseus.] In *pl.*, A group of meteors which appear to radiate from the constellation Perseus. Also *attrib.*

1876 G. F. CHAMBERS *Astron.* 799 The meteors of the shower were first named Perseids by Schiaparelli in the year 1866. **1893** KIRKMAN in *Astron. & Astro-Physics* xii. 791 History of the great comet of 1862, and of the thence derived shower of Perseid meteors.

perseity (pə'siːɪtɪ). [ad. med.L. *persēitās* (Duns Scotus *c* 1300), f. *per sē* by itself = Gr. καθ' αὑτό, as used by Aristotle, *Anal. Poster.* i. 4; see PER *prep.* 9. In F. *perséité.*] The quality or condition of existing independently, or of being predicated essentially of a subject.

1694 R. BURTHOGGE *Reason & Nat. Spirits* ix. 269 Subsistence is a mode of Existence, to which it adds Perseity. **1876** *Contemp. Rev.* XXVIII. 1006 One novelty.. in philosophy—the exclusion of the *per-se-ity* and *must-be-ity*, which cut such a figure in what goes for metaphysics.

perseiue, obs. form of PERCEIVE.

persel, persely, perseline, perseneppe, obs. ff. PARSLEY, PURSLANE, PARSNIP.

†persen'tiscency. *Obs. rare.* [f. L. *persentiscent-em*, pr. pple. of *persentiscĕre* to perceive clearly, f. PER- 2 + *sentiscĕre* to perceive, detect.] Direct or intuitive perception of truth and certainty.

1712 *H. More's Antid. Ath.* Schol. on App. VI. §7 Let him consider that this very Persentiscency is one of our faculties... This internal Persentiscency may in some measure, though at a great distance, imitate that divine.. Certitude.

persepcion, obs. form of PERCEPTION.

†'persequent, *a. Obs.* [ad. L. *persequent-em*, pr. pple. of *persequī* to follow after, to pursue.] Following after, pursuing.

1650 ASHMOLE *Chym. Collect.* 60 Made after this manner, lest the fugient should first fly away, before the Fire could any way bring forth the persequent thing. **1677** GALE *Crt. Gentiles* II. IV. 494 Divine grace is termed by the Greek Fathers..persequent or actuating and conservant grace.

perservation, perserve, obs. ff. PRESERVATION, PRESERVE.

perseu, obs. Sc. var. PURSUE *v.*

perseuerance, -aunce, obs. forms of PERCEIVERANCE, PERSEVERANCE.

†**per'severable**, *a. Obs. rare*⁻¹. [ad. post-cl. L. *persevērābilis*, f. *persevērā-re* to PERSEVERE: see -ABLE.] Constant, enduring.

c **1450** tr. *De Imitatione* II. vii. 47 The loue of a creature is failyng & unstable; þe loue of iesu is true and perseuerable.

perseverance (pɜːsɪ'vɪərəns). [a. F. *persévérance* (12th c. in Hatz.-Darm.), ad. L. *persevērāntia* steadfastness, constancy, perseverance, f. *persevērānt-em*: see next and -ANCE. Formerly (pə'sɛvərəns): see Note to PERSEVERE.]

1. The fact, process, condition, or quality of persevering; constant persistence in a course of action, purpose, or state; steadfast pursuit of an aim; tenacious assiduity or endeavour.

a **1340** HAMPOLE *Psalter* xxxvi. 8 Loke þat þe ese of ill stire not þe fra perseueraunce. *c* **1374** CHAUCER *Troylus* I. 44 Biddeth ek for hem that ben at ese, That god hem graunte ay goode perseueraunce [*rime* plesaunce]. *c* **1420** LYDG. *Assembly of Gods* 1094 With Vertew hys rerewarde came Good Perseueraunce [*rime* dysplesaunce]. **1557** N. T. (Genev.) *Eph.* vi. 18 Watch thereunto with all perseuerance [WYCL. bysynesse, TINDALE instance and supplication]. **1606** SHAKS. *Tr. & Cr.* III. iii. 150 Perseuerance, deere my Lord, Keepes honor bright; to haue done, is to hang Quite out of fashion. **1671** MILTON *P.R.* I. 148 Job, Whose constant perseverance overcame Whate're his cruel malice could invent. **1796** BURKE *Corr.* (1844) IV. 400 There is nothing which will not yield to perseverance and method. **1838** DICKENS *Nich. Nick* xxii, They kept on with unabated perseverance. **1854** MILMAN *Lat. Chr.* VIII. v, Perseverance which hardened into obstinacy.

b. *transf.* of things: Persistence.

1866 GROVE *Addr. Brit. Assoc.* in *Corr. Phys. Forces* (1867) 321 If species be said to be a perseverance of type incapable of blending itself with other types.

†**c.** Remaining, abiding (in existence). *Obs.*

1657 TOMLINSON *Renou's Disp.*, Places them..in vessels ..for present use or perseverance, till occasion serves.

2. *Theol.* Continuance in a state of grace leading finally to a state of glory.

final perseverance, perseverance of the saints: the doctrine that those who are elected to eternal life, justified, adopted, and sanctified, will never permanently lapse from grace or be finally lost: one of the 'Five points of Calvinism', and thus stated in the Westminster Confession of Faith xvii. §1: 'They whom God hath accepted in his Beloved, effectually called and sanctified by his Spirit, can neither totally nor finally fall away from the state of grace, but shall certainly persevere therein to the end, and be eternally saved'.

a **1555** BRADFORD *Let. to Traves* in Foxe *A. & M.* (1583) 1663/1 The perseuerance of Gods grace, with the knowledge of his good will, encrease with you vnto the ende. **1562** T. NORTON tr. *Calvin's Inst.* Table s.v., A confutation of the most wycked error, that Perseuerance is geuen of God according to the Merit of men. [Cf. CALVIN *Inst.* II. v. §3 Ipsa perseverantia donum Dei est; *transl. by Norton*, Contynuance yt selfe ys the gyfte of God.] **1628** WITHER *Brit. Rememb.* II. 54 Nor helpes it those Who perseverance of the Saints oppose. **1751** WESLEY *Wks.* (1872) X. 291 The Apostle was at that time fully persuaded of his own perseverance. **1852** HOOK *Ch. Dict.* (1871) 579 According to the Calvinistic system, the elect receive the grace of perseverance, so that when grace has once been received, they cannot finally fall away from it.

perseverance, -aunce, obs. ff. PERCEIVERANCE.

perseverant (pɜːsɪ'vɪərənt), *a.* Now *rare.* [a. F. *persévérant* (12th c. in Hatz.-Darm.), pr. pple. of *persévérer* to PERSEVERE. Formerly (pə'sɛvərənt).] Steadfast, persistent, persevering.

[**1340**: implied in PERSEVERANTLY.] **1413** *Pilgr. Sowle* (Caxton) I. xii. (1859) 9 He hath been perseuerant in good purpoos. **1552** ABP. HAMILTON *Catech.* (1884) 9 Ane constant and perseverent lufe. **1616** J. LANE *Cont. Sqr.'s T.* VII. 549 Not one perseverant mutinous hee spaerd. **1660** H. MORE *Myst. Godl.* II. viii. 45 That assuredly at the last, Passive and Perseverant Vertue shall ascend her Triumphant Chariot. **1710** WHITBY *Disc. Election* II. ii. iv. 333 Christ's coming..was not to save the Elect, but under conditions of Repentance and perseverant Faith. **1854-6** PATMORE *Angel in Ho.* I. XII. i. 64 When a bold youth so swift pursues, And siege of tenderest courtesy With hope perseverant, still renews. **1903** *Athenæum* 18 July 81/2 The ..perseverant zeal with which he has prosecuted this pious work.

†**b.** *transf.* Lasting, enduring, permanent. *Obs.*

1453 in *Epist. Acad. Oxon.* (O.H.S.) I. 322 Oure seid worke shall endure unto you and youre progeny a perseveraunt memorialle. **1510** *Howers Bl. Virg.* 84 Haile, starre of the sea most radiant,..A pure virgin alway perseverant.

perse'verantly, *adv.* Now *rare.* [f. prec. + -LY², or directly after the OF. adv. *perseveranment* (12th c. in Hatz.-Darm.).] In a persevering manner; perseveringly; persistently; continually.

1340 *Ayenb.* 210 Huanne þou woldest bidde god and acsi wisliche and diligentliche, þet is ententifliche and perseuerantliche. *c* **1450** tr. *De Imitatione* III. xxxv. 103 Where is þy feiþe? stande stedfastly & perseuerantly. **1533** MORE *Answ. Poysoned Bk.* Wks. 1068/1 And so dwelleth in Chryst & Christ in him perseuerantly. **1656** STANLEY *Hist. Philos.* VI. (1701) 271/1 Go perseverantly thro' it, for it is of great glory. **1826** C. BUTLER *Vind. Bk. Rom. Cath. Ch.* 56 By communicating perseverantly with the Churches in which these oaths of allegiance and disclaimer have been taken.

perseverate (pə'sɛvəreɪt), *v. Psychol.* [Back-formation from PERSEVERAT(ION; cf. L. *persevērāre* to persevere.] *intr.* To repeat a response after the cessation of the original stimulus, in various senses of PERSEVERATION 2.

1915 *Brit. Jrnl. Psychol.* VII. 388 The varying degree in which their ideas after disappearing from consciousness continue to 'perseverate' unconsciously. **1927** C. SPEARMAN *Abilities of Man* xvii. 293 They seem not even to have cared to inquire whether..he who perseverates in one kind of operation may be expected to do so..in others. *Ibid.* 306 A tendency for mental processes to have a certain lag or inertia and in this meaning to 'perseverate'. **1968** P. MCKELLAR *Experience & Behaviour* xii. 324 One subject started to draw an analogy with a gramophone record, and perseverated. **1976** SMYTHIES & CORBETT *Psychiatry* vii. 105 He may be talkative but difficult to understand, and perseverates—that is replies to questions with responses appropriate to previous questions. **1977** *Word 1972* XXVIII. 214 Often, the archiunit is one which was used appropriately some time ago in the conversation. It then pops up again and again —both in the patient's own speech and in his misunderstanding of the speech which he hears. In the latter case, the patient is said to *perseverate* on the archiunit.

Hence **per'severating** *ppl. a.*; **per'severative** *a.*; **per'severator**, one who perseverates.

1915 *Brit. Jrnl. Psychol.* VII. 389 This inhibition of a succeeding by the effect of a preceding experience must also be expected to reveal itself in the relative slowness of the perseverator. **1923** E. JONES *Papers on Psycho-Anal.* (ed. 3) xxxiii. 445 The perseverating influence of this last reaction is also to be noticed in the next succeeding one. **1924** R. M. OGDEN tr. *Koffka's Growth of Mind* iv. §5. 178 This 'perseverative tendency' of certain methods deserves special consideration. **1927** C. SPEARMAN *Abilities of Man* xvii. 292 The perseverator has been assumed to be stable in his emotions and steadfast in his purposes. **1943** H. READ *Educ. through Art* v. 150 On the other hand we have slight ability to direct attention, inclination to concentrate on colour to the neglect of form, perseverative talent—all symptoms of the tetanoid type. **1964** M. CRITCHLEY *Developmental Dyslexia* vi. 23 Words may be repeated in a perseverating fashion, e.g. *The cat the cat.* **1972** *Science* 16 June 1227/1 Attempts to reproduce such effects [*sc.* of medial temporal lesions] in animals have been largely fruitless; perseverative or disinhibitory effects have been the most frequent outcome. **1977** *Lancet* 10 Dec. 1227/2 She had a generalised memory disorder, momentary confusion, and mental and motor inertia and perseverative responses.

perseve'ration. [a. OF. *perseveration, -acion* (13th c. in Godef.), ad. L. *persevērātiōn-em*, n. of action from *persevērāre* to PERSEVERE.]

1. Persevering, perseverance.

1612 *Pasquil's Night-Cap* (1877) 61 Shee said, his faith and long perseueration, Had almost forc't her to commiseration. **1685** COTTON tr. *Montaigne* III. vi, [He] in this siege manifested the utmost of what suffering and perseveration can do. **1915** *Brit. Jrnl. Psychol.* VII. 388 The 'Perseveration'-qualities of character, *i.e.* perseverance or persistency of will. **1971** *Where* Nov. 333/2 The *Pinky and Perky* annual shows this nauseating little pair in stories, pictures, strip cartoons, puzzles, crosswords and as objects to paint. Faced by this merciless perseveration, an adult reader can be excused for thinking longingly of an efficient bacon-slicer.

2. *Psychol.* **a.** The tendency for an activity to be persevered with or repeated after the cessation of the stimulus to which it originally responded, studied as an aspect of behaviour.

[**1901** *Brain* XXIV. 620 G. E. Müller and Pilzecker have shown that an image..that has occupied consciousness tends to rise again to consciousness spontaneously,..a tendency to which they give the name 'Perseveration-tendenz'.] **1915** *Brit. Jrnl. Psychol.* VII. 388 Is Perseveration a general factor,—comparable with General Ability, influencing the entire range of mental activity? **1916** A. A. BRILL tr. *Freud's Leonardo da Vinci* v. 96 We call such a repetition a perseveration. It is an excellent means to indicate the affective accentuation. **1927** C. SPEARMAN *Abilities of Man* iv. 42 He [*sc.* Müller] writes: 'Consistency of thought and action that extends beyond the immediately given is based to an essential degree upon perseveration.' *Ibid.* 52 As most fundamental of all concepts involved, we may pick out that of 'perseveration'. **1951** J. C. FLUGEL *Hundred Yrs. Psychol.* (ed. 2) xi. 322 One of the most remarkable [general characteristics] concerns a factor known as *p* ('perseveration'), manifesting itself as a general inertia, which..makes it difficult for the subject to pass rapidly from one kind of mental operation to another. **1963** T. ALCOCK *Rorschach in Pract.* xi. 172 He is also showing some perseveration of theme on winged objects, whether creatures or emblems. **1973** P. E. VERNON in J. R. Royce *Multivariate Anal. & Psychol. Theory* 127 Tests of different kinds of perseveration, inertia or rigidity, often showed little or no correlation with one another.

b. The mechanical and involuntary repetition of a motor or verbal response, despite a change of stimulus, as a result of brain damage or organic malfunction; usu. distinguished from the stereotypy associated with schizophrenia.

1910 *Lippincott's New Med. Dict.* 715/1 *Perseveration*, the senseless repetition of a word just pronounced or an act accomplished: either a functional or an exhaustion psychosis. **1937** *Jrnl. Mental Sci.* LXXXIII. 144 Perseveration, an extremely common symptom of organic disease..can be present in various degrees, and may extend to words, phrases, actions or to the total behaviour. **1961** W. R. BRAIN *Speech Disorders* v. 62 Perseveration may lead to difficulties, the whole or part of a previous word being repeated and thus persisting to contaminate the new word which should be evoked. **1966** I. B. WEINER *Psychodiagnosis in Schizophrenia* iv. 36 In 'fixed concept' perseveration a response that accurately corresponds to a blot when first given is repeated on subsequent blots without regard for actual blot qualities. **1976** M. HAMILTON *Fish's Schizophrenia* (ed. 2) iii. 58 Perseveration consists in continuing to carry out a goal-directed activity after the need for this activity has ceased. It..is different from a stereotypy because it has been initiated by a goal-directed activity.

persevere (pɜːsɪ'vɪə(r)), *v.* Forms: α. 4-5 per'seuere, 5-7 -'seuer, -'sever, 5-6 -'ceuer, 5 -'seyuer, 6 per'cever, -'ceyver, -'ceauer, par'seuer. β. 4-5 perse'wer, 4-6 -se'uere, 6 -sy'uere, -se'ueir, -si'ueir, 5- perse'vere. [a. F. *persévére-r*, ad. L. *persevērā-re* to abide by strictly, continue steadfastly, persist, persevere, f. *persevērus* very strict, f. PER- 4 + *sevēr-us* strict, severe. The usual Eng. pronunciation, down to the middle of the 17th c. or later, was (pər'sɛvər). The form *perse'vēre* appears to have been used from an early period by Scottish writers, and isolated examples appear in Eng. writers in 15th (rarely in 16th c.). Shaks. used only *per'sever*; Quarles, 1624, used both forms in the same poem; Milton always *perse'vēre*, which became universal by *c* 1680. So with the derivatives *perse'verance*, *perse'vērance*, etc.

The two forms arise from the shifting stress in L. *persevē'rāre* and *perse'vērat*, F. *persévé'rer* and *persé'vère*. Milton's use was doubtless determined by Latin quantity.]

1. *intr.* To continue steadfastly in a course of action (formerly, also, in a condition, state, or purpose), esp. in the face of difficulty or obstacles; to continue staunch or constant. Const. *in, with.*

α. *c* **1374** CHAUCER *Troylus* I. 951 He hasteþ wel þat wysly kan a-byde,..Be lusty, fre, perseuere yn þyn seruyse. *c* **1400** *Apol. Loll.* 17 Who euer deserue to tak þe sentence of daming, if he wele perseyuer in his wit, no man mai relesse him. **1523** LD. BERNERS *Froiss.* I. 418 To take advyse howe they shulde perceyver in their warr. **1568** GRAFTON *Chron.* II. 892 That he should manfully and courageously perceauer and proceede in this..enterprise. **1594** SPENSER *Amoretti* xxxviii. 9 But in her pride she dooth persever still. **1605** SHAKS. *Lear* III. v. 23, I will perseuer in my course of Loyalty. **1624** QUARLES *Job* Medit. vii, A rare Affection of the soule..doth perseuer [*rime* Neuer; but cf. 1624 in β]. **1678** *Yng. Man's Call.* 409 Nor priest nor jesuit could ever Move him, but he did still persever Like a house founded on a rock.

β. *c* **1375** *Sc. Leg. Saints* iii. (*Andreas*) 631 Quhen þu seis me In hard torment persewer, Lowand myn god with gladsum cher. *c* **1375** *Sc. Leg. Saints* xxxii. (*Justin*) 256 Bot cypriane ȝet þan but were In his foly cane perseuere. *c* **1430** LYDG. *Min. Poems* (Percy Soc.) 178 To persevere in virginal clennesse. **1484** CAXTON *Curiall* 2 Now late vs graunte that thou woldest perseuere in vertue. *c* **1500** *Lancelot* 1564 He thinkith no worschip to conquere, Nore in the weris more to persyuere. **1500-20** DUNBAR *Poems* lxxx. 7 God gif to the.. grace ay for to perseveir, In hansell of this guid new ȝeir. **1533** GAU *Richt Vay* 82 He techit thayme..quhow thay suld persiueir and be constant in prayer. **1624** QUARLES *Job* Medit. xv, The Iust and Constant mind, that perseueres.. neuer fears. **1667** MILTON *P.L.* VII. 632 Thrice happie if they know Thir happiness, and persevere upright. **1783** WATSON *Philip III*, IV. (1839) 231 If the Morescoes should persevere in their present resolution. **1828** SCOTT *F.M. Perth* x, Your Grace is best judge whether they have been long enough persevered in. **1856** FROUDE *Hist. Eng.* I. ii. 140 He was determined to persevere at all costs.

†**b.** Const. *to* with infin.: To continue *to. Obs.*

1580 SIDNEY *Ps.* XLIV. xi, Why to hid thy face persever? **1614** LODGE *Seneca* 131 Let Fortune persever to be so equally favourable unto him. **1745** ELIZA HEYWOOD *Female Spect.* No. 13 (1748) III. 28 What the duty of a wife bound me to while living, I persevere to observe in death. **1796** MRS. M. ROBINSON *Angelina* II. 209 Persevere to cultivate her friendship.

†**c.** with adj. or sb. complement: To remain, continue to be. *Obs.*

1513 BRADSHAW *St. Werburge* I. 3009 Who-so perceuers in herte and mynde true. **1563-7** BUCHANAN *Reform. St. Andros* Wks. (1892) 11 In thys college nayne sal persever regent in humanite abuve the space of vij or viij ȝeir. *c* **1600** DONNE *Elegies on Mrs. Boulstred* ii. 61 Had she persever'd just, there would have bin Some that would sinne, misthinking she did sinne. **1653** BAXTER *Chr. Concord* xix. B iij, If he persevere impenitent.

†**d.** To proceed steadily on one's way. *Obs.*

1515 BARCLAY *Egloges* iv, Who doth persever, & to this Towre attayne, Shall have great pleasure to see the building olde. **1596** DALRYMPLE tr. *Leslie's Hist. Scot.* I. 37, I wil begin at the west cost of Lorne, quhair I left offe, and thairfra Northerlie wil perseueir, vpon the Sey coste.

e. *Theol.* To continue in a state of grace. Cf. PERSEVERANCE 2. ? *Obs.*

[*c* **1450** tr. *De Imitatione* I. xxv. 23 There was a man in gret hevynesse, ofte tymes doutinge bitwene drede & hope..; þis he þouȝte in his mynde, wolde god I wiste þat I shulde perseuere.] **1751** WESLEY *Wks.* (1872) X. 291 This does not prove that every believer shall persevere.

f. To persist, insist, in speech or argument. *Obs.* or *arch.*

1560 DAUS tr. *Sleidane's Comm.* 184 Davalus..sayd he could not fynd nothing, and herin persevered. **1691** BEVERLEY *Mem. Kingd. Christ* 7 Above all I persevere, that within the Six next Summers, viz. in 97, the Kingdom of Christ shall be in its Succession. [**1859** LANG *Wand. India* 328 'Ah! And crime—much crime!' his lordship persevered.]

†**2. a.** To continue, remain, stay in a place, or in a state or condition (implying no active effort).

c **1401** LYDG. *Flour Curtesye* 174 For ever to persever Ther she is set, and never to dissever. **1483** CAXTON *Gold. Leg.* 261/1 Luke recordeth in his wrytynges sayeng that all they were by one courage perseueryng with the Vyrgyne Marye. *a* **1550** in *Dunbar's Poems* (S.T.S.) 318 Quharfor in Scotland come I heir With ȝow to byde and perseveir. **1596**

DALRYMPLE tr. *Leslie's Hist. Scot.* I. 77 Quhil now in peace thay daylie perseueirit. **1784** *Unfortunate Sensibility* I. 74, I would not..that my children should persevere in infantine ignorance till, quite grown up, they find themselves [etc.].

†**b.** Of things: To continue, last, endure. *Obs.*

c **1407** LYDG. *Reson & Sens.* 4386 Thilke fruyt as thou maist se, Perseuereth ay in hys beaute. **1485** *Rolls of Parlt.* VI. 343/1 That the said Graunte or Grauntes, and Lettres Patentes..stand and persevere in their full strength. **1523** LD. BERNERS *Froiss.* I. 714 Wherby the good love and affectyon that hath bene bytwene you & the Comons of Flaunders shulde perceyver. **1549–62** STERNHOLD & H. *Ps.* CXIX. 91 Even to this day we may well se, how all thinges persevere. **1612** *Enchir. Med.* II. 37 The fourth day, if the disease doe as yet perseuer. **1633** G. HERBERT *Temple, Heaven* 10 Light, joy, and leisure; but shall they persever? Echo, Ever. **1696** WHISTON *Th. Earth* I. (1722) 1 All Bodies will persevere for ever in that state..in which they once are.

†**3.** *trans.* To maintain or support continuously; to cause to continue; to keep constant, preserve.

1502 *Ord. Crysten Men* (W. de W. 1506) III. iii. 152 Obstinates & perseueryinge theyr malyce. **1534** MORE *Comf. agst. Trib.* I. Wks. 1159/1 That the fauoure of God perseuered hym. **1655** GURNALL *Chr. in Arm.* verse 13. viii. §4 (1669) 143/2 Such want a principle of Divine life to draw strength from Christ to persevere them in their course.

Hence **perse'vering** (†-'**evering**) *vbl. sb.*

c **1386** CHAUCER *Sec. Nun's T.* 117 Round and hool in good perseuerynge. **1596** DALRYMPLE tr. *Leslie's Hist. Scot.* I. 70. **1667** MILTON *P.L.* VIII. 639, I in thy persevering shall rejoyce.

persevering (pɜːsɪ'vɪərɪŋ), *ppl. a.* [-ING[2].] That perseveres: see the vb.

1650 FULLER *Pisgah* IV. v. 91 Such was his persevering beauty..that it lasted unto his old-age. **1659** *Gentl. Calling* Pref., Their persevering Impieties. **1798** ISABELLA WILSON *Diary* in *Mem.* (1825) 131 All glory be to God for persevering grace. **1816** SOUTHEY *Poet's Pilgr.* I. x, The persevering Spaniard girt it round. **1836** T. HOOK *G. Gurney* (L.), He trusted more to steady and persevering industry.

Hence **perse'veringly** *adv.*, in a persevering manner, steadfastly, persistently.

1611 COTGR., *Constamment*, constantly..perseueringly. **1678** CUDWORTH *Intell. Syst.* I. iv. 568 Promising.. everlasting life to those who believe in Christ, and perseveringly obey him. **1798** *Hull Advertiser* 4 Aug. 3/3 He ..has perseveringly refused to answer any interrogatory. **1858** FROUDE *Hist. Eng.* IV. xx. 229 The ambassadors..had found Henry perseveringly moderate. **1865** PUSEY *Truth Eng. Ch.* 70.

persew, persewer, perseyte, perseyve, obs. ff. PURSUE, PERSEVERE, PERCEIT, PERCEIVE.

persh, *sb.* (*a.*) *Obs.* exc. *dial.* Also 4 persche. [Origin unascertained.] A flexible twig; a withe.

1398 TREVISA *Barth. De P.R.* XVII. clxx[i]v. (Bodl. MS.), Persche hiȝt vimen viminis, and is a nesche ȝerde... Of persche beþ nedefulle bondes and knyttels made to binde vp vines and hopes..for tonnes. **1890** *Gloucester Gloss.*, *Persh*, osier. 'Persh bed.'

b. As *adj.* Pliant; flexible.

1398 TREVISA *Barth. De P.R.* XVII. cxliii. (1495) Tiv/2 Some wylowes ben..more smale and plyaunt than other: and..ben persh. And ben so plyaunt that they breke not.

per-sheeting: see PER III. 2 b.

Pershing ('pɜːʃɪŋ). The name of J. J. *Pershing* (1860–1948), U.S. General of the Armies, applied *attrib.* and *absol.* to a type of U.S. short-range surface-to-surface ballistic missile, so called in his honour.

1958 *N.Y. Times* 22 Jan. 1/4 The committee moved..to make available an extra $40,000,000 for the new Pershing and other short-range Army missiles. *Ibid.*, The Pershing will replace the 200-mile Redstone. **1965** *Guided Missiles Volume & Sales Directory* (U.S. Govt. Data Publ.) 200 The Army's Pershing missile is a selective range, surface-to-surface ballistic missile system. **1983** *Listener* 13 Oct. 4/1 President Andropov may offer to liquidate a number of SS-20s in return for a delay in deployment of Tomahawks and Pershings. **1985** D. JONES *Barbarossa Red* 9 The removal of the Pershings and the cruise missiles.

Persian ('pɜːʃən), *a.* and *sb.* Forms: 4 **Percien, -sien,** 5 **-cynne, -syn, -sen; -san, -sante,** 6– **Persian,** (7 **-cian**); *pl.* 6 **-sience, -sianis.** [orig. ME. *Persien*, a. F. *persien* = It. *persiano*:—L. type **Persiānus*, f. *Persia*, name of the country, in Gr. Περσίς, OPers. *Pārsa*, mod.Pers. *Pārs*, Arab. *Fārs*. In 16th c. conformed to the Eng. type in -IAN; sometimes also to F. *persan*.]

A. *adj.* **1.** Of or pertaining to Persia (mod. Iran), or its inhabitants or language. Also, of or pertaining to a Persian cat.

a **1400–50** *Alexander* 2885 þe pure propure name in percynne tonge. **1587** HARRISON *England* II. xxii. (1877) I. 338 Our men are..become..through Persian delicacie crept in among vs altogither of straw. **1605** SHAKS. *Lear* III. vi. 85, I do not like the fashion of your garments. You will say they are Persian. **1737** POPE *Hor. Epist.* II. ii. 265 Robes of Persian dye. **1841** ELPHINSTONE *Hist. Ind.* I. 287 In Persian poets..a long description of inanimate nature is rarely met with. **1889** H. WEIR *Our Cats* 28 Tabby is not a Persian colour. **1972** ING & POND *Champion Cats of World* II. 73 When the two varieties [*sc.* the Angora and the Persian] were mated together by the early fanciers it was found that the Persian characteristics were dominant, so gradually all the Longhairs were classified as 'Persian'.

2. a. In the specific names of productions, natural or artificial, found in or imported from Persia, or attributed to that country or its people; e.g. ***Persian carpet, (flower) pattern, cyclamen, iris, jasmine, lilac, poplar, ranunculus***, etc.

Persian bed = DIVAN 3; **Persian berries**, the unripe fruit of *Rhamnus infectorius*, coming from Persia; also commercially applied to those of other species grown in Southern Europe; **Persian blinds** = PERSIENNES; **Persian cat**, a long-haired cat, formerly one belonging to a variety introduced from Persia, distinguished by broad, round heads, small ears, stocky bodies, and thick, rather woolly fur; **Persian cord**: see quot.; **Persian drill**, a hand drill operated by the movement of a nut backward and forward on the thread of a revolving screw, which carries the drill; **Persian earth** = *Indian red* (see INDIAN A. 4); **Persian fire**, *Path.* = ANTHRAX 1 (*Persicus ignis*, in tr. *Blancard's Phys. Dict. 1693*); †**Persian fruit** (in Sylvester), opium; **Persian insect-powder**, an insecticide made of the flowers of *Pyrethrum roseum*; **Persian lamb**, the skin or pelt of the karakul lamb, which has a silky, tightly-curled appearance; a coat made from this fur; **Persian lilac**, a shrub, *Syringa persica*, of the family Oleaceæ, bearing panicles of fragrant, mauve or white flowers; **Persian lily**, a species of fritillary (*Fritillaria persica*); **Persian lynx** = CARACAL; **Persian morocco**, a kind of morocco leather, used in bookbinding, made from the skin of a hairy sheep called the Persian goat; **Persian sheep**, a southern African breed of sheep, kept for the meat it produces; also called the blackhead Persian; **Persian silk** = B. 4; **Persian tick**, a parasitic mite, *Argas persicus*, found in houses in some parts of Persia; **Persian ware**, name given to a variety of glazed pottery; **Persian wheel**, a wheel for raising water: (*a*) a *bucket-wheel* (see BUCKET *sb.*[1] 6), a NORIA; (*b*) a wheel having chambers formed by curved or radial partitions, which lift up water as they are submerged and discharge it near the level of the axis; **Persian Yellow (rose)**, a variety of the Austrian briar, *Rosa foetida* var. *persiana*, which bears fragrant, double, yellow flowers and was brought back to England from Persia by Sir Henry Willock in 1837.

1616 T. ROE *Jrnl.* 11 Mar. in *Embassy to Court of Gt. Mogul* (1899) I. 143 Vnder foote it is layd with good *Persian Carpetts of great lardgnes. **1621** J. CHAMBERLAIN *Let.* 10 Nov. in *Mem. Amer. Philos. Soc.* (1939) XII. II. 406 The Moscovie ambassador..brought divers presents of ermins, sables, blacke foxe, Persian carpetts wrought with gold.. besides a faire Persian tent. **1632** B. JONSON *Magn. Lady* IV. iii, Spread on the sheets Under a brace of your best Persian carpets. **1844** A. W. KINGLAKE *Eothen* xxvii. 394 A few Persian carpets (which ought to be called Persian rugs, for that is the word which indicates their shape and dimension,) are sometimes thrown about near the divan. **1969** *Times* 12 Dec. (Kenya Suppl.) p. viii/3 A friend..drove all the way to Rhodesia, with her savings invested in a dozen Persian carpets supporting three dogs in the back of a station wagon. **1978** *Times* 22 Nov. 2/1 Public auction sale of genuinely rare and valuable Persian Carpets on behalf of foreign creditors. **1821** BYRON *Don Juan* III. xviii. 157 Two parrots, with a *Persian cat and kittens, He chose from several animals he saw. **1824** M. R. MITFORD *Our Village* I. 289 The white kitten..has succeeded to his lamented grandfather, our beautiful Persian cat. **1889** H. WEIR *Our Cats* 24 The Persian cat..differs somewhat from the Angora. **1894** LYDEKKER *Nat. Hist.* I. 428 The most celebrated of all the Asiatic breeds is the Persian, or Angora cat... These cats are characterised by their large size, their long silky hair,..and the thick bushy tail. **1903** F. SIMPSON *Bk. of Cat* vii. 98/1 In classing all long-haired cats as Persians I may be wrong, but the distictions between Angoras and Persians are of so fine a nature that I must be pardoned if I ignore the cat commonly called Angora, which seems gradually to have disappeared from our midst... It is my intention to confine my division of cats to long-haired or Persian cats, and short-haired or English and foreign cats. **1935** E. B. SIMMONS *Cats* xxvii. 133 In the beginning there were Persian cats..and Angora cats... Interbreeding has made the two one. **1972** ING & POND *Champion Cats of World* II. 72 Eventually all Angora and Persian cats were referred to as Longhairs. **1873** *Young Englishwoman* June 312/1 Two good merinos, one Russell or *Persian cord. **1882** CAULFEILD & SAWARD *Dict. Needlework*, *Persian cord*, a material for women's dresses, resembling rep, made of cotton and wool. **1875** KNIGHT *Dict. Mech.* 1671/2 A hand-drill..sometimes known as the *Persian drill..is frequently used for fine work and in dentistry. **1735** *Dict. Polygraph.* II. Kk v b, Indian-red, or *Persian-earth, is what we improperly call English-red. *a* **1618** SYLVESTER *Panaretus* 1303 That soft *Persian Fruit (so deer) Banefull at home, and little better here. **1889** *Persian lamb [see LAMB *sb.* 5 b]. **1892**, **1899** [see BROADTAIL]. **1937** J. LAVER *Taste & Fashion* xv. 215 All kinds of combinations of furs were tried: squirrel collared with fox, Persian lamb trimmed with mink kolinsky. **1959** J. LUDWIG in *Tamarack Rev.* Summer 6 She..walks..not in her Persian lamb..but in that worn cloth coat. **1972** C. DRUMMOND *Death at Bar* v. 123 Mrs. Gaukroger, wearing a purple pyjama suit under her Persian lamb coat. **1640** J. PARKINSON *Theatrum Botanicum* 1468 This Persian Iasmine (or *Persian Lilac, whether you will) is a shrub, or shrubby plant. **1712** [see LILAC 1 b]. **1800** *Curtis's Bot. Mag.* XIV. 486 The Persian Lilac is a shrub of much humbler growth than the common sort. **1847** F. A. KEMBLE *Let.* 12 Dec. in *Rec. Later Life* (1882) III. 301 Her maid has been with me this morning, with..a bunch of delicious Persian lilac. **1861** [see LILAC 1 b]. **1959** A. MOOREHEAD *No Room in Ark* ii. 62 The incredibly sweet scent of Persian lilac hung in the air. **1975** V. NABOKOV *Tyrants Destroyed* 47 A bright breeze ruffled the Persian lilacs. **1597** GERARDE *Herbal* I. xcv. 152 This *Persian Lillie..is nowe made.. a denizon in some fewe of our London gardens. **1870** D. ROCK *Textile Fabrics* p. lxvi, Though there be seen the 'homa', the 'cheetah', and other elements of *Persian patterns, still the discordant two-handled vase..betrays the textile to be not Persian, but Syrian. **1895** *Montgomery Ward Catal.* Spring & Summer 37/2 Ladies' Shirt Waists... New fancy Persian patterns. **1971** *Guardian* 30 Mar. 9/2 Printed Crimplene sweaters in a Persian flower pattern. **1912** R. LYDEKKER *Sheep & its Cousins* x. 209 The *Persian fat-rumped sheep..is a well-known breed, which has been carried to Cape Colony and Rhodesia, where it is now bred to a considerable extent. **1932** S. ZUCKERMAN *Social Life Monkeys* xii. 206, I have seen Chacma baboons playing about and foraging in the midst of a flock of Persian sheep. **1966** E. PALMER *Plains of Camdeboo* xvi. 256 'I guess it is a black-head Persian from the Karoo.' 'You're right,' replied Sir Abe [Baily] with delight. 'It is Karoo Persian.' When he travelled he took with him live Persian sheep from the Karoo to be slaughtered when he needed them. **1696** J. F. *Merchant's Ware-ho.* 34 There is one sort of Indian Silk more, called *Persian Silk, or Persian Taffety, which of all Silk that comes from the East Indies is of most use. **1903** M. L. SOLON *Hist. Old French Faïence* iv. 52 This..bears a distant likeness to the *Persian ware. **1971** L. A. BOGER *Dict. World Pott. & Porc.* 165/1 The earliest extant examples of Persian underglaze blue and white wares date from the 15th century. **1972** H. HODGES *Pottery* 53 Throughout the twelfth century the larger part of Byzantine polychrome pottery is best seen as a poor copy of Persian wares. **1704** *Dict. Rust. et Urb.*, **Persian-Wheel*..for overflowing of..Land lying on the borders or banks of Rivers or Streams. **1829** *Nat. Philos.* I. ii. 6 (Usef. Knowl. Soc.). **1864** J. A. GRANT *Walk across Afr.* xvii. 403 The Persian wheel, with its hanging earthen jars, overhangs the river [Nile] and..raises the water to the heights of the fields and gardens. **1843** *Gardeners' Chron.* 25 Feb. 121/1 The new *Persian Double Yellow Rose..is an entirely different variety from *Rosa Harrisonii*; it is very like the old double yellow. **1848** W. PAUL *Rose Garden* 97 Persian Yellow; flowers of the deepest yellow, large and full; form, globular... Introduced from Persia by Sir H. Willock in 1837. **1898** M. A. VON ARNIM *Elizabeth & her German Garden* 17 The Persian Yellows look as though they intended to be big bushes. **1911** E. WILLMOTT *Genus Rosa* II. 271 It is easy to understand the popularity of the beautiful Persian Yellow Rose. **1971** 'L. BLACK' *Death has Green Fingers* iv. 37 Two other strains of roses were added to the family tree, one species called the Persian Yellow.

b. In names of colours associated with Persia or its products, e.g. ***Persian blue, green, red.***

1869 *Bradshaw's Railway Manual* XXI. 460/2 (Advt.), Reds..Persian Red..Venetian Red. **1873** *Young Englishwoman* Aug. 390/1 Bright but delicate shades, such as sky blue, Persian green, and blush rose. **1886** H. C. STANDAGE *Artists' Man. Pigments* v. 51 Besides the Persian red obtained from the ochres, there is another which is a chromate of lead. **1903** M. L. SOLON *Hist. Old French Faïence* ix. 139 Some of the earliest pieces are painted upon Persian blue ground. **1934** H. HILER *Notes Technique Painting* ii. 116 *Persian green*, synonym for emerald green. **1951** R. MAYER *Artist's Handbk.* ii. 57 *Persian orange*, lake made of aniline colour on a barytes or blanc fixe base. Not permanent. **1963** tr. *Kornerup & Wanscher's Handbk. Colour* 177/1 *Persian blue*, the colour of Persian procelain... Before about 1912, this name referred to the colour of certain Persian fabrics dyed with indigo blue. *Ibid. Persian orange*, this name probably corresponds to Persian yellow, a pigment derived from a compound of arsenic and sulphur.

3. *Arch.* (See quots.)

1727–41 CHAMBERS *Cycl.*, *Persian*, or *Persic*,..a name common to all statues of men, serving instead of columns, to support entablatures. *Ibid.* s.v. *Order*, Persian Order, is that which has figures of Persian slaves, instead of columns, to support the entablature.

B. *sb.* **1.** A native or inhabitant of Persia.

(In ME. also PERSE.)

c **1374** CHAUCER *Boeth.* II. pr. ii. 35 þe kyng of perciens. **1390** GOWER *Conf.* I. 27 Persiens gon under fote. *c* **1489** CAXTON *Sonnes of Aymon* xxiv. 502 He..smote vpon the persans and dommaged theim sore. **1568** BIBLE (Bishops') *Dan.* vi. 8 The lawe of the Medes and Persians whiche altereth not. **1776** GIBBON *Decl. & F.* viii. (1788) I. 319 Zoroaster, the ancient prophet and philosopher of the Persians. **1841** LANE *Arab. Nts.* I. 77 The tale..was related to me by a Persian.

2. The native language of Persia.

1634 SIR T. HERBERT *Trav.* 170, I adde a little of their language..the English and Persian explayning one the other. **1777–80** RICHARDSON *Persian Dict.* Diss. p. viii, In Hindostan..two thirds of the Persian..is pure Arabic.

3. *Arch.* A male figure dressed in the ancient Persian manner serving instead of a column or pilaster to support an entablature: cf. A. 3.

1823 P. NICHOLSON *Pract. Build.* 590.

†**4.** A thin soft silk, usu. used for linings. Also called *Persia* or *Persian silk*. *Obs.*

1696 J. F. *Merchant's Ware-ho.* 34 There is of those Persians several lengths. **1704** *Lond. Gaz.* No. 3992/3 East-India Goods,..consisting of..Persians, Pudisways, Paunches. **1777** MME. D'ARBLAY *Early Diary* 7 Apr., She had an exceeding pretty..dress, made of pink persian. **1853** MRS. GASKELL *Ruth* I. ii. 39 Miss Hilton! where have you put the blue Persian? **1876** PLANCHÉ *Cycl. Costume* I. 394 *Persian*, a thin silk, used principally for lining coats, gowns, and petticoats, in the seventeenth century.

attrib. **1710** *Lond. Gaz.* No. 4700/4 Stolen.., A strip'd Persian riding Gown. **1818** M. EDGEWORTH *Let.* 8 Sept. (1971) 85 Little Lady Louisa flying about with her green persian sash floating. **1838** DICKENS *Nich. Nick.* x, Green persian lining.

5. = PERSIENNES.

Also pl. in Sp. form *persianas*, It. *persiane* (erron. *-ani*). **1786** tr. *Beckford's Vathek* (1823) 75 Through blinds of Persian, they perceived large soft eyes. **1856** MRS. BROWNING *Aur. Leigh* VII. 662 The closed persiani threw Their long-scored shadows on my villa-floor. **1860** *Merc. Marine Mag.* VII. 222 With green persianas or shutters. **1861** MRS. BROWNING *Parting Lovers* ii, Did I undo The persian?

6. = *Persian cat* in sense A. 2.

1871 *Graphic* 22 July 75/3 A Persian, direct from Persia, ..'a very amiable beast'. **1879** M. E. BRADDON *Vixen* III. i. 52, I have a Persian who has been my attached companion for the last ten years. **1902** A. BENNETT *Anna of Five Towns* vii. 152 The Persian with one ear met them in the lobby, his tail flying. **1921** C. VAN VECHTEN *Tiger in House* i. 15 Jessie Pickens had a very remarkable brown tabby Persian. **1934** M. V. HUGHES *London Child of Seventies* x. 113 The parlour cats were Persians, sat on laps and best chairs. **1956** G. DURRELL *My Family* ix. 116 The consul was a great cat-lover, and he possessed three large and well-fed Persians to prove it. **1972** ING & POND *Champion Cats of World* II. 72 The fur texture also differed, that of the Angoras being soft, fine and silky, while the Persians were more woolly.

7. Other misc. ellipt. or substantival uses, esp. = *Persian carpet* in sense A. 2.

1897 [see FLORAL *sb.* 2]. **1903** W. D. ELLWANGER *Oriental Rug* (1904) ii. 15 The Persians came first, and perhaps in the following order of excellence: Kirman, Sehna, [etc.]. **1905** *Daily Chron.* 9 Sept. 3/2 'Persians' and other East Indian skins are stripped of their original tannage, and then finished as morocco. **1915** J. WEBSTER *Dear Enemy* 43 New rugs on the floor (my own prized Persians). **1957** M. MCCARTHY *Memories Catholic Girlhood* viii. 197 In the winter, she would have on her mink or her Persian or her squirrel or her broadtail. **1960** *News Chron.* 12 Sept. 6/4 Persians can be geometric or floral. **1964** *House & Garden* Dec. 42/3 The rugs are Persians and Kelims. **1970** *Times* 12 May 11/8 The design of the print is a combination of paisley and persian.

C. *Comb.* as ***Persian-looking*** adj.; **Persian-like** *a.* or *adv.*, like a Persian (in quot. a Parsee).

1679 *Confinement, a Poem* 54 He never.. rising Sun, can Persian-like adore. **1902** *Daily Chron.* 1 Nov. 8/3 Persian-looking ribbon passementerie.

Hence **Persiana** (pəsɪˈɑːnə), a dress material: see quot. 1882; **ˈPersianist**, a professed student of Persian, a Persian scholar; **ˈPersianize** *v.*, *trans.* to make Persian in customs, language, etc.; *intr.* to act like or play the Persian.

1827 *Perils & Captivity* (Constable's Misc.) 327 A velvet petticoat.. of *Persiana. **1882** CAULFEILD & SAWARD *Dict. Needlework*, *Persiana*, a silk stuff decorated with large flowers. **1903** *Nation* (N.Y.) 12 Mar. 212/1 The Arabist, in the rarest of cases, has been a *Persianist. **1816** W. TAYLOR in *Monthly Rev.* LXXIX. 193 The Pythagoreans, as the *Persianizing Greeks were called. **1882** FLOYER *Unexpl. Baluchistan* 330 They are most of them half Persianized.

Persianization (ˌpɜːʃənaɪˈzeɪʃən). [f. PERSIAN *a.* + -IZATION.] The process of making Persian in appearance, structure, or other attributes.

1910 *Encycl. Brit.* XIII. 479/2 This extreme Persianization of Urdu was due rather to Hindu than to Persian influence. **1916** G. A. GRIERSON *Linguistic Survey India* IX. I. 45 This extreme Persianisation of Hindōstānī is not.. the work of conquerors ignorant of the tongue of the people. *Ibid.*, Like Urdū it [*sc.* Dakhinī] is written in the Persian character, but is much more free from Persianisation. **1924** P. BROWN *Indian Painting under Mughals* 18 The earlier Mughal emperors.. introduced the art of miniature painting into Hindustan from Persia. Their action.. represents.. only one comparatively small item in a fairly wide movement. From the nature of this movement it may be termed the 'Persianization' of Northern India. **1937** *Scrutiny* V. 446 Mr. Chib.. attributes the Persianization of Urdu and the Sanskritization of Hindi to communal jealousy. **1948** D. DIRINGER *Alphabet* II. vi. 362 *Hindi* is the modern development of Hindustani which is free from Persianization.

ˈPersic, *a.* and *sb.* [ad. L. *Persic-us* Persian.]

A. *adj.* = PERSIAN *a.*

1606 B. JONSON *Masque Hymen* Wks. (Rtldg.) 558 On their heads they wore Persic crowns. **1738** NEAL *Hist. Purit.* IV. 179 Printed in the vulgar Latin, Hebrew, Greek,.. and Persick languages. **1771** SWINTON in *Phil. Trans.* LXI. 354 *note*, The letters of the antient Persic alphabet. **1835** BROWNING *Paracelsus* v. 187 Oh Persic Zoroaster, lord of stars!

B. *sb.* **1.** The Persian tongue: = PERSIAN *sb.* 2.

1753 HANWAY *Trav.* (1762) I. III. xlvii. 216 He could read and write persic. **1850** J. BROWN *Disc. our Lord* (1852) I. iv. 209 A word borrowed from the Persic.

†**2.** [L. *persicum*.] A peach. *Obs.* In quot. *attrib.*

1599 A. M. tr. *Gabelhouer's Bk. Physicke* 141/2 Take Persick stones, and contund them to pouldre.

Hence **ˈPersicize** *v. trans.*, to turn into Persian.

1881 SIR W. HUNTER in *Encycl. Brit.* XII. 731/1 'India', .. derived.. from the Persicized form of the Sanskrit *sindhu*, a 'river', pre-eminently the Indus.

‖**persicaria** (pɜːsɪˈkɛərɪə). *Herb.* [med. or mod.L. (also It.), f. L. *persicum* (*mālum*) peach: cf. med.L. *persicārius* peach-tree, and PEACHWORT.] The plant *Polygonum Persicaria*, Dead Arsesmart, or Peachwort; also, with defining words, applied to other species of *Polygonum*; the garden species is *P. orientale*.

1597 GERARDE *Herbal* II. cix. 361 Dead Arsmart is called *Persicaria*, or Peach-woort, of the likenesse that the leaues haue with those of the Peach tree. **1663** BOYLE *Usef. Exp. Nat. Philos.* II. ii. 79 A Load of Persicaria or Arsmart, brought to him by some of the Country People. **1824** MISS MITFORD *Village* Ser. I. (1863) 101 Buck-wheat,.. the delicate pink-white of the flower, a paler persicaria. **1883** *Good Words* 710 Orach and fleabane, the yellow toadflax and pink persicaria.

ˈpersicary. Anglicized form of prec.

c **1400** *Lanfranc's Cirurg.* 83 Þe ius of þe leeues of pechis, or ellis persicarie. **1687** J. CLAYTON in *Phil. Trans.* XLI. 146 They take the biting Persicary, and chew it. **1938** M. HADFIELD *Everyman's Wild Flowers & Trees* 131 Spotted Persicary, *Polygonum Persicaria*... A branching annual up to 2 ft. high... Pale persicary.. is a very similar plant. **1952** *Common Farm Weeds Illustr.* (Plant Protection Ltd.) I. 60 Willow-weed (*Polygonum persicaria*). Other names: Redshank, Persicary. **1972** R. ADAMS *Watership Down* xlv. 375 The weeds of harvest—knot-grass and pimpernel.. heartsease and persicary.

persico, persicot (ˈpɜːsɪkəʊ). [a. 17th c. F. *persico*, now *persicot*, a. It. *persico*, L. *persicum* peach.] A kind of cordial prepared by macerating the kernels of peaches, apricots, etc., in spirit.

1709 MRS. MANLEY *Secret Mem.* (ed. 2) I. 108 Tincture of Saffron, Barbadoes-Water, Persico. **1712** ADDISON *Spect.* No. 328 ¶1. **1889** DOYLE *Micah Clarke* 9 Powders and confects, cordials and persico. **1893** *Syd. Soc. Lex.*, *Persicot*.

†**perˈside**, *v. Obs. rare*$^{-0}$. [ad. L. *persidē-re* to continue sitting, f. PER- 1 + *sedēre* to sit.]

1656 BLOUNT *Glossogr.*, *Perside*,.. to sit by, to abide still.

Persie: see PERSE, PARSEE.

‖**persiennes** (pɜːʃɪˈɛnz, ‖pɛrsjɛn), *sb. pl.* [Fr., pl. fem. of adj. *persien* Persian.] Outside window-shutters or blinds, made of light laths horizontally fastened in a frame, so as to be movable, like those of Venetian blinds.

1842 LOUISA S. COSTELLO *Pilgr. Auvergne* I. 90 Throwing the persiannes wide open. **1865** tr. *Erckmann-Chatrian's Waterloo* (1870) 24 The Jews and Lutherans behind their persiennes up above.

persiflage (ˈpɜːsɪflɑːʒ, ‖pɛrsiflaʒ). [Fr., f. *persifler* to banter or rally slightly: see -AGE.] Light banter or raillery; bantering, frivolous talk; a frivolous manner of treating any subject.

1757 CHESTERF. *Lett.* (1774) IV. 103 Upon these delicate occasions you must practise the ministerial shrugs and persiflage. **1799** HAN. MORE *Fem. Educ.* (ed. 4) I. 15 The cold compound of irony, irreligion, selfishness, and sneer, which make up what the French.. so well express by the term *persiflage*. **1814** W. TAYLOR in *Ann. Rev.* II. 308. **1827** SCOTT *Jrnl.* 13 Jan., There is a turn for persiflage, a fear of ridicule among them. **1853** KINGSLEY *Hypatia* xxi, All his smooth and shallow persiflage, even his shrewd satiric humour, had vanished. **1893** A. DOBSON *H. Walpole* ix. 254 The element in which his easy persiflage delights to disport itself.

persiflate (ˈpɜːsɪfleɪt), *v. rare*$^{-1}$. [f. F. *persifler* to banter lightly: see -ATE^{3}.] *intr.* To use or practise persiflage; to talk banteringly.

[**1848** THACKERAY *Van. Fair* xiv, Osborne was quite savage. The little governess patronised him and *persifflèd* him.] **1849** —— *Let.* in *Scribner's Mag.* (1887) I. 551/1 We talked and persiflated all the way to London.

‖**persifleur** (pɛrsɪflœr). [Fr., agent-noun f. *persifler*: see prec.] One who is addicted to persiflage, who indulges in frivolous, quizzical talk.

1840 CARLYLE *Heroes* i, They felt that if *persiflage* be the great thing, there never was such a *persifleur* [as Voltaire]. **1879** HARE *B'ness Bunsen* I. v. 147 He would have been a consummate persifleur.

persil, -sile, obs. forms of PARSLEY.

persimmon (pəˈsɪmən). Forms: 7 **putchamin, pessemmin, posimon,** 8 **pitchumon, pishamin, phishimon, porsimmon,** 8–9 **persimon,** 9 **-siman, -simmen,** 8– **persimmon.** [Corruption of the native name in the Powhatan dialect (Algonkin of Virginia). The exact form of the first element is uncertain; the second is the suffix *-min*, common to many names of grains or small fruits in Algonkin dialects: cf. *mondamin*, *shahbomin*, in Longfellow's 'Hiawatha'. The stress was orig. not on the second syllable, *persiˈmin* or *ˈpersimin* being earlier than *perˈsimmon*.]

1. The plum-like fruit of the tree *Diospyros virginiana*; the American Date-plum, of yellowish orange colour, an inch or more in diameter, with from six to eight stony seeds; it is very astringent even when ripe, but becomes sweet and edible when softened by frost. Also, The large red fruit of the Chinese and Japanese species *D. Kaki*.

1612 CAPT. SMITH *Map Virginia* 12 The fruit like medlers; they call *Putchamins*, they cast vppon hurdles on a mat, and preserue them as Pruines. **1612** W. STRACHEY *Trav. Virginia* x. (Hakl. Soc.) 119 They have a plomb which they call pessemmins, like to a medler, in England, but of a deeper tawnie cullour. **1670** D. DENTON *Descr. New York* (1845) 3 The Fruits natural to the Island are Mulberries, Posimons,.. Huckelberries. **1705** BEVERLEY *Hist. Virginia* II. iv. (1722) 112 Of stoned Fruits, I have met with three good Sorts, *viz.* Cherries, Plums, and Persimmons. **1731** CATESBY *Nat. Hist. Carolina* I. p. x, Phishimons, whorts, and some other fruit. **1760** J. LEE *Introd. Bot.* App. 322–3 Persimon Plum,.. Pishamin Plum, *Diospyros*. **1785** J. BELKNAP in *M. Cutler's Life*, etc. (1888) II. 235, I enclose you the seeds of the Persimmon, a fruit natural to Pennsylvania. **1859** *All Year Round* No. 1. 17 The [Chinese] persiman is like a large egg-plum, but containing half a dozen stones. **1863** ALCOCK *Capital Tycoon* I. 323 Apples, pears, plums, peaches, chestnuts, persimmons, oranges,.. all are here. **1887** *Century Mag.* Oct. 859/2 Away! Away!.. to where the purple and golden persimmons hang low from the boughs.

2. (More fully ***persimmon-tree***.) The tree *Diospyros virginiana* (N.O. *Ebenaceæ*); a native of North America, which produces the fruit described in 1, and yields a fine hard wood valuable for turning. Also applied to other species, as Black or Mexican P., *D. Texana*, which has a small black insipid fruit, and Japanese P., *D. Kaki*.

1737 WESLEY *Wks.* (1872) I. 62 In the moistest part of this land some porsimmon-trees grow. **1788** REES *Chambers' Cycl.*, *Plum, Indian date*, pishamin, persimon, or pitchumon, *diospyros*,.. a genus of the *polygamia dioecia* class. **1876** BANCROFT *Hist. U.S.* I. ii. 47 They brought.. loaves made of the fruit of the persimmon. **1882** *Garden* 7 Jan. 1/2 There are.. fruiting Japan Persimmons, American Persimmons.

3. In various phrases. *U.S. colloq.* and *slang.* ***to be a huckleberry to*** (or ***over***) ***someone's persimmon***: see HUCKLEBERRY 4.

1827 DE QUINCEY *Murder* Wks. 1854 IV. 50 Why or with what view, it passes my persimmon to tell you. **1841** *Spirit of Times* 18 Dec. 499 They had not forgotten that the game little mare had put Sarah up to 7:45–7:40, in March last, and it seemed as if it was now their turn to 'shake down the persimmons'. **1844** in Sperber & Trittschuh *Amer. Pol. Terms* (1962) 313/2 David Tod should go there and repeat that original remark of his about the longest pole knocking down the persimmons. **1845** *Knickerbocker* XXV. 425 Wall now, that are's a jump above my tallest persimmons. **1857** *Call* (San Francisco) 3 Apr. 4/2 He will deal himself four aces and his opponent four queens, so that your honor will perceive he must 'rake the persimmons'. **1861** in W. H. Russell *My Diary North & South* (1863) II. iii. 62 Let both parties meet where there will be no interruption at the scalping business, and the longest pole will knock the persimmon. **1889** FARMER *Americanisms* s.v., 'To rake up the persimmons.'—To pocket the stakes or spoils. *Ibid.*, 'The persimmon above one's huckleberry',.. an avowal of disbelief in one's ability to perform.. a given task or undertaking. **1896** *Daily News* 5 June 5/3 There is.. in the Southern States, a proverb.. 'The longest pole knocks the persimmon', i.e. success falls to him who has the most advantages. **1900** F. P. DUNNE *Mr. Dooley's Philos.* 68 'I'll jus' move me music back a mile,' he says, 'an' peg away, an' th' longest gun takes th' persimmons,' he says. **1901–2** FARMER & HENLEY *Slang* s.v., That's persimmon (or all persimmon) = 'That's fine'. **1903** CUTCLIFFE HYNE *McTodd* 40 No use taking four bites at a persimmon. **1946** *California Folklore Q.* July 240 That's the ripe persimmon. That is just right, or taken at the best moment.

4. *U.S.* **a.** The colour of persimmon fruit, yellow to red-orange. **b.** The colour of persimmon wood, reddish brown. Also *attrib.* and *Comb.*

1928 S. V. BENÉT *John Brown's Body* 150 Grievin' yaller gals always does all right. Next time I'se gwine to git me a coal-black gal. I'se tired of persimmon-skins. **1975** *Vogue* Dec. 103 Persimmon lipstick. **1977** *Time* 27 June 50/1 The thickly painted figures with features eroded by light, the sharp eupeptic color—emerald, persimmon, rust, ultramarine. **1977** *New Yorker* 10 Oct. 132/2 They looked forward eagerly to sporting their persimmon outfit, say, in the first round of the club championship.

5. *attrib.*, as ***persimmon-beer, -bush, -wood***.

1737 J. BRICKELL *Nat. Hist. N. Carolina* 38 The following are made in the Country, *viz.* Cyder, Persimon-Beer, made of the Fruit of that Tree, [etc.]. **1860** BARTLETT *Dict. Amer.* (ed. 3), *Persimmon Beer*, a kind of domestic beer whose principal ingredient is persimmons. *a* **1941** P. B. BARRINGER *Natural Bent* (1949) xxvi. 189 In the early seventies alcohol was everywhere in the South, and cut glass decanters stood on every sideboard... Beer was just coming, unless we except 'persimmon beer' and 'locust beer' made on every plantation and in many village homes. **1950** *Publ. Amer. Dial. Soc.* XIV. 51 *Persimmon beer*, a beverage made from ripe persimmons. **1643** *Virginia Stat.* (1823) I. 250 Skowen's damms and Persimon Ponds. **1892** *Joseph Gardner & Sons' Monthly Circular* 1 Oct., Persimmon Wood, £3 to £3 10s. per ton. **1786** G. WASHINGTON *Diary* 8 Aug. (1925) III. 102 A parcel of small Persimon bushes. **1944** G. WILSON *Passing Institutions* 177 Many an upland field not good for cultivation formerly had its flock of sheep, browsing among the sassafras and persimmon bushes.

Persism (ˈpɜːsɪz(ə)m). [f. Gr. περσίζειν to speak Persian: see -ISM.] A Persian idiom.

1760 BYROM *Jrnl. & Lit. Rem.* (1857) II. I. 619 The Arabisms, Persisms and Tyriasms that the learned observe in it [New Testament].

persist (pəˈsɪst), *v.* [ad. L. *persist-ĕre* to continue steadfastly, to persist, f. PER- 2 + *sistĕre* to stand. Cf. F. *persister* (14th c. in Hatz.-Darm.).]

1. *intr.* To continue firmly or obstinately *in* a state, opinion, purpose, or course of action, esp. against opposition, or remonstrance. Formerly also with *infin.*

1538 ELYOT *Dict.*, *Consto*, to persyste or abyde in a thynge. *Ibid.*, *Obstino*, to be obstinate, or persist firme, in one sentence or purpose. **1555** EDEN *Decades* Pref. (Arb.) 53 To persist in frowarde stoobernesse. **1574** tr. *Marlorat's Apocalips* 43 Whosoeuer persisteth in Gods truth to the ende, there is no cause why he should feare the euerlasting death. **1606** SHAKS. *Tr. & Cr.* II. ii. 186 Thus to persist In doing wrong, extenuates not wrong. **1668** CULPEPPER & COLE *Barthol. Anat.* 372 Farewel most learned Bartholine, And persist to love me. **1779** SHERIDAN *Monologue Garrick*, Can we persist to bid your sorrows flow? **1858** DICKENS *Lett.* (1880) II. 75 They persisted in going to the room last night.

b. To be insistent or urgent in a statement or question; to persist in saying or asserting.

1698 FRYER *Acc. E. India & P.* 389 The Droger.. persists; What comfort can I reap from your disturbance? *a* **1774** GOLDSM. *Hist. Greece* II. 256 [Callisthenes] persisted in his innocence to the last. **1838** LYTTON *Alice* I. vi, 'Mr. Aubrey is not severe', persisted Evelyn.

†**2.** To remain or continue to be (something or of some quality). *Obs.* or merged in 1.

1539 *Act 31 Hen. VIII*, c. 5 The saide Indenture shall persiste continue and abide.. in full strength and vertue. **1590** MARLOWE *2nd Pt. Tamburl.* IV. i, I will persist a terror to the world. **1606** HOLLAND *Sueton.* 2 They persisted earnest suiters still for him. **1671** MILTON *Samson* 249 But they persisted deaf, and would not seem To count them things worth notice. **1722** WOLLASTON *Relig. Nat.* v. 78 [Matter] will always persist uniformly in its present state, either of rest or motion, if nothing stirs, diverts, accelerates, or stops it.

†**3.** To remain standing (against opposing force); to stop short (at some point). *Obs. rare.*

1643 SIR T. BROWNE *Relig. Med.* I. §18 Those that hold that all things are governed by Fortune, had not erred, had they not persisted there. **1646** —— *Pseud. Ep.* VII. xviii. 381 He was able to persist erect upon an oyled planke, and not to bee removed by the force..of three men.

4. To remain in existence; to last, endure.

1760 J. LEE *Introd. Bot.* I. xi. (1765) 26 The Calyx.. Persisting, till the Fruit is come to Maturity. **1866** TATE *Brit. Mollusks* iv. 147 Bulimus has persisted since the period of..the Upper Eocene. **1898** A. C. HADDON *Study of Man* p. xxvii, Among the pigmy peoples..we find many infantile characters persisting in the adults.

persistence (pəˈsɪstəns). Also 6–9 **-ance.** [In 16th c. a. F. *persistance* (cf. *resistance*); subseq. changed to -ENCE after L. *persistentem*: cf. next.]

1. The action or fact of persisting; firm or obstinate continuance in a particular course in spite of opposition. Also, The quality of being persistent; = PERSISTENCY.

1546 BALE *1st Exam. Anne Askewe* 1 A faste membre of Christ by her myghtye persystence in hys veryte. **1633** BP. HALL *Hard Texts* Jer. xiii. 23 After so long and obstinate persistance in your wickednesse. **1786** BURKE *W. Hastings* Wks. 1842 II. 156 Such further evils, as must have been consequent on a persistance therein. **1844** MARG. FULLER *Wom. 19th C.* (1862) 24 Persistence and courage are the most womanly no less than the most manly qualities. **1874** GREEN *Short Hist.* viii. §2. 472 The refusal of supplies was met by persistence in the levy of Customs.

2. a. Continued existence in time or (*rarely*) in space; endurance; continuous occurrence.

1621 RACHEL SPEGHT *Frailty of Life*, Man is in sacred writ compar'd to grasse,..Of short persistance, like an Aprill showre. **1849** MURCHISON *Siluria* v. 103 A geological band of great persistence. **1879** H. GEORGE *Progr. & Pov.* Introd. (1881) 11 Political economy..does not explain the persistence of poverty amid advancing wealth. **1880** CARPENTER in *19th Cent.* Apr. 599 The persistence of a.. number of cretaceous types..through the whole of the Tertiary period.

b. spec. *persistence of an impression*: the continuance of a sensible impression after the exciting cause is removed, esp. of a visual impression upon the retina of the eye, the cause of many phenomena in optics. *persistence of force* or *energy*, *persistence of matter*, names for the two principles of the conservation of energy and the permanence of matter. *persistence of an impression* (also simply *persistence*): used chiefly with reference to vision (so *persistence of vision*).

1862 H. SPENCER *First Princ.* II. viii. 251 *note*, I expressed to..Prof. Huxley my dissatisfaction with the current expression—'Conservation of force'... Huxley suggested *persistence*. *Ibid.* (1867) 189 By the persistence of Force, we really mean the persistence of some Power which transcends our knowledge and conception... In other words, asserting the persistence of Force, is but another mode of asserting an Unconditioned Reality. **1869** TYNDALL *Notes Lect. Light* 27 An electric spark is sensibly instantaneous; but the impression it makes upon the eye remains for some time after the spark has passed away... Wheatstone's Photometer is based on this persistence. **1883** A. BARRATT *Phys. Metempiric* 81 The persistence of matter and energy, and the law..that events happen equally well in all parts of space where their conditions occur, prove that time and space have no real existence, but are only forms of arrangement of phenomena. **1902** *Encycl. Brit.* XXVII. 95/1 Cinematograph... This apparatus shows in rapid sequence a series of views representing closely successive phases of a moving object, and persistence of vision creates the illusion that the object is in motion. **1924** J. P. C. SOUTHALL tr. *H. von Helmholtz's Treat. Physiol. Optics* II. 228 The best way to realize this persistence of the impression is to turn the eye to a perfectly dark field after it has been gazing at bright objects. **1944** R. W. MONCRIEFF *Chem. Senses* iii. 56 Although it has not been measured the persistence of odour must be short like that of taste. **1952** PIRENNE & ABBOTT tr. *Piéron's Sensations* IV. iii. 283 It is generally stated that visual sensations have a persistence of a tenth of a second. **1966** C. W. WILMAN *Seeing & Perceiving* vi. 52 Persistence of vision is one reason..why a series of pictures presented at short intervals produces a satisfactory effect in the cinema.

c. (The duration of) the emission of light by a luminescent substance after the cause of the luminescence has ceased; *persistence characteristic* (see quot. 1950[1]).

1917 *Physical Rev.* IX. 297 It appears that the persistence of luminescence is due to the consistency of the substance and disappears as the fluidity increases. **1935** *Proc. IRE* XXIII. 1325 Slight changes in either the screen material or the method of manufacture may result in large changes..in the persistence with which the light continues to emanate from the excited portion of the screen after the electron beam has been removed. *Ibid.*, Screens which have a short persistence are desired for recording on moving film. *Ibid.* 1341 The persistence characteristic is taken by the use of some form of stroboscopic apparatus by means of which one is able to measure the relative brilliance of the screen at definite times after excitation. **1950** RIDER & USLAN *Encycl. Cathode-Ray Oscilloscopes* vii. 157/1 A plot of the brightness ..versus the decay time of the phosphorescence is termed the persistence characteristic of the screen. **1950** H. W. LEVERENZ *Introd. Luminescence of Solids* v. 150 For (conventional) luminescence emissions, all persistences longer than about 10^{-8} sec are called phosphorescence to indicate an abnormal delay. **1967** *Electronics* 6 Mar. 127/1 In the 710B, the top scope is coated with P7 phosphor for good persistence.

persistency (pəˈsɪstənsɪ). [f. L. *persistent-em*: see next and -ENCY; cf. prec.]

1. The quality of persisting or being persistent; firmness or obstinacy in adhering to a course, purpose, or opinion; also = PERSISTENCE 1.

1597 SHAKS. *2 Hen. IV*, II. ii. 50 Thou think'st me as farre in the Diuels Booke..for obduracie and persistencie. *a* **1672** T. HORTON *Serm., Ps.* cxxxiii. 1 (1679) 195 This is also pertaining to the love and concord of brethren, a perseverance and persistency in it. **1833** SARAH AUSTIN *Charac. Goethe* II. 209 *note*, He did this with the more ardour and persistency. **1879** TROLLOPE in *19th Cent.* Jan. 36 Clever young men, ambitious but idle and vacillating, are met every day, whereas the gift of persistency in a young man is uncommon.

2. The quality or condition of continuing in existence; = PERSISTENCE 2.

1833 LYELL *Princ. Geol.* III. 331 Not to place implicit reliance on the alleged persistency of the same mineral characters in secondary rocks. **1866** THIRLWALL *Rem.* (1878) III. 304 It has only undergone a series of transformations, which has not interrupted its persistency.

persistent (pəˈsɪstənt), *a.* [ad. L. *persistent-em*, pr. pple. of *persistĕre* to persist. In F. *persistant*; cf. PERSISTENCE.]

1. Persisting or continuing firmly in some action, course, or pursuit, esp. against opposition or remonstrance, or in spite of failure.

1830 HERSCHEL *Stud. Nat. Phil.* 81 Our resistance against the destruction of..prejudices..of sense, is commonly more violent at first, but less persistent, than in the case of those of opinion. **1868** E. EDWARDS *Ralegh* I. xvi. 332 His greed, no less than his ambition,..made him a persistent colonizer. **1888** F. HUME *Mme. Midas* I. i, Her suitors were numerous and persistent as those of Penelope.

2. Existing continuously in time; enduring.

1853 KANE *Grinnell Exp.* xxxix. (1856) 360 There is a something about this persistent day antagonistic to sleep. **1864** H. SPENCER *Biol.* I. III. viii. §144. 404 This assumption of a persistent formative power, inherent in organisms, and making them unfold into higher forms. **1866** TATE *Brit. Mollusks* iv. 169 A marked and persistent variety. **1871** L. STEPHEN *Playgr. Eur.* iv. (1894) 94 A persistent screen of stormy cloud drove up the valley.

b. Of an action or condition: Continued, continuous, constant; constantly repeated.

1857 *G. Bird's Urin. Deposits* 289 The persistent occurrence of deposits of the earthy phosphates in the urine. **1872** HUXLEY *Phys.* iv. 100 The persistent breathing of such air tends to lower all kinds of vital energy.

3. *spec.* **a.** *Zool.* and *Bot.* Of parts of animals and plants (as the horns, hair, leaves, calyces, etc.): Remaining after the period at which such parts in other cases fall off or wither; permanent; continuing; opp. to *deciduous* or *caducous*.

1826 KIRBY & SP. *Entomol.* IV. 344 *Persistent*... Legs which the insect has in all its states. Ex. The legs attached to the trunk. **1830** LINDLEY *Nat. Syst. Bot.* 206 Crowned by the persistent lobes of the calyx. **1835** KIRBY *Hab. & Inst. Anim.* II. xxiv. 502 Lastly, come the Ruminants, whose horns are hollow and naked, but persistent. **1872** OLIVER *Elem. Bot.* II. 199 Called 'Everlastings' from their dry, scarious, persistent involucres. **1880** GRAY *Struct. Bot.* iii. (ed. 6) 86 Leaves..may be..persistent, when they remain through the cold season..during which vegetation is interrupted. **1888** ROLLESTON & JACKSON *Anim. Life* 348 In some Mammalia the teeth grow from persistent pulps.

b. *Geol.* Of a stratum: Extending continuously over the whole area occupied by the formation; not thinning out or disappearing.

1833 LYELL *Princ. Geol.* III. 173 The individual strata are rarely persistent for a great distance. **1839** MURCHISON *Silur. Syst.* I. xxix. 372 The bed is persistent only for a few yards. **1865** GEIKIE *Scen. & Geol. Scot.* vi. 138 Even with such doubtful forms, the two main systems remain tolerably persistent.

Hence **perˈsistently** *adv.*, in a persistent manner, with persistence or continuously repeated action.

1859 SMILES *Self-Help* 323 Gentleness in society..pushes its way quietly and persistently. **1880** C. R. MARKHAM *Peruv. Bark* iii. 276 A fair recompense has been persistently refused.

perˈsister. [f. PERSIST *v.* + -ER[1].] **a.** One who persists. *rare.*

1748 RICHARDSON *Clarissa* (1811) II. viii. 44 Each of them tends to the exclusion of that ungenerous persister's visits.

b. *Biol.* A bacterium which continues to live in the presence of enough antibiotic to kill almost all members of its species.

1944 J. W. BIGGER in *Lancet* 14 Oct. 498/1 These abnormal cocci have been termed 'persisters', to denote their power of surviving in the presence of sufficient penicillin to be lethal for the normal forms. **1949** E. CHAIN et al. in H. W. Florey et al. *Antibiotics* II. xxxv. 1143 The proportion of persisters in cultures of staphylococci is not constant, and the factors governing their numbers are not yet fully understood. **1970** *Jrnl. Med. Microbiol.* III. 669 Another type of persister is a cell in a non-replicating phase on which the antibiotic cannot act because of the absence of cell-wall synthesis. **1977** *Lancet* 15 Oct. 822/2 Electron microscopy was the only technique to demonstrate successfully the presence of small numbers of bacterial persisters in the vegetations of this treated case of streptococcal endocarditis.

perˈsisting, *vbl. sb.* [f. as prec. + -ING[1].] The action of the vb. PERSIST; persistence.

a **1694** TILLOTSON *Serm., John* iii. 19 Wks. 1717 II. 602 Another usual concomitant of Infidelity, is..pertinacious persisting in Error. **1800** *Asiat. Ann. Reg., Misc. Tracts* 22/1 Convinced that his persisting was to little purpose.

perˈsisting, *ppl. a.* [f. as prec. + -ING[2].] That persists, persistent; *spec.* = PERSISTENT 3.

1552 HULOET, Persistyng, *constans, manens.* **1626** BACON *Sylva* §902 It may make him..more confident and persisting then otherwise he would be. **1774** CURTIS *Flora Lond.* i. (1777) 12 Pimpernel..Calyx persisting. **1899** *Allbutt's Syst. Med.* VIII. 484 Columns separated by the persisting collagenous tissue.

Hence **perˈsistingly** *adv.*, persistently.

1854 *Tait's Mag.* XXI. 451 He..pursues persistingly an idea. **1885** L. WINGFIELD *Barbara Philpot* III. iv. 92 That the interesting schemer should so persistingly cling to a Cause that was hopeless.

perˈsistive, *a.* [f. PERSIST *v.* + -IVE.] Characterized by persisting, tending to persist.

1606 SHAKS. *Tr. & Cr.* I. iii. 21 The protractiue trials of great Ioue, To finde persistiue constancie in men. **1757** HOME *Douglas* II, For chance and fate are words: Persistive wisdom is the fate of man. **1896** *Q. Rev.* Oct. 354 The King's plan was of no effect against his persistive constancy.

Hence **perˈsistively** *adv.*, **perˈsistiveness.**

1847 J. SHEPPARD *Life J. Foster* II. 500 These evils ought to be boldly and persistively exposed. **1864** A. LEIGHTON *Myst. Leg. Edinburgh* (1886) 238 Persistiveness draws, as it were, a power from the wearing out of resistiveness.

persiueir, obs. Sc. form of PERSEVERE.

persive, obs. form of PIERCIVE.

†**perske,** obs. Sc. form of (?) PARCH *v.*

1565 *Randolphes Phantasey* 784 in *Satir. Poems Reform.* i, The hills of highest hight are sonest perskt with sone; The Silver streames with somers drowght are letten oft to Rone.

perske, obs. variant of PERSE *a.*, blue, bluish.

persley, -lie, -ly, persoley, -oly, obs. forms of PARSLEY.

persnepe, obs. f. PARSNIP.

persnickety (pəsˈnɪkɪtɪ), *a.* (*adv.*) *U.S. colloq.* Also **perˈsnikity.** Altered f. PERNICKETY *a.* Hence **perˈsnicketiness.**

1905 *Dialect Notes* III. 63 *Persnickety*,..disagreeable, or snippy. 'They acted mighty *persnickety*.' **1915** *Ibid.* IV. 215 Fern is more persnikity about her clothes than either of the other girls. **1922** W. STEVENS *Let.* 5 May (1967) 227, I have no desire to be persnickety about the arrangement of the group. **1940** *Sat. Even. Post* 10 Feb. 25 Dad was too old to begin being what he called 'persnickety'. **1960** WENTWORTH & FLEXNER *Dict. Amer. Slang* 384/1 *Persnickety, pernickety* adj., fussy; fastidious; punctilious; snobbish. Since *c.* 1890. 'Pernickety' is now obs.; 'persnickety', once dial., is now colloq. **1967** R. STEIN *Great Cars* 222/1 That archetype of persnickety Yankee toolmakers. **1977** *Time* 17 Oct. 48/2 Billy compensates for his brother's sweet-eyed psalm-singing and persnicketiness.

persolution (pɜːsəʊˈl(j)uːʃən). *Chem.* [See PER- 5.] A solution of the highest strength.

1854 J. SCOFFERN in *Orr's Circ. Sc., Chem.* 461 Solutions of tin may..come under the notice of the chemists as protosolutions and persolutions.

†**perˈsolve,** *v. Obs.* [ad. L. *persolv-ĕre* to release, discharge completely, f. PER- 2 + *solvĕre* to loosen, to pay.] *trans.* To pay in full; to fulfil or discharge completely.

a **1548** HALL *Chron., Edw. IV* 230 b, .l.M. crounes, yerely to be persolued & paied within the toure of London. **1550** BALE *Apol.* 83 If all thynges muste be persolued, that hathe bene promysed in papisme.

person (ˈpɜːrs(ə)n), *sb.* Forms: α. 3–4 **persun,** 3–6 **persone,** (4 **persoyne**), 4–5 **persoon(e,** (5 **persown**), 5–6 **persoun(e, personne,** 4– **person.** β. 4 **parsoun,** 4–7 **parson,** 5–6 **parsone,** 6 **parsonne.** [a. OF. *persone* (12th c. in Littré), mod.F. *personne*, a personage, a person, a man or woman, = Pr., It. *perˈsona*:—L. *persōna* a mask used by a player, a character or personage acted (*dramatis persona*), one who plays or performs any part, a character, relation, or capacity in which one acts, a being having legal rights, a juridical person; in late use, a human being in general; also in Christian use (Tertullian *c* 200) a 'person' of the Trinity. Generally thought to be related to L. *personāre* to sound through; but the long *ō* makes a difficulty. The sense *mask* has not come down into Eng.; and the other senses did not arise here in logical order, the earliest being 1, 2, 4 b, and 7. See also PARSON, a differentiated form of the same word.]

I. 1. A character sustained or assumed in a drama or the like, or in actual life; part played; hence function, office, capacity; guise, semblance; one of the characters in a play or story. (Now chiefly of the *dramatis personæ* or characters in a drama, and in phr. *in the person* *of* = in the character of, as representing.) †***to put on a person***, to assume a character (cf. PERSONAGE 7 b). Also, ***persons of the drama*** [tr. DRAMATIS PERSONÆ] *lit.* or *fig.*

The strict dramatic use does not appear in Eng. so early as the transferred use: cf. quot. 1590.

a **1225** *Ancr. R.* 126 þe pellican..is euer leane... Dauid efnede him þerto in ancre persone, and ine ancre stefne. **1377** LANGL. *P. Pl.* B. XVIII. 333 In my paleys paradys in persone of an addre, Falseliche þow fettest þere þynge þat I loued. **1538** CDL. POLE in Strype *Eccl. Mem.* I. App. lxxxiv. 219 Never heard of the like in Christendom, against ony that bear that person, that I do at this time. **1559** W. CUNNINGHAM *Cosmogr. Glasse* 11 Whan as he speaketh vnder the parson of Phebus. **1560** DAUS tr. *Sleidane's Comm.* 107 They susteyne the persones of intercessours. **1590** SHAKS. *Mids. N.* III. i. 62 He comes to disfigure, or to present the person of Moone-shine. **1600** —— *A.Y.L.* IV. i. 92 Well, in her person, I say I will not haue you. **1607** *Lingua* II. iv, Hee's bold to bring your person vpon the Stage. **1608** [see PERSONATOR]. **1653** JER. TAYLOR *Serm. for Year* I. xxi. 278 No man can long put on a person and act a part, but his evill manners will peep through the corners of the white robe. *a* **1656** HALES *Gold. Rem.* (1688) 184 And put on a kind of surly and sullen Person, of Purpose to deter her. **1665** LLOYD *State Worthies* (1670) 14 To fit them by degrees for the person they are to sustain. **1712** ADDISON *Spect.* No. 542 ¶1 Had I always written in the person of the Spectator. **1779–81** JOHNSON *L. P., Lyttelton* Wks. IV. 313 The names of his [Lyttelton's] persons too often enable the reader to anticipate their conversation. **1803–6** WORDSW. *Intim. Immort.* vii, Filling..his 'humourous stage' With all the persons, down to palsied Age. **1895** G. B. SHAW *Our Theatres in Nineties* (1932) I. 39 The persons of the drama belong rather to the world of imagination than of reality. **1948** M. SHARP *Flowering Thorn* II. iii. 72 Thus admitted, so to speak, among the persons of the drama, the young American rose to his feet.

II. 2. a. An individual human being; a man, woman, or child. (In earliest use, The human being acting in some capacity, personal agent or actor, person concerned.)

a **1225** *Ancr. R.* 316 Abuten sunne liggeð six þinges þet hit heliep..person, stude, time, manere, tale, cause. Persone, þe þet dude þeo sunne, oðer mid hwam me dude hire. **13..** *Cursor M.* 26684 (Cott.) To tell þe nam o þat person es na man halden wit resun. **13..** *Coer de L.* 3317 Fyftene persons in Acres toun, He gaff hem clothis gret foyson. *c* **1340** HAMPOLE *Prose Tr.* 11 The fifte comandement es þat thou slaa na man..And also here es forboden vn-ryghtwyse hurtynge of any persone. **1467** in *10th Rep. Hist. MSS. Comm.* App. v. 304 That this acte be not prejudicial ne hurt to no parson nor parsones. ?**1507** *Communyc.* (W. de W.) A iij, In Noes tyme bycause of synne..Saue viij. persones drowned were all. **1611** BIBLE *Luke* xv. 7 Ninety and nine iust persons. **1727** FIELDING *Love in Sev. Masques* III. x, There is a certain person in the world, who in a certain person's eye, is a more agreeable person than any person, amongst all the persons, whom persons think agreeable persons. **1827** JARMAN *J. J. Powell's Devises* (ed. 3) II. 337 The bequest did not spring from a parent or person standing in the place of a parent.

b. Emphatically, as distinguished from a thing, or from the lower animals. (Cf. 3.)

1481 CAXTON *Myrr.* I. xiv. 43 Her [nature's] werke is alway hool..be it in persones or in bestes. **1665** BOYLE *Occas. Refl.* IV. xi. (1848) 233 My Opinions, whether of Persons or things, I cannot in most cases command my self. *a* **1713** SPRAT (J.), A zeal for persons is far more easy to be perverted, than a zeal for things. **1766** BLACKSTONE *Comm.* II. ii. 16 The objects of dominion or property are things, as contradistinguished from persons. **1893** PATMORE *Relig. Poet.* 107 In every person who has a right to be called a person, as distinguished from an animal, there are two distinct consciences.

c. A man or woman of distinction or importance; a personage. (Usually with qualifying word or words expressing this.)

(Outside English this was an earlier sense than 2.)

c **1400** *Rom. Rose* 3202 On hir heed she hadde a crown, Hir semede wel an high persoun. **1579** *Reg. Privy Council Scot.* III. 205 Johnne Cheisholme, comptrollar and secund persoun of the artailyeirie. **1604** E. G[RIMSTONE] *D'Acosta's Hist. Indies* v. viii. 348 If it were a person of qualitie, they gave apparrell to all such as came to the interrement. *a* **1648** LD. HERBERT *Hen. VIII* (1649) 154 Charles Duke of Bourbon, whom I find so considerable a Person at this time. **1672** DRYDEN *Assignation* I. i, A man of my parts and talents, though he be but a *valet de chambre*, is a person. **1769** ROBERTSON *Chas. V*, VI. Wks. 1813 VI. 81 Immediately the chief persons in the state assembled. **1845** M. PATTISON *Ess.* (1889) I. 22 The Bishop..whose great popularity at Tours ..made him a person of much consideration.

d. Used contemptuously or slightingly of a man. Also, of a woman.

1782 MISS BURNEY *Cecilia* VI. i, Do you suppose a young lady..would want to take advantage of a person in trade? *Ibid.* ii, Miss Beverley, if this person wishes for a longer conference with you, I am sorry you did not appoint a more seasonable hour for your interview. **1935** *Punch* 18 Dec. 678 This Pearl person has neglected to say whether [etc.]. **1939** *Punch* 23 Aug. 198/1 She was a sort of secretary person down at the works.

e. ***young person***: a young man or young woman (L. *juvenis*); now esp. used of the latter, when the speaker does not desire to specify her position as 'girl', 'woman', or 'lady'.

1535 COVERDALE *Judith* vii. 12 Then came the men and women, yonge personnes and children all vnto Osias. **1743** J. MORRIS *Serm.* vii. 181 Highly criminal in young persons. **1759** SARAH FIELDING *C'tess of Dellwyn* II. 217 This young Person had been left at her Parents' Death. **1793** W. ROBERTS *Looker-on* No. 72 (1794) III. 125 There lived a young person at Loudun from whom he could not resolve to be separated. **1801** *Lusignan* I. 21 Her daughter, a young person of seventeen. **1820** SCOTT *Monast.* xviii, There be some flashes of martial spirit about this young person [Halbert Glendinning]. **1885** W. S. GILBERT *Mikado* I, They are not young ladies, they are young persons. **1893** MRS. F. H. BURNETT *One I knew best of all* xv, The Small Person blushed, because she was of the Small Persons who are given to superfluous blushing.

f. Used (*a*) as a substitute for MAN *sb.*[1] (esp. sense 4 p: also for BOY *sb.*[1], etc.) as second element in numerous *Combs.* relating to offices which may be held by a member of either sex, as ***chairperson, salesperson***; (*b*) with preceding defining word, as ***marketing person***, and in other fanciful formations of this type, as ***henchperson***.

In practice usually employed to avoid alleged sexual discrimination and widely regarded as having amusing connotations.

1971 *Sci. News* 11 Sept. 166 A group of women psychologists thanked the board for using the word 'chairperson' rather than 'chairman'. **1971** *Sci. Amer.* Dec. 37/1 (Advt.), If there is any doubt at the counter, let him show the salesperson this ad. **1972** *Listener* 24 Aug. 232/1 Two young black women will almost certainly join Representative Shirley Chisholm in Congress..putting up the number of black 'Congresspersons' to at least 14. *Ibid.*, Yvonne Brathwaite Burke..the stunning and extremely saucy 'Vice-Chairperson'. **1973** *Ibid.* 1 Mar. 286/3 Chairperson Mitchell and her henchpersons looked at the way education brainwashes girls. **1974** *Black Panther* 23 Feb. 9/2 Brother Malcolm Kelley, chairperson for the Committee for Justice for Tyrone Guyton. **1976** 'L. BLACK' *Healthy Way to Die* ii. 19 You're a newspaperwoman—or, as we have to say in these days of female emancipation, a newspaper person. **1976** *Publishers Weekly* 16 Feb. 81/1 The author [*sc.* Jeanne Wilson] is a solid craftsperson who tells her old-fashioned story in a winning manner. **1976** *Oxford Times* 23 July 32 (Advt.), Builders' merchants require yardperson. **1976** *Jrnl. R. Soc. Arts* CXXIV. 510/1 The exercise known amongst marketing men, or should I say marketing persons, as market segmentation. **1977** *Times Lit. Suppl.* 29 Apr. 506/5 A pair of homosexual network anchorpersons. **1977** C. SAGAN *Dragons of Eden* ii. 41 A group of literary Englishpersons, immobilized in the Alps by inclement weather. **1978** *Amat. Photographer* 29 Nov. 119/3 We saw nothing in cine to rival the spectacular application of high-technology design to still cameras for everyman (sorry, everyperson).

g. With defining word, as ***cat person, dog person***, etc.: one who is characterized by a preference or liking for the thing specified; a lover or enthusiast. (Used much as the combining form -PHIL, -PHILE.)

1971 'D. HALLIDAY' *Dolly & Doctor Bird* i. 6, I am not.. a 'night person', and had no desire to see a..niterie. **1976** T. HEALD *Let Sleeping Dogs Lie* i. 23, I should say you're more of a cat person. Or even a parrot person. **1986** R. LITTELL *Sisters* II. vii. 152 Millie is basically a dog person.

3. In general philosophical sense: A self-conscious or rational being.

1659 PEARSON *Creed* (1839) 436 All which words are nothing else but so many descriptions of a person, a person hearing, a person receiving, a person testifying. **1877** E. R. CONDER *Bas. Faith* ii. (1884) 72 We can address God as a Person, and sustain..relations [with Him] such as are possible only between persons.

III. 4. a. The living body of a human being; either (*a*) the actual body as distinct from clothing, etc., or from the mind or soul, or (*b*) the body with its clothing and adornment as presented to the sight of others; bodily frame or figure. Usually with *of* or possessive.

c **1374** CHAUCER *Troylus* II. 652 (701) Troylus persone She knew by sighte and ek by gentillesse. *c* **1400** *Destr. Troy* 2139 To proffer our persons & our pure goodes, To venge of our velany and our vile harme. *c* **1460** FORTESCUE *Abs. & Lim. Mon.* vi. (1885) 121 His highnes shall þan haue therfore a bouute his persone..lordes, knyghtes, and sqviers. **1526** TINDALE *Col.* ii. 1 As many as have not sene my parson in the flesshe. **1606** SHAKS. *Ant. & Cl.* II. ii. 202 For her owne Person, It beggerd all description. **1692** DRYDEN *St. Euremont's Ess.* 30 The Senate..sent to advise Pyrrhus to take care of his Person. **1732** LAW *Serious C.* iv. (ed. 2) 61 It is very possible for a man that is proud of his estate..to disregard his dress and person. **1766** GOLDSM. *Vic. W.* xxxi, It was her fortune, not her person, that induced me to wish for this match. **1876** GEO. ELIOT *Dan. Der.* I. iii, One of his advantages was a fine person.

b. (With qualifying adj.) A human (or quasi-human) being considered in reference to bodily figure or appearance; a man or woman of (such and such) a figure. ? *Obs.*

c **1330** R. BRUNNE *Chron. Wace* (Rolls) 14913 'Alas!' he sayde, 'so fair mankynde,..So fare persones, so bright of ble.' *c* **1386** CHAUCER *Sqr.'s T.* 17 A fair persone he was and fortunat. **1539** BIBLE (Great) *Gen.* xxxix. 6 And Josep[h] was a goodly persone, & a well fauored. **1610** SHAKS. *Temp.* I. ii. 416. **1667** MILTON *P.L.* II. 110 Belial, in act more graceful and humane; A faire person lost not Heav'n. **1768** STERNE *Sent. Journ.* (1775) II. 137 (*Maria*), I asked her if she remembered a pale thin person of a man. **1797–1805** S. & HT. LEE *Canterb. T.* V. 27 'What person of a man?' 'Very handsome, if he was not so pale.'

5. a. The actual self or being of a man or woman; individual personality. With *of* or possessive: ***his*** (***own***) ***person*** = himself; ***your person*** = yourself, you personally. †Formerly often used by way of respect: e.g. ***the king's person*** for 'the king'.

1362 LANGL. *P. Pl.* A. III. 172 þou knowest Concience, I com not to chyde, Ne to depraue þi persone with a proud herte. *c* **1386** CHAUCER *Wife's T.* 305 Ffor gentillesse nys but renomee Of thyne auncestres,..Which is a strange thyng to thy persone. **1470–85** MALORY *Arthur* I. xxi. 67 Ye are the falsest lady of the world and the most traitresse vnto the kynges person. **1523** CROMWELL in Merriman *Life & Lett.* (1902) I. 37, I am so extremely desyrows that the noble parson yf [*sic*: ? of] my saide Prynce showlde tarry withyn Hys Realme. **1605** BACON *Adv. Learn.* I. vii. §5 Traian..was for his person not learned. **1643** in Neal *Hist. Purit.* (1736) III. 35 The charge..shall..be either given to their persons, or left at their houses. *a* **1715** BURNET *Own Time* I. 368 His circumstances may deserve that his character should be given, though his person did not. **1824** SCOTT *Redgauntlet* ch. xxiii, Let me first..see your Majesty's sacred person, in such safety as can now be provided for it. **1853** MAURICE *Proph. & Kings* ix. 148 Asserting the dignity of his own person, or at all events of his own office. **1876** MOZLEY *Univ. Serm.* iii. (ed. 2) 54 We observe..to begin with, that our bodies are not we,—not our proper persons.

fig. **1651** HOBBES *Leviath.* I. xv. 75 Robbery and Violence, are Injuries to the Person of the Common-wealth.

†b. Expressing bodily presence or action; presence or action 'in person'. *Obs.* exc. as in 11.

1480 CAXTON *Chron. Eng.* ccxliii. (1482) 289 Whan they were y wedded..the kyng his owne persone brought and ladde this worthy lady to the bisshops place of wynchestre. **1509** HAWES *Past. Pleas.* xxx. (Percy Soc.) 146 Up than I went where as her person stode. **1557** *Order of Hospitalls* D iv b, The President..without his persoun, shall no waightie matters be determined or agreed on. **1585** T. WASHINGTON tr. *Nicholay's Voy.* III. x. 86 [They] do wrastle before his person two and two. **1605** SHAKS. *Macb.* III. iv. 128 How say'st thou that Macduff denies his person At our great bidding? [**1732** LEDIARD *Sethos* II. IX. 309, I hope to be of service..with my troops and person.]

IV. 6. *Law.* **a.** A human being (***natural person***) or body corporate or corporation (***artificial person***), having rights and duties recognized by the law.

1444 *Rolls of Parlt.* V. 75/1 And þey [the Master & Brethren of the Hospital] by that same name mowe be persones able to purchase Londez and Tenementz of all manere persones. **1475** *Ibid.* VI. 150/1 Any persone Temporell, corporat or not corporat. **1704** J. HARRIS *Lex. Techn.* I. s.v., A Writ that lies for Prebendaries, or other Spiritual Persons. **1765** BLACKSTONE *Comm.* I. i. 123 Natural persons are such as the God of nature formed us; artificial are such as are created and devised by human laws for the purposes of society and government; which are called corporations or bodies politic. **1768–74** TUCKER *Lt. Nat.* (1834) II. 188 A crowd is no distinct existence,..but if the same people be erected into a corporation, there is a new existence superadded; and they become a person in law capable to sue and be sued [etc.]. **1833** *Act 3 & 4 Will. IV*, c. 74 §1 The word 'Person' shall extend to a Body Politic, Corporate, or Collegiate, as well as an Individual.

b. Euphemistically, the genitals.

1824 *Act 5 Geo. IV* c. 83 §4 Every Person wilfully, openly, lewdly and obscenely exposing his Person in any Street, Road or public Highway, or in View thereof, or in any place of public Resort, with intent to insult any Female.., shall be deemed a Rogue and Vagabond within the true Intent and Meaning of this Act. **1853** MR. JUSTICE MAULE in *Law Jrnl. Rep.* XXXI. III. 123/1 What do you mean in law by exposing his *person*? The indictment should have been for exposing his *private parts*. **1911** *Straits Times* (Singapore) 13 June 7/3 He let go my arms, held me round the waist with his right arm and used his left hand. He stooped to do it. He put his hand on my person. **1973** R. E. MEGARRY *Second Miscellany-at-Law* ii. 165 Few readers of the newspapers can be unaware of the curious convention whereby for many years past the word 'person' was used anatomically in prosecutions for indecency.

V. 7. *Theol.* **a.** Applied to the three distinctions, or modes of the divine being, in the Godhead (Father, Son, and Holy Spirit) which together constitute the Trinity. (Cf. ESSENCE *sb.* 4 b, HYPOSTASIS 5, SUBSTANCE.)

c **1250** *Gen. & Ex.* 55 For ðhre persones and on reed, On miȝt and on godfulhed. *c* **1315** SHOREHAM vii. 143 Wat may þe holy gost nou be? Persone þrydde in trynyte. **1340** HAMPOLE *Pr. Consc.* 14 The sam God..That woned ever in his godhede, And in thre persons and anhede. *a* **1425** *Cursor M.* 288 (Trin.) þerfore he is þe trinite þat is o god and persones þre. **1529** MORE *Dyaloge* I. Wks. 145/1 If yᵉ one beleued in all the thre parsones of the trinite, yᵉ father yᵉ sone & the holy gost. **1663–70** SOUTH *Serm.* (1727) IV. vii. 284 A Plurality of Persons, or Personal Subsistences in the Divine Nature, is a great Mystery, and so to be acknowledged by all who really are, and profess themselves Christians. **1768–74** TUCKER *Lt. Nat.* (1834) II. 188 The divine persons differ in another manner than human persons. **1833** J. H. NEWMAN *Arians* II. ii. (1876) 155 The mysteriousness of the doctrine evidently lies in our inability to conceive a sense of the word *person*, such, as to be more than a mere character, yet less than an individual intelligent being. *Ibid.* v. i. 365 The word *Person* which we venture to use in speaking of those three distinct and real modes in which it has pleased Almighty God to reveal to us His being.

†b. Substance: = HYPOSTASIS 3. *Obs. rare*$^{-1}$.

1548 GEST *Pr. Masse* in H. G. Dugdale *Life* (1840) App. I. 87 Semblable though the sayd body [of Christ] be presented in the bred, howbeit it is not become one person therwith.

c. The personality of Christ, esp. as uniting the two natures, divine and human; = HYPOSTASIS 5 (*d*).

1562 *Articles of Religion* ii, Two whole and perfect Natures..were joined together in one Person. **1855** LYNCH *Lett. to Scattered* ii. 34 Christianity shows itself in immense breadths of time and life, which imply Profundity in the Person of Christ.

VI. 8. *Gram.* Each of the three classes of personal pronouns, and corresponding distinctions in verbs, denoting or indicating respectively the person speaking (***first person***), the person spoken to (***second person***), and the person or thing spoken of (***third person***); each of the different forms or inflexions expressing these distinctions.

[Gr. πρόσωπον in Dionysius Thrax; L. *persōna* in Varro.] **1520** WHITINTON *Vulg.* (1527) 8 b, Ye verbe shal be ye fyrst persone. **1530** PALSGR. Introd. 27 This tong hath thre parsones in bothe the nombres of theyr verbes. *Ibid.*, Euery substantyue is onely of the thyrde parson. **1672** PETTY *Pol. Anat.* (1691) 97 The Quakers..speak to one another in the second Person and singular Number. **1764** W. PRIMATT *Accentus Redivivi* 111 The Dorians penacuted verbs ending ον,..that is, provided they were third persons plural. **1845** STODDART in *Encycl. Metrop.* (1847) I. 62/1 In many Languages the person is necessarily expressed by a pronoun. This is universally the case in the Chinese,..the verb being alike in all the persons. *c* **1850** [see APOCOPATE *ppl. a.*]. **1905** [see THOU *pers. pron.* 2 b]. **1951** V. NABOKOV *Speak, Memory* i. 17 In addressing me, a small boy, he used the plural of the second person. **1962** J. G. BENNETT *Witness* xxv. 333 She never said 'I', but always referred to herself in the third person as 'Madame' or even 'she'. **1966** J. DERRICK *Teaching Eng. to Immigrants* ii. 89 The teacher must proceed slowly and patiently, and again has good reason for confining questions to 1st and 2nd person forms only at first.

VII. 9. *Zool.* Each individual of a compound or 'colonial' organism, having a more or less independent life, and often specialized in form or function; a zooid.

1878 BELL *Gegenbaur's Comp. Anat.* 117 In the Pennatulidæ..some, and at times many, persons in a colony are less well-developed. *Ibid.*, 123 When the persons of a colony are dimorphic, those which are the more developed are at the same time those which are functionally sexual.

VIII. *Phrases and Comb.*

10. ***in*** one's (***own***) ***person***, formerly also ***in*** (one's) ***proper person*** (= L. *in propriâ personâ*): †**a.** = in person (see 11). *Obs.* **b.** In one's own character (not as representing another): see sense 1.

a. [**1292** BRITTON I. i. § 1 Pur ceo qe nous ne suffisums mie en nostre propre persone a oyer et terminer totes les quereles del poeple. *trans.* Inasmuch as we are not sufficient in our proper person to hear and determine all the complaints of our said people.] **1340** HAMPOLE *Pr. Consc.* 4958 For to sytte in dome in proper parsoun. *c* **1380** WYCLIF *Sel. Wks.* III. 443 Aftur þat a man deserves in his owne persoyne schal he be rewardid. **1390** GOWER *Conf.* I. 5 The which noman in his persone Mai knowe. **1472–3** *Rolls of Parlt.* VI. 52/1 That the said John Myrfeld, Richard Ledys, and either of theym, in their propre persone and persones appere. **1526** *Pilgr. Perf.* (1531) 13 He wolde be in his owne persone, the example of our hole iourney. **1560** DAUS tr. *Sleidane's Comm.* 375 They haue ofte intreated you, sometime by their Ambassadours, and somtime in their own persons.

b. 1692 WASHINGTON tr. *Milton's Def. Pop.* M.'s Wks. 1738 I. 503 Not such as the Poet would speak, if he were to speak in his own person. **1875** JOWETT *Plato* (ed. 2) III. 266 The poet is speaking in his own person. [See sense 1.]

11. ***in person***: with or by one's own action or bodily presence; personally; oneself.

1568 GRAFTON *Chron.* II. 631 King Iames..then beyng there in person. **1597** SHAKS. *2 Hen. IV*, II. i. 127 (Quarto), You haue..made her serue your vses both in pwrse and in person. **1671** MILTON *Samson* 851 Princes of my country came in person, Solicited, commanded, threatn'd, urg'd. **1748** *Anson's Voy.* II. vi. 205 To return him thanks in person. **1782** PRIESTLEY *Corrupt. Chr.* II. x. 260 Charlemaigne excused the bishops from serving in person. **1868** FREEMAN *Norm. Conq.* II. ix. 310 Others crossed the sea in person.

12. ***in the person of*** (***in his*** or ***her person***).
a. In the character of, as the representative of, as personally representing. See sense 1.
b. Embodied or invested in; impersonated in; (as) personally represented by.

1582–3 *Reg. Privy Council Scot.* III. 541 A power strange and unsufferabill to be in the persoun of ony inferior subject. **1678** DRYDEN *All for Love* Pref., Persecuting Horace and Virgil in the persons of their successours. **1809** KENDALL *Trav.* I. vii. 60 The company still subsists in the person of the state. **1859** TENNYSON *Enid* 216, I will avenge this insult, noble Queen, Done in your maiden's person to yourself.

13. ***to accept*** (†***take***), ***respect*** (†***behold***, †***look on***) ***persons***, or ***the person of*** any one: to look upon with favour, to favour, to show partiality, esp. on personal or improper grounds. (*Scriptural.*)

Person here represents L. *personam* of the Vulgate (which however has in some places *faciem*), the Gr. being πρόσωπον 'face, countenance, person', usually in the comb. προσωποληπτεῖν 'to accept the face of', rendering Heb. *nāsā' pānīm* 'to lift up or accept the face' (prob. orig. to lift up the face of one prostrated in humility or supplication).

a **1300** *Cursor M.* 19944 (Cott.), I se he [Petre] said..þat godd, þat mad for us ranscun, Bihaldes noght mans persun. **1382** WYCLIF *Luke* xx. 21 Thou takist not persoone of man, but thou techist in treuth the wey of God. —— *Rom.* ii. 11 For accepciouns of persoones [*gloss*, that is, to putte oon bifore another withoute desert] is not anentis God. **1535** COVERDALE *1 Sam.* xxv. 35 Behold I haue herkened vnto thy voyce, and accepted thy personne [Vulg. *honoravi faciem tuam*]. —— *Ps.* lxxxi. 2 How longe wil ye geue wronge iudgment & accepte the persounes of the vngodly? **1539** BIBLE (Great) *Acts* x. 34 There is no respecte of parsones wyth God [*Vulg.* Non est personarum acceptor Deus; 1382 WYCLIF not acceptour of persoones; *Rhem.* not an accepter ..; 1526 TINDALE God is not parciall; 1611 God is no respecter of persones]. [See also ACCEPT *v.* 2, ACCEPTER, ACCEPTION 2, RESPECT *sb.* and *v.*, RESPECTER.]

14. *Comb.* **a. person-object** (*a*) *Gram.*, a personal object of a verb; (*b*) in psychoanalytic theory, the choice of a person as the object of one's libidinal energy; also *attrib.*; **person-oriented** *a.*, of that in which interest or concern is centred on the person as contrasted with (by implication) a theory or thing; **person-perception**, perception which leads to or constitutes awareness and understanding of another person or persons.

1647 FULLER *Good Th. in Worse T.* (1841) 132 When we are time-bound, place-bound, or person-bound. **1873** MISS M. BLIND tr. *Strauss' Old Faith & New* xlii. 169 The impersonal but person-shaping All. **1928** H. POUTSMA *Gram. Late Mod. Eng.* (ed. 2) I. I. iii. 176 It will, therefore, often be useful to distinguish person-objects and thing-objects. Even when both objects, considered apart from the context, are the names of things, one of them more or less distinctly suggests, through its connexions, thoughts of personal qualities. **1949** M. MEAD *Male & Female* vii. 154 The distinction between mother's body and the own body.. in person-object terms, is an important one. **1954** *Essays in Crit.* IV. 316 The pre-Hellenic nature cults are accused..of failing to own that the person-to-person drive must push on past the person-object situation to find a response which plays back. **1958** TAGIURI & PETRULLO (*title*) Person perception and interpersonal behaviour. *Ibid.* p. x, We propose using the term *person perception* whenever the perceiver regards the object as having the potential of representation and intentionality. **1964** M. ARGYLE *Psychol. & Social Probl.* iii. 36 Person perception has been made the object of considerable research. **1964** E. BECKER in I. L. Horowitz *New Sociol.* 123 The schizophrenic is..someone who has been accustomed to relating to symbol-objects rather than to person-objects. **1967** M. L. KING JR. in *Freedomways* VII. 114 We must rapidly begin the shift from a 'thing-oriented' society to a 'person-oriented' society. **1972** *Encycl. Psychol.* II. 336/1 An object of experience, especially a 'person-object'. **1972** *Jrnl. Social Psychol.* LXXXVI. 135 The concept of dependency has been used.. to describe person-oriented behavior. *Ibid.* LXXXVI. 23 Accurate person perception is repeatedly identified as an essential component of effectiveness in the research literature concerned with interpersonal functioning. **1973** J. LYONS *Experience* IV. viii. 241 Its major practitioners [*sc.* of encountering], who are likely to be ex-theologians, teachers, counselors, actors..—whatever field can furnish perceptive, person-oriented leaders—rather than formally trained psychotherapists.

b. With a period of time, as ***person-day***, ***-month***, units equivalent to one day, month, of one person's work or life. Cf. MAN *sb.*[1] 20 b.

1970 *Sci. Amer.* Feb. 91 In that year people in California spent some 235 million person-days in specified outdoor recreational activities, primarily swimming, picnicking, fishing and boating. **1975** *Nature* 30 Oct. 733/2 Under an agreement signed recently in Stockholm, scientists and experts from the two countries will exchange visits of 10 person-months a year.

† **'person**, *v. Obs. rare.* [f. prec.: cf. late L. *persōnāre* to represent.] = PERSONATE *v.* 5.

1643 MILTON *Divorce* II. xiv, Or let us person him like some wretched itinerary Judge.

person, obs. form of PARSON.

‖**persona** (pəˈsəʊnə). The Latin word for PERSON, q.v., used in certain phrases:

1. persona grata [late L.], an acceptable person or personage; originally applied to a diplomatic representative who is personally acceptable to the personage to whom he is accredited; **persona non grata** (pl. **personæ non gratæ**), an unacceptable or unwelcome person.

1882 *Standard* 20 Dec. 5 At a supper of criminals in full work in their profession he might be welcomed as a *persona grata*. **1884** E. W. HAMILTON *Diary* 2 Sept. (1972) II. 679 Malet did well at Versailles and is a *persona grata* to Bismarck, who was intimate with Malet's mother. **1904** CONRAD *Nostromo* I. vi. 86 See that, Mr. Gould? *Persona non grata*. That's the reason our government is never properly informed. **1928** 'BRENT OF BIN BIN' *Up Country* iv. 52 He was admirably suited to his calling at that time, and his education and personality made him *persona grata* to all his superiors, from the Surveyor-General downwards. **1928** D. L. SAYERS *Lord Peter views Body* vi. 151 Oh, I'll keep out of it... I shan't be exactly persona grata, don't you know. **1935** H. EDIB *Clown & his Daughter* xlii. 238 The fact that he is his father's son makes him *persona grata* in the Sultan's eyes. **1958** *Oxford Mail* 15 Feb. 1/2 The BMC management should have known that the introduction of two or three people who are persona non grata with the other 350 men in the shop would create difficulty. **1964** M. GOWING *Britain & Atomic Energy, 1939–1945* v. 172 He made it clear that Mr Akers was *persona non grata* to the Americans on account of his industrial connections with I.C.I. **1965** C. D. EBY *Siege of Alcázar* (1966) i. 30 At such times Army officers were *personae non gratae*. **1968** *Listener* 7 Nov. 603/3 Gandhi was..always *persona grata* with the high-ups. **1972** *Daily Tel.* 2 June 3/3 Your recent book has..caused a lot of annoyance here, and you would not be *persona grata* at Eton on the Fourth of June. **1973** *Times* 15 Feb. 7/8 In view of Pakistan's 'violation', the spokesman added, the Iraq Government had decided to retaliate by declaring the Pakistan Ambassador and a Second Secretary as *personae non gratae* and warning them against returning to Iraq. **1974** *Times* 23 Jan. 15/1 Moscow intercepts a Peking-bound Chinese diplomat..claims he is carrying espionage material, and declares him persona non grata. **1976** A. GREY *Bulgarian Exclusive* xvi. 109 With half a dozen telephone calls..you will be *persona non grata*..throughout Eastern Europe.

2. ***in propria persona***: see IN *Lat. prep.*

3. ***persona designata*** [Law L.], a specified person; one who is individually denominated, as opp. one who is included in a legal category or class consisting of several persons.

1875 *Law Rep. Chancery Appeal Cases* X. 359 The legatees in this case, although described as a class, are in fact *personæ designatæ* as much as if they were mentioned by name. **1876** H. S. THEOBALD *Conc. Treat. Construction of Wills* xiii. 114 My nephew Joseph is clearly *persona designata*, and the question then is whom did the testator mean to point out? **1955** *Times* 4 May 4/3 It was against him as the person designated to carry out certain functions prescribed by Act of Parliament of laying before each House of Parliament a draft scheme, and that was done as a *persona designata*. **1973** *Deb. Senate Canada* 19 June 4889/1 There have been examples of an appeal court challenging the actions of an appellate court judge when he was acting *persona designata*.

4. Pl. **personæ, personas. a.** A character deliberately assumed by an author in his writing; also *transf.*

1909 E. POUND (*title*) Personae. **1958** *Times Lit. Suppl.* 20 June 345/1 To this extent, Lewis Eliot is, as it were, a convenient and comfortable persona for his author. **1962** W. NOWOTTNY *Lang. Poets Use* ii. 42 So far as a particular kind of *persona* is necessary to the poem, the poet's diction must create it. **1963** AUDEN *Dyer's Hand* 401 The more closely his [*sc.* Byron's] poetic *persona* comes to resemble the epistolary *persona* of his letters to his male friends..the more authentic his poetry seems. **1976** *Gramophone* Dec. 965/3 George Logan and Patric Fyffe in the *personae* of Dr Evadne Hinge and Dame Hilda Bracket are on EMI One-Up OU2125 (7/76).

b. In Jungian psychology, the set of attitudes adopted by an individual to fit himself for the social role which he sees as his; the personality an individual presents to the world; also *loosely*. Opp. ANIMA.

1917 C. E. LONG tr. *Jung's Coll. Papers Analytical Psychol.* (ed. 2) xv. 466 The persona is always identical with a *typical* attitude, in which *one* psychological function dominates, *e.g.* feeling, or thought, or intuition. **1923** [see ANIMA]. **1931** H. G. WELLS *Work, Wealth & Happiness of Mankind* (1932) viii. 298 A man's guiding and satisfying idea of himself is what Jung calls his '*persona*'. *Ibid.* xii. 617 There was nothing in their personas to prevent it. **1935** *Trans. Philol. Soc.* 66 We are born individuals. But to satisfy our needs we have to become social persons, and every social person is a bundle of rôles or *personæ*. **1936** 'M. INNES' *Death at President's Lodging* iii. 51 In the Dean's *persona* the episcopal idea had of late been rapidly developing. **1940** H. G. WELLS *Babes in Darkling Wood* IV. ii. 333 Some austerer element in his make-up was putting his *persona* on trial. **1966** COX & ROLFE tr. *Herzog's Psyche & Death* xv. 193 The dreamer has to answer for himself in his own right—he cannot claim the protection of the persona of his office. **1972** *Observer* 30 Jan. 9/6 He can be a pompous, contentious man, yet his private persona sometimes contrasts sharply with his more abrasive public image... He has also kept his dignity, consistently refusing to exploit or trivialise his public persona in the lucrative entertainment field.

personable (ˈpɜːsənəb(ə)l), *a.* [f. PERSON *sb.* + -ABLE: cf. 16th c. F. *personnable.*]

1. Having a well-formed person or body; well-made, handsome; good-looking, comely, presentable. (Now chiefly in literary use.)

c **1430** *Syr Gener.* (Roxb.) 1552 His bodie so personable and plesaunt, So feir and so wel y-wroght. **1540–1** ELYOT *Image Gov.* 102 One woman..hath manie children, of theym some be fayre and personable, some ill fauoured and croked. **1622** S. WARD *Life of Faith in Death* (1627) 69 The most personable Creature that euer the Sunne saw. **1723** SWIFT *Cook Maid's Lett.* Wks. 1755 III. II. 205 My master is a personable man, and not a spindle-shank'd hoddy-doddy. **1815** *Sporting Mag.* XLV. 79 She was..too personable and attractive a nymph to be without a swain. **1890** BESANT *Armorel of Lyonesse* I. vi, Certainly, he was a personable young man.

†**2.** *Law.* Having the status of a legal person (PERSON 6), and as such competent to maintain a plea in court, or to take anything granted or given. *Obs.*

1544 tr. *Littleton's Tenures* 68 Whan he is made abbot he is as a man personable [LITTLETON *edd.* 1481–1530 vn home ou person; *ed.* 1557 parsonable] in the lawe, alonly to purchase and to haue landes and tenementes..to the vse of his house, & nat to his owne proper vse. **1607** COWELL *Interpr.* s.v., The tenent pleaded that the wife was an alien borne in Portingall... The plaintife saith: shee was made personable by Parlament, that is, as the Ciuilians would speake it, *habere personam standi in iudicio*. Personable is also as much, as to be of capacitie to take any thing graunted or giuen. *Ibid.* s.v. *Personal*, The demaundant was judged personable to maintaine this action. **1660** SHERINGHAM *King's Suprem.* vii. (1682) 68 All agreed that the King was Personable, and discharged from all attainder in the very act that he took the Kingdom upon him.

†**3.** = PERSONAL. *Obs.*

1632 *Virginia Stat.* (1823) I. 172 Exempted from theire personable service in the warrs.

Hence **'personableness**, personal handsomeness.

1604 T. WRIGHT *Passions* V. iv. 223 An apt figure, and personablenes of body. **1654** R. CODRINGTON tr. *Iustine* I. 21 Darius besides his personableness and his vertue, was of neer relation in blood to the ancient Kings. *c* **1815** JANE AUSTEN *Persuas.* iii, I know no other set of men but what lose something of their personableness when they cease to be quite young.

†**'personably**, *adv. Obs.* [f. prec. + -LY[2].]

1. Like a personage of importance; in grand style.

1481 CAXTON *Reynard* xix. (Arb.) 47 Yf ye had seen reynart how personably he wente wyth hys male and palster on his sholder [*Du.* hoe persoenliken hi doe ghinc].

2. = PERSONALLY. [Cf. OF. *personablement* = *personnellement*.]

1483 CAXTON *Gold. Leg.* 371 b/1 He myght not hym self entende personably vnto hys thynges. **1538** FITZHERB. *Just. Peas* 125 Upon payn of forty pounds personably to appere before the kinge.

personage (ˈpɜːsənɪdʒ). [a. OF. *personage*, *-ounage* (13th c. in Godef.), mod.F. *personnage*

= Pr. *personatge*, It. *personaggio*, med.L. *persōnāticum* (1057 in Du Cange), *-āgium*, deriv. of *persōna* PERSON: see -AGE.]

†**1.** A representation or figure of a person; an image or effigy; a statue or portrait. *Obs.*

1483 in *Lett. Rich. III & Hen. VII* (Rolls) I. 6 There was a personage like to the symilitude of the king in habet royall crowned with the crown oon his hede. **1588** PARKE tr. *Mendoza's Hist. China* 186 The gate was wrought of masons warke of stone..full of figures or personages. **1601** HOLLAND *Pliny* VII. xxxviii, Alexander streightly forbad.. That no man should draw his pourtrait in colours but Apelles the painter: that none should engraue his personage but Pyrgoteles the grauer. **1604** E. G[RIMSTONE] *D'Acosta's Hist. Indies* V. xxix. 420 Upon this litter they set the personage of the idoll, appoynted for the feast. **1607-12** BACON *Ess., Beauty* (Arb.) 210 Apelles, or Albert Durere,.. Whereof the one would make a Parsonage by Geometricall proporcions, the other, by takeing the best partes out of divers faces to make one excellent.

†**2.** The body of a person; chiefly with reference to appearance, stature, etc.; bodily frame, figure; personal appearance: = PERSON *sb.* 4. (In quot. 1785 humorously for the 'person' or 'body'.) *Obs.*

1461 *Rolls of Parlt.* V. 463/1 The beaute of personage that it hath pleased Almyghty God to send You. *c* **1559** R. HALL *Life Fisher* in *Fisher's Wks.* (E.E.T.S.) II. p. lxiij, Doctor Ridley (who was a man of verie little and small personage). **1606** BRYSKETT *Civ. Life* 32 Well borne, vertuous, chaste, of tall and comely personage, and well spoken. **1680** MORDEN *Geog. Rect.* (1685) 344 The Armenians are..of comely Personage. **1701** C. WOLLEY *Jrnl. New York* (1860) 57 Of a Gentile Personage, and a very agreeable behaviour in conversation. **1785** COWPER *Let. to Lady Hesketh* 20-24 Dec., Half a dozen flannel waistcoats..to be worn..next my personage.

fig. **1593** G. HARVEY *Pierce's Super.* Wks. (Grosart) II. 103 His stile addeth fauour, and grace to beauty; and in a goodly Boddy representeth a puissant Soule. How few verses carry such a personage of state?

†**b.** A person of (such and such a) figure or appearance: = PERSON *sb.* 4 b. *Obs.*

1568 GRAFTON *Chron.* II. 594 Hee being a tall and hardie personage. **1653** HOLCROFT *Procopius, Goth. Wars* III. 75 He was a beautifull personage, tall, and of the goodliest countenance that could be seen. **1706** PHILLIPS, *Personage*, the same with Person; as She was a comely Personage. **1807** WORDSW. *Wh. Doe* III. 145 The monumental pomp of age Was with this goodly Personage.

3. A person (man or woman) of high rank, distinction, consideration, or importance; a person of note. (Originally always with *great* or the like qualification, which in the 19th c. began to be implied in calling any one 'a personage'.)

1503-4 *Act 19 Hen. VII*, c. 25 *Preamble*, Honorable personages to have joint..power with the seid persones rehersed. **1532** SIR J. RUSSELL in Ellis *Orig. Lett.* Ser. II. I. 301 As for the greate personages that be taken..none of them shalbe as yet put to no raunsome. **1654** EARL MONM. tr. *Bentivoglio's Warrs Flanders* 42 The Councel of Spain was then full of many eminent personages. **1683** *Brit. Spec.* 268 Her Majesty, is a Personage endowed with rare Perfections both of Mind and Body. **1812** LD. MILTON *Sp. Ho. Com.* 1 Dec., The Great Personage at the Head of the Government. **1845** D'ISRAELI *Sybil* vii, Sir John Warren bought another estate, and picked up another borough. He was fast becoming a personage. **1893** F. F. MOORE *I Forbid Banns* (1899) 120 Lady Ashenthorpe was a Personage. That she had become a Personage, proved that she possessed a large amount of tact.

b. In weakened or generalized sense: A person; a man or woman (whose status the speaker does not know, or does not desire to specify).

Sometimes applied ironically or laughingly to a self-important person, who considers himself 'a personage'; also with mixture of other senses.

a **1555** BRADFORD *Let. to Lady Vane* in Foxe *A. & M.* (1583) 1648 Many whiche were in comparison of Peter, but rascall personages. **1668** LLOYD (*title*) Memoires of the Lives..of those Personages who Suffered for the Protestant Religion. **1766** GOLDSM. *Vic. W.* xxx, The personage whom we had long entertained as a harmless amusing companion. **1786** MRS. A. M. BENNETT *Juvenile Indiscr.* II. 56 The Seraphic Miss Franklin, was, in his present opinion, a very disgusting personage. **1818** R. SHARP *Lett. & Ess.* (1834) 54 Your shrewd, sly, evil-speaking fellow is generally a shallow personage. **1879** GEO. ELIOT *Theo. Such* ii. 28 No impassioned personage wishes he had been born in the age of Pitt. **1890** 'R. BOLDREWOOD' *Col. Reformer* (1891) 215 That ready-witted and helpful personage.

†**4.** The quality of being a person or persons; personality. *Obs. rare.*

1526 *Pilgr. Perf.* (W. de W. 1531) 198 b, For here is no consubstancialite nor personage, whiche is in yͤ deite.

†**5.** Personal identity, personality, individual self. ***our personages***, ourselves. *Obs.*

1531 ELYOT *Gov.* III. xxv, Any thinge wherby our wittes may be amended and our personages be more apte to serue our publike weale. **1650** BULWER *Anthropomet.* 179 Acts of his personage and not of ours.

†**6.** The sort of person any one is, or is represented to be, in respect of character, rank, etc. *Obs.*

1534 WHITINTON *Tullyes Offices* I. (1540) 43 Poetes iudge comly what soeu[e]r becometh a man by his personage. **1560** COLE *Lett. to Jewell* ii, The greater personage you beare, the lesse cause haue ye to be put to answer. **1576** FLEMING *Panopl. Epist.* 242 Instruments whereʷᵗ he obteined estimation, and wonne worship conuenient for his proper personage. **1598** BARRET *Theor. Warres* IV. iv. 115 Many good parts ought to be in the parsonage of a Sergeant Maior.

7. One of the persons or characters of a drama (*dramatis personæ*), or of a dramatic poem, story, etc.; also one of the actors on the stage of history.

1573 in Cunningham *Acc. Revels Crt.* (Shaks. Soc. 1842) 32, Patternes for personages of Men & Women in strange attyer. **1579** E. K. in *Spenser's Sheph. Cal.* Ep. to Harvey §1 His [Spenser's] dewe obseruing of Decorum everye where, in personages, in seasons, in matter, in speach. **1594** in Ellis *Orig. Lett.* Ser. I. III. 33 There being in that Tragœdie sondry personages of greatest astate, to be represented in auncient princely attire. **1751** JOHNSON *Rambler* No. 156 ⁋6 Only three speaking personages should appear at once upon the stage. **1828** D'ISRAELI *Chas. I*, I. Pref. 7 The motives of the personages are sometimes as apparent as their actions. **1862** TROLLOPE *Orley F.* xix, I intend that Madeline Staveley shall..be the most interesting personage in this story.

b. Hence, the impersonation or acting of such a character, the part (acted); in the phrases, *to* ***take upon oneself, put on, play, assume the personage of***; also *fig.* and *transf.*, in ***to represent the personage of***.

1559 *Mirr. Mag.* (1563) B ij, I will take upon me the personage of the last,..full of woundes, miserably mangled, with a pale countenaunce, and grisly looke. **1582** MULCASTER *1st Pt. Elem.* Pref., Her Majestie representeth the personage of the hole land. **1632** J. HAYWARD tr. *Biondi's Eromena* 37 You have hitherto represented the personage of one, whom you are not. **1641** LD. J. DIGBY *Sp. in Ho. Com.* 21 Apr. 3 Judges wee are now, and must put on another personage. **1651** tr. *De-las-Coveras' Don Fenise* 78 Every one of us played so well his personage in this Comedy. **1685** COTTON tr. *Montaigne* I. xix. (1877) I. 75 Whatsoever personage a man takes upon himself to perform, he ever mixes his own part with it. **1901** *Pall Mall G.* 27 Feb. 6/1 It is common for tragedians to shut themselves up in their dressing-rooms between the acts of a play, and to reassume their personage immediately on being called.

†**c.** Assumed or pretended character; acting; semblance. *Obs.*

1572 tr. *Buchanan's Detect. Q. Mary* M iv, At Setons sche threw away all hir disguisit personage of mourning.

8. Phrases. †***in one's own personage***, in person (PERSON 10), personally (*obs.*). ***in the personage of***, †**a.** in the character of, as representing (*obs.*); **b.** as represented by; personified in; = *in the person of* (PERSON 12 a, b).

1534 CRANMER *Misc. Writ.* (Parker Soc.) II. 291 In case I had so spoken the same unto you in my own personage. *Ibid.* 294 To examine in your own personage the said misdoers. **1553** KENNEDY *Compend. Tract.* in *Wodrow Soc. Misc.* (1844) 153 Spekying unto his Apostolis in the personage of the rest of the ministeris of the Kirk of God. **1888** J. PAYN *Prince of Blood* I. i. 30 'Circumstances over which she had no control', in the personage of her brother Ernest, were impelling her.

personage, obs. form of PARSONAGE.

personal (ˈpɜːsənəl), *a.* (*sb.*) Also 4-5 -el, etc., 6 parsonal(l. [a. OF. *personal* (12th c. in Hatz.-Darm.), *-el* (mod.F. *-onnel*), ad. L. *persōnāl-is* of or pertaining to a person (in Law or Gram.), f. *persōna* PERSON: see -AL[1].]

A. *adj.* **1. a.** Of, pertaining to, concerning, or affecting the individual person or self (as opposed, variously, to other persons, the general community, etc., or to one's office, rank, or other attributes); individual; private; one's own. Rarely in reference to an animal (quot. 1796).

personal EQUATION, *personal* IDENTITY: see these words.

1387 TREVISA *Higden* (Rolls) III. 115 Seruius Tullius.. ordeyned first personal tribute [L. *censum*] to þe Romayns. **1565** CALFHILL *Answ. Treat. Crosse* vi. 135 Examples be daungerous to be followed..bycause they be sometime but personall. **1601** SHAKS. *Jul. C.* II. i. 11, I know no personall cause, to spurne at him, But for the generall. **1683** *Col. Rec. Pennsylv.* I. 236 Know no reason why they might not give their personal bills to such as would take them as money to pass. **1782** LD. AUCKLAND *Let.* 22 Aug. (1861) I. 29 Lord North, too, could on *very easy* terms answer for thirty or forty, quite as personal friends and followers. *a* **1794** GIBBON *Mem.* (1796) I. 71 Mr. Allamand, Minister at Bex, was my personal friend. **1796** HUNTER tr. *St.-Pierre's Stud. Nat.* (1799) I. 79 Even the instincts of animals appear to be less adapted to their own personal utility, than to that of Man. **1818** CRUISE *Digest* (ed. 2) III. 182 Although dignities are now become little more than personal honours; yet they are still classed under the head of real property. **1845** M. PATTISON *Ess.* (1889) I. 18 It required all the personal influence of the king to check the turbulence of his irritated followers. **1853** C. BRONTË *Villette* I. xv. 304 Had that audience numbered as many personal friends and acquaintance for me, as for him, I know not how it might have been. **1915** T. F. A. SMITH *Soul of Germany* 54 Opponents are often personal friends, but that makes no difference. **1938** AUDEN & ISHERWOOD *On Frontier* I. i. 24 The Valerian School..will educate your dear little kiddies in Patriotism and Personal Hygiene. **1970** *Guardian* 17 Aug. 7/5 Much propaganda about 'personal hygiene' is on the wrong track... Why the obsession with stopping *fresh* perspiration? **1979** D. ATTENBOROUGH *Life on Earth* xi. 248 The sloth..pays such little attention to its personal hygiene that green algae grow on its coarse hair.

b. Const. *to* (cf. *proper to, peculiar to*).

a **1768** ERSKINE *Inst. Law Scot.* I. iv. §12. 58 The jurisdiction annexed to the principality is not heritable, but personal to the King's eldest son. **1844** LINGARD *Anglo-Sax. Ch.* (1858) I. ii. 61 The authority..was personal to Augustine, and not intended to descend from him to his successors. **1874** S. WILBERFORCE *Ess.* I. 376 This is personal to himself.

c. Designating an official or employee attached to one's person in a subordinate capacity, as ***personal assistant, maid***, etc.

1928 *Radio Times* 2 Nov. 301/3 My personal maid..[was] sent to service at 11 years. **1941** in G. Howell *In Vogue* (1975) 162 A personal maid..is absent, on munitions. **1956** *Times* 21 Jan. 7/5 An adequate type of skilled secretarial assistant could be ensured by certain responsible bodies.. holding examinations for executive secretaries/personal assistants (as opposed to company secretaries). **1958** P. SCOTT *Mark of Warrior* I. 21 'These chaps are your personal servants,' the receiving officer explained. **1964** M. LASKI in S. Nowell-Smith *Edwardian Eng.* iv. 144 Personal servants at least must wait up until their masters and mistresses chose to go to bed. **1972** T. P. MCMAHON *Issue of Bishop's Blood* iv. 44 Frank Velandi..three arrests for assault... Said at one time to be Streppelli's personal bodyguard. **1977** A. SCHOLEFIELD *Venom* v. 198 M. Michel Blanchet, the hotel millionaire wanted a personal maid for his new wife. **1978** W. GARNER *Möbius Trip* i. 21 Hand over the mouthpiece she called 'Prime Minister's personal assistant'.

2. a. Done, made, performed, held, etc. in person; involving the actual or immediate presence or action of the individual person himself (as opposed to a substitute, deputy, messenger, etc.). Of a reciprocal action or relation, Carried on or subsisting between individual persons directly.

c **1388** in *Wyclif's Sel. Wks.* III. 493 þai sayne, þat no persone ne vicare ne prelate is excusud fro personele residense to be made in þer beneficys. **1494** FABYAN *Chron.* II. an. 1407 (R.) With great dyffyculte he pacyfyed them agayn..and brought them to personall communycacion. **1588** SHAKS. *L.L.L.* II. i. 32 Tell him, the daughter of the King of France..Importunes personall conference with his grace. **1630** *R. Johnson's Kingd. & Commw.* 387 The one was their personall presence and travelling to the wars. **1733** C. COOTE 13 Dec. in *Swift's Lett.* (1768) IV. 59 Your allowing me to some degree of personal acquaintance with you. **1844** THIRLWALL *Greece* lxiv. VIII. 263 The wealthier citizens..bound by law to personal service in the cavalry. **1880** L. STEPHEN *Pope* iv. 85 Pope..did not enjoy the honour of any personal interview with royalty.

†**b.** Present or engaged in person. *Obs.*

1596 SHAKS. *1 Hen. IV*, IV. iii. 88 When hee was personall in the Irish Warre. **1600** E. BLOUNT tr. *Conestaggio* 152 Kings ought to be personall in their enterprises. **1617** MORYSON *Itin.* II. 211 None but we that are personall actors therein..can thorowly apprehend [etc.].

3. Of or pertaining to one's person, body, or figure; bodily: **a.** as an action or quality. †***personal oath*** (quot. 1577-87): = ***bodily*** or ***corporal oath*** (see CORPORAL *a.* 5 a).

a **1400-50** *Alexander* 5142 A purtrayour..scho prays with þam to pas, And his personele proporcions in perchemen hire bring. **1577-87** HOLINSHED *Chron.* III. 1 He tooke his personall oth before the altar of S. Peter at Westmister, to defend the holie church, and rulers of the same. **1597** SHAKS. *2 Hen. IV*, IV. iv. 8 Our Nauie is addressed, our Power collected... Onely wee want a little personall Strength. **1620** BRATHWAIT *Five Senses* in *Archaica* II. 82 It is..a personal comeliness, adds honour to our clothing. **1716** ADDISON *Freeholder* No. 21 ⁋3 A Princess whose Personal Charms..were now become the least part of her Character. **1865** LUBBOCK *Preh. Times* 21 The personal ornaments of the Bronze age consist principally of bracelets,..pins,..and rings.

b. as something affecting or having reference to one's person or body.

1591 HORSEY *Trav.* (Hakl. Soc.) 165 The Russ Emperor flies with his..personall guard of 20 thowsand gonnors, towards a stronge monesterie. **1765** BLACKSTONE *Comm.* I. i. 141 Three great and primary rights, of personal security, personal liberty, and private property. **1782** MISS BURNEY *Cecilia* VIII. iv, Turning their attention to her personal safety. **1796** MORSE *Amer. Geog.* I. 228 Designed..for the purpose of personal defence. **1824** SCOTT *Redgauntlet* ch. xvi, He shall have no personal ill-usage. **1861** MILL *Utilit.* (1862) 65 It is..considered unjust to deprive any one of his personal liberty.

4. a. Having an individual person as object; relating to a person in his individual capacity; directed to, aimed at, or referring to some particular person or to oneself personally, *spec.* in a disparaging or offensive sense or manner.

1614 T. LORKIN *Let.* in *Crt. & Times Jas. I* (1848) I. 346 If they had..not proceeded to personal invectives, and mutinous and seditious speeches against his majesty,..his favourites, and..the Scots in general. *a* **1729** J. ROGERS (J.), Publick reproofs of sin are general..; but in private conversations the application may be more personal. **1801** *Med. Jrnl.* V. 264 A dispute, which, by the conduct of my opponent, has degenerated into personal abuse. **1844** DICKENS *Mart. Chuz.* xi, He asked him distinctly,..as a personal favour too,..not to play. **1863** H. COX *Instit.* I. iv. 19 Private Acts of Parliament are divided into those which are *personal* and those which are *local*. **1888** J. INGLIS *Tent Life in Tigerland* 236, I seemed to take it as a personal insult that anybody..amid all the depressing surroundings, should dare to be cheerful.

b. Const. *to* (cf. *relative to*, etc.).

c **1680** HICKERINGILL *Hist. Whiggism* I. Wks. 1716 I. 56 The Earl of Arundel was restrained for a Misdemeanour, which was Personal to his Majesty. **1814** SCOTT *Wav.* xliii, He [the Prince] had a different and good natured motive, personal to our hero, for prolonging the conference.

c. Having oneself as object; directed to oneself.

1778 MISS BURNEY *Evelina* xxx, They have every one of them so copious a share of their own personal esteem. **1830** D'ISRAELI *Chas. I*, III. iv. 60 The strong personal vanity of the man.

d. *transf.* Making a personal remark, reflection, or attack; addicted to such remarks, etc.

1607 B. JONSON *Volpone* Ded., Where have I been particular? where personal? except to a mimic, cheater [etc.]. **1855** TENNYSON *Maud* I. x. ii, And therefore splenetic, personal, base, A wounded thing with a rancorous cry. **1882** PEBODY *Eng. Journalism* xxiii. 187 *Punch*..is racy, frank, and personal to a degree that often perplexes foreigners.

e. Of newspaper advertisements: small, on private matters (see also quot. 1902); esp. in ***personal column***.

1888 W. WHITMAN *Daybks. & Notebks.* (1978) II. 448 Letter from J. G. Bennett, N.Y. Herald, ask'g me to write for 'Personal' col Herald. **1902** *Encycl. Brit.* XXXI. 173/2 'Personal journalism', *i.e.*, paragraphs about the private life or personal appearance of individuals..of note or notoriety in society or public affairs, has become far more marked. **1936** *Discovery* Dec. 386/1 The 18th century 'personal' advertisement, dealing with such wants as wives, lost umbrellas, or menservants 'of black complexion and sound principles'. **1948** *Chicago Daily News* 30 Aug. 19/3 German newspapers have 'personal' columns filled with advertisements for mates. **1966** *Listener* 6 Jan. 14/2 Most of its members were gathered by putting an advertisement in the personal column of a daily newspaper. **1978** J. WAINWRIGHT *Ripple of Murders* 11 A small ad. in the Personal Column..will read 'J.D. Message received'.

f. Of a letter or other communication: intended for the attention of a particular recipient.

1934 G. B. SHAW *Too True to be Good* II. 50 Is this a personal letter to be sent on to him, or is it a dispatch? **1940** R. S. LAMBERT *Ariel & all his Quality* ix. 244 A letter was delivered..addressed 'H. Brown, Esq., Broadcasting House'. It was not marked 'Personal' or 'Private'. **1973** 'D. JORDAN' *Nile Green* i. 9 A stack of letters was open on my desk including..two which must have been marked 'Personal' on the envelope. **1978** J. SYMONS *Blackheath Poisonings* v. 241 The rectangular package was addressed..to Mr George Collard, and marked *Personal*.

g. Of a (transistor) radio or television: small (see quot. 1962).

1962 *Which?* Feb. 36/1 The two main categories are: personal radios, which will slip into a pocket—or are just too large to do so—and portable radios, which have to be carried. **1973** *Philadelphia Inquirer* 7 Oct. 16 (Advt.), Personal size 16" diagonal screen.

h. Of a computer: designed for use by an individual, esp. in an office or business environment.

1976 *Byte* May 90/2 You can do such modelling..using the personal computer as a central element. **1979** *Personal Computer World* Nov. 44/3 Denmark's personal computer industry has software for us. **1983** *Your Computer* (Austral.) Aug. 4 A personal computer..is a microprocessor-based machine with integrated video circuitry (or even screen) and keyboard, which is dedicated to use by a single person, and the software for which reflects the needs of a single person and not an organisation. **1985** *Listener* 17 Jan. 22/3 There are 400 word processor programs to choose from, and a vast range of personal computers.

5. a. Of, pertaining to, or characteristic of a person or self-conscious being, as opposed to a thing or abstraction.

1651 HOBBES *Leviath.* III. xxxiii. 206 If the Church be not one person, then it hath no authority at all,..nor has any will, reason nor voice: for all these qualities are personal. **1659** PEARSON *Creed* (1839) 435 Grief is certainly a personal affection, of which a quality is not capable. **1835** URE *Philos Manuf.* 5 At least double the amount of personal industry is engaged in the arts, manufactures, and trade, to what is engaged in agriculture. **1877** E. R. CONDER *Bas. Faith* i. 26 This unity is not..possessed of what we call personality; incapable therefore of sustaining any personal relation to man.

b. Having the nature of a person; that is a person, not a thing or abstraction.

a **1860** J. A. ALEXANDER *Gosp. Jesus Christ* xxxvi. (1861) 533 It is not before a mere abstraction that man trembles, but before a personal avenger. **1860** PUSEY *Min. Proph., Amos* v. 21 Worshipping 'nature', not a holy, Personal, God. **1880** HAUGHTON *Phys. Geog.* i. 1 Imagining..a personal creator of themselves and of the universe.

6. *Law.* Opposed to *real*: †**a.** originally, in ***personal action*** (or ***plea***), an action wherein the claim was not the restitution of a specific thing (since the thing might be destroyed, concealed, or transported beyond the reach of the law) but the recovery from the *person* concerned of compensation, i.e. of damages; distinguished from a *real action*, which claimed the restitution of the thing itself (being something indestructible and irremovable), and from a *mixed* action in which both restitution and damages were demanded. (This distinction is *Obs.*, real actions having fallen out of use early in 17th c., and been formally abolished in 1833. See Sweet *Dict. Eng. Law* 24.) Hence **b.** ***personal property*** (***estate***, etc.), things recoverable in the personalty or by a personal action, i.e. chattels and chattel interests in land, etc., as opposed to *real property* (*estate*, etc.), i.e. things recoverable in the realty, or by a real action; viz. land (in the legal sense: see LAND 4 c), and rights attached to the possession of land. ***personal property*** therefore includes generally all property except land and those interests in land which pass on the owner's death to his heir; corresponding in general (though not entirely) to the *movables* of Scotch, Continental, and Anglo-Indian law.

Personal and *real action* represent L. *actio in personam* and *actio in rem* of the Roman law, in which actions were distinguished by the nature of the right thereby asserted; the terms were taken by Bracton into English Law, but employed in a different way, to distinguish actions according to the process of execution obtained, that is, in reference not to the right asserted but to the relief afforded therein. The thing sought by Britton's *actio in rem* was restitution of a specific thing which the law was always able to lay hold of and hand over; this limited it to land and rights exercisable over or in respect of land. But land and its rights were hereditary possessions, descending to the owner's heirs, hence *real property* became coextensive with or equivalent to heritable property, and *personal property* came to include all other property; this again reacted upon the definition, inasmuch as the question whether any particular property was hereditary and passed to the heir, or was non-hereditary and passed to the executors or administrators, became the test whether the property or estate was real or personal; so that certain rights attached to land, came to be treated as *real* or *personal*, not according to the original application of these words, but according to the rule which had been established as to the descent of these rights severally. Thus leases, of whatever duration, as well as mortgages and securities for money affecting lands or heritable property, which in Scotland are themselves heritable and descend to the heir, in England go to the personal representative, and are classed as personal estate. (See T. Cyprian Williams in *Law Quarterly* IV. (1888); Pollock and Maitland *Hist. Eng. Law* II. 179–80, 568–70.)

a. [*c* **1250** BRACTON III. iii. §2 Personales vero actiones sunt quæ competunt contra aliquem ex contractu, vel quasi. **1292** BRITTON II. i. §1 Personels pletz pledables par attachementz de cors ou destresces des biens moebles. *a* **1294** HENGHAM *Summa Parva* i. (1616) 81 Post defaltam in actione Reali, non competit in personali.] **1448** *Shillingford's Lett.* (Camden) App. 139 Any action real personall and myxte apon any person or persons. *c* **1450** *Godstow Reg.* 304 Relesed to them and pardoned all accions reals and personels of eny maner cause I-begonne. **1544** tr. *Littleton's Tenures* III. iv. 73 b, Also as to accyons parsonels, tenauntes in comon ought to haue suche accyons parsonels Ioyntly in all theyr names. **1768** BLACKSTONE *Comm.* III. viii. 117 Personal actions are such whereby a man claims a debt, or personal duty, or damages in lieu thereof: and, likewise, whereby a man claims a satisfaction in damages for some injury done to his person or property. **1888** T. C. WILLIAMS in *Law Quarterly Rev.* IV. 401 Before the year 1832, the plaintiff in a personal action could never obtain final judgment against the defendant in default of appearance.

b. [*a* **1481** LITTLETON *Tenures* §497 En mesme le manere est de choses personelx. **1481** *Year-bk. 21 Edw. IV* (1599) 83 b, Cest annuitie est un chose personal.] **1544** tr. *Littleton's Tenures* III. iv. 74 There be possessyons and propertyes of Chatell reall and Chatell parsonal. **1622** BACON *Hen. VII* 123 Jewels, household-stuff, stocks upon his grounds, and other personal estate exceeding great. **1650** in *Bury Wills* (Camden) 226 The rest and residue of all my goods and personall estate whatsoeuer..I doe will vnto my executours towards the payment of my debts and legacies aforesaid. **1766** BLACKSTONE *Comm.* II. i. 13 In personal estates the father may succeed to his children; in landed property he never can be their immediate heir, by any the remotest possiblility. *Ibid.* xxiv. 385 But things personal, by our law, do not only include things moveable, but also something more: the whole of which is comprehended under the general name of chattels. **1838** W. BELL *Dict. Law Scot.* 735 In the law of England, the distinction between real and personal property, is almost, but not entirely, the same as the distinction between heritable and movable property in the law of Scotland. **1844** WILLIAMS *Real Prop.* (1875) 8 Funded property is personal. **1888** [see PERSONALTY]. **1895** MAITLAND *Bracton & Azo* (Selden Soc.) 173 It has been suggested that had Bracton looked a little deeper, we might have had no talk of 'real' and 'personal' property. **1895** POLLOCK & MAITLAND *Hist. Eng. Law* II. 180 When our orthodox doctrine has come to be that land is not owned, but that 'real actions' can be brought for it, while no 'real action' can be brought for just those things which are the subjects of 'absolute ownership', it is clear enough that the 'personalness' of 'personal property' is a superficial phenomenon.

c. ***personal contract, injury, law, representative***: see quots.

1796 A. ANSTRUTHER *Reports* I. 131 The personal representative is *in general* considered as trustee of the property devised from the testator, undisposed of, *as belonging to him*. **1832** RUSSELL & MYLNE *Rep. Cases Chancery* 1829–30 I. 589 The ordinary sense of the words 'personal representatives' is, executors and administrators. **1882** C. SWEET *Dict. Eng. Law* 200 A personal contract is one which depends upon the existence, or the personal qualities, skill, or services of one of the parties: such as a contract of marriage, or a contract to paint a picture. It follows from the nature of a personal contract that it cannot be assigned, and that it is discharged by the death of the party on whose personality it is founded. *Ibid.* 602 A personal injury is an injury to the person of an individual, such as an assault, as opposed to an injury to his property, such as a trespass. *Ibid.*, A system of laws is said to be personal, when its operation is limited to one of several races inhabiting a state, as in the case of India. **1883** *Wharton's Law Lex.* 725/1 An heir-at-law or devisee is a real representative; an executor or administrator is a personal representative. [But the executor has been made a 'real representative' for some purposes, by the Land Transfer Act, 1897 (Sir F. Pollock).] **1967** E. RUDINGER *Wills & Probate* 40 The people who deal with what you own when you die are called your personal representatives.

d. ***personal diligence, personal execution*** (Scots Law): (*a*) the process for enforcing performance of civil obligations by imprisonment of the debtor (opposed to diligence or execution against estate heritable or movable); now abolished, exc. in exceptional cases; (*b*) also used to include attachment of debtor's movables, as well as imprisonment (opposed to *real* diligence, i.e. against heritable estate).

a **1768** ERSKINE *Inst. Law Scot.* IV. iii. §24 The power of staying the execution of personal diligence might, if abused, greatly impair the right competent to creditors for the recovery of their debts. **1838** W. BELL *Dict. Law Scot.* 304 Personal diligence comprehends, 1st. Letters of Horning and of Caption..2d...the *meditatio fugæ* warrant..3d. The Border Warrant. **1861** *Ibid.* 287/2 The use of these letters [of Horning] is almost entirely superseded by the Personal Diligence Act, 1 and 2 Vict., c. 114, which authorizes warrant to charge, arrest, and poind to be inserted in extract decrees. **1886** GOUDY *Law of Bankruptcy* 644 By the Debtors' Act, 1880, and the Civil Imprisonment Act, 1882, personal diligence has been, with a few unimportant exceptions, altogether abolished.

7. *Gram.* Of or pertaining to the three persons; denoting one of these: see PERSON *sb.* 8. *spec.* **a.** said of a verb that has inflexions for all three persons (opp. to *impersonal*: now *rare*); **b.** used as the distinctive appellation of those pronouns which denote the first, second, and third persons respectively, viz. (in English) *I, thou, he*, in their various genders, numbers, and cases.

1530 PALSGR. 4 Verbes..as well personall as *il prent*..as impersonall as *il couient*. **1590** STOCKWOOD *Rules Construct.* 6 A verbe personal agreeth with his nominatiue case in number and person. **1668** WILKINS *Real Char.* 305 The Personal Pronouns, and any of the rest being us'd Substantively, are capable of Number and Case. **1871** ROBY *Lat. Gram.* II. xvii. §562 In the perfect indicative the personal suffix has dropped off altogether. **1879** FARRAR *St. Paul* I. 579 The needlessly frequent prominence of the first personal pronoun. **1889** MORFILL *Gram. Russ. Lang.* III. 53 Sometimes personal verbs are used impersonally by an idiom in which all the Slavonic languages share, as [*mne khóchetsya*], I wish, lit. it wishes itself to me.

†**8.** *Theol.* Of or pertaining to substance (see PERSON *sb.* 7 b): = HYPOSTATIC 1. *Obs.*

1548 GEST *Pr. Masse* in H. G. Dugdale *Life* (1840) App. I. 87 Soch..is the personal presence of christes godheade in hys manhode. **1624** GATAKER *Transubst.* 168 When as by personal union with himselfe, he giveth to the same body a far higher and more inconceivable manner of being.

¶**9.** Often (by confusion) for PERSONABLE *a.* 1.

1658 *Topsell's Four-f. Beasts* 40 A goodly well proportioned and personal [*ed.* 1607 personable] Prince. *c* **1760** *Charlton Ho. Papers* in *Sussex Archæol. Collect.* X. 47, I am told that the lad is very personal with his own hair. **1888** MRS. LYNN LINTON *Thro' Long Night* I. viii, She..made him out at last to be really quite personal and presentable.

10. Special collocations, as ***personal appearance***, (*a*) the appearance or presence of an individual (esp. a celebrity) in person; (*b*) the visual aspect or looks of a person, considered in terms of dress, grooming, and expression; ***personal bill***, a private bill (BILL *sb.*[3] 3) usu. introduced in the House of Lords, relating to the estate, status, or other personal concern of an individual (see also quot. 1844); ***personal call***, a telephone call in which the caller specifies to the operator the person to whom he wishes to speak, and only the time so spent is charged for (in addition to a fixed service charge); ***personal caller***, a prospective client who establishes personal contact with a business; ***personal explanation***, a statement made by a Member of the House of Commons in explanation or mitigation of recent conduct; ***personal god***, a god possessing personal attributes; ***personal government***, autocratic rule in which effective power is vested in the person of a monarch (commonly associated with the reign of George III); ***personal idealism***, philosophical idealism which emphasizes the essential role of the conscious person in relation to perception of external reality and, usu., also in relation to God as supreme Person; akin to PERSONALISM b; hence ***personal idealist***; ***personal loan***, a loan made to an individual for his private requirements by a finance company or bank; ***personal name***, the name by which an individual (occas. a thing) is distinguished or identified; ***personal shopper***, one who shops in person, as opposed to by mail-order; ***personal touch***, a personal element introduced into something otherwise institutional or impersonal.

1610 S. RID *Martin Mark-all* sig. A 3, They presently send to the Beadle of the Hall to make his personal appearance at the Swan with five necks in Kings Streete. **1736** M. W. MONTAGU *Let.* Dec. (1966) II. 111 Halfe those aspirations to the B.V. would deserve her personal appearance to encourrage so sincere a Votary. **1842** DICKENS *Amer. Notes* I. viii. 277 Comparing notes on my personal appearance with as much indifference as if I were a stuffed figure. **1883** [see APPEARANCE 2]. **1914** G. B. SHAW *Fanny's First Play* 152 Mr Trotter..assisted the make-up by which Mr Claude King so successfully simulated his personal appearance. **1951** S. J. PERELMAN in *New Yorker* 2 June 26/3, I caught your personal appearance at the Mastbaum in Philly. **1962** L. DEIGHTON *Ipcress File* xvi. 92 A cinema where a nineteen-year-old rock-an'-roll singer was making a personal appearance for £600. **1972** *N.Y. Law Jrnl.* 22 Aug. 8/1 *Personal Appearances*..Ping Keun Chu v. Jade Fountain of Paramus, Inc. [etc.]. **1976** T. HEALD *Let Sleeping Dogs Die* i. 7 She had little time for clothes and cared nothing for her personal appearance. [**1683** Personal bill: see PERSONAL *a.* 1 a.] **1844** T. E. MAY *Treat. Parliament* xxviii. 457 All private bills, during their progress in the commons, are known by the general denomination of private bills; but in the lords the term 'private' is applied *technically* to estate bills only, all other bills being distinguished as 'local' or 'personal', although in the standing orders no such distinction is expressed. **1929** G. F. M. CAMPION *Introd. Proc. House of Commons* ix. 274 Personal Bills, *i.e.* Estate, Divorce, Naturalisation, Restitution and Name Bills.. always originate in the Lords. **1973** *Jrnl. House of Lords* (1974) 14 Nov. CCVI. 29/2 Personal Bills: Select Comee appointed. **1930** *Telegr. & Telephone Jrnl.* XVI. 70/2 Another important event of the past year was the introduction of the 'personal' call system in the Inland and Anglo-Continental trunk services. **1947** AUDEN *Age of Anxiety* (1948) ii. 43 To be held waiting in A packed lounge for a Personal Call From Long Distance. **1960** [see PERSON-TO-PERSON *adj.* (and *adv.*) *phr.* a]. **1967** E. LEMARCHAND *Death of Old Girl* ii. 21 There's a phone call for you... A personal call from London. **1978** F. DURBRIDGE *Tim Frazer gets Message* iv. 61 Can Miss Thackery take a personal call? **1966** *Listener* 25 Aug. 291 (Advt.), Send now for a free copy... For personal callers —235 Grand Buildings, Trafalgar Sq., W.C.2. Tel.: WHItehall 8377. **1976** *Norwich Mercury* 19 Nov. 12/5 (Advt.), Personal callers will be welcomed by a receptionist at Prospect House. **1844** T. E. MAY *Treat. Parliament* xi. 195 (*heading*) Personal explanation. **1857** *Sat. Rev.* 14 Feb. 152/2 That green oasis in the desert of legislation—that dainty morsel in the sessional banquet—a personal explanation, which, in Mr. Disraeli's hands, was pretty sure to include also a personal attack. **1886** J. BAILEY *Let.* 11 Apr. (1935) 24, I might say a good deal on this subject but as the House of Commons has lately made personal explanations vulgar, I don't think I will. **1974** *House of Commons Man. Procedure Publ. Business* (ed. 11) viii. 116 By the indulgence of the House, a Member may make a personal explanation, although there is no question before the House, but in this case no debatable matter may be brought forward, and no debate can arise. **1860** Personal God [see sense 5 b]. *a* **1902** S. BUTLER *Way of All Flesh* (1903) xlix. 225 There is not one of you here who doubts the existence of a Personal God. **1921** G. B. SHAW *Back to Methuselah* p. xlii, We had been so oppressed by the notion that everything that happened in the world was the arbitrary personal act of an arbitrary personal god of dangerously jealous and cruel personal character, so that even the relief of the pains of childbed and the operating table by chloroform was objected to as interference with his arrangements which he would probably resent, that we just jumped at Darwin. **1963** J. A. T. ROBINSON *Honest to God* iii. 48 The difference.. can perhaps best be expressed by asking what is meant by speaking of a *personal* God. Theism.. understands by this a supreme Person, a self-existent subject.., who enters into a relationship with us comparable with that of one human personality with another. **1976** P. HILL *Hunters* vi. 73 An allegedly all-powerful and personal God. **1909** W. TOYNBEE *Glimpses of Twenties* i. 1 George the Third.. ascended the throne with a fixed determination to re-establish 'personal government', which quickly aroused the misgivings of even his best-affected subjects. **1954** *Proc. Brit. Acad.* XXXVIII. 225 We no longer believe that George III's system of personal government came to an end in 1784, and that power was then transferred from the King to the Prime Minister. **1901** G. H. HOWISON (*title*) The limits of evolution, and other essays illustrating the metaphysical theory of personal idealism. **1921** *Encycl. Relig. & Ethics* XII. 229/2 Where personal idealism means spiritual pluralism of a theistic type, the concept of purpose applied to the interpretation of the universe yields a conclusion that satisfies. **1966** F. COPLESTON *Hist. Philos.* VIII. III. xiii. 296 It is so often religiously minded people who are attracted in the first instance to personal idealism. **1902** H. STURT *Personal Idealism* p. vi, Naturalism and Absolutism, then, are the adversaries against whom the personal idealist has to strive. **1966** F. COPLESTON *Hist. Philos.* VIII. III. xiii. 296 Unless the personal idealist equates ultimate reality with the system of finite selves, as McTaggart did, he must be a theist. **1914** *Laws State of N.Y.* II. 1435 When authorized by the superintendent of banks.. three or more persons.. may form a corporation to be known as a personal loan company. **1957** D. KARP *Leave me Alone* v. 80 Individual enterprisers offered.. dry cleaning, baked goods.. personal loans. **1958** *Times* 29 Aug. 8/7 Barclays are after all to be the first of the banks to bring a personal loans scheme into operation. **1961** *Which?* May 103/1 The banks have started 'Personal Loan' schemes, whereby you can borrow money from a bank without providing security. **1979** *Guardian* 5 Feb. 15/4 Basically the clearing banks offer three kinds of packages: overdraft facilities; loan accounts, and personal loans. **1748** B. MARTIN *Institutions of Lang.* 27 Of nouns or names there are three sorts, common, proper or personal, and relative... Proper or personal names are such as denote the individuals of each species; as Cæsar,.. London, Paris, &c. **1871** E. B. TYLOR *Primitive Culture* I. viii. 276 Up from this savage level the same childlike habit of giving personal names to lifeless objects may be traced, as we read of Thor's hammer, Miölnir. **1911** J. G. FRAZER *Golden Bough*: *Taboo* (ed. 3) vi. 318 (*heading*) Personal names tabooed. **1925** O. JESPERSEN *Mankind, Nation & Individual* ix. 172 The Araukans carefully conceal their personal-name from strangers. **1950** *Funk's Stand. Dict. Folklore* II. 782/2 It is believed that if one is sick one's name is possibly not agreeing with one, hence the name is 'washed off', and a new personal name given. **1972** *Harrods Christmas Catal.* 58/1 *Fresh pâté de foie gras*... For personal shoppers only. **1976** *Field* 18 Nov. 1023/2 (Advt.), Send SAE for descriptive leaflet of our full range including a How-to-find-us map for personal shoppers. **1887** S. A. BARNETT *Let.* 12 Oct. in H. Barnett *Canon Barnett* (1918) II. xxxiii. 63 We talked of how workmen could be made at home in Toynbee. I am sure that attractions won't bring them, but only the personal touch. **1936** A. CHRISTIE *ABC Murders* i. 11, I had various affairs to see to in England that I felt could only be successful if a personal touch was introduced. **1967** A. HUNTER *Gently Continental* vi. 75 We try to make people feel they belong here. The personal touch, you know. **1976** 'O. JACKS' *Assassination Day* iii. 48 Butcher hadn't overplayed his hand. He'd been crafty, relying on the personal touch.

B. *sb.* †**1.** A personal being; a person. *Obs.*

1678 C. HATTON 18 June in *H. Corr.* (Camden) I. 163 Soe yt neither I nor any personells shall receive any prejudice by what I shall disclose to you.

2. a. *pl.* Things belonging to an individual person; personal matters or things. †*spec.* Personal goods or property, personalty.

1724 *Briton* No. 24. 106 The Personals of the Nation belong not to this Enquiry. **1748** RICHARDSON *Clarissa* (1811) I. xxxi. 219 Shall my vanity extend only to personals? **1751** ELIZA HEYWOOD *Betsy Thoughtless* I. 13 All his personals, which were very considerable in the bank,.. should be equally divided. **1824** SOUTHEY *Bk. of Ch.* vi. (1841) 57 The personals he distributed among the poor.

b. *pl.* Personal remarks or statements, 'personalities'.

1742 RICHARDSON *Pamela* III. 227 We are going into Personals again, Gentlemen and Ladies, said the Earl. **1843** LYTTON *Last Bar.* II. iii, Must I go bonnet in hand and simper forth the sleek personals of the choice of her kith and house?

c. An item in a newspaper about a person or group of persons; a classified advertisement addressed to an individual person. orig. *U.S.*

1861 in A. Sterling *Belle of Fifties* (1904) 238, I inclose you a 'personal' from Brother Clement, published in yesterday's *Enquirer*. **1873** F. HUDSON *Journalism in U.S.* 472 Take the 'personals' of the *Herald* any day, and they will set one to thinking. **1875** J. G. HOLLAND *Sevenoaks* viii. 103 Returning.. to look over the papers, his eye was attracted, among the 'personals', to an item [etc.]. **1888** *Pall Mall G.* 22 June 14/1 What they call 'personals' across the ocean. **1901** *Daily Colonist* (Victoria, B.C.) 16 Oct. 7/1 (*heading*) Personals. **1913** *Collier's* 1 Feb. 17/3 He inserts a 'personal' in a New York newspaper under her initials. **1968** L. DURRELL *Tunc* III. 166 He had invented what he called the mnemon which he insisted was a literary form... *Times* Personals of a slightly surrealist tinge. **1977** R. E. HARRINGTON *Quintain* viii. 76 The classified section was his favorite part of the paper. He enjoyed reading the disguised, plaintive little cries for help in the Personals.

3. *Gram.* Short for *personal pronoun*: see A. 7. *rare.*

1824 L. MURRAY *Eng. Gram.* (ed. 5) I. 234 These personals are superfluous. **1845** STODDART in *Encycl. Metrop.* (1847) I. 45/1 It might, perhaps, have been better.. if the words which we are now considering had been arranged in a class between the personals and the article.

4. = PERSONNEL. *rare.* ? *Obs.*

1818 *Blackw. Mag.* IV. 159 The personal of the establishments to be under the joint direction of the founder [etc.]. **1833** *Westm. Rev.* Apr. 308 The personal of the army or navy.

5. A personal friend. *colloq.*

1961 *Listener* 21 Dec. 814/3 Reynard La Spoon, the choreographer—he's a close personal, ent he, Jule?

6. *Basketball.* A foul involving bodily contact with an opponent.

1961 in WEBSTER. **1969** *Eugene* (Oregon) *Register-Guard* 3 Dec. 1D/3 Love played only the first eight or nine minutes of the first half before collecting his third personal. **1974** *State* (Columbia, S. Carolina) 3 Mar. 2-D/1 He fouled out in the game's final minute after playing almost 13 minutes with four personals.

personalia (pɜːsəˈneɪlɪə), *sb. pl.* [ad. L. *persōnālia*, neut. pl. of *persōnālis* personal.] Personal matters; personal allusions; personal mementoes.

1903 'SIGMA' (*title*) Personalia: political, social, and various. **1909** H. G. WELLS *Tono-Bungay* III. ii. 314 My aunt received these personalia cheerfully. **1920** *Glasgow Herald* 27 Mar. 8 His speech on Wednesday contained some quite superfluous personalia. **1928** J. BAILEY *Let.* 26 Oct. (1935) 292 The best letters of you, as of other masters of the art epistolary, are the ones full of personalia—*from you to me, etc.* **1969** *Daily Tel.* 25 Oct. 8/1 On the theme of Ruskin and Venice this exhibition includes watercolours and drawings by him, various editions of his works and personalia. **1974** M. Z. LEWIN *Enemies Within* xxxi. 140 That lovely desk, which I would have filled to the brim with personalia. **1974** *Nature* 3 May 6/1 With pieces of original equipment.. and personalia including Marconi's swordstick.

personalism (ˈpɜːsənəlɪz(ə)m). [f. PERSONAL *a.* (*sb.*) + -ISM.] **a.** The quality or character of being personal: variously used to denote some theory, doctrine, principle, system, method, characteristic, etc. that is, or involves something that is, personal.

a **1846** *Q. Rev.* cited in WORCESTER. **1865** J. GROTE *Explor. Philos.* I. 146 The idealism, personalism, or whatever it may be called, which lies at the root of all that I have said. **1887** W. M. ROSSETTI *Life Keats* 208 Personalism of a wilful and fitful kind pervades the mass of his handiwork. **1890** *Atlantic Monthly* June 770/2 Hampered by this impotent system of personalism.. the party in possession of the executive power soon begins to drift helplessly upon a sea of troubles. **1901** CALDECOTT *Philos. & Relig.* xii. 81 Against the claim that Reason is the sole faculty of supersensible apprehension, Personalism opposes its assertion that here also Feeling and Will come into action.

b. A philosophical view, usually theistic and positing God as supreme Person, that reality has meaning only through the conscious minds of persons; a view of social organization that places primary emphasis on the person and his involvement in it rather than on the material means necessary for achieving such organization.

1908 B. P. BOWNE (*title*) Personalism. *Ibid.* iii. 111 We have now to consider the phenomenality of the physical world. This is the next step in the establishment of personalism. **1917** *Encycl. Relig. & Ethics* IX. 771/2 Aristotle laid the foundation for personalism by affirming self-consciousness as the highest being. **1938** tr. *Mounier's Personalist Manifesto* i. 1 Personalism is for us at present a sort of general pass-word. We are using it as an inclusive term for various doctrines that in our present historical situation can be made to agree upon the elementary physical and metaphysical conditions of a new civilization. **1947** *Partisan Rev.* XIV. 396 Berdyaev developed into one of the outstanding religious writers of our time, preaching a synthesis of socialism, personalism, and corporate Christianity. **1957** M. P. FOGARTY *Christian Democracy* iii. 29 Personalism, as distinct from individualism, is held by Christian Democrats to imply a certain 'solidarist' conception of the individual's responsibility to and for the society around him. **1959** *Pacific Affairs* XXXII. 77 Since 1956 the Ngo brothers and officials high and low in the government have referred to Personalism (and humanism) as the philosophical basis of the national revolution. **1966** F. COPLESTON *Hist. Philos.* VIII. III. xiii. 296 The basic tenet of personalism has been stated as the principle that reality has no meaning except in relation to persons; that the real is only in, of or for persons. **1971** A. R. CAPONIGRI *Hist. Western Philos.* V. VI. v. 349 He [*sc.* the person] finds the plenitude of his self-affirmation and of the affirmation of his vertical relation to God in the recognition of, and cooperation with, other persons. This has been called the social dimension of Stefanini's personalism.

c. Allegiance to a person, esp. a political leader, rather than to a party or ideology.

1937 *Times* 4 Sept. 11/6 Personalism is a characteristic of Argentine politics. A party is the personal following of a man. **1964** M. C. NEEDLER *Polit. Syst. Lat. Amer.* xxi. 518 Personalism stands in inverse relation to permanence of party organization, the extreme case of personalism being found in the party organized solely to support the candidacy of one individual. **1970** N. A. VICTORIA in I. L. Horowitz *Masses in Lat. Amer.* xv. 557 One of the conditions which may favor the emergence of such leadership is an element of 'personalism', or the extraordinary extension of the personal and emotional sphere. **1976** *Encounter* June 79 General Franco instinctively sensed something of the communal dangers inherent in Spanish personalism ('individualism' is the conventional term, but it fails to convey the whole meaning).

So **ˈpersonalist**, (*a*) a writer of personal notes, anecdotes, etc.; (*b*) a believer in or advocate of personalism (in any sense); also *attrib.*; **personaˈlistic** *a.*, of or pertaining to a person considered as different and separate from other people, esp. of the psychological study of the individual in relation to his personal experience (see quots.); also occas. **personaˈlistics** *sb. pl.* (treated as *sing.*).

1876 *Nation* (N.Y.) 15 June 382 As a witty and slashing political personalist,.. he was considered by friend and foe as without an equal. **1901** CALDECOTT *Philos. & Relig.* xii. 85 If, however, a Personalist is found.. secretly relying upon some peremptory intellectual or moral deliverances really universal in character, these must be brought to light, and he is passed from the school of pure Personalism to some other, accordingly. **1917** *Encycl. Relig. & Ethics* IX. 771/2 In this sense Eucken, Howison, Bergson, James.., and others of the modern school may be called personalists. **1937** *Times* 4 Sept. 11/6 The Radicals who remained faithful to the 'Chief' were known as Personalist or Irigoyenist Radicals. **1938** tr. *Mounier's Personalist Manifesto* i. 1 We shall apply the term *personalist* to any doctrine or any civilization that affirms the primacy of the human person over material necessities and over the whole complex of implements man needs for the development of his person. **1929** H. KLÜVER in G. Murphy *Hist. Introd. Mod. Psychol.* xxv. 424 But returning.. to personalistic theory, some further implications of the 'psychophysical neutrality' of 'person' should be considered. **1936** *Mind* XLV. 247 The 'personalistic' Psychologists go so far as to insist on the uniqueness of every combination of dispositions. **1938** G. REAVEY tr. *Berdyaev's Solitude & Society* 33 Personalist philosophy, as I understand it, has nothing in common with the subjectivist, individualist, empirical or nominalist currents of to-day. **1938** H. D. SPOERL tr. *Stern's Gen. Psychol. from Personalistic Standpoint* p. vii, In spite of this basic concern with the whole fabric of psychological specialties, our book will maintain a thoroughly distinctive and novel point of view... This is the *personalistic* point of view, which here finds its first occasion to demonstrate its fitness to formulate and interpret a particular empirical science. *Ibid.* xxvii. 494 The author.. points to this personalistic basis of transfer without knowing anything about personalistics. **1939** *Brit. Jrnl. Psychol.* XXIX. 411 Stephenson.. proposed to substitute a modified system of his own, which, he maintains, should lead to 'an entirely new branch of psychometry, for which the term Personalistics may be coined'. *Ibid.* XXX. 65 The roots of 'personalistics' clearly go back to the classical researches embodied in the *Differentielle Psychologie.* **1956** *Jrnl. Theol. Stud.* VII. 165 He [*sc.* Luther] maintains a thoroughly personalistic idea of grace, which is received by faith alone. **1962** S. E. FINER *Man on Horseback* ix. 131 Paraguay.. the parties—Colorados and Azules—are personalist cliques. **1969** C. DAVIDSON in Cockburn & Blackburn *Student Power* 359 The hippy movement has served to make many of our people withdraw into a personalistic, passive cult of consumption. **1970** B. BREWSTER tr. *Althusser & Balibar's Reading Capital* (1975) II. viii. 172 This is a stumbling-block for all the interpretations of Marxism as a 'philosophy of labour', whether ethical, personalist or existentialist. **1970** D. GOLDRICH et al. in I. L. Horowitz *Masses in Lat. Amer.* v. 190 APRA.. the personalist party of former dictator General Odría. **1976** H. A. WILLIAMS *Tensions* vi. 99 Personalist pastors, perhaps more than public campaigners, sometimes try (unsuccessfully) to impose a totalitarian tyranny upon scholars and thinkers.

‖**personalismo** (persona'lizmo). [Sp. and Pg.] = PERSONALISM c.

1962 G. BLANKSTEN in M. A. Kaplan *Revolution in World Politics* III. v. 120 *Personalismo* may be regarded as the custom of following or opposing a political leader on the basis of his personality rather than on ideological grounds. **1964** L. B. LOTT in M. C. Needler *Polit. Syst. Lat. Amer.* xii. 244 A strong tendency on their [*sc.* the people's] part to associate themselves with powerful personalities rather than with programs and issues. This tendency we may label *personalismo.* **1969** *Language* XLV. 464 Joshua Fishman's comparison of those two categories in terms of cross-cultural indices reveals a most interesting association between linguistically heterogeneous polities and 'personalismo' or 'charisma' in follower-leader relationships. **1969** J. Mander *Static Society* i. 66 Mexico has cast off the incubus of *personalismo.*

personality (pɜːsəˈnælɪtɪ). Also 4 -ite. [a. OF. *personalité* (14th c. in Hatz.-Darm.), now *personn-*, ad. med. Schol. L. *persōnālitās*, f. *persōnāl-is* PERSONAL: see -ITY.]

1. a. The quality, character, or fact of being a person as distinct from a thing; that quality or principle which makes a being personal. Also in reference to a corporate body: see PERSON *sb.* 6.

c **1380** Wyclif *Sel. Wks.* II. 296 Al þe personalite of man stondiþ in þe spirit of him. **1655** H. More *Antid. Ath.* xii. §5 App. (1662) 219 For a time he loses the sense of his own personality, and becomes a mere passive instrument of the deity. **1692** Bentley *Boyle Lect.* v. 152 We must be wary lest we ascribe any Personality to this Nature or Chance. **1802** Paley *Nat. Theol.* xxiii. (1819) 362 These capacities constitute personality, for they imply consciousness and thought. **1836** Emerson *Nature, Idealism* Wks. (Bohn) II. 164 Religion includes the personality of God; Ethics does not.

b. The condition ascribed to the Deity of consisting of distinct persons (see PERSON *sb.* 7).

1492 Ryman *Poems* xlii. 3 in *Archiv. Stud. neu. Spr.* LXXXIX. 209 Ay thre in personalite, In deite but oon. **1624** Gataker *Transubst.* 173 If a perfect substance or nature (as was the humanity of Christ) could want the naturall personality and subsistence thereof, supplyed by the divine person and *hypostasis* of the Sonne of God. **1752** J. Gill *Trinity* iv. 81 Personality is the bare mode of subsisting. **1833** J. H. Newman *Arians* II. ii. (1876) 154 The apparent Personality ascribed to them [the Word, and the Spirit] in the Old Testament, is changed for a real Personality. **1870** —— *Gram Assent* I. v. 120 The Almighty God, instead of being One Person only, which is the teaching of Natural Religion, has three Personalities.

c. Personal existence, actual existence as a person; the fact of there being or having been such a person; personal identity.

1835 Thirlwall *Greece* I. viii. 337 This inference.. would lead to other conclusions affecting the personality of Lycurgus. **1849** Ruskin *Sev. Lamps* vi. §2. 164 The age of Homer is surrounded with darkness, his very personality with doubt. **1870** Freeman *Norm. Conq.* II. App. 673 There are others..whose personality can be identified in Domesday.

2. a. That quality or assemblage of qualities which makes a person what he is, as distinct from other persons; distinctive personal or individual character, esp. when of a marked or notable kind. Also *fig.* in reference to a thing. Also in phr. ***to have personality***, to have qualities or traits of character to an unusual or noteworthy degree.

1795 *Jemima* II. 167 Marmontel observes that even a French girl of sixteen, if she has but a little personality, is a Machiavel. **1847** Emerson *Repr. Men, Napoleon* Wks. (Bohn) I. 367 Mirabeau, with his overpowering personality, felt that these things, which his presence inspired, were as much his own, as if he had said them. **1882** Farrar in *Contemp. Rev.* XLII. 807 The almost indescribable charm which his sermons derived from his personality. **1902** W. D. Howells *Lit. & Life* 249 How many houses now have character—personality? **1934** C. Fox in *Proc. 1st Internat. Congr. Prehist. & Protohist. Sci.* 27 Position, outline, and structure..; the climate resulting from position, and the soil derived from structure, determine the vegetable life which she nourishes and the animal life which she harbours. The whole represents Man's environment, and Britain's 'Personality'. **1940** R. S. Lambert *Ariel & all his Quality* iv. 116 To attract a solid core of permanent readers to any literary paper presupposes that that paper shall have a 'personality' to distinguish it from others of its kind. *a* **1960** E. M. Forster *Maurice* (1971) xxxiv. 155 So he was in a way, but evidently he had personality. **1973** *Times* 31 Jan. (Mediterranean Suppl.) p. i/3 The Mediterranean islands could easily lose their personality in a short time.

†**b.** (with *pl.*) A personal quality or characteristic; an individual trait. *Obs. rare.*

1748 Richardson *Clarissa* (1811) II. 138 In return [I] fall to praising those qualities and personalities in Lovelace, which the other never will have.

c. *Psychol.* and *Sociol.* The unique combination of psychophysical qualities or traits, inherent and acquired, that make up each person as observable in his reactions to the environment or to the social group; also, psychological study concerned with such aspects of the person, and with the similarities and differences that exist between persons.

1879 H. Maudsley *Path. of Mind* (ed. 3) i. 12 It is this physiological unity of organic functions, which is something deeper than consciousness and constitutes our fundamental personality. **1906** M. Prince (*title*) The dissociation of a personality. *Ibid.* i. 3 A more correct term is *disintegrated* personality, for each secondary personality is a part only of a normal whole self. **1921** Park & Burgess *Introd. Sci. of Sociol.* ii. 144 In sociology, personality is studied, not only from the subjective stand-point of its organization, but even more in its objective aspects and with reference to the rôle of the person in the group. **1930** *Psychol. Bull.* XXVII. 677 The methods and problems of contemporary research in personality. **1947** G. Murphy *Personality* p. x, The approach to personality is made chiefly in terms of origins and modes of development on the one hand, interrelations or structural problems on the other. **1949** Kluckhorn & Murray *Personality* i. 6 In trying to remedy these failures, there emerged the first comprehensive dynamic theory of personality—psychoanalysis. **1950** E. Frenkel-Brunswick in T. Wiesengrund-Adorno et al. *Authoritarian Personality* ix. 291 (*heading*) An approach to the prejudiced personality. **1964** J. Strachey et al. tr. *Freud's New Introd. Lect.* xxxi, in *Compl. Psychol. Wks.* XXII. 57 (*title*) The dissection of the psychical personality. **1969** J. W. Getzels in Lindzey & Aronson *Handbk. Social Psychol.* (ed. 2) V. xlii. 463 A social psychology of education is concerned with the interaction of role and personality in the school or classroom. **1975** J. Plamenatz *K. Marx's Philos. of Man* xiv. 401 There are ideas of love and freedom common to liberal 'bourgeois' society and to its Utopian critics which differ from these older ties and forms. There are ideas of personality, of personal relationships, and of their social conditions, peculiar to this society and to its critics.

3. a. A personal being, a person. (In first quot. applied to the distinct 'persons' in the Godhead: cf. PERSON *sb.* 7 a.)

1678 Cudworth *Intell. Syst.* I. iv. 597 The Platonists thus distinguishing, betwixt οὐσία and ὑπόστασις, the Essence of the Godhead, and the Distinct Hypostases or Personalities thereof. *Ibid.* v. 750 Humane Souls, Minds, and Personalities, being unquestionably Substantial Things and Really Distinct from Matter. **1851** Hawthorne *Ho. Sev. Gables* xi, By its remoteness, it melts all the petty personalities, of which it is made up, into one broad mass of existence. **1895** W. H. Hudson *Spencer's Philos.* 209 We cannot think of an infinite personality. Personality implies limitation, or it means nothing at all.

b. A person who stands out from others either by virtue of strong or unusual character or because his position makes him a focus for some form of public interest.

1889 G. B. Shaw in *Church Reformer* Mar. 68/1 Individuality is concentrated, fixed, gripped in one exceptionally gifted man, who is consequently what we call a personality, a man pre-eminently himself, impossible to disguise. **1919** V. Woolf *Night & Day* iv. 46 I've only seen her once or twice, but she seems to me to be what one calls a 'personality'. **1933** *Radio Times* 14 Apr. 82/3, I apply what may seem a whimsical test to broadcasting personalities. I ask myself if I would care to meet and talk with them in the flesh. **1947** *Sat. Rev. Lit.* (U.S.) 26 Apr. 4/1 In Elizabeth Ann McMurray, John McGinnir, Jimmie Albright, and Lon Tinkle, it harbors four of the outstanding personalities in the American book world. **1959** *Language Learning* IX. IV. 79 It is used with the greatest aplomb and ease by radio and T.V. personalities. **1962** *Listener* 22 Mar. 503/1 He is a local councillor in a small town, and one of its prominent personalities. **1973** *Birmingham* (Alabama) *News* 10 June E-7/4 More recently she has tried, fairly unsuccessfully, for a career as television personality. **1973** D. Miller *Chinese Jade Affair* xviii. 176 The woes of being a secret policeman during the visits of V.I.P. personalities. **1976** *National Observer* (U.S.) 13 Nov. 1/1 'In movies they buy personalities,' says Billy Dee.

4. Bodily parts collectively; body, person. Also in *pl.* in same sense. *rare.*

1842 Gen. P. Thompson *Exerc.* VI. 413 It might bait a rat-trap; though a well-fed rat would hardly risk his personalities for such a pittance. **1884** Malleson *Battle-fields Germany* vi. 161 Notwithstanding that he was the possessor, at the age of thirty-three, of little more than half of his original personality, he was as active, as daring, as efficient, as the strongest and soundest-limbed man in his army.

5. a. The fact of relating to an individual person, or to particular persons; *spec.* the quality of being directed to or aimed at an individual, esp. in the way of disparagement or unfriendly reference.

1772 *Ann. Reg.* 33/1 By specifying and applying their charges to individuals, to incur the censure of a mean and malicious personality. **1786** Cumberland *Observer* No. 93 III. 325 There is yet another topic, which he has been no less studious to avoid, which is personality. **1814** D'Israeli *Quarrels Auth.* (1867) 283 Personality in his satires, no doubt, accorded with the temper and the talent of Pope. **1856** Froude *Hist. Eng.* (1858) II. vi. 41 He had attacked Wolsey himself with somewhat vulgar personality. **1865** Trollope *Belton Est.* v. 49 Never referring with clear personality to those who had been nearest to her when she had been a child.

b. (Usu. in *pl.*) A statement or remark aimed at or referring to an individual person, usually of a disparaging or offensive kind. (In quot. 1811 (*pl.*) used for 'personal attentions or compliments'.)

1769 Sir W. Draper in *Junius Lett.* xxvi. (1772) I. 187 Cannot political questions be discussed without descending to the most odious personalities? **1811** Miss L. M. Hawkins *C'tess & Gertr.* (1812) III. lix. 262 When occupied at home, she put by his personalities, by trying to interest him in a plan of diligence. *a* **1850** Calhoun *Wks.* (1874) III. 250 The Senator resorted to personalities. **1891** C. Lowe in *19th Cent.* Dec. 859 The Court cannot and will not stand.. journalistic personalities about its members.

†**c.** The fact of being personal, or done by a person himself. *Obs.*

1648 Fairfax, etc. *2nd Remonstr.* 36 The King comes in with the reputation..of having long sought it [Peace] by a Personal Treaty:..the truth is, neither the Treaty, nor the Personality of it have advanced the businesse one jot.

6. *Law.* †**a.** = PERSONALTY a. *Obs.* **b.** = PERSONALTY b; *gen.* personal belongings. *rare.*

1658 Phillips, *Personality*, (a Law-Term) an abstract of personal, as the action is in the personalty [1661 Blount personality; 1704 J. Harris *Lex. Techn.* I, Personality]; that is, brought against the right person. **1752** Dodson in *Phil. Trans.* XLVII. 334 The interest or dividends of many personalities in the stocks. **1858** Hawthorne *Fr. & It. Note-Bks.* II. 72 Michael Angelo's..old slippers, and whatever other of his closest personalities are to be shown.

c. The quality of concerning persons (in phr. ***personality of laws*** = F. *personnalité des statuts*).

1834–46 J. Story *Confl. Laws* i. §16 (1883) 19 By the personality of laws foreign jurists generally mean all laws which concern the condition, state, and capacity of persons; by the reality of laws, all laws which concern property or things; *quæ ad rem spectant.*

7. *attrib.* and *Comb.*, as ***personality assessment, clash, defect, disorder, problem, test, theory***; **personality cult**, devotion to a leader that is deliberately fostered by the emphasis placed on certain aspects of his personality; **personality dynamics**, a term used for the active, though not necessarily conscious, adaptation effected by a person of his personality to his environment; **personality factor**, a trait considered as sufficiently distinct and general in the study of personality to be measurable by factor analysis; **personality integration** (see quot. 1970); **personality inventory**, a questionnaire designed to assess personality traits; **personality pattern**, the pattern of personality that is formed by the inherited and acquired traits of an individual; **personality structure**, the combination of traits that make up a personality; **personality system**, a sociological term for individual personality in its dynamic social context; **personality trait**, a particular feature or characteristic that can be considered as relatively stable in an individual personality; **personality type**, a classification of personality according to the preponderant features or traits found either in a person or in a society; **personality variable** = *personality factor.*

1956 G. G. Stern et al. (*title*) Methods in personality assessment. **1964** *Eng. Stud.* XLV. 50 The intellectual and personality assessment of boys. **1969** *Playboy* July 102/1 These range from personality clashes..to on-the-job incompetence. **1956** *Canadian Forum* May 25/1 The spread of the 'personality cult' diminished the role of collective leadership within the party and sometimes led to serious defects in our work. **1957** *Economist* 21 Sept. 912/2 The election campaign was marked by a personality cult, but its inspiration and techniques owed infinitely more to Madison Avenue than to Dr. Goebbels. **1959** *Encounter* July 80/2 The emphatic condemnation of the 'personality cult' at the 20th Congress of the CPSU by Mr. Krushchev. **1960** *20th Cent.* Apr. 342 A big factor in the sale of the more popular 'name' records is the personality cult. **1971** *Black Scholar* Apr.–May 7/2 We must be careful to avoid the tendency of building personality cults around specific individuals. **1971** I. Deutscher *Marxism in our Time* (1972) xv. 290 The crudities and cruelties of the 'personality cult' must have made him shudder more than once. **1973** *Times* 4 Dec. 16/7 Signs of new trouble in the Kremlin are evident in the rapid growth of the Brezhnev personality cult. **1927** *New Republic* 21 Sept. 129/1 The understanding thus gained spreads to all the slighter estrangements, the problems of discipline,..the normalization of those with personality deficits or defects. **1936** W. S. Sadler *Theory & Pract. Psychiatry* xxiv. 393 About one-quarter of all school children carry definite personality defects. **1970** 'T. Coe' *Wax Apple* (1973) vii. 56 A naturally offensive man who had found a way..to turn a personality defect to advantage. **1938** L. P. Thorpe *Psychol. Found. Personality* viii. 338 Investigators..have attempted to ascertain the degree of relationship obtaining between glandular disturbances and personality disorders. **1969** *Guardian* 22 July 11/7 The 11-year old girl..sentenced to life detention..for strangling two small boys..suffers from ..a severe personality disorder, for which there is no organic cause. **1976** Smythies & Corbett *Psychiatry* xvii. 290 Some patients who ask his help..suffer from a different kind of illness—a personality disorder. **1954** B. R. Sappenfield (*title*) Personality dynamics: an integrative psychology of adjustment. **1958** M. Argyle *Relig. Behaviour* v. 48 M. B. Smith and others (1956) distinguish those people whose attitudes are primarily an adjustment to group standards from those whose attitudes are based more on internal personality dynamics. **1960** J. C. Coleman (*title*) Personality dynamics and effective behavior. **1932** P. M. Symonds *Diagnosing Personality & Conduct* xi. 438 The creatinine concentration of the urine was also found by Rich to be associated with personality factors. **1957** R. B. Cattell *Personality & Motivation* ix. 335 A personality factor will have a series of predictive validities against specific cultural performances. **1971** Lanyon & Goodstein *Personality Assessment* iv. 89 A system of five relatively orthogonal (independent) and easily interpreted personality factors. **1938** L. P. Thorpe *Psychol. Found. Personality* ix. 434 (*heading*) Definition and nature of personality integration. **1970** G. A. & A. G. Theodorson *Mod. Dict. Sociol.* 297 *Personality integration*, the harmonious coordination of the various aspects of the personality with each other, and of the personality as a whole with its environment... Perfect personality integration is.. certainly not normal for persons in social interaction. **1932** P. M. Symonds *Diagnosing Personality & Conduct* v. 208 An integration of these various questionnaires designed to measure adjustment has been effected in a 'Personality Inventory' constructed by Bernreuter. **1933** *Jrnl. Social Psychol.* IV. 389 The test which was constructed has been entitled the Personality Inventory and is referred to herein as the P-I test. **1950** E. A. Suchman in S. A. Stouffer *Measurement & Prediction* v. 162 Evidence of the quasi-scale pattern in the case of personality inventories, information tests, and measures of intensity of feeling. **1968** Blum & Naylor *Industr. Psychol.* iv. 113 Numerous reasons have been suggested to account for the general lack of success in industrial situations of personality inventories. **1971** 'D. Halliday' *Dolly & Doctor Bird* xiii. 193 I've done an Eysenck personality inventory on you both... You wouldn't suit. **1949** C. E. Thompson *Thematic Apperception Test: Manual* 3 When cultural prejudices or antagonisms are part of the personality pattern of the Negro they are likely to reduce the subject's identification with the white figures of the TAT. **1960** R. F. Peck et al. *Psychol. of Character Devel.* iv. 89 There are distinct personality patterns which characterize each type group, and which differentiate one group from another. **1973** E. B. Hurlock *Personality Devel.* (1974) ii. 19 The personality pattern is not the product of learning exclusively or of heredity exclusively..it comes from an interaction of the two. **1963** A. Heron *Towards Quaker View of Sex* 51 Symptoms of deeper personality problems. **1939** R. Linton in A. Kardiner *Individual & his Society* p. vi, Basic personality structure, as the term is used here, represents the constellation of personality characteristics which would appear to be congenial with the total range of institutions comprised within a given culture. It..is, therefore, an abstraction of the same order as culture itself. **1947** G. Murphy *Personality* xxviii. 664 Problems of generality of the conditioned response being interwoven with problems of personality structure in the true sense. **1957** R. B. Cattell *Personality & Motivation* viii. 281 A comparatively new world of personality structure..has become visible to psychologists... On this foundation of measurable functions, the psychology of the second half of the twentieth century may proceed to build its laws and theories of personality. **1972** *Jrnl. Social Psychol.* LXXXVI. 151 Individuals will be encouraged to hold attitudes of intolerance largely irrespective of their basic personality structure. **1951** Parsons & Shils *Toward Gen. Theory Action* II. i. 55 A personality system is a system of action... Social systems, personality systems, and cultural systems are critical subject matter for the theory of action. **1961** L. Thompson *Toward Sci. of Mankind* I. iv. 68 The personality system and the core values function as covert connecting links between the other four systems. **1971** F. Hollis in Roberts & Nee *Theories Social Casework* 59 This means attention to both the interpersonal system—parent-child, husband-wife, family—and to the personality systems of the individuals who compose the interpersonal system. **1927** *Psychol. Bull.* XXIV. 419 A battery containing a mixture of intelligence and personality tests was used by Gallup. **1964** M. Argyle *Psychol. & Social Probl.* xi. 139 The contribution of psychology..has been to devise various objective tests and measures which are better able to select those who are good at the job. These include intelligence tests, personality tests, [etc.]. **1957** Hall & Lindzey *Theories of Personality* xiv. 538 It seems appropriate..to pause and attempt to identify general trends which exist in spite of the tremendous differences among personality theories. **1977** R. Holland *Self & Social Context* v. 131 The emergence of new personality theories is accompanied by ambivalence towards predecessors as the new theorists filter out what they need from the past and construct around it a new position. **1921** F. H. & G. W. Allport in *Jrnl. Abnormal Psychol.* XVI. 6 (*title*) Personality traits: their classification and measurement. **1931** T. H. Pear *Voice & Personality* ii. 18 In the speech of some persons, there are sounds which really symbolise personality-traits. **1948** *Mind* LVII. 511 The gesture in question is a personality trait of a given individual if it is performed by him, say, six out of every ten times when he might have performed it. **1972** *Jrnl. Social Psychol.* LXXXVI. 30 We deduced that the personality traits of leaders would be more varied in the non-conformity than in the conformity situation. **1919** *Psychol. Rev.* XXVI. 374 Personality-type A..is an individual rated as especially intelligent, prompt, persistent, ..sensitive, not at all loquacious. **1936** W. S. Sadler *Theory & Pract. Psychiatry* liv. 845 The most important etiologic factor..is to be found in the personality type of these patients. **1949** MacIver & Page *Society* iii. 58 These studies have rather convincingly demonstrated..that each culture tends to create and is supported by a 'basic personality type'. **1966** *Philosophy* XLI. 299 Different social norms result in different modal personality-types. **1968** A. Etzioni *Active Society* xxi. 627 Most studies of efforts to affect 'deep' personality variables—especially psychoanalysis, 'brainwashing', and psychological experiments—show these efforts to have little effect. **1972** *Encycl. Psychol.* II. 385/1 Such personality variables as aggression, anxiety or authoritarianism. **1972** *Jrnl. Social Psychol.* LXXXVI. 121 Choosing groups dichotomized along some single personality variable, such as aggression, would allow far too many sources of variance.

personalization (ˌpɜːsənəlaɪˈzeɪʃən). [f. next + -ation.] The action of personalizing; representation or embodiment in a person; personification; impersonation.

1880 Fairbairn *Stud. Life Christ* Introd. (1881) 27 He was the personalization of its genius, the heir of its work. **1884** *Pop. Sci. Mo.* XXV. 458. **1888** S. McComb in *Pulpit Treasury* (N.Y.) Mar. 696 Luther was the personalization of tendencies..that threatened the very life of the papacy. **1911** W. W. Fowler *Relig. Experience Roman People* vii. 149 It is not..*a priori* probable that the process of personalisation (if I may coin the word) should have proceeded..so far as to ascribe to these named deities..the characteristics of human beings. **1957** R. Hoggart *Uses of Literacy* vi. 163 The quite unusual degree of 'personalisation' in the newspapers designed particularly for working-class people. **1968** S. Brittan *Left or Right* viii. 172 The personalisation of politics round the leaders. **1973** *Times* 24 Jan. (Security Printing Suppl.) p. i/9 A developing sphere of operation for the security printer is in the realm of cheque printing and personalization. The latter is the process whereby the account holder's name and initials are printed on to the cheque.

personalize (ˈpɜːsənəlaɪz), *v.* [f. personal *a.* + -ize: cf. mod.F. *personnaliser*.] *trans.* To render personal; to represent as personal, personify; to embody in a person, impersonate; to make (some impersonal object or thing) more obviously related to, or identifiable as belonging to, a particular individual; also *fig.*

1747 Warburton *Notes Shaks., Hen. VIII*, I. iv, Danger is personalized as serving in the rebel army, and shaking the established government. **1754** A. Murphy *Gray's Inn Jrnl.* No. 82 The Poets are fond of personalizing both physical and moral Qualities. **1886** *Sat. Rev.* 31 July 167/2 Imagination is here a general term, an abstraction,..a personalized abstraction of the most surprising character. **1893** Fairbairn *Christ in Mod. Theol.* I. ii. §1. 48 What sort of religious ideal did He personalize? **1935** *Advt. for Mohawk Sheets* (Miller & Rhoads, Richmond, Va.), Now personalized with smart needlecrest initials. **1947** *Amer. Speech* XXII. 71/1 Personalize your luggage, personalized stationery. **1961** *Daily Tel.* 28 Feb. 24/6 He [*sc.* Mr. Gaitskell] probably appreciates that any further move towards 'personalising' the defence issue would merely play into Mr Crossman's hands. **1966** *Electronics* 31 Oct. 42/3 In the CP and EP, the memory is a plug-in unit that can be replaced in a few minutes, so that the design of either model can be quickly personalized for a special application. **1967** *Autocar* 27 Dec. 9/2 All the multitude of accessories offered (and bought) for the embellishment of ordinary cars is enough to show that many buyers want, in the American phrase, to 'personalize' their transport. **1970** *Daily Tel.* (Colour Suppl.) 13 Nov. 21 (*caption*) Dealer delegate is chatted up by an oil executive... Moments like these help to 'personalise' a giant company with the employees. **1972** *Daily Tel.* 24 Nov. 6/7 Outstandingly clever children often pass through school unnoticed by their teachers... 'One major reason is the failure in schools to personalise the learning environments which they provide.' **1977** *New Yorker* 9 May 143/2 Crossman blames the mass media for personalizing politics.

Hence **ˈpersonalized** *ppl. a.*; **ˈpersonalizing** *vbl. sb.* and *ppl. a.*

1727–41 Chambers *Cycl.*, *Personifying*, or *Personalising*, the feigning a person; or attributing a person to an inanimate being. *a* **1834** Coleridge in *Lit. Rem.* (1839) IV. 430 The individual will or personalizing principle of free agency..is the factor. **1947** *Forum* (Johannesburg) 26 Apr. 46/1 (Advt.), Fare is inclusive of personalised steward service throughout journey. **1957** R. Hoggart *Uses of Literacy* vi. 165 As the 'personalising' technique becomes yearly more machine-tooled, so a good instinct is pulled out of shape. **1959** *Economist* 4 Apr. 68/1 A 'personalised' cheque, one that carries an identifying account number and so can be used only by the owner of the account. **1961** *Daily Tel.* 28 Feb. 24/6 (*heading*) No witch hunt. Against 'Personalising'. **1974** *Times* 14 Dec. 24/6 Personalized crystal glasses, initials, names, dates, crests, etc., hand engraved to your requirements. **1976** *National Observer* (U.S.) 13 Mar. 11/2 (Advt.), Personalized attention, experienced tutors, relaxed atmosphere. **1977** *Theology* LXXX. 191 The man Jesus Christ as the personalized instrument..of the self-expressive activity of God. *Ibid.* Such a union would be marked by *eudokia*, or divine good-pleasure, and by *synapheia* or true and personalizing relationship. *a* **1977** *Harrison Mayer Ltd. Catal.* 39/3 The Cerama-pen is a fibre tip pen filled with precious metal ink. Ideal for thin line decorating and personalising work. **1978** *Bull. Amer. Acad. Arts & Sci.* Jan. 10 Scholars with no prior knowledge of computers will be able to obtain a personalized index to the material most relevant to their particular researches.

personally (ˈpɜːsənəlɪ), *adv.* [f. personal *a.* + -ly².] In a personal manner, capacity, etc.

1. In the way of personal presence or action; in person: = (by) himself, themselves, etc.

1398 Trevisa *Barth. De P.R.* xiv. xxxv. (Bodl. MS.), Aboute þe foote of þis mounte þe Hebrues..were worþi to see god in fuyre and in a cloude and to here hym speke personallich. **1495** *Act 11 Hen. VII*, c. 7 That they appere personelly at the next general sessions of the peas. **1568** Grafton *Chron.* II. 933 He personally toke his ship at Douer,..and sailed to Calice. **1665** Manley *Grotius' Low C. Warres* 576 Being very moderate, both in Sleep and Recreations, he did more Personally, than by his Servants and Ministers. **1765** Blackstone *Comm.* I. xiv. (1793) 431 If the servant, going along the street with a torch, by negligence sets fire to a house..he..must himself answer the damage personally. **1863** H. Cox *Instit.* III. vii. 682 The Treasurer acted personally at the Exchequer. **1900** F. H. Stoddard *Evol. Eng. Novel* 96 History in Scotland is edited, or I may say personally conducted, to this day by Walter Scott.

b. In objective sense, expressing the relation of an action, feeling, etc. to the actual person mentioned: = himself, themselves, etc. (as object of some action, etc.).

1483 Caxton *Gold Leg.* H viij, He shold be punysshed personaly vii fold more. *a* **1562** G. Cavendish *Wolsey* (1893) 277 To se hyme personally deade. **1684** T. Hockin *God's Decrees* 342 This great truth is confirm'd and more personally applied in answer to S. Peters question. **1722** De Foe *Plague* 94 They had given me a great deal of ill Language too, I mean Personally. **1891** *Law Times* XC. 409/1 The amended writ ought to have been served on them personally.

2. As a person; in the form or character of an individual person.

1597 Hooker *Eccl. Pol.* v. lii. §3 Christ is..a person divine, because he is personallie the Sonne of God, humane, because he hath reallie the nature of the children of men. *Ibid.* liv. §5 Christ..is man, but man with whome deitie is personally ioyned. *a* **1729** J. Rogers (J.), The converted man is personally the same he was before. **1860** Pusey *Min. Proph.* 128 As God the Word, when He took human nature, came into it personally, so that the fulness of the Godhead dwelt bodily in it. *Mod.* In Christian theology, God is conceived as personally existing and acting.

3. In one's personal capacity; as an individual person (as distinct from others); individually; in oneself; as regards oneself; *esp.* 'for myself', 'as far as I am concerned'.

1849 Macaulay *Hist. Eng.* vii. II. 226 Howe had, like Baxter, been personally a gainer by the recent change of policy. **1878** Lecky *Eng. in 18th C.* I. i. 128 None of the Tory leaders were personally popular. **1902** W. E. Norris *Credit of County* xxii, Personally I don't despair. **1903** R. Ellis *Lect. Commonit. Orientius* 17 To myself personally the work has a peculiar interest. *Mod.* Personally I am in favour of the change.

4. *Comb.* ***personally conducted***, conducted by some one in person: see sense 1.

1884 *Pall Mall G.* 6 Sept. 4/1 Where Mr. Cook has not yet led swarms of personally-conducted tourists. **1892** Dobson *18th C. Vignettes* 223 A flying visit of..an hour, with a miscellaneous and 'personally-conducted' party.

ˈpersonalness. *rare.* [f. as prec. + -ness.] The quality of being personal.

1879 P. Brooks *Influence Jesus* iii. 194 It is this personalness of all His moral enthusiasms..that keeps us from ever feeling or fearing in Jesus any of that moral pedantry. **1895** [see personal *a.* 6 b].

personalty (ˈpɜːsənəltɪ). *Law.* [ad. late AF. *personaltie* = med.L. *persōnālitās* personality: cf. *reality*, *realty*.]

†**a.** See quots. 1607, 1888. **b.** Personal goods, personal estate: see personal A. 6; also *gen.* personal belongings. **c.** = personality 6 c. *rare.*

a **1481** Littleton *Tenures* §315 III. iv. (1516) D v b, Pur ceo qe laccion est en le personalte & nemye en le realte. **1544** *translation*, Bycause that the accyon is in the parsonalte and nat in the realte. **1607** Cowell *Interpr.*, *Personalty* (*Personalitas*), is an abstract of personall. The action is in the personalty,..that is to say, brought against the right person, or the person against whome in lawe it lieth. **1766** Blackstone *Comm.* II. xxiv. 385 Our courts now regard a man's personalty in a light nearly, if not quite, equal to his realty: and have adopted a more enlarged and less technical mode of considering the one than the other. **1827** Jarman *J. J. Powell's Devises* (ed. 3) II. 163 The intention to confine the word 'estate' to personalty was inferred by the subsequent specification. **1845** Stephen *Comm. Laws Eng.* (1874) I. 167 Things personal, (otherwise called personalty,) consist of goods, money, and all other moveables, and of such rights and profits as relate to moveables. **1865** *Look Before You Leap* I. 12 His gay jacket, his horses, and a few personalties. **1880** Gladstone *Speech* 15 Mar., You will find that the duties on personalties of half a million or one million are comparatively insignificant; and so it is in regard to rates. **1888** T. C. Williams in *Law Quarterly Rev.* IV. 405 Actions were said to be or to sound *in the realty* or *in the personalty*, according to the nature of the relief afforded therein. Next the terms, *the realty*, *the personalty* were applied to the things recoverable in real or personal actions respectively. Such things were then distinguished as real or personal things.

†**personar**, obs. Sc. form of parcener.

1385 in *3rd Rep. Hist. MSS. Comm.* 410/2 To prowe gif the forsayde personaris walde seke hym othir with tretys, grace, or lauch. **1489** *Acta Audit.* (1839) 146/1 William chancellare & marioune Inglis personaris of þe landis of Richertoune.

personate (ˈpɜːsənət), *a.* [ad. L. *persōnāt-us* masked, feigned, f. *persōna* mask: see -ate².]

†**1.** Personated, feigned, pretended, counterfeit. *Obs.*

1597–8 Bp. Hall *Sat.*, *Defiance to Envie* 103 Or whether list me sing so personate My striving selfe to conquer with my verse. **1607** Topsell *Four-f. Beasts* 483 A stranger,..seeing the counterfeit personate asse-Lyon,..knewe it for an asse in a lion's skin. **1640** R. Baillie (*title*) Canterburians Self-conviction... With a Postscript to the Personat Jesuite Lysimachus Nicanor. **1822** Lamb *Elia* Ser. I. *Decay of Beggars*, Under a personate father of a family, think..that thou hast relieved an indigent bachelor.

†**2.** Of the nature of a person, personal; embodied in a person, impersonated. *Obs.*

1612 Brerewood *Lang. & Relig.* 189 They held indeed but one personate nature to be in Christ, resulting of the union of two natures not personated. **1633** T. Adams *Exp. 2 Peter* i. 4 But if there be not always a personate devil, there is always a personal devil. **1689** *Col. Rec. Pennsylv.* I. 314 A Pattern and instance of personate humble deference, Submission and Obedience.

3. *Bot.* Mask-like; applied to a two-lipped corolla having the opening between the lips closed by an upward projection of the lower lip, as in the snapdragon. (Distinguished from *ringent*.)

[**1706** Phillips, *Personati*, a Term us'd by some Herbalists for such Flowers as express the gaping Mouths of some living Creatures.] **1760** J. Lee *Introd. Bot.* II. xvii. (1765) 107 Such as have a simple Stigma, and personate Corolla. **1785** Martyn *Rousseau's Bot.* iv. (1794) 42 Personate or masked flowers. **1870** Hooker *Stud. Flora* 261 Linaria, Toadflax..Corolla personate.

4. *Zool.* **a.** Having a masked or disguised form (as compared with the perfect form); larval. **b.** Having mask-like markings on the head.

personate (ˈpɜːsəneɪt), *v.* [f. ppl. stem of late L. *persōnāre* to represent, bear the character of (Boethius: *De Duab. Nat. Christi* iv, 'persona dicta a personando, circumflexa penultima'), f. *persōna* mask, etc.: see person *sb.* Cf. It. *personare* 'to personate, to act or play the part of any person' (Florio 1598).]

1. *trans.* To act or play the part of (a character in a drama or the like); to act, play (a drama, etc.); to represent or exhibit dramatically.

1598 [see etym. above]. **1602** Marston *Ant. & Mel.* Induct., *Alb.* Whome doe you personate? *Pie.* Piero, Duke of Venice. **1647** Trapp *Comm. Matt.* vi. 2 They [i.e. Stage players] can act to the life those whom they personate. **1774** Warton *Hist. Eng. Poetry* (1775) II. 203 Profane characters were personated in our pageants, before the close of the fourteenth century. **1873** Symonds *Grk. Poets* vii. 190 It was one of the chief actors of Marathon and Salamis who composed the Prometheus, and personated his own hero on the stage.

b. To assume the character of; to 'play'.

1704 SWIFT *T. Tub* ix. 177 The Elder Brutus only personated the Fool and Madman, for the Good of the Publick. **1709** —— *Proj. Adv. Relig.* Wks. 1841 II. 177/1 The proudest man will personate humility. **1795** SOUTHEY *Joan of Arc* III. 210 Upon the throne Let some one take his seat and personate My presence, while I mingle in the train.

c. *absol.* To play or act a part; to masquerade.

1642 R. WATSON *Serm. Schisme* 28 We pull off that false vizard wherein their zeal too often personates. **1646** BUCK *Rich. III*, III. 76 *margin* He wrote..sundry petty Comedies, and Enterludes, oftentimes personating with the Actors. **1679** J. GOODMAN *Penitent Pard.* III. i. (1713) 251 Even those..that had raised the tragedy personate so well as to take upon them to be his comforters. **1895** SIR H. IRVING in *Westm. Gaz.* 21 Aug. 3/3 The actor's first duty..is to be the man of his part—to represent the personage, to personate.

2. To assume or counterfeit the person of (another), usually for the purposes of fraud; to pretend to be, pass oneself off as.

1613 R. CAWDREY *Table Alph.* (ed. 3), *Personate*, to counterfait anothers person. **1634–5** BRERETON *Trav.* (Chetham Soc.) 81 The Countess of Oxford personated the Queen and deceived the child. **1694** in Wood *Life* 10 July (O.H.S.) III. 460 A yong woman in man's apparel, or that personated a man. **1769** BLACKSTONE *Comm.* IV. x. 128 By statute 4 W. & M. c. 4. to personate any other person before any commissioner authorized to take bail in the country is also felony. **1879** DIXON *Windsor* II. xiii. 141 Having with him the deposed King's confessor..to personate the King. *absol.* **1855** MACAULAY *Hist. Eng.* xviii. IV. 245 He wandered..about Ireland and England, begging, stealing, cheating, personating, forging.

†**b.** *refl.* with complement: To feign oneself to be (some one). *Obs. rare.*

1708 SWIFT *Abolit. Chr.* Wks. 1755 II. I. 93 Instructions to personate themselves members of the several prevailing sects. **1710** *Lond. Gaz.* No. 4759/4 Convicted for..personating her self the Widow of Thomas Smith.

†**c.** *transf.* To cause to personate; to put forward in a feigned character. *Obs. rare.*

1621 BURTON *Anat. Mel.* III. ii. III. iv. (1676) 302/2. I personated mine own servant to bring in a present from a Spanish Count..as if he had been the Counts servant.

†**3.** To feign, counterfeit (a quality). *Obs.*

1630 B. JONSON *New Inn* III. ii, Tut, she dissembles; all is personated And counterfeit comes from her! **1633** MASSINGER *Guardian* I. i, Hear him, madam; His sorrow is not personated.

†**4.** To imitate, mimic; to imitate the example of, follow. *Obs. rare.*

1646 J. HALL *Horæ Vac.* 73 [Children's] tongues are more flexible to personate any pronunciation. **1647** TRAPP *Comm. Rom.* iv. 12 [To] personate and expresse him to the life, as Constantines Children..did their father.

†**5.** To represent (a person, etc.) in writing (as being of such and such a kind, or *esp.* as saying so and so); to describe; sometimes, to describe allegorically, indicate symbolically, symbolize. *Obs.*

1591 SPENSER *M. Hubberd* Ded., Simple is the deuice, and the composition meane, yet carrieth some delight, euen the rather because of the simplicitie & meannesse thus personated. **1641** MILTON *Animadv.* Ad sect. xiii. 58 That false Shepheard..under whom the Poet lively personates our Prelates, whose whole life is a recantation of their pastorall vow. **1667** WATERHOUSE *Fire Lond.* 124 Jerusalem is personated to cry out,..'Is it nothing to you all yee that pass by?' **1693** DRYDEN *Juvenal* (1697) 3 Our Poet..brands ev'n the living, and personates them under dead mens Names.

6. To be or stand as an emblem or representative of; to stand for, represent, symbolize, typify, signify; to represent vicariously or officially, stand in the place of; to embody in a personal form, impersonate. Now *rare* or *Obs.*

1611 SHAKS. *Cymb.* v. v. 454 The lofty Cedar, Royall Cymbeline Personates thee. **1640** FULLER *Joseph's Coat* (1867) 74 These Elements, which personate and represent Christ's body. **1700** C. NESSE *Antid. Armin.* (1827) 81 On the behalf of those whom he personated on the cross. **1850** T. M'CRIE *Mem. Sir H. Agnew* xiii. (1852) 196 Those rude and vulgar men..for a time personated religion in power.

†**7.** To represent as a person, personify. *rare.*

1612 SELDEN *Illustr. Drayton's Poly-olb.* ii. 35 The fruitfull bedde of this Poole, thus personated as a Sea Nymph. **1791–1823** D'ISRAELI *Cur. Lit.* (1858) III. 323 Time seemed always personated in the imagination of our philosopher.

†**8.** To mention personally or by name; to name: = INDIVIDUALIZE 2. *Obs. rare.*

1651 *Fuller's Abel Rediv., Bolton* (1867) II. 344 In reproving sin he never personated any man to put him to shame. **1662** GURNALL *Chr. in Arm.* verse 19. x. §3 (1669) 507/1 The Minister is to reprove the sins of all, but to personate none.

'personated, *ppl. a.* [f. prec. + -ED[1].]

1. Dramatically represented or acted; feigned, pretended; fictitious, imaginary: see the verb.

1606 B. JONSON *Masque Hymen* Wks. (Rtldg.) 553/1 Betwixt these a personated bride, supported, her hair flowing, and loose sprinkled with gray. **1711** ADDISON *Spect.* No. 92 ¶5 Whether or no they are real Husbands or personated ones I cannot tell. **1790** BURKE *Fr. Rev.* 120 They could not bear even the hypothetical proposition of such wickedness in the mouth of a personated tyrant.

†**2.** ? Embodied in a person. *Obs. rare.*

1635 PAGITT *Christianogr.* I. ii. (1636) 62 They affirme two natures to be united in Christ:..one personated nature to be made of the two natures not personated, without mixtion or confusion.

'personately, *adv. rare.* [f. PERSONATE *a.* + -LY[2].] In a personate manner; in an assumed character, feignedly.

1610 DONNE *Pseudo-martyr* 56 If he wore this maske and disguise cleane through the Epistle, then he spoke personately, and dissemblingly. **1611** W. SCLATER *Key* iii. 303 Ouer great heat in pressing obiections, though but personately.

'personating, *vbl. sb.* [f. PERSONATE *v.* + -ING[1].] The action of the verb PERSONATE, q.v. *personating agent* = Personation agent.

1607 SHAKS. *Timon* v. i. 35 It must be a personating of himselfe. **1695** J. EDWARDS *Perfect. Script* 365 The personating of a Christian and a Jew by way of dialogue. **1879** *Law Rep.* 4 *C.P.D.* 193 At the polling-station in which the respondent acted as personating agent.

'personating, *ppl. a.* [f. as prec. + -ING[2].] That personates: see the verb.

1612 SELDEN *Illustr. Drayton's Poly-olb.* i. A ij, In winding steps of personating fictions. **1851** MRS. BROWNING *Casa Guidi W.* I. 30 Some personating Image, wherein woe Was wrapt in beauty from offending much.

personation (pɜːsə'neɪʃən). [n. of action from PERSONATE *v.*] The action of personating.

1. The action of assuming the person of another, or of passing oneself off as some one else (usually for fraudulent purposes).

1622 BACON *Hen. VII* 113 One of the strangest Examples of a Personation, that euer was in Elder or Later Times. **1856** DICKENS *Let. to W. Collins* 13 July, The admirable personation of the girl's identity.

2. The dramatic representation of a character.

1697 COLLIER *Ess. Mor. Subj.* II. (1698) 119 Men will not be..consider'd by the Height of their Character, but for the Decency of Personation. **1841** D'ISRAELI *Amen. Lit.* (1867) 542 He [Shakespeare] was fortunate in the personation of his characters.

3. *concr.* A person or thing that represents some other, dramatically or in the way of pretence.

1851 MRS. BROWNING *Casa Guidi W.* I. 47 'Tis easier to gaze long On personations, masks and effigies, Than to see live weak creatures crushed by strong.

4. Representation or embodiment of some quality, etc. in a person; the person as embodying such quality, etc.; impersonation.

1837 DICKENS *Pickw.* v, Mr. Pickwick was the very personation of kindness and humanity. **1853** LYTTON *My Novel* x. xxv, A very personation of the beauty and magnificence of careless, luxurious, pampered, egotistical wealth.

5. *attrib.*, as **personation agent**, an agent employed by a candidate at an election to detect attempted personation of voters.

1885 *Times* (weekly ed.) 18 Dec. 10/4 Personation agents for the Nationalist Candidates. **1886** *Pall Mall G.* 15 July 2/1 Had I been a personation agent I should most certainly have protested against every alternate voter.

personative ('pɜːsəneɪtɪv), *a. rare.* [f. as PERSONATE *v.* + -IVE.] Having the quality of personating; involving dramatic representation.

1789 T. TWINING *Aristotle's Treat. Poetry* (1812) I. 31 Immediate and obvious resemblance, we shall find..only in Dramatic—or to use a more general term—Personative Poetry. **1898** T. HARDY *Wessex Poems* p. viii, The pieces are in a large degree dramatic or personative in conception.

personator ('pɜːsəneɪtə(r)). Also 7 -er. [agent-n. from PERSONATE *v.*: suffix orig. Eng., subseq. Latin.] One who personates (in various senses).

1608 B. JONSON *Hue & Cry Cupid* Pref., Expressing..a most reall affection in the personaters, to those, for whose sake they would sustayne these persons. **1654** GAYTON *Pleas. Notes* III. xi. 144 Passions conterfeited long..have so alter'd the personaters. **1863** LYTTON *Caxtoniana* II. 160 In the drama William Tell is the personator of the Swiss liberties. **1872** E. W. ROBERTSON *Hist. Ess.* 187 Was he a personator of the betrayed Ætheling?

persone, obs. form of PARSON, PERSON.

personed ('pɜːsənd), *a. rare.* [f. PERSON *sb.* + -ED[2].] †**a.** United in one person or substance. *Obs.* †**b.** Seated in or belonging to a person, personal, individual. *Obs.* **c.** In parasynthetic comb.: Having a person or bodily figure (of a specified kind).

1548 GEST *Pr. Masse* in H. G. Dugdale *Life* (1840) App. I. 86 Soch a presence of Christes body in the bread, wherwyth they both shuld be unseverably personed and have al theyr condicions and properties common. **1565** HARDING in Jewel *Def. Apol.* (1611) 632 The Pope..may erre by personed error, in his own priuate iudgement, as a man, and as a particular Doctor in his own opinion. **1615** CHAPMAN *Odyss.* x. I. 456 This man, So goodly person'd, and so match'd with mind.

personeity (pɜːsə'niːɪtɪ). *rare.* [Arbitrarily f. PERSON, app. after the etymologically formed *corporeity*: cf. also *hæcceity*, *ipseity*.] Used by Coleridge app. for **a.** That which constitutes a person; the being or essence of a person, personship. **b.** *concr.* A being of the nature of a person, a personal being. (App. intended in both uses to avoid some of the connotations of *personality*, as applied to a human being or to one of the persons of the Trinity.) Hence affected by some later writers in different senses of PERSONALITY and PERSONAGE.

1822 COLERIDGE *Lett. Convers.*, etc. II. 146 Our own wandering thoughts may be..the most effective viceroys, or substitutes of that dark and dim personëity, whose whispers and fiery darts holy men have supposed them to be. *a* **1834** —— in *Lit. Rem.* (1839) IV. I, I cannot meditate too often..on the personeity of God, and his personality in the Word. *Ibid.* 166. *Ibid.* 232 Who can comprehend his own will; or his own personeity, that is, his I-ship (*Ichheit*)? **1836** *Fraser's Mag.* XIV. 411 Σῶμα..expressing indifferently either personeity or corporeity. **1873** M. COLLINS *Miranda* I. 179 That illustrious personeity was nothing loth.

†**personer,** obs. form of PARCENER.

1387–8 T. USK *Test. Love* II. ii.

personhood. [f. PERSON *sb.* + -HOOD.] The quality or condition of being an individual person.

1959 *Times Lit. Suppl.* 3 Apr. 197/3 From there he proceeds to the machine-like properties of animals and so on up to responsible human personhood. **1971** *Time* 13 Dec. 36 The United Church of Christ has in hand a statement written by six Christian education executives which maintains that sex is moral if the partners are committed to the 'fulfilling of each other's personhood'—pointedly omitting marriage as a prerequisite. **1973** *Austral. Humanist* XXVI. 10/1 The locus of power needs to move from institutionalization towards man in his personhood, thus freeing man to respond to life with his own body, his own thinking, feeling and acting, expressing his abilities by working creatively with his human, natural and material environments. **1973** *Black World* Mar. 71 'Collage' defines her Black womanhood first in relation to her personhood, selfhood, or humanness and then in relation to her femininity. **1974** K. MILLETT *Flying* (1975) I. 34 There is something healing in her talk: its religious care for personhood. **1976** *Church Times* 12 Nov. 9/1 My unreflective believers have been denied the home atmosphere which encourages them to find their own personhood and value it.

personifiable (pə'sɒnɪfaɪəb(ə)l), *a. rare.* [f. PERSONIFY + -ABLE.] Capable of being personified.

1890 *Harper's Mag.* June 48/1 Outraged domesticity is not a personifiable quality.

personifiant (pə'sɒnɪfaɪənt), *a. rare*[−1]. [ad. F. *personnifiant*, pr. pple. of *personnifier* to PERSONIFY: see -ANT.] Personifying.

1856 RUSKIN *Mod. Paint.* III. IV. viii. §6 A full third..of the works of Tintoret and Veronese..are entirely symbolical or personifiant.

personification (pəsɒnɪfɪ'keɪʃən). [n. of action f. PERSONIFY: so in mod.F. (1835 in *Dict. Acad.*).] The action of personifying, or something in which such action is embodied.

1. Attribution of personal form, nature, or characteristics; the representation of a thing or abstraction as a person: esp. as a rhetorical figure or species of metaphor. Also in art, the representation of a thing or abstraction by a human figure.

1755 JOHNSON, *Personification*, prosopopœia; the change of things to persons: as, 'Confusion heard his voice.' **1776** MICKLE tr. *Camoens' Lusiad* VI. 263 *note*, Poetry delights in Personification. **1795** BURKE *Regic. Peace* iv. Wks. IX. 11 Therefore comes in abstraction and personification..'Make your peace with France'. **1865** TYLOR *Early Hist. Man.* xi. 324 A personification of the phenomena of nature. **1875** JOWETT *Plato* (ed. 2) I. p. xiv, The personifications of church and country as females.

b. An imaginary or ideal person conceived as representing a thing or abstraction.

1850 M'COSH *Div. Govt.* I. i. (1874) 22 The Stoic divinities are just a personification of the stern method of the Stoic character. **1869** TOZER *Highl. Turkey* II. 321 Scylla, who is the personification of the whirlpool. **1885** CLODD *Myths & Dr.* I. iii. 44 Among the Aztecs..the bird-serpent, was a personification of the wind.

2. The embodiment of a quality, idea, or other abstraction, in a real person (or, by extension, in a concrete thing); usually applied to the actual person (or thing) as embodying the quality, etc., or exemplifying it in a striking manner or degree; an impersonation, 'incarnation' (*of* something).

1807–8 W. IRVING *Salmag.* i. (1860) 20 A fair damsel, who looked for all the world like the personification of a rainbow. **1819** SCOTT *Ivanhoe* ii, The large-jointed heavy horses,..which, placed by the side of those Eastern coursers, might have passed for a personification of substance and of shadow. **1855** MACAULAY *Hist. Eng.* xi. III. 76 He was popularly regarded as the personification of the Latitudinarian spirit.

3. A dramatic representation, or literary description, of a person or character. *rare.*

1814 D'ISRAELI *Quarrels Auth.* (1867) 307 He was creating new dramatic existences in the exquisite personifications of his comic characters. **1848** THACKERAY *Van. Fair* liii, The beautiful and accomplished Mrs. Rawdon Crawley's admirable personifications.

So **per'sonifi,cative** *a.*, having the quality of personifying; **per'sonifi,cator** = PERSONIFIER.

1834 SOUTHEY *Doctor* xxxiii. (1862) 79 Michael Drayton, ..as determined a personificator as Darwin himself. **1864** *Press* 9 July 669 He is a perfect personificator of the travelling mountebank. **1890** *Cent. Dict.*, *Personificative.*

personified (pəˈsɒnɪfaɪd), *ppl. a.* [f. PERSONIFY + -ED[1].]

1. Represented, spoken of, or figured as a person.

1833 HT. MARTINEAU *Fr. Wines & Pol.* i. 16 Alms issuing from an English merchant's pocket..in the name of a personified vineyard. **1870** LUBBOCK *Orig. Civiliz.* vii. (1875) 350 The worship of personified principles, such as Fear, Love, Hope, &c.

2. Made into a person; in human form. *rare.*

1851 GALLENGA *Italy* I. II. ii. 146 The poem of Dante was to Italy what the spark of the sun was to the personified clay of Prometheus. **1899** *Harper's Mag.* Feb. 385 A fierce battle raged between the personified geese who hissed and the men who resented the offence.

personifier (pəˈsɒnɪfaɪə(r)). [f. as prec. + -ER[1].] One who personifies: **a.** A speaker or writer who uses personification; **b.** One who personates or acts the part of another.

1768–74 TUCKER *Lt. Nat.* (1834) II. 464 As I am a great personifier, I have..addressed that virtue as a person. **1871** G. MEREDITH *Harry Richmond* xiii, Captain Welsh could not perceive in Temple the personifier of Alcibiades. **1900** R. J. DRUMMOND *Apost. Teaching* vi. 235 He ventured on personification which became at times so vivid as to impose on the personifier himself.

personify (pəˈsɒnɪfaɪ), *v.* [app. a. F. *personnifier* (in Boileau, 17th c.), f. L. type **persōnificāre*: see PERSON and -FY.]

1. *trans.* To figure or represent (a thing or abstraction) as a person; to attribute a personal nature or personal characteristics to, by way of metaphor, in thought, or esp. in speech or writing; in art, to symbolize by a figure in human form.

1727–41 CHAMBERS *Cycl.* s.v., The poets have personified all the passions; and made divinities of them. *Ibid.*, Personifying is essential to poetry, especially the epopœia. **1783** H. BLAIR *Lect.* viii. I. 147 We can personify any object that we chuse to introduce with dignity. **1834** McMURTRIE *Cuvier's Anim. Kingd.* 1 It is in this latter sense..that we usually personify Nature. **1875** JOWETT *Plato* (ed. 2) IV. 376 Like mythology, Greek philosophy has a tendency to personify ideas.

2. To embody (a quality, etc.) in one's person or self; to be an embodiment or concrete type of; to exemplify in a typical manner; to impersonate. Chiefly in *pa. pple.* = embodied, 'incarnate'.

1803 WELLINGTON in Gurw. *Desp.* (1837) II. 404 The natives of this country are rashness personified. **1849** MACAULAY *Hist. Eng.* ii. I. 246 In this man the political immorality of his age was personified.

3. To make or turn into a person; to give a human form or nature to. (Cf. PERSONIFIED 2.)

1768 [W. DONALDSON] *Life Sir B. Sapskull* II. xxi. 174 Men possessed of that plastic virtue to personify, and even make gentlemen out of the most stubborn and clownish ingredients.

4. To assume the person of, to personate. *rare.*

1824 HOGG *Conf. Sinner* 257, I blessed myself, and asked whom it was his pleasure to personify to-night? **1851** GALLENGA *Italy* i. 33 There were adroit men about him, who did not scruple to personify him.

Hence **perˈsonifying** *vbl. sb.* and *ppl. a.*

1886 *Athenæum* 27 Feb. 290/1 Full of that personifying tendency. **1898** ROBERTSON *Poetry & Relig. Ps.* xi. 276 The personifying theorists.

personize (ˈpɜːsənaɪz), *v.* ? *Obs.* [f. PERSON or L. *persōna* + -IZE.]

1. *intr.* To assume a character; to act a part.

1593 G. HARVEY *Pierce's Super.* 197 It was nothing with him [Dr. Perne] to Temporise *in genere*, or *in specie*..that could so formally and featly Personise *in individuo*.

2. *trans.* To represent as a person, to personify.

1734 J. RICHARDSON *On Milton's P.L.* II. 964 Milton has Personiz'd them and put them in the Court of Chaos. **1757** *Herald* No. 1 (1758) I. 3 If the purity of the Christian system admits not of her being personized and worshiped externally in shrines. **1762** GOLDSM. *Cit. W.* lxx, If you would make Fortune your friend, or, to personize her no longer, if you desire, my son, to be rich.

Hence **personiˈzation** *rare*$^{-0}$, the action of personizing; personification; impersonation.

1890 in *Cent. Dict.*

ˈpersonless, *a.* [f. PERSON *sb.* + -LESS.]

a. Unrecognized as a person; denied individuality. **b.** Making no distinction of persons.

1909 E. HILL in Hill & Shafer *Gt. Suffragists* 11 The slaves of ancient empires, like women of to-day, were not recognised as 'persons', but they built the hanging gardens of Babylon and her mammoth buildings, and the material glory of Athens, just as the 'personless persons' of to-day weave the great moral fabric of the universe and, departing, bequeath their ideals to the willing souls ready to receive them. **1932** H. S. WALPOLE *Fortress* IV. ii. 607 He was by temperament intensely cautious and by training suspicious, and, mingled with these two strains, there was an odd element of personless, rather noble philanthropy.

personne, obs. form of PARSON, PERSON.

personnel (pɜːsəˈnɛl, pɛrsɔnɛl). [mod.F., sb. use of *personnel* adj., personal, as contrasted with *matériel* material, e.g. *le matériel et le personnel d'une armée*. In earlier use anglicized; see PERSONAL B. 4.] **1. a.** The body of persons engaged in any service or employment, esp. in a public institution, as an army, navy, hospital, etc.; the human as distinct from the *matériel* or material equipment (*of* an institution, undertaking, etc.).

In quot. 1834 used in the French sense of 'the sum of qualities which make up the character': but this can hardly be considered as more than an isolated use in Eng.

[**1834** *Edin. Rev.* LIX. 329 In their hands..the *personnel* of the robbers [became] more truculent.]

1837 J. S. MILL in *Westm. Rev.* XXVIII. 25 In moments of general enthusiasm it is enough that a party carries the favourite banner; but in the intervals between those moments, its importance depends upon the confidence inspired by its *personnel*. **1857** S. OSBORN *Quedah.* xv. 200 Captain Warren was favourably impressed with the *matériel* and *personnel* of the native army co-operating with us. **1861** THACKERAY *Four Georges* 142 He knew the *personnel* of the Universities. **1863** P. BARRY *Dockyard Econ.* 39 It is not here recommended that the *personnel* of the English dockyards should be remodelled on the French plan. **1886** LD. BRASSEY *Nav. Annual* 3 From the *personnel* we pass to the *materiel* of the [English] fleet. **1886** STUBBS *Lect. Study Hist.* iv. 89 To study the drama in its plot and personnel. **1894** C. N. ROBINSON *Brit. Fleet* 315 The personnel—the body of men, that is, who themselves constitute our Navy. **1899** H. JAMES *Awkward Age* x. xxxvii. 397 The *personnel*, as the newspapers say, of the saloon will shift and change. **1943** *R.A.F. Jrnl.* Aug. 3 The new basis of distribution is one copy to every twenty-five personnel. **1944** *Return to Attack* (Army Board, N.Z.) 15/1 British forces then rushed the landing ground..capturing nineteen aircraft together with a number of somewhat bewildered air-force personnel. **1969** [see JAWAN]. **1972** J. MOSEDALE *Football* v. 56 Sammy Baugh of the Washington Redskins, playing with inferior personnel overall, lasted 16 years.

b. *spec.* The members of an orchestra, band, etc.

1956 *Gramophone* June 25/1 The sleeve [of a record] gives personnels. **1962** *Oxford Mail* 19 Feb. 6/5 The personnel of the nine bands on this important release includes many of the most famous names in jazz. **1967** *Melody Maker* 16 Dec. 10/5 It is certainly a very good band with above average solo strength and a personnel which includes a mass of arranging talent. **1968** *Blues Unlimited* Nov. 10 It is owing to him that personnels and dates for so many blues/gospel recordings by this company are now wellknown. **1973** *Melody Maker* 4 Aug. 50/6 When the Humphrey Lyttelton Band makes an appearance at the Lancastrian Hall, Swinton, Manchester, ..the personnel will include Kathy Stobart (tenor), [etc.].

c. (Usu. with capital initial.) = *personnel department*.

1960 M. SPARK *Ballad of Peckham Rye* v. 86 I'm just mentioning a factor that Personnel keep stressing. **1970** 'D. CRAIG' *Young Men may Die* xviii. 127, I rang Personnel at the office and asked for Stephen's full name. **1973** *Clarendonian* XXVII. I. 21 It was not therefore surprising that when a vacancy occurred, J. L. A. asked for her in Personnel.

2. Personal appearance. *rare.*

1861 T. MCWEENEY in D. Crow *Theresa* (1966) xvi. 182 Mrs Yelverton is still in the possession of an exceedingly agreeable personnel, and, without being positively handsome, she is most prepossessing and ladylike. **1909** W. DE MORGAN *It never can happen Again* I. x. 139 Contrast it with the dowdy personnel and awkward manners of the political gentleman's wife.

3. *attrib.* and *Comb.*, as ***personnel audit, car, carrier, department, management, manager, officer, policy, procurement, secretary, transfer capsule***; ***personnel-designating*** adj.; ***personnel-wise*** advb.

1967 COULTHARD & SMITH in Wills & Yearsley *Handbk. Managem. Technol.* 211 *Personnel audit*—in the same way that a firm's accounts are audited, or the stockrooms checked periodically, it is desirable to maintain an accurate analysis of the company's personnel needs—in managerial, clerical, sales, and manufacturing areas—together with an assessment of its strengths, as made up by the individuals concerned. **1914** *Illustr. London News* 17 Oct. 540/2 The personnel-car of the Schneider gun-train. **1945** *Finito! Po Valley Campaign* (15th Army Group) 51 A German convoy of two 170 mm cannon pulled by prime movers and followed by personnel carriers swung out of a side road. **1975** *N.Y. Times* 8 Sept. 2/2 A modern armored personnel carrier is one of Israel's obvious military needs. **1976** *Globe & Mail* (Toronto) 24 Sept. 9/1 The Post Office says there are now 908 'mailmobiles' or 'personnel carriers' operating across Canada. **1977** *Time* 25 July 37/1 A wave of Soviet tanks and armored personnel carriers rolls across the northern German plain. **1943** J. B. PRIESTLEY *Daylight on Saturday* vi. 32 Mr. Cheviot..was very keen on the personnel department and welfare generally. **1962** S. E. GODFREY *Retail Selling & Organization* vii. 55 The personnel department is also responsible for keeping detailed records of each employee and for authorizing salary payments. **1973** E. PACE *Any War will Do* (1974) i. 15 All the famous benefits the personnel department was always talking about. **1963** F. G. LOUNSBURY in S. Koch *Psychol.* VI. 570 Lexical units in kinship terminologies can differ, as between different societies, in two aspects of their meanings: the 'personnel-designating' aspect and the 'role-symbolizing' aspect. **1957** CLARK & GOTTFRIED *University Dict. Business & Finance* 265/1 *Personnel management*, the branch of business management concerned with the administration and direction of all of the relations between a company and its employees. **1959** *Cambr. Rev.* 6 June 575/1, I have heard personnel management described as a career that the liberal-minded, not unintellectual arts graduate of this university can take up without being accused of selling himself to mammon. **1973** 'M. UNDERWOOD' *Reward for Defector* v. 38 He would need a bread and butter job... He mentioned personnel management. **1926** M. S. LEUCK *Fields of Work for Women* vii. 74 (*heading*) Personnel manager. **1951** J. B. PRIESTLEY *Festival at Farbridge* I. i. 21, I have a friend.. who's now the personnel manager at Whatmore's. **1973** Personnel manager [see *labour relations* s.v. LABOUR *sb.* 8]. **1957** C. SMITH *Case of Torches* xi. 132 The women's personnel officer was tall, smart and superior. **1958** A. WILSON *Middle Age of Mrs Eliot* III. 430 Old Shuffler suggested that I got a job as secretary to a personnel officer at some big works in the London area. **1976** M. HINXMAN *End of Good Woman* x. 139 'Work your way up, lad,' the personnel officer told him. **1949** M. MEAD *Male & Female* xvii. 349 The personnel policy is protecting the firm, not the married men and women. **1950** *N.Y. Times* 20 Apr. 1/3 Donald Dawson, an administrative assistant responsible for personnel procurement, who has the never-ending task of seeking and investigating candidates for important vacancies. **1923** H. CRANE *Let.* 10 June (1965) 136, I don't know many at the office yet..but I've already been invited out to tea by the personnel secretary. **1965** *Tuscaloosa* (Alabama) *News* 11 Sept. 8/1 Doctors say a swift rise to the surface would probably be fatal. So the aquanauts will enter a special personnel transfer capsule that will take them to the surface where they will enter a decompression chamber on the mother ship's deck. **1975** *Offshore* Aug. 54/3 The personnel transfer capsule (PTC) was launched from the YDT to carry out open sea dives to 1,000 ft. **1963** R. I. McDAVID *Mencken's Amer. Lang.* 250 The practice [of forming adverbs from nouns by adding *-wise*] quickly spread from the admen to the bureaucrats and the educationists and soon yielded *curriculumwise*,.. *personnelwise* and *weatherwise*.

personology (pɜːsəˈnɒlədʒɪ). *Psychol.* [f. PERSON *sb.* + -OLOGY.] A term sometimes used for the study of personality. So **personoˈlogical** *a.*; **persoˈnologist**, one who studies personality.

1926 J. C. SMUTS *Holism & Evolution* x. 262 Personality is, in fact, largely an unexplored subject and requires a discipline to itself as a real factor in the universe. 'Characterology' has been suggested as a name for the new discipline, but there are objections to it, and Personology is suggested as a better name. The 'Person' is a concept of the Roman law, not of Greek philosophy, and the hybrid is therefore justified. **1938** H. A. MURRAY *Explorations in Personality* i. 4 The branch of psychology which principally concerns itself with the study of human lives and the factors that influence their course, which investigates individual differences and types of personality, may be termed 'personology' instead of 'the psychology of personality' a clumsy and tautological expression. *Ibid.* 8 Since the latter [*sc.* psychic impulses] are intangible, personologists must imagine them. **1951** J. S. BRUNER in Blake & Ramsey *Perception* v. 121 The perception-centered approach takes as its primary focus of interest the variables of perception and studies the way these are affected by various learnings, motivational states, personological structures, etc. **1957** HALL & LINDZEY *Theories of Personality* v. 157 The focus of this theory is upon the individual in all his complexity and this point of view is highlighted by the term 'personology'. **1967** R. R. HOLT in Lazarus & Opton *Personality* 48 Personologists have increasingly begun to recognize that all the error-terms of standard psychological equations are their own happy hunting grounds. *Ibid.* (*heading*), The logic of the Romantic point of view in personology. **1980** *Underground Grammarian* Mar., Since personology must be too subtle a science for the likes of us, we cannot explain how 'personological' variables might be different from differences in persons.

ˈpersonship. *rare.* [f. PERSON *sb.* + -SHIP.] Personality, individuality.

1645 USSHER *Body Div.* 78 Though one may communicate his nature with one, he can not communicate his personship with another. *Ibid.* 165 One naturall person-ship, which..in ordinary men maketh a perfect person.

person-to-ˈperson, *adj.* (and *adv.*) *phr.*

a. Designating a personal telephone call: see *personal call* s.v. PERSONAL *a.* 10. orig. and chiefly *U.S.*

1919 *N.Y. City Telephone Directory* 20/2 A Person-to-Person Toll Call is one made by name for a particular person reached through a telephone which is located outside the local service area and at a point to which there is a person-to-person toll rate. **1933** *Sat. Even. Post* 11 Feb. 57 There are two classes of Long Distance calls: station-to-station and person-to-person... When the caller asks the operator for a specific individual, the person-to-person rate applies. **1960** C. FITZ GIBBON *When Kissing had to Stop* viii. 128 I've put through a personal call, what they call a person-to-person call over there. **1973** C. EGLETON *Seven Days to Killing* xx. 222 They stopped by the call-box..and Tarrant got the operator to put through a person-to-person call. **1973** *Sat. Rev. Society* (U.S.) Mar. 70/2 Person-to-person calls are, of course, more expensive than station-to-station calls. **1977** *Transatlantic Rev.* LX. 50 A representative of the Columbus Police Department placed a person-to-person call to Dr. Edward Hudson in Padananim.

b. Taking place directly between individuals; interpersonal.

1951 R. FIRTH *Elem. Social Organiz.* i. 30 Some anthropologists have argued that a social structure is the network of all person-to-person relations in a society. **1954** [see *high-potential* s.v. HIGH *a.* 22 a.]. **1960** *Times* 12 Feb. 4/6 Person-to-person communication between specialists is much less satisfactory in applied science. **1965** H. KAHN *On Escalation* xiii. 248 The person-to-person meeting of Khrushchev and Kennedy. **1970** *Hospital Tribune* 26 Jan., Person-to-person spread probably accounted for the introduction of new cases into communities. **1977** *Proc. R. Soc. Med.* LXX. 553/1 Leukaemia and Hodgkin's disease are unusual among neoplastic disorders in man in often having aroused suspicion of person-to-person transmission or an infective aetiology.

As *adv. phr.* (usu. without hyphens).

1971 G. CUTTLE in B. de Ferranti *Living with Computer* i. 4 This does not mean that in future all contact will be person-to-person over the telephone and viewing screen. **1977** B. LUCAS tr. *C. De Foucauld's Lett. from Desert* vii. 128 Apostolic work..as I envisage it consists in talking person to person with infidels.

persoon(e, -oun(e, -own, obs. ff. PARSON, PERSON.

persorption (pəˈsɔːpʃən). *Chem.* [f. PER(MEATION + SORPTION.] Sorption in which molecules of a gas enter pores in a solid that are only a little larger than themselves.

1930 MCBAIN & BRITTON in *Jrnl. Amer. Chem. Soc.* LII. 2220 The sorbed molecules of nitrogen must be so intimately surrounded by the atoms of carbon with which they are in contact that the designation 'adsorption', which implies a surface, becomes a misnomer. There is very little difference in such a case between adsorption and absorption; and if a precise word to describe sorption by charcoal were required, the new term 'persorption' might be coined. **1948** GLASSTONE *Textbk. Physical Chem.* (ed. 2) xiv. 1204 It is probable that persorption is operative in the highly active charcoals, and perhaps to some extent in silica gel; the occlusion of hydrogen by palladium..may well be an extreme case of combined activated adsorption and persorption. **1960** A. W. ADAMSON *Physical Chem. of Surfaces* xi. 523 What might be considered to be a limiting or extreme case of persorption is the formation of clathrate compounds.

persour, persowr, obs. ff. PIERCER.

persp. (pɜːsp). Also persp (without full point). Colloq. abbrev. of PERSPIRATION 4.

1923 WODEHOUSE *Inimitable Jeeves* ii. 24 The good old persp. was bedewing my forehead by this time in a pretty lavish manner. **1966** —— *Plum Pie* i. 19 It was with quite a few beads of persp bedewing the brow that I went back to the dining room. **1974** —— *Aunts aren't Gentlemen* ii. 12 He said 'Phew' and removed a bead of persp. from the brow.

†**per'spection.** *Obs.* [ad. L. *perspectiōn-em*, n. of action from *perspicĕre* to look through, look closely into, view, behold, f. PER- 1 + *specĕre* to look.] A looking through, into, or at something; view, sight, inspection, contemplation; regard, respect; insight; outlook, look-out. (*lit.* and *fig.*)

1549 *Compl. Scot.* viii. 72 O quhat vanhap..is this that..hes blyndit ȝour ene fra the perspectione of ȝour extreme ruuyne? **1621** T. WILLIAMSON tr. *Goulart's Wise Vieillard* 177 Such perspection and contemplation of faith is not..a vaine imagination. **1650** BULWER *Anthropomet.* 72 Not only made..for ornament unto the eye, but for perspection. **1682** BUNYAN *Holy War* i, Eye-gate was the place of perspection.

perspectival (pəˈspɛktɪvəl), *a.* [f. PERSPECTIV(E *sb.* + -AL[1].] Of or pertaining to perspective, esp. in a *fig.* sense of a mental perspective. Hence **per'spectivally** *adv.*

a **1866** J. GROTE *Exploratio Philosophica* (1900) II. xii. 121 The '*perspectival*' fact (so to call it) of fore-shortening..is opposed to his argument in one respect. **1932** H. H. PRICE *Perception* vii. 196 The group would be a *series* of shapes having a certain limit... The series will consist primarily of perspectival distortions. **1957** *Scottish Jrnl. Theol.* X. 126 It is now clear that all historiography is perspectival, originating from some given point in the economic, political, cultural and moral structures of society and in the course of history itself. **1967** *Philos. Rev.* LXXVI. 193 Seeming to behold our universe(s) *from a place*, perspectivally. **1970** TODES & DREYFUS in J. M. Edie et al. *Patterns of Life-World* xviii. 363 Corresponding to each of these ideas of truth is a certain degree of awareness that knowledge is 'perspectival', i.e., that what we know reflects our ways and means of knowing it. **1977** *Dædalus* Summer 75 The perspectival view from the infrastructure may be at least as false as any superstructural cosmology.

perspective (pəˈspɛktɪv), *sb.* [ad. med.L. *perspectīva* (sc. *ars*), the science of optics, fem. of *perspectīvus*: see next; cf. F. *la perspective* (14th c.).]

I. †**1.** The science of sight; optics. (Also in *pl.*)

c **1380** WYCLIF *Sel. Wks.* II. 299 As tellin men of perspectif, þer ben þree maner of bodili siȝt. **1387** TREVISA *Higden* (Rolls) III. 365 He [Aristotle] made..problemys of perspective and of methaphesik. **1398** —— *Barth. De P.R.* III. xvii. (Tollem. MS.), þe auctor of þe science of perspectiue [*scientiæ perspectivæ*], þat is þe science of þe syȝte. **1570** DEE *Math. Pref.* Bj, Perspectiue, is an Art Mathematicall, which demonstrateth the maner, and properties, of all Radiations Direct, Broken, and Reflected. **1577** HARRISON *England* II. iii. (1877) I. 78 Skill in the perspectiues. **1625** N. CARPENTER *Geog. Del.* I. vii. (1635) 177 The Angle of Vision, as we finde it taught in the Perspectiues. **1658** PHILLIPS, *Perspective*,..the art of advantaging the sight by the contrivance of glasses, being a branch of Opticks.

†**2.** An optical instrument for looking through or viewing objects with; a spy-glass, magnifying-glass, telescope, etc. Also *fig.*, esp. in such phrases as ***to look through the wrong end of the perspective*** = to look upon something as smaller or of less consequence than it is. *Obs.*

In early use applied to various optical devices, as arrangements of mirrors etc. for producing some special or fantastic effect, e.g. by distortion of images. (Cf. also 4 b.)

[In the Chaucer quotation, the word in all the ancient MSS. has the prefix contracted, the Hengwrt, Corpus, and Lansdowne having (according to the Six-text ed.) the contraction *p* for *per*, the Ellesmere, Cambridge, Petworth, and Harleian 7334, having that for *pro-*, which is also the form in the 16th c. printed edd. Notwithstanding this preponderance of MS. testimony, there can be little doubt that the correct reading is *perspective*, as shown by the history of the two words; *prospective*, as a genuine word, having arisen only *c* 1590.]

c **1386** CHAUCER *Sqr.'s T.* 226 (Hengwrt MS.) They speke of Alocen and Vitulon Of Aristotle þat writen in hir lyues Of queynte Mirours and of perspectyues. *a* **1529** SKELTON *Wks.* (1843) I. 25 Encleryd myrroure and perspectyue most bryght. *c* **1532** DU WES *Introd. Fr.* in *Palsgr.* 1045 The perspectif or glasse in the whiche the kindes [*printed* kindnes] and symilitudes of thynges ben shewed. **1601** SHAKS. *All's Well* v. iii. 48 Contempt his scornefull Perspectiue did lend me, Which warpt the line of euerie other fauour. **1634** SIR T. HERBERT *Trav.* Ded. A ij b, Like an ill-sighted man, who sees with Spectacles or Perspectives. **1634-5** BRERETON *Trav.* (1844) 60 W[m]. Daviseon offered to furnish me with a couple of these perspectives, which shew the new-found motion of the stars about Jupiter. **1646** BUCK *Rich. III* Ded., To looke at other mens actions and memory by the wrong end of the perspective. **1668** PEPYS *Diary* 13 July, To Reeves's; and there saw some [books], and bespoke a little perspective, and was mightily pleased with seeing objects in a dark room. **1692** DRYDEN *St. Euremont's Ess.* 280 By the means of Great Perspectives, which Invention becomes more perfect every Day, they discover new Planets. **1709** STEELE & ADDISON *Tatler* No. 103 ¶13, I..refused him a Licence for a Perspective, but allowed him a Pair of Spectacles. **1716** CIBBER *Love's Last Shift* I. i, If we look thro' Reason's never-erring Perspective. **1748** *Anson's Voy.* II. vi. 195 By means of our perspectives..we saw an English flag hoisted. **1789** BURNS *Let. to Mrs. Dunlop* 4 Mar., As a snail pushes out his horns, or as we draw out a perspective.

II. 3. a. The art of delineating solid objects upon a plane surface so that the drawing produces the same impression of apparent relative positions and magnitudes, or of distance, as do the actual objects when viewed from a particular point. (Formerly also *pl.* in same sense.) See also 6 b.

Without qualification, usually denoting ***linear perspective***, an application of projective geometry, in which the drawing is such as would be made upon a transparent vertical plane (*plane of delineation*) interposed in the proper position between the eye and the object, by drawing straight lines from the position of the eye (*point of sight*) to the several points of the object, their intersections with the plane of delineation forming the corresponding points of the drawing.

AERIAL *p.*, ISOMETRIC *p.*, LINEAR *p.*, PARALLEL *p.*: see these words. ***angular perspective*** = *oblique p.* ***conical p.***, that in which objects are delineated as if projected upon the surface of a vertical cone from a point in its axis, the surface being then unrolled into a plane: so ***cylindrical p.*** ***gauche p.***, that in which the surface of delineation is not a plane. ***oblique p.***, that in which neither side of the principal object is parallel to the plane of delineation, so that the horizontal lines meet at a vanishing point.

1598 R. HAYDOCKE tr. *Lomazzo* Pref. 8 A Painter without the Perspectiues was like a Doctor without Grammer. **1601** HOLLAND *Pliny* xxxv. xi. II. 547 So excellent he was in this perspectiue, that a man would say, his euen, plaine, and flat picture were embossed and raised work. **1694** DRYDEN *To Sir G. Kneller* 39 Yet perspective was lame, no distance true, But all came forward in one common view. **1702** ADDISON *Dial. Medals* iii, They have represented their buildings according to the rules of perspective. **1704** J. HARRIS *Lex. Techn.* I, *Aerial Perspective* is a Proportionable Diminution of the Teints and Colours of a Picture, when the Objects are supposed to be very remote. **1783** MASON *Art of Painting* 163 Yet deem not, Youths, that Perspective can give Those charms complete by which your works shall live. **1822** IMISON *Sc. & Art* II. 385 The method of drawing a building ..in oblique perspective. **1859** RUSKIN *Perspective* Introd. 3 Every picture drawn in true perspective may be considered as an upright piece of glass on which the objects seen through it have been thus drawn.

b. *transf.* The appearance presented by visible objects, in regard to relative position, apparent distance, etc.

1826 FARADAY *Exp. Res.* xxxvii. (1859) 216 The convergence of the rays to one spot..was merely an effect of perspective. **1834** MRS. SOMERVILLE *Connex. Phys. Sc.* xxxvii. (1849) 431 The stars, from the effects of perspective alone, would seem to diverge in the direction to which the solar system was going. **1881** ATKINSON tr. *Helmholtz's Lect. Sci. Subjects* Ser. II. III. i. 87 Aerial perspective. By this we understand the optical action of the light, which the illuminated masses of air, between the observer and distant objects, give.

c. *Mod. Geom.* = HOMOLOGY 4.

1857 CAYLEY *Coll. Math. Papers* III. 5 Triangles are in perspective when the three lines joining the corresponding angles meet in a point, or, what is the same thing, when the three points of intersection of the corresponding sides lie in a line. **1881** CASEY *Sequel to Euclid* 77 Triangles whose corresponding vertices lie on concurrent lines have received different names from Geometers... Townshend and Clebsch call them triangles in *perspective*, and the point *O* and the line *XYZ* the *centre* and the *axis of perspective*. **1885** LEUDESDORF *Cremona's Proj. Geom.* iv. 20.

d. *fig.* The relation or proportion in which the parts of a subject are viewed by the mind; the aspect of a matter or object of thought, as perceived from a particular mental 'point of view'. Hence the point of view itself; a way of regarding (something).

1605 BACON *Adv. Learn.* II. viii. §1 We have endeavoured in these our partitions to observe a kind of perspective, that one part may cast light upon another. **1613** DRUMM. OF HAWTH. *Cypress Grove* Wks. (1711) 120 All, that we can set our eyes on in these intricate mazes of life, is but vain perspective and deceiving shadows, appearing far otherwise afar off, than when..gazed upon at a near distance. **1813** SHELLEY *Q. Mab* II. 250 The events Of old and wondrous times..were unfolded In just perspective to the view. **1841** MYERS *Cath. Th.* IV. xxxv. 359 Clearly no method can be satisfactory but that which preserves the perspective of history true. **1894** H. DRUMMOND *Ascent of Man* 11 Evolution..has thrown the universe into a fresh perspective. **1907** H. ADAMS *Educ. Henry Adams* ii. 20 Time and experience, which alter all perspectives. **1934** M. BODKIN *Archetypal Patterns in Poetry* 307 Writing from the psychological standpoint, I intend this statement less as criticism than as recognition of the limitations of the vital perspective present in these essays. **1949** R. K. MERTON *Social Theory* III. ix. 262 Mannheim's inconsistency..stems from an indefinite distinction between incorrectness (invalidity) and perspective ('onesidedness'). **1963** J. T. WATERMAN (*title*) Perspectives in linguistics. **1964** GOULD & KOLB *Dict. Social Sci.* 262/1 There has been much discussion from many perspectives as to the origins and 'causes' of fascism.

e. An apparent spatial distribution or extent in perceived sound. Freq. preceded by a qualifying word, as ***auditory***, ***sound***, etc.

1934 STEINBERG & SNOW in *Electrical Engineering* (N.Y.) Jan. 12/1 An audience..senses the spatial relations of the instruments of the orchestra. This spatial character of the sounds gives to the music a sense of depth and of extensiveness, and for perfect reproduction should be preserved. In other words, the sounds should be reproduced in true auditory perspective. **1949** FRAYNE & WOLFE *Elem. Sound Recording* xxxii. 674 Adjustment of the gain of the individual channels also helps in preserving the acoustic perspective. **1961** G. MILLERSON *Technique Television Production* i. 17 He can warn boom operators against dipping into shot..while assisting them in achieving sound perspective to suit the transmitted picture. **1963** *Times* 12 Jan. 11/3 The sound is all too full and forward, and badly lacking in aural perspective.

4. *concr.* **a.** A drawing or picture in perspective; a 'view'; *spec.* a picture so contrived as seemingly to enlarge or extend the actual space, as in a stage scene, or to give the effect of distance.

1644 EVELYN *Diary* 27 Feb., In the upper walkes are two perspectives, seeming to enlarge the allys. *Ibid.* 1 Mar., A little Garden, which, tho' very narrow, by the addition of a well-painted perspective, is to appearance greatly enlarged. **1648** in *Bury Wills* (Camden) 217, I give him alsoe my two perspectives of Saint Marke, hanging in the chamber of my laboritary. **1651** J. JANE (*title*) Εικων Ακλαστος. The Image Vnbroken. A Perspective of the Impudence, Falshood [etc.] in a Libell entitled Εικονοκλαστης against Εικων Βασιλικη. **1664** POWER *Exp. Philos.* Pref. 18 Outside Fallacies; like our Stage-scenes or Perspectives, that shew things inwards, when they are but superficial paintings. **1680** AUBREY in *Lett. Eminent Persons* (1813) III. 501, I have a curious designe of his to drawe a landskip or perspective. **1703** OLIVER in *Phil. Trans.* XXIII. 1404 A Perspective of the late King of Denmark's Family, the Queen's Face being in the middle, and eight Princes and Princesses round her. **1858** HAWTHORNE *Fr. & It. Note-Bks.* II. 77 A vista of cypress-trees, which were indeed an illusory perspective, being painted in fresco. **1861** THACKERAY *Four Georges* I. (1862) 60 Hogarth's lively perspective of Cheapside.

†**b.** A picture or figure constructed so as to produce some fantastic effect; e.g. appearing distorted or confused except from one particular point of view, or presenting totally different aspects from different points. *Obs.*

1593 SHAKS. *Rich. II*, II. ii. 18 For sorrowes eye..Diuides one thing intire, to many obiects, Like perspectiues, which rightly gaz'd vpon Shew nothing but confusion, ey'd awry, Distinguish forme. **1601** —— *Twel. N.* v. i. 224 One face, one voice, one habit, and two persons, A naturall Perspectiue, that is, and is not. **1610** B. JONSON *Alch.* IV. iv, Hee'll shew a perspectiue, where on one side You shall behold the faces, and the persons Of all sufficient yong heires, in towne,..On th' other side, the marchants formes, and others That..will trust such parcels: In the third square, the verie street, and signe Where the commoditie dwels. [Cf. **1661** J. POWELL *Hum. Industry* vi. 76; and **1686** PLOT *Staffordsh.* ix. §100, where perspectives are described, but not named.]

†**c.** So, in similar senses, ***piece of perspective***. (Sometimes = *peep-show*.) *Obs.*

1599 B. JONSON *Ev. Man out of Hum.* IV. iv, To view 'hem (as you'ld doe a piece of Perspectiue) in at a key-hole. **1621** BURTON *Anat. Mel.* II. ii. IV. (1624) 233 Those excellent landskips and Dutch-workes,..such pleasant peeces of perspective. **1662** J. DAVIES tr. *Olearius' Voy. Ambass.* 16 A Walking-Staff, Vermilion Gilt, in which was a piece of Perspective. **1662** STILLINGFL. *Orig. Sacr.* II. v. §8 To direct them in those excellent pieces of Perspective, wherein by the help of a Prophetick glass they might see the Son of God fully represented. **1665** SIR T. HERBERT *Trav.* (1677) 151 Besides these upon the same Mountains some pieces of Perspective are elaborately and regularly cut, resembling the noblest sort of ancient structure. **1755** YOUNG *Centaur* vi. Wks. 1757 IV. 262 As in some pieces of perspective, by the pressure of the eye..the magnificent prospect is opened, and aggrandized, still more and more.

5. a. A visible scene; a (real) view or prospect; *esp.* one extending in length away from the spectator and thus showing distance, a vista.

(In mod. use associated with sense 3.)

1620 SHELTON *Quix.* III. xiv. 94 He saw the self-same Face,..the same Aspect, the same Physiognomy, the same Shape, the same Perspective of the Batchelor Samson Carrasco. **1652** LOVEDAY tr. *Calprenede's Cassandra* III. 156 The frontispeece did discover it selfe in perspective through a long walk of goodly trees. **1686** DRYDEN *To Mem. Mrs. Anne Killigrew* 115 Of lofty trees, with sacred shades And perspectives of pleasant glades. **1712** *Spect.* No. 524 ¶5 At the end of the Perspective of every strait Path,..appeared a high Pillar. **1770** GRAY *Let. to Wharton* 18 Apr., The lofty towers and long perspectives of the church. **1791** MRS. RADCLIFFE *Rom. Forest* ii, Dark hills, whose outline appeared distinctly upon the vivid glow of the horizon, closed the perspective. **1859** JEPHSON *Brittany* ii. 21 Mysterious perspectives among pillars and arches.

b. *fig.* A mental view, outlook, or prospect, esp. through an imagined extent of time, past or (usually) future; hence sometimes = expectation, 'look-out'.

1762 GOLDSM. *Cit. W.* xxx, I saw a long perspective of felicity before me. **1796** H. HUNTER tr. *St. Pierre's Stud. Nat.* (1799) I. 438 This perspective of a divine felicity, here below, would throw us into a lethargic rapture. **1879**

FARRAR *St. Paul* II. 255 The concluding words of this section..open a glorious perspective of ultimate hope for all whose hearts are sufficiently large and loving to accept it. **1965** *Economist* 6 Mar. 989/2 Only a general negotiation can offer the perspective of a return to peace and a real independence.

6. Phr. ***in perspective***. **a.** In mental view; in prospect, looked for, expected: see 5 b. ? *Obs.*

(In quot. 1633 the sense is doubtful.)

1633 G. HERBERT *Temple, Sinne* ii, Yet as in sleep we see foul death, and live: So devils are our sinnes in perspective. **1640** C. HARVEY *Synagogue* xiv. *Bible*, 'Tis heaven in perspective, and the bliss Of glory here. **1849** C. BRONTE *Shirley* xi, Take care of this future magistrate, this churchwarden in perspective.

b. Drawn or viewed in accordance with the rules or principles of perspective; also *fig.*: see 3.

1655 MRQ. WORCESTER *Cent. Inv.* §97 An instrument whereby an ignorant person may take any thing in Perspective, as justly, and more then the skilfullest Painter can do by his eye. **1806** *Med. Jrnl.* XV. 10 My delineations ..together with one done by a friend in perspective. **1821** CRAIG *Lect. Drawing* v. 282 The tops of the trees..receding in perspective into the distance. **1902** *Daily Chron.* 16 July 3/2 The engraver said he must..'put it in proper perspective'.

c. *Mod. Geom.* = *in* HOMOLOGY: see 3 c.

III. †**7.** The action of looking into something, close inspection; the faculty of seeing into a thing, insight, penetrativeness. *Obs.*

? *a* **1586** Q. ELIZ. *Let. to Jas. VI* (Camden) 173, I haue not so smal a parspectiue in my neighbors actions, but I haue foresene some wicked euent to folowe a careles gouvernement. **1622** BACON *Hen. VII* 23 Doubting that there would bee too neare looking, and too much Perspectiue into his Disguise, if he should show it here in England; he..sailed with his scholar into Ireland. **1643** MILTON *Divorce* II. xvi, And this also will be somewhat above his reach, but yet no lesse a truth for lack of his perspective. *a* **1649** DRUMM. OF HAWTH. *Poems* Wks. (1711) 24 To me this world did once seem sweet and fair, While senses light minds perspective kept blind.

IV. 8. *attrib.* ***perspective control***; ***perspective-free***, ***-suggesting*** adjs.; **perspective shell** [in allusion to its markings], the depressed conical shell of the gastropod mollusc *Solarium perspectivum*; also called *sundial shell* and *staircase shell*.

1971 C. BONINGTON *Annapurna South Face* App. F. 285, I used 2 Nikon bodies, with 24-mm. and 35-mm. perspective-control lenses, [etc.]. **1966** R. L. GREGORY *Eye & Brain* ix. 163 It would be interesting to bring animals up in a perspective-free environment. **1890** *Cent. Dict.*, Perspective shell. **1880** W. JAMES *Let.* 12 Dec. in R. B. Perry *Tht. & Char. W. James* (1935) I. 727 Metaphors and epigrams which, witty and striking and perspective-suggesting as they often are,..may be in danger of having the changes rung on them too long.

Hence **per'spective** *v. trans.*, to set in perspective; also *intr.*, to draw a plan of the perspective of a drawing, etc. Hence **per'spectived** *ppl. a.*, placed or drawn in perspective; **per'spectiveless** *a.*, devoid of perspective, drawn without regard to perspective (in quot. *fig.*); †**per'spectiver**, †**perspec'tivian**, one who treats of perspective.

1598 R. HAYDOCKE tr. *Lomazzo* II. 197 The Perspectiuers call it, the Center, Marke, Point, Terme, and the Cone of the Pyramis. **1569** J. SANFORD tr. *Agrippa's Van. Artes* 34 b, The Geometricians and Perspectiuians. **1812** B. R. HAYDON *Jrnl.* 4 Apr. in *Autobiogr.* (1853) I. x. 171 Began my picture —perspectived the greater part of the day—felt a sort of check in imagination at the difficulties I saw coming. **1874** H. R. REYNOLDS *John Bapt.* vii. 420 Blended in one dazzling but perspectiveless picture. **1902** *Westm. Gaz.* 12 Sept. 2/1 Towers, battlements, cypresses, statues all perspectived not merely for the eye but for the imagination. **1908** *Ibid.* 8 Aug. 4/1 A certain aimlessness, casualness almost, has suddenly been perspectived into purpose and plan. **1949** BROOKS & WARREN *Mod. Rhetoric* xiii. 442 It is the prose of a mind which is arranging its world, by delicate adjustments and careful discriminations, into a perspectived pattern. **1970** *Nature* 4 July 93/1 From the perspectiveless drawing of the Ancient Egyptians to the deliberate mixing of contradictory signs of depth by Hogarth and later artists. **1978** *Gramophone* July 181/1 These arrangements even make more comfortable and perspectived listening than the harpsichord originals.

perspective (pəˈspɛktɪv), *a.* [ad. late L. *perspectīv-us* (Boeth.), f. *perspect-*, ppl. stem of *perspicĕre*: see PERSPECTION and -IVE; cf. F. *perspectif*, *-ive* (14th c.).]

I. †**1.** Relating to sight; optical. *Obs.*

1432-50 tr. *Higden* (Rolls) III. 365 This saide Aristotill.. made..problemes perspective [*perspectiva problemata*] and metaphisicalle. **1477** NORTON *Ord. Alch.* v. in Ashm. *Theat. Chem. Brit.* (1652) 61 Science Perspective giveth great evidence, To all the Ministers of this Science. **1530** PALSGR. 320/2 Perspectyfe, beholdyng or regarding with the eye, *perspectif*. **1551** RECORDE *Pathw. Knowl.* Pref. Archimedes ..dyd also by arte perspectiue (whiche is a parte of geometrie) deuise such glasses within the towne of Syracusæ, that dyd bourne their enemies shyppes a great way from the towne. **1592** R. D. *Hypnerotomachia* 27 The entrie, which was by my perspective judgement twelve paces.

†**2.** Used for looking or viewing; serving to look through, or to assist the sight: applied to various optical instruments or devices. Also *fig. Obs.* Almost always in phr. ***perspective glass*** = prec. 2.

1570 DEE *Math. Pref.* Bj, He may wonderfully helpe him selfe, by perspectiue Glasses. **1594** PLAT *Jewell-ho.* III. 6 A perspectiue Ring that will discouer all the Cards that are neere him that weareth it on his finger. **1613** FLETCHER, etc. *Honest Man's Fort.* IV. i, This vizard wherewith thou wouldst hide thy spirit Is perspective to shew it plainlier. **1614** RALEIGH *Hist. World* I. vii. §2 (1634) 85 A worthy Astrologer now living [Galileo] who by the helpe of perspective Glasses hath found in the Starres many things unknowne to the Ancients. *c* **1619** WOTTON *Let. to Bacon* in *Reliq.* (1651) 414 He [Kepler] applies a long perspective-trunke..with the convexe glasse fitted to the said hole. *a* **1626** BACON *New Atl.* (1650) 30 We have also Perspective-Houses, where we make Demonstrations of all Lights, and Radiations: And of all Colours. **1674** *Lond. Gaz.* No. 931/4 To be sold at the Sign of the Royal Exchange,..all sorts of Perspective Glasses, as well Telescopes as Microscopes. **1727** POPE, etc. *Art of Sinking* II. v, His eyes should be like unto the wrong end of a perspective glass, by which all the objects of nature are lessened. **1729** SAVAGE *Wanderer* I. 144 If tubes perspective hem the spotless prize. [**1837** WHEWELL *Hist. Induct. Sc.* v. (1857) I. 300 Observed by Galileo Galilei ..by the assistance of a perspective glass.] **1852** THACKERAY *Esmond* II. x. 174 We have but to change the point of view, and the greatest action looks mean; as we turn the perspective-glass, and a giant appears a pigmy. **1859** DICKENS *T. Two Cities* v. 59 If a girl..swoons within a yard or two of a man's nose, he can see it without a perspective-glass. **1867** *Atlantic Almanac 1868* 9 So thought Lonson Nash,..who saw it [*sc.* a sea-serpent] through a perspective-glass in the year 1817.

II. 3. a. Of or pertaining to perspective (see prec. 3); drawn according to perspective; showing the effect of distance, as a picture or actual scene (cf. prec. 4, 5). †***perspective piece*** = piece of perspective: see prec. 4 c (*obs.*).

1606 DEKKER *Sev. Sinnes* I. (Arb.) 17 You may behold now in this Perspectiue piece which I haue drawne before you, how deadly and dangerous an enemy to the State this Politick Bankruptisme hath bin, and still is. **1617** MORYSON *Itin.* I. 84 The painting of the arched-roof, rare for perspectiue Art, and the chiefe of that kinde. **1628** BURTON *Anat. Mel.* II. ii. IV. 259 Brokes, riuers, trees..with many pretty landskips, and perspectiue peices. **1731** W. HALFPENNY *Perspective* 1 To find the Perspective Plan of a Square or Cube fixt above the Eye, whose Point of Sight is in a Right Line, with the Middle of the Object. **1777** P. THICKNESSE *Year's Journey* I. p. xiii, I might raise..money sufficient to pay for engraving a perspective view of Montserrat. **1813** SCOTT *Trierm.* III. xxviii, A fair arcade, In long perspective view display'd. **1850** LEITCH tr. *C. O. Müller's Anc. Art* §99 (ed. 2) 67 The art of painting..made such progress, especially in the perspective treatment of subjects, as enabled it to appear in great perfection at the very beginning of the next period. **1871** MRS. GATTY *Parables fr. Nature* Ser. v. 67 That far-off visionary point where all perspective lines converge. **1871** J. R. DICKSEE *Perspective* i. 1 Perspective drawing is so termed, because in the study of it, all objects are supposed to be seen through a transparent plane. **1911** *Encycl. Brit.* XX. 470/2 A fresco of 'The Flood' at Florence is even more naive in its parade of the painter's [*sc.* Uccello's] newly won skill in perspective science. *Ibid.* XXI. 257/2 A horizontal plane on which we suppose the objects to rest of which a perspective drawing is to be made. **1935** *Burlington Mag.* Apr. 200/1 This artist's work, including his portraits, perspective pieces and genre subjects. **1942** D. D. RUNES *Dict. Philos.* 230/2 In epistemology: the perspective predicament, the limited though real viewpoint of the individual; the plight of being confined to the experience of only part of actuality. **1959** W. C. LOUNSBURY *Backstage from A to Z* 34 Perspective drawings of sets executed to dimension can be of great value, but avoid misleading, haphazard drawings which merely confuse. **1959** P. & L. MURRAY *Dict. Art & Artists* 236 The basic assumption of all perspective systems is that parallel lines never meet, but that they appear to do so. **1961** *Architect & Building News* 21 June 822/2 The perspective drawing realistically illustrates this interesting feature of the design. **1961** G. MILLERSON *Technique Television Production* iii. 31 (*caption*) Viewing from too close or too far makes its perspective look unnatural. This is termed perspective distortion. **1970** *Oxf. Compan. Art* 843/1 Shortly after Brunelleschi made his perspective demonstrations his fellow architect Alberti devised a perspective construction for the special use of painters, which he described in detail in his famous treatise *On Painting* (1436)... This is the first known written account of a fully scientific perspective construction. **1972** *Jrnl. Social Psychol.* LXXXVII. 143 The average number of illusion supporting responses was scored for each of five geometric illusions... Muller-Lyer ..; Sander parallelogram..; perspective drawing.

b. *Mod. Geom.* Belonging to perspective (prec. 3 c) or homology; homologous, homological.

1885 LEUDESDORF *Cremona's Proj. Geom.* 3 We are said to project from a centre (or vertex) S a given figure σ upon a plane of projection σ'. The new figure σ' is called the perspective image or the central projection of the original one.

¶**4.** ? Misused for PROSPECTIVE. (But cf. prec. 6 a.)

1709 MRS. MANLEY *Secret Mem.* (1736) III. 274 My Hand, unable to support the Pen, drops in perspective Extasies. **1796** J. BIDLAKE in *New Ann. Reg.* 155 O blindness to the future! That kindly veils sharp pain's perspective ills.

perspectively (pəˈspɛktɪvlɪ), *adv.* [f. PERSPECTIVE *a.* + -LY².]

†**1.** Optically; as through an optical instrument. (Sometimes with allusion to those producing fantastic effects: see PERSPECTIVE *sb.* 2.) *Obs.*

1552 HULOET, Perspectyuelye, *optice*. **1599** SHAKS. *Hen. V*, v. ii. 347 Yes my lord, you see them perspectiuely: the Cities turn'd into a Maid; for they are all gyrdled with Maiden Walls.

†**2.** Clearly, evidently. (Cf. L. *perspecte* adv.)

1598 R. HAYDOCKE tr. *Lomazzo* II. 198 No otherwise than that which it seeth beholding it Perspectiuely. **1632** LITHGOW *Trav.* v. 223 Which Houses haue stood on pillars ..: the infinite number whereof, as may as yet bee, (aboue and below the Sands) perspectiuely beheld.

3. According to perspective; in perspective (see PERSPECTIVE *sb.* 3).

1703 MOXON *Mech. Exerc.* 252 If more Fronts than one be shewn Perspectively in one Draught. **1853** *Blackw. Mag.* LXXIV. 95 Atmospheric light..perhaps not quite perspectively true to the actual distances.

b. *Mod. Geom.* So as to be 'in perspective' or homologous: see PERSPECTIVE *sb.* 3 c, *adj.* 3 b.

1865 CAYLEY *Coll. Math. Papers* V. 480 Two triangles, ABC, $A'B'C'$ which are such that the lines AA', BB', CC' meet in a point, are said to be in perspective..the triangle $A'B'C'$ is said to be perspectively inscribed in the triangle ABC.

perspectivic (pəˈspɛktɪvɪk), *a. rare.* [f. PERSPECTIV(E *sb.* + -IC.] = PERSPECTIVE *a.* 3.

1949 KOESTLER *Insight & Outlook* xxii. 315 The laws of perspectivic geometry make the painter *see* differently.

perspectivism (pəˈspɛktɪvɪz(ə)m). [f. PERSPECTIV(E *sb.* + -ISM.] **1.** *Philos.* The theory that knowledge of a subject is inevitably partial and limited by the individual perspective from which it is viewed; also, the partiality and limitation inherent in knowledge on this view.

1910 T. COMMON tr. *Nietzsche's Joyful Wisdom* 299 Fundamentally our actions are in an incomparable manner altogether personal, unique and absolutely individual—.. but as soon as we translate them into consciousness, they do not appear so any longer... This is the proper phenomenalism and perspectivism as I understand it. **1949** R. K. MERTON *Social Theory* ix. 261 Mannheim's conception of 'perspectivism' is substantially the same as the Rickert-Weber conception of *Wertbeziehung* (which holds that values are relevant to formulation of the scientific problem and choice of materials but are not relevant to the validity of the results). **1954** A. HUXLEY *Let.* 17 Jan. (1969) 693 Von Bertalannfy..calls it 'Perspectivism', and points out that the unity of science is to be sought..in the isomorphy of explanatory laws in the different fields and disciplines of science. **1965** A. DANTO *Nietzsche* iii. 80 Does Perspectivism entail that Perspectivism itself is but a perspective, so that the truth of this doctrine entails that it is false? **1969** C. O. SCHRAG *Experience & Being* viii. 276 Is it possible for a philosophy of experience..to proceed beyond the perspectivism of point of view philosophizing? **1973** J. P. STERN *On Realism* v. 64 This perspectivism to which all experience is subject.

2. The practice of regarding and analysing a situation, work of art, etc., from different points of view and on different levels.

1948 L. SPITZER *Linguistics & Lit. Hist.* ii. 50 We may assume that the linguistic perspectivism of Cervantes is reflected in his invention of plot and characters... Cervantes' perspectivism, linguistic and otherwise, would allow him qua artist to stand above, and sometimes aloof from, the misconceptions of his characters. **1949** WELLEK & WARREN *Theory of Lit.* xii. 158 The unsound thesis of absolutism and the equally unsound antithesis of relativism must be superseded and harmonized in a new synthesis which makes the scale of values itself dynamic, but does not surrender it as such. 'Perspectivism', as we have termed such a conception, does not mean an anarchy of values, a glorification of individual caprice, but a process of getting to know the object from different points of view which may be defined and criticized in their turn. **1962** M. MCLUHAN *Gutenberg Galaxy* 125 The habit of a fixed..'point of view' ..gave popular extension to the avant-garde perspectivism of the fifteenth century.

perspectivist (pəˈspɛktɪvɪst). [f. PERSPECTIV(E *sb.* + -IST.] An artist who specializes in perspective effects; one who studies the principles of perspective.

1942 *Burlington Mag.* Jan. 24/2 In the case of Fouquet the traditional methods of the master of the Bedford Hours.. gives way to the influence of Fra Angelico, of Jacopo Bellini and of the Florentine perspectivists. **1955** H. READ *Icon & Idea* 149 The 'Commentaries' of Ghiberti.., which are a kind of commonplace book in which we find all the ancient texts and recorded observations that occupied the minds of these fifteenth-century perspectivists, depend a good deal on Arabic sources. **1958** R. MYERSCOUGH-WALKER *Perspectivist* i. 7 A perspectivist never, under any condition, begins with an image behind the transparency. *Ibid.* 11 There are very few professional perspectivists in England at this moment. **1970** M. H. PIRENNE *Optics, Painting & Photogr.* vii. 85 On 'perspectivists', that is artists who made such illusionistic paintings [*sc.* painted ceilings], see Maffei. .. This interesting article..does not refer to the works of perspectivists extant in Great Britain.

perspectivistic (pəˌspɛktɪˈvɪstɪk), *a.* [f. PERSPECTIV(E *sb.* + -ISTIC.] Of or pertaining to perspectivism.

1948 L. SPITZER *Linguistics & Lit. Hist.* 67 We are offered basically the same perspectivistic pattern that we have noted in the case of the *baciyelmo*. **1950** J. MESERVE tr. E. Auerbach in *Partisan Rev.* May–June 416 And so the excursus does not begin until two lines later, when Eurycleia has discovered the scar—the possibility for a perspectivistic connection no longer exists, and the story of the wound becomes an independent and exclusive present.

perspectivity (pəspɛkˈtɪvɪtɪ). [f. PERSPECTIV(E *sb.* + -ITY.] The quality or condition of being limited by or confined to a particular perspective or point of view.

1910 A. M. LUDOVICI tr. *Nietzsche's Will to Power* II. 20 (*heading*) Biology of the instinct of knowledge. Perspectivity. **1930** A. O. LOVEJOY *Revolt against Dualism* iii. 92 The necessary diversity of the characters experienced by percipients having different standpoints, we may call 'perspectivity'. **1933** *Jrnl. Philos.* XXX. 63 Such perspectivity is what the organism escapes to the extent that it becomes aware of..the logical dimension of nature. **1969**

C. O. SCHRAG *Experience & Being* viii. 276 In becoming clear about the meaning of perspectivity, a rather firmly entrenched prejudice needs to be suspended.

perspectograph (pəˈspɛktəgrɑːf, -æ-). [f. L. *perspect-*, ppl. stem (see PERSPECTIVE *a.*) + -GRAPH.] 'An instrument for the mechanical drawing of objects in perspective' (Francis *Dict. Arts*, 1842).

1875 *Carpentry & Join.* 137 As a practical means of teaching perspective the perspectograph will be found a very handy instrument.

So ˌ**perspecˈtography** (*rare*$^{-0}$), the art or theory of drawing in perspective.

1864 in WEBSTER.

Perspex (ˈpɜːspɛks). Also **perspex**. [Irreg. f. L. *perspect-*, ppl. stem of *perspicere* to look through (1st pers. perfect *perspexī*), f. PER *prep.* + *specere* to look (at).] A proprietary name for polymerized methyl methacrylate, a tough transparent thermoplastic that is much lighter than glass and does not splinter. Freq. *attrib.* and in *Comb.*

In the U.S. sold under the names of PLEXIGLAS and LUCITE.

1935 *Trade Marks Jrnl.* 9 Jan. 48/2 Perspex... Synthetic resins sold in the form of sheets, rods, tubes and shaped pieces, and as moulding powders. I.C.I. (Fertilizer & Synthetic Products) Limited, London,.. manufacturers. **1937** *Nature* 20 Feb. 336/1 The lenses.. were made of a particular form of the plastic material known by the trade name of 'Perspex'. **1943** L. CHESHIRE *Bomber Pilot* i. 9, I asked Percy to dim his light; it reflected on the perspex in front and I couldn't see out. **1946** *Electronic Engin.* XVIII. 224 The needle holder is in the form of a small perspex block. **1951** *Official Gaz.* (U.S. Patent Office) 13 Nov. 336/1 Imperial Chemical Industries Limited, London... Perspex. .. Claims use since 1934; and since November 1949 in commerce between Great Britain and the United States. **1957** *Times* 21 Dec. 9/7 The sculpture is dominated by.. designs for a fountain and a triptych in Perspex. **1959** G. FREEMAN *Jack would be Gent.* i. 13 There were two large, ornate chandeliers made of wrought iron and bits of Perspex. **1960** *Practical Wireless* XXXVI. 397/1 Behind a small sheet of perspex screwed to the front above the speaker aperture. **1961** *Lancet* 23 Sept. 680/2 After infection, groups of mice were kept in air-tight 'Perspex' boxes. **1963** *Times* 11 May 4/7 The perspex windscreen is faired down almost to the driver's seat. **1975** N. LUARD *Travelling Horseman* iii. 81 A damn great Perspex-faced wall map of London.

† **ˈperspicable**, *a. Obs.* [ad. late L. *perspicābilis* that may easily be beheld (Ammianus, Augustine), f. **perspicārī* = *perspic-ĕre* to see through, look closely into, perceive, behold. Cf. L. *conspicābilis*, f. *conspicārī* beside *conspicĕre*.]

1. That can be seen through, transparent.

1615 T. ADAMS *Spir. Navigator* 5 This is 'mare vitreum' a sea of glasse more cleare perspicable and transparent.

2. Capable of being beheld; visible; in view.

1660 F. BROOKE tr. *Le Blanc's Trav.* 237 Eight parts, which are all perspicable from the middle station of the Town. **1665** SIR T. HERBERT *Trav.* (1677) 142 There be but nineteen Pillars at this day extant, yet the fractures and bases of other one and twenty more are perspicable.

perspicacious (pɜːspɪˈkeɪʃəs), *a.* [f. L. *perspicāx*, *-cācem*, having the power of seeing through, sharp-sighted, f. *perspicĕre*: see PERSPECTION and -ACIOUS. Cf. F. *perspicace* (1546 in Hatz.-Darm.).]

1. Of clear or penetrating sight; clear-sighted. (Often passing into 2.) *arch.*

1616–61 HOLYDAY *Persius* (1673) 327 And can'st thou with a perspicacious sight Discern the shew of truth from truth? **1751** JOHNSON *Rambler* No. 102 ⁋4 An expanse of waters.. covered with so thick a mist, that the most perspicacious eye could see but a little way. **1879** MISS M. A. SPRAGUE *Earnest Trifler* xi. (1880) 117 Like the brilliant perspicacious stare of the critical world.

2. Of persons, their faculties, etc.: Of clear or penetrating mental vision or discernment.

1640 HOWELL *Dodona's Gr.* (1645) 52 He was rarely quick and perspicacious. **1721** STRYPE *Eccl. Mem.* III. App. xx. 59 [These] testify the man to be of a most perspicacious wit. **1873** H. ROGERS *Orig. Bible* iii. 121 He was far too perspicacious to be imposed upon by any such false analogy.

¶ **3.** *erron.* Clear, translucent, perspicuous. *rare.*

a **1820** SHELLEY *Pr. Wks.* (1888) I. 415 The genuine doctrine of 'political Justice', presented in one perspicacious and impressive river.

Hence **perspiˈcaciously** *adv.*, with clear vision, clearly; **perspiˈcaciousness**.

1727 in BAILEY vol. II, *Perspicaciousness*. **1750** JOHNSON *Rambler* No. 43 ⁋13 He that.. too perspicaciously foresees obstacles. **1779–81** —— *L.P.*, *Denham* Wks. II. 78 The particulars of resemblance are so perspicaciously collected.

perspicacity (pɜːspɪˈkæsɪtɪ). [ad. L. *perspicācitās*, f. *perspicāx*: see prec. and -ITY: cf. F. *perspicacité* (15–16th c. in Hatz.-Darm.).]

1. Keenness of sight. *Obs.* or *arch.*

1607 TOPSELL *Four-f. Beasts* 493 From these fables of Lynceus came the opinion of the singular perspicacity of the beast Linx. **1646** SIR T. BROWNE *Pseud. Ep.* I. ii. 5 Nor can there any thing escape the perspicacity of those eyes which were before light, and unto whose opticks there is no opacity. **1774** GOLDSM. *Nat. Hist.* (1862) II. II. vii. 55 The barn-owl.. watches in the dark, with the utmost perspicacity and perseverance.

2. Clearness of understanding or insight; penetration, discernment.

1548 BECON *Solace of Soule* Wks. (1560) II. 115 Thou shalte neuer by the perspycacyte and quyckenes of thy owne reason perceyue how it maye be possible. **1663** BP. PATRICK *Parab. Pilgr.* xxviii. (1668) 323 The greatest wits want perspicacity in things that respect their own interest. **1779–81** JOHNSON *L.P.*, *Blackmore* Wks. III. 173 [This] is the only reproach which all the perspicacity of malice.. has ever fixed upon his private life. **1809–10** COLERIDGE *Friend* (1865) 153 A masterpiece of perspicacity as well as perspicuity. **1838** PRESCOTT *Ferd. & Is.* (1846) III. xvi. 183 She showed the same perspicacity in the selection of her agents. **1876** GLADSTONE *Homeric Synchr.* 61 Lessing, in his Laocoon, has discussed with luminous perspicacity [etc.].

† **ˈperspicacy.** *Obs.* [f. L. *perspicāc-em* PERSPICACIOUS: see -ACY 1.] = prec.

1599 B. JONSON *Ev. Man out of Hum.* v. ii, Nay, lady, doe not scorne us, though you haue the gift of perspicacie aboue others. **1658** SIR T. BROWNE *Pseud. Ep.* VII. xviii. 463 It was a very great mistake in the perspicacy [*ed.* 1646 perspicacity] of that Animal. *a* **1693** *Urquhart's Rabelais* III. xliii. 355 In blunting the perspicacy of the Eyes of the Wise.

† **perˈspicience.** *Obs.* [ad. L. *perspicientia*, f. *perspicient-em*, pr. pple. of *perspicĕre* to see through: see PERSPECTION and -ENCE.] Keen or clear perception; insight.

1661 FELTHAM *Resolves* II. iii. (1677) 163 Though it [Faith] be set in a heighth, beyond our Humane Perspicience, I can believe it rather super-elevated, then contradictive to our Reason. **1721–90** in BAILEY. **1768** [W. DONALDSON] *Life Sir B. Sapskull* II. xx. 163 His conducting this perplexing affair with so much judgment and perspicience.

† **ˈperspicil.** *Obs.* [ad. med. or mod.L. *perspicillum*, f. *perspic-ĕre* to see through + *-illum*, dim. and instrumental suffix: cf. *aspergillum*.] An optic glass; a lens; a telescope or microscope.

1614 TOMKIS *Albumazar* I. iii, Sir, 'tis a perspicil.. With this I'll read a leaf of that small Iliad.. Twelve long miles off. **1625** N. CARPENTER *Geog. Del.* I. iv. (1635) 87 It is manifest out of the experiment of the new Perspicils, that the bodies of the Sunne and Jupiter haue at least a double motion. **1661** GLANVILL *Van. Dogm.* 174 The Perspicil, as well as the Needle, hath enlarged the habitable World. **1680** *Counterplots* 29 There is no such mirrour so clear and true to look in, no such optick or perspicil to see with.

fig. **1611** S. PAGE *Commendatory Verses* in *Coryat's Crudities*, And give the world in one Synoptick quill Full proofe that he is Brittaine's Perspicill. **1675** SIR E. SHERBURNE tr. *Manilius* Pref. 2 That the Galaxie is a Congeries of Numberless small stars was by the sole Perspicil of Reason discovered by the Ancients.

† **perˈspicuate**, *a. Obs. rare*$^{-1}$. [f. as next + -ATE[2].] Transparent: = PERSPICUOUS 1.

1477 NORTON *Ord. Alch.* v. in Ashm. *Theat. Chem. Brit.* (1652) 64 Every cleere thinge perspicuate and fayre.

† **perˈspicuate**, *v. Obs. rare*$^{-1}$. [f. L. *perspicu-us* PERSPICUOUS + -ATE[3].] *trans.* To render perspicuous, clear, or transparent.

1634 *Simple Reasons* in *Harl. Misc.* (Malh.) IV. 181 Our faith in God, and loyalty to the King, are.. emblazoned, perspicuated, cognominated, propagated, and promulgated.

perspicuity (pəspɪˈkjuːɪtɪ). [ad. L. *perspicuitās*, f. *perspicu-us* (see below and -ITY): cf. F. *perspicuité* (16th c. in Godef. *Compl.*).]

† **1.** Transparency, translucency. *Obs.*

1477 NORTON *Ord. Alch.* iii. in Ashm. *Theat. Chem. Brit.* (1652) 42 A goodly stone glittering with perspecuitie. **1594** PLAT *Jewell-ho.* I. 4 Glasses through whose perspicuitie.. one may discern weekly in what plight they are. **1601** HOLLAND *Pliny* II. 609 Pretious stones which are commended for their perspicuity and transparent clearenesse. **1691** RAY *Creation* II. (1692) 122 The aqueous Humor of the Eye.. hath the Perspicuity and Fluidity of common Water. **1750** tr. *Leonardus' Mirr. Stones* 35 To declare in what Manner Perspicuity or Opacity happens in Stones.

2. Clearness of statement or exposition; freedom from obscurity or ambiguity; lucidity.

1546 LANGLEY *Pol. Verg. De Invent* I. x, The perfection of an History resteth in matter and wordes... The tenor of the wordes asketh a brief perspicuite. **1611** BIBLE *Transl. Pref.* 8 The translation of the Seuentie dissenteth from the Originall in many places, neither doeth it come neere it, for perspicuitie, grauitie, majestie. **1711** STEELE *Spect.* No. 2 ⁋3 The Perspicuity of his Discourse gives the same Pleasure that Wit would in another Man. **1833–6** J. H. NEWMAN *Hist. Sk.* (1873) II. II. xii. 295 Greek.. is celebrated.. for its perspicuity, and its reproductive power. **1834** SOUTHEY *Doctor* lviii. (1862) 127 There is nothing more desirable in composition than perspicuity; and in perspicuity precision is included.

† **3.** Distinctness to the sight; conspicuousness. *Obs. rare.*

1609 B. JONSON *Masque of Queens* Wks. (Rtldg.) 575/2 After it, succeeded their third dance... Wherein, beside that principal grace of perspicuity, the motions were so even and apt [etc.]. **1634** SIR T. HERBERT *Trav.* 88 A high imperious mountaine.. eminent for height and perspicuitie.

¶ **4.** *improp.* Discernment, insight, perspicacity.

1662 GAUDEN in Chr. Wordsw. *Doc. Suppl.* (1825) 37 There are no eyes I more justly dread than your's for the acuteness and perspicuity, yet none to which I more willingly present.. myself, and what I do. **1680** MORDEN *Geog. Rect.* (1685) 458 When the Pupil can read the Alcoran with perspicuity. **1720** GORDON & TRENCHARD *Independ. Whig* (1728) 120 It may well be expected from Persons of their Penetration and Perspicuity. **1806** H. SIDDONS *Maid, Wife, & Widow* III. 211 That worthy man could read hearts with great perspicuity. **1865** DICKENS *Mut. Fr.* I. xv, Mr. Wegg made a smiling demonstration of great perspicuity here.

† **perˈspiculative**, *a. Obs. rare*$^{-0}$. [irreg. f. L. *perspic-ĕre* to see through, see clearly.]

1623 COCKERAM, *Perspiculatiue*, which may be seen.

† **perˈspiculous**, *a. Obs. rare.* [Erroneous formation from L. *perspicu-us* PERSPICUOUS.] Clear, lucid. Hence † **perˈspiculously** *adv.*

1565 T. STAPLETON *Fortr. Faith* 122 b, S. Basill.. (whose pleasaunt perspiculous eloquence who haue read his workes in greke, can not but wonder at). **1662** PAGITT *Heresiogr.* (ed. 6) 220 A thing most perspiculously evident this day.

perspicuous (pəˈspɪkjuːəs), *a.* [f. L. *perspicu-us* transparent, clear, evident (f. *perspic-ĕre* to see through) + -OUS.]

† **1.** Transparent, translucent. *Obs.*

1477 NORTON *Ord. Alch.* v. in Ashm. *Theat. Chem. Brit.* (1652) 64 Christall hath Water declyning toward Ayer, Wherefore it is cleere, perspicuous and faire. **1599** H. BUTTES *Diets Dry Dinner* P iv b, [Tabacco] of a tawny colour, somewhat inclining to red: most perspicuous and cleare. **1660** BOYLE *New Exp. Phys. Mech.* xxxvii. (1682) 158 Water turning from perspicuous to white. **1669** WORLIDGE *Syst. Agric.* (1681) 293 Represented to our sight through the perspicuous body of the Air. **1750** tr. *Leonardus' Mirr. Stones* 224 Sapphire is a Stone of a yellow or Skie-blue Colour, perspicuous like the most pure Azure.

2. Clear or easy to be understood; clearly expressed, lucid; evident.

1586 B. YOUNG *Guazzo's Civ. Conv.* IV. 190 Whereupon the Queene commaunded him.. he should make that intricate sentence more perspicuous. **1624** GATAKER *Transubst.* 87 The proofe is so plaine, and his meaning so perspicuous. **1668** DRYDEN *Dram. Poesy* Ess. (ed. Ker) I. 77 The reason is perspicuous, why no French plays, when translated, have, or ever can succeed on the English stage. **1741** WATTS *Improv. Mind* I. viii. §6 Wheresoever he writes more obscurely, search out for some more perspicuous passages in the same writer. **1791** BOSWELL *Johnson* an. 1754 (1831) I. 243 The most perspicuous and energetick language. **1872** MINTO *Eng. Prose Lit.* Introd. 13 Rules can be laid down for the perspicuous construction of paragraphs.

b. Of persons: Clear in statement or expression.

1593 R. HARVEY *Philad.* 10 Or if Dianaes Priest be commonly obscure.. cannot it be, that hee should be perspicuous at anie one time? **1611** DEKKER *Roaring Girle* Wks. 1873 III. 211 Prethee maister Captaine Iacke, be plaine and perspicuous with mee. **1776** ADAM SMITH *W.N.* I. iv. (1869) I. 30, I am always willing to run some hazard of being tedious in order to be sure that I am perspicuous. **1791** in Boswell *Johnson* Aug. an. 1783, He [Johnson] was always most perfectly clear and perspicuous.

3. Easily or distinctly seen, conspicuous. ? *Obs.*

1586 FERNE *Blaz. Gentrie* II. 102 Set in the chiefe of the Coate, as in the most perspicuous place. **1615** G. SANDYS *Trav.* 22 The ruines that are now so perspicuous,.. stand foure miles South-west from the aforesaid place. *c* **1710** CELIA FIENNES *Diary* (1888) 50 Ely-minster.. so Lofty built yᵗ its perspicious above ye town. **1805** FOSTER *Ess.* II. ii. 140 An exceedingly distinct and perspicuous aspect.

b. *fig.* Eminent, distinguished, conspicuous.

1634 *Malory's Arthur* Pref., The never-dying fame of the illustrious Trojan Hector is perspicuous. *a* **1674** CLARENDON *Surv. Leviath.* (1676) 274 The person of every Soveraign Prince, is too notorious and perspicuous to need any such demonstration.

¶ **4.** *improperly.* Discerning, perspicacious. *rare.* † **b.** Clear-sighted (*obs.*).

1584 R. SCOTT *Discov. Witchcr.* Ep. Ded. to Sir R. Manwood, I know you to be perspicuous, and able to see downe into the depth and bottome of causes, &c. **1650** GENTILIS *Considerations* 224 That character.. is not seene many times by the most perspicuous sight. **1652–62** HEYLIN *Cosmogr.* III. (1673) 9/1 From one of the summits or tops thereof, a man of perspicuous eyes may discern the Euxine on the one hand, and the Mediterranean on the other. **1865** SWINBURNE *Atalanta* 221 The gods are heavy on me.. and my perspicuous soul Darken with vision.

perˈspicuously, *adv.* [f. prec. + -LY[2].]

1. In a perspicuous manner; clearly, evidently, lucidly.

1592 WYRLEY *Armorie*, *Ld. Chandos* 3 It is of importance that they be known.. by al, and that so perspicuously, that .. the meanest and simplest common soldier may thereby know euerie particular officer. **1637** HEYWOOD *Dial.*, *Procus & Puella* Wks. 1874 VI. 123 Thy minde by myne I see perspicuously. **1713** STEELE *Guard.* No. 15 ⁋4 He will express himself perspicuously. **1833** J. H. NEWMAN *Arians* II. v. (1876) 225 Dionysius.. declares perspicuously the principle of the orthodox teaching.

¶ **2.** *improperly.* With perspicacity. *rare.*

1600 W. WATSON *Decacordon* (1602) 317 This doctrine [of the Jesuits] when princes and other men of learning, iudgement, and experience in such pragmatical platformes do perspicuously looke into: [they] perceiue [etc.].

perˈspicuousness. [f. as prec. + -NESS.] The quality of being perspicuous; perspicuity.

1727 in BAILEY vol. II. **1787** W. MARSHALL *Norfolk* II. To Rdr. 6 With any degree of accuracy and perspicuousness. **1862** MERIVALE *Rom. Emp.* (1871) V. xli. 126 *note*, Nowhere else are his stories told with such vivacity and perspicuousness.

perspirable (pəˈspaɪərəb(ə)l), *a.* (*sb.*) [f. PERSPIRE *v.* + -ABLE. Cf. F. *perspirable* (in Paré 1561).]

1. Capable of perspiring; allowing the passage of perspiration; liable to perspire.

† *perspirable veins*, an old name of the arteries, as the supposed channels of the 'vital spirits'.

1604 F. HERING *Mod. Defence* A iv b, Womens bodies being more soft, tender, and perspirable. 1684 tr. *Bonet's Merc. Compit.* VI. 158 The Bloud, as it.. passes to and fro, through the perspirable Veins. 1690 BOYLE *Chr. Virtuoso* I. 63 Who would believe that the Poyson.. should be able.. to continue in the warm and still perspirable Body of the bitten person? 1744 tr. *Boerhaave's Inst.* III. 309 The whole Surface of the human Body.. is perspirable. 1860–1 FLOR. NIGHTINGALE *Nursing* 65 The skin absorbs the water and becomes softer and more perspirable.

†**b.** Capable of breathing forth or emitting an effluvium. *Obs. rare.*

1646 SIR T. BROWNE *Pseud. Ep.* II. iv. 79 For Electricks will not commonly attract, except they grow hot or become perspirable. 1656 BLOUNT *Glossogr.*, *Perspirable*,.. that may, or is able to breathe through.

c. Of, pertaining to, or attended with perspiration; *perspirable point*, point of perspiration.

1805 W. SAUNDERS *Min. Waters* 496 To bring down the animal heat to the perspirable point. 1822 *Examiner* 380/2 Her fan, which.. he is essaying to pick up by a puffing and perspirable exertion.

†**2.** Liable to be blown through; exposed to air or the wind, airy. *Obs.*

c 1624 CHAPMAN *Homer's Epigr.* x, [Ida] Where every tree Beares up in aire such perspirable heights. 1660 R. COKE *Power & Subj.* 57 Joyning this perspirable region with the celestial and intelligible. 1669 WORLIDGE *Syst. Agric.* (1681) 197 Let the Doors and Windows be stopp'd with Clay, that the House be not perspirable with Wind or Air.

3. a. Capable of being thrown off in perspiration (insensible or sensible). †**b.** Capable of being exhaled or emitted in vapour (*obs.*). †**c.** Allowing of the passage of perspiration (*obs.*).

1646 SIR T. BROWNE *Pseud. Ep.* V. xxi. 270 The Amnios is a generall investment, containing the sudorous or thin serosity perspirable through the skin. *c* 1720 W. GIBSON *Farrier's Guide* I. i. (1738) 5 Porous for the passage of Sweat, or other perspirable Matter. 1744 BERKELEY *Siris* §88 Perspirable humours not discharged will stagnate and putrefy. 1800 *Med. Jrnl.* IV. 9 Speculations concerning the perspirable Fluids of Human Bodies. 1822–34 *Good's Study Med.* (ed. 4) IV. 417 A copious discharge of perspirable matter.

B. as *sb.* in *pl.* Perspirable matters.

1797 J. DOWNING *Disord. Horned Cattle* 30 A regular discharge, or secretion of perspirables.

Hence **perspiraˈbility**, capability of perspiring; liability to perspire.

1744 MITCHELL in *Phil. Trans.* XLIII. 145 On account of the Perspirability of their Bodies. 1805 W. SAUNDERS *Min. Waters* 529 A salutary relaxation and perspirability of the skin.

†**perspirant.** *Obs. rare.* [ad. L. *perspīrānt-em*, or F. *perspirant*, pr. pple. of L. *perspīrāre* or F. *perspirer* to PERSPIRE: see -ANT.] A perspiring duct; a sweat-duct.

1745 FRANKLIN *Let. to Cadwal. Colden* Wks. 1887 II. 5 That they [i.e. absorbent ducts] should communicate with the veins, and the perspirants with the arteries only seems natural enough.

perspirate (ˈpɜːspɪreɪt), *v. rare.* [f. L. *perspīrāt-*, ppl. stem of *perspīrāre*: see PERSPIRE and -ATE³. Perh. a back-formation from next.] = PERSPIRE. Hence **ˈperspirating** *ppl. a.*

1822 *New Monthly Mag.* VI. 504 The perspirating surface of the leaf. 1843 THACKERAY *Carmen Lilliense* III. i, The sun bursts out in furious blaze, I perspirate from head to heel.

perspiration (pɜːspɪˈreɪʃən). [a. F. *perspiration* (in Paré 1561), n. of action from *perspirer*, ad. L. *perspīrāre*: see PERSPIRE.] The action of perspiring, in various senses.

†**1.** Breathing out or through. *Obs.*

1611 COTGR., *Perspiration*, a perspiration, or breathing through. 1681 CHETHAM *Angler's Vade-m.* iii. §16 (1689) 27 It's convenient to bore small holes in it for their better perspiration. 1710 SHAFTESB. *Charac.* III. *Adv. Author* i, He wou'd find the Air perhaps more rarefy'd and sutable to the Perspiration requir'd, especially in the case of a Poetical Genius.

†**2.** Evaporation, exhalation. *Obs.*

1652 FRENCH *Yorksh. Spa* vii. 70 This Spaw water is strongest.. in Winters frost, by reason of the earth being the more bound up, and the said spirits being thereby kept from perspiration. 1707 MORTIMER *Husb.* (1721) II. 329 Cover'd only with a loose Cover, that there may be a free Perspiration of the Volatile Spirit of your Must.

3. The excretion of moisture through the pores of the skin (originally applied to the insensible excretion, now also to the sensible); sweating.

1626 BACON *Sylva* §680 Much of the matter of hair in the other parts of the body [than the head] goeth forth by insensible perspiration. 1656 BLOUNT *Glossogr.*, *Perspiration* is as it were a breathing or vaporing of the whole body through the skin. 1704 SWIFT *Mech. Operat. Spirit* ii. Misc. (1711) 293 These [Caps] when moisten'd with Sweat, stop all Perspiration. 1740 BAYNARD *Health* (ed. 6) 21 For thro' a constant dilatation, The spirits spend by perspiration. 1804 ABERNETHY *Surg. Obs.* 186 His feet put into warm water in hopes of procuring perspiration. 1842 ABDY *Water Cure* (1843) 159 He returns to his bed, and drives out the enemy by renewed perspiration.

†**b.** The exhalation of vapour or moisture through the pores of plants. *Obs.*

1664 POWER *Exp. Philos.* I. 29 That all Vegetables have a constant perspiration, the continual dispersion of their odour makes out. 1674 GREW *Veget. Trunks* ii. §7 Part of the Sap, remitted, in perspirations, back again into the Aer. 1796 MORSE *Amer. Geog.* I. 673 The perspiration of vegetables of all kinds.. fills the air with moisture.

4. *concr.* That which is perspired; sweat.

1725 N. ROBINSON *Th. Physick* 72 It yields an Excrement call'd Perspiration, which is the last Digestion the Blood undergoes. 1759 ELLIS in *Phil. Trans.* LI. 211 Their covering was not thick enough to keep in their perspiration. 1884 F. M. CRAWFORD *Rom. Singer* I. 21 The next minute the perspiration stands on your forehead.

5. *Comb.*

1849 E. B. EASTWICK *Dry Leaves* 5 It is no holiday-work climbing that steep, craggy, perspiration-exciting.. Pinnacle. 1899 *Westm. Gaz.* 29 Nov. 2/1 His red-brown perspiration-bathed arms.

perspirative (pəˈspaɪərətɪv, ˈpɜːspɪreɪtɪv), *a. rare.* [f. L. *perspīrāt-*, ppl. stem of *perspīrāre* to PERSPIRE + -IVE.] Promoting or subservient to perspiration; = next.

1730–6 BAILEY (folio), *Perspirative*, of or pertaining to perspiration or breathing or exhaling through. 1755 JOHNSON, *Perspirative*, performing the act of perspiration. [Hence in later dicts.] *a* 1776 R. JAMES *Diss. Fevers* (1778) 157 It is a very common error in practice,.. to administer very heating and perspirative medicines, with an intent to drive out the measles as it is called.

perspiratory (pəˈspaɪərətərɪ), *a.* [f. L. *perspīrāt-* (see prec.) + -ORY².]

1. Subservient to, leading to, or producing perspiration.

1725 CHEYNE *Health & Long Life* 15 Besides the Air that gets through the perspiratory Ducts into the Blood, whenever we Eat, Drink, or Breath, we are taking into our Bodies such Air as is about us. 1732 J. B. tr. *Belloste's Hosp. Surg.* ii, Eliminate them out of the body by the perspiratory passages. 1748 *Phil. Trans.* XLV. 294 Deposited.. in the very perspiratory pores of its bark. 1791 E. DARWIN *Bot. Gard.* I. Notes 101 Concerning the use of the leaves of plants. Some have contended that they are perspiratory organs. *c* 1865 J. WYLDE in *Circ. Sc.* I. 428/2 Substances, which.. will close the perspiratory pores. 1900 *Pilot* 17 Nov. 632/2 The temperature was distinctly perspiratory.

2. Of, pertaining to, or of the nature of perspiration.

1805 W. SAUNDERS *Min. Waters* 501 This is fulfilled.. by establishing the perspiratory excretion in the fullest manner. 1874 BLACKIE *Self-Cult.* 51 To stimulate the natural perspiratory action of the skin.

perspire (pəˈspaɪə(r)), *v.* [ad. L. *perspīrā-re*, etymologically, to breathe through (f. PER- 1 + *spīrāre* to breathe), but in ancient L. used only in the senses 'to breathe', and 'to blow constantly (of the wind)'. This verb is not retained in the modern Romanic langs.]

†**1.** *intr.* Of the wind: To breathe or blow gently through. *Obs. rare.*

1648 HERRICK *Hesper, Farewell Frost*, What gentle winds perspire! As if here Never had been the northern plunderer To strip the trees.

†**2.** *intr.* Of any volatile substance: To pass out or escape in the form of vapour through pores (in the human body or any porous body or substance); to escape by evaporation; to evaporate; to exhale. *Obs.* (or *arch.*)

1646 SIR T. BROWNE *Pseud. Ep.* 196 A man in the morning is lighter in the scale, because in sleep some pounds have perspired. 1664 POWER *Exp. Philos.* I. 29 The Effluvium's that continually perspire out of all Plants whatsoever. 1669 WORLIDGE *Syst. Agric.* (1681) 7 This *Spiritus Mundi*.. in some places perspires more freely than in other, and causes that different verdant colour of the Grass in certain rings or circles, where the Country people fancy the Fairies dance. 1676 —— *Cyder* (1691) 137 The cork being.. porous, part of the spirits.. perspire. 1695 WOODWARD *Nat. Hist. Earth* III. i. (1723) 161 [Heat] perspiring-forth at the same Outlets with the Water. 1799 G. SMITH *Laboratory* I. 436 The water will perspire through the pores of the cup.

†**b.** *fig.* To transpire; to come out, become public; to 'get wind'. *Obs. rare.*

1766 ENTICK *London* I. 142 It never perspired what the.. sum amounted unto. *Ibid.* 265 The affair perspiring.

3. *intr.* Of a person (or the animal body): To give out watery fluid through the pores of the skin. Originally of insensible perspiration; later including sensible perspiration or sweating. (Now the ordinary sense.)

1725 N. ROBINSON *Th. Physick* 180 Dropsical People are generally observ'd to sweat much, but perspire little. 176. WESLEY *Serm. 1 Cor.* xiii. 9 During a night's sleep, a healthy man perspires one part in four less when he sweats, than when he does not. 1791 *Gentl. Mag.* LXI. II. 1099 It is well known that for some time past, neither man, woman nor child.. has been subject to that gross kind of exudation which was formerly known by the name of *sweat*;.. now every mortal, except carters, coal-heavers and Irish Chairmen.. merely *perspires*. 1799 *Med. Jrnl.* II. 394 A child is much more liable to perspire than an adult. 1841 LANE *Arab. Nts.* I. 121 The heat causes him immediately to perspire profusely.

4. *trans.* †**a.** To breathe out; to exhale; to emit or give off (air, gas, vapour, fire). *Obs.* (or *fig.* of b.) **b.** To give off (liquid) through pores, either insensibly as vapour, or sensibly as moisture: said of organic bodies.

a. 1680 MORDEN *Geog. Rect.* (1685) 329 The Grotta.. famous for those pestilential Vapors which it perspires. 1683–4 ROBINSON in *Phil. Trans.* XXIX. 483 The various Effluvia perspir'd out of our Globe. *a* 1711 KEN *Preparatives* Poet. Wks. 1721 IV. 54 To make Love infinite perspire Devouring Fire. *a* 1774 GOLDSM. *Surv. Exp. Philos.* (1776) II. 39 The vapours perspired by the clove tree.

b. 1707 FLOYER *Physic. Pulse-Watch* 88 But when the great quantity of Chyle is perspir'd,.. the Spirits are more increas'd, and the Blood is well rarify'd. 1759 tr. *Duhamel's Husb.* III. xii. (1762) 385 To perspire off the crudities of the sap. 1799 *Med. Jrnl.* II. 141 The matter he perspired generally smelt sour. 1807 J. E. SMITH *Phys. Bot.* 67 The liquor perspired becomes sensible to us by being collected from a branch introduced into any sufficiently capacious glass vessel. 1837 *Penny Cycl.* IX. 18 After the blossom unfolds it perspires a sweet honey-like fluid.

Hence **perspired** (-ˈaɪəd) *ppl. a.*; **perˈspiring** *vbl. sb.* and *ppl. a.* (whence **perˈspiringly** *adv.*); **perˈspiry** *a.* (*colloq.*), full of perspiration.

1664 H. MORE *Myst. Iniq.*, *Apol.* III. xv. 503 An Atmosphere of perspired vapours. 1699 BENTLEY *Phal.* xiii. 392 Like the perspiring Bodies of living Creatures. 1733 TULL *Horse-Hoeing Husb.* ii. 19 *note*, As soon as the perspiring State returns. 1857 *G. Bird's Urin. Deposits* (ed. 5) 163 If.. an organic acid.. be an element of the perspired fluid. 1860 *All Year Round* No. 63. 302 Two seedy old women,.. with.. black, perspiry old gloves. 1864 *Evening Standard* 26 May, A Jack-in-the-Green.. disporting himself, perspiringly, for the sake of a hardly-earned copper. 1897 MARY KINGSLEY *W. Africa* 689 Conscientiously rolled in your blanket until the perspiring stage is well over. 1899 *Allbutt's Syst. Med.* VIII. 725 In health, an actively perspiring skin is usually a flushed skin.

†**perˈspoil**, *v. Obs. rare*⁻¹. [f. PER- 2 + SPOIL *v.*] *trans.* To spoil or destroy completely.

1523 SURREY in Ellis *Orig. Lett.* Ser. I. I. 234 To kepe theym togidder unto the tyme that I shall knowe the Duks army bee perspoiled.

perssh(e, obs. forms of PERISH, PIERCE.

perssouar, obs. Sc. form of PURSUER.

†**perˈstand**, *v. Obs. rare.* [app. a confusion of *perceive* and *understand*.] *trans.* To understand.

a 1577 GASCOIGNE *Flowers* Wks. (1587) 44 First then you must perstand, I am no stranger I But English boy, in England borne. 1599 PEELE *Sir Clyom.* Wks. (Rtldg.) 492/1 Say what is your will, that it I may perstand.

†**perˈstimulate**, *v. Obs. rare*⁻⁰. [f. ppl. stem of L. *perstimulāre*, f. PER- 2 + *stimulāre* to stimulate.] *trans.* To stimulate exceedingly.

1623 COCKERAM, *Perstimulate*, to prouoke.

†**ˈperstinate**, *v. Obs. rare*⁻⁰. [f. ppl. stem of L. *perstināre*, an erroneous reading of *præstināre* to buy, purchase.]

1623 COCKERAM, *Perstinate*, to set price on a thing.

†**perˈstreperous**, *a. Obs. rare.* [f. L. *perstrepĕre* to make much noise: cf. *obstreperous*.] Making much noise; noisy.

1628 FORD *Lover's Mel.* II. i, You're too perstreperous, sauce-box.

perstriction (pəˈstrɪkʃən). [ad. L. (post-class.) *perstrictiōn-em* a rubbing, friction, n. of action f. *perstringĕre*: see PERSTRINGE.]

†**1.** The action of perstringing; sharp censure; criticism; stricture. *Obs. rare.*

1681 H. MORE *Exp. Dan.* Pref. 67 A free perstriction of the disorders observable in the Reformed Churches. *Ibid.* ii. 48 There is only a slight perstriction or brief intimation of them.

2. *Surg.* An operation for stopping hæmorrhage by compression or tightly drawn ligature of the artery.

1893 in *Syd. Soc. Lex.*

So †**perˈstrictive** *a. Obs.*, of the nature of or tending to censure or reprimand.

1659 GAUDEN *Tears Ch.* III. xxi. 333 They.. make no perstrictive or invective stroke against it.

perstringe (pəˈstrɪndʒ), *v.* [ad. L. *perstring-ĕre* to bind tightly, draw together, graze, rub, blunt, make dull, touch slightly, glance at, touch or wound slightly with words, censure, reprimand; f. PER- 2 + *stringĕre* to tie, bind.]

†**1.** *trans.* To bind tightly; to constrain. *rare.*

1684 T. GODDARD *Plato's Demon* 343 These proportionate arguments.. whilst they perstringe the mind, do not constrain the body.

2. To censure; to take to task; to pass strictures upon; to criticize adversely, find fault with.

1549 in *Latimer's Serm. bef. Edw. VI*, ii. Pref. (Arb.) 54 He [Latimer] so frankely and liberallye taxed perstringed and openly rebuked.. yᵉ peculiar fauts of certayne of his auditours. 1699 EVELYN *Acetaria* 168 So was I glad to find it [the lazy life of friars] justly perstring'd and taken notice of by a learned Person. 1831 DE QUINCEY *Parr* Wks. 1857 VI. 113, I am endeavouring with the gentlest of knoutings quietly to 'perstringe' your errors. Sam Parr!.. Perstringing, which was a favoured word of your own, was a no less favoured act. 1880 *Edin. Rev.* Apr. 382 One of them, by name Marcellus, is lightly perstringed as 'praetenuis meriti'.

†**3.** To touch on; to glance at; to hint at. *Obs.*

a 1619 FOTHERBY *Atheom.* (1622) Pref. 8 They passe ouer them so sleightly, and perstringe them so briefely, that all of them may be truly affirmed to haue beene.. rather touched then handled. **1653** H. MORE *Conject. Cabbal.* III. iii. (1713) 228 But that.. these parts of Knowledge should be perstringed by Moses in this History, it seems to me not to have the least probability in it. **1697** BURGHOPE *Disc. Relig. Assemb.* 114 To observe when our neighbour is perstring'd by such a doctrine. **1706** PHILLIPS, To *Perstringe*, to touch lightly, or to glance at a thing in discourse. **1797** T. GREEN *Diary Lover of Lit.* (1810) 43 The prefaces and notes perstringe.. whatever has, of late years, obtained celebrity in politics or literature.

†**4.** To blunt or dull (the eyes, or light); to dazzle; to dim. *Obs.*

1603 HOLLAND *Plutarch's Mor.* 644 The interrogations also and demaunds [ought to be] nothing darke or intricate: lest they doe perstringe and dazzle their eies, who are not quicke sighted. **1657** W. MORICE *Coena quasi Κοινὴ* xxii. 216 The Sun.. by his matchless light perstringeth and eclipseth all other starrs. **1664** H. MORE *Myst. Iniq.* I. I. vii. 21 The Golden splendour and magnificency of them did, it seems, so perstringe the eyes of the simple sort.

Hence **per'stringing** *vbl. sb.*; also **per'stringement**, censure, stricture, criticism.

1676 *Doctrine of Devils* 88 A perstringing of the eyes might delude them. **1891** *Sat. Rev.* 12 Dec. 669/2 One more perstringement and we have done.

†**per'struct**, *v. Obs. rare*⁻¹. [f. L. *perstruct-*, ppl. stem of *perstruĕre* to build up completely, f. PER- 2 + *struĕre* to build.] *trans.* To construct, put together, fashion.

1547 BOORDE *Brev. Health* cclxxiv. 91 b, The mattere perstructed in dewe order and fashion.

persuadable (pə'sweɪdəb(ə)l), *a.* Also 6 -yble. [f. PERSUADE *v.* + -ABLE; but in earlier form ad. L. type **persuādibilis*, f. *persuādēre*.]

†**1.** Having the quality of persuading, persuasive: = PERSUASIBLE 1. *Obs.*

c **1530** L. COX *Rhet.* (1899) 41 The ryght pleasaunt and parsuadyble arte of Rhetoryke.

2. Of a person: Capable of being persuaded; easy to persuade: = PERSUASIBLE 2.

1598 FLORIO, *Suasibile*, perswadable, that may be perswaded. **1679** J. GOODMAN *Penit. Pard.* III. iii. (1713) 310 He requires a perswadable, counsellable temper. **1788** CLARA REEVE *Exiles* III. 89, I was rejoiced to find him so rational and persuadable. **1877** MRS. OLIPHANT *Makers Flor.* x. 252 They had no easy or persuadable ruler in their new Prior.

†**3.** Of a thing: That may be recommended to acceptance: = PERSUASIBLE 3. *Obs. rare.*

1617 COLLINS *Def. Bp. Ely* II. vii. 275 You confesse your selfe that it is persuadeable, but by inducements, namely what others haue obserued, found, and experienced.

Hence **persuada'bility** (-i'bility), **per'suadableness; per'suadably** *adv.*

1797 SOUTHEY *Let. to J. May* 26 June in *Life* (1849) I. 317 There was a time when I believed in the *persuadibility of man, and had the mania of man-mending. **1871** Persuadability [see PERSUASIBILITY, quot. 1860]. **1889** J. M. ROBERTSON *Ess. Crit. Method* 71 The impulse to the struggle is the notion of persuadibility. **1742** RICHARDSON *Pamela* IV. 277 From what you intimate of Mr. H.'s Good Humour, and his *Persuadableness, if I may so say. **1889** *Blackw. Mag.* Apr. 569 Extraordinary candour and persuadableness. **1611** COTGR., *Persuasiblement*, *persuadeably. **1632** in SHERWOOD. [Hence 1818 in TODD, and in Mod. Dicts.]

persuade (pə'sweɪd), *v.* Also 6–8 **perswade**, (6 *Sc.* **-swaid, -suaid, -suaed**). [ad. L. *persuādēre* to bring over by talking, induce, f. PER- 1 or 2 + *suādēre* to advise, recommend, urge as desirable: see SUADE, SUASION; perh. immediately from F. *persuader*, in Oresme 14th c., but not in general use until 16th c.]

I. To persuade *a person*.

1. a. *trans.* To induce (a person) to believe something; to lead to accept a statement, doctrine, fact, etc.; to win to a belief or assurance. Const. *that* (a thing is so), formerly sometimes acc. and inf. (a thing *to be* so); *of* (a fact, etc.), rarely *into*, †*to*, *out of*, †*from* (a belief, etc.). Somewhat *arch.*

1513 MORE *Rich. III* Wks. 40 In youth,.. which is lighte of beliefe and sone perswaded. **1538** STARKEY *England* I. ii. 29 Yf hyt [i.e. the will] be persuadyd that gud ys yl, and yl gud. *a* **1555** RIDLEY *Lament. Churche* (1566) B viij, They are perswaded it to be truth. **1581** MULCASTER *Positions* vi. (1887) 41, I would take paines to perswade them by argumentes. **1600** J. PORY tr. *Leo's Africa* III. 156 These.. perswade women that they can foretell them their fortune. *c* **1637** A. WRIGHT in *Hist. Papers* (Roxb.) I. Introd. 6 The villanous humour of Jago when he persuades Othello to his jealousy. **1647** TRAPP *Comm. 1 Cor.* viii. 7 No mans speech .. shall ever perswade me from that opinion. **1651** HOBBES *Leviath.* II. xxv. 132 To perswade their Hearers of the Utility.. of following their advise. **1691–8** NORRIS *Pract. Disc.* (1711) III. 39 Men must oftentimes be persuaded out of their Senses, before they can be persuaded into Sense. **1777** SHERIDAN *Sch. Scand.* III. iii, They'll persuade me presently I'm at Bengal. **1796** H. HUNTER tr. *St.-Pierre's Stud. Nat.* (1799) I. Pref. 31 He could not be persuaded that it actually was only the 24th of January. **1823** T. C. GRATTAN *Father's Curse* i, I could not have been persuaded to the contrary by a host of cynical philosophers. **1844** LADY G. C. FULLERTON *Ellen Middleton* xi, We could persuade her out of those notions.

b. *refl.* To bring oneself to believe, convince oneself; to arrive at a certain or assured belief; to become or be sure.

1542 UDALL in *Lett. Lit. Men* (Camden) 4, I cannot persuad myself that your maistershipp hateth in me.. any thyng excepte vices. **1557** N. T. (Genev.) *Heb.* vi. 9 We haue perswaded our selues better things of you [**1611** BIBLE, Wee are perswaded better things of you]. **1604** SHAKS. *Oth.* II. iii. 223, I perswade my selfe, to speake the truth Shall nothing wrong him. *c* **1625** MILTON *On Death of Fair Infant* v, Yet can I not perswade me thou art dead. **1718** J. CHAMBERLAYNE *Relig. Philos.* Pref. (1730) 28 Perswading themselves.. that their own Hypotheses will serve them. **1873** BLACK *Pr. Thule* ii, Persuading oneself that men and women are to be studied in that fashion.

c. *pa. pple.* Led to believe, brought to the belief; 'convinced', assured, certain, sure.

1553 EDEN *Treat. Newe Ind.* (Arb.) 24 The hole nacion is persuaded that they greatly excel all other men. *c* **1595** CAPT. WYATT *R. Dudley's Voy. W. Ind.* (Hakl. Soc.) 9 Wee had sight of a saile.. the which wee weare perswaded was one of our consorts. **1678** BUNYAN *Pilgr.* I. 152, I have a Key .. that will, I am persuaded, open any Lock in Doubting Castle. **1703** MAUNDRELL *Journ. Jerus.* (1732) 15 Fully persuaded of the truth of it themselves. **1790** PALEY *Horæ Paul.* Rom. i. 10 No one, I am persuaded, will suspect that this clause was put into St. Paul's defence. **1852** H. ROGERS *Ecl. Faith* (1853) 282, I am thoroughly persuaded that the notion.. is a fallacy.

d. *absol.* To convince, be convincing, carry conviction; to use persuasion.

1673 O. WALKER *Educ.* (1677) 174 Such as perswade as well as delight. **1714** *Steele's Poet. Misc.* 29 The charming Youth Perswades with so much Eloquence and Truth. **1892** STEVENSON & L. OSBORNE *Wrecker* 269 His strong sterling face progressively and silently persuaded of his full knowledge.

2. a. To induce or win over (a person) to an act or course of action; to draw the will of (another) to something, by inclining his judgement or desire to it; to prevail upon, or urge successfully, to do something. Const. *to* with *inf.* (formerly sometimes *that* with *subord. cl.*); *to, unto, into* (an action, etc.); also *from, out of* (= to dissuade successfully); *away from* (a belief, etc.), *down to* (a place, etc.), *off* (an intention, place, etc.).

1513 MORE *Rich. III* Wks. 41 The Quene being in this wise perswaded, such woorde sente vnto her sonne, and vnto her brother. **1526** TINDALE *Matt.* xxvii. 20 The chefe preestes.. had parswaded the people that they shulde axe Barrabas. **1579** W. WILKINSON *Confut. Familye of Loue* 6 Yet saw he not a reason to perswade him to let Israell go. **1585** T. WASHINGTON tr. *Nicholay's Voy.* I. xii. 14 [He] vsed al the meanes he coulde to perswade me from it. **1586** A. DAY *Eng. Secretary* I. (1625) 70 To perswade him to the use thereof. *a* **1648** LD. HERBERT *Hen. VIII* (1683) 218 He had accorded divers other conditions, which no other persons could have persuaded him unto. **1771** T. HULL *Sir W. Harrington* I. 121 To persuade the lady into a private marriage. *a* **1774** GOLDSM. *Hist. Greece* I. 381 To persuade the young and old against too much love for the body. **1777** C. REEVE *Champion of Virtue* 30 Let it be kept from my two cousins.., if they offer to be of the party I will persuade them off it. **1857** GEO. ELIOT *Scenes Clerical Life, Janet's Repentance* vii, Persuading my clients away from me. **1865** DICKENS *Mut. Fr.* I. vi, Be persuaded into being respectable and happy. **1875** JOWETT *Plato* (ed. 2) I. 128 The man was persuaded to open the door. **1895** 'G. MORTIMER' *Like Stars that Fall* ii. 17, I wish you'd just try to persuade Lou off a silly idea she's just got hold of. **1941** A. L. ROWSE *Tudor Cornwall* xiv. 348 The object of which was to persuade him away from his stand for catholicism. **1959** M. SHADBOLT *New Zealanders* 12 He.. persuaded his brother off the waterfront to look after the herd for six months. *Ibid.* 218 I've been trying to persuade Izzy down to the city for the last five years.

b. *absol.* (See also 8.)

1577 EARL OF LEICESTER in Ellis *Orig. Lett.* Ser. I. II. 373 We all do what we can, to persuade from any progress at all. **1602** DANIEL *Civ. Wars* II. xxv, A sufficient motive to persuade. **1846** G. F. GRAHAM *Eng. Synonyms* (1862) 216 In order to persuade, we address the feelings and the imagination. In order to convince, we address the reasoning faculty.

c. To get by or as by persuasion, to 'coax'. *nonce-use.*

1887 NICOLAY & HAY *A. Lincoln* I. i. (1890) 25 It required .. earnest and intelligent industry to persuade a living out of those barren hillocks and weedy hollows.

†**3.** To seek to induce (a person) to (or from) a belief, a course of action, etc.; to assure, try to convince, 'impress upon' (one) *that*; to urge, plead with, advise or counsel strongly; with *from*, etc., to advise against a course, to dissuade. Const. as in 1 and 2. *Obs.*

1525 ABP. WARHAM in Ellis *Orig. Lett.* Ser. III. I. 371 In caas they finde any maner of sticking or difficultie in thayme, not to wade verey far to persuade thayme. **1538** STARKEY *England* I. ii. 52 Men of gret wytt.. began to persuade the rest of the pepul to forsake that rudnes and vncomly lyfe. **1590** SIR J. SMYTH *Disc. Weapons* 6 They perswaded him with great vehemence, that it was verie meete and conuenient. **1675** WOOD *Life* (O.H.S.) II. 332, I persuaded the society to set it above the arches, but I was not then heard. **1796** COLERIDGE *Lett., to T. Poole* (1895) 186 That I should find you earnestly and vehemently persuading me to prefer Acton to Stowey. **1801** —— *to Southey* 362 Dr. Fenwick has earnestly persuaded me to try horse-exercise.

II. To persuade *a thing*.

†**4.** To induce belief of (a fact, statement, opinion, etc.); to lead one to think or believe; to prove, demonstrate. Const. with *simple obj.*, or *obj. cl.* (with *that*, or *acc.* and *inf.*); and with *to, unto*, or simple dative of person. *Obs.*

1528 G. DE CASSALIS, etc. *Let. Wolsey* in Strype *Eccl. Mem.* I. App. xxiii. 46 It was wel known and persuaded to the Kings Highnes and your Gr. of the gret zeal, love, and affection that his Holynes bearith towards them both. *Ibid.* 49 It hath been persuaded to the Pope,.. that there is no way to delyver Italy of war, but to commence it in some other place. **1553** T. WILSON *Rhet.* (1580) 225 We shall.. perswade theim the rather the truthe of our cause. **1581** J. BELL *Haddon's Answ. Osor.* 292 b, Surely if Osorius can perswade that to be true, he shall beare the bell away. *a* **1643** LD. FALKLAND, etc. *Infallibility* (1646) 97 The grossest errours, if they.. be but new, may be perswaded to the multitude. **1685** tr. *Bossuet's Doctr. Cath. Ch.* ii. 3 This is what they endeavour to perswade.

5. To induce the doing or practice of (an act, course of action, etc.) by argument, entreaty, or the like; to lead one to do or practise; to urge successfully upon one; to induce or lead to by reasoning, etc. Const. *simple obj.*, rarely *obj. cl.*; with *to, unto*, or simple dative of person. *arch.*

1538 BALE *Thre Lawes* 11 Perswadynge all truth, dyssuadynge all iniury. **1542** UDALL *Erasm. Apoph.* 18 b, A philosophier.. perswadyng the contempte of golde & siluer. **1560** WHITEHORNE *Arte Warre* (1573) 65 To perswade or to diswade a thing vnto fewe is verye easie. **1593** SHAKS. *3 Hen. VI*, III. iii. 176 Your King.. Sends me a Paper to perswade me Patience? **1647** N. BACON *Disc. Govt. Eng.* I. lx. (1739) 118 The Taxes.. were rather perswaded than imposed upon them. *a* **1677** BARROW *Contentedness* (1714) 43 Rational considerations, apt.. to persuade Contentedness. **1753** L. M. *Accomplished Woman* II. 294 But what need.. of so many arguments to persuade that which is so conformable to their disposition? **1840** J. H. NEWMAN *Ch. of Fathers* vii. 104 (tr. Let. of St. Basil), I know letters are but feeble instruments to persuade so great a thing.

†**6.** To commend (a statement, opinion, etc.) to acceptance, to urge as credible or true; to inculcate; to go to prove, make probable. Const. as in 4. *Obs.*

1537 tr. *Latimer's 1st Serm. bef. Convoc.* A vij, They haue a wonderfulle prety example, to perswade this thynge. **1542** UDALL *Erasm. Apoph.* 234 Thei persuaded not to hym the thynge that were false. **1553** KENNEDY *Compend. Tract.* in *Wodrow Soc. Misc.* (1844) 105 The Jewis perswaded circumcisioun to be necessare with Baptime. **1588** PARKE tr. *Mendoza's Hist. China* 128 There was none that better coulde.. perswade with His Majestie the great importance of that ambassage. **1611** BIBLE *Acts* xix. 8 Disputing and perswading the things concerning the Kingdom of God. *a* **1677** HALE *Prim. Orig. Man.* I. vi. 127 Evidences of probability strongly perswading the same Truth. **1687** TOWERSON *Baptism* 113 The former of these perswading Men's being under sin from some inward principle.

†**7.** To commend to adoption, advise, counsel, advocate, recommend (an act, course of action, etc.). Const. as in 5. *Obs.*

1525 ABP. WARHAM in Ellis *Orig. Lett.* Ser. III. I. 371 Muche medling and persuading this Matier to come to effecte. **1586** T. B. *La Primaud. Fr. Acad.* I. (1594) 584 Megabyses.. perswaded the oligarchicall government. **1656** RIDGLEY *Pract. Physick.* 44 Physicians perswade that.. the Artery shall be cut crosse asunder. **1668** CULPEPPER & COLE *Barthol. Anat.* Manual I. vi. 312 In Diseases of the Head (if the Circulation did not perswade the contrary) the opening of the Cephalick Vein would help a little more. **1781** MADAN *Thelyph.* III. 326 He always perswades a public marriage.

III. 8. *intr.* To use persuasion; to plead, expostulate, use inducements to win over to some opinion or some course of action; to do this successfully, to succeed in bringing over or inducing.

1526 *Pilgr. Perf.* (W. de W. 1531) 84 He wyll make other persones to couer his offence.. or perswade & entreate for hym. **1532** BECON *Pomaunder of Prayer* Wks. (1560) II. 215 The world perswaded vnto vanytyes. **1603** SHAKS. *Meas. for M.* v. i. 93 How I perswaded, how I praid, and kneel'd. **1684** tr. *Bonet's Merc. Compit.* VI. 176 Barber-Chirurgeons sometimes perswade to it. **1798** LANDOR *Gebir* I. 72 He went, nor slumber'd in the sultry noon When viands, couches, generous wines, persuade.

IV. *to persuade with.* †**9. a.** To use persuasion with, expostulate with, plead with; sometimes, to prevail with. *Obs.*

1581 RICH *Farewell* (1846) 179 Not doubtyng but.. that he hymself would so perswade with his brother, that she should bee heard to speake in her owne defence. **1593** NASHE *Christ's T.* 2 Iesus, whom hee sent from Heauen to perswade with these Hus-band-men. **1596** SHAKS. *Merch. V.* III. ii. 283 The Magnificoes Of greatest port haue all perswaded with him. **1636** E. DACRES tr. *Machiavel's Disc. Livy* I. 235 A good man may easily have the meanes to perswade with a licentious and tumultuous people, and so reduce them to reason. **1684** BUNYAN *Pilgr.* II. 62 Whoever they could perswade with, they made so too.

b. *fig.* Of a thing: To have influence or weight with; to prevail or avail with. *Obs.*

1618 *Let.* in Rushw. *Hist. Coll.* (1659) I. 10 You and I well know, that this stile most perswades with them. **1622** MABBE tr. *Aleman's Guzman d'Alf.* I. 146, I saw.. that neither perswasions, nor protestations would perswade with her. **1643** TRAPP *Comm. Gen.* xxxiv. 23 Profit perswades mightily with the multitude.

†**10. a.** with clause (with *that* or equivalent) in senses 4 and 6. *Obs.*

1535 CRANMER *Let. to Cromwell* in *Misc. Writ.* (Parker Soc.) II. 304, I cannot perswade with myself that he so much tendereth the king's cause as he doth his own. **1553** T. WILSON *Rhet.* (1580) Pref., These.. perswaded with them what was good, what was bad, and what was gainfull for mankinde. **1651** R. VAUGHAN in *Ussher's Lett.* (1686) 561 This Evidence doth perswade with me, that Cadwalader went to Rome far before Anno 680.

b. with obj. clause or infin. expressing purpose, in sense 7. *Obs.*

c **1540** tr. *Pol. Verg. Eng. Hist.* (Camden) I. 161 Quendreda.. wente abowte to persuade with her husbande that he should murthere Ethelbertus. **1565** T. STAPLETON *Fortr. Faith* 59 S. Augustin persuadeth with him to leaue the Manichees. **1603** HOLLAND *Plutarch's Mor.* 406 His friends perswaded with him that voluntarily, he would.. give over this violent and lordly rule. **1637** HEYLIN *Brief Answ. Burton* 61 His Doctors..perswaded with him..to vent that humour.

†**per'suade**, *sb. Obs. rare.* [f. prec.] An act of persuading; persuasion.

1590 T. WATSON *Eglogue Death Walsingham* 421 Thy learnd persuades command my sorrow cease. **1626** *Faithful Friends* I. i, The king's entreats, Persuades of friends..can [not] move him.

persuaded (pəˈsweɪdɪd), *ppl. a.* [f. as prec. + -ED[1].] Prevailed upon; convinced; having an assured opinion; †proved, demonstrated (*obs.*); induced by persuasion: see the verb, esp. 1 c.

1538 ELYOT *Dict.*, *Impulsus*, perswaded, prouoked, inforced. **1561** T. NORTON *Calvin's Inst.* I. vii. §5 Let this..stand for a certainly persuaded truthe. **1638** WILKINS *New World* ix. (1707) 72 This Answer..rather bewrays an obstinate, than a perswaded Will. **1837** HT. MARTINEAU *Soc. Amer.* II. 104 Thoroughly persuaded persons. **1860** RUSKIN *Mod. Paint* VIII. i. §17 A persuaded or voluntarily yielded obedience.

Hence **per'suadedly** *adv.*; **per'suadedness**.

1638 FORD *Fancies* I. i, He's our own; Surely, nay most persuadedly. **1648** BOYLE *Seraph. Love* i. (1700) 8 From Persuadedness that nothing can be a greater Happiness than her Favour.

persuadend (pəˈsweɪdɛnd). *nonce-wd.* [ad. L. *persuādendus*, gerundive of *persuādēre* to PERSUADE.] A person who is to be persuaded.

1865 GROTE *Plato* II. xxiv. 255 That the topics insisted on by the persuader shall be adapted to the feelings..of the persuadend.

persuader (pəˈsweɪdə(r)). [f. PERSUADE *v.* + -ER[1]. Cf. obs. F. *persuadeur* (15–16th c.).] **a.** One who or that which persuades. Const. *of* a person, formerly also *of* an action, etc.: see the verb.

1538 ELYOT *Dict.*, *Persuasor*, a perswader or inducer to do a thynge. **1550** BALE *Apol.* 86 b, Neyther is S. Paule..a persuader of vowes makynge. **1580** *Reg. Privy Council Scot.* III. 281 Blamit as the persuaderis of his Hienes in sindrie thingis. **1603** KNOLLES *Hist. Turks* (1638) 148 The euill persuaders of rebellion preuailed with him. **1654** R. CODRINGTON tr. *Iustine* xxxviii. 458 His friend..was both his Companion, and his perswader to undertake this journey. **1718** ROWE tr. *Lucan* vi. 94 The sweet Perswader speaks. **1838** FR. A. KEMBLE *Resid. in Georgia* (1863) 35 The canoes..are very inviting persuaders to this species of exercise.

b. *slang.* Something used to compel submission or obedience, as a weapon, spurs, etc.

1796 GROSE *Dict. Vulg. T.* (ed. 3), *Persuaders*, spurs. **1833** MARRYAT *P. Simple* xii, He never appeared on deck without his 'persuader', which was three rattans twisted into one, like a cable. **1844** DICKENS *Mart. Chuz.* xxxiv, I didn't admire his carryin' them murderous little persuaders, and being so ready to use 'em. **1862** *N.Y. Tribune* 3 June 3/5 In the South heavy guns are called persuaders. **1871** 'M. LEGRAND' *Cambr. Freshm.* xiv, 'Don't you go in "persuaders"—spurs, you know?' Mr. Pokyr explained. **1884** W. L. REDE *Sixteen String Jack* II. iv. 14/2 It's no use resisting, 'cause ve has the persuaders. *Ibid.*, Dick, out vith your persuader! (Draggle puts a pistol to his head.) **1900** ADE *More Fables* 54 The Colonel arose and pulled his Persuader, expecting to make it a Case of Justifiable Homicide. **1925** FRASER & GIBBONS *Soldier & Sailor Words* 221 *Persuader*, a nickname for the club, or knob-kerry, carried by trench raiders. Also, bayonet. **1930** *Detective Fiction Weekly* 10 May 48/1 Papers..held down by what crooks call a 'sap' or a 'persuader'. **1935** A. J. POLLOCK *Underworld Speaks* 87/1 *Persuader*, a pistol. **1964** L. DEIGHTON *Funeral in Berlin* xlii. 258 'Do you have a pistol or a knife or a persuader?' 'I have a persuader... Two hundred dollars in singles.' **1974** P. CAVE *Mama* (new ed.) xiv. 113 'How the hell are you gonna persuade the guy to pull off the road?' asked Ethel... 'I've thought of that,' answered Mama coldly. 'And that's one of the little changes. .. I'm gonna have to take along a little persuader.'

c. *Printing.* A tool used as a lever by a compositor when type matter and furniture is being fitted into a chase.

1898 J. SOUTHWARD *Mod. Printing* I. xli. 257 Fit the quoins, using the 'persuader' to squeeze in the pages, and tap up all round. The 'persuader' is usually a tool made by the compositor himself... The tool is a lever whereby the space between the type matter and the chase can be expanded.

d. *Television.* An electrode in the image orthicon camera tube which deflects the returning beam of scanning electrons into the electron multiplier. Freq. *attrib.*

1946 *RCA Rev.* VII. 361 The persuader electrode is tied electrically to the first stage. *Ibid.* 362 There is no need to adjust the persuader voltage for controlling uniformity of gain. **1953** AMOS & BIRKINSHAW *Television Engin.* I. 108 The persuader potential can be set to any value up to +300 volts. **1967** H. A. COLE *Basic Televison* I. 56 When they get near the electron gun, the returning electrons are diverted on to the first dynode of the electron multiplier by an electrode aptly named the persuader grid.

persuadibility, variant of PERSUADABILITY.

per'suading, *vbl. sb.* [f. as prec. + -ING[1].] The action of the verb PERSUADE; persuasion.

1530 PALSGR. 253/2 Persuadyng, *persuasion.* **1535** COVERDALE *Acts* xix. 26 This Paul turneth awaye moch people with his persuadyng. *a* **1614** DONNE *Βιαθανατος* (1644) 198 This perswading to his destruction. **1651** HOBBES *Leviath.* III. xlii. 289 There was then no government by Coercion, but only by Doctrine, and Perswading.

per'suading, *ppl. a.* [f. as prec. + -ING[2].] That persuades; persuasive.

1581 J. BELL *Haddon's Answ. Osor.* 8 His Epistle is..altogether of the perswading kinde. **1613** SHAKS. *Hen. VIII*, IV. ii. 52 He was..Exceeding wise, faire spoken, and perswading. *a* **1641** BP. MOUNTAGU *Acts & Mon.* iii. (1642) 173 An argument, and perswading motive. **1745** T. RANDALL in *Sc. Paraphr.* XI. vi, Though all men's eloquence adorn'd My sweet persuading tongue.

Hence **per'suadingly** *adv.*, persuasively.

1552 HULOET Perswadynglye, *persuasibiliter.* **1614** J. COOKE *Tu Quoque* in Dodsley *O. Pl.* VII. 71 Some fitter time Shall bring me more persuadingly unto her.

persuance, obs. form of PURSUANCE.

†**per'suase.** *Obs. rare.* [ad. L. *persuāsus* (-*u* stem), f. ppl. stem of *persuādēre*.] Persuasion.

1599 PORTER *Angry Wom. Abingd* v. Kj, He may perswade as long as his perswase Is backt with reason and a right-full sute. *Ibid.* K ij, What say you vnto my perswase?

persuasibility (pəsweɪsɪˈbɪlɪtɪ). [f. next: see -ITY.] The quality of being persuasible; capability of being, or readiness to be, persuaded.

1627 DONNE *Serm.* v. 49 When thou shalt have..infused a perswasibility into them and a perswasivenesse into me, by thy Spirit. **1842** W. IRVING in *Life & Lett.* (1866) III. 236 Maria Christina miscalculated..on the persuasibility, if I may use the term, of Espartero. **1860** HAWTHORNE *Marb. Faun* xxvii. II. 177 The young count's good-nature and easy persuasibility [*so ed.* 1865; *edd.* 1871, '79, '84, *etc.*, persuadability] were among his best characteristics.

persuasible (pəˈsweɪsɪb(ə)l), *a.* [ad. L. *persuāsibil-is*, f. *persuās-*, ppl. stem of *persuādēre* to PERSUADE: see -BLE.]

†**1.** Having the power to persuade; persuasive. *Obs.*

1382 WYCLIF 1 *Cor.* ii. 4 Not in persuable [*v.r.* persuasible, *Vulg.* persuasibilibus; 1388 suteli sturyng] wordis of mannis wysdom. **1532** MORE *Confut. Barnes* VIII. Wks. 810/2 One..by hys persuasible wordes had turned the waueringe people. **1580** HARVEY in *Spenser's Wks.* (Grosart) I. 39 The best and persuasiblest Eloquence. **1647** TRAPP *Comm. Col.* xi. 4 With probable and persuasible speeches.

2. Capable of being, or ready to be, persuaded; open to persuasion.

1502 *Ord. Crysten Men* (W. de W. 1506) IV. xxi. 278 That suche infante fereth & loueth god and were persuasyble. **1620** T. GRANGER *Div. Logike* 374 One that is rather perswaisable by mens authoritie, then by reason. **1854** *Blackw. Mag.* LXXVI. 46 His wife being a persuasible woman, who will hear reason after all.

†**3.** Capable of being commended for acceptance; credible, plausible. *Obs.*

1628 JACKSON *Creed* IX. xxxvi. §2 The latter opinion is in itself persuasible. *a* **1643** LD. FALKLAND, etc. *Infallibility* (1646) 127 Nor [is] Mahumetisme at any time so perswasible as Christian religion.

Hence **per'suasibleness**, persuasibility; **per'suasibly** *adv.*, in a persuasible manner; †persuasively.

1555 in Foxe *A. & M.* (1583) 1802 This man did..speake ..earnestly and perswasibly, as euer I heard any. **1755** JOHNSON, *Persuasibleness*, the quality of being flexible by persuasion. [Hence 1818 in TODD; and in mod. Dicts.]

persuasion (pəˈsweɪʒən). Also 6–8 **persw-**; 4 **-cioun**, 6 **-cion**, **-tio(u)n.** [ad. L. *persuāsiōn-em*, n. of action from *persuādēre* to persuade: perh. through F. *persuasion* (14th c. *persuacion* in Oresme, *persuacioun* in Gower).]

1. The action, or an act, of persuading or seeking to persuade; the presenting of inducements or winning arguments; the addressing of reasonings, appeals, or entreaties to a person in order to induce him to do or believe something.

1382 WYCLIF *Gal.* v. 8 Forsoth this persuacioun, or softe mouynge, is not of hym that clepide 3ou. **1477** EARL RIVERS (Caxton) *Dictes* 133 Ther may no persuasions nor holsom counseil auaile. **1555** EDEN *Decades* 24 Seduced by theyr perswasions and prouocations. **1595** SHAKS. *John* v. v. 11 The English Lords By his perswasion, are agaıne falne off. **1697** POTTER *Antiq. Greece* I. iii. (1715) 10 These, he, by his Persuasions, appeas'd. **1788** GIBBON *Decl. & F.* xlv. (1869) II. 674 The arts of persuasion were tried without success. **1856** FROUDE *Hist. Eng.* (1858) I. v. 472 Promises and persuasions being unavailing, they tried threats. **1867** FREEMAN *Norm. Conq.* I. iv. 257 By force or persuasion, he gained over to his side the Princes of Aquitaine.

†**b.** Something tending or intended to induce belief or action; an argument or inducement. *Obs.*

c **1384** CHAUCER *H. Fame* II. 364 How thenketh the my conclusyon... A goode persuasion Quod he hyt is. *c* **1450** tr. *De Imitatione* III. vii. 72 He wil not bileue þe wily persuasions of þe enemy. **1532** MORE *Confut. Tindale* Wks. 695/2 An other that serueth more honest, or that hath better perswasions, than he. **1598–9** [E. FORDE] *Parismus* I. (1661) 42 A sufficient perswasion to all that the Prince..was murdered. **1624** CAPT. SMITH *Virginia* III. 63 For his relation we gaue him many toyes, with perswasions to goe with vs.

c. Power of persuading, persuasiveness.

1601 SHAKS. *Twel. N.* III. iv. 383 Ist possible that my deserts to you Can lacke perswasion? **1759** STERNE *Tr. Shandy* I. xix, Persuasion hung upon his lips, and the elements of Logic and Rhetoric were so blended up in him. **1858** LYTTON *What will he do* VIII. i. *note*, No printer's type can record his decorous grace, the persuasion of his silvery tongue. **1868** M. PATTISON *Academ. Org.* v. 166 For teaching there is required a persuasion as well as for advocacy, though of a different kind.

2. a. The fact or condition of being persuaded, convinced, or assured of something; conviction, assurance, full belief.

1534 MORE in Ellis *Orig. Lett.* Ser. I. II. 51 The knowledge of your trew graciouse persuation in that behalfe. **1601** DENT *Pathw. Heaven* 242 In the verie Elect, and in those which are growen to the greatest perswasion. **1667** MILTON *P.L.* XI. 152 Perswasion in me grew That I was heard with favour. **1777** PRIESTLEY *Matt. & Spir.* (1782) I. Pref. 8 My doubts were..converted into a full persuasion. **1855** BREWSTER *Newton* II. xx. 221 He intimated to Newton ..his persuasion of Flamsteed's fitness for the work.

b. With *pl.* That of which one is persuaded; what one is led to believe; a belief, conviction.

c **1510** MORE *Picus* Wks. 14/1 This is a very deadly & monstrous perswacion, which hath entred, the mindes of men. *a* **1687** PETTY *Pol. Arith.* (1690) Pref., Examin the following Perswasions, which I find too currant in the World. **1737** WATERLAND *Eucharist* 175 My Perswasion.. is, that the Passage relates not at all to the Eucharist. **1860** W. COLLINS *Wom. White* I. viii, It will always remain my private persuasion that [etc.].

3. *spec.* Religious belief or opinion; a form or system of religious belief, a creed. Rarely used for political opinion. Hence, **b.** A body of persons holding a particular religious belief; a sect, a denomination.

In *Hebrew* or *Jewish persuasion*, often loosely or humorously put for 'race'; hence app. the humorous use in c.

[**1588** *Marprel. Epist.* (Arb.) 24 The said Iohn Cant. hath many things in him, which euidently shew a catholike perswasion.] **1623** DONNE *Encænia* Ep. Ded., Any matter of Controuersie betweene vs and those of the Romane Perswasion. **1656** A. WRIGHT *Five Serm.* To Chr. Rdr., Those of the Episcopal perswasion. **1662** *Bk. Com. Prayer* Pref., All his Subjects of what perswasion soever. **1684** *Scanderbeg Rediv.* ii. 16 Their then received Religion (which was as still it is, the Lutheran Perswasion). **1687** LUTTRELL *Brief Rel.* (1857) I. 404 Persons of the congregational persuasion in the city of Norwich. **1769** BLACKSTONE *Comm.* IV. viii. 104 The Church of England.—The clergy of her Persuasion. **1779** SHERIDAN *Critic* II. ii, While we, You know, the Protestant persuasion hold. **1794** PALEY *Evid.* I. v. §3 (1817) 93 The exertions of the Founder [of Christianity] and his followers in propagating the new persuasion. **1807–8** SYD. SMITH *Plymley's Lett.* ix, I detest that state of society which extends unequal degrees of protection to different creeds and persuasions. **1813** HOBHOUSE *Journey* (ed. 2) 622 Many of them, being of the Roman Catholic persuasion. **1862** TROLLOPE *Orley F.* xiii, Nor at first sight would it probably have been discerned that he was of the Hebrew persuasion. **1879** M. ARNOLD *Irish Cath.* Mixed Ess. 101 Men of any religious persuasion might be appointed to teach anatomy or chemistry. **1888** SAINTSBURY *Ess. Eng. Lit.* (1891) 184 His political satires would have galled Tories,.. and could hardly be read by persons of that persuasion with such complete enjoyment.

b. **1727** SWIFT *What passed in London* Wks. 1755 III. I. 190 All the different persuasions kept by themselves. **1844** S. WILBERFORCE *Hist. Prot. Episc. Ch. Amer.* (1846) 308 A field of battle on which each persuasion sought to obtain the mastery. **1863** WHYTE MELVILLE *Gladiators* III. 11 These were the Essenes, a persuasion that reject pleasure as a positive evil.

c. *slang* or *burlesque.* Nationality; sex; kind; sort; description.

[**1863** ALFORD in *Gd. Words* 199 We constantly read of the 'Hebrew persuasion', or the 'Jewish persuasion'. I expect soon to see the term widened still more, and a man of colour described as 'an individual of the negro persuasion'.] **1864** *Daily Tel.* 1 Apr. 5 Brawny, vituperative-tongued females, of the Irish persuasion. **1885** 'F. ANSTEY' *Tinted Venus* vii. 78 She said she thought it was..a gentleman in the hair-cutting persuasion. **1890** *Amer. Naturalist* XXIV. 236, I have a canary of the feminine persuasion. **1902** R. HICHENS *Londoners* 33 A sinister moustache of the tooth-brush persuasion. **1903** B. HARRADEN *Kath. Frensham* 28 A dark little man, evidently of French persuasion, came into the room. *Mod.* (*humorous.*) No one of the male persuasion was present.

persuasive (pəˈsweɪsɪv), *a.* and *sb.* Also 7–8 **persw-.** [ad. med. Scholastic L. *persuāsīv-us*, f. L. *persuās-*, ppl. stem: see PERSUASIBLE and -IVE. Cf. F. *persuasif*, *-ive* (15th c. in Hatz.-Darm.; in Cotgr.), perh. the immediate source.]

A. *adj.* Having the power of persuading; tending or fitted to persuade; winning.

1589 GREENE *Menaphon* (Arb.) 22 With such perswasiue arguments Democles appeased the distressed thoughtes of his doubtful countrimen. *a* **1639** SPOTTISWOOD *Hist. Ch. Scot.* (1677) 385 A most persuasive Preacher. **1718** POPE *Iliad* XIV. 251 Persuasive speech, and more persuasive sighs, Silence that spoke, and eloquence of eyes. **1814** CARY *Dante's Inf.* II. 66 Thy eloquent persuasive tongue. **1884** W. J. COURTHOPE *Addison* v. 97 The most powerful and persuasive advocate of Virtue in fiction.

B. *sb.* Something adapted or intended to persuade; a motive or inducement presented.

1641 T. WARMSTRY *Blind Guide Forsaken* 45 A strong perswasive to carry us along to the throne of grace. **1680** ALLEN (*title*) A Perswasive to Peace and Unity among Christians. **1751** JOHNSON *Rambler* No. 175 ⁋2 What are treatises of morality, but persuasives to the practice of duties? **1855** PRESCOTT *Philip II*, I. I. iii. 40 Persuasives in the form of gold chains, gold crowns and other compliments.

persuasively (pə'sweɪsɪvlɪ), *adv.* [f. prec. + -LY².] In a persuasive manner; with a persuasive air; so as to persuade.

1667 MILTON *P.L.* IX. 873 The Serpent wise..with mee Perswasively hath so prevaild, that I Have also tasted. **1695** LD. PRESTON *Boeth., Life* 32 Sometimes perswasively gliding to that which is to follow. **1875** JOWETT *Plato, Apol.* (ed. 2) I. 349 They almost made me forget myself—so persuasively did they speak.

per'suasiveness. [f. as prec. + -NESS.] Persuasive quality; power of persuasion.

1611 FLORIO, *Persuasibilità*, perswasiuenesse. **1655** FULLER *Ch. Hist.* III. i. §34 The best perswasiveness of his flattery, consisted in down-right arguments of gold and silver. **1715–20** POPE *Iliad* III. 271 *note*, Nestor's Eloquence ..consisted in Softness and Persuasiveness. **1881** W. COLLINS *Bl. Robe* I. iv. 164 There was a tender persuasiveness in her tones.

per'suasory, *a.* Now *rare* or *Obs.* [ad. med. or mod.L. *persuāsōri-us* (f. L. *persuāsor* persuader: see -ORY²), whence also F. *persuasoire* (Ch. Estienne *Dict.* 1552).] = PERSUASIVE *a.*

1576 FLEMING *Panopl. Epist.* 43 *margin*, In this his persuasorie speach, he giueth a testimonie of the..affection which he did beare to the Vniuersitie of Cambridge. **1608–11** BP. HALL *Epist.* v. i, Their very silence is perswasorie. **1646** SIR T. BROWNE *Pseud. Ep.* IV. v. 188 But neither is this [conceit] perswasory. **1748** RICHARDSON *Clarissa* (1811) I. xx. 142 The last persuasory effort that is to be attempted. **1838** SIR H. TAYLOR *Autobiog.* I. xv. 247 The persuasory and recommendatory process may appear more conciliatory.

†**'persue.** *Venery. Obs.* Also 6 parcy, parsee, parsie, 7 pursue. [app. orig. **parcee*, **percee*, a. F. *percée* act of piercing (or *percé*, *-ée* pa. pple. pierced, struck by an arrow, etc.). After a series of corruptions, finally confused with *pursue.*] The track of blood left by a stricken deer or other wounded beast of the chase. *to draw parcy, by parsie*, etc., to follow the track of blood.

1530 PALSGR. 739/1, I stryke a dere or any other wylde beest as a huntar dothe whan he draweth parcy, *je enferre.* I have strykyn him, let go your blodhounde, *je lay enferré,.. laissez aller vostre limier.* **1590** SPENSER *F.Q.* III. v. 28 By tract of blood, which she had freshly seene To have besprinckled all the grassy greene: By the great persue which she there perceav'd Well hoped shee the beast engor'd had beene. **1592** WARNER *Alb. Eng.* VII. xxxvi. (1612) 175 A fell fleet Dog, that hunts my Heart by parsee each-wheare found. *Ibid.* Prose Add. 345 Ascanius and his Companie drawing by Parsie after the Stagge. *a* **1619** FLETCHER *Bonduca* v. ii, Now h' as drawn pursue on me he hunts me like a devil. **1661** FELTHAM *Disc. Eccles.* II. 11 Resolves, etc. (1677) 351 As pursue in a strucken Deer, they fall from us like blood, and make us to be hunted to death.

persue, persuit, obs. ff. PURSUE, PURSUIT.

persulphate (pə'sʌlfət). *Chem.* [PER- 5 b.] That sulphate which contains the greatest proportion of oxygen, or of the sulphuric acid radical SO_4; as ***persulphate of iron***, now more systematically named *ferric sulphate*, $Fe_2(SO_4)_3$; ***persulphate of mercury***, now *mercuric sulphate*, $HgSO_4$.

1813 T. THOMSON *Ann. Philos.* II. 452 If instead of the sulphate of iron we were to make choice of the persulphate of iron. **1880** GARROD & BAXTER *Mat. Med.* 39 A mixed solution of sulphate and persulphate of iron. **1893** *Syd. Soc. Lex.*, Persulphate of mercury, mercuric sulphate.

persulphide (pə'sʌlfaɪd). *Chem.* [PER- 5.] That sulphide of any element or basic radical which contains the greatest proportion of sulphur. Originally called PERSULPHURET. Now usually more definitely named, as *trisulphide*, *pentasulphide*, etc.; e.g. *persulphide* or *persulphuret of arsenic*, or *arsenious sulphide* = *arsenic trisulphide*, As_2S_3.

1856 MILLER *Elem. Chem.* II. 585 Persulphide of Hydrogen (HS_5?)—In order to procure this compound it is usual to prepare first a persulphide of calcium (CaS_5), which may be formed by boiling equal weights of slacked lime and powdered sulphur in water.

persulpho-: see PER- 5, 5 b and SULPHO-.

1836 BRANDE *Chem.* (ed. 4) 658 *Persulphocyanuret of Iron* ..may be obtained in the form of a deliquescent uncrystallizable mass, of a red colour. **1880** *Nature* XXI. 363/1 On persulphocyanate of silver.

per'sulphuret. *Chem.* = PERSULPHIDE.

1836 BRANDE *Chem.* (ed. 4) 755 *Persulphuret of Arsenic...* When sulphuretted hydrogen is passed through a concentrated solution of arsenic acid, a yellow precipitate falls, which resembles orpiment in colour. **1853** W. GREGORY *Inorg. Chem.* (ed. 3) 135 The formation of persulphuret of ammonium. **1854** J. SCOFFERN in *Orr's Circ. Sc., Chem.* 347 This process yields..persulphurets of the base radical.

So **persul'phuric** *a.* [PER- 5 a], in ***persulphuric acid***, the acid $H_2S_2O_8$, containing the largest known proportion of oxygen in combination with sulphur; ***persulphuric oxide***, the anhydride of this acid, S_2O_7, discovered by Berthelot in 1878. †**per'sulphurous** *a. Obs.* = HYPOSULPHUROUS.

1819 J. G. CHILDREN *Chem. Anal.* 432 A peculiar acid, which he proposed to call the persulphurous, but afterwards changed the name to that of hyposulphurous acid. **1883** *Athenæum* 16 June 767/2 The formation of Berthelot's persulphuric acid.

persul'tation. *Path. rare*⁻⁰. [ad. L. *persultātio*, n. of action from *persultāre* to leap through.] An eruption of blood from an artery.

1706 PHILLIPS, *Persultation*, ..in Surgery..is taken for a bursting of Blood thro' the Vessels, occasion'd by their Thinness. [**1853** DUNGLISON *Med. Lex.*, *Persultatio.*]

persun, obs. form of PARSON, PERSON.

persure, persute, obs. ff. PIERCER, PURSUIT.

†**per'swage,** *v. Obs. rare.* [app. f. PER- 2 + SWAGE *v.*: cf. ASSUAGE.] *trans.* To assuage, lessen, diminish, dim.

[Cf. *c* **1485** *Digby Myst.* (1882) II. 1977 *Rex.* A! we may syyn and wepyn also þat we have for-gon þis lady fre... *Regina.* þat doth perswade [? perswage] all my ble þat swete sypresse þat she wold so.] **1503** HAWES *Examp. Virt.* VI. iii, Of cruell deth a dolfull ymage That all her beaute dyd perswage.

†**per'sway,** *v. Obs. rare.* In 7 perssway. App. = prec.

1614 B. JONSON *Barth. Fair* II. vi, The creeping venome of which subtill serpent,..neither the cutting of the perillous plant [tobacco] nor the drying of it, nor the lighting, or burning, can any way perssway or asswage.

persyle, persyuere, obs. ff. PARSLEY, PERSEVERE.

pert (pɜːt), *a.* (*sb.*, *adv.*) Forms: α. 3– pert, 4–7 perte, (6 perth, *Sc.* pairt). β. 5–6 (9 *dial.*) peert, 5–7 (9 *dial.*) peart, 6 peirt(e, pearte, pierte, 6–7 (9 *dial.*) piert. [Aphetic f. APERT, and, like it and OF. *apert*, partly repr. L. *apertus*, partly = OF. *aspert*, *espert*, L. *expertus.*

From 15th c. evidenced with a long vowel, *peert*, later *peart*, *piert* (pɪərt, piːrt), retained dialectally and in U.S., esp. in sense 6, as distinguished from the ordinary general English sense (4) of *pert.* Hence *peart* and *pert* are sometimes viewed as different words.]

A. *adj.* **I.** †**1. a.** Open, unconcealed; manifest, evident; = APERT *a.* 1, 2. Often opposed to *privy. Obs.*

In quot. 1330, *aperte folie* ought perh. to be read, but the Petyt MS. has it as printed.

α. *c* **1330** R. BRUNNE *Chron.* (1810) 216 Hardely dar I say he did a perte folie. *c* **1350** *Will. Palerne* 4930 þer come menskful messageres..from hire broþer partendo þat was hire pert broþer. **1387–8** T. USK *Test. Love* III. iii. (Skeat) I. 163 By no waie maie it be then through perte necessite. *c* **1460** ROS *La belle Dame* 174 (MS. Harl.) In hir failed nothyng..prive, or perte. **1579** SPENSER *Sheph. Cal.* Sept. 162 Or priue or pert yf any bene, We han great Bandogs will teare their skinne.

β. **1529** in *Vicary's Anat.* (1888) App. xiv. 255 That no persons..from hensforth occupye eny maner Shavyng, priuy or peirt on the Sondayes.

†**b.** Open of countenance, frank. *Obs.*

1567 DRANT *Horace Epist.* xviii. F vj, Be perte, and cleare in countinaunce, Not malipert, and light.

†**2.** Of personal appearance. **a.** (in early use) Beautiful. **b.** (later) Smart, spruce, dapper. *Obs.*

α. *c* **1400** *Destr. Troy* 542, I haue pittye of your person & your pert face. *Ibid.* 14039 Pyrrus, the pert kyng put vnto dethe Pantasilia the prise qwene, pertest of ladies. **1684** OTWAY *Atheist* III. iii, He's so very little, pert and dapper. **1952** W. G. HARDY *Unfulfilled* III. v. 246 Actually, as he looked her over, she was rather cute—slim young body and pert young breasts.

β. **1596** COLSE *Penelope* (1880) 167 A thousand prettie damsels peart. **1608** DAY *Law Trickes* II. (1881) 28 What think you of this Lady? would she not make a prettie peart Dutches? **1611** COTGR., *Godinet*, prettie, dapper, feat, peart. ..*Godinette*, a prettie peart lasse.

II. 3. †**a.** Expert, skilled; ready: = APERT 4. *Obs.*

c **1250** *Gen. & Ex.* 3292 Ðor quiles he weren in ðe desert, God taȝte hem weie, wis and pert. *c* **1330** *King of Tars* 18 Hire to seo was gret preyere Of princes pert in play. *c* **1500** *Melusine* xxxviii. 303 But geffray, that was pert in armes, smote with hys clubbe suche a stroke vpon the flayel, that he made it to flee out of the geantis handes.

b. Quick to see and act, sharp, intelligent; adroit, clever. *Obs.* since 17th c. exc. in dial. form *peart.*

α. **1375** BARBOUR *Bruce* x. 531 Ane william francass, Wicht and pert, viss and curtass. *c* **1400** *Destr. Troy* 12044 Cassandra..Priams pure dughter, pertist of wit. **1484** CAXTON *Fables of Æsop* ad fin., The mayster that was perte and quyck was anone promoted to a benefyce. *c* **1500** *Melusine* xix. 105 So pert & swyft they were. **1628** FELTHAM *Resolves* II. [1.] xcii, Thus we see for Morality, Nature still is something pert and vigorous. **1644** MILTON *Areop.* (Arb.) 71 The acutest, and the pertest operations of wit and suttlety.

β. **1586** J. HOOKER *Hist. Irel.* in *Holinshed* II. 96/2 Perceiving that rough nets were not the fittest to take such peart birds. **1640** R. BAILLIE *Canterb. Self-convict.* ii. 12 Of so obscure and intricate a nature, that..our Assembly was to peart to make any determination about them. **1850** *N. & Q.* 1st Ser. II. 276/2 'I beant peart at making button-holes', said a needle woman. **1852** MRS. STOWE *Uncle Tom's C.* xxi, She's such a peart young un, she won't take no lookin' arter.

III. 4. a. Forward in speech and behaviour; unbecomingly ready to express an opinion or give a sharp reply; saucy, bordering upon 'cheeky'; malapert: = APERT 5. Said usually of children, young people, or persons in inferior position, such as are considered to be too 'uppish' or forward in their address. Now the ordinary sense.

α. *c* **1386** CHAUCER *Reeve's T.* 30 (Corpus MS.), And sche was proud and pert as is a pye [so 4 MSS.; 3 peert]. *a* **1450** *Knt. de la Tour* xiii. 18 Y saide y wolde not of her, for she was so pert and so light of maners. *a* **1529** SKELTON *Bowge of Courte* 71 And sayde I was to blame To be so perte to prese so proudly uppe. **1530** PALSGR. 320/2 Perte saucy or homly, *malapert.* **1552** HULOET, Perte in makynge aunswere, *argutus et argutulus.* **1654** JER. TAYLOR *Real Pres.* iv. 73 S. Hierome reproving certain pert Deacons for insulting over Priests. **1741** RICHARDSON *Pamela* I. 36 Says Mrs. Jervis, Pamela, dont be pert to his Honour. **1826** DISRAELI *Viv. Grey* II. xiv, As pert a genius as the applause of a common-room ever yet spoiled. **1835** SOUTHEY in *Corr. w. C. Bowles* (1881) 319 Mrs. Barbauld was cold as her creed: her niece.. pert as a pear-monger. **1858** TRENCH *Stud. Words* v, We have been obliged to make 'pert' do double duty, that of 'malapert' and its own. As some word is plainly wanting, not so strong as 'insolent', we have been led to employ 'pert' exclusively in an unfavourable sense.

β. *a* **1430** Peert [see quot. *c* 1386 in α]. **1515** BARCLAY *Egloges* iii (1570) C ij b/2 Some be forgetfull, some peart, some insolent. **1593** DONNE *Sat.* i. Poems (1630) 325 Though a briske perfum'd piert Courtier Deigne with a nod, thy courtesie to answer. **1835** C. F. HOFFMAN *Winter in Far West* I. 212 He looks so peert whenever he comes in.

b. Of behaviour, speech, etc.

1681 GLANVILL *Sadducismus* Pref., With a pert and pragmatique Insolence they censure all. **1702** *Eng. Theophrast.* 6 We admire the pert talk of children, because we expected nothing from them. **1835** LYTTON *Rienzi* IV. i, The grave officer could not refrain a smile at the pert.. answer of the boy. **1898** G. B. SHAW *Candida* I. 82 In a black merino skirt and a blouse, rather pert and quick of speech, and not very civil in her manner. **1924** —— *St. Joan* vi. 87 We are not so foolish as you think us. Try to resist the temptation to make pert replies to us.

†**c.** As a vague expression of disfavour. *Obs.*

a **1704** T. BROWN *Imit. Persius' Sat.* i, Here a pert sot, with six months pain, brings forth A strange, misshapen, and ridiculous birth. **1711** SWIFT *Jrnl. to Stella* 15 July, We had a sad pert dull parson at Kensington to-day. **1728** POPE *Dunc.* II. 39 With pert flat eyes she window'd well its head, A brain of feathers and a heart of lead. **1752** H. WALPOLE *Let. to R. Bentley* 5–12 Aug., The Fairfaxes have fitted up a pert bad apartment in the fore-part of the Castle.

5. Bold (esp. in a blameworthy sense); forward; audacious, presumptuous. *Obs.* (exc. as merged in 4.)

1535 STEWART *Cron. Scot.* (1858) I. 169 That none.. Durst be so pert as to stryk with ane wapyn. *Ibid.* II. 15 That ony Pecht sould be so perth to preve, To pas that wall without the legatis leve. **1590** MARLOWE *Edw. II*, I. iv, But this I scorne that one so basely borne Should by his soueraignes fauour grow so pert. **1673** CHAS. II in *Lauderdale P.* (1885) III. 2 Now they are not so perte on that subiect as they were.

β. **1535** LYNDESAY *Satyre* 2914 Ye are over peart with sik maters to mell. **1570** LEVINS *Manip.* 211/15 Pearte, *audax, impudens.*

6. a. Lively; brisk, sprightly; in good spirits, cheerful, 'jolly'. Since 17th c. only *dial.*; often used of the state of an invalid: 'bright', 'perky', 'chirpy', as opposed to 'depressed', 'down' (esp. in form *peart*: see β).

1581 NUCE *Seneca's Octavia* I. i, Syr Phœbus pert with spouting beame From dewy neast doth mount apace. **1590** SHAKS. *Mids. N.* I. i. 13 Awake the pert and nimble spirit of mirth. **1634** MILTON *Comus* 118 And on the Tawny Sands and Shelves, Trip the pert Fairies and the dapper Elves. **1693** *Humours Town* 116 A young, pert, blooming Girl. **1696** *Verney Mem.* (1899) IV. 477, I watched last night with him and I thought him fine and pert in the morning but hee fell off again in the afternoone as hee doth most Daies. *a* **1732, 1738** [see PEARMONGER]. **1774** P. V. FITHIAN *Jrnl.* (1900) 241 Ben seems a little more pert today. **1872** R. B. MARCY *Border Rem.* 252 Wa'al, now, straanger,..I war middlin' sort o' pert yesterday, but..I'ze powerful weak to-day. **1891** L. T. MEADE *Sweet Girl Graduate* xxii. 187 I'll be glad to lie down... I'll be as pert as a cricket in the morning.

β. *dial.* and *U.S.* (often viewed as a distinct word).

'No word in literary English precisely expresses the idea of *peart*; least of any does *pert. Peart* conveys the impression of sprightly liveliness, of a joyous, healthy, fresh, happy condition, in the person or animal to which it is applied.' F. T. Elworthy in *N. & Q.* 9th ser. IV. (1899) 525.

1500–20 DUNBAR *Poems* lxxv. 10 He wes townysche, peirt, and gukit. **1565** [see PEARMONGER]. **1578** GOSSON in *Sch. Abuse* (Arb.) Notes 78 When he perceyues Don Cortes here so pearte. **1661** LOVELL *Hist. Anim. & Min.* 2 They are very peart in the new of the Moon, and sad in the conjunction. **1828** J. HALL *Lett. fr. West* 304 These little fixens..make a man feel right peart, when he is three or four hundred miles from any body or any place. **1832** W. IRVING *Jrnl.* 10 Nov. (1919) III. 171 My horse goes quite peart. **1857** HUGHES *Tom Brown* I. iii, And watched the hawks soaring, and the 'peert' bird. **1859** W. WARNER *Albion's Eng.* II. xxxi. 135 As peart as bird. **1863** KINGSLEY *Water-Bab.* i, For which reason he [Tom] was as piert as a game-cock. **1869** BLACKMORE *Lorna D.* xlv, Quick she had always been and 'peart', as we say on Exmoor. **1873** A. J. MUNBY *Diary* 11 July in D. Hudson *Munby* (1972) 335 Sir Arthur Helps with his bristling white hair and 'peart' white face, so like Mazzini. **1889** HURST *Horsham, Gloss. Sussex Words* s.v., I'm sure the child is better to-day, she looks so peart. **1943** *Amer. Speech* XVIII. 67/2 *Peart* (lively, in good health, especially of older people).

b. Of plants: Fresh, flourishing, verdant.

1727 S. SWITZER *Pract. Gard.* II. xii. 95 Provided it [a melon] ripens well whilst the leaves and stalk are pert and green. **1772** in *Maryland Hist. Mag.* (1919) XIV. 272 The Corn looks pert & green. **1883** in *Hampsh. Gloss.*

c. Of liquor: Brisk, pleasantly sharp to the taste.

a **1722** LISLE *Husb.* (1757) I. 377 Oat-malt and barley-malt equally mixed..makes a very pretty, pert, smooth drink. [Cf. quot. *c* 1825 s.v. PERTISH.]

B. *sb.* (*absol.* use of the adj.) A pert person or thing: in various senses. † *in pert*, openly (*obs.*).

c **1400** *Destr. Troy* 13725 Pirrus of þat pert was pristly enamurt. *c* **1450** HOLLAND *Howlat* 60 For schame of my schape in pert till appeir. **1784** COWPER *Task* IV. 145 No powdered pert, proficient in the art Of sounding an alarm, assaults these doors.

C. *adv.* or quasi-*adv.*: in various senses of the adj.

1399 LANGL. *Rich. Redeles* IV. 88 Some parled as perte as prouyd well after. *a* **1400–50** *Alexander* 2295 And Bedels & bailȝais he bad a-none crye, Before hys peple so pert. **1485** *Waterf. Arch.* in *10th Rep. Hist. MSS. Comm.* App. v. 321 That..will goo among them prevy or peart for his propre besynes. **1528** ROY *Rede me* (Arb.) 48 Morover that no clarcke be so bolde, Prevy or pearte with hym to holde. **1530** PALSGR. 841 Privy or perte, *en privé ou en apert.* **1795** COWPER *Pairing Time* 28 A last year's bird, who ne'er had tried What pairing means, thus pert replied. **1859** J. REDPATH *Roving Editor* 248 'Now hold up your head and walk pert... Quick—come—pert—only there already? pert!' jerked out the mulatto, to hasten the boy's steps. **1902** W. N. HARBEN *Abner Daniel* 230 Well, I'm glad I won't have to go furder'n Darley... By ridin' peert I can let you out before sundown. **1972** *News & Observer* (Raleigh, N. Carolina) 30 Dec. 4/3 We aren't journey proud, and few of us get the big head or act pert.

† **pert**, *v.* *Obs. rare.* [In sense 2, f. PERT *a.* 4; in 1, app. a phonetic variant of PERK *v.*; but the relation between these words is obscure.]

1. *trans.* with *up.* To raise briskly: = PERK *v.*[1] 3.

1611 BEAUM. & FL. *Knt. Burn. Pestle* I. i, Didst thou ever see a prettier child? How it behaves it selfe..And speaks and looks, and pearts up the head?

2. *intr.* To behave pertly: = PERK *v.*[1] 1 b.

1637 POCKLINGTON *Altare Chr.* 158 If..allowed to piert upon the Canons of the Church, and crow over her authority. **1661** GAUDEN *Anti-Baal-Berith* 292 Hagar perted against Sarah, and lifted herself up against her superiours.

pert, obs. form of PART.

pertain (pəˈteɪn), *v.* Forms: 4–6 par-, pertene, -teyne, 5 -tyne, -tiene, -tine, 5–6 -teigne, -tayne, 6 partein, 6–7 pertaine, 4 -tein(e, 7 -tayn, 6– pertain. [ME. *par-, pertene, -teyne*, a. OF. *parten-ir* (3rd pres. Norman *parten-t*, *parten-ent*, subj. *partene*, *-teigne*: cf. CONTAIN) = Pr. *pertener*, It. *pertenere* to belong:—L. *pertinēre* to extend, stretch, tend (to), belong (to), f. PER- 1 + *tenēre* to hold.]

1. *intr.* To belong, be connected (in various ways); e.g. as a native or inhabitant, as part of a whole, as an appendage or accessory, as dependent. Const. *to.*

c **1350** *Will. Palerne* 1419 All þe grete, Of lordes & ladies þat to þat lond partened. **1387** TREVISA *Higden* (Rolls) II. 121 From þat tyme þe citee and þe see of Dorchestre perteyned and longede to þe prouince of Mercia. **1483** *Act 1 Rich. III*, c. 6 §1 To euery of the same Feyres is of right perteynyng a court of Pepowders to mynystre to theim due Justice. **1532** FRITH *Mirror* i. Wks. (1829) 266 Whether they be outward gifts or inward, pertaining either to the body or soul. **1546** *Reg. Privy Council Scot.* I. 28 The samin [house] and landis pertenand thairto. **1611** SHAKS. *Wint. T.* v. iii. 113 If she pertaine to life, let her speake too. **1850** GROVE *Corr. Phys. Forces* (ed. 2) 89, I have purposely avoided this subject, as pertaining to a department of science to which I have not devoted my attention. **1859** C. BARKER *Assoc. Princ.* iii. 62 Scenes which pertain to an age happily passed away.

† **b.** *spec.* To belong as a possession, legal right, or privilege. *Obs.*

c **1380** WYCLIF *Serm.* Sel. Wks. I. 140 þe sheep perteynen not to him. **1425** *Rolls of Parlt.* IV. 298/1 Suche service as pertienneth of honeste to my said Lord. **1526** TINDALE *Mark* xii. 17 Geve to Cesar that which belongeth to Cesar: and geve God that which perteyneth to God. **1592** DAVIES *Immort. Soul* VII. iii. (1714) 46 To create, to God alone pertains. **1609** SKENE *Reg. Maj.* 11 The persewer may alledge the lands to perteine to him. **1630** PRYNNE *Anti-Armin.* 144 The real intention, benefit, and application of his death..pertains not vnto all.

c. To belong as one's care or concern. *to pertain to*: to matter to, to concern. *Obs.* or *arch.*

1382 WYCLIF *Mark* iv. 38 Maistre, perteneth it nat to thee, that we perishen? **1470–85** MALORY *Arthur* XVI. xi. 679 But thow wenest to rescowe a mayde whiche perteyneth no thynge to the. **1549** LATIMER *3rd Serm. bef. Edw. VI* (Arb.) 85 Thy syluer is drosse... What pertained that to Esay? *c* **1696** PRIOR *Love Disarmed* 27 To me pertains not, she replies, To know or care where Cupid flies. **1870** BRYANT *Iliad* I. VI. 207 The cares of war Pertain to all men born in Troy.

d. To belong as an attribute, fitting adjunct, or duty; to be appropriate *to.*

1375 BARBOUR *Bruce* XIII. 728 In that tuelf moneth suld he Cum and clayme it, and tharfor do To the king that pertenyt thar-to. **1423** JAS. I *Kingis Q.* cvii, Though It to me pertene In lufis lawe the septre to gouerne. **1447** BOKENHAM *Seyntys* (Roxb.) 44 Anne is as myche to seyn as grace..worthyly thys appellacyoun To hyr pertenyth. **1552** *Bk. Com. Prayer, Order. Deacons*, It perteineth to thoffice of a Deacon..to assist the Prieste. **1577–87** HOLINSHED *Chron.* III. 2/2 Requiring at your hands the things which pertaine to peace. **1688** R. HOLME *Armoury* III. 321/1 There are..these Tools and Instruments pertaining to the Iron Workers. **1773–83** HOOLE *Orl. Fur.* XIX. 522 Weapons that pertain to war. **1861** M. PATTISON *Ess.* (1889) I. 47 To keep an iron helmet and harness, and all arms pertaining to a complete furnishing for war.

2. To have reference or relation; to relate *to.*

c **1400** MAUNDEV. (Roxb.) xxxiv. 152 Spicery and all maner of oþer gudez, and namely þat partenez to mannez lyflade. **1432–50** tr. *Higden* (Rolls) IV. 417 William Malmesbur..supposenge the writenge of that ston to perteyne to Marius the consul of Rome. **1526** TINDALE *2 Pet.* i. 3 All thynges that pertayne vnto lyfe. **1611** BIBLE *Transl. Pref.* 2 Specially if it pertaine to Religion. *a* **1770** JORTIN *Serm.* (1771) III. iii. 47 This law pertains, first to vows made to God himself and confirmed by an oath. **1841** BORROW *Zincali* I. i. 233 We..discoursed on matters pertaining to our people.

† **3.** In both senses (1 and 2), formerly sometimes with an indirect (dative) object without *to.* Cf. BELONG *v.* 3. *Obs.* or *dial.*

1472–3 *Rolls of Parlt.* VI. 52/1 Answere in and to all such Writte and Writtes, Bille and Billes,..perteynyng any of the premisses. **1535** LYNDESAY *Satyre* 3354 My coattis, and my offrands, With all that dois perteine my benefice. **1553** in *Maitl. Cl. Misc.* (1840) I. 41 *note*, I, wyth all ffreindis pertening me. **1628** (*title of MS.*) Booke of the Land perteyninge the Famyly of the Twysdens in Kent.

† **4.** The 3rd pers. sing. impersonally, and the pres. pple. were used in the phrases ***as pertains to, as pertaining to*** = as regards, as concerns, in regard to, in relation to. *Obs.* (or *arch.*)

1526 TINDALE *Rom.* iv. 1 Abraham oure father, as pertayninge [so 1611; 1881 *R.V.* according] to the flesshe. —— *Heb.* ix. 9 Gyftes and sacrifises are offered which cannot make them that minister parfect, as pertaynynge to [1881 *R.V.* as touching] the conscience. **1568** BIBLE (Bishops') *Rom.* ix. 3 My kinsmen as parteyneth to the fleashe.

Hence **perˈtaining** *vbl. sb.* (also pl. in concr. sense = 'belongings') and *ppl. a.*

1591 PERCIVALL *Sp. Dict.*, *Pertenencia*, perteining. **1869** BUSHNELL *Wom. Suffrage* v. 90 These things are duly considered as pertainings of a woman's lot. **1889** *Electrical Rev.* 29 Nov. 607/1 Seven houses and their pertainings. **1898** E. PHILLPOTTS *Childr. of Mist* I. v, The pertaining farm already had a tenant.

perˈtainment. *rare.* [f. prec. + -MENT.] A belonging, an appurtenance.

1897 *Contemp. Rev.* Sept. 415 [They] possess some of the finest pertainments of the human race.

pertake, pertane, perte, pertene, pertener, obs. forms of PARTAKE, PARTAN (crab), PART, PERTAIN, PARTNER.

† **perˈterebrate,** *v.* *Obs. rare*$^{-0}$. [f. ppl. stem of L. *perterebrāre* to bore through, f. PER- 1 + *terebrāre* to bore.] *trans.* (See quots.)

1623 COCKERAM, *Perterebrate*, to wimble. **1656** BLOUNT, *Perterebrate*, to peirce or bore thorow with a wimble.

So † **pertereˈbration**, a boring through.

1658 PHILLIPS, *Perterebration*, a boring through with a wimble. [Hence in Bailey, Johnson, and mod. Dicts.]

† **perˈterrify,** *v.* *Obs. rare*$^{-0}$. [f. PER- 2 + TERRIFY, after L. *perterrefacĕre* to frighten thoroughly.] *trans.* To terrify thoroughly.

1623 COCKERAM, *Perterifie*, to fright.

perterych, obs. form of PARTRIDGE.

† **perˈtexed,** *ppl. a.* *Obs. rare*$^{-0}$. [ad. L. *pertext-us*, pa. pple. of *pertexĕre* to weave throughout.]

1623 COCKERAM, *Pertexed*, weaued out.

perteyne, perteyner, -or, obs. ff. PERTAIN, PARTNER.

Perthes(') disease (ˈpɜːtəz). *Med.* [Named after Georg Clemens *Perthes* (1869–1927), German surgeon, who described the condition in 1910.] A disease of the hip occurring in children, probably owing to an interrupted blood supply, in which necrosis of part of the head of the femur leads to progressive deformity of the joint.

1915 *Amer. Jrnl. Orthopedic Surg.* XII. 557, I shall try to reproduce these features which give a character of its own to Perthes disease, and to describe it as a new and typical disease of the hip. *Ibid.* 564 One must conclude that Perthes disease has a tendency to spontaneous reparation and that all treatment is useless. **1958** *Jrnl. Bone & Joint Surg.* XL-B. 173 Stigmata of pre-existing Perthes' disease: a large [femoral] head, decreased height of the epiphysis, slight subluxation, shortening or broadening of the femoral neck. **1974** *Israel Jrnl. Med. Sci.* X. 230 The results may indicate that the deformity of the acetabulum in Perthes disease, generally recognized as secondary to femoral head deformity, may in fact develop in the initial stages of the disease.

perthite (ˈpɜːθaɪt). *Min.* [Named by T. Thomson (1832) after Perth, Ontario, where found: see -ITE[1].] (See quot. 1868.)

1832 C. U. SHEPARD *Min.* I. 232 (Chester). **1868** DANA *Min.* (ed. 5) 356 *Perthite*, a flesh-red aventurine feldspar, consisting of interlaminated albite and orthoclase.

Hence **perˈthitic** *a.*, pertaining to, resembling, or containing perthite; **perˈthitically** *adv.*, in the manner of perthite.

1905 in N.E.D. **1906** J. P. IDDINGS *Rock Minerals* II. 236 Perthitic intergrowth. **1930** PEACH & HORNE *Geol. Scotl.* 112 The alkali-felspar includes both orthoclase and albite, which may be present separately, perthitically intergrown. **1949** *Econ. Geol.* XLIV. 174 In the diorite facies the microcline is generally only slightly perthitic..whereas in the syenitic rock it is ordinarily highly perthitic. *Ibid.* 179 The sodic solutions soaked into the microcline and replaced it perthitically by albite and then by grains along margins and fractures. **1965** G. J. WILLIAMS *Econ. Geol. N.Z.* xiii. 208/2 A radioactive biotite-granite with quartz, perthitic orthoclase, microcline and 20 per cent of dark minerals was also found in the Big River area.

perti, pertie, obs. forms of PARTY.

† **ˈpertical,** *a.* *Obs. rare.* [ad. L. *perticāl-is*, f. *pertica* pole, PERCH *sb.*[2]] Of, pertaining to, or done by means of the measuring-rod or surveyor's staff.

1625 NORDEN *England* Pref. Addr., For want of perticall demensuration, I have beene enforced to borrow the helpe ..of mine owne maps. **1656** BLOUNT *Glossogr.*, *Pertical*, belonging to, or serving for a Perch or Pole.

perticat, -e, perticular, -er(e, pertiliche, obs. ff. PARTICATE, PARTICULAR, PERTLY.

† **pertinace,** *a.* *Obs.* Also 5 -nax. [a. OF. *pertinace*, also *pertinax* (14–15th c.), in It. *pertinace*, Sp. *pertinaz*, ad. L. *pertināx*, *-ācem* very tenacious, f. PER- 4 + *tenax* tenacious.] = next.

14.. in *Rel. Ant.* I. 192 Olde maisterez war noȝt bisie ne pertinacez in sekyng and serchyng of this forsaide cure. **1491** CAXTON *Vitas Patr.* (W. de W. 1495) II. 301/1 Seeyng that he was pertynax & obstynate.

Hence † **pertinacely** *adv.*, pertinaciously.

1526 *Pilgr. Perf.* (W. de W. 1531) 224 Pertynacely expownynge the holy scripture wrong, they fell in to heresyes.

pertinacious (pɜːtɪˈneɪʃəs), *a.* Also 7 -atious, 7–8 -aceous. [f. L. *pertināci-*, stem of *pertināx* (see PERTINACE) + -OUS.] Persistent or stubborn in holding to one's own opinion or design; resolute; obstinate. Chiefly as a bad quality.

1626 MEADE in Ellis *Orig. Lett.* Ser. I. III. 224 You will perceive my Lord Digby's pertinacious importunity to come to Parliament. *a* **1635** NAUNTON *Fragm. Reg.* (Arb.) 21 Given to any violent or pertinatious dispute. **1655** FULLER *Ch. Hist.* III. vi. §43 To dispight them, who are.. pertinacious worshippers of one God. **1794** SULLIVAN *View Nat.* V. 191 Pertinaceous bigotry may chuse to adhere to it. **1805** FOSTER *Ess.* I. iv. 55 As pertinacious as ivy climbing a wall. *a* **1859** MACAULAY *Biog.* (1867) 16 Atterbury became the most factious and pertinacious of all the opponents of the government.

b. Obstinately or persistently continuing; *spec.* of disease, etc., not yielding to treatment.

1646 H. LAWRENCE *Comm. Angells* 60 Put them into a pertinacious and constant state of ill. **1675** GREW *Disc. Tasts Plants* v. §6 The Barque of the Root..impresseth a pertinaceous and diffusive Taste. **1684** tr. *Bonet's Merc. Compit.* VIII. 279 The Flux..is sometimes so pertinacious, that it is impossible to stop it. *a* **1785** GLOVER *Athenaid* I, Recumbent, not reposing, there Consumes the hours in pertinacious woe, Which sheds no tear. **1878** BROWNING *Poets Croisic* xlix, Its pertinacious hues Must fade.

pertinaciously (pɜːtɪˈneɪʃəslɪ), *adv.* [f. prec. + -LY[2].] In a pertinacious manner; resolutely; persistently; obstinately, stubbornly.

1637–50 ROW *Hist. Kirk* (1842) 58 The Assemblie condemnes this proposition as erroneous, false, and, if pertinaciouslie maintained, hereticall. **1751** HUME *Princ. Morals* i. 1 Disputes with Persons, pertinaciously obstinate in their Principles, are, of all others, the most irksome. **1830** D'ISRAELI *Chas. I*, III. v. 66 He kept cautiously and pertinaciously to the laws. **1876** HOLLAND *Sev. Oaks* xi. 145 It returned and returned again so pertinaciously that he was glad to order his horses and ride to the factory.

pertiˈnaciousness. [See -NESS.] = next.

1651 JER. TAYLOR *Holy Dying* v. viii. (1719) 249 Fearing lest the pertinaciousness of her Mistress's Sorrows shou'd cause her Evil to revert, or her Shame to approach. *a* **1711** KEN *Psyche* Poet. Wks. 1721 IV. 200 In a mistaken way With Pertinaciousness I stray. **1837** T. HOOK *Jack Brag* xix, The pertinaciousness with which Mr. Levert adhered to his opinion.

pertinacity (pɜːtɪˈnæsɪtɪ). [a. F. *pertinacité* (1419 in Godef.), ad. L. type **pertinācitās* (perh. in mod.L. for *pertinācia*), in mod.It. *pertinacità* (cf. L. *tenācia* and *tenācitās*), f. L. *pertināc-em*: see PERTINACE.] The quality of being pertinacious; resolute or stubborn adherence, as to an opinion, purpose, design, course of action, etc.; persistency; usually in a bad sense: perverse obstinacy or stubbornness; evil persistence.

1504 ATKYNSON tr. *De Imitatione* I. ix. 159 It is a synne of pertynacite & pryde. **1570–6** LAMBARDE *Peramb. Kent* (1862) 179 Thomas Becket..having by froward disobedience and stubborne pertinacitie, provoked King Henrie the Seconde to indignation against him. *c* **1620** MORYSON *Itin.* IV. v. iv. (1903) 482 The mere Irish..haue singular and obstinate pertinacity in retayning their old manners and Customes. **1639** N. N. tr. *Du Bosq's Compl. Woman* II. 9 Constancy is but for good things, pertinacity for the bad. **1759** JOHNSON *Idler* No. 55 ¶3, I have collected materials with indefatigable pertinacity. *a* **1832** MACKINTOSH *Rev. of 1688*, Wks. 1846 II. 87 The pertinacity of the heretic. **1845** SARAH AUSTIN *Ranke's Hist. Ref.* IV. i. II. 343 The imperialists carried on the siege of Marseilles with great pertinacity. **1880** HAUGHTON *Phys. Geog.* iii. 118 The propriety of the term is shewn by the pertinacity with which the lines AA and CC cling to the water and avoid the land.

†**ˈpertinacy.** *Obs.* Also 7 -tenacy. [= Pr., It., Sp. *pertinacia*, ad. L. *pertinācia*, f. *pertināx*, *-ācem*: see PERTINACE. Cf. prec.]

= PERTINACITY: being the earlier word; very common in 17th c. Mostly in an evil sense.

c**1386** CHAUCER *Pars. T.* ⁋330 Pertinacie is whan man deffendeth hise folies and trusteth to muchel in his owene wit. **1387–8** T. USK *Test. Love* II. i. (Skeat) l. 46 Holy faders ..proved..her pertinacie to distroy. **1548** UDALL, etc. *Erasm. Par. Matt.* xii. 71 The pertinacye and stubbernesse of the Iewes. **1577** HARRISON *England* II. i. (1877) I. 17 In cases of heresie, pertinacie, contempt, and such like. **1605** B. JONSON *Volpone* IV. ii, My breeding is not so coarse..to offend with pertinacy. **1656** BLOUNT *Glossogr.*, *Pertinacy*.. some-times..taken in the good part for perseverance, constancy. **1686** GOAD *Celest. Bodies* II. iii. 192 Justifying it self by the Pertinacy of the Constitution throughout all the Term. **1751** *Affect. Narr. of Wager* 96 Reflecting on..the Disgrace arising to himself, by his Ignorance and Pertinacy.

†**ˈpertinate,** *a.* *Obs.* [An irreg. formation, perh. on the mistaken analogy of *intimate, intimacy*, and the like; or originating in a misreading of *pertinace*.] = PERTINACE, PERTINACIOUS.

c**1534** T. THEOBOLD in Ellis *Orig. Lett.* Ser. III. III. 128 This Friar..yn his symple opynnion somwhat pertynate. **1545** JOYE *Exp. Dan.* vi. 88 Oh how pertinate and styfe are the vngodly lawers and act makers. **1552** LYNDESAY *Monarche* 5730 All pertinat wylfull Arratykis.

Hence †**ˈpertinately** *adv.* = PERTINACIOUSLY.

c**1400** *Apol. Loll.* 42 To defend þe contrary pertinatly is heresy, contrary to þe feiþ. **1545** JOYE *Exp. Dan.* xii. 211 These abominacions when thei be defended pertinatly of the enemies of the gospel, then their stifnecked pertinacie inflammeth discordis.

pertinence (ˈpɜːtɪnəns). Also 5–6 -tenaunce, 6 -tenance, -tynense. [In sense 1, a. OF. *partenance, partinance, pertinence*, f. *partenant*, pr. pple. of *partenir* to belong; cf. PURTENANCE; in 3, from PERTINENT: see -ENCE.]

†**1.** Something which belongs or is an appendage to another larger thing; = PURTENANCE, APPURTENANCE 1 and 2. *Obs.*

a. *Law.* An adjunct to property: cf. PERTINENT *sb.* a.

1432–50 tr. *Higden* (Rolls) VIII. 509, I, Henricus, duke.., clayme and take..the crowne of Ynglonde with the pertinence. **1455** *Rolls of Parlt.* V. 320/1 The manoir of Whitgift, with the pertinences. **1525** TINDALE *Marg. Notes on Matt.* xiv. 1. Wks. (Parker Soc.) II. 233 Jewry, with her pertenance, was then divided into four lordships.

†**b.** The offal of a carcase; = PURTENANCE 2.

1535 COVERDALE *Exod.* xii. 9 His heade wᵗ his fete and pertenaunce [*Bps'., Geneva*, 1611 purtenance].

†**c.** *pl.* Belongings, appendages, trimmings of a dress. *Obs.*

1552 *Inv. Ch. Surrey* (1869) 32, j vestement of blacke damaske with the pertynenses.

†**2.** The fact of pertaining or being attached *to*. *Obs. rare.*

c**1611** CHAPMAN *Iliad* XIV. 434 Wounding him in that part ..Betwixt the short ribs and the bones that to the triple gut Have pertinence.

3. The fact of being pertinent; = PERTINENCY 1.

1659 H. THORNDIKE *Wks.* (1846) II. 665 The agreement of them with other copies, together with the..pertinence of sense. a**1693** SOUTH *1st Serm. on Eccles.* v. 2 Serm. 1737 II. 96 A due ordering of our words..; which is done by pertinence and brevity of expression. **1837–9** HALLAM *Hist. Lit.* II. viii. §8 Montucla calls him [Commandin] the model of commentators for the pertinence and sufficiency of his notes.

pertinency (ˈpɜːtɪnənsɪ). [f. L. *pertinēnt-em* PERTINENT: see -ENCY.]

1. The quality of being pertinent or pertaining to the matter in hand; relevancy; appositeness.

1598 FLORIO, *Pertenenza*, pertinency. **1603** —— *Montaigne* I. xxv. (1632) 73 Making choice of his reasons, loving pertinency, and by consequence brevitie. a**1652** J. SMITH *Sel. Disc.* vii. 316 Because of their pertinency and usefulness in the matter now in hand. **1701** NORRIS *Ideal World* I. vi. 320 The pertinency of it to our present concern. **1794** PALEY *Evid.* I. ii. II. i. (1817) 354 Still less is there of pertinency in Mr. Hume's eulogium. **1865** CARLYLE *Fredk. Gt.* xxi. vii. (1872) X. 128 Innumerable things, of no pertinency to us, are wearisomely told.

†**b.** With *pl.* An instance of this. *Obs.*

1654 WHITLOCK *Zootomia* 208 On occasion to draw out Pertinencies to some emergent. **1665** WITHER *Lord's Prayer* Preamble, Made forth explicitely in every Essential and Circumstantial pertinency thereof.

†**2.** = PERTINENCE 1, APPURTENANCE 1. *Obs.*

1651 G. W. tr. *Cowel's Inst.* 105 Nor can a prescription be of those pertinencies whose principles have not a perpetuall and durable continuance. [**1872** E. W. ROBERTSON *Hist. Ess.* 127 The thanage of Kintore which was made over in 1375 'saving the pertinencies [*pertinenciis*] and our kanes' by Robert II to John de Dunbar, Earl of Moray.]

pertinent (ˈpɜːtɪnənt), *a.* and *sb.* Also 6 par-. [Ultimately from L. *pertinēnt-em*, pr. pple. of *pertinēre* to PERTAIN; but in early use immed. a. OF. *partenant* (1246 in Godef.), *pertenant*, pr. pple. of OF. *partenir*; the latinized *pertinent* is cited by Hatz.-Darm. from Chr. de Pisan c1400.]

A. *adj.* †**1.** Pertaining or belonging (*to*): **a.** as a possession, dependency, or appendage; **b.** as a part, constituent, or function. See PERTAIN *v.* 1.

[**1278** *Rolls of Parlt.* I. 11/1 Les autres terres, purtinauntz a Tillebury.] c**1407** LYDG. *Reson & Sens.* 5157 Any maner herbe fynde,..Greyn or gomme, rynde and roote, Pertinent vnto physike. **1412–20** —— *Chron. Troy* I. vii. (1555), An yle to Grekes pertinent. **1586** A. DAY *Eng. Secretary* I. (1625) 32 Whatsoeuer is pertinent to folly. **1635** SWAN *Spec. M.* iv. §2 (1643) 63 This was a work pertinent unto the third day.

†**2.** Appropriate, suitable in nature or character.

1413 *Pilgr. Sowle* (Caxton 1483) III. iii. 51 Many peynes pertynent to dyuers synnes. **1432** JAS. I *Kingis Q.* cxxxviii, Lat me se Gif thy remede be pertynent to me. **1539** *Act 31 Hen. VIII.* c. 5 A..beautifull and princely manour..mete and partinent to his royall maiestie. **1567** MAPLET *Gr. Forest* A vj, Proper or pertinent to earths are many and sundrie kindes. **1658** A. FOX *Wurtz' Surg.* III. xiii. 255 To apply pertinent remedies for such Symptomes. **1697** POTTER *Antiq. Greece* IV. xi. (1715) 270 My Parents to the Match will not consent, Therefore desist, it is not pertinent.

3. Pertaining or relating to the matter in hand; relevant; to the point; apposite. Const. *to*.

c**1380** WYCLIF *Sel. Wks.* II. 13 þei..seiden, þat þei hadden no breed, how were it þanne pertinent to telle hem of sour douȝ? **1532** MORE *Confut. Tindale* Wks. 608/2 Lettyng..the remenant passe, as nowe not pertinent properlye to this matter. **1631** GOUGE *God's Arrows* I. Ded. 9 Pertinent therefore to the present times are the Treatises following. **1647** CLARENDON *Hist. Ref.* IV. §309 A most pertinent instance of the Tyranny, and Injustice of that time. a**1713** ELLWOOD *Autobiog.* (1714) 353 Books and Papers, pertinent to the case in Hand. **1875** JOWETT *Plato* (ed. 2) V. 131 He..prefers a few good judges who make pertinent remarks on the case.

B. *sb.* Something which pertains, belongs, or forms an appendage, to another; a minor property, appurtenance. Usually in *pl.*

a. *Law.* (Chiefly *Sc.*) Anything belonging to an estate, the ownership of which it follows.

1396 in *Scott. Antiq.* (1900) XIV. 217 Al his landys of the Murtclauch..lyand within the schyrraydome of Banfe with the pertinents. c**1450** *Godstow Reg.* 35 The mylle of dudekesford, with the pertynentis. **1495** *Rolls of Parlt.* VI. 501/1 The Manours of Wodstock, Hanburgh and Stonefeld, of the Hundred of Wotton, with the pertinentes, in the Countie of Oxon'. a**1649** DRUMM. OF HAWTH. *Fam. Ep.* Wks. (1711) 157 His said lands,..with houses, biggings, yards, parts, pendicles, and pertinents thereof. **1813** N. CARLISLE *Topog. Dict. Scot.* II. s.v. *Hassendean*, The Church of Hassendean, with its pertinents,..were granted to Walter, Earl of Buccleugh. **1864** CARLYLE *Fredk. Gt.* xv. xiv. IV. 211 Torgau and pertinents now his.

b. *generally.* Belongings; apparatus; dependencies. Now *Sc.*

1526 *Pilgr. Perf.* (W. de W. 1531) 103 Whiche tree he.. offreth..with all the fruytes & partynentes to the same. **1554** KNOX *Let.* in *Sel. Writ.* (1845) 337 Make not your members pertinents to sin. a**1657** R. LOVEDAY *Lett.* (1663) 111 Great ones love at such solemn troubles to have their servants presence signifie they have such pertinents. **1774** PENNANT *Tour Scot. in 1772*, 318 Boats with nets and other pertinents for fishing. **1854** H. MILLER *Sch. & Schm.* xxi. (1858) 468 As if its thinking part had no other vocation than simply to take care of the mouth and its pertinents.

ˈpertinently, *adv.* [f. prec. + -LY².] In a pertinent manner; suitably, appropriately; appositely, to the point or purpose.

1596 DRAYTON *Leg.* iv. 103 And to be alwaies pertinently good, Followes not still the greatnesse of our Bloud. **1626** T. H[AWKINS] *Caussin's Holy Crt.* 15 Nor yet will I touch what might pertinently be disputed. a**1688** CUDWORTH *Immut. Mor.* (1731) 230 This Aristotle hath observed very pertinently to our Purpose. **1738** NEAL *Hist. Purit.* IV. 4 [They] expounded some parts of the Scripture..pertinently to the occasion. **1885** *Spectator* 8 Aug. 1048/1 There is nothing new in this article, but the points are pertinently put.

So **ˈpertinentness**, pertinence. *rare*$^{-0}$.

1727 in BAILEY vol. II. Hence in JOHNSON and later Dicts.

pertiner, obs. form of PARTNER.

†**perˈtingency.** *Obs.* [f. as PERTINGENT: see -ENCY.] The fact or condition of reaching to so as to touch.

1656 H. MORE *Enthus. Tri.* (1712) 3 The Outward Senses, which upon the pertingency of the Object to the Sensitive Organ cannot fail to act. **1706** PHILLIPS, *Pertingency*, (in Philos.) a reaching to.

†**perˈtingent,** *a.* *Obs.* [ad. L. *pertingent-em*, pr. pple. of *pertingĕre* to stretch out, reach, extend, f. *per* through (see PER- 1) + *tangĕre* to touch; see -ENT.] Touching; in contact; reaching to.

1656 BLOUNT *Glossogr.*, *Pertingent*, extending, reaching or joyning near unto. **1658** PHILLIPS, *Pertingent* lines in Heraldry, vide *Entire*. *Ibid.*, *Entire pertingents*, are lines that run the longest way of the sheilds position, without touching the Center.

pertisan, -ant, -en, -on, obs. ff. PARTISAN.

pertish (ˈpɜːtɪʃ), *a.* [f. PERT *a.* + -ISH¹ 3.] Somewhat pert, inclined to be pert; in quot. c1825, rather brisk or sharp to the taste.

c**1825** *Houlston Tracts* II. xlviii 12 A sup of pertish beer. **1836** T. HOOK *G. Gurney* II. 287 A rather pertish, forward-looking young man.

pertition, obs. form of PARTITION *sb.*

pertlike (ˈpɜːtlaɪk), *a.* and *adv.* [f. PERT *a.* + -LIKE 2 a and b.] †**a.** *adj.* Pert-looking, pert. *Obs.* **b.** *adv.* Pertly, briskly, cheerfully. *dial.*

1582 STANYHURST *Æneis* II. (Arb.) 54 The pertlyke Greeks thee flamd citty with ruthlesse victorye ransack. **1756** in *Daily Chron.* (1905) 7 Jan. 3/2, I saw the Countess of Coventry at Ranelagh. I think she is a pert-like husy going about with her face up to the sky.

U.S. *dial.* **1879** TOURGEE *Fool's Err.* vii. 29 I've managed to pull through thus far tollable peart-like.

†**ˈpertling.** *Obs. rare.* [f. PERT *a.* + -LING¹ 2.] A pert or sharp child.

1581 MULCASTER *Positions* xlii. (1887) 257 What a pleasure would the maister take in such a perfit perteling?

pertly (ˈpɜːtlɪ), *adv.* Forms: see PERT *a.*; also 5 partly. [f. PERT *a.* + -LY².] In a pert manner.

†**1.** Openly, without concealment; plainly; evidently, manifestly. (Opposed to *privily*.) *Obs.*

13.. *E.E. Allit. P.* B. 244 A payne þer-on put & pertly halden. c**1350** *Will. Palerne* 97 þere pried he in priuely and pertiliche biholdes. **1468** *Maldon Essex Liber B.* lf. 13 b (MS.), Noo ducheman ner other alion shall bere no manere wepyn of werre, priuily ner pertly. **1533** in *10th Rep. Hist. MSS. Comm.* App. v. 406 He..shuld buy or bargayne for the same hides pertly or oppenlye. a**1670** SPALDING *Troub. Chas. I* (1829) 21 He began to kyth in Strathaven, and pertly and avowedly travelled through the country.

†**2.** Expertly, skilfully; cleverly, adroitly. *Obs.*

a**1400** *Pistill of Susan* 355 þis prophete so pertly proues his entent. a**1440** *Sir Eglam.* 753 The worme ys slayne, That hathe a knyȝt done hym selfe allone, Pertly be my fay. **1640** R. BAILLIE *Canterb. Self-convict.* ii. 11 In Edinburgh Master Sydserfe did peartly play his part.

3. Smartly, sharply; briskly; promptly; readily; quickly. Now *dial.* and *U.S.* (chiefly in form *peartly*).

1377 LANGL. *P. Pl.* B. v. 23 How pertly afore þe poeple resoun gan to preche. c**1400** *Destr. Troy* 1033 To Pelleus pertly þen past he agayne. c**1450** *Cast. Persev.* 1598 þerfor, spede now þy pace pertly to ȝone precyouse place. **1610** SHAKS. *Temp.* IV. i. 58 Now come my Ariell, bring a Corolary,..appear, and pertly.

β. **1515** *Scot. Field* 109 The King was glade of that golde, ..And promised him full peertly, his part for to take. **1596** DALRYMPLE tr. *Leslie's Hist. Scot.* II. 163 The Romanis persues peirtlie the flieris. **1856** G. D. BREWERTON *War in Kansas* 383 To 'get along' in a happy-go-lucky sort of way, which he calls 'a-doin'-right-peartly'. **1857** T. H. GLADSTONE *Englishman in Kansas* 46 I'll teach these..Free-soilers a lesson right peartly.

4. In a forward saucy manner; boldly, audaciously; over-confidently.

c**1400** *Laud Troy Bk.* 11215 He sat pertly bolde vp-right As man that hadde ben In his myght. **1523** COVERDALE *Old God & New* (1534) H, To se how pertely he percheth forth of his neste. **1540** HYRDE tr. *Vives' Instr. Chr. Wom.* II. xi. §21 Any worde or dede of yᵉ childe, dooen lewdely,.. naughtily, wantonly or piertlye. **1606** SHAKS. *Tr. & Cr.* IV. v. 219 Yonder wals that pertly front your Towne,..Must kisse their owne feet. **1699** BENTLEY *Phal.* Pref. 31 To my surprize he answer'd me very pertly. a**1748** WATTS *Educ. Children* ix, The children of our age will pertly reply,..must we turn Puritans again? **1852** THACKERAY *Esmond* I. xiii, The words were said lightly and pertly by the girl. **1874** C. GEIKIE *Life in Woods* iv. 68 They carry their heads so pertly.

†**ˈpertly,** *a.* *Obs.* [f. PERT *a.* + -LY¹.] ?Experienced, skilled, expert.

1465 in Tytler *Hist. Scot.* (1864) II. 388 Lord fleming sal adwis the kyng at al his pertly power wytht his gud cunsail. **1589** NASHE *Anat. Absurd.* Wks. (Grosart) I. 51 Translated by his toyle from the Parrish good man Webbe,..to a pertly Gentleman in the Court. **1596** DALRYMPLE tr. *Leslie's Hist. Scot.* VI. 319 Duncan, King Malcolme his bastard sone, a man..stout, bauld and pertlie.

pertness (ˈpɜːtnɪs). [f. PERT *a.* + -NESS.] The quality of being pert.

†**1.** Smartness or elegance of person; beauty.

c**1400** *Destr. Troy* 9205 On what wise in this world wilne shuld I hir..Of Rent, & of Riches, rankir þan I, And passes of pertnes pure wemen all?

2. Briskness, liveliness, sprightliness, confidence.

1560 ROLLAND *Crt. Venus* II. 30 Ane spark of peirtnes in his breist than grew. **1616** *Rollock's Lect. Passion* Ep. Ded., He was dumb before the earthly judge that thou might have boldness and peartnesse in thy prayers. **1741** WATTS *Improv. Mind* I. v, There is indeed amongst them a lively pertness, a parade of literature.

U.S. *dial.* **1885** C. F. HOLDER *Marvels Anim. Life* 224 'That kinder tuck the peartness aout of us, so to speak'.

3. Forward boldness in behaviour or speech; sauciness; smartness bordering upon impudence: esp. in inferiors or young people.

1573 TWYNE *Æneid* XII. Mmj, This peartnes Phegeus might not bide, nor pride of stomack bold. a**1658** J. DURHAM *Exp. Rev.* II. iii. (1680) 67 A symptom of that peartnesse and impudencie. **1741** RICHARDSON *Pamela* xxiv, Provided she humble herself,..and is sorry for her pertness. **1773** MRS. CHAPONE *Improv. Mind* (1774) II. viii. 103 Nothing is so disgusting in youth as pertness and self-conceit. **1881** RUSKIN *Love's Meinie* I. iii. §82. 86 [The parrot] is mostly gay in plumage, often to vulgarity, and always to pertness.

†**4.** Pungency of taste. *Obs.*

1756 *Gentl. Mag.* 572 The Holy Well [at Malvern] drank on the spot leaves a pertness in the throat approaching the taste of brass or allum. **1777** SHERIDAN *Sch. Scand.* III. iii, Spa-water..has all the pertness and flatulency of champagne, without its spirit.

†**per'tolerate**, *v.* *Obs. rare*$^{-0}$. [f. ppl. stem of L. *pertolerāre* to bear out: see PER- 2.]

1623 COCKERAM, *Pertolerate*, to endure to the end.

†**per'tract**, *v.*[1] *Obs. rare.* [ad. L. *pertract-āre* to feel over, handle, f. PER- 1, 2 + *tractāre* to handle, treat.] To treat *of* (in narration).

1542 BOORDE *Dyetary* xiii. (1870) 264, I wyl fyrst wryte & pertract of hen-egges. **1547** *Ibid.* Pref., The which doth pertract howe a man shuld order him selfe.

†**per'tract**, *v.*[2] *Obs. rare.* [f. L. *pertract-*, ppl. stem of *pertrahĕre* to draw out or on, f. PER- 2 + *trahĕre* to draw, drag.] *trans.* To protract, prolong (time).

a **1548** HALL *Chron., Edw. IV* 237 b, He..kepte with theim a long communicacion to pertracte the tyme.

†**pertrac'tation.** *Obs. rare*$^{-1}$. [ad. L. *pertractātiōn-em*, n. of action from *pertractāre*: see PERTRACT *v.*[1]] Handling, manipulation.

1597 A. M. tr. *Guillemeau's Fr. Chirurg.* 46 b/1 The sharpe ossicles or bones..in the pertractatione of the same [limb] might pricke the Fleshe.

†**per'transible,** *a. Obs. rare*$^{-1}$. [f. L. *pertransī-re* to pass through, cross (f. PER- 1 + *transīre* to go across) + -BLE.] Capable of being traversed or passed through; traversable.

1656 STANLEY *Hist. Philos.* VI. (1701) 249/1 Infinite is that which is pertransible without end.

†**per'transient,** *a. Obs. rare*$^{-0}$. [ad. L. *pertransient-em*, pr. pple. of *pertransīre*: see prec.] Passing quite through, crossing from side to side.

1658 PHILLIPS, *Entire pertransient*, is in Heraldry a line which crosseth the middle of a shield, and runs diametrically the longest way of her position. *Ibid., Intersecants*, in Heraldry, are pertransient lines which crosse one another. **1706** *Ibid., Pertransient*, passing or striking through as a Colour does in a precious Stone. Hence **1721** in BAILEY; **1755** in JOHNSON; and in mod. Dicts.

So †**pertran'sition**, a passing through, traversing. *Obs. rare*$^{-1}$.

1653 R. G. tr. *Bacon's Hist. Winds* 359 Let the fifteenth Motion be the Motion of Pertransition, or the Motion according to the issues or holes by which the vertues of bodies are more or lesse hindred or forwarded.

pertre, obs. f. PEARTREE.

pertrek, -trich(e, -trick, -trige, -trik, etc., obs. ff. PARTRIDGE.

†**per'trouble**, *v. Obs.* Chiefly *Sc.* In 5-6 perturble, 6 -trubil, -troubil. [a. OF. *per-, partroubler*, f. PER- 2 + *troubler* to TROUBLE. For the *-turble* form (L. type **perturbulāre*), cf. DISTURBLE.] *trans.* To perturb, trouble greatly.

c **1470** HARDING *Chron.* LXXXV. iv. (MS. Ashm. 34), Fortune..whare men wolde ay leven in charyte Thou doste perturble [*v.r.* perturbe] wiþ mutabilyte. **1485** CAXTON *Chas. Gt.* 17 For this thyng I am noo thyng perturbled in my courage. **1513** DOUGLAS *Æneis* VII. vii. 16 That..scho suld perturble [*ed.* **1553** pertroubil] all the toun. **1819** W. TENNANT *Papistry Storm'd* (1827) 38 But mair pertrubill'd was his case, Whan..They cam a' round him in a fluther.

So †**pertroublance**, mental disturbance, perturbation. *Obs. rare*$^{-1}$.

1513 DOUGLAS *Æneis* XII. xi. 119 As first the schaddois of pertrublans [*ed.* **1553** pertroublance] Was dryve away, and hys remembrans The lycht of ressoun has recouerit agane.

pertryche, -trycke, -tryk(e, obs. ff. PARTRIDGE.

pertuisan, -zan, obs. ff. PARTISAN[2].

†**pertund**, *v. Obs. rare*$^{-1}$. [ad. L. *pertund-ĕre*, f. PER- 2 + *tundĕre* to beat, hammer.] *trans.* To break through, perforate.

1657 TOMLINSON *Renou's Disp.* 206 A Pyrotick..breaks the impostume and pertunds the swellings.

perturb (pəˈtɜːb), *v.* [a. OF. *per-, partourber, -turber* (14th c. in Godef.), ad. L. *perturbare*, f. PER- 2 + *turbāre* to disturb, confuse.]

1. a. *trans.* To disturb greatly (physically or externally); to cause disorder or irregularity in; to unsettle, confuse, derange, throw into confusion.

c **1386** CHAUCER *Knt.'s T.* 48 What folk been ye that at myn hom comynge Perturben [*v. rr.* perturbe, -tourbe(n; *Camb. MS.* disturblen] so my feste with criynge. **1490** CAXTON *Eneydos* i. 13 The force and strengthe of the troyians was thenne so perturbed by the pryckynge of fortune. **1568** GRAFTON *Chron.* II. 69 Notyng in him arrogancy and wilfulnesse, in perturbyng and refusyng such an honest order of agreement. **1599** JAS. I *Βασιλ. Δωρον* To Rdr., Rash-headed Preachers, that thinke it their honour to contend with kinges and perturbe whole kingdomes. **1646** SIR T. BROWNE *Pseud. Ep.* VI. vi. 295 Perturbing the Chaldean and Ægyptian Records with fabulous additions. **1874** MORLEY *Compromise* iii. 96 To perturb the pacific order of society either by active agitation or speculative restlessness.

b. *Astron.* (Cf. PERTURBATION 2 b.)

1879 PROCTOR *Pleas. Ways Sc.* iii. 68 The members of the sun's family perturb each other's motions in a degree corresponding with their relative mass. *Ibid.* 69 The earth plays..but a small part in perturbing the planetary system.

2. To disturb greatly (mentally), to trouble; to disquiet, agitate, discompose.

c **1374** CHAUCER *Troylus* IV. 533 (561) ȝit drede I moste hire herte to perturbe With vyolence ȝif I do swych a game. *c* **1430** LYDG. *Min. Poems* (Percy Soc.) 16 No child be falce iniquité Purturbed never his felicité. **1552** LYNDESAY *Monarche* 5094 Gretlye it doith perturbe my mynde. **1632** B. JONSON *Magn. Lady* I. i, I do neuer feel myself perturb'd With any general words 'gainst my profession. **1826** SCOTT *Woodst.* v, His childish imagination was perturbed at a phenomenon for which he could not account.

absol. *c* **1470** [see PERTROUBLE]. **1558** PHAER *Æneid* VI. R iij b, Thy greuous ghost, Perturbing in my dremes hath me compeld to see this coast. **1902** *Daily Chron.* 23 Apr. 3/3 It is the unexpected that perturbs.

3. *Physics* and *Math.* To subject (a physical system, or a set of equations, or its solution) to a perturbation (sense 4).

1901, etc. [implied in PERTURBED *ppl. a.* 2]. **1931** *Physical Rev.* XXXVIII. 875 The $^3P_2{}^0$ sequence is perturbed by $X^3P_2{}^0$. **1973** *Nature* 17 Aug. 416/1 If the initial potential is that of a hard sphere, this can be 'perturbed' into a realistic form by adding an attractive term and softening the repulsion.

Hence **per'turbing** *vbl. sb.* and *ppl. a.*

c **1386** CHAUCER *Sompn. T.* 546 Whan þat þe weder is fair With-outen wynd, or perturbynge of Air. **1647** WARD *Simp. Cobler* 46 Distracted Nature calls for distracting Remedies; perturbing policies for disturbing cures. **1796** W. TAYLOR in *Monthly Mag.* II. 464 A mean to conjure away this perturbing spirit. **1862** H. SPENCER *First Princ.* II. v. §56 (1875) 182 The maintenance of a circular orbit by any celestial body, implies..that there are no perturbing bodies.

per'turbable, *a.* [f. PERTURB *v.* + -ABLE: cf. OF. *perturbable* (14-15th c. in Godef.).] Liable to be perturbed. Hence **per,turba'bility**.

1800 W. TAYLOR in *Monthly Mag.* VIII. 599 The characteristic feature of the Russian constitution is the substitution of military rank, perturbable at the will of the prince, to hereditary or professional distinction. **1882** OGILVIE, *Perturbable, Perturbability.*

†**per'turbance.** *Obs.* [a. OF. **perturbance*, f. *perturber* to PERTURB: see -ANCE.] The action of perturbing; the fact of being perturbed; great disturbance; molestation; perturbation.

c **1407** LYDG. *Reson & Sens.* 5326 And somme gaf perseueraunce Ageyn al maner perturbaunce. **1426** —— *De Guil. Pilgr.* 21474 And whyl I lay thus in A trance, In gret Anoy and perturbaunce. **1575** R. B. *Appius & Virginia* in Hazl. *Dodsley* IV. 133 No let, no stay, nor ought [of] perturbance. **1610** HEALEY *St. Aug. Citie of God* XIX. xvii. (*title*), Peace which no perturbances can seclude from the law of nature. *a* **1714** ABP. SHARP *Serm.* Wks. (1754) III. ix. 158 Some sudden passion and perturbance of mind.

per'turbancy. *rare.* [f. as prec.: see -ANCY.]

a. Perturbed or unsettled condition, disturbance. **b.** The action or quality of perturbing.

1654 EARL MONM. tr. *Bentivoglio's Warrs Flanders* 216 By reason of the great perturbancie of the Confederate Provinces. **1880** W. ORD in *Brit. Med. Jrnl.* 31 Jan. 156/1 Structures of equal—here, perhaps, of greater—power of perturbancy.

per'turbant, *a.* and *sb. rare.* [ad. L. *perturbānt-em*, pr. pple. of *perturbāre* to PERTURB.]

a. *adj.* Disturbing. **b.** *sb.* A disturbing agent.

1875 NEWTON *Dict. Birds* (1893) 548 Open to the influence of many perturbants.

perturbate (see next), *a.* [ad. L. *perturbāt-us*, pa. pple. of *perturbāre*: see PERTURB.]

1. Disturbed, put out of order; in *Math.* = INORDINATE 4 a.

1570 BILLINGSLEY *Euclid* v. def. xix. 136 This kinde of proportionalitie is called inordinate or perturbate. **1773** HORSLEY in *Phil. Trans.* LXIV. 232 By equi-distance perturbate, CB : Cb = Cꞓ.βꞓ. **1788** T. TAYLOR *Proclus Comm.* I. 106 The doctrine of perturbate proportions, which Apollonius has copiously handled. **1823** BENTHAM *Not Paul* 190 The perturbate mode of his operation in this field [chronology]. **1862** TODHUNTER *Euclid* 280 In 19 he defines ordinate proportion, and in 20..perturbate proportion.

2. Perturbed.

1860 RUSSELL *Diary in India* I. 294 How dreary is a siege unless when the enemy are active and strong, and make one uneasily perturbate.

perturbate, *v. rare.* (For pronunciation, see CONFISCATE, COMPENSATE.) [f. ppl. stem of L. *perturbāre* to PERTURB.] *trans.* = PERTURB. Hence **perturbated, perturbating** *ppl. adjs.*

1547 BOORDE *Brev. Health* cxix. 45 The humour discendynge, doth perturbate the hert. **1631** J. DONE *Polydoron* 5 Happy is hee whose Mind is not perturbated beyond his Reason. **1771** MRS. GRIFFITH *Hist. Lady Barton* I. 84 The distresses of my perturbated mind. **1790** WILDBORE in *Phil. Trans.* LXXX. 528 This last-mentioned perturbating force vanishes. **1891** SIR R. BALL *Ice Age* 78 Unaltered in so far..as the more important class of perturbating effects are concerned.

perturbation (pɜːtɜːˈbeɪʃən). [a. OF. *perturbacion* (14th c. in Littré), ad. L. *perturbātiōn-em*, n. of action f. *perturbāre* to PERTURB.]

1. The action of perturbing; the fact or condition of being perturbed; disturbance, disorder, commotion; mental agitation or disquietude; trouble.

c **1374** CHAUCER *Boeth.* I. pr. v. 16 (Camb. MS.), Thilke passyuns þat ben woxen hard in swellynge by perturbasyouns fflowyng in to thi thowht. *c* **1380** WYCLIF *Sel. Wks.* III. 401 Freris ben cause..of perturbacioun in Cristendom. **1460** *Rolls of Parlt.* V. 382/2 Outrageous and ymmesurable perturbation and violence of the peas. **1555** *Sc. Acts Mary* (1814) II. 500/1 Gif ony wemen or vthers.. singand makis perturbatioun to the Quenis liegis in the passage throw Burrowis and vthers landwart townis. **1594** SHAKS. *Rich. III*, v. iii. 161 Richard, thy Wife,..Now filles thy sleepe with perturbations. **1667** MILTON *P.L.* x. 113 Love was not in thir looks,..but apparent guilt, And shame, and perturbation, and despaire. **1719** DE FOE *Crusoe* I. xiii, The Perturbation of my Mind was very great. **1870** J. H. NEWMAN *Gram. Assent* I. v. 105 These various perturbations of mind, which are characteristic of a bad conscience.

2. a. Disturbance of the regular order or course; irregular variation, disorder.

1567 MAPLET *Gr. Forest* 10 Auaylable against diseases and consumption of the Splene, and other perturbations Melancholike. **1621** BURTON *Anat. Mel.* To Rdr. (1624) 11, I require a fauourable censure of all faults omitted.. Perturbations of Tenses, numbers [etc.]. **1722** WOLLASTON *Relig. Nat.* v. 85 The magnificence of the world admits of some perturbations; not to say, requires some variety. **1848** MILL *Pol. Econ.* III. iii. §2 Perturbations of value during a period which cannot exceed the..time necessary for altering the supply. **1881** HUXLEY in *Nature* 11 Aug. 344/1 Disease ..is a perturbation of the normal activities of a living body.

b. *Astron.* The deviation of a heavenly body from its theoretically regular orbit, caused by the attraction of bodies other than its primary, or by the imperfectly spherical form of the latter.

1812 WOODHOUSE *Astron.* xix. 216 The perturbation of the Earth caused by the attracting force of the Moon and planets. **1834** MRS. SOMERVILLE *Connex. Phys. Sc.* iii. (1849) 25 Neptune produces a periodical perturbation in the motion of Uranus. **1853** HERSCHEL *Pop. Lect. Sc.* iii. §25 (1873) 114 The calculation of the planetary perturbations.. had then been brought to great perfection. **1946** H. & B. S. JEFFREYS *Methods Math. Physics* xvi. 464 Without the disturbance due to other planets, the motion of any planet would be an ellipse, specified by six constants... To allow for perturbations these constants are taken as variables.

3. A cause or factor of disturbance or agitation.

1597 SHAKS *2 Hen. IV*, IV. v. 23 Why doth the Crowne lye there, vpon his Pillow, Being so troublesome a Bed-fellow? O pollish'd Perturbation! Golden Care! **1614** R. TAILOR *Hogge hath lost Pearle* v. G ij, Cressus royall selfe..is not tortured there as Poets feine With molton Gold and sulphrie flames of fire Or any such molesting perturbation.

4. *Physics* and *Math.* A slight alteration of a physical system, esp. of the conditions which a solution of Schrödinger's equation must satisfy, or of a set of equations, from a relatively simple form to one which is to be studied by comparison with the simpler form. Freq. *attrib.*, as ***perturbation calculation, expansion, method, series***; **perturbation theory**, the method of investigating solutions of equations of state by relating them to solutions of similar but simpler equations which can be solved directly.

[**1868** *Phil. Mag.* XXXVI. 135 The motions [of molecules] are, however, not altogether free from perturbation.] **1899** *Q. Jrnl. Math.* XXX. 47 In this paper it is proposed to follow the theory of perturbations in the problems of mechanics in the order of its historical development from Lagrange to Lie. **1926** *Proc. R. Soc.* A. CXI. 301 If the [magnetic] field is weak we may use perturbation theory, according to which the change of energy of the stationary states is given, to the first order, by the constant term in the Fourier expansion of the energy of the perturbation in terms of the uniformising variables for the undisturbed system. **1937** E. C. KEMBLE *Fund. Princ. Quantum Mech.* xi. 380 In quantum mechanics, as in the Bohr theory, perturbation methods are of fundamental importance due to the fact that so few problems can be rigorously solved by direct methods. *Ibid.* xiv. 526 The usual method of approach to the problem of the many-electron atom is through a perturbation calculation in which the unperturbed problem..is of the central-field type. **1956** R. H. ATKIN *Math. & Wave Mech.* xi. 241 The method of perturbations is a practical technique for approximating to such solution. **1957** *Technology* Apr. 73/2 Perturbation theory and electron spin are studied, and used to explain the periodic table of elements and chemical bonds. **1961** POWELL & CRASEMANN *Quantum Mech.* xi. 381 We shall begin by deriving..the result of Section 5-8, giving the effect of a small perturbation on the energy levels of a system with discrete stationary states. *Ibid.* 403 A system subject to a weak time-dependent perturbation can be described approximately by a Hamiltonian of the form $H = H^0 + V(t)$. *Ibid.*, Since the perturbation is time-dependent, the system does not, in general, have stationary states. **1968** FOX & MAYERS *Computing Methods for Scientists & Engineers* ii. 17 We accept the 'solution'..and try to find a 'neighbouring' problem, a 'perturbation' of the given problem. **1972** G. E. BROWN *Many-Body Probl.* ii. 25 The two types of perturbation theory most commonly used are the Brillouin-Wigner perturbation expansion and the Rayleigh-Schrödinger one. **1973** ALONSO & VALK *Quantum Mech.* v. 202 Expressions (5.8-19) through (5.8-23) constitute the Rayleigh-Schroedinger perturbation series.

Hence **perturbation-theoretic, -theoretical** *adjs.*, of, pertaining to, or involving perturbation theory.

1964 *Physical Rev.* CXXXIII. A1070 (*heading*) Perturbation theoretic calculation of polaron mobility. **1968** C. G. KUPER *Introd. Theory Superconductivity* i. 2 Early attempts to construct a perturbation-theoretical model based on Fröhlich's interaction encountered severe mathematical difficulties.

pertur'bational, *a.* [f. prec. + -AL[1].] Of, pertaining to, or of the nature of perturbation.
1849 HERSCHEL *Astron.* Pref. 5 That very delicate and obscure part of the perturbational theory. **1881** *Athenæum* No. 2811. 343/1 A perturbational inequality of two hundred and forty years period in the motions of the earth and Venus.

†**pertur'batious**, *a.* *Obs.* *rare*$^{-1}$. [f. PERTURBATION: see -IOUS.] Causing perturbation; characterized by disturbing.
1630 TAYLOR (Water P.) *Heauens Bless. & Earths Ioy* Wks. III. 116/1 And for the auoyding of the troublesomenesse of Boats and Wherries, and other perturbatious multitudes there was a lists or bounds, made with Lighters, Hoyes, and other great Boates, to the number of 250 or thereabouts.

perturbative (pəˈtɜːbətɪv, ˈpɜːtɜːbeɪtɪv), *a.* [ad. late L. *perturbātīv-us*, f. ppl. stem. of *perturbāre* to PERTURB: see -IVE.] Causing or apt to cause perturbation or disturbance. ***perturbative function*** (*Astron.*), a function expressing the potential of the attractions which cause perturbation in the motion of a planet: see PERTURBATION 2 b.
1638 *Gen. Demands conc. Covenant* 7 All such bands are declared to be seditious, and perturbative of the publick peace. **1823** *Ann. Reg.* 176 Journals edited in a manner not less dangerous and perturbative. **1833** HERSCHEL *Astron.* xi. 321 The perturbative effect in this case..is equal to the whole attraction of the moon on the earth. **1881** *Nature* XXV. 72 Development of the principal part of the perturbative function. **1971** *Ann. Physics* LXIV. 383 The change in the initial set of site amplitudes is sufficiently small so that a perturbative solution of the set of equation[s] remains valid. **1973** *Physics Bull.* Dec. 734 A perturbative approach to the valence charge density in tetrahedrally bonded semiconductors.
Hence **'perturbatively** (or *pertur'batively*) *adv.*
1977 *Nature* 21 July 205/2 Since α is about 1/127, things may be calculated perturbatively.

perturbator (ˈpɜːtɜːbeɪtə(r)). Now *rare*. [a. late L. *perturbātor* (Ambrose, Sulpicius Severus), agent-n. f. *perturbāre* to PERTURB: perh. through OF. *perturbateur* (1418 in Godef. *Compl.*)] A disturber, troubler; = PERTURBER.
1539 CROMWELL in Merriman *Life & Lett.* (1902) II. 169 To be bruted suspected or noted as a perturbatour of peax. **1657–83** EVELYN *Hist. Relig.* (1850) II. 259 The no less perturbators of the quiet and beauty of that Christian charity. **1753** *Scots Mag.* XV. 60/2 Perturbators of the public repose. **1848** *Fraser's Mag.* XXXVII. 392 That perturbator of kingdoms..the terrible Palmerston.

perturbatory (pəˈtɜːbətərɪ), *a. rare.* [f. prec., or L. *perturbāt-*, ppl. stem of *perturbāre* to PERTURB: see -ORY[2].] **a.** *adj.* Having the quality of perturbing; perturbative. **b.** *sb.* A name given to the alleged power of certain persons to deflect a divining-rod, or the like, by magnetic or other influence residing in their fingers.
1866 A. FLINT *Princ. Med.* (1880) 139 Not to continue perturbatory measures with a view to promote absorption too long. **1885** *Jrnl. Franklin Instit.* Feb. 112 The passive perturbatory is a high degree of expansive, and the active perturbatory in like manner a powerful compressive.

perturbatress. *rare.* [See -ESS.] A female perturbator or disturber. So **pertur'batrix** [a. L. *perturbātrix*, fem. of *perturbātor*].
1623 WODROEPHE *Marrow Fr. Tongue* 325/2 Beautie is the Perturbatresse of publicke Peace. **1730–6** BAILEY (folio), *Perturbatrix*, [a disturber, a troublesome person] in the female sex. **1882** OGILVIE (Annandale), *Perturbatrix*.

perturbed (pəˈtɜːbd, *poet.* -bɪd), *ppl. a.* [f. PERTURB *v.* + -ED[1].] **1.** Disquieted, agitated, restless; confused, deranged.
1512 *Helyas* in Thoms *Prose Rom.* (1828) III. 45 Matabrune was ful sorye and perturbed of these tidings. **1602** SHAKS. *Ham.* I. v. 183 Rest, rest, perturbed Spirit. **1656** tr. *Hobbes' Elem. Philos.* (1839) 166 Whether the proportions in both orders be successively answerable to one another, which is called ordinate proportion, or not successively answerable, which is called perturbed proportion. **1799** KIRWAN *Geol. Ess.* 283 The perturbed state of the strata. **1871** MACDUFF *Mem Patmos* xii. 159 The perturbed spirit of the spectator is calmed.
2. *Physics* and *Math.* Subjected to a perturbation (sense 4).
1901 *Phil. Mag.* II. 268 By a kinematical analysis he (Stoney) shows that such perturbed elliptic motion may be regarded as resultant of two or more circular motions of different amplitudes and frequencies. **1927** *Proc. R. Soc.* A. CXIII. 639 The wave equation of the perturbed system. **1937** E. C. KEMBLE *Fund. Princ. Quantum Mech.* xi. 380 We designate the problems based on the two operators H_0 and H as the unperturbed and the perturbed problems, respectively. **1949** *Q. Jrnl. Math.* XX. 155 (*heading*) Perturbed functional equations. **1968** FOX & MAYERS *Computing Methods for Scientists & Engineers* ii. 17 We can often say that we have obtained an *exact* solution of the perturbed problem.
Hence **per'turbedly** (-ɪdlɪ) *adv.*, in a perturbed manner, confusedly, distractedly.
1842 LYTTON *Zanoni* I. i, Music..wanders perturbedly through the halls and galleries of the memory. **1860** W. COLLINS *Wom. White* I. iii, Perturbedly picking up the broken pieces of a teacup.

perturber (pəˈtɜːbə(r)). [f. PERTURB *v.* + -ER[1].]
1. A disturber, troubler.
1485 *Rolls of Parlt.* VI. 295/1 Many evill doers, and perturbers of the pees. *a* **1533** LD. BERNERS *Gold. Bk. M. Aurel.* (1546) Hh iij b, To put awaie the perturbers of peace. **1602** T. FITZHERBERT *Apol.* 18 Perturbers, and enemies of the common wealth. *a* **1700** in Grant *Burgh Sch. Scotl.* (1876) II. v. 195 [Forbidding them to be] perturbers, vaguers—[wandering from place to place].
2. *Physics.* A particle which interacts with a radiating atom or ion, affecting the wavelength of the emitted radiation.
1932 *Physical Rev.* XL. 401 R_1 means, crudely speaking, the distance of closest approach between the excited Hg-atom and its perturber. **1962** M. BARANGER in D. R. Bates *Atomic & Molecular Processes* xiii. 505 It often happens that the interaction of the perturbers with the atom in the lower state of a given line is much weaker than their interaction with the upper state. **1974** H. R. GRIEM *Spectral Line Broadening by Plasmas* ii. 72 The principal difference between the broadening of neutral-atom and positive-ion lines lies in the presence of the long range Coulomb interactions between radiators and charged perturbers.

perturble, variant of PERTROUBLE *Obs.*

per'turbment. *rare.* [f. PERTURB *v.* + -MENT. Cf. OF. *perturbement* (1300 in Godef.).] Perturbing, perturbation.
1901 H. S. MERRIMAN *Velvet Glove* v, He had travelled without perturbment.

per'tusate, *a. Bot. rare.* [f. as next + -ATE[2].] 'Pierced at the apex' (Webster 1879).

pertuse (pəˈtjuːs), *a. rare.* [ad. L. *pertūs-us*, pa. pple. of *pertundĕre* to punch or bore into a hole, f. PER- 1 + *tundĕre* to beat, hammer.]
1. (See quot.)
1721 BAILEY, *Pertuse*, beaten to Pieces, bored thro', having Holes.
2. *Bot.* Of a leaf: see quots.
1828–32 WEBSTER, *Pertuse*, *Pertused*..2. In botany, full of hollow dots on the surface, as a leaf. **1866** *Treas. Bot.*, *Pertuse*, having slits or holes. **1887** in *Nicholson's Dict. Gardening*.
So **per'tused** *a.* = prec.
1755 JOHNSON, *Pertused*, bored, punched, pierced with holes. *Dict.* [Cf. quot. 1721 in PERTUSE 1.] **1828–32** [see PERTUSE 2]. **1858** MAYNE *Expos. Lex.*, *Pertusus*,..*Bot.* applied to leaves that are pierced with large holes and distributed irregularly..: pertused.

†**per'tusion.** *Obs.* [ad. late L. *pertūsiōn-em*, n. of action from *pertundĕre*: see prec.]
1. The action of punching or boring.
a **1735** ARBUTHNOT (J.), The manner of opening a vein in Hippocrates's time was by stabbing or pertusion, as it is performed in horses.
2. A hole punched or bored.
1626 BACON *Sylva* §470 And the better, if some few Pertusions be made in the Pot. **1657** AUSTEN *Fruit Trees* III. 19 Not so much because of the pertusions or holes in the Pot.

pertussal (pəˈtʌsəl), *a.* [irreg. f. next + -AL[1].] Of or pertaining to pertussis or hooping-cough.
1890 in *Cent. Dict.* **1905** *Brit. Med. Jrnl.* 25 Feb. 452 His work on Pertussal Glycosuria.

‖**pertussis** (pəˈtʌsɪs). *Path.* [mod.L., f. PER- 4 + *tussis* cough.] = HOOPING-COUGH.
[**1772** T. KIRKLAND (*title*) Dissertatio Inaug. de Pertussi.] **1799** HOOPER *Med. Dict.*, *Pertussis*, the hooping cough. **1880** GARROD & BAXTER *Mat. Med.* 361 Spasmodic coughs, as pertussis and asthma.

perty, pertycion, pertyculer, pertyner, obs. ff. PARTY, PARTITION, PARTICULAR, PARTNER.

Perugian (pəˈruːdʒɪən), *sb.* and *a.* [f. *Perugia* the name of a city and province in central Italy + -AN.] **A.** *sb.* A native or inhabitant of Perugia. **B.** *adj.* Of or pertaining to Perugia; *spec.* of or relating to a division of the Umbrian school of painting having Perugia as its centre.
1759 A. BUTLER *Lives Saints* IV. 62 He with several others was carried away prisoner by the Perugians. *c* **1863** MRS. GASKELL *Lett.* (1966) 934 The first thing..[is] to tell you how capitally our Perugian journey answered. **1864** CROWE & CAVALCASELLE *New Hist. Painting Italy* II. vii. 187 The fragment of a recovered fresco..explains the rise and progress of the Perugian school out of that of Gubbio. **1885** *Encycl. Brit.* XVIII. 680/1 In the centre rises the great marble fountain constructed about 1277 by Bevignate, Frate Alberto (both Perugians), and Boninsegna (a Venetian). **1887** A. H. LAYARD *Kugler's Handbk. Painting: Italian Schools* (ed. 5) I. vii. 212 That branch of the Umbrian school which we may term the 'Perugian', was developed at a later period.. it culminated in *Raphael*. **1914** BROWN & RANKIN *Short Hist. Italian Painting* II. 155 Pleasing as is this early phase of Perugian painting, it is chiefly valuable as a factor in the education of less local men. **1934** E. BOWEN *Cat Jumps* 193 Over the bed hung a panel of leafy Perugian damask. **1936** G. F.-H. & J. BERKELEY *Italy in Making* II. vii. 108 Dr. Luigi Masi..was a young Perugian. **1970** A. P. OPPÉ *Raphael* ii. 29 The irregularity of Raphael's advance is shown in the two pictures of the Madonna which alone give certain evidence of the characteristics of his Perugian period.

Peruginesque (pəruːdʒɪˈnɛsk), *a.* [f. *Perugino* (see below) + -ESQUE.] Resembling the style of the Italian painter Pietro Vannucci (*c* 1450–1523), known as Pietro *Perugino* after the town Perugia.
1842 tr. *Kugler's Handbk. Hist. Painting* I. iv. iv. 172 The figures are beautiful and dignified, but without constraint or Peruginesque mannerism. **1863** G. M. HOPKINS *Let.* 10 July (1956) 202 There are the most deliciously graceful Giottesque ashes..here—I do not mean Giottesque though, Peruginesque, Fra-Angelical(!), in Raphael's earlier manner. **1874** E. EASTLAKE tr. *Kugler's Handbk. Painting: Italian Schools* (ed. 4) I. IV. ii. 297 Various pictures, more or less weak, of a Peruginesque class, bear his name. *Ibid.*, His [*sc.* Lo Spagna's] style is a mixture of the Peruginesque and Raphaelesque. **1936** *Burlington Mag.* Sept. 130/1 The two saints..have indeed something Umbrian, even late Peruginesque, in them. **1956** K. CLARK *Nude* vi. 232 Drawings in a Peruginesque style, which show the holy women weeping over the stretched-out body of the dead Christ.

peruke (pəˈruːk), *sb.* Forms: 6–7 **perruke**, 6–9 **perruque**, 7 **perruck, -ucke, perru'ke, perrucq**; 6 **perug**, 7 **perucke**, 6– **peruke, peruque.** See also other early forms under PERIWIG. [a. F. *perruque* (end of 15th c., in Diez and Littré), ad. It. *perruca* or *parrucca*, of obscure origin. Cf. Romanian *paróc̨e*, Sp. *peluca*, Pg. *peruca*, *-uqua*, in same sense; also Sardinian *pilucca*, Lomb. *peluch* shock, lock, or large tuft of hair, Piedm. *pluch*, Genoese *pellucco* hair, thread. Generally conjectured to be derived from L. *pilus*, It. *pelo*, OF. *pel* hair; but the phonetic difficulties are considerable: see Diez and Littré; Hatz.-Darm. say 'origin unknown'.
The earlier Eng. stress was '*perruke*, found in verse down to 1812; but Cotton has *pe'ruke* a 1659.]
†**1.** A natural head of hair. *Obs.* [So F. *perruque* in 16th c.]
1548 ELYOT *Dict.*, *Capillamentum*..the heare of a mannes head..a perruke. **1590** C'TESS PEMBROKE *Antonie* 1284 Who ..Is not amazed at Perruque gray Olde rustie Charon weareth.
2. (In early use, distinguished as a *false* or *artificial* peruke.) A skull-cap covered with hair so as to represent the natural hair of the head; a periwig or wig. (In quot. 1661–2 app. a 'heart-breaker'.)
(Fairholt makes the *peruke* 'a less cumbrous article' than the periwig, which 'came into fashion in the time of Charles II'; but the name is found 120 years earlier than that, and identical in sense with *periwig*.)
1565–73 COOPER *Thesaurus*, *Capillamentum*.., a false perruke. **1581** MULCASTER *Positions* xxxix. (1887) 211 She.. must neede haue an vnnaturall perug, to set forth her fauour, where her owne [hair] had been best. **1606** HOLLAND *Sueton.* 228 Wearing by reason of thin haire a perrucke [*margin*] Or counterfeit cap of false haire. **1613** HAYWARD *Norm. Kings* 281 When their owne hair failed, they set artificiall Peruques, with long locks upon their heades. **1645** G. DANIEL *Poems* Wks. (Grosart) II. 63 My Perru'ke is as neat An Equipage as might Become a wooer. *a* **1659** COTTON *Burlesque Gt. Frost* Poems (1689) 99 Perukes now stuck so firm and stedfast, They all were riveted to headfast. **1661–2** PEPYS *Diary* 24 Mar., By and by comes La Belle Pierce to see my wife, and to bring her a pair of peruques of hair. **1668** EVELYN *Corr.* 27 Aug., The use of their monstrous Perrucqs. **1757** WESLEY *Wks.* (1872) IX. 230 A fair peruke may adorn a weak head. **1812** COMBE *Picturesque* IV. (Chandos) 14 His chin well shaved, his peruke dressed. **1852** THACKERAY *Esmond* I. v, Perruques of different colours. *Ibid.* II. xv, The generals in their perukes made way for him. **1878** BROWNING *Poets Croisic* lxxx, If it be worthy praises or rebukes, My poem, from these Forty old perukes!
b. A (heraldic) representation of peruke.
1610 GUILLIM *Heraldry* III. xxv. (1611) 174 He beareth argent a cheueron gules between three peruques sable.
3. *attrib.* and *Comb.*, as ***peruke-block, -man***.
1654 GAYTON *Pleas. Notes* III. xiii. 159 Mr. Barber..was a Peruke-man by profession. **1713** SWIFT *Frenzy J. Dennis* Wks. 1755 III. I. 145 Mr. John Dennis..snatched up a peruke-block that stood by the bedside.
Hence **pe'rukeless** *a.*, without a peruke.
1875 DOWDEN *Shaks., His Mind & Art* vii. 346 That a most Christian king should each morning receive his peruke inserted upon a cane through an aperture of his bed-curtains is entirely correct; for the valet cannot retain faith in a perukeless grand monarch.

pe'ruke, *v. rare.* [f. prec. sb.] *trans.* To furnish with a peruke.
1669 *Address hopeful young Gentry Eng.* 32 Observe how fashion has prevail'd against nature to perruque all complexions with the fairest hair.

pe'ruked, *a.* [f. PERUKE *sb.* + -ED[2].] Wearing a peruke, having a peruke on.
1632 MASSINGER *Maid of Hon.* I. ii, He has been all this morning In practice with a peruked gentleman-usher. **1856** KAYE *Sir J. Malcolm* I. xiii. 343 Lord Lake in full uniform ..powderd and peruqued. **1858** CARLYLE *Fredk. Gt.* VI. vi. II. 97 The little peruked ribanded high gentleman.

pe'ruke-,maker. A wig-maker.
a **1697** AUBREY *Lives*, *Gregory* (1898) I. 274 Gregorie, famous peruq-maker, buryed at St. Clement Danes church. **1753** HOGARTH *Anal. Beauty* vi. 31 A Roman general, dress'd by a modern tailor and peruke-maker for tragedy is a comic figure. **1817** tr. *Bombet's Haydn & Mozart* 225 Chance threw in his way a peruke-maker. **1905** T. AUDEN *Shrewsbury* viii. 201 Brought up at Manchester as a barber and peruke-maker, he adopted the Jacobite principles. **1966** J. S. COX *Illustr. Dict. Hairdressing* 111/2 s.v. Peruke 'Riot', As the distressed peruke-makers marched through the streets it was seen that most of them were without wigs themselves.

perukier (pɛrəˈkɪə(r)). *rare.* [Anglicized form of PERRUQUIER.] A wig-maker. Hence **peru'kier-**

ship (*nonce-wd.*), the office or art of a wig-maker.

1822 PYNE *Wine & Walnuts* (1824) II. iv. 26 It certainly was a skilful piece of perukiership. **1892** W. B. SCOTT *Autobiog. Notes* I. 44 On one side was a perukier with an imposing assembly of law-wigs.

perule ('pɛr(j)ʊl). *Bot.* [a. F. *pérule*, ad. mod.L. *pērula*, dim. of *pēra*, a. Gr. πήρα purse, wallet.] †**a.** The covering of a seed. *Obs.* **b.** Applied, after Mirbel and Zuccharini, to the scaly covering of a leaf-bud. **c.** Applied, after L. C. Richard, to a kind of sac formed by the adherent bases of the two lateral sepals in certain Orchideæ.

1825 HAMILTON *Dict. Terms Art, Perule*, in *Botany*, the cover of a seed. **1856** HENSLOW *Bot. Dict.* 133 *Perula* (a little pouch), a sac formed in some Orchideæ by the prolonged and united bases of two of the segments of their perianth. The cap-like covering of buds, formed by the abortion of their outer leaves. **1866** *Treas. Bot., Perule*, the covering of a leaf-bud formed by scales; also a projection in the flower of the orchids formed by the enlargement of two lateral sepals.

Hence '**perulate** *a.*, having a perule.

1858 MAYNE *Expos. Lex.*

perusable (pə'ruːzəb(ə)l), *a.* [f. PERUSE *v.* + -ABLE.] Capable of being perused.

1829 BENTHAM *Justice & Cod. Petit.* Advt. 9 In this way it [printed matter] is perusable by any number of persons at the same time. **1845** *Blackw. Mag.* LVIII. 374 The Rosciad is.. not now perusable without an accompanying feeling akin to contempt.

perusal (pə'ruːzəl). [f. PERUSE *v.* + -AL[1].]

1. Survey, examination, scrutiny. *Obs.* or *arch.*

1602 SHAKS. *Ham.* II. i. 90 He fals to such perusall of my face, As he would draw it. **1653** H. MORE *Antid. Ath.* I. i. (1712) 9 Permitting a freer perusal of matters of Religion than in former Ages. **1710** ADDISON & STEELE *Tatler* No. 265 ⁋2 The Jury, after a short Perusal of the Staff, declared .. That the Substance was British Oak. **1845** JUDD *Margaret* II. vi, He.. gave her a close perusal with his eye.

2. A reading through or over.

c **1600** SHAKS. *Sonn.* xxxviii. If ought in me, Worthy perusal stand against thy sight. **1644** MILTON *Areop*, (Arb.) 73 The book.. being publisht to the world,.. by him who both for his life and for his death deserves, that what advice he left be not laid by without perusall. **1711** STEELE *Spect.* No. 27 ⁋5 What could be observed of them from a Perusal of their private Letters. **1867** SMILES *Huguenots Eng.* i. (1880) 12 To the thoughtful, the perusal of the Bible gave new views of life and death.

peruse (pə'ruːz), *v.* [Found first in 15th c. In sense 1, f. PER- 1 or 2 + USE *v.*; the connexion of the other senses with this is not very obvious, and there may have been two distinct formations; in the second, the sense of the *per-* element is prominent, the notion being generally that of 'go *through*' lit. or fig.; but the element *-use* is not so easy to account for.]

I. †**1.** *trans.* To use up; to wear out by use.

a **1483** *Liber Niger* in *Househ. Ord.* (1790) 18 Fees of bestes, and also fees of other stuffe perused, or otherwise occupied within the court, and towching it. **1485** *Naval Acc. Hen. VII* (1896) 57 Saile twyne.. Spent & perused in a voiage into Lumbardye. **1536** in Strype *Cranmer* (1694) II. App. 26 Six and thirty old chysybils.. some of them perused. **1570** LEVINS *Manip.* 195/6 To peruse, *peruti*.

II. To go through.

2. †**a.** *trans.* To go through (a series of things or persons) so as to deal with one after another; to handle, deal with, describe, or examine (a number of things) one by one. *Obs.*

1479 in *Eng. Gilds* (1870) 414 The Maire, first.. to name and gyve his voice.., and after hym the Shiref, and so all the house perusid in the same, euery man to gyve his voice as shall please him. **1523** FITZHERB. *Husb.* §40 Let the shepeherde.. take those [sheep] that nede any handling, and put them into the lyttell folde. And thus peruse them all tyll he haue doone. **1581** W. STAFFORD *Exam. Compl.* ii. (1876) 63, I pray you peruse these sortes.. one by one, and by course. **1669** RAY in *Philos. Lett.* (1718) 32, I have perused the dried Plants you sent me, and.. added names to such as wanted. *a* **1716** SOUTH *Serm.* (1744) VIII. iii. 76 Let us peruse the obligations that lay upon him [Adam] as a man.

†**b.** To go through by name; to name or recount in order. *Obs.*

1534 MORE *Comf. agst. Trib.* I. Wks. 1154/1 It were a long worke to peruse euery comforte that a man maye well take of tribulacion. *c* **1550** *Disc. Common Weal* (1893) 47, I praie youe pervse those sortes.. one by one and by cours.

c. To survey, inspect, examine, or consider in detail. *arch.* (now associated with 5).

1533 ELYOT *Cast. Helthe* Pref. (1539) 1 When I had eftsones perused that little fortresse. **1577** HARRISON *England* II. xxiv. (1877) I. 361 If you should happen to peruse the thickenesse and maner of building of those wals and borowes. **1592** SHAKS. *Rom. & Jul.* V. iii. 74 Let me peruse this face. **1667** MILTON *P.L.* VIII. 267 My self I then perus'd, and Limb by Limb Survey'd. **1726** POPE *Odyss.* XXI. 439 He.. disdain'd reply; The bow perusing with exactest eye. **1847** TENNYSON *Princ.* II. 54 At those high words, we, conscious of ourselves, Perused the matting. **1866** G. MACDONALD *Ann. Q. Neighb.* xiii. (1878) 252 By this time I had perused his person, his dress, and his countenance.

d. To travel or journey through observingly or scrutinizingly. *Obs.* exc. *dial.*

1523 *St. Papers Hen. VIII*, IV. 38, I have also well perused and vewed this towne and castell. **1549** PAGET in Froude *Hist. Eng.* (1860) V. 182 Make a progress this hot weather, till you have perused all those shires that have offended. **1600** J. PORY tr. *Leo's Africa* II. 67 This prouince I perused in the companie of my deere friend Sidi Iehie. **1887** *Hereford Gloss., Peruse*, to explore the fields or woods.

3. *intr.* †To go from one to another of a series, to proceed, continue (*obs.*); to travel (*humorous*).

1523 FITZHERB. *Husb.* §30 Let hym caste out the .x. shefe in the name of god, and so to pervse from lande to lande, tyll he haue trewely tythed all his corne. *Ibid.* §124. **1523** —— *Surv.* xix. (1539) 40 To peruse from house to house till he come to saint Magnus churche. **1895** KIPLING in *Windsor Mag.* 124 Unluckily, you cannot peruse about the Hugli without money.

†**4. a.** *trans.* To go over (a writing, etc.) again; to revise, reconsider. *Obs.*

a **1529** SKELTON *P. Sparowe* 813 Wherfore hold me excused If I haue not well perused Myne Englyssh halfe abused. **1560** DAUS tr. *Sleidane's Comm.* 42 The Printers shall Print nothinge but the same shall be fyrste perused. **1604** BACON *Apol.* Wks. 1879 I. 440 It was perused, weighed, censured, altered, and made almost a new writing. **1632** SHERWOOD, To peruse, *revoir, reveoir, revisiter*. Perused, *reveu, revisité*. A perusing, *reveuë*.

b. To go through (a book) critically; to review, criticize; also, to set forth or expound critically. *Obs.*

1533 MORE *Answ. Poysoned Bk.* I. i. Wks. 1039/2, I wyll good reader peruse the remanant of his booke after this first part answered. *Ibid.* II. i. 1078/1. **1551** GARDINER *Explic. Cath. Faith* 76 Thus hauinge perused the effecte of the thyrde booke, I will likewise peruse the fourth.

5. a. To read through or over; to read thoroughly or carefully; hence (loosely) to read. Also *absol.* or *intr.*

1532 ELYOT *Let.* in *Gov.* (1883) Pref. 79 Thei.. doo peruse every daye one chapitre of the New Testament. **1591** SHAKS. *1 Hen. VI*, V. i. 1 Haue you perus'd the Letters from the Pope, The Emperor, and the Earle of Arminack? **1647** CLARENDON *Hist. Reb.* I. §7 Having carefully perused the Journals of both Houses. **1709** STEELE *Tatler* No. 51 ⁋5, I will show what to turn over unread and what to peruse. **1802** MAR. EDGEWORTH *Moral T.* (1816) I. xii. 99 H. put the paper.. into his hands, and waited.. whilst he perused the case. **1886** HARDY *Mayor Casterbr.* II. xviii. 254, I have tried to peruse and learn all my life; but the more I try to know the more ignorant I seem. **1887** BOWEN *Virg. Eclogue* vi. 10 If any who love me there be This poor verse to peruse. **1909** H. G. WELLS *Ann Veronica* i. 25 Her father.. appeared not to observe her entry. 'Sit down,' he said, and perused.. for some moments.

†**b.** Const. *over.* (Cf. *read over.*) *Obs.*

1561 DAUS tr. *Bullinger on Apoc.* (1573) 85 Let vs peruse ouer stories, and see if there be not such warres to be founde. **1579** in W. Wilkinson *Confut. Familye of Loue* Pref. Note *j b, Perusing ouer this little treatise. **1595** SHAKS. *John* V. ii. 5 Perusing ore these notes.

Hence **pe'rused** *ppl. a.*, in quot. in sense 1, used up, worn out; **pe'rusing** *ppl. a.*

a **1483** *Liber Niger* in *Househ. Ord.* (1790) 83 If they be perused clothes, so that with honestye they will noe longer serve. **1887** T. HARDY *Woodlanders* iv. 26 Our new neighbour is a strange deep perusing gentleman.

pe'ruse, *sb.* [f. prec. vb.] †**a.** Perusal; study; examination. *Obs.*

1578 BANISTER *Hist. Man* I. 1 The diligent peruse of this History of Bones. **1594** SOUTHWELL *M. Magd. Fun. Teares* (1823) 120, I will pound these spices, and dwell a while in the peruse of thy resolute fervour. **1600** W. WATSON *Decacordon* (1602) 358 The onely peruse of his bookes.

b. *Sailors' colloq.* Exploration, a 'look round' ashore. 'Come for a bit of peruse, Jack.'

peruser (pə'ruːzə(r)). [f. PERUSE *v.* + -ER[1].] One who peruses (in various senses: see the verb).

1549 BALE *Leland's N. Years Gift* D v, No lesse profytable to vs.. than were Strabo, Pliny, Ptholome, and other Geographers to their perusers. **1622** R. PRESTON *Goodly Man's Inquis.* Ep. Ded. 3 Be no seuere examiner, but a mild pervser. **1704** SWIFT *T. Tub* Pref., It will be absolutely impossible for the candid peruser to go along with me in a great many bright passages. **1758** JOHNSON *Idler* No. 7 ⁋8 The most eager peruser of news is tired. **1824-9** LANDOR *Imag. Conv.* Wks. 1846 I. 199 Swift.. was a peruser of rare books.

pe'rusing, *vbl. sb.* [f. PERUSE *v.* + -ING[1].] The action of the verb PERUSE.

†**1.** A using up. *Obs.*

1488 *Naval Acc. Hen. VII* (1896) 6 Delivueree perusing & other wyse demeanyng of the said shipps. *Ibid.* 35 Deliuerances perusynges & other wise demeaninges of the said Shipps. **1495** *Ibid.* 159.

†**2.** Inspection in succession or detail; examination, scrutiny: = PERUSAL 1. *Obs.*

1587 R. HOVENDEN in *Collect* (O.H.S.) I. 220 Upon the perusing, it received.. good liking. **1648-60** HEXHAM *Dutch Dict., Een Overzieninge*, an Overseeing, a Per-using, or a Conferring.

3. Reading through: = PERUSAL 2.

1585 JAS. I *Ess. Poesie* (Arb.) 20, I was moued by the oft reading and perusing of them, with a restles and lofty desire. **1644** MILTON *Areop.* (Arb.) 47 Arminius was perverted meerly by the perusing of a namelesse discours writt'n at Delf. **1764** HARMER *Observ.* Pref. 14 The perusing of Travels is to most people a very delightful kind of reading. **1808** *Med. Jrnl.* XIX. 85 [It] is well worth perusing, though some of the instructions are not new to the English reader.

Peruvian (pə'ruːvɪən), *a.* (*sb.*) [f. mod.L. *Perūvia*, Latinized name of the country + -AN.]

A. *adj.* **a.** Of, pertaining to, or native to Peru, in South America; in the names of natural productions of that country, as ***Peruvian balsam*** (= BALSAM of Peru), ***bat, cinnamon, cotton, emerald, heliotrope, ipecacuanha, mastic tree, nutmegs, sheep***, etc.; ***Peruvian lily*** = ALSTRŒMERIA.

Peruvian province, a zoogeographical subregion or province consisting of the coast of Peru and Chile with the island of Juan Fernandez.

1747 tr. *Astruc's Fevers* 148 The Peruvian balsam is commonly used in fumigations only. **1748** *Anson's Voy.* I. vi. 68 Vicunnas or Peruvian sheep. **1781** PENNANT *Hist. Quad.* II. 554 Bat, Peruvian. **1796** H. HUNTER tr. *St.-Pierre's Stud. Nat.* (1799) II. 89 The French or Peruvian heliotrope. **1819** *Pantologia, Peruvian Mastic Tree.* **1842** BRANDE *Dict. Sci.*, etc., *Peruvian balsam*, the produce of the *Myroxylon Peruvianum*... It is obtained by boiling the twigs in water. **1847** CRAIG, *Peruvian mastic-tree*, or Mulli, the tree Schinus mulli, a native of Brazil and Peru. **1866** *Treas. Bot.*, Daffodil, Peruvian, *Ismene Amancaes*. **1866** *Ibid.* s.v. *Laurelia*, The aromatic seeds of the Chilian species, *L. sempervirens*, are used as a spice in Peru, and are often called Peruvian Nutmegs. **1883** W. ROBINSON *Eng. Flower Garden* 10/1 Alstrœmeria (Peruvian Lily)... One or two kinds.. are hardy and charming as any flowers on warm soil. **1890** *Cent Dict.* s.v. *Heliotrope, H. Peruvianum*, the Peruvian heliotrope, has long been a favorite garden-plant, on account of the fragrance of its flowers. **1931** M. E. STEBBING *Hardy Flower Gardening* v. 100 *Alstrœmerias*, called 'Peruvian Lilies', do curiously well in Scotland, considering they come from such a warm climate. **1970** *Sunday Tel.* 3 May 19/2 Among many plants which can be grown out of doors for cut flowers, excitement has been aroused by the new Peruvian lilies, or alstroemerias, bred in Holland.

b. Peruvian bark, the bark of the Cinchona tree: see BARK *sb.*[1] 7, CINCHONA.

1663 BOYLE *Usef. Exp. Nat. Philos.* II. iii. 67 That Peruvian Bark, that now begins to be somewhat taken notice of, under the name of The Jesuits Powder. **1870** YEATS *Nat. Hist. Comm.* 234 Peruvian bark is usually imported in packages, or serons, made of dried cow-hides.

c. Peruvian Jew = sense B. 2 below.

1899 in C. Pettman *Africanderisms* (1913) 370 Peddling Peruvian Jews were mulcted in sums from £10 downwards .. and compelled to contribute to the Pretorian war-chest.

B. *sb.* **1. a.** A native or inhabitant of Peru. **b.** *pl.* Peruvian stocks, bonds, etc.

1776 MICKLE tr. *Camoens' Lusiad* Introd. 30 *note*, He [Pizarro] massacred the Peruvians, he said, because they were barbarians. **1865** G. MEREDITH *Rhoda Fleming* iii. I. 47, I see bonds in all sorts of colours,.. Peruvians—orange, Mexicans—red as the British army.

2. [Prob. f. acronym *P.R.U.* Polish and Russian Union.] In South Africa, a contemptuous name for a Jew, esp. from Central or Eastern Europe.

1898 L. SEARELLE *Tales of Transvaal* 4 A 'Peruvian' standing by, whose name was Schadrach Levi. **1900** *Rand Daily Mail* (Pettman), Behold one of the most striking types of Johannesburg life—the Peruvian. **1936** 'IDLER' *Rolling Home* 385 He called me one day to a little Jew of the worst type which comes from Eastern Europe—the type of 'Peruvian' in South Africa. **1956** H. M. BATE *S. Afr. without Prejudice* iii. 59 Kruger and other equally stubborn of his advisers saw in this a deliberate move by Rhodes to dominate the polls with mine employees and, as they so ungallantly added, 'Peruvians' (a term of contempt which is applied to Jews of low class). **1972** E. ROSENTHAL *Let.* 23 May in *Voorloper* (1976) 638 According to Max Sonnenburg, the expression originated in the early days of Kimberley, where a body was set up, called 'The Polish and Russian Union', the initials of which 'P.R.U.', gave rise to the word 'Peruvian'.

peruvin ('pɛruvɪn). *Chem.* [f. PERUV-IAN + -IN[1].] An alcohol ($C_9H_{10}O$) distilled from the balsam of Peru: STYRYLIC alcohol, or STYRONE.

1847 CRAIG, *Peruvine.* **1857** MILLER *Elem. Chem.* III. 477 **1866-77** WATTS *Dict. Chem.* IV. 381 *Peruvin.* Syn. with *Styrone* or *Cinnylic Alcohol*.

perv (pɜːv), *v.* *Austral. slang.* Also **perve.** [f. PERVERT *sb.*] *intr.* To act as or like a sexual pervert; to indulge in eroticism. Phr. ***to perv at, on***: to look at with sexual or erotic interest. Hence '**perving** *vbl. sb.*

1941 BAKER *Dict. Austral. Slang* 53 *Perve, to*, to act as a sexual pervert. **1944** L. GLASSOP *We were Rats* xxxiii. 183 'Doing a bit of perving again?' I asked, looking at the gallery of nudes he had gathered from all sorts of magazines. **1959** BAKER *Drum* 134 *To perve at* (a girl), to extract pleasure from looking at her, esp. if she is scantily dressed as on a beach. **1964** B. HESLING *Dinkumization* vi. 116 What they get you for, perving? **1966** BAKER *Austral. Lang.* (ed. 2) vii. 154 *Perve on*, to contemplate with erotic interest. **1969** *Truth* (Melbourne) 18 Oct. 2/3 They caught me perving on the nurses at the Austin Hospital. **1972** I. HAMILTON *Thrill Machine* iii. 17 She's a cheap thrill machine for the boys to stare at and perve on. **1973** A. BROINOWSKI *Take One Ambassador* iii. 30 'Paper'd fold without me.' 'Yeah, I'll bet. Nothing for old Hastings to perve at.' **1974** K. COOK *Bloodhouse* 65 The little poofter perving on her hand ought to have his balls kicked in.

perv (pɜːv), *sb.* *Austral. slang.* Also **perve.** [Shortened from PERVERT *sb.*] A sexual pervert. Also *attrib.* or as *adj.*

1944 L. GLASSOP *We were Rats* xxxi. 177 Bluey brought a perv book back from Cairo with him. **1949** R. PARK *Poor Man's Orange* (1950) v. 51 That dirty old cow, always making up to kids... Merv, Merv, the rotten old perv. **1959** E. LAMBERT *Glory Thrown In* 18 He was a perv. Special attention given to small boys. **1964** B. HESLING *Dinkumization* vi. 116 Two cops, according to the inquiry, booked nearly two hundred 'pervs' a year. **1967** H. STOREY in *Coast to Coast 1965-66* 203 It's that bloody old perve from next door. **1968** D. IRELAND *Chantic Bird* x. 101 He might have been a perve or a copper's nark. **1973** A. BROINOWSKI *Take One Ambassador* x. 163 My god, the number of pervs there must be in this country.

2. Someone given to 'perving'; the act of 'perving'.

1963 J. CANTWELL *No Stranger to Flame* 15 'Never even saw him. Might have been a spook.' She did up the top button on the green blouse. 'Even spooks like a bit of a perv.' **1974** STACKPOLE & TRENGROVE *Not just for Openers* 38 After the next bowl had been bowled, the blokes' heads would turn around unobtrusively so they could have a 'perv' at a bird in a mini-skirt walking down the aisle.

pervade (pəˈveɪd), *v.* [ad. L. *pervādĕre* to go or come through, pass or spread through, f. PER- 1 + *vādĕre* to go, walk.]

1. *trans.* To pass through; to flow or extend through; to traverse. Now *rare.*

1656 BLOUNT *Glossogr.*, *Pervade*, to go and enter over all, thorow or into; to scape or pass through or by. **1725** POPE *Odyss.* XXIV. 18 So cowering fled the sable heaps of ghosts, ..And now pervade the dusky land of dreams. **1775** R. CHANDLER *Trav. Greece* (1825) II. 192 A cave in Paphlagonia... It was long and wide and pervaded by cold water, clear as crystal. **1858** HAWTHORNE *Fr. & It. Note-bks.* (1871) II. 122 Mr. Powers and I pervaded the whole universe. **1892** A. K. H. BOYD *25 Yrs. St. Andrews* II. xvii. 54, I pervaded Westminster Hall and looked into most of the Courts.

2. To extend or diffuse itself throughout; to spread through or into every part of; to permeate, saturate. (Of things material and immaterial.)

1659 H. MORE *Immort. Soul* II. xv. §5. 274 There is a vitall Aire that pervades all this lower world. **1704** NEWTON *Optics* II. III. iii. Substances soaked in such liquors as will intimately pervade their little pores, become by that means more transparent than otherwise. **1791** HAMILTON *Berthollet's Dyeing* I. Translator's Pref., An ardent spirit of enquiry pervaded..Europe. **1876** GLADSTONE *Homeric Synchr.* 102 That powerful sentiment of nationality, which pervades the Poems.

b. *intr.* To diffuse itself, permeate. Now *rare.*

1653 H. MORE *Antid. Ath.* (1662) 153 Here union pervades through all. **1796** MRS. E. PARSONS *Myst. Warning* IV. 186 A general air of concern pervaded through the whole party. **1809** PINKNEY *Trav. France* 105 In England, the manners, habits and dress of the capital, pervade to the remotest angle of the kingdom. **1889** GEIKIE in *Nature* 19 Sept. 492/1 We find certain well-defined principles, or one may term them natural laws, pervading everywhere.

Hence **per'vadence**, the action of pervading; **per'vader**, one who or that which pervades.

1838 G. S. FABER *Inquiry* 580 A pervadence of the world both universal and complete. **1883** MONIER-WILLIAMS *Relig. Th. Ind.* ii. 39 Fire [according to Indian laws of thought] is the pervader, smoke the pervaded. *Ibid.* 46 Vishnu..his function is that of a divine Pervader, infusing his Essence..into created things, animate and inanimate.

per'vading, *ppl. a.* [f. prec. + -ING².] That pervades, or runs through.

1732 POPE *Ess. Man* I. 31 Of this frame the bearings [etc.] has thy pervading soul Look'd thro'? **1841** MYERS *Cath. Th.* III. ix. 32 The preliminary and pervading assumption of these pages. **1871** SMILES *Charac.* ii. (1876) 40 A pervading atmosphere of cheerfulness, contentment, and peace.

Hence **per'vadingly** *adv.*, in a pervading manner; **per'vadingness.**

1851 KITTO *Bible Illustr.* (1858) III. 122 The Eastern mind is so pervadingly regal that to be without a sovereign is scarcely an intelligible state of things to an Oriental. **1872** LIDDON *Elem. Relig.* ii. 64 An inner self into which..evil penetrates so constantly and so pervadingly. **1862** F. HALL *Hindu Philos. Syst.* 64 In the matter of omnipresence,—or, rather, all-pervadingness,—he possesses it indeed.

pervagate (ˈpɜːvəgeɪt), *v.* [f. L. *pervagāt-*, ppl. stem of *pervagārī* to wander about, f. PER- 1 + *vagārī* to wander.] *trans.* To wander through.

1871 M. COLLINS *Mrq. & Merch.* I. ii. 65 Lord Waynflete ..was in the habit of pervagating the neighbourhood. *a* **1876** —— *Th. in Gard.* (1880) I. 42 To lose myself in it, to pervagate it, to find out its beauties without guidance.

So **perva'gation,** wandering about.

1656 BLOUNT *Glossogr.*, *Pervagation*, a straying up and down, a wandring through or about. **1876** M. COLLINS *Midnight to Midn.* III. xi. 187 'The retort', said Albany, stopping in his polar bear pervagation, 'would be in the words of an old proverb.'

pervaginal (pɜːvəˈdʒaɪnəl), *a.* [f. PER-¹ + VAGINAL *a.* and *sb.*] Done or performed along the vagina.

1922 JOYCE *Ulysses* 483, I have made a pervaginal examination and..I declare him to be *virgo intacta*.

pervaporation (pəvæpəˈreɪʃən). *Chem.* [f. PER(MEATION + E)VAPORATION.] The evaporation of a liquid through a semi-permeable membrane with which it is in contact.

1917 P. A. KOBER in *Jrnl. Amer. Chem. Soc.* XXXIX. 944 My assistant..called my attention to the fact that a liquid in a collodion bag, which was suspended in the air, evaporated, although the bag was tightly closed... Further experiments ..soon forced us to the conclusion that the aqueous vapor is given off through the membrane, as though the water were suspended as a solid without any membrane present. This phenomenon we have named pervaporation. **1934** H. N. HOLMES *Introd. Colloid Chem.* ii. 19 Dilute hydrochloric acid solutions were concentrated by pervaporation to the acid of constant boiling point. **1956** *Science* 13 July 77/2 We have used pervaporation to dehydrate mashed potatoes. **1964** *New Scientist* 26 Nov. 591/1 For the separation of mixtures of non-ionic liquids considerable interest is being shown in what is called the method of 'pervaporation' using thin polymer films. **1968** *Encycl. Polymer Sci. & Technol.* VIII. 629 In pervaporation a mixture of liquids, often heated, on the upstream side of a membrane is driven through the film by a vacuum applied to the downstream side.

Hence **per'vaporate** *v. trans.* and *intr.*, to evaporate in this way; **per'vaporated, per'vaporating** *ppl. adjs.*

1917 *Jrnl. Amer. Chem. Soc.* XXXIX. 944 After fanning these containers with an ordinary office fan for 24 hours the aqueous layer had pervaporated to dryness. *Ibid.* 945 The pervaporating surface decreased with the sinking of the water level. *Ibid.* 947 A similar container was filled with.. sodium chloride solution and pervaporated. **1934** H. N. HOLMES *Introd. Colloid Chem.* ii. 18 A protein digestion residue containing strong hydrochloric acid, histidine, and enough humin to make it black was pervaporated. **1956** *Science* 13 July 77/3 The filtrate from a mixture of mashed potato, ethanol, and water was pervaporated... In pervaporating solutions containing class-I solutes, the percentage of water in the pervaporated vapor varied somewhat.

pervasion (pəˈveɪʒən). [ad. late L. *pervāsiōn-em*, n. of action from *pervādĕre* to PERVADE.] The action of pervading; the condition of being pervaded; permeation; penetration.

1661 BOYLE *Fluidity* xvii, Both those kinds or manners of fluidity..will appear to be caused by the pervasion of a foreign body. **1802** PALEY *Nat. Theol.* vii. (1819) 74 Roots and stalks..hard and tough as they are, yield to its powerful pervasion. **1881** CLELAND *Evolution* i. 4 The general, if not altogether universal pervasion of sexual distinction.

pervasive (pəˈveɪsɪv), *a.* [f. L. *pervās-*, ppl. stem of *pervādĕre* to PERVADE + -IVE.] Having the quality or power of pervading; permeative.

c **1750** SHENSTONE *Economy* III. 107 The works of frost, Pervasive, radiant icicles. **1794** W. ROBERTS *Looker-on* No. 49 II. 224 A pervasive beauty without name, description, or place. **1886** SYMONDS *Renaiss. It., Cath. React.* (1898) I. v. 235 In Italy the disintegrating process had been..far more subtle and pervasive.

Hence **per'vasively** *adv.*, in a pervasive manner; **per'vasiveness,** quality of pervading.

1879 *Christian World* 14 Nov. 732/5 Seldom..have we read discourses more *pervasively and distinctively Christian. **1895** R. F. HORTON *Teaching of Jesus* II. 240 He would Himself be pervasively present, working powerfully on the hearts of men. **1876** GLADSTONE *Homeric Synchr.* 253 The *pervasiveness of the idea of Sun-worship in Egypt. **1880** L. OLIPHANT *Gilead* xiv. 386 The oneness and pervasiveness of the Deity is the prominent feature of the Druse religion.

pervay, erron. form of *prevay*, PRIVY *a.*

perveance (ˈpɜːvɪəns). *Electronics.* [Perh. f. the sound of PERVIOUS *a.* + -ANCE (after *resistance*, *conductance*, *permittance*, etc.).] A valve parameter which in the case of a diode is equal to the anode current divided by the three-halves power of the anode voltage.

1928 Y. KUSUNOSE in *Res. Electrotechn. Lab.* (Japan) No. 237. 3 The constant *G* which is called 'perveance' may be determined from the electrode configurations. **1951** D. V. GEPPERT *Basic Electron Tubes* iv. 155 The perveance of a parallel-plane tetrode is equal to the perveance of the triode portion of the tube considering the screen grid as the plate. **1962** C. SUSSKIND *Encycl. Electronics* 229/2 It is convenient to classify electron guns in terms of their perveance, a parameter that remains invariant when the gun is geometrically scaled. **1973** FERRARI & JONSCHER *Probl. Physical Electronics* i. 20 It is interesting to note that the ratio $\Delta V/V_0$..depends upon the beam perveance $P = I_0 V_0^{-3/2}$ but not upon the beam radices, suggesting that the quantity *P* is the deciding factor as to whether a beam will be perturbed by its own space charge, independently of any particular beam geometry.

pervenche (pɛrvɑ̃ʃ). [Fr., = PERIWINKLE¹.]

1. A shade of light blue, resembling the colour of the flowers of the periwinkle. Also *pervenche blue.*

1899 *Westm. Gaz.* 30 Mar. 3/1 Pervenche and navy are the opposite points of the cold tone of blue. **1909** *Daily Chron.* 6 July 4/5 She wore a beautiful dress of blue embroidered net in a shade of pervenche blue. **1923** *Daily Mail* 26 Apr. 9 The Queen wore a gown of pervenche blue.

2. = PERIWINKLE¹ 1.

1948 E. POUND *Pisan Cantos* (1949) lxxvi. 44 And in spite of hoi barbaroi Pervenche and a sort of dwarf morning-glory.

†**per'vene,** *v. Obs. rare.* [ad. L. *pervenīre* to arrive at, reach (a place), f. PER- 2 + *venīre* to come: cf. F. *parvenir* to arrive.] *intr.* To reach; to get *to*, get access *to*.

1692 BENTLEY *Boyle Lect.* 227 Effluvia and spirits that are emitted from the one, and pervene to the other.

†**per'venient.** *Obs. rare.* [ad. L. *pervenient-em*, pr. pple. of *pervenīre*: see prec.] The number which comes as the result of multiplying one number by another; the product.

c **1400** *Art Nombryng* 8 The .3 nombre, the whiche is clepide product or pervenient,..as twyes .5 is .10., 5. the nombre to be multipliede, and .2. the multipliant, and .10. as before is come therof.

pervenke, obs. form of PERIWINKLE¹.

perverse (ˈpɜːvəs, pəˈvɜːs), *sb. Geom.* [f. next: cf. PERVERSION 2 a.] A figure or image in which the right and left directions of the original are reversed: such are the impression taken from any figured surface, and the image of anything seen in a plane mirror.

1895 in *Funk's Standard Dict.*

perverse (pəˈvɜːs), *a.* Also 4–6 peruers. [a. F. *pervers, -e*, ad. L. *perversus* turned the wrong way, awry, perverse, pa. pple. of *pervertĕre* to turn about, subvert, PERVERT.]

1. Turned away from the right way or from what is right or good; perverted; wicked.

c **1369** CHAUCER *Dethe Blaunche* 813 The false trayteresse peruerse [*v.r.* peruers]. **1426** LYDG. *De Guil. Pilgr.* 19003 An hunte [Satan] stoode with his horne Off chere and looke ryght pervers. **1484** CAXTON *Fables of Æsop* I. ix, The decepcion and flaterye of the peruers and evylle folke. **1526** TINDALE *Acts* xx. 30. **1568** BIBLE (Bishops') *Matt.* xvii. 17 O faythlesse and peruerse nation, howe long shal I be with you? *a* **1631** DONNE *Serm.* cxxxi. V. 352 It is the perversest assertion that God gives man temporall things to ensnare him. **1742** YOUNG *Nt. Th.* VII. 866 Man's perverse, eternal War with Heav'n! **1873** BLACK *Pr. Thule* xiii, A perverse fancy that you are different from the people you meet.

b. Not in accordance with the accepted standard or practice; incorrect; wrong.

a **1568** ASCHAM *Scholem* I. (Arb.) 25 Peruerse iudgement, both of wordes and sentences. **1850** H. ROGERS *Ess.* (1874) II. iv. 194 Perverse transfers of uncongenial idiom. **1856** STANLEY *Sinai & Pal.* Introd. (1858) 47 Massive walls and colonnades, irregular and perverse in all their proportions.

c. *spec.* Of a verdict: Against the weight of evidence or the direction of the judge on a point of law.

1854 SIR J. T. COLERIDGE in Ellis & Blackb. *Reports* (1855) III. 952 We shall grant a new trial if the verdict is perverse, but not if the evidence is merely conflicting. **1884** SIR J. STEPHEN in *Law Rep. 12 Q. Bench Div.* 285 If..a jury in a criminal case give a perverse verdict, the law has provided no remedy.

2. Obstinate or persistent in what is wrong; selfwilled or stubborn (in error).

1579 LYLY *Euphues* (Arb.) 107 If women be not peruerse they shall reape profite. **1609** BIBLE (Douay) *Wisd.* xvi. 5 They were destroyed with the bytings of perverse serpents. **1641** WILKINS *Math. Magick* II. vi. (1648) 192 A blind and perverse incredulity. **1751** JOHNSON *Rambler* No. 87 ⁋2 Perverse neglect of the most salutary precepts. **1860** EMERSON *Cond. Life, Consid.* Wks. (Bohn) II. 423 The steady wrongheadedness of one perverse person irritates the best.

3. Untoward, froward; disposed to go counter to what is reasonable or required; hence, wayward, petulant, cross-grained, ill-tempered, peevish.

1412–20 LYDG. *Chron. Troy* II. x. (1555), This lady [Fortune] wilfull and rechles As she that is froward and peruers. **1568** GRAFTON *Chron.* II. 754 He was with mischarging of a speare, by fortunes peruerse countenaunce pittifully slayne. **1592** SHAKS. *Rom. & Jul.* II. ii. 96 Ile frowne and be peruerse, and say thee nay. **1660** F. BROOKE tr. *Le Blanc's Trav.* 313, I married the most perverse woman in the world. **1754** RICHARDSON *Grandison* IV. iv. 28, I touched first one hand, then the other, of the perverse baby with my lips. **1873** HAMERTON *Intell. Life* x. v. (1875) 389 It is difficult for a man who feels cheerful and refreshed..to write anything morbid or perverse.

absol. **1748** RICHARDSON *Clarissa* (1811) VI. 23, I expected that the dear perverse would begin with me with spirit and indignation.

†**b.** Of things or events: Adverse, unpropitious.

c **1440** *Partonope* 2377 So this batayle ys perversse. **1671** MILTON *Samson* 737 Though the fact more evil drew In the perverse event then I foresaw. **1713** SWIFT *Cadenus & Vanessa* Wks. 1755 III. II. 29 Though by one perverse event Pallas had cross'd her first intent.

†**per'verse,** *v. Obs.* [ad. obs. F. *perverser*, f. *pervers* adj.: see prec.] *trans.* To pervert; to turn away from that which is good, right, or true.

1574 HELLOWES *Gueuara's Fam. Ep.* (1577) 339 Such are ..accursed of God, and hated of men, who..confound iustice with tyrannie, peruerse equitie with iniquitie. **1653** T. BLAKE (*title*) Covenant of God entered with Man-kinde .., with the Scripture texts perversed by Mr. Tombes vindicated.

†**per'versed,** *ppl. a.* Chiefly *Sc. Obs.* Also 6–7 perverst. [f. L. *pervers-us*, pa. pple. with Eng. suffix -ED¹.] Perverted; = PERVERSE *a.* 1.

1508 DUNBAR *Tua Mariit Women* 249 Sa, that my preching may pers your perverst hertis. *a* **1535** FISHER *Wks.* (E.E.T.S.) II. 437 By the errour of false doctrines and of peruersed heresies. **1552** ABP. HAMILTON *Catech.* (1884) 33 To fall into a perversit mynde. **1632** LITHGOW *Trav.* I. 19 All the hypocriticall crew, of these peruers'd Iebusites.

Hence †**per'versedly** *adv.*, perversely; †**per'versedness,** perverseness.

a **1535** FISHER *Wks.* (E.E.T.S.) II. 444 To all them that be nat ouer peruersedly drowned in the heresies of Luther. **1568** *Reg. Privy Council Scot.* I. 624 Continewand in his formar perversednes. **1632** LITHGOW *Trav.* VIII. 373 Hauing past the peruerstnesse of this calamity. *Ibid.* x. 488 Whose empty Sculles..your selues peruerstly vexe.

perversely (pəˈvɜːslɪ), *adv.* [f. PERVERSE *a.* + -LY².] In a perverse manner; with perversity; in a way obstinately contrary to what is proper, true, or good; untowardly, vexatiously, crossly.

1526 *Pilgr. Perf.* (W. de W. 1531) 189 b, In no wyse to doubt therof, nor peruersly to impugne it. *c* **1559** R. HALL *Life Fisher* in *Fisher's Wks.* (E.E.T.S.) II. p. liii, Had not he bene other-wise perversly bent. **1663** COWLEY *Verses Sev. Occas.*, *To Royal Soc.* iv, From Words, which are but

Pictures of the Thought, (Tho' we our Thoughts from them perversely drew). **1727** HARTE *Statius' Thebaid* VI. 1090 The chiefs perversely blind Neglect the sign, nor see th' event behind. **1847** EMERSON *Poems* (1857) 91 Stream could not so perversely wind But corn of Guy's was there to grind.

perverseness (pəˈvɜːsnɪs). [f. as prec. + -NESS.] The quality of being perverse; the disposition or tendency to act in a manner contrary to what is right or reasonable; obstinate wrongheadedness; refractoriness; corruption, wickedness.

1561 T. NORTON *Calvin's Inst.* I. 1 Our owne ignorance,.. weaknesse, perversenesse, and corruption. **1644** MILTON *Judgm. Bucer* Wks. 1851 IV. 338 To enforce the innocent and faultles to endure the pain and misery of anothers perversnes. **1741** RICHARDSON *Pamela* I. 36, I am likely to suffer in my Reputation by the Perverseness and Folly of this Girl. **1814** CARY *Dante, Paradise* XXVII. Argt., The perverseness of man, who places his will on.. perishable things. **1880** E. WHITE *Cert. Relig.* 60 Corruption.. brought in.. through the interested perverseness of false teachers.

b. Contrariness, adverseness; unfavourableness.

1748 *Anson's Voy.* II. iii. 152 They were.. delayed by the perverseness of the winds. **1777** SHERIDAN *Sch. Scand.*, *Portrait*, By fate's perverseness, she alone Would doubt our truth.

†**perˈverser.** *Obs.* Also 5 -our. [app. orig. agent-noun in L. or AF. form from L. *pervertĕre* or obs. F. *perverser* to pervert; in form *perverser* referred to PERVERSE *v.*] One who perverts; a corrupter, perverter.

1482 *Monk of Evesham* (Arb.) 90 Not beyng rectors and faders, but peruersours and destroyers of her sowlys. *a* **1564** BECON *Demands Holy Script.* Pref., Such professors, or rather perversers of the gospel, are like to that son whych promised his father to work.., and wrought nothyng at al.

perversion (pəˈvɜːʃən). [ad. L. *perversiōn-em*, n. of action f. *pervertĕre* to PERVERT: cf. F. *perversion* (16th c. in Littré and Hatz.-Darm.).]

1. a. The action of perverting or condition of being perverted; turning the wrong way; turning aside from truth or right; diversion to an improper use; corruption, distortion; *spec.* change to error in religious belief (opp. to CONVERSION 8); *transf.* a perverted or corrupted form *of* something.

1388 WYCLIF *Prol.* 45 If the speche of holi writ seme to comaunde peruersion of soule.. it is figuratijf speche. **1563** FOXE *A. & M.* (1583) 1674 *Suffr[agan]*. We seeke not thy bloud but thy conuersion. *Shet[erden]*. Then shall you proue my peruersion first before you condemn me. **1619** CORNWALLIS *Let. to Digby* in *Select. Harl. Misc.* (1793) 362 Contrariwise, there might be great danger of the infanta's perversion. **1622** BACON *Holy War* Wks. 1879 I. 528/2 Women to govern men,.. slaves freemen,.. being total violations and perversions of the laws of nature and nations. **1713** DERHAM *Phys.-Theol.* II. iii. 45 Miraculous Perversions of the Course of Nature. **1790** BURKE *Fr. Rev.* Wks. V. 261 The perversion of history, by those, who, for the same nefarious purposes, have perverted every other part of learning. **1847** EMERSON *Repr. Men, Swedenborg* Wks. (Bohn) I. 331 To what a painful perversion had Gothic theology arrived, that Swedenborg admitted no conversion for evil spirits. **1873** BLACK *Pr. Thule* xi, The statement was an audacious perversion of the truth. **1877** ROBERTS *Handbk. Med.* (ed. 3) I. 11 Perversion of the functions of digestion, assimilation, and nutrition.

b. *Psychol.* A disorder of sexual behaviour in which satisfaction is sought through channels other than those of normal heterosexual intercourse.

1892 D. H. TUKE *Dict. Psychol. Med.* II. 1156/2 *Sexual perversion*, an innate perversion or 'inversion' of the sexual feelings with consciousness of its morbid nature... A passion for the sex to which the sufferer belongs, instead of the normal inclination to the opposite sex. **1894** H. ELLIS *Man & Woman* xvi. 365 Sexual perversions, again, are more common in men than in women. **1937** J. S. PLANT *Personality* II. viii. 223 A perversion in sexual expression has nothing at all to do with the form of the act but only with its purpose. **1948** A. C. KINSEY et al. *Sexual Behavior Human Male* viii. 264 Perversions are defined as unnatural acts, acts contrary to nature, bestial, abominable, and detestable. Such laws are interpretable only in accordance with the ancient tradition of the English common law which.. is committed to the doctrine that no sexual activity is justifiable unless its objective is procreation. **1949** J. STRACHEY tr. *Freud's Three Ess. Theory of Sexuality* i. 28 Even in the most normal sexual process we may detect rudiments which, if they had developed, would have led to the deviations described as 'perversions'. *Ibid.* 37 Extreme cases of masochistic perversion. **1967** BRUSSEL & CANTZLAAR *Chambers's Dict. Psychiatry* 88 *Exhibitionism*, a form of sexual perversion in which erotic gratification is obtained from the exposure of parts of the body that have sexual significance. **1968** C. RYCROFT *Crit. Dict. Psychoanal.* 88 Masochism, sexual perversion in which the subject claims to get erotic pleasure from having pain inflicted upon himself. **1973** I. SINGER *Goals of Human Sexuality* 156 It would be erroneous to assume that the so-called perversions are merely alternative attitudes, as desirable as any other sexual possibility.

2. a. *Geom.* The formation of the perverse of a figure; the perverse itself.

1881 MAXWELL *Electr. & Magn.* II. 415 They are geometrically alike in all respects, except that one is the perversion of the other, like its image in a looking glass. **1900** LARMOR *Æther & Matter* 208 The change from a molecule to its enantiograph involves.. perversion of its orbital configuration.

b. *Med.* and *Surg.* See quots.

1842 DUNGLISON *Med. Lex.*, *Perversion*, one of the four modifications of function in disease: the three others being augmentation, diminution, and abolition. The Humorists used the term also, to designate disorder or morbid change in the fluids. **1858** MAYNE *Expos. Lex.* 920/1 Diastremma, or distortion of a part: a perversion. **1899** *Allbutt's Syst. Med.* VII. 693 A sensory perversion or defect.

†**perˈversionate,** *a. Obs. rare.* [f. L. *perversiōn-em*, or F. or Eng. *perversion* + -ATE[2] 2. Cf. *affectionate*, *passionate*.] Affected with perversion; perverted.

c **1450** *Mankind* 187 in *Macro Plays* 8 Yf we wyll mortyfye owur carnall condycyon, Ande owur voluntarye dysyres, þat euer be pervercionatt.

†**perversiˈose,** *a. Obs. rare.* [f. L. *pervers-us* + -OSE: perh. meant for **perversuose*.] Perverse.

c **1450** *Mankind* 744 in *Macro Plays* 27 Thys peruersyose ingratytude I can not rehers.

perversity (pəˈvɜːsɪtɪ). [a. F. *perversité* (12th c. in Littré), ad. L. *perversitās*, f. *pervers-us* PERVERSE *a.*] The quality or character of being perverse: = PERVERSENESS.

1528 ROY *Rede me* (Arb.) 55 He hath falce farises and scrybes,.. Full of fraudes and perversite. **1549** COVERDALE, etc. *Erasm. Par. Titus* iii. 31 b, An errour commynge onelye of the fraylenes of man, is remedied by one or two warnynges, but peruersitie is incurable and made worse by puttyng to of remedies. **1687** NORRIS *To Dr. Plot on Staffordsh.* i, What strange Perversity is this of Man! When 'twas a Crime to tast th' inlightning Tree He could not then his hand refrain. **1831** CARLYLE *Sart. Res.* I. iv, It is in this peculiarity.. that all these short-comings, over-shootings, and multiform perversities, take rise. **1865** *Pall Mall G.* 4 Oct. 2/2 The most flagrant instances of juratorial perversity. **1871** R. ELLIS *Catullus* Pref. 9 The experiments of the Elizabethan writers [in classical metres].. by that strange perversity which so often dominates literature, were as decidedly unsuccessful from an accentual, as the modern experiments from a quantitative point of view.

perversive (pəˈvɜːsɪv), *a.* [f. L. *pervers-*, ppl. stem of *pervertĕre* to PERVERT + -IVE.]

†**1.** Having the quality or tendency of turning awry or distorting. *Obs. rare.*

a **1693** *Urquhart's Rabelais* III. xxxi. 256 A perversive Wriness and Convulsion of the Muscles.

2. Having the character or quality of perverting in nature, character, or use.

1817 G. S. FABER *Eight Dissert.* (1845) I. 73 A Scheme of Pseudo-Theology characterised by inculcating a series of perversive and usurpative Messiahships. **1818** in TODD. **1824** LANDOR *Imag. Conv.* xxi. Wks. 1846 I. 126 An institution perversive of those on which the government of America is constructed. **1862** LYTTON *Str. Story* 171 Discourteously perversive of the obvious intention of the quotation.

pervert (pəˈvɜːt), *v.* Also 6 par-, -wert, -vart. [ad. F. *pervert-ir* = Pr. and Sp. *pervertir*, Pg. *perverter*, It. *pervertere*, ad. L. *pervert-ĕre* to turn round or about, turn the wrong way, overturn, turn to error or ruin, undo, corrupt; f. PER- 2, 3 + *vertĕre* to turn: cf. *convert*, *divert*, etc.]

†**1.** *trans.* To turn upside down; to upset, overthrow; to subvert, ruin. *Obs.*

c **1374** CHAUCER *Boeth.* II. pr. i. 20 (Camb.) Fortune.. hath peruertyd the clernesse and the estat of thi corage. *c* **1450** *Mankind* 379 in *Macro Plays*, All þe menys xull be sought. To perverte my condycions, & brynge me to nought. **1543** JOYE *Confut. Gardiner* 9 So setting the carte before the horse, and.. like an vngodly gardener to peruert and turne the rotes of his plantes and herbes vpward. *c* **1560** A. SCOTT *Poems* (S.T.S.) xxxiv. 53 ȝour play [is] sone peruertit. **1604** R. CAWDREY *Table Alph.*, *Peruert*, ouerthrowe, or turne up side downe. **1656** in BLOUNT *Glossogr.*

2. To turn aside from its right course, aim, etc.

a. To turn aside from justice, right order, etc.

1382 WYCLIF *Deut.* xxvii. 19 Cursid [is he] that peruertith doom of comlynge, faderles child, and widewe. **1483** *Rolls of Parlt.* VI. 240/2 The ordre of all politique Rule was perverted. **1526** TINDALE *Acts* xiii. 10 Thou ceasest not to pervert the strayght wayes off the lorde. **1620** VENNER *Via Recta* (1650) 297 If we pervert the order of Nature, as to sleep in the day and wake in the night. **1650** BULWER *Anthropomet.* 254 The Symetry whereof being causally [? casually] or purposely perverted. **1783** POTT *Chirurg. Wks.* II. 76 The peristaltic motion of the whole canal is disturbed or perverted. **1868** FREEMAN *Norm. Conq.* (1877) II. vii. 127 They perverted the course of justice.

b. To turn from the proper use, purpose, or meaning; to misapply, misconstrue, wrest the purport of.

c **1386** CHAUCER *Melib.* ¶ 223 If thou do hem bountee they wol peruerten it in to wikkednesse. **1413** *Pilgr. Sowle* (Caxton) II. xliii. (1859) 49 They peruertyn hooly Scripture by fals vnderstandynge. **1542-5** BRINKLOW *Lament.* (1874) 86 The Supper of the Lorde is peruerted and not vsed after Christes institucion. **1593** NASHE *Christ's T.* 83 They peruert foundations, and will not bestow the Bequeathers free almes. **1630** PRYNNE *Anti-Armin.* 118 It peruerts, it disanulls the very series, and substance of the Scripture. **1700** DRYDEN *Pref. Fables* Wks. (Globe) 506 He has perverted my meaning by his glosses. **1849** COBDEN *Speeches* 9 What I stated with reference to the great mass of the French people last year was perverted.

†**c.** To turn, divert. *Obs. rare*[−1].

1611 SHAKS. *Cymb.* II. iv. 151 Let's follow him, and peruert the present wrath He hath against himselfe.

d. *intr.* for *refl.* To become perverted. *rare.*

1635 QUARLES *Emblems* I. i. 7 Blessings unus'd pervert into a Wast, As well as Surfeits.

3. *trans.* To turn (a person, the mind, etc.) away from right opinion or action; to lead astray; to corrupt.

c **1375** *Sc. Leg. Saints* xli. (*Agnes*) 237 Hir.. þat þis wichcrafte has done, & peruertis thocht and wil Of al þat treutht giffis hir til. *c* **1380** WYCLIF *Sel. Wks.* II. 318 þei witen not how many men ben pervertid bi þer lore. *c* **1440** *York Myst.* xxvi. 113 He pervertis oure pepull. **1593** in Ellis *Orig. Lett.* Ser. II. III. 172 Seminarie Priests, Jhesuits.. sent hither to pervert such as are dutiefull and well inclyned. **1667** MILTON *P.L.* x. 3 How He [Satan] in the Serpent had perverted Eve, Her Husband shee. **1710** STEELE *Tatler* No. 111 ¶2 A Mind that is not perverted and depraved by wrong Notions. **1859** MILL *Liberty* ii, When we forbid bad men to pervert society by the propagation of opinions which we regard as false and pernicious.

b. *spec.* To turn (any one) aside from a right to a false or erroneous religious belief or system (i.e. to what the speaker or writer holds to be such).

13.. *S. Erkenwolde* 10 in Horstm. *Altengl. Leg.* (1881) 266 þe Saxones.. peruertyd alle þe pepul þat in þat place dwellide. **1480** CAXTON *Chron. Eng.* IV. (1520) 38 b/2 He was perverted by the heresy of the Ariens. **1579** W. WILKINSON *Confut Familye of Loue, Brief Descr.*, To peruert and turne from the truth xii godly Christians which were martyred. **1666** E. MOUNTAGU in *12th Rep. Hist. MSS. Comm.* App. v. 8 If the young Lord was a strict and a grounded Papist there was some danger my Lady Dorothy might bee perverted. **1770** J. R. FORSTER tr. *Kalm's Trav. N. Amer.* (1772) II. 106 It seems that they have been rather perverted than converted. **1849** MACAULAY *Hist. Eng.* vi. II. 87 Walker.. with some fellows and undergraduates whom he had perverted, heard mass daily in his own apartments.

c. *intr.* To turn aside from the right course; to become a pervert.

1387-8 T. USK *Test. Love* I. ix. (Skeat) I. 127 So that in nothinge thy kynde from his wil decline, ne from his nobley perverte. **14..** in *Lett. Marg. Anjou & Bp. Beckington* (Camden) 167 Then I wente to Rome, and from Rome to Rodes, and I perverted to the Sowden in feythe. **1890** *Graphic* 11 Oct. 420/3, 1593, the year when Henry perverted to Roman Catholicism.

4. *Geom. trans.* To reverse the right and left directions of; to form the perverse of (see PERVERSE *sb.*).

1900 LARMOR *Æther & Matter* 209 Enantiomorphy [of a molecule] reverses the signs of all its electrons and perverts their relative position.

Hence **perˈverting** *vbl. sb.* and *ppl. a.*

c **1380** WYCLIF *Wks.* (1880) 386 Peruertynge of goddis ordynance. **1533** TINDALE *Supper of Lord* Wks. (1573) 460 A great tunne full of Mores mischief and pernicious peruertyng of Gods holy worde. **1665** BOYLE *Occas. Refl.* IV. xii. (1848) 241 Of so perverting a Nature, is so high a Station. **1680** HICKERINGILL *Meroz* 33 The Converting of a Turk has a better Reward than the perverting of one that is a Christian already. **1712** PRIDEAUX *Direct. Ch.-wardens* (ed. 4) 22 A perverting of the Statute.

†**perˈvert,** *a. Obs.* [? shortened from *perverted*: cf. CONVERT *a.*] Perverted; perverse; wicked.

c **1470** HARDING *Chron.* XLVII. v. (Ashm. MS. 34), Brytons.. Afore þat were paynims and also perverte. *c* **1500** *Lancelot* 1471 Fore thow to gode was frawart and perwert. **1512** *Act 4 Hen. VIII.* c. 19 *Preamble*, Abydyng in his seid indurat & pervart opynyons. **1549-62** STERNHOLD & H. *Ps.* xxviii. 3 Repute me not among the sort Of wicked and peruert. *c* **1550** R. WEVER *Lusty Juventus* B j, God which hath geuen me the knowledge To know his doctrine from the false and peruarte.

pervert (ˈpɜːvət), *sb.* [app. absolute use of prec., with shifted stress: cf. CONVERT *sb.*] **1.** One who has been perverted; one who has forsaken a doctrine or system regarded as true for one esteemed false; an apostate.

1661 BLOUNT *Glossogr.* (ed. 2), *Pervert*, one that is turned from good to evil; as Convert is the contrary. **1716** M. DAVIES *Athen. Brit.* II. 316 A Popish pervert and a Protestant convert are, indeed, two different provisionals. **1845** DE QUINCEY *Coleridge & Opium* Wks. 1862 XI. 95 Relapsing perverts (such is the modern slang). **1860** THACKERAY *Round. Papers* i. (1863) 4 That notorious 'pervert' Henry of Navarre and France. **1879** FARRAR *St. Paul* I. 329 That this audacious pervert [Paul] should not only preach, but preach to the heathen.. filled them with rage.

2. *Psychol.* One who suffers from a perversion of the sexual instinct.

1897 H. ELLIS *Stud. Psychol. Sex* I. i. 11 A pervert whom I can trust told me that he had made advances to upwards of one hundred men. **1906** *Jrnl. Abnormal Psychol.* Apr. 28 Subconscious feelings which represent, in embryo, the grosser manifestations of the most abandoned sexual perverts. **1924** D. BRYAN tr. *Freud's Hysterical Phantasies* in *Coll. Papers* II. v. 51 The strange conditions under which certain perverts carry out their sexual gratifications—either in imagination or in reality. **1972** *Encycl. Psychol.* II. 388/1 In psychoanalytic theory it is postulated that the child shows perversions or is a 'polymorphous pervert'. **1977** *Gay News* 24 Mar. 27/1 The word 'pervert' hardly seems apt to describe Douglas, in the light of such facts.

perverted (pəˈvɜːtɪd), *ppl. a.* [f. PERVERT *v.* + -ED[1].] Turned from the right way, from the proper use, from truth to error, etc.; wicked; distorted; misapplied.

1667 MILTON *P.L.* XII. 547 To dissolve Satan with his perverted World. **1728** YOUNG *Love Fame* vi, But own I must, in this perverted age, Who most deserve, can't always most engage. **1844** W. H. MILL *Serm. Tempt. Christ* v. 113 That perverted self-consciousness which constitutes pride. **1866** ROGERS *Agric. & Prices* I. xxix. 693 Exhibitions of perverted intellectual activity.

Hence **perˈvertedly** *adv.*; **perˈvertedness.**

1816 G. S. FABER *Orig. Pagan Idol.* I. 61 The idolatry.. was all borrowed *pervertedly from the Israelites. **1860** PUSEY *Min. Proph.* 374 All pervertedly imitate Thee, who remove far from Thee. **1828** —— *Hist. Enq.* I. p. ix, The shallowness and *pervertedness of [such] enquiries. **1881** M. A. LEWIS *Two Pretty G.* I. 209 Suffering from..the pride of intellect and from voluntary pervertedness.

perverter (pə'vɜːtə(r)). [f. PERVERT *v.* + -ER[1].] One who perverts, or turns from right to wrong; one who misinterprets or corrupts.

1546 LANGLEY *Pol. Verg. De Invent.* VII. i. 131 The deuil, peruerter of all good thinges. **1648** JENKYN *Blind Guide* i. 6 He is a soul perverter. **1779–81** JOHNSON *L.P., Pope* Wks. IV. 98 Perverters of epistolary integrity. **1807** G. CHALMERS *Caledonia* I. II. vi. 302 This story is retold by Buchanan, and by the other perverters of the Scottish history. **1889** DOYLE *Micah Clarke* xviii. 175 The crown which he had wrested.. from the Popish perverter.

pervertible (pə'vɜːtɪb(ə)l), *a.* [f. L. type **pervertibilis*, f. *pervertĕre* (see -BLE): cf. obs. F. *pervertible* (16th c.).] Capable of being perverted.

1611 COTGR., *Corrompable*, corrumpable, corruptible, peruertable, deprauable. **1651** DAVENANT *Gondibert* Pref. (1673) 15 Armies, if they were not pervertible by Faction, yet are to Commonwealths like Kings Physitians to poor Patients. **1711** SHAFTESB. *Charac., Moralists* I. iii, The Depravity of Minds..dependent on such pervertible Organs. **1888** BRYCE *Amer. Commw.* II. III. lxiv. 473 New immigrants, politically incompetent, and therefore easily pervertible.

Hence **perverti'bility**, capability of being perverted; **per'vertibly** *adv.*, in a pervertible manner.

1850 ROBERTSON *Serm.* Ser. IV. xiii, That part of human pervertibility is an awful fact and mystery. **1642** *Animadv. on Observator's Notes* 4 The Parliament is the Vniversall unerring and unpervertibly just body of the Kingdome.

per'vertive, *a. rare.* [f. PERVERT *v.* + -IVE.] = PERVERSIVE 2.

1901 H. MCINTOSH *Is Christ infallible*, etc. (1902) 153 Their whole conception..is based upon a false and pervertive subjectivity.

†**per'vertness.** *Obs.* [f. PERVERT *a.* + -NESS.] The quality of being pervert; perversity.

1581 MARBECK *Bk. of Notes* 494 Not yt there is anie frowardnesse or peruertnesse in God.

†**per'vestigate**, *v. Obs.* [f. L. *pervestīgāt-*, ppl. stem of *pervestīgāre* to trace out, f. PER- 2 + *vestīgāre* to track, trace.] *trans.* To trace out, investigate diligently; to find out by research.

1610 W. FOLKINGHAM *Art of Survey* I. iii. 4 It would be also peruestigated, whether it [the soil] be light, loose, softe, fatt. *Ibid.*, Obseruation to peruestigate the Pregnance wherewith the Earth is imbowelled. **1688** R. HOLME *Armoury* III. 139/1 *Pervestigate*, to seek out, or diligently to observe.

†**pervesti'gation.** *Obs.* [ad. L. *pervestīgātiōn-em*, noun of action from *pervestīgāre*: see prec.] The action of 'pervestigating'; diligent research or investigation.

1610 W. FOLKINGHAM *Art of Survey* I. xi. 44 The peruestigation of the secrets of Agriculture. **1638** CHILLINGW. *Relig. Prot.* I. ii. §55. 74 The pervestigation of the true and genuine Text. **1715** tr. *Pancirotlus' Rerum Mem.* II. xvii. 380 In the pervestigation of this curious Theory.

†**'perviable**, *a. Obs. rare.* [f. rare L. *perviā-re* (f. PER- 1 + *via* way) + -BLE.] Capable of being passed through; pervious.

1610 W. FOLKINGHAM *Art of Survey* I. vi. 13 For woods, how peruiable, how penetrable, how enterlaced, as Timber with Tinsell, Coppice, or vnderwood.

†**'pervial**, *a. Obs. rare.* [f. L. *pervi-us* (see PERVIOUS) + -AL[1].] Pervious; hence, easily seen through, clear.

1595 CHAPMAN *Ovid's Banquet* Ded., That Poesie should be as pervial as oratory, and plainness her special ornament, were the plain way to barbarism. *c*1611 —— *Iliad* XIV. Comm. 199 Yet all peruiall enough (you may well say) when such a one as I comprehend them.

Hence †**'pervially** *adv. Obs.*, clearly.

*c*1611 CHAPMAN *Iliad* II. Comm. 34 Since a man may peruially (or as he passeth) discerne all that is to be vnderstood. *Ibid.* XIII. 187 Imagining his vnderstanding Readers eyes more sharpe, then not to see peruially through them.

perviance, -aunce, obs. forms of PURVEYANCE.

†**'perviate**, *v. Obs. rare*⁻¹. [f. L. *pervi-us* (see PERVIOUS) + -ATE[3].] *trans.* To make a way through; to penetrate, perforate.

1657 TOMLINSON *Renou's Disp.* 392 [Galls] nodose, solid and perviated with no holes.

pervicacious (pɜːvɪ'keɪʃəs), *a.* [f. L. *pervicāx, -cāc-em* stubborn, headstrong (f. root *pervic-* of *pervincĕre* to carry one's point, maintain one's opinion, f. PER- 1 + *vincĕre* to conquer, prevail against) + -IOUS.] Very obstinate or stubborn; headstrong, wilful; refractory.

1633 AMES *Agst Cerem.* II. 93 Pervicatious contending, without reason and measure. **1672** H. STUBBE *Justif. Dutch War* 66 The Dutch..grew more pervicacious in opposition to His Majesties Officers. **1748** RICHARDSON *Clarissa* (1811) I. 167 One of the most pervicacious young creatures that ever was heard of. **1853** G. J. CAYLEY *Las Alforjas* II. 174 The pursuit of pervicacious donkeys who diverged into the green barley. **1973** *Daily Tel.* 16 Apr. 13/4 Are audiences the only thing wrong with the theatre?.. At once funky and firm, a pervicacious horde of floating voters, they rush confidently to support the worst candidate on offer. **1973** *N.Y. Law Jrnl.* 7 Aug. 4 The language of the bureaucrats and administrators must needs be recognized as an outgrowth of legal parlance. There is no other way to explain its pervading, pervicacious and pernicious meanderings. **1978** W. M. SPACKMAN *Armful of Warm Girl* 37 Must she like a pervicacious angel think that because he loved her with every beat of his heart, [etc.].

Hence **pervi'caciously** *adv.*; **pervi'cacious-ness.**

1650 CHARLETON *Paradoxes* 83 The phansy of an Animal pervicaciously surviving death, is impressed not onely upon the blood: but also [etc.]. **1692** BENTLEY *Boyle Lect.* vi, But if God hath actually created those intelligent substances ..'tis pervicaciousness to deny that he created matter also. **1822** T. TAYLOR *Apuleius, Golden Ass* II. xx. 35 This man being confused by the pervicaciousness of all those who were looking at him.

pervicacity (pɜːvɪ'kæsɪtɪ). Now *rare.* [f. L *pervicāc-em* (see prec.) + -ITY; cf. late L. *pervicācitās* (*Gloss. Philox.*) for ancient L. *pervicācia*: see next.] The quality or state of being pervicacious; obstinacy; wilfulness.

1604 PARSONS *3rd Pt. Three Convers. Eng.* 175 Was heere constancy or pertinacity, perseuerance or peruicacity? **1660** H. MORE *Myst. Godl.* VII. ix, Which constancy of theirs he calls *pervicaciam & inflexibilem obstinationem*, a Pervicacity and inflexible Obstinacy. **1825–9** MRS. SHERWOOD *Lady of Manor* III. xx. 178, I never could account..for the strange pervicacity of his humour in rejecting every kind of refinement. **1837** C. LOFFT *Self-formation* I. 197 Every man by patience and pervicacity may frame himself intellectually to what he pleases.

†**pervicacy** ('pɜːvɪkəsɪ). *Obs.* [ad. L. *pervicācia* steadfastness, stubbornness, obstinacy, It. *pervicacia*, f. L. *pervicāc-em*: see PERVICACIOUS.] = PERVICACITY (being the earlier word).

1537 CROMWELL in Merriman *Life & Lett.* (1902) II. 87 This princely goodnes, myght haue brought that desperat rebell from his so stourdy malice, blyndnes and pervicacie. **1610** HOLLAND *Camden's Brit.* II. 127 Least his peevish pervicacy should be more and more enkindled. **1711** in *10th Rep. Hist. MSS. Comm.* App. v. 113 Pharo and..his people of Egypt..fatally payed for their pervicacy. **1748** RICHARDSON *Clarissa* II. vi. 31 If you persist in your pervicacy. Shall I be a pedant Miss for this word?

†**per'vigilate**, *v. Obs. rare*⁻⁰. [f. ppl. stem of L. *pervigilāre* to remain awake, watch all night, f. PER- 1 + *vigilāre* to watch.]

1623 COCKERAM, *Peruigilate*, to watch.

So †**pervigi'lation** *Obs.* [L. *pervigilātio*], a watching through the night, keeping of vigil.

1623 COCKERAM *Pervigilation*, a watching. **1721** BAILEY.

pervincle, -vink(e, -kle, obs. ff. PERIWINKLE[1].

pervious ('pɜːvɪəs), *a.* [f. L. *pervi-us* that has a way or passage through (f. PER- 1 + *via* way) + -OUS; in It. *pervio*.]

1. Allowing of passage through; passable; affording passage or entrance; lying open (*to*).

*a*1631 DONNE *Obseq. Ld. Harrington's Bro.* 6 If looking up to God; or down to us, Thou finde that any way is pervious, 'Twixt heav'n and earth. **1659** STANLEY *Hist. Philos.* XI. (1701) 466/2 Every Country is pervious to a wise Man; for the whole World is the Country of a wise Soul. **1725** POPE *Odyss.* IV. 1056 The bolted Valves are pervious to her flight. **1781** GIBBON *Decl. & F.* lviii. (1869) III. 445 So large a circuit must have yielded many pervious points. **1859** MASSON *Brit. Novelists* iii. 172 A time when the Highlands were much less pervious..to Lowland tourists.

b. *esp.* Allowing of passage through its substance; permeable.

1627 MAY *Lucan* IV. (1631) 5 Make the strooke earth to deluge pervious. **1661** BOYLE *Examen* iii. (1682) 24 Glass also is pervious to the Air. **1779** COWPER *Pineapple & Bee* 10 The frame was tight, And only pervious to the light. **1807** VANCOUVER *Agric. Devon* (1813) 22 A coarse argillaceous gravel pervious to water. **1871** TYNDALL *Fragm. Sc.* (1879) I. ii. 40 Melloni..found crystals of sulphur to be highly pervious to radiant heat.

c. *fig.* (*a*) That can be penetrated by the mental sight; fully intelligible, 'transparent'. (*b*) Of a person or the mind: Accessible to influence or argument.

*a*1614 DONNE *Βιαθανατος* (1644) 98 In exposition of places of Scripture, which he alwaies makes so liquid, and pervious. **1684** T. BURNET *Th. Earth* I. 307 Sees all things from top to bottom, as pervious and transparent. **1867** EMERSON *May-Day*, etc. Wks. (Bohn) III. 480 The solid, solid universe Is pervious to Love. **1902** *Scotsman* 17 Jan. 4/6 The Boer mind..pervious to reason and the logic of facts.

d. *Zool.* and *Bot.* Open, patent, patulous: opposed to *impervious*.

1806 GALPINE *Brit. Bot.* 14* Primula... *Cor.* throat pervious, tube cylindrical. **1874** COUES *Birds N.W.* 373 The nostrils are very large and pervious, whereas those of the true Vultures are separated by an impervious septum.

2. Having the quality of passing through, penetrating, or permeating; pervasive. Now *rare.*

1684 *Contempl. St. Man* II. v. (1699) 180 They [bodies of saints] have an agility to move from place to place,..like light; to have their way free and pervious through all places, and can penetrate wheresoever they please. **1718** PRIOR *Solomon* III. 622 What is this little agile, pervious Fire, This flutt'ring motion, which we call the mind? *a*1849 H. COLERIDGE *Poems* (1850) II. 344 His mortal clay Abolish'd quite, or blent with pervious air.

'perviousness. [f. prec. + -NESS.] The quality of being pervious; penetrability.

1669 HOLDER *Elem. Speech* 78 The Italians..make the Occluse Appulse, especially the Gingival, softer than we do, giving a little of perviousness. **1672** BOYLE *Disc. Perviousness Glass* Exp. iii, The perviousness we above observed in glass. **1871** TYNDALL *Fragm. Sc.* (1879) I. iii. 88 On account of its extreme perviousness to the visible rays. **1882** —— in *Longman's Mag.* I. 39 The very meaning of transparency is perviousness to the luminous rays.

pervise, obs. form of PARVIS.

[**pervise** *v.*, editorial and dictionary error for *peruise*, PERUSE.

1549 *St. Paper* 18 May in *Bradford's Wks.* (Parker Soc.) II. 369 Clare Hall, the state whereof these two days we have thoroughly pervised [*orig. MS.* perused]. **1577** *Bk. Univ. Kirk Scotl.* (1839) 163 Their haill travells and work..sould be revysit and pervysit [*MS.* pervisit = peruisit, perused] be some brethren.]

per'vulgate, *v. rare.* [f. ppl. stem of L. *pervulgāre*, f. PER- 2 + *vulgāre* to make known.] *trans.* To make public, make known.

1586 FERNE *Blaz. Gentrie* Ep. Ded., I did pervulgate the same treatise vnto some of my familiars and acquaintance.

Hence **pervul'gation**, the action of making public; advertisement. *rare.*

1832 I. TAYLOR *Saturday Even.* (1833) 79 Religious principles undergo a far more extended pervulgation than those of any secular science.

pervy ('pɜːvɪ), *a. slang.* [f. PERV(ERTED *ppl. a.* + -Y[1].] Sexually perverted; erotic.

1944 L. GLASSOP *We were Rats* xxxi. 178 Listen to this... 'He buried his head in the warm fragrance of her bosom.' So-and-so, so-and-so. It gets pervy again here. 'His hungry kisses were returned with passionate abandon.' **1970** G. F. NEWMAN *Sir, You Bastard* viii. 223 Twenty maximum security, the lights never out, pervy screws watching every movement.

perwanah, -wanna, etc., var. PURWANAH.

perwick(e, -wig, -wyke, obs. ff. PERIWIG.

perwinckle, -winkle, -wyncle, -wynke, obs. ff. PERIWINKLE[1], [2].

pery, -e, obs. ff. PERRIE, PERRY[1], [2], PIRRIE.

perylene ('pɛrɪliːn). *Chem.* [ad. G. *perylen* (R. Scholl et al. 1910, in *Ber. d. Deut. Chem. Ges.* XLIII. 2202), f. *per(i-di-naphth)ylen*, f. *peri-* PERI- (used in a spec. chemical sense) + *di-* DI-[2] + *naphthylen* NAPHTHALENE.] A yellow, crystalline hydrocarbon, $C_{20}H_{12}$, consisting of five fused aromatic rings, which occurs in coal tar and from which certain organic pigments are derived.

1910 *Jrnl. Chem. Soc.* XCVIII. I. 616 To establish the constitution as a *peri*-derivative, 1:8-naphthalenediamine was converted into the azimide, this into 8-iodo-α-naphthylamine, and further into 1:8-di-iodonaphthalene, which last when heated with copper powder yielded..peri-dinaphthalene, which it is proposed to term perylene. **1946** *Nature* 10 Aug. 209/2 It has also been found that the position and number of fluorescence bands of anthracene, perylene, phenanthrene and naphthacene in benzene are independent of the wave-length of the exciting radiation. **1966** *New Scientist* 29 Dec. 735/3 An electron donor such as perylene (which consists of a series of fused benzene rings) is combined with an electron acceptor such as iodine. **1974** *Environmental Sci.* IX. 352/2 A one-year study of the amount of..benzo(*a*)pyrene, benzo(*k*)fluoranthrene, and perylene, was carried out for the particulate matter collected at the York [Ontario] sampling station.

†**peryng**, *ppl. a. Obs.* [f. *pere*, PEAR *v.* + -ING[2].] Appearing.

1562 TURNER *Herbal* II. M iv, A stalk half a cubit hyghe.. about the whiche com furthe certayn furth peryng thynges ..which looke toward the roote. [*Ibid.*, Ye thynges that appere out in ye stalk in..Horminum look downwarde.]

peryngall, variant of PAREGAL *Obs.*

peryr, variant of PERER *Obs.*, pear-tree.

peryshing, obs. form of PARISHEN.

perysshe, obs. form of PERISH, PIERCE.

perywig, perywinkle, etc., obs. forms of PERIWIG, PERIWINKLE.

‖**pes** (piːz). Pl. pedes ('pɛdiːz). [The L. word *pēs* foot, used technically in Comparative Anatomy, Botany, etc.]

1. *Comp. Anat.* The terminal segment of the hind limb of a vertebrate animal, corresponding to the human foot. Opposed to MANUS hand, applied to the corresponding part of the fore limb.

1842 DUNGLISON *Med. Lex.*, *Pes*, the inferior extremity of the abdominal member. **1875** HUXLEY & MARTIN *Elem. Biol.* (1877) 161 Thickenings, or callosities, of the integument, however, occur beneath the joints of the digits, both in the pes and the manus.

2. *Bot.* A footlike part or organ; a base of support; a peduncle.

3. *Pros.* A name for each of the two quatrains forming the first part of a sonnet.

1880 *Macm. Mag.* No. 253. 46 The sonnet..we find that its volta occurs after the eighth line, that it has two pedes of four lines each, and a cauda of six.

pes, obs. form of PEACE, PEASE, PIECE.

† **'pesable**, *a. Obs. rare.* [a. OF. *pesable*, f. *peser* to weigh, PEISE: see -ABLE.] Capable of being weighed; in quot., Weighed; evenly balanced.

c **1400** tr. *Secreta Secret, Gov. Lordsh.* 93 And a pesable right [L. *iusticia ponderata*] and mesuryd ys, to byholde vpon statys by þe self vnderstondyng.

‖ **Pesach** ('pɛsax). [Heb.] = PASSOVER 1.

1613 PURCHAS *Pilgrimage* II. xviii. 173 From the second night of their Pesach they number to their Pentecost fifty daies inclusively. **1887** [see HAGGADAH 2]. **1893** I. ZANGWILL *Ghetto Tragedies* 94 'Passover is over,' she said.. 'Is *Pesach* over?' he said mournfully. **1905** [see MAROR]. **1928** *Daily Express* 9 Apr. 10 Passover, or 'Pesach', is the most interesting ceremony in the Jewish calendar. **1950** M. HAY *Foot of Pride* iii. 77 The date of Easter corresponded approximately to the period of the Jewish *Pesach* when Jews were obliged by their law to eat unleavened bread. **1960** *Jewish Chron.* 8 Apr. 35/1 The Rev. S. Black..told the boys and girls of Pesach and its meaning. **1970** I. SIEFF *Mem.* ii. 20 On the eve of this great day, the most cherished of Jewish holidays, called the *Pesach*, a great family *Seder* is held. **1972** [see MAROR]. **1973** *Jewish Chron.* 19 Jan. 43/3 (Advt.), Book now for Pesach & Summer season.

‖ **pesade** (pəzad). [F. *pesade*, altered (under influence of *peser* to poise) from earlier *posade* (1579 in Hatz.-Darm.), ad. It. *posata*, lit. 'pause, resting', *posate* 'arests which a horse doth make in aduancing his forepart' (Florio 1598), f. *posare* to PAUSE, rest.] (See quot.)

1727–41 CHAMBERS *Cycl.*, *Pesade*, or *Pesate*, in the manage, that action taught a horse, wherein he rises with his fore feet, and bends them up to his body, without stirring the hind feet. The Pesade is the first lesson taught a horse, in order to bring him to curvetts, &c.

pesage, variant of PEISAGE *Obs.*

‖ **pesame** ('pesame). *Obs.* [Sp. phrase *pesa me* 'it grieves me', hence as sb. 'a compliment of condolence'.] An expression of condolence: in phrase ***to give*** or ***receive the pesame***.

1676 LADY FANSHAWE *Mem.* (1830) 225, I waited upon the Queen to give her Majesty *pesame* of the King's death. **1678** PHILLIPS (ed. 4), *Pesame* (Sp.), a word often used by Travellers, and to give one the Pesame, is to condole with any one for his loss, or sorrow.

pesan, -ane, obs. variant of PISANE.

† **pesant**. *Obs. rare.* [a. F. *pesant* (11th c. in Littré), pr. pple. of *peser* to weigh, PEISE; also as sb. 'weight'. Cf. PEISANT *a.*]

1. The amount that a thing weighs; weight.

c **1500** *Melusine* xxi. 142, I shall gyue hym hys pesaunnt or weyght of syluer. *Ibid.* xxxvii. 300 Al gaf you to eyther of vs your pesaunt or weyght of fyn gold.

2. ? Name of a coin or weight. (Or ? BEZANT.)

1577 HELLOWES *Gueuara's Chron.* x. 35 That he should.. giue 100000 pesants of golde [*pesantes de oro*] to paye the armie.

pesant, obs. f. PEASANT; var. PEISANT *a. Obs.*

† **pesanteur, -ture**. *Obs. rare.* [a. F. *pesanteur* (12th c. in Littré), f. *pesant*: see prec.] Heaviness, weight.

1480 CAXTON *Ovid's Met.* XIV. xii, For the weighte & pesanteur of the fruyt. **1689** G. HARVEY *Curing Dis. by Expect.* viii. 61 The pesanture of a Stone of compass.

Pesaro (pɛ'sɑːrəʊ). The name of a city in northern Italy, used *attrib.* to designate majolica made there in the fifteenth and sixteenth centuries, and the potters who made it.

1856 O. JONES *Gram. Ornament* xvii. 12 *Renaissance ornament.* As early as 1486 the Pesaro ware was considered so superior to all other Italian ware, that a protection was granted to it by the lord of Pesaro. **1885** [see GUBBIO]. **1960** R. G. HAGGAR *Conc. Encycl. Cont. Pott. & Porc.* 345/1 A Pesaro potter, Jacomo de Pesaro, was working in Venice in 1542.

pesaunt, var. PEISANT *Obs.*; obs. f. PEASANT.

pesayne, obs. variant of PISANE.

pescod, -code, -codde, obs. ff. PEASECOD.

pese, obs. f. PEACE, PEASE, PIECE *sb.* and *v.*; var. PEISE, PECE *Obs.*

pesen, obs. var. PISANE; obs. pl. of PEASE.

pesent, obs. f. PEASANT.

peseta (pə'seɪtə, pə'seːtə, ‖pe'seta). [Sp., dim. of *pesa* weight; cf. *peso* Spanish dollar.] A modern Spanish silver coin, equivalent to the French franc and Italian lira; now (since Oct. 1868) the unit of value in Spain. It is divided into 100 centimos.

1811 P. KELLY *Cambist* II. 188 Silver Coins..Spain.. Mexican Peceta (1774) [Value in Sterling] 1*s.* 0¾*d.*.. Peceta Provincial of two Reals of new plate (1775)..0*s.* 10*d.* **1860** *All Year Round* No. 45. 445 The honest burgher who.. climbed up from penury to affluence by maravedis and pesetas at a time. **1882** BITHELL *Counting-ho. Dict.* (1893) 225 The peseta of Peru is also ⅕ of the silver sol, and equal to the French franc. **1893** T. B. FOREMAN *Trip to Spain* 55 We have each to pay a peseta (10*d.*) for a cup of coffee.

pesewa (pɛ'siːwə). [Fante *pesewa* penny.] A monetary unit of Ghana, equivalent to one hundredth of a cedi.

1965, **1970** [see CEDI]. **1976** M. BIRMINGHAM *Heat of Sun* iv. 52, I paid him the few pesewas he asked.

‖ **peshcush, -kash** ('peːʃkʌʃ). *E. Ind.* Forms: 7 **pish-, piscash**, 7–8 **pishcush**, 8 **peiscush**, 8– **peshcush**, 9 **paish-, pescush, peshkash, peshkesh.** [Pers. *pēshkash* first drawn, first fruits, tribute, f. *pēsh* before, in front + *kash* drawing.] An offering; a present; tribute, quit-rent, fine.

1634 SIR T. HERBERT *Trav.* 156 The Sultans and Chans bestow Pishcashes, or gifts one on another. **1753** HANWAY *Trav.* (1762) II. XIV. vii. 371 A peiscush, or present from an inferior to a superior. **1804** WELLINGTON in Gurw. *Disp.* (1844) II. 1159 The payment of the peshcush and the pensions due at Hyderabad. **1811** KIRKPATRICK *Tippoo's Lett.* 9 The Paishcush, or tribute, which he was bound..to pay to the Government of Poonah. **1844** H. H. WILSON *Brit. India* II. II. xi. 491 A peshkash, or tribute, of seven lakhs of rupees a year had hitherto been paid to the Nizam by the Company, for the northern Circars.

peshe, obs. form of PEACH.

‖ **Peshito** (pə'ʃiːtəʊ), **Peshitta** (pə'ʃiːtta), *a.* and *sb.* Also 8–9 **Peschito**, 9 **Peshitto**. [Syriac *p'shītâ*, *-tô*, *p'shīttâ*, *-tô*, 'the Simple' or 'Plain'.] The name given to the principal version of the Old and New Testaments in the ancient Syriac tongue, sometimes styled the Syriac Vulgate.

The two Syriac forms are respectively masc. and fem. of the adj. in the emphatic state, the latter agreeing with *mappaqtâ*, *-tô*, 'version'. (The final *â* and *ô* represent the same vowel in Eastern and Western Syriac pronunciation respectively.) So far as is known the name appears first in Moses Bar Kepha, 813–903. The date of the Peshito has been variously put; the prevalent opinion is that the translation of the O.T. was made from Hebrew at an early date, and that the Peshito N.T. was a revision or recension made early in the 5th c., of a translation going back, in part at least, to the 2nd c., earlier forms of which are preserved in the Sinaitic and Curetonian MSS. Later versions, more verbally rendering the Greek, were the Philoxenian and Heraclean.

1793 H. MARSH tr. *Michaelis' Introd. N.T.* II. i. 5 It is called by the Syrians Peshito, that is the literal. **1821** T. H. HORNE *Introd. Crit. Study Holy Script.* II. 192 The most celebrated of them is the Peschito or Literal (versio Simplex). **1842** *Penny Cycl.* XXIII. 477/2 The Peshito (*literal*) Version, also called 'The Old Syriac Version', is one of the most ancient and valuable translations of the Bible. **1903** F. C. BURKITT in *Encycl. Bibl.* 5001/1 To Rabbūla is due both the publication of the Peshitta and the suppression of the Diatessaron. *Ibid.* 5025/1 In the OT. the Syriac Vulgate, commonly called Pĕshiṭta, is a translation made direct from the Hebrew. **1904** *Athenæum* 22 Oct. 543/2 It seems to be certain that the Syriac Vulgate, known by the name of Peshitta, dates, so far as the New Testament is concerned, from the earlier part of the fifth century, and that Rabbula, Bishop of Edessa from 411 to 435, is mainly responsible for its redaction.

‖ **peshwa** ('peːʃwaː). Forms: 7 **peshua**, 8 **paish-**, 9 **peish-, peesh-, peshwa(h.** [Pers. *pēshwā* chief.] The appellation of the chief minister of the Mahratta princes (from *c* 1660), who made himself in 1749 the hereditary sovereign of the Mahratta state.

The princes descended from *Sevajī* became *rois fainéants*, the administration being in the hands of the peshwa; in 1749 the holder of the office, Balajī Bishenāth, seized the sovereignty and, without changing his official title, made it hereditary in his family. In 1818 his descendant Bajerow surrendered his power to the British, and the government of the Peshwa came to an end.

1698 FRYER *Acc. E. India & P.* 79 The English have audience of Sevaji. He referred our Business to Moro Pundit his Peshua, or Chancellour, to examine our Articles. **1782** *Ann. Reg.* 5 Assuming no other title or character than that of Paishwa, or prime minister. **1804** CASTLEREAGH in Owen *Wellesley's Desp.* 254 It appears hopeless to attempt to govern the Mahratta empire through a feeble and perhaps disaffected Peishwa. **1841** MACAULAY *Ess.*, *W. Hastings* (1887) 653 The Mahratta states..acknowledged, by words and ceremonies, the supremacy of the heir of Sevajee, a *roi fainéant*,..and of his Peshwa, or mayor of the palace, a great hereditary magistrate. **1862** BEVERIDGE *Hist. India* II. v. v. 399 The object of contest was the office of peshwa—in other words, the sovereign power.

Hence **'peshwaship**, the office or rule of a peshwa.

1782 *Ann. Reg.* 5 From this change, the empire of the Ram-Rajah has been distinguished only by the appellation of the Paishwaship, or otherwise the government of Poonah. **1883** *Encycl. Brit.* XV. 291 The first collision with the English..arose from a disputed succession to the pèshwaship.

† **peskan**. *Obs.* A French spelling of PEKAN.

1773 *Hist. Brit. Dom. in N. Amer.* 215 Other furs.. martins,..sables;..peskans, or wild cats;..and musk-rats.

peske, obs. form of PEACH.

pesky ('pɛskɪ), *a. colloq.* (orig. *U.S.*). [Origin uncertain. (It has been conjectured to be an alteration of **pesty*, f. *pest* = plague, which suits the sense exactly.)]

a. 'Plaguy', 'confounded'; annoying, disagreeable; hateful, abominable.

1775 S. DEANE in *Connecticut Hist. Soc. Coll.* (1870) II. 224 What reply, think ye, these heroes of five companies of the invincible Royal Irish, gave to this pesky Yankey? **1830** *Massachusetts Spy* 13 Oct. 4/1 I'm plagu'd most to death with these ere pesky sore eyes. *a* **1848** DOWNING *May-day New York* 36 (Bartlett), I found [looking for houses] a pesky sight worse job than I expected. **1859** W. P. TOMLINSON *Kansas in 1858*, 207 At Fort Scott the ruffians have..a large telescope,..to prevent themselves from being surprised by the pesky 'abolitionists'. **1860** HOTTEN *Dict. Slang* (ed. 2) 189 *Pesky*, an intensitive expression, implying annoyance. **1878** MRS. STOWE *Poganuc P.* xxiv. 214 'Taint nothin' but one o' these 'ere pesky spring colds she's got. **1885** G. ALLEN *Babylon* i, To cuff him about the head for his pesky idleness. [In *Eng. Dial. Dict.* from Oxf. and Bucks., etc., but app. only on the authority of late 19th c. novelists; not in any of the dialect glossaries.] **1901** M. FRANKLIN *My Brilliant Career* xiii. 113 He had always considered Harold as too sensible to neglect his business to stand grinning at a pesky youngster in short skirts and a pigtail. **1909** L. M. MONTGOMERY *Anne of Avonlea* xxvii. 318 Them pesky hens are in my pansy bed again. **1942** E. PAUL *Narrow St.* xxiii. 193 Sometimes I wish he would take over this pesky garden and let me manage the restaurant. **1956** D. KARP *All Honorable Men* 252 Just stay away from reporters. And if you can't—you have no comment. If they get real pesky, thell them to talk to me. **1959** I. & P. OPIE *Lore & Lang. Schoolch.* ix. 161 Juvenile repugnance continues to be expressed by the old standbys: ..pesky [etc.]. **1974** *Times* 23 Jan. 1/8 Dr Benjamin Spock ..says that an inability to be firm with their children is the commonest problem of parents in America today, and that it can lead to a child's personality becoming 'balkier and peskier' as the months and years go by. **1974** *Sunday Express* 30 June 6/4 The pesky thing didn't come anywhere near to working. **1977** *Time* 8 Aug. 39/2 But a pesky psychological climate is overhanging the securities markets.

b. as *adv.* = PESKILY; 'plaguy'.

1845 S. JUDD *Margaret* 305 (Bartlett) So pesky slow, we shan't get through to-night. **1855** HALIBURTON *Nat. & Hum. Nat.* II. ii. 64 Don't be so pesky starch. **1901** *Harper's Mag.* Dec. 228 Pesky few Democrats ever I see. **1939** L. M. MONTGOMERY *Anne of Ingleside* xxii. 153 O' course I don't believe in fairies.. I've heard they were pesky mischievous.

Hence **'peskily** *adv.*, 'plaguily', 'confoundedly'.

1834 C. A. DAVIS *Lett. J. Downing* 139 The Post Office accounts was the next bother; and that puzzled all on us peskily. **1835** HALIBURTON *Clockm.* (1862) 65 He looked so peskily vexed. **1855** —— *Nat. & Hum. Nat.* I. v. 153 When a feller is so peskilly sleepy as I be. **1877** *Atlantic Monthly* July 77/2 It does rile him peskily.

pesle mesle, obs. form of PELL-MELL.

‖ **peso** ('peso). Also 6 **peaso**, 7 **pezo**. [Sp. *peso* weight, a certain weight of precious metal, a coin of this weight:—L. *pensum*: see PEISE *sb.*] The name of a coin, either of gold (*peso de oro*) or silver (*peso de plata*), formerly current in Spain and its colonies; now, of a standard silver coin = (in 1905) 5 francs or 3*s.* 11½*d.*, used in most of the S. American republics. The Mexican silver peso (then = 5·43 francs, or 4*s.* 3½*d.*) is known as the *Mexican dollar*.

1555 EDEN *Decades* 87 Those pieces of golde which they caule Pesos or golden Castellans. *Ibid.* 145 The weyght of eight thousand Pesos. **1595** *Drake's Voy.* (Hakl. Soc.) 12 The whole..was yielded unto them for twenty-four thousand peasos, five shillings and sixpence a peece, to be payde in pearles. **1654** WHITLOCK *Zootomia* 399 They gave 1500. Pezos of Gold for a Horse. **1777** ROBERTSON *Hist. Amer.* I. Pref., In mentioning sums of money, I have uniformly followed the Spanish method of computing by pesos. **1850** PRESCOTT *Peru* II. iv. 86 On some days articles of the value of thirty or forty thousand *pesos de oro* were brought in, and occasionally of the value of fifty or even sixty thousand *pesos*. **1901** *Scotsman* 11 Sept. 5/8 Colombia's financial straits are extreme, and the paper peso is worth less than three cents in gold.

† **peson**. *Obs. rare.* [a. F. *peson*, a balance weight on a spindle, the balance knob on the end of a balance, a weighing instrument with fixed counterpoise and movable fulcrum; deriv. of OF. *peis*:—Rom. *pēso*, L. *pensum* weight.] A kind of weighing-machine: see quot. 1847, and cf. AUNCEL.

1459 *Paston Lett.* I. 474 In primis, a peson of gold, it fayleth v. balles, weiyng xxiij. unces gold. **1847–78** HALLIWELL, *Peson*, an instrument in the form of a staff, with balls or crockets, used for weighing before scales were employed.

peson, -e, obs. ff. *peasen*, pl. of PEASE.

pess. *Obs.* exc. *dial.* [Derivation obscure: cf. BASS *sb.*² 2, and PASSOCK.] A hassock or cushion to rest the feet on, or to kneel on, esp. in church.

1575 *Gamm. Gurton* I. iii, My gammer sat her downe on her pes, & bad me reach thy breches. **1623–4** in Willis & Clark *Cambridge* (1886) II. 96 Sixe pesses for the Chappell 0 1 4. **1633** AMES *Agst. Cerem.* II. 182 A pesse, hassok, or cushin may be called holy, because it is used to kneel upon. **1702–3** in Willis [as above] 211 Mats and pesses in the Chappel. *a* **1825** FORBY *Voc. E. Anglia*, *Pess*, a hassock to kneel on at church.

pess, obs. Sc. f. PACE *sb.*², PASCH; obs. f. PEASE, PIECE.

pessant, variant of PEISANT *Obs.*

pessary ('pɛsərɪ). [ad. med.L. *pessārium*, f. L. *pess-um*, *-us*, a. Gr. *πεσσός* (pl. *πεσσά*, as if from *πεσσόν*), an oval stone used in playing a game like draughts; hence, a medicated plug, as here.]

†**1.** *Med.* A medicated plug of wool, lint, etc., to be inserted in the neck of the womb, or other aperture of the body, for the cure of various ailments; a suppository. *Obs.*

c **1400** *Lanfranc's Cirurg.* 339 A medicyn..þat is putt in binepe wiþ a clisterie, ouþer wiþ a pessarie for to make clene a mannes lymes wiþinne. **1562** TURNER *Herbal* II. 25 b, The floures of the wilde grape..are good to put in pessaries to stanche blode. **1681** *Phil. Trans.* XII. 18, I thought I had sufficiently arm'd my Senses against it,..my Ears with Cotton, my Nose with Pessaries, my mouth with Sponges, all dipt in Vinegars and Treacles. **1718** QUINCY *Compl. Disp.* 113 It is..used outwardly in the Form of a Pessary. **1860** TANNER *Pregnancy* iii. 137 A very efficient medicated pessary.

2. *Surg.* An instrument of elastic or rigid material worn in the vagina to prevent or remedy various uterine displacements.

1754–64 SMELLIE *Midwif.* I. 418 Different kinds of pessaries..of a triangular, quadrangular, oval, or circular shape. **1805** *Med. Jrnl.* XIV. 98 A case of Prolapsus Uteri, in which the sponge pessary seems to have a decided and manifest superiority. **1846** BRITTAN tr. *Malgaigne's Man. Oper. Surg.* 556 Pessaries..some..are called *vaginal pessaries*; the others, called *uterine pessaries*. **1861** HULME tr. *Moquin-Tandon* II. III. ii. 81 The manufacture of artificial teats, pessaries, and other surgical instruments.

3. A contraceptive device which is placed in the vagina, now *esp.* a suppository.

1886 H. A. ALLBUTT *Wife's Handbk.* (ed. 2) vii. 48 Dr. Mensinga, of Flensburg, has invented a preventive pessary, to be worn by the woman, which..will,..properly adjusted, be a real preventive of conception. **1922** *Brit. Med. Jrnl.* 19 Aug. 327/2 In cases unable to maintain themselves or their children the woman should be temporarily sterilized by compulsion..—for example, by the insertion of the spring wish-bone pessary. **1935** H. B. WHITEHOUSE *Eden & Lockyer's Gynæcol.* (ed. 4) 211 Of mechanical devices to prevent conception three are in common use to-day, the male sheath or condom.., the female vaginal occlusive pessary.., and the cervical cap pessary. **1957** T. N. A. JEFFCOATE *Princ. Gynaecol.* xxxviii. 583 Some pessaries dissolve to form a 'foam' which creates a mechanical barrier between the spermatozoa and the cervix. **1973** B. LAW *Family Planning in Nursing* ii. 44 Pessaries, vagitories and foaming tablets are other forms in which spermicides are presented.

†**pesse.** *Med. Obs.* (?)

1464 *Mann. & Househ. Exp.* (Roxb.) 280 Put it in a fayre clothe and wrynge owt the watyr therof into a pesse, and put it to the sore yhe and it shall make it hole. **1562** TURNER *Herbal* II. 89 A stirryng stik may be made of them fit to prepare pesses and medicines to swage werines.

pessen(e, obs. form of *peasen*, pl. of PEASE.

pesshe, obs. form of PEACH.

pesshoner, variant of PESSONER *Obs.*

pessimism ('pɛsɪmɪz(ə)m). [mod. f. L. *pessim-us* worst + -ISM, after *optimism*: in F. *pessimisme*.]

†**1.** The worst condition or degree possible or conceivable; the state of greatest deterioration: antithetical to OPTIMISM 2. *Obs.*

1794 COLERIDGE *Lett.* (1895) 115 'T is almost as bad as Lovell's 'Farmhouse', and that would be at least a thousand fathoms deep in the dead sea of pessimism. **1803** SYD. SMITH *Wks.* (1850) 35 It is well to be acquainted with the boundaries of our nature on both sides; and to Mr. Fievée we are indebted for this valuable approach to pessimism. **1812** SOUTHEY *Lett.* (1856) II. 253 An age when public criticism is upon works of fine literature at the very point of pessimism.

2. The tendency or disposition to look at the worst aspect of things; the habit of taking the gloomiest view of circumstances: antithetical to OPTIMISM 3.

1815 *Q. Rev.* XIV. 230 This savours of pessimism. **1835** *Edin. Rev.* LX. 291 Violent extremes either way—optimism or pessimism..must be pernicious. **1889** *Times* 12 Apr. 5/1 There was a fear of the contagion of that moral evil which was visiting the end of the 19th century—namely pessimism.

3. The name given to the doctrine of Schopenhauer, Hartmann, and other earlier and later philosophers, that this world is the worst possible, or that everything naturally tends to evil: opp. to OPTIMISM 1. [= Ger. *pessimismus* (Schopenhauer 1819), F. *pessimisme* (Dict. Acad. 1878).]

1878 DOWDEN *Stud. Lit.* 20 The pessimism of our own day aspires to be constructive. **1878** R. J. LLOYD (*title*) Pessimism, a study in contemporary Sociology. **1880** GOLDW. SMITH in *Atlantic Monthly* No. 268. 195 The established optimism is confronted by pessimism, which, by the mouths of Schopenhauer, Hartmann, and their school, proclaims that the world, the estate of man, and the powers from which they emanate, are evil. *Ibid.* 196 Pessimism, which affirms the definitive ascendency of evil. **1892** W. S. LILLY *Gt. Enigma* 32 Pessimism, in..its contemporary presentation, is irreconcileable with any form of the Theistic idea.

pessimist ('pɛsɪmɪst), *sb.* (*a.*) [f. as prec. + -IST; cf. F. *pessimiste* (1835 in *Dict. Acad.*).]

A. *sb.* **a.** One who habitually takes the worst view of things; **b.** One who holds the metaphysical doctrine of pessimism. Antithetical to OPTIMIST.

1836 SMART, *Pessimist*, a complainer on all subjects, as opposed to an optimist. **1858** BAILEY *Age* 174 Holding God and man both pessimists. **1879** H. SPENCER *Data Ethics* iii. 27 The pessimist says that he condemns life because it results in more pain than pleasure. **1880** GOLDW. SMITH in *Atlantic Monthly* No. 268. 202 The writer of patriotic lyrics, however melancholy is their tone, can hardly have been a consistent pessimist.

B. *adj.* (the sb. used *attrib.*) Characterized by pessimism; pessimistic.

1861 *Times* 23 July, If the pessimist sentiments of hon. members who had spoken to-night [on the British Museum] were to be generally adopted. **1868** M. E. G. DUFF *Pol. Surv.* 9 [They] must have thought that I had taken a pessimist view of the situation. **1878** R. J. LLOYD *Pessimism* (1880) 9 At the hands of the Pessimist philosophy. **1884** *Manch. Exam.* 2 Sept. 5/2 The amusements of the people are often the theme of pessimist laments.

pessimistic (pɛsɪ'mɪstɪk), *a.* [f. prec. + -IC.] Pertaining to, of the nature of, or characterized by pessimism; disposed to take the worst view of circumstances.

1868 *Chronicle* 4 Jan. 5 The press itself was at first sceptical, oppositional, and pessimistic with regard to Baron Beust's system. **1880** GOLDW. SMITH with *Atlantic Monthly* No. 268. 202 Arthur Schopenhauer, the originator of the pessimistic philosophy as distinguished from mere pessimistic sentiment. **1889** *Times* 13 Dec. 5/4 The feeling here..is day by day becoming more pessimistic.

pessimistical (pɛsɪ'mɪstɪkəl), *a.* [f. as prec. + -ICAL.] = prec. Hence **pessi'mistically** *adv.*

1885 *American* X. 297 The pessimistical teaching of the English economists. **1888** *Spectator* 15 Sept. 1296/2 Dealing with what is the chief dread of Unionists pessimistically inclined. **1900** *Pall Mall G.* 27 Sept. 2/1 He..spoke pessimistically of our coast defences.

'pessimize, *v. rare.* [f. L. *pessim-us* worst + -IZE, after *pessimism*.] *trans.* To make the worst of; to take the most unfavourable view of.

1862 *Daily Tel.* 5 Sept., The rabid rage of a losing cause precipitating and pessimising its own loss. *a* **1873** *Sat. Rev.* cited by F. Hall in *Mod. Eng.* 194.

pessimum ('pɛsɪməm). [neut. sing. of L. *pessimus* worst.] The most unfavourable condition in the habitat of an animal or plant. Also *attrib.* and *transf.*

1931 R. N. CHAPMAN *Animal Ecol.* viii. 189 It is possible ..to conceive of survival potential as representing the actual position on the temperature scale where a species would experience its optimum and pessimum conditions. **1937** *Nature* 16 Oct. 663/2 The first part [of the Russian book under review] contains..a clear presentation of basic ecological principles, namely, factors of existence, ecological valency, optimum and pessimum, habitat concept, biological types (life-forms) and biocœnoses. **1947** N. BALCHIN *Lord, I was Afraid* 180 Assume that the radius of effectiveness..is 100 feet for a two-ton bomb—which is in many ways the pessimum hypothesis. **1976** *Nature* 19 Feb. 537/2 Above ~10 Ci s (4 rad to 1 kg) there is a '*pessimum*' number of particles.

†**'pessomancy.** *Obs.* [f. Gr. *πεσσός* oval pebble + -MANCY.] Divination by means of pebbles.

1727 in BAILEY vol. II, whence in mod. Dicts.

†**'pessoner.** *Obs.* Also 4 **pesshoner.** [app. repr. an AF. **pessoner*, *peiss-* = OF. *poissonnier* (13th c. in Littré), f. AF. *pessoun* (Britton) = OF. *peisson*, *poisson* = Pr. *peisso*, It. *pescione*:—pop.L. **pisciōn-em*, deriv. of *pisc-is* fish.] A fishmonger.

1310 (Jan. 13) in *Cal. Let. Bk. D Lond.* (1902) 45 [John Gerard de Leuesham] pesshoner [admitted]. **1415** in *York Myst.* Introd. 20 Pessoners [*glossed* Fysshmongers] and Mariners. Noe in Archa.

pessular ('pɛsjʊlə(r)), *a.* [f. L. *pessul-us* (see next) + -AR.] Pertaining to or having the character of the pessulus.

In mod. Dicts.

‖**pessulus** ('pɛsjʊləs). *Anat.* [L. *pessulus* a bolt.] **a.** A bolt-like bone: see quot. 1805. **b.** In some birds, the cartilaginous or bony bar extending vertically across the lower end of the windpipe, and forming part of the syrinx.

1805 A. CARLISLE in *Phil. Trans.* XCV. 204 The stapes in these animals [guinea-pig, marmot] is formed with slender crura, constituting a rounded arch, through which an osseous bolt passes, so as to rivet it to its situation. This bolt I have named *pessulus*. **1890** in *Cent. Dict.* [in sense b]. **1896** NEWTON *Dict. Birds* 983 Before the septum has been reduced to the pessulus marking the beginning of the bronchi.

†**pe'ssundate**, *v. Obs.* [ad. L. *pessundat-*, ppl. stem of *pessundare* (*pessum dare*) to ruin, destroy, f. *pessum* adv. to the ground, to the bottom + *dare* to give, put.] *trans.* To ruin, cast down, destroy. Hence †**pessun'dation** *Obs.*

1656 BLOUNT *Glossogr.*, *Pessundate*, to tread or cast under feet, to put down or to the worst. **1658** PHILLIPS, *Pessundation*,..a putting to the worst, a casting under foot.

pest (pɛst). [a. F. *peste* (R. Estienne 1539), ad. L. *pest-is* plague, pestilence, contagious disease.]

1. a. Any deadly epidemic disease; pestilence; *spec.* the bubonic plague: the common name of this in Sc. in the 16th–17th c. Now *rare.*

1568 SKEYNE *The Pest* A ij b, Ane pest is the corruption or infection of the Air. *a* **1572** KNOX *Hist. Ref.* Wks. 1846 I. 204 Moreover, within the Castell was the pest, (and diverse thairin dyed). *a* **1613** OVERBURY *Newes, Answ. Countrey Newes* Wks. (1856) 179 Living neere the church-yard, where many are buried of the pest. **1631** GOUGE *God's Arrows* I. §47. 83 In Latine *pestis* importeth as much, whence the Scots call this sicknesse the pest. **1637–50** ROW *Hist. Kirk* (Wodrow Soc.) 468 After he had been but one yeare in Mr John Russell's house the pest came to Edinburgh. **1715–20** POPE *Iliad* I. 192 Let fierce Achilles, dreadful in his rage, The god propitiate and the pest assuage. *a* **1839** PRAED *Poems* (1864) II. 108 There came a dark infectious pest To break the hamlet's tranquil rest.

b. In imprecation: ***pest on*** or ***upon*** = may a plague light upon. [= F. (*la*) *peste soit de..*, *peste de...*]

1553 *Respublica* v. ii. in Collier *Illustr. O.E. Lit.* I. 54 *Res.* Yea, bothe Mercie and Verytee. *Avar.* A peste on them bothe, saving my charitee. **1843** LYTTON *Last Bar.* IV. vi, 'Pest on these Burgundians', answered Clarence.

2. Any thing or person that is noxious, destructive, or troublesome; a bane, 'curse', 'plague': **a.** a thing.

1621 T. WILLIAMSON tr. *Goulart's Wise Vieillard* 64 Tortured with particular passions, and diuerse diseases, and pestes of the minde. **1632** LITHGOW *Trav.* VI. 260, I would ..haue eaten of them; but the Friers forbade me, saying; they were the onely pest of Death vnto a stranger. **1755** JOHNSON *Dict.* Pref. (*ad fin.*), The great pest of speech is frequency of translation. **1844** LD. BROUGHAM *Brit. Const.* xvii. (1862) 282 Putting down the pest of corruption.

b. a person or animal. (Now the more usual application.)

1609 JAMES I *Sp. at White-hall* Wks. (1616) 531 They that perswade them the contrary, are vipers, and pests, both against them and the Commonwealth. **1676** LISTER in *Ray's Corr.* (1848) 125 This sort of men being the bane and pest of learning. **1709** STEELE *Tatler* No. 135 ¶1 The Pests of Society, the Revilers of Humane Nature. **1852** MISS YONGE *Cameos* I. xl. 340 Philippe IV, the pest of France. **1865** LIVINGSTONE *Zambesi* vi. 152 To extirpate these destructive pests [cockroaches]. **1899** *Allbutt's Syst. Med.* VIII. 867 Mosquitoes, harvest bugs, and similar pests.

3. *attrib.* and *Comb.*, as ***pest-angel***, ***control***, ***place***, ***spot***, ***-worm***; ***pest-free*** adj.; †**pest-cart**, the cart to carry away the bodies of the dead during a plague or pestilence; †**pest-coach**, a vehicle used to convey the infected to the PEST-HOUSE; †**pest-man**, †**pest-master**, one in charge of the infected, or of the arrangements for getting rid of the plague; **pest officer**, one who is responsible for the control or extermination of animal pests; **pest-ship**, †(*a*) a ship for the reception of those suffering from the pest; (*b*) a ship having any infectious disease on board.

1613 PURCHAS *Pilgrimage* (1614) 216 In a generall pestilence they write..strange characters and wonderfull names, which (they say) are the names of *Pest-angels. **1603** DEKKER *Wonderful Year* Wks. (Grosart) I. 111 After the world had once run vpon the wheeles of the *Pest-cart. **1841** W. H. AINSWORTH *Old St. Paul's* II. 68 The doleful bell announcing the approach of the pest-cart. **1665** PEPYS *Diary* 3 Aug., They got one of the *pest-coaches, and put her into it, to carry her to a pest-house. **1931** J. S. HUXLEY *What dare I Think?* i. 30 Dr Tillyard, now in charge of *pest control. **1947** *Nature* 4 Jan. 32/1 The use of a highly refined petroleum oil for application to orchard trees..is firmly established as a valuable pest-control treatment with citrus. **1978** A. HUXLEY *Illustr. Hist. Gardening* v. 179 Pest control by chemicals is often called warfare. **1944** J. S. HUXLEY *On Living in Revolution* x. 111 Once more the goal is in sight.., the goal of *pest-free stores and stored materials. **1950** *Mind* LIX. 161 An apple..of pleasing taste, high vitamin content and pest-free. **1613** T. GODWIN *Rom. Antiq.* (1625) 181 Three *Pest-men, which were to oversee those that lay infected with any contagious sickenesse. **1642** *Fore-runner Revenge* in *Select. Harl. Misc.* (1793) 275 He hath conferred with the skilfullest *pest-masters..who visit the bodies of those that die of the venom of the pest. **1963** *Times* 9 Mar. 12/4 The hunting of deer was likely to be a more economic and efficient way of controlling them if the hounds were followed only by a small number of qualified foresters or *pest officers. **1976** A. PRICE *War Game* I. vi. 115 He was.. a cross between a high class refuse collector and the municipal pest officer. **1665** EVELYN *Diary* 7 Sept., A *pest-ship, to wait on our infected men. **1895** *Edin. Rev.* Apr. 263 The horrors of the holds of the pest-ship. **1872** BAKER *Nile Tribut.* viii. 110, I believe in holy shrines as the *pest spots of the world. **1848** ELIZA COOK *My Own* xiv, Do we not see the *pest-worm steal The rose of Beauty to destroy?

pesta ('pɛstə). [Malay, f. Pg. *festa* feast.] In Malaysia, a festive gathering, a festival.

1964 K. G. TREGONNING *Hist. Mod. Malaya* xiv. 298 The dominant Malay element..was gathered together in a highly successful three day *Pesta* or Festival. **1972** S. BACKHOUSE *Singapore* iv. 95 In 1966 the first *Pesta Sukan*, the festival of sport took place, and now accompanies the National Day celebrations held in August. *Ibid.* 96 The *Pesta Sukan* holds two chess tournaments. **1972** *Malay Mail* (Kuala Lumpur) 27 May 2/5 The pesta will have 50 games stalls run by the various societies in the university. **1972** M. SHEPPARD *Taman Indera* 93 The Cultural Festival, or 'Pesta', organized in Kuala Lumpur in 1956.., gave a fresh stimulus to older dance forms.

Pestalozzi (pɛstəˈlɒtsɪ). The name of Jean Henri *Pestalozzi* (see PESTALOZZIAN *a.*) used *attrib.* in ***Pestalozzi (children's) village*** to designate any of several communities of refugee and homeless children established on Pestalozzian principles in Switzerland and elsewhere in Europe after the war of 1939–45.

1947 *Internat. Child Welfare Rev.* I. 253 Pro Juventute.. on two occasions made collections in favour of the Pestalozzi Village. **1949** D. MACARDLE *Children of Europe* xv. 219 The most lasting of Swiss projects for child victims of the war was initiated in 1946 and opened in October in Trogen... The Pestalozzi Children's Village is a great experiment in education for peace. **1950** T. BROSSE *Homeless Children* i. 5 In Switzerland,..in the Canton of Appenzell, a Children's Village was built in 1946, on the initiative of Walter Robert Corti. *Ibid.* ii. 16 The Pestalozzi School-Town was founded in January 1945 [in Florence]. **1969** *Guardian* 8 Mar. 5/3 The 20 Tibetan children from the Pestalozzi village in Sussex came to dance in traditional style. **1974** *Radio Times* 14 Mar. 25/4 *Down Your Way.* Brian Johnston recently visited Pestalozzi Children's Village, Sedlescombe, Sussex.

Pestalozzian (pɛstəˈlɒtsɪən), *a.* (*sb.*) [f. surname *Pestalozzi* + -AN.] Of or pertaining to the system of elementary education introduced by Jean Henri Pestalozzi (1746–1827), a Swiss educational reformer, who held the chief end of education to be the development of the faculties in natural order, the perceptive powers being the first to be developed. For this he made much use of object-lessons.

1826 C. MAYO *Mem. Pestalozzi* (1828) 22 Elementary education..on the Pestalozzian system..is an organic development of the human faculties, moral, intellectual, and physical. **1847** EMERSON *Repr. Men, Uses Gt. Men* Wks. (Bohn) I. 286 Is it a reply..to say society is a Pestalozzian school: all are teachers and pupils in turn? **1859** *Encycl. Brit.* (ed. 8) XVII. 479/1 The Pestalozzian arithmetic was introduced at a very early period, into the Dublin model schools.

B. *sb.* An adherent of the system of Pestalozzi.

1868 R. H. QUICK *Ess.* vii. 178 The scandals which arose out of the dissensions of the Pestalozzians.

Hence **Pestaˈlozzianism**, the system of education instituted by Pestalozzi.

1859 H. BARNARD (*title*) Pestalozzi and Pestalozzianism.

peste (pɛst), *v.* [a. F. *pester* to utter the imprecation of *peste de*, f. *peste* PEST, as an imprecation.] *trans.* To invoke a plague or mischief upon; *intr.* to give vent to angry imprecations; to exclaim *pest!* Now *rare* exc. as a curse or exclamation of annoyance (*arch.*).

1768 STERNE *Sentimental Journey* I. 143 La Fleur..began to search for the letter..*Diable!*—then sought every pocket ..not forgetting his fob—*Peste!*—then La Fleur emptied them upon the floor. **1815** SOUTHEY *Lett.* (1856) III. 9 So instead of pesting the ode (that French word is better than either our synonyme in c or in d), I set about it. **1824** in *Spirit Pub. Jrnls.* (1825) 280 In vain we clamour, curse, and peste, Our viands are like all the rest. **1835** W. IRVING *Tour Prairies* 24 In spite of all the pesteing and bedevilling of Tonish. **1858** THACKERAY *Virginians* I. ii. 15 Peste! I don't know why my father gave up such a property. **1896** G. A. HENTY *Through Russian Snows* x. 193 *Peste!* these Russians are obstinate brigands. **1898** S. WEYMAN *Shrewsbury* xlv. 393 '*Peste!*' he said, taking snuff with a droll expression of chagrin. 'Will anyone else ask a question.' **1932** G. HEYER *Devil's Cub* xv. 240 'But I do not know!' cried madame... 'Oh, *peste!*' said Léonie impatiently.

pestelet, variant of PISTOLET *Obs.*

pester (ˈpɛstə(r)), *v.*[1] Also 6–7 pestre, pesture. [app. short for EMPESTER, IMPESTER, or F. *empestrer*, with which it is synonymous in its first sense; used by Cotgrave to translate *empestrer*. In later use influenced by PEST; hence the sense 'plague'.

But several points in the history are obscure: *pester* itself is found much earlier than *empester* or *impester*; and the prefix *em-* was generally dropped through an intermediate *a-*, as in *em-, impair, apair*, PAIR *v.*[2], *em-, impeach, apeach*, PEACH *v.*; but no parallel series appears for *pester*.]

†**1.** *trans.* To clog, entangle, embarrass, obstruct the movements of; to encumber as by overloading or the like. *lit.* and *fig.* *Obs.*

*c*1536 SIR J. RUSSELL *Let. to Visct. Lisle* 29 Aug. in *L. Papers* VII. 36 (P.R.O.) You are daily pestered with business. **1542** UDALL *Erasm. Apoph.* 159 That we maye not with to many thynges pestre & cloye the reader. **1577–87** HOLINSHED *Chron.* I. 25/1 The Romane soldiers were.. pestered with their heavie armour and weapons. **1608** CAPT. SMITH *True Relation* 28 The Indians seeing me pestred in the O[o]se, called to me. **1611** COTGR., *Empestrer*, to pester, intricate, intangle, trouble, incomber. **1653** HOLCROFT *Procopius, Persian Wars* I. 29 Seing him pestred in a narrow passage. **1676** HOBBES *Iliad* XVI. 328 Cleobulus then pester'd in the throng By little Ajax taken was alive.

†**2.** To obstruct or encumber (a place) by crowding; to crowd to excess, overcrowd. *Obs.*

*a*1548 HALL *Chron., Hen. VI* 103 b, Whether also fled so many Englishemen, that the place was pestured, and..thei wer..likely to be famished. **1572** *Act 14 Eliz.* c. 5 The common gaoles..are like to bee greatly pestered with a more number of prisoners than heretofore hath beene. **1573** TUSSER *Husb.* (1878) 106 Some pester the commons, with iades and with geese. **1588** LAMBARDE *Eiren.* IV. xiii. 544 It is not my meaning to pester this Booke with Precedents. **1625** SIR J. GLANVILLE *Voy. Cadiz* (Camden) 10 That noe parte of the Harbor might bee over pestred. **1719** DE FOE *Crusoe* II. ix, I shall not pester my Account..with Descriptions of Places. **1748** *Anson's Voy.* II. x. 246 Her hands..are as few as is consistent with the safety of the ship, that she may be less pestered with the stowage of provisions.

†**3.** To crowd or huddle (persons or things *in* or *into*). *Obs.*

1579 GOSSON *Sch. Abuse* (Arb.) 22 They..whom Anthony admitted were expelled agayn, pestred in gallies and sent into Hellespont by Marcus Aurelius. **1634** MILTON *Comus* 6 Men..Confin'd, and pester'd in this pin-fold here. **1686** tr. *Chardin's Coronat. Solyman* 154 With several great Trees pester'd one within another.

b. *intr.* for *refl.* To crowd, press. *Obs.*

1610 E. SKORY *Extr. Hist. Hen. IV of France* 15 This villaine..to that purpose pestered somewhat neere his Person.

4. To annoy, trouble, plague. **a.** Of noxious things, vermin, wild beasts, etc.: To infest. Now merged in b.

1562 *Burn. Paules Ch.*, Howe was this Realme pesterd with straunge rulers, straunge Gods..and howe is it now peaceablye ridde of theym all. **1625** A. HATCH in Purchas *Pilgrims* X. iii. 1701 The climate is..not much pestred with infectious or obnoxious ayres. **1664** POWER *Exp. Philos.* I. 20 These Vermin that pester the outside of Animals. **1727** A. HAMILTON *New Acc. E. Ind.* II. xxxiii. 4 There are no Inhabitants on those Islands, for they are so pestered with Tigers. **1796** MORSE *Amer. Geog.* II. 559 [Malabar] is rich and fertile, but pestered with green adders.

b. To trouble with petty and reiterated vexations, as with questions or requests; to vex, annoy, trouble persistently, plague. (The current sense.)

1586 A. DAY *Eng. Secretary* I. (1625) 63 You are pestered with some troubles. **1592** WYRLEY *Armorie, Ld. Chandos* 82 He was perplext and pesterd in his hed. **1600** C'TESS ESSEX in Ellis *Orig. Lett.* Ser. I. III. 57, I..had never ceased to pester you with my complaints. **1683** MOXON *Mech. Exerc., Printing* xvii. ¶3 The hollow..pesters the Workman to get the Letter out of the Mold and Matrice. **1795** JEFFERSON *Writ.* IV. 124, I pestered him with questions. **1825** COBBETT *Rur. Rides* 179 You are pestered to death to find out the way to..get from place to place. **1849** C. BRONTE *Shirley* ii, These gossips..will keep pestering me about being married. **1877** A. B. EDWARDS *Up Nile* xiii. 349 The boys pester us to buy wretched half-dead chameleons.

Hence **ˈpestered** *ppl. a.*

1570 FOWLER *Let. to Cecil* 25 Feb. in *Cal. St. Papers, For.* 192 The air is so evil in this pestered prison that [etc.]. **1586** FERNE *Blaz. Gentrie* 71 In the city amongst the pestered habitations of artificers. **1605** SHAKS. *Macb.* v. ii. 23 Who then shall blame His pester'd Senses to recoyle, and start? **1712** W. ROGERS *Voy.* 8 Very much crouded and pester'd ships.

pester (ˈpɛstə(r)), *v.*[2] [ad. Romany *pessa* to pay.] To pay. So **ˈpestering** *vbl. sb.*

1936 J. CURTIS *Gilt Kid* v. 53 She had to pester up herself out of the pound you give her. *Ibid.* viii. 88 Tell him to go out and get me a new shirt... Tell him to pester about seven and six for it. *Ibid.* xi. 116 'It's his flat. He pays the rent.' 'Sure. I know he does the pestering.'

pester (ˈpɛstə(r)), *sb.* Also 7 pesture. [f. PESTER *v.*[1]]

†**1.** Obstruction; encumbrance. *Obs.*

1585 J. JANES *Voy. J. Davies* in *Hakluyt's Voy.* III. 102 A very faire entrance or passage,..altogether void of any pester of ice. **1614** RALEIGH *Hist. World* v. ii. §8 (1634) 604 Being without carriage, pester or other impediment.

2. Annoyance, trouble, bother; nuisance, plague.

1613–18 DANIEL *Coll. Hist. Eng.* 98 To the great pesture and disturbance of that people. **1873** HOLLAND *A. Bonnic.* xii. 205 As likely as any way he was a plague and a pester.

†ˈ**pesterable**, *a.* *Obs.* Also 7 pestar-, -turable. [f. PESTER *v.*[1] + -ABLE.] Of such a nature as to obstruct or cumber; obstructing, cumbersome; troublesome. ***pesterable wares***: see quots.

1540 *Act 32 Hen. VIII*, c. 14 For the freight of euery tunne marchandises..(pesterable wares only excepted). **1560** in *Hakluyt's Voy.* (1599) I. 306 It must goe either shaken and bounde vp or else emptie, which will bee pesterable. **1622** MALYNES *Anc. Law-Merch.* 141 Pesterable wares which take a great deale of roome are excepted, and must be agreed for. [**1867** SMYTH *Sailor's Word-bk.*, *Pessurable*, or *Pestarable*, of our old statutes, implied such merchandise as take up much room in a ship.]

†ˈ**pesterance.** *Obs. rare.* In 6 pestreaunce. [f. PESTER *v.*[1] + -ANCE.] **a.** Pestering, obstruction, overcrowding. **b.** Encumbrance.

1548 UDALL *Erasm. Par. Luke* v. 52 b, That a man while he teacheth the ghospell, maie stande quiete and safe from pestreaunce of the people, cloustreyng and throngyng together. *Ibid.* xvii. 134 b, Castyng awaie from hym al pestreaunce and heauie carriage.

pesteˈration. *nonce-wd.* [f. PESTER *v.*[1] + -ATION.] The action of pestering; that which pesters or troubles; 'botheration'.

1802 A. WILSON in *Poems & Lit. Prose* (1876) I. 92 To banish every pedantic pesteration.

pesterer (ˈpɛstərə(r)). [f. PESTER *v.*[1] + -ER[1].] One who pesters: see the verb.

1611 COTGR., *Embarasseur*, an intricator, pesterer, comberer. **1733** MILLNER *Compend. Jrnl.* 182 To keep that Side of the Country clear of Pesterers. *c*1817 HOGG *Tales & Sk.* V. 22 Of all pesterers..he was the most insufferable. **1893** F. ADAMS *New Egypt* 20 He has seriously damaged his ..walking-stick on the fore-arm of some street-pesterer.

ˈ**pestering,** *vbl. sb.* [f. PESTER *v.*[1] + -ING[1].] The action of the verb PESTER, in various senses.

1552 *Reg. Privy Council* in *Sussex Archæol. Collect.* X. 199 Without sume hinderaunce to the cuntrie, and pestering of the trayne. *c*1595 CAPT. WYATT *R. Dudley's Voy. W. Ind.* (Hakl. Soc.) 59 Makinge the decks..cleare of anie pesteringe or impediments. **1598** MANWOOD *Lawes Forest* x. (1615) 73 For that the pestring of the Forest with many houses, are noysome to the Forest. **1832** MARRYAT *N. Forster* xxviii, Clacking of pattens and pestering of sweepers.

ˈ**pestering,** *ppl. a.* [f. as prec. + -ING[2].] That pesters, in various senses of the verb.

1606 BIRNIE *Kirk-Buriall* B iv b, Our Kirk-courtes or yardes..being ordinarly bedunged by pestring and pasturing brute. **1641** MILTON *Animadv.* 51 All the hell pestering rabble of Sumners and Apparitors. **1716** [see PESTIFY]. **1868** MRS. WHITNEY *P. Strong* xi. (1869) 125 Her raw girl and her pestering stove.

Hence ˈ**pesteringly** *adv.*, in a pestering way.

1805 W. TAYLOR in Robberds *Mem.* II. 93 How pesteringly I can scribble when there is business to agitate. **1875** TENNYSON *Q. Mary* v. i, Unalterably and pesteringly fond!

pesterment (ˈpɛstəmənt). *Obs.* exc. *dial.* [f. PESTER *v.*[1] + -MENT.] The action of pestering or fact of being pestered, in various senses of the verb: †overcrowding (*obs.*); annoyance, worry.

1593 *Pass. Morrice* (1876) 51 An armie might have lodged therein without pesterment. **1652** J. WRIGHT tr. *Camus' Nat. Paradox* vi. 124 How joyfull were they to see themselves rid of the pesterment of their Companions. **1729** FRANKLIN *Ess.* Wks. 1840 II. 26, I have all the trouble and pesterment of children, without the pleasure of calling them my own. **1828** *Craven Gloss.*, *Pesterment*, embarrassment.

pesterous (ˈpɛstərəs), *a. rare.* Also 6 pestreous. [f. PESTER *v.*[1] or *sb.* + -OUS.] Having the quality of pestering; cumbersome; troublesome.

1548 UDALL *Erasm. Par. Luke* v. 52 b, Remoued from the pestreous throngyng of the multitude. **1578** T. N. tr. *Conq. W. India* (1596) 197 Pesterous wares..that is to say stone, timber, lime, bricke [etc.]. **1622** BACON *Hen. VII* 216 Gaoling of them,..which was chargeable, pesterous and of no open example. **1825** HOGG *Q. Hynde* 47 When petulant and pesterous Wene Kneel'd on the Sand.

pestersome (ˈpɛstəsəm), *a.* [f. PESTER *v.*[1], *sb.* + -SOME[1].] Annoying, troublesome.

1843 *Amer. Pioneer* II. 439 All innocent enquiries, by infants and children..should be indulged and encouraged, how pestersome soever they may seem. **1906** *Dialect Notes* III. 150 *Pestersome*, bothersome, annoying.

†ˈ**pestful,** *a.* *Obs.* [f. PEST + -FUL.] Pestiferous, pestilential.

1608 SYLVESTER *Du Bartas* II. iv. IV. *Schisme* 417 The Lybians pest-full and un-blest-full shore. **1794** COLERIDGE *Destiny of Nations*, Long and pestful calms, With slimy shapes, and miscreated life Poisoning the vast Pacific.

ˈ**pest-house.** [f. PEST + HOUSE *sb.*] A hospital for persons suffering from any infectious disease, esp. the plague; a lazaretto. Also *attrib.*

1611 in *Vicary's Anat.* (1888) App. iii. 166 Helpinge such persons as come to the Pesthowse. **1617** MORYSON *Itin.* I. 73 They have a Pest house called *Lazaretto*, and two like houses for Lepers. **1665** PEPYS *Diary* (1879) III. 199. **1722** DE FOE *Plague* (1840) 37 Some people being removed to the pest-house beyond Bunhill fields. **1830** MISS MITFORD *Village* Ser. IV. (1863) 265 He..shunned ball-rooms and drawing-rooms as if they were pest-houses. **1890** *Times* 20 Jan. 9/2 [The prisons] were pesthouses in which gaol-fever annually claimed a multitude of victims.

fig. *a*1613 OVERBURY *Charac., Prison* Wks. (1856) 155 It is an infected pest-house all the yeare long: the plague-sores of the law, are the diseases here wholely reigning. **1833** CARLYLE *Misc. Ess., Cagliostro* (1840) IV. 352 A painful search, as through some spiritual pest-house. **1840** DICKENS *Barn. Rudge* lxv, In all the crime..of the great pest-house of the capital, he stood alone.

pesticide (ˈpɛstɪsaɪd). [f. PEST + -I- + -CIDE I.] A substance for destroying pests, esp. insects.

1939 *70th Ann. Rep. Entomol. Soc. Ontario* 16 A special committee..known as the Pesticide Supply Committee is being set up. **1943** *Farm Jrnl. & Farmer's Wife* Sept. 71/1 A new word, 'pesticide', has crept into garden literature this year. **1947** *Times* 9 May 10/1 The demand for 'Gammexane', a pesticide which we discovered, has grown rapidly. **1955** *Sci. News Let.* 24 Sept. 197/3 A pesticide that kills injurious plant mites, but leaves beneficial honeybees and other insects alive has been developed. **1958** *Manch. Guardian* 13 Sept. 2/5 Chemical weed-killers should generally be regarded only as elements in a management programme, not as specific pesticides to to be used when weeds became a nuisance. **1964** *Daily Tel.* 3 Jan. 19/2 Pesticide residues in the fat of birds, animals and human beings were absorbed into the body and gradually built up in the body fat. **1969** *Times* 8 May 12/7 The chief threat to birds of prey is the use of pesticides. **1971** *Power Farming* Mar. 5/1 Shell, like most other companies in this field, recognize that the indiscriminate use of pesticides is highly undesirable. **1978** *Dædalus* Spring 43 The development of a specific sweetener, pesticide, or weapon could be prevented with little generalized effect.

Hence **pestiˈcidal** *a.*

1950 in WEBSTER Add. **1956** *Nature* 25 Feb. 350/1 The United States Department of Agriculture has a list of thirty thousand pesticidal formulations. **1971** *Ibid.* 3 Sept. 72/1 The properties, functions, utility and contributions of pesticidal chemicals to human welfare.

†**'pestiduct.** *Obs.* [f. L. *pesti-s* plague + *duct-us* DUCT *sb.*] A channel of the plague, or of any infectious epidemic.

1624 DONNE *Devotions*, etc. (ed. 2) 89 They may be made instruments, and pestiducts, to the infection of others, by their comming. **1672** W. DE BRITAINE *Interest Eng. Dutch War* 11 They begin to be look'd upon as the Pesti-ducts of Europe, the scorn and indignation of every good man.

†**pestifere,** *a. Obs. rare.* [a. F. *pestifère.*] = PESTIFEROUS.

1490 CAXTON *Eneydos* xxvii. 95 Yf her moeuyng [*i.e.* of the course celestial] were irryted ayenste vs by pestyfere influences.

pestiferous (pɛˈstɪfərəs), *a.* [f. L. *pestifer, -fer-us* plague-bringing, f. *pesti-s* plague + *-fer*, stem of *fer-re* to bear, bring: see -FEROUS. In F. *pestifère*. In sense 3, f. F. *pestiféré*.]

I. 1. Bringing or producing pest or plague; destructive to health; noxious, deadly; of the nature of a pest, pestilent, pestilential.

1542 BOORDE *Dyetary* xxvii. (1870) 289 An ordre to be vsed in the Pestyferous tyme. **1551** ROBINSON tr. *More's Utop.* I. (1895) 55 Sendynge amonge the shepe that pestiferous morreyn. **1601** HOLLAND *Pliny* I. 183 Vexed at certain houres..with the pestiferous heats and shaking colds of the feuer. **1632** LITHGOW *Trav.* VI. 256 [No] Trees, or Bushes, grow neere to Sodome..such is the consumation of that pestiferous Gulfe. **1726** LEONI *Alberti's Archit.* I. 3/1 We affirm the Air to be pestiferous, where there is a continued Collection of thick Clouds and stinking Vapours. **1830** MISS MITFORD *Village* Ser. IV. (1863) 229 Having lost many children in the pestiferous climate of Barbadoes. **1830** HERSCHEL *Stud. Nat. Phil.* I. iii. 56 Regions almost desolated by pestiferous exhalations.

b. Of animals: Hurtful; noxious.

c **1600** *Timon* III. iii, These women are a pestiferous kinde of animals. **1731** *Gentl. Mag.* I. 12 The depredations of Locusts, Palmer-worms, and other pestiferous vermin. **1894** *Chicago Advance* 27 Dec. 438/1 As pestiferous a creature as could be allowed to roam at large.

2. *fig.* Bearing moral contagion; hurtful to morals or society; mischievous; pernicious.

1458 in *Pecock's Repr.* (Rolls) I. Introd. 55 *note*, The damnable doctrine and pestiferous sect of Reynold Pecock exceedeth in malice and horribility all other heresies and sects of heretics. **1523** *St. Papers Hen. VIII*, VI. 124 Moche bounde to Allmyghty God, that the Popes Holynes is rid of so pestiferous a Counsailour. **1630** *R. Johnson's Kingd. & Commw.* 111 Done by the perswasions of the pestiferous Jesuites. *a* **1715** BURNET *Own Time* (1766) I. 2 One of the most pestiferous forms of calumny. **1824** *Hist. Gaming* 16 Those pestiferous hordes of gamblers, black-legs, and sharpers. **1885** *Manch. Exam.* 18 July 5/3 They are said to pursue their pestiferous occupation unchecked.

II. 3. [= F. *pestiféré*.] Plague-stricken; smitten with a contagious disease.

1665 EVELYN *Diary* 11 Oct., I was environ'd with multitudes of poore pestiferous creatures begging almes. **1858** FABER tr. *Life Xavier* 369 A malady contracted in attending on the pestiferous.

Hence **pe'stiferously** *adv.*, pestilentially, noxiously, 'plaguy'; **pe'stiferousness**.

1727 BAILEY vol. II, *Pestiferousness*. **1847** WEBSTER, *Pestiferously*. **1863** GEO. ELIOT *Romola* xlv, Melema, you are a pestiferously clever fellow.

†**pe'stifugous,** *a. Obs. rare.* [f. L. *pesti-s* plague + *-fug-*, stem of *fugĕre* to flee, *fugāre* to put to flight + -OUS.] Having the property of driving away or dispelling the plague.

1684 tr. *Bonet's Merc. Compit.* VI. 215 The business may be done by Pestifugous Alexitericks.

†**'pestify,** *v. Obs.* [f. L. *pesti-s* plague + -FY.] To cause or produce a pest. Hence †**'pestifying** *ppl. a.*, plague-bringing.

1716 M. DAVIES *Athen. Brit.* III. *Arianism* 30 Scatter them about with his wonted pestifying and pestring Air of Assurance.

pestilence ('pɛstɪləns), *sb.* (*adv.*) Also 4–6 **pestilens, -elence,** 5 **pestlens,** 5–6 **pestylens, -ylence,** 6 **-elens,** 6–7 **pestlence.** [a. F. *pestilence*, ad. L. *pestilentia*, sb. of condition f. *pestilent-em* PESTILENT: see -ENCE.]

1. Any fatal epidemic disease, affecting man or beast, and destroying many victims.

1303 R. BRUNNE *Handl. Synne* 1370 Yn Rome fyl a grete moreyne..A pestelens of men. **1377** LANGL. *P. Pl.* B. xx. 97 Many kene sores, As pokkes and pestilences. *c* **1440** *Gesta Rom.* XXXVII.* 360 (Add. MS.) In the Citee of Rome befille a grete pestilence of men and bestes. **1538** STARKEY *England* I. iii. 83 Lyke as a pestylens..destroyth a grete nombur of the pepul wythout regard of any person had, or degre. **1539** BIBLE (Great) *Ps.* xc[i]. 6 The pestilence that walketh in darkness. **1548–9** (Mar.) *Bk. Com. Prayer, Litany*, From plage, pestilence, and famine,..Good lorde deliuer us. **1600** J. PORY tr. *Leo's Africa* VIII. 326 About an hundred yeeres ago, all the monks of this monasterie died of a pestilence. **1796** H. HUNTER tr. *St.-Pierre's Stud. Nat.* (1799) II. 485 Should a pestilence come, and sweep off one half of the people. **1845** BUDD *Dis. Liver* 394 In the winter of 1830–31 ..in some of the midland, eastern, and southern countries, where the pestilence was most rife, the existing race of sheep was almost entirely swept off. **1865** *Cornh. Mag.* May 591 To be entitled to the name of pestilence, a disease must be unusually fatal, very rapid in its operation, and must destroy great numbers of victims.

b. *spec.* The bubonic plague, the plague *par excellence*; = PEST 1.

[**1350–1** *Rolls of Parlt.* II. 225/2 Et puis en cea ad il este destourbe, primes per la dit Pestilence.] **1362** LANGL. *P. Pl.* A. x. 185 Mony peire seþþen þe pestilence han pliht hem togedere. **1466** in *Archæologia* (1887) L. 1. 50 Men and women and children ȝonge and olde of other parissches than ther owne infecte in pestilence the which sekenes euery man escheweth. **1556** *Chron. Gr. Friars* (Camden) 6 This yere was the iij. great pestelens. *Ibid.* 22 [Edw. IV] xvij°... Thys yere..was..the terme deferrd from Ester to Myhylmas be cause of the grete pestelens. **1564** BULLEYN *Dial. agst. Pest.* (1888) 8, I met with wagones..full laden with yong barnes, for fear of the blacke Pestilence. **1579** *Reg. Privy Council Scot.* III. 229 The infectioun and plague of the pistolence. **1706** PHILLIPS, *Pestilence* or *Plague*, a Disease arising from an Infection in the Air, accompany'd with Blotches, Boils, and..other dreadful Symptoms. **1823** MRS. MARKHAM *Hist. Eng.* xviii. (1853) 160 During the great pestilence he bought a piece of ground, which he gave for a burying-ground for those who died in London of that dreadful disease.

2. *fig.* That which is morally pestilent or pernicious; moral plague or mischief, evil conduct, wickedness; that which is fatal to the public peace or well-being. Now *rare*.

a **1340** HAMPOLE *Psalter* i. 1 In þe chaiere of pestilens he noght sate. *c* **1374** CHAUCER *Boeth.* IV. met. iii. 95 (Camb. MS.) Mercurie..hath vnbownded hym fro the pestelence of his oostesse [Circes]. **1406** HOCCLEVE *Misrule* 260 O flaterie! o lurkyng pestilence! **1577** NORTHBROOKE *Dicing* (1843) 97 Such players of enterludes..are so noysome a pestilence to infect a common wealth. **1604** SHAKS. *Oth.* II. iii. 362 Ile powre this pestilence into his eare. **1634** *Documents agst. Prynne* (Camden) 6 Clemens Alexandrinus, Tertullian, and Ste Chrisostome, call playe howses the state of pestilence. **1875** MANNING *Mission H. Ghost* ix. 258 The fashions of the day, the pestilence of bad literature.

†**3.** That which plagues, injures, or troubles in any way; a cause of trouble or injury; a plague.

c **1374** CHAUCER *Boeth.* I. pr. iv. 8 (Camb. MS.), For þat the gouernementus of Citees..ne sholde nat bryngen in pestelence and destruccion to goode fookk. **1456** SIR G. HAYE *Law Arms* (S.T.S.) 3 [To] put this travailland warld in pes and rest that now is put in grete pestilence. **1538** STARKEY *England* I. iv. 106 In no cuntrey may be any grettur pestylens..then cyuyle warre. **1555** EDEN *Decades* 274 [Norway] hath also a peculiar pestilence which they caule Leem or Lemmer..a lyttle foure footed beaste abowte the byggenesse of a ratte with a spotted skynne.

†**4.** As an imprecation: ***a pestilence on*** or ***upon*** ...*!* may a plague or mischief light upon ...! Cf. PEST 1 b, DEVIL 17, PLAGUE. ***the pestilence of*** (a penny), not a penny: cf. DEVIL 21, FIEND 2 b. ***with a pestilence***, with a vengeance, so as to plague or trouble, much more than one wishes. *Obs.*

c **1386** CHAUCER *Nun's Pr. T.* 590 A verray pestilence vp-on yow falle. **1568** NORTH *Gueuara's Diall Pr.* IV. viii. 129 The pestilens of penny he hath in his purse to blesse him with. **1594** NASHE *Unfort. Trav.* F ij, He interpreted to vs with a pestilence. **1594** GREENE & LODGE *Looking Glasse* G.'s Wks. (Rtldg.) 120/1 We..clap a plaster to him, with a pestilence, that mends him with a very vengeance. **1602** SHAKS. *Ham.* V. i. 196 A pestlence on him for a mad Rogue! **1612** CHAPMAN *Widow's Tears* II. D j b, Has giuen me a Bone to tire on with a pestilence.

5. *attrib.* and *Comb.*, as ***pestilence ill, planet, time; pestilence-bringer, -causer; pestilence-laden, -stricken*** adjs.; **pestilence-weed**, Dr. Prior's name for PESTILENCE-WORT.

1362 LANGL. *P. Pl.* A. XI. 59 To plese with þis proude men seþþe pestilence tyme. *c* **1475** *Pict. Voc.* in Wr.-Wülcker 801/30 *Hic saturnus*, a pestlens planyt. **1552** HULOET, Pestilence brynger or causer, *fatifer, pestifer*. **1819** SHELLEY *Ode West Wind* I. 5 Pestilence-stricken multitudes. **1899** *Month* Mar. 300 Striking across pestilence-laden swamps.

†**B.** as *adv.* 'Plaguy', 'pesky', 'tarnation'. *colloq.*

1614 B. JONSON *Barth. Fair* II. i, The Fair's pestilence dead methinks. **1633** —— *Tale of Tub* IV. ii, Diogenes. A mighty learned man, but pestilence poor.

†**'pestilence,** *v. Obs.* [f. prec.] *trans.* To make pestilent, infect with disease. Also *fig.*

1593 NASHE *Christ's T.* (1613) 151 From our redolentest refined compositions, ayre pestilenzing stinkes..shall issue. **1598** TOFTE *Alba* (1880) 96 Loue (pestilenzing) doth infect my Soule.

†**'pestilence-wort.** *Herb. Obs.* Also 7- **pestilent-wort.** [ad. Ger. *pestilenzwurz, pestwurz*, from its repute against the Plague.] A bookname for the Butterbur, *Petasites vulgaris*.

α. [**1548** TURNER *Names of Herbes* (E.D.S.) 61 Petasites is called in the South partes of Englande a Butter bur,..the duch cal it pestilentz kraute [**1562** —— *Herbal* II. 83 Pestilentz wurtz]. **1578** LYTE *Dodoens* I. xiii. 21 In Englishe Butter Burre: in high Douch *Pestilentz-wurtz*: in base Almaigne..*Pestilentie wortel*.] **1640** PARKINSON *Theat. Bot.* Table 1742 Pestilence wort is the Butter Burre. **1841** W. H. AINSWORTH *Old St. Paul's* I. 232 He likewise collected a number of herbs and simples, as Virginian snake weed, contrayerva, pestilence-wort, angelica, elicampane.

β. **1597** GERARDE *Herbal* Table Eng. Names, Pestilent woorts, that is water Burre Docke. **1617** MINSHEU *Ductor*, *Pestilent woorts*..i. herba pestilentialis: quia radix huius multum valet contra pestem. **1766** *Museum Rust.* VI. 450 Butter-bur or Pestilent-wort, resembles Colt's-foot in many respects; but the flowers are purple, and grow in a thyrse.

pestilent ('pɛstɪlənt), *a.* (*sb., adv.*) [ad. L. *pestilens, -ent-em*, a deriv. of participial form from *pestis* plague, or *pestilis* of the nature of a plague; also *pestilentus*: cf. *gracilentus, macilentus*.]

1. Destructive to life; fatal; deadly; poisonous.

1432–50 tr. *Higden* (Rolls) III. 293 Socrates..was compellede to eite an herbe pestilente in the name of goddes, and he was dedde anoone. **1564** GOLDING *Justine* XIX. (1570) 99 Hamilco..sodainly by the influence of a pestilent planet, lost all his men of warre. **1606** SHAKS. *Ant. & Cl.* III. xiii. 194 The next time I do fight Ile make death loue me: for I will contend Euen with his pestilent Sythe. **1784** COWPER *Task* III. 494 A pestilent and most corrosive steam. **1880** *Our Nat. Responsibility for Opium Trade* 14 The English merchant empoisons China with pestilent opium.

2. Producing or tending to produce infectious disease; infectious as a disease or epidemic; pestilential. Now *rare*.

1613 R. CAWDREY *Table Alph.*, *Pestilent*, contagious, hurtfull. **1615** MARKHAM *Eng. Housew.* II. i. (1668) 7 The Pestilent Feaver..a continual Sickness full of infection and mortality. **1667** MILTON *P.L.* x. 695 Vapour, and Mist, and Exhalation hot, Corrupt and Pestilent. **1685** TEMPLE *Ess. Gard.* Wks. 1731 I. 188 *The Lice of the Vine*. This is of all others the most pestilent Disease of the best Fruit-trees.

3. *fig.* Injurious or dangerous to religion, morals, or public peace; noxious; pernicious.

1513 MORE *Rich. III*, Wks. 39/1 Suche a pestilente serpente is ambicion and desyre of vaineglorye and soueraintye. **1526** TINDALE *Acts* xxiv. 5 We have founde this man a pestilent felowe. **1655** *Nicholas Papers* (Camden) II. 208 There is one Mowbray if possible more pestilent of his tongue then euer. **1758** JORTIN *Erasm.* I. 129 The works of Erasmus are reckoned amongst those pestilent books. **1823** SCOTT *Peveril* vii, 'The man, bating he is a pestilent Roundhead and Puritan, is no bad neighbour'. **1855** PRESCOTT *Philip II*, I. IV. i. 398 One [Corsair] distinguished ..for the pestilent activity with which he pursued the Spaniards.

4. That pesters or annoys; troublesome; plaguy. Often used ***humorously***.

1592 SHAKS. *Rom. & Jul.* IV. v. 147 What a pestilent knaue is this same. **1602** *2nd Pt. Return fr. Parnass.* IV. v, O that Ben Jonson is a pestilent fellow, he brought vp Horace giuing the Poets a pill. **1625** K. LONG tr. *Barclay's Argenis* III. ii. 187 That old Woman, that Hagge, of a most pestilent Wit. **1798** WOLCOTT (P. Pindar) *Tales of Hoy* Wks. 1812 IV. 409 All the servants agree that he is a pestilent man for a rhyme. **1806–7** J. BERESFORD *Miseries Hum. Life* (1826) I. Introd., I have some pestilent affairs upon my hands. **1873** T. W. HIGGINSON *Oldport Days* i. 18 Now and then a man comes here..with a pestilent desire to do something.

†**B.** *sb.* A pestilent thing or person; a pestilence; an injurious person. *Obs.*

1567 *Triall Treas.* (1850) 29 We have sene..this cancard pestilent Corrupting our realme to our great decaie, Ambition, I meane. **1583** BABINGTON *Commandm.* vi. (1637) 53 The translation..of the Hebrew word *Lezim*, mockers, into *pestilents*, pestilent fellows and hurtfull, for so they are indeed, even the plagues of a Common-weale.

†**C.** *adv.* Confoundedly; 'plaguy': = PESTILENTLY 2.

1567 *Triall Treas.* in Hazl. *Dodsley* III. 273 By the mass, but Hugh Howlit is pestilent witty. **1604** SHAKS. *Oth.* II. i. 251 A pestilent compleat knaue, and the woman hath found him already. **1641** SUCKLING *Ballad on Wedding* Wks. (1709) 30 Amongst the rest, one Pest'lent fine. *a* **1700** B. E. *Dict. Cant. Crew*, *Pestilent-fine*, Tearing-fine.

†**'pestilent,** *v. Obs. rare*$^{-1}$. [f. prec. adj.] *trans.* To infect fatally; to poison, corrupt.

1613 T. MILLES tr. *Mexia's Treas. Anc. & Mod. T.* I. 27/2 So hurtfull are the Serpents teeth, they pestilent the blood.

pestilential (pɛstɪˈlɛnʃəl), *a.* Also 5–6 **-cial.** [ad. med.L. *pestilentiāl-is*; also in F. *pestilentiel* (1549 in Hatz.-Darm.), It. †*pestilenziale, -tiale* (Florio), f. L. *pestilentia* PESTILENCE: see -AL[1].]

1. Producing or tending to produce pestilence or epidemic; noxious to life or health; pestiferous.

1398 TREVISA *Barth. De P.R.* XI. i. (Bodl. MS.), Nyȝnes of careyns and of mareis for bi corrupcion þereof aier is infecte and roted and ymade pestilencial. **1597** A. M. tr. *Guillemeau's Fr. Chirurg.* 18/1 The matter beinge venomous or pestilentialle. **1646** SIR T. BROWNE *Pseud. Ep.* III. vii. 119 Plagues or pestilentiall Atomes have beene conveyed in the ayre from different Regions. **1663** COWLEY *Garden* v, All th Uncleanness which does drown In Pestilential Clouds a populous Town. **1727** SWIFT *What passed in London* Wks. 1755 III I. 187 A pestilential malignancy in the air, occasioned by the comet. **1796** MORSE *Amer. Geog.* II. 417 The Campagna di Roma..is now almost pestilential. **1882** 'OUIDA' *Maremma* I. 174 In the sultry pestilential mists of a summer day in Maremma.

†**b.** Said of pernicious animals. *Obs.*

1697 DRYDEN *Virg. Georg.* III. 636 Snakes..of pestilential Kind To Sheep and Oxen, and the painful Hind.

2. Of the nature of or pertaining to pestilence or infectious and deadly disease; *spec.* of the nature of or pertaining to bubonic plague. †***pestilential fever***, old name of typhus fever (*Syd. Soc. Lex.*).

1530 PALSGR. 157 *Vne charboncle*, a carboncle, a sore pestylenciall. *a* **1548** HALL *Chron.*, *Hen. IV* 26 In this sommer, the Pestilenciall plage..infected the Citie of London and the countrei round about. **1612** WOODALL *Surg. Mate* Wks. (1653) 76 Antimonium..is good against pestilential fevers in their beginning. **1671** SALMON *Syn. Med.* III. xxii. 400 The Figs open the Lungs,..ripen Pestilential tumours. **1704** J. HARRIS *Lex. Techn.* I, *Pestilential Feever*..differs from the Plague, as a Species or sort from the Genus or Kind; because a *Pestilence* may sometimes happen without a *Feaver*. **1706** PHILLIPS, *Pestilential Bubo*, a Plague-sore, or Botch. **1781** GIBBON *Decl. & F.* lvi. (1869) III. 373 That camp was soon afflicted with a pestilential disease. **1789** W. BUCHAN *Dom. Med.* xx. (1790) 195 Of the malignant, putrid, or spotted fever. This may be called the *pestilential fever* of Europe, as in many of its symptoms it bears a great resemblance to that dreadful disease the plague. **1807–26** S. COOPER *First Lines Surg.* (ed.

5) 69 The carbuncle of the plague is called symptomatic or pestilential.

†**b.** Used as a specific against plague or pestilence. *Obs.*

1460-70 *Bk. Quintessence* 24 Vse in þe dayes two or þre smale pelotis pestilenciales in oure 5 essencia.

†**c.** Infected with plague or pestilence; plague-stricken. *Obs.*

1568 SKEYNE *The Pest* (1860) 32 Quhasoeuir findis tham seltis pestilenciall, incontinent tak ane iniectione.

3. Morally baneful or pernicious.

1531 ELYOT *Gov.* III. vi, Corrupted with pestilenciall auarice or ambicion. **1651** JER. TAYLOR *Serm. for Year* I. iii. 34 So pestilential, so infectious a thing is sin, that it scatters the poison of its breath to all the neighbourhood. **1782** PRIESTLEY *Corrupt. Chr.* II. IX. 187 John..pronounced it to be a pestilential..doctrine. **1857** BUCKLE *Civiliz.* I. xiii. 725 Bossuet had been taught that Mohammedanism is a pestilential heresy.

†**4.** ***Pestilential Doctors***, a humorous appellation of those Doctors of Divinity who were created at Oxford, without performance of Acts, during the visitation of the Plague. *Obs.*

After the appellation *Royal Doctors* with which those were dignified who were similarly created at the King's visit.

1654 GATAKER *Disc. Apol.* 42 If ever I took the Degree of Doctor [of Divinity], I would so do it, as that I would not be styled either a Royal, or a Pestilential Doctor; which by-names were in common speech given unto those that had taken that Degree, at either of those times.

Hence **pesti'lentially** *adv.*, after the manner of a pestilence; **pesti'lentialness** (Bailey, vol. II, 1727).

1643 TUCKNEY *Balme of G.* 35 Englands present disease.. is grown pestilentially malignant. **1830** *Fraser's Mag.* II. 417 Useless, nay, pestilentially unclean.

†**pestilentious**, *a. Obs.* [ad. F. *pestilencieux*, †*-tieux* (15th c. in Godef.) = It. *pestilenzioso*, †*-tioso* (Florio), ad. post-cl. L. *pestilentiōsus*, f. *pestilentia* PESTILENCE: see -OUS.]

1. = PESTILENTIAL *a.* 1, 2.

1533 BELLENDEN *Livy* III. iii. (S.T.S.) I. 249 þe ȝere [was] richt pestilentius baith to burgh & land, to na less mortalite of man þan beist. **1589** R. BRUCE *Serm.* (1843) 164 The disease..was a pestilentious boil. **1632** LITHGOW *Trav.* VI. 256 This contagious and pestilentious Lake [the Dead Sea]. **1694** *Lond. Gaz.* No. 2948/2 The Pestilentious Distemper which had for a long while reigned in that Island. **1745** tr. *Columella's Husb.* I. iv, The owner of a pestilentious, though very fertile and fat land.

2. Noxious, pernicious; = PESTILENTIAL *a.* 3.

1533 BELLENDEN *Livy* I. xxii. (S.T.S.) I. 125 Tarquinius sixtus..come armit on me þis last nycht, And has reft fra me ..all my joy and solace to his pestilentius plesser. **1546** *Reg. Privy Council Scot.* I. 63 The pestilencious hereseis of Luther. *a* **1586** SIDNEY *Arcadia* III. (1622) 332 Such a pestilentious influence poysoned the time of my natiuitie. **1689** tr. *Buchanan's De Jure Regni* 45 Nothing..is given us of God..more Pestilentious than a wicked King. **1748** H. BROOKE *Last Speech J. Good* Poems & Plays 1789 II. 117 In the days of old there were Giants.., people of magnitude,.. of prodigious deeds, and of pestilentious atchievements.

Hence †**pesti'lentiousness.**

1748 tr. *Vegetius' Distemp. Horses* 25 The Pestilentiousness of the Disease.

pestilently ('pɛstɪləntlɪ), *adv.* [f. PESTILENT *a.* + -LY².] In a pestilent manner.

1. Perniciously, noxiously, mischievously.

1528 TINDALE *Obed. Chr. Man* Wks. (1573) 128 Would he spare..to alleage, and to wrest other doctors pestilently, which feareth not for to iugle wyth the holy scripture? **1563-83** FOXE *A. & M.* 56 Some..haue most pestilently abused the authoritie of the holy and auncient fathers. **1653** H. MORE *Antid. Ath.* III. ix. §7 The smell nevertheless encreased, and became above all measure pestilently noisome.

2. Annoyingly; intolerably; excessively, outrageously, 'plaguily'.

1567 *Trial Treas.* in Hazl. *Dodsley* III. 271 But some-time they cumber me pestilently. **1670** EACHARD *Cont. Clergy* 35 The pretence of making People sagacious, and pestilently witty. **1883** *Standard* 16 May 5/8 The most pestilently annoying bird in the world.

So '**pestilentness**, the character of being pestilent.

1727 in BAILEY vol. II; and in later Dicts.

pestilent-wort: see PESTILENCE-WORT.

pestilenze: see PESTILENCE *v.*

pestilet, obs. form of PISTOLET.

†**pe'stility.** *Obs. rare.* [ad. L. *pestilitās*, n. of quality f. *pestilis* pestilential (f. *pestis* plague): see -ITY.] Pestilential visitation, pestilence, plague.

1570 FOXE *A. & M.* (ed. 2) 95/1 Latyn writers..making mencion of the sayde pestilitie, declare how the beginning thereof..came..out of Ethiope, and from the hot countries.

pestill, -illation, var. PISTIL, PISTILLATION.

pestle ('pɛs(ə)l, 'pɛst(ə)l), *sb.* Forms: 4-7 **pestel**, 5 **-tylle**, 5-6 **-telle**, 5-7 **-tell**, **-til** (8-9 *dial.*), 6-7 **-till**, 7 **-sel(l**, **-teell**, 8 **pistil**, 5- **pestle**. [ME. a. OF. *pestel*, *-eil* = It. *pestello*:—L. *pistillum*, *-us* (med.L. also *pestillum*) pounder, pestle, dim. of **pistrum*, f. *pinsĕre*, *pist-um* to pound, bray, crush.]

1. An instrument (usually club-shaped) for bruising or pounding substances in a mortar. ***pestle and mortar***, esp. those used by the apothecary in triturating and compounding drugs; hence taken as the symbol of the profession.

Used by Wyclif (1 Chron. xxi. 23) also to render L. *tribula* threshing-instrument.

[**1272** in Rogers *Agric. & Prices* II. 566/2 Mortar cum pestelello.] **1382** WYCLIF *Exod.* xvi. 14 It [the manna] aperid in wildernes lassid, and as with a pestel pownyd, into the lyknes of an hoore frost vpon the erthe. **1388** —— *Prov.* xxvii. 22 Thouȝ thou beetist a fool in a morter, as with a pestel smytynge aboue dried barli: his foli schal not be don awei fro him. *c* **1400** *Lanfranc's Cirurg.* 347 Make clene þe morter; & þan leie þeron camphore..þan do þerto oile, & grinde hem wel togidere wiþ þe pestel. *c* **1440** *Promp. Parv.* 395/1 Pestel, of stampynge, *pila, pistillus.* **1584** COGAN *Haven Health* (1636) 107 Beat them small in a woodden mortar, or marble, with a pestill of wood. **1711** STEELE *Spect.* No. 52 ¶3 The renowned British Hippocrates of the Pestle and Mortar. **1850** W. IRVING *Goldsmith* vi. 85 His medical science..could not gain him the management of a pestle and mortar.

fig. **1589** *Pappe w. Hatchet* D, Then haue I a pestle so to stampe his pistles, that Ile beate all his wit to powder. *a* **1839** PRAED *Poems* (1864) I. 282 Beat up by poetic pestle. **1849** D. G. MITCHELL *Battle Summer* (1852) 232 He will pound their pamphlets with his pestle of a pen.

2. Applied to various mechanical appliances for pounding, stamping, pressing, etc.; e.g.

a. The vertically moving bar in a stamping-mill; a stamp. **b.** The beater or pounder in a fulling-mill. **c.** The stamper in an oil-mill. †**d.** The piston of a pump (*obs.*).

1604 E. G[RIMSTONE] *D' Acosta's Hist. Indies* IV. xiii. 247 The difference of these engins is, that some goe with sixe pestels, some with twelve, and others with foureteene. **1659** LEAK *Waterwks.* 3 The Pestle A may be put therein, which shall be like to those which are used for Pumps and Forcers of water; and..well invironed with leather. **1678** EVELYN *Diary* 24 Aug., They stamp them [rags] in troughs to a papp with pestles or hammers like the powder-mills. **1727-41** CHAMBERS *Cycl.* s.v. *Fulling*, The principal parts of the Fulling-mill are..the pestles, or stampers. The pestles and troughs are of wood. **1772** *Ann. Reg.* 213 Discontinuing the use of pestles in making gunpowder at his mills. **1800** tr. *Lagrange's Chem.* I. 234 Nitrate of potash, mixed with.. charcoal and..sulphur, forms gunpowder. These three substances are pounded by means of pestles or a grinding-stone. **1825** J. NICHOLSON *Operat. Mechanic* 450 (Oil mill) When the workman wants to stop a pestle, he pulls at the rope 18, during the rise of the pestle. When this is at its greatest height, the detent is horizontal, and prevents the pestle from falling, by means of a pin projecting from the side of the pestle, which rests upon the detent.

3. The leg of certain animals, used for food, *esp.* the ham or haunch of the pig (occasionally, the foreleg); also, the human leg. Now *dial.*

(Cf. Ger. *keule* a club, pestle, leg of pork, mutton, etc.)

1326 *Wardr. Acc. Edw. II* 31/17 (MS.) Un pestel de pork, 3½*d.* ? *c* **1390** *Form of Cury* in Warner *Antiq. Culin.* 13 The fyletes buþ two, that buþ take oute of the pestels. **14..** *Anc. Cookery* in *Househ. Ord.* (1790) 437 Take the pestelles of the chekyns and couche hom in dysshes. *c* **1440** *Promp. Parv.* 395/1 Pestelle, of flesche, *pestellus.* *a* **1529** SKELTON *E. Rummyng* 423 Her legges..were sturdy and stubbed Myghty pestels and clubbed. **1563** B. GOOGE *Eglogs* etc. *Cupido* (Arb.) 123 A Belye byg..and Pestels two, lyke Postes. **1568** WITHALS *Dict.* 48 b/2 A pestel of bacon, *perna suilla.* **1611** COTGR., *Faucille*,..the bought..or pestle of the thigh [of a horse]. **1777** HOOLE *Comenius' Vis. World* (ed. 12) 71 He dresseth a swine with..scalding water, and maketh gamons, pistils, and flitches. **1828** *Craven Gloss.* (ed. 2), *Pestil*,..also the shank end of a ham or pork. **1886** ELWORTHY *W. Som. Word-bk.* s.v., 'Pestle o' pork.' So called, when cooked fresh, instead of being salted for ham o' pork.

†**b.** Phr. ***the pestle of a lark***: *fig.*, a trifle, something very small. So ***a pestle of a portigue***, humorously used for a piece of gold. *Obs.*

1597-8 BP. HALL *Sat.* IV. iv. 29 Yet can I set my Gallio's dieting, A pestle of a larke or plouers wing. **1622** FLETCHER *Sea Voy.* I. iv, *Fran.* Oh I am hungry... *Tib.* Here's a pestle of a Portigue, Sir: Tis excellent meat with soure sauce: And here's two chaines, suppose 'em sausages. *a* **1661** FULLER *Worthies, Rutland.* II. (1662) 346 Rutlandshire is..called by Mr. Cambden *Angliæ Provinciola minima.* Indeed it is but the Pestel of a Lark, which is better than a quarter of some bigger bird, having the most cleanly profit in it. **1712** STEELE *Spect.* No. 326 ¶5 Sometimes..a Wheat Ear or the Pestle of a Lark were chearfully purchased.

†**4.** A constable's truncheon or club. *Obs. rare.*

1611 CHAPMAN *May-Day* IV. i, To trie whether this chopping knife or their pestels were the better weapons.

†**5.** *Bot.* Early form of PISTIL, q.v.

6. *attrib.* and *Comb.*: **pestle-frame**, the structure in a pestle-mill which supports the pestles and the machinery which operates them; †**pestle-head**, a blockhead; **pestle-mill**, a stamping-mill, a powder-mill; **pestle-pie** *dial.* (see quot.).

1825 J. NICHOLSON *Operat. Mechanic* 450 Profile of the *pestle-frame. **1591** PERCIVALL *Sp. Dict.*, *Majadero*, a pestill, a dolt, a *pestill head, a beetle head. **1773** *Act 13 Geo. III*, c. 13 An Act to enable certain persons..to continue to work a *Pestle Mill,..in making Battle Gunpowder, at Old Forge Farm, in the parish of Tonbridge. **1777** *Horæ Subsecivæ* 323 (E.D.D.) A '*pestle pye', a large standing pye, which contains a whole gammon, and sometimes a neat's tongue also, together with a couple of fowls, and if a turkey not the worse. A noted dish at country fairs and wakes, and some-times a Xtmas treat.

'**pestle**, *v.* [a. OF. *pesteler* to bray, pound, f. *pestel*: see prec.]

1. *trans.* To beat, pound, or triturate, with or as with a pestle. Also *fig.*

1413 *Pilgr. Sowle* (Caxton 1483) III. ii. 51 So were they.. cast in to the fire where they were with grete cheynes pesteled and beten. **1659** HOWELL *Lexicon, Fr. Prov.* 25 A morter, wherein Garlicke hath been pestelled in, cannot be so washed, but that it will still retain some smell thereof. **1855** TENNYSON *Maud* I. I. xi, To pestle a poison'd poison. **1884** SALA *Journ. due South* I. xiv. (1887) 186 The black-eyebrowed assistant..[was] pestling something in a huge mortar. **1891** *Chamb. Jrnl.* 20 June 385/2 She has been put into a mortar and is being pestled into shape.

2. *intr.* To use or work with a pestle.

1866 HOWELLS *Venet. Life* 336 His apprentice pestles away at their prescriptions. **1871** —— *Wedd. Journ.* 62 The apothecary..gaily pestled away at a prescription.

Hence '**pestling** *ppl. a.*

1609 B. JONSON *Sil. Wom.* III iii, It will be such a pest'ling deuice,..It will pound all your enemies practises to poulder.

pesto ('pɛstəʊ). [a. It. *pesto*, contracted form of *pestato*, pa. pple. of *pestare* to pound, to crush.] A pasta sauce of crushed herbs, garlic, and olive oil.

1937 M. MORPHY *Good Food from Italy* 166 When used with pastes, such as macaroni,..the *pesto* is diluted with 3 or 4 tablespoons of boiling water. **1953** R. HOWE *Italian Cooking* 61 Prepare a vegetable soup..just before it is ready stir into it a garlic paste or *pesto*. There are several recipes for making *pesto*. **1954** E. DAVID *Italian Food* 288 (*heading*) Pesto. *Ibid.*, 1 large bunch of fresh basil, garlic, 1 handful of pine nuts, 1 handful of grated Sardo or Parmesan cheese, 1½-2 oz. of olive oil... When the *pesto* is a thick purée start adding the olive oil. **1962** M. SOPER *Encycl. European Cooking* 398 Pesto is a sauce of Genoese origin... Any left-over pesto may be placed in a small jar, covered with olive oil and kept for some days. **1976** R. CONDON *Whisper of Axe* I. x. 59 Enid grew basil for making *pesto*. **1976** *Times* 6 Mar. 12/3 Home-made pesto followed by aïoli garni at the Carved Angel in Dartmouth. **1976** *Publishers Weekly* 20 Sept. 83/1 Sauces such as pesto, aioli, mayonnaise.

'**pestoid**, *a. rare.* [f. L. *pest-is* plague + -OID.] Resembling the pest or plague.

1890 *Cent. Dict.*, Pestoid fever.

pestology (pɛ'stɒlədʒɪ). [f. L. *pest-is* PEST + -OLOGY.] The scientific study of pests and methods of dealing with them. Hence **pesto'logical** *a.*, of or pertaining to pestology; **pe'stologist**, an expert or specialist in pestology.

1921 *Glasgow Herald* 26 Nov. 6 Lieut.-Colonel Nathan Raw, M.P., has become President of the newly formed Institute of Applied Pestology. **1927** *Daily Express* 23 Sept. 3/3 The pestological exhibition and conferences..opened yesterday... There were insect powders, sprays, pastes and —this will show you how far a pestologist goes—automatic fire-arms. **1927** *Times* 27 Sept. 12/5 An exhibition organized by the College of Pestology..was opened on Thursday. **1971** *New Scientist* 3 June 554/2 Our war-weary pestologists may perhaps become disenchanted with the scientific approach.

pesture, obs. f. PESTER.

pesty ('pɛstɪ), *a. U.S. colloq.* [f. PEST + -Y¹.] Obnoxious, troublesome, annoying.

1962 E. LACY *Freeloaders* iv. 65 My last pesty question —can you spare a hundred bucks? **1974** *Spartanburg* (S. Carolina) *Herald* 24 Apr. (Sky City Advt. Suppl.) 5 Twin flaming torches $3⁹⁹ pr... Kills pesty bugs and mosquitoes. For outdoor lighting, everywhere. **1976** B. BOVA *Multiple Man* (1977) xiii. 139 Our pesty friend here..has found out.

pesyble, obs. f. PEACEABLE.

pesyn, obs. f. *peasen*, pl. of PEASE.

pet (pɛt), *sb.*¹ Also 6 pette, 8 pett. [Originally Sc. and north. Eng.; of unknown origin. Ir. *peat* and Gael. *peata* are from Sc.

From the history, app. not related in origin to PEAT *sb.*², though the words may at times have been confused.]

1. a. Any animal that is domesticated or tamed and kept as a favourite, or treated with indulgence and fondness; esp. applied to 'a lamb' (or kid) 'taken into the house, and brought up by hand, a cade lamb' (Johnson). (The latter is the ordinary literal sense in Sc. and north. Eng.)

1539 *Acc. Ld. High Treas. Scot.* in Pitcairn *Crim. Trials* I. *299 *Item*, to Thomas Melvillis Wiffe, in Falkland, at þe Kingis command, for keping of certane Pettis, and nurising of þe samyn. [*note.* These *Pets* consisted of Parroquets, monkeys, peacocks, swans, &c., &c.] **1674-91** RAY *N. C. Words, Pet*, and *Pet-lamb*, a cade lamb. **1710** STEELE *Tatler* No. 266 ¶2 The other has transferred the amorous Passions of her first Years to the Love of Cronies, Petts and Favourites [a dog, monkey, squirrel, parrot]. **1808** JAMIESON s.v. *Pet* vb., Pet..denotes..more generally, any creature that is fondled and much indulged. **1825** BROCKETT *N.C. Gloss.*, *Pet*, a domesticated lamb. **1828** *Craven Gloss.* (ed. 2), *Pet*, a cade or house lamb. [So **1869** *Lonsdale Gloss.*] **1830** [see CADE *sb.*² 2]. **1837** M. DONOVAN *Dom. Econ.* II. 119 The animal is cleanly in its habits, and is reared in the houses rather as a pet.

b. Applied to a plant artificially reared.

1842 in J. Aiton *Domest. Econ.* (1857) 154 The pet having been brought to this its first state of existence, must be put in the window. At first it will be a stout thread, whitish, and covered with tiny scales; then the scales will expand a little, and the end will become greener.

2. a. An indulged (and, usually, spoiled) child.

1508 DUNBAR *Flyting w. Kennedie* 247 Herretyk, lunatyk, purspyk, carlingis pet. **17..** *Scotch Prov.*, He has fault of a wife who marries mam's pet. **1788** W. MARSHALL *Yorksh. Gloss.*, *Pet*, a child spoilt by improper indulgence. **1824** MACTAGGART *Gallovid. Encycl.* 380 A *pet* is always a dangerous creature; thus, a child *petted* by its parents, plays the devil some day in the world; a sheep *petted* is apt to turn a *duncher* [= butter, one which butts].

b. Any person who is indulged, fondled, or treated with special kindness or favour; a darling, favourite; a sweet or obliging person; †also as a name for a favourite boxer (*obs.*). Also *transf.* of a thing. Phr. ***teacher's pet***: a derogatory term for a teacher's favourite pupil; also *transf.*

[**1755** JOHNSON, *Peat*, a little fondling; a darling; a dear play-thing. It is now commonly called *pet*.] **1825** BROCKETT *N.C. Gloss.*, *Pet*, . . a fond designation for a female favourite. **1826** DISRAELI *Viv Grey* IV. i, Patronise him! he is my political pet! **1833** T. CREEVEY in *C. Papers*, etc. (1904) II. 260 He made himself a real pet of mine. **1841** DICKENS *Let.* 9 Feb. (1969) II. 208 'The Pet of the Fancy', or 'the Slashing Sailor Boy', or 'Young Sawdust'. **1848** THACKERAY *Van. Fair* xxxiv. 303 James Crawley had met the Tutbury Pet, who was coming to Brighton to make a match with the Rottingdean Fibber; and enchanted by the Pet's conversation, had passed the evening in company with that . . man. **1859** J. BLACKWOOD *Let.* 8 July in *Geo. Eliot Lett.* (1954) III. 113 A dive kept . . by Dick Curtis the pet of the Fancy. **1872** BLACK *Adv. Phaeton* xxx, No place was so much the pet of fortune as the Blue Bell Inn. **1881** BESANT & RICE *Chapl. of Fleet* I. x, I was once the pet and plaything of ladies, a sort of lapdog. **1902** R. HICHENS *Londoners* 11 You are the pet of society. **1914** B. TARKINGTON *Penrod* xii. 89 'Teacher's pet!' whispered Penrod hoarsely. He had nothing but contempt for Georgie Bassett. **1922** WODEHOUSE *Girl on Boat* iv. 82 Do be a pet and go and talk to Jane Hubbard. I'm sure she must be feeling lonely. **1930** J. DOS PASSOS *42nd Parallel* III. 237 The other employees in the department hated her and nick-named her Teacher's Pet. **1952** S. KAUFFMANN *Philanderer* (1953) xii. 199 He was not only the 'teacher's pet', he was the 'rich kid'. He was doubly isolated. **1957** J. KIRKUP *Only Child* xi. 139 So immediately after lessons were over, I would not linger in the classroom 'sucking up to teacher' as the 'teacher's pets' did. **1968** *Guardian* 16 Mar. 11/5 The anxious child was usually the conventional teacher's pet, always well dressed and obedient. **1976** T. HEALD *Let Sleeping Dogs Die* ix. 184 Be a pet and fetch me a Tom Collins. **1976** H. WILSON *Governance of Britain* i. 12 It [*sc.* the phrase 'prime minister'] was used to denote 'court favourite', with connotations similar to 'teacher's pet'.

c. = ***pet-day***, 'a day too fine to last': see 3 d.

1825 JAMIESON s.v., It is commonly said 'I fear this day will be a pet', Renfrew.

d. Used as a term of endearment or familiar vocative.

1849 J. RUSKIN *Let.* 24 Apr. in M. Lutyens *Ruskins & Grays* (1972) xxi. 185 Do you know, pet, it seems almost a dream to me that we have been married. **1939** L. M. MONTGOMERY *Anne of Ingleside* xxxvii. 293 There is a parcel I want to send up to Thomasine Fair. . . Will you run up with it this afternoon, pet? **1972** G. SERENY *Case M. Bell* I. ii. 33 Mary smiled and asked to see Martin. I said, 'No, pet, Martin is dead.' **1975** J. WAINWRIGHT *Square Dance* 186 He . . spoke to the policewoman on duty. . . 'Now then, pet—can you help me?' **1977** *Daily Mirror* 22 Mar. 24 Sounds like just the job for you, pet, eh?

3. *attrib.* and *Comb.* **a.** *attrib.* or as *adj.* Of an animal: Kept as a pet or favourite: orig. applied to a lamb brought up by hand, a CADE *lamb*.

1584 *Wills & Inv. N.C.* (Surtees) II. 99 One pette sheipe 4s. **1674–91** *Pet-lamb* [see 1] **1800** WORDSW. (*title of poem*) The Pet Lamb. **1851** D. JERROLD *St. Giles* xi. 105 [He] may keep his pet-lamb safe from London wolves. **1863** BATES *Nat. Amazon* I. 82 A favorite pet-bird of the Brazilians. **1890** D. G. MITCHELL *Lands, Lett., & Kings* iii. 124 [Herrick] kept a pet goose at the vicarage, also a pet pig. **1897** *Westm. Gaz.* 30 July 1/2 Threatening, abusive, and coaxing letters from pet-dog owners.

b. Of a person, or more usually *transf.* of a thing (material or immaterial): Specially cherished; for which one has a particular fondness or weakness; favourite. Also (jocularly or ironically) ***pet aversion***, that which one specially dislikes; also, ***pet hate***; ***pet peeve***: see PEEVE *sb.*

1826 *Blackw. Mag.* XX. 53/1 Men of the most different habits and characters in other respects, resemble each other in the practice of nursing in secret some pet superstition. **1832** MANNING *Let* in Purcell *Life* (1895) I. 97 My pet iron bed . . I shall want at Merton. **1845** MIALL in *Nonconf.* V. 25 The success of his pet financial scheme. **1846** H. ROGERS *Ess.* (1860) I. 192 Philosophers are apt to be blindly fond of their pet theories. **1870** DICKENS *E. Drood* iii, The pet pupil of the Nuns' House is Miss Rosa Bud. **1877** MRS. FORRESTER *Mignon* I. 242 This pet weakness of her sex is not to be scored against Olga. **1880** 'MARK TWAIN' *Tramp Abroad* xxvi. 262 For years my pet aversion had been the cuckoo clock. **1890** *Times* 14 Jan. 12/2 Prince Metternich was her pet aversion. **1898** G. B. SHAW *Plays* II. *Candida* 117 My own particular pet scrubbing brush has been used for blackleading. **1920** [see ASSASSINATE *v.* 3]. **1939** *Sun* (Baltimore) 21 Apr. 28/2 Hill-passers, he said, were one of his 'pet hates'. **1949** *Proc. Inst. Electr. Engin.* XCVI. II. 629/1 Engineers will always have their pet ideas and want their special sizes of cables. **1969** *Morning Star* 19 Nov. 4 Many of you will have your own pet dishes. . . With your help we could give the cookery column a real international flavour. **1974** 'R. TATE' *Birds of Bloodied Feather* vi. 118 No doubt you have one of your pet theories. **1977** *National Observer* (U.S.) 22 Jan. 12/2 Another pet hate is the 'News Flash' that breaks into a program with total disregard for its distracting impact on the show.

c. Expressing fondness, endearing: chiefly in **pet-form**, an adaptation of a name used as a pet-name; **pet name** (often hyphened), a name expressing fondness or familiarity, as the various abbreviated and altered forms, diminutives, etc., of Christian names; a hypocoristic name; hence **pet-name** *v. trans.*, to give (a person) a pet name; to call by a pet name.

1829 LYTTON *Devereux* III. v, Call me only by those pretty pet words by which I know you will never call any one else. **184.** MRS. BROWNING *Sonn. fr. Portuguese* xxxiii, Yes, call me by my pet-name! let me hear The name I used to run at, when a child, From innocent play. **1875** JOWETT *Plato* (ed. 2) III. 359 A lover who uses these pet names. **1892** *Spectator* 5 Mar. 331/2 They invent pet-names [for their parents] usually tinged with a comic irreverence. **1915** E. CORRI *30 Yrs. Boxing Ref.* 183 Men of the most human type are usually pet-named by the public in some way. **1932** E. WEEKLEY *Words & Names* X. 138 *Christopher* may have implied stupidity, as its German pet-form *Stoffel* is synonymous with blockhead. **1942** C. MORLEY *Thorofare* (1943) xix. 66 He had pet-named the two funnels for his twin daughters, Alma and Sophie. **1956** *Archivum Linguisticum* VIII. 70 *Ned* and *Nanny* are . . mere pet-forms like *Ted*. **1960** P. H. REANEY *Orig. Eng. Place-Names* i. 8 We must believe . . that *Brihtling* was a pet-form for *Brihtric*. **1973** *Times Lit. Suppl.* 1 June 608/3 His young bride Nadia petnamed him Klop (which is Russian for 'bug').

d. *Comb.*: ***pet-vendor***; **pet cemetery** = *pets' cemetery*; **pet-day**: see quots.; **pet-food**, food for pet animals; **petland**, the realm of pets; **pet-lover**, a lover of domestic pets; **pets' cemetery**, a burial-ground for domestic pets; **pets' corner**, a part of a display, zoo, etc., reserved for the display of animals normally kept as pets or suitable for keeping as pets; **pet-shop**, a shop selling animals to be kept as pets.

1967 A. LEWIN *Unaltered Cat* II. viii. 180 He telephoned the *pet-cemetery. . . Mr Carpenter agreed to pick up the cat-corpse. **1973** *Post-Herald* (Birmingham, Alabama) c1/1 The Los Angeles Pet Cemetery has a small 'slumber room' where owners may view their pet lying in state on a blue satin covered stand. **1823** GALT *Gilhaize* III. viii. 63 The lown of that time was as a *pet day in winter. **1882** W. MARRIOTT in *Standard* 26 Dec. 7/4 They are generally accompanied by weather 'too fine to last', or what in Scotland is known as a 'pet-day'. **1939** L. M. MONTGOMERY *Anne of Ingleside* ii. 14 Such a lovely day. . . I'm afraid it's a pet day though—there'll be rain to-morrow. **1961** A. WILSON *Old Men at Zoo* i. 48 If I'd been made Director, Beard would be getting a thumping great subsidy from some of those big *pet food people. **1968** *Observer* (Colour Suppl.) 25 Feb. 35/1 Pet foods come sixth in the consumer top ten. Baby food lags way behind. **1973** R. HILL *Ruling Passion* II. vi. 132 A man was unloading trays of meat and made-up pet food from a blue van. **1884** WOOD (*title*) *Petland Revisited. **1904** *Contemp. Rev.* Aug. 230 Pet lions were only one example of the aberrations of *pet-lovers in ancient Rome. **1908** HARDY *Let.* 23 Dec. in *One Rare Fair Woman* (1972) 138 Our very old cat 'Comfy' died two days ago. . . He is buried in our *pets' cemetery. **1948** E. WAUGH *Loved One* 27 He took a job at the pets' cemetery. **1940** *Pets' corner [see DUMB *a.* 1 b]. **1961** *Guardian* 5 May 15/4 In the children's corner [of the park] there is . . a pets' corner. **1968** J. RATHBONE *Hand Out* xiv. 113 Gee, Elmer, it's better'n pets' corner back home. **1976** *Star* (Sheffield) 29 Oct. 14/6 Now he is hoping to open a pet's corner and leisure centre there, with a pride of lions as the star attraction. **1928** KIPLING *Limits & Renewals* (1932) 47 Mr. Wilham's fashionable West End *pet-shop. **1942** D. POWELL *Time to be Born* (1943) xii. 295 In front of the pet-shop window a man stood watching half a dozen infant Siamese kittens. **1976** W. GREATOREX *Crossover* 35 He called at the pet shop. . . There were whining puppies and mewing kittens. **1924** *Glasgow Herald* 21 Nov. 10/7 A London *pet-vendor has had about 2,500 snakes through his hands within the last few months.

pet (pɛt), *sb.*[2] Also 7–8 pett. [In use since end of 16th c., first app. in the phrase 'to take the pet'; origin obscure.

It has naturally been associated with PET *sb.*[1], as being a characteristic habit of a 'pet' or indulged and spoiled child; but the connexion of sense is not very clear or simple, esp. in the early phrase 'to take the pet'. It is also to be noted that in the 16th, 17th, and early 18th c., PET *sb.*[1] was still an exclusively northern word, while PET *sb.*[2] has been app. Southern English also from the first.]

Offence at being (or feeling) slighted or not made enough of; a fit of ill humour or peevishness from this cause: now usually implying one of a slight or childish kind. ***to take (the) pet***, to take offence and become ill-humoured or sulky.

1590 LODGE *Euphues Gold. Leg.* Wks. (Grosart) IV. 90 Some while they thought he had taken some word vnkindly, and had taken the pet. **1606** CHAPMAN *Mons. D'Olive* II. i, Fled backe as it came and went away in Pett. **1611** COTGR., *Se mescontenter de*, to take the pet, or pepper in the nose, at. **1621** LAUD *Serm. on Ps.* xxi. 6 When they may haue a blessing and will not, it is a sullen pet. **1625** MASSINGER *New Way* I. ii, But what's this to your pet against my lady? **1640** SANDERSON *Serm. on Ps.* cxix. 75 §10 Jonas took pet at the withering of the gourd. **1647** *Let. of Intelligence* 16 Aug. (Clarendon MSS. 2576), The Lords . . in a pet did adjourn their House. **1660** PEPYS *Diary* 6 Dec., Which did vex me . . and so I took occasion to go up and to bed in a pet. **1707** *Reflex. upon Ridicule* 199 Who takes Pett at things that are lightly said. **1725** RAMSAY *Gentle Sheph.* I. ii. song iii, The dawted bairn thus takes the pet, Nor eats tho' hunger crave. **1830** SCOTT *Jrnl.* 23 May, About a year ago I took the pet at my Diary, chiefly because I thought it made me abominably selfish. *c* **1850** *Arab. Nts.* (Rtldg.) 11 She went back to the house in a pet, shut herself up, and cried the whole night. **1894** R. H. ELLIOT *Gold*, etc. *Mysore* 102 They [tigers] take the pet in a case of failure and go off in disgust.

†**pet**, *sb.*[3] *Obs. rare.* [a. F. *pet* (13th c. in Littré) = It. *petto*:—L. *pēdit-us*, in med.L. *pettus*.] A breaking wind; = FART *sb.*

1515 BARCLAY *Egloges* iv. (1570) C vj, Though all their cunning scantly be worth a pet.

pet (pɛt), *v.*[1] [f. PET *sb.*[1]; in early use Sc.]

a. *trans.* To make a pet of, treat as a pet; to indulge; to fondle.

1629 Z. BOYD *Last Battell* 324 Grosse euill thoghts fedde and petted with yeelding and consent. **1788** W. MARSHALL *Yorksh. Gloss.*, *Pet*, to indulge; to spoil by over-indulgence. **1818** TODD, *Pet*, to treat as a pet; to fondle; to indulge. **1824** [see PET *sb.*[1] 2 a]. **1846** D. JERROLD *Mrs. Caudle* xxxvi, Get another wife to study you and pet you up as I've done. **1847** HELPS *Friends in C.* (1861) I. 127 The truth is, . . we cannot pet anything much without doing it mischief.

b. *intr.* To have erotic physical contact with another person by kissing, caressing, and sexual stimulation. orig. *U.S.*

1924 P. MARKS *Plastic Age* vi. 53 I'm a bad egg. I drink and gamble and pet. I haven't gone the limit yet . . —but I will. **1953** A. C. KINSEY et al. *Sexual Behav. Human Female* ix. 389 The most responsive females may be the ones who most often pet to orgasm before marriage. **1959** N. MAILER *Advts. for Myself* (1961) 230 The game she cherished was to play the bobby-soxer who petted with a date in the living room and was finally seduced. **1969** E. M. BRECHER *Sex Researchers* (1970) v. 113 Some lower-level boys also occasionally pet. **1977** C. STORR *Tales Psychiatrist's Couch* 84 Haven't you ever reached a climax when you've been out with a boy? When you'd be petting?

pet (pɛt), *v.*[2] [f. PET *sb.*[2]] *intr.* To be in a pet; to take offence at one's treatment; to sulk.

1629 GAULE *Holy Madn.* 239 Jonas pets for his Gourd. **1661** FELTHAM *Resolves* II. ii, He sure is queasie stomack t, that must pet and puke at such a trivial circumstance. *c* **1685** SIR P. HUME *Narr. Occurr.* (1809) 40 The Erle petting at it, forbare and stayed there. **1837** CARLYLE *Fr. Rev.* II. v. i, The loyal Right Side sat . . as it were pouting and petting.

b. *trans.* To cause to take offence. *dial.*

1814 W. NICHOLSON *Peacock* IV. *Poems* 104 Shou'd some passage pet or pout them, They ken best if the bonnet suit them.

pet, petach, obs. forms of PEAT, PIT, PATACHE.

peta- (ˈpɛtə), *prefix.* [Said to be f. PE(N)TA-, the mode of formation having been suggested by TERA-/TETRA-.] Prefixed to the names of units to form the names of units 10^{15} times larger (symbol P).

1975 *Physics Bull.* Mar. 105/1 The Committee [*sc.* the International Committee of Weights and Measures (CIPM)] also agreed to recommend that the 15th and 18th powers of 10 be assigned the names 'peta' (symbol P) and 'exa' (symbol E) respectively. **1975** *B.S.I. News* Dec. 13/3 The Conference [*sc.* the General Conference of Weights and Measures (CGPM)] . . adopted the name peta, symbol P, for 10^{15} and exa, symbol E, for 10^{18}.

petal (ˈpɛtəl), *sb.* [= F. *pétale*, Sp., It. *petalo*, ad. mod.L. *petal-um*, in Fabio Colonna 1649 (Hatz.-Darm.); in ancient L. in sense 'metal plate', a. Gr. πέταλον thin plate, lamina, leaf, neuter of πέταλος adj. outspread, f. root πετ- to spread.]

1. *Bot.* Each of the divisions (modified leaves) of the corolla of a flower (see COROLLA 2), esp. when separate. (Strictly, distinguished from the *sepals* or leaves of the calyx, but often including these when coloured or petaloid.) At first used in mod.L. form *petalum*, pl. *-a*.

1704 J. HARRIS *Lex. Techn.* I, *Petala*, is a Term in Botany, signifying those fine coloured Leaves that compose the Flowers of all Plants. **1726** *Flower Gard. Displ.* (ed. 2) Introd., *Petals*, Leaves of a Flower; so called to distinguish them from the Green Leaves of the Plant. **1776** WITHERING *British Plants* (1796) I. 18 [It] contains Blossoms of one Petal; and this Petal is fixed beneath the Germen. **1793** COLERIDGE *Rose* i, Within the petals of a rose A sleeping Love I spied. **1857** HENFREY *Elem. Bot.* §177 The petals are either distinct, and then the corolla is called *polypetalous*, or they are coherent more or less, and the corolla is *monopetalous* [or *gamopetalous*]. **1866** GEO. ELIOT *F. Holt* i, Petals fell in a silent shower. **1883** G. ALLEN in *Knowledge* 9 Mar. 143 The spring snowflake . . has three sepals or calyx-pieces, and three petals or corolla-pieces; only . . these two whorls exactly resemble one another.

fig. **1837** LYTTON *E. Maltrav.* I. vii, Love opens all the petals of the soul. *a* **1887** JEFFERIES *Field & Hedgerow* (1889) 6 From the sweet delicious violets think out fresh petals of thought and colours, as it were, of soul.

2. *Zool.* In Echinoids: A petaloid ambulacrum, or the dilated end of one. (Oftener in L. form.)

1888 ROLLESTON & JACKSON *Anim. Life* 557 In the *Cassidulidæ* the peristomial ends of the ambulacra dilate into petala or *phyllodes*, forming a figure known as *floscella*.

3. *Comb.*, as ***petal-shower***, ***-tambourine***; ***petal-like***, ***-soft*** adjs.; ***petal-wise*** adv.; **petal collar**, a collar on a woman's garment cut in the shape of petals; **petal ware**, a type of pottery (see quot. 1960).

1957 M. B. PICKEN *Fashion Dict.* 74/1 *Petal collar*, collar made of overlapping petals of fabric. **1969** *Times* 24 Mar. 13/8 (Advt.), A button-through coat dress for Spring into Summer. Short sleeves, petal collar. **1830** LINDLEY *Nat. Syst. Bot.* 145 The two coloured lateral petal-like bodies. **1862** ANSTED *Channel Isl.* II. ix. (ed. 2) 238 Petal-like tentacles . . furnished with cupping glasses. **1828–32** WEBSTER, *Petal-shaped*, having the shape of a petal. *a* **1918** W. OWEN *Coll. Poems* (1963) 117 Stirs Of leaflets in the gloom; soft petal-showers. **1945** P. LARKIN *North Ship* 4 Whose every hell The light as music fills, and on your face Shines petal-soft. **1947** *Sun* (Baltimore) 6 Aug. 9 (Advt.), Generously cut to the new hem lengths . . and pretty as you please, Colony Club's pettiskirt. . . In petal-soft Bur-Mil rayon crepe, white, pink or black. **1922** BLUNDEN *Shepherd* 26 And petal-tambourines shall earn A largess this May morn. **1930** D. T. RICE *Byzantine Glazed Pott.* 9 In dealing with the Constantinople finds,..six main groups were distinguished; plain glazed ware; stamped ware; white inscribed or sgraffito ware; 'petal' ware [etc.]. **1952** —— *Eng. Art 871–1100* viii. 248 The glazes, however, are of a type not so far known from Germany, and suggest, rather Byzantine prototypes; one group, indeed, where the glaze is thick and dark, and where a decoration of blobs has been added, is extremely close to a Byzantine group, usually classed as 'petal' ware. **1960** R. G. HAGGAR *Conc. Encycl. Cont. Pott. & Porc.* 345/2 '*Petal' ware*, ware found at Constantinople, characterized by the addition of horizontal bands of lumps of clay, pressed firmly to the body at one end but left free at the other, which resemble crude petals, hence the name. **1882** G. ALLEN in *Nature* 17 Aug. 374/1 The mere fact that the stamens are opposite to the lobes of the calyx,..in itself shows that a petal-whorl has been suppressed. **1880** W. WATSON *Prince's Quest*, etc. (1892) 62 Doubtful as a dream that lies Folded within another, petal-wise.

petal ('pɛtəl), *v. poet.* [f. the sb.] *trans.* To provide or scatter with petals. Also *fig.*

1907 *Westm. Gaz.* 3 June 2/3 Sigh, little wind.., Winnow the lilacs pink and white, Petal the shining grass. **1930** E. POUND *XXX Cantos* iv. 17 Saffron sandal so petals the narrow foot. **1955** —— *Section: Rock-Drill* (1957) xci. 76 The water-bug's mittens petal the rock beneath.

petaled: see PETALLED.

petaliferous (pɛtə'lɪfərəs), *a.* [f. mod.L. type **petalifer*, f. *petal-um* PETAL *sb.* + *-fer-us* bearing: see -FEROUS.] Bearing petals.

1864 in WEBSTER. **1870** HOOKER *Stud. Flora* 79 Tetramorphic flowers occur; petaliferous large. **1882** G. ALLEN in *Nature* 17 Aug. 374/1 *Scleranthus* or *Mercurialis*, known descendants of petaliferous forms.

petaliform ('pɛtəlɪfɔːm), *a. rare.* ?*Obs.* [ad. mod.L. *petaliform-is*, f. *petal-um* PETAL *sb.*: see -FORM.] Having the form of a petal; petaloid.

1806 GALPINE *Brit. Bot.* 3* Iris..alternate petals reflexed. *Stig.* petaliform. **1858** in MAYNE *Expos. Lex.*

petaline ('pɛtəlaɪn, -lɪn), *a.* [ad. mod.L. *petalinus*, f. L. *petal-um* PETAL *sb.*: see -INE[1,2].] Pertaining to a petal; situated on a petal; consisting of petals; resembling a petal, petaloid.

1793 MARTYN *Lang. Bot.*, *Petalinum nectarium*, a petaline nectary. **1858** MAYNE *Expos. Lex.*, *Petalinus*, *Bot.*, that which relates to a petal..petaline. **1879** G. ALLEN *Col.-Sense* iv. 65 The corolla, or petaline whorl, forms in most flowers the main attractive organ.

petalism ('pɛtəlɪz(ə)m). *Anc. Hist.* [ad. Gr. πεταλισμός, f. πέταλον leaf: see PETAL *sb.* and -ISM. In mod.F. *pétalisme* (Littré).] A method of temporary banishment (for five years) practised in ancient Syracuse, in imitation of the OSTRACISM of Athens, but effected by writing the name of the person on an olive-leaf.

1612 *North's Plutarch, Dionysius* 1141 The other Lords made a law called Petalisme, to meete with this practise. *Ibid.*, By meanes of this Petalisme, the Lords banished one another, so that in the end, the people became Lord. **1768** HUME *Ess.*, *Balance of Power* xxix. 199 The Ostracism of Athens and Petalism of Syracuse. **1900** F. M. CRAWFORD *Rulers of South* I. 99 For their own safety the Syracusans introduced the law of petalism corresponding almost exactly to the ostracism of the Athenians.

petalite ('pɛtəlaɪt). *Min.* [mod. (d'Andrada, 1800) f. Gr. πέταλον leaf + -ITE.] A silicate of aluminium and lithium, occurring in whitish or greyish masses having leaf-like cleavage.

1808 T. ALLAN *Names of Min.* 51 Petalite..a Swedish mineral named by Dandrada. **1818** W. PHILLIPS *Outl. Min. & Geol.* (ed. 3) Advt., Petalite..composed, in round numbers, of 80 parts of silex, 17 of alumine and 3 of lithion. **1850** DAUBENY *Atom. The.* xii. (ed. 2) 408 Minerals which are destitute of water..Petalite.

petalled, petaled ('pɛtəld), *a.* [f. PETAL *sb.* + -ED[2].] **a.** Furnished or adorned with or as with petals; having petals. Also, formed like or resembling a petal or petals.

1793 MARTYN *Lang. Bot.*, *Petalodes flos*, a petalled flower. **1823** BEDDOES *Romance of Lily* Poems 145 The other curls, and bends its bell Petalled inwards as it fell. **1845** T. COOPER *Purgatory of Suicides* (1877) 109 The purple eye petalled with snow. **1862** G. M. HOPKINS *Vision of Mermaids* (1929), Betwixt ten thousand petall'd lips. **1888** SWINBURNE in *19th Cent.* XXIII. 318 Fledged not as birds are, but petalled as flowers. **1929** G. C. ALLEN *Oxf. Poetry* 1 Let's pick the petals of all joy apart, And launch them uncontrolled on the wind-stream With gleam of petalled gold. **1937** BLUNDEN *Elegy* 74 The petalled cloud and the blue brook aflow. **1975** G. HOWELL *In Vogue* 30 Delysia looking curious in a petalled evening dress.

b. In parasynthetic compounds, as *crimson-petalled*, *large-petalled*, *six-petalled*, etc.

1776 WITHERING *Brit. Plants* (1796) I. 160 Bloss. 2-petaled. **1868** GEO. ELIOT *Sp. Gipsy* I. 51 The ripe-cheeked fruits, the crimson-petalled flowers. **1870** HOOKER *Stud. Flora* 44 Viola... Flowers often dimorphic, the large-petalled flowering early..; the small-petalled or apetalous flower late.

petalless ('pɛtəllɪs), *a.* [f. PETAL *sb.* + -LESS.] Destitute of petals; apetalous.

1825 *Greenhouse Comp.* II. 83 Petalless Pomaderris, a shrub from New Holland. **1882** G. ALLEN in *Nature* XXVI. 373 It has tiny green petalless axillary flowers.

petally ('pɛtəlɪ), *a. nonce-wd.* [f. as prec. + -Y.] Having or resembling petals.

1888 FENN *Man w. Shadow* III. iii. 30 It darted from her petally lips to the poisonous gum.

petalocerous (pɛtə'lɒsərəs), *a. Entom.* [f. mod.L. *Petalocera*, neut. pl. of *petalocerus* (f. Gr. πέταλον leaf, plate + -κερος, -ως horned, f. κέρας horn) + -OUS. In F. *pétalocère*.] Having laminated antennæ, as the beetles of the division *Petalocera* or *Lamellicornes*; lamellicorn.

1826 KIRBY & SP. *Entomol.* III. xxxv. 568 Its *mesosternum* in its direction and appearance resembles that of many Petalocerous beetles. *Ibid.* IV. xlvii. 398 [He] discovered that the thalerophagous and saprophagus Petalocerous beetles resolved themselves..into a circle.

petalodic (pɛtə'lɒdɪk), *a. Bot.* [f. Gr. πεταλώδ-ης leaf-like (cf. PETALODY) + -IC.] Exhibiting petalody.

1909 W. BATESON *Mendel's Princ. Heredity* xi. 198 In the hose-in-hose *Campanula*, which has the sepals petaloid, the well-formed anthers contain plenty of pollen (some may be petalodic).

petalodont ('pɛtələʊdɒnt), *a.* and *sb. Palæont.* [f. mod.L. *Petalodūs* (-*odont*-), name of the typical genus, f. Gr. πέταλον leaf + ὀδούς, ὀδοντ- tooth.] **a.** *adj.* Belonging to the extinct family *Petalodontidæ* of sharks, having compressed teeth forming a pavement. **b.** *sb.* A shark of this family. So **petalo'dontid**; **petalo'dontoid** *a.* and *sb.*

1889 NICHOLSON *Palæont.* II. III. xlvii. 929 *Family Petalodontidæ.*—The Petalodonts form a family exclusively Carboniferous.

petalody ('pɛtələʊdɪ). *Bot.* [f. Gr. type *πεταλώδεια, f. πεταλώδης leaf-like, f. πέταλον leaf: see -ODE[1].] The condition of having other organs or parts of the flower modified into the form of petals; e.g. the stamens in most 'double' flowers, or the calyx-lobes in some species of *Primula*, *Campanula*, etc.

1882 MASTERS in *Jrnl. Bot.* XI. 40 This specimen affords an instance of true doubling or petalody of the stamens.

petaloid ('pɛtəlɔɪd), *a.* [ad. mod.L. *petaloideus*, f. Gr. πέταλον, L. *petal-um* PETAL *sb.*: see -OID: in mod.F. *pétaloïde*.]

1. *Bot.* Of the form of, or resembling, a petal: applied to parts or appendages of the flower when 'coloured' (i.e. not green) and of thin expanded form and delicate texture, like an ordinary petal.

1730 STACK in *Phil. Trans.* XXXVI. 463 Where the Tube expanded itself, it divided into more than forty petaloid Segments. **1845** LINDLEY *Sch. Bot.* iv. (1858) 25 Flowers unsymmetrical, with 2 petaloid and 3 herbaceous sepals. **1875** BENNETT & DYER tr. *Sachs' Bot.* 470 The contrast of structure referred to is frequently wanting, both whorls being either sepaloid, as in Juncaceæ, or both petaloid, as in Lilium; in Helleborus, Aconitum, and some other species, the outer whorl or calyx alone is petaloid, the inner whorl or corolla being transformed into nectaries. **1882** G. ALLEN in *Nature* 27 July 300/2 All stamens show a great tendency easily to become petaloid.

b. Belonging to the *Petaloideæ*, a division of Monocotyledons having normally flowers with ordinary coloured petals or petaloid parts, as lilies, orchids, etc. (not spadiceous, as arums, nor glumaceous, as grasses and sedges).

1836 *Penny Cycl.* V. 248 Under the name of Asphodels he [Lobel] grouped the principal part of modern petaloid monocotyledons. **1872** OLIVER *Elem. Bot.* I. v. 58 Monocotyledons..with a perianth of petal-like leaves, hence called..Petaloid (*Petaloideæ*).

2. *Zool.* Applied to the ambulacra of certain Echinoids, which have a dilated portion and a tapering extremity, suggesting petals of a flower.

1862 DANA *Elem. Geol.* 160 As this portion has..some resemblance to the petals of a flower, the ambulacra are then said to be *petaloid*. **1888** ROLLESTON & JACKSON *Anim. Life* 558 Fascioles surrounding the petaloid ambulacra.

So **peta'loidal** *a.* (in quot. = sense 2); **peta'loideous** *a.* = sense 1 b.

1872 NICHOLSON *Palæont.* 109 Ambulacra composed of simple pores, not petaloidal.

‖**petalon** ('pɛtələn). [a. Gr. πέταλον leaf of metal, etc.] The plate of pure gold worn on the linen mitre of the Jewish high priest. Also in L. form *petalum*.

1678 PHILLIPS (ed. 4), *Petalum*, a certain kind of ornament which Priests formerly used to wear on their heads. **1874** *Supernat. Relig.* II. III. ii. 406 The Apostle John wore the mitre and petalon of the High Priest. **1882** FARRAR *Early Chr.* I. xviii. 363 The High Priest..wearing the name Jehovah on the golden *petalon* upon his forehead.

petalostichous (pɛtə'lɒstɪkəs), *a. Zool.* [f. mod.L. *Petalosticha*, neut. pl. of *petalostichus* (f. Gr. πέταλ-ον leaf + στίχος row) + -OUS.] Having petaloid ambulacra; belonging to the division *Petalosticha* of Echinoids.

petalous ('pɛtələs), *a. rare*$^{-0}$. [f. L. *petal-um* PETAL *sb.* + -OUS.] Having petals: the opposite of *apetalous*. Cf. *monopetalous*, *polypetalous*, etc.

1730–6 BAILEY (folio), *Petalous*, having flower leaves. **1755** in JOHNSON. **1858** MAYNE *Expos. Lex.*, *Petalodes*, having, or full of leaves or petals;..petalous.

petamar(e, variants of PATTAMAR.

petance, obs. form of PITTANCE.

‖**pétanque** (petɑ̃k). [Fr.] A game, resembling bowls, played orig. and chiefly in southern France. Also *attrib.* Cf. BOULE[4] 2.

1955 *Times* 8 Aug. 8/7 No longer the fraternal glass of pastis..no longer..the earnest game of *pétanque*, that travesty of bowls. **1956** N. RYAN tr. *Simenon's My Friend Maigret* vii. 112 Two old men were playing bowls, *pétanque* style, that is without sending the jack more than a few yards from their feet. **1963** N. FREELING *Because of Cats* vii. 105 Cunning little French butane stoves and the chi-chi of le camping, huge rubber water-wings, pétanque sets and elaborate German beach toys. **1967** G. BELLAIRS *Single Ticket to Death* i. 7 Littlejohn and Dorange were playing *pétanque*... The players, with a twist of the wrist, hurled their steel balls at the small wooden jack. **1972** A. H. HAYNES *Story of Bowls* i. 7 In..Petanque..a small marker ball is thrown a distance of up to ten yards; occasionally the distance is doubled and in this event, remarkable skill is demonstrated by the players in putting top and side spin on the heavy steel balls bowled under-arm towards the marker ball. **1977** *Times* 25 Apr. 16/7 The finals of the London pétanque championship.

petara(h, varr. PITARAH.

‖**peta'rade**. *Obs.* [Fr., ad. Pr. *petarrada*, f. *petarra*, f. *petar*, F. *péter*, f. *pet* PET *sb.*[3]]

[**1611** COTGR., *Petarrade*, gunshot of farting.] **1658** PHILLIPS, *Petarrade*,..a yerking out of a horse behind, commonly accompanied with farting. *a* **1693** *Urquhart's Rabelais* III. v. 54 In discharging of their Postern Petarades.

petard (pɪ'tɑːd, pɪ'tɑː(r)), *sb.* Also 7 **petar, -arr(e, -arh, -arde, -arra, patar, pettar, pittar, -ard.** [a. F. *pétard*, †*-art*, pl. *-ars* (1580 in Littré) (= It. *petardo* (Florio 1598); obs. Sp. *petar* 'a kinde of Artillery to batter, lately invented' (Minsheu 1599), mod.Sp. *petardo*), f. *péter* to break wind, f. *pet*: see PET *sb.*[3] and -ARD.]

1. A small engine of war used to blow in a door or gate, or to make a breach in a wall, etc.; originally of metal and bell-shaped, later a cubical wooden box, charged with powder, and fired by a fuse. (Now *Hist.*)

1598 FLORIO, *Petardo*, a squib or petard of gun powder vsed to burst vp gates or doores with. **1604** SHAKS. *Ham.* III. iv. 207 (2nd Quarto) For tis the sport to haue the enginer Hoist with his owne petar. **1609** B. JONSON *Sil. Wom.* IV. v, He has made a petarde of an old brasse pot, to force your dore. **1611** COTGR., *Petart*, a Petard, or Petarre; an Engine (made like a Bell, or Morter) wherewith strong gates are burst open. **1614** CAMDEN *Rem.* (ed. 2) 241 Petronils, Pistoll, Dagge, &c. and Petarras of the same brood lately inuented. **1627** DRAYTON *Agincourt* xxxviii, The Engineer providing the Petar [*rimes* are, far] To breake the strong Percullice. **1637–50** ROW *Hist. Kirk* (Wodrow Soc.) 511 The noblemen, with a pittard brake up the utter gate of the Castle of Edinburgh. **1670** COTTON *Espernon* Table, Montereau Faut-Yonne taken by Petarr. **1721** DE FOE *Mem. Cavalier* (1840) 113 By the help of a petard, we broke open the gate. **1849** MACAULAY *Hist. Eng.* iii. I. 322 A third had defended his old house till Fairfax had blown in the door with a petard.

b. *fig.* (See also HOISE *v.* 2 b.)

1639 MASSINGER *Unnat. Combat* I. i, Give but fire To this petard, it shall blow open, madam, The iron doors of a judge. **1642** FULLER *Holy & Prof. St.* v. ii. 364 His very name being a Petrard to make all the city-gates fly open. **1678** BUTLER *Hud.* III. i. 745 Eternal Noise and Scolding. The Conjugal Petard, that tears Down all Portcullices of Ears. **1878** STEVENSON *Inland Voy.* 133, I never saw such a petard of a man.

2. A kind of firework that explodes with a loud report; a cracker.

[**1611** COTGR., *Petard*, as *Petart*; also, a Squib.] **1668** J. WHITE *Rich Cab.* (ed. 4) 111 Standing launces are commonly made with hollow wood, to contain sundry petards or rockets. **1884** *St. James' Gaz.* 25 July 4/2 Fusees, petards, and crackers, fired off unintermittingly..form an indispensable accompaniment of a festive occasion in China.

†**3.** ? Some kind of cheating at dice. *Obs.*

1662 J. WILSON *Cheats* IV. i. (1664) 46 Did not I..teach you..the use of Up-hills, Down-hills, and Petarrs?.. And, generally, instructed you from Prick-penny, to Long Lawrence?

pe'tard, *v.* Also 7 petar, -arre. [a. F. *pétarder* (1603 in Hatz.-Darm.), f. *pétard* sb.: see prec.]

†**1.** *trans.* To blow open, or make a breach in, with a petard. *Obs.*

1603 FLORIO *Montaigne* I. lvi. (1632) 176 To scale a Castle, ..to pettard a gate. **1603** KNOLLES *Hist. Turks* (1621) 1307 They resolved to petarde the Castle. **1670** COTTON *Espernon* II. v. 201 To Petarre one of the Gates of the City.

†**b.** *transf. Obs.*

1654 Z. COKE *Logick* Pref., The prayers of the Saints ascending with you, will Petarr your entrances through heavens Portcullis.

2. *intr.* To fire off petards (sense 2). *rare.*

1837 CARLYLE *Fr. Rev.* I. III. ix, A 'wicker Figure'..is promenaded..then solemnly consumed by fire..with such petarding and huzzaing.

petardeer, -ier (pɛtəˈdɪə(r)). [a. F. *pétardier*, f. *pétard*: see -EER¹, -IER.] A soldier who manages and fires a petard.

1632 SHERWOOD, A Petardier, *petardier.* **1706** PHILLIPS, *Petardeer*, he that manages or applies a Petard. **1707** J. CHAMBERLAYNE *St. Eng.* III. 656 Ordnance..Mates to the Master-Gunner..Chief Petardier. **1715** *Jrnls. Ho. Comm.* 41 Wages to the..Fire-masters, Fire-workers, Petardiers, Bombardiers, &c. daily attendant and employed in the Office at the Tower [etc.].

†**peˈtarder.** *Obs.* = prec.

1611 COTGR., *Petardier*, a Petarder; one that vses, or shoots off, a Petard.

petarrero, obs. var. PEDRERO, a small gun.

petary, variant of PEATERY, peat-bog.

†**petasite.** *Herb. Obs.* [ad. Bot.L. *Petasītēs*, Gr. πετασίτης, f. πέτασος PETASUS.] The Butterbur or Pestilence-wort, *Petasites vulgaris*.

1771 *Gentl. Mag.* XLI. 521/1 The autumnal fevers..have gone off very easy this season, by the use of Petasite root.

petasma (pɛˈtæzmə). *Zool.* [a. Gr. πέτασμα something spread out.] In prawns of the family *Penæidea*, a membranous appendage attached to the first pair of pleopods.

1888 C. S. BATE in *Rep. Sci. Results Voy. H.M.S. Challenger*: *Zool.* XXIV. 230 The pleopods [of *Penæus*] are large and powerful, terminatng in two foliaceous branches in every pair except the first, which in the male carries attached to the base a large membranous appendage that I call 'petasma'. **1909** A. E. SHIPLEY in A. Sedgwick *Student's Text-bk. Zool.* III. v. 527 In *Penæus*, *Leucifer* and *Sergestes* a lobe projects inwards from the base of the first pleopods in the male, and may unite with its fellow to form the petasma (or curtain). **1966** *McGraw-Hill Encycl. Sci. & Technol.* V. 105/1 The male [genital] system [of Eumalocostraca] consists of the testis, vas deferens, ductus ejaculatorius, and sometimes a penis, modified thoracic limbs (pleopods), or petasma.

‖**petasus** (ˈpɛtəsəs). [L., a. Gr. πέτασος, f. root πετ- spread out: cf. *petal*.] A low-crowned broad-brimmed hat worn by the ancient Greeks, and frequently represented as worn by the god Hermes or Mercury; hence, also, the winged hat which Hermes is represented as wearing in later art.

1599 B. JONSON *Cynthia's Rev.* v. iii, A *Petasus* or Mercuriall hat. **1601** —— *Forest* x, Though he would steal his sisters' Pegasus, And rifle him; or pawn his petasus. **1842** J. YATES in *Proc. Philol. Soc.* (1854) I. 9 The dress..consists of boots,..a scarf..., and a petasus tied under the chin. **1873** SYMONDS *Grk. Poets* xi. 350 A boy emerging into manhood leaves his petasos and strigil and chlamys to Hermes, the god of games.

petaunce, etc., obs. forms of PITTANCE, etc.

petaurine (pɪˈtɔːraɪn), *a.* and *sb.* *Zool.* [ad. mod.L. *Petaurīnæ* fem. pl., f. *Petaurus*: see next, 2.] **a.** *adj.* Belonging to or having the characters of the *Petaurinæ*: see next, 2. **b.** *sb.* One of the *Petaurinæ*; a petaurist.

petaurist (pɪˈtɔːrɪst). [ad. Gr. πεταυριστής a performer on the πέταυρον or spring-board.]

†**1.** An acrobat, tumbler, rope-dancer. *rare*$^{-0}$.

1656 BLOUNT *Glossogr.*, *Petaurist*, a Dancer on the Ropes, a Tumbler, a runner upon Lines. **1658** in PHILLIPS.

2. *Zool.* Any marsupial of the genus *Petaurista* or subfamily *Petaurinæ* (= the old genus *Petaurus*), most of which have a patagium or parachute by which they are enabled to take flying leaps; a flying phalanger, Australian flying-squirrel, flying-opossum, or opossum-mouse.

1835 KIRBY *Hab. & Inst. Anim.* II. xvii. 159 The petaurists, or flying squirrels. **1839-47** TODD *Cycl. Anat.* III. 262/2. **1868** OWEN *Anat. Vertebr.* III. 416 In the Koala, which is, perhaps, a more strictly vegetable feeder than the Petaurists or Phalangers, the cæcum..is more than three times the length of the animal.

Hence **petauˈristic** *a.*: see quot.; **petauˈristine** *a.* and *sb.* = PETAURINE; so also **peˈtaurite** *a.*

1656 BLOUNT *Glossogr.*, *Petauristick*, tumbling, vaulting, running upon ropes. **1890** *Cent. Dict.*, *Petauristine*, *Petaurite*.

petchary (ˈpɛtʃərɪ). [Onomatopœic, from the bird's cry.] The grey king-bird or chicheree of the West Indies (*Tyrannus dominicensis* or *griseus*).

1860 GOSSE *Rom. Nat. Hist.* 17 Then the petchary, from the top of a tall cocoa-palm, cackled his three or four rapid notes, 'OP, PP, P, Q'.

pet-cock. [app. f. PET *sb.*¹ or ? *sb.*³ + COCK *sb.*¹ 12.] A small plug-cock fastened in a pipe or cylinder, as in a pump or a steam-engine, for purposes of draining or testing.

1864 in WEBSTER. **1875** in KNIGHT *Dict. Mech.* 1672/2. **1888** HASLUCK *Model Engin. Handybk.* (1900) 107 The pet-cock often fixed to a feed pump barrel is used to test the action of the pump (to see whether it is drawing water), and to draw off confined steam or air.

Pete, pete (piːt). [Dimin. of the name *Peter* (see PETER *sb.*).] **1.** *slang.* (With small initial.) **a.** A safe. Cf. PETER *sb.*¹ 6 b.

1911 G. BRONSON-HOWARD *Enemy to Society* iv. 73 All the time a man equipped with burglar's tools would be kneeling behind the safe and drilling it open; those 'petes'—as cracksmen call them—in people's houses are generally very easy to open. **1932** WODEHOUSE *Hot Water* i. 32 Show me the pete I can't open with my eye-teeth and a pin, and I'll eat it. **1938** D. RUNYON *Furthermore* viii. 153 This is a very soft pete. It is old-fashioned, and you can open it with a toothpick. **1951** WODEHOUSE *Old Reliable* x. 129 You think I'm scared to bust that pete?

b. Nitroglycerine, as used for safe-breaking.

1931 D. W. MAURER in *Writer's Digest* Oct. 29/2 *Soup*, nitroglycerine or 'pete'. **1948** MENCKEN *Amer. Lang.* Suppl. II. 668 Among the cant terms of the *jug-heavies* are..*soup* or *pete*, nitroglycerine.

c. *attrib.* and *Comb.*, as **pete box** = sense 1 a; **pete-man** = PETERMAN 3 c.

1931 D. RUNYON *Guys & Dolls* (1932) iv. 77 Nobody opens pete boxes for a living any more. They make the boxes too good, and they are all wired up with alarms. **1911** G. BRONSON-HOWARD *Enemy to Society* v. 105 You've already caught four 'pete-men' who attempted to drill the safe. **1931** *Everyman* 21 May 522/1 All my safe-blower pals used ..'pete-men'.

2. (With capital initial.) Used in various mild exclamations and phrases expressive of exasperation or annoyance; esp. in phr. ***for Pete's sake***.

1924 *Dialect Notes* V. 274 For the love of Pete, for Pete's sake. **1942** N. BALCHIN *Darkness falls from Air* ix. 170 Why in the name of Pete didn't you say so? **1949** N. MARSH *Swing, Brother, Swing* iv. 59 Carlisle heard Mr. Bellairs whisper under his breath: 'For the love of Pete!' **1959** W. GOLDING *Free Fall* vi. 129 Marry me, Taffy, for Pete's sake marry me. **1973** 'B. MATHER' *Snowline* xviii. 223 For Pete's sake don't ask bloody fool questions. **1975** *Listener* 24 July 115/1 For Pete's sake when will so-called 'experts'..get it into their noddles that rising wages and prices *are* inflation.

pete, obs. form of PEAT, PITY.

‖**petechia** (pɪˈtiːkɪə); usually in pl. **petechiæ** (-kiː). *Path.* [mod.L., a. It. *petecchia* 'a specke, or freckle or spot in ones face', pl. *petecchiè* 'the meazels or Gods markes' (Florio 1598); thence also F. *pétéchie* (1741 in Hatz.-Darm.). Ulterior history obscure: conjectures in Diez, Scheler, Littré; Hatz.-Darm. say 'd'origine inconnue'.] A small red or purple spot in the skin caused by extravasation of blood, occurring in certain fevers, etc.

[**1582** HESTER *Secr. Phiorav.* III. xvii. 32 This is the true and perfect Unction, that helpeth Petecchie, a disease so called in the Italian.] **1794-6** E. DARWIN *Zoon.* (1801) I. 434 Hence the oozing of blood from every part of the body, and the *petechiæ* in those fevers which are termed putrid. **1891** C. CREIGHTON *Hist. Epidem. Brit.* 588 There were small spots or petechiae like those often seen in the plague.

petechial (pɪˈtiːkɪəl), *a.* [ad. mod.L. *petēchiālis*, f. *petēchia*: see prec.] Of the nature of, pertaining to, or characterized by petechiæ.

1710 T. FULLER *Pharm. Extemp.* 129 In..petechial Fevers..it is accounted destructive. **1842** ABDY *Water Cure* (1843) 16 Attacked by spotted or petechial fever with violent epistaxis. **1866** A. FLINT *Princ. Med.* (1880) 1124 True petechiae are to be distinguished from the characteristic eruption of typhus fever, which is often called petechial.

petechiate (pɪˈtiːkɪət), *a.* [f. mod.L. *petēchia* + -ATE¹.] Marked or affected with petechiæ.

1890 in *Cent. Dict.* **1893** in *Syd. Soc. Lex.*

peˈtechio-, combining form of PETECHIA, as in ***petechio-erythematous*** adj. (See quot.)

1897 *Allbutt's Syst. Med.* II. 192 *Petechio-erythematous Rashes.*—These are formed as the name implies by a combination of petechial and erythematous eruptions.

†**peteˈcure, -ˈcurie.** *Obs.* [AF. for OF. *petite keuerie* (see CURY); cf. *Petty Cury*, name of a street in Cambridge.] 'Small cookery', cookery on a small or simple scale.

c **1420** *Liber Cocorum* (1862) 42 Of petecure I wylle preche; What falles þer to ȝow wylle I teche.

peteekot, peteet, obs. ff. PETTICOAT, PETIT.

petefull, obs. f. PITIFUL.

petegre, -greu, etc., obs. ff. PEDIGREE *sb.*

petelade: see PASTELADE.

†**ˈpetenˌlair.** *Obs.* [a. F. *pet-en-l'air* (petɑ̃lɛr), f. *pet* PET *sb.*³, *en l'air* in the air.] A jacket reaching down to the waist.

1753 A. MURPHY *Gray's Inn Jrnl.* No. 24 Two very ugly Monkeys, dressed out..with Paris Caps, and well chosen Petonlair and Petticoat. **1754** *Connoisseur* No. 25 (1774) I. 195 Hence it is, that sacks and petenlairs may be seen at Moorfields and White-chapel. **1761** FOOTE in *Brit. Mag.* II. 315 English cloths, Irish linens, and French peténlairs.

peteous, obs. form of PITEOUS.

Peter (ˈpiːtə(r)), *sb.*¹ Forms: 1-2 **Petrus**, 2- **Peter**; also 3-5 **Petir**, 4-5 **Petre**; 7- **peeter** (in senses 4-6). [In 12th c. *Peter*, ad. L. *Petrus*, a. Gr. Πέτρος, lit. 'Stone', translating Syriac *kēfā* (*Cephas*) 'stone', the surname conferred by Christ upon one of his disciples, Simon Peter, historically known as St. Peter, in honour of whom it subsequently became a noted Christian name, in many local forms, e.g. It. *Pietro*, *Pedro*, Sp. Pg. *Pedro*, Pr. *Peire*, OF. *Pierres*, in regimen *Pierre*, F. *Pierre*, AF. *Piers*, *Pers*, *Pierce*; OE. *Petrus*, gen. *Pet(e)res*, dat. *Pet(e)re*, acc. *Petrus*, *-um*; in Hatt. Gosp. nom. *Petrus*, *Peter*, dat. acc. *Petre*, ME. 3-5 *Petir*, 4-5 Wyclif *Petre*.]

A male Christian name; hence in many transferred uses, mostly referring directly or indirectly to St. Peter.

1. †**a.** As an exclamation or quasi-oath. *Obs.* (Cf. *Mary! Marry!* etc.)

c **1350** *Will. Palerne* 681 He wende ful witerly sche were in is armes: Ac peter! it nas but is puluere. **1362** LANGL. *P. Pl.* A. VI. 28 'Knowest þou ouht A Corseynt Men calleþ Seynt Treuþe'..'Peter!' quod a Plouȝ-Mon..'I knowe him as kuyndeliche, as Clerk doþ his bokes'.

b. [Imitative.] The cry of various tits.

1874 C. M. YONGE *Lady Hester* ii. 28 The tomtits were calling 'peter' in the trees. **1892** —— *Old Woman's Outlook* ii. 37 Sunshine, setting the thrushes and robins to sing, and the ox-eyes to cry Peter.

2. Used in proverbial phrases in conjunction with *Paul*; esp. in ***to rob*** (†***borrow from***, †***unclothe***) ***Peter to pay*** (†***clothe***) ***Paul***, to take away from one person, cause, etc. in order to pay, or confer something on, another; to discharge one debt by incurring another.

In quot. *c* 1400 we might think that there was a mere conjunction of two well-known alliterating names (cf. *Jack and Jill*); but something is prob. due to the association of St. Peter and St. Paul, as leading apostles and saints, and as fellow-martyrs at Rome. The phrase 'to rob Peter, etc.' may have no more specific origin; at least, the current explanation (quoted by Heylin in 1657-61) is in its details set aside by the chronology, as well as by the occurrence of the phrase in French also: cf. **1611** COTGR. s.v. *Pol*, *Descouvrir S. Pierre pour couvrir S. Pol*, to build, or inrich one Church with the ruines, or reuenues of another; also in mod.F., *décoiffer Saint Pierre pour coiffer Saint Paul*.

c **1400** *Lanfranc's Cirurg.* 331 Sum medicyne is for peter þat is not good for poul, for þe diuersite of complexioun. **1515** BARCLAY *Egloges* i, Fewe Princes geue that which to them selfe attayne... They robbe saint Peter therewith to cloth S. Powle. **1562** J. HEYWOOD *Prov. & Epigr.* (1867) 131 Rob Peter and pay Poule, thou sayst I do: But thou robst and poulst Peter and Poule too. **1581** PETTIE *Guazzo's Civ. Conv.* III. (1586) 168 b, That in my iudgement is a shamefull thing..to uncloath Peter to cloath Paule. **1657-61** HEYLIN *Hist. Ref.* (1674) 121 The Lands of Westminster so dilapidated by Bishop Thirlby..the rest laid out for Reparation to the Church of St. Paul; pared almost to the very quick in those days of Rapine. From hence first came that significant By-word (as is said by some) of Robbing Peter to pay Paul. **1692** R. L'ESTRANGE *Fables* clxxvi. (1714) 215 Those that Rob Peter, as we say, to Pay Paul, and take the Bread out of their Masters Mouths to give it to Strangers. *a* **1693** *Urquhart's Rabelais* III. iii. 35 You may make a shift by borrowing from Peter to pay Paul. **1926** *Times* 7 Jan. 9/6 Martin and Martin had been in low water for a long time and had recourse to the method of robbing Peter to pay Paul. **1961** D. WOODWARD tr. *Simenon's Premier* iii. 84 After the disastrous experiments made by previous governments, which had lived from day to day, robbing Peter to pay Paul, the only solution was a large-scale devaluation. **1976** *Star* (Sheffield) 29 Oct. 13/7 A Sheffield man who tried to set up a travel agency business was accused of 'robbing Peter to pay Paul', at Sheffield Bankruptcy Court.

†**3.** A name for the cowslip: = *herb Peter* (see HERB *sb.* 7 b). *Obs.*

a **1400-50** *Stockh. Med. MS.* 192 Peter or cowsloppe, *herba Petri*.

†**4.** A kind of wine: ? = PETER-SEE-ME. *Obs.*

a **1625** FLETCHER *Chances* v. iii. (*Song*) By old Claret I enlarge thee, By Canary thus I charge thee, By Britain, Mathewglin, and Peeter, Appear and answer me in meeter.

†**5.** 'Some kind of cosmetic' (Halliwell). *Obs.*

1689 *Disc. Van. Modish Women* iii. 43 Our fickle Ladies no less blush (I mean if their Peeter would give them leave). *Ibid.* xi. 175 Then her boxes of Peeter, and Patches, and all her Ornamental knacks and dresses.

6. a. *Thieves' Cant* and *Taxi-drivers' slang.* A portmanteau or trunk; a bundle or parcel of any kind.

1668 HEAD *Eng. Rogue* I. *Canting Vocab.*, *Peter*, a Portmantua. *a* **1700** B. E. *Dict. Cant. Crew*, *Flick the Peeter*, cut off the Cloak-bag or Port-manteau. **1828** P. CUNNINGHAM *N.S. Wales* II. 231 'Three peters cracked and frisked', made a frequent opening of the morning's log. **1894** A. MORRISON *Mean Streets*, etc. 261 People sat defiantly on piles of luggage at the railway stations, and there was never a peter to touch for. **1930** 'A. ARMSTRONG' *Taxi* xii. 164 'Peters' are pieces of luggage,—a threepenny extra for the driver. **1939** H. HODGE *Cab, Sir?* III. xv. 221 The driver calls each package a 'Peter'.

b. *Criminals' slang.* A safe or cash-box; a cash register, a till.

1859 G. W. MATSELL *Vocabulum* 66 *Peter*, a portmanteau; a travelling-bag; a trunk; an iron chest; a cash-box. **1862** [see *peter-cutter*, sense 8 a]. **1868** [see *peter-screwing*, sense 8 a]. **1869** *Macm. Mag.* Oct. 506/1 After we left the course, we..got a peter (cashbox) with very near a century of quids in it. **1889** CLARKSON & RICHARDSON *Police!* xxv. 351 In order to 'ready' these places, they watch the shops at closing time, to learn if the swag is placed in the 'Peter', or safe. **1935** A. J. POLLOCK *Underworld Speaks* 87/1 *Peter*, a cash drawer; a money box; cash register. **1936** J. CURTIS *Gilt Kid* xvii. 171 There was no safe. 'There ain't no peter.' 'No.' **1943** *Penguin New Writing* XVII. 66 He pushed me over one more double gin which he only pretended to ring up on the peter, but there wasn't a chance to talk. **1945** BAKER *Austral. Lang.* viii. 140 *To tickle the peter*, to rob a till. **1958** F. NORMAN *Bang to Rights* III. 121 If some poor unsuspecting manageing [*sic*] director left his peter open well, I ask you? **1965** M. SHADBOLT *Among Cinders* xvi. 143 'Did he tickle the peter?'..'To the tune of two thousand quid.' **1967** K. GILES *Death & Mr Prettyman* v. 98 But level, old boy, was Prettyman tickling the peter? **1970** G. F. NEWMAN *Sir, You Bastard* viii. 211 There was s'posed to be some dough in the Peter. **1978** *Daily Mail* 25 Jan. 12/2 While most of the country's police call the safe a 'peter', in London it's a 'gas'.

c. *slang.* A cell in a prison, a police station, a court of law, etc.; a lock-up. orig. *Austral.*

1890 BARRÈRE & LELAND *Dict. Slang* II. 125/1 *Peter* ..(Australian prison), punishment cell. **1953** K. TENNANT *Joyful Condemned* vi. 55 The doors of the peters just crash open at the name of McGarty. **1955** D. NILAND *Shiralee* 69 They could throw you in the peter stone-cold sober. **1958** F. NORMAN *Bang to Rights* I. 9, I turned and walked down the stairs to the peter under the court. **1960** C. HATTON in *Pick of Today's Short Stories* XI. 147 He snapped up any likely bloke just as soon as he..had come out of the peter. **1965** *Guardian* 10 Oct. 21/6 'Hurry up and slop out'—'Get back in your f—— Peter'. **1973** 'J. PATRICK' *Glasgow Gang Observed* ix. 81 He..had spent the first night in a police cell (or 'peter' as they call it).

d. *U.S. slang.* A stupefying drug.

1899 'J. FLYNT' *Tramping with Tramps* IV. 396 'Knockout drops' are also 'peter'. **1933** *Amer. Speech* VIII. II. 27/1 Among the addicts dope in general is known as *gow, junk*, or *peter* (any kind of *knockout drops*). **1971** E. E. LANDY *Underground Dict.* 148 *Peter*..Chloral hydrate.

e. *slang.* The penis.

1902 FARMER & HENLEY *Slang* V. 177/1 *Peter*... 4. (venery).—The *penis*: also *St. Peter.* **1928** *Dialect Notes* VI. 61 The proper name *Peter*..is so universally used by children and facetious adults as a name for the penis that it never quite loses this significance. Very few natives of the Ozarks will consider naming a boy *Peter*. **1940** C. MCCULLERS *Heart is Lonely Hunter* I. ii. 18 There was one fellow who had had his peter and his left leg blown off in a boiler explosion. **1970** R. D. ABRAHAMS *Positively Black* ii. 41, I fuck your mammy on a red hot heater; I miss her pussy and burn my peter. **1975** M. KENYON *Mr Big* v. 48 In New Jersey peter was childhood slang for penis, equivalent to willie and john thomas. **1977** J. WAMBAUGH *Black Marble* (1978) vi. 75 If you look very closely you can see a gerbil's dick, but not a parakeet's peter.

7. Blue Peter: see BLUE *a.* 13 (also *Naut.* and in *Whist* simply *Peter*). In *Bridge*, = ECHO *sb.* 8.

1803 *Naval Chron.* IX. 417 She has had Blue Peter's flag flying at the fore, as a signal..for sailing. **1885** PROCTOR in *Longm. Mag.* VI. 606 The signal or Peter consists in playing an unnecessarily high card to a trick. **1891** KIPLING *Barrack-Room Ballads* (1892) 205 See the shaking funnels roar, with the Peter at the fore. **1939** [see ECHO *sb.* 8]. **1945** PHILLIPS & REESE *How to play Bridge* III. xiii. 115 East's play of the 8 is the commencement of what is known as a 'peter'. **1959** *Listener* 27 Aug. 334/2 There are those who advocate the peter to indicate length at virtually all times in defence. **1966** *Sunday Tel.* 14 Aug. 9/6 Every bridge player knows the principle of high-low defence as a signal of encouragement. Generally known as the 'peter' in Britain and the 'echo' or 'come-on' in America, it is most frequently used against an opponent's trump contract to indicate strength or a doubleton. **1974** *Country Life* 28 Mar. 750/3 South played a Diamond to the King, East starting a peter.

8. *Comb.* **a.** † **Peter-corn**: see quot.; **Peter-fish** = *St. Peter's fish* (see b); † **petergrass (-grys)**, app. a name for wild thyme; **Peter Grievous** (also **Peter Grievance**), one who complains; a whining child; freq. *attrib.* or as *adj.*, complaining, fretful, miserable (*dial.* and *slang*); **Peter Gunner**, 'an amateur gun' (Farmer *Slang*; but cf. *Peter* = saltpetre); † **Peterlock** (?); **Peternet**, a kind of fishing net; **Peter-pastoral** *adj.*, derisive expansion of *pastoral.* Also *slang* in sense 6, as ***peter-claiming, -cutter, -hunting, -lay, -popping, -ringer, -screwing*** (see quots.). See also PETER-BOAT, -MAN, -PENNY.

1894 A. MORRISON *Mean Streets*, etc. 258 From this, he ventured on *peterclaiming, laying hands nonchalantly on unconsidered parcels and bags at railway stations. **1736** DRAKE *Eboracum* I. vii. 332 One thrave of corn out of every carucate of land..in the bishopric of York; which to this day is called **Peter corn.* **1862** MAYHEW *Lond. Labour* IV. 339 Some cracksmen have what is called a *petter-cutter, that is, a cutter for iron safes. *a* **1682** SIR T. BROWNE *Tracts* iii. 99 The fish called..by some, a *Peter or Penny-fish..having two remarkable round spots upon either side, these are conceived to be the marks of St. Peter's fingers. *c* **1425** *Voc.* in Wr.-Wülcker 645/2 *Hoc sirpillum*, *petergrys. [**1724** (*title of play*) Valentine and Orson, with the comical whining humours of Peter Pitiful.] **1774** F. HOPKINSON (*title*) A pretty story written in the year of Our Lord 2774. By *Peter Grievous, Esq. **1777** H. L. THRALE in *Thraliana* (1942) I. 155 Cradocke had written a Tragedy a very *deep* one they said..We'll call it *Peter* said he—the scene was in Russia, at least said I let it be *Peter Grievous.* **1875** W. D. PARISH *Dict. Sussex Dial.* 86 *Peter-grievous*, fretful; whining. 'What a peter-grievous child you are! Whatever is the matter?' **1894** *Southward Ho!* I. 338 (E.D.D.), A peter-grievous wot shrapes an makes a rookery, an a ranky chimley be pettigues fer to send a feller in de crazy-house. **1896** G. F. NORTHALL *Warwickshire Word-bk.* 172 *Peter Grievous, sb.* A grumbler: a grievance-monger. Oxf. (*Peter Grievance*, a cross, fretful child). The word is used as an adjective also, as 'He's a regular peter-grievous fellow.' Glouc., Worc. **1932** E. WEEKLEY *Words & Names* vii. 90 *Peter grievous*, a lachrymose individual, belongs to the class of *simple Simon.* **1615** *Cold Yeare 1614*, C ij, It was a shame that poore harmelesse Birds could not be suffered in such pittifull cold weather to save them-selues under a Bush..but that euery paltrie *Peter-gunner must fart Fire and Brimstone at them. **1633** SHIRLEY *Witty Fair One* II. ii, I smell powder,..this peter-gunner should have given fire. **1811** *Lexicon Balatr.*, *Peter Gunner*, who will kill all the birds that died last summer. **1812** J. H. VAUX *Flash Dict.*, **Peter-hunting*, traversing the streets or roads for the purpose of cutting away trunks, &c. from travelling carriages. **1725** *New Cant. Dict.*, **Peter-Lay*, Rogues who follow Petty Thefts, such as cutting Portmanteaus, &c. from behind Coaches. **1397–8** in *36th Rep. Dep. Kpr.* (1875) App. II. 90 [Nine locks with nine keys, called] *petrelokes. **1584** in *Descr. Thames* (1758) 63 Treat Nets, *Peter Nets, must be two Inches large in the Meish. **1880–4** DAY *Fishes Gt. Brit. & Irel.* I. p. ci, *Peter-nets* have floats along the upper rope and weights along the foot-line, one end is attached on shore, and the other anchored out at sea on a right line with the coast. **1821** *Blackw. Mag.* VIII. 672 Water-gruel sonnets on the *peter-pastoral ruralities of the Serpentine. **1960** *Observer* 24 Jan. 5/2 The expertise of *peter-popping consists in knowing just how much gelignite to use on the safe in question. **1863** *Once a Week* 7 Nov. 555/2 Well, my friend, a *Peter-ringer is one who tries to get his living by stealing carpet-bags. **1868** *Temple Bar* XXIV. 537 'What do you mean by "lobster-sneaking", and "Peter-screwing"?' 'Why, "lob" means the till, and "Peter" means a safe. Stealing the till and opening the safe is what we call "lob-sneaking" and "Peter-screwing".'

b. Combinations with *Peter's*: † **(St.) Peter's barge, bark, boat, ship**, allusive names for the Christian or Catholic Church; † **St. Peter's corn**, the single-grained wheat, *Triticum monococcum* (Linn.); † **Peter's cress**, a name for Samphire: see quot.; **(St.) Peter's fish**, a name given to several fishes (as the John Dory, the haddock, etc.) having a mark on each side near the pectoral fin, affirmed in legend to have been made by St. Peter's thumb and finger when he caught the fish for the tribute-money (Matt. xvii. 27); **Peter's penny**: see PETER-PENNY.

c **1440** CAPGRAVE *Life St. Kath.* IV. 1214 Ye shal leden hem on-to *peteres barge. **1597** GERARDE *Herbal* I. xlvii. §1. 68 *Briza Monococcos*, after L'Obelius;..in English *Saint Peters Corne. **1884** MILLER *Plant-n.*, St. Peter's Corn, *Triticum monococcum.* **1866** *Treas. Bot.* 347 **Cress, Peter's*, an old name for *Crithmum maritimum. Ibid.* 348 Thus a herb properly enough called Rock-cress from its growing in the crevices of rocks, came to be known as Peter's cress. **1611** COTGR., *Dorée*, the Dorce, or *Saint Peters fish. **1668** WILKINS *Real Char.* 137 Doree, St. Peters fish. **1857** WRIGHT *Dict.* II. 738/1 *Peter's-fish*, the haddock. Haddock has spots on either side, which are said to be marks of St. Peter's fingers, when he caught that fish for the tribute. **1678** *Donna Olimpia* 188 The only man judged capable of governing *St. Peter's Ship in so boisterous time.

c. St. Peter's wort (also **St. Peterwort, Peterwort**), a name for several plants: (*a*) the Cowslip, *Primula veris* (= Herb Peter); (*b*) certain species of *Hypericum* or St. John's wort, esp. *H. quadrangulum*; also of the kindred American genus *Ascyrum*; (*c*) Feverfew, *Pyrethrum Parthenium.*

? **1516** *Grete Herball* cccl. T v, Primula veris is called prymerolles. Some call it saynt peterworte. **1552** ELYOT, *Ascyrum*,..of some is called Peter worte: other wolde haue it to be Tutson; some think it to be a kind of S. Iohns worte, and that is most lykely, and may be called square S. Iohns grasse. **1578** LYTE *Dodoens* I. xi. 19 It [Feverfew] is called.. of some Whitewurte, also S. Peters wurt. *Ibid.* xlv. 66 It is hoate and dry like S. Iohns grasse, or S. Peters wurte. **1597** GERARDE *Herbal* II. cli. 434. **1733** MILLER *Gard. Dict.*, *Ascyrum*, S. Peter's wort. **1785** MARTYN *Rousseau's Bot.* xxv. (1794) 373 Another wild sort..growing in moist hedges and woods, and called Saint Peter's wort.

Hence **'peterkin, 'peterling** *nonce-wds.* [dim. of *Peter*], a petty claimant to the spiritual position of St. Peter and his reputed successors the Popes.

c **1662** F. KERBY in *P. Heywood's Diaries*, etc. (1883) III. 30 Proud peter-lings vouchsafe the crown to bles. **1892** HUXLEY *Ess. Controverted Quest.* 15 Setting up Lutheran, Zwinglian, and other Peterkins, in the place of the actual claimant to the reversion of the spiritual wealth of the Galilean fisherman.

Peter ('piːtə(r)), *sb.*[2] The name of Dr. Laurence Johnston *Peter* (b. 1919), Canadian-born U.S. educationalist and author, used *attrib.* in ***Peter principle*** (see quot. 1968). Also ***Peter's principle.***

1968 L. J. PETER *Peter Principle* (1969) i. 25 My analysis of hundreds of cases of occupational incompetence led me on to formulate *The Peter Principle*: In a Hierarchy Every Employee Tends to Rise to His Level of Incompetence. **1969** *Sunday Times* (Colour Suppl.) 21 Dec. 30/2 What is now called the Peter Principle: the system by which a man is always promoted until he reaches a job which he cannot do. **1970** *Guardian Weekly* 25 July 6 Much blame must attach to the administrative system,..which religiously follows the Peter Principle of promoting mediocrities. **1976** *Publishers Weekly* 15 Mar. 58/3 Most flibbertigibbet corporate president (maybe the Peter Principle applies here). **1978** *Jrnl. R. Soc. Arts* CXXVI. 273/2 In in-company situations, assessment centres can hopefully help avoid Peter's principle, whereby everyone is promoted to his level of incompetence. **1980** *Observer* 27 Jan. 4/3 There is a school of Westminster and Belfast thought which sees Mr Atkins as a classic example of the Peter Principle—promoted above his level of competence.

† **peter**, *v.*[1] [f. PETER *sb.*[1] 5.] *trans.* To apply cosmetics to, to 'paint'.

1656 EARL MONM. tr. *Boccalini's Advts. fr. Parnass.* 161 My face is now so fresh and ruddy, because people have peter'd it, and coloured it with lakes.

'peter, *v.*[2] *slang* or *colloq.* [Origin unknown.]

1. *trans.* To cease, stop, leave off. *slang.*

1812 J. H. VAUX *Flash Dict.*, *Peter that*, synonymous with *stow that.*

2. a. *intr.* (orig. *U.S. Mining colloq.*) To diminish gradually and cease; to run out and disappear (as a stream, a vein of ore); to die out, give out, fail, come to an end. Usu. const. *out.* Hence **'petering-out** *vbl. sb.*

1846 *Quincy* (Illinois) *Whig* 6 Jan. 1/4 When my mineral petered why they all Petered *me.* If so be I gets a lead, why I'm Mr. Tiff again. **1854** H. H. RILEY *Puddleford* vi. 84 He 'hoped this 'spectable meeting war n't going to Peter-out'. *a* **1865** A. LINCOLN in McClure *Life* (1896) 133 The store in which he clerked was 'petering out'—to use his own expression. **1865** S. BOWLES *Across Continent* 133 Humboldt River..runs west and south from three hundred to five hundred miles, and then finds ignominious end in a 'sink', or ..quietly 'peters out'. **1881** RAYMOND *Mining Gloss.*, *Peter* or *peter out*, to fail gradually in size, quantity, or quality. **1883** STEVENSON *Silverado Sq., Childr. Israel* i, But the luck had failed, the mines petered out. **1892** *Sat. Rev.* 9 Jan. 45/1 Human effort of all kinds tends..to 'peter out'. **1923** R. MACAULAY *Told by Idiot* III. 221 The year and the government petered towards their end. **1926** E. F. SPANNER *Naviators* 100 Lucky your engine petered out, Sterne. **1944** F. CLUNE *Red Heart* 6 The fabulous silver-lead wealth..has enticed a city of 15,000 inhabitants to arise in the desert wastes—and there they will continue to dwell until the lode peters. **1949** 'J. TEY' *Brat Farrar* xix. 170 The..petering-out of the poorer suburbs. **1955** *Times* 28 June 3/3 With the end of this partnership, however, the innings virtually petered out. **1976** *Quoddy Tides* (Eastport, Maine) 13 Aug. 4/4 Hurricane 'Belle'..petered out before reaching the Quoddy area.

b. *trans.* To exhaust; to cause or allow to peter out; const. *away*, to squander. Freq. as ppl. adj.

1869 *Overland Monthly* III. 127 After a long desert journey the oxen become much 'petered'. **1878** C. HALLOCK *Amer. Club List & Sportsman's Gloss.* p. viii/1 *Peter-out*, to fail; to exhaust; to collapse. **1943** *Amer. Speech* XVIII. 67/2 *Petered out* (exhausted), S.C., N.C., Tenn., La., Tex. **1956** B. HOLIDAY *Lady sings Blues* (1973) vi. 58 He wouldn't give us nothing but a lecture on how he saved his money and how we petered ours away. **1971** 'D. HALLIDAY' *Dolly & Doctor Bird* xvi. 228 It was another petered-out trail.

3. *intr. Whist* and *Bridge.* To play a high card followed by a low one. Cf. PETER *sb.*[1] 7.

1887 *N. & Q.* 29 Oct. 356/1 The Blue Peter..is..used when a ship is about to start... Calling for trumps at whist or 'petering' is derived from this source. **1901** C. J. MELROSE *Bridge Whist* 38 Another whist convention, which may occasionally be employed with advantage in Bridge..is known variously as 'Petering', the 'trump signal' or the 'call for trumps'. **1939** N. DE V. HART *Bridge Players' Bedside Bk.* 141 At one time..a player petered to show two cards only of a suit. **1961** *Times* 7 June 8/3 My partner had not petered in hearts. **1976** *Country Life* 22 Jan. 202/1 West started by cashing two top diamonds, on which East petered.

4. *slang.* **a.** *intr.* (See quot. 1925.) **b.** *trans.* To blow open (a safe).

1925 *Flynn's* 7 Mar. 192/1 *Peter, v.*, to use knock-out drops; to use nitroglycerine. **1962** B. KNOX *Little Drops of Blood* iii. 65 The Dolman boys are going to peter a pawnshop safe tonight.

peter, variant of PETRE, saltpetre, etc.

peteraro, obs. var. PEDRERO, a small gun.

'peter-boat. [app. f. PETER *sb.*[1] + BOAT *sb.*: cf. *Peterman.*] Local name (chiefly on the Thames and adjacent coasts) for a decked fishing-boat smaller than a smack or yawl; also for a dredgerman's double-ended boat, travelling equally well bow or stern foremost.

1540 in R. G. Marsden *Sel. Pl. Crt. Adm.* (1894) I. 99, I ..being in a certeyn petyr boat comyng toward the towne of Lye. **1607** DEKKER & WEBSTER *Northw. Hoe* II. i. Wks. 1873 III. 20 If we haue but good draughts in my peeter-boate. **1769** *Chron.* in *Ann. Reg.* 69/1 Discovered by the people of a peterboat, on the shore somewhere below Gravesend. **1851** MAYHEW *Lond. Labour* (1861) II. 148 The boats of the dredgermen are of a peculiar shape. They have no stern, but are the same fore and aft. They are called Peter boats. **1862** *Catal. Internat. Exhib.* II. XII. 18 Model of 'Peterboat', used in the whitebait fishery.

Peterborough[1] ('piːtəbʌrə). *N. Amer.* Also Peterboro. The name of a town in Ontario used *attrib.* and *ellipt.* to designate a type of canoe (orig. built there), made entirely of wood.

1882 *Forest & Stream* 2 Nov. 277/1 There is the open Peterboro' canoe, so familiar to the Canadian eye. **1895** *Rudder* Sept. 215 Eleven paddling canoes—eight Peterboro's and three Rushton—and the Cruiser, complete the fleet. **1897** J. W. TYRRELL *Across Sub-Arctics of Canada* ii. 20 We launched our handsome 'Peterboroughs' in the great stream. **1901** *Daily Colonist* (Victoria, B.C.) 30 Oct. 6/2 We portaged around it on the way up by packing our Peterboro up a hill one hundred feet high, taking us a whole day. **1966** *Canad. Geogr. Jrnl.* Sept. 78/3 John Stephenson ..later came up with the excellent cedar rib craft known the world over as the Peterborough Canoe. **1973** D. ANDERSEN *Ways Harsh & Wild* iii. 86, I set a net in an eddy and later paddled Ted's Peterborough canoe down to check.

Peterborough[2] ('piːtəbʌrə). The name of a town in eastern England, site of a phase of the Neolithic Age: used to denote the type of civilization of that period, and the materials or people associated with its culture.

1910 *Archaeologia* LXII. 346 The characteristic decoration of the drinking-cup or beaker is well known, and full justice has been done to the Peterborough series by our

Fellow, Mr. Praetorius. **1922** *Antiquaries Jrnl.* II. 231 The Peterborough pottery seems to bear all the signs of its makers advancing in ceramic skill by gradual stages. **1935** HUXLEY & HADDON *We Europeans* vii. 237 The 'Peterborough' ware was brought from the Baltic by long-headed people who buried their dead in long barrows. **1939** V. G. CHILDE *Dawn European Civilization* (ed. 3) xviii. 306 In Norfolk and even Wiltshire Peterborough folk..were associated with its exploitation. *Ibid.* 317 Skara Brae and Peterborough traditions survived. **1943** J. & C. HAWKES *Prehist. Brit.* ii. 47 These are the Peterborough people, largely descendants of the old Mesolithic inhabitants of Britain, who, while adopting certain Neolithic accomplishments such as potting, herding and simple husbandry, continued to follow the old mode of life as hunters and fishers. **1947** V. G. CHILDE *Dawn European Civilization* (ed. 4) xviii. 323 In the standard Peterborough ware the rims are thickened and the shallow bowls are richly decorated. **1951** *Proc. Prehist. Soc.* XVII. 119 The associations and chronology of these Group VI factories and their products are firmly fixed in the Neolithic with emphasis in favour of the Peterborough phase. **1954** S. PIGGOTT *Neolithic Cultures* xi. 303 We can now see that Peterborough pottery is distinctive of only one variant within a group of Secondary Neolithic cultures. *Ibid.* 312 (*heading*) Relationships of the Peterborough culture. **1967** *Antiquaries Jrnl.* XLVII. 201 Its sharply formed tripartite upper half, and the decoration of this so lavishly by whipped-cord impression, support those traits in strongly recalling Neolithic antecedents, among the Mortlake bowls ..of British 'Peterborough' ware.

peterera, -ro, var. PEDRERO, a small gun.

† **'peterish**, *a.* *Obs.* [f. PETRE + -ISH[1].] Containing saltpetre.

1690 in R. W. Cochran-Patrick *Med. Scotl.* iv. (1892) 65 When peterish earth shall be found, to dispose thereof for the convenience of the gun-powder factories.

peterman ('pi:təmən). [app. f. PETER *sb.*[1] (in allusion to the occupation of Simon Peter).]

1. A fisherman; formerly, app. one who practised a particular kind of fishing.

c **1400** *Act Comm. Council London* in C. Welch *Tower Bridge* (1894) 88 An Acte concernyng Petermen and other fysshing in the Thames [decrees that] none fish in the Thames with anglys nor other engines, but only with nets of assize and only at times seasonable, nor near any wharf of the bridge. **1500** *Acc., ibid.*, Fines of Petermen for fishing and rugging at the bridge, and with their nets and engines daily hurting the same contrary to divers acts thereof made. **1624** HEYWOOD *Captives* IV. i, *Clowne.* But [resolve mee] feythefully. *Fisher.* As I am honest peeterman. **1629** H. BURTON *Truth's Triumph* 230 The troubled sea, where Romes Peter-men finde the best fishing. **1630** in *Descr. Thames* (1758) 68 No Peter-men shall..fish or work with any Manner of Net upon the said Water. *a* **1825** FORBY *Voc. E. Anglia, Peterman*, a fisherman; a fellow-craftsman of the Apostle Peter. **1894** C. WELCH *Tower Bridge* 73 Crowded with devout citizens, from the dignified Alderman to the rough-clad peterman. (*Historical.*)

† **2.** Some kind of beer. *Obs.*

1767 S. PATERSON *Another Trav.* II. 51 To give him a dram, or a glass of peterman.

3. a. *Thieves' Cant.* [f. PETER *sb.*[1] 6.] A thief who steals portmanteaus from vehicles.

1812 *Sporting Mag.* XXXIX. 209 As good a cracksman or peter-man as any in the ring. **1863** *Story of Lanc. Thief* 9 (Farmer) Sometimes he'd turn peterman, and he had been generally lucky at it.

b. (See quots.) *slang.*

1897 ELDRIDGE & WATTS *Our Rival* xi. 289 The rogue's name for the professional users of 'knockout drops' is Petermen or Peter-players. **1904** 'No. 1500' *Life in Sing Sing* 2-6/2 *Peter man*,..person who administers a drug for the purpose of robbery. **1908** *Sun* (N.Y.) 2 Mar. 2/2 A peterman is one who uses knockout drops as an aid to robbery.

c. A safe-blower. *slang.*

1900 'FLYNT' & 'WALTON' *Powers that Prey* 176 Sliger's record, both as 'peter-man' and convict, was produced. **1936** J. G. BRANDON *Pawnshop Murder* i. 5 Your flash 'peterman' is as gentle-natured as the average curate. **1950** R. CHANDLER *Let.* 18 May in *R. Chandler Speaking* (1966) 80 Opening a good safe (without a time lock) requires expensive and heavy tools, the finest drills either to drill out the lock or to get in the nitro if he is a peterman. **1960** *Observer* 24 Jan. 5/1 Gelignite in plastic sticks..was the British peterman's basic material. **1968** P. N. WALKER *Carnaby & Gaolbreakers* i. 13 Well, you'd never be a peter man, or a breaker in a month of Sundays. **1973** 'B. GRAEME' *Two & Two make Five* vii. 68 The wall safe..would [not] have presented much difficulty to an expert peterman. **1977** J. WAINWRIGHT *Nest of Rats* I. vii. 46 The genuine peterman —the safe-breaker who takes a personal pride in pitting his wits against those of the safe-makers.

† **'Petermas.** *Obs. rare.* [f. PETER *sb.*[1] + MASS *sb.*[1]] The feast of St. Peter ad Vincula, 1 Aug. (Cf. PETER-PENNY 1, quot. 1747.)

c **1000** WULFSTAN *Hom.* l. 272 Romfeoh ȝelæste man æȝhwilce ȝeare be Peteres mæssan. **1548** *Aberdeen Regr.* XX. (Jam.), Petermas nixt cumis.

petermorel, obs. var. *petty morel*: see MOREL.

Peter Pan. [The name of the boy hero of J. M. Barrie's play *Peter Pan, the boy who wouldn't grow up* (1904).] **1.** Used *attrib.* to designate various styles of clothing, esp. **Peter Pan collar** (also with lower-case initials), a flat collar with rounded ends, often white or light-coloured.

1908 S. FORD *Side-Stepping with Shorty* iv. 60 She was sportin' a Peter Pan peekaboo that would have made Comstock gasp. **1909** *Westm. Gaz.* 10 July 15/1 The collars and cuffs are what we call 'Peter Pan'.., edged with Valenciennes. **1923** *Daily Mail* 12 June 1 (Advt.), Can also be had with Robespierre or Peter Pan collar. **1933** M. LUTYENS *Forthcoming Marriages* 204 She was wearing a white Peter Pan collar over a little blue cape. **1948** 'J. TEY' *Franchise Affair* xiv. 148 Miss Tuff had worn peter-pan collars over her dark frock for twenty years. **1958** *Vogue* Sept. 133 Clothes for children with puff sleeves, peter pan collars. **1960** *Times* 15 Jan. 14/3 A white silk shirt with a frilled Peter Pan collar. **1975** *Listener* 10 July 46/1 The maids, they used to wear what we call their print dresses in the mornings. In the afternoon they changed into blue alpaca or black, with white Peter Pan collar and little cuffs.

2. Used allusively for an immature adult (usu. a man); one who is emotionally (occas. physically) retarded. Also *attrib.*

1914 G. B. SHAW *What I really wrote about War* (1930) ii. 109 It is frightful to think of the powers which Europe..left in the hands of this Peter Pan [*sc.* the Kaiser]. **1927** A. HUXLEY *Proper Stud.* 163 An electorate composed in a great part of mental Peter Pans. **1931** J. S. HUXLEY *What dare I Think?* ii. 62 The Peter Pan type of semi-dwarf who, though perfectly proportioned, never grows up fully. **1956** I. BROMIGE *Enchanted Garden* II. iii. 99 'Fiona..has the wide-eyed simplicity of eternal youth.' 'A Peter Pan.' **1958** *Sunday Express* 15 June 15/2 Bogarde has still got his hooks into the Peter Pan racket... He is still prowling the screen, demanding mother love from his millions of female fans. **1971** *Guardian* 21 Oct. 6/4 Professor Desmond Pond... Professor of psychiatry at the London Hospital,..told of highly-educated students who became 'Peter Pans' and never managed to leave adolescence. **1976** J. WAINWRIGHT *Bastard* v. 76 He is something of a museum-piece..Peter Pan, in person. The fink who never grew up..never acknowledged the responsibilities of adulthood. **1978** *Time* 3 July 48/2 Warren's conquests of women are not totally successful... But the Peter Pan quality in Warren is very attractive to some. He teaches them to fly, and they have extraordinary experiences with him. Then they grow up and go on, and he keeps flying. Like Peter Pan, he always comes back to another little girl who's ready to fly off with him to never-never land.

Hence **Peter 'Panic** (*nonce*) [joc. f. PANIC *sb.*[2]], confused, childish behaviour; also as *adj.* [-IC], characteristic of a Peter Pan; **Peter 'Pan(n)ish** *a.* [-ISH[1]] = *Peter Panic* adj.; hence ***Peter Pan(n)ishness***; **Peter 'Pannery, Peter-Pannery**, immaturity; childish quality or behaviour; **Peter 'Panning** (see quot. 1974).

1914 'I. HAY' *Knight on Wheels* (ed. 2) xiv. 143 Mr. Mablethorpe remained as incorrigibly Peter Pannish as ever. Although his hair was whitening..he declined to grow up. **1928** F. E. BAILY *Golden Vanity* xvi. 252 They were all in the early twenties except Joe, and he had an eternal Peter Pan-ish-ness which made the passage of time as marked by the calendar quite immaterial in his case. **1934** R. CAMPBELL *Broken Record* 160 Though not predisposed to this Peter Panic, I had considerable time to see it at work at first hand. **1937** *Times Lit. Suppl.* 10 July 502/3 If we are seeking to know what gives a thinness to much of his fiction ..it was not 'Peter Pannishness' in the sense of shrinking from adult reality. **1958** *Listener* 12 June 987/3 The Peter-Panish English is not entirely the fault of the translator. **1960** *Spectator* 2 Sept. 345 An occasional embarrassing lapse into peter-pannery. **1962** A. HUXLEY *Island* ix. 152 A year in jail won't cure a Peter Pan of his endocrine disbalance... For Peter Panic delinquency, what you need is early diagnosis. **1962** *John o' London's* 2 Aug. 115/3 General air of Peter Pannery. **1974** *Daily Tel.* 12 Mar. 3/2 So many people have invented fictitious children to evade income tax that Inland Revenue officials have introduced their own catch phrase for it 'Peter Panning'. **1975** *Listener* 9 Oct. 464/3 To use one's children's slang is Peter Pannish. **1978** *Radio Times* 28 Jan. 13/4 You could say that Lewis was a latter-day Lewis Carroll... There is a Peter Panishness to his heroes and echoes of Ratty and Badger in his anthropomorphics.

'Peter-,penny, Peter's penny. Usu. in pl. 'Peter-,pence, Peter's pence. [f. PETER *sb.*[1] (in reference to the claim of the see of Rome to the patrimony of St. Peter) + PENNY.]

1. *Hist.* An annual tax or tribute of a penny from each householder having land of a certain value, paid before the Reformation to the papal see at Rome; also, a similar tribute paid by several northern lands.

The institution of Peter's pence has been attributed to Ine king of Wessex, 688–728, and to Offa king of Mercia, 755–94. It is mentioned as due by ancient law in a (Latin) letter of Canute in 1031. It was discontinued by statute in 1534.

c **1205** LAY. 31964 Inne wes þe uormeste mon þe Peteres peni bigon. **1297** R. GLOUC. (Rolls) 10139 Fram rome he broȝte and heste þat me here nome Petres peni of ech hous þat smoke out of come. [Cf. 9720 Peires panes þat me gadereþ manion.] *c* **1380** *Antecrist* in Todd *Three Treat. Wyclif.* (1851) 147 Antecrist makiþ hise [priests] knowen.. bi peterpens gederynge. *a* **1491** J. ROUS *Hist. Reg. Angl.* (1716) 72 Denarius Petri, Anglice Petir pens, vel Romscot. **1535** COVERDALE *Bible* Ded., I passe ouer his pestilent pykynge of Peter pens out of youre realme. **1647** N. BACON *Disc. Govt. Eng.* I. lxvi. (1739) 148 The Roman Tribute of Peter-pence was allowed by the Conqueror's Law to the Bishops Court. **1660** R. COKE *Power & Subj.* 183 Every one who shall have thirty pence of current money in his house, of his own property..shall pay a Peter-penny. **1747** CARTE *Hist. Eng.* I. 274 Being paid at the rate of a penny by every family that had thirty pence annual rent in land, every year on the first of August, the feast of St. Peter ad vincula, [it] was thence called Peter-pence. **1882** *Encycl. Brit.* XIV. 668/1 Linköping..it was at a council held in this town in 1153 that the payment of Peter's pence was agreed to at the instigation of Nicholas Breakspeare.

2. Applied to the voluntary contributions of Roman Catholic peoples to the papal treasury since 1860.

1884 *Times* (weekly ed.) 26 Sept. 12/1 The more ignorant believers who were asked to contribute to Peter's Pence. **1902** *Encycl. Brit.* XXV. 483/2 He [Antonelli, 1870] obtained from the Italians payment of the Peter's pence (5,000,000 lire) remaining in the papal exchequer.

† **,Peter-see-'me.** *Obs.* Also **Peter-sa-meene, -se-mea**, (?) **-semine.** [A corruption of *Pedro Ximenes*, the name of a celebrated Spanish grape, so called after its introducer: see quot. 1846, and Notes to Dekker in Pearson's ed. 1873.] A kind of Spanish wine.

1617 BRATHWAIT *Law of Drinking* 80, I am phlegmaticke as may be, Peter see me must inure me. **1623** J. TAYLOR (Water P.) *Praise of Hempseed* 5 Peeter-se-mea, or head-strong Charnico, Sherry, nor Rob-o-Dauy here could flowe. **1623** MIDDLETON & ROWLEY *Sp. Gipsy* III. i. (1653) E j b, Peter see me shall wash thy nowle. **1630** DEKKER *2nd Pt. Honest Wh.* Wks. 1873 II. 160 A pottle of Greeke wine, a pottle of Peter sa meene. **1631** HEYWOOD *1st Pt. Fair Maid of West* III. Wks. 1874 II. 301 Peter-see-mee, Canary, or Charnico. [**1846** FORD *Gatherings fr. Spain* 152 The *Pedro Ximenez*, or delicious sweet-tasted grape which is so celebrated, came originally from Madeira, and was planted on the Rhine, whence about two centuries ago one Peter Simon brought it to Malaga.]

Petersen grab ('pi:təsən). *Marine Biol.* [Named after its inventor, Carl Georg Johan *Petersen* (1860–1928), Danish marine biologist, who first described it in 1911 (*Rep. Danish Biol. Station* XX. 47).] A kind of grab for obtaining a sample of the bed of a body of water, consisting of two jaws semicircular in vertical cross-section and hinged along the top, arranged so as to close automatically on contact with the bottom.

1923 *Sci. Investigations, 1922* (Fishery Board Scotland) III. 1 (*title*) Preliminary survey of the Scottish waters of the North Sea by the Petersen grab. **1950** *Biol. Rev.* XXV. 309 The Petersen grab will only produce reliable results on the softer bottoms. **1970** tr. *J. Schwoerbel's Methods Hydrobiol.* iv. 118 In larger rivers the Petersen grab can be used... The grab weighs 40 kg.

Petersen graph ('pi:təsən). *Math.* [Named after Julius *Petersen* (1839–1910), Danish mathematician, who first devised it (*L'Intermédiaire des Mathématiciens* (1898) V. 227).] A graph having ten vertices and fifteen lines, which may be drawn as a pentagram disposed symmetrically within a pentagon, each vertex of the latter being joined by a line to the nearest vertex of the former.

1947 *Proc. Camb. Philos. Soc.* XLIII. 460 The 5-cage is the 'Petersen graph'. **1962** O. ORE *Theory of Graphs* xv. 240 The so-called Petersen graph has the form indicated in Figure 15.1.3. It is regular of degree 3 and order 10. It was first introduced by Petersen as an illustration of a graph with $\rho = 3$ which is not the sum of 3 subgraphs of first degree. **1976** *Sci. Amer.* Apr. 127/1 The other class of uncolorable trivalent maps Tait missed are all nonplanar (impossible to draw on the plane without at least one intersecting edge). The simplest example, known as the Petersen graph, is shown in the upper illustration at the right.

Petersham ('pi:təʃəm). [Named after Viscount Petersham, *c* 1812.] (*attrib.*, or *ellipt.* as *sb.*)

a. Name for a kind of heavy overcoat or breeches formerly fashionable; also for the cloth of which such overcoats are made.

1812 *Sporting Mag.* XL. 95 What crowding and jostling to get a side view Of my Petersham breeches and coat of sky-blue. **1819** *Hermit in London* III. 82 Put on my dowlas Petershams, half-stockings, and dicky. **1863** GRONOW *Recollect.* II. 154 The Viscount [Petersham] was likewise a great Mæcenas among the tailors, and a particular kind of great-coat when I was a young man was called a Petersham. **1864** *Athenæum* 29 Oct. 558/3 We deal with less disputable matters when we come to Petersham coats, so called from the head of the 'Dandies' of half-a-century ago, who afterwards became Earl of Harrington. **1904** *Woollen Draper's Terms* in *Tailor & Cutt.* 4 Aug. 479/3 Petersham Cloth: A heavy woollen cloth having a round nap surface; used for heavy overcoats.

b. Name for a thick kind of ribbon of ribbed or corded silk used for strengthening the waists of women's dresses, and for belts and hatbands.

1873 *Young Englishwoman* Mar. 147/2 Waistband *Petersham*, and all the odds and ends of needlework. **1930** V. SACKVILLE-WEST *Edwardians* ii. 62 Miss Wace..affected a dress of heliotrope serge with a stiff petersham belt. **1957** *Terms & Definitions* (Textile Inst.) (ed. 3) 82 *Petersham ribbon* (*millinery*), a ribbon usually with silk or rayon warp and having single picks of relatively coarse weft. *Ibid.*, *Petersham ribbon* (*skirt*), a narrow-fabric having a pronounced rib weft-way composed of one or more picks per rib and having lateral stiffness. **1972** *Daily Tel.* 18 May 9/2 The jacket was edged in navy petersham and fastened with navy and gold buttons.

c. A style of hat.

1825 H. WILSON *Mem.* III. 65 His little Petersham hat seemed to have been remit de nouveau, for the third time, at least.

Petertide ('pi:tətaid). [f. PETER *sb.*[1] + TIDE *sb.*] The 29th of June (the feast of St. Peter in the Church of England and of St. Peter and St. Paul in the Roman Catholic Church), or the period round about it.

1912 C. MACKENZIE *Carnival* xxxiv. 349 Well, being in the city, I suppose we must follow city manners, but darn 'ee, I never thought to go gazing at dancing like maidens at Petertide. **1974** *Daily Tel.* 3 July 16 Southwark..has worked out a fair system. This accounts for the large number of ordination candidates over Petertide. **1975**

Church Times 7 Mar. 12/5, I look forward to my ordination at Petertide conscious of the numerous people who have made it possible.

Peterwort: see PETER *sb.*[1] 8 c.

petewous, -wus, obs. forms of PITEOUS.

ˈpetful, *a. rare.* [f. PET *sb.*[2] + -FUL.] Pettish.
1861 SALA *Dutch Pict.* xx. 315 Sitting, with petful impatience, in the parlour.

peth, pether, dial. forms of PITH, PEDDER.

pethidine (ˈpɛθidiːn). *Pharm.* [f. P(IPER)IDINE with insertion of *eth* from ETHYL, METHYL.] A narcotic analgesic (usu. given, orally or intramuscularly, as the hydrochloride, a colourless crystalline compound) which has actions similar to those of morphine but of shorter duration and is less addictive; ethyl 1-methyl-4-phenylpiperidine-4-carboxylate, $C_{15}H_{21}NO_2$.
1942 *Lancet* 22 Aug. 234/2 Pethidine hydrochloride, a synthetic compound closely allied to morphine in composition, and combining the analgesic effect of morphine with the spasmolytic effect of the atropine group and papaverine, is issued by Roche Products. **1942** *Ibid.* 24 Oct. 487 Fairly recent.. is the carboxylic acid ethyl ester of 1-methyl-4-phenylpiperidine, officially named pethidine by the GMC a year ago and known on the continent as 'Dolantin' and in the United States as 'Demerol'. **1947** *Daily Tel.* 1 Mar. 3/4 Several bottles found in the man's room were marked 'pethidine'. **1955** *Times* 2 July 4/3 The annual Government report to the United Nations.. estimates that there are 317 known drug addicts... Heroin and pethidine were used by 17 per cent. and 16 per cent. respectively. **1962** [see MEPERIDINE]. **1972** *Nature* 15 Dec. 411/2 Hysterotomy patients received pethidine 100 mg postoperatively for analgesia. **1974** M. C. GERALD *Pharmacol.* xiii. 247 Meperidine or pethidine, as this drug is more commonly called outside the United States, was fortuitously discovered in 1939 as the result of a search for atropine-like agents possessing antispasmodic activity. This compound was the first totally synthetic narcotic analgesic agent.

†pethrow, obs. corrupt form of PEDRERO.
1630 J. TAYLOR (Water P.) *Brave Sea-fight* Wks. III. 42 Ordnance of whole Cannon, Demy-Cannon, Cannon Pethrow, whole Culuering, and Demy-Culuering.

pethwind, variant of BETHWINE.

petiaguay, -augre, obs. corrupt ff. PIRAGUA.

peticoot, -cote, obs. forms of PETTICOAT.

peti degree, petiegre, -grew: see PEDIGREE *sb.*

petie, obs. form of PETTY, PITY.

petifactor: see PETTIFACTOR.

†ˈpetifoot, *rare.* Pl. petifeet. [For *petty feet*; rendering L. *pediculus*, dim. of *pes* foot.] Little foot: in quot. = peduncle or pedicle (of an apple).
c **1420** *Pallad. on Husb.* III. 902 Let her petifeet downward be wende, And touche hem not vntil they schal be spende.

petigre(e, -grue, etc., obs. forms of PEDIGREE *sb.*

†petigrew, pettigree. *Obs.* Also 6 **petygrew, petigrue, -gre(e.** [f. PETIT, PETTY *a.* + Pr. *greù, agreù* holly (also *grevel, agreveu, agrafel, agrafuelh*, Mistral) = Gascon *agreu*, Cat. *grevol* (Körting):—L. *acrifolium* holly (f. *acri-s* sharp, piercing + *folium* leaf): cf. *aquifolium* (for **acui-, acifolium*) holly. *Petit greù* may itself occur in Pr., as the equivalent of F. *petit houx* 'little holly', synon. of *brusc*, butcher's broom.]
A name for Butcher's Broom (*Ruscus aculeatus*).
1538 TURNER *Libellus, Ruscus*.. Humile officinæ uocant bruscum, angli Butchers broome, & Petygrew. **1548** —— *Names of Herbes* 69 Petigrue groweth in Kent wilde by hedge sydes. **1597** GERARDE *Herbal* II. cccxxiv. 760 It is called..in English Kneeholme..and Petigree. **1611** COTGR., *Petit houx*, Kneeholme, Pettigree, Butchers Broome.

‖**pétillant** (petijɑ̃), *a.* [Fr.] Crackling, sparkling, lively; *spec.* of semi-sparkling wine (see quot. 1965).
1881 C. C. HARRISON *Woman's Handiwork* III. 215 Permit your wood-fire to sink into the *pétillant* stage upon the tiled hearth. **1902** G. MEREDITH *Let.* 19 Apr. (1970) III. 1440, I wish I were about in the world to give you communications more *pétillantes*. **1938** *Times Lit. Suppl.* 15 Jan. 43/1 Her spirit is..more fiery, its flame richer, more consuming and far less *pétillant* than before. The sparkle, which made her such an entertaining, quick-witted..character on her first appearance has now almost vanished. **1955** A. LICHINE *Wines of France* (ed. 2) 214 Mousseux and pétillant wines are rarely imported into the United States, largely because these lesser wines carry the same high duty as fine Champagnes, and the resulting prices make them poor value. **1959** *Times* 14 Nov. 9/7 The light pétillant white wines of Neuchâtel are famous. **1960** *House & Garden* Aug. 71/3 It [*sc.* a wine] has a slight prickle—it is what the French call *pétillant*. **1965** O. A. MENDELSOHN *Dict. Drink* 257 *Pétillant*, French term, meaning crackling or sparkling, applied to slightly sparkling wines, much less heavily charged than mousseux. **1971** *Homes & Gardens* Aug. 102/1 These pétillant wines are now all the rage in France. **1974** *Times* 16 Feb. 15/4 The only successful *pétillant* (semi-sparkling) wine so far produced in the Eastern Mediterranean is Bellapais.
So **pétillance** *sb.*
1951 R. POSTGATE *Plain Man's Guide to Wine* iv. 87 *Pétillance* occurs when the wine in bottle is still working, and produces some natural gas. **1974** *Times* 18 May (Summer Drinking Suppl.) p. i/2 A good muscadet..with its faint *pétillance*, more felt than seen. **1975** *Times* 28 June 13/3 A deliciously fragrant rosé... There is a slight liveliness, verging on *pétillance*.

ˈpetillate, *v. nonce-wd.* [f. F. *pétiller* (dim. of *péter* to break wind): see -ATE[3] 7.] *intr.* To crepitate, to effervesce (as an aerated liquid).
1852 *Blackw. Mag.* LXXI. 622 Sparkling Hock and petillating Moselle.

†petiˈlodemenage. *Obs. rare.* = Petty lodemanage: see LODEMANAGE.
1622 MALYNES *Anc. Law-Merch.* 138 Primage, Petilodeminage, and sometimes Pilotage, according to the accustomed manner in the like Voyages.

petimorel, obs. var. *petty morel*: see MOREL.

petinine (ˈpɛtɪniːn, -naɪn). *Chem.* [f. Gr. πετειν-ός volatile + -INE[5].] A synonym of *isobutylamine*, $CH(CH_3)_2{\cdot}CH_2{\cdot}NH_2$.
1853 *Pharmac. Jrnl.* XIII. 134 The sulphates of.. chinoline, picoline, petinine are..insoluble. **1857** MILLER *Elem. Chem.* III. 212. **1868–77** WATTS *Dict. Chem.* V. 737 Petinine, a volatile base obtained by Anderson from the most volatile portion of bone-oil, is..isomeric, or perhaps identical, with tetrylamine.

petioˈlaceous, *a. rare*$^{-0}$. [f. L. *petiolus* PETIOLE + -ACEOUS.] = PETIOLATE.
1858 MAYNE *Expos. Lex.*, *Petiolaceus*..petiolaceous.

petiolar (ˈpɛtɪəʊlə(r)), *a.* [f. L. *petiolus* PETIOLE + -AR.] Of, pertaining to, of the nature of a petiole.
1760 J. LEE *Introd. Bot.* III. xv. (1765) 204 Petiolar Buds. **1793** MARTYN *Lang. Bot.*, *Petiolaris cirrus*, a petiolar tendril, proceeding from the petiole of a leaf. **1830** LINDLEY *Nat. Syst. Bot.* 169 The genus Eriogonum in which there is no petiolar sheath. **1884** BOWER & SCOTT *De Bary's Phaner.* 376 In the glandular ends of the petiolar appendages of Passifloræ.
Also **ˈpetiolary** *a.*, in same sense. *rare*$^{-0}$.
1828 WEBSTER, *Petiolar, Petiolary.*

petiolate (ˈpɛtɪəʊlət), *a.* [ad. mod.L. *petiolāt-us*, f. *petiol-us* PETIOLE: see -ATE[1]. In F. *pétiolé.*] Having or furnished with a petiole; stalked; borne or growing upon a petiole or stalk. **a.** *Bot.*
1753 CHAMBERS *Cycl. Supp.* s.v. *Leaf, Petiolate Leaf*, one affixed to a plant by means of a peculiar pedicle. **1785** MARTYN *Rousseau's Bot.* xvi. (1794) 183 The lower ones [leaves] petiolate, the upper sessile. **1861** BENTLEY *Man. Bot.* (1870) 133 When a leaf arises from the stem by means of a petiole it is said to be stalked or petiolate.
b. *Zool.*: see PETIOLE 2; *spec.* in *Entom.* Belonging to the division *Petiolata* of hymenopterous insects, with a stalked abdomen, as bees, wasps, etc.
1826 KIRBY & SP. *Entomol.* xliii. IV. 185 Insects that have a petiolate abdomen. **1856–8** W. CLARK *Van der Hoeven's Zool.* I. 350 Abdomen always petiolate.
Also **ˈpetiolated** *a.*, in same senses.
1756 *Phil. Trans.* XLIX. 835 The leaves..of this species are constantly petiolated. **1856–8** W. CLARK *Van der Hoeven's Zool.* I. 641 Branchiopoda.—Two eyes petiolated and a frontal ocellus sessile.

petiole (ˈpɛtɪəʊl). *Nat. Hist.* [= mod.F. *pétiole*, ad. L. *petiol-us* little foot, stem, stalk of fruit: specialized by Linnæus:
1751 LINNÆUS *Philos. Bot.* 41 *Petiolus, Pedunculus, Pediculus* antecessoribus Synonymi fuere, nobis autem minime. Petiolus promit folium, et Pedunculus Fructificationem.]
1. *Bot.* The footstalk of a leaf, by which it is attached to the stem; a leaf-stalk.
1753 CHAMBERS *Cycl. Supp.*, *Petiole, petiolum*, among botanists, expresses that stalk which supports the leaves,.. as the peduncle does the fructifications. *Ibid.* s.v. *Leaf*, The oppositely pinnated..folioles stand opposite to one another on the common petiole. **1870** HOOKER *Stud. Flora* 250 Leaves,..gradually narrowed into long winged petioles.
2. *Zool.* Applied to a slender stalk-like structure supporting some part, as the eye-stalk in certain Crustacea, or the stalk connecting the abdomen and thorax in wasps, ants, and other insects.
1782 ANDRÉ in *Phil. Trans.* LXXII. 441 *note*, Crabs, whose eyes are placed on petioles, or stalks, and are moveable. **1856–8** W. CLARK *Van der Hoeven's Zool.* I. 243 Filaments of branchiæ numerous, placed on a petiole twisted spirally.

petioled (ˈpɛtɪəʊld), *a.* [f. prec. + -ED[2].] Furnished with a petiole; petiolate.
1793 MARTYN *Lang. Bot.*, *Petiolatum folium*, a Petiolate or Petioled leaf. **1877–84** F. E. HULME *Wild Fl.* p. xiii, Stem-leaves shortly petioled or sessile.

petiolule (pɛtɪˈɒljuːl). *Bot.* [ad. mod.L. *petiolul-us*, dim. of *petiolus* PETIOLE; also in mod.F. (Littré).] A partial or secondary petiole; the footstalk of a leaflet in a compound leaf.
1832 LINDLEY *Introd. Bot.* I. ii. 94 In all truly compound leaves the petiole is articulated with each petiolule. **1861** BENTLEY *Man. Bot.* (1870) 167 The divisions of the petiole ..are then called petiolules, stalklets, or partial petioles.
Hence **petiˈolular** *a.* [= F. *pétiolulaire*], pertaining to a petiolule; **petiˈolulate** *a.* [= F. *pétiolulé*], having, or borne upon, a petiolule.
1858 MAYNE *Expos. Lex.*, Petiolular. **1881** BAKER in *Jrnl. Linn. Soc.* 267 Leaflets 7,..alternate, petiolulate.

petious, obs. form of PITEOUS.

petipanik, *petty panic*: see PETTY *a.* 5.

petit (†ˈpɛtɪt, ‖pəti), *a.* (*sb.*) Also 6 **petyt**, 7 **pettit**; *β.* 5–6 **petyte**, 5–8 **-ite**, 7 **pettite**; *γ.* 7 **peteet, -e.** [a. F. *petit.* fem. *petite* (11th c.) = Pr. and Cat. *petit*, OIt. *petitto, pitetto* (both in Florio, 1611). Found in Anglo-Fr. phrases or combs. from 13th c., and as an Eng. adj. in 14th c.; but before 1400 written also *pety*, later *petty*, which became the proper English form; but, beside this, *petit* continued in use, being still common in the 17th c., though little used in the 18th c., exc. as retained in legal phrases, or as influenced by modern French (in some phrases from which it still occurs). While it was still a living Eng. word the final *t* was pronounced, as shown by the frequent 16–17th c. spelling *petite, -yte* (in Eng. only a spelling-variant, not distinctively fem. as in Fr.). The stress varied; the alliteration and rhythm in *Piers Plowman* shows *ˈpetit* (as does the surname *Pettit*); while the spellings *peteet, -eete*, show final stress.
The origin of F. *petit* is uncertain: 'the primitive type appears to have been **pitittum* or **pettittum*' (Darmest.), and as there is no such form in L., many scholars think it a derivative of a Celtic root *pett-* 'part, piece, bit', whence also It. *pezza*, F. *pièce*, Eng. *piece*. Cf. Diez s.v. *Pito*, Thurneysen *Keltoroman.* s.v. *Pezza*, Körting (1901), stem *pett-*, No. 7106.]
A. *adj.* **†1.** Of small size, small; also occas. Few or small in number. *Obs.*
α. **1377** LANGL. *P. Pl.* B. XIV. 242 Pouerte nis but a petit þinge appereth nouȝt to his naule. **1420** *E.E. Wills* (1882) 46, I petit brase morter. **1569** T. NORTON *To Q.'s deceived subjects N.C.* D iij, The number is great agaynste you, infinitely exceedyng your petit multitude. **1665** NEEDHAM *Med. Medicinæ* 193 That sort of petit Animals. **1671** F. PHILLIPS *Reg. Necess.* 356 Which declared the number of his Servants not to be small, petit, or inconsiderable. [**1854** H. MILLER *Sch. & Schm.* xv. (1858) 323 A really handsome man,..with..an erect though somewhat petit figure.]
β. **1567** DRANT *Horace* To his Bk. R viij, Stamering age to petyte laddes in corners al wil reede thee. **1638** SIR T. HERBERT *Trav.* (ed. 2) 113 Kishmy a pettite castle not farre from Tasques. **1650** FULLER *Pisgah* I. xii. 40 Many other petite tracts of ground. **1671** GREW *Anat. Plants* I. vii. §16 As in cutting a petite and Infant-Bean, may be seen.
γ. **1660** tr. *Amyraldus' Treat. conc. Relig.* I. i. 6 The fortuitous concourse of infinite peteet Atomes. **1675** TEONGE *Diary* (1825) 114 At the south east corner of this peteete building.
†2. Of little importance or value; insignificant, trifling: = PETTY *a.* 2. *Obs.*
α. **1362** LANGL. *P. Pl.* A. VIII. 60 His pardoun In purgatorie is petit, I trowe. **1554** in Strype *Eccl. Mem.* III. xvi. 139 It was not meet..that the Bishop [Bonner] should debase himself to such petit Functions of Preaching. **1599** THYNNE *Animadv.* (1865) 52 But on these and suche petit matters, I will not nowe longe insiste. *a* **1716** SOUTH *Serm.* (1717) V. 492 Their grand Subject was Truth, and consequently above all petit Arts, and poor Additions. *a* **1734** NORTH *Lives* (1826) III. 275 His name..confined to some petit cycle in a musty genealogy. **1759** DILWORTH *Pope* 99 [His] taste..was turned entirely towards the grand; he hated everything petit.
β. **1565** JEWEL *Repl. Harding* (1611) 135, I passe by other petite faults. **1610** T. ABBOTT *Old Way* 25 By a petite reason [marg. *absurda ratiuncula*] of Pelagius he was driuen to speake absurdly thereof. *a* **1637** B. JONSON *Underwoods, Eupheme* ix, In all her petite actions, so devote. **1691** WOOD *Ath. Oxon.* (1817) III. 1203 In translating..and other petite employments.
†3. a. Subordinate, minor, on a small scale: = PETTY *a.* 3. Sometimes as opposed to *grand*. *Obs.*
α. **1531** *Dial. on Laws Eng.* II. li. S v b, To scour the see of pyrates & petyt robbers of the see. **1552** HULOET, Petit brybar, *furcifer*... Petit bribarye, *latrocinium*. *a* **1661** FULLER *Worthies, Hereford.* II. (1662) 35 Milfred (a petit Prince of that Country). **1722** J. RICHARDSON *Statues*, etc. *Italy* 273 The Stiff, Petit Style of Painting, the Remnant of Gothicism. **1724** BP. NICOLSON in Ellis *Orig. Lett.* Ser. II. IV. 335 All our pedlers and petit merchants are confederating..against the currency of them. [**1897** *Genealog. Mag.* Oct. 365 In it [manor court of Teignmouth] were anciently tried all petit cases relating to the inhabitants.]
β. **1570–6** LAMBARDE *Peramb. Kent* (1826) 11 Kent was then divided into foure petite kingdomes. **1588** —— *Eiren.* IV. xx. 619 To deliuer the gaoles of..idle poor folkes, petite theeues, and some others. **1613** PURCHAS *Pilgrimage* III. ii.

196. **1641** HEYLIN *Help to Hist.* (1671) 4 Those inferiour and petite Kings, being in tract of time worn out.

b. Hence *petit-bribing* adj., practising 'petit bribery': cf. quot. 1552 in 3 *a*. *Obs.*

1634 CANNE *Necess. Separ.* 143 The petitbribing Sumner rideth foorth laden with excommunications.

4. In special collocations (rarely hyphened), as an earlier form or variant of *petty*: **petit custom**: see PETTY *a.* 5; **Petit Bag, canon, captain, officer**: see PETTY BAG, PETTY CANON, PETTY CAPTAIN, PETTY OFFICER; also, *petit* CAPE, CHAPMAN, CONSTABLE, JUROR, JURY, LARCENY, SERGEANTY, -TRY, SESSIONS, TREASON.

‖**5.** In some mod. French collocations adopted in English, as **petit battement (sur le cou-de-pied, sur le talon)** (see quots. 1957); **petit baume**, a liquor distilled from *Croton balsamiferum* in the West Indies; **petit beurre**, a sweet butter biscuit; **petit bleu**, a telegram in France, esp. one sent by the pneumatic post in Paris; **petit choux** (see quot.); **petit déjeuner**, breakfast in France, and by extension, elsewhere; **petit four**, a small fancy cake, biscuit, or sweet, usu. served with the dessert course of a meal; also *fig.*; **petit nègre** (see quots.); **petit nom**, a pet-name; **petit pain**, a small bread roll; **petit point** (see quot.); **petit poussin**, a young chicken; **petits paquets**, name of a game of some kind; **petits** (erron. **petit**) **pois**, young sweet green peas; **petits soins**, small attentions or services [*lit.* small cares]; **petit suisse**, a cream cheese (see quot. 1966); **petit tranchet** (*Archæol.*), a small stone artefact whose blade is produced by transverse-flaking; **petit verre**, a glass of liqueur [*lit.* a small glass]. Also PETIT-MAÎTRE, PETIT SOUPER.

1914 *Petit battement [see *pas de chat* s.v. PAS 2]. **1930** CRASKE & BEAUMONT *Theory & Pract. Allegro in Classical Ballet* 66 Bring the right foot *sur le cou de pied devant* and execute four *petite battements devants* (that is, beaten without passing). **1957** G. B. L. WILSON *Dict. Ballet* 48 *Petit Battement sur le Talon*, lit. small beating on the heel, a movement in which the danseuse, on the point and supported by her partner, lightly beats the heel of the supporting foot with the sole of the working foot. *Ibid.*, *Petit Battement sur le Cou-de-pied*, an exercise at the bar in which the dancer beats lightly with the working foot, which may be fully extended or partially relaxed, to the front and back of the cou-de-pied of the supporting leg. **1858** HOGG *Veg. Kingd.* 658 The distilled plant furnishes the liquor called *eau de mantes*, or *petit baume*, in the West Indies. **1906** *Mrs. Beeton's Bk. Househ. Managem.* facing p. 1432 Biscuits... Cream Toast... Wine... *Petit Beurre. **1913** C. MACKENZIE *Sinister St.* I. I. ix. 130 They all sat down at midnight,.. not at all too much tired to sip grenadine sucrée and to crunch Petit Beurre biscuits. **1937** J. BETJEMAN *Continual Dew* 22 He gives his Ovaltine a stir And nibbles at a 'petit beurre'. **1958** I. MURDOCH *Bell* ii. 39 She indicated a large biscuit tin. .. 'No more Petit Beurre,' Peter Topglass was saying meditatively to himself. **1967** V. NABOKOV *Speak, Memory* (rev. ed.) ii. 46 A couple of broken Petit-Beurre biscuits she had found on a plate. **1975** *Times* 13 Mar. 14/7 An expensive-looking parcel.. revealed a pound of *petit beurre* biscuits. **1908** W. S. MAUGHAM *Magician* x. 171 The note.. was a *petit bleu sent off from the Gare du Nord. **1920** D. H. LAWRENCE *Touch & Go* 7 It may be that coal-owners are like the *petit bleu* arrangement, a system of vacuum tubes for whooshing Bradburys about from one to the other. **1924** W. J. LOCKE *Coming of Amos* xvi. 204 She had just finished dressing when a *petit-bleu*—a letter sent by pneumatic post, was delivered. **1933** 'G. ORWELL' *Down & Out* vi. 44 An agency.. sent me a *petit bleu*. **1978** R. GRAYSON *Murders at Impasse Louvain* xvi. 113 He had sent her.. a 'petit bleu' or message by the pneumatic telegraph. **1706** PHILLIPS, *Petits Choux*, a sort of Paste for garnishing, made of fat Cheese, Flower, Eggs, Salt, etc. bak'd in a Pye-pan, and Ic'd over with fine Sugar. **1895** E. DOWSON *Let.* 9 Dec. (1967) 326 After a *petit déjeuner at the Crémerie I get hungry again. **1909** W. J. LOCKE *Septimus* iii. 37, I skip afternoon tea and dinner and supper, and *petit déjeuner*. **1914** R. BROOKE *Lett.* (1968) 561 Up at 6 and bathe. *Petit déjeuner* of coffee and fruit 6.45. **1926** F. W. CROFTS *Inspector French & Cheyne Mystery* xv. 213 The 4.50 fr. for *petit dejeuner* suggested a fairly good hotel. **1936** J. BUCHAN *Island of Sheep* xii. 228 The fashion of the household was for a skimpy *petit déjeuner* and then an elaborate midday meal. **1963** N. MARSH *Dead Water* (1964) v. 125, I took my *petit dejeuner* in my room. **1972** L. BACHMANN *Ultimate Act* v. 39 Your *petit déjeuner* is waiting. **1884** L. TROUBRIDGE *Life amongst Troubridges* (1966) 172 We all went to Charbonnel.. for iced coffees and *petits fours. **1898** H. A. DE SALIS *Housewife's Referee* 266 *Petits Fours*, small fancy biscuits. **1904** H. JAMES *Golden Bowl* II. xlii. 367 Amerigo.. selected for presentation to the other visitor a plate of *petits fours*. **1908** [see CRYSTALLIZED *ppl. a.* 3]. **1948** *Good Housek. Cookery Bk.* 59 *Petits fours*, very small fancy cakes, iced cakes and biscuits served at the end of the formal dinner. Crystallised fruits, and caramellised and fondant-coated fruits are often included in the petits fours. **1961** [see KUGELHUPF]. **1970** *New Yorker* 19 Sept. 31/1 The French served champagne and *petits fours*. **1974** *Publishers Weekly* 25 Mar. 55/2 Reichler's little prose petit fours accompanying the book's 100-plus photos.. are toothsome and on-the-nose. **1964** E. PALMER tr. *Martinet's Elem. Gen. Linguistics* v. 156 '*Petit nègre*' is the nearest equivalent in French to pidgin. **1972** J. L. DILLARD *Black English* i. 22 Pidgin versions of French (still represented in West Africa by *Petit Nègre*) and English began developing in the factories. *Ibid.* iii. 78 Pidgin French (called *Petit Nègre*).. came to the New World at about the same time. **1974** *Times* 7 Jan. 16/3 Many [immigrants] get by on a pidgin language which the French call 'petit negre'. **1867** O. LOGAN in *Galaxy* Aug. 442 'Well, you see,' replied he, referring to her familiarly by her *petit nom, 'Leo hates the leg business as much as anybody but, bless you, nothing else pays now-a-days; so what can she do? **1939** W. FORTESCUE *There's Rosemary* lxxi. 368 After dinner she said gaily: 'And now for your important business with B. D. (her *petit nom* for General Long).' **1841** THACKERAY in *Fraser's Mag.* June 718/2 I.. swallow.. the greater portion of my *petit pain, too, before my second dish arrives. **1924** A. D. SEDGWICK *Little French Girl* I. i. 3 The long buttered *petits pains*. **1963** J. CREASEY *Depths* vi. 47 Sitting on the terrace, eating croissants or *petits pains*. **1977** E. AMBLER *Send no more Roses* vii. 141, I had one of the petits-pains just delivered by the village bakery. **1882** CAULFEILD & SAWARD *Dict. Needlework* 32/1 *Tent Stitch*, this stitch is also known as '*petit point' and 'perlenstich'. **1902** *Petit poussin [see *milk chicken* s.v. MILK *sb.* 10]. **1926–7** *Army & Navy Stores Catal.* 69/1 Poultry.. Petit Poussin (English)—each 3/-. **1927** *Daily Express* 1 Apr. 5, English poultry is dear, but there are spring chicken and petits poussins, ducklings and plovers' eggs. **1961** *Harrods Food News* 16/2 Poultry.. English Petit Poussin. **1821** M. EDGEWORTH *Let.* 19 Dec. (1971) 298 Went to the *hall of the marble table* and there played at **petits paquets* (not time to describe) a great deal of running and laughing among pretty men and pretty maids. **1874** L. TROUBRIDGE *Life amongst Troubridges* (1966) 88 After tea we .. played at Petit Pacquet in the field outside. **1820** M. EDGEWORTH *Let.* 4 June (1979) 144, I give you one dinner.. 2d service—œufs au jus—*petits pois (stewed)—lettuce (ditto). **1855** F. DUBERLY *Jrnl.* 21 Mar. in E. E. P. Tisdall *Mrs. Duberly's Campaigns* (1963) v. 134 We made purchases of chickens, carrots, *petits pois verts* and various other necessaries. **1916** A. BENNETT *Lion's Share* xi. 87, I shall like very much to hear the details of this story of *petits pois*. **1951** *Good Housek. Home Encycl.* 591/1 Peas vary in size from the small 'petit pois' to large ones. **1952** A. GRIMBLE *Pattern of Islands* 81 An exquisite little shoulder of frozen lamb, *and* some onions, *and* potatoes, AND a tiff of real French petits pois. **1961** J. CREASEY *Follow Toff* xx. 171 He served the duck.. the *petit pois*, tiny new potatoes. **1820** A. OPIE *Tales of Heart* IV. 292 Melville dined at home that day, and paid her voluntarily all those **petits soins* which she had demanded of Arthur. **1825** H. WILSON *Mem.* III. 50, I never .. heard of one.. who was so eternally au [*sic*] petits soins, and paid a woman the unremitting attention which I received from Worcester. **1847** F. A. KEMBLE *Let.* 17 Dec. in *Rec. Later Life* (1882) III. 318 The 'small attentions', *les petits soins* of affection. **1857** C. KINGSLEY *Two Yrs. Ago* II. iii. 59 Elsley showed Lucia no *petits soins*. **1959** *Times* 31 Oct. 7/4 All the barometer ever gets in the way of *petits soins* is this allegedly deleterious tapping. *c* **1906** A. JOHN *Let.* in *Listener* (1972) 6 July 10/1 He is always asking for *petits-suisses which are unheard of in this country. **1951** [see GERVAIS]. **1962** J. BRAINE *Life at Top* iii. 53 He selected a piece of Gorgonzola, then.. pointed out a *petit Suisse*. **1966** P. V. PRICE *France: Food & Wine Guide* 284 *Petit Suisse*, a small, round, fresh cream cheese, evolved by a farmer's wife ..near Gournay, about the middle of the nineteenth century. **1979** H. MCCLOY *Smoking Mirror* ii. 12 A delicious cream cheese called *petit suisse*. **1939** W. B. WRIGHT *Tools & Man* ix. 76 The microliths are predominantly trapezes or **petit tranchets* for use as arrow heads. **1949** *Proc. Prehist. Soc.* XV. 127 A flint assemblage including petit-tranchet derivative arrowheads and one leaf-arrowhead. **1954** S. PIGGOTT *Neolithic Cultures* ii. 44 An arrowhead of the 'derived *petit-tranchet*' type. **1963** H. N. SAVORY in Foster & Alcock *Culture & Environment* iii. 33 In South Wales, the main overlap of this new element was with the Western Neolithic rather than the Beaker Culture, as is shown by the regular appearance of *petit-tranchet* derivatives in surface collections where leaf arrowheads predominate. *a* **1855** C. BRONTË *Professor* (1857) I. viii. 141 They proposed a '*petit verre', I declined. **1860** *Once a Week* 23 June 606/2 He must be an unfortunate Frenchman indeed who cannot contrive to get a *bouillon* and a *petit verre* at the railway station. **1862** THACKERAY *Philip* xix, He summoned the waiter, and paid for his *petit verre*. **1895** *Cornh. Mag.* Nov. 521 [He] sipped his *petit verre*. **1939** AUDEN & ISHERWOOD *Journey to War* 292 Self-confident among the laughter and the *petits verres*.

B. *sb.* †**1.** A little boy in a grammar-school; a junior schoolboy. Also *transf. Obs.*

1460–70 *Ipswich Sch. Reg.* in *Trans. R. Hist. Soc.* (1902) XVI. 166 Petytis vocati Apeseyes and Song. **1531** ELYOT *Gov.* III. xxv, Some.. be as who sayeth petites and unethe lettered. **1534** MORE *Comf. agst. Trib.* I. xix. Wks. 1165/2 A teacher of children (or as they call suche one in the grammer scoles) an vsher or a mayster of the petytes. **1571** FULKE *Confut. Popery* 127 You haue discouered such a solemne secret to the yong petits of Popery. **1691** tr. *Emilianne's Observ. Journ. Naples* 19 They.. count them [classes] backward; for that which receives the Petits at first, is called the seventh Classis.

†**2.** A variety of domestic pigeon. *Obs. rare.*

1725 BRADLEY *Fam. Dict.* s.v. *Pigeon*, Many sorts of Pigeons, such as Carriers,.. Barbs, Petits, owls, spots [etc.].

‖**petit bourgeois** (pəti burʒwa). Also fem. **petite bourgeoise**; pl. **petits bourgeois**; fem. **petites bourgeoises**. [Fr., lit. 'little citizen': see BOURGEOIS *sb.*[1] and *a.*] A member of the middle or commercial classes in a society; freq. in derogatory use, one judged to have conventional or conservative political and social attitudes. Also *fig.* and (freq. with hyphen) *attrib.* or as *adj.* See also PETTY BOURGEOIS.

1853 C. BRONTË *Villette* III. xliii. 338 Should you object to beginning with three petite bourgeoises, the Demoiselles Miret? **1859** M. ARNOLD *England & Italian Question* iii. 16 How indignant he was with the townspeople, the *petits bourgeois*. **1887** F. ENGELS in Moore & Aveling tr. *Marx's Capital* I. i. 39 It is, of course, highly desirable in the eyes of the petit bourgeois, for whom the production of commodities is the ne plus ultra of human freedom and individual independence, that the inconveniences resulting from this character of commodities not being directly exchangeable, should be removed. *Ibid.* ii. 59 We may form an estimate of the shrewdness of the petit-bourgeois socialism, which, while perpetuating the production of commodities, aims at abolishing the 'antagonism' between money and commodities, and consequently,.. at abolishing money itself: We might just as well try to retain Catholicism without the Pope. **1897** G. B. SHAW *Our Theatres in Nineties* (1932) III. 79 She suddenly drops from an Egyptian warrior queen into a naughty English *petite bourgeoise*. **1931** *Times Lit. Suppl.* 1 Oct. 755/1 'Elise Hermann'.. takes the reader into a *petit bourgeois* world. **1939** S. SPENDER tr. *Toller's Pastor Hall* II. 82 We called freedom a petit bourgeois phrase, so little did we know what slavery is. **1942** E. WAUGH *Put out More Flags* iii. 216 The provincial *petit-bourgeois* youth floundering and groping in the gloom of Teutonic adolescence. **1943** C. GRAY *Contingencies* (1947) i. 11 Arthur Rimbaud.. sought refuge in the existence of a typical French *petit bourgeois* from the terrible and terrifying realities which confronted him. **1954** KOESTLER *Invis. Writing* 25 Revulsion against this code was a sign of sentimental *petit-bourgeois* prejudice. **1958** *Times Lit. Suppl.* 19 Sept. 525/3 Comrade Nemeth is an ambitious bureaucrat, anxious to allay the guilt of his *petit bourgeois* birth by utter conformity to proletarian party standards. **1959** N. MAILER *Advts. for Myself* (1961) 163 Sam and Eleanor do not think of themselves as really belonging to a class, and they feel that the Sperbers and Rossmans are petit-bourgeois. **1973** *Sat. Rev.* (U.S.) 25 Sept. 22/3 The children of an ideology dominated by *petit bourgeois* sexual repression. *a* **1974** R. CROSSMAN *Diaries* (1976) II. 160 His [*sc.* Harold Wilson's] natural modesty has remained unchanged. So have his modest tastes, his simple liking of high tea, his completely unaffected petit-bourgeois habits. **1975** A. BEEVOR *Violent Brink* iii. 56 She was a fraud; a *petit* [*sic*] *bourgeoise* in revolt.. for emotional reasons. **1976** J. M. BROWNJOHN tr. *Kirst's Time for Payment* iii. 58 You're putting a petit bourgeois cat among the pigeons.

Hence **petite** (erron. **petit**) **bourgeoisie** (pətit burʒwazi), the middle classes collectively (see BOURGEOISIE, PETTY BOURGEOISIE).

1916 A. E. GALLATIN *Certain Contemporaries* 53 In all his studies of bohemians, vagabonds and the *petite bourgeoisie*, there exists only tenderness and sympathy. **1928** F. STARK *Let.* 26 Oct. (1974) I. 179 They are all good—Scotch of the very petite bourgeoisie—city folk. **1930** *N. & Q.* 10 May 325/1 The intellectual man is.. frequently drawn from the peasantry or the *petite bourgeoisie*. **1949** N. MARSH *Swing, Brother, Swing* xi. 250 He.. and our Mr. Eton-and-Oxford Detective-Sergeant Salis got into a discussion about the *petit bourgeoisie*. **1950** A. L. ROWSE *England of Elizabeth* v. 174 The petite-bourgeoisie were a strong element in Cromwell's support. **1970** *Times* 11 Mar. 11/2 There is today a strong Conservative government in power, to which the petite bourgeoisie naturally looks. **1976** *Brit. Jrnl. Sociol.* XXVII. 50 It is a good idea to bear in mind Rosenberg's taunt: 'Amateur sociologists have generally concluded that the petit-bourgeoisie was that mysterious class with the aid of which Hitler and Mussolini won their victory.'

petit degree, obs. erron. form of PEDIGREE *sb.*

‖**petite** (pəˈtiːt), *a.* [In sense 1, obs. var. of prec.; now only as Fr. fem. of *petit* adj.: see PETIT *a.* (*sb.*)]

†**1.** A variant of PETIT, q.v. (used without reference to gender or sex). *Obs.*

2. a. Now, of a woman or girl: Little, of small stature or size, tiny. Also used *absol.*

1784 J. BARRY in *Lect. Paint.* iii. (1848) 132 His [Raphael's] women in general are either charged and heavy ..or dry and petite. **1794** GODWIN *Cal. Williams* 51 Her person was petite and trivial. **1829** *Yng. Lady's Bk.* 290 The style of dress suitable to.. the pretty and petite. **1875** W. S. HAYWARD *Love agst. World* 48, I know that Florence's slender petite figure cannot compare with mine. **1901** [see JAPANESEY, JAPANESY *a.*] **1935** H. EDIB *Clown & his Daughter* vii. 33 Durnev Hanim did come in, a *petite* person with large innocent brown eyes and very black eyebrows. **1958** *Times Lit. Suppl.* 10 Oct. 573/3 Being American, of course, fifteen-year-old Franzie, petite and bouncy, has begun her sentimental education long before she meets the 'surf-bums' on Malibu beach. **1960** *News Chron.* 12 Sept. 6/1 The dress is from a newish range for the petite. **1972** M. KAYE *Lively Game of Death* ii. 9 Some men would probably dismiss her as 'small'... 'Petite' is *le mot juste*.

b. Used of small sizes in women's clothing. Also used *absol.*

1929 *Radio Times* 8 Nov. 439/2 This Stylish Coat.. From Petite to Matrons' Sizes. **1960** *Harper's Bazaar* Oct. 5 Afternoon dress.. in 'petite' sizes for the 5′2″ and under. **1974** *Times* 26 Apr. 7/7 The tights.. are in three sizes—Petite, Medium or Large. **1978** *N.Y. Times* 29 Mar. A6 (Advt.), You'll find whatever you're looking for in misses (6 to 18), petites (6 to 16), juniors (5 to 13) and women's ($16\frac{1}{2}$ to $24\frac{1}{2}$) in the brightest spring colors.

3. In certain French collocations often used in Eng., as **petite amie** (see quot. 1966); **petite culture**, small farming; **petite marmite**, soup of meat and vegetables served in a marmite; **petite morale**, minor morals, the ethics of every-day details; **petite noblesse**, the lesser nobility in France; **petite pièce**, a minor performance; in *pl.*, the minor writings of an author (formerly as Eng. *petite pieces*); **petite vitesse**, slow train.

1712 BUDGELL *Spect.* No. 341 ¶9 [The French] always close their Tragick Entertainments with what they call a *Petite Piece*. **1797** *Encycl. Brit.* (ed. 3) VI. 155/2 The petite pieces of this eminent writer [Dryden].. are too numerous to specify here. **1825** JEFFREY *Ess.* (1844) I. 265 [They] composed a variety of petite pieces, and novels of polite gallantry. **1832** *Edin. Rev.* July 521 The duties, and decencies, and charities, which are, after all, the *petite morale* of a home. **1848** MILL *Pol. Econ.* I. I. ix. 179 The working of the *petite culture* cannot be fairly judged where the small cultivator is merely a tenant. **1883** C. M. YONGE *Stray Pearls* I. iv. 32 He had only known of two ladies who had followed their husbands to the wars, and both of them only belonged to the *petite noblesse*. **1884** SEELEY *H. Walpole* viii. 192 This country is.. hardened against the *petite morale*. **1887** F. ENGELS in Moore & Aveling tr. *Marx's Capital* II. xxvi. 739 The labourers of the towns [in Northern Italy] were driven *en masse* into the country, and gave an impulse ..to the *petite culture*, carried on in the form of gardening. *Ibid.* xxvii. 741 Japan, with its purely feudal organisation of landed property and its developed *petite culture*, gives a much truer picture of the European middle class than all our history books. **1896** E. Dowson *Let.* c 24 Apr. (1967) 355 Here, I have no petites Amies. **1905** *Spectator* 7 Jan. 13/2 France is notoriously a country of *petite culture*. **1906** A. Filippini *Internat. Cook Bk.* 250 Petite Marmite... It is very important that during the two and a half hours it should simmer exceedingly slowly. **1913** T. E. Lawrence *Home Lett.* (1954) 277 [The source has some illegible words, followed by]...on a railway with one train a day in four hours should take three days and *petite vitesse* ten days is a mystery. **1921** Beerbohm *Lett. to R. Turner* (1964) 258, I.. told him that you had ordered the book for me, and that I expected it had been sent by *petite vitesse*. **1923** A. Huxley *Let.* 2 Sept. (1969) 219 The bulk of the luggage..is still on its way from England, coming by *petite vitesse* which appears to be extremely petite. **1924** Petite noblesse [see haute bourgeoisie]. **1945** A. L. Simon *Conc. Encycl. Gastron.* vii. 93 *Petite marmite*, the name given in restaurants to a *consommé*..served in the earthenware pot in which it was made. **1966** A. J. Bliss *Dict. Foreign Words & Phrases* 279 *Petite amie*.., the female friend of a middle-aged man. 20c. Always with the implication that the friendship is not wholly Platonic. **1972** R. Mayne *Europeans* v. 102 Gay Paree.. home of the *grisette*, the *petite amie*, the bedroom farce. **1978** W. Garner *Möbius Trip* v. 111 His *petite amie*..had raised the subject of marriage. **1978** G. Vidal *Kalki* viii. 191, I narrowly avoided a lapful of petite marmite as one bemused agent's ladle missed the soup plate.

4. *Biol.* Used, freq. as *sb.*, to designate certain variant strains of yeast that are characterized by the cytoplasmically heritable lack of mitochondrial constituents and tend to form small colonies. [The sense is due to B. Ephrussi et al., who used F. *petite colonie* (*Annales de l'Inst. Pasteur* (1949) LXXVII. 64).]

1951 *Genetics* XXXVI. 572 In many strains of yeast apparently non-genetic, cytochrome-deficient variants exhibiting a single strong alpha absorption band at 550 mu occur frequently ('petites'). **1968** *Jrnl. Molecular Biol.* XXXVII. 493 In cytoplasmic petite mutants no changes were observed in the major band. **1971** D. J. Cove *Genetics* viii. 115 It is possible to get mutant strains of yeast which are incapable of metabolising sugars oxidatively; such strains grow almost as well as the wild type on glucose, which they ferment, but on carbon sources such as acetate, which can only be metabolised oxidatively by the tricarboxylic acid cycle, they are unable to grow. These strains, called petite, can often be shown to be abnormal in their mitochondrial constituents. Some have certain mitochondrial enzymes and cytochromes absent, and others have the relative proportions of these components altered. **1978** *Nature* 23 Feb. 750/2 Cytoplasmically inherited respiratory deficient mutants termed *petites*, were first described in baker's yeast over 20 years ago.

petite degree, obs. erron. form of pedigree *sb.*

petiteness (pəˈtiːtnɪs). [f. petite + -ness.]

†**a.** Smallness, small size (*obs.*). **b.** Finicking or dainty littleness; puniness (*contemptuous*).

a **1677** Hale *Prim. Orig. Man.* iii. vi. 276 In respect of the smallness and petiteness of these little Animals. **1796** *Mod. Gulliver's Trav.* 50, I could not manage their box, (from its petiteness), so as to play with distinct fairness. **1887** *Pall Mall G.* 18 June 11 A sombreness and roughness of dress and a petiteness of person about a number of them [Irish Members].

‖**petitio** (pɪˈtɪʃɪəʊ, pəˈtiːtɪəʊ). [L.: see next.] The Latin word for 'asking, begging, petitioning, petition', used in some phrases: esp.

‖**petitio induciarum**, *Law* = imparlance 2.

1706 in Phillips. **1847** Craig s.v. *Petition, Petitio induciarum*, the same in the civil law as *imparlance* in the common law; namely, a motion made to the declaration of the plaintiff by the defendant, whereby he craves respite, or another day, to put in his answer.

‖**petitio principii** (pɪˈtɪʃɪəʊ prɪnˈsɪpɪaɪ), *Logic* [lit. begging or taking for granted of the beginning or of a principle], a logical fallacy which consists in taking for granted a premiss which is either equivalent to, or itself depends on, the conclusion, and requires proof; an instance of this; a 'begging the question'.

1531 Tindale *Expos. 1 John* v. 1-3 Wks. (1573) 420/1 Which kynde of disputyng schole men call *Petitio principii*, the prouyng of two certaine thynges, eche by the other, and is no prouyng at all. **1565** Jewel *Repl. Harding* Wks. 1848 II. 339 This argument is called *petitio principii*, which is, when a thing is taken to make proof, that is doubtful, and standeth in question, and ought itself to be proved. **1646** Sir T. Browne *Pseud. Ep.* i. iv. (1686) 11. **1668** Dryden *Def. Ess. Dram. Poesy* Ess. (ed. Ker) I. 132 Here you see, instead of proof, or reason, there is only *petitio principii*. **1761** Sterne *Tr. Shandy* IV. Introd., Had it not been for a *petitio principii*..the whole controversy had been settled at once. **1827** Whately *Logic* iii. §3. 142. **1887** Fowler *Deduct. Logic* (ed. 9) viii. 145 The argument in a circle is the most important case of the fallacy called *Petitio Principii* (or, as it is more properly called, *Petitio Quæsiti*, begging the question).

petition (pɪˈtɪʃən), *sb.* Also 4-7 -cion, 4-6 -cioun, -cyon, etc. [a. F. *pétition*, in OF. *peticiun* (12th c. in Littré), ad. L. *petitiōn-em*, n. of action f. *petĕre* to aim at, seek, lay claim to, ask, beg.]

1. The action of formally asking, begging, supplicating, or humbly requesting; esp. in phr. ***to make petition***, to ask, supplicate, or formally beg.

1417 in Ellis *Orig. Lett.* Ser. ii. I. 57 He was forced againste his will to make peticion to have yor Peace by indenture. **1509** Hawes *Past. Pleas.* xxxvi. (Percy Soc.) 187 We thought to her we made peticion. **1555** Eden *Decades* 169 The instant peticion of any other person. **1611** Bible *Esther* vii. 3 Let my life be giuen me at my petition. **1673** Temple *Observ. United Prov.* Wks. 1731 I. 37 Petition signifying barely asking or demanding, tho' implying the Thing demanded to be wholly in the Right and Power of them that give. **1817** Cobbett *Addr. Men Bristol* Wks. XXXII. 64 Petition, peaceable petition, is the course. **1872** Yeats *Growth Comm.* 212 The company's charter could be renewed only on petition and payment of a fine.

†**b.** ***petition of the principle***: begging of the question; = petitio *principii*. *Obs.*

1579 Fulke *Heskins' Parl.* 223 He must haue an easie aduersarie, or else he shall gaine litle by such petition of principles. **1618** Chapman *Hesiod* Ded., Or if the allusion (or petition of the Principle) begge with too broad a Licence in the Generall. **1829** Landor *Imag. Conv., Diogenes & Plato* Wks. 1853 I. 458/1 Those terms are puerile, and imply a petition of a principle.

2. A supplication or prayer; an entreaty; *esp.* a solemn and humble prayer to the Deity, or to a sovereign or superior; also, one of the clauses of a prayer, e.g. of the Lord's prayer.

c **1330** R. Brunne *Chron.* (1810) 299 Nede behoued him grante to clerke & baroun, & hold þam þe conante of ilk peticioun. c **1385** Chaucer *L.G.W.* 363 (MS. Gg. 4. 27) And here compleyntys & petyciouns. **1470-85** Malory *Arthur* vii. i. 214 Now syre this is my petycyon for thys feest, that ye wylle gyue me mete and drynke suffycyauntly for this twelue moneth. **1552** *Bk. Com. Prayer, Communion*, Then shall the priest saye the Lordes prayer, the people repeating after him euery peticion. **1671** Milton *Samson* 650 This one prayer yet remains, might I be heard, No long petition, speedy death. **1697** Dryden *Virg. Georg.* iv. 733 What shou'd he do, who twice had lost his Love? What Notes invent, what new Petitions move? **1750** Gray *Long Story* 49 My Lady heard their joint petition. **1885** Ruskin *Pleas. Eng.* 136 Our petition in the Litany, against sudden death, was written originally to her [St. Barbara].

b. *transf.* The matter of the petition; the thing asked or entreated: as in ***to have*** or ***receive one's petition, to grant a petition***.

c **1440** *Gesta Rom.* xxxviii. 154 (Harl. MS.) Sithe I shall dye, I aske the law of yow, *scil.* þat I may have iij. peticiouns or I deye. **1480** Caxton *Chron. Eng.* iv. (1520) 31 b/2 He sayde..he sholde haue somwhat of his petycyon. **1526** Tindale *1 John* v. 15 We knowe thatt we shall have the peticions that wee desyred of hym. **1601** Shaks. *Jul. C.* ii. i. 58 O Rome, I make thee promise, If the redresse will follow, thou receiuest Thy full Petition at the hand of Brutus.

3. A formally drawn up request or supplication; *esp.* a written supplication from an individual or body of inferiors to a superior, or to a person or body in authority (as a sovereign or legislature), soliciting some favour, privilege, right, or mercy, or the redress of some wrong or grievance.

[**1314-15** *Rolls of Parlt.* I. 297/1 La dite Prohibition, dount les transescryt est cosu a ceste petitioun.] **1450** *Ibid.* V. 186/1 Agreith to this Petition of Resumption, and the same accepteth. **1544** tr. *Littleton's Tenures* (1574) 17 They haue none other remedy but to sue vnto the lorde by peticion. **1601** Shaks. *All's Well* v. i. 19 That it will please you To giue this poore petition to the King. **1631** *Star Chamb. Cases* (Camden) 8 The petition of Philip Bushell, whose Father was unjustly condemned, soe is the title. **1736** Sheridan in *Swift's Lett.* (1768) IV. 161 Thus this great affair has ended like the Yorkshire petition, which has been the chief business of the house of commons this session. **1812** J. Smyth *Pract. of Customs* (1821) 386 Goods are said to be delivered by Petition, when they are returned for some legal purpose, and are allowed to be imported without the tedious form of an entry. **1844** H. H. Wilson *Brit. India* III. 550 They prepared a petition to the House against the Bill.

†**b.** *spec.* The form in which the Houses of Parliament formerly presented a measure for the king's granting: now represented by the passing of a bill for the royal assent. *Obs.* exc. *Hist.*

[**1367** *Act 36 Edw. III*, c. 2 Sachiez nous avoir resceu la peticion baillez a nous par la commune de notre realme, en cest present parlement en la forme qui sensuyt.] **1414** *Rolls of Parlt.* IV. 22 þe kyng of his grace especial graunteþ þat fro hens forþ no þyng be enacted to þe Peticione of the Comune, þat be contrarie of hir askyng, wharby þey shuld be bounde wiþoute their assent. **1439** *Ibid.* V. 9/1 A Petition putte up to the Kyng in this Parlement, by the Communes of this londe. **1512** *Act 4 Hen. VIII*, c. 11 Everything..byfore rehersed declared and expressed in this bill of peticion. **1681** Nevile *Plato Rediv.* 111 Another Act..by which it was provided, That no Parliament should be dismist, till all the Petitions were answered; That is, in the Language of those times, till all the Bills..were finished. **1818** Cruise *Digest* (ed. 2) V. 3 It became..fully established in the reign of Rich. III. that no award could be made on a private petition, without a formal and complete act of the whole legislature.

c. ***Petition and Advice*** (*Eng. Hist.*): the Remonstrance presented by Parliament to Cromwell on 4 Apr. 1657.

1657-76 Whitelock *Mem.* (1732) 655/2 A Writing which they stiled, The humble Petition and Advice of the Parliament of England, Scotland, and Ireland to his Highness. *Ibid.*, This Petition and Advice was presented to his Highness by the House. **1827** Hallam *Const. Hist.* (1876) II. x. 258, 266. **1845** Carlyle *Cromwell* (1871) IV. x. 245 This 'Remonstrance' of Pack's.., under the name 'Petition and Advice presented to his Highness,' became famous to the world in those spring months. **1884** C. H. Firth in Low & Pulling *Dict. Eng. Hist.* 818/1 On the whole the Petition and Advice established a far more workable distribution of political power than the instrument of government.

d. ***Petition of Right***: the parliamentary declaration of the rights and liberties of the people, set forth in the form of a petition to King Charles I, which was finally assented to by the king in 1628. Although not a formal statute or ordinance, 'it has ever been accepted as having the full force of law'. (See also 4 a.)

1627 *Act 3 Chas. I* (*title*) The Peticion exhibited to His Majestie by the Lordes Spirituall and Temporall and Comons in this present Parliament assembled concerning divers Rightes and Liberties of the Subjectes. [Conclusion] All which they most humblie pray of your most Excellent Majestie as their Rightes and Liberties. **1647** Clarendon *Hist. Reb.* i. §8 Yet all these provocations and many other.. produced no other resentment than the Petition of Right. a **1676** Whitelock *Mem.* (1732) 10/2 The King gave another Answer to the Petition of Right,..which satisfy'd the Commons,..and so that excellent Law passed. **1768** Blackstone *Comm.* III. 134 This drew on a parliamentary enquiry, and produced the petition of right, 3 Car. I. **1824** Mackintosh *Sp. Ho. Com.* 1 June, The illustrious Judge on this occasion appeals to the Petition of Right. **1827** Hallam *Const. Hist.* (1876) I. vii. 391 The Petition of Right, as this statute is still called, from its not being drawn in the common form of an act of parliament. **1844** Ld. Brougham *Brit. Const.* xv. (1862) 228 The Petition of Right, whereby the Lords and Commons obliged the King to declare the illegality of requiring loans without Parliamentary sanction.

4. *Law.* **a.** ***petition of right***: an ancient Common Law remedy against the Crown for obtaining possession or restitution of real or personal property: in Law Fr. *pétition de droit*, L. *petitio justitiæ*. (*Encycl. Laws Eng.*)

1467-8 *Rolls of Parlt.* V. 575/1 By Writte or Writtes, or by Petition or Petitions of right sued. **1473** *Ibid.* VI. 72/2 Any Castelles..or Enheritamentes..wherof any persone or persones have had restitution by auctorite of Parlement, or restitution by Travers, Petition of Right, Lyvere, or any Recovere by the cours of the commen lawe. **1658** tr. *Coke's Rep.* iv. 55 a (1826) II. 428. **1768** Blackstone *Comm.* III. xvii. 256. [**1797** *Encycl. Brit.* (ed. 3) XIV. 242/2 *Petition*..is used for that remedy which the subject hath to help a wrong done by the king..: In which sense it is either general that the king do him right..: Or it is special, when the conclusion and indorsement are special, for this or that to be done, &c.] **1840** *Penny Cycl.* XVIII. 34/1 In modern practice the petition of right is not resorted to, except in cases to which neither a traverse of office nor a monstraunce de droit applies, or after those remedies have failed... The Latin term 'petitio justitiæ' shows that the words are used in the sense of a 'petition *for right*'. **1898** *Encycl. Laws Eng.* s.v. *Petition of Right*, Stated in general terms, the only cases in which a petition of right is available are where the land or goods or money of a subject have found their way into the possession of the Crown.

b. A formal application in writing made to a court (*a*) for judicial action concerning the matter of a suit then pending before it (formerly called a ***cause petition***); (*b*) for something which lies in the jurisdiction of the court without an action, as a writ of *habeas corpus*, an order in bankruptcy, etc.; (*c*) in some forms of procedure initiating a suit or its equivalent: see quot. 1872.

1737 Reclaiming Petition [see reclaiming *vbl. sb.* b]. **1802-12** Bentham *Ration. Judic. Evid.* (1827) II. 366 Petition is the name given to the instrument by which, in cases of bankruptcy, claims are preferred to the Lord Chancellor sitting in a judicial capacity superordinate to that of the commissioners of bankruptcy. **1818** Cruise *Digest* (ed. 2) VI. 541 Lord Hardwicke... I did not think fit to determine the matter upon a petition, but thought it proper for a bill. **1838** W. Bell *Dict. Law Scot.* 735 In the judicial procedure of the Court of Session, a petition and complaint is the form in which certain matters of summary and extraordinary jurisdiction are brought under the cognisance of the Court. **1840** *Penny Cycl.* XVIII. 33/1 A petition is an application in writing, addressed to the lord chancellor, the master of the rolls, or to the Equity side of the Court of Exchequer, in which the petitioner states certain facts as the ground on which he prays for the order and direction of the court... A cause petition is a petition in a matter of which the court has already possession by virtue of there being a suit concerning the matter of the petition; and the petitioner is generally either a party to such suit, or he derives a title to some interest in the subject matter of the suit from a party to it. When there is no suit existing about the matter of the petition, it is called an *ex parte* petition. *Ibid.* 33/2 A petition may be presented for the appointment of guardians to infants, and for an allowance for their maintenance. **1848** Wharton *Law Lex.* 518/1 A petition is the proper mode of coming before the court for the relief of insolvent debtors. **1872** *Wharton's Law Lex.* (ed. 5) 729/2 Divorce and matrimonial suits, and suits instituted under the Legitimacy Declaration Act, are commenced by petition. *Ibid.*, Municipal Election Petitions are tried by a barrister under the Municipal Corporations Act, 1882.

†**5.** *Math.* A postulate; an axiom. *Obs.*

1529 More *Dyaloge* i. Wks. 149/1 These two thinges seme to me two as true pointes, and as plaine to a christen man, as any peticion of Euclidis geometry is to a resonable man. **1570** Billingsley *Euclid* i. post. i. 6 After the definitions.. now follow petitions, which are the second kynd of principles. *Ibid.*, Petitions..are certain general sentences, so plain, and so perspicuous, that they are perceiued to be true as soone as they are vttered. **1656** tr. *Hobbes' Elem. Philos.* (1839) 37 Also certain petitions are commonly received into the number of principles; as, for example, that a straight line may be drawn between two points. **1709** J. Ward *Yng. Math Guide* (1734) 11 Postulate or Petition. That any Number may be diminished..by taking another Number from it. **1795** Hutton *Math. Dict.* II. 270/1 *Postulate*, a demand, petition, or a problem of so obvious a nature as to need neither demonstration, nor explication, to render it more plain or certain.

6. *attrib.* and *Comb.*, as ***petition-form***, ***-monger***, ***-writer***; **petition crown**, a pattern crown-piece presented to Charles II by Thomas Simon, and bearing his request for its comparison with the work of John Roeter by whom he had been superseded at the mint.

1853 *Numismatic Chron.* XVI. 135 Simon's 'Trial Piece' .. There exist four varieties... that which has on the edge Simon's Petition to Charles II. to be employed on his new coinage, and which is consequently known by the name of the Petition Crown. **1903** *Daily Chron.* 6 Nov. 5/2 The Petition Crown piece, of which a specimen was sold on Wednesday for £310, was the famous Simon's protest against foreign labour. **1887** BULLOCH *Pynours* v. 46 This brave document was inspired by some petition-monger. **1900** *Daily News* 30 Apr. 6/2 We have to bribe magistrates, clerks, and petition-writers to get a hearing.

petition (pɪ'tɪʃən), *v.* [f. PETITION *sb.*: cf. mod.F. *pétitionner* (1792 in Hatz.-Darm.).]

1. *trans.* To address or present a petition to; to make a humble request or supplication to; *spec.* to address a formal written petition to (a sovereign, a legislative body, person in authority, or court).

1607 SHAKS. *Cor.* II. i. 187 You haue, I know, petition'd All the Gods for my prosperitie. **1637** *Documents agst. Prynne* (Camden) 72 Sondaie last the parishieners petitiond his Majestie that their church might not be pulld downe. **1765** BLACKSTONE *Comm.* I. i. 143 There still remains a fourth subordinate right, appertaining to every individual, namely, the right of petitioning the king, or either house of parliament, for the redress of grievances. **1818** CRUISE *Digest* (ed. 2) V. 161 Lord Pembroke petitioned the House of Lords for a bill to set aside an amendment made in a fine, levied in the Court of Great Sessions in Wales. **1845** SARAH AUSTIN *Ranke's Hist. Ref.* II. 273 To petition the emperor to hold an ecclesiastical council in the German nation. **1857-8** SEARS *Athan.* II. ii. 186 They petition Pilate for a guard.

b. To solicit, ask, beg for (a thing).

1631 HEYLIN *St. George* 86 The picture of some state or Country, petitioning..the ayde and helping-hand of so great a Saint. **1812** CRABBE *Tales* XVI. *Confidant*, All that I hope, petition, or expect.

2. *absol.* or *intr.* To address or present a petition, to make petition, to make a humble request or entreaty, to ask humbly (*for* something).

1634 HEYWOOD *Maidenhead Lost* I. Wks. 1874 IV. 108 You petition heere For Men and Money! **1751** LABELYE *Westm. Br.* 25 Westminster Bridge was petitioned for. **1766** ENTICK *London* IV. 71 The method of gaining admission into this hospital is by petitioning to the committee. **1838** LYTTON *Alice* IV. v, The Colonel petitioned for three days consideration. **1847** TENNYSON *Princ.* VI. 300 Then Violet.. Petition'd too for him.

Hence **petitioned** (pɪ'tɪʃənd) *ppl. a.*

1894 H. HUNT in *Daily News* 11 June 8/2 That the petitioned should not misunderstand us.

petitionable (pɪ'tɪʃənəb(ə)l), *a.* [f. PETITION *sb.* + -ABLE.] That allows, justifies, or involves, the making of a petition.

1898 *Westm. Gaz.* 14 Mar. 2/1 A few suggestions for amending the Bankruptcy Act... 1. Reduce the petitionable amount from fifty pounds to five.

petitional (pɪ'tɪʃənəl), *a. rare.* [f. PETITION *sb.* + -AL[1]. Cf. *conditional*, etc.] Of, pertaining to, or of the nature of a petition.

1600 W. WATSON *Decacordon* (1602) 120 A very formall letter, petitionall or supplicatiue. **1641** BURROUGHS *Sion's Joy* 37 A voice hath come from the Citie, a petitionall voice, graciously accepted by you. **1847** BUSHNELL *Chr. Nurt.* II. viii. (1861) 393 Working toward a grand petitional harmony with them.

pe'titionarily, *adv. rare.* [f. next + -LY[2].] In a petitionary manner: (in quot. 1646) by way of *petitio principii* or unproved assumption.

1604 *Supplic. Masse Priests* § 1 Ever lowelie to solicite, yea petitionarily to importunate your Maiestie, for the happy grant of so manifold, farre-spreading..a blessednesse. **1646** SIR T. BROWNE *Pseud. Ep.* IV. v. 191 This doth but petitionarily inferre a dextrality in the heavens.

petitionary (pɪ'tɪʃənərɪ), *a.* [ad. med.L. *petītiōnāri-us*, f. *petītiōn-em* PETITION: see -ARY[1]: cf. F. *pétitionnaire* (1792 in Hatz.-Darm.).]

1. Of the nature of, consisting of, containing or characteristic of a petition.

1579 J. STUBBES in *Harington's Nugæ Ant.* (ed. Park 1804) I. 162 These fewe petitionarye lynes. **1597** HOOKER *Eccl. Pol.* v. xlviii. § 2 Petitionarie prayer belongeth onely to such as ..stand in need of reliefe from others. **1611** B. JONSON *Catiline* IV. i, It is our base petitionary breath That blows 'hem to this greatnesse. **1738** NEAL *Hist. Purit.* IV. 139 Dr. Gauden presented a Petitionary Remonstrance. **1855** TENNYSON *Brook* 113 Claspt hands and that petitionary grace Of sweet seventeen subdued me ere she spoke.

2. Of persons: Suppliant, entreating, petitioning. *Obs.* or *arch.*

1604 MARSTON *Malcontent* I. v. sig. B4 Petitionarie vassailes licking the pauement with their slauish knees. **1607** SHAKS. *Cor.* v. ii. 82, I..coniure thee to pardon Rome, and thy petitionary Countrimen. **1820** LAMB *Elia* Ser. I. *Two Races of Men*, To say no to a poor petitionary rogue.

†**3.** Containing an unproved assumption or *petitio principii*. *Obs. rare*$^{-1}$.

1646 SIR T. BROWNE *Pseud. Ep.* IV. xiii. 227 From plaine and naturall principles, the doubt may be fairely salved, and not clapt up from petitionary foundations and principles unestablished.

†**pe'titionate**, *v. Obs. rare.* [f. L. *petītiōn-em* PETITION + -ATE[3]: cf. *ambitionate*, etc.] **a.** *trans.* To address with petitions, supplicate, petition. **b.** *intr.* To make petition; to address or present a petition.

1624 BP. MOUNTAGU *Immed. Addr.* 120 Their more then probabilitie to preuaile in whatsoeuer they shall petitionate God for mee. **1625** in *Cosin's Corr.* (Surtees) I. 76 It will be time enough to heare from you agayne, and in no case time to petitionate till something be don.

petitionee (pɪˌtɪʃə'niː). *U.S. Law.* [f. PETITION *v.* + -EE.] The person or party against whom a petition is filed, and who is required to answer and defend.

1764 *Conn. Col. Rec.* (1881) XII. 262 Unless the petitioner would..execute notes of hand to the petitionee for the whole added together. **1767** *Ibid.* 618 Under the circumstances the petitioner ought not in equity to be holden to answer the same to the petitionee. **1828-32** WEBSTER, *Petitionee*, a person cited to defend against a petition. **1895** in *Funk's Stand. Dict.*

petitioner (pɪ'tɪʃənə(r)). [f. PETITION *sb.* + -ER[2]: cf. *pensioner*, *commissioner*, etc., and med.L. *petītiōnārius* beggar, f. *petītiōn-em* PETITION.

In earlier use than PETITION *v.*, but, after the introduction of the latter, naturally viewed as its agent-n. in -ER[1].]

1. One who presents a petition; one who petitions.

For quot. 1414, cf. PETITION *sb.* 3 b.

1414 *Rolls of Parlt.* IV. 22 Consideringe that the Comune of youre lond..ben as well Assentirs as Peticioners. **1553** T. WILSON *Rhet.* Ep. A ij b, I shal be a continuall peticioner vnto almyghtye God for your preseruation. **1647** WARD *Simp. Cobler* 14, I would be understood..an humble Petitioner, that ignorant and tender conscienced Anabaptists may have due time and means of conviction. **1792** *Anecd. W. Pitt* I. viii. 182 The relief desired by the petitioners. **1855** MACAULAY *Hist. Eng.* xvi. III. 714 Some petitioners asked to be heard by counsel.

b. *Hist.* One of those who signed the address, also called Addressers (cf. quot. 1681 s.v. ADDRESSER) to Charles II in 1680, petitioning for the summoning of Parliament. Opposed to ABHORRER 2.

1757-1870 [see ABHORRER 2].

2. *Law.* **a.** A plaintiff in an action commenced by petition. **b.** A petitioning creditor.

1503 *Rolls of Parlt.* VI. 526/1 By whiche longe tracte of tyme, the said Sueters and Peticioners were and shulde be discomforted. **1593** SHAKS. *2 Hen. VI*, I. iii. 26 Alas Sir, I am but a poore Petitioner of our whole Towneship. **1764-7** [see PETITIONEE]. **1845** POLSON *Eng. Law* in *Encycl. Metrop.* II. 835/1 Praying his lordship to issue his fiat, authorizing the petitioner, as such creditor, to prosecute his complaint in her Majesty's Court of Bankruptcy. **1876** BANCROFT *Hist. U.S.* IV. li. 286 The question as presented by Dunning was already decided in favor of the petitioners. *Mod. Rep. Divorce Crt.*, The judge pronounced a decree *nisi*, the petitioner to have the custody of the children.

pe'titioning, *vbl. sb.* [f. PETITION *v.* + -ING[1].] The action of making or presenting a petition.

a **1649** DRUMM. OF HAWTH. *Declar.*, etc. Wks. (1711) 210 They could not be induced..to acknowledge the smallest error, either in the matter of their petition or in the manner of their petitioning. **1769** BLACKSTONE *Comm.* IV. 147 Nearly related to this head of riots is the offence of tumultuous petitioning. **1849** MACAULAY *Hist. Eng.* v. II. 658 James..had treated modest petitioning as a crime.

pe'titioning, *ppl. a.* [f. as prec. + -ING[2].] That petitions; supplicating, humbly begging.

petitioning creditor, one who applies for an adjudication in bankruptcy against his debtor (*Wharton*).

1615 BRATHWAIT *Strappado* (1878) 111 This priuiledge and Knightly honour; Which hauing got by long petitioning suite. **1649** MILTON *Eikon.* iv. Wks. 1851 III. 361 Unarm'd and Petitioning People. **1845** POLSON *Eng. Law* in *Encycl. Metrop.* II. 835/1 Proof being given before them [commissioners of the Court of Bankruptcy] of the petitioning creditor's debt..and of the act of bankruptcy, the trader is declared a bankrupt. **1849** E. B. EASTWICK *Dry Leaves* 4 A pony standing on his hind legs like a petitioning poodle.

pe'titionist. *nonce-wd.* [See -IST.] One who makes a practice of petitioning; a professional or professed petitioner.

1822 LAMB *Let. to Coleridge*, I met a venerable old man, not a mendicant,—but thereabouts; a look-beggar, not a verbal petitionist.

petitive ('pɛtɪtɪv), *a.* [f. L. *pĕtītus* pa. pple. of *pĕtĕre* to ask: see -IVE.] Of, relating to, or expressing a prayer or request; = PRECATIVE *a.*

1923 J. S. HUXLEY *Ess. Biologist* vii. 297 Although the value of prayer persists in so far as it is meditative and a self-purification of the mind, yet its commonly accepted petitive value must fall to the ground. **1964** E. A. NIDA *Toward Sci. Transl.* ix. 201 Mode (or mood), which defines the psychological background of the action, involves principally such categories as possibility..necessity..and desire (desiderative, optative, and petitive). **1977** *Maledicta* Summer 33 The more active attitude of seeking or desiring we call *petitive*.

‖**petit-maître** (pətimɛtr). [Fr., lit. little master.] **1.** An effeminate man; a dandy, fop, coxcomb. Also as *adj.*

1711 ADDISON *Spect.* No. 83 ¶5 All his Men were *Petits Maitres*, and all his Women *Coquets*. **1744** H. WALPOLE *Lett. to Mann* 22 July, A little, pert petit-maître figure. **1754** RICHARDSON *Grandison* (1781) II. v. 88 Do you pretend, in such an age of petit maitres, to live single? **1820** T. MITCHELL *Comm. Aristoph.* I. p. cliii, A boon companion for the *petits-maitres* of the Ilyssus. **1843** JAMES *Forest Days* (1847) 37 The long and hanging sleeves of the loose coat he wore were..one of the distinguishing marks of a petit maître of that day. **1880** SHORTHOUSE *J. Inglesant* xxxviii. 537 He had..the look of a petit maître, and even, what is more contemptible still, of a petit-maître priest. **1883** C. M. YONGE *Stray Pearls* I. x. 115 He would be ashamed to count kindred with that effeminate *petite maître*! *c* **1905** E. NEWMAN in H. Van Thal *Fanfare for E. Newman* (1955) x. 145 It is the *petit-maître* Mozart, tripping along with his manneristic little elegancies of walk and gesture but scarcely conscious of the bigness of the world around him or of the real nature of the humanity that strives in it. **1939** 'A. BRIDGE' *Four-Part Setting* vi. 63 His manners were slightly *petit-maître*. **1948** D. CECIL *Two Quiet Lives* 88 At moments ..one is tempted to dismiss him [*sc.* Horace Walpole] as an affected petit-maître who happened to be gifted with a talent for letter writing.

2. A 'minor master' with reference to musicians, writers, etc. (usu. derog.).

1856 J. B. WARING in O. Jones *Gram. Ornament* (1865) xviii. 132 As regards another main feature in Elizabethan ornament, viz. the complicated and fanciful interlaced bands, we must seek its origin in the..designs of the class of engravers known as the 'petits maîtres' of Germany and the Netherlands. **1934** C. LAMBERT *Music Ho!* III. 168 Liadoff, a real petit-maître, produced at rare intervals a few miniatures of extraordinary felicity. **1960** *Times* 8 Mar. 4/7 Michel is accounted a *petit-maître* and in French comparison does not reach the same height as Théodore Rousseau. **1963** *Listener* 3 Jan. 45/3 He [*sc.* Puccini] was a musician of great artistic integrity who clearly recognized his limitations... But such awareness does not make him a *petit maître* any more than it did Chopin, Bizet, Ravel. **1975** *Daily Tel.* 10 June 11/4 Pierre Prins is one of those French petits maitres whom, if we only saw their best work, we would rate rightly.

Hence (*nonce-wds.*) **petit-'maitreship**, **petit-'maitreism**. So ‖**petite-maîtresse**, the female counterpart of a dandy, an *élégante*.

1818 LADY MORGAN *Fl. Macarthy* (1819) II. i. 68 (Stanf.) At the head of these pious petite maitresses stood Miss Crawley. **1822** *New Monthly Mag.* IV. 110 None of the petit-maitreship of the art. **1824** *Ibid.* X. 518 We..begin to give up our old ideas of their coxcombry, gaiety, and petit-maitreism. **1823** SCOTT *Peveril* xxx, 'You stand excused, Master Empson', said the petite maitresse, sinking back on the downy couch. **1840** *Penny Cycl.* XVIII. 167/1 (*Pinkerton*) The Frenchified style of thinking and air of *petit-maitre-ship* affected by the quondam laborious antiquary.

‖**petit mal** (pəti mal). [Fr., = the little evil.] The milder or imperfectly developed form of epilepsy, when the fits are abortive or incomplete: there is only momentary confusion or unconsciousness without general convulsions or other major manifestations.

[**1842**: see GRAND MAL.] **1874** J. CUNNINGHAM *New Theory of Knowing* 173 Some persons afflicted with the *petit mal* continue their work..after they have sunk into unconsciousness. [**1878** tr. *H. von Ziemssen's Cycl. Med.* XIV. 190 From consideration of the 'little attacks' (*petit mal*).] **1879**, etc. [see GRAND MAL]. **1891** *Daily News* 1 May 5/5 It is impossible in one examination to say whether a man suffers from petit mal. **1899** *Allbutt's Syst. Med.* VII. 910 The attacks of petit mal which may accompany head-nodding. *Ibid.* VIII. 97 Paroxysmal vertigo in hysterical patients has been called hysterical petit-mal. **1927** *Daily Express* 6 Aug. 7/6 She was suffering from a disease known as petit mal, which occasionally makes persons unconscious of their surroundings, and they then perform normal actions. **1957** L. DURRELL *Justine* III. 160 An occasional headache only proved him to be a victim of *petit mal*—or some other such customary disease of the rich and idle. **1974** *Daily Tel.* (Colour Suppl.) 18 Jan. 19/1 In a 'Petit Mal' a child looking out of the window may see the nose of a passing bus come into his line of vision and then, straight away, the disappearing tail of the same bus. The only ill effect is that he probably gets ticked off for daydreaming.

†**pe'titor.** *Obs. rare.* [a. L. *petītor* a candidate, agent-n. from *petĕre* to seek.] A seeker, applicant, candidate.

1613 T. GODWIN *Rom. Antiq.* (1674) 144 The Roman Petitors or Suitors for bearing office. **1655** FULLER *Ch. Hist.* XI. ii. § 48 A very potent (I cannot say competitor, the Bishop himself being never a petitor for the place, but) desirer of this office.

petitory ('pɛtɪtərɪ), *a.* [ad. late L. *petītōri-us*, f. *petītor*: see prec. and -ORY.]

1. Characterized by asking, soliciting, or begging; petitionary, supplicatory. Now *rare.*

1579 G. HARVEY *Letter-bk.* (Camden) 62, I suppose it needlesse extraordinarilye to procure any noblemans petitory or commendatorye letters in any sutch private respectes. **1651** JER. TAYLOR *Holy Dying* iii. § 2 (1727) 63 The proper voices of sickness are expressly vocal and petitory in the ears of God. **1720** *Wodrow Corr.* (1843) II. 518 The opinion of friends at London, that no petitory clause for protection and favour should be in. **1864** BURTON *Scot. Abr.* I. v. 299 As an equivalent to some petitory lines ..there were verses.

2. *Law.* Characterized by laying claim to something; in ***petitory action***, etc., an action claiming title or right of ownership, as distinct from mere possession, in anything; **b.** *spec.* in *Sc. Law*: see quot. 1773.

1602 FULBECKE *2nd Pt. Parall.* 48 In our Law it is held, that there is no diuersitie, where a man selleth land depending a writ petitorie of the same land, or doe giue it depending the writ. **1773** ERSKINE *Inst. Law Scot.* IV. i. § 47. 655 Petitory actions are so called,..because some demand is made upon the defender, in consequence either of a right of property or credit in the pursuer. Thus, actions for restitution of moveables, actions of poinding, of forthcoming, and indeed all personal actions upon contracts, or *quasi* contracts, which the Romans called *condictiones*, are petitory. **1847** in Aiton *Domest. Econ.* (1857) 339 The action should contain declaratory conclusions as well as petitory conclusions, adapted to bring out the Sheriff's views. **1880** MUIRHEAD *Gaius* IV. §92 The petitory formula is that in which the pursuer asserts that the thing in dispute is his. **1901** *Scotsman* 9 Mar. 11/1 A petitory action by the..Patents Company..for payment of £1500.

3. That involves a *petitio principii*. *rare*.

1832 SIR W. HAMILTON *Discuss.* (1852) 63 The fact of the external reality is not only petitory but improbable. **1836–7** —— *Metaph.* (1877) II. xxvi. 142 Any hypothesis is probable in proportion as..it involves nothing petitory, occult, supernatural.

‖**petit pâté.** Now only as Fr. (pəti pɑte). Also 5 **pety-petty**, 7 **petty-patty**, **pettit pasté**, **petipete**, 8 **petty patee**. [F. *petit* little, and *pâté* pasty, pie.] A small patty or pie.

c **1440** *Anc. Cookery* in *Househ. Ord.* (1790) 450 Payn puffe, and pety-pettys and cuspis and doucettes. *a* **1625** FLETCHER *Women Pleased* II. vi, Shall I make petty patties of him? **1678** T. BAKER *Tunbridge Wells* 12 (Stanf.) A Treat of *pettit Pasté* and Brandy. **1688** R. HOLME *Armoury* III. iii. 84/1 *Petipetes* are Pies made of Carps and Eels, first roasted and then minced, and with Spices made up in Pies. **1787** P. BECKFORD *Lett. Italy* (1805) I. 29 Mademoiselle G——, lost the heart of..Lord W—— G——, by eating too many *petits patés*. Petits patés were at that time very much in fashion. **1812** *Sporting Mag.* XXXIX. 163 Sausages are admitted with petit patés.

‖**petits chevaux** (pəti ʃəvo). [Fr., lit. little horses.] A gambling game in which bets are placed on the performance of mechanically operated horses made to spin round a flag placed at the centre of a specially prepared circular table.

1891 *Clown* 9 June 13/2 Some of the most naughty of us will go and tempt fortune with the 'petit[s] chevaux'—at Dieppe. **1905** W. J. LOCKE *Morals M. Ordeyne* xii. 147 She has a consuming passion for *petits chevaux*. I speak sagely of the evils of gambling. **1911** [see BOULE[4] 1]. **1912** 'SAKI' *Chron. Clovis* 181 It was just before *petits chevaux* had been supplanted by *boule*. **1929** R. ALDINGTON *Death of Hero* III. vi. 330 He disapproved of baccarat, roulette, and *petits chevaux*. **1964** C. MACKENZIE *My Life & Times* III. i. 22, I do not know what the rules are to-day for *petits chevaux* but in 1900 horse number 5 of the 9 horses meant that the bank won. **1964** A. WYKES *Gambling* ix. 211 Other variations of roulette..*Petits chevaux*—which still flourishes in Northern France and Ireland.

‖**petit souper** (pəti supe). [F. *petit* little, and *souper* supper.] A little supper; an unceremonious supper to which a few intimates are admitted; orig. in reference to the French court in the 18th century.

1765 *Ann. Reg.* II. 56 Those *petit-soupers* of which the king [of France] is so fond. **1819** SHELLEY *Peter Bell* v. i, Among the guests who often staid Till the Devil's petits-soupers. **1849** LONGF. in *Life* (1891) II. 149 After the concert a petit-souper.

'petkin, 'petling, nonce-diminutives of PET[1].

1863 HOLME LEE *Annie Warleigh* II. 2 She tried to nurse Katherine's tiny petkin. **1837** *New Monthly Mag.* LI. 183 Be-scented and be-lioned petlings!

‖**peto** ('peto). [Sp.] A padded or stuffed protective covering for a picador's horse.

1957 A. MACNAB *Bulls of Iberia* v. 52 The number of pics is not rigid..for with the *peto* the contact may last some time, and not be broken at once as in the pre-*peto* days. **1967** MCCORMICK & MASCAREÑAS *Compl. Aficionado* ii. 35 Before 1928, when the peto was introduced, the work of the picador was more prominent than it is in the modern corrida. **1968** *Economist* 17 Feb. 32/1 It was she [*sc.* Queen Victoria Eugenia] who insisted on the use of the *peto*, the ugly mattress-like covering that protects picadors' horses, though not infallibly, from disembowelment.

petong, obs. form of PAKTONG.

petous(s, petowiss, obs. Sc. forms of PITEOUS.

petralogy, etc., erron. f. PETROLOGY, etc.

petranel, obs. form of PETRONEL.

Petrarchal (pɪ'trɑːkəl), *a.* [f. *Petrarch*, It. *Petrarca*, personal surname + -AL[1].] Of, pertaining to, characteristic of, or in the style of the Italian poet Petrarca or Petrarch (1304–74). So **Pe'trarchan** *a.* (also as *sb.* = *Petrarchist*), **Petrar'chesque, Pe'trarchian** *adjs.*; **Petrarchism** ('piːtrɑːkɪz(ə)m), imitation of the style of Petrarch; **'Petrarchist,** an imitator of Petrarch; **Petrar'chistical** *a.*, imitative of Petrarch; **'Petrarchize** *v. intr.*, to imitate Petrarch's style.

1818 KEATS *Let.* Wks. 1889 III. 159 Were it my choice, I would reject a *Petrarchal coronation. **1827** BEDDOES *Let.* Apr., Poems (1851) p. lxix, The sonnets, &c. are much more to my taste than that *Petrarchan 'eau d'Hippocrène sucrée'. **1881** *Athenæum* 28 May 714/2 Conforming the structure of his sonnet to the Petrarchan type. **1904** *Q. Rev.* July 5 Wyatt..leaned upon the forms of Italy—the porcelain sonnet of the Petrarchans, the satiric *terza rima* of the Alamanni. **1839** HALLAM *Hist. Lit.* II. v. §11 *note*, It is ..**Petrarchesque* in a high degree. *a* **1801** R. GALL *Poems* (1819) 12 His sweet *Petrarchian lay. **1881** *Encycl. Brit.* XIII. 506/1 From this period [14th century] also dates that literary phenomenon known under the name of *Petrarchism. **1823** ROSCOE *Sismondi's Lit. Eur.* (1846) I. xv. 438 He ridiculed both the pedants and *Petrarchists. **1897** W. P. KER *Epic & Rom.* 233 The ideal of Petrarch was formulated and abused by the Petrarchists. **1603** FLORIO *Montaigne* II. x. (1632) 228 Fantasticall, new fangled, Spagniolized, and *Petrarchisticall elevations. **1593** HARVEY *Pierce's Super.* Wks. (Grosart) II. 93 All the noblest Italian, French, and Spanish Poets, haue in their seuerall Veines *Petrarchised. **1611** COTGR., *Petrarquiser*, to Petrarkise it, to write like a passionate louer. **1902** *Q. Rev.* Oct. 440 That was the direction in which he [Surrey] Petrarchised.

petrary ('pɛtrərɪ). Now only *Hist.* [ad. med.L. *petrāria* fem. (Du Cange), f. *petra* stone = OF. *perrière*. Cf. also It. *petriero* masc. (Florio) = Sp. *pedrero*, F. *pierrier*, all in same sense.] A mediæval military engine for discharging stones: = PEDRERO, PERRIER.

1610 HOLLAND *Camden's Brit.* I. 400 On the East-side there was planted one Petrarie and two Mangonells. **1795** SOUTHEY *Joan of Arc* VIII. 250 Charging with huge stones the murderous sling Or petrary. **1854** *Blackw. Mag.* LXXV. 530 The trebuchet, the matafunda, the ribaudequin, and the petrary, were special machines for discharging..rocks.

petre ('piːtə(r)). Also 7 **peeter**, 7–9 **peter**. [In sense 1, abbreviation of SALTPETRE; in sense 2, ad. L. *petra*, Gr. πέτρα rock.]

1. = SALTPETRE. (Now only *technical colloq.*)

1594 [see c below]. **1626** BACON *Sylva* §120 A Mixture of Petre and Sulphur without Coale. **1644** NYE *Gunnery* (1670) 6 Certainly if Gunpowder were only made of peter, that would be more strong than powder made of peter, Coal and Brimstone. **1667** T. HENSHAW in *Phil. Trans.* II. 470 To see whether it will shoot into Chrystals of Peeter. **1869** BLACKMORE *Lorna D.* i, The fire of candle lays hold of the peter with a spluttering noise and a leaping.

†**b.** Also *petre-salt*. *Obs.*

1708 *Brit. Apollo* No. 78. 2/1 The Peter-salt is that which is chrystalliz'd last, is fix'd as Sea-salt. **1728** WOODWARD *Meth. Fossils* 36 *note*, Nitre, while..in its native State, is call'd Petre-Salt; when refin'd, Salt-Petre. **1763** *Museum Rust.* I. 53 To let the lye drain off from the petre-salt.

c. *attrib.*, as †**petre man**, a manufacturer of saltpetre (*obs.*).

1594 PLAT *Jewell-ho.* I. 47 That salt, whereof the Peter men doo gather a bushell or two at the most, from thirty tunnes of earth.

†**2.** *oil of petre*: rock-oil, petroleum. *Obs.*

1653 WALTON *Angler* viii. 172 A small piece of Scarlet.. soked in, or annointed with Oyl of Peter, called by some, Oyl of the Rock. **1697** *Phil. Trans.* XIX. 544 There is likewise Distilled from this Stone, an Oil which may be used for Oil of Petre. **1741** *Compl. Fam.-Piece* I. i. 58 Take red and unsophistical Oil of Petre, and anoint therewith..the Part affected.

petrean (pɪ'triːən), *a.* (and *sb.*) Also **petræan**. [f. L. *petræ-us* (= F. *pétrée*, It. *petreo*, a. Gr. πετραῖος rocky, stony, f. πέτρα rock) + -AN. (Hence the name *Arabia Petræa*, Arabia the rocky.)] **1.** Rocky; of or pertaining to rocks or stones; of Arabia Petræa. *rare*. ? *Obs.*

1632 LITHGOW *Trav.* v. 210 Arabia Petrea..diuideth the true Syria from Canaan; this Petrean countrey it selfe, deualling euen downe to the limits of Iacobs bridge. **1803** G. S. FABER *Cabiri* II. 448 We have already found in that country the ancient petrean worship established. **1849** J. FORBES *Physician's Holiday* xx. 294 The same petræan desert continues beyond Swarenbach.

2. (With capital initial.) Of or pertaining to Petra, a city in ancient Arabia Petræa. Also as *sb.*, an inhabitant of Petra.

1852 E. A. ANDREWS *Copious Latin-Eng. Lex.* 1133/2 *Pĕtra*,..a city in Arabia Petraea, now the ruins of Wadi Musa... Hence..*Pĕtreus*, a, um, adj., Petrean. **1923** A. FORDER *Petra: Perea: Phœnicia* 10 One would gather from Bible records that the Petreans were always a proud and turbulent people. *Ibid.* 20 A feasible explanation..was given to me by a modern Petrean. **1925** A. B. W. KENNEDY *Petra* iii. 34 Very little is known about the religion of the Nabataeans as a nation, and even less, perhaps, about the religion of those of the nationality whom we may call particularly Petraeans, and who are responsible for the monuments of Petra. *Ibid.* 35 We know from the dated tombs at Madaïn Salih that the most complex and highly developed of the Petraean designs were already in existence before the commencement of our era. **1957** *Encycl. Brit.* XVII. 652/2 The chief god of Petra was Dhūsharā..he was worshipped under the form of a black rectangular stone, a sort of Petraean Ka'ba. **1965** N. GLUECK *Deities & Dolphins* (1966) x. 331 The Petraean feminine figure on a sea animal could..be identified with an Atargatis or Aphrodite mounted on a fish-tailed Capricornus.

petrefact ('pɛtrɪfækt). Also **petrifact**. [f. L. *petra* rock, stone, after *artefact*.] An object made of stone; also *fig.*, something that has become hardened or fixed.

1911 BEERBOHM *And Even Now* (1920) 39 He..does strive, by day and by night, poor petrefact, to rip off these fell and clownish integuments... He forgets that after all he is only a statue. **1932** *Brit. Jrnl. Psychol.* Apr. 313 Those in whom space perception is still of the early, plastic form frequent among children, in whom the later 'petrefacts' have not yet been crystallized out..should be primary colour perceptors. **1975** *Encounter* Sept. 86 In Germany, in any case, he destroyed numerous outdated structures, did away with old classes, smashed to pieces revered petrifacts.

petreity (pɪ'triːɪtɪ). [ad. med.Schol.L. *petræitās*, f. *petræ-us*: see PETREAN *a.* (and *sb.*) and -ITY. Cf. *paneity*.] The essential quality of being a stone, stoniness.

1711 tr. *Werenfelsius' Disc. Logomachys* vi. 101 Hæcceitys, Ecceitys, Petreitys, Quidditys, Identitys [*petreitates, quidditates, identitates*]..and whole Cart-loads of Qualitys. **1902** M. H. DZIEWICKI *Wyclif's Misc. Philos.* I. p. lxxvii, What makes a stone to be a stone? Petreity. Therefore igneity, petreity, are substantial forms.

petrel ('pɛtrəl). Also 7 **pitteral**, 8 **pittrel**, **petril**, **petteril**, 8–9 **peterel**. [Occurs in 1676 as *pitteral*, in 1703 spelt *petrel* by Dampier, who says that the name was derived from that of St. Peter: see quot. If this was so, *petrel* may have been a formation analogous to *cockerel*, *dotterel*, *hoggerel*, *pickerel*; or might represent a Latin dim. of *Petrus* (e.g. *Petrillus*, *Petrellus*).

The name appears first in Eng.; it occurs in F. (*pétrel*) as a term of Ornithology in Brisson 1760; to Buffon 1782 it was app. an Eng. word requiring explanation. The Norwegian *Soren Peders*, and *Peders fugl* (Brunnich 1764), and Ger. *Peters vogel* are also later than the Eng. and app. suggested by it; they support Dampier's explanation. (But it is of course possible that the word had some other source, represented by *pitteral*, and that the association with *Peter* was due to popular etymology.)]

A small sea-bird, *Procellaria pelagica*, with black and white plumage and long wings; hence extended (with qualifications) to any species of the genus *Procellaria* (distinctively called Storm-Petrels or Stormy Petrels), or of the family *Procellariidæ*, or order *Tubinares*, esp. of the subfamily *Procellariinæ*. See quot. 1894.

1676 FLAWES *Jrnl. Voy. Nova Zembla* in *Acc. Voy.* I. (1694) 181 Saw many Pitterals about the Ship. **1703** DAMPIER *Voy.* III. I. 97 As they fly..they pat the Water alternately with their Feet, as if they walkt upon it; tho' still upon the Wing. And from hence the Seamen give them the name of Petrels, in allusion to St. Peter's walking upon the Lake of Gennesareth. **1748** *Phil. Trans.* XLV. 166 The Pittrel or Storm-Fink. **1767** CARTERET in Hawkesworth *Voy.* (1773) I. 318 The peterels, to which sailors have given the name of Mother Carey's Chickens. **1768** PENNANT *Zool.* II. 431 The whole genus of Petrels have a peculiar faculty of spouting from their bills, to a considerable distance, a large quantity of pure oyl. **1776** *Ibid.* (ed. 4) II. 467 Stormy petrel. **1802** BARRINGTON *Hist. N.S. Wales* viii. 270 The sooty petrel had appropriated a certain grassy part of the island to herself. **1825** WATERTON *Wand. S. Amer.* II. i. 85 When it blows a hard gale of wind, the stormy Petrel makes its appearance. **1838** POE *A. G. Pym* Wks. 1864 IV. 123 Mother Carey's geese, or the great peterel... The great peterel is as large as the common albatross and is carnivorous. **1843** YARRELL *Hist. Brit. Birds* III. 514 The Storm Petrel,.. exhibiting the deep keel of a Swift, and possessing accordingly enduring powers of flight. *a* **1879** in *Poems Places, Br. America*, etc. 90 Pied petrels coursed about the sea. **1894** NEWTON *Dict. Birds* s.v., The true Petrels, *Procellariinæ*, in which..are combined forms so different.. as the Diving-Petrels, *Pelecanoides* or *Halodroma*, the Storm-Petrels, *Procellaria*, the Flat-billed Petrels, *Prion*, the Fulmar, the Shearwaters and others... The common Storm-Petrel, *Procellaria pelagica*..Seamen hardly discriminate between this and others nearly resembling it.., such as Leach's or the Fork-tailed Petrel, *Cymochorea leucorrhoa*,..and Wilson's Petrel, *Oceanites oceanicus*, the type of the Family *Oceanitidæ*... The Cape-Pigeon or Pintado Petrel, *Daption capensis*, is one that has long been well known.

fig. **1862** *Sat. Rev.* 13 Sept. 321 M. Hugo..is the petrel of literature, revelling in the storms of passion, and the conflict of the elements that determine human action.

b. Locally applied to the Kittiwake.

1770 PENNANT *Zool.* IV. 26 [The] Kittiwake..inhabits the romantic cliffs of Flamborough head. [*Note*] Where it is called Petrel.

petrel, var. PEITREL *Obs.*

petrenall, obs. f. PETRONEL.

petreol, obs. f. PETROL.

petrera, -ro, obs. var. PEDRERO, a small gun.

petrescent (pɪ'trɛsənt), *a.* ? *Obs.* [f. L. *petra* rock, stone + -ESCENT.] Properly, Becoming converted into stone or petrified; but usually, Having the quality of petrifying, petrifactive. (In quot. 1757, Tending to form 'stone' or calculus.)

1663 BOYLE *Usef. Exp. Nat. Philos.* II. ii. 32 A Liquor abounding with petrescent parts may..turn Wood (as I have observ'd in a petrifying Spring) into a kind of Stone. **1676** HODGSON in *Phil. Trans.* XI. 766 Concerning petrescent Springs. **1757** *Phil. Trans.* L. 216 The petrescent quality of his urine was..destroyed. **1763** *Brit. Mag.* IV. 216 He thought it possible to make oysters and mussels breed pearls by feeding them with a proper petrescent water. **1819** H. BUSK *Banquet* II. 456* Round the lapideous tuft,..petrescent tendrils curl.

So **pe'trescence, pe'trescency,** the process of petrifaction; formation of calculus.

1662 J. CHANDLER *Van Helmont's Oriat.* 246 That which I have said..of the Disease of the Stone, concerning the stony seed, and so of petrescency or the manner of making in stones. **1663** BOYLE *Usef. Exp. Nat. Philos.* II. ii. 35 None of the enumerated ways of Petrescency..deserves to be look'd upon as satisfactory. **1799** KIRWAN *Geol. Ess.* 140 It proves..that petrifactions are carried on in appropriate circumstances in modern times, and the successive process of petrescence.

Petri ('pɛtrɪ, 'piːtrɪ). Also **petri**. [Name of R. J. *Petri* (1852–1922), German bacteriologist, who first proposed the use of such a dish (*Centralbl. f. Bacteriol. und Parasitenkunde* (1887) I. 279).] *Petri* (or †*Petri's*) *dish*: a shallow, circular, flat-bottomed glass (or plastic) dish with vertical sides and with a cover of the same shape but

slightly larger, which is used particularly for growing cultures of bacteria or the like. Also *fig.*
1892 A. C. Abbott *Princ. Bacteriol.* viii. 87 Petri's dishes are flat, double dishes of glass. *Ibid.* xx. 212 Place the tissue in a sterilized Petri dish. **1897** Muir & Ritchie *Man. Bacteriol.* 57 The latter are known as Petri's dishes. **1903** *Univ. Nebraska Stud.* Oct. 2 The hydroids were cut..into the desired lengths and placed in watch glasses, petri-dishes, finger bowls, etc. **1946** F. Schneider *Qualitative Organic Microanalysis* vii. 187 Stopper the flask with a small cork, place the side arm in the petri dish, and fill the latter with alkaline permanganate solution. **1973** J. Goodfield *Courier to Peking* xv. 211 I've got a test I want to do. Get me a Petri dish smeared with gelatine and the following serums. **1976** *Nature* 24 June 701/1 Both cell types were plated on plastic Petri dishes (5 cm diameter).

petrichor (ˈpɛtrɪkɔ(r)). [f. petr(o- + ichor.] A pleasant, distinctive smell that frequently accompanies the first rain after a long period of warm, dry weather in certain regions; in quot. 1975, applied to an oily substance obtained from the ground in which this smell was concentrated.
1964 Bear & Thomas in *Nature* 7 Mar. 993/2 The diverse nature of the host materials has led us to propose the name 'petrichor' for this apparently unique odour which can be regarded as an 'ichor' or 'tenuous essence' derived from rock or stone. This name, unlike the general term 'argillaceous odour', avoids the unwarranted implication that the phenomenon is restricted to clays or argillaceous materials; it does not imply that petrichor is necessarily a fixed chemical entity but rather it denotes an integral odour. **1971** *Listener* 4 Nov. 612/3 No matter what kind of rock or earth was used, the oily essence always possessed the aroma of petrichor—the smell of rain falling on dry ground. **1975** *Sunday Mail* (Brisbane) 2 Nov. 32/2 CSIROs Melbourne mineral chemistry division discovered that it was not fungi or dead vegetation which produced the smell, but small yellowish-gold oily globules. The globules, nicknamed 'petrichor' or 'essence of rock' by the researchers, contained at least 50 different compounds, not unlike a perfume and were absorbed into the ground from the air.

petricolous (pɪˈtrɪkələs), *a. Zool.* [f. mod.L. **petricola* (f. *petra* rock + *col-ĕre* to inhabit) + -ous; in mod.F. *pétricole* (Littré).] Inhabiting rocks; saxicolous; lithodomous.
1858 Mayne *Expos. Lex.*, *Petricolus*..shells found in more or less hard rocks which their animals pierce: petricolous.

pétrie (ˈpeɪtriː), *v. Massage.* [ad. F. *pétri-r* to knead, in OF. *pestrir*:—L. type **pistūrīre*, f. *pistūra* pounding.] *trans.* To knead in massage.
1887 D. Maguire *Art Massage* iv. (ed. 4) 57 Grasping between his thumb and four fingers those of the patient, he pétries all the circumference for a few minutes. *Ibid.* 58 Presses strongly while he petries the centre of the hand.

petrifaction (ˌpɛtrɪˈfækʃən). Also 8–9 erron. petre-. [f. petrify, after *satisfaction*, *stupefaction*, from *satisfy*, *stupefy*, L. *satisfacĕre*, *stupefacĕre*, etc., instead of the etymological form petrification.]
1. The action of petrifying, or condition of being petrified; conversion into stone or stony substance; in *Path.* formation of 'stone' or calculus.
1646 Sir T. Browne *Pseud. Ep.* ii. v. 91 That corall is soft under water, but waxeth hard as soon as it arriveth unto the ayre,..we have some reason to doubt,..from so sudden a petrifaction, and strange induration. **1704** J. Harris *Lex. Techn.* I, *Petrifaction*, is properly the changing of a mix'd Body into a Stony Substance, when it had no such Nature before; and the Action by which this is performed, is called, *Petrification.* **1802** Playfair *Illustr. Hutton. The.* 117 What are called petrifactions or the formation of stony substances by means of water. **1885** G. Denman in *Law Rep. 14 Q.B. Div.* 951 Pearson..[had made a] well for the convenient petrifaction of barristers' wigs and other interesting objects. **1896** *Allbutt's Syst. Med.* I. 195 Dead tissues lying in the midst of living tissues are prone to calcification and petrifaction.
b. *fig.*: cf. petrify 2.
1722 Wollaston *Relig. Nat.* vi. §17 The principle of compassion..broke through his petrifaction, and would shew that it could not totally be eradicated. **1820** Hazlitt *Lect. Dram. Lit.* 253 This is making a petrefaction both of love and poetry. **1868** Hawthorne *Amer. Note-Bks.* (1879) II. 148 To my horror and petrifaction. **1874** Deutsch *Rem.* 172 The common assumption that Islam is identical with mental and religious petrifaction.
2. *concr.* Something petrified, or formed by conversion into stone; a stony concretion formed by the petrifying of an organic body, as in fossils, or by the deposition of mineral substance from solution in water or other liquid, as in stalactites and stalagmites.
1686 Plot *Staffordsh.* 190 So far are these stones from being petrifactions. **1692** Ray *Disc.* ii. iv. (1732) 155 His curious Collection of Petrifactions. **1758** J.S. *Le Dran's Observ. Surg.* (1771) 259 A Disposition in the Blood to form Concretions and Petrefactions. **1812** *Chron.* in *Ann. Reg.* 142 There was discovered under the cliffs..the complete petrifaction of a crocodile, seventeen feet in length. **1848** Dickens *Dombey* xxiii, Curling and twisting like a petrifaction of an arbour over the threshold. **1872** Nicholson *Palæont.* 2 Fossils, or, as they are often termed, petrifactions.
fig. **1818** Hazlitt *Eng. Poets* v. (1870) 128 He gives you the petrifaction of a sigh. **1856** Stanley *Sinai & Pal.* xiv. (1858) 449 The House of Loretto is the petrifaction, so to speak, of the 'Last Sigh of the Crusades'.

petrifactive (pɛtrɪˈfæktɪv), *a.* [f. stem of *petrifact-ion* + -ive: cf. *stupefactive.*] Having the quality of petrifying; causing petrifaction.
1646 Sir T. Browne *Pseud. Ep.* iii. xxiii. 167 The Lapidescencies, and petrifactive mutations of hard bodies. **1778** W. Pryce *Min. Cornub.* 103 The petrifactive quality of water. **1857** H. Miller *Test. Rocks* iii. 145 The famous fossil-man of Guadaloupe, locked up by the petrifactive agencies in a slab of limestone.

petrifiable (ˈpɛtrɪfaɪəb(ə)l), *a. rare*⁻⁰. [f. petrify + -able.] Capable of being petrified.
In mod. Dicts.

petrific (pɪˈtrɪfɪk), *a.* Now *rare.* [ad. med.L. *petrific-us*, f. *petra* rock, stone: see -fic.]
1. Having the quality of petrifying; making something into stone, or as hard as stone; petrifactive, petrifying; in *Path.* causing the formation of 'stone' or calculus.
1667 Milton *P.L.* x. 293 The aggregated Soyle Death with his Mace petrific..As with a Trident smote. **1670** W. Simpson *Hydrol. Ess.* 136 Indued with a deopilative, and (if I may so say) antipetrifick property. **1695** Congreve *Taking of Namure* xi, Wing'd Perseus, with Petrifick shield Of Gorgon's head. **1746** Simon in *Phil. Trans.* XLIV. 308 Convinced of the petrific Quality in some Parts of the Lough. **1811** W. Taylor in *Monthly Mag.* XXXI. 448 The progress of petrific conversion may be traced to a considerable depth in contiguous..strata. **1839** De Quincey *Recoll. Lakes* Wks. 1862 II. 44 Stiffened, as by the petrific touch of Death.
fig. **1729** Savage *Wanderer* i. 56 [Winter's] Breath A nitrous Damp, that strikes petrific Death. **1782** Miss Burney *Cecilia* vi. ii, A look meant to be nothing less than petrific. **1837** De Quincey in *Tait's Mag.* IV. 69 No society is..so cheerless and petrific in its influence upon others.
2. Loosely in passive sense: Petrified, stony.
1804 Anna Seward *Mem. Darwin* 214 Marble and other petrific substances. **1888** F. P. Noble in *Chicago Advance* 10 May 290 In Heidelberg, Calvinism is plastic, Scriptural, dynamic; in Westminster, petrific, scholastic, dogmatic.

† **peˈtrificate**, *v. Obs. rare*⁻¹. [f. L. type **petrificāre* (It. *petrificare*, F. *pétrifier*): see -ate³.] = petrify. So † **peˈtrificant** *a.*, petrifying.
1603 Florio *Montaigne* ii. xxxvii. (1632) 437 There was some grettie or petrificant qualitie. **1647** J. Hall *Poems* ii. 96 Though our hearts petrificated were, Yet causedst thou thy law be graven there.

petrification (ˈpɛtrɪfɪˈkeɪʃən). Now *rare.* [a. F. *pétrification* (16th c. in Hatz.-Darm.) = It. *petrificazione*, †*-atione* (Florio), L. type (prob. in mod.L.) **petrificātio*, n. of action from **petrificāre*, *pétrifier*, petrify. For this the non-etymological *petrifaction* has been substituted.]
1. = petrifaction 1.
1611 Cotgr., *Petrification*, a petrification; a making stonie, a turning into stone. **1646** Sir T. Browne *Pseud. Ep.* ii. v. 91 We have..visible petrification of wood in many waters. **1665–6** *Phil. Trans.* I. 320 Much has been already said and written of Petrification. **1776** G. Semple *Building in Water* 132 It is the Lime alone, that creates the Petrification. **1882** Geikie *Text-bk. Geol.* v. 611 The only true petrification..consists in the abstraction of the organic substances, molecule by molecule, and in their replacement by precipitated mineral matter.
b. *fig.* = petrifaction 1 b.
1678 Cudworth *Intell. Syst.* i. iv. §1. 193 Mortification or petrification of the soul. **1681** H. Hallywell *Melampron.* Introd. B, This state and condition he terms..a Petrification or Mortification of the Mind. **1865** Dickens *Mut. Fr.* i. x, A widowed female glaring petrification at her fellow creatures. **1891** *Daily News* 28 Apr. 6/2 The misfortune was that the contagion of petrification had spread to the free churches.
2. *concr.* = petrifaction 2.
1677 Plot *Oxfordsh.* ii. §26 Incrustations are petrifications, made by such waters as let fall their stony particles. **1762** tr. *Busching's Syst. Geog.* III. 579 Great numbers of petrifications, more particularly of marine shells and plants, are found among them. **1794** Sullivan *View Nat.* I. 61 Flints never having been found to contain petrifications, or the marks of any organized body.

petrified (ˈpɛtrɪfaɪd), *ppl. a.* [f. petrify *v.*]
1. a. Changed into stone or stony substance. Esp. in phr. ***petrified forest.***
1667 H. Stubbe in *Phil. Trans.* II. 499 Upon those other Plants with petrified roots there gathers a Lime-stone. **1776** G. Semple *Building in Water* 40 Some of the Piers were much more petrified than others. *Ibid.* 52 We met with very large Cakes of the petrified Sand. **1813** Bakewell *Introd. Geol.* (1815) 442 Petrified fish have been discovered in solid rocks in the very attitude of seizing and swallowing their prey. **1830** *Illinois Monthly Mag.* Oct. 31 The earth's surface is literally covered with stumps, roots and limbs of petrified trees; presenting the appearance of a 'Petrified Forest'. **1841–71** T. R. Jones *Anim. Kingd.* (ed. 4) 649 The countless petrified remains known by the names of Hamites, Lituites, Orthoceratites, Cyrtoceratites. **1873** S. W. Cozzens *Marvellous Country* 76 We came upon the remains of a petrified forest,..converted by some chemical process into specimens of variegated jasper. **1937** M. Huxley *Let.* 13 Oct. in *Lett. A. Huxley* (1969) 425 We drove through all the view places and the petrified forests and the grand-canyons. **1969** E. H. Pinto *Treen* 196 Petrified wood. The most interesting and highly prized results of wood transformed into rock, are examples from the several petrified forests which exist in various parts of the world. *Ibid.* 197 Two of the most famous of the petrified forests are situated in the U.S.A.—one at the Yellowstone National Park.., the other in Chalcedony Park, Arizona.

b. *transf.* and *fig.* Represented or embodied in stone.
1634 Habington *Castara* (Arb.) 50 Spencer hath a Stone; and Draytons browes Stand petrified ith'wall, with Laurell bowes Yet girt about. **1889** Hissey *Tour in Phaeton* 106 Our cathedrals, abbeys, and ancient churches are truly petrified poems.
2. *fig.* Hardened, stiffened, 'paralysed' with surprise, etc.; terrified, extremely frightened; also const. *of.* See petrify *v.* 2.
1720 Welton *Suffer. Son of God* II. xix. 533 Melt the Petrified Obduracy of this Harden'd Heart! **1790** Han. More *Relig. Fash. World* (1791) 210 How would the petrified enquirer be astonished. **1863** Geo. Eliot *Romola* xxxvi, This petrified coldness was better than a passionate, futile opposition. **1869** 'Mark Twain' *Innoc. Abr.* xlvi. 481 A great herd of curious-looking Syrian goats and sheep were gratefully eating gravel. I do not state this as a petrified fact. I only *suppose* they were eating gravel, because there did not appear to be any thing else for them to eat. **1870** Max Müller *Sc. Relig.* (1873) 67 A careful interpretation of the petrified language of ancient India and Greece. **1875** —— *Sk. New & Old* 219 Here, here, you petrified fool. **1963** R. Wolff *I, Keturah* (1964) ii. xvii. 229, I was petrified of all the gadgets. **1968** *Observer* 7 Jan. 28/6 [They] *think* they want the foreign flavour; but actually couldn't be more petrified of it. **1974** W. J. Burley *Death in Stanley St.* xi. 186 He was trying to get at the gun... I was petrified!

petrifier (ˈpɛtrɪfaɪə(r)). [f. as prec. + -er¹.] One who or that which petrifies.
1891 Abbott *Philomythus* Introd. 16 Almighty God, reported as a Petrifier of unlawfully dressed fowls.

petrify (ˈpɛtrɪfaɪ), *v.* Also 7 erron. petrefie. [a. F. *pétrifi-er* (16th c. in Godef. *Compl.*) = It. *petrificare* 'to grow hard as a stone' (Florio), ad. L. type **petrificāre* (prob. in early mod.L.), f. *petra* rock, stone: see -fy.]
1. *trans.* To convert into stone or stony substance; *spec.* to turn (an organic body) into a stony concretion by replacing its original substance by a calcareous, siliceous, or other mineral deposit; also, *loosely*, to encrust with such a deposit, as may be done by a stream of water holding the mineral in solution. Also *absol.*
1594 Plat *Jewell-ho.* i. 22 Wood that is both metalized and petrified in clay groundes. **1611** Florio, *Insassire*,..to enstone, to petrifie. **1668** R. L'Estrange *Vis. of Quev.* (1708) 103 A Man would swear the whole Woman to be directly Petrify'd. *a* **1697** Aubrey *Lives* (1898) I. 131 At the foot..runnes a fine cleare stream which petrifies. **1750** tr. *Leonardus' Mirr. Stones* 30 Albertus gives an account of a tree..with a nest and birds petrified. **1805–17** R. Jameson *Char. Min.* (ed. 3) 229 Wood is petrified with an earthy mineral, as in wood-stone and wood-opal. **1869** Tozer *Highl. Turkey* I. 148 The eight caryatides..were supposed to have been petrified by..magic.
2. *fig.* To change as if into stone. **a.** To deprive of feeling, vitality, capacity of change or development, etc., to harden, benumb, deaden, stiffen.
1626 Donne *Serm.*, *Luke* ii. 29 (1640) 34 Doe not petrifie and harden thy Conscience against these holy suggestions. *a* **1711** Ken *Hymnarium* Poet. Wks. 1721 II. 82 All Hell let loose..to blind And petrify the unrelenting Mind. **1742** Pope *Dunc.* iv. 264 Full in the midst of Euclid dip at once, And petrify a Genius to a Dunce. **1892** Westcott *Gospel of Life* 57 It is..possible to petrify a doctrine into an outward formula.
b. To deprive of movement by a sudden emotion; to make motionless or rigid with astonishment, horror, or the like; to paralyse, stupefy, strike dumb, confound. (Chiefly *passive.*)
1771 Goldsm. *Haunch of Venison* 108 With looks that quite petrified enter'd the maid. **1786** Mme. D'Arblay *Diary* 2 Aug., I was almost petrified with horror at the intelligence. **1814** Col. Hawker *Diary* (1893) I. 96 Mr. Cudmore petrified the whole neighbourhood with his astonishing pianoforte playing. **1880** G. Meredith *Tragic Com.* 287 She had stood petrified before him, as if affected by some wicked spell.
3. *intr.* (for *pass.*) To become converted into stone or stony substance; to undergo petrifaction.
1646 Sir T. Browne *Pseud. Ep.* ii. i. 50 When wood and many other bodies doe petrifie..wee do not usually ascribe their induration to cold. **1730** A. Gordon *Maffei's Amphith.* 272 Cement like that of the Ancients, which petrified. **1776** G. Semple *Building in Water* 40 Those Piers did not petrify at all that lay on Beds that were not gravelly.
b. *fig.*: cf. 2.
1685 Dryden *Threnod. August.* 8 Like Niobe we marble grow, And petrify with grief. **1721** Amherst *Terræ Fil.* No. 12 (1754) 62 A director, or scull of a college..petrifies in fraud and shamelessness. **1868** J. H. Blunt *Ref. Ch. Eng.* I. 29 The minds of men had petrified in certain forms of theological language.

ˈpetrifying, *vbl. sb.* [f. prec. + -ing¹.] The action of petrify *v.*; also *concr.* = petrifaction 2.
1712 J. James tr. *Le Blond's Gardening* 214 Rock-Works, Congelations, Petrifyings, and Shell-Works.

ˈpetrifying, *ppl. a.* [f. as prec. + -ing².] That petrifies (see the verb); petrifactive.
1652 French (*title*) The Yorkshire Spaw..the Dropping, or Petrifying Well. **1660** R. Coke *Justice Vind.* 21 Some is of a petrifying quality. **1705** J. Taylor *Journ. Edenborough* (1903) 48 The water is of a petrifying nature and as it falls

turns the moss into stone. **1878** HUXLEY *Physiogr.* 170 Such springs are vulgarly called *petrifying springs*..all that such springs are able to do is to simply cover the objects which receive the water with a crust of carbonate of lime.

b. *fig.*

1667 *Decay Chr. Piety* xvii. ¶6 A kind of petrifying crime, which induces that induration, to which the fearful expectation of wrath is consequent. **1800** MRS. HERVEY *Mourtray Fam.* II. 112 She seemed..surprised to see Mrs. Mourtray, to whom, with petrifying civility, she made a few speeches on her recovery. **1814** MRS. J. WEST *Alicia de Lacy* IV. 249 That petrifying horror which, by benumbing every faculty, renders them all incapable of useful exertion.

Petrine ('piːtraɪn), *a.* [f. L. *Petr-us* PETER + -INE: cf. PAULINE, also Gr. πέτρινος stony, rocky.] **1.** Of, pertaining to, or characteristic of the Apostle Peter. ***Petrine liturgy***, the Roman liturgy traditionally ascribed to St. Peter.

Petrine claims, claims of the Popes, based on their traditional succession from St. Peter.

1846 S. DAVIDSON in *Eclectic Rev.* May 529 Another hypothesis is that of Baur..followed by Billroth, [that] there were, properly speaking, but two parties in the Corinthian church, the Pauline and the Petrine. **1853** J. MARTINEAU *Stud. Chr.* (1858) 252 The 'Tübingen romance'..that the antagonism between the Petrine and Pauline, the Hebrew and the Hellenic Gospel..continued into the second century. **1865** LITTLEDALE *North Side of Altar* 5 The early Christian liturgies, inclusive of the Petrine or Roman family. **1885** tr. *Pfleiderer's Influence Paul* iii. 142 The moderate Jewish Christians (the Petrine section). **1930** tr. *F. von Hügel's Some Notes on Petrine Claims* vii. 30 Four contentions which make up the Catholic Petrine claims.

2. Of, pertaining to, or characteristic of Peter I the Great (1672–1725), czar and emperor of Russia.

1908 R. N. BAIN in *Cambr. Mod. Hist.* V. xvii. 549 At least half the Senate (though that was a purely Petrine institution). **1927** E. M. ALMEDINGEN in *Magnificat* Mar. 235/2 No really great men of letters lived in Peter's time: Theophanus..and Prince Kantemir..were the two men who left any mark at all in the annals of Petrine literature. **1956** E. MUNZER *Solovyev* iii. 41 It was he [*sc.* the Patriarch Nikon] who paved the way to the Petrine perversion, or pseudomorphosis, of the Russian soul. **1964** *Listener* 5 Mar. 392/1 [Alexis] Tolstoy's Peter the Great modifies the Petrine myth in accordance with an up-to-date and almost professional conception of history. **1974** *Times Lit. Suppl.* 13 Sept. 984/3 No extracts on eastern Europe;..none on Russia, where the Petrine reforms were nothing if not military.

Hence **Petrinism** ('piːtrɪnɪz(ə)m), the doctrine of (or attributed to) St. Peter, Petrine theology or teaching; **'Petrinize** *v. trans.*, to make Petrine, imbue with Petrinism.

1857 M. PATTISON *Ess.* (1889) II. 230 The development of Christianity through the antagonism of Petrinism and Paulinism. **1883** SCHAFF *Hist. Ch.* I. III. xxii. 212 He has not ..brought upon the stage either a Paulinised Peter, or a Petrinised Paul. **1902** J. SMITH *Integr. Script.* 78 Baur's tendency theory of a conflict between Petrinism and Paulinism in the primitive Church..no longer commands belief.

Petrinist ('piːtrɪnɪst). [f. PETRINE *a.* + -IST.] A follower of St. Peter; a student of Petrine theology.

1922 JACKSON & LAKE *Beginn. Christianity* II. I. v. 123 Gfrörer thought that the compiler of Acts..used a collection of unhistorical legends arranged by a zealous Petrinist.

‖**pétrissage** (petrisaʒ). [Fr., f. *pétrir* to knead.] A kneading process used in massage.

1886 W. MURRELL *Massage* iii. 11 Next [after *effleurage*] comes *pétrissage* which is more important and is by no means easy to acquire. **1906** *Practitioner* Dec. 769 *Pétrissage* is performed by grasping the tissues to be operated on, lifting the mass thus seized, and alternately loosening and tightening the grasp. **1957** *Encycl. Brit.* XV. 32/1 Pétrissage ..consists of a seizure by the hands of muscles or other tissues which are then subjected to a process of kneading. **1961** [see MALAXATION c].

Petrist ('piːtrɪst). [ad. L. *Petrista*, f. the personal name *Petrus*, PETER: see -IST.] A follower or disciple of Petrus Lombardus (Peter the Lombard), a schoolman of the Twelfth Century, called 'Master of the Sentences' (died 1164).

1600 W. WATSON *Decacordon* (1602) 140 Petrists, Thomists, Scotists, and other schoolemen.

petro-[1] (pɛtrəʊ), properly combining form of Gr. πέτρος stone or πέτρα rock, as in PETROGLYPH, -GRAPH, etc. In *Anat.* used to form adjectives descriptive of parts connected with the petrous portion of the temporal bone and some other part indicated by the second element (most of which may also be used *ellipt.* as substantives): as **petro'hyoid, petro'mastoid, petro-oc'cipital (petroccipital), petropha'ryngeal, petro-'sphenoid, -sphe'noidal, petro-squa'mosal, -'squamous, petrotym'panic.**

1875 HUXLEY & MARTIN *Elem. Biol.* (1877) 243 The hyoid bone..from it a slip of muscle (*petrohyoid) will be seen passing up towards the occipital region of the skull. **1848** OWEN *Archetype & Homol. Vertebr. Skel.* 29 The coalescence of the primitively distinct mastoid with the ossifying capsule of the labyrinth is very speedy,..and a composite '*petromastoid' bone is thus formed. *Ibid.* 31 In the walrus..the mastoid, or petromastoid, forms as large a proportion of the outer lateral walls of the cranium as does the squamosal. **1831** R. KNOX *Cloquet's Anat.* 85 The first part of this line is named the *Petro-occipital suture. **1893** *Syd. Soc. Lex.*, **Petro-sphenoid ligament*... *Petro-sphenoidal suture.* **1842** DUNGLISON *Med. Lex.*, *Petro-sphenoidal. **1899** *Allbutt's Syst. Med.* VII. 507 There was a small opening into the skull along the *petro-squamosal suture. **1879** *St. George's Hosp. Rep.* IX. 240 A line of fracture.. extended from left *petro-squamous junction backwards along the parieto-occipital suture as far as the sagittal suture. **1854** OWEN *Skel. & Teeth* in *Circ. Sc., Org. Nat.* I. 238 [In the giraffe] the *petrotympanic is a separate bone, as in all ruminants. **1877** BURNETT *Ear* 42 The petrotympanic fissure.

petro-[2] ('pɛtrəʊ), combining form of PETROLEUM, in recent formations as ***petro-politics, -power, -resources, -wealth***; freq. with ref. to revenue, esp. foreign exchange, deriving from petroleum exports, as ***petro-billion, -naira, -pound***; **petro-currency**, the currency of a petroleum-exporting country, of which the exchange rate varies chiefly with the fluctuations of the petroleum market. Also PETRODOLLAR. Cf. PETRO-CHEMISTRY 2.

1973 *Time* 3 Dec. 44/1 The energy crisis..may have been artificially imposed, but its implications stretch far beyond petropolitics. **1974** *Time* (U.S. ed.) 17 June 83 (*heading*) The petrocurrency peril. **1974** *Newsweek* 7 Oct. 52/3 Top Arab leaders have now decided not to put their petro-billions into U.S. Treasury bonds..but to invest in American industry instead. **1975** *Economist* 8 Mar. 86/3 Some members [of OPEC]..want their own petro-currencies put into the basket of IMF special drawing rights. **1975** *Publishers Weekly* 19 May 99/1, I understand they're rolling in petropounds since oil was discovered in the North Sea. **1976** *Ibid.* 5 Jan. 60/1 An Arab emirate saturated with petro-resources. **1976** *Daily Times* (Lagos) 5 May 7/1 As the tenth largest oil producer in the league, Nigeria has every reason to tout her petro-wealth. **1976** *Daily Colonist* (Victoria, B.C.) 20 June 35/1 'There are two kinds of power,' he said, 'petropower and agripower.' **1976** *Daily Times* (Lagos) 20 July 7/1 Nigeria's foreign exchange reserve zoomed to N2,047 million through oil boom, thus projecting an over-sized petro-naira bubble which beclouded the vision of some former military rulers. **1977** *Time* 11 July 36/3 The Saudis can be expected to wield their petropower prudently. **1979** *Daily Tel.* 5 July 21 Industrialists are ill-prepared for Britain's 'petro-currency' era. **1986** *Tablet* 19 Apr. 405/1 As a petrocurrency of a country with a Conservative government, it [*sc.* sterling] was probably bound to strengthen when oil prices soared.

Petrobrusian (pɛtrəʊ'bruːsɪən). *Ch. Hist.* [ad. L. *Petrobrusiani* pl., f. name of Pierre de Bruys (*Petrus Brusianus*), f. Bruys (*Brusium*).] A member of a sect founded by Peter or Pierre de Bruys in the South of France early in the 12th century, who rejected infant baptism, transubstantiation, and the worship of the cross, and opposed the building of churches, the observance of fasts, sacred music, etc.

c **1559** R. HALL *Life Fisher* in *Fisher's Wks.* (E.E.T.S.) 135 Petrus Clinacensis against the..Petrobrussians. **1686** HORNECK *Crucif. Jesus* xv. 357 Petrus Cluniacensis having understood of the Petrobrusians, that they had a communion but once a year, thus expostulates with them. **1727–41** CHAMBERS *Cycl.* s.v., F. Langlois objects manicheism to the Petrobrussians. **1889** W. B. CARPENTER *Perm. Elem. Relig.* iii. 116 The Petrobrusians, the Apostolical brethren, and the Waldenses have been recognised as possessing common aims.

petrochemical (pɛtrəʊ'kɛmɪkəl), *a.* and *sb.* Also **petro-chemical.** [f. next, after *chemistry, chemical.*] **A.** *adj.* **a.** Of or pertaining to petrochemistry (sense 1).

1913 *Chem. Abstr.* VII. 3949 (*heading*) Petrochemical studies. **1952** *Geochim. et Cosmochim. Acta* II. 283 (*heading*) A petrochemical study of the Tertiary lavas of north-east Ireland. **1960** *Internal Geol. Rev.* II. 273 (*heading*) Petrochemical study of the Cenozoic basaltic rocks in eastern China. **1975** *Nature* 27 Feb. 691/1 Another study of the intrusion was initiated in the hope that new geo-physical and petrochemical techniques might provide the added insight needed to resolve some of these questions.

b. Of or pertaining to petrochemistry (sense 2) or petrochemicals.

1942 *Oil & Gas Jrnl.* 30 Apr. 47 The long experience of the Badger Company..enables it..to meet the requirements of the rapidly expanding Petro-Chemical Industry. **1947** *Chem. & Engin. News* 8 Dec. 3634/1 Increasing demands for organic chemicals..have led to rapid development of the petrochemical industry. **1959** *Times Rev. Industry* Sept. 99/3 The Monsanto Chemical Company..will build a petro-chemical factory..to produce styrene monomer from which polystyrene plastics are made. **1961** G. R. CHOPPIN *Exper. Nucl. Chem.* xi. 185 Further reduction is effected by using solvents of petro-chemical origin. **1969** *Times* 30 Apr. 23/2 (Advt.), Dutch-American firm, specialising in design and fabrication of unusual petrochemical heat transfer equipment,..seeks experienced man. *a* **1974** R. CROSSMAN *Diaries* (1976) II. 290 There was a likelihood of petro-chemical and associated development in the Invergordon area.

B. *sb.* Any chemical compound or element obtained or derived industrially from petroleum or natural gas. Freq. *attrib.* in *pl.*

1942 *Oil & Gas Jrnl.* 25 June 180 (Advt.), Typical 'petro-chemicals' already in production: alcohols, butadiene, benzol, [etc.]. **1950** *N.Y. Times* 19 Nov. 1F/3 Petrochemicals which are derived from the vast supplies of petroleum and natural gas available in the South, are the bellwether of the country's economy. **1959** *Engineering* 2 Jan. 24/1 The new petrochemicals plant at the Fawley refinery of Esso. **1967** *New Scientist* 16 Feb. 385/3 Chemical engineering has now advanced to the point whereby the idea of using this gas [*sc.* carbon monoxide] as the key building block for petrochemicals—such as plastics and pesticides..—is no longer a pipe-dream. **1972** HARKER & ALLEN *Fuel Sci.* iii. 35 Crude oil also provides the source of raw material for the rapidly growing petro-chemicals industry. **1975** *Petroleum Rev.* XXIX. 381/2 (*caption*) 65,000 tons of petrochemicals.. are stored under an inert blanket.

Hence **petro'chemically** *adv.*

1952 *Trans. Edin. Geol. Soc.* XV. 82 Ophitic texture is the result of delayed crystallisation of augite from magma characterised petrochemically by marked undersaturation in the pyroxene-components. **1963** *Economist* 28 Sept. 1140, 60 per cent of world nitrogen is petrochemically derived. **1973** *Nature* 27 Apr. 566/1 'Petrographically' the dredged lavas are typically submarine fine grained, vesicular and porphyritic basalts... 'Petrochemically' the basalts are classified as tholeiites according to the Yoder and Tilley normative scheme.

petrochemistry (pɛtrəʊ'kɛmɪstrɪ). [f. PETRO- (in sense 2 repr. *petroleum*: cf. PETRO-[2]) + CHEMISTRY.] **1.** *Geol.* The chemistry of the composition and formation of rocks (as distinct from minerals, ore deposits, etc.), esp. igneous and metamorphic ones.

1937 *Bull. Volcanologique* I. 59 (*heading*) Petro-chemistry of the Scottish Carboniferous-Permian igneous rocks. **1958** *Q. Jrnl. Geol. Soc.* CXIII. 393 (*heading*) The petrochemistry of the Ardara aureole. **1971** *Internat. Geol. Rev.* XIII. 561/2 In petrochemistry we are often required to compare associations of rocks of different regions and assign them to definite petrographic groups. **1974** *Nature* 18 Oct. 581/2 There is, as yet, insufficient documentation of the relationship between precisely measured Sr isotope ratios and the petrochemistry of Icelandic rocks.

2. The chemistry of petroleum and natural gas, and of their refining and processing.

1942 *Oil & Gas Jrnl.* 18 June 96/1 The section in next week's Journal devoted to petro-chemistry is something you'll not want to miss. **1954** *Chem. & Engin. News* 20 Sept. 3719/3 Entrance of one company into field of petro-chemistry in 1925 was followed by dozens of others. **1959** *Ibid.* 22 June 41 (Advt.), Exciting new products through petro-chemistry.

petrodollar ('pɛtrədɒlə(r)). [f. PETRO-[2] + DOLLAR.] A notional unit of currency available in a petroleum-exporting country. Freq. *attrib.* of the surplus of petroleum exports over imports of all other goods, and in *pl.*

1974 *Globe & Mail* (Toronto) 27 Aug. 7/1 What emerged in Washington..was a growing concern over the swiftly accelerating petrodollar holdings of the Arabs. (Petro-dollars are defined as the excess foreign-exchange assets of the oil-producing countries)... There simply isn't sufficient data on the flow of petrodollars. *Ibid.* 7/6 Still, the question of petrodollars and their potential recycling into U.S. industries..is something officials and analysts are studying. **1974** LD. GLADWYN in *Hansard Lords* 5 Nov. 310 The loan to Italy, the sugar deal, which they approved; the beginning of petro-dollar recycling are all instances in point. **1974** *Financial Times* 21 Nov. 23/3 The size of the 'petrodollar' surplus—defined as the current earnings of the OPEC countries over and above what they can spend on imports —has been estimated at about $60 bn. [*sc.* thousand million] this year. **1975** *Times* 8 Jan. 1/6 Two suggested schemes for recycling surplus petrodollars to deficit countries. **1976** *Time* 27 Dec. 21/1 Problems of inflation, devaluation and petro-dollars intimately bind our economy and that of other nations into a common system. **1977** *Time* 18 July 39/1 In Aspen, Colo. the Empress..danced away the Fourth of July at a local night-spot and dropped some petrodollars in Aspen shops.

petrodrome ('pɛtrəʊdrəʊm). *Zool.* [ad. mod.L. *Petrodromus*, f. Gr. πέτρος stone + -δρομος runner.] An insectivorous animal of the genus *Petrodromus* of elephant-shrews, esp. *P. tetradactylus* of Mozambique.

petrofabrics (pɛtrəʊ'fæbrɪks), *sb. pl. Geol.* [f. PETRO- + FABRIC *sb.*: see -IC 2.] The texture and microscopic structure of a rock or rocks, or the study of these, esp. as guides to the movements to which they have been subjected. Cf. PETROTECTONICS *sb. pl.*

1934 B. SANDER in *Amer. Jrnl. Sci.* XXVIII. 37 (*heading*) Petrofabrics (Gefügekunde der Gesteine) and orogenesis. *Ibid.*, Petrofabrics denotes the study of the internal space relations of a rock. **1949** *Q. Jrnl. Geol. Soc.* CV. 111 The greatest contribution of the Sander-Schmidt school of petrofabrics has been its emphasis on the movements influencing fabric rather than on the forces responsible for the movements. **1960** *Liverpool & Manch. Geol. Jrnl.* II. 503 (*heading*) New work on petrofabrics. **1974** *Nature* 12 Apr. 621/3 Papers on..the petrofabrics of the peridotite suite xenoliths.

So **petro'fabric** *a.*

1934 B. SANDER in *Amer. Jrnl. Sci.* XXVIII. 38 Petro-fabric analysis is..important for purely petrographic investigations that seek only descriptive characteristics of rocks. **1942** M. P. BILLINGS *Structural Geol.* xviii. 341 Many petrofabric diagrams show the attitude of the cleavage rather than the orientation of the optic axes. **1956** E. W. HEINRICH *Microsc. Petrogr.* vii. 208 Petrofabric studies reveal that the optic axes of the quartz grains usually are well oriented in one of several patterns. **1968** B. BAYLY *Introd. Petrol.* xxv. 303 There is..a large field known as petrofabric analysis, in which the orientation of many individual grains is studied.

Petro-Forge ('pɛtrəʊfɔədʒ). Also -forge. [f. PETRO- (taken as repr. PETROL) + FORGE *sb.*] A forging machine powered by a petrol engine.

1964 *Engineering* 2 Oct. 438/2 A session at the fifth MTDRC was devoted entirely to high energy rate forming. .. The paper read last: 'Petro-Forge Mk I-DRD',.. gave evidence of industry's keen interest in the development of a method of high energy operation which uses the internal combustion process for its power source. **1965** *Economist* 18 Dec. 1354/3 The Petro-Forge has been sufficiently developed (it started under a DSIR grant in 1962) to show that even when working at slow speeds it will be cheaper and better than existing forging machinery. **1970** DAVIES & AUSTIN *Devel. High Speed Metal Forming* II. i. 54 Multi-blow operation at one second intervals is..possible and enables the Petro-Forge to be used for large volume production of components. **1973** E. C. ROLLASON *Metall. for Engineers* (ed. 4) vii. 129 In the Petro-forge the energy is derived from the combustion of a fuel/air mixture in the cylinder of an internal combustion engine.

petrogenesis (pɛtrə'dʒɛnɪsɪs). *Petrol.* [f. PETRO- + -GENESIS. Cf. G. *petrogenese* (R. Th. Simler *Ueber die Petrogenese* (1862)); *petrogenesis* was used by F. Zirkel (*Lehrb. der Petrogr.* (1866) I. 159).] (The study of) the formation of rocks, esp. igneous and metamorphic rocks.

1901 *Q. Jrnl. Geol. Soc.* LVII. p. lxv, Hutton was in advance of his time on matters relating to petrogenesis. **1911** *Geol. Mag.* Decade V. VIII. 248 (*heading*) The fundamental problems of petrogenesis, or the origin of the igneous rocks. **1956** *Nature* 14 Jan. 68/1 He has achieved high distinction for his researches on petrogenesis, notably on rock transformations in the granitic suite. **1960** *Times* 13 Feb. 8/4 Lyell Medal to Dr. Doris Reynolds for her work on the rocks of Northern Ireland and her contributions to petrogenesis. **1971** *Nature* 24 Sept. 260/1 Romey..suggests that theories of lunar petrogenesis are developing too fast. **1977** A. HALLAM *Planet Earth* 313 *Petrogenesis*, an envelope term embracing all aspects and features of the formation of rocks.

Hence ˌ**petroge'netic** *a.*, **-ge'netically** *adv.*

1911 *Geol. Mag.* Decade V. VIII. 251 Such a conception exists, but we can oppose to it several geological data and petrogenetic considerations. **1950** A. K. WELLS in F. H. Hatch et al. *Petrol. Igneous Rocks* (ed. 10) 5 The modern tendency to explain many petrogenetic problems in terms of emanations, ionic migration and 'granitization'. **1954** *Jrnl. Geol.* LXII. 172 (*heading*) The trace elements of the plutonic complex of Loch Doon..and their petrogenetic significance. **1970** *Mineral. Abstr.* XXI. 77/1 Petrogenetically it is suggested that a basalt differentiated to produce an olivine-augite peridotite which subsequently assimilated a potassic granite.

petrogeny (pɪ'trɒdʒɪnɪ). *Petrol.* [f. PETRO- + -GENY.] = PETROGENESIS. Chiefly in *petrogeny's residua system.*

1888 TEALL *Petrography* Gloss. 448 *Petrogeny*, that department of geology which treats of the formation of rocks. **1937** N. L. BOWEN in *Amer. Jrnl. Sci.* CCXXXIII. 1 It is concluded..that in mixtures containing all of these (SiO_2, Al_2O_3, iron oxide, CaO, MgO, Na_2O and K_2O) the residual liquid from fractional crystallization will show this same character of great enrichment in alkali-alumina silicate. Since the oxides listed above make up some 97 per cent of the composition of the average igneous rock the alkali-alumina silicate system ($NaAlSiO_4$-$KAlSiO_4$-SiO_2) is here referred to as petrogeny's 'residua system'. **1948** [see MAGMATISM a]. **1950** E. E. WAHLSTROM *Introd. Theoret. Igneous Petrol.* i. 3 Petrogeny places emphasis on the manner of origin or genesis of rocks. **1966** *Jrnl. Petrol.* VII. 115 It is necessary to know something of the residual liquids that might be produced in the course of crystallization of silicate melts, and a considerable part of the efforts of experimental petrology has been directed to this end. The classic system in this regard is 'petrogeny's residua system', $NaAlSiO_4$-$KAlSiO_4$-SiO_2..but..even this is a residua system only for liquids in which the alkali/alumina ratio [*printed* ration] is unity.

Hence **petro'genic** *a.* = PETROGENETIC *a.*

1908 *Amer. Jrnl. Sci.* CLXXVI. 45 In a fully represented petrogenic cycle at a batholithic area..the oldest intrusion should be a rock of gabbroid (basaltic) composition. **1947** A. KNOPF *Pirsson's Rocks & Rock Minerals* (ed. 3) vi. 144 A period in which a genetically related series of igneous rocks was formed is called a petrogenic epoch, and as this concept is more definite than 'petrographic province', it is supplanting the older idea. **1971** I. G. GASS et al. *Understanding Earth* 12 The rise of understanding of rocks, and particularly of petrogenic processes, was initially highly dependent on the way in which microscopy assisted in the study of the constituent minerals.

petroglyph ('pɛtrəglɪf). [ad. mod.F. *pétroglyphe*, f. Gr. πέτρα rock + -γλυφή carving.] A rock-carving (usually prehistoric).

1870 *Athenæum* 12 Feb. 233 The peculiar cup-shaped depressions and concentric rings rudely sculptured on certain stones in this locality. In addition to these petroglyphs there are menhirs, cairns, and duns, while crannoges occur in most of the lochs. **1883** IM THURN *Among Ind. Guiana* xix. 403 Richard Andrée..has described and figured a very large number of examples of 'petroglyphs', as he calls rock-drawings. **1952** V. G. CHILDE *New Light Most Anc. East* ii. 23 Petroglyphs, like microliths, attest hunting over many areas now uninhabitable. **1955** *Sci. News Let.* 9 July 31/2 The crescent is not a common figure among petroglyphs and pictographs of northern Arizona. **1958** E. A. ARMSTRONG *Folklore of Birds* i. 10 In the Californian deserts I have seen petroglyphs made by Red Indian initiands. **1972** *Sci. Amer.* June 91/1 The use of a line to depict a contour may well have been one of the earliest developments in art, as exemplified by the 'line drawings' in the pictographs and petroglyphs of prehistoric artists. **1974** *Environmental Conservation* I. 8/2 The desert is dotted with ..fossil remains..of domestic animals whose present range lies well outside the areas of the petroglyphs.

So **petro'glyphic** *a.*, belonging to or of the nature of a petroglyph; **petroglyphy** (pɪ'trɒglɪfɪ), the art or process of carving upon rocks.

In Dicts.

petrograph ('pɛtrəgrɑːf, -æ-). (*erron.* **petra-**.) [f. Gr. πέτρα rock + -GRAPH.] A writing (or what is supposed to be such) carved upon a rock; a rock-inscription.

1814 SOUTHEY *Lett.* (1856) II. 366 The rock-manuscript, Petragraph, or Ogham Inscription. **1888** *Science* 27 July 40/2 Mr. Cushing's party found on the rocks of neighbouring mountains petrographs, or crude etchings.

petrographer (pɪ'trɒgrəfə(r)). [f. as PETROGRAPHY + -ER.] One versed in petrography; one who scientifically describes or studies rocks.

1881 JUDD *Volcanoes* ix. 265 Some petrographers..have maintained the principle [etc.]. **1882** GEIKIE in *Nature* XXVII. 26/1 What is known to petrographers by the name of 'fluxion-structure'.

petrographic (pɛtrəʊ'græfɪk), *a.* [f. as PETROGRAPHY + -IC.] Of or pertaining to petrography. ***petrographic province***: see PROVINCE 6 b.

1864 in WEBSTER. **1875** tr. *Schmidt's Desc. & Darw.* 73 The petrographic character of the oolitic strata. **1892** *Nation* (N.Y.) 22 Dec. 474/3 Neglect of petrographic methods by the members of the Pennsylvania Survey.

petro'graphical, *a.* Also 7 erron. **petra-**. [f. as next + -AL[1].] Relating to, engaged in, or dealing with petrography; also = petrographic. ***petrographical province***: see PROVINCE 6 b.

1651 BIGGS *New Disp.* 100 In their petragraphicall character of the qualities of it [Bezoar-stone], they make many a voyage wide of the Æquator. **1845** NEWBOLD in *Jrnl. Asiat. Soc. Bengal* XIV. 285 The petrographical characters of the Marhatta beds. **1880** *Nature* XXI. 287/1 To prepare his petrographical description of the Caucasian region. **1895** T. DWIGHT *Rep. Yale Univ.* 74 The rapidly increasing petrographical collections.

Hence **petro'graphically** *adv.*, in relation to petrography.

1845 NEWBOLD in *Jrnl. Asiat. Soc. Bengal* XIV. 286 Petrographically speaking, the rock passes from a green chloritic schist. **1875** tr. *Schmidt's Desc. & Darw.* v. 96 The deposit..may be divided into about 40 petrographically distinguishable layers.

petrography (pɪ'trɒgrəfɪ). (In 7 erron. **petra-**.) [mod. f. Gr. πέτρα rock + -GRAPHY.] The scientific description of the composition and formation of rocks; descriptive petrology.

1651 BIGGS *New Disp.* 99 They who have written hitherto of this stone [Bezoar-stone],..have steer'd by the compasse or Lant-skip only of others petragraphy and description. **1858** MAYNE *Expos. Lex.*, *Petrographia*, term for a history or description of rocks: petrography. **1885** J. J. H. TEALL in *Nature* XXXI. 444/2 Descriptive petrography..concerns itself with the chemical, mineralogical and physical characters of the individual rocks. **1888** —— *Brit. Petrography* 5 It is necessary to remark that petrography is a branch of geology, and not merely a department of mineralogy.

petroil ('pɛtrɔɪl). [f. PETR(OL + OIL *sb.*[1]] = MIXTURE 3 e. Freq. *attrib.*

1927 A. W. JUDGE *Mod. Motor Engineer* III. vi. 164 In the case of two-stroke engines using the 'petroil' (i.e. petrol and oil mixture) system of lubrication, it is important to keep the float chamber and filter clean. **1959** *Motor* 21 Oct. 344/1 The petroil system of lubrication has been so refined that only one pint of oil need be added to each 5 gallons of petrol. **1967** P. E. IRVING *Two-Stroke Power Units* vii. 129 With crankcase compression, it is manifestly impossible to have large quantities of oil splashing around inside the engine... The most generally accepted way out of this situation is to dissolve a small amount of oil in the fuel, the resulting mixture being termed 'petroil' (in England, anyway). **1972** J. STEVENS *Scooter* iv. 98 Another cut in running costs comes from the scooters which run on a petroil mixture containing only 2% of oil. **1977** *Good Motoring* Oct. 8/1 Mixed a gallon of petroil to fill the tank of a two-stroke motor cycle.

petrol ('pɛtrəl). Also 7 **petroll, -eol, -iol**(**l**, 9 **-ole**. [a. F. *pétrole* (13th c., Hatz.-Darm.), *petrolle* (16th c.), f. med.L. PETROLEUM, q.v.]

†**1.** = PETROLEUM. *Obs.*

1596 LODGE *Margarite of America* (Hunter. Cl.) 52 As the clay petrol draweth fire, so the lookes do gather affection. **1616** BULLOKAR *Eng. Expos.*, *Petroll*, a substance strained out of the naturall Bitumen... It is for the most part white, and somtime black, and being once set on fire can hardly be quenched. **1669** STURMY *Mariner's Mag.* v. xiii. 85 These Ingredients being mingled with Oyl of Petriol. **1678** PHILLIPS (ed. 4), *Petreol*, a certain Liquor that falls from the Fields near Modena, like Oyl extracted out of a Rock. **1796** KIRWAN *Elem. Min.* (ed. 2) II. 43 Petrol is evidently nothing else but Naphtha, altered by the action of the air. **1811** PINKERTON *Petralogy* II. 147 Naphtha, or pure rock oil, as fluid and transparent as water; petrol, which is less fluid and pure, when it is yet more impure it becomes mineral tar.

2. *Chem.* A hydrocarbon (C_8H_{10}) occurring in petroleum.

1866–77 WATTS *Dict. Chem.* IV. 381.

3. a. [Reintroduced from mod.Fr.] A name for refined petroleum as used in motor-cars, etc.

For an attribution of the Eng. word to Frederick Simms, 1893, see E. Liveing *Pioneers of Petrol* (1959) 42. However *pétrole* was current in Fr. by 1892 (cf. G. Richard *Les nouveaux Moteurs à Gaz et à Pétrole* (1892)).

[**1895** SIR D. SALOMONS *Horseless Carriage* 14 Benzine of a certain density, known in France under the name of *essence de pétrol*,..is the material employed to run the engines.] **1895** F. R. SIMMS in *Sat. Rev.* 3 Aug. 144/1 The Daimler carriage can easily take a gradient of 1 in 10... The fuel used is rectified petroleum or petrol or benzoline, of a specific gravity of 0·680 to 0·705, which has many advantages over common petroleum, and is obtainable almost any-where. **1897** *Westm. Gaz.* 23 July 7/1 To prevent the sale in this country of a French preparation known as 'Petrol', the fumes of which are said to be extremely explosive and very easily ignited. *Ibid.* 26 July 5/1 The death by fire of a lady in a hairdresser's shop while having her hair dressed with a preparation known as petrole. *Ibid.* 24 Nov. 7/3 [The car] was worked on the Daimler principle, the motive power used being petrol, or refined petroleum. **1900** *Daily News* 24 Apr. 7/5 How largely petroleum spirit (familiarly known as 'petrol'), holds favour may be seen by stating that there were three steam cars, and but one driven by heavy oil. Eighty.. were 'petrol' cars.

b. *attrib.* and *Comb.* ***petrol adjustment, bicycle, bowser*** [BOWSER[2]], ***bus, can,*** †***car, consumption, costs, cycle, engine, feed, -filler, fumes, lamp, motor, omnibus, pipe, ration, rationing, tank, tanker, tap, tin, vapour***; ***petrol-driven, -engined, -propelled*** adjs.; **petrol attendant**, one who attends to the petrol pumps at a petrol station; **petrol blue**, a shade of blue similar to the colour of petrol; **petrol coupon**, a petrol rationing coupon; **petrol-electric** *a.*, (*a*) driven by electric motors powered by current from a generator, which in turn is driven by a petrol engine (cf. *diesel-electric* adj.); (*b*) applied to a petrol-driven electricity generator; **petrol gauge**, a meter indicating the quantity of petrol in a tank; **petrol injection**, fuel injection, where the fuel is petrol; **petrol lighter**, a cigarette lighter employing petrol; **petrol pump**, (*a*) a pump at a petrol station for supplying motor vehicles with petrol; (*b*) a pump which delivers petrol from the petrol tank of a motor vehicle or aircraft to the engine; **petrol sniffer**, one who inhales petrol fumes for a narcotic effect; hence **petrol-sniffing**, the activity of a petrol-sniffer; **petrol station** = *filling station* s.v. FILLING *vbl. sb.* 4.

1920 Petrol adjustment [see IDLE *v.* 4a]. **1963** M. LEVINSON *Taxi!* iv. 47 He can very easily get a part-time job ..as a petrol attendant. **1975** *Evening Herald* (Dublin) 8 May 12/3 (Advt.), Petrol attendants required. **1895** Petrol bicycle [see *petrol cycle* below]. **1949** *Dict. Colours Interior Decoration* (Brit. Colour Council) III. 21/1 *Petrol blue*, a colour name introduced into seasonal ranges by B.C.C. in 1943. **1971** *Sunday Mirror* 21 Mar. 15/1 You can't sell them bright or pastel colours. In summer they just want petrol blue, bottle green or navy. **1973** *Guardian* 10 Apr. 13/3 (*caption*) Chunky petrol blue mohair cardigan. **1943** T. R. ST. GEORGE *C/o Postmaster* 58 We learned, presently, that it wasn't a gas station at all, for that matter, but a 'petrol bowser'. **1943** P. BRENNAN et al. *Spitfires over Malta* 24 A petrol bowser on the perimeter track caught fire..and blazed fiercely. **1911** *Chambers's Jrnl.* Jan. 77/1 The electrically propelled vehicle..is smoother in running, more silent, and more convenient to handle than the petrol-bus. **1966** M. WOODHOUSE *Tree Frog* xxii. 159 The jeep bounced. .. Yancy cursed the petrol cans fluently. **1975** M. RUSSELL *Murder by Mile* xiv. 151 The petrol cans that she's just been emptying. **1900** Petrol car [see sense 3a]. **1902** A. C. HARMSWORTH et al. *Motors* x. 183 (*heading*) The petrol car. **1908** *Westm. Gaz.* 16 June 4/2 Petrol-consumption is a factor which is taken into serious consideration by purchasers of cars nowadays. **1936** 'N. BLAKE' *Thou Shell of Death* ii. 37 Your defence planes of the future..must, above all, have a very low petrol consumption. **1974** A. ROSS *Bradford Business* 15 We covered the hundred and seventy miles..at an average speed of 91·5 miles an hour... The petrol consumption was..sixteen imperial gallons. **1955** *Times* 10 May 6/3 Their petrol costs, according to a branch official, are being met by some of the voluntary miners' funds. **1939** *Times* 14 Oct. 5/3 (*heading*) Supplementary petrol coupons. **1963** D. HUGHES in Sissons & French *Age of Austerity* IV. 86 Forged petrol coupons changed hands at half a crown a time. **1971** A. DIMENT *Think Inc.* iv. 59 This man concerned himself with rough copies of ration books and petrol coupons. **1973** T. ALLBEURY *Choice of Enemies* viii. 35 Bring..your car—we'll see you get enough petrol coupons. **1895** *Times* 28 Nov. 11/5 The Germans had also attempted petrol cycles. Mr. Pennington of New York had invented a petrol bicycle. **1899** *Westm. Gaz.* 10 June 7/2 The 'Delahaye' four-wheel petrol-driven phaeton. **1905** *Ibid.* 2 Jan. 2/1 Purely petrol-driven auto-cars on exactly the same principle as a road automobile. **1937** BLUNDEN *Elegy* 50 The televisionary world to come, The petrol-driven world already made. **1960** *Farmer & Stockbreeder* 22 Mar. (Suppl.) 8/1 You can pay as little as 33gs for a 14in petrol-driven mower. **1964** J. J. WALSH *Understanding Paraplegia* xvi. 113 Popularity of the fast and more powerful petrol-driven tricycle. **1903** *Motoring Annual* 248 The power is derived from the Fischer petrol-electric combination in which a petrol engine works a dynamo and charges an accumulator. **1905** *Westm. Gaz.* 2 Jan. 2/1 The North-Eastern, Great Northern, and Brighton Railways. The first-named has some petrol-electric coaches. **1909** *Installation News* III. 117/2 The petrol electric set..is increasing in popularity every day; at the moment however the danger does not present itself..as a source of loss to the Central Station. **1930** *Times* 25 Mar. 25/1 With regard to the replacement of our motor omnibuses,..the petrol-electric machine..has given us very good service. **1940** *Chambers's Techn. Dict.* 631/1 *Petrol-electric generating set* (Elec. Eng.), a small generating plant using a petrol engine as the prime-mover. **1902** R. J. MECREDY in A. C. Harmsworth *Motors* vii. 105 'Petrol Engine' is a slang term for an engine driven by a series of explosions of a mixture of the vapour of a light spirit of petroleum with air. **1916** A. GARRARD (*title*) Gas, oil, and petrol engines. **1933** Petrol engine [see INJECTION 1 b]. **1974** *Country Life* 3 Oct. 948/1 Daimler's petrol engine was used in vehicles constructed between 1885 and 1888. **1906** *Daily Chron.* 27 June 3/5 The invention of a petrol-engined torpedo-boat. **1936** *Discovery* Sept. 289/1 The new L.M.S. 'Coventry' petrol-engined railcar. **1971** *Daily Tel.* 28 Jan. 3/1 A regulation requiring new petrol-engined vehicles to be fitted with means to prevent fumes escaping from the crank-case is to be laid before Parliament. **1913** *Autocar Handbk.* (ed. 5) iii. 67 (*caption*) Exhaust pressure petrol feed. **1928** *Manch. Guardian Weekly* 10 Aug. 107/4 They experienced trouble with the petrol feed and turned back. **1935** C. DAY LEWIS *Time to Dance* 34 They..rose and flew on to Paris, and there Trivially were delayed—a defective petrol feed—Three days. **1977** J. CLEARY *High Road to China* v. 145 One of the petrol feed pipes had been dented... Fuel had been getting to the engine only in a trickle. **1907** *Westm. Gaz.* 22 Nov. 10/1 The latest thing in petrol-fillers, horns and sirens. **1970** *Country Life* 31 Dec. 1278/2 A conical petrol-filler with a spout that he got from a local garage. **1908** *Lancet* 29 Feb. 658/2 He was only able to find in the literature one other case relating to the toxic effects of petrol fumes. **1912** KIPLING *Let.* 10 Dec. in C. E. Carrington *Rudyard Kipling* (1955) xvi. 420 A rather shrill stink..like chlorine gas on top of petrol fumes... That's the stink of the aeroplane. *a* **1930** D. H. LAWRENCE *Last Poems* (1932) 32 The weather in town is always benzine, or else petrol fumes. **1974** N. FREELING *Dressing of Diamond* 45 The summer night..was still tainted with petrol fumes. **1976** M. HINXMAN *End of Good Woman* vii. 94 She had stood on traffic intersections..inhaling petrol fumes. **1913** *Autocar Handbk.* (ed. 5) iii. 66 As the tank is arranged near the occupants a simple form of petrol gauge can be fitted. **1938** N. MARSH *Artists in Crime* xiii. 198 The petrol gauge ..registered only two gallons. **1974** D. KYLE *Raft of Swords* xiv. 156 He glanced down at the petrol gauge, saw the tank was roughly half empty. **1940** *Chambers's Techn. Dict.* 249/2 *Direct petrol injection* (I.C. Engs.), a method of operating a petrol engine by injecting liquid petrol directly into the induction pipe or cylinder during the suction-stroke, thus dispensing with a carburettor; in aero engines it avoids carburettor freezing troubles. **1972** K. NEWTON et al. *Motor Vehicle* (ed. 9) xvii. 379 Even in the U.S.A., where..very high-powered vehicles are the rule, petrol injection seems to make little headway. **1977** *Economist* 3 Sept. 51/1 (Advt.), Petrol injection makes for cleaner..combustion than the conventional carburettor. **1917** W. OWEN *Let.* 9 Feb. (1967) 432 Last night I burnt a petrol lamp under my bed! **1957** L. DURRELL *Justine* I. 14 The boys stir uneasily at their backgammon under the petrol-lamps. **1978** G. SIMS *Rex Mundi* vii. 45 We sped with..straining sails and hissing petrol lamps. **1926–7** *Army & Navy Stores Catal.* 88/1 Automatic 'Petrol' Lighter..With Nickel Case—each 1/3. **1930** SAYERS & 'EUSTACE' *Documents in Case* I. 151, I hunted through my pockets for a petrol lighter. **1978** D. BLOODWORTH *Crosstalk* iv. 35 The end of his cigarette trembling in the tiny spluttering flame of an almost extinct petrol lighter. **1900** BEAUMONT *Motor Vehicles & Motors* xiv. (*heading*), Light Petrol Motor Vehicles. *Ibid.* xv, Petrol Motor cycles. **1904** T. H. WHITE (*title*) Petrol motors and motor cars: a handbook for engineers, designers and draughtsmen. **1912** *Motor Manual* (ed. 14) i. 1 The modern motorcar has been a gradual development since the introduction of the petrol motor or light internal-combustion engine by Benz, Levassor and Daimler. **1900** *Daily News* 7 Sept. 6/5 The two petrol omnibuses now running had taught them some valuable lessons. **1907** *Westm. Gaz.* 9 July 4/2 Wright's breakdown in the race.. was variously ascribed to a broken valve, a seized piston, a choked petrol-pipe. **1925** *Morris Owner's Manual* ii. 33 Clean petrol filter and petrol pipe. **1963** R. F. WEBB *Motorists' Dict.* 170 *Petrol pipe*, the flexible or copper tube carrying petrol from the petrol tank to the petrol pump or carburettor. **1908** *Westm. Gaz.* 14 Apr. 4/2 Both the Wolseley and Thornycroft motors are masterpieces of engineering skill and ingenuity, and are taking us along as fast as applied science will admit towards the petrol-propelled battle-ship. **1922** JOYCE *Ulysses* 703 A scheme for the development of Irish tourist traffic in and around Dublin by means of petrolpropelled riverboats. **1928** *Manch. Guardian Weekly* 19 Oct. 301/2 A hideous outbreak of advertisement hoardings, petrol pumps..and gaunt new motor-tracks. **1932** J. BUCHAN *Gap in Curtain* ii. 96 They had to make a forced landing..on the skirts of Ruwenzori, where they found that something had gone wrong with the petrol pump and that some of the propeller and cylinder bolts had worked loose. *Ibid.* iv. 210 We want to get past the garages and petrol pumps and county council cottages to the ancient rustic England. **1963** R. F. WEBB *Motorists' Dict.* 170 When the float chamber of the carburettor is filled, the petrol pump encounters pressure and this opens a valve which stops further supplies of fuel being pumped up to the carburettor until the level of the reserve has dropped slightly. **1970** 'D. HALLIDAY' *Dolly & Cookie Bird* iv. 48 A black and white petrol-pump sign. **1976** 'W. TREVOR' *Children of Dynmouth* i. 16 His sister was..employed as a petrol-pump attendant on the fore-court of the Smiling Service Filling Station. **1939** *Times* 14 Oct. 5/3 Owners of vehicles and industrial plant who have been issued with only one month's additional petrol ration from the divisional petroleum office, should now apply for a further allowance for the second month if this is needed for essential purposes. **1948** G. V. GALWEY *Lift & Drop* v. 107 He's very scrupulous about his petrol ration being for professional purposes only. **1973** *Country Life* 6 Dec. 1892/1 Last week ..motorists were beginning to queue for their petrol-ration books. **1948** M. LASKI *Tony Heaven* iv. 59, I take it..that there's no petrol rationing for A's? **1973** *Times* 4 Dec. 10/7 One or two people involved in industry said they were not worried about petrol rationing..they would..buy one or two more cars, draw the coupons, and sell the cars when rationing ended. **1958** W. SANSOM *Cautious Heart* 53 Do you know what a petrol-sniffer is?.. It's quite serious really, it's an addiction to the smell of petrol—like any other narcotic. People who work among petrol fumes get the habit. **1973** *Black World* June 47/2 The..escapism..is 'petrol-sniffing', which produces a coma-like state. **1926** *Times* 6 May 1/4 (Advt.), Wanted, hard, ambitious, and independent worker with £750, to erect and operate new petrol station under exceptionally favourable supply contract. **1954** *Coast to Coast 1953–54* 145 A petrol-station at the far end. **1969** *Listener* 15 May 669/3, I suspect that Penguins and other paperbacks wouldn't sell at all well at petrol stations. **1972** 'J. & E. BONETT' *No Time to Kill* v. 52 He was approaching a petrol station... He drew up beside a row of pumps. **1902** KIPLING *Traffics & Discov.* (1904) 189 At Pigginfold, after ten minutes, we refilled our petrol tank and lavishly oiled our engines. **1973** J. LEASOR *Host of Extras* viii. 142 Drugs in spare tyres, dummy petrol tanks.. windscreen washer tanks. **1974** *Country Life* 21 Nov. 1579/2 The petrol-tank capacity of 9·9 gallons was small for such a car. **1975** J. RATHBONE *Kill Cure* I. i. 7 His eyes returned to the road and the back of the large petrol tanker. **1908** *Autocar Handbk.* (ed. 2) xix. 148 The petrol tap having been turned on, the float may be agitated so as to flood the carburetter. **1925** *Morris Owner's Manual* i. 9 The petrol tap is at the bottom of the tank, under the dashboard. **1916** J. BUCHAN *Greenmantle* xvi. 217, I got out the petrol tins and spare tyres and cached them among some rocks on the hillside. **1940** 'GUN BUSTER' *Return via Dunkirk* I. x. 76 First name out of the petrol tin was Turner's. **1966** M. WOODHOUSE *Tree Frog* vi. 49 Petrol vapour clawed its way harshly into my lungs. **1974** J. DYSON *P.M.'s Boat is Missing* xl. 209 He could smell the strong petrol vapour.

4. = *petrol blue.*

1927 *Daily Express* 22 Feb. 6 (Advt.), White, Phlox, Cardinal, Red, Black, Brown, Navy, Bois de Rose, Lavender, Petrol, New Blue, Grey. **1971** *Vogue* 15 Sept. 129/1 Coat..sizes 10–16; colours: black, purple, green, brown, petrol. **1971** *Guardian* 18 Sept. 11/1 Dress and coat ..Brown..Petrol, Grotto or Tomato.

Hence **'petrol** *v. trans.*, to supply with petrol; **'petrolage**, the pouring of petroleum in a thin film over stagnant water and puddles, in order to prevent the breeding of mosquitoes; **'petrolless** *a.*, having no petrol.

1902 *Daily Mail* 23 Apr. 3/6 The [motor-] cars can be fed, groomed, and petrolled for a nominal charge. **1904** *Brit. Med. Jrnl.* 17 Sept. 630 It seems to me that this method should take from the first this form—namely drainage—and that it is not wise to substitute for it petrolage. *Ibid.* 633 He is evidently sparing of oil for petrolage. **1908** *Daily Chron.* 31 July 4/3 The foolish virgins, with their oilless lamps, have found a latter-day analogue in the petrolless taxi-cabby. **1944** DYLAN THOMAS *Let.* 27 July (1966) 265 The well-off people were dry and thin and grieved over their petrolless motorcars.

petrol, obs. form of PATROL.

‖**petro'latum.** *Pharm.* [mod.L., f. PETROL + *-ātum* in *acetatum*, *sulphatum*, etc.: see -ATE[1] c.] The official name in U.S. Pharm. for pure Vaseline, called in the British Pharm. *paraffinum molle*; = *petroleum jelly.*

1887 *Sci. Amer.* (N.Y.) 7 May 293/3 With a silk handkerchief apply petrolatum evenly. **1890** WEBSTER s.v., Petrolatum is the officinal name for the product. Cosmoline and vaseline are commercial names for substances essentially the same, but differing slightly in appearance and consistence or fusibility. **1959** *Industr. Wood Processes* VII. 15 (*heading*) The effect of petrolatum on the strength of glued joints. **1972** *Materials & Technol.* V. xiv. 520 Other plasticizers derived from petroleum are: petrolatum, paraffin waxes,..and asphalts. **1976** *Lebende Sprachen* XXI. 151/2 Lubricate sparingly with petrolatum/white petroleum before destructive testing.

petrol bomb. [f. PETROL + BOMB *sb.* 2.] A bomb, usu. home-made and thrown by hand, consisting of a petrol-filled bottle and a wick; a Molotov cocktail.

1958 [see *flick-knife* s.v. FLICK *sb.*[1] 4]. **1963** *Times* 20 Feb. 11/3 It will be imposed where petrol bombs or inflammatory liquid or explosives are used against persons. **1969** *Guardian* 13 Aug. 1/1 The rioters threw petrol bombs. **1971** *Peace News* 10 Sept. 7/1 The effects of petrol bombs, CS gas and searchings were tragically obvious in the children. **1976** P. FERRIS *Detective* ii. 24 A petrol bomb was thrown.

Hence **'petrol-bomb** *v. trans.*, to throw a petrol bomb at; to destroy or damage with a petrol bomb; **'petrol bomber**, one who throws a petrol bomb; **'petrol-bombing** *vbl. sb.*, throwing of a petrol bomb.

1963 *Times* 23 Feb. 7/4 Sir Edgar Whitehead, said that unless the Government dropped the provision making the death sentence for petrol bombing compulsory, the Opposition 'with all the constitutional means at our disposal will fight this Bill clause by clause to the bitter end'. **1969** *Guardian* 16 Aug. 9/1 The Catholics who were petrol-bombed out of their homes. **1971** *Daily Tel.* 4 Jan. 7/6 Other odd areas [of Paris] that are patrolled include the Chad Embassy (petrol-bombed a year ago). **1974** J. MITCHELL *Death & Bright Water* vii. 60 All he had to worry about now was the petrol bombers he'd seen. **1976** *Times* 23 Dec. 10/5 The dockyard boys had petrol-bombed the rent office.

petrolean (pɪ'trəʊlɪən), *a.* *nonce-wd.* [f. PETROLE-UM + -AN.] Using petroleum (for incendiary purposes: see PÉTROLEUR).

1893 GOLDW. SMITH *Ess.* 2 Satanism manifests itself.. under various forms and names, such as Nihilism, Intransigentism, Petrolean Communism.

petrolene ('pɛtrəʊliːn). *Chem.* [a. F. *pétrolène*, f. *pétrole* or PETROL-EUM + -ENE.] Boussingault's name for the oily volatile constituent of asphalt or compact bitumen.

1838 T. THOMSON *Chem. Org. Bodies* 721 This name [Petrolene] has been given by M. Boussingault to a substance which he extracted from the bitumen of Bechelbronn... Petrolene, thus obtained, has a pale yellow colour, little taste, but a bituminous odour. **1863–72** WATTS *Dict. Chem.* I. 426 According to Boussingault..asphalt or compact bitumen is a mixture of two definite substances, viz. *asphaltene*, which is fixed and soluble in alcohol, and *petrolene*, which is oily and volatile.

petroleous (pɪ'trəʊlɪəs), *a.* [f. PETROLE-UM + -OUS.] Abounding in or containing petroleum.

1762 tr. *Busching's Syst. Geog.* III. 61 The petroleous wells of Saffo..are observed to become very turbid. **1876** M. COLLINS *Midnight to Midnight* III. ix. 154 If he had been able to command more champagne, howsoever petroleous, ..he might have been happy.

petroleum (pɪ'trəʊlɪəm). Also 6–8 -ium. [a. med.L. *petroleum*, f. L. *petra* (Gr. πέτρα) rock + *oleum* oil.] **a.** A mineral oil, varying from light yellow to dark brown or black, occurring in rocks or on the surface of water in various parts of the world; in modern times of great economic importance, esp. as a source of oils for illumination and mechanical power; rock-oil. Also in extended use (see quots.).

Usually distinguished from the more limpid oils called *naphtha* and the more viscid called *maltha* or mineral tar, but sometimes used to include one or both of these.

[**1348–9** *Accts. Exch.*, *K. R.* Bundle 391. No. 15. m. 18 Domino Regi de precepto suo..in Cameram suam apud Caleys..viij lb. de petroleum. **14..** *Sloane MS.* 5 lf. 10/2 Petroleum..oleum est factum de petra..G[allice] petroille.] **1526** *Grete Herball* xxvi. (1529) Bv, Make a decoccyon in oyle petrolium. **1543** TRAHERON *Vigo's Chirurg.* (Straunge Wds.), Petrolium is vsed for naphtha which droppeth out of a babilonyke lyme. **1578** LYTE *Dodoens* II. cvii. 296 The garden Angelica..smelleth almost like to Petroleum. **1601** HOLLAND *Pliny* XXXI. vii. II. 415 In Babylon..is a certain liquid Bitumen or Petroleum, an oleous substance [*bitumen liquidum oleo simile*]. **1607** MARKHAM *Caval.* I. (1617) 42 If you annoint..with the oile Petrolium. **1695** WOODWARD *Nat. Hist. Earth* IV. (1723) 217 The Bitumen..found floating in Form of an Oyl upon the Surface of the Water..called by Naturalists Naphtha, and Petroleum. **1761** W. LEWIS *Mat. Med.* (ed. 2) 445 Fine petroleum catches fire on the approach of a flaming body. **1800** *Misc. Tracts* in *Asiat. Ann. Reg.* 320/2 This oil is a genuine petroleum, possessing all the properties of coal tar, being in fact the self-same thing. **1826** *Amer. Jrnl. Sc.* X. 5 The other [well] discharges..vast quantities of petroleum, or, as it is vulgarly called, 'Seneca oil'. **1842** BRANDE *Dict. Sc.*, etc., *Petroleum*, a brown liquid bitumen, found in several parts of Europe, in Persia, and in the West Indies. **1861** *Times* 21 Jan. 7/6 In November 1859 in the State of Pennsylvania wells were sunk for the purpose of pumping petroleum or rock oil. **1871** ROSCOE *Elem. Chem.* 331 This volatile hydro-carbon also exists in the light oils from American petroleum, as well as in coal oils. **1938** A. W. NASH in A. E. Dunstan et al. *Sci. of Petroleum* I. 1. 12/1 Petroleum may contain, or be composed of,..compounds in the gaseous, liquid, and/or solid state, depending on the nature of these compounds and the existent conditions of temperature and pressure. **1960** J. W. AMYX et al. *Petroleum Reservoir Engin.* i. 1 Virtually all petroleum is produced from the earth in either liquid or gaseous form. **1960** C. GATLIN *Petroleum Engin.* i. 1/1 Petroleum may be defined as a naturally occurring mixture of hydrocarbons which may be either gas, liquid, or solid. *Ibid.* 4/2 (*heading*) Gaseous petroleum (natural gas). **1967** J. R. HUGHES *Storage & Handling Petroleum Liquids* 3 Petroleum, by legal definition (Petroleum (Consolidation) Act, 1928) 'includes crude petroleum, oil made from petroleum, or from coal, shale, peat or other bituminous substances, and other products of petroleum'... The term may also include natural gas found in petroleum-bearing formations.

b. *attrib.* and *Comb.*, as ***petroleum-burner***, ***-car***, ***-filter***, ***-furnace***, ***-lamp***, ***-motor***, ***-ointment***, ***-spring***, ***-still***, ***-stove***, ***-thrower*** (cf. PÉTROLEUR), ***-well***; ***petroleum-bearing***, ***-driven*** adjs.; **petroleum coke**, the solid, non-volatile residue left after the distillation and cracking of petroleum; **petroleum-ether**, a volatile oil obtained from petroleum, also called *naphthalic ether*; **petroleum geology**, the branch of geology concerned with the search for oil and natural gas and with their formation, occurrence, and exploitation; so **petroleum geologist**; **petroleum jelly**, a soft, greasy, semi-solid mixture of hydrocarbons obtained from petroleum, used as an ointment and lubricant; cf. PETROLATUM, VASELINE; **petroleum-oil** = petroleum; in mod. use *spec.* applied to those varieties whose vapour ignites or 'flashes' at higher temperatures, as distinguished from **petroleum-spirit**, whose vapour flashes at lower temperatures.

1882 E. O'DONOVAN *Merv Oasis* I. ii. 37 Proprietors of large tracts of *petroleum-bearing ground. **1963** D. W. & E. E. HUMPHRIES tr. *Termier's Erosion & Sedimentation* xi. 231 The evolution of petroleum-bearing sediments is brought to its final stages by diagenetic processes. **1875** KNIGHT *Dict. Mech.*, *Petroleum-burner, a burner contrived to vaporize and consume liquid petroleum fed to it from a reservoir. *Ibid.*, *Petroleum-car, one for transporting petroleum in bulk. **1877** BLACK *Green Past.* xiii, And drank *petroleum-champagne at 4 dollars a bottle. **1881** *Jrnl. Chem. Soc.* XL. 239 (*heading*) Products from *petroleum coke. **1971** *Materials & Technol.* II. x. 638 Since 1920 petroleum coke has become a plentiful by-product of petroleum cracking. *Ibid.* xi. 655 The high graphitizability of the petroleum coke results from the formation of large polycyclic aromatic molecules, which assists carbon crystallite alignment during the coking operation. **1900** *Westm. Gaz.* 28 Feb. 9/2 *Petroleum drinking is on the increase in France. **1896** *Ibid.* 16 Nov. 9/1 In the *petroleum-driven cars there is an odour, which would be more acceptable if it were perfumed. **1866** *Intell. Observ.* No. 51. 231 A volatile essential oil..termed *petroleum ether. **1917** *Bull. Geol. Soc. Amer.* XXVIII. 157 *Petroleum geology is..a new profession. *Ibid.*, (*heading*) Ethics of the *petroleum geologist. **1928** E. R. LILLEY *Geol. Petroleum & Nat. Gas* i. 8 The main work of the petroleum geologist until recently was that of locating areas in which anti-clinal folds showed in the outcropping strata. **1973** R. E. CHAPMAN *Petroleum Geol.* ii. 22 A study of petroleum geology suggests that the construction of boreholes in the 20th century has not contributed sufficiently to modern geological thought, and that some of the difficulties . . are due to the extension of the concepts developed from surface geology to the subsurface. *Ibid.* 27 The chemistry of petroleum . . is low on the petroleum geologists' list of priorities. **1902** *Westm. Gaz.* 8 May 3/1 At a recent inquest the *petroleum inspector of the London County Council stated that within a fortnight there had been eleven sufferers from the use of low-flash oil! **1897** *Sears, Roebuck Catal.* 27/2 *Petroleum Jelly. This is another name for the preparations called Vaseline, Cosmoline, etc., all made from Petroleum. **1906** T. E. HERBERT *Telegraphy* xxii. 782 As the cable passes into the pipe it is heavily anointed with petroleum jelly. **1922** D. T. DAY *Handbk. Petroleum Industry* II. 360 The official petrolatum of the United States Pharmacopœia, otherwise known as petroleum jelly, or 'Vaseline'. **1966** J. S. COX *Illustr. Dict. Hairdressing* 112/1 *Petroleum jelly*, (Petrolatum, Vaseline, Paraffin Jelly), a purified mixture of semi-solid hydrocarbons, chiefly of the Methane series. **1903** *Daily Chron.* 11 Dec. 6/6 The *petroleum motors . . show that a very distinct advance has been made during the twelve months. **1799** G. SMITH *Laboratory* I. 41 Mealed powder . . mixed with rock-oil, or *petroleum oil. **1874** J. H. COLLINS *Metal Mining* (1875) 121 Within the last few years, lamps for burning paraffin and petroleum oils underground have been devised. **1898** *Daily News* 14 July 6/6 To adopt a flash point of 100 degrees (Abel close test) as the dividing line between petroleum oil and petroleum spirit. **1881** WATTS *Dict. Chem.* VIII. 1509 Artificial Turpentine-oil, *Petroleum-spirit, Polishing Oil: distillate between 120°–170°. **1900** *Daily News* 17 Apr. 7/4 Petroleum spirit still holds the field as a propelling force, both in the cars exhibited here and in those seen in London streets. **1900** *Regulations Storage, etc., Petrol* 15 May (Home Office), The expression 'Petroleum spirit' shall mean the petroleum to which the Petroleum Act, 1871, applies. **1877** RAYMOND *Statist. Mines & Mining* 21 Some ten years ago *petroleum-springs were discovered in California. **1875** KNIGHT *Dict. Mech.*, *Petroleum-still, a still for separating the hydrocarbon products from crude petroleum, etc., in the order of their volatility. **1800** *Misc. Tracts* in *Asiat. Ann. Reg.* 315 An Account of the *Petroleum Wells, in the Burmah Dominions.

‖**pétroleur** (petrɔlœr). [Fr. (in *Dict. Acad.* 1878), f. *pétrole* + *-eur*, ending of masc. agent-nouns.] A (male) incendiary who uses petroleum. Also ‖**pétroleuse** (petrɔlœz) [fem. of this], a female who does the same; esp. applied to the women who set fire to public buildings in Paris by means of petroleum, during the Commune in May 1871.

1871 *Standard* 7 Sept. 4 The judgment recorded against the five Petroleuses, or petroleum-throwers, tried this week. **1871** RUSKIN *Fors Clav.* vii. (1896) I. 138 His daughter had made a petroleuse of herself. **1878** DOWDEN *Stud. Lit.* 466 The petroleuse dragged like a chained beast through the scorching streets of Paris. **1902** *Daily Chron.* 13 May 6/6 His looks suggested the pétroleur more than the littérateur.

petrolic (pɪˈtrɒlɪk), *a.* [f. PETROL + -IC.] Of or pertaining to petrol or petroleum; also, relating to the use of petrol motor-cars.

petrolic ether, one of the four products into which crude petroleum is refined, being that which comes over at a temperature of 40° to 70° Fahr., and has a specific gravity of ·640 to ·650.

1899 *Allbutt's Syst. Med.* VIII. 497 *Recipe*, spirits of wine 200 grammes; petrolic ether, 5 grammes. **1902** *Autocar* 19 July 69/1 The Swiss War Office have . . [provided] for the purchase of an automobile for the petrolic instruction of army officers.

petroliferous (pɛtrəʊˈlɪfərəs), *a.* [f. PETROLEUM or PETROL + *-i-ferous*, -FEROUS, q.v.] Producing or yielding petroleum.

1890 in *Cent. Dict.* **1898** *Nature* 5 May 20/2 Subterranean petroliferous strata. **1900** *Pop. Sci. Monthly* Mar. 610 The new oil rock had proved petroliferous.

petrolin (ˈpɛtrəʊlɪn). Also *erron.* -ine. [f. PETROLEUM or PETROL + -IN.] Christison's name for a substance obtained by him from Rangoon petroleum, identical with *paraffin*. **b.** A trade name for an oil obtained from petroleum.

1831 SIR R. CHRISTISON in *Trans. R. Soc. Edin.* (1836) XIII. 121, I find that the crystalline principle of petroleum differs materially from that of coal-tar, . . and I shall therefore beg leave to denominate it *Petroline*. **1838** [see PARAFFIN 1]. **1842** BRANDE *Dict. Sc.* etc., *Petroline*, a substance obtained by distilling the petroleum of Rangoon. **1884** *Health Exhib. Catal.* 77/2 Illuminating Oils, viz. Petroline or Crystal Oil.

ˈpetrolist. [f. PETROL-EUM + -IST.] = PÉTROLEUR, PÉTROLEUSE.

1890 in *Cent. Dict.* **1905** *Dundee Advertiser* 10 Jan. 8 It cannot be said that Louise Michel directly proposed the institution of the Petrolists.

petrolization (ˌpɛtrəlaɪˈzeɪʃən). [f. PETROLIZ(E *v.* + -ATION.] The oiling of water in order to kill mosquito larvæ.

1901 L. O. HOWARD *Mosquitoes* 193 The petrolization of mosquito-breeding pools is one of the most important measures to be taken in the warfare against mosquitoes. **1930** [see next].

petrolize (ˈpɛtrəʊlaɪz), *v.* [f. PETROL, PETROLEUM + -IZE.]

1. *trans.* To set on fire by means of petroleum: cf. PÉTROLEUR, PÉTROLEUSE.

a **1876** M. COLLINS *Th. in Garden* (1880) I. 130 The communists . . petrolising clubs and palaces, upsetting columns.

2. To make like petroleum; to imbue with the character of petroleum.

1890 *Cent. Dict.* cites URE.

3. = OIL *v.* 1 c. So **ˈpetrolizing** *vbl. sb.*

1901 L. O. HOWARD *Mosquitoes* 193 To the Italians we are indebted for a useful expression, which we might just as well adopt, namely to 'petrolize', meaning to treat waters with kerosene. **1903** *Boston Even. Transcript* 28 Apr. 9/2 All the breeding places [of the mosquito] treated last year will again be petrolized this year. **1906** *Westm. Gaz.* 21 Apr. 16/1 Marshes are drained; ponds are petrolised or stocked with fish. **1930** I. J. KLIGLER *Epidemiology & Control of Malaria in Palestine* vii. 144 Petrolization and petrolizing mixtures.—One of the most important and useful methods of antilarval control is the oiling of the surface of breeding-places.

petrology (pɪˈtrɒlədʒɪ). [f. Gr. πέτρα rock + -OLOGY: orig. formed erron. as *petralogy*.]

a. That branch of geology which deals with the origin, structure, and composition of rocks.

1811 PINKERTON (*title*) Petralogy, A Treatise on Rocks. **1876** PAGE *Adv. Text-bk. Geol.* xx. 440 The whole petralogy of the period . . is a thing taking place beneath and around us. **1876** *Academy* 21 Oct. 410/3 German monographs dealing with microscopic petrology.

b. The petrological features *of* something or somewhere.

1880 *Nature* XXI. 259 A valuable memoir on the petrology of Rodriguez by Mr. N. S. Maskelyne. **1954** *Geol. Mag.* XCI. 44 (*heading*) Further data on the petrology of the pelitic hornfelses of the Carn Chuinneag-Inchbae region, Ross-shire. **1975** *Sci. Amer.* Jan. 29/1 The mineralogy, the content of trace elements and gas, the petrology and so on of literally hundreds of different meteorites have been measured.

So **petroˈlogic** (chiefly *U.S.*), **petroˈlogical** *adjs.*, pertaining or relating to petrology; **petroˈlogically** *adv.*, in relation to petrology; **peˈtrologist**, one versed in petrology; one who studies rocks scientifically.

1811 PINKERTON *Petralogy* I. p. xvii, This unavoidable uncertainty has been well illustrated by the greatest of petralogists. **1814** *Edin. Rev.* XXIII. 64 By reading through this petralogical performance. **1845** NEWBOLD in *Jrnl. Asiat. Soc. Bengal* XIV. I. 283 The schists . . of Kittoor resemble, petrologically, the jaspideous schists of Bellary and Sondur. **1864** J. B. JUKES in *Reader* IV. 678/2 The lithological composition and petrological structure of the rocks immediately beneath it. **1874** LYELL *Elem. Geol.* xxviii. 497 Rocks containing an excess of silica are termed by many Petrologists acid rocks. **1879** WEBSTER, Suppl., *Petrologic*, pertaining to petrology, or the science or investigation of rocks. **1936** H. L. ALLING *Interpretative Petrol. Igneous Rocks* p. vii, The portions of the book devoted to petrologic history. **1972** *Science* 3 Nov. 497/1 Approximately one-third of the book is devoted to mineralogic and petrologic attributes of sandstones.

petro-mastoid: see PETRO-[1].

‖**Petromyzon** (pɛtrəʊˈmaɪzən). *Ichth.* [mod.L. (Linnæus, 1735), f. Gr. πέτρο-ς stone + μύζων 'sucking, sucker', pr. pple. of μύζ-ειν to suck, lit. 'stone-sucker', formed on the explanation of late or med.L. *lampetra*, from *lambĕre* to lick + *petra* stone: see LAMPREY.] Name of a genus of lampreys, now restricted to those of the northern hemisphere. Hence **petroˈmyzont**, any member of the *Petromyzontidæ* or lamprey family; **petromyˈzontoid** *a.*, related to the lampreys; also *sb.*

1753 CHAMBERS *Cycl. Suppl.*, *Petromyzon*, the stone-sucker, in the Linnæan system of zoology, the name of a genus of fishes of the chondropterygii order, comprehending the lamprey, &c. **1854** BADHAM *Halieut.* 438. **1878** BELL *Gegenbaur's Comp. Anat.* 448 In Petromyzon two enlargements which contain the auditory organ are attached to the sides of this capsule.

†**petron**, variant of PECTRON *Obs.*

1590 BARWICK *Breefe Disc. Weapons* xviii. K iv, There is ten to one armed more vpon the head then vpon the petron.

petronel (ˈpɛtrənəl). Now *Hist.* or *arch.* Also 6–7 -ell, (6 petrenall, petranel(l, petternel, 7 petronil, pewternel, *Sc.* puitternell). [a. F. *petrinal* (Paré 16th c.), dial. form of *poitrinal* (*poict-*, *pot-*, Godef.), sb. use of *poitrinal* adj. 'of or belonging to the breast or chest', f. *poitrine* breast, chest:—pop.L. **pectorīna*, f. *pectus*, pl. *pectora* breast. So called because in firing it, the butt end rested against the chest.] A kind of large pistol or carbine, used in the 16th and early 17th century, esp. by horse-soldiers.

a **1577** GASCOIGNE *Weedes* Wks. (1587) 186 Their peeces then are called Petronels. **1586** R. LANE *Let. to Ralegh* in *Hakluyt's Voy.* (1600) III. 263 Being by the way shot thwart the buttocks by mine Irish boy with my petronell. **1598** BARRET *Theor. Warres* v. ii. 143 A Petranell, or horsemans peece. **1602** *Aberdeen Regr.* (1848) II. 224 Hauing and vsing of ane pistoll and puitternell . . and presenting the same, to hawe schott at Andro Hay. **1611** CORYAT *Crudities* 341 Most of the horsemen being well appointed with muskets or pewternels ready charged. **1656** BLOUNT *Glossogr.*, *Petronel*, a horsemans peece, . . which were always hanged at the Brest, ready to shoot, as they do now at the Horses Brest. **1663** BUTLER *Hud.* I. ii. 787 But he with petronel upheaved, Instead of shield, the blow received. **1813** SCOTT *Rokeby* I. xix, 'Twas then I fired my petronel, And Mortham, steed and rider, fell. **1824** *Ann. Sporting* VI. 200 Another engine, called a petronel or poitrinal, which, according to Fauchet, was the medium between the harquebuss and the pistol. Nicot, however, says it was . . when discharged . . rested on the breast of the person who used it. **1838** *Hist. Rec. 4th Dragoon Guards* Introd. 2 The Cuirassiers were armed Cap-a-pie, and their Arms were a sword and a pair of large pistols, called petrenels. **1881** GREENER *Gun* 35 The German 'Ritters' were the first to employ 'petronels' or hand-bombardes, on horseback.

†**b.** *transf.* = PETRONELLIER *Obs.*

1598 BARRET *Theor. Warres* v. ii. 142 The Petronell and Pistolier is . . weaponed with a Petronell peece, which is with a snap-haunce. **1602** *2nd Pt. Return fr. Parnass.* I. ii. 160 There be neuer an ale-house in England, . . but sets forth some poets petternels or demilances to the paper warres in Paules Church-yard. **1622** F. MARKHAM *Bk. War* III. i. §5. 82 The third sort which are Carbines, are armed Petronels.

Petronella (pɛtrəˈnɛlə). Also with lower-case initial. [? the feminine name *Petronella*.] A Scottish country dance.

1897 *Ball Room* Nov. 11/1 The country dances of twenty-five or thirty years ago were being quite forgotten. 'Sir Roger', 'Triumph', 'Pettonella' [*sic*], the 'Saraband', [etc.]. **1905** F. H. NORMAN *Compl. Dance Instructor* 50 Petronella. **1907** N. MUNRO *Daft Days* xxx. 251 Our dances at the inn are not like city routs: Petronella, La Tempête, and the reel have still an honoured place in them. **1924** *Glasgow Herald* 1 Sept. 8 Despite the grumbles of old-timers who lament the passing of the schottisch, the lancers, and the polka—not to speak of petronella and 'La Va'—the dancing world is eminently conservative. **1935** N. MITCHISON *We have been Warned* I. i. 17 You and I danced Strip the Willow and Petronella. **1978** A. DUNNETT *No Thanks to Duke* xii. 175 We danced the whole night . . Petronella, Strip the Willow, . . Foursome Reel.

†**petronellier.** *Obs.* [a. obs. F. *petrinalier* (also *poit-*, *poict-*, *pest-*), f. *pet-*, *poitrinal*: see PETRONEL and -IER.] A soldier armed with a petronel.

a **1577** GASCOIGNE *Weeds* Wks. (1587) 186 Or of the stone wherwith the lock doth strike, Petronelliers, they called are by like. **1590** BARWICK *Breefe Disc. Weapons* G iv, Sir Iohn Smith dooth commend the Long bowes and the Cros-bowes, to serue on horsebacke, to be better wepons then either the Petronelliers or the Pistolliers [= s'].

petro-occipital, -pharyngeal: see PETRO-[1].

petrophysics (pɛtrəʊˈfɪzɪks), *sb. pl.* (const. as *sing.*). *Geol.* [f. PETRO + PHYSICS.] The study of the physical properties and behaviour of rocks.

1950 G. E. ARCHIE in *Bull. Amer. Assoc. Petroleum Geologists* XXXIV. 942 'Petrophysics' is suggested as the term pertaining to the physics of particular rock types, whereas geophysics pertains to the physics of larger rock systems composing the earth. The petrophysics of reservoir rocks is discussed here. **1959** *Times* 28 July 2/6 (Advt.), They [*sc.* applicants] should also be fully conversant with modern petrophysics methods. **1976** *Nature* 19 Feb. 607/2 Esoteric accounts of palaeotemperature analysis, coal metamorphism, petrography of volcanic rocks, petrophysics of chalk, and intimate analyses of stratigraphic boundaries.

So **petroˈphysical** *a.*; **petroˈphysicist**, a specialist or expert in petrophysics.

1950 G. E. ARCHIE in *Bull. Amer. Assoc. Petroleum Geologists* XXXIV. 961 A tentative petrophysical system . . is presented. **1956** *Geol. Mag.* XCIII. 112 The petrophysical characteristics of sedimentary and igneous rocks are important . . in . . deformation. **1972** *Bull. Amer. Assoc. Petroleum Geologists* LVI. 1906/2 Petrophysical analysis utilizing digital-log information has recently become a recognized tool in the search for oil and gas. **1975** G. ANDERSON *Coring* vii. 128 Most discussions on wireline logs define shale as a nonporous rock as compared to porous reservoir rocks, a point worth remembering in geological discussions with petrophysicists and the like.

petrosal (pɪˈtrəʊsəl), *a.* (*sb.*) *Anat.* [f. L. *petrōsus* stony, rocky + -AL[1].] **a.** Applied to the petrous portion of the temporal bone (*petrosal bone*, med.L. *os petrōsum*), and parts belonging to or connected with it; and to some branches derived from the facial and glossopharyngeal nerves that pass through the petrosal bone, and to the inferior ganglion of the glossopharyngeal nerve, situated in a notch in this bone.

1741 MONRO *Anat. Bones* (ed. 3) 118 A Vein . . returns to the superior petrosal Sinus. **1835–6** TODD *Cycl. Anat.* I. 739/2 The petrosal ridges form the sides of the triangle. **1854** OWEN *Skel. & Teeth* in *Circ. Sc.*, *Org. Nat.* I. 192 It is excavated in front to lodge the petrosal cartilage. **1872** HUXLEY *Phys.* viii. 198 The essential organ of the sense of Hearing . . [is] lodged in the midst of a dense and solid mass of bone (from its hardness called *petrosal*), forming a part of the temporal bone. **1881** A. L. RANNEY *Appl. Anat. Nervous Syst.* II. 179 (*caption*) A diagram of the branches of the facial nerve. . . 3, orifice of aqueduct of Fallopius; 4, large petrosal nerve; 5, small petrosal nerve; 6, external petrosal nerve. **1888** W. R. GOWERS *Man. Dis. Nervous Syst.* II. 250 The tympanic nerve of Jacobson (arising from the enlargement on the glosso-pharyngeal, termed the 'petrosal ganglion'), forms, with the sympathetic, the tympanic plexus in the wall of the middle ear. **1934** L. B. AREY *Developmental Anat.* (ed. 3) xvi. 438 The sensory fibres of the glossopharyngeal nerve arise from two ganglia, the superior ganglion closer to the brain and the petrosal ganglion farther peripherad on the trunk. **1972** M. L. BARR *Human Nervous Syst.* viii. 128/2 The sensory fibres in question [*sc.* those for taste] leave the facial nerve in the greater petrosal branch at the level of the geniculate ganglion.

b. *absol.* as *sb.* = Petrosal bone.

1848 OWEN *Archetype & Homol. Vertebr. Skel.* 13, I have substituted for 'pars petrosa' or 'os petrosum' the substantive term 'petrosal'... 'Petrosal' has appeared to me to be the best English equivalent of Cuvier's 'rocher'. **1878** BELL *Gegenbaur's Comp. Anat.* 458 In all birds and Reptiles the petrosal (prootic) lies in front of the ex-occipital.

†**pe'trose**, *a. Obs. rare*$^{-1}$. [ad. L. *petrōs-us*, f. *petra* rock, stone: see -OSE.] Rocky, stony.

1661 LOVELL *Hist. Anim. & Min.* 232 Diphilus makes them equal to the guilt-head, if living in petrose places.

petroseline ('pɛtrəsɪlaɪn), *a.* [f. L. *petroselīnum*, a. Gr. πετροσέλῑνον rock-parsley, f. πέτρα rock + σέλῑνον parsley.] Of or related to parsley.

1727 S. SWITZER *Pract. Gard.* VI. xlviii. 246 The *apium*, comprehending the whole of the petroseline family. **1760** J. LEE *Introd. Bot.* App. 322 Petroseline Wortle, *Apium*.

petrosilex (pɛtrəʊ'saɪlɛks). *Min.* [mod.L., f. *petr-us* stone or *petr-a* rock + *silex* flint, pebble; also in Fr. (1753 D'Holbach *Min. de Walerius* I. 176, in Hatz.-Darm.).] A hard rock; an early name for compact feldspar, now called Felsite; in Dana given as a synonym of albite and orthoclase.

1770 *Cronstedt's Min.* I. 68 Petro-silex, Lapis Corneus. The Hornstein of the Germans. **1791** BEDDOES in *Phil. Trans.* LXXXI. 63 It forms molten currents of petrosilex and flint exactly the same as our gun-flints. **1794** SULLIVAN *View Nat.* I. 437 Porphyries, properly so called, and jaspers, but more ambiguously petro-silices and felt spar. **1815** J. SMITH *Panorama Sc. & Art* II. 463 Petrosilex, or Chert occurs most frequently in beds of limestone. **1855** LYALL *Man. Geol.* xxviii. (ed. 5) 476 Compact Felspar, which has also been called Petrosilex,..is allied to clinkstone, but is harder, more compact, and translucent. It is a varying rock, of which the chemical composition is not well defined. **1865** LUBBOCK *Preh. Times* iv. (1869) 77 The type of the felspathic extreme of the series of trap rocks is..petrosilex..the average composition of which is 25 parts quartz and 75 felspar.

petrosiliceous (ˌpɛtrəʊsɪ'lɪʃəs), *a.* [f. prec. after *siliceous*.] Consisting of or containing petrosilex.

1799 KIRWAN *Geol. Ess.* 174 Vast layers of porphyry.. either argillaceous, or petrosiliceous. **1804** WATT in *Phil. Trans.* XCIV. 298 A species of petrosilex is found..in Corsica, which contains radiated petrosiliceous glands, from half a line to an inch in diameter. **1879** J. J. YOUNG *Ceram. Art* 60 Mineralogically, it is to be classed with petrosilicious felspar.

petro-sphenoid, -squamous, etc.: see PETRO-^{1}.

petrostearin (pɛtrəʊ'stiːərɪn). [f. PETRO-^{1} + STEARIN.] A name for ozocerite, a mineral resembling stearin.

1879 WEBSTER, Suppl., *Petro-stearine*.., a solid unctuous material of which certain kinds of candles are made. **1893** in *Syd. Soc. Lex.*

petrotectonics (ˌpɛtrəʊtɛk'tɒnɪks), *sb. pl.* (const. as *sing.*). *Geol.* [f. PETRO- + TECTONICS, repr. G. *petrographische tektonische analyse*.] The study of the structure of rocks, esp. as a guide to the movements to which they have been subjected. Cf. PETROFABRICS *sb. pl.*

1933 *Amer. Jrnl. Sci.* XXV. 433 (*heading*) Petrotectonics. *Ibid.* 439 Sander uses the word petrotectonics to express the branch of the investigation that deals with the relation of the oriented microscopic fabric of deformed rocks to their tectonic history. **1937** *Q. Jrnl. Geol. Soc.* XCIII. 581 The science of *Gefügekunde*, variously translated as petrofabrics, petrotectonics, or structural petrology, is understood to comprise a study of all the spatial data, macroscopic and microscopic, which go to form a complete vector-picture so far as this is legible in the make-up of the rock. **1974** *Nature* 10 May 107/3 Evidence supporting the composite nature of Asia has been adduced from palaeomagnetism, palaeontology, geology and petrotectonics.

So ˌpetrotec'tonic *a.*

1933 *Amer. Jrnl. Sci.* XXV. 470 The ultimate test..will be the study by petrotectonic methods of material that has been deformed under known stress conditions. **1970** *Internat. Geol. Rev.* XII. 361/2 The internal petrotectonic structure of the intrusive body, which was established by systematic study of the orientations of the planar and linear parallelism, primary jointing, chromite and durite segregations and so forth, is folded and..corresponds to the folding of the host rocks.

petro-tympanic: see PETRO-^{1}.

petrouille, -ville, obs. forms of PATROL.

petrous ('pɛtrəs), *a.* [f. L. *petrōs-us* stony, rocky: cf. F. *pétreux, -euse* (15th c. in Godef.).]

1. Of the nature of, or as hard as, stone or rock; stony, rocky: in *Anat.* spec. applied to a part of the temporal bone (in some animals a separate bone), remarkable for its density and hardness, and forming a protective case for the internal ear or labyrinth; med. L. *os petrosum*, F. *os pétreux* (Paré); also = PETROSAL.

[*c* **1400** *Lanfranc's Cirurg.* 110 þese boonys..ben ful hard þere as þe hole of þe eere passiþ þoruȝ, & þei ben clepid petrosa.] **1541** R. COPLAND *Guydon's Quest. Chirurg.* D iv b, The .v. and the .vj. be yᵉ bones [of the head] that are called Petrous, for they are harde as a stone. **1657** *Physical Dict.*, *Petrous*, rocky. **1741** MUNRO *Anat. Bones* (ed. 3) 100 The inferior petrous Part is thick. **1800** SIR A. COOPER in *Phil. Trans.* XC. 154 The probe struck against the petrous portion of the temporal bone. **1869** HUXLEY *Phys.* viii. 228 The bony labyrinth, as this collection of cavities in the petrous bone is termed, is perfectly closed.

absol. **1899** *Allbutt's Syst. Med.* VII. 596 Small abscess size of Barcelona nut found in petrous.

2. ? Pertaining to rock or stone; ? petrifying.

a **1851** MOIR *Miner of Peru* Poet. Wks. 1852 II. 172 By death unchanged So strong had been the power preservative, Mineral or petrous, of the charmed flood.

pe-tsai (peɪ'tsaɪ). Also **Pe-Tsai**. [Older transliteration of Chinese *báicài*, f. *bái* white + *cài* vegetable; cf. PAK-CHOI.] A Chinese species of cabbage, *Brassica pekinensis*. Also *attrib.*

1795 W. WINTERBOTHAM *Hist., Geogr., & Philos. View Chinese Empire* v. 221 The Chinese make provision of *pe-tsai* for winter; pickling of it, and mixing it with their rice. **1845** *Encycl. Metrop.* XVI. 588/1 The *Pe-tsai*, or white herb, a kind of mustard,..is cultivated in large fields, and eaten either fresh or pickled, like the German *Sauer-kraut*. **1885** [see *Chinese cabbage* s.v. CHINESE *a.* 2]. **1900** L. H. BAILEY *Cycl. Amer. Hort.* I. 178/2 Pe-tsai cabbage. *Ibid.*, The Pe-tsai, or Chinese cabbage, is no longer a novelty in American gardens, though it does not appear to be well known, and its merits are not understood. **1960** *Farmer & Stockbreeder* 8 Mar. (Suppl.) 11/2 The celery-cabbage (Pe-Tsai) is worth trying, too. The heads are crisp and tender. **1969** *Oxf. Bk. Food Plants* 154/1 Pe-Tsai (*Brassica pekinensis*) is grown mostly for use as an autumn and winter vegetable... Pe-tsai has soft green, prominently veined leaves... The rather loose, elongated head bears some resemblance to a cos lettuce. **1972** *Homes & Gardens* Aug. 104/1 Chinese cabbage, or pe-tsai, is a new vegetable to this country. It comes from Israel and looks like a cross between a very pale whitish-green cos lettuce and a head of celery, although it is larger and considerably heavier than both. **1972** *Country Life* 14 Dec. 1676/3 Last autumn's drought delayed the growth of Chinese Pe-Tsai cabbage, sown in August, so.. they are being cooked now.

petsywetsy (ˌpɛtsɪ'wɛtsɪ). *nonce-wd.* [f. PET *sb.*^{1}: see -SY.] A fanciful extension of PET *sb.*^{1} 2.

1928 D. H. LAWRENCE *Lady Chatterley* xvii. 305 I'm not content to be any man's little petsywetsy.

pett, obs. form of PEAT, PET, PIT.

pettable ('pɛtəb(ə)l), *a.* [f. PET *v.*^{1} + -ABLE.] Suitable for petting. Hence **petta'bility**.

1934 WEBSTER, Pettable. **1962** *Times* 17 Sept. 15/3 There is scarcely a 'pettable' creature that has not been adopted by my family. **1963** F. E. SPARSHOTT *Structure of Aesthetics* iii. 74 'Handsome'..is applied to things whose appearance stirs the imagination—but by suggestions of vigour rather than of pettability. **1978** *Chicago* June 50/2 In the large Children's Zoo, youngsters can walk into a petting area and be surrounded by pettable domestic animals.

‖**pettah** ('pɛtə). [ad. Tamil *pēṭṭai* (Yule & Burnell).] A town or village lying outside of or around a fort, but itself sometimes partially fortified. Also *attrib.*

1763 R. ORME *Milit. Trans. Indostan* I. II. 151 The pagoda served as a citadel to a large pettah. **1803** WELLINGTON in Gurw. *Desp.* II. 193 The Pettah wall was very lofty and defended by towers. **1845** STOCQUELER *Handbk. Brit. India* (1854) 383 The harbour is protected by a fort..encircling the town, and separated from the pettah, a part of Galle inhabited by natives and government servants, by an esplanade. **1876** JAS. GRANT *Hist. India* I. lxxi. 369/1 The pettah was taken on the 24th.

pettaill, var. PEDAILE *Obs.*

pettar-, petteraro, var. PEDRERO *Obs.*, a small gun.

pette, obs. f. PET, PIT.

petted ('pɛtɪd), *ppl. a.* [f. PET *v.*^{1} + -ED^1.] Treated as a pet or favourite, made a pet of, made much of; indulged, spoiled by petting or indulgence.

In sense often approaching the next, since the indulged child is specially apt to take offence at supposed slights.

1724 RAMSAY *Tea-t. Misc.*, *Bonny Bessie* iii, Petted things can nought but teez ye. **1821** GALT *Ann. Parish* xii. (1850) 50 She began to cry and sob, like a petted bairn. **1826** DISRAELI *Viv. Grey* III. vi, The wind was capricious and changeable as a petted beauty. **1828** SCOTT *F.M. Perth* xxx, We are but like petted children, who break and throw from them the toys they have wept themselves sick for. **1852** MRS. STOWE *Uncle Tom's C.* ii, Eliza had been brought up by her mistress, from girlhood, as a petted and indulged favourite. **1877** BRYANT *3rd November 1861* ii, Tenderly the season.. Spared the petted flowers that the old world gave the new. **1887** *Poor Nellie* (1888) 143 The petted hobby of two distinguished Ministers.

petted ('pɛtɪd), *a.* [f. PET *sb.*^{2} + -ED^2.] In a pet; offended or sulky at feeling slighted or ill-used; piqued; given to taking pet, pettish.

1760 H. BROOKE *Fool of Qual.* (1809) I. 149, I was petted at their neglect of us during our long illness. **1814** WORDSW. *Excursion* I. 580 Poverty brought on a petted mood And a sore temper.

Hence '**pettedly** *adv.*, pettishly; '**pettedness**.

1858 R. S. SURTEES *Ask Mamma* lxiv. 287 Take off his nightcap! cried Jack, pulling pettedly at the strings of the hood. **1893** *Whitby Gaz.* 6 Oct. 3/5 Though I do not wish to show any pettedness I have now no alternative but to say that I have no proposition to make.

pettegre, -grye, obs. forms of PEDIGREE *sb.*

petter ('pɛtə(r)), *sb.* [f. PET *v.*^{1} + -ER^1.] **1.** One who pets or indulges.

1863 *N. & Q.* 3rd Ser. III. 240 The author must..be a petter of all kinds of pets.

2. One who pets (PET *v.*^{1} b); one who engages in petting (PETTING *vbl. sb.* 2).

1925 *College Humor* Aug. 77/1 Have a nice evening? Jean's some high-type petter, isn't she? **1930** F. DELL *Love in Machine Age* ix. 170 Science's adjuration to the petters is only: 'You really *must* get *some* food and sleep, my dears!' **1931** F. L. ALLEN *Only Yesterday* v. 101 The vendors of another picture promised 'neckers, petters, white kisses, red kisses, pleasure-mad daughters, sensation-craving mothers'. **1931** *Brit. Jrnl. Psychol.* Oct. 183 One finds oneself extremely dubious about this contention that the modern adolescent 'petter' and 'demi-vierge' have discovered for themselves a satisfactory way of acquiring the adequate pre-marital emotional education. **1942** BERREY & VAN DEN BARK *Amer. Thes. Slang* §443/13 Heavy necker *or* petter.

petter ('pɛtə(r)), *v.* [Echoic: cf. PITTER.] To emit the sound natural to a grasshopper.

1849 *Tait's Mag.* XVI. 106 The grasshopper was pettering his monotonous contralto.

petternel, pettestale, obs. ff. PETRONEL, PEDESTAL.

petti- ('pɛtɪ). Combining form of PETTI(COAT *sb.*, designating garments having some of the characteristics or functions of a petticoat.

1922 JOYCE *Ulysses* 360 He could see her other things too, nainsook knickers, the fabric that caresses the skin, better than those other pettiwidth, the green, four and eleven, on account of being white. *Ibid.* 544 Lifting up her pettigown and folding a half sovereign into the top of her stocking. **1923** *Dialect Notes* V. 246 *Pettibockers*, n. pl. A loose garment for girls, worn under skirts: contamination of *petticoat* and *knickerbockers*. **1939** JOYCE *Finnegans Wake* IV. 611 His yellow saffron pettikilt. **1942** BERREY & VAN DEN BARK *Amer. Thes. Slang.* §87/27 *Pettibockers*, women's old-fashioned knickerbockers. **1960** *Harper's Bazaar* Apr. 11 Nightdresses, slips, pettiskirts, panties. **1963** *Seventeen* Aug. 32 A new word in lingerie. Pettisets (a petti-top matched with petti-pants as well as a petticoat). **1964** *N.Y. Post* 7 Oct. 13 Perfect under your swinging skirts, pettipants fashioned with a divided skirt. **1968** J. IRONSIDE *Fashion Alphabet* 71 *Pettipants*, petticoat and pants combined. **1970** N. ARMSTRONG et al. *First on Moon* vi. 126 They found a present for Jan's friend—pettipants edged with green lace. **1972** *Daily Tel.* (Colour Suppl.) 13 Oct. 16/1 On top of this I wore a petti-blouse (which is a blouse and a petticoat).

pettiagua, -auger, etc., corrupt ff. PIRAGUA.

pettichaps ('pɛtɪtʃæps). Also 7-9 **pettychaps**; 9 *dial.* **pettichap.** [f. PETTY *a.* + ? CHAP *sb.*^{2} or ^{3}. Locally used in Yorkshire and Lancashire: a specimen of the bird was sent from Sheffield to Willughby *c* 1670, under this name, which thus entered into ornithological nomenclature; but app. never in general Eng. use, and still chiefly a book-name.] A name of the Garden Warbler (*Sylvia hortensis*). Also applied to other species of warblers, as ***lesser pettichaps***, the chiff-chaff (*Phylloscopus rufus*); *dial.* the long-tailed titmouse (*rare*).

1674 RAY *Collect. Words, Eng. Birds* 86 Pettichaps: *Ficedula Septima* Aldrov. **1678** —— *Willughby's Ornith.* 206 Mr. Jessop shot this bird in Yorkshire, and sent it us by the name of Pettychaps. **1785** *Phil. Trans.* LXXV. 10 The male and female..are both larger than the Pettychaps described by Willoughby. **1829** KNAPP *Jrnl. Nat.* 211 The quantities of cherries and raspberries that the blackcap and pettichaps will eat are surprising. **1833** SELBY in *Proc. Berw. Nat. Club* I. 20 The greater pettichaps (*Curruca hortensis*) and wood-wren..are considerably later. **1843** H. DOUBLEDAY in *Zoologist* I. 13 In the spring of 1841 the redstart..lesser pettychaps and garden warbler were very numerous. **1851** T. STERNBERG *Dial. & Folk-lore of Northants.*, *Pettichap*, the long-tailed titmouse.

petticoat ('pɛtɪkəʊt), *sb.* (*a.*) Forms: α. 5 **pety coote**, 6 **pety cote**, 7 **petty coat**, **pettie coat.** β. 5 **pettecote**; 5-7 **pety-**, 6-7 **peti-**, **pettycote**; 6 **peteekot**; **peticoot**, **petticoit(e**; 6-7 **petti-**, **pettycoate**; **pette-**, **peticoate**; 7 **peticoat**, **pettie-coat**, 7-8 **pettycoat**, **petty-coat**; 6- **petticoat**. [Orig. two words, *petty coat*, lit. little or small coat (cf. OF. *cote*, mod.F. *cotte* petticoat, *cotte simple* under-petticoat). From an early period written as one word, or less usually hyphened.]

1. †**a.** A small coat worn by men beneath the doublet; in quot. 1412-20 app. a short coat worn as armour. *Obs.* **b.** *dial.* (from 17th c.) A waistcoat.

a. 1412-20 LYDG. *Chron. Troy* III. xxii. (1555), The famous knyghtes arme them in yᵉ place... A payre gussettes on a pety coote. *c* **1440** *Promp. Parv.* 395/1 Petycote, *tunicula*. *c* **1460** J. RUSSELL *Bk. Nurture* 872 Se that youre souerayne haue clene shurt & breche, A petycote, a dublett, a longe coote. **1474** *Acc. Ld. High Treas. Scot.* I. 26, j elne of skarlete for a petticote to the King..Ls. **1542** BOORDE *Dyetary* viii. (1870) 249 Next your sherte vse to were a petycote of skarlet.

b. 1674 RAY *S. & E.C. Words* (1691) 109 A Petticoat, is in some places used for a Mans Wastcoat. **1736** J. LEWIS *Isle Tenet* Gloss. (E.D.S.), *Petty-coat*, a man or boy's waistcoat. [Hence in PEGGE *Kenticisms*.] **1834** PLANCHÉ *Brit. Costume* 181. **1887** in *Kent. Gloss.*

2. *gen.* A garment worn by women, girls, and young children (perh. orig. a kind of tunic or chemise, but) usually a skirt dependent from the waist. Also used as the equivalent for some similar Greek or Roman female garment.

(Of the following early quots., several prob. belong to the specific senses a and b.)

1464 *Mann. & Househ. Exp.* (Roxb.) 544 Item, for makenge of ij. petycotes for mastres Marget and m. Anne, iiij.*d.* **1520** Sir R. Elyot *Will* in *Elyot's Gov.* (1883) I. App. A. 312 Every of their wifes a white petycote. **1530** Palsgr. 253/2 Petycote, *corset simple, cotte simple, chemise de blanchet.* *c* **1532** Du Wes *Introd. Fr.* in *Palsgr.* 906 The petycote, *la cotte simple.* **1558** *Aberdeen Regr.* (1844) I. 309 For the wrangous reiffing and away taking fra hir of ane plyd, ane petticoitt [etc.]. *a* **1586** Sidney *Arcadia* III. (1629) 235 Sixe maides, all in one liuerie of scarlet peticotes, which were tucked vp almost to their knees. **1661** Evelyn *Tyrannus* 10 Those who sacrific'd to Ceres put on the pettycoat with much confidence. **1858** Hawthorne *Fr. & It. Note-bks.* I. 98 A statue of Minerva, with a petticoat of red porphyry.

spec. **a.** A skirt as distinguished from a bodice, worn either externally, or beneath the gown or frock as part of the costume, and trimmed or ornamented; an outer, upper, or show petticoat.

1602 Marston *Ant. & Mel.* III. Wks. 1856 I. 39 The fringe of your sattin peticote is ript. *a* **1641** Suckling *Poems* (1646) 38 Her feet beneath her Petticoat Like little mice stole in and out. **1662** Pepys *Diary* 18 May, She was in her new suit of black sarcenet and yellow petticoate very pretty. **1711** Addison *Spect.* No. 129 ¶8 A Lady..entered..in..a hoop'd Petticoat. **1711** Steele *ibid.* No. 145 ¶7 There is not one of us but has reduced our outward Petticoat to its ancient Sizable Circumference, tho' indeed we retain still a Quilted one underneath. **1712** *Spect.* No. 277 ¶13 The Puppet was dressed in a Cherry-coloured Gown and Petticoat. **1716** Lady M. W. Montagu *Let. to C'tess Mar* 14 Sept., Their Whalebone petticoats outdo ours by several yards' circumference. **1724** De Foe *Mem. Cavalier* II. 248 One of my Comerades in the Farmer's Wife's Russet Gown and Petticoat, like a Woman. **1796** Jane Austen *Pride & Prej.* viii, I hope you saw her petticoat, six inches deep in mud,..and the gown which had been let down to hide it not doing its office. **1815** *Zeluca* I. 78 Her figure would best be displayed in the vandyke petticoat. **1816** J. Scott *Vis. Paris* (ed. 5) 109 Their boddices contrasted against their petticoats with the judgement of a painter. **1824** Scott *Redgauntlet* ch. ix, A skirt, or upper petticoat, of camlet. **1881** *Truth* 19 May 686/2 One of her Court dresses has the bodice of sky-blue satin... The petticoat is of net, covered with silver lace.

b. An under-skirt of calico, flannel, or other material.

(In early quotations not easily separable from a.)

1596 Shaks. *Tam. Shr.* II. i. 5 But for these other goods, Vnbinde my hands, Ile pull them off my selfe, Yea all my raiment, to my petticoate. **1625** Meade in Ellis *Orig. Lett.* Ser. I. III. 201 She came out of her bedchamber in her petticoat. **1662** Pepys *Diary* 21 May, Saw the finest smocks and linnen petticoats of my Lady Castlemaine's. **1712** Addison *Spect.* No. 295 ¶10 He would..have presented her ..with the Sheering of his Sheep for her Under-Petticoats. **1812** *Poet. Sk. Scarborough* (ed. 2) 138 While Kate was like a crouching goddess, In only petticoat and boddice. **1836–9** Dickens *Sk. Boz, Mr. Watkins Tottle* i, I said, jokingly, that when I went to bed I should wrap my head in Fanny's flannel petticoat. **1844** Mrs. Sherwood *Hist. J. Marten* xv. 205 A good flannel petticoat ought to be little the worse for one year's wear. **1848** [cf. crinoline 4].

†**c.** The skirt of a woman's riding-habit. *Obs.*

1663 Pepys *Diary* 13 July, The..Queene..in..a white laced waistcoate and a crimson short pettycoate,..mighty pretty; and the King rode hand in hand with her. **1666** *Ibid.* 12 June, The Ladies of Honour dressed in their riding garbs, with coats and doublets.., with perriwigs and with hats; so that, only for a long petticoat dragging under their men's coats, nobody could take them for women. **1711** Steele *Spect.* No. 104 ¶2. **1824** Scott *Redgauntlet* ch. ix, A skirt, or upper petticoat, of camlet, like those worn [in 18th c.] by country ladies of moderate rank when on horseback.

d. Applied also to the rudimentary garment worn by women among primitive peoples, e.g. the 'grass petticoat' of Papuan women.

1698 Fryer *Acc. E. India & P.* 156 Over their Lower Parts a Petticoat or Lungy, their Feet and Legs without Stockins. *a* **1704** T. Brown *Walk round London* (1709) 41 Our good Grandmother Eve might have sav'd her self a great deal of trouble in tacking together Primitive Green Petticoat and Wastcoat. **1712** E. Cooke *Voy. S. Sea* 336 The Women have short Petticoats made of Silk Grass.

3. *pl.* Skirts collectively, upper and under; also, skirts worn by children, including young boys: chiefly in phrase (said of a young boy) ***in petticoats.***

1600 Shaks. *A.Y.L.* I. iii. 15 They are but burs,..if we walke not in the trodden paths, our very petty-coates will catch them. **1650** Howell *Giraffi's Rev. Naples* I. (1664) 78 He commanded also that all women..shold tuck their petticoats somwhat high. **1727** Swift *Country Post* Wks. 1755 III. I. 176 A mouse..took shelter under Dolly's petticoats. **1818** I. Taylor *Scenes Europe* (1821) §67 A young Dutch [peasant] girl in her holiday suit,..with petticoats only half down the leg. **1833** Ht. Martineau *Three Ages* iii. 85 The country was chalky, and whitened the hems of her petticoats. **1837** Marryat *Dog-fiend* xiv, The old woman.. executed her parental authority as if he were still in petticoats. **1877** Mrs. Forrester *Mignon* I. 253, I have known him ever since he was in petticoats. **1887** *Daily News* 23 Sept. 5/1 Both in batting and bowling, however, petti-coats are decidedly hindering, especially in windy weather. **1898** *Cycling* xii. 72 Petticoats, which only hamper the action of the knees, must absolutely be discarded.

4. (chiefly *pl.*) As the characteristic or typical feminine garment; hence as the symbol of the female sex or character. ***to wear*** or ***be in petticoats***, to be a woman, to behave as befits a woman. ***a Nero*** (or other male) ***in petticoats***, a female counterpart to Nero, or other man specified.

1593 Shaks. *3 Hen. VI*, v. v. 23 That you might still haue worne the Petticoat, And ne're haue stolne the Breech from Lancaster. **1702** Addison *Medals* ii. Misc. Wks. 1726 III. 36 It is a great compliment methinks to the sex,..that your Virtues are generally shown in petticoats. *a* **1715** Burnet *Own Time* I. (1724) 83 A saying that went of her [Lady Falconbridge], that those who wore breeches deserved petticoats better, but if those in petticoats had been in breeches, they would have held faster. **1766** Chesterf. *Lett. to Godson* (1898) 210 Ignorance is only pardonable in petty-coats. **1828** Scott *F.M. Perth* xi, Since she wears a petticoat..I will answer for her protection as well as a single man may. **1853** Kingsley *Misc., Shelley & Byron* (1859) I. 321 Beatrice Cenci is really none other than Percy Bysshe Shelley himself in petticoats. **1880** Ouida *Moths* I. 39 She was a sort of Wesley in petticoats.

b. (*sing.*) The wearer of a petticoat; a female; the female sex.

1600 Shaks. *A.Y.L.* II. iv. 7 But I must comfort the weaker vessell, as doublet and hose ought to show it selfe coragious to petty-coate. *a* **1657** R. Loveday *Lett.* (1663) 118 The *Maistre de Hostell* still keeps his state with the better sort of petticoats. **1728** Young *Love Fame* v, Vain is the task to petticoats assign'd, If wanton language shews a naked mind. **1776** J. Adams in *Fam. Lett.* (1876) 155 Rather than give up this, which would completely subject us to the despotism of the petticoat, I hope [etc.]. **1864** G. Meredith *Emilia* xxv, Must give up business to-day. Can't do business with a petticoat in the room. **1898** *Daily News* 1 Aug. 4/7 There was as much force as brutality in his [Bismarck's] exclamation that the Emperor Frederick's death would put an end to the rule of 'petticoats in politics'.

5. A wide outer garment, made of oilskins or rough canvas, worn by fishermen in warm weather, and reaching below the knee, often undivided: cf. *petticoat trousers* in 9. *U.S.*

1890 in *Cent. Dict.* **1895** in *Funk's Stand. Dict.*

b. Applied humorously or contemptuously to the skirts of a scholar's or clergyman's gown; also descriptively to the kilt of the Highlander or Highland regiments, the fustanella of the Greek, and similar male garments.

c **1730** Burt *Lett. N. Scot.* (1754) II. xxii. 189 That they [Highlanders] would not be so free to skip over the Rocks and Bogs with Breeches, as they are in the short Petticoat. **1849** Mrs. Mortimer *Near Home, Turkey* 357 It would astonish you to see how fast they [dancing dervishes] turn round in their full white petticoats. **1849** Macaulay *Hist. Eng.* xiii. (1871) II. 34 Artists and actors represented Bruce and Douglas in striped petticoats.

6. *transf.* **a.** A toilet-table cover reaching down to the floor. **b.** A sheeting hung round a yacht while being launched, to hide its outlines. **c.** A projecting fringe-like part forming the foot of a tankard, etc. **d.** *Archery.* 'The ground of a target beyond the white'; the *spoon*. **e.** = *petticoat insulator*: see 9.

1864 Webster, *Petticoat*, the outer space or surface of a target. [*Eng.*] **1875** *Encycl. Brit.* II. 378/2 *Petticoat*, or *Spoon*, the ground of the target beyond the white. **1880** Baring-Gould *Mehalah* xii. (1884) 164 The dressing-table had a pink petticoat with gauze over it. **1899** *Westm. Gaz.* 24 June 7/2 Shamrock is to be launched 'in petticoats' on Monday. **1899** *Daily News* 27 June 7/3 A long curtain or 'petticoat' hung over the stern of the boat, and, reaching to the ground, effectually prevented any view of the keel and lower part of the yacht. **1903** P. Macquoid in *Burlington Mag.* Apr., In about 1640..the tankard becomes plain and high with a so-called petticoat shooting out at the bottom.

II. *attrib.* and *Comb.*

7. *simple attrib.* Of a petticoat or petticoats.

1587 *Acc. Bk.* in *Antiquary* XXXII. 118, vj yeardes of petecote lace, xviijd. **1834** *Tait's Mag.* I. 663/1, I would warrant every knave of them to kiss the hem of the petticoat-tail of the smallest member of the sacred conclave. **1844** Mrs. Sherwood *Hist. J. Marten* xv. 217 It was flannel petticoat time [i.e. for a clothing club distribution]. *a* **1844** Campbell *Ep. to Hor. Smith*, In his breeches of petticoat size..his garb is a fair compromise 'Twixt a kilt and a pair of small-clothes. **1872** *Routledge's Ev. Boy's Ann.* 664/2 To give you the horrors with, in petticoat days. **1886** Dr. Richardson in *Pall Mall G.* 27 Sept. 6/2 A petticoated generation could never do the full work of a generation whose limbs were free of petticoat encumbrance.

8. *attrib.* (often = *adj.*). **a.** In petticoats, wearing petticoats; that is a woman, female; womanish. (Often hyphened.) Now *rare*.

1625 Hart *Anat. Ur.* II. vi. 85 The ignorant Empiricke, the peticoate or woman-physitian. **1706** E. Ward *Wooden World Diss.* (1708) 10 Many a Heccatomb of humble Prayers, does he offer to appease this Petticoat-Deity. **1712** Addison *Spect.* No. 305 ¶4 A Seminary of Petticoat Politicians, who are to be brought up at the Feet of Madam de Maintenon. **1725** Bailey *Erasm. Colloq.* (1878) I. 186 What does this Petticoat-Preacher [*concionatrix*] do here? **1797** Mrs. M. Robinson *Walsingham* II. 213 To ridicule the petticoat pedant. **1813** Moore *Post-bag* (1818) App. iv. 108 A Petticoat Pope in the Ninth Century.

b. Of, belonging, or relating to a woman or women, as the wearers of petticoats; executed, performed, wielded by a woman; female, feminine.

1660 Hickeringill *Jamaica* (1661) 30 The Petticoat Sex. **1690** Dryden *Amphitryon* I. i, Venus may know more than both of us, For 'tis some petticoat affair. **1800** *Proc. E. Ind. Ho.* in *Asiat. Ann. Reg.* 63/2 He thought this petticoat influence in the India Company, a most curious circumstance! **1806** *Francis Lett.* (1901) II. 638, I will not go to Petticoat Parties. **1828** Scott *F.M. Perth* xi, He will obey you in making a weapon, or in wielding one, but he knows nothing of this petticoat service. **1850** Kingsley *Alt. Locke* xxvii, The coarsest allusions to petticoat influence. **1901** *Westm. Gaz.* 23 May 4/2 Miss Gertrude Elliott has the only petticoat part [in a play].

9. Special combs: **petticoat body**, a body attached to or worn with a petticoat; **petticoat breeches**, loose wide breeches with legs resembling skirts, fashionable during the earlier part of the reign of Charles II; **petticoat insulator**, an inverted cup-shaped insulator of porcelain or the like that supports a telegraph wire; **petticoat-maker**, a maker of petticoats, esp. of farthingales; †**petticoat-monger**, ? a whore-monger; **petticoat-pensioner**, a man paid by a woman, a woman's 'fancy-man'; **petticoat-pipe**, a bell-mouthed pipe in the chimney of a locomotive into which the exhaust-steam enters and which serves to equalize and strengthen the draught; **petticoat-trousers**, (*a*) a New England colloquial name for wide baggy trousers; (*b*) = 5; (*c*) the wide-seated trousers worn by Muslim women; **petticoat-wise** *adv.*, in the manner of a petticoat.

1862 *Eng. Wom. Dom. Mag.* IV. 238/2 Patterns of the newest and most fashionable under-linen, including.. petticoat band, *petticoat body. **1891** Flo. Marryat *There is no Death* xii. 116 She had not got on 'Rosie's' petticoat body. **1658** R. Holme in Fairholt *Costume in Eng.* (1860) 255 A short-waisted doublet and *petticoat-breeches, the lining lower than the breeches tied above the knee. **1860** Fairholt *Ibid.* Gloss. 399 Towards the end of the reign of Charles the petticoat breeches were discarded. **1552** Huloet, *Peticote maker, *indusiarius*. **1783** Ainsworth *Eng. Lat. Dict.* **1605** *Tryall Chev.* v. ii. in Bullen *O. Pl.* III. 347 You pick-hatch Cavaliero *petticote-monger. *a* **1700** B. E. *Dict. Cant. Crew*, **Pettycoat-Pensioner*, a Gallant, or one Maintain'd for secret Service. **1825** Knapp & Baldw. *Newgate Cal.* IV. 327/1 He became a petticoat-pensioner. **1864** Webster, **Petticoat pipe*, one of a series of short conical pipes, in a smoke-box, to equalize the draught. **1878** *Engineer* XLVI. 57/3 A good modification of the well-known American petticoat pipe. **1753** *N. Jersey Archives* XIX. 291 He took with him..two Pair of *Petticoat Trowsers. **1761** *Ibid.* XX. 597 Run away ..an English servant lad... Had on..long petticoat trowsers, much worn. **1867** Smyth *Sailor's Word-bk.*, *Petticoat trowsers*, a kind of kilt formerly worn by seamen in general, but latterly principally by fishermen. **1885** Burton *Arab. Nts.* II. 6 The strings of her petticoat-trowsers. **1903** *Daily Chron.* 31 Mar. 10/2 Overcoats slung round the loins, *petticoat-wise.

b. **petticoat government**: (undue) rule or predominance of women in the home, or in politics. So **petticoat-governed** *a.*, ruled by a woman, hen-pecked.

1702 J. Dunton (*title*) Petticoat-Government. *Ibid.* 70 By Petticoat-Government, I mean when Good Women Ascend the Throne, and Rule according to Law, as is the case of the present Queen. Again, by Petticoat-Government, I mean the discreet and housewifely Ruling of a House and Family. **1702** (*title*) The Prerogative of the Breeches: an answer to Petticoat-Government, written by a True-born English Man. **1731** Fielding *Grub-St. Op.* I. i, Petticoat-government is a very lamentable thing indeed. **1825** Cobbett *Rur. Rides* (1885) I. 365 He, being under strict petticoat government..was compelled to get home that night. **1836–9** Dickens *Sk. Boz, Boarding-Ho.* i, Mr. Calton seized the hand of the petticoat-governed little man. **1884** *Chr. World* 19 June 453/1 This..would throw electoral power into the hands of women, and petticoat government would prevail.

'petticoat, *v. rare.* [f. prec. sb.] **a.** *trans.* To clothe in petticoats, put petticoats on; *fig.* to treat as a woman. **b.** *intr.* To wear, or posture in, petticoats. Hence **'petticoating** *vbl. sb.*

1850 Browning *Christmas Eve* xxii, Let us hope That no worse blessing befall the Pope, Turned sick at last of to-day's buffoonery, Of posturings and petticoatings. **1895** J. Winsor *Mississ. Basin* 175 The Shawnees..were restless in being what was termed 'petticoated' by the Iroquois.

petticoated ('pɛtɪkəʊtɪd), *a.* [f. petticoat *sb.* + -ed[2].] Having or wearing petticoats; female.

1748 Richardson *Clarissa* (1811) VII. 49, I will contrive to be the man, petticoated out, and vested in a gown and cassock. **1820** Scott *Monast.* xiv, Here, dame,..is a letter from your petticoated baron, the lord-priest yonder. **1824** Miss Mitford *Village* Ser. I. (1863) 155 Days of every variety of falling weather..too bad to admit the possibility that any petticoated thing..should stir out. **1859** G. Meredith *R. Feverel* II. iii. 22 A lady who..was the petticoated image of her admirable ancestor. **1871** —— *H. Richmond* xliv, She..was..in the squire's phrase, 'a petticoated parsimony'. **1871** M. Collins *Mrq. & Merch.* I. iv. 131 She wanted to make this..School a petticoated Rugby. **1900** *Queen Cycling Bk.* 1 To see a petticoated woman [cyclist] struggling along on a windy day.

b. *transf.* Having a 'petticoat' or enclosing pendent fringe: see petticoat *sb.* 6.

1858 Lytton *What will he do* I. xix, This petticoated divan suddenly closed round the painter. **1880** Baring-Gould *Mehalah* xii. (1884) 169 [His] gilt balcony and petticoated dressing-table.

c. (See *petticoat insulator*, petticoat 9.)

1900 *Engineering Mag.* XIX. 754/2 They are supported on strong porcelain insulators, triple-petticoated.

petticoatery, -ie. *nonce-wd.* [f. petticoat + -ery (with punning allusion to *coterie*).] A petticoated company or coterie; wearers of petticoats collectively.

1849 *Blackw. Mag.* LXV. 680 The whole coterie (which, in this instance, is an undiluted petticoatery) assembles for consultation. **1884** *Punch* 22 Nov. 252/1 Astounding both to the old-fashioned petticoaterie and the new-fangled divided skirtists.

ˈpettiˌcoatie. *Sc.* [dim.] A little petticoat.
1794 Burns *Coming through the Rye* i, She draiglet a' her petticoatie, Coming through the rye.

Petticoat Lane. A popular name given to Middlesex Street (formerly Hog Lane) in the City of London, where dealers in second-hand clothes and other commodities congregate. Also *attrib.*
1602 in *Calendar of Cecil MSS.* 168 in *Parl. Papers 1910* (Cd. 5291) XXXIV. 1, I understand by Udall that Eccleston is a gentleman dwelling near Knowsely, but has left his habitation, and abides altogether in London, in Peticote Lane. **1631** B. Jonson *Devil an Ass* i. i. 60 We will suruay the Suburbs, and make forth our sallyes, Downe Petticoate-lane, and vp the Smock-allies, To Shoreditch, Whitechappell, and so to Saint Kathernes. **1909** W. W. Hutchings *London Town* II. xc. 967/1 This street formerly Petticoat Lane, and in yet earlier days Hog Lane, has of late years been rebuilt, but it is still largely inhabited by dealers in second-hand clothes, and still on Sundays it is thronged by those who come to buy other people's cast-off garments. **1967** M. Waddell *Otley Pursued* xii. 109 It was 6.42 by my Petticoat Lane watch, give or take ten minutes or so. **1972** *Police Rev.* 17 Nov. 1495/3 The man who had been given the licence had described the street..as 'Petticoat Lane'. Section 21 (1) required that the particular street must be named, and Petticoat Lane has become Middlesex Street. **1976** *Oadby & Wigston Advertiser* 26 Nov. 10/1 Glen Parva Borstal was like a 'small Petticoat Lane' with items being offered for sale all the time, Rutland magistrates heard on Monday.

ˈpetticoatless, *a.* [f. petticoat *sb.* + -less.] Without a petticoat, not wearing petticoats.
1888 *Macm. Mag.* Aug. 306 The graceful curves of her slight, petticoatless figure. **1896** *Godey's Mag.* Apr. 447/1 Men declare that the petticoatless female has unsexed herself and has left her modesty behind.
b. *fig.* Without female characters.
1892 *Longm. Mag.* Aug. 435 Mamie is perhaps the best petticoat among Mr. Stevenson's rather petticoatless tales.

petticoat tails. *Sc.* [Origin uncertain: see quot. 1825.] 'The name given to a species of cake baked with butter, used as tea-bread' (Jamieson 1825).
? *a* **1800** *Collect. Receipts* 3 (Jam.) For Petticoat tails, take the same proportion of butter as for Short Bread. **1818** Scott *Br. Lamm.* xxvi, Never had there been..such making of car-cakes and sweet scones, Selkirk bannocks, cookies, and petticoat-tails—delicacies little known to the present generation. **1825** Jamieson s.v., The general idea is, that this kind of cake is denominated from its resemblance to a section of a petticoat. For a circular cake, when a smaller circle has been taken out of the middle, is divided into eight quarters. But a literary friend has suggested that the term has probably a French origin, q. *petit gasteau*, a little cake. The old form of this word is *petit gastel.* **1870** Ramsay *Remin.* vi. (ed. 18) 247. **1887** *Pall Mall G.* 27 Dec. 5/2 Yorkshire Parkin, Simnel cake, and Scotch petticoat tails are to be found among a host of local delicacies.

ˈpetticoaty, *a.* [f. petticoat *sb.* + -y.] Like or akin to a petticoat.
1883 G. H. Boughton in *Harper's Mag.* Mar. 522/2 He wears a pair of baggy breeches..very voluminous and petticoaty. **1885** *Pall Mall G.* 21 May 4 When men took to wearing a long, petticoaty style of coat..some of them took to wearing stays also.

†**pettifactor, petifactor.** *Obs. rare.* [app. = *petty factor*: cf. petty *a.* and factor *sb.* 3.]
? A legal agent who undertakes small cases. Cf. pettifogger.
1586 Ferne *Blaz. Gentrie* 92 Thereby, the number of pleaders and petifactors be so far increased that although the common-wealth is wonderfully torn with the litigiousnes of clyents notwithstanding their purchase is not worth their rent. **1633** T. Nash *Quaternio* 41 How difficult a thing it is for a petifactor to rayse himselfe, without a great deale of jugling and false-dealing.

pettifog (ˈpɛtɪfɒg), *v.* [app. a back-formation from pettifogger: cf. fog *v.*³ and pettifogging.]
1. *intr.* To act as a pettifogger; to plead or conduct a petty case in a minor court of law; to practise legal chicanery; also *transf.*, to wrangle or quibble about small petty points.
1611 Cotgr., *Chicaner*, to wrangle, or pettifog it; to spoyle, or perplex a cause with craftie, or litigious pleading. **1628** Wither *Brit. Rememb.* vii. 738 And cogge, And lie, and prate of Law, and pettifogge As craftily (sometimes) as many a one Who divers yeares hath studied Littleton. *a* **1680** Butler *Rem.* (1759) II. 165 He will..rather pettyfog and turn common Barreter, than be out of Employment. *c* **1867** Symonds in *Life* (1895) II. 133 They accepted the whole, and were not trafficking or pettifogging about a portion. **1895** *Westm. Gaz.* 18 June 1/3 'But what is this about a woman lifting up her voice in a law-court and pleading?' —'Oh, in America you can do that in a local police-court; in a mayor's court women may pettifog.'
2. *trans.* **a.** To plead (a case) with legal chicanery. †**b.** *loosely.* To take by petty larceny.
1759 D. Mallet *Wks.* I. 22 He pettyfogs a scrap from authors dead. **1858** *N. York Tribune* 23 Oct. 4/5 [He] saw fit..to address to the Editor..a letter pettifogging the hard case of his master.

†**ˈpettifog,** *a.* and *sb.*¹ *Obs.*
a. *adj.* = Pettifogging. **b.** *sb.* = Pettifogger.
1647 Lilly *Chr. Astrol.* clxxxv. 821 That he shall have both the Civill and Common Lawyer and the pettifog Atturney against him. **1796** Charlotte Smith *Marchmont* III. 44 T'wont do this time—you must try again, old pettifog.

†**ˈpettifog,** *sb.*² *Obs.* Used as a paronomasia on *petty fog* = mist, and *pettifogging.*
1641 Milton *Prel. Episc.* 19 And thus much for this cloud I cannot say rather then petty-fog of witnesses, with which Episcopall men would cast a mist before us.

pettifogger (ˈpɛtɪˌfɒgə(r)). Also 6–7 pety-, 6–9 petty-fogger; 6 petifoger, 7 *dial.* -voguer, petty foger. [Orig. sometimes as two words, *petty fogger*, and later often hyphened, *petti-fogger*, etc. First element petty *a.*, second obscure: cf. fogger¹ (but this was perhaps only a shortening of *petty-fogger*). The general sense seems to be the same as in pettifactor, of about the same age.]
1. A legal practitioner of inferior status, who gets up or conducts petty cases; *esp.* in an opprobrious sense, one who employs mean, sharp, cavilling practices; a 'rascally attorney'.
1564–78 Bulleyn *Dial. agst. Pest.* (1888) 19, I knowe theim verie well; they are two Pettifoggers in the Lawe. **1576, 1577** Pettie fogger [see fogger¹ 1]. **1584** *Leycesters Commw.* (1641) 178 A most wicked Promoter, and wretched Petifoger, enriched himself by other mens ruines. **1592** Nashe *P. Penilesse* (ed. 2) 6 Sergeant, Bencher, Counsailor, Atorney or petifoger. **1602** Carew *Cornwall* 4 b, The worst conditioned and least cliented Petivoguers. **1612** Dekker *If it be not good* Wks. 1873 III. 274 We must all turne petti-foggers, and instead of gilt rapiers, hang buckram bags at our girdles. **1645** Milton *Colast.* Wks. 1851 IV. 365 A meer and arrant petti-fogger, who lately was so hardy, as to lay aside his buckram wallet, and make himself a fool in Print. **1746** H. Walpole *Corr.* (1846) II. 142 He behaved so like an attorney the first day, and so like a pettifogger the second. **1841** Macaulay *W. Hastings* Ess. (1851) 623 The ravenous pettifoggers who fattened on the misery and terror of an immense community. **1873** Longf. *Wayside Inn* iii. *Rhyme Sir Christopher* 35 Morton of Merry Mount, That pettifogger from Furnival's Inn.
†**b.** Sometimes app. a professional name. *Obs.*
1688 R. Holme *Armoury* iii. 63/2 Officers of the Palatinate Courts in Chester. Assizes.. The Sollicitor. The Petty Fogers. Constable of the Castle [etc.]. **1721** *MS. Par. Reg. Campton, Beds.*, 5 Apr., Bur[ied] John Street of Shefford (Pettyfogger).
2. *transf.* A petty practitioner in any department; a tyro; an empiric, pretender.
1602 Herring tr. *Oberndoerffer's Anat.* 41 Laying open the Packe and Fardle of these circumferaneous Iugglers, and pedling Pettifoggers in Physicke. **1670** Eachard *Cont. Clergy* 22 He had much better commit himself to an approved-of cobler or tinker,..than to be only a disesteemed petti-fogger, or empyrick in divinity. **1711** Puckle *Club* §215. 41 That such petty-foggers and retailers of news and politicks..should pretend to teach their rulers how to govern.
3. *Nailmaking.* See quot. and cf. fogger¹ 3.
1871 A. S. Harvey in *Gd. Words* 610 A large proportion of the trade is in the hands of middlemen, called 'foggers', —those who truck being known as 'pettifoggers',—each of whom employs a certain number of nailmakers.
4. A local name of a fish, the rockling.
1880–4 Day *Fishes Gt. Brit. & Irel.* I. 315 *Pettifogger* and *baud* are said to have been two local names in Cornwall for some species of *Motella* [Rockling].
5. *Comb.*, as *pettifogger-like* adj.
1729 Mrs. Delany in *Life & Corr.* 205 It is saucy, impertinent, unmannerly, and pettyfogger-like, to be making comparisons that are odious.

pettifoggery (ˈpɛtɪˌfɒgərɪ). [f. prec. + -y.] Pettifogging practice; legal chicanery.
1653 Milton *Hirelings* 62 The last and lowest sort of thir arguments, that men purchas'd not thir tithe with thir land, and such like pettifoggerie, I omitt. *a* **1693** *Urquhart's Rabelais* iii. xxxvi. 306 Under-hand tricky..Cavilling, Petti-foggery. **1871** *Athenæum* 28 Jan. 83 Code-making..is going on with vigour in South America: and this is not surprising, for the Spaniards left them a legacy of miscellaneous pettifoggery.

pettifogging (ˈpɛtɪfɒgɪŋ), *vbl. sb.* [f. as pettifog *v.* + -ing¹.] The action of a pettifogger; legal trickery; chicanery, pettifoggery; quibbling.
1580 Hollyband *Treas. Fr. Tong, Chicanerie*, pety-fogging. **1611** Cotgr., *Chicanerie*, wrangling, pettifogging; litigious or craftie pleading. **1630** *R. Johnson's Kingd. & Commw.* 171 (France) This Chiquanery (Petti-fogging) and multiplicitie of Pleaders, came first from the Popes Court, when his seat was at Avignon, (as my Author saith). **1651** tr. *De-las-Coveras' Don Fenise* 129, I was forced to spend the greatest part of my goods in suites and pettifoggings, untill I was forced to leave my country. **1843** H. Rogers *Ess.* (1860) III. 80 Number Ninety [Tract for the Times], that singular monument of logical pettifogging.

pettifogging (ˈpɛtɪfɒgɪŋ), *ppl. a.* [f. as prec. + -ing².] Acting as a pettifogger or rascally attorney; mean, shifty, quibbling; also, pertaining to or characteristic of pettifoggers.
1603 Florio *Montaigne* ii. xxxvii, Petty-fogging Lawyer. **1604** T. Wright *Climact. Years* (ed. 2) 12 He was..a petty-fogging Phisitian at his owne costs, as they be petty-fogging Lawyers thorow theyr owne sutes. **1649** Milton *Eikon.* iv, To see some store of their Friends, and in the Roman, not the pettifogging sense, their Clients so neer about them. **1673** Dryden *Amboyna* i. i, This Fiscal, who was..an ignorant Advocate in Rotterdam, such as in England we call a Petty-fogging Rogue. **1759** Sterne *Tr. Shandy* I. xl, The character of this last man, said Dr. Slop,..seems to have been taken from some pettifogging lawyer amongst you. **1837** Dickens *Pickw.* liii, 'You are', continued Mr. Pickwick,..'a well-matched pair of mean, rascally, pettifogging robbers'. **1874** L. Stephen *Hours in Library* (1892) II. iv. 117 The pettifogging cunning which supposes the gossips of lobbies..to be the embodiment of statesmanship.

pettiˈfogulize, *v. nonce-wd.* [f. pettifogger.] *intr.* To quibble. Hence **pettiˈfogulizer.**
1853 De Quincey *Autobiog. Sk.* Wks. I. 59 So far from seeking to 'pettifogulise'—i.e. to find evasions for any purpose in a trickster's minute tortuosities of construction. *Ibid.* 60, I showed so much scrupulosity about the exact value and position of his words, as finally to draw upon myself the vexatious reproach of being habitually a 'pettifoguliser'. **1872** Minto *Eng. Prose Lit.* i. i. 77 This 'petti-fogulising'.

pettigree, obs. form of pedigree *sb.*

†**pettilashery, -lasserie,** obs. corrupt forms of *petty* larceny: cf. larcery.
1591 Greene *Connie Catch.* ii. Wks. (Grosart) X. 118 Commonly..called pilfering or petulacerie. **1592** —— *Black Book's Messenger* ibid. XI. 10 Filching, pettilashery, and such trifling toyes. **1613** R. Cawdrey *Table Alph., Petti-lasserie*, stealing of things of no great value.

pettiloon, colloq. perversion of pantaloon.
1858 Whyte Melville *Tilbury Nogo* 174 Two pair of flannel 'pettiloons', as people call them now, thick winter trousers.

pettily (ˈpɛtɪlɪ), *adv.* [f. petty *a.* + -ly².] In a petty, mean, paltry, or trivial way or manner.
1840 Gen. P. Thompson *Exerc.* (1842) V. 86 Nothing has been too grandly mischievous, or too pettily vexatious, for their doing. **1858** M. Pattison *Ess.* (1889) II. 18 We should rather endeavour a unity of doctrine and spirit among Christians than pettily insist on establishing certain ceremonies. **1883** Stevenson *Silverado Sq.* (1886) 62 They are..pettily thievish, like the English gipsies.

pettiness (ˈpɛtɪnɪs). [f. petty *a.* + -ness.] The quality of being petty; triviality, insignificance; little-mindedness; an instance of this, a petty trait; formerly, a petty or trivial object.
1581 Mulcaster *Positions* ii. (1887) 6 A petie companion, I confesse, but till some better do deale, why may not my petinesse fullwell take place? **1599** Shaks. *Hen. V*, iii. vi. 136 His ransome, which must proportion the losses we haue borne..which in weight to re-answer, his pettinesse would bow vnder. **1660** H. More *Myst. Godl.* v. xv. 175 These pettinesses being below the Divine Majesty to catch at. **1845** Browning *Pictor Ignotus* ad fin., See their faces, listen to their prate, Partakers of their daily pettiness. **1872** Stubbs in *Mem. W. de Coventria* (Rolls) II. Pref. 15 A mean reproduction of all the vices and of the few pettinesses of his family.

ˈpetting, *ppl. a.* [f. pet *v.*¹ + -ing².] That pets. Hence **ˈpettingly** *adv.*, in a petting manner.
1895 Kipling *2nd Jungle Bk.* 180 'Aowa! Aowa!' said Mowgli pettingly, 'I have killed one striped ape.'

petting (ˈpɛtɪŋ), *vbl. sb.* [f. pet *v.*¹ + -ing ¹.]
1. Indulgence, fondling.
1873 Black *Pr. Thule* iii, The young man escaped a great deal of the ordinary consequences of this petting. **1883** Bp. Thorold *Yoke of Christ* (1884) 37 A little tender petting does her a great deal of good. **1889** *Athenæum* 27 Apr. 534/1 His fatherly affection for his children..takes the form of unreasonable petting.
2. In the sense of pet *v.*¹ b: the action of amatory caressing and fondling; non-coital sexual activity. Also *attrib.* See also *heavy petting* s.v. heavy *a.*¹ 13.
1920 [see sense 3 below]. **1922** S. Lewis *Babbitt* xviii. 228 Babbitt had heard stories of what the Athletic Club called 'goings-on' at young parties; of girls 'parking' their corsets in the dressing-room, of 'cuddling' and 'petting', and a presumable increase in what was known as Immorality. **1928** J. P. McEvoy *Show Girl* 11 They have no time to perfect their petting technique. **1929** B. Russell *Marriage & Morals* xii. 126 There is so much 'petting' and 'necking' that the absence of complete intercourse can only be viewed as a perversion. **1933** Auden *Dance of Death* 25 Gay girl to whom petting Matters so much Poor kid, the reason's You're out of touch With flowers and such. **1947** *Partisan Rev.* XIV. 273 When the couple finally reached the stage of mild petting in the living room, Ruth in the kitchen listened with a mixture of pleasure and distaste. **1948** A. C. Kinsey et al. *Sexual Behavior in Human Male* xvi. 531 This behavior is known to the younger generation as petting, although certain other terms are applied to certain types of contacts. Those which are confined to latitudes not lower than the neck are sometimes known as necking, and petting is distinguished from the heavy petting which involves a deliberate stimulation of the female breast, or of the male or female genitalia. *Ibid.*, In the present volume the term 'petting' has been applied to any sort of physical contact which does not involve a union of genitalia but in which there is a deliberate attempt to effect erotic arousal. **1956** S. Ertz *Charmed Circle* 62 Indulging in a pastime that was highly popular with the young... They had been 'necking' or 'petting'. **1958** M. Argyle *Relig. Behaviour* x. 123 '*Petting to climax*' was as common among Kinsey's devout men as for the non-religious. A smaller proportion of Kinsey's devout female sample reported this, but Chesser's devout women reported as much 'petting' as the others. **1960**, etc. [see heavy *a.*¹ 13]. **1971** A. F. Guttmacher *Understanding Sex* iv. 52 There are many degrees of petting, from holding each other in your arms to mutually manipulating the genitals..without actually having sexual intercourse. **1976** *N.Y. Rev. Bks.* 13 May 20/4 Since the time of Kinsey there have been some important changes:.. a decline in petting..and an increase in copulation.

3. *Comb.*, as **petting party**, a social gathering at which petting is the principal activity.

1920 F. SCOTT FITZGERALD *This Side of Paradise* I. ii. 64 That great current American phenomenon, the 'petting party'. **1926** A. HUXLEY *Jesting Pilate* IV. 265 Hymns and the movies and Irving Berlin. Petting Parties and the First Free United Episcopal Methodist Church. Jazz it up! **1934** R. CHANDLER in *Black Mask* Oct. 28/1 The prowl car takes a slant down it [*sc.* the old road] now and then looking for petting parties. **1946** [see *half-virgin* s.v. HALF- II n]. **1973** A. MACVICAR *Painted Doll Affair* viii. 91 Drinking parties, drug parties, petting parties. Mostly youngsters.

pettish ('pɛtɪʃ), *a.* [f. PET *sb.*² + -ISH¹.

But the earliest quots. precede our first example of the sb., and are not clearly connected with it in sense.]

Subject to 'pets' or fits of offended ill humour; in a pet; proceeding from, pertaining to, or of the nature of, a pet; impatiently angry; peevish, ill-humoured, petulant; easily 'put out'.

[**1552** HULOET, Petyshe, *impetuosus*. **1570** LEVINS *Manip.* 145/44 Pétish, *effrænis, iracundus.*] *a* **1591** R. GREENHAM *Wks.* (1599) 12, I am pettish, I am vncomfortable and vnquiet with them, with whom I liue. *a* **1641** BP. MOUNTAGU *Acts & Mon.* iv. (1642) 272 He became pettish, wayward, frantick, bloudy. **1653** SCLATER *Civ. Magistracy* 17 The pettish Israelites (a people seldom if ever, pleased with God's present Providencies) who murmured under Moses. **1666** PEPYS *Diary* 6 Aug., I checked her, which made her mighty pettish. **1794** MRS. RADCLIFFE *Myst. Udolpho* xii, She received the apology with the air of a pettish girl. **1838** LYTTON *Alice* III. vii, This was a very pettish speech in Evelyn. **1873** J. R. GREEN *Letters* (1901) I. 7, I was.. too weak and pettish for the rougher horse-jokes of stronger boys.

† '**pettiship.** *Obs. nonce-wd.* [f. PETTY *a.* + -SHIP.] Littleness; pettiness.

1581 MULCASTER *Positions* xxxviii. (1887) 178 Some petie lowlinges.. will needes seeme like, where their petieship cannot light.

'**pettishly,** *adv.* [f. PETTISH + -LY².] In a pettish manner; peevishly, petulantly.

a **1619** FLETCHER *Mad Lover* III. ii, Poorly, and pettishly, ridiculously To fling away your fortune? **1762** STERNE *Tr. Shandy* V. xxxiii, He kept his fore-finger in the chapter:—not pettishly,—for he shut the book slowly. **1879** MISS BRADDON *Clov. Foot* xii, 'Drip, drip, drip', cried Celia, pettishly, 'one of these odious Scotch mists'.

'**pettishness.** [f. as prec. + -NESS.] The quality of being pettish; peevishness, petulance.

1645 BP. HALL *Remedy Discontents* xiv, To see his bounty contemned out of a childish pettishnesse. **1782** MISS BURNEY *Cecilia* III. iii, Cecilia [was] offended at her pettishness and folly. **1806** *Edin. Rev.* VIII. 162 The.. pettishness of disappointed selfishness. **1865** MRS. WHITNEY *Gayworthys* xxiii. (1879) 228 Her very little pettishnesses and vanities were like the spring breeze.

pettit(e, obs. forms of PETIT.

pettitoes ('pɛtɪtəʊz), *sb. pl.* Rarely in *sing.* Forms: α. *sing.* 6 **pettytoe, petitoe,** 8–9 **pettitoe;** β. *pl.* 6 **pettie toes, petitose,** 6–7 **petitoes,** 7 **petti-,** 7–8 **petty-toes, pettytoes,** 6– **pettitoes.** [Of uncertain origin; but before 1600 taken as PETTY *a.* and *toes*, pl. of TOE. See Note below.]

1. The feet of a pig, esp. as an article of food; pig's trotters; in earlier use the word seems to have included the heart, liver, lungs, etc., not only of the pig, but of calves, sheep, and other animals.

α. **1555** BRADFORD in Strype *Eccl. Mem.* (1721) III. App. xlv. 133 Yf ye haue.. halfe a Loyn of lean mutton: a Pygges Pettytoe, with half a dossen of grene salletts. **1597** *Bk. Cookerie* 53 b, The first course at Supper. A Sallet, a Pigs Petitoe, powdered Beefe sliced. **1725** BRADLEY *Fam. Dict.* s.v. *Pig's pettitoes*, Take Pettitoes.. cut them into halves, and let every Pettitoe be tyed up together.

β. **1589** *W. Darrell's Exp.* in H. Hall *Eliz. Soc.* (1887) 218 For dressinge ye mutton, rabbettes and a pigges pettie toes. **1597** *2nd Pt. Gd. Hus-wiues Iewell* B j b, For a Goose gibluts and pigges petitose. **1598** FLORIO, *Peduccij*, all manner of feete, or petitoes drest to be eaten, as calues, sheepes, neates, or hogs feete, or pigs petitoes. **1607** BEAUMONT *Woman Hater* I. ii, Like the Table of a countrey Justice,.. sprinkled over with all manner of cheap Sallads, sliced Beef, Giblets, and Petitoes. **1683** E. HOOKER *Pref. Pordage's Mystic Div.* 56 To giv the Pettitoes in alms wil not.. satisfi for stealing the Pig. **1793** WOLCOTT (P. Pindar) *Ep. to Pope* Wks. 1812 III. 203 Calves' Heads, Pigs Pettitoes, perform as well. **1861** GEO. ELIOT *Silas M.* x, We can send black puddings and pettitoes without giving them a flavour of our own egoism. *c* **1875** M. JEWRY *Model Cookery* 79/2 When pettitoes are fried they should be first boiled.

† **b.** *fig.* in expressions of contempt. *Obs.*

1644–7 CLEVELAND *Char. Lond. Diurn.* 7 Brereton and Gell; two of Mars his Petty-toes, such snivelling Cowards, that it is a favour to call them so. **1647** WARD *Simp. Cobler* 26 Futilous womens phansies; which are the very pettitoes of infirmity, the gyblets of perquisquilian toyes. **1648** JENKYN *Blind Guide* i. 17 Rather than this petty-toes of a Pope can erre an haires breadth.

2. The feet of a human being, esp. of a child; in quot. 1589 of an ape.

1589 R. HARVEY *Pl. Perc.* (1860) 7 The medling Ape.. did wedge in his pettitoes, so fast betwixt the two clefts that he stucke by the feete for a saie. **1592** LYLY *Midas* III. iii, And you, Cælia, that would fain trip on your petitoes. **1611** SHAKS. *Wint. T.* IV. iv. 619. **1708** T. WARD *Eng. Ref.* (1716) 146 His Grace.. Stood therefore up on Petty-toes. **1884** SALA *Journ. due South* I. xxiv. (1887) 323 The osseous structure of the tiny creature is yet perfect, even to the bones of the pettitoes.

fig. **1653** GAUDEN *Hierasp.* 109 Particular congregations; which are, but as the Pettitoes or little Fingers of the church.

Hence † **pettitoe** *v. intr.* (with *it*), to dance, move about on the toes (*obs.*).

1651 OGILBY *Æsop* (1665) 180 Not in prophaner Arts, like Popish Pigs, To pettitoe-it on the Organs Jigs.

[Note. *Petitoe, -toes*, was in 17th c. taken by some (e.g. Skinner, 1671) as = F. *petite oie* (lit. 'little goose') the giblets of a goose, which is thus given in Cotgrave: '*La petite oye*, the giblets of a Goose; also, the bellie, and inwards or intralls, of other edible creatures.' The extended sense in the second part of this definition is not mentioned by Littré (who has a number of transferred senses of a different kind), and it may really have been an English extension, and may show the actual way in which a word meaning the giblets of a goose was extended to the analogous parts cut off in dressing a pig or other animal. Among these were the feet, to which the pl. *petitoes* would seem naturally to point, and to which it may soon have been appropriated (cf. the quot. from Florio 1598). But if this is the history, it must have taken place within the space of a generation, since the first example of 'a pyges pettytoe' is of 1555, and *pettytoes* was evidently applied to toes or feet by 1589. It is to be noted that Cotgr. has also '*Petitose* [Fr.], the garbage of fowle (an old word)'; but this is not given by Godefroy, and may be some error. It may be worth inquiring whether *petitoe* was not orig. a simple adoption of OIt. *petitto* little, petty, small (Florio), quasi 'petties', petty items.]

pettle ('pɛt(ə)l), *v. Sc.* and *north. dial.* [dim. or freq. of PET *v.*¹: see -LE.]

1. *trans.* To pet, fondle, indulge.

1719 RAMSAY *Answ. to Hamilton* 10 July iv, Sae roos'd by ane of well-kend mettle, Nae sma' did my ambition pettle, My canker'd critics it will nettle. **1781** J. HUTTON *Tour Caves* (ed. 2) Gloss., *Pettle*, to coax, play or toy with. **1808** JAMIESON, *Pet, Pettle*, to fondle, to indulge, to treat as a pet. **1818** SCOTT *Hrt. Midl.* xviii, They harle us to the correction-house in Leith Wynd, and pettle us up wi' bread and water, and siclike sunkets. **1882** J. WALKER *Jaunt Auld Reekie*, etc. 181 Auld Scotland's muse I've coaxed and pettled. **1889** NICHOLSON *Folk-Sp. E. Yorks.* 77.

2. *intr.* To nestle; to cuddle (see CUDDLE *v.* 2).

1855 ROBINSON *Whitby Gloss.*, To *pettle*, to cling to the mother's bosom as a young child. **1876** *Mid-Yorks. Gloss.* s.v., Of a lamb and a sheep together, it will be said of the former, that 'it pettles with its head against the old one'.

pettle, var. PATTLE *sb.*, a plough-staff.

‖ **petto** ('pɛtəʊ). [It. *petto*:—L. *pectus* breast.] The breast: *in petto* (It.), (*a*) in one's own breast or private intention; in contemplation; undisclosed; ¶ (*b*) by confusion with PETTY *a.* (*sb.*¹): in short, in miniature, on a small scale.

1674 BLOUNT *Glossogr.* (ed. 4), *In Petto* (Ital.), in design, in the breast or thought, and not yet put in execution. **1679** J. SMITH *Narrat. Pop. Plot* 2 They reserved them in their *Petto*, to be made use of upon occasion. **1712** S. SEWALL *Diary* 29 Feb., I ask'd the Govr. to take a Copy of it: He said No, It should remain yet in Petto.. and put it in his Pocket. **1712** *Lond. Gaz.* No. 5015/1 There are Seven Cardinals still remaining in Petto, whose Names the Pope keeps Secret. **1772** *Hartford Merc., Suppl.* 18 Sept. 1/1 His Majesty nominated some new Counsellors and Senators, declaring.. that he kept two in *petto*. **1838** EMERSON *Jrnl.* 19 Sept. (1911) V. 53 Such ostentation *in petto* I never did see. **1844** DISRAELI *Coningsby* I. II. ii. 185 He commenced a discourse, which was in fact, one of his 'slashing' articles in petto on Church Reform. **1845** —— *Sybil* IV. xiv, Great constitutional movements in petto. *a* **1846** B. HAYDON *Autobiogr.* (1853) I. 247 Away we marched, my little guide wearing a red night-cap.. till we came in sight of the height, when my grenadier in petto turned round. **1894** W. S. HADLEY *Euripides' Hecuba* p. x, The effect thus produced within the compass of a single play is comparable to that brought about on a larger scale by the older trilogy... This trilogy *in petto* may be regarded as an experiment made by the youngest of the three great tragedians. **1901** KIPLING *Kim* xiii. 341 He represents *in petto* India in transition—the monstrous hybridism of East and West. **1924** T. E. LAWRENCE *Let.* 1 Jan. (1938) 450 Yes, it will be revised, but only in petto. No good cuts or noble changes, no rewriting: just punctuation and insect-blemishes removed. **1937** L. BROMFIELD *Rains Came* II. ii. 258 Mr. Bannerjee's house and garden were a kind of India *in petto*, overcrowded, confused, swarming with noisy life. **1979** *Country Life* 29 Mar. 947/4 In small (or, as people now cheerfully and wrongly say, *in petto*).

pettrel, variant of PEITREL *Obs.*

petty ('pɛtɪ), *a.* (*sb.*¹) Forms: 4–7 **pety, petti,** 6–7 **pettie, petie, pittie,** (6 **peti, pyty**), 6– **petty.** [In late ME. *pety*; phonetic spelling, after Fr. pronunciation, of PETIT, which finally took the place of the earlier form.]

A. *adj.* † **1.** Small (in size or stature); below the ordinary or normal size. *Obs.* exc. in special collocations (see 5).

1393 LANGL. *P. Pl.* C. XVII. 84 And pouerte is a pety [*B.* petit] þyng apereþ nat to hus nauele. *c* **1430** LYDG. *Min. Poems* (Percy Soc.) 45 Go pety quaier, and war where thou appere. **1592** GREENE *Def. Conny Catch* Wks. (Grosart) XI. 68 The Ale-wife vnles she nicke her Pots and Conny-catch her guestes with stone Pottes and petty Cannes, can hardly paye her Brewer.

2. Of small importance, inconsiderable, insignificant, trivial; little-minded, 'small'.

1581 MULCASTER *Positions* Ep. Ded. (1887) 7, I know your Maiesties pacience to be exceeding great in verie petie arguments. **1582** T. WATSON *Centurie of Loue* Ep. Ded., In turning out this my pettie poore flocke vpon the open common of the wide world. **1591** SHAKS. *Two Gent.* IV. i. 52 And I [was banished] for such like petty crimes as these. **1596** —— *Merch. V.* I. i. 12 Your Argosies with portly saile.. Do ouer-peere the pettie Traffiquers. **1597–8** BACON *Ess.*, *Expence* (Arb.) 54 Commonly it is lesse dishonourable to abridge pettie charges then to stoupe to pettie gettings. **1649** JER. TAYLOR *Gt. Exemp.* II. Disc. ix. 124 Extirpate petty curiosities of apparell, lodging, diet. **1666** DRYDEN *Ann. Mirab.* ccxiii, His birth perhaps some petty village hides. **1713** STEELE *Guard.* No. 20 ⁋8 Our petty animosities. **1779–81** JOHNSON *L.P.*, *Denham* Wks. II. 81 Most of these petty faults are in his first productions. **1824** W. IRVING *T. Trav.* II. 112 Those petty evils which make prosperous men miserable. **1871** R. ELLIS *Catullus* i. 4 You of old did hold them Something worthy, the petty witty nothings. **1875** WHITNEY *Life Lang.* viii. 142 It is rather petty to link such an element to the name of an Italian doctor. **1890** GROSS *Gild Merch.* I. 149 General dealers in petty wares.

3. a. Of persons or things in expressed or implied comparison with others: Minor, inferior; of secondary rank or importance; subordinate; on a small scale.

Sometimes hyphened or combined with a sb. as *petyking, pettifalconer, pettie-inne, petty-saint, petty-sphere*, etc. See esp. PETTY BAG, PETTY CANON, and the others mentioned in 5.

1523 in *10th Rep. Hist. MSS. Comm.* App. v. 328 The marchant cheapell of the pittie rode [crucifix] within the cathedral church. **1526** *Pilgr. Perf.* (W. de W. 1531) 22 The principall braunches, the vij gyftes of the holy goost; the iiij pety braunches, the iiij cardynall vertues. **1552** in *Vicary's Anat.* (1888) App. xvi. 313 Suspicious men.. as shalbe thought to bee petie pickers. **1570** FOXE *A. & M.* (ed. 2) 204/2 He [Edgar] being at Chester, viii. kinges (called in histories *Subreguli*) to wit, petykings, or vnderkings, came and did homage to him. **1570** LEVINS *Manip.* 112/7 Petie, *secundarius*. **1575** TURBERV. *Falconrie* 354 The petifalconers and novices which know not what it meaneth. **1613** PURCHAS *Pilgrimage* (1614) 284 Aden and Zibyth, two pettie Kingdomes in Arabia. **1649** G. DANIEL *Trinarch.*, *Rich. II*, ccxxxiv, Now the Machine moues on euery wheele, And Petty-Sphærs contribute to the whole. **1655** FULLER *Ch. Hist.* III. vi. §14 William Wickwane, Arch-Bishop of York.. esteemed a petty-saint in that Age. **1659** WOOD *Life* Mar. (O.H.S.) I. 273 An alehouse or pettie-inne for travellers, called The Chequer. **1665** BOYLE *Occas. Refl.* IV. xvii. (1848) 268 Those petty Thefts for which Judges condemn Men. **1711** ADDISON *Spect.* No. 70 ⁋4 The Barons, who were then so many petty Princes. **1764** GOLDSM. *Trav.* 392, I fly from petty tyrants to the throne. **1831** J. W. CROKER in *C. Papers* 5 Apr., Petty shopkeepers and small farmers. **1879** FROUDE *Cæsar* viii. 70 Mithridates was once more a petty Asiatic prince existing upon sufferance.

† **b.** *petty (petit, pety-) school*: a school for little boys [see B. 1]; a junior or preparatory school. So *petty (petty-) form*, the junior form.

1555–6 *Louth Rec.* (1891) 140 Item paide.. at suche tyme as the petie scole was in making, xls. [**1580** FULKE *Martiall Confut.* IV. Wks. (Parker Soc.) II. 163 Which.. he would not have done in his petite School at Winchester.] **1590** in *Hakluyt's Voy.* (1904) VI. 361 All private and pety-schooles. **1674** *Will J. Storie* (MS.), Poor children taught at a petty school.. till they can go to Wakefield Free School. **1718** HICKES & NELSON *J. Kettlewell* I. ii. 9 He was first put to a petty School. **1746** *Brit. Mag.* 112 He was placed.. near the Bottom of the Petty-Form. **1818** BENTHAM *Ch. Eng.* 116 The career.. from the petty form at Eton or Westminster, up to the examining Chaplain's study.

† **4.** repr. F. *petit*, in *petty master* = PETIT-MAÎTRE; *petty nephew, son* = great-nephew, grandson. *Obs.*

1611 SPEED *Hist. Gt. Brit.* IX. xxiv. §32 One being Petty Nephew, the other Grand-child of Francis the first. **1625** LISLE *Du Bartas, Noe* 124 Joktan, the double Pety-son of Sem, that is whose double grandfather Sem was. **1707** *Reflex. upon Ridicule* 200 A sort of Petty Master, that thinks himself very Modish.

5. In special collocations, as **petty apartheid**, apartheid as exercised in everyday life; racial segregation in its trivial applications (see APARTHEID); **petty average**: see quots. and AVERAGE *sb.*² 2; † **petty boy**: see quot.; † **petty brain** = BRAINLET; † **petty budget**, a small bag; applied attrib. to a lawyer; cf. *petifactor, pettifogger*; **petty cash**, small cash items of receipt or expenditure; also *attrib.*, esp. *petty cash-book*; † **petty coy** = *petty-cotton*: see COTTON *sb.* 7, and quot.; **petty custom, -s**, duty charged upon goods coming to market: see *parva custuma* in CUSTOM *sb.* 4; **petty dancers**, the Northern Lights; **petty exchange**: see quot.; † **petty farm**, the farming of the petty customs; † **petty gladen**, obs. name of Gladiolus; † **petty John**, a small point; **petty orders** = minor orders: see ORDER *sb.* 6; **petty pan**, a small pan (with various local definitions); † **petty panic**, Turner's name for Canary-grass, *Phalaris canariensis*; **petty-point** *Sc.*, some kind of stitch, ? = tent-stitch; **petty rice** = QUINOA; † **petty watch**, an old name of coast-guards; **petty weal**, a petty state, province, etc. [suggested by *common weal*]; † **petty-world**, a microcosm. Also PETTY BAG, PETTY CANON, PETTY CAPTAIN, PETTY GOD, PETTY OFFICER, q.v. as Main words; and *petty* CAPE, CHAPMAN, -WOMAN, CONSTABLE, JUROR, JURY, LARCENY, SERGEANTY, -TRY, SESSION, SINGLES, TALLY, TITHE, TREASON, VIEW, and names of plants, as *petty* COTTON, MADDER, MOREL, MUGWORT, MULLEIN, SPURGE, WHIN: for which see these sbs.

1966 *Cape Argus* 8 Apr. 14 While separate development proceeds so slowly, the Government, for home consumption, makes demonstrations of strength on the *petty apartheid front. 1971 *Rand Daily Mail* 10 June 12 You can just imagine what it feels like when you have to use a lift which is marked 'Goods only'; when you have to wait for the train in a cage-like sort of place, packed like sardines; when you have to buy food at a snack bar only through a window at the back. I think all these are what a sound mind can classify as petty apartheid. 1974 *Black Panther* 9 Feb. 15/4 Last week the Johannesburg City Council announced measures to eliminate what is called here 'petty apartheid'. These are practices of discrimination against the city's Blacks and coloreds not imposed by national law. 1977 *Time* 27 June 20/1 There have been some changes in 'petty apartheid'. Whites boast that 'international' hotels have been opened to blacks, and that blacks now participate in white sports, which has great symbolic meaning. 1848 ARNOULD *Mar. Insur.* III. v. (1866) II. 829 Small charges occurring regularly in the usual course of the voyage..are called *petty averages. 1865 [see AVERAGE *sb.*[2] 2]. 1867 SMYTH *Sailor's Word-bk.*, *Petty average*, small charges borne partly by a ship, and partly by a cargo, such as expenses of towing, &c. 1688 R. HOLME *Armoury* III. 292/1 A *Petty Boy, or a Shoomakers petty Boy..Instruments belonging to the Cordwiners Occupation: and are used generally for their burnishing and smoothing down the Stitches, and to pair pieces of Leather upon. 1668 CULPEPPER & COLE *Barthol. Anat.* III. Introd. 127 The contained [parts] are the Brain, the *Petty-brain, and the Marrow. *c*1550 *Wyll of Deuyll* (1825) B iv, To euery of these *Pety bouget men of law and Tearmers, a couple of Geldynges. 1834 J. BOWRING *Min. Mor.*, *Perseverance* 139 Jonas kept what is called the *petty cash in the merchant's counting-house, that is, he was charged with the payment of all the small sums for the ordinary expenses of the business. 1839 DICKENS *Let.* *c* 18 Feb. (1965) I. 509 He was not quite correct in the facts of the 'petty cash' story, the realities of which are far more honorable to the noble fellows concerned. 1858 SIMMONDS *Dict. Trade*, *Petty Cash-book*, a book for entering small receipts and payments. 1886 A. W. THOMSON *Text-bk. Princ. & Pract. Bk.-Keeping* iii. 37 When a number of small payments need to be made..a separate book called the Petty Cash Book is kept for recording such payments. 1922 JOYCE *Ulysses* 171 He went towards the window and, taking up the petty cash book, scanned its pages. 1974 *Terminol. Managem. & Financial Accountancy* (Inst. Cost and Managem. Accountants) 57 *Petty cash book*, a separate record of small cash receipts and payments. 1736 AINSWORTH, *Petty coy (herb), *Gnaphalium minus* [app. meaning *Filago minima*]. 1442 *Rolls of Parlt.* V. 63/1 Your grete Customes and *petit Customes there. 1450 *Ibid.* 188/1, xl li. in the pety Custume of London. 1482 *Ibid.* VI. 200/2 Of oure petite Custume in oure Port of London. 1723 *Lond. Gaz.* No. 6154/1 An Act..for discontinuing Payment of the Petty-Port Customs [at Edinburgh]. 1635 L. FOXE *Voy. N. West* (Hakl. Soc.) II. 313 At clocke 12, there was *Pettiedancers or henbanes (as some write them) North in the firmament, betokening a storme, to follow within 24 houres. 1888 A. H. MARKHAM in *Gd. Words* Feb. 118/2 These luminous patches occasionally seen with auroræ are, I think, the same so frequently alluded to by the old navigators as the 'pettie dancers'. 1682 SCARLETT *Exchanges* 2 This Exchange is two-fold, viz. An Exchanging of Monyes for Monyes, one Coyn or sort for another; and a giving of Money upon Exchange for a Bill, &c. The former of these is *Petty Exchange, the latter Real. 1707 E. CHAMBERLAYNE *Pres. St. Eng.* III. III. 384 Commissioners..have the whole Charge and Management of all her Majesty's Customs, (the *Petty-farms excepted) in all the Ports in England. 1601 HOLLAND *Pliny* II. 92 The *pety Gladen or Sword-grasse. *Ibid.* 99 In the range of these bulbous and onion-rooted plants, some place the root of Cyperus, that is to say, of Gladiolus (*i.* Petie-gladen, Flags, or Sword-wort). 1640 BROME *Sparagus Gard.* II. iii, I have a many small jests, *petty Johns, as I call 'hem. 1644–7 CLEVELAND *Char. Lond. Diurn.*, etc. Poems, etc. (1677) 104 It is a Maxime..That the only way to win the Games is to play Petty Johns. 1679 V. ALSOP *Melius Inquirend.* II. v. 291 To call them [i.e. Christ's institutions] the Circumstantials, the Accidents, the minutes, the Punctilios, and, if need be, the Petty-Johns of Religion. 1727–41 CHAMBERS *Cycl.* s.v. *Orders*, The *petty, or minor Orders, are four: viz. those of door-keeper, exorcist, reader, and acolyth... Those in petty orders may marry without any dispensation. 1714 MRS. MANLEY *Adv. Rivella* 62 The Daughter of a poor *Petty-pan Merchant. 1825 JAMIESON, *Pettie-pan*, *s.* a white-iron mould for pastry. 1905 *Eng. Dial. Dict.* Suppl., *Petty pon*, a small, round, earthenware pan in which mince-pies and other tarts are baked. 1562 TURNER *Herbal* II. 85, I haue as yet heard no English name of Phalaris, but for lak of a better name it may be called *peti panik, of the likenes that it hath with the ryght panic. 1632 in *14th Rep. Hist. MSS. Comm.* App. III. 235 Ane waistcott of grein taffitie, wroght with *pettie-point. 1825 JAMIESON, *Pettie-point*, a particular kind of sewing stitch. 1858 SIMMONDS *Dict. Trade*, *Petty-rice*, a name in Peru for the white seeds of *Chenopodium quinoa*. 1372 *Rolls of Parlt.* II. 314/2 De chescun Hundred des Countees sur la Mer sont trovez sur la garde de Mier pur Enemys aliens certeins gentz q'est appelle *Petti-Wacche. 1628 WITHER *Brit. Rememb.* 202 Should the Common-wealth herself oppose These corporations..it would scarce obtaine That pow'r which could these *Petty-weales restraine. 1605 CAMDEN *Rem.* 7 A *pettie world within himselfe.

B. *sb.* **1.** †**a.** A little boy at school; a boy in a lower form; a junior schoolboy. *Obs.*

1589 NASHE *Martins Months minde* To Rdr. 7 Some of them..were the Petties and Punies of that schoole, whereof old Martin was the master. 1600 HOLLAND *Livy* III. xliv. 117 There were the schooles for peties kept, of reading and writing. 1607 *Stat.* in *Hist. Wakefield Gram. Sch.* (1892) 71 This schole is not ordained for petties but for grammarians. 1617 MINSHEU *Ductor*, A Petie in his crosse rowe..an ABC scholler. *a*1670 HACKET *Abp. Williams* I. (1692) 37 Mr. Lamb..came by holding fast to Fortune's middle finger, from a schoolmaster that taught petties, to a Proctor in Christian Courts. 1855 THACKERAY *Newcomes* iv, A junior ensign being no more familiar with the Commander-in-Chief at the Horse Guards..than the newly-breeched infant in the Petties with a senior boy in a tailed-coat.

fig. 1613 JACKSON *Creed* II. xiv. §8 The School of Christ, in which all in this life are but 'parvuli', petties or children. 1619 W. SCLATER *Exp. 1 Thess.* (1630) 26 Euen of such petties amongst vs, Papists haue taken notice so farre, as by them to make our Church odious.

b. A school or class for small boys.

*c*1810 W. HICKEY *Mem.* (1913) I. ii. 13, I however soon got out of that disgraceful and ignorant form, passed with rapidity and *eclat* the under and upper petty, and entered into the upper first. 1961 R. WILLIAMS *Long Revolution* 133 The 'petties' or 'ABCs' were proper schools.

2. A privy or latrine; = *little-house* (LITTLE *a.* 13).

Widely prevalent in familiar use.

1848 M. J. STANLEY *Let.* 27 Sept. in N. Mitford *Ladies of Alderley* (1938) 206 If these houses had been built by his Lordship every one would have had his *petty*, at all events dividing the odour. 1961 E. WILLIAMS *George* I. vii. 87 It was a nice little cottage.., with a lot of neglected garden and a tumbledown petty. *Ibid.* II. xi. 151 Mam..hated the petty for being attached to next door's.

petty ('pɛtɪ), *sb.*[2] Familiar abbrev. of PETTICOAT *sb.*

1915 T. BURKE *Nights in Town* 63 There..was young Beryl, superintending her aunt's feverish struggles with paint and powder-jars, frocks, petties,..and wraps. 1939 JOYCE *Finnegans Wake* I. 87 The litigants..were egged on by their supporters in the shape of betterwomen with bowstrung hair of Carrothagenuine ruddiness, waving crimson petties and screaming from Isod's towertop. 1971 *Guardian* 24 Aug. 9/1 The language of lingeries..petties and pretties, and frillies.

petty-auga, -auger, corrupt ff. PIRAGUA.

Petty Bag, petty-bag. *Obs.* exc. *Hist.* [See quot. 1658.] An office formerly belonging to the Common Law jurisdiction of the Court of Chancery, for suits for and against solicitors and officers of that court, and for process and proceedings by extents on statutes, recognizances, *scire facias*, to repeal letters patent, etc.: see also CLERK 6 c.

1631 in *Crt. & Times Chas. I* (1848) II. 102 Some forty officers more of the same court, as cursitors, filazers, petty bags, hanaper, &c. 1631 WEEVER *Anc. Fun. Mon.* 440 Clarke of the Petit Bagge. 1648 C. WALKER *Hist. Independ.* I. 83 Mr. Pury the Petty-bag Office, besides 1000*l.* formerly given him. 1654 GATAKER *Disc. Apol.* 45 A Gentleman, one of the Petti-Bag, who pretended a Title. 1658 PHILLIPS s.v., Clerks of the Petit bag, three officers of Chancery who record the return of all inquisitions out of every Shire, all liveries granted in the Court of Wards, make all Patents of Customes, Gaugers, Controllers, etc., each record being put in a petit or little leather bag; whence they had the denomination of Clerks of the Petit bag. 1797 *Monthly Mag.* III. 48 The specification of this bridge, as enrolled in the Petty bag office. 1852 DICKENS *Bleak Ho.* i, Maces, or petty-bags, or privy-purses..all yawning. 1896 SCARGILL-BIRD *Guide Pub. Rec.* (ed. 2) Introd. 14 By Stat. 11 & 12 Vict., c. 94, the Clerks of the Petty Bag were reduced to a single Clerk, and the office was finally abolished in 1889.

petty 'bourgeois. [f. PETTY *a.* (*sb.*[1]) as anglicization of Fr. *petit* + BOURGEOIS *sb.*[1] and *a.*] = PETIT BOURGEOIS. Also (occas. with hyphen) *attrib.* or as *adj.*

1888 S. MOORE tr. *Marx & Engels's Manifesto of Communist Party* 24 In countries where modern civilization has become fully developed, a new class of petty bourgeois has been formed. *Ibid.* 26 German Socialism recognised..its own calling as the bombastic representative of the petty bourgeois socialism. 1904 in R. C. K. Ensor *Mod. Socialism* xx. 289, I reckon, the life of the petty bourgeois,..is an unhappy one. 1906 E. M. AVELING tr. *Plechanoff's Anarchism & Socialism* iii. 26 His [*sc.* Max Stirner's] 'League of Egoists' is only the Utopia of a petty bourgeois in revolt. *Ibid.* iv. 35 Proudhon was the most typical representative of petty bourgeois socialism. 1931 *Times Lit. Suppl.* 26 Feb. 141/3 It is for its intellectual critics, whom it first degrades by the question-begging epithet 'petty-bourgeois', that Bolshevism reserves its cruellest penalties. 1936 'M. INNES' *Death at President's Lodging* vii. 133 Our Inspector's petty-bourgeois passion for the till. 1943 H. READ *Politics of Unpolitical* 15 According to Dr. Fromm, Hitler succeeded so well because he was able to combine the qualities of a resentful petty-bourgeois..with those of an opportunist ready to serve the interests of the German industrialists and Junkers. 1951 C. W. MILLS *White Collar* I. ii. 30 It is..a feature of such petty-bourgeois life that extreme repression is often exercised in its patriarchal orbit. 1958 I. MURDOCH in N. Mackenzie *Conviction* 230 This mass is now quiescent, its manner of life largely suburban and its outlook 'petty bourgeois'. 1960 D. LESSING *In Pursuit of English* I. 13 These are not the real working-class. They are the lumpen-proletariat, tainted by petty-bourgeois ideology. 1974 J. WHITE tr. *Poulantzas's Fascism & Dictatorship* III. ii. 111 The Nazi Party was filling the whole State apparatus..with members of petty-bourgeois origin and with their own quite specific petty-bourgeois ideology. 1977 *Time* 24 Jan. 14/3 Italian Communist Party..spokesmen have denounced the leftists as 'petty bourgeois' hoodlums. 1978 *Encounter* Feb. 36/2 The 'people' is what the petty bourgeois of the spirit transform all men and women into.

'petty bourgeoi'sie. [f. as prec. + BOURGEOISIE.] = PETIT BOURGEOISIE.

1850 *Red Republican* 16 Nov. 171/1 The petty Bourgeoisie, the inferior ranks of the middle-class, the small manufacturers, merchants, tradesmen, and farmers, tend to become Proletarians. 1920 F. E. GREEN *Hist. Eng. Agric. Labourer 1870–1920* v. 125 The farmers and the petty bourgeoisie took possession of the Parish and the Rural District Councils. 1924 G. B. SHAW *Saint Joan* Pref. p. xiii, In short, much more of a young lady, and even of an intellectual, than most of the daughters of our petty bourgeoisie. 1930 tr. *Marx & Engels's Communist Manifesto* iii. 56 In the countries where modern civilization flourishes, a new petty bourgeoisie has come into being. This class hovers between the proletariat and the bourgeoisie. 1956 C. W. MILLS *Power Elite* xiv. 329 Classic conservatism has required the spell of tradition among such surviving elements of pre-industrial societies as an aristocracy of noble men, a peasantry, a petty-bourgeoisie with guild inheritances. 1957 R. N. C. HUNT *Guide to Communist Jargon* 118 Generally speaking, Marx and Engels understood by the petty-bourgeoisie the small traders who, they contended, were being driven down into the proletariat by the monopolist capitalists. 1969 A. G. FRANK *Latin Amer.* xix. 312 The next layer may be termed the middle class of petty bourgeoisie. It comprises a large variety of economic walks of life—small landowner, professional, merchant, clergy, government and white collar worker, small politician—but it affords considerable lateral mobility within it, from one occupation to another. 1975 *Times Lit. Suppl.* 14 Mar. 270/4 In Havana in 1827,..a higher proportion of coloureds were legitimately married than of whites. This black 'petty bourgeoisie' was, however, dispersed..in the repression of 1844 and the terms of the racial stratification system were redefined to the advantage of the whites.

†**'petty 'canon, ,petti'canon.** *Obs.* Also 6 **petichanon**, 7 **peticanon**, 8 **petit-canon**. A Minor Canon: see CANON *sb.*[2] 2.

1530 PALSGR. 253/2 Pety cannon, *uicaire*. 1546 *Mem. Ripon* (Surtees) III. 15, ix Chauntries..the Incumbentes wherof be bounde to be presente in the Quere of the saide Churche at all the service..and be named Petichanons. 1556 *Chron. Gr. Friars* (Camden) 71 Thei..went in to the pettycannons and fowte there. 1661 J. BARNARD *Praelat. Ch. Eng.* 25 That the Vicars, Peticanons, singing men and boyes, with the rest be turned into Schollers. 1769 *De Foe's Tour Gt. Brit.* III. 136 One Dean, and seven Prebendaries..besides Petit-canons, Singing-men, and Choristers.

†**'petty 'captain, ,petti'captain.** *Obs.* Also 5 **pety-capteyne**, 6–7 **petit-capteyn**, etc.: see PETTY, PETIT, CAPTAIN. An officer below a captain; a lieutenant. Also formerly used to render various ancient titles, e.g. centurion.

*c*1420 LYDG. *Assembly of Gods* 635 As for pety capteyns many mother wase. *Ibid.* 1093 Whyle these pety-capteynes susteyned thus the feelde. 1489 CAXTON *Faytes of A.* III. ix. 185, I telle the that the pety captayne whiche is vndre the captayne princypall may not godely doo this. 1526 TINDALE *Matt.* xxvii. 54 When the pety Captayne..sawe the erth quake. 1548 *Privy Council Acts* (1890) II. 160 Every captain to give yearely ij[s]; every petit-captein xij[d]. 1563 GOLDING *Cæsar* (1565) 30 The old beaten soldiers, and the peticapteynes [*centuriones*], and those that had the charge of the men of armes, were sore troubled. 1586 J. HOOKER *Hist. Irel.* in *Holinshed* II. 95/1 Holland, petit Captaine to the earle of Salisbury. 1633 T. STAFFORD *Pac. Hib.* I. i. 12 Two shillings by the day for a petty Captaine.

pettycoite, -cote, obs. forms of PETTICOAT.

†**petty 'fidian.** *Obs. nonce-wd.* [f. PETTY *a.* + L. *fid-ēs* faith + -IAN.] One 'of little faith'.

1647 TRAPP *Comm. Matt.* viii. 26 *O ye of little faith.* Ye petty fidians; He calleth them not nullifidians. *Ibid.* xiv. 31 Thou petty-fidian, small-faith: Christ chides Peter, and yet helps him.

†**'petty 'god, 'pettigod.** *Obs.* Also 6 **petit God**, **petigod**, **petti-god**, etc. [f. PETTY *a.* + GOD.] A minor or inferior deity, a demigod. So †**,petty'goddess.**

1581 J. BELL *Haddon's Answ. Osor.* 508 Renouncing the necessary helpes of pettygodds and pettygoddesses, intercession is made here onely vnto Christ. 1585 FETHERSTONE tr. *Calvin on Acts* viii. 13 This man, whom the Samaritans counted a petit God. 1600 J. PORY tr. *Leo's Africa* I. 39 They honour those doctours and priests,..as if they were petie-gods. 1610 BP. HALL *Apol. Brownists* xlv, The maiestie of Romish petti-gods..was long agone, with Mithra and Serapis, exposed to the laughter of the vulgar. *a*1716 BLACKALL *Wks.* (1723) I. 504 Putting up Prayers to the Saints departed, as to a sort of petty Gods in Heaven.

petty-'minded, *a.* [MINDED *ppl. a.* III.] Having or characteristic of a mind that dwells on the trivial and ignores what is important. So **petty-'mindedness.**

1909 *Daily Chron.* 10 June 7/4 Weakness and petty-mindedness were fostered by the narrow sphere and limited outlook that..such tasks necessitated. 1927 V. WOOLF in *Forum* (N.Y.) May 707 It was all so paltry, weak-blooded, and petty-minded to care so much at her age. 1954 T. S. ELIOT *Confid. Clerk* I. 25 He's not petty-minded—though nothing escapes him. 1963 W. SOYINKA *Dance of Forests* 57 Is the nation to ignore the challenge of greatness because of the petty-mindedness of a few cowards and traitors. 1978 *Times* 24 Jan. 14/5 This..petty-minded change of policy.

petty-oager, corruption of PIRAGUA.

petty officer. [PETTY *a.* 3.]

1. *generally.* A minor or inferior officer.

1577–87 HOLINSHED *Chron.* I. 53/2 Petie officers to oversee and overrule the people. 1598 BARRET *Theor. Warres* III. ii. 45 There be many petie officers vsed amongst vs. 1603 SHAKS. *Meas. for M.* II. ii. 112.

2. *spec.* An officer in the navy corresponding in rank to a non-commissioned officer in the army.

1760 C. JOHNSTON *Chrysal* (1822) III. 14, I need not describe to you the situation of a petit officer. 1768 J. BYRON *Narr. Patagonia* (ed. 2) 28 It was very hard upon us petty officers. 1840 R. H. DANA *Bef. Mast.* xx. 60 He had been a petty officer on board the British frigate Dublin. 1867 SMYTH *Sailor's Word-bk.*, *Petty officer*, a divisional seaman of the first class, ranking with a sergeant or corporal.

petuis, obs. Sc. form of PITEOUS.

petulacerie: see PETTILASHERY.

petulance ('pɛtjʊləns). [a. F. *pétulance* (1529 in Hatz.-Darm.), ad. L. *petulāntia*: see next and -ANCE. (In sense 2, influenced by *petted, pettish,* etc.)] The fact or quality of being petulant.

1. Wanton, pert, or insolent behaviour or speech; self-assertiveness; wantonness, immodesty; sauciness, insolence; rudeness. Now *rare* or *Obs.*

1610 B. JONSON *Masque Oberon* 159 Satyrs, leave your petulance, And go frisk about and dance. **1656** STANLEY *Hist. Philos.* VI. (1701) 243/1 Behave not your self towards Greece Tyrannically or Loosely, for one argues Petulance, the other Temerity. **1728** YOUNG *Love Fame* II. 105 But time his fervent petulance may cool; For tho' he is a wit, he is no fool. **1791** BOSWELL *Johnson* an. 1738 (1816) I. 94 The Petulance with which obscure Scribblers..treat men of the most respectable character and situation. **1816** J. GILCHRIST *Philos. Etym.* 196 To repel the petulance of hollow upstart pretension. **1818** SCOTT *Hrt. Midl.* x, With the petulance of youth she pursued her triumph over her prudent elder sister.

b. A petulant or saucy expression.

1741 in *Richardson's Pamela* (ed. 2) I. Introd. 26 Naughty contains, in one single significant petulance, twenty thousand inexpressible delicacies! **1851** CARLYLE *Sterling* II. iii. (1872) 112 At times too he could crackle with his dexterous petulances, making the air all like needles round you.

2. Peevish or pettish impatience of opposition or restraint; peevishness, pettishness.

1784 COWPER *Task* I. 456 The spleen is seldom felt where Flora reigns; The low'ring eye, the petulance, the frown. **1820** W. IRVING *Sk. Bk.* I. 102 The same weakness of mind that indulges absurd expectations, produces petulance in disappointment. **1848** W. H. KELLY tr. *L. Blanc's Hist. Ten Y.* I. 251 Charles X.'s appearance was tranquil,..but the sight of a bit of tricoloured ribbon, or a slight neglect of etiquette, was enough to excite his petulance. **1876** J. SAUNDERS *Lion in Path* iv, Her face wore something of a disappointed child's wistfulness and petulance.

petulancy ('pɛtjʊlənsɪ). [ad. L. *petulāntia*, n. of quality f. *petulānt-em* PETULANT: see -ANCY.]

†**1.** = PETULANCE 1. *Obs.*

1559 W. CUNNINGHAM *Cosmogr. Glasse* 38 So folishe (whether it sprong of petulancye, or ignoraunce, I knowe not) as to affirme the Heauens to be flat. **1598** MERES *Pallad. Tamia* 275 b, Lasciuiousnesse and petulancie in poetrie mixt with profitable and pleasing matters is very pestilent. **1604** R. CAWDREY *Table Alph.*, *Petulancie*, wantonnes, saucines. **1646** J. HALL *Horæ Vac.* 152 Pride and petulancy are inseparable companions of victory. **1673** *Lady's Call.* II. ii. §14 God..will not make acts of repeal to satisfie the petulancy of a few masterless women. **1712** STEELE *Spect.* No. 528 ¶1 A certain lascivious Manner which all our young Gentlemen use in Publick, and examine our Eyes with a Petulancy in their own, which is a downright Affront to Modesty. **1748** CHESTERF. *Lett.* (1774) I. 350 The frequentation of Courts checks this petulancy of manners.

2. = PETULANCE 2. *rare.*

1712 STEELE *Spect.* No. 370 ¶1 The Petulancy of a peevish old Fellow, who loves and hates he knows not why, is very excellently performed by..Mr. William Penkethman. **1884** TENNYSON *Becket* I. iii, Thou goest beyond thyself in petulancy!

petulant ('pɛtjʊlənt), *a.* (*sb.*) Also 7-8 erron. **petulent.** [a. F. *pétulant* (1350 in Hatz.-Darm.), ad. L. *petulānt-em*, pr. pple. of **petulāre*, dim. of *petĕre* to aim at, seek, quasi 'to aim at or assail in jest'. In sense 3, which is not found in L. or Fr., app. influenced by *petted, pettish.*]

1. Forward or immodest in speech or behaviour; wanton, lascivious. Now *rare.*

1599 MARSTON *Sco. Villanie* III. xi, Deride me not, though I seeme petulant To fall into thy chops. *a* **1625** FLETCHER & MASS. *Laws Candy* II. i, I have been both nurs'd and train'd up to Her petulant humours, and been glad to bear them. **1683** TRYON *Way to Health* 277 Corrupted..amongst Lascivious and Petulent Men and Women, through various sorts of Vncleannesses, which are against God's Law. **1783** HAILES *Antiq. Chr. Ch.* ii. 20 Amongst the lively, petulant, and licentious inhabitants of Alexandria. **1859** G. MEREDITH *R. Feverel* III. v. 128 The air of petulant gallantry.

2. Pert; saucy; insolent; rude. Now *rare.*

1605 B. JONSON *Volpone* III. ii, Look, see, these petulant things, How they have done this! *c* **1611** CHAPMAN *Iliad* XIX. 27 The petulent swarm Of flies. **1650** BULWER *Anthropomet.* 256 A kind of Back-biting mockery, proceeding from mans petulant wit and invention. **1693** DRYDEN *Disc. Orig. & Progr. Satire* Ess. (Ker) II. 23 The petulant scribblers of this age. **1729** T. COOKE *Tales, Proposals*, etc. 124 Mr. Theobald is treated in so unhandsome, foolish, and petulant, a Manner, thro the Dunciad. **1849** MACAULAY *Hist. Eng.* vii. II. 175 He is..as fair a mark as factious animosity and petulant wit could desire.

3. Displaying peevish or pettish impatience and irritation, especially on slight occasion.

1755 JOHNSON, *Peevish*, petulant, waspish, easily offended. **1782** MISS BURNEY *Cecilia* v. iii, He was grown so ill-humoured and petulant. **1830** D'ISRAELI *Chas. I*, III. v. 72 Laud was petulant, passionate, and impatient of contradiction. **1856** EMERSON *Eng. Traits, Manners* Wks. (Bohn) II. 46 The Englishman is very petulant and precise about his accommodation at inns, and on the road. **1874** GREEN *Short Hist.* viii. §2. 470 The address was met by a petulant scolding from James. **1888** HUME *Mme. Midas* I. iii, With a petulant gesture she hurled the rose out of the window.

B. *sb.* A petulant person (esp. in sense A. 3).

1682 SHADWELL *Lanc. Witches* I. Wks. 1720 III. 225 Come, good petulant, Mr. Chop-logick, pack up your few books..And leave my house. **1755** *Man* No. 2. 4 Can satire be too sharp for such petulants? **1893** T. M. HEALY in *Westm. Gaz.* 2 Nov. 2/1 Hostile journalists..pursued Mr. Parnell at the outset of his Parliamentary career as a bore, a blunderer, and a petulant.

'**petulantly,** *adv.* [f. prec. + -LY².] In a petulant manner; insolently, wantonly; pertly; with peevish or pettish impatience.

1610 HEALEY *St. Aug. Citie of God* I. i. (1620) 2 Those.. most petulantly insulting ouer Christs seruants. **1717** PARNELL *Homer's Batrachom.* II. Poems (1722) 88 My flow'ry Wreaths they petulantly spoil, And rob my chrystal Lamps of feeding Oil. **1838** EMERSON *Misc. Papers, Milton* Wks. (Bohn) III. 300 Johnson petulantly taunts Milton with 'great promise and small performance'. **1881** W. COLLINS *Bl. Robe* ii, I am sorry I spoke so petulantly and so unfairly.

petulate ('pɛtjuːleɪt), *v. rare*⁻¹. [f. PETUL(ANT *a.* + -ATE³.] *trans.* To make petulant or peevish. In quot. as *ppl. adj.*

1897 [see HYPERSENSITIZE *v.*].

†**pe'tulcous,** *a. Obs. rare.* [f. L. *petulcus* butting, wanton, frisky (f. *petĕre* to aim at, assail, etc.: cf. *hiulcus* gaping, f. *hiāre* to gape) + -OUS.] Butting; wantonly aggressive.

1661 CANE *Fiat Lux* iii. §13 (1665) 151 The Pape.. whistles him and his fellow petulcous rams in order by charitable admonition.

So †**pe'tulcity,** offensive forwardness or temerity.

1628 T. MORTON *Let. to Bp. Hall* in H.'s Wks. 1837 IX. 408, I do, therefore, much blame the petulcity of whatsoever author, that should dare to impute a Popish affection to him.

‖**petun** (pɪ'tʊn, 'pɛtʊn), *Obs.* Forms: 6-8 **petum,** 7 **pitum,** 7- **petun.** [a. F. *petun* (in 16th c. also *petum*), a. Guarani *petỹ* (nasalized *y*, nearly = F. *un*).] A native South American name of tobacco, formerly partially in English use.

[**1547-55** tr. *Captivity H. Stade* II. xxii. (Hakl. Soc.) 147 The soothsayer..fumigates it with a herb which they call Bitún.] **1577** FRAMPTON *Joyful News* II. 42 b, Many haue giuen it the name, *Petum*, which is in deede the proper name of the Hearbe, as they whiche haue traueiled that Countrey can tell. **1600-14** *Newe Metamorphosis* (N.), Petun [*erron.* Puten]..Tobacco cald, most soveraigne herbe approved, And nowe of every gallant greatly loved. **1616** SURFL. & MARKH. *Country Farme* 219 To make triall of this hearbe, caused the wound of a dogge to be rubbed with sublimate, and then presently after to be applied the juice of Petum, together with the substance and all. **1630** J. TAYLOR (Water P.) *Wks.* (1630) (N.), Whereas..the hearb (alias weed) ycleped tobacco, (alias) trinidado, alias, petun, alias, necocianum, a long time hath been in continuall use and motion. **1763** tr. *Charlevoix' Acc. Voy. Canada* 239 (Stanf.) A sort of Petun, or wild tobacco, grows everywhere in this country. [**1874** BURTON in *Captivity H. Stade* (Hakl. Soc.) Introd. 65 In the Brazilian tongue the terminal -y was pronounced mostly like the Greek ypsilon and the French U. Thus, Pity, tobacco, was phonetically written Betum and Pitun. **1893** *Syd. Soc. Lex.* s.v., When they [the Caribs] smoked it, they called it tabaco, and when they snuffed it, petun.]

pe'tuncle. *rare.* [a. F. *pétoncle* (1555 in Hatz.-Darm.), ad. L. *pectuncul-us*, dim. of *pecten* a scallop.] A small scallop-shell.

1854 BADHAM *Halieut.* 42 The best nidus for all kinds of coquillages, oysters, scallops, the petuncles (whence we derive our purples).

petune (pɪ'tjuːn), *v.* [a. F.*petune-r* (1612 in Hatz.-Darm.) to smoke tobacco, f. *petun*: see PETUN.] *trans.* To spray (tobacco) with a liquid intended to produce flavour or aroma.

1902 in WEBSTER *Suppl.*

petunia (pɪ'tjuːnɪə). *Bot.* [mod.L. (Jussieu 1789), f. PETUN: so called from its close botanical affinity to the tobacco plant.]

1. A genus of ornamental herbaceous plants (N.O. *Solanaceæ* or *Atropaceæ*) nearly allied to tobacco, natives of South America; they bear white, violet or purple, and variegated funnel-shaped flowers. Also, a plant or flower of this.

1825 *Curtis's Bot. Mag.* LII. 2552 *Petunia Nyctaginiflora.* Large-flowered Petunia... Found by Commerson on the shores of Rio de Plata. **1846** LINDLEY *Veg. Kingd.* 621 Solanaceæ... Genera..ii. Petunia. **1861** WHYTE MELVILLE *Good for Nothing* II. 169 A splendid confusion of verbena, petunia, anemone, and calceolaria spangled with spots of gold. **1882** *Garden* 25 Mar. 202/3 The Petunia, although a perennial, may also be successfully grown as an annual.

2. The dark violet or purple colour of the petunia. Also *attrib.*

1891 *Daily News* 19 Jan. 3/1 Woollen materials..in dark tones of red, russet,..violet, pansy, dahlia, petunia, &c. **1892** *Ibid.* 18 June 3/3 The yoke was of petunia velvet with a deep frill of lace. **1894** *Westm. Gaz.* 26 June 8/2 The Duchess wore a very rich costume of petunia and black.

‖**petuntse** (peɪ'tʊntsə, pɪ'tʌntsə). Also 8-9 **petunse, petuntze,** 9 **pehtuntse.** [Chinese (Mandarin) *pai-tun-tzə*, f. *pai* (dial. *peh, pe*) white, *tun* a mound, stone + *-tzə*, a formative ending. Also in F. *pétunsé.*] A white earth, prepared in China by pulverizing and levigating a partially decomposed granite, probably a mixture of kaolin with quartz and felspar; used in combination with kaolin in the manufacture of Chinese porcelain. The name has also been applied to similar earths prepared in other countries. Also *attrib.*

1727-41 CHAMBERS *Cycl.* s.v. *Porcelain*, There are two kinds of earths..used in the composition of porcelain..the second, called petunse, is a plain white, but exceedingly fine, and soft to the touch. *Ibid.*, For the finer porcelains, they use equal quantities; four parts of kaulin to six of petunse for moderate ones; and never less than one of kaulin to three of petunse, for the coarsest. **1764** CROKER *Dict. Arts & Sc.* s.v. *China-Ware*, The preparation of petunse is by pounding the stone till it be reduced to a very fine powder. **1794** SULLIVAN *View Nat.* I. xxix. 440 Felt spar, or petuntze, is generally opaque. **1868** DANA *Min.* (ed. 5) 475 The petuntze (peh-tun-tsz) of the Chinese..is a quartzose feldspathic rock, consisting largely of quartz. **1879** J. J. YOUNG *Ceram. Art* 53 The manufacture of hard porcelain was begun at Sèvres in 1769, the quarries of St. Yrieix supplying both the kaolin and petuntse. **1883** *Binns' Guide Worc. Porcelain Wks.* 14 Petuntse is the decomposed granite rock found in Cornwall. Composed of quartz, felspar partially decomposed, and a talcose material.

petuous, petwys, obs. forms of PITEOUS.

petwood ('pɛtwʊd). [Corruption of Burmese name *hpet-wŭn* or *pet-woon* (Watt *Dict. Econ. Prod. Ind.* 1889).] A large timber tree, *Berrya Ammonilla* or *mollis*, N.O. *Tiliaceæ*, found in Burma, Southern India, Sri Lanka, the Philippines; also its timber, called also *Trincomalee wood.*

1866 *Treas. Bot.*, Petwood, *Berrya mollis.* [**1902** J. S. GAMBLE *Man. Ind. Timbers* (ed. 2) 107 The Trincomali Wood... Petwŭn, Burm.; Halmillila, halmilla, Cingh. (whence the specific name).]

pety, petyte, obs. forms of PETTY, PETIT.

petycioun, -cyon, obs. forms of PETITION.

petygre, -grewe, -gru, obs. ff. PEDIGREE *sb.*

petygree, butcher's broom: see PETTIGREE.

†**petypernaunt, petyperny.** *Obs.* Usually in *pl.* Forms (pl.): 5 **pety (peti) perna(u)ntes, perneis, perneux, perneys, pernollys, pernys.** [Derivation of second element uncertain: perh. *pernant* = *prenant*, pr. pple. of *prendre* to take.] A kind of pastry, app. akin to *pain puff* (PAIN *sb.*²).

The *n* has often been printed as *u* (*v*) by editors, etc.

c **1390** *Form of Cury* (1780) 89 The Pety Pernaunt [*printed* -uaunt.]. Take male Marow..powdour of Gyngur,..datis mynced, raisons of coraunce,..& loke þat þou make þy past with ȝolkes of Ayren, & þat no water come þerto; and fourme þy coffyn, and make up þy past. *c* **1430** *Two Cookery-bks.* 50 *Pety Pernollys.*.. Take marow of bonys, to or .iij. gobettys, & cowche in þe cofynn; þan take pouder Gyngere, Sugre, Roysonys of coraunce, & caste a-boue [etc.]. *Ibid.* 51 Pety Pernauntes. *Ibid.* 58, 59 (Bills of fare) Pety perneux. *c* **1450** *Ibid.* 74 *Auter peti pernantes.* Take and make thi Coffyns as hit is a-for said [etc.]. *c* **1460** J. RUSSELL *Bk. Nurture* 499 Kut of þe toppe of a payne puffe..Also pety perneys be fayre and clene. *Ibid.* 748 Pety perneis may not be exiled. **1513** *Bk. Keruynge* in *Babees Bk.* 271 Gelly, creme of almondes,.. petypernys, quynces bake.

petzite ('pɛtsaɪt). *Min.* [Named 1845 by W. Haidinger, after W. Petz, a chemist, who analysed it: see -ITE¹ 2.] Telluride of silver, containing a variable amount of gold.

1849 J. NICOL *Min.* 477 The petzite of Haidinger is the same species. **1868** DANA *Min.* 51 Petzite... Differs from hessite in gold replacing much of the silver... Color between steel-gray and iron-black, sometimes with pavonine tarnish.

peucedaneous (pjuːsɪ'deɪniːəs), *a. Bot.* [f. mod.L. *Peucedaneæ*, f. *Peucedanum*, a. Gr. πευκέδανον the herb hog's fennel (f. πεύκη pine + ἔδανον eatable, food): see -EOUS.] Belonging to the *Peucedaneæ*, a suborder of *Umbelliferæ*, having the genus *Peucedanum* for type.

1858 in MAYNE *Expos. Lex.* **1866-77** WATTS *Dict. Chem.* IV. 386 Umbelliferous plants of the peucedaneous tribe.

peucedanin (pjuː'sɛdənɪn). *Chem.* [f. *Peucedan-um* (see prec.) + -IN¹.] A neutral substance ($C_{12}H_{12}O_3$) contained in the root of masterwort, *Peucedanum* (*Imperatoria*) *Ostruthium*, and other umbelliferous plants; also called *imperatorin.*

1840 *Penny Cycl.* XVIII. 51/1 *Peucedanin*, a peculiar principle obtained from the *peucedanum officinale*, or sea sulphur-wort... The name of peucedanin was given by Schlatter. **1866-77** WATTS *Dict. Chem.* IV. 386 Peucedanin crystallises in light, transparent, colourless, shining prisms.

peucyl ('pjuːsɪl). *Chem.* [f. Gr. πεύκη pine + -YL.] An oily hydrocarbon obtained from turpentine-oil: also called *terebilene.*

1857 MILLER *Elem. Chem.* III. 442 The liquid hydrochlorate has been termed hydrochlorate of peucyl. **1866-77** WATTS *Dict. Chem.* IV. 387 *Peucyl*, syn. with *Terebilene.*

peuish, peule, obs. ff. PEEVISH, PULE.

Peulh (pɜːl), *sb.* and *a.* Also 8 Pholey, 9 Pul(ah), Púl(l)o, 9– Peul, Pul(l)o; Peuhl. [Native name; prop. the sing. of FULAH.] = FULAH *sb.* and *a.*

[**1611** BIBLE *Isaiah* lxvi. 19, I will send those that escape of them unto the nations, to Tarshish, Pul and Lud.] **1799** M. PARK *Trav. Afr.* (ed. 2) ii. 17 The Foulahs (or Pholeys)..are chiefly of a tawny complexion, with soft silky hair, and pleasing features. **1858** H. BARTH *Trav. N. & Cent. Afr.* II. xxxiv. 414 A Mohammedan kingdom engrafted upon a mixed stock of pagan tribes,—the conquest of the valorous and fanatic Púllo chieftain, A'dama, over the great pagan kingdom of Fúmbiná. *Ibid.* IV. lvii, 143 If any African tribe deserves the full attention of the learned European, it is that of the Fúlbe (*sing.* Púllo), or Fula, as they are called by the Mandingoes. **1876** G. A. L. REICHARDT *Gram. Fulde Lang.* p. xiii, (*heading*) Indroduction to a grammar of the Pul language... The proper and indigenous name for the Fulahs, as we have called them, is Pulo. *Ibid.* p. xiv, We find a strong Pulo empire in a northwesterly direction, from the upper course of the Jaliba. **1883** R. N. CUST *Mod. Lang. Afr.* I. x. 158 This language..is known by many names, Fula,..Púlo, Pulah,..; its meaning is said to be 'light brown', as opposed to that of the neighbouring people, Wolof or 'black'. **1898** A. J. BUTLER tr. *Ratzel's Hist. Mankind* III. v. xi. 296 Fulbe or Fulah (sing. Pullo, Peul) is the Mandingo name, Fellani the Houssa... These names seem to indicate the lighter colour of their skin. **1915** A. WERNER *Lang. Families Afr.* vi. 100 We have..referred to the Fula language... The people who speak it call themselves Ful-be (in the singular, Pulo). **1921** F. W. TAYLOR *First Gram. Adamawa Dial. of Fulani Lang.* 6 The people whose language is the subject of this book call themselves Pullo in the singular and Fulbe in the plural. **1931** W. B. SEABROOK *Jungle Ways* III. ii. 199 Women walked in groups, with long black robes and faces of pale ivory, cameo-cut... These special women, notoriously beautiful as a race,..were Peuhls. **1932** W. L. GRAFF *Lang.* 154 Peul, Wolof, and Serere, three languages of the above-mentioned African group. **1935** G. GORER *Africa Dances* II. 159 The Peulh women were remarkable for their lighter skin and sharper features. **1959** *Encounter* Sept. 36/1 M. Diallo belongs to the Peulhs, a fascinating people..spread throughout the sub-Saharan regions of Africa. **1973** *Guardian* 19 June 18/1 The Tuareg and Peul nomads have ..watched the bulk of their scrawny animals die.

‖**peulvan, -ven** (pølvɑ̃). *Archæol.* [Fr. *peulven* (1837 in Ernault, 1876 in *Compl. Dict. Acad.*), *peulven* or *peulvan* (1879 in *Dict. Acad.*), a. Breton *peûlvan* (Le Pelletier 1752), dial. Quiberon *palwen* (Ernault), f. *peûl* stake, pillar (= Welsh *pawl*, L. *pālus*) + *van*, mutate of *man* appearance, figure, statue (Le Pelletier, Legonidec, etc.), or ? *ven*, mutate of *men* stone, or ? merely formative suffix (Loth, Ernault).] An upright long stone, an undressed stone pillar of prehistoric age; properly applied to those existing in Brittany.

1851 SIR F. PALGRAVE *Norm. & Eng.* I. 469 When will Druidical archæologists be convinced that menzhir and peulven, cromlech and kistvaen tell us nothing? **1859** JEPHSON *Brittany* xi. 182 It would puzzle many an engineer of the present day to..balance a peulvan or rocking-stone. **1889** *Jrnl. Anthrop. Inst.* XIX. 73 An 'inclined dolmen', and four peulvens, or small upright stones, 1 m. 45 to 3 m. high.

peun, pe-une, obs. forms of PEON.

peur(e, obs. forms of POOR, PURE.

Peutingerian (pjuːtɪnˈdʒɪərɪən), *a.* [f. proper name *Peutinger* (ˈpɔɪtɪŋər) + -IAN.] Of or belonging to Peutinger: in ***Peutingerian table***, a map on parchment of the military roads of the ancient Roman empire, supposed to be a copy of one constructed about A.D. 226.

This was found in the 15th c. in a library at Speyer, and came into the possession of Konrad Peutinger of Augsburg (1465–1547), in whose family it remained till 1714; it is now in the Imperial library at Vienna.

1796 MORSE *Amer. Geog.* I. 23 An ancient set of maps, called the Peutingerian Table or map [*note*, found by Conrad Celtes, and purchased by Conrad Peutinger a burgomaster of Augsburg, from whom it derives its name]. **1834** *Encycl. Brit.* (ed. 7) X. 391/2 The Peutingerian Table ..forms a map of the world, constructed on the most singular principles. *Ibid.*, The Peutingerian Table serves as a specimen of what were called *Itinera Picta*, the 'painted roads' of the ancients, intended for the clearer direction of the march of their armies.

peutral, -il, variants of PEITREL *Obs.*

†**peve'rade.** *Obs. Cookery.* Also 4–5 -arde; 4 pevorat, pevrate. [app. f. ONF. *peivre* pepper + -ADE.] A sauce of which pepper was an important ingredient: cf. POIVRADE.

c **1390** *Form of Cury* in Warner *Antiq. Culin.* 25 Pevorat for veel and venyson. **14..** *Anc. Cookery* ibid. 64 Pevrate sause. *Ibid.* 79 Boor in peverarde, or braune in peverarde. *c* **1430** *Two Cookery-bks.* 11 Brawn en Peuerade. *c* **1450** *Ibid.* 71 Brawne in peu[er]ard.

pevett, obs. form of PIVOT.

pew (pjuː), *sb.*[1] Forms: 4 puwe, 5 pywe, peawe, 5–7 pewe, 5–9 pue, 7 piew(e, 6– pew. [Late ME. *puwe, pywe, pewe*, app. orig. identical in form with OF. *puye, puie, poye* fem., parapet, balustrade, balcony:—L. *podia*, pl. of *podium* elevated place, height, also, balcony, parapet, balcony in the Roman theatre where the emperor sat, a. Gr. πόδιον base, pedestal, dim. of πούς, ποδ- foot. The Lat. sing. *podium* gave OF. *pui, poi, puz, pou, peu* height, hill, mount, hillock, mole-hill, mod.F. *puy* hill, mount. But there are gaps alike in the form-history and sense-history of the word: see *Note* below.]

†**1.** A raised standing-place, stall, or desk in a church, to enable a preacher, reader, or other officiant to be seen and heard by the congregation; often with defining word, as ***minister's pew***, a pulpit, ***prayer*** or ***praying pew***, ***reading*** or ***reader's pew***, the desk at which the service is read, a lectern, ***shriving pew***, a confessional seat, a ***pew for penance***, etc. *Obs.*

Quot. 1470–85 is obscure; it has been suggested to mean a chantry chapel.

[**1470–85** MALORY *Arthur* XIV. iii. 644 He fonde a preest redy at the aulter, And on the ryght syde he sawe a pewe closyd with yron.] **1479** *Bury Wills* (Camden) 50 My body to be beryed in the pariche cherche of Euston be for the chaunsell dore by syde the pue. **1487–8** *Rec. St. Mary at Hill* 130 Item, for naylles for þe schryvyng peawe, ob. **1529** MORE *Dyaloge* I. Wks. 127 Vpon yᵉ sondaye at high masse time..for fulfillinge of hys penance, vp was the pore soule set in a pew, that yᵉ peple might wonder on him and hyre [sic] what he sayd. **1548** *Churchw. Acc. St. Michael, Cornhill* in Heales *Hist. Pews* I. 43 Payd to the Ioyner for takynge downe the Shryuyng pew. **1550** BALE *Eng. Votaries* II. 31 b, To laye stones of great wayghte vpon the roufe beames of the temple ryght ouer hys prayenge pewe, and to lete them fall vpon hym to hys vtter destruccyon. **1568** *Churchw. Acc. St. Peter, Chepe* in Heales 38 Paid for ii matts for the pewe wherein Mʳ Parson saithe the service. **1640** FULLER *Joseph's Coat, Christning Serm.* 170 Passe from the Font to the Ministers pue. **1640** C. HARVEY *Synagogue* xii, I doubt their preaching is not alwaies true, Whose way to th' Pulpit's not the reading Pue. **1641–1848** [see READING *vbl. sb.* 10 b]. **1646** BP. MAXWELL *Burd. Issach.* in *Phenix* (1708) II. 264 Two always speak, the first from the Reader's Desk or Pew, the other in some other place distant from him. **1662** *Bk. Com. Prayer, Commination*, The Priest shall, in the Reading-Pew or Pulpit, say: [1549–1604 shall go into the pulpit and say thus:]. **1692** BURNET *Sarum Visit. Art.* in Heales *Hist. Pews* I. 39 Have you in your said Church or Chappel a convenient seat or Pew for your minister to read Divine Service in?

2. a. A place (often enclosed), usually raised on a footpace, seated for and appropriated to certain of the worshippers, e.g. (in early use) for women only, for a great personage (***patron's***, ***royal***, ***lord's***, ***squire's pew***) or for a family (***family pew***); in the latter case often a quadrangular enclosure or compartment containing a number of seats.

1393 LANGL. *P. Pl.* C. VII. 144 Among wyues and wodewes ich am ywoned sitte Yparroked in puwes. **1427–8** *Rec. St. Mary at Hill* 67 For certeyne pavynge & mevynge of pewes in the cherche. **1453** *Will Wm. Wyntringham* (Lambeth), Et volo quod in muro ad sedile vocatum anglice *pewe* nuper dicte Katerine fiat scriptura sculpta in auricalco ex opposito sepulturam meam. *c* **1460** J. RUSSELL *Bk. Nurture* 917 Prynce or prelate..or any oþer potestate, or he entur in to þe churche, be it erly or late, perceue all þynge for his pewe þat it be made preparate, boþe cosshyn, carpet, & curteyn, bedes & boke, forgete not that. **1479–81** *Rec. St. Mary at Hill* 100 For the makynge of a nywe pywe. **1494–5** *Ibid.* 215 For makyng of the pewes for the pore pepull, and j pew at the Northe dorre, and ij benches, and the pewes in Sent steven Chapell. **1496–7** *Ibid.* 225, xij foot of borde, elmyn, to kneyl on In the pews. **1511** FABYAN *Will* in *Chron.* Pref. 3, I will that my Corps be buried atwene my pewe and the highe awter wᵗʰin the qwere of the parisshe churche of Alhalowen of Theydon Gardon. **1517–18** in Swayne *Sarum Churchw. Acc.* 59 For the pewys thys yere xs. vd. **1529** WOLSEY in Ellis *Orig. Lett.* Ser. I. II. 10 Goyng this day owt of my pue to sey masse, your lettres..wer delyueryd vnto me. **1540** *Ludlow Churchw. Acc.* (Camden) 6 Ffor whiche pewe the seide baylifes have awardede that the seide Richarde Langforde shalle content and paye to the Churche wardeyns..the some of vis. viijd. **1572** *Wills & Inv. N.C.* (Surtees) I. 369 My bodye to be buried wᵗʰin the parishe churche of thorneton in the strett in the closyd or pew wherin I vse to sitt. **1625** BACON *Apophth.* Wks. 1879 I. 328/1 Sir Thomas More..did use, at mass, to sit in the chancel; and his lady in a pew. And because the pew stood out of sight, his gentleman-usher..came to the lady's pew, and said 'Madam, my lord is gone'. **1637** POCKLINGTON *Altare Chr.* iv. 28 The prophanenesse that is, and may be, committed in close, exalted Pewes. **1644** EVELYN *Diary* 6 Mar., The rest of the congregation on formes and low stooles, but none in pewes as in our Churches, to their greate disgrace. **1663–4** PEPYS *Diary* 28 Feb., St. Pauls..The Bishop of London..sat there in a pew made a' purpose for him by the pulpitt. *a* **1696** AUBREY *Lives* (1898) I. 273 Under the piewes (*alias* hogg-sties) of the north side of the middle aisle. **1766** BLACKSTONE *Comm.* II. xxviii. 429 Pews in the church..may descend by custom immemorial (without any ecclesiastical concurrence) from the ancestor to the heir. **1842** F. E. PAGET *Milf. Malv.* 211 Asking your consent to the removal of your pew, and the substitution of an open sitting in its place. **1845** G. A. POOLE *Churches* vii. 74 A man has no right, because he is rich,..to perch his coronet on the top of his canopied pue. *Ibid.* xiv. 143 The close-hearted worshipper in a canopied pue, with tables and a fire-place, behind crimson curtains. **1865** TROLLOPE *Belton Est.* i, The squire was once more seen in the old family pew at church. **1904** H. LITTLEHALES in *Rec. St. Mary at Hill* I. Introd. Note 22 As early as 1496 it was customary for certain parishioners to have pews allocated to them... There were special pews for the poor people,..pews for men,..and for women.

fig. **1653** MILTON *Hirelings* 85 His Sheep oft-times sit the while to as little purpose of benefiting as the Sheep in thir Pues at Smithfield.

b. Now commonly applied to the fixed benches with backs, each seating a number of worshippers (usually four to six or eight), with which the area of a church or chapel is now usually filled, except for the passages affording access to these seats.

In most churches these have now superseded the earlier 'family pew' (see 2); but in the earlier quotations it is often uncertain which are meant.

Pew, as the place of a layman or member of the congregation, is often opposed to *pulpit*: cf. c.

1631 WEEVER *Anc. Fun. Mon.* 573 Dead bodies of the Nobilitie whose funerall trophies are wasted with deuouring time and..seates or Pewes for the Townesmen, made ouer their honorable remaines. **1654** WHITLOCK *Zootomia* 139 You may take away the Pewes, where all the Pulpitarians. **1665–9** BOYLE *Occas. Refl.* III. vi. (1848) 159 As if all that belongs to Ministers, and their Flocks, could be perform'd in the Pulpit, and the Pew. **1691** *Weesils* I. 5 The Neighboring Wives already slight me too, Justle to the Wall, and take the Upper Pew. **1706–7** FARQUHAR *Beaux' Strat.* II. ii, The Verger..Inducts me into the best Pue in the Church. **1868** DICKENS *Let. to Miss Dickens* 18 Jan., It was very odd to see the pews crammed full of people.

c. *transf.* The people who occupy the pews, the worshippers or congregation; the hearers as opposed to the preacher.

1882 J. PARKER *Apost. Life* I. 74 How can we preach to a people unprepared to hear?—A prepared pulpit should be balanced by a prepared pew. **1901** *Contemp. Rev.* Mar. 323 As is the pew, so is the pulpit.

d. Loosely, a seat, esp. in phr. *take a pew*. *colloq.*

1898 BELLOC *Mod. Traveller* i. 5 Be seated; take a pew. **1903** WODEHOUSE *Prefect's Uncle* xvi. 230 The genial 'take a pew' of one's equal inspires confidence. **1914** C. MACKENZIE *Sinister St.* II. III. vii. 652 Come in, you chaps... I don't know any of your names, but take pews, take pews. **1926** I. MACKAY *Blencarrow* xiii. 116 'Have a pew?' he offered, making himself as small as possible on the red plush car seat. **1939** R. LEHMANN *No More Music* 90 Colonel: (drawing up a chair) Take a pew. **1958** B. HAMILTON *Too Much of Water* xi. 232 Have the pew. I'll squat on the bed. **1974** K. ROYCE *Trap Spider* ii. 30 Sit down, Spider. Take a pew.

†**3. a.** A raised seat or bench, for persons sitting in an official capacity, as judges, lawyers, etc.; a rostrum used by public speakers or by academic disputants, etc.; an elevated station, 'stump', or stand for persons doing business in an exchange or public place; a 'box' in a theatre. *Obs.* exc. as transf. from 2.

1558 PHAER *Æneid* VII. Tj, This was both minster, court and hall, Here stoode theyr offryng pewes, and many a slaughter downe did fall [Virgil VII. 175 Hoc illis curia templum, Hæ sacris sedes epulis]. *c* **1600** *Timon* II. iv, From whence doe yee hale him? from the pewes of most wicked iudges. **1600** HOLLAND *Livy* III. lxiv. 132 Duillius then.. caused the Consuls to be called into their owne pues and seates. **1629** WADSWORTH *Pilgr.* iii. 15 Six other of their companions disputing three against three in two pewes one ouerthwart the other. **1644** EVELYN *Diary* 3 Feb., One side is full of pewes for the Clearkes of the Advocates, who swarme here [the Palais, Paris] (as ours at Westminster). *a* **1661** HOLYDAY *Juvenal* x. 187 But ne're Did silly lawyers blood the pew besmear. **1668–9** PEPYS *Diary* 15 Feb., Did get into the play:..but I sat so far I could not hear well, nor was there any pretty woman that I did see, but my wife, who sat in my Lady Fox's pew with her. **1678** BUTLER *Hud.* III. iii. 623 To this brave Man, the Knight repairs For Counsel, in his Law-affairs; And found him mounted, in his Pew. **1894** SALA *London up to Date* 80 In the seventeenth century ..there were shops inside the Hall [Westminster Hall] itself; and scriveners had their desks, and usurers their 'pews'.

b. *transf.* Station, situation; allotted place.

c **1400** *Pety Job* 555 in *26 Pol. Poems* 139 Ye lat me peyne here in a peynfull pewe, That ys a place of grete doloures. **1607** DEKKER *Knts. Conjur.* ix. (1842) 72 The Elisian Gardens... The very Pallace wher Happines her selfe maintaines her Court... Women!..scarce one amongst fiue hundred has her pewe there. **1673** *Char. Quack-Astrologer* B iij b, And placing the Planets in their respectiue Pues.

4. *attrib.* and *Comb.*, as ***pew-bench***, ***-cushion***, ***-desk***, ***-door***, ***-end***, ***-holder***, ***-keeper***, ***-mate***, ***-opener***, ***-seat***, ***-shutter***, ***-woman***; **pew-chair**, †**pew-dish**: see quots.; **pew-gallery**, a gallery of pews; **pew group** *Pottery*, figures on a high-backed bench, usu. in salt-glazed stoneware; **pew-mate**, a fellow occupant of a pew, a 'pewfellow'. Also PEWFELLOW, -RENT, etc.

1898 *Westm. Gaz.* 4 June 4/2 The grave is nearly covered by a *pew bench. **1875** KNIGHT *Dict. Mech.*, **Pew-chair*, a seat affixed to the end of a pew so as to occupy a part of the aisle when seats in excess of the pew accommodation are required. **1862** H. MARRYAT *Year in Sweden* II. 260 Some idle boy had carved his initials on the *pew-desk. **1654** GATAKER *Disc. Apol.* 67 Pleading for the setled and immoveable Font.., which the Presbyterians, he saith, have brought to a moveable and unsettled *Pue-dish. **1491–2** *Rec. St. Mary at Hill* 173 For a peyre of henges for the *pewe dore. **1520** *Will G. Gough* in *Surrey Archæol. Jrnl.* 184 My body to be buried in erth at my pew dore within our Lady Chapell of my parish Church. **1713** STEELE *Guardian* No. 65 ¶1 Clattering the pewdoor after them. **1803** G. COLMAN *John Bull* I. i. 4 Troth! and myself..was brought up to the church... I opened all the pew doors at Belfast. **1842** Pew-door [see UNACCOMMODATED *ppl. a.*]. **1874** MICKLETHWAITE *Mod. Par. Churches* 34 *note*, Fantastically-shaped *pew-ends. **1848** B. WEBB *Cont. Ecclesiol.* 173 There was a kind of *pew-gallery on each side of the chancel. **1906** G. W. & F. A. RHEAD *Staffs. Pots* xiv. 170 The British Museum '*pew group'..is one of four known pieces of the kind, all evidently by the same hand. **1942** *Burlington Mag.* Oct. 260/1 Most dangerous are the increasingly skilful fakes of Astbury and Whieldon figures, first betrayed by the marks of Wedgwood on a pew group and Ralph Wood on a figure of similar origin. **1961** L. G. G. RAMSEY *Connoisseur New Guide Antique Eng. Pott., Porc. & Glass* 39 Aaron Wood (1717–85), to whom have been attributed also the vigorous and amusing salt-glaze 'Pew Groups', modelled in the round and representing a man and woman courting, a pair of musicians, etc. **1976** *Country Life* 5 Feb. 278/1 These.. Staffordshire salt-glaze groups are still referred to as pew groups, where everyone by now is aware that these people.. are not seated in church..but are on a wooden settle. **1845** *Ecclesiologist* IV. 257 The *pue-holder may lock up his pue and absent himself from Church. **1887** A. Abbott in Gladden *Parish Problems* 70 A double organization, the communicants or spiritual body..being one, and the congregation of pewholders..the other or secular body. **1742** Richardson *Pamela* III. 233 Where..it might be more likely seen by the *Pew-keepers. **1596** Colse *Penelope* (1880) 165 But if you needes will puling sit, A *pew-mate for you am I fit. **1782** Miss Burney *Cecilia* IX. v, To perform her promise with the *Pew Opener. **1853** 'C. Bede' *Verdant Green* I. vi, Seeing no beadle, or pew-opener..to direct him to a place. **1886** Ruskin *Præterita* I. 282 There was no beadle to lock me out of them [churches], or *pew-shutter to shut me in. **1810** S. Green *Reformist* II. 17 He..would have given the *pew-woman a shilling to have let him into a pew.

[*Note.* The phonological relation of *puwe, pywe, pewe,* to OF. *puye, puie,* offers difficulties. For the sense, cf. 16th c. Dutch (Brabantish) *puye* or *puyde* (which must have been taken from OF.). Plantin 1573 has '*een Puye,* vn lieu eleué au marché, ou contre l'hostel de la ville, pour proclamer arrests, ou publier ordonnances'; Kilian 1599, '*Puye, puyde,* podium, pulpitum, suggestus, suggestum, rostra, suggestus lapideus'; Hexham 1678, '*Puye,* a Pue, or place elevated in a Market, to Proclaim or to Cry of any thing'; cf. mod.Du. *de pui* the front of a town-hall or other building. Of the L. sing. *podium,* Du Cange gives one of the mediæval senses as 'Lectrum, analectrum in ecclesia, ad quod gradibus ascenditur', i.e. a lectern or reading-desk in a church, to which one ascends by steps; in Italian, Florio (1598) has '*poggio,* a hill or mounting side of a hill, a blocke to get vp on horsebacke'. (So occasionally in Eng. *horse-pew* = horse-block: see *N. & Q.* 10th s. IV. 27, 8 July 1905.) These point to the series of senses: base or raised structure to mount or stand on; raised place to stand on in making a public speech or proclamation, 'stump', rostrum; esp. in a church, a raised lectern, reading-desk, pulpit, or the like; whence, generally, place elevated above the floor for any purpose; particularly, sitting place on a raised base. But it is not impossible that this last sense, which seems to be peculiar to Eng., may have originated in that of 'balcony, balustrade' (see the Etymology), esp. if the name was first applied to a range of seats raised against the wall.]

pew, *sb.*² [a. OF. *peu,* var. of *pel,* pl. *peus,* mod.F. *pieu* a pointed stake, a large stick shod with iron.] A long-handled pointed prong, for handling fish, blubber, etc.

1861 L. de Boileau *Recoll. Labrador Life* 29 The Fish are not taken out [of the seine] by hand, but by an instrument called 'a pew', which is a prong with one point. **1883** *Fisheries Exhib. Catal.* 197 Fish forks and pews used in storing and handling the catch.

pew, *sb.*³ *Sc.* [Onomatopœic: partly echoic, partly expressive of the action: cf. PEW *v.*²]

† **1.** The thin cry of a bird, esp. of the kite. *Obs.*

c **1470** Henryson *Mor. Fab.* XIII. (*Frog & Mouse*) xix, The gled..pyipand with mony pew. **1513** Douglas *Æneis* VII. Prol. 125 The soir gled quhislis loud wyth mony ane pew. **1552** Lyndesay *Monarche* 1451 Byrdis, with mony pietuous pew Afferitlye in the air thay flew.

2. A fine stream of breath forced through an aperture in the lips; a thin stream of air or smoke.

1824 Mactaggart *Gallovid. Encycl.* (1876) 389 There's no a pue o' reek in a' the house. **1895** Crockett *Men of Moss-Hags* xviii. 126 Sending up a heartsome pew of reek into the air, that told of the stir of breakfast. *Ibid.* xliv. 312 With a pew of blue smoke, blowing from its chimney.

3. *to play pew*: to make the slightest sound, utterance, or exertion. (Always with negative expressed or implied.) Cf. PAW *sb.*²

1728 Ramsay *Last Sp. Miser* xxix, He never mair play'd pew. **1808–18** Jamieson s.v., *He canna play pew,* he is unfit for any thing. **1819** Scott *Br. Lamm.* xxiv, I couldna hae played pew upon a dry humlock.

pew, *v.*¹ [f. PEW *sb.*¹]

1. *trans.* To furnish or fit up with pews.

1449 [see *pewing* below]. **1634–5** Brereton *Trav.* (Chetham Soc.) 81 St. Nichol-church..as neat pewed..as any..in England. **1686** in A. Laing *Lindores Abbey* xx. (1876) 242 It was agreed that the Kirk be pewed. **1766** *Hist. Pelham, Mass.* (1898) 119 The Town Has agreed on a Method to Pew or Repair the Meeting House. **1861** Freeman in *Life & Lett.* (1895) I. v. 321 The Normans are inferior to the Gascons in this, that they pew their churches and sometimes lock them. **1894** *Speaker* 12 May 524/2 The ..benchers plastered it and pewed it and galleried it and whitewashed it [the Temple Church].

2. To shut up in or as in a pew.

1609 W. M. *Man in Moone* (1857) 100 To pick a pocket, or pervert some honest man's wife he would on purpose be pued withall. **1831** *Examiner* 71/1 The same men who were as willingly pewed in the parish church as their sheep were in night folds. **1855** Bailey *Mystic* 59 Order loftier than the mind of man Pews in its petty systems.

Hence **pewed** *ppl. a.*; ˈ**pewing** *vbl. sb.* (also *concr.* pews collectively).

1449 in Heales *Hist. Pews* I. 33 In..makyng of pleyn desques & of a pleyn Radeleft and in puying of the said chirch nouȝt curiously but pleynly. **1454** in *Test. Vetusta* 289 To the fabric of the churche of Herne, viz. to make seats called puyinge, x marks. **1840** W. Dyott *Diary* 31 July (1907) II. 322, I visited the old church at Ashbourne to admire the new pewing and other highly ornamental improvements. **1848** B. Webb *Contin. Ecclesiol.* 77 A most miserable pued and galleried preaching-room. **1874** Micklethwaite *Mod. Par. Churches* 32 The pewed part of the church. **1884** J. Cubitt in *Contemp. Rev.* XLVI. 113 Nothing in his [Wren's] parish churches..impresses common observers more unpleasantly than the pewing. **1970** H. Braun *Parish Churches* i. 20 The Victorian church, ..packed with pewing and comfortably behassocked.

pew, pue (pjuː), *v.*² [Echoic: cf. PEW *sb.*³ 1.] *intr.* To cry in a plaintive manner, as a bird.

1398 Trevisa *Barth. De P.R.* XII. xxvi. (Tollem. MS.), The kyte..whan he hungreþ, he secheþ his mete pewynge [*ed.* 1535 wepynge] with voyce of pleynynge and of mone. **1530** Lyndesay *Test. Papyngo* 698 We sall gar cheknis cheip, and geaslyngis pew. *Ibid.* 763, I maye nocht pew, my panes bene sa fell. **1549** *Compl. Scot.* vi. 39 The chekyns began to peu quhen the gled quhissillit. *a* **1586** Sidney *Arcadia* III. (1622) 398 The birds likewise with chirps, and puing could Cackling, and chattering, that of Ioue beseech.

†**pew,** *int. Obs.* Also **peugh.** An utterance of contempt or derision: = POOH, PHEW.

a **1625** Fletcher *Noble Gent.* III. i, Pew, nothing, the law Salicke cuts him off. **1638** Ford *Lady's Trial* II. i, Hang Dutch and French,.. Christians and Turks. Pew-waw, all's one to me!

pewage (ˈpjuːɪdʒ). Also **puage.** [f. PEW *sb.*¹ + -AGE.] The arrangement or provision of pews; rent paid for a pew or pews.

1684 J. Wade in Nichols *Coll. Top. & Gen.* (1836) III. 317 For pewage, Sʳ Lionel Jenkin £1 5 0. **1836** Nichols *ibid.* 316 The presents or gratuities which he received in addition to the 'pewage money'. **1841** G. Poulson *Hist. Holderness* II. 288 The former pewage was very ancient; two pews bore the inscription 1590. **1842** *Ecclesiologist* Nov. 62 The puage of all these churches is exceeding bad. **1866** *Guardian* 27 Dec. 1327/1 The incumbent..objecting..that the services might damage his income, arising almost entirely from 'pewage'.

pewdom (ˈpjuːdəm). [f. as prec. + -DOM.] The system or prevalence of pews in churches; the condition or rank of being a pew.

1866 *Ch. & St. Rev.* 24 Aug. 530 Dilapidated chancels, shabby altars, dreary hebdomadal services, and general pewdom and beadledom. **1876** *Mr. Gray & Neighb.* I. 143 The seats..where the aged poor sat, had little doors to them, to make them as much like pews as was possible without giving them the full dignity of pewdom. **1888** E. J. Parr in *Ch. Times* 30 Nov. 1044/2 The crusade against Pewdom.

pewee (ˈpiːwiː). *U.S.* and *Canada.* [Echoic: cf. PEWIT.] A name applied by some to small olivaceous fly-catchers of the family *Tyrannidæ,* and so identified with PEWIT 3; by others restricted to the genus *Contopus,* as *Contopus virens,* the ***wood-pewee*** of the United States and Canada.

1810 A. Wilson in *Poems & Lit. Prose* (1876) I. 199 A pewee had fixed her nest on a projecting shelf of the rock. **1839–40** W. Irving *Wolfert's R.* (1855) 19 The Pe-wit, or Pe-wee or Phœbe-bird; for he is called by each of these names, from a fancied resemblance to the sound of his monotonous note. **1869** J. Burroughs in *Galaxy Mag.* Aug., The common pewee excites..pleasant emotions, both on account of its plaintive note and its exquisite mossy nest. **1870** Lowell *Study Wind.* (1886) 19 The pewee is the first bird to pipe up in the morning. **1874** S. F. Baird, etc. *N. Amer. Birds* II. 357 *Contopus virens,* Wood Pewee. **1875** Whitney *Life Lang.* vii. 120 The cuckoo and the peewee and the toucan were named from their notes. **1883** *Century Mag.* Sept. 685/1 The wood pewee builds an exquisite nest.

†**pewewe.** *Obs.* [Echoic: cf. PEW *sb.*³] Imitation of the plaintive cry of some birds.

c **1450** Holland *Howlat* 642 The Pitill and the Pype Gled cryand pewewe.

†ˈ**pewˌfellow.** *Obs.* [f. PEW *sb.*¹ + FELLOW.] One who has a seat in the same pew; a fellow-worshipper; one of the same communion, persuasion, or sect; a companion, an associate.

c **1524** Wolsey in J. Hooker *Hist. Irel.* in *Holinshed* (1587) II. 85/1 It hath plesed some of your pufellows to report that I am a professed enimie to all nobilitie, & namelie to the Geraldines. **1533** More *Debell. Salem* Wks. 948/2 The frere, that as he was preaching in the country, spyed a poore wyfe of the paryshe whyspering wyth her pewfellow. **1579** W. Wilkinson *Confut. Familye of Loue* 44 b, Fayne would they their toyes were pewefellowes with the sacred truth of God. *a* **1600** Hooker *Eccl. Pol.* VI. iv. §10 To please their pew-fellows, the disciples of Novatian. **1630** Massinger *Picture* III. iv, If you spend this way too much of your royal stock, Ere long we may be puefellows. **1673** *Lady's Call.* I. v. §48 These sit down to talk and laugh with their Pew-fellows [in church].

pewful (ˈpjuːfʊl). [f. as prec. + -FUL.] As many persons as will fill a pew.

1641 E. Udall *Commun. Comlinesse* 4 So many..as there be Pewfulls in the Church. **1938** M. Muggeridge *In Valley* iv. 23 The congregation, a few pewfuls, nodded to his words.

pew-gaff (ˈpjuːgæf). [f. PEW *sb.*² + GAFF *sb.*¹]

1884 Knight *Dict. Mech., Suppl., Pew-gaff* (Fishing), a hook on a staff, used in handling and pitching fish.

†**pew-glede.** *Obs. rare.* [f. PEW *sb.*³ + GLEDE.] The Kite: see GLEDE.

1615 Markham *Pleas. Princes* v. (1635) 25 Made of a fine greene floxe, and the wings of..a Pew-glead.

pewit, peewit (ˈpiːwɪt, ˈpjuːɪt). Forms: α. 6 puwit, 6–7 puet, 6–9 puit, 7–8 puett. β. 6 pewitt, 7–8 pewet, 8 peevit, pievit, 6– pewit, 8– peewit. [Echoic, from the cry of the bird; cf. *pee-weep, peesweep*; also Flem. *piewit-voghel* (Kilian), Du. *kieviet* (*kieuit* Kil.), MLG. *kivit,* LG. *kiwit,* Ger. *ki(e)bitz, kiwitz* (Grimm), MHG. *gîbitz,* etc.; all of echoic origin. The original Eng. type was prob. (ˌpiːˈwiːt), whence by stress-shift (ˈpiːwiːt, ˈpiːwɪt, ˈpjuːɪt). Parallel names with initial *t* (*teewit,* etc.) are also found both in England and on the Continent: cf. popular F. *dix-huit,* MLG. *tîvit* (Gramm).]

1. A widely-diffused name of the Lapwing (*Vanellus vulgaris* or *cristatus*): the usual name in Scotland, and in Eng. Dial. Dict. cited as used from Northumberland to Berkshire.

a **1529** Skelton *P. Sparowe* 430 The culuer, the stock-dowue, With puwyt the lapwyng, The versycles shall syng. **1570** Levins *Manip.* 87/34 A Puet, *phalaris. Ibid.* 149/36 Puit, *phalaris.* **1612** in *Naworth Househ. Bks.* (Surtees) 29 Sʳ George Dawlston's man bringing 20 puetts. **1688** R. Holme *Armoury* II. 254/2 A..Pewet..in the North of England..is called a Tewit, or Bastard Plover. **1725** Bradley *Fam. Dict.* s.v. *Spring,* The Snipe and Woodcock, Pewit, or the like. *c* **1730** Burt *Lett. N. Scotl.* (1818) I. 129 The green plover or pewit..is therein said to be the ungrateful bird. **1821** Clare *Vill. Minstr.* II. 121 The startling peewits, as they pass, Scream joyous whirring over-head. **1842** Tennyson *Will Waterpr.* 230 To come and go..Returning like the pewit [*rime* cruet].

b. The thin wailing cry of this bird.

1812 *Sporting Mag.* XXXIX. 106 The shrilly sounding cry of Pe-wit. **1876** Smiles *Sc. Natur.* xiii. (ed. 4) 260 You could now hear..the pleasant *peewit* of the Lapwing.

2. (In full **pewit gull.**) The black-headed Gull (*Larus ridibundus*): from its cry.

1678 Ray *Willughby's Ornith.* 347 The Pewit or Black-cap, called in some places, The Sea-Crow and Mire-Crow: *Larus cinereus.* **1686** Plot *Staffordsh.* 231. **1768** Pennant *Zool.* II. 426 The Pewit Gull... The notes of these gulls distinguish them from any others; being like a hoarse laugh. **1885** Swainson *Brit. Birds* 209 Puit or Peewit gull.

3. In *U.S.* A name given to various species of Tyrant Flycatchers, as the Common Pewit, *Sayornis fusca* or *S. phœbe,* and the Black Pewit, *S. nigricans,* small birds of 6 or 7 inches long.

1839–40 [see PEWEE]. **1890** *Cent. Dict.* s.v., The common pewit abounds in eastern North America. **1894** Newton *Dict. Birds* 711 The name Pewit..was given from the bird's cry, as it is in North America to one of the Tyrant-birds, *Sayornis fusca,* which is a general favourite there as a recognized harbinger of summer.

4. ***pewit's eggs,*** a name for certain shells.

1776 Da Costa *Conchology* 173 The sixth family is the Nuces seu Bullæ, commonly called the *Pewit's Eggs.*

5. *Comb.,* as ***pewit-ground, -land*** (poor undrained land), ***pewit-pool,*** etc. (where pewits breed); **pewit-gull** (see 2).

1686 Plot *Staffordsh.* 231 At which Moss they continued about three years, and then removed to the old pewit pool again. **1894** Newton *Dict. Birds* 710 The great Pewit-pool at Norbury in Staffordshire..had ceased to be occupied by the end of the last century.

pewk(e, pewl, obs. forms of PUKE, PULE.

pewless (ˈpjuːlɪs), *a.* [f. PEW *sb.*¹ + -LESS.] Without pews; having no pew.

a **1857** D. Jerrold *Pew-opener* Wks. 1864 IV. 233 Glancing coldly at his pewless brother standing in the crowded aisle. **1874** Micklethwaite *Mod. Par. Churches* 29 The fashion for pewless churches. **1887** Anna Forbes *Insulinde* 236 Farther back, in a pewless space, native dames in smothering veils [etc.].

pewne, pewpe, pewre, obs. ff. PAWN *sb.*¹, POOP, PURE.

ˈ**pew-ˌrent.** The rent paid for a pew, or for sittings in a church. Hence ˈ**pew-ˌrental,** ˈ**pew-ˌrenter**; ˈ**pew-ˌrented,** ˈ**pew-ˌrenting** *adjs.*

1840 *Penny Cycl.* XVIII. 52/2 Pew-rents, under the church-building acts, are exceptions to the general law. **1843** *Ecclesiologist* II. 15 A fashionable pue-rented chapel. **1872** Talmage *Serm.* 105 The building is..untrammelled by the pew-rental system. *Ibid.* 168 Pew-renting churches and free churches. **1885** *Truth* 11 June 929/1 Let the plates go round To take the mites of affluent pew-renters.

pewtene, Sc. var. PUTAIN *Obs.,* a whore.

pewter (ˈpjuːtə(r)). Forms: 4–5 **peutre,** 4–6 **pewtre,** 4–8 **peuter,** 4– **pewter** (also 5 **peautyr, pewtyr(e,** 5–7 **peauter,** 6 **pewtur,** 6–7 **puter,** 7–8 **pewther**); 4 **peudur, -yr,** 5 **-dre, peauder,** 5–6 (–9 *dial.*) **pewder.** [ME. a. OF. *peutre, peautre, peaultre, pialtre,* etc. (from 12th c. in Godef.), repr. an earlier *peltre = It. *peltro,* Sp. *peltre.* In later OF. also *espiautre, espeautre*; in Du. *piauter,* and *spiauter* (in Kilian, *peauter, speauter*), Ger. *spiauter,* LG. *spialter.* The mutual relations of these forms and the origin of the word are unascertained: see Diez (s.v. *peltro*), Körting (s.v. *peltrum), Littré, Hatz.-Darm., Franck (s.v. *Piauter*), Skeat; and cf. SPELTER. The form with *d* (*pewder*) is still in dialect use.]

1. a. A grey alloy of tin and lead, usually containing one fifth of its weight of lead, for which other metals are sometimes substituted, partly or entirely, in the composition of different varieties.

[**1292** Britton I. xvi. §6 Qi mauveise chose vendent pur bone, sicum peutre pur argent ou latoun pur or.] **1370** *Bury Wills* (Camden) 1 In vasis de pewtre debil. iiijs. ijd. **1387** in *E.E. Wills* (E.E.T.S.) 2 The lauour of peuter with the basyn of led. **1388–9** *Abingdon Acc.* (Camden) 57, j charg' de peudur. *c* **1425** *Pol. Rel. & L. Poems* (1903) 311 Do thi licour in a vessel of peauder, or of leed, or of glas. *c* **1450** in *Cal.*

Let. Bk. D. City of Lond. (1902) 202 Alle the pottis of peuter that ye fynde not aselyd. **1552–3** *Inv. Ch. Goods Staffs.* in *Ann. Lichfield* IV. 17 A cruett of puter. **1552** *Inv. Ch. Goods York*, etc. (Surtees No. 97) 18, ij crewettes of pewder. **1602** *Narcissus* (1893) 277 Whose head doth shine with bright hairs white as pewter. **1782** PRIESTLEY *Corrupt. Chr.* II. VI. 35 A chalice of gold, or silver, or at least of pewter. **1833** HT. MARTINEAU *Three Ages* i. 9 The service of pewter made a grand display. **1839** URE *Dict. Arts* 952 The English tradesmen distinguish three sorts, which they call plate, trifle, and ley pewter; the first and hardest being used for plates and dishes; the second for beer-pots; and the third for larger wine measures. **1879** *Cassell's Techn. Educ.* I. 55 A small proportion of antimony combined with tin forms hard pewter.

b. Pewter utensils collectively; pewter ware.

1573 TUSSER *Husb.* (1878) 175 That pewter is neuer for manerly feastes, That daily doth serue so vnmanerly beastes. **1596** SHAKS. *Tam. Shr.* II. i. 357 Pewter and brasse, and all things that belongs To house or house-keeping. **1596** — *1 Hen. IV*, II. iv. 51 Fiue yeares: Berlady a long Lease for the clinking of Pewter. **1604** *Knaresborough Wills* (Surtees) I. 244 All the pewther as yt standes. **1717** RAMSAY *Elegy on Lucky Wood* iv, Her pewther glanc'd upo' your een Like siller plate. **1807** SOUTHEY *Espriella's Lett.* II. 72 We ate off pewter, a relic of old customs.

c. The colour of the alloy, a bluish or silver grey.

1971 *Vogue* Nov. 81/1 One size tights in palest pewter. **1979** *Guardian* 28 Apr. 32/2 Single-leg stocking tights... Colours: Dark Tan, Mink, American Tan, Pewter, Black.

2. †**a.** Applied to armour: cf. *pewter coat* in 5.

1611 BEAUM. & FL. *Philaster* v. iv, And every man trace to his home again, And hang his pewter up.

b. A pewter pot. Also *fig.*

a **1839** PRAED *Poems* (1864) II. 233 Now drinking from the pewter. **1853** G. J. CAYLEY *Las Alforjas* II. 54 A huge glass mug with a handle, as big as a pewter. **1861** HUGHES *Tom Brown at Oxf.* xi, Stopping in the bar to lay hands on several pewters full of porter.

c. *slang.* A tankard or 'cup' given as a prize; prize-money; money.

1829 P. EGAN *Boxiana* 2nd Ser. II. 90 The exertions of *Jack's* fists and his tongue were both rewarded by a shower of *browns*, and also a little *pewter* into the bargain. **1842** EGAN *Macheath, Bould Yeoman* v. (Farmer), Hand up the pewter, farmer, you shall have a share. **1873** *Slang Dict.*, *Pewter*,.. the pots for which rowing men contend are often called pewters. **1888** *Academy* 24 Mar. 202/1 The anxiety for 'pewter' or prize money, which.. animated our officers and men.

†**3.** A pale yellow alloy of gold and silver; = ELECTRE 1, ELECTRUM 2. *Obs.*

Perhaps only a traditional entry in successive vocabularies, founded orig. on some misunderstanding.

c **1425** *Voc.* in Wr.-Wulcker 653/12 *Hoc Electrum*, pewtyre. *c* **1440** *Promp. Parv.* 395/2 Pewtyr, metalle, *electrum, secundum communem scolam.* **1483** *Cath. Angl.* 277/2 Pewdyr, *electrum.* **1552** HULOET, Pewter, *electrum*, or it is a kynde of mettall, halfe golde, halfe siluer, or parte.

4. A polishing medium used by marble-workers, made by the calcination of tin.

1875 in KNIGHT *Dict. Mech.*

5. a. *attrib.* passing into *adj.* Made or consisting of pewter; also *humorously*, in **pewter coat** (quot. 1584), a cuirass, coat of mail; †**pewter language** (quot. 1615), pothouse talk.

c **1400** *Lanfranc's Cirurg.* 192 Leie it in a peuter disch. **1422–3** *Abingdon Acc.* (Camden) 94, j pewderpot de potel. **1522** in *Bury Wills* (Camden) 115 A grett pewter basen. **1525–6** *Rec. St. Mary at Hill* 333 A pewtur pott for watur for the preistes. **1584** LYLY *Campaspe* v. iii, These pewter coates canne neuer sitte so wel as satten dublets. **1615** BRATHWAIT *Strappado* (1878) 1 Mounsieur Bacchus,.. singuler Artist in pewter language. **1631–2** in Swayne *Sarum Churchw. Acc.* (1896) 316 A quarte and a pinte of pewter pottes. **1688** in Willis & Clark *Cambridge* (1886) III. 384 Two and twenty peauter Trenchers plaits. **1707** MORTIMER *Husb.* (1721) I. 272 Placing a large Pewter-platten under the Cluster of Bees. **1816** SCOTT *Antiq.* iv, With a pewter badge on the right arm. **1840** DICKENS *Barn. Rudge* ii, A table decorated with a white cloth, bright pewter flagons. **1894** *Daily News* 10 Feb. 5/2 The old familiar pewter pot is disappearing from London public-houses, and its place is being taken by the Continental glass.

b. Of the colour of pewter.

1922 JOYCE *Ulysses* 46 Galleys of the Lochlanns ran here to beach,.. their bloodbeaked prows riding low on a molten pewter surf. **1972** 'H. BUCKMASTER' *Walking Trip* 135 They stood silently looking at the pewter water and pewter sky. **1975** B. GARFIELD *Death Sentence* (1976) xxix. 137 The sky had thickened and gone pewter.

6. *Comb.*, as *pewter-maker, -making*; *pewter-buttoned, -like, -topped* adjs.; **pewter-carrier**, one who serves in an ale-house, a potman; **pewter-case**, a case for holding pewter utensils; **pewter grey** = sense 1 c; **pewter-mill**, a lapidary's wheel made of pewter, used with rotten-stone and water for polishing gems of medium hardness (amethyst, agate, cornelian); **pewter-solder**, soft solder, of similar composition to pewter, but containing a greater proportion of lead. Also PEWTERWORT.

1779–81 JOHNSON *L.P., Dryden* III. 110 It haunts me worse than a *pewter-buttoned serjeant does a decayed cit. **1833** MARRYAT *P. Simple* ii, I say, you *pewter-carrier, bring us another pint of ale. **1789** *Chron.* in *Ann. Reg.* 214/1 The fluid passed from the bell to the *pewter-case, and spent its force there. **1973** J. ROSSITER *Manipulators* xiii. 134 Lampett Street was long.. its *pewter-grey length made residential by the planting of trees. **1975** 'D. JORDAN' *Black Account* xxxviii. 193 The White Nile is no longer white but pewter grey. **1874** BOUTELL *Arms & Arm.* ii. 38 Leggings formed of a *pewter-like metal. **1902** *Stirling Nat. Hist. & Archæol. Soc.* 22 Robert was a *pewter-maker. **1888** HASLUCK *Model Engin. Handybk.* 138 Using ordinary 'soft' or *pewter solder for uniting surfaces that are already tinned. **1891** *Pall Mall G.* 29 Oct. 2/2 Shouting and gesticulating, in front of the long, *pewter-topped barrier.

pewterer ('pjuːtərə(r)). Forms: 4 **peautrer**, 5 **pewtrer(e, -terere**, 5–6 **peuterer**, 6 **pewtrer, peauterer**, (7 **peatterer**), 8 *Sc.* **peudrar, peutherer**, 6– **pewterer**. [ME. *peautrer*, in AF. *peautrer* = OF. *peautrier* (1300 in Godef.), *peaultrier* = It. *peltraio, peltraro* (:—**peltrario*), f. OF. *peau(l)tre*, It. *peltro*, PEWTER.] A worker in pewter; one who makes pewter utensils.

1348 in Riley *Mem. Lond.* (1868) 244 [Stephen Lestraunge and John Syward,] Peautrers. **1402** *Rolls of Parlt.* III. 519/2 Peuterers. *c* **1440** *Promp. Parv.* 395/2 Pewtrere, *electuarius*, vel *stannarius.* **1503** *Act 19 Hen. VII*, c. 6 The Pewterers and Brasiers of the Cities of London and York. **1530** PALSGR. 253/2 Pewtrer, *pottier destain, peavltrier.* **1597** SHAKS. *2 Hen. IV*, III. ii. 281 Hee shall charge you, and discharge you, with the motion of a Pewterers Hammer. **1660** BOYLE *New Exp. Phys. Mech.* xx. 146 We caus'd a skilful Pewterer.. to close it up.. with Soder. **1839** URE *Dict. Arts* 120 Bismuth, with tin, forms a compound more elastic and sonorous than the tin itself, and is therefore frequently added to it by the pewterers. **1930** *Aberdeen Press & Jrnl.* 14 Oct. 6 Pewterers nowadays are making their articles tougher and more shock-resisting. **1955** *Times* 16 June 9/6 The pewterer's craft is a peculiarly English one. **1976** *New Yorker* 15 Nov. 73/2 (Advt.), Our attention to detail and un-excelled workmanship have earned us a Royal Title—a distinction no other pewterer in the world can claim.

pewternel, obs. variant of PETRONEL.

pewterwort ('pjuːtəwɜːt). *Herb.* [f. PEWTER + WORT.] A name given to the plant *Equisetum hyemale* on account of its use in polishing pewter and other utensils.

1597 GERARDE *Herbal* II. ccccxlii. 958 Italian rushie Horse taile... Women.. scowre their pewter and wooden things of the kitchen therewith,.. and thereupon some of our huswiues do call it Pewterwoort. **1657** W. COLES *Adam in Eden* xxxiii. 69 The rougher kind hereof, called in English Shave-grass,.. hath been by some of them called Pewterwort. **1883** JEFFERIES in *Longm. Mag.* June 195 One the moist banks jointed pewterwort.

pewtery ('pjuːtərɪ), *sb. rare.* [f. PEWTER + -Y.] **a.** Pewter utensils collectively. **b.** An apartment in a house, in which the pewter is kept.

1645 *Inv. of Kimbolton* in Dk. Manchester *Crt. & Soc. Eliz. to Anne* (1864) I. 374 Pewtery. **1864** DK. MANCHESTER *Ibid.* I. 368 There is an array of pewtery which suggests an idea of a spectacle next in brilliancy to a silversmith's. *Ibid.* 373 Seven dozen of trenchers in the pantry, and the pewter chargers and dishes in the Pewtery.

'**pewtery**, *a.* [f. PEWTER + -Y.] Of the nature of, or characteristic of, pewter.

1864 in WEBSTER.

pewy ('pjuːɪ), *a. Hunting slang.* [f. PEW *sb.*[1] + -Y.] Of country: Divided into small enclosures by fences, as a church is into pews.

1828 *Sporting Mag.* XXII. 359 The largest portion of our Eastern sportsmen.. would prove cock-tails in a pewey and stiff country. **1885** *Daily Tel.* 11 Dec. (Farmer), Sixty or seventy years since the fences were stronger, the enclosures smaller, the country more pewy.

pex, obs. variant of PAX: cf. *peax*, PEACE.

†'**pexity.** *Obs. rare*$^{-0}$. [ad. L. *pexitās*, f. *pex-us*, lit. combed, hence, having the nap on it.]

1658 PHILLIPS, *Pexity*, the roughnesse of the web.

-pexy (pɛksɪ), terminal element repr. Gr. -πηξια, πῆξις a fixing or putting together (f. πηγνύναι to join or fix), used in the names of surgical operations for fixing organs in position; as *hysteropexy* (s.v. HYSTERO-[1]), *orchidopexy* (s.v. ORCHIDO-).

†**pey, peyae**, obs. forms of PAY, PEAI.

1613 PURCHAS *Pilgrimage* (1614) 831 They call this Deuill Peyae, with whom the men haue often conference.

peyce, variant of PEISE *Obs.*; obs. f. PIECE.

peyckes, peyer, obs. ff. PICKAXE, PAIR *sb.*

Peyerian (paɪ'ɪərɪən), *a. Anat.* [f. proper name *Peyer*: see below + -IAN.] Of, pertaining to, or named after the Swiss anatomist Johann Konrad Peyer (1653–1712): as the ***Peyerian*** (or ***Peyer's***) ***glands*** or ***patches***, groups of follicles in the wall of the small intestine.

1799 HOOPER *Med. Dict.*, *Peyer's glands*, the glands of the intestines. See *Brunner's glands.* **1831** *Encycl. Brit.* (ed. 7) II. 816/2 Peyerian glands. **1858** R. G. MAYNE *Expos. Lex. Med. Sci.* (1860) 924/1 Peyer's glands, Peyer's patches. **1870** *Trans. Path. Soc.* XXI. 391 There were no leuchæmic nodules in the liver or kidneys, and the tonsils, like Peyer's patches, were remarkably inconspicuous. **1885** KLEIN *Micro-Organisms* 86 In the inflamed Peyer's glands, in the mesenteric glands, larynx, and lungs of patients dead of typhoid fever. **1886** C. H. FAGGE *Princ. & Pract. Med.* I. 183 If in a Peyer's patch, it is usually elongated in the direction of the axis of the intestine. **1893** *Syd. Soc. Lex.*, *Peyerian.* **1955** *Sci. News Let.* 23 July 51/1 Polio antibodies in the blood.. build up their response to polio while the virus is still multiplying in the tonsils and the Peyer's patches of the small intestine. **1974** PASSMORE & ROBSON *Compan. Med. Stud.* III. xii. 46/1 Enteric or typhoid fevers. .. Hyperplasia and mononuclear infiltration lead to swelling of the intestinal lymphoid tissue, especially the Peyer's patches of the lower ileum.

peyet: see PIET.

peyl(l, obs. Sc. f. PEEL *sb.*[1]

peyn(e, obs. f. PAIN.

peyneyes, obs. pl. of PENNY.

peyni, peynim, -yme: see PAYENY, PAYNIM.

peynt, etc., obs. ff. PAINT, etc.

peyote (peɪ'jəʊteɪ). Also **payote, pellote, pelotte, peyoti, peyotl**, etc. [Amer. Sp. *peyote*, a. Nahuatl *peyotl.*] **1.** = MESCAL 3 a.

[**1859** BARTLETT *Dict. Amer.* (ed. 2) 509 *Whiskey-root*, a plant of the Cactus species possessing intoxicating properties, which is thus described by a correspondent of the New Orleans Picayune: 'It is what the Indians call Pie-o-ke.'] **1885** *Proc. U.S. Nat. Museum* VIII. 521 It is principally as an intoxicant that the Peyote has become noted, being often added to 'tizwin' or other mild fermented native drink to render it more inebriating. **1898** J. MOONEY in *17th Ann. Rep. U.S. Bureau Amer. Ethnol. 1895–96* I. 238 The worship of the peyote.. is comparatively modern with the Kiowa. **1911**, etc. [see MESCAL 3 a]. **1927** *Daily News* 28 Sept. 8/7 M. R. Desille.. said that a herb.. known as peyotl 'produced remarkable hallucinations of undoubted psychic value'. **1955** *Sci. News Let.* 2 July 4/1 Mescaline is extracted from the Mexican plant better known as peyote. **1969** D. WENIGER *Cacti of Southwest* 95/2 The insignificant members of this genus [sc. *Lophophora*].. are the sacred plants of the Indians best known by the ancient Indian name, *peyotl*, which has become the peyote of modern usage. **1977** LEWIS & ELVIN-LEWIS *Med. Bot.* xviii. 405/2 Peyote is usually eaten as mescal buttons, the dried, brown pieces of the above-ground part of the cactus. Occasionally fresh green pieces are used. *Ibid.* 407/1 Peyote is also brewed and the tea drunk.

2. = MESCAL 3 b.

1849 J. W. AUDUBON *Western Jrnl.* (1906) 186 Out of these acorns the Indians make their 'payote', a kind of paste. **1913** [see *mescal button*]. **1915** *Jrnl. Heredity* VI. 295/2 The majority from the *peyote* and the wine were unable to utilize their legs. **1916** *Jrnl. Amer. Med. Assoc.* 15 Jan. 194/2 Among the menaces.. to which some of the American Indians are said to be exposed.. is the use of a natural product variously known as mescal buttons, peyote or pellote. **1953** [see HIGH *sb.* 1 h]. **1975** *High Times* Dec. 49/3 Many natural hallucinogens—peyote is a good example—are supposed to trigger nausea by their direct pharmacological actions.

3. *attrib.* and *Comb.*, as ***peyote cactus, high***; **peyote button** = *mescal button*; **peyote cult** = PEYOTISM.

1921 M. R. HARRINGTON *Relig. & Ceremonies of Lenape* viii. 185 *(caption)* Peyote 'Button'. Diameter 1·9 in. **1966** G. BAXT *Queer Kind of Death* (1967) xiv. 204 The stupid bastard must have cut himself a peyoti button. **1975** 'S. MARLOWE' *Cawthorn Journals* (1976) II. xi. 88 Have you ever eaten peyote buttons? **1953** A. HUXLEY *Let.* 21 June (1969) 678 The most extraordinary fact about mescaline—the active principle in the peyotl cactus used by the North American Indians..—is that it is almost completely non-toxic. **1974** M. C. GERALD *Pharmacol.* xvii. 327 Among the plants the Spanish conquistadors observed to be worshipped by the Mexican natives was the peyote cactus. **1920** *Univ. Calif. Publ. Amer. Archaeol. & Ethnol.* XVI. 437 It was quite customary to eat peyote during the day in the early days of the peyote cult. **1970** *Times Lit. Suppl.* 18 Dec. 1480/5 Now coca.. became the basis of a kind of peyote cult. **1953** Peyote high [see HIGH *sb.* 1 h].

peyotism ('peɪjətɪz(ə)m). [f. PEYOT(E + -ISM.] A religious cult of American Indians in which peyote is taken sacramentally. Hence **pe'yotist**, one who practises this religion.

1934 V. PETRULLO *(title)* The diabolic root: a study of peyotism, the new Indian religion, among the Delawares. *Ibid.* II. 126 The original Peyote people claim that one cannot be a Christian and a Peyotist at the same time. **1953** A. HUXLEY *Let.* 17 Aug. (1969) 683 No craving.. even among people who have been peyotists for forty or fifty years. **1957** P. WORSLEY *Trumpet shall Sound* 223 Henceforth the Indians turned.. to pacific cults like peyotism. **1971** E. SHORRIS *Death of Great Spirit* iii. 34 God may change the peyotist, but the peyotist.. has no hope of changing God. *Ibid.* 38 Apologists for peyotism say, 'It is the only thing we have left that is Indian.'

peyr, obs. f. PAIR, PEAR *sb.* and *v.*

Peyronie's disease ('peɪrəniːz). *Path.* [Named after François de La *Peyronie* (1678–1747), French physician, who described the condition in 1743 (*Mém. Acad. r. de Chirurgie* I. 425).] (See quot. 1974.)

1903 *Boston Med. & Surg. Jrnl.* CXLVIII. 245/1 *(heading)* Peyronie's disease. **1949** H. C. ROLNICK *Pract. Urol.* I. xi. 173 In Peyronie's disease or plastic induration of the corpora cavernosa the incurvation becomes noticeable on erection. **1974** PASSMORE & ROBSON *Compan. Med. Stud.* III. xxvii. 13/1 Fibrous cavernositis (Peyronie's disease) is a condition in which fibrous plaques develop near the glans or on the dorsum of the penis, and cause curvation, swelling, pain on erection and interference with coitus.

peys, obs. f. PEACE; obs. Sc. pl. of PEE *sb.*[1]

peysan, -a(u)nt, obs. ff. PEASANT, PEISANT.

peyse, peyss(e, obs. ff. PEISE, PEACE, PIECE.

peyssant, var. PUSANE *Obs.*

ˈpeytral, *sb. Obs.* exc. *Hist.* Forms: 4 (9–) **peytral**, 4–5 **-elle**, 4–7 **-el**, 5–6 **-ell**; 6 **-erel**, 7 **-il**; 6–7 **peit(t)rel(l**; 4 **paytrel**, 5–6 **-ell(e**, **-ylle**, **paitrell**, **patrelle**, 6 **pattrell**; (5 **pettryll**), 6 **petrel(l**, **-il**, **-al**, **peterell**, 6–7 **pet(t)rel(l**, (6 **pewtrell**, **peutral**, **-il**). [ME. a. AF. *peitrel* = OF. *peitral* (mod.F. *poitrail*) = Sp. *petral*, It. *petrale*:—L. *pectorāle* breast-plate, neuter of *pectorālis* adj., f. *pectus*, *pector-* breast: see PECTORAL.] A piece of armour to protect the breast of a horse (often richly ornamented, and retained for ornament after its defensive use had passed away); occas. also applied to a breast-collar: = POITREL.

13.. *Coer de L.* 5713 Hys crouper heeng al full off belles, And hys peytrel, and hys arsoun. *c* **1380** *Sir Ferumb.* 3665 Brydel & paytrel & al þe gere Wiþ fyn gold y-harneysed were. *c* **1386** Chaucer *Can. Yeom. Prol.* & *T.* 11 Aboute the peytrel stood the foom ful hiȝe. **1483** *Cath. Angl.* 271/2 A Patrelle, *antela, pectorale.* **1513** Douglas *Æneis* VII. v. 194 Thair brusit trappouris and patrellis. **1552** Huloet, Pewtrell for a horse, *antela.* **1555** Eden *Decades* 271 When theyr peitrels or drawynge collers are put on them. **1556** Withals *Dict.* (1568) 39 a/1 A peterell, *antilena.* **1558** Phaer *Æneid* VII. T ij, Horses..Their brestes embroydryd gylt, their paitrells pendant compasfolde. *a* **1586** Sidney *Arcadia* III. (1629) 272 His petrell and raines, were embrodered with feathers sutable vnto it. **1600** F. Walker *Sp. Mandeville* 143 b, Besides the ordinary gyrths and peutrals, comming ouer their breast and belly. **1607** Topsell *Four-f. Beasts* (1658) 240 That neither girths, peytril, sturrops, trappings, or crupyard, fall betwixt the Back and Saddle. **1653** Urquhart *Rabelais* I. v, It is enough to break both girths and pettrel. **1656** Blount *Glossogr.*, *Petrel*, see *Pectoral.* *Ibid.*, *Pectoral*, a brest-plate or defence for the brest, a Peitrel, Poitrel, or Stomacher. **1894** H. A. L. Dillon in W. J. Loftie *Authorised Guide to Tower of London* (ed. 2) 147 Note also the horse armour consisting of the chanfrein for the head, the crinet for the neck, and the bard protecting the body, that is, the peytral on the chest, the flanches on the sides, and the crupper covering the hinder portion of the horse. **1926** *Fine Armour* (Christie's Sale Catal. 29 June) 4 A Peytrel for the Horse, of three plates of plain bright steel. *Ibid.* 15 A Horse Chanfron and Peytrel Plates. **1929** *Archaeologia* LXXIX. 242 The two sales of the armoury of Prince Radziwill..included no less than 22 chanfrons and 15 peytrals of Maximilian date. **1953** *Proc. Prehistoric Soc.* XIX. 175 The object was claimed to be a 'peytrel' or chest ornament for a small horse. **1962** J. Mann *Wallace Coll. Catal.: European Arms & Armour* I. 12 *Peytral* of five large plates. **1967** *Punch* 29 Nov. 809/3 If some hulking great brute..were to straddle an already overburdened war-horse, the whole caboodle would collapse in a sorry ruin of pauldron and salade, breastplate and roundel, cantle, crupper, greave, flanchard, peytral, chanfron and crinet.

Hence †ˈ**peytral** *v. trans.*, to put a peytral on. *Obs.*

1393 Langl. *P. Pl.* C. v. 23 Sette my sadel vppon soffre-til-ich-see-my-tyme; Let peitrel hym and pole hym. **1688** R. Holme *Armoury* III. xix. (Roxb.) 165/1 Mounted on a Pettrelled or Barded courser.

peyvee, **peyze**, obs. forms of PAVIE, PEISE.

pezant, obs. form of PEASANT.

†**peˈzantic**, *a. Obs. nonce-wd.* [f. *pezant*, PEASANT + -IC.] Of the character of a peasant; boorish, clownish.

1613 Sir E. Hoby *Countersnarle* 66 To defile my fingers with such a Pezantique Fugitiue, who is ashamed of his Fathers name.

pezazz, var. PIZZAZZ.

†**peze**, obs. form of PEISE *v.*, to weigh, balance.

1595 *Alcilia* (1879) 29 Twixt Hope, and Feare in doubtfull ballance pezed.

‖**Peziza** (pɪˈzaɪzə). *Bot.* [mod.L. (Dillenius); cf. L. *pezica* or *pezita*, f. Gr. πέζις a stalkless mushroom.] A large genus of discomycetous fungi, of cup-like or saucer-like shape, and often of brilliant colour, growing on the ground or on decaying wood, etc.; various species are called *cup-mushrooms*, *fairy-cups*, etc.

[**1623** Cockeram, *Pezite*, a Mushrompe. **1706** Phillips, *Pezica*, a sort of Mushroom.] **1861** Miss Pratt *Flower. Pl.* III. 55 The yellow hairy sessile Peziza. **1887** W. Phillips *Brit. Discomycetes* 126 This beautiful little peziza adheres by a claw at the base to the putrid stems of decayed plants in moist places near rills of water. *Ibid.* 361 In its young state it is truly Peziza-like, and very beautiful.

Hence **peˈziziform** (*erron.* **-æform**), **peˈzizoid** *adjs.*, of the form of or resembling a Peziza.

1857 Berkeley *Cryptog. Bot.* 199 A pezizæform body figured by Greville. **1887** W. Phillips *Brit. Discomycetes* 17 Pileus deflexed even from the first, not pezizoide.

pezle mezle, obs. form of PELL-MELL.

pezo, **pezzant**, obs. forms of PESO, PEASANT.

Pfaffian (ˈpfæfɪən), *a.* and *sb. Math.* [f. proper name *Pfaff* (see below) + -IAN.]

A. *adj.* Pertaining to, discussed by, or named after, the German mathematician Johann Friedrich Pfaff (1765–1825): applied to certain differential equations, etc. **B.** *sb.* Name given by Cayley to a species of function occurring in Pfaff's investigation of differential equations.

1852 Cayley *Coll. Math. Papers* II. 19 The permutants of this class (from their connexion with the researches of Pfaff on differential equations) I shall term 'Pfaffians'. **1860** *Ibid.* IV. 600 A skew symmetrical determinant of any even order is the square of a Pfaffian.

†**Pfalzgrave.** *Obs.* = PALSGRAVE; hence †**Pfalzgraviate**, a (German) palatinate.

1762 tr. *Busching's Syst. Geog.* V. 197 The town..is the origin of the Pfalzgraviate of Swabia.

Pfalzian (ˈpfæltsɪən), *a.* (*sb.*) *Geol.* Also **Pfälzian**. [ad. G. *Pfälzische* (F. Kühne 1922, in *Jahrb. Preuss. Geol. Landesanst.* XLIII. 433), f. *Pfalz*, the (Rhineland) Palatinate (ult. f. L. *palatium* imperial residence: see PALACE *sb.*[1]): see -IAN.] Pertaining to or designating a minor orogenic episode in Europe which is believed to have occurred in the Permian period, later than the SAALIAN. Also *ellipt.* as *sb.*

1931 Gregory & Barrett *Gen. Stratigr.* 19 Pfalzian. Between Trias and Permian. **1932** T. W. E. David *Explan. Notes to accompany New Geol. Map Austral.* 73 While the epi-Permian movement as a whole seems nearly to correspond with the Pfalzian of Europe and the Appalachian of U.S.A., it would seem that in eastern Australia it continued, in places, for some little time after Pfalzian and Appalachian disturbance had ended. **1937** A. L. Du Toit *Our Wandering Continents* viii. 164 At the close of the Permian, during the Pfalzian Phase, the central plateau of France and the Saar region were upheaved along an E.–W. axis. **1974** [see SAALIAN *a.*].

‖**Pfannkuchen** (ˈpfankuːxən). Also **pfannekuchen**. [G.] In Germany and other German-speaking areas, a pancake.

1877 [see KRAPFEN]. **1906** *Cosmopolitan* XLII. 547/1 Do you sometimes haf *pfannekuchen* for supper? **1964** L. Deighton *Funeral in Berlin* xl. 242 'You got rid of your tail?' ..'He got a lapful of *Pfannkuchen* and scalding coffee.'

‖**Pfefferkuchen** (ˈpfɛfərkuːxən). Also **pfefferkuchen**. [G., lit. 'pepper cake'.] In Germany and other German-speaking areas, a spiced cake, gingerbread.

1870 *Western Monthly* Jan. 29/1 One long room..being gay with bright Christmas trees loaded with nuts, apples, sugar-plums, and all sorts of jolly-looking figures in honey-cake and *pfeffer-kuchen*. **1961** J. Heller *Catch-22* (1962) xxiv. 249 Pumpernickel and *Pfefferkuchen* from Berlin. **1977** G. Butler *Brides of Friedberg* v. 136 Underneath I put little dishes of Pfefferkuchen, Nüsse and Stolle.

Pfeiffer (ˈpfaɪfə(r)). *Bacteriol.* The name of Richard *Pfeiffer* (1858–1945), German bacteriologist, used in the possessive and *attrib.* to designate: **a.** The specific lysis of the cholera vibrio in the presence of antibody and complement as described by him (in *Zeitschr. für Hygiene und Infektionskrankh.* (1893) XIV. 59).

[**1895** E. Metchnikoff in *Ann. de L'Inst. Pasteur* IX. 438 La découverte de la destruction extracellulaire des microbes dans le liquid péritonéal, ou de ce qu'on peut appeler le 'phenomène de Pfeiffer', suggère toute une série de questions touchant le problème général de l'immunité.] **1897** Muir & Ritchie *Man. Bacteriol.* xvii. 393 A striking change is observed microscopically in the vibrios when injected along with the protective serum into the peritoneal cavity of another guinea-pig—Pfeiffer's reaction. **1929** Topley & Wilson *Princ. Bacteriol. & Immunity* II. lxi. 905 Pfeiffer's phenomenon is of great value in the identification of the cholera vibrio. **1970** *Science* 3 Apr. 141/2 (*heading*) A new application of the Pfeiffer phenomenon.

b. A species of bacterium, *Hæmophilus influenzæ*, described by him (in *Deutsch. med. Wochenschr.* (1892) 14 Jan. 28) as the causal agent of influenza, but now known not to be.

1900 H. J. Curtis *Essent. Pract. Bacteriol.* 287/1 (Index), Pfeiffer's influenza bacillus. **1910** Hiss & Zinsser *Text-bk. Bacteriol.* xxxvii. 528 The bacillus of influenza (Pfeiffer bacillus) is an extremely small organism, about 0·5 micron long. **1936** *Lancet* 12 Dec. 1383/1 The illness produced by introducing virulent cultures of Pfeiffer's bacillus into a healthy person is not genuine epidemic influenza. **1953** J. Ramsbottom *Mushrooms & Toadstools* xxiii. 278 The insensitive Pfeiffer's bacillus..in the respiratory tract is usually associated with organisms highly sensitive to penicillin.

pfella (ˈ(p)fɛlə). Also **pfeller**. Repr. Austral. Aborigines' pronunc. of FELLOW *sb.* Cf. FELLA, FELLAH. In Austral. Pidgin often used as a marker of an adjective, demonstrative, or numeral.

1908 'G. Seagram' *Bushmen All* 310 Now you go longa Warrego an' big pfella pleeseman hang you longa rope. **1921** A. B. Paterson *Man from Snowy River* (new ed.) 74 What parson tellin' you, Ole Mister Dodd, Tell you in Sunday-school? Big pfeller God! **1936** M. Franklin *All that Swagger* iii. 38 That one sit down longa white pfella—all same as white pfella. *Ibid.* iv. 46 Danny had established himself as a superman, a big pfella chief. *Ibid.* vii. 65 Minetinkit, that pfella budgery! **1936** I. L. Idriess *Cattle King* xxix. 257 How much would you want to make a big pfella flood, Paddy?

‖**pfennig**, **-ing** (ˈpfɛnɪg, -ɪŋ). Forms: 6 **phenyng**, **penning**, 6–7 **phenning**, 7–8 **pfening**, 8 **phen(n)ig**, 7– **pfenning**, 9 **pfennig**: see also FENNIN. [Ger. *pfennig*, OHG. *pfenning*:—WGer. **pani(n)g*, whence Eng. PENNY.] A small copper coin of Germany, formerly of varying value, now the hundredth part of a mark (see MARK *sb.*[2] 4 b). Also *Comb.*

1547 Boorde *Introd. Knowl.* xiv. (1870) 161 They haue Norkyns, Halardes, Phenyngs, Crocherds, Stiuers, and halfe styuers. **1575** *Brief Disc. Troubles Frankford* (1846) 157 Thirteene not Dalers but hallers or phenninges. **1617** Moryson *Itin.* I. 287 At Nurnberg..two haller make one pfenning, fiue pfening make one finfer. **1756–7** tr. *Keysler's Trav.* (1760) I. 196 A small copper-piece, whose real worth was scarce a pfening, went for a dollar silver-money, which is equal to half a German rix-dollar. **1897** Ouida *Massarenes* xxxix, You haven't got a pfennig to spend. **1909** *Daily Chron.* 15 July 4/7, I have an actual pfennig-piece before me as I write, which was coined in 1894. **1979** R. Cox *Auction* iii. 75 Pouring pfennig pieces into a coinbox.

pfft (ft, pft). Also **pfft**, **phfft**, **phtt**, etc. [Echoic.] = PHUT *int.* (*adv.*, *sb.*)

1923 Kipling *Irish Guards in Gt. War* I. 5 One..rifle-bullet landed with a *phtt* in the chalk between two officers. **1934** *Amer. Speech* IX. 313/2 Then it all goes pffft. **1942** Berrey & Van den Bark *Amer. Thes. Slang* §360/2 *Divorce*, ..go pfft,—pffft *or* phut,..pfft, phffft, phut. **1954** Wodehouse *Jeeves & Feudal Spirit* iii. 29 It wouldn't take much to make the Stilton-Florence axis go p'fft again. **1972** F. Warner *Lying Figures* I. 6 Commuters' corset till sixty-five, then pppfft! the six by four. **1975** *Washington Post* 10 Mar. B1 A voice..said 'Thank you, Barbra' and, phffft! The hour was over. **1977** *Ibid.* 13 Jan. C1/3 Senatorial marriages of 5, 23 and 35 years were going pfffffft, as the Hollywood columnists used to write. **1977** *Rolling Stone* 16 June 11/2 Nothin' serious; $500 in bail, phffffftttt.

Hence **pfft** *v. intr.* (*U.S. journalists' slang*), to come to an abrupt end, to collapse; of a couple, to become estranged, to separate, to divorce; also *transf.* and as *ppl. adj.*

1930 *Vanity Fair* (N.Y.) Jan. 48/3 Mr. Walter Winchell.. exercises a tremendous power for mischief with impassive diablerie: 'the so-and-sos have phffft!' **1938** W. Winchell in *Baltimore News-Post* 16 Mar. 16/2 Have Lionel Stander and the films phffft? **1938** —— in *Ibid.* 21 Mar. 10/1 Burton Rascoe and Dorothy Parker have phffft! **1939** *Time* 28 Aug. 13 Gossip columnists took this as renewed notice that the Franklin D. Jrs. are not *phphpht* as gossiped. **1940** *New Yorker* 13 July 22/3 International Politics, March 29, 1937. 'Adolf and Benito have phffft! The break will be announced soon enough.' **1946** J. T. Shipley in W. S. Knickerbocker *20th Cent. English* 136 To indicate the collapse of a project ..the columnist declares that it has pfft. **1957** *Chicago Amer.* 9 Feb. 17/8 Alan and Joanne Rio, who were dating, have pffft.

pfui (ˈfuːɪ, ‖ˈpfui), *int.* [G.: cf. PHOO *int.*, PHOOEY *int.* (*sb.*)] (Orig. in Germany or among German-speaking people) an exclamation of contempt or disgust. Hence **pfuiteufel** (ˈpfuːɪtɔɪfəl) [G. *teufel* devil], emphatically in same sense.

1866 C. M. Yonge *Dove in Eagle's Nest* I. x. 206 Christina heard Friedel say..'I think I shall be a priest, Ebbo.' To which Ebbo only answered, 'Pfui!' **1871** Geo. Eliot in *Macm. Mag.* July 185 Pfui! The time was, I drank that home-brewed wine. **1920** D. H. Lawrence *Touch & Go* 6 The plays are good... What about your *good* plays? Whose good? *Pfui* to your goodness! **1922** Joyce *Ulysses* 184 Out on't! *Pfuiteufel!* **1934** R. Macaulay *Going Abroad* xxxiii. 281 Pfui, my poor Pierre, you are a fool. **1935** C. Isherwood *Mr. Norris changes Trains* iv. 52 You men are all alike; from seventeen to seventy... *Pfui!* I'm surprised at you. **1937** Wyndham Lewis *Blasting & Bombardiering* 100 Why should one be asked to meet such people? It is absurd that a Bennett should be referred to, for anything except the time of a train or the cost of a bicycle lamp! Pfui! **1943** E. M. Almedingen *Frossia* II. 107, 'I trusted you. Pfui,' he spat on the paper-strewn floor. **1949** R. Stout *Second Confession* xiii. 134 'I didn't get him to. As it says, he wrote and signed it of his own free will.' 'Pfui. I know what it says. But why should I believe that when I don't believe anything in it?' **1966** —— *Death of Doxy* (1967) vi. 71 Pfui. A prodigy on a treadmill. Take him off. **1972** *Human World* May 96 Brutal to give a little girl a doll? Brutal to bring children up? Pfui! Not all the madmen are in the madhouses. **1974** Wodehouse *Aunts aren't Gentlemen* ix. 163, I don't mind criticism, but I will not endure vulgar abuse. 'Pfui,' I said. It is an expression I don't often use, but Nero Wolfe is always saying it with excellent results.

Pfund (fʊnt). *Physics.* The name of A. Herman *Pfund* (1879–1949), U.S. physicist, used *attrib.* to designate a series of lines in the infra-red part of the spectrum of atomic hydrogen, with wave numbers represented by $R(1/5^2 - 1/m^2)$ (where R is the Rydberg constant and $m = 6, 7, \ldots$), of which the first line has a wavelength of 7·46 micrometres and the series limit is at 2·28 micrometres.

1934 H. L. Brose tr. *Sommerfeld's Atomic Struct. & Spectral Lines* (ed. 3) ii. 73 A. H. Pfund found an infra-red line belonging to hydrogen at $\lambda = 7{\cdot}40\mu$, which is the first member of a 'Pfund series' and corresponds to $n = 5$, $m = 6$. **1970** D. W. Tenquist et al. *University Optics* II. ii. 43 Lines in the infra-red part of the spectrum are caused by transitions terminating at $n = 3$ (Paschen series), $n = 4$ (Brackett series) and $n = 5$ (Pfund series).

ph, a consonantal digraph, having usually the phonetic value of F. It was the combination used by the Romans to represent the Greek letter Φ, ϕ or φ, named Φῖ, *Phī*. This letter, cognate with Skr. *bh* (and so with Germanic *b*), was in early Greek written ΠΗ, and was a real aspirated *p*; it was subsequently often written ΠΦ, πϕ, and had then prob. nearly the same sound as German *pf*; but by the second century

B.C. it had sunk into a simple sound, prob. the *bilabial* spirant (the sound made in blowing through the lips). As the Roman F was dentilabial, like mod. Eng. *f*, the Romans in earlier times represented the Greek Φ not by F, but by PH; in the time of the Emperor Severus, however, the two began to be confused, and from *c* 400 were treated as identical. Hence in late popular and mediæval Latin, and in the Romanic languages, *f* was often substituted, as it is now regularly in Italian and Spanish (e.g. *fantasia, filosofia, Filippo, fotografico*). This was also the case to a great extent in Old French, and in Old and early Middle English (see PHARISEE, PHILISTEE, PHANTOM, PHEASANT); but here, under the influence of the Latin forms, most words so written were subsequently altered back to *ph*, the preponderance of which is particularly notable in Gower. Exceptionally the *f* remains in mod. Eng., as in *fancy* (= *phantasy*), *fantastic*. In all modern words of Greek derivation (e.g. in *phano-, philo-, phospho-, photo-, phyto-*) *ph* is alone found.

One consequence of these conditions was that in the 15th, 16th, and 17th c., *ph* was frequently substituted for *f* in words not of Greek origin, esp. in words that were somewhat rare, the scribes apparently taking *ph* as a more learned, and thus presumably more correct, spelling. Many instances of this will be found under F, and among the cross-references given below, as in *phalucco, phan, phane, phang, pharman, philaser, philhorse, philimot*, etc. This spelling is often retained in *philabeg* = *filibeg*, and in certain interjections, *phew! pho! phoo!* where perhaps it may have been adopted to express the simple bi-labial ('lip-breath') consonant (the sound made in blowing) as distinct from the labio-dental *f*. Modern phonologists, e.g. Mr. A. J. Ellis in his 'Palæotype', have used *ph* as the symbol of the bi-labial sound. Greek had the initial combination *φθ-*, in Roman spelling *phth-*. This was difficult for the Roman nations, and in the only early word of this class, *phthisicus*, was reduced to *pht, th*, or simple *t*. See PHTHISIC, etc. In mod.F. words in *phth* are now normally pronounced *ft-*; in Eng. the *ph* is generally mute and the *th* pronounced; but in scientific words many scholars pronounce (fθ-), a combination which is quite as easy as (sf-) in *sphere*.

Ph (pronounced *f*) is also used to represent Hebrew פ (without dagesh), and even initial פּ (according to the Masoretic pointing, with dagesh) in proper names which have come to us through a Greek form with Φ: see PHARAOH, PHILISTINE, SERAPH. In the Roman spelling of Indian languages *ph* represents the true aspirated *p* (फ of Sanskrit), and this is occasionally the origin of *ph* in alien words: cf. PHULKARI.

pH (piː'eɪtʃ). Formerly p_H, P_H. [Introduced (in Ger.) as p_H by S. P. L. Sörensen 1909, in *Biochem. Zeitschr.* XXI. 134, the *p* repr. G. *potenz* power and H· the hydrogen ion.]

1. A measure of the acidity or alkalinity of a solution, equal to the logarithm to the base 10 of the reciprocal of the effective concentration (activity) of hydrogen ions (in moles per litre).

A pH of 7 corresponds to a neutral solution, one less than 7 to an acidic solution, and one greater than 7 to an alkaline solution.

1909 *Jrnl. Chem. Soc.* XCVI 861 The optimal concentration was p_H = 4·4 to 4·6. **1920** W. M. CLARK *Determination Hydrogen Ions* i. 26 As a matter of typographical convenience we shall adopt pH in place of P_{H+}. **1921** *Jrnl. Nat. Dental Assoc.* VIII. 653/1 He uses agar with a P_H value of 8·1 as a basis for blood agar. **1935** W. A. KOEHLER *Princ. & Applic. Electro-Chem.* II. xiv. 359 The bulb dips into the solution of unknown P_H. **1937** PIERCE & HAENISCH *Quantitative Analysis* viii. 121 Acid-base indicators are highly colored organic dyes which exhibit a change in color when the *p*H of a solution is changed. **1952** C. E. L. PHILLIPS *Small Garden* iii. 25 For general garden purposes in this country best results come from a neutral or slightly acid *p*H reading. **1970** *Pure & Appl. Chem.* XXI. 33 In all existing national standards the definition of pH is an operational one. *Ibid.*, The difference between the pH of two solutions having been defined as above, the definition of pH can be completed by assigning a value of pH at each temperature to one or more chosen solutions designated as standards. **1974** P. SVENDSEN *Introd. Animal Physiol.* xiii. 143 The maximum acidity of the wine is about pH 4·5.

2. *attrib.* and *Comb.*, as ***pH meter, scale, value***; ***pH-dependent*** adj.; **pH-stat**, a device for automatically maintaining a solution at constant pH.

1960 *Jrnl. Bacteriol.* LXXIX. 734 (*heading*) Temperature and pH-dependent changes of electrophoretic mobility of *Pasteurella pestis*. **1972** *Brit. Jrnl. Nutrition* XXVIII. 389 The pH-dependent rearrangements have also to be borne in mind when performing administration experiments with formylfolates in metabolic studies. **1940** REILLY & RAE *Physico-Chem. Methods* (ed. 3) xii. 493 The Beckman *p*H meter.. uses the principle of the potentiometer system in which the voltage of the electrode system is balanced against that of a standard cell. **1968** PASSMORE & ROBSON *Compan. Med. Stud.* I. vi. 3/1 The pH measured electrometrically by a glass electrode and a pH meter is not in fact a precise measure of actual hydrogen ion concentration. **1920** W. M. CLARK *Determination Hydrogen Ions* ii. 41 It is advantageous to show the position of the several indicators on the pH scale. **1973** F. G. SHINSKEY *pH & pIon Control in Process & Waste Streams* iii. 57 The pH scale is not bound to the limits of 0 to 14. **1957** *Methods Biochem. Anal.* IV. 174 A pH-stat consists of an appropriate cell.. connected with a suitable pH-meter which in turn is connected with an adjustable controlling device. **1974** SAWYER & ROBERTS *Exper. Electrochem. for Chemists* ix. 417 In general autotitrators that work with a preset endpoint lend themselves to application as pH-stats. **1920** W. M. CLARK *Determination Hydrogen Ions* ii. 38 To a series of test tubes are added, seriatim, 10 cc. of each of a series of standard solutions whose pH values are known. **1932** T. P. FRANCIS *Mod. Sewage Treatm.* 252 The pH values for filter effluents should not differ by more than ·6. **1946** J. W. DAY *Harvest Adventure* iii. 44 Every acre of arable land has had a dressing of chalk. In all.. some 30,000 tons have been put down, the idea being to maintain a *p*H-value of 5. **1974** *Encycl. Brit. Macropædia* X. 606/1 Some volcanic lakes are extremely acid, however, with pH values below 4, and some lakes with very high pH values, such as Lake Nakuru, Kenya, also occur in nature.

phacelia (fə'siːlɪə). [mod.L. (A. L. Jussieu *Genera Plantarum* (1789) 129), f. Gr. φάκελος bundle, in reference to the clustered flowers.] An annual herb of the genus so called, belonging to the family Hydrophyllaceæ, usually native to western North America and bearing clusters of blue, violet, or white flowers.

1818 A. EATON *Man. Bot.* (ed. 2) II. 354 *Phacelia.. bipinnatifida* (phacelia..). **1835** *Edwards's Bot. Reg.* XX. 1696 (*heading*) Tansy-leaved Phacelia. **1898** A. M. DAVIDSON *California Plants* 119 There are many kinds of Phacelias; the flowers vary very much in size and in color and form, but they always grow in clusters that last a long time. **1903** M. AUSTIN *Land of Little Rain* 145 Larkspur in the *coleogyne*, and for every spinosa the purpling coils of phacelia. **1911** A. E. SPEER *Annual & Biennial Garden Plants* 206 The Phacelias are a family of hardy annuals useful for edgings or groups, and are all natives of either California, Texas, or Mexico. **1935** *Times Educ. Suppl.* 9 Mar. (Home and Classroom Suppl.) p. iv/3 Phacelia is a lovely little plant of which the colour rivals that of the Gentians. **1962** *Amat. Gardening* 24 Mar. 9/2 My own favourite hardy annuals are.. phacelia,.. escholtzia.

phacellate (fə'sɛlət), *a. Zool.* [f. mod.L. *phacellus*, pl. *-i*, ad. Gr. φάκελος bundle + -ATE[2].] Having *phacelli* or groups of filaments within the central gastric cavity, as certain Hydrozoa.

1890 in *Cent. Dict.*

phacoanaphylaxis (ˌfækəʊænəfɪ'læksɪs). *Ophthalm.* Also **phako-**. [mod.L., f. Gr. φακό-ς lentil + ANAPHYLAXIS.] Allergic reaction to protein released from the crystalline lens of the eye.

[**1922** VERHOEFF & LEMOINE in *Trans. Internat. Congr. Ophthalm.* 274 Certain individuals are hypersensitive to lens protein... When in such individuals rupture of the lens capsule takes place through injury or operation or spontaneously, a characteristic inflammatory reaction may properly be termed endopthalmitis phacoanaphylactica.] **1948** *Amer. Jrnl. Ophthalm.* XXXI. 1006/2 Verhoeff and Lemoine conceived the idea of phacoanaphylaxis in order to explain the postoperative inflammatory reaction of the eyes with extracapsular extraction. **1962** D. G. COGAN in A. Pirie *Lens Metabolism Rel. Cataract* 291 The lens.. becomes invaded by polymorphonuclear cells, especially in the immunological reactions known as phakoanaphylaxis. **1964** *Arch. Ophthalm.* LXXII. 14/2 Sympathetic ophthalmia and phacoanaphylaxis are both manifestations of autoimmune reactions, the former to uveal pigment and the latter to lens protein.

So **ˌphacoanaphy'lactic** *a.*, of, pertaining to, or involving phacoanaphylaxis.

1922 *Trans. Internat. Congr. Ophthalm.* 280 Intraocular inflammation resulting from rupture of a Morcagnian cataract is not usually phacoanaphylactic in nature. **1966** *Amer. Jrnl. Ophthalm.* LXI. 1431/1 The phacoanaphylactic reaction was seen in full bloom.

phacochœre ('fækəkɪə(r)). *Zool.* Also **-chere**. [= F. *phacochère* (Littré), ad. mod.L. *phacochœrus*, f. Gr. φακός lentil, wart + χοῖρος pig.] A wart-hog.

1842 *Penny Cycl.* XXIII. 246/2 In the locomotive organs the true hogs and the Phacochœres bear the greatest resemblance to each other. **1849** *Sk. Nat. Hist., Mammalia* III. 85 The range of the South African phacochœre, or Vlacke Vark, does not appear to be precisely determined.

So **phaco'chœrid (-cher-)**, an animal of the family *Phacochœridæ*; **phaco'chœrine (-cher-)** *a.*, belonging to the family *Phacochœridæ*; **phaco'chœroid** *a.* = *phacochœrine*; *sb.* = *phacochœrid*.

In modern Dictionaries.

phacocyst ('fækəsɪst). *Bot.* Also **phako-**. [ad. mod.L. *phacocystē*, f. Gr. φακός lentil + κύστις CYST.] The lenticular nucleus of a cell.

1835 LINDLEY *Introd. Bot.* (1848) II. 234 Each cell contains two phakocysts. **1858** MAYNE *Expos. Lex.*, *Phacocyst*.

phacoid ('fækɔɪd), *a. rare*[−0]. [ad. mod.L. *phacoïdēs* (applied by Vesalius to the crystalline lens), in F. *phacoïde*, f. Gr. φακός lentil: see -OID.] Lentil-shaped. Hence **pha'coidoscope** = PHACOSCOPE.

1858 MAYNE *Expos. Lex.*, *Phacoides*.. resembling a lentil in shape: phacoid. **1864** tr. *Donders' Anom. Accomm. Eye* Note 16, I have given to it in this form the name of phacoidoscope, which word fully expresses its object.

phacoidal (fə'kɔɪdəl), *a. Petrogr.* [f. as PHACOID *a.* + -AL.] **a.** Lens-shaped, lenticular. **b.** Characterized by the presence of lenticular inclusions.

1901 *Rep. Brit. Assoc. Adv. Sci.* 617 The basic dykes.. appear frequently as phacoidal masses amid the reconstructed gneiss. **1920** [see EYE *sb.*[1] 12 f]. **1956** E. W. HEINRICH *Microsc. Petrogr.* vii. 185 In phacoidal rocks the characteristic textural feature consists of ellipsoidal or lensoid units in a finer-grained matrix that is brecciated and sheared. *Ibid.* 186 Some mechanically metamorphosed conglomerates also possess the phacoidal texture. **1959** W. W. MOORHOUSE *Study of Rocks in Thin Section* xxviii. 463 Granites, syenites, and granodiorites show some foliation and a lenticular, 'phacoidal' form of quartz and feldspar grains.

phacolite ('fækəlaɪt). In sense 1 also **phako-**. [f. Gr. φακός lentil: see -LITE.] **1.** *Min.* [ad. Ger. *phakolit* (Breithaupt).] A colourless variety of CHABAZITE, occurring in crystals of lenticular form.

1843 PORTLOCK *Geol.* 219 Levyne (? Phakolite) occurs in double six-sided prisms. **1880** *Academy* 21 Aug. 139/1 The occurrence of the zeolites, phacolite, and phillipsite, in cavities of basaltic rocks containing liquid.

2. *Geol.* = next.

1909 A. HARKER *Nat. Hist. Igneous Rocks* iii. 77 A concurrent influx of molten magma will.. find its way along the crests and troughs of the wave-like folds. Intrusive bodies corresponding more or less closely with this ideal case are common in folded districts. Since some distinctive name seems to be needed, we may call them phacolites... The intrusions.. are not, like true laccolites, the cause of the attendant folding, but rather a consequence of it. **1937** WOOLDRIDGE & MORGAN *Physical Basis Geogr.* viii. 109 Phacolites are lens-shaped masses of rock occupying the saddles of anticlines or the heels of synclines, places where rigid rock sheets naturally gape apart in the folding process. **1946** [see LACCOLITE].

phacolith ('fækəʊlɪθ). *Geol.* [Alteration of prec.: see -LITH.] An intrusive mass of igneous rocks situated between consecutive strata at the top of an anticline or the bottom of a syncline.

1910 LAKE & RASTALL *Text-bk. Geol.* xiii. 225 These long narrow intrusions are called by Mr. Harker phacolites (more correctly phacoliths). **1947** S. J. SHAND *Study of Rocks* (ed. 2) ii. 16 The phacolith might be described as a saddle-shaped laccolith;.. but there is this important difference between a laccolith and a phacolith that the former is the cause of the folding of its country rocks while the latter is a consequence of folding. [*Ed.* 1 (1931): phacolite, laccolite.] **1971** B. W. SPARKS *Rocks & Relief* iii. 93 Laccoliths are approximately circular, but phacoliths are not, except in the rare case of their being formed in a dome. Usually they are elongated in the direction of the axes of the folds. **1977** A. HALLAM *Planet Earth* 68 Phacoliths are curved sill-like intrusions emplaced in the crests and troughs of folded rocks.

phacometer (fæ'kɒmɪtə(r)). In quots. **phako-**. [mod. f. Gr. φακό-ς lentil, lens + -METER.] An instrument for measuring the power of lenses.

1876 *Catal. Sci. App. S. Kens.* 117. **1893** *Syd. Soc. Lex.*, *Phakometer*.

phacoscope ('fækəskəʊp). Also **phako-**. [mod. f. as prec. + -scope.] An apparatus for observing the changes in form of the crystalline lens of the eye in accommodation to objects at different distances.

1890 in *Cent. Dict.* **1893** in *Syd. Soc. Lex.*

Phæacian (fiː'eɪʃən). [f. L. *Phæacia*, Gr. Φαιακία, the isle of Scheria (Corcyra) + -AN.] One of the inhabitants of Scheria, noted for their luxury; hence (= L. *Phæax*, Horace), a gourmand.

1788 LEMPRIÈRE *Classical Dict.* (1826) 510/2 The Phæacians.. were naturally dull, effeminate, and so affectatious, that the ancients gave them the name of parasites. **1899** *Speaker* 28 Oct. 85/1 He was a bon vivant, declined into a fat Phaeacian.. and latterly did nothing.

phæism ('fiːɪz(ə)m). *Biol.* [f. Gr. φαι-ός dusky + -ISM.] A dusky or dark variety of coloration, which falls short of melanism.

1891 *Athenæum* 12 Dec. 804/3 Mr. Jenner-Weir exhibited two dark specimens of *Zygæna minos*.. [he] expressed an opinion that the specimens were not representatives of complete melanism, and suggested that the word 'phæism' .. would be a correct word to apply to this and similar departures from the normal coloration of a species. **1899** *Cambr. Nat. Hist.* VI. 337.

phænigm, erron. spelling of PHŒNIGM *Obs.*

phænocarpous (fiːnəʊ'kɑːpəs), *a. Bot. rare*[−0]. [mod. f. Gr. φαινο- showing + καρπός fruit + -OUS.] 'Bearing a fruit which has no adhesion with surrounding parts' (*Treas. Bot.* 1866).

1858 MAYNE *Expos. Lex.*, *Phænocarpus*.. phenocarpous.

phænogam, phe- ('fiːnəgæm). *Bot.* [f. mod.L. *phænogama*, sc. *vegetabilia* (Willdenow 1804), or *phænogamæ* (sc. *plantæ*), f. Gr. φαινο- showing + γάμος marriage, sexual union; in Ger. *phanogamen* sb. pl. (Rudolphi 1807).] A flowering plant; = PHANEROGAM. So **phæno'gamian, phæno'gamic** (fɛ-) *adjs.* = PHANEROGAMIC; **phæ'nogamous** *a.*, producing flowers, flowering; = PHANEROGAMOUS.

1846 LINDLEY *Veg. Kingd.* Pref. 17 The substitution of the words Monocotyledons,.. Cryptogams, *Phænogams, etc., for Monocotyledones,.. Cryptogamæ, Phænogamæ, &c. **1857** BERKELEY *Cryptog. Bot.* §8. 13 The word Phænogams is very generally used as a collective term for flowering plants. **1828–32** WEBSTER, **Phenogamian*, having the essential organs of fructification visible. **1808** S. F. GRAY in *Monthly Mag.* XXIV. 612 *Phœnogamic [*sic*], or phænogamous, is a word much used by the German botanists in contradistinction to cryptogamic, and from its convenience begins to be adopted here. **1841** Douglas in *Proc. Berw. Nat. Club* I. 249 Additions to the phenogamic Flora of the district. **1808** *Phænogamous [see *phænogamic* above]. **1814** R. Brown *Bot. Terra Austral.* 4 Phænogamous plants. **1821** S. F. Gray *Nat. Arr. Brit. Pl.* I. 43 Phenogamous..the sexual organs very distinct and visible. **1830** Sir W. Hooker (*title*) British Flora, comprising the Phænogamous, or Flowering Plants, and Ferns. **1885** Goodale *Physiol. Bot.* (1892) 3 Division of the vegetable Kingdom..into..Phaenogamous (or Phanerogamous) or Flowering, and Cryptogamous or Flowerless Plants.

phænology, phænomenon: see pheno-.

phænotype, obs. var. phenotype.

phænozygous (fiːˈnɒzɪgəs), *a. Anthropol.* Also pheno-. [mod. f. Gr. φαινο- showing + ζυγόνα joining + -ous.] Of a skull: Having the zygomatic arches visible from immediately above the centre; of a person: having such a skull.

1878 Bartley tr. *Topinard's Anthrop.* II. iii. 288 When the angle is positive, the zygomatic arches are called phenozygous. **1888** *Jrnl. Anthrop. Inst.* Aug. 7 The male is distinctly phænozygous, but the female is not.

phæochrome (ˈfiːəʊkrəʊm), *a. Histology.* Also pheo-. [f. Gr. φαιός dusky + χρῶμα colour.] = chromaffin *a.*

1909 Bailey & Miller *Text-Bk. Embryol.* xv. 43 The medulla is composed of irregularly arranged sympathetic ganglion cells and other granular cells which, after treatment with chrome salts, acquire a peculiar brownish color. The brown cells are known as chromaffin (or phæochrome) cells and their granules as chromaffin (or phæochrome) granules. **1929** M. A. Goldzieher *Adrenals* v. 223 The phæochrome tumors produce an excessive amount of adrenalin. **1941** R. G. Hoskins *Endocrinol.* ii. 51 A tumor made up of pheochrome cells..may be situated in either the adrenal medulla or in one of the paraganglia. **1956** Robson & Keele *Recent Adv. Pharmacol.* (ed. 2) i. 29 Phæochrome tumours..are benign in nearly 90 per cent of cases.

phæochromocyte (fiːəʊˈkrəʊməʊsaɪt). *Med.* Also pheo-. [ad. G. *phäochromocyte* (H. Poll 1906, in O. Hertwig *Handb. d. vergleich und exper. Entwickelungslehre d. Wirbeltiere* III. 460), f. *phäochrom* phæochrome: see -cyte.] A chromaffin cell, esp. one in the adrenal medulla.

1929 *Arch. Path.* VII. 229 The final stage of differentiation brings forth the mature pheochromocytes, which are large, irregular or polyhedral cells, with each a round or ovoid vesicular nucleus, containing a loose chromatin network, and a well formed nucleolus. *Ibid.* 230 The pheochromocytes have the peculiar property of staining brown with chromic salts. **1948** Martin & Hynes *Clin. Endocrinol.* vii. 144 Phæochromocytomata... The tumours consist of mature phæochromocytes and 90 per cent are benign. **1975** *Nature* 27 Nov. 342/1 Pheochromocytoma cells exhibit properties of both pheochromocytes and neurones as a manifestation of neoplasia.

ˌphæochromocyˈtoma. *Path.* Also pheo-. Pl. -omas, -omata. [mod.L., ad. G. *phäochromocytom* (L. Pick 1912, in *Berlin. klin. Wochenschr.* 1 Jan. 21/2): see prec. and -oma.] A tumour arising from chromaffin cells of the adrenal medulla. Cf. paraganglioma.

1929 *Arch. Path.* VII. 228 (*heading*) Chromaffin cell tumor of the suprarenal medulla (pheochromocytoma). **1929** *Trans. Assoc. Amer. Physicians* XLIV. 298 Pheochromocytomas are a rare tumor. **1931** W. Boyd *Path. Internal Dis.* ix. 482 Chromaffin cell tumor..is also known as a paraganglioma, a pheochromocytoma and a chromaffinoma. **1943** J. M. Beattie et al. *Textbk. Path.* (ed. 4) xxiv. 847 The chromaphil (or so-called 'chromaffine') tumour or phæochromocytoma is a growth affecting especially adults and is usually benign, although malignant varieties are recorded. **1944** *Surg. Clinics N. Amer.* Aug. 932 The terms 'chromaffinoma' and 'pheochromocytoma' have by common consent been used to describe suprarenal tumors of this type insomuch as they almost exclusively produce the clinical phenomena of hyperadrenalism. The term 'paraganglionoma' is reserved for extra-adrenal chromaffinomas, such as tumors of the carotid body. **1948**, **1956** [see paraganglioma]. **1974** Passmore & Robson *Compan. Med. Stud.* III. xxiii. 55/2 Histologically phaeochromocytomata closely resemble normal chromaffin tissue.

phæodarian (fiːəʊˈdɛərɪən), *a.* and *sb. Zool.* [f. mod.L. *Phæōdāria* neut. pl. (Haeckel), f. *phæōdium*, f. φαίος dusky + *-odium* (see -ode[1]).]

A. *adj.* Belonging to the *Phæodaria*, a division of Radiolarians characterized by a mass of dark pigment (*phæodium*), containing rounded granules (*phæodellæ*), surrounding the central capsule. **B.** *sb.* A radiolarian of this division.

[**1880** *Nature* XXI. 450/1 The extra-capsular-soft substance of all Phæodaria is distinguished by..the mass of Phæodella or 'dark pigment granules' which it contains.] **1888** Rolleston & Jackson *Anim. Life* 875 The spicules being..disposed..radially only in the Phaeodarian family *Aulocanthida.* **1900** *Jrnl. Quekett Micros. Club* Apr. 265 The central capsule is generally almost entirely imbedded in the phæodium.

phæophorbide (fiːəʊˈfɔːbaɪd). *Biochem.* Also pheo-. [ad. G. *phäophorbid* (Willstätter & Stoll 1911, in *Ann. d. Chem.* CCCLXXVIII. 25), f. as phæophytin + Gr. φορβή pasture, food: see -ide.] Either of two compounds (orig. not distinguished) formed by the action of a strong acid on chlorophyll or phæophytin, having the structure of the latter except for the replacement of the phytol group by a hydrogen atom: phæophorbide *a*, $HOOC\cdot C_{32}H_{32}N_4O\cdot COOCH_3$, or phæophorbide *b*, $HOOC\cdot C_{32}H_{30}N_4O_2\cdot COOCH_3$. Also, an ester of one of these compounds (as phæophytin).

1911 *Chem. Abstr.* V. 873 The following nomenclature is now adopted: for the free tricarboxylic acid, the basis of chlorophyll, the name chlorophyllin is retained, the monomethyl ester is called chlorophyllide and the deriv. free from Mg, pheophorbide. **1950** J. Bonner *Plant Biochem.* xxx. 470 Hydrolysis of pheophytin with stronger acid removes the phytol group to yield pheophorbides *a* and *b*, which are both monocarboxylic acids and which can be esterified..to yield the alkyl pheophorbides. **1956** I. L. Finar *Org. Chem.* II. xix. 697 These phytyl phæophorbides are also known as phæophytins *a* and *b*. *Ibid.* 702 When phytyl phæophorbide-*a*..is hydrolysed with acid, the phytyl group is removed to form phæophorbide-*a*. **1963** R. P. Dales *Annelids* ii. 56 The intestine..is apparently absorptive. It is this region that has a deep green colour, just as that of Chaetopterus has, and for the same reason, for in both the colour is due to phæophorbides—breakdown products of chlorophylls presumably derived from the food. **1975** *Nature* 24 Jan. 241/1 Sudden heating [of leaf juice] inactivates chlorophyllase and so prevents the formation of phaeophorbide.

phæophyll (ˈfiːəfɪl). *Bot.* [mod. f. Gr. φαιός dusky + φύλλον leaf: after chlorophyll.] Name proposed for the brown colouring-matter, composed of phycophæin and phycoxanthin, found in sea-weeds of the orders *Fucaceæ* and *Phæosporeæ*.

1890 in *Cent. Dict.* **1893** *Syd. Soc. Lex.*, *Phæophyll*, the brown colouring-matter of the Fucoïdeæ; also called *Phyllophæin.*

phæophytin (fiːəʊˈfaɪtɪn). *Biochem.* Also pheo-. [a. G. *phaeophytin* (now *phäo-*) (Willstätter & Hocheder 1907, in *Ann. d. Chem.* CCCLIV. 207), f. Gr. φαιός dusky + φυτόν plant: see -in[1].] Either of two brownish compounds (orig. not distinguished) formed by the action of a weak acid on chlorophyll, having the structure of the latter except that the magnesium atom is replaced by two hydrogen atoms; a phytyl ester of phæophorbide: phæophytin *a*, $C_{20}H_{39}OOC\cdot C_{32}H_{32}N_4O\cdot COOCH_3$, or phæophytin *b*, $C_{20}H_{39}OOC\cdot C_{32}H_{30}N_4O_2\cdot COOCH_3$.

1907 [see phytol]. **1950**, **1956** [see phæophorbide]. **1967** *Oceanogr. & Marine Biol.* V. 269 The increase of the pigment ratio in deep water has to be ascribed in part to the persistence of yellow pigments and phaeophytin in decomposing plankton and in excrements.

†**phæoplast** (ˈfiːəplɑːst, -plæst). *Obs. Bot.* [a. G. *phaeoplast* (now *phäo-*) (A. F. W. Schimper 1885, in *Jahrb. für wissensch. Bot.* XVI. 34), f. Gr. φαιός dusky + πλαστ-ός formed, moulded; cf. chloroplast.] A chromoplast of a brown alga.

1886 *Jrnl. R. Microsc. Soc.* VI. 640 For the chromoplasts of the Phæophyceæ the author proposes the term phæoplasts. **1904** *Amer. Naturalist* XXXVIII. 378 The chromatophores of the higher brown Algæ (Phæophyceæ)..have the discoid form characteristic of chloroplasts. They might be called phæoplasts..if one wished to classify plastids according to their color.

phaeton (ˈfeɪtən, ˈfeɪtən). [a. Gr. φαέθων shining, used in Gr. mythology as proper name of the son of Helios and Clymene, famous for his unlucky driving of the sun-chariot.]

†**1.** *allusively.* A rash or adventurous charioteer like Phaethon; any charioteer; something that, like Phaethon, sets the world on fire.

1593 Nashe *Four Lett. Confut.* Wks. (Grosart) II. 242 That hee should talke of gnashing of teeth, yong Phaetons, yong Icari, yong Chorebi, young Babingtons. **1629** *Leather* 13 Euerie priuate Gentleman now is a *Phæton*, and must hurrie with his thundring Caroch along the Streetes. **1692** Watson *Body of Div.* 862 Sin is the Phaeton that sets the World on Fire. **1747** *Gentl. Mag.* XVII. 94 If the hackney-man should grumble, I fear our Phaeton must tumble.

2. A species of four-wheeled open carriage, of light construction; usually drawn by a pair of horses, and with one or (now generally) two seats facing foward; but applied to carriages variously modified and distinguished as *Stanhope, mail, park, dog-cart, pony phaeton*, etc.

[**1735** *Machines approuvées par l'Acad. Sc.* VI. 3 Chaise de Poste dont on peut faire un Phaeton.] **1742** Young *Nt. Th.* v. 819 Like Nero,..drives his phaeton, in female guise. **1747** Miss Talbot *Lett., to Miss Carter* 18 Aug. (1809) I. 201 A fashionable post chaise or phaeton. **1794** Felton *Carriages* (1801) II. 68 The sizes and constructions of Phaetons are more various than any other description of carriages. **1844** *Act 7 & 8 Vict.* c. 91 Sched., Every horse..drawing any coach,..barouche, chaise, phaeton, vis-a-vis, calash. **1872** Black (*title*) Strange Adventures of a Phaeton. **1880** Mrs. Forrester *Roy & V.* II. 16 Are you going to drive your phaeton this afternoon?

†**3.** A name for the planet Jupiter. (So in French.)

1631 Widdowes *Nat. Philos.* 11 Jupiter is a bright Plannet ..being neere the earth, of which he is called Phaeton.

4. *attrib.* and *Comb.*

1679 J. Goodman *Penit. Pard.* I. v. (1713) 125 Fancy gets the ascendant, and Phaeton-like, drives on furiously and inconsistently. **1883** *Standard* 7 Feb. 2/5 The carriage was described as a phaeton-wagonette.

Hence **phaetoˈneer** [cf. *charioteer*], driver of a phaeton; **phaeˈt(h)onian** = sense 1; **phaeˈthonic**, †**phaeˈthonical**, †**phaeˈthontal**, **phaeˈthontic**, †**phaeˈthontical** *adjs.*, belonging to, characteristic of, or resembling, Phaethon (see etymology above).

1890 *Sat. Rev.* 23 Aug. 244/1 A merry time had our *phaetoneer. **1784** Macneill *Poet. Wks.* (1812) I. 69 No female *Phaetonians then Surpassed the boldest of our men In gesture, look and straddle. **1708** *Brit. Apollo* No. 7. 2/2 Or would'st with *Phaetonick Pride, Within the Solar Chariot Ride? *c* **1630** Risdon *Surv. Devon* §45 (1810) 52 Which *phæthonical fact of his deserves the name of Nody. *a* **1649** Drumm. of Hawth. *Poems* Wks. (1711) 37 Po burns no more with *Phaetontal fire. **1658** J. Jones tr. *Ovid's Ibis* 1st Ded., How *Phaetontick spirits break their necks. **1829** Lamb *Let. to Gilman* Dec., I fear their steed, bred out of the wind without father..hot, phaetontic. **1630** *R. Johnson's Kingd. & Commw.* 509 Achmat..is left at this present to manage the Horses of this *Phaëtonticall Chariot.

phage (feɪdʒ). *Biol.* [Shortening of bacteriophage.] A virus which attacks bacteria, entering the cell and either multiplying at its expense until the cell is lysed and the phage particles released, or becoming attached to the bacterial genome as a prophage and replicating synchronously with it; = bacteriophage. Also *collect.*

[**1925** *Lancet* 1 Aug. 234/2 The musical comedy spirit which reduces 'bacteriophage' to its final syllable.] **1926** *Encycl. Brit.* I. 302/1 If a tube of suitable diluted phage, inoculated with *B. dysenteriae*, is incubated for three hours, and a loop of it then inoculated on agar, confluent growth of the bacteria may be obtained with a number of small, round, clear areas where no growth of bacteria has occurred. **1936** Topley & Wilson *Princ. Bacteriol. & Immunity* (ed. 2) x. 238 Phages acting on one or other of the normal or pathogenic intestinal bacteria can almost always be isolated from fæces, from sewage, or from polluted water supplies. **1939** *Nature* 24 June 1073 Lowering of virulence can..be induced by incubating phage with bacteria in media containing neither calcium nor magnesium salts. **1949** Abraham & Heatley in H. W. Florey et al. *Antibiotics* I. ii. 89 A thin layer of agar containing an organism susceptible to lysis by the phage was spread on the plate and incubation was continued. **1960** *New Biol.* XXXI. 77 Like other viruses, phages multiply by causing the host cells to synthesize the components of the virus. **1968** H. Harris *Nucleus & Cytoplasm* ii. 22 Infection of *E. coli* with phage λ, however, allows β-galactosidase synthesis to continue almost until the time of lysis. **1972** *Nature* 21 Jan. 129/1 Carcinogens..were tested for mutagenic activity in conventional assay systems, involving the use of bacteria or phage as target organisms. **1975** E. Nnochiri *Med. Microbiol. in Tropics* xi. 306/2 Temperate phages..fail to lyse the cells they infect but continue, nevertheless, to reproduce synchronously with the bacterial host for many generations.

b. *attrib.* and *Comb.*, as ***phage genome***, ***particle***, ***replication***; ***phage-infected***, ***-related***, ***-resistant***, ***-specific*** adjs.; **phage type** *sb.*, a division of a bacterial species characterized by a common susceptibility to a particular group of phages; so **phage-typing** *vbl. sb.* the determination of the phage type of a bacterium; **phage-type** *v. trans.*

1969 A. M. Campbell *Episomes* i. 5 We conclude that a phage genome can indeed multiply in two different states. **1964** G. H. Haggis et al. *Introd. Molecular Biol.* xii. 315 Although these first experiments were made on phage-infected, evidence has also been found in normal bacteria for an RNA fraction with rapid turnover. **1957** C. E. Clifton *Introd. Bacterial Physiol.* 380 The number of phage particles adsorbed per bacterium can vary with experimental conditions. **1957** *Virology* II. 256 (*heading*) Production of phage-related structures during multiplication of phages T2 and T4. **1968** J. D. Watson *Double Helix* xvii. 121 André [Lwoff] was very keen about the role of divalent metals in phage replication. **1951** Whitby & Hynes *Med. Bacteriol.* (ed. 5) xxiv. 436 Phage-resistant mutants of undiminished virulence may replace the originally susceptible bacteria. **1973** R. G. Krueger et al. *Introd. Microbiol.* xviii. 479/2 The bacterial cell wall contains phage-specific receptor sites that undergo chemical union with the attachment apparatus of the virus. **1942** *Jrnl. Infectious Dis.* LXXI. 165/2 A series of mouse passage tests resulted in cultures of the same phage type as the original strains. **1961** *Lancet* 29 July 248/1 The second distinctive feature in Australia is an apparently great prevalence of antibiotic-resistant staphylococci, including phage-types 47 and 80. **1975** E. Nnochiri *Med. Microbiol. in Tropics* xi. 307/1 If a particular phage-type of *Salmonella typhi* is the cause of an outbreak of typhoid infection, a search is made for carriers of organisms of the same phage-type. **1938** *Canad. Publ. Health Jrnl.* XXIX. 493 (*heading*) The limitations of phage typing *B. typhosus.* **1949** *Brit. Med. Jrnl.* 10 Sept. 565/2 Staphylococci isolated from a series of 100 cases of infection occurring in this hospital have all been tested for penicillin sensitivity and phage-typed to see if the two could be correlated. **1961** *Lancet* 2 Sept. 506/2 All strains of *Staph. aureus* were tested for sensitivity to eight antibiotics, and a small number were phage-typed. **1942** *Jrnl. Infectious Dis.* LXXI. 161/1 Phage typing of typhoid culture has been employed quite extensively in Canada as an aid in tracing the origin of typhoid fever outbreaks. **1970** Passmore & Robson *Compan. Med. Stud.* II. xviii. 70/2 There are a number of phages with specific affinities for different staphylococci and it is therefore possible to identify strains of staphylococci by their phage-sensitivity patterns. This is the basis of phage-typing which is of great use in the investigation of outbreaks of staphylococcal sepsis.

‖**phagedæna, -ena** (fædʒɪˈdiːnə, fægɪ-). *Path.* Also 7 *erron.* **phagadena.** [L., a. Gr. φαγέδαινα an eating ulcer, cancer, f. φαγεῖν to eat, devour.] An eating sore; an ulcer that spreads and corrodes the neighbouring parts; spreading erosion occurring in an ulcer or sore.

1657 *Physical Dict.*, *Phagadena*, a running canker or pock. **1676** Wiseman *Surgery* II. x. 193 *Phagedæna*,..is an Ulcer with swelled Lips, that eats the Flesh and neighbouring Parts in the bottome and edges of the Ulcer. **1891** *Lancet* 3 Oct. 751 Formerly diseases peculiar to a hospital were the terror of the surgeon. Phagedæna attacked wounds even of the most trivial kind.

phagedænic, -enic (fædʒɪˈdiːnɪk, -ˈdɛnɪk, fægɪ-), *a.* (*sb.*) [ad. L. *phagedænic-us*, Gr. φαγεδαινικ-ός, f. φαγέδαινα: see prec.]

1. *Path.* Of the nature of, characterized by, or affected with, phagedæna or spreading ulcer.

[**1563** T. Gale *Antidot.* II. 65 It..is approued in eatynge vlcers called Phagedenica, &c.] **1656** Blount *Glossogr.*, *Phagedenick.* **1754** Gooch in *Phil. Trans.* XLVIII. 815 He had an ulcer upon his leg, of the phagedænic kind. **1816** A. C. Hutchison *Pract. Obs. Surg.* (1826) 194 On hospital gangrene, and the sloughing phagedenic ulcer, which occurs on board ships of war and in naval and military hospitals. **1897** Mary Kingsley *W. Africa* 618 The great prevalence there of phagedænic ulcers.

†**2.** *Med.* Applied to a corrosive liquid preparation used for destroying proud flesh, or for cleansing ulcers. Also *ellipt.* as *sb. Obs.*

1704 J. Harris *Lex. Techn.* I, *Phagadenick Water*, is made by dissolving a Dram of Sublimate Corrosive in a Pound of Lime Water. **1727–41** Chambers *Cycl.* s.v., Phagedænic medicines..are used to eat off fungous, or proud flesh. **1766** *Complete Farmer* s.v. *Poll-evil*, Some wash with the phagædenic water. **1799** Hooper *Med. Dict.*, *Phagedænics*, medicines that destroy fungous flesh.

So †**phageˈdænical** (**-den-**), **phageˈdænous** *a.*

1635 Read *Tumors & Vlcers* 273 A..phagedænicall and cancerous ulcer of the head. **1725** Bradley *Fam. Dict.* s.v. *Wounds*, It is called by Farriers..the Phagedenical Water. **1659** Hickman *Justif. Fathers* 15 Phagedænous and eating sores. **1895** *Times* 18 Feb. 13/5 The phagedenous ulcer has, by some miracle, become the source of nourishment.

phagocytable (ˈfægəsaɪtəb(ə)l), *a. Biol.* [f. phagocyt(e *v.* + -able.] Susceptible to phagocytosis. Hence **ˌphagocytaˈbility.**

1911 *Jrnl. Amer. Med. Assoc.* 11 Nov. 1579/2 Pneumonic leukocytes would take up more easily phagocytable pneumococci than normal leukocytes. **1915** Thomas & Ivy *Appl. Immunol.* i. 15 An ingenious..laboratory method was devised whereby the measure of the ratio of phagocytability could be determined and this was styled the 'opsonic index'. **1921** Wright & Colebrook *Technique Teat & Capillary Glass Tube* (ed. 2) ix. 208 (*heading*) Requirements in the matter of the number and phagocytability of the microbes employed in opsonic testing. **1927** *Jrnl. Bacteriol.* XIII. 40 Microbic dissociation *in vivo* would serve to transform a virulent but non-phagocytable organism into a non-virulent but phagocytable organism. *Ibid.*, The frequent correlation between S type culture, high virulence and non-phagocytability on the one hand, and, on the other, the correlation between R type culture, non-virulence and phagocytability, are emphasized.

phagocyte (ˈfægəsaɪt), *sb. Physiol.* [mod. f. (Metschnikoff) Gr. φαγο- eating, devouring + -cyte.] A leucocyte (white blood-corpuscle or lymph-corpuscle) which, under certain conditions, has the power of absorbing and destroying pathogenic microbes by a process of intracellular digestion, and thus of guarding the system against infection. More widely, any cell in the body that phagocytoses bacteria or foreign particles.

1884 *Q. Jrnl. Microsc. Sc.* XXIV. 110 Amœboid cells were frequently budded off from the ectoderm to join the other devouring cells (phagocytes) in the body. **1889** E. R. Lankester *Adv. Sci.* (1890) II. App. A. 112 [Metschnikoff's] theory is that by accustoming these corpuscles, which he calls 'phagocytes', to tolerate a weak form of the poison produced by pathogenic Bacteria, we 'educate' them, so that they are able subsequently to resist and eventually to attack and destroy the same pathogenic Bacterium..in a stronger and deadly form. **1898** P. Manson *Trop. Diseases* i. 26 This body [the flagellated organism of malaria] seems to have a powerful attraction for the phagocyte. **1939** F. A. Knott *Clin. Bacteriol.* iii. 45 The lining cells of the hepatic spaces (Küpffer cells) and the reticular cells of the cells of the spleen and lymph glands and the septal cells lining the pulmonary alveoli..can all be shown..to be active phagocytes and capable of ingesting pathogenic bacteria. **1972** R. Hartenstein *Princ. Physiol.* xi. 494 Reticular cells differentiate into various forms of phagocytes including the fixed dust cells of vertebrate lungs, cellular linings of sinuses within glands, fixed Kupffer cells in the capillary sinusoids of liver.

Hence **phagocytal** (-ˈsaɪtəl), **phagocytic** (-ˈsɪtɪk), **-ical** *adjs.*, pertaining to, or having the nature or function of, a phagocyte; ***phagocytic index***, any of various indices of phagocytic activity; **phagoˈcytically** *adv.*; **phagocytism** (ˈfægəʊsaɪtɪz(ə)m), **phagocytosis** (ˌfægəʊsaɪˈtəʊsɪs), the process by which a cell engulfs or absorbs bacteria or foreign particles so as to isolate or destroy them; **phagoˈcytoblast**, the embryonic form of a phagocyte.

1888 *Nature* 24 May 91/2 'Phagocitism'—that is, the intracellular digestive process. **1889** *Q. Jrnl. Microsc. Sc.* Dec. 298 *note*, To attribute very direct phagocytical properties to the outer layer of trophoblast cells. **1891** *Times* 13 Aug. 5/2 Dr. Metschnikoff had elaborated and supported by great research his theory of *phagocytosis*, according to which there was a veritable struggle for existence, a battle *à outrance* between the cells of the body and the invading micro-organisms. **1892** *Pop. Sci. Monthly* XLI. 631 Influences which are associated in aiding phagocytic action. **1896** *Allbutt's Syst. Med.* I. 87 Inflammation is to be regarded, on the whole, as a phagocytic reaction of the organism against irritants. **1904** Wright & Douglas in *Proc. R. Soc.* LXXIII. 129 The phagocytic index given below..represents in each case the average number of bacteria ingested by the individual P.W.B.C. The number of polynuclear white blood corpuscles which have furnished the index is in each case inserted in brackets. **1908** R. W. Allen *Vaccine Therapy* (ed. 2) xii. 199 The phagocytic index appears to be depressed for three to six weeks after commencing treatment. **1911** *Jrnl. Amer. Med. Assoc.* 11 Nov. 1580/1 So far as staphylococci are concerned, the cells with one nucleus are more active phagocytically and those with four least active. **1937** E. E. Hewer *Text-bk. Histol.* 7 This property of phagocytosis is shown by the blood leukocytes, osteoclasts, and all the histiocyte cells scattered throughout the body. **1963** R. P. Dales *Annelids* ii. 55 Kermack also found that food particles in the stomach were taken up phagocytically by certain epithelial cells. **1970** *Times Lit. Suppl.* 23 Oct. 1221/2 Amoebocytes..tend to be of variable shape and to engulf particles in their environment by the process of phagocytosis. **1971** Herbert & Wilkinson *Dict. Immunol.* 139 *Phagocytic index*, a measure of the activity of the reticulo-endothelial system of the body. It is usually represented by a constant K that characterizes the rate of carbon clearance..from the blood and is inversely proportional to the dose of carbon injected. **1972** F. Spencer *Aspects Human Biol.* iv. 112 As performed by such primitive cells as the protozoon amoeba, phagocytosis or engulfment represents a normal feeding mechanism. In the higher animals..phagocytosis is a highly developed activity, as exemplified by the granular leucocytes, and the cells of the reticulo-endothelial system. **1974** *Brit. Jrnl. Haematol.* XXVIII. 542 The phagocytic index was the average number of particles per neutrophil. **1977** P. B. & J. S. Medawar *Life Sci.* xiii. 100 *Phagocytosis*, a process in which antigenic particles are engulfed into and very often digested by, or in any case rendered harmless by, 'macrophages' and 'polymorphs'.

phagocyte (ˈfægəsaɪt), *v. Biol.* [f. the sb.] *trans.* = phagocytose *v.* So **ˈphagocyting** *ppl. a.*

1906 *Jrnl. Exper. Med.* VIII. 676 With a dilution of 1:20 not more than four or five staphylococci are taken up by the phagocyting cells. *Ibid.*, This possibility that a second substance besides the opsonins may determine the number of organisms phagocyted, also exists in the case of normal blood serum. **1933** M. Fernán-Núñez tr. *S. Ramón y Cajal's Histol.* xxi. 547 The Kupffer cells..phagocyte senile and injured erythrocytes. **1961** H. Chantrenne *Biosynthesis of Proteins* iii. 88 The low residual incorporation observed in enucleate *Amoeba proteus* is due to the activity of micro-organisms recently phagocyted by the *Amoeba*.

phagocytize (fægəˈsaɪtaɪz), *v. Biol.* [f. phagocyt(e *v.* + -ize.] *trans.* = phagocytose *v.*

1925 *Physiol. Rev.* V. 195 The ink particles so carried into the liver were readily phagocytized by the Kupffer cells of that organ. **1956** *Arch. Path.* LXI. 165/2 Many of the spores were phagocytized early in the normal rabbit. **1973** R. G. Krueger et al. *Introd. Microbiol.* xxiii. 582/1 This cell type [*sc.* the macrophage] is characterized by its large size, ability to migrate, and its ability to phagocytize foreign materials.

So **ˈphagocytized, -izing** *ppl. adjs.*, **ˈphagocyˌtizable** *a.*

1923 *Johns Hopkins Hosp. Bull.* XXXIV. 328/1 The Kupffer cells..were filled with phagocytized ink particles. **1924** *Physiol. Rev.* IV. 559 No evidence..of the true endothelium of the blood- and lymph-vessels and the heart ..producing wandering, phagocytizing cells in inflammation. **1948** *Biol. Skrift. K. Danske Videnskabernes Selskab* IV. vii. 82 In histological sections from animals which have received injections of phagocytizable material, such as India ink, some of the sinusoid lining cells contain ink and some do not.

phagocytose (fægəˈsaɪtəʊz, -s), *v. Biol.* Also **-oze.** [Back-formation from phagocytosis.] *trans.* To engulf or absorb (a cell or particle) like a phagocyte, so as to isolate or destroy it.

1912 R. W. Allen *Vaccine Therapy* (ed. 4) i. 32 The number of bacteria phagocytozed in a certain number of corpuscles were counted. **1943** Papanicolaou & Traut *Diagnosis Uterine Cancer by Vaginal Smear* iii. 16 Endometrial cells which are being phagocytized by histiocytes. **1973** *Nature* 21 Sept. 50/2 These cells phagocytosed 'Zymosan' particles for at least 6 weeks. **1973** R. G. Krueger et al. *Introd. Microbiol.* xxiii. 582/1 The neutrophil..is capable of actively phagocytozing foreign material.

Hence **ˈphagocytosed, ˈphagocyˌtosing** *ppl. adjs.*

1912 R. W. Allen *Vaccine Therapy* (ed. 4) i. 42 The phagocytosed bacteria should stain clearly. **1958** J. K. Frost in E. & E. R. Novak *Gynecol. & Obstetr. Path.* (ed. 4) xxxv. 626 (*heading*) Hypersecretory vacuoles filled with phagocytosing neutrophils. **1970** *Nature* 1 Aug. 511/1 These cells did not contain any phagocytosed particles, such as aluminium phosphate. **1972** *Science* 2 June 1040/1 [They] have reported that phagocytosing leukocytes take up inorganic iodide.

phagology (fæˈgɒlədʒɪ). *nonce-wd.* [f. Gr. φαγο- eating + -logy.] The subject of eating or feeding; dietetics.

1837 *Blackw. Mag.* XLII. 231 His having so accurately studied the phagology of robins.

phagolysis (fæˈgɒlɪsɪs). *Med.* [mod.L., ad. F. *phagolyse* (E. Metchnikoff 1895, in *Ann. de l'Inst. Pasteur* IX. 441), f. *phagocyte* phagocyte: see -lysis.] **a.** Lysis of phagocytes. **b.** Lysis by phagocytes.

1898 W. S. L. Barlow *Man. Gen. Path.* ix. 403 Attack directed from the German schools and advancing knowledge have obliged Metchnikoff to assume that under certain circumstances the phagocytes become dissolved (phagolysis) in the body fluids. *Ibid.*, The phagocytes, chiefly by phagocytosis, but partly by phagolysis, are responsible for immunity, natural and acquired. **1905** F. G. Binnie tr. *Metchnikoff's Immunity in Infective Dis.* x. 534 Phagolysis (so I termed this transitory damage to the phagocytes) is indispensable for the manifestation of Pfeiffer's phenomenon in the peritoneal fluid. **1963** *Antibiotiki* VIII. 465 (*heading*) Effect of Levomycetin..on phagolysis of Flexner dysentery bacteria resistant to this antibiotic.

phagolysosome (fægəʊˈlaɪsəʊsəʊm). *Biol.* [f. next + lysosome.] A structure formed in the cytoplasm of a cell by the fusion of a phagosome and a lysosome, in which the foreign particle is digested.

1963 W. Straus in de Reuck & Cameron *Lysosomes* 166 The term 'phagosomes' was used to characterize the segregating ability of granules; the term 'lysosomes' was used to indicate the contents of hydrolytic enzymes in the granules.., and the terms 'lyso-phagosomes' or 'phago-lysosomes' were used when both these properties were described for the same granules. **1964** *Jrnl. Histochem. & Cytochem.* XII. 470/2 The foreign protein..was segregated in small and large 'phagosomes'. These later fused with pre-existing lysosomes. The gradual digestion of the injected protein in the 'phago-lysosomes'..could be followed by double staining. **1973** R. G. Krueger et al. *Introd. Microbiol.* xxiii. 584/1 The phagolysosome, containing the remains of the foreign object is then either eliminated from the cell or is left in the cytoplasm. **1977** *Lancet* 29 Oct. 929/2 These organelles are probably secondary lysosomes (phagolysosomes), common in actively feeding cells.

Hence **ˌphagolysoˈsomal** *a.*

1975 *Nature* 3 July 48/2 The phagolysosomal membrane was invariably applied closely to the surface of the enclosed yeast cell.

phagosome (ˈfægəʊsəʊm). *Biol.* [f. phagocyte + -some[4].] A vacuole formed in the cytoplasm of a cell when a particle is phagocytosed and enclosed within a part of the cell membrane.

1958 W. Straus in *Jrnl. Biophysical & Biochem. Cytol.* IV. 548 The uptake of proteins is probably the function of certain intracellular granules related to the droplets of kidney cells. The term 'phagosomes' is suggested for these granules. (If these granules, characterized by segregating ability, are found to be identical with the 'lysosomes', the latter term can be used as a common nomenclature.) **1974** *Nature* 22 Nov. 305/2 If these processes engage in phagocytosis, phagosomes containing groups of cone disks should be observed within their cytoplasm.

Hence **phagoˈsomal** *a.*

1975 *Nature* 17 Apr. 600/2 Possibly the living bacteria produce a factor which inhibits fusion between phagosomal and lysosomal membranes and thereby prevent the discharge of putatively bactericidal lysosomal contents into the bacterial environment.

-phagous, *suffix*, f. L. *-phag-us*, Gr. -φαγ-ος eating (in F. *-phage*) + -ous: as *anthropophagous, ichthyophagous, phytophagous, sarcophagous*; also in humorous nonce-words. Also **-phagy**, ad. Gr. -φαγία eating (*sb.*); as *anthropophagy, ichthyophagy.*

†**Phaˈgyphany.** *Obs. rare*[−1]. [prob. repr. a med.L. **phagyphania*, f. Gr. φαγ-εῖν to eat, -φαγ-ος eating + -φανια, see -phany.] The festival of the miraculous feeding of the five thousand, celebrated on the fourth Sunday in Lent.

14.. *Ephyphanye* in *Tundale's Vis.* (1843) 121 With loves v,..Fyve thousand..he dyd fede; Of the whych myracle.. Thys day is named Phagyphanye, Lyke as hyt was fyrst called Ephyphanye. For thys word *phagy*..Is seyd of fedyng of ellis refeccion.

phah (fɑː), *int.* [Cf. pho, phoo, faugh.] An ejaculation expressing contempt or disgust.

1592–3 G. Harvey *Pierce's Super.* Wks. (Grosart) II. 118, I wonder, his owne mouth can abide it without a phah.

phaine, variant of phane.

†**phairse, pheirs.** *Sc. Obs.* Also **phraisse, phrasse, frais.** [Variant forms of *fairss, fairce* = farce partly with metathesis of *r.*] A farce, in earlier sense: = interlude 1.

a **1578** Lindesay (Pitscottie) *Chron. Scot.* (S.T.S.) I. 379 Greit treumph and blythnes of phrassis and playis maid to hir at hir hame comming... Wpoun the eist syde thair was maid to her ane trieumphant frais [*MSS.* pheirs] to Schir Dawid Lyndsay of the Mont. *Ibid.* 381 Greit triumph, phraissis maid and playis wnto the queins grace. *Ibid.* II. 125 Singing playing dansing and pheirsis.

phakellite, var. facellite.

phakic ('feɪkɪk), *a. Ophthalm.* [f. Gr. φακ-ός lentil + -IC.] Of an eye: having a crystalline lens (as in the normal organ). Cf. APHAKIC *a.*

1918 J. H. PARSONS *Dis. Eye* (ed. 3) xxiv. 495 It is easy to calculate the amount of axial myopia of a phakic eye which is 31 mm. long. **1961** *Lancet* 22 July 169/1 Two perforating grafts have been performed in phakic eyes, and although the appearance of the cornea has improved the results are not as good as in the aphakic cases. **1975** R. N. SHAFFER in D. R. Anderson et al. *Symposium on Glaucoma* xiv. 250 In the phakic eye pupillary block is caused by apposition of the iris to the lens.

phako: see PHACO-.

phakoanaphylaxis, var. PHACOANAPHYLAXIS.

‖**phalæna** (fə'liːnə). *Entom.* [mod.L., a. Gr. φάλαινα, prop. φάλλαινα a moth.] A moth: used by Linnæus as a generic name for all moths; afterwards for all below the *Sphingina*, or for the *Geometrina*; not now used with any entomological value.

1658 ROWLAND tr. *Moufet's Theat. Ins.* 958 There are those that interpret this Phalaina to be the Cicindela or Glow-worm, but not rightly. *Ibid.* 1110 The Phalenæ that come from thence stick by the feet to the roofs of houses. **1752** J. HILL *Hist. Anim.* 77 The antennæ of the Phalæna are attenuated to the point... The species of this genus are very numerous. **1800** *Asiat. Ann. Reg.* 5/2 The phalæna, a species of which is to be found in a treatise published in France on foreign butterflies.

Hence **pha'lænian** *a.*, of or pertaining to a phalæna; *sb.* one of the *Phalænæ*, a moth, esp. a geometrid moth; **pha'lænoid** *a.*, akin to a phalæna; moth-like; *sb.* a moth-like insect.

1887 *Science* Apr. 318/2 Some of the Phalaenian larvae have 12 legs, and some even 14. **1858** MAYNE *Expos. Lex.* 928/1 Phalenoid.

phalænopsid (fæliː'nɒpsɪd). *Bot.* [ad. mod.L. *Phalænopsis*, f. Gr. φάλαινα moth + ὄψις appearance.] An orchid of the East Indian epiphytic genus *Phalænopsis*; a moth-orchid or moth-plant.

[**1846** LINDLEY *Veg. Kingd.* 181 Order LII. Orchidaceæ.. Genera..iii. Vandeæ... Phalænopsis.] **1880** BURBIDGE *Gard. Sun* iv. 54 The phalænopsids and other epiphytes are less ambitious. **1882** *Garden* 11 Feb. 97/1 The Phalænopsids at Rendlesham are specially distinguished by the size and number of their leaves. *Ibid.*, Fine plants of Phalænopsis are in full bloom.

phalangal (fə'læŋgəl), *a. rare.* [f. L. *phalanx*, *phalang-*, PHALANX + -AL[1].] = PHALANGEAL. Also **pha'langar** *a.*

1848 QUAIN *Elem. Anat.* (ed. 5) I. 174 The last two phalangal bones of the little toe. **1893** *Syd. Soc. Lex.*, *Phalangar process* [in the organ of Corti]. *Ibid.*, The phalangar bar on the outside of the ring in which lies the head of the twin cell of Corti.

phalange[1] ('fælændʒ). Also 6 falange, fallange; phalangue, 7 phalang. [a. Fr. *phalange*, in 13th c. *phalenge* (Hatz.-Darm.), = It. *falange*, ad. L. *phalange-m*, acc. of PHALANX.]

†**1.** = PHALANX 1. *Obs.*

1560 WHITEHORNE *Arte Warre* (1573) 29 b, Calld, of the Romanes, a Legion; of Greekes, a Fallange. **1569** STOCKER tr. *Diod. Sic.* II. xxxix. 90 He placed..the Elephantes.. before the Phalange or maine battail. **1585** T. WASHINGTON tr. *Nicholay's Voy.* III. iii. 73 The Macedonian Phalangue. **1689** PLUNKET *Char. Gd. Commander*, etc. 29/1 The Macedons still march'd in great Phalanges, And kept that order several Parasanges.

2. = PHALANX 3, 4.

1864 H. SPENCER *Biol.* III. §135 Here is a digit with its full number of phalanges, and there a digit, of which one phalange has been arrested in its growth. **1864** SALA in *Daily Tel.* 25 Feb., The delicate and taper finger of woman is plunged up to its topmost phalange into every political pie. **1893** *Syd. Soc. Lex.*, *Phalange*... Also, in *Entomol.*, a joint of the tarsus in Insecta. Also, in *Bot.*, a mass of stamens partly joined together by their filaments.

phalange[2]. Also 6 phalanga, phalang. [= F. *phalange*, It. *falangio*, ad. L. *phalangium*, a. Gr. φαλάγγιον, in same senses.]

†**1.** = PHALANGIUM I. *Obs.*

1551 TURNER *Herbal* I. D iv, Good against the bytinges of phalanges & scorpiones. **1587** GREENE *Carde of Fancie* Wks. (Grosart) IV. 112 He that is venomed by the *Phalanga*, feeleth such painefull passions, as he runneth mad. **1666** J. DAVIES *Hist. Caribby Isles* 82 Other kinds of great Flies..in these Islands, and which some call Phalanges. **1694** MOTTEUX *Rabelais* IV. lxvii. (1737) 265 Phalangs, Sloe-worms, Horn-worms.

2. An arachnid of the genus PHALANGIUM, or family *Phalangidæ*; a phalangid.

1876 E. SCHUYLER *Turkistan* xi. II. 123 The phalange (*Solpuga araneoides* and *S. intrepida*) is of a yellowish or reddish brown, also with long hair, and when walking seems as large as one's two fists.

phalangeal (fə'lændʒɪəl), *a. Anat.* and *Zool.* [f. mod.L. *phalange-us*, f. *phalanx*, *phalang-* + -AL[1].] Pertaining to, or of the nature of, a phalanx or phalanges (PHALANX 3).

1831 R. KNOX *Cloquet's Anat.* 159 The anterior or phalangeal extremity of this bone,..also named the head. **1878** T. BRYANT *Pract. Surg.* I. 179 The disease involves the last phalangeal joint or bone. **1893** *Syd. Soc. Lex.*, *P[halangeal] process*, the same as *Phalangar process*.

Also **pha'langean** *a. rare*$^{-0}$.

1882 in OGILVIE. **1893** in *Syd. Soc. Lex.*

phalanger (fə'lændʒə(r)). *Zool.* [a. mod.L. (Buffon), also mod.F., f. Gr. φαλάγγιον 'spider's web', in reference to the webbed toes of the hind feet.] A quadruped of the genus *Phalangista*, or of the subfamily *Phalangistinæ*, Australian marsupials of arboreal habits, containing numerous genera and species, usually of small size, with thick woolly fur; the typical genera (Australian 'opossums') have prehensile tails; the ***flying phalangers*** (called also *flying opossums*, *flying-squirrels*, or *petaurists*) have non-prehensile tails and a flying-membrane or parachute.

1774 GOLDSM. *Nat. Hist.* (1862) I. VII. i. 515 The Phalanger, so-called by Mr. Buffon,..about the size of a rat, and has..been called the Rat of Surinam. **1780** SMELLIE tr. *Buffon's Nat. Hist.* (1785) VII. 175 We have called it the phalanger, because its phalanges are very singularly constructed. **1876** *Forest & Stream* 13 July 375/2 The native bear, the vulpine phalanger, the wombat. **1885** M. R. O. THOMAS in *Encycl. Brit.* XVIII. 727/2 Buffon gave to a pair of cuscuses examined by him the name..'Phalanger', on account of the peculiar structure of the second and third toes of the hind feet, which are united in a common skin up to the nails. **1890** 'R. BOLDREWOOD' *Miner's Right* xxvii. 249 The rustle of the phalangers and the smaller marsupials.

pha'langial, *a. rare*$^{-0}$. = PHALANGEAL.

1864 in WEBSTER.

phalangian (fə'lændʒɪən), *a.* (*sb.*) [In sense 1, f. Gr. φάλαγξ, φαλαγγ- PHALANX; in 2, f. mod.L. (PHALANX 3) + -IAN; in 3, f. PHALANGIUM + -AN.]

1. *Gr. Antiq.* Belonging to a (military) phalanx: see PHALANX 1.

1843 *Fraser's Mag.* XXVIII. 696 The long spear of the phalangian soldier.

2. *Anat.* = PHALANGEAL. *rare*$^{-0}$.

1853 in DUNGLISON *Med. Lex.*

3. *Zool.* Belonging to the arachnid genus *Phalangium* or order *Phalangidea*; as *sb.* = PHALANGID.

1835 KIRBY *Hab. & Inst. Anim.* II. xv. 39 Some [crabs] imitating spiders, and others phalangians.

phalangic (fə'lændʒɪk), *a. rare.* [f. Gr. φάλαγξ, φαλαγγ- PHALANX + -IC.]

1. Pertaining to or of the nature of a (military) phalanx.

1846 H. W. TORRENS *Rem. Milit. Hist.* 45 A modern tactician much given to prize the phalangic or columnar formation for troops.

2. *Anat.* = PHALANGEAL. *rare*$^{-0}$.

1858 MAYNE *Expos. Lex.*, *Phalangicus*.., of or belonging to the *phalanges*: phalangic. **1893** *Syd. Soc. Lex.*, *Phalangic*, belonging to the *Phalanges*.

phalangid (fə'lændʒɪd). *Zool.* [f. mod.L. *Phalangidæ*, f. PHALANGIUM: see -ID[3].] An arachnid of the family *Phalangidæ* or order *Phalangidea* (typical genus *Phalangium*), related to the mites, but more resembling spiders, without spinnerets or poison-glands, and usually with very long and slender legs; the common species are known as *harvest-spiders* or *harvestmen*, and in U.S. as *daddy-long-legs*. So **pha'langidan**; **phalan'gidean** *a.*, belonging to the *Phalangidea*.

1835 KIRBY *Hab. & Inst. Anim.* II. xix. 303 The Class consists of two Orders..Pseudo Scorpions and Phalangidans. **1875** CAMBRIDGE in *Encycl. Brit.* II. 278/2 Phalangids..popularly known by the name of 'Harvest-men'. **1888** ROLLESTON & JACKSON *Anim. Life* 528 A Scorpion has been found in Silurian strata, and a Phalangid in the Solenhofen slates (Mesozoic).

pha'langiform, *a. Bot.* and *Anat.* [f. PHALANX or PHALANGIUM + -FORM.] Having the form of a phalanx.

1858 MAYNE *Expos. Lex.*, *Phalangiformis*..*Bot.*, applied by Nees von Esenbeck to vegetable hairs which are provided with transverse *septa* with a contraction at the outside of the *septa*, as in the *Tradescantia*: phalangiform. **1875** NEWTON in *Encycl. Brit.* III. 710/2 The rest of the second post-oral is reduced to..an elegant ridged phalangiform basi-hyal.

pha'langigrade, *a. Zool.* [ad. mod.L. *Phalangigrad-us*, f. as prec. + L. *gradus* step; cf. DIGITIGRADE, PLANTIGRADE.] Walking on the phalanges; belonging to the (now disused) division *Phalangigrada*, comprising the camel and llama.

1891 FLOWER & LYDEKKER *Mammals* ii. 50 Two forms, to which the terms 'phalangigrade' (as the Camel) and 'sub-plantigrade' (as in most Carnivora) are applied.

†**pha'langious,** *a. Obs.* [f. L. *phalangi-um* + -OUS.] Of the nature of a PHALANGIUM (sense 1).

1646 SIR T. BROWNE *Pseud. Ep.* III. xxvii. 177 Red Phalangious spiders like Cantharides mentioned by Muffetus.

phalangist[1] (fə'lændʒɪst, 'fæləndʒɪst). *Zool.* [ad. mod.L. *Phalangista*, substituted by Cuvier 1800 for Buffon's term *Phalanger*.] = PHALANGER.

1835 KIRBY *Hab. & Inst. Anim.* II. xvii. 159 The phalangists, or flying opossums. **1892** *Daily News* 4 Jan. 5/6 The Sooty Phalangist—the brown opossum from Tasmania.

So **pha'langistine** *a.*, belonging to the subfamily *Phalangistinæ*; *sb.* a marsupial of this subfamily, a phalangist.

Phalangist[2] ('fæləndʒɪst, fə'lændʒɪst). [ad. Sp. *falange*: see FALANGE.] **1.** A member of the Spanish FALANGE. Also *attrib.* or as *adj.*

1936 *Times* 17 Aug. 10/1 The main attack was delivered by a force of some 3,000 men, including the Foreign Legion, Moroccan troops, and 'Phalangists' or insurgent militia, divided into two columns. **1937** KOESTLER *Spanish Testament* i. 20 He [*sc.* a foreigner in Vigo] notes, during his hour's walk through the town, that it is chockfull of troops —Legionaries, Carlists, Phalangists, but no Moors. **1938** *Ann. Reg. 1937* 240 It was substantially the Phalangist programme which was adopted as the basis of the proposed Constitution for 'Nationalist' Spain. **1938** G. T. GARRATT *Shadow Swastika* vii. 192 The improved prospects of the Phalangists.

2. *transf.* A member of a right-wing, mainly Christian party in Lebanon. Also *attrib.* or as *adj.*

1972 *Daily Tel.* 20 June 4/3 Leaders of the mainly Christian Phalangist party are calling for an end to the 1969 Cairo agreement providing a Lebanese sanctuary for the commandos. **1975** *Times* 28 June 4/5 The Prime Minister-designate..is trying to reconcile differences between the mainly Christian Phalangists and..the influential socialist leader. **1977** *Time* 8 Aug. 29/1 The results were clearly joyous to a crowd including Israeli border police and flag-bearing Lebanese Christian Phalangist soldiers allowed on Israeli territory for the occasion. **1979** *Guardian* 9 Apr. 7/5 Iran's young Guerillas..find themselves increasingly out of step with the..'Phalangists' as the Left-wing has dubbed the country's new theocracy.

phalangite ('fælændʒaɪt). [ad. L. *phalangīta* or *-ites*, a. Gr. φαλαγγίτης, f. φάλαγξ PHALANX: see -ITE.] A soldier belonging to a phalanx.

[**1600** HOLLAND *Livy* XXXVII. cxl. 967 Hee had of Macedonians sixteene thousand footemen, heavily armed after their manner, called *Phalangitæ*.] **1839** THIRLWALL *Greece* xlviii. VI. 147 The phalangite soldier wore the usual defensive armour of the Greek heavy infantry. **1856** GROTE *Greece* II. xcii. XII. 77 The phalangites were drawn up in files generally of sixteen deep, each called a Lochus.

phalangitis (fælæn'dʒaɪtɪs). *Path.* [f. *phalanges*, pl. of PHALANX (sense 3) + -ITIS.] Inflammation of the phalanges.

1877 J. D. HOOKER in L. Huxley *Life J. D. Hooker* (1918) II. 142 [I get home] with a crick in my shoulder and 'phalangitis' from pump-handling some 500 people. **1903** *Lancet* 30 May 1526/1 He regarded the case as one of phalangitis of syphilitic origin.

‖**phalangium** (fə'lændʒɪəm). Pl. -ia. [L., a. Gr. φαλάγγιον a kind of venomous spider, also a plant, spiderwort.]

†**1.** Name for venomous spiders of various kinds.

1601 HOLLAND *Pliny* II. 360 These venomous spiders Phalangia, which the Greeks distinguish..by the name of Lupus. **1658** ROWLAND tr. *Moufet's Theat. Ins.* 1061 Grievous symptomes follow the bitings of Pismire Phalangium. **1671** *Phil. Trans.* VI. 3002 Whether the Tarantula be not a Phalangium (that is, a six-eyed skipping Spider)?

b. *Zool.* A genus of non-venomous arachnids having very long slender legs: see PHALANGID.

1848 JOHNSTON in *Proc. Berw. Nat. Club* II. 292 This mite lives on the Phalangia..or long-legged spiders.

†**2.** A former name for various liliaceous and iridaceous plants. *Obs.*

1664 EVELYN *Kal. Hort.* (1729) 208 June..Flowers in Prime, or yet lasting..Phalangium Allobrogicum. **1741** *Compl. Fam.-Piece* 380 Asphodels, Phalangiums, Smilax.

†**pha'langy.** *Obs.* Anglicized form of PHALANGIUM (sense 1).

1608 TOPSELL *Serpents* (1658) 770 There be many sorts of Spiders found in very cold Countries, but no Phalangies at all. **1659** STANLEY *Hist. Philos.* XII. (1701) 480/2 Athenagoras..felt no Pain at the biting of Scorpions, or Phalangies.

†**phalanque,** obs. form of PALANK.

1685 *Lond. Gaz.* No. 2055/2 This day the Enemy have abandoned a Phalanque.

‖**phalanstère** (falɑ̃stɛr). [mod.F., arbitrarily composed of *phalanx* with the ending of *monastère* monastery.] = PHALANSTERY.

1844 HENNELL *Soc. Syst.* 203 Mr. Owen's community is to be located in a Parallelogram, Fourier's in a Phalanstère. **1853** LYTTON *My Novel* IV. viii, Tracts which..substituted in place thereof Monsieur Fourier's symmetrical phalanstere, or Mr Owen's architectural parallelogram.

phalan'sterial, *a.* [f. as next + -AL[1].] = next, A.

1843 *Blackw. Mag.* LIII. 811 Should..the Phalansterial system of Fourier preferably suit their taste, they will be entitled to enter into the 'phalanx of harmony'.

phalansterian (fælæn'stɪərɪən), *a.* and *sb.* [ad. F. *phalanstérien*, f. *phalanstère*: see -IAN.]

A. *adj.* Of, pertaining or relating to a phalanstery, or the system of phalansteries.

1844 HENNELL *Soc. Syst.* 211 Two thousand colonists who intended to establish a Phalansterian Society at St. Catherine. **1875** *N. Amer. Rev.* CXX. 186 Unless children are to be afterwards reared and educated like chickens in an Egyptian oven upon Phalansterian principles.

B. *sb.* **a.** A member of a phalanstery. **b.** An advocate of the system of phalansteries; a Fourierist.

1843 *Fraser's Mag.* XXVIII. 341 Members of secret societies, clubbists, phalansterians. **1895** LAYARD in *19th Cent.* June 1069 Now, we are not Phalansterians. Phalansteries have been tried and failed.

Hence **phalan'sterianism**, the phalansterian system, Fourierism; so **phalansteric** (-'ɛrɪk) *a.*, pertaining to or characterized by phalansteries; **'phalanste,rism** = *phalansterianism*; **'phalanste,rist** = *phalansterian*, B. b.

1848 *Tait's Mag.* XV. 706 The world once fixed, and *phalansterianism universally adopted, Fourier's first care is to pay the English national debt. **1884** G. ALLEN *Strange Stories* 320 The final outcome..of all our modern *phalansteric civilization. **1877** *Echo* 28 Sept. 1/4 *Phalansterism or Fourierism. **1882** *Standard* 2 Aug., Social *phalansterists, who look upon all forms of aristocracy as deplorable survivals of a dark age.

phalanstery ('fælænstərɪ). [Anglicized form of F. *phalanstère* (mod.L. type **phalansterium*).]

a. In Fourier's scheme for the reorganization of society, A building or set of buildings occupied by a *phalanx* or socialistic community; hence, such a community itself, numbering about 1,800 persons, living together as one family, and holding property in common.

1846 *Knickerbocker* XXVIII. 16 And are all your slaves productive workers? This is contemplated, I believe, in all the *Phalansteries* of Unitative Associationists. *a* **1850** MARG. FULLER *Life Without* (1860) 148 Visions of phalansteries in every park. **1852** HAWTHORNE *Blithedale Rom.* II. ii. 26 One of our purposes was to erect a Phalanstery..after Fourier,.. where the great and general family should have its abiding-place. **1882** BRACE *Gesta Christi* 415 Christianity..has no sympathy with Socialism..in..its methods of dividing the returns from labour, or its phalansteries or communities. **1963** V. NABOKOV *Gift* iv. 235 Let us dream of the phalanstery living in a palace: 1,800 souls—and all happy! *attrib.* **1884** G. ALLEN *Strange Stories* 301 They sat together in a corner of the beautiful phalanstery garden.

b. *transf.* Applied allusively to associations or groups of persons, or the places where they dwell.

1850 KINGSLEY *Alt. Locke* viii, Every room..held its family, or its group of families—a phalanstery of all the fiends. **1856** EMERSON *Eng. Traits, Land* Wks. (Bohn) II. 15 England is a huge phalanstery, where all that man wants is provided within the precinct. **1883** HYNDMAN *Hist. Basis Socialism* xiii. 449 The tendency now exhibiting itself to turn workhouses into wholesome phalansteries.

phalanx ('fælæŋks). Pl. 'phalanxes, ‖phalanges (fə'lændʒiːz). Also 7 falanx. [a. L. *phalanx*, *-angem*, Gr. φάλαγξ, -αγγα.]

1. *Gr. Antiq.* A line or array of battle; *spec.* a body of heavy-armed infantry drawn up in close order, with shields joined and long spears overlapping; especially famous in the Macedonian army. Hence **b.** sometimes applied to a compact body of troops in later times.

1553 BRENDE *Q. Curtius* IV. (1565) 95 The square (whiche the Macedons call phalanx). *a* **1619** FLETCHER *Bonduca* II. iv, Youth and fire Like the fair breaking of a glorious day Guilded their Falanx. **1697** POTTER *Antiq. Greece* III. vi. II. 63 The Macedonians..; Their Phalanx is describ'd by Polybius to be a square Battail of Pike-men, consisting of sixteen in Flank, and five-hundred in Front. **1766** GIBBON *Decl. & F.* (1869) I. i. 26 The strength of the phalanx was unable to contend with the activity of the legion. **1838–42** ARNOLD *Hist. Rome* xxxvii. (1846) II. 491 The phalanx when once broken became wholly helpless. **1874** REYNOLDS *John Bapt.* vi. i. 367 Amid the serried phalanxes of Rome. **b. 1814** *Columbian Centinel* (Boston) 15 June 2/3 On Monday the Charlestown Warren Phalanx paraded. **1862** GRATTAN *Beaten Paths* I. 185 Noble veterans.., the remnant of those phalanxes which maintained the pride and power of England in so many a hard-fought field. *attrib.* **1838** ARNOLD *Hist. Rome* I. 71 The phalanx order of battle was one of the earliest improvements in the art of war. **1861** MUSGRAVE *By-Roads* 305 They massed them in phalanx form.

2. a. *transf.* A compact body of persons or animals (more rarely things) massed or ranged in order, as for attack, defence, united movement, etc.

1733 POPE *Ess. Man* III. 108 Who forms the phalanx [of migrating storks], and who points the way? **1785** COWPER *Needless Alarm* 48 The sheep..All huddling into phalanx, stood and gaz'd. **1837** W. H. AINSWORTH *Crichton* I. 237 A dense phalanx of cavaliers and dames of every age and rank. **1891** 'L. FALCONER' *Mlle. Ixe* 25 Sheltered from the north by high red walls and a phalanx of elms.

b. *fig.* A number or set of persons, etc. banded together for a common purpose, esp. in support of or in opposition to some cause; a 'united front'; the union or combination of such (in phr. *in phalanx*, unitedly, in combination, 'solidly').

1600 W. WATSON *Decacordon* (1602) 239 To encounter this Hispanised Camelion Parsons, with all his Africanian phalanges and Iesuiticall forces. **1772** *Pol. Reg.* XI. 168 The ministerial phalanx, it seems, is to be irreparably weakened by your loss. **1817** JAS. MILL *Brit. India* III. i. 32 On this occasion, the crown lawyers opposed in phalanx.

c. In Fourier's social organization, A community of persons living together in a PHALANSTERY, q.v.

1843 [see PHALANSTERIAL].

3. *Anat.* and *Zool.* Each of the bones, arranged in series or rows, forming the distal segment of the skeleton of each limb, beyond the metacarpus or metatarsus; each bone of the digits (fingers and toes, or homologous parts). Usu. in pl. *phalanges* (rarely *phalanxes*).

1693 tr. *Blancard's Phys. Dict.* (ed. 2), *Phalanx*, the Order and Rank, observed in the Finger-Bones. **1741** MONRO *Anat. Bones* (ed. 3) 271 Their Articulations with the first *Phalanx* of the Fingers is by *Enarthrosis*. *Ibid.* 274 Three *Phalanges*. **1807** *Med. Jrnl.* XVII. 347 It was necessary to amputate the phalanges of the fingers. **1808** BARCLAY *Muscular Motions* 375 Certain animals can, without clavicles, lay hold of objects with the digital phalanxes. **1872** MIVART *Elem. Anat.* iv. 152 Each digit consists of three rather elongated bones termed phalanges.

b. *Entom.* Each joint of the tarsus of an insect.

c. *Anat.* Each of certain processes in the organ of Corti in the internal ear; a phalangar process.

4. *Bot.* A bundle of stamens united by their filaments.

1770 *Phil. Trans.* LX. 519 The stamina..divided into five distinct phalanges, or bundles. **1880** GRAY *Struct. Bot.* vi. §3 (ed. 6) 205 Phalanges or united stamen-clusters.

5. *Taxonomy.* A group in classification, higher than a genus, but of no fixed grade.

1774 GOLDSM. *Nat. Hist.* (1776) II. 313 We should find it difficult..to place many that lie at the out-skirts of this phalanx. **1785** MARTYN *Rousseau's Bot.* xvi. (1794) 209 These are of another phalanx, having five petals to the corolla.

†**6.** = PHALANGIUM I. *Obs.*

1608 TOPSELL *Serpents* (1658) 769 The Phalangium or Phalanx Spider. *Ibid.*, This kinde of Phalanx is often found among Spiders webs.

Hence **'phalanxed** (-ŋkst) *a.*, drawn up or ranged in a phalanx; also in *Comb.*, as *close-phalanxed*.

1766 G. CANNING *Anti-Lucretius* IV. 245 The close-phalanx'd order of its course. **1812** BYRON *Ch. Har.* I. lxxx, Though now one phalanxed host should meet the foe. **1904** A. AUSTIN in *Standard* 13 Oct. 2/5 A pall of smoke penetrated only by phalanxed chimneys.

†**pha'laric.** *Rom. Antiq. Obs.* [a. F. *falarique*, ad. L. *phalārica*, erroneous spelling of *falārica* (in same sense), deriv. of *fala* (said to be Etruscan) a scaffolding from which missiles were thrown in sieges.] A javelin or dart wrapped in tow and pitch, set on fire, and thrown by the catapult or by hand, in order to set fire to a fortified place, a ship, etc.

1608 SYLVESTER *Du Bartas* II. iv. IV. *Decay* 964 With Brakes and Slings, and Phalariks they play, To fire their Fortresse, and their Men to slay. [**1685** COTTON tr. *Montaigne* I. xlviii. (1711) I. 440 They called a certain kind of *Javeline*..*Phalarica*.]

†**Pha'larical,** *a. Obs. rare.* erron. Phalerical. [f. *Phalaris* (see PHALARISM) + -ICAL.] Like that of Phalaris; inhuman: cf. PHALARISM.

1600 W. WATSON *Decacordon* (1602) 245 How many millions of men, women, and children, they haue there murthered: and that with such inhumane barbarousnesse, and much more then Phalericall cruelty.

phalaris ('fælərɪs). [L., f. Gr. φαλαρίς, Pliny's name for a similar grass; adopted by Linnæus in his *Hortus Cliffortianus* (1737) 23 as the name of a genus.] A grass of the genus so called, which includes canary-grass and some species useful for grazing.

1911 *Agric. Gaz. N.S.W.* XXII. 407 *Phalaris* and Kentucky Blue are spreading well. **1942** *Austral. Vet. Jrnl.* XVIII. 182 In three districts in South Australia the grazing of stock on pastures consisting almost exclusively of *Phalaris* has resulted in the occurrence of a 'staggers' syndrome. **1946** *Ibid.* XXII. 92/1 The general technique has been to select.. areas of pasture in which phalaris was dominant. **1956** *Brit. Vet. Jrnl.* CXII. 390 When the disease is noticed early the sheep are moved to a fresh pasture containing no phalaris and the nervous condition soon improves. **1966** *New Scientist* 25 Aug. 412/1 Nervous disfunction of sheep grazing phalaris has been recognized for many years. **1977** *Weekly Times* (Melbourne) 19 Jan. 10/5 Some stands of the sub clover and phalaris have been harvested for seed.

2. phalaris staggers, a nervous disorder of sheep and cattle caused by the consumption of the perennial grass, *Phalaris tuberosa*.

1946 I. W. MCDONALD in *Austral. Vet. Jrnl.* XXII. 91/2 A disease of sheep and cattle characterized by profound nervous symptoms and degenerative changes in the central nervous system was described. The disease was associated with the consumption of the perennial grass *Phalaris tuberosa* and thus had become colloquially known as 'phalaris staggers'. **1966** *Ibid.* XLII. 279/1 Neurological disorders of sheep grazing *Phalaris tuberosa* have hitherto been grouped under the term 'phalaris staggers'. **1970** JUBB & KENNEDY *Path. Domestic Animals* (ed. 2) II. vii. 387/2 The lesser syndrome, known as phalaris staggers, occurs when the plant is in lush growth and in 3–10 days after animals are given access to such pasture. Affected sheep appear normal when quiet, but, when disturbed, they show stiffness, incoordination, a staggering gait, and a tendency to fall.

†**'Phalarism.** *Obs.* Also 7 Phalerism. [ad. Gr. φαλαρισμ-ός cruelty like that of Phalaris, the tyrant of Agrigentum, who caused those condemned to death by him to be roasted alive in a brazen bull, the maker himself being the first victim.] Inhuman cruelty; pleasure in the infliction of torture.

1581 J. BELL *Haddon's Answ. Osor.* 278 b, This so great slaughter and bootchery,..so execrable Phalarisme and Tyranny. **1604** PARSONS *3rd Pt. Three Convers. Eng.*, *Relation Trial* 47 Two bookes of the Atheismes, and Phalerismes..of the ghospellers of our tymes. **1699** BENTLEY *Phal.* Pref. 41 There's a certain Temper of Mind, that Cicero calls *Phalarism*, a Spirit like Phalaris's.

phalarope ('fælərəʊp). *Ornith.* [a. F. *phalarope* (Brisson 1760), irreg. ad. mod.L. *Phalaropus* (ibid.), f. Gr. φαλαρίς a coot (φαλᾱρός having a patch of white) + πούς, ποδ- foot, intended to render Edwards's designation *Coot-footed* Tringa (1741).]

A name applied to several small wading and swimming birds of the family *Phalaropodidæ*, order *Limicolæ*, related to the snipes. They include the ***grey*** or ***red phalarope***, *Phalaropus fulicarius*, noted for its great seasonal changes of plumage, the ***red-necked*** or ***northern phalarope***, *P.* (*Lobipes*) *hyperboreus*, both occasional in Great Britain, and ***Wilson's phalarope***, *P.* (*Steganopus*) *Wilsoni*, of America.

1776 PENNANT *Zool.* (ed. 4) II. 413 Phalarope [*ed.* 1 Grey scollop toed Sandpiper]... This is about the size of the common Purre, weighing one ounce. **1843** YARRELL *Hist. Birds* III. 48 In its habits the Red-necked Phalarope very closely agrees with the Grey Phalarope, but is..much more rare in England, and more common on the northern islands of Scotland. **1894** NEWTON *Dict. Birds* 712 In the Phalaropes, as in the Dotterel and the Godwits, that sex [the male] undertakes the duty of incubation.

‖**phalera** ('fælərə). *Gr.* and *Rom. Antiq.* Also 7 phaler. [L. *phalera*, in pl. *phaleræ*, orig. *-a*, a. Gr. φάλαρα pl., in same sense.] A bright metal disk or boss worn on the breast as an ornament by men, or used to adorn the harness of horses.

1606 HOLLAND *Sueton.* 193 Attended..with a multitude of Mazaces and Curreurs gaily set out with their bracelets and riche Phalers. **1886** *Athenæum* 31 July 148/3 Four large bronze phaleræ such as are usually supposed..to belong to horse-harness.

†**'phalerate,** *a. Obs.* In 8 phalarate. [ad. L. *phalerāt-us*, pa. pple. of *phalerāre* to adorn with trappings, f. *phaleræ*: see prec.] Ornamented, decorated. In quot. *fig.*

1702 C. MATHER *Magn. Chr.* IV. iv. (1852) 93 A sort of harangue finely laced and guilded with such phalarate stuff as plainly discovers the vanity of them that jingle with it.

So †**'phalerated** *a. Obs.*

1656 BLOUNT *Glossogr.*, *Phalerated*,..trapped, or dressed with Trappings, as horses use to be.

Phaleucian (fə'l(j)uːsɪən), *a.* Also 6 -sian. [f. L. *Phaleucius*, properly *Phalæci-us* (f. *Phalæcus*) + -AN.] Of or pertaining to Phalæcus, an ancient Greek poet: applied to an ancient metre consisting of a spondee, a dactyl, and three trochees.

1571 GOLDING *Calvin on Ps.* vi. 1 As if a man woold terme it a Saphicke, or Phaleusian verse. **1639** SHIRLEY *Maids Revenge* I. i. B iij b, I can..sting with Phaleucians [*printed* Phalenciums], whip with Saphicks. **1658** PHILLIPS, *Phaleucian verse*. **1836** LANDOR *Pericles & Aspasia* Wks. 1846 II. 373, I think she has injured the phaleucian verse, by transposing one foot, and throwing it backward. **1903** *Scott. Hist. Rev.* Oct. 38 The fourth epitaph is described as in 'Phaleucian verse' that is in lines of eleven syllables.

So †**Pha'leucic, -'leusic, -'leuciac** *a. Obs.* = prec.: also *absol.* as *sb.*

a **1586** SIDNEY *Arcadia* (1622) 228 [He] neuer left intreating her, til she had (taking a *Lyra Basilius* held for her) sung these Phaleuciakes. **1656** BLOUNT *Glossogr.*, *Phaleusick Verse* (*phaleuceum carmen*).

‖**phallalgia** (fæ'lældʒɪə). *Path.* [f. Gr. φαλλ-ός penis + -ALGIA.] (See quots.) Hence **pha'llalgic** *a.*

1853 DUNGLISON *Med. Lex.*, *Phallalgia*. **1858** MAYNE *Expos. Lex.*, *Phallalgia*..term for pain in the *membrum virile*: phallalgy... *Phallalgicus*..of or belonging to *Phallalgia*: phallalgic.

phallephoric (fælɪ'fɒrɪk), *a. rare.* [f. Gr. φαλληφορία the phallus-bearing (f. φαλλός + -φόρος bearing) + -IC.] Of or pertaining to the bearing of the phallic emblems.

1876 A. WILDER in *R. P. Knight's Symbolic Lang.* 55 *note*, Venus Erycina..worshipped by the Roman women, who every first of April made a phallephoric procession to her temple.

phallic ('fælɪk), *a.* [mod. ad. Gr. φαλλικός, f. φαλλός penis: in F. *phallique* (*Dict. Acad.* 1878).] Of or relating to the phallus or phallism; symbolical of the generative power in nature. Also in special collocations as ***phallic stage***

Psychoanal., *phallic symbol*; and in adj. phr. as *phallic-centred, -shaped*.

1789 TWINING *Aristotle's Treat. Poetry* 72 Those *Phallic* songs, which, in many cities, remain still in use. **1850** GROTE *Greece* II. lxvii. VIII. 446 The exuberant revelry of the phallic festival and procession. **1873** SYMONDS *Grk. Poets* v. 118 The Phallic Hymn, from which comedy took its origin, was a mad outpouring of purely animal exultation. **1891** T. HARDY *Tess* (1892) 368 Myriads of loose white flints in bulbous, cusped, and phallic shapes. **1907** G. B. SHAW *John Bull's Other Island* II. 38 The view that the Round Towers are phallic symbols. **1923** *Internat. Jrnl. Psycho-Anal.* IV. 383 Charlie Chaplin as phallic symbol. **1927** *Ibid.* VIII. 468 Freud postulated a 'phallic' stage in female development corresponding with that in the male. **1928** D. H. LAWRENCE *Let.* 15 Mar. (1962) II. 1046 It is a nice and tender phallic novel. **1949** J. STRACHEY tr. *Freud's Three Ess. Theory of Sexuality* ii. 77 This phase..is differentiated from the final organization of sexual maturity... For it knows only one kind of genital: the male one. For that reason I have named it the 'phallic' stage of organization. **1952** C. THOMPSON *Psychoanal.* iii. 69 A phallic character comes from sublimation of the phallic stage. Such a person is..insolent, domineering, and aggressive. **1959** E. POUND *Thrones* xcix. 49 That man's phallic heart is from heaven a clear spring of rightness. **1963** A. HERON *Towards Quaker View of Sex* iii. 23 Males are very phallic-centred. **1964** P. F. ANSON *Bishops at Large* ix. 358 The 'forces' and 'vibrations' within this phallic-shaped building. **1968** R. & G. BLANCK *Marriage & Pers. Devel.* ii. 9 The anal character is greedy; the anal character is stubborn and parsimonious; the phallic character is exhibitionistic and competitive. **1968** M. ELLMAN *Thinking about Women* ii. 46 It is through this identification that phallic criticism regularly and rapidly shifts from writing by women, which can be dismissed as innocuous, to their vicious influence upon writing by men. **1972** C. SHORT *Naked Skier* xxiv. 137, I switched my mind to contemplation of the Eiffel Tower. It too was a phallic symbol. **1975** C. REGISTER in J. Donovan *Feminist Lit. Crit.* 9 A second exercise in Phallic Criticism is to admit grudgingly to the literary value of works by women, and then to deny that it is consciously attained. **1977** *Spare Rib* Sept. 13/2 Now we [*sc.* women] can have the phallic freedoms to screw where and when we want. **1978** *Amer. Poetry Rev.* July/Aug. 19/1 If you riffle the pages from back to front you will see one block of pattern divide, while another phallic-shaped pattern slowly enters it.

So **'phallical** *a.*

1900 W. SENIOR *Pike & Perch* 11 Among the fishes of fancy are..a phallical pike with golden fins; a pike begotten by the west wind.

phallically ('fælɪkəlɪ), *adv.* Also **phallicly**. [f. PHALLIC, PHALLICAL *adjs.*: see -ICALLY.] In a manner resembling a phallus.

1967 E. GRIERSON *Crime of one's Own* i. 9 In the distance Brunelleschi's dome and Giotto's tower rose phallically towards the Tuscan sky. **1971** *Daily Tel.* (Colour Suppl.) 11 June 27/4 *Bomb Release*, Dennis's own work that lights up and changes colour while it erects phallicly. **1978** J. UPDIKE *Coup* (1979) iii. 102 Abrasive ointments phallically packaged and chemically fortified.

phallicism ('fælɪsɪz(ə)m). [f. PHALLIC *a.* + -ISM.] The worship of the phallus, or of the organs of sex, as symbols of the generative power in nature.

1884 H. JENNINGS *Phallicism* iii. 38 It expressed deified phallicism in perplexing but convincing forms. **1890** A. H. LEWIS in *Outlook & Sabb. Quarterly* (U.S.) 145 Phallicism ..was the lowest phase of that cult [sun-worship].

So **'phallicist**, one who studies, or is versed in, phallicism.

1924 *Jrnl. R. Anthrop. Inst.* LIV. 49 The phallicists of the seventies, Burton, Fergusson,..and Westropp.

phallin ('fælɪn). *Chem.* Also -ine. [a. G. *phallin* (R. Kobert 1891, in *St. Petersb. med. Wochenschr.* XVI. 472/2), f. mod.L. *phalloides* (see PHALLOIDIN): see -IN[1], -INE[5].] A hæmolytic substance present in the death cap toadstool, *Amanita phalloides*, and formerly thought to be its poisonous principle.

1897 *Trans. Brit. Mycol. Soc.* I. 27 Professor Kobert..has given the name of phalline to the poisonous substance present in *Amanita phalloides*, Fries. *Ibid.* 28 Phalline is a very powerful agent..in causing the dissolution of the red corpuscles of the blood. **1930** *Lancet* 1 Feb. 228/1 The toxin of tetanus is checked by La Bourboule water and not by Mont Dore, phallin poison by Mont Dore water and not by La Bourboule. **1965** BELL & COOMBE tr. *Strasburger's Textbk. Bot.* 508 Familiar Agaricaceae:..*Amanita phalloides* .., deadly poisonous with toxic glucosides (phallin) and peptides (phalloidin, amanitin). **1972** T. & O. WIELAND in S. J. Ajl et al. *Microbial Toxins* VIII. x. 252 A hemolytic agent..was obtained from *A. phalloides* as early as 1891 by Kobert and was called 'phallin'. It has recently been reinvestigated by Fiume (1967), who..stated that, in addition to a hemolytic action, a cytotoxic effect on cultures of cells of KB line and of human amnion cells occurred. This substance, whose chemical nature has not yet been established, is presumably destroyed in the gastrointestinal tract and, therefore, cannot be responsible for lethality of the mushroom.

phallism ('fælɪz(ə)m). [f. Gr. φαλλ-ός PHALLUS + -ISM.] = PHALLICISM.

1879 M[c]CLINTOCK & STRONG *Cycl. Bibl. Lit.* VIII. 55 The religion of Baal, openly denounced by the prophets, was a sort of phallism..which the Jews too often imitated. **1928** A. HUXLEY *Point Counter Point* x. 165 Civilized lasciviousness is the same as the healthy—what shall I call it? —phallism..of the ancients... Worshipping with the body —that's the genuine phallism. **1950** *Funk's Stand. Dict. Folklore* II. 863/2 Among some ethnic groups phallism, also often called sex worship, is the worship of the male sexual organ.

So **'phallist** = PHALLICIST.

‖**phallitis** (fæ'laɪtɪs). *Path.* [f. PHALL-US + -ITIS.] (See quot.)

1853 in DUNGLISON *Med. Lex.* **1867** C. A. HARRIS *Dict. Med. Terminol.*, *Phallitis*, inflammation of the penis.

phallocentric (fæləʊ'sɛntrɪk), *a.* [f. Gr. φαλλός penis + -CENTRIC.] Centred on the phallus. Hence **phallocen'tricity, phallo'centrism**.

1927 *Internat. Jrnl. Psycho-Anal.* VIII. 459 There is a healthy suspicion growing that men analysts have been led to adopt an unduly phallo-centric view of the problems in question. **1951** *Brit. Jrnl. Psychol.* XLII. 382 The phallocentric tendencies of early psychology. **1970** G. GREER *Female Eunuch* 48 The enormous hoo-ha about the strange impalpable results of vasectomy..results from.. phallocentricity. **1977** *Spare Rib* June 46/4 She capitulates, without too much struggle, to an individual solution of phallocentric romantic love. **1977** A. SHERIDAN tr. *Lacan's Écrits* vi. 198 The phallocentrism produced by this dialectic is all that need concern us here. **1977** R. HOLLAND *Self & Social Context* viii. 254 Wilden's critique of Lacan, whose valuable exposition of the Imaginary does not allow him to escape its vicissitudes, as can be seen by his phallocentrism and his elitist conceptual violence.

phallocrat ('fæləkræt). [f. as prec. + -CRAT: cf. Fr. *phallocrate*.] One who advocates or assumes the existence of a male-dominated society; a man who argues his superiority over women because of his masculinity. Also *attrib.* or as *adj.* So **pha'llocracy, phallo'cratic** *a.*

1977 *Gay News* 24 Mar. 11/3 The march was backed up by members of the Groupe de Liberation Homosexuel.. shouting the slogan 'with women against phallocracy'. **1977** *Times Lit. Suppl.* 10 June 699/3 That feeble tyrant, the reincarnation of her father—the 'phallocrat' male. **1977** *Radical Philos.* Summer 9/2 It would be a mystery how the jury of 1971 could have escaped the effects of this phallocratic unconscious. *Ibid.*, Her phallocrat of a husband or lover letting her deal with all the domestic chores. **1977** *Ibid.* Autumn 1, I do myself think that the style of at least some of those 'great texts' is indeed phallocratic. **1978** *Times Lit. Suppl.* 24 Mar. 342/5 By a species of reification no more excusable than that dictated by the phallocrats, they have consecrated a ready-made caricature of Woman which serves to reduce all women to an absolute type.

phalloid ('fælɔɪd), *a.* [f. PHALLUS + -OID.]

1858 in MAYNE *Expos. Lex.* **1893** *Syd. Soc. Lex.*, *Phalloid* ..resembling the penis in appearance. **1967** A. EDWARDES in R. E. L. Masters *Sexual Self-Stimulation* 308 Arab and Israeli girls of prepubertal age..masturbate..with fingers or some phalloid object.

phalloidin (fæ'lɔɪdɪn). *Chem.* Also -ine. [a. G. *phalloidin*, given its present meaning by U. Wieland 1938 (*Ann. d. Chem.* DIII. 100) following its coinage as F. *phalloïdine* by A. Gubler 1877 (*Bull. de l' Acad. de Méd.* VI. 879) to denote an 'amorphous toxic principle' obtained from *A. phalloides* by P. C. Oré; f. mod.L. *phalloides*, specific epithet (f. Gr. φαλλός penis: see -OID): see -IN[1], -INE[5].] The principal phallotoxin, $C_{35}H_{48}N_8O_{11}S$.

1938 *Chem. Abstr.* XXXII. 3456 Toxin II has been crystd. (needles) and is designated as phalloidin. **1955** *Sci. News Let.* 23 Apr. 265/2 The two amanitines and phalloidine in mushrooms affect the liver, kidney and heart. **1961** *Lancet* 16 Sept. 630/2 More than a century of investigation, mainly in Germany and France, has led to the isolation of five crystalline toxins from *Amanita phalloides* (α, β, and γ amanitin, phalloin, and phalloidin). **1972** *Science* 1 Sept. 808/1 The principal phallotoxin is phalloidin. **1977** R. JEFFRIES *Troubled Deaths* xiii. 101 The normal symptoms of phalloidine poisoning.

phalloin ('fæləʊɪn). *Chem.* [a. G. *phalloin* (Wieland & Mannes 1957, in *Angewandte Chem.* LXIX. 389/1), f. mod.L. *phallo-ides* (see prec.) + -IN[1].] One of the phallotoxins, $C_{35}H_{48}N_8O_{10}S$.

1959 *Chem. Abstr.* LIII. 18880 Chromatographic sepn. of the enriched poison mixt. of the amanita mushroom on neutral Al_2O_3 in H_2O-satd. BuOH + 10% EtOH mixt. gave another toxin, called phalloin. **1961** [see PHALLOIDIN]. **1968** [see PHALLOTOXIN].

phallophoria (fæləʊ'fɔrɪə). [f. Gr. φαλλοφορ-εῖν to bear a phallus + -IA[1] or ad. Gr. φαλληφόρια (see PHALLEPHORIC *a.*) influenced by the root φαλλό-ς.] The carrying of a phallus, esp. as part of a festival of Dionysus in ancient Greece. Hence **phallo'phoric** *a.* = PHALLEPHORIC *a.*

The Gr. word φαλληφόρια is a neuter plural, but the English form *phallophoria* is usu. const. as a sing.

1903 J. E. HARRISON in *Jrnl. Hellenic Stud.* XXIII. 322 We have established..that a phallophoria formed a part of Dionysiac mysteries. **1950** *Funk's Stand. Dict. Folklore* II. 864/1 The carrying of phalli in public processions (*phallophoria*). **1964** *New Statesman* 13 Mar. 398/1 The puppets looked more phallophoric than the Beatles themselves. As the taped Beatle music rose to a pitch, the jiggling became an almost indecent enactment of sexual rhythm. **1967** A. L. LLOYD *Folk Song in England* ii. 93 The randy animal-guiser song of the 'Derby Ram'..a song that is the lyrical equivalent of those phallophoric dances that survive in farming communities in Europe, intended to celebrate and stimulate the powers of reproduction.

phallophorus (fæləʊ'fɔrəs). Also -phoros. Pl. -phori, -phoroi. [ad. Gr. φαλλοφόρος bearing a phallus.] One who carries a phallus, esp. as part of a festival of Dionysus in ancient Greece.

1854 C. D. YONGE tr. *Athenæus' Deipnosophists* III. XIV. 992 Semos the Delian says in his book about Pæans... 'And those,..who are called Ithyphalli, wear a mask representing the face of a drunken man... And the Phallophori..wear no masks, but they put on a sort of veil of wild thyme... The Phallophorus..marched straight on, covered with soot and dirt'. **1885** H. M. WESTROPP *Primitive Symbolism* 54 The periphallia..carried long poles with phalli hung at the end of them: they were crowned with violets and ivy... These men were called phallophori. **1909** L. R. FARNELL *Cults Gk. States* V. v. 210 It may be that Semos of Delos is describing something that happened in the later Attic festival when —according to Athenaeus—he speaks of 'the ithyphalloi'.. and of the phallophoroi without masks entering through the central doors of the theatre. **1927** A. W. PICKARD-CAMBRIDGE *Dithyramb Tragedy & Comedy* iii. 234 The phallophorus proper had his face disguised with soot. (Probably he carried, but did not wear, the phallus). *Ibid.* 235 Possibly the ceremony of the phallophori was of a common type, differing little from town to town. **1931** A. NICOLL *Masks, Mimes & Miracles* i. 26 Bethe thinks that the *phallophoroi* were Delians; for this there is no proof.

‖**phallos** ('fæləs). Pl. -oi. [Gr. φαλλός penis.] = PHALLUS. Also *attrib.* and *Comb.*

1928 D. H. LAWRENCE *Lady Chatterley* x. 161 The man dwindled to a..mere phallos-bearer, to be torn to pieces when his service was performed. **1950** *Funk's Stand. Dict. Folklore* II. 862/1 The Greek satyrs of the Dionysiac *orgia* stamped and capered with gigantic phalloi and artificial breasts—a symbol of self-fructification. **1963** AUDEN *Dyer's Hand* III. 102 If all round hills were suddenly to turn into breasts, all caves into wombs, all towers into phalloi, we should not be pleased..we should be bored. **1972** *Times Lit. Suppl.* 19 May 565/3 Golden phalloi of superb craftsmanship and considerable avoirdupois. **1978** K. J. DOVER *Greek Homosexuality* III. 133 The 'phallos-bird', which has the legs, body and wings of a bird but a neck and head in the form of a curved penis with the foreskin rolled back and an eye on the glans.

phallotoxin (fæləʊ'tɒksɪn). *Chem.* [f. mod.L. *phallo-ides* (see PHALLOIDIN) + TOXIN.] Any of several closely related poisonous peptides present in the death cap toadstool, *Amanita phalloides*, all of which have the same ring structure of seven amino-acids bridged by a sulphur atom.

1968 *Science* 1 Mar. 949/1 The phallotoxins include phalloidin, phalloin, [etc.]. **1972** *Ibid.* 1 Sept. 808/1 The rapidly acting phallotoxins..are responsible for the gastrointestinal phase of the poisoning. **1975** *Sci. Amer.* Mar. 95/1 In the phallotoxins the cyclopeptide ring has seven amino acids; in the amatoxins it has eight.

‖**phallus** ('fæləs). Pl. -i. [L. *phallus*, a. Gr. φαλλός penis: so in mod.F. (1835 in *Dict. Acad.*).]

1. a. An image of the male generative organ, symbolizing the generative power in nature, venerated in various religious systems; *spec.* that carried in solemn procession in the Dionysiac festivals in ancient Greece. In later times commonly worn as an amulet or protection against the evil eye.

1613 PURCHAS *Pilgrimage* (1614) 79 Two substantiall witnesses, besides others, affirming the same, namely two Phalli, or Priapi (huge Images of the priuie part of a man). *Ibid.* 579 This yard, which they called Phallus, was vsually made of Figge-tree. **1797** *Encycl. Brit.* (ed. 3) XIV. 266/2 *Phallus*, among the Egyptians, was the emblem of fecundity. **1895** ELWORTHY *Evil Eye* 148 In compounded amulets the commonest of all objects was the phallus or some other suggesting the ideas conveyed by it.

b. The male generative organ, often in the context of its symbolical significance; in psychoanalysis, in the context of the pre-genital phase of sexual development.

By some writers used in the specific sense 'erect penis'.

1924 J. RIVIERE tr. *Freud's Infantile Genital Organization* in *Coll. Papers* II. 245 The primacy reached is..not a primacy of the *genital*, but of the *phallus*. *Ibid.* 247 The significance of the castration complex can only be rightly appreciated when its origin in the phase of the primacy of the phallus is also taken into account. **1935** M. BALINT *Primary Love & Psycho-Anal. Technique* (1952) iii. 56 The same is true of the phenomena of the phallic period: belief in the non-existence of the female genital organs..or in the existence of mothers with a phallus. **1935** R. V. STORER *Sexual Technique* xxi. 274 Effective virility therefore depends on erectile capacity; that is, the penis must be able to become a phallus (as the erect male organ in action is called). **1951** FORD & BEACH *Patterns of Sexual Behavior* ii. 22 The bodily adjustments that give rise to these sensations involve merely insertion of the phallus followed by piston-like thrusts within the vagina. **1960** J. RODNEY *Handbk. Sex Knowledge* iv. 45 In its simplest—and crudest—form, copulation consists of the entrance of the erect penis or phallus into the vagina, followed by certain movements which produce an ejaculation of male semen into the vaginal cavity. **1961** C. & W. M. S. RUSSELL *Human Behaviour* vi. 271 A welter of key stimuli independent of the individual's personality, of breasts and phalluses, hands and feet. **1963** A. HERON *Towards Quaker View of Sex* iii. 35 The experience is thus phallus-centred and produces excitement without deep commitment. **1972** *Times Lit. Suppl.* 29 Sept. 1156/5 A phallus is a prerequisite of intercourse and, being so, has a social significance..whereas a penis can never have more than a biological significance. **1974** H. S. KAPLAN *New Sex Therapy* i. 21 The female sexual response transforms the tight, dry vaginal potential space into a well-lubricated, open receptacle for the phallus. **1977** *Times* 18 Feb. 11/7 Fat villains sporting Old Comedy phalli.

2. *Bot.* A genus of gasteromycetous fungi, so called from their shape; of which one species, *P. impudicus*, is the common stink-horn.

1857 Henfrey *Elem. Bot.* §636 In *Phallus* the volva is more strikingly developed. **1953** J. Ramsbottom *Mushrooms & Toadstools* xvi. 182 A violet-scented *Phallus* would certainly be exceptional. **1976** G. C. Ainsworth *Introd. Hist. Mycology* iii. 38 There is a figure of the stink-horn (both 'egg' and fruit-body) which in 1562 had been described and illustrated by the Dutch physician Adriaen Jonghe (H. Junius) who gave the name 'Phallus' to it in the first independently published mycological monograph.

3. *Comb.*, as ***phallus-worship***.

1850 Carlyle *Hudson's Statue* in *Latter-Day Pamphlets* vii. 43 Kings and Papas flying like detected coiners; and in their stead Icaria, Red Republic,..Literature of Desperation curiously conjoined with Phallus-Worship too clearly heralding centuries of bottomless Anarchy. **1880** Stallybrass tr. *Grimm's Teut. Mythol.* I. 213 *note*, Phallus-worship..must have arisen out of an innocent veneration of the generative principle.

†**phalucco**, obs. erroneous form of felucca.

1615 G. Sandys *Trav.* 227 A Phalucco arriueth at the place.

†**phan**, obs. erroneous spelling of fan.

1539 *MS. Acc. St. John's Hosp., Canterb.*, Payd for a phan a[t] Baluerley ixd.

‖**Phanar** (ˈfænɑː(r)). Also 9 **Fanar**. [Turkish *fanar*, ad. Gr. φανάριον (mod.Gr. φανάρι) lighthouse, lantern (dim. of φανός torch, lamp, lantern).] A quarter of Constantinople (so called from a lighthouse on the Golden Horn), which became the chief Greek quarter after the Turkish Conquest; hence put for the Greek official class under the Turks, through whom the affairs of the Christian population in the Ottoman Empire were largely administered. Also, the seat of the Patriarch of Constantinople after the Ottoman conquest. Also *transf.*

1819 T. Hope *Anastasius* I. ii. 42 He..plunged head-long into all the intrigues of the Fanar. **1838** *Penny Cycl.* X. 194/2, The bankers of the Fanar. **1878** Disraeli in G. E. Buckle *Life* (1920) VI. 320 A perfect Greek of the Fanar. **1886** *Encycl. Brit.* XX. 20/1 The Fanar quarter of Constantinople. **1897** R. Davey *Sultan & his Subjects* II. iii. 112 The noble Greek families which returned after the siege and settled in that quarter of Constantinople, known as the Phanar. **1900** 'Odysseus' *Turkey in Europe* vi. 276 One small Slavonic Church, however, that of Montenegro, resisted Hellenism and the Phanar as successfully as the Government withstood the Turks. **1901** *Dundee Advertiser* 3 May 6 All candidates for the post who did not show Russophile tendencies have been eliminated. Whoever is appointed, he will be hostile to pretensions of the Phanar. **1911** E. Pears *Turkey & its People* vii. 118 The patriarch of Constantinople..resides at the Phanar, a district in Constantinople... As there was much intrigue and bribery ..under the sultans, Phanariot came to be a synonym for a man of unscrupulous political intrigue. **1936** H. Luke *Making of Mod. Turkey* iv. 97 It was only in 1850 that the Phanar, reluctantly and under Russian pressure, recognized the Church of the Greek kingdom as independent. **1961** D. Attwater *Christian Churches of East* II. iii. 22 in 1766 the Phanar obtained from the sultan Mustafa III an order for the suppression of the Serbian independent church. **1964** P. F. Anson *Bishops at Large* viii. 281 No Christian Church would be able to offer such..ceremonial as this new one with its '*phanar*' or '*curia*' in Holloway.

Hence **Phanariot** (fəˈnærɪɒt). Also 9 **Fanariote**. [ad. mod.Gr. φαναριώτης: see prec. and -ot².], a resident in the Phanar quarter of Constantinople; one of the class of Greek officials residing there; also as *adj.*

1819 T. Hope *Anastasius* I. iv. 74 The persons of the Fanariote grandees were of a piece with their habitations. *Ibid.* 82, I had my share of the second hand insolence, which the Fanariotes take very quietly from the Turks. **1838** *Penny Cycl.* X. 194/2 A crowd of Fanariotes always followed the new Hospodars. **1856** tr. *F. Perthes' Mem.* I. xxxiii. 411 The cruel exactions of the Greek princes, and insatiable Fanariotes. **1862** G. Finlay in W. R. W. Stephens *Freeman's Life & Lett.* (1895) I. 281 If..phanariots and the nominees of diplomatists are not intruded. **1880** Donaldson in *Encycl. Brit.* XI. 125/2 Many of them were phanariots, accustomed to double dealing, ambitious and avaricious. **1899** in *Daily News* 20 July 6/4 A masterpiece of Phanariot perfidy.

phanatic, -ik, -ique, etc., obs. ff. fanatic, etc.

phanatron, var. phanotron.

phancie, -y, obs. forms of fancy.

phane, an early spelling of fane *sb.*¹ 2: = vane.

1387–8 T. Usk *Test. Love* ii. i. (Skeat) l. 23 Some saine that loue shulde be in windy blastes, that stoundemele tourneth as a phane. *c* **1407** Lydg. *Reson & Sens.* 6180 They turne nat as doth a phane With vnwar wynde. **1500–20** Dunbar *Poems* lxvi. 95 This fals failȝeand warld..That ever more flytis lyk ane phane. **1601–2** in Willis & Clark *Cambridge* II. 629 For a phaine for the peremint of the Coundite.

phane, obs. erron. form of fane *sb.*²

†**phanekill**. *Sc. Obs.* [dim. of fane *sb.*¹ 1.] A little flag or vane.

1538 *Aberdeen Regr.* XVI. (Jam.), The ferd part of vj elnis of tapheit, quhilk wes maid ane phanekill of.

phanelle, obs. form of fannell.

†**ˈphanerite**, *a.* *Geol. Obs. rare.* [f. Gr. φανερ-ός (see next) + -ite¹.] (See quots.)

a **1857** J. Fleming *Lithol. Edinb.* v. (1859) 51 The Phanerite series consists of deposits produced by causes in ordinary operation, and respecting the circumstances under which they have been produced little obscurity prevails. **1859–65** Page *Handbk. Geol. Terms, Phanerite Series*..the upper-most stage of the modern epoch, as consisting of deposits..whose origin is evident, as compared with the brick-clays and boulder-clays..which lie beneath.

phanero- (ˈfænərəʊ), before a vowel **phaner-**, combining form of Gr. φανερός visible, evident (opposed to crypto-): used in a few technical terms.

phaneroˈbranchiate *a.*, having evident *branchiæ* or gills; **phaneroˈcarpous** *a.* [Gr. καρπός fruit] (see quots.); **ˌphanerocoˈdonic** *a.* [Gr. κώδων a bell], bell-shaped: said of the gonophores of hyrdrozoans, when possessing a developed umbrella; **phaneroˈcrystalline** *a.*, of evident crystalline structure; **phaneroˈglossal, -ˈglossate, -ˈglossous** *adjs.* [Gr. γλῶσσα tongue], having a distinct tongue: used of a family of Frogs; **phaneˈromerous** *a.* [Gr. μέρος part], **ˈphaneroˈpneumonous** *a.* [Gr. πνεύμων lungs] (see quots.).

1858 Mayne *Expos. Lex., Phanerocarpus*..applied by Eschenholtz to a section..of the Acalepha Discophora, comprehending those in which the reproductive corpuscles are perceived across the body: *phanerocarpous. **1871** Allman *Gymnobl. Hydroids* 195 The *phanerocodonic and the adelocodonic gonophores. **1862** Dana *Man. Geol.* 72 *Phanero-crystalline or distinctly crystalline. **1858** Mayne *Expos. Lex., Phaneroglossus*..*phaneroglossous. **1888** Teale *Petrography* Gloss. 443 **Phaneromerous*..a term applied to coarse crystalline rocks. **1858** Mayne *Expos. Lex., Phaneropneumonus*..applied by Gray to an Order..of the *Gasteropodophora*, which corresponds..to the *Pulmonea Operculata* of Férussac: *phaneropneumonous.

phanerogam (ˈfænərəʊˌgæm). *Bot.* [a. F. *phanérogame* (*adj.* Ventenat 1799, De Candolle 1813; *sb.* Brongniart 1828), in mod.L. *phanerogam-us* adj. f. Gr. φανερό-ς, phanero- + γάμος marriage, sexual union.] A phanerogamic or flowering plant. (Opposed to cryptogam.) Chiefly in plural.

In pl. *phanerogams* = mod.L. *Phanerogamæ, plantæ phanerogamæ* (Humboldt, *Nova Gen. et Sp. Plant.*, 1815).

1861 L. Stephen tr. *Berlepsch's Alps* 47 The weak soft cellular tissue of nearly all the other phanerogams. **1889** J. S. Van Cleve in *Literature* (N.Y.) 2 Feb. 261 The flora.. includes 1080 phanerogams and 1800 cryptogams.

‖**Phanerogamia** (ˌfænərəʊˈgæmɪə). *Bot.* [mod.L., sing. fem. abstr. f. *phanerogam-us*: see prec.] A primary division of the vegetable kingdom, comprising plants having obvious reproductive organs, i.e. stamens and pistils; the sub-kingdom of flowering plants: opposed to cryptogamia.

Actually a noun singular, but often erron. treated as pl., after such Zoological neuter plurals as *Mammalia*, = *phanerogams*: for this some have used a plural form *phanerogamiæ*; but the only L. plural is *phanerogamæ*: see prec.

1821 *Elem. Philos. Plants* (tr. De Candolle & Sprengel) 87 Plants whose parts of fructification are manifest, Phanerogamia. [**1847** W. E. Steele *Field Bot.* p. vi, The acknowledged division of plants into those with stamens and pistils, Phanerogamiæ, and those without, Cryptogamiæ. **1848** Carpenter *Anim. Phys.* xv. (1872) 553 The gemmæ of Phanerogamia may be developed in connexion with the parent structure.] **1857** Henfrey *Bot.* § 395 The vegetable kingdom. Subkingdom I. Phanerogamia, or flowering plants.

Hence **ˌphaneroˈgamic** *a.*, of or belonging to the division *Phanerogamia*; = next.

1830 Lyell *Princ. Geol.* I. 123 In the continent of India ..the proportion of ferns to the phanerogamic plants is only as one to twenty-six. **1862** Ansted *Channel Isl.* ii. viii. (ed. 2) 198 These latter islands..show no essential difference in their phanerogamic flora. **1894** *Naturalist* 93.

phanerogamous (fænəˈrɒgəməs), *a.* *Bot.* [f. F. *phanérogame* adj. or mod.L. *phanerogam-us* (see phanerogam) + -ous.] Having stamens and pistils: flowering. (The earliest word of the group in Eng.: opposed to cryptogamous.)

1816 J. Bigelow in *N. Eng. Jrnl. Med. & Surg.* V. 335 Humboldt affirms that..the phanerogamous plants, which have been recognized as natives of the tropical regions of both continents, are extremely few. **1881** *Nature* XXIII. 264/2 The phanerogamous Flora of Silesia.

phanerophyte (ˈfænərəʊfaɪt). *Bot.* [ad. Da. *fanerofyt* (C. Raunkiaer 1904, in *Bot. Tidsskr.* XXVI. p. xiv), f. phanero- + -phyte.] A plant which bears its dormant buds well above the surface of the ground.

1913 W. G. Smith in *Jrnl. Ecol.* I. 17 Phanerophytes have their dormant buds on branches which project freely into the air; they are the trees and shrubs. **1932** Fuller & Conard tr. *Braun-Blanquet's Plant Sociol.* xii. 295 The more northern phanerophytes are characterized by special bud protection. **1934** H. Gilbert-Carter tr. *Raunkiaer's Life Forms of Plants* ii. 19 By Phanerophytes I mean plants whose buds and apical shoots destined to survive the unfavourable period of the year project into the air on stems which live for several, often for many, years. **1952** [see *chamæphyte* s.v. chamæ-]. **1976** Bell & Coombe tr. *Strasburger's Textbk. Bot.* (rev. ed.) 191 Phanerophytes.. bear their resting buds more than 50 cm above the soil surface.

phaneˈropterid, *a.* and *sb.* *Zool.* **a.** *adj.* Belonging to the genus *Phaneroptera* [f. phanero- + Gr. πτερόν wing] or family *Phaneropteridæ* of grasshoppers. **b.** *sb.* A grasshopper of this family.

1895 *Camb. Nat. Hist.* V. xiii. 323 Two specimens of a little Phaneropterid..brought from the Soudan.

phanerozoic (ˌfænərəʊˈzəʊɪk), *a.* [f. phanero- + Gr. ζωή life + -ic.]

1. *Ecol.* Describing those animals living in exposed conditions above the surface of the ground. Cf. cryptozoic *a.* 1.

1896 A. Dendy in *Natural Sci.* July 8 Cryptozoic fauna imperceptibly blends with what by way of contrast may be called the 'phanerozoic'. **1911** A. Willey *Convergence in Evolution* iii. 23 Phanerozoic or diurnal animals are positively heliotropic. **1922** Flattely & Walton *Biol. of Sea-Shore* i. 7 We thus have two great sub-realms: the phanerozoic and the cryptozoic.

2. *Geol.* (With capital initial.) Of, pertaining to, or designating the whole of the geological time since the beginning of the Cambrian period, as contrasted with the Pre-Cambrian (Cryptozoic); (so named in allusion to its abundant evidence of life). Also *absol.*

1930 G. H. Chadwick in *Bull. Geol. Soc. Amer.* XLI. 48 The following classificatory scheme is offered for criticism. .. Phanerozoic or Phanerobiotic 45%... Cryptozoic or Cryptobiotic (Precambrian) 55%. **1958** R. C. Moore *Introd. Hist. Geol.* (ed. 2) iv. 59/2 It is convenient also to designate the Cryptozoic rocks as Precambrian, a commonly used term indicating age older than the Cambrian Period, first division of the Paleozoic Era and of the Phanerozoic Eon. **1963** *Q. Jrnl. Geol. Soc.* CXIX. 137 The rocks concerned range in age from 1055 to 1700 m.y. (radiometric dating), spanning more time than the whole of the Phanerozoic. **1971** *Nature* 25 June 498/1 All stratigraphic methods of correlation..that are used for Phanerozoic rocks should be extended as far as possible in the Pre-Cambrian part of the stratigraphic column. **1974** *Ibid.* 18 Oct. 568/2 It is no coincidence that the three faunally defined eras of Phanerozoic time, the Palaeozoic, Mesozoic and Cainozoic, are divided by these two so-called crises in the history of life. **1977** A. Hallam *Planet Earth* 189 The later Proterozoic Grenville belt of southern Canada..is a linear belt with more similarities to the younger mountain belts of the Phanerozoic.

phanerozonate (fænərəʊˈzəʊneɪt), *a.* *Zool.* [f. mod.L. order name *Phanerozonia* (W. P. Sladen in Thomson & Murray *Rep. Sci. Results Voy. H.M.S. Challenger: Zool.* (1889) XXX. p. xxvi), f. phanero- + Gr. ζώνη girdle + -ia²: see -ate².] Characteristic of or comprising certain starfishes grouped in the order Phanerozonia, distinguished by conspicuous marginal plates.

1889 W. P. Sladen in *Rep. Sci. Results Voy. H.M.S. Challenger: Zool.* XXX. p. xxvi, I consider that the Phanerozonate group is older than the Cryptozonate. **1906** E. W. MacBride in *Cambr. Nat. Hist.* I. xvi. 454 In a very large number of Asteroidea the supero- and infero-marginal ossicles are represented by squarish plates even when the rest of the skeleton is reticulate; this is the so-called 'phanerozonate' structure. **1923** *Nature* 13 Jan. 47/1 What these specialists are impressed by is the 'phanerozonate' character of the Astropectinidae, that is, the edging of the arms with a series of broad plates termed the 'marginals'. **1966** J. W. Durham et al. in R. C. Moore *Treat. Invertebr. Paleont.* U. I. u36/2 Some Cryptozonia have a phanerozonate stage in ontogeny.

phanerozone (ˈfænərəʊzəʊn), *a.* (*sb.*) *Zool.* [see prec.] = prec. Also as *sb.*

1962 D. Nichols *Echinoderms* iii. 51 *Petraster* is a true phanerozone starfish. *Ibid.* 53 There is a thick aboral membrane for protection instead of the paxillate condition normally associated with the phanerozones. **1964** *Oceanogr. & Marine Biol.* II. 394 Spencer..describes the transition from the early somasteroid stock to the phanerozone asteroids.

phang, phanged, obs. erron. ff. fang, fanged.

†**phangle**, obs. erron. form of fangle *sb.*¹

1648 E. Sparke in *Shute's Sarah & Hagar* Pref. b j, Any new Phangles of these wilder times.

phanopœia (ˌfænəʊˈpiːjə). [f. Gr. φανό-ς light, bright, f. φαίνειν to shine, give light + ποι-εῖν to make, after melopœïa: see -ia¹.] (See quot. 1929.)

1929 E. Pound in *N.Y. Herald-Tribune* 20 Jan. xi. 5/4 There are three 'kinds of poetry': Melopoeia... Phanopoeia, which is a casting of images upon the visual imagination... Logopoeia. *Ibid.* 6/1 In phanopoeia we find the greatest drive toward utter precision of word. **1934**, **1957** [see logopœia]. **1961** [see modernist 5].

phanotron (ˈfænətrɒn). *Electronics.* Also **phanatron**. [f. *phano-* (? f. Gr. φαίνειν to bring to light, cause to appear) + -tron.] A thermionic diode rectifier utilizing an arc discharge in mercury vapour or gas at very low pressure.

Formerly a proprietary name in the U.S.

1931 *Thomas' Reg. Amer. Manuf., 1931–32* (ed. 22) *Leading Trade Names* 447 Phanotron vacuum tubes, General Electric Co., Schenectady, N.Y. **1933** J. H. Morecroft *Electron Tubes* viii. 193 In the Phanotron a low temperature filament must be used, because the mercury vapor has not enough density to prevent the evaporation of the filament. **1939** H. J. REICH *Theory & Applications Electron Tubes* xii. 430 The construction of the type FG-166 phanatron. **1966** *McGraw-Hill Encycl. Sci. & Technol.* VI. 62/1 Typical phanotrons have average current ratings from 1·25–10 amperes and peak inverse voltage ratings of 10,000–22,000 volts. **1975** YEAGER & GOURLEY *Introd. Electron & Electromech. Devices* (1976) xiv. 283 We will discuss two types of gaseous discharge: arc discharge and glow discharge... Arc discharge tubes are commonly called thermionic gas tubes; for example the gas diode (phanotron) and the gas triode (thyratron).

phansie, -y, early forms of FANCY.

‖**Phansigar** (ˈp(h)ɑːnsigɑː(r)). [Hindī *phānsigār* strangler, noose-man, f. *phānsi* noose.] An East Indian professional robber and assassin, one of a gang who strangled and robbed travellers and others; a thug.

1813 J. FORBES *Orient. Mem.* IV. xxxvii. 13 A tribe called *phanseegurs*, or stranglers. **1841** C. MACKAY *Mem. Pop. Delusions* I. 371 Murderers, who, under the name of Thugs, or Phansigars, have so long been the scourge of India.

phantascope (ˈfæntəskəʊp). [irreg. f. Gr. φαντ-ός visible + -SCOPE: cf. PHANTOSCOPE.] A name independently given to different optical instruments.

1. A contrivance for exhibiting phenomena of binocular vision by an arrangement of slit cards, through which two figures seen at a certain distance converge into one combined image.

1866 BRANDE & COX *Dict. Sci.*, etc. II. 880/1 *Phantascope*, the name given by Professor Locke, of the United States, to an apparatus for enabling persons to converge the optical axis of the eyes, or to look cross-eyed, and thereby observe certain phenomena of binocular vision. **1875** KNIGHT *Dict. Mech.* 1677/2 *Phantascope*.. A pair of objects on the base-board is viewed through the perforations of both cards, and by viewing the index the optical axes of the eyes are converged and the objects are reduplicated, and eventually a merged image appears in the central position.

2. = PHENAKISTOSCOPE.

1876 BERNSTEIN *Five Senses* 117 The persistence of these incidental images is the basis of.. the phantascope or magic disc, on which various figures are seen in motion. **1881** *Oracle* 12 Nov. 306 The optical toy, which has been variously called Phantascope, Phantasmascope, and Phenakistoscope.

phantasia, another form of FANTASIA.

phantasiast (fænˈteɪzɪæst). [ad. eccl. Gr. Φαντασιασταί, pl. of φαντασιαστής, f. φαντασία appearance: see FANTASY.]

1. *Eccl. Hist.* A name given to those of the Docetæ (also called *Phantasiodocetæ*, Φαντασιοδοκηταί) who held that Christ's body was only a phantasm, not a material substance.

1680 BAXTER *Answ. Stillingfl.* xxxiv. 57 Phantasiasts. **1852** BP. FORBES *Nicene Cr.* 221 The Docetae, or Phantasiasts, and those who asserted our Lord was only in appearance dead. **1863** LONGF. *Wayside Inn* I. *Interlude* v. 51 The creed of the Phantasiasts, For whom.. Christ [was but] a phantom crucified!

2. One who deals in or treats of phantasies.

1855 SMEDLEY, etc. *Occult Sc.* 88 Ben Jonson, who had some experience as a phantasiast, thus invokes the fairer creations of this power in his 'Vision of Delight'.

Hence **phantasiˈastic** *a.*, of or characteristic of the Phantasiasts; of the nature of a phantasm.

1826 G. S. FABER *Diffic. Romanism* (1853) 102 *note*, The same line of argument is adopted by Tertullian against Marcion and his phantasiastic brethren. **1838** —— *Inquiry* 176 The Manicheans.. denied that Christ had any proper material body; the form, which was seen, having been purely phantasiastic.

†**phantasim(e.** *rare.* [Cf. It. '*fantasima* or *fantasma*' (Florio 1611).] A fantastic being.

1588 SHAKS. *L.L.L.* IV. i. 101 This Armado is a Spaniard that keeps here in court A Phantasime, a Monarcho, and one that makes sport To the Prince and his Booke-mates. *Ibid.* V. i. 20, I abhor such phanaticall phantasims, such insociable and poynt deuise companions.

ˈ**phantasist.** *rare.* [f. *phantasy*, FANTASY; or a. F. *fantaisiste*, f. *fantaisie*.] = FANTAST 1.

1864 ALGER *Future Life* 660 The 'Vision of Annihilation' depicted by the vermicular, infested imagination of the great Teutonic phantasist.

phantasm (ˈfæntæz(ə)m). Forms: α. 3 **fantesme**, 5–7 **fantasme**, 7, 9 **fantasm**. β. 6– **phantasm**, (7–8 **phantasme**). [Orig. a. F. *fantasme* (OF. also *-esme*), ad. L. *phantasma*, a. Gr. φάντασμα: see next. From 16th c. gradually conformed to the Latin spelling with *ph-*.]

I. 1. a. *gen.* Illusion, deceptive appearance. Cf. PHANTOM 1. *Obs.* or *arch.*

a **1225** *Ancr. R.* 62 Louerd, seið Dauid, wend awei mine eien vrom þe worldes dweole, & hire fantesme [cf. Ps. cxix. 37]. **1460** *Lybeaus Disc.* 1432 Wyth fantasme, and fayrye, Thus she blerede hys yye. **1483** CAXTON *Gold. Leg.* 289/1 The deuylle appered to them in guyse of a maronner in a shippe of fantasme. **1656** STANLEY *Hist. Philos.* VIII. (1701) 303/1 Phantasm is that, to which we are attracted by that frustraneous attraction, which happens in Melancholy, or Mad persons. **1860** EMERSON *Cond. Life, Illusions* Wks. (Bohn) II. 446 'Tis all phantasm.

b. With *a* and *pl.* An illusion, an appearance that has no reality; a deception, a figment; an unreal or imaginary being, an unreality; a phantom.

1426 LYDG. *De Guil. Pilgr.* 10890 Yt are but fantasmes that ye speke. **1483** CAXTON *Gold. Leg.* 175 b/2 He [St. Germayn] dyd so many myracles that yf his merytes had not goon before they shold haue ben trowed fantasmes. **1614** RALEIGH *Hist. World* I. xi. §8 They beleeve, and they beleeve amisse, because they be but Phantasmes or Apparitions. **1644** MILTON *Areop.* 10 Or else it was a fantasm bred by the feaver which had then seis'd him. **1678** CUDWORTH *Intell. Syst.* I. ii. §8. 68 The Minds of men strongly possess'd with Fear, especially in the Dark, raise up the Phantasms of Spectres, Bug-bears, or affrightful Apparitions to them. **1778** MISS BURNEY *Evelina* (1791) I. xxx. 156, I will not afflict you with the melancholy phantasms of my brain. **1843** CARLYLE *Past & Pr.* II. i, Peopled with mere vaporous Fantasms. **1843** PRESCOTT *Mexico* (1850) I. 119 The allegorical phantasms of his religion, no doubt, gave a direction to the Aztec artist, in his delineation of the human figure.

c. An illusive likeness (*of* something), a 'ghost' or 'shadow'; a counterfeit.

1638 BAKER tr. *Balzac's Lett.* (vol. II) 113 It is fit to stay ones selfe upon the true vertue, and not to follow the vaine Phantasmes of holinesse. **1699** BURNET *39 Art.* xxvi. (1700) 297 If these are no true Sacraments which they take for such, but only the Shadows and the Phantasms of them. **1870** DISRAELI *Lothair* xlviii, There is only one Church and only one religion, all other forms and phrases are mere phantasms. **1876** GEO. ELIOT *Dan. Der.* lviii, Every phantasm of a hope was quickly nullified by a more substantial obstacle.

†**d.** One who is not what he appears or pretends to be; a counterfeit, an impostor. *Obs.*

1622 BACON *Hen. VII* 24 The People were in furie, entertayning this Airie bodie or phantasme [Lambert Simnel] with incredible affection. **1638** BAKER tr. *Balzac's Lett.* (vol. II) 229 Farre from being a Plagiary, [he] refuseth that which is his own, and suffers a Phantasme, to receive those acclamations and praises which belong to himselfe. **1641** MILTON *Prel. Episc.* 23 Rather to make this phantasme an expounder, or indeed a depraver of Saint Paul, then Saint Paul an examiner, and discoverer of this impostorship.

2. An apparition, a spirit or supposed incorporeal being appearing to the eyes, a ghost. Now only *poet.* or *rhet.*

c **1410** LOVE *Bonavent. Myrr.* xxvii. (1510) Hiij b, The discyples supposynge that it had ben a fantasme cryed for drede. *c* **1550** CHEKE *Matt.* xiv. 26 His discipils seing him walking on yᵉ see weer trobled saieng, yᵗ it was a phantasm. **1643** SIR T. BROWNE *Relig. Med.* I. §37 That those phantasms.. do frequent Cemeteries, Charnel-houses, and Churches, it is because these are the dormitories of the dead. **1667** MILTON *P.L.* II. 744 Why.. thou call'st Me Father, and that Fantasm call'st my Son? **1863** P. S. WORSLEY *Poems & Transl.* 7 Like the erring phantasm of a man Slain traitorously and cast into the deep.

b. *Psychics.* The supposed vision or perception of an absent person, living or dead, presented to the senses or mind of another.

1884 *Proc. Soc. Psychical Research* I. v. 44 Phantasms, as we call them, in order to include under a term more general than phantoms, impressions which may be not visual only, but auditory, tactile, or purely mental in character. **1886** GURNEY, etc. *Phantasms of Living* I. Introd. 35 We propose .. to deal with all classes of cases where.. the mind of one human being has affected the mind of another.. by other means than through the recognized channels of sense. **1887** C. L. MORGAN in *Mind* Apr. 281 Where.. the phantasm includes details of dress or aspect which could not be supplied by the percipient's mind, Mr. Gurney thinks it may be attributed to a conscious or sub-conscious image of his own appearance.. in the agent's mind, which is telepathically conveyed as such to the mind of the percipient.

II. 3. *Philos.* A mental image, appearance, or representation, considered as the immediate object of sense-perception: as distinct (*a*) from the external thing represented, or (*b*) in Platonic philosophy, from the true form or essence, perceptible by thought only and not by sense.

1594 CAREW *Huarte's Exam. Wits* iv. (1596) 38 Brute beasts with the temperature of their braine, and the fantasmes which enter thereinto by the fiue sences.. partake those abilities. **1620** T. GRANGER *Div. Logike* 108 Memorie is a facultie of retaining well the phantasmes of things. **1669** GALE *Crt. Gentiles* I. III. i. 19 Homer, and Hesiod.. busied themselves about the phantasmes or pictures of Truth, but regarded not the Truth it self. **1751** HARRIS *Hermes* Wks. (1841) 221 It is then on these permanent phantasms that the human mind first works. **1785** REID *Intell. Powers* I. i. 25 When they are objects of memory and of imagination, they get the name of phantasms. **1880** *Academy* 26 June 469 The phantasm or idea which awakens feeling in accordance with an appetence is not abstract but concrete and generally single.

†**b.** An idea, a concept. *Obs.*

a **1619** FOTHERBY *Atheom.* II. ii. §8 (1622) 210 God is a fantasme, that can fill the fantasie.

4. †**a.** Imagination, fancy. *Obs.*

1490 CAXTON *Eneydos* xxii. 82 She saw also, to her semynge, two sonnes shynynge one by another, that presente hemself by symulacyon wythin the fantasme of her entendement. **1656** RIDGLEY *Pract. Physick* 252 Proceeding from a melancholic Phantasme. **1689** EVELYN *Let. to Pepys* 4 Oct., Y subject of my wild phantasme.. naturally leading me to something which I lately mention'd.

b. An imagination, a fancy: now always with emphasis on its unreality (cf. 1 b).

1672 SIR T. BROWNE *Let. Friend* §17 His Female Friends were irrationally curious so strictly to examine his Dreams, and in this low state to hope for the Fantasms of Health. **1738** H. BROOKE *Tasso* I. 60 Ambitious phantasms haunt his idle brain. **1856** R. A. VAUGHAN *Mystics* I. Pref. 5 Is it well to recal from Limbo the phantasms of forgotten dreamers?

5. *attrib.*

1831 CARLYLE *Sart. Res.* I. iii, Visible and tangible objects in this phantasm world. **1843** —— *Past & Pr.* III. i, From highest Phantasm apex to lowest Enchanted basis. **1871** MORLEY *Carlyle* in *Crit. Misc.* Ser. I. (1878) 180 Why then should not the royalist assume.. that the Protector was a usurper and a 'phantasm captain'?

phantasma (fænˈtæzmə). Also 7 **fantasma.** Pl. **-as, -ata** (7 **-aes**). [a. It. *fantasma* = L. *phantasma*, a. Gr. φάντασμα appearance, mere appearance, phantom, image, f. φαντάζ-ειν to make visible, present to (or as to) the eye, f. φαντ-ός visible, f. stem φαν- of φαίν-ειν to show, appear, bring or come to light. See also PHANTASM and PHANTOM, which are forms of the same word through Fr.] **a.** An illusion, vision, dream; **b.** an apparition, a spectre: = PHANTASM 1 b and 2.

1598 SYLVESTER *Du Bartas* II. ii. III. *Colonies* 338 Round about the Desart Op, where oft By strange Phantasma's Passengers are scoft. **1599** MARSTON *Sco. Villanie* In Lect. prorsus indignos, Shall this Fantasma, this Colosse peruse And blast with stinking breath my budding Muse? **1607** —— *What you Will* Introd., Wks. 1856 I. 221 Skru'd about With each slight touch of od phantasmatas. **1607** WALKINGTON *Opt. Glass* 149 He shall see.. strange phantasmaes. **1631** J. TAYLOR (Water P.) *Turn Fort. Wheel* Pref., Dreames and phantasmas full of contradictions. **1765** GOLDSM. *Ess.* Misc. Wks. 1837 I. 227 All was a phantasma, and a hideous dream of incoherent absurdities. **1816** SCOTT *Antiq.* x, At length these crude phantasmata arranged themselves into something more regular. **1849** ROBERTSON *Serm.* Ser. IV. ix. (1876) 78 These were all an illusion and a phantasma, a thing that appeared, but did not really exist.

phantasmagoria (fæntæzməˈgɔərɪə). [f. Gr. φάντασμα PHANTASM + (?) ἀγορά assembly, place of assembly.

(But the inventor of the word prob. only wanted a mouth-filling and startling term, and may have fixed on *-agoria* without any reference to the Greek lexicon.)]

1. A name invented for an exhibition of optical illusions produced chiefly by means of the magic lantern, first exhibited in London in 1802. (Sometimes erroneously applied to the mechanism used.)

In Philipstal's 'phantasmagoria' the figures were made rapidly to increase and decrease in size, to advance and retreat, dissolve, vanish, and pass into each other, in a manner then considered marvellous.

1802 *Gentl. Mag.* June 544 Dark rooms, where spectres from the dead they raise—What's the Greek word for all this *Goblinstoria*? I have it pat—It is Phantasmagoria. *Ibid.* (end of vol.), An awful sound proclaims a spectre near, And full in sight behold it now appear.. Such are the forms Phantasmagoria shows. **1805** MRS. CREEVEY in *C. Papers*, etc. (1904) I. 67 The Baron is preparing a phantasmagoria at the Pavillion. **1831** BREWSTER *Nat. Magic* iv. 80 An exhibition depending on these principles was brought out by M. Philipstal in 1802, under the name of the Phantasmagoria... Spectres, skeletons, and terrific figures .. suddenly advanced upon the spectators, becoming larger as they approached them, and finally vanished by appearing to sink into the ground. **1883** *Encycl. Brit.* XV. 207 Philipstal gave a sensation to his magic lantern entertainment by lowering unperceived, between the audience and the stage, a sheet of gauze, upon which fell the vivid moving shadows of phantasmagoria.

b. Extended to similar optical exhibitions, ancient and modern.

1830 SCOTT *Demonol.* ii. 59 The Almighty substituted, for the phantasmagoria intended by the witch, the spirit of Samuel. **1832** GELL *Pompeiana* I. v. 98 Machines by which phantasmagoria and oracular prestiges were played off. **1834** LYTTON *Pompeii* II. ix.

2. A shifting series or succession of phantasms or imaginary figures, as seen in a dream or fevered condition, as called up by the imagination, or as created by literary description.

[**1803** *Europ. Mag.* XLIII. 186 'The Phantasmagoria' (title of a series of articles consisting of sketches of imaginary characters).] **1828** LANDOR *Imag. Conv.* Wks. 1853 I. 345/2 The army seemed a phantasmagoria. **1835** W. IRVING *Newstead Abbey* in *Crayon Misc.* (1863) 347 Such was the phantasmagoria that presented itself for a moment to my imagination. **1875** E. WHITE *Life in Christ* II. xii. (1878) 133 Milton's genius has filled the atmosphere with a brilliant phantasmagoria of contending angels.

3. *transf.* A shifting and changing external scene consisting of many elements.

1822 HAZLITT *Table-t.* Ser. II. v. (1869) 121 A huddled phantasmagoria of feathers, spangles, etc. **1853** KANE *Grinnell Exp.* ix. (1856) 68 The wildest frolic of an opium-eater's revery is nothing to the phantasmagoria of the sky tonight. **1880** SHORTHOUSE *J. Inglesant* xxiii, Without was a phantasmagoria of terrible bright colours, and within a mental chaos and disorder without a clue.

b. A phantasmagoric figure, or something compared thereto.

1821 BYRON *Vis. Judgm.* lxxvii, The man was a phantasmagoria in Himself—he was so volatile and thin.

4. *attrib.*

1841 MISS MITFORD in L'Estrange *Life* (1870) III. viii. 130 There was no background to form a phantasmagoria deception, since the part plainest to be seen was the figure as it rose and sank above the paling. **1873** E. SPON *Workshop Receipts* Ser. I. 295/1 By the aid of a gas microscope attached to a powerful phantasmagoria lantern the image can be reflected on to a screen.

Hence †**phantasmagoriacal** (-ˈaɪəkəl), **phantasmaˈgorial** (whence **-ally** *adv.*), **phantasmaˈgorian, phantasmagoric** (-ˈgɒrɪk), **phantasmaˈgorical** *adjs.*, of, pertaining to, or of the nature of a phantasmagoria; hence, visionary, phantasmal; **phanˈtasmaˌgorist**, one who produces or exhibits a phantasmagoria.

1823 *Blackw. Mag.* XIII. 537 Deucalion sees a *phantasmagoriacal shadow of what..forms the history of the ancient world. **1828** SCOTT *Jrnl.* 17 Apr., In this *phantasmagorial place [London], the objects of the day come and depart like shadows. **1822** *Blackw. Mag.* XII. 86 A thousand other scenes..come up *phantasmagorially or panorama-wise before us. **1827** *Examiner* 212/2 The Will-o'-the-wisp is painted..with shadowy and *phantasmagorian power. **1870** *Contemp. Rev.* XIV. 180 It will ever elude his grasp like..the phantasmagorian images on the canvas. **1818** COLERIDGE in *Lit. Rem.* (1836) I. 139 All Rabelais' personages are *phantasmagoric allegories. **1883** SYMONDS *Shaks. Predec.* i. (1900) 5 The phantasmagoric brilliancy of shows at Court. **1852** HAWTHORNE *Blithedale Rom.* Pref. (1879) 6 To establish a theatre..where the creatures of his brain may play their *phantasmagorical antics. **1816** J. LAWRENCE in *Monthly Mag.* XLII. 298 Whether..it can possibly be worth while..for our chemists, or rather for our *phantasmagorists to repeat any of the old palingenesian experiments? **1862** LYTTON *Str. Story* lxxi, Those arch phantasmagorists, the philosophers who would leave nothing in the universe but their own delusions.

phantasmagory (fænˈtæzməgɒrɪ). [Cf. F. *phantasmagorie.*] = PHANTASMAGORIA.

1837 CARLYLE *Fr. Rev.* III. I. iv, This dim Phantasmagory of the Pit. **1865** —— *Fredk. Gt.* XXI. iii. (1872) IX. 304 The thing is reality; but it reads like a Phantasmagory produced by Lapland Witches. **1873** M. ARNOLD *Lit. & Dogma* (1876) 79 The phantasmagories of more prodigal and wild imaginations.

phantasmal (fænˈtæzməl), *a.* [f. PHANTASM or PHANTASMA + -AL¹.] Of the nature of a phantasm; spectral; having no material existence, unreal, imaginary; passing like a phantasm.

1813 SHELLEY *Q. Mab* VI. 192 All that chequers the phantasmal scene That floats before our eyes in wavering light. **1817** COLERIDGE *Biog. Lit.* vii. (1882) 56 The phantasmal chaos of association. **1870** LOWELL *Study Wind.* 230 No confirmation has been found for the story, fathered on a certain phantasmal Mr. Buckley. **1880** SHORTHOUSE *J. Inglesant* (1882) II. xvi. 320 With such phantasmal imaginations he filled Inglesant's ears.

b. *Psychics*: see PHANTASM 2 b.

1886 GURNEY, etc. *Phantasms of Living* I. Introd. 65 Between the moment of death and the phantasmal announcement thereof to a distant friend.

Hence **phantasˈmalian** *a.*, relating to what is phantasmal; **phantasˈmality**, the quality of being phantasmal.

1841 LYTTON *Nt. & Morn.* III. viii, The idea grows up, a horrid phantasmalian monomania. **1875** LEWES *Probl. Life & Mind* II. II. ii. §38. 45 Between the reality of our waking sensations, and the phantasmality of our dream perceptions ..the contrast is marked. **1903** *Critic* XLIII. 354/1 His is the spirit that cries for delivery from the tyranny of his senses, the phantasmality of the world.

phanˈtasmally, *adv.* [f. prec. + -LY².] In a phantasmal manner or form; as a phantasm.

1855 MISS COBBE *Intuit. Mor.* 103 The belief that this causation descends into the sensible world, and takes place therein not phantasmally, but actually. **1886** GURNEY, etc. *Phantasms of Living* II. 530 Persons are phantasmally seen or heard very soon before their actual appearance in the flesh.

phantasmascope (fænˈtæzməskəʊp). [irreg. f. PHANTASMA + -SCOPE.] = PHENAKISTOSCOPE.

1835 KIRBY *Hab. & Inst. Anim.* I. App. 350 They appear as if..a hundred [legs] were revolving and so form a kind of natural Phantasmascope. **1844** OLMSTED *Rud Nat. Philos.* viii. 558 The Phantasmascope consists of disks bearing on their margin a variety of figures, which are so related to each other, that each..figure shall afford a continuation of the preceding. *c* **1865** J. WYLDE in *Circ. Sc.* I. 77/2.

phantasˈmatic, *sb. Eccl. Hist.* [f. Gr. φαντασματ- (see PHANTASMA) + -IC.] = PHANTASIAST.

1701 tr. *Le Clerc's Prim. Fathers* (1702) 322 The Phantasmaticks..who pretended that Christ had not a true Body.

phantasˈmatic, *a.* [as prec.] = next.

1858 MAYNE *Expos. Lex.*, *Phantasmaticus*.., of or belonging to Phantasma: phantasmatic.

†**phantasˈmatical**, *a. Obs.* [f. as prec.: see -ICAL.] Pertaining to or of the nature of a phantasm; phantasmal. Hence †**phantasˈmatically** *adv.*

1642 H. MORE *Song of Soul* Notes Q ij, In our corporeall spirit: For that is the matter that the soul raiseth her phantasmaticall forms in. **1658** BROMHALL *Treat. Specters* VII. 364 The Angels moving..with a locall motion, by the phantasmaticall body which they took [etc.]. *a* **1688** CUDWORTH *Immut. Mor.* IV. i. (1731) 143 So are the Cogitations that we have of Corporeal things usually both Noematical and Phantasmatical together, the one being as it were the Soul, and the other the Body of them. *Ibid.* 144 By a Rose considered thus Universally and Phantasmatically, we mean a Thing which so affects our Sense in respect of Figure and Colour.

phanˌtasmaˈtography. *rare*⁻⁰. [f. as prec. + -(O)GRAPHY.] (See quot.)

1730–6 BAILEY (folio) Pref., *Phantasmatógraphy*,..a Treatise or Discourse of celestial Appearances, as the Rainbow. **1823** in CRABB *Technol. Dict.* **1864** in WEBSTER.

phantasmic (fænˈtæzmɪk), *a.* [f. PHANTASM or PHANTASMA + -IC.] Of, pertaining to, or of the nature of a phantasm; unreal; imaginary. So **phanˈtasmical** *a.*

1825 *New Monthly Mag.* XIII. 185 His shadowy monarch is assailed by ideal conspirators, and their phantasmic high treason he will have atoned for by substantial flesh and blood. **1857–8** SEARS *Athan.* vi. 49 The spectacle..was not phantasmic, but real. **1863** A. B. DAVIDSON *Bibl. & Lit. Ess.* (1902) 16 A species of Doketism akin to giving Christ a phantasmical body.

phanˈtasmically, *adv.* [f. PHANTASMICAL *a.* + -LY².] = PHANTASMALLY *adv.*

1906 *Daily News* 2 Jan. 6 If I stretch out my hand to a touch, will it not surely melt under my fingers?—melt and form again phantasmically.

phanˈtasmist. *rare*⁻¹. [f. as PHANTASMIC *a.* + -IST.] One who maintains something to be a phantasm; a PHANTASIAST.

1823 COLERIDGE *Table-t.* 6 Jan., It was real blood,..and not a mere celestial ichor, as the Phantasmists allege.

phanˌtasmoˈgenesis. *rare.* [f. Gr. φάντασμα PHANTASM + GENESIS.] The causation or origination of phantasms.

1890 in *Cent. Dict.* **1893** in *Syd. Soc. Lex.*

So **phantasmogenetic** (fænˌtæzməʊdʒɪˈnɛtɪk) *a.*, producing phantasms or apparitions; *esp.* creating or producing a phantasm (sense 2 b); **phanˌtasmogeˈnetically** *adv.*

1886 GURNEY, etc. *Phantasms of Living* II. 279 A Phantasmogenetic impulse conveyed directly from mind to mind. **1890** *Cent. Dict.*, *Phantasmogenetically*. **1903** F. W. H. MYERS *Hum. Personality* I. Gloss., *Phantasmogenetic centre*, a point in space so modified by the presence of a spirit that it becomes perceptible to persons materially present near it.

phantasˈmognomy. [f. as prec. + Gr. γνώμη means of knowing: cf. *physiognomy*.] (See quot.)

1855 SMEDLEY, etc. *Occult Sc.* 296 Phantasmognomy.. teaches men to foresee and to foretell future or distant events from the images which fancy presents to the mind.

phantasˈmology. [f. as prec. + -LOGY.] The scientific study of phantasms. Hence **phantasmoˈlogical** *a.*

1890 in *Cent. Dict.*

phantast, -ic, -ical, etc., obs. or rare variants of FANTAST, -IC, -ICAL, etc.

phantastica (fænˈtæstɪkə). [f. *phantastic*, var. FANTASTIC *a.* and *sb.* + *-a* (cf. -A 4).] Hallucinogenic drugs collectively; ¶ also, one such drug.

1931 L. LEWIN *Phantastica, Narcotic & Stimulating Drugs* 31 Phantastica; hallucinating substances. This series comprises a number of substances of vegetable origin, varying greatly in their chemical constitution, and to these belongs in its proper sense the name Phantastica, or Drugs of Illusion. *Ibid.* 92, I mean the action of chemical substances capable of evoking such transitory states without any physical inconvenience for a certain time in persons of perfectly normal mentality who are partly or fully conscious of the action of the drug. Substances of this nature I call Phantastica. They..influence particularly the visual and auditory spheres as well as the general sensibility. **1958** *Sci. News* XLVII. 31 The two groups of drugs on which most attention has been focused recently have been: (*a*) those that tend to make normal people appear to be psychotic (hallucinogens, psychotomimetic drugs or phantastica), and (*b*) those that are mostly intended to have the opposite effect. **1967** M. M. GLATT et al. *Drug Scene* i. 9 The three principal drugs in this group are mescaline, psilocybin, and lysergic acid diethylamide (LSD 25 or LSD). These drugs are also designated as phantastica, psychedelic, and psychotomimetic drugs. **1968** J. BLACKBURN *Young Man from Lima* v. 51 Marcus tried to remember what he knew about modern hallucinogenics... Lysergine..was probably the most powerful phantastica known to man.

phantastikon (fænˈtæstɪkɒn). *poet.* [f. Gr. φανταστικόν imaginative faculty, neut. of φανταστικός (see FANTASTIC *a.* and *sb.*).] Imagination.

1917 E. POUND *Lustra* 187 Shall I claim; Confuse my own phantastikon Or say the filmy shell that circumscribes me Contains the actual sun. **1933** —— *Let.* 15 Jan. (1971) 243 As fer yr. final pp., that is about the kind of mess that has been trespassin on my phantastikon for several weeks.

phantastron (fænˈtæstrɒn). *Electronics.* [f. alteration of FANTASTIC *a.* and *sb.*: see -TRON.] A circuit in which a brief triggering pulse produces at one electrode a longer pulse whose duration is proportional to an applied control voltage, and at another electrode a linear sweep voltage of the same duration (which can then be used to generate another pulse that will occur at a definite interval after the triggering pulse).

1943 (*title*) An adaptation of the phantastron delay multivibrator circuit to the 6SA7 tube. (M.I.T. Radiation Laboratory Rep. 63-21.) **1947** L. J. HAWORTH in L. N. Ridenour *Radar Syst. Engin.* xiii. 500 The phantastron of Fig. 13·17 is a flip-flop..which serves as a timing circuit maintaining its calibration to about one per cent. **1953** *Electronic Engin.* XXV. 143/1 The position of the selector pulse in the time scale depends on the delay produced by the phantastron and is controlled by R_{13}. **1964** R. BLITZER *Basic Pulse Circuits* vi. 215 A linear sawtooth voltage generator similar to the Miller sweep circuits of Sec. 6·11 is called the phantastron... Besides the sawtooth waveshape being used as a sweep, the phantastron is also often used as a delay circuit.

ˈphantastry (ˈfæntæstrɪ). Also 8 **fantastry**. [f. FANTAST, PHANTAST + -RY.] **a.** Fantastic display or show; ostentation, affectation. Also *concr.* Showy trappings. **b.** Visionary delusion. **c.** Illusory character, deceptiveness.

1656 H. MORE *Enthus. Tri.* §47. 47 This strong spirit of Phantastrie..breaths in Paracelsus his books. **1670** GLANVILL *Way Happiness* iv. §3. 139 The indiscretions..of some preachers, the phantastry and vain babble of others. *a* **1677** BARROW *Serm.* (1686) III. 429 There shall they stand bare and devested of all their phantastry. **1678** CUDWORTH *Intell. Syst.* 47 There is something in us superiour to Sense, which judges of it, detects its Phantastry, and condemns its Imposture. **1710** R. WARD *Life H. More* 28 Fantastry and Levity..is so much seen to abound amongst us. *Ibid.* 51 Against Fantastry and Enthusiasm it self. **1870** *Contemp. Rev.* XIII. 1 It [*sc.* the Church] must have its pomp and phantastry, its tributes and taxes. **1922** HARDY *Late Lyrics* 72 So white her drape..I could not guess what phantastry it meant.

phantasy, variant of FANTASY (where see the Note, as to its frequent use in some senses).

†**phantic, -ike.** *Obs. rare.* [? Syncopated for *ˈphanatick*, FANATIC 2.] A possessed person.

1598 SYLVESTER *Du Bartas* II. i. II. *Imposture* 234 So doth the Phantike (lifting vp his thought On Sathan's wing) tell with a tongue distraught Strange Oracles. **1656** BLOUNT *Glossogr.*, *Phantick*.

phantom (ˈfæntəm), *sb.* Forms: α. 4–7 **fantosme**, 4–8 **-om(e**, (4 **-oum, -eme, -ime, -umme, -on, faintum**, 4–5 **fantum**, 6 **fantone**). β. 6–8 **phantome**, (7 **-ôm(e)**, 7–8 **phantosme**, 7– **phantom**. [ME. *fantosme*, *fantome*, a. OF. *fantosme* (12th c. in Hatz.-Darm.) = Pr. *fantasma*, *-auma*, Cat. *fantarma*, Sp., It. *fantasma*:—L. *phantasma*, a. Gr. φάντασμα: see PHANTASMA. (The *o* of the Fr. (and Eng.) form has not been satisfactorily accounted for.)]

†**1. a.** Illusion, unreality; vanity; vain imagination; delusion, deception, falsity. *Obs.*

a **1300** *Cursor M.* 55 Hit neys bot fantum [*v.rr.* fanton, fantom] for to say, To day it is, to moru away. *Ibid.* 22160 Wiþ iugulori þai sal be wroght, And fantum [*v.rr.* faintum, fantom] be, and elles noght. *a* **1300** *E.E. Psalter* iv. 3 Whi love yhe fantom [L. *vanitatem*] and lighinge speke? *c* **1384** CHAUCER *H. Fame* I. 493 (Fairf. MS) Fro Fantome, and Illusion Me save. **1390** GOWER *Conf.* III. 172 Josaphat was in gret doute, And hield fantosme al that he herde. *c* **1425** *Hampole's Psalter* Metr. Pref., Copyed has þis Sauter ben of yuel men of lollardry:..Hur fantom hath made mony a fon. *c* **1500** *Melusine* xli. 311, I byleue it is but fantosme or spyryt werke of this woman. **1692** R. L'ESTRANGE *Fables* ccccxliv. (1714) 481 The whole Entertainment of his Life was Vision and Phantome.

b. With *a* and *pl.* An instance of this; an illusion, a delusion; a deception; a figment, a lie. *Obs.*

c **1325** *E.E. Allit. P.* B. 1341 Honoured he not hym þat in heuen wonies, Bot fals fantummes of fendes, formed with handes. *a* **1340** HAMPOLE *Psalter*, etc. 505 þe deuyl sayd,.. i. sall take þaim wiþ snarys of sere temptaciouns, and many fald errours & fantoms. *c* **1420** *Avow. Arth.* ii, This is no fantum, ne no fabulle. **1483** *Cath. Angl.* 122/2 A Fantum, *fantasma.* **1628** WITHER *Brit. Rememb.* 155 The tricks And Fantosmes wherewithall our Schismaticks Abuse themselves and others. **1686** tr. *Chardin's Coronat. Solyman* 50 The Express which they assure us to have been dispatched ..is a meer Fantome.

2. a. Something that appears to the sight or other sense, but has no material substance; an apparition, a spectre; a spirit, a ghost.

1382 WYCLIF *Matt.* xiv. 26 Thei, seeynge hym walkynge aboue the see, weren distourblid, seyinge, For it is a fantum. *c* **1500** *Melusine* xli. 311 It is som spyryt, som fantosme or Illusyon that thus hath abused me. **1621** MOLLE *Camerar. Liv. Libr.* IV. ii. 265 An Abbesse in Spaine, whose place a phantosme held in the Church..while shee lay with a wicked spirit that maried her. **1693** SMALLRIDGE *Jul. Cæsar* in *Dryden's Plutarch* IV. 484 The Phantôm which appear'd to Brutus. **1746** SMOLLETT *Tears Scot.* 31 The pale phantoms of the slain Glide nightly o'er the silent plain. **1859** TENNYSON *Elaine* 1016 Hark the Phantom of the house That ever shrieks before a death. **1887** BOWEN *Virg. Æneid* VI. 292 The phantoms are thin apparitions, clothed in a vain Semblance of form.

b. Something having the form or appearance, but not the substance, of some other thing; a (material or optical) image *of* something.

1707 *Curios. in Husb. & Gard.* 325 When a Body is.. reduc'd into Ashes, we find again in the Salts, extracted from its Ashes, the Idea, the Image, and the Phantom of the same Body. **1817** SHELLEY *Rev. Islam* VI. xxxiii. 5 As twin phantoms of one star that lies O'er a dim well, move, though the star reposes. **1819** —— *Prometh. Unb.* III. iii. 52 The forms Of which these are the phantoms. **1856** T. B. BUTLER *Philos. Weather* iv. 63 (Funk) The thirsty wanderer is deluded by the phantom of a moving, undulating, watery, surface. **1882** P. G. TAIT in *Encycl. Brit.* XIV. 582/1 Another curious phenomenon..the phantoms which are seen when we look at two parallel sets of palisades or railings, one behind the other... The appearance..is that of a magnified set of bars..which appear to move rapidly as we slowly walk past.

c. *fig.* Applied to that which is a 'vain show', or to a person, institution, etc., that has the name and show of power but none of the substance, or to one which remains a 'ghost of his (or its) former self'; a cipher. Cf. GHOST *sb.* 9.

1661 EVELYN *Tyrannus* 23 Exorcising these Apparitions and Fantosm's of a Court and Country. **1707** *Reflex. upon Ridicule* 75 The Husband is only a Fantom. **1781** GIBBON *Decl. & F.* xxxi. III. 260 The caprice of the Barbarians.. once more seated this Imperial phantom [Maximus] on the throne. **1818** HALLAM *Mid. Ages* (1872) II. vi. 131 They annihilated the phantom of authority which still lingered with the name of Khalif at Bagdad. **1874** GREEN *Short Hist.* viii. §6. 530 'If I granted your demands', replied Charles, 'I should be no more than the mere phantom of a king'. **1901** C. B. MOUNT in *N. & Q.* 15 June 465 This little phantom of a village [Temple, Cornwall]..dwindled to nothing..in the eighteenth century.

3. a. A mental illusion; an image which appears in a dream, or which is formed or cherished in the mind; also, the thought or apprehension of anything that haunts the imagination.

1590 SPENSER *F.Q.* II. xii. 47 Who wondrous things concerning our welfare, And straunge phantomes doth lett us ofte foresee. **1706** ADDISON *Rosamond* II. i, Farewel sorrow, farewel fear, They're fantoms all! **1758** JOHNSON *Idler* No. 32 ¶11 We suffer phantoms to rise up before us, and amuse ourselves with the dance of airy images. **1804** WORDSW. '*She was a Phantom*', She was a Phantom of delight When first she gleamed upon my sight. **1849** DE QUINCEY *Eng. Mail Coach* III. v, Sister unknown..a thousand times, amongst the phantoms of sleep, have I seen thee entering the gates of the golden dawn. **1879** B. TAYLOR *Stud. Germ. Lit.* 127 There is the phantom of an implacable Fate behind all those dreadful deeds.

b. The mental image or concept of an external object (considered as having a merely subjective existence).

1681 GLANVILL *Sadducismus* I. (1682) 3 The notion they have of him is but a phantôme and conceit. **1842** EMERSON *Lect., Transcend.* Wks. (Bohn) II. 280 How easy it is to show him [the Materialist] that he also is a phantom walking and working amid phantoms. **1865** GROTE *Plato* II. xxv. 270 When you contemplate many similar objects, one and the same ideal phantom or Concept is suggested by all.

4. The visible representative, image, or figure of some incorporeal person or body politic.

1690 LOCKE *Govt.* II. xiii. §151 So [the supreme executor of the law] is to be consider'd as the Image, Phantom, or Representative of the Commonwealth.

5. Technical uses. **a.** A model of an infant used in obstetric demonstrations: cf. MANIKIN 2 c.

1882 in OGILVIE. **1902** *Rep. Gen. Med. Council on Exam. Univ. Durham* 17 Candidates were required to demonstrate on the 'phantom' the application of the forceps. **1904** *Brit. Med. Jrnl.* 10 Sept. 605 A good description is given of the various forms of 'phantom'.

b. *Angling.* An artificial bait made to resemble live-bait.

1883 *Fisheries Exhib. Catal.* 52 Patent Soleskin Phantoms, and Artificial Baits. **1892** G. R. LOWNDES *Camping Sk.* 181 The 'phantom' had still less effect. *Ibid.* 207 Of a phantom the boss had no opinion at all.

c. *Telegr.* and *Teleph.* An additional circuit obtained by using each of two other circuits as one of its two conductors, the two wires of each of the other circuits being effectively in parallel. Usu. *attrib.*

1883 G. BLACK in *Operator & Electr. World* 3 Feb. 71/1 The method of telephonic transmission was discovered by myself in 1878, while experimenting to get rid of telegraphic induction in telephones. I found that my apparatus gave me a new 'phantom' circuit over a telegraph wire. **1920** J. G. HILL *Telephonic Transmission* ix. 192 If one of the side circuits in a phantom circuit is out of order, the phantom necessarily fails with it. **1924** W. AITKEN *Automatic Telephone Syst.* III. xlviii. 229 In using phantom or superimposed circuits on automatic systems great care must be exercised to prevent impulse and other currents in one physical circuit affecting the mate physical circuit by way of the phantom loop. **1943** A. L. ALBERT *Fund. Telephony* x. 258 A phantom circuit is obtained by repeating coils.. installed at each end of two pairs of wires constituting the phantom group. This arrangement gives three telephone channels: one over each side circuit and one channel over the phantom circuit. **1957** W. FRASER *Telecommunications* v. 123 The additional circuits may be provided by utilising pairs of phantom circuits to produce other phantom circuits.

d. *Radiology.* A life-size model of part of the body made of material which absorbs radiation in a similar way, used in investigations into the character and absorption of a beam of radiation.

1922 tr. *Kroenig & Friedrich's Princ. Physics & Biol. Radiation Therapy* I. 33 Perthes had to employ a solid substance, namely aluminium, as phantom material... These aluminium phantoms have general use in practice on account of their convenience. **1950** WALTER & MILLER *Short Textbk. Radiotherapy* iv. 99 Water is not always an ideal medium in which to insert small ionization chambers... A suitable phantom can be made of layers of pressed wood fibre which can be obtained of unit density. Suitable holes ..enable the ionization chamber to be inserted. **1974** RAFLA & ROTMAN *Introd. Radiotherapy* iii. 35/1 A plastic material .., which simulates water (and soft tissues), has been described. If such a material is placed around a bony skeleton, then a phantom that simulates the body with its bones more accurately than water alone can be built.

6. *appositive* or *adj.* That is a phantom; merely apparent, spectral, illusive. Also in more general use: imaginary; false; devised by way of pretence, imitation, or deceit. (Sometimes hyphened.)

c **1425** WYNTOUN *Cron.* VI. xviii. 2206 Syne þai herd, þat Makbeth aye In fantown Fretis had gret Fay. *c* **1450** *St. Cuthbert* (Surtees) 1861 þe fantom fyre it vanyst sone. **1671** F. PHILLIPS *Reg. Necess.* 478 To assert their phantosme or feigned soveraignty. **1726** POPE *Odyss.* XXII. 233 The adverse host the phantom-warrior ey'd. **1762** KAMES *Elem. Crit.* xix. (1833) 344 Such phantom similes are mere witticisms. **1822–56** DE QUINCEY *Confess.* Wks. 1897 III. 284 Phantom cavalry careered, flying and pursuing. **1850** S. DOBELL *Roman* ii, Phantom ship to skim aërial waves Or desert mirage. **1872** LIDDON *Elem. Relig.* ii. 47 That phantom-god who, as we are told, is only a pale reflection of human vanity. **1885** KIPLING *Phantom 'Rickshaw* (1889) 25 The phantom 'rickshaw and I went side by side along the Chota Simla road in silence. **1897** W. B. YEATS *Let.* 24 Dec. (1954) 293 He did not come because of the phantom sore throat. **1909** *Westm. Gaz.* 19 Aug. 8/1 There was more phantom work on the Downs yesterday. **1927** H. CRANE *Let.* 7 Jan. (1965) 283 The 'ships' [in a poem] should meet and pass in line and type—as well as in wind and memory, if you get my rather unique formal intentions in this phantom regatta seen from Brooklyn Bridge. **1931** *Daily Express* 28 Apr. 11/4 The ball was centred, and the eleven men, playing a phantom team, swept down the pitch to the unguarded goal. **1934** *Sun* (Baltimore) 5 Apr. 1/3 The steel industry was indulging in a monopolistic form of price boosting and price fixing which included the writing into its price structure of so-called 'phantom' freight rates which the consumer pays, but which find their way into the manufacturers' coffers and not those of the railroads. **1951** M. MCLUHAN *Mech. Bride* (1967) 143/2 They are not rooted in any concept of civilized society but are merely a blind drive toward the phantom security of subrational collectivism. **1952** *Times* 12 Dec. 12/3 Lot 90 was not a phantom beaver coat, or indeed a beaver coat at all, but a phantom racoon coat. **1958** *Times* 29 Sept. 13/1 The duvetyn coat with a phantom beaver collar. **1976** *National Observer* (U.S.) 29 May 9/2 A 'phantom', or dummy, fluorescent tube that reduces the amount of electricity used by standard two-tube fixtures.

7. *attrib.* and *Comb.* **a.** Simple attrib., as ***phantom-land, -nation, -shape, -tribe, -warning; phantom-life***; **b.** similative, as ***phantom-fair, -white*** adjs.; objective, as ***phantom-chaser***; also ***phantom-like*** adj. and adv.; ***phantom-wise*** adv.

1954 KOESTLER *Invisible Writing* ii. 34 The *phantom-chaser..who discovers Helen's image in each beloved face. **1855** TENNYSON *Daisy* 65 *Phantom-fair Was Monte Rosa. *a* **1849** MANGAN *Poems* (1859) 42 Roams the *phantomland for ever. **1907** *Folk-Lore* June 147 Cuchulain was recalled to *phantom-life on one occasion by St. Patrick. *c* **1820** S. ROGERS *Italy, Venice* 141 *Phantom-like, vanish with a dreadful scream. **1860** T. MARTIN *Horace* 55 Before thee evermore doth Fate Stalk phantomlike. **1725** POPE *Odyss.* x. 627 The *Phantome-nations of the dead. *c* **1820** S. ROGERS *Italy* (1839) 70 Two *phantom-shapes were sitting side by side. **1812** W. TENNANT *Anster F* VI. lxxix, Oberon, the silver-scepter'd fay, That rules his *phantom-tribes with gentle force. **1850** TENNYSON *In Mem.* xcii, Tho' the months..Should prove the *phantom-warning true. **1871** 'L. CARROLL' *Through Looking-Glass* 223 Still she haunts me, *phantomwise.

8. Special combinations and collocations: **phantom corn, phantom corpuscle**: see quots.; **phantom-fish**, the transparent young of the common conger; **phantom flesh**: see quot.; **phantom-larva**, the transparent larva of a dipterous fly of the genus *Corethra*; **phantom limb**, a sensation of the presence of an amputated limb; **phantom minnow** (cf. 5 b); **phantom pain**, pain perceived as in a phantom limb; **phantom tumour**, a rounded abdominal swelling of temporary nature having the appearance of an actual tumour.

1674 RAY *N.C. Words*, **Fantome corn*, lank or light Corn. .. Phantome Corn is Corn that has as little bulk or solidity in it as a Spirit or Spectre. **1899** CAGNEY tr. *Jaksch's Clin. Diagn.* vii. (ed. 4) 258 They [i.e. red-blood corpuscles in urine] may retain their proper form, or they may appear as pale yellowish rings (*phantom corpuscles of Traube). **1879** *Bull. Essex Inst.* (Cent. Dict.), Conger eels and their curious transparent young—*phantom fish—are occasionally seen. **1674** RAY *N.C. Words*, **Fantome flesh*, when it hangs loose on the Bones. **1900** MIALL & HAMMOND *Harlequin Fly* ii. 78 The *phantom-larva (Corethra), which poises itself in the middle depths of clear water. [**1872** S. W. MITCHELL *Injuries of Nerves* xiv. 349, I recently faradised a case of disarticulated shoulder... As the current affected the brachial plexus of nerves, he suddenly cried aloud, 'Oh, the hand, the hand!' and attempted to seize the missing member. The phantom I had conjured up swiftly disappeared.] **1879** G. H. LEWES *Probl. Life & Mind* (ser. 3) II. 336 The '*phantom limb', of which Weir Mitchell speaks, is only one detail in the general picture mentally formed of the body. **1937** *Lancet* 8 Aug. 314/1 After amputation it was usual for the patient to experience sensations as if his limb were still present. These phantom limbs might be painless or painful. **1955** *Sci. News Let.* 13 Aug. 104/3 Phantom limb pains, a troublesome affliction in amputation cases, and pains in amputation stumps can be relieved in many cases by ultrasound treatment. **1974** *Nature* 26 Apr. 731/1 Phantom limbs occur in 95 to 100% of all poeple who have had a limb or part of a limb amputated. **1883** *Fisheries Exhib. Catal.* 212 Flexible Minnows.. Caledonian Minnows..*Phantom Minnows. **1900** *Daily News* 13 Oct. 8/2 A bewildering 'eenstrument', as the Highland gillie called a phantom minnow. **1960** I. A. STANTON *Dict. for Med. Secretaries* 115/2 *Phantom pain. **1964** *N.Y. State Jrnl. Med.* LXIV. 2907/2 Many theories have been advanced to explain the mechanism of phantom pain. **1973** *Daily Colonist* (Victoria, B.C.) 11 Apr. 34/7 It's pretty weird to have a pain in a foot that has been amputated. .. The person [is] suffering from 'phantom pains' as they are called. **1857** SIR T. WATSON *Princ. & Pract. Physic* (ed. 4) II. lxvii. 415 The tumour which she had presented to the notice of the surgeon was what has been called a *phantom tumour. **1897** *Allbutt's Syst. Med.* II. 1137.

Hence (mostly *nonce-words*) **'phantom** *v. trans.*, to haunt as a phantom; **phanto'matic** [cf. *phantasmatic*] *a.*, phantom-like, unreal; **phan'tomic, phan'tomical** *adjs.*, of the nature of or resembling a phantom; **phan'tomically** *adv.*, as or in the form of a phantom; **'phantomish** *a.*, akin to or suggestive of phantoms; **'phantomishly** *adv.* (in 5 **fantomysliche**), in the manner of or by means of phantoms; **'phantomry**, phantoms collectively; **'phantomship**, the personality of a phantom.

1899 *Harper's Mag.* Feb. 356, I had tried..the cure-all of hard work, but there was that ghost of the heart *phantoming everything sadly. **1818** COLERIDGE in *Lit. Rem.* (1836) I. 177 The love of Adam and Eve in Paradise is ..not *phantomatic, and yet removed from every thing degrading. **1877** T. SINCLAIR *Mount* (1878) 63 Their libraries of volumes..are but *phantomic. **1687** MRS. BEHN *Emperor of Moon* II. i, Whether they appear'd in solid bodies, or *fantomical, is yet a question. **1882** *Gd. Words* 602 Thus she appeared *phantomically [*pr.* -mimically] to her slumbering parents. **1832** *Blackw. Mag.* May 803/1 The time was late, the place was *phantomish. *c* **1420** *Chron. Vilod.* st. 1142 þus visiones nere not *fantomysliche ydo. **1835** ANSTER tr. *2nd Pt. Faustus* III. (1887) 159 Did the anguish of my spirit Shape the wild *phantomry? **1713** C'TESS WINCHELSEA *Misc. Poems* 22 Of her *Phantomship requested, To learn the Name of that close Dwelling. **1853** MISS E. S. SHEPPARD *Ch. Auchester* xvi. (1875) 68 This ghost of an aphorism stalked forth from my brain,..and to lay its phantomship, I am compelled to submit it to paper.

'phantomist. [f. prec. + -IST.] One who professes some doctrine or theory as to phantoms; in quot., one holding the Docetic theory of Christ's body, a phantasiast. Also *attrib.* or as *adj.*

1895 *Edin. Rev.* Jan. 212 The reality of Christ's sufferings, which those who held the phantomist theory denied.

'phantomize, *v. rare.* [f. as prec. + -IZE.] *trans. lit.* To make a phantom of, reduce to a phantom; in quots. used polemically for, To explain away by interpreting in a 'spiritual' or figurative sense. Hence **'phantomizer.**

1860 WOLFF *Trav. & Adv.* I. xii. 377 The system of interpreting..unfulfilled prophecy in a phantomizing, or, what is commonly called spiritual manner. *Ibid.* 379 Against the spiritual interpreters, that is, the phantomizers, of the 3rd and 4th verses. *Ibid.* II. 121 Christians who phantomize the clear sense of prophecy.

[phantomnation. Explained as: Appearance of a phantom; illusion. Error for *phantom nation.*

[**1725** POPE *Odyss.* x. 627 The Phantome-nations of the dead.] Entered as one word in **1820** JODRELL, in accordance with his method of writing compounds: *Phantomnation*, a multitude of spectres. Hence the following entries: **1860** WORCESTER, *Phantomnation*, illusion. *Pope.* **1864** WEBSTER, *Phantomnation*, appearance as of a phantom; illusion. (*Obs.* and *rare.*) *Pope.* So in OGILVIE (Annandale) and *Cassell's Encycl. Dict.*]

†**'phantomy,** *sb. Obs.* In 5 **fantomye.** [f. PHANTOM + -Y: cf *villainy*, etc.] Illusion; fantasy; the practice of illusion, deception.

c **1440** *Gesta Rom.* xcii. 421 (Add. MS) Now ye mow se the sothe, that it is false and vntrew, and fantomye.

'phantomy, *a. rare.* [f. PHANTOM + -Y.] Of the nature of or characteristic of a phantom; phantasmal; *dial.* thin, reduced to a 'shadow'.

1877 E. LEIGH *Cheshire Gloss.* (E.D.D.), Horses are very phantomy at this time of year. **1893** *Temple Bar Mag.* XCVII. 240 A phantomy pair of thick black brows.

phantoscope ('fæntəskəʊp). [f. Gr. φαντός visible + -SCOPE: cf. PHANTASCOPE.]

1. A modification of the kaleidoscope.

1894 *Westm. Gaz.* 14 Sept. 8/1 This new invention, called the phantoscope, and patented by Mr. W. S. Simpson, differs from the traditional kaleidoscope as..any object whatever can, through an aperture at the end, be placed within it—a bee, for instance, a butterfly, a spray of maiden-hair fern, or a sprig of heather, producing a complex vision of quite inconceivable beauty.

2. = PHANTASCOPE.

1902 in WEBSTER *Suppl.*

†**phanun,** obs. form of FANON.

c **1475** *Voc.* in Wr.-Wülcker 755/27 *Hic Phano*, phanun.

-phany, repr. Gr. -φανία, -φάνεια appearance, manifestation, f. stem φαν- of φαίνειν to show, appear; as in *angelophany, epiphany, theophany.*

†**phaometer** (feɪ'ɒmɪtə(r)). *Obs.* [f. Gr. φάος light + -METER.] An apparatus for determining the intensity of light; a photometer.

1747 *Phil. Trans.* XLIV. 495 M. de Buffon, being asked if it might be possible to invent a Phaometer, or Machine for measuring the Intensity of Light.

Pharaoh ('fɛərəʊ). Forms: 1 **Pharaon,** 4 **Pharaone, Pharaoe, Farao,** 4–7 **Pharao,** 7 **Pharoh,** 8 **Pharoah,** 7– **Pharaoh.** [orig. ad. L. *Pharaō, Pharaōn-em* (whence F. *Pharaon*), a. Gr. Φαραώ, a. Heb. *parʿōh*, ad. Egypt. *pr-ʿo* great house. The later Eng. spelling takes the final *h* from Heb.]

1. The generic appellation of the ancient Egyptian kings; an Egyptian king, *esp.* that one under whom Joseph flourished, and those in whose time the oppression and Exodus of Israel took place.

c **893** K. ÆLFRED *Oros.* I. iv. §2 Hiora þeaw wære þæt hi ealle hiora cyningas hetan Pharaon. **1362** LANGL. *P. Pl.* A. VIII. 150 Hit fel as þe Fader seide In Pharaones tyme. **1382** WYCLIF *Gen.* xli. 1 After two ȝeer Pharao [**1388** Farao] sawe a sweuen. *a* **1555** LATIMER *Serm. & Rem.* (Parker Soc.) 177 After that he came at the Red sea, Pharao with his power followed at his back. **1614** SELDEN *Titles Hon.* 73 The Egyptian Kings in holy writ vntill Salomons time are all calld Pharaoh's. It was no proper name, but a title which euery one of them had. **1877** A. B. EDWARDS *Up Nile* xiv. 385 Rameses the Second..remains to this day the representative Pharaoh of a line of monarchs whose history covers a space of fifty centuries.

b. *fig.* Used as a name for any tyrant or task-master.

c **1630** SANDERSON *Serm. Prov.* xix. 21 §34 Scattering such proud Pharaohs in the imagination of their hearts. **1846** MRS. GORE *Sk. Eng. Char.* (1852) 69 The Sundays..by permission of his Pharaoh of the mill, were usually spent in wandering with his sisters about the green lanes by Gadesbridge, or Gaddesden.

†**2.** (Also **Pharaon, Pharoan, Pharo.**) A gambling game played with cards: = FARO[1]. *Obs.*

1717 GAY *To Pulteney* 79 Nannette last night at tricking Pharaon play'd. **1739**, **1748** [see FARO[1] 1]. **1782** [T. VAUGHAN] *Fashionable Follies* II. cclxii. 212 She..spent whole days, and even nights, at whist and pharoan. **1792** WOLCOTT (P. Pindar) *Odes Import., Resignation* xii, Behold, a hundred coaches at her door, Where Pharo triumphs in his mad career.

attrib. **1721** MRS. CENTLIVRE *Artifice* I, He belongs to a Pharaoh-table, I us'd to see him tally sometimes. **1729** GAY *Polly* II, For some time I kept a Pharaon bank with success. **1796** COLQUHOUN *Police of Metropolis* p. x, [Houses] where Pharo Banks are kept. *a* **1843** SOUTHEY *Comm.-pl. Bk.* (1849) IV. 416 A party were at the pharo-table.

†**3.** A kind of strong ale or beer; also known as 'Old Pharaoh', 'Stout Pharaoh'. Cf. FARO[2]. *Obs.* or *dial.*

1683 G. MERITON *Praise Yorks. Ale* (1685) 3 Lac'd Coffee, Twist, Old Pharoh, and Old Hoc, Juniper, Brandy and Wine de Langue-Dock. **1702** T. BROWN *Lett. fr. Dead* Wks. 1760 II. 286 A morning's draught of three-threads and old Pharoah. **1839** W. H. AINSWORTH *J. Sheppard* II. v, Don't muddle your brains with any more of that Pharaoh.

4. In names of animals, plants, etc.; as **Pharaoh hound**, a short-coated, tan-coloured hunting dog with large, pointed ears, belonging to the breed so called; **Pharaoh's ant**, the little red ant (*Monomorium pharaonis*); **Pharoah's beans**, nummulites found in the rock of the pyramids, etc.; **Pharaoh's chicken**, the Egyptian vulture (*Neophron percnopterus*); **Pharaoh's corn**, *Triticum compositum*, the grains of which have been found in mummy-cases; mummy-wheat; **Pharaoh's fig**, †(*a*) some species of the genus *Musa*; (*b*) *Sycomorus antiquorum*; **Pharaoh's hen** = *Pharaoh's chicken*; **Pharaoh's mouse**, or **rat**, the ichneumon; **Pharaoh's pence** = *Pharaoh's beans*; **Pharaoh's serpent** [cf. Exod. vii. 9], a chemical toy composed of sulpho-cyanide of mercury, which fuses in a serpentine form; **Pharaoh's worm** = GUINEA-WORM.

1967 R. GLYN *Champion Dogs of World* 191/2 The Ibizan Hound. Also known as the *Pharaoh Hound. **1969** V. CANNING *Queen's Pawn* xiii. 240 Raikes sat..reading an article about the revival of interest in Pharaoh hounds from Malta. **1974** A. G.-I. BROWNE *Hamlyn Guide to Dogs* 180 Pharaoh Hound... Although in the opinion of many people they belong to one and the same breed, the FCI [*sc.* Fédération Cynologique Internationale] recognizes the Pharaoh Hound as well as the Podenco Ibicenco [or Ibizan hound]... It is supposed that the Pharaoh Hound came to Gozo and Malta with the seafaring Phoenicians. **1910** W. M. WHEELER *Ants* i. 10 Some of them [*sc.* tropical ants], like *Pharaoh's ant.., have been carried by commerce to all the inhabited regions of the globe. **1939** METCALF & FLINT *Destructive & Useful Insects* (ed. 2) xxi. 770 Pharaoh's ant, *Monomorium pharaonis*... This tiny, slender, yellowish-red ant..generally nests in inaccessible places about the foundations and in the walls of buildings, from which it forages indoors the year round in search of food. **1978** *Times* 24 Apr. 2/2 Ministry of Agriculture scientists have devised a way to get rid of one of the more serious modern hospital pests, the Pharaoh's ant. **1884** *Leisure Ho.* 236/1 Those round discs..known as *Nummulites*, and which Strabo was informed were petrified beans—'*Pharaoh's beans'. **1840** MACGILLIVRAY *Hist. Brit. Birds* III. 166 *Neophron percnopterus*, the white neophron. Egyptian vulture. *Pharaoh's chicken. **1753** CHAMBERS *Cycl. Supp.* App., **Pharaoh's Fig*,..a genus of plants called by authors *musa*. **1884** MILLER *Plant-n.*, *Sycomorus antiquorum*, Pharaoh's Fig. **1876** *Helps Study Bible, Birds* s.v. *Eagle*, The 'Egyptian vulture' or '*Pharaoh's hen', common in Asia and all parts of Africa. **1607** TOPSELL *Four-f. Beasts* (1658) 427 The Indian Mouse, or *Pharaohs Mouse (as some learned later Writers do write) is no other then the Ichneumon. **1598**, **1886** *Pharaoh's rat [see RAT *sb.*[1] 1 b]. **1865** *Pall Mall G.* 18 Nov. 5, I have found that one half of a 6*d.* *Pharaoh's serpent is sufficient to poison a large sized rabbit.

5. *attrib.* and *Comb.*, as ***Pharaoh-like*** adj.

1647 FULLER *Good Th. in Worse T.* (1841) 84 That I may seasonably drown this Pharaoh-like procrastination in the sea of repentance. **1899** *Westm. Gaz.* 23 Nov. 3/1 For a while he shows a Pharaoh stubbornness.

Hence †**Pharaonian** (fɛəreɪ'əʊnɪən), **Pharaonic** (-'ɒnɪk), †**Phara'onical** *adjs.*, of or pertaining to, of the nature or character of, or like Pharaoh.

1673 PENN *The Chr. a Quaker* xviii. 577 *Pharaonian Task-Master. **1853** KANE *Grinnell Exp.* xlii. (1856) 387 Barriers, grander and more massive than the *Pharaonic rubbish of the Ramesium. **1899** SAYCE *Early Israel* v. 149 The Pharaonic Egyptians are the Egyptians of history. **1958** L. DURRELL *Mountolive* i. 17 Forgotten Pharaonic frescoes of light and darkness. **1972** *Nature* 14 Apr. 324/1 A travelling exhibition of works of art dating from both Pharaonic and Islamic times. **1976** *Sci. Amer.* Aug. 38/2 It is interesting to note that in the earliest Pharaonic era, that of the Old Kingdom, the Egyptians showed a lively interest in domesticating local animals. *c* **1528** *Impeachm. Wolsey* in Furnivall *Ballads fr. MSS.* I. 352 Where he dyd well, thowe doste Amys by thy *pharon[i]call mynde. **1632** *High Commission Cases* (Camden) 266 It was a Pharaonical thing to deny her choice of a midwife.

pharate ('færeɪt), *a. Ent.* [f. Gr. φᾶρ-ος cloak + -ATE[2].] (See quot. 1946.)

1946 H. E. HINTON in *Nature* 27 Apr. 553/1 The term 'pharate'..is proposed to designate the place of an instar which is enclosed within the cuticle of the previous instar. **1957** RICHARDS & DAVIES *Imms's Gen. Textbk. Entomol.* (ed. 9) 222 There may be an appreciable interval between the two events, during which the instar within the old cuticle is known as the pharate instar. **1971** *Nature* 12 Feb. 490/1 The developing adult inside the pupal cuticle (the pharate adult) can also move the spiracles. **1973** W. S. ROMOSER *Sci. of Entomol.* viii. 242 The pharate condition..is where the adult is fully formed but is still within the confines of the pupal cuticle.

pharbitin (fɑː'baɪtɪn). *Chem.* [f. Bot. L. *Pharbīt-is* + -IN.] A purgative resin obtained from the KALADANA resin-plant *Pharbitis* (or *Ipomæa*) *Nil*; also called **phar'bitisin**.

1873 DRURY *Usef. Plants Ind.* 337 Dr. G. Bidie prepared a resin from the seeds called *Pharbitisin*, which is a safe and efficient purgative. **1887** MOLONEY *Forestry W. Afr.* 389. **1893** *Syd. Soc. Lex.*, *Pharbitin.*

phare (fɛə(r)). [a. F. *phare* (1553 in Hatz.-Darm.), ad. L. *phar-us*, a. Gr. φάρος: see PHAROS.]

1. A lighthouse; = PHAROS[1] 2. Also *fig.*

1656 BLOUNT *Glossogr.*, *Phare*,..a Tower or high place by the Sea coast, wherein were continually lights and fires, which served Seamen to see the Haven. **1668** SMITH *Voy. Constantinople* in *Misc. Cur.* (1708) III. 23 On the Sandy Banks stands the Phare or Watch-tower. **1835** BROWNING *Paracelsus* v. 386 Sun!..what care If lower mountains light their snowy phares At thine effulgence, yet acknowledge not The source of day? **1845** —— *Lett.* (1899) I. 18 Like the light in those crazy Mediterranean phares I have watched at sea.

†**2.** A strait or channel lighted by a pharos; the Strait of Messina: cf. FARE *sb.*[3] *Obs.*

1615 G. SANDYS *Trav.* 246 The Phare of Messina (for so these streights are now called of the Lanterne that stands on the point of Pelorus). **1652** HOWELL *Giraffi's Rev. Naples* II. Proem, The flames thereof flew ore the Phare of Messina into Calabria. **1723** *Lond. Gaz.* No. 6176/1 Near the Phare of Messina.

phareis, pl. of *pharie*, obs. form of FAIRY.

†**Pharian** ('fɛərɪən), *a.* and *sb. Obs.* [f. L. *Pharius* of Pharos, Egyptian.] **A.** *adj.* Of or pertaining to the island of Pharos; *poet.* Egyptian, Nilotic. **B.** *sb.* An Egyptian.

1591 SYLVESTER *Du Bartas* I. i. 500 The Ephesian Temple and high Pharian Tower. **1624** MILTON *Paraphr. Ps.* cxiv, And past from Pharian fields to Canaan land. **1718** ROWE tr. *Lucan* x. 778 He chears the drooping Pharians with success. *a* **1729** CONGREVE tr. *Ovid's Art of Love* III. Wks. 1773 III. 271 If pale, let her the crimson juice apply; If swarthy, to the Pharian varnish fly.

Pharisæan (færɪ'siːən), *a.* Also **-ean.** [f. L. *Pharisæ-us* PHARISEE + -AN.] = next, 1.

1645 MILTON *Colast.* Wks. 1851 IV. 367 All of them Pharisæan disciples, and bred up in their Doctrin. **1891** CHEYNE *Orig. Psalter* viii. 415 The Second Book of Maccabees approaches much more closely to the Pharisæan theology.

Pharisaic (færɪ'seɪɪk), *a.* [ad. L. *Pharisaïc-us* (Jerome), a. Gr. φαρισαϊκ-ός, f. φαρισαῖ-ος: see PHARISEE and -IC. Cf. F. *Pharisaïque* (Calvin).]

1. Of or belonging to the Pharisees.

1643 MILTON *Divorce* II. vi, He..removes the Pharisaick mists rais'd between the Law and the peoples eyes. **1678** CUDWORTH *Intell. Syst.* I. i. §4. 6 The Pharisaick Sect amongst the Jews. **1879** C. GEIKIE *Christ* 22 The bitterest persecutions of the Pharisaic party.

2. Resembling the Pharisees in being strict in doctrine and ritual, without the spirit of piety; laying great stress upon the external observances of religion and outward show of morality, and assuming superiority on that account; hypocritical; formal; self-righteous.

The particular connotation varies according as one or other of the aspects in which the Pharisees appear in the Gospels is emphasized; the present tendency being to emphasize that of self-righteousness.

a **1618** SYLVESTER *Alls not gold* xxiv, Wee are so Punctuall and Precise In Doctrine (Pharisaik-wise). **1771** FLETCHER *Checks* Wks. 1795 II. 13 He sets up pharisaic self, instead of Christ. **1795** SOUTHEY *Soldier's Funeral* 56 O my God! I thank thee, with no Pharisaic pride I thank thee, that I am not such as these. **1884** *Congregational Year Bk.* 86 There is something worse than Pharisaic respectability. There is Pharisaic vice.

Pharisaical (færɪ'seɪɪkəl), *a.* [f. as prec. + -AL[1].] †**1.** = PHARISAIC 1. *Obs.*

1538 BALE *Thre Lawes* 1604 As Cayphas ones sayd in counsell pharysaycall. **1613** PURCHAS *Pilgrimage* (1614) 124 The want of which office Christ obiected to another of his Pharisaicall hostes. **1831** BURTON *Eccl. Hist.* viii. (1845) 189 The Pharisaical part of the Council declared him to be innocent.

2. = PHARISAIC 2.

1531 TINDALE *Exp.* 1 *John* ii. 3 (1537) 37 Our pharisaycall doctours haue no doctrine to knowe when a man is in the state of grace. **1625** BACON *Ess., Superstition* (Arb.) 347 The Causes of Superstition are:..Excesse of Outward and Pharisaicall Holinesse. **1794** G. ADAMS *Nat. & Exp. Philos.* II. xx. 371 The pharisaical self-sufficiency of the modern infidel. **1835** J. H. NEWMAN *Par. Serm.* (1837) I. xi. 161 There are vast multitudes of Pharisaical hypocrites among baptized Christians.

Hence **Phari'saically** *adv.*; **Phari'saicalness.**

1599 *Broughton's Let.* vii. 21 So farre houen with surquedrie and self-loue,..Pharisaically..to annihilate all others. **1679** PULLER *Moder. Ch. Eng.* xvii. 489 Their many kinds of Superstitions, and Pharisaicalness. **1884** *Bookseller* 6 Nov. 1177/2 He, pharisaically, in the interests of morality, gets the thief, whom he taught, committed to prison.

Pharisaism ('færɪseɪɪz(ə)m). [f. mod.L. *Pharisaïsm-us*, in 16th c. F. (Calvin) *Pharisaïsme*, f. Gr. φαρισαῖ-ος PHARISEE + -ISM.]

1. The doctrine and practice of the Pharisees; the fact of being a Pharisee.

1610 BP. HALL *Apol. Brownists* iv. 9 Paul was (ἀφωρισμένος) separated, which some would haue allude to his Pharisaisme. **1727–41** CHAMBERS *Cycl.* s.v. *Pharisee*, Pharisaism is still the prevailing doctrine in the Jewish religion. **1882** FARRAR *Early Chr.* I. 519 It was the desire to preserve that Law intact which..formed the nobler side of Pharisaism.

2. The character and spirit of the Pharisees; hypocrisy; formalism; self-righteousness.

1601 W. WATSON *Import. Consid.* (1831) 27 You should not be seduced by Pharisaism, hypocrisy, and plausible persuasions. **1711** *Reflect. on Wall's Hist. Inf. Bapt.* 351 What at length, do you find, but a kind of men mad with Pharisaism, bewitching with traditions? **1874** PUSEY *Lent. Serm.* 167 Of all the Pharisaisms of the day, our Church-going seems to me the masterpiece. **1879** FARRAR *St. Paul* iii. I. 46 When we speak of Pharisaism we mean obedience petrified into formalism, religion degraded into ritual, morals cankered by casuistry.

Pharisaist ('færɪseɪɪst), *a.* [After PHARISAISM, f. PHARISEE *sb.* + -IST.] = PHARISAIC *a.*

1918 P. T. FORSYTH *This Life & Next* xi. 112 Its idea of resurrection means something very much more than the repristination of the old life under happier circumstances. That..is but Jewish, and the Pharisaist, and Moslem.

Pharisean: see PHARISÆAN, PHARISIAN.

Pharisee ('færɪsiː), *sb.* Forms: α. 1–2 **fari-, phariseus,** 3 **pharisewus, farisew,** 4 **phariseu, -isew, -ysu, farizeu,** 5 **pharysew.** β. (3 **pharise**), 4 **far-,** 4–6 **pharise, -isey;** 4– **pharisee.** γ. *pl.* 5 **pharisen, -ysen.** [α. OE. *fari-, phariseus* (gen. sing. *-ees*, pl. *-eas*), in 13th c. *pharisewus*; thence ME. *farisew, pharisew, -eu*, etc. (cf HEBREW). β. ME. *pharise, -ee*, a. OF. *pharise* (13th c. in Godef.). The OE. and OF. were both ad. L. *pharisæus, -ēus*, a. Gr. φαρῖσαῖος, pl. -αῖοι, ad. Aramaic *p'rīshaiyā* emph. pl. of *p'rīsh* = Heb. *pārūsh*, separated, hence separatist.]

1. One of an ancient Jewish sect distinguished by their strict observance of the traditional and written law, and by their pretensions to superior sanctity.

α. *c* **897** K. ÆLFRED *Gregory's Past. C.* xlvii. 362 Ða Fariseos ʒeliefdon ðære æriste. *c* **1000** *Ags. Gosp.* Luke vii. 37 He sæt on þæs fariseus [*c* **1160** *Hatton* farisees] huse. *Ibid.* xi. 43 Wa eow fariseum [*Hatt.* fariseen, xiv. 3 farisean]. *Ibid.* xviii. 11 Ða stod se fariseus [*Hatt.* phariseus]. *c* **1200** ORMIN 16862 Forr Farisew bitacneþþ uss Shædning onn Ennglissh spæche. *Ibid.* 19658 Þa laþe Farisewess. *a* **1225** *Ancr. R.* 328 Nout ase was þe Pharisewus þet tolde his god deden. *a* **1300** *Cursor M.* 13588 Þaa phariseus [*v.rr.* -eseus, -aseus] þat war ful fell. **1303** R. BRUNNE *Handl. Synne* 11647 Do nat as þe pharysu Preyde Gode aȝens hys pru. **1340** *Ayenb.* 175 Zuyche weren þe farizeus of þe godspelle. *c* **1450** *Cov. Myst.* xxiii. 215 Herke, sere pharysew, and sere scrybe.

β. [*c* **1290** *S. Eng. Leg.* I. 365/27 A-mong men of pharise þat luþere weren, he cam.] *c* **1380** WYCLIF *Serm.* Sel. Wks. I. 223 Cunne we wel Goddis lawe, and loke wher Fariseis grounden hem in it. *Ibid.* II. 36 Essey, Saducey and Pharisey. **1382** —— *Luke* xviii. 10 Oon a Pharise [**1388** a Farisee] and the tothir a pupplican. **1390** GOWER *Conf.* I. 14 The Scribe and ek the Pharisee. ? *a* **1500** *Chester Pl.* xiii. 117 (MS. 1607) To the pharisies these wordes say [*v.rr.* pharaseres, pharasittes]. **1526** TINDALE *Luke* vii. 36 He cam in to the pharises housse. **1590** GREENWOOD *Collect. Sclaund. Art.* E iv b, He was a Pharisey. *Ibid.* F iij b, Blynde Pharesies. **1673** MILTON *True Relig.* 6 The Pharisees and Saduces were two Sects. **1841** TRENCH *Parables, Two Debtors*, The true spirit of a Pharisee betrays itself.

γ. *c* **1400** *Rom. Rose* 6893 Upon the chaire of Moyses.. Sitte Scribes and Pharisen.

2. A person of Pharisaic spirit or disposition; a self-righteous person; a formalist; a hypocrite.

1589 G. HARVEY *Advt. Pappe Hatchet* Wks. (Grosart) II. 168 Reprobates,..tyrants, pharises, hypocrites, false prophets. **1593** NASHE *Four Lett. Confut.* Wks. (Grosart) II. 193 Though he play the Pharisie neuer so in iustifying his owne innocence, theres none will beleeue him. **1599** *Broughton's Let.* ii. 8 Not the nation, but the affection makes a Pharisee. **1682** TATE *Abs. & Achit.* II. 788 Whom laws convict, and only they, shall bleed, Nor Pharisees by Pharisees be freed. **1781** COWPER *Truth* 59 The peacock, see —Mark what a sumptuous Pharisee is he! **1901** 'LUCAS MALET' *Sir R. Calmady* II. iii, I was a self-righteous little Pharisee—forgive me.

3. Usu. in *pl.*: app. a dialectal alteration of *fairies*, pl. of FAIRY *sb.*

[**1807** SOUTHEY *Lett. from Eng.* III. liv. 37 The man observed..that the fairies were never seen now, as they used to be in old times... The man persisted [to the priest], —'It is no longer ago than last Sunday you read about the Scribes and *Pharisees*.'] **1850** H. ELLIS *Brand's Observations on Pop. Antiquities* (ed. 4) II. 504 The calf is rid every night by the *farisees.* **1852** J. ALLIES *Antiquities & Folk-Lore Worcestershire* (ed. 2) xii. 418 According to tradition,.. Oseberrow..Rock..was a favourite haunt of the fairies (*vulgo* pharises). **1854** M. A. LOWER *Contributions to Lit.* 157 It's very hard to say how them rings do come, if it isn't the Pharisees that makes 'em. **1884** *Contemp. Rev.* Aug. 329 Among the peasants of the South Downs a belief in the existence of fairies, or as they call them, 'Pharisees', has not died out. **1906** KIPLING *Puck of Pook's Hill* 264 'Pharisees,' cried Una. 'Fairies? Oh, I see!' **1930** M. ALLINGHAM *Mystery Mile* iv. 49 Seven Whistlers... No one knows if they be ghosts or Pharisees—that be fairies. **1947** E. MEYNELL *Sussex* ix. 243 The belief in fairies—though few of the old Sussex people would dream of using such an 'outland' word, it is as pharisees they are known—also continued late in the county. **1948** L. SPENCE *Fairy Tradition in Brit.* iv. 82 'Pharisees', a term used to denote the fairies in Suffolk.

4. *attrib.* and *Comb.*

1611 COTGR., *Pharisien*, hypocriticall, Pharisie-like. **1822** J. MACDONALD *Mem. J. Benson* 153 Did he Pharisee-like bless God that he was not as other men? **1874** PUSEY *Lent. Serm.* 24 His may have been a respectable, decorous, Pharisee religion. **1900** G. SWIFT *Somerley* 25 Perhaps..I did not mix the ingredients in their proper quantities: a little too much Pharisee-tincture, I expect.

†**'Pharisee**, *v. Obs. rare.* [f. prec. sb.] *intr.* To play the Pharisee; *refl.* to take credit to oneself for piety.

1598 TOFTE *Alba* (1880) 51. I loue not I to pharisie, nor praise My selfe, for to her owne selfe I appeale. **1648** C. WALKER *Hist. Independ.* I. 30 Some of them..acknowledge the Scripture, but..only..to Pharisee themselves, and Publican all the world besides.

Phariseeism ('færɪsiːɪz(ə)m). [f. PHARISEE + -ISM.] = PHARISAISM.

1585 FETHERSTONE tr. *Calvin on Acts* xv. 7. 355 There remained no phariseisme in Paul. **1865** L. OLIPHANT *Piccadilly* VI. (1870) 221 The force and despotic power of the Phariseeism of the present day.

†**Pharisian.** *Obs.* Forms: 4 farisen, -ysen, 6 pharisean, -esian(e, -isan, 6–7 -isian(e. [In earlier forms a. F. *pharisien* (13th c. in Hatz.-Darm.); subseq. conformed to L. types *Pharisæān-us*, *-iānus*: see PHARISÆAN.] A Pharisee.

c **1394** *P. Pl. Crede* 486 He..founded hem on Farysens feyned for gode. *Ibid.* 547 Beþ nouȝt þise i-lyke Fully to þe Farisens in fele of þise poyntes? **1533** GAU *Richt Vay* 108 Yᵉ phariseans and pyntid ypocritis quhilk vald mak thair selff richtwis throw thair aune varkis. **1552** ABP. HAMILTON *Catech.* (1884) 63 The pridful Pharisiane. **1567** *Gude & Godlie B.* (S.T.S.) 193 Wo be to ȝow, Pharesianis, That Regnis ȝit lyke hie Capitanis.

†**'pharmacal**, *a. Obs.* [f. L. *pharmac-um*, a. Gr. φάρμακ-ον poison, drug + -AL¹.] Of the nature of, or dealing with, drugs; pharmaceutical.

1638 T. WHITAKER *Blood of Grape* 22 Our pharmacall compositions. **1694** WESTMACOTT *Script. Herb.* 214 Brandy ..too often is used in its stead, by the Pharmacal Artist.

pharmaceutic (fɑːmə'sjuːtɪk, -'kjuːtɪk), *a.* and *sb.* [ad. L. *pharmaceutic-us*, a. Gr. φαρμακευτικ-ός, f. φαρμακευτής = φαρμακεύς poisoner, druggist, f. φάρμακ-ον poison, drug, medicine.]

A. *adj.* Pertaining or relating to pharmacy; pharmaceutical. Now *rare.*

1656 STANLEY *Hist. Philos.* v. (1701) 164 Medecine is of five kinds. Pharmaceutic, cureth diseases by application of Medecine. **1775** SIR E. BARRY *Observ. Wines* 356 The pharmaceutic cure of several diseases. **1830** SCOTT *Demonol.* x. 403 A user of pharmaceutic enchantments.

B. *sb.* (Usually in pl. **pharmaceutics.**) The science of pharmacy; that branch of medical science which relates to the use of medicinal drugs. Also *concr.*, a medicinal drug; = PHARMACEUTICAL *sb.*

1541 R. COPLAND *Galyen's Terap.* 2 A j b, The parties of the art of Medycyne (yᵗ is to wyt dyetityke, pharmaceutyke, and cyrurgery). **1670** H. STUBBE *Plus Ultra* 67 Whosoever shall enquire into the ill consequences of the two Pharmaceutics, will say, that..the Galenical..is always the most safe. **1869** *N. Syd. Soc. Year-bk. Med.* 442 General Pharmaceutics. **1927** *Daily Express* 11 May 11/4 The agreement will later be extended to include artificial silk,.. fertilisers, pharmaceutics, and many other products. **1974** *Nature* 6 Sept. p. xi/1 (Advt.), Applications are invited for the post of Senior Lecturer in the Department of Pharmaceutics commencing January 1, 1975.

pharma'ceutical (see prec.), *a.* (*sb.*) [f. as prec. + -AL¹.] **A.** *adj.* Pertaining to or engaged in pharmacy; relating to the preparation, use, or sale of medicinal drugs.

1648 PETTY *Adv. Hartlib* 16 Some good pharmaceuticall, Botanick and Chymicall Institutions. **1799** *Med. Jrnl.* II. 108 Remarks on the concentration of vinegar, and on some pharmaceutical preparations formed from this acid. **1836–41** BRANDE *Chem.* (ed. 5) 24 The foundations of chemical science are to be found in the medical and pharmaceutical writers of the sixteenth century. **1868** *Act 31 & 32 Vict.* c. 121 It shall be unlawful for any Person to ..use the title 'Chemist and Druggist'..unless such Person shall be a Pharmaceutical Chemist. **1904** *Daily Chron.* 26 Feb. 9/6 The 'Pharmaceutical Journal', which is the official organ of the Pharmaceutical Society of Great Britain.

B. *sb.* A pharmaceutical preparation; a medicinal drug.

1881 B. S. PROCTOR in *Pharmaceut. Jrnl.* 219 The association of trade in pharmaceuticals from extraneous sources with the practice of pharmacy and trade in pharmaceuticals made at home is a matter of convenience both to the pharmacist and the public. **1955** T. STERLING *Evil of Day* iv. 39 The night-table..was prominently littered with pharmaceuticals. **1958** *Times* 5 Dec. 3/3 An international company manufacturing surgical and orthopaedic dressings, pharmaceuticals and proprietary medical products.

Hence **pharma'ceutically** *adv.*, in relation to, or from the point of view of, pharmacy.

1770 *New Dispens.* p. v, Many..articles I have examined pharmaceutically. **1880** GARROD & BAXTER *Mat. Med.* 116 A solid mass is produced, rendering the combination pharmaceutically incompatible. **1882** *Med. Temp. Jrnl.* LI. 109 No alcohol has been administered..either dietetically, pharmaceutically or medicinally.

pharma'ceutist (see above). [irreg. f. Gr. φαρμακευτ-ής (see PHARMACEUTIC) + -IST: ? after *chemic*, *chemist.*] A pharmaceutical practitioner; a pharmacist, druggist.

1836 J. M. GULLY *Magendie's Formul.* (ed. 2) 193 M. Leroux, a pharmaceutist of Vitry-le Français. *c* **1865** WYLDE in *Circ. Sc.* I. 20/2 This..has been taken advantage of by sugar-refiners and pharmaceutists.

†**phar'macian.** *Obs.* [f. late L. *pharmacīa* PHARMACY + -AN, app. after F. *pharmacien* (17th c. in Hatz.-Darm.).] = next.

1720 BLAIR in *Phil. Trans.* XXXI. 31 By the unanimous Consent of all Physicians and Pharmacians.

pharmacist ('fɑːməsɪst). [f. PHARMACY + -IST: cf. *botanist.*] A person skilled or engaged in pharmacy; one who prepares or dispenses medicines; a druggist or pharmaceutical chemist.

1834 LYTTON *Pompeii* I. ii, Unskilful pharmacists! pleasure and study are not elements to be thus mixed together. **1875** H. C. WOOD *Therap.* (1879) 437 He used two samples of the alkaloid prepared by different pharmacists. **1898** *Rev. Brit. Pharm.* 29 The Pharmacopœia, generally a stickler in legality, speaks of 'pharmacists', which, strictly speaking, chemists and druggists are not.

†**'pharmacize**, *v. Obs. rare*⁻¹. [f. as prec. + -IZE.] *trans.* To treat with drugs, to 'physic'.

1609 BP. W. BARLOW *Answ. Nameless Cath.* 108 That Religion should bee Pharmacized with such Drugs.

†**'pharmack.** *Obs. rare*⁻¹. [a. obs. F. *pharmaque* (Cotgr.), ad. med.L. *pharmacum*, a. Gr. φάρμακ-ον drug, medical or poisonous.] A drug, a medicine.

1643 *Decl. Lords & Com., Reb. Irel.* 39 It is one sicknesse, and one Pharmack will suffice.

pharmaco-, repr. Gr. φαρμακο-, comb. form of φάρμακον drug, medicine, poison, a formative of technical words, as in the following:

ˌ**pharmacody'namic** *a.*, relating to the powers or effects of drugs (*Cent. Dict.* 1890); hence ˌ**pharmacody'namically** *adv.*; ˌ**pharmacody'namics** *sb. pl.*, the science or subject of the powers or effects of drugs; **pharma'cognosist**, an expert in pharmacognosy; ˌ**pharmaco'gnostic** *a.*, of or pertaining to pharmacognosy; **pharmacognosy** (fɑːm 'kɒgnəsɪ) (also in L. form **-'gnosia**, and less correctly **-'gnosis**), the knowledge of drugs, pharmacology; esp. as a branch of natural history relating to medicinal substances in their natural or unprepared state; so **pharmaco'gnostical** *a.*, pertaining to pharmacognosy (whence **pharmaco'gnostically** *adv.*); **pharmaco'gnostics** = *pharmacognosy*; **pharma'cography**, a description of drugs (Ogilvie 1882); ˌ**pharmacoki'netics** *sb. pl.* (const. as *sing.*), the branch of pharmacology concerned with the movement of drugs within the body; so ˌ**pharmacoki'netic** *a.*, **-ki'netically** *adv.*; ˌ**pharmaco'mania**, a mania or craze for using or trying drugs (Dunglison *Med. Lex.* 1853); so ˌ**pharmacoma'niacal** *a.*, madly or irrationally addicted to drugs (Mayne *Expos. Lex.* 1858); **pharma'comathy** = *pharmacognosy* (Ogilvie 1882); **pharma'cometer**, a vessel or contrivance for measuring medicines; **pharmaco'morphic** *a.*, see quot.

1906 *Jrnl. Infectious Dis.* III. 572 (*heading*) *Pharmacodynamic action due to ions. **1951** A. BURGER *Medicinal Chem.* I. xxi. 386 Certain cholinergic agents (Doryl) can add to the analgetic effect produced by injected epinephrine. The pharmacodynamic mechanism..is as yet uncertain; it may be that the para-sympathomimetic drug stimulates the output of epinephrine by the adrenal gland which can then enhance the peripheral adrenergic vasoconstrictor effect. **1929** MITCHELL & HAMILTON *Biochem. Amino Acids* vii. 363 It is a fact of great significance that histidine, a substance entirely indifferent *pharmacodynamically, should be transformable by simple decarboxylation into such an active substance as histamine. **1959** K. H. BEYER in Waife & Shapiro *Clin. Eval. New Drugs* ii. 19 Some compounds are so active that no chemical or isotopic method may be suitable to follow them at pharmacodynamically effective dosages. **1842** DUNGLISON *Med. Lex.*, **Pharmacodynamics*, a division of pharmacology, which considers the effects and uses of medicines. **1867** R. HUGHES (*title*) Manual of Pharmaco-dynamics. **1867** R. E. SCORESBY-JACKSON *Note-Bk. Materia Med.* I. 3 Pharmacology..is divided into General Pharmacology and Special Pharmacology, and is subdivided into Pharmacognosy, Pharmacy, and Pharmacodynamics. **1925** E. NOVAK in *Gynecol. & Obstetr. Monogr.: Appendix* 22 The study of the pharmacodynamics of the various forms of ovarian extract has until recent years yielded unimpressive results as regards the generative system. **1974** M. C. GERALD *Pharmacol.* i. 9 Pharmacodynamics, a basic experimental science, is a study of where a drug acts in the body..and how it acts (what is its mechanism of action in physiological and/or biological terms). **1842** DUNGLISON *Med. Lex.*, **Pharmacognosia*, a division of pharmacology, which treats of simples or unprepared medicines. **1868** M. PATTISON *Academ. Org.* v. 190 Special Botany, *pharmacognosis, inorganic botany. **1901** tr. Dieterich (*title*), Analysis of Resins, Balsams and Gum-resins: their Chemistry and Pharmacognosis. **1934** WEBSTER, *Pharmacognosist. **1939** *Nature* 1 Apr. 540/2 The complete pharmacognosist is a man of many parts. His preliminary training in botany, zoology, chemistry and physics furnishes him with a foundation on which to build experience in the technique of microscopy, histology, morphology, [etc.]. **1972** *Ibid.* 21 Jan. 134/1 Some people may have thought of pharmacognosists as witch doctors in that their methods of selection of plants for study have relied to some extent on folklore and ancient custom. **1961** WEBSTER, *Pharmacognostic. **1974** *Nature* 13 Sept. 169/1 While familiarising himself with the natural history of the islands, Linnaeus was instructed particularly to look for plants.. with pharmacognostic value. **1890** *Cent. Dict.*, **Pharmacognostical.* **1884** F. B. POWER (*title*) The Cinchona Barks *pharmacognostically considered. **1858** MAYNE *Expos. Lex.*, *Pharmacognostica*..*pharmacognostics. **1890** *Cent. Dict.*, **Pharmacognosy.* **1901** *Chemist & Druggist* 7 Sept., Pharmacopedia is..a commentary on the botany, chemistry, pharmacognosy, and pharmacy of the medicines recognised by the British Pharmacopœia. [**1874** FLÜCKIGER & HANBURY (*title*) *Pharmacographia: a History of the Principal Drugs of Vegetable Origin met with in Great Britain and British India.] **1964** *Antibiotica et Chemotherapia* XII. p. viii/1 A list of symbols for the use in *pharmacokinetic models. **1976** *Lancet* 9 Oct. 808/1 Pharmacokinetic analysis indicates that binding is unlikely to be a major problem in vivo when less than 75–85% of the drug is bound. **1972** *Nature* 28 Apr. 434/2 The leaching of DDT from fatty tissue after exposure to abnormally large controlled doses of DDT appears to be *pharmacokinetically similar to the uptake process. **1960** *Jrnl. Amer. Pharmaceutical Assoc.* XLIX. 311 (*heading*) Dosage schedule and *pharmacokinetics in chemotherapy. **1971** R. E. NOTARI *Biopharmaceutics & Pharmacokinetics* i. 4 Since the movement of drug from the site of administration to the site of action requires time, the overall process may best be analyzed by what is called pharmacokinetics. **1973** *Nature* 22 June p. xvi (Advt.), A graduate with experience in pharmacokinetics and drug metabolism. **1830** *Edin. Rev.* L. 516 Impossible to light upon proper *pharmacometers. **1890** BILLINGS *Nat. Med. Dict.* II. 326 **Pharmacomorphic*, pertaining to the form or appearance of drugs.

ˌ**pharmacoge'netics**, *sb. pl.* (const. as *sing.*). *Pharm.* [ad. G. *pharmakogenetik* sb. (F. Vogel 1959, in *Ergebnisse d. inneren Med. und Kinderheilkunde* XII. 117): see PHARMACO-, GENETIC *a.*, and -IC 2.] The study of the effect of genetic factors on reactions to drugs.

1960 *Times* 11 Nov. 17/2 This development of pharmacogenetics may affect quite considerably our methods of treating patients. **1962** W. KALOW (*title*) Pharmacogenetics: heredity and the response to drugs. **1965** FINGL & WOODBURY in Goodman & Gilman *Pharmacol. Basis Therapeutics* (ed. 3) i. 25/2 The objectives of pharmacogenetics include not only identification of differences in drug effects that have a genetic basis but also development of simple methods by which susceptible individuals can be recognized before the drug is administered. **1974** M. C. GERALD *Pharmacol.* iii. 58 Among the newest subdivisions of pharmacology is that of pharmacogenetics which is the study of the influence of genetic factors on the drug response.

Hence ˌ**pharmacoge'netic** *a.*, **-ge'neticist.**

1962 *Pharmaceutical Jrnl.* CLXXXIX. 282/3 Pharmacogenetic studies. **1970** PASSMORE & ROBSON *Compan. Med. Stud.* II. xxxi. 11/1 Not all pharmacogenetic studies are prompted by the occurrence of adverse effects. **1971** *Sci. News* 26 June 439 Some pharmacogeneticists advocate screening individuals who are to receive succinylcholine before surgery for their pseudocholinesterase activity. **1974** M. C. GERALD *Pharmacol.* iii. 59 Pharmacogenetic differences, in part, account for the development of resistant strains of bacteria and insects.

pharmacolite ('fɑːməkəʊˌlaɪt). *Min.* [Named by Karsten 1800, f. Gr. φάρμακο-ν poison + -LITE.] Hydrous arsenate of calcium, occurring usually in silky fibres. ***magnesian pharmacolite***, a synonym of BERZELIITE (Dana *Min.* (1844) 239).

1805 R. JAMESON *Syst. Min.* II. 483 Pharmacolite.. occurs as a coating. **1815** W. PHILLIPS *Outl. Min. & Geol.* (1818) 27 Lime combined with the arsenic acid, forms a mineral called Pharmacolite. **1850** DANA *Min.* (ed. 4) 220

Picropharmacolite of Stromeyer..is probably impure pharmacolite.

pharmacology (fɑːməˈkɒlədʒɪ). [ad. mod.L. *pharmacologia* (W. Harris 1683): see PHARMACO- and -LOGY.] That branch of medical science which relates to drugs, their preparation, uses, and effects; the science or theory of pharmacy.

1721 BAILEY, *Pharmacology*, a Treatise concerning the Art of preparing Medicines. **1800** *Med. Jrnl.* III. 576 This work ..answers the requisites of a good practical Pharmacology. **1875** H. C. WOOD *Therap.* (1879) 17 *Pharmacology* is the general term employed to embrace these three divisions [Pharmacy, Therapeutics, Materia Medica]. **1883** *Nature* XXVII. 542/2 The knowledge of the action of remedies, or Pharmacology.

Hence **ˌpharmacoˈlogical** *a.*, pertaining or relating to pharmacology (whence **ˌpharmacoˈlogically** *adv.*); **ˌpharmacoˈlogic** *a.* (chiefly *U.S.*) = PHARMACOLOGICAL *a.*; **pharmaˈcologist**, a person versed in pharmacology.

1901 T. SOLLMANN *Text-bk. Pharmacol.* 8 The organic poisons..often require *pharmacologic experience for their recognition. **1973** *Sci. Amer.* Sept. 123/3 Psychiatry..has two faces, one represented by treatment at the psychosocial level and the other by treatment at the pharmacologic level. **1851–9** HOOKER in *Man. Sci. Enq.* 421 Upon *pharmacological subjects Lindley's *Flora Medica*..will be found valuable. **1873** J. W. LEGG in *St. Barth. Hosp. Rep.* IX. 163 Operations..done in the pharmacological laboratory. **1900** *Lancet* 8 Dec. 1644/2 The aldehydes are *pharmacologically active. *a* **1728** WOODWARD *Fossils* (J.), The osteocolla is recommended by the *pharmacologists as an absorbent and conglutinator of broken bones. **1881** HUXLEY in *Nature* XXIV. 346/2 Sooner or later, the pharmacologist will supply the physician with the means of affecting, in any desired sense, the functions of any physiological element of the body.

pharmacopedia (ˌfɑːməkəʊˈpiːdɪə). Also in anglicized form **pharmacopedy** (-ˈkɒpɪdɪ). [mod. f. PHARMACO- + Gr. παιδεία instruction: cf. *cyclopædia*. (Introduced in 1901–2 as a substitute for MATERIA MEDICA in sense 2: see *Pharmaceut. Jrnl.* 29 Mar. 1902, p. 254.)] The art of imparting instruction or information about drugs, or a work containing such information; the sum of scientific knowledge concerning drugs and medicinal preparations. So **ˌpharmacoˈpedic** (-ˈpiːdɪk) *a.*, relating to the study of drugs; **ˌpharmacoˈpedics** *sb. pl.*, the scientific study of drugs and medicinal preparations.

1901 E. WHITE & J. HUMPHREY (*title*) Pharmacopedia. **1901** *Pharmaceut. Jrnl.* 28 Dec. 730/1 Pharmacopedics, as the scientific study of drugs and medicinal preparations may fitly be termed. *Ibid.*, A valuable addition to pharmacopedic literature. **1902** *Ibid.* 1 Mar. 177/2 Pharmacopedy (*materia medica*), galenic pharmacy, prescription reading, and dispensing. *Ibid.* 26 Apr. 346/2 Works on chemistry or pharmacopedy.

pharmacopœia (ˌfɑːməkəʊˈpiːə). Also 7 **-pea**, (erron. **-pæa**, **-pæia**), 7–8 **-pœa**, 8–9 **-peia**. [mod.L., a. Gr. φαρμακοποιία, the art of a φαρμακοποι-ός or preparer of drugs, f. φαρμακο- PHARMACO- + -ποιος making, maker.]

1. A book containing a list of drugs, with directions for their preparation and identification; *spec.* such a book officially published by authority and revised at stated times.

1621 BURTON *Anat. Mel.* II. iv. I. i, That infinite variety of medicines which I find in every Pharmacopea. *Ibid.* II. v. I. iii. 466 Our new London Pharmacopæa. *a* **1648** LD. HERBERT *Life* (1886) 55 Pharmacopaeias or antidotaries of several countries. **1800** *Med. Jrnl.* IV. 98 The medicine obtained a place in the Pharmacopeia of the Swedes. **1866** BRANDE & COX *Dict. Sci.* II. 881/1 Previous to the year 1863, three Pharmacopœias were extant in Great Britain, viz. those of the Colleges of Physicians of London, Edinburgh, and Dublin. In 1863 a British Pharmacopœia was compiled by the Medical Council of the kingdom, and sanctioned as a substitute for its predecessor. **1868** A. K. H. BOYD *Less. Mid. Age* 37 All the doctors in Britain and all the medicines in the pharmacopœia could make nothing of such a case.

2. A collection or stock of drugs. Also *fig.*

1721 BAILEY, *Pharmacopœa*, a Dispensary or Collection of Medicines. **1807** J. BERESFORD *Miseries Hum. Life* xx. (ed. 5) II. 246 Then moistens her dewlaps With..each panacea From the Pharmacopeia. **1814** SCOTT *Wav.* xxiv, An opiate draught administered by the old Highlander from some decoction of herbs in his pharmacopeia. **1877** F. HEATH *Fern W.* 42 Ferns have..a greater repute as items in the pharmacopoeia of the herbalist.

†**3.** A chemical laboratory. *Obs. rare*⁻⁰.

1864 in WEBSTER. Hence in later Dicts.

Hence **pharmacoˈpœist**, the compiler of a pharmacopœia.

1900 H. G. GRAHAM *Soc. Life Scot. 18th C.* (1901) II. 480 The Pharmacopaeist of 1737 protests against the worthless farragoes made and sold in the shops.

pharmacoˈpœial, *a.* [f. prec. + -AL¹.] Pertaining to a pharmacopœia; *spec.* recognized in, or prepared, administered, etc. according to the directions of, the official Pharmacopœia.

1858 in MAYNE *Expos. Lex.* **1864** *N. Syd. Soc. Year-bk. Med.* 435 Two only..reached the standard of pharmacopœial strength. **1881** *Times* 14 Apr. 6/3 He was in the habit of treating his patients..with pharmacopœial remedies in ordinary pharmacopœial doses.

pharmacopœian (-ˈpiːən), *a.* and *sb. rare.* [f. as prec. + -AN.]

A. *adj.* †**a.** Versed in the pharmacopœia; acquainted with the use of drugs. *Obs.* **b.** = prec.

1670 MAYNWARING *Physician's Repos.* 77 The Pharmacopœian Physicians are but very few. **1890** *Daily News* 8 May 5/5 The spirit used in many of the pharmacopœian tinctures is rectified.

†**B.** *sb.* A person versed in the pharmacopœia.

1668 MAYNWARING *Compl. Physician* 83 The most renowned Physitians..were Pharmacopœians..diligent and careful in the preparing of their own Medicines. **1671** —— *Anc. & Mod. Pract. Physick* 25 He that is not a Pharmacopœian, is but half a Physician, and the worst half.

†**ˌpharmacopoiˈetic**, *a. Obs. rare*⁻¹. [f. PHARMACO- + Gr. ποιητικός making, productive.] Pertaining to the making or compounding of drugs. Also †**ˌpharmacopoiˈetical** *a. Obs.*

1670 MAYNWARING *Physician's Repos.* 86 Pharmacopoietick operations and tryals of Medicines. *Ibid.* 88 For want of knowledge in the Pharmacopoietical part.

†**ˈpharmacoˌpole.** *Obs.* Also 8 **-pol**, and 6 in L. form **-pola**. [ad. L. *pharmacopōla*, a. Gr. φαρμακοπώλης dealer in drugs: see -POLE. So in Fr. (Furetière 1690).] = PHARMACOPOLIST.

1541 R. COPLAND *Galyen's Terap.* 2 A j b, With the apotycaries, wherof they haue yᵉ name of pharmacopoles. **1597** *1st Pt. Return fr. Parnass.* I. i. 241 The carle lyeth here, att the house of this Pharmacopola. **1790** E. DARWIN *Lett.* (1879) 39 Thus have I emptied my quiver of the arts of the Pharmacopol.

So †**ˌpharmacoˈpolic** (-ˈpɒlɪk) *a.*, drug-selling; †**ˌpharmacoˈpolitan** [irreg. after *metropolitan*, etc.] = next.

1775 S. J. PRATT *Liberal Opin.* cxxxiii. (1783) IV. 207 With the assistance of our pharmacopolic friends. **1657** TOMLINSON *Renou's Disp.* 153 Something that neither the Pharmacopolitan's shops nor gardens afford.

pharmacopolist (fɑːməˈkɒpəlɪst). Now *rare*. [f. as prec. + -IST.] A seller of drugs; an apothecary, a druggist.

1651 BIGGS *New Disp* §64 The family of Pharmacopolists. **1764** FOOTE *Mayor of G.* I. i, Not only a pharmacopolist, or vender of drugs, but likewise a chirurgeon. **1822** SCOTT *Nigel* ii. **1852** TH. ROSS *Humboldt's Trav.* II. xxiv. 440 That self-sufficient air and tone of pedantry of which the pharmacopolists of Europe were formerly accused.

†**pharmacopoly.** *Obs. rare*⁻¹. [f. PHARMACOPOLE + -Y, as if from a F. **pharmacopolie*.] A place where drugs are sold; an apothecary's shop.

1657 TOMLINSON *Renou's Disp.* 498 Simple Syrup is made in every Pharmacopoly.

pharmacosiderite (ˌfɑːməkəʊˈsaɪdəraɪt). *Min.* [Named by Hausmann, 1813, f. Gr. φάρμακον in sense 'poison' + σίδηρ-ος iron + -ITE.] Hydrous arsenate of iron, occurring in minute greenish or brownish crystals of cubic or tetrahedral form; also called *cube-ore*.

1835 C. U. SHEPARD *Min.* II. 102 Pharmacosiderite. (See Cube-Ore.) **1877** *Min. Mag.* I. 17 The pharmacosiderite occurs in the usual cubical forms.

‖**ˌpharmacoˈtheon.** *Obs.* [ad. Gr. type *φαρμακοθεῖον (f. φάρμακον medicine + θεῖον divine), in med. or mod.L. *pharmacothēum*, 'medicamentum divinum' (Jos. Laurentius *Amalthea Onomastica* 1640).] A divine medicine.

a **1633** AUSTIN *Medit.* (1635) 113 By a generall Pharmacotheon, when he gave his Body full of all these vertues in the Sacrament, to make his Sufferings ours.

pharmacy (ˈfɑːməsɪ). Forms: 4–5 **fermacie**, **-cye**, 5 **farmasye**, **(formacie)**, 7 **pharmacie**, 8– **pharmacy**. [a. OF. *farmacie* (13–14th c. in Hatz.-Darm.), *pharmacie* (16th c.), a. late L. *pharmacīa* (Cælius Aur., Isidore), a. Gr. φαρμακεία the practice of the φαρμακεύς or druggist.]

†**1.** A medicine or medicinal potion. *Obs. rare*⁻¹.

c **1386** CHAUCER *Knt.'s T.* 1855 Somme hadden salues and somme hadden charmes, Fermacies of herbes.

2. The use or administration of drugs or medicines. (Now chiefly *poet.* or *rhet.*, or as a vague extension of next sense.)

c **1400** *Lanfranc's Cirurg.* 83 A walkynge vlcus is heelid wiþ fleobotomie & formacie [*v.r.* ffarmasye]. **1704** F. FULLER *Med. Gymn.* Pref., We ought not to be so eager after Courses of Pharmacy in all Cases. **1718** POPE *Iliad* XVI. 38 Their pain soft arts of pharmacy can ease. **1850** BLACKIE *Æschylus* II. 40 They..did slowly..waste away for lack of pharmacy. **1895** ELWORTHY *Evil Eye* 445 Pharmacy consisted in divination by means of medicated drugs.

3. The art or practice of collecting, preparing, and dispensing drugs, esp. for medicinal purposes; the making or compounding of medicines; the occupation of a druggist or pharmaceutical chemist.

[**1597** A. M. tr. *Guillemeau's Fr. Chirurg.* 1 b/1 *Pharmacia* instructed vs how to compownde our medicaments.] **1651** WITTIE tr. *Primrose's Pop. Err.* I. xi. 40 A physician ought.. to be skilfull in Pharmacie, which consists in choice, preparation, and composition of simple Medicaments. **1717** GARTH *Ovid's Met.* XIV. 275 So nice her Art in impious Pharmacy! **1830** HERSCHEL *Stud. Nat. Phil.* 112 The vaunts of Paracelsus..and his open condemnation of the ancient pharmacy. **1878** HUXLEY *Physiogr.* 76 A substance long known in pharmacy as 'red precipitate'.

attrib. **1882** *Chemist & Druggist* 1 Feb. 51/1 The Poison Schedule of the Pharmacy act.

4. A place where medicines are prepared or dispensed; a drug-store or dispensary.

1833 *Fraser's Mag.* VII. 321 Attached to the church..is a pharmacy, where medicine is dispensed gratis. **1842** *Blackw. Mag.* LII. 494 The 'Pharmacy' is large, airy, and well-filled with ancient blue and white jars. **1875** H. C. WOOD *Therap.* (1879) 554 Bonjean's ergotin is that usually kept in our pharmacies.

‖**pharmakos** (ˈfɑːməkɒs). Pl. **pharmakoi.** [Gr. φαρμακός scapegoat.] In ancient Greece, a scapegoat chosen in atonement for a crime or misfortune. Also *transf.* in allusive use.

1903 J. E. HARRISON *Proleg. Study Greek Relig.* iii. 104 The pharmakos is killed then, not because his death is a vicarious sacrifice, but because he is so infected and tabooed that his life is a practical impossibility. **1923** A. LE MARCHANT *Greek Relig. to Time of Hesiod* iv. 25 A ceremony in which two men called Pharmakoi, decked with branches, were led out of the city. **1926** J. BUCHAN *Dancing Floor* ii. 42 You have your purgation herbs like buckthorn and agnus castus, and you have your *pharmakos*, your scapegoat, who carries away all impurities. **1957** N. FRYE *Anat. Crit.* 41 The figure of a typical or random victim begins to crystallize in domestic tragedy as it deepens in ironic tone. We may call this typical victim the *pharmakos* or scapegoat.

†**pharman, -maund, -mond,** early forms of FIRMAN.

1698 FRYER *Acc. E. India & P.* 115 The Pharmaund (or Charter) granted..from their Emperors. *Ibid.* 354 If the Petition be granted, he wears the Pharmond open in his Turbat.

Pharo, Pharoan: see PHARAOH 2.

†**pharol.** *Obs. rare.* [ad. It. *farolo*, 'the lanterne of a galley or ship; also a beacon' (Florio), dim. of *faro, pharo*, PHAROS¹.] A ship's light (lantern or lamp).

1660 HOWELL *Parly of Beasts* 10 His ears are the two chief scuttles, his eyes are the pharols, the stowage is his mouth.

pharology (fɛəˈrɒlədʒɪ). *erron.* **pharonology.** [f. PHAROS¹ + -LOGY.] The art or science which treats of lighthouses and signal lights.

1847 A. G. FINDLAY in *Trans. Soc. Arts* LV. 262 The term Pharology was first introduced by the late Mr. Purdy. **1867** SMYTH *Sailor's Word-bk.*, *Pharonology* denotes the study of, and acquaintance with light-houses. **1879** WEBSTER *Suppl.*, *Pharology.*

Pharos¹ (ˈfɛərɒs). Also 6–7 (9) **pharus**, 7 **pharo**, **-oe**, **(faro)**; *pl.* 7 **phari**, 9 **-oses.** [a. L. *Pharos, -us*, a. Gr. Φάρος; It. *faro* (occas. in Eng.).]

1. The name of an island off Alexandria, on which stood a famous tower lighthouse, built by Ptolemy Philadelphus: hence the lighthouse itself.

1575 LANEHAM *Let.* (1871) 48 Az it wear the Egiptian Pharos relucent vntoo all the Alexandrian coast. **1601** HOLLAND *Pliny* v. xxxi. I. 110 The second [island] is Pharus, which is joined to Alexandria by a bridge:..now by fires from a watch-tower saylers are directed in the night, along the coast of Ægypt. *Ibid.* XXXVI. xii. II. 578 A great name there is of a tower built by one of the kings of Ægypt within the Island Pharos, and it keepeth and commaundeth the haven of Alexandria. **1617** MORYSON *Itin.* I. 141 A most high Tower, like to the Pharo of Alexandria, out of which light was hung out by night, to direct the ships. **1799** *Naval Chron.* I. 52 We saw the Pharos of Alexandria.

2. Any lighthouse or beacon to direct mariners.

a **1552** LELAND *Itin.* IV. 81 This Towre is a Pharos to all Partes about from the Hilles. **1610** HOLLAND *Camden's Brit.* I. 70 Lanternes or light-towers standing by haven sides—commonly called Phari. **1638** SIR T. HERBERT *Trav.* (ed. 2) 4 Her high peak Teyda..serves as an excellent Pharoe, exceeding those at Cayro on the other side of Nylus. **1769** *De Foe's Tour Gt. Brit.* (ed. 7) I. 177 Dover Castle is very large, and situated upon a Rock... But the greatest Curiosity is the Pharos, or Roman Watch-tower. **1807** J. BARLOW *Columb.* IX. 13 Each high pharos double flames provides. **1850** LEITCH tr. *C. O. Müller's Anc. Art* §296 (ed. 2) 333 The Harbours of the ancients,..with their moles, pharoses, outer bays and inner basins.

attrib. **1871** FARRAR *Witn. Hist.* iv. 153 Like Pharos-lights which deceived and wrecked the vessels they were meant to save.

b. *fig.*

1596 FITZ-GEFFRAY *Sir F. Drake* B i j b, Fames stately Pharus, map of dignitie. **1606** SYLVESTER *Du Bartas* II. iv. II. *Trophies* 894 Their eyes sweet splendor seems a Pharos bright. **1679** J. GOODMAN *Penit. Pard.* II. i. (1713) 140 Repentance is the Pharos or watch-tower, which gives light by night to those who are bewildered by their own vanity. **1795** MRS. E. PARSONS *Myst. Warn.* I. ix. 137 To be held up as a pharos to warn unthinking youth of the miseries attending a too hasty connexion. **1896** W. K. LEASK *Boswell* i. 14 Henry Dundas,..that Pharos of Scotland, as Lord Cockburn calls him.

3. *transf.* Applied to any conspicuous light; a ship's lantern; a candelabrum; a lamp.
1759 FALCONER *Descr. Ninety-gun Ship* 26 Her stern displays, And holds a Pharos of distinguish'd blaze. **1844** LINGARD *Anglo-Sax. Ch.* (1858) I. vi. 244 *note*, The *pharus* was a contrivance for the suspension of lights in the church. **1862** J. THRUPP *Anglo-Sax. Home* vii. 212 Above [the altars] ..were suspended three rows of nine lamps in a pharus of the largest dimensions. **1870** LOWELL *Study Wind.* (1886) 49, I could see these tiny pharoses..flash out.

‖**pharos**² ('fɛərɒs). [a. Gr. φᾶρος.] A cloak.
1871 BROWNING *Balaust.* 685 Suppose a rider furls a cloak About a horse's head,..he goes his gait To journey's end; then pluck the pharos off!

pharsang, obs. var. FARSANG, PARASANG.

phary, obs. Sc. f. FAIRY; variant of FARY *Obs.*

pharyngal (fə'rɪŋgəl), *a.* (and *sb.*) [f. mod.L. *pharynx* PHARYNX + -AL¹.] = next. Hence as *sb.* = pharyngal vowel or consonant.
1835 KIRBY *Hab. & Inst. Anim.* I. x. 303 The wheel animals in which Ehrenberg detected pharyngal ganglions. **1867** A. J. ELLIS *E.E. Pronunc.* I. iii. 71 The widening of the pharyngal aperture. **1887** BENSON *Univ. Phonogr.* 11 The vowels [may be divided] into Five Pharyngals: Five Orals: Five Diphthongs. *Ibid.* 12 The Pharyngals in Et, At, Aht, Ot, Ut, are heard. *Ibid.* 13 All these Pharyngal vowels are best uttered with the mouth quite open. **1925** W. H. T. GAIRDNER *Phonetics of Arabic* iv. 27 [ħ]..is a pharyngal unvoiced fricative. **1925** W. H. T. GAIRDNER *Phonetics of Arabic* iv. 27 We are faced with two difficulties in regard to the two pharyngals ħ and ʕ. **1931** G. NOËL-ARMFIELD *Gen. Phonetics* (ed. 4) xviii. 107 Two very difficult plosive sounds for English people..are the Arabic (or Hebrew) *qaf* and its voiced correspondent. They are somewhat similar to [k] and [g] respectively... These consonants, though usually termed uvular, would be better regarded as pharyngal. **1950** D. JONES *Phoneme* p. xiii, ħ, breathed pharyngal fricative. **1964** *Language* XL. 501 A series of pharyngal stops, plain and labialized, aspirated and glottalized.

Hence pha'ryngalization = PHARYNGEALIZATION; **pha'ryngalized** *ppl. a.* = PHARYNGEALIZED *ppl. a.*
1931 G. NOËL-ARMFIELD *Gen. Phonetics* (ed. 4) 186 (Index), Pharyngalised consonants. **1949** *Trans. Philol. Soc.* 1948 148 All the *gh* spellings..are realized as long slightly pharyngalized vowels. **1964** R. KINGDON in D. Abercrombie et al. *Daniel Jones* 115 Secondary articulations such as..pharyngalization.

pharyngalgia: see PHARYNGO-.

pharyngeal (fə'rɪndʒɪəl), *a.* (and *sb.*) [f. mod.L. *pharynge-us* (f. *pharynx, pharyng-em*) + -AL¹.]

A. *adj.* Of, pertaining to, or connected with the pharynx; *spec.* of speech-sounds: applied to those vowel sounds produced by resonance in the pharynx; also applied to consonantal sounds articulated with obstruction of the air-stream at the pharynx.
1828 STARK *Elem. Nat. Hist.* I. 445 Maxillary front teeth conical, the pharyngeal blunt. **1835–6** TODD *Cycl. Anat.* I. 70/2 The..pharyngeal muscles. **1884** F. J. NOTT in *Harper's Mag.* Aug. 443/2 Nasal, pharyngeal, laryngeal, and bronchial catarrh. **1968** CHOMSKY & HALLE *Sound Pattern Eng.* 305 Ubykh, a Caucasian language, distinguishes pharyngeal, uvular, velar, and perhaps also palatal obstruents. **1978** *Studies in Eng. Lit.: Eng. Number* (Tokyo) 159 Part III consists of two chapters, the first of which is concerned with the phonological characterisation of pharyngeal consonants.

B. *sb.* **1.** Short for *pharyngeal artery, bone*, etc.: esp. applied to the pharyngeal bones in fishes.
1834 MᶜMURTRIE *Cuvier's Anim. Kingd.* 210 The inferior pharyngeals strongly dentated. **1880** GÜNTHER *Fishes* 23 Fishes with the lower pharyngeals coalesced into one bone.

2. *spec.* designating speech-sounds: (see sense A above); also, a pharyngeal consonant.
1968 CHOMSKY & HALLE *Sound Pattern Eng.* 305 The consonants where the primary constriction is formed with the body of the tongue..: the palatals, velars, uvulars, and pharyngeals. **1976** *Archivum Linguisticum* VII. 91 Nor is it [*sc.* preaspiration] necessarily a pharyngeal..but may be realized as a spirant formed at some other point of articulation.

Hence **pha'ryngealization**, obstruction of the air-stream at the pharynx; modification into a pharyngeal sound; **pha'ryngealized** *ppl. a.*, produced by pharyngealization.
1947 K. L. PIKE *Phonemics* xvi. 219 Pharyngealized consonants which are phonemically distinct from nonpharyngealized consonants would..need a special symbol. **1968** CHOMSKY & HALLE *Sound Pattern Eng.* 309 We know of no languages that exhibit parallel variations in degree of narrowing concomitant with palatalization or pharyngealization. **1968** P. M. POSTAL *Aspects Phonol. Theory* iv. 82 Consonants are normally non-Pharyngealized. Hence there are no languages with only Pharyngealized consonants. **1977** J. C. CATFORD *Fund. Probl. Phonetics* ix. 182 Pharyngealized vowels involve a compression of the pharynx simultaneously with a primary vowel articulation. .. Such vowels occur in several Caucasian languages of Dagestan.

pharyngectomy (færɪn'dʒɛktəmɪ). [f. Gr. φάρυγξ, φαρυγγ- PHARYNX + ἐκτομή cutting out.] Excision of the pharynx.
1890 in *Cent. Dict.* **1893** in *Syd. Soc. Lex.*

pharyngic (fə'rɪndʒɪk), *a. rare*⁻¹. [f. as prec. + -IC.] Of the pharynx; = PHARYNGEAL.
1822–34 *Good's Study Med.* (ed. 4) II. 110 Pharyngic quinsy.

‖**pharyngitis** (færɪn'dʒaɪtɪs). *Path.* [mod.L., f. as prec. + -ITIS.] Inflammation of the pharynx.
1844 in DUNGLISON *Med. Lex.* **1880** A. FLINT *Princ. Med.* 451 Simple acute pharyngitis..is an affection of frequent occurrence.

Hence **pharyngitic** (-'ɪtɪk) *a.*, pertaining to or affected with pharyngitis.
1858 in MAYNE *Expos. Lex.* **1893** in *Syd. Soc. Lex.*

pharyngo- (fə'rɪŋgəʊ), before a vowel sometimes **pharyng-**, combining form of PHARYNX, in various terms of anatomy, pathology, zoology, etc.

‖**pharyn'galgia**, also **'pharyngalgy** [Gr. -αλγία pain], pain in the pharynx; hence **pharyn'galgic** *a.* (Mayne *Expos. Lex.* 1858). **pha'ryngobranch** (-bræŋk) *a.*, belonging to the *Pharyngobranchii* (or *Leptocardii*), the lowest group of vertebrates, characterized by the pharynx being perforated by the branchial slits; *sb.* an animal of this group, an *Amphioxus* or lancelet; so **pharyngo'branchial** *a.*, (*a*) = prec. adj.; (*b*) see quot. 1846; **pharyngo'branchiate** *a.* = *pharyngobranch* adj. **pha'ryngocele** (-siːl) [Gr. κήλη tumour], an abnormal enlargement at the base of the pharynx or top of the œsophagus, in which food sometimes lodges. **pha,ryngocon'junctival** *a.*, epithet of a syndrome that is characterized by conjunctivitis, pharyngitis, and fever and occurs chiefly in epidemics among children. **pha,ryngo-epi'glottic** *a.*, pertaining to the pharynx and epiglottis: applied to a fold of mucous membrane on each side of the epiglottis, continuous with the wall of the pharynx. **pha,ryngo-'glossal** *a.* [Gr. γλῶσσα tongue], pertaining to the pharynx and the tongue; glossopharyngeal. **pha'ryngognath** [Gr. γνάθος jaw] *a.*, belonging to the order *Pharyngognathi* of fishes, having the inferior pharyngeal bones ankylosed; *sb.* a fish belonging to this order; so **pharyngognathous** (færɪŋ'gɒgnəθəs) *a.* **pharyngography** (færɪŋ'gɒgrəfɪ) [-GRAPHY], a description of the pharynx; hence **pharyngographic** (fə,rɪŋgəʊ'græfɪk) *a.*, pertaining to pharyngography (*Syd. Soc. Lex.*). **pharyngo-laryngeal** (-lə'rɪndʒɪəl) *a.*, pertaining to the pharynx and larynx: applied to the lower cavity of the pharynx, below the soft palate. **pharyngology** (færɪŋ'gɒlədʒɪ) [-LOGY], that part of physiology which treats of the pharynx; hence **pharyngological** (fə,rɪŋgəʊ'lɒdʒɪkəl) *a.*, pertaining to pharyngology (*Syd. Soc. Lex.*). **pha,ryngo-'nasal** (-'neɪzəl) *a.*, pertaining to the pharynx and nose: applied to the upper cavity of the pharynx (*nasopharynx*), above the soft palate; now *rare* or *obs.* (cf. *nasopharyngeal* adj. s.v. NASO-). **pha,ryngo-œso'phageal** *a.*, pertaining to the pharynx and œsophagus (*Syd. Soc. Lex.*). ‖**pha,ryngo-œ'sophagus**, a structure combining or representing pharynx and œsophagus. **pha,ryngo-'oral** *a.* [L. *ōs, ōr-is* mouth], pertaining to the pharynx and the mouth: applied to the middle cavity of the pharynx (*oropharynx*), into which the mouth opens. **pha,ryngo-'palatine** *a.*, pertaining to the pharynx and the palate; palato-pharyngeal. **pharyn'gopathy** [-PATHY], disease of the pharynx. **pha'ryngo,plegy** [Gr. πληγή stroke], paralysis of the muscles of the pharynx; hence **pha,ryngo'plegic** *a.* **pha,ryngo'pleural** *a.* [see PLEURAL], pertaining to the pharynx and the lateral body-wall (of *Amphioxus*). **pha,ryngo'pneustal** *a.* [Gr. -πνευστ-ος, f. πνέ-ειν to blow, breathe], of or pertaining to the *Pharyngopneusta*, a group proposed by Huxley, comprising the ascidians and the *Enteropneusta*. **pha,ryngo-rhi'noscopy** [Gr. ῥίς, ῥίν nose, σκοπεῖν to view], 'visual examination, by means of a small mirror, of the posterior nares and upper part of the pharynx' (*Syd. Soc. Lex.*). **pha'ryngoscope** [-SCOPE], an instrument for inspecting the pharynx; so **pharyngoscopy** (færɪŋ'gəʊskəpɪ), inspection of the pharynx. **pha'ryngo,spasm**, spasm of the pharynx (Mayne *Expos. Lex.* 1858). **pha'ryngotome** [Gr. -τομος cutting], an instrument for making an incision into the pharynx; so **pharyngotomy** (færɪŋ'gɒtəmɪ), incision into the pharynx. **pha,ryngo-'typhoid** *a.*, applied to typhoid fever combined with an affection of the pharynx.
1846 OWEN *Comp. Anat. Vertebr.* 116 To the epibranchial of the second and third arches is commonly attached a shorter and broader bone beset with teeth, the *pharyngobranchial. **1844** DUNGLISON *Med. Lex.*, **Pharyngocele.* **1878** tr. *H. von Ziemssen's Cycl. Med.* VIII. 57 It has been..termed a hernia of the mucous membrane (pharyngocele). **1955** J. A. BELL et al. in *Jrnl. Amer. Med. Assoc.* 26 Mar. 1092/2 Study of the clinical, etiological, and epidemiological attributes of a newly recognized communicable disease entity has appeared to differentiate one disease entity from the poorly defined mass of undifferentiated respiratory illnesses generally known as the common cold, catarrhal fever, nonstreptococcic sore throat, or acute respiratory disease. We suggest that this disease entity be named *pharyngoconjunctival fever. **1974** PASSMORE & ROBSON *Compan. Med. Stud.* III. xii. 18/1 (*heading*) Pharyngo-conjunctival syndrome. **1976** *Lancet* 6 Nov. 990/2 Respiratory illness and pharyngoconjunctival fever are commonly associated with adenovirus infections. **1872** COHEN *Dis. Throat* 51 From which is given off on either side a *pharyngo-epiglottic fold of mucous membrane. **1844** DUNGLISON *Med. Lex.*, **Pharyngo-glossal.* **1865** *Nat. Hist. Rev.* 21 He [Günther]..omits..the soft-finned *Pharyngognaths of Müller. **1844** DUNGLISON *Med. Lex.*, **Pharyngography*, anatomical description of the pharynx. **1890** BILLINGS *Nat. Med. Dict.*, **Pharyngo-laryngeal cavity.* **1897** *Allbutt's Syst. Med.* IV. 802 Tickling sensations..in the pharyngo-laryngeal region. **1844** DUNGLISON *Med. Lex.*, **Pharyngology.* **1861** G. D. GIBB tr. *Czermak's On Laryngoscope* iii. 25 The principle of the laryngoscopic method could be equally applied to the inspection of..the superior parts of the pharynx (*pharyngo-nasal vault). **1893** *Syd. Soc. Lex.*, *Pharyngo-nasal cavity.* **1894** J. W. DOWNIE *Clin. Man. Study Dis. Throat* i. 29 These growths..may attain to such a size as to completely block the pharyngo-nasal cavity, thereby hindering nasal respiration. **1843** R. J. GRAVES *Syst. Clin. Med.* xxvii. 346 The arches of the palate hang very low down, the glosso-palatine higher than the *pharyngo-palatine. **1872** COHEN *Dis. Throat* 133 The pharyngo-palatine muscles. **1858** MAYNE *Expos. Lex.*, *Pharyngopathia*..*pharyngopathy. *Ibid.*, *Pharyngoplegia*..*pharyngoplegy. *Ibid.*, *Pharyngoplegicus* ..*pharyngoplegic. **1888** E. R. LANKESTER in *Encycl. Brit.* XXIV. 184/2 The fluted *pharyngo-pleural membrane. **1877** HUXLEY *Anat. Inv. Anim.* xii. 679 The Tunicata and the Enteropneusta..constitute the *Pharyngopneustal Series. **1870** T. HOLMES *Syst. Surg.* (ed. 2) IV. 516 Moura-Bourouillon describes, in his treatise on Laryngoscopy, an instrument which he names the '*Pharyngoscope'. **1863** *N. Syd. Soc. Year-bk. Med.* 297 Rhinoscopy and *Pharyngoscopy. **1730–6** BAILEY (folio), **Pharyngotomy.* **1844** DUNGLISON *Med. Lex.*, *Pharyngotomy*, some authors have used this word synonymously with œsophagotomy... It means, also, scarification of the tonsils, or an incision, made for opening abscesses there. **1897** *Allbutt's Syst. Med.* IV. 840 Thyrotomy, or subhyoid pharyngotomy..offers the best chance of getting rid of the whole disease. **1896** *Ibid.* I. 833 *Pharyngo-typhoid, laryngo-typhoid..instances of mixed infection.

pharynx ('færɪŋks). *Anat.* Also 8 **pharinx.** [a. mod.L. *pharynx, pharyng-em*, a. Gr. φάρυγξ, φάρυγγ-α throat, pharynx: cf. φάραγξ cleft, chasm. So F. *pharynx* (Paré 1560).] The cavity, with its enclosing muscles and mucous membrane, situated behind and communicating with the nose, mouth, and larynx, and continuous below with the œsophagus; forming a passage from the mouth for the food and drink, and from the nasal passages for the breath.
1693 tr. *Blancard's Phys. Dict.* (ed. 2), *Pharynx*, the upper part of the Gullet, consisting of Three pair of Muscles. **1714** MANDEVILLE *Fab. Bees* (1733) II. 100 This destroying of manhood..has a considerable influence..on the pharinx, the glands and muscles of the throat. **1794–6** E. DARWIN *Zoon.* (1802) I. 49 When the pharinx is irritated by agreeable food, the muscles of deglutition are brought into action by association. **1848** CARPENTER *Anim. Phys.* iv. (1872) 176 The teeth of fishes are often set..upon the surface of the palate and even in the pharynx or swallow. **1879** G. PRESCOTT *Sp. Telephone* 50 The resonance of the air..in the cavity behind the tongue, comprehending the pharynx and larynx.

b. A more or less corresponding cavity in many invertebrates, forming a continuation of the mouth or beginning of the alimentary canal.
1826 KIRBY & SP. *Entomol.* III. xxxiii. 359 *Pharynx*... The opening into the gullet. **1828** *Ibid.* xxxiv. 456 On the upper side of the tongue..is the pharynx, or aperture by which the food passes from the mouth to the œsophagus. **1888** ROLLESTON & JACKSON *Anim. Life* 103 The pharynx [of an Ascidian] has thus a respiratory function. *Ibid.* 633 (Rotifera) The mouth leads into an œsophagus, followed.. usually directly by a muscular pharynx or mastax.

phasalle, obs. form of VASSAL.

‖**Phascogale** (fæ'skɒgəliː), **Phascologale** (fæskəʊ'lɒgəliː). *Zool.* [mod.L., f. Gr. φάσκωλ-ος leathern bag, purse + γαλῆ weasel.] A genus of small insectivorous marsupials of the family *Dasyuridæ*, diffused over Australia and New Guinea, commonly known as pouched or kangaroo mice.
1836 WATERHOUSE in *Trans. Zool. Soc.* (1841) II. 152 The skull of *Myrmecobius*, however, differs in several points from that of *Phascogale.* **1852** J. WEST *Hist. Tasmania* I. 324 The Phascogales are small insectivorous animals, found on the mountains and in the dense forest parts of the island.

phascolome ('fæskəʊləʊm). *Zool.* [ad. mod.L. *Phascōlomys*, f. as prec. + Gr. μῦς mouse.] An animal of the marsupial genus *Phascolomys*, containing the three species of the WOMBAT.

1838 *Encycl. Brit.* (ed. 7) XVII. 705/2 The phascolome, a species of rat from Australia, which possesses an abdominal pouch. **1842** OWEN in *Ann. Nat. Hist.* XI. 7 The largest fossil..indicating rather an extinct gigantic Phascolome.

phase (feɪz), *sb.* [ad. mod.L. *phasis*, a. Gr. φάσις: see PHASIS; = F. *phase* (Furetière *a* 1688), Sp., It. *fase*, Pg. *phase*, Ger. *phase*. In Eng. originally used in L. form *phasis*, pl. *phasēs*. The English use of *phase* appears to have arisen in the 19th c. from taking mod.L. pl. *phasēs* (which was more in use than the sing.) for an Eng. plural, and deducing from this a sing. *phase*; which would be natural to any one who knew that the French forms are *phase, phases*.

It results from this that *phases* is the written pl. both of *phasis* and of *phase*, and that in many instances it is not possible to say to which singular it is meant to belong.]

1. Each of the aspects or appearances presented by the moon or any planetary body, according to the amount of its illumination: = PHASIS 1.

Thus the crescent moon, half moon, gibbous moon, and full moon, are phases; but the term is commonly applied to the points of new moon, first quarter, full moon, and last quarter.

1812 WOODHOUSE *Astron.* xxx. 295 The period of the Moon's phases. *Ibid.* xxxv. 350 To the greatest phase, that is, to the greatest quantity of the eclipsed disk. **1854** MOSELEY *Astron.* lxii. (ed. 4) 187 All those varieties of phase which characterize the changes of the moon. **1868** LOCKYER *Elem. Astron.* iii. §229 Let us now explain what are called the phases of the Moon.

2. a. Any one aspect of a thing of varying aspects; a state or stage of change or development; = PHASIS 2. Esp. in phr. ***phase one*** (or ***two***, etc.): the first (or second, etc.) planned stage of a process, series of events, etc.

1841 CATLIN *N. Amer. Ind.* I. x. 78 These clay-formed hills..are..subjected to continual phases, more or less, until ultimately their decomposition ceases. **1843** LYTTON *Last Bar.* III. ii, He saw her in the most attractive phase of her character. *a* **1862** BUCKLE *Civiliz.* III. iii. 190 Unfolding the successive phases of their mighty career. **1875** JOWETT *Plato* (ed. 2) IV. 226 To enter into each successive phase of the discussion which turns up. **1883** LEIFCHILD in *Contemp. Rev.* XLIII. 54 Shakespeare has painted every phase of antagonism to the world. **1957** *Economist* 5 Oct. 24/2 There was little..to suggest that the government expects Britain to be a very active combatant in 'Phase Two' of another war. Mr. Butler's emphasis was solely on Phase One. **1974** *Times* 1 Apr. 21/1 A contract..for phase one of a new district general hospital. **1977** *Whitaker's Almanack 1978* 580/1 The Chancellor of the Exchequer, other ministers, and the T.U.C. economic committee opened negotiations for a Phase 3 pay policy.

b. *Zool.* A particular period of an animal's life, distinguished by a characteristic form, colour, or type of behaviour. Also *attrib.*

1873 [see *form-genus* (FORM *sb.* 22)]. **1921** B. P. UVAROV in *Bull. Entomol. Res.* XII. 153 We are yet far from knowing whether the transformation of one form [of locust] into the other is due to some immediate external influence or to some yet unknown internal cause; I think therefore, that the term 'phase'..suggested to me by Dr. G. A. K. Marshall is more appropriate [than 'morpha']. *Ibid.* 155 The swarming phases [of locusts] enable the species to extend at one stroke its area of distribution. **1937** *Ann. Reg. 1936* 54 Phase variation was found in grasshoppers. **1947** *New Biol.* III. 10 It is now a recognised fact that all true locusts occur in two phases—the solitary and the swarming, or gregarious as it is usually called. **1956** *Nature* 28 Jan. 167/2 Dr. M. L. Roonwal's work has been concerned..with phase-transformation and population dynamics of the desert locust. **1964** L. S. CRANDALL *Managem. Wild Mammals in Captivity* 368 It [*sc.* the jaguarundi]..occurs in two color phases, dark gray and reddish brown. **1966** B. P. UVAROV *Grasshoppers & Locusts* I. 386 The ideas behind the phase theory are being followed by workers on other insects. **1973** *Nature* 24 Aug. 484/1 Phase transformation in locusts refers to the changes induced when solitary hoppers (juvenile locusts) become gregarious. **1977** *Times* 18 Aug. 14/5 A slate-black falcon..was agreed to have all the field-clues of the dark phase of Eleanora's falcon, one of Europe's rarest predators.

c. A temporarily difficult or unhappy period or stage of development, esp. of adolescents; freq. in ***to go*** (or ***pass***) ***through a phase***.

1913 W. J. LOCKE *Stella Maris* xix. 258 'What's the matter with her, for pity's sake?' asked Herold... 'Perhaps it's a phase. Young girls often pass through it.' **1932** R. LEHMANN *Invitation to Waltz* I. ii. 27 Mrs. Curtis was silent: a pregnant silence. Kate was going through a phase. Best not to take too much notice. **1960** *Times* 28 May 7/4 'It's only a phase', we say uncertainly when our children sulk, fight, or burst into tears for no reason. **1971** [see CROWD *sb.*[3] 2 c]. **1971** H. MCCLOY *Question of Time* I. iii. 36 Whenever Pel or Mél get into trouble, Mrs Heron always says: 'It's just a phase they're going through.'

3. a. *Physics.* A particular stage or point in a recurring sequence of movements or changes, e.g. a vibration or undulation, considered in relation to a particular reference position or time. Also *transf.* ***in phase***, in the same phase; having the same phase at the same time; const. *with*; ***out of phase***, not in phase.

1861 *Phil. Mag.* XXI. 163 Two series of undulations traversing the same space do not combine into one resultant as two attractions do, but produce an effect depending on relations of *phase* as well as intensity. **1863** E. ATKINSON tr. *Ganot's Elem. Treat. Physics* VII. viii. 474 Fig. 362 represents two waves issuing from the same source of light, and meeting at *a*, under a very acute angle in the same phases [*ed.* 2 (1866): in the same phase], while fig. 363 represents the coincidence of two waves in opposite phases of undulation. **1874** SPOTTISWOODE *Polaris. Lt.* iii. 32 The distance whereby one set of waves is in advance of another is called the difference of phase. **1875** *Encycl. Brit.* I. 101/2 Two particles which are in the same stage of vibration..and are moving in the same direction and with equal velocities, are said to be in the same phase. **1879** THOMSON & TAIT *Nat. Phil.* I. I. §54 The Phase of a simple harmonic motion at any instant is the fraction of the whole period which has elapsed since the moving point last passed through its middle position in the positive direction. **1891** J. W. URQUHART *Dynamo Construction* xvi. 239 If switched when not 'in phase', the fresh machine would..be quickly pulled into unison. **1892** *Lightning* Spec. Suppl. 3 Mar. *Gloss. Electr. Terms* s.v., The phase of an alternating current or electro-motive force, is the proportion of the whole period which has elapsed since last alternating into the direction considered positive. **1903** T. SEWELL *Elem. Electr. Engin.* (ed. 2) xvii. 337 The current flowing in the circuit, whether it be in or out of phase with the e.m.f., is indicated by the ammeter. **1931** MOYER & WOSTREL *Radio Handbk.* II. 74 In a circuit containing only non-inductive resistance the current and voltage are in phase. **1936** L. S. PALMER *Wireless Engin.* x. 403 The plate and outer grid may be indirectly connected by any device..which changes the phase of the output with respect to the input by 180°. **1953** *Economist* 14 Nov. 505/2 To keep the supply of raw materials in phase with productive capacity. **1973** *Sci. Amer.* June 47 The light is reflected from a system of mirrors and arrives either in phase or out of phase at the second Kerr cell, depending on the length of the light path between the cells.

b. *Electr. Engin.* Each of the windings of a polyphase machine.

1904 M. B. FIELD in M. Maclean *Mod. Electr. Pract.* II. I. vi. 28 If one of the phases of a Δ-connected system is disconnected, the remaining two can still supply a three-phase current, but with a diminished efficiency. **1931** G. C. BLALOCK *Princ. Electr. Engin.* xviii. 243 The power in any polyphase circuit must of necessity be the sum of the powers in the component phases. It is usually more convenient, however, to determine polyphase power in terms of line voltage and current. **1962** *Newnes Conc. Encycl. Electr. Engin.* 787/2 The phases are interlinked in star connection. **1972** SMITH & HOSIE *Basic Electr. Engin. Sci.* ix. 244 Symmetrical delta-connected systems... The power developed in the generator, when supplying a balanced load, is three times that developed in each phase. *Ibid.* 254 Each phase of a 3-ph star-connected load is a coil of resistance 20 Ω.

4. A physically distinct and homogeneous form of matter that may be present in a system, characterized by its composition and state and when present separated by a bounding surface from other forms.

1875 J. W. GIBBS in *Trans. Connecticut Acad.* III. 152 We may call such bodies as differ in composition or state, different phases of the matter considered, regarding all bodies which differ only in quantity and form as different examples of the same phase. **1916** C. A. EDWARDS *Physico-Chem. Properties of Steel* iv. 47 From the phase rule we know that three phases can coexist in equilibrium, in a binary system, only at one temperature. At the Ar_1 point there are three phases—namely, α-iron, carbide of iron, and the solid solution of the eutectoid composition. **1931** MAASS & STEACIE *Introd. Princ. Physical Chem.* ix. 135 Every liquid has a vapour pressure and will evaporate and enter the gas phase. **1967** J. WILKS *Properties of Liquid & Solid Helium* i. 6 Both solid ^{3}He and ^{4}He exist in three phases with different crystal structures. **1971** I. G. GASS et al. *Understanding Earth* iii. 55/1 These two phases, sand and clay, are very effectively separated from each other by deposition or sedimentation from water.

5. *attrib.* and *Comb.*, as (sense 3) ***phase difference, doctrine, relation(ship), reversal***; ***phase-sensitive*** adj.; (sense 4) ***phase boundary***; **phase advancer** *Electr. Engin.*, a device for improving the power factor of an induction motor by generating a magnetizing current in the rotor circuit which leads the main rotor current in phase; **phase change**, a change in the phase of a wave (PHASE 3) or of a substance (PHASE *sb.* 4); **phase changer** *Electr. Engin.* = *phase converter*; **phase contrast**, the technique in microscopy of introducing a phase difference between parts of the light supplied by the condenser so that interference causes the outlines of the sample, or the boundaries between parts of differing optical density, to appear more prominent; usu. *attrib.*, esp. in ***phase-contrast microscope, microscopy***; **phase converter, convertor** *Electr. Engin.*, a device which converts an alternating current into one having a different number of phases but the same frequency; **phase diagram** *Chem.*, a diagram which represents the limits of stability of the various phases of a chemical system at equilibrium with respect to two or more variables (commonly composition and temperature); an equilibrium diagram; **phase displacement** *Electr.*, a difference in phase; **phase distortion**, distortion of a waveform caused by components of different frequencies being propagated at different speeds, so that their phase relations are altered; **phase inverter, invertor** *Electr.*, a phase splitter which produces two signals 180 degrees out of phase; **phase-lock** *sb. Electronics*, the stabilization of the frequency of an oscillator with respect to that of another, stable, oscillator of lower frequency, by means of a circuit in which any variation in the higher frequency generates a phase difference which produces an automatic correction to that oscillation; freq. *attrib.*; so **phase-lock** *v. trans.*, to stabilize (an oscillation or a device) in this way; **phase-locked** *ppl. a.*, **-locking** *vbl. sb.*; **phase microscope** *Biol.*, a phase-contrast microscope; so **phase microscopy**; **phase modulation** *Telecommunications*, modulation of a wave by variation of its phase; hence **phase-modulated** *ppl. a.*, (as a back-formation) **phase-modulate** *v. trans.*; **phase reaction** *Chem.*, a chemical or physical change which involves the transfer of material between phases, or the appearance or disappearance of a phase; **phase rotation** *Electr. Engin.* = PHASE SEQUENCE 1; **phase rule, Phase Rule** *Physical Chem.* (see quots. 1913, 1966); **phase separation** *Physical Chem.*, the separation of one phase into two, esp. the separation of a mixture by partition between two phases, or the coacervation of a colloidal solution; **phase shift**, a change in the phase of a waveform; **phase-shifter** *Electr.*, a circuit or device which introduces a change in the phase of an oscillation; orig. *spec.* a transformer which alters the power factor in an a.c. circuit by changing the phase relationship of voltage and current; so **phase-shifted, -shifting**, *ppl. adjs.*; **phase space** *Physics*, a multi-dimensional space in which each axis corresponds to one of the co-ordinates (spatial or other) required to specify the state of a physical system, all the co-ordinates being thus represented so that a point in the space corresponds to a state of the system; **phase-splitter** *Electr.*, a circuit or device which splits a single-phase voltage into two or more voltages differing in phase; so **phase-splitting** *ppl. a.* and *vbl. sb.*; **phase transition**, a change in the phase of a substance (PHASE *sb.* 4); **phase velocity**, the speed of propagation of a sine wave or a sinusoidal component of a complex wave, equal to the product of its wavelength and frequency (cf. *group velocity*); **phase-wound** *a. Electr. Engin.*, having a secondary in the form of windings rather than a squirrel-cage.

1909 M. WALKER in *Jrnl. Inst. Electr. Engin.* XLII. 611 The author believes that it is possible to devise a new type of machine to act as an exciter in the manner proposed by M. Leblanc... Such a machine might be called a 'phase advancer'. **1920** *Whittaker's Electr. Engineer's Pocket-bk.* (ed. 4) 521 Should the speed be increased above synchronism, the reactance attains a negative value (*i.e.* the phase-advancer acts as a capacity), with the result that the current is advanced and the leading component of it compensates for the magnetizing current of the induction motor, thereby relieving the system. **1962** *Newnes Conc. Encycl. Electr. Engin.* 596/1 Many different types of phase advancer have been developed but they are only rarely used because of the high maintenance required. **1952** *New Biol.* XII. 99 The adsorption of simple organic molecules from the atmosphere or from solutions at the surface of phase boundaries may have been of far greater importance. Suitable phase boundaries occur..at the surface of crystals of inorganic minerals. **1914** *Physical Rev.* III. 126 At high pressures we are concerned with phase changes of only two types, from the fluid to the solid (or crystalline) phase, and from one solid phase to another. *Ibid.* 354 Methods..for determining the phase change produced by reflection from the surfaces of metals. **1956** *Nature* 4 Feb. 240/1 The rate of diffusion in the plane of the layers for each phase-change is equal in all directions. **1962** A. NISBETT *Technique Sound Studio* 254 Noise..is strongly discriminated against [by frequency modulation], though it does produce phase-change effects which cannot be eradicated. **1974** *Times* 4 Feb. 14 It was once thought that deep earthquakes marked the simultaneous collapse of many cubic kilometres of rock from one atomic structure to another—a so-called phase change. **1900** *Jrnl. Electr., Power & Gas* Oct. 81/2 (*heading*) An induction motor phase changer. **1935** *Discovery* Nov. 326/1 Phase changers and automatic regulators have worked perfectly [in locomotives of Hungarian railways]. **1934** F. ZERNIKE in *Monthly Notices R. Astron. Soc.* XCIV. 377 (*heading*) Diffraction theory of the knife-edge test and its improved form, the phase-contrast method. **1942** *Jrnl. Sci. Instrum.* XIX. 71 (*heading*) Phase-contrast microscopy. **1947** *Nature* 21 June 829/2 Mr. Taylor has made and described a new phase-contrast microscope in which a controlled variable amplitude for the 'direct-light' component is obtained. **1961** M. FRANÇON *Progress in Microsc.* ii. 65 Originally used by its inventor [*sc.* Zernike] for inspecting telescope mirrors, the phase contrast technique was applied to microscopy shortly afterwards. **1966** *McGraw-Hill Encycl. Sci. & Technol.* VIII. 399/2 The phase contrast microscope is the routine instrument for the examination of living cells. **1970** E. M. SLAYTER *Optical Methods in Biol.* xiii. 288 The phase contrast microscope is a device which renders differences in refractive index between regions of a specimen visible as differences in intensity. **1971** *Nature* 17 Sept. 198/1 Parasitaemia was estimated by examination of fresh blood preparations by phase contrast microscopy..every 2–3 days. *Ibid.* 26 Nov. 227/2 Cytological characters and chromosomal behaviour during mitosis were studied in live cultures under phase contrast. **1916** *Trans. Amer. Inst. Electr. Engin.* XXXV. 1318 No. 4 is in general respects the same as No. 2 with the addition of a relatively new development known as the 'phase converter' which preserves the balance of the system even when large blocks of single-phase power are taken from the system. **1935** *Discovery* Nov. 326/1 The phase converter is usually regarded as the most complicated part of the locomotive. **1967** C. V. Jones *Unified Theory Electr. Machines* xviii. 241 As a final example of induction motor performance, its operation as a phase converter will be briefly considered. **1911** *Chem. Abstr.* V. 1219 (*heading*) Phase diagram of silver iodide. **1926** *Jrnl. Iron & Steel Inst.* CXIII. 655 The phase diagram is characterised by a solid solution of tin in iron with a maximum of 18 per cent tin, and by two compounds. **1972** *McGraw-Hill Yearbk. Sci. & Technol.* 350/2 The most apparent departure from conventional behavior is seen in the phase diagram of solid He^3 shown in Fig. 2. **1889** J. A. Fleming *Alternate Current Transformer* I. iv. 291 θ is the angle of phase difference of the currents. **1962** *Symp. Zool. Soc.* No. 7. 10 It has been generally supposed until recently that for man..phase differences are of no account. But we now realize that if changes of phase of particular components occur at a sufficiently rapid state, then differences of sound-quality are in fact heard. **1907** H. H. Norris *Introd. Study Electr. Engin.* iv. 120 (*heading*) Phase displacement of alternating quantities. **1933** Phase displacement [see balanced *ppl. a.* 6]. **1928** *Bell Syst. Techn. Jrnl.* VII. 195 For relatively short distances the deleterious effects of phase distortion are not appreciable. **1961** G. Millerson *Technique Television Production* iii. 43 Certain video distortions, from phase-distortion to signal reflections, can also be the reason for poor definition in a picture. **1970** J. Earl *Tuners & Amplifiers* ii. 43 For high quality all the significant sideband signals must be handled by the i.f. channel to avoid phase distortion and treble attenuation. **1904** *Westm. Gaz.* 23 Apr. 12/2 Roozeboom, who applied the phase doctrine to all kinds of equilibrium, is the founder of a new branch of physical chemistry. **1942** A. Hund *Frequency Modulation* xi. 178 Figure 49 shows a balanced reactance-tube modulator where a phase inverter replaces the push-pull input transformer. **1951** *Electronic Engin.* XXIII. 64 Phase-invertors using resistance-loaded triode valves are well known. **1960** E. N. Lurch *Fund. Electronics* xv. 353 A circuit arrangement to produce balanced voltages which are 180° out of phase for the grids of the push-pull stage is termed a phase inverter. **1953** W. A. Edson *Vacuum-Tube Oscillators* xiv. 342 The question of time delay or phase lock arises in all methods of frequency composition. **1957** *Electronic & Radio Engineer* XXXIV. 141/2 The simple phase-lock loop is effectively a position control servo-mechanism operated by a d.c. error voltage from the phase-sensitive detector. **1973** *Wireless World* Dec. 605/1 The device contains a phase-locked loop which I have found suitable for demodulating teleprinter f.s.k. signals because it requires only a small input signal for phase lock. **1974** Harvey & Bohlman *Stereo F.M. Radio Handbk.* iv. 65 When 'phase-lock'is achieved the in-phase detector registers this by providing a d.c. output. **1955** *Proc. IRE* XLIII. 869/1 A circuit has been developed with which microwave oscillators may be phase-locked to weak but stable reference signals. **1967** *Electronics* 6 Mar. 6/2 (Advt.), The generator frequency can be phaselocked to an external standard frequency. **1959** *Proc. IRE* XLVII. 1137/2 A phase-locked oscillator can serve as a filter of arbitrarily narrow bandwidth. **1976** *Gramophone* Aug. 354/2 A quartz crystal controlled phase-locked servo circuit holds speed drift within 0.002% and is independent of any changes in line voltage or frequency. **1955** *Proc. IRE* XLIII. 872/2 This phase-locking circuitry may also be used to make a divider of particular use in the microwave region where no other kind exists. **1963** *Electronics* 19 Apr. 45/2 Because phase-locking is used, the offset between channels is affected only by the frequencies assigned to the i-f reference oscillators. **1977** *Proc. R. Soc. Med.* LXX. 379/2 Temporal information depends on phase-locking; the nerves fire at a particular phase of the stimulating wave-form so that for sinusoids the time intervals between firings are approximately integral multiples of the period of the wave-form. **1946** *Trans. Amer. Microsc. Soc.* LXV. 129 (*heading*) Phase microscopy. *Ibid.*, The Phase Microscope reveals detail in transparent materials having regions of slightly differing absorption or with different indices of refraction. **1949** *World-Herald* (Omaha, Nebraska) 4 Dec. 19-A, The phase microscope can see the interior of a cell in bright or dark contrast to bring hidden parts into view. **1964** N. S. Cohn *Elem. Cytol.* ii. 22 The observation of living cells has been greatly facilitated by the development of phase microscopy and related optical systems. **1970** O. W. Richards in J. E. Blair et al. *Man. Clin. Microbiol.* 24/1 The phase microscope has an annular stop in the condenser to limit the lighting to a symmetrical hollow cone. **1930** *Proc. IRE* XVIII. 633 (*heading*) The effect of frequency or 'phase'modulation upon signal quality. **1936** Phase-modulated [see frequency-modulated *ppl. a.*]. **1941** *Electronic Engin.* XIV. 537/3 Phase modulation possesses much the same advantages as frequency modulation. Signal-to-noise ratio is greater than for amplitude modulation..though it is less than for frequency modulation since the triangular noise spectrum effect is absent because noise itself phase modulates the carrier. **1962** J. H. & P. J. Reyner *Radio Communication* iii. 140 Whereas with phase modulation the modulation index *m* is simply proportional to the amplitude of the modulating signal, with frequency modulation it is *also* inversely proportional to the modulation frequency. **1968** B. P. Lathi *Communication Syst.* iv. 213 If we integrate the modulatory signal $f(t)$ first and then allow it to phase-modulate the carrier, we obtain a frequency-modulated carrier. **1974** Harvey & Bohlman *Stereo F.M. Radio Handbk.* ii. 36 It is a characteristic of phase modulation that the amount of frequency swing introduced is proportional not only to the amplitude of the modulating signal but also to its frequency. **1976** *Sci. Amer.* June 62/3 The antenna transmits a phase-modulated radio signal that carries scientific and engineering data from the spacecraft to the radio tracking stations on the earth. **1920** D. A. Clibbens *Princ. Phase Theory* i. 3 If the temperature is raised,..a transference of material from one phase to another will, in general, occur; such a transference is known as a phase reaction. **1923** A. C. D. Rivett *Phase Rule* iv. 72 Until the temperature reaches that of x_1,..cooling does not bring about any phase reaction. **1938** S. T. Bowden *Phase Rule & Phase Reactions* i. 6 A phase reaction is a physical or chemical change which involves the appearance or disappearance of a phase. **1878** *Proc. R. Soc. Edin.* IX. 604 They may be so related in phase that at one of the instants of maximum pressure of one of the constituents there is also maximum pressure of the other constituent. The same phase-relation, if the harmonic numbers of the constituent tones be odd, will give also coincident minimums. **1896** S. P. Thompson *Dynamo-Electr. Machinery* (ed. 5) xxvi. 708 (*heading*) Phase-relations in transformers. **1962** A. Nisbett *Technique Sound Studio* xii. 218 The phase relationship between the sounds. **1898** *Daily News* 12 May 6/3 The features of Mr. Wood's phase reversal and silver zone plates. **1938** *Science* 4 Mar. 213/2 [They] misinterpret the situation still more by referring to.. the setting of gelatine as involving phase-reversal. **1957** *Practical Wireless* XXXIII. 539/2 There is a phase reversal across the common emitter circuit. **1962** A. Nisbett *Technique Sound Studio* 244 *Cardioid microphone*, microphone with a heart-shaped polar diagram (arrived at by adding omnidirectional and figure-of-eight responses together, taking into account the phase reversal at the back of the latter). **1918** K. Edgcumbe *Industr. Electr. Measuring Instruments* (ed. 2) 254 The direction of phase rotation of the secondary pressures and currents may conveniently be checked by a phase rotation indicator. **1922** [see phased *ppl. a.* 1]. **1962** *Newnes Conc. Encycl. Electr. Engin.* 572/2 A simple portable instrument to indicate phase rotation. **1896** *Jrnl. Chem. Soc.* LXX. ii. 415 Only at some one definite temperature would all four salts tend to coexist in an unchanged condition. This point is, in the case of solutions of the salts, a sextuple point in the sense of the phase rule. **1904** A. Findlay (*title*) The Phase Rule and its Applications. **1913** Bloxam & Lewis *Bloxam's Chem.* (ed. 10) 338 The Phase Rule of Willard Gibbs..is expressed in the equation P + F = C + 2,..where P is the number of phases, F the number of degrees of freedom, and C the number of components. **1935** *Discovery* Sept. 258/2 A system so complex as to baffle the most ardent exponent of the phase rule. **1966** *McGraw-Hill Encycl. Sci. & Technol.* V. 55/1 If a system consists of P phases and C distinguishable components, there are $C + 2$ thermodynamic variables (C chemical potentials μ_i, plus the temperature and pressure) which are interrelated by an equation for each phase. Since there are P independent equations relating the $C + 2$ variables, one needs to fix only $F = C + 2 - P$ variables to define completely the state of the system at equilibrium; the other variables are then beyond control. This relation for the number of degrees of freedom F, or variance, is called the Phase Rule and was first derived by Willard Gibbs in 1873. **1957** Phase-sensitive [see *phase-lock* sb. above]. **1963** B. Fozard *Instrumentation Nucl. Reactors* xi. 135 This requires the provision of a phase-sensitive rectifier at the output. **1941** *Nature* 27 Sept. 373/1 We have sought to replace the customary phase separation of 'crude carotene' and xanthophylls by using the same chromatographic technique for the removal of xanthophylls as well as of non-carotene chromogens from the petrol ether solution. **1947** *Jrnl. Polymer Sci.* II. 90 The phase separation in solutions of high polymers in the same solvent (technically known as incompatibility) has been studied for fourteen high polymers..dissolved in thirteen solvents. **1948** [see hæm, heme b]. **1960** P. A. Albertson *Partition of Cell Particles* ii. 13 Bungenberg de Jong & Kruyt ..coined the term 'coacervation' for the general phenomenon of phase separation of colloid mixtures. **1970** [see coacervation 3]. **1971** *Materials & Technol.* II. vi. 340 Devitrification of glass is the formation of crystals (phase separation) in a glass. **1927** *Wireless World* 1 June 686/2 In order to give a high-grade telephone line such an extended characteristic, special equipment for the equalisation of attenuation and of phase shift had to be devised. **1929** J. A. Ratcliffe *Physical Princ. Wireless* iii. 37 If a beam of light is focussed on to a point and then allowed to spread out on the other side of the focus, the total phase-shift is π. **1960** *Practical Wireless* XXXVI. 411/2 While a simple phase-shift oscillator..may be used coupled into a suitable amplifier installation, a neater method is to build the complete practice set together with power supply, speaker and controls into a self-contained unit. **1976** *Gramophone* Feb. 1398/1 Either we must accept some loss of loudness of rearward sources in mono playback, or a certain amount of phase-shift between the signals coming from the two loudspeakers in stereo. **1965** *Wireless World* Aug. 396/2 If the gate voltage is phase-shifted with respect to the anode voltage, the firing point is delayed by the appropriate time. **1908** *Electrician* 11 Dec. 341/2 In Fig. 1, which shows diagrammatically a phase shifter for a two-phase supply, AB and CD are the terminals of the two phases. **1951** *Engineering* 23 Feb. 221/2 The first method enables the point in each cycle at which the anodes become conducting to be delayed..by a double-wound phase-shifter. **1959** K. Henney *Radio Engin. Handbk.* (ed. 5) xiv. 16 In the microwave region, a matched transmission line or slotted line may be used as a phase shifter. **1908** *Electrician* 11 Dec. 341/1 (*heading*) The use of a phase-shifting transformer for wattmeter and supply meter testing. **1929** *Phil. Mag.* VIII. 168 Thus the artificial line has zero attenuation at all frequencies, and is a pure phase-shifting network. **1965** *Wireless World* July 332/1 Thin film circuits..may be more useful where passive networks only are required—for attenuators, RC phase shifting networks, etc. **1927** R. C. Tolman *Statistical Mech.* iii. 32 To follow the behavior of such a system..it is very convenient to think of its phase as given by the position of a representative point..in a $2m$-dimensional space (phase space) corresponding to the $2m$ coordinates and momenta whose values are to be specified. **1970** G. K. Woodgate *Elem. Atomic Struct.* vi. 98 The exclusion principle states, in this context, that not more than two electrons are allowed in each volume of size h^3 in phase space. **1974** G. Reece tr. *Hund's Hist. Quantum Theory* vi. 80 Ehrenfest attempted to interpret the radiation formulae by means of a weight function in phase space. **1896** D. C. & J. P. Jackson *Alternating Currents* 652 Special starting devices must be included in the design and construction [of single-phase induction motors]. As a rule, this takes the form of what is called a Phase Splitter. **1965** *Wireless World* Aug. 72 (Advt.), A pentode triode ideally suited for use as a voltage amplifier and phase splitter. **1970** J. Earl *Tuners & Amplifiers* ii. 54 The collector and emitter outputs..are equal in amplitude but opposite in phase, rather like the signals from a single valve phase-splitter circuit. **1895** S. P. Thompson *Polyphase Electric Currents* iv. 99 (*caption*) Phase-splitting device. **1947** *Wireless World* Aug. 274/1 The advantages of resistance-capacitance circuits for phase-splitting in push-pull amplifiers are now well recognized. **1969** R. W. Smeaton *Motor Applic. & Maintenance Handbk.* xviii. 14 A simple phase-splitting device could be rigged up..so that the motors could be used on 120 volts, 60 cycles, single-phase. **1975** G. J. King *Audio Handbk.* iv. 84 Some form of 'phase-splitting' stage is necessary to drive common-pair output stages. **1939** *Jrnl. Chem. Physics* VII. 1019/1 A first-order phase transition. **1968** R. A. Lyttleton *Mysteries Solar Syst.* ii. 71 *L* is the energy per unit mass required for the phase-transition from solid to liquid. **1977** A. Hallam *Planet Earth* 11 Such a phase transition does not involve differences in chemical composition but only a spatial rearrangement of the atoms in the silicate structure. **1932** Ladner & Stoner *Short Wave Wireless Communication* iii. 34 For the case of a group of waves passing through an ionised medium, therefore, the phase velocity will be greater than *c*, the velocity of light in a pure dielectric,..but the group velocity will be less than *c*. **1968** M. S. Livingston *Particle Physics* iii. 49 Consider a pulse of water waves originating from the point where a stone strikes the water, and focus on a particular wave crest. ..The velocity with which the general disturbance moves is the group velocity; the velocity of the wave crest relative to the water is the phase velocity. **1907** H. H. Norris *Introd. Study Electr. Engin.* x. 290 The phase-wound motor has very satisfactory starting qualities and draws little excess starting current.

phase, obs. erron. form of pasch, pace *sb.*[2]; an error in various Dicts. (Webster 1828–64, etc.) for prase, *Min.*

phase, erroneous spelling of faze *v.*, to discompose, disturb.

1889 'Mark Twain' *Yankee at Crt. K. Arthur* (Tauchn.) II. 154 His spirit—why, it wasn't even phased. **1898** R. B. Townshend in *Westm. Gaz.* 19 Nov. 2/1 It don't seem to 'phase' him in the very slightest.

phase (feɪz), *v.* [f. the sb.] **I. 1.** *trans.* To adjust the phase of; to bring into phase, synchronize.

1938 A. E. Greenlees *Amplification & Distribution of Sound* x. 154 Wherever two or more loudspeakers are used, these must be properly phased so that all the diaphragms move in the same direction at the same time. **1951** S. Deutsch *Theory & Design Television Receivers* xvi. 502 A phasing control is needed in order to phase the oscilloscope sweep so that the beam goes from left to right when the sweep frequency goes from its lowest to highest extremes. **1967** *Electronics* 6 Mar. 67/2 Researchers have succeeded in phasing the lasers. **1970** J. Earl *Tuners & Amplifiers* vi. 131 The two speakers of a stereo pair..can be correctly phased initially with little danger of the phasing being upset subsequently. **1974** *Sci. Amer.* Jan. 118/2 One can also 'phase'the drum and the mirror by interrupting the circuit of the drum motor momentarily.

2. To organize or carry out gradually in planned stages or instalments.

1949 [implied in phased *ppl. a.* 2]. **1955** *Bull. Atomic Sci.* Jan. 9/3 The British-French proposals were directed primarily to the problem of phasing the controls. **1963** *Ann. Reg. 1962* 97 The British members of the Commission preferred a merger phased over five years. **1969** *Daily Tel.* 8 Jan. 22/7 New tenants will face rent increases of as much as £1 a week, while increases will be phased over three years for existing tenants.

II. With adverbs: **3. phase down**: to reduce or decrease (something) gradually or in planned stages.

1970 *Times* 6 Nov. 8 The secretary said that the programme to phase down American operations in Indo-China..'is solidly based'. **1972** *Physics Bull.* Feb. 76/1 If the innovation manager is truly perceptive, he can phase down his work *without* human suffering. **1974** *Daily Tel.* 11 Feb. 2/8 Production had been cut to 60 per cent of normal. It would be phased down further for two months, when virtually no steel would be produced.

4. phase in. a. *intr.* To come into phase. *rare.*

1929 *Proc. IRE* XVII. 1787 The separate multiple echoes from a given set of pulses phase in and out at different rates. ..Part of the observed phasing must be due to changes in optical path.

b. *trans.* To introduce or incorporate (something) gradually or in planned stages. Also *intr.*, to be so introduced.

1955 *Bull. Atomic Sci.* Feb. 57 New weapons must be 'phased in' gradually to our existing weapons systems. **1959** *Time* 9 Feb. 11 It would be dangerous to phase out obsolescent weapons too slowly. But it would be exceedingly wasteful to phase in too heavily the newer weapons. **1971** *Farmer & Stockbreeder* 23 Feb. 7/3 The levies should be phased in over a one-year period. **1972** [see sense 5 d below]. *a* **1974** R. Crossman *Diaries* (1976) II. 472 As for national superannuation, we shouldn't try and bring it forward but phase it in in 1975, when a large number of existing pensioners will be dying off.

5. phase out. †**a.** *Electr. Engin.* To eliminate phase differences between (parts of polyphase equipment that are to be connected together). *Obs.*

1921 W. S. Ibbetson *Motor & Dynamo Control* viii. 283 The synchronising of two- and three-phase generators may be performed by connecting the synchronising lamps across one phase only, provided the alternators are correctly connected up to the bus bars. To phase out such connections before a machine may be paralleled the following operations may be performed. **1939** —— *Electric Power Engineers' Handbk.* vi. 151 If the leads were not correctly phased out so that the phases of all the machines were in the same sequence, interchange of current between the alternators would occur.

b. To eliminate by adjustments of phase. *nonce-use.*

1921 *Wireless World* 6 Aug. 287/2 The interfering note can be completely 'phased out' by adjusting bellows and tube to equal length.

c. *intr.* To become out of phase. *rare.*

1929 [see 4 a above].

d. *trans.* To remove, eliminate, or take out *of* gradually or in planned stages. Also *intr.*, to disappear gradually.

1954 *Quartermaster Rev.* July–Aug. 159/1 We in Defense are phasing out the support of basic research for the general welfare. **1955** *Sun* (Baltimore) (B ed.) 25 Apr. 8/5 The old propellor-driven Mustangs.. will be 'phased out'on August 1—which means that replacement parts will have become so scarce that they cannot longer be operated in safety. **1959** [see sense 4b above]. **1959** *New Scientist* 17 Sept. 446/2 Finding a way to phase out the jet lift as forward speed generates lift in the wings. **1967** *Guardian* 9 Jan. 6/4 We could safely decide to phase out the carrier fleet by 1970. **1969** J. GARDNER *Compl. State of Death* ix. 172 It's been a tricky job phasing out these people. **1969** *Daily Tel.* 13 Dec. 13/1 While he was 'phasing out' from the public view, he said, he was not shirking his duties as an MP. **1970** *Ibid.* 30 Sept. 1/6 The Jaguar 420G range of cars is to be gradually phased out of production. **1971** *Nature* 1 Oct. 299/1 Five top level scientific committees.. have recommended that the pesticide be phased out of domestic use. **1972** *Lebende Sprachen* XVII. 135/1 In a research organization projects do phase in and phase out all the time. **1975** *Times* 22 Sept. 3/3 The Government wants to phase out pay beds. **1977** B. PYM *Quartet in Autumn* xii. 102 The whole department was being phased out and only being kept on until the men working in it reached retirement age. **1979** *Time* 2 Apr. 59/1 It has been generally thought that Ford would start phasing out after Sept. 4, 1980, when he turns 63.

†**6. phase up** *Electr. Engin.*: to synchronize, bring into phase. *Obs. rare.*

1904 W. R. BOWKER *Dynamo, Motor & Switchboard Circuits* v. 99 In connecting two-phase generators for parallel running it is necessary to synchronise both phases the first time the machines are paralleled. After they have once been 'phased-up' synchronising one phase is sufficient. Fig. 101 shows the connections for properly 'phasing up' two two-phase generators.

'phaseal, *a.* [irreg. f. PHASE *sb.* + -AL[1].] = PHASIC.

1847–9 TODD *Cycl. Anat.* IV. 667/1 The law.. is one of a phaseal quantitative degradation.

phase angle. [f. PHASE + ANGLE *sb.*[2]] **1.** An angle representing a difference in phase, 360 degrees (2π radians) corresponding to one complete cycle.

1889 J. A. FLEMING *Alternate Current Transformer* I. iii. 110, OP.. is called the amplitude or maximum value, and POM the phase angle of the motion. **1936** *Discovery* Mar. 80/2 By phase-angle changes so produced.. any of our mean amplitudes may be much reduced and the real importance of a periodicity [in the weather] accordingly masked proportionately. **1947** R. LEE *Electronic Transformers & Circuits* v. 127 These waves indicate that the phase angle encountered in audio transformers does not of itself introduce much distortion in a lightly loaded triode. **1966** BROSAN & HAYDEN *Adv. Electr. Power & Machines* vii. 279 The voltage will be alternating, and.. in general, $e = E_m \sin \omega t$. If the coil is connected to an external circuit, a current will flow, given by $i = I_m \sin(\omega t - \psi)$ where ψ is the internal phase angle.

2. *Astr.* The angle between the lines joining a given planet to the sun and to the earth.

1926 H. N. RUSSELL et al. *Astron.* I. ix. 234 How much of the illuminated hemisphere can be seen from the earth depends upon the angle at the planet between lines to the earth and to the sun. Where this phase angle is always very small, as it is from the most distant planets, there is never any perceptible deviation from a circular disk. **1974** R. H. STOY *Everyman's Astron.* vi. 203 The apparent brightness of any minor planet varies inversely both as the square of its distance from the Earth and as the square of its distance from the Sun. It also depends on the phase angle, that is on the angle between the lines joining the minor planet to the Sun and to the Earth.

phased (feɪzd), *ppl. a.* [f. PHASE *v.* + -ED[1].] **1.** Synchronized; adjusted to be in phase.

1922 GLAZEBROOK *Dict. Appl. Physics* II. 936/2 If these two readings give zero reading, the transformers are correctly phased... If readings are obtained across EE' and FF' then polarity or phase rotation is incorrect. **1929** *Photoplay* (Chicago) Apr. 31/2 *Phased*, or *interlocked*, all motors of sound and picture recording equipment lined up in readiness to start out in perfect step together. **1951** S. DEUTSCH *Theory & Design Television Receivers* xiii. 435 When the sync pulse is near the center of the saw-tooth retrace, there can be no doubt that the picture is correctly phased with respect to the horizontal sweep. **1958** *Listener* 9 Oct. 558/1 Zoning, road classification, phased traffic lights. **1969** *Focal Encycl. Film & Television Techniques* 544/1 The associated synchronizing pulse trains are locked together and correctly phased. **1971** *Hi-Fi Sound* Feb. 71/2 It can be difficult for the newcomer to hi-fi to know whether the loudspeakers are correctly phased or not.

b. ***phased array***: an array of aerials that is made to transmit or receive at a variable angle by delaying the signals to or from each one by an amount depending on its position in relation to the others.

1938 *Television* XI. 644/3 None of these changes.. affect the description of the phased array. **1960** *Proc. IRE* XLVIII. 1715 Phased arrays can provide scanning patterns and scanning rates which are impossible to attain with mechanically scanned antennas. **1966** *Electronics* 3 Oct. 173 The satellite transponder will receive signals on 149.2 Mhz with an 8-element phased array. **1970** *New Scientist* 10 Sept. 534/1 The beams formed by phased arrays can be steered electronically, and can be scanned up to several hundred million times a second.

2. Planned or carried out in stages or by degrees.

1949 *Archit. Rev.* CV. 225/2 A phased building programme for all developments proposed for the accommodation of population and industry from London. **1953** *Manch. Guardian* 12 May 1/3 Mr Dulles issued a statement that the United States Government favours a 'phased' withdrawal of British troops from the Canal Zone. **1956** *Sun* (Baltimore) (B ed.) 30 Nov. 1/6 Lord Salisbury.. declared: 'Our policy is that of a phased withdrawal.' This supposedly means a step by step withdrawal.. rather than a quick overall pullout. **1967** D. WILSON in Wills & Yearsley *Handbk. Managem. Technol.* iii. 49 The phased implementation of new procedures. **1972** *Daily Tel.* 4 Mar. 32/6 A policy to end imprisonment without trial by a phased programme of releases of every detainee and internee. **1976** *Glasgow Herald* 26 Nov. 3 The council who are planning 800 phased redundancies in the department next year. **1976** *Broadcast* Dec. 1/1 There will have to be a phased introduction of any changes that are agreed in pay structures and conditions of service.

phase-down ('feɪzdaʊn). [f. PHASE *v.* 3.] A gradual reduction or planned decrease.

1968 *Times* 12 Feb. 17 The best scope for achieving economies in clerical staff will probably come on the female side, where the turnover is rapid and any required phasedown can thus be acquired easily in a relatively short time. **1972** *Lebende Sprachen* XVII. 135/1 The systems division has reported the phase-down of its program office. **1973** *Times* 10 Oct. 19/8 An employee has a progressively shorter working year (the phase-down being at the rate of one, two or perhaps three weeks per annum).

phaseless ('feɪzlɪs), *a. rare.* [f. PHASE *sb.* + -LESS.] Having no phases, of unchanging aspect.

a **1849** POE *Ragged Mount.* Wks. 1865 II. 311 A phaseless and unceasing gloom.

†**phasels, phaselles, phasiols,** var. FASELS *Obs.*, kidney-beans.

1562 WARDE tr. *Alexis' Secr.* II. 13 Take.. Peason, Phasiols, Lintelles, and such like. **1562** TURNER *Baths* 5 b, All kindes of pulse as beanes, peasen, phaselles and ciches. **1694** MOTTEUX *Rabelais* v. xxix, Beans, Pease, Phasels or Long-peasen.

phasemeter ('feɪzmiːtə(r)). *Electr.* [ad. G. *phasenmeter*, †*phasometer* (M. von Dolivo-Dobrowolsky 1894, in *Elektrotechnische Zeitschr.* XV. 351): see PHASE and METER *sb.*[3]] An instrument which measures the phase difference between two oscillations having the same frequency, esp. that between an alternating current and the corresponding voltage (hence giving the power factor).

1894 *Electrician* 21 Sept. 610/1 The phasemeter here described is essentially an ampere meter measuring the idle current. **1903** G. D. A. PARR *Electr. Engin. Measuring Instruments* vii. 194 The phasemeter now under consideration, made by the Electrical Co., Ltd., of London, is an instrument for measuring directly the value of the wattless current in an inductive alternating-current circuit. **1974** *Physics Bull.* Oct. 477/1 The circuitry of the phasemeter has been designed to reduce the effects of errors introduced by crossover distortion and noise in the input signal, which are the most common sources of inaccuracy.

phaseolin (fəˈsiːəʊlɪn). *Biochem.* [f. L. *phaseolus* kidney-bean; see -IN[1].] **a.** A crystalline globulin found in the seeds of the kidney bean.

1893 T. B. OSBORNE in *17th Ann. Rep. Connecticut Agric. Exper. Station* IV. 187, I have been able to identify and obtain in a state of comparative purity, two distinct proteids, one, the most abundant, having quite the properties of a globulin, which I shall designate phaseolin. **1921** *Nature* 21 July 666/2 Little or no cystines in a protein has also an effect upon the growth of rats. This has been most clearly demonstrated in the case of the protein, phaseolin, of the navy bean. **1964** *Chem. Abstr.* LXI. 10938 The enzymic hydrolysis of phaseolin with trypsin was affected by addn. of the azo dye, amaranth, at pH 8.

†**b.** = PHASEOLLIN. *Obs.*

1963 CRUICKSHANK & PERRIN in *Life Sci.* II. 680 The isolation is now reported of a further phytoalexin of the *Leguminosae*, sub-family *Papillionaceae*. This substance, for which we propose the trivial name, phaseolin, has been obtained by inoculation of detached, opened pods of the French bean, *Phaseolus vulgaris* L., using a spore suspension of [the fungus] *Monilinia fructicola* (Wint.). **1964** [see PHASEOLLIN].

phaseolite (fəˈsiːəʊlaɪt). *Palæont.* [ad. mod.L. *Phaseolites*, f. *phaseolus* kidney-bean: see -ITE[1] 2 a.] (See quot.)

[**1859** PAGE *Geol. Terms* (1865), *Phaseolites*,.. a genus of leguminous plants found in the Tertiary fresh-water formation of Aix.] **1882** OGILVIE, *Phaseolite.*

phaseollin (fəˈsiːəʊlɪn). *Biochem.* [f. PHASEOLIN with inserted *l*: see quot. 1964[1].] A fungitoxic phytoalexin produced by the kidney bean plant, which has been isolated as a white, crystalline heterocyclic compound, $C_{20}H_{18}O_4$.

1964 D. R. PERRIN in *Tetrahedron Lett.* VIII. 438 The author's attention has been drawn to the prior use of the term phaseolin to denote a protein from *Phaseolus vulgaris*. Accordingly the name of the phytoalexin from *P. vulgaris* is now changed to phaseollin. **1964** CRUICKSHANK & PERRIN in J. B. Harborne *Biochem. Phenolic Compounds* xiii. 530 Phaseollin is similar in its biological properties to pisatin. **1967** R. K. S. WOOD *Physiol. Plant Path.* xiv. 497 Another phytoalexin, closely related to pisatin and called phaseollin has now been obtained from pods of French bean (*Phaseolus vulgaris*) inoculated with conidia of *S*[*clerotinia*] *fructicola*. **1973** *Nature* 20 Apr. 533/1 The phytoalexin phaseollin does accumulate in hypersensitive responses in leaves of French bean.. caused by avirulent bacteria but this substance has little or no effect on growth of bacteria.

†**pha'seolous,** *a. Obs. rare.* [f. L. *phaseol-us* (see PHASEOLITE) + -OUS.] Related to the kidney-bean or scarlet runner.

1681 GREW *Musæum* II. 233 It is neither of the Phaseolous, nor Fabaceous, but of the Peas-kind.

phaseomannite (feɪsiːəʊˈmænaɪt). *Chem.* [f. *phaseo*(*lus* (see above) + MANNITE.] Another name of INOSITE.

1859 *Fownes' Man. Chem.* 355 *Inosite*.. is identical with phaseomannite, which occurs in unripe beans (*Phaseolus*). **1862** MILLER *Elem. Chem.* (ed. 2) III. 783.

phaseometer (feɪzɪˈɒmɪtə(r)). *Electr.* [f. Gr. φάσις, gen. φάσε-ως PHASE *sb.* + -O)METER.] An instrument for indicating the phase of an electric current.

1898 *Engineering Mag.* XVI. 142/2 A Direct Indicating Phaseometer.. which resembles a double Watt-meter, with two movable bobbins.

phase-out ('feɪzaʊt). [f. PHASE *v.* 5 d.] A gradual removal or planned elimination. Also *attrib.*

1958 *Time* (Atlantic ed.) 6 Oct. 26 The Moroccans countered a request for a three-year phase-out. **1960** *Economist* 8 Oct. 126/1 Britain has thus given *de facto* recognition to the Norwegian twelve-mile limit, but the ten year phase-out period for fishing in the outer six miles will do something to cushion the blow to Hull and Grimsby. **1961** *Ann. Reg. 1960* 298 There was a planned phase-out in the field of economic aid. **1969** *New Scientist* 28 Aug. 421/1 The RAF.. is to assign more strike aircraft to cover Britain's seaward approaches as the phase-out of the Navy's carriers proceeds. **1972** *Science* 12 May 618/3 In 1971 Shell announced the phase-out of the Emeryville station. **1975** *Daily Tel.* 7 May 8/5 Unless the Government abandoned some [Bills], there seemed little chance of beginning the pay-beds phase-out until 1976 at the earliest.

phase sequence. [f. PHASE *sb.* + SEQUENCE.] **1.** *Electr. Engin.* The sequence in which the different lines of a polyphase system attain their maximum voltage.

1918 K. EDGCUMBE *Industr. Electr. Measuring Instruments* (ed. 2) 257 A simple method of determining phase sequence when a rotation indicator is not available has been described. **1971** A. SYMONDS *Electr. Power Equipment* vi. 91 There are three essential conditions to be met before two transformers can be connected in parallel: (a) Secondaries must have the same phase sequence. This can be checked by a phase-sequence indicator.

2. *Psychol.* A hypothetical sequence of cellular activity in the brain initiated by a sensory stimulus, suggested by D. O. Hebb as an explanation of motivated behaviour.

1946 D. O. HEBB in *Psychol. Rev.* LIII. 269/1 Let us designate the specific pattern of cellular activity throughout the thalamo-cortical system, at any one moment, as a 'phase'. Behavior is directly correlated with a phase sequence which is temporally organized. **1954** *Brit. Jrnl. Psychol.* XLV. 189 Hebb (1949) expresses the belief that the mental processes corresponding to cortical processes ('phase-sequences') will be most rewarding.. when the phase-sequences are in the course of being built up. **1964** COFER & APPLEY *Motivation* viii. 407 The theory presented .. was essentially.. that nerve cells in the brain when more or less simultaneously excited constitute assemblies of mutually facilitating, and to some extent stimulating, elements, a series of such cell assemblages acting one after another constitute a 'phase sequence'. **1970** C. TAYLOR in Borger & Cioffi *Explanation in Behavioural Sci.* 77 Hebb.. presents mechanisms, the 'cell assembly' and 'phase sequence', which although expressed in neurological terms are not based on any direct supporting neurological evidence.

phasianic (feɪsɪˈænɪk), *a. rare*[−1]. [f. Gr. φασιαν-ός pheasant + -IC.] Of or pertaining to pheasants.

1884 *Pall Mall G.* 4 Apr. 4/2 The formation of coverts, food and management, and all other points and details of phasianic economy.

So **phasianid** ('feɪsɪənɪd) *a.*, of or pertaining to the *Phasianidæ* or pheasant family of gallinaceous birds; **phasianine** ('feɪsɪənaɪn) *a.*, of or pertaining to the *Phasianinæ*, a sub-family of the *Phasianidæ*, including the pheasants proper; **'phasianoid** *a.*, allied in form to the pheasants, phasianid; **phasianomorphic** (ˌfeɪsɪeɪnəʊˈmɔːfɪk) *a.*, of or pertaining to the *Phasianomorphæ* [Gr. μορφή form], in Sundevall's classification of birds, a cohort of *Gallinæ* containing some of the *Phasianidæ* with the *Turnicidæ* (*Hemipodii*).

1868 *Proc. Zool. Soc.* 14 May 299 The great series of Galline, Pavonine, Phasianine, and Tetraonine birds.

phasic ('feɪzɪk, -sɪk), *a.* [f. Gr. φάσ-ις PHASE *sb.* + -IC.] **1.** Of, pertaining to, or of the nature of a phase or phases; presenting phases.

1890 *Chamb. Jrnl.* 13 Sept. 588/2 It is not.. the mere phasic change of the moon that influences the weather. **1898** *Allbutt's Syst. Med.* V. 417 The number [of lymphocytes] in the blood undergoes phasic variation. **1947** *Sci. News* V. 24 Gjessing concluded that the phasic disturbance of nitrogen metabolism constituted the fundamental pathology of the disorder, the mental changes being merely the outward symptoms. **1975** *Nature* 6 Nov. 81/1 Action potential firing of individual endocrine cells falls into two principal categories: most fire continuously and randomly at 1–2 spikes s^{-1}, while the rest have a phasic pattern of firing, periods of bursting activity alternating over 10–60 s with periods of silence.

2. *Physiol.* Responding to a change in environment, rather than to a constant stimulus.

1906 C. S. SHERRINGTON *Integrative Action Nervous Syst.* viii. 302 The very muscles that to the observer are most obviously under excitation by the *tonic* system are those most obviously inhibited by the *phasic* reflex system. **1956** *Jrnl. Physiol.* CXXXIV. 48 A temperature receptor.. has.. a high coefficient of phasic discharge to temperature change or a high coefficient of tonic discharge to maintained temperatures. **1973** *Sci. Amer.* May 97/1 Many human receptors, such as the ones that sense pressure on the skin, are phasic; if they were not, one would be constantly conscious of such things as a wristwatch or a shirt.

Hence **'phasically** *adv.*

1975 *Nature* 6 Nov. 81/1 We found that, during bilateral occlusion of the common carotid arteries, supraoptic neurones are excited and that this activation is confined almost exclusively to phasically active neurones.

phasing ('feɪzɪŋ), *vbl. sb.* [f. PHASE *sb.* or PHASE *v.* + -ING[1].] **1.** The action of adjusting or eliminating a phase difference.

1896 *Trans. Amer. Inst. Electr. Engin.* XII. 514 The condenser in this combination fills two very important functions, first assists in the phasing, and second prevents the lag upon the line. **1922** GLAZEBROOK *Dict. Appl. Physics* II. 935/2 Before connecting any two polyphase transformers in parallel it is necessary to ensure that the phase rotation is correct, and this can only be done by phasing out. The term 'phasing out'is applied to the procedure adopted for determining the correct junction of the terminals of two or more transformers. **1940** *Amat. Radio Handbk.* (ed. 2) v. 72/2 Let it be assumed that the parallel capacity C_4 has been balanced by the phasing condenser K. **1949** FRAYNE & WOLFE *Elem. Sound Recording* xxx. 627 The process of choosing the optimum position is known as the phasing of the speakers. **1959** R. L. SHRADER *Electronic Communication* xvi. 525 Another entirely different method of producing a single-sideband suppressed-carrier emission is to use 90° phasing networks. **1960** *Times* 12 Jan. 15/6 Pedestrians are ignored in the phasing of traffic lights at many T-junctions. **1978** *Hi-Fi News* Sept. 179/1 Phasing is.. produced by mixing a direct signal with the same signal when passed through a phase-shift network.

b. The relationship between the phases of two or more periodic phenomena having the same frequency.

1929 [see PHASE *v.* 4a]. **1938** A. E. GREENLEES *Amplification & Distribution of Sound* x. 154 Each loud-speaker should have one terminal marked.. so that when all these are connected to one line wire and the remaining terminals connected to the other, correct phasing is assured. **1951** S. DEUTSCH *Theory & Design Television Receivers* xiii. 435 Incorrect phasing is illustrated in Fig. 13-7, where the picture signal begins before the horizontal sweep has ended. **1962** A. NISBETT *Technique Sound Studio* 264 Correct phasing of speakers is.. vital to true stereo reproduction. **1968** *Radio Communication Handbk.* (ed. 4) xiii. 61/1 If two such aerials are erected horizontally in the form of a *V*.., and if the phasing between them is correct, the two pairs of lobes will add fore and aft. **1970** [see PHASE *v.* 1].

2. The action of PHASE *v.* 2. Chiefly in ***phasing in, out,*** a gradual planned introduction or elimination (cf. PHASE *v.* 4b, 5d).

1955 *Sun* (Baltimore) (B ed.) 25 Apr. 8/5 The 'phasing out'will end the official approval for even this operation. **1962** *Times* 8 Dec. 5/4 The phasing-out schedule for Thor.. ballistic missiles. **1964** *Ann. Reg. 1963* 1 Whitehall was still preoccupied with.. the phasing-in of British farm subsidies into the European system. **1964** G. L. COHEN *What's Wrong with Hospitals?* iii. 45 There exist new hospitals of greater efficiency than this one (for the Government's 'phasing'policy has entailed some incredible botching). **1967** *Boston Sunday Globe* 23 Apr. 20/4 The report recommends a gradual phasing out of these incinerators by 1985. **1969** *Daily Tel.* 18 Nov. 16 In Zambia the currency went decimal.. overnight without any phasing-in of coins over two years. **1971** *Guardian* 7 June 11/4 The French.. want to discuss the phasing out of sterling as a reserve currency. **1971** *Daily Tel.* 14 Aug. 13/7 The phasing of the new plants depends on the CEGB's planning timetable. **1977** *Air Mail* Spring 27/1 The Command is now coming to the end of another extensive re-equipment programme which will have seen the introduction of the Jaguar and the phasing out of the Lightning. **1977** *Time* 30 May 24/3 Carter said that he was 'committed to the phasing-in of a national health insurance system' and would send the legislation to Congress early next year.

phasiols: see PHASELS, FASELS.

‖**phasis** ('feɪzɪs, 'feɪsɪs). Pl. **phases** ('feɪziːz, 'feɪsiːz). [mod.L., a. Gr. φάσις appearance, phase, f. root φα-, φαν- of φαίν-ειν to show, appear.

As *phases* is the plural both of *phasis* and *phase*, it is often impossible to allot it to its proper singular. But all instances before 19th c. necessarily belong to *phasis*.]

1. Each of the aspects presented by the moon or any planetary body, according to the extent of its illumination. Now usually *phase* (PHASE *sb.* 1).

1660 BOYLE *New Exp. Phys. Mech.* xxxiii. 242 May vary according to.. the phases of the Moon. **1665-6** *Phil. Trans.* I. 69 This Author cannot conceive, how Saturn could.. have no difference in its Phasis. *a* **1677** HALE *Prim. Orig. Man.* IV. vi. 341 The Figure that discovers the Phasis of the Moon. **1727-41** CHAMBERS *Cycl.* s.v. *Moon*, The earth will present all the same phases to the moon, as the moon does to the earth. *Ibid.* s.v. *Phases*, To determine the phasis of an Eclipse for any given time. **1792** SIBLY *Occult Sci.* I. 138 One phasis contains ten degrees, and every sign three phases.

b. The first appearance of the new moon.

1880 *Ch. Times* XVIII. 855 The phasis or reappearance of the moon after her conjunction with the sun takes place in about eighteen hours. **1899** *Expositor* Nov. 363 After the phasis, i.e. after the first appearance of the moon's disk.

2. The aspect presented by a person or thing; appearance; *esp.* any one aspect of a thing of varying appearances; a state or stage of change or development. Now usually *phase* (PHASE *sb.* 2).

1665 GLANVILL *Scepsis Sci.* Address 20 The Phasies of the Universe. *c* **1800** H. K. WHITE *Time* 406 Through every phasis still 'Tis shadowy and deceitful. **1834** L. RITCHIE *Wand. by Seine* (1835) 4 This agreeable scene assumed a new phasis at every turning. **1836** SIR W. HAMILTON *Discuss.* (1852) 268 Some exercise, and consequently develope, perhaps, one faculty on a single phasis. **1862** CARLYLE *Fredk. Gt.* XI. i. (1872) IV. 15 A second and contemporaneous phasis of Friedrich's affairs. **1886** BLACKIE in *19th Cent.* Apr. 528 It is.. only a new phasis of an old thing.

phasitron ('feɪzɪtrɒn). *Electronics.* [f. PHAS(E + -I- + -TRON.] An electron tube suitable for phase-modulating a wave by large amounts, in which a pattern of beams emitted radially from a central cathode passes through a slotted cylindrical anode to a coaxial second anode, the pattern of beams being both rotated at a steady rate by a three-phase supply and modulated by a varying axial magnetic field that advances and retards the beams and thereby also the phase of the current at the second anode.

1946 *Electronics* Oct. 108/2 The carrier frequency.., after one stage of amplification, is used to drive a phase-splitting network to provide three-phase voltages for the input deflector grids of a 'Phasitron' tube. *Ibid.* 111/2 Since the Phasitron is modulated by a magnetic field, fields other than those produced by the audio input will cause noise modulation of the carrier. **1966** *McGraw-Hill Encycl. Sci. & Technol.* V. 514/1 An improvement in the phase-modulation method is provided by a special tube called the phasitron, which is capable of increasing the amount of phase shift.

phasm ('fæz(ə)m). [ad. L. *phasma*, a. Gr. φάσμα spectre, apparition, phantom, f. φάω I shine, give light, or φαίν-ειν to show, pass. to appear. At first in Gr.-L. form *phasma*, pl. *phasmata*.]

†**1.** An extraordinary appearance, esp. of brilliant light in the air; a meteor. *Obs.*

1635 SWAN *Spec. M.* v. §2 (1643) 82 Fierie [Meteors].. such as onely seem to burn, which are therefore called Phasmata. **1656** STANLEY *Hist. Philos.* VI. (1701) 253/2 Hence are also Phasmes, such as are called, gulfs, chasmes, bloody colours, and the like. **1686** GOAD *Celest. Bodies* II. xiv. 358 What have we to say of Phasmes and Apparitions in the Air?

2. Anything visionary or imaginary; a phantom, apparition. *Obs.* or *arch.*

1659 HAMMOND *On Ps.* lxxiii. 20 Splendid nothings, meer phasmes. **1665** SIR T. HERBERT *Trav.* (1677) 374 After a small space the lights.. extinguish, and.. the Phasma having assumed a bodily shape or other false representation accompanies her. **1667** *Decay Chr. Piety* v. ¶18 Such phasmes, such apparitions are most of those excellencies which men applaud in themselves. **1822** W. TENNANT *Thane Fife* II. 64 Flinging their phasms fantastically high.

‖**phasma** ('fæzmə). [See prec.]

1. Earlier form of PHASM, q.v.

2. *Zool.* A genus of cursorial orthopterous insects, typical of the family *Phasmidæ*, known from their appearance as Spectre-insects, or Walking-sticks. Hence **'phasmid**, any insect of the *Phasmidæ*.

1872 DOMETT *Ranolf* xiii. 209 A span-long Phasmid then he knew, Stretching its fore-limbs like a branching twig. **1888** BELT *Nat. in Nicaragua* xxi. 382 Another insect.. had a wonderful resemblance to a piece of moss... It is the larval stage of a species of *Phasma*. **1899** *Westm. Gaz.* 19 Apr. 2/2 Another singular-looking group are the Phasmidæ, which bear a remarkable resemblance to vegetable structures. Some.. look exactly like sticks or stems of grass; some might be mistaken for moss-grown twigs.

phasor ('feɪzər). *Electr.* [f. PHAS(E + *-or*, after VECTOR.] A line whose length and direction represent a complex electrical quantity with no spatial extension. Freq. *attrib.*

1944 *Proc. IRE* XXXII. 181/3 The instantaneous angular velocity of the voltage phasor may, in a special case of particular interest, be of the form $\omega_t = \omega + \Delta\omega \cos \Omega t$, where Ω is the angular velocity of the frequency deviation. **1958** W. D. COCKRELL *Industr. Electronics Hand-bk.* I. 249 The term 'phasor'is in the process of replacing the time-honored term 'vector'. **1962** F. DE LA C. CHARD *Power Syst. Engin.* i. 4 Phasor impedance can be shown on phasor diagrams and treated mathematically as a true complex quantity, but it differs from phasor voltage and current in the important respect that its value is invariable with time. **1973** M. R. WARD *Electr. Engin. Princ.* iii. 47. The phasors are drawn of length proportional to the r.m.s. **1975** R. F. W. COATES *Mod. Communication Syst.* i. 2 The phasor conveys the essential information regarding amplitude and phase of a fixed frequency sinusoid.

†**'phassachate.** *Obs.* [ad. mod.L. *phassachātēs*, f. Gr. φάσσα ring-dove, cushat + ἀχάτης agate.] The lead-coloured agate.

[**1753** CHAMBERS *Cycl. Supp.*, *Phassachates*, in the natural history of the antients, the name of a species of agate.] **1828** WEBSTER, *Phassachate*. Hence in mod. Dicts.

†**phat(e**, obs. erron. form of FAT *sb.*[1], vat.

1678 *Phil. Trans.* XII. 1063 As the Brine runs from the Salt after it is laded out of the Phats.

†**'phatagin.** *Obs.* Also **phataguin.** [f. Gr. φαττάγης a beast mentioned by Ælian, supposed to be a species of *Manis* or pangolin.] The Short-tailed or Five-fingered Pangolin (*Manisbrachyura*).

1774 GOLDSM. *Nat. Hist.* (1862) I. VI. iii. 469 Of this animal [the Pangolin] there is a variety which is called the Phatagin, much less than the former.

phatic ('fætɪk), *a.* [f. Gr. φατός spoken, or φατικ-ός assertory, f. φάναι to say: see -IC.] Of or pertaining to speech or verbal expression; *spec.* in ***phatic communion***, a term applied by B. Malinowski (see MALINOWSKIAN *a.*) to speech communication as used to establish social relationships rather than to impart information. Hence used *gen.* to denote formal or trivial verbal contact.

1923 B. MALINOWSKI in Ogden & Richards *Meaning of Meaning* 478 There can be no doubt that we have here a new type of linguistic use—*phatic communion* I am tempted to call it, actuated by the demon of terminological invention —a type of speech in which ties of union are created by a mere exchange of words. **1929** I. A. RICHARDS *Pract. Crit.* IV. i. 318 It would be an excellent thing if all the critical chitchat.. were universally recognised to be what it is, social gesture, 'phatic communion'. **1942** T. C. POLLOCK *Nature of Lit.* ix. 167 Phatic communion is one of the important ways in which men use language. **1954** W. LA BARRE *Human Animal* xv. 306 A surprisingly large part of every culture is merely the phatic sharing of common emotional burdens, and has no relevance at all to the outside world. **1959** *20th Cent.* Nov. 379 The magic words of phatic chat that fell from my falsely smiling lips. **1964** *Listener* 15 Oct. 603/3 How many of the youthful roarers of Parry's *Jerusalem* know that Blake's 'dark satanic mills'are not factories but churches?.. But the whole evening was warmly phatic, providing an image of British teenagers as less delinquent than jingoistic. **1971** J. SPENCER *Eng. Lang. W. Afr.* 29 Phatic expressions and greeting and leave-taking formulae never precisely match across cultural borders. **1972** *Scholarly Publishing* Apr. 282/2 The reader on a committee who blandly and thoughtlessly says, 'You really ought to get this study published' (in the same phatic way he says, 'Good morning'). **1976** *Archivum Linguisticum* VII. 86 Those illocutionary acts for which there might seem, on the face of it, to be no propositional content at all: 'greet' for example ..or 'phatic communion' of various sorts. **1977** *Time* 21 Mar. 67/1 Many Western ears will find it hard to tell whether Merwin is being vatic or phatic.

†**phaune**, obs. erron. form of FAWN *v.*[1]

1562 BULLEYN *Bulwark, Sick Men* 75b, Thei will.. phaune upon theim, waggyng their tailes.

pheal ('fiːəl). Also **pheale, pheeal.** [Imitative.] The cry of the jackal when hunting.

1879 F. POLLOK *Sport Brit. Burmah* I. 117 The peculiar cry of the jackal, which is generally called the 'pheale', so unlike the unearthly nightly howl of that animal. **1895** KIPLING *2nd Jungle Bk.* 176 It was what they call in the Jungle the Pheeal, a kind of shriek that the jackal gives when he is hunting behind a tiger.

phear(e, var. FERE *sb.*[1], companion, mate.

†**phearse**, var. FERS *Obs.*, the queen in chess.

a **1577** GASCOIGNE *Flowers* Wks. (1587) 45 Prepare hymselfe to saue his pawne, or else to leese his phearse.

pheasant ('fezənt). Forms: α. 3, 6 **fesaund**, (4 *pl.* **-auns**), 4-6 **-aunt, -e**, 4-7 **-ant**, 5 **-antt, -annte, -awnt, -awante, -auntt, fasand, feisaunt, feysaund, -aunt**, *pl.* **-aunce**, 5-6 **fesande, -aund(e, -ante**; 6 **faysanne, -sant, feisant, fezant, feasaunt, -e**, *Sc.* **fasiane**; 6-7 **feasant**, 7 **feasan**, 9 (*dial.*) **fezen, fezzan**. β. 4, 7-8 **phesant**, 6 **phesaunt, -ante**, 7 **phasi-, phais-, pheis-, pheys-, pheazant**, 6- **pheasant**. [ME. a. AF. *fesant, fesaunt*, OF. *fesan* (13th c. in Hatz.-Darm.), F. *faisan* = Pr. and Sp. *faisan*, It. *fagiano*:—L. *phāsiān-us*, Gr. φᾱσιᾱνός (sc. ὄρνις) the Phasian bird, sb. use of φᾱσιᾱν-ός of or pertaining to Φᾶσις, the Phasis, a river of Colchis, whence the pheasant is said to have spread into the west. The final *-t* is found also in OHG., MHG. *fasant* (also *fasân*, Ger., Da., Sw. *fasan*), Du. *fazant*, all of Romanic origin.]

1. a. The name of a well-known game-bird, *Phasianus colchicus*, long naturalized in Britain and other parts of Europe; by extension, applied to all the species of *Phasianus*, and to some related genera. (See 2.)

[**1059** *Inv. Sanctæ Crucis apud Waltham* (1861) 16 Unicuique canonico.. ii. perdices aut unus phasianus.]

α. **1299** *Durham Acc. Rolls* (Surtees) II. 498 In xxvj perdicibus et uno fesaund empt. *c* **1320** *Orfeo* 296 Of game they fonde grete haunt, Fesaunt, heron, and cormerant. *c* **1350** *Will. Palerne* 183 Wiþ fesauns & feldfares and oþer foules grete. *c* **1450** HOLLAND *Howlat* 158 In a mornyng, Come four Fasandis full fair. ?*c* **1475** *Sqr. lowe Degre* 322 With fesauntes fayre, theyr were no wane. *c* **1489** CAXTON *Sonnes of Aymon* iv. 124 Dyuerse pertryches and feysauntes. **1515** BARCLAY *Egloges* i, The crane, the fesant, the pecocke and curlewe. **1535** FISHER *Wks.* (1876) 370 It is a more goodly beinge.. of a goodly Fesaund. **1543** TRAHERON tr. *Vigo's Chirurg.* II. VI. vii. 75 Of chyckens, of hennes, of capones, of faysannes. **1588** KYD *Househ. Philos.* Wks. (1901) 246 For the desire of Feisants or Partrich. **1596** DALRYMPLE tr. *Leslie's Hist. Scot.* I. 39 Sumthing les than the fasiane. **1662** J. DAVIES tr. *Olearius' Voy. Ambass.* 321 Patridges and Feasants are common. **1697** *View Penal Laws*

122 None shall take Fesants or Partridges with Engins. **1877** *N.W. Linc. Gloss.*, *Fezzan*, a pheasant.

β. **1390** Gower *Conf.* III. 76 A Phesant cam before here yhe. **1530** Palsgr. 254/1 Phesaunt a byrde, *faisant*. **1603** Owen *Pembrokeshire* (1892) 268 The Phesant and Partridg. **1611** Shaks. *Wint. T.* iv. iv. 770, I haue no Pheazant, Cock nor Hen. **1635** Heywood *Hierarch.* i. Comm. 41 Figured like a Wood-hen or shee-pheasant. **1645** G. Daniel *Poems* Wks. (Grosart) II. 37 Fair as the Phasiant. *a* **1653** —— *Idyll., Landskip* 5 Fame, a peircht Phaisant and the Quest of Kings, Keepes her at Bay. **1750** Gray *Long Story* 48 A wicked imp..Bewitch'd the children of the peasants,..And suck'd the eggs, and kill'd the pheasants. **1873** 'Mrs. Alexander' *Wooing o't* xxvii, She enjoyed occasionally startling a pheasant as it rose with a sudden whirr.

b. Locally applied to various birds of other families, as the Ruffed Grouse (*Bonasa umbellata*) of the U.S.; the Mallee-bird (*Lipoa ocellata*) of Australia; in South Africa, applied to certain francolins, esp. *Francolinus capensis*, and other birds belonging to the family Phasianidæ.

1637 T. Morton *N. Eng. Canaan* (1883) 194 A kinde of fowles which are commonly called Pheisants, but whether they be pheysants or no, I will not take upon me to determine. **1766** W. Stork *Acc. East Florida* 51 The pheasant is in size like the European, its plumage like that of our partridge. **1785** G. Forster tr. *Sparrman's Voy. Cape Good Hope* I. iv. 153, I found here two new species of the genus of *tetrao*, one of which is called *partridge* and the other *pheasant*: either sort being nearly of the size of our partridges. **1805** Pike *Sources Mississ.* (1810) 31 Killed three prairie hens, and two pheasants. **1837** N. Polson *Subaltern's Sick Leave* v. 119 There is also a bird, general all over the Colony, styled 'pheasant', though about as like a pheasant of England as a Dutch Boer is to a Bond-street exquisite. **1855** Longf. *Hiaw.* v. 20 He..Heard the pheasant, Bena, drumming. **1883** C. F. Adams in *T. Morton's N. Eng. Canaan* 194 *note*, The Pheasant of Morton and other early writers has been supposed by ornithologists to be the Prairie Hen or Pinnated Grouse (*Cupidonia cupido*). **1893** Newton *Dict. Birds* 541 Known in England as the Mallee-bird, but to the colonists as Lowan and 'Native Pheasant'—the *Lipoa ocellata*. **1896** R. Wallace *Farming Industries Cape Colony* i. 15 No true pheasant..is found in Africa... Several species of francolins belonging to the same family..are known as pheasants. **1970** *Stand. Encycl. S. Afr.* II. 345/1 Most of the birds of the open veld are well camouflaged, for example the pheasants, partridges and quails, the bustards and korhaans.

c. The bird or its flesh as an article of food.

1377 Langl. *P. Pl.* B. xv. 455 He fedde hem with no venysoun ne fesauntes ybake. **14..** *Chaucer's Dreme* 354 The second apple..You nourishes in pleasaunce, Better than partridge or fesaunce. **1533** Elyot *Cast. Helthe* (1539) 29b, Fesaunt excedeth all fowles in swetenesse and holsomnesse. *c* **1645** Howell *Lett.* (1650) II. 114 One past makes up the prince and peasan, Though one eat roots, the other feasan. **1681** Dryden *Abs. & Achit.* ii. 472 To what would he on Quail and Pheasant swell That even on tripe and carrion could rebel?

2. *Ornith.* **a.** With defining words, applied to particular species of the genus *Phasianus* and allied *Phasianinæ* (as *Thaumalea*, *Euplocamus*), and *Pavoninæ* (as *Polyplectron*, *Argus*); also to some other birds in some way resembling the pheasant.

(Lady) **Amherst's p.**, of Szechuen, China, *Thaumalea amherstiæ*; **Argus p.**, *Argus giganteus*: see Argus 2; **bar-tailed p.** = *Reeve's p.*; **blood p.**, the Sanguine Partridge, *Ithaginis geoffroyi*; **cheer p.**, of N. India, *Phasianus wallichii*; **copper p.**, of Japan = *Sœmmering's p.*; **eared p.**, of China and Tibet, any species of the genus *Crossoptilon*; **Elliot's p.**, of China, *Phasianus ellioti*; **firebacked p.**, of the Malay archipelago, etc., *Euplocamus ignitus*; **gold** or **golden p.**, of China and Tibet, *Thaumalea picta* or *Chrysolophus pictus*; **lyre-** or **lyre-tailed p.**, of Australia = lyre-bird; **peacock-p.** or **pea-p.**, any species of *Polyplectron*, akin to *Pavo*; **reed-p.**, the bearded Titmouse, *Panurus panarmicus*; **Reeves's p.**, of N. China, *Phasianus* or *Syrmaticus reevesi*; **ring-necked p.**, of China, *Phasianus torquatus*; **Siamese p.**, *Euplocamus prælatus*; **silver p.**, of China, *Euplocamus nycthemerus*; **snow p.** = *eared p.*; **Sœmmering's p.**, of Japan, *Phasianus sœmmeringii*; **swamp p.**, the Pheasant Coucal of New South Wales, *Centropus phasianus*; **water p.**, the pheasant-tailed Jacana, *Hydrophasianus chirurgus*.

1819 *Pantologia* s.v. *Phasianus*, *Argus pheasant... Inhabits Chinese Tartary, and is as large as a turkey. **1743** G. Edwards *Hist. Birds* 69, I have three Sorts of *Chinese Cock Pheasants, and the Hens of two of them. **1894** Newton *Dict. Birds* 716 Two other species of Pheasant have been introduced to the coverts of England, *P. reevesi* from China, remarkable for its very long tail, white with black bars, and the *Copper Pheasant, *P. sœmmerringi*, from Japan. **1796** Sir G. L. Staunton *Macartney's Embassy China*, Plates, No. 13 The *Fire-backed Pheasant of Java. **1770** *Chron.* in *Ann. Reg.* 97 A *gold pheasant was sold for 20 guineas. **1819** *Pantologia* s.v. *Phasianus*, The *golden pheasant of China, the most beautiful of this genus. **1885** 'Wanderer' *Beauteous Terr.* 60 And have we no visions pleasant Of the playful *lyre-tailed pheasant? **1864** Jerdon *Birds of India* ii. II. 508 Near the Peafowl should be placed the genus *Polyplectron*, or *Pea-pheasants; often called Argus pheasants. **1770** *Chron.* in *Ann. Reg.* 98 A *peacock pheasant [was sold] for 40 guineas. **1871** Darwin *Desc. Man* ii. xiv. 137 The species and sub-species of Polyplectron..so far resemble this bird [peacock] that they are some-times called peacock-pheasants. **1831–48** *Reed pheasant [see reed *sb.*[1] 14]. **1894** Newton *Dict. Birds* 779 Reed-pheasant is the local name in East Anglia for the unhappily called Bearded Titmouse. **1834** *Proc. Zool. Soc.* ii. 34 A second male specimen of the *Reeve's Pheasant, *Phasianus veneratus*, Temm., had also been sent to the Menagerie by John Reeves, Esq. **1838** *Encycl. Brit.* (ed. 7) XVI. 610/1 The *ring-pheasant (*Ph. torquatus*), characterized by a more or less completed circle of white around the lower portion of the neck. **1819** *Pantologia* s.v. *Phasianus*, *Ringed pheasant. Collar white. **1838** *Encycl. Brit.* (ed. 7) XVI. 610/1 The gold and *silver pheasants of our aviaries. **1840** *Penny Cycl.* XVIII. 61/2 The rare and elegant *Sœmmering's Pheasant ..a native of Japan. **1847** Leichhardt *Jrnl.* iii. 60 A Centropus phasianellus (the *Swamp pheasant of Moreton Bay) was shot.

b. sea pheasant, †(*a*) the Turbot; (*b*) the Pintail Duck, *Dafila acuta*.

1633 Hart *Diet of Diseased* i. xxi. 89 Turbot..yeeldeth good and wholesome nourishment..and is called therefore by some the Sea-pheasant. **1674** Ray *Collect. Words, Water Fowl* 96 The Sea Pheasant: *Anas caudacuta*. **1837** *Penny Cycl.* IX. 180/1 *Dafila caudacuta*. The Pintail Duck. This is ..the Sea Pheasant, or Cracker, of Willughby.

3. *attrib.* and *Comb.*, as ***pheasant-colour***, ***-driving***, ***-mew***, ***-poult***, ***-rearer***, ***-shooting***; ***pheasant-plumed***, ***-tailed*** adjs.; **pheasant-cock**, the male pheasant; **pheasant-coucal**, **-cuckoo** = *swamp pheasant* (see 2); **pheasant-duck** = *sea pheasant* (b) (see 2b); **pheasant-finch**, *Astrilda undulata*, of Africa; **pheasant-grouse**, ? a species of Sharp-tailed Grouse, *Pediœcetes phasianellus*; **pheasant-hen**, the female pheasant; **pheasant-Malay**, a variety of the domestic fowl; **pheasant-wood** = partridge-wood 1.

?*c* **1325** in *Rel. Ant.* I. 168 Partrich, fesaunt hen, and *fesant cocke. *c* **1420** *Liber Cocorum* (1862) 36 Þo fesaunt kok, but not þo henne. **1626** Bacon *Sylva* §852 The Pea-cocke, and Phesant-Cocke, and Gold-Finch-Cocke, have glorious and fine Colours. **1849** D. J. Browne *Amer. Poultry Yd.* (1855) 42 The beauty of the breed is with the hens, which are of a *pheasant-color in all parts of the body, with a velvety-black neck. **1873** *Pheasant Coucal [see coucal]. **1908** E. J. Banfield *Confessions of Beachcomber* i. iii. 103 The swamp pheasant, or pheasant coucal..is also an early bird. **1935** [see coucal]. **1944** A. Russell *Bush Ways* ii. 17 The cuckoos, with the single exception of the pheasant-coucal, build no nests of their own. **1965** *Austral. Encycl.* VII. 90/2 Pheasant, a name formerly applied in Australia to the lyrebird and still in general use for the pheasant-coucal or swamp pheasant (*Centropus phasianinus*). **1846** J. L. Stokes *Discov. Australia* I. vi. 125, I enjoyed some very fair sport; especially with the *pheasant-cuckoo. **1892** Greener *Breech-Loader* 224 *Pheasant-driving is pursued..for the object of obtaining sporting shots. **1871** Darwin *Desc. Man* ii. xiv. 101 The black-cock, capercailzie, *pheasant-grouse ..are, as is believed, polygamists. ?*c* **1325** *Fesaunt hen [see *pheasant cock*]. **1601** Holland *Pliny* x. xlviii. I. 296 The Fesant hens of Colchis. **1849** D. J. Browne *Amer. Poultry Yd.* (1855) 28 The cross between the *pheasant-Malay and the Spanish produces a particularly handsome fowl. **1829** *Sporting Mag.* XXIII. 392 A county..which..has degenerated..into a mere hare-warren and *pheasant-mew. **1849** D. J. Browne *Amer. Poultry Yd.* (1855) 41 The dark *pheasant-plumed breed, both of Bantams and common poultry. **1575** E. Hake *Newes out of Powles Ch.-yd.* iv. Dij b, Fat *Pheasaunt Powt, and Plouer base for them that after come. **1694** Motteux *Rabelais* iv. lix. (1737) 243 Phesants, and Phesant poots. **1819** *Pantologia*, *Pheasant-pouts*, young pheasants. **1889** *Cent. Dict.* s.v. *Jacana*, The *pheasant-tailed jacana of India, *Hydrophasianus chirurgus*..has a very long tail. **1884** Miller *Plant-n.*, **Pheasant-wood*, another name for Partridge-wood.

pheasant-eye: see pheasant's eye 3.

pheasant-eyed (ˈfɛzəntˈaɪd), *a.* [Parasynthetic f. *pheasant-eye* + -ed[2].] Marked like the eye of the pheasant: applied to certain flowers.

1733 Miller *Gard. Dict.* s.v. *Caryophillus*, The Damask Pink,..Pheasant's ey'd Pink. **1754** *Catal. Seeds* in *Fam. Rose Kilravock* (Spalding Cl.) 428 Annuals to be sowed in the open ground in the spring..Columbine. Sea ragwort. Pheasant-eyed Pink [etc.]. **1899** *Daily News* 19 May 5/2 The ..pheasant-eyed narcissus.

pheasantry (ˈfɛzəntrɪ). [f. pheasant + -ry.] A place where pheasants are reared or kept.

1725 *Lond. Gaz.* No. 6360/2 His Majesty's Pheasantry in Bushy-Park. **1856** W. White *On Foot thro' Tyrol* xiv. 300 There are pleasant woods behind the palace, and a pheasantry.

pheasant's eye. A name of certain plants: cf. pheasant-eyed.

1. The common name of plants of the genus *Adonis*, esp. *A. autumnalis*: = Adonis 2.

1733 Miller *Gard. Dict.*, *Adonis*, or *Flos Adonis*, Bird's-Eye, or Pheasant's-Eye. **1854** S. Thomson *Wild Fl.* iii. (ed. 4) 209 The pheasant's eye,..with its bright scarlet flowers.

2. The common white Narcissus (*N. poeticus*).

1872 *Routledge's Ev. Boy's Ann.* May 362/2 The Pheasant's eye (*Narcissus poeticus*). **1898** *Westm. Gaz.* 30 Aug. 2/1 The 'pheasant's eye'narcissus grows wild upon these vine-covered hill-sides.

3. (Also **pheasant-eye**, **pheasant's eye pink**): the ring-flowered variety of the Garden Pink (*Dianthus plumarius* var. *annulatus*).

1753 Chambers *Cycl. Supp.*, App., Pheasant's-eye Pink. **1824** Loudon *Encycl. Gard.* (ed. 2) 860 The pink is considered..to have proceeded from *D. deltoides*,..and the pheasant-eye pinks from *D. plumarius*. **1884** Miller *Plant-n.*, Pink, Pheasant's-eye.

pheasant-shell. A shell of the gastropod genus *Phasianella*, of the Australian seas; named from the brilliantly coloured and polished surface.

pheal, variant of pheal.

pheer, variant of fere *sb.*[1], companion, mate.

pheering, var. feering *vbl. sb.*, marking out of land for ploughing.

1812 Souter *Agric. Surv. Banffs.* App. 4 (Jam.) There ought to be a small interstice left between the two furrows, to facilitate the next pheering. **1896** J. Lumsden *Poems* 23 It stands as plain's a pheerin pole.

pheese, pheeze, obs. forms of feeze *sb.*

pheidiac, -an: see phid-.

pheirs, var. phairs, obs. Sc. f. farce *sb.*[2]

†**pheldifare**, obs. or dial. form of fieldfare.

1594 Barnfield *Affect. Sheph.* ii. x, Pit-falls for the Larke and Pheldifare.

phellandrene (fɛˈlændriːn). *Chem.* [f. Bot. L. *Phellandr(ium* + -ene.] A terpene occurring in the seeds of the Water Hemlock, *Phellandrium aquaticum*, and other plants.

1893 *Syd. Soc. Lex.*, *Phellandrene*, name given by Pisci to a terpene occurring in Elemi, in the seeds of *Phellandrium aquaticum* [etc.]. **1898** *Rev. Brit. Pharm.* 50.

phellem (ˈfɛləm). *Bot.* [a. G. *phellem* (F. von Höhnel 1877, in *Sitzungsber. Math.-Naturw. Classe K. Akad. Wissenschaften (Wien)* LXXVI. 600), f. Gr. *φελλ-ός* cork + *-em* as in *phloem*.] = cork *sb.*[1] 5.

1887 W. Hillhouse tr. *Strasburger's Handbk. Pract. Bot.* xiv. 153 A meniscus..produces externally colourless cells, which become rounded..and internally cork-cells, or Phellem. **1925** Eames & MacDaniels *Introd. Plant Anat.* ix. 206 The cells constituting phellem, commonly known as cork cells, are for the most part uniform in shape. **1953** K. Esau *Plant Anat.* xiv. 327 The type of phellem used for bottle cork consists of thin-walled, air-filled cells. **1971** A. Cronquist *Introd. Bot.* (ed. 2) xxiv. 455/2 Cork is also called phellem.

phello- (fɛləʊ), combining form of Gr. *φελλός* cork. **ˈphelloderm** *Bot.* [Gr. *δέρμα* skin], a layer of parenchymatous cells containing chlorophyll, formed in the stems of some plants from the inner cells of the phellogen; hence **phelloˈdermal** *a.*, of or pertaining to the phelloderm. **ˈphellogen** *Bot.* [see -gen], the layer of meristematic cells from which the cork-cells are formed, the cork-cambium; so **phellogeˈnetic** *a.*, producing cork, of the nature of phellogen; **phelloˈgenic** *a.*, of the nature of or pertaining to phellogen.

1875 Bennett & Dyer *Sachs' Bot.* 90–1 In some cases the phellogen of the periderm gives rise not only to cork-cells.. but..[to] permanent parenchyma-cells containing chlorophyll..which Sanio terms the suberous cortical layer (Phelloderm)... In such cases the phellogen lies between the periderm and the phelloderm, the outer of its daughter-cells producing cork-cells, the inner phelloderm. **1884** Bower & Scott *De Bary's Phaner.* 545 The periderm consists of the phellogenetic meristem [= phellogen], and the tissues..derived from it, which..include a..stratum of Cork-cells..to which usually, but not always, phellogenic or peridermal parenchyma, the Phelloderm of Sanio, is added. *Ibid.* 549 The number of the phellodermal layers..is in most species very small, in comparison with the cork-layers which appear in the same space of time.

phelloˈplastic. [See prec. and plastic.] A cork model or figure; the art of cutting figures or models in cork (also **phelloˈplastics**).

1802 W. Taylor *Let.* 26 July in Robberds *Mem.* I. 416 In print, in copper-plate, in painting or in fello-plastic (you have seen the cork-model of Rome). **1848** Richter *Levana* 13 An intellectual imitation in cork (a *phelloplastic*, according to Böttiger's retranslation into Greek). **1864** Webster, *Phelloplastics*, the art of forming models in cork.

pheme (fiːm). [ad. Gr. *φήμη* words, speech.] A term used by the American philosopher, C. S. Peirce (1839–1914), for words in an utterance as they make up a grammatical unit in language, contrasted with words used in speech to convey sense (see rheme, seme).

1906 C. S. Peirce in *Monist* XVI. 506 By a *Pheme* I mean a Sign which is equivalent to a grammatical sentence, whether it be Interrogative, Imperative, or Assertory... Such a Sign is intended to have some sort of compulsive effect on the interpreter of it. **1923** Ogden & Richards *Meaning of Meaning* 438 We are introduced to Semes, Phemes, and Delomes. **1931** G. Stern *Meaning & Change of Meaning* iii. 31 Meaning is a property peculiar not only to what we traditionally call words, but also to parts of words, *e.g.* the genitive ending in *man's*... As a comprehensive term ..Vendryes..has proposed *sémantème*, and C. S. Peirce, quoted by Ogden-Richards..has *seme* and *pheme*. **1955** J. L. Austin *How to do Things with Words* (1962) viii. 97 The same pheme (token of the same type) may be used on different occasions of utterance with a different sense or reference, and so be a different rheme... The pheme is a unit of *language*... But the rheme is a unit of *speech*.

phememe (ˈfiːmiːm). *Linguistics.* [f. prec.: see -eme.] A term used by Leonard Bloomfield for the smallest linguistic unit.

1933 L. Bloomfield *Language* xvi. 264 The parallelism of lexical and grammatical features can be exhibited in a set of terms like the following: (1) Smallest and meaningless unit of linguistic signaling: *phememe*; (a) lexical: *phoneme*; (b) grammatical: *taxeme*. **1936** J. R. Kantor *Objective Psychol. Gram.* xi. 149 The reader will notice the three hierarchical steps or classes: phememe, glosseme, and linguistic form. **1955** J. L. Austin *How to do Things with Words* (1962) vii. 92 A 'pheme' (as distinct from the phememe of linguistic theory).

phen-, pheno-, formative element in *Chem.*, (for *phæn(o-)* f. Gr. φαινο- shining, φαίν-ειν to bring to light, cause to appear, show; φαίν-εσθαι to come to light, appear. First used by the French chemist Laurent, 1841, in 'hydrate de phényle' and 'acide phénique', names which he applied to the substance subsequently called PHENOL. These names referred to the fact that the substance was a coal-tar product, arising from the manufacture of *illuminating* gas. Hence *phen-*, *pheno-* was gradually used as the basis of the names of all the bodies derived from benzene (i.e. phenyl hydride, which French chemists proposed to call *phène*). See PHENE, PHENIC, PHENOCOLL, PHENOL, etc. below; also the following:

phenacetin (fɪˈnæsɪtɪn), the acetyl derivative of phenetidin, the ethylic ether of paramidophenol, hence called also *para-acet-phenidin*, $C_6H_4{\cdot}OC_2H_5{\cdot}NH(CH_3CO)$; it occurs in white shining crystals, without taste or odour, and is used as an antipyretic. †**phenamide** (ˈfɛnəmaɪd), a synonym of phenylamide or aniline. †**pheˈnamylol**: see quot. **pheˈnanthraquiˌnone**, a substance, $(C_6H_4{\cdot}CO)_2$, related to phenanthrene, crystallizing in shining orange yellow needles. **pheˈnanthrene**, a solid hydrocarbon, $(C_6H_4{\cdot}CH)_2$, prepared from crude anthracene (with which it is isomeric), crystallizing in colourless shining laminæ. **ˈphenazine**, $C_6H_4{\cdot}N_2{\cdot}C_6H_4$, crystallizing in long yellowish needles. **ˈphenazon**, a febrifuge prepared from coal-tar, called also antipyrin. **pheˈnetidin**, the ethyl derivative of amidophenol. **ˈphenetole** (also -OL) [a. G. *phenetol* (A. Cahours 1850, in *Ann. d. Chem. u. Pharm.* LXXIV. 314)], ethyl phenyl ether, or phenate of ethyl, $C_2H_5{\cdot}OC_6H_5$, a volatile aromatic-smelling liquid; hence *phenetole red* = COCCININ, $C_{14}H_{12}O_3$.

1889 *Pall Mall G.* 29 Apr. 3/1 The coal-tar 'analgesic' ..*Phenacetin, a..white powder, which has direct action on ..neuralgia, and which presumably is a narcotic. **1891** *Lancet* 3 Oct. 771. **1896** *Allbutt's Syst. Med.* I. 242 The newer analgesics—antipyrin, antifebrin, and phenacetin. **1857** MILLER *Elem. Chem.* III. 570 Phenate of amyl, *Phenamylole. **1881** *Athenæum* 26 Mar. 433/1 On the Action of Aldehydes on *Phenanthraquinone in presence of Ammonia. **1882** *Ibid.* 16 Dec. 818/2 A new acid and a new compound,..the desoxybenzoin of *phenanthrene. **1899** *Allbutt's Syst. Med.* VII. 751 Some of the synthetic analgesics—*phenazone or phenacetin—are of value. **1865** MANSFIELD *Salts* 377 The probability..is enhanced by the production by the same chemist of '*Phenetidine', an epibase containing C_2H_2 more than Anisidine. **1899** CAGNEY tr. *Jaksch's Clin. Diagn.* vii. (ed. 4) 401 The presence of phenetidin may be shown by changing it [the urine] into its diazo compound. **1850** *Q. Jrnl. Chem. Soc.* III. 78 *Phenetol is a colourless, very mobile liquid, lighter than water; and having an agreeable, aromatic odour. **1857** MILLER *Elem. Chem.* III. 570 Phenate of ethyl, or Phenetole. **1972** *Materials & Technol.* IV. 306 Reaction [of phenol] with dimethyl or diethyl sulphate in a weakly alkaline solution gives anisole,..or phenetole, $C_6H_5OC_2H_5$ respectively.

phenacaine (ˈfɛnəkeɪn). *Pharm.* Formerly also **phenocain(e**. [f. PHEN- + *-a* + *-caine* after COCAINE.] Holocaine.

1907 *Brit. Pharmaceutical Codex* 260 Many synthetic substitutes for cocaine have been suggested for use as local anæsthetics, including..phenacaine (Holocaine). **1911** *Ibid.* 312 Phenocaine. **1920** MARTINDALE & WESTCOTT *Extra Pharmacopœia* (ed. 17) I. 331 Holocain Hydrochloride. ..*Syn.* Phenocain. **1946** *Brit. Jrnl. Pharmacol.* I. 99 Pethidine, phenacaine and papaverine possess both aromatic and basic groups and have a quinidine-like action. **1968** [see HOLOCAINE].

phenacite (ˈfɛnəsaɪt) *Min.* -kite (-kaɪt). [Named, 1833, f. Gr. φέναξ, φένακ-α cheat (on account of its having been mistaken for quartz) + -ITE[1].] A silicate of glucinum, occurring in quartz-like transparent or translucent crystals, colourless, wine-yellow, or brown.

1834 *Phil. Mag.* Ser. III. V. 102 Phenakite, a new mineral from the Ural. **1861** H. W. BRISTOW *Gloss. Min.* 282 Phenacite..transparent to opaque. **1879** LONGF. in *Life* (1891) III. 304 The precious stones in the 'Iron Pen' are a white Phenacite from Siberia, a yellow zircon from Ceylon, and a red Tourmaline from Maine. **1881** *Nature* XXIV. 89/2 The rare mineral phenakite..sometimes used as a gem.

phenagle, var. FINAGLE *v.*

phenakism (ˈfɛnəkɪz(ə)m). *rare.* [ad. Gr. φενακισμός deception, f. φενακίζειν: see next.] Deception, cheating, trickery; equivocation.

1818-60 WHATELY *Commpl. Bk.* (1864) 135 At least they regard phenakism as a peccadillo. *Ibid.* 170 Who avow and openly defend the system of what is called, in modern phraseology, phenakism, double-doctrine, economy, or reserve.

phenakistoscope (fɛnəˈkɪstəskəʊp). Also **phenakistiscope**. [mod. f. Gr. φενακιστ-ής cheat, impostor, f. φενακίζ-ειν to cheat, trick + -SCOPE.] A scientific toy, consisting of a disk with figures upon it arranged radially, representing a moving object in successive positions; on turning it round rapidly, and viewing the figures through a fixed slit (or their reflexions in a mirror through radial slits in the disk itself), the persistence of the successive visual images produces the impression of actual motion. Hence **phenakistoˈscopic** *a.*, resembling or reminiscent of a phenakistoscope.

1834 *Edin. Rev.* LIX. 160 The ingenious improver of that beautiful instrument called the Phenakistoscope. **1838** BREWSTER in *Encycl. Brit.* (ed. 7) XVI. 512/2 The phenakistoscope..was, we believe originally invented by Dr. Roget, and improved by M. Plateau, at Brussels, and Mr. Faraday. **1882** *Life J. C. Maxwell* ii. 36 A scientific toy ..called by the names phenakistoscope, stroboscope or magic disc. **1934** V. M. YEATES *Winged Victory* 162 It was gone, and beyond a phenakistoscopic veil he saw the flying moons and spheres caught in webs and dragged away. **1955** *Times* 18 July 3/4 The exhibition takes us back to beyond the origins of the cinema proper, to Plateau's Phénakistiscope, in which pictures, mounted on the inside of a circular revolving drum and viewed through slits, first created the illusion of continuous movement. **1961** *Glasgow Herald* 13 July 6/4 The thaumatrope, the phenakistiscope, the zoetrope, and the tachyscope..are the steps by which the modern cinema climbed to its present perfection. **1978** *Radio Times* 4-10 Mar. 4/4 A phenakistoscope and other Victorian toys.

phenanthroline (fɪˈnænθrəliːn). *Chem.* [ad. G. *phenanthrolin* (Z. H. Skraup 1882, in *Ber. d. Deut. Chem. Ges.* XV. 895), f. *phenanthr-en* phenanthrene (s.v. PHEN-, PHENO-) + *chinoline* CHINOLINE, QUINOLINE.] An organic compound, $C_{12}H_8N_2$, whose molecule is a tricyclic phenanthrene ring system in which one CH group in each of the two outer rings is replaced by a nitrogen atom, and the *ortho* isomer of which is used esp. as an indicator for iron, with which it forms a red-orange complex.

1882 *Jrnl. Chem. Soc.* XLII. 1111 Phenanthroline,.. obtained by the action of glycerol and sulphuric acid on metadiamidobenzene, crystallises in transparent plates (m.p. 79°). **1909** *Chem. Abstr.* III. 2571 The terms *o-*, *m-* and *p-phenanthroline* are suggested in place of isophenanthroline, phenanthroline and pseudophenanthroline. **1935** *Chem. Rev.* XVI. 113 The development of the use of *o*-phenanthroline-ferrous complex..constitutes one of the most outstanding advances of recent years in the field of analytical chemistry. Its application to many new procedures of analytical chemistry immediately followed. **1966** *McGraw-Hill Encycl. Sci. & Technol.* IV. 273/1 Certain organic compounds, such as 1,10-phenanthroline, also catalyze the drying of oils and have been used for this purpose. **1978** *Sci. Amer.* July 120/2 After the bromine color disappears mix in one milliliter of ·025-molar phenanthroline ferrous sulfate (a dye sometimes called ferroin).

phenate: see under PHENIC.

phencyclidine (fɛnˈsaɪklɪdiːn). *Pharm.* [f. PHEN- + CYCL(O- + PIPER)IDINE, constituent parts of the systematic name.] A powerful analgesic and anæsthetic whose use is now chiefly restricted to veterinary medicine on account of its hallucinogenic effects; 1-(1-phenylcyclohexyl)piperidine hydrochloride, $C_{17}H_{25}N.HCl$. Abbrev. PCP.

1959 *Antibiotic Med.* VI. 84 Phencyclidine, when given to patients with anxiety symptoms, appeared to be most effective in mild to moderately severe reactions. **1963** *Lancet* 16 Feb. 392/2 Phencyclidine was used to relieve the pain of multiple rib fractures in a 57-year-old male who had bronchitis. **1973** *Daily Tel.* 20 Dec. 3 A new drug called 'angel dust' which causes people to believe they have been reduced to the size of Tom Thumb is to be brought to the attention of the authorities... The drug, known as phencyclidine or PCP, was not covered by the Dangerous Drugs Act. **1974** M. C. GERALD *Pharmacol.* xvii. 330 Phencyclidine (Sernyl) is employed therapeutically as a veterinary anesthetic agent. *Ibid.*, Compounds purported to be mescaline, LSD, psilocybin, and THC..have often been chemically identified as phencyclidine. **1979** *Tucson (Arizona) Citizen* 20 Sept. 7c/1 Seven men have been charged by a federal grand jury with conspiracy to manufacture and distribute phencyclidine, and for possession of the drug.

†**phene** (fiːn). *Chem. Obs.* [a. F. *phène*: see PHEN-.] An early name proposed for BENZENE. So **ˈphenene**, in same sense; **ˈphenenyl**, the radical C_6H_3 of phenylene compounds.

1857 MILLER *Elem. Chem.* III. 564 Benzole; Benzine, or Phene. **1866** ODLING *Anim. Chem.* 35 Here..we have the series of aromatic hydrocarbons:—C_6H_6 Phenene, C_7H_8 Benzoene. *Ibid.* 94 Both phenene C_6H_6, and phenol or carbolic acid C_6H_6O, are producible by transmitting the vapour of alcohol or fusel oil through red-hot tubes.

phenelzine (fəˈnɛlziːn). *Pharm.* [f. the systematic name 2-*phene*thyl*hydrazine*, f. PHEN- + ETHYL + HYDRAZINE.] A monoamine oxidase inhibitor that is used as an anti-depressant, usu. in the form of the sulphate, $C_6H_5CH_2CH_2NHNH_2.H_2SO_4$, a white crystalline solid with a pungent odour.

1959 *Amer. Jrnl. Psychiatry* CXVI. 64/1 Twenty-five patients with depression who entered this hospital on the female service were assigned alternately to Phenelzine and ECT. **1961** *Lancet* 16 Sept. 622/2 A housewife, aged 56, with depression, had for five months been taking phenelzine ..when she suddenly got pruritis, pain behind the eyes, and anorexia, and noticed that she was becoming yellow. **1965** [see PARNATE]. **1971** G. G. LUCE *Body Time* iii. 85 Other drugs sometimes used to combat depression, such as phenelzine, have an opposite effect and shorten the sleep cycle.

Phenergan (ˈfɛnəgən). *Pharm.* Also **phenergan**. A proprietary name for promethazine.

1947 (Sept. 16) [registered in Canada as a trade mark, no. 112/28759]. **1948** *Canad. Med. Assoc. Jrnl.* LIX. 322/2 The name phenergan (3,277 R.P.) has been given to the N-dimethylaminopropyl derivative of phenothiazine. **1949** *Trade Marks Jrnl.* 8 June 499/1 Phenergan... Pharmaceutical preparations consisting of or containing benzine or its derivatives for human use and veterinary use. May & Baker Limited, Dagenham, Essex; manufacturing chemists. **1956** *Jrnl. Amer. Med. Assoc.* 3 Mar. 755/1 From these studies, several drugs have emerged that provide significant protection against motion sickness. These.. include..promethazine (Phenergan) hydrochloride. **1958** A. HUXLEY *Let.* 4 Jan. (1969) 841 He has been experimenting with..a mixture of aspirin, chlorpromazine and phenergen [*sic*] compounded a year or so ago by some French physicians and used for producing a form of hibernation. **1977** *Detroit Free Press* 11 Dec. 18-B/2 It takes down about 10 percent of the cold-remedy business with its Dristan and Phenergan lines.

phenethicillin (fəˌnɛθɪˈsɪlɪn). *Pharm.* [f. PHEN- + ETH(YL + PEN)ICILLIN.] The compound 6-(2-phenoxypropionamido)penicillanic acid, $C_{17}H_{20}N_2O_5S$, which is a semi-synthetic penicillin active when given by mouth and is usu. employed in the form of the white, crystalline, potassium salt.

1960 *Brit. Med. Jrnl.* 1 Oct. 994/2 When phenethicillin (6-(α-phenoxypropionamido)penicillanic acid) was marketed as 'broxil', it was claimed that this preparation would give blood levels at least equal to those after intramuscular injection of corresponding doses of penicillin G. **1965** G. T. STEWART *Penicillin Group of Drugs* iii. 25 In scientific medical circles, the advent of phenethicillin as the first offspring of the new biosyntheses was something of an anticlimax. *Ibid.* iv. 34 As prepared at present, phenethicillin is a racemic mixture containing 55-75% of the L-isomer and 25-45% of the D-isomer. **1970** *Daily Tel.* 23 Oct. 13/3 The first semi-synthetic penicillin, phenethicillin, introduced in 1959, became widely used for the infections treated by family doctors.

phenetic (fəˈnɛtɪk), *a. Taxonomy.* [f. Gr. φαίν-ειν to appear + *-etic* as in PHYLETIC *a.*] (See quot. 1960.) So **pheˈnetically** *adv.*, showing similar characteristics; **pheˈneticism**, taxonomy that stresses classifications based on obvious resemblances; **pheˈneticist**, a taxonomist using classifications of this type.

1960 CAIN & HARRISON in *Proc. Zool. Soc.* CXXXV. 3 Following a suggestion made by Mr. H. K. Pusey, we shall refer to the arrangement by overall similarity, based on all available characters without any weighting as phenetic, since it employs all observable characters (including of course genetic data when available). *Ibid.*, When a good fossil record is available..the whole evolutionary dendrite can be worked out for that group simply by putting those forms together that are most alike phenetically. **1963** DAVIS & HEYWOOD *Princ. Angiosperm Taxon.* iv. 112 The separation of phenetic and phylogenetic classifications is not generally accepted today. **1968** *Nature* 9 Nov. 547/1 The school of the pheneticists, one of the branches of numerical taxonomy. They deliberately set out to 'make' taxa on the basis of calculated overall similarity. *Ibid.*, The phenetic approach has been most useful when applied to groups with immature classifications..and to those with numerous non-redundant characters. **1971** *Virology* XLV. 357/2 To be useful, a classification of viruses..must be based on many characters, not few... This will give a classification based on the general resemblance of the phenotypic characters of the viruses (a 'phenetic classification'). **1972** *Nature* 21 Apr. 412/2 Extreme pheneticism is equally criticized.

phenetidin, phenetol: see PHEN-.

phenformin (fɛnˈfɔːmɪn). *Pharm.* [f. PHEN- + FORM(ALDEHYDE + IMINO(-), constituent parts of the alternative name *phen*ethyl*form*amidinyl*imino*urea.] A white crystalline solid, 1-phenethylbiguanide hydrochloride, $C_{10}H_{15}N_5$ .HCl, which is used in the oral treatment of diabetes. Also *phenformin hydrochloride*.

1959 *Canad. Med. Assoc. Jrnl.* LXXX. 773/1 In 1957 Ungar, Freedman and Shapiro reported that hypoglycæmic properties had been discovered in a synthetic diguanide compound, N′-β-phenethylformaminyliminourea hydrochloride, subsequently designated DB1 or phenformin. **1960** [see BIGUANIDE]. **1961** *Lancet* 9 Sept. 566/1 Phenformin is clearly a potent hypoglycæmic substance effective in most diabetics we have tested. **1967** *Martindale's Extra Pharmacopoeia* (ed. 25) 675/2 Phenformin hydrochloride is contra-indicated in acidosis, coma, infections, [etc.]. **1974** M. C. GERALD *Pharmacol.* xxv. 441 It appears that phenformin may act by accelerating the intracellular oxidation of glucose, a process which is depressed in the absence of insulin. Phenformin is used alone for the treatment of maturity-onset diabetes and in combination with insulin in juvenile diabetes. **1977** *Lancet* 22 Jan. 191/2 Metformin is replacing phenformin as the biguanide of choice in the treatment of obese maturity-onset diabetics because of the association between phenformin therapy and lacticacidosis.

phengite ('fɛndʒaɪt). *Min.* Also 8 **fengite**; and in Gr.-L. form **phengites** (fɛn'dʒaɪtiːz), also corruptly **fingites**. [ad. L. *phengītēs*, a. Gr. φεγγίτης phengite, selenite, or crystallized gypsum, f. φέγγο-ς light, lustre, moonlight: see -ITE[1] 2 b.]

1. A transparent or translucent kind of stone known to the ancients; 'probably crystallized gypsum or modern selenite' (Dana *Min.* (1868) 640).

1601 HOLLAND *Pliny* XXXVI. xxii. II. 592 In which regard (for that it is so resplendent) it hath found a name to be called Phengites: of this stone the said Emperour [Nero] caused the Temple of Fortune to be built called Seia. **1750** tr. *Leonardus' Mirr. Stones* 103 Fingites, is of a white Colour, hard as Marble, and transparent like Alabaster. **1776** R. CHANDLER *Trav. Greece* lxiii, The gallery is illuminated with pieces of the transparent marble called Phengites, fixed in the wall in square compartments, and shedding a yellow light. **1828** WEBSTER, *Phengite*, a beautiful species of alabaster, superior in brightness to most marbles.

2. A modern name for muscovite, a strongly doubly-refractive species of mica.

1868 DANA *Min.* Index, Phengite, 309. [*Ibid.* 309 Muscovite. Common Mica; Potash Mica.. Phengit *v. Kob.* Taf., 62, 1853.] **1882** OGILVIE, *Phengite*, same as *Muscovite*.

phenic ('fiːnɪk, 'fɛnɪk), *a. Chem.* [f. PHENE + -IC; in F. *phénique* (Laurent 1841).] Pertaining or related to phenyl or to benzene; = PHENYLIC. ***phenic acid***, another name of PHENOL or carbolic acid. Its salts are '**phenates**.

1852 *Chemical Gaz.* X. 136 St. Evre suspected a connexion between his acid and phenic acid (phenole, phenylous acid), $C^{12}H^6O^2$. **1857** MILLER *Elem. Chem.* III. 564 Benzole.. belongs to a group called the phenic series. *Ibid.* 570 Phenic, or carbolic acid.. Phenate of methyl, or anisole. **1866** ROSCOE *Elem. Chem.* xxxix. 336 Phenol.. dissolves in the alkalies, forming a phenate. **1876** HARLEY *Mat. Med.* (ed. 6) 354 It is the first of the Phenic series. **1884** *Health Exhib. Catal.* 96/1 Phenate of Soda solution. An antiseptic application for burns, scalds, &c.

phenicine, -in ('fɛnɪsaɪn, -ɪn). *Chem.* [Etymologically *phœnicin(e*, f. Gr. φοῖνιξ a purple-red, purple, or crimson, lit. a Phœnician (in reference to Tyrian purple) + -IN.] A colouring matter produced by the action of nitro-sulphuric acid on phenylic alcohol; indigo carmine.

1826 HENRY *Elem. Chem.* II. x. 282 From the property, possessed by this substance, of becoming purple coloured on the addition of certain salts, Mr. Crum terms it phenecin. **1838** T. THOMSON *Chem. Org. Bodies* 379 Acids have no effect in preventing the precipitation of phenicin by salts. **1866–77** WATTS *Dict. Chem.* IV. 388 Phenicine.. dyes silk and wool without the intervention of a mordant.

phenindione (fɛnɪn'daɪəʊn). *Pharm.* [f. PHEN- + IN(DO-[2] + -DIONE.] A white crystalline solid, 2-phenylindan-1,3-dione, $C_{15}H_{10}O_2$, which is a vitamin K analogue used as an anticoagulant, esp. in the treatment of thrombosis.

1955 *Proc. Soc. Exper. Biol. & Med.* LXXXIX. 81/1 In an investigation of the effect of phenindione (PID) on the coagulation mechanism.., it was discovered that patients who had received this anticoagulant for more than about 30 days developed a distinctly prolonged glass clotting time. **1962** *Lancet* 13 Jan. 104/2 Treatment with heparin and phenindione was begun, but after six hours the patient suddenly became unconscious and pulseless, though slow voluntary respirations persisted. **1974** R. H. HAMMER in W. O. Foye *Princ. Med. Chem.* xviii. 409/1 Phenindione is the most commonly used 1,3-indandione anticoagulant... The chief disadvantage of phenindione is its toxic side effects.

pheniprazine (fə'nɪprəziːn). *Pharm.* [f. PHEN- + I(SO- + PR(OPYL + HYDR)AZINE.] The compound 1-phenyl-2-hydrazinopropane, $C_9H_{14}N_2$, which was formerly used (as the hydrochloride) for the treatment of depression, angina, and hypertension.

1960 *Jrnl. Amer. Med. Assoc.* 2 Apr. 1554/1 Mackinnon and co-workers used pheniprazine to treat a series of 28 patients with the anginal syndrome. **1961** *Lancet* 16 Sept. 622/2 It seems probable that pheniprazine was the cause of the jaundice; the total dose was 560 mg. given over sixty days. **1971** L. E. HOLLISTER in Melmon & Morrelli *Clin. Pharmacol.* (1972) xi. 459/1 The first hydrazide drug was iproniazid... A later member of the series was pheniprazine (Catron). Both have subsequently been removed from the market because of intolerable toxicity.

phenix, variant of PHŒNIX.

phenmetrazine (fɛn'mɛtrəziːn). *Pharm.* [f. PHEN(YL + *-metr-* (f. MET(HYL + HYD)R(O-) + AZINE, constituent parts of the systematic name *2-phenyl-3-methyl-tetrahydro-1,4-oxazine*.]

3-Methyl-2-phenylmorpholine, $C_{11}H_{15}NO$, the hydrochloride of which, a white powder, has been used as an appetite suppressant and is a stimulant of the central nervous system similar to (though weaker than) amphetamine, to which it is chemically related.

1956 *Amer. Jrnl. Digestive Dis.* I. 155 Phenmetrazine has been used clinically in Germany in the management of obesity. **1959** *Lancet* 22 Aug. 152/1 Phenmetrazine ('Preludin'), a sympathomimetic drug discovered by Thomae and Wick, was first used in 1954 in the treatment of obesity. Since then it has been given in asthma, in parkinsonism, and as a euphoriant. **1962** [see HERNIATION]. **1970** [see PRELUDIN].

phennig, -ing, obs. forms of PFENNIG.

pheno ('fiːnəʊ), colloq. abbrev. of PHENOBARBITAL, PHENOBARBITONE.

1966 J. PEARL *Crucifixion P. McCabe* (1967) viii. 118 Take a couple of my phenos and sack in early. **1968** 'E. TREVOR' *Place for Wicked* vi. 82 She'd just managed to catch the chemist open for some phenos:.. after the plane journey she wouldn't be able to sleep properly. **1971** *Where* Dec. 360/2 He agreed that she did not need such a heavy dose and suggested a quarter grain of pheno twice a day only if she was under the weather.

pheno-, formative element: see PHEN-.

phenobarb (fiːnəʊ'bɑːb). Also **pheno barb** and with final point. Abbrev. of PHENOBARBITAL, PHENOBARBITONE, used *colloq.* and in *Pharm.*

1956 M. MCMINNIES *Flying Fox* III. iv. 223 Whatever next? Not with all that phenobarb inside you. **1961** *Lancet* 22 July 205/2 Finally my colleague pleaded: 'If you won't take that phenobarb. yourself, for Heaven's sake dish it out to the rest of us.' **1971** *Where* Dec. 360/1 When Sarah got her sight back.. she came back to us on a dose of one grain of pheno barb twice a day. **1972** J. MANN *Mrs. Knox's Profession* x. 82 She picked up a small bottle and said, 'Phenobarb?' **1977** N. ADAM *Triplehip Cracksman* xii. 125 The phenobarb and the adrenalin, the swallowed capsule and the upcoming junket.

phenobarbital (fiːnə-, fɛnə'bɑːbɪtəl). *Pharm.* [f. PHENO- + BARBITAL.] The equivalent in the U.S. Pharmacopeia of PHENOBARBITONE; also, a tablet of this.

[**1918** *New & Nonofficial Remedies* (Amer. Med. Assoc.) p. vi, In accordance with the action of the Federal Trade Commission, New and Nonofficial Remedies recognizes.. Phenylbarbital as the official name for the product first introduced as luminal.] **1919** *Ibid.* 84 Phenobarbital is claimed to be a useful hypnotic in nervous insomnia. **1938** [see AMPHETAMINE]. **1950** M. LOWRY *Let.* Jan. (1967) 189, I must have had one too many phenobarbital. **1974** M. C. GERALD *Pharmacol.* ii. 18 Barbiturates, such as phenobarbital, cause depression. *Ibid.* xi. 202 Barbital was widely used for about a decade until the introduction of phenobarbital (Luminal) in 1912.

phenobarbitone (fiːnə-, fɛnə'bɑːbɪtəʊn). *Pharm.* [f. PHENO- + BARBITONE.] A white crystalline compound, 5-ethyl-5-phenylbarbituric acid, $C_{12}H_{12}N_2O_3$, which is widely used as a sedative, hypnotic, and anticonvulsant, often in the form of its sodium salt. So ***phenobarbitone sodium***. Cf. LUMINAL *sb.*

1932 *Brit. Pharmacopœia* 330 Phenobarbitone is 5-phenyl-5-ethylbarbituric acid, and may be obtained by the condensation of ethyl phenylethylmalonate with urea. **1943**, etc. [see ANTI-CONVULSANT *a.* and *sb.*]. **1954** *Newsweek* 12 Apr. 90/2 To 'keep their interest up', he [*sc.* a rowing coach].. reportedly prescribed phenobarbitone pills for a good night's sleep on the eve of the race. **1970** 'D. HALLIDAY' *Dolly & Cookie Bird* vi. 85 She has an Attitude to Life which would drive a phenobarbitone pill up the wall. **1975** CAWSON & SPECTOR *Clin. Pharmacol. in Dentistry* vi. 106 The main disadvantage of phenobarbitone is that as well as anti-anxiety (anxiolytic) properties, it is strongly sedative.

phenocain(e), obs. varr. PHENACAINE.

phenocoll ('fiːnəʊkɒl). *Chem.* [f. PHENO- + ending of GLYCOCOLL.] A derivative of phenacetin (= *amido-aceto-para-phenetidin*); in pharmacy, applied to the hydrochloride, as a febrifuge.

1891 *Lancet* 9 May 1060/2 A new antipyretic, hydrochlorate of phenocoll, a white crystalline powder which is readily soluble in water. **1898** P. MANSON *Trop. Diseases* vi. 121, I have never seen benefit in any way approaching that of quinine from.. phenocol, parthenium, .. or any of the many drugs.. recommended in malaria.

phenocopy ('fiːnəʊkɒpɪ). *Biol.* [ad. G. *phänokopie* (R. Goldschmidt 1935, in *Zeitschr. für induktive Abstammungs- und Vererbungslehre* LXIX. 46): see PHEN-, PHENO- and COPY *sb.*] An individual showing features characteristic of a genotype other than its own, but induced by a modified environment.

1938 R. GOLDSCHMIDT *Physiol. Genetics* ii. 14 The production of phenocopies in Drosophila succeeded only if the temperature shock was applied at a definite time in development, the sensitive period. **1957** *Amer. Naturalist* XCI. 86 The production of phenocopies succeeded more readily in organisms which were heterozygous for a recessive mutant gene with homologous morphological effects. **1971** D. J. COVE *Genetics* xii. 172 A wild-type organism which has been subjected to such a heat treatment may develop so that it resembles closely an organism with a particular mutation. These environmentally induced abnormal organisms are called phenocopies.

phenocryst ('fiːnəkrɪst). [ad. mod.F. *phénocryste*, irreg. f. Gr. φαίνειν to show + κρύστ(αλλος crystal.] Each of the large or conspicuous crystals in a porphyritic rock.

1893 GEIKIE *Textbk. Geol.* II. (ed. 3) 155 Two phases of consolidation.. to be observed, the first (porphyritic) marked by the formation of large crystals (phenocrysts) which were often broken and corroded by mechanical and chemical action. **1903** H. B. GUPPY in *Daily Chron.* 7 Nov. 3/3 The pyroxene phenocrysts usually are represented by separate crystals of the monoclinic as well as the rhombic type.

phenogam, etc., variants of PHÆNOGAM, etc.

phenogenetics (ˌfiːnəʊdʒə'nɛtɪks), *sb. pl.* (const. as *sing.*). *Biol.* [ad. G. *phänogenetik* (V. Haecker *Entwicklungsgeschichtliche Eigenschaftsanalyse* (1918) i. 4): see PHEN-, PHENO-, GENETIC *a.*, and -IC 2. Cf. next.

Haecker previously called it *phänogenese* (*Zeitschr. f. induktive Abstammungs- und Vererbungslehre* (1915) XIV. 260).]

(See quots.)

1938 R. GOLDSCHMIDT *Physiol. Genetics* ii. 23 It becomes imperative to know the details of development that distinguish the mutant types from the wild type. Studies of this type have been called.. phenogenetics, a term that is not necessary but is sometimes useful. **1962** I. H. HERSKOWITZ *Genetics* xxx. 262/2 How does the mutant change normal development to produce the new morphological result? The answer to the latter question deals with learning how phenotypes (of any type) come into being via gene action, and is the subject of phenogenetics, a study which is of broader scope than developmental genetics. *Ibid.* 269 Phenogenetics starts out as a study of the developmental genetics of morphology.

phenol ('fiːnɒl). *Chem.* [f. Gr. φαινο- (see PHEN-) + -OL 1 (= alcohol).] **a.** A hydroxyl derivative of benzene, $C_6H_5(OH)$, commonly known as CARBOLIC *acid*, q.v. (also *phenic* or *phenylic acid*, *phenyl hydrate*).

1852 [see PHENIC]. **1857** MILLER *Elem. Chem.* III. 568 Phenic, or Carbolic Acid.. Phenole.. is the most abundant acid product of the distillation of pit-coal. **1866** ODLING *Anim. Chem.* 123 Castoreum.. contains phenol, or coal-tar kreosote. **1878** ROSCOE *Elem. Chem.* 338 If one atom of hydrogen [in benzene] be replaced by hydroxyl an alcohol-like substance termed phenol is obtained. *Ibid.* 341 Phenol is sometimes called phenyl-alcohol, but it differs from a true alcohol in several respects;.. it is not readily oxidized and yields neither an aldehyde, a ketone, nor an acid. **1890** *Nature* 4 Sept., The important and universally-known antiseptic and disinfectant, carbolic acid, or phenol.

b. A hydroxyl derivative of the aromatic or benzene series of hydrocarbons; also, applied to derivatives of phenol, in which one or more of the hydrogen atoms are replaced by other radicals, the names of which are usually prefixed; e.g. *bromophenols* or *bromophenic acids* (C_6H_5BrO, etc.), *chlorophenols, iodophenols, nitrophenols* ($C_6H_5(NO_2)O$, etc.), *diazo-nitrophenols* ($C_6H_3N_3O_3$), etc.

1857 MILLER *Elem. Chem.* III. 568 The so-called phenols or alcohols derived from hydrocarbons of the benzene series by the displacement of an atom of hydrogen in the C_6 group by the group OH. **1868** JONES & WATTS *Fownes' Man. Elem. Chem.* (ed. 10) III. 646 A xylylic phenol is mentioned by Hugo Müller as occurring in coal-tar. **1877** WATTS *Ibid.* (ed. 12) II. 477 These latter compounds, including the hydroxyl-derivatives of benzene, are called Phenols. *Ibid.* 478 Monatomic Phenols... The phenols exhibit acid as well as alcoholic characters. *Ibid.* 488 Eight-carbon Phenols. **1952** L. N. FERGUSON *Electron Struct. Org. Molecules* viii. 189 For the same type of dissociation of a phenol.. the large increase in dissociation constant can be attributed largely to the effects of resonance. **1964** N. G. CLARK *Mod. Org. Chem.* xxi. 431 The acidity of a phenol is increased by a nitro group located *ortho* and/or *para* to the functional group.

c. *attrib.* and *Comb.*, as ***phenol compound, group, poisoning***; ***phenol-forming*** adj.; **phenol-formaldehyde**, used *attrib.* and *absol.* to designate plastics, resins, etc., made by condensation of phenols with formaldehyde; **phenol oxidase, pheno'loxidase** *Biol.* [ad. G. *phenoloxydase* (Battelli & Stern 1912, in *Biochem. Zeitschr.* XLVI. 396): see OXIDASE] = PHENOLASE; **phenol red** = *phenolsulphonphthalein* in sense d; **phenol resin**, a phenolic resin (see PHENOLIC *a.* b).

1897 *Allbutt's Syst. Med.* IV. 33 Phenol compounds. **1912** *Jrnl. Industr. & Engin. Chem.* IV. 737/2 (*heading*) Phenol-formaldehyde condensation products. **1933** *Archit. Rev.* LXXIII. 1 The most modern and significant group consists of the synthetic plastics of which the two best known and most fully developed are the Phenol-formaldehyde and the Urea-formaldehyde types. **1965** *Wireless World* Sept. 32 (Advt.), New 10 pin (Decal) based valves type B10B, moulded in polypropylene and phenol formaldehyde. **1972** *Materials & Technol.* V. 95 All types of phenol formaldehyde glue are resistant to organic solvents, bacteria and fungi. *Ibid.* 96 The largest use of phenol formaldehyde resin adhesives is in gluing wood. **1899** CAGNEY tr. *Jaksch's Clin. Diagn.* vii. 346 A considerable portion of phenol-forming substance. **1899** CAGNEY tr. *Jaksch's Clin. Diagn.* vi. (ed. 4) 240 When the volatile fatty acids and phenol group have passed over in the process of distillation. **1913** *Chem. Abstr.* VII. 796 The authors [*sc.* Battelli & Stern] recommend that the term phenolase be dropped and the term phenoloxidase be used instead. **1920** *Biochem. Jrnl.* XIV. 539 The oxidase (synonymous with laccase, phenoloxidase and phenolase) of the pear and potato. **1931** E. C. MILLER *Plant Physiol.* xiii. 769 Substances which give the same or similar reactions as laccase toward the phenol compounds.. have been named collectively the 'laccases', the 'phenol oxidases', or the 'phenolases'. **1971** I. ZELITCH *Photosynthesis* v. 136 Phenol oxidase activity is responsible for the familiar 'browning' observed in plant cells after injury. **1897** *Allbutt's Syst. Med.* II. 948 An antidote to phenol poisoning. **1916** CLARK & LUBS in *Jrnl. Washington Acad. Sci.* VI. 488 Phenol red and cresol red are undoubtedly the most reliable indicators of the series. **1956** WHITBY & HYNES *Med. Bacteriol.* (ed. 6) xi. 151 Collect the supernatant fluid, add a drop of phenol red solution, neutralize with N NaOH, and centrifuge. **1974** D. H. KAY in W. O. Foye *Princ. Med. Chem.* xxxvii. 816/2 This dye is also known as phenol red and is official as phenolsulfonphthalein (U.S.P.). **1912** J. W. AYLSWORTH *U.S. Pat. 1,020,593* The fusible anhydrous resinous condensation product..(hereinafter termed a 'phenol resin') is first prepared by causing a reaction between suitable amounts of phenol and formaldehyde. **1923** *Industr. & Engin. Chem.* July 677/1 The phenol resins continue to find wider applications in the industries on account of their physical and chemical properties. R. NAUTH *Chem. & Technol. Plastics* ii. 16 (*caption*) The dark rings which look like grain are..an effect produced by the phenol resin between the laminated veneers. **1973** *Materials & Technol.* VI. viii. 591 Phenol resins are widely used in the furniture and woodworking industries.

d. In comb. with other chemical terms, denominating substances containing or derived from phenol, as ***phenol-sulphuric*** acid, $C_6H_6{\cdot}SO_4$, ***phenol-sulphate*** of potassium, $C_6H_5{\cdot}K{\cdot}SO_4$, ***phenol-sulphonic*** acid, $C_6H_4{\cdot}SO_3{\cdot}OH$, etc.; ˌ**phenolcar'boxylic** (or **phenol carboxylic**) **acid**, any acid which contains a carboxyl group and a hydroxyl group bonded to the same benzene ring; ˌ**phenolsulphon'phthalein** [SULPHON(E + PHTHALEIN], a red crystalline solid $C_{19}H_{14}O_5S$, which is used as an indicator in the pH range 6·7 (yellow) to 8·3 (red), and in medicine is given intravenously as a test of kidney function.

1899 *Collective Index Trans. & Abstr. Chem. Soc. 1873–82* II. 471/1 Phenolcarboxylic acid. *See* Hydroxybenzoic acids and Salicylic acid. **1946** *Thorpe's Dict. Appl. Chem.* (ed. 4) VII. 285/1 All the compounds of this sub-series have been shown to be phenol carboxylic acid derivatives.., and the majority belong to the depsides. **1956** [see DEPSIDE]. **1975** D. JARVIS tr. *Hess's Plant Physiol.* 128 Phenol carboxylic acids, such as protocatechnic acid and gallic acid, occur widely. **1881** *Med. Temp. Jrnl.* XLVI. 99 Phenol naphthaline changed color both with acids and alkalies. **1876** HARLEY *Mat. Med.* (ed. 6) 356 Dry powder of phenol-sodium. **1898** M. D. SOHON in *Amer. Chem. Jrnl.* XX. 263 Phenolsulphonphthalein, $C_{19}H_{14}SO_5$..was obtained as a bright red crystalline powder, somewhat soluble in water. **1960** I. A. STANTON *Dict. for Med. Secretaries* 116/1 Phenolsulphonphthalein is injected intramuscularly or intravenously and should normally appear in the urine in 10 or 15 minutes. **1974** [see *phenol red* in c]. **1878** KINGZETT *Anim. Chem.* 237 Phenol-sulphuric acid.

phenolase ('fiːnəleɪz, -s). *Biol.* [a. G. *phenolase* (F. Czapek 1906, in *Jahrb. f. wissensch. Bot.* XLIII. 380), f. *phenol* PHENOL: see -ASE.] Any of a class of copper-containing enzymes found esp. in plants, which oxidize phenols to quinones; = *phenol oxidase* s.v. PHENOL c.

1911 *Jrnl. Chem. Soc.* C. I. 824 The phenolase was prepared from *Lactarius vellerius*. **1931** E. C. MILLER *Plant Physiol.* xiii. 768 The oxidases of plants that have been studied have been grouped into two main classes according to the substances upon which they act. These are the laccases or phenolases and the tyrosinases. **1956** *Nature* 14 Jan. 79/1 The phenolase complex, widely distributed throughout the phylogenetic scale, consists of two enzymic activities, phenol *o*-hydroxylase..and *o*-diphenol dehydrogenase. **1964** *Oceanogr. & Marine Biol.* II. 408 Isolation of the amoebocytes from the fluid brings about more rapid oxidation, suggesting that an inhibitor to phenolase activity may exist in the coelomic fluid. **1975** D. JARVIS tr. *Hess's Plant Physiol.* 83 Cytochrome oxidase a_3 makes direct contact with oxygen and is therefore known, together with a few other enzymes, (peroxidases, catalases, and phenolases), as a 'direct'oxidase.

phenolate ('fiːnəleɪt). *Chem.* [f. PHENOL + -ATE¹.] = PHENOXIDE.

1885 I. REMSEN *Introd. Study Compounds of Carbon* xv. 270 Potassium phenolate, $C_6H_5.OK$, made by dissolving potassium in phenol, and by treating phenol with caustic potash. **1913** A. R. WARNES *Coal Tar Distill.* viii. 79 Owing to the pressure of the C_6H_5 radicle the ·OH group (hydroxyl) possesses slight acid properties.., and..reacts with the caustic alkalies, forming salts known as phenolates. **1963** F. G. BORDWELL *Org. Chem.* v. 159 (*caption*) Resonance in the phenolate ion. **1974** R. S. CAHN *Introd. Chem. Nomencl.* (ed. 4) vi. 95 Salts of alcohols and phenols should receive the ending -olate, as in sodium methanolate .., sodium phenolate.., but names such as..the abbreviated methoxide,..and phenoxide are extremely common.

phenolic (fɪ'nɒlɪk), *a.* and *sb. Chem.* [f. PHENOL + -IC.] **A.** *adj.* **a.** Of the nature of, belonging to, derived from, or containing a phenol; *esp.* containing or being a hydroxyl group bonded directly to a benzene ring.

1872 WATTS *Dict. Chem.* VI. 916 Phenolic ethers. **1880** FRISWELL in *Jrnl. Soc. Arts* 16 Apr. 446 A naphthol was substituted for the phenolic or amido portion of the molecule. **1898** *Naturalist* 183 Antiseptic tannic and phenolic bodies. **1932** *Ann. Rep. Chem. Soc.* XXVIII. 236 Marrian had identified the substance $C_{18}H_{24}O_3$ as a trihydric alcohol with one phenolic hydroxyl. **1951** I. L. FINAR *Org. Chem.* I. xxvii. 533 Phenolic aldehydes..are very important compounds, and contain an aldehyde group and one or more hydroxyl groups directly attached to the nucleus. *Ibid.* xxviii. 557 It should be noted that only half the phenol is converted into the phenolic acid. **1964** N. G. CLARK *Mod. Org. Chem.* xxi. 430 The crude oily phenolic layer is separated from the aqueous liquor, and purified by distillation. *Ibid.* 431 The formation of simple ethers in this manner is a convenient way of 'protecting'a phenolic group. **1970** *Watsonia* VIII. 3 Chromatographic investigation.. into the intraspecific variation of phenolic and other compounds is proving to have interesting results. **1973** *Nature* 20 July 132/1 A serine hydroxyl..makes a hydrogen bond to a phenolic hydroxyl hydrogen, the oxygen of which bonds to another phenolic hydroxyl.

b. Designating a large class of usu. thermosetting polymeric materials that have wide industrial applications as plastics or resins and are prepared from phenols by condensation with aldehydes in the presence of acid or base catalysts; as ***phenolic plastic*** or ***resin***.

1910 J. W. AYLSWORTH *U.S. Pat. 1,020,593*, I..have made a certain new and useful Invention in Phenolic Condensation Products and Methods of Preparing Same. **1917** *Chem. Abstr.* XI. 693 (*heading*) Insoluble phenolic resins. **1931** *Product Engin.* Nov. 503/2 Cast phenolic plastics are softer than the ordinary phenolic materials. **1944** *Electronic Engin.* XVII. 35/1 A skilful combination of a polyvinyl acetal resin..with a thermo-setting phenolic resin has enabled 'Thermex'enamel to be produced from wholly synthetic sources. **1963** *House & Garden* Feb. 8/2 (*caption*) Mural panel in polished copper and black phenolic resin. **1968** *Wall St. Jrnl.* 26 July 28/1 Prices of phenolic molding compounds, among the more widely used plastics, will be raised one cent a pound by Union Carbide Corp. **1973** *Materials & Technol.* VI. viii. 589 The starting materials for the manufacture of phenolic plastics are mainly phenols and formaldehyde.

B. *sb.* **a.** Phenolic plastic or resin.

1935 *Industr. & Engin. Chem.* Oct. 1141/1 Certain plastics, particularly the cast phenolics, have unusual qualities for the passage and reflection of light. **1946** H. A. TAYLER *Plastics Explained* iv. 90 Cast phenolics are resistant to moisture, weak acids, oils and organic solvents. **1960** *Times Rev. Industry* Mar. 57/1 British plastics production.. total was divided as: thermosetting materials 195,000 tons (alkyds 50,000 tons; aminoplastics 55,000 tons; phenolics 75,000 tons) and thermoplastics 300,000 tons. **1968** *Wall St. Jrnl.* 26 July 28/1 (*heading*) Phenolics price boost is planned by Union Carbide. **1973** *Sci. Amer.* July 42/3 The matrix in glass-reinforced composites may be either a thermoset plastic, such as polyester, phenolic or epoxy, or any of a number of thermoplastic resins, such as nylon, polyethylene or polystyrene.

b. Chiefly *Biochem.* Any compound containing a hydroxyl group bonded directly to a benzene ring, esp. one that occurs in plants.

1956 *Chem. & Industry* 9 June 478/2 Ellagic acid occurs in 43 families of dicotyledons, and is usually accompanied by the other vicinal-trihydroxy phenolics myricetin and leucodelphinidin. **1960** A. H. WILLIAMS in J. B. Pridham *Phenolics in Plants* 1. 3 Phloridzin, the principal phenolic of apple leaf and bark is absent from the flesh of the fruit. **1970** J. VAN BUREN in A. C. Hulme *Biochem. Fruits* I. xi. 298 Varieties of fruits high in phenolics are more astringent than varieties low in phenolics. **1976** *Which?* Aug. 185/2 The household disinfectants you'll usually find in your shop will be either phenolics or hypochlorites.

phenolized ('fiːn-, 'fɛnəlaɪzd), *ppl. a.* Chiefly *Med.* [f. PHENOL + -IZ(E + -ED¹.] Treated with phenol; *spec.* (of vaccines, cell samples, etc.) suspended in a dilute solution of phenol. So **phenoli'zation**.

1921 DORLAND *Med. Dict.* (ed. 11) 791/1 *Phenolization*, treatment of infected wounds by subjecting them to the energetic action of strong carbolic acid. **1922** *Jrnl. Amer. Vet. Med. Assoc.* LXI. 40 The vaccination consists of a single injection of a large dose of phenolized fixed virus. **1949** RHODES & VAN ROOYEN *Textbk. Virol.* xxv. 226 The most popular method [of reducing the potency of rabies vaccine] is the use of phenolized virus... A common practice is to issue a vaccine consisting of a 4 to 5 per cent suspension of infected nervous tissue with 0·5 per cent phenol. **1961** *Amer. Jrnl. Med.* XXX. 804/2 Phenolized and acetone-extracted vaccines were ineffective in preventing clinical disease but probably modified the course of illness. **1975** *Nature* 24 July 277/1 Pure MS2 A-protein was obtained by isolation of the A-protein—RNA complex.., phenolisation, chromatography..and further separation. **1976** *Lancet* 9 Oct. 764/2 Granulomas were not transmitted by either frozen (−25°C) or phenolised sarcoid or Crohn's tissue homogenates.

phenological (fiːnəʊ'lɒdʒɪkəl), *a.* Also phæn-. [f. *pheno-* (in *phenomenon*) + *-logical* (in *meteorological*, etc.): rendering Ger. *phänologisch*, used by Dr. C. Fritsch in *Jahrb. d.k.k. Central-Anstalt für Meteorologie*, 1853, Vienna 1858.]

Of or pertaining to phenology or to the objects of its study. So **pheno'logic** *a.*; **phenology** (fɪ'nɒlədʒɪ), the study of the times of recurring natural phenomena (see quot. 1884), esp. in relation to climatic conditions; **phe'nologist**, one who studies phenology.

1875 (*title*) Instructions for the Observation of Phenological Phenomena, published by the Council of the Meteorological Society. **1883** *Nature* 4 Jan. 234/2 The most important feature of the phenological year was the mild winter. **1884** *Ibid.* 9 Oct. 558/2 Phenology, the observation of the first flowering and fruiting of plants, the foliation and defoliation of trees, the arrival, nesting, and departure of birds, and such like, has attracted the attention of naturalists from time to time for nearly 150 years. **1894** *Naturalist* 241 Phenological notes and statistical tables of rainfall and temperature. **1897** WILLIS *Flower. Pl.* I. 155 The study of the periodic phenomena of vegetation..is termed *phaenology*. **1947** [see ISOPHANE, ISOPHENE]. **1974** *Nature* 1 Mar. 42/1 This proposed sequence of major volcanic eruptions followed by several years of cold summers and then by glacial advance is supported by historic and phenologic data.

† **phenoloid** ('fiːnəʊ-, 'fɛnəʊlɔɪd), *sb.* and *a. Obs.* [f. PHENOL + -OID.] **A.** *sb.* A phenoloid substance, *spec.* phenoloid oil. **B.** *adj.* Of the nature of, containing, or resembling phenols; ***phenoloid oil***, a form of creosote obtained from the distillation of coal, esp. as a by-product from blast-furnace gases.

1907 V. B. LEWES *Liquid & Gaseous Fuels* 99 The oil obtained from blast furnaces is also sometimes used locally for fuel purposes under the name of 'Phenoloid', or blast furnace oil. **1911** *Med. Ann.* 758 Phenoloid Disinfectant. —This contains 66 per cent phenoloid, with high carbolic acid coefficient. **1913** V. B. LEWES *Oil Fuel* 129 Another variety of oil is obtained from blast furnaces, and is known as blast furnace oil, or 'phenoloid oil'. **1920** J. M. FORTESCUE-BRICKDALE *Text Bk. Pharmacol.* ix. 74 Phenoloids are bodies having similiar properties [to cresols], and are obtained from the distillation of coke. Cyllin, izal, and kerol are mainly composed of phenoloids. **1929** *Encycl. Brit.* VI. 668/2 The mixture of phenol and phenoloid substances derived..from coal, wood, blast furnace, and other tars. *Ibid.* 669/1 Blast-furnace creosote, sometimes known also as 'phenoloid' resembles vertical-retort tar. **1961** *Brit. Med. Dict.* 1092/1 *Phenoloid*..a term, now becoming obsolete, describing substances of phenolic character such as cresols and xylenols.

phenolphthalein (fiːnɒl'fθeɪliːn). [f. PHENOL + PHTHALEIN.] A whitish or yellowish crystalline solid,

$$(HO{\cdot}C_6H_4{\cdot})_2C{\cdot}C_6H_4{\cdot}CO,\quad \underbrace{\qquad}_{O}$$

which is used in alcoholic solution as an indicator in the pH range 8 to 10, in which it changes from colourless to red, and is also used medically as a laxative.

1875 *Jrnl. Chem. Soc.* XXVIII. 67 When phenol is gently warmed with phthalic anhydride and sulphuric acid the mixture assumes a brownish yellow colour, from the formation of phenol-phthalein. **1881** J. ATTFIELD *Chem.* (ed. 9) 658 In delicate experiments turmeric, 'eosin', 'phenolphthalein', etc., may be used instead of litmus. **1893** *Photogr. Ann.* 287 For testing the alkalinity of sulphites... The best [indicator] is phenol-phthalein in alcoholic solution. **1946** *Nature* 23 Nov. 744/2 Back titration of the solution immediately after the substance had dissolved, using phenolphthalein as an indicator, indicated an apparent equivalent weight of 325. **1951** R. MAYER *Artist's Handbk.* ii. 97 Acids and alkalis are detected by the use of litmus, phenolphthalein, or other indicators. **1974** M. C. GERALD *Pharmacol.* ii. 31 In some laxatives, such as Ex-Lax and Feen-A-Mint, the active ingredient is phenolphthalein.

† **'phenomen, -mene.** *Obs. rare.* Anglicized form of PHENOMENON [= F. *phénomène*].

1644 DIGBY *Nat. Bodies* xxxi. §2. 271, I apply them to the seuerall Phoenomens which Mr. Hall shewed me. **1652** H. L'ESTRANGE *Amer. no Jewes* 44 These fancies and phenomenes in their braine.

phenomena: as erron. sing. form (see PHENOMENON 1 *β*).

phenomenal (fɪ'nɒmɪnəl), *a.* (*sb.*) Also phæn-. [f. PHENOMEN-ON + -AL¹: so mod.F. *phénoménal* (1875 in Littré).]

1. a. Of the nature of a phenomenon; consisting of phenomena; cognizable by the senses, or in the way of immediate experience; apparent, sensible, perceptible; *Psychol.*, of or relating to a phenomenon as it is directly perceived or sensed, esp. as compared with its objective reality; also in special collocations, as ***phenomenal regression***, the tendency for a shape, esp. a perspective, to be perceived as nearer to the shape of a related and known object than it actually is. (Opposed to *real*, *absolute*, etc., and in Philosophy to *noumenal*.) Also *absol.*, ***the phenomenal***, that which is cognizable by the senses.

1825 COLERIDGE *Aids Refl.* (1848) I. 205 The Mosaic narrative thus interpreted gives a just and faithful exposition of the birth and parentage and successive movements of phenomenal sin (*peccatum phænomenon*; *crimen primarium et commune*). **1836** EMERSON *Nature, Idealism* Wks. (Bohn) II. 165 Seen in the light of thought, the world always is phenomenal. **1843** MILL *Logic* I. iii. §7 All that we know is therefore phænomenal—phænomenal of the unknown. **1847** LEWES *Hist. Philos.* (1867) II. 534 If a path of transit from the phenomenal to the noumenal world could be found.. should we not then be quickly in possession of the truth? **1865** J. GROTE *Explor. Philos.* I. i, The ideal is the subjective, the phenomenal the objective. **1874** SIDGWICK *Meth. Ethics* II. iii. 120 The Phenomenal is the Real: there is no other real that we can distinguish from it. **1881** [see PHENOMENALIZATION]. **1884** J. TAIT *Mind in Matter* (1892) 3 When the positivist demands acceptance of the phenomenal as the ultimate, the position is felt to be inadmissible. **1922** K. KOFFKA in *Psychol. Bull.* XIX. 569 A field, reflecting a certain amount and quality of light, depends for its phenomenal color-quality upon the ground on which it appears. **1931** R. H. THOULESS in *Brit. Jrnl. Psychol.* XXI. 340 The shape reported by the subject as seen by him may be called the 'apparent shape'or 'phenomenal shape'. *Ibid.* 344 As a general name for this tendency, in whatever kind of perceptual character it is found, we may use the term *phenomenal regression to the 'real' object* or, more shortly, *phenomenal regression*. **1948** *Jrnl. R. Aeronaut. Soc.* LII. 467/1 The factor of phenomenal regression was a quantity differing widely among different people. **1951** G. R. WENDT in S. S. Stevens *Handbk. Exper. Psychol.* xxxi. 1208/2 We lack words in our language to distinguish phenomenal motion from the physical event. **1969** C. O. SCHRAG *Experience & Being* I. i. 19 The phenomenal field, according to Merleau-Ponty, is neither an 'outer world'of objectively reconstituted properties..nor is it an abstracted 'inner world'.

b. Of, relating to, or concerned with phenomena, esp. with the phenomena of any science.

1840 Whewell *Philos. Induct. Sc.* x. ii. §4. II. 103 Descriptive or Phenomenal geology. *Ibid.* §7. 109 We must have a Phenomenal science preparatory to each Ætiological one. **1888** A. J. Balfour in *Pall Mall G.* 2 Oct. 1/2 The belief in a future state is one of the most striking differences between phenomenal and supernatural religion.

c. as *sb. pl.* Things of the nature of phenomena.

1878 G. D. Boardman *Creative Week* 289 (Cent.) In the matter of elementals, the new earth will be identical with the old; in the matter of phenomenals, the new earth will be different from the old.

2. Of the nature of a remarkable phenomenon (phenomenon 3); very notable or remarkable, extraordinary, exceptional; 'prodigious'.

a **1850** Rossetti *Dante & Circ.* I. (1874) 23 To afford a glimpse of the phenomenal fact that the bosom of the Church was indeed for a time the refuge of this shorn lamb [Cecco]. **1862** B. Taylor *Home & Abr.* Ser. II. II. ix. 190 Others have been found, showing that the tree is not phenomenal in its appearance. **1882** *Athenæum* 7 Jan. 19/2 The success of Miss Kate Greenaway's 'Birthday Book' was phenomenal.

pheˈnomenaˌlism. [f. prec. + -ism.] **a.** That manner of thinking which considers things from the point of view of phenomena only. **b.** The metaphysical doctrine that phenomena are the only objects of knowledge, or the only realities; externalism.

1865 J. Grote *Explor. Philos.* I. i, I shall call then by the name of 'phenomenalism' that notion of the various objects of knowledge which go to make up the universe which belongs to the point of view of physical science. **1865** *Reader* 8 July 29 It seems..to have no clear superiority over the law of gravity, or any other generalization of phenomenalism. **1877** E. Caird *Philos. Kant* II. ix. 402 Kant's Phenomenalism... The doctrine that the objects of our knowledge are merely phenomenal.

So **pheˈnomenalist**, one who holds or advocates phenomenalism; also as *adj.*, of or pertaining to phenomenalism or a phenomenalist; hence **phenomenaˈlistic** *a.*; **phenomenaˈlistically** *adv.*, as regards or in terms of phenomenalism. Also **phenomenalistically-minded** *a.*

1856 Dove *Logic Chr. Faith* I. ii. II. §1. 83 We must conclude that both the materialist and phenomenalist are wrong. **1865** J. Grote *Explor. Philos.* I. 92 A view more or less phenomenalistic is natural from the first to our manner of existence here. **1880** T. C. Murray *Orig. & Growth Ps.* ix. 285 He [G. H. Lewis] differs from the modern phenomenalist alone in his result. **1885** W. James *Coll. Ess. & Rev.* (1920) 277 Modern thinkers..for the most part obey a common drift..towards a phenomenalistic or idealistic creed. **1904** Phenomenalistic [see ante rem]. **1909** Webster, Phenomenalistically. **1914** C. D. Broad *Perception* iii. 166 Berkeley, whose argument is properly phenomenalistic. *Ibid.* 171 The phenomenalist position has to be stated as follows. **1934** A. C. Ewing *Idealism* vii. 294 A sense which cannot..be analysed phenomenalistically. **1943** *Mind* LII. 340 But surely it ought to worry a phenomenalistically-minded philosopher; and Mr. Smith does not seem to be sufficiently worried by it. **1956** E. H. Hutten *Lang. Mod. Physics* ii. 64 It is..said that a thing-language, or a phenomenalist language, e.g. one taking sense-data as a key-concept, represents an empiricist language. **1963** Phenomenalistic [see *direct realism*]. **1975** *New Left Rev.* Nov.–Dec. 33 Knowledge is restricted to what is known for certain; it is then shown, in a phenomenalistic analysis of perception, that what is known in perception is certain; only perception gives knowledge of things (principle of empiricism); hence knowledge must be what is given in perception.

phenomeˈnality. [f. as prec. + -ity.] The quality of being phenomenal; something that is phenomenal, a phenomenon.

1882 J. B. Stallo *Concepts & The. Mod. Physics* 201 Phenomenalities are the deliverances of sense. **1884** tr. *Lotze's Metaph.* 380 With respect to the Phenomenality of Space, I have argued..that the appearance both of Space itself and of the changes which take place in it, is to be referred to real events which do not take place in Space. **1884** W. James in R. B. Perry *Tht. & Char. W. James* (1935) I. 580 To see whether the object thus given be itself only more subjectivity, more phenomenality, more experience than the instant. **1917** A. S. Pringle-Pattison *Idea of God* xi. 211 This organic point of view delivers us..from the difficulties which so sorely afflict modern philosophy as to the relativity, or subjectivity, or phenomenality, of knowledge. **1933** *Jrnl. Theol. Stud.* XXXIV. 314 The notion that all phenomenality including the self is illusory.. finally became..the foundation of Sankara's philosophy. **1969** T. F. Torrance *Theol. Sci.* i. 21 Modern philosophy in its preoccupation with phenomenality.

pheˈnomenalize, *v.* [f. as prec. + -ize.] *trans.* To render phenomenal; to conceive or represent as phenomenal. Hence **pheˌnomenaliˈzation,** the action of phenomenalizing.

1870 J. C. Simon in *Contemp. Rev.* XIII. 405 This doctrine [of Hegel] that the Whole of Being is phenomenal —consisting of the process which we commonly call Thought or Thinking, and which..we may call Phenomenalization. **1878** S. H. Hodgson *Philos. of Reflection* I. 213 What *was* the Thing-in-itself has been phenomenalised and relegated to this possible world. **1881** Fraser *Berkeley* 73 Phenomenalisation not being possible in the absence of sense-conscious spirits, the world, it is argued, could not have existed before man.., if its reality is only phenomenal. *Ibid.* 112 Berkeley phenomenalises finite things, but not finite persons. **1921** Hannay & Collingwood tr. *G. de Ruggiero's Mod. Philos.* III. ii. 274 Bradley..fails to see that the true absolute is..appearance itself, in so far as it is the absolute process of appearing, the phenomenalization of the absolute.

phenomenally (fɪˈnɒmɪnəlɪ), *adv.* [f. as prec. + -ly².] In a phenomenal manner or degree. **a.** In relation to phenomena. **b.** Extraordinarily, notably, surprisingly.

1826–7 De Quincey *Lessing* Wks. 1859 XIII. 291 Fixed bodies..or individual things he [Homer] paints only phenomenally, or through their participation in these fluent actions. **1886** *Manch. Exam.* 15 Mar. 5/4 Describing the weather as phenomenally severe for the season.

phenomene: see phenomen.

†phenoˈmenic, *a. Obs. rare.* Also phæn-. [f. phenomen-on + -ic.] Of the nature of a phenomenon: = phenomenal 1. So **†phenoˈmenical** *a. Obs.*, relating to phenomena: = phenomenal 1 b.

1851 *Fraser's Mag.* XLIII. 497 The 'palpable' is not the 'real', but the 'actual',—the 'phænomenic', if you must needs have a big, vague Latin or Greek word for it. **1858** W. R. Pirie *Inquiry Hum. Mind* ix. 503 The mind in sleep being directed rather to its phenomenical states..than to its own subjective existence.

phenomenism (fɪˈnɒmɪnɪz(ə)m). *Philos.* Also phæn-. [f. phenomen-on + -ism.] = phenomenalism b. So **pheˈnomenist**, a holder or advocate of phenomenism; also *attrib.* or as *adj.*; hence **phenomeˈnistic** *a.*

1830 J. Douglas *Errors Relig.* 231 His philosophy was still phenomenism. **1852** Bp. Forbes *Nicene Cr.* 107 Some have maintained a pure idealism, others a pure materialism, and a third party pure phaenomenism. **1865** J. Grote *Explor. Philos.* I. 182 The notion of an unknowable noumenism with which phænomenism..is contrasted. **1871** *Dublin Rev.* Oct. 309 No one will doubt, either that the phenomenist school professes the general doctrine we have ascribed to it, or that Mr. Mill habitually identifies himself with this school. *Ibid.*, The phenomenistic doctrine is such as this: that an ascertained truth, means a truth experienced or inferred from experience. **1871** W. G. Ward *Ess. Philos. Theism* (1884) I. 1 English philosophers..may be divided into two sharply contrasted classes, whom we may call objectivists and phenomenists respectively. **1893** W. Ward *W. G. Ward & Cath. Revival* 328 We would thus..address some phenomenistic opponent.

pheˈnomenize, *v.* [f. phenomenon + -ize.] *trans.* To make phenomenal or apparent to the senses or mind; to treat as a phenomenon.

1860 J. Young *Prov. Reason* 33 The ego of consciousness is only the manifested, the phenomenized ego. *Ibid.* 245 Phenomena are phenomena of something actual behind them, which they phenomenize, and thereby reveal.

phenomenological (fɪˌnɒmɪnəˈlɒdʒɪkəl), *a.* [f. phenomenolog(y + ical.] Of or pertaining to phenomenology; dealing with the description and classification of phenomena, not with their explanation or cause; ***phenomenological method***, the method outlined by Husserl for the description and analysis of phenomena as they are directly experienced (cf. phenomenology b).

1858 in Mayne *Expos. Lex.* **1866** J. Martineau *Ess.* I. 26 Phenomenological, as opposed to ontological. **1891** tr. *De La Saussaye's Man. Sc. Relig.* i. 8 We proceed to treat the phenomenological facts. **1923** Ogden & Richards *Meaning of Meaning* 419 It is important for the understanding of Husserl's terminology to realise that everything he writes is developed out of the 'Phenomenological Method and Phenomenological Philosophy'. **1931** W. R. B. Gibson tr. *Husserl's Ideas* 14 There..grows up, on the pure basis of inner intuition, of the intuition of the soul's own essence, a phenomenological psychology. **1956** A. A. Townsend *Struct. Turbulent Shear Flow* iii. 33 The success of this approach has led to the present tendency to approach the problem of turbulence by examining the dynamics of the turbulent motion itself in preference to using phenomenological theories which do not attempt to describe the turbulent motion but only its effects on the mean flow. **1963** J. Wild in A. L. Fisher tr. *Merleau-Ponty's Struct. Behaviour* (1965) p. xvi, The phenomenological thinking of this book cuts through the traditional oppositions between ..body and soul, sense and reason, and subjectivism and objectivism. **1965** *Math. in Biol. & Med.* (Med. Res. Council) IV. 131 These difficulties..may be largely responsible for the fact that neurophysiologists..have often been hesitant to go beyond reporting raw data in a somewhat phenomenological manner. **1968** C. G. Kuper *Introd. Theory Superconductivity* i. 4 Long before the physics of superconductivity was understood, a number of phenomenological theories had been proposed. **1976** T. Eagleton *Crit. & Ideology* i. 24 He rejected, naturally, the political consequences..but the phenomenological basis of that criticism was of peculiarly direct relevance to him. **1977** *Dædalus* Summer 63 Processual analysis has undoubtedly gained from the phenomenological critique of positivist anthropology.

pheˌnomenoˈlogically, *adv.* [f. prec. + -ly².] In terms of, or as regards, phenomena or phenomenology.

1891 M. E. Lowndes tr. *Höffding's Outl. Psychol.* ii. 63 Phenomenologically, he [*sc.* Lotze] thus places himself at the standpoint of the natural interaction. **1909** W. M. Urban *Valuation* i. 18 Ideals of a supernatural character are the product, phenomenologically speaking, of individual and racial appreciative constructions. **1942** *Amer. Jrnl. Physiol.* CXXXV. 736 Phenomenologically, the muscular reactions during a tonic-clonic response to electrical stimulation of the motor cortex have for a long time been recognized as analogous to those in Jacksonian or in grand-mal epilepsy. **1958** *Times Lit. Suppl.* 23 May p. xii/3 These images can be observed and described phenomenologically and by the means of psychology. **1975** *Sci. Amer.* June 56/3 If the collision yields an electron-positron pair, the annihilation and rebirth of such a pair is phenomenologically indistinguishable from the mere elastic scattering of the incident electron and positron. **1977** P. Johnson *Enemies of Society* xvii. 227 When we enter a cathedral, and examine its various axial tendencies and its symmetrical, and asymmetrical forms, we perceive it phenomenologically; the approach to music is, in all essentials, the same.

phenomenologist (fɪnɒmɪˈnɒlədʒɪst). [f. phenomenolog(y + -ist.] One who makes a study of, or adheres to the doctrines of phenomenology, esp. a philosopher or psychologist. Also *attrib.*

1865 J. H. Stirling *Secret of Hegel* I. i. 19 He who shall make it his business to watch the gathering of the materials for the seething..will be the Phaenomenologist or Historian of the Seething. **1910** *Mind* XIX. 287 Another line of derivation from Kant leads..to Nelson and to the phenomenologists (Gomperz). **1951** *Scottish Jrnl. Theol.* IV. 175 Most modern Existentialists are phenomenologists. They do not however totally deny the existence of external reality. **1957** H. Whitehall in N. Frye *Sound & Poetry* 135 The Polish critic-philosopher, Roman Ingarden, using the phenomenologist techniques of Husserl, banished the form-content dichotomy. **1967** J. F. Corso *Exper. Psychol. Sensory Behavior* i. 9 Those psychologists who emphasize the importance of experience in psychology and use subjective..terms to describe experience are called phenomenologists. **1975** *Listener* 25 Dec.–1 Jan. 857/2, I regard myself as a phenomenologist—that is, someone who is studying the phenomena of the human mind in an existential way. **1977** *Dædalus* Summer 63 The phenomenologists, notably Schutz, insisted that the social world is in many important respects a cultural construct, an organized universe of meaning in the form of what Harold Garfinkel calls a series of 'typifications' of the objects within it.

phenomenology (fɪnɒmɪˈnɒlədʒɪ). [f. phenomenon + -logy.] **a.** The science of phenomena as distinct from that of being (ontology). **b.** That division of any science which describes and classifies its phenomena; in *Philos.*, the theory, put forward by the German philosopher Edmund Husserl (1859–1938) and his followers, to the effect that the pure and transcendental nature and meaning of phenomena, and hence their real and ultimate significance, can only be apprehended subjectively; the method of reduction, based by Husserl on Descartes's method, whereby all factual knowledge and reasoned assumptions about the phenomenon as object and the experiencing 'ego' are set aside so that pure intuition of the essence of the phenomenon may be rigorously analysed and studied.

1797 J. Robison in *Encycl. Brit.* (ed. 3) s.v. *Philosophy* §47 This part of philosophy may be called Phenomenology. **1836–7** Sir W. Hamilton *Metaph.* vii. (1877) 121 If we consider the mind merely with the view of observing and generalising the various phænomena it reveals..we have one..department of mental science; and this we call the phænomenology of the mind..; we might call it phænomenal psychology. **1840** Whewell *Philos. Induct. Sci.* x. ii. (1847) II. 464 Each Palætiological Science, when complete, must possess three members: the Phenomenology, the Ætiology, and the Theory. **1875** Mansel *Gnostic Heresies* i. 3 Between the real and the apparent, between ontology and phenomenology. **1914** *Mind* XXIII. 588 Phenomenology, then, if I have understood it right, is the science of the essential connexions of vital experiences, as rooted in their nature or their character; not, for example, of their causal connexions as events in time. **1931** W. R. B. Gibson tr. E. Husserl (*title*) Ideas: general introduction to pure phenomenology. *Ibid.* 11 Under the title 'A Pure or Transcendental Phenomenology', the work here presented seeks to found a new science..a science covering a new field of experience, exclusively its own, that of 'Transcendent Subjectivity'. **1938** G. Reavey tr. *Berdyaev's Solitude & Society* 57 For this reason Husserl's Phenomenology fails to be an Existential philosophy although it exercised a considerable influence on Heidegger. **1949** H. F. Mins tr. G. Lukács in R. W. Sellars et al. *Philos. for Future* 572 Modern phenomenology is one of the..philosophical methods which seek to rise above both idealism and materialism by discovering a philosophical 'third way', by making intuition the true source of knowledge. **1957** H. E. Barnes tr. *Sartre's Being & Nothingness* p. xlvi, Phenomenology is anything but a nominalism. **1974** D. Carr *Phenomenology & Probl. of Hist.* I. 33 The 'common' subject matter of phenomenology and psychology, consciousness, is subjected in phenomenology to an essential rather than a factual consideration.

c. *Psychol.* The methods of description and analysis developed from philosophical phenomenology applied to the subjective experiencing of phenomena and to consciousness, esp. in the fields of Gestalt psychology, existential analysis and psychiatry.

1930 W. B. Wolfe tr. *Wexberg's Individual Psychol.* 8 Phenomenology prepared the way for the decisive step toward a comparative and contextual point of view in psychology. **1935** K. Koffka *Princ. Gestalt Psychol.* iii. 73 For us phenomenology means as naïve and full a description of direct experience as possible. **1958** H. F. Ellenberger in R. May et al. *Existence* I. iii. 92 There is a wide gap between the philosophical phenomenology of Husserl and the psychiatric phenomenology of Minkowski. *Ibid.* 101 Phenomenology can also use a 'categorical'frame of reference... The two basic categories of inner experiences are considered to be time ('temporality') and space ('spatiality'). **1959** A. W. LEVI *Philos. & Mod. World* II. x. 405 The phenomenology of the human condition.. in which inescapable situations constitute the historical determination in its four forms of death, suffering, conflict, and guilt. **1969** C. O. SCHRAG *Experience & Being* I. ii. 65 Psychiatric phenomenology has contributed interesting and revealing studies on the nature of psychological space and.. time in their pathological expressions.

phenomenon (fɪˈnɒmɪnən). Pl **-a**. Forms: *Sing.* 7 phain-, 7–9 phæn-, 7– phenomenon; (*β. erron.* 8–9 -omena). *Pl. α.* 7– -omena; *β.* 7–9 -omenons; *γ. erron.* 7–8 -omenas (-a's). [a. L. (post-cl.) *phænomenon*, pl. *-a*, a. Gr. *φαινόμενον*, pl. *-μενα* (absol. use of pr. pple. passive of *φαίνειν* to show, pass. to be seen, to appear) appearing, apparent (to the senses or mind), hence *τὰ φαινόμενα* things that appear, appearances, phenomena. Cf. F. *phénomène* (1570 in Hatz.-Darm.), It., Sp. *fenomeno*, Pg. *phenomeno*; Ger. *phänomen*.]

1. a. In scientific and general use: A thing that appears, or is perceived or observed; an individual fact, occurrence, or change as perceived by any of the senses, or by the mind: applied chiefly to a fact or occurrence, the cause or explanation of which is in question.

a **1639** WOTTON *Life Dk. Buckhm.* in *Reliq.* (1651) 102 Somwhat I must note in this strange Phainomenon. **1692** BENTLEY *Boyle Lect.* 203 The most considerable phænomenon belonging to terrestrial bodies is the general action of gravitation. **1727** DE FOE *Syst. Magic* I. ii. (1840) 45 Observing an unusual and surprising phenomenon, viz. a star at Noonday, moving in a particular orbit. **1785** REID *Intell. Powers* 618 That every phaenomenon must have a cause, was always taken for granted. **1816** PLAYFAIR *Nat. Phil.* II. 63 Any phenomenon, the beginning or end of which is seen at the same instant by observers under different meridians, affords the means of determining the difference of longitude. **1878** HUXLEY *Physiogr.* 75 Every one is familiar with the common phenomenon of a piece of metal being eaten away by rust.

β. (*erron.*) **1576** TOLDERVY *Hist. 2 Orphans* IV. 79 The landlady being so strange a phaenomena as to be Conscientious. **1783** J. WOODFORDE *Diary* 8 Jan. (1926) II. 54, I went.. to see a wonderful Phœnomena in Nature a Heifer 3 years old with two distinct Heads. **1856** OLMSTED *Slave States* 285 A phenomena of pregnant importance. **1947** GERTH & MILLS *From M. Weber: Ess. in Sociol.* iii. 73 In this conception of freedom as a historically developed phenomena,.. Weber represents humanist and cultural liberalism rather than economic liberalism. **1969** *Daily Progress* (Charlottesville, Va.) 5 Feb. 1/7 'They have an image now,'said Dr. Granville C. Fisher, University of Miami psychologist, 'and many others will follow the same route. It is a phenomena that will keep spreading.' **1970** *Nature* 31 Oct. 405/2 His work is fundamental to the concept of 'frozen'lines of magnetic force being held inside a plasma, a phenomena of great importance to any understanding of the processes occurring in the magnetosphere. **1972** *Real Estate Rev.* Winter 6/1 In some of our major cities, the abandonment phenomena to be witnessed is unlike anything that can be found in the United States outside the ghost towns of the old West.

b. Plural.

α. **1605** BACON *Adv. Learn.* II. ix. §1 It is not repugnant to any of the *phainomena*. **1653** H. MORE *Antid. Ath.* II. v, Those more large Phænomena of Day and Night, Winter and Summer. **1877** E. R. CONDER *Bas. Faith* iii. 104 The shifting phenomena of sensation.

β. **1707** *Curios. in Husb. & Gard.* 55 The efficient Cause of the several Phænomenons. **1708** *Brit. Apollo* No. 102. 2/1 The two Phænomenons, which you question. **1735** JOHNSON tr. *Lobo's Voy. Abyssinia* x. 105 How many empty Hypotheses and idle Reasonings, the Phænomenons of this River [Nile] have put Mankind to the expence of. **1865** [see 3].

γ. (*erron.*) **1635** (*title*) Atlas Cœlestis, Containing the Systems and Theoryes of the Planets,.. and other Phenomenas of the Heavens. **1685** BOYLE *Enq. Notion Nat.* 17 In the Ascension of Water in Pumps, and in other Phænomena's of that kind. **1751** *Guide to Stage* 29 Phenomena's which have appear'd nowhere but upon our theatres. **1767** MRS S. PENNINGTON *Lett.* III. 13 All the phenominæ of Nature.

†**c.** Phr. *to save* (or *salve*) *the phenomena* (tr. Gr. *σώζειν τὰ φαινόμενα*): to reconcile the observed and admitted facts with some theory or doctrine with which they appear to disagree. *to solve a phenomenon*: to explain or account for an observed fact (so *solution of a phenomenon*). *Obs.*

1625 BACON *Ess., Superstition* (Arb.) 345 Like Astronomers, which did faigne Eccentricks and Epicycles, and such Engines of Orbs, to save the Phenomena; though they knew, there were no such Things. **1643** MILTON *Divorce* I. i, To save the phenomenon of our Saviours answer to the Pharises. **1646** SIR T. BROWNE *Pseud. Ep.* II. ii, Conceits of eminent use to salve magneticall Phenomena's. **1662** STILLINGFL. *Orig. Sacr.* III. i. §9 To solve the Phænomena of nature. **1681** NEVILE *Plato Rediv.* 214 The Phenomena of Government cannot be salved. **1704** SWIFT *T. Tub* ix. (1709) 105 An original solution of this phaenomenon. **1748** HUME *Ess. & Treat.* (1777) II. 134 The solution of their phænomenon is obvious.

2. In philosophical use: That of which the senses or the mind directly takes note; an immediate object of perception (as distinguished from substance, or a thing in itself). (Opposed to NOUMENON.)

1788 REID *Active Powers* I. vi. 43–7. **1836** EMERSON *Nature, Idealism* Wks. (Bohn) II. 160 It is the uniform effect of culture in the human mind.. to lead us to regard nature as phenomenon, not as substance. **1877** E. R. CONDER *Bas. Faith* iv. 184 Self, therefore, is not a phenomenon, nor yet a bundle of phenomena. **1895** HUXLEY in *19th Cent.* Mar. 536 The doctrine that the subject-matter of knowledge is limited to phenomena.. is common to all I have mentioned [Hume, Berkeley, Locke]. **1895** A. J. BALFOUR *Found. Belief* (ed. 2) 7 Its leading doctrines are that we may know 'phenomena' and the laws by which they are connected, but nothing more [etc.].

3. Something very notable or extraordinary; a highly exceptional or unaccountable fact or occurrence; *colloq.* a thing, person, or animal remarkable for some unusual quality; a prodigy.

1771 *Junius Lett.* lvii. (1772) II. 257 From whatever origin your influence in this country arises, it is a phænomenon in the history of human virtue. **1796** MORSE *Amer. Geog.* I. 605 Here, such occurrences are considered as phenomena. **1803** WELLINGTON in Gurw. *Desp.* (1837) II. 411 In short, the only conclusion to be drawn.. is, that, the British Government in India is a phenomenon. **1838** DICKENS *Nich. Nick.* xxiii, 'This, Sir', said Mr. Vincent Crummles, bringing the maiden forward, 'this is the infant phenomenon—Miss Ninetta Crummles'. **1865** *Cornh. Mag.* May 631 People do not usually feel the same affection for phenomenons, however curious, that they do for perfectly commonplace human creatures. **1877** E. R. CONDER *Bas. Faith* (1884) App. I. iii. §8 *note*, The perversion of this word 'phenomenon'into the sense of 'prodigy'. Even educated people may be found speaking of a remarkable occurrence as 'Quite a phenomenon'.

†**4.** That which appears or seems to a person to be the correct view; one's (own) notion, opinion, or theory. *Obs. rare.*

1677 GALE *Crt. Gentiles* II. III. 21 Self love produceth in us al a fond conceit of and regard unto our own phænomena and principles. *Ibid.* 22 Dogmatising opiniatretie, which makes men to abandon Truth for the preservation of their own Phænomena.

†**pheˈnomenous**, *a. Obs. rare*$^{-1}$. [f. prec. + -OUS.] = PHENOMENAL 2.

1754 FIELDING *J. Wild* II. xii, To account for many occurrences of the phænomenous kind.

†**phenoˈmethol.** *Chem.* [f. PHENO- + METH(YL + -OL 1.] An obs. name of ANISOL.

1857 MILLER *Elem. Chem.* III. 492 If anisic acid be distilled with an excess of caustic baryta, it yields a compound termed *anisole*, or *phenomethole*.

phenon (ˈfɛnɒn). [f. Gr. *φαίνειν* to appear + *-on*.] **a.** *Biol.* A group of apparently similar plants or animals.

1943 CAMP & GILLY in *Brittonia* IV. 335 Phenon: a species which is phenotypically homogeneous and whose individuals are sexually reproductive, but which is composed of intersterile segments. **1969** E. MAYR *Princ. Systematic Zool.* i. 5 There is no generally accepted technical term for a phenotypically reasonably uniform sample, but it may be designated as a phenon. *Ibid.* 10 A phenon is not necessarily a population in the biological sense.

b. *Taxonomy.* A grouping of plants or animals established by techniques of numerical analysis.

1962 SNEATH & SOKAL in *Nature* 3 Mar. 860/1 How should we name the groups which are established by numerical taxonomy?.. We call the groups simply 'phenons'. **1963** DAVIS & HEYWOOD *Princ. Angiosperm Taxon.* iv. 136 Sneath & Sokal have introduced the concept of a phenon for the definition of groups obtained by cluster analysis... In practice a phenon defines groups by drawing lines horizontally across the dendrograms. **1963** SOKAL & SNEATH *Princ. Numerical Taxon.* ix. 251 The phenon nomenclature... Phenons are groups which approach natural taxa more or less closely, and.. they can be of any hierarchic rank or of indeterminate rank. **1966** *New Scientist* 20 Jan. 151/3 These groups are called *phenons*... If the original taxa are species each of the three new phenon taxa might represent a sub-genus or genus. **1973** SNEATH & SOKAL *Numerical Taxon.* v. 294 The term phenon is intended to be general, to cover the groups produced by any form of cluster analysis.

phenosafranine (fiːnəˈsæfrəniːn, -ɪn). *Chem.* Formerly also **-in**. [ad. G. *phenosafranin* (O. N. Witt: see R. Nietzki in *Ber. d. Deut. Chem. Ges.* (1883) XVI. 466), f. *pheno-* PHENO- + *safranin* SAFRANIN.] A synthetic red dye, $C_{18}H_{15}N_4Cl$, which is used in photography as a desensitizer; also, any of the derivatives of this compound.

1883 *Jrnl. Chem. Soc.* XLIV. 731 Phenosafranine,.. obtained by Witt by oxidising a mixture of aniline (2 mols.) and paraphenylenediamine (1 mol.).., forms beautifully crystalline salts. **1921** [see DESENSITIZE *v.*]. **1937** *Thorpe's Dict. Appl. Chem.* (ed. 4) I. 571/2 Nietzki showed that the same phenosafranine may be obtained (*a*) by condensing phenyl-*m*-phenylenediamine with phenyl-*p*-phenylenediamine, or (*b*) from diphenyl-*m*-phenylenediamine.. and *p*-phenylenediamine. **1970** *Amat. Photographer* 11 Mar. 63/3 The phenosafranines and allied desensitising dyes are not suitable for papers as they stain badly.

phenose (ˈfiːnəʊs). *Chem.* [f. PHEN- + -OSE².] A sweetish amorphous deliquescent compound formed by the action of hypochlorous acid on benzene, and having the general formula $C_6H_{12}O_6$ of the carbohydrates.

1878 KINGZETT *Anim. Chem.* 402 Phenose, as this body is termed, is not fermentible, but if its production.. be hereafterwards confirmed, it is of the greater importance, since it directly connects the so-called carbohydrates with the benzene series and with the fatty acid series. **1892** MORLEY & MUIR *Watts' Dict. Chem.* III. 838 Phenose $C_6H_{12}O_6$. Formed by the action of aqueous ClOH on benzene in the dark,.. also by the electrolysis of toluene mixed with alcohol and dilute H_2SO_4.

phenothiazine (fiːnəʊ-, fɛnəʊˈθaɪəziːn). *Pharm.* Formerly also **phenthiazine.** [f. PHENO- + THI(O- + AZINE.] **a.** A green, crystalline, heterocyclic compound, $C_{12}H_9NS$, which is used in veterinary medicine in the treatment of parasitic infestations. **b.** Any of various derivatives of this, which constitute an important class of tranquillizing drugs used esp. in the treatment of mental illnesses.

1894 G. M'GOWAN tr. *Bernthsen's Text-bk. Org. Chem.* (ed. 2) 539 Nile Blue springs from naphtho-phenoxazine; and the thionine dyes from phen-thiazine. **1917** *Chem. Abstr.* XI. 3903 (Index), Phenothiazine. **1926** H. G. RULE tr. *J. Schmidt's Text-bk. Org. Chem.* 709 Phenthiazine, thio-diphenylamine,.. is also the parent compound of a number of dye-stuffs. **1940** *Nature* 17 Aug. 232/2 Since phenothiazine is a new and valuable vermifuge, its effect on animal tissues is of some general interest. **1959** *Times* 14 Sept. 19/4 The nodula worm of sheep has been completely eliminated.. by the use of pheno-thiazine during the period of winter housing. **1969** *Daily Tel.* 1 Nov. 2/7 Large doses of phenothiazines induce a Zombi-like rigidity. **1974** M. C. GERALD *Pharmacol.* iv. 71 The phenothiazine nucleus has proved.. a rather versatile progenitor of pharmacologically useful compounds. *Ibid.* xvi. 301 Chlorpromazine (Thorazine), the most commonly employed phenothiazine.

phenotype (ˈfiːnəʊtaɪp). *Biol.* Also †**phænotype.** [ad. G. *phaenotypus* (W. Johannsen *Elem. der exakten Erblichkeitslehre* (1909) vii. 123): see PHEN-, PHENO- and -TYPE.] A type of organism distinguishable from others by observable features; the sum total of the observable features of an individual, regarded as the consequence of the interaction of its genotype with its environment. Cf. GENOTYPE *sb.*²

1911 W. JOHANNSEN in *Amer. Naturalist* XLV. 132, I have proposed the terms 'gene'and 'genotype'and some further terms, as 'phenotype'and 'biotype', to be used in the science of genetics. *Ibid.* 134 All 'types'of organisms, distinguishable by direct inspection or only by finer methods of measuring or description may be characterized as 'phenotypes'. **1931** S. J. HOLMES *Life & Evolution* xiv. 277 A study of our checkerboard indicates that there are four phaenotypes. **1958** *Antiquity* XXXII. 207 The Neolithic people were mostly of a different phenotype. **1964** G. H. HAGGIS et al. *Introd. Molecular Biol.* vii. 193 In this scheme the bodily characteristics, or phenotype, are jointly determined by the environment on the one hand and by the inherited chromosomal complement, or genotype, on the other. **1969** *Times Lit. Suppl.* 20 Nov. 1341 Darwinian selection acts on phenotypes. **1971** D. J. COVE *Genetics* iv. 45 It is usual to refer to the genetic constitution of a strain as its genotype, and to its appearance as its phenotype. **1973** *Listener* 28 June 851/1 Whether or not the average phenotypes of such races can be shown to differ significantly in IQ is beside the point. **1976** SMYTHIES & CORBETT *Psychiatry* iv. 36 A number of different subgroups based on different biochemical lesions.. all.. end up with a similar clinical picture. In other words many different genotypes can end up with a very similar phenotype.

Hence **phenoˈtypic, phenoˈtypical** *adjs.*, of or pertaining to the observable features of, or differences between, organisms (often used with the implication 'not genotypic'); **phenoˈtypically** *adv.*

1911 *Amer. Naturalist* XLV. 148 The phenotypically distinct and even diversely localized 'characters' convey easily the impression that they are the reactions of different genes. *Ibid.* 156 The merely phenotypical phenomena of alternative variability first pointed out by De Vries. **1929** R. R. GATES *Heredity in Man* ii. 26 There are cases where two or more factors combined to produce a single phenotypic character. **1930** *Biol. Bull.* LVIII. 85 (*heading*) Phenotypical variation in body and cell size of *Drosophila melanogaster*. **1935** *Proc. Nat. Acad. Sci.* XXI. 22 A rare phenomenon —the recurrence of phaenotypically the same scute mutation. **1942** *Endeavour* I. 18/2 Many geneticists have.. attempted to discover the processes involved in the mechanism by which the genes of the genotype bring about phenotypic effects. **1964** M. CRITCHLEY *Developmental Dyslexia* x. 64 His present study lent no support to the hypothesis that specific dyslexia, mental deficiency,.. and speech defects were different phenotypical manifestations of the same hereditary taint. **1964** *Punch* 28 Oct. 652/2 Earlier [sheep] breeders.. chose their stock phenotypically, that is, by the look of them. **1970** *Sci. Amer.* Feb. 62/3 It seems likely that the highlanders have derived their special qualities from acclimatization—in short, that their response to their environment is phenotypic rather than genotypic. **1977** J. L. HARPER *Population Biol. of Plants* viii. 239 Parts of a clone or shoots on a tree will differ phenotypically, e.g. in age and size.

phenotyping (ˈfiːnətaɪpɪŋ), *vbl. sb.* [f. prec. + -ING¹.] Allocation to a phenotype.

1964 *Jrnl. Dairy Sci.* XLVII. 1262/1 That agreement in phenotyping exists is valuable in.. establishing a uniform nomenclature of the genetic variants. **1977** *Lancet* 8 Jan. 82/1 The variants so recognised are labelled alphabetically in the protease-inhibitor (Pi) phenotyping system.

phenoxide (fɪˈnɒksaɪd). *Chem.* [f. PHEN-, PHENO- + OXIDE *sb.*] A salt of phenol, containing the anion $C_6H_5O^-$; = PHENATE, PHENOLATE.

1888 *Jrnl. Chem. Soc.* LIV. 586 (*heading*) Compounds of phenoxides with cuprous and mercurous chlorides. **1906** J. J. SUDBOROUGH *Bernthsen's Org. Chem.* (rev. ed.) xxiv. 405 The phenols possess the character of weak acids, and they form salts with alkalis.. known as phenates or phenoxides.

1936 L. J. DESHA *Org. Chem.* 185 Phenoxides, sometimes called phenates, are formed from phenols either by the action of the strongly positive free metals such as sodium or by dissolving in aqueous alkalies such as solutions of sodium hydroxide. **1966** RAKOFF & ROSE *Org. Chem.* xviii. 594 Phenols..are stronger acids than water; they will react with sodium hydroxide to form water and sodium phenoxide. **1974** [see PHENOLATE].

phenoxy(-) (fɪ'nɒksɪ), *prefix* and *a.* (*sb.*) *Chem.* and *Pharm.* [f. PHEN- + OXY-.] (Before a vowel formerly also **phenox-**.) An inseparable formative element in names of compounds which contain the group $-O{\cdot}C_6H_5$, as in **phe,noxya'cetic** (or †**phenoxacetic**) **acid**, a colourless, crystalline solid, $C_6H_5O{\cdot}CH_2COOH$; also, any of the chlorinated derivatives of this, which are widely used as weedkillers; **phe,noxymethylpeni'cillin** a white powder, 6-phenoxyacetamidopenicillanic acid, $C_{16}H_{18}N_2O_5S$, which is a semisynthetic penicillin.

1879 *Jrnl. Chem. Soc.* XXXVI. 322 The author [*sc.* P. Fritzsche]..has undertaken the investigation of oxyphenylacetic acid,..which was discovered and described by Heintz.., and named by him phenoxacetic acid. *Ibid.* 642 (*heading*) Phenoxypropionic acid. **1880** *Ibid.* XXXVII. 318 The preparation of phenoxyacetic acid is described at length. **1900** E. F. SMITH tr. *V. von Richter's Org. Chem.* (ed. 3) II. 146 Phenoxyacetone,..$C_6H_5O.CH_2.CO.CH_3$, boiling at 230°, is condensed by concentrated sulphuric acid to methyl cumarone. **1926** D. W. MACARDLE *Use of Solvents in Synthetic Org. Chem.* iv. 62 Marvel and Tanenbaum found that if in the preparation of phenoxybutyl alcohol, ethyl alcohol dried over lime was used as solvent, yields of not over 45% were obtained. **1946** LONG & BRENCHLEY *Suppression of Weeds* (ed. 2) xiii. 62 As a result of the work carried out..at Jealott's Hill Research Station a range of phenoxyacetic acid products were discovered, of which Methoxone (4-chlor-2-methylphenoxyacetic acid) was finally chosen as being a most efficient weed killer with selective properties. **1948** O. K. BEHRENS et al. in *Jrnl. Biol. Chem.* CLXXV. 798 Phenoxymethylpenicillin—N - (2 - Hydroxyethyl) - phenoxyacetamide (150 mg. per liter).. was used as the precursor for this penicillin. **1954** W. J. HICKINBOTTOM in E. H. Rodd *Chem. Carbon Compounds* IIIA. viii. 426 By the action of alcoholic potash, phenoxyacetylene is formed, an unstable oil. **1959** *Jrnl. Exper. Bot.* X. 33 (*heading*) Factors controlling the uptake of phenoxyacetic acids by *Lemna minor*. **1959** *Times* 6 Mar. 13/6 A preparation of penicillin—penicillin V, or phenoxymethylpenicillin—was produced which was not destroyed by the acid contents of the stomach. **1969** *New Scientist* 9 Jan. 61/2 Even the relatively innocuous phenoxyacetic acid compounds..have already caused significant ecological damage by destroying natural mangrove associations. **1970** HOOVER & STEDMAN in A. Burger *Medicinal Chem.* (ed. 3) I. xviii. 382/1 Phenoxymethylpenicillin (penicillin V) is now the only important biosynthetic penicillin in use.

B. In Combs. in which *phenoxy* may be used *attrib.* (without hyphen) or joined by a hyphen to the second element. **1.** Containing or being the group $-O{\cdot}C_6H_5$.

1896 *Jrnl. Chem. Soc.* LXIX. 161 (*heading*) On γ-phenoxy-derivatives of malonic acid and acetic acid. **1923** *Chem. Abstr.* XVII. 3864 (*heading*) Phenoxy derivatives of propane. **1926** *Jrnl. Amer. Chem. Soc.* XLVIII. 2748 The method chosen for the synthesis of these compounds was first to prepare the phenoxy alcohols and then to convert them into the chlorides. **1926** *Biochem. Jrnl.* XX. 1083 Replacement of the two phenoxy-groups by bromine. **1928** *Chem. Abstr.* XXII. 769 (*heading*) Influence of the phenoxy group and its derivatives upon the halochromism of known chromogens. **1964** L. J. AUDUS *Physiol. & Biochem. Herbicides* v. 195 The effects of the halogenated aliphatic acids on total soil populations are as diverse as those of the phenoxy herbicides. **1964** W. A. WATERS *Mechanisms Oxidation Org. Compounds* ix. 139 In aqueous solution the phenoxy radical itself has a mean lifetime of about 10^{-3} second. **1974** *McGraw-Hill Yearbk. Sci. & Technol.* 330/2 The phenoxy herbicides (2,4-D and 2,4-T), aminotriazole.., and pidoram are frequently used in forestry.

2. Designating thermoplastics characterized by a linear molecule containing recurring phenoxy groups, which are usu. made by condensation of epoxides, esp. epichlorhydrin, with certain phenols. Also as *sb.*

1962 *Mod. Plastics* Nov. 169 (*heading*) Phenoxy—a new thermoplastic. *Ibid.*, Phenoxy materials are a new family of thermoplastic resins that can be chemically cross-linked to impart thermosetting properties. **1963** *Aeroplane* 21 Feb. 29/2 Ventilating ducts in the Boeing 727 are fabricated from self-extinguishing phenoxy resin. **1967** *Times Rev. Industry* May 76/2 There has also been progress in the currently lower tonnage plastics such as nylon and polyester in film laminates for packaging processed foods, phenoxy polymer in blown bottles, and polycarbonate for sterilizable containers. **1969** L. S. MOUNTS in W. R. R. Park *Plastics Film Technol.* v. 141 Phenoxy films are rigid transparent films with high impact strength. **1970** W. G. POTTER *Epoxide Resins* ii. 19 The 'phenoxies' are in fact to be regarded as high-M thermoplastic materials and have been used either as surface-coating binder resins.., or as thermoplastics for blow moulding, injection moulding, [etc.].

phenozygous, variant of PHÆNOZYGOUS.

phenthiazine, obs. var. PHENOTHIAZINE.

phentolamine (fɛn'tɒləmiːn). *Pharm.* [f. PHEN-, PHENO- + TOL(YL + AMINE.] A white or cream-coloured heterocyclic solid, $C_{17}H_{19}N_3O$, which is used (in the form of its salt) as a vasodilator, esp. in the treatment of hypertension caused by phæochromocytoma.

1953 *Jrnl. Amer. Med. Assoc.* 15 Aug. 1533/2 Phentolamine hydrochloride, a salt of phentolamine base, is suitable for oral administration and acts as a potent adrenergic blocking agent, producing adrenolytic and sympatholytic effects. **1961** L. MARTIN *Clin. Endocrinol.* (ed. 3) vi. 182 Phentolamine is the most reliable of the adrenolytic substances both for diagnosis of phæochromocytoma and for use during its removal. **1968** J. H. BURN *Lect. Notes Pharmacol.* (ed. 9) 8 Patients with a high blood pressure may suffer from an adrenal medullary tumour which secretes noradrenaline and adrenaline into the blood. This can be diagnosed by injecting phentolamine intravenously. **1972** *Materials & Technol.* V. xxi. 810 Alpha receptor blockers such as tolazoline may be used in the treatment of peripheral blood vessel spasm, while phentolamine is used to treat hypertensive (high blood pressure) crises.

phenyl ('fiːnaɪl, 'fiːnɪl, 'fɛnɪl). *Chem.* [f. PHEN- + -YL, lit. 'radical of benzene (*phene*)'.]

1. The monovalent organic radical C_6H_5 (also symbolized Ph), which exists in the free state as DIPHENYL, $H_5C_6{-}C_6H_5$, and enters as a radical into benzene (***phenyl hydride***), phenol (***phenyl hydroxyl***), aniline (***phenylamine***), and a very extensive series of organic compounds.

1850 DAUBENY *Atom. The.* viii. (ed. 2) 238 A compound radical called phenyle, a name given by Laurent to the supposed base of the volatile liquid, obtained by compressing oil gas, which was first examined by Faraday, and denominated by him benzole. **1857** MILLER *Elem. Chem.* III. 563 Compounds..have been formed, which appear to contain oxide of phenyl in combination with acids. **1862** *N. Syd. Soc. Year-bk. Med.* 441 On some applications of Carbolic Acid or Oxide of Phenyle. **1880** CLEMINSHAW *Wurtz' Atom. The.* 220 Phenyl..wants but one atom of hydrogen to become benzene.

2. *attrib.* and *Comb.*, as ***phenyl acetate***, ***carbonate***, ***cyanide***, ***ether***, ***ketones***, ***oxide***, ***phosphate***, ***sulphide***; ***phenyl compounds***, ***derivatives***, etc.; **phenyl-blue**, dimethyl-amido-phenylimide of quinone; **phenyl-brown**, a colouring matter, possessing explosive properties.

1866 ODLING *Anim. Chem.* 123 This relationship of salicic and phenyl compounds. **1872** WATTS *Dict. Chem.* VI. 918 Phenyl carbonate... Phenyl phosphates [etc.]. **1875** *Ibid.* VII. 945 The explosive character of the phenyl-brown is.. due to the dinitrophenol. **1899** CAGNEY tr. *Jaksch's Clin. Diagn.* vii. (ed. 4) 400 The exhibition of salol (phenyl-æther of salicylic acid).

b. Freely combined (hyphened or written connectedly) with other chemical terms, denominating compounds into which phenyl enters as a radical, often replacing hydrogen or other monovalent element or group; such are, e.g.

phenyl-a'cetamide = ACETANILIDE. **phenyl-a'cetic** *a.*: see quot. 1877. **phenyl-a'cetylene**: see quot. 1872. **,phenylar'sonic** *a.* [ARSONIC *a.*], in ***phenylarsonic acid***, a colourless, toxic, crystalline solid, $C_6H_5AsO(OH)_2$, which is used as a trypanocide; also, any derivative of this; **phenyl-'glycol**, a diatomic alcohol, $C_6H_5{\cdot}CHOH.CH_2OH$. **phenyl-'hydrazine**: see quot. 1902. **phenyl'hydrazone** [ad. G. *phenylhydrazon* (O. Rudolph 1888, in *Ann. d. Chem. u. Pharm.* CCXLVIII. 99): see HYDRAZONE], any of a class of compounds formed by condensation of an aldehyde or ketone with phenylhydrazine, which are usu. crystalline solids and are used to characterize the parent aldehyde or ketone; **phenyl'mercury**, used *attrib.* or *absol.* to denote compounds which contain a phenyl group bonded directly to a mercury atom; so **,phenylmer'curic** *a.*, as ***phenylmercuric acetate***, a white crystalline solid, $CH_3COOHgC_6H_5$, used mainly as a fungicide and herbicide; ***phenylmercuric nitrate***, a white crystalline solid, $C_6H_5HgNO_3.C_6H_5HgOH$, used mainly as a fungicide and disinfectant. **,phenylpy'ruvic** *a.*, ***phenylpyruvic acid***, a colourless crystalline solid, $C_6H_5CH_2CO{\cdot}COOH$, which in phenylketonuria is produced by the metabolism of phenylalanine and excreted in the urine; hence **,phenylpy'ruvate**, a salt or the anion of this acid. **phenyl-sul'phuric** *a.*, sulphocarbolic: see quot. 1880. **,phenyl,thio'carbamide**, a white, crystalline solid, $NH_2{\cdot}CS{\cdot}NH{\cdot}C_6H_5$, which has a bitter taste to persons possessing a certain dominant gene and is tasteless to those lacking it. **,phenylthiou'rea** (-,θaɪəʊjʊ'riːə) = *phenylthiocarbamide* above.

1866 WATTS *Dict. Chem.* IV. 418 *Phenyl-acetamide or Acetanilide..Produced by the action of aniline upon acetic anhydride or chloride of acetyl. **1885–8** FAGGE & PYE-SMITH *Princ. Med.* (ed. 2) I. 205 Antifebrin (..phenyl-acetamide) is said to be more useful, more agreeable, and more safe than any. **1877** WATTS *Fownes' Chem.* (ed. 12) II. 528 Alpha-toluic or *phenyl-acetic acid, $C_6H_5{\cdot}CH_2{\cdot}CO_2H$. **1885** KLEIN *Micro-Organisms* 73 Antiseptics, such as carbolic acid..strong solutions of phenyl-propionic acid and phenyl-acetic acid. **1872** WATTS *Dict. Chem.* VI. 920 *Phenyl-acetylene. Syn. with Acetenyl-benzene. **1885** REMSEN *Org. Chem.* (1888) p. ix, Phenyl-acetylene and Derivatives. **1905** *Amer. Chem. Jrnl.* XXXIII. 104 The reduction takes place with equal ease in the aromatic series, monophenyl arsine..being obtained from *phenyl arsonic acid. **1937** *Thorpe's Dict. Appl. Chem.* (ed. 4) I. 488/1 The introduction of an amino group into the para-position in phenylarsonic acid decreases its toxicity and increases its trypanocidal activity. **1959** *Times* 7 Dec. (Agric. Suppl.) p. vii/1 So far as arsenicals are concerned, two phenylarsonic acids have received attention [as growth stimulants for poultry]. **1897** *Allbutt's Syst. Med.* III. 213 The property of *phenyl-hydrazin to form with grape-sugar a characteristic crystalline compound called phenyl-glucosagon. **1902** *Encycl. Brit.* XXVI. 721/2 E. Fischer [in] 1884, made the all-important discovery of phenylhydrazine, $C_6H_5{\cdot}NH.NH_2$ or $Ph.NH.NH_2$. **1889** *Jrnl. Chem. Soc.* LVI. 251 (*heading*) *Phenylhydrazones. **1938** [see HYDRAZONE]. **1966** *McGraw-Hill Encycl. Sci. & Technol.* VII. 62/2 When the starting material is the phenylhydrazone of acetone, the product is 2-methylindole. **1920** *Chem. Abstr.* XIV. 2181 There at once sep. leaflets of *phenylmercuric chloride, PhHgCl, m. 250°. **1921** F. C. WHITMORE *Org. Compounds Mercury* iii. 65 Phenyl mercuric acetate reacts with ammonium hydroxide giving a substance $(C_6H_5Hg)_2NH_2OAc$. *Ibid.* ix. 177 Phenylmercuric nitrate forms rhombic tablets, insoluble in cold water. **1951** A. GROLLMAN *Pharmacol. & Therapeutics* xxv. 510 The first of these compounds used as an antiseptic was phenylmercuric chloride but..this was supplanted by the more soluble basic phenylmercuric nitrate. **1966** *McGraw-Hill Encycl. Sci. & Technol.* I. 483/1 The most important of the organic mercurials are phenylmercuric nitrate and acetate. **1972** Phenylmercuric [see *phenylmercury* below]. **1931** *Jrnl. Infectious Dis.* XLIX. 440 *Phenyl-mercury-nitrate was first prepared by Otto in 1870, but its biologic characteristics have..never been studied. **1955** G. J. ROSE *Crop Protection* vi. 103 Bacterial canker of cherries has been controlled by applications of a formulation containing the phenyl mercury salt of naphthyl methane sulphonic acid. **1969** JOHNELS & WESTERMARK in Miller & Berg *Chem. Fallout* x. 224 There is no indication..that the use of..phenylmercury from 1930 to 1940 has caused an increase in the mercury content of these terrestrial bird species. **1971** *Nature* 20 Aug. 535/1 The death of birds in Sweden was traced to the use of phenylmercury compounds in the pulp and paper industry. **1972** F. MATSUMURA *Environmental Toxicol. Pesticides* 532 In the U.S. the source of contamination of many rivers has been suspected to be by phenylmercuries, because of the extensive use of phenylmercuric acetate as a slime treatment agent in paper mills. **1932** *Jrnl. Biol. Chem.* XCVI. 628 In one experiment, after 2·5 gm. of sodium *phenylpyruvate had been fed for 2 successive days, it was possible to isolate from the urine 0·4 gm. of phenaceturic acid. **1970** R. W. MCGILVERY *Biochem.* xvii. 387 People with phenylketonuria also excrete some other aromatic compounds.., representing aberrations of the normal process of metabolism due to the high concentration of phenylpyruvate. **1887** *Jrnl. Chem. Soc.* LII. 142 The author ..advances the view that the compound is probably *phenylpyruvic acid. **1935** [see PHENYLKETONURIA]. **1968** PASSMORE & ROBSON *Compan. Med. Stud.* I. xi. 24/2 Presence of phenylpyruvic acid in the blood leads to mental retardation. Arrangements to test the urine of every child soon after birth for phenylpyruvic acid have been made in many places. **1880** GARROD & BAXTER *Mat. Med.* 177 Sulphocarbolic or *phenylsulphuric acid is formed by the direct union of pure carbolic acid with sulphuric acid. **1879** *Jrnl. Chem. Soc.* XXXVI. 804 Mono- and di-*phenylthiocarbamide..are soluble in caustic soda or potash. **1932** [see *PTC* s.v. P II]. **1976** *Nature* 20 May 223/2 This report concerns two dermatoglyphic traits, fingerprint pattern index and total ridge-count, both strongly heritable. In addition, phenylthiocarbamide (PTC) taster ability.. and skin colour were studied. **1896** *Jrnl. Chem. Soc.* LXIX. 857 If dilute hydrochloric acid be now added to the clear solution, a white solid at once separates, which..forms white prisms..consisting of *phenylthiourea. **1959** *Listener* 3 Dec. 968/2 People who can taste phenylthiourea seem to be slightly more liable to get one form of thyroid disease and slightly less liable to get another. **1971** J. Z. YOUNG *Introd. Study Man* xxxviii. 553 A minimal yet striking example [of genetic variation of the nervous system] is the inheritance of the capacity to taste the substance phenylthiourea.

Hence **pheny'lamic** *a.* = ANILIC. **'phenyla,mide** = ANILIDE. **'phenyla,mine**, the systematic name of ANILINE (*monophenylamine*), $NH_2{\cdot}C_6H_5$, and of a large series of compounds of the same type, 'organic bases derived from ammonia by the substitution of one or more atoms of phenyl for an equivalent quantity of hydrogen' (Watts); e.g. ***diphenylamine***, $NH(C_6H_5)_2$, ***triphenylamine***, $N(C_6H_5)_3$; so ***azophenylamine***, $NH_2{\cdot}C_6H_2N$, ***bromophenylamine***, $NH_2{\cdot}C_6H_4Br$, ***chloro-***, ***iodo-***, ***nitro-phenylamine***, etc. **'phenylate**, a salt of phenylic acid. †**phe'nylia**, obs. synonym of *phenylamine* (aniline). **phenylic** (fɪ'nɪlɪk) *a.*, of or derived from phenyl; ***phenylic acid***, ***alcohol***, other names for Phenol or Carbolic acid; also formerly called **'phenylous acid**. **'phenyli,mide** (IMIDE): see quot. 1866. **pheny'lurea** = CARBANILAMIDE.

1866 WATTS *Dict. Chem.* IV. 419 **Phenylamic acids*. Anilic acids. **1857** MILLER *Elem. Chem.* III. 255 Aniline, Kyanol, *Phenylamide, Phenylia, Crystalline, or Benzidam ($C_{12}H_7N$)... This remarkable base may be prepared from several sources, and by a variety of reactions. **1866** ROSCOE *Elem. Chem.* xxxix. 338 Aniline has been called *Phenylamine..but it cannot be prepared like an amine. **1880** FRISWELL in *Jrnl. Soc. Arts* 16 Apr. 442/1 The earliest violets obtained by artificial means were those produced by the action of pure aniline, or phenylamine, on roseine. **1880** *Athenæum* 27 Nov. 713/1 The authors..have thus prepared aluminic methylate,..*phenylate, &c. **1857** *Phenylia [see *phenylamide*]. **1858** THUDICHUM *Urine* 339 *Phenylic acid was discovered, by Runge, in tar obtained by the distillation of coal. **1897** *Allbutt's Syst. Med.* II. 944 Carbolic acid is obtained from phenic acid or phenylic alcohol, a product of coal-tar distillation. **1866** WATTS *Dict. Chem.* IV. 419 *Phenylimides or Anils, tertiary monamides.. which.. may be regarded as aniline in which 2 atoms of H[ydrogen] are replaced by a diatomic radicle: e.g. $C_6H_5 \cdot (C_4H_4O_2)'' \cdot N$, phenyl-succinimide. **1852** *Phenylous acid [see PHENIC]. **1857** MILLER *Elem. Chem.* III. 616 *Phenyl-urea (carbanilamide).

phenylalanine ('fɛnɪl-, fiːnaɪl'æləniːn). *Biochem.* [ad. G. *phenylalanin* (Erlenmeyer & Lipp 1883, in *Ann. d. Chem. u. Pharm.* CCXIX. 186), f. *phenyl* PHENYL + *alanin* ALANINE.] A colourless, crystalline amino-acid, $C_6H_5CH_2 \cdot CH(NH_2)COOH$, which, in its lævorotatory form, is widely distributed in plant proteins and is an essential constituent of the human diet.

1883 *Jrnl. Chem. Soc.* XLIV. 992 Phenyl-α-amidoproprionic acid (phenylalanine),.. obtained as a hydrochloride by pouring the crude product of the action of ammonia on phenylethylidine cyanhydrin into hydrochloric acid, and boiling the mixture. **1934** *Times Lit. Suppl.* 1 Nov. 758/3 Whether this represents a real ability to synthesize the amino-acid for all purposes, or simply a power to use dietary phenylalanine, remains an open question. **1955** *Sci. News Let.* 22 Jan. 52/1 Since phenylalanine poisoning caused the mental deficiency, Dr. Woolf decided to try devising a diet that would not contain this amino acid. **1956** [see DOPA]. **1970** *Observer* 12 Apr. 25/4 Because he lacks a single pair of genes out of all those thousands, his liver cannot convert a chemical in his diet, called phenylalinine, into another chemical, tyrosine, and soon after birth he will start sliding down into severe mental retardation unless his diet is strictly controlled. **1970** [see PHENYLKETONURIA].

phenylbutazone (fɛnɪl-, fiːnaɪl'bjuːtəzəʊn). *Pharm.* [f. PHENYL + BUT(YL + AZ(O- + -ONE.] A white or cream-coloured crystalline solid which is used as an analgesic, esp. for the relief of rheumatic pain, and as an antipyretic; 4-butyl-3,5-dioxo-1,2-diphenylpyrazolidine, $C_{19}H_{20}N_2O_2$.

1952 *Jrnl. Amer. Med. Assoc.* 21 June 729/1 Phenylbutazone.. is one of a group of pyrazole derivatives developed by the chemists of the J. R. Geigy Co., of Basel, Switzerland. **1963** *Lancet* 5 Jan. 21/2 She was given phenylbutazone ('Butazolidin') for five days, with immediate relief of her joints. **1974** *Daily Colonist* (Victoria, B.C.) 1 June 1/3 The U.S. tests on the hard, round, black pills have apparently shown the presence of aminopyrine and phenylbutazone, two drugs legally available in Canada only on prescription. **1974** M. C. GERALD *Pharmacol.* xiv. 273 Phenylbutazone is a potent analgesic, anti-pyretic, and anti-inflammatory agent.

phenylene ('fɛnɪliːn). [f. PHENYL + ENE.]

a. The hydrocarbon C_6H_4.

1866 WATTS *Dict. Chem.* IV. 480 Phenylene. C_6H_4. A liquid having this composition and boiling at 91° was found by Church among the products of the distillation of phenylic chloride with sodium-amalgam.

b. phenylene blue, a blue dye (see INDAMINE); **phenylene brown** = *Bismarck brown* (s.v. BISMARCK 1), VESUVIN; **ˌphenylene'diamine,** any of three isomeric, toxic, crystalline solids, $C_6H_4(NH_2)_2$, or their alkylated derivatives, which are widely used in the dye industry, as photographic developers, and (in the case of the *para* isomer) as an additive in rubber to prevent oxidation.

1876 *Athenæum* 16 Dec. 806/1 'Phenylene-diamine' obtained from dinitro-benzene by the action of reducing agents. **1889** G. M'GOWAN tr. *Bernthsen's Text-bk. Org. Chem.* 356 The simplest member of this class is the indamine 'Phenylene Blue', $C_{12}H_{11}N_3$,.. which results from the oxidation of a mixture of aniline and *p*-phenylenediamine. **1903** [see INDAMINE]. **1952** K. VENKATARAMAN *Chem. Synthetic Dyes* II. xxv. 762 The indamines (e.g., Phenylene Blue) are obtained by oxidizing a neutral solution of.. a *p*-diamine.., and.. a monamine (e.g. aniline) having a free *p*-position. **1867** *Chem. News* 12 July 24/2 The phenylene-brown consists chiefly of a new base of the composition $C_{12}H_{13}N_5$. **1885** [see BISMARCK 1]. **1922** A. CLARKE *Coal-Tar Colours in Decorative Industries* iii. 43 The colours most suitable for this method are:—On White Earth—..Phenylene Brown, Crystal Violet and Methyl Violet. **1862** A. W. HOFMANN in *Proc. R. Soc.* XI. 519 The idea very naturally suggested itself, to look to dinitrobenzol as the source from which phenylene-diamine might reasonably be expected to arise. **1918** *Jrnl. Chem. Soc.* CXIV. II. 69 The authors have investigated the.. binary systems formed between phenol.. and the three phenylenediamines. **1972** *Materials & Technol.* V. xiv. 522 Only the.. *p*-phenylene diamines and dihydroquinolines give good ozone protection [to rubber]. **1973** D. A. SPENCER *Focal Dict. Photogr. Technol.* 440 *Phenylenediamines*, generic name for compounds derived from ortho-phenylenediamine and para-phenylenediamine which act as photographic developing agents.

phenylephrine (fɛnɪl-, fiːnaɪl'ɛfrɪn, -iːn). *Pharm.* [f. PHENYL + EPIN)EPHRINE.] The lævorotatory form of 1-(*m*-hydroxyphenyl)-2-methylaminoethanol, $HO \cdot C_6H_4 \cdot CH_2OH \cdot NH \cdot CH_3$, which is used (usu. as the hydrochloride) as an anti-hypotensive agent and nasal decongestant. Cf. NEO-SYNEPHRINE.

1947 *New & Non-Official Remedies* 225 Phenylephrine hydrochloride is a vasoconstrictor and is active as a vasopressor when administered orally. **1950** *Jrnl. Amer. Pharmaceut. Assoc.* XXXIX. 50/1 Phenylephrine N.N.R. (Neo-Synephrine) is a sympathomimetic amine in general use. **1963** *Lancet* 19 Jan. 138/2 Our experience and published reports suggest that, of the vasoconstrictors, phenylephrine and noradrenaline are probably the most satisfactory. **1974** [see NEO-SYNEPHRINE]. **1975** *Sci. Amer.* Nov. 117/1 On one of her visits she had her pupils artificially dilated with the drug phenylephrine hydrochloride. **1976** [see PHENYLPROPANOLAMINE].

phenylketonuria (ˌfɛnɪl-, ˌfiːnaɪlkiːtəʊ'njʊərɪə). *Path.* [f. PHENYL + KETONURIA.] An inherited inability to metabolize phenylalanine normally, which if untreated in children leads to mental deficiency.

1935 *Lancet* 27 July 192/2 Phenylpyruvic amentia, more conveniently termed phenylketonuria. *Ibid.* 193/1 Dr. J. H. Quastel.. suggested the name phenylketonuria. **1958** *Observer* 23 Mar. 9/8 An estimated 30 babies are born every year with an unsuspected 'metabolic' disorder called phenylketonuria. **1958** *New Biol.* XXV. 22 Phenylketonuria is a chemically definable character inherited as a Mendelian recessive, and accounting for perhaps 1 per cent of certifiable mental defect. **1965** *New Statesman* 10 Dec. 922/1 The classic examples here are phenylketonuria and galactosaemia, in which the lack of a single gene means that the body cannot use or break down normal substances in the diet.. so that toxic products accumulate and poison the brain. **1970** PASSMORE & ROBSON *Compan. Med. Stud.* II. xxv. 40 In phenylketonuria the hereditary deficiency of the enzyme phenylalanine hydroxylase in the liver cells retards or deletes the normal oxidation of phenylalanine to tyrosine. **1977** *Jrnl. R. Soc. Arts* CXXV. 186/2 The 'inborn error of metabolism', phenylketonuria.. is a simply inherited defect which causes mental retardation, due to accumulation of toxic products from birth onwards.

Hence **ˌphenylketo'nuric** *sb.*, an individual with phenylketonuria; *a.*, affected with or pertaining to this disorder.

1937 *Biochem. Jrnl.* XXXI. 270 Experiments were carried out.. to determine the effects of feeding phenylalanine to a phenylketonuric on a low protein diet. **1961** *Lancet* 26 Aug. 465/2 This suggests that there is no biochemical reason why any phenylketonuric woman should not have normal children. *Ibid.*, Exposure to a phenylketonuric environment while in utero. **1975** *Nature* 4 Dec. 462/3 Even if an observed difference is genetic it does not mean that a trait cannot be altered substantially by an appropriate environmental change. An example is the treatment of phenylketonurics.

phenylpropanolamine (ˌfiːnaɪl-, ˌfɛnɪlprəʊpə'nɒləmiːn). *Pharm.* [f. PHENYL + PROPANOL + AMINE.] = *norephedrine* s.v. NOR-1 a.

1947 LORHAN & MOSSER in *Ann. Surg.* CXXV. 171 (*heading*) Phenylpropanolamine hydrochloride: a vasopressor drug, for maintaining blood pressure during spinal anesthesia. **1968** W. C. BOWMAN et al. *Textbk. Pharmacol.* xxix. 750 Phenylpropanolamine, or norephedrine, is known commercially as Propadrine. **1969** [see COLD *sb.* 5 c]. **1976** *Which?* Mar. 53/1 Some pills and capsules are intended to help your nose feel less blocked up (they contain phenylephrine or phenylpropanolamine for this).

phenytoin ('fɛnɪtəʊɪn). *Pharm.* [f. PHENY(L + HYDAN)TOÏN.] 5,5-Diphenylhydantoin, $C_{15}H_{12}N_2O_2$, an anticonvulsant widely used in the treatment of epilepsy (usu. in the form of its sodium salt, a white powder).

1942 *Jrnl. Amer. Med. Assoc.* 4 Apr. 1209/2 While phenytoin sodium (sodium diphenyl hydrantoinate, or dilantin sodium) was effective in protecting animals from electrically induced convulsions it produced little sedative effect. **1952** A. H. DOUTHWAITE *Hale-White's Materia Medica* (ed. 29) 193 When grand mal and petit mal occur in the same patient phenobarbitone and troxidone should be used together: phenytoin must not be employed. **1961** *Lancet* 23 Sept. 683/2 Since then, she has had post-encephalic epilepsy which is controlled by phenobarbitone and phenytoin sodium. **1969** *New Scientist* 10 July 57/3 Patients who had received phenobarbitone or phenytoin showed a dramatic reduction in DDE levels. **1973** [see MYSOLINE].

pheon ('fiːɒn). Also 5 **feon.** [Origin unknown. Identity has been suggested with OF. *foine, foene*, mod.F. *fouine*, a pitchfork, or trident for catching fish, etc., the regular Eng. repr. of which is FOIN; but the *pheon* is never a fork, and the *fouine* is not essentially barbed.]

1. *Her.* 'A charge representing a broad barbed arrow, or head of a javelin' (Fairholt). Either identical with the figure called the broad arrow, or differing only in being engrailed on the inner edge.

1486 *Bk. St. Albans, Her.* B v, Feons be calde in armys brode arow hedys. **1562** LEIGH *Armorie* 175 A Pheon Azure, whiche signifieth the hedd of a Darte. **1610** GUILLIM *Heraldry* IV. xiv. (1611) 228 The pheon is the head of an instrument of the missile sort which we call a dart. **1864** BOUTELL *Her. Hist. & Pop.* ix. 49 Unless the contrary be specified, the point of the Pheon is blazoned to the base.

2. As the name of an actual weapon: see quots.

a **1618** SYLVESTER *Job Triumph.* IV. 599 Canst thou his Skin with barbed pheons pierce? [**1860** FAIRHOLT *Costume in Eng.* (ed. 2) Gloss., *Pheon*, a barbed javelin, carried by sergeants-at-arms in the king's presence as early as Richard I's time.]

pheophorbide, -phytin, varr. PHÆOPHORBIDE, -PHYTIN.

‖**pheran** ('fɛːrən, 'pɛːrən). [Kashmiri, prob. ad. Pers. *pairáhan* a shirt.] (See quots.)

1882 *Encycl. Brit.* XIV. 12/1 The Kashmíris, both men and women, wear commonly a kind of loose gown with sleeves, called *phéran* (Pers., *pairáhan*, 'a robe'). **1895** W. R. LAWRENCE *Valley of Kashmir* xix. 464/2 Tunic worn by all Kashmíris.. *Pheran.* **1922** *Chambers's Jrnl.* Nov. 760/2 He is robed in the national Kashmiri dress—the pheran—a loose, flowing garment of white lawn or silk. **1953** R. GODDEN *Kingfishers catch Fire* ii. 18 He wore a grey *pheran*—the loose robe that most Kashmiri men and women wore. **1976** R. KALAPESI *Catal. Pageant of Indian Costumes* 29 In Kashmir, the long pant is called the 'salwar' and is worn with a loose shirt, called the 'pheran', with its typical embroidered Sassanian neckline and square armholes.

phere, var. FERE *sb.*[1] companion, *sb.*[2] company.

Pherecratean (ˌfɛrɪkrə'tiːən), *a.* (*sb.*) *Gr.* and *Lat. Pros.* [f. L. *Pherecratius*, a. Gr. φερεκράτειος (f. Φερεκράτης name of a Greek poet) + -AN.] Name of a logaœdic metre or verse consisting of three feet, normally a spondee, dactyl, and spondee (or trochee), but admitting of some variations. Also called **Pherecratian** (-'kreɪʃ(ɪ)ən), **Pherecratic** (-'krætɪk).

1788 LEMPRIÈRE *Classical Dict.* (1826) 511/1 He [Pherecrates] invented a sort of verse, which from him has been called *Pherecratian.* **1797** *Encycl. Brit.* (ed. 3) XIV. 456/2 Pherecrates.. was author of a kind of verse called, from his own name, *Pherecratick*... This verse of Horace (..*Quamvis pontica pinus*) is a Pherecratick verse. **1861** HADLEY *Greek Gram.* §921 Pherecratean verses are sometimes combined in systems: but much more frequent are Glyconic systems closing with a Pherecratean.

† **'pheretrer,** obs. form of FERETRAR.

1555 W. WATREMAN *Fardle Facions* I. v. 77 Certaine Pheretrers, whose facultie it is to sette for the burialles.

pheromone ('fɛrəʊməʊn). *Biol.* [f. Gr. φέρ-ειν to convey + -O + ὁρμῶν, pres. pple. of ὁρμᾶν to set in motion, urge on (after *hormone*).] Any substance that is secreted and released by an animal (usu. in minute amounts) and causes a specific response when detected by another animal of the same (or a closely related) species.

1959 KARLSON & LÜSCHER in *Nature* 3 Jan. 55/2 We propose.. the designation 'pheromone' for this group of active substances... Pheromones are defined as substances which are secreted to the outside by an individual and received by a second individual of the same species, in which they release a specific reaction, for example, a definite behaviour or a developmental process... Having stated that pheromones act on individuals of the same species, they must be differentiated from other stimulating substances, like.. scents of flowers and insect repellents... Strict species-specificity is not required; certain overlaps between closely related species may occur. **1962** *New Scientist* 19 Apr. 86/2 The queen substance of honey-bees, which inhibits ovary development and profoundly affects behaviour in workers, is a pheromone; and pheromones of various kinds are supposed to affect caste differentiation and colony structure in termites. **1965** *Listener* 14 Jan. 57/2 Our observation of ant colonies.. has led us to believe that as few as ten pheromones, transmitted singly or in combination, might suffice for the total organization of ant society. **1971** *Nature* 17 Dec. 415/2 We now describe a case in which male attraction to females of the same species is inhibited by a pheromone emitted from females of a closely related species. Our tests were conducted with the Indian meal moth *Plodia interpunctella* (Hübner) and the almond moth *Cadra cautella* (Walker), both phycitid species. **1973** H. O. BOX *Organisation in Animal Communities* viii. 200 Examples.. include the blocking of pregnancy in the females of some strains of mice by a pheromone in the urine of a strange male mouse. **1975** D. S. HILL *Agric. Insect Pests of Tropics* iii. 23 Behavioural control with several types of pheromone may be possible, but attention has been focused on pheromones causing aggregation for mating, feeding or oviposition. **1977** *Sci. Amer.* May 104/3 It now appears that certain insects take chemicals from the plants they eat, store the chemicals and later emit them for defense, as 'aggregation pheromones' or perhaps as sex attractants.

Hence **phero'monal** *a.*, of, pertaining to, or being a pheromone or pheromones.

1959 *Ann. Rev. Entomol.* IV. 39 Pheromonal secretion need not occur in definite glands (though that is the case normally). **1971** *New Scientist* 25 Feb. 413/1 Much of this would be speculation alone if research had not produced an intriguing instance of human communication which might just possibly prove to be pheromonal. Recently, Dr Martha McClintock of Harvard.. has investigated the menstrual cycles of women students in a hall of residence... Her investigation threw up the bizarre observation that, precisely as in mice, the cycles of close friends.. fall into synchrony. **1971** *Nature* 16 Apr. 432/1 Odour fingerprinting techniques and gas chromatography now make the detection and preparation of human pheromonal agents feasible if they exist. **1975** *Sci. Amer.* May 59/1 The physiological causes, possibly pheromonal ones, for the synchrony of births remain to be determined, and it will not be easy to determine them with lions in the wild.

† **phese,** obs. form of FEEZE *v.*

1606 SHAKS. *Tr. & Cr.* II. iii. 215 And a be proud with me, ile phese his pride.

phesike, obs. form of PHYSIC.

phesycion, phetonesse, pheuterer, obs. ff. PHYSICIAN, PYTHONESS, FEWTERER.

phew (fjuː, fjʊ), *int.* (*v.*, *sb.*) Also 7 (pheut), pfew, 8 phu, 9 phugh: see also PHO, PHOO [Representing the action of puffing or blowing away with the lips.] A vocal gesture expressing impatience, disgust, discomfort, or weariness.

1604 MARSTON & WEBSTER *Malcontent* I. iv, Pheut, I'll not shrink. **1633** FORD *Love's Sacr.* IV. i, Phew, sir, do not stand upon that. **1727** VANBR. & CIB. *Journ. Lond.* I. i, Phu! a fig for his money. **1856** BOKER *Poems* (1857) II. 133 As for your share,—phew! **1866** GEO. ELIOT *F. Holt* i, Phew-ew! Jermyn manages the estate badly, then. **1889** E. DOWSON *Let.* 30 June (1967) 88, I think it is possible for the feminine nature to be reasonably candid & simplex, up to the age of 8 or 9. Afterwards—phugh! **1892** H. HUTCHINSON *Fairw. Isl.* 16 'Phugh! and isn't it hot?'

b. (*nonce-uses*) as *vb. intr.* to utter the exclamation 'phew!'; as *sb.* an utterance of this.

1858 FARRAR *Eric* II. ii, Eric only 'phewed' again two or three times, and thought of Montagu. **1904** ADA CAMBRIDGE *Sisters* 70 Soon Rose heard sighs and phews, and sudden rustlings and slappings.

phi (faɪ). [The name of ϕ, Φ, the 21st letter of the Greek alphabet (in Gr. called φεῖ).]

1. *Petrol.* The negative of the logarithm to base 2 of the diameter in millimetres of a particle. Freq. *attrib.*, as ***phi scale***, and written as ϕ.

1934 W. C. KRUMBEIN in *Jrnl. Sedimentary Petrol.* IV. 76, ξ is the numerical value of the diameter... The substitution $\phi = -\log_2 \xi$, or $\xi = (\frac{1}{2})^\phi$, is made in part for typographical convenience, but also to introduce a convenient symbol that may be used for expressing grain diameters. **1936** —— in *Ibid.* VI. 38/1 One immediately apparent advantage accruing from the ϕ-scale is the elimination of unwieldy fractions or decimals, such as 1/1024 mm. (0·00098 mm.). *Ibid.* 45/1 The use of ϕ as the new independent variable.. makes available a series of statistical measures based on the moments of the distributions. **1949** *Ibid.* XIX. 76/1 The sieve interval of one phi unit is too large to make the true and nominal mean diameters reasonably equal for all size fractions. **1961** *Ibid.* XXXI. 205/2 Comparison of the mean diameters of each pair of beach-dune samples.. shows that there is little difference between the two. In these comparisons, 48 are within 0·2 phi of each other. **1971** E. F. MCBRIDE in R. E. Carver *Procedures Sedimentary Petrol.* vi. 110 The Phi scale is now used almost exclusively for computation and is gradually replacing the millimeter scale. **1978** *Nature* 14 Sept. 100/2 The sediments.. have mean sizes of 1·6–0·125 mm (−0·7 to 3·0 phi: very coarse to fine sand)... These sands exhibit good sorting, with standard deviations that are generally less than 0·8 phi units.

2. ***phi coefficient*** (Statistics): A synonym for the product-moment coefficient of correlation (see PRODUCT *sb.*[1]) used when each of the observed variables has only two possible values.

[**1904** K. PEARSON in *Drapers' Co. Res. Mem.: Biometric Ser.* I. 6, I shall call $\phi^2 = \chi/N$ the mean square contingency. **1913** *Biometrika* IX. 214 We do not agree with him, but it is singular that if he thinks so, he should not have rejected the use of ϕ, the 'theoretical value of the correlation'.] **1950** S. A. STOUFFER *Measurement & Prediction* x. 410 [This] is the Pearson r or the so-called phi-coefficient of the latent fourfold table, which appears here as a mere algebraic byproduct. **1968** BLUMLER & MCQUAIL *Television in Politics* iv. 75 All the phi coefficients of ·30 or higher (a level which is most unlikely to be reached by chance) were picked out. **1975** MOREHOUSE & STULL *Statistical Princ. Physical Educ.* xi. 235 The phi coefficient is also related to chi-square... $\phi = \sqrt{(\chi^2/N)}$, where N = number of observations. *Ibid.* 237 The phi coefficient is often recommended for use in the analysis of test items in which the items are scored as correct or incorrect, pass or fail.

3. *Nuclear Physics.* In full ***phi meson***. A neutral meson that has the same quantum numbers as the omega meson (OMEGA 3 b), is observed as a resonance, has a mass of 1019 MeV (1995 times that of the electron), and on decaying usu. produces two kaons or three pions. Freq. written ϕ.

1962 J. J. SAKURAI in *Physical Rev. Lett.* IX. 472/1 In a recent issue of this journal a Brookhaven-Syracuse group reports the possible presence of a narrow resonance ($\Gamma \approx 20$ MeV) in the $K\bar{K}$ system with mass $\approx$1020 MeV in the reactions $K^- + p \to K^+ + K^- + \Lambda$, $K^0 + \bar{K}^0 + \Lambda$. In discussing the quantum numbers of the resonating $K\bar{K}$ pair, which we tentatively refer to as the ϕ meson, [etc.]. *Ibid.* 474/1 We would like to suggest that this discrepancy is due to mixing between ω and ϕ arising from the fact that the ω and ϕ have the same quantum numbers as far as spin-parity, isospin, and G-parity are concerned. **1968** J. BERNSTEIN *Elem. Particles* vi. 86 Since these objects, the ρ, ω^0, ϕ^0, are very short-lived ($\tau \sim 10^{-23}$ sec), it is not really correct, in a rigorous sense, to treat them as if they were stable particles. **1971** *Sci. Amer.* July 100/2 Three vector mesons with zero strangeness are currently known: the rho, the omega and the phi. **1974** *Nature* 6 Dec. 438/2 Another well established meson, called the phi, also has electromagnetic decays to e^+e^-. **1975** *Sci. Amer.* Oct. 48/2 Zweig's rule was formulated to explain the decay of the phi meson, which is made up of a strange quark and a strange antiquark and has a mass of about 1 GeV. The two particles are closely analogous, but the decay of the J is appreciably slower than that of the phi.

phi-: see PHY-.

phial ('faɪəl), *sb.* Forms: α. 4 fiol, 4–5 **fyole**, 5 **fyoll(e, fialle**, 6 **fyol**, 7 **fiole**. β. 4 **phyall(e**, 6 **phiall**, 7 **phiole**, **phyal**, 7– **phial**. See also VIAL. [ME. a. F. *fiole* (12th c. in Hatz.-Darm.), also *phiole* (13th c. in Littré), in Cotgr. *fiole*, *phiole* = Pr. *fiola*, It. *fiala*, ad. late L. *phiola*, L. *phiala*, ad. Gr. φιάλη a broad flat vessel.]

A vessel for holding liquids, esp. drinks; formerly variously applied; now usually a small glass bottle, esp. for liquid medicine. † ***Leyden phial*** = Leyden jar: see LEYDEN. ***Bologna phial***: see BOLOGNA.

13.. *E.E. Allit. P.* B. 1476 Fyoles fretted with flores & fleez of golde. **1382** WYCLIF *Num.* vii. 84 Silueren fiols [1388 viols] twelue, golden morters twelue. **1483** *Cath. Angl.* 129/2 A Fialle, *ampulla, fiola*. **1490** CAXTON *Eneydos* xiii. 47 The fyole fulle of the holi libacion. **1609** BIBLE (Douay) *Amos* vi. 6 You..that drinke wine in phials [1611 bowls]. **1656** BLOUNT *Glossgr.*, *Phial*, a plain pot with a wide mouth, whereout a man might drink enough. **1669** BOYLE *Contn. New Exp.* II. (1682) 12 A Glass Phial filled with Mercury. **1747** FRANKLIN *Let.* Wks. 1840 V. 194 Set the electrified phial on one, and then touch the wire. **1806** *Med. Jrnl.* XV. 433 Very little of it will be lost, provided the phial be properly shaken. **1820** SCORESBY *Acc. Arctic Reg.* I. 235 The phial was suddenly corked and inverted. **1846** JOYCE *Sci. Dial.* VII. vi. (1849) 461 We will describe what is usually called the Leyden phial. **1873** HALE *In His Name* iii. 16 What is the elixir in your phial?

b. *fig.* (See Rev. v. 8, xvi. 1.) Cf. VIAL.

1649 JER. TAYLOR *Gt. Exemp.* II. Disc. xi. 12 That my Prayers being..presented in the Phial of the Saints may ascend..Where thy glory dwells. **1742** YOUNG *Nt. Th.* I. 53 The Phial of thy Vengeance, pour'd On this devoted Head. *a* **1881** ROSSETTI *House of Life* xc, Wait the turning of the phials of wrath For certain years.

c. *attrib.* and *Comb.*, as ***phial-book***, ***-glass***; ***phial-like*** adj.

1826 KIRBY & SP. *Entomol.* III. xxix. 81 Eggs..of a long phial-like form. **1851** *Blackw. Mag.* June 688 The homoeopathist pulling out..his phial-book.

Hence **'phial** *v. trans.*, to store or keep in a phial, to bottle up; **'phialful**, as much as fills a phial.

a **1763** SHENSTONE *Love & Hon.* 164 Full on my fenceless head its phial'd wrath May Fate exhaust. **1769** LANE in *Phil. Trans.* LIX. 219 The liquor being shaken, and another phial-full taken up soon after.

phialine ('faɪəlɪn, -aɪn), *a. rare.* [f. PHIAL *sb.* + -INE[2].] Resembling a phial or that of a phial.

1881 H. B. BRADY in *Jrnl. Microsc. Sc.* Jan. 62 A thin peripheral border, surmounted by a stout sessile phialine lip.

Phi Beta Kappa (faɪ 'biːtə (or 'beɪtə) 'kæpə). *U.S.* [f. the initials of Gr. φιλοσοφία βίου κυβερνήτης philosophy (the) guide of life.] An honorary society to which distinguished undergraduate, and occas. graduate, scholars may be elected; a member of this society. Also *attrib.*

[**1776** in *William & Mary College Q.* (1896) Apr. 214 A list of Members who have been Initiated into the S.P. *alias* ΦBK Society.] **1831** *N.Y. Mirror* 3 Sept. 71/2 Chancellor Kent will deliver an oration before the Phi Beta Kappa Society, at the annual commencement of Yale College. **1894** *Harper's Mag.* June 34/1 I've got to read the Phi Beta Kappa poem at Harvard next week. **1912** M. NICHOLSON *Hoosier Chron.* 278 Sylvia..just walked through everything and would be chosen for the Phi Beta Kappa. **1929** *Chicagoan* 17 Aug. 21/3 Harvard University Phi Beta Kappa conventions. **1932** W. FAULKNER *Light in August* xix. 419 A Harvard graduate, a Phi Beta Kappa. **1949** *Newsweek* 5 Dec. 54/2 Selby won a Phi Beta Kappa key at Northwestern. **1954** W. STEVENS *Let.* 29 Jan. (1967) 816, I am going to read a Phi Beta Kappa poem..at Columbia. **1968** *Wall St. Jrnl.* 19 Feb. 1/1 Mr. Kahn, a Phi Beta Kappa member in his junior year. **1974** 'I. DRUMMOND' *Power of Bug* x. 144 The other was collegiate too, but not an athlete, a Phi Beta Kappa. **1976** *National Observer* (U.S.) 10 July 11/1 Phi Beta Kappa was founded as a secret society at the College of William and Mary on Dec. 5, 1776, and it featured, along with an oath of secrecy, mottoes in Latin and Greek, a code of laws, elaborate initiation rites, a badge, a seal, and a special handclasp. **1978** *Detroit Free Press* 16 Apr. 23A/1, I notice you wearing your Phi Beta Kappa Key from Barnard.

Phidiac ('faɪdɪæk), *a.* Also Pheidiac. [ad. L. *Phīdiac-us*, Gr. Φειδιακός, f. Φειδίας, Phīdias.] Of, pertaining to, or like the work of Phidias, the most famous sculptor of ancient Greece. So **Phi'diacan** *a.*; also **'Phidian** (**'Pheidian**) *a.*

1809 BYRON *Bards & Rev.* liii, Let Aberdeen and Elgin.. Waste useless thousands on their Phidian freaks. **1823** —— *Juan* XIII. cx, Phidian forms cut out of marble. **1870** EMERSON *Soc. & Solit.* xi. 271 Features that explain the Phidian sculpture. **1883** *Century Mag.* XXVII. 175 Throughout all the works of Pheidiac art which have come down to us. **1885** F. B. VAN VORST *Without a Compass* 8 He had endeavoured to breathe into that most refractory of all materials..Phidiacan forms.

phife, obs. form of FIFE.

Phil (fɪl), colloq. abbrev. PHILHARMONIC *sb.* b. Also *attrib.*

1949 E. COXHEAD *Wind in West* iii. 84 Alan was a violinist. He played in the Northern Phil. **1963** *Times* 25 Jan. 14/7 The 'Phil' audience, as regular and loyal as any in London. **1977** *Listener* 28 Apr. 564/3 A 'great' orchestra such as the New York Phil or the Concert-gebouw. **1978** J. GALLWAY *Autobiogr.* xiv. 162, I thought the fellows in the Berlin Phil a marvellous bunch.

phil (fɪl), *a. rare.* [The suffix -PHIL used as a separate word.] Having a love or leaning (towards something).

1915 [see PHOBE *a.*].

phil-, form of PHILO- used before a vowel or *h*.

-phil (fɪl), **-phile** (faɪl), combining element repr. Gr. φίλος loving, dear. In Greek, found only in certain personal names, where it means 'dear, beloved', as Δίφιλος (dear to Zeus), Θεόφιλος (dear to God). In med. and mod.L. often used as a second element in form *-philus*, *-phila*, with sense 'lover, loving' (e.g. *botanophilus* (Linn.) lover of plants, amateur botanist, *Ammophila*, generic name). Hence in French words *-phile*, in Eng. *-phile* or later *-phil*, as *Anglophil(e*, *Russophil(e*, *Slavophil(e*, *Turcophil(e*, for which forms with the prefix PHILO- are more correct etymologically; so *conchophil(e* (shell-loving), *gastrophil(e*, *oxyphil(e*, etc.; *spec.* in *Biol.* and *Med.* in the sense 'having an affinity for (a certain substance or class of substances)', as in EOSINOPHIL *a.* and *sb.*, *neutrophil(e* adj. and sb. (s.v. NEUTRO-). Hence also -PHILOUS, q.v.

philabeg, erroneous form of FILIBEG, a kilt.

Philadelphia (fɪlə'dɛlfɪə). The name of the city in Pennsylvania, U.S.A., used *attrib.* in **Philadelphia chromosome**, an abnormal small chromosome sometimes found in the leukocytes of patients suffering from leukæmia, esp. chronic granulocytic leukæmia; **Philadelphia lawyer**, a lawyer of great ability, esp. one expert in the exploitation of legal technicalities; a shrewd or unscrupulous lawyer.

[**1961** I. S. TOUGH et al. in *Lancet* 25 Feb. 411/2 In this paper the abnormal chromosome, for the sake of brevity, is referred to by the symbol Ph[1]. This is chosen as it indicates the geographical location, Philadelphia in the United States, of the laboratories in which the chromosome was first noted, and thus it accords with the recommendations on the nomenclature of abnormal chromosomes of the Denver conference.] **1963** WALTER & ISRAEL *Gen. Path.* iii. 45 Some of the leucocytes show replacement of one of their small autosomes by a minute chromosome (the 'Philadelphia chromosome'). This is generally assumed to be 21. **1977** R. B. THOMPSON *Disorders of Blood* xxxv. 566/1 The Philadelphia chromosome usually arises by a translocation from G22 to C9. **1788** *Columbian Mag.* Apr. 182 They have a proverb here [in London], which I do not know how to account for;—in speaking of a difficult point, they say, *it would puzzle a Philadelphia lawyer*. **1803** *Balance* (Hudson, N.Y.) 15 Nov. 363/1 It would (to use a Yankee phrase) *puzzle a dozen Philadelphia lawyers* to unriddle the conduct of the democrats. **1834** W. G. SIMMS *Guy Rivers* II. i. 23 You would have made a prime counsellor..worthy of the Philadelphia lawyers. **1896** *N.Y. Weekly Witness* 30 Dec. 13/1 Not even a Philadelphia lawyer would have been able to pick the winners [in an election contest]. **1901** *Daily Tel.* 6 Nov. 5/4 What entertainment is afforded by a horse-race run 'in camera', only a Philadelphia lawyer would be able to explain. **1909** L. M. MONTGOMERY *Anne of Avonlea* xxvi. 306, I won't undertake to answer Davy's questions... I'm not an encyclopedia, neither am I a Philadelphia lawyer. **1947** *Daily Times* (Chicago) 28 Nov. 14/3 The new violation ticket will be in quadruplicate, and traffic officials say it takes a 'Philadelphia lawyer' to fix it. **1977** *Washington Post* 25 Mar. D18/2 President Carter has made it clear that he understands how complex the income tax laws are. To head IRS, he has picked a Philadelphia lawyer.

Philadelphian (fɪlə'dɛlfɪən), *a.* and *sb.* [In sense 1, f. Gr. φιλαδελφία brotherly love (f. φιλάδελφος loving one's brother or sister, f. PHILO- + ἀδελφός brother, ἀδελφή sister) + -AN; in sense 2 in part, and in 3, 4, f. Gr. Φιλαδέλφεια, *Philadelphia* (i.e. the city of Ptolemy Philadelphus).]

A. *adj.* **1.** Brother-loving; loving the brethren.

1615 BYFIELD *Exp. Coloss.* i. 10 We must get that philanthropian love of men into our hearts, but especially philadelphian, the love of the brethren. **1868** *Sat. Rev.* 13 June 778/2 His unfortunate brother must..suffer for the blasphemous philadelphian piety of his profane advocate.

2. Of or pertaining to the Philadelphians: see B. 2, and cf. Rev. iii. 7–13.

1693 BEVERLEY *True St. Gosp. Truth* Pref. A ij, That Philadelphian State, to which Christ hath opened a Door, which none can shut. **1697** (*title*) *State of Philadelphian Society*. *Ibid.* 5 Where are these Pillars of the Philadelphian Temple? **1764** MACLAINE tr. *Mosheim's Eccl. Hist.* (1844) II. 282/2 A notion that her [Jane Leadley's] Philadelphian society was the true kingdom of Christ. **1874** J. H. BLUNT *Dict. Sects*, etc. (1886) s.v., The Philadelphian Society contributed largely to the spread of that mystical piety which is so conspicuous in the works of..William Law, and which affected in no small degree the early stages of Methodism.

3. Of or pertaining to the ancient city of Philadelphia, to Philadelphia in Pennsylvania, or to any other place of the name.

1775 *Short View of Lord High Admiral's Jurisdiction* 35 A Philadelphian ship might be tried with a fairer chance of condemnation at Halifax than at Philadelphia. **1855** H. A. MURRAY *Lands of Slave & Free* I. xiv. 360 The only peculiarity in the Philadelphian mint is a frame-work for counting the number of pieces coined. **1930** R. MACAULAY *Staying with Relations* i. 14 She loved her little Philadelphian aunt. **1975** *Country Life* 2 Jan. 21/3 Rococco mirrors and girandoles attributed to the Philadelphia craftsman James Reynolds... The majority of the other pieces in the house are also Philadelphian.

4. Of or pertaining to Ptolemy Philadelphus.

B. *sb.* **1.** (See quot.)

1656 BLOUNT *Glossogr.*, *Philadelphia*, a womans name, and signifies brotherly or sisterly love. And lovers of Brothers or Sisters, are stiled *Philadelphians*.

2. (*pl.*) A religious society or party organized in England towards the end of the 17th c. under the name of the ***Philadelphian Society***.

The name appears to have combined a reference to the sense of the Gr. φιλαδελφία brotherly love, with one to the church of Philadelphia, Gr. Φιλαδέλφεια, in Rev. iii. 7–13.

1693 BEVERLEY *True St. Gosp. Truth* Pref. A ij, That.. none should take their Crown, who are true Philadelphians. **1697** *Princ. Philadelphians* 1 There has lately appeared in England.. a Sect or certain number of People, who attribute to themselves an extraordinary Sanctity... They seem to derive themselves from a Sect long since started up.. the Family of Love, now stiling themselves Philadelphians, or the little Virgin Church of Philadelphia. *a* **1700** B. E. *Dict. Cant. Crew*, *Philadelphians*, a new Sect of Enthusiasts, pretenders to Brotherly Love. **1710** STEELE & ADDISON *Tatler* No. 257 ¶ 10. **1860** J. GARDNER *Faiths World* II. 654/2 A small body of Philadelphians existed for a short time also in Holland.

3. a. A native or inhabitant of the ancient city of Philadelphia in Asia Minor.

1725 E. COMTE tr. *Huet's Weakness of Human Understanding* 117 Herodotus, the Tutor of Sextus Chaeronensis, was a Philadelphian. **1904** W. M. RAMSAY *Lett. Seven Churches* xviii. 249 The writer seems not to have loved the Ephesians as he did the Smyrnaeans and Philadelphians.

b. A native or inhabitant of the city of Philadelphia in Pennsylvania.

1744 A. HAMILTON *Itinerarium* (1907) 164, I dined with Mr. Fletcher in the company of two Philadelphians. **1789** J. MORSE *Amer. Geogr.* 332 The Philadelphians have exerted their endeavours.. to prevent the intemperate use of spirituous liquors. **1803** *Lit. Mag.* (Philadelphia) Dec. 170 A Philadelphian.. told us, he could not, after repeated trials, find a chaise. **1841** J. S. BUCKINGHAM *America* II. 84 The Philadelphians have the reputation of being cold, formal, and difficult of approach. **1891** L. J. JENNINGS *Philadelphian* I. i. 11 The reputation of Mr. Snapper for integrity stood deservedly high, and in entrusting his capital to the hands of the Philadelphian, Pendleton incurred no more than the ordinary and legitimate risks of commercial affairs. **1901** *Chambers's Jrnl.* Jan. 31/2 One enterprising Philadelphian has been trying to form a Snake Trust. **1947** *Harper's Mag.* Sept. 200/2 The Proper Bostonian is a very well-defined type—more so.. than the Proper Baltimorean, the Proper Philadelphian, or the Proper person of any other city. **1976** *Amer. Speech 1974* XLIX. 213 The Philadelphian is also judged the richest and least friendly of the group and seventh in politeness. **1977** *Sci. Amer.* Nov. 30/2 Redheffer took his device to New York (but only after the ingenious Philadelphians had made up and showed him their own perpetual-motion machine).

Hence **Phila'delphianism** (from sense 2).

1697 *State Philadelph. Soc.* 5 If You please to read the Charter of Philadelphianism in the Epistle to that Church.

philadelphite (fɪlə'dɛlfaɪt). *Min.* [Named 1880, from Philadelphia in Pennsylvania, near which it is found; see -ITE[1] 2 b.] A kind of vermiculite akin to jefferisite.

1880 H. C. LEWIS in *Proc. Acad. Nat. Sc. Philad.* 313. **1896** CHESTER *Dict. Min.*, *Philadelphite*, a brownish-red, micaceous mineral, closely related to jefferisite.

philadelphus (fɪlə'dɛlfəs). [mod.L. (C. Bauhin *Πιναξ Theatri Botanici* (1623) 398, adopted by Linnæus in *Systema Naturæ* (1735) as a generic name), f. Gr. φιλάδελφος loving one's brother, used as a plant name.] A shrub of the genus so called, belonging to the family Saxifragaceæ, native to southern Europe, North America, or Asia, and generally bearing white or cream flowers, often fragrant; also called mock orange or syringa.

1783 [see SYRINGA]. **1797** *Bot. Mag.* XI. 391 (*heading*) Philadelphus Coronarius. Common Philadelphus, or Mock-Orange. **1899** G. JEKYLL *Wood & Garden* iii. 22 How extremely dense and hard is the wood of Philadelphus! as close-grained as Box. **1938** M. HAWORTH-BOOTH *Flowering Shrub Garden* xvi. 158 When a Philadelphus.. is grown in the open, say as a specimen set in the turf, such [drastic] pruning is unnecessary. **1970** *Times* 14 July 10/7 Notcutts nurseries show large flowered philadelphus. **1975** C. NESBITT *Little Love & Good Company* xvii. 220, I used to think the lilac tree had the sweetest scent, till the philadelphus came with summer and was still sweeter.

†**phila'delphy.** *Obs. rare.* [ad. Gr. φιλαδελφία: see above.] Brotherly love.

a **1677** BARROW *Serm.* (1683) II. x. 152 That charity, which in respect to others is called philanthropy.. in regard to [Christians] is named philadelphy (or brotherly affection).

philagrain, -green, -grin, obs. forms of FILIGRANE.

philamort, -mot, obs. ff. FILEMOT.

philander (fɪ'lændə(r)), *sb.* [ad. Gr. φίλανδρος adj., loving or fond of men, (of a woman) loving her husband, f. φιλο-, PHILO- + ἀνήρ, ἄνδρ-α man, male, husband; hence used as a proper name in story, drama, dialogue; in later use esp. for a lover (perh. misunderstood as = a loving man).

Thus in Ariosto's *Orlando Furioso*, Filandro was the youth beloved and ruined by the lustful Gabrina; and in Beaumont and Fletcher's *Laws of Candy*, one of the personages is 'Philander Prince of Cyprus, passionately in love with Erota'; but the name seems to have been more particularly matched with *Phillis*, as in quot. 1682. Cf. PHILLIS.]

†**1. a.** A lover; one given to making love. *Obs.*

[*a* **1682** (*title of Ballad*) The faithful Lovers Downfal: or, The Death of Fair Phillis Who Killed her self for loss of her Philander. *Ibid.*, Philander, ah Philander! still the bleeding Phillis cries, She wept awhile, And she forc't a Smile, then clos'd her eyes and dyes.] **1700** CONGREVE *Way of World* v. i, I'll couple you! yes, I'll baste you together, you and your Philander. [**1709** TATLER No. 13 ¶ 1 Enter'd Philander, who is the most skilful of all Men in an Address to Women.] **1794** C. PIGOT *Female Jockey Club* 99 Those philanders of former times once led Captivity Captive, too happy to be bound in her fetters. **1813** MOORE *Post-bag* viii, Bring thy best lace, thou gay Philander!

b. A love-making or philandering.

1898 G. B. SHAW *Philanderer* I. 78 It was nothing but a philander with Julia—nothing else in the world, I assure you.

2. A name given to certain marsupial animals (also FILANDER).

[From the name of *Philander de Bruyn*, who saw in 1711 in the garden of the Dutch governor of Batavia the species named after him (in a), being the first member of the family known to Europeans. (Morris *Austral Eng.*)]

a. A small wallaby (*Macropus brunnii*) first described by Philander de Bruyn. **b.** A South American opossum (*Didelphys philander*). **c.** An Australian bandicoot (*Perameles lagotis*).

1737 [see FILANDER[2]]. **1753** CHAMBERS *Cycl. Supp.*, *Didelphis*, the name by which Linnæus calls the animal called philander by other writers. **1866** *List Anim. Zool. Soc.* (ed. 9) 215 *Didelphys philander*,.. Philander Opossum.

†**philander,** obs. f. FILANDER[1], intestinal worm in hawks.

1596 HARINGTON *Metam. Ajax* D iv, You feare shee hath the philanders.

phi'lander, *v.* Also 9 **filander.** [f. PHILANDER *sb.*; lit. 'to act or do the Philander'.]

1. *intr.* To make love, especially in a trifling manner; to flirt; to dangle after a woman.

1737 [implied in PHILANDERING]. **1788** *Disinterested Love* I. 53, I must disguise my sentiments, or I shall get none of the pretty fools to philander with. *a* **1805** A. CARLYLE *Autobiog.* 92, I passed the day.. between disputing with my landlord, and walking about and philandering with the ladies. **1826** DISRAELI *Viv. Grey* II. i, The military M.P. fled to the drawing-room to philander with Mrs. Grey. **1875** MRS. RANDOLPH *W. Hyacinth* I. iii. 58 You surely don't expect me to go philandering about the woods playing Corydon to my cousin Phyllis. **1881** MISS BRADDON *Asph.* I. 191 [To] cure him of this inclination to philander.

†**2.** *trans.* To pay court to, make love to. *Obs.*

1792 *Elvina* II. 61, I could have Philandered the daughter, and complimented the father.

Hence **phi'landering** *vbl. sb.* and *ppl. a.*

1737 MRS. A. GRANVILLE in *Mrs. Delany's Life & Corr.* I. 597, I was extremely diverted with the philandering you gave me an account of.. Bath is not a place to keep lovers a secret. **1860** THACKERAY *Four Georges* ii. (1876) 48 Henrietta Howard accepted the noble old earl's philandering. **1884** *Sat. Rev.* 7 June 736/2 Sham piety and philandering religiousness.

phi'landerer. [f. prec. + -ER[1].] One who philanders; a male flirt.

1841 HOR. SMITH *Moneyed Man* I. v. 136 The imputation of being a dangler, a Philanderer. **1877** BLACK *Green Past.* x. (1878) 80 Worse still, a philanderer—a professor of the fine art of flirtation.

†**phi'lanthropal,** *a. Obs. rare.* [f. Gr. φιλάνθρωπ-ος (see next) + -AL[1].] Beneficent or friendly to mankind.

1648 J. RAYMOND *Il Merc. Ital.* Introd. 21 A Rimarra is a Philanthropall creature in forme like a Lyzzard. **1656** BLOUNT *Glossogr.*, *Philanthropal*, ful of love to mankind.

philanthrope ('fɪlænθrəʊp). [ad. Gr. φιλάνθρωπ-ος (adj.) loving mankind (said of gods, men, animals), humane, benign or useful to man, f. φιλο-, PHILO- + ἄνθρωπος man. Cf. F. *philanthrope* (in *Dict. Acad.* 1762; Oresme *a* 1400, has *philantropos* pl.).] = PHILANTHROPIST.

a **1734** NORTH *Lives* (1826) II. 44 He had a goodness of nature.. in so great a degree that he may be deservedly styled a philanthrope. **1810** BERESFORD *Bibliosophia*, &c. 22 Calling on the Philanthrope to counteract their balefulness. **1883** R. F. BURTON in *Academy* 26 May 366/3 If only we govern like men, not like philanthropes and humanitarians.

†**philan'thropian,** *a. Obs.* [f. L. (post cl.) *philanthrōpia* + -AN.] Of the nature of philanthropy; philanthropic.

1615 BYFIELD *Exp. Coloss.* i. 10 [see PHILADELPHIAN *a.* 1].

philanthropic (fɪlæn'θrɒpɪk), *a.* (*sb.*) [ad. F. *philanthropique* (Mirabeau, 18th c.), f. Gr. φιλάνθρωπ-ος (see PHILANTHROPE) + -IC (cf. Gr. ἀνθρωπικ-ός, f. ἄνθρωπος).] Characterized by philanthropy; actuated by love of one's fellow-men; benevolent; humane.

1789 (*title*) First Report of the Philanthropic Society instituted in London, Sept. 1788, for the prevention of Crimes. **1799** *Med. Jrnl.* I. 263 The philanthropic intentions of a man so zealous in the cause of humanity. **1824** L. MURRAY *Eng. Gram.* (ed. 5) I. 507 The eloquent Burke.. in his eulogium of the philanthropic Howard. **1874** GREEN *Short Hist.* x. §1. 716 The religious and philanthropic movement, which bears the name of Wesley.

B. *sb.* (*nonce-uses.*) A philanthropic person or practice: = PHILANTHROPIST, PHILANTHROPY.

a **1845** HOOD *Smithfield Market* xv, Great philanthropics! pray urge these topics! **1899** *Daily News* 11 Apr. 2/3 The Councils may be led astray in their philanthropics.

philanthropical (fɪlæn'θrɒpɪkəl), *a.* Now *rare* or *Obs.* [f. as prec. + -AL[1].] Relating to or concerned with philanthropy; = PHILANTHROPIC *a.*

1818 in TODD. *a* **1845** HOOD *Black Job* iii, A knot of very charitable men Set up a Philanthropical Society. **1856** MRS. BROWNING *Aur. Leigh* IV. 1016 Romney's school Of philanthropical self-sacrifice.

philan'thropically, *adv.* [f. prec. + -LY[2].] In a philanthropic manner; benevolently, humanely. Also *Comb.*

1787 'G. GAMBADO' *Acad. Horsemen* (1809) 29 *note*, The author is here philanthropically amiable. **1803** GODWIN *Chaucer* liv. II. 535 Philanthropically disposed. **1976** 'D. FLETCHER' *Don't whistle 'Macbeth'* 20 Various philanthropically-minded and prestige-seeking business and industrial concerns. **1980** J. ROSE *Elizabeth Fry* vi. 105 A number of philanthropically-minded ladies.

philanthropine (fɪ'lænθrəpɪn). [ad. Ger. *Philanthropin* (latinized *-inon*, *-inum*), a. Gr. φιλανθρώπιν-ον, neuter of φιλανθρώπιν-ος adj., rare parallel form of φιλάνθρωπος philanthropic (after ἀνθρώπινος human).] Anglicized form of the name given to the school founded in 1774 by John Bernhard Basedow or Bassedau (1723–90) at Dessau, Germany, for the education of children by his 'natural system', in the principles of philanthropy, natural religion, and cosmopolitanism; also any similar institution.

1802 tr. *De Luc's Lett. conc. Educ. Infancy* in *Guardian of Educ.* 26 Establishments.. afterwards multiplied in Germany under the title of *Philanthropines*; a specious name. **1805** MRS. TRIMMER in Southey *Life A. Bell* (1844) II. 135 M. De Luc.. gives there the history of the origin of the Philanthropines, which have done so much mischief. **1865** M. PATTISON *Ess.*, *F. A. Wolf* 356 These reformers,.. setting up an insitution of their own—the Philanthropinum at Dessau... Education was no longer to bear the stamp of the convent.

Hence **philan'thropinism** [ad. Ger. *philanthropinismus*], the educational system of the philanthropine.

1842 in BRANDE *Dict. Sci.*, etc.

philanthropinist (fɪlæn'θrəʊpɪnɪst), *sb.* (*a.*) [f. prec. + -IST.] An advocate of the 'natural system' of education of Basedow; also, a pupil at a philanthropine. Also *attrib.* or as *adj.* Of or pertaining to philanthropinism.

1842 BRANDE *Dict. Sci.*, etc. 920/2 The influence of the labours of the Philanthropinists has undoubtedly entered largely into the modern system of education. **1865** M. PATTISON *Ess.*, *F. A. Wolf* 358 Trapp was.. himself one of the Philanthropinists. **1868** QUICK *Educ. Reformers* vi. 152 It would soon be seen what was the value of Philanthropinist Latin. *Ibid.* 156 Philanthropinists, when they left school, were not in all respects the superiors of their fellow-creatures.

philanthropism (fɪ'lænθrəpɪz(ə)m). [f. as next + -ISM.] The profession or practice of philanthropy; a philanthropic theory or system.

1835 *Fraser's Mag.* XI. 102 A time of Tithe Controversy, Encyclopedism, Catholic Rent, Philanthropism, and the Revolution of Three Days! **1849** CLOUGH *Poems*, etc. (1869) I. 301 The more enlightened philanthropism of England resorts to the formation of charitable societies, to district-visiting, distribution of tracts, and teaching in charity schools. **1859** GEN. P. THOMPSON *Audi Alt.* II. xci. 68 'Philanthropism' then is up again, and all Reformers are Philanthropists, and all Philanthropists Reformers.

philanthropist (fɪ'lænθrəpɪst). [f. PHILANTHROPY + -IST.] One who practises philanthropy; one who from love of his fellow-men exerts himself for their well-being. Formerly, with the more general sense of 'friend or lover of man', and so applied to the Deity, and also to friendly animals.

1730–6 BAILEY (folio), *Philanthropist*,.. a lover of mankind. **1742** YOUNG *Nt. Th.* IV. 602 Thou great Philanthropist! Father of Angels! but the Friend of Man! **1769** PENNANT *Zool.* III. 49 The Dolphin.. was celebrated in the earliest time for its fondness of the human race, was honored with the title of the Sacred Fish, and distinguished by those of Boy-loving and Philanthropist. **1797** *Anti-Jacobin* 11 Dec. (1852) 19 Tom Paine the philanthropist. **1804** *Med. Jrnl.* XII. 209 The man of letters, philosopher, and philanthropist. **1829** I. TAYLOR *Enthus.* vii. 178 The spirit that should actuate a Christian philanthropist. **1875** HELPS *Soc. Press.* iii. 44 A great philanthropist has astonished the world by giving it large sums of money during his lifetime.

Hence **philanthro'pistic** *a. rare*, pertaining to or characteristic of a philanthropist; of the nature of philanthropism.

1851 CARLYLE *Sterling* I. v, Mere darkness with philanthropistic phosphorescences, empty meteoric lights.

philanthropize (fɪ'lænθrəpaɪz), *v.* [f. as prec. + -IZE.]

1. *intr.* To play or perform the part of the philanthropist; to practise philanthropy.

1826 *Blackw. Mag.* XIX. 464 Why do they not buy all the land in a single island, and missionize and philanthropize at their own expense? **1836** *New Monthly Mag.* XLVI. 71 Away she went philanthropising till nine in one place, playing three-card loo till twelve in another.

2. *trans.* To treat philanthropically; to make (persons) objects of philanthropy.

1830 *Fraser's Mag.* II. 563 A convention..met for the purpose of philanthropising the blacks. **1859** W. CHADWICK *De Foe* iv. 236 De Foe again returns to the attack upon Sir Humphrey Mackworth's bill for philanthropizing the poor by deceiving and robbing the rich. **1894** *Westm. Gaz.* 27 June 2/3 Till they get them [votes], we look jealously at these attempts to philanthropise woman *malgré lui.*

3. To make philanthropic in character, cause to become a philanthropist.

1891 B. E. MARTIN *Footpr. C. Lamb* 61 Basil Montagu, the philanthropized courtier.

philanthropoid (fɪˈlænθrəpɔɪd). orig. *U.S.* [f. PHILANTHROP(IST + -OID, joc. after ANTHROPOID *a.* and *sb.*] A professional philanthropist, a worker for a charitable or grant-awarding institution. Also *attrib.* or as *adj.* Hence **phiˌlanthroˈpoidal** *a.*; **phiˌlanthroˈpoidally** *adv.*

1949 *Harper's Mag.* Mar. 9/1 Edwin R. Embree..calls himself a 'philanthropoid', a term which he and Frederick Keppel of the Carnegie Corporation coined some years ago to describe a person who gives away other people's money. **1957** *Britannica Bk. of Year* 512/1 Coinages with a more colloquial or individualistic ring were..*philanthropoid*, one who disburses the money of a philanthropic institution or foundation. The adjectival and adverbial forms *philanthropoidal* and *philanthropoidally* also occurred. **1959** *Fortune* May 110/2 Philanthropoid is what Jonathan King cheerfully calls himself. King has spent most of his adult life giving away money. **1966** *Economist* 31 Dec. 1391/3 All of this brings a danger that there will be in-breeding of ideas, grants going round in circles... Representatives of the best foundations try to avoid this... Indeed, most of these complaints about 'philanthropoid man' are well on the way to being out of date. **1977** *Daily Tel.* 13 Jan. 17/3 I'm not playing the role of the hard-headed tycoon who thinks all philanthropoids are Socialists and all university professors are Communists.

†**phiˈlanthropos.** *Herb. Obs.* [a. Gr. φιλάνθρωπος cleavers (from its sticking to men).] An old name of Cleavers (*Galium Aparine*); by some applied to Agrimony (*Agrimonia Eupatoria*).

c **1000** *Sax. Leechd.* I. 306 Ðas wyrt man phylantropos nemneþ, þæt ys on ure ȝeþeode menluȝiȝende, forðy heo wyle hrædlice to ðam men ȝeclyfian. **1597** GERARDE *Herbal* II. ccxxx. 575 Agrimonie..Named..of some *Philanthropos*, of the cleauing qualitie of the seedes, hanging to mens garments. **1601** HOLLAND *Pliny* II. 273 It is ready to catch hold of folkes clothes as they passe by, and to stick unto them [*Marg.*] Whereupon they cal it *Philanthropos*, i. a louer of man.

philanthropy (fɪˈlænθrəpɪ). Also 7 in L. form **philanˈthropia.** [ad. late L. *philanthrōpia* (in earlier Eng. use), a. Gr. φιλανθρωπία love to mankind, f. φιλάνθρωπος: see PHILANTHROPE. So F. *philanthropie* (1567 in Hatz.-Darm.).] Love to mankind; practical benevolence towards men in general; the disposition or active effort to promote the happiness and well-being of one's fellow-men.

α. [**1607–12** BACON *Ess., Goodness* (Arb.) 198 The affecting of the Weale of Men: which is that the Græcians call Philanthropia.] **1608** TOPSELL *Serpents* (1658) 781, I should first begin with the commendation of their..*Philanthropia.* **1678** *Yng. Man's Call.* 133 That orient pearl, that Cyrus in his time so highly delighted in..to attain the study of a due philanthropia (for that was his own very word) toward all. β. **1623** COCKERAM, *Phylanthropie*, Humanitie. *c* **1650** JER. TAYLOR *Serm., Matt.* v. 20 Wks. 1831 III. 255 That godlike excellency, a philanthropy and love to all mankind. **1693** DRYDEN *Charac. Polybius* in Shears *Polyb.* I. B v b, This Philanthropy (which we have not a proper word in English to express) is every where manifest in our Author. **1704** J. HARRIS *Lex. Techn.* I, *Philanthropy*, is a generous Love for Mankind in General, or an Inclination to promote Publick Good. **1749** FIELDING *Tom Jones* VI. i, In friend-ship, in parental and filial affection, and indeed in general philanthropy, there is a great and exquisite delight. **1827** LYTTON *Falkland* I. 26 While I felt aversion for the few whom I knew, I glowed with philanthropy for the crowd which I knew not. **1849** R. I. WILBERFORCE *Holy Bapt.* (1850) 23 He first taught the lessons of universal Philanthropy.

†**b.** *spec.* The love of God to man. *Obs.*

[Cf. *Titus* iii. 4 ἡ χρηστότης καὶ ἡ φιλανθρωπία..τοῦ σωτῆρος ἡμῶν θεοῦ, 1611 The kindenesse and loue of God our Sauiour toward man.]

1631 R. H. *Arraignm. Whole Creature* i. 4 His Philanthropie and good will to Man, which our Sauiour Christ especially manifested. **1643** TRAPP *Comm. Gen.* xvi. 10 He is oft (out of his meer Philanthropie) found of them that sought him not. *a* **1711** KEN *Hymnarium* Poet. Wks. 1721 II. 112 The blessed Three..In co-immense Philanthropy conspire.

c. *pl.* Philanthropic actions, movements, or agencies.

1884 R. R. BOWKER in *Harper's Mag.* Apr. 776/1 To be.. the head of a great hospital and many philanthropies, demands..devotion. **1890** *Spectator* 24 May, Tedious toil in connection with all manner of philanthropies.

philarchaist, etc.: see PHILO-.

philarea, obs. erron. form of PHILLYREA.

†**phiˈlargyry.** *Obs.* Also 7 **-gury.** [ad. Gr. φιλαργυρία, n. of quality from φιλάργυρ-ος fond of money, f. φιλ(ο-, PHIL(O + ἄργυρος silver, money.] Love of money; avarice, covetousness.

1570–6 LAMBARDE *Peramb. Kent* (1826) 249 The Popes laboured more and more with this incurable disease of Philargyrie. **1631** R. H. *Arraignm. Whole Creature* xviii. 320 That Philargury or love of money which is called Covetousnesse. **1652** URQUHART *Jewel* Wks. (1834) 212 In matter of philargyrie, or love of money.

So †**phiˈlargyrist**, a lover of money, a covetous person; †**phiˈlargyrous (gurous)** *a.*, money-loving, covetous.

1633 T. ADAMS *Exp. 2 Peter* iii. 18 If he did hoard up his knowledge, as a..philargyrist his coin, we might still be poor. **1654** H. L'ESTRANGE *Chas. I* (1655) 138 They were thought Philargyrous, and over solicitous of filthy lucre. **1663** STILLINGFL. *Shecinah* Ded., The progging attempts of an ambitious phylargyrist.

philaser, obs. form of FILACER.

philately (fɪˈlætɪlɪ). [ad. F. *philatélie*, f. Gr. φιλ(ο-, PHILO- + ἀτελής free from tax or charge, ἀτέλεια exemption from payment (ἐξ ἀτελείας without payment, free, *franco*). Proposed by M. Herpin, a postage-stamp collector, in *Le Collectionneur de Timbres-poste* (15 Nov. 1864).

(When a letter was 'carriage-free' or carriage-prepaid by the sender, it was formerly in various countries stamped FREE, or FRANCO; the fact is now indicated by the letter bearing an impressed receipt stamp, or its substitute an adhesive label (commonly called a postage-stamp), for the amount; the Greek ἀτελής, being a passable equivalent of *free* or *franco*, has for the purpose of word-making been employed to express the *freimarke, franco-bollo*, franco-mark, frank-stamp, or 'postage-stamp', and so to supply the second element in *philatélie.*)]

a. The pursuit of collecting, arranging, and studying the stamped envelopes or covers, adhesive labels or 'postage-stamps', postcards, and other devices employed in different countries and at different times, in effecting the prepayment of letters or packets sent by post; stamp-collecting.

1865 *Stamp.-Coll. Mag.* 1 Dec. 182/2 He [M. Herpin] proposes the word *philatélie*, which we anglicise into 'philately'... Twelve months have glided on..and the French terms *philatéle* and *philatélie*, as well as their English equivalents 'philately', 'philatelist', and 'philatelic'..have become household words in the postage-stamp collecting world. *Ibid.* Advts., The works of the Philatelic Society of France. **1867** *Philatelist* I. 37 A poser to the non-initiated in philately. **1881** *Athenæum* 1 Oct. 431/2 It is possibly a question whether the science should properly be called philately or timbrophily.

b. Stamps collectively.

1930 *19th Cent.* Dec. 785 The small-bourgeois quality of English philately remained untarnished with sham elegance.

Hence **philatelic** (fɪləˈtɛlɪk) *a*, relating to or engaged in philately; so **philaˈtelical** *a.*; hence **philaˈtelically** *adv.*; **phiˈlatelism**, philately; **phiˈlatelist**, a person devoted to philately, a stamp-collector (whence **philateˈlistic** *a.*); **phiˌlateloˈmaniac**, one with whom stamp-collecting has become a mania.

1865 Philatelic, Philatelist [see above]. **1866** (*title*) The Philatelist: An Illustrated Monthly Magazine for Stamp Collectors. **1871** *Routledge's Ev. Boy's Ann.* Suppl. Apr. 7/1 A manuscript Philatelic Magazine. **1871** E. L. PEMBERTON in *Stamp-Coll. Mag.* IX. 130 The faults..incident to American philatelism. **1872** —— (*title*) The Philatelical Journal. **1882** *Sat. Rev.* 15 Apr. 472/2 Many a parent..will now hasten to provide him instead with the records of philatelism. **1884** *Boston* (Mass.) *Jrnl.* 26 July, It is valued at about $1000 by philatelomaniacs. **1890** *Times* 20 May 5 On May 19. 1890, an exhibition was opened of postage stamps collected by the London Philatelic Society. **1890** *Standard* 25 Apr. 5/6 The philatelistic scholar. **1893** *Westm. Gaz.* 18 Oct. 3/1 Of the exhibition itself..we shall not attempt to speak..philatelically.

philaterie, -ory, obs. ff. PHYLACTERY.

philautian (fɪˈlɔːtɪən), *a. rare*$^{-1}$. [f. as PHILAUTY + -AN.] Selfish.

1811 SHELLEY *Let.* 25 July (1964) I. 98 This is entirely a *philautian* argument.

†**phiˈlauty.** *Obs.* Also in Gr. form **philautia.** [ad. Gr. φιλαυτία, n. of state f. φίλαυτος loving oneself, f. φιλ(ο-, PHIL(O- + αὐτόν oneself.] Self-love; undue regard for oneself or one's own interests; self-conceit; selfishness.

c **1525** TINDALE *Obed. Chr. Man* Pref., Wks. (1573) 103 They will say yet more shamefully, that no man can vnderstand the Scriptures without Philautia, that is to say Philosophy. A man muste first bee well seene in Aristotle, yer he can vnderstand the Scripture, say they. **1564–5** LEDINGTON *Let. to Cecil* 28 Feb. in Tytler *Hist. Scot.* (1864) III. 401 Phylautye which maketh us fancy too much our own conceptions. **1577–87** HOLINSHED *Chron.* (1807) II. 148 There we see philautie or selfe-love, which rageth in men so preposterouslie. *a* **1592** GREENE *Jas. IV*, III. ii, Such as giue themselues to Philautia, as you do, maister. **1651** BIGGS *New Disp.* §72 And will have philautie to be natures first-born. **1721** BAILEY s.v. *Geese*, This Proverb intimates that an inbred Philauty runs through the whole Race.

philazer, obs. form of FILACER.

philberd, -bert, -bud, obs. forms of FILBERT.

-phile: see -PHIL.

†**philed**, obs. form of FILED.

1578 T. PROCTOR *Gorg. Gallery, Lover approv. Lady unkinde*, Your Phrases fine philed, did force mee agree.

philemort, obs. f. FILEMOT = FEUILLEMORTE.

philery, philet(t, obs. ff. PHILLYREA, FILLET.

philetism: see PHYLETISM.

philharmonic (fɪlhɑːˈmɒnɪk), *a.* and *sb.* [a. F. *philharmonique* (1739), after It. *filarmonico*, f. Gr. φιλ(ο-, PHIL(O- + ἁρμονικός HARMONIC.]

A. *adj.* Loving harmony; fond of or devoted to music; also used characteristically in the names of symphony orchestras.

Philharmonic Society, name of various musical societies, *esp.* that founded in London in 1813 for the promotion of instrumental music; hence ***Philharmonic concert***, one given by the Philharmonic Society.

1813 *Philharmonic Soc.* I. 1 Several Members of the Musical Profession have associated themselves, under the title of The Philharmonic Society;..to procure the performance, in the most perfect manner possible, of the best and most approved Instrumental Music. **1823** *New Monthly Mag.* VIII. 127 The most philharmonic ear is at times deeply affected by a simple air. **1862** *Times* in Grove *Dict. Mus.* II. 700/2 The successful completion of the 50th year of the Philharmonic Society. *Ibid.* 701/1 The forty-ninth series of the Philharmonic Concerts. [**1895** G. B. SHAW in *Daily Chron.* 6 Nov. 6/5 Every violoncellist in the Philharmonic orchestra [*sc.* the Philharmonic Society orchestra] used to dread the trio of the third movement.] **1898** STAINER & BARRETT *Dict. Mus. Terms* 362/1 The pitch of Costa's Philharmonic Orchestra..was A. 452·5. **1923** *Gramophone* Apr. 14/1, I prefer the old rendering [of Beethoven's C minor Symphony] conducted by Nikisch with the Berlin Philharmonic Orchestra. **1937** N. SLONIMSKY *Music since 1900* I. 371, 1934... German State Philharmonic Orchestra of the German Soviet Republic of the Volga basin is established... *Fifth Symphony* of Arnold Bax is performed..by the London Philharmonic Orchestra. **1940** GRANT & HETTINGER *America's Symphony Orchestras* iii. 70 The New York Philharmonic, Philadelphia, and Boston symphony orchestras..have been grouped together as Group I. **1944** B. GEISSMAR *Baton & Jackboot* 25 The Berlin Philharmonic Orchestra unanimously voted for Furtwängler. **1961** *N.Y. Times* 17 Nov. 38 In recent years Anna Xydis has played with the New York Philharmonic. **1974** *Encycl. Brit. Micropædia* I. 927/1 Beecham..founded the Royal Philharmonic Orchestra in London (1947).

B. *sb.* **a.** A lover of harmony; a person devoted to music. **b.** *colloq.* Short for *Philharmonic Society, Orchestra, concert*: see above.

1762 tr. *Busching's Syst. Geog.* III. 86 The place in which the society or academy of the philharmonics assemble. **1843** COL. HAWKER *Diary* (1893) II. 239 A Philharmonic of blackbirds and thrushes. **1855** GEO. ELIOT in *Fraser's Mag.* July 51/1 When a symphony of Beethoven's was first played at the Philharmonic, there was a general titter among the musicians in the orchestra. **1862** *Times* in Grove *Dict. Mus.* II. 701/1 Mr. Sterndale Bennett—an old member of the 'Philharmonic'. **1880** *Ibid.*, At the close of the season of 1866 Professor Bennett resigned the conductorship, and his place at the Philharmonic was filled by Mr. W. G. Cusins. **1897** [see PERFORMING *vbl. sb.* 4 b]. **1931** *Gramophone* Apr. 526/2 Even the famous New York Philharmonic..must, I think, take second place. **1933** M. BAUER *20th Cent. Music* iv. 40 Spohr..was the first to conduct an orchestra, the London Philharmonic (1820) with a baton and without the aid of a piano. **1944** B. GEISSMAR *Baton & Jackboot* 24 Arthur Nikisch..had been permanent conductor..of the Hamburg Concerts with the Berlin Philharmonic since 1897. **1951** J. H. MUELLER *Amer. Symphony Orchestra* iii. 63 A century of uninterrupted orchestral programs of the New York Philharmonic affords an extraordinary view of changes in musical taste. **1961** J. WILLIAMS *Forger* i. 12 The artist is like a fragment of a mosaic—no, he is more than that, a virtuoso performer in some vast philharmonic. **1977** *Time* 10 Oct. 17/3 Her orchestral works have been performed by the Philadelphia Orchestra and the Los Angeles and New York Philharmonics.

philhellene (ˈfɪlhɛliːn), *a.* and *sb.* Also **-en.** [ad. Gr. φιλέλλην adj., loving the Greeks, f. φιλ(ο-, PHIL(O- + Ἕλλην HELLENE, Greek; so mod.F. *philhellène.*] **a.** *adj.* = PHILHELLENIC. **b.** *sb.* = PHILHELLENIST. (In quot. 1827, A lover of Greek language or literature.)

c **1825** MOORE *Ghost Miltiades* 23 And, poor, dear ghost, how little he knew The jobs and the tricks of the Philhellene crew! **1827** J. SYMMONS in Barker *Parriana* (1828) I. 547 As a Philhellen, I was received, entertained, and introduced into the house. **1865** *Pall Mall G.* 25 Aug. 11/2 If nobody were to talk about Greece, there would be no philhellenes. **1882** *Athenæum* 5 Aug. 172/3 He is enthusiastically Philhellene as to the present inhabitants of the country.

philhellenic (fɪlhɛˈliːnɪk, -ˈɛnɪk), *a.* [f. as prec. + HELLENIC.] Loving, friendly to, or supporting the cause of, Greece or the Greeks (esp. in relation to national independence). So **philhellenism** (fɪlˈhɛliːnɪz(ə)m), the principle of supporting the Greeks; **philhellenist** (fɪlhɛˈliːnɪst), a friend or supporter of Greece (also *attrib.*).

1830 MAUNDER *Dict.*, *Philhellenic. **1852** GROTE *Greece* II. lxx. IX. 96 So emphatically did he [Klearchus] pledge himself for the good faith and philhellenic dispositions of the satrap. **1862** G. FINLAY in *Freeman's Life & Lett.* (1895) I. 281, I feel again a return of *philhellenism. **1869** TOZER *Highl. Turkey* II. 304 The suggestion was..decried as striking at the root of all Phil-hellenism. **1811** BYRON *Rem. on Romaic* Wks. (1846) 793/2 The reply of the *Philhellenist

I have not translated. **1842** MRS. BROWNING *Grk. Chr. Poets* 98 But if by chance an Attic voice be wist, They grow softhearted straight, philhellenist.

philhippic, -hymnic: see PHILO-.

philhorse, obs. f. *fill-horse*: see FILL *sb.*[2]

‖**philia** (ˈfɪlɪə). [ad. Gr. φιλία friendship.] Amity, friendship, liking.

1953 J. A. K. THOMSON *Ethics of Aristotle* VIII. 202 The subject of the eighth and ninth books is *Philia*, the feeling which friends have for one another. *Ibid.*, Without this discussion of *Philia* the *Ethics* would have nothing to say on the subject of love. **1960** C. S. LEWIS *Four Loves* iv. 69 The very tone of the admission, and the sort of acquaintanceships which those who make it would describe as 'friendships', show clearly that what they are talking about has very little to do with that *Philia* which Aristotle classified among the virtues. **1963** AUDEN *Dyer's Hand* 143 From that moment on his relationship with Passepartout ceases to be impersonal; *philia* is felt by both. **1977** *Christian* IV. 137 For everybody, whatever his or her sexual orientation.., life can include all the elements of love: eros, philia, and agape. *Ibid.*, Philia, affection, as we have seen, is not easily expressed in public in our society, and it is most difficult for gay men.

-philia (ˈfɪlɪə), ad. Gr. φιλία friendship, fondness, forming abstract sbs. (usu. corresp. to an adj. in -PHIL, -PHILE, -PHILIC, or -PHILOUS), with the senses 'affinity for' (as in EOSINOPHILIA), 'undue inclination towards' (as in HÆMOPHILIA, SPASMOPHILIA), 'love of or liking for' (as in ANGLOPHILIA, *necrophilia* s.v. NECRO-).

philiamort, philimot, var. FILEMOT.

philibeg, var. FILIBEG.

philibert, obs. f. FILBERT.

-philic (ˈfɪlɪk), f. -PHIL, -PHILE + -IC (cf. Gr. φιλικός), used to form adjs. with the sense 'having an affinity for, attracted by, liking', as in LYOPHILIC, *mesophilic* s.v. MESO-, *neutrophilic* s.v. NEUTRO-. Cf. -PHILOUS.

philigrain, -grin, obs. ff. FILIGRANE.

Philip (ˈfɪlɪp). Also 5 phelipp, 6 phylyp, 7 phillip. [A personal name, in F. *Philippe*, L. *Philippus*, a. Gr. Φίλιππος, lit. lover of horses.]

1. A man's name: well known as that of the king of Macedon, father of Alexander, referred to in the expression 'to appeal from Philip drunk to Philip sober': see quot., and cf. Valer. Max. VI. ii.

[Cf. **1509** BARCLAY *Shyp of Folys* (1874) I. 95, I am no traytoure, apele I woll certayne From dronken Alexander tyll he be sober agayne. **1568** NORTH *Gueuara's Diall Pr.* IV. xviii. (1582) 439 After he had geuen iudgement.. against a poore widow woman, she aunswered streight.. I appeale to king Philip which is now drunk: yt when hee is sober, he returne to geue sentence.] **1886** MRS. LYNN LINTON *Paston Carew* i, Not even appealing from Philip drunk to Philip sober.

b. Philip, the Evangelist: see Acts viii. 26–40.

1607 HIERON *Wks.* I. 299 God encrease the number of such Philips, and make vs all such as the eunuch was in this particular.

†**2.** Name of certain old French, Spanish, and Burgundian coins, of gold and silver, issued by kings or dukes of this name. *Obs.*

1482 *Cely Papers* (1900) 126 Item an phellypus.. iijs iiijd fls. **1617** MORYSON *Itin.* I. 286 A Rhenish Gold Gulden.. the siluer Phillips Doller, was of the same value. **1632** LITHGOW *Trav.* x. 454 Eleauen Philippoes or Ducatons. **1769** *Ann. Reg.* 135/2 The damage as yet is estimated at four millions of philippis.

3. A name formerly given to a sparrow: also PHIP (perh. in imitation of its chirp). *Obs.* exc. *dial.*: also *dial.* applied to the hedge-sparrow (Swainson *Prov. Names Brit. Birds*).

a **1529** SKELTON *Ph. Sparowe* 26 Nothynge it auayled To call Phylyp agayne, Whom Gyb our cat hath slayne. **1595** SHAKS. *John* I. i. 231 *Gour.* Good leaue good Philip. *Bast.* Philip, sparrow, Iames. **1612** *Pasquil's Night-Cap* (1877) 103 Let chirping Philip learne to catch a flie. **1865** *Cornh. Mag.* July 36 The house-sparrow is still in many parts Skelton's 'Philip', the Philip of the Elizabethan dramatists, and of Cartwright.

†**4.** *Philip and Cheyney*. **a.** An expression for two (or more) men of the common people taken at random (cf. 'Tom, Dick, and Harry'). Also *Philip, Hob, and Cheyney*. *Obs.*

1542 UDALL *Erasm. Apoph.* II. *Pompeius* 280 It was not his entente to bryng vnto Silla philip and cheiny moo then a good meiny, but to bryng hable soudiours of manhood approued and well tryed. *a* **1563** BECON *Display Popishe Masse* Wks. III. 47 Ye praye for Philippe and Chenye, mo than a good meany, for the soules of your great grand Sir and of your olde Beldame Hurre. **1573** TUSSER *Husb.* Ep. Ded. (1878) 8 Loiterers I kept so meanie, Both Philip, Hob, and Cheanie.

†**b.** Name for a kind of worsted or woollen stuff of common quality (erroneously *Phillipine, Cheny*): see CHEYNEY. *Obs.*

c **1614** FLETCHER, etc. *Wit at Sev. Weap.* II. i, Thirteene pound... 'Twill put a Lady scarce in Philip and Cheyney, With three small Bugle Laces, like a Chamber-maid. **1633** in *Naworth Househ. Bks.* (Surtees) 298, 12 yeardes of Philip and cheyney.. for a coate for Mrs. Marie Howard. **1641** *Canterb. Marriage Licences* (MS.), Peter Donnaing.. Phillipp and Chainey weaver. **1650** *Will of J. Brooke* (Somerset Ho.), My red bed of Phillipp and China. **1668** HEAD *Eng. Rogue* II. xii. (1671) 112 [To] muster up the names of their stuffs,.. there's your Parragon, Burragon, Phillipine, Cheny, Grogrum, Mow-hair.

philip, obs. f. FILLIP.

philipende, philipendula, obs. erron. ff. VILIPEND, FILIPENDULA.

Philippic (fɪˈlɪpɪk), *sb.* (*a.*) Also philippic. [ad. L. *Philippic-us*, a. Gr. φιλιππικός, f. Φίλιππος Philip (of Macedon). So mod.F. *philippique*.]

1. Name for the orations of Demosthenes against Philip king of Macedon in defence of Athenian liberty; hence applied to Cicero's orations against Antony, and *gen.* to any discourse of the nature of a bitter attack, invective, or denunciation.

1592 G. HARVEY *Foure Lett.* iii. Wks. (Grosart) I. 210 What honest Eloquence is not furnished with Catilinaries and Philippiques against Vice? **1603** HOLLAND *Plutarch* Explan. Wds., Invective orations made by Demosthenes.. against Philip king of Macedony,.. heereupon all invectives may be called Philippicke, as those were of M. Tullius Cicero against Antonie. **1693** DRYDEN *Juvenal's Sat.* x. (1697) 255, I rather wou'd be Mævius.. Than that Philippique fatally Divine, Which is inscrib'd the Second, should be mine. **1798** JEFFERSON *Writ.* (1859) IV. 227 Mr. Harper and Mr. Pinckney pronounced bitter philippics against France. **1813** WELLINGTON in Gurw. *Desp.* (1838) X. 443 Then follows the usual Philippic against England. **1864** BURTON *Scot Abr.* II. i. 29 *note*, Lord North, sound asleep during one of Burke's philippics on him.

†**2.** Used to render Gr. φιλίππειον, 'a gold coin coined by Philip of Macedon, worth £1 3*s.* 5*d.* of our money' (Liddell & Scott). *Obs.*

1651 JER. TAYLOR *Serm. for Year* I. viii. 99 Æsops picture was sold for two talents, when himself was made a slave at the price of two Philippicks. **1771** RAPER in *Phil. Trans.* LXI. 462 Some.. have supposed the Roman Aureus to have been heavier than the Greek Philippic.

B. *adj.* **a.** Of or pertaining to any person called Philip (in quot. 1650, Sir Philip Sidney); **b.** of Philippi; **c.** of the nature of a philippic or invective.

a **1614** D. DYKE *Myst. Self-deceiving* (ed. 8) 356 Though the Phillippick Preachers preached of enuy and vaine-glory, yet.. what was that to Paul? **1627** tr. *Bacon's Life & Death* (1651) 16 She survived the Philippick Battaile sixty-four yeares. **1650** MILTON *Eikon.* i. (1770) 29 What I tell them for a truth, that this philippic prayer is no part of the Kings goodes. **1707** TOLAND (*title*) A Phillippick Oration to incite the English against the French.

Hence **Phiˈlippicize** (-saɪz) *v. intr.*, to utter a philippic or invective; also *trans.*, to bring or put *into* some condition by doing this.

1799 SOUTHEY *Let. to G. C. Bedford* 21 Dec. in *Life* (1850) II. 33 However, I need not philippicise, and it is too late to veer about. **1839** *Blackw. Mag.* XLVI. 173 We have Philippicized ourselves into a perspiration.

†**Phiˈlippical**, *a. Obs.* [f. as prec. + -AL[1].] Of or belonging to Philip (in quot. Devoted to Philip II of Spain).

1600 O. E. *Repl. Libel* I. viii. 191 All loue of that king to her Maiestie, which this philippical parasite so much pretendeth, was altogether extinguished.

philippina (fɪlɪˈpiːnə), **philopœna**. Also phillipina, philopena, philippine, fillipeen, philopœne. [Understood to repr. Ger. *vielliebchen*, dim. of *viellieb* much loved, very dear (cf. *liebchen* darling), altered into *Philippchen*, whence F. *Philippine*, Du. *filippine*, Da. *filipine*, Sw. *filipin*, Eng. *fillipeen, philippina*, etc.] A custom or game reputed to be of German origin: see quot. 1848. Also applied to the double nut or kernel, and to the present claimed or given, as mentioned.

The greeting in German is *Guten Morgen, Vielliebchen!* in F. *Bon jour, Philippine!* See Flügel, Muret-Sanders, Littré.

1839 C. F. BRIGGS *Adventures H. Franco* II. xiv. 143 There would be.. scandal by the wholesale, besides sugar kisses, and phillippinas [at the party]. **1848** BARTLETT *Dict. Amer.*, *Fillipeen* or *Phillipina*. There is a custom common in the Northern States at dinner or evening parties when almonds or other nuts are eaten, to reserve such as are double or contain two kernels, which are called fillipeens. If found by a lady, she gives one of the kernels to a gentleman, when both eat their respective kernels. When the parties again meet, each strives to be the first to exclaim, Fillipeen! for by so doing he or she is entitled to a present from the other. **1854** MARION HARLAND *Alone* ix, 'Miss Ida', said Charles Dana, across the table, 'Will you eat a philopœna with me?' [*a* **1857** Remembered in England with the form *Philippine*.] **1864** WEBSTER, *Philippine*, the same as *Philopena*. **1879** G. F. PENTECOST *Vol. of the Book* x, Bibles which somebody gave you.. for a philopoena present. **1905** *Daily Chron.* 14 Feb. 4/7 In those days Valentines were as expensive as philopœnes. **1917** H. H. RICHARDSON *Fortunes R. Mahony* III. v. 213 She had won a pair of gloves in a philippine with Mr. Urquhart.

Philippine (ˈfɪlɪpiːn), *a.*[1] and *sb.* Also Filippine, and *sb. pl.* in It. form Philippini. [f. the name of St. *Philip* Neri (1515–95), founder of the Congregation of the Fathers of the Oratory at Rome + -INE[1].] Of, pertaining to, or characteristic of the Oratorians or the Oratory of St. Philip Neri (ORATORY *sb.*[1] 5). **B.** *sb.* A father or priest of this Oratory; also, a female novice (see quot. 1773).

1773 *Encycl. Brit.* III. 476/2 *Philippines*, a religious society of young women, at Rome; so called from their taking St. Philip de Neri for their protector: they consist of an hundred poor girls, who are brought up till they are of age to be married, or become nuns. **1848** F. W. FABER *Let.* 17 Feb. in J. E. Bowden *Life & Lett. F. W. Faber* (1869) viii. 337 Father Superior has now left us, all in our Philippine habits with turndown collars, like so many good boys brought in after dinner. **1852** —— *Let.* 14 Jan. in M. Trevor *Newman: Pillar of Cloud* (1962) 578 F. Rossi.. declares.. that he has acted in a manner unworthy of a Filippine *in re Achilli*. **1856** J. H. NEWMAN *Let.* 2 Jan. in M. Trevor *Newman: Light in Winter* (1962) 99 The Philippine house is one large vault. *Ibid.* 7 Jan. 101 The brief half-hour we had for going to the Philippini. **1863** —— *Let.* 27 Dec. in W. Ward *Life J. H. Newman* (1912) I. xix. 612 Since 1846 or 1847,.. since I went to Propaganda and came back a Philippine. **1959** J. C. CHAPIN tr. *Giovannetti's We have Pope* v. 111 Patriarch Roncalli thought it proper to cede to the Filippine Institutes (now run by the Brethren of the Christian Schools) the splendid Villa Fietta.

Philippine (ˈfɪlɪpiːn), *a.*[2] [ad. Sp. *Filipino*: see FILIPINO *sb.* and *a.*] Of or pertaining to a Filipino, or to the Philippine islands (now the Republic of the Philippines). Also *Comb.*

1812 W. MARSDEN *Gram. Malayan Lang.* p. xxi, The dictionaries of *Tagala, Bisaya, Pampagna*, and other Philippine languages are voluminous. **1815** J. F. STEPHENS in G. Shaw *Gen. Zool.* IX. I. 190 Philippine Woodpecker... About eleven inches in length... It is said to make a great noise with its beak. **1832** R. BAIRD *View of Valley of Mississippi* xxiv. 287 The Philippine or ribband cane is rapidly supplanting this species of cane. **1899** W. JAMES *Talks to Teachers* x. 98 What a help is our Philippine war at present in teaching geography! **1932** W. L. GRAFF *Language* 423 The Philippine-Formosa group [of languages]. **1941** *Sun* (Baltimore) 12 Aug. 17/2 A considerable quantity of Philippine mahogany also will be used in the construction of the hulls. **1945** C. L. B. HUBBARD *Observer's Bk. Dogs* 115 Though not recognized by The American Kennel Club, Philippine Dogs are generally bred to a type. **1947** J. C. RICH *Materials & Methods Sculpture* x. 292 Philippine mahogany is not a true mahogany. The name is applied to at least a half-dozen species of the dipterocarp family. Most of the woods referred to as Philippine mahogany are fairly soft and carve well. **1948** F. H. TITMUSS *Conc. Encycl. World Timbers* 72 Lauan.. is sometimes exported under the title of Philippine Mahogany, but is not a member of the true Mahogany family. **1964** P. F. ANSON *Bishops at Large* xi. 530 Only one Philippine-born priest, a *mestico*, was raised to the episcopate. **1976** E. S. GRUSON *Checklist Birds of World* 77 *Picoides maculatus* Philippine Pygmy Woodpecker. **1977** *Time* 12 Dec. 27/1 Manila-born Emerson Coseteng, by contrast, is a 46-year-old naturalized Philippine citizen and a major stockholder in the Mariwasa group of companies.

philippinite (fɪlɪˈpiːnaɪt). *Geol.* [f. prec. + -ITE[1].] Any tektite from the tektite field of the Philippine Islands.

1951 H. E. SUESS in *Geochim et Cosmochim. Acta* II. 76 So-called 'gas-rich' philippinites, tektites from the Philippines, which are exceptionally rich in bubbles of various sizes. **1961**, **1964** [see JAVAITE]. **1969** *New Scientist* 30 Oct. 237/1 We find ages of indochinites and philippinites to lie between 0·6 and 0·7 m.y.

Philippist (ˈfɪlɪpɪst). *Ch. Hist.* [f. PHILIP = Gr. Φίλιππ-ος + -IST.] A follower of Philip Melanchthon; one of the party of moderate Lutherans or ADIAPHORISTS. Also *attrib.*

1727–41 CHAMBERS *Cycl.*, *Philippists*, a sect or party among the Lutherans; the followers of Philip Melanchthon. **1764** MACLAINE tr. *Mosheim's Ch. Hist.* (1844) II. 90/1 Matthew Flacius, the virulent enemy of Melancthon, and all the Philippists. **1873** MCCLINTOCK & STRONG *Cycl. Bibl. Lit.* V. 670/1 In 1574 the Philippist party was overthrown in Electoral Saxony, and its heads imprisoned.

So **ˈPhilippism**, the doctrine or practice of Melanchthon or the Philippists; **Philiˈppistic** *a.*, like or pertaining to the Philippists.

1882–3 *Schaff's Encycl. Relig. Knowl.* II. 1042/1 Hunnius.. contributed much to suppress all Philippistic traditions [at Wittenberg]. *Ibid.* III. 1827 The elector did so, not from any preference for Philippism, but [etc.].

†**Phiˈlippizate**, *v. Obs. rare*[−1]. [f. Gr. φιλιππίζειν (see next) + -ATE[3].] = next.

1612 *North's Plutarch* 1134 Demosthenes had it often in his mouth, that the Prophetes [Pythia] did Philippizate, to wit, fauoured Philips affaires.

Philippize (ˈfɪlɪpaɪz), *v.* Also philippize. [ad. Gr. φιλιππίζειν (Demosthenes), f. Φίλιππος Philip: see -IZE.] *intr.* To favour, or take the side of, Philip of Macedon (cf. PHILIPPIC); also *gen.* to speak or write as one is corruptly 'inspired' or influenced: see quots.

1646 SIR T. BROWNE *Pseud. Ep.* I. x. 40 What jugling there was therein, the Oratour plainely confessed, who.. could say that Pythia Phillippised. **1675** J. SMITH *Chr. Relig. Appeal* I. 26 Demosthenes said Apollo's Priestess did Philippize: as.. if he had said, Philip had corrupted the Oracle, and put words into the Prophetesses mouth. **1790** BURKE *Fr. Rev.* 13 Caballers.. set him up as a sort of oracle; because, with the best intentions in the world, he naturally philippizes.. in exact unison with their designs. **1831** DE QUINCEY *Whiggism & Lit.* Wks. 1857 V. 124 If the oracle at Hatton philippized, the oracle of Göttingen philippized no less. **1875** HELPS *Ess.*, *Advice* 46 The oracles will Philippize, as long as Philip is the master.

¶ Erron. used for: To utter a philippic; also *trans.* to utter a philippic against.
1804 D. WEBSTER *Let.* 17 Sept., Priv. Corr. 1857 I. 179, I philippize against that employment now. **1837** *Tait's Mag.* IV. 163 What a certain set of young literateurs have been lately philippizing against me. **1845** S. JUDD *Margaret* iii. (Cent.), He argued with us, philippized us, denounced us.

Hence ˈ**Philippizing** *ppl. a.*; also ˈ**Philippizer**, one who philippizes, a partisan of Philip.
1826 *Blackw. Mag.* XX. 358 An Æschines, or a Midias, or the other Philippizers. **1853** GROTE *Greece* II. lxxxviii. XI. 455 The philippising party in that city [Olynthus]. **1856** *Ibid.* xcvi. XII. 484 He acted with Æschines and the Philippizers.

philippy: see PHILO-.

Philips, var. PHILLIPS[1].

† **philiser**, obs. form of FILACER.
1447 *Rolls of Parlt.* V. 138/2 To be entrid ther of Recorde, by the Philiser of the Shire.

philism (ˈfɪlɪz(ə)m). *rare.* [The termination of such words as NEGROPHILISM and ANGLOPHILISM, used as a noun.] A feeling of friendliness towards another race or nation.
1917 *Edin. Rev.* July 127, Germany is the home of such movements..and many other 'philisms' and 'phobisms'. **1923** *Contemp. Rev.* Sept. 325 Tzankoff..is not credited with 'philism' or 'phobism' toward any particular country.

† **Phili'stean**, *a. Obs.* Also Phy-. [f. L. *Philist(h)æus* (see next) + -AN.] = PHILISTINE *a.*
1623 COCKERAM, *Phylistean embrace*, is to picke ones purse, and cut his throat. **1667** MILTON *P.L.* IX. 1061 So rose..Herculean Samson, from the Harlot-lap Of Philistean Dalilah, and wak'd Shorn of his strength.

† **Philistee.** *Obs.* Also 5 Phil-, Filistei, 6 Phylystee. [ad. L. *Philisthæ-us* (Vulg.), Gr. Φιλιστιαῖος: see PHILISTINE.] = PHILISTINE *sb.* 1.
1382 WYCLIF *1 Sam.* xvii. 3 And Philisteis [**1388** Filisteis, Vulg. *Philisthiim*] stoden vpon the hil. *Ibid.* 23 That bastard man, Goliath by name, Philistee of Geth [Vulg. *Philisthæus*; **1388** a Filistei of Gath]. —— *1 Chron.* x. 1 Philisteis [**1388** Filisteis] forsothe fouȝten aȝeinus Yrael. **1508** FISHER *Penit. Ps.* vi. Wks. (1876) 4 Whan Israhell sholde make batayle agaynst the phylystees.

‖ **philister** (fɪˈlɪstər). [The German word for Philistine, f. L. *Philistæus*, *-ēus* or Heb. *p'lishtī.*] A name applied by the students at German universities to the townsmen, or to all persons not students; an outsider; hence, an unenlightened uncultured person; = PHILISTINE *sb.* 3, 4.
Said to have originated at Jena in 1693, in a sermon from the text *Philister über dir, Simson!* 'The Philistines be upon thee, Samson!' preached by Pastor Götze at the funeral of one of the students, who had been killed by the townsmen in a quarrel between 'town and gown'. (See *Quarterly Rev.*, Apr. 1899, 438 note.)
1828 CARLYLE *Let.* 7 Mar. in Froude *Biog.* I. xxii. 425 He went to Mill (the British India Philister). **1833** *Fraser's Mag.* VIII. 658 Need is there that compassion should be had on the poor infatuated philister! **1859** HELPS *Friends in C.* Ser. II. (ed. 2) II. 136 If there were a stupid man amongst us, or what the Germans call a Philister.

Philistia (fɪˈlɪstɪə). In 6 Philistea. [med.L. *Philistia* = late L. *Philistæa* (*-thæa*) in Jerome = Gr. Φιλιστία, -ιαία; ult. repr. Heb. *p'lesheth*: see PHILISTINE.]
1. The country occupied by the Philistines, in the south-west of Palestine. Also, the people or nation of the Philistines.
1535 COVERDALE *Ps.* lix. [lx.] 8 Philistea shal be glad of me. **1611** BIBLE *Ps.* lxxxvii. 4 Behold Philistia, and Tyre, with Ethiopia.
2. The class or community of 'Philistines', i.e. unenlightened or commonplace people; or the locality they inhabit. Cf. PHILISTINE *sb.* 4.
1857 KINGSLEY *Two Y. Ago* x, Yet have Philistia and Fogeydom neither right nor reason to consider him a despicable or merely ludicrous person. **1889** *Pall Mall G.* 31 July 3/2 The homage paid by virtue to vice, or, rather, by Philistia to Bohemia. **1894** *Nation* (N.Y.) 21 June 473/2 The requirements of a novel as understood by literary Philistia.

Philistian (fɪˈlɪstɪən), *sb.* and *a.* Forms: 3-4 Philistien, 4- -an. [a. OF. *Philistien*, ad. med.L. *Philistiān-us*, f. PHILISTIA: see -AN.]
† **A.** *sb.* = PHILISTINE 1, 2. *Obs.*
a **1300** *Cursor M.* 7091 Vnder philistiens þan war þe Iuus halden, þat si-quar. *c* **1340** *Ibid.* 7150 (Cott.) Agh i for to haue na wite, To do philistens [*other texts* -iens] despite. **1375** (MS. *c* 1487) BARBOUR *Bruce* IV. 753 Quhen saull abasit [wes] Of the philistianis [*MS. E.* (1489) felystynys] mycht. **1382** WYCLIF *1 Sam.* xvii. 4 A bastard man wente out fro the tentis of Philistiens [1388 Filisteis, *Vulg.* Philisthinorum]. *c* **1656** *Roxb. Ball.* VII. 402 'Tis neither Pagan, Turk, nor Jew, nor any proud Philistians [*rime* Christians].
B. *adj.* Of or pertaining to Philistia or the Philistines.
1671 MILTON *Samson* 1371 But who constrains me to the Temple of Dagon, Not dragging? the Philistian Lords command. **1836** KEBLE in *Lyra Apost.* (1849) 198 By proud Philistian hosts beset.

Philistine (ˈfɪlɪstaɪn, -tɪn, fɪˈlɪstɪn), *sb.* and *a.* Forms: α. 4 (**Philisten, Palisten, -estine**), 4-6 **Philistyne**, (5 **Felystyne**, 7 **Philistin**), 6- **Philistine**. β. 6-7 **Philistim** (*pl.* -im, -ims), 7 -thiim, -time. Also with lower-case initial. See also PHILISTEE, PHILISTIAN. [a. F. *Philistin*, ad. late L. *Philistīnus*, usually in pl. *Philistīnī* (*-thīnī*, *thiim*, *Palæsthīnī*, all in Vulg.), ad. late Gr. Φιλιστῖνοι, Παλαιστῖνοι (both in Josephus); found beside L. *Philisthiīm* = Gr. Φυ-, Φιλιστιείμ (LXX in Hexateuch), ad. Heb. *p'lishtīm* (or *-iīm*). Cognate with *p'lesheth*, PHILISTIA, Palestine, Assyrian *Palastu*, *Pilistu*. (The word has been very doubtfully explained as = 'wanderers, immigrants'; but was more probably a native name of the people, appearing in Egyptian as *Palusata* or *Purusati*.)
The Gr., L., Eng. forms in -είμ, *-im*, directly represent the Heb. pl.; with *Philistims* cf. *Anakims*, *cherubims*, etc. Several other forms appear, e.g. late Gr. Φιλιστιαῖοι (Aquila), Φυλ- (Symm.), L. *Philistæi*, *-thæi*, *-tēi*, *Phyl-*, ME. PHILISTEE; late L. *Philistiāni*, OF., ME. *Philistien*, Eng. PHILISTIAN. (The pronunciation (fɪˈlɪstɪn) occurs chiefly in U.S.)]

A. *sb.* **1.** One of an alien warlike people, of uncertain origin, who occupied the southern sea-coast of Palestine, and in early times constantly harassed the Israelites. Also *fig.*
[*c* **1340** Philisten; **1375–1489** Felystynys: see PHILISTIAN.] **1382** WYCLIF *Amos* ix. 7 Wher Y made not Yrael for to stye vp of..Egypt, and Palistens of Capadocie [1388 Palestines; *Vulg.* Palæstinos; 1611 the Philistines from Caphtor]. —— *Zech.* ix. 6 Y shal distruye the pride of Philistynes [1388 Filisteis, *Vulg.* Philisthinorum]. **1535** COVERDALE *1 Sam.* xvii. 10 Am not I a Philistyne? **1611** BIBLE *ibid.* 26 Who is this vncircumcised Philistine? **1812** LADY GRANVILLE *Lett.* (1894) I. 40, I feel a little like 'The Philistines are upon thee, Samson'.
β. **1560** BIBLE (Genev.) *1 Sam.* v. 1 Then the Philistims toke the Arke of God. **1609** BIBLE (Douay) *Ecclus.* xlvii. 8 He ..rooted out the Philisthijms. **1620** BP. HALL *Hon. Mar. Clergy* II. §9 Like a Philistim, he hath pulled out the eyes of this Samson. **1637** R. ASHLEY tr. *Malvezzi's David Persecuted* 217 The Philistimes pitch their tents in Shunem. **1642** CUDWORTH *Lord's Supper* i. (1676) 4 Concerning the Philistims when they had put out Sampson's eyes.
2. *fig.* Applied (humorously or otherwise) to persons regarded as 'the enemy', into whose hands one may fall, e.g. bailiffs, literary critics, etc.; formerly, also, to the debauched or drunken.
1600 DEKKER *Gentle Craft* D iij b, Looke here Maggy help me Firk, apparrel me Hodge, silke and satten you mad Philistines, silke and satten. **1687** DRYDEN *Hind & P.* II. 2 Times are mended well Since late among the Philistines you fell. **1688** MIEGE *Fr. Dict.*, *Philistins*, for lewd (or drunken) people, *des Debauchez*. *a* **1700** B. E. *Dict. Cant. Crew*, *Philistines*, Serjeants Bailiffs and their Crew; also Drunkards. **1738** SWIFT *Pol. Conversat.* 14 They say, you went to Court last Night very drunk; Nay, I'm told for certain, you had been among Philistines. **1752** FIELDING *Amelia* v. vi, If he had fallen into the hands of the Philistines (which is the name given by the faithful to bailiffs). **1775** SHERIDAN *Rivals* v. i, Above all, there is that blood thirsty Philistine, Sir Lucius O'Trigger. **1777** *N. Jersey Archives* Ser. II. I. 392 On Monday last we had a brush with the Philistines, killing three lighthorsemen, four Highlanders, and one Lieut. Colonel. **1847** MRS. GORE *Castles in Air* I. 286 [To] be pinched and kicked, in order to afford sport for the Philistines.
3. = PHILISTER, applied by German students to one not a student at a university.
1824 J. RUSSELL *Tour Germ.* (1828) I. iii. 128 The citizens he denominates Philistines. **1826** BEDDOES *Let.* Poems (1851) p. lix, A little inn with a tea-garden, whither students and Philistines (i.e. townsmen who are not students) resort on Sundays. **1840** *Blackw. Mag.* XLVIII. 757 The people read it with great interest, from the fiery youths to the cautious old Philistines. [**1863** M. ARNOLD *Ess. Crit.*, *Heine* (1865) 157 Efforts have been made to obtain in English some term equivalent to *Philister* or *épicier*: Mr. Carlyle has ..'respectability with its thousand gigs',..well, the occupant of every one of those gigs is, Mr. Carlyle means, a *Philistine*.]
4. Hence: A person deficient in liberal culture and enlightenment, whose interests are chiefly bounded by material and commonplace things.
But often applied contemptuously by connoisseurs of any particular art or department of learning to one who has no knowledge or appreciation of it; sometimes a mere term of dislike for those whom the speaker considers 'bourgeois'.
1827 CARLYLE *Misc. Ess.* (1872) I. 58 [The partisans of Illuminism] received the nickname of *Philistern* (Philistines) which the few scattered remnants of them still bear. **1827** *Examiner* 70/2 If Germans require that species of assistance, the obtuseness of a mere English Philistine we trust is pardonable. **1831** [see PHILISTINISM]. **1839** A. H. EVERETT *Addr. Germ. Lit. at Hanover, U.S.A.* 40 Released from the importunity of this Philistine [Wagner],—to use an expressive German term,—Faust relapses into his former gloom. **1851** CARLYLE *Sterling* I. vii. (1872) 41 At other times, Philistines would enter, what we call bores, dullards, Children of Darkness. **1864** FROUDE *Short Stud.*, *Sci. Hist.* 31 A professor at Oxford..spoke of Luther as a Philistine.. meaning an.. enemy of men of culture or intelligence such as the professor himself. **1869** M. ARNOLD *Cult. & An.* 20 The people who believe most that our greatness and welfare are proved by our being very rich, and who most give their lives and thoughts to becoming rich, are just the very people whom we call the Philistines. **1879** L. STEPHEN *Hours in Library* III. 306 In common phraseology he [Macaulay] is a Philistine—a word which I understand properly to mean indifference to the higher intellectual interests. **1890** T. B. SAUNDERS tr. *Schopenhauer's Wisd. Life* (1891) 44 A man who has no mental needs, because his intellect is of the narrow and normal amount, is, in the strict sense of the word, a philistine—..one who is not a son of the Muses.
B. *adj.* **1.** Of or pertaining to the people of Philistia.
1842 LONGF. *Warning* 6 The Israelite..at last led forth to be A pander to Philistine revelry.
b. *transf.*
1596 NASHE *Saffron Walden* Wks. (Grosart) III. 132 So did he by that Philistine Poem of *Parthenophill and Parthenope*, which to compare worse than it selfe, it would plunge all the wits of France, Spaine, or Italy.
2. Characteristic of, or of the nature of, the modern 'Philistine'; uncultured; commonplace; prosaic. (Of persons and things.)
1831 CARLYLE *Germ. Poetry* in *Misc. Ess.* (1872) III. 241 To a German we might have compressed all this long description into a single word. Mr. Taylor is simply what they call a *Philister*; every fibre of him is Philistine. **1848** T. SINCLAIR *Mount* 57 The philistine division of our own critics. **1869** SWINBURNE *Ess. & Stud.* (1875) 216 Byron.. had in him a cross of the true Philistine breed. **1871** B. TAYLOR *Faust* (1875) I. Notes 235 Critics consider that he symbolizes the Philistine element in German life,—the hopelessly material, prosaic and commonplace.
C. *Comb.*
1817 COLERIDGE *Fire, Famine*, etc. Apol. Pref., Afterward this philistine-combatant went to London, and there perished of the plague. **1903** *Westm. Gaz.* 8 Oct. 4/1 What purpose some of them serve would be but a Philistine-like question.

Hence ˈ**philistinely** *adv.*, like or after the manner of a social Philistine. Also **philistinian** (-ˈtɪnɪən) *a.* = B. 1; **philistinic** (-ˈtɪnɪk) *a.* = B. 2; **philistinish** (ˈfɪlɪstaɪnɪʃ, -ɪnɪʃ) *a.* = B. 2.
1881 *Society* 1 June 9/2 A dress of black cashmere, *philistinely tight. **1773** J. ROSS *Fratricide* I. 636 (MS.) The *Philistinean stride of him of Gath. **1882–3** *Schaff's Encycl. Relig. Knowl.* III. 1829 The name of the Philistine harbor, Majuma, is entirely Egyptico-Philistinian. **1869** BLACK *In Silk Attire* I. 114 The audience..applauding *Philistinic politics over their raw chops. **1883** *Gd. Words* Aug. 493/1 There are some among us, nowadays, who sneer at all common-sense as philistinic. **1881** *Standard* 30 Aug. 5/2 Unhappily, we live in *Philistinish times. **1903** *Edin. Rev.* Oct. 407 His work sometimes lacks distinction..but it is never Philistinish.

philistinism (ˈfɪlɪstɪnɪz(ə)m, fɪˈlɪstɪnɪz(ə)m). [f. PHILISTINE + -ISM.] The opinions, aims, and habits of social Philistines (see prec. A. 4); the condition of being a social Philistine.
1831 CARLYLE *Sart. Res.* II. v, One 'Philistine'; who even now, to the general weariness, was dominantly pouring-forth Philistinism (*Philistriositäten*). **1856** R. A. VAUGHAN *Mystics* (1860) II. 248 The Romanticists were..the sworn foes..of that low-minded, prosaic narrowness which Germany calls *Philistinism*. **1863** M. ARNOLD *Ess. Crit.*, *Heine* (1865) 157 Philistinism! we have not the expression in English. Perhaps we have not the word because we have so much of the thing. **1890** *Spectator* 29 Nov. 760/2 British Philistinism is extremely overbearing. **1899** *Q. Rev.* Apr. 438 'Philistinism', after all, stands for two great habits, decency and order.

So **philistinize** (ˈfɪlɪst-, fɪˈlɪstɪnaɪz) *v. trans.*, to render Philistine; to imbue with the tastes, habits, and opinions of those termed Philistines.
1880 G. MEREDITH *Tragic Com.* xvi. (1892) 224 Children ..are secretly Philistinizing the demagogue,..turning him into a slow-stepping Liberal. **1891** ZANGWILL *Bachelors' Club* 164 She has not been philistinised by a refined education.

philizer, obs. form of FILACER.

phillaber, obs. f. PILLOW-BERE.

phillarea, phillerey: see PHILLYREA.

phillet, obs. f. FILLET.

phillibeg, var. FILIBEG.

philliberd, obs. f. FILBERT.

† **phillida**, variant of FILLADY *Obs.*
1620 J. MASON *Newfoundland* 4 The fowles are..Butters, blacke Birds with redd breastes, Phillidas.

philligree, phillip, obs. ff. FILIGREE, FILLIP.

Phillipine: see PHILIP 4 b.

Phillips[1] (ˈfɪlɪps). Also **Philips**. [The name of Henry F. *Phillips*, of Portland, Oregon.] A proprietary name used *attrib.* to designate screws having a slot in the form of an equal-armed cross, and corresponding screwdrivers.
1935 *Iron Age* 7 Nov. 42/3 American Screw Co., Providence, R.I., announces a line of case-hardened sheet metal screws featuring a new 'Phillips' recessed, self-centering head in place of the conventional screw-slot. *Ibid.*, The geometric pattern of the Phillips head provides that the screw shall hold to the taper point of the driver and may be brought into position with one hand. **1938** *Official Gaz.* (U.S. Patent Office) 18 Oct. 517/2 Henry F. Phillips, Portland, Oreg... Phillips Recessed Head. For screws. Claims use since Dec. 15, 1934. **1952** *Trade Marks Jrnl.* 20 Feb. 159/1 Phillips Recess... Screws of common metal. Guest, Keen & Nettlefolds Limited,.. Smethwick; manufacturers. *Ibid.* 161/1 Phillips Recess... Screwdrivers. Guest, Keen & Nettlefolds Limited,.. Smethwick; manufacturers. **1956** A. P. MORGAN *Woodworking Tools* ii. 37 Phillips head screws require a Phillips screwdriver. **1962** E. AMBLER *Light of Day* viii. 172 He had used an ordinary screwdriver on the Phillips heads. **1966** *Official Gaz.* (U.S. Patent Office) 18 Oct. TM119/1 Phillips Screw Company, Natick, Mass. Filed April 14, 1966. Phillips... For screws and allied fasteners. First use 1933. **1972** *Practical Motorist* Oct. 209/3 For Philips screws, you may be able to get by with one screwdriver but it's better to buy a large and a small one. **1976** *Practical Householder* Nov. 55/1 The kit

comprises the Impact Driver, bit holder, two cross points for Philips screws, two ordinary screw-driver bits for slotted screws and instructions for use, all packed in a strong metal case.

'Phillips[2]. The name of A. W. H. Phillips (1914–75), New Zealand economist, used *attrib.* or in the possessive in ***Phillips*** (or ***Phillips'***) ***curve***, a supposed inverse relationship between the level of unemployment and the rate of inflation.

1969 *Times* 5 May (Wall St. Suppl.) p. i/4 The Phillips curve was mentioned frequently during last year's presidential campaign, usually with the assumption that a Nixon Administration would tolerate a higher level of unemployment and thereby bring about a lower rate of inflation than would the opposition party. **1974** *Times* 23 Mar. 13/1 Many have come to doubt whether any such choice—between unemployment and inflation as expressed in the traditional Phillips's curve—exists at all. **1977** *Dædalus* CVI. IV. 90 The observation that prices start to rise long before the real GNP reaches full employment levels led to the Phillips curve hypothesis.

phillipsite ('fɪlɪpsaɪt). *Min.* [Named 1825 after the English mineralogist, J. W. Phillips: see -ITE[1].] A hydrous silicate of aluminium, calcium, and potassium, found in cruciform twin crystals of a white colour.

1825 *T. Thomson's Ann. Philos.* Ser. II. X. 362, I propose the name of phillipsite in honor of Mr. J. W. Phillips. **1850** DANA *Min.* (ed. 3) 306 Phillipsite occurs in large translucent crystals.

Phillis ('fɪlɪs), *sb.* Also 9 **Phyllis.** [a. L. *Phyllis*, a girl's name in Virgil, Horace, etc., a. Gr. *Φυλλίς* female name, lit. foliage of a tree, f. *φύλλον* leaf. The English spelling appears to be influenced by association with words in *phil-*, *philo-*.] A generic proper name in pastoral poetry for a comely rustic maiden, or for a sweetheart (cf. PHILANDER); also applied (after Milton) to a pretty or 'neat-handed' table-maid or waitress.

1632 MILTON *L'Allegro* 86 Hearbs, and other Country Messes, Which the neat-handed Phillis dresses. *a* **1700** SEDLEY *Song* Wks. 1778 I. 94 Phillis is my only joy, Faithless as the Winds or Seas. **1700** T. BROWN *Amusem. Ser. & Com.* 116 At the Bar the good Man always places a charming Phillis or two. **1768–74** TUCKER *Lt. Nat.* (1834) II. 574 Having perpetually filled their head with ideas of Strephons and Phillises. **1842** BARHAM *Ingol. Leg.* Ser. II. *Black Mousquetaire* II, As his Patients came in, certain soft-handed Phyllises Were at once set to work on their legs, arms, and backs. **1848** THACKERAY *Van. Fair* xxiv, If you have any Phillis to console.

Hence †**'Phillis** *v.* (*nonce-wd.*) *trans.*, to address in pastoral verses.

1699 GARTH *Dispens.* I. 148 He pass'd his easie Hours, instead of Prayer, In Madrigals, and Phillising the Fair.

phillosella, philly, erron. ff. FILOSELLA, FILLY.

phillumenist (fɪ'lju:-, fɪ'lu:mənɪst). Also **philumenist.** [f. PHIL- + L. *lūmen* light + -IST.] A collector of match-box or match-book labels. Hence **phi'llumeny**, the collecting of such labels.

Quot. 1943, supplied by a private correspondent, is from an unverifiable source.

1943 M. S. EVANS in *Floyd's Label Rev.* May 4, I have been wondering.. if we could not have a better name than 'labelists'... Under luminary in the dictionary I found the Latin word Lumen (light) and under philately the Greek word Philos (loving), also came across the Latin word Lucus (light). These suggest Phillumenist and Philucist. **1949** *This Week* 23 Oct. 24/2 Phillumenists (the word properly fits those who collect labels from wooden-match boxes, but also is applied to the paper-book fans) are outnumbered among hobbyists only by stamp collectors. **1951** *Britannica Bk. of Year* 686/2 *Phillumeny*, the hobby of collecting match-box covers. **1960** *News Chron.* 18 Feb. 4/5 Are phillumeny, meadopholy, tegestology and fromology as popular as they were? **1960** W. MILLER *Russians as People* 178 Some matchbox designs, among the hundreds which now make Russia a philumenist's paradise, have a charming simplicity suited to their size. **1967** *Listener* 13 Apr. 493/3 Little did John Walker foresee that his invention would become a great blessing to mankind, or that it would give rise to a popular hobby—phillumeny. **1976** *Weekend Mag.* (Montreal) 18 Dec. 8/1 Phillumenists go weak in the knees at the prospect of a rare matchbook cover.

Philly ('fɪlɪ). Also **Phillie.** U.S. slang abbrev. *Philadelphia* (see PHILADELPHIA and PHILADELPHIAN *a.* 3).

1891 W. DE VERE *Tramp Poems of West* 79 Draw up a chair 'thatch', I'll tell you a story, That happened in 'Philly' some twenty years since. **1899** 'J. FLYNT' *Tramping with Tramps* IV. 396 *Phillie*, Philadelphia. **1930** *Sat. Even. Post* 5 Apr. 46/2, I hope and trust that you do all right for yourself in Philly. **1961** *Rogue* May 14/3 After a while, Kitty murmured something to Cappy, and he held her close, answering, 'We'll just have to wait till we pull into Philly, honey.' **1971** *Black World* Apr. 65 To what hospital you goin?.. Back down in Philly. **1972** L. NEAL in A. Chapman *New Black Voices* 308 Remembering the time in Philly/the cops crashing the hotel room. **1976** 'D. HALLIDAY' *Dolly & Nanny Bird* vii. 90 Philly socialites. **1977** *Time* 31 Jan. 52/1 Nicky.. has shot a bookie and is holed up in a fleabag Philly hotel, going crazy.

phillygenin (fɪ'lɪdʒɪnɪn). *Chem.* [f. PHILLYRIN with ending of *saligenin.*] A resinous crystallizable substance ($C_{21}H_{24}O_6$), polymeric with saligenin, obtained from phillyrin by boiling with hydrochloric acid, or by lactic fermentation.

1862 [see PHILLYRIN].

‖**Phillyrea** (fɪ'lɪri:ə, fɪlɪ'ri:ə). *Bot.* Also 7 **phillyræa, phyl(l)area, phyleria,** 7–8 **phyllerea, philarea,** 8 **phyl(l)yrea, -ræa, phillarea, phyllirea, -ra, philyræa, -rea;** also *β.* in anglicized forms: 7–8 **philery, phillerey,** (8 **ffilleroy**). [Bot. L. *phyllyrea* (Tournefort; Linnæus *Philos. Bot.* 175), erroneously for *philyrea*, a. Gr. *φιλυρέα* (Theophr.), app. a deriv. of *φιλύρα* linden tree. There are many erroneous spellings in *phyll-* and *phyl-*. Also F. *phillyrée* (1572 in Godef.); cf. Cotgr. '*phillyrée*, mocke-priuet; a shrub'; thence the *β*-forms.]

A genus of ornamental evergreen shrubs (N.O. *Oleaceæ*), natives of the Mediterranean region and the East, with opposite leaves and inconspicuous greenish-white flowers in axillary clusters; also called *jasmine-box* or *mock privet*. *P. latifolia* is considered to be the *φιλυρέα* of Dioscorides and Theophrastus.

Cape phillyrea, a name for the S. African shrub *Cassine capensis* (N.O. *Celastraceæ*). (Treas. Bot. 1866.)

1664 EVELYN *Sylva* xxiv, All the Phillyreas are yet more hardy. **1678** PHILLIPS (ed. 4), *Philyræa*, see Privet. **1691** J. GIBSON in *Archæol.* XII. 188 In his garden he has four large round philareas, smooth clipped. **1699** M. LISTER *Journ. Paris* 210 Lentiscus's and Phylarea's in as great abundance, as Hazel or Thorn with us. **1706** J. GARDINER tr. *Rapin's Gardening* II. 89 Line The walls with Phylyrea fresh and fine. *c* **1710** CELIA FIENNES *Diary* (1888) 71 Cut box and ffilleroy and Lawrell. **1720** STRYPE *Stow's Surv.* (1754) I. I. xx. 112 Against the stone walls are planted Phillereys. **1785** MARTYN *Rousseau's Bot.* xvi. (1794) 207 This shrub [Alaternus] is frequently confounded with Philyrea, from which it may be known at all times by the position of the leaves. **1866** *Treas. Bot.*, *Phillyrea*, evergreen shrubs and trees introduced from the shores of the Mediterranean.

attrib. *c* **1665** LADY MARY WARWICK in C. F. Smith *Life* (1901) 325 Upon the phyllerea hedge that grew before the great parlour door. **1683–4** WOOD *Life* Jan.–Feb. (O.H.S.) III. 88 Frost.. killed laurel, bayes, philery hedges. **1747** WESLEY *Prim. Physic* (1762) 107 Gargle often with Phyllyrea leaves boiled with a little Allum. **1748** RICHARDSON *Clarissa* (1749) III. xvii. 100 The rushing of a little dog.. through the phyllerea hedge.

phillyrin ('fɪlɪrɪn). *Chem.* [f. prec. + -IN[1].] A white crystallizable bitter substance ($C_{27}H_{34}O_{11}$) obtained from the bark of *Phillyrea latifolia.*

1858 *Penny Cycl.* 2nd Suppl. 135/1 *Phillyrine* is a non-azotised compound, crystallising in silver scales and of a bitter taste. **1862** MILLER *Elem. Chem.* (ed. 2) III. 568 Phillyrin.. when submitted to lactic fermentation yields phillygenin and sugar, phillygenin containing the elements of 3 atoms of saligenin.

†**philm(e**, obs. erron. form of FILM.

1572 J. JONES *Bathes of Bath* II. 18 A skinne, pellicle, or philme. **1730** BURDON *Pocket Farrier* (1735) 48 A Philm grows over the Eye.

philo- (fɪləʊ), before a vowel (or *h*) usually **phil-** (fɪl), repr. Gr. *φιλο-*, *φιλ-*, combining form from root of *φιλ-εῖν* to love, *φίλ-ος* dear, friend (cf. *μισο-*, *miso-*, from *μῑσ-εῖν* to hate, *μῖσ-ος* hate, hatred). The number of compounds so formed in Greek was very great; usually they were adjs., having derived sbs. and other words, and capable themselves also of being used as sbs.; e.g. *φιλόσοφος* loving wisdom, a lover of wisdom, whence *φιλοσοφία*, *φιλοσοφικός*, *φιλοσοφεῖν* to philosophize, etc.; *φίλορνις* fond of birds, *φιλορνῖθία* fondness for birds, etc. Among these were some formed on national names, as *φιλέλλην* loving the Hellenes or Greeks, *φιλολάκων* loving the Lacedæmonians. Many of the Greek compounds have come down (frequently through Latin, and usually with formative suffixes) into English; and, on the model of these, *philo-* (*phil-*) has been employed to form new compounds, the second element of which is properly Greek, but often Latin, and even, esp. in nonce-words, English or in Eng. use. *Philo-* has thus become a living element, esp. with national names, as *philo-German*, *philo-Russian*, *philo-Turk*, and the like.

Examples are: ***phil-aristocracy***, ***-athlete***, ***-athletic*** [cf. Gr. *φιλαθλητής*], ***-hymnic*** [Gr. *φίλυμνος*] (loving hymns), ***-orthodox***; ***philo-botanic***, ***-botanist***, ***-cathartic***, ***-catholic***, ***-dramatic***, ***-dramatist***, ***-felon***, ***-garlic***, ***-irenist***, ***-mathematic(al***, ***-musical***, ***-mystic***, ***-mythology*** (love of fables), ***-mythy*** [Gr. *φιλομυθία* love of talk], ***-pagan***, ***-peristeronic*** (pigeon-fancying), ***-pig***, ***-poet***, ***-publican***, ***-radical***, ***-tadpole***, ***-theorist*** [cf. Gr. *φιλοθέωρος*], etc. Among those formed on national names are ***phil-African***, ***-Arabian***, ***-Arabic***, ***-Athenian***; ***philo-Athenian*** [cf. Gr. *φιλαθήναιος*], ***-French***, ***-Gallic*** (***-ism***), ***-German*** (***-ism***), ***-Greek***, ***-Hindu***, ***-Jew***, ***-Laconian*** [Gr. *φιλολάκων*], ***-Peloponnesian***, ***-Pole***, ***-Polish***, ***-Slav***, ***-Teuton*** (***-ism***), ***-Turk*** (***-ish***, ***-ism***), ***-Yankee*** (***-ist***), ***-Zionist***, etc. Among humorous nonce-words are ***philo-destructiveness***, ***-financitive***, ***-foxhuntingness***, ***-legislativeness***, in ridicule of the phrenological ***philoprogenitiveness***. Also **philarchaist** (-'ɑ:keɪɪst) [see ARCHAIST, and cf. Gr. *φιλάρχαιος*], a lover of what is ancient, an antiquary. **phil'hippic** *a.* [Gr. *ἵππος* horse: cf. Gr. *φίλιππος*], fond of or interested in horses; so **phi'lippy** [after *philanthropy*: cf. Gr. *φιλιππία*], love for or kindness to a horse or horses. **philo'brutish** *a.*, characterized by love of or kindness to the brutes or lower animals; so **philo'brutist**, a lover of brutes. **philocalist** (fɪ'lɒkəlɪst) [Gr. *φιλόκαλος*, f. *καλός* beautiful], a lover of beauty; so **phi'localy**, love of beauty. **phi'locomal** *a.* [cf. Gr. *φιλόκομος*, f. *κόμη* hair], characterized by love of or attention to the hair. **phi'locubist** [Gr. *φιλόκυβος* fond of dice (Aristophanes)], a lover of dice-play. **philocynic** (-'sɪnɪk) [Gr. *κύων*, *κυν-* dog: see CYNIC; after *philanthropic*] *a.*, loving dogs, fond of dogs; *sb.* a lover of dogs; so **philo'cynical** *a.*; **phi'locynism, phi'locyny**, love of dogs. **philodemic** (-'dɛmɪk) *a.* [Gr. *φιλόδημος*, f. *δῆμος* the people], loving the people. **philo'dendrist** [cf. Gr. *φιλόδενδρος* tree-loving, f. *δένδρον* tree], a lover of trees. **philoepiorcian** (-ɛpɪ'ɔ:sɪən) *a.* [Gr. *ἐπιορκία* false oath], loving false oaths. **philofelist** (fɪlɒ'fi:lɪst) [L. *fēles*, *-is* cat], a lover of cats. **phi'logalist** [Gr. *γαλέη*, *γαλῆ* pole-cat, taken as = cat], = prec. **philo'gastric** *a.* [Gr. *γαστήρ* belly], loving the stomach, indulging the appetite. **philogenitive** (-'dʒɛnɪtɪv) *a.* [see GENITIVE], inclined to procreation, or to sexual indulgence; hence **philo'genitiveness. philo'kleptic** *a.* [Gr. *κλέπτης* robber], fond of thieves or robbers. **philo'melanist** [Gr. *μελαν-* black] a Negrophile. **philomuse** ('fɪləʊmju:z) *a.* [Gr. *φιλόμουσος*], loving the Muses. **philonoist** (fɪ'lɒnəʊɪst) [Gr. *νόος*, *νοῦς* mind, understanding], a lover of knowledge. †**philo'plutary** [cf. Gr. *φιλόπλουτος*], a lover of wealth; so †**philoplu'tonic** *a.* (erron. for *philoplutic), loving wealth. **philo'pogon** [Gr. *πώγων* beard], a lover of beards. **philopo'lemic** *a.* [cf. Gr. *φιλοπόλεμος*, f. *πόλεμος* war], fond of war or strife; so **philopo'lemical** *a.* **philo'pornist** [cf. Gr. *φιλόπορνος*, f. *πόρνη* harlot], a lover of harlots. **philorchi'daceous** *a.*, fond of orchids. **philornithic** (-ɔ:'nɪθɪk) *a.* [cf. Gr. *φίλορνις*, f. *ὄρνις*, *ὀρνῖθ-* bird], fond of birds. **philo-'Semite**, one who is favourable to or who supports the Jews; also as *adj.*; so **philo-Se'mitic** *a.*; **philo-'Semitism**, theory, action, or practice directed in favour of the Jews. **philothaumaturgic** (-θɔ:mə'tɜ:dʒɪk) *a.* [see THAUMATURGIC], loving works of wonder. **philotheism** ('fɪləʊθi:ɪz(ə)m) [cf. Gr. *φιλόθεος*, f. *Θεός* God], love of God; so **'philotheist**, a lover of God; hence **philothe'istic** *a.* **philo'therian** *a.* and *sb.* [Gr. *θήρ* wild beast], (a person) that loves wild animals; so **philo'therianism**, love of wild animals. †**philoxygenous** (-ɒk'sɪdʒɪnəs) *a.*, having an affinity for oxygen (*obs.*). **philozoic** (-'zəʊɪk) *a.* [Gr. *ζῷον* animal, after *philanthropic*], loving or showing kindness to animals; so **philo'zoist** (erron. **-zoonist**), a lover of animals.

1897 *Current Hist.* (Buffalo, N.Y.) VII. 224 The *Phil-african Liberators' League is an association.. to work for the extinction of the African slave trade. **1750** *Student* I. 42 The *Phil-Arabians think that.. theirs [Arabic].. may be made very instrumental in illustrating the present Hebrew text. **1652** URQUHART *Jewel* Wks. (1834) 211 New Palestine, as the Kirkomanetick *Philarchaists would have it [Scotland] called. **1820** *Examiner* No. 612. 1/1 Ready to put a grave panegyrical face on his elderly Odes and *philaristocracy. **1908** *Westm. Gaz.* 19 Aug. 4/3 Are we to suspect a *phil-Athenian bias in the story? **1922** S. LESLIE *Oppidan* xi. 133 The *Philathlete and the Philistine. **1864** TREVELYAN *Compet. Wallah* (1866) 14 The *Phil-athletic club at Harrow. **1890** *Sat. Rev.* 13 Dec. 672/1 Every sport known to the philathletic Briton. **1905** *Blackw. Mag.* Dec. 811/2 Pick out an untrained but philathletic young Englishman. **1922** S. LESLIE *Oppidan* iii. 42 In an anti-musical philathletic school he was always anxious to impress the new boys. **1929** *Observer* 17 Nov. 11/2 The Sixth Form cricket ground and the Philathletic field of the School have been zoned as residential areas. **1886** *World* 24 Feb. 11 The state-carriage horses.. excited much admiration in a very *philhippic population. **1861** *Longman's List* Oct., Hymnologia Christiana: Psalms and Hymns.. Selected or Contributed by *Philhymnic Friends. **1799** E. DU BOIS *Piece Family Biog.* II. 146 The old Welchman in pure *philippy, took his horse out of the road. **1922** JOYCE *Ulysses* 574 Modern *philirenists, notably the tsar and the King of England, have invented arbitration. **1865** W. WHITMAN *November Boughs* (1888) 106 He will not countenance at all the demand of the extreme *Philo-African element of the North. **1850** GROTE

Greece II. lxi. (1862) V. 343 The tone of feeling in Lesbos had been found to be decidedly *philo-Athenian. **1856** DELAMER *Fl. Gard.* (1861) Pref., To volunteer as gate-opener to other fields of *Philobotanic Literature. **1824** BENTHAM *Mem. & Corr.* Wks. 1843 X. 543, I am glad to hear your master has turned *Philo-Botanist at last. **1826** *Sporting Mag.* XVIII. 137 These days of *philo-brutish refinement. *Ibid.* XVII. 124 The *Philobrutists may carry their humanity too far. **1861** J. BROWN *Horæ Subs.* (1862) 353 This poor..creature was a *philocalist: he had a singular love of flowers and of beautiful women. **1891** *Sat. Rev.* 24 Jan. 113/2 His '*philocaly' is ..destitute of vigour. **1822** SYD. SMITH *Wks.* (1859) II. 2/1 If..the apothecary, the druggist, and the physician, all called upon him to abandon his *philocathartic propensities. **1893** SWINBURNE *Stud. Prose & Poetry* (1894) 108 The *philocatholic whiggery of Macaulay and Tom Moore. **1869** *Daily Tel.* 14 Jan. 5/4 To consider the present state of the *philocomal art. **1822** T. MITCHELL *Aristoph.* II. 179 You Amynias there —hist!—A *philocubist?—Miss'd. **1815** MOORE *Life Byron* (1833) III. 143 *note*, You, who are one of the *philocynic sect. **1887** *Sat. Rev.* 21 May 730/2 The philanthropic and the philocynic zeal of Lord Harrowby and Lord Mount-Temple. *c* **1843** M. J. HIGGINS *Ess.* (1875) 87, I admired my ingenious friend's *philo-cynical treaty with Mr. William Sykes. **1865** *Spectator* 4 Mar. 240/2 Miss Baker's *philocynism rose into a passion for a particular bull-dog. **1839** *Blackw. Mag.* XLV. 478 Our *philocyny developed itself at the earliest possible period. **1870** LOWELL *Study Wind.* 44 This..does too much mischief to the trees for a *philodendrist to take unmixed pleasure in. **1841** J. T. HEWLETT *Parish Clerk* I. 101 The organ of *philo-destructiveness would have been found strongly developed. **1833** *Fraser's Mag.* VIII. 42 James Smith may indeed be well called a *philo-dramatic poet. **1817** COLERIDGE *Biog. Lit.* xxiii. (1882) 274 The enlightened and patriotic assemblage of *philodramatists. **1838** G. S. FABER *Inquiry* 239 They must have borrowed their *philŏepiorcian maxim from some lurking remnant of the Priscillianists, who flourished in Spain in the time of Augustine. *a* **1843** SOUTHEY *Doctor, Fragm.* (1848) 681/2 The Laureate, Dr. Southey, who is known to be a *philofelist, and confers honours upon his Cats according to their services. *Ibid.* 684/2 He made himself acquainted with all the philofelists of the family. **1831** —— in *Q. Rev.* XLIV. 277 A monument.. of Jeremy's philosophico-*philofelon philanthropy. **1829** *Blackw. Mag.* XXVI. 743 Never having heard of a *philo-financitive bump, we fear it can be nothing better than acquisitiveness. **1828** *Sporting Mag.* XXII. 271 An impression on the organ of *philo-foxhuntingness..not very easily to be effaced. **1894** in *Daily News* 3 Nov. 5/6, I believe he is not so much *philo-French as Prussophobe. **1821** SOUTHEY *Lett.* (1856) III. 240 You, Grosvenor, who are a *philogalist, and therefore understand more of cat nature than has ever been attained by the most profound naturalists. **1870** *Daily News* 19 Nov., Mr. Carlyle's fierce philo-Germanism is as dangerous a sentiment as the blind *philo-Gallicism against which he lifts up his voice. **1847** DE QUINCEY *Spanish Nun* ix, With these *philo-garlic men Kate took her departure. **1884** *West. Daily Press* 16 Dec. 7/3 The *philogastric propensities of boys. **1816** *Gentl. Mag.* LXXXVI. I. 255 If he be given to mystery, Or fond of individuality, Or *philo-genitive, or whatsoe'er His passion be. **1823** BYRON *Juan* XII. xxii, I say, methinks that '*Philo-genitiveness' Might meet from men a little more forgiveness. **1852** *Fraser's Mag.* XLII. 482 No sentimental *philo-Hindoo. **1865** *Pall Mall G.* 22 June 9 What will the Italian Government say to such a *philokleptic proceeding on our part? **1850** GROTE *Greece* II. lxi. (1862) V. 345 The active *philo-Laconian party. **1832** *Fraser's Mag.* VI. 733 Sawing through your organ of *philolegislativeness. *c* **1670** SETTLE in Johnson *L.P., Dryden* (1781) II. 36 Poor Robin, or any other of the *philomathematicks, would have given him satisfaction in the point. **1700** MOXON *Math. Dict.* 67 The Philo-Mathematick Reader. **1734** BERKELEY *Analyst* Query 55 Those *philomathematical physicians, anatomists, and dealers in the animal economy. **1833** DE QUINCEY *Rev. Greece* Wks. 1862 X. 120 *note*, The original (or *Philomuse society)..adopted literature for its ostensible object. **1811** BUSBY *Dict. Mus.* (ed. 3), **Philomusical.* **1752** H. WALPOLE *Lett. to Montagu* l, A true born Englishman and *philomystic. **1612** T. SCOT (*title*) *Philomythie, or *Philomythologie, wherein Outlandish Birds, Beasts, and Fishes, are Taught to Speake True English. **1804** COLERIDGE *Lett., to R. Sharp* (1895) 448 Philologists, *Philonoists, Physiophilists, keen hunters after knowledge and science. **1850** GROTE *Greece* II. lxi. (1862) V. 343 The *philo-Peloponnesian party. **1828** SOUTHEY *Epistle to A. Cunningham* 336 Who in all forms Of pork, baked, roasted, toasted, boil'd or broil'd,..Profess myself a genuine *Philopig. *a* **1876** M. COLLINS *Pen Sk.* (1879) II. 72 He likes to outdo his *philoplutonic brethren in his wife's rank and silks, in the splendour of his house. **1720** SWIFT *Lett. Yng. Poet.* 1 Dec., Wks. 1841 II. 300/2 A multitude of poetasters, poetitoes, parcel-poets, poet-apes, and *philo-poets. **1875** R. F. BURTON *Gorilla L.* (1876) I. 205 Whatever absurdity in hair may be demanded by the trichotomists and *philopogons of modern Europe. **1794** T. TAYLOR *Pausanias* III. 242 She [Minerva] is called..*Philopolemic, as uniformly ruling over the opposing natures which the world contains. **1827** SYD. SMITH *Wks.* (1859) II. 127/2 The increasing arrogance of the Americans, and our own *philopolemical folly. **1893** SWINBURNE *Stud. Prose & Poetry* (1894) 122 To the mealy-mouthed modern *philopornist the homely and hardy method of the old poet ..may seem rough and brutal. **1896** A. B. BRUCE in *Expositor* Sept. 225 They called Him a drunkard, a glutton and a *philo-publican. **1884** *World* 30 Apr. 6 A *phil-orchidaceous peer. **1862** *Ibis* July 289 The smart game-bags and neat bird-cages testify at least to the *philornithic taste of the natives in one direction or another. **1888** J. H. OVERTON & ELIZ. WORDSW. *Chr. Wordsworth* 387 The love which you, so noble, so *philorthodox, so philhellenic, have displayed. **1946** KOESTLER *Thieves in Night* 275 If the Jews were as the *philosemites describe them, there would be no reason for this Return. **1948** WYNDHAM LEWIS *Let.* 25 Oct. (1963) 467, I am not philosemite. **1976** C. BERMANT *Coming Home* I. ii. 28 All *goyim* were presumed to be *antisemitten* unless they showed definite proof to the contrary, whereupon they were pronounced *Judenfreint*—philosemites. **1962** *Observer* 27 May 28/2 *Philo-semitic authors can be no whit less tedious than anti. **1977** *Daily Tel.* 31 May 16 Both Jews and philo-Semitic people have been made aware of the ghastly similarities between the 'old' form of anti-Semitism and its 'modern' euphemism [*sc.* 'anti-Zionism']. **1965** *New Statesman* 16 Apr. 617/3 He calls attention to the scale and cohesion of the *philo-semitism now current in the cultural life of America. **1976** M. J. LASKY *Utopia & Revolution* (1977) viii. 301 Philo-Semitism was a natural by-product of the enthusiasm with which the Puritan generation returned to the old books of the Bible for inspired guidance. **1886** *Pall Mall G.* 14 Dec. 2/2 We see the real cause..and realize some hidden dangers which have nothing to do with *Philo-Slavism or Slavo-philism. **1862** LOWELL *Biglow P.* Ser. II. 80 The thing was done, the tails were cropped, And home each *philotadpole hopped. **1891** ABBOTT *Philomythus* ix. 235 Useless to the *philothaumaturgic soul. **1870** SWINBURNE *Ess. & Stud.* (1875) 82 Baudelaire always kept in mind that Christianity ..was not and could not be a creature of philanthropy or *philotheism, but of church and creed. **1829** LANDOR *Imag. Conv.* Wks. 1853 I. 506/1 Polemics can never be philosophers or *philo-theists. *a* **1843** SOUTHEY *Doctor* ccxiii. (1848) 577 The speculation, or conception (as the *Philotheistic philosopher himself called it) of Giordano Bruno. **1809–10** COLERIDGE *Friend* (1818) III. 176, I distinguish, first, those whom you indeed may call *Philotheorists, or Philotechnists, or Practicians, and secondly those whom alone you may rightly denominate Philosophers, as knowing what the science of all these branches of science is. **1906** *Times* 24 Aug. 1/2 The terrible cruelties practised on quadrupeds..have been..denounced by..that noble and devoted *philotherian. **1909** *Athenæum* 23 Oct. 494/3 An indulgence having been accorded to persons..purchasing, perusing, or subscribing to any philotherian publication. *Ibid.* 495/1, I ask myself why the practice of charity, in the shape of *philotherianism, should be left out of sight. **1838** *New Monthly Mag.* LIV. 132 Mr. Urquhart..is a *Philo-Turk. **1895** *Eclectic Mag.* Oct. 565 An anti-Russian and *philo-Turkish policy. **1799** BEDDOES *Contrib. Phys. & Med. Knowl.* 223 Should it be discovered that oxygen enters into their composition the terms *philoxygenous and misoxygenous must be changed. **1818** SYD. SMITH in Lady Holland *Mem.* (1855) II. 166, I.. believe that I am to the full as much a *Philoyankeeist as you are. **1897** *19th Cent.* Oct. 628 The *Philo-Zionists recognise the mission: but they recognise the misery as well. **1868** *Daily News* 15 Oct., The Society..is animated by, as we cannot say philanthropic, let us say *philozoic motives. **1887** HUXLEY *Ess., Progr. Sc.* I. 122 Unless the fanaticism of philozoic sentiment overpowers the voice of humanity. **1831** *Examiner* 219/2 That *philozoonist would certainly have introduced into his bill against 'cruelty to animals' a special clause. **1899** *Pop. Sci. Monthly* May 140 Inconsistent philozoists.

philobiblic (fɪləʊˈbɪblɪk), *a.* [f. Gr. φιλόβιβλος fond of books (f. φιλο- PHILO- + βίβλος book) + -IC.] Fond of books; devoted to literature. Cf. *Philobiblon*, name of book by R. de Bury, 1344, and of a modern society. So **philoˈbiblian** *a.*; **philoˈbiblist**, a lover of books. (All more or less *nonce-wds.*)

1755 *Connoisseur* No. 86 ¶2 My method has since been to visit the Philobiblian libraries. **1824** J. COLE (*title*) Bibliographical..Tour..to the Library of a Philobiblist. **1845** LD. CAMPBELL *Chancellors* (1857) I. xiii. 200, I am rather surprised that a 'De Bury' club has not yet been established by Philobiblists. **1864** BOHN *Bibliogr. Manual* (Lowndes) VI. 82 *Philobiblon Society.* Composed of Persons interested in the History, Collection, or Peculiarities, of Books. Instituted in London, 1853. **1885** *Spectator* 23 May 676 It has been known in philobiblic circles..for some years.

philoˈbiblical, *a.* [f. as prec. + -AL[1]: in sense b, after *biblical*.] **a.** = prec. **b.** Devoted to the study of the Bible.

1880 *Encycl. Brit.* XI. 475/1 [Hermann von der Hardt] had founded at Leipsic a philobiblical society, with the object of determining the sacred text. **1896** *Blackw. Mag.* Mar. 253 The philobiblical physician has always his favourite prescription.

philobotanic to **-dendrist**: see PHILO-.

‖**philodendron** (fɪləʊˈdɛndrən). *Bot.* Also **-um.** [mod.L. (Schott 1830), a. Gr. φιλόδενδρον, neuter of φιλόδενδρος fond of trees (f. φιλο- PHILO- + δένδρον tree), in reference to its climbing upon trees.] A genus of tropical American climbing shrubs (N.O. *Araceæ*), some species of which are cultivated as stove-plants.

1877 F. W. BURBIDGE *Propag. Cult. Pl.* 190 Some hybrid Philodendrons and Anthuriums. **1899** RODWAY *Guiana Wilds* 28 Everywhere were long cords dangling from the rosettes of philodendrums, which had to be waved aside.

philoˈdespot. *rare.* [ad. Gr. φιλοδέσποτ-ος adj., loving one's master, f. φιλο- PHILO- + δεσπότης master; in b. directly f. PHILO- + DESPOT.]

†**a.** (See quot. 1656.) *Obs. rare*⁻⁰. **b.** One who favours despots or despotism (quot. 1796).

1656 BLOUNT *Glossogr.*, *Philodespot*.., he that loveth his Master. **1796** COLERIDGE in Mrs. Sandford *T. Poole & Friends* (1888) I. 140 As bad as the most..rampant Philodespot could wish in the moment of cursing.

philodine (ˈfɪlədaɪn). *Zool.* [f. PHILO- + Gr. δῖνος whirling, rotation.] A rotifer of the genus *Philodīna* or family *Philodīnidæ*. So **philoˈdinid**; **philoˈdinoid** *a.*, resembling this familly.

1883 H. J. SLACK in *Knowledge* 15 June 358/2 The Philodines, of which the common Rotifer, *R. vulgaris*, is the most abundant. **1895** *Funk's Stand. Dict.*, *Philodinid* ..*Philodinoid.*

philodox (ˈfɪlədɒks). *rare.* [ad. Gr. φιλόδοξ-ος adj. (Plato), loving fame or glory, f. φιλο- PHILO- + δόξα glory (also opinion, etc.).] Properly, One who loves fame or glory; but taken (after *orthodox*) as = One who loves his own opinion; an argumentative or dogmatic person. So **philoˈdoxical** *a.*

1603 FLORIO *Montaigne* II. xii. (1632) 303 No people are lesse Philosophers..than Platoes Philodoxes, or lovers of their owne opinions. **1852** DAVIES & VAUGHAN tr. *Plato's Republic* v. (1866) 196 Philodoxical rather than philosophical, that is to say, lovers of opinion rather than lovers of wisdom. **1872** *Nonconf.* 27 Mar. 326/2 The lover of argument, the *philodox*—to revive an old word—..is less likely to listen to it.

philo-dramatic to **-Germanism**: see PHILO-.

philogenesis, -genetic, etc. erron. ff. PHYLO-.

philograph (ˈfɪləgrɑːf, -æ-). [f. Gr. φιλο- PHILO- + -γραφος writing, writer, delineator.] A device for facilitating the production of an outline drawing.

1892 *Echo* 9 Feb. 2/4 By the use of an instrument called the 'Philograph', an absolutely correct representation can be obtained of any organic form. **1892** G. HAKE *Mem. 80 Years* lxviii. 292 Photographs in my early days were not in use, so philographs must be produced in their stead. **1894** *Times* 1 Mar. 6/5 The philograph, in which an exact picture was sketched on glass or celluloid of the objects seen through it, was useful and accurate, and excellent in its perspective.

†**philoˈgrobolise**, *v. Obs. rare.* [ad. F. *philogroboliser*.] (See quot.)

1653 URQUHART *Rabelais* II. x, All-to-be-dunced and philogrobolised in their braines.

philogynist (fɪˈlɒdʒɪnɪst). [f. Gr. φιλογύν-ης, in pl. -γύναικ-ες, fond of women, φιλογυνία love of women, f. φιλο- + γυνή woman.] A lover or admirer of women. So **philogynæcic** (-ˈiːsɪk), **phiˈlogynous** *adjs.*, fond of women; **phiˈlogyny** (also irreg. **philogyˈneity**), love of women.

1870 *Sat. Rev.* 2 July 24/2 The philanthropic or *philogynæcic brain of one of the most benevolent of mortals. **1884** *N. & Q.* 6th Ser. X. 277, I would object to much of philanthropy, but I must say that such *philogyneity as this closely borders on the ridiculous. **1865** HUXLEY *Lay Serm.* (1870) 21 There are *philogynists as fanatical as any 'misogynists'. **1892** M. O'CONNOR MORRIS *Memini* p. xxxv, Dean Swift was most *philogynous. **1623** COCKERAM, **Phyloginie*, a doating on women. **1754** FIELDING *Jonathan Wild* I. x, We will..draw a curtain over this scene, from that philogyny which is in us. **1892** *Pall Mall G.* 25 Feb. 2/1 False demagoguy and sentimental philogyny.

philo-Hindu, philokleptic, etc.: see PHILO-.

philologaster (fɪlɒləʊˈgæstə(r)). *nonce-wd.* [f. L. *philolog-us* (see below) + -ASTER.] A petty or would-be philologist. So **philoloˈgastry**, petty or blundering philology.

1880 F. HALL in *19th Cent.* Sept. 442 The doings of American philologasters are, in truth, a curious study. **1893** —— in *Nation* (N.Y.) 16 Feb., He is quite capable of such an enormity of philologastry.

philologer (fɪˈlɒlədʒə(r)). [f. PHILOLOGY + -ER: cf. *astrologer*.]

1. = PHILOLOGIST 1. Now *rare* or *Obs.*

1588 J. HARVEY *Disc. Probl.* 63 Antiquaries, philologers, schoolemen, and other learned discoursers. **1659** HEYLIN *Examen Hist.* I. 129 John Selden, of the Inner Temple,.. that renown'd Humanitian and Philologer, sometime a Commoner of this House. **1706** PHILLIPS, *Philologer*, an Humanist, a Man of Letters. **1847** J. W. DONALDSON *Vind. Protest. Princ.* 96 All competently educated and impartial philologers would derive, from a careful examination of the whole Jewish and Christian Scriptures, the views which we have now set forth respecting the person of the Deity.

2. = PHILOLOGIST 2.

1660 HOWELL *Lexicon* Pref. *heading*, To the tru Philologer, Touching the English (or Saxon) with the three Sororian Toungs, French, Italian, and Spanish. **1755** JOHNSON, *Philologer*, one whose chief study is language; a grammarian; a critick. **1840** ARNOLD *Let.* in Stanley *Life* (1858) II. 174 Donaldson, the author of the new Cratylus, and almost the only Englishman who promises, I think, to be a really good philologer. **1882** FREEMAN in *Longm. Mag.* I. 83 The word 'American', as applied to language, means, in the mouth of a comparative philologer, the native languages of the American Continent.

philologian (fɪləʊˈləʊdʒɪən). [f. L. *philologia* PHILOLOGY + -AN.] = PHILOLOGIST 2.

1830 PUSEY *Hist. Enq.* II. x. 349 Philologians we have perhaps not a few, and not unlearned. **1844** J. CAIRNS *Let.* in *Life* viii. (1895) 165 The brothers Grimm, the philologians. **1869** FARRAR *Fam. Speech* ii. (1873) 42 The researches of the philologian into dead and existing tongues.

philologic (fɪləʊˈlɒdʒɪk), *a.* [ad. mod.L. *philologic-us*, f. *philologia*: see -IC. Cf. F. *philologique* (1668 in Hatz.-Darm.).] = next.

1669 GALE *Crt. Gentiles* I. Introd. 2 Their choisest Notions and Contemplations, both Philologic and Philosophic. **1776** BURNEY *Hist. Mus.* I. 225 *note*, The common foundation of most modern philologic systems, etymologies. **1847** DE QUINCEY *Secret Soc.* Suppl. Note, Wks. VI. 305 Depositaries of all the erudition—archæologic, historic, and philologic—by which a hidden clue could be sought.

philological (fɪləʊˈlɒdʒɪkəl), *a.* [f. as prec. + -AL[1].] Of, pertaining to, concerned with, or devoted to the study of, philology (in the wider or, now usually, the restricted sense: see PHILOLOGY).

1621 Bp. Mountagu *Diatribæ* 9 You are much vpon the by, to bring in your Philologicall obseruations. **1659** Bp. Walton *Consid. Considered* 230 Though the controversy [about the Hebrew points] be in itself grammatical, or philological, yet it had its rise from a question theological. **1741** Watts *Improv. Mind* I. xx. §26 Those studies which are wont to be called philological, such as history, language, grammar, rhetoric, poesy, and criticism. **1797** *Monthly Mag.* III. 486 The Philological Society, at Bath, for educating and placing out the sons of poor clergymen and mechanics (instituted in 1792). **1832** (*title*) Philological Museum [Contents of Vol. I] On the names of the Days of the Week. On the number of Dramas ascribed to Sophocles. On the early Ionic Philosophers. **1842** *Proc. Philol. Soc.* I. 7 The author considered the adoption of an improved system of orthography by the Editors of the Philological Journal (Camb. 1832) an example worthy of imitation on the part of the Philological Society. **1851** D. Wilson *Preh. Ann.* (1863) II. iv. i. 185 Philological relations traceable between Cymri and Gael.

Hence **philo'logically** *adv.*, in accordance with or in relation to philology.

1622 Peacham *Compl. Gent.* (1661) 263 See learned *Hieron-Mercurialis* in his books *De Arte Gymnastica*: where this matter is fully handled, both Physically..and Philologically. **1794** Mathias *Purs. Lit.* (1798) 332 There is no passage..which will not at last admit of such an illustration or explanation, I mean philologically or critically, as may put to silence the ignorance of foolish men. **1884** H. D. Traill in *Macm. Mag.* Oct. 442/1, I have never yet met a man..who was philologically qualified for a seat on the bench.

philologist (fɪ'lɒlədʒɪst). [f. PHILOLOGY (? or Gr. φιλόλογ-ος) + -IST.] A person versed in or devoted to philology.

1. One devoted to learning or literature; a lover of letters or scholarship; a learned or literary man; a scholar, *esp.* a classical scholar. Now *less usual* (cf. PHILOLOGY 1).

1648 E. Sparke in *Shute's Sarah & Hagar* Pref. b j, For his Method, let no nice Philologist distaste it, as too Calvinistical. *a* **1682** Sir T. Browne *Tracts, Plants Script.* §25 Why the Rods and Staffs of the Princes were chosen for this decision Philologists will consider. **1799** Mrs. J. West *Tale of Times* III. 388 Philologists dispute the revealed will of God. **1841** Spalding *Italy & It. Isl.* I. 125 This labour ..is least irksome to the professed philologist, who, in the purity of the style and the bold structure of the versification, can forget the weary barrenness of the matter.

2. A person versed in the science of language; a student of language; a linguistic scholar.

1716 M. Davies *Athen. Brit.* III. *Diss. Drama* 12 He pass'd for an Excelling Philologist, especially as to the Greek Roots. **1770** Baretti *Journ. fr. London* I. 160 Old Facciolati the philologist. **1865** Tylor *Early Hist. Man.* ii. 15 We know so little about the origin of language, that even the greatest philologists are forced..to avoid the subject altogether. **1865** Max Müller *Chips* (1880) I. i. 21 The Comparative Philologist ignores altogether the division of languages according to their locality.

philologize (fɪ'lɒlədʒaɪz), *v. rare.* [f. Gr. φιλόλογ-ος + -IZE.] *intr.* To play the philologist; to deal in philology (i.e. either literary scholarship, or linguistic science). Also *trans.* to bring *into* some condition by philologizing.

1664 Evelyn *Sylva* III. vi, It is not here that I design to enlarge, as those who have philologiz'd on this occasion *de Sycophantis*, and other curious Criticismes. **1868** *Contemp. Rev.* VIII. 165 It cannot be criticized or philologized into nothingness, like written record. **1877** F. Hall *On -able and reliable* 25, I have spoken of the unscientific philologizing which has recently become so rife.

philologue ('fɪlɒlɒg). *rare.* Also 7 -log, -loge. [a. F. *philologue* (Rabelais 16th c.), ad. L. *philologus* man of letters, a. Gr. φιλόλογ-ος: see PHILOLOGY.] = PHILOLOGIST. Also *attrib.* or *adj.* (quot. 1611) = PHILOLOGICAL.

1594 R. Ashley tr. *Loys le Roy* 110b, Philologves or serchers of antiquitie, and proprietie of tongues. **1611** Chapman *Paneg. Verses to Coryat's Crudities*, To the Philologe Reader. **1646** Gillespie *Malè Audis* A ij, Great philologs will tell him that *maledico* is taken in a good sense as well as in a bad. **1653** Urquhart *Rabelais* Prol. (Rtldg.) 17 Homer,..the paragon of all philologues. **1851** Carlyle *Sterling* I. iv. (1872) 29 One cannot..conceive of Sterling as a steady dictionary philologue. **1862** R. G. Latham *Elem. Comp. Philol.* II. i. 704 The effect of some philological force which it is the business of philologues to elucidate.

philology (fɪ'lɒlədʒɪ). [In Chaucer, ad. L. *philologia*; in 17th c. prob. a. F. *philologie*, ad. L. *philologia*, a. Gr. φιλολογία, abstr. sb. from φιλόλογος fond of speech, talkative; fond of dicussion or argument; studious of words; fond of learning and literature, literary; f. φιλο- PHILO- + λόγος word, speech, etc.]

1. Love of learning and literature; the study of literature, in a wide sense, including grammar, literary criticism and interpretation, the relation of literature and written records to history, etc.; literary or classical scholarship; polite learning. Now *rare* in *general* sense except in the U.S.

[*c* **1386** Chaucer *Merch. T.* 490 Hoold thou thy pees thou poete Marcian That writest vs that ilke weddyng murie Of hire Philologie and hym Mercurie. (Martianus Capella, 5th cent. wrote 'De nuptiis Philologiæ et Mercurii'.)]

1614 Selden *Titles Hon.* Ded. A ij, This of Mine dealing with *Verum* chiefly, in matter of Storie and Philologie. **1637** Heylin *Antid. Lincoln.* II. 108 Your Grammer learning being showne, we must next take a turne in your Divine and Theologicall Philology. *a* **1661** Fuller *Worthies* I. (1662) 26 Philology properly is Terse and Polite Learning, *melior literatura*... But we take it in the larger notion, as inclusive of all human liberal Studies. **1669** Gale *Crt. Gentiles* I. I. x. 50 Philologie, according to its original, and primitive import ..implies an universal love, or respect to human Literature. **1776** G. Campbell *Philos. Rhet.* I. I. v. 125 All the branches of philology, such as history, civil, ecclesiastic, and literary: grammar, languages, jurisprudence, and criticism. **1818** Hallam *Mid. Ages* IX. ii, Philology, or the principles of good taste, degenerated through the prevalence of school-logic. **1892** *Athenæum* 25 June 816/1 The fact that philology is not a mere matter of grammar, but is in the largest sense a master-science, whose duty is to present to us the whole of ancient life, and to give archæology its just place by the side of literature. **1922** O. Jespersen *Language* iii. 64 In this book I shall use the word 'philology' in its continental sense, which is often rendered in English by the vague word 'scholarship', meaning thereby the study of the specific culture of one nation. **1925** L. Bloomfield in *Language* I. 4 That noblest of sciences, philology, the study of national culture is..greater than a misfit combination of language plus literature... The British use of 'philology' for linguistics leaves no name for the former subject. **1931** J. W. Spargo tr. *Pedersen's Linguistic Sci. 19th Cent.* iv. 79 One may define philology briefly as a study whose task is the interpretation of the literary monuments in which the spiritual life of a given period has found expression. *Ibid.* 80 The use of 'philology' as a mere synonym for 'linguistics' is to be avoided. **1939** L. H. Gray *Foundations of Lang.* 3 A more serious objection to the term [*sc.* comparative philology] lies in the fact that 'philology', strictly speaking, denotes not only the study of language, but also of literature and of all the civilisational phenomena of a people. *a* **1941** B. L. Whorf in *Ann. Rep. Board of Regents Smithsonian Inst. 1941* (1942) 502 As the major linguistic difficulties are conquered, the study becomes more and more philological; that is to say, subject matter, cultural data, and history play an increasing role... This is philology. But at the base of philology we must have linguistics. **1947** E. H. Sturtevant *Introd. Linguistic Sci.* i. 7 Philology is a word with a wide range of meaning. I use it here to designate the study of written documents. **1954** F. G. Cassidy *Robertson's Devel. Mod. Eng.* (ed. 2) 424 *Philology*, the study of thought and culture as embodied in literary monuments; in a narrower sense, the study of language (but for this sense, the term linguistics is now preferred). **1964** R. H. Robins *Gen. Linguistics* i. 6 In German,..*Philologie* refers more to the scholarly study of literary texts, and more generally to the study of culture and civilization through literary documents... This meaning..is matched by..the use of *philology* in American learned circles. **1980** *Yale Rev.* Winter 312 Philology meant, and still ought to mean, the general study of literature.

†**2.** Rendering Gr. φιλολογία love of talk, speech, or argument (as opposed to φιλοσοφία love of wisdom, philosophy). *Obs.*

1623 Cockeram, *Phylologie*, loue of much babling. **1654** Whitlock *Zootomia* 195 Whereas hee [Seneca] complaineth Philosophy was turned into Philology; may not we too sadly complain, most of our Christianity is become Discoursive noise? **1678** R. L'Estrange *Seneca's Mor.* (1702) 387 By which Means Philosophy is now turn'd to Philology.

3. *spec.* (in mod. use) The study of the structure and development of language; the science of language; linguistics. Now usu. restricted to the study of the development of specific languages or language families, esp. research into phonological and morphological history based on written documents. (Really one branch of sense 1.)

This sense has never been current in the U.S. *Linguistics* is now the more usual term for the study of the structure of language, and, with qualifying adjective or adjective phrase, is replacing *philology* even in the restricted sense.

comparative philology: see COMPARATIVE 1 b.

1716 M. Davies *Athen. Brit.* III. 102 Harduin has there several erudite Remarks upon Philology: especially upon the Pronunciation and Dialects of the Greek Tongue. **1748** Hartley *Observ. Man* I. iii. 353 Philology, or the Knowledge of Words, and their Significations. **1838** Winning (*title*) Manual of Comparative Philology. **1843** H. H. Wilson in *Proc. Philol. Soc.* I. 22 The publication of the grammar of the late Sir Charles Wilkins constitutes an important era in the annals of Sanskrit philology. **1852** Blackie *Stud. Lang.* 7 Philology unfolds the genesis of those laws of speech, which Grammar contemplates as a finished result. **1964** R. H. Robins *Gen. Linguistics* i. 6 In British usage philology is generally equivalent to comparative philology, an older and still quite common term for what linguists technically refer to as comparative and historical linguistics. **1968** J. Lyons *Introd. Theoret. Linguistics* i. 22 The term 'comparative philology', which I shall use to refer to this period of linguistics [*sc.* the nineteenth century].., though less commonly used these days by linguists themselves (who tend to prefer 'comparative and historical linguistics'), is not infrequently met in general books on language and, like many other unsuitable terms, has been perpetuated in the titles of university chairs and departments and of prescribed courses of study. **1974** R. Quirk *Linguist & Eng. Lang.* v. 84 'Developmental' and 'general' philology—or, as we would usually call them today, historical and general linguistics.

philomath ('fɪləmæθ). [ad. Gr. φιλομαθής fond of learning, f. φιλο- PHILO- + μαθ-, root of μανθάνειν to learn: cf. MATHEMATIC.] A lover of learning; a student, esp. of mathematics, natural philosophy, and the like; formerly popularly applied to an astrologer or prognosticator.

a **1643** W. Cartwright *Loves Convert* IV. ii, I hate a scholar:..I'm only a Philomath, sweet Lady. **1695** Congreve *Love for L.* II. v, An Entertainment for all the Philomaths, and Students in Physick and Astrology, in and about London. **1751** Chesterf. *Lett.* (1774) III. ccxii. 132 Ask my friend, L'Abbé Sallier, to recommend to you some meagre philo-math to teach you a little geometry and astronomy. **1755** *Connoisseur* No. 99 ¶1 Complete Ephemerides &c. drawn up by Partridge..and the rest of the sagacious body of Philomaths and Astrologers. **1873** Doran *Lady of last Cent.* vii. 192 The aged philomath might have been the original of the legendary mathematician. **1927** A. Huxley *Proper Stud.* 132 It is precisely for the philomaths that universities ought to cater. **1955** *Sci. Amer.* May 114/3 John Whiblin, the carpenter and 'philomath' who was 'ingenious at models'. **1977** R. V. Hudson in Bond & McLeod *Newslett. to Newspaper* II. 120 The philomath responsible for it..was selected to receive the shafts of Franklin's wit.

So **philo'mathic** [= F. *philomathique*], **philo'mathical** *adjs.*, devoted to learning; of, pertaining to, or consisting of 'philomaths' (in quot. 1828, 'mathematical'); also, astrological; **philomathy** (fɪ'lɒməθɪ) [Gr. φιλομάθεια, -μαθία], love of or devotion to learning. (All now *rare.*)

1797 *Monthly Mag.* III. 462 Girod Chantrans read lately to the *Philomathic Society of Paris, an observation which he had made on the *conferva bullosa.* **1839** Lady Lytton *Cheveley* (ed. 2) I. x. 221 His work..was meant to be statistical, philological,..philomathic, and political. **1709** Steele *Tatler* No. 11 ¶5 Partridge..is dead and gone, who ..*Philomathical as he was, could not read his own Destiny. **1828** T. C. Croker *Fairy Leg. S. Ireland* II. 86 Too much whiskey..might occasionally prevent his walking the chalked line with perfect philomathical accuracy. **1623** Cockeram, **Phylomathie*, the loue of learning. **1901** *Daily Chron.* 17 Sept. 5/6 With a pure view to philomathy, I should much like some veracious 'average' husband to inform your readers what he does..to alleviate the insufferable monotony..of the 'average' domesticated wife.

Philomel ('fɪləʊmɛl), **Philomela** (fɪləʊ'miːlə). *poet.* Forms: 5–6 **phylomene**, 6 **Philumene**; 6 **Philomele**, 7– **Philomel**; 6– **Philomela**. [a. F. *philomèle*, ad. L. *philomēla*, a. Gr. φιλομήλα the nightingale, supposed to be f. φιλο- PHILO- + μέλος song, with vowel lengthened; but cf. φιλόμηλος fond of apples. The early form in *-mene* appears to have been due to some error.] A poetic name for the nightingale. (In later use always as proper name, with capital P, usually with reference to the ancient myth of Philomela metamorphosed into a nightingale. Hence properly feminine, and involving the error of attributing song to the hen bird.)

[*c* **1385** Chaucer *L.G.W.* 2274 That Philomene he wyfes suster myghte On Proigne hys wyfe but ones haue a syght. **1390** Gower *Conf.* II. 326 The ferst into a nyhtingale Was schape, and that was Philomene.] **1423** Jas. I *Kingis Q.* cx, Vnlike the cukkow to the phylomene. **1576** Gascoigne *Philomene* 129 To vnderstande the notes of Phylomene (For so she hight, whom thou calst Nightingale). **1579** Spenser *Sheph. Cal.* Nov. 141 And Philomele her song with teares doth steepe. **1591** —— *Daphn.* 475 But I will wake and sorrow all the night With Philumene, my fortune to deplore. **1599** *Pass. Pilgr.* xv, While Philomela sits and sings. **1634** Milton *Il Pens.* 56. *a* **1639** Wotton *Descr. Spring* 12 The Groves already did rejoyce In Philomels triumphing voyce. *c* **1790** Cowper *Catharina* vi, By Philomel's annual note To measure the life that she leads. **1798** Coleridge *Nightingale* 39 O'er Philomela's pity-pleading strains.

Hence †**philo'melian** *a. poet. Obs.*, pertaining to the nightingale.

1621 Quarles *Argalus & P.* (1708) 101 The winged choristers of night..sweetly warbling out Their philomelian air.

philomot, obs. erroneous form of FILEMOT.

philomuse, philomystic, etc.: see PHILO-.

Philonian (faɪ'ləʊnɪən), *a.* [ad. L. *Philōniānus*, f. *Philo, -ōn-em*, ad. Gr. Φίλων, a man's name: see -AN.] Of or pertaining to the Jewish philosopher Philo, who flourished at Alexandria about the beginning of the Christian era. So **Philonic** (faɪ'lɒnɪk) *a.*, in same sense; **Philonism** ('faɪləʊnɪz(ə)m), the system of Philo; **'Philonist**, a follower of Philo; **'Philonize** *v. intr.*, to imitate Philo.

1874 *Supernat. Relig.* II. III. i. 288 The *Philonian Epistle to the Hebrews. **1892** E. P. Barrow *Regni Evang.* 51 Hebraic, Philonian or Gnostic teaching. **1854** Emerson *Lett. & Soc. Aims, Quot. & Orig.* Wks. (Bohn) III. 214 Reverence..claimed for it [the Bible] by the prestige of *philonic inspiration. **1900** R. T. Drummond *Apost. Teaching* vi. 224 The Philonic resolution of Old Testament personages, events and rites into philosophic abstractions. **1883** *Athenæum* 23 June 793/3 The Egyptian city where Platonism and *Philonism had imbued Christianity with a peculiar character. **1833** J. H. Newman *Arians* I. iv. (1876) 101 The discriminative view of heathen philosophy which the *Philonists had opened. **1610** Healey *St. Aug. Citie of God* XVII. xx. *Vives' note*, It was a proverbe, Philo either Platonized or Plato *Philonized. **1812** J. Adams *Wks.* (1856) X. 18 The opinions..appear to me to resemble the platonizing Philon, or the philonizing Plato, more than the genuine system of Judaism. **1882-3** *Schaff's Encycl. Relig. Knowl.* III. 1832 Either Philo platonizes, or Plato philonizes, says Suidas.

†**phi'lopater.** *Obs. rare.* [ad. Gr. φιλοπάτωρ loving one's father, or φιλόπατρις loving one's fatherland.] A lover of one's father, or (*transf.*) of one's country.

1641 R. Harris *Abner's Funerall* 21 Wise, Learned, Pious, Philosopher, Philopater, and the like. **1643** Prynne *Sov. Power Parl.* Ded. A ij, Eternally Renowned Senators, and most cordiall Philo-paters to Your bleeding, dying dearest

Country. *Ibid.* I. Pref. (ed. 2) A ij b, The cordiallest Endevours, of a reall unmercenary Philo-pater.

philoplutary to **-pornist**: see PHILO-.

philoproge'neity. *rare*⁻¹. [irreg. f. PHILO- + L. *progeniēs* PROGENY, with ending of *homogeneity*.] Love of progeny or offspring: cf. next.

1888 *Science* 14 Sept. 124/1 Sexual differentiation, including philoprogeneity, hybridity, etc.

philoprogenitive (ˌfɪləʊprəʊˈdʒɛnɪtɪv), *a.* [irreg. f. PHILO- + L. *progenit-*, ppl. stem of *progignĕre* to beget + -IVE.]

1. Inclined to production of offspring; prolific.

1865 tr. *Strauss' New Life Jesus* II. II. lvii. 41 To assimilate him to the philoprogenitive Gods of the heathen. **1884** *Public Opinion* 11 July 33/1 Its ['native' oyster's] place will be taken by the less philoprogenitive but not less delicate bivalve of Baltimore or of Portugal.

2. *Phrenol.* Loving one's offspring; of or pertaining to love of offspring.

1876 H. SPENCER *Princ. Sociol.* III. xi. (1879) 767 Among brutes the philoprogenitive instinct is occasionally suppressed by the desire to kill, and even to devour, their young ones. **1894** D. C. MURRAY *Making of Novelist* 183 The pellet..hit him..on the philoprogenitive bump, and he swore audibly.

ˌphilopro'genitiveness. *Phrenol.* [f. as prec. + -NESS: see quot. 1815.] Love of offspring; the instinct or faculty of love for one's children, or for children (and animals) in general. Its organ is located by phrenologists just above the middle of the cerebellum.

1815 J. G. SPURZHEIM *Physiogn. Syst.* Pref. 10, I am aware that the name..ought to indicate love of producing offspring. As however progeny means offspring; philoprogeny, love of offspring, and Philoprogenitiveness, the faculty of producing love of offspring, I have adopted that term. **1826** *Edin. Rev.* XLIV. 269 Why therefore should we not have a separate principle of Philoprogenitiveness? **1856** OLMSTED *Slave States* 425 The nurse was a kind-looking old negro woman, with, no doubt, philoprogenitiveness well developed.

philorchidaceous, -ornithic, etc.: see PHILO-.

philosoph, -ophe (ˈfɪləʊsɒf, -ˈzɒf). *Obs.* or only as Fr. Forms: 1 philosoph; 4 filosofe, -zofe, -sophe; 8–9 philosoph(e. [In OE. ad. L. *philosoph-us*, a. Gr. φιλόσοφ-ος lover of wisdom, philosopher, f. φίλος loving + σοφός wise, a sage; in ME. a. OF. *filosofe, philosophe* ad. L.] = PHILOSOPHER 1; now often = PHILOSOPHIST 2. Also *attrib.* or as *adj.* and *transf.*

c **893** K. ÆLFRED *Oros.* III. vii. §2 þæm stro[n]gan cyninge & þæm ȝelæredestan philosophe. **1340** *Ayenb.* 77 Alle the wyse clerkes, and þe greate filosofes. *Ibid.* 126 Filozofes. *Ibid.* 164. **1721** RAMSAY *Content* 404 Two Busbian philosophs put in their claims. [**1774** H. WALPOLE *Let.* 28 Sept. (1904) IX. 59 Madame du Deffand hates *les philosophes.*] **1779** —— *Let.* 7 July (1904) X. 441 The *philosophes*, except Buffon, are solemn, arrogant, dictatorial coxcombs. **1827** PRAED *Poems* (1865) II. 214, I danced with a female philosophe, Who was not quite a bore. **1830** J. P. COBBETT *Jrnl. Tour in Italy* 286 Guard us ye powers.. against all that calls itself '*liberal*' or '*philosophe*'! **1840** J. S. MILL in *London & Westm. Rev.* Mar. 270 Those writers were as much cried down among the *philosophes* themselves. **1868** W. WHITMAN *Poems* 87 See..superior judges, philosophs, Presidents, emerge, dressed in working dresses. **1932** *Scrutiny* I. 122 Two things appeared to Bentham's *philosophe* mind to be necessary. **1961** *Times* 25 Mar. 3/7 He [*sc.* Raymond Williams] is not a politician so much as a prophet really, a sort of English *philosophe*. **1969** *Listener* 9 Jan. 37/2 All the *philosophes*, all the Encyclopedists, shared the Baconian belief that science could save mankind. **1977** *N.Y. Rev. Bks.* 13 Oct. 8/3 Despite his genuine and profound erudition, Gibbon was a *philosophe* far more than a philosopher, though he hankered after being a philosopher of history.

Hence **philo'sophedom**, the domain or realm of philosophs.

1833 CARLYLE *Misc., Diderot* (1857) III. 216 They entertain their special ambassador in Philosophedom, their lion's-provider to furnish spiritual Philosophe-provender.

† **phi'losophable,** *a. Obs. rare.* [a. OF. *philosophable*, ad. med.L. type **philosophābilis*, f. *philosophārī*: see PHILOSOPHATE.] Able to philosophize.

c **1400** tr. *Secreta Secret., Gov. Lordsh.* 96 þanne comes to him a strengh shewable, or Philosophable [*in Fr. transl.* force demostrable ou philosophable], þat byholdys shappys vndirstandable.

philosophaster (fɪlɒsəʊˈfæstə(r)). [a. L. *philosophaster*, in It. *filo-, philosofastro*, f. L. *philosoph-us*: see -ASTER.] A shallow or pseudo-philosopher; a smatterer or pretender in philosophy.

1611 FLORIO, *Philosofastro*, a smatterer in Philosophy, a foolish, pedanticall Philosophaster. **1650** H. MORE *Observ.* in *Enthus. Tri.*, etc. (1656) 72 Superficiall Philosophasters. **1737** BRACKEN *Farriery Impr.* (1757) II. 95 A Philosophaster, or Quack-Doctor. **1894** HUXLEY *Evolution & Ethics* 26 The philosophy of philosophasters and..the moralizing of sentimentalists.

Hence **philoso'phastering** *ppl. a.*, acting the philosopher, philosophizing pretentiously; **philoso'phastry**, shallow or pseudo-philosophy.

1897 *Q. Rev.* Oct. 355 His philosophastering or martial strains are at best neutral. **1904** SAINTSBURY in *Daily Chron.* 22 Sept. 3/3 You cannot bridge the gulf that a God has set by any philosophastering theory. **1850** *Fraser's Mag.* XLI. 104 A little of the old leaven, pedantry and philosophastry. **1899** M. M. SNELL in *Dublin Rev.* July 41 Victories over the philosophast[r]y of the Encyclopædia.

† **phi'losophate,** *v. Obs.* Also 7 -phat. [f. L. *philosophāt-*, ppl. stem of *philosophārī* to do the philosopher, philosophize, f. *philosoph-us*: see PHILOSOPH. Perh. immed. f. F. *philosopher* in Montaigne: see -ATE³ 6.]

1. *intr.* To reason as a philosopher; to philosophize.

1603 FLORIO *Montaigne* II. iii. (1632) 193 If as some say, to philosophate be to doubt. **1649** H. LAWRENCE *Some Considerations* 15 These..perhaps could Philosophate as mysteriously as their neighbours. **1765** STERNE *Tr. Shandy* VII. xxxviii, So I sat me down upon a bench by the door, philosophating upon my condition.

2. *trans.* To philosophize upon (a thing).

1649 H. LAWRENCE *Some Considerations* 34 These Sectaries..even so Philosophating the Gospel, as they made it [etc.].

Hence † **phi'losophating** *vbl. sb.* and *ppl. a.* Also † **philoso'phation**, philosophizing.

1644 G. PLATTES in *Hartlib's Legacy* (1655) 204 There need no other or further philosophation concerning the same. **1649** H. LAWRENCE *Some Considerations* 3 A carnall and vaine Philosophating about spirituall things. **1681** GLANVILL *Sadducismus* I. (1726) 78 Our Philosophations touching an Incorporeal Being. **1802** in *Spirit Pub. Jrnls.* VI. 244 Jobbing may be associated with [the ideas] of fame and honour in our philosophating age!

philosopheme (fɪˈlɒsəfiːm). [ad. late L. *philosophēma* (Boethius), a. Gr. φιλοσόφημα a demonstrative syllogism, philosophical doctrine or principle, f. φιλοσοφεῖν to love or pursue knowledge, philosophize, f. φιλόσοφ-ος: see PHILOSOPH.] A philosophic conclusion or demonstration; a philosophical statement, theorem, or axiom.

1678 GALE *Crt. Gentiles* III. 51 An evasion, which not only Reason and Scripture but even Pagan Philosophemes contradict. **1741** WATTS *Improv. Mind* I. ix. §2 Perhaps you may derive some useful philosophemes or theorems, for your own entertainment. **1804** W TAYLOR in *Crit. Rev.* Ser. III. III. 540 Only sagas and philosophemas, which..contain no pure history. **1818** J. BROWN *Psyche* 115 Without our running to extremes, Or deeming flights philosophemes. **1862** F. HALL *Hindu Philos. Syst.* (1897) 152 This passage bears upon more than one Hindu philosopheme.

philosopher (fɪˈlɒsəfə(r)). Forms: α. 4 philosofre, -zofre, filosofre, -sophre, (philisophre), 4–5 philosophre, (5 phili-, philesofre, 6 phylosophre). β. 4 filosopher, philosipher, phylozopher, 4– philosopher, (4 fylesofer, 5 philosoffer, -sofer, -sofyr, -sophir, -sophyr, -saphir, phylosofer, -sophyr; phili-, fili-, fylysofer; philsophir, fylzofyr, 5–6 philosophier, 5–7 phylosopher, 6 -phar, philosephur). γ. 4 phylosy-, philysophere, 5 philosophere, philesofere, fillosophere, filis(o)phere. δ. 5 filo-, 5–6 phylosophour. [In 14th c. *philosophre, filo-, -sofre*, an Anglo-Fr. or OF. var. of *philosophe* PHILOSOPH (cf. *legiste, legistre*, etc.), the ending being subseq. identified in Eng. with that of agent-nouns in -ER; sometimes with those in *-our*, -OR. The original stress was *philo'sofre*, which prevailed to the close of the ME. period, in which however there are also instances of the later stressing; *philoso'phour* is certain in Dunbar *c* 1500, and *phi'losopher* appears to have prevailed from the 16th c.]

1. a. A lover of wisdom; one who devotes himself to the search of fundamental truth; one versed in philosophy or engaged in its study; formerly in a wide sense, including men learned in physical science (physicists, scientists, naturalists), as well as those versed in the metaphysical and moral sciences, but now chiefly confined to the latter. Also with defining word, as ***moral philosopher, political philosopher***; ***natural philosopher*** (= physicist).

c **1325** *Chron. Eng.* 5 This philosofres us doth towyte, Ase we findeth ywryte. **1340** HAMPOLE *Pr. Consc.* 1901 Bot þe payn of dede þat al sal fele A philosopher þus discrived wele. *Ibid.* 7567 Als a gret philisiphir þat hyght Rabby Moyses telles ryght. **1340–70** *Alex. & Dind.* 1070 In fablus of philozofrus olde. *c* **1375** *Sc. Leg. Saints* v. (*Johannes*) 89 A phylosyphere of gret renowne þat cratone hecht. **1382** WYCLIF *Acts* xvii. 18 Forsothe summe Epicureis, and Stoycis, and philosofris [**1388** filosofris] disputiden..with him. **1393** LANGL. *P. Pl.* C. XXIII. 38 Filosofres for-soken welthe, for þei wolde be neody. *c* **1400** *Destr. Troy* 1484 Of his sonnes..the fourth was a philosoffer, a fyne man of lore. *c* **1420** LYDG. *Assembly of Gods* 272 And that I recorde of all philosophres That lytyll store of coyne kepe in her cofres. *a* **1440** *Sir Degrev.* 1450 There was purtred in ston The fylesoferus everychon. *c* **1440** *Gesta Rom.* xl. 159 (Harl. MS.) Amonge the wiche was master Virgile, þe philesofere. *c* **1449** PECOCK *Repr.* I. iii. 14 Hethen philsophiris bi her studie in natural witt founden..alle hem to be doon. **14..** *Nom.* in Wr.-Wülcker 680/32 *Hic philosofus*, a fylysofer. **1477** EARL RIVERS (Caxton) *Dictes* 2 The saynges or dictis of the Philosophers. **1483** *Cath. Angl.* 130/2 A Filosophur, *philosophus.* **1500–20** DUNBAR *Poems* lxiii. 5 Divinouris, rethoris, and philosophouris, Astrologis, artistis, and oratouris. **1538** STARKEY *England* I. i. 4 The old and antique phylosopharys..applyd themselfys to the secrete studys and serchyng of nature. **1540–1** ELYOT *Image Gov.* (1549) 136 Numa Pompilius.., beyng an excellent philosophier,..was chosen to be kyng. **1596** SHAKS. *Merch. V.* I. ii. 53, I feare hee will proue the weeping Phylosopher [Heraclitus] when he growes old. **1664** POWER *Exp. Philos.* Pref. 18 Without some such Mechanical Assistance, our best Philosophers will but prove empty Conjecturalists. **1728** PEMBERTON *Newton's Philos.* 2, I drew up the following papers, to give a general notion of our great philosopher's [Newton's] notions. **1734** POPE *Ess. Man* IV. 390 Thou wert my Guide, Philosopher, and Friend. **1776** ADAM SMITH *W.N.* I. i. (1869) I. 11 Philosophers or men of speculation, whose trade is not to do anything, but to observe everything. **1809** COLERIDGE *Friend* (1866) 290 Pythagoras..is said to have first named himself philosopher or lover of wisdom. **1827** WHATELY *Logic* IV. iii. §2 The Philosopher's [business is] to combine and select known facts or principles, suitably for gaining from them conclusions which though implied in the Premises, were before unperceived. **1872** GEO. ELIOT *Middlem.* lxvii, A philosopher fallen to betting is hardly distinguishable from a Philistine under the same circumstances.

† **b.** *the Philosopher*, spec. applied to Aristotle.

[**1340** *Ayenb.* 120 Huerof þe filosofe zayþ þet yefþe is yeuynge wyþoute ayen-yefþe.] *c* **1385** CHAUCER *L.G.W.* Prol. 381 This is the sentens of the philysophre, A kyng to kepe hise lygis in iustise. *c* **1449** PECOCK *Repr.* III. v, For the philsophir feelid bettir than so, seiyng that richessis ben instrumentis of vertu. **1672** WILKINS *Nat. Relig.* 41 It is laid down by the philosopher as the proper way of reasoning from authority, that what seems true to some wise men, may upon that account be esteemed somewhat probable. [*a* **1850** ROSSETTI *Dante & Circ.* I. (1874) 108 This the Philosopher says in the Second of the Metaphysics.]

c. A member of a class called 'Philosophers' in certain Jesuit schools and colleges.

1711 in E. H. Burton *Life Bishop Challoner* (1909) I. iii. 32 Ye Superiors had inculcated..ye two pair of beads to be said every week by one of ye Philosophers. **1712** in *Ushaw Mag.* (1904) Mar. 20 Ye Littanies of ye Saints, every night our Ladyes wch are solemnly sung every Saturday, ye two pair of beads to be said every week by one of ye Philosophers, ye fasting before our Ladyes dayes and ye like. **1809** in *Edmundian* (1948) Summer 9 The boys in the higher classes viz. Philosophers and Rhetoricians have separate rooms. **1915** *Ushaw Mag.* Dec. 292 The new furniture..is to be arranged and then the Divines and Philosophers can take possession.

† **2.** An adept in occult science, as an alchemist, magician, diviner of dreams, weather-prophet, etc.

In ME. often not separable from sense 1, the notions being popularly identified.

1377 LANGL. *P. Pl.* B. xv. 351 With clerkes also Han no believe to þe lifte, ne to þe lore of philosofres. *c* **1386** CHAUCER *Prol.* 299 But al be that he was a Philosophre, Yet hadde he but litel gold in cofre. —— *Frankl. T.* 833 Allas that I bihighte Of pured gold a thousand pound of wighte Vn to this Philosophre [*v.r.* -ofre]. **1470–85** MALORY *Arthur* V. iv. 165 The kynge..was sore abasshed of this dreme And sente anone for a wyse philosopher commaundynge to telle hym the sygnyfycacion of his dreme. [**1869** LECKY *Europ. Mor.* I. ii. 327 Many great families [in Rome] kept a philosopher.]

3. One who regulates his life by the light of philosophy and reason; one who speaks or behaves philosophically.

1599 SHAKS. *Much Ado* v. i. 35 For there was neuer yet Philosopher That could endure the tooth-ake patiently. **1700** FARQUHAR *Constant Couple* II. iii, I'll beat him with the temper of a philosopher. **1855** TENNYSON *Maud* I. IV. ix, Be mine a philosopher's life in the quiet woodland ways. **1871** E. F. BURR *Ad Fidem* ix. 165 Most men are not philosophers. *Mod.* He was too great a philosopher to be disturbed by this incident, unexpected though it was.

† **4.** Phrases. ***egg*** (or ***eye***) ***of philosophers*** = PHILOSOPHERS' STONE: see also *philosophers' egg* in 5 b. ***oil of philosophers*** = ***brick oil*** (BRICK *sb.*¹ 3).

c **1400** tr. *Secreta Secret., Gov. Lordsh.* 87 Of þe stoon, þe Eye of Philosophers. *Ibid.* 88 þe Eyrn, þat ys to say þe Eye of Philosophers. **1547** BOORDE *Brev. Health* 20 To anoynt the stomake with the oyle of Philosophers, named in latin *Oleum philosophorum.* **1651** FRENCH *Distill.* iii. 81 Oil made out of Tile-stones called the Oile of Philosophers. **1706** PHILLIPS, *Oil of Philosophers*, a Chymical Preparation of pieces of Brick heated red hot, soak'd in Oil of Olives, and afterwards distill'd in a Retort.

5. *attrib.* and *Comb.*, chiefly appositive, as ***philosopher-courtier, -king, -poet, -politician, -scientist***; also ***philosopher-like*** adj. and adv.

1471 RIPLEY *Comp. Alch.* III. vi. in Ashm. *Theat. Chem. Brit.* (1652) 140 Than Phylosopher-lyke usyd ys hyt. **1579–80** NORTH *Plutarch* (1676) 44 To speake Laconian-like, was to be Philosopher-like. **1664** H. MORE *Myst. Iniq.*, *Apol.* IV. vi. 508 The Gentleman Atheist or Philosopher Infidel. **1885** PATER *Marius* III. xv, Under the full sanction of the philosopher-pontiff. **1923** A. HUXLEY *Let.* 12 Nov. (1969) 222 One determined Poincaré can defeat..ten philosopher-kings. *a* **1937** J. L. STOCKS *Reason & Intuition* (1939) v. 68 The philosopher-scientist of the nineteenth century had certainly no place for chance. **1945** R. G. COLLINGWOOD *Idea of Nature* II. iii. 128 A philosopher-scientist like Whitehead can restate Hegel's theory (not knowing that it is Hegel's, for he does not appear to have read Hegel). **1962** *Listener* 25 Jan. 163/1 It is doubtful whether Socrates and the philosopher-kings of the Republic could have lived peaceably together. **1979** *Guardian* 3 Sept. 10/1 The TUC's last philosopher-king, George Woodcock.

b. Combinations with *philosophers'*, *-'s*: † **philosophers' egg**, a medicine used to cure the plague, compounded of yolk of egg and saffron; † **philosophers' game** (L. *ludus philosophorum*, *Arithmomachia*, *Rythmomachia*), an intricate game, played with men of three different forms, round, triangular, and square, each marked with a number, on a board resembling two chess-boards united; called also **philosophers' table**; **philosopher's philosopher** [after *poet's poet* s.v. POET 1 c], a philosopher whose works appeal, or are intelligible, primarily to another philosopher; † **philosophers' tower**, a chemical furnace in the form of a tower; † **philosophers' tree** = *Tree of Diana*: see DIANA 2, ARBOR 2; **philosophers' vinegar** (L. *acetum philosophorum*), the supposed universal solvent; † **philosophers' wheel** (*wheel of philosophy*, *of elements*, etc.): see WHEEL; † **philosophers' wool**: see WOOL *sb.* 2 b; † **philosophers' work** = PHILOSOPHERS' STONE.

c **1500** *MS. Sloane* 1592, lf. 151 b [154 b], A proved medicine againste the pestilence called A *philosophres Egge. Take Firste an egge and breake a hole in one ende.. and do out the white.. take hole safron and fille the shelle therewith by the yolcke [etc.]. [Cf. **1653** C'TESS OF KENT *Choice Manual* (ed. 2) 139.] [*c* **1407** LYDGATE *Reson & Sens.* 2414 The play he kan of Ryghtmathye (*margin* Rihtmachia est ludus philosophorum et consistit in arsmetrica et proporcionibus numerorum).] **1563** FULKE (*title*) The Most Ancient and learned Playe called the *Philosophers Game invented for the honest recreation of Students. **1621** BURTON *Anat. Mel.* II. ii. IV. (1676) 172/2 The ordinary recreations which we have in Winter.. are Cards, Tables and Dice, Shovel-boord, Chess-play, the Philosophers game. **1787** TWISS *Chess* 65 The board of this Philosopher's game, is eight squares in breadth, and sixteen in height. There are twenty-four men on a side, represented as flat pieces of wood, cut in the form of circles, triangles, and squares. The king is a square on which is a triangle and a circle. **1937** A. H. MURRAY *Philos. of James Ward* ii. 45 Bradley may have been a *philosopher's philosopher, but much of what he describes and analyses in the tendency to unity inherent in thought is part of the direct experience of thinkers—and of other people. **1957** J. PASSMORE *100 Yrs. Philos.* iv. 81 McTaggart was a philosopher's philosopher, if ever there has been one. **1971** *Classical Rev.* XXI. 224 Aristotle, a philosopher's philosopher. **1974** A. W. LEVI *Philos. as Social Expression* v. 298 That *déformation professionnelle*.. has produced the doctor's doctor, the lawyer's lawyer, and the philosopher's philosopher. **1584** R. SCOT *Discov. Witchcr.* XI. x. (1886) 159 A childish and ridiculous toie, and like unto childrens plaie at *Primus secundus*, or the game called The *philosophers table. **1688** R. HOLME *Armoury* III. xx. (Roxb.) 228 The *Philosophers Tower,.. a kind of Tower furnace, wherewith a man may distill both water and oyle with one only fire. **1704** J. HARRIS *Lex. Techn.* I, **Philosophers Tree*, see *Diana's Tree.* **1727–41** CHAMBERS *Cycl.*, *Philosophers Tree*, a chymical preparation, called also *arbor dianæ*, *diana's tree.* **1610** B. JONSON *Alch.* II. iii, *Svb.*.. Ha' you set the oile of Luna in kemia? *Fac.* Yes, sir. *Svb.* And the *philosophers vinegar? *Fac.* I. *Ibid.* I. i, Paines Would twise haue won me the *philosophers worke.

Hence (*nonce-wds.*) **phi'losophercraft** (-krɑːft, -æ-), after *priestcraft*; **phi'losopherling**, a young or embryo philosopher, a smatterer in philosophy.

1865 DE MORGAN *Budget of Paradoxes* (1872) 378 There is philosophercraft as well as priestcraft, both from one source, both of one spirit. **1833** LYTTON *Eng. & Engl.* IV. x, He is Snap, the academical philosopherling. *Ibid.*, Nine times out of ten our philosopherling is the son of a merchant.

philosopheress (fɪˈlɒsəfərɪs), **-phress** (-frɪs). [f. prec. + -ESS[1].] A female philosopher; also, the wife of a philosopher; = PHILOSOPHESS.

1631 CHAPMAN *Cæsar & Pompey* V. i, She's a Philosophresse, Augure, and can turne Ill to good as well as you. **1797** D. SIMPSON *Plea Relig.* (1808) 27 The philosopher dies, and leaves the philosopheress his wife to the protection of a friend. **1851** ROBERTSON in *Life & Lett.* (1882) II. 31 Thou meditatest, mighty philosopheress! on nitrogen and carbon.

philosophership (fɪˈlɒsəfəʃɪp). [f. as prec. + -SHIP.] The office or function of a philosopher; also, the personality of a philosopher.

1549 CHALONER *Erasm. on Folly* D iv b, His too muche philosophership made hym odious and hatefull to the people. **1874** HUXLEY in *Daily News* 3 Aug. 2 He held the duties of his manhood and the duties of his citizenship to be vastly superior to those of his philosophership.

philosophers' stone. [tr. med.L. *lapis philosophorum*, the stone of the philosophers (see PHILOSOPHER 2), also *lapis philosophicus*, *-icalis*; in F. *pierre philosophale*, Ger. *der Stein der Weisen*. See Note below.]

1. A reputed solid substance or preparation supposed by the alchemists to possess the property of changing other metals into gold or silver, the discovery of which was the supreme object of alchemy. Being identified with the ELIXIR, it had also, according to some, the power of prolonging life indefinitely, and of curing all wounds and diseases.

c **1386** CHAUCER *Can. Yeom. Prol. & T.* 309 The Philosophres stoon, Elixer clept, we sechen faste echoon. **1590** NASHE *Pasquil's Apol.* Wks. (Grosart) I. 219 The Philosophers stone to turne mettles into gold is yet to seeke. **1611** BIBLE *Transl. Pref.* 3 Men talke.. of the Philosophers stone, that it turneth copper into gold. **1670** PETTUS *Fodinæ Reg.* 44 Henry VI.. did then grant 4 successive Patents and Commissions to several Knights.. and Mass-priests.. to find out the Philosophers stone. **1706** PHILLIPS, *Transmutation of Metals*, among Alchymists, is what they call the Grand Operation or Secret of finding the Philosophers-Stone, which they give out to be so curious an Universal Seed of all Metals, That if any Metal be melted in a Crucible, and then a little of this Stone or *Powder of Projection*, be put into the melted Metal, 'twill immediately change it into Gold or Silver. **1768–74** TUCKER *Lt. Nat.* (1834) II. 79 How many profitable discoveries in chymistry have taken birth from that whimsical notion of finding the philosopher's stone? **1864** BURTON *Scot Abr.* I. iii. 145 He was in search of the philosopher's stone.

b. *transf.* and *fig.*

1610 B. JONSON *Alch.* I. i, I will haue A booke, but barely reckoning thy impostures Shall proue a true philosophers stone, to printers. **1643** SIR T. BROWNE *Relig. Med.* I. §46, I am half of opinion that Antichrist is the Philosopher's Stone in Divinity. **1856** R. A. VAUGHAN *Mystics* (1860) II. 94 [Behmen] declared that the true Philosopher's Stone.. was 'the new life in Christ Jesus'.

2. An artificial gem so called.

1879 *Cassell's Techn. Educ.* IV. 310/1 France is clever at producing.. shams, and a perfect thing called the *philosopher's-stone* which.. has a very beautiful and gem-like appearance, is imported from there.

[Note. *Lapis philosophorum* occurs in works attributed to Raymund Lully (1234–1315), and in those of Arnoldus de Villa Nova (1240–1314). Probably it was used earlier; it appears in various mediæval works of uncertain age or doubtful authenticity; e.g. in the *Clavis Majoris Sapientiæ* attributed to Artefius or Artesius, whose date has been put by some *c* 1130. In some of these also we find *lapis philosophicus*, *l. philosophicalis*. But the earlier works (e.g. the mediæval Latin *De Investigatione Perfecti Magisterii*), passing as translated from Geber (Abu Musa Ja'far al-Sufi), usually refer to it simply as *Lapis* 'the Stone', or *noster lapis* 'our stone'. Albertus Magnus (1205–82), who doubted the transmutation of metals, refers to it as *lapis quem philosophi laudant ubique*, 'the stone which the philosophers everywhere laud', and *lapis quem honorant philosophi*. It is thus possible that *philosophorum* originated later, as an identifying adjunct to *lapis*, as if 'the Stone, of which all the philosophers speak', 'the Stone of the philosophers', and that the descriptive phrase grew at length into a specific name or title. It will be seen that the correct form is not *philosopher's*, but *philosophers' stone*.]

philosophess (fɪˈlɒsəfɪs). [a. F. *philosophesse* (*a* 1518 in Godef.), f. *philosophe*: see PHILOSOPH and -ESS.] = PHILOSOPHERESS.

1668 ST. SERFE *Taruga's Wiles* 23, I hope none.. will be offended that my neighbour here Clubs his cloven Philosophess. **1821** W. TAYLOR in *Monthly Rev.* XCIV. 497 Remember me to my philosophess. **1875** M. COLLINS *Midnight to Midn.* II. ii. 222 There were peers and peeresses; there were philosophers and philosophesses.

† **philosophiant.** *Obs.* [a. OF. *philosophiant*, pr. pple. of *philosophier* to practise philosophy; but perh. altered from OF. *philosophien* (L. type **philosophiān-us*) a philosopher.] = PHILOSOPHER 1.

c **1400** tr. *Secreta Secret.*, *Gov. Lordsh.* 88 Oure ffader Hermogenes, þat ys full fayr in Philosophie and wel faire Philosophiant.

‖ **philosophia perennis** (fɪləʊˈsɒfɪə pəˈrɛnɪs). [L., = perennial philosophy.] An alleged central core of philosophical truths that are generally accepted regardless of time or place, usu. taken to be exemplified by Aristotle and St. Thomas Aquinas.

[**1540** A. STEUCHUS (*title*) De perenni philosophia.] **1858** A. C. FRASER *Rational Philos.* ii. 116 The long line of what an old writer calls *philosophia perennis.* **1933** W. R. INGE *God & Astronomers* i. 13 The classical tradition of Christian philosophy, which Roman Catholic scholars call the *philosophia perennis.* **1941** *Mind* L. 166 The tradition of Nominalism, Naturalism, Materialism, which has always haunted the *Philosophia Perennis* like a shadow. **1960** H. KRAEMER *World Cultures & World Relig.* vi. 150 A.. career of proclaiming in America, England and Europe the glorious universality of Vedanta as the philosophia perennis. **1965** *Listener* 1 July 14/1 Like the *philosophia perennis* which it reflects, his [*sc.* Dante's] poem just goes on applying to the human situation year after year.

‖ **philosophia prima** (fɪləʊˈsɒfɪə ˈpriːmə). [L., = first philosophy.] The study of the most general and universal truths of all science, (so called by Aristotle, followed by Francis Bacon and others); also, more specifically, the study of the divine and eternal.

1605 BACON *Adv. Learning* II. fol. 20ᵛ Therefore it is good, before wee enter into the former distribution, to erect & constitute one vniuersal Science by the name of *Philosophia Prima*, *Primitive* or *Svmmarie Philosophie*, as the Maine and common way, before we come where the waies part. [**1641** DESCARTES (*title*) Meditationes de prima philosophia, in qua Dei existentia, & animæ immortalitas demonstratur.] **1651** HOBBES *Leviathan* IV. xlvi. 371 There is a certain *Philosophia prima*, on which all other Philosophy ought to depend; and consisteth principally, in right limiting of the significations of such Appellations, or Names, as are of all others the most Universall. **1865** J. S. MILL *Exam. Hamilton's Philos.* xxiv. 464 What is inappropriately termed the Philosophia Prima.. would be more properly called *ultima*, since it consists of the widest generalizations respecting the laws of Existence and Activity. **1890** G. T. LADD *Introd. Philos.* (1891) 14 Yet a *prima philosophia* is in some sort recognized, which is nothing more than a mixture of definitions of the more fundamental conceptions. **1945** *Mind* LIV. 209 An author who calls himself a positivist had better show cause that he is in earnest when he protests his concern for *philosophia prima.*

philosophic (fɪləˈsɒfɪk), *a.* (*sb.*) [ad. post-cl. L. *philosophic-us*, a. Gr. *φιλοσοφικ-ός (implied in φιλοσοφικῶς adv.), f. φιλοσοφία PHILOSOPHY: see -IC. Cf. F. *philosophique* (*c* 1500 in Hatz.-Darm.).]

A. *adj.* **1. a.** Of or pertaining to philosophers or philosophy: = PHILOSOPHICAL 1.

1644 MILTON *Areop.* 24, I have sat among their lerned men,.. and bin counted happy to be born in such a place of Philosophic freedom as they suppos'd England was. **1704** HEARNE *Duct. Hist.* (1714) I. 415 They went to Megara, where Euclid who had been a Disciple of Socrates, had erected a Philosophick School. *a* **1734** NORTH *Life Ld. Guildford* (1742) 284 This resignation to philosophic studies spoiled the lawyer. **1736** BUTLER *Anal.* Diss. I. 303 In the proper philosophick Sense of the Word *same.* **1802** MAR. EDGEWORTH *Moral T.* (1816) I. xiv. 110 Questions, which he.. imagined scarcely admitted of philosophic doubt. **1872** MORLEY *Voltaire* (1886) 9 Philosophic candour and intelligence. **1879** A. J. BALFOUR (*title*) A Defence of Philosophic Doubt, being an Essay on the Foundations of Belief.

b. = PHILOSOPHICAL 1 b; scientific. Now *rare.* ***philosophic cotton***: see COTTON 7. ***philosophic stone***: see PHILOSOPHERS' STONE. ***philosophic wool***: see WOOL *sb.* 2 b.

1686 W. HARRIS tr. *Lemery's Chym.* I. xiii. (ed. 3) 340 Antient Chymists have given the Epithete Philosophick to all preparations wherein they have used Brick. **1687** DRYDEN *Hind & P.* II. 113 Every saint has to himself alone The secret of this Philosophic stone. **1784** COWPER *Task* III. 229 Philosophic Tube, That brings the planets home into the eye Of Observation. **1825** *Inscr. on statue of Jas. Watt in Westm. Abbey*, An original genius, early exercised in philosophic research.

2. Of persons, etc.: = PHILOSOPHICAL 2.

1711 STEELE *Spect.* No. 2 ¶ 6 He is a Clergyman, a very Philosophick Man, of general Learning. **1796** KIRWAN *Elem. Min.* (ed. 2) I. 15 For the discovery.. we are indebted to that celebrated philosophic artist Mr. Wedgewood. **1845** GRAVES *Rom. Law* in *Encycl. Metrop.* II. 735/1 The history of legal systems is a subject of great interest to philosophic minds. **1890** E. R. LANKESTER *Adv. Sc.* 286 Speculations which have a historical value for the philosophic biologist.

3. = PHILOSOPHICAL 3.

a **1700** DRYDEN (J.), Among mankind so few there are, Who will conform to philosophick fare. **1700** W. KING *Transactioneer* 34, I call him the Philosophick Sancho, and he me Don. **1781** COWPER *Retirement* 429 What early philosophic hours he keeps. **1816** JANE AUSTEN *Emma* II. xvi. 304 The philosophic composure of her brother on hearing his fate. **1822** DE QUINCEY *Confess.* 110 The poor are far more philosophic than the rich... They show a more ready and cheerful submission to what they consider as irremediable evils. **1927** E. O'NEILL *Marco Millions* II. i. 85 The expression has grown mask-like, full of philosophic calm. *a* **1953** —— *Touch of Poet* (1957) II. 86, I flatter myself I have preserved a philosophic poise. **1977** D. AITKIN *Second Chair* xxiv. 227 She was composed and philosophic, aware that I did not blame her.

4. ***philosophic radical*** (also with capital initials) = *philosophical radical*; hence ***philosophic radicalism.***

1834 J. S. MILL in *Monthly Repos.* VIII. 309 Few of the results of the Reform Bill have fallen more short of our hopes, than the conduct of the little band of enlightened and philosophic Radicals. **1837** —— in *Westm. Rev.* XXVII. 67 Those whom.. we call philosophic radicals, are those who in politics observe the common practice of philosophers—that is, who, when they are discussing means, begin by considering the end, and when they desire to produce effects, think of causes. *a* **1854** —— *Early Draft Autobiogr.* (1961) 114 Almost every debate was a bataille rangée between the philosophic radicals & the Tory lawyers. *Ibid.* 157 The foundation of a periodical organ of philosophic radicalism. **1882** A. BAIN *John Stuart Mill* iv. 124 In the days when he was heading the philosophic radicals, he was conscious of the weakness of his position in not being himself in the House of Commons. **1911** *Encycl. Brit.* XVI. 661/1 In April 1835 he [*sc.* William Molesworth] founded, in conjunction with Roebuck, the *London Review*, as an organ of the 'Philosophic Radicals'. **1969** D. BEALES *From Castlereagh to Gladstone* I. iv. 68 Bentham.. was the most productive.. of a group which was of great importance in that it had some influence on public opinion at large, more on political leaders, and more still.. on practical administration. They were known as the Philosophic Radicals.

B. *sb.* (in *pl.*) Studies, works, or arguments pertaining to philosophy.

a **1734** NORTH *Life Sir D. North* (1744) 200 So much Latin as to make him take pleasure in the best classics, especially in Tully's philosophics. **1867** 'OUIDA' *Idalia* xiv. 190 A woman had enthralled him, and his philosophics were dead.

philosophical (fɪləˈsɒfɪkəl), *a.* (*sb.*) [f. as prec. (perh. immediately from F. *philosophique*) + -AL[1]: see -ICAL.]

A. *adj.* **1. a.** Of or pertaining to a philosopher or philosophy; of the nature of, consonant with, or proceeding from philosophy or learning; in earlier usage including 'scientific', but now restricted in the same way as PHILOSOPHER and PHILOSOPHY, q.v.

1500–20 DUNBAR *Poems* lxv. 11 The naturall science philosophicall. **1530** PALSGR. 320/2 Phylosophycall, belongyng to a phylosopher, *philosophal.* **1538** STARKEY *England* I. i. 21 Phylosophycal resonys out of nature drawne. **1570** DEE *Math. Pref.* *iij, This most subtile and frutefull, Philosophicall Conclusion. **1617** MORYSON *Itin.* I. 32 In the valley.. towards the City [Heidelberg], is a pleasant walk, of the sweetnes called the Phylosophicall way. **1668** WILKINS *Real Char.* 299 Capable of being stated and fixed according to a Philosophical method. **1728** PEMBERTON *Newton's Philos.* 1 The manner, in which Sir Isaac Newton has published his philosophical discoveries. **1736** BUTLER *Anal.* Diss. I. 303 A strict and philosophical Manner of Speech.

1775 JOHNSON *Western Isl.* Wks. X. 406 The cuddy is a fish of which I know not the philosophical name. **1830** COLERIDGE *Table-t.* 30 Apr., My mind is in a state of philosophical doubt as to animal magnetism. **1880** MCCARTHY *Own Times* IV. lxvii. 537 He has treated history on a large scale and in the philosophical spirit.

b. Pertaining to, or used in the study of, natural philosophy, or some branch of physical science; physical, scientific. Now *Obs.* or *arch.*

1471 RIPLEY *Comp. Alch.* Pref. iv. in Ashm. *Theat. Chem. Brit.* (1652) 125 The second Water phylosophycall. **1594** PLAT *Jewell-ho.* II. 17 A philosophicall contrition of oiles. **1651** tr. *Glauber* (*title*) Description of New Philosophical Furnaces, or a New Art of Distilling. **1774** GOLDSM. *Nat. Hist.* I. 110 This we must..call pure water; but even this is far short of the pure, unmixed, philosophical element. **1843** *Penny Cycl.* XXVII. 136/2 *note*, Young Watt..exhibiting a box of philosophical toys to the students..at Glasgow. *Mod.* A Philosophical Instrument-maker.

2. Of persons, or their faculties, etc.: Skilled in or devoted to philosophy or learning (formerly including science); learned.

Formerly common, and still retained in the titles of scientific societies, institutions, journals, etc., e.g. the *Philosophical Transactions* (of the Royal Society), the *American Philosophical Society*, the *Edinburgh Philosophical Journal*, a *Literary and Philosophical Institution*, etc.

c **1374** CHAUCER *Troylus* v. 1857 (Campsall MS.) O moral Gower, þis boke I directe To þe, and þe Philosophical Strode. **1553** EDEN *Treat. Newe Ind.* (Arb.) 8 The same to a philosophical head is apparent by suche ryches and presentes. **1570** DEE *Math. Pref.* *iv b, Such as haue modest and earnest Philosophicall mindes. **1601** SHAKS. *All's Well* II. iii. 2 They say miracles are past, and we haue our Philosophicall persons, to make moderne and familiar things supernaturall and causelesse. **1662** STILLINGFL. *Orig. Sacr.* III. i. §12 Some of the wisest and most Philosophical men of Greece and Rome. **1798** (*title*) The Philosophical Magazine. *a* **1810** in *Sir J. Sinclair's Corr.* (1831) II. 43 Like our American Philosophical Society, it is voluntary, and unconnected with the public. **1813** SIR H. DAVY *Agric. Chem.* i. (1814) 26 A philosophical chemist would probably make a very unprofitable business of farming. **1838** THIRLWALL *Greece* II. xii. 137 He also attacked several doctrines of his philosophical contemporaries or predecessors.

3. Characterized by practical philosophy or wisdom; befitting or characteristic of a philosopher; wise; calm; temperate; frugal.

1638 SIR T. HERBERT *Trav.* (ed. 2) 203 His patience was more Philosophicall than his Intellect. **1717** POPE *Let. to Lady M. W. Montagu* June, What with ill-health and ill-fortune, I am grown so stupidly philosophical as to have no thought about me that deserves the name of warm or lively. **1833** HT. MARTINEAU *Charmed Sea* ii. 18 Alexander gazed with a grave countenance of philosophical curiosity.

4. In special collocations: ***philosophical logic***, logic pertaining to philosophy (opp. *mathematical logic*); ***philosophical radical*** (also with capital initials), a member of a group of early 19th-century radicals whose advocacy of reform was based on the utilitarian theories of Bentham and James Mill; hence ***philosophical radicalism***.

† ***philosophical candle*** or ***lamp***, a lighted jet of hydrogen; † ***p. egg***, a kind of alembic or retort; † ***p. oil*** = *brick oil* (BRICK *sb.*[1] 3); † ***p. stone*** = PHILOSOPHERS' STONE; † ***p. tree*** = Tree of Diana: see DIANA 2, ARBOR 2; † ***p. vinegar*** = *philosophers' vinegar*: see PHILOSOPHER 5 b; ***p. wool***: see WOOL *sb.* 2 b.

1822 IMISON *Sc. & Art* II. 51 On this principle is constructed the *philosophical candle, which cannot be easily blown out. Fill with hydrogen gas, a bell glass, furnished with a capillary tube; compress the gas,.. apply a lighted taper to the upper extremity of the tube; the gas will take fire, and exhibit a candle, which will burn till all the gas is exhausted. [**1893** *Syd. Soc. Lex.*, Philosophic candle.] [**1611** COTGR. s.v. *Oeuf, Oeuf des Philosophes*, the vessell wherein Alchymists put the stuffe which they hope will yeeld the Philosophers stone.] **1660** BOYLE *New Exp. Phys. Mech.* xx. 144 A great Glass-bubble, with a long neck; (such as Chymists..call a *Philosophical Egg). **1704** J. HARRIS *Lex. Techn.* I. **1903** B. RUSSELL *Princ. Math.* ii. 32 It remains a question for *philosophical logic whether there is not a quite different notion of the disjunction of individuals. **1921** C. K. OGDEN *Let.* 5 Nov. in B. Russell *Autobiogr.* (1968) II. ii. 121, I am still a little uneasy about the title [of Wittgenstein's *Tractatus*] and don't want to feel that we decided in a hurry on *Philosophical Logic.* **1952** *Mind* LXI. 57 That philosophical logic is concerned with form is the traditional and still prevalent view. **1967** P. STRAWSON *Philos. Logic* 1 Wittgenstein's suggestion does not itself belong to formal logic. It belongs to philosophical logic. **1807** T. THOMSON *Chem.* (ed. 3) II. 443 Oil, thus distilled, was formerly distinguished by the name of *philosophical oil. **1834** J. S. MILL in *Monthly Repos.* VIII. 174 Those who aspire to be..distinguished as the instructed and *philosophical Radicals. **1855** in T. Woollcombe *Notices of Late Sir W. Molesworth* (1857) 36 They were generally known by the rather ambitious title of philosophical radicals. **1873** H. GROTE *Personal Life G. Grote* vi. 56 The 'Philosophical Radicals' as the followers of Bentham were designated. **1885** W. HARRIS *Hist. Radical Party* vii. 130 The so-called Philosophical Radicals, following the methods and sharing the conclusions of Bentham, performed the duty of proving that the political reforms.. were not the mere creations of disaffected ignorance, but were founded on great moral and social laws. **1945** B. RUSSELL *Hist. Western Philos.* (1946) III. xxi. 746 The romantic revolt..passes on, somewhat softened, to the philosophical radicals in England. **1974** *Encycl. Brit. Macropædia* XII. 197/2 The *Westminster Review*..was the organ of the philosophical radicals. **1910** *Ibid.* V. 351/2 Carlyle had some expectation of the editorship of the *London Review*.., an organ of *philosophical radicalism. **1935** A. HUXLEY *Let.* 13 Jan. (1969) 390 Bertrand Russell's book on 19th century history..was excellent if regarded as a series of essays on different aspects of the time—Marxism, Philosophical Radicalism and so forth. **1966** F. COPLESTON *Hist. Philos.* VIII. I. i. 3 The philosophical radicalism which is associated with the name of Jeremy Bentham and which had already been expressed by him in the closing decades of the eighteenth century. **1638** MARCOMBES in *Lismore Papers* (1888) Ser. II. III. 283 Euery one thinks yt because I belong to my Lord of Corke I must haue ye *Philosophical stone. **1791–1823** D'ISRAELI *Cur. Lit., Six Follies Sc.*, The Quadrature of the Circle; the Multiplication of the Cube; the Perpetual Motion; the Philosophical Stone; Magic; and Judicial Astrology. **1706** PHILLIPS, **Philosophical Tree.* See Diana's Tree. **1694** SALMON *Bate's Dispens.* (1713) 568/2 That Vinegar which Quercetan calls in his Writings, *Philosophical Vinegar.

† **B.** *sb.* (in *pl.*) The subjects of study in a course of philosophy. Cf. LOGICALS. *Obs.*

1691 WOOD *Ath. Oxon.* I. 10 John Colet..spent seven years in Logicals and Philosophicals. **1716** M. DAVIES *Athen. Brit.* II. 328 He was educated in Grammaticals in Wikeham-School near Winchester, in Logicals and Philosophicals in New College Oxon.

philo'sophically, *adv.* [f. prec. + -LY[2].] **a.** In a philosophic or philosophical manner; according to philosophical rules or principles; as befits a philosopher; from a philosophical point of view.

1580 G. HARVEY 3 *Lett.* Wks. (Grosart) I. 64 Partly Philosophically, partly Theologically set downe. **1598** BARCKLEY *Felic. Man* (1631) 717 If I have written anything over-much philosophically that dissenteth from the true professed Religion. **1741–3** WESLEY *Extract of Jrnl.* (1749) 81 Who will either disprove this fact or philosophically account for it. **1825** MACAULAY *Ess., Milton* (1887) 12 But, though philosophically in the wrong, we cannot but believe that he was poetically in the right. **1873** HARDY *Pair of Blue Eyes* III. iii. 75 The practical husbands and wives who take things philosophically are very humdrum, are they not? **1888** *Daily News* 16 July 4/7 Philosophically indifferent as to the question of who are in power. **1898** G. B. SHAW *Widowers' Houses* (rev. ed.) II. 46 Trench..tries to take his disenchantment philosophically. **1933** E. O'NEILL *Ah, Wilderness!* I. 43 *Mrs. Miller.* (stares after him worriedly—then sighs philosophically). **1971** *Countryman* Autumn 112 Suddenly the third member of the brood swooped down from its perch in a nearby spruce and flew back to the tree with the worm in its beak. The hen [blackbird] philosophically started again. **1977** K. O'HARA *Ghost of T. Penry* xi. 97 He..switched off Joe's lamp. Philosophically coiling down the cord, Joe said 'Exactly.'

b. *Comb.*, as ***philosophically-minded*** adj.

1942 R. G. COLLINGWOOD *New Leviathan* xliii. 365 We know too much about the Bogomils to be content with a Gibbonesque, eighteenth-century picture of them as simple, philosophically minded innocents. **1955** *Sci. Amer.* July 73/1 Only a few scientists had been philosophically minded, but today physicists are almost all philosophers.

philo'sophicalness. *rare.* [f. as prec. + -NESS.] The quality of being philosophical.

1661 RUST *Origen* in *Phenix* I. 8 According to the Philosophicalness of his excellent Spirit. **1664** H. MORE *Myst. Iniq., Apol.* 481 The Philosophicalness of this present Age.

philosophi'cation. *nonce-wd.* [f. assumed **philosophicate* vb., f. *philosophic* (cf. *sophisticate*): see -ATION.] The action of philosophizing.

1851 SIR F. PALGRAVE *Norm. & Eng.* I. 237 Philosophications meaningless as the melodious moanings of the Æolian harp.

philosophicide (fɪləʊ'sɒfɪsaɪd). *nonce-wd.* [f. L. *philosoph-us* philosopher + -CIDE[1].] One who would put an end to philosophers or philosophy.

1804 COLERIDGE *Lett., to Southey* (1895) 465 This dim-headed prig of a philosophocide. **1812** SOUTHEY *Ess.* (1832) I. 149 Philosophists on one side..and..philosophicides on the other.

philo'sophico-, combining form (used advb.) of Gr. *φιλοσοφικό-ς PHILOSOPHIC, PHILOSOPHICAL: = philosophically-, philosophical and..; as in ***philosophico-chorographical*** (pertaining to physical geography), ***-historic, -juristic, -legal, -lexicological, -linguistic, -psychological, -religious, -scientific*** adjs.

1743 PACKE *Ancographia* (title-p.), The Origine..Of all The Valleys, Hills, Brooks and Rivers of East-Kent, as an explanation Of a New Philosophico-Chorographical Chart. **1903** *Daily Chron.* 20 Mar. 3/2 The International Association of Academies has..agreed to the admission of the association [British Academy] as a constituent Academy in the philosophico-historic section. *a* **1866** J. GROTE *Exam. Utilit. Philos.* ix. (1870) 157 The Roman Stoic or philosophico-juristic notion of *jus.* **1924** C. K. OGDEN tr. *Vaihinger's Philos. of 'As If'* 140 We will not embark here on a philosophico-lexicological excursus. **1967** C. L. WRENN *Word & Symbol* 2 A creative fundamental philosophico-linguistic re-assessment. **1899** *Allbutt's Syst. Med.* VIII. 406 Developed from a specially philosophico-psychological point of view. **1934** WEBSTER, Philosophicoreligious. **1960** PARTRIDGE *Charm of Words* 96 Rosenkreuz..founder..of a philosophicoreligious secret society. **1977** *Times Lit. Suppl.* 18 Feb. 190/1 The problem of 'life'..is so fraught with philosophico-religious profundities. **1847** W. SMITH tr. *Fichte's Characteristics Present Age* 242 The Philosophico-scientific character of the Third Age has been already set forth.

philosophing: see PHILOSOPHYING.

philosophism (fɪ'lɒsəfɪz(ə)m). [a. F. *philosophisme* (1690 in Littré), f. Gr. φιλόσοφ-ος (see PHILOSOPH): cf. *sophism.*] Philosophizing, or a philosophizing system; usually, in a hostile sense, affectation of philosophy; applied esp. to the system of the French Encyclopædists.

1792 R. VALPY *Progr. Morality* (1793) 47 *note*, Would the philologer..be offended, if the term *Philosophism* were hazarded, to express the abuse, or the reverse, of Philosophy? **1799** KETT *Prophecy* (1805) II. 206 The power which trained in the Schools of Philosophism, assumed the dress of mildness, virtue, and religion. **1799** COLERIDGE *Lett., to Southey* (1895) 307 And so philosophisms fly to and fro, in series of imitated imitations. **1813** EUSTACE *Class. Tour* (1821) III. ix. 353 To replace the bullion of ancient wisdom by the tinsel of Gallic *philosophism.* **1843** CARLYLE *Past & Pr.* IV. i, The Dryasdust Philosophisms and enlightened Scepticisms. **1848** J. H. NEWMAN *Loss & Gain* I. ix. (1858) 62 His father had always held up Pope's Universal Prayer to him as a pattern specimen of shallow philosophism.

philosophist (fɪ'lɒsəfɪst). Now *rare.* [In form, a deriv. of *philosophize*; but app. in sense 1, from L. *philosophia* or PHILOSOPHY + -IST: see -IST 2. In sense 2 = F. *philosophiste* (1760 in Littré).]

† **1.** = PHILOSOPHER 1. *Obs.*

1589 PUTTENHAM *Eng. Poesie* I. iv. (Arb.) 25 As they [Poets] were the first obseruers of all naturall causes and effects..they were the first Astronomers and Philosophists.

2. In depreciative use: One who philosophizes or speculates erroneously; applied polemically to the French Encyclopædists, and hence to rationalists and sceptics generally.

1798 W. TAYLOR in *Monthly Rev.* XXVI. 529 With the rash ridicule of a French philosophist, who does not.. hesitate to extinguish hope, to withdraw consolation, or to abolish restraint. **1799** HAN. MORE *Fem. Educ.* (ed. 4) I. 44 The same allurement..which was employed by the first philosophist to the first sinner—Knowledge. **1829** K. DIGBY *Broadst. Hon.* I. *Godefridus* 9 Infidel philosophists and men of the new wisdom who know of nothing beyond the senses and their little reign. *a* **1849** H. COLERIDGE *Ess.* (1851) I. 266 Let the Yankee-Gallico-philosophists work their will in the House of Commons and the Court of Chancery, they can hardly make them much worse than they have been.

† **phi'losophister.** *Obs. nonce-wd.* [f. prec. + -ER, after earlier words in *-istre*, -ISTER.] = prec. 2.

1797 D. SIMPSON *Plea Relig.* (1808) 103 What would they have said to the Philosophisters of the present day? *Ibid.* 257 Mr. Paine, and our other vaunting Philosophisters.

philosophistic (fɪlɒsəʊ'fɪstɪk), *a.* [f. PHILOSOPHIST + -IC; cf. *Calvinist-ic*, etc.] = next.

1828 in WEBSTER.

philosophistical (fɪlɒsəʊ'fɪstɪkəl), *a. rare* or *Obs.* [f. as prec. + -ICAL.] Of the nature of or pertaining to philosophists; rationalistic, sceptical.

1805 T. HARRAL *Scenes of Life* I. 22 In the garden of Eden —if our philosophistical gentry will admit that such a place ever existed. **1812** SOUTHEY *Ess.* (1832) I. 80 Against this Goliath of the philosophistical Canaanites, Mr. Malthus stept forth. **1820** —— *Wesley* II. xxvi. 401 He brought away a taint of that philosophistical infidelity which was then beginning to infect half-learned men.

philosophistry (fɪ'lɒsəfɪstrɪ). *nonce-wd.* [f. PHILOSOPHIST + -RY: cf. *sophist-ry, casuistry.*] The 'trade' or method of philosophists; shallow philosophy.

1880 W. M. TORRENS in *19th Cent.* Nov. 777 Whereupon philosophistry curls its official lip.

philo-'sophistry. *nonce-wd.* [f. PHILO- + SOPHISTRY.] Love of sophistry.

1894 *Nat. Observer* 6 Jan. 199/1 Nor are Burton's notes.. always to be taken for genuine..any more than his 'chaff' and his philo-sophistry.

philosophization (fɪ,lɒsəfaɪ'zeɪʃən). [f. next + -ATION, after *civilization*, etc.] The action of philosophizing; philosophical treatment.

1800 BENTHAM *Mem. & Corr.* Wks. 1843 X. 347 In the choice of the subject-matter of philosophization, the principle of utility..has been my guide. **1891** *Harper's Mag.* Oct. 800/2 We..find her philosophization of Browning scanty.

philosophize (fɪ'lɒsəfaɪz), *v.* [f. Gr. φιλόσοφ-ος philosopher: see PHILOSOPH and -IZE 1.]

1. a. *intr.* To play the philosopher; to think, reason, or argue philosophically; to speculate, theorize; to moralize.

1594 CAREW *Huarte's Exam. Wits* (1616) 27 To the end the reasonable soule may discourse and Philosophize. **1653** H. MORE *Antid. Ath.* III. xii. (1662) 125 My intent is not to Philosophize concerning the nature of Spirits, but onely to prove their Existence. **1690** BURNET *Th. Earth* III. 44 It is a great question whether..Moses did either philosophize or astronomize in that description. **1785** REID *Intell. Powers* I. iii. 234 When men first began to Philosophize it was very natural for them to indulge conjecture. **1836–7** SIR W. HAMILTON *Metaph.* iv. (1859) I. 65 Man philosophises as he lives. He may philosophise well or ill, but philosophise he must. **1841** D'ISRAELI *Amen. Lit.* (1867) 654 Bacon.. presumed not to establish a philosophy, but to show how we should philosophize.

b. *trans.* To bring (*into*) by philosophizing.

1737 *Wks. of Learned* I. 67 He endeavoured to philosophize himself into a Belief, that Animals were mere Machines. **1844** *North Brit. Rev.* I. 71 To philosophize our starving operatives into a quiet endurance.

2. *trans.* To render philosophic; to conform to the principles of philosophy; to explain, treat, or construct philosophically; also, to say or comment philosophically.

1800 COLERIDGE in C. K. Paul *W. Godwin* (1876) II. 10, I wish you to philosophize Horne Tooke's system. **1806** FESSENDEN *Democr.* I. 72 To kill one half mankind were best, And then philosophize the rest. **1818** COLERIDGE in *Lit. Rem.* (1836) I. 154 [Dante] philosophized the religion and Christianized the philosophy of Italy. **1856** R. A. VAUGHAN *Mystics* (1860) I. III. iv. 77 This endeavour to philosophise superstition. **1922** JOYCE *Ulysses* 203 The will to live, John Eglinton philosophised, for poor Ann, Will's widow, is the will to die. **1977** J. WAINWRIGHT *Do Nothin'* vi. 97 'It takes all sorts,' I philosophise.

Hence **phi'losophized** *ppl. a.*, **phi'losophizing** *vbl. sb.* and *ppl. a.*; **phi'losophizer**, one who philosophizes.

1594 CAREW *Huarte's Exam. Wits* (1616) 95 This manner of Philosophising will not sticke much in the soul. **1676** H. MORE *Remarks* Contents, The fond humour of the Philosophizers of this age. *Ibid.* xxxvii. 148 Nothing else but a certain modified mass of Philosophizing matter. **1772** NUGENT tr. *Hist. Friar Gerund* I. 544 That philosophised orator who suspected [etc.]. **1805** W. TAYLOR in *Ann. Rev.* III. 250 Simplicity of expression in which these French philosophizers excel. **1850** MAURICE *Mor. & Met. Philos.* (1854) 27 This early form of..philosophized Christianity. **1855** MILMAN *Lat. Chr.* IX. viii. (1864) V. 380 No philosophising Christian ever organised or perpetuated a sect. **1856** MASSON *Ess.* 455 The philosophizings of a Spinoza.

†**philosophling.** *Obs. rare.* [f. PHILOSOPH or F. *philosophe* + -LING.] A petty philosopher; a tyro in philosophy; = PHILOSOPHASTER.

1815 JAS. GILCHRIST *Labyrinth Demolished* 8 Bewildered bewildering Aristotelian philosophlings. *Ibid.* 24 If the intellectual philosophling trouble the world with any more of his familiar notions.

philoso'phobia. [f. Gr. φιλόσοφ-ος + -PHOBIA.] Dread of philosophy or philosophers.

1853 J. MARTINEAU *Stud. Chr.* (1873) 235 The greatest sufferer from philosophobia.

philoso'phocracy. [f. as prec. + -CRACY.] Government by philosophers; the rule of philosophy.

1798 W. TAYLOR in *Monthly Mag.* VI. 110 That philosophocracy, the live-long hope of the sage, and still the pursuit of the philanthropist.

philosophress, variant of PHILOSOPHERESS.

philoso'phuncule. *nonce-wd.* [f. L. type **philosophuncul-us*, dim. of *philosophus* philosopher: cf. *homuncle*, and see -UNCLE, -UNCULE.] A petty or insignificant philosopher. So **philoso'phunculist.**

[**1817** *Blackw. Mag.* I. 470 The sagacity of the sapient philosophunculi.] **1840** *Fraser's Mag.* XXI. 588 The unsettled races of the north..are Scotch philosophunculists and Irish savages.

philosophy (fɪ'lɒsəfɪ), *sb.* Forms: 3 **philosofie**, 4 **-fye**, 4–6 **-sophye**, 4–7 **-sophie**, 5–6 **-sophi**, 6–7 **phylosophy(e**, **-sophie**, 6– **philosophy**. *β.* 4 **filosofie**, **-zofe**, 5 **-sofi**, **-sophi**, **sofye**, 5–6 **filo-**, **fylosophye**. [ME. a. OF. *filosofie* (12th c. in Hatz.-Darm.), *philosophie* (13th c.) = Pr., Pg. *philosophia*, Sp. *filosofia*, It. *filosofia* (also Du. *filozofie*, Ger. *philosophie*, Da., Sw. *filosofi*), ad. L. *philosophia*, a. Gr. φιλοσοφία, n. of condition f. φιλόσοφ-ος philosopher: see PHILOSOPH.]

1. a. (In the original and widest sense.) The love, study, or pursuit of wisdom, or knowledge of things and their causes, whether theoretical or practical.

The definition of Cicero, *De Officiis* II. ii. §5, was considered authoritative: Nec quicquam aliud est philosophia, si interpretari velis, praeter studium sapientiae; sapientia autem est rerum divinarum et humanarum causarumque quibus eae res continentur scientia. Cf. quot. 1586.

1340 *Ayenb.* 126 Vor filozofé is ase moche worþ ase loue of wysdome. *Ibid.* 251 þet is þe heȝeste wyt of man, wel to knawe his sseppere and him louie mid al his herte. Vor wyþoute þise filosofie alle oþre wyttes ys folye. *Ibid.* 164 Filozofie. *c* **1430** LYDG. *Min. Poems* (Percy Soc.) 175 With philosophres speke of philosophie. **1483** *Cath. Angl.*, Filosophi, *philosophia.* **1586** T. B. *La Primaud. Fr. Acad.* I. (1594) 38 Philosophie is a love or desire of wisedome: or otherwise, it is a profession, studie, and exercise of that wisedome, which is the knowledge of divine and humane things. **1603** HOLLAND *Plutarch's Mor.* 804 Aristotle and Theophrastus, with the Peripateticks,..divide Philosophie in this maner; namely, into Contemplative and Active. **1607–12** BACON *Ess., Atheism* (Arb.) 330 Certainely a litle Philosophie inclineth to Atheisme, but depth in Philosophie bringeth Men about to Religion. **1669** GALE *Crt. Gentiles* I. I. x. 50 Al human wisdome may be reduced to these two Heads of Philologie, and Philosophie. **1775** HARRIS *Philos. Arrangem.* Wks. (1841) 247 Philosophy, taking its name from the love of wisdom, and having for its end the investigation of truth, has an equal regard both to practice and speculation.

†**b.** Sometimes used especially of practical wisdom. *Obs.* Cf. 9.

From the time of the post-Aristotelian philosophy of the Stoics and Epicureans this had become a usual employment of the Gr. and L. word.

1557 NORTH *Gueuara's Diall Pr.* III. l. 332 The chiefe of all philosophy consisteth to serve God, and not to offend men. **1679** PENN *Addr. Prot.* I. viii. (1692) 37 Famous for her Virtue and Philosophy, when that word was understood not of vain Disputing but of Pious Living. **1750** *Phil. Trans.* XLVI. 750 The original meaning of the Word Philosophy was rightly applied to moral Wisdom.

2. That more advanced knowledge or study, to which, in the mediæval universities, the seven liberal arts were recognized as introductory; it included the three branches of ***natural, moral,*** and ***metaphysical philosophy***, commonly called ***the three philosophies***. Hence the degree of ***Doctor of Philosophy***.

1387–8 T. USK *Test. Love* III. i. (Skeat) l. 54 Philosophie is knowinge of deuinly and manly thinges ioyned with studie of good liuing... The firste spece of Philosophye is naturel... The seconde spece is morall, whiche in order of liuing maners techeth..Prudence, Justice, Temperaunce, and strength... The thirde spece tourneth in to reason of vnderstanding, al thinges to be said soth and discussed, and that in two thinges is deuided: one is art, another is rhetorique. **1393** LANGL. *P. Pl.* C. XVIII. 115 Doctours of decree..That shoulde þe seuene ars conne..Bote þei faille in fylosophye. **1605** BACON *Adv. Learn.* II. v. §2 Out of which several inquiries there do arise three knowledges, divine philosophy, natural philosophy, and human philosophy, or humanitie. **1895** RASHDALL *Univ. of Europe in Mid. Ages* II. 452 At Oxford..importance was attached to keeping up the theory that a University Arts course included the *Trivium* and *Quadrivium* of the earlier Middle Ages, as well as the 'three Philosophies' introduced by the rediscovery of Aristotle in the thirteenth century.

3. a. (= *natural philosophy*.) The knowledge or study of nature, or of natural objects and phenomena; 'natural knowledge': now usually called *science*. Now *rare* or *Obs.*

1297 R. GLOUC. (Rolls) 2748 þe clerkes sede þat it is in philosofie yfounde, þat þer beþ in þe eyr an hey ver fram þe grounde, As a maner gostes wiȝtes as it be. **1471** RIPLEY *Comp. Alch.* v. xxv. in Ashm. *Theat. Chem. Brit.* (1652) 154 No Multeplyers but Phylosophers callyd wyll they be, Whych naturall Phylosophye dyd never rede nor see. **1681** RAY *Corr.* (1848) 130, I hope you [the naturalist Dr. Sloane] persist in your resolution of making your discoveries and observations public, for..the advancement of real philosophy. **1728** PEMBERTON *Newton's Philos.* 2 It is..to be wished, that the whole of his [Newton's] improvements in philosophy might be universally known. **1784** COWPER *Task* I. 712 Where finds Philosophy her eagle eye [telescope], With which she gazes at yon burning disk Undazzled? **1813–26** (*title*) Annals of Philosophy; or Magazine of Chemistry, Mineralogy, Mechanics, Natural History, Agriculture and Arts.

†**b.** *spec.* (In early use) Magical or occult science; magic; alchemy. *Obs.*

c **1386** CHAUCER *Can. Yeom. Prol. & T.* 505, I wol yow teche pleynly the manere How I kan werken in Philosophie. ?*a* **1550** *Freiris Berwik* 406 in *Dunbar's Poems* (S.T.S.) 298 Ane man of gret science,..Hes brocht ws heir throw his knawlege in filosophie.

4. (= *moral philosophy*.) The knowledge or study of the principles of human action or conduct; ethics.

c **1400** *Rom. Rose* 5664 In Boece of Consolacioun, Where it is maked mencioun Of our countree pleyn at the eye, By teching of philosophye. **1481** CAXTON *Myrr.* III. xii. 160 After cam Boece..And compiled..plente of fair volumes aourned of hye and noble philosophye. **1556** G. COLVILLE (*title*) The boke of Boecius, called the comforte of philosophye, or wysedome. **1592** SHAKS. *Rom. & Jul.* III. iii. 55 Ile giue thee Armour to keepe off that word, Aduersities sweete milke, Philosophie, To comfort thee, though thou art banished. **1634** MILTON *Comus* 476 How charming is divine Philosophy! *a* **1751** BOLINGBROKE *Stud. & Use Hist.* ii. (1777) 25 History is Philosophy teaching by example. **1816** SHELLEY *Alastor* 71 The fountains of divine philosophy Fled not his thirsting lips.

5. (= *metaphysical philosophy*.) That department of knowledge or study which deals with ultimate reality, or with the most general causes and principles of things. (Now the most usual sense.)

1794 J. HUTTON *Philos. Light*, etc. 121 Now, philosophy is that general knowledge by which the works of nature are understood in seeing the wisdom of design. **1852** SIR W. HAMILTON *Discuss.* 622 The Philosophical Society of Cambridge ought not, however, to be so entitled, if we take the word Philosophy in the meaning attached to it everywhere out of Britain. **1857** FLEMING *Vocab. Philos.* 381 Underlying all our inquiries into any of these departments [God, nature, or man], there is a first philosophy, which seeks to ascertain the grounds or principles of knowledge, and the causes of all things. Hence philosophy has been defined to be the science of causes and principles. It is the investigation of those principles on which all knowledge and all being ultimately rest. **1862** H. SPENCER *First Princ.* §37 Philosophy is completely unified knowledge. **1865** J. GROTE *Explor. Philos.* xi, Philosophy, by which I mean the study of thought and feeling..as we understand, think, feel them of ourselves and from within. **1880** J. CAIRD *Philos. Relig.* 2 Whatever is real is rational, and with all that is rational philosophy claims to deal... So far from resting in what is finite and relative, the peculiar domain of philosophy is absolute truth. **1887** *Edin. Rev.* Jan. 95 That philosophy only means psychology and morals, or in the last resort metaphysics, is an idea slowly developed through the eighteenth century, owing to the victorious advances of science. **1891** LADD *Introd. Philos.* i. 27 Philosophy—we define to be—the progressive rational system of the principles presupposed and ascertained by the particular sciences, in their relation to ultimate Reality. **1902** H. SIDGWICK *Philos.* 10, I regard Philosophy then..as the study which 'takes all knowledge for its province'.

6. a. Sometimes used especially of knowledge obtained by natural reason, in contrast with revealed knowledge.

(Cf. Ger. *Weltweisheit* opp. to *Gottesweisheit*.)

1388 WYCLIF *Col.* ii. 8 That no man disseyue ȝou bi filosofie [**1382** philosofye] and veyn fallace, aftir the tradicioun of men, aftir the elementis of the world and not aftir Crist. *c* **1449** PECOCK *Repr.* I. i. 7 Se ȝe that no man bigile ȝou bi philosophi and veyn falsnes. **1605** BACON *Adv. Learn.* II. vi. §1 Concerning Divine Philosophie, or Naturall Theologie, It is that knowledge..concerning God, which may be obtained by the contemplation of his Creatures. **1640** QUARLES *Enchirid.* IV. xci, Let Phylosophy not be asham'd to be confuted. **1850** TENNYSON *In Mem.* liii, Hold thou the good: define it well: For fear divine Philosophy Should push beyond her mark, and be Procuress to the Lords of Hell.

†**b.** *spec.* of the sceptical or rationalistic views current in France and elsewhere in the 18th c. *Obs.*

1749 SMOLLETT *Gil Blas* IV. viii, Our mistress is also a little tainted with philosophy. **1790** HAN. MORE *Relig. Fash. World* (1791) 16 Philosophy..(as Unbelief..has lately been pleased to call itself) will not do nearly so much mischief to the present age, as its great apostles intended. **1795** BURKE *Corr.* (1844) IV. 308 He is certainly a man of parts; but one who has dealt too much in the philosophy of France.

7. With *of*: The study of the general principles *of* some particular branch of knowledge, experience, or activity; also, less properly, of those *of* any subject or phenomenon.

1713 STEELE *Englishman* No. 7. 48 What Beau knows the Philosophy of the Perfume which emboldens him to appear amongst the Ladies? **1791** BURKE *Let. to Member Fr. Nat. Assembly* Wks. VI. 32 The great professor..of the philosophy of vanity [Rousseau]. **1800** *Med. Jrnl.* III. 385 The different problems which ought to be solved by a Philosophy of Nature. **1823** SCOTT *Let.* 5 Oct. (1935) VIII. 104, I would defer to the very last what is always taught first namely the philosophy as it hath been termd [*sic*] of history. **1835** URE (*title*) The Philosophy of Manufactures: or, an Exposition of the Scientific, Moral, and Commercial Economy of the Factory System. **1835** J. S. MILL in *London Rev.* I. I. 106 The evidence of history..leaves the philosophy of society in exactly the state in which physical science was, before the method of experiment was introduced. **1843** —— *Logic* I. I. v. 119 The notion..seems to me one of the most fatal errors ever introduced into the philosophy of Logic. **1847** J. D. MORELL *Hist. View Philos.* (ed. 2) II. v. 15 We have already shown in the case of Reid, that the philosophy of perception was well commenced, but not fully completed. **1852** *Westm. Rev.* Oct. 435 (*heading*) The philosophy of style. **1853** LYTTON *My Novel* IV. xxxv. 283 Levy is a man who has admitted the fiercer passions into his philosophy of life. **1863** W. PHILLIPS *Speeches* v. 87, I believe I understand the philosophy of reform. **1865** J. S. MILL *Auguste Comte* 54 The philosophy of science consists of two principal parts; the methods of investigation, and the requisites of proof. **1878** LECKY *Eng. in 18th C.* II. v. 73 To trace the causes, whether for good or ill, that have made nations what they are is the true philosophy of history. **1880** J. CAIRD *Philos. Relig.* 1 A philosophy of religion starts with the presupposition that religion and religious ideas can be taken out of the domain of feeling or practical experience and made objects of scientific reflection. **1890** W. JAMES *Princ. Psychol.* I. xiv. 585 We see in the philosophy of desire and pleasure, that such nascent excitements..may become potent mental stimuli and determinants of desire. **1896** W. CALDWELL *Schopenhauer's Syst.* iii. 162 A philosophy of life must make some broad assertion about reality as a whole. **1919** G. B. SHAW *Heartbreak House* p. xxvii, It is impossible to estimate what proportion of us..grasped the war and its political antecedents as a whole in the light of any philosophy of history or knowledge of what war is. **1940** F. J. E. WOODBRIDGE *Essay on Nature* i. 53 Expressions like 'philosophy of science', 'philosophy of history', 'philosophy of government', 'philosophy of law', 'philosophy of religion', and so forth creep into the language, indicating that after scientists, historians, statesmen, jurists, priests, and the rest have said all they have to say, there is still need of a special kind of knowledge to inform us what it is all about. **1957** G. RYLE in C. A. Mace *Brit. Philos. in Mid-Cent.* 243 We do systematically construe 'name' on the model of 'proper name'. The assumption of the truth of this equation has been responsible for a large number of radical absurdities in philosophy in general and the philosophy of logic in particular. **1960** H. L. BOND *Lit. Art E. Gibbon* vii. 138 Gibbon's well-defined manner of speaking and the details of his style reflect..his whole philosophy of life. **1966** J. J. KATZ *Philos. Lang.* i. 4 Philosophy of language is an area in the philosophical investigation of conceptual knowledge, rather than one of the several branches of contemporary philosophy such as philosophy of science, philosophy of mathematics, philosophy of art, and so forth. **1976** *Hiroshima Stud. Eng. Lang. & Lit.* XXI. 60 This is a study of D. H. Lawrence's *The Man Who Loved Islands* with a view to locating the spot it occupies in a series of works descriptive of his unique philosophy of life. **1977** P. A. FRENCH et al. (*title*) Studies in the philosophy of language.

8. (With *a* and *pl.*) A particular system of ideas relating to the general scheme of the universe; a philosophical system or theory. Also, more generally, a set of opinions, ideas, or principles; a basic theory; a view or outlook.

1390 GOWER *Conf.* III. 48 Of Tholome thastronomie, Of Plato the Philosophie. **1573** G. HARVEY *Letter-bk.* (Camden) 10 Mi chefist propositions against Aristotles philosophi. **1602** SHAKS. *Ham.* I. v. 167 There are more things in Heauen and Earth, Horatio, Then are dream't of in our Philosophy. **1674** GREW *Disc. Mixture* §1, I shall endeavour to conform to the Phylosophy, which this Society doth profess; which is, Reasoning grounded upon Experiment, and the Common Notions of Sense. **1841** ELPHINSTONE *Hist. Ind.* I. 237 The Indian philosophy resembles that of the earlier rather than of the later Greeks. *a* **1866** J. GROTE *Exam. Utilit. Philos.* xvi. (1870) 249 The special doctrines of other philosophies. **1898** G. B. SHAW *Plays Unpleasant* p. xix, It is quite possible for a piece to enjoy the most sensational success on the basis of a complete misunderstanding of its philosophy. **1899** O. WILDE *Ideal Husband* I. 12 *Mrs. Cheveley.* I don't know that women are always rewarded for being charming. I think they are usually punished for it! Certainly, more women grow old nowadays through the faithfulness of their admirers than through anything else! At least that is the only way I can account for the terribly haggard look of most of your pretty women in London! *Sir Robert Chittern.* What an appalling philosophy that sounds! **1901** G. B. SHAW *Three Plays for Puritans* p. xxxii, It is the philosophy, the outlook on life, that changes, not the craft of the playwright. *Ibid.*, Such men must rewrite all the old plays in terms of their own philosophy. **1903** —— *Man & Superman* p. v, Here is your play! .. Its profits, like its labor, belong to me: its morals, its manners, its philosophy, its influence on the young, are for you to justify. *Ibid.* III. 126 Yes, Juan: we know the libertine's philosophy. Always ignore the consequences to the woman. **1922** JOYCE *Ulysses* 629 You have every bit as much right to live by your pen in pursuit of your philosophy as the peasant has. **1946** E. O'NEILL *Iceman Cometh* (1947) I. 45 You pretend a bitter, cynic philosophy, but in your heart you are the kindest man among us. **1959** *Economist* 12 Sept. 836/1 Rival policies—or at least rival philosophies, for they barely reached the stage of practical policies—were very much in the centre of public attention. **1962** G. COOPER in *Into Orbit* 30 The entire philosophy had to be revised once we got involved with manned flights. **1973** *B.S.I. News* Dec. 32/2 Philosophy of control assignment on keyboards... Outlines the general philosophy for the positioning of areas for control keys, in relation to 'graphic' areas, of..keyboards for office machines. **1975** J. PLAMENATZ *K. Marx's Philos. of Man* i. 4 It is not surprising, then, that these ideas, derived from philosophies alien to them, should be less interesting to Marxists and students of Marxism outside the West. Even if they have similar ideas in their native philosophies, they are ideas differently expressed, and so such similarities as there may be go unrecognized.

9. a. The system which a person forms for the conduct of life. **b.** The mental attitude or habit of a philosopher; serenity under disturbing influences or circumstances; resignation; calmness of temper.

1771 CHESTERF. *Lett., to Bp. Waterford* 12 Aug., Philosophy, and confidence in the mercy of my Creator, mutually assist me in bearing my share of physical ills. **1774** J. ADAMS in *Fam. Lett.* 12 May, My own infirmities, the account of the return of yours, and the public news coming altogether have put my utmost philosophy to the trial. **1832** LYTTON *Eugene A.* I. v, Philosophy has become another name for mental quietude. **1877** SPARROW *Serm.* ii. 26 And as to philosophy, alas! it may answer some of the lighter purposes of life, but can never pillow the soul in death.

10. *attrib.* and *Comb.*, as ***philosophy-dreamer***, ***-hater***; †**philosophy-game**: see PHILOSOPHER 5 b.

1621 BURTON *Anat. Mel.* II. i. IV. 348 The like I may say of Cl. Bruxers Phylosophy game. *a* **1628** F. GREVIL *Sidney* (1652) 18 To turn the barren Philosophy precepts into pregnant Images of life. **1653** *Nicholas Papers* (Camden) II. 19 This Gentleman..is desirous to have the place of Philosophy Professor at Breda. **1670** COTTON *Espernon* II. v. 236 Proceeding to publick Lectures, he became Philosophy Reader. **1711** SHAFTESB. *Charac.* (1737) III. 159 Here, methinks, the ridicule turns more against the philosophy-haters than the virtuosi or philosophers. **1796–1803** COLERIDGE *Let.* (in *Sotheby's Catal.* 20 Nov. (1899) 17), Your philosophy dreamers from Toth, the Egyptian, to Taylor the English Pagan.

Hence †**phi'losophyship** *Obs.*, a mock title for a philosopher.

1798 CHARLOTTE SMITH *Yng. Philos.* III. 13 Is your philosophyship disinterested enough to give a letter of recommendation to your elder brother? *Ibid.* IV. 47, [I], of whose libertinism his philosophyship has such terrible ideas.

†**philosophy,** *v. Obs.* Also 4 philosofien. [f. prec. sb.: cf. obs. F. *philosophier* (15–16th c. in Godef.).] *intr.* = PHILOSOPHIZE *v.* I.

1382 WYCLIF *Bible* Pref. Ep. vi. 67 Other..among 3ong wymmen philosofien of holi lettres [1388 talken as filosoferes of hooly lettris among 3onge wymmen]. **1584** R. SCOT *Discov. Witchcr.* xv. xxxiii. (1886) 383 Salomon did philosophie about all things. *a* **1614** DONNE *Βιαθανατος* ii. §2 (1644) 46 Ambrose Philosophying divinely in a contemplation of Bees. **1654** FLECKNOE *Ten Years Trav.* 134 You see..how I Philosophy on every thing.

Hence †**phi'losophying** *vbl. sb.* and *ppl. a.*

1577 tr. *Bullinger's Decades* 1113 Those townes by reason of ye Philosophying [L. *philosophantibus*; edd. 1587–92 Philosophing] Leuites, were called Leuitical. **1591** SPARRY tr. *Cattan's Geomancie* Ep. Ded. A ij, By the philosophying upon the compilation, lines, and proportion of the handes. **1648** H. GRESBY tr. *Balzac's Prince* 250 A most perfect manner of Philosophying.

†**philostorgy** ('fɪləstɔːdʒɪ). *Obs. rare*$^{-0}$. [ad. Gr. φιλοστοργία tender love, f. φιλόστοργος tenderly loving, f. φιλο- PHILO- + στοργή affection.] Natural affection, such as that of parents and children.

1623 COCKERAM, *Philostorgie*, parents loue towards their children. **1656** in BLOUNT *Glossogr.*

philotechnic (fɪləʊ'tɛknɪk), *a.* [f. Gr. φιλότεχνος fond of art, f. φιλο- PHILO- + τέχνη art: so mod.F. *philotechnique* (*Dict. Acad.* 1835).] Fond of or devoted to the arts, esp. the industrial arts.

1825 *Gentl. Mag.* XCV. I. 348/2 British Philotechnic Society. Proposals have been issued for the establishment of a society under the above title. **1887** *Pall Mall G.* 6 Oct. 11/1 Organization of popular education in the evenings in Paris:—III.—The Philotechnic Association.

So **philo'technical** *a.* (*rare*$^{-0}$) = prec.; **philo'technist**, a lover of the practical arts.

1809–10 COLERIDGE *Friend* (1818) III. 176, I distinguish, first, those whom indeed you may call Philotheorists, or Philotechnists, or Practicians, and secondly those whom alone you may rightly denominate Philosophers. **1846** WORCESTER, *Philotechnic, Philotechnical*, fond of the arts; friendly to the arts.

philothaumaturgic, etc.: see PHILO-.

philothion (fɪləʊ'θaɪən). *Biochem. Obs.* exc. *Hist.* [a. F. *philothion* (J. de Rey-Pailhade 1888, in *Compt. Rend.* CVI. 1684), f. Gr. φιλο- (see PHILO-) + θεῖον sulphur.] = GLUTATHIONE.

1888 *Jrnl. Chem. Soc.* LIV. 1101 It follows that the substance, to which the author gives the name *philothion*, exists in animal tissues in a form different from that in which it exists in yeast. It stands to sulphur in the same physiological relation as hæmoglobin to oxygen, that is to say, it renders it soluble and assimilable. **1900** [see HYDROGENASE]. **1921** [see GLUTATHIONE]. **1954** T. WIELAND in S. Colowick et al. *Glutathione* 45 In 1888 de Rey-Pailhade ..described a substance containing sulfur which he had been able to isolate from yeast in an impure state and which he called 'philothion'.

†**philotimy.** *Obs. rare.* [ad. G. φιλοτιμία, f. φιλότιμος, f. φιλο- PHILO- + τιμή honour.] Love of honour, ambition.

1593 R. HARVEY *Philad.* 24 These honourable Rulers approued their Princely Magnificence, and Philotimy in a braue maner. **1656** in BLOUNT *Glossogr.*

-philous (fɪləs), repr. med. and mod.L. *philus*, Gr. -φιλος, for examples of which see -PHIL. So **-philist** = -PHIL; **-phily** (-fɪlɪ), in derivatives of adjectives formed with *-phil*, *-philous*, denoting the quality or condition of loving, being devoted to, or favouring the person or thing denoted by the first element of the compound.

b. In *Biol.* forming adjs. with the sense 'having an affinity for or thriving in (a particular kind of habitat or environment)', as in *dendrophilous* s.v. DENDRO-, HYDROPHILOUS, *hygrophilous* s.v. HYGRO-.

phi'loxenist. [f. Gr. φιλοξενίζειν (f. φιλόξενος loving hospitality, f. φιλο- PHILO- + ξένος stranger): see -IST.] A lover of hospitality to strangers.

1822 T. MITCHELL *Aristoph.* II. 179 And Nicostratus trips, For I see that his lips To themselves are philoxenist framing.

So †**phyloxeny, -ie.** *Obs. rare*$^{-0}$.

1623 COCKERAM, *Phyloxenie*, loue of hospitalitie.

philoxygenous to **philozoonist**: see PHILO-.

philter, obs. form of FILTER: var. PHILTRE.

'philterer. *rare.* [f. PHILTRE *sb.* or *v.* + -ER[1].] One who makes or administers philtres.

1676 *Doctrine of Devils* 105 What more consonant to this Etymon, than a Poysoner, Philterer, Jugler, Cheater, or Deceiver. *Ibid.* 106.

philtre, philter ('fɪltə(r)), *sb.* Also 7 filtre; 7–8 in L. form **philtrum** (pl. **-a** or **-ums**). [a. F. *philtre* (1568 in Hatz.-Darm.), ad. L. *philtrum*, a. Gr. φίλτρον love-charm, love-potion, f. φιλ-, stem of φιλεῖν to love, φίλος dear, loved, loving + -τρον, suffix of instrument.]

1. A potion or drug (rarely, a charm of other kind) supposed to be capable of exciting sexual love, esp. towards a particular person; a love-potion or love-charm. Sometimes *loosely*, a potion or drug to produce some magical effect, a magic potion. Also *fig.*

? **1587** NEWTON *Tryall Man's owne selfe* (1602) 116 in Brand *Pop. Antiq.* (1870) III. 261 By any secret sleight or cunning, as Drinkes, Drugges, Medicines, charmed Potions, Amatorious Philters, Figures, Characters, or any such like paltering Instruments, Devises, or Practises. **1609** B. JONSON *Sil. Wom.* IV. i. (1620) I, If I should make 'hem all in loue with thee afore Night! *Daup.* I would say thou had'st the best Philtre. *a* **1618** SYLVESTER *Maydens Blush* 798 The hellish Philtree made of Stygian Wave. **1621** BURTON *Anat. Mel.* I. ii. I. iii, They can make friends enemies, and enemies friends, by philters. **1700** S. L. tr. *Fryke's Voy. E. Ind.* 347, I threw all over-board, for fear some trick or philter should have been play'd with them. **1868** TENNYSON *Lucretius* 16 A witch Who brew'd the philtre.

β. *c* **1610** RANDOLPH *Eclogue Two Doctors* Wks. 1875 II. 604 Love-sick Amyntas, get a philtrum here, To make thee lovely to thy truly dear. **1732** BERKELEY *Alciphr.* VI. §25 That demons..assist in making philtrums and charms.

†**2.** See quots. *Obs.* [So It. *philtro* (Florio 1598), F. *philtre* (Cotgr. 1611).]

1653 R. SANDERS *Physiogn.* 278 A mole on the philtrum or hollow of the upper lip, under the nostrils. **1706** PHILLIPS, *Philter* or *Philtrum*... Among some Anatomists, it is taken for the Hollow that divides the upper Lip.

3. Comb., as ***philtre-bred***, ***-charmed*** adjs.

1598 SYLVESTER *Du Bartas* II. i. II. *Imposture* 511 Not philtre-charm'd nor by Busiris prest. **1876** GEO. ELIOT *Dan. Der.* IV. xxxii. (heading), The philtre-bred passion of Tristan.

'philtre, 'philter, *v.* [f. prec. sb.]

1. *trans.* To charm with a philtre or love-potion; *fig.* to bewitch.

1674 *Govt. Tongue* vi. §34 Let [them] not..shew themselves philter'd and bewitch'd by this. *a* **1711** KEN *Hymnotheo* Poet. Wks. 1721 III. 378 Hearts philtred by Concupiscence impure. **1888** LOWELL *Endymion* II. 32 Soon, like wine, Her eyes, in mine poured, frenzy-philtred mine.

2. *intr.* To prepare a philtre or magic potion.

1768 [W. DONALDSON] *Life Sir B. Sapskull* II. xxv. 213, I thought my chymical chiromancers were philtering to charm the devil.

†**philtrous** ('fɪltrəs), *a. Obs.* [f. as prec. + -OUS.] Of the nature of a philtre.

1653 A. WILSON *Jas. I* 57 With Philtrous powders and such drugs he works upon their persons. **1664** H. MORE *Myst. Iniq.* II. I. xii. 276 *heading*, That it is a Philtrous Cup.

philyrea: see PHILLYREA.

‖**phimosis** (faɪ'məʊsɪs). *Path.* Also 7 **phy-**. [mod.L., a. Gr. φίμωσις muzzling. So in Fr. (16th c. in Paré).] Contraction of the orifice of the prepuce, so that it cannot be retracted.

1674–7 J. MOLINS *Anat. Obs.* (1896) 22, I cut the Phymosis, and he did well. **1804** *Med. Jrnl.* XII. 20 With the dysuria he had a complete phimosis. **1878** T. BRYANT *Pract. Surg.* (1879) II. 161 Phimosis is a congenital affection.

Hence **phimosed** ('faɪməʊzd) *a.*, affected with phimosis; **phimotic** (faɪ'mɒtɪk) *a.*, pertaining to or of the nature of phimosis.

1899 *Allbutt's Syst. Med.* VIII. 837 The irritation of retained smegma beneath a phimosed prepuce. **1822–34** *Good's Study Med.* (ed. 4) II. 47 Phimotic Phlegmon.

phinnock, phinoc, obs. ff. FINNOC *Sc.*, white trout.

phioll, variant of FILIOLE[1] *Obs.*

†**phip.** *Obs.* An imitation of the chirp of a sparrow; hence formerly used as name for a sparrow. Also PHILIP.

1377 LANGL. *P. Pl.* B. XI. 41 '3ee, farewel phippe [C. XII. 310 fyppe]!' quod fauntelte. *a* **1529** SKELTON *Ph. Sparowe* 138 And whan I sayd, Phyp, Phyp, Than he wold lepe and skyp. *a* **1577** GASCOIGNE *Praise P. Sparrow* Wks. (1587) 285 As if you say but Fend cut Phip, Lord, how the peat will turne and skip.

phiph(e, -er, obs. ff. FIFE, FIFER.

phirman, phirmaund, var. FIRMAN.

phiscall, obs. f. FISCAL.

phisick, phisician, -itian, etc., obs. ff. PHYSIC, PHYSICIAN.

phisionomy, phisnomy, etc., obs. ff. PHYSIOGNOMY.

phit (fɪt). An imitation of various sounds, esp. that made by a rifle-bullet.

1894 *Outing* (U.S.) XXIV. 420/1 He [a bear] gave a soft 'phit!' of startled recognition, pricked up his ears and turned his head askew. **1896** *Daily Chron.* 25 Aug. 3/5 The pert crack of the Lee-Metford, the 'phit' of whose bullet is lost in the whirr of a lead-coated stone from the Matabele arsenal. **1898** DOYLE *Trag. Korosko* iv. 80 The air was full of the phit-phit-phit of the bullets.

phiton, -es, etc., obs. ff. PYTHON, -ESS, etc.

phiz (fɪz). *humorous colloq.* Also 7 **phis**, 7–8 **phyz, phys**, 8 **phizz**, (fiz). [Colloq. abbreviation of *phiznomy*, PHYSIOGNOMY.]

Face, countenance; expression or aspect of face.

1688 SHADWELL *Sqr. Alsatia* V. i, In deed your magnanimous Phyz is somewhat disfigur'd by it, captain. **1691** *New Discov. Old Intreague* xxvii, Next Cousin Will,.. With Aukward Phys. **1693** CONGREVE *Old Bach.* IV. viii, What a furious phiz I have! **1762** CHURCHILL *Ghost* IV, Savour'd in talk, in dress, and phyz, More of another World than this. **1774** GOUV. MORRIS in Sparks *Life & Writ.* (1832) I. 21 Grave phizes are grinned out of countenance. **1868** W. S. GILBERT *Bab Ballads, Only Dancing Girl*, And her painted, tainted Phiz.

b. *Comb.*, as ***phiz-maker***, one who makes 'faces' or grimaces.

1742 J. YARROW *Love at first Sight* Prol., Mass John the Phiz-Maker with zealous Cant.

phiz, phizz, obs. ff. FIZZ.

phizgig ('fɪzgɪg). *Austral. slang.* Also **phizzgig.** = FIZGIG 6. Hence as *v. intr.*, to act as an informer.

1941 in BAKER *Dict. Austral. Slang.* **1955** V. KELLY *Shadow* i. 10 The boys suspect he's been phizgigging. *Ibid.* iv. 45 Prior passed the word along to phizgigs that the police would appreciate information about the identity of the counterfeiters. **1973** *Nation Rev.* (Melbourne) III. No. 49. 2/2 Lenny..was described in his biog as a former 'phizzgig' (police informer).

phizitian, phizononomye, obs. ff. PHYSICIAN, PHYSIOGNOMY.

phizog ('fɪzɒg). *joc. colloq.* Also **fizzog, phisog, physog, phyzog.** [f. as PHIZ.] = PHIZ. Cf. PHYSIOG.

1811 *F. Grose's Lexicon Balatronicum, Physog*, the face. A vulgar abbreviation of physiognomy. **1829** P. EGAN *Boxiana* 2nd Ser. II. 706 A certain melancholy cast was taking possession of Tom's *phisog*. **1846** *Swell's Night Guide* 127/2 *Phizog*, the face. **1850** C. KINGSLEY *Alton Locke* II. iii. 37 He had received an anonymous letter, 'a'thegither o' a Belgravian cast o' phizog,' containing a bank-note for twenty pounds. **1912** W. OWEN *Let.* 12 Jan. (1967) 110 Unable to get out and see anything better in the way of physogs. **1922** JOYCE *Ulysses* 297, I saw his physog do a peep in and then slidder off again. **1939** *Airman's Gaz.* Dec., One observer 'snapped' Adolph's phisog. **1946** B. MARSHALL *George Brown's Schooldays* iv. 16 The prefect shuts the door in their physogs. **1959** I. & P. OPIE *Lore & Lang. Schoolch.* x. 194 'Shut yer face'—'fizzog'—'flycatcher'—or, 'gate'. **1980** *Radio Times* 5–11 Jan. 15/1 The phizog is definitely familiar... 'I get recognised wherever I go,' he says.

phleam, obs. form of FLEAM *sb.*[1]

phleb-, before a consonant PHLEBO-, combining form of Gr. φλέψ, φλεβ- vein, an element in terms of physiology, pathology, etc.

‖**phlebectasia** (flɛbɛk'teɪsɪə), ‖**phlebectasis** (flɪ'bɛktəsɪs), **phlebectasy** (flɪ'bɛktəsɪ) [Gr. ἔκτασις extension], abnormal dilatation of a vein, varix. **phlebectopy** (flɪ'bɛktəpɪ) [Gr. ἐκ out of, τόπος place], displacement or abnormal situation of a vein.

1842 DUNGLISON *Med. Lex.*, **Phlebectasia*, dilatation of a vein, or portion of a vein. **1849–52** TODD *Cycl. Anat.* IV. 1397/2 *Phlebectesis may conveniently be divided into several forms. **1858** MAYNE *Expos. Lex.* 938/2 *Phlebectasy .. *Phlebectopy.

phlebenterate (flɪ'bɛntərət), *a.* (*sb.*) *Zool.* [ad. mod.L. *Phlebenterāta*, f. Gr. φλέψ, φλεβ- vein + ἔντερον intestine: see -ATE[2] 2.] Belonging to the *Phlebenterata*, a former division of gastropod molluscs, characterized by processes of the alimentary canal extending into processes of the body-wall. **b.** *sb.* One of the *Phlebenterata*. So **phlebenteric** (flɛbɛn'tɛrɪk) *a.*, characterized by such processes as those of the *Phlebenterata*; **phlebenterism** (flɪ'bɛntərɪz(ə)m), the condition of having processes of the alimentary canal extending into processes of the body-wall, as in the *Phlebenterata*, or into the legs, mandibles, etc., as in the *Pycnogonidæ*; the opinion that such processes have a circulatory function.

1857 E. C. OTTÉ tr. *Quatrefages' Rambles Nat.* I. 351 Phlebenterism was declared to be entirely exploded, and characterised as a mere chimera.

‖**phlebitis** (flɪ'baɪtɪs). *Path.* [mod.L., f. Gr. φλεψ, φλεβ- vein: see -ITIS.] Inflammation of the walls of a vein.

1822–34 *Good's Study Med.* (ed. 4) II. 11 The inflammation of veins, by some writers called Phlebitis, has of late occupied more attention. **1878** T. BRYANT *Pract. Surg.* I. 425 Phlebitis is the chief evil to be feared from an injury to a vein.

Hence **phlebitic** (flɪ'bɪtɪk) *a.*, pertaining to or affected with phlebitis.

1899 *Allbutt's Syst. Med.* VI. 170 Paget..contended for the primarily phlebitic nature of thrombosis in gout.

phlebo-, combining element: see PHLEB-.

phlebolite ('flɛbəlaɪt), **'phlebolith** (-lɪθ) [Gr. λίθος stone: see -LITE], a morbid calcareous concretion in a vein, a vein-stone; hence **phlebolitic** (-'lɪtɪk), **-lithic** (-'lɪθɪk) *a.*, of the nature of, or pertaining to, a phlebolite. **phlebology** (flɪ'bɒlədʒɪ) [-LOGY], that part of physiology or anatomy which treats of the veins; hence **phlebo'logical** *a.*, pertaining to phlebology. ‖**phlebometritis** (ˌflɛbəʊmɪ'traɪtɪs) [Gr. μήτρα womb: see -ITIS], inflammation of the veins of the womb (Mayne *Expos. Lex.* 1858). ‖**phleborrhagia** (flɛbəʊ'reɪdʒɪə), **phleborrhage** ('flɛbərədʒ) [Gr. -ραγία, from ῥήγνυναι to burst; cf. *hæmorrhage*], hæmorrhage from rupture of a vein. ‖**phleborrhexis** (flɛbəʊ'rɛksɪs) [Gr. ῥῆξις bursting], rupture of a vein (Dunglison *Med. Lex.* 1842). ‖**phlebosclerosis** (ˌflɛbəʊsklɪ'rəʊsɪs) [Gr. σκλήρωσις induration, f. σκληρός hard], morbid thickening and hardening of the wall of a vein; hence **phlebosclerotic** (-'ɒtɪk) *a.*, pertaining to phlebosclerosis. ‖**phlebostenosis** (ˌflɛbəʊstɪ'nəʊsɪs) [Gr. στένωσις contraction], abnormal contraction of a vein or veins (Dunglison 1853). ‖**phlebothrom'bosis**, thrombosis in a vein. in mod. use a venous thrombosis in which inflammation of the vein is absent or of only secondary significance. Also PHLEBOTOMY, etc.

1842 DUNGLISON *Med. Lex.*, **Phlebolite*, a loose concretion, varying in size from a currant to that of a pea, occasionally found in the veins. **1874** VAN BUREN *Dis. Genit. Org.* 217 Certain concretions found in the dilated veins.. and known as phlebolites. **1847–9** TODD *Cycl. Anat.* IV. 89/2 *Phleboliths originate in clots in the interior of the vessels. **1858** MAYNE *Expos. Lex.* 939/2 *Phlebolithic, *Phlebolitic. **1893** *Syd. Soc. Lex.*, **Phlebological*, belonging to Phlebology. **1842** DUNGLISON *Med. Lex.*, **Phlebology*, the part of anatomy which treats of the veins. **1693** tr. *Blancard's Phys. Dict.* (ed. 2), **Phleborragia*, the breaking of a Vein. **1842** DUNGLISON *Med. Lex.*, *Phleborrhagia*. **1899** *Allbutt's Syst. Med.* VI. 331 The sclerotic process may affect the veins also—**phlebo-sclerosis*. *Ibid.* 220 *Phlebo-sclerotic thrombosis. **1893** *Syd. Soc. Lex.*, **Phlebothrombosis*, venous thrombosis. **1939** A. OCHSNER in *Surgery* VI. 129 In considering intravascular clotting, it is important to distinguish between those lesions which are associated with an inflammatory process in the vessel wall, a true thrombophlebitis, and those in which there is intravascular clotting without the associated inflammatory lesion which can be termed a '*phlebothrombosis'. **1956** P. MARTIN et al. *Peripheral Vascular Disorders* xv. 628 Phlebothrombosis occurs frequently in both legs yet one side only may progress to thrombophlebitis. **1974** PASSMORE & ROBSON *Compan. Med. Stud.* III. xvii. 33/1 There are two types of venous thrombosis depending upon whether the wall of the vein is inflamed (thrombophlebitis) or not inflamed (phlebothrombosis).

phlebogram ('flɛbəgræm). [f. PHLEBO- + -GRAM] **1.** A diagram (sphygmogram) of the pulsations of a vein (*Syd. Soc. Lex.* 1893). Now *rare.*

1885 W. STIRLING tr. *Landois's Text-bk. Human Physiol.* I. II. 194 In order to interpret the various events of the phlebogram it is most important to record simultaneously the events that take place in the heart. **1923** W. D. REID *Heart in Mod. Pract.* iii. 59 The nodal extrasystole is not common. It gives rise to an exaggerated wave in the phlebogram. **1964** HOCHSTEIN & RUBIN *Physical Diagnosis* xix. 266 The *c* wave, although inscribed on a phlebogram, is not seen by clinical inspection of the neck veins, either because it is an artifact of the phlebogram due to the adjacent carotid pulse, or because the *c* wave of the right atrial pressure pulse is too small in magnitude to be reflected visually in the jugular pulse.

2. *Med.* An X-ray photograph of a vein.

1933 *Lancet* 18 Nov. 1144/2 The speed of circulation is very different in the brain as compared with other parts of the head... We have ascertained this fact by studying the arteriograms and phlebograms of diverse cases. **1969** D. SUTTON *Textbk. Radiol.* xxxi. 602 (*caption*) Adrenal vein phlebogram showing small Conn's tumour in the adrenal. Other investigations including angiography and air insufflation had failed to show the lesion. **1977** *Lancet* 1 Jan. 49/2 Evidence for a 50% frequency of a minor degree of iliac-vein compression was based on phlebograms.

phlebography (flɪ'bɒgrəfɪ). [f. PHLEBO- + -GRAPHY]

1. A description of the veins.

1842 DUNGLISON *Med. Lex.*, *Phlebography*, description of the veins.

2. *Med.* The recording of the pulse in a vein. *rare.*

1915 DORLAND *Med. Dict.* (ed. 8) 731/2 *Phlebography*, the graphic recording of the venous pulse. **1966** R. B. REES in H. F. Conn et al. *Current Diagnosis* XII. 521/2 The Trendelenburg test, Perthes's test, phlebography and other tests of venous competence are sometimes useful in determining whether vein surgery is indicated.

3. *Med.* Radiography of a vein, carried out after the introduction into it of a contrast medium.

1937 L. J. FRIEDMAN *Text-bk. Diagnostic Roentgenol.* 612/2 (Index), Phlebography (see Angiography). **1946** E. V. ALLEN et al. *Peripheral Vascular Dis.* xxv. 619 Theoretically the amount and location of organic obstruction to the veins in the limb can be determined with great accuracy by means of indirect phlebography (intra-arterial injection). The technic of this procedure, however, is rather difficult and .. it is not advisable to attempt it during the acute stage of thrombophlebitis. The technic of direct phlebography is much simpler, but with this procedure only a portion of the venous tree can be visualized. **1972** *Lancet* 27 May 1134/2 A small-calf-vein thrombosis confirmed by phlebography.

So **'phlebograph**, an instrument (sphygmograph) for recording diagrammatically the pulsations of a vein; **phlebo'graphical** *a.*, pertaining to phlebography.

1902 *Brit. Med. Jrnl.* 21 June 1571 Dr. J. Mackenzie will demonstrate his Clinical Polygraph and Phlebograph. **1893** *Syd. Soc. Lex.*, *Phlebographical*, belonging to Phlebography.

phleboidal (flɪ'bɔɪdəl), *a.* [f. PHLEB- + -OID + -AL[1].] Resembling a vein or veins: see quot.

1876 *Encycl. Brit.* IV. 87/1 The tissue composed of these moniliform vessels has been denominated *phleboidal*.

†**phle'botomer.** *Obs. rare.* In 6 **-thomer.** [f. PHLEBOTOMY + -ER.] = PHLEBOTOMIST.

1564–78 BULLEYN *Dial. agst. Pest.* (1888) 26 Let vs.. take our Phlebothomer with us to let hym bloud.

phlebotomic (flɛbəʊ'tɒmɪk), *a. rare.* [ad. Gr. φλεβοτομικός (φλεβοτομική sb., the phlebotomic art), f. φλεβοτομία PHLEBOTOMY.] Of or pertaining to phlebotomy. So **phlebo'tomical** *a.*; hence **phlebo'tomically** *adv.*, in relation to phlebotomy.

1799 in *Spirit Pub. Jrnls.* III. 148 President of the phlebotomic college. **1858** MAYNE *Expos. Lex.* 940/2 Phlebotomical. **1869** E. C. RYE in *Student* II. 185 The 'mosquito' cannot be said to exist specifically, though phlebotomically it has an entity.

phlebotomist (flɪ'bɒtəmɪst). [f. PHLEBOTOMY (or its source), see -IST: cf. F. *phlébotomiste* (1732 in *Dict. Trévoux*).] Orig., one who practises phlebotomy; a surgeon who bleeds patients; a blood-letter. In mod. use, someone trained to take blood from a person for subsequent examination or transfusion.

1657 G. STARKEY *Helmont's Vind.* 256 A just reward for a butcherlike Phlebotomist. **1816** KIRBY & SP. *Entomol.* iii. (1818) I. 63 The cupping glasses of the phlebotomist. **1974** N. M. ABELSON *Topics in Blood Banking* vi. 124 The skill of the phlebotomist. **1976** I. CHANARIN et al. *Blood & its Dis.* ix. 78 Venous blood samples are required. These may be collected by either laboratory staff, medical staff, nursing staff or phlebotomists. **1977** *Age & Ageing* VI. 85 Blood was taken, usually by a phlebotomist, after the skin had been prepared.

phleˌbotomi'zation. [f. next + -ATION.] The action of phlebotomizing; blood-letting.

1597 A. M. tr. *Guillemeau's Fr. Chirurg.* 49/2 We may not, in Phlebotomizatione, be to timorouse and fearfull. **1837** SIR F. PALGRAVE *Merch. & Friar* v. (1844) 199 A general phlebotomization at stated and regular periods.

phlebotomize (flɪ'bɒtəmaɪz), *v.* Also 6 **-thomize.** [a. F. *phlébotomise-r* (16th c.), in med.L. *flebotomizāre* (Du Cange), f. *phlebotomus*, Gr. φλεβότομος: see next and -IZE.] **a.** *intr.* To practise phlebotomy; to let blood by opening a vein. **b.** *trans.* To bleed (a person, or a part of the body); also *transf.* and *fig.* **c.** *intr.* for *pass.* To undergo phlebotomy, to be bled (quot. 1652).

1596 NASHE *Saffron Walden* Ep. Ded., Wks. (Grosart) III. 12 Phlebothomize them, sting them, tutch them. **1597** A. M. tr. *Guillemeau's Fr. Chirurg.* 27 b/1 To phlebotomize aright, is oftentimes a difficulte matter. **1644** HOWELL *England's Tears* in *Dodona's Gr.* etc. 160 Body politiques, .. as well as the frayle bodies of men .. must have an evacuation for their corrupt humours, they must be phlebotomiz'd. **1652** BENLOWES *Theoph.* XI. xxiv. 196 Post for physick's skill Phlebotomize he must, and take the vomit pill. **1796** J. ANSTEY *Pleader's Guide* Poet. Wks. 192 *Bother.* You took some blood, Sir, from him. *Tench.* Plenty—Phlebotomiz'd him ounces twenty. **1873** BROWNING *Red Cott. Nt.-cap* III. 135 The while I blister and phlebotomize! **1876** R. F. BURTON *Gorilla L.* I. 131 At night the mosquitoes phlebotomized us.

Hence **phle'botomized** *ppl. a.*; **-izing** *vbl. sb.*

1597 A. M. tr. *Guillemeau's Fr. Chirurg.* 2 b/2 Phlebotomisinge or blood-lettinge. **1631** R. H. *Arraignm. Whole Creature* v. 36 Yea, they would..make Bread and Cates of the Blood of their Phlebotomized bullockes. **1835** ANSTER tr. *Faust* (1887) 292 For spirits sinking, spirits rising The one cure is phebotomising. **1865** *Pall Mall G.* 14 Aug. 11 These phlebotomizing days are now, however, long gone by.

phlebotomy (flɪ'bɒtəmɪ). Forms: 5 **fleobotomie, -ye, (flo-, flabotomye),** 5–6 **flebotomye,** (9 **-y),** 6 **fleubothomy(e, flebothomie, -y, phlebothomy, -tomye,** 6–7 **-tomie,** (7 **-thomie),** 6– **phlebotomy.** [a. OF. *flebothomie* (13th c. in Godef.), mod.F. *phlébotomie*, It. *flebotomia*, ad. L. *phlebotomia*, a. Gr. φλεβοτομία, the opening of a vein, f. φλεβότομος that opens a vein, f. φλεβο- PHLEBO- + -τομος -cutting, -cutter.]

1. The action or practice of cutting open a vein so as to let blood flow, as a medical or therapeutical operation; venesection, blood-letting, bleeding.

c **1400** *Lanfranc's Cirurg.* 83 A walkynge vlcus is heelid wiþ fleobotomie [*v.r.* flebotomye] & formacie. **1413** *Pilgr. Sowle* (Caxton) I. xxii. (1859) 24 The nature of thy maladye wyl aske sothely a flobotomye. **1542** BOORDE *Dyetary* xxiii. (1870) 287 Clense it with stufes or by fleubothomye. **1621** BURTON *Anat. Mel.* II. v. I. ii. (1651) 384 Phlebotomy is promiscuously used before and after Physick. **1780** JOHNSON *Let. to Mrs. Thrale* 24 Aug., Gentle purges, and slight phlebotomies, are not my favourites; they are pop-gun batteries, which lose time and effect nothing. **1877** KHORY *Princ. Medicine* 60 Marks of leech bites, and of phlebotomy.

2. *transf.* and *fig.* The drawing of blood in any way (*lit.* or *fig.*); *esp.* bloodshed (i.e. scourging, slaughter, etc.), or other violent or destructive means used for the cure of moral, social, or political disorder; 'bleeding' in purse or pocket.

1589 [? NASHE] *Almond for Parrat* 3 b, O it is a haire-brande whooresonne, and well seene in Phlebotomie. **1646** J. HALL *Horæ Vac.* 151 Warre is the Phlebotomy of the Body Politique. **1827** *Gentl. Mag.* XCVII. II. 539 Fiscal Phlebotomy was unknown, as a science, to our ancestors.

†**3.** An instrument for phlebotomy; a lancet. *Obs.* [Gr. φλεβότομον.]

1477 EARL RIVERS (Caxton) *Dictes* 33 Ypocras .. holding in his honde a flabotomye of munycion for latyng blood.

‖**Phlegethon** ('flɛgɪθɒn, 'flɛdʒ-). *Gr.* and *Lat. Myth.* Also 4 **Flegeton,** 6 **Phlegeton.** [a. Gr. Φλεγέθων, -οντ = lit. 'burning, blazing', hence as here.] Name of a fabled river of fire, one of the five rivers of Hades.

1390 GOWER *Conf.* II. 164 He wolde swere his commun oth, Be Lethen and be Flegeton. **1590** SPENSER *F.Q.* II. vi. 50 Nor damned ghoste In flaming Phlegeton does not so felly roste. **1701** tr. *Le Clerc's Prim. Fathers* (1702) 299 T'is certain, that the Pagans, who first used the word Phlegethon, denoted by it not a River of the Elysian Fields .. but of Hell and the Place of Torments. **1860** EMERSON *Cond. Life, Behaviour* Wks. (Bohn) II. 391 No phlegethon could be found that would burn him.

Hence **phlege'thontal, phlege'thontic** *adjs.*, of or pertaining to Phlegethon; burning, fiery.

1600 TOURNEUR *Transf. Metam.* Prol., To feele the smart of Phlegetontike sight. *a* **1649** DRUMM. OF HAWTH. *Poems* Wks. (1711) 34 Blaz'd with phlegethontal fires. **1651** BIGGS *New Disp.* ⁋ 121 Phlegetontal and direfull evils. **1821** BYRON *Juan* IV. liii, Cogniac! Sweet Naïad of the Phlegethontic rill!

phlegm (flɛm). Forms: see below. [ME. *fleem, fleume, fleme*, a. OF. *fleume, flemme* (13th c. in Littré), mod.F. *flegme* (dial. *fleume, flême, flume*) = Pr. *flegma, flemma*, Cat. *fleuma*, Sp. *flema*, It. *flemma*:—L. (post-cl.) *phlegma* clammy humour of the body, phlegm, a. Gr. φλέγ-μα inflammation, heat, morbid clammy humour (as the result of heat), f. φλέγ-ειν to burn, blaze. In 16–17th c. conformed in spelling to Gr.-L. original.]

A. Illustration of Forms.

α. 4–6 **fleume, flewme**; 4 **fleem**, 5–7 **fleme**, 6–7 **fleame, fleam**, 8 **fle'me**.

1387 TREVISA *Higden* (Rolls) II. 147 þey hadde moche fleem. **1390–1563** Fleume [see B. 1 a]. **1398** TREVISA *Barth. De P.R.* IV. ix. (Add. MS. 27944), Flewme is an humour kyndeliche colde & moiste. **1422** tr. *Secreta Secret., Priv. Priv.* 245 Agarik Purgyth fleme and malencoly. **1508** DUNBAR *Tua Mariit Wemen* 91 Ane bag full of flewme. *c* **1532** DU WES *Introd. Fr.* in *Palsgr.* 904 The fleame, *le flegme*. **1586** BRIGHT *Melanch.* ii. 4 The second is fleume, next to bloud in quantitie. **1645** MILTON *Colast.* 12 What if fleam and choler..come instead? **1650** HOWELL *Giraffi's Rev. Naples* 130 They answered prudently and with fleme. **1709** POPE *Ess. Crit.* 662 Our Critics..judge with fury, but they write with fle'me.

β. 6–7 **flegme, fleagm(e**, 7 **fleugme**, 7–8 **flegm**.

1547–64 BAULDWIN *Mor. Philos.* (Palfr.) 44 The rest of him flegme & cholier. **1587** GOLDING *De Mornay* x. (1592) 141 Agarick purgeth Fleagme. *a* **1618** RALEIGH *Sceptick* in *Rem.* (1651) 8 Abounding with Fleagm. **1621** SANDERSON *3rd Serm., 1 Kings* xxi. 29 §26 Abundance of melancholy, tough flegm. **1659** STANLEY *Hist. Philos.* III. II. 134 Hence are generated Choler and Flegme. **1726** LEONI *Alberti's Archit.* I. 24/2 The superfluous Flegm and Humidity.

γ. 6 **phleume, phleugme**; 6–7 **phlegme**, 7– **phlegm**; 7–8 **phleam, phleme**.

1541 R. COPLAND *Galyen's Terapeut.* 2 G iv, To purge yᵉ humours coleryke or melancolyke, or els phleume. **1565–73** COOPER *Thesaurus* s.v. *Consisto, Cursus pituitae consistit*, the course of the phleugme is stayed. *a* **1592** GREENE *Mamillia* II. Wks. (Grosart) II. 223 The naturall constitution of women is Phlegme, and of men Choller. **1605** TIMME *Quersit.* I. vii. 29 A certaine watry elementary phleme. **1617** *Janua Ling.* 100 Phleame expelleth choler. **1660–** Phlegm [see B. 2]. **1669** WORLIDGE *Syst. Agric.* 5 Phlegme distilled from Salt of Tartar. **1684** EARL ROSCOM. *Ess. Transl. Verse* (1709) 301 Write with Fury, but correct with Phleam.

‖ δ. 6 **phlegma**, 7 **phlegma**.

1527 ANDREW *Brunswyke's Distyll. Waters* B vij, Onely the flegma of the grene herbes is dystylled. **1610** Phlegma [see B. 2]. **1657** *Physical Dict., Phlegma*.. is used for any distilled water which hath no spirit, as rose-water.

B. Signification.

1. The thick viscid fluid or semifluid substance secreted by the mucous membranes, esp. of the respiratory passages; mucus.

a. In old physiology, regarded as one of the four bodily 'humours', described as cold and moist, and supposed when predominant to cause constitutional indolence or apathy.

1387 [see A. α]. **1390** GOWER *Conf.* III. 99 The moiste fleume with his cold Hath in the lunges for his hold Ordeined him a propre stede. **1502** *Ord. Crysten Men* (W. de W. 1506) IV. xxvii. 318 An armony..of the foure humours, that is to knowe of yᵉ blode, of the colour, of the fleume, and of yᵉ malancoly. **1533** ELYOT *Cast. Helthe* I. i. (1541) 8 b, Natural fleume is a humour cold and moyst, whyte and swete, or without taste. **1563** *Mirr. Mag., Rivers* lxvi, They turned theyr blud to melancholick fleume. **1615** G. SANDYS *Trav.* I. 72 Fleame hath the predominancy in his complexion. **1731** ARBUTHNOT *Aliments* VI. vii. (1735) 188 Phlegm amongst the Ancients signified a cold viscous Humour, contrary to the Etymology of the Word. **1860** WHEWELL *Philos. Discov.* IV. vi. 35 The doctrine of the Four Humours (Blood, Phlegm, Yellow Bile and Black Bile).

b. In modern (or corresponding early) use; esp. when morbid or excessive, and discharged by cough, etc. Now chiefly in popular use, and no longer applied to the mucus of the nasal passages. So mod.F. *flegme* (dial. *fleume, flume*).

1486 *Bk. St. Albans* C vj b, And makyth flewme fall owte of the brayne. **1508** DUNBAR *Tua Mariit Wemen* 274 Ane hair hogeart, that hostit out flewme. **1549** *Compl. Scot.* vi. 67 Ysope, that is gude to purge congelit fleume. **1601** HOLLAND *Pliny* II. 277 Wormwood..dischargeth the brest of tough fleagme. **1732** ARBUTHNOT *Rules of Diet* in *Aliments* 267 To dissolve viscid Phlegm, and excite a Cough. **1843** R. J. GRAVES *Syst. Clin. Med.* xx. 229 The principal annoyance the patient suffers is in getting up the phlegm in the morning. **1877** ROBERTS *Handbk. Med.* (1894) 400 The discharge of various substances, technically termed expectoration or *sputum*, and popularly known as phlegm.

†**c.** With *a* and *pl.* A collection or mass of phlegm, or of any mucous secretion. *Obs.*

1561 HOLLYBUSH *Hom. Apoth.* 15 If thou wilt..purge the head and breste..of all slymye fleumes and fylth. **1584** COGAN *Haven Health* cxxxiv. (1636) 136 [It] doth take away Flewmes of the Eyes. **1688** MIEGE *Fr. Dict.* s.v. *Bring*, To bring up a phlegm, *cracher*. **1727** *Philip Quarll* (1816) 16 A phlegm sticking in my throat, I happened to hem pretty loud.

†**d.** In figurative use. *Obs.*

1565 JEWEL *Def. Apol.* (1611) 153 In danger to be choaked with the flegme & humour of his sins. **1633** G. HERBERT *Temple, Church-porch* xvi, O England! full of sinne, but most of sloth; Spit out thy flegme, and fill thy brest with glorie. **1655** H. VAUGHAN *Silex Scint.* II. *Proffer* viii, Spit out their phlegm, And fill thy brest with home.

e. See SAUCEFLEME.

†**2.** *Old Chem.* One of the five 'principles' of bodies, also called *water*; any watery inodorous tasteless substance obtained by distillation. *Obs.*

1471 RIPLEY *Comp. Alch.* III. iv. in Ashm. *Theat. Chem. Brit.* (1652) 140 Fyrst wyth moyst Fyre and after wyth the dry: The flewme by Pacyence owt drawyng. **1610** B. JONSON *Alch.* II. v, Rectifie your menstrue, from the phlegma. **1660** SHARROCK *Vegetables* 130 Seeds steeped..in Spirit of Urine mixt with phlegm of Elder-berries. **1686** HARRIS tr. *Lemery's Chym.* 5 Water which is called Phlegm..comes in distillation before the Spirits when they are fixt, or after them when they are volatile. **1707** *Curios. in Husb. & Gard.* 335 Three Principles of which all things are form'd; that is to say, the Flegm, the Grease and the Ashes. The Flegm is the Mercury. **1718** QUINCY *Compl. Disp.* 9 Phlegm or Water, is the common Vehicle or Diluter of all solid Bodies. **1791** HAMILTON *Berthollet's Dyeing* I. I. I. v. 78 The gall-nut yields, by distillation, a limpid phlegm. **1812** SIR H. DAVY *Chem. Philos.* 51 The attempts made to analyse vegetable substances previous to 1720 merely produced their resolution into the supposed elements of the chemists of those days—viz. salts, earths, phlegm and sulphur.

3. The character supposed to result from predominance of phlegm (sense 1 a) in the bodily constitution; phlegmatic temperament or disposition; want of excitability or enthusiasm; coldness, dullness, sluggishness, apathy; coolness, calmness, self-possession, evenness of temper.

1578 T. N. tr. *Conq. W. India* 198 There are few nations of so much fleame or sufferance [as the Mexicans]. **1642** HOWELL *For. Trav.* (Arb.) 52 He that hath to deale with that Nation, must have good store of Phlegme and patience. **1668** TEMPLE *Let. to Ld. Arlington* Wks. 1731 II. 50 Monsieur de Wit defended their Cause..with great Phlegm, but great Steddiness. **1765** T. HUTCHINSON *Hist. Mass.* I. 223 A man of more phlegm, and not so sensibly touched. **1836** SIR W. HAMILTON *Discuss.* (1852) 281 The mathematical genius requires much phlegm, moderation, attention and circumspection. **1871** G. MEREDITH *H. Richmond* xvi, The patience of the people was creditable to their phlegm.

phlegmagogue ('flɛgməgɒg). [a. F. *phlegmagogue*, OF. *fleumagogue* (14th c. in Hatz.-Darm.), ad. med.L. *phlegmagōgus*, a. Gr. φλεγμαγωγός, f. φλέγμα PHLEGM + ἀγωγός drawing forth.] A medicine for expelling phlegm. Now *rare*.

[**1657** *Physical Dict., Phlegmagogon*, purgers of flegm.] **1671** SALMON *Syn. Med.* III. li. 570 Electuary of Jallap..is a good Phlegmagogue. **1737** BRACKEN *Farriery Impr.* (1757) II. 248 Phlegmagogues or those [medicines] which draw off pitious Matter or Phlegm by Stool.

So **phlegmagogal** (-'gəʊgəl) *a.*, having the property of expelling phlegm; **phlegmagogic** (-'gɒdʒɪk), *a.* = prec.; *sb.* = *phlegmagogue*.

1657 TOMLINSON *Renou's Disp.* 115 Some are called Phlegmagogall which purge Phlegme. **1684** tr. *Bonet's Merc. Compit.* 144 Mercury..with..some phlegmagogick Extract.

‖**phlegmasia** (flɛg'meɪsɪə, -zɪə). *Path.* Pl. -æ. [mod.L., a. Gr. φλεγμασία (Hippocr.) inflammation. Cf. F. *phlegmasie*.] Inflammation, *esp.* inflammation accompanied by fever.

phlegmasia dolens, or ***phlegmasia alba dolens***, inflammation of the veins of the leg, with severe pain, swelling, hardness, and whiteness, occurring in women after childbirth; also called *milk-leg* or *white-leg*.

1706 PHILLIPS, *Phlegmasia*, an Inflammation. **1753** CHAMBERS *Cycl. Supp., Phlegmasia*, a word used by some of the medical writers for an inflammation. **1800** J. HULL (*title*) An Essay on Phlegmasia Dolens. **1859** SEMPLE *Diphtheria* 1 The mucous tissue..is also the seat of very different kinds of phlegmasiæ.

phlegmatic (flɛg'mætɪk), *a.* (*sb.*) Forms: see PHLEGM; also 4–6 **flum-**, 6–7 **flugm-**; 4–6 **-etyke, -ytyck(e, -ytek**. [ME. *fleumatike*, a. OF. *fleumatique* (12–13th c. in Hatz.-Darm.), ad. L. *phlegmatic-us*, a. Gr. φλεγματικός, f. φλέγμα, φλεγματ-: see PHLEGM.]

1. Of the nature of or abounding in phlegm.

a. (In sense pertaining to PHLEGM 1.) Of the nature of the 'humour' or secretion called phlegm; mucous. Of the human body, its organs, etc.: Having a predominance of phlegm in the constitution or 'temperament' (see also 2). Of diseases, etc.: Characterized or caused by excess of phlegm. Now *rare* or *Obs.*

1340 *Ayenb.* 157 þe dyevel..asayleþ stranglakest þane colrik mid ire and mid discord..þane fleumatike: mid glotonye and be sleaupe. **1398** TREVISA *Barth. De P.R.* IV. ix. (Tollem. MS.) A verry flewmatike man is in the body lustles, heuy and slow. *Ibid.* VII. lix. (Bodl. MS.), As þe brayne dischargeþ hym silfe of flewmatike humoures and of fumosite. *c* **1400** tr. *Secreta Secret., Gov. Lordsh.* 86 If it be yn tokenynge ffleumetyke. **1527** ANDREW *Brunswyke's Distyll. Waters* F ij, To spette and putte oute the flegmatyke matter. **1542** BOORDE *Dyetary* viii. (1870) 245 A flemytycke man may slepe .ix. houres or more. **1562** BULLEYN *Bulwark, Bk. Simples* 3 b, It is good in the meates of them whiche be Flugmatike. **1563** T. GALE *Antid.* II. 84 In phlegmaticke bodyes they maye forbeare their supper. **1741** BETTERTON *Eng. Stage* v. 63 Persons of a flegmatic Constitution are slow in turning of their Eyes. **1875** H. C. WOOD *Therap.* (1879) 22 The phlegmatic person is no more easily moved by medicinal than by other agencies.

†**b.** (In sense pertaining to PHLEGM 2.) Of the nature of the 'principle' called phlegm; watery and insipid. Of bodies in general: Abounding in 'phlegm'; and hence, producing phlegm (PHLEGM 1 a or b) when taken as food, etc. *Obs.*

1502 ARNOLDE *Chron.* (1811) 172 For as mych as all fisshes aftir water ben flewmatike therfore they be better rost than soden. **1533** ELYOT *Cast. Helthe* (1541) 2 b, Where colde with moysture preuayleth, that body is called Fleumatike, wherein water hath preeminence. **1567** MAPLET *Gr. Forest* 77 She [the Carp] is of very soft flesh and phlegmatike. **1669** WORLIDGE *Syst. Agric.* (1681) 5 Standing Waters..by reason of the constant waste of the Phlegmatique vapour that constantly rises from it. **1747** LANGRISH in *Phil. Trans.* (1748) XLIV. II. [4] The watery or phlegmatic Principle abounds so much as to be nearly 13/14 Parts of the whole Mass.

2. Having or showing the mental character or disposition formerly supposed to result from predominance of phlegm among the bodily 'humours'; not easily excited to feeling or action; lacking enthusiasm; cold, dull, sluggish, apathetic; cool, calm, self-possessed.

1574 HELLOWES *Gueuara's Fam. Ep.* 30 The Numantines of their naturall condition, were more flegmatike than cholerike. **1622** MASSINGER *Virg. Mart.* IV. i, Cold, phlegmatike bastard, th'art no brat of mine. **1756–82** J. WARTON *Ess. Pope* (ed. 4) I. v. 276 Raphael never received a more flegmatic Eulogy. **1825** WATERTON *Wand. S. Amer.* IV. i. (1879) 288 Cold and phlegmatic must he be who is not warmed into admiration by the surrounding scenery. **1888** F. HUME *Mme. Midas* I. iv, Selina resumed her knitting in a most phlegmatic manner.

†**B.** *sb.* A phlegmatic person. *Obs. rare.*

1541 R. COPLAND *Guydon's Quest. Chirurg.* M iij, The fleumatykes, & them that are wont to diseases of colde maladyes. **1629** MAXWELL tr. *Herodian* (1635) 120 He contemned Iulian, as an abject Fellow: and Niger as a dull Flegmaticke.

So †**phleg'matical** *a.* = *phlegmatic*; **phleg'matically**, †**phleg'maticly** *adv.*, in a phlegmatic manner; **phleg'maticness**, the quality of being phlegmatic.

1586 Q. ELIZ. in *Leycester Corresp.* (Camden) 243 What *flegmaticall reasons soever were made you. **1684** tr. *Bonet's Merc. Compit.* VI. 235 They that have a phlegmatical Ague. **1828–32** WEBSTER, **Phlegmatically*. **1838–9** HALLAM *Hist. Lit.* IV. iv. §76 The most phlegmatically impudent of the whole school. **1870** *Daily News* 5 Oct., The videttes phlegmatically continued their circling. **1673** *S' too him Bayes* 56 This is..so hal'd in, and so *phlegmatickly apply'd. **1727** WARBURTON *Prodigies* 80 All the rest [of the story] is phlegmaticky past over. **1659** FELTHAM *Low-Countries* 42 Being full of humours, that is her cradle, which luls and rocks her to a dull *phlegmatickness.

'**phlegmatism.** *rare*⁻¹. [f. as prec. + -ISM.] Phlegmatic character. So †'**phlegmatist** [-IST], a person of phlegmatic constitution.

1599 H. BUTTES *Dyets drie Dinner* D vij b, Pistake Nuts... In cold weather, for flegmatists. **1797** GODWIN *Enquirer* 436 The phlegmatism of..Sir Robert Walpole's..conduct.

'**phlegmatous,** *a.* *rare*⁻¹. [f. as prec. + -OUS.] 'Inflamed or much inflamed' (*Syd. Soc. Lex.*).

1878 A. M. HAMILTON *Nerv. Dis.* 133, I have already spoken of peripheral phlegmatous troubles.

phlegme, erron. form of FLEAM *sb.*¹, lancet.

1612 WOODALL *Surg. Mate* Wks. (1653) 11 Phlegmes..to launch and cut the gums. **1850** R. G. CUMMING *Hunter's Life S. Afr.* (1902) 99/1 Before starting I gave Johannus my phlegme, and a hasty lesson in the art of bleeding.

†**phlegmed** (flɛmd), *a.* *Obs. rare*⁻¹. [f. PHLEGM + -ED².] Imbued with 'phlegm' (sense 2).

1683 *Phil. Trans.* XIV. 503 This [oil of Vitriol] as highly phlegm'd..as any usually is.

phlegmless ('flɛmlɪs), *a.* *rare.* [f. as prec. + -LESS.] Devoid of or free from phlegm.

1663 BOYLE *Usef. Exp. Nat. Philos.* II. v. vii. 175 One distillation..will bring it over from Wine it self, so pure and flegmless, as to burn all away. **1768** J. ROSS *Ode on loss of Friend* Wks. 224 (MS.) Philomel, Whose shrill harmonious note So swells her phlegmless throat.

phlegmon ('flɛgmən). *Path.* Also 4–7 **fleg-**. [ME. *flegmon*, a. L. *phlegmon* or *phlegmona* (Plin.), a. Gr. φλεγμονή inflammation, a boil, deriv. of φλέγ-ειν to burn: cf. OF. *fleugmon* (13–14th c. in Hatz.-Darm.) = mod.F. *phlegmon*.] An inflammatory tumour, a boil or carbuncle; inflammation, esp. of the cellular tissue, tending to or producing suppuration; an acute local inflammation with marked redness and swelling.

1398 TREVISA *Barth. De P.R.* VII. lix. (Bodl. MS.), Suche swellinge hatte Apostema, & somtyme it comeþ..of a semple humoure as of blood and hatte flegmone. **1541** R. COPLAND *Galyen's Terapeutyke* 2 B ij b, Yf ecchymosis, or vicere, or erisipelas, or putryfaction, or phlegmone be in any parte. **1599** A. M. tr. *Gabelhouer's Bk. Physicke* 364/1 [A prescription] For the Flegmone or Felon of the Fingers. **1651** WITTIE *Primrose's Pop. Err.* II. 81 It may also be a phlegman, or erysipelas of some part. **1782** A. MONRO *Compar. Anat.* 14 These parts..may be subject to..phlegmon. **1788** J. C. SMYTH in *Med. Commun.* II. 191 The Phlegmon is the inflammation of the cellular membrane. **1899** *Allbutt's Syst. Med.* VI. 256 This bacillus is identical with one subsequently found..in gaseous phlegmons.

Hence **phlegmonic** (flɛg'mɒnɪk), '**phlegmonous** *adjs.*, pertaining to or of the nature of a phlegmon; **'phlegmonoid** *a.*, resembling a phlegmon.

1758 J. S. *Le Dran's Observ. Surg.* (1771) 170 A Man.. had a *Phlegmonick Erysipelas upon the Right Arm. **1875** H. WALTON *Dis. Eye* 185 In phlegmonic inflammation, pulsation has been felt, as from an aneurism. **1755** *Gentl. Mag.* XXV. 12 It appeared more like the erysipelatous than *phlegmonoide kind. **1835-6** TODD *Cycl. Anat.* I. 455/2 External inflammation resembling phlegmonoid erysipelas. **1666** G. HARVEY *Morb. Angl.* xi. (1672) 31 It's..generated ..out of the dregs and remainder of a *Phlegmonous or Oedematick tumour. **1849-52** TODD *Cycl. Anat.* IV. 850/2 Phlegmonous inflammation of the areolar tissue.

phlegmy ('flɛmɪ), *a.* Forms: see PHLEGM. [f. PHLEGM + -Y.]

1. Of the nature of or consisting of phlegm, mucous; containing or characterized by phlegm.

c **1550** LLOYD *Treas. Health* I j, The stoppynges of the leuer that comethe of grosse and fleymy humors. **1620** VENNER *Via Recta* iii. 57 It..breedeth a clammy, and fleamy nourishment. **1678** ANNE BRADSTREET *Poems* (1875) 16 The flegmy constitution I uphold. **1739** R. BULL tr. *Dedekindus' Grobianus* 209 Now from thy Lungs hawk up the phlegmy Load. **1891** *Daily News* 26 Dec. 5/5 A cold, accompanied by a phlegmy cough.

†**b.** Watery; moist: cf. PHLEGM 2. *Obs.*

1599 H. BUTTES *Diets Drie Dinner* P iv, [The mid-air] spits out watry reums amaine, As phleamy snow, and haile, and sheerer raine. **1683** TRYON *Way to Health* 83 The gross phlegmy part of Grass.

2. Of mental disposition: = PHLEGMATIC 2.

1607 MARKHAM *Caval.* I. 25 Such as out of their flemye womanishnesse seeke for such secrets. **1645** MILTON *Colast.* Wks. 1851 IV. 362 Rather then spend words with this fleamy clodd of an Antagonist. **1892** *Pall Mall G.* 29 Dec. 1/2 Mild as milk, they hobnob with the phlegmy Saxon.

phleme, variant of FLEAM *sb.*[1], lancet.

phlizz (flɪz). [Fanciful.] In Lewis Carroll's book *Sylvie and Bruno*, a fruit or flower that has no real substance; hence, allusively, anything without meaning or value, a mere name.

1889 'L. CARROLL' *Sylvie & Bruno* vi. 75 Bruno..picked a fruit... 'It hasn't got no taste at all!' he complained. 'It was a *Phlizz*,' Sylvie gravely replied. *Ibid.* xx. 294 They *will* be sorry when they find them [*sc.* flowers] gone!.. The nosegay was only a *Phlizz*. **1899** *Johnson Club Papers* 188 We crown the musicians with flowers that, like poor Bruno's in the fairy tale, are but a phlizz. **1926** GALSWORTHY *Silver Spoon* II. ix. 187 What was his image of her but a phlizz, but a fraud? *Ibid.* xii. 218 Was Foggartism a phlizz? **1931** —— *Maid in Waiting* iv. 20 The thing's a phlizz. Just a low type of Homo Sapiens.

phlobaphene ('flɒbəfiːn). *Chem.* Also -en. [a. F. *phlobaphène*, f. Gr. φλό-ος = φλοι-ός bark + βαφή dye + -ENE.] Name for a class of brown or red colouring matters, of complex composition, occurring in the bark of various trees and shrubs.

1880 WATTS *Dict. Chem.* VIII. 1568 *Phlobaphene*,..name ..applied to certain red bodies, formed, together with glucose, when many tannins are heated with dilute sulphuric acid. **1887** *Athenæum* 10 Dec. 787/2 It [tannin] is decomposed into glucose, gallic acid, and a substance analogous to phlobaphen. **1895** *Naturalist* 23 It [the hawthorn] yields a phlobaphene with acids.

phloem ('fləʊɛm). *Bot.* [a. G. *phloëm* (C. W. Nägeli *Beiträge zur wiss. Bot.* (1858) I. 9), f. Gr. φλόος = φλοιός bark + -ημα, passive suffix.] Collective name for the cells, fibres, and vessels forming the softer portion of the fibrovascular tissue, as distinct from the *xylem* or woody portion; the bast with its associated tissues. Also *attrib.*, as ***phloem-bundle***, ***-island***, ***-layer***, ***-sheath***, ***-strand***, etc.

1875 BENNETT & DYER tr. *Sachs' Bot.* 94 The different forms of tissue of a differentiated fibro-vascular bundle may be classified into two groups, which Nägeli calls the *Phloëm-* (Bast) and *Xylem-* (Wood) portion of the bundle... In many bundles the phloëm is formed on one, the xylem on the other side of the procambium. *Ibid.* 95 These horizontal elements ..may be generally designated as rays; within the xylem they are called xylem-rays, within the phloëm, phloëm-rays. **1876** *Encycl. Brit.* IV. 85/2 Found in the bast or phloëm layers of ordinary trees. **1882** VINES *Sachs' Bot.* 440 [In Ferns] A single layer or several layers of cells may often be found at the periphery of the phloëm lying just inside the true bundle-sheath. Russow regards this structure as belonging..to the ground tissue, and he terms it the phloëm-sheath. **1889** Phloem-island, -strand [see *interxylary* adj. s.v. INTER- 6]. **1891** *Ann. Bot.* V. 178 The phloëm-islands are produced centrifugally by the cambium. **1914** M. DRUMMOND tr. *Haberlandt's Physiol. Plant Anat.* xiv. 656 The various tissues that are comprised in the general category of secondary phloem are usually arranged in more or less distinct tangential layers. **1951** MCLEAN & IVIMEY-COOK *Textbk. Theoret. Bot.* I. xxi. 922 Phloem Islands..are formed by the enclosure of portions of the normal phloem by short arcs of secondary cambium. **1953** K. ESAU *Plant Anat.* xii. 265 The phloem is the principal food-conducting tissue of the vascular plants. **1969** [see *interxylary* adj. s.v. INTER- 6]. **1975** J. D. HAYNES *Botany* xx. 314 The vascular tissue is the transport tissue of the plant, and is composed of two major tissue types, the xylem and the phloem. **1978** J. UPDIKE *Coup* (1979) iii. 95 Some substratum in the phloem or xylem savored smartly of those little glossy red American candies.

phlogistian (fləʊ'dʒɪstɪən). [f. PHLOGISTON + -IAN.] A believer in the existence or theory of phlogiston.

1799 SIR H. DAVY in Beddoes *Contrib. Phys. & Med. Knowl.* 67 The phlogistians were obliged to consider all combustible bodies as combinations of different.. substances with the undemonstrated phlogiston.

phlogistic (fləʊ'dʒɪstɪk, -'gɪstɪk), *a.* (*sb.*) [In sense 1, mod. f. PHLOGISTON: cf. mod.L. *phlogisticus*, F. *phlogistique* (1762 in *Dict. Acad.*); in senses 2, 3, immediately f. Gr. φλογιστ-ός inflammable, inflamed + -IC.]

I. 1. *Chem.* Of the nature of or consisting of phlogiston; †containing phlogiston, combustible (*obs.*); connected with or relating to phlogiston.

1733 *Phil. Trans.* XXXVIII. 63 [In Phosphorus] The Phlogistic Part is so slightly connected with the other Principles, that the least..Friction or Warmth, sets it on fire. **1774** PRIESTLEY *Observ. Air* I. 188 Common air.. deprived of its fixed air by phlogistic processes. *Ibid.* 50 Plants imbibing the phlogistic matter with which it is overloaded. **1789** HIGGINS (*title*) Comparative View of the phlogistic and antiphlogistic Theories. **1794** G. ADAMS *Nat. & Exp. Philos.* II. xxi. 400 Bodies that are eminently luminous..contain a certain species of matter..this is called phlogistic inflammable or combustible matter. **1830** HERSCHEL *Stud. Nat. Phil.* III. iv. 300 The phlogistic doctrines of Beccher and Stahl.

†**b.** as *sb.* A phlogistic principle or substance.

1733 *Phil. Trans.* XXXVIII. 61 This red Earth retains so much of an unctious Phlogistic, that [etc.].

II. 2. *Path.* Inflammatory.

1754-6 *Connoisseur* No. 53 ¶9 Blotches and breakings out ..owing to a kind of a phlogistic humour in her blood. **1813** J. THOMSON *Lect. Inflam.* 71 Cases of acute or active inflammation preceded by what is called the phlogistic diathesis. **1854** JONES & SIEV. *Pathol. Anat.* (1875) 321 The phlogistic process in the pericardium.

†**3.** Burning, fiery, heated, inflamed (*lit.* and *fig.*). *Obs.* (Chiefly in rhetorical use.)

1791 E. DARWIN *Bot. Gard.* I. I. 136 Ethereal Powers! you ..Gem the bright Zodiac, stud the glowing pole, Or give the Sun's phlogistic orb to roll. **1802-3** tr. *Pallas' Trav.* (1812) I. 83 The phlogistic mountains of that neighbourhood. **1821** *Blackw. Mag.* X. 407 A sorry imitator of that whole-sale dealer in phlogistic curses. **1855** SMEDLEY, etc. *Occult Sc.* 59 Much phlogistic correspondence was discovered.

phlo'gisticate, *v. Chem. Obs.* exc. *Hist.* [f. prec. + -ATE[3]: cf. F. *phlogistiquer.*] *trans.* To render phlogistic; to combine with phlogiston. Chiefly in **phlo'gisticated** *ppl. a.* [F. *phlogistiqué.*]

†***phlogisticated air*** or ***gas***, names for nitrogen in the phlogistic theory. †***phlogisticated alkali***, name for prussiate (hydrocyanate) of potash.

1774 PRIESTLEY *Observ. Air* I. 178 *note*, It might not be amiss to call air that has been..made noxious by any of the processes above mentioned..by the common appellation of *phlogisticated air*. **1776** —— in *Phil. Trans.* LXVI. 242 The nitrous air..lost a great proportion of its power of diminishing, that is, phlogisticating, common air. **1789** *Ibid.* LXXIX. 146 It is also natural to suppose, that..the dephlogisticating principle..[being] expelled, the phlogisticating principle should enter. **1805** W. SAUNDERS *Min. Waters* 160 Almost intirely phlogisticated air, or, as it is now termed, azotic gas. **1846** GROVE *Contrib. Sc.* in *Corr. Phys. Forces* (1874) 325 Priestley..was led to believe that water was convertible into nitrogen (phlogisticated air).

So †**phlogisti'cation** [also in Fr. 1777], combination with phlogiston: the name in the phlogistic theory for the process now called *deoxidation*.

1774 PRIESTLEY *Observ. Air* (1775) I. 189 This air.. without any previous phlogistication, is purified by agitation in water. **1794** SULLIVAN *View Nat.* II. 86 The power of the loadstone..is increased by cooling, by a regeneration of iron, or phlogistication of its calx, and by the action of acids upon iron. **1801** WOLLASTON in *Phil. Trans.* XCI. 432 In the precipitation of copper by silver, [we see] an instance of de-oxidation (or phlogistication) by negative electricity.

phlogiston (fləʊ'dʒɪstən, -'gɪstən). *Chem.* [mod.L., a. Gr. φλογιστόν, neuter of φλογιστός burnt up, inflammable, vbl. adj. from φλογίζ-ειν to set on fire, f. φλόξ, φλογ- flame, ablaut deriv. of φλεγ-, root of φλέγ-ειν to burn.] A hypothetical substance or 'principle' formerly supposed to exist in combination in all combustible bodies, and to be disengaged in the process of combustion; the 'principle of inflammability'; the matter of fire, conceived as fixed in inflammable substances.

This use of the term and the theory connected with it were introduced by Stahl in 1702, in his ed. of Beccher's *Physica Subterranea* of 1669. The phrase '*esse φλογιστὸν*' had been used by Sennert (in 1619) in the sense of 'the being inflammable', inflammability or combustibility as a *quality* of some substances, but not regarded as a substance or principle. The existence of phlogiston was denied by Lavoisier in 1775, and though stoutly maintained by Priestley, the belief in it was generally abandoned by 1800.

[**1619** SENNERTUS *De Chym. Consensu ac Dissensu* 283 At Colores, Odores, Sapores, esse φλογιστὸν & similia alia, mineralibus, metallis, gemmis lapidibus, plantis, animalibus insunt. **1702** STAHL *Spec. Beccherianum* I. I. xvi. 19 in *B.'s Phys. Subterr.* (1732), Ad substantiam ipsam mixti, ut ingrediens..ut materiale principium, et pars totius compositi constitutiva, concurrit, materia et principium ignis, non ipse ignis: Ego Phlogiston appellare cœpi.]

[**1730** GODFREY in *Phil. Trans.* XXXVI. 288 By the Solution of crude Mercury united with the *Phlogiston Vini*, or other Vegetables.] **1733** A. G. HANCKEWITZ *ibid.* XXXVIII. 69 We produce the Phlogiston out of fat Substances, and from the Phlogiston a Fuligo, or Soot, and from the Fuligo an urinous Salt. **1750** *Elaboratory laid Open* Introd. 74 The sulphureous principle, or phlogiston, which is the proper essence of all oils. **1774** PRIESTLEY *Observ. Air* (1775) I. 65 Considering inflammable air as air united to or loaded with phlogiston. **1785** —— in *Phil. Trans.* LXXV. 280 Mr. Lavoisier is well known to maintain, that there is no such thing as what has been called phlogiston. **1794** G. ADAMS *Nat. & Exp. Philos.* I. ix. 360 Phlogiston..may be considered as a treasure..of light and heat, to be dispensed in the absence of the sun. **1794** J. HUTTON *Philos. Light*, etc. 12 There is truly in bodies a substance, which may be properly named phlogiston, as being the cause of that light and heat which accompany burning. **1800** PRIESTLEY (*title*) The Doctrine of Phlogiston established, and that of the Composition of Water refuted. **1822** IMISON *Sc. & Art* II. 98 The existence of phlogiston is no longer believed in. **1861** WILSON & GEIKIE *Mem. E. Forbes* iv. 117 Jameson [left college 1802] had heard the last dying echoes of the battle between the partisans of the phlogiston and the antiphlogiston camp.

†**b.** *fig.* Energy, 'fire'. *Obs.*

1792 A. YOUNG *Trav. France* 171 Moni. Faujas pleases me much; the liveliness, vivacity, phlogiston of his character, do not run into pertness, foppery, or affectation.

phlogogenetic (,flɒgəʊdʒɪ'nɛtɪk), *a. Path.* [f. Gr. φλογο-, comb. f. φλόξ flame + -GENETIC.] Producing inflammation. Also **phlogogenic** (-'dʒɛnɪk), **phlo'gogenous** *adjs.* in same sense.

1893 *Syd. Soc. Lex.*, *Phlogogenic*..*Phlogogenous*. **1896** *Allbutt's Syst. Med.* I. 156 There are several species [of bacteria] which are phlogogenetic. **1904** *Brit. Med. Jrnl.* 3 Dec. 1508 Certain species of bacteria..possess in their cell bodies a phlogogenic poison.

phlogopite ('flɒgəpaɪt). *Min.* [Named 1841 (in Ger. *Phlogopit*), f. Gr. φλογωπός fiery (f. φλογ- flame + ὤψ, ὠπ- face, look) + -ITE[1].] A magnesia mica, found in crystalline limestone and serpentine, usually of a brownish-yellow or brownish-red colour, with pearly, often submetallic (coppery) lustre.

1850 DANA *Min.* (ed. 3) 359 It agrees in atomic proportions with the phlogopite. **1879** RUTLEY *Stud. Rocks* x. 135 Phlogopite crystallises in the same system, and has the same cleavage as muscovite.

‖**phlogosis** (fləʊ'gəʊsɪs). *Path.* Pl. **-es** (-iːz). [mod.L., a. Gr. φλόγωσις inflammation, f. φλόξ, φλογ- flame. In F. *phlogose.*] Inflammation.

1693 tr. *Blancard's Phys. Dict.* (ed. 2), *Phlogosis*, the same that *Phlegmone*. **1710** T. FULLER *Pharm. Extemp.* 284 Sometimes..the Mercury..causeth a great Phlogosis..in the Part. **1845** G. E. DAY tr. *Simon's Anim. Chem.* I. 299 A circumstance which..characterizes the phlogoses.

Hence **phlogosed** (-'əʊzd) *ppl. a.*, affected with phlogosis, inflamed; **phlogosin** (-'əʊsɪn) *Chem.*, name for a product of cultures of certain bacteria, which produces acute local inflammation; **phlogotic** (-'ɒtɪk) *a.*, of the nature of or tending to phlogosis, inflammatory.

1872 GROSS *Syst. Surg.* (ed. 5) II. 884 The..*phlogosed condition of the penis. **1896** *Allbutt's Syst. Med.* I. 521 Leber obtained *phlogosin from the staphylococcus aureus. **1822-34** *Good's Study Med.* (ed. 4) II. 41 A mark of high entonic health, or a *phlogotic diathesis. *Ibid.* 50 Like the push [the boil] is found in persons of an entonic or phlogotic habit.

†**phlome.** *Obs. rare.* [ad. Bot.L. *Phlomis*, a. L. *phlomis*, *phlomos* (Plin.), a. Gr. φλομίς, φλόμος mullein.] A plant of the genus *Phlomis* (N.O. *Labiatæ*), comprising herbs and shrubs with wrinkled leaves, often thick and woolly.

(*Phlomis fruticosa* is Jerusalem Sage; *P. Lychnites* is Lamp-wick.)

[**1706** see PHLOMIS.] **1715** PETIVER in *Phil. Trans.* XXIX. 243 These Leaves differ from the Broad Phlome in being thicker.

phlomis ('flɒmɪs). [mod. L. (J. P. de Tournefort *Institutiones Rei Herbariæ* (1700) I. 178), a. Gr. φλομίς a name used by Dioscorides.] A shrub or herb of the large genus so called, belonging to the family Labiatæ, and native to temperate parts of Asia and southern Europe, esp. *Phlomis fruticosa*, the Jerusalem sage, which has pale green leaves with white, hairy undersides, and whorls of deep yellow flowers.

1706 PHILLIPS, *Phlomis*, a kind of Flower, which some take for a Primrose. **1789** W. AITON *Hortus Kewensis* II. 307 Broad-leav'd shrubby Phlomis, or Jerusalem Sage. **1908** G. JEKYLL *Colour in Flower Garden* ix. 80 Further back among the flowers are..some grey bushes of Phlomis and a silvery leaved Willow. **1961** *Times* 25 Nov. 11/4 Phlomis, verbascums, and many more, can be brought into service for such [dry, sunny] positions. **1974** *Country Life* 21 Mar. 627/3, I particularly like the bold groups of golden foliage.. and woolly, silvery phlomis with the purple nut. **1976** *Daily Tel.* 9 Oct. 6/2 Here..I would grow the pink-flowered Italian phlomis, which has come into garden centres in recent seasons, as well as the old Jerusalem one,..which.. has yellow flowers, in addition to the silvery, woolly leaves characteristic of the group.

phloramine to **phloretin**: see PHLORO-.

phlorizin (flɒˈraɪzɪn, ˈflɒrɪzɪn). *Chem.* Also phlo(r)rhizin, phloˈridzin († -ine), † phloˈridzin(e. [a. G. *phloridzin* (L. de Koninck 1835, in *Ann. der Pharm.* XV. 76; *phlorrhizin* suggested there by the editor as the proper form of the word, f. Gr. φλό-ος, φλοι-ός bark + ῥίζα root + -IN.] A bitter substance ($C_{21}H_{24}O_{10}$), crystallizing in silky needles, obtained from the bark of the root of the apple, pear, plum, and cherry trees. Also formerly called † **phloˈridzite**. Hence **phlorizein** (flɒˈraɪziːɪn), a bitter reddish-brown uncrystallizable solid ($C_{21}H_{30}N_2O_{13}$), a combination of oxygen and ammonia with phlorizin.

1835 *Amer. Jrnl. Sci.* XXVIII. 383 (*heading*) Phloridzin, a new substance. **1838** T. THOMSON *Chem. Org. Bodies* 714 The bark of apple-tree root..yields about 3 per cent. of phloridzite. *Ibid.*, Phloridzite thus obtained, has a dull white colour, with a shade of yellow, and is crystallized in silky needles. **1840** *Penny Cycl.* XVIII. 98/2 Phlorizin is by various processes, described by M. Stass, converted into phlorizein, phloretin, and phloretic acid. **1867** BLOXAM *Chem.* 478 Phloridzine..is extracted from the bark of the apple, pear, plum, and cherry tree. **1873** WATTS *Fownes' Chem.* (ed. 11) 641 Phlorizin is a substance bearing a great likeness to salicin. **1895** *Naturalist* 26 There is no.. phlorizin (the glucoside of the apple tree) in any part of the organism. **1900** *Amer. Jrnl. Physiol.* IV. p. xi, If a well fed milch goat be made to fast two days and phlorhizin be administered three times daily during the two days, the milk flow stops entirely. **1927** M. BODANSKY *Introd. Physiol. Chem.* ix. 232 The experimental production of this condition [*sc.* renal diabetes] was accomplished in 1886 by von Mering upon injecting into animals phlorizin, a glucoside which is found in the root bark of the cherry, apple, pear and plum tree. **1947** E. BALDWIN *Dynamic Aspects Biochem.* vii. 199 Both phlorrhizin and iodoacetate are known to be powerful inhibitors of fermentation and glycolysis. **1968** PASSMORE & ROBSON *Compan. Med. Stud.* I. xi. 21/1 Phlorizin poisons the renal tubules. **1969** DATTA & OTTAWAY *Biochem.* (ed. 2) viii. 154 Active absorption of sugars can be inhibited specifically by low concentrations of phlorrhizin. **1970** A. L. LEHNINGER *Biochem.* xxii. 491 Such a net conversion of tricarboxylic cycle intermediates is also observed in animals treated with the toxic glycoside phloridzin. **1970** R. W. MCGILVERY *Biochem.* xvii. 399 Phlorhizin is a polyphenolic glycoside.

phlorizinized (flɒˈraɪzɪnaɪzd), *ppl. a.* Forms: see prec. [f. prec. + -IZE + -ED[1].] That has been given phlorizin. So **phloˈrizinize** *v. trans.*

1900 *Amer. Jrnl. Physiol.* IV. p. x, A well phlorhizinized muscle begins to go into rigor within five minutes after death. **1912** A. E. TAYLOR *Digestion & Metabolism* vi. 393 In the phloridzinized dog, it is assumed that no sugar is burned and that neither sugar nor nitrogen is stored. **1927** M. BODANSKY *Introd. Physiol. Chem.* ix. 220 Mandel and Lusk gave phlorizinized dogs lactic acid and recovered it as extra glucose in the urine. **1954** CANTAROW & SCHEPARTZ *Biochem.* xvii. 434 Under ordinary dietary conditions, the body stores of carbohydrate are never depleted to the point where fat and protein catabolism are significantly increased, as they are in the phlorizinized animal. **1965** DATTA & OTTAWAY *Biochem.* xi. 199 It was observed many years ago that when single amino acids were fed to diabetic or phlorrhizinized animals, some caused the excretion of extra glucose in the urine, others the excretion of extra ketone bodies.

Also **phloˌriziniˈzation**, the action of making, or state of being, phlorizinized.

1917 *Amer. Jrnl. Med. Sci.* CLIII. 330 Maximal phloridzin poisoning with feeding of nothing but fat, or the longest possible phloridzination on diet free from carbohydrate and high in fat, has failed to produce in dogs anything resembling diabetic lipemia. **1959** W. B. WHALLEY in J. W. Fairbairn *Pharmacol. Plant Phenolics* 30 The glucosuria in phlorizinisation is to be attributed to the rapid loss of glucose through the kidney.

phloro-, before a vowel **phlor-**, used in *Chem.*, to form names of substances connected with PHLORIZIN, as

phloramine (ˈflɒrəmaɪn) [AMINE], the amine ($C_6H_7NO_2 = C_6H_5O_2{\cdot}NH_2$) obtained in thin shining films by the action of ammonia on phloroglucin (Watts *Dict. Chem.* IV. 488). **phloretin** (ˈflɔərɪtɪn), a sweet crystalline substance ($C_{15}H_{14}O_5$) produced by the action of dilute acids on phlorizin; hence **phloretic** (flɒˈrɛtɪk) *a.*, applied to an *acid* ($C_9H_{10}O_3$) obtained from phloretin by the action of potash; also to ethers (*phloretic ethers*) in which an organic radical takes the place of 1 atom of hydrogen in phloretic acid (Watts *Dict. Chem.* IV. 491). Its salts are ˈ**phloretates**. **phloroglucinol** (flɒrəʊˈgluːsɪnɒl), † **phloroglucin**, † **phloroglucol**, [Gr. γλυκ-ύς sweet + -IN[1]: cf. GLUCOSE], a colourless or yellowish crystalline, intensely sweet substance ($C_6H_6O_3$), obtained from phloretin, and occurring widely distributed in plants; also a derivative of this, as *nitrophloroglucin*, etc.; hence **phloroˈglucic** *a.*, **phloroˈglucide**: see quots. **phlorol** (ˈflɒrɒl), a phenol, an oily substance ($C_8H_{10}O$) obtained from salts of phloretic acid, or from creosote. **phlorone** (ˈflɒrəʊn), a yellow crystalline substance ($C_8H_8O_2$), homologous with quinone, obtained by distillation of beech-wood and coal-tar.

1840 *Phloretic, *Phloretin [see PHLORIZIN]. **1866–77** WATTS *Dict. Chem.* IV. 489 Phloretic acid [is] produced, together with phloroglucin, by the action of caustic potash on phloretin. **1857** MILLER *Elem. Chem.* III. 511 Phloridzin, when boiled with weak acids, is decomposed into grape sugar, and a resinous matter termed *phloretin*. Phloretin crystallizes in microscopic almost insoluble plates. **1881** WATTS *Dict. Chem.* VIII. 1572 **Phloroglucic Anhydride*, or **Phloroglucide*, $C_{12}H_{10}O_5$..is obtained: 1. by the action of heat on phloroglucol. **1866–77** WATTS *Dict. Chem.* IV. 495 *Phloroglucin is sweeter than common sugar,..permanent in the air at ordinary temperatures. **1893** *Syd. Soc. Lex.*, *Phloroglucin*..is found widely distributed in nature, mainly in combination as the complex body phloroglucide, but partly also in the free state. **1881** WATTS *Dict. Chem.* VIII. 1570 **Phloroglucol*, $C_6H_6O_3$..*Phloroglucin*. **1895** *Naturalist* 24 A red-brown phlobaphene which fused with potass gives protocatechnic acid and phloroglucol. **1879** *Jrnl. Chem. Soc.* XXXVI. 633 By this synthesis, the aromatic nature of *phloroglucinol is definitely established. **1949** E. CHAIN in H. W. Florey et al. *Antibiotics* II. xix. 758 They also tested a large number of chemicals for their ability to stimulate the production of penicillin... Among the ineffective substances were sodium azide,..phloroglucinol, naphthol, [etc.]. **1963** [see FILICIC *a.*]. **1872** WATTS *Dict. Chem.* VI. 928 *Phlorol or phloryl alcohol.. is one of the constituents of beech-tar creosote. **1873** —— *Fownes' Chem.* (ed. 11) 798 Phlorol, an oily liquid obtained by the dry distillation of the barium salt of phloretic or oxethyl-benzoic acid. **1881** —— *Dict. Chem.* VIII. 1572 *Phlorol*... This phenol, first noticed as a constituent of beech-tar creosote. **1866–77** *Ibid.* IV. 496 **Phlorone*. $C_8H_8O_2$. **1872** *Ibid.* VI. 928 Phlorone crystallises in golden-yellow oblique rhombic prisms, which when heated give off a pungent odour.

phlox (flɒks). *Bot.* [a. L. *phlox* (Plin.), a. Gr. φλόξ a plant (prob. *Silene*), lit. flame. Taken into Bot. as a generic name by Dillenius.] A North American genus of herbaceous (rarely shrubby) plants (N.O. *Polemoniaceæ*), with clusters of salver-shaped flowers of various colours, usually showy: many cultivated forms are found in gardens.

[**1601** HOLLAND *Pliny* II. 92 The Panse, called in Latine Flammea, and in Greeke Phlox, I meane the wild kind onely.] **1706** PHILLIPS, *Phlox*,..a Flower of no Smell, but of a fine Flame-colour. **1788** REES *Chambers' Cycl.*, *Phlox*, lychnidea, or bastard lychnis, in Botany, a genus of the pentandria monogynia class. **1856** BRYANT *Maiden's Sorrow* iii, There, in the summer breezes, wave Crimson phlox and moccasin flower. **1866** BRANDE & COX *Dict. Sc.* etc. II. 887/1 The garden Phloxes being all productions of the florist, and of a most ornamental character. **1895** MRS. H. WARD *Bessie Costrell* i. 8 Phloxes and marigolds grew untidily about their doorways.

b. *attrib.*, as **phlox family**, **phloxworts** (Lindley), names for the Natural Order *Polemoniaceæ*; **phlox-worm**, the larva of an American moth, *Heliothis phlogophagus*, which feeds upon phloxes.

1846 LINDLEY *Veg. Kingd.* 635 Order ccxliii. Polemoniaceæ, Phloxworts. **1863** J. H. BALFOUR *Man. Bot.* §952 Polemoniaceæ, the Phlox family. **1898** WATTS-DUNTON *Aylwin* II. xiii, Among the geraniums, phlox-beds, and French marigolds.

phloxine (ˈflɒksiːn). *Chem.* Also **phloxin** (-ɪn). [f. Gr. φλόξ flame + -IN[1].] A red coal-tar dye-stuff resembling eosin.

1890 in *Cent. Dict.* **1899** CAGNEY tr. *Jaksch's Clin. Diagn.* vi. (ed. 4) 210 This observer recommends that the nutrient medium be stained with phloxin-red or benzo-purpurin. **1954** MARTIN & HYNES *Clin. Endocrinol.* (ed. 2) i. 10 A preliminary eosinophil count is made by the method of Randolph. [*Note*] By Randolph's method blood is diluted in a white cell pipette with a fluid composed of phloxine and methylene blue dissolved in equal parts of propylene glycol and water. The eosinophils are counted directly per c.mm. on a counting chamber. **1956** KIRK & OTHMER *Encycl. Chem. Technol.* XV. 141 The Phloxines are chlorinated derivatives of Eosine. *Ibid.*, The two Phloxines are used interchangeably as biological stains and have also been used in lake and pigment manufacture. **1967** KARCH & BUBER *Offset Processes* vii. 269 Phloxine or eosine lakes are brilliant reds with a 'bluish' or 'purplish' cast or undertones not fast to light.

phlyaˈrologist. *nonce-wd.* [f. Gr. φλύαρο-ς silly talk + -LOGY + -IST.] A talker of nonsense.

1867 *Athenæum* 12 Oct. 459/1, I would not meddle with such a phlyarologist.

‖**phlyctena, -æna** (flɪkˈtiːnə). *Path.* [mod.L., a. Gr. φλύκταινα a blister (Hippocr.), f. φλύειν, φλύζ-ειν to swell.] An inflammatory vesicle, pimple, or blister upon the cuticle or the eye-ball.

1693 tr. *Blancard's Phys. Dict.* (ed. 2), *Plyctæna*, a Pimple in the Skin; also a little Ulcer in the corneous Tunick of the Eye. **1813** J. THOMSON *Lect. Inflam.* 511 The cuticle often separates in some points from the skin, and the vesications termed phlyctenæ are formed. **1899** *Allbutt's Syst. Med.* VIII. 466 The vesication may be so..complete, as to rise from the skin like a pemphigus, bulla, or phlyctena.

Hence **phlycˈtenar**, **phlycˈtenous** (-æn-) *adjs.*, pertaining to or of the nature of a phlyctena; characterized by or affected with phlyctenæ; **phlycˈtenoid** (-æn-) *a.*, resembling a phlyctena; **phlycˌtenophˈthalmy**, phlyctenular ophthalmia (Mayne *Expos. Lex.* 1858); ‖**phlycˈtenula** (-æn-), pl. **-æ** [mod.L. dim. of *phlyctena*], also in anglicized form **phlycˈtenule**, a small phlyctena, esp. upon the conjunctiva or cornea of the eye; whence **phlycˈtenular** (-æn-) *a.*, pertaining to, of the nature of, or characterized by phlyctenules.

1842 DUNGLISON *Med. Lex.*, *Phlyctenoid. **1869** E. A. PARKES *Pract. Hygiene* (ed. 3) 107 An eruption.. phlyctenoid in character. **1822–34** *Good's Study Med.* (ed. 4) II. 342 He adds to the two varieties of red and white miliaria a third, which he distinguishes by the name of *phlyctenous. **1842** DUNGLISON *Med. Lex.*, **Phlyctænula*. **1869** G. LAWSON *Dis. Eye* (1874) 33 One or more small phlyctenulæ close upon the margin of the cornea. **1843** SIR T. WATSON *Princ. & Pract. Physic* xix. I. 309 For relieving strumous or *phlyctenular ophthalmia. **1899** *Allbutt's Syst. Med.* VIII. 746 Similar *phlyctenules appear on the mucous membrane of the mouth, tongue, and palate.

‖**phlyzacium** (flɪˈzeɪʃɪəm, -sɪəm). *Path.* Also -ion; pl. -ia. [mod.L., a. Gr. φλυζάκιον a little blister (Hippocr.), f. φλύζ-ειν to swell.] A red, usually large, pustule on a hard inflamed base and terminating in a dark scab; also = PHLYCTENA. Hence **phlyzacious** (-ˈeɪʃ(ɪ)əs) *a.*, pertaining to or of the nature of a phlyzacium.

1693 tr. *Blancard's Phys. Dict.* (ed. 2), *Phlysacium*, the same with *Phlyctæna*. **1818–20** E. THOMPSON tr. *Cullen's Nosol. Method.* (ed. 3) 330 An eruption of the inflamed pustules, termed phlyzacia. **1870** T. HOLMES *Surg.* (ed. 2) I. 704 The phlyzacious pustules induced by the external application of tartar emetic. **1893** *Syd. Soc. Lex.*, *Phlyzacion*,..was Willan's term for the largest of his four varieties of Pustules.

pho, phoh (fəʊ, fəʊh), *sb. int. rare.* [A variant of PHEW, PHOO *sb.*, representing the action of blowing away. See also FOH.] An exclamation expressing contemptuous rejection or making light of anything.

1601 MARSTON *Pasquil & Kath.* IV. 166 *Sir Ed.* Daughter, giue mee your hand. With your consent I giue you to this gentleman. *Came.* Marie, phoh! Will you match me to a foole? **1738** G. LILLO *Marina* II. ii. 32 Pho! those are our best customers. **1800** MRS. HERVEY *Mourtray Fam.* II. 56 Pho! pho! there is no fear of their knowing any thing of the matter. **1908** S. WEYMAN *Wild Geese* xx. 304 Pho! Take my word for it, he's no man to bear malice! **1942** BERREY & VAN DEN BARK *Amer. Thes. Slang* §151/11 *Nonsense!*; *it is ridiculous!..pho!*

† **phob**, obs. erron. f. FOB *sb.*[2], small pocket.

a **1687** COTTON *Poet. Wks.* (1765) 133 And brought his Gods away in 's Phob.

phobanthropy (fɒˈbænθrəpɪ). *nonce-wd.* [f. Gr. φόβ-ος fear + ἄνθρωπος man: cf. *philanthropy*.] Morbid dread of mankind.

1848 *Westm. Rev.* Oct. 164 The evil of Ireland..is her seven millions of a cottier population—and the phobanthrophy (to coin a word) of the other, not over-wise, noble lords.

phobe (fəʊb), *a. rare.* [The suffix -PHOBE used as a separate word.] Having a hatred or aversion (towards someone or something).

1915 *Times* 5 Apr. 5/6 The Italian people is not, and cannot be at this moment, either phil or phobe regarding any other people.

-phobe, a. Fr. *-phobe*, ad. L. *-phob-us*, a. Gr. -φόβος -fearing, -dreading, adj. ending, f. φόβος fear; as in ὑδροφόβ-ος, *hȳdrophob-us*, *hydrophobe*, lit. 'one who has a horror of water'. Also in modern words formed in Fr. or Eng. by analogy, as *Anglophobe*, *Russophobe*.

phobia (ˈfəʊbɪə). Also 9 phoby. [The prec. suffix used as a separate word.] Fear, horror, or aversion, esp. of a morbid character. In *Psychol.*, an abnormal and irrational fear or dread which is caused by a particular object or circumstance.

1786 *Columbian Mag.* Nov. 110/1, I shall begin, by defining Phobia in the present instance, to be a fear of an imaginary evil, or an undue fear of a real one. **1801** COLERIDGE in *Sir H. Davy's Rem.* (1858) 92, I..have a perfect phobia of inns and coffee-houses. **1875** W. CORY *Lett. & Jrnls.* (1897) 409 Against management by phobies, either Tory phobies or popular phobies. **1887, 1895** [see -PHOBIA]. **1897** tr. *T. Ribot's Psychol. of Emotions* II. ii. 215 We can easily see that many phobias come under this category. **1899** *Allbutt's Syst. Med.* VIII. 157 Specific means..to dissipate the 'phobias' or the obsessions. **1907** S. A. K. WILSON tr. *Meige & Feindel's Tics* iv. 88 Prominent among the mental anomalies of the subjects of tic are found different sorts of phobia. **1909** A. A. BRILL tr. *Freud's Sel. Papers on Hysteria* v. 123 Thus far the processes are the same in hysteria, in phobias and obsessions, but from now on their ways part. *Ibid.* 127 Thus..freed anxiety, the sexual origin of which can not be recalled, attaches itself to the common primary phobias of man. **1954** R. F. C. HULL tr. *Jung's Devel. of Personality* in *Coll. Wks.* XVII. iv. 74 The latter [*sc.* the mother] projected all her phobias onto the child. **1974** E. B. MCNEIL *Psychol. of being Human* ix. 232 Phobias are symptoms issuing from unacceptable basic urges that have been repressed from consciousness. When repression is effective, phobia symptoms need not exist. **1978** *New York* 3 Apr. 85/2 (Advt.), Swim-o-phobia? Cure it forever. Our private lessons by professional instructors will have you phobia-free and swimming in no time.

So ˈ**phobist** *nonce-wd.*, one who has a horror of or morbid aversion to anything.

1883 *Church Quarterly* XV. 394 Men, who refuse to give up their liberty at the dictation of 'phobists' of any denomination.

-phobia, a. L. *-phobia*, a. Gr. -φοβία, forming abst. sbs. from the adjs. in -φόβος (see -PHOBE) with sense 'dread, horror'; as in ὑδροφοβία, *hydrophobia* 'horror of water'. Also in modern words formed in Eng. by analogy, as *Anglophobia*, *Gallophobia*, *Germanophobia*, *Russophobia*, some of them imitating Fr. forms in *-phobie*. The following exemplify the uses to which *-phobia* has been put:

1547- [see HYDROPHOBIA]. **1803** Gallophobia [see GALLO-[1] *in comb.*]. **1803** ANNA SEWARD *Lett.* (1811) VI. 94 He is a very laconic personage, and has upon him the penphobia. **1824** SOUTHEY in *Life* (1849) I. 125 She laboured under a perpetual dustophobia; and a comical disease it was. **1843** *Blackw. Mag.* LIV. 245 That powerful..writer..depicts the same regiphobia as raging among the Parisian *Charlatanerie*. **1861** RAMSAY *Remin.* i. 41 The account given me by my correspondent of the Fife swinophobia is as follows. **1887** *Pall Mall G.* 17 Dec. 1/1 Confounding it with 'Germanophobia', 'Francophobia', or as many 'phobias' as you like! **1890** *Cent. Dict.*, *Phobophobia*, morbid dread of being alarmed. **1895** tr. *Max Nordau's Degeneration* 242 It was unnecessary for Magnan to give a special name to each sympton of degeneration, and to draw up in array.. the host of 'phobias' and 'manias'. *Agoraphobia* (fear of open space), *claustrophobia* (fear of enclosed space), *rupophobia* (fear of dirt) [etc.]. **1896** *Westm. Gaz.* 6 June 2/2 The cycling craze has produced the antagonistic disease of cyclophobia. **1902** *Ibid.* 21 Oct. 2/3 There were symptoms in the City attitude of a certain amount of L.C.C.-phobia [= dread of the London County Council].

Hence **-'phobic** forming *adjs.*, **-'phobiac**, **-phobist** forming *sbs.*

1900 *Daily News* 15 Aug. 3/1 The professional Anglophobiac. **1902** *Daily Chron.* 13 Oct. 5/5 Several Anglophobic deputies have announced their intention of appearing in their official scarves.

phobic ('fəʊbɪk), *a.* and *sb.* [f. PHOB(IA + -IC.] **A.** *adj.* Pertaining to, or characterized by a phobia. **B.** *sb.* A person suffering from a phobia.

1897 tr. *T. Ribot's Psychol. of Emotions* II. ii. 215 For 'phobic' subjects it is (at least potentially) a permanent state, ready to arise when suggested by some association. **1930** *Brit. Jrnl. Med. Psychol.* X. 46 (*heading*) A phobic case. *Ibid.* 66 Recall and reunion may simply give the phobic mechanism a chance to dominate the normal system. **1964** GOULD & KOLB *Dict. Social Sci.* 466/2 Hysteria, obsession-compulsion, and phobic reactions..tend to restrict the scope of the neurotic's behaviour. **1968** *N.Y. Rev. Bks.* 29 Feb. 32/4 She has small regard for the population of South Vietnam which she sees as an unpleasant amalgam of cynical self-seekers, stooges, and phobics (i.e., people who fear Communism). **1970** *Daily Tel.* (Colour Suppl.) 4 Sept. 11/4, I..learned that phobics all over the country were undergoing such unlikely cures as yoga, hypnosis, acupuncture and shock treatment. *Ibid.* 12/2 'Desensitisation' thus involves a simple-sounding cure: the phobic patient is taught right habits again. **1976** J. PAYNE *All in Mind* 47/1 A bird phobic would initially be talked to by therapist about phobia, then about birds, then (with a relaxing injection if necessary) pictures of birds would be introduced... It is a very gradual process by which the phobic is helped to overcome the object of irrational fear.

phobism ('fəʊbɪz(ə)m). *rare.* [f. as PHOBIA + -ISM.] A morbid fear of or aversion to anything.

1917, 1923 [see PHILISM].

phoby ('fəʊbɪ), colloq. shortening of HYDROPHOBIA 2 (*rare*).

1843 DICKENS *Mart. Chuz.* (1844) xvii. 223 A jug and ewer, that might have been mistaken for a milk-pot and slop-basin... 'They've certainly got a touch of the 'phoby, sir.'

‖**phoca** ('fəʊkə). *Zool.* Pl. **phocæ** ('fəʊsiː), **phocas**. [L. *phōca*, a. Gr. φώκη seal: so It., Sp. *foca*, F. *phoque*.] A seal (chiefly in transl. from Latin or Greek); any aquatic mammal of the *Phocidæ*, or seal and walrus family of *Carnivora*; in modern zoology, restricted to the genus typified by the Common Seal, *P. vitulina*.

[**1398** TREVISA *Barth. De P.R.* XIII. xxii. (Bodl. MS.), þe fissche þat hatte Foca & þe fissche þat hiȝt Delphinus.] **1599** NASHE *Lenten Stuffe* 57 Neptunes phocases that scard the horses of Hippolitus. **1678** DRYDEN *All for Love* I. i, Here monstrous phocæ panted on the shore. **1791** COWPER *Odyss.* IV. 493 The Phocæ also rising from the waves. **1800** *Med. Jrnl.* III. 389 M. Riegels intends successively to treat..on rats, the phocas, the mole, the frog and lizard. **1816** SCOTT *Antiq.* xxx, A *phoca* or seal lying asleep on the beach. —— *Ibid.* xxxv, xxxviii. **1822-34** *Good's Study Med.* (ed. 4) I. 429 The deepest tones are struck by animals that have the largest glottis, as the phoca, the ox, the *ardea stellaria*.

Hence **pho'cacean** *a.*, of or pertaining to the *Phocidæ* or seal family; *sb.* a member of this family; **pho'caceous** *a.*, of the nature of a seal; phocacean; **'phocal** *a.*, of or pertaining to a seal.

1842 BRANDE *Dict. Sc.* etc., *Phocaceans*,..the name of the family of carnivorous and amphibious Mammals of which the seal (Phoca) is the type. **1858** MAYNE *Expos. Lex.*, Phocaceous. **1860** GOSSE *Romance Nat. Hist.* 351 This is.. in favour of a mammalian, and of a phocal nature.

Phocæan (fəʊ'siːən), *sb.* and *a.* Also 7 **Phocean**. [f. Gr. Φώκαι-α, the place-name Phocæa, or L. *Phocaei* Phocæans + -AN.] **A.** *sb.* A native or inhabitant of the ancient city of Phocæa, the most northern of the Ionian cities on the west coast of Asia Minor.

1600 HOLLAND tr. *Livy's Romane Hist.* XXXVIII. 1007 The Phocæans had both their owne lands restored unto them.. , and also libertie to live under their auncient lawes. **1784** W. MITFORD *Hist. Greece* I. vii. 297 The Phocæans, hard pressed, obtained a truce for a day. **1797** *Encycl. Brit.* XIV. 613/1 The Phocaeans were expert mariners. **1899** R. MUNRO *Prehistoric Scotl.* i. 2 At a subsequent date (600 B.C.) the Phocæans founded Massilia. **1909** W. W. FOWLER *Social Life at Rome* i. 9 At a later time of deep depression Horace could fancifully suggest that the Romans should leave their ancient home like the Phocaeans of old. **1962** J. M. COOK *Greeks in Ionia & East* iv. 59 Phocaea lacked good arable land... But the Phocaeans had the benefit of a magnificent harbour.

B. *adj.* Of or relating to Phocæa or its inhabitants.

1614 A. GORGES tr. *Lucan's Pharsalia* v. 168 And to Massilians (Cæsars spoyle) They freely gave the Phocean soyle. **1797** *Encycl. Brit.* XIV. 613/2 The Massilienses, a Phocaean colony, interposed, and with much difficulty, assuaged the anger of the senate. **1929** CARY & WARMINGTON *Anc. Explorers* ii. 22 The last stage of the Phocaean track was marked by a colony at Maenace. **1957** E. HYAMS *Speaking Garden* 163 Italy and France could have had wine and vines from one or both of two sources: Phœnician.., or Greek, by way of the Phocaean colony in Marseilles. **1966** G. E. BEAN *Aegean Turkey* v. 119 The Phocaean adventurers arrived hoping to establish a city.

phocænine (fəʊ'siːnaɪn), *a.* *Zool.* [f. Zool. L. *Phōcæna* (a. Gr. φώκαινα porpoise, deriv. of φώκη seal) + -INE[1].] Of or pertaining to the *Phocænina*, a group of Cetacea containing the true porpoises; resembling a porpoise.

1890 in *Cent. Dict.*

phocenic (fəʊ'siːnɪk, -'sɛnɪk), *a.* *Chem.* [For **phocænic*, f. Zool. L. *Phōcæna* (see prec.) + -IC.] Applied to an acid obtained by Chevreul in 1817, from porpoise- or dolphin-oil, originally called DELPHINIC, and subsequently identified with VALERIC acid, $(CH_3)_2.C_2H_3.CO_2H$. So **'phocenate**, a salt of phocenic acid; **'phocenil**, **'phocenin**, glyceryl valerate, or trivalerin, $C_3H_5(C_5H_9O_2)_3$ = DELPHIN *sb.* 2.

1836-9 TODD *Cycl. Anat.* II. 234/2 When this oil is saponified, it yields..a peculiar volatile acid..termed phocenic acid. *Ibid.*, The phocenate of baryta forms efflorescent prismatic crystals. *Ibid.*, Phocenine is a peculiar fatty substance contained in the oil of certain species of porpoise. *c* **1865** LETHEBY in *Circ. Sc.* I. 99/1 Many of the animal oils..contain a volatile fat, which gives them their peculiar odour. In..whale and seal oils, this is called phocenine.

Phocian ('fəʊsɪən), *sb.* and *a.* Also 5 **Phocean**, 6 **Phocayan**. [f. Gr. Φωκί-ς the place-name Phocis, or L. *Phocii* Phocians + -AN.] **A.** *sb.* A native or inhabitant of the ancient region of Phocis in central Greece.

a **1490** J. SKELTON tr. *Diodorus Siculus' Bibliotheca Historica* (1956) I. I. 57 In Boecia the streme callyd Cifissus that cometh fro the Phoceans [*Note*] MS.: Thophoceans. **1567** A. GOLDING tr. *Ovid's Metamorphoses* XI. 141 Commes ronning thither all in haste and almost out of breth Anætor the Phocayan who was Pelyes herdman. **1612** SELDEN *Illustr. Drayton's Poly-olb*, x. 168 A colony of Phocians. **1774** GOLDSMITH *Grecian Hist.* II. ii. 55 The first cause of the rupture, (which was afterwards called the Sacred War) arose from the Phocians having ploughed up a piece of ground belonging to the temple of Apollo at Delphos. **1797** *Encycl. Brit.* XIV. 615/1 The Phocians afterwards formed themselves into a commonwealth. **1845** *Encycl. Metrop.* IX. 617/2 The Amphictyonic council..found themselves induced to impose on the Phocians a heavy fine for their impiety. **1951** J. B. BURY *Hist. Greece* (ed. 3) ix. 357 At the same time the Phocians entered into the alliance of Athens. **1967** H. W. PARKE *Oracles of Zeus* vii. 139 The Phocians had just occupied the Delphic sanctuary. **1968** V. EHRENBERG *From Solon to Socrates* 419 The Phocians heard the rustling of the leaves under the feet of the Persians before they could see them.

B. *adj.* Of or relating to Phocis or its inhabitants.

1614 A. GORGES tr. *Lucan's Pharsalia* v. 174 A garland greene of Laurell dight, With Phocian vaile of lawne pure white. **1774** GOLDSMITH *Grecian Hist.* II. ii. 72 Philip.. went on, according to his agreement with the Thebans, to put an end to the Phocian war. **1790** W. MITFORD *Hist. Greece* II. xiv. 160 Not only Delphi was again brought under Lacedæmonian influence, but the Phocian people were gained to the Lacedæmonian interest. **1845** *Encycl. Metrop.* IX. 618/2 Philomelus, the Phocian general, was succeeded by Onomarchus. **1911** *Encycl. Brit.* XXI. 448/2 The Dorian population of Delphi constantly strove to establish its independence and about 590 B.C. induced a coalition of Greek states to proclaim a 'Sacred War' and free the oracle from Phocian supervision. **1970** *Oxf. Classical Dict.* (ed. 2) 943/2 The *Second Sacred War* was precipitated by a Phocian seizure of Delphi.

phocic, phocin. *Chem.* = PHOCENIC, PHOCENIN.

1861 HULME tr. *Moquin-Tandon* II. III. 189 The oil of the porpoise..contains..much more phocine. **1866** ODLING *Anim. Chem.* 36 Diatomic Fatty Acid Series. $C_5H_{10}O_3$ Phocic. *Ibid.* 120 Phocine.

phocid ('fəʊsɪd). *Zool.* [f. Zool. L. *Phōcidæ*, f. *phōca*: adopted as the name of a genus by Linnæus in his *Systema Naturæ* (ed. 10, 1758) I. 37: see -ID[3].] Any member of the *Phocidæ* or seal family. Also as *adj.*, of or pertaining to the family Phocidæ. So **'phociform** *a.*, having the form or structure of a seal, phocoid; **'phocine** *a.*, pertaining to the sub-family *Phocinæ*, containing the seals proper; *sb.*, a member of this sub-family; **'phocoid** *a.*, allied in structure to the seals.

1846 WORCESTER, *Phocine* (citing *Penny Cycl.*). **1880** J. A. ALLEN *Hist. N. Amer. Pinnipeds* (U.S. Geol. Survey Misc. Publ. No. 12) 421 All the Phocids or Earless Seals known to systematic writers were referred to the common seal. *Ibid.* 470 Some supposed Phocine remains were described. *Ibid.* 740 It [*sc.* the hooded seal] is commonly described as the most courageous and combative of the Phocids. **1930** A. B. HOWELL *Aquatic Mammals* ii. 34 The otariids have descended from the bears and the phocids from the otters. *Ibid.* xi. 283 No great significance can be attached to details of the phocid tarsal bones. **1958** V. B. SCHEFFER *Seals, Sea Lions & Walruses* v. 87 Thirteen genera of phocids are recognized. **1970** *Sci. Jrnl.* Apr. 69/2 The so-called 'true' or phocid seals (which lack external ears and have small pectoral flippers) are not such rapid swimmers but can dive for longer times. **1976** H. L. GUNDERSON *Mammalogy* v. 122 The otariids and the phocids may have a common ancestor.

phocodont ('fəʊkədɒnt), *a.* (*sb.*) *Zool.* [f. Gr. φώκη seal + ὀδούς, ὀδοντ- tooth.] Of or pertaining to the *Phocodontia*, an extinct sub-order of *Cetacea*, furnishing connecting links with the *Phocidæ* or seals. **b.** *sb.* Any member of the *Phocodontia*. So **phoco'dontic** *a.* = PHOCODONT *a.*

phocomele ('fəʊkəʊmiːl). *Teratology*. [mod. f. Gr. φώκη seal + μέλος limb. So in Fr. (Littré).] A monster having limbs so short as to resemble or suggest the flappers of a seal.

1861 *N. Syd. Soc. Year-bk. Med.* 404.

Hence **phoco'melous** *a.*

1902 *Brit. Med. Jrnl.* 15 Mar. 672 Whether the Harpy owes its origin to the occurrence of a phocomelous fetus.

phocomelia (fəʊkəʊ'miːlɪə). *Med.* Also **phokomelia**. [mod.L., f. Gr. φώκ-η seal + -o + μέλ-ος a limb + -IA[1].] A congenital defect of the limbs (see quot. 1892).

1892 F. P. FOSTER *Med. Dict.* IV. 2567/2 *Phocomelia*, a monstrosity in which one or both of the hands or feet, or all four of those members, or rudimentary semblances of them, are attached to the trunk like flippers, with little or no intervening structures. **1932** H. CUMMINS in *Practitioners Libr. Med. & Surg.* I. i. 20 In phocomelia the extremity is abbreviated, through reduction or absence of the proximal and intermediate segments, the hands and feet approaching normal. **1947** *Arch. Path.* XLIV. 521 The majority of the homozygous Creeper embryos die on the fourth day... Those which survive have phokomelia. **1968** *Brit. Med. Bull.* XXIV. 207/1 The demonstration of an association between phocomelia and thalidomide. **1974** *Jrnl. Embryol. & Exper. Morphol.* XXXI. 732 Embryos showing almost the complete absence of humerus, radius, and ulna, described previously as phocomelia. **1978** *Sci. Amer.* Oct. 130/3 The drug thalidomide could cause phocomelia..in a fetus when it was taken by a pregnant woman.

Hence **phoco'melic** *a.*, exhibiting or characteristic of phocomelia; also *ellipt.* as *sb.*

1942 *Jrnl. Exper. Zool.* LXXXIX. 104 These transplants differentiated into 'phocomelic' limbs. **1947** *Arch. Path.* XLIV. 521 In eyes of homozygous Creeper embryos transplanted to the flanks of normal embryos colobomas develop similar to those of phokomelic embryos. **1959** *Jrnl. Exper. Zool.* CXLII. 635 The lethal period of phocomelics. **1962** *Lancet* 1 Dec. 1155/2 No firm rule should guide schooling for phocomelic children. **1978** *Time* 20 Feb. 69/3 Children who are born legless or armless, their limbs amputated by a tangled umbilical cord, are sometimes hard to tell from true phocomelics, or seal-children, with vestigial hands and feet attached directly to the torso.

‖**Phœbades** ('fiːbədiːz), *sb. pl.* [L. pl. of *Phœbas*, a. Gr. Φοιβάς, pl. -βαδες, priestess of Phœbus.] Priestesses of Phœbus or Apollo; persons possessed by a spirit of divination.

1585 FETHERSTONE tr. *Calvin on Acts* xvi. 16. 394 They said that those who wer possessed wer inspired with the spirit of Python, and peradventure they wer thervpon called Phoebades in honor of Apollo. **1613** CHAPMAN *Maske Inns Court, Description*, Attir'd like Virginean Priests, by whom the Sun is there ador'd; and therfore called the Phoebades.

Phœbe[1] ('fiːbɪ). [a. L. *Phœbe*, a. Gr. Φοίβη, fem. of φοῖβος bright, radiant: cf. PHŒBUS.] **1.** The name of Artemis or Diana as goddess of the moon; the moon personified. *poet.*

[**1390** GOWER *Conf.* II. 110 Thus this lusti Cephalus Preide unto Phebe and to Phebus The nyht in lengthe forto drawe.] **1590** SHAKS. *Mids. N.* I. i. 209 To morrow night, when Phœbe doth behold Her siluer visage, in the watry glasse. **1681** COTTON *Wond. Peak* 28 Nor yet does Phœbe with her silver horns..Push into crowded tides the frighted waves.

2. *attrib.* and *Comb.*, as **Phœbe lamp** *N. Amer. Hist.* (see quots. 1935 and 1970).

1935 *Colony of Connecticut* (Conn. Board Educ.) (Senate Doc. 53, 74th Congr., 1st Sess.) 15 Phoebe lamps:..These were similar to Betty lamps in shape... Some had double wicks from a nose on either side. **1970** G. PAYTON *Webster's Dict. Proper Names* 525/2 *Phoebe lamp*, American pioneers' name for a primitive tallow-and-wick lamp of the type used down the ages, e.g. by the Ancient Greeks. **1972** F. VAN W. MASON *Roads to Liberty* 182 Betty..lit a Phoebe lamp with a splinter from the fire.

phœbe[2] ('fiːbɪ). Also **phebe**. [A name imitative of the bird's call, but accommodated in spelling to prec.] A small North American flycatcher of the genus *Sayornis*, esp. *S. phœbe*, which is common in the eastern part of the continent. Also called PEWIT (3), PEWEE.

1700 J. GREEN *Jrnl.* 4 Mar. In *Essex Inst. Hist. Coll.* (1866) VIII. 216 Cloudy & rainy. heard a Phebe and other birds sing. **1782** 'J. H. ST. JOHN DE CRÈVECŒUR' *Lett. from Amer. Farmer* ii. 40 That [*sc.* a nest] of a swallow was affixed in the corner next to the house; that of a phebe in the other. **1839–40** W. IRVING *Wolfert's R.* (1855) 19 Another of our feathered visitors..is the Pe-wit, or Pe-wee, or Phœbe-bird; for he is called by each of these names, from a fancied resemblance to the sound of his monotonous note... They arrive early in the spring... Their first chirp spreads gladness through the house. 'The Phœbe-birds have come!' is heard on all sides. **1893** *Scribner's Mag.* June 765/2 Plain, dull-colored peewee or phœbe, sitting on the house-gable or on a dead branch..catching insects, or reiterating his own name, 'phœbe, phœbe'. **1947** E. B. WHITE *Lett.* (1976) 284, I haven't been doing much of anything—just..watching phoebes through binoculars, and mixing drinks. **1961** O. L. AUSTIN *Birds of World* (1962) 209/1 Another flycatcher that announces itself is the Phoebe, the pert olive-grey bird that plasters its mud and moss nest under bridges over country streams.

Phœbean (fiːˈbiːən), *a.* Also 7 -ian. [f. L. *Phœbēus*, a. Gr. Φοίβειος adj., f. Φοῖβος Phœbus + -AN.] Of, pertaining to, or characteristic of Phœbus or Apollo as the god of poetry.

a **1621** B. JONSON *Leges Convivales* Wks. (Rtldg.) 727/2 'Tis the true Phœbian liquor, Cheers the brains, makes wit the quicker. **1632** SHIRLEY *Changes* Prol., Able to distinguish straines that are Cleare, and Phebean, from the popular. **1873** SYMONDS *Grk. Poets* Ser. I. ii. (1877) 43 His long Phœbean locks.

Phœbus (ˈfiːbəs). Forms: 4–9 Phebus, 6– Phœbus. [a. L. *Phœbus*, a. Gr. Φοῖβος, lit. bright, shining, radiant.] A name of Apollo as the Sun-god; the sun personified. Chiefly *poet.*

c **1386** CHAUCER *Man of Law's Prol.* 11 By the shadwe he took his wit That Phebus which þat shoon so clere and brighte Degrees was fyue and fourty clombe on highte. **1423** JAS. I *Kingis Q.* lxxii, Till phebus endit had his bemes bryght. **1559** W. CUNNINGHAM *Cosmogr. Glasse* 54 Phebus with his golden beames. *a* **1649** DRUMM. OF HAWTH. *Poems* Wks. (1711) 15 Phœbus arise, And paint the sable skies With azure, white, and red. **1726** POPE *Odyss.* XVII. 30 With riper beams when Phœbus warms the day. **1742** GRAY *Death of West*, Redd'ning Phœbus lifts his golden fire.

b. Apollo as the god of poetry and music, presiding over the Muses: hence, the genius of poetry.

1776 G. CAMPBELL *Philos. Rhet.* (1801) II. 63 The figure which the French Phebus is capable of making in an English dress.

phœnicean (fɪˈnɪsɪən, -ˈɪʃɪən), *a.* [f. L. *phœnīceus* (Plin.) (a. Gr. φοινίκεος adj., f. φοῖνιξ purple-red, crimson: see PHŒNICIAN) + -AN.] = next.

1857 *Fraser's Mag.* LVI. 579 The wings are of a phoenicean colour, that is to say, reddish verging upon fulvous.

phœniceous (fiːˈnɪʃiːəs), *a.* Also phenicious. [f. as prec. + -OUS.] Applied to a bright red.

[**1398** TREVISA *Barth. De P.R.* XIX. xxv. (1495) 877 Colour that highte *Pheniceus*: therwyth the cheyf and pryncypall letters of bokes ben wryten.] **1866** *Treas. Bot.*, *Phœniceous*, pure lively red, with a mixture of carmine and scarlet.

Phœnician (fɪˈnɪʃ(ɪ)ən), *sb.* and *a.* Forms: 4 Feniceonne, Phenicien, 7– Phœnician, 9 Phenician. [a. F. *phénicien*, f. L. *Phœnīcia* (sc. *terra*), synon. with L. *Phœnīcē*, Gr. Φοινίκη the country, f. Φοῖνιξ, Φοινῖκ-, *sb.* and *a.* Phœnician: see -AN.

Gr. φοῖνιξ also meant 'purple-red or crimson' (*a.* and *sb.*), the PHŒNIX, and the date (fruit and tree). It is generally held that these are all senses of the same word; but their mutual relations and the primary sense are uncertain. Some start with Φοῖνιξ, Phœnician, as a foreign ethnic name; others take the primary sense as 'red', and see in φοινίκη 'the red land', perh. the land of the sunrise, or in Φοῖνιξ 'a red man'. *Phœnicia* could hardly be (as some have suggested) 'the land of the date'.]

A. *sb.* **1.** A native or inhabitant of Phœnicia, an ancient country consisting of a narrow strip of land on the coast of Syria, to the north-west of Palestine, which contained the two famous cities of Tyre and Sidon; also of any Phœnician colony (of which there were many on the shores of the Mediterranean).

1387 TREVISA *Higden* (Rolls) I. 129 For Pheniciens were þe firste fynderes of lettres, ȝit we writeþ capital lettres wiþ reed colour. **1432–50** tr. *Higden* ibid., Phenix the sonne of Agenoris toke to these Feniceonnes somme redde letters. **1606** SHAKS. *Ant. & Cl.* III. vii. 65 Let th' Egyptians And the Phœnicians go a ducking. **1667** MILTON *P.L.* I. 438 Astoreth, whom the Phœnicians call'd Astarte, Queen of Heav'n. **1727** DE FOE *Syst. Magic* I. ii. (1840) 40 Cadmus was a Phoenician, but went from his own country and settled in Greece, where, as they say, he built the city of Thebes, .. having brought 16 letters of the Greek alphabet among them. **1808** MITFORD *Hist. Greece* x. §1 Britain, .. excepting the Phenicians, unknown among civilized nations. **1843** THIRLWALL *Greece* liii, Many..costly and useful productions of India..were very early known in the west, chiefly..through the commercial activity of the Phœnicians.

2. The language spoken by this people.

1836 *Encycl. Brit.* (ed. 7) XIII. 83/1 The Phœnician is only known from a few coins and inscriptions found chiefly in Cyprus and Malta. **1836** N. WISEMAN *Twelve Lect. on Connexion betw. Sci. & Revealed Relig.* I. i. 53 Cadiz, or *Gadir*, as it was originally called, must no longer signify, as the word does graphically in Phenician, *the island* or *peninsula*. **1861** *Dublin Rev.* Feb. 400 Joseph Scaliger demonstrated that the well-known passage of the Pœnulus of Plautus was a fragment of genuine Phœnician. **1948** E. POUND *Pisan Cantos* (1949) lxxix. 76 'Prepare to go on a journey.' Or to count sheep in Phoenician. **1965** *Illustr. London News* 13 Feb. 22/3 Three thin rectangular sheets of gold leaf... One of them is inscribed in Phoenician, the other two in Etruscan.

B. *adj.* Of or pertaining to ancient Phœnicia, or its inhabitants or colonists; hence, Punic, Carthaginian.

1601 HOLLAND *Pliny* I. 100 All that sea yet, which beateth vpon that coast, beareth the name of the Phœnician sea. **1808** MITFORD *Hist. Greece* x. §1 The large projection of Africa, over-against Sicily, could not fail..to fix the attention of the Phœnician navigators. **1878** GLADSTONE *Homer* (*Primer*) vii. 96 It appears that the Phœnician name in Homer stands to a great extent for that of foreigner in general.

Hence **Phœˈnicianism**; also **Phœnicize** (phen-) *v.*, to make Phœnician in language, nationality, etc.

1878 GLADSTONE *Homer* (*Primer*) vii. 96 There is in Homer a very general and pervading association between a group of marks of which a portion are Phœnicianism [etc.]. **1846** GROTE *Greece* II. xviii. 453 Strabo describes these towns..as altogether phenicised.

phœnicine, *Chem.*, variant of PHENICINE.

phœnicistic (fiːnɪˈsɪstɪk), *a. Path.* [f. mod.L. *phœnicismus*, name given by Plouquet to Rubeola or measles (f. Gr. φοῖνιξ purple-red, crimson): see -ISM, -ISTIC.] Of or pertaining to measles.

1858 MAYNE *Expos. Lex.*, Phenicistic. **1893** *Syd. Soc. Lex.*, *Phoenicistic*.

phœnicity (fiːˈnɪsɪtɪ). [ad. med. Schol. L. *phœnīcitās* (in Wyclif *fēnīcitās*), f. *phœnix*, *phœnīc-em* PHŒNIX: see -ITY.] The quality or condition of being a phœnix.

1901 DZIEWICKI in *Wyclif's Repl. de Univers.* 136 *margin*, Suppose there is but one phoenix in the world; there are the universal and the singular phoenicities, the former naturally prior to the latter, which is neither Phoenicity in itself nor not. For if it were, then it would be the same as the Universal on which it depends; and if it were not, there would be more than one phoenicity, which contradicts the hypothesis.

ˈphœnicle. *rare*$^{-1}$. [ad. med. or mod.L. *phœniculus*.] Contemptuous dim. of PHŒNIX.

1710 tr. *Werenfels's Disc. Logom.* 140 He introduces Heinsiolus (as he ridiculously calls..the great Heinsius) as the Phœnicle (not the Phœnix..) of the Age.

phœnicochroite (fiːnɪˈkɒkrəʊaɪt). *Min.* [Named 1839, f. Gr. φοῖνιξ, φοινικο- purple-red, crimson + -χροος -coloured + -ITE[1].] Basic chromate of lead, found in deep red tabular crystals.

1849 J. NICOL *Min.* 388 Phoenikochroite..occurs in veins in limestone. **1868** DANA *Min.* (ed. 5) 630 As the color is red, ..Glocker changed it [the name] to Phoenicochroite.

phœnicopter (fiːnɪˈkɒptə(r)). *Ornith.* [ad. F. *phœnicoptère* (Rabelais) or ad. L. *phœnīcopterus* (Plin.), a. Gr. φοινικόπτερος flamingo, lit. red-feathered, f. φοῖνιξ, φοινικ- crimson + πτέρον feather, wing.] Adapted form of the Greek and Latin name of the flamingo of Southern Europe (*Phœnicopterus roseus* or *antiquorum*).

1570 FOXE *A. & M.* (ed. 2) 83/2 Some daies his [Heliogabalus'] companye was serued at meale with..a straunge fowle called Phenocapterie. **1627** HAKEWILL *Apol.* (1630) 388 The fowle which they [Romans] specially hunted and most delighted in were phænicopters, peacockes, thrushes, and pigeons. [**1646** SIR T. BROWNE *Pseud. Ep.* III. xii. 136 The luxurious Emperour..had at his table many a Phœnicopterus.] **1653** URQUHART *Rabelais* I. xxxvii, Flamans, which are phœnicopters or crimson-winged sea-fowles. **1692** SOUTH *Serm., Prov.* i. 32 (1718) IV. 79 Their Lucrinian oysters, their phœnicopters, and the like. **1875** MERIVALE *Gen. Hist. Rome* lvi. (1877) 452 It was for their rarity only that peacocks and nightingales and the tongues and brains of phœnicopters (possibly flamingoes) could be regarded as delicacies.

Hence **phœniˈcopterid** *Ornith.*, any bird of the *Phœnicopteridæ* or flamingo family; **phœniˈcopteroid** *a.*, resembling the flamingo in structure; **phœniˈcopterous** *a.*, related to the flamingoes; also in *Entom.*, having red wings (Mayne *Expos. Lex.* 1858).

phœniˈcurous, *a. Zool.* [f. Gr. φοινίκουρος red-tailed, spec. the redstart.] Having a red tail.

1858 in MAYNE *Expos. Lex.*

† **phœnigm.** *Obs.* [ad. med.L. *phœnigmus*, a. Gr. φοινιγμός irritation of the skin by rubefacients, f. φοινίσσειν to redden, f. φοῖνιξ crimson: cf. F. *phénigme*.] Reddening of the skin; also, a medicinal application causing this.

[**1646** SIR T. BROWNE *Pseud. Ep.* 109 Which Topically applied become a Phænigmus or Rubifying medicine.] **1657** TOMLINSON *Renou's Disp.* 203 It is called a Phœnigm, that is, a rubrifying medicament. **1684** tr. *Bonet's Merc. Compit.* III. xii. 71 The Ancients frequently used Phænigms and Sinapisms. **1710** T. FULLER *Pharm. Extemp.* 359 It is a.. Phaenigm which the Antients used much. [**1858** MAYNE *Expos. Lex.*, *Phœnigmus*.]

phœnix[1], **phenix** (ˈfiːnɪks). Forms: 1, 4–6 fenix, 4–6 fenyx, 5 phenes, 6 phenex, -yx, fenyce, 6– phœnix, phenix (7 phænix). [OE. and OF. *fenix*, a. med.L. *phēnix*, L. *phœnix*, a. Gr. φοῖνιξ the mythical bird, identical with φοῖνιξ Phœnician, purple-red, crimson: see Note below. In OF. also *fenis, fenisces*; Sp. *fenix*, It. *fenice*; Du. *feniks*, MLG. *fenix*, Ger. *phönix*, Da., Sw. *fönix*. The Eng. spelling was in 16th c. assimilated to the L. (*fenyce* was after It.).]

1. A mythical bird, of gorgeous plumage, fabled to be the only one of its kind, and to live five or six hundred years in the Arabian desert, after which it burnt itself to ashes on a funeral pile of aromatic twigs ignited by the sun and fanned by its own wings, but only to emerge from its ashes with renewed youth, to live through another cycle of years.

(Variations of the myth were that the phœnix burnt itself on the altar of the temple at Heliopolis: and that a worm emerged from the ashes and became the young phœnix. See also PHŒNIX[2].)

a **900** *Phœnix* 86 in *Exeter Bk.*, Ðone wudu weardaþ wundrum fæȝer fuȝel feþrum se is fenix haten. *c* **1000** ÆLFRIC *Gram.* ix. (Z.) 70 *Hic Fenix* (swa hatte an fuȝel on arabiscre ðeode, se leofað fif hund ȝeara and æfter deaðe eft arist ȝeedcucod). **1398** TREVISA *Barth. De P.R.* XII. xv. (Bodl. MS.), þis brid Fenix is a brid wiþoute make and leueþ þre hundred oþer fyue hundred yere. *c* **1400** MAUNDEV. (Roxb.) vii. 25 A fewle þat men calles Fenix; and þer es bot ane..þis fewle liffes fyue hundreth ȝere; and at þe fyue hundreth ȝere end he commes to þe forsaid temple and apon þe awter he brynnes him self all to powder. **14..** *Nominale* in Wr.-Wülcker 702/17 *Hic phenix*, a phenes. **1526** *Pilgr. Perf.* (1531) 202 b, There is one byrde called a Fenyce, & but onely one of that kynde in the worlde. **1555** EDEN *Decades* 216 The Phenyx the which I knowe no man that euer hath seene. **1593** SHAKS. *3 Hen. VI*, I. iv. 35 My ashes, as the Phœnix, may bring forth A Bird, that will reuenge vpon you all. **1601** HOLLAND *Pliny* XIII. iv. I. 387 The bird Phœnix, which is supposed to haue taken that name of this Date tree (called in Greeke φοῖνιξ) for it was assured to me, that the said bird died with that tree, and reuiued of it selfe as the tree sprung againe. **1610** SHAKS. *Temp.* III. iii. 23 A liuing Drolerie: now I will beleeue That..in Arabia There is one Tree, the Phœnix throne, one Phœnix At this houre reigning there. **1661** LOVELL *Hist. Anim. & Min.* Introd., Birds..the fabulous are, the gryphin, harpie, .. phœnix, cinnamologus. *a* **1700** DRYDEN *Ovid's Metam.* XV. 527 All these receive their Birth from other Things; But from himself the Phœnix only springs: Self-born, begotten by the Parent Flame In which he burn'd, Another and the Same. **1809** BYRON *Eng. Bards & Scotch Rev.* 961 And glory, like the phœnix 'midst her fires, Exhales her odours, blazes, and expires. **1882** FARRAR *Early Chr.* I. 103 He [Clemens Romanus] illustrates [the] possiblity [of the Resurrection] by natural analogies, especially by the existence and history of the Phœnix! **1885** BIBLE (R.V.) *Job* xxix. 18 Then I said, I shall die in my nest, and I shall multiply my days as the sand [*margin*, Or, the phœnix].

2. *transf.* and *fig.* **a.** A person (or thing) of unique excellence or of matchless beauty; a paragon.

13.. *E.E. Allit. P.* A. 430 Now for synglerte o hyr dousour We calle hyr fenyx of Arraby. *c* **1369** CHAUCER *Dethe Blaunche* 982 Trewly she was to myn eye, The Soleyn Fenix of Arabye. *a* **1548** HALL *Chron., Hen. V* 33 b, This Prince [Henry V] was almost the Arabicall Phenix. **1549** LATIMER *1st Serm. bef. Edw. VI* (Arb.) 42 For goddes loue, let not him be a Phenix, let him not be alone. **1603** KNOLLES *Hist. Turks* (1621) Ded., Her late sacred Majestie, .. the rare Phœnix of her sex, who now resteth in glorie. **1669** STURMY *Mariner's Mag.* VI. iii. 128 The Phœnix of Astronomy Ticho-Braghe. **1775** WESLEY *Wks.* (1872) IV. 50 He seems to think himself a mere Phenix. **1838–9** HALLAM *Hist. Lit.* I. I. iii. §96. 209 Picus of Mirandola..so justly called the phœnix of his age.

b. That which rises from the ashes of its predecessor.

1591 SHAKS. *1 Hen. VI*, IV. vii. 93 From their ashes shal be reard A Phœnix that shall make all France affear'd. **1632** HEYWOOD *1st Pt. Iron Age* I. Ep. Ded., Out of her ashes hath risen two the rarest Phœnixes in Europe, namely London and Rome. **1867** H. MACMILLAN *Bible Teach.* xvi. (1870) 329 The phœnix of new institutions can only arise out of the conflagration and ashes of the old.

3. The figure of the phœnix in Heraldry, or as an ornament.

Heraldically represented as rising in the midst of flames.
c **1420** LYDG. *Assembly of Gods* 810 A fenyx on hys helme stood. So forthe gan he fare. **1887** *Pall Mall G.* 24 Oct. 13/2 The button is surrounded by seven gold phœnixes, of which each is inlaid with seven large and twenty-one small pearls and a cat's eye.

4. *Astr.* One of the southern constellations.

1674 MOXON *Tutor Astron.* I. iii. §10 (ed. 3) 19 Twelve Constellations..added by Frederico Houtmanno..who.. named them as follows, 1 The Crane, 2 The Phenix, 3 The Indian [etc.]. **1774** M. MACKENZIE *Maritime Surv.* I. v. 51 When it appears in a horizontal Line with the Foot of the Cross, or the Head of the Phenix. **1868** LOCKYER *Guillemin's Heavens* (ed. 3) 335.

5. *attrib.* and *Comb.*: (*a*) simple attrib. (of the phœnix), as ***phœnix life, nest, plume, pride, riddle, wing***; also passing into adj. (= phœnix-like; as of a phœnix), as ***phœnix-birth, -life, -pyre, -resurrection, -tinder***; (*b*) appositive (that is a phœnix: sense 2) passing into adj. (= phœnix-like), as ***phœnix bride, family, -fuel, grace, mercy, -moon, opinion, parson, queen, sect, she, -world***; (*c*) parasynthetic, as ***phœnix-feathered*** adj.; also **phœnix-like** *a.* and *adv.*, like or after the manner of a phœnix; † **phœnix-man**, a fireman in the employ of the old Phœnix Insurance Office (founded 1681: see quot. 1700, also Phillips, ed. Kersey 1706).

1946 R. CAMPBELL *Talking Bronco* 69 The proud Alcazar caught the fire Which gave that splendour *phoenix-birth. **1977** *Listener* 10 Nov. 617/1 His radio ballads, combining actuality voices, music and sound effects were a pheonix birth at a dark hour. **1814** MRS. J. WEST *Alicia de Lacy* II. 289 The Earl.. was too austere, cold, and misanthropic to be a meet companion for his *Phœnix bride. **1805** SURR *Winter in Lond.* (1806) II. 141 That *phœnix family the Rosevilles—alias the Dickenses. **1596** FITZ-GEFFRAY *Sir F. Drake* (1881) 21 Into whose soule sweete Sidney did infuse The essence of his *Phœnix-feather'd Muse. **1936** R. CAMPBELL *Mithraic Emblems* 50 True *phoenix-fuel whom no burning mars. **1671** FLAVEL *Fount. of Life* ii. 32 Faith is the *Phenix-Grace, as Christ is the Phenix-Mercy. *a* **1957** R. CAMPBELL tr. *Quevedo's On Lisi's Golden Hair* in *Coll. Poems* (1960) III. 83 Out of their ash to fan new *phoenix-lives. **1612** *Two Noble K.* I. iii, *Phenix like They dide in perfume. **1654** WHITLOCK *Zootomia* 544 Abraham saw..a Phœnix-like Resurrection of his Son, as possible with God. **1865** H. PHILLIPS *Amer. Paper Curr.* II. 11 When from the ruins of a State, Phœnix-like, a new one arises. *a* **1700** B. E. *Dict. Cant. Crew*, **Phenix-men*, the same as *Fire-drakes*. [*Fire-drakes*, men with a Phenix for their Badge, in Livery, and Pay from the Insurance-Office, to extinguish Fires.] **1934** L. B. LYON *White Hare* 29 The *phoenix moon with molten breast. **1594** NASHE *Unfort. Trav.* Wks. (Grosart) V. 62 Her high exalted sunne beames haue set the *phenix neast of my breast on fire. **1630** *R. Johnson's Kingd. & Commw.* 113 The Pope himselfe shall gratifie him with a *Phenix plume. **1930** R. CAMPBELL *Adamastor* 78 And now from the wet earth reborn, All Africa his *phoenix pyre. **1583** STUBBES *Anat. Abus.* II. (1882) 8 Such a vertuous Ladie and *Phenix Queene. **1963** L. TRILLING in N. Frye *Romanticism Reconsidered* 88 When he [*sc.* Keats] is 'consumed in the fire', they will contrive his *Phoenix-resurrection. *a* **1631** DONNE *Canonization* in *Poems* (1633) 203 The *Phoenix ridle hath more wit By us, we two being one, are it. *a* **1720** SHEFFIELD (Dk. Buckhm.) *Wks.* (1729) 132 That *Phenix-She deserves to be beloved. **1939** R. CAMPBELL *Flowering Rifle* III. 74 So their black chaos is but welcome fuel And *phoenix-tinder to this fierce renewal. **1657** EVELYN *Diary* 17 Sept., Habits of curiously-colour'd and wrought feathers, one from the *phœnix wing as tradition goes. **1944** W. TEMPLE *Let.* 22 Feb. (1963) 147 The reforms necessary for the arising of that brave new *phoenix-world on which we have set our hearts.

Hence **phœnixity** *nonce-wd.*, the quality of being a phœnix or unique.

1886 G. B. SHAW *Cashel Byron* (1889) 268 She, poor girl! cannot appreciate even her own phœnixity.

[*Note.* The relation of *Phœnix* to other senses of Gr. φοῖνιξ is obscure: see note to PHŒNICIAN. It could hardly be 'the Phœnician bird', since it was at Heliopolis in Egypt, where the cult of the phœnix (in Egypt. *bennu*) was coeval with the city, that Herodotus learned the legend about it. It might perh. be 'the red', with reference to the prevailing colour of its body (τὰ μὲν χρυσόκομα τῶν πτερῶν, τὰ δὲ ἐρυθρὰ ἐς τὰ μάλιστα, Herod. II. 73), or, as some think, as an emblem of the sun in its perpetual setting and rising again. See Roscher *Lexikon d. griech. u. röm. Mythologie*, s.v.]

‖**phœnix²** ('fi:nɪks). *Bot.* [mod.L. (Linnæus), a. Gr. φοῖνιξ the date palm, a date: see PHŒNICIAN.

Various speculations connecting the date-tree with the mythical bird, PHŒNIX¹, were current from the time of Pliny or earlier: see quots. here, also 1601 in PHŒNIX¹ 1, and the Latin *Carmen de Phœnice*, attributed to Lactantius (*a* 325). Some have supposed a much earlier connexion: the Egyptian name of the phœnix was *bennu*, that of the date (fruit and tree) *benr* or *benra*, whence Coptic *benne*. But Egyptologers hold the two words to be unconnected. Some would explain φοῖνιξ the date, as 'the red fruit'.]

The name of a genus of palms, distinguished by their pinnate leaves; the most important species is *P. dactylifera*, the Date Palm.

[*a* **900** *Phœnix* 174 in *Exeter Bk.*, Beam..þone hatað men fenix on foldan of þæs fugles noman. **1398** TREVISA *Barth. De P.R.* (Bodl. MS.) XVII. cxvi, For he [*palma*] dureþ & is grene..longe tyme, þerfore bi liknes of þe brid Fenix þat lyueþ longe tyme þere, hatte Fenix amonge þe Grees. *Ibid.* (1495) 679 In the south countree is a manere palme that is alone in that kynde: and none other spryngeth ne comyth therof: but whan this palme is so olde that it faylyth all for aege: thenne ofte it quyknyth and spryngyth ayen of itself; therfore men trowe that Fenix that is a byrde of Arabia hath the name of this palme of Arabia, for he dieth and quiketh efte as the foreseide palme dothe, as Plinius seith. **1727–41** CHAMBERS *Cycl.* s.v., Hence the Phœnicians gave the name *phœnix* to the palm-tree, by reason when burnt down to the very root, it rises again fairer than ever.] **1895** *Westm. Gaz.* 18 Apr. 1/3 To sit under the waving feathers of the date and phœnix palms.

phokomelia, var. PHOCOMELIA.

pholad ('fəʊləd). *Zool.* [Anglicized form of PHOLAS.] A mollusc of the *Pholas* family, *Pholadidæ*. So **pho'ladean**, **'pholadid**, one of the *Pholadidæ*; †**'pholadite**, a fossil pholad or the like; **'pholadoid** *a.*, resembling the genus *Pholas*.

1835 KIRBY *Hab. & Inst. Anim.* I. viii. 245 The *Pholads or stone-borers. **1842** BRANDE *Dict. Sci.* etc., **Pholadeans*, ..the family of Lamellibranchiate Bivalves of which the genus Pholas is the type. **1828–32** WEBSTER, **Pholadite*, a petrified shell of the genus Pholas. *Jameson.*

‖**pholas** ('fəʊləs). *Zool.* Pl. pholades ('fəʊlədi:z). [mod.L., a. Gr. φωλάς, φωλαδ- adj. lurking in a hole (φωλεός), hence, a mollusc inhabiting holes in stone.] A genus of boring bivalve molluscs; an animal of this genus, a piddock.

1661 LOVELL *Hist. Anim. & Min.* 241 Pholas..They are pleasant to the pallate, but of evil juyce... They live in hollow places, and so amongst stones, that they can hardly be perceived. **1774** GOLDSM. *Nat. Hist.* (1776) VII. 68 Thus immured, the pholas lives in darkness, indolence, and plenty. **1802** PLAYFAIR *Illustr. Hutton. Th.* 452 The marble columns of the temple of Serapis..are..perforated by pholades, to the height of sixteen feet above ground. **1868** WOOD *Homes without H.* v. 101 One of the British species, the Paper Pholas..has a peculiarly thin and delicate shell.

pholcid ('fɒlsɪd). *Zool.* [f. mod.L. *Pholcidæ*, f. *Pholcus*, a. Gr. φολκός bandy-legged.] A spider of the family *Pholcidæ* (typical genus *Pholcus*), having long legs, and inhabiting dark places. So **pholcoid** ('fɒlkɔɪd) *a.*, allied to the genus *Pholcus*.

pholerite ('fɒləraɪt). *Min.* [a. F. *pholérite* (named 1825), irreg. f. Gr. φολίς, φολιδ-, horny scale: see -ITE¹.] A hydrous silicate of aluminium closely allied to or identical with KAOLINITE, occurring in minute scales with a pearly lustre.

1826 *Q. Jrnl. Lit.*, etc. XXI. 406 Pholerite or silicate of Alumina. **1892** DANA *Min.* (ed. 6) 686 Pholerite has been separated..but there can be little doubt of its identity with kaolinite.

Pholey, var. PEULH *sb.* and *a.*

pholidolite (fəʊ'lɪdəʊlaɪt). *Min.* [Named 1890, f. Gr. φολίς, -ιδ- scale + -LITE.] A hydrous silicate of aluminium, magnesium, and potassium, occurring in minute scales.

1890 *Amer. Jrnl. Sc.* Ser. III. XLIV. 335 Pholidolite, a mineral allied to the chlorites.

‖**pholidosis** (fɒlɪ'dəʊsɪs). *Zool.* [mod.L., f. Gr. φολίς, φολιδ- scale + -OSIS.] Arrangement of the scales, esp. in *Reptilia*.

1884 *Ann. & Mag. Nat. Hist.* Aug. 117 The classifications ..founded to a great extent on characters of pholidosis and physiognomy.

pholidote ('fɒlɪdəʊt), *a. Zool. rare⁻⁰*. [ad. Gr. φολιδωτ-ός, f. φολίς, φολιδ- scale.] Covered with scales, scaly. Also **pholi'dotous** *a.*

1858 MAYNE *Expos. Lex.* 945/2 Pholidotous. **1890** *Cent. Dict.*, *Pholidote*.

pholque (fɒlk). *Zool. rare.* [= F. *pholque*, ad. mod. Zool. L. *Pholcus* (Walckenaer 1805), a. Gr. φολκός bandy-legged.] A spider of the genus *Pholcus*: see PHOLCID.

1835–6 TODD *Cycl. Anat.* I. 201/2 The thorax of a pholque.

phon (fɒn). [a. G. *phon* (H. Barkhausen 1926, in *Zeitschr. für techn. Physik* VII. 601/1), f. Gr. φωνή sound.] A unit of loudness (strictly, loudness level), defined so that the loudness in phons of any sound is numerically equal to the intensity in decibels of a pure 1000 Hz tone judged to be equally loud. Formerly = DECIBEL.

1932 *B.B.C. Techn. Tables & Gloss.* 63/2 Two noises may be compared in strength in sensation units or phons by comparing the attenuations necessary to reduce each to the threshold of audibility. **1932** *Engineering* 9 Sept. 314/3 For quantitative measurements we turn to a unit called the decibel. [*Note*] Called the 'phon' in Germany. **1935** *Sunday Times* 13 Oct. 18/3 Now a machine exists which measures units of noise in 'phons', and no vehicle will be allowed after a certain date to make more than 90 phons of noise at a speed of 30 m.p.h. **1937** A. H. DAVID *Noise* iv. 46 Originally a 'phon' had been used in Germany as a four-fold power ratio. Later it was employed as an equivalent of the decibel. *Ibid.*, Limitation of the decibel to intensity ratios and the phon to loudness scales has been adopted by the British Standards Institution. **1942** *Wireless World* June 132/2 The magnitude of these upper intensity levels in terms of loudness can be expressed by writing phons for decibels, since they are equal, in the range here considered. **1959** G. R. PARTRIDGE *Princ. Electronic Instruments* xvi. 303 A loudness of 70 phons requires 80 db intensity at 70 cycles. **1962** A. NISBETT *Technique Sound Studio* 264 Phons equal decibels at 1000 c/s, and at other frequencies are related to this scale by contours of equal loudness. **1963** JERRARD & MCNEILL *Dict. Sci. Units* 104 The loudness of a jet aircraft engine is about 140 phon, whereas the noise of a steam railway locomotive is less than 100 phon. **1974** *Daily Colonist* (Victoria, B.C.) 22 Nov. 16/5 Tokyo metropolitan government standards set permissible noise levels at 40 phon (sound measurement) in the morning and evening and at 45 phon during the day.

phonæstheme ('fəʊnɪsθi:m). *Linguistics.* Also **phonaestheme, phonestheme.** [f. PHONE *sb.*¹ + ÆSTH(ETIC *a.* and *sb.* + -EME.] A phoneme or group of phonemes with recognizable semantic associations due to recurrent appearance in words of similar meaning.

1930 J. R. FIRTH *Speech* vi. 50 The *slack* etymeme belongs to a much bigger group of habits we may call the *sl* phonæstheme. *Ibid.* vi. 53 The habit background of *wirl*.. probably includes the *tw* and *irl*, *-url* phonæsthemes. **1946** *Word* II. 83 Phonestheme is defined as a phoneme or cluster of phonemes shared by a group of words which also have in common some element of meaning or function, tho [*sic*] the words may be etymologically unrelated. **1957** *Gen. Linguistics* II. 55 Previous studies have erred in attempting to separate the long consonant phonesthemes from the other phonesthemes of the language. **1969** *Language* XLV. 284 The term 'phonaestheme' has been used, but it seems to mean different things for those who have used it. **1972** M. L. SAMUELS *Linguistic Evol.* iii. 46 The phonaestheme /sl-/ may be assigned the values 'slippery' or 'falling' in *slide, slip, slime, slush*..; and it may also be assigned the closely related values 'inactive', 'degenerate' or 'morally worthless' in *slow, sloth, sleep(y), slumber, slack, slouch,* [etc.]. **1974** *Amer. Speech 1971* XLVI. 129 The word-initiating segments *sn-* and *sl-* (as in *snit* and *slit*), which, because they are not readily identifiable as morphemes or other grammatical units, are often referred to as 'phonesthemes'. **1977** *Word 1972* XXVIII. 305 Phonesthemes are considered to have meaning through their occurrence in words of a particular meaning.

Hence **phonæsthesia** (fəʊnɪs'θi:sɪə, -zɪə) [ÆSTHESIA], **phonæsthesis** (fəʊnɪs'θi:sɪs, -zɪs) [ÆSTHESIS], sound symbolism; the use of phonæsthemes; **phonæsthetic** (fəʊnɪs'θɛtɪk) [ÆSTHETIC *a.*] *a.*, of or pertaining to phonæsthemes; **phonæs'thetically** *adv.*

1930 J. R. FIRTH *Speech* vi. 52 The phonæsthetic habits.. are much more than 'blends'..and are of general importance in speech. *Ibid.* 54 Play on phonæsthetic habits gives much of the pleasure of alliteration, assonance, and rhyme. **1950** *Archivum Linguisticum* II. 97 Phonaesthesia or sound symbolism. **1965** *Language* XLI. 347 Morphophonemics, phonesthesis, and paralanguage she wholly ignores. **1971** *Archivum Linguisticum* New Ser. II. 43 Some verbs, for example, do not occur without aspectival.. or directional..extension; *shamble*, for instance, requires the 'complementation' of *off, on, up, down, across*, etc., a fact to which its phonaesthetic overtones of *amble, shuffle*,..may or may not relate. **1972** M. L. SAMUELS *Linguistic Evol.* iii. 48 The growth of phonaesthetic patterns is of importance as a special type of linguistic change. *Ibid.* xiii. 161 In some verbs where a short vowel had been developed phonetically, it was phonaesthetically suited for the expression of point-action. **1977** *Maledicta* Summer 65 (*heading*) Phonesthesis and scatology.

phonal ('fəʊnəl), *a. rare.* [f. Gr. φωνή voice + -AL¹.] Pertaining to vocal sound; phonetic.

1868 MAX MÜLLER *Stratif. Lang.* 42 The Tibetan is near [the Chinese] in phonal structure as being tonic and monosyllabic. **1883** D. H. WHEELER *By-Ways of Lit.* xi. 227 Family life requires a minimum of phonal breath.

phonascetics (fəʊnə'sɛtɪks), *sb. pl. rare⁻⁰*. [f. Gr. φωνασκητ-ής one who exercises the voice, f. φωνασκεῖν to exercise the voice, f. φωνή voice + ἀσκεῖν: see ASCETIC.] (See quots.)

1864 WEBSTER, *Phonascetics*, a method of treatment for restoring the voice. **1890** *Cent. Dict.*, *Phonascetics*, systematic practice for strengthening the voice; treatment for improving or restoring the voice.

phonate ('fəʊneɪt), *v. Physiol.* [f. Gr. φωνή voice + -ATE³.] *intr.* To utter vocal sound; to produce the tone which constitutes voice by vibration of the vocal cords; *trans.* to sound vocally.

1876 BRISTOWE *Th. & Pract. Med.* (1878) 475 Undue expenditure of breath during forcible expiration, as when the patient attempts to phonate or coughs. **1894** *Brit. Med. Jrnl.* 26 May 81/2 The patient could phonate, but not articulate. **1897** *Allbutt's Syst. Med.* IV. 783 On phonating 'eh! eh!' the vocal cords should come into symmetrical apposition in the middle line.

phonation (fəʊ'neɪʃən). *Physiol.* [f. Gr. φωνή voice + -ATION: in mod.L. *phonātio*, F. *phonation* (Littré).] The production or utterance of vocal sound: usually, as distinguished from *articulation*, or the division of the tone so produced into the elements of speech by the other vocal organs. Also *spec.* the process or act of producing voice (VOICE *sb.* 1 g); sometimes *gen.* vocal utterance, voice-production.

1842 DUNGLISON *Med. Lex.*, *Phonation*, the physiology of the voice. **1866** A. FLINT *Princ. Med.* (1880) 285 Movements concerned in phonation. **1879** LEWES *Study Psychol.* 29 Aphasia may be due to a defect of Phonation. **1892** R. L. GARNER *Speech Monkeys* iv. 41 The phonation of a species is generally uniform. **1931** *Musical Times* Jan. 18/2 The simplest act of speech involves the co-ordination of three very complicated sets of muscles: those of inspiration and expiration; those of phonation (the intra- and extra-laryngeal muscles); and those of articulation. **1935** *Jrnl. Mental Sci.* LXXXI. 837 The muscles of respiration, phonation, and articulation. **1956** J. WHATMOUGH *Language* ix. 157 It [*sc.* language] is now articulated (i.e. jointed) phonation, though originally simple and reflex. **1959** E. PULGRAM *Introd. Spectrogr. of Speech* iv. 43 Many experiments have been performed..to measure subglottic pressure during phonation. *Ibid.* xviii. 140 *Fig. 30* illustrates four phonations of the vowel [i]. **1962** A. C. GIMSON *Introd. Pronunc. Eng.* ii. 9 The action of the vocal cords which is most characteristically a function of speech consists in their role as a *vibrator* set in motion by lung air—the production of *voice*, or *phonation*. **1964** J. C. CATFORD in D. Abercrombie et al. *Daniel Jones* 28 Various components of speech-sound pronunciation, including phonation-types. **1970** *Language* LXVI. 313 The human larynx is so constructed that the fundamental frequency of phonation is a function of both the transglottal air pressure drop and the tensions of the laryngeal muscles. **1976** *Canad. Jrnl. Linguistics* XXI. 1. 118 A most informative explanation of air-stream mechanisms and phonation times, including voice-onset-time.

Hence **pho'national** *a.* = PHONATORY *a.*

1939 L. H. GRAY *Foundations of Lang.* i. 5 Persons whose phonational and auditory apparatus are normal. *Ibid.* ii. 18 This condition..is the auditory counterpart of the pathological forms of the phonational soliloquy. **1947** *Word* III. 2 The phonational act..gives rise, in the hearer, to an acoustic image which is distinct from the physical sound.

phonatory ('fəʊnətərɪ), *a.* [f. PHONATE: see -ORY.] Pertaining or relating to phonation.

1895 WOLFENDEN tr. *Joal's Respiration in Singing* 137 These two muscular groups..in their phonatory functions. **1897** *Allbutt's Syst. Med.* IV. 814 Both vocal cords are very apt to become fixed more or less in the phonatory position.

phonautograph (fəʊˈnɔːtəgrɑːf, -æ-). [= F. *phonautographe* (1855), f. Gr. φωνή voice + αὐτο- self + -GRAPH -writer (i.e. recorder).] An apparatus for automatically recording the vibrations of sound, by means of a membrane set in vibration by the sound-waves, and having a point attached which makes a tracing upon a revolving cylinder.

1859 *Times* 22 Sept. 9/2 (Brit. Assoc.) Section A. Phonautograph [*mispr.* -anto-], or Apparatus for the Self-Registering of the Vibrations of Sound. By Messrs. Scott and Kœnig... These splendid results of the powers of the phonautograph were never seen before the Aberdeen meeting. **1879** tr. *Du Moncel's Telephone* 11 This telephone ..is based on the vibrating membrane of which Mr. L. Scott made use in his phonautograph, in 1855. **1879** G. PRESCOTT *Sp. Telephone* 67 For some time I carried on experiments with the manometric capsule of Köenig and the phonautograph of Léon Scott. **1894** DICKSON *Edison* 124 The phonautograph, a machine used for the delineations of the sound waves.

Hence **phoˈnautogram** [cf. *telegram*], a record or tracing made by a phonautograph; **phonautoˈgraphic** *a.*, of or pertaining to a phonautograph; **phonautoˈgraphically** *adv.*, by means of a phonautograph.

1877 *Nature* 3 May 12/2 The capabilities of various membranes of taking impressions from vocal sounds for phonautographic purposes. **1888** *Jrnl. Franklin Inst.* Jan. 53 The method..of reproducing sounds recorded phonautographically. **1890** *Cent. Dict., Phonautogram.*

phone (fəʊn), *sb.*[1] *Phonetics.* [ad. Gr. φωνή voice.] **1.** An elementary sound of spoken language; a simple vowel or consonant sound. Also = ALLOPHONE.

In quot. 1892 used for one of the sounds uttered by monkeys, supposed by the writer to express certain ideas (corresponding to *words* in human speech).

a **1866** J. GROTE in *Jrnl. Philol.* (1872) IV. 55 When I mean words as sounded I shall use the term *phone* (like *zone*, φωνή, ζώνη). **1890** in *Cent. Dict.* **1892** R. L. GARNER *Speech Monkeys* xiii. 137 There is a difference in the phones of all different genera. **1896** R. J. LLOYD in *Jrnl. Anat. & Physiol.* XXXI. 233 The movable units of which the sounds called words are composed may be called phones... A phone which either by itself constitutes a syllable or is the strongest phone in a syllable is called a vowel. The weaker connective phones are called consonants. **1899** —— *North. Eng.* §2 A logical alphabet has one letter for each phone and one phone for each letter. **1924** H. E. PALMER *Gram. Spoken Eng.* I. 1 A phone may be a simple sound, such as [f]..or it may be an intimate combination of simple sounds, such as [tʃ]... On the other hand, sounds such as non-significant glides are not phones. **1942** *Language* XVIII. 8 A phone is a member of a phoneme. **1950** *Ibid.* XXVI. 90 In the latter meaning, the term 'phone' is a shorter equivalent of 'allophone'. **1957** [see ALLOPHONE]. **1959** E. PULGRAM *Introd. Spectrogr. of Speech* xix. 145 All those phones, that is, events of articulation, which are linguistically identifiable with one another though not acoustically identical with one another, belong to the same class, which we call phoneme. **1961** W. R. BRAIN *Speech Disorders* 9 A phone is the name for a single isolable sound made in the course of speech by a speaker. **1964** [see ALLOPHONE]. **1971** D. CRYSTAL *Linguistics* iv. 178 The term 'phoneme' had been used in the nineteenth century, but it referred to a unit of sound (that is, a phonetic unit—what we would usually these days call a 'phone'), and not to any abstract notion involving contrastivity. **1975** L. M. HYMAN *Phonology* 8 The units of phonetic description are sound segments (or *phones*), while the units of phonological description are *phonemes.* **1976** *Language* LII. 317 In the early distinctive-feature model, phonemes are redundancy-free versions of the corresponding phones.

2. Special Combs., as **phone-type**, a speech-sound considered as a purely phonetic event.

1961 F. W. HOUSEHOLDER in Saporta & Bastian *Psycholinguistics* 19/2 Biuniqueness..means that to any given phone-type in a given environment there must correspond only one possible phoneme, and to any phoneme in a given string there must correspond only one phone-type. *Ibid.*, It is frequently simpler and more elegant to have units so chosen that a given phone-type in one environment may be an allophone of one such phoneme, but in another an allophone (or the only allophone) of a different one. **1965** R. L. KELLOGG in Besinger & Creed *Medieval & Linguistic Stud.* 67 We might add that the fixed formula is to the abstract pattern of which it is a manifestation as the phonetype is to the phoneme.

phone (fəʊn), *sb.*[2] Also 'phone. **1.** Colloq. abbreviation of TELEPHONE *sb.* Also, a telephone call.

1884 *Sci. Amer.* 19 July 43/2, I made a telephone as shown in the *Scientific American*, Supplement, No. 142. The phones are made of ebony, and are perfect. **1899** *Westm. Gaz.* 18 Apr. 2/1 The receiver of this 'phone' consisted of a horizontal cylinder divided vertically by a diaphragm which projected several inches beyond the front orifice. **1900** *N.B. Daily Mail* 3 Jan. 6 In the matter of calling up the Exchange and ringing off, the Postmaster General says these should be done by taking off and hanging up the phone. **1903** *Architect* 24 Apr. Suppl. 28/2 'Jersey City is on the 'phone'. **1922** J. REITH *Diary* 6 Nov. (1975) i. 87 Many phones from the National Liberal Headquarters asking for speakers. **1942** BERREY & VAN DEN BARK *Amer. Thes. Slang* §808/5 *Telephone call,*..phone. **1943** J. THURBER *Men, Women & Dogs* 105 If I called the wrong number, why did you answer the phone? **1949** N. SPAIN *Death goes on Skis* III. viii. 186 For an intellectual she seems to be quite illiterate..saying 'phone for telephone. **1960** K. AMIS *Take Girl like You* xxvii. 306 A telephone was ringing... 'Jenny, someone on the phone for you.' **1974** M. SPARK *Abbess of Crewe* i. 30 Mildred treads softly over the green carpet..and answers the phone. **1976** *Daily Tel.* 13 Nov. 17/3 A 19-year-old youth made an estimated 1,000 fraudulent telephone calls.. and was on the 'phone for 63 hours.

2. Colloq. abbrev. of *ear-phone* s.v. EAR *sb.*[1] 17, HEAD-PHONE. Usu. *pl.*

1913 *Wireless World* May p. v (Advt.), High resistance 'phones. **1926** R. MACAULAY *Lett. to Sister* (1964) 27 No longer..does the husband have to sit in the evenings and listen to inanities from his wife..; he and she can now both sit in silence, with the phones on their ears. **1948** *Electronics* Aug. 88/2 A person listening to sound through a binaural system has the illusion that the sound originates in the room rather than in the phones. **1962** A. NISBETT *Technique Sound Studio* 256 Some degree of control of volume can be achieved with telephone receiver type phones by moving them a little off the ear. **1970** J. EARL *Tuners & Amplifiers* iii. 76 It also pays for the amplifier etc. to carry a loudspeaker switch to cut the speakers when listening on 'phones. **1977** *Rolling Stone* 24 Mar. 79/2 Played back over the phones part of the system..the sense of space and realism of sound is unbelievable.

3. *attrib.* and *Comb.* (in sense 1), as ***phone bell, call, caller, exchange*** [EXCHANGE *sb.* 10c], ***installation, jack*** [JACK *sb.*[1] 15d], ***kiosk, message, operator*** [OPERATOR 5a], ***order, receiver, wire***; ***phone-answering*** ppl. adj. and vbl. sb.; **phone bill**, an account for the cost of hire of a telephone and of calls made from it; **phone book**, a telephone directory; **phone booth, box**, a box-like kiosk in which a public telephone is installed; **phonecard**, a pre-paid card designed for use with a cardphone; **phone number**, the identifying call-number assigned to a telephone, line, etc.; **phone patch** [PATCH *sb.*[1] 6f], a temporary radio link made to establish communication between a radio operator and a telephone user; **phone-tapping** *vbl. sb.* = *telephone-tapping* vbl. sb.; so **phone-tap** *sb.* and *v. trans.*; **phone-tapper**.

1976 *New Yorker* 23 Feb. 30/2 The Silverstein headquarters..has a phone-answering machine that will deliver a tape-recorded message from the candidate. **1977** E. AMBLER *Send no more Roses* v. 111 Business accommodation services which provided mail-forwarding and phone-answering. **1937** M. ALLINGHAM *Dancers in Mourning* xxv. 300 The 'phone bell alone was silent and everyone..was waiting for that shrill, familiar alarum. **1950** T. WALSH *Nightmare in Manhattan* (1951) III. 86 The phone bell had given him a first intuitive comprehension. **1972** 'H. HOWARD' *Nice Day for Funeral* v. 82 It was the phone bell that prodded me awake. **1965** N. FREELING *Criminal Conversation* I. ix. 63 Sounds like your night for collecting a phone bill. Why not do this in the office—then you wouldn't have to pay for them? **1972** *Guardian* 24 Aug. 20/5 He..had to sell his camera to pay his phone bill. **1925** F. SCOTT FITZGERALD *Great Gatsby* (1926) ix. 198 Meyer Wolfshiem's name wasn't in the phone book. **1963** 'E. MCBAIN' *Ten Plus One* (1964) ii. 23 Carella picked up the phone book and looked up the number. **1977** G. SCOTT *Hot Pursuit* vi. 56 Give us a ring. We're in the phone book. **1927** W. R. JAMES *Cow Country* vii. 199 He came back in the hotel and went in the phone-booth and there he proceeded to call them up, one after another. **1952** S. KAUFFMANN *Philanderer* (1953) xi. 186 He had to fret away three or four minutes outside the busy phone booth. **1976** 'M. DELVING' *China Expert* vi. 72 One of the phone booths across the street. **1954** M. STEWART *Madam, will you Talk?* xvi. 127 There's a phone box a mile or so along the road. **1968** 'R. RAINE' *Night of Hawk* xiv. 75 Henry made an anonymous call to the police from a near-by phone box. **1977** D. JAMES *Spy at Evening* ix. 61, I left the hot-house atmosphere of the phone box. **1929** D. HAMMETT *Dain Curse* (1930) xv. 166, I wasn't convinced that my phone call was of any importance. **1959** N. MAILER *Advts. for Myself* (1961) 198 About a month later, this letter was followed by a phone call. **1977** W. MCILVANNEY *Laidlaw* xxxviii. 179 There had been a funny phone-call for me when I got back..checking that I could still be reached here. **1972** J. PHILIPS *Vanishing Senator* (1973) II. ii. 67 Some of those letter writers and phone callers might be willing to help. [**1980** *Brit. Telecom Jrnl.* I. II. p. xxi. (Advt.), Call up the future with Phonocard. Pre-paid card public telephone box.] **1982** *Brit. Telecommunications Engineering* Apr. 9/1 A public-service trial began in July 1981 of 200 payphones which accept as means of payment, instead of coins, a pre-paid phone card. **1983** *Ambit* July 11/3 The regular payphone user may well buy the special phone-cards, but casual users probably won't. **1986** *Daily Tel.* 19 Nov. 1/3 Payment will be by phonecards which will be sold in buffet cars and from train trolleys. **1939** R. CAMPBELL *Flowering Rifle* v. 131 In the munition-works, the 'phone-exchange. **1924** H. CRANE *Let.* 29 Jan. (1965) 173 Putting down money for a phone installation. **1946** P. CARTER in *Astounding Sci. Fict.* Aug. 49/2 He pulled out the phone jack, plugged it in elsewhere. **1973** *New Yorker* 14 Apr. 32/2 It will have phone jacks, so the staff will be able to answer queries without going back to a central desk. **1976** M. MACHLIN *Pipeline* ii. 31 There was a phone jack just behind his chair in the dining room. **1968** R. V. BESTE *Repeat Instructions* xv. 154 He.. went out to the phone kiosk and arranged to see King. **1977** G. MARKSTEIN *Chance Awakening* lv. 169 That silent street corner by the 'phone kiosk. **1930** M. ALLINGHAM *Mystery Mile* xxiii. 217 He overheard a 'phone message. **1955** *Times* 23 July 4/4 Norbury knows nothing about this. In all the 'phone messages I have impersonated him. **1978** M. BIRMINGHAM *Sleep in Ditch* 117 He has no address now, just gets a phone message once a month telling him where to send a money order. **1911** G. STRATTON-PORTER *Harvester* xvii. 393, I want Dr. Frank Harmon... I don't know the 'phone number. **1960** C. MACINNES *Mr. Love & Justice* 51 I'm a seaman... I've got stacks of foreign phone numbers in my diary. **1971** R. RENDELL *One Across* vi. 51 One day he'd walk in..to find the lot of them gone and a note on the table with a Chigwell phone number on it. **1973** E. HYAMS *Final Agenda* vi. 82 Call that phone operator and make sure she knows English, French or German. **1932** *New Yorker* 4 June 7 (Advt.), Mail and phone orders filled. **1975** *Ibid.* 20 Oct. 38/1 Martin finds phone-patch relays difficult; he forgets to say 'Over' when it's time for his father to speak, and he can't get used to the idea of not being able to interrupt. **1976** PERKOWSKI & STRAL *Joy of CB* xii. 142 A phone patch links a mobile rig to a land line through a base station. The mobile user contacts a base station with a phone patch. The base station operator then places the call, and connects the land line to the base's rig, placing the telephone handset in a cradle device or otherwise establishing an electrical connection with the rig. Once the connection is made, a voice-operated transmitter relay or a switch operated by the base station operator transmits the voice of the land-line party through the base transmitter. **1970** R. LOWELL *Notebk.* 191 He's trying to part his hair on the phone-receiver. **1959** *Daily Tel.* 10 Dec. 1/8 Motion of censure on 'phone tap'. **1966** 'G. BLACK' *You want to die, Johnny?* vii. 130, I didn't think he'd known about the phone tap. **1973** J. WAINWRIGHT *Pride of Pigs* 169 No sweat, princess. They don't phone-tap too easily in this country, so we're okay. **1976** W. GREATOREX *Crossover* 193 Meade had just told him of the phone-tap report. *Ibid.* 191 She said it in Russian knowing that the phone tappers would have to send the tape to the linguists. **1957** *Times* 12 June 9/5 We are thus, it seems, to have phone-tapping on suspicion. **1976** R. PERRY *One Good Death* v. 68 Phone-tapping had become one of the essential props of modern government. **1951** Phone wire [see PHONEVISION]. **1964** L. DEIGHTON *Funeral in Berlin* xxxvii. 227 Two G.P.O. phone wires had been brought in..and could be attached to the handset. **1978** R. HILL *Pinch of Snuff* v. 44 The phone wire was cut.

phone (fəʊn), *v. colloq.* Also 'phone. [Abbrev. TELEPHONE *v.*] **a.** *trans.* = TELEPHONE *v.* 1c. Also const. *up* and with advbs.

1889 *Telephone* 1 Feb. 56/1 The expression 'I telephoned So-and-So', is often rendered 'I phoned So-and-So.' **1900** *Westm. Gaz.* 26 Sept. 8 (Advt.) Wire, phone, or write Publisher, 'Westminster Gazette', Tudor House, Tudor Street, E.C. **1901** *Ibid.* 4 Sept. 4/2 Mr. Higgins was promptly "phoned". **1909** *Daily Chron.* 10 Dec. 7/2 He could 'phone up Scotland Yard for a detective. **1910** 'W. LAWTON' *Boy Aviators on Secret Service* ii. 22 Wait a minute while I go to 'phone my resignation. **1962** I. MURDOCH *Unofficial Rose* xvi. 159 Was it really necessary to phone me? **1963** L. DEIGHTON *Horse under Water* xliv. 181, I couldn't have Charley phoning up the police. **1974** A. ROSS *Bradford Business* 146 [He] offered me a tuppenny piece... 'Take it,' he said testily, 'and phone her back.' **1976** *Daily Tel.* 2 Nov. 17/2, I 'phoned Paris, and explained what had happened.

b. *intr.* = TELEPHONE *v.* 1a. Freq. with particle as phrasal verb or with advbs.

1925 F. SCOTT FITZGERALD *Great Gatsby* viii. 193 Gatsby ..left word with the butler that if any one phoned word was to be brought to him at the pool. **1926** E. O'NEILL *Great God Brown* III. i. 73 Shall I phone for a doctor? **1927** *Rev. Eng. Stud.* Oct. 433 Phrases like *e.g. phone through* and *come across* no more represent 'degradation' than do *give up, give in, ring up, send off, think out.* **1932** T. S. ELIOT *Sweeney Agonistes* 13 She says will you ring up on Monday... All right, Monday you'll phone through. **1946** E. O'NEILL *Iceman Cometh* IV. 231 It was Hickman himself phoned in and said we'd find him here around two. **1955** *Times* 11 June 4/3 If you will 'phone for an appointment when the strike is over, I will try to fix a convenient date. **1959** I. JEFFERIES *Thirteen Days* viii. 105 He phoned around and..within an hour I had a motley but effective army. **1962** L. DEIGHTON *Ipcress File* xvii. 101 Phone in this time tomorrow. **1972** C. FREMLIN *Appointment with Yesterday* vii. 56 You've hardly been in the place two hours, and she has to phone up. **1977** F. BRANSTON *Up & Coming Man* xiii. 147 Andy and I took turns to phone round... Nearly every news desk called back.

c. *trans.* Const. *in.* = TELEPHONE *v.* 1b.

1972 *Radio Times* 28 Dec. 53/1 Parents phone in their questions on the three Rs to Miss Edith Biggs..and Ronald Palmer. **1973** *Black World* Mar. 15 (*caption*) Tell him to hurry up—I've got to phone in a bomb threat. **1977** *Gay News* 24 Mar. 20/1 We have many flats and bedsits with understanding landlords available now. (Landlords, please phone in your vacancies!)

Hence **ˈphoner** = TELEPHONER; also ***phoner-in***; **ˈphoning** *vbl. sb.* = TELEPHONING *vbl. sb.*

1908 *Daily Chron.* 10 Aug. 7/1 So graphically had Enid done her bit of descriptive 'phoning that he was under no illusions as to what he had to do. **1942** BERREY & VAN DEN BARK *Amer. Thes. Slang* §808/3 *Telephoner*, phoner. **1957** 'A. GARVE' *Narrow Search* iii. 80 I'll have to do a bit of phoning in the morning. **1972** *Listener* 27 Jan. 124/1 An excellent job of training phoners to that programme by classic reward and punishment methods. **1975** *Times* 26 Apr. 8/5 Radio 4's *The Forbidden Subject* was..a phone-in. .. The phoners-in, with two exceptions, were all women. **1977** *Belfast Tel.* 24 Jan. 3/5, I hope that phoners-in are not an accurate cross-section of the population. **1977** *Times* 12 Feb. 12/1 This is your late night phone-in programme... Mr. Jenkins..says you phoners are ignorant, pathetic and moronic.

-phone (fəʊn), ad. Gr. φων-ή voice, φῶν-ος sounding. **1.** Used in the sense 'sound' in the names of various instruments (scientific and musical), as GRAMOPHONE, MAGNETOPHONE, MEGAPHONE, MELLOPHONE, MICROPHONE, VIBRAPHONE.

2. Used in the sense 'speaker of' or '-speaking' in the formation of nouns and adjectives from Latinate combining forms of names of peoples and languages, as *Anglophone, Bulgarophone,* FRANCOPHONE *sb.* and *a.*, *Turcophone.*

1900 Anglophone [see FRANCOPHONE *sb.* and *a.*]. **1937** Bulgarophone [see EXARCHIST]. **1977** *Times Litt. Suppl.* 18 Mar. 295/5 His description of Turcophones in Iran (of whom he is one) as a 'nation'.

phone freak, var. PHONE PHREAK *sb.* and *v.*

phoneidoscope (fəʊˈnaɪdəskəʊp). [f. Gr. φωνή voice + εἶδο-ς form, figure + -SCOPE. Cf. *kaleidoscope.*] An instrument for exhibiting the colour-figures produced by the action of sound-vibrations upon a thin film, e.g. of soap-solution.

1878 *Cassell's Fam. Mag.* 576/1 By means of a recently constructed instrument known as the Phoneidoscope. **1893** *Athenæum* 4 Feb. 159/1 Prof. Sedley Taylor.. produced an instrument he unhappily named the 'Phoneidoscope', which was contrived to exhibit the 'crispations' of a soap film set in vibration by a vocal sound.

Hence **phoneidoscopic** (-'skɒpɪk) *a.*

1880 *Nature* 8 Jan. 243/1 M. Guébhard.. proceeded to show that.. the fleeting films condensed from the breath may exhibit phoneidoscopic properties.

phone-in ('fəʊnɪn). [f. phr. *to phone in*, f. PHONE *v.* + IN *adv.*; for sense 1 see also -IN[3].] **1.** A protest in the form of mass telephone calls of complaint.

1967 *New Statesman* 17 Mar. 356/3 In San Francisco.. Mrs. Whitehouse has perfected the phone-in. **1973** *Times* 8 Feb. 6/1 Actress Dame Peggy Ashcroft plans to join a massive 'phone-in'.. aimed at jamming the switchboard of the Department of the Environment.

2. A 'live broadcast' radio or television programme during which listeners telephone the studios to ask questions or express their views. Also, this type of broadcasting. Also *attrib.*

1968 *Time* 29 Mar. 16 He proposed reducing transit fares for San Franciscans over 65 to 5¢ and, on a subsequent TV 'phone-in', said he would try to get buses closer to the curb at pickup. **1971** *Listener* 30 Dec. 915 One of the most exciting potentials this year has been the phone-in. **1972** *Guardian* 13 Mar. 11/2 Duke Miller of St. Petersburg asked him on a phone-in show.. how voters were expected to forgive him for his part in the escalation of the war. **1974** *Daily Tel.* 30 Jan. 13/1 The arrival of phone-in conveniently coincided with the fashion for public 'participation and access' in broadcasting. *Ibid.* 11 Feb. 5/5 There will be a daily 55-minute 'phone-in' on Radio 4 to 13 leading figures from the main Parties. **1977** B. PYM *Quartet in Autumn* xiv. 118 Listening to a phone-in programme on the radio she had heard a question about holidays for people on their own.

†**phonel**, obs. erron. form of FUNNEL.

1426 LYDG. *De Guil. Pilgr.* 12988 He me gaff.. Thys sak also, and thys phonel Wyth wych my wynes I vp tonne.

phonematic (fəʊnɪ'mætɪk), *a.* and *sb. Linguistics.* [f. Gr. φωνήματ- stem of φώνημα sound made + -IC.] **A.** *adj.* **a.** = PHONEMIC *a.*

1936 *Proc. 2nd Internat. Congr. Phonetic Sci.* 50, Z, considered as a phonematic unit, has a value very different from the value it has when considered as a grammatical unit. **1936** *Language* XII. 311 Professor J. Vendryes.. announced that competent legal opinion indicated the desirability of organizing separate national groups.. for the advancement of phonological (phonematic) studies. **1949** *Trans. Philol. Soc. 1948* 129 We may speak of a five-vowel or seven-vowel phonematic system. **1952** A. COHEN *Phonemes of Eng.* i. 12 An implication is the replacing of one phoneme by another under definite phonematic conditions. **1956** J. WHATMOUGH *Language* v. 84 The strange words that a language adopts are adapted to its own phonematic and other patterns. **1958** *Proc. 8th Internat. Congr. Linguists.* 763 Quechua, a language with a phonematic system of 3 vowels only. **1962** P. S. RAY in F. A. Rice *Study of Role of Second Lang. in Asia, Afr. & Lat. Amer.* 101 Even one who prefers to write 'phonemic' rather than 'phonematic' is doing a bit of prescriptive intervention. **1977** A. SHERIDAN tr. *Lacan's Ecrits* iv. 126 The elements of the language (*langue*) at its different levels, from the phonematic pair of oppositions to the compound expressions to disengage the stable forms of which is the task of the most modern research.

b. In 'prosodic analysis', designating a segmental element of vowel or consonant features which combines with prosodies (see PROSODY 3).

1949 [see PROSODY 3]. **1964** R. H. ROBINS *Gen. Linguistics* iv. 159 *Prosodic analysis*, as it is usually called, is a brief title for a method of phonological analysis that employs as fundamental concepts two types of element, not reducible to a common type, prosodies and phonematic units. **1968** J. LYONS *Introd. Theoret. Linguistics.* iii. 129 The sequence of phonematic units constitutes the segmental 'infrastructure' of the word, whereas the prosodies form its 'superstructure'. **1972** HARTMANN & STORK *Dict. Lang. & Linguistics* 187/2 At first sight phonematic units and prosodies seem to be equivalent to segmental and suprasegmental phonemes of the traditional phonemic analysis, but in a prosodic analysis, features which would be assigned to segmental phonemes in a phonemic analysis are sometimes assigned to prosodies, e.g. such features as palatalisation, nasalisation or lip rounding.

B. *sb. pl.* [see -IC 2.] **a.** Phonemics.

1936 *Proc. 2nd Internat. Congr. Phonetic Sci.* 49 By *phonematics* I understand a science which treats phonemes exclusively as elements of language. **1939** L. H. GRAY *Foundations of Lang.* iii. 62 The phoneme.. is.. regarded as ..a point in the linguistic (grammatical) pattern ('phonematics'). **1949** *Amer. Speech* XXIV. 54 It [*sc.* the term *phonemics*] has replaced in American usage the terms *phonology* and *phonematics*. **1953** W. J. ENTWISTLE *Aspects of Lang.* iii. 94 The chapter-heading *Sounds* is used to cover.. questions affecting the pattern (phonematics, not the ungrammatical 'phonemics'). **1960** J. VACHEK *Dict. de Linguistique de l'École de Prague* 61/1 *Phonologie* (Phonemics; less frequently, Phonematics/Phonology..). **1961** *Brno Studies in English* III. 55 In his well-known compendium of diachronistic phonematics,.. A. Martinet rightly insists on the presence in any language of two opposed forces. **1964** E. PALMER tr. *Martinet's Elem. Gen. Linguistics.* i. 30 They form a chapter entitled prosody distinct from phonematics, which treats of the units of the second articulation.

b. That part of 'prosodic analysis' which deals with phonematic units.

1971 *Archivum Linguisticum* New Ser. II. 68 'Phonematics' (a term which bears only etymological resemblance to 'phonemics').

So **phone'matically** *adv.*, in relation to phonemes or phonematic units; according to the theory of phonemes or phonematic units; **phonemati'zation**, advancement from allophonic to phonemic status; **phonema'tology**, phonemics, phonematics (sense a).

1949 *Archivum Linguisticum* I. 41 There is, further, a well-known problem in English phonematology. **1950** *Ibid.* II. 181 The book [*sc.* D. Jones's *The Phoneme*] is.. essentially a hand-book of phonematology. **1951** S. ULLMANN *Princ. Semantics* ii. 47 With reference to phonematically constituted word-engrams. **1956** *Trans. Philol. Soc.* 34 There are distinctions in the written language which are phonematically motivated. **1956** J. WHATMOUGH *Language* i. 11 If you hear *pwivate* 'private' from a few speakers [w] is a variant, phonematically speaking, of [r]. **1958** A. S. C. ROSS *Etym.* i. 24 Phonematology has one extremely practical application, that is, the construction of alphabets for languages hitherto unwritten. **1962** *Canad. Jrnl. Linguistics* VII. II. 79 When such adaptations become loanwords, however, they sometimes are phonematically homophonous with native words. **1964** *Amer. Speech* XXXIX. 70 Phonematization of /ü/ in eastern dialects of Basque resulted from changes [o] → [u], [u] → [ü]. **1971** *Archivum Linguisticum* New Ser. II. 85 With the exception of the 3 sg. general tense ending.., all the endings can be analyzed phonematically as the same for each person regardless of tense. **1977** *Word 1972* XXVIII. 250 Automatic nasalization of vowels in contact with nasal consonants is a general characteristic of languages in which there are no phonematically nasalized vowels. **1978** *Language* LIV. 231 Phonematization relies on the examination of contrasts.

phoneme ('fəʊniːm, formerly fəʊ'niːm). [= F. *phonème*, ad. Gr. φώνημα a sound, f. φωνεῖν to sound.] **1. a.** = PHONE *sb.*[1] *rare.*

1894 G. DUNN in *Classical Rev.* Mar. 95/1 The problem remains to determine whether there are any Phonemes which may be regarded as the representatives of these hypothetical and analogically deduced long sonants.

b. A phonological unit of language that cannot be analysed into smaller linear units and that in any particular language is realized in non-contrastive variants. Also *attrib.* See ALLOPHONE.

Although its exact nature is disputed, and the existence of an abstract phonemic level (and hence the abstract phoneme as a constituent of morphemes) is controversial in phonological theory, the phoneme remains a standard taxonomic unit in the description of speech. The phoneme of structural linguistics is sometimes called the ***autonomous*** or ***taxonomic phoneme*** by generative phonologists, and distinguished from the ***systematic phoneme***.

1896 R. J. LLOYD in *Die Neueren Sprachen* III. 615 There are a few of these terms which the author [*sc.* J. Baudouin de Courtenay] still thinks valuable and retains. One of these is the term *phoneme*, invented by Kruszewski... I take it that the various sounds which are accepted as identical by any speaking community are one *phoneme*, though they may differ considerably in actual sound. **1917** D. JONES in *Trans. Philol. Soc. 1917–20* (1932) 99 The Sechuana language appears to contain twenty-eight phonemes, i.e. twenty-eight sounds or small families of sounds which are capable of distinguishing one word from another. **1928** I. C. WARD *Phonetics of English* 61 Care must be taken not to confuse the various members of the phoneme with the different pronunciations heard from different people. The latter may be termed *variant pronunciations*; the different sounds constituting a phoneme occur in *one* person's pronunciation. **1933** L. BLOOMFIELD *Language* v. 80 The phonemes of a language are not sounds, but merely features of sound which the speakers have been trained to produce and recognize in the current of actual speech-sound. **1935** G. K. ZIPF *Psycho-Biol. of Lang.* i. 20 A word may consist of a single phoneme.. or it may represent a phoneme-sequence of considerable magnitude. **1936** *Amer. Speech* XI. 109 When in a given language two sounds occur in the same phonological conditions and neither of the two sounds may be substituted for the other without changing the meanings of the words, the two sounds are capable of differentiating two words and are realizations of two different phonemes. **1939** L. H. GRAY *Foundations of Lang.* iii. 61 The exact nature of the phoneme is disputed. It is variously regarded as 1) a mere grouping of sounds.. 2) as a point in the psychological pattern (.. Sapir and the Prague School); or 3) as a point in the linguistic (grammatical) pattern. **1950** D. JONES *Phoneme* ii. 10 A phoneme is a family of sounds in a given language which are related in character and are used in such a way that no one member ever occurs in a word in the same phonetic context as any other member. *Ibid.* 12 Some phoneticians have employed the term phoneme to mean anything that may serve to effect a minimal distinction.. between one word and another. **1958** K. AMIS *I like it Here* i. 6 To cut Sinatra off in mid-phoneme was not such uproarious fun. **1961** W. R. BRAIN *Speech Disorders* i. 10 The letters of an alphabet transcribe with more or less precision the phonemes of speech, of which standard English has about thirty-two. **1962** A. C. GIMSON *Introd. Pronunc. Eng.* v. 44 It is possible to establish the phonemes of a language by means of a process of commutation or the discovery of *minimal pairs*, i.e. pairs of words which are different in respect of only one sound segment. **1968** R. T. HARMS *Introd. Phonological Theory* 14 In this presentation the term 'phoneme' is used in the sense of systematic phoneme. **1968** *Language* XLIV. 723 A consideration of the taxonomic phonemes of a language may.. be of use in determining the orthographic peculiarities of a scribe. **1970** F. BRENGELMAN *Eng. Lang.* p. viii, The concept of the phoneme is used here because the author believes that the English spelling system can be described best with reference to a segmented representation. **1971** D. CRYSTAL *Linguistics* iv. 183, I have spent so much space on the phoneme concept because of its unequalled status as a concept for organizing people's thinking in the first half of this century. **1975** *Jrnl. Linguistics* XI. I. 40 This phonologically motivated structure is given in terms of systematic phonemes. **1975** L. M. HYMAN *Phonology* 82 It would be worthwhile to briefly examine the kind of argument given against what has come to be known as the 'autonomous' or 'taxonomic' phoneme. **1977** *Language* LIII. 241 He rejects the orthodox neo-Bloomfieldian motto 'Once a phoneme, always a phoneme'. **1978** *Ibid.* LIV. 173 With one of his main points (that the taxonomic phoneme is not dead), I would naturally agree.

2. *Psychol.* [ad. G. *phonem* (C. Wernicke *Grundriss der Psychiatrie* (1896) II. 126).] (See quot. 1911.)

1905 A. J. ROSANOFF tr. *J. Rogues de Fursac's Man. Psychiatry* I. ii. 44 Phonemes (the verbal auditory hallucinations of Séglas) have.. a special significance, inasmuch as they consist of 'words representing ideas'. **1911** W. A. WHITE *Outl. Psychiatry* (ed. 3) vi. 47 The more complicated hallucinations which are conceived by the patient to be 'voices'—verbal auditory hallucinations—are known as phonemes.

Hence ˌ**phonemi'zation** = *phonemicization.*

1959 E. PULGRAM *Introd. Spectrogr. of Speech* xi. 78 (*heading*) Phonemization. **1960** *Amer. Speech* XXXV. 218 The Middle English phonemization of the Old English allophones of the postdental spirant.

phonemic (fəʊ'niːmɪk), *a.* and *sb. Linguistics.* [f. PHONEME 1 b + -IC.] **A.** *adj.* Of or pertaining to phonemes or phoneme theory; analysable in terms of phoneme theory.

1933 L. BLOOMFIELD *Language* v. 85 The laboratory phonetician usually knows, from other sources, the phonemic character of the speech-sounds he is studying. **1933** E. SAPIR in *Encycl. Social Sci.* IX. 155/2 Not only are all languages phonetic in character; they are also 'phonemic'. *Ibid.*, Languages differ very widely in their phonemic structure. **1942** BLOCH & TRAGER *Outl. Linguistic Analysis* ii. 36 For nearly all purposes it is better to use a *Phonemic* transcription, which represents the sounds of the language organized into a few dozen distinctive units. **1947** E. H. STURTEVANT *Introd. Linguistic Sci.* xi. 122 No scholar has a right to demand.. that we discard the familiar and convenient word *phonemic* for the reason that if an ancient Greek had coined an adjective from the noun *phōnēma* he would probably have produced *phōnēmaticos*. **1950** R. A. HALL *Linguistics & Your Lang.* vi. 96 Then, when he has gotten the best phonetic and phonemic analysis possible for the language he is working on, the linguist is ready to go ahead and analyze its grammatical structure. **1950** D. JONES *Phoneme* ii. 9 The more general use of the term [*sc.* language] covers the speech of people who speak in ways differing considerably from each other—who use different sounds, or who use sounds in such a way that a different phonemic classification is called for. **1955** *Q. Jrnl. Speech* XLI. 254/1 The variation is non-significant, of course, but belongs on the morphemic rather than the phonemic level. **1958** *Times Lit. Suppl.* 13 June 334/5 The earlier lessons, which offer a phonemic transcription with the ordinary spelling of words, ask for hard work both in the classroom and outside. **1964** M. A. K. HALLIDAY et al. *Linguistic Sci.* 300 Transformation grammar has thus taken over, but reversed, the hierarchical relation among levels that is characteristic of phonemic-morphemic theory. **1965** CHOMSKY & HALLE in *Jrnl. Linguistics* I. 98 We suggested the names *systematic phonemic and systematic phonetic* for these levels of representation. *Ibid.*, We called these *taxonomic phonemic theories* so as to bring out their reliance on procedures of segmentation and classification and their essential independence of 'higher levels'. **1967** *Ibid.* III. 3 The advantage of introducing a systematic phonemic level is that it enables us to generalize the phonological description beyond the limits of one speaker. *Ibid.* 25 Given a taxonomic phonemic system, it can always be 'translated' into distinctive feature terms. **1968** CHOMSKY & HALLE *Sound Pattern Eng.* 11 We will make no further mention of 'phonemic analysis' or 'phonemes' in this study and will also avoid terms such as 'morphophonemic' which imply the existence of a phonemic level. **1968** P. M. POSTAL *Aspects Phonol. Theory* iv. 90 It is natural to view autonomous phonemic representations as being exactly like phonetic representations except that certain 'redundant', 'predictable', 'noncontrastive', etc., features of the phonetic representation have been eliminated. **1971** *Language* XLVII. 503 Some of the theoretical discussions dealing with generative phonology have been concerned with demonstrating that a *phonemic* level of representation could not be motivated within phonological descriptions and that the only relevant levels were the morphophonemic and the phonetic. **1972** M. L. SAMUELS *Linguistic Evol.* iii. 31 Phonemic shifts are.. often extensive and involve a large part of the vocalic or consonantal systems. **1973** A. H. SOMMERSTEIN *Sound Pattern Anc. Greek* i. 2 An autonomous phonemic description of classical Attic. **1974** tr. *Wertheim's Evolution & Revolution* iii. 74 At present China could lead the way in introducing 'phonemic spelling'.

B. *sb. pl.* (const. as *sing.*). [See -IC 2.] The study of phonemes and phoneme systems; phonemic analysis.

1936 W. F. TWADDELL in *Language* XII. 294 These [t]s, in the practice of every writer on phonemics, are considered as one phoneme. **1940** *Ibid.* XVI. 247 In English we have the incomparably superior term *phonemics*, which leaves us free to use *phonology* in its old and widely established usage as a general term for all the phenomena concerned with the production and use of sounds. **1949** G. L. TRAGER *Field of Linguistics* 5 The description of the phonemes of a language, and of their occurrence and arrangement, is the phonemics of that language. **1952** A. COHEN *Phonemes of Eng.* i. 4 Phonemics.. must concern itself with studying distinctive oppositions existing between sounds or sound features. **1957** N. CHOMSKY *Syntactic Struct.* i. 11 A linguistic level, such as phonemics, morphology, phrase structure, is essentially a set of descriptive devices that are made available for the construction of grammars. **1964** —— *Current Issues in Linguistic Theory* 74 It seems necessary to conclude that systematic phonemics and systematic phonetics are the only two levels of representation that appear in structural descriptions provided by the phonological component. *Ibid.* 75 Let us coin the term 'taxonomic phonemics' to refer to this body of doctrine.

1968 P. M. Postal *Aspects Phonol. Theory* iv. 89 Traditional autonomous phonemics was able to maintain a natural relation between phonetic and phonemic organization in the absence of any universal rules of the type required by systematic phonemics simply because its phonemic and phonetic systems were so close. **1968** *Language* XLIV. 723 The concept of taxonomic phonemics in linguistics.. arose in part as a result of traditional orthographic practices. **1972** M. L. Samuels *Linguistic Evol.* i. 4 There has been justifiable insistence, in recent decades, that graphetics and graphemics must in the first instance be studied separately, before their relationship with phonetics and phonemics can be considered. **1975** L. M. Hyman *Phonology* 82 Systematic phonemics.. goes beyond proposing an abstract morphophonemic level.

Hence **pho'nemically** *adv.*, with regard to phonemes; in terms of phoneme theory; **phonemicist** (fɒ'niːmɪsɪst), a specialist in or student of phonemics.

1934 *Language* X. 123 If a set of phonemic elements only occur together, they constitute a phonemically unitary complex; thus, the stop and the aspiration in English initial f. **1935** *Ibid.* XI. 97 The technique of analyzing phonemically the structure of a dialect. **1942** Bloch & Trager *Outl. Linguistic Analysis* iii. 46 If a language has only five vowel phonemes, the best way of representing them phonemically—regardless of their phonetic nature—is by the letters *a, e, i, o, u*. *Ibid.* 49 The affricates in *chain* and *Jane* are treated by many phonemicists as unit phonemes, often written /č, ǰ/. **1951** *Language* XXVII. 219 The English affricates *ch* and *j* have generally been regarded as double sounds by phoneticians; but phonemicists have vacillated back and forth. **1966** N. Chomsky in *Current Trends in Linguistics* III. 49 The notion of 'complementary distribution'.. permits analyses that are not acceptable to the taxonomic phonemicist (or to anyone else). **1967** C. L. Wrenn *Word & Symbol* 5 The multifarious and phonemically divergent regional dialects spoken in the Chinese Republic. **1975** *Amer. Speech 1972* XLVII. 246 We list all the contrasting ways of beginning an English stressed syllable (in utterance-initial) that every classical phonemicist would have agreed must be a 'cluster' rather than a single 'segmental phoneme'.

phonemicize (fəʊ'niːmɪsaɪz), *v. Linguistics.* [f. phonemic *a.* and *sb.* + -ize.] **1.** *trans.* To classify, analyse, or describe in terms of phoneme theory. Also *absol.* or *intr.*

1940 *Language* XVI. 354 Lorimer made no attempt to phonemicize here. **1951** *Ibid.* XXVII. 340 We are forced to phonemicize as /patadak/ and /padatak/. **1953** *Ibid.* XXIX. 81 It is difficult to explain to a communications engineer what we mean by phonemicizing. **1953** *Internat. Jrnl. Amer. Linguistics* XIX. 166 Each long nucleus has been phonemicized as a cluster of two phonemes. **1957** *Publ. Amer. Dial. Soc. 1956* xxvi. 46 In these terms learning the sound system of another language could be described as a phonemicizing of diaphones. **1960** *Amer. Speech* XXXV. 234 Would lead to a rapid collection of vast body of contemporary speech by uniform procedures yielding easily phonemicized data. **1960** Z. S. Harris *Structural Linguistics* vii. 71 Such is the question of how to phonemicize long vowels. **1963** F. G. Lounsbury in S. Koch *Psychol.* VI. 567 This process is called 'phonemicizing' the transcription. **1965** *Language* XLI. 480 It would seem possible to phonemicize [nt·] as a cluster *nht. **1972** H. Kurath *Stud. Area Linguistics* 31 When two or more plans of phonemicizing the data seem feasible, preference is given to the one that facilitates the comparison of the dialects. **1975** *Amer. Speech 1972* XLVII. 240 Does 'phonemically different' imply 'different phonemes'? This is a catch-question I put to my students at a certain point as they are learning to 'phonemicize'. **1976** *Language* LII. 307 Once the surface redundancy has been lost, the forms which violate the lost constraint may be phonemicized as having the impermissible sequence.

2. a. *trans.* To advance from allophonic to phonemic status.

1972 M. L. Samuels *Linguistic Evol.* iii. 35 The split of one phoneme into two is clearly mechanical in origin: what are at first allophones of a single phoneme are 'phonemicised', or attain the status of separate phonemes. **1976** *Archivum Linguisticum* VII. 184 One could postulate.. another old series of labials and dentals which changed *u to o and which then joined with the other dentals and labials, 'phonemicizing' the old allophone.

b. *intr.* To attain phonemic status.

1973 J. M. Anderson *Struct. Aspects Lang. Change* 142 The reduction of the labiovelars allowed these fronted allophones to phonemicize.

Hence **pho,nemici'zation**, (*a*) classification into phonemes, description in terms of phoneme theory; phonemic transcription or an instance of this; (*b*) development from allophonic to phonemic status.

1942 C. F. Hockett in *Language* XVIII. 20 Grammatical work is carried on, of course, in cases where phonological information is incomplete... But many of the gaps and ambiguities in such grammar have their source directly in the lack of complete phonemicization. **1948** —— in *Ibid.* XXIV. 123 He should make his phonemic interpretation clearly recognizable.. by including for every form cited.. a possible phonemicization. **1957** *Trans. Philol. Soc.* 22 There is no difficulty about the phonemicization, since there is contrast in such pairs as ker.. and kar,.. pe·r-.. and pa·r. **1972** M. L. Samuels *Linguistic Evol.* iii. 37 It is still possible to argue that what appears to us as coincidental is in fact nothing of the sort, and that the functional pressures towards phonemicisation are more important than the mechanical. **1975** N. Chomsky *Logical Struct. Linguistic Theory* vi. 163 There is no need to think of phonemes as literally occurring in sequence, each with its distinctive physical properties, in the stream of speech. Any attempt to maintain such a view will lead to very artificial phonemicization.

phonendoscope (fəʊ'nɛndəskəʊp). [f. Gr. φωνή voice + ἔνδον within + -scope.] An apparatus for rendering small sounds in the human body, or in solid bodies in general, more distinctly audible.

1895 *Specif. Patent* No. 10223 (p. 1, 1. 35) If this 'phonendo-scope' be brought into contact with any solid body.. the tone-vibrations in that solid body will communicate themselves to the point of contact. **1897** L. Robinson *Wild Traits in Tame Anim.* 262, I took my phonendoscope (.. a form of stethoscope somewhat on the microphone principle).

phone phreak ('fəʊn friːk), *sb.* and *v.* Also **phone freak**. [f. phone *sb.*² + phreak *sb.* and *v.*]

A. *sb.* (See quot. 1972².)

1972 *Daily Tel.* 15 Apr. 3 The Post Office are trying to break up a ring of 'phone phreaks' who are cheating the telephone service. *Ibid.* 9 Oct. 13/6 Detectives and Post Office officials investigating 'phone phreaks'—people who make free telephone calls all over the world by using an electronic device—raided a flat in Hammersmith. **1973** *New Scientist* 5 Apr. 23 The challenge of beating the telephone system to get long distance calls for the 2p price of a local call is not restricted to the so-called 'phone-phreaks'. **1973** *Guardian* 1 June 10/1 Andy first heard the news of Edie Sedgwick's death from a fellow phone-freak on the West Coast. **1976** 'O. Bleeck' *No Questions Asked* xiv. 156 He's a monster phone freak... He knows all the phone company jargon.

B. *v. intr.* To use an electronic device to make telephone calls without payment. Only as **'phone phreaking** *vbl. sb.*

1972 *Daily Tel.* 9 Oct. 13/6 Scotland Yard and the Post Office have been investigating phone phreaking since January. **1973** *Guardian* 22 Jan. 5/3 'Phone phreaking'—making free calls with the use of electronic gadgets—is a growing international problem. **1974** W. Garner *Big enough Wreath* xiii. 197 'What is it? Some kind of calculator?' Bip began with technicalities, ended with a complete exposition of phone freaking. **1976** *Computing Europe* 2 Sept. 5/2 There are a lot of Post Office employees and the recent 'phone phreaking' cases have shown that at least some of them can have criminal inclinations.

‖**phonesis** (fəʊ'niːsɪs). [a. Gr. φώνησις a sounding, f. φωνεῖν to sound.] Utterance of vocal sounds.

1878 Latham *Outl. Philol.* 55 Accent underlies the Monosyllabic system, and belongs to Phonesis. **1883** D. H. Wheeler *By-Ways of Lit.* xi. 221 The same principles involve consonantal phonesis in a perpetual diversity.

phonetic (fəʊ'nɛtɪk), *a.* and *sb.* [ad. mod.L. *phōnĕtic-us* (Zoega 1797), a. Gr. φωνητικός adj., f. φωνητός to be spoken, f. φωνεῖν to utter voice, speak. In F. *phonétique* (Dict. Acad. 1878).]

A. *adj.* **1.** Representing vocal sounds: applied to signs or characters which represent the sounds, esp. the individual or elementary sounds, of speech, or which express the pronunciation of words.

Applied *spec.* **a.** to characters in ancient writing (orig. Egyptian) representing sounds, opposed to the *ideographic* or *pictorial*; and **b.** to systems of spelling in which each letter represents invariably the same spoken sound, e.g. to systems proposed for reform of English spelling, as opposed to the traditional (*historical* or *etymological*) method.

a. [**1797** G. Zoega *De Origine et Usu Obeliscorum* 454 Superest quinta classis notarum phoneticarum, quem ad aenigmaticam referri posse jam monui.] **1826** *Edin. Rev.* XLV. 104 The picture-writers, seeking for the first time to express sounds, and so to render their work Phonetic. **1831** M. Russell *Egypt* xi. (1853) 434 To George Zoega also belongs the merit of employing (1797) the term phonetic. **1851** D. Wilson *Preh. Ann.* (1863) II. iv. iv. 285 The derivation of.. phonetic symbols from a primitive system of pictorial writing. **1879** Renouf *Orig. Relig.* 16 The key to hieroglyphic decipherment [consists] in the knowledge of the simultaneous use of both phonetic and ideographic signs.

b. **1848** A. J. Ellis (*title*) A Plea for Phonetic Spelling. **1848** —— *Esenʃalz ov Fωnetics* p. ii, Key to the Phonetic spelling employed in this work... A copious account of the English phonetic alphabet is furnished.. pp. 87–105. **1864** Max Müller *Sci. Lang.* II. iii. 108 A new system of 'Brief Writing and True Spelling', best known under the name of the *Phonetic Reform*. **1864** *Soc. Sci. Rev.* 223 The Phonetic alphabet.. consists of thirty-four letters, twenty-two being consonants and twelve vowels. These.. fairly represent every important sound in our language.

2. a. Of, pertaining or relating to the sounds of spoken language; consisting of vocal sounds.

1861 Max Müller *Sc. Lang.* I. ii. 40 Two processes which should be carefully distinguished...—1. Dialectical Regeneration. 2. Phonetic Decay. **1867** Miss Broughton *As a Flower* xiii. 125 A whistle, from which unfeminine phonetic exercise she however refrained. **1875** Whitney *Life Lang.* iv. 53 This.. is itself an example of phonetic change. **1884** J. Tait *Mind in Matter* (1892) 183 Advanced languages are 'evolved' chiefly by plagiarism and by phonetic corruption.

b. Involving vibration of the vocal cords (as opp. to mere breath or whisper). Cf. phonate.

1880 M. Mackenzie *Dis. Throat & Nose* I. 443 His voice was weak, but phonetic.

c. *Comb.* (= phonetico-), as *phonetic-linguistic*, *-morphological*, *-phonemic*, *-semantic* adjs.

1961 L. F. Brosnahan *Sounds of Language* v. 101 The criteria.. are of phonetic-linguistic nature. **1921** E. Sapir *Language* viii. 185 In other words, on this particular point it took German at least three hundred years to catch up with a phonetic-morphological drift that had long been under way in English. **1966** M. Pei *Gloss. Linguistic Terminol.* p. ix, A specialist in descriptive linguistics and phonetic-phonemic description. **1931** L. Bloomfield in *Language* VII. 205 Some linguistic forms bear no partial phonetic-semantic resemblance to other forms. **1966** M. Pei *Gloss. Linguistic Terminol.* 204 There is a partial phonetic-semantic resemblance in all forms containing a particular phonestheme.

†**3.** *Entom.* Applied to the collar or prothorax of hymenopterous insects when its posterior angles cover the mesothoracic or so-called vocal spiracles.

1826 Kirby & Sp. *Entomol.* IV. 331 Collar... 5. Phonetic.. When its posterior angles approaching the wings, cover the vocal spiracles. Ex. *Hymenoptera*.

B. *sb.* An element of a Chinese character which is itself the character for another word, adopted as part of the new character because of the words' identity or similarity of sound. = primitive *sb.* 6.

1842 J.-M. Callery *Encycl. Chinese Lang.* 3 The phonetic is in itself one of the characters of primitive formation, which cannot be annexed to any of the preceding orders, and which must therefore be looked on as indivisible. **1874** S. W. Williams *Syllabic Dict. Chinese Lang.* p. lvi/1 That part of a character which is not the radical, has no name among the Chinese, but foreigners have termed it the *primitive* or *phonetic*. **1907** W. Hillier *Chinese Lang.* i. 6 It is possible.. by learning these phonetics, or primitives as they are sometimes called, to make a very close guess at the sound of any Chinese character. **1948** R. A. D. Forrest *Chinese Lang.* ii. 38 In many cases the connection of the phonetic element, whether in sound or shape, with a word still existing independently, or with the same phonetic in other characters, has become much more obscure through changes in sound or in written form. **1968** P. Kratochvíl *Chinese Lang. Today* v. 151 The former was the borrowed phonetic.. and the latter the radical added as an indication that the whole form was borrowed and denoting something connected with manual action. **1973** *Sci. Amer.* Feb. 54/2 There are characters that are not pronounced like their phonetic, often for reasons of historical change.

Hence **pho'netical** *a.* (*rare*), phonetic; **pho'netically** *adv.*, in a phonetic manner; in relation to vocal sound; according to sound or pronunciation; **phonetician** (fəʊnɪ'tɪʃən), one versed in speech-sounds, a phonetist; **phoneticism** (fəʊ'nɛtɪsɪz(ə)m), (*a*) phonetic quality, or the phonetic system, of writing or spelling; (*b*) phonetic spelling; an example of this; (*c*) use of the criterion of phonetic similarity to determine the phonemes of a language; **pho'neticist** (-sɪst), (*a*) an advocate of phonetic spelling; (*b*) = *phonetician*; **phoneticization** (-saɪ'zeɪʃən), phonetic spelling; an example of this; (greater) correlation of symbol and sound (in a writing system); **pho'neticize** (-saɪz) *v. trans.*, to render phonetic, to write phonetically.

1845 Ellis *Plea Phonotypy & Phonography* 4 *note*, In this pamphlet, we only recommend Phonography upon the score of its giving a correct *phonetical representation of the English language. **1867** Burton *Hist. Scot.* (1873) I. v. 188 By a distinct phonetical and grammatical pedigree. **1826** *Edin. Rev.* XLV. 120 Characters employed by the Egyptians.. *phonetically in representing foreign combinations of sound. **1876** T. Hill *Order Studies* 108 Bad spelling.. usually arises from an attempt to spell phonetically with the common alphabet. **1848** A. J. Ellis *Esenʃalz ov Fωnetics* 88 A practist *fωnetiʃan. **1859** A. Holbrook *Normal Meth.* 34 The most approved views of Phoneticians have been made subservient. **1877** Sweet *Handbk. Phonetics* 20 The first and indispensable qualification of the phonetician is a thorough practical knowledge of the formation of the vowels. **1933** L. Bloomfield *Language* v. 75 The phonetician can study either the sound-producing movements of the speaker.. or the resulting sound-waves. **1964** D. Abercrombie *Eng. Phonetic Texts* 14 It is not, in the nature of things, possible for a 'standard' mode of transcription of English, suitable for all purposes and all audiences, to be agreed on by phoneticians. **1975** *Amer. Speech 1973* XLVIII. 111 To do so is perfectly sound phonemically, though Phoneticians use a modified symbol (with hook) for the *r*-colored vowel. **1885** G. L. Gomme *Hist. T. Hickathrift* p. iv, There are too few *phoneticisms and dialect words to make it probable that the print in the Pepysian collection is the one directly derived from popular tradition. **1938** *Better English* Nov. 44/1 Phoneticism is not a noble progressive movement. It is only an annoying attack on a superior language which will never give up its proud fundamental structure. **1939** *Amer. Speech* XIV. 148/1 The author condemns phoneticism as contrary to language structure. **1952** A. Cohen *Phonemes of Eng.* ii. 24 The same objection to phoneticism in phonemic analysis can be raised against Trubetzkoy's handling of the problem how to decide whether we have to do with one or more phonemes. **1977** *Daily Tel.* 24 Feb. 18 Probably the most bizarre example of phoneticism I have ever come across was an 11-year-old's spelling of the word 'usual'—'yousyouall'. **1849** *Fraser's Mag.* XL. 423 To the consistent *phoneticist, we need only observe that the new code.. would be as arbitrary as the old. **1932** G. K. Zipf *Sel. Stud. Princ. Relative Frequency in Lang.* I. 4 All phoneticists agree about it; it is at once evident to anyone listening to a native of Peking speak. **1935** —— *Psycho-Biol. of Lang.* (1936) 96 The highly important work of the experimental phoneticist. **1954** Pei & Gaynor *Dict. Linguistics* 168 *Phoneticist*, a person who studies or is skilled in phonetics. **1915** *Spectator* 21 Aug. 235/1 To turn the Russian genitive plural termination into 'off', as is sometimes done, is to go in for an exaggerated *phoneticization. **1959** *Brno Studies in English* I. 14 Voices demanding reforms of traditional spellings usually regard 'phoneticization' of such spellings as the only effective remedy. **1970** *Language* XLVI. 959 For a primitive logographic system can develop into a full system of writing only if it succeeds in attaching to a sign a phonetic value independent of the meaning which this sign has as a 'word'; this is phoneticization. **1975** *Daily Colonist* (Victoria, B.C.) 22 Aug. 5/1 The common direction of phoneticization for all written languages in the world must be followed. **1848** A. J. ELLIS *Esenſalz ov Fωnetics* Pref., Mr. Isaac Pitman first propounded the idea..of *phoneticizing the English language. **1881** J. FRYER in *Nature* XXIV. 54/2 [To] phoneticise the foreign term, using the sounds of the Mandarin dialect.

phonetico- (fəʊˈnɛtɪkəʊ), combining form (on Greek analogy) of PHONETIC, as in **phoˌneticograˈmmatical** *a.*, relating to the phonetic part of grammar; **phoˌnetico-hieroˈglyphic** *a.*, of or belonging to hieroglyphics with a phonetic value; **phonetico-ideoˈgraphic** *a.*, of or pertaining to ideographs having a phonetic value; **phonetico-phoˈnemic** *a.*, employing both phonetic and phonemic criteria.

1879 WHITNEY *Sanskrit Gram.* p. x, A number of phonetico-grammatical treatises. **1826** *Edin. Rev.* XLV. 141 The high antiquity of the phonetico-hieroglyphic system in Egypt. **1891** C. LOMBROSO *Man of Genius* III. ii. 189 This mixture of letters, hieroglyphics, and figurative signs, constitutes a kind of writing recalling the phonetico-ideographic stage through which primitive peoples (the Mexicans and Chinese certainly) passed, before the discovery of alphabetic writing. **1952** A. COHEN *Phonemes of Eng.* iv. 85 M. Swadesh..distinguished between the two categories [*sc.* long and short vowels] on a mixed phonetico-phonemic basis.

phonetics (fəʊˈnɛtɪks), *sb. pl.* [See PHONETIC and -ICS.] That department of linguistic science which treats of the sounds of speech; phonology; the phonetic phenomena (of a language or dialect). Now usu. restricted to the study of speech sounds as physical phenomena, and distinguished from *phonology*.

1841 LATHAM *Eng. Lang.* II. ii. 113 Phonetics..determines (amongst other things) the systematic relation of Articulate Sounds..Between sounds like *b* and *v*, *s* and *z*, there is a connexion in Phonetics. **1848** A. J. ELLIS (*title*) Esenſalz ov Fωnetics [= Essentials of Phonetics]. **1871** EARLE *Philol. Eng. Tongue* § 138 Provincial phonetics go still further, and call a gown *gownd*. **1875** WHITNEY *Life Lang.* iv. 60 Phonetics, as a branch of linguistic science. **1924** O. JESPERSEN *Philos. Gram.* ii. 35 It would, perhaps, be advisable to restrict the word 'phonetics' to universal or general phonetics and to use the word *phonology* of the phenomena peculiar to a particular language (e.g. 'English Phonology'), but this question of terminology is not very important. Some writers would discriminate between the two words by using 'phonetics' of descriptive (static), and 'phonology' of historical (dynamic) 'lautlehre', but this terminology is reversed by some (de Saussure, Sechehaye). **1937** J. ORR tr. *Iordan's Introd. Romance Linguistics* 287 Generally, 'phonetics' is used to designate the physiology of sounds, and 'phonology' the history of sounds. Saussure reverses the use of the two terms. **1953** J. B. CARROLL *Study of Lang.* ii. 25 General phonetics, in fact, is virtually a science in its own right, with two chief branches, *motor phonetics* (or *articulatory phonetics*) and *acoustic phonetics*. **1962** A. C. GIMSON *Introd. Pronunc. Eng.* I. i. 2 Our primary concern will be the production, transmission, and reception of the sounds of English—in other words, the *phonetics* of English. **1964** P. STREVENS in D. Abercrombie et al. *Daniel Jones* 120 There seem to be two main kinds of use of the term... 'Phonetics' for some means 'making sounds', while for others it refers to a component of the discipline of linguistics. **1970** G. C. LEPSCHY *Survey Structural Linguistics* iii. 59 Trubeckoj mentions a number of linguists who preceded him..in distinguishing between sound and phoneme, and thus between phonetics and phonology.

phonetism (ˈfəʊnɪtɪz(ə)m). [f. Gr. φωνητός (see PHONETIC) + -ISM.] Phonetic representation; reduction to a phonetic system of writing or spelling.

1879 RENOUF *Orig. Relig.* 16 *note*, Champollion strongly insists upon the necessity of phonetism, for otherwise how could foreign names, for which no symbolism existed, be expressed in writing? **1880** *Address Philol. Soc.* 38 They had no scruple in sacrificing exact phonetism, if they could thereby express their sense more distinctly. **1891** A. B. EDWARDS *Pharaoh's Fellahs* 241 Pictorial phonetism registers the second stage in the art of writing.

phonetist (ˈfəʊnɪtɪst). [f. as prec. + -IST.]

1. A person versed in phonetics; one who studies the sounds of speech.

1864 in WEBSTER. **1875** WHITNEY *Life Lang.* iv. 73 The phonetist is never able to put himself in an 'à priori' position. **1896** *Voice* (N.Y.) 20 Aug., The phonetists of to-day make a careful distinction.

2. An advocate or user of phonetic spelling; a phoneticist.

1875 *N. Amer. Rev.* CXX. 475 We do not remember ever to have seen the case of the phonetists so happily and strongly put. **1878** J. A. H. MURRAY in *Encycl. Brit.* VIII. 396/1 The author of the *Ormulum* was a phonetist, and employed a special spelling of his own to represent not only the quality but the quantity of vowels and consonants.

ˈ**phonetize**, *v. rare*⁻¹. [f. as PHONETIST + -IZE.] *trans.* To write or spell (a word) phonetically.

1875 LOWELL *Spenser* Prose Wks. 1890 IV. 347 *note*, Just as one would spell it who wished to phonetize its sound in rural New England.

Hence **phonetiˈzation**, the representation of vocal sounds by phonetic characters; also = PHONETICIZATION.

1860 WORCESTER cites *The Athenæum*. **1952** I. J. GELB *Study of Writing* iii. 66 The need for indicating grammatical elements was of no great importance in the origin of phonetization. *Ibid.* 67 Phonetization..arose from the need to express words and sounds which could not be adequately indicated by pictures or combinations of pictures. **1976** *Visible Language* Winter 20 Phonetization of the alphabet and other writing systems is a province of orthoepy.

Phonevision (ˈfəʊnvɪʒən). [f. PHONE *v.* + VISION *sb.*] The proprietary name of a pay-as-you-view television system (see quot. 1951).

1950 *N.Y. Times* 10 Feb. 42/3 The Zenith plan involves the use of so-called 'phonevision'. By this method, special programs are televised in scrambled form so they cannot be picked up on any ordinary receiver. A subscriber, however, can receive the program by telephoning his local exchange and establishing a connection between the television set and the telephone system. **1951** *Life* 5 Feb. 43/1 Phonevision, or PV,..offers a way of bringing movies straight into the family parlor. Under PV, a television set owner learns that a certain movie is being scheduled at a given time. It goes out over a TV channel and shows on his set as a confusion of blurs. If he calls the Phonevision switchboard, an unscrambling device on his set, which is hooked up to the phone wires, is turned on and the blurs become a clear picture. **1953** *Official Gaz.* (U.S. Patent Office) 8 Sept. 281 Zenith Radio Corporation—Phonevision. For Radio and Television Transmitting and Receiving Operations and Parts Thereof. Claims use since June 13, 1947. **1975** *New Trends in Cable Television* (Com Quest Corp.) iii. 51 Zenith Radio Corporation developed the first commercially used pay-television/broadcasting equipment under the tradename Phonevision. **1978** *CATV Market* (Frost & Sullivan, Inc.) iv. 65 This Phonevision service was offered under a special permit from the F.C.C.

phoney, phony (ˈfəʊnɪ), *a.* and *sb.* orig. *U.S.* [Of uncertain origin.] **A.** *adj.* That has no real existence; fake, sham, counterfeit; false; insincere.

1900 ADE *More Fables* 138 'Overlook all the Phoney Acting by the Little Lady, Bud,' said the Fireman. **1916** C. SANDBURG *Chicago Poems* 63 You're only shoving out a phoney imitation of the goods. **1924** *Scribner's Mag.* Aug. 204/1 Hope you didn't mind when I gave you a phony name. **1933** *Sun* (Baltimore) 2 May 8/7 A line of argument..which I have long suspected is quite phoney. **1935** C. DAY LEWIS *Time to Dance* 60 You funny old, phoney old bogus man! **1949** *Chicago Tribune* 17 Sept. III. 18/3 Stop moaning about that phony blonde and her phonier lawsuit. **1951** J. D. SALINGER *Catcher in Rye* II. 19 They had this headmaster, Mr. Haas, that was the phoniest bastard I ever met in my life. **1956** W. SLIM *Defeat into Victory* ix. 181 On our side we had the somewhat phoney propaganda that followed Wingate's raid and the more solid influence of General Giffard's character. **1970** *Daily Tel.* 10 Nov. 12/4 Like his singing, he is gentlemanly: no long hair, exaggerated clothes, or phony emotionalism. **1974** E. BRAWLEY *Rap* (1975) I. x. 169 My parole officer violated me on another phony beef.

b. Special collocations, as **phoney war**, the period of comparative inaction at the beginning of the war of 1939–45; also *transf.* and *fig.*; so ***phoney peace***.

1940 *Times* 19 Apr. 7/2 When the Allies seemed slow at getting off the mark,..it was whispered to the American public that this was a 'phoney' war. **1940** *Manch. Guardian Weekly* 12 July 25 During the eight months of the 'phoney' war everything seemed to be running smoothly between Great Britain and France. **1940** G. GREENE *Lost Childhood* (1951) 115 This can never at any time have been a 'phoney' war: from the word go, these famous individuals were on the job. **1944** J. S. HUXLEY *On Living in Revolution* 9 The inadequacy of British production and planning during the Chamberlain 'phony war' period. **1947** *Partisan Rev.* XIV. 347 Within each state the necessary psychological atmosphere would be kept up by complete severance from the outer world, and by a continuous phony war against rival states. **1954** N. COWARD *Future Indefinite* III. 114 The Germans invaded Norway and Denmark... The reaction of the Americans to the break-up of what they themselves had christened the 'Phoney War' would be interesting to observe. **1960** O. MANNING *Great Fortune* xv. 199 This sort of phoney war can't go on for ever. Someone's going to move some time and we'll be trapped. **1964** *New Statesman* 4 Sept. 301/2 The electoral phoney war is almost over. **1972** *Daily Tel.* 29 Mar. 2/6 A curious 'phoney war' atmosphere has pervaded Ulster during the past few days. **1977** *Guardian Weekly* 27 Feb. 9/2 At this stage of phoney peace, the Americans are being careful to say or do nothing that might alarm Israel.

B. as *sb.* A phoney person or thing.

1902 C. L. CULLEN *Six Ex-Tank Tales* 99 If youse tinks f'r a minnit dat youse is goin' t' git away wit' a phony like dat wit' me youse is got hay in y'r hemp, dat's wot. **1916** *San Francisco Call & Post* 28 Nov. 12 'Don't Mr. Jenks know a lot of people?' 'They're all phonies.' **1938** E. AMBLER *Cause for Alarm* xi. 170 He's probably gone to the trouble to check the first lot and found that they're phoneys. **1952** S. C. ARMSTRONG *Black-Eyed Stranger* i. 5 Lynch is no international jewel thief. He's a tired old phony. **1958** K. AMIS *I like it Here* xvi. 200 The kind of prancing, posturing phoney who'd say he was better than Fielding. **1971** F. FORSYTH *Day of Jackal* II. xv. 262 'Leave the others to continue checking the remainder, just in case there is another phoney among the bunch,' instructed Thomas. **1971** S. E. MORISON *European Discovery Amer.: Northern Voy.* iii. 79 Adolf Rieth..tells of European false runic inscriptions and other famous phonies, one of which, the 'turkey frieze' in Schleswig Cathedral, pertains to America. **1977** *New Yorker* 27 June 79/1 This simple test—a way of telling the phonies from the truly committed.

Hence ˈ**phoneyness, phoniness**, the state or quality of being phoney; deceitfulness, unreality, insincerity; ˈ**phonily** *adv.*, in a phoney manner; falsely; insincerely.

1942 BERREY & VAN DEN BARK *Amer. Thes. Slang* § 315/1 Fakeness, phoniness. **1947** D. M. DAVIN *Gorse blooms Pale* 212 You felt a sort of phoneyness in your power. **1949** D. SMITH *I capture Castle* ix. 139 Am I just trying to rationalize my phoniness? **1959** *Times Lit. Suppl.* 17 Apr. 224/4 A racket is phoneyness organized. **1961** C. J. ROLO in *Webster* s.v., Phonily flamboyant amours and impossible deeds of derring-do. **1961** W. C. BOOTH *Rhetoric of Fiction* II. vii. 193 Though attracted by youth and freshness, he can see the phoniness of the American worship of Hollywood's idea of youthfulness. **1976** T. GIFFORD *Cavanaugh Quest* (1977) iii. 51 Tim didn't have any phoniness about him; he was what we used to call a regular guy. **1976** *Economist* 16 Oct. 15/2 Name another [parliamentary democracy] that could pass through the past 18 months and still have a parliament doing business phonily as usual. **1978** P. McCUTCHAN *Blackmail North* iv. 38 He brightened rather phonily. 'It could have been worse.'

phoney, phony, *v. slang* (chiefly *U.S.*). [f. the adj.] *trans.* and *intr.* To counterfeit, falsify, make *up*. (See also quot. 1950.)

1942 BERREY & VAN DEN BARK *Amer. Thes. Slang* § 207/12 *Disguised*,..phonied up. **1950** H. E. GOLDIN *Dict. Amer. Underworld Lingo* 156/1 *Phony up*, to counterfeit; to set up an impressive front or agency for purposes of swindling; to alter the amount of money indicated on a check; to change the serial number of a stolen bond or commit any similar criminal act; to turn traitor to the underworld. 'I got a chill on (doubt the courage of) this dude we're working with. He might phony up on a drop (under police pressure coincident with arrest).' **1952** *New Yorker* 26 July 43, I ain't phoneying them woids. **1963** 'E. McBAIN' *Ten plus One* (1964) xv. 173 I'll phony it up, stall him. **1968** 'G. BAGBY' *Another Day* iii. 53 He..made no effort to phony up an excuse. **1972** B. F. CONNERS *Don't embarrass Bureau* (1973) II. 200 It's tough for a cop to stay completely honest... It's like an agent who won't phoney his overtime. **1977** *Daily Tel.* 8 Dec. 3/7 Furs are often not clearly labelled. Cat skins could be passed off as 'bunny'. You can phoney anything up.

phoniatric (fəʊnɪˈætrɪk), *a. Med.* [f. Gr. φων-ή voice + ἰατρικ-ός of or for a doctor.] Of or pertaining to phoniatrics (logopedics).

1938 *Jrnl. Speech & Hearing Disorders* III. 286 (*heading*) Phoniatric aspects of unilateral recurrent paralysis. **1947** *Folia Phoniatrica* I. 14 Patients often receive wrongly and unsuccessfully treatment for chronic laryngitis, whereas, only phoniatric treatment..is promising. **1960** F. TROJAN *Current Probl. Phoniatrics & Logopedics* I. 53 Further research will enable this problem to be solved both from the surgical and the phoniatric point of view.

Hence **phoniaˈtrician, phoˈniatrist** (fəʊˈnaɪətrɪst), an expert or specialist in phoniatrics; **phoniˈatrics** *sb. pl.* (const. as *sing.*), **phoˈniatry** (fəʊˈnaɪətrɪ) = LOGOPEDICS *sb. pl.*

1947 *Folia Phoniatrica* I. 5 Phoniatry deals with the..sciences of the voice, speech and speech training, the problem of the deaf and dumb and musical problems and technique. **1950** *Ibid.* II. 175 Phoniatrics is practically inexistent. *Ibid.* 182 There exists no preparation or control for the Phoniatrist's profession. **1950** S. POTTER *Our Language* 186 Ward is more concerned with phoniatry and the rectification of faulty pronunciation in the speech of English children. **1959** *Amer. Speech* XXXIV. 55 Conscientious report on the articulatory organs, functions, and theories as they would interest the phoniatrician rather than the phonetician. **1960** F. TROJAN *Current Probl. Phoniatrics & Logopedics* I. 67 The relation of phoniatry to laryngeal surgery has two aspects. *Ibid.*, Surgical operations upon professional voice users should be undertaken by the phoniatrist. **1961** L. F. BROSNAHAN *Sounds of Language* vi. 144 Speech therapists and phoniatricians. **1962** *Folia Phoniatrica* XIV. 81 If we accept that phoniatrics means the 'medicine and medical art of phonation' it is clear that we limit ourselves to the medical aspects of impaired phonation.

phonic (ˈfəʊnɪk, ˈfɒnɪk), *a.* (*sb.*) [f. Gr. φωνή voice + -IC. Cf. F. *phonique* (Dict. Acad. 1835).]

A. *adj.* **1.** Of or pertaining to sound in general; acoustic; ***phonic wheel*** [tr. F. *roue phonique* (P. Lacour 1878, in *Compt. Rend.* LXXXVII. 500)], a toothed disc or rotor of magnetic material which is caused to rotate at a constant speed by an electromagnet energized by alternating, or interrupted direct, current (orig. derived from a tuning fork vibrating against a contact and sustained by another electromagnet); also ***phonic motor***.

1823 WHEATSTONE in *Ann Philos.* Aug. 81 On the Phonic Molecular Vibrations. **1857** MAYNE *Expos. Lex.*, *Phonic*, of or belonging to sound or the voice... The point where is found either the person who speaks, or the body which emits the sound is called the *phonic* centre. **1878** *Smithsonian Inst. Rep.* 492 The axis of the phonic ray will be deflected upwards. **1878** *Telegraphic Jrnl.* VI. 476/2 M. Paul la Cour has succeeded in causing a phonic wheel to maintain its uniform rate of rotation when acted upon by an accelerating or retarding force of one kilogramme-metre-minute. **1884** KNIGHT *Dict. Mech.* Suppl., *Phonic Apparatus*. **1906** T. E. HERBERT *Telegraphy* 838 Fig. 493 is a general view of the transmitter. At the back may be seen the rectangular frame of a La Cour phonic wheel motor that drives the transmitter. **1924** *Jrnl. Sci. Instruments* I. 162 By making use of a device known as a phonic motor—invented by the late Lord Rayleigh—a wheel is constrained to rotate at a constant speed controlled by an electromagnetically maintained tuning-fork. **1930** A. B. WOOD *Textbk. Sound* II. 129 The phonic motor provides a very convenient and accurate method of determining the frequencies of electrically-maintained forks. **1956** *IRE Trans. Electronic Computers* V. 159/1 The clock frequency is 50 kc, obtained from a phonic wheel on the drum.

2. a. Of or pertaining to vocal sounds: = PHONETIC 2; ***phonic method***, a method of teaching reading by correlating alphabetic symbols and sounds (= PHONICS *sb. pl.* 4).

1843 (*title*) The First Phonic Reader. *Ibid.* 101 Under the phonic method, the sound of each letter is taught by means of an object in which that sound occurs. **1844** CROKER in *Q. Rev.* June 38 With no other guide than Dr. Kay

Shuttleworth's 'Phonic Lessons', we are perfectly satisfied that no child could ever learn at all. **1875** T. Hill *True Order Stud.* 104 Pronounce the phonic elements.. separately. **1875** G. C. Mast *Primer of Phonic Method* p. iv, For years it had been his [*sc.* the Author's] wish to introduce in this country the German, or Phonic method of teaching reading and writing simultaneously. **1896** R. J. Lloyd in *Jrnl. Anat. & Physiol.* XXXI. 234 The usefulness of a vowel depends also upon its distinct phonic character. **1928** Ward & Roscoe *Approach to Teaching* ix. 110 The Phonic Method ..has the undoubted advantage that the children, if properly taught, are from the first not afraid to attack new words. **1954** *Language* (Ministry of Educ.) v. 56 The alphabetic method was superseded generally in British schools by the *phonic* method. **1966** J. Derrick *Teaching Eng. to Immigrants* v. 184 English is not a 'phonic' language —the sounds represented by certain letters or groups of letters do not all fit neatly into readily observed and easily learnt patterns (like those of Italian, or Welsh, for instance). **1968** J. Lyons *Introd. Theoret. Linguistics* ii. 62 Whatever other factors may have influenced the development of human speech, it is clear that phonic substance (that range of sound which can be produced by the human speech organs and falls within the normal range of human hearing) satisfies the conditions of availability and convenience fairly well. **1973** D. Rockey *Phonetic Lexicon* ii. 36 For many years reading theories have been polarised between two extremes—the phonic method and the so-called 'Look-and-Say'. **1976** *Amer. Speech 1974* XLIX. 12 As understood here, a *phonic transcription* includes the broad phonetic transcription presently favored by European phoneticians, the unsystematic simplification of phonetic forms often used by American dialectologists under the term *diaphone*, and the systematic broad phonics of Bloch and Trager..that is called 'classical phonemics' by generative apologists.

b. *Physiol.* (*a*) Applied to a nerve-centre which excites the organs of speech. (*b*) Produced or accompanied by vibration of the vocal cords: = PHONETIC 2 b.

1878 tr. *H. von Ziemssen's Cycl. Med.* XIV. 650 This reflex centre..we shall term the basial phonic centre. **1897** *Allbutt's Syst. Med.* IV. 851 The cough and sometimes the laugh are phonic.

†**B.** *sb.* A body that emits sound, a sonorous body. *Obs.*

1823 C. Wheatstone in *Ann. Philos.* Aug. 81 Bodies, which, being properly excited, make those sensible oscillations, which have been thought to be the proximate causes of all the phenomena of sound. These bodies..I have termed Phonics. *Ibid.* 82 The points of division in linear phonics are called nodes. **1836–9** Todd *Cycl. Anat.* II. 565/1 The body by which the sound is produced, denominated by Professor Wheatstone a *phonic*, occasions in the surrounding air vibrations or oscillations, corresponding in number and extent to those which exist in itself.

Hence **'phonically** *adv.*, in respect of vocal sound; in the form of speech sounds.

1959 *Brno Studies in English* I. 12 The spoken norm of language is a system of phonically manifestable language elements. **1962** S. R. Levin *Linguistic Struct. in Poetry* v. 50 The occurrence of phonically or semantically equivalent forms in equivalent positions, either syntagmatically or conventionally defined. **1965** [see HIGH *a.* 4 b]. **1977** *Word 1972* XXVIII. 310 The values assigned to the sequences may be analyzed with exclusive regard to the semantic qualities associated with these phonically polar vowels.

phonics ('fəʊnɪks, 'fɒnɪks), *sb. pl.* [f. as prec. + -ICS.]

1. The science of sound in general; acoustics. *Obs.*

1683–4 *Phil. Trans* XIV. 473 Three parts of our Doctrine of Acousticks: which are yet nameless, unless we call them Acousticks, Diacousticks, and Catacousticks, or (in another sence, but to as good purpose) Phonicks, Diaphonicks, and Cataphonicks. **1774** Goldsm. *Nat. Hist.* (1862) I. vii. 191 We are neither giving a treatise of optics or phonics, but a history of our own perceptions. **1842** Brande *Dict. Sci.* etc. s.v., The science [of] direct, reflected, and refracted sound. In allusion to the corresponding branches of optics, these have been denominated phonics, cataphonics, and diaphonics.

2. The science of spoken sounds; phonetics.

1844 Croker in *Q. Rev.* June 26 (*title of article*) Shuttleworth's Phonics. **1870** C. G. Smith tr. *Domesday Bk.* p. xlvii, Their knowledge of phonics must have guided them in spelling. **1961** *Amer. Speech* XXXVI. 93 (*title*) Phonemics and phonics in historical phonology. **1976** [see PHONIC *a.* (*sb.*) 2].

†**3.** 'The art of combining musical sounds' (Busby *Dict. Mus.* 1811). *Obs.*

4. The correlations between sound and symbol in an alphabetic writing system; used *spec.* with reference to a method of teaching reading by associating letters or groups of letters with particular sounds (cf. *phonic method* s.v. PHONIC *a.* (*sb.*) 2).

1908 E. B. Huey *Psychol. & Pedagogy of Reading* III. xiv. 280 Too often the line between phonics and reading is not drawn. **1960** J. R. Newton *Reading in your School* iv. 63 Phonics is that part of phonetics which is used in reading and spelling. **1966** K. De Hirsch et al. *Predicting Reading Failure* viii. 82 Five auditorily gifted children who read well had been intensively trained in phonics. **1966** *New Statesman* 30 Dec. 962/3 *Look and Say, Phonics* and *The Sentence Method* are all at the moment acting as smokescreens which obscure a simple fact known to most mothers but few reading research experts. The most important thing in a reading beginner's life is a willing listener. **1973** *Daily Tel.* 10 Apr. 18, I believe that most teachers of remedial reading would agree that more attention to phonics when teaching children to read would be an excellent thing. **1976** *Sci. Amer.* July 8/2 They replaced the teaching of reading by phonics with the 'look-see' method.

phonily, phoniness: see PHONEY, PHONY *a.* and *sb.*

phono ('fəʊnəʊ), colloq. abbrev. of PHONOGRAPH *sb.* (sense 3). Chiefly *U.S.*, exc. as applied to a type of plug (and the corresponding socket) used with audio equipment, in which one conductor is cylindrical and the other is a central prong that extends beyond it. Freq. *attrib.* and in *Comb.*

1948 F. Brown *Dead Ringer* 9 You can play the phono. **1956** C. Fowler *High Fidelity* x. 203 Interconnections to and from preamp-control units are made via so-called 'phono plugs'. *Ibid.*, Hum is almost inevitable when the control unit is switched to the phono channel and the bass tone control is fully advanced. **1970** J. Earl *Tuners & Amplifiers* iii. 70 American 'phono' sockets are commonly used for the tape signals. **1971** *Computers & Humanities* VI. 95 Such multi-media materials as broadsides, films, filmstrips, and phono-records. **1973** *Washington Post* 13 Jan. H7/5 (Advt.), Automatic portable phono. **1975** *Hi-Fi Answers* Feb. 74/3 Some amplifiers do not have a DIN socket for tape recording, there being only phono types. **1975** *Physics Bull.* May 229/1 These can be substituted for permanent magnets in phonocartridges. **1976** *Gramophone* May 1835/1 The controls on the front panel are a large selector knob for phono, tuner, auxiliary, tape 1 and tape 2. [Etc.] **1978** *N.Y. Times* 30 Mar. C10/1 Mounting a phono cartridge in a tone arm..invariably makes me think I'm in the wrong trade.

phono- (fəʊnəʊ), before a vowel **phon-**, combining form of Gr. φωνή voice, sound, used as a word-element in Gr., as in φωνασκός 'one who exercises the voice', φωνόμῑμος 'that imitates voice or voices', and extensively employed in recent technical terms, as PHONOGRAPH, PHONOLOGY, etc.; also in the following: **phono'dynamograph** [cf. DYNAMOGRAPH] (see quot.); **,phono-electro'cardioscope** *Med.*, an instrument for registering simultaneously the sounds and the electrical changes caused by the heart, or one of these together with the pulse; **phono-la'ryngoscope** (-dʒəʊskəʊp), an apparatus for observing the operation of the larynx in the production of speech sounds; so **phonolaryngo'scopic** *a.*; †**'phonomime** [cf. Gr. φωνόμῑμος adj., imitating voice], a musical instrument imitating a chorus of voices; so **phono'mimic** *a.* [F. *phonomimique*], applied to a system of teaching in which each of the elementary sounds of speech is associated with an appropriate onomatopœic gesture; **phono'motor** [MOTOR], a scientific toy in which the force of sound-vibrations, acting through a diaphragm and spring, is caused to drive a wheel; **'phonophote** [Gr. φώς, φωτ- light], an electrical apparatus by which sound-vibrations are converted into light; **,phonophoto'graphically** *adv.*; **,phonopho'tography**, photographic recording of the physical parameters of speech or singing; hence **,phonophoto'graphic** *a.*; **'phonoreception** *Biol.*, perception of sound by a living organism; hearing; so **'phonoreceptor**, a sensory receptor for sound; ‖**pho'norganon, pho'norganum** [mod.L., f. Gr. ὄργανον: see ORGAN], an instrument imitating the sounds of the voice, a speaking-machine; †**'phonovision**, a system of television in which the signals were stored on gramophone records to be reproduced at will.

1882 *Nature* XXVI. 331/1 Mr. W. B. Cooper has lately brought before the Franklin Institute a device for increasing the dynamic effect of the vibrations of diaphragms..called a *phonodynamograph. **1942** *Lancet* 26 Dec. 759/2 In what he calls by the rather cumbersome name of a *phono-electrocardioscope, G. E. Donovan has introduced an instrument which holds out high promise of useful service to the clinician. *Ibid.*, The most obvious application of the phono-electrocardioscope is in the teaching of auscultation. **1943** G. E. Donovan in *Jrnl. Inst. Electr. Engin.* XC. III. 39/1 The present apparatus incorporates a double-beam cathode-ray oscilloscope with a fluorescent screen of long afterglow. This permits the simultaneous direct visual observation of two phenomena such as the phonocardiogram and electrocardiogram, or sphygmogram and phonocardiogram, etc., at the patient's bedside. The amplified heart sounds can be heard at the same time. The instrument is called a phono-electrocardioscope. **1950** *Electronic Engin.* XXII. 90/2 In order to time accurately the events of the cardiac cycle, an electrocardiogram occurring simultaneously should accompany a phonocardiogram, and his [*sc.* Donovan's] apparatus, the phonoelectrocardioscope, is designed on these principles. **1953** L. F. Brosnahan *Some Old Eng. Sound Changes* 11 The production of each of the Dutch vowels, as observed with Russell's '*phono-laryngoscope'. **1934** *Amer. Speech* IX. 226/2 A *phonolaryngoscopic examination of the position and function of the various organs of the larynx. **1834** *New Monthly Mag.* XLII. 389 A very singular musical instrument has been lately invented by a mechanic at Vienna. This instrument..is called a *phonomime..the inventor has found a method, by means of numerous pipes and machinery, to cause it to emit the sound of a fine chorus of male voices. **1835** *Musical Library* Suppl. II. 19 The phonomime and performers were placed in a room adjoining... Every one thought that the piece was sung by an excellent choral band. **1884** J. C. Gordon in *Amer. Ann. Deaf & Dumb* Apr. (1885) 135 Each of the 32 sounds of the French language is associated with an appropriate gesture. .. This process for teaching children to read was called by Mr. Grosselin [the inventor] the *Phonomimic method. **1888** Payne tr. *Compayre's Hist. Pedagogy* (1888) §146. 135 Is not this already the very essence of the phonomimic processes brought into fashion in these last years? **1884** Knight *Dict. Mech.* Supp., *Phonomotor, *Phonophote. **1928** M. Metfessel *Phonophotogr. in Folk Music* 22 All the twists, quavers, trills, breaks in the voice, quick slurs, erratic tempi and other similar features..are.. what *phonophotography will reveal. *Ibid.* 19 There was no simple ready-made *phonophotographic camera, nor had there ever been any studies which required the detailed reading of the sound wave photographs. **1931** T. H. Pear *Voice & Personality* 17 Dr. Milton Metfessel..has recorded 'phonophotographically' the turns..of the 'Jubilee voice' of the negro. **1933** *Brit. Jrnl. Psychol.* Apr. 408 Seashore's claim..that his phonophotographic methods constitute an objective approach to the study of the beautiful,..in the performance of vocal music. **1935** *Amer. Speech* X. 312/2 By means of phonophotography the readings of several distinguished poets were analyzed for pitch, loudness and duration in an effort to solve some of the fundamental problems of verse. **1939** *Ibid.* XIV. 228/1 The application for the first time of phono-photographic technics to study of melody in isolated southern districts of the United States. **1968** P. Oliver *Screening Blues* 10 Phonophotography and voice-prints may give an accurate translation of certain characteristics of the voice in graphic form. **1940** *Biol. Rev.* XV. 108 The substitution of the term '*phonoreception' for hearing evades the real issue. **1960** *Neurology* X. 662/1 Photoreception and phonoreception provide the principal means of association between the individual and his external environment. **1968** D. W. Wood *Princ. Animal Physiol.* ix. 188 Phono-reception is really a specialized case of mechano-reception, and it is not always easy to distinguish between the two. *Ibid.*, It is probably simpler to include vibration reception in phonoreception and to define the latter as the perception of any mechanical disturbance external to the animal that involves regular repetition. **1961** Webster, *Phonoreceptor. **1968** D. W. Wood *Princ. Animal Physiol.* ix. 191 The most primitive phonoreceptor in vertebrates is the lateral line organ-system of fishes and a few amphibians. **1892** Ogilvie (Annandale), *Phonorganon. **1927** *Punch* 7 Sept. 253/3 Mr. J. L. Baird, the inventor of television and *phonovision, is reported as saying that some faces sound like a gargle. **1935** *Times* 16 May 9/3 The new system of 'Phonovision' demonstrated some years ago in which wax-disk records of television signals were employed in much the same way.

phonocamptic (fəʊnəʊ'kæmptɪk), *a.* Now *rare.* [f. PHONO- + Gr. καμπτ-ός, -ικ-ός, f. κάμπτειν to bend: see -IC. In F. *phonocamptique* (Littré).] Having the property of reflecting sound, or producing an echo; relating to the reflexion of sound, cataphonic. Hence **phono'camptics**, that part of acoustics which treats of reflected sounds; cataphonics, catacoustics.

1668 Evelyn *Let. to Dr. Beale* 27 Aug., Besides what the Masters of the Catoptrics, Phonocamptics, Otacoustics, &c., have don. **1694** R. Burthogge *Ess. Reason*, etc. 155 In the Phonocamptick Center. **1857** Mayne *Expos. Lex.* 946/1 The phonocamptic centre is the situation where is placed the ear destined to receive reflected sounds. *Ibid.*, *Phonocamptica*..a branch of Physics which treats of the phænomena of the reflection of sound: phonocamptics.

phonocardiogram (fəʊnəʊ'kɑːdɪəʊgræm). *Med.* [f. PHONO- + *cardiogram* s.v. CARDIO-.] A tracing of the sounds made by the heart.

1912 *Heart* IV. 161 In many of our phonocardiograms it is very possible that we should have discovered initial vibrations. **1942** *Lancet* 26 Dec. 759/2 Permanent photographic records can be obtained of the phonocardiogram, electrocardiogram or sphygmogram. **1974** *Physics Bull.* Feb. 70/2 Incompatibility between echo signals and phonocardiograms.

phonocardiograph (fəʊnəʊ'kɑːdɪəʊgrɑːf, -æ-). *Med.* [f. PHONO- + *cardiograph* s.v. CARDIO-.] An apparatus used for registering phonocardiograms.

1926 *Amer. Heart Jrnl.* I. 721 (*caption*) Phonocardiograph record of human heart. **1943** *Jrnl. Inst. Electr. Engin.* XC. III. 43/1 The phonocardiograph employed by Einthoven possessed a simple but crude sort of high-pass acoustic filter. **1977** *Lancet* 19 Mar. 646/1 Records of the beat can be taken with an apex-cardiograph/phonocardiograph transducer attached to a commercial electrocardiograph.

phonocardiography (,fəʊnəʊkɑːdɪ'ɒgrəfɪ). *Med.* [f. PHONO- + *cardiography* s.v. CARDIO-.] The investigation and interpretation by means of a phonocardiograph of the sounds made by the heart.

1921 *Jrnl. Amer. Med. Assoc.* 12 Feb. 434/1 Such a conception will explain a murmur of regurgitation in early systole... The first sound, as has been observed in phonocardiography, is held to be present, but its initial components may be masked by the murmur. **1926** *Amer. Heart Jrnl.* I. 717 (*heading*) Phonocardiography of the human fetus. **1961** *Lancet* 16 Sept. 644/1 Lewis et al. have shown by intracardiac phonocardiography that a similar murmur can be recorded in the main pulmonary artery of all healthy subjects. **1971** *Nature* 25 June 542/3 The basic principles of auscultation and phonocardiography are dealt with in the first chapter.

Hence **,phonocardi'ographer**, one who operates a phonocardiograph or is expert in phonocardiography; **,phonocardio'graphic, -'graphical** *adjs.*, of, pertaining to, or involving phonocardiography; ˌ**phonocardioˈgraphically** *adv.*

1935 *Amer. Heart Jrnl.* X. 458 We suggest that further phonocardiographic studies be performed along these lines. **1943** *Jrnl. Inst. Electr. Engin.* XC. III. 52/1 Certain frequency components..which are met with in routine phonocardiographical clinical work. **1967** M. E. TAVEL *Clin. Phonocardiography* i. 15 The phonocardiographer..is usually presented with a complex array of sounds, murmurs, and pulses. **1973** *Brit. Heart Jrnl.* XXXV. 1276/1 Both major components of the first sound were demonstrated phonocardiographically. **1974** *Circulation* XLIX. 5/2 Phonocardiographers are often faced with the difficult problem of telling the auscultator what he is hearing. *Ibid.* 434/1 We have delineated the phonocardiographic.. characteristics of the mitral prosthesis.

phonofiddle (ˈfəʊnəʊfɪd(ə)l). *Mus.* Also **Phonofiddle.** [f. PHONO- + FIDDLE *sb.*] A type of violin in which the usual body of the instrument is replaced by a mechanism connected with an amplifying horn. Also *attrib.*

1923 *Ashore & Afloat* Aug. (Advt.), Zither Banjos, Houson Phonofiddles, Strohviols, One String Fiddles. **1930** *Stage* 3 Apr. 9/4 A string of merry jokes and just sufficient phono-fiddle work to add to their appeal. **1955** *Oxf. Compan. Mus.* (ed. 9) 995/2 The Phonofiddle is sometimes played with a plectrum. **1977** *Early Music* Apr. 265/3 Susan Baker plays and talks about the..phonofiddle, [etc.].

phonofilm (ˈfəʊnəʊfɪlm). *Obs.* exc. *Hist.* Also **Phonofilm.** [f. PHONO- + FILM *sb.*] A cinema film having a sound-track.

Orig. a proprietary name in the U.S.

1921 *Official Gaz.* (U.S. Patent Office) 8 Nov. 391/2 Phonofilm... Claims use since Jan. 1, 1921. **1922** *Radio Broadcast* Dec. 96 De Forest's Phono-film. **1923** *Weekly Dispatch* 13 May 5 In so far as it eliminates the use of a gramophone..the new phono-film..would appear to mark a decided step forward. **1928** *Manch. Guardian Weekly* 17 Aug. 134/4 The Prime Minister for a quarter of an hour delivered to an audience of half a dozen people and two phonofilm cameras a farewell address. **1930** A. B. WOOD *Textbk. Sound* v. 495 A somewhat similar process is used in the production of phonofilms or 'speaking pictures'. **1973** *Listener* 7 June 744/3 There we were, south of San Francisco... Just down the road, De Forest had invented the radio valve and the phonofilm.

phonogenic (fəʊnəʊˈdʒɛnɪk, -ˈdʒiːnɪk), *a.* [f. PHONO- + -GENIC b.] With pleasing voice qualities; well suited to mechanical reproduction of sound; of or pertaining to pleasing recorded sound.

1945 *Office Economist* June 10 (*heading*) Are you *Phonogenic*? **1947** *Red Barrel* Feb. 22 She shows how to be phonogenic by what not to do. **1957** MANVELL & HUNTLEY *Technique Film Music* v. 205 Roman Vlad..claims that he prefers to use a chamber music orchestra for what he calls 'phonogenic' reasons..('the possibilities of obtaining a clearer sound are superior'). **1977** *Gramophone* Jan. 1131/2 Perhaps hers is not a 'phonogenic' voice; the vibrations which are part of its appeal in a large house might appear too prominently in recording.

phonogram (ˈfəʊnəgræm). [f. PHONO- + -GRAM; in sense 2, after *telegram.*]

1. A written character or symbol representing a spoken sound; *spec.* a letter or symbol of (Pitman's) Phonography.

1860 I. PITMAN *Man. Phonography* (ed. 10) §17. 21 *Phonogram*, a written letter or mark, indicating a certain sound, or modification of sound; as —*k*, ·*ah*. **1883** I. TAYLOR *Alphabet* I. i. 22 It is probable that the..step by which the advance was made from ideograms to phonograms arose out of the necessity of expressing proper names. **1895** HOFFMAN *Beginn. Writ.* 173 A phonogram is the graphic representation of a sound. An alphabetic character is a phonogram.

2. The sound-record or tracing made by a phonograph, or the sounds reproduced or reported by means of it; a phonographic record or message.

1879 *Telegraphic Jrnl.* VII. 233/1 M. Delecheneau has succeeded in getting phonograms on zinc and brass cyclinders. **1884** *Jrnl. Educ.* XIX. 267 Dr. Zintgraff..will use the instrument to obtain foil phonograms of the speech and melodies of the natives [of Africa]. **1887** *Spectator* 22 Oct. 1407 The phonograph reports music with absolute exactness, and..the phonogram will keep for a hundred years. **1967** A. L. LLOYD *Folk Song in England* i. 65 Dr. Walker Fewkes made phonogram recordings among North American Indians in 1889. **1976** *Daily Tel.* 10 July 4/8 To celebrate the centenary of sound recording next year major record companies in more than 60 countries are to present a programme of events... This was announced yesterday by the International Federation of Producers of Phonograms and Videograms. **1977** *Gramophone* Apr. 1527/2 It is not a laughing matter that it has taken so long and so much effort to establish the recording, the phonogram, as a serious creative art form in its own right.

3. A telegram that the sender dictates over the telephone. Freq. *attrib.*

1911 D. MURRAY in *Jrnl. Inst. Electr. Engin.* Aug. 451 Economic necessity will..lead to a great increase in telephone-telegrams, or, as the British Post Office already calls them, 'phonograms'. **1932** *Telegraph & Telephone Jrnl.* Oct. 2/1 Any telephone subscriber can hand over and receive his telegrams by telephone (phonogram service). **1968** E. H. JOLLEY *Introd. Telephony & Telegr.* i. 16/2 Nowadays small offices generally dictate their telegrams over the telephone to an appointed office. The appointed office receives the traffic from a group of minor offices..and is provided with special phonogram equipment designed to facilitate the handling of calls from the various offices. **1969** *West Australian* 5 July 66/2 (Advt.), Postmaster-General's Department has vacancies for phonogram operator (Perth). **1976** R. N. RENTON *Telegraphy* ix. 246/1 As far as the method is reversible, a telegram is delivered to the recipient over the same medium used for handing in, e.g. via phonograms, printergrams or leased teleprinter circuit. **1976** *Sydney Telephone Directory*, Phonograms. To save time, telephone your telegrams. The usual telegram charges will be debited to your telephone account.

Hence **phonogramic** (-ˈgræmɪk) *a.* [irreg. f. prec. + -IC], of the nature of a phonogram, or consisting of phonograms (sense 2); **phonoˈgramically** *adv.*, by means of phonograms; **phonograˈmmatic** *a.*, consisting of phonograms (sense 1) = PHONOGRAPHIC 1.

1861 *Proc. Amer. Phil. Soc.* VIII. 279 A phonogrammatic system of telegraphic symbols. **1888** *Times* 27 June 12/1 In the several long phonogramic communications. **1888** *Standard* 17 Sept. 2/7 All new music worthy of reproduction will be thus phonogramically published.

phonograph (ˈfəʊnəgrɑːf, -æ-), *sb.* [f. Gr. φωνή voice (see PHONO-) + (in sense 1) -(ό)γραφος written, (in sense 2) -γράφος writing, writer: see -GRAPH.]

†**1.** A character representing a sound: = PHONOGRAM 1. *Obs. rare.*

1835–40 HINCKS *On Hieroglyphics* (MS. B.M., Egypt. Antiq., 19 *e*), Hieroglyphic characters are either ideographs, that is, representations of ideas, or phonographs, that is, representations of sounds. **1845–57** PITMAN *Man. Phonogr.* 19 *Phonograph*, a written letter, or mark, indicating a certain sound, or modification of a sound; as, ·*e*, — *k*. [Later called *phonogram*.]

2. † **a.** Another name for the PHONAUTOGRAPH. *Obs.*

b. *electro-magnetic phonograph*: see quot.

1863 *Jrnl. Soc. Arts* 16 Oct. 747/1 *Electro-magnetic phonograph*. This machine is capable of being attached to pianofortes, organs, and other keyed musical instruments, by means of which they are rendered melographic, that is, capable of writing down any music..played upon them.

3. a. (spec. ***talking phonograph.***) An instrument, invented by Thomas A. Edison in 1877 (patented 30 July), by which sounds are automatically recorded and reproduced. In Britain the word is retained only for early cylinder machines, but in N. Amer. it has become synonymous with *record player*, *record deck*, etc., corresponding to the British *gramophone*. Also *attrib.*

The aerial sound-vibrations enter a mouth-piece, and cause vibration in a thin metal diaphragm having attached to it a steel point, which makes tracings (as in the PHONAUTOGRAPH) upon a sheet of soft metal or hard wax fixed upon a revolving cylinder; by means of these tracings the diaphragm, whose vibrations originally produced them, may be caused (by again turning the cylinder) to repeat these vibrations, and thus reproduce (more or less perfectly) the original sounds.

1877 *Sc. Amer.* 17 Nov. 304 Whoever may speak into the mouthpiece of the phonograph. **1877** EDISON *Specif. U.S. Patent* 24 Dec., Improvement in phonograph or speaking machines. **1878** *Examiner* 2 Mar. 283/1 The Phonograph is now in England; all doubts as to the reality of the invention are at an end. The instrument has spoken in our hearing. **1878** G. B. PRESCOTT *Speaking Telephone* x. 305 Having provided thus for the durability of the phonograph plate, it will be very easy [etc.]. *Ibid.* 430/2 (Index), The talking phonograph record. **1879** G. PRESCOTT *Sp. Telephone* 306 The talking phonograph is a natural outcome of the telephone. **1885** F. HARRISON *Choice Bks.* (1886) 178 The old man's laugh..comes up to us as out of a phonograph. **1909** *Jrnl. Industr. & Engin. Chem.* Mar. 157/2 Phonograph records have been made with it [*sc.* Bakelite]. **1913** [see GRAMOPHONE]. **1927** *Jrnl. Abnormal Psychol.* XXII. 13 Several of the major phonograph companies maintain 'race record' departments. **1929** E. WILSON *I thought of Daisy* i. 15 Somebody turned on the phonograph which began jigging a popular fox-trot. **1946** *Fortune* Oct. 158/2 Home phonographs rarely compare in precision with professional studio equipment. **1949** *Reader's Digest* Dec. 139/1 Sixteen million American phonograph owners are bewildered and unhappy. **1952** [see GRAMOPHONE]. **1956** C. FOWLER *High Fidelity* i. 9 Time was when a phonograph made by one of the big companies was automatically considered low-fidelity. **1960** C. HANSEN in A. Dundes *Mother Wit* (1973) 507 The advertisements of..phonograph record companies. **1967** A. L. LLOYD *Folk Song in England* i. 65 Singers.. whom Percy Grainger recorded on phonograph cylinders as early as 1904. **1975** *Daily Tel.* 17 Jan. 8/6 An Edison phonograph of about 1905 obtained £240. It was sold with 38 cylinder records. **1975** *New Yorker* 29 Sept. 64/2 Mrs. Santana turned off the TV, turned on the phonograph to its top volume, and went into the kitchen.

b. *fig.* Applied to a person or thing that exactly reproduces the utterances of some other.

1884 *Pall Mall G.* 3 Apr. 1/2 All those whose humble office it is to act as phonographs of the tittle-tattle which forms the staple of the ordinary conversation of Society. **1890** 'R. BOLDREWOOD' *Miner's Right* (1899) 29/2, I heard it all in memory's wondrous phonograph.

c. *Comb.*

1891 F. M. WILSON *Primer on Browning* 214 That phonograph-like conservation of force, heredity.

Hence **ˈphonograph** *v. trans.*, (*a*) to report in (Pitman's) phonography; (*b*) to record or reproduce by or as by a phonograph.

1857 J. H. GIHON *Geary & Kansas* 219 It is a great loss to the world that their speeches were not phonographed and preserved for future generations. **1883** G. ROGERS in Spurgeon *Treas. Dav.* Ps. cxxxix. 2–4 Whether it be so or not, they are phonographed in the mind of God.

phonographer (fəʊˈnɒgrəfə(r)). [f. PHONOGRAPHY + -ER[1].]

1. One who writes according to sound, i.e. spells phonetically; a phonetist. *rare*$^{-1}$.

1851 TRENCH *Study Words* vii. 215 The word 'temps'; from which the phonographers eject the *p* as superfluous.

2. *spec.* One who uses phonography (sense 2); a shorthand writer (in Pitman's system).

1845 I. PITMAN *Man. Phonogr.* 49 Phonographers who wish to become reporters, should, from the commencement, cherish reporting habits. **1863** *Cornh. Mag.* Jan. 99 The.. phonographers that reported its deliberations were sworn to secrecy.

3. 'One who uses or is skilled in the use of the phonograph' (*Cent. Dict.*). *rare.*

phonographic (fəʊnəʊˈgræfɪk), *a.* [f. as prec. + -IC: see -GRAPHIC.]

1. Representing, or consisting of characters representing, spoken sounds; phonetic.

1847 WEBSTER, *Phonographic, phonographical*, descriptive of the sounds of the voice. **1866** *Reader* No. 164. 177/1 Chinese phonographic devices. **1883** I. TAYLOR *Alphabet* I. i. 6 Although our own writing has reached the alphabetic stage, yet we still continue to employ a considerable number of phonographic and ideographic signs.

2. Of, pertaining to, or using phonography (Pitman's system of phonetic shorthand).

1840 I. PITMAN *Phonography* 6 The Phonographic signs for the simple articulations. **1842** —— *Man. Phonogr.* 5 The pupil should first learn the Phonographic Letters, taking them in the natural order of pronunciation. **1853** —— (*title*) Phonographic Reporter's Companion.

3. Of, pertaining to, or produced by a phonograph. Also *fig.*

1878 T. A. EDISON in *N. Amer. Rev.* CXXVI. 532 They are required to do no more by the phonographic method. **1878** G. B. PRESCOTT *Speaking Telephone* x. 303 (*heading*) Tracings from phonographic records. **1898** H. G. WELLS *Let.* 22 Jan. in *G. Gissing & H. G. Wells* (1961) 79 A beautiful phonographic newspaper with a leathery flat voice. **1900** *Westm. Gaz.* 31 May 2/3 The Vienna Academy of Sciences is..going to set up phonographic archives. There are to be three sections of phonograms. **1976** *Times* 2 Nov. 5/2 The British phonographic industry.

So **phonoˈgraphical** *a. rare.*

1846 WORCESTER, *Phonographic, Phonographical.* **1974** *Country Life* 12 Dec. 1857/3 The two-volume CBS Astaire solo anthology..are transfers of old Brunswick 78s and therefore more satisfying in purely phonographical terms.

phonoˈgraphically, *adv.* [f. PHONOGRAPHIC: see -ICALLY.] In a phonographic manner.

1. According to or by means of phonography (Pitman's system of shorthand).

1845 I. PITMAN *Man. Phonogr.* 42 If we write phonographically, we must, at least, name our letters phonetically.

2. By means of the phonograph. Also *fig.*

1879 *Sat. Mus. Rev.* 6 Sept. 568/2 Mr. Sankey's voice in 'Hold the Fort', phonographically preserved on a sheet of tinfoil. **1882–3** *Schaff's Encycl. Relig. Knowl.* 1446 A volume of his sermons, phonographically reported.

phonographist (fəʊˈnɒgrəfɪst). [f. next + -IST.] = PHONOGRAPHER 2.

[**1847** WEBSTER, *Phonographist*, one who explains the laws of the voice.] **1864** *Ibid.*, *Phonographist*, one who is versed in phonography; a phonographer. **1897** *Daily News* 20 Feb. 10/6 Young lady seeks Engagement as Typist and Phonographist, Remington or Caligraph. Speed 60 and 100.

phonography (fəʊˈnɒgrəfɪ). [f. Gr. φωνή voice (see PHONO-) + -GRAPHY.]

1. The art or practice of writing according to sound, or so as to represent the actual pronunciation; phonetic spelling. ? *Obs.*

1701 J. JONES (*title*) Practical Phonography: or, the new Art of Rightly Spelling and Writing Words By the Sound thereof, and of Rightly Sounding and Reading Words By the Sight thereof. **1851** TRENCH *Study Words* vii. 215 The same attempt to introduce phonography has been several times made.

2. *spec.* The system of phonetic shorthand invented by Isaac Pitman in 1837: so named by him in 1840; Pitman's shorthand.

1840 I. PITMAN (*title*) Phonography, or writing by sound; being a natural method of writing, applicable to all languages, and a complete system of short hand. **1847** —— *Hist. Shorthand* in *Man. Phonography* §15 (1889) 8 Phonography is not adapted to the wants of the reporter alone, but is..well suited for letter-writing and general composition.

3. The automatic recording of sounds, as by the PHONAUTOGRAPH, or the recording and reproduction of them by the PHONOGRAPH; the construction and use of phonographs.

1861 WHYTE MELVILLE *Mkt. Harb.* xxi. 247 Savage..was explaining to Sawyer..a new discovery termed phonography, by which sounds or vibrations of air are to be taken down, as they arise, upon the principle of the photograph. **1886** *Cassell's Encycl. Dict.*, *Phonography*... 3. The art of using, or registering by means of, the phonograph; the construction of phonographs.

†**4.** The scientific description of sound, or of the voice; = PHONOLOGY. *Obs. rare*$^{-0}$.

1847 in WEBSTER. **1858** in MAYNE *Expos. Lex.*

phonolite (ˈfəʊnəlaɪt). *Min.* Also **-lyte** (Dana). [f. PHONO- + -LITE; in F. *phonolithe* (1812 in

Hatz.-Darm.).] Name for various volcanic rocks which ring when struck; clinkstone.

1828–32 WEBSTER, *Phonolite*, sounding stone; a name proposed as a substitute for *klingstein* (jingling stone). **1832** DE LA BECHE *Geol. Man.* (ed. 2) 251 Rolled masses of trachyte, phonolite, basalt, or volcanic cinders. **1868–80** DANA *Min.* 359 *Phonolyte* (or clinkstone), a compact grayish rock, often containing crystals of glassy feldspar, and having a zeolite in the base along with orthoclase.

Hence **phonolitic** (fəʊnəʊˈlɪtɪk) *a.*, pertaining to or consisting of phonolite.

1852 TH. ROSS *Humboldt's Trav.* I. ii. 99 The phonolitic ejections of the Peak of Teneriffe. **1875** A. SMITH *New Hist. Aberdeen.* I. 644 Clinkstone or phonolitic felspar.

phonology (fəʊˈnɒlədʒɪ). [f. Gr. φωνή voice (see PHONO-) + -LOGY. So F. *phonologie* (Littré).] Orig., the science of vocal sounds (= PHONETICS), esp. of the sounds of a particular language; the study of pronunciation; *transf.* the system of sounds in a language. Now, that branch of linguistics which deals with sound systems, or with sound systems and phonetics; the study of the sound system of a particular language.

The domain of phonology is variously limited by different linguists and linguistic schools of thought. In the writings of the Prague school it is used to mean phonemics.

1799 E. FRY *Pantographia* (title-p.), Specimens of all well authenticated oral languages; forming a comprehensive digest of phonology. **1828** in WEBSTER. **1845** *Proc. Amer. Phil. Soc.* IV. 168 Observations on General Phonology and alphabetical notation. **1862** MARSH *Eng. Lang.* 64 In our enquiries into extinct phonologies we have no such guide. **1879** *Addr. Philol. Soc.* 1 Contributions to Old English Phonology and Etymology. **1924**, etc. [see PHONETICS *sb. pl.*]. **1933** L. BLOOMFIELD *Language* viii. 138 The description of a language, then, begins with phonology, which defines each phoneme and states what combinations occur. **1937** J. ORR tr. *Iordan's Introd. Romance Linguistics* iv. 287 The great majority of linguists and all the phoneticians.. use 'phonetics' for the physiology of sounds, and although all do not adopt the term 'phonology' for their historical study, those who use the term 'phonetics' for the latter avoid confusion by speaking of 'historical phonetics'. *Ibid.* 288 This matter of terminology has become complicated still further by the special meaning given to 'phonology' by the Prague philologists. **1939** *Language* XV. 1 We use the term phonology to refer to alternations (synchronic phonology) or changes (historical, diachronic phonology) in sounds, rather than for the theory of the nature and permutations of the sounds. The latter we call phonemics. Those who use 'phonology' in this sense.. deprive themselves of a convenient means of distinguishing two fundamentally distinct subjects. **1949** G. L. TRAGER *Field of Linguistics* 5 The phonetics and phonemics of a language are its phonological systems, its phonology. **1953** J. B. CARROLL *Study of Lang.* ii. 43 Some languages have only a limited number of phonemes, while some others appear to possess extremely complex phonologies, offering a large number of finely differentiated phonemes. **1962** E. F. HADEN et al. *Resonance-Theory for Linguistics* iii. 29 Phonology is the true-structure whose contributing members are phonemics and phonotactics. **1968** CHOMSKY & HALLE *Sound Pattern Eng.* p. vii, In the course of this detailed investigation of English sound patterns and their underlying structure, certain rules of English phonology are developed. **1972** M. L. SAMUELS *Linguistic Evol.* i. 3 For some, at present, phonology is less important than grammar or lexis.

Hence **phoˈnologer** (*rare*$^{-0}$) = *phonologist*; **phonoˈlogic, phonoˈlogical** *adjs.*, of, pertaining or relating to phonology; **phonoˈlogically** *adv.*, in respect of phonology; **phoˈnologist**, one learned in phonology; **phonologiˈzation**, (*a*) shift to phonemic status; (*b*) development (of a phonetic feature) to the status of the distinguishing feature in a phonemic opposition.

1864 WEBSTER, *Phonologer, one versed in phonology; a phonologist. **1846** WORCESTER, *Phonologic. **1875** A. J. ELLIS *E.E. Pronunc.* xi. 1336 Indian Phonologic Alphabet. **1936** *Amer. Speech* XI. 110 A 'phonologic system' is defined as the ensemble of phonologic oppositions proper to a given language. **1955** [see MINIMAL *a.* b (*a*)]. **1970** *Language* XLVI. 312 Some phonologic features are closely related to an articulatory maneuver that involves a specific muscle. **1977** *Archivum Linguisticum* VIII. 50 'Generative grammar' in the second sense is concerned with the description of rules for sentence-structures which include the phonologic level as well as the semantic one. **1818** *Trans. Amer. Philos. Soc.* I. 246 These modifications.. may be distinguished in a *phonological alphabet by particular signs. **1880** E. L. BRANDRETH in *Academy* 19 June 459/2 The Prakrits.. are separated from Sanskrit by very important phonological and other changes. **1888** *Athenæum* 26 May 657/3 Modern Kentish.. is strikingly different *phonologically from the language of the same district as written in the fourteenth century. **1818** *Trans. Amer. Philos. Soc.* I. 241 This *Sheva*, the English *phonologists (if I may be allowed to use the name) have almost uniformly represented by *u* short. **1880** R. G. WHITE *Every-Day Eng.* 137 Alexander Ellis, whose preeminence as a phonologist is questioned by no one. **1936** *Proc. 2nd Internat. Congr. Phonetic Sci.* 63 The *phonologization of Middle English voiced spirants is an isolated process in the development of Germanic languages. **1964** B. TRNKA in D. Abercrombie et al. *Daniel Jones* 190 The phonologization of voice of spirants. **1976** *Archivum Linguisticum* VII. 95 Preaspiration.. was consequently inadmissible in *kampur*, etc., but since it had been distinctive its loss was accompanied by phonologization of the devoicing of the sonant.

phonometer (fəʊˈnɒmɪtə(r)). [f. Gr. φωνή sound (see PHONO-) + μέτρον measure. Cf. F. *phonomètre* (Dict. Acad. 1878).] An instrument for measuring or automatically recording the number or force of sound-waves.

1823 *New Monthly Mag.* VIII. 20 We should not be surprised to see this uncertainty brought, in time, under mathematical controul, by the invention of a musical Phonometer, to indicate the precise strength of sound. **1880** *Libr. Univ. Knowl.* (N.Y.) V. 268 [Mentioned.. among the inventions of Edison]. **1885** *Pall Mall G.* 6 June, The Ministry are the most perfect phonometer in the world. Their decisions faithfully record the comparative strength of the noise that can be made by either of two conflicting sections.

Hence **phonometric** (fəʊnəʊˈmɛtrɪk) *a.*, pertaining to a phonometer, or to the measurement of sound; **phonoˈmetrically** *adv.*, using the methods of phonometry.

1895 E. B. TITCHENER tr. *Külpe's Outl. Psychol.* I. iii. 156 The phonometric determination of sound intensity in psychophysical experiments is.. usually carried out upon a principle similar to that employed in photometry. **1938** *Amer. Speech* XIII. 282 Taking the long vowels of German which, merely for the sake of illustration, we shall assume are a phonometrically unclassifiable residue. *Ibid.* 278 This typical example of phonometric technique has clearly a considerable bearing upon both phonology and dynamic philology. **1965** *Jrnl. Appl. Physiol.* XX. 302/2 Pressure determinations were made at the same time as the phonometric ones.

phonometrics (fəʊnəʊˈmɛtrɪks), *sb. pl.* (const. as *sing.*) [f. PHONOMETRIC *a.*: see -IC 2.] The study and practice of phonometry.

1957 H. J. ULDALL in Hjelmslev & Uldall *Outl. Glossematics* I. 16 In linguistics, phonometrics, experimental phonetics, and word counting. **1970** H. BLUEHME tr. *E. & K. Zwirner's Princ. Phonometrics* 4 Phonometrics is based on the assumption that the description and the synchronic or diachronic comparison of languages can be extended beyond what would be possible on the basis of the mere mastery of language by speaking, listening, or writing. **1972** HARTMANN & STORK *Dict. Lang. & Linguistics* 175 *Phonometrics*, the analysis and description of the spoken language by phonological (linguistic) and phonetic (instrumental) as well as statistical means.

phonometry (fəʊˈnɒmɪtrɪ). [ad. G. *phonometrie* (E. & K. Zwirner, *Grundfragen der Phonometrie* (1936)).] A method of investigating language by the statistical analysis of instrumentally measured speech sounds and informants' responses to the same data.

1936 *Amer. Speech* XI. 358 The first volume.. seeks to provide the historical and the theoretical bases for the methods of 'Phonometry'. The *raison d'être* of this venture is the conviction that the problems of comparative and historical linguistics are susceptible of further solution than has yet been achieved if one applies to these problems the technique known in biology as the statistics of variations. **1938** *Ibid.* XIII. 275 The chief concern of phonometry to date has been the empirical study of the variation of speech sounds, or, more precisely stated, the attributes of speech sounds, such as, for example, that of the duration of vowels. **1964** *Phonetica* XI. 151 Phonometry always works with recordings of connected speech.

phonon (ˈfəʊnɒn). [f. PHONO- + -ON[1].]

1. *Physics.* A quantum or quasiparticle associated with compressional waves, such as sound or those in a crystal lattice.

1932 J. FRENKEL *Wave Mech.* vi. 267 It is possible to associate the acoustical waves with certain particles which we shall call 'phonons', and to replace the study of the heat oscillations forming these waves by the study of the motion of the corresponding 'phonons'. [*Note*] It is not in the least intended to convey hereby the impression that such phonons have a real existence. **1953** C. KITTEL *Introd. Solid State Physics* v. 82 If the forces between atoms were purely harmonic, there would be no mechanism for collisions between different phonons, and the mean free path would be limited solely by collisions of a phonon with the crystal boundary, and by lattice imperfections. **1968** C. G. KUPER *Introd. Theory Super-conductivity* i. 2 In field-theoretical language the mechanism responsible for electrical resistance is scattering of electrons, with associated emission or absorption of quanta ('phonons') of the acoustic vibration field of the medium. **1969** *New Scientist* 2 Jan. 32/3 They calculated that 100 W of the light were converted into coherent phonons. **1974** H. E. HALL *Solid State Physics* ii. 67 It is often convenient to treat lattice vibrations in an analogous way, and introduce the idea of phonons of energy $\hbar\omega$ as quanta of excitation of the lattice. Our normal modes are plane waves extending throughout the crystal lattice, and correspondingly the phonons are not localized particles. *Ibid.*, Like photons, phonons are bosons and are not conserved.

2. *Linguistics.* In stratificational grammar, a phonetic feature which is capable of distinguishing phonemes. Cf. *distinctive-feature* s.v. DISTINCTIVE *a.* 1 b. Hence **phoˈnonic** *a.*

1964 S. M. LAMB in Romney & Andrade *Transcultural Stud. in Cognition* (Amer. Anthropologist: special publication) 60 The elementary units of which the phoneme, the morpheme, the lexeme, and the sememe are composed may be called the *phonon*, the *morphon*, the *lexon*, and the *semon* respectively. **1965** *Language* XLI. 200 Units that Lamb calls 'phonons' but that I shall call distinctive features. **1966** S. M. LAMB *Outl. Stratificational Gram.* ii. 29 The phononic alternation pattern specifies alternations involving phonological components. *Ibid.* iii. 57 The following symbols.. may be used for hypophonemic signs, hypophonemes, and phonons. **1967** C. F. HOCKETT *Lang., Math. & Linguistics* 83 The pair 'pit' and 'bit' attests to a minimal difference,.. but that difference is between voicelessness and voicing, not between /p/ and /b/. We shall follow Lamb in calling the terms of such minimal differences *phonons*. **1969** *Language* XLV. 300 The use of phonons in stratificational phonology is compared with the use of marked vs. unmarked features by transformationalists. **1975** *Amer. Speech 1972* XLVII. 248 In many, most, or all languages there are recurrent bundles of phonons which it is convenient to represent in a linear rotation by single letters.

phonophore (ˈfəʊnəfɔə(r)). *Physiol.* [f. PHONO- + -PHORE.] Name for the small bones of the ear, or auditory ossicles, as transmitting the vibrations of sound to the labyrinth or internal ear.

1882 COUES in *Amer. Jrnl. Otology* IV. 19.

So **phonophorous** (fəʊˈnɒfərəs) *a.*, transmitting sound-vibrations, as the auditory ossicles.

phonopore (ˈfəʊnəpɔə(r)). [f. PHONO- + Gr. πόρος passage.] Name of an apparatus by means of which electrical impulses produced by induction, as in a telephone, may be used to transmit messages along a telegraph wire, without interfering with the current by which ordinary messages are simultaneously transmitted.

1886 *Pall Mall G.* 27 May 3/1 The phonopore, the principle of which consists in employing the electrical 'induction noises' as motive power to work telegraph instruments, or transmit the voice, or do both at once, is far more remarkable. **1891** C. LANGDON-DAVIES *Explan. Phonopore* 14, I.. called the cable coil instrument a Phonopore (or sound passage). **1892** *Pall Mall G.* 27 Apr. 7/2 By means of the phonopore,.. the carrying capacity of the existing telegraph wires can be.. increased tenfold.

Hence **phonoporic** (-ˈpɒrɪk) *a.*, of or pertaining to the phonopore.

1886 *Manch. Exam.* 31 May 5/5 So completely is the phonoporic current under control. **1889** *Times* (weekly ed.) 29 Mar. 5/2 Phonoporic messages can be transmitted and received through an ordinary line wire by the phonopore [*printed* -phoric, -phore]. **1892** *Pall Mall G.* 27 Apr. 7/2 The phonoporic system is as applicable to telephony as it is to telegraphy. By its means a phonopore telephone service may be established on any existing telegraph wire on which ordinary telegraph instruments are already at work, without the two systems in any way interfering with one another.

phonoscope (ˈfəʊnəskəʊp). [f. PHONO- + -SCOPE.]

1. An apparatus for testing the quality of musical strings, shown by M. Koenig at the International Exhibition, in 1862.

2. Name for various instruments or devices by means of which sound-vibrations are indicated or represented in a visible form.

1884 KNIGHT *Dict. Mech.* Suppl., *Phonoscope*, an instrument invented by Henry Edmunds for producing figures of light from vibrations of sound. It consists essentially of three parts, an induction coil, an interrupter, and a rotary vacuum tube. **1888** *Amer. Ann. Deaf* Jan. 84 *Forchhammer's Phonoscope.* Mr. E. Walther.. says that it solves the problem of the optical representation of the pitch of the voice in the simplest and clearest manner. The instrument is of service in correcting the unnatural pitch of the voice in which some pupils speak. **1890** *Cent. Dict.*, *Phonoscope*, a machine for recording music as it is played or sung.

3. = MICROPHONE.

phonostylistics (fəʊnəʊstaɪˈlɪstɪks), *sb. pl.* (const. as *sing.*) [f. PHONO- + STYLISTIC *sb.*]

a. The study of the stylistic implications of phonetic variation. **b.** (See quot. 1972[1].) Hence **phonostyˈlistic** *a.*

1968 M. SHAPIRO *Russian Phonetic Variants & Phonostylistics* p. vii, Phonetic free variation in Russian is treated in the present monograph not only for itself but as the material of a new subdiscipline of phonology which I have called phonostylistics after Trubetzkoy. *Ibid.* ii. 9 For the purposes of a special investigation, be it phonostylistic or otherwise, one cannot adopt the uneconomical view. **1969** *Computers & Humanities* III. 252 Linguistic features of style may be classified under *phono-stylistics* (meter, rhyme), *morphostylistics*,.. and *syntactostylistics*. **1972** HARTMANN & STORK *Dict. Lang. & Linguistics* 175/2 *Phonostylistics*, that branch of stylistics which investigates the expressive function of sounds, e.g. the use of onomatopoeia in poetry. **1972** *Language* XLVIII. 350 It is of interest to note the phonostylistic correlates of these alternate pronunciations.

phonotactics (fəʊnəʊˈtæktɪks), *sb. pl.* (const. as *sing.*) *Linguistics.* [f. PHONO- + TACTICS.] That part of phonology which comprises or deals with the rules governing the possible phoneme sequences in a language. So **phonoˈtactic, phonoˈtactical** *adjs.*; **phonoˈtactically** *adv.*

1956 E. HAUGEN in M. Halle et al. *For Roman Jakobson* 216 The key to our understanding of the syllable lies in the development of phonotactics, or the study of phonemic distribution. **1958** [see MORPHOTACTICS *sb. pl.*]. **1958** A. A. HILL *Introd. Linguistic Struct.* viii. 116 Such a form reaches the maximum sequence which is pronounceable without breaking English phonotactic sequences. **1962** E. F. HADEN et al. *Resonance-Theory for Linguistics* iii. 24 Phonotactics.. deals with the order of phonic entities. The field of phonotactics is phonemes-in-sequence. **1964** E. BACH *Introd. Transformational Gram.* ii. 23 A restatement of the rules in which there is a clean break between phonotactic and allophonic rules will require a longer description. **1965** W. WINTER *Evidence for Laryngeals* 210 We do not yet know enough about the phonotactics of Proto-Tocharian to rule out the possibility that.. *ssk and *tsk were reduced to *sk* and *tk*. **1967** D. STEIBLE *Conc. Handbk. Linguistics* 96 Phonotactical description defines the phoneme classes which occur in a language. **1970** *Language* XLVI. 211 Young Binis..pronounce the word *epich*, deliberately violating Bini phonotactic rules (which forbid closed syllables). **1972** *Ibid.* XLVIII. 465 Prenasalized stops are found in many languages, and are not usually subject to such stringent phonotactical restrictions; in Albanian, for example, they occur both initially and as first members of clusters. **1973** D. ROCKEY *Phonetic Lexicon* ii. 28 Tests for phoneme recognition should be designed with the aim of determining whether the patient has grasped the phonotactic rules of the language, that is, whether he knows the phonemes and their combinations. **1973** *Word 1970* XXVI. 108 Monosyllabic nonsense forms, phonotactically Russian. **1975** *Canad. Jrnl. Linguistics* XX. I. 61 Portuguese phonotactics generally does not tolerate word-final stops. **1976** *Ibid.* XXI. I. 38 Many of the morphological rules which are proposed by linguists, whether morphophonemic or phonotactic in presumed character, are posited primarily, if not solely, in order to capture certain kinds of supposed 'lexical redundancies'. **1977** *Ibid.* XXII. I. 45 R2 and R3 are phonotactically motivated P-rules; they 'conspire' to prevent occurrences of *ss*-sequences on the surface.

phonotype ('fəʊnətaɪp), *sb.* [f. PHONO- + TYPE.] A character or letter of a phonetic alphabet adapted for printing; (without *a* or *pl.*), phonetic print or type. Hence **'phonotype** *v. trans.* to print in phonotype; **phonotyper** = *phonotypist*; **phonotypic** (-'tɪpɪk), **-ical** *adjs.*, pertaining or relating to phonotype or phonotypy (whence **phono'typically** *adv.*); **'phonotypist** (-taɪpɪst), an advocate or user of phonotype; **'phonotypy** (-taɪpɪ), a method or system of phonetic printing.

1844 *Phonotypic Jrnl.* III. 2 Aspirate *h*, as in *heap*; *Phonotype—H. **1845** I. PITMAN *Man. Phonogr.* 19 *Phonotype*, a printed letter, or sign, indicative of a particular sound, or modification of sound. **1848** A. J. ELLIS *Esenf. Fωnetics* 241 Pica phonotypes. **1881** *Kansas Hist. Coll.* II. 162 Phonotype was with him both a theory and a practice. **1850** *Fonetic Jrnl.* 133/2 The only way to preserve the language from further arbitrary changes is to *phono-type it. **1845** A. J. ELLIS *Plea Phonot.* 28 The *phonotyper.. having acquired a habit of reading phonotypy..will soon be able to read heterotypy with ease. **1843** (*title*) The *Phonotypic Journal. **1858** *N.Y. Tribune* 2 July 3/2 Many of those who are interested in the Phonotypic 'movement' advocate the entire abandonment of the old orthography. **1845** A. J. ELLIS *Plea Phonot.* 5 The *phonotypical representation of the sounds. **1875** —— *E.E. Pronunc.* 1182 *note*, Phonetic Essays which I published in [the Phonotypic] Journal..1846 (all printed *phonotypically). **1850** *Fonetic Jrnl.* 74/1 The Spelling Reform which Phonographers and *Phonotypists are endeavouring to effect, would confer incalculable benefits on society. **1844** ELLIS in *Phonotypic Jrnl.*, A Key to *Phonotypy or printing by sound. **1880** *Academy* 9 Oct. 255 It is printed in semi-phonotypy—in a system of spelling intended to bridge over the transition.

phonus-bolonus ('fəʊnəs bə'ləʊnəs). *U.S. slang.* Also **phonus bolognus**. [f. PHON(EY, PHON(Y *a.* and BALON(EY, BOLON(EY + the meaningless syllable *-us*.] Nonsense, exaggeration, ostentation, an insincere statement; fraud, trickery; goods not up to specification; a swindling transaction. Also as *adj.*

1929 D. RUNYON in *Hearst's International* July 58/1 Of course this message is nothing but the phonus bolonus. **1936** WODEHOUSE *Laughing Gas* xviii. 202 Sure. It was just a bit of phonus-bolonus. I was stringing you along so's I could get hold of that notebook. I'd be a fine sap giving you money. **1947** —— *Full Moon* vi. 115 His little friend had scouted the idea that there was any phonus-bolonus afoot between Veronica Wedge and this prominent Anglo-American snake. **1948** in Wentworth & Flexner *Dict. Amer. Slang* (1960) 386/1 The phonus-bolonus which gums up the average backstage musical. **1950** R. STARNES *Another Mug for Bier* xviii. 121 Who was..the one who engineered the phonus-bolonus deal? **1955** *Sun* (Baltimore) 3 Feb. 3/1 'Phonus Bolognus!' whipped back Charles Hess.

phony: see PHONEY *a.* and *sb.*, *v.*

phoo (fuː), *int.* [Another form of PHEW, PHO.] A vocal gesture expressing contemptuous rejection, cursory dismissal (of a proposition, idea, etc.) or reproach, and discomfort or weariness (cf. PHEW *int.*).

1672 VILLIERS (Dk. Buckhm.) *Rehearsal* IV. i. (Arb.) 105 Phoo! that is to raise the character of Drawcansir. —— *Chances* v. iv. (1682) 61 Phoo! y' are always abusing me. **1673** [R. LEIGH] *Transp. Reh.* 20 Phoo! reply'd a Friend of the Transprosers. **1814** JANE AUSTEN *Mansf. Park* I. xv. 305 Phoo! Phoo! Do not be so shamefaced. **1840** HOOD *Up Rhine* 46, I..enquired how the untoward event had originated. 'Originated!—*phoo, phoo*—no such thing, it was done on purpose.' *c* **1874** D. BOUCICAULT in M. R. Booth *Eng. Plays of 19th Cent.* (1969) II. 171 Phoo! How my arms ache! **1960** J. STROUD *Shorn Lamb* xviii. 201 I'm fed up o' lodgings... Feet orf my sofa, no smokin' in front o' children —phoo! **1978** 'J. LYMINGTON' *Waking of Stone* i. 26 She.. dropped on the seat and went, 'Phooo!'

Hence **pho(o)-pho(o)** *v. trans.*, to ridicule, = POOH-POOH *v.* Also *absol.*

1865 *Cornh. Mag.* June 755 He pho-pho'd the poor ghost. **1866** *Ibid.* Aug. 141 It is easy to blame and to phoo-phoo.

phooey ('fuːɪ), *int.* (*sb.*) orig. *U.S.* Also **phooie**. [f. PHOO *int.* + -Y[6], or ad. PFUI *int.*] An expression of strong disagreement with or disapproval of something said. Also as *sb.*, applied to the thing said: nonsense, 'baloney'.

1929 *Sun* (Baltimore) 11 July 11/1 Girls are described as weenies, janes, dames and broads. A mad-man is phooey, crackers or blooey. **1936** O. NASH *Primrose Path* 185 And I'll say, 'Phooie!' or something of the sort. **1940** R. CHANDLER *Farewell, my Lovely* xix. 95 'Ten o'clock at The Belvedere Club,' I said. Somebody said: 'Phooey'. **1946** —— *Let.* 29 Jan. in *R. Chandler Speaking* (1966) 45 So let's not have any more of that phooey about 'as literature my stuff still stinks'. **1951** J. B. PRIESTLEY *Festival at Farbridge* I. ii. 55 Oh phooey, Benny... This don't count as a drink. **1957** J. BRAINE *Room at Top* x. 94 'Keep right on believing that, and it won't be long before I see your name in the Sunday papers.' 'Phooey,' I said. 'It's a simple straightforward transaction.' **1967** *Boston Globe* 30 Mar. 18/2 The governor's advisers, spoilsports, have said 'Phooey' to the technicalities. **1972** R. LOCKRIDGE *Something up Sleeve* (1973) x. 135 The answer to that was simple. It was 'Phooey!' **1975** A. PRICE *Our Man in Camelot* v. 94 'Oh—phooey.' She scowled at him.

phooka, the same as POOKA.

‖**phoolwa**, variant spelling of FULWA.

c **1865** LETHEBY in *Circ. Sc.* I. 95/1 Similar fats are obtained from the seeds of *Bassia latifolia*,..and *Bassia butyracea*,..the latter [is named] *Phoolwa*, or *vegetable butter*.

phoonghie, -gyee, etc.: see POONGHIE.

phorate ('fɔːreɪt). [f. phos*phor*odithio*ate*, f. PHOSPHORO- + DI-[2] + THIO- + -ATE[1].] A systemic and soil insecticide that is effective against a wide range of insects and is also poisonous to man on contact or ingestion; *O,O* - diethyl - *S* - (ethylthio)methylphosphorodithioate, $(C_2H_5O)_2PS{\cdot}S{\cdot}CH_2SC_2H_5$.

1959 *Jrnl. Econ. Entomol.* LII. 1032 Changes in common names of insecticides... Name to be used..phorate. **1962** *New Scientist* 7 June 508/3 Disyston (thiodemeton) and Thimet (phorate)..gave the best control of aphids and the most improved yield. **1973** *Pesticide Sci.* IV. 90 Phorate has been effective for the control of two-spotted spider mite. *Ibid.* 97 Foliar application of phorate results in moderate initial residues on mint hay which disappear rapidly.

phorbol ('fɔːbɒl). *Chem.* [a. G. *phorbol* (Flaschenträger & Boehm 1927, in *Ber. über die ges. Physiol. und exper. Pharmakol.* XLII. 585), f. Gr. φορβή fodder, forage (f. φέρβειν to feed): see -OL.] A tetracyclic compound, $C_{20}H_{28}O_6$, some of the esters of which are cocarcinogens and are present in croton oil.

1935 *Chem. Abstr.* XXIX. 2533 Phorbol ($C_{20}H_{28}O_6$ or $C_{20}H_{30}O_6$) with very dilute H_2SO_4 in N_2 gives 38% crotophorbolon. **1939** *Thorpe's Dict. Appl. Chem.* (ed. 4) III. 434/2 Phorbol and the product of its benzoylation are physiologically inactive, but the (? tetra-)acetate is highly toxic. **1967** *Chem. & Engin. News* 16 Oct. 42/1 A possible absolute configuration of phorbol, polyfunctional parent alcohol of tumor-promoting compounds in croton oil, has been determined. **1978** *Nature* 17 Aug. 640/2 The most powerful known tumour promotors are the phorbol esters, which are not carcinogenic in themselves but can induce tumour growth after a subthreshold dose of carcinogen.

-phore (fɔə(r)), in F. *-phore*, mod.L. *-phorus*, *-phorum*, a. Gr. -φόρος, -ον bearing, bearer, f. φέρ-ειν to bear. A formative of various technical and scientific words, as *carpophore*, *semaphore*, *gonophore*, *phonophore*. Hence -PHOROUS, q.v.

phoresis (fɒ'riːsɪs). *Med.* Now *rare* or *Obs.* [ad. Gr. φόρησις being carried; cf. CATAPHORESIS, ELECTROPHORESIS.] = CATAPHORESIS a.

1902 HERDMAN & WILLEY in *Jrnl. Physical Therapeutics* III. 125 In view of this fact that certain substances are actuated to seek the anode while others are moved toward the cathode when a difference of potential is established in the liquid in which they are dissolved, or suspended, it would seem that a generic term, as *phoresis*, should be chosen to designate the therapeutic employment of this physical action of a direct electric current, a term which would comprehend in its meaning the moving power of the current in whatever direction upon particles suspended in it or held in solution by it, while the specific terms, *cataphoresis* and *anaphoresis* would, as now, indicate the direction taken by certain of these substances. **1911** C. S. POTTS *Electr.* (1912) ii. 50 The [ionic] migration will take place even through a porous barrier or membrane, in which case it is known as electric osmosis or phoresis. **1936** H. H. U. CROSS *Electr. in Therapeutics* vii. 184 The essential distinction between the modern ionic medication and the older cataphoresis (or simply phoresis).

-phoresis (-fɒ'riːsɪs), *suffix* [f. as prec.], forming sbs. which describe the movement of small particles by some agency, as CATA-, ELECTRO-, IONO-, IONTO-, PHOTOPHORESIS.

phoresy (fɒ'riːsɪ, 'fɒrəsɪ). Also **phoresis**. [a. F. *phorésie* (P. Lesne 1896, in *Bull. Soc. Ent. France* 164), f. Gr. φόρησις being carried.] An association in which one organism is carried by another, without being a parasite upon it. Hence **pho'retic** *a.*, of or pertaining to an association of this type.

1923 L. O. HOWARD in *Entomol. News* XXXIV. 90 (*heading*) An interesting new case of phoresie. **1927** —— in *Ibid.* XXXVIII. 145 In 1896 P. Lesne..proposed the name *phorésie*..to describe the carriage of small insects by larger insects without the actual feeding of the smaller upon the larger in the adult stage... It is proposed to give it the English form, *phoresy*. Apparently, in this form it has not occurred in the English language, although the word *phoresis* is used by electricians to express the conduction of substances dissolved in a liquid through a membrane by means of a current. **1942** E. O. ESSIG *College Entomol.* xxxiv. 663 The remarkable phenomenon of phoresy occurs in the case of *Rielia manticida* Kieffer, the adult females of which attach themselves to the body of the praying mantid. **1962** J. D. SMYTH *Introd. Animal Parasitol.* i. 3 Phoresis. This term is used for a particular type of association in which one organism merely provides shelter, support or transport for another organism of a different species. *Ibid.*, In phoresis.. there is no metabolic dependence of either of the associates on the other. **1965** B. E. FREEMAN tr. *Vandel's Biospeleol.* xv. 245 Phoresy or epizoism, that is to say the fixation of a plant or animal species on to the surface of another organism without the first living at the expense of the second. *Ibid.* 248 The ciliates may be divided into internal parasites, and epizoic or phoretic types which do not live at the expense of their hosts. **1969** R. F. CHAPMAN *Insects* xvii. 327 An association in which an animal of one species provides transport for another species is known as phoresy.

phoria ('fɔːrɪə). *Ophthalm.* [f. prec.] A tendency for the eyes to be directed towards different points in the absence of a visual stimulus.

1891 *Trans. Amer. Ophthalm. Soc.* VI. 136, I..then record the 'phoria' or 'heterophoria' found. **1937** *Times* 23 July 18/5 Every discovered phoria with a history of flying trouble was not for certain the absolute root cause. **1975** *Nature* 20 Nov. 202/2 Now phorias, or tendencies to strabismus, are common in infancy.

-phoria ('fɔːrɪə), comb. form f. Gr. φόρος bearing (f. φέρειν to bear: see -IA[1]), used in *Ophthalm.* to form terms denoting a tendency to squint, as ESOPHORIA, *heterophoria* s.v. HETERO-.

‖**phorminx** ('fɔːmɪŋks). [mod.L., a. Gr. φόρμιγξ.] A stringed instrument of the harp class; a kind of cithara or lyre used by the ancient Greeks as an accompaniment to the voice.

1776 BURNEY *Hist. Mus.* I. 344 The cithara may in ancient times have been thought inferior to the *phorminx*, as the modern guitar is esteemed at present a trivial and effeminate instrument, when compared with the double harp. **1856** MRS. BROWNING *Aur. Leigh* I. 979 We beat the phorminx till we hurt our thumbs.

phormium ('fɔːmɪəm). *Bot.* [mod.L. (J. R. & G. Forster *Characteres Generum Plantarum* (1776) 47), f. Gr. φορμίον, dim. of φορμός mat, basket, in reference to the use made of the fibres of the leaves.] An evergreen plant of the genus so called, belonging to the family Liliaceæ, native to New Zealand, and distinguished by long, tough leaves in tufts at the base and large, erect panicles of dull red or yellow flowers; = *New Zealand flax* s.v. NEW ZEALAND I.

1821 J. YULE in *Edin. Philos. Jrnl.* V. 345 The following results..manifest the comparative superiority in strength of the fibres of the Phormium. **1852** DE BOW *South. & West. States* I. 84 The phormium would doubtless succeed in the rich bottoms of the Mississippi Valley. **1905** [see MILLABLE *a.*]. **1933** W. J. BEAN *Trees & Shrubs Hardy in Brit. Isles* III. 274 Strictly speaking, the phormiums are, I suppose, 'herbs', but they are genuinely evergreen. **1955** *Sci. News Let.* 2 Apr. 213/2 Four fiber crops also under study for use on American farms are ramie, kenaf, sanseveria, and phormium. **1972** S. EMBERTON *Year in Shrub Garden* III. 150 The tall, snow-trapping evergreen leaf blades of the phormiums (New Zealand Flax) never regain their poise once their stiff backs have been broken by the weight of snow. **1976** *Country Life* 26 Feb. 478/1 Shrubs like.. phormiums, variegated osmanthus, carefully chosen hebes.

phorometer (fɒ'rɒmɪtə(r)). *Ophthalm.* [f. Gr. -φόρος bearing, f. φέρ-ειν to bear + -METER.] Any instrument for measuring the degree to which the eyes tend to be differently directed.

1888 G. T. STEVENS in *Med. Rec.* 5 May 511/1 New instruments. A phorometer... This instrument is designed to assist in the determination of the visual lines to each other. *Ibid.* 511/2, I have now used the phorometer during several months past. **1941** *Arch. Ophthalm.* XXV. 483 As a part of the flight surgeon's equipment there is a phorometer trial frame with an adjustable bracket and a tripod stand, a rather complex and impressive piece of equipment. **1970** *Jrnl. Gen. Psychol.* LXXXII. 111 The apparatus consisted of ..(*b*) a head rest, (*c*) American Optical phorometer, [etc.].

phorone (fɒ'rəʊn). *Chem.* [Shortened (by Gerhardt) from CAMPHORONE.] †**a.** A substance, $C_9H_{14}O$, obtained by distilling calcium camphorate; now called *camphorphorone*; **b.** An isomer of this substance, *diisopropylidene acetone*, a colourless oil with aromatic odour.

1859 FOWNES *Man. Chem.* 527 Phorone contains $C_{18}H_{14}O_2$. **1863-72** WATTS *Dict. Chem.* I. 733 *Camphorone*, Phorone (Gerhardt)..$C_9H_{14}O$..a colourless or yellowish oil, very mobile, lighter than water.

Hence **pho'ronic** *acid*, $C_{11}H_{18}O_5$, a crystallizable acid obtained from camphic acid.

1881 WATTS *Dict. Chem.* VIII. 1574.

phoronomy (fɒ'rɒnəmɪ). *Physics.* [ad. mod.L. *phoronomia* (Hermann 1716) = Ger., F. *phoronomie*, f. Gr. φορά motion (f. φέρ-ειν to bear, carry) + *-nomia*: cf. *astronomia* ASTRONOMY.] The purely geometrical theory of motion; the branch of mechanics that treats of the motion of bodies considered absolutely; kinematics.

[**1716** HERMANN (*title*) *Phoronomia, seu de Viribus et Motibus Corporum solidorum et liquidorum.*] **1877** E. CAIRD *Philos. Kant* II. xii. 489 Matter quantitatively defined, is the moveable in space. In this point of view it is the object of a science we may call 'Phoronomy'. **1892** *Nature* 24 Mar. 486/2 The letter of Dr. Besant..suggests strong reasons for employing the word phoronomy in the place of kinematics.

Hence **phoro'nomic** *a.*, of or belonging to phoronomy, kinematic; **phoro'nomics** *sb.* = *phoronomy*; **phoro'nomically** *adv.*, in respect of or in relation to phoronomy; kinematically.

1842 BRANDE *Dict. Sc.* etc., *Phoronomia* or *Phoronomics*, a term sometimes used to denote the science of motion. **1858** MAYNE *Expos. Lex.* 946/2 Phoronomic. **1893** MCCORMACK tr. *Mach's Sc. Mechanics* 166 Phoronomically similar structures.

phoroscope ('fɒrəskəʊp). [f. Gr. φορό-ς adj. bearing + σκόπος view, sight.] An instrument for reproducing a visual image at a distance by means of electricity.

1890 in *Cent. Dict.*

-phorous (fərəs), combining element, f. mod.L. *-phor-us*, Gr. -φόρ-ος, F. *-phore* + -OUS, forming adjs. related to sbs. in -PHORE, with the sense '-bearing'; synonymous with -FEROUS, but properly used only in words derived from Gr., e.g. *carpophorous*, *cladophorous*, *oophorous*, *phonophorous*, *phragmophorous*, etc.

phoro'zooid. *Zool.* [f. Gr. φορό-ς bearing + ZOOID.] One of the 'foster forms' in the sexual generation of Ascidians of the order *Thaliacea.*

1888 HERDMAN in *Encycl. Brit.* XXIII. 615/2 Foster forms (phorozooids), which..do not become sexually mature, but..are set free as cask-shaped bodies with eight muscle bands and a ventral outgrowth..formed of the stalk by which the body was formerly united to the nurse.

†**phos-.** *Chem. Obs.* [a. Gr. φῶς light.] Used by Sir H. Davy, to form names of chemical compounds, into which he considered light to enter as an element. Such were **pho'sacid**, **phos'muriate**, **phosmuri'atic** *a.*, **phos'nitric** *a.*, **pho'soxyd**, **pho'soxydable** *a.*, **pho'soxydate** *v.*, **pho'soxygen**, **pho'soxygenate** *v.*, etc.: see the quots.

1799 SIR H. DAVY in Beddoes *Contrib. Phys. & Med. Knowl.* 89 All the combinations of phosoxygen that have acid properties are denoted by the names of phosacids. *Ibid.* 90 The different quantities of phosoxygen entering into the composition of the phosoxyds and phosacids. *Ibid.* 96 It is evident..that phosnitric acid is a compound of light, oxygen and nitrogen. *Ibid.* 108 Phosmuriate of Potash is compounded of phosmuriatic acid and potash. *Ibid.* 71 The phosoxydable base remains pure. *Ibid.* 116 Gold becomes phosoxydated by attracting light and oxygen from the muriatic phosacid. *Ibid.* 109 Muriatic acid is never phosoxygenated. **1879** *Cassell's Techn. Educ.* IV. 314/2 'Phosoxygen' (such was the name he [Davy] put upon the ordinary oxygen of the atmosphere).

phos, phoss, also phos., foss, slang or colloq. abbreviation of PHOSPHORUS: now esp. applied to phosphorus necrosis: see PHOSSY.

1811 *Lex Balatr.*, *Phos bottle*, a bottle of phosphorus: used by housebreakers to light their lanthorns. *Ding the phos*; throw away the bottle of phosphorus. **1812** J. H. VAUX *Flash Dict.*, *Foss* or *phos*, a phosphorus bottle used by cracksmen to obtain a light.

1892 *Star* 18 Jan. 2/5 The manager denied she had 'got the phos.' and refused any money.

Phosfon ('fɒsfɒn). Also **Phosphon** and with lower-case initial. A proprietary name for an organophosphorus compound used to retard the growth of chrysanthemums and certain other garden plants. Also *Phosfon-D.*

1961 *Official Gaz.* (U.S. Patent Office) 22 Aug. TM104/2 Virginia-Carolina Chemical Corporation, Richmond, Va. Filed June 1, 1960. Phosfon-D for chemical height-retardant for chrysanthemums. First use Feb. 25, 1960. **1962** *Economist* 21 Apr. 248/2 The size of plants can be regulated by two new chemicals (one of which, phosfon-D, is already on the market) so that lilliputian Easter lilies and dwarf hydrangeas are possible. **1962** *Official Gaz.* (U.S. Patent Office) 2 Oct. TM7/1 Virginia-Carolina Chemical Corporation, Richmond, Va. Filed Feb. 8, 1962. Phosfon... For chemical height retardant for garden chrysanthemums. First use Jan. 1, 1962. **1968** *New Scientist* 10 Oct. 84/2 Studies in Israel have shown that another retardant, 2-4-dichlorobenzyltributyl phosphonium chloride (Phosfon) gives better control of the Oleander aphid. **1969** *Trade Marks Jrnl.* 23 Dec. 2098/2 Phosfon... Chemical substances..for use in agriculture and horticulture, being or containing compounds of phosphorus. Mobil Oil Corporation.., New York City.., United States of America; manufacturers and merchants. **1975** *Adv. Agronomy* XXVII. 116 Other chemicals which reduce stomatal aperture such as phosphon-D..tend to protect against smog injury.

phosgene ('fɒsdʒiːn). *Chem.* Also -gen (-dʒɛn). [f. Gr. φῶς light + *-gene*, -GEN (in *hydrogen(e*, etc.). In F. *phosgène.*] A name for the gas carbon oxychloride, $COCl_2$, originally obtained by exposing equal volumes of chlorine and carbonic oxide to the sun's rays; used as a poison gas in the war of 1914–18, and now as an intermediate in the manufacture of some synthetic resins and organic chemicals. Also called *phosgene gas.*

1812 J. DAVY in *Phil. Trans.* 6 Feb. 151 It will be necessary to designate it by some simple name. I venture to propose that of phosgene, or phosgene gas; from φως, light, and γινομαι, to produce, which signifies formed by light. **1826** HENRY *Elem. Chem.* I. 362 Being produced by the agency of light, it was called by Dr. [John] Davy phosgene gas, but as it exhibits distinctly acid properties, it has since been better termed *chloro-carbonic acid.* **1898** G. MCGOWAN tr. *Meyer's Hist. Chem.* 425 Carbon oxychloride or phosgene ..was first prepared by Davy in 1811. **1918** M. PLOWMAN *Right to Live* 3 They have been poisoned with phosgene. **1919** C. P. THOMPSON *Cocktails* 26 The laboratory where the Corps chemists pored over the latest phials of German phosgene. **1938** *Encycl. Brit. Bk. of Year* 144/1 Phosgene has a faint smell of musty hay; and it tends to work its way down into cellars and 'dug-outs'. **1953** KIRK & OTHMER *Encycl. Chem. Technol.* X. 397 Throughout 1917, phosgene was the gas used in largest tonnage by all belligerents. However, mustard gas was introduced by the Germans in 1917 and gradually supplanted phosgene. **1967** SIMONDS & CHURCH *Encycl. Basic Materials for Plastics* 432/1 Both sodium hydroxide and sodium promote the bisphenol A—phosgene reaction to form polyacrylcarbonates. Phosgene is produced catalytically from chlorine and carbon monoxide. **1978** A. PRICE *'44 Vintage* i. 12 His father..had been with him in the trenches and came back with a lungful of phosgene.

phosgenite ('fɒsdʒɪnaɪt). *Min.* [Named 1820; f. prec. + -ITE[1].] A mineral consisting of nearly equal parts of carbonate and chloride of lead, occurring in tetragonal crystals.

1849 NICOL *Min.* 379 Phosgenite, Breithaupt; Corneous lead, Jameson. **1868** DANA *Min.* (ed. 5) 703 Phosgenite.. Dissolves with effervescence in nitric acid. **1896** CHESTER *Dict. Min.*, *Phosgenite*, chloro-carbonate of lead, occurring in brilliant, white or yellow crystals.

phosmuriate to **phosoxygen**: see PHOS-.

phosph- = PHOSPHO-, combining form of PHOSPHORUS in Chem.; hence *phospham*, *-ate*, *-ide*, *-ine*, *-ite*, *-onium*, *-ure*, *-uret*, *-yl*, etc.

phosphagen ('fɒsfədʒən). *Biochem.* [f. PHOSPHA(TE + -GEN.] An organic phosphate in muscle tissue (in vertebrates, creatine phosphate) whose phosphate group is readily released and transferred to adenosine diphosphate, thereby forming the triphosphate needed for muscular contraction.

1927 P. & M. G. EGGLETON in *Nature* 5 Feb. 194/2 There appears to be in muscle tissue an organic phosphorus compound which, by reason of its great instability in acid solution, has been confused hitherto with inorganic phosphate... The confusion is increased by the fact that this substance, the organic phosphorus compound which we have designated 'phosphagen', is intimately connected with the chemical mechanism of contraction. **1937** BEST & TAYLOR *Physiol. Basis Med. Pract.* liii. 971 In the presence of oxygen the phosphoric acid and creatine are resynthesized to phosphagen. **1965** *New Scientist* 18 Feb. 445/1 So far, animal tissues have been found to contain organic compounds, N-phosphorylated guanidines, whereas plants and microorganisms contain only inorganic polyphosphates. This clear distinction between the two characteristic types of 'phosphagen' seems to offer a basis for deciding whether a particular organism is a plant or an animal. **1972** J. A. WILSON *Princ. Animal Physiol.* v. 141/1 Several other phosphagens have been found in the annelids.

phospham ('fɒsfæm). *Chem.* [f. PHOSPH- + AM(MONIA).] The nitril of phosphoric acid (PHN_2); a white, reddish, or yellowish-red powder.

1866–77 WATTS *Dict. Chem.* IV. 497 Phospham..is a bulky powder, white if moisture has been carefully excluded during its preparation, reddish in the contrary case.

phosphatæmia (fɒsfæ'tiːmɪə). *Physiol.* Also **phosphatemia.** [f. PHOSPHAT(E + Gr. αἷμα blood: see -IA[1].] The concentration of phosphates (and other compounds of phosphorus) in the blood. Less commonly = *hyperphosphatæmia* s.v. HYPER- IV.

1926 *Jrnl. Amer. Med. Assoc.* 6 Feb. 451/1 Phosphatemia and fibroma.—Dalsace and Guillaumin noted an exaggerated amount of phosphorus in the blood of women with a fibroma. **1928** *Q. Cumulative Index Medicus* III. 163/1 Glycemia and phosphatemia following intravenous injection of defibrinated blood. **1961** *Lancet* 22 July 215/1 In a control group of 20 normal adult men the average value for serum-phosphate was 3·43 mg. per 100 ml.,..so we can take 2·6 mg. per 100 ml. as the lower limit of normal phosphataemia. **1973** *Ann. d'Endocrinol.* XXXIV. 621 (*heading*) Role of the fœtal parathyroids in the regulation of calcemia and phosphatemia of the rat fœtus.

phosphatase ('fɒsfəteɪz, -s). *Biochem.* [f. PHOSPHAT(E + -ASE.] **a.** Any enzyme which catalyses the synthesis or hydrolysis of an ester of phosphoric acid.

H. Euler (in *Zeitschr. für physiol. Chem.* (1911) LXXVII. 14) coined the G. *phosphatese*, having proposed that the termination *-ase* be restricted to enzymes which decompose substrates, and *-ese* be used for enzymes which synthesize. Hence quot. 1911.

[**1911** *Jrnl. Chem. Soc.* C. I. 1051 There is no evidence that the enzyme which synthesises carbohydrate phosphoric acid esters has any splitting action. The term *phosphatese* is suggested.] **1912** *Chem. Abstr.* VI. 2084 Expts. with pepsin, trypsin, and animal organ exts. failed to show conclusively the presence of phosphatase. **1931** *Times Lit. Suppl.* 2 Apr. 274/3 There are two mechanisms at work in calcification: (*a*) a phosphatase mechanism which produces in the matrix fluid, by hydrolysis of phosphoric ester, a condition of supersaturation with respect to the bone phosphate. **1951** WEST & TODD *Textbk. Biochem.* xiv. 471 The acid and the alkaline phosphatases of serum are so called because of optimum activity at an acid and at an alkaline pH respectively. **1968** [see ISOENZYME]. **1973** B. J. WILLIAMS *Evolution & Human Origins* iv. 67/1 Red cell acid phosphatase provides a good illustration of the fact that alleles at a single locus can produce a 'continuous' trait in the manner described.

b. phosphatase test, a test applied to dairy products to find whether they have been adequately pasteurized.

1933 KAY & GRAHAM in *Jrnl. Dairy Res.* V. 70 If..the cream was pasteurised, its phosphatase content was completely or almost completely destroyed. This suggested to us the possibility that the phosphatase test might also be used for determining whether a given sample of butter had been made from fresh or from pasteurised cream. **1960** JUDKINS & KEENER *Milk Production & Processing* xiv. 256 The phosphatase test is very sensitive and will show very small variations in the time and temperature of pasteurization. As little as 0·1 per cent raw milk in pasteurized milk is also easily detected by this test. **1975** J. W. G. PORTER *Milk & Dairy Foods* xi. 55 The phosphatase test shows whether the proper temperature has been reached during pasteurization.

phosphate ('fɒsfət), *sb. Chem.* Also 8–9 **phosphat.** [a. F. *phosphate* (G. de Morveau *Nomencl. Ch.* 1787), f. PHOSPH- + -ATE[4].]

1. a. A salt, ester or other organic derivative of a phosphoric acid; esp. in *Biochem.*, any of these derivatives of sugars, nucleosides, etc., which occur widely in living organisms. Also, a radical or group derived from a phosphoric acid. Also *attrib.*

1795 PEARSON in *Phil. Trans.* LXXXV. 335 The siderite of Bergman; which is now believed to be phosphate of iron. **1799** *Med. Jrnl.* I. 280 The phosphat of mercury has long been known as a chemical preparation. **1826** HENRY *Elem. Chem.* I. 590 Phosphate of lime derives importance from its being the principal ingredient of animal bones, of which it constitutes about 86 per cent. **1869** ROSCOE *Elem. Chem.* (1871) 219 Calcium phosphate, or bone phosphate. **1895** *Jrnl. Chem. Soc.* LXVIII. I. 639 The liquid separates into two layers, the upper of which seems to contain triallylic phosphate. **1930** CAVEN & LANDER *Systematic Inorg. Chem.* ix. 237 Soluble phosphates, e.g. those of sodium,..show marked hydrolysis in solution. **1953** *Nature* 25 Apr. 737/1 The bases are on the inside of the helix and the phosphates on the outside. *Ibid.* 741/2 The phosphate groups lie on the outside of the structural unit, on a helix of diameter about 20 A. **1953** FRUTON & SIMMONDS *Gen. Biochem.* xix. 422 In the formulae for the sugar phosphates, the phosphoric acid residue is written in the undissociated form. **1954** A. WHITE et al. *Princ. Biochem.* xvi. 381 Enzymes which catalyze transfer of phosphate from ATP to an acceptor are designated kinases. **1957** *Encycl. Brit.* XVII. 780/2 Considerable tonnages of other phosphates such as $(NH_4)H_2PO_4$ and $(NH_4)_2HPO_4$ are also used in the fertilizer industry. **1964** N. G. CLARK *Mod. Org. Chem.* xxi. 433 Triphenyl phosphate..is used as a plasticizer for various cellulose and vinyl plastics. **1968** A. WHITE et al. *Princ. Biochem.* (ed. 4) xv. 315 Three classes of high-energy phosphate compounds are known: acid anhydrides, phosphate esters of enols, and derivatives of phosphamic acid $R-NH-PO_3H$. **1972** FARAGO & LAGNADO *Life in Action* v. 129 The starting material, glucose, is converted into phosphate derivatives which then go through a series of molecular gyrations, and are finally broken down to three-carbon units. **1976** *Nature* 1 July 45/1 Adsorption of phosphate on hydrous metal oxides is of considerable importance in soil fertility and eutrophication studies.

b. Applied esp. to the phosphates of lime or iron and alumina, as constituents of cereals, etc., and to that of lime (calcium) as a mineral.

1849 *Q. Jrnl. Geol. Soc.* V. p. lxxxiv, We find such phosphates surrounding some fossils, such as crustaceans from the London clay, leading us to infer a connexion between the animal matter and this substance. **1858** CARPENTER *Veg. Phys.* §32 One great source of the value of guano,..and many artificial manures, is the phosphates they supply to the soil. **1870** YEATS *Nat. Hist. Comm.* 37 Soils derived from rocks devoid of phosphates cannot produce cereals. **1891** F. WYATT *Phosphates of Amer.* iii. 28 The principal phosphate mines of Canada have been located on those positions of the pyroxenite belt in which, at the surface, the apatite has shown signs of predominating. **1892** *Amer. Jrnl. Sci.* XLIII. 403 The South Carolina phosphates are nodular in form. **1893** *Syd. Soc. Lex.*, *Phosphates, saccharated wheat*,..the organic phosphates and cerealin dissolved out of bran, and mixed with milk-sugar. **1936** J. C. BROWN *India's Mineral Wealth* (ed. 2) x. 225 The problem of the utilization of Indian rock phosphates demands more research than it appears yet to have received. **1954** K. B. CUMBERLAND *Southwest Pacific* ii. 42 In the central Pacific province the only mining is that of phosphate. **1976** *Nature* 10 June 452/3 If Abbott's Booby were found nesting in the group, this could be of crucial importance for the species, which is now reduced to about 2,000 pairs threatened by phosphate mining on Christmas Island. **1977** *Radio Times* 1 Jan. 54/4 The Banabans of Ocean Island..claim that they have been exploited..for 76 years because their island turned out to be full of phosphate.

2. Special Comb.: **phosphate bond** *Biochem.*, a bond between a phosphate group and another part of a molecule, esp. such a bond in an adenosine phosphate which is hydrolysed to provide energy in living organisms; **phosphate glass,** a glass of which the major constituent is phosphorus pentoxide or a phosphate;

phosphate island, an island consisting largely of phosphate rock; **phosphate rock**, rock containing a substantial amount of calcium phosphate (usu. in the form of apatite).

1940 *Jrnl. Biol. Chem.* CXXXIV. 463 Since pyruvic acid was found to promote adenylic acid phosphorylation, any such intermediate must contain an energy-rich phosphate bond. **1953** FRUTON & SIMMONDS *Gen. Biochem.* xv. 355 It has become the custom to refer to phosphate bonds whose hydrolysis is accompanied by the liberation of 8000 to 16,000 cal per mole.. as 'high-energy' phosphate bonds.., whereas the ester phosphate bonds (as in glucose-6-phosphate) are termed 'low-energy' phosphate bonds. **1962** I. ASIMOV *Life & Energy* xxi. 291 The two phosphate groups at the end away from the adenosine portion are more easily hydrolyzed than phosphate bonds generally are. **1977** *Sci. Amer.* Mar. 147/2 It now seems that fast direct-energy release by the splitting of high-energy phosphate bonds supplies our initial power, up to half of the overall oxygen debt. **1937** *Glass* XIV. 519/1 This work originated from the observation that a phosphate glass.. turns red on exposure to soft X-rays. **1950** J. E. STANWORTH *Physical Properties Glass* i. 8 It has long been known that phosphate glasses may be made which resist the attack of hydrofluoric acid solution or gas. **1959** W. A. WEYL *Coloured Glasses* i. 36 Phosphate glasses..offer certain unique features when used as a base for coloured glasses. **1925** *Econ. Geol.* XX. 276 The next change is when a phosphate island is elevated by earth movements. **1936** *Discovery* Aug. 260/1 He [sc. A. F. Ellis] 'discovered' Nauru as a phosphate island. **1870** F. S. HOLMES *Phosphate Rocks S. Carolina* 87 The Ashley Phosphate-rock is used in the manufacture of their fertilizer. **1915** W. S. BAYLEY *Minerals & Rocks* I. ii. 71 Phosphate rock is a mixture of apatite, phosphorite and various hydrated phosphates. **1923** A. B. SEARLE *Sands & Crushed Rocks* I. iv. 199 Coprolite and Phosphorite are natural phosphate rocks which are produced by the accumulation of organic remains. **1965** E. T. DEGENS *Geochem. Sediments* iii. 149 Phosphate rocks owe some of their rare metals to co-existing organic matter and sulfides rather than to phosphates themselves.

phosphate ('fɒsfeɪt), *v.* [f. the sb. Cf. PHOSPHATED *a.*] *trans.* = PHOSPHATIZE *v.* 2.

1939 BURNS & SCHUH *Protective Coatings for Metals* xvi. 374 'Coslettizing' was..used in England for phosphating the steel parts of bicycles. **1963** H. R. CLAUSER *Encycl. Engin. Materials* 477/1 The fabricated parts are cleaned.., phosphated and rinsed thoroughly.

Hence **'phosphating** *vbl. sb.*

1940 J. C. HUDSON *Corrosion of Iron & Steel* vi. 136 The proprietary phosphating processes, such as Parkerising and Bonderising. **1948** H. SILMAN *Chem. & Electro-Plated Finishes* v. 166 In the presence of accelerators the phosphating process is completed rapidly. **1956** WERNICK & PINNER *Surface Treatm. & Finishing of Aluminium & Alloys* vi. 213 As distinct from chemical oxidation, phosphating is carried out on a clean surface, and the work is therefore degreased before immersing..in the phosphating solution. **1976** J. A. VON FRAUNHOFER *Basic Metal Finishing* xiii. 146 The simplest phosphating treatment is immersion in hot dilute orthophosphoric acid solution for up to 30 min. but many proprietary solutions and commercial processes are in use.

phosphated ('fɒsfeɪtɪd), *a. Min.* [f. PHOSPHATE *sb.* + -ED[1].] Converted into a phosphate; combined with or containing phosphoric acid.

1802 *Med. Jrnl.* VIII. 551 Sulphat and sulphite... I should propose to render these terms into the adjectives sulphated and sulphitous: [so] phosphat and phosphite will form phosphated and phosphitous. **1858** in MAYNE *Expos. Lex.* **1888** *Nature* 20 Dec. 192/1 On the phosphated deposits of Montay and Forest. **1893** *Syd. Soc. Lex., Phosphated*,.. applied in Mineralogy to a base that has become converted into a phosphate by combining with phosphoric acid.

phosphatic (fɒs'fætɪk), *a.* [f. PHOSPHATE *sb.* (or mod.L. *phōsphāt-um*) + -IC.]

1. Of the nature of, characterized by the presence of, or containing a phosphate.

p. diathesis, a bodily condition predisposing to the excretion of phosphates in the urine; cf. PHOSPHATURIA. ***p. nodules***, hard rounded lumps containing phosphate of lime, of fossil origin, found in certain strata, now used as manure.

1843 R. J. GRAVES *Syst. Clin. Med.* iv. 50 Certain derangements of the urinary functions, such as the phosphatic and lithic diatheses. **1847–9** TODD *Cycl. Anat.* IV. 83/2 The tonsils are not unfrequently the seat of phosphatic deposit. **1859** DARWIN *Orig. Spec.* x. (1878) 287 The presence of phosphatic nodules..in some of the lowest azoic rocks, probably indicates life at these periods. **1866** *Reader* 7 July 635 The dark phosphatic nodules are usually named coprolites.

†**2.** ***phosphatic acid***, 'a name applied to the syrupy mixture of phosphoric and phosphorous acids, produced by the slow combustion of phosphorus in moist air', formerly supposed to be a distinct acid; also called *hypophosphoric acid*. *Obs.*

1826 HENRY *Elem. Chem.* I. 370 The acid thus obtained is a mixture of phosphorous and phosphoric acids, &c. Dulong..believes it to be a distinct compound, for which he has proposed the name of phosphatic acid. **1836–41** BRANDE *Chem.* (ed. 5) 489. **1866–77** WATTS *Dict. Chem.* IV. 499.

phosphatide ('fɒsfətaɪd). *Biochem.* Also †-id. [f. PHOSPHAT(E + -IDE.] Formerly = PHOSPHOLIPID; now *esp.* a fatty acid ester of glycerol phosphate in which a nitrogen base is linked to the phosphate group.

1884 J. L. W. THUDICHUM *Treat. Chem. Constitution Brain* i. 4 According to the result of this revision the phosphorised substances [in the brain] are not glycerides at all, as commonly defined, and have nothing in common with fats considered as glycerides, except that some of them contain fatty acids also present in fats... In accordance with this new knowledge, I have termed the phosphorised substances phosphatides, that is to say, substances which are similar to (but not by any means identical with) phosphates, on the assumption that their basal or principal joining radicle is that of phosphoric acid and that in this acid one, two, or three molec[u]les of hydroxyl may be replaced by radicles of alcohols, acids, or bases. **1910** [see PHOSPHOLIPIN]. **1918** [see HEPARIN]. **1921** B. HARROW *Vitamines* 43 A number of very complicated substances—the phosphatids—are found in larger quantities in the brain than in other parts of the body. **1927** [see PHOSPHOLIPIN]. **1944** L. F. & M. FIESER *Org. Chem.* xix. 490 In the more active tissues (brain, liver, kidney, etc.) they [*sc.* fats] usually occur in a form more complex than depot fats, which are mainly glycerides... These fats can be divided into two classes, phosphatides and cerebrosides. The former on hydrolysis yield fatty acids, a nitrogenous base, phosphoric acid, and usually glycerol. **1951** H. J. DEUEL *Lipids* I. i. 4 Phospholipids or Phosphatides. The former term is most generally employed in the United States while the latter one is favored in English and German literature. **1953** FRUTON & SIMMONDS *Gen. Biochem.* xxii. 509 Evidence has been presented for the occurrence, in the..brain, of a phosphatide that contains inositol. **1954** A. WHITE et al. *Princ. Biochem.* v. 87 The next large class of lipids..is the phospholipids, more usually called phosphatides... The members of this group all contain a nitrogenous base. **1968** *Ibid.* (ed. 4) iv. 69 The larger groups of naturally occurring phospholipids are termed phosphatides.

phosphatidic (fɒsfə'taɪdɪk, -'tɪdɪk), *a. Biochem.* [f. prec. + -IC.] ***phosphatidic acid***: any of the esterified derivatives of glycerol phosphate in which the hydrogen atoms in both hydroxyl groups are replaced by fatty acid radicals.

1927 CHANNON & CHIBNALL in *Biochem. Jrnl.* XXI. 1115 It seems to us preferable to keep to Thudichum's original definitions [of *phosphatide* and *cerebroside*]. If this is done the diglyceridephosphoric acid and its salts are phosphatides. Since the acid is chemically the parent acid of the two more commonly occurring phosphatides lecithin and kephalin, we propose to call it phosphatidic acid. **1954** A. WHITE et al. *Princ. Biochem.* v. 88 The phosphatides of known structure which contain one atom of N per atom of P may be regarded as derivatives of phosphatidic acid. **1964** W. G. SMITH *Allergy & Tissue Metabolism* viii. 87 Once these fatty acids are converted to fatty acyl CoA they could be incorporated immediately into diglyceride formed from 1-glycerophosphate via phosphatidic acid. **1967** [see *phosphoglyceride* s.v. PHOSPHO-]. **1979** *Sci. Amer.* Jan. 49/1 Two molecules of a fatty acid..are transferred from a donor to a molecule of glycerol phosphate, forming the most primitive phospholipid, phosphatidic acid.

Hence **phosphatidyl** (fɒsfə'taɪdaɪl, -ɪl, fɒs'fætɪdaɪl, -ɪl), the univalent radical of phosphatidic acid formed by the loss of a hydrogen atom from the phosphate group; usu. *attrib.* or in *Comb.* in the names of esters (phospholipids), as ***phosphatidyl choline, ethanolamine, serine***.

1941 J. FOLCH in *Jrnl. Biol. Chem.* CXXXIX. 973 In a recent paper it was shown that cephalin prepared in the usual manner..did not contain..all of its nitrogen in the form of ethanolamine, but that from 40 to 70 per cent was in the form of a β-hydroxyamino acid... The cephalin fraction containing the amino acid has now been isolated, and the amino acid crystallized as..*l*(+)-serine. We shall call this phosphatide 'phosphatidyl serine'. **1942** —— in *Ibid.* CXLVI. 35 Cephalin prepared from brain by the classical methods has..been separated into three fractions: (*a*) phosphatidyl ethanolamine so called because it has its nitrogen as ethanolamine and its P as glycerophosphoric acid, [etc.]. **1954** A. WHITE et al. *Princ. Biochem.* v. 88 Phosphatidyl choline, or lecithin, has the following formula. **1964** *Oceanogr. & Marine Biol.* II. 173 Among the phospholipids of vertebrates is a class known as plasmalogens. These are closely related to the classical lecithin (phosphatidyl choline) and cephalin (phosphatidyl ethanolamine). **1967** *Information Bull. Internat. Union Pure & Appl. Chem.* XXX. 23 The term 'lecithin' is permitted but not recommended to designate a 1,2-diacyl-*sn*-glycero-3-phosphorylcholine. The recommended generic term for such compounds is 3-*sn*-phosphatidylcholine. **1971** M. F. MALLETTE et al. *Introd. Biochem.* ix. 324 Phosphatidylserine..is another phospholipid isolated from plant and animal sources.

phosphatize ('fɒsfətaɪz), *v.* [f. as PHOSPHATIC *a.* + -IZE.] **1.** *trans.* To convert into a phosphate. Usu. as PHOSPHATIZED *ppl. a.*

1883 *Nature* XXVIII. 433/2 The majority of the Jurassic fossils are not phosphatised at all. **1884** *Science* 16 May 587/1 These fossils are phosphatized more or less completely. **1885** *Q. Jrnl. Geol. Soc.* XLI. 80 There this process of phosphatizing the coral has been in operation on a most extensive scale.

2. To treat with a phosphate; to coat (metal) with a phosphate to protect it against corrosion.

1939 *Metal Treatment* IV. 172 A modern phosphatising process for sheet steel work comprises the following steps:—1. degrease, 2 phosphatise, 3 chromate rinse, 4 dry off. **1961** *Engineering* 23 June 855/2 The skin which forms protects it from sprays used to clean and phosphatise the panels.

Hence **phosphati'zation**, the action of phosphatizing; the fact or condition of being phosphatized; **'phosphatizing** *ppl. a.* and *vbl. sb.*

1875 *Q. Jrnl. Geol. Soc.* XXXI. 362 At the Berwyn mine this process of phosphatization is most complete. **1883** *Nature* XXVIII. 433/2 That the phosphatisation of the Upware coprolites was effected at some distance from their present billet. **1900** *Proc. Geologists' Assoc.* XVI. 385 The 'rock phosphates' are phosphatised portions of the underlying Eocene and Miocene limestones... What was the nature of the phosphatising agent? **1939** *Automobile Engineer* XXIX. 460/1 Phosphatisation converts the work surfaces to a porous but adherent coating of iron phosphate. *Ibid.* 460/3 Specimens having the full treatment of phosphatising and chromate rinse showed markedly superior performance. **1965** G. J. WILLIAMS *Econ. Geol. N.Z.* xvi. 262/2 Reed believed the phosphatization to have occurred during the deposition of the Miocene beds. **1976** J. R. DUNCAN tr. *Barton's Protection against Atmospheric Corrosion* v. 114 Chemical pre-treatment methods have come into use as an answer to the problem of finding methods for rust stabilization... Phosphatizing is the most frequently used of these methods. **1977** A. HALLAM *Planet Earth* 173 The phosphatization produced nodules and pellets up to 2 cm..in diameter.

phosphatized ('fɒsfətaɪzd), *ppl. a.* [f. PHOSPHATE + -IZE + -ED[1].] **1.** Converted into a phosphate; = PHOSPHATED *a.*

1875 *Q. Jrnl. Geol. Soc.* XXXI. 361 The shales..are rich in organic remains. These..are all more or less phosphatized. **1935** *Jrnl. R. Anthrop. Inst.* LXV. 345 It was much sought after years ago for its contained rolled lumps of phosphatized clay—the so-called 'coprolites'. **1976** *Nature* 12 Feb. 473/2 They are characterised by..phosphatised fish debris and faecal pellets.

2. Treated or coated with a phosphate.

1939 *Metal Treatment* IV. 170 Phosphatised work, when successfully effected, was superior to work having the protective coating alone. **1976** J. R. DUNCAN tr. *Barton's Protection against Atmospheric Corrosion* v. 114 There is greater resistance to under-rusting of phosphatized substrates under cracked or mechanically damaged layers.

‖**phosphaturia** (fɒsfə'tjʊərɪə). *Path.* [f. PHOSPHATE *sb.* (or mod.L. *phōsphāt-um*) + *-ūria*, f. Gr. οὖρον urine.] A morbid state evidenced by the excess of phosphates in the urine. Hence **phospha'turic** *a.*

1876 HARLEY *Mat. Med.* (ed. 6) 92 Hydrochloric acid may be used in phosphaturia. **1897** *Allbutt's Syst. Med.* III. 254 Much the same symptoms as the polyuric and phosphaturic classes. **1899** CAGNEY tr. *Jaksch's Clin. Diagn.* vii. (ed. 4) 378 A phosphatic sediment does not imply phosphaturia.

phosphazene ('fɒsfəziːn). *Chem.* Also -ine. [ad. G. *phosphazin* (Staudinger & Meyer 1919, in *Helv. Chim. Acta* II. 619), f. *phosph-in* PHOSPHINE + *azin* AZINE.] Any compound containing the group $-N{=}P{<}$, esp. as a repeating unit of a ring or chain in which two substituents are attached to each phosphorus atom. Cf. PHOSPHONITRILE, PHOSPHONITRILIC *a.*

1920 *Jrnl. Chem. Soc.* CXVIII. 105 Tertiary phosphines combine more or less readily with the most varied aliphatic diazo-compounds, yielding derivatives, for which the name phosphazines is proposed, in accordance with the scheme $CR_2{:}N{:}N + PR_3 \rightarrow R_2C{:}N{-}N{:}PR_3$. **1958** J. R. VAN WAZER *Phosphorus & its Compounds* I. vi. 341 The compound $(C_6H_5)_3PNN{=}C(C_6H_5)_2$, a typical phosphazine, is a yellow, stable solid with slightly basic properties. **1961** *Inorganic Polymers* (Chem. Soc. Special Publ. No. 15) 115 The family of polymers, which are called variously phosphinic nitrides, phosphonitriles, and phosphazenes. These names all describe a bonding system characterized by the repeating unit $-PR_2{=}N-$. **1970** *New Scientist* 5 Nov. 275/1 The cyclic nitrogen and phosphorus compounds known as phosphazenes will make life easier for textiles manufacturers in the UK and the US... Phosphazenes, which are incorporated into viscous rayon during the spinning process,..are ideal for flame proofing. **1974** *Nature* 29 Nov. 427/3 A simple survey of the structural chemistry of the phosphazines.

phosphene ('fɒsfiːn). [mod. (F. *phosphène*) irreg. f. Gr. φῶς light + φαίν-ειν to make to appear.] An appearance of rings of light produced by pressure on the eyeball, due to irritation of the retina.

1872 HUXLEY *Phys.* ix. 222 Pressure on any part of the retina produces a luminous image, which lasts as long as the pressure, and is called a phosphene. **1881** LE CONTE *Sight* I. iv. 67 Press the finger into the internal corner of the eye: you perceive a brilliant colored spectrum in the field of view on the opposite or external side,..[having] a deep-steel-blue center, with a brilliant yellow border... These colored spectra have been called phosphenes.

phospher, obs. form of PHOSPHOR.

phosphethyl ('fɒs,fɛθɪl). *Chem.* [f. PHOSPH- + ETHYL.] A compound of phosphorus and ethyl. Hence **phosphe'thylic** *a.*

1859 *Fownes' Man. Chem.* 387 Phosphethyl.—The compounds of ethyl and phosphorus. **1857** MILLER *Elem. Chem.* III. 147 On decomposing this salt cautiously by the addition of sulphuric acid, the phosphethylic acid is liberated. **1866–77** WATTS *Dict. Chem.* IV. 589 Ethylphosphoric Acid, also called *Phosphethylic* or *Phosphovinic acid*, $C_2H_7PO_4$.

phosphide ('fɒsfaɪd). *Chem.* [f. PHOSPH- + -IDE.] A combination of phosphorus with another element or a radical. (Earlier name *phosphuret*.)

1849 D. CAMPBELL *Inorg. Chem.* 65 *Phosphides*.—Compounds of phosphorus with the other elements are very numerous. *c* **1865** WYLDE in *Circ. Sc.* I. 371/2 It may be..prepared from the phosphide of calcium. **1881** *Metal World* No. 12. 186 The phosphide of iron only begins to be decomposed after all silicon and carbon is gone.

phosphine ('fɒsfaɪn). *Chem.* [f. PHOSPH- + -INE[5], used to form a term analogous to AMINE.]

1. A name for phosphuretted hydrogen gas, PH_3 (as an analogue of ammonia, NH_3).

1873 WATTS *Fownes' Chem.* (ed. 11) 225 Phosphine is analogous in some of its chemical relations to ammoniacal gas.

2. A phosphorus ammonia; a compound having the structure of an *amine*, with phosphorus in place of nitrogen: e.g. ***monoethyl phosphine***, $C_2H_5 \cdot P \cdot H_2$, ***diethyl phosphine*** $(C_2H_5)_2 \cdot P \cdot H$, ***triethyl phosphine*** $(C_2H_5)_3 \cdot P$, etc.

1871 ROSCOE *Elem. Chem.* xxxi. 340 The following table shows the similarity between amines and phosphines. *Ibid.*, Phosphine iodide, $PC_2H_5H_3I$. **1898** G. MCGOWAN tr. *Meyer's Hist. Chem.* 469 The phosphines and phosphonium bases first became known through the classical and comprehensive researches of A. W. Hofmann.

Hence **phos'phinic** *a.*, of, pertaining to, or derived from phosphine; in ***phosphinic acid***, any one of various acids formed from the primary and secondary phosphines by fixation of 3 and 2 atoms of oxygen respectively.

1875 WATTS *Dict. Chem.* VII. 956 *Phosphinic acids.* **1881** *Ibid.* VIII. II. 1581 The phosphinic acids of the fatty series have already been described.

phosphite ('fɒsfaɪt). *Chem.* [a. F. *phosphite* (G. de Morveau *Nomencl. Ch.* 1787), f. PHOSPH- + -ITE[1].] A salt or ester of phosphorous acid.

1799 HOOPER *Med. Dict., Phosphites*,.. salts formed by the combination of the phosphorous acid with different bases; thus, *aluminous phosphite, ammoniacal phosphite*, &c. **1808** SIR H. DAVY in *Phil. Trans.* XCIX. 88 In one case sulphurets, and sulphites, and in the other phosphurets, and phosphites of potash, are generated. **1808** HENRY *Epit. Chem.* (ed. 5) 203 The phosphites differ considerably in their characters from phosphates. **1866** ROSCOE *Elem. Chem.* 133 Phosphorous acid, or hydric phosphite, H_3PO_3. **1890** *Jrnl. Chem. Soc.* LVIII. 858 Ethyl phosphite, $P(OEt)_3$, is obtained,.. when phosphorus trichloride is gradually added to finely divided sodium ethoxide, covered with ether. **1966** J. CASON *Princ. Mod. Org. Chem.* xxxiii. 603 Phosphorus trichloride reacts with alcohols to give phosphite esters... Only the tri-esters of phosphorous acid are known. **1970** *Encycl. Polymer Sci. & Technol.* XII. 748 Tertiary phosphites are among the most efficient groups of materials which have been used as poly(vinyl chloride) stabilizing agents.

phospho- ('fɒsfəʊ), before a vowel PHOSPH-, combining form, shortened from PHOSPHORUS.

phospho'chalcite *Min.* = PHOSPHOROCHALCITE; †**,phosphoco'zymase** *Biochem.* [COZYMASE] = *NAD(P)* s.v. N II. 1; **phospho'creatine** *Biochem.*, creatine phosphate, $HOOC \cdot CH_2 \cdot N(CH_3) \cdot C(NH) \cdot NH \cdot PO(OH)_2$, the phosphagen of vertebrate muscle; **,phosphodi'ester** (-daɪ'ɛstə(r)) *Biochem.*, used *attrib.* to designate a bond of the kind joining successive sugar molecules in a polynucleotide or oligonucleotide, in which a molecule of phosphoric acid links a hydroxyl group in one molecule to a hydroxyl group in the next with the loss of two molecules of water (giving the sequence $-O \cdot PO(OH) \cdot O-$ between carbon atoms); **,phosphodi'esterase** (-daɪ'ɛstəreɪz, -s) *Biochem.* [a. G. *phosphodiesterase* (S. Uzawa 1932, in *Jrnl. Biochem.* (Japan) XV. 22)], any enzyme that breaks a phosphodiester bond in an oligonucleotide; **,phospho,enolpy'ruvate** *Biochem.*, the anion $CH_2{:}C(O \cdot PO(OH)_2) \cdot COO^-$ derived from the phosphate ester of the enol of pyruvic acid; **phospho'ferrite** *Min.* [ad. G. *phosphoferrit* (Laubmann & Steinmetz 1920, in *Zeitschr. für Kryst. und Min.* LV. 569)], a hydrated phosphate of ferrous iron and bivalent manganese (the former predominating), $(Fe,Mn)_3(PO_4)_2 \cdot 3H_2O$, which forms an isomorphous series with reddingite and occurs as pale green, translucent or transparent, orthorhombic crystals; **,phospho,fructo'kinase** *Biochem.*, an enzyme that catalyses the phosphorylation of fructose phosphate to fructose diphosphate; **,phospho,gluco'mutase** *Biochem.*, an enzyme that catalyses the transfer of a phosphate group between the first and the sixth carbon atoms of a molecule of glucose phosphate; **phospho'glycerate**, a salt of phosphoglyceric acid = *glycerophosphate*; **phosphogly'ceric** *acid* = *glycerophosphoric acid* (see GLYCERO-); **phospho'glyceride** *Biochem.*, any phospholipid with a structure based on glycerol phosphate; **phosphoi'nositide** *Biochem.*, any phospholipid in which inositol is linked to the phosphate group; **phospho'kinase** *Biochem.* = KINASE b; **phospholite**, synonym of **phosphomo'lybdate**, a salt of phosphomolybdic acid; **phosphomo'lybdic** *acid*, or *permolybdic phosphate* $(2P_2O_5 \cdot 48MoO_3 \cdot 6H_2O)$, a lemon-yellow salt produced by the action of molybdic trioxide on phosphoric acid; **,phosphomono-esterase** (-mɒnəʊ'ɛstəreɪz, -s) *Biochem.* [a. G. *phosphomonoesterase* (S. Uzawa 1932, in *Jrnl. Biochem.* (Japan) XV. 20)], any enzyme that removes a terminal phosphate group from an oligonucleotide or a mononucleotide; **phospho'phyllite** *Min.* [ad. G. *phosphophyllit* (Laubmann & Steinmetz 1920, in *Zeitschr. für Kryst. und Min.* LV. 566), f. Gr. φύλλον leaf, in allusion to its perfect cleavage], a brittle, almost colourless secondary mineral that is a hydrated phosphate of zinc, iron, and manganese, $Zn_2(Fe,Mn)(PO_4)_2.4H_2O$, and occurs as tabular, monoclinic crystals; **phospho'protein** *Biochem.*, any protein that contains phosphorus other than in a nucleic acid or a phospholipid; **phospho'silicate**, any substance which contains phosphate and silicate anions, or consists largely of the corresponding oxides; freq. *attrib.*; **phospho'tungstic** ***acid***, an acid of the form $P_2O_5{\cdot}xWO_3{\cdot}yH_2O$; †**phospho'vinic** ***acid***, old synonym of *ethyl-phosphoric acid*, $(C_2H_5)H_2PO_4$, a colourless, inodorous, viscid oil, with a biting sour taste, produced by the action of phosphoric acid on alcohol or ether; **phospho-wol'framic** *a.* = *phosphotungstic.*

1946 *Nature* 24 Aug. 275/2 It was found with a preparation of cozymase and *phosphocozymase received from Prof. Otto Warburg that only one pentose was found for two phosphorus atoms. **1964** Phosphocozymase [see COZYMASE]. **1927** FISKE & SUBBAROW in *Science* 22 Apr. 402/2 Our main evidence for the existence of '*phosphocreatine' in muscle is of a quite different nature. **1950** G. A. BAITSELL *Human Biol.* (ed. 2) xiv. 243 The energy for the resynthesis of phosphocreatine, following contraction, comes indirectly from the oxidation of glucose in the muscle cells. **1969** J. I. ROUTH et al. *Essent. Gen., Org. & Biochem.* xxxiv. 666 Creatine.. is especially abundant in muscle tissue, where it is combined with phosphoric acid as phosphocreatine, or creatine phosphate. **1953** FRUTON & SIMMONDS *Gen. Biochem.* vii. 190 The products obtained from PNA preparations have been shown to be chains of nucleosides linked by 3',5'- (or 2',5'-)*phosphodiester bonds. **1975** *Sci. Amer.* July 25/3 A DNA strand is a chain of nucleotides... The individual nucleotide building blocks are connected by phosphodiester bonds between the carbon atom at position No. 3 on one sugar and the carbon atom at position No. 5 on the adjacent sugar. [**1932** *Chem. Abstr.* XXVI. 2994 (*heading*) The phosphormonoesterase and the phosphordiesterase.] **1937** *Ibid.* XXXI. 10078/1 *Phosphodiesterase. *See* Phosphatases. **1967** *Biochim. & Biophys. Acta* CXLII. 111 (*heading*) The action of snake venom phosphodiesterase on liver ribosomal ribonucleic acids. **1968** J. H. BURN *Lect. Notes Pharmacol.* (ed. 9) 65 Cyclic AMP is broken down by phosphodiesterase to the inactive 5-AMP. **1968** Phosphodiesterase [see *phosphomonoesterase* below]. **1956** W. F. H. M. MOMMAERTS in O. H. Gaebler *Enzymes* xiv. 319 The system consists.. of a hydrolyzing enzyme (actomyosin), a common substrate (ATP), a resynthesizing enzyme (pyruvate kinase), and a reservoir substrate (*phosphoenol pyruvate or PEP). **1970** *New Scientist* 23 Apr. 168/1 The last step in the glycolytic pathway, from phosphoenolpyruvate to pyruvate, is effectively irreversible... But in liver and kidney there is a carboxylation reaction which reverses the step. **1921** *Mineral. Abstr.* I. 125 **Phosphoferrite* from Hagendorf, as cloudy-white or greenish, crystalline masses with greasy lustre; H. 4–5, sp. gr. 3·156. **1955** *Ibid.* XII. 562 Phosphoferrite $(Fe,Mn)_3(PO_4)_2.3H_2O$ and reddingite $(Mn,Fe)_3(PO_4)_2.3H_2O$ have recently been found in the south pegmatite quarry at Hagendorf, Bavaria, as hydrothermal alteration products of triphylite. They are orthorhombic and isomorphous, the former.. of cubo-octahedral or tabular (on 001) habit. **1974** *Nature* 27 Sept. 305/2 The evidence clearly points to a complete solid solution series between $Fe_3{}^{2+}(H_2O)_3[PO_4]_2$ (phosphoferrite) and $Fe_3{}^{3+}(OH)_3[PO_4]_2$ (kryzhanovskite). **1947** *Federation Proc.* VI. 297 (*heading*) The purification of *phosphofructokinase from rabbit muscle. **1970** AMBROSE & EASTY *Cell Biol.* xiii. 246 Fructose-6-phosphate is phosphorylated by ATP to form fructose-1,6-diphosphate in a reaction catalyzed by a specific phosphofructokinase... This phosphorylation is also essentially irreversible and is an important control point in metabolism. **1938** G. T. CORI et al. in *Jrnl. Biol. Chem.* CXXIV. 543 A study of the enzyme which causes a migration of the phosphate group from carbon atom 1 to the spacially [*sic*] adjacent carbon atom 6; the enzyme will be referred to as *phosphoglucomutase. **1964** A. WHITE et al. *Princ. Biochem.* (ed. 3) xxi. 403 The best-studied mutase is phosphoglucomutase, which has been obtained in pure form from rabbit muscle, yeast, and several bacterial species. **1901** *Westm. Gaz.* 5 Jan. 7/2 Aged patients.. dosed with glycerophosphate of sodium and *phosphoglycerate of lime and other chemical combinations. **1857** W. A. MILLER *Elem. Chem.* III. 378 *Phosphoglyceric acid exists ready formed in the yolk of the egg. **1954** A. WHITE et al. *Princ. Biochem.* xxxii. 800 These phosphatides include *phosphoglycerides, phosphosphingosides, and the phosphoinositides. **1967** *Information Bull. Internat. Union Pure & Applied Chem.* XXX. 22 The term 'phosphoglyceride' signifies any derivative of glycerophosphoric acid that contains at least one *O*-acyl, or *O*-alkyl, or *O*-alk-1'-en-1'-yl group attached to the glycerol residue... The term ' phosphatidic acid' signifies a derivative of glycerophosphoric acid in which both remaining hydroxyl groups of glycerol are esterified with fatty acids. **1970** A. L. LEHNINGER *Biochem.* x. 195 The most abundant phosphoglycerides in higher plants and animals are phosphatidyl ethanolamine and phosphatidyl choline. **1954** *Phosphoinositide [see *phosphoglyceride* above]. **1961** WEST & TODD *Textbk. Biochem.* (ed. 3) vi. 154 Two different types of phosphoinositides have been described which are differentiated by the inositol derivatives yielded upon hydrolysis. One type found in heart, liver, soybean, and wheat germ yields inositol monophosphate, fatty acids, and α-glycerol phosphate..; it.. is phosphatidyl inositol... Another type of phosphoinositide found in brain.. yields inositol-m-diphosphate, glycerol, and fatty acids. **1971** D. G. BISHOP in Johnson & Davenport *Biochem. Lipids* xx. 411 Although phosphoinositides have been recognized as important constituents of brain lipids for some time, their occurrence in nature is now known to be widespread. **1946** DIXON & NEEDHAM in *Nature* 28 Sept. 435/1 Needham has given reasons for believing that the component of the pyruvate oxidase system which is inhibited may be a phosphate-transferring enzyme belonging to the same group as hexokinase. We suggested the name '*phosphokinase' for this small but important group of enzymes. **1953** *Brit. Med. Bull.* IX. 110/2 The phosphokinases all seem to have the common property that they require the presence of Mg^{++} for their activity. **1962**, **1964** Phosphokinase [see KINASE b]. **1856** W. A. MILLER *Elem. Chem.* II. 783 The *Phosphomolybdate of Soda is an extremely delicate test for the presence of salt of ammonium in solution. **1878** KINGZETT *Anim. Chem.* 207 A mixture of sulphuric and nitric acids with *phosphomolybdic acid. [**1932** *Phosphomonoesterase: see *phosphodiesterase* above.] **1933** *Chem. Abstr.* XXVII. 1020 (*heading*) Phosphomonoesterase of animal organs and especially of the blood. **1968** PASSMORE & ROBSON *Compan. Med. Stud.* I. xii. 25/1 The combined action of the depolymerases, phosphodiesterases and phosphomonoesterases is to degrade RNA and DNA to the state of nucleosides. **1921** *Mineral. Abstr.* I. 125 **Phosphophyllite* from Hagendorf, colourless to pale-blue, well-developed, monoclinic crystals,.. with perfect micaceous cleavage and lamellar twinning both parallel to *c* (001); H. 3–4, sp. gr. 3·081. **1968** *Mineral. Mag.* XXXVI. 624 In both phosphophyllite and hopeite.. the P—O tetrahedron shares one oxygen with six-coordinated zinc (Zn^{vi}) and three with four-coordinated zinc (Zn^{iv}). **1908** *Jrnl. Biol. Chem.* IV. p. l, Joint Recommendations of the Physiological and Biochemical Committees on Protein Nomenclature... **Phosphoproteins.* Compounds of the protein molecule with some, as yet undefined, phosphorus containing substance other than a nucleic acid or lecithin. **1929** R. A. GORTNER *Outl. Biochem.* xvi. 391 Casein of milk and vitellin of egg yolk are the two most important phosphoproteins. **1968** H. HARRIS *Nucleus & Cytoplasm* i. 14 Synthesis of a specific plasma phosphoprotein induced in male chickens by the administration of diethylstilboestrol. **1964** *IBM Jrnl. Res. & Devel.* VIII. 378/2 The importance of the *phosphosilicate layer for transistor stabilization has also been shown by the examination of production transistors after life tests. **1966** *Solid-State Electronics* IX. 1009 An i.r. spectrophotometer.. detects accurately the presence of the phosphosilicate layer. **1975** *Physics Bull.* Jan. 14/1 A team at Southampton University has also achieved very low losses with a new type of fibre—a phosphosilicate (P_2O_5/SiO_2) glass core contained in a pure silica cladding. **1975** *Nature* 27 Feb. 722/2 Except for the chemical analysis of minerals such as viseite and wilkeite, few systematic studies of phosphosilicates have been made. **1884** *Athenæum* 26 Apr. 584/3 With regard to strychnine..*phosphotungstic acid will give a distinct precipitate with one-two-hundred-thousandth of a grain. **1899** CAGNEY tr. *Jaksch's Clin. Diagn.* vii. (ed. 4) 369 Kreatinin is a base which forms highly characteristic compounds with acids, such as phosphotungstic and phosphomolybdic. **1838** T. THOMSON *Chem. Org. Bodies* 186 Phosphovinate of barytes was the salt which M. Pelouze chiefly studied, and by means of which, he determined the composition of *phosphovinic acid. **1866–77** WATTS *Dict. Chem.* IV. 589 Ethylphosphoric Acid, also called *Phosphethylic* or *Phosphovinic acid.* **1878** KINGZETT *Anim. Chem.* 276 By precipitation of its hydrochloric acid solution with *phosphowolframic acid.

phospholipase (fɒsfəʊ'lɪpeɪz, -s). *Biochem.* [a. G. *phospholipase* (H. Udagawa 1935, in *Jrnl. Biochem.* (Japan) XXII. 324): see next and -ASE.] Any enzyme that hydrolyses lecithin (phosphatidyl choline) and similar phospholipids; = LECITHINASE.

1945 *Jrnl. Biol. Chem.* CLVII. 643 A method is described for following the partial hydrolysis of phospholipids by the phospholipase of moccasin venom. **1965** HANAHAN & BROCKERHOFF in Florkin & Stotz *Comprehensive Biochem.* VI. iii. 91 Through the use of quite specific enzymes, called the phospholipases (or lecithinases), the phosphatidyl choline (lecithin) molecule can be effectively degraded in a stepwise manner... The enzyme, phospholipase A, is found in high concentration in many species of snake venom... Phospholipase C has been found in high concentration in plant tissues, such as carrots, spinach and cabbage leaves whereas phospholipase D occurs mainly in bacteria. **1974** DUNN & BONDY *Functional Chem. of Brain* iv. 84 Lecithin (phosphatidyl-choline) may be hydrolyzed by phospholipase A to lysolecithin (lecithin lacking its β-fatty acid).

phospholipid (fɒsfəʊ'lɪpɪd). *Biochem.* Also -ide (now *rare*). [f. PHOSPHO- + LIPID.] Any compound whose products of hydrolysis include fatty acids, phosphoric acid, and (with some writers) a nitrogen base; *esp.* one that is an ester of glycerol phosphate; in recent use applied more widely to any lipid containing phosphoric acid, esp. ones having a structure based on glycerol phosphate.

1928 *Industr. & Engin. Chem.* (*News Ed.*) 10 Sept. 3 The Commission [on the Reform of Biological Chemical Nomenclature].. proposes the following classification of the group lipides... The term *phosphatides* is abolished. It is replaced by the terms *phospholipides* and *phosphoaminolipides.* Phospholipides are the lipides which contain phosphorus (in the form of the phosphoric radical). Phosphoaminolipides are the lipides which contain both phosphorus.. and nitrogen. **1929** *Jrnl. Biol. Chem.* LXXXII. 117 (*heading*) The rôle of the phospholipids of the intestinal mucosa in fat absorption. **1946** *Nature* 27 July 119/2 These results indicated strongly that the vaccinia and ectromelia hæmagglutinins were composed of a virus antigen plus a phospholipid component, the latter being responsible for union with the surface of the cell. **1951** [see

PHOSPHATIDE]. **1951** E. A. ZELLER in Sumner & Myrbäck *Enzymes* I. xxx. 987 The fact that the hemolysis caused by many animal poisons is connected with the breakdown of lecithin considerably stimulated the investigation of the metabolism of phospholipides. **1953** FRUTON & SIMMONDS *Gen. Biochem.* xxii. 511 In the plasma of mammals.. nearly all the phospholipid contains choline, and is therefore largely composed of lecithins and sphingomyelins. **1967** I. L. FINAR *Org. Chem.* (ed. 5) I. xi. 292 One subgroup of the phospholipids is the phosphatides... Another group of phospholipids is the sphingolipids. These are not glycerides... Sphingolipids are also known as sphingomyelins. **1967** *Information Bull. Internat. Union Pure & Appl. Chem.* XXX. 26 The term 'phospholipid' may be used for any lipid containing a radical derived from phosphoric acid. **1971** M. F. MALLETTE et al. *Introd. Biochem.* ix. 321 The phospholipids can be defined as those lipids which contain phosphate esters of acylated glycerol.. or sphingosine. **1972** D. J. HANAHAN in F. Snyder *Ether Lipids* ii. 27 Structure (7) is the unusual diether phospholipid found in an extremely halophilic bacterium. **1973** S. J. EDELSTEIN *Introd. Biochem.* xii. 210 Phospholipids are composed of fatty acids linked to a glycerol backbone. **1976** *Daily Colonist* (Victoria, B.C.) 31 Mar. 18/4 Liposomes are balls made from fatty substances called phospholipids, found in the membranes of animal cells.

† **phospholipin** (fɒsfəʊˈlɪpɪn). *Biochem. Obs.* [f. PHOSPHO- + LIPIN.] = prec.

1910 J. B. LEATHES *Fats* i. 41 Compounds of fatty acids containing phosphorus and nitrogen... Thudichum gave the name 'phosphatides' to a number of such substances... The indefinite nature of the term has led to its application frequently to substances that are not compounds of fatty acids at all. And it is indeed impossible to say what kind of substances should be regarded as phosphatides... In these pages, therefore, for the compounds of fatty acids containing phosphorus and nitrogen the term phospholipine will.. be used. **1915** *Jrnl. Biol. Chem.* XX. 404 Preparations of phospholipins, *i.e.*, lecithin, the alcohol-soluble compound, and kephalin, the alcohol-insoluble compound, were made. **1927** M. BODANSKY *Introd. Physiol. Chem.* iii. 55 The phosphatides (also called phospholipins) are present in every animal and vegetable cell and are especially abundant in the brain, heart, muscles, liver, and eggs. On hydrolysis these substances yield fatty acids, a nitrogenous base, phosphoric acid, and usually glycerol. **1948** *New Biol.* V. 38 Their [*sc.* microsomes'] principal constituents are phospholipins (complex fatty molecules containing phosphoric acid and organic acids and bases) and nucleo-proteins.

Phosphon: see PHOSFON.

phosphonitrile (fɒsfəʊˈnaɪtraɪl). *Chem.* [f. PHOSPHO- + NITRILE.] = PHOSPHAZENE.

1921 J. R. PARTINGTON *Text-bk. Inorg. Chem.* xxxi. 625 At 175–200°, ammonia and phosphorus pentachloride form a mixture of six phosphonitrile chlorides: $(PNCl_2)_3$, $(PNCl_2)_4$, [etc.]. **1943** *Chem. Rev.* XXXII. 102 Most investigators have accepted the designation phosphonitrile for the PN group, since it is looked upon as a group resembling the CN or nitrile radical. **1961** [see PHOSPHAZENE]. **1972** H. R. ALLCOCK *Phosphorus-Nitrogen Compounds* i. 3 The cyclo- or polyphosphazenes (phosphonitriles) are probably the best known and most intensively studied phosphorus-nitrogen derivatives.

phosphonitrilic (ˌfɒsfəʊnaɪˈtrɪlɪk), *a. Chem.* [f. as prec. + -IC.] Containing the phosphonitrile group, $-N{=}P\lessgtr$. Cf. PHOSPHAZENE.

1895 H. N. STOKES in *Amer. Chem. Jrnl.* XVII. 278, (*d*) is a polymer of an acid $N{\equiv}P(OH)_2$, which we may call phosphonitrilic acid. **1943** *Chem. Rev.* XXXII. 119 The phosphonitrilic chlorides form as complete a polyhomologous series as is known in the realm of chemistry. *Ibid.* 122 The phosphonitrilic halides undergo reactions of hydrolysis to yield partially and completely hydroxylated products—the latter being known as the phosphonitrilic acids. **1956** H. H. SISLER in Sneed & Brasted *Comprehensive Inorg. Chem.* V. i. ii. 134 All the phosphonitrilic chlorides, when heated to about 300°C, are converted to an elastic product, possessing many of the properties of rubber. **1974** D. E. C. CORBRIDGE *Struct. Chem. Phosphorus* xii. 333 Phosphonitrilic compounds, or phosphazenes, are characterized by the presence of the group $P{=}N-$.

phosphonium (fɒsˈfəʊnɪəm). *Chem.* [f. PHOSPH(ORUS + ending of AMMONIUM.]

A combination of hydrogen and phosphorus, PH_4, analogous to ammonium, entering as a monovalent radical into many compounds, as ***phosphonium iodide***, PH_4I; also applied to compounds in which the hydrogen is replaced by organic radicals, as ***tetramethylphosphonium***, $P(CH_3)_4$, ***tetrethylphosphonium***, $P(C_2H_5)_4$, ***methyltriethylphosphonium***, $P(CH_3)(C_2H_5)_3$, etc.

1866–77 WATTS *Dict. Chem.* IV. 607 Monophosphoniums, of the type R_4PI, analogous to iodide of tetrethylammonium. *Ibid.* 615 (*heading*) Ethylphosphoniums. *Ibid.* 620 Diphosphoniums. **1871** ROSCOE *Elem. Chem.* xxxi. 339 Obtained.. by acting upon phosphonium iodide, PH_4I, with ethyl iodide in presence of zinc oxide.

Hence **phosˈphonic** *a.* [cf. *sulphonic*], in ***phosphonic acid***, any one of several compounds derived from phosphoric acid by the replacement of hydroxyl (OH) by a hydrocarbon group: e.g. ***benzene phosphonic acid***, $C_6H_5.P(OH)_2O$. Sometimes called *phosphinic*, or *phosphenilic* acid.

phosphor (ˈfɒsfə(r)), *sb.* (*a.*) Also 7 -pher, -fer, 8 -phore. [ad. L. *phōsphor-us* PHOSPHORUS. Cf. F. *phosphore* (1680 in Hatz.-Darm.), Ger. *phosphor*.]

1. (With capital P.) The morning star; the planet Venus when appearing before sunrise; Lucifer. Also *fig.* Now only *poet.*

1635–56 COWLEY *Davideis* II. 763 They saw this Phosphors infant-light, and knew It bravely usher'd in a Sun as New. **1656** STANLEY *Hist. Philos.* v. (1701) 178/1 *Plato's Epigram on Aster*, A Phospher 'mongst the Living, late wert thou, But Shin'st among the Dead a Hesper now. **1734** WATTS *Reliq. Juv.* (1789) 257 Still Phosphor glitters, and still Syrius burns. **1850** TENNYSON *In Mem.* cxxi, Bright Phosphor, fresher for the night. **1871** M. COLLINS *Mrq. & Merch.* I. x. 309 That which men have seen in early skies, Ere Phosphor in the abyss of perfect purple dies.

2. Anything that phosphoresces, or emits light without sensible heat: = PHOSPHORUS 2. In mod. use [after G. *phosphor* (Lenard & Klatt 1904, in *Ann. der Physik* XV. 226)], any substance exhibiting phosphorescence or fluorescence, esp. one that is an artificially prepared solid. Also *attrib.* and *Comb.*

The more restricted meaning in quot. 1950 is not usual.

1705 HAUKSBEE in *Phil. Trans.* XXIV. 2131 Shewing that it requires not so thin a Medium, as.. in the Torricillian Experiment, to produce the Mercurial Phosphore. *a* **1711** KEN *Edmund* Poet. Wks. 1721 II. 288 No Light was there but what the Phosphors raise. **1819** KEATS *Lamia* 152 Her eyes in torture fix'd, and anguish drear,.. Flashed phosphor and sharp sparks. **1910** *Sci. Abstr.* A. XIII. 269 Different phosphores consisting of an alkaline earth sulphide and heavy metal. **1914** *Chem. Abstr.* VIII. 3751 For Sa-Ca-'phosphor'.. the rate of decay of the phosphorescence increases with increasing temp. **1943** *Endeavour* Jan. 25/1 Phosphors are principally used for the fluorescence which they exhibit. **1950** H. W. LEVERENZ *Introd. Luminescence of Solids* v. 147 The generic term *luminophor* is subclassified into fluorophors.. (fluorescent materials) and phosphors (phosphorescent materials). **1960** CHALMERS & QUARRELL *Physical Examination of Metals* (ed. 2) xvi. 777 Sodium iodide, activated with a trace of thallium.. combines a number of properties which make it one of the most important tracer scintillation phosphors. **1961** G. MILLERSON *Technique Television Production* ii. 21 By applying the video signal to regulate the picture-tube's beam, a pattern of light and shade can be built up on the screen's phosphor, corresponding to the light distribution in the studio scene. **1971** D. POTTER *Brit. Eliz. Stamps* ii. 25 Phosphor bands are practically invisible in normal light. **1975** *New Yorker* 5 May 51/3 Television pictures are produced by a flow of electrons moving in straight lines across the phosphorcoated surface of a cathode-ray tube.

3. = PHOSPHORUS (sense 3); esp. in ***phosphor-bronze***, ***-copper***, ***-tin***, ***-zinc***, alloys of phosphorus with the metals named: see BRONZE, etc.

†**B.** as *adj.* Light-bearing, light-giving; phosphorescent. *Obs.* (Also *hyphened.*)

1804 CHARLOTTE SMITH *Conversations*, etc. I. 127 Steady and clear thy phosphor brilliance burns. **1811** W. R. SPENCER *Poems* 185 Some gleams of phosphor-light it shews. *c* **1820** S. ROGERS *Italy, Como* 21 And now appear as on a phosphor-sea Numberless barks.

† **ˈphosphoraˈmide.** *Chem. Obs.* = PHOSPHAMIDE.

1866 ODLING *Anim. Chem.* 17 If we replace them by amidogen we obtain phosphoramide.

† **phosphoˈrana.** *Chem. Obs.* Term applied by Davy to a combination of one part of phosphorus with two of chlorine (Mayne *Expos. Lex.*).

1812 SIR H. DAVY *Chem. Philos.* 111 Phosphorus burnt in chlorine in excess, forms a white volatile substance, which I have named *phosphorana*. **1815** W. HENRY *Elem. Chem.* (ed. 7) II. xv. 14 Both these compounds were discovered by Sir H. Davy, who has termed the latter *phosphorane* and the former *phosphorana*.

phosphorane (ˈfɒsfəreɪn). *Chem.*

†1. A compound of one part of phosphorus with one of chlorine.

1815 [See PHOSPHORANA].

2. *Chem.* [after *methane*, *ethane*, etc. (-ANE 2 b).] Any compound that is regarded as a derivative of PH_5, the phosphorus having five covalencies.

1952 *Chem. & Engin. News* 2 June 2336/2 Ph_5 is phosphorane (not phosphane, as the latter name is used in the series diphosphane, triphosphane, and so on..). **1963** *Q. Rev. Chem. Soc.* XVII. 411 Stable phosphoranes of the formula $Ph_3P{:}CXY$ (X, Y = CN, CO_2R, COR) can be obtained. **1970** *Nature* 25 July 335/2 Examples of the utility of phosphoranes in the Wittig olefin synthesis were numerous. **1971** P. A. T. HOYE in *Mellor's Comprehensive Treat. Inorg. & Theoret. Chem.* VIII. Suppl. III. xxxiii. 881 Pentaphenylphosphorane was first obtained by Wittig and Rieber by the reaction of tetraphenylphosphonium iodide with phenyl lithium... The phosphoranes $(C_6H_5)_4PC(C_6H_5)_3$ and $p\text{-}CH_3{\cdot}C_6H_4P(C_6H_5)_4$ are prepared similarly.

† **ˈphosphorate**, *sb. Chem. Obs.* = PHOSPHATE *sb.*

c **1865** in *Circ. Sc.* I. 334/2 We find in this liquid.. phosphorates.. of the alkalies.

phosphorate (ˈfɒsfəreɪt), *v. Chem.* [f. PHOSPHOR-US + -ATE[3].] Orig. and chiefly in *ppl. a.* **ˈphosphorated** (= F. *phosphoré*).

1. *trans.* To combine or impregnate with phosphorus.

1789 WALKER in *Phil. Trans.* LXXIX. 210 The frigorific mixture.. composed of phosphorated natron and nitrated ammonia dissolved in the diluted nitrous acid. **1791** PEARSON *ibid.* LXXXI. 334 The liquid.. seemed to contain a little phosphorated lime. **1836** SMART, *Phosphorate* v. **1858** MAYNE *Expos. Lex.*, *Phosphorated*,.. having or imbued with phosphorus. **1893** in *Syd. Soc. Lex.*

2. To render phosphorescent.

1827 *Perils & Captivity* (Constable's Misc.) 59 Aware that the sea is sometimes phosphorated.

phosphoreal (fɒsˈfɔəriːəl), *a.* Also 9 (less correctly) -ial. [f. (doubtful) L. *phōsphore-us* (f. *phōsphor-us*) + -AL[1].] Of or pertaining to phosphorus; resembling that of phosphorus. Also *fig.*

1745 MORTIMER in *Phil. Trans.* XLIII. 479 The kindling the phosphoreal Fire in them. **1794** G. ADAMS *Nat. & Exp. Philos.* IV. xlix. 331 Its smell is strongly phosphoreal or sulphureous. **1816** W. TAYLOR in *Monthly Mag.* XLI. 329 Phosphorial lustre beaming from their hair. **1891** G. MEREDITH *One of our Conq.* xix, Delphica's phosphorial enthusiasm for our galaxy of British Poets.

phosphorent (ˈfɒsfərənt), *a. rare.* [f. PHOSPHOR-US + -ENT.] = PHOSPHORESCENT *a.*

1841 *Fraser's Mag.* XXIV. 25 Where, shining as brightly as phosphorent ling, The forefinger flashes the Fisherman's ring.

phosˈphoreous, *a. rare.* [f. as prec. + -OUS.] Of the nature of phosphorus; resembling that of phosphorus; phosphorescent.

1777 PENNANT *Zool.* (ed. 4) IV. 26 The Mollusca.. by their phosphoreous quality illuminate the dark abyss, reflecting lights to the heavens. **1822** *Blackw. Mag.* XI. 187 Their phosphoreous effulgence.. drew our admiration.

phosphoresce (fɒsfəˈrɛs), *v.* [f. PHOSPHOR-US + L. *-ēscĕre*, formative of inceptive vbs.: perh. inferred from *phosphorescent*, found earlier.] *intr.* To emit luminosity without combustion (or by gentle combustion without sensible heat); to exhibit phosphorescence: to shine in the dark.

1794 G. ADAMS *Nat. & Exp. Philos.* I. App. 546 Fluats.. when heated, phosphoresce. **1848** E. FORBES *Naked-eyed Medusæ* 76 When the *Pelagia* phosphoresces, it seems like a great globe of fire in the water. **1879** DANA *Man. Geol.* (ed. 3) 58 When powdered and thrown on a shovel heated nearly to redness, it phosphoresces brightly.

fig. **1799** W. TAYLOR in *Monthly Rev.* XXVIII. 182 Luminous trains of idea which kindle and phosphoresce along its track. **1858** CARLYLE *Fredk. Gt.* v. vii. I. 618 Mines of native Darkness and Human Stupidity, capable of being made to phosphoresce and effervesce.

Hence **phosphoˈrescing** *vbl. sb.* and *ppl. a.*

1796 KIRWAN *Elem. Min.* (ed. 2) I. 79 It has not the phosphorescing quality. **1895** *Times* 21 Jan. 15/1 Able to dissipate.. luminosity of a phosphorescing body.

phosphorescence (fɒsfəˈrɛsəns). [f. next: see -ENCE. Cf. F. *phosphorescence* (in Buffon, *a* 1788; *Dict. Acad.* 1835).] The condition or quality of being phosphorescent; the action of phosphorescing or shining in the dark without combustion or sensible heat. In scientific use now distinguished from fluorescence on techn. grounds (see quots.); (the various definitions are all broadly equivalent).

1796 KIRWAN *Elem. Min.* (ed. 2) I. 27 [Internal characters of earths and stones:] Phosphorescence. **1836** MACGILLIVRAY tr. *Humboldt's Trav.* x. 125 All the meteors left luminous traces,.. the phosphorescence of which lasted seven or eight seconds. **1838** T. THOMSON *Chem. Org. Bodies* 627 When two pieces of sugar are rubbed against each other in the dark, a strong phosphorescence is visible. **1848** CARPENTER *Anim. Phys.* 303 A large proportion of the lower classes of aquatic animals possess the property of luminosity... The phosphorescence of the sea.. is due to this cause. **1874** tr. *Lommel's Light* 192 This power of shining in the dark after having been exposed to light is termed phosphorescence. **1949** P. PRINGSHEIM *Fluorescence & Phosphorescence* 5 A photoluminescence process of this type, involving the passage through a metastable level, is called phosphorescence. *Ibid.*, It is no longer possible to define some arbitrary duration of the emission process as the boundary between fluorescence and phosphorescence. *Ibid.* iv. 292 The duration of a fluorescence process is essentially independent of external conditions insofar as this duration is determined by internal transition probabilities... The duration of a real phosphorescence is fundamentally a function of temperature. **1950** H. W. LEVERENZ *Introd. Luminescence of Solids* iv. 124 If the excitation and emission process occurs in times approximating the natural lifetimes of excited nonmetastable isolated atoms (about 10^{-8} sec for optical transitions), the process is called fluorescence, whereas longer-duration processes are called phosphorescence. **1954** C. ZWIKKER *Physical Prop. Solid Materials* xiii. 228 Fluorescence is the process in which the radiating electron falls back from the same energy level to which it was raised by the impinging photon..; phosphorescence is that in which the electron, after being raised to a higher energy level, first moves to a metastable level from where it can only be moved by external interference. **1971** *Physics Bull.* Oct. 577/2 The terms fluorescence and phosphorescence denote allowed and partially forbidden transitions respectively, though the practical distinction based on lifetimes is largely arbitrary. **1973** *Sci. Amer.* June 51/3 Today the definition is more technical, fluorescence corresponding to 'spin-allowed' electric dipole transitions and phosphorescence to 'spin-disallowed' transitions.

phosphorescent (fɒsfəˈrɛsənt), *a.* (*sb.*) [f. PHOSPHOR-US: see -ESCENT. So in Fr. (*Dict. Acad.* 1835).] Having the property of shining in the dark; luminous without combustion or without sensible heat; self-luminous.

1766 DA COSTA in *Phil. Trans.* LVI. 39 It detonates with small phosphorescent sparks. **1805–17** R. JAMESON *Char. Min.* (ed. 3) 313 Fluor-spar, when heated, becomes phosphorescent, or occasionally exhibits this property after having been exposed to the sun's rays. **1833** M. SCOTT *Tom Cringle* xvi. (1859) 421 The sea in our neighbourhood was strongly phosphorescent. **1881** SPOTTISWOODE in *Nature* 13 Oct. 571/1 Certain parts of the interior surface of the tube become luminous with phosphorescent light.

fig. **1855** I. TAYLOR *Restor. Belief* 19 A man sits surrounded with the books of all ages; among these he has passed the best years of his life..the books are phosphorescent in the view of their possessor. **1859** RUSKIN *Arrows of Chace* I. 194 Dim, phosphorescent, frightful superstitions.

B. *sb.* A phosphorescent substance.

1863 ATKINSON tr. *Ganot's Physics* VII. vii. 465 The best phosphorescents are..diamonds..fluorspar [etc.]. **1889** *Philos. Mag.* Ser. v. XXVIII. 428 All of them fusible at the temperatures at which the phosphorescents are prepared.

Hence **phosphoˈrescently** *adv.*

1848 DICKENS *Dombey* i, The buttons sparkled phosphorescently in the feeble rays. **1857** *Chamb. Jrnl.* VIII. 308/2 Content with such political and judicial lights as gleam, as it were phosphorescently, from the decayed and rotten *caput mortuum* of eight centuries ago.

phosphoret, -etted *Chem.*, obs. var. PHOSPHURET, -ETTED.

phosphoretic (fɒsfəˈrɛtɪk), *a. rare.* [f. PHOSPHORET or mod.L. *phosphorēt-um* + -IC.]

†**1.** = PHOSPHORESCENT *a. Obs.*

1794 G. ADAMS *Nat. & Exp. Philos.* II. xxi. 395 Oyster-shells possessed the phosphoretic quality. *Ibid.* 396 A phosphoretic appearance, produced by putrefied materials from fish and vegetables.

2. Of the nature of a phosphuret; combined with phosphorus.

1883 *Daily News* 19 Sept. 3/2 Adapting the phosphoretic Cleveland ores to the making of steel.

phosphorgummite (fɒsfərˈgʌmaɪt). *Min.* [Named 1859, f. Ger. *phosphor* phosphorus + *gummit* GUMMITE.] A gummite or hydrate of uranium containing phosphorus.

1868 DANA *Min.* (ed. 5) Index, *Phosphorgummite*, 179. **1896** CHESTER *Dict. Min.*, *Phosphorgummite.*

phosphorial: see PHOSPHOREAL.

phosphoric (fɒsˈfɒrɪk), *a.* [ad. F. *phosphorique*: see PHOSPHOR and -IC.]

1. Pertaining to or of the nature of a phosphorus (sense 2); phosphorescent. [F. *phosphorique* 1765.]

1784 MORGAN in *Phil. Trans.* LXXV. 209 Phosphoric bodies are very different..a shell may be made to lose all its light by exposure to heat. **1786** tr. *Beckford's Vathek* (1868) 110 Those phosphoric meteors that glimmer by night in places of interment. **1835** KIRBY *Hab. & Inst. Anim.* I. ix. 292 They [violet snails] are vividly phosphoric in the night. **1870** DISRAELI *Lothair* lvii, A phosphoric light glittered in her Hellenic eyes.

fig. **1830** ALFORD in *Life* (1873) 56 A thousand phosphoric sparks of poetry leaping about in my mind. **1847** H. MILLER *First Impr.* ii. (1857) 27 The phosphoric light of genius. **1900** *Pilot* 16 June 497/1 That phosphoric brilliance of decay which brightened the court of the second Charles. **1929** A. E. COPPARD in *Legion Bk.* 61 Baxter and Brabazon ..had been subjected to some phosphoric comments by the magistrate.

2. *Chem.* Of or pertaining to the element phosphorus; *spec.* applied to compounds in which phosphorus has its higher valency (pentavalent), as opp. to PHOSPHOROUS; esp. in ***phosphoric acid*** = ***orthophosphoric acid*** s.v. ORTHO- 2a trihydrogen phosphate, H_3PO_4 = $P(OH)_3O$, a colourless, inodorous, intensely bitter acid [F. *acide phosphorique, Nomencl. Chimique*, 1787]; also applied *loosely* to phosphorus pentoxide, P_2O_5, as a constituent of minerals and fertilizers, and (freq. in *pl.*) to any of the common acids (meta-, ortho-, and pyrophosphoric acid) which contain pentavalent phosphorus.

phosphoric anhydride = phosphorus pentoxide, P_2O_5, a white amorphous powder. ***phosphoric chloride*** = phosphorus pentachloride, PCl_5, a yellowish solid substance. ***phosphoric glass***: see quot. 1807.

1791 TENNANT in *Phil. Trans.* LXXXI. 182 When phosphoric acid is combined with calcareous earth, it cannot be decomposed by distillation with charcoal. **1800** tr. *Lagrange's Chem.* I. 65 Nitrous gas almost always detects some hundredth parts of oxygen contained in the residuum of the phosphoric eudiometer. **1807** T. THOMSON *Chem.* (ed. 3) II. 181 At a red heat it assumes the form of a transparent liquid, and when cooled resembles the purest crystal. In this state it is known by the name of phosphoric glass. This glass is merely phosphoric acid totally deprived of water. **1876** HARLEY *Mat. Med.* (ed. 6) 64 Phosphoric anhydride may be readily obtained by burning phosphorus in dry air or oxygen. **1881** LOCKYER in *Nature* 25 Aug. 397 Complex groups..like phosphoric chloride. **1912** J. W. MELLOR *Mod. Inorg. Chem.* xxx. 597 The three phosphoric acids and their salts are distinguished by the difference in their behaviour towards silver nitrate. **1941** *Thorpe's Dict. Appl. Chem.* (ed. 4) V. 69/2 These phosphates have a range of from about 25–32% of phosphoric acid (P_2O_5). **1950** N. V. SIDGWICK *Chem. Elements* I. 745 Esters of all three types of phosphoric acid are known. **1952** W. H. WAGGAMAN *Phosphoric Acid, Phosphates & Phosphatic Fertilizers* (ed. 2) i. 13 The term phosphoric acid..has been, and still is used very loosely... In the fertilizer industry the term phosphoric acid refers to phosphorus pentoxide... To the chemical manufacturer and distributor phosphoric acid means orthophosphoric acid.

†**phosˈphorical**, *a. Obs. rare.* [f. as PHOSPHORIC *a.* + -AL[1].] Light-bearing.

1753 CHAMBERS *Cycl. Supp.* s.v. *Column, Phosphorical column*, a light-house; or a hollow column, built on a rock,.. or other eminence, to serve as a lantern to a port.

phosphoriferous (fɒsfəˈrɪfərəs), *a. rare.* [f. PHOSPHOR-US + -(I)FEROUS.] Yielding or containing phosphorus.

1881 *Metal World* No. 12. 186 After the removal of the phosphoriferous cinder, spiegeleisen was..added, in order to reduce any oxide of iron..dissolved in the fluid metal.

phosphorism (ˈfɒsfərɪz(ə)m). [a. F. *phosphorisme* (Buffon, *a* 1788): see -ISM.]

†**1.** = PHOSPHORESCENCE. *Obs.*

1790 *Monthly Rev.* III. 547 (Mem. Phil. Soc., Lausanne) On the Phosphorism of Fossil Substances, excited by Friction. **1792** in *Phil. Trans.* LXXXII. 28 From this time I find nothing relative to the phosphorism of bodies, till the beginning of the sixteenth century.

2. *Path.* A diseased state of the system caused by phosphorus; chronic phosphorus poisoning.

1897 *Allbutt's Syst. Med.* II. 921 Phosphorus poisoning may be acute or chronic. The latter malady, known as *phosphorism*, is principally met with in those who are engaged in the manufacture of matches. *Ibid.* 924 Children of parents engaged in the manufacture of matches and tainted with phosphorism.

phosphorist (ˈfɒsfərɪst). [ad. Sw. *fosforist*, f. Sw. *fosforos* PHOSPHORUS + -IST: see quot.] One of a school of poetic, idealistic, and romantic Swedish writers at the beginning of the 19th century.

1887 GOSSE in *Encycl. Brit.* XXII. 757/1 These young men had at first to endure bitter opposition..but they.. answered back in their magazines '*Polyfem*' and '*Fosforos*' (1810–13). They were named 'Fosforisterna' (Phosphorists) from the latter... Among the Phosphorists, Atterbom was the man of most genius.

phosphorite (ˈfɒsfəraɪt). *Min.* [Named 1796, f. PHOSPHOR-US + -ITE[1].] A name originally applied by Kirwan to APATITE, or native phosphate of lime; now restricted to a non-crystallized variety from Estremadura, Spain, and elsewhere.

1796 KIRWAN *Elem. Min.* I. 129 1st Family. Phosphorite, Apatite of Werner. **1854** BUSHNAN in *Orr's Circ. Sc., Org. Nat.* I. 43 The phosphate of lime exists..under two forms —namely, apatite and phosphorite. **1876** PAGE *Adv. Text-bk. Geol.* xi. 196 The system yields..phosphorite containing 45 to 64 per cent phosphate of lime. **1882** *Academy* 27 May 382/1 Mammalian remains found in the phosphorite deposits of Quercy.

Hence **phosphoˈritic** *a.*, of, pertaining to, or of the nature of phosphorite.

1858 in MAYNE.

phosphorize (ˈfɒsfəraɪz), *v.* [a. F. *phosphoriser* (Lavoisier), f. PHOSPHOR-US: see -IZE.]

1. *trans.* To combine or impregnate with phosphorus; orig. and chiefly in *ppl. a.* **ˈphosphorized.**

1799 SIR H. DAVY in Beddoes *Contrib. Phys. & Med. Knowl.* 143 The luminous appearance..which Lavoisier supposed to be occasioned by phosphorised hydrogen. **1807** T. THOMSON *Chem.* (ed. 3) II. 393 This phosphorized alcohol exhales the odour of phosphureted hydrogen gas. **1836** J. M. GULLY *Magendie's Formul.* (ed. 2) 185 He has.. seen benefit derived from frictions with phosphorized ointment. **1898** *Westm. Gaz.* 4 June 7/1, I had just come from the bedside of a girl..whose breath was phosphorised and so offensive as to prevent her family living in the same room.

2. To make phosphorescent; to cause to phosphoresce. Hence **ˈphosphorizing** *vbl. sb.*

1837 *New Monthly Mag.* XLIX. 59 He did not, like Sterne, bid the 'lights of science' phosphorize corruption. **1895** *Daily News* 21 Jan. 2/3 Experiments to prove the phosphorising of non-phosphorescent materials by immersion in liquid air at low temperature were made in the dark.

phosphoro-, combining form of PHOSPHORUS, entering into the formation of chemical and other terms: e.g. **phosphorochalcite** (ˌfɒsfərəʊˈkælsaɪt) *Min.* [Gr. χαλκ-ός copper], hydrous phosphate of copper, closely related to Dihydrite and Ehlite. **phosphorogenic** (-ˈdʒɛnɪk), *a.*, causing phosphorescence; *spec.* applied to those rays of the spectrum which excite phosphorescence in certain objects. **phosphorograph** (ˈfɒsfərəʊˌgrɑːf, -æ-) [-GRAPH], an evanescent picture obtained by projecting a luminous image upon a phosphorescent surface; used in particular to obtain an impression of the invisible rays of the spectrum; hence **phosphoroˈgraphic** *a.*; **phosphoˈrography**, the process of making phosphorographs.

1868 DANA *Min.* (ed. 5) 569 Pseudomalachite of Hausmann is the earliest of the names of this species, and is as short and as good as the later *Phosphorochalcite of Glocker. **1854** J. SCOFFERN in *Orr's Circ. Sc., Chem.* 96 The *phosphorogenic rays of an electric spark..are intercepted by glass. **1863** ATKINSON *Ganot's Physics* VII. iv. 408 The phosphorogenic rays..have the property of rendering certain objects self-luminous in the dark after they have been exposed for some time to the light. **1881** *Smithsonian Inst. Rep.* 368 J. W. Draper has obtained what he calls a *phosphorograph of the solar spectrum, and has compared it with a photograph of the same spectrum. **1886** *Nature* 4 Mar. 431/2 *Phosphorographic studies for the photographic reproduction of the stars. **1886** *Athenæum* 18 Sept. 375/2 Mr. Ch. V. Zenger brought before the Academy of Sciences on August 30th a paper entitled '*Phosphorography applied to the Photography of the Invisible'.

phosphorolysis (fɒsfəˈrɒlɪsɪs). *Biochem.* [f. PHOSPHOR(US or PHOSPHOR(YLATION + HYDR)OLYSIS.] A form of hydrolysis in which a bond in an organic molecule is broken and an inorganic phosphate group becomes attached to one of the atoms previously linked.

1937 *Enzymologia* II. 160 Phosphorolysis is an enzymic process. **1946** *Nature* 23 Nov. 746/2 It was suggested that the coenzyme in muscle, while taking up two hydrogen atoms in the pyridine nucleus through the addition of free phosphate, undergoes a phosphorolysis and is split into pyridin[e] nucleotide and adenosine diphosphoric or triphosphoric acid. **1970** R. W. MCGILVERY *Biochem.* xv. 296 Glycogen is mainly degraded by a simple phosphorolysis of the 1 → 4 glucosidic bonds to form glucose-1-phosphate... The primary reaction is catalyzed by the enzyme, phosphorylase.

Hence ˌ**phosphoroˈlytic** *a.*

1937 *Enzymologia* II. 154 Phosphorolytic decomposition of glycogen. **1970** A. L. LEHNINGER *Biochem.* xv. 328 (*caption*) Phosphorolytic removal of a glucose residue from the nonreducing end of a glycogen chain by phosphorylase.

phosphoroscope (ˈfɒsfərəskəʊp). [-SCOPE.]

a. An apparatus for observing and measuring the duration of phosphorescence in such substances as emit light for a very short period; **b.** A scientific toy consisting of an arrangement of glass tubes containing various phosphorescent substances, each of which glows with a different coloured light.

1860 W. A. MILLER *Elem. Chem.* (ed. 2) I. 152 An ingenious instrument has been devised by E. Becquerel for the purpose of observing phosphorescence of very brief duration... This *phosphoroscope*, as he terms it. **1869** *Academy* 11 Dec. 77/2 M. Becquerel has modified his phosphoroscope in order to examine the phosphorescence caused by rays of various refrangibility. **1881** J. E. H. GORDON *Electr. & Magn.* II. 116 Alumina..glowing with a rich red colour in the phosphoroscope.

phosphorous (ˈfɒsfərəs), *a.* [f. L. *phōsphorus* PHOSPHORUS + -OUS; in sense 2, ad. F. *phosphoreux* (*Nomencl. Chimique* 1787): see -OUS c.]

1. = PHOSPHORESCENT *a.*

1777 PENNANT *Zool.* (ed. 4) IV. 50 Their phosphorous quality is well known; nor was it overlooked by the antients. **1883** C. F. HOLDER in *Harper's Mag.* Jan. 185/2 MM. Edoux and Soulezet collected some of the phosphorous substance.

2. *Chem.* Abounding in phosphorus; *spec.* applied to compounds into which phosphorus enters in its lower valency (trivalent), as opp. to PHOSPHORIC; esp. in ***phosphorous acid*** = trihydrogen phosphite, H_3PO_3 = $P(OH)_3$, obtained from phosphorus, usually in the form of a thick uncrystallizable syrup, but also in crystalline form.

phosphorous anhydride = phosphorus trioxide, P_2O_3, a white non-crystalline powder, produced by the slow combustion of phosphorus in the air; ***phosphorous chloride*** = p. trichloride, PCl_3, a colourless strongly fuming liquid.

1794 SULLIVAN *View Nat.* I. 259 All urine contains some animal earth, or lime combined with phosphorous acid. **1815** J. SMITH *Panorama Sc. & Art* II. 440 The spontaneous combustion of phosphorus at the temperature of the atmosphere, forms, in the first instance, phosphorous acid, which contains less oxygen than the phosphoric; but as phosphorous acid acquires an additional quantity of oxygen from the atmosphere, it is speedily converted into the phosphoric. **1866** ROSCOE *Elem. Chem.* xv. 133 Phosphorous Anhydride..forms a white non-crystalline powder which combines with great energy with water, forming thereby phosphorous acid.

phosphor-roesslerite (fɒsfəˈrøsləraɪt). *Min.* Also **phosphorrösslerite**. [ad. G. *phosphorrösslerit* (Friedrich & Robitsch 1939, in *Zentralbl. für Min., Geol., und Paläont.* A. 143), f. *phosphor* PHOSPHORUS: see ROESSLERITE.] A hydrated acid phosphate of magnesium, $MgH(PO_4).7H_2O$, that is isomorphous with rösslerite and occurs as monoclinic crystals that are usually discoloured by impurities and that lose water on exposure to air.

1939 *Mineral. Abstr.* VII. 316 Mud in old workings in the gold mines at Schellgaden (in Salzburg) shows glistening crystals of the new mineral phosphor-rösslerite... The water-clear crystals, usually yellow from iron staining, are monoclinic. **1951** C. PALACHE et al. *Dana's Syst. Min.* (ed. 7) II. 713 Phosphorroesslerite.

‖**phosphoruria** (fɒsfəˈjʊərɪə). *Path.* [mod.L., f. PHOSPHOR-US + *-uria*, f. Gr. οὖρον urine.]

a. = PHOSPHATURIA. **b.** A morbid condition of the urine, which is phosphorescent on emission.

1858 MAYNE *Expos. Lex., Phosphorūria*,..term for the presence of phosphorus in the urine. **1893** *Syd. Soc. Lex., Phosphoruria*... 1. Photuria. 2. Phosphaturia.

phosphorus (ˈfɒsfərəs). Also 7–8 -os. [a. L. *phōsphorus* the morning star (Mart.), a. Gr. φωσφόρος adj. (f. φῶς light + -φόρος bringing); hence as sb. (sc. ἀστήρ) the morning star. Sense 2 was taken independently from the Gr. adj., and thence sense 3.]

I. 1. (with capital P): The morning star: = PHOSPHOR 1. Also *fig.* Now *rare.*

1629 T. ADAMS *Medit. Creed* Wks. (1630) 1209 John Baptist was that Phosphorus or Morning Starre, to signifie the Sunnes approching. **1676** TOWERSON *Decalogue* 7 Though it be not the sun, yet it is the Phosphorus to it. **1694** CONGREVE *Double Dealer* II. i, He wants nothing but a blue ribbon and a star to make him shine the very phosphorus of our human sphere. **1715** M. DAVIES *Athen. Brit.* I. 39 Throughout the whole Protestant Reformation, whereof he [Erasmus] was the brightest Phosphoros. **1878** NEWCOMB *Pop. Astron.* III. iii. 290 It [Venus] was known to the ancients by the names of Hesperus and Phosphorus.

2. Any substance or organism that phosphoresces or shines of itself (naturally, or when heated, etc.); *esp.* (in later use) a substance that absorbs sunlight, and shines in the dark. Pl. †**phosphoruses**, †**-'s**, **phosphori**. Now *rare.*

Baldwin's phosphorus, calcium nitrate that has been strongly heated: discovered by Baldwin in 1674. ***Bolognian*** or ***Bononian phosphorus***, ***Montalbano's phosphorus***, barium sulphide or heavy spar from Monte Paterno, which becomes phosphorescent by calcination; its property was discovered in 1602 by Casciolorus, a shoemaker of Bologna. ***Canton's phosphorus***, calcium sulphide that has been strongly heated; its phosphorescence was discovered by Marggraf in 1750, who obtained it by calcining gypsum with combustible matter; Canton prepared it in 1768 by igniting oyster shells with sulphur. ***Homberg's phosphorus***, calcium chloride that has been fused; its property was discovered by Homberg in 1693. ***mercurial phosphorus***: see quot. 1710.

1645 EVELYN *Diary* May, Dr. Montalbano..he who invented or found out the composition of the *lapis illuminabilis*, or phosphorus. He shew'd me their property.. being to retain the light of the sun for some competent time, by a kind of imbibition, by a particular way of calcination. **1680** BOYLE *Aerial Noctiluca* Wks. 1772 IV. 380 Phosphoruses may well be distinguished into two sorts; those that may be stiled natural, as glow-worms, some sorts of rotten wood and fishes..and those that are properly artificial. **1705** HAUKSBEE in *Phil. Trans.* XXIV. 2129 Several Experiments on the Mercurial Phosphorus, made before the Royal Society. **1710** J. HARRIS *Lex. Techn.* II, *Mercurial Phosphorus*, is a Light arising from the shaking of Mercury in *Vacuo*. **1727–41** CHAMBERS *Cycl.* s.v., *Natural Phosphori* are matters which become luminous at certain times. **1753** —— *Cycl. Supp.* s.v., There is a vast variety of *phosphori* in the animal kingdom. **1756–7** tr. *Keysler's Trav.* (1760) IV. 406 A kind of amethysts, which may be used as a phosphorus, if laid on a hot stove: and I do not question, but that, with a suitable process, a sort of Bononian stone may be made of them. **1794** G. ADAMS *Nat. & Exp. Philos.* II. xxi. 396 Phosphori..may be considered as bodies giving light; though more properly they are those bodies which give a faint light, visible only in the dark. **1800** HENRY *Epit. Chem.* (1808) 52 Bodies, gifted with this property [of absorbing the rays of light in their totality] are called *solar phosphori*. **1807** T. THOMSON *Chem.* (ed. 3) II. iii. 533 When thus reduced to a submuriate, it has the property of shining in the dark, as Homberg first observed: hence it has been called the phosphorus of Homberg. **1834** MRS. SOMERVILLE *Connex. Phys. Sc.* xxviii. (1849) 326 Sulphuret of calcium, known as Canton's phosphorus. **1866** BRANDE & COX *Dict. Sc.* etc. II. 139 *Homberg's Phosphorus*. **1898** SIR W. CROOKES *Addr. Brit. Assoc.* 23 The energy thus absorbed reappears in the form of light, and the body is said to phosphoresce... The best known *phosphori* belong to certain well-defined classes, such as the sulphides of the alkaline-earthy metals, and some of the so-called rare earths.

3. *Chem.* One of the non-metallic elements, a yellowish translucent substance resembling wax, widely distributed in nature in combination with other elements; it is extremely inflammable, undergoing slow combustion at ordinary temperatures, and hence appearing luminous in the dark. (Chemical symbol P.)

Accidentally obtained from urine in 1669 by Brandt, an alchemist of Hamburg, in the course of his search for the philosophers' stone. He communicated his discovery and method of obtaining it to the chemist Kunkel; hence the early name ***Kunkel's phosphorus***, the substance being classed with the phosphorescent bodies in sense 2. The method of its production was not made public till 1737. About 1750 it began to be named *phosphorus* par excellence.

1680 BOYLE *Aerial Noctiluca* Wks. 1772 IV. 381 This substance [shown by Mr. Daniel Kraft, a German chemist] ..was at least as yielding as bees-wax in summer... On the score of its uninterrupted action, it is called by some in Germany, the constant noctiluca; which title it does not ill deserve, since this phosphorus is much the noblest we have yet seen. **1681** *Phil. Trans.* XII. 9 Concerning the Noctiluca or Phosphoros of Dr. Kunkelius. **1685** EVELYN *Diary* 10 Dec., This matter or phosphorus was made out of human blood and urine, elucidating the vital flame or heate in animal bodys. **1758** REID tr. *Macquer's Chem.* I. 34 From the Marine Acid combined with a Phlogiston results a kind of Sulphur..that..takes fire of itself upon being exposed to the open air. This combination is called English Phosphorus, Phosphorus of Urine, because it is generally prepared from urine, or, only Phosphorus. **1774** GOLDSM. *Nat. Hist.* (1776) VIII. 175 In the dark they send forth a kind of shining light resembling that of phosphorus. [**1787** DE MORVEAU *Nomencl. Chimique* 131 Nom ancien, *Phosphore de Kunkel*: Nom nouveau *Phosphore*.] **1799** *Med. Jrnl.* I. 173 Sulphur and phosphorus merely attract oxygen; they form in this combination peculiar acids, and thereby disengage..heat and light which appear in the form of flame. **1827** E. TURNER *Elem. Chem.* II. 224 It is remarkable that the slow combustion of phosphorus does not take place in pure oxygen, unless its temperature be about 80°F. **1855** BAIN *Senses & Int.* I. ii. § 2 Phosphorus abounds more in the brain than in any other tissue. **1866** BRANDE & COX *Dict. Sc.* etc. II. 890/2 As a result of exposure to heat or light, phosphorus sometimes acquires a red colour, and this red substance is allotropic or amorphous phosphorus. Schrötter made the discovery of this variety of phosphorus in 1848. **1876** BRISTOWE *The. & Pract. Med.* (1878) 529 Fatty degeneration..is sometimes observed..in poisoning by phosphorus.

4. *attrib.* and *Comb.*, as ***phosphorus cachexia***, ***liver***, ***matches***, ***poison***, ***poisoning***; in Chem. = of phosphorus, as ***phosphorus oxychloride***, ***pentachloride***, ***trichloride***, ***trihydride***; ***phosphorus-containing*** adj.; **phosphorus-bottle**, †(*a*) a bottle containing phosphorus, used for igniting sulphur matches; (*b*) a bottle containing a small quantity of phosphorus dissolved in olive oil, which emits light on being uncorked in the dark; †**phosphorus box**, a box containing matches tipped with chlorate of potash, with phosphorus on which to ignite them; †**phosphorus-lamp** = *phosphorus-bottle* b; **phosphorus necrosis**, gangrene of some part of the jaw-bone, due to the fumes of phosphorus, a disease affecting persons engaged in the manufacture of lucifer matches; **phosphorus paste**, a paste containing phosphorus, used to kill vermin.

1814 *Chron.* in *Ann. Reg.* 324 Brimstoned matches, and *phosphorus boxes were fireworks. **1881** G. W. CABLE *Mme. Delphine* xi. 62 She softly laid the phosphorus-box out of her hands. **1897** *Allbutt's Syst. Med.* II. 930 So long as profound *phosphorus cachexia remains. **1896** *Ibid.* I. 165 Certain *phosphorus-containing substances in the body. **1869** ROSCOE *Elem. Chem.* 118 Acting upon *phosphorus iodide with water. **1899** CAGNEY tr. *Jaksch's Clin. Diagn.* vii. (ed. 4) 396 The typical *phosphorus-liver leads to alimentary glycosuria. **1898** *Westm. Gaz.* 16 July 3/3 If the manufacture of yellow *phosphorus matches can be proved to be fatal, nay, even injurious to human life,..then let the Government take action. *Ibid.* 3 June 4/3 Forty-seven cases of *phosphorus necrosis have developed among our workpeople. **1860** URE *Dict. Arts* (ed. 5) III. 439 *Phosphorus paste, for the destruction of rats and mice. **1873** WATTS *Fownes' Chem.* (ed. 11) 227 *Phosphorus Pentachloride or Phosphoric Chloride, is formed when phosphorus is burned in excess of chlorine. **1878** T. BRYANT *Pract. Surg.* I. 539 Necrosis of the jaws, as a result of the *phosphorus poison, is now rarely seen. **1897** *Westm. Gaz.* 24 Mar. 9/2 Death was due to phosphorus poison. **1897** *Allbutt's Syst. Med.* II. 923 In Pardieu's second form of *phosphorus poisoning the symptoms are referable from the outset to the nervous system. **1873** WATTS *Fownes' Chem.* (ed. 11) 225 *Phosphorus Trihydride is analogous in some of its chemical relations to ammoniacal gas.

phosphoryl (ˈfɒsfərɪl, -aɪl). *Chem.* [f. PHOSPHOR(US + -YL.] **a.** The usu. trivalent radical PO. **b.** The univalent phosphate radical, $-PO(OH)_2$.

1871 *Jrnl. Chem. Soc.* XXIV. 1161 In the first case, ordinary phosphoryl trichloride is produced: $P_2O_3Cl_4 + PCl_5 = 3POCl_3$. **1912** J. W. MELLOR *Mod. Inorg. Chem.* xxx. 586 Phosphoryl fluoride, POF_3, as well as the other phosphoryl compounds can be made by the action of phosphorus pentoxide, P_2O_5, on the halogen acid. **1962** S. G. WALEY in A. Pirie *Lens Metabolism Rel. Cataract* 360 In the enzymatic reaction, there is a direct transfer of the phosphoryl $\left(O{=}P{\lt}^{OH}_{OH}\right)$ group from phosphoenolpyruvate to ATP. **1964** N. G. CLARK *Mod. Org. Chem.* 553 Phosphoryl chloride ('phosphorus oxychloride'), $POCl_3$, is a colourless liquid..which reacts slowly with water giving phosphoric acid. **1964** W. G. SMITH *Allergy & Tissue Metabolism* viii. 82 Thus the synthesis of glycerophosphatide is dependent on the availability of these phosphoryl bases as well as diglyceride. **1979** *Science* 7 Dec. 1151/1 Figure 7, from this work, represents a hypothetical example in which phosphoryl is conducted from ATP on the left to a substrate S on the right.

phosphorylase (fɒsˈfɒrɪleɪz, -s, ˈfɒsfərɪleɪz, -s). *Biochem.* [f. prec. + -ASE.] An enzyme that introduces a phosphate group into an organic compound.

1939 G. T. CORI et al. in *Jrnl. Biol. Chem.* CXXVII. 771 Various mammalian tissues..contain an enzyme which can be extracted with water and which forms glucose-1-phosphoric ester..from glycogen and inorganic phosphate... This enzyme, which will be referred to as phosphorylase, initiates the degradation of glycogen. **1955** *Sci. News Let.* 7 May 297/1 Use of muscle to do work and its recovery depends upon the chemical action of an enzyme, phosphorylase, which is found in muscle. **1970** [see PHOSPHOROLYSIS]. **1971** *Nature* 19 Feb. 529/1 The breakdown of glycogen, in accordance with instantaneous energy requirements, is controlled by the activity of glycogen phosphorylase. This enzyme exists in two states: phosphorylase *b*..is a form of low concentration... Under the action of phosphorylase kinase it is phosphorylated at one serine residue in each of the four subunits, to give the highly active phosphorylase *a*.

phosphorylation (ˌfɒsfɒrɪˈleɪʃən). *Biochem.* [f. as prec. + -ATION.] The introduction of a phosphate group into an organic molecule.

1925 *Chem. Abstr.* XIX. 3278 Dry yeast..did cause the formation of phosphoric ester with glucose. Slight phosphorylation occurred with yeast ext. **1931** [see DEPHOSPHORYLATION]. **1960** *Radio Times* 22 Jan. 38/4 From the latest work it appears that the capacity to transform the light energy absorbed by chlorophyll into the energy of phosphate bonds (photosynthetic phosphorylation) is its unique feature. **1962** H. A. KREBS in A. Pirie *Lens Metabolism Rel. Cataract* 351 Owing to the obligatory coupling between the electron transport from substrate to oxygen and oxidative phosphorylation, oxidations cannot take place unless ADP and phosphate are available. **1973** R. G. KRUEGER et al. *Introd. Microbiol.* viii. 254/2 Let us.. consider the mechanism of the electron transport system and of oxidative phosphorylation. The cell uses these mechanisms to capture energy from reduced coenzymes (NADH and NADPH) to store in ATP.

So **phos'phorylate** *v. trans.*, to introduce a phosphate group into; **phos'phorylated**, **phos'phorylating** *ppl. adjs.*

1931 *Jrnl. Biol. Chem.* XCII. 765 Phosphorylated sugars. **1937** *Nature* 20 Feb. 309/2 Prof. Verzár attributes these observations to the fact that glucose is rapidly phosphorylated in the cells of the living mucous membrane. **1937** *Biochem. Jrnl.* XXXI. 329 (*heading*) Competition between phosphorylating enzymes in muscle extract. **1962** R. VAN HEYNINGEN in A. Pirie *Lens Metabolism Rel. Cataract* 399 In general, carbohydrate metabolism in animal tissues proceeds by way of phosphorylated intermediates. **1970** R. W. MCGILVERY *Biochem.* x. 197 Racker has.. suggested that the non-heme iron, that is, iron not associated with porphyrins,..may also be associated with the phosphorylating complex rather than with the electron transfer system. **1971** [see PHOSPHORYLASE].

phosphosiderite (fɒsfəʊˈsɪdəraɪt). *Min.* [Named 1890, f. PHOSPHO- + SIDERITE.] Hydrous ferric phosphate, found in transparent red prismatic crystals.

1890 *Amer. Jrnl. Sc.* Ser. III. XL. 336 Phosphosiderite.. is orthorhombic and occurs in prismatic crystals.

phosphuranylite (fɒsfjʊˈrænɪlaɪt). *Min.* [f. PHOSPH(O- + URANYL + -ITE.] Hydrous phosphate of uranium, occurring as a yellow pulverulent incrustation.

1879 *Amer. Jrnl. Sc.* Ser. III. XVIII. 153 A new species called by the describer phosphuranylite. **1892** DANA *Min.* 859 Phosphuranylite..occurs as a pulverulent incrustation.

†**'phosphure.** *Chem. Obs.* Also 8 **phosphur.** [a. F. *phosphure* (*Nomencl. Chimique* 1787), f. PHOSPH(O-: see -URE.] = PHOSPHIDE: cf. next.

[**1787** DE MORVEAU, etc. *Nomencl. Chimique* 205 Phosphure, *Phosphoretum*: combinaison de phosphore non oxigéné, avec différentes bases.] **1792** *Phil. Trans.* LXXXII. 304 This compound..some of my chemical friends have called fulminating hepar of phosphorus... In the new system of chemistry it will be called *phosphur of lime*. **1799** W. CLAYFIELD in Beddoes *Contrib. Phys. & Med. Knowl.* 438 Both barytes and strontian combine with phosphorus and exhibit similar appearances to the phosphure of lime. **1801** *Monthly Rev.* XXXV. 527 Bertrand Pelletier..made several experiments on metallic phosphures.

†**phosphuret** (ˈfɒsfjʊərɛt). *Chem. Obs.* Also -oret. [ad. mod.L. *phosphorētum*; altered to *phosphuret* after F. *phosphure*: see prec. and -URET.] = PHOSPHIDE.

1799 HOOPER *Med. Dict., Phosphurets*.., combinations of phosphorus, not oxygenated, with different bases, as *phosphuret of copper, phosphuret of iron*, &c. **1826** HENRY *Elem. Chem.* II. 49 Phosphuret of cadmium has a grey colour and a feeble metallic lustre. **1893** *Syd. Soc. Lex., Phosphoret*, old term for *Phosphide*.

phosphuretted, -eted (ˈfɒsfjʊərɛtɪd), *a. Chem.* Also phosphor-. [f. prec. + -ED.] Combined chemically with phosphorus.

phosphuretted hydrogen = PHOSPHINE, phosphorus trihydride, PH_3, a poisonous gas of disgusting smell, produced by the decomposition of animal substances. When arising from water, it contains traces of the vapour of a liquid hydride, and is then spontaneously inflammable, giving rise (it is believed) to the phenomenon known as *ignis fatuus* or *will o' the wisp*.

1807 T. THOMSON *Chem.* (ed. 3) II. 41 Phosphureted hydrogen gas is emitted, which takes fire as soon as it comes to the surface of the water. **1808** HENRY *Epit. Chem.* (ed. 5) 205 Phosphuretted hydrogen gas. **1826** —— *Elem. Chem.* II. 510 No mixture..of oxygen, nitrous oxide, or chlorine with phosphureted hydrogen. **1858** CARPENTER *Veg. Phys.* §32 During the decomposition of animal and vegetable substances, they enter into combination with hydrogen, forming sulphuretted and phosphuretted hydrogen.

β. **1865–72** WATTS *Dict. Chem.* III. 200 Spontaneously inflammable phosphoretted hydrogen. **1880** BASTIAN *Brain* ii. 28 These tissues..are composed, in the main, of water, of phosphoretted fats, and of protein compounds.

‖**phos'phuria.** *Path.* = PHOSPHORURIA.

1858 MAYNE *Expos. Lex., Phosphuria*, see *Phosphoruria*. **1885** W. H. DICKINSON *Renal & Urinary Affect.* III. xxi. 1233 (Running title) Phosphuria.

phosphyl (ˈfɒsfɪl). *Chem.* [f. PHOSPH- + -YL.] The univalent radical PO_2.

1898 G. MCGOWAN tr. *Meyer's Hist. Chem.* 462 Organic compounds containing the group phosphyl (PO_2) were also prepared a few years ago.

phossy (ˈfɒsɪ), *a. colloq.* Also fossy. [f. PHOS, colloq. abbreviation of *phosphorus* + -Y.]

Characterized or affected by the presence of phosphorus; in **phossy jaw**, the popular name of the disease phosphorus necrosis of the jaw.

1889 *Pall Mall G.* 4 Apr. 2/3 The public knows nothing of the 'fossy jaw' which is one of the familiar dangers of life to the East-end match girl. **1893** *Brit. Med. Jrnl.* 1 Apr. 706/1 The match girls' 'leprosy' and phossy jaw demand our attention. **1897** *Allbutt's Syst. Med.* II. 928 The work people suffer from necrosis of the bone, sometimes called in this country 'phossy jaw' and in France 'mal chimique'... The 'mixers' and 'dippers' are particularly liable to suffer from 'phossy jaw'.

phot (fəʊt). *Physics.* [a. F. *phot*, f. Gr. *φῶς, φωτ-* light.] †**a.** A unit of the product of illumination and duration, equal to one lux maintained for one second. *Obs.*

1894 tr. A. Blondel in *Electrician* 28 Sept 634/2 Some years ago the photographers..established under the presidency of eminent *savants* (MM. Abney, Cornu, Janssen, Sébert, Violle, &c.), a unit of time-illumination (*illumination*) specially applicable to photography, the 'phot'.

b. A unit of illumination equal to one lumen per square centimetre (equivalent to 10,000 lux).

1917 *Trans. Illuminating Engin. Soc.* (U.S.) XII. 440 Using the centimeter as the unit of length, the unit of illumination is one lumen per square centimeter, for which Blondel has proposed the name 'phot'. One millilumen per square centimeter (milliphot) is more useful as a practical unit. **1939** [see *metre-candle* s.v. METRE *sb.*[2] b]. **1953** AMOS & BIRKINSHAW *Television Engin.* I. 280 The phot is rather a large unit, and its submultiple the milliphot (equal to 10^{-3} phot) is frequently used.

‖**phota.** *Obs.* Also 7 foota. [a. Pers. *fūtah* loin-band, bathing-cloth.] An East Indian fabric, included in lists of piece-goods; cf. LUNGI.

1616 B. FARIE *Let.* in *E. Ind. Comp. Rec.* (1900) IV. 306 If you have..lunges and footaes..ship them away for this place [Ayuthia (Siam)]. **1725** *Lond. Gaz.* No. 6388/2 The following Goods, viz...Herba Taffaties,..Photaes. **1813** MILBURN *Orient. Comm.* II. xxi. 221 Piece goods form the staple commodity of Bengal... The following are the kinds imported... Percaulahs, Photaes, Pulicat handkerchiefs.

photal ('fəʊtəl), *a. rare.* [f. Gr. *φῶς, φωτ-* light + -AL[1].] = PHOTIC.

1877 E. R. CONDER *Bas. Faith* iii. (1884) 121 Physical forces—gravitation, cohesion, molecular vibration, photal vibration, and so forth.

photelectric: see PHOTO-ELECTRIC.

Photian ('fəʊʃən), *sb.* and *a.* [f. *Photius*, the name of a ninth-century Patriarch of Constantinople + -IAN.] **A.** *sb.* A follower or supporter of Photius. **B.** *adj.* Of or pertaining to Photius or the schism in which he took a part. Hence **'Photianism**; **'Photianist** *a.* and *sb.*

1849 D. ROCK *Church of our Fathers* I. I. ii. 90 Not only the united or orthodox Greeks..but the Photians or separated Greeks, and the other sects in the East living apart, by schism and heresy, from Rome, entirely agree with her and the Latins upon Transubstantiation. **1850** Æ. McD. DAWSON tr. *J. M. de Maistre's The Pope* IV. iii. 307 The Photian churches are preserved in the midst of Mahometanism, as an insect is preserved in amber. *Ibid.* x. 340 Among the Photians, on the contrary, as among all other Protestants, there is no unity. **1854** J. H. NEWMAN *Lect. Hist. Turks* III. ii. 183 The unhappy city..which had been successively the seat of Arianism, of Nestorianism, of Photianism. **1864** in E. S. Purcell *Life & Lett. A. P. de Lisle* (1900) I. xv. 388 Photianism and Anglicanism are two forms of the same true Christian religion. **1907** *Catholic Encycl.* II. 45/1 The mutual bitterness which was evinced in Constantinople by the contending parties of Photians and Anti-Photians was reflected here in Athens... Sabbas, who succeeded Anastasios, was likewise a Photian. **1948** F. DVORNIK *Photian Schism* I. i. 27 The Fathers had listened to the Photianist bishops Zachary and Theophilus. *Ibid.* ii. 46 The anti-Photianist Collection...contains all the documents against Photius and served the extreme Ignatians as an armoury in their struggle against the Photianists. **1967** *New Catholic Encycl.* XI. 328/2 We have only..an extract in Greek, preserved in the anti-Photianist collection. *Ibid.*, The Photian legend grew in the West, picturing the patriarch as the father of schism and the archenemy of papal primacy.

photic ('fəʊtɪk), *a.* [f. Gr. *φῶς, φωτ-* light + -IC.] **a.** Pertaining or relating to light (orig. applied to a supposed 'fluid' constituting the matter of light; cf. *electric fluid*). So †**'photicated** *a. Obs.*, ? impregnated with 'photic fluid'; **'photics** *sb. pl.*, (*a*) the science of light and its intrinsic properties (sometimes used instead of *optics*, which properly denotes the science of sight); (*b*) see quot. 1875.

1843 *Mech. Mag.* XXXVIII. 47 The photic fluid may be regarded as the base of all other traversing fluids. *Ibid.* 6 The photicated ether..I presume to pervade all nature. **1858** MAYNE *Expos. Lex.*, *Photica*, term for the doctrine of the nature and appearance of light: photics. **1875** KNIGHT *Dict. Mech.*, *Photics*...the term originated in the United States Patent Office, and is there applied to that class of mechanical inventions embracing lamps, gas-light arrangements, and illuminating apparatus generally. **1919** *Jrnl. Exper. Zool.* XXIX. 254 Tactile receptors, photic receptors, and chemoreceptors [of chitons] are physiologically distinct. **1957** G. E. HUTCHINSON *Treat. Limnol.* I. xiii. 757 The rather feeble photic requirements of the purple bacteria. **1971** *Nature* 30 Apr. 579/2 The clam has just been placed on its side and, in response to both tactile and photic disturbance (a shadow cast on the exposed tissues), has tightly closed its valves. **1973** *Black Panther* 18 Aug. 8/3 The photic driver..uses flashing infrared light and pulsing ultrasonic noise to pull brain waves from their normal frequency. The subjected individual sees and hears nothing, becomes lethargic, dizzy, perhaps nauseous, and may suffer epileptic fits.

b. Applied to the parts of the oceans penetrated by sufficient sunlight for the growth of plants.

1903 W. R. FISHER tr. *Schimper's Plant-Geogr.* 782 Three chief stages of brightness may be distinguished: 1. The photic or bright region, in which the intensity of light is sufficient for the normal development of macrophytes. **1972** A. LAURIE *Living Oceans* iv. 88 For small, slow-moving animals the twilight zone is also a safer habitat than the photic zone, which is the home of many active predators, especially fast-moving fish. *Ibid.* vi. 126 The photic zone of the oceans reaches down to a depth of 650 feet below the surface, which is deeper than the continental shelf. The entire shelf sea lies within the photic zone.

Hence **'photically** *adv.*, by light.

1960 *Recent Adv. Biol. Psychiatry* II. 181 Photically evoked cerebral patterns have been studied. **1971** *Jrnl. Gen. Psychol.* LXXXIV. 22 Later components of the photically evoked cortical potential.

Photinian (fəʊ'tɪnɪən), *a.* and *sb. Ch. Hist.* [ad. late L. *Phōtīniānī* (pl.), Isidore 5th c., f. *Phōtīnus*, in Gr. *Φωτεινός*, a man's name (from *φωτεινός* shining, bright, luminous).] **a.** *adj.* Of or pertaining to Photinus, Bishop of Sirmium, who held that Jesus Christ was not essentially divine, but became so by a divine emanation which descended upon him: his doctrines were condemned by various councils between 336 and 351. **b.** *sb.* A follower of Photinus.

1648 OWEN *Toleration* Wks. 1851 VIII. 179 [Grotianus] granted liberty to all sects but Manichees, Photinians and Eunomians. **1720** WATERLAND *Eight Serm.* 9 A celebrated Writer abroad, has openly espoused this Photinian Notion. **1853** M. KELLY tr. *Gosselin's Power Pope in Mid. Ages* I. 79 In this edict he condemns by name the Photinians, Arians, and Eunomians. **1864** BRYCE *Holy Rom. Emp.* vi. (1889) 82 It was becoming more and more alienated from the West by the Photinian schism. **1884** EDNA LYALL *We Two* xxiv, A few years ago he was an atheist, now he's a mere Photinian.

Hence **Pho'tinianism**, the doctrine or heresy of the Photinians.

1655 OWEN *Vind. Evang.* Wks. (1853) XII. 8 Of the Socinian religion there are two main parts: the first is Photinianism, the latter Pelagianism. **1865** *Union Rev.* III. 440 Socinus, the reviver of a modified Arianism or rather Photinianism in the West.

photism ('fəʊtɪz(ə)m). *Psychics.* [ad. Gr. *φωτισμός* illumination, f. *φωτίζειν* to shine, illuminate, f. *φῶς, φωτ-* light.] A hallucinatory sensation or vision of light.

1892 D. H. TUKE *Dict. Psychol. Med.* II. 1126/1 Most sound photisms are projected on externality. **1902** *Athenæum* 19 July 82/3 The alleged accompanying vision of a great light, a 'photism' Mr. James calls the phenomenon. **1903** F. W. H. MYERS *Hum. Personality* I. Gloss. s.v. *Secondary Sensations*, With some persons every sensation of one type is accompanied by a sensation of another type; as, for instance, a special sound may be accompanied by a special sensation of colour or light (*chromatisms* or *photisms*). **1903** A. LANG *Valet's Trag.* 205 Her [Jeanne d'Arc's] thoughts..presented themselves in visual forms..attended by an hallucinatory brightness of light (a 'photism').

pho'tistic, *a. rare*$^{-1}$. [ad. Gr. *φωτιστικ-ός* enlightening, f. *φωτιστής* an enlightener, f. *φωτίζειν*: see prec.] Of, pertaining to, or of the nature of illumination.

1885 J. MARTINEAU *Types Eth. Th.* II. II. i. 356 When, from the dull sense..the photistic thrill disengages itself as something different from the rest, it will not be denied that this is a perceptive gain, i.e. an accession not only to the creature's sensory store, but to his life-relations with reality.

photo ('fəʊtəʊ).

1. Colloquial abbreviation of PHOTOGRAPH.

1860 QUEEN VICTORIA *Let.* 24 Oct. in R. Fulford *Dearest Child* (1964) 275 She is waiting to know..about the photo. *Ibid.* 28 Nov. 286, I send you (*to look at only*) a wonderful photo: of the Queen of Naples. **1861** D. G. ROSSETTI *Let.* 11 July (1965) II. 411 The only way I know about Scott's photos, is to send you a set I have. **1870** MISS BRIDGMAN *Ro. Lynne* II. x. 215, I should like her photo. **1877** PRINCESS ALICE in *Mem.* (1884) 357, I send you the last photos done of the children. **1893** ROMANES in *Life* 313 The photos.. make me realise what splendid work the buildings are.

2. Colloquial (technical) abbreviation for PHOTOGRAPHIC: see also PHOTO- 2.

1889 *Nature* 31 Oct. 647/2 Corrected for photo work. **1890** *Anthony's Photogr. Bull.* III. 271, I have written so often to the various year books and photo papers on this subject.

b. = PHOTO-FINISH. Also *attrib.*

1937 *N.Y. Times* 3 Jan. S7/3 Kindred Spirit survived a hair-raising finish to take a photo decision at 18-1 under Jimmy Start. **1946** *Sun* (Baltimore) 2 Oct. 15 War Trophy ..closed with a belated rush..to earn the photo. **1950** *Ibid.* 1 June 21/8 (*heading*) Tar wins in photo. **1976** *Scottish Daily Express* 23 Dec. 10/6 Brigadier General Preston Gilbride's ex-Irish colt..collared Gambling Prince..smoothly in the closing stages to win by four lengths..with the photo showing Bronson to have held O'Conna out of third spot.

3. *attrib.* and Comb., as ***photo-frame, -stand***, etc.; **photo opportunity** orig. *U.S.*, an opportunity provided for press and television photographers to take photographs of a celebrity or celebrities.

1879 MRS. A. E. JAMES *Ind. Househ. Managem.* 27 Odds and ends in the way of photo-stands [etc.]. **1902** *Daily Chron.* 5 Sept., Fancy leather and photo-frame work. **1974** RATHER & GATES *Palace Guard* III. xx. 242 Photographers and reporters already had been alerted..that the 'photo opportunity' would be coming off momentarily. **1977** *Guardian Weekly* 2 Oct. 16/1 This maneuvering leaves open whether a Geneva conference would be a mere 'photo opportunity' or whether..it could be a prelude to..serious bilateral bargaining. **1984** *Sunday Times* 14 Oct. 19/7 'Photo opportunities', where television cameras are ushered in to record the president carrying out his formal duties.

Hence as *v. trans.*, to photograph; also **'photo'd**, **'photoed**, *pa. pple.* and *ppl. a.*

1868 D. G. ROSSETTI *Let.* 21 Feb. (1965) II. 653, I shall be anxious to have a set of his admirable photo'd drawings. **1870** CARLYLE *Let. Anderson* 20 Mar., No mask that has it not..can be accepted to engrave from or be thought worth photoing. **1889** J. K. JEROME *Three Men in Boat* xviii. 291 We had no objection to being photo'd full-length. **1928** A. HUXLEY *Let.* 12 Dec. (1969) 304 The type is photoed on to sheets of jelly..and printed from the jelly. **1973** A. BEHREND *Samarai Affair* xi. 109 O.K. sarge. Do we..wait till you've had him photoed?

photo- (fəʊtəʊ), before a vowel properly **phot-** (but often in full form *photo-* in Eng. compounds), repr. Gr. *φωτο-*, combining form of *φῶς, φωτ-* light.

1. Words in which *photo-* simply denotes 'light'.

photoab'sorbing *ppl. a.*, that absorbs light; capable of absorbing a photon; **photoab'sorption**, absorption of a photon; **photoact** ('fəʊtəʊækt) *Biochem.* = next; **'photoaction** *Biochem.*, a molecular event caused by light; **photo'activate** *v. trans.*, to induce a change in or render active by means of light; hence **photo'activated** *ppl. a.*; **,photoacti'vation**, activation by means of light; **photo'active** *a.*, capable of or involving a chemical or physical change in response to illumination; hence **,photoac'tivity**, the degree to which a substance or system is photoactive; **photo-æs'thetic** *a.* [see ÆSTHETIC], perceptive of light; **photoa'ffinity** *a. Biochem.*, applied to a technique of labelling large molecules (esp. proteins) at specific sites by means of molecules which initially form loose complexes at the active sites and are then photochemically converted *in situ* to reactive forms which immediately bond more permanently; so ***photoaffinity label*** sb. and vb. trans.; **photo'allergy**, an allergy brought about by light; hence **photo-a'llergic** *a.*; **,photoassimi'lation** *Biol.*, photo-synthetic assimilation; so **photoa'ssimilate** *v. trans.*; **,photoauto'trophic** *a. Bot.* [after G. *photoautotrophie* sb. (E. G. Pringsheim 1932, in *Naturwiss.* XX. 479/1)], autotrophic and obtaining energy from light; so **photo-'autotroph**, a photoautotrophic organism; **photobac'terium**, a phosphorescent bacterium; **photobi'ology**, the study of the effects of light on living things; so **,photobio'logical** *a.*, **photobi'ologist**; **photobiotic** (-baɪ'ɒtɪk) *a.* [see BIOTIC], *Bot.*, 'living in the light; an epithet for certain vegetable cells' (*Syd. Soc. Lex.*); **photo'bleaching**, a loss of colour when illuminated; **,photocon'version** *Biochem.*, any reversible chemical change effected by light, esp. that of one form of phytochrome to the other; hence **,photocon'vert** *v. trans.*, to change by photoconversion; **,photocon'vertible** *a.*, capable of undergoing photoconversion; **'photocurrent**, an electric current induced by illumination; **'photodamage**, damage caused by (esp. ultraviolet) light; **,photodensi'tometer**, an instrument for measuring the density of a photographic negative or the opacity of a fluid; hence **,photodensi'tometry**; **photoder'matic** *a.* [Gr. *δέρμα* skin], having a skin sensitive to light; **photode'struction**, destruction brought about by light; **photode'tachment** *Physics*, detachment *of* an electron from an atom caused by an incident photon; **'photodetector**, a device that responds to incident light, esp. one whose operation depends on the electrical effect of individual photons; so **,photode'tection**; **,photodisinte'gration** *Nuclear Physics*, the breaking up of a nucleus by the action of a gamma ray; **'photodrome** [Gr. *-δρομος* -running, -runner, f. *δρόμος* running], an instrument for producing optical effects by flashes of light thrown upon revolving disks bearing figures or devices (Knight *Dict. Mech.* Supp. 1884); **'photoeffect** *Physics*, a photoelectric effect, esp. the emission of an electron from an atom or of a nucleon from a nucleus by the action of a photon; **photoe'jection**, ejection (of an electron from an atom) as a result of the absorption of a photon; **ˌphotoelectro'chemical** *a.*, of, pertaining to, or designating an electrochemical cell in which the electrode potential or the current flowing depends upon the degree of illumination of the cell; **ˌphotoelectromag'netic** *a. Physics* = *photomagnetoelectric* adj. below; **'photoenˌvironment**, the environment formed by light; **photoenzyme** ('fəʊtəʊɛnzaɪm) *Biol.*, an enzyme that catalyses a photochemical reaction; hence **ˌphotoenzy'matic** *a.*, **-enzy'matically** *adv.*; **photo-'epinasty** *Bot.*, 'epinasty consequent upon exposure to bright light' (*Syd. Soc. Lex.*); hence **ˌphoto-epi'nastic** *a.*, pertaining to or of the nature of photo-epinasty; ˌphoto-epi'nastically *adv.*; **ˌphoto-equi'librium**, state of equilibrium in regard to the vibrations of light; **ˌphoto-exci'tation** *Physics*, excitation (sense 5) caused by light or by a photon; so **ˌphotoex'cited** *ppl. a.*; **'photofabriˌcation**, the manufacture of integrated circuits by photo-lithography; **'photofission** *Nuclear Physics*, fission of an atomic nucleus caused by a gamma-ray photon; **'photoformer** *Electronics*, an apparatus for generating a voltage corresponding to a given curve, incorporating a cathode-ray tube, a photo-electric cell, and an intervening opaque mask with an edge cut to the shape of the curve; **ˌphotohetero'trophic** *a. Bot.* [after G. *photoheterotrophie* sb. (E. G. Pringsheim 1932, in *Naturwiss* XX. 479/1)], heterotrophic and obtaining energy from light; hence **ˌphotohetero'trophically** *adv.*; also **photo'heterotroph**, a photoheterotrophic organism; **photo-'hyponasty** *Bot.*, 'hyponasty consequent upon exposure to intense light following upon an arrest of growth' (*Syd. Soc. Lex.*); hence **ˌphoto-hypo'nastic** *a.*, **ˌphoto-hypo'nastically** *adv.*; **ˌphotoinacti'vation** *Biochem.*, destruction by light of the biological activity of an enzyme or other substance; **photo'labile** *a.*, unstable in the presence of light; opp. *photostable* adj. below; hence **photola'bility**; **photo'lithotroph**, a photolithotrophic organism; **photo'lithotrophy** *Bot.* [Gr. λίθος stone + τροφή nourishment], a form of nutrition in which energy is obtained photosynthetically from inorganic compounds; so **ˌphotolitho'trophic** *a.*, characterized by photolithotrophy; **ˌphotomag'netic** *a.*, (*a*) applied to certain rays of the spectrum having, or supposed to have, a magnetic influence; (*b*) = *photomagnetoelectric*; so **photo'magnetism**, photomagnetic property or character; that branch of physics which deals with the relations between light and magnetism; **ˌphotomagˌnetoe'lectric** *a. Physics*, of, pertaining to, or designating an effect observed in some solids, whereby illumination of a solid subjected to a magnetic field parallel to its surface gives rise to a voltage at right angles to both the direction of the field and that of the illumination; **'photomask** *Electronics*, in the manufacture of microcircuits, a photographic pattern through which a photoresist is irradiated with ultraviolet light in order to transfer the pattern on to it; **photo'meson** *Nuclear Physics*, a meson emitted from a nucleus as a result of the interaction of a gamma-ray photon with it; hence **photo'mesic** *a.*, **'photomixer** *Physics*, a device that acts as a mixer (MIXER 2 c) for light waves; so **'photomixing** *vbl. sb.*, the mixing of light waves in a heterodyne or homodyne process; **photo'neutral** *a.*, unaffected in some respect by light; **photo'neutron** *Nuclear Physics*, a neutron released from a nucleus by the action of a gamma-ray photon; **photo'nuclear** *Nuclear Physics*, of or pertaining to the interaction of a photon with an atomic nucleus; **ˌphotoor'ganotroph**, a photoorganotrophic organism; **ˌphoto-organo'trophically** *adv.*; **ˌphotoorga'notrophy** *Bot.* [Gr. τροφή nourishment], a form of nutrition in which energy is obtained photosynthetically from organic compounds; so **ˌphotoorgano'trophic** *a.*, characterized by photoorganotrophy; **pho'topathy** [Gr. -πάθεια, πάθος suffering], the behaviour of an organism towards light, in moving towards or away from an illuminated region; hence **photo'pathic** *a.*; **photope'rimeter** = PERIMETER 2; **'photophil** (also **-phile**) *a.* [-PHIL], loving light, tending towards a lighted region; thriving best in abundant light; *spec.* [after G. *photophil* (E. Bünning 1944, in *Flora* CXXXVIII. 95)], applied to a phase of the circadian cycle of a plant or animal during which light tends to stimulate reproductive activity; **photo'philic** *a. Biol.* = next; **pho'tophilous** *a. Biol.*, light-loving; thriving best in abundant light; **pho'tophily**, the state of being photophilous; **photophob, -e** *a.* [-PHOBE], having an aversion to light, given to retreating into the darkness; **ˌphotophospho'rescent** *a.*, 'becoming phosphorescent from the action of light' (*Syd. Soc. Lex.*); **photo'physical** *a.*, belonging to the physical effect of light (opp. to PHOTOCHEMICAL); so **photo'physics** *sb. pl.* (const. as *sing.*); **'photopigment** *Biol.*, a pigment (e.g. in the eye) whose chemical state depends on its degree of illumination; **'photopile**, an apparatus, resembling a thermopile, sensitive to light, as the sensitive selenium cells in the receiver of a photophone; **ˌphotopola'rimeter**, †(*a*) [ad. F. *photopolarimètre* (A. Cornu in *Compt. Rend. Assoc. Française pour l'Avancement des Sci. 1882* 253)], an apparatus for measuring the proportion of polarized light in a given beam (*rare*⁻⁰); (*b*) a telescopic apparatus for photographing distant objects (as planets) and measuring the polarization of light from them; hence **ˌphotopolari'metric** *a.*, **-pola'rimetry**; **'photo-potential**, an electric potential generated by light; **'photoprocess**, a (biological or chemical) process involving light; **'photoproduct**, a product of the chemical action of light; **'photoproduction**, production by light or by a single incident photon; so **'photoproduced** *ppl. a.*; **photo'protein** *Biol.*, any protein active in the emission of light by a living creature; **photo'proton** *Nuclear Physics*, a proton released from a nucleus by the action of a gamma-ray photon; **pho'topsia, 'photopsy** [Gr. ὄψις vision], 'a subjective sensation of light' (*Syd. Soc. Lex.*); **'photoreaction**, a photochemical reaction; **photore'covery** *Biol.* = PHOTOREACTIVATION; **photo'regulate** *v. trans.*, to regulate (a biological process) by means of light; so **photo'regulated** *ppl. a.*; **ˌphoto-regu'lation**, the act of photoregulating; **photo'regulator**, a biological mechanism that regulates a process according to the duration, intensity, etc., of the light which it detects; **'photorepair** *Biol.*, repair of tissue brought about by the action of (visible or ultraviolet) light; so **photore'pairable** *a.*; **ˌphotore'sistance** *Physics*, (an) electrical resistance that is light-dependent; also, a photoresistor; **ˌphotore'sistive** *a.*, exhibiting photoresistance; **'photoresistor**, a resistor whose resistance varies according to its degree of illumination; **'photoresponse**, a response to light; *esp.* a response of a plant mediated otherwise than through photosynthesis; so **photore'sponsive** *a.*, **-re'sponsiveness**; **photore'versal**, reversal of a (biological) process by the action of light; **photore'versible** *a. Biol.*, capable of being reversed by the action of light; (of a substance) changing from one form into another and back again as the degree of illumination increases and decreases; hence **ˌphotoreversi'bility**; **photo-'sensor**, a sensor that responds to light; **photo'sensory** *a. Biol.*, pertaining to or involving the perception of light; **'photo-shock** *Psychiatry* [ad. F. *photo-choc* (Cossa & Gastaut 1949, in *Ann. Médico-Psychologiques* CVII. 187)], a flash or series of flashes of light given as part of shock therapy; **photo'stable** *a.*, stable in the presence of light; opp. *photolabile* adj. above; so **photosta'bility**; **photo'stationary** *Chem.*, applied to a state of equilibrium in a photochemical reaction in which the rate of dissociation of the reactants equals their rate of recombination; **ˌphotostimu'lation**, stimulation by means of light; so **photo'stimulate** *v. trans.*, **photo'stimulated** *ppl. a.*, **-'stimulating** *vbl. sb.*; also **photo'stimulator**, an apparatus used for photostimulation; **ˌphotostimu'latory** *a.*, pertaining to or involving photostimulation; **'photosurface** *Electr.*, a surface which emits electrons when illuminated; **ˌphotota'chometer** (-tə'kɒmɪtə(r)) [Gr. τάχος swiftness, ταχύς swift: see -METER], an apparatus for determining the velocity of light; so **ˌphototacho'metric, -ical** (also **-tachy-**) *adjs.*, relating to the measurement of the velocity of light; **ˌphotota'chometry**, the measurement of the velocity of light; **'phototele'legraphy**, 'electric reproduction of pictures, writings, etc., at a distance; telephotography' (Funk *Stand. Dict.*); in mod. use, a system of facsimile telegraphy in which variations of tone are adequately preserved; hence **ˌphototele'graphic** *a.*; also **photo'telegram**, a telegram sent by photo-telegraphy; **photo'telegraph**, an apparatus used for phototelegraphy; **photo'telephone** = PHOTOPHONE; **ˌphotothera'peutic** *a.* [see THERAPEUTIC], pertaining to **ˌphotothera'peutics** or **photo'therapy**, a system of treatment of certain skin diseases by exposure to particular light-rays, introduced by N. R. Finsen of Copenhagen; **photo'thermic** *a.* [Gr. θέρμος heat], pertaining to the heating effect of light-rays; **phototo'xicity**, the property of causing a harmful reaction to sunlight; so **photo'toxic** *a.*; **ˌphototransfor'mation**, a transformation (of a chemical compound) effected by light; **photo'transient** *Chem.*, a short-lived molecular species produced by irradiation; **'phototroph** *Bot.*, a phototrophic organism; **photo'trophically** *adv.*; **'phototrophy** *Bot.* [Gr. τροφή nourishment], nutrition in which sunlight is utilized as a source of energy; so **photo'trophic** *a.*, characterized by phototrophy; **ˌphotovol'taic** *a.*, pertaining to, exhibiting, or utilizing the generation of an e.m.f. by light incident on an interface between certain pairs of substances; **photovol'taics** *sb. pl.* (const. as *sing.*), the branch of science and technology concerned with photovoltaic effects and devices; hence **photovol'taically** *adv.*

1966 PHILLIPS & WILLIAMS *Inorg. Chem.* II. xx. 87 A biological system obtains energy from the oxidation of organic substrates or from the action of light on its *photo-absorbing pigments. **1977** I. M. CAMPBELL *Energy & Atmosphere* viii. 252 (*heading*) The generation of the photoabsorbing species and their relative significance. **1966** *Physical Rev.* CXLIX. 55/1 (*caption*) Charge distribution of ions resulting from *photoabsorption primarily in the 3*d* shell of krypton. **1976** *Physics Bull.* Dec. 544/2 The continuum states of two electron atoms and ions can be studied by electron scattering or by photoabsorption. **1971** *Nature* 5 Feb. 372/1 The second possibility is that the mechanism of photosynthesis switches from a reaction involving two photosystems to a simpler form involving but one *photoact. **1971** R. GREGORY *Biochem. of Photosynthesis* ii. 36 Eight separate 'photoacts' are involved, so that we should expect 2500/8, say 300 chlorophyll molecules to be associated with each reaction centre. **1957** *Plant Physiol.* XXXII. 397/2 Since the most probable photoreceptor is the oxidized form of the flavoprotein, the *photoactions are effective in its return to the reduced form. **1965** HENDRICKS & BORTHWICK in T. W. Goodwin *Chem. & Biochem. Plant Pigments* xv. 409 Reversibility of light action .. indicates that the photoactions are conversions of molecular configuration. **1926** *Ann. Rep. Progr. Chem.* XXII. 340 In the case of chlorine,.. W. Taylor draws the conclusion that only absorption within the continuous absorption band will *photoactivate the gas. **1959** *Mycologia* LI. 87 Pigmentation was photo-activated. Light of wave lengths between 390 and 513 mμ stimulated the production of colour. **1926** *Ann. Rep. Progr. Chem.* XXII. 360 In general, the 'electron-loosening' mechanism of Stark .. describes the state of a *photo-activated molecule better than the other conceptions put forward by photochemists. **1954** *Jrnl. Res. Nat. Bureau of Standards* (U.S.) LIII. 125 (*heading*) Catalytic photoactivated polymerization of tetrafluoroethylene. **1925** *Phil. Mag.* XLIX. 1116 (*heading*) A note on the *photo-activation of chlorine. **1974** *Physiologia Plantarum* XXXII. 228 (*heading*) Action spectrum for photoactivation of the water-splitting system in plastids of intermittently illuminated wheat leaves. **1908** *Physical Rev.* XXVI. 541 A study of *photo-active effects produced by illuminating one electrode only, no external electromotive force being applied. **1951** *Sci. News* XXII. 75 Perhaps indeed the carotenoids were the primaeval photoactive pigments which in the course of evolution of green plants and algae have been functionally although not physically replaced by .. chlorophyll. **1975** *Nature* 10 Apr. 507/2 The properties of an organic photovoltaic cell in which the photoactive material is microcrystalline chlorophyll-*a*. **1915** *Physical Rev.* V. 45 This value of current was used in comparing the *photo-activity of solutions. **1970** *Biochim. & Biophys. Acta* CCXXIII. 444 The photoactivity was measured by observation of the blue-shift. **1880** ALLMAN in *Jrnl. Linn. Soc., Zool.* XV. 137 Ascribing to the marginal bodies of the Hydroid Medusae a *photo-aesthetic function. **1970** H. KIEFER et al. in *Prov. Nat. Acad. Sci.* LXVII. 1688 The method of affinity labeling is in widespread use for attachment of covalent labels at the active sites of protein molecules. The usual affinity-labeling reagent has the structure R—X, where R is the portion of the molecule that binds specifically and reversibly to the active site under study, and X is a chemically reactive group, such as diazonium or haloacyl... In *photo-affinity labeling, a reagent R—P is used, where P is a group that is ordinarily unreactive, but which can be converted by photolysis to an exceedingly reactive intermediate P*. Those molecules of R—P that are reversibly bound to the active sites react instantaneously upon conversion to R—P* before they can dissociate from the site. **1970** *Proc. Nat. Acad. Sci.* LXVII. 1694 Binding sites of similar specificities in the same membrane preparation .. may be photo-affinity labeled by the same reagents. **1976** *Nature* 29 Apr. 802/1 Without irradiation the photoaffinity label reversibly inhibited the potassium conductance .. whereas the sodium conductance was not affected. **1978** *Nature* 12 Jan. 157/1 The modified pheromone is radioactively labelled, and since the carbene is generated photolytically, the process is called photoaffinity labelling. **1939** *Jrnl. Investigative Dermatol.* II. 45 (*heading*) Mechanism of the *photoallergic reaction. **1968** HJORTH & FREGERT in A. J. Rook et al. *Textbk. Dermatol.* I. 300/1

Photo-allergic reactions can resemble sunburn. **1976** *Lancet* 20 Nov. 1116/1 Chloroquine.. is also used in.. photoallergic reactions. **1939** S. Epstein in *Jrnl. Investigative Dermatol.* II. 45 These experiments demonstrate a true allergic type of photosensitivity (*photoallergy). As far as I can see, this is the first report of this particular type of photosensitization and the first experimental proof of the allergic nature of this form of light sensitivity. **1976** *Arch. Dermatol.* CXII. 1124/1 The diphenhydramine photoallergy was elicited by long-wave ultraviolet light. **1922** *Jrnl. Soc. Dyers & Colourists* XXXVIII. 8/1 The green pigment chlorophyll has been shown by Willstätter to be an equilibrium mixture of chlorophyll A and chlorophyll B... This equilibrium is not appreciably altered when *photo-assimilation of CO_2 is taking place. **1975** *Nature* 9 Oct. 490/2 The ability of the cyanobacterium to *photoassimilate CO_2 in reactions driven by photosystem I alone and using Na_2S was demonstrated ..; no photoassimilation was observed in the absence of sulphide or light. **1951** J. W. Foster in Werkman & Wilson *Bacterial Physiol.* 363 *Photoautotrophs are those which utilize light. **1974** *Encycl. Brit. Macropædia* X. 896/1 A green plant is a typical example of a photoautotroph. **1943** *Physiol. Rev.* XXIII. 350 This.. implies that the organism so operating must be capable of carrying out conversions of organic compounds. Theoretically it should even be able to grow heterotrophically on the proper organic substrates. Many of the *photo-autotrophic organisms have yielded to this treatment. **1975** *Nature* 25 Dec. 715/1 Manganese is required for the photoautotrophic growth of O_2-evolving organisms. **1977** A. Hallam *Planet Earth* 189 This may bear some relation to the rapid evolution of photoautotrophic organisms such as blue-green algae. **1900** *Lancet* 13 Oct. 1087/1 The peculiar greenish glow seen upon stale haddocks and other sea fishes is produced by this remarkable *photo-bacterium... By protracted exposure they [photobacteria] may be photographed by their own light. **1907** *Chem. Abstr.* I. 190 (*heading*) The *photobiological sensitizers and their proteid compounds. **1976** *Sci. Amer.* Feb. 119/1 The results of the experiment.. also rule out for the wasp any model of a clock in which light induces, or starts, diapause or development by photobiological means other than mere entrainment. **1958** *Plant Physiol.* XXXIII. 447/1 Robert Bruce Withrow died on April 8, 1958... With his passing this country lost one of its prominent *photobiologists. **1973** *Nature* 6 July 37/1 Wald has therefore suggested that photobiologists should plot spectral functions on a frequency scale. **1935** *Science* 31 May 526/2 The cure of rickets by ultra-violet light constitutes one of the most interesting chapters in *photo-biology. **1941** H. F. Blum *Photo-dynamic Action* i. 3 Although.. the phenomenon has been found to have a more limited significance in photobiology, the name photodynamic action has persisted. **1968** *New Scientist* 5 Dec. 579/2 This Penguin survey is a valuable guide to the present knowledge and research work in photobiology. **1937** *Ann. Rep. Progr. Chem.* XXXIII. 426 Considerations of the *photo-bleaching of fluorescent dyes in an oxygen-free atmosphere by the action of ferrous salts. **1974** *McGraw-Hill Yearbk. Sci. & Technol.* 127/2 Light conversion in photo-active chlorophyll is accompanied by photobleaching and by the simultaneous appearance of a free or unpaired electron. **1952** *Jrnl. Chem. Soc.* 4524 The *photoconversion of (I) and (III) into coloured forms does not occur with light of wave-lengths greater than about 540 mμ. **1964** *Photochem. & Photobiol.* III. 521 The absorption spectra of the two forms of phytochrome show, in addition to the major absorption bands in the red and far-red regions, minor bands in the blue and near u.v. which are also effective in the photoconversions of phytochrome, $P_R \rightleftharpoons P_{FR}$. **1971** *Nature* 27 Aug. 602/1 The implication is that acetylcholine is involved in electrical changes in the plant which presumably follow the photoconversion of phytochrome. **1962** *Jrnl. Physical Chem.* LXVI. 2476/1 Any X formed from B being immediately *photoconverted into A. **1970** *Nature* 15 Aug. 666/1 The axis of orientation of the chromophores is parallel to the plasmalemma surface in the P_R form, but is changed to an orientation at 90° to the surface of the plasmalemma when photoconverted to P_{FR}. **1962** *Jrnl. Physical Chem.* LXVI. 2469/2 Only this isomer is *photoconvertible into the spiropyran by visible light. **1913** H. S. Allen *Photo-Electricity* x. 127 The proportionality factor between light absorption and *photocurrent is only independent of the angle of incidence ϕ for an electric vector.. vibrating at right angles to the plane of incidence. **1913** *Physical Rev.* I. 74 The photocurrent-potential curve was almost identical with that furnished by the mercury lamp. **1936** *Discovery* May 151/2 This type of light-sensitive cell.. requires no battery to obtain the photo-current. **1974** *Nature* 26 Apr. 804/1 Light-induced release of protons might thus provide an alternative mechanism for generation of the photocurrents. **1973** *Nature* 12 Jan. 133/1 This demonstrates the potential importance of the excited states of tryptophan as intermediates in lens *photodamage. **1977** I. M. Campbell *Energy & Atmosphere* ix. 348 The link between DNA photodamage in living tissue cells and carcinogenesis by radiation is somewhat empirical. **1928** *Jrnl. Optical Soc. Amer.* XVI. 222 A self-registering *photodensitometer has been described in which the direct-reading method and a thermocouple are employed. **1949** *Jrnl. Appl. Physics* XX. 129/2 The specimen containing the diffused Na^{24} was placed directly on the emulsion for one-half hour... The plate was then developed and analyzed in a photo-densitometer. **1971** *Nature* 19 Feb. 572/1 For most plant shoots, however, the change in methylene blue concentration is far too small to be accurately measured using standard photodensitometers. **1971** *Ibid.* 16 July 185/1 The haloes were also evident in a photodensitomer profile across a cloud bank image, and extended 1 km from the cloud edge. **1965** *Biochemistry* (Easton, Pa.) IV. 1653/2 Sometimes absorption optics are used on the ultracentrifuge, and in this event concentrations are measured by *photo-densitometry. **1889** *Nature* 15 Aug. 384/2 Although these mollusks possess no eyes, they display extreme sensibility to light... It also appears that the *photodermatic (receptive) function is stimulated by luminous vibrations from without. **1964** *Jrnl. Cell Biol.* XXII. 448/2 The most conspicuous structural change in the plastids during the 1 to 3 hours of *photodestruction of the pigments is the formation of stacked lamellar structures. **1977** I. M. Campbell *Energy & Atmosphere* ix. 371 The minimum in the altitude concentration profile of nitric oxide with altitude near to 70 km is evidently a reflection more of the variation of production rate with altitude than of the variation of the photodestruction rate. **1943** *Phil. Trans. R. Soc.* A. CCXXXIX. 278 (*heading*) *Photodetachment of electrons from normal O^- ions. **1973** *Nature* 26 Oct. 450/2 The profiles.. confirmed the hypothesis that the daytime D region of the ionosphere below 80 km may be formed by photo-detachment of electrons. **1959** *Rev. Sci. Instruments* XXX. 593/1 The application of the parametric amplifier principle to *photodetection. **1972** S. S. Charschan *Lasers in Industry* ix. 523 In direct photodetection, all optical frequency and phase information is lost. **1947** *Proc. Nat. Electronics Conf. 1946* 171 (*heading*) *Photodetectors for ultraviolet, visible and infrared radiation. **1959** *Proc. IRE* XLVII. 1475/1 Until the early 1950's, the development of infrared photodetectors revolved principally around polycrystalline films of PbS, PbSe, or PbTe. **1967** *New Scientist* 16 Nov. 416/1 The infrared radiation falls on the photodetector and produces visible radiation from the photoemitter. **1972** S. S. Charschan *Lasers in Industry* ix. 529 Quantum or photo-detectors depend on the action of light quanta on a single electron rather than on the absorption and distribution of energy over an entire macroscopic body. **1935** *Proc. R. Soc.* A. CLI. 481 The next point of interest is the probability of the '*photo'-disintegration. *Ibid.* 482 The effect of the γ-rays of radium in producing the photo-disintegration was also examined. **1942** J. D. Stranathan *'Particles' of Mod. Physics* xi. 444 Another illustration of photodisintegration is that of $_4Be^9$. This reaction is $_4Be^9 + h\nu \rightarrow {}_4Be^8 + {}_0n^1$. **1968** D. D. Clayton *Princ. Stellar Evolution & Nucleosynthesis* vii. 519 What happens then, as the temperature rises, may be described as a redistribution of loosely bound nucleons into more tightly bound states. We choose to call this process.. photodisintegration rearrangement. **1903** *Encycl. Brit.* XXXV. 729/4 (Index), *Photo-effect. **1913** H. S. Allen *Photo-Electricity* i. 8 For substances which show only a 'normal' photo-effect the specific photo-electric activity increases continuously as the wave-length diminishes. **1938** R. W. Lawson tr. *Hevesy & Paneth's Man. Radioactivity* (ed. 2) x. 123 These [γ-]rays are able to bring about nuclear photo-effects by the ejection of neutrons from the nuclei of various elements. **1960** R. H. Bube *Photoconductivity of Solids* i. 2 Two new photoeffects were discovered in the early 1930s. In 1931, Dember.. reported that a potential difference was developed in cuprous oxide in the direction of the light. **1974** *Encycl. Brit. Macropædia* XV. 439/2 The photoeffect probability goes as approximately the fifth power of the atomic number of the absorbing material. **1966** *Physical Rev.* CXLIX. 55/1 *Photoejection of a $3d$ electron. **1977** I. M. Campbell *Energy & Atmosphere* i. 2 The photoejection of electrons from a metal surface irradiated with monochromatic.. light. **1972** *Nature* 7 July 37/2 If the energy of light is used effectively in an electrochemical system, it should be possible to decompose water with visible light. Here we describe a novel type of *photo-electrochemical cell which decomposes water in this way. **1976** *Ibid.* 9 Sept. 100/1 Better and cheaper means of storing electricity.. remain desirable, and hence the practical importance of photo-electrochemical decomposition of water into hydrogen and oxygen. **1953** *Proc. Physical Soc.* B. LXVI. 743 If the slab [of germanium] is placed in a magnetic field perpendicular to the direction of illumination, a voltage is produced at right angles to both field and illumination (*photoelectromagnetic effect). **1965** K. F. Hulme in C. A. Hogarth *Materials used in Semiconductor Devices* vi. 153 The theory and the constructional details and performance of a practical room-temperature photo-electromagnetic detector have been given. **1965** M. Evenari in E. J. Bowen *Recent Progress in Photobiol.* v. 161 The ocean of light which constitutes the *photoenvironment. **1973** *Nature* 6 July 37/1 The adrenal cortex, thyroid and pineal of birds are affected by the photoenvironment. **1962** *Jrnl. Gen. Physiol.* XLV. 703 (*heading*) *Photoenzymatic repair of ultraviolet damage in DNA. **1975** *Nature* 17 Apr. 627/1 If ultraviolet biological damage can be reversed by true photoenzymatic repair, then dimers have a major role in the production of that damage. **1966** *Adv. Radiation Biol.* II. 23 A *photoenzymatically reversible competitive inhibition of transforming DNA repair *in vitro*. **1960** *Photoenzyme [see photoreactivating *ppl. a.*]. **1966** *Adv. Radiation Biol.* II. 19 This type of PR [*sc.* photoreactivation] does not result from the same type of photoenzyme. **1890** *Cent. Dict.*, **Photo-epinastic... *Photo-epinastically... *Photo-epinasty.* **1924** H. S. Taylor *Treat. Physical Chem.* II. xviii. 1239 With constant illumination, between reaction temperatures of 50 and 800° C., the *photo-equilibrium is the same, regardless of the gas temperature. This indicates that the temperature coefficient of the two photo-processes is the same. **1962** *Jrnl. Physical Chem.* LXVI. 2472/2 In reversible photoisomerizations photoequilibrium is established when the rates of the two opposing photoreactions A ⇌ B under the action of the particular photoactive light used, are equal. **1974** *Chem. Soc. Rev.* III. 332 As the sensitizer energy is reduced the efficiency of sensitization of the *cis*-isomer falls below that of the *trans*. As a result there is a region where the *trans*-isomer is selectively excited and the proportion of *cis*-isomer at photoequilibrium is greater. **1918** *Physical Rev.* XI. 485 Having followed the kathodo phosphorescence for 300 seconds by the usual well-known method of a single excitation and determined the form of the curve of decay, the relation of this curve to that obtained by *photoexcitation is of importance. **1946** *Nature* 2 Nov. 603/2 In the large gap region it was necessary to increase the stress above that calculated, to provide the required photoexcitation. **1975** *McGraw-Hill Yearbk. Sci. & Technol.* 357/1 In photoconductors the carriers can be generated internally by photoexcitation. **1954** *Ann. Rev. Plant Physiol.* V. 277 In basic solvents like pyridine, *photoexcited chlorophyll can be reduced by ascorbate. **1970** *Physics Bull.* Nov. 488/2 The migration of photoexcited electrons out of regions of high optical excitation to be entrapped in regions of low optical excitation. **1967** *Sci. Amer.* Apr. 47 *Photofabrication starts with drawings and by chemistry and optics transforms them into the objects, usually with a linear reduction in scale. **1968** *Physics Bull.* Dec. 423/1 The application of holography to.. the photofabrication of microcircuits. **1939** *Physical Rev.* LVI. 449/2 We can form an estimate of the cross section for *photo-fission by comparison with the yields of photoneutrons. **1974** *Encycl. Brit. Macropædia* XIV. 299/2 More complicated [photonuclear] interactions involve either the emission of heavier particles.., many particles, or photofission. **1949** *Electronics* Feb. 100/1 The *Photoformer, as it is called since it generates waveshapes through the use of a cathode-ray tube and phototube, is fed with a sawtooth voltage of the desired frequency. **1965** *Math. in Biol. & Med.* (Med. Res. Council) i. 38 Figure 3 shows how an analogue computer is used to resolve such a curve into its components... A voltage generated from the curve by a photoformer is compared with the sum of exponentials generated in the computer. **1951** J. W. Foster in Werkman & Wilson *Bacterial Physiol.* 364 The above two classes of autotrophs have their counterparts in the heterotrophic bacteria. Thus there are chemoheterotrophs and *photoheterotrophs... The latter are a specialized photosynthetic group which is capable of using for growth both radiant energy and preformed organic matter. **1963** *Studies on Microalgae & Photosynthetic Bacteria* (Jap. Soc. Plant Physiologists) 465 Two characteristic facultative photoheterotrophs.. have been examined for response to nitrate under various conditions of growth. **1945** E. I. Rabinowitch *Photosynthesis* I. v. 106 The metabolism of the '*photoheterotrophic' bacteria—that is, bacteria which require light for the assimilation of organic nutrients, seemed at first to be quite different from that of the 'photautotrophic' bacteria. **1975** *Nature* 18 Dec. 631/1 Typical purple bacteria produce large quantities of molecular hydrogen during photoheterotrophic growth on organic acids. **1972** *Science* 27 Oct. 404/3 Under anaerobic conditions in the light, cultures [of flexibacteria] grow *photoheterotrophically. **1938** *Recueil des Travaux bot. Néerlandais* XXXV. 12 The decrease of the curvature with auxin-a by light must be ascribed to the *photo-inactivation of the auxin-a-lactone. **1973** *Biochemistry* (Easton, Pa.) XII. 2540/2 Studies.. on the photoinactivation of a purified bovine kidney mutarotase were undertaken. **1937** *Nature* 25 Sept. 545/1 In the chicken retina, which contains principally cones, attempts to identify *photo-labile pigments heretofore have failed. **1975** *Ibid.* 31 Jan. 316/2 Some photolabile metabolite accumulates until a threshold concentration is reached. **1961** Webster, *Photolability. **1968** *Arch. Biochem. & Biophysics* CXXIII. 109 (*heading*) Formation and photolability of a methyl cobalamin enzyme. **1958** R. Y. Stanier et al. *Gen. Microbiol.* 669 The most familiar examples of the *photolithotrophs are the green plants, which use water as a hydrogen donor in photosynthesis. **1971** J. S. Poindexter *Microbiol.* xxi. 473 Ectotrophic mycorrhizae are found in many forest trees... Generally, these trees are photolithotrophs as adults, and their seeds contain sufficient organic nutrients to provide the energy for germination and development of photosynthetic capacity. **1976** *Nature* 18 Mar. 200/2 Photolithotrophs such as *Thiorhodaceae* or purple sulphur bacteria and *Chlorobacteriaceae* or green sulphur bacteria, learned, through photochemical promotion, to use inorganic reductants as electron donors. **1958** R. Y. Stanier et al. *Gen. Microbiol.* xiv. 292 For the enrichment of chemolithotrophic and *photolithotrophic organisms, organic compounds must be omitted from the medium, and CO_2 or bicarbonate must be used as the only source of carbon. **1972** Goodwin & Mercer *Introd. Plant Biochem.* i. 3 The phototrophic bacteria are subdivided into photolithotrophic bacteria (e.g. green and purple sulphur bacteria) whose growth is dependent on exogenous inorganic hydrogen donors.. and photo-organotrophic bacteria (e.g. purple, non-sulphur bacteria) whose growth is dependent on exogenous organic hydrogen donors. The biochemistry of photolithotrophic bacteria is related to that of green plants. **1947** *Cold Spring Harbor Symp. Quant. Biol.* XI. 302 The following terminology is hereby proposed to characterize nutritional types [of microorganism]... A. *Phototrophy* . Energy chiefly provided by photochemical reaction. 1. *Photolithotrophy. Growth dependent on exogenous inorganic H-donors. 2. Photoorganotrophy. Growth dependent on exogenous organic H-donors. B. *Chemotrophy*. Energy provided entirely by dark chemical reaction. **1969** F. E. Round *Introd. Lower Plants* i. 2 Photolithotrophy is the common photosynthesis of plants possessing chlorophyll a and using water as the hydrogen donor. **1858** Mayne *Expos. Lex.* 948/2 **Photomagnetic.* **1959** R. A. Smith *Semiconductors* viii. 315 From equations (309) and (328) we may obtain an expression for the ratio of the photo-magnetic current per unit magnetic field to the photo-conductive current per unit electric field. **1975** *Physics Bull.* Jan. 15/1 The materials in which such 'photomagnetic' phenomena have been observed so far are magnetic insulators or semiconductors. **1864** Webster, **Photomagnetism*, the relation of magnetism to light. *Faraday*. **1934** *Physik. Zeitschr. der Sowjetunion* V. 597 (*heading*) On the explanation of the *photomagnetoelectric effect in semi-conductors. **1967** R. H. Bube in Willardson & Beer *Semiconductors & Semimetals* III. xi. 473 The photomagnetoelectric (PME) effect provides a technique for the determination of minority-carrier lifetimes. **1965** W. R. Runyan *Silicon Semiconductor Technol.* iv. 76 Silicon dioxide is very convenient to use as a mask since it can be easily delineated by standard *photomask techniques. **1977** *Sci. Amer.* Sept. 114/3 Thus each photomask, typically a glass plate about five inches on a side, has a single pattern repeated many times over its surface. **1952** R. E. Marshak *Meson Physics* iii. 104 The *photomesic production process probably leads, in the majority of cases, to excited states of the final nucleus having smaller spins than 4. **1974** (*title*) Photomesic and photonuclear reactions and investigation methods with synchrotrons. **1950** A. S. Bishop *Photoproduction of Mesons from Hydrogen* (Univ. of Calif. Radiation Lab., UCRL-874) 40 By definition, $\sigma(E_{ph})$, the excitation function at 90° for *photo-meson production from protons, constitutes the probability that a photon of energy E_{ph}, interacting with a proton, will produce a meson at 90° in the laboratory system. **1951** *Physical Rev.* LXXXI. 189/1 The angular dependence of the nuclear cross section for photo-meson production.. yields fairly direct information concerning the momentum distribution with[in] the nucleus. **1954** *Ibid.* XCV. 592/2 (*heading*) Negative-to-positive ratio of photomesons from deuterium. **1955** *Ibid.* XCIX. 1694/2 It is in the photoelectric mixing tube, or *photomixer,..that the beat frequency is generated. **1975** *Nature* 13 Feb. 515/1 We have built a heterodyne spectrometer using.. a HgCdTe photodiode as a photomixer. **1962** *Appl. Optics* I. 51/1 This paper reports the observation of microwave signals produced by *photomixing of near-neighbour axial mode components in the output spectrum of a ruby optical maser. **1966** M. Ross *Laser Receivers* iv. 125 Photomixing has been successfully achieved under laboratory conditions. However, no operational receiver incorporating photomixing has yet been announced. **1950** CURTIS & CLARK *Introd. Plant Physiol.* xx. 630 Some plants are evidently highly indifferent to the photoperiod with respect to their flowering behavior and will flower over almost any photoperiod ranging from a 5-hr daily exposure to a 24-hr, or continuous, exposure. Some of the plants that fall into this indeterminate, or *photoneutral, group are buckwheat, sunflower, tomato, cotton, and dandelion. **1975** *Nature* 25 Dec. 712/2 Natural populations of *D. melanogaster* and *D. pseudoobscura* are photoneutral in general, but respond rapidly to selection for positive or negative phototactic behaviour. **1935** *Proc. R. Soc.* A. CLI. 488 The angular distribution of the *photo-neutrons from beryllium was investigated. **1975** K. G. MCNEILL et al. in Jochim & Ziegler *Interaction Stud. in Nuclei* 451 Predictions have been made of the angular distributions of the photoprotons emitted from ^{40}Ca and going to the ground state of ^{39}K..and of the distribution of ground state photoneutrons. **1949** *Science* 2 Dec. 579/1 There is an appreciable background of *photonuclear stars and proton tracks. **1959** DEUTSCH & KOFOED-HANSEN in E. Segrè *Exper. Nucl. Physics* III. x. ii. 305 Photonuclear reactions are sometimes used for the detection of high-energy gamma-rays and for the measurement of their energies. **1973** *Physics Bull.* Nov. 694/3 The program will cover effective interactions in light nuclei, photonuclear reactions, neutron scattering below 15 MeV, [etc.]. **1965** A. H. ROSE *Chem. Microbiol.* iii. 40 Thus we arrive at the following four nutritional categories of micro-organisms based on their energy-yielding metabolism: photolithotrophs, *photoorganotrophs, chemolithotrophs and chemoorganotrophs. **1976** *Nature* 18 Mar. 200/2 Photo-organotrophs such as purple non-sulphur bacteria use as electron donors in the light, in anaerobic conditions, those organic electron donors which were used by fermenters in the dark. **1958** R. Y. STANIER et al. *Gen. Microbiol.* xiv. 292 Since the *photoorganotrophic bacteria require various growth factors, a small amount of yeast extract is generally added to the enrichment medium. **1972** Photoorganotrophic [see *photolithotrophic* adj. above]. **1971** J. S. POINDEXTER *Microbiol.* xiii. 154 The few types of algae that can grow *photoorganotrophically are aerobes. **1947** *Photoorganotrophy [see *photolithotrophy* above]. **1897** C. B. DAVENPORT *Exper. Morphol.* I. 185 A phototactic or *photopathic response has not hitherto been certainly observed in this group. **1897** *Ibid.* 180 Control of the Direction of Locomotion by Light—Phototaxis and *Photopathy. [*Note.*] The second includes the wandering of organisms into a more or less intensely illuminated region. **1897** C. B. DAVENPORT *Exper. Morphol.* I. 181 According as the migration is towards or from the more intensely illuminated area, we can distinguish positive (+) and negative (−) photopathy; and correspondingly we.. speak of the organisms themselves as *photophil or photophob. In this nomenclature I follow Graber. *Ibid.* 194 Among Echinodermata, Asteracanthion rubens..appears to be photophil, and Asterina gibbosa..to be photophob. **1952** *Physiologia Plantarum* V. 81 Bünning concluded that light is favourable to flowering during the 'rising' or photophile phase of the leaf movement, and inhibiting during the falling or scotophile phase. **1964** E. BÜNNING *Physiol. Clock* xiv. 122 During the long dark period the plants endogenously reach a second 'photophil' state. **1965** *Plant Physiol.* XL. 873/1 Light during the photophil phases may stimulate flowering to such an extent that..nearly every bud on the plant responds. **1975** D. VINCE-PRUE *Photoperiodism in Plants* v. 170 He [*sc.* Bünning] proposed that photoperiodism involves a regular oscillation of phases or half-cycles with different sensitivity to light, and postulated that transfer to light sets in motion a *photophile* (or light-loving) phase, which is followed about twelve hours later by a *skotophile* (dark-loving) phase, also of twelve hours duration. **1900** A. J. EWART tr. *Pfeffer's Physiol. Plants* I. vii. 358 Even for light-loving (*photophilic) plants bright diffuse daylight seems as a general rule to be preferable to strong sunlight. **1967** M. E. HALE *Biol. Lichens* v. 72 Photophilic algae as *Pleurococcus*, when lichenized would be inhibited by reduced light. **1905** I. B. BALFOUR tr. *C. E. von Goebel's Organogr. Plants* II. 463 They [*sc.* geophilous shoots]..are united by many intermediate stages with '*photophilous' shoots. **1967** M. E. HALE *Biol. Lichens* vii. 87 The photophilous (light-loving) characteristics of most lichens. **1934** WEBSTER, *Photophily. **1960** *Cold Spring Harbor Symp. Quantitative Biol.* XXV. 241/1 The phase of strongest responsiveness to temperature in both types coincides with maximum responsiveness to light..: with maximum photophily in long-day plants and maximum scotophily in short-day plants. **1974** *Biol. Abstr.* LVII. 762/1 An ecological scale of photophily was developed. **1897** *Photophob [see *photophil adj.* above]. **1888** MELDOLA *Chem. Photogr.* i. (1889) 8 *Photo-physical changes requiring more or less time for their completion. **1889** *Athenæum* 26 Oct. 562/3 The author discriminates between photo-physical changes, that is, those in which the chemical composition of the substance exposed to light is in no way altered, and photo-chemical changes. **1914** S. E. SHEPPARD *Photo-Chem.* p. vii, There exists..some difference of opinion as to the desirability of incorporating a discussion of photo-physical and radiation phenomena and laws in a work on photo-chemistry. **1971** *Physics Bull.* Sept. 546/1 (Advt.), A comprehensive treatment is given of the interactions of low energy electrons with atoms and molecules, and photophysical processes. **1976** *Nature* 15 Apr. 654/2 Two chapters deal with photophysical processes: the first is a brief survey of the electronic spectroscopy of complexes. **1961** M. CALVIN in McElroy & Glass *Symposium on Light & Life* 317 A discussion of some of the photochemistry and *photophysics of porphyrins. **1970** J. B. BIRKS *Photophysics of Aromatic Molecules* p. vii, There are six related subjects concerned with the interaction of radiation with molecular systems: photophysics, photochemistry and photobiology, which deal with optical non-ionizing radiation; and radiation physics, radiation chemistry and radiation biology, which deal with ionizing radiation. Photophysics is the keystone of the structure, since it is an integral constituent of each of the other five subjects. **1937** *Nature* 25 Sept. 545/2 The familiar Purkinje effect, for which clearly the extracted *photo-pigments form an adequate chemical basis. **1964** S. DUKE-ELDER *Parsons' Dis. Eye* (ed. 14) xxiv. 364 It [*sc.* colour blindness] is an inherited condition,..and is probably due to the absence of one of the two photopigments normally found in the foveal cones. **1970** HAND & DAVENPORT in P. Halldal *Photobiol. of Microorganisms* ix. 278 The photopigment responsible for photoaxis and photokinesis is probably flavin. **1884** C. LOCK *Workshop Receipts* Ser. III. 180/1 The resistance of the whole *photopile is reduced to a minimum. **1884** KNIGHT *Dict. Mech.* Supp. 675 (title of Fig. 1908) Bell's Photo-pile of Receiver. **1971** *Time* 15 Mar. 46 Light measurements by Pioneer's imaging *photo-polarimeter will enable computers on earth to construct about ten pictures of the planet [*sc.* Jupiter] that will show features as small as 250 miles across. **1972** *Daily Colonist* (Victoria, B.C.) 25 Feb. 5/2 In the last 20 hours before closest approach, the spacecraft's imaging photopolarimeter will take 100 pictures of the planet. **1974** *Nature* 6 Sept. 18/1 The imaging photopolarimeter of Gehrels *et al.* contained a 2·5 cm telescope which made maps of Jupiter. **1971** *Icarus* XV. 454 (*heading*) *Photopolarimetric observations of the minor planet Flora. **1974** *Sci. Amer.* Feb. 43/1 More detailed knowledge of the planet's atmosphere awaits analysis of *photopolarimetry measurements. **1914** *Physical Rev.* IV. 229 The results as a whole confirm the point of view adopted by Richardson and Compton in regard to the relation between *photo- and contact potentials. **1924** *Jrnl. Physical Chem.* XXVIII. 333 Becquerel was the first to observe that the photo-potential of the silver iodide electrode: electrolyte cell was not always positive. **1976** *Nature* 9 Sept. 99/2 If we want to use a semiconductor with an optical bandgap, so as to give optimal utilisation of solar radiation.., the maximum photopotential attainable will be ~0·4 eV. **1924** *Photoprocess [see *photo-equilibrium* above]. **1926** *Trans. Faraday Soc.* XXI. 560 Weigert sees in the photosensitisation of ozone decomposition by chlorine, the simplest possible photoprocess. **1959** W. H. KLEIN in R. B. Withrow *Photoperiodism* III. 207 (*heading*) Interaction of growth factors with photoprocess in seedling growth. **1974** *Photochem. & Photobiol.* XIX. 441/2 The versatility of flavins as photosensitizers in numerous photoprocesses. **1953** *Physical Rev.* XCI. 480/2 The cross section obtained in this way is modified principally by the presence of terms describing the multiple scattering of the *photo produced mesons. **1973** *Physics Bull.* July 431/1 Modulation excitation (ME) spectrophotometry is a technique to measure the absorption spectra of short lived photoproduced transients, such as excited states of molecules. **1926** E. MAYER *Clin. Applic. Sunlight* iii. 30 This action of small doses of radiant energy may be due to toxic '*photo-product'. **1941** *Brit. Jrnl. Psychol.* XXXII. 79 The rate of dark adaptation is supposed..to be determined by the concentration of photoproduct present at each moment. **1977** *Nature* 17 Feb. 660/2 Comparison of spectra taken before and after prolonged irradiation..showed no change in the relative position or intensity of the shoulder, eliminating a permanent photoproduct generated by the high intensity pulse as the species responsible for the shoulder. **1950** *Federation Proc.* IX. 544/1 (*caption*) *Photoproduction of H_2 from succinate by *Rhodopseudomonas gelatinosa*. **1950** A. S. BISHOP *Photoproduction of Mesons from Hydrogen* (Univ. of Calif. Radiation Lab., UCRL-874) 5 From the measured energy distribution of the mesons at 90°..it is possible to determine the excitation function for photoproduction of mesons at 90°. **1961** *Nature* 13 May 602/1 Photoproduction of hydrogen gas by photosynthetic cells was first observed..in the green alga *Scenedesmus*. **1974** FRAUENFELDER & HENLEY *Subatomic Physics* xii. 326 (*caption*) Total cross sections for the photoproduction of neutral and charged pions from hydrogen, as a function of the incident photon energy. **1966** SHIMOMURA & JOHNSON in Johnson & Haneda *Bioluminescence in Progress* 495 Solutions of the protein, for which the general term '*photoprotein' is suggested, show a fluorescence maximum at 458 mμ when excited at 350 mμ. *Ibid.* 497 As a convenient, general designation of the active component in the hydromedusan and *Chaetopterus* type of system, to which the terms 'luciferin' and 'luciferase' do not apply in their usual meaning, we propose the term 'photoprotein'. **1975** *Nature* 17 July 236/2 The photoprotein aequorin (molecular weight about 30,000) isolated from the bioluminescent jellyfish *Aequorea aequorea* emits blue light. **1935** CHADWICK & GOLDHABER in *Proc. R. Soc.* A. CLI. 480 The experimental arrangement for the detection of the protons released from deuterium, which we may for convenience call '*photo'-protons, was as follows. *Ibid.*, An estimate of the energy of the photoprotons can be deduced from the measurement of the size of the oscillograph kicks. **1975** Photoproton [see *photoneutron* above]. **1844** DUNGLISON *Med. Lex.*, *Photopsia. **1858** MAYNE *Expos. Lex.* 649/1 Photopsy. **1889** *Lancet* 28 Dec. 1331/1 In the optic nerve these conditions cause photopsia or flashes of light, flames, sparks, and stars. **1909** *Jrnl. Chem. Soc.* XCV. 442 That most remarkable *photo-reaction which Marckwald..has named phototropy. **1925** H. S. ALLEN *Photo-Electricity* (ed. 2) xiv. 235 Perrin has developed..the view that 'ordinary' chemical reactions may be regarded as due to radiation, *i.e.* they are photo-reactions. **1975** D. VINCE-PRUE *Photoperiodism in Plants* iv. 146 The photoreactions which control the induction of flowering in LDP [*sc.* long-day plants] and SDP [*sc.* short-day plants] are remarkably similar. **1950** *Proc. Nat. Acad. Sci.* XXXVI. 626 The *photorecovery after ultra-violet radiation, manifested by the *Arbacia* egg, seems in all ways parallel to the 'photoreactivation' in fungi and bacteria. **1974** *Encycl. Brit. Macropædia* XV. 390/1 It is probable that photorecovery mechanisms are continually operative in some plants exposed to direct action of sunlight. **1969** *Proc. Nat. Acad. Sci.* LXIV. 1103 The enzymic activity of acetylcholinesterase can be *photoregulated through the mediation of photochromic inhibitors of the enzyme. **1957** *Bot. Gaz.* CXVIII. 207/2 Flowering, seed germination, and certain other *photoregulated phenomena. **1970** *Proc. Nat. Acad. Sci.* LXVI. 853 A systematic study of the interaction of naturally occurring carotenoids with various enzyme systems might provide information useful for an understanding of photoregulated processes found in nature. **1968** *Science* 27 Dec. 1487 (*heading*) *Photoregulation of an enzymic process by means of a light-sensitive ligand. **1970** *Proc. Nat. Acad. Sci.* LXVI. 850 A possible role in photoregulation is suggested for naturally occurring carotenoids. **1959** R. J. DOWNS in R. B. Withrow *Photoperiodism* ii. 129 The woody plant thus appears to be running two different systems with the same *photoregulator. **1970** *Nature* 22 Aug. 778/1 Bieth *et al.* conjecture that carotenoids of animals and plants..might function as photoregulators, controlling diurnal and seasonal changes in metabolic levels. **1967** *Mutation Res.* IV. 22 The impossibility of attaining complete *photorepair of lethal and mutagenic damage raises the important question of whether there is a qualitative difference between damage which is photoreactivable and damage which is not. **1978** *Nature* 31 Aug. 891/1 Forward mutations at a variety of loci in *rad* 1-1 yeast are also subject to photorepair. **1966** *Adv. Radiation Biol.* II. 49 The number of *photorepairable lethal lesions in..DNA. **1978** *Nature* 31 Aug. 890/2 As many as 80% of the extra *lys*$^+$ revertants are photorepairable and therefore dimer-associated in origin. **1925** *Astrophysical Jrnl.* LXII. 317 (*heading*) Apparent *photoresistance effects. **1957** *Chem. Abstr.* LI. 7134 At low levels of ionizing radiation CdS photoresistances exhibited considerable inertness. **1970** *New Scientist* 14 May 335/1 The rate at which the charge of any photo-element leaks away between sweeps depends upon the value of the photo-resistance. **1978** *Nature* 23 Mar. 315/1 The light rays impinged on the photoresistances L_1 and L_2, which formed a bridge circuit with the variable resistances R_1 and R_2. **1933** *Jrnl. Inst. Electr. Engin.* LXXIII. 437/1 The first step towards the conversion of the picture into electrical energy was taken by May in 1873, with his discovery of the *photo-resistive property of selenium. **1973** *Sci. Amer.* Jan. 116/3 Selenium and cadmium photocells are more sensitive, but they are of the photoresistive type and require an external source of power. **1959** *Chem. Abstr.* LIII. 13793 (*heading*) Germanium *photoresistors. **1965** LINDMAYER & WRIGLEY *Fund. Semiconductor Devices* x. 384 Photoresistors made from nearly intrinsic polycrystalline thin films are very sensitive detectors for the average intensity of a wide source spectrum. **1969** *New Scientist* 18 Sept. 568/3 Shamer and Fox observed no fringe shift using..sensitive photoresistors to detect the fringe positions. **1977** J. HEDGECOE *Photographer's Handbk.* 21 (*in figure*) Cds photo-resistor cell. **1950** *Ann. Rev. Plant Physiol.* I. 43 The *photoresponses of plants at different ages or stages of development may be opposite. **1955** HENDRICKS & BORTHWICK in *Proc. 1st Internat. Photobiol. Congr.* i. 23 Photoresponses controlling etiolation of plants and germination of seeds are also examples [of photoperiodism]. **1971** *Jrnl. Appl. Physics* XLII. 568/2 Additional silver increases the photoresponse. **1976** *Nature* 19 Aug. 680/2 For photoresponse spectra, electrodes were illuminated by 400-Hz chopped, monochromatic radiation. **1955** HENDRICKS & BORTHWICK in *Proc. 1st Internat. Photobiol. Congr.* i. 31 Flowering in *photo-responsive plants can be controlled through a single leaf in the presence of other leaves. **1974** *Nature* 26 Apr. 800/2 If the cells of *D. discoideum* are broken gently in a Dounce homogenizer, the photoresponsive pigment sediments with the mitochondrial fraction collected by differential centrifugation between 6,000 and 10,000 g. **1972** *Science* 27 Oct. 421/2 Severance of the optic nerve in immature male ducks decreased the *photoresponsiveness to one-fifth of the normal. **1954** *Bot. Gaz.* CXV. 216/2 (*heading*) *Photoreversal of promotion and inhibition of germination of Grand Rapids lettuce seed at 20°C. after irradiation at 26° and 6°-8°. **1966** *Adv. Radiation Biol.* II. 20 The direct nonenzymatic photoreversal of UV damage to DNA. **1954** HENDRICKS & BORTHWICK in D. Rudnick *Aspects of Synthesis & Order in Growth* vii. 159 Some further details about the several *photoreversibilities. **1955** *Plant Physiol.* XXX. 468 (*heading*) Photoreversibility of leaf and hypocotyl elongation of dark grown red kidney bean seedlings. **1975** D. VINCE-PRUE *Photoperiodism in Plants* iv. 108 Extracts of leaves of several species have been found to show photoreversibility. **1954** HENDRICKS & BORTHWICK in D. Rudnick *Aspects of Synthesis & Order in Growth* vii. 154 The cuticle coloration response..is *photoreversible. **1966** *Adv. Radiation Biol.* II. 21 The photoreversible effects of UV on cytoplasmic entities of cells..formerly suggested RNA damages. **1972** W. SHROPSHIRE in Mitrakos & Shropshire *Phytochrome* p. v, Phytochrome is a photoreversible pigment which can exist in two principal forms. **1962** *Instrument Pract.* XVI. 1519/2 (*heading*) Subminiature *photosensors. **1964** *New Scientist* 4 June 594/2 The photo-sensor is simply a detector which changes light into an electrical signal... Several types exist, such as photo-emissive cells, photo-conductors, photo-voltaic cells, and photo-transistors. **1975** *Physics Bull.* Feb. 82/3 The solid state cameras..replace the bulky Vidicon tube normally used by an array of 10^4 photosensors, which have a broad spectral response. **1919** *Jrnl. Gen. Physiol.* I. 556 The *photosensory responses of an animal like *Mya*. **1972** *Internat. Jrnl. Neurosci.* III. 145 (*heading*) Photosensory cell of the flatworm ocellus. **1953** *Amer. Jrnl. Psychiatry* CIX. 744/1 Although the method for producing convulsions (*photoshock) presented here may be considered similar to that of Metrazol shock, it is our impression that this modified procedure has several possible advantages. **1955** *Sci. News Let.* 21 May 325/1 Instead of electric current, a flashing light is used for 'photo-shock' treatment. **1936** *Jrnl. Gen. Physiol.* XX. 52 The ammoniacal retina bleaches more slowly than the neutral tissue. This difference cannot be ascribed to induced *photostability in the visual purple itself. **1965** J. B. THOMAS *Primary Photoprocesses in Biol.* iv. 85 The acid-resistance as well as the photostability of suspensions of such native chlorophyll are much higher than those of dissolved chlorophyll. **1977** *Protecting World's Crops* (Shell Internat. Petroleum Co.) 2 Recently, however, compounds have been synthesized which combine with photostability remarkable activity against insects. **1921** *Jrnl. Gen. Physiol.* III. 380 The filters are quite *photostable. But in order to avoid any possible bleaching effect, a shutter is placed between the light source and the filter. **1973** Photostable [see *photocatalysed* ppl. adj. s.v. PHOTOCATALYSE *v.*]. **1924** *Trans. Faraday Soc.* XX. 112 The decomposition of sulphur dioxide gas under the action of light radiated from a uviol mercury lamp has been investigated, and the resulting *photostationary state, characteristic of a given set of conditions, determined, using a number of different light filters. **1972** W. HAUPT in Mitrakos & Shropshire *Phytochrome* xxi. 561 Whenever a randomly distributed population of phytochrome molecules is irradiated, light is absorbed by P_r and P_{fr} to different extents... This difference leads to a photostationary state of P_{fr}/P which depends only on the wavelength and which can therefore be predicted precisely. **1956** *Nature* 21 Jan. 143/1 Attempts to *photostimulate tropical birds have been rare, and the results confusing. **1971** *New Scientist* 29 July 255/1 Since it seems that the timing of a light stimulus rather than its duration might be important it is conceivable that a bird could be photostimulated with even very small daily doses of light that would normally be non-stimulatory. **1959** D. S.

FARNER in R. B. Withrow *Photoperiodism* x. 729 In domestic ducks.. both ocular and encephalic receptors are involved in *photostimulated testicular development. **1970** *Proc. Nat. Acad. Sci.* LXVI. 850 *(caption)* Photostimulated *cis-trans* isomerism. **1967** *Ibid.* LVIII. 2129 The initial *photostimulating step.. is postulated as being followed at some stage by release of a 'hormone', the hypothetical 'florigen'. **1937** *Jrnl. Exper. Biol.* XIV. 86 Many shallow-water teleosts,.. when blinded, show a pigmentary response to *photostimulation. **1955** *Sci. News Let.* 21 May 325/1 The flashing light shock is given after patients have had injected into their veins the drug, Azozol... Results were compared with..another group given less intensive 'photostimulation', in which smaller quantities of the drug were used and the light flashes were interrupted oftener. **1959** D. S. FARNER in R. B. Withrow *Photoperiodism* x. 724 These investigations suggest that photostimulation of gonadal development does not involve entirely the same receptors as are involved in vision. **1967** *Psychol. Abstr.* XLI. 1499/1 The role of intermediary structures of the brain in the formation of certain functional relationships in the human CNS was studied, employing single, rhythmic, and interrupted photostimulation in Ss with lesions of the diencephalic region and brain stem. **1971** *Nature* 18 June 465/1 The lamp of the *photo-stimulator was above and behind an animal's head at 110 cm from the centre of the hemisphere. **1976** *Ibid.* 3 June 423/2 *Photostimulatory cues ..influence the hypothalamic input to the pars intermedia. **1939** *Jrnl. Inst. Electr. Engin.* LXXXV. 472/2 The optical picture to be transmitted is focused on a continuous transparent *photo-surface. **1952** *Electronic Engin.* XXIV. 302/1 The spectral response curves of these photosurfaces are compared. **1970** *Proc. IEEE* LVIII. 1794/1 The AgOCs photocathode, the only photosurface to give appreciable response beyond 1 micron until recently. **1886** *Athenæum* 3 July 21/1 An account of Prof. Newcomb's determination.. of the velocity of light. The apparatus employed, to which the name of '*phototachometer' was given. **1882** HARKNESS in *Nature* 30 Nov. 117/2 The solar parallax..cannot be regarded as exactly known until the results obtained from trigonometrical,..and *phototachymetrical methods are in perfect harmony. **1929** *Telegraph & Telephone Jrnl.* XVI. 3/2 *Photo-telegrams will have to be charged by space measurement instead of the number of words. **1948** *Post Office Guide* 283 A reply voucher issued with a phototelegram may be used to prepay an ordinary telegram. **1968** *Guardian* 10 Apr. 8/3 To quote the bleak prose of Her Majesty's Post Office, 'Telex—no service. Phototelegrams —no service. Telephone—no service.' **1909** *Electrical Mag.* XII. 249/1 *(heading)* The Sémat *phototelegraph. **1949** *Post Office Electr. Engineers' Jrnl.* XLI. 189 *(heading)* The Post Office phototelegraph service to Europe. **1959** J. W. FREEBODY *Telegr.* xiii. 538/2 *(heading)* The Muirhead-Jarvis photo-telegraph equipment. **1909** *Electrical Mag.* XI. 57/1 New York, Chicago, and other cities are now about to commence *photo-telegraphic trials. **1940** *Wireless World* Sept. 398/3 The clarity of reception, at a distance of 12,000 miles, of photographs transmitted from the West Base of the U.S. Navy Antarctic Expedition, is attributed to the use of a recently developed phototelegraphic technique to counteract selective fading of the carrier frequency. **1886** W. GEMMILL *Brit. Pat. 4841* 6 It will be seen that the system of *photo-telegraphy opens up an entirely new field in telegraphy, namely the actual reproduction of photographs through the medium of electrically conducting wires. **1930** *Post Office Electr. Engineers' Jrnl.* XXIII. 1/2 British newspapers using photo-telegraphy transmit to and from London and their provincial offices using 'Four-Wire' telephone circuits. **1976** R. N. RENTON *Telegr.* iv. 60/1 Telephone circuits are used as the 'bearer' circuits for multiplex telegraph systems and for phototelegraphy. **1904** *Daily Chron.* 26 Sept. 5/5 Further experiments in *phototherapeutics dealt with the bactericidal effects of concentrated violet rays in cases of lupus. **1899** *Allbutt's Syst. Med.* VIII. 796 The latest addition to our practical resources is the '*photo-therapy' of Finsen of Copenhagen. **1903** *Westm. Gaz.* 24 June 9/1 The new cure of lupus by phototherapy has been most successful. **1891** *Anthony's Photogr. Bull.* IV. 359 The *photothermic energy in the luminous spectrum. **1942** S. EPSTEIN in *Jrnl. Investigative Dermatol.* V. 290, I propose the term '*phototoxicity' for the primary, non-allergic photosensitivity, and '*phototoxic reaction' for the effect produced by this mechanism... Phototoxic reactions apply indiscriminately to all individuals. **1974** M. C. GERALD *Pharmacol.* xxvii. 471 Demeclocycline has been shown to cause phototoxicity in some patients, where severe burns develop when susceptible patients are exposed to sunlight. **1976** *Arch. Dermatol.* CXII. 327/1 The duration of methoxsalen's phototoxic potentiality, after its application to skin, varied in direct proportion to chemical concentration. **1962** *Jrnl. Physical Chem.* LXVI. 2470 The results indicate the occurrence of consecutive and concurrent *phototransformations and thermal interconversions between stereoisomers of the colored modification. **1975** D. VINCE-PRUE *Photoperiodism in Plants* vi. 215 The general conclusion..is that the phototransformation of phytochrome may very rapidly lead to an alteration of membrane properties. **1973** *Physics Bull.* July 431/1 It is obvious that for light induced species with large lifetimes, a simple DC method would suffice to measure their absorption. However, with the short lifetimes associated with excited states, the changes occurring in DC current by the absorption of the *phototransient will be much smaller than the noise. **1975** *Nature* 25 Dec. 767/2 Evidence was obtained that this phenomenon is a consequence of an overlap from a shorter lived phototransient (maximum about 530 nm) which is the precursor of the 410-nm species. **1941** R. P. HALL in Calkins & Summers *Protozoa in Biol. Res.* ix. 477 Some [chlorophyll-bearing protozoa] appear to be obligate *phototrophs. **1965** A. H. ROSE *Chem. Microbiol.* iii. 39 Only a minority of micro-organisms including algae and photosynthetic bacteria and protozoa are able to utilize directly the energy of solar radiation. These organisms are described as phototrophs to distinguish them from chemotrophs. **1975** *Nature* 7 Aug. 463/2 This versatility would give it a clear advantage over other blue-green algae (mostly obligate phototrophs) as well as over bacteria. **1939** H. W. HARVEY in P. D. Trask *Recent Marine Sediments* II. 145 Although plants are occasionally found down to considerable depths, they can only grow and increase down to a depth to which sufficient light penetrates. In clear blue-green water of temperate regions this *phototrophic zone may extend down to 30 or 50 meters in summer time. **1965** PELCZAR & REID *Microbiol.* (ed. 2) vi. 496/2 Phototrophic organisms are regarded as the most important plankton organisms since they are the primary producers of organic matter via photosynthesis. **1972** Phototrophic [see *photolithotropic* adj. above]. **1973** *Biochim. & Biophys. Acta* CCCXXX. 80 *(heading)* Membrane differentiation in *phototrophically growing *Rhodospirillum rubrum* during transition from low to high light intensity. **1947** *phototrophy [see *photolithotrophy* above]. **1959** LAMANNA & MALLETTE *Basic Bacteriol.* (ed. 2) xi. 467 *(heading)* Phototrophy. **1923** *Jrnl. Physical Chem.* XXVII. 601 The terms 'Becquerel effect' and '*photo-voltaic effect' have been used to distinguish between the light-sensitive systems of the electrode-electrolyte type and the well known 'Hallwachs effect' or 'photo-electric effect'. Cells having one or more light-sensitive electrodes of the former type are able to convert radiant energy into electrical energy and have been called 'photo-voltaic cells'. **1943** D. H. JACOBS *Fund. Optical Engin.* xxiii. 377 Some problems in instrument design call for vacuum or gas-filled photoemissive cells, and some call for photovoltaic cells. **1953** AMOS & BIRKINSHAW *Television Engin.* I. iii. 41 An electrode may, however, be sensitive to light in other ways; for example, it may be photo-voltaic, i.e., develop e.m.f.s when illuminated. **1957** *Proc. Inst. Electr. Engin.* CIV. B. 467/1 In 1839 Becquerel had found that, when light fell on two metal electrodes immersed in an electrolyte, a potential difference was established between them; this is now known as the photo-voltaic effect. **1964** *Oceanogr. & Marine Biol.* II. 359 Clark (1933) demonstrated the correlation between diurnal migration of plankton and changes in submarine irradiation by means of a photo-voltaic cell. **1977** *Undercurrents* June–July 8/2 A comparison of fast breeder reactor technology with photo-voltaic (solar cell) technology neatly illustrates the two poles of opinion. **1978** *Solar Energy* (Shell Internat. Petroleum Co.) 5 A second way of using sunlight is *photovoltaically—the direct conversion of sunlight into electricity. **1973** *Physics Bull.* Jan. 53/3 Papers are invited on the following areas: *photovoltaics, thermoelectrics, electrochemical conversion, [etc.]. **1978** *Telegraph* (Brisbane) 16 May 6/2 Photovoltaics is the dream form of solar power—a single cell without moving parts, silent, reliable and pollution free. **1978** *Nature* 13 July 117/1 The United States administration is clearly determined to make a success of photovoltaics.

2. Words in which *photo-* indicates connexion with photography, or some photographic process; being sometimes (esp. in *nonce-wds.*) practically equivalent to PHOTOGRAPHIC, as in ***photo-chart, -cyclist, -equipment, -miniature, -process, -revolver, -survey, -tracing, -transfer.***

photo-'aquatint: see quots.; **,photo-bibli'ography**, description of books by the aid of photography; **'photo-call**, a summoning (cf. CALL *sb.* 6 h) of theatrical performers or the like to be photographed; the session at which they are photographed; **,photo-ce'ramic** *a.*, ceramic (work) decorated by photographic processes; also as *sb.* (*pl.*); hence **photo-'ceramist**, an artist in photoceramic work; **'photo,charger**, a device for photographically recording details of books loaned from a library; so **'photo,charging** *vbl. sb.*; **,photocli'nometry** [CLINO-], the process of deriving topographical information about a region from measurements of the brightness distribution in aerial photographs of it; **photo-'collotype**: see quot.; **photo-'crayon** *a.*, produced by a photographic process giving the effect of crayons, or by crayon-work on a photographic groundwork: see quot.; **,photo-e'lectrotype**: see quot.; so **,photo-e'lectrotyping**; **'photo-,essay**, an essay or short biography consisting of text matter and (numerous) photographs; **photo-'etch** *v. trans.*, to etch by a photographic process, as in photogravure; **'photo-,etcher**, one who employs a photographic process in etching; so **photo-'etching**; **photofac'simile**, facsimile in which the likeness is reproduced in photographic form; usu. *attrib.*; **photo-'filigrane**: see quot.; **photo'fluorogram**, a photograph of a fluoroscopic X-ray image; **photo'fluorograph** *sb.* = prec.; *v. trans.*, to examine by photofluorography; **,photofluo'rography**, photography of a fluoroscopic X-ray image; hence **,photofluoro'graphic** *a.*, **,photofluoro'graphically** *adv.*; **photo'fluoroscope**, an instrument for taking photofluorograms; **,photofluo'roscopy** = *photofluorography* above; **photo'gastroscope**, 'an arrangement for photographing the inside of the stomach' (Woodbury *Encycl. Phot.* 1892); **photo-'gelatin** *a.*, applied to any photographic process in which gelatin is used; **,photogoni'ometer**, (*a*) an instrument for measuring angles indirectly from photographs of an area; (*b*) an instrument for photographically recording the X-rays diffracted at known angles by a crystal or substance; hence **,photogonio'metric** *a.*, **-goni'ometry**; **photo'graphotype**, a method of producing blocks for letter-press printing by the aid of photography and electrotyping; **photo-'hyalotype** = HYALOTYPE; **,photo-'ink** *a.*, produced by photography so as to be printed in ink; **,photo-in'taglio** (-'tɑːljəʊ), a design in intaglio produced by a photographic process; also *attrib.*; **,photointerpre'tation**, the interpretation of aerial photographs; so **photo-in'terpreter**; **photoin'terpretative**, **-in'terpretive** *adjs.*; **photo'journalism**, the use of photographs in journalism; so **photo'journalist**; **photo-'lithotype**, a picture produced by photolithography; **'photo-magazine**, a magazine containing many photographs; **'photomap**, a map consisting of or drawn on a photograph or photomosaic of the area concerned; **photo-'mapping**, the mapping (of the stars, etc.) by photography; so **photo-'mapper**, an instrument for this; **,photo-me'tallograph**, a photozincograph or analogous engraving; so **,photo-meta'llography**; **photo-'mezzotype** (also abbrev. **photo-mezzo**), a photo-mechanical printing process similar to collotype; a print produced by this; **photomo'saic** = MOSAIC *sb.* 3 d; **photo'mural**, a mural consisting of a photograph or photographs; **photo-'nephograph** [Gr. νέφος cloud: see -GRAPH], an apparatus for taking a succession of simultaneous photographs of a cloud from two points at some distance apart, in order to ascertain the height and movement of the cloud; also called **photo-'nephoscope**; **photo'nymograph** *Cartography* [Aeolic Gr. ὄ-νυμ-α name], an instrument used in map production for producing printed names photographically; **,photo-pa'pyrograph**, a plate or print made by **,photo-papy'rography**, a modification of photolithography, in which paper is used as the support, instead of a stone or a metal plate; **'photophane**: see quot.; **'photoplate**, a photographic plate (PLATE *sb.* 5 c); **'photo-'print**, a print produced by a photo-mechanical process; so **'photo-'printing**; **photo'radiogram**, a picture, diagram, or the like transmitted by radio; (formerly a proprietary name in the U.S.); **'photo-,recce**, colloq. abbrev. of next; **photore'connaissance**, reconnaissance by means of aerial photography; **'photo-re'lief**, an image in relief produced by a photographic process; also *attrib.*; **,photo-repor'tage** = *photojournalism* above; also, a report that uses photographs; so **'photo-reporting**; **photo-'rocket**: see quot.; **'photo-scanning** *vbl. sb. Med.*, photography of the pattern of radiation from the body following the internal administration of a radio-isotope (e.g. to locate tumours); so **'photoscan**, a photograph so obtained; **'photoscanner**, an apparatus for taking such photographs; **photo-'sculpture** *sb.*, a process in which the subject is photographed simultaneously from a number of different points of view all round, and the photographs are used to trace successive outlines on a block of modelling clay, which is afterwards finished by hand; hence **photo-'sculptural** *a.*, pertaining to or produced by photo-sculpture; **photo-'sculpture** *v. trans.*, to produce by photo-sculpture; **,photo-spec'troscopy**, the application of photography to spectroscopy; so **,photo-spectro'scopic** *a.*, pertaining to photo-spectroscopy; **photo'stereogram**, a stereophotograph; **photo'stereograph**, an instrument for the observation, measurement, and interpretation of pairs of stereophotographs for surveying purposes; so **,photostereo'graphic** *a.*; **'photo,story**, a story with accompanying photographs; **photo-'telescope**, a telescope with photographic apparatus, used for photographing stars or other heavenly bodies; **,photo-the'odolite**, an instrument for the performance of triangulation by means of photographs; **'photo-,timer**, (*a*) (see quot. 1942); (*b*) (see quot. 1949); **'phototint**, a photo-mechanical printing process similar to collotype, used *c* 1875 (Woodbury *Encycl. Phot.*); **photo-'vitrotype** [L. *vitrum* glass: see TYPE], a photograph printed on glass; **photo-xylography** (-zaɪ'lɒgrəfɪ) [XYLOGRAPHY], a process of employing photography in the preparation of wood blocks for printing from.

1892 WOODBURY *Encycl. Phot.* 503 **Photo-Aquatint*, a process for printing pictures from intaglio copperplates. **1897** *Daily News* 4 Oct. 6/4 The bichromate process, to which has been given the name 'Photo-Aquatint' because there is practically nothing used but pure water-colour fixed by the effect of light acting through a negative. **1878** H. STEVENS *(title)* *Photo-Bibliography, or a Word on Printed Card Catalogues of Old, Rare, Beautiful and Costly Books, etc., with reduced facsimiles of some famous Works issued during the Sixteenth and Seventeenth Centuries. **1891** *Athenæum* 10 Jan. 53/2 The subject of photo-bibliography was one of his [H. Stevens's] pet hobbies. **1958** L. Vining in *Newnes Compl. Amat. Photogr.* xx. 182 Theatre photography can be divided into two classes—*photo calls when you have control of the actors and lights, and photographing from the stalls during the performance, when you have no control of anything. **1966** 'S. Harvester' *Treacherous Road* i. 22 A string of camels kept motionless against the burnt yellow sky, well-trained as pop singers on a photo-call. **1971** *Times* 8 Sept. 3 Sir Bernard, who plays Iago, promised that the official photocall next week would reveal all of Miss Stevenson, and a very lyrical and beautiful sight it would be. **1977** J. Hedgecoe *Photographer's Handbk.* 93 Most photography of theatrical productions takes place under one of two distinct sets of conditions—during an actual public performance, or during a dress rehearsal or specially staged 'photo-call'. **1895** *Daily News* 9 May 3/6 The Princess of Wales has consented to lend her Collection of *Photo-Ceramics to the Exhibition of Photography. **1894** *Amer. Ann. Photog.* 143 A *photo-ceramist of no ordinary merit. **1959** L. M. Harrod *Librarians' Gloss.* (ed. 2) 208 **Photo-charger*, an electrical machine for recording the loan of books on microfilm. **1967** L. V. Paulin in W. L. Saunders *Librarianship in Brit. Today* i. 4 The introduction of more photochargers. **1955** W. Ashworth *Handbk. Special Librarianship* xii. 319 Such devices as audio-charging..and *photo-charging..have been used in America in public libraries. **1967** C. R. Eastwood *Mobile Libraries* ix. 94 Photocharging is widely used on American mobile libraries but not in Britain. **1894** *Athenæum* 4 Aug. 165/3 Comparing the present *photo-charts [of stars] with others obtained by the same processes after the lapse of several years. **1967** *Surveyor III* (U.S. Nat. Aeronaut. & Space Admin. SP-146) iii. 16 *(caption)* *Photoclinometric profiles of the Surveyor III landing site. Profiles were calculated from photometric measurements of Lunar Orbiter III photograph H154..(*photoclinometry by H. E. Holt and S. G. Priebe). **1974** *Nature* 10 May 132/1 The development of inferred topography on the basis of the brightness distribution in the image of a surface exhibiting diffuse reflection, and a knowledge of the quantitative law of light scattering for the kind of surface under scrutiny, has been called photoclinometry by common agreement over the past few years. (The word 'photoclinometry' is due to J. F. McCauley...) An operational photoclinometric theory adapted to light scattering properties peculiar to the Moon was worked out..several years ago. **1975** *Times* 18 June 2/2 A group..specializing in lunar and planetry sciences at Lancaster University..is using a method known as photoclinometry to measure the profiles and heights of hills, craters, ridges and cliffs [on Mercury]; the process depends on assessing subtle changes in brightness of the ground and rocks on the pictures. **1881** Abney *Photogr.* 186 By a *photo-collotype process is meant a 'surface printing' process, by which prints are obtained from the surface of a film of gelatine, or other kindred substance. **1873** E. Spon *Workshop Receipts* Ser. i. 270/1 *Photo-Crayon Portraits. **1892** Woodbury *Encycl. Phot.* 503 *Photo Crayon Process*, a photographic transparency on glass..[was] afterwards backed up with white paper, on which a number of lines, hatchings, or stippling were lithographed, giving the portrait the appearance of a crayon work. **1898** *Westm. Gaz.* 13 July 8/1 A *photo-decorated tile company in Staffordshire. **1875** Knight *Dict. Mech.*, **Photo-electrotype*, a process in which a photographic picture is produced in relief so as to afford, by electro-deposition, a matrix for a cast, from which impressions in ink may be obtained. **1865** in *Abridgm. Specif. Patents, Photogr.* (1872) 118 An improved *photo-electro-typing process. **1891** *Anthony's Photogr. Bull.* IV. 427 A dozen African explorers could be fitted out with the now indispensable *photo-equipment. **1976** *Publishers Weekly* 2 Aug. 104/1 Mexican landscape architect Luis Barragán..in a major book... Seven of his most characteristic works—each briefly prefaced and explored at length in a *photo-essay. *Ibid.* 4 Oct. 65/3 Seven sumptuous photo-essays (more than 300 pictures, many in color). **1977** C. McFadden *Serial* (1978) ix. 24/2 Michael Bry would..do this photo essay on her. **1889** *Photo-etch [see photo-engraving]. **1900** *Athenæum* 21 July 92/1 The plates..have been photo-etched from the author's drawings. **1889** *Year Bk. Photogr.* 158 One difficulty which *photo-etchers have to contend against in the City is the vibration caused by the incessant traffic. **1896** *Daily News* 19 Dec. 3/5 A skilful *photo-etching..after the picture of 'The Ferry'. **1959** K. Henney *Radio Engin. Handbk.* (ed. 5) xxiii. 1 *Photofacsimile systems reproduce the subject copy on photographic papers or films. **1971** *Science* 6 Aug. 529/2 These transmissions, known as the DRIR (direct readout infrared) data, can be displayed on a photofacsimile recorder, which produces a continuous strip image. **1973** *Nature* 16 Feb. 434/2 His youthful German collaborator made a fair copy of Copernicus's precious autograph (now splendidly reproduced in photofacsimile). **1883** *Athenæum* 27 Jan. 124/2 A new process..named '*photo-filigrane', for producing the water-mark in paper by a photographic process. **1942** *Radiology* XXXVIII. 453/2 The initial scrutiny of routine *photofluorograms by the staff radiologist will provide him with an objective means of determining which of all patients..should be referred for searching x-ray examination of the chest. **1975** B. W. Gayler in E. J. Potchen *Current Concepts in Radiol.* II. vii. 131 For many years, mass survey and screening chest radiographs were taken as 70 mm photofluorograms. **1941** *Med. Jrnl. Austral.* I. 267/2 The method of focusing is to make *photofluorographs of a wire mesh mounted immediately in front of the fluorescent screen holder. **1972** *Science* 16 June 1186/3 The American public would be exposed to hundreds of thousands of unnecessary chest photofluorographs each year. **1945** *Amer. Jrnl. Roentgenology* L. 405/2 A subject 20 cm. in thickness *photofluorographed with the roentgen machine operating at 90 kv. **1957** *Ibid.* LXXVII. 1079/1, 101 persons were photofluorographed. **1941** *Med. Jrnl. Austral.* I. 267/2 The four inches by five inches *photofluorographic unit incorporates a special 14 inches by 17 inches fluorescent screen. **1954** *Brit. Jrnl. Radiol.* XXVII. 459/1 An attempt to reduce cost of routine examinations..by employing the photofluorographic method. **1972** J. E. Cullinan *Illustr. Guide X-Ray Technics* i. 24/1 A photofluorographic unit is a quick, efficient way to accomplish mass survey chest radiography. **1949** *Amer. Jrnl. Roentgenology* LXI. 186/1 All patients above the age of forty..will be examined *photofluorographically. **1941** *Med. Jrnl. Austral.* I. 266/1 *Photofluorography opens up a new avenue of examination to the wage-earning class. **1974** *Encycl. Brit. Macropædia* XV. 462/2 Photofluorography and television observation can take place simultaneously by means of separate apertures, and thus observation of what is being photographed is achieved. **1896** J. M. Bleyer in *N.Y. Med. Jrnl.* LXIII. 540/1 The *photo-fluoroscope is an instrument which differs from all other fluoroscopes in the fact that it allows a direct shadow picture to be taken from the screen on the fluoroscope, after it is focused through the screen, and the image is seen on the ground glass in the photographic focusing box. **1933** O. Glasser *Sci. of Radiol.* i. 10 J. M. Bleyer of New York built his photofluoroscope which was destined to become the predecessor of the roentgen moving picture camera. **1955** G. L. Clark *Appl. X-Rays* (ed. 4) ix. 197 *(heading)* *Photofluoroscopy (indirect radiography). **1966** *McGraw-Hill Encycl. Sci. & Technol.* XI. 302/2 The photography of the fluorescent image, as in mass chest examinations, is called photofluoroscopy. **1875** Knight *Dict. Mech.*, **Photo-gelatine Process*, one in which gelatine, prepared chemically, usually by the bichromate of potash, is made to receive a photographic image. **1926** A. W. Judge *Stereoscopic Photogr.* xviii. 218 The effect of tilting and swinging the plate in the *photogoniometer is such as to render the angular measurements..the same as if the view had been taken on a vertical plate. **1927** *Jrnl. Sci. Instruments* IV. 273 *(heading)* A universal X-ray photogoniometer... Combining: apparatus for single crystal rotation photographs—Laue photographs—X-ray spectrometry—powder photographs—photographs of crystal aggregates, metals, materials, etc. **1933** A. R. Hinks *Maps & Survey* (ed. 3) xii. 243 The machines which have been developed during the last few years all utilise..the principle of the *Bildmesstheodolit*, otherwise called the Photogoniometer, in which the plates are viewed through objectives identical with those which took them. **1939** *Geogr. Jrnl.* XCIII. 150 The American Geographical Society first of all made a photogoniometer (*Bild-Theodolit*) on a somewhat novel principle. **1970** *Chem. Abstr.* LXXIII. 305/2 A single-circle universal photogoniometer with vertical crystal-bearing attachment,..was devised. **1939** *Geogr. Jrnl.* XCIII. 242 The first extensive photographic survey was that of the stars, made by Kapteyn..with a *photogoniometric machine he built about 1890. **1968** *Chem. Abstr.* LXIX. 6626/2 *(heading)* Photogoniometric investigation of a crystal surface. *Ibid.*, A goniometric study of crystals is rarely made because labs. often have no goniometer. The goniometric method in many cases can be replaced by photogoniometry. **1939** B. B. Talley *Engin. Applic. Aerial & Terrestr. Photogrammetry* ii. 9 *(caption)* *Photogoniometry by the method of Porro and Koppe. **1874** *(title)* Specimens of *Photo-Graphotype Engraving. **1875** Knight *Dict. Mech.*, **Photo-hyalotype*. **1888** *Athenæum* 14 July 69 Reproduced, with no remarkable success, by the *photo-ink process. **1875** Knight *Dict. Mech.*, **Photo-intaglio Engraving*, a process in which, by photographic means, lines are etched in a plate to be subsequently filled with ink and printed by the copperplate printing-press. **1891** *Anthony's Photogr. Bull.* IV. 181 An early photo-intaglio process. **1923** *Photogrammetric Engin.* VIII. 27 The ..function of exploiting and developing the intelligence from the aerial photos falls within the sphere of *photo interpretation units. **1959** *Proc. Geologists' Assoc.* LXX. 144 It may be necessary..to complete a preliminary photo-interpretation before planning ground traverses. **1966** *Daily Tel.* 20 Aug. 14/5 These pictures will form stereo-pairs and can be analysed by standard techniques of photo-interpretation to give maximum information about the terrain on which American astronauts may land. **1973** *Sci. Amer.* Feb. 21/2 The cost of hardware and manpower for photo-interpretation..will remain high. **1959** *Proc. Geologists' Assoc.* LXX. 144 The best practice is a judicious combination of *photo-interpretative methods and geological field mapping. **1942** *Photogrammetric Engin.* VIII. 26 While the aerial camera sees all, it is the *photo interpreter who must know all and tell all. **1957** *Ibid.* XXIII. 933 A mathematical proof is presented for the statement that differential parallaxes smaller than 0·001 inch cannot be detected by average photo-interpreters. **1977** *Sci. Amer.* Sept. 57/1 Only the wide curve it must make on slopes betrays it to the photointerpreter. **1967** *Boston Sunday Herald* 26 Mar. (Comic Section), I subjected the film to the usual *photo-interpretive analysis. **1944** K. Hubschmann in A. Kraszna-Krausz *Photogr. as Career* 118 My friend proved an excellent teacher of the essentials of *photo-journalism. **1958** M. F. Harker in *Newnes Compl. Amat. Photogr.* xiii. 140 The present trend of photo-journalism which attempts to put over human stories in pictures rather than words. **1976** *National Observer* (U.S.) 11 Sept. 20/1 This colorful chap is Nelson Wadsworth, who teaches photojournalism, magazine writing, and investigative reporting at Brigham Young University in Utah. **1977** *Time* 12 Dec. 60/2 World War II was the longest-running story in the history of *Life*, the magazine that practically invented photojournalism. **1959** C. B. Neblette *Photogr. Lens Manual* ii. 25 After the 50 mm, the 35 mm medium wide-angle, or wide-field lens is undoubtedly the most useful to.. the *photojournalist. **1963** A. E. Woolley *Creative 35mm Techniques* III. 113/2 At all times a photojournalist is aware of the maximum emotion or conflict of the subject of the story. **1974** *Nat. Geographic* Aug. 252 At last I am here in North Korea, the first American photojournalist to gain entry into a country cloistered from the non-Communist world for a quarter of a century. **1978** *New York* 3 Apr. 32/3 Micha Bar Am/Harold Edgerton/Frank Rinehart—Begin and Sadat by this Mid-East photojournalist. **1859** *Sat. Rev.* 26 Feb. 243/1 A process well worth attention..its result may be called a *Photo-litho-type. **1960** *News Chron.* 10 Oct. 4/1 Paris-Match, the most powerful *photo-magazine in Europe. **1969** *Amat. Photographer* 28 May 26/3 Few of the present-day casual photographers and snapshotters do their own processing. The photographic trade and the photo-magazines do not encourage it. **1939** B. B. Talley *Engin. Applic. Aerial & Terrestr. Photogrammetry* xix. 521 When this becomes economically feasible encouragement should be given to the development of '*photo-maps' to which may be added contours. **1955** *Times* 1 Aug. 6/1 The first 200 photographic sky charts..are being sent to observatories all over the world, and when the atlas is completed in 1956 it will include 1,758 such 'photomaps'. **1969** *Nature* 16 Aug. 668/1 *(caption)* Satellite photomap of the Tucson, Arizona, area with transport network superimposed. The map is based on a photograph taken..from Gemini V. **1870** H. M. Parkhurst *Amer. Jrnl. Sci.* Ser. ii. XLIX. 38 The motion of the diaphragm may be produced..by the star-key of my star-mapper; and this constitutes the *Photo-mapper. *Ibid.* 39 In *photo-mapping I place the prism always in the meridian. **1899** *Daily News* 6 June 8/4 The photo-mapping of the heavens by the Astrographic Equatorial. **1875** Knight *Dict. Mech.*, **Photo-metallograph*, see *Photo-zincograph*. **1859** *Sat. Rev.* 26 Feb. 242/2 *Photo-metallography. **1890** *Pall Mall G.* 4 Aug. 6/2 A *photomezzotype of Mrs. General Booth. **1891** *Anthony's Photogr. Bull.* IV. 428 That perfected form of collotype which the company has christened 'photomezzotype'. **1893** *Nation* (N.Y.) 13 July 34/1 The..photomezzotype plates give us pictures of the Great Barrier Reef..of the greatest beauty. **1958** *New Scientist* 13 Nov. 1247/3 The *photomosaic is being assembled now. **1962** *Times* 17 May 10/3 The leading aircraft, navigating on a photo-mosaic. **1973** *Sci. Amer.* Dec. 132/3 This is the planet Mars, drawn from *Mariner 9* photomosaics. **1977** *Time* 17 Oct. 45/1 Among the pictures released by NASA: a photomosaic of the planet's north pole, showing a concentric pattern of striations in the ice cap. **1935** W. D. Morgan et al. *Leica Manual* 469 *(caption)* *Photomurals with the Leica. **1937** *Archit. Rev.* LXXXI. 86 The true photo-mural... This new process of mural decoration, which can now be said to have passed the experimental stage, has its chief virtue in that the design is projected direct on to the wall surface. The surface is first sprayed with photo-sensitive emulsion, and the photograph printed on it much in the same way as an ordinary camera enlargement. **1960** *House & Garden* Oct. 65/1 For ease of hanging, these photomurals are printed on lightweight white base paper. **1976** *National Observer* (U.S.) 24 Apr. 24/2 Once inside, the visitor encounters giant photomurals, three-quarter mock-ups of building exteriors, [etc.]. **1890** *Athenæum* 29 Mar. 408/2 Reference was..made to Mr. J. B. Jordan's form of sunshine recorder, and to Capt. Abney's *photo-nephograph. **1933** J. S. A. Salt *Simple Method Surveying from Air Photogr.* xi. 130 The names..are printed photographically in a *Photonymograph... Names may be printed in a variety of sizes and styles on a strip of sensitized paper. The alphabet..and any other signs..are contained on a master-disc. With the disc in position, each letter in turn is brought into position and an exposure made. .. The strips are developed and fixed..and then show a series of names in various sizes and styles. **1963** *Record* (Oxf. Univ. Press) Dec. 2/3 The Drawing Office has installed a 'photonymograph' (a device whose development was in fact sponsored by the Cartographic section) to produce its lettering and so free draughtsmen for drawing. **1971** Monkhouse & Wilkinson *Maps & Diagrams* (ed. 3) i. 64 The new model..of the Photonymograph (developed from a machine which appeared in its earliest form over thirty years ago) is made by Barr and Stroud, Ltd. **1862** *Catal. Internat. Exhib.* II. xiv. 53 Plans reduced by photography, photozincographs, and *photopapyrographs. **1862** Scott & James *Photo-zincography* Pref. 6 The discovery of the art of *Photo-papyrography was the result of an accident. **1889** *Anthony's Photogr. Bull.* II. 427 *Photophane is a photo-mechanical process allied (but superior) to collotype. **1918** *Physical Rev.* XI. 137 *(heading)* Images on silvered *photo-plate. **1974** *Nature* 20 Dec. 698/2 Organochlorine compounds may be identified at low concentrations in crude extracts of natural samples by a high resolution mass spectrometric method involving photoplate detection. **1888** Ld. R. Gower *(title)* 'Bric-a-brac', or some *Photoprints illustrating Art Objects at Gower Lodge, Windsor. **1889** *Athenæum* 20 July 91/2 The book is embellished with six photoprint illustrations. **1884** Knight *Dict. Mech.* Supp., **Photo-printing Process*. **1875** *Ibid.*, **Photo-processes*. **1897** *Daily News* 1 Apr. 5/4 Photo-process classes for the instruction of all comers actually engaged in any branch of the photo-mechanical, photographic, designing, lithographic, engraving, and printing crafts. **1924** *Glasgow Herald* 13 Dec. 9 The signature was that of Sir Robert Kindersley, whose *photo-radiogram read—'My warmest greetings.—R. M. Kindersley.' The message and signature accompanied a radio photo of Sir Robert. **1925** *Official Gaz.* (U.S. Patent Office) 26 May 803/1 Radio-corporation of America, New York, N.Y. Filed Jan. 13, 1925. *Photoradiogram*... Pictures, drawings, and facsimiles transmitted by radio. Claims use since Nov. 30, 1924. **1926** *Daily News* 1 May 5/6 Most of the photoradiograms sent from this side during the night will appear in American newspapers today. **1927** *Daily Express* 16 Dec. 1, December 21 is the latest date for handing in Christmas photo-radiograms at Marconi offices. **1946** *War Report* (B.B.C.) vi. 149 Then on Sunday evening one of our *photo-recce Spitfires was shot down in German territory. **1971** *N.Y. Times* 13 June iv. 37 We have a high priority requirement for night photorecce of key motorable routes in Laos. **1944** *Sci. News Let.* 19 Aug. 117/3 *Photo reconnaissance supplies information regarding the strength of enemy troops. **1951** A. C. Clarke *Sands of Mars* xvi. 209 I'm going to suggest a photo-reconnaissance of all the..forests. **1973** *Sci. Amer.* Feb. 14/2 The main restrictions imposed by both of the SALT I agreements can be..monitored largely by means of sensors carried on board such orbiting photoreconnaissance systems. **1875** tr. *Vogel's Chem. Light* xv. 230 The Production of *Photo-Reliefs. **1881** Abney *Photogr.* xxvii. 186 Mr. Dallas..has produced photo-relief blocks for the reproduction of half-tone prints. **1892** Woodbury *Encycl. Phot.* 538 The Woodbury process is often termed a photo-relief one. **1960** *Spectator* 17 June 886 The great *photo-reportage magazines have now..largely relinquished their commanding position to television. **1960** L. Durrell *Spirit of Place* (1969) 162, I remember seeing a photo-reportage in *Life* magazine once which dealt with the extraordinary changes in physique which immigrants to the U.S.A. underwent. **1966** *Punch* 6 Apr. 498/1 One of the many technical hazards which are endemic in photo-reportage are bound to materialise in full force. **1957** T. L. J. Bentley *Man. Miniature Camera* (ed. 5) iv. 41 The few models which incorporate a motor drive create totally new possibilities of rapid-sequence pictures which may be quite invaluable in.. records of sporting events and *photo-reporting for journalistic purposes. **1886** *Pall Mall G.* 4 Oct. 10/1 Instantaneous photographs of Russian life, taken by the *photo-revolver invented by K. Brandil, photographer to the Warsaw Imperial University. **1889** *Pall Mall G.* 11 Jan. 6/2 A curious photographic apparatus, in which a camera is raised by a rocket and lowered by a parachute... For securing bird's-eye views the *photo-rocket offers several important advantages over balloon photography. **1956** *Radiol.* LXVI. 737/2 (*heading*) *Photoscan (superimposed on roentgenogram) shows lesion to be thyroid tissue rather than metastasis from breast. **1974** *Cancer Res.* XXXIV. 1/1 The photoscans showed an increased uptake of radioactivity over the tumors. **1959** *Internat. Jrnl. Appl. Radiation & Isotopes* IV. 154 (*heading*) A versatile, high-contrast *photoscanner for the localization of human tumors with radioisotopes. **1966** *Sci. News* 12 Nov. 400 The gamma rays coming from the abnormal portions of bone are detected by a photoscanner that is passed externally over the body. Any portion of bone that gives off gamma rays is considered diseased. X-rays, in contrast, work by showing changes in bone density. **1956** *Internat. Jrnl. Appl. Radiation & Isotopes* I. 137/1 A *photo scanning device has been devised which presents a 150% increase in picture density as the result of a 10% increase in count rate. **1967** *Times* 19 Sept. 9 Photo-scanning using radioactive isotopes can tell us if cancer is present in such organs as the thyroid gland, the liver and the brain. **1974** *Cancer Res.* XXXIV. 1/1 Radiolabeled nonantibody components of heterospecific IgG can be localized in certain tumors and normal tissues by photoscanning. **1883** *Pall Mall G.* 6 Dec. 5/1 Comparing some of the originals with the *photosculptural copies. **1863** in *Abridgm. Specif. Patents, Photogr.* (1872) 70 [This invention (of François Willème) relates to] *photo-sculpture. **1864** *Round Table* 18 June 12/2 Busts and figures in clay, modeled by a new process called Photosculpture, exhibiting a new and charming development of heliographic art. **1875** tr. *Vogel's Chem. Light* xv. 231 This photo-sculpture, as it is called, can only be carried out imperfectly. **1881** Abney *Photogr.* 282 The spectroscope and camera are rigidly connected one with another... This completes the *photo-spectroscopic arrangement. *Ibid.* 263 *Photo-spectroscopy..has two aspects: in one it is the study as to the sensitiveness of compounds to the influence of different portions of the spectrum; in the other, the study of the spectrum itself. **1913** *Chem. Abstr.* VII. 3862 App[aratus] for copying the surface of a solid body from a *photostereogram. **1939** B. B. Talley *Engin. Applic. Aerial & Terrestr. Photogrammetry* xix. 526 (*caption*) The Nistri *photostereograph. **1963** W. K. Kilford *Elem. Air Survey* xi. 265 (*caption*) The photostereograph (Beta/2) coupled with coordinate computer on the left and plotting table and coordinate plotter on right. **1933** A. R. Hinks *Maps & Survey* (ed. 3) xii. 243 (*heading*) Recent developments in *photostereographic surveying. **1940** *War Illustr.* 19 Jan. 627 (*heading*) *Photo-story of the life and death of a U-boat. **1972** *Guardian* 24 Mar. 12/6 The photo-story in 7 Days left one with a powerful impression. **1973** D. Matias tr. C. Metz in *Screen* Spring/Summer 197 Image-languages.. figurative drawing,..television, photography, the photo-story etc. **1891** *Anthony's Photogr. Bull.* IV. 236 Join a society which has undertaken the '*photo-survey' of its district, and do your part. **1893** Fichel in *Chatauquan* XIII. 318 The photo-connecting lens of 33 inch diameter being placed over the 36 inch telescope, thus turning it into a *phototelescope. **1894** *Athenæum* 10 Feb. 183/2 The Compton 8-inch photo-telescope has been used for photographing stars suspected of variation. **1892** *Ibid.* 5 Mar. 311/3 A *photo-theodolite, an instrument equally well adapted for geodetic and astronomical measurements, and invaluable for taking panoramic views of mountain regions. **1942** *Amer. Jrnl. Roentgenology* LXVIII. 220/1 A new instrument, a photoelectric timing mechanism, capable of regulating automatically the length of roentgenographic exposure time has been developed... The photoelectric timing mechanism, or *phototimer, is a modification of the roentgenographic exposure meter. **1949** *Britannica Bk. of Year* 687/2 *Photo-timer*, an electrical device which photographs the finish of a race and supplies the elapsed time from start to finish. **1958** *Times* 22 Aug. 4/1 The race ..should be started farther back from the bend, in spite of the cost of moving the electrical photo-timer. **1892** Woodbury *Encycl. Phot.* 531 A little *photo-transfer ink is mixed with turpentine. **1875** Knight *Dict. Mech.*, *Photo-vitrotype. **1865** *Chambers's Encycl.* VII. 510/1 *Photo-Xylography*, is the application of photography to wood-engraving.

3. Prefixed to the names of chemical salts, etc., and of chemical processes, to express the effect of light in changing the molecular constitution of the salt, etc. (by virtue of which it is capable of being employed in photography). Thus: **'photo-decompo'sition**, decomposition due to the action of light; **ˌphotodegra'dation**, degradation of a substance caused by light; so **photode'gradable** *a.*; **photo'dimer** *Chem.*, a dimer formed by photochemical action; so **photodi'meric** *a.*; also **ˌphotodimeri'zation**, the formation of, or conversion into, a photodimer; **photo'dimerize** *v. trans.* and *intr.*, to dimerize by the action of light; **ˌphotodissoci'ation** *Chem.*, dissociation of a chemical compound by the action of light; so **photodi'ssociate** *v. trans.*, to dissociate by means of light; **photo-oxi'dation**, oxidation due to the action of light; **photo-'oxidative** *a.*, involving or characterized by photo-oxidation; **photo-'oxidize** *v. trans.*, to oxidize photochemically; hence **photo-'oxidizable** *a.*, **-'oxidized** *ppl. a.*; **ˌphotophosphory'lation** *Biochem.*, the process by which light energy is utilized by a plant or micro-organism to convert adenosine diphosphate to adenosine triphosphate without the reduction of oxygen to water that occurs in oxidative phosphorylation; **photo'polymer**, a polymer produced photochemically; **ˌphoto-polymeri'zation** *Chem.*, polymerization brought about by the action of light; so **photo'polymerize** *v. trans.*, to polymerize photochemically; **photo'polymerized** *ppl. a.*; also **photo'polymerizable** *a.*, capable of being photopolymerized; **ˌphotopolymeriza'bility**; **'photo-ˌsalt**, a general term for any salt modified by light; so ***photo-bromide***, ***photo-chloride***, ***photo-iodide***, ***photo-sulphate***, etc.

1888 *Chem. Photogr.* (1889) 52 It is known that moisture accelerates the photo-decomposition. **1972** *New Scientist* 5 Oct. 41/2 (*heading*) Photo-degradable plastic carriers. **1975** Rånby & Rabek *Photodegradation* ix. 361 The development of methods for making plastics which are photodegradable to form harmless and biologically useful chemical compounds is of great interest. **1962** J. T. Marsh *Self-Smoothing Fabrics* xviii. 303 The resin exerts a considerable protective influence even in presence of those vat dyes whose action accelerates photo-degradation of cellulose. **1975** *Physics Bull.* Apr. 164/1 (Advt.), The fundamental photochemical reactions involved in photodegradation of polymers. **1936** *Trans. Faraday Soc.* XXXII. 521 The photodimer of thiophosgene. **1970** J. B. Birks *Photophysics of Aromatic Molecules* vii. 322 If..photodimers of other anthracene derivatives are irradiated with ultraviolet photons of sufficient energy..photolysis occurs and the dimer reverts to the original pair of individual molecules. **1952** *Chem. Rev.* LI. 19 The nonoccurrence of the photodimeric products of the previously mentioned anthracene derivatives is probably due to their thermolability. **1936** *Trans. Faraday Soc.* XXXII. 517 A photodimerisation of 9–10-diphenyl anthracene has not yet been observed. **1972** DePuy & Chapman *Molec. Reactions & Photochem.* iv. 65 Naphthalenes, anthracenes, and polyacenes in general undergo photodimerization. **1955** *Jrnl. Chem. Soc.* 315, 3-Bromothionaphthen 1:1-dioxide was photodimerised in order to ascertain whether angular.. or linear dimerisation was favoured. **1969** *Organic Photochem.* II. 75 Acyclic α, β-unsaturated ketones photodimerize when substituted with an aromatic group in the beta position. **1970** J. B. Birks *Photophysics of Aromatic Molecules* vii. 321 There are a large group of other 9-substituted and 9, 10-disubstituted anthracenes which also photodimerize. **1962** F. I. Ordway et al. *Basic Astronautics* vi. 249 Water vapor is constantly being photodissociated by the action of sunlight. **1969** *Nature* 22 Nov. 756/2 NH_3, H_2O and H_2CO can all be photodissociated by ultraviolet photons of $E < 13{\cdot}6$ eV. **1925** *Phil. Mag.* XLIX. 1166 It becomes of interest..to investigate the relation between the activation, and the frequency of the illumination;..only recently has a similar investigation been made on the photo-dissociation of sulphur dioxide. **1974** *Sci. Amer.* June 29/1 Atomic iodine is prepared in the proper excited state by the photodissociation of gaseous compounds such as iodotrifluoromethane (CF_3I) with xenon flash lamps. **1977** *Jrnl. R. Soc. Arts* CXXV. 766/2 The high spectral brightness of lasers can be used resonantly to obtain selective photodissociation. **1888** *Chem. Photogr.* (1889) 269 The photo-oxidation of lead compounds, of mercurous oxide,..and of sulphides, proceeds more rapidly in the red than in the violet rays. **1941** *Jrnl. Gen. Physiol.* XXV. 309 The ultimate cause of the extra oxygen absorption after or during irradiation consists of photoxidation processes sensitized mainly by chlorophyll. **1956** *Nature* 17 Mar. 513/2 The Bituminous Binder Research Unit has completed a preliminary investigation of photo-oxidation in the weathering of binders on the road. **1971** *Jrnl. Oil & Colour Chemists' Assoc.* LIV. 846 Bleaching by sunlight may be due to photo-oxidation of double bonds. **1937** *Ann. Rep. Progr. Chem.* XXXIII. 431 There is little doubt that this element [*sc.* manganese] can affect the chlorophyll content of leaves, and probably also its photo-oxidative properties. **1976** *Nature* 13 May 169/2 A film exposed under high vacuum showed a dose response almost identical to that of one exposed in air, and indicates the photolytic rather than the photo-oxidative nature of the process. **1949** *Chem. Abstr.* XLIII. 5391 (*heading*) Photoöxidizable derivatives of helianthrene. **1974** *Photochem. & Photobiol.* XIX. 35/1 Dye-sensitized photo-oxidation..permitting preferential destruction of the photo-oxidizable amino-acid residues of proteins. **1941** *Adv. Enzymol.* I. 232 Artificially added substances whose oxidation products can be recognized by their color are actually photo-oxidized in plants. **1975** *Nature* 9 Oct. 490/2 It seems that *O. limnetica* photo-oxidises S^{2-} quantitatively to S^0. **1973** *Biochem.* XII. 2540/2 The tryptophan content of the native and the photooxidized enzyme was measured. [**1954** D. I. Arnon et al. in *Nature* 28 Aug. 394/1 Evidence has now been obtained that whole chloroplasts..have the ability to carry out.. photosynthetic phosphorylation, a term which we use for the conversion of light energy into the high-energy phosphate bonds of adenosine triphosphate (ATP), without the participation of respiration.] **1956** *Plant Physiol.* XXXI. p. xxx/2 (*heading*) The mechanism of cell-free, bacterial photophosphorylation. **1956** *Federation Proc.* XV. 260/2 Photophosphorylation depends upon an inductive reduction. **1971** M. F. Mallette et al. *Introd. Biochem.* xviii. 646 Photosystem 1, the longer wave length photosystem, has been associated with the reduction of $NADP^+$ and with photophosphorylation. Photosystem 2 is related to dissociation of water and the evolution of oxygen. **1973** R. G. Krueger et al. *Introd. Microbiol.* viii. 271/1 Photophosphorylation occurs in the reduction of cytochrome c with the generation of ATP from ADP and inorganic phosphate. The electron initially emitted from chlorophyll is ultimately returned to chlorophyll in a cyclic fashion; hence, the entire process of converting light energy to ATP (chemical energy) is termed cyclic phosphorylation. .. In plants and algae, a noncyclic type of photophosphorylation also occurs. **1932** *Canad. Jrnl. Res.* VII. 479 The photo-polymer of vinyl butyl ether was purified. **1953** *Jrnl. Res. Nat. Bureau of Standards* (U.S.) LI. 327 Teflon and tetrafluoroethylene photopolymers, on pyrolysis in a vacuum at 423·5° to 513·0° C, yield almost 100 percent of monomer. **1961** *Printing News* 16 Feb. 10 The first complete 4-colour magazine to be produced from 'Dycril' photo-polymer (light-sensitive plastic) printing plates. **1974** *Clarendonian* XXVIII. 1. 41 There are plans afoot to convert other letterpress 'classics' to this type of plate should photopolymers prove the equal of our now traditional hot-moulded plastic plates. **1932** *Canad. Jrnl. Res.* VII. 473 The photo-polymerizability is practically the same as that of the butyl ether. *Ibid.*, Comparison with the closely related vinyl esters.. shows that, in the absence of catalysts, the latter are much more readily photo- and thermo-polymerizable. **1973** *Materials & Technol.* VI. ix. 664 The photopolymerisable amide-compositions are used for the production of letterpress printing plates. **1920** *Chem. Abstr.* XIV. 4427/1 (Index), Photopolymerization. **1924** *Jrnl. Amer. Chem. Soc.* XLVI. 1614 It is concluded that in the photopolymerization of anthracene, a single molecule is activated by absorption of blue light and then proceeds to react with an unactivated molecule to form the polymer. **1970** H. L. Needles in R. F. Reinisch *Photochem. Macromolecules* 129 Both oxygen and hydrogen donors effect riboflavin-sensitized photopolymerizations of aqueous acrylamide. **1921** *Jrnl. Chem. Soc.* CXIX. 1028 Whether the same explanation does not apply to all carbohydrates and to chlorophyll, namely, that under the influence of light of very short wave-length they are decomposed to carbon dioxide, which is photosynthesised to formaldehyde, and this in its turn photopolymerised to sugars. **1933** *Jrnl. Amer. Chem. Soc.* LV. 577 Ethyl acetate does not react with Wijs solution; nor does the polymerized product, since..solid photopolymerized vinyl acetate gave iodine values as low as 9·5 and 6·3, corresponding to 96 and 98% polymerized. **1974** *Sci. Amer.* Oct. 119/2 They are made by first crystallizing the molecules of an appropriate monomer and then photopolymerizing the monomer crystal with ultra-violet light or gamma rays. **1887** Carey Lea in *Amer. Jrnl. Sc.* 352 As these substances have been hitherto seen only in the impure form in which they are produced by the continued action of light on the normal salts, it might be convenient to call them photosalts, photochloride, photobromide, and photoiodide, instead of red or coloured chloride, etc. **1890** *Anthony's Photogr. Bull.* III. 395 Photo-sulphate of iron solution was for a long time the only developer used.

photoabsorbing to **photobacterium**: see PHOTO- 1.

ˌphotobi'ography. [f. PHOTO- 2 + BIOGRAPHY.] A person's life shown in a series of photographs.

1944 *Spectator* 3 Mar. 188/1 A 'photobiography', consisting of 250 scenes from Woodrow Wilson's life, with 150 pages of letterpress..is in an advanced stage of preparation. **1951** C. Beaton (*title*) Photobiography. **1952** *N.Y. Times Bk. Rev.* 1 June 12 A 'photobiography' that does not seem likely to lose the general votes in the future.

photobiological to **-bleaching**: see PHOTO- 1.

photoblepharon (fəʊtəʊ'blɛfərɒn). [mod.L. (M. Weber *Siboga Expeditie* (1902) I. 108), f. PHOTO- 1 + Gr. βλέφαρον eye.] A small luminous fish of the genus so called, found in the Red Sea and the Indian Ocean.

1920 E. N. Harvey *Nature Animal Light* i. 18 Leaving out of account..the use for bait, in fishing, of the luminous organ of a fish, *Photoblepharon*, by the Banda islanders, we find that luminous bacteria are of value for certain purposes in the laboratory. **1928** C. M. Yonge in Russell & Yonge *Seas* viii. 193 Light organs are apparently commonest in fish which live in the upper 500 metres of the warmer seas, although there are notable exceptions, for example, a..fish ..called Photoblepharon found in pools of fresh water in quarries and the craters of extinct volcanoes in Malaya. **1964** *Oceanogr. & Marine Biol.* II. 356 In *Photoblepharon* the glow may be hidden by an opaque screen. **1978** *Nat. Geogr. Mag.* Nov. 722 Despite its name, *Photoblepharon* has no real eyelid.

photo-call: see PHOTO- 2.

photocatalyse (fəʊtəʊ'kætəlaɪz), *v. Chem.* Also (*U.S.*) -yze. [f. PHOTO- 1 + CATALYSE *v.*] *trans.* To subject to photocatalysis.

1921 *Jrnl. Chem. Soc.* CXIX. 1034 The photosynthesis of formaldehyde from carbon dioxide and water can be photocatalysed by certain coloured basic substances... The photosynthesis then takes place in visible light. *c* **1955** *Proc. 1st Internat. Photobiol. Congr.* *1954* ii. 137 Ferric chloride photocatalyses the reduction of..methylene blue by citrate in water. **1970** *Nature* 22 Aug. 832/2 The decomposition of N_2O photocatalysed both by metal free and Cu-phthalocyanine.

Hence **photo'catalysed** *ppl. a.*

c **1955** *Proc. 1st Internat. Photobiol. Congr.* *1954* ii. 135 The observed total reaction consists of a photocatalysed reaction between leucoindophenol and air plus a dark reaction between leucoindophenol and peroxide. **1973** *Biochem.* XII. 4154/1 Although sensitive to photocatalyzed degradation, these reagents readily react with thiol compounds..yielding photostable covalent derivatives.

photocatalysis (fəʊtəʊkə'tælɪsɪs). *Chem.* †Also with hyphen. [f. PHOTO- 1 + CATALYSIS. The words of this group originated with the Ger. adj. (see below).] The acceleration of a reaction by light; the catalysis of a photochemical reaction.

1913 *Jrnl. Chem. Soc.* CIV. II. 653 (*heading*) Photo-catalysis. **1916** W. C. McC. Lewis *Syst. Physical Chem.* II. III. i. 420 Another instance of photo-catalysis in solution is the decomposition of aqueous sodium hypochlorite. **1970** *Nature* 22 Aug. 832/2 (*heading*) Homogeneous photocatalysis by organic dyes in the liquid phase.

So **ˌphotocata'lytic** *a.* [ad. G. *photokatalytisch* (J. Plotnikow *Photochemie* (1910) II. 72)], pertaining to or exhibiting photocatalysis; **ˌphotocata'lytically** *adv.*; **photo'catalyst**, † **-'catalyser**, a substance that acts as a catalyst in a photochemical reaction.

1913 H. S. Allen *Photo-Electricity* xiv. 198 We may conveniently divide..photo-chemical reactions into three main classes. To the first class may be assigned the so-called photokatalytic reactions, in which light only accelerates an irreversible process. **1914** S. E. Sheppard *Photo-Chem.* vii. 293 The kations Fe, Mn, Ce were peculiarly effective photo-catalysts for the reaction. **1923** *Jrnl. Chem. Soc.* CXXIII.

189 The synthesis takes place photocatalytically by the influence of visible light when the carbonic acid is in loose combination with a coloured base, such as malachite green. **1926** E. MAYER *Clin. Applic. Sunlight* viii. 160 Metallic compounds, especially iron salts, act as photocatalyzers. For example, benzoic acid under the influence of light will change very quickly to salicylic acid if an iron salt be present. **1945** E. I. RABINOWITCH *Photosynthesis* I. iii. 56 Chlorophyll is a photocatalyst, since no decrease in the concentration of chlorophyll in leaves has been observed after intense photosynthesis. **1959** *Ann. Rev. Plant Physiol.* X. 56 (*heading*) Photocatalytic activities of bacterial chromatophores. **1971** E. GURR *Synthetic Dyes* 108 Crystal violet is one of the dyes used by Binding (1970) as a photocatalyst. **1978** *Nature* 3 Aug. 508/1 The concentration of Ru (about 8×10^{-5} M) changed by less than 5%, so the complex was acting as a photocatalytic agent.

photocathode (fəʊtəʊˈkæθəʊd). *Electronics.* Also **photo-cathode**, **†-kathode**. [a. G. *photokathode* (P. Selényi 1929, in *Physik. Zeitschr.* XXX. 933/1): see PHOTO- 1 and CATHODE.] A cathode which emits electrons when illuminated, thereby allowing an electric current to pass.

1930 *Sci. Abstr.* A. XXXIII. 525 (*heading*) Red-sensitive sodium photo-kathodes (photo-electric cells). **1931** *Physics* I. 343 If a silver surface is first oxidized in an electrical discharge, and then baked in the presence of caesium vapor, it may be converted into a photo-cathode of remarkable sensitivity. **1957** *Proc. Inst. Electr. Engin.* CIV. B. 470/2 The photo-electric surface developed by Koller in 1929, consisting of a complex mixture of silver, oxygen and caesium, was the first of the really efficient modern photo-cathodes and it is still in use, especially when red or infra-red sensitivity is required. **1969** *New Scientist* 10 July 21/1 An image tube consists of a photo-cathode which emits electrons in direct proportion to the amount of light falling on it.

photocell (ˈfəʊtəʊsɛl). Also **photo-cell**, **photo cell**. [f. PHOTO- 1 + CELL *sb.*[1]] A device which generates an electric current or voltage dependent on its degree of illumination.

1891 *Phil. Mag.* XXXI. 232 The effect of this connexion with the Daniell is to develop between the poles of the photo cell a difference of potential opposed in sign to that which light produces. **1913** *Physical Rev.* I. 74 When..the spark gap was pulled six feet away from the photo-cell the positive potential slowly fell to 1·6 volts. **1932** *Discovery* Apr. 112/1 By passing the film between a light and..a photocell the film can be turned into speech again. **1938** G. H. SEWELL *Amateur Film-Making* ii. 21 The photo-cell meter is recognized as the most accurate light-measuring device normally available. **1958** *New Statesman* 23 Aug. 214/2 There will be a system of photo-cells, which, sensitive to infra-red and visible rays, will scan the hidden side of the moon, as the rocket-probe spins on its axis. **1973** *Daily Tel.* 10 Dec. 7/3 When fog distorts the light path, it alters the pattern being received by the photocell, which is then electronically translated into distance of visibility.

photocharger, -charging: see PHOTO- 2.

photochemical (fəʊtəʊˈkɛmɪkəl), *a.* [f. PHOTO- + CHEMICAL.] Of or pertaining to the chemical action of light; ***photochemical smog***, a condition of the atmosphere attributed to the action of sunlight on hydrocarbons and nitrogen in it and characterized by the presence of aerosols and increased ozone and nitrogen oxides and by effects that include irritation of the eyes, damage to plants, and visibility reduced to a mile or less.

1859 *Sat. Rev.* 26 Feb. 242/1 The use of that bichromate of potassium to which we alluded before as the foundation of so many of these ingenious combinations of photochemical changes and mechanical inventions. **1888** MELDOLA *Chem. Photogr.* i. (1889) 7 By a photo-chemical action must be understood a chemical change produced by the action of light. **1957** *Rep. Air Pollution Foundation* (U.S.) No. 21. 1 It is now realized that Los Angeles' smog is primarily a reaction between organic matter and nitrogen oxides in the presence of sunlight. The need for irradiation to produce the reaction has led to the designation 'photochemical' smog. **1972** *Daily Colonist* (Victoria, B.C.) 13 Feb. 27/5 His studies of animals show that Vitamin E serves as an antioxidant to protect lung tissue from damage by the ozone in photochemical smog. **1972** *Nature* 18 Feb. 360/1 There is no doubt that motor vehicles are the principal outlets for photochemical smog in large cities. **1976** *New Yorker* 16 Feb. 74/2 Los Angeles is perhaps the best-known victim of the bus and the automobile; photochemical smog, the distinctive pollutant of these vehicles, made its first recorded appearance in Los Angeles in 1943.

Hence **photoˈchemically** *adv.*; **photoˈchemist**, one versed in photochemistry; **photoˈchemistry**, that part of chemistry which deals with the chemical action of light.

1867 M. CAREY LEA in *Amer. Jrnl. Sci.* Ser. 2. XLIV. 71 The nature of the action of light upon iodid of silver,..the most important..of all the facts of photochemistry. **1881** *Phil. Mag.* XII. 21 The impression of an electromotive force upon a film possessing, as do all photochemically active bodies, electrolytic conductivity, will tend to produce at least partial electrolysis. **1898** *Daily News* 15 Apr. 5/6 It works photo-chemically. **1926** *Trans. Faraday Soc.* XXI. 438 Stark's views undoubtedly did not receive from photochemists the attention they deserved. **1941** S. H. BARTLEY *Vision* i. 5 The photochemist has given increasing attention to the cycle of changes that occur in the eye in response to light. **1961** G. R. CHOPPIN *Exper. Nucl. Chem.* xii. 194 It is tempting to seek to relate photochemistry and radiation chemistry by considering that ionization is the ultimate state of excitation. **1967** MARGERISON & EAST *Introd. Polymer Chem.* iv. 184 The process is started by the decomposition of an initiator induced thermally, photochemically or by admixture of another substance. **1972** DEPUY & CHAPMAN *Molec. Reactions & Photochem.* i. 6 Photochemistry is the study of the chemistry of electronically excited molecules produced by the absorption of electromagnetic radiation. **1973** *Sci. Amer.* Apr. 68/2 Photochemists have measured the probability that ultraviolet photons will destroy particular molecules. **1978** *Nature* 23 Feb. 733/1 Photochemically produced sulphate aerosols can, in certain circumstances, account for a large proportion of total particulate mass in the 0·1–1·0 μm size range.

photo-chloride: see PHOTO- 3.

photochromatic (ˌfəʊtəʊkrəʊˈmætɪk), *a.* [f. PHOTO- + CHROMATIC.] Of or pertaining to the chromatic or colouring action of light; pertaining to or produced by photochromy.

1888 MELDOLA *Chem. Photogr.* viii. (1889) 322 Other investigators..have confirmed the general result that silver chloride can be made susceptible of *photochromatic impressions. *Ibid.* 324 The photochromatic property apparently belongs to the reduction product, which we now have good reasons for believing to be an oxychloride.

So **ˈphotochrome**, name for a coloured photograph; **ˌphotochroˈmography**, a method of colouring photographs, or of producing photochromes; **ˌphoto-chromoˈlithograph**, a chromolithograph in the production of which photographic processes have been used; **photoˈchromoscope**, an optical apparatus by which photographic or stereoscopic views are exhibited in their natural colours; **photo-ˈchromotype** *sb.*, a picture in colours printed from plates prepared by a photo-relief process; also = *photo-chromotypy*; whence **photo-ˈchromotype** *v. trans.*, to reproduce in photo-chromotype; **photo-ˈchromotypy**, the art or process of producing pictures in this way; **ˈphotochromy**, (*a*) the art or process of colouring photographs; (*b*) the art of photographing objects in their natural colours; colour-photography; (*c*) [ad. F. *photochromie*] = PHOTOCHROMISM.

1880 *Illustr. Lond. News* 24 Jan. 82/1 The new invention of *photo-chrome will cause a revolution in the art of portrait-taking. **1894** *Westm. Gaz.* 1 Jan. 3/1 Judging by a series of photochroms sent to us..it is now possible to reproduce, photographically, all the most striking tints in a landscape. **18..** M. C. C. *Photo-Chromography* 4 *Photo-Chromography..will..maintain the foremost place amongst the various modes of painting photographs. **1870** *Eng. Mech.* 14 Jan. 428/2 Mr Griggs has..applied photo-lithography successfully to the production of *photo-chromolithographs. **1881** *Eng. Mechanic* 27 May 294/3 Five-guinea *Photochromoscope,..adds Nature's beauteous tints to any glass transparency. **1893** *Brit. Journ. Photogr.* XL. 798 Which could be used like the stereoscope or the photo-chromoscope. **1895** *Current Hist.* (Buffalo) V. 963 By means of an instrument to which has been given the name 'photochromoscope', a stereoscopic effect is produced in which the original tints stand out faithfully. **1886** *Sci. Amer.* 24 July 49/3 [They] produce by a new process colored prints, so-called '*photo-chromotypes', which are made in the printing press. **1896** *Idler* Mar. 239/1 A design for a Christmas annual, which is to be reproduced in 'photochromotype'. **1894** *Brit. Jrnl. Photogr.* XLI. 53 *Photo-chromotypy is in its experimental stage, but no doubt there is a great future before it. **1888** MELDOLA *Chem. Photogr.* (1889) 326 To deal with the chemical principles of *photochromy. **1891** *Daily News* 15 May 7/1 An exhibition illustrative of photochromy, or the science of producing colour in combination with photography. **1951** *Chem. Abstr.* XLV. 10059 (*heading*) Photochromy in the bianthrone series. **1963** *Adv. Photochem.* I. 282 Photochromy and thermochromy are mutually exclusive properties in crystalline salicylidine-anilines.

photochromic (fəʊtəʊˈkrəʊmɪk), *a.* and *sb.* [f. as next + -IC.] **A.** *adj.* Of, pertaining to, or displaying photochromism.

1953 *Jrnl. Chem. Physics* XXI. 1619/2 In those compounds which exhibit both thermochromism and photochromism the thermochromic and the photochromic colors are in each case spectroscopically identical. **1965** *New Scientist* 29 Apr. 291/3 Silver halide particles dispersed through this sheet of 'photochromic' glass..cause the glass to darken on exposure to light, and clear again within minutes. **1971** H. MEIER in K. Venkataraman *Chem. Synthetic Dyes* IV. vii. 427 The photochromic reaction of aqueous solutions of the leucosulfite of parafuchsine could be used as a UV dosimeter for the measurement of the UV radiation of sky light. **1974** *Observer* (Colour Suppl.) 13 Oct. 18/4 Photochromic lenses that automatically change the darkness of their tint to match the prevailing brightness.

B. *sb.* A photochromic substance.

1965 *Guardian* 13 Apr. 14/5 Sunglasses which are clear in ordinary daylight but which darken progressively in increasing sunlight, were among the practical applications of photochromics described in London yesterday. **1970** *Physics Bull.* Nov. 487/1 Two other classes of material which have been developed recently as promising photochromics..are the alkaline earth fluorides and titanates.

Hence **ˌphotochroˈmicity** = PHOTOCHROMISM.

1966 *Applied Optics* V. 946/2 The size of the silver halide microcrystals embedded in the glass matrix determines not only the photochromicity but also the character of the unexposed material (transparent, translucent, and opaque).

photochromism (fəʊtəʊˈkrəʊmɪz(ə)m). [f. as next + -ISM.] The phenomenon whereby certain substances undergo a reversible change of colour or shade when illuminated with light of appropriate wavelength.

1951 *Physics Abstr.* A. LIV. 204/2 (*heading*) Photochromism in the bianthrone series. **1953** [see PHOTOCHROMIC *a.*]. **1960** *New Scientist* 2 June 1424/1 This new kind of reversible colour change in organic compounds was first described by me [*sc.* Yehuda Hirshberg] in 1950, and I called it 'photochromism'. *Ibid.* 1425/3 Another recent development in photochromism is the discovery that many compounds which undergo reversible colour changes by exposure to ultraviolet light show the same effect when subjected to high-energy electrons or to any ionizing radiation. **1972** *Nature* 31 Mar. 245/2 Photochromism is an effect associated with compounds which reversibly change their absorption spectra on illumination with light.

photochronograph (fəʊtəʊˈkrɒnəgrɑːf, -æ-). [f. PHOTO- + CHRONOGRAPH, or (in a.) from the Gr. elements of this.] **a.** An instrument for taking a series of instantaneous photographs at regular short intervals of time; also, each of the photographs so taken. **b.** An instrument by which a beam of light is caused to produce a photographic image at some precise instant of time, e.g. so as to show the exact time at which a star crosses the meridian. So **ˌphotochronoˈgraphic** *a.*, pertaining to photochronography; **ˌphotochronoˈgraphically** *adv.*, by means of photochronography; **ˌphotochroˈnography** (-krəʊˈnɒgrəfɪ), the art or process of taking instantaneous photographs at regular intervals (see a. above).

1887 *Nature* 15 Sept. 480/1 Photochronography applied to the dynamic problem of the flight of birds, by M. Marey. *Ibid.*, On the photochronograph are measured all the displacements of the mass of the bird on the wing, together with the velocity of these movements. **1891** *Pall Mall G.* 13 July 6/3 The photo-chronograph..causes a star to record the time of its own transit across the meridian. **1892** *Ibid.* 14 Oct. 5/1 The Jesuit Father Fargis,..the inventor of the photochronograph for measuring star transits. **1897** *Westm. Gaz.* 19 May 6/2 At the receiving end the polarising photochronograph of Lieutenant Squier and Professor Crehore completes the work, allowing a beam of light to register itself on a rapidly revolving sensitive plate.

photoclinometry: see PHOTO- 2.

ˌphotocoaguˈlation. *Ophthalm.* [f. PHOTO- 1 + COAGULATION.] The surgical technique of using an intense beam of light to coagulate small areas of tissue, esp. of the retina.

1961 *Times* 16 Jan. 11/7 Today by surgery and the use of electro or photo-coagulation successful reposition..is achieved. **1971** G. N. WISE et al. *Retinal Circulation* xv. 446/1 Photocoagulation is an effective method of destroying individual features of proliferative diabetic retinopathy. **1972** T. N. WAUBKE in Michaelson & Berman *Causes & Prevention of Blindness* 313/1 Most of our patients did not realize the defects in the visual field which occur after photocoagulation.

Hence **ˌphotocoˈagulate** *v. trans.*, to treat by this technique; **ˌphotocoˈagulating** *ppl. a.*; **ˌphotocoˈagulator**, an apparatus which produces the light beam used for photocoagulation.

1967 *New Scientist* 30 Mar. 679/3 The sharply focused beam caused only minimal scars to surrounding tissue. Ultimately they hope to develop more versatile laser photocoagulators. **1969** *Sci. Jrnl.* July 16 When the retina is subjected to a photocoagulating laser pulse..the transient pressure waves which reverberate through the eyeball resemble the seismic records following an earthquake. **1972** L. M. AIELLO in Michaelson & Berman *Causes & Prevention of Blindness* 317/2 A ruby laser photocoagulator. *Ibid.* 318/2 Control studies are important..in order..to control our eagerness to photocoagulate every eye of all diabetics.

photo-collotype: see PHOTO-.

photocomposing (ˌfəʊtəʊkəmˈpəʊzɪŋ), *vbl. sb. Printing.* Also with hyphen. [f. PHOTO- 2 + COMPOSING *vbl. sb.*] **1.** The setting of text by the projection of images of letters or symbols on to photographic film, which is then used in the preparation of the printing surface; filmsetting. Freq. *attrib.*

1929 *N.Y. Times* 30 Jan. 11/1 There is another great revolution coming in the printing industry... That is the use of photo-composing instead of metal composing. Instead of producing a column of metal type, we will have a machine which produces a strip of film. **1929** *Times* 29 Oct. (Printing Suppl.) p. xii/7 The Typary machine..though not strictly a photo-composing machine, was directly inspired by the desire to abolish typesetting. **1948** *Sci. News Let.* 4 Dec. 362/1 Several photocomposing machines are in experimental use. **1955** *Times* 5 July 6/5 This is the first time that..photo-composing machines have been on view at Olympia as working exhibits. **1961** *Spectator* 14 Apr. 509/3 Technical advances, particularly in photo-composing and the printing of matter from film, rather than metal, are reaching a stage where their place in the British industry must be decided. **1973** S. JENNETT *Making of Bks.* (ed. 5) v. 83 All three hot-metal composing-machine companies in Britain, and others abroad, have introduced photo-composing machines.

2. The manufacture of printing plates directly from photographic images for the production of multiple copies of illustrations, designs, etc.

1929 W. C. HUEBNER in *Trans. Amer. Soc. Mech. Engin.* L. PI. 21/2 Photo composing or photo-mechanical imposition is..the art of making printing plates wherein original designs are photographed directly on the press plate. **1953** *Composition Manual* (Printing Industry of Amer.) VIII. 296/1 It [*sc.* photo-typesetting] should not be confused with 'photo-composing' because the latter has been definitely applied, for a number of years, to machines that are used for the multiple-printing of photographic images in offset lithography and other process work... The word 'photo-composition', sometimes used in current writing to denote photo-typesetting, has likewise been a source of some confusion.

So ˌ**photocomˈpose** *v. trans.*, **-comˈposed** *ppl. a.*; ˌ**photocomˈposer**, a machine for carrying out photocomposition.

1929 W. C. HUEBNER in *Trans. Amer. Soc. Mech. Engin.* L. PI. 21/2 The results attained by photo-composed plates indicate the wide range of work that can be done economically. *Ibid.* 22/1 All sizes of work..are photo-composed successfully. *Ibid.* 23/1 The photocomposer can do it [*sc.* produce several copies of a plate] better. **1948** *Sci. News Let.* 4 Dec. 362/1 One company known for typesetting machinery has its photocomposer in day-by-day use. **1965** *Economist* 22 May (Press Ahead Suppl.) p. xvi/2 Two photocomposers were installed. **1969** *Physics Bull.* Jan. 24/1 The *Current Papers* will be photocomposed for printing under computer control. **1970** A. CAMERON et al. *Computers & Old Eng. Concordances* 7 Photo-composed pages can look very handsome indeed. **1972** *Computers & Humanities* VI. 153 Computerized photocomposers may be divided into three stages of development or three generations of machine in use today.

photocomposition (ˌfəʊtəʊkɒmpəˈzɪʃən). *Printing.* [f. PHOTO- 2 + COMPOSITION.] = PHOTOCOMPOSING *vbl. sb.* Also *attrib.*

1929 *N.Y. Times* 30 Jan. 11/1 (*heading*) Publisher..tells of a photo-composition machine that will do away with metal composition. **1949** H. O. SMITH *Rotophoto Process* 5 With the commercial advent of mechanical photocomposition the future will undoubtedly see more print changing over to photographic methods of reproduction. **1953** [see PHOTOCOMPOSING *vbl. sb.* 2]. **1957** E. LINKLATER *Private Angelo* 238 (*colophon*) Of this book, first published by Jonathan Cape in 1946, two thousand copies were printed at Christmas 1957 for Sir Allen Lane and Richard Lane... The book was composed entirely without metal type: it is the first to have been produced in Great Britain by means of photocomposition. **1967** D. G. HAYS *Introd. Computational Linguistics* iv. 67 Early photocomposition devices..used photosensitive stock and stored negative images of characters. **1968** A. BLUHM *Photosetting* i. 3 These two terms [*sc.* photosetting and filmsetting], and also photocomposition and phototypesetting, are all currently used to mean exactly the same thing, namely the composition of letters and symbols by photographic exposure from a set of transparent master characters for subsequent reproduction by any printing process. **1975** *Times* 4 Sept. 1/1 The printing unions were told..that labour-saving photocomposition techniques would be introduced. **1977** *Times* 14 May 1/2 The plans also involve..Fleet Street production by the new technology of photocomposition.

ˌ**photoconˈductance.** *Physics.* [f. PHOTO- 1 + CONDUCTANCE.] = PHOTOCONDUCTIVITY.

1939 *Jrnl. Chem. Physics* VII. 426/2 Photovoltaic experiments indicate the release of photoconductance electrons. **1959** *Bell Syst. Techn. Jrnl.* XXXVIII. 750 Measurements..of work functions, photoconductance, surface conductivity and field effect have indicated that there is a large density of surface states.

ˌ**photoconˈducting,** *ppl. a. Physics.* Also with hyphen. [f. PHOTO- 1 + CONDUCTING *ppl. a.*] Exhibiting or utilizing a decrease in electrical resistance when illuminated.

1929 *Sci. Abstr.* A. XXXII. 638 (*heading*) Thallium photo-conducting cells. **1932** HUGHES & DUBRIDGE *Photoelectric Phenomena* viii. 329 Cuprous oxide..was found to be photoconducting. **1974** *Encycl. Brit. Macropædia* XI. 184/2 Zinc sulfide phosphors..are photoconducting, which means that many excited electrons are lifted to the conduction band.

ˌ**photoconˈduction.** *Physics.* Also with hyphen. [f. PHOTO- 1 + CONDUCTION.] = PHOTOCONDUCTIVITY.

1929 CAMPBELL & RITCHIE *Photoelectric Cells* ii. 20 Our present knowledge of photo-conduction is largely due to the work of Gudden and Pohl. **1955** *Proc. IRE* XLIII. 1819 (*heading*) Photoconduction in germanium and silicon. **1965** PHILLIPS & WILLIAMS *Inorg. Chem.* I. vi. 209 Excitation of electrons in semiconductors can also be brought about by absorption of light, the phenomenon of photo-conduction. **1971** SMITH & THOMSON *Optics* xxiii. 334 In another type of television camera tube, the basic effect is photoconduction instead of photo-emission.

ˌ**photoconˈductive,** *a. Physics.* Also with hyphen. [f. PHOTO- 1 + CONDUCTIVE *a.*] Photoconducting; of or pertaining to the property of being photoconducting.

1929 CAMPBELL & RITCHIE *Photoelectric Cells* i. 1 Selenium cells might be termed photo-conductive. **1933** *Product Engin.* Aug. 289/1 With each of the three general types of cells, photo-voltaic, photo-emissive and photo-conductive, it is possible to use a wide variety of auxiliary equipment. **1957** *Proc. Inst. Electr. Engin.* CIV. B. 467/1 In 1873, Smith discovered the change in conductivity of selenium when sunlight fell upon it—the photo-conductive effect. **1960** *Time* 8 Mar. 2/3 The effects of light, X and gamma radiation on photoconductive materials. **1971** *Sci. Amer.* June 13/3 (Advt.), An advantage of photovoltaic detectors is that no external power supply is required to produce the photosignal, whereas photoconductive detectors must be activated.

Hence ˌ**photoconducˈtivity**, the property of being photoconductive.

1929 CAMPBELL & RITCHIE *Photoelectric Cells* ii. 20 The effect of the radiation appears as an increase of conductivity of the material rather than as a current flowing from it. This is the ultimate principle of selenium and other photo-conductivity devices. **1932** HUGHES & DUBRIDGE *Photoelectric Phenomena* viii. 329 Coblentz studied the photoconductivity of the halides of thallium, lead, and silver. **1974** *Encycl. Brit. Macropædia* XIII. 817/2 The most outstanding physical property of crystalline selenium is its photoconductivity: on illumination, the electrical conductivity increases more than 1,000-fold.

ˌ**photoconˈductor.** *Physics.* Also with hyphen. [f. PHOTO- 1 + CONDUCTOR.] A photoconducting substance or device.

1929 *Sci. Abstr.* A. XXXII. 638 Detailed instructions for constructing photo-conductors. **1947** *Sun* (Baltimore) 1 Jan. 6/2 A newly developed photoconductor cell, the size of a peanut, has already spotted things never seen before on Venus and Saturn. **1967** E. CHAMBERS *Photolitho-Offset* xiv. 203 The two most common photoconductors used are selenium and zinc oxide. **1973** *Focal Dict. Photogr. Technol.* 445 Photoconductors are available whose respective sensitivities cover between them all wavelengths from 450 to 7,000 nm.

photoconˈtrol. [f. PHOTO- 1, 2 + CONTROL *sb.*]
1. Control by light.

1954 *Bot. Gaz.* CXV. 360 (*heading*) Oxygen consumption of lettuce seed in relation to photocontrol of germination. **1975** *Nature* 10 Apr. 512/2 Many aspects of plant development are subject to photocontrol by way of the chromoprotein photoreceptor phytochrome.

2. *Surveying.* (Also as two words.) A control (i.e. a system of precisely surveyed points in terms of which subordinate local surveys are carried out) consisting of points that can be identified on aerial photographs.

1956 *Nature* 3 Mar. 419/1 Good progress was made with geodetic surveys, and the triangulation and photocontrol work over twenty thousand square miles..was completed. **1967** F. H. MOFFITT *Photogrammetry* (ed. 2) v. 126 The rigid requirements for precision photo control for analytic control extension, for cadastral surveys, and for certain types of highway design mapping, make it necessary to pre-mark a great deal of the control points. **1974** P. R. WOLF *Elem. Photogrammetry* xi. 223 According to this rule, a map being plotted with a contour interval of 10 feet requires vertical photo control accurate to within ± 2·0 feet.

photoconversion to **-convertible:** see PHOTO- 1.

photocopier (ˈfəʊtəʊkɒpɪə(r)). Also (*rare*) -copyer. [f. next + -ER[1].] **a.** An apparatus for making photocopies.

1934 in WEBSTER. **1959** *Economist* 21 Mar. 1087/1 For more than 20 to 25 copies it will prove cheaper to use some kind of duplicator than even the cheapest type of photocopyer. **1964** D. FRANCIS *Nerve* xvi. 210, I made ten copies of this statement and then on the photocopier printed ten copies each of the statements. **1973** *Daily Colonist* (Victoria, B.C.) 29 July 4/5 They're electioneering day by day with their photocopiers reeling out these miles of guff. **1978** 'L. BLACK' *Foursome* xi. 104 There was a public photo-copier in the main post office..coin-operated, 5p per one copy of one sheet.

b. One who operates a photocopying machine.

1977 *Daily Tel.* 26 Nov. 15/2 A fourth man,..who had worked at Somerset House as a photocopier, was jailed for nine months.

photocopy (ˈfəʊtəʊkɒpɪ), *v.* [f. PHOTO- 2 + COPY *v.*[1]

In quot. 1924 the formation is prob. *photo + copying machine* rather than *photocopy + -ing + machine*.]

trans. To make a photocopy of. So ˈ**photocopied** *ppl. a.*, ˈ**photocopying** *vbl. sb.* and *ppl. a.*

1924 C. W. HACKLEMAN *Commerc. Engraving & Printing* (rev. ed.) 792 Photo copying machines. In Fig. 2015 is shown a machine for making copies of records, drawings,.. flat merchandise, etc., by a simplified method of photography, the copies being made in enlarged, reduced or natural size directly upon sensitized paper. *Ibid.* 793 (*caption*) Prints as made with a photo copying machine. **1942** H. H. FUSSLER *Photogr. Reproduction for Libraries* xi. 192 Less expensive papers can be used in many instances for enlargement printing than are required in the original photocopying machines. **1948** *Library Assoc. Rec.* Feb. 37/1 There are private photocopying firms in most cities. **1952** I. GRAHAM *Encycl. Advertising* 350/1 The original subject may be photocopied in actual, enlarged, or reduced size; the finished photocopy may be black on a white background (called a 'positive') or white on a black background (called a 'negative'). **1958** S. HYLAND *Who goes Hang?* xxxix. 184 Neat files of photo-copied documents. **1958** H. R. VERRY *Document Copying* vii. 40 Photocopying processes are..able to copy material which cannot be reproduced on the typewriter, such as drawings, half-tone and line illustrations. **1966** *McGraw-Hill Encycl. Sci. & Technol.* X. 142/2 Photocopying processes may be somewhat arbitrarily divided into seven classes: silver halide photocopying, transfer processes, thermography.., plan copying, electrostatic processes, the electrolytic process, and microfilming. **1968** *Brit. Med. Bull.* XXIV. 222/1 Many laboratories..have used photocopying or laboratory record cards as a means of reporting their results. **1972** A. PRICE *Col. Butler's Wolf* vi. 55 He passed the sheets to Butler. Anonymous, greyish photocopying paper; the reproduction of a letter. **1973** *Nature* 16 Mar. 147/2 Advance copies of the technical report are available in photocopied form. **1976** P. HILL *Hunters* v. 47 Here's the questionnaire, get it photocopied.

photocopy (ˈfəʊtəʊkɒpɪ), *sb.* [f. prec. or f. PHOTO- 2 + COPY *sb.*] A copy of documentary material made by any of various processes (usu. involving the chemical or electrical action of light on a specially prepared surface) in a copying machine and usu. the same size as the original.

1934 in WEBSTER. **1952** [see prec.]. **1958** S. HYLAND *Who goes Hang?* xxii. 97 A simple photo-copy, in black and white, of a..drawing. **1966** *Lancet* 24 Dec. 1414/1, I was flattered enough to have some photocopies made of my modest contribution. **1971** *Physics Bull.* Nov. 682/1 In the USA, theses are readily available either on microfilm or as photocopies. **1973** 'C. AIRD' *His Burial Too* xiv. 130 The photocopy..had been folded neatly inside a telephone directory.

photocurrent, -damage: see PHOTO- 1.

photodegradable, -degradation: see PHOTO- 3.

photodensitometer to **-detector:** see PHOTO- 1.

photodimer to **-dimerize:** see PHOTO- 3.

photodiode (fəʊtəʊˈdaɪəʊd). *Electronics.* Also with hyphen. [f. PHOTO- 1 + DIODE *a.*, *sb.*] A semiconductor diode which generates a potential difference or changes its electrical resistance when illuminated.

1945 S. BENZER *Photoelectric Effects in Germanium* (U.S. Dept. of Commerce, Office of Publication Board PB 28644) 3 In exploring germanium samples for their rectification at different points, uncommon current-voltage characteristics are sometimes observed. There are two types which are of particular interest because of their sensitivity to light... K. Lark-Horovitz has given the descriptive names 'photodiode' and 'photopeak' to these characteristics. *Ibid.* 4 Even in the most highly saturated photodiodes, the current continues to rise somewhat as the voltage is raised. **1959** [see PHOTOTRANSISTOR]. **1962** *Jrnl. Optical Soc. Amer.* LII. 1237/1 Large-area photodiodes have been in use for a number of years as solar cells for the conversion of solar radiation to electrical power. **1971** *Nature* 20 Aug. 540/1 The photometers are protected from excessive light levels by protective photodiodes which disconnect the high voltage supply at times when the light level is above a minimum value. **1975** D. G. FINK *Electronics Engineers Handbk.* XI. 67 Figure 11-55 is a cross-sectional diagram of a metal semiconductor (Schottky barrier) photodiode. **1978** *Gramophone* Jan. 1322/2 A light beam from a heliumneon laser scans the track and the reflected light is directed towards a photodiode which converts the light variations into a corresponding electrical signal for decoding and relaying to the aerial socket of a standard TV set for viewing and listening.

photodisintegration: see PHOTO- 1.

photodissociate, -dissociation: see PHOTO- 3.

photodynamic (ˌfəʊtdaɪˈnæmɪk), *a.* [f. PHOTO- 1 + DYNAMIC *a.*]

a. Pertaining or relating to the energy of light.

1893 *Syd. Soc. Lex.*, *Photodynamic*, belonging to the energy of light-rays.

b. [after G. *photodynamisch* (H. von Tappeiner 1904, in *Münch. med. Wochenschr.* 19 Apr. 714/1).] Involving or causing a toxic response to light, esp. ultraviolet light.

1909 *Jrnl. Chem. Soc.* XCVI. II. 925 Extracts in methyl alcohol of various etiolated plants invariably showed a distinct photodynamic action on suspensions of red-blood corpuscles. **1937** *Ann. Reg. 1936* 59 Advance was made in the understanding of the photodynamic inactivation of viruses and bacteria. **1965** SELIGER & MCELROY *Light* v. 327 Calcutt (1954) found a large group of carcinogens, other than the polycyclic hydrocarbons, that was also photodynamic. **1973** *Daily Colonist* (Victoria, B.C.) 16 Nov. 5/5 The 'photodynamic therapy' may provide a new approach to treating several human cancers. **1974** *Nature* 9 Aug. 504/1 Light of wavelengths between 400 nm or 500–600 nm causes lesions through photodynamic action of porphyrin in the skin. **1977** *Ibid.* 3 Nov. 15/3 The use of dye photosensitisers in research on the so-called photodynamic effect is an area in which an important role for $^1\Delta_g O_2$ is beyond dispute.

Also ˌ**photodyˈnamical** *a.*; ˌ**photodyˈnamically** *adv.*; ˌ**photodyˈnamics**, that part of physics which deals with the energy of light, esp. in relation to growth or movement in plants.

1890 GARNSEY & BALFOUR tr. *Sachs' Hist. Bot.* III. iii. 535 The movements of swarm-spores..must be ranked with these photodynamical phenomena. *Ibid.* 554 [Normal growth and the movements of protoplasm] two phenomena which also fall within the province of photodynamics. **1926** E. MAYER *Clin. Applic. Sunlight* v. 87 With the exception of toluene-red and indigo-carmine, all dyes which stained staphylococci well, and were not toxic for them, were photodynamically active. **1954** *Jrnl. Bacteriol.* LXVIII. 125/2 Photodynamically inactivated phage. **1967** J. M. HOSKINS *Virol. Procedures* xiii. 181 Neutral red is a photodynamically active dyestuff, and infected cells incubated in its presence in the light fail to yield normal plaques.

photo-effect, -ejection: see PHOTO- 1.

photoelastic (fəʊtəʊɪˈlæstɪk), *a.* Also with hyphen. [f. PHOTO- 1 + ELASTIC *a.* and *sb.*] Employing or exhibiting the property of becoming birefringent when mechanically stressed, so that polarized light passed through such a substance gives rise to interference fringes that display the stress patterns in it.

1911 E. G. COKER in *Trans. Inst. Naval Archit.* LIII. 265 (*heading*) The determination, by photo-elastic methods, of the distribution of stress in plates of variable section, with some applications to ships' plating. **1920** *Flight* XII. 399/1 On arrival..they were welcomed by the Superintendent, and later attended the lecture of Professor Coker on his photo-elastic method of measuring stresses in materials. **1936** *Jrnl. R. Aeronaut. Soc.* XL. 472 To analyse quick variations of internal stresses, *e.g.*, in vibrating specimens or in impact phenomena, kinematography or [*read* of] photo-elastic fringes at very high speeds was devised. **1953** FAIRMAN & CUTSHALL *Mech. of Materials* xiii. 372 A third method of experimental stress analysis involves the transmission of polarized light through transparent models and is known as the photoelastic method. **1958** *New Scientist* 2 Oct. 953/2 The 'photo-elastic technique'..enables the movements of stresses inside the gear teeth under load to be seen. **1965** HAWKES & HOLISTER in Zienkiewicz & Holister *Stress Anal.* xii. 267 In the photoelastic coating technique, sheets of birefringent plastic are bonded, using a reflective cement, to the surface of the body being studied. When the body is strained under load, the strain is conveyed through the cement to the coating where isoclinic and isochromatic fringes appear, when the coating is viewed through a reflection polariscope. **1970** *New Scientist* 3 Dec. 377/2 The photoelastic plastic generally indicated higher stresses than did the strain gauges.

So ˌ**photoelaˈsticity**, the photoelastic method (of stress analysis).

1911 E. G. COKER in *Engineering* 6 Jan. 1/1 (*heading*) Photo-elasticity. **1950** DOLAN & MURRAY in M. Hetényi *Handbk. Exper. Stress Anal.* xvii. 829 His [*sc.* E. G. Coker's] introduction of celluloid for models and the use of monochromatic light have led to the modern laboratory methods which make photoelasticity a powerful engineering tool. **1959** R. R. ARCHER et al. *Introd. Mech. of Solids* iv. 157 The three most widely used methods of measuring strain are 1. Photoelasticity. 2. Brittle coatings. 3. Wire or foil strain gages.

ˌ**photo-eˈlectric**, *a.* Also **photelectric.** [f. PHOTO- + ELECTRIC.]

†**a.** = PHOTO-GALVANIC. *Obs.* Now usu. written as one word. **b.** Pertaining to, furnishing, or employing electric light. **c.** Of or pertaining to photo-electricity (see below); producing an electric effect by means of light. pertaining to or employing a photoelectric effect; ***photoelectric absorption***, the absorption of light by an atom which then emits an electron; ***photoelectric cell*** = PHOTOCELL; ***photoelectric effect*** (see quot. 1973); ***photoelectric emission***, the emission of electrons by an illuminated surface. **d.** Used for taking photographs by electric light.

a. 1863 *Boston Commw.* (U.S.) 30 Oct., A specimen of what is called the 'Photelectric engraving', according to a new art called 'the Dallas process'. **1905** *Daily Chron.* 14 Mar. 3/7 The early photo-electric engravings by the Pretsch process are not half a century old.

b. 1863 ATKINSON *Ganot's Physics* VII. v. 441 Photoelectric Microscope. This is nothing more than the solar microscope,..illuminated by the electric light. **1875** KNIGHT *Dict. Mech.* 1679/1 *Photo-electric Lamp*, a name for the electric lamp.

c. 1880 *Athenæum* 20 Nov. 679/1 Prof. Minchin showed by experiment the photo-electric current set up by a beam of light falling on a sheet of tinfoil immersed in a solution of acid carbonate of calcium. **1891** *Phil. Mag.* XXXI. 231 The seleno-aluminium cells differ from all other photoelectric cells that I have constructed in their great sensitiveness to all parts of the spectrum. **1892** *Photogr. Ann.* II. 113 As a rule a much greater photo-electric effect is produced by the more refrangible rays than by the less refrangible. **1903** A. R. WALLACE *Man's Place in Universe* 290 Experiments on the Electrical Measurement of Starlight by means of a photo-electric cell. **1912** *Physical Rev.* XXXIV. 475 Photoelectric cells containing sodium or potassium..give a current on illumination which is strictly proportional to the intensity of the exciting light. **1921** *Jrnl. R. Soc. Art* 16 Dec. 85/1 The electrons so detached are called photoelectrons and the action photoelectric. **1949** *Jrnl. Brit. Interplanetary Soc.* VIII. 115 The photo-electric telescope, which can amplify faint images. **1955** *Sci. News Let.* 12 Mar. 168/3 The instrument, known as a photoelectric polarimeter, measures polarization of skylight with the aid of polarizing prisms. **1958** W. K. MANSFIELD *Elem. Nucl. Physics* i. 10 The electrons can gain this energy by absorbing electromagnetic radiation which gives rise to photo-electric emission of electrons. *Ibid.* v. 44 In photo-electric absorption the γ-ray interacts with an atom as a whole, ejecting an electron. **1960** R. W. MARKS *Dymaxion World of B. Fuller* 25/1 In 1927, seeking photo-electric cells and relay-actuated devices, he wrote to his brother. **1961** G. R. CHOPPIN *Exper. Nucl. Chem.* iii. 30 The photo-electric effect is the predominant mode of interaction in aluminium for gamma rays below 60 kev. **1970** O. DOPPING *Computers & Data Processing* xi. 161 In the photo-electric reader, a lamp sends light beams onto a number of photo cells through the holes in the tape. **1973** J. YARWOOD *Electricity & Magnetism* xv. 594 There are three main photoelectric effects: (*a*) the photoemissive effect or surface photoemission, in which electrons are emitted from the surface of a material when radiation falls upon it; (*b*) the photoconductive effect, concerned when the incident radiation causes electrons to be released within the material (a non-metallic solid) and so increase its conductivity; (*c*) the photovoltaic effect, in which the radiation absorbed in a device causes an e.m.f. to be set up at a discontinuity..at a barrier between two different materials.

So ˌ**photo-eˈlectrical** *a.* = *photo-electric* (*Cent. Dict.* 1890); ˌ**photoeˈlectrically** *adv.*; ˌ**photo-elecˈtricity**, electricity generated or affected by light.

1877 *Nature* 25 Oct. 558/2 Some interesting experiments on the photo-electricity of fluorspar. **1888** A. RIGHI in *Phil. Mag.* XXV. 315 The system of the two metals, when receiving the radiation, behaves then as a voltaic cell, and can be called a photoelectrical cell. **1911** *Physical Rev.* XXXII. 631 A platinum cathode film on glass is photo-electrically active even when of the utmost tenuity. **1923** GLAZEBROOK *Dict. Appl. Physics* IV. 563/2 One of the most interesting phases of the inquiry into the laws and constants of radiation is the confirmatory data which one obtains from a consideration..of photo-electrical action. **1941** MILLMAN & SEELY *Electronics* iii. 101 The number of electrons released photoelectrically from any part of the photocathode depends upon the intensity of the light at that point. **1974** *Physics Bull.* May 204/1 The work functions of polycrystalline films of aluminium..were measured photoelectrically.

photoelectrochemical, -electromagnetic: see PHOTO- 1.

photoelectron (ˈfəʊtəʊɪlɛktrɒn). *Physics.* Also with hyphen. [f. PHOTO- 1 + ELECTRON[2].] An electron released from an atom by the interaction of a photon with it; *esp.* one emitted from a solid surface by the action of light.

1912 *Phil. Trans. R. Soc.* A. CCXII. 206 The law connecting the maximum emission velocity of the photo-electrons with the wave-length has been investigated by Ladenburg for Cu, Zu and Pt, and by Kunz for Na-K alloy and Cs. **1934** [see COMPTON]. **1962** H. D. BUSH *Atomic & Nucl. Physics* ix. 209 An electron bound in an atom may absorb the whole of the energy of an incident γ-ray photon, being ejected from the atom as a photo-electron. *Ibid.* 210 The photoelectrons..will have a short range in the absorbing material, and so unless the material is very thin they are likely to be reabsorbed. **1965** *Wireless World* Sept. 442/1 The process by which the energy of the particles is converted first into photons and then into photo-electrons at the cathode of a photo-multiplier tube is very inefficient. **1975** J. R. LAMARSH *Introd. Nuclear Engin.* iii. 76 The kinetic energy of the ejected photoelectron is equal..to the energy of the photon less the binding energy of the electron to the atom.

Hence ˌ**photoelecˈtronic** *a.*, of or pertaining to a photoelectron, or the interaction of light with electrons; ˌ**photoelecˈtronics** *sb. pl.* (const. as *sing.*), the study of photoelectronic phenomena.

1922 *Physical Rev.* XX. 195 (*heading*) Symmetry of emergent and incident photoelectronic velocities. **1940** *Chambers's Techn. Dict.* 638/1 Photo-electronics. **1947** *Jrnl. Optical Soc. Amer.* XXXVII. 430/1 The lower limit of usable voltage or gain in the photomultiplier tube in a pulse-counting application is reached when the photo-electronic output pulse becomes reduced..to the point where there is confusion from the tube noise and the thermal noise of the coupling resistor. **1957** *Proc. Inst. Electr. Engin.* CIV. B. 480/1 The photo-electric effect is the fundamental basis of the generation of television signals, since this depends on the conversion of light energy into electrical energy. A detailed account of this branch of photo-electronics is beyond the scope of this review. **1963** *Adv. Photochem.* I. 276 The second fundamental photo-electronic mechanism often producing photochromism is charge transfer (photoionization). **1966** N. S. KAPANY *Fiber Optics* (1967) viii. 206 One important application of fiber optics in photoelectronics lies in the coupling of image intensifier stages. **1970** *Sci. Jrnl.* Aug. 90/1 Modern photoelectronic devices can detect or produce radiations over the whole electromagnetic spectrum. **1977** *Gramophone* Apr. 1629/1 The auto-stop and pickup return at the end of a record is sensed by photo-electronic means, involving no side pressures.

photo-electrotype: see PHOTO- 2.

photoemission (ˈfəʊtəʊɪmɪʃən). *Physics.* Also with hyphen and † as two words. [f. PHOTO- 1 + EMISSION.] The emission of electrons from a surface by the action of light incident on it.

1916 *Physical Rev.* VII. 383 (*heading*) Theories of photo emission. **1923** *Ibid.* XXII. 578 It is evident..that the gases given off by the copper-oxide cylinder during the baking out of the tube and the glowing of the filament, have a pronounced effect upon the photo-emission. **1961** G. R. CHOPPIN *Exper. Nucl. Chem.* iii. 35 Tertiary electrons may be produced by photoemission resulting from the photons of the secondary ionization process. **1971** SMITH & THOMSON *Optics* xxiii. 334 In another type of television camera tube, the vidicon, the basic effect is photoconduction instead of photoemission.

So ˈ**photoemitted, -emitting** *ppl. adjs.*; **photoeˈmissive** *a.*, exhibiting, employing, or pertaining to photoemission; ˈ**photoemitter**, a photoemissive body or substance.

1932 *Electronics* Jan. 19/2 The necessary condition arises to develop a photoemissive surface which..gives satisfactory emission. **1933** *Jrnl. Inst. Electr. Engin.* LXXIII. 439/1 The equilibrium potential of the element is defined by (*a*) the velocity of the beam [of electrons] and (*b*) the secondary emission from the photo-emitting substance due to bombardment by the electrons. **1957** *Ibid.* CIV. B. 467/1 Hertz discovered the photo-emissive effect—the loss of negative electric charges from metal surfaces which are illuminated. **1957** *Proc. Inst. Electr. Engin.* CIV. B. 468/2 The earliest photo-emitters were common metal surfaces. **1959** *Control* Feb. 92/2 The spectral response of photoemissive cells depends on the cathode coating. **1970** *Nature* 3 Oct. 6/1 Two new spectroscopes using synchroton radiation and photoemitted electrons are singled out for special mention. **1971** SMITH & THOMSON *Optics* xxiii. 333 Semiconductors are widely used as photoemitting surfaces. **1973** [see PHOTO-ELECTRIC *a.* c]. **1975** *Physics Bull.* Feb. 65/2 For the first time in a commercial instrument the simultaneous measurement of the energy and angular distribution of photoemitted or secondary electrons can be made.

ˌ**photo-enˈgraving.** [f. PHOTO- + ENGRAVING.] A common name for processes in which, by the action of photography, a matrix is obtained from which prints in ink can be taken; also, a print or engraving so made. (Usually restricted to those cases in which the matrix is in relief, as distinguished from PHOTOGRAVURE, in which it is usually in intaglio.) Also *attrib.* So **photo-enˈgrave** *v. trans.*; **photo-enˈgraver**, one who practises photo-engraving.

1872 *Nature* 8 Feb. v. 285/2 Some results of early photo-engraving. **1881** *Times* 4 Jan. 3/6 The very first true photographic process discovered by Niépce..is again practised for photo-engraving. **1881** *Athenæum* 19 Mar. 401/3 A photo-engraving..enlarged from a photograph.., which is a fine example of photo-engraving. **1889** *MacKellar's Amer. Printer* (ed. 17) 37 Three distinct methods of photo-engraving are employed in the United States; namely, swelled gelatine, photo-etching, and wash-out. **1892** WOODBURY *Encycl. Phot.* 506 Producing photo-engraved plates by the bitumen process. **1902** *Daily Chron.* 24 Mar. 3/4 Her drawings should give the photo-engraver no trouble.

photoenvironment to **-fabrication:** see PHOTO- 1.

photo-essay to **-filigrave:** see PHOTO- 2.

photo-ˈfinish. Also **photo finish.** [f. PHOTO- 2 + FINISH *sb.*] The finish of a race in which competitors are so close that the result has to be determined by reference to a photograph of the situation. Also *attrib.* and *fig.*

1936 *N.Y. Times* 1 July 36/6 New..tests will be made tomorrow at Pimlico on the photo finish device. *Ibid.* 2 July 16/8 At Belmont Park thirty pictures were called for. Of this number the photo finish awarded the decision to sixteen horses racing on the outside, with fourteen on the inside. **1938** D. RUNYON *Take it Easy* xv. 283, I will take a chance on Nicely-Nicely against anything on four legs, except maybe an elephant, and at that he may give the elephant a photo finish. **1940** *Sun* (Baltimore) 22 Nov. 1/2 Gov. Payne H. Ratner..emerged a photo-finish leader tonight in the complete unofficial count of ballots cast sixteen days ago. **1944** J. H. FULLARTON *Troop Target* 160 'We've got to choose between security and progress.' 'Personally,' said MacVaughan, 'I'm for security—but it's a photo finish.' **1951** *Sport* 7–13 Jan. 4/2 Combination 'B' looks like proving a photo-finish between Plymouth and Chelsea, with Charlton holding an outside chance. **1961** *Times* 22 July 3/2 Jones..snatched second place through a photo-finish from Radford. **1973** D. FRANCIS *Slay-Ride* iv. 55 Sixteen hundred metres for staying two-year-olds... There was a photo-finish. **1974** *Times* 6 May 1/3 A photo finish was predicted by the last two public opinion polls. The final one showed M Mitterrand..winning on the second ballot by a short head. **1976** *Guardian Weekly* 19 Sept. 7/2 The Zia coup was a photofinish affair just four days after another army putsch that is popularly supposed to have been backed by India. **1976** *Norwich Mercury* 19 Nov. 10/1 A number of very close contests took place in Division Two, but Thetford British Legion B and Saints E were involved in a 'photo-finish' which the Legion won by a whisker.

photofission: see PHOTO- 1.

photofit (ˈfəʊtəʊfɪt). Also **Photo-Fit.** [f. PHOTO- 2 + FIT *sb.*[4]] Name of a method of building up an identikit picture (cf. IDENTIKIT) by assembling a number of photographs of individual facial features; a picture so formed. Freq. *attrib.*

1970 *Guardian* 23 Apr. 6/4 The Home Office believes it has a 'promising development' at its disposal with the introduction of a new system of criminal identification—the Photo-Fit. By using photographs instead of line drawings, the new technique will enable the police to build up..many ..composite faces. *Ibid.* 6/5 Photo-Fit is a product of the invention of Mr Jacques Penry..and the manufacturing facilities of John Waddington Ltd. of Leeds. **1971** *Daily Tel.* 5 Mar. 2/8 Photo-Fit and Identikit pictures have been issued to police throughout London. **1973** *Oxf. Times* 10 Aug. 1/9 Thames Valley Police have issued a photofit picture and a description of a man they wish to interview. **1974** J. GARDNER *Corner Men* xiv. 233 They showed..a straight and recent picture of Peppe, together with some photofits put together to show the [Mafia] don in a permutation of disguises. **1976** *Daily Record* (Glasgow) 4 Dec. 13/2 Police are so anxious to capture him that they applied for special permission from the Lord Advocate to issue this photofit picture.

photoflash (ˈfəʊtəʊflæʃ). Also with hyphen. [f. PHOTO- 2 + FLASH *sb.*[2]] A flash of light produced to enable a photograph to be taken; a device for producing such a flash. Freq. *attrib.*

1930 *N.Y. Times* 24 Oct. 21/2 Noiseless and smokeless photoflash lamp devised. **1946** L. E. O. CHARLTON *R.A.F. & U.S.A.A.F. July 1943 to Sept. 1944* vii. 156 (*caption*) This night photograph shows huge volumes of smoke pouring from targets bombed at Duesseldorf which have been illuminated by a photo flash bomb. **1946** *R.A.F. Jrnl.* May 170 (*caption*) A Lancaster Master-Bomber on a night raid dropping a photo-flash. **1956** A. H. COMPTON *Atomic Quest* I. 58 The question is one of straightforward thermodynamics, which I had myself used several years before in calculating..the forces that cause bursting of photoflash bulbs. **1964** L. DEIGHTON *Funeral in Berlin* vii. 46 Photo-flashes sliced instants from eternity. **1972** *Gloss. Electrotechnical, Power Terms (B.S.I.)* IV. iii. 15 *Photoflash lamp*, lamp giving..a single high light output for a very brief period, for lighting objects to be photographed. **1975** N. FREELING *What are Bugles blowing For?* iv. 17 An expressionless face for the photo-flash.

photoflood (ˈfəʊtəʊflʌd). [f. PHOTO- 2 + FLOOD *sb.*] A very bright flood-light used in photography and cinematography. Freq. *attrib.*

1933 *Pop. Sci. Monthly* Feb. 76/1 The ordinary bulb in the reading light was removed and a photoflood bulb substituted.. The photoflood is so strong that it will give the proper effect during the brief time the shutter is open for the flash. **1937** *Discovery* Feb. 57/2 A photoflood bulb gives an intensity of the same order at close range. **1962** *Which?* May 133/2 The Type A photoflood version of Kodachrome. **1972** *Amat. Photographer* 12 Jan. 38 A most popular light source with amateur photographers, photofloods have a colour temperature of 3,400° K and a very high light output. **1977** J. HEDGECOE *Photographer's Handbk.* 34 A larger 'No. 2' photoflood bulb..offers longer life but is more expensive.

photofluorogram to **-fluoroscopy**: see PHOTO- 2.

photoformer: see PHOTO- 1.

photog (fəʊˈtɒg). Also fotog. N. Amer. colloq. abbrev. of PHOTOGRAPHER.

1913 *Technical World* XIX. 395/1 The elements of the air ..and a dozen other things may make the newspaper 'fotog' ready to throw up the sponge. **1934** H. N. ROSE *Thes. Slang* 51/2 Photographer: *a photog.* **1952** *Daily News* (N.Y.) 21 Aug. C4 The Swedish fotogs were actually saving film. **1968** *Globe & Mail* (Toronto) 17 Feb. 35 (Advt.), A photog's delight! **1973** R. PARKES *Guardians* vi. 104 You'll like that fashion photog of ours—what's her name.

ˌphotogalˈvanic, *a.* Also **photo-galvanic**. [f. PHOTO- 2 + GALVANIC.] **1.** = PHOTO-GALVANOGRAPHIC; cf. PHOTOELECTRIC *a.* a.

1852 JOUBERT in *Journal Soc. Arts* 26 Nov. in *Circ. Sc.* (*c* 1865) I. 241/1 This process will be found extremely valuable..for photogalvanic plates.

2. *Physics.* Designating or utilizing the generation of a potential difference between two electrodes by a photo-chemical reaction in the electrolyte containing them.

1940 E. RABINOWITCH in *Jrnl. Chem. Physics* VIII. 551/1 The term 'photogalvanic effect' is used in the present series of papers to denote a special case of the so-called Becquerel effect, in which the influence of light on the electrode potential is due to a photochemical process in the body of the electrolyte (as distinct from photo-chemical or photoelectric processes in the surface layer of the electrode..). *Ibid.* 553/2 The top curve shows *L* [*sc.* the intensity of illumination] as a function of time... The lower curve represents the simultaneous changes in the potential of a Pt-electrode placed in the solution—the 'photogalvanic effect'. *Ibid.* 560 The oxidation-reduction system thionine-iron..provides an extremely sensitive photogalvanic cell. **1956** *Nature* 21 Jan. 110/2 Electrical processes for the direct conversion of radiation to electricity, including thermoelectric generators, photo-voltaic cells and *p-n* junctions and photogalvanic cells. **1976** *Interdisciplinary Sci. Rev.* I. 132/2 The irradiation of an electrode/electrolyte system produces a change in the electrode potential (on open circuit) or in the current flowing (on closed circuit). The cause of this may be a photochemical reaction in bulk solution, the products of which are electroactive, in which case the cell is commonly called a photogalvanic cell.

ˌphoto-galvaˈnography. [f. PHOTO- 2 + GALVANOGRAPHY.] A process of obtaining from a positive photograph on glass or paper, or a drawing on translucent paper, by means of a gutta-percha impression from a relief negative in bichromated gelatine, an electrotype plate capable of being used as in copper-plate printing.

See *The Engineer* 25 Apr. 1856, 227; *Art Jrnl.* VIII. 215. The name was given by Mr. D. C. Dallas, by whom the process, invented by Mr. Paul Pretsch of Vienna, was perfected in 1855.

Hence **ˌphoto-galˈvanograph**, a print thus formed; **ˌphoto-galvanoˈgraphic** *a.*, of, pertaining to, or produced by photo-galvanography.

1855 (*title*) The Patent Photo-galvanographic Company. **1856** P. PRETSCH *Paper before Soc. Arts* 23 Apr., The name of 'photo-galvanography, or engraving by light and electricity' has been given to the new art by Mr. Duncan Campbell Dallas. *Ibid.*, The impressions from the photo-galvanographic plates. **1870** *Eng. Mech.* 7 Jan. 405/3 Previous to the invention of the photo-galvanographic process by Herr Paul Pretsch, no satisfactory permanent prints in carbon from plates had been obtained by means of photography. **1875** KNIGHT *Dict. Mech.* 1679/2 *Photogalvanograph.*

photogastroscope, -gelatin: see PHOTO- 2.

photogen (ˈfəʊtədʒən). [f. Gr. φῶς, φωτ- light (PHOTO- 1) + -GEN, used as = 'producing'. In mod.F. *photogène*.]

1. Name for a kind of paraffin oil; kerosene.

a **1864** GESNER *Coal, Petrol.*, etc. (1865) 93 Wagenman applied himself to the oils derivable from turf, Crown coal, and bituminous slate, from which he obtained photogen, solar oil, and paraffin. **1880** *Pall Mall G.* 10 May 12/1 The American raw petroleum gave about two-thirds of its weight of photogen, while the Russian only gives about one-third photogen, but a greater proportion of fatty oils.

2. See quot.

1858 *Soc. Arts Jrnl.* VI. App. I. Catalogue 10th exhibit. inventions 31, No. 166 Patent Photogen, or Light Generator, to be used for taking Photographs at Night.

3. A light-producing organ in an animal.

1896 *Cambr. Nat. Hist.* II. 296 In *Tomopteris* there is..a brightly-coloured spherical organ, which for a long time was regarded as an eye, but from its structure appears to be a 'photogen'.

photogene (ˈfəʊtədʒiːn). [mod. f. Gr. type *φωτογενής light-produced: see PHOTO- 1, -GEN 2.]

1. *Physiol.* A visual impression (usually negative, i.e. having the complementary colours and shades) continuing after the withdrawal of the object which produced it; an after-image.

1864 H. SPENCER *Biol.* §62 In youth, the visual apparatus is so quickly restored to its state of integrity, that many of these photogenes, as they are called, cannot be perceived.

†**2.** A 'photogenic drawing', photograph. *Obs.*

1851 CRABB *Techn. Dict.* 541/2 *Photograph*,..also called *photogene*,..signifying what is generated or delineated by the help of light.

photogenetic (ˌfəʊtəʊdʒɪˈnɛtɪk), *a. rare*⁻¹. [f. PHOTO- 1 + GENETIC.] Having the property of producing or emitting light, luminiferous.

1896 *Allbutt's Syst. Med.* I. 530 The phosphorescence observed on the surface of sea-water, or on decomposing meat or fish, is due to photogenetic bacteria.

photogenic (fəʊtəʊˈdʒɛnɪk, -dʒiːnɪk), *a.* [f. as PHOTOGENE + -IC: in F. *photogénique* (Talbot in *Comptes Rendus* VIII. 341, 4 Mar. 1839). (In sense 3, not etymologically used.)]

1. Produced or caused by light.

1855 H. SPENCER *Princ. Psychol.* III. iv. 310 The darkening of the skin caused by long exposure to sunshine. .. In transparent and semi-transparent creatures any such photogenic effect must pervade the whole body. **1954** *Brain* LXXVII. 234 Photic excitation has been subjected to intense study in electroencephalographic laboratories... Yet clinical descriptions of photogenic epilepsy are few. **1962** *Times* 30 June 12/2 Self-induced photogenic epilepsy in children. **1972** NAQUET & MELDRUM in D. P. Purpura et al. *Exper. Models of Epilepsy* xv. 373 (*heading*) Photogenic seizures in baboon.

2. *spec.* Produced by, or pertaining to, the chemical action of light on a sensitized surface; an earlier word for *photographic. Obs.* exc. *Hist.*

photogenic drawing, the term originally used by W. H. Fox Talbot for photography, or for a photograph; *spec.* a photograph of a flat translucent object (as a drawing on translucent paper, a leaf, etc.), obtained by placing it under glass in contact with a sensitive film. (Hence F. *photogénique*.)

1839 (Jan. 31) TALBOT in *Proc. Roy. Soc.* IV. 120 (*title*) Some account of the Art of Photogenic Drawing, or the Process by which Natural Objects may be made to delineate them-selves without the aid of the Artist's Pencil. **1839** *Athenæum* 2 Feb. 96/2 Mr. Talbot proposes for this new art the name of Photogenic Drawing. **1839** TALBOT in *Lond. & Edin. Philos. Mag.* Mar. 1839 This paper, if properly made, is very useful for all ordinary photogenic purposes. **1839** *Proc. Scot. Soc. Arts* 27 Mar. in *Edin. New Phil. Jrnl.* XXVII. 418 Dr. Fyfe V.P. described Mr. Talbot's process of Photogenic Drawing. **1840** *Penny Cycl.* XVIII. 113 *Photogenic drawings*, facsimile representations of objects produced according to the recent discovery of M. Daguerre. **1841** BRANDE *Chem.* (ed. 5) 200 Many improvements in these photogenic drawings, as they have been termed, have been effected more especially by Mr. Fox Talbot, Sir John Herschel, and Mr. Alfred Taylor. **1842** *Blackw. Mag.* LI. 388 They were having their portraits taken by the photogenic process. **1849** FROUDE *Nemesis of Faith* 124 Like the prepared mirror of the photogenic draughtsman. **1867** J. HOGG *Microsc.* I. ii. 157 On this screen is placed a sheet of photogenic paper. **1973** *Times* 22 May 28/5 (Advt.), Early photographs and related material, including..calotypes by William Henry Fox Talbot; early photogenic drawings; [etc.].

3. = PHOTOGENETIC.

1863 *Q. Rev.* CXIV. 310 There are Grecian and Gothic lighthouses,..but even then we forget these absurdities in contemplating the beauty and perfection of their photogenic arrangements. **1865** *Spectator* 14 Jan. 49 A surrounding envelope of photogenic matter. **1876** G. F. CHAMBERS *Astron.* 711 Those portions of the Moon's surface which are illumined by a very oblique ray from the Sun possess so little photogenic power that [etc.]. **1877** HUXLEY *Anat. Inv. Anim.* vii. 440 According to Schulze the males of *Lampyris splendidula* possess two photogenic organs.

4. Of a person or thing: that is a good subject for photography; that shows to good advantage in a photograph or film. Also in Fr. form *photogénique*. orig. *U.S.*

1928 *Reflex* June 91/1 The mere doll-face, the photogenic type which thrived on 'fan' adulation, will be a thing of the past. **1931** S. GOLDWYN in *Sat. Rev.* 14 Feb. 220/1 An actor may be 'photogenic' and have personality and appearance, but that is not enough. **1931** *Daily Express* 13 Mar. 19/4 Look at..Pamela Nickalls, with her perfect oval face and high, photogenic forehead. **1935** *Times Lit. Suppl.* 10 Oct. 631/4 Spain is very probably the most *photogénique* country in Europe. **1940** *New Statesman* 19 Oct. 379 The thrills in *Foreign Correspondent* are massive and photogenic to a degree. **1948** E. WAUGH *Loved One* 5 Her legs were never *photogénique*. **1958** *Newnes Compl. Amat. Photogr.* 143 Take two common 'photogenic' subjects, a scene of hills and sky, and a child playing in a flower garden. *Ibid.* 150 It is a fact that very few faces are symmetrical, regular or photogenic. **1974** M. HASTINGS *Dragon Island* viii. 74 She was a good-looking girl; photogenic..and with the right bone structure.

Hence **photoˈgenically** *adv.*; also †**ˈphotogenize** *v. trans.* = PHOTOGRAPH *v.* (*obs.*); **photogenous** (fəʊˈtɒdʒɪnəs) *a.* = PHOTOGENETIC; †**phoˈtogeny** = PHOTOGRAPHY (*obs. rare*).

1839 MEMES tr. *Daguerre's Photogenic Drawing* (ed. 3) 53 It was I [Daguerre] who first pointed out iodine..as the sensitive coating upon which the image was to be created *photogenically. **1841** MOORE *Mem.* (1856) VII. 297, I found grouped..upon the grass before the house, Kit Talbot, Lady E. Fielding, Lady Charlotte and Mrs. Talbot, for the purpose of being *photogenized by Henry Talbot, who was busy preparing his apparatus. **1888** *Nature* 20 Sept. 512/2 To reconcile their theory of *photogenous fermentation with the hypothesis of the oxidation of a phosphorated substance. **1840** *Penny Cycl.* XVIII. 113/1 *Photogenic Drawings*, facsimile representations of objects produced according to the recent discovery of M. Daguerre. .. Such apparatus is named after its inventor the Daguerreotype, and the process itself either *photogeny, photography, or heliography (sun-drawing). **1959** *Times* 23 Feb. 10/6 There were nets drying photogenically in the sun. **1974** *Daily Tel.* 9 Aug. 13/2 The director..does score photogenically in the action scenes.

photogeology (fəʊtəʊdʒiːˈɒlədʒɪ). Also with hyphen. [f. PHOTO- 2 + GEOLOGY.] (See quot. 1941.)

1941 H. C. REA in *Bull. Amer. Assoc. Petroleum Geologists* XXV. 1796 For this little known branch of geology the writer suggests the term 'photogeology', which is defined as the geologic interpretation of aerial photographs. **1970** *Nature* 24 Jan. 322/1 The long range aim is to establish an absolute lunar time scale directly related to relative ages obtained by photogeology over the whole lunar surface. **1976** *Jrnl. R. Soc. Arts* CXXIV. 639/2 British scientists [in the Antarctic] possess an impressive array of modern techniques: airborne magnetometry,..satellite photogeology, [etc.].

Hence **ˌphotogeoˈlogic, -ˈlogical** *adjs.*, of or pertaining to photogeology; **ˌphotogeoˈlogically** *adv.*, by photogeological means; **photoˈgeologist**, an expert or specialist in photogeology.

1941 *Bull. Amer. Assoc. Petroleum Geologists* XXV. 1796 A photogeologic map would be a map produced from a stereoscopic study of the aerial photos. *Ibid.* 1797 It proved that a trained photogeologist could produce a map which would agree very favorably with actual field observations. **1949** *Ibid.* XXXIII. 1251 During 1947, more than 110,000 square miles in the Rocky Mountain region were covered photogeologically. **1950** *Ibid.* XXXIV. 2285 Mutual checking of photogeological and field work should be just as apt to lead to corrections of the one as the other whenever discrepancies are found. **1962** F. I. ORDWAY et al. *Basic Astronautics* v. 206 The first remotely conducted photogeologic experiment of another world was remarkably successful. **1966** E. BURGESS *Assault on Moon* ii. 43 The Army Map Service produced a general photogeologic map of the Moon in the late 1950s. **1967** *Q. Jrnl. Geol. Soc.* CXXIII. 255 It is possible to define the geometry of photogeologically observed large folds by plotting..dip and strike values on a stereographic net. **1972** *Science* 2 June 976/3 Deposits of basin ejecta concentric about Imbrium are termed the Fra Mauro Formation by photogeologists. **1977** A. HALLAM *Planet Earth* 111 Photogeological interpretation assist rapid production of geological maps from aerial photographs.

photoglyph (ˈfəʊtəglɪf). [f. PHOTO- 2 + Gr. γλυφή: see GLYPH.] An engraved plate, such as can be printed from, produced by the action of light. So **photoˈglyphic, photoˈglyptic** *adjs.*; **ˈphotoglyˈphography, ˈphotoglyphy**, the art or process of engraving by means of the action of light and certain chemical processes; the production of photoglyphic plates and photoglyphs or photogravures.

1852 TALBOT in *Ure's Dict. Arts* III. 444 The liquid [solution of perchloride of iron] penetrates the gelatine wherever the light has not acted on it, but it refuses to penetrate those parts upon which the light has sufficiently acted. It is upon this remarkable fact that the art of photoglyphic engraving is mainly founded. **1856** *Chambers's Encycl.* VII. 511/1 Photo-Glyphography is a process, invented by Mr. Fox Talbot, for etching a photograph into a steel plate. **1859** *Sat. Rev.* 22 Jan. 97/2 (*title*) Phototypes and Photoglyphs. *Ibid.* 98/1 To review the points in which these various processes of photoglyphy and phototypy concur. *Ibid.* 26 Feb. 242/1. **1892** WOODBURY *Encycl. Phot.* 517 Photoglyphic Engraving, a process of photo-etching invented by Fox-Talbot [1852].

photogoniometer to **-metry**: see PHOTO- 2.

photogram (ˈfəʊtəgræm). [f. PHOTO- 2 + -GRAM (as in *telegram*): see etym. note to PHOTOGRAPH *sb.*] **1.** = PHOTOGRAPH. Now *rare.*

1859 LUARD in *Archæol. Cantiana* II. 4 A lithographic drawing, from a photogram. **1859** (*title*) Photograms of an Eastern Tour, including Greece, Palestine, Egypt. **1874** H. T. GRIFFITH in *Cowper's Poems* I. Introd. 15 Not reproduced with the mechanical and soulless exactitude of the photogram. **1894** *Brit. Jrnl. Photogr.* XLI. 144/2 Portraits like these, such perfect photograms. **1935** *Amer. Mineral* XX. 476 Montmorillonite was *x*-rayed..and its lines..agree with the powder spectrum photograms of other investigators. **1961** (*title of periodical*) New photograms.

†**2.** A photograph, picture, diagram, or other facsimile transmitted by wireless or ordinary telegraphy. *Obs.* (Now called a phototelegram (see PHOTO- 1).)

1928 *Observer* 24 June 23 The wireless photogram service ..has been extended. **1928** *Times* 6 Sept. 11/6 The Postal Telegraph Company put into commercial operation to-day a new telephoto and facsimile message service, which it calls photograms. **1929** *Telegraph & Telephone Jrnl.* XVI. 4/1 Suppose that transmissions of photo-grams by modified television apparatus can take place at the rate of 30 per second.

3. A photograhic picture made without a camera (see quots.). Also †***photogramme***.

1934 *Archit. Rev.* LXXV. 12/2 As a photographer he [*sc.* Moholy-Nagy] has been a pioneer in the photogramme (the cameraless photography which he regards as the art-form of the future). **1948** J. H. GABLE *Compl. Introd. Photogr.* III. xvii. 209 The first photogram was probably made by Fox Talbot by placing lace on a sheet of his calotype paper and exposing it to light. **1958** *Newnes Comp. Amat. Photogr.* III. xxvii. 241 Photograms can also be made with the aid of a torch bulb. **1972** *Sci. Amer.* Dec. 115/1 A photogram is made without a camera by exposing photographic paper to a point light source, the leaf or the fruit being placed directly on the paper. **1978** J. H. COOTE *Focalguide to Cibachrome* 175 You can easily make photograms in colour, directly from leaves, flowers and any other translucent objects.

photogrammeter (fəʊtəʊˈgræmɪtə(r)). [f. prec. + -METER.] A photographic camera combined with a theodolite, for use in surveying, or for taking pictures for use in map-making; a phototheodolite.

1891 *Nature* 3 Sept. 426/2 One other instrument, quite recently added to the apparatus of the surveyor, is the photographic camera, converted for his especial benefit into a photogrammeter. **1893** *Athenæum* 25 Nov. 737/3 With respect to [lunar distances] the camera or photogrammeter yields more trustworthy results than does the sextant. **1898** *Nature* 14 Apr. 563/1 In the earliest form of surveying camera or photogrammeter,..the instrument consisted of little more than an ordinary bellows camera, set on a horizontal circle, and moving about a vertical axis.

photogrammetry (fəʊtəʊˈgræmɪtrɪ). [f. as prec. + -METRY.] The technique of using photographs to ascertain measurements relating to what is photographed, esp. in surveying and mapping.

1875 tr. *Vogel's Chem. Light* xiv. 170 All these circumstances militate against the application of photogrammetry, as this mode of measurement has been called by Meyenbauer. **1894** *Brit. Jrnl. Photogr.* XLI. 55 Balloon photogrammetry. **1933** *Jrnl. R. Aeronaut. Soc.* XXXVII. 386 Most of the continental plotting machines.. were designed originally for terrestrial photogrammetry, where each goniometer in the plotter can be set to a known orientation. **1934** *Ibid.* XXXVIII. 257 (*heading*) Photogrammetry of landing speeds. **1948** *Sci. News* VII. Pl. 25, After the church had been destroyed..the essential dimensions were deduced from a pre-war snapshot... The science of deducing dimensions from photographs is called Photogrammetry. **1959** F. H. MOFFITT *Photogrammetry* i. 1 The term *aerial photogrammetry* denotes that branch of photogrammetry wherein photographs of the terrain..are taken by a precision camera mounted in an aircraft... The term *terrestrial photogrammetry* denotes that branch.. wherein photographs are taken from a fixed, and usually known, position on or near the ground and with the camera axis horizontal or nearly so. *Ibid.* 2 Terrestrial photogrammetry embraces also the use of cameras at ground stations in known positions for the following purposes: To reproduce plan and elevation views of buildings and structures... By means of motion-picture photography, to make measurements involving transitory phenomena such as wave motion,..moving machinery, [etc.]. **1965** *New Scientist* 18 Nov. 507/1 Photogrammetry is now being explored for use on large microwave aerials, to check the accuracy of construction, and to measure deformations under wind loads. **1978** *Jrnl. R. Soc. Arts* CXXVI. 473/1 Ankara, particularly at the Middle East Technical University, was early in the field in the use of photogrammetry for mass recording.

Hence **photograˈmmetric**, **photograˈmmetrical** *adjs.*, of or pertaining to photogrammetry; **photograˈmmetrically** *adv.*; **photoˈgrammetrist**, an expert or specialist in photogrammetry.

1891 *Athenæum* 11 July 67/1 He maintains that every explorer should provide himself with a photogrammetrical apparatus. **1906** J. A. FLEMER *Elem. Treat. Phototopogr. Methods* i. 5 The theoretical principles upon which photogrammetric methods are primarily based were known to J. H. Lambert.., who published a work on perspective in 1759. *Ibid.* xii. 397 If differences in the elevations of points of the terrene are to be deduced photogrammetrically within a limit of error not exceeding one meter, the pictured length ..of a meter..should not appear shorter than 0·1 mm. **1939** B. B. TALLEY *Engin. Applic. Aerial & Terrestr. Photogrammetry* i. 6 For photogrammetrical purposes photographs may be classified as either aerial or terrestrial, depending on whether the taking camera was borne aloft or ..on the surface of the earth. *Ibid.*, Photogrammetry.. should never be considered as an end in itself. Such consideration is the stumbling block of photogrammetrists. **1950** *Antiquity* XXIV. 85 With the use of Photogrammetric Tables, extreme accuracy was possible in determining and measuring the exact position on the ground of crop-mark sites visible in the air photographs. **1957** *Oxf. Mag.* 21 Nov. 131/1 The search for oil today requires the organisation of teams of specialists: surveyors, palaeontologists, photogrammetrists, geophysicists and geochemists. **1970** J. A. HOWARD *Aerial Photo-Ecol.* ix. 98 Vertical photographs are simple to use photogrammetrically, as a minimum of mathematical correction is required. **1975** *Sci. Amer.* Jan. 130/3 In 1962..he organized a modern aerial photogrammetric survey of the site from 4,000 feet.

photograph (ˈfəʊtəgrɑːf, -æ-), *sb.* [f. Gr. φῶς, φωτο- light (PHOTO- 1) + -γραφος written, delineated (cf. AUTOGRAPH, PARAGRAPH): as to origin, see PHOTOGRAPHY. Cf. Ger. *photograph*, F. *photographe*, photographer, f. Gr. -γράφος writer, delineator: see -GRAPH.

English has also in *telegraph* (from Fr.) and its likes, examples of *-graph* Gr. -γράφος) in the agent sense, which have been complemented by forms in *-gram* (e.g. *telegram*) in the passive or resultant sense; influenced by which, some have used PHOTOGRAM, after *telegram*, instead of *photograph*; but this has not found general acceptance.]

a. A picture, likeness, or facsimile obtained by photography.

1839 (Mar. 14) SIR J. HERSCHEL in *Proc. Roy. Soc.* IV. 132 Pure water will fix the photograph by washing out the nitrate of silver. [*Note*, Twenty-three specimens of photographs, made by Sir John Herschel, accompany this paper; one a sketch of his telescope at Slough fixed from the image in a lens.] **1840** (Mar. 5) *Ibid.* 207 Hence are deduced ..secondly, the possibility of the future production of naturally coloured photographs. **1841** TALBOT *Specif. Patent* No. 8842. 4 It is possible to strengthen and revive photographs. **1861** MUSGRAVE *By-roads* 238 As evanescent as a photograph, which grows faint and fainter in tint the longer it remains exposed to the sun and air. **1875** tr. *Vogel's Chem. Light* xiv. 158 A photograph taken from a photograph is never so fine as an original picture. **1901** *Munsey's Mag.* XXV. 649/1 The first man to obtain a permanent photograph, in the modern sense of the word, was Nicephore Niepce, a Frenchman, who died in 1833.

b. *fig.* A picture, *esp.* a mental or verbal image or delineation; a description having the exact detail of a photograph.

1852 BAILEY *Festus* xx. (ed. 5) 336 A photograph of pre-existent light Or Paradisal sun. **1869** GOULBURN *Purs. Holiness* x. 94 [In the gospels] you have four photographs of Our Lord in different postures. **1876** FREEMAN *Norm. Conq.* V. xxiv. 403 While Domesday gives us a photograph, the compilers of codes give us an artistic picture.

c. *attrib.* and *Comb.*, as ***photograph album***, ***book***, ***camera***, ***frame***, ***gallery***; ***photograph-like*** adj.

1858 *N.Y. Tribune* 4 Nov. 1/2 The first number of *The Photograph News* appeared last Friday. **1858** F. J. COOK *Let.* 19 Sept. in F. G. Bascom *Lett. Ticonderoga Farmer* (1946) 46, I..visited..Brady's celebrated photograph gallery. **1870** O. LOGAN *Before Footlights* 258 The only thing worth carrying away was a decent sort of photograph album. **1872** E. WORDSWORTH in E. Romanes *C. M. Yonge* (1908) ix. 150, I found her armed with a large photograph-book of friends and relations. **1873** *Young Englishwoman* Feb. 94/2 Photograph frame in leather work. **1888** MRS. H. WARD *R. Elsmere* I. iii. 76 Mrs. Seaton was severely turning over a photograph book. **1896** *Westm. Gaz.* 26 Sept. 3/2 The inimitable sketches of life in that little country town were at once recognised for their photograph-like fidelity. **1900** *Daily News* 19 Apr. 7/1 The photograph camera can be the biggest liar on the face of the earth. **1940** T. S. ELIOT *East Coker* v. 14 The evening with the photograph album. **1949** *Chicago Tribune* 18 Sept. 27/4 Andrew Burgess..bought and operated Brady's national photograf gallery in Washington.

photograph (ˈfəʊtəgrɑːf, -æ-), *v.* [f. prec. sb.]

1. a. *trans.* To take a photograph of.

1839 SIR J. HERSCHEL *MS. Mems.* (on 2 Negatives) 'Photographed Feb. 17 /39. Hyp. Sod.'—'Hyp. So., Hy. Su.; J.F.W.H. Photogr. Feb. 17 /39'. *a* **1846** *Monthly Rev.* cited in WORCESTER. **1861** MUSGRAVE *By-roads* 25 Mons. Souquet has photographed it. **1883** *Hardwich's Photogr. Chem.* (ed. Taylor) 201 When a distant landscape is photographed, a large number of rays of light are concentrated upon the film. **1898** WATTS-DUNTON *Aylwin* I. vi, One Raxton fair-day I induced Winnie to be photographed.

b. *absol.* or *intr.* To practise photography, take photographs. Also *fig.*

1857 C. KINGSLEY *Two Yrs. Ago* III. i. 37 If any one will ensure me a poor two thousand a year, I will promise to photograph no more. **1861** CARLYLE *Let.* in *Trench's Lett. & Mem.* (1888) I. 332 That charming bit of 'Diary'... It is.. faithful as a picture by the sun;..*photographing* for us in that manner.

c. *intr.* (for *passive*). To undergo being photographed; to 'take' (well or badly).

1893 *Chamb. Jrnl.* 28 Oct. 676/1, I do not photograph at all well. **1919** *Conquest* Nov. 24/1 The red leaves of autumn photograph as black. **1931** F. L. ALLEN *Only Yesterday* vi. 126 He photographed well and the pictures of him in the rotogravure sections won him affection and respect. **1949** E. COXHEAD *Wind in West* i. 10 A creamily handsome young woman..Hedy Lamarr type, would photograph, summed up Tony at a glance. **1965** *Listener* 18 Nov. 817/2 Wales photographs beautifully: the short, slated roofs, the coal-tips and the valleys, the terraced houses on grey streets—none of them loses much in black and white reproduction. **1974** 'E. LATHEN' *Sweet & Low* xix. 183, I don't like the way he photographs. Yours is the face I want.

2. *trans. fig.* To portray vividly in words; to fix or impress on the mind or memory.

1862 LADY MORGAN *Mem.* I. 21 These wild, incredible, and apparently fabulous scenes..are indelibly photographed on a memory from which few things..have been effaced. **1865** BUSHNELL *Vicar. Sacr.* III. v. 296 In the twenty-fifth chapter of Matthew He photographs the transaction in a scene of judgment.

Hence **ˈphotographed** *ppl. a.*, **ˈphotographing** *vbl. sb.*

1864 *Daily Tel.* 14 June, Who are all these photographed people? *c* **1865** J. WYLDE in *Circ. Sc.* I. 140/2 All attempts at photographing must..fail. *Ibid.* 157/2 The contrast of light and shade, on which depends the beauty of all photographed productions. **1883** *Harper's Mag.* Jan. 241/2 Albums of photographed hands are fashionable. **1889** *Anthony's Photogr. Bull.* II. 149 Photographing, or 'Light drawing' is both a physical and a chemical process.

photographable (ˈfəʊtəgrɑːfəb(ə)l, -æ-), *a.* [f. prec. + -ABLE.] Capable of being photographed.

1896 *Westm. Gaz.* 18 July 2/3 When Thought is photographable! **1897** O. NORTH in *Strand Mag.* XIV. 513 It would not have been photographable. **1939** [see ABSORPTIOMETER 2]. **1962** C. WALSH *From Utopia to Nightmare* i. 20 Some artists..have created..nothing remotely photographable. **1973** 'E. MCBAIN' *Hail to Chief* i. 13 A blush which, if not quite kissable, is at least photographable.

photographee (ˌfəʊtəgrɑːˈfiː, -æ-). [f. as prec. + -EE: correl. to PHOTOGRAPHER.] The person who is photographed.

1859 *All Year Round* No. 30. 79 Picking up sorry crumbs as photographees, sitting as models. **1889** *Anthony's Photogr. Bull.* II. 21 When there is a contract between the photographer and the photographee.

†**photoˈgrapheme.** *Obs. rare.* [f. PHOTOGRAPH *sb.* + *-eme* as if f. Gr. -ημα (cf. -EME).] A photograph.

1864 G. M. HOPKINS *Further Lett.* (1956) 211 She *comprehood* who I was by my photographeme which you strangely said was not like me. **1888** *Ibid.* 291 It is not altogether as I should wish it either as a portrait or as a.. photograph, photogram, photographeme, φωτογράφημα, a work of the photographic camera.

photographer (fəˈtɒgrəfə(r)). [f. PHOTOGRAPHY + -ER[1]: cf. *geographer*, etc.] One who takes photographs; *esp.* one who practises photography as a profession or business. Also *attrib.*

1847 [J. E.] *Photography* 43 Photographers have seldom operated therewith for portraits. **1862** B. TAYLOR *Home & Abr.* Ser. II. 387 A photographer on board took two or three views. **1879** *Cassell's Techn. Educ.* III. 1 To train a special body of men as photographers. **1902** *Westm. Gaz.* 28 July 4/2 There is no training-school for the photographer-journalist.

photographic (fəʊtəʊˈgræfɪk), *a.* [f. as PHOTOGRAPHY + -IC: see -GRAPHIC. (As to origin, see PHOTOGRAPHY.)] **a.** Of, pertaining to, used in, or produced by photography; engaged or skilled in photography.

1839 (Mar. 14) HERSCHEL in *Proc. Roy. Soc.* IV. 131 His attention was first called to the subject of M. Daguerre's concealed photographic process, by a note dated the 22nd of January last. **1839** (April 10) A. FYFE in *Edin. New Phil. Jrnl.* XXVII. 147 The use of the camera obscura for Photographic purposes. **1841** TALBOT *Specif. Patent* No. 8842. 4 It should be taken on common photographic paper. *a* **1845** HOOD *Daguerr. Portrait* i, Her nose, and her mouth, with the smile that is there, Truly caught by the Art Photographic! **1859** JEPHSON *Brittany* vi. 74 He insisted on my photographic friends..dining with him. **1883** *Hardwich's Photogr. Chem.* (ed. Taylor) 39 It is gradually formed in the Photographic Nitrate Bath.

b. *fig.* Accurately portraying life or nature; minutely accurate; mechanically imitative.

1864 *Reader* 26 Nov. 665/3 Amongst novels of the photographic order we should assign a very high place to 'Broken to Harness'. **1883** RUSKIN *Art of Eng.* 30 Ouida's photographic story of 'A Village Commune'. **1890** *Chicago Advance* 24 July, Not..to be taken as pragmatical, photographic prose.

c. ***photographic memory***: a memory that records visual perceptions with the accuracy of a photograph.

1940 in *Chambers's Techn. Dict.* 638/1. **1948** 'J. TEY' *Franchise Affair* vii. 73 She has a photographic memory... She would remember what she saw. **1964** M. CRITCHLEY *Developmental Dyslexia* ix. 62 He is perhaps a person weak in visual imagery and visual memory of all types, the opposite of the person with eidetic imagery and photographic memory. **1974** A. MORICE *Killing with Kindness* iv. 37 I've got what they call a photographic memory and I don't visualise her wearing a wedding ring.

photographica (fəʊtəʊˈgræfɪkə), *sb. pl.* [f. PHOTOGRAPHIC *a.*: see -A 4.] Books, albums, or collections of photographs; items connected with photography.

1973 *Country Life* 20 Sept. (Suppl.) 76 (Advt.), Photographs and Photographica. **1976** *Times Lit. Suppl.* 25 June 804/3 Photographica, which until recently accounted for a minute part of each year's offerings at book auctions in the United States, was the subject of no less than three large sales this spring. **1976** *National Observer* (U.S.) 4 Dec. 20/3 There can be no doubt that this is one of the most remarkable collections of American photographica.

photographical (fəʊtəʊˈgræfɪkəl), *a.* [f. as PHOTOGRAPHIC *a.* + -AL[1].] Dealing with or relating to photography.

1846 in WORCESTER. **1871** PROCTOR *Light Sc.* 294 At a recent meeting of the Photographical Society.

photographically (fəʊtəˈgræfɪkəlɪ), *adv.* [f. prec. + -LY[2].] In a photographic manner; by means of or in reference to photography; from a photographic point of view.

1842 J. F. W. HERSCHEL in *Phil. Trans. R. Soc.* CXXXII. 194 The retina itself may be *photographically* impressible by strong lights. **1847** [J. E.] *Photography* 45 The object.. photographically pictured. **1856** *Engineer* 25 Apr. 227/2 The possibility of producing photographically..a printing surface of relievo and intaglio parts. **1859** GULLICK & TIMBS *Paint.* 118 The solution which renders the ivory photographically sensitive. **1882** YOUNG *Sun* 262 Violet rays, which are photographically the most active. **1968** R. A. LYTTLETON *Mysteries Solar Syst.* iv. 119 Comet Borelly showed photographically as many as nine tails.

fig. **1862** M. B. EDWARDS *John & I* xx. (1876) 159 This afternoon I have seen my life photographically, as it were. **1869** T. W. WOOD in *Student* II. 83 The chrysalides of butterflies.., their shells being photographically sensitive for a short time after the caterpillars' skins have been shed, so that each individual assumes the colour most prevalent in its immediate vicinity.

photographist (fəˈtɒgrəfɪst). Now *rare.* [f. PHOTOGRAPHY + -IST: cf. *geologist*, *botanist*, etc.] = PHOTOGRAPHER.

1843 W. H. T. *Photogr. Manip.* 3 One of the chief endeavours of the Photographist. **1848** *Art-Union Jrnl.* Jan. 18 The greatest difficulty the photographist has to contend

with. **1872** TALMAGE *Serm.* 71 There are some faces so mobile that photographists cannot take them.
fig. **1851** E. HITCHCOCK *Relig. Geol.* xii. 393 What if it should turn out that sable night..is an unerring photographist!

photographize (fəʊˈtɒɡrəfaɪz), *v. rare.* [f. as prec. + -IZE.] *trans.* = PHOTOGRAPH *v.*
1860 KINGSLEY *Misc.* II. 8 Nothing is possible but to photographize everybody and everything.

photographometer (ˌfəʊtəɡrəˈfɒmɪtə(r)). [f. as PHOTOGRAPH + -(O)METER, -METER.]
1. An instrument for ascertaining the degree of sensitiveness of photographic films to the chemical action of light; an actinometer.
1849 *Art Jrnl.* 96 With the photographometer of Mr. Claudet this is easily ascertained. **1853** R. HUNT *Man. Photogr.* 149 M. Claudet turned his attention to contrive an apparatus by which he could test at the same time the sensitiveness of the daguerreotype plate and the intensity of light. This instrument he called a Photographometer.
2. A photographic apparatus for automatically recording the angular position of objects around a given point.
1884 KNIGHT *Dict. Mech.* Suppl. 673/2.

photographophone (fəʊtəʊˈɡræfəfəʊn). [f. as PHOTOGRAPH + Gr. φωνή sound, voice, -φωνος sounding.] An instrument for recording and reproducing sounds by means of kinematographic photographs of a sensitive flame which are caused to affect a selenium cell, with telephones attached.
1901 *Westm. Gaz.* 19 June, Dr. Ruhmer, of Berlin, has invented what he calls a 'photographone', a new scientific marvel, with which he expects to be able to record a series of sounds of the human voice. **1902** *Harper's Mag.* Feb. 498 Another invention..known as the photographophone.

photographotype: see PHOTO- 2.

photography (fəʊˈtɒɡrəfɪ). [f. Gr. φῶς light, PHOTO- + -γραφία writing, delineation: see -GRAPHY.
So far as is known, *photography* was introduced, along with *photographic* and *photograph*, by Sir John Herschel, in a paper read before the Royal Society on 14 March 1839. (They may have suggested themselves to him as combining the approved elements of Talbot's *photo* genic and Niepce's héliograph*ie*, and as being more suitable than either.) They gradually took their place as the general terms: in French, *art photographique* appears in the *Comptes Rendus* of the *Académie des Sciences*, VIII. 714, 6 May 1839; *photographie* and *photographique* were the terms used, for the subject generally, by Arago, in his *Rapport* to the Chamber of Deputies on the project of Daguerre's pension, 3 July 1839; they are in common use in tome IX of the *Comptes Rendus* (July to Dec. 1839): see the Table des Matières.]
The process or art of producing pictures by means of the chemical action of light on a sensitive film on a basis of paper, glass, metal, etc.; the business of producing and printing such pictures.
1839 (Mar. 14) HERSCHEL in *Proc. R. Soc.* IV. 131 Note on the Art of Photography, or the application of the Chemical Rays of Light to the purpose of Pictorial Representation. **1839** (Mar. 27) A. FYFE in *Proc. Scot. Soc. Arts* 419 Paper smeared with the solution [of lunar caustic] is darkened... Hence the process of photogenic drawing [as pub. in May, in *Edin. New Phil. Jrnl.* XXVII. 145, altered to Hence the art of *Photography*]. **1839** *Ed. N.P.J.* XXVII. 156 (*Article*) Notes on Daguerre's Photography. By Sir John Robison. [Word not used in article.] **1840** (Mar. 5) HERSCHEL (as above) IV. 206 A method of precipitating on glass a coating possessing photographic properties, and of accomplishing a new and curious extension of the art of photography. **1841** TALBOT *Specif. Patent* No. 8842. 7 For the purposes of economy in the processes of photography. **1864** H. SPENCER *Biol.* I. i. §13 Light..which works those chemical changes utilized in Photography. **1872** PROCTOR *Ess. Astron.* xxxiii. 395 Within the last few years solar photography has made a progress which is very promising..as an aid to exact astronomy. **1893** *Brit. Jrnl. Photogr.* XL. 796 Just now a great deal of attention is being given to chromo-photography, in which transparent colours are necessary.

photograver (ˈfəʊtəʊˌɡreɪvə(r)). [f. PHOTO- 2 + GRAVER.] A photo-engraver; an artist in photogravure.
1888 *Pall Mall G.* 20 Dec. 3/1 The Typographic Etching Company,..the photogravers of these and many other choice volumes.

photogravure (ˌfəʊtəʊɡræˈvjʊə(r)), *sb.* [a. F. *photogravure*, f. PHOTO- + *gravure* engraving.] Photo-engraving; *esp.* the process of preparing a plate or matrix by transferring a photographic negative of a drawing, painting, or object to a metal plate, and then etching it in; a picture produced by this process. Also *attrib.*
1879 *Daily Tel.* 28 July 2/4 Photogravure reproductions in course of publication. **1880** A. S. MURRAY in *Academy* 4 Dec. 411 The perfection of photogravure with which the plates have been executed. **1883** *Pall Mall G.* 1 Nov. 3/2 Several photogravures of the graceful recent pictures of Sir Frederick Leighton. **1890** *Jrnl. Soc. Arts* 19 Dec. 72 Both painter and public..must prefer a photogravure to the hard, formal..character of the line engraving.
Hence **photograˈvure** *v. trans.*, to reproduce by photogravure; **photograˈvurist**, an artist or operator in photogravure.
1884 *Pall Mall G.* 17 Nov. 9/1 The work will be taken to Paris to be photogravured. **1889** *Anthony's Photogr. Bull.* II. 251 A lithographer, or photogravurist, steps in and robs me of the result of my thought, skill and labor, without saying 'by your leave'.

photoheliograph (fəʊtəʊˈhiːlɪəʊɡrɑːf, -æ-). [f. PHOTO- + Gr. ἥλιο-ς sun + -GRAPH: cf. HELIOGRAPH.] A photographic telescope adapted for taking photographs of the sun: = HELIOGRAPH 2.
1861 W. FAIRBAIRN *Address Brit. Assoc.*, The careful registering of the appearances of the sun by the photo-heliograph of Sir John Herschel. **1884** *Brit. Almanac*, Comp. 20 The great photoheliograph with which Mr. De la Rue took sun-pictures during the eclipse in Spain in 1860. **1899** *Westm. Gaz.* 24 Aug. 8/2 This novel instrument will be practically a horizontal photo-heliograph, giving images of the moon exceeding a foot in diameter.
So **ˌphotohelioˈgraphic** *a.*, pertaining to a photoheliograph or to **ˌphotoheliˈography**, the art or process of taking photographs of the sun; **photoˈhelioscope** [see -SCOPE] = *photoheliograph.*
1865 *Reader* No. 141. 292/1 Perfection attained in photo-heliography. **1871** HERSCHEL *Outl. Astron.* (ed. 11) 261 Photographic representations of the spots have been made ..with a 'photohelioscope' at Kew. **1890** *Cent. Dict.*, *Photo-heliographic.* **1905** *Athenæum* 29 Apr. 535/1 The volume of 'Greenwich Observations' for the year 1902..together with ..'Magnetical and Meteorological Observations', and 'Photoheliographic Results'.

photoheterotroph to **-inactivation:** see PHOTO- 1.

photoinduce (ˌfəʊtəʊɪnˈdjuːs), *v.* Also with hyphen. [f. PHOTO- 1 + INDUCE *v.*] *trans.* To induce by the action of light; esp. in *Plant Physiol.*, to induce reproductive behaviour in a plant by an appropriate sequence of light and darkness (used with the behaviour or the plant as obj.).
1949 *Bot. Gaz.* CX. 495/1 If one part of the plant was kept completely in the dark and some other part above it was photoinduced to flower, then the part in the dark also flowered. **1952** *Ann. Rev. Plant Physiol.* III. 269 If a plant is photoinduced and then is grafted on to an individual kept on the noninductive conditions, the latter plant will also initiate flowers. **1974** *Photochem. & Photobiol.* XIX. 163/1 It is..of importance to determine if an electron transfer reaction of this type can be photoinduced in a model system.
So **photoinˈduced** *ppl. a.*, induced by the action of light; also **photoinˈducible** *a.*, capable of being photoinduced.
1947 *Bot. Gaz.* CIX. 121/1 Buds develop and flower only on the photoinduced portion or one node beyond. **1961** *Jrnl. Appl. Physics* XXXII. 1901/2 The photoinduced current.. is equal to the diode current with the bias voltage zero. **1970** DORION & WIEBE *Photochromism* i. 9 The reversible or self-bleaching feature distinguishes photochromism from the well-known irreversible photoinduced reactions. **1970** GRESSEL & GALUN in G. Bernier *Cellular & Molecular Aspects Floral Induction* x. 154 Some fungal systems are reported to be photoinducible by ultraviolet light as short as 230 mμ with no sporulation beyond 340 mμ. **1974** *Nature* 26 Apr. 801/1 We have not obtained a cell-free system from *P*[*hycomyces*] *blakesleeanus* which shows the photoinducible changes. **1977** I. M. CAMPBELL *Energy & Atmosphere* ix. 344 It is generally considered that erythema is the least serious of a series of photoinduced skin complaints.

photoinduction (ˌfəʊtəʊɪnˈdʌkʃən). [f. PHOTO- 1 + INDUCTION.] The action or process of induction by light, esp. of reproductive behaviour in plants.
1947 *Bot. Gaz.* CIX. 131/2 A reduction in total reproductive activity in relation to reduced photoinduction. **1971** *New Scientist* 9 Sept. 558/1 Flowering..occurred about 20 days after this photoinduction. **1975** D. VINCE-PRUE *Photoperiodism in Plants* vi. 229 Endogenous cytokinins may..be involved in the process of photoinduction.

photoinductive (ˌfəʊtəʊɪnˈdʌktɪv), *a. Bot.* [f. PHOTO- 1 + INDUCTIVE *a.*] Tending to induce flowering or other activity in plants by means of a regime of alternating periods of light and darkness; ***photoinductive cycle***, a circadian cycle of one period of light and one of darkness.
1940 *Bot. Gaz.* CI. 667 (*caption*) Effect of duration and intensity of light during seven photoinductive cycles on subsequent initiation of a floral primordia by Biloxi soybean. **1956** *Plant Physiol.* XXXI. 280/2 A measure of the amount of stimulation afforded by photoinductive treatments. **1971** *New Scientist* 9 Sept. 558/2 Flowering was ..enhanced if the plants got a drenching during the photoinductive period. **1975** D. VINCE-PRUE *Photoperiodism in Plants* i. 42 In the SD [*sc.* short-day] grass, *Rottboellia exaltata*..a minimum of six photoinductive cycles are necessary for flowering.

photo-interpretation to **-interpretive:** see PHOTO- 2.

photo-ionization (ˌfəʊtəʊaɪənaɪˈzeɪʃən). *Physics.* Also without hyphen. [f. PHOTO- 1 + IONIZATION[2].] Ionization produced by electro-magnetic radiation.
1914 S. E. SHEPPARD *Photo-Chem.* ix. 356 (*heading*) Photo-ionization of gases. **1955** *Jrnl. Brit. Interplanetary Soc.* XIV. 18 From its effect in lowering the D layer, H. Friedman deduced that the intensity of the sun's radiation in the Lyman alpha wave-length must increase a thousand fold during solar flares. He added that it creates the D region by photo-ionization of nitrous oxide. **1975** D. H. BURRIN in Williams & Wilson *Biologist's Guide to Princ. & Techniques Pract. Biochem.* v. 166 Alternatively, strong electric fields.. or ultraviolet light (photoionization) may be employed to ionize the sample.
So **photoˈionize** *v. trans.*, to ionize by means of electromagnetic radiation; **photoˈionized, -ˈionizing** *ppl. adjs.*
1953 MEEK & CRAGGS *Electr. Breakdown of Gases* i. 15 Photoionizing radiations. **1962** *Jrnl. Optical Soc. Amer.* LII. 1241/1 Different responses at short wavelengths result from the different thicknesses of the surface layer from which the photo-ionized carriers must diffuse before recombination. **1974** *Rev. Sci. Instruments* XLV. 662/2 The approach consists of photoionizing some species in a field-free region and extracting a portion of the photo-electrons thus produced into a beam. **1977** *Jrnl. R. Soc. Arts* CXXV. 767/1 A second laser beam was..used to photoionize the excited magnesium atoms.

photoisomer (ˌfəʊtəʊˈaɪsəmə(r)). *Chem.* [f. PHOTO- 1 + ISOMER.] An isomer formed by irradiation of a different, often more stable, form of a compound.
1960 *Jrnl. Amer. Chem. Soc.* LXXXII. 3642/2 Colchicine ..on prolonged exposure to sunlight gave three photoisomers. **1965** SELIGER & MCELROY *Light* v. 307 The temperature..of the solution affected the stability of the various photoisomers that were formed upon initial irradiation of the room-temperature stable material. **1973** *Tetrahedron* XXIX. 3869/1 This new photoisomer is formed from heptachlor epoxide exposed to sunlight on bean leaves only in the presence of a photosensitizer.
Hence **ˌphotoisoˈmeric** *a.*, of or pertaining to a photoisomer or photoisomers; **ˌphotoiˈsomerism**, the fact of being or having a photoisomer.
1955 *Jrnl. Chem. Physics* XXIII. 1367/1 The final photoisomeric equilibrium was always independent of the isomeric composition before irradiation. **1965** SELIGER & MCELROY *Light* ii. 144 The photoisomerism of 11-*cis* retinene.

photoisomeriˈzation (fəʊtəʊaɪs-). *Chem.* [f. PHOTO- 1 + ISOMERIZATION.] The formation of a photoisomer.
1926 H. A. SPOEHR *Photosynthesis* v. 285 They tried to detect the photoisomerization of the chlorophyll-carbonic acid complex. **1956** H. A. BORTHWICK et al. in A. Hollaender *Radiation Biol.* III. x. 494 The relative biological response, such as internode elongation, seed germination, or flowering, is limited by the photoisomerization of the pigment. **1965** SELIGER & MCELROY *Light* v. 305 When rhodopsin in the retina is exposed to white light, the result is a photoisomerization to the yellow-colored all-*trans* form through several intermediate steps. **1976** H. CAMPION et al. in B. E. C. Nordin *Calcium, Phosphate & Magnesium Metabolism* xii. 452 Ergocalciferol itself can, under prolonged irradiation, undergo irreversible photoisomerization.
So **ˌphotoiˈsomerize** *v. intr.*, to undergo photoisomerization.
1963 *Adv. Photochem.* I. 325 Simple tropolones also photoisomerize. γ-Tropolone methyl ether..gives the bicyclic photoisomer..on irradiation in aqueous solution.

photojournalism, -ist: see PHOTO- 2.

photokinesis (ˌfəʊtəʊkaɪˈniːsɪs, -kɪˈniːsɪs). *Biol.* [mod.L. ad. G. *photokinese* (T. W. Engelmann 1883, in *Archiv. f. ges. Physiol.* XXX. 95): see PHOTO- 1 and KINESIS.] An undirected movement of an organism in response to the effect of light.
1905 [see KINESIS 2]. **1940** *Jrnl. Compar. Psychol.* XXIX. 448 Photokinesis (the activating effect of light) is particularly a function of the visual receptor. This characteristic accounts for the excitation of the ants at daybreak. **1967** *Oceanogr. & Marine Biol.* V. 361 Aggregation [of polyzoan larvae] in a shaded area may.. perhaps best be explained in terms of low photokinesis. **1970** W. NULTSCH in P. Halldal *Photobiol. of Microorganisms* viii. 219 The photokinetic action of light absorbed by photosynthetic pigments has led to the conclusion that photokinesis may be linked with photosynthesis.
Hence **photokiˈnetic** *a.*, pertaining to or exhibiting photokinesis; **photokiˈnetically** *adv.*
1900 *Amer. Jrnl. Physiol.* III. 291 Light may cause gatherings of animals... By a reaction of the animal to sudden changes in the intensity of illumination... Such animals Loeb calls 'Unterschiedsempfindlich', photokinetic. **1907** *Jrnl. Exper. Zool.* V. 72 The purpose.. is to consider the phototactic movement of planarians, as distinct from their photokinetic behavior. **1957** G. E. HUTCHINSON *Treat. Limnol.* I. ix. 617 Oxygen uptake in the clear bottles is actually higher than in the black... This is presumably due to a photokinetic effect on the zooplankton in the bottles. **1967** *Oceanogr. & Marine Biol.* V. 361 It seems probable that polyzoan larvae display photokinetic responses. **1970** W. NULTSCH in P. Halldal *Photobiol. of Microorganisms* viii. 218 As the ultraviolet region of the spectrum is photokinetically effective, too, this effectiveness must be due to another photoreceptor of unknown chemical structure.

photolabile, -lability: see PHOTO- 1.

photolith, photolitho (also photo-litho), abbreviations of PHOTOLITHOGRAPH, PHOTOLITHOGRAPHIC *a.*, PHOTOLITHOGRAPHY.
1864 *Autographic Mirror, Shaks. No.*, A Photo-Litho Portrait of Shakspeare, taken from the print by Martin

Droeshout. **1870** *Holbein Soc. Publ.* (*title*) The Mirrovr of Maiestie, or Badges of Honovr Conceitedly Emblazoned, a photo-lith facsimile reprint from the only perfect copy in existence.. A.D. 1618. **1896** *Photographic Jrnl.* XX. 278 In photo-litho in line a perfect transfer must be as follows, the lines must be perfectly firm and free from rottenness, the ink forming the image must be hard... For photo-litho transfers in half-tone the smooth gradations of the photograph must be broken up by the discriminating reticulation of gelatine. **1907** C. SALTER tr. *Andés' Treatment of Paper* xvii. 191 Ordinary transfer paper for photolitho work is liable to stretch in the press. **1921** *Brit. Printer* Nov. 163/1 From an economic aspect photo-litho easily holds its own when compared with letterpress printing. **1946** *Nature* 28 Dec. 929/1 This volume.. is published in photo-litho. **1960** G. A. GLAISTER *Gloss. Bk.* 306/1 Various methods were attempted to produce workable photo-lithos by copying direct on stone. *Ibid.*, Photo-lithography at the end of the 19th century was dominated by Eugen Albert's photo-litho paper. **1973** S. JENNETT *Making of Bks.* (ed. 5) x. 162 Like letterpress.. photo-litho can print only an even film of ink.

2. photo-litho offset (see quot. 1934).

1931 A. ESDAILE *Student's Man. Bibliogr.* v. 170 Photo-litho-offset in various processes is now largely used for the cheap production of unaltered reprints of books. **1934** H. CURWEN *Processes of Graphic Reproduction in Printing* I. 64 Under offset printing must be mentioned the very wide use made of 'photo litho offset'. As the name implies, this is printing by lithography via a rubber blanket, from printing surfaces prepared by photographic methods. **1948** H. MISSINGHAM *Student's Guide Commercial Art* II. 129 Photo-litho offset.. is a method of printing by lithography, in which the design is photographed on to zinc plate. **1960** G. A. GLAISTER *Gloss. Bk.* 306/1 The negative is copied on to a photo-lithographic plate from which printing is done by photo-litho offset.

photolithograph (ˌfəʊtəʊˈlɪθəgrɑːf, -æ-), *sb.* [f. PHOTO- 2 + LITHOGRAPH.] A print produced by photolithography.

1855 *Civil Engineer & Architects Jrnl.* 390 Prof. Ramsay .. described a process by which Mr. Robert Macpherson, of Rome, had succeeded in obtaining beautiful photo-lithographs. **1870** *Eng. Mech.* 14 Jan. 428/2 Much has been done.. to aid the production.. of photo-lithographs. **1877** *Archæol. Journal* XXXIII. 305 The greatly reduced scale of the photolithograph.

Hence **photoˈlithograph** *v. trans.*, to produce or copy by photolithography.

1864 (*title*) Shakespeare's Much Ado about Nothing, 1600. Photo-lithographed by R. Preston. **1872** PROCTOR *Ess. Astron.* xxviii. 346 This chart is now completed.. with photolithographed keymaps. **1874** MAX MÜLLER *Addr. Congress of Orientalists* Sel. Ess. II. 30 Three valuable MSS. .. have been photolithographed at the expense of the Indian Government.

photolithographer (ˌfəʊtəʊlɪˈθɒgrəfə(r)). [f. PHOTOLITHOGRAPHY, after LITHOGRAPHER.] One who practises photolithography.

1857 *Encycl. Brit.* (ed. 8) XIII. 514/2 Specimens which we have seen by photo-lithographers in Paris, Munich, and Rome. **1875** tr. *Vogel's Chem. Light* xix. 281 We see very few heliographers and photolithographers.

photolithographic (ˌfəʊtəʊlɪθəʊˈgræfɪk), *a.* [f. as prec., after LITHOGRAPHIC.] Pertaining to or produced by photolithography. So **photolithoˈgraphically** *adv.*

1863 *Rep. Juries Internat. Exhib.* Class XIV. 5. The following may be considered as a classification of photolithographic processes. **1867** MURCHISON *Siluria* xi. (ed. 4) 251 *note*, I received.. photolithographic representations. **1873** E. SPON *Workshop Receipts* Ser. I. 289/1 A photo-lithographic impression of a negative. **1880** *Nature* XXI. 358 A reduced photolithographic reproduction of Tunstall's 'Ornithologia Britannica'. **1886** *Sci. Amer.* 24 July 49/3 From the original or negative.. a photo-lithographic plate is taken. **1945** H. BARRON *Mod. Plastics* xxv. 523 Photolithographic printing plates are now being made with surfaces based on polyvinyl alcohol. **1965** *Wireless World* July 338/2 The original pattern to be photolithographically reproduced was formed by.. winding plastic strip round pegs. **1972** *Physics Bull.* Dec. 743/2 By employing photolithographic techniques.. IRD has produced simple arrays of detectors. **1977** *Sci. Amer.* Sept. 76/1 Areas to be doped.. are defined photo-lithographically.

photolithography (ˌfəʊtəʊlɪˈθɒgrəfɪ). [f. PHOTO- 2 + LITHOGRAPHY.] The art or process of producing, by photography, designs upon lithographic stone (or a similar substance), from which prints may be taken as in ordinary lithography; esp. a planographic printing process using plates prepared from photographic negatives, usually printed by offset methods.

1856 W. A. MILLER *Elem. Chem.* II. Index, Photolithography. **1858** *Proc. Amer. Phil. Soc.* VI. 328 Specimens of photo-lithography executed by Mr. Rehn of Philadelphia. **1875** tr. *Vogel's Chem. Light* xv. 251 Photography.. entered into competition with lithography. It was Poitevin who allied the two by inventing photo-lithography. **1929** *Times* 29 Oct. (Printing Suppl.) p. xii/7 The process of photo-lithography through the growing importance of the offset process directed fresh attention to the subject [of composing textual matter without the use of type]. **1948** *Science News* VII. 100 Photographic prints on metal are the basis of another major industry—photo-lithography—and here again war-time researches have made possible considerable simplifications in the working procedures. **1966** *Listener* 22 Sept. 422/3 The two [books].. have now reappeared, beautifully reproduced by modern photo-lithography. **1972** *Guardian* 25 Nov. 14/3 Photo-lithography is ousting other methods [of making prints] in the commercial market.

photolithotroph to **-trophy**: see PHOTO- 1.

photo-lithotype: see PHOTO- 2.

photology (fəʊˈtɒlədʒɪ). *rare.* [f. Gr. φῶς light, PHOTO- 1 + -LOGY.] The science of light; optics. Hence **photoˈlogic**, **photoˈlogical** *adjs.*, pertaining to photology, optical; **phoˈtologist**, one versed in photology.

1828 WEBSTER, *Photologic, Photological... Photology* (citing MITCHILL). **1833** HERSCHEL *Absorption of Light* in *Fam. Lect. Sc.* (1866) 477 The phœnomena of absorption.. have always appeared to me to constitute a branch of photology *sui generis*. *Ibid.* 479 The question 'What becomes of light?' which appears to have been agitated among the photologists of the last century. *a* **1866** —— *Light* in *Ibid.* 265 The painter should never forget that his notion of colour (as compared with that of the photologist) is a negative one. **1865** *All Year Round* 11 Mar. 149/1 Photological phenomena are made known to us by.. the sense of sight.

ˌphotolumiˈnescence. *Physics.* †Also with hyphen. [ad. G. *photoluminescenz* (E. Wiedemann 1888, in *Ann. d. Physik und Chem.* XXXIV. 447): see PHOTO- 1 and LUMINESCENCE.] Luminescence caused by visible light or by infra-red or ultraviolet radiation.

1889 tr. E. Wiedemann in *Phil. Mag.* XXVIII. 151 According to the mode of excitation I distinguish Photo-, Electro-, Chemi-, and Tribo-luminescence. In particular, photo-luminescence, including fluorescence and a number of cases of phosphorescence, is defined as those phenomena in which the incident light excites vibrations within the molecule of a body which produce directly an emission of light. **1913** H. S. ALLEN *Photo-Electricity* xi. 147 By means of this hypothesis [*sc.* of light quanta] Einstein sought to explain such phenomena as the photo-electric effect, the ionisation of gases by ultra-violet light, photo-luminescence, and the theory of specific heat. **1930** *Times Lit. Suppl.* 6 Mar. 195/2 A masterly account.. including the theory of atomic and molecular structure and spectra, and photoluminescence. **1968** *McGraw-Hill Yearbk. Sci. & Technol.* 345/1 Little effort has been put into using semiconductors in powder phosphor applications for photoluminescence and cathodoluminescence, because efficient powder phosphors are already available to cover the entire visible spectrum.

Hence **ˌphotolumiˈnescent** *a.*

1909 in *Cent. Dict.* Suppl. **1958** *Sci. News* XLVII. 14 The difference between photoluminescent materials, e.g., those used in fluorescent lamps, and most electroluminescent phosphors is thus primarily a difference in the mode of electron excitation. **1968** H. T. MINDEN in S. L. Marshall *Laser Technol. & Applic.* v. 102 Before describing the GaAs injection electroluminescent spectra, it is instructive to study the more conventional photoluminescent spectrum.

photolyse (ˈfəʊtəlaɪz), *v.* Also (chiefly *U.S.*) -lyze. [f. PHOTOLYSIS, after *analysis*, *analyse*.] **a.** *trans.* To decompose or dissociate by irradiation with light. **b.** *intr.* To undergo photolysis.

1956 *Jrnl. Amer. Chem. Soc.* LXXVIII. 6229/1 Pure liquid ethyl iodide was photolyzed at several light intensities and for varying times. **1970** *Nature* 7 Mar. 928/2 In our experiments the Xe lamp not only photolysed ICN but also excited it to the $B^2\Sigma$ state. **1978** *Ibid.* 21 Sept. p. xv/2 The detector senses any halogen-containing compound which will photolyse in the presence of UV light.

Hence **ˈphotolysed** *ppl. a.*

1960 *Jrnl. Chem. Soc.* 977 No electron-spin resonance absorption could be detected with the photolysed glasses. **1973** *Nature* 6 July 49/2 A washed and concentrated suspension of bacteria (for example, *Proteus mirabilis*) caused a conversion of photolysed rhodopsin to isorhodopsin.

photolysis (fəʊˈtɒlɪsɪs). [f. PHOTO- 1 + Gr. λύσις loosening: cf. *electrolysis*.] **1.** *Bot.* General term for the movements of protoplasm (esp. that containing chlorophyll-granules) under the influence of light, distinguished as APOSTROPHE EPISTROPHE. **2.** *Chem.* Decomposition or dissociation of molecules by the action of light; ***flash photolysis***; see FLASH *sb.*² 14 b.

1911 *Chem. Abstr.* V. 1705 When the action is prolonged the decomp[osition] products may also undergo a partial photolysis. **1938** *Phil. Trans. R. Soc.* A. CLXIV. 151 (*heading*) The theory of the photolysis of silver bromide and the photographic latent image. **1955** *Jrnl. Amer. Chem. Soc.* LXXVII. 6457/2 Most of the photolyses were carried out at room temperature. **1965** *New Scientist* 29 Apr. 291/1 Fission of the molecule (photolysis) occurs. **1972** R. A. JACKSON *Mechanism* iv. 61 Radicals may be introduced into reaction systems by photolysis or pyrolysis of a suitable molecule.

Hence **photoˈlytic** *a.*, produced by or being photolysis; **photoˈlytically** *adv.*

1934 WEBSTER, Photolytic. **1938** *Phil. Trans. R. Soc.* A. CLXIV. 151 (*heading*) Direct photolytic reduction of silver halides. **1946** *Nature* 7 Sept. 345/1 Both the reducing hydrogen and the hydroxyl radicals were supposed to be photolytic products of water. **1951** *Sci. News* XXII. 78 Carbon dioxide is not directly reduced to formaldehyde by the photolytically produced hydrogen. **1970** *Photochem. & Photobiol.* XII. 228 One is led to the conclusion that the chemically reactive intermediate in these photolytic systems is $^3SO_2$. **1977** I. M. CAMPBELL *Energy & Atmosphere* viii. 227 It.. allows nitrogen dioxide to be photolytically dissociated within the troposphere.

photomacrography (ˌfəʊtəʊmæˈkrɒgrəfɪ). [f. PHOTO- 2 + μακρός large + PHOTO)GRAPHY.] = MACROPHOTOGRAPHY.

1936 J. DESCHIN *New Ways in Photogr.* xiv. 208 A type of photography.. which has recently gained.. general favor among hobbyists is that known as photomacrography. **1942** *Ilford Man. Photogr.* (ed. 2) xxiii. 407 These are low-power magnifications mainly concerned with the surface detail of opaque objects and to this type of work the term photomacrography is applied. **1967** [see MACROPHOTOGRAPHY]. **1972** *Sci. Amer.* Jan. 68 (Advt.), Photomacrography at magnifications in the vicinity of 2–3× with conventional equipment has been practically impossible. **1976** *Publishers Weekly* 27 Sept. 82/2 'Photomacrography'—a photo technique obtaining an image the size of the object photographed, or larger.

So **photoˈmacrograph** = MACROPHOTOGRAPH; **ˌphotomacroˈgraphic** *a.*

1948 J. H. GABLE *Compl. Introd. Photogr.* II. xi. 117 Photomacrography is a method whereby this image can be made many times larger than the object, and a picture so made is called a photomacrograph. **1961** WEBSTER, Photomacrographic. **1966** A. FEININGER *Compl. Photographer* VIII. 309 A photograph in which the subject is rendered in natural or larger than natural size on the film.. is called a 'photomacrograph'. **1972** *Sci. Amer.* Jan. 68 (Advt.), It makes superb large-format, widefield photomacrographs all the way from 40× down to ½×. **1978** *Nature* 21 Sept. p. xii/3 The Polaroid MP-4 camera is a copy, photomacrographic and photomicrographic recording system.

photo-magazine, -mapping: see PHOTO- 2.

photo-magnetic to **-mask**: see PHOTO- 1.

ˌphoto-magnetograph (-mægˈniːtəgrɑːf). [f. PHOTO- 2 + MAGNETOGRAPH.] An instrument by which records of the fluctuations of the magnetic needle are obtained photographically.

1893 SIR R. BALL *Story of Sun* 228 Facts of magnetic perturbations taken from the photo-magnetographs of the United States Naval Observatory. *Ibid.* 230 A magnetic storm described as very strong was also recorded by the photomagnetographs.

Photomaton (fəʊˈtɒmətən). orig. *U.S.* [f. PHOTO- 2 + AUTO)MATON.] The proprietary name of a machine that takes photographs automatically; a photograph taken by such a machine. Also abbrev. as ***ˈPhotomat***.

1927 *N.Y. Times* 28 Mar. 1/3 Henry Morgenthau.. and a group of business associates announced yesterday that they had purchased the control of the Photomaton—the quarter-in-the-slot automatic photographing device which has been in use in this city since last September. **1927** *Bulletin* (Glasgow) 28 Mar. 3/3 Anatol Josephs, the inventor of the Photomaton machine, sold the rights yesterday to a syndicate.. for 1,000,000 dollars. **1928** *Daily Express* 22 Feb. 11/5 Mr. O'Connor.. tried his luck with the 1s. in the slot Photomaton with successful results. **1936** G. GREENE *Gun for Sale* iii. 104 I'll wire home for a better likeness. I've got a whole strip of Photomatons at home. Her face from every angle. You couldn't have a better lot of photos for newspaper purposes. **1963** *Trade Marks Jrnl.* 22 May 691/1 Photomaton... Photographic apparatus and parts thereof.. Cyril Astor Photomaton (London) Limited,.. Rhyl,.. North Wales; manufacturers and merchants. **1966** L. COHEN *Beautiful Losers* (1970) III. 237 The Photomat was broken; it accepted quarters but returned neither flashes nor pictures. **1966** J. BETJEMAN *High & Low* 48 The enlarged Photomaton—that's the latest. **1973** M. A. SINCLAIR tr. *Simenon's Maigret & M. Charles* iv. 92 A small passport photograph taken in a Photomat.

Hence **phoˈtomaton** *v. trans.*, to photograph (someone) by means of a Photomaton.

1933 V. WOOLF *Let.* 19 Feb. (1979) V. 161 I've got to be photomatoned tomorrow.

ˌphoto-meˈchanical, *a.* [PHOTO- 2.] Combining a photographic and mechanical process.

1889 [see *photophane*, PHOTO- 2]. **1892** WOODBURY *Encycl. Phot.* 533 The term photo-mechanical is applied to all processes in which the action of light upon chemical substances becomes the means of preparing printing surfaces from which many impressions can be made without any further assistance of light.

photomesic, -meson: see PHOTO- 1.

photometer (fəʊˈtɒmɪtə(r)), *sb.* [f. Gr. φῶς light, PHOTO- + -METER: in mod.L. *photometrum*, 1760.] **1.** The name of instruments (of many kinds) for measuring the intensity of light, or for comparing the relative intensities of light from different sources.

[**1760**: see PHOTOMETRY.] **1778** *Phil. Trans.* LXVIII. 487 We wish for an Hygrometer, an Electrometer, a Photometer. **1793** RUMFORD *ibid.* LXXXIV. 73, I have now brought the principal instrument to such a degree of perfection, that, if I might without being suspected of affectation, I should dignify it with a name, and call it a photometer. *c* **1865** LETHEBY in *Circ. Sc.* I. 92/2 Leslie and Wheatstone have also invented photometers. **1893** *Brit. Jrnl. Photogr.* XL. 811 Very many different patterns of photometers have been introduced and used during the last thirty years.

2. Special Combs.: **photometer bench**, an apparatus similar to an optical bench for the support of a photometer and light sources; cf. *photometric bench*; **photometer head**, the part of a photometer by means of which the comparison or measurement is effected.

1900 W. M. STINE *Photometrical Measurements* iii. 104 The Reichanstalt photometer bench is commonly made for a maximum working distance between the light sources of either 200 or 250 centimetres. **1966** LARGE & WILMAN in Hewitt & Vause *Lamps & Lighting* vii. 89 An appropriate calibrated lamp is..mounted on the photometer bench. **1907** SHEPPARD & MEES *Investigations Theory Photogr. Process* I. ii. 27 Simmance and Abady's new flicker photometer possibly forms the best of the bench photometer heads. **1966** LARGE & WILMAN in Hewitt & Vause *Lamps & Lighting* vii. 89 Distance between the photometer head and lamps may be adjusted and accurately measured. *Ibid.*, The photometer head may consist of either a photocell or a visual device such as the Lummer-Brodhun Contrast Head. **1973** W. THOMAS *SPSE Handbk. Photographic Sci. & Engin.* ii. 153 Photometer heads are used in conjunction with some means for varying the luminance of one or both surfaces in a known manner so that a photometric balance may be obtained.

pho'tometer, *v.* [f. the sb.] *trans.* To measure the brightness of (a light source or an illuminated surface) by means of a photometer. Hence **pho'tometered** *ppl. a.*, **pho'tometering** *vbl. sb.*

1900 *Jrnl. Franklin Inst.* CXLIX. 291 The leading makers now photometer each and every lamp, and the practice of photometering a few and picking out the remainder by the eye is past. **1917** *Physical Rev.* X. 695 The photographs taken thus far are not suitable for photometering, but arrangements are complete for taking such photographs, and for measuring the intensity of the lines. **1923** *Amer. Jrnl. Sci.* CCV. 459 The films were photometered with a microphotometer at the Bureau of Standards. *Ibid.* 460 No high precision was sought in the photometering. *Ibid.* 461 The photometered maximum in the mixture lies between the positions of the two simple maxima. **1966** D. G. BRANDON *Mod. Techniques Metallogr.* iii. 127 The minimum area that can be photometered is principally limited by the size of the diffraction image of the spot selected for photometry.

photometric (fəʊtəʊ'mɛtrɪk), *a.* [f. PHOTOMETRY + -IC.] Of or pertaining to photometry. *photometric bench* = *photometer bench*.

1849 *Lit. Gaz.* 24 Feb. 132/1 He [Grove] had tested by the photometric method of equality of shadows the intensity of the light as compared with a common wax candle. **1869** DUNKIN *Midn. Sky* 175 Interesting photometric experiments..on the relative light of the principal stars. **1875** BENNETT & DYER *Sachs' Bot.* 663. **1894** G. W. & M. R. PATTERSON tr. *Palaz's Treat. Industr. Photometry* iv. 178 The photometric bench is an optical bench strongly and carefully constructed. **1966** LARGE & WILMAN in Hewitt & Vause *Lamps & Lighting* vii. 89 Where measurements involving direction and distance are concerned a photometric bench is required.

So **photo'metrical** *a.*, dealing with photometry; made or measured by a photometer; **photo'metrically** *adv.*, according to photometry, by means of a photometer; **photometrician** (-'trɪʃən), **photometrist** (-'tɒmɪtrɪst), one who practises photometry.

1833 HERSCHEL *Astron.* xii. 375 A numerical estimate, grounded on precise *photometrical experiments, of the apparent brightness of each star. **1864** *Daily Tel.* 16 Sept., The photometrical standard [of gas-light] is more than twice as high in many other places than it is in London. **1854** BREWSTER *More Worlds* v. 95 In measuring *photometrically the light of these three different structures. **1883** *Athenæum* 16 June 766/2 Method of determining the magnitudes of stars photometrically. **1870** PROCTOR *Other Worlds* v. 143 The estimates of Zöllner, the eminent *photometrician, serve to show..that Jupiter sends more light to us..than a planet of equal size and constituted like Mars, the moon, or the earth, could possibly reflect to us if placed where Jupiter is. **1867** W. R. BOWDITCH *Coal Gas* iii. 67 The best way for a *photometrist to be certain of his instruments is to test them himself.

photometry (fəʊ'tɒmɪtrɪ). [ad. mod.L. *phōtometria* (1760), f. Gr. φῶς, φωτο- light, PHOTO- + -μετρία measuring, -METRY.] Measurement of light; comparison of the intensity of light from different sources; the use of a photometer.

[**1760** LAMBERT *Photometria* 7 Optandum certe esset, ut excogitaretur Photometrum thermometro analogum, quod lumini exposituim ejus intensitatem atque claritatem indicaret.] **1824** R. WATT *Biblioth. Brit.* s.v. *J. H. Lambert*, Photometry. **1830** *Encycl. Brit.* (ed. 7) *Prelim. Dissert.* 637/2 The eighteenth century created a new branch of optical science, destined to measure or compare the intensities of different lights, and therefore termed Photometry. **1865** *Daily Tel.* 24 Nov. 4/6 So far as photometry is concerned, the metropolitan [gas] companies have usually complied with the law. **1876** G. F. CHAMBERS *Astron.* VI. i. 480 The subject of the photometry of stars..has received but little attention from practical astronomers.

photo-mezzotype: see PHOTO- 2.

photomicrograph (fəʊtəʊ'maɪkrəgrɑːf, -æ-). [f. PHOTO- 2 + Gr. μικρό-ς small, MICRO- + -GRAPH: cf. MICROGRAPH.] A photograph of a microscopic object on a magnified scale. So **photo'microgram** in same sense; **photomi'crographer**, one who takes photomicrographs; ,**photomicro'graphic** *a.*, pertaining to photomicrography; used for taking photomicrographs; **photomi'crographist**. ,**photomi'crography**, the art of obtaining photographs of microscopic objects on a magnified scale.

1858 G. SHADBOLT in *Sutton's Photogr. Notes* III. 208 The word microphotograph originated, I believe, with my-self, and is applied, I think correctly, to very small photographs, not to photographs of small objects, which would more correctly be photomicrographs. **1862** *Catal. Internat. Exhib.* II. XIV. 53 A photo-micrographic camera..for taking photographs of..microscopic objects. **1865** *Chambers's Encycl.* VII. 510/2 Photo-Micrography consists in the enlargement of microscopic objects, by means of the microscope, and the projection of the enlarged image on a sensitive collodion film. **1866** J. J. WOODWARD *Amer. Jrnl. Sci.* Ser. II. XLII. 190 The paper..is illustrated by photomicrographs reproduced by photolithography. **1870** R. J. FOWLER in *Eng. Mech.* 4 Feb. 501/3 By uniting the photomicrographic object glass..with the eyepiece.., the apparatus becomes a dioptric compound microscope. **1887** *Jrnl. R. Microsc. Soc.* VII. 358 As an evidence of progress in another direction, perhaps equally important to the photomicrographer, the negatives which accompany the *Amphipleura* specimens may not be without interest. **1889** *Anthony's Photogr. Bull.* II. 156 The admitted advantage which Photomicrography offers to the microscopist for recording the images seen under the microscope. **1893** *Brit. Med. Jrnl.* 26 Aug. 487 Illustrated by..photomicrographs of affected nerves. **1896** *Nature* 24 Sept. 490/1 Excellent stained preparations of bacteria, taken by..well-known photomicrographers. **1903** *Nation* (N.Y.) 21 May 417/1 It would have been better..to keep the photomicrograms and the delineations of the trunk-bark separate. **1937** *Discovery* Sept. 283/1 (*heading*) Dufaycolor for the photo-micrographist. **1958** *Newnes Compl. Amat. Photogr.* 6 Nowadays the photographer can take his camera underwater, and record the life of the seabed; amateur photomicrographists can explore the world of nature. **1971** *Sci. Amer.* Dec. 37/1 (Advt.), The complaints will now cease that when we speeded up Kodachrome Film we robbed the photomicrographer of some of his resolving power.

,**photomicro'scopic,** *a.* [PHOTO- 2.] Produced on a microscopic scale by photography.

1870 *Daily News* 7 Dec., The thousands..of private photomicroscopic telegrams from all parts of the country brought in [to Paris] by pigeon post.

photomixer, -mixing: see PHOTO- 1.

photomontage (,fəʊtəʊmɒn'tɑːʒ). Also with hyphen. [f. PHOTO- 2 + MONTAGE.] Montage (MONTAGE 2) using photographs or photographic negatives, a picture made by this method.

1931 *Times Lit. Suppl.* 25 June (Arts Suppl.) p. iv/3 'Photomontage', the use of stripped negatives in futurist compositions to convey the effect of simultaneous ideas,.. made its first success in the U.S.S.R. **1936** [see COLLAGE]. **1944** K. VAUGHAN in *Penguin New Writing* XXII. 153 Attempts at combining modern type faces with drawing and photomontage..have more often been made by certain branches of publicity. **1958** N. MARSH *Singing in Shrouds* (1959) ii. 19 They could see her reflection in the window-pane, like a photomontage richly floating across street lamps and the façades of darkened buildings. **1971** P. GRESSWELL *Environment* 231 A series of photo-montages should be prepared. **1972** *Daily Tel.* 8 Mar. 16 Not all the illustrations, which range from drawings to photomontage, come from people known primarily as artists. **1975** *Times Lit. Suppl.* 9 May 519/3 Ingeniously chosen illustrations and designs—notably the surrealistic photomontages of Benjamin Palencia. **1978** *Nature* 26 Jan. 359/1 (*caption*) Super-imposed photomontages from serial frontal sections of Procion yellow-stained horizontal cells contrasting sharply against the autofluorescing background tissue.

,**photomorpho'genesis.** *Bot.* [f. PHOTO- 1 + MORPHOGENESIS.] (See quots. 1964.)

1959 A. W. GALSTON in R. B. Withrow *Photoperiodism* ii. 139 Further knowledge of this substance..will help elucidate the details of photomorphogenesis. **1964** *Biol. Rev.* XXXIX. 87 By the term *photomorphogenesis* we designate the control which may be exerted by visible radiation over growth, development and differentiation of a plant, independently of photosynthesis. *Ibid.* 506 Photomorphogenesis concerns the regulation of plant growth and morphology by light. **1975** *Nature* 10 Jan. 94/2 Profound changes in the activity of many plant enzymes occur during photomorphogenesis, the response of dark-grown plants to light.

So ,**photo,morphoge'netic, -'genic** *adjs.*, of or pertaining to the effects of light on plants; ,**photo,morphoge'netically, -'genically** *advs.*

1956 *Plant Physiol.* XXXI. 279/1 This same reversible photoreaction was also established for the control of flower initiation of Xanthium..and photomorphogenic effects such as leaf expansion. **1959** A. W. GALSTON in R. B. Withrow *Photoperiodism* ii. 139 We have been concerned with the photomorphogenic reaction and auxin metabolism. *Ibid.* 153 Certain experiments have suggested that the cofactor is transformed, by photomorphogenically active light, into the inhibitor. **1960** *Chem. Abstr.* LIV. 25090 Some expts. indicated that *V*..is converted to *I* by photomorphogenetically active light. **1962** *Plant Physiol.* XXXVII. 142 (*heading*) Photomorphogenetic responses of sporelings of *Marsilea vestita*. **1971** *Nature* 27 Aug. 602/1 Acetylcholine, when given to dark grown seedlings, mimicked the effect of red light in certain photomorphogenic responses. **1975** D. VINCE-PRUE *Photoperiodism in Plants* iv. 119 Some experiments suggest that..the photomorphogenetic response occurs because P_{fr} operates *via* a threshold type of mechanism.

photomosaic: see PHOTO- 2.

photo'multiplier. Also with hyphen. [f. PHOTO- 1 + MULTIPLIER.] Also *photomultiplier tube*. A phototube in which the small current from the photocathode is multiplied by a succession of secondary electrodes, so that light of very low intensity can be detected.

1940 *Rev. Sci. Instruments* XI. 226/1 In the photo-multiplier the original electron current is supplied by a photo-cathode. **1955** *Sci. News* XXXVI. 21 A photo-multiplier, in which an initial small pulse of light is converted into a cascade of electrons. **1961** G. R. CHOPPIN *Exper. Nucl. Chem.* vii. 93 Normally, in scintillation systems it is not the phosphor or photomultiplier tube that determines the resolving time, but rather it is the electronic system. **1968** *Brit. Med. Bull.* XXIV. 261/1 Light from the spot is imaged onto the specimen.., and a photomultiplier positioned so as to read the intensity of the transmitted light. **1975** D. H. BURRIN in Williams & Wilson *Biologist's Guide to Princ. & Techniques Pract. Biochem.* v. 137 Photomultiplier tubes are more sensitive than simple photocells. **1977** *Dædalus* Fall 42 Photo-multipliers convert the light pulses into electric pulses.

photomural: see PHOTO- 2.

photon[1] ('fəʊtɒn). *Physics.* [f. PHOTO- 1 + -ON[1]. In senses 1 and 2 the ending *-on* may be merely arbitrary.]

†**1.** = TROLAND. *Obs.*

1916 L. T. TROLAND in *Trans. Illuminating Engin. Soc.* (U.S.) XI. 950, I have..found it very convenient to express all intensity measures in terms of a unit of retinal illumination which I have called the photon. **1929** *Bureau of Standards Jrnl. Res.* (U.S.) II. 445 If the rods initiate the nerve activity responsible for the blue arcs a pure spectral stimulus of wave length, say, 640 mμ, would have to be at a much higher illumination (measured in photons..) than a stimulus of wave length less than, say 550 mμ. **1934** *Jrnl. Gen. Physiol.* XVII. 241 With the present apparatus, which has a pupil area of 2·54 sq. mm. the maximal retinal illumination available in the central test area when it is not interrupted is very nearly 6000 photons. **1944** [see TROLAND]. **1949** J. H. PRINCE *Visual Devel.* I. vi. 85 Feldman ..has estimated that, whereas a rod requires only 0·00025 photons to stimulate it, a cone requires 0·025 photons. **1953** H. H. EMSLEY *Visual Optics* (ed. 5) II. xviii. 232 A surface of luminance one millilambert observed through a 4 mm. diameter pupil gives a retinal illumination of $2{\cdot}5 \times 4^2 = 40$ photons.

†**2.** (See quot.) *Obs. rare.*

1921 J. JOLY in *Proc. R. Soc.* B. XCII. 226 In the foregoing pages.. the unit light stimulus discharged by a single visual fibre is frequently referred to. It represents a very small amount of energy... It must not be confused with the quantum of energy... I propose to designate it a photon. *Ibid.* 228 The stimulus value of the three colour sensations in such proportions as to give white light is nine photons.

3. A quantum of light or other electro-magnetic radiation, the energy of which is proportional to the frequency of the radiation.

1926 G. N. LEWIS in *Nature* 18 Dec. 874/1, I therefore take the liberty of proposing for this hypothetical new atom, which is not light but plays an essential part in every process of radiation, the name *photon*. **1929** *Jrnl. Amer. Chem. Soc.* LI. 2850 In 1906, Einstein showed that the photo-electric effect and many photochemical reactions could be explained in terms of the Quantum Theory if light itself consisted of discrete particles of energy or quanta, now usually called photons. **1934** *Discovery* May 125/1 Photons (quanta or packets of electro-magnetic energy) are in general more efficient in bringing about atomic changes than particles of corresponding energy. **1942** J. D. STRANATHAN '*Particles' of Mod. Physics* viii. 357 The ejection of a β particle might leave the new nucleus in an excited state. In this case one would expect the disintegration to be followed by the radiation of a γ-ray photon having an energy equal to the excitation energy. **1948** *Sci. News* VI. 75 In the quantum theory a light signal cannot be sub-divided indefinitely, but consists of finite units, so-called light quanta, or 'photons', each carrying an amount of energy proportional to the frequency of the light wave of which they form part. **1959** [see COMPTON]. **1968** M. S. LIVINGSTON *Particle Physics* v. 96 In particle physics, the individual photons entering or emerging from interactions are treated as particles with zero rest mass, velocity *c*, energy $E = h\nu$, and momentum $p = E/c$. **1971** *Nature* 2 July 67/2 The dark-adapted human eye is capable of detecting a pulse of less than a hundred photons. **1977** *Dædalus* Summer 26 On the subnuclear level the gluons are the analogues of the photons or quanta of the electromagnetic field for atomic processes.

4. Special Comb.: **photon rocket**, a rocket propelled by the backward ejection of photons.

1949 *Jrnl. Brit. Interplanetary Soc.* VIII. 242 Two possible schemes for utilizing nuclear energy are then considered, the first using a nuclear 'boiler' to heat a working fluid which is then expanded through a nozzle in the normal way and the second using the energy direct in a 'photon' rocket. **1958** C. C. ADAMS et al. *Space Flight* 347 Others ponder photon rockets driven by parallel beams formed by properly designed reflectors.

Hence **pho'tonic** *a.*

1938 R. W. LAWSON tr. *Hevesy & Paneth's Man. Radioactivity* (ed. 2) v. 61 In the production of the former the whole of the energy of the γ-quantum or photon..is transmitted to the electron, whereas in the production of recoil electrons only a fraction of the photonic energy is handed over to the recoil electron. **1952** R. E. MARSHAK *Meson Physics* iii. 98 The first observations on the photonic production of charged π mesons were made in 1949. **1952** *Jrnl. Brit. Interplanetary Soc.* XI. 59 Whether the 'jet propulsion engine' concerned is of a type that consumes air, burns chemical propellants, utilizes nuclear power, or represents some form of electronic or photonic drive. **1958** C. C. ADAMS et al. *Space Flight* 348 The best we can do is to base our calculations on highly developed systems using atomic, ionic, or photonic particles. **1969** AUDEN *City without Walls* 97 His light is felt as a friendly presence not a photonic bombardment. **1970** *Science* 30 Jan. 618/2 The rocks were analyzed by photonic microscopy (transmitted and reflected light).

Photon[2] ('fəʊtɒn). [f. PHOTO- 2 + -*n*.] The proprietary name of a range of photocomposing equipment (see quot. 1958). Also *attrib.*

1953 *Publishers' Weekly* 7 Feb. 756/2 'The Wonderful World of Insects' is the first volume to be composed with the revolutionary Higgonet-Moyroud [*sic*] photographic type-composing machine, more commonly called Photon. **1953** *Newsweek* 16 Feb. 82/3 Last week the Photon made its formal debut... Dr. Bush presented..the first Photon-composed book, 'The Wonderful World of Insects'. **1958** *Times Lit. Suppl.* 11 Apr. 200/2 This apparatus was invented in 1944 by two French engineers, MM. Higonnet and Moyroud, who sold their plans to the Graphic Arts Foundation of Cambridge, Mass., which has developed their invention since 1949 under the name of Photon. The machine prints letters on to film by stroboscopic flashes of light which pass through a continuously revolving disc, upon which are carried sixteen founts of ninety letters each. *Ibid.* 200/3 The first Photon book was *The Wonderful World of Insects*, by Albro Gaul, published by Rinehart & Company Inc. in New York in 1953. **1967** C. J. DUNCAN in Cox & Grose *Organiz. Bibliogr. Rec. by Computer* 11. 45 In the Photon 540 or the Intertype, the characters are held on a disc.

photonegative (fəʊtəʊˈnɛgətɪv), *a.* Also with hyphen. [f. PHOTO- 1 + NEGATIVE *a.*] **1.** *Zool.* Of an animal: tending to move away from light.

1914 S. O. MAST in *Biol. Zentralblatt* XXXIV. 662 In place of positively or negatively phototropic, geotropic, etc., we might use photo-, geo-, negative or positive, etc. **1923** *Jrnl. Exper. Zool.* XXVIII. 120 Insects with one eye blinded usually turn, in non-directive light, toward the functional eye if they are photopositive and toward the blinded eye if they are photonegative. **1945** T. H. SAVORY *Spiders Brit. Isles* (ed. 2) 143 They [*sc.* harvestmen spiders] are strongly photonegative and collect in the darkest corner of their cage. **1975** *Nature* 25 Dec. 712/2 Flies entering the maze..receive phototactic scores ranging from 1·0 (highly photonegative) to 16·0 (highly photopositive).

2. *Physics.* Pertaining to or exhibiting a decrease in electrical conductivity when illuminated.

1915 *Physical Rev.* V. 62 For certain regions of the spectrum these cells were photo-negative, while for longer wave-lengths they were photo-positive. **1925** H. S. ALLEN *Photo-Electricity* (ed. 2) vi. 95 In some instances an apparent *rise* in resistance has been observed on exposure to light. This type of response is said to be 'photo-negative'. **1932** [see PHOTOPOSITIVE *a.* 2].

Hence ˌ**photonegaˈtivity**.

1962 *Jrnl. Insect Physiol.* VIII. 253 There is a less pronounced shift towards photonegativity in the later instars. **1974** *Marine Biol.* XXV. 313/2 Photokinesis and phototaxis were deliberately confounded in this measure, since there was no way to predict which behavioural element might respond to selection for photonegativity in the tidal pool.

photo-nephograph: see PHOTO- 2.

photoneutral, -neutron: see PHOTO- 1.

photonics (fəʊˈtɒnɪks), *sb. pl.* [f. PHOTON: see -IC 2.] The study of the applications of the particle properties of light.

1952 *Jrnl. Brit. Interplanetary Soc.* XI. 58 From the fundamental domains of photonics, electronics, nuclear physics, atomic physics and physical chemistry, our interest passes without interruption, via thermodynamics and gas kinetics, to aerodynamics and the physics of solid bodies. **1976** *Physics Bull.* Mar. 126/1 The term 'photonics', by analogy with electronics, describes the application of the photon to the transmission of information, and includes such topics as photon beam production, waveguiding, deflection, modulation, amplification, image processing, storage and detection. **1978** *Daily Tel.* 11 Mar. 10/6 According to the commentary..we can expect the new science of photonics to be comparable to electronics. We shall be making telephone calls by laser and watching three dimensional films on television.

photonuclear: see PHOTO- 1.

photonymograph: see PHOTO- 2.

photo-offset (ˌfəʊtəʊˈɒfsɛt). [f. PHOTO(LITHOGRAPHY + OFFSET.] A planographic printing process in which a photographic negative is used as the basis of the printing surface; also called *photolitho offset*. Also *attrib.* Cf. OFFSET *sb.* 10 b.

1926 F. B. WIBORG *Printing Ink* ix. 122 During the last few years a number of photo-offset processes have been perfected... By means of some of these processes it is now possible to photograph a design directly upon the surface of a prepared metal plate, and then to mechanically etch the plate for printing. **1947** R. MESSNER *Selling Printing & Direct Advertising* vi. 140 Both the simplest black-and-white pieces and the most elaborate productions in many colors may thus be 'photo' 'offset' lithography. **1957** *Times Lit. Suppl.* 20 Dec. 780/3 The time is surely ripe for general agreement upon a standard set of [bibliographical] terms designed to cover modern processes, including the now commonly used method of photo-offset reproduction. **1970** O. DOPPING *Computers & Data Processing* xxiii. 377 Multiple copies can be produced by means of carbon, stencil, offset, or photo offset. **1976** *Sat. Rev.* (U.S.) 4 Sept. 7/1 The Folio Society..does not mass-produce huge editions by photo-offset.

photoorganotroph to **-organotrophy:** see PHOTO- 1.

photo-oxidation to **-oxidized:** see PHOTO- 3.

photoperiod (ˈfəʊtəʊpɪərɪəd). *Biol.* [f. PHOTO- 1 + PERIOD *sb.*] The period of daily illumination which an organism receives; also, the value of this period which optimally stimulates reproduction or some other function.

1920 GARNER & ALLARD in *Jrnl. Agric. Res.* XVIII. 603 The term *photoperiod* is suggested to designate the favorable length of day for each organism, and *photoperiodism* is suggested to designate the response of the organism to the relative length of day and night. **1932** FULLER & CONARD tr. *Braun-Blanquet's Plant Sociol.* v. 102 Photoperiod affects growth as well as flowering of plants. **1937** *Ann. Reg. 1936* 58 The photoperiod of a plant can be modified by temperature. **1957** *New Biol.* XXIII. 10 The profound importance which the daily photoperiod may have in controlling the time of transition from vegetative growth to flowering was discovered more than forty years ago. **1972** *Sci. Amer.* Aug. 27/1 It is likely..that temperature rather than photoperiod directly influences the duration of incubation [of mallard eggs]. **1976** *Nature* 1-8 Jan. 41/1 The fish were maintained in aquaria at 22–24°C, on a light-dark (LD) 12:12 photoperiod.

Hence ˌ**photoperiˈodic** *a.*, of, pertaining to, or influenced by photoperiods; ˌ**photoperiˈodically** *adv.*, by means of or with regard to photoperiods; ˌ**photoperioˈdicity** = PHOTOPERIODISM (see quot. 1945[1]).

1923 *Jrnl. Agric. Res.* XXIII. 873 The wide extent and great variety in form of the photoperiodic response verifies ..the modern view..that environment through its action on internal conditions governs the form of expression in the plant. **1936** *Q. Rev. Biol.* XI. 373/2 It is open to question whether they are true cases of sexual photoperiodicity. **1940** *Bot. Gaz.* CI. 815 These differences..indicated that young leaves were photoperiodically more effective than old ones. **1945** *Science* 6 Apr. 353/2 Botanists refer to this phenomenon as 'photoperiodism', while most zoologists use the term 'photoperiodicity'. *Ibid.* 354/1 'Photoperiodicity' ..has now come to include any periodic or rhythmic process controlled by photoperiods. It is not only reproduction controlled photoperiodically, but includes pelt cycles, plumage cycles in birds and migrations also. **1971** *Canad. Jrnl. Zool.* XLIX. 109 Two morphological variations of *Davainea tetraoensis* were found... Changes in diet and changes in photoperiodicity do not seem to effect any change from one form to the other. **1972** *Country Life* 16 Mar. 630/4 Wild rock doves are photoperiodic..and cease to breed when day lengths become shortened in winter. **1974** *Nature* 10 May 183/2 The data showed that different strains produced F1 hybrids photoperiodically intermediate between the parents. **1976** *Sci. Amer.* Feb. 114/2 It has.. been demonstrated that the insect's eye is not involved in its photoperiodic response.

photoperiodism (fəʊtəʊˈpɪərɪədɪz(ə)m). *Biol.* [f. prec. + -ISM.] The phenomenon whereby many plants and animals are stimulated or inhibited in breeding and other functions by the lengths of the daily periods of light and darkness to which they are subjected. Cf. PHOTOPERIODICITY.

1920 [see PHOTOPERIOD]. **1929** WEAVER & CLEMENTS *Plant Ecol.* xiii. 328 Knowledge of photoperiodism, as these responses to length of day are called, should aid the plant breeder. **1971** *Country Life* 30 Dec. 1854/1 The commercial production of chrysanthemums has been revolutionized by the application of the principles of photo-periodism. **1976** *Sci. Amer.* Feb. 114/2 Most of the early investigations of photoperiodism in insects were concerned with the nature and location of the photo-receptors and the effector system.

photophil to **-philous:** see PHOTO- 1.

‖**photophobia** (fəʊtəʊˈfəʊbɪə). *Path.* Also anglicized **-phoby**. [mod.L., f. Gr. φῶς light, PHOTO- + -PHOBIA.] Dread of or shrinking from light, esp. as a symptom of diseases of the eyes.

1799 HOOPER *Dict. Med.*, *Photophobia*, such an intolerance of light, that the eye, or rather the retina, can scarcely bear it's irritating rays. **1858** MAYNE *Expos. Lex.*, *Photophobia*,..photophoby. **1869** G. LAWSON *Dis. Eye* (1874) 15 The lids are then red, swollen, and spasmodically closed, from the excessive photophobia. **1899** *Allbutt's Syst. Med.* VIII. 708 The retina [in albinos] is unprotected, and there is consequent photophobia.

Hence **photophobic** (-ˈfɒbɪk) *a.*, pertaining to or affected with photophobia; dreading light; ‖ˌ**photophobophˈthalmia** (-fɒbɒfˈθælmɪə) [mod.L.], ophthalmia attended with photophobia.

1842 DUNGLISON *Med. Lex.*, Photophobophthalmia. **1858** MAYNE *Expos. Lex.*, *Photophobicus*, of, or belonging to Photophobia: photophobic. *Ibid.*, Ophthalmy, with excessive intolerance of the light: photophobophthalmy. **1878** T. BRYANT *Pract. Surg.* I. 89 The affection is attended with photophobic pain about the orbit and sclerotic injection.

photophone (ˈfəʊtəʊfəʊn). [f. Gr. φῶς light, PHOTO- + -φωνος sounding, sounder, φωνή voice, sound.] Any apparatus in which sounds are transmitted by light; *esp.* that invented by A. Graham Bell and Sumner Tainter in 1880, by means of which sound-vibrations are conveyed to a distance by means of a beam of light reflected from a mirror and received upon a sensitive selenium cell by means of which the sounds are reproduced. See RADIOPHONE.

1880 A. GRAHAM BELL in *Jrnl. Franklin Inst.* CX. 246 We have named the apparatus for the production and reproduction of sound in this way 'The Photophone', because an ordinary beam of light contains the rays which are operative. **1880** *Athenæum* 25 Sept. 405/2 The sensibility of the metal selenium to the action of the solar spectrum recommends it as the most favourable substance for use in the 'photophone', as the new instrument is called. **1889** PREECE & MAIER *Telephone* 104 Bell and Sumner Tainter have constructed an apparatus, to which they gave the name of 'photophone', which enabled them to reproduce words at a distance by the aid of luminous rays.

Hence **photophonic** (-ˈfɒnɪk) *a.*, pertaining to or produced by the photophone; **photophony** (fəʊˈtɒfənɪ), the use of the photophone; the conveyance of sound-vibrations by means of light.

1880 A. GRAHAM BELL in *Athenæum* 4 Dec. 747/3 (*title of paper*) On Methods of preparing Selenium and other Substances for Photophonic Experiments. **1881** S. P. THOMPSON in *Nature* 17 Feb. 366/2 An elegant series of researches in photophony. **1882** *Nature* 16 Feb. 377/1 Yielding radiophonic and photophonic sounds when illuminated by intermittent beams of different kinds.

photophore (ˈfəʊtəfɔə(r)). [mod. ad. Gr. φωτοφόρος light-bearing or -bringing: see PHOTO- and -PHORE.]

1. An apparatus with an electric light, used for examination of internal organs of the body and for other purposes.

1885 *Athenæum* 12 Dec. 773/3 Mr. J. Mayall, jun., exhibited the Helot-Trouvé electric photophore, which had been recommended as an excellent illuminant for microscopical purposes. **1893** *Syd. Soc. Lex.*, *Photophore*, the name for an electric light for use in laryngoscopy, adapted to a forehead-band, so as to be reflected by the laryngoscopic mirror into the mouth and throat under examination.

2. A luminiferous organ in certain animals.

1898 *Nature* 23 June LVIII. 192/1 The new bathybial fish from Lord Howe Island,..*Æthoprora perspicillata*,.. distinguished..by the presence of a pair of supernumerary photophores between the upper angle of the eye and the ante-orbital. **1934** *Bull. N.Y. Zool. Soc.* XXXVII. 193/1, I [*sc.* W. Beebe] suddenly saw the amazing beauty of the photophores [of the constellation fish, *Bathysidus pentagrammus*]. There were five rows of these. **1963** P. H. GREENWOOD *Norman's Hist. Fishes* (ed. 2) x. 168 There are typically two rows of organs, or photophores, on either side of the fish [*sc.* a wide-mouth]. **1964** *Oceanogr. & Marine Biol.* II. 354 In each of these groups of prawns the pattern of the photophores is similar. **1974** *Nature* 18 Jan. 155/2 The ventral photophores of some mesopelagic fishes in the upper regions of the sea may produce bioluminescence.

photophoresis (fəʊtəʊfɒˈriːsɪs). *Physics.* Also with hyphen. [ad. G. *photophorese* (F. Ehrenhaft 1918, in *Ann. der Physik* LVI. 93): see PHOTO- 1 and -PHORESIS.] The motion of small particles under the influence of a beam of light.

1919 *Sci. Abstr.* A. XXII. 275 (*heading*) Mechanical and osmotic actions of radiation on the media passed through. Theory of photophoresis. **1950** *Engineering* 14 Apr. 407/1 The generation of such heat would probably introduce difficulties due to thermal currents and photo-phoresis effects. **1972** *Sci. Amer.* Feb. 64/3 In the case of photophoresis single particles would be heated asymmetrically by the light and would as a result move through the surrounding medium.

Hence **photophoretic** (-fɒˈrɛtɪk) *a.*, of or pertaining to photophoresis.

1924 *Sci. Abstr.* A. XXVII. 397 Especially through it [*sc.* this hypothesis] is the fact of the small dependence of the photophoretic force on pressure made understandable. **1941** *Physical Rev.* LX. 169/2 The possibility of finding an explanation of the cause of the Earth's magnetism in terms of the photophoretic influence will be discussed. **1976** *Chem. Abstr.* 23 Feb. 404/2 Est[imatio]n of the value and direction of photophoretic velocity was made.

photophosphorescent to **-salt:** see PHOTO-.

photophosphorylation: see PHOTO- 3.

photophthalmia (ˌfəʊtɒfˈθælmɪə). *Ophthalm.* [f. PHOTO- 1 + OPHTHALMIA.] Inflammation of the cornea produced by ultraviolet light, causing blindness or defective vision.

1907 J. H. PARSONS *Dis. Eye* x. 211 Electric Light Ophthalmia (Photophthalmia).—The ultraviolet rays of the electric light, especially of the arc lamp, may cause extreme burning pain, lacrymation, photophobia, blepharospasm, and swelling of the palpebral conjunctiva and retrotarsal folds, coming on a few hours later. **1916** *Proc. Amer. Acad. Arts & Sci.* LI. 641 An ordinary case of photophthalmia completely disappears in less than a week and repair is going on all through this period. **1947** *Med. Jrnl. Austral.* 26 Apr. 524/2 Solar photophthalmia occurred in summer months among convoy drivers in the Northern Territory. **1969** *Amer. Jrnl. Optometry* XLVI. 569 The radiation below 305 nm required to produce marked photophthalmia was approximately 2×10^6 ergs/cm^2.

Hence ˌ**photophˈthalmic** *a.*, of or pertaining to photophthalmia.

1913 *17th Internat. Congr. Med.* IX. 1. 204 The flash of a short circuit is extremely rich in ultra-violet rays, and to these are to be attributed the photophthalmic symptoms. **1947** *Med. Jrnl. Austral.* 26 Apr. 524/2 Duke Elder considers the name 'snow blindness'..as thoroughly unsatisfactory, since the photophthalmic symptoms are not caused by snow, but by solar energy partly reflected by snow.

photophysical, -physics: see PHOTO- 1.

photopic (fəʊˈtɒpɪk, fəʊˈtəʊpɪk), *a. Physiol.* [f. PHOT(O- 1 + -OPIA + -IC.] Of or pertaining to vision in levels of illumination similar to daylight, believed to involve chiefly the cones of the retina.

1915 J. H. PARSONS *Introd. Study of Colour Vision* ii. 17 If the eye has been exposed to bright light it is said to be light-adapted. I shall speak of vision under these circumstances as photopia, and the light-adapted eye as a photopic eye. **1921** *Phil. Mag.* XLI. 298 The entire luminosity curve of photopic vision will be shifted towards the red end of the spectrum. *Ibid.*, The photopic luminosity curve does not quite coincide with the scotopic luminosity curve. **1960** *Electronic Engin.* XXXII. 145/1 For the comparison of camera versus visual estimates of relative luminance, it is convenient to have inscribed on the graticule to photopic curve. **1965** J. E. CROUCH *Functional Human Anat.* xix. 597/1 The cones are photopic or discriminative and enable us to see details of form, structure, and color. **1975** J. P. THOMAS in Carterette & Friedman *Handbk. Perception* V. vii. 238 At photopic levels of illumination, acuity is highest when the target is viewed with the center of the fovea and decreases rapidly as the image of the target is displaced toward the periphery.

photopigment: see PHOTO- 1.

photoplate: see PHOTO- 2.

photoplay ('fəʊtəʊpleɪ). orig. *N. Amer.* Also **photo-play.** [f. PHOTO- 2 + PLAY *sb.*] A cinematic representation of a play or drama; a motion picture. Also *attrib.* and *Comb.*

1910 *Moving Picture World* 12 Nov. 1103/2 (*heading*) The Barnstormer in the photoplay. **1911** *Daily Colonist* (Victoria, B.C.) 1 Apr. 11/1 (Advt.), Romano Photo-play Theatre. The Aristocrat of Picturedom. Continuous performances daily from noon to 11 p.m. **1912** *Everybody's Mag.* Oct. 505/2 The clever photoplays that dramatize the hard, dry facts into living stories. **1913** [see *film studio* s.v. FILM *sb.* 7 c]. **1914** [see CREDIT *sb.* 13 d]. **1918** V. O. FREEBURG (*title*) The art of photoplay making. *Ibid.* 57 The filming and projection of a photo-play. **1920** *Chambers's Jrnl.* Mar. 188/1 Los Angeles.. is the scene of many well-known and popular photo-plays. **1930** *Times Educ. Suppl.* 22 Feb. 81/1 The historical accuracy of the photoplays is vouched for by specialists. **1950** BLESH & JANIS *They all played Ragtime* iii. 59 The ragtimers' repertory, finally, included descriptive overtures. These prefigured the early photoplay interpretation of the nickelodeon pianos. **1975** *Language for Life* (Dept. Educ. & Sci.) xxii. 319 Some [children] have made photoplays to illustrate a story or give a visual interpretation of a piece of music.

photopolarimeter to **-metry**: see PHOTO- 1.

photopolymer to **-polymerized**: see PHOTO- 3.

photopositive (fəʊtəʊ'pɒzɪtɪv), *a.* Also with hyphen. [f. PHOTO- 1 + POSITIVE *a.* and *sb.*]

1. *Zool.* Of an animal: tending to move towards light.

1914 [see PHOTONEGATIVE *a.* 1]. **1923** *Jrnl. Exper. Zool.* XXVIII. 194 The photopositive reactions of insects under normal conditions usually result in their escape from places of danger. **1964** *Oceanogr. & Marine Biol.* II. 482 The larvae [of *Spirorbis*] may settle or may resume their pelagic existence, again becoming photopositive for a short time. **1975** [see PHOTONEGATIVE *a.* 1].

2. *Physics.* Pertaining to or exhibiting an increase in electrical conductivity when illuminated.

1915 [see PHOTONEGATIVE *a.* 2]. **1932** HUGHES & DUBRIDGE *Photoelectric Phenomena* viii. 328 The effect of light [on photoconducting substances] is usually to increase the conductivity (the photopositive effect..), but occasionally it is found that light apparently diminishes the conductivity (the photonegative effect..). The photonegative effect occurs above a critical voltage whose value depends on the temperature.

Hence **photo'positively** *adv.*; **,photoposi'tivity.**

1946 *Nature* 13 July 58/2 When behaving photopositively *Hydra* orientates itself klinokinetically. **1962** *Jrnl. Insect Physiol.* VIII. 251 Photopositivity declines continuously within each instar, but shows an increase after each moult.

photopotential to **-production**: see PHOTO- 1.

photopro'tection. *Biol.* [f. PHOTO- 1 + PROTECTION.] The process whereby illumination of living matter with visible light can protect it from being harmed by subsequent ultraviolet irradiation.

1958 J. JAGGER in *Bacteriol. Rev.* XXII. 100/1 'Post-UV-photoprevention' would describe completely what is here called photoreactivation. In addition, this term would distinguish the present effect from photoprotection ('pre-UV-photoprevention'). **1962** *Photochem. & Photobiol.* I. 256 Photoprotection is found to require, at an ultraviolet survival level of 2 per cent, about three times as much radiation energy as photoreactivation. **1975** *Nature* 17 Apr. 628/1 We..conclude that photoprotection does not contribute to the increased survival of HSV in Jay Tim cells treated with photoreactivating light.

photopro'tective, *a.* [f. PHOTO- 1 + PROTECTIVE *a.* (*sb.*)] **a.** Of or pertaining to protection conferred by light (as in photoprotection). **b.** Of or pertaining to protection against harmful effects of light.

1961 *Jrnl. Bacteriol.* LXXXI. 526/2 Visible light irradiation of *Nocardia corallina* was found to render the culture more resistant to subsequent X irradiation... The results appear to be attributable only to a photoprotective action. **1975** *Sci. Amer.* July 73/1 Patients with the disease complain at first of a burning sensation in areas of the skin that are exposed to sunlight... The symptoms of the disease can be ameliorated by administering photoprotective agents such as carotenoids. **1976** *Nature* 12 Feb. 507/1 The melanosome has long been considered a passive cellular organelle. Its considered role as a photoprotective agent in the skin and other illuminated areas, could not explain its presence and function in the non-illuminated areas (for example, the midbrain).

photoprotein, -proton: see PHOTO- 1.

photoptic (fəʊ'tɒptɪk), *a. Physiol.* [f. PHOT(O- 1 + Gr. ὀπτικ-ός OPTIC *a.*] = PHOTOPIC *a.*

1949 *Amer. Jrnl. Bot.* XXXVI. 198/2 The scattered red light was just on the threshold of photoptic vision for the dark-adapted eye. **1955** C. W. ALLEN *Astrophysical Quantities* v. 103 (*heading*) Relative visibility K_λ for normal brightness.., the photoptic curve (International) (cone vision at fovea).

photoradiogram, -reaction: see PHOTO- 2, 1.

photore'activate, *v. Biol.* [f. PHOTO- 1 + REACTIVATE *v.*] *trans.* To repair by photoreactivation.

1954 *Biochim. & Biophys. Acta* XV. 471 They [*sc.* the systems studied] are then photoreactivated and the reactivated complexes are again exposed to UV in order to determine their UV sensitivity. **1975** *Nature* 13 Mar. 160/1 Even though cells of the higher plants can photo-reactivate ultraviolet damage.., the absence of dark-repair capability could be a significant disadvantage.

So **photore'activated, -re'activating** *ppl. adjs.*; ***photoreactivating enzyme***, any enzyme which catalyses photoreactivation. Also **,photoreactiva'bility**, the potential for photoreactivation; **photore'activable** *a.*, (of a biological system) capable of displaying photoreactivation; (of damage caused by ultraviolet irradiation) capable of being photoreactivated.

1953 *Jrnl. Bacteriol.* LXV. 252 (*heading*) Growth, respiration and nucleic acid synthesis in ultraviolet-irradiated and in photoreactivated *Escherichia coli.* **1958** *Jrnl. Gen. Physiol.* XLI. 463 (*heading*) Subcellular nature of the photoreactivating system. **1960** *Ibid.* XLIII. 592 This photoreactivating enzyme (PRE) is interesting for two reasons. First, it is a photoenzyme, and few enzymes involved in photochemical reactions are known at present. Second, it acts on DNA *in vitro* without depolymerizing it. **1961** J. A. SCHIFF et al. in Christensen & Buchmann *Progress in Photobiol.* vi. 290 Photoreactivability of the cells falls off rapidly when the cells are permitted to divide. Under non-dividing conditions, the cells remain completely photoreactivable indefinitely. **1965** J. JAGGER in E. J. Bowen *Recent Progress in Photobiol.* ii. 61 Evidence for the photoreactivability of RNA. **1975** *Nature* 13 Mar. 160/1 Some types of excisable ultraviolet-induced DNA damage are not photoreactivable. **1975** [see PHOTOREACTIVATION].

,photoreacti'vation. *Biol.* [f. PHOTO- 1 + REACTIVATION.] The process whereby illumination of living matter with visible light can counteract the destructive effects of previous ultraviolet irradiation.

1949 A. KELNER in *Jrnl. Bacteriol.* LVIII. 511 The effect of reactivating light will be referred to in this paper as *photoreactivation.* [*Note.*] The use of this term was suggested by Dr. Max Delbrück. **1962** [see PHOTOPROTECTION]. **1966** *Adv. Radiation Biol.* II. 21 These photoreactivations may result from DNA inactivations repairable by the mechanisms already described here. **1969** A. C. GIESE in F. Urbach *Biol. Effects Ultraviolet Radiation* 63 With protozoans..even UV radiation as well as blue-violet visible light are effective for photoreactivation, while yellow visible light during or after UV exposure is ineffective. **1975** *Nature* 11 Sept. 133/1 Photoreactivation is a DNA repair process in which the photoreactivating enzyme (PRE) monomerises pyrimidine dimers induced by ultraviolet light.

photorealism ('fəʊtəʊ'riːəlɪz(ə)m). *Art.* Also **Photorealism, Photo-Realism.** [f. PHOTO- (in *photographic*, etc.) + REALISM.] Detailed and unidealized representation in art, characteristically of the banal, vulgar, or sordid aspects of life. So **,photo-'realist** *a.* and *sb.*

1961 J. WILLIAMS *Forger* i. 6 A gigantic exhibition that will span everything..from extreme abstract expressionism to extreme photorealism. **1973** *Art Internat.* Mar. 49/1 Curators, critics, teachers, and writers all over the world, who come to it looking for women's art of every sort from photo-realist to conceptual. **1973** *Guardian* 11 Apr. 10 There's something a bit pompous..about the claims made for Photorealism, the kick-off show at the Serpentine... Photorealist sculpture is there too. **1975** *New Yorker* 19 May 11/3 (Advt.), The paintings, done in an authoritative Photo-Realist style, dramatically illustrate Photo-Realism's strange ability to invest ordinary, ugly, even disgusting objects of our Pop culture with an appearance of home truth that borders on beauty. **1976** *Ibid.* 26 Apr. 137/1 There are Abstract Expressionist, Conceptual, and even Photo-Realist photographs being made. **1977** *It* June 5/4 About a foot away from it..hover a ghastly mob of poofs, lesbians, photo realists and deviants of every conceivable kind. **1977** *Jrnl. R. Soc. Arts* CXXV. 272/1 America, which Hockney visited towards the end of the '60s, brought him to some of his major paintings. In these he had used extensive photographic material for a variety of purposes—for information, for realistic detail, for inspiration, the result yielding a new photo-realism of strictly integrated design.

photo-recce: see PHOTO- 2.

photoreceptor ('fəʊtəʊrɪsɛptə(r)). *Biol.* Also with hyphen. [f. PHOTO- 1 + RECEPTOR.] Any living structure which responds to incident light, esp. a cell in which light is absorbed and converted to a nervous or other signal.

1906 C. S. SHERRINGTON *Integrative Action Nervous Syst.* ix. 334 The free-swimming Ascidia with fin-like motor organs and semi-rigid aerial notochord..bears at its anterior end a well-formed photo-receptor organ (eye) and a well-formed otocyst (head proprio-ceptor). **1944** *Electronic Engin.* XVII. 189/3 The retina consists of ten layers, in the third of which are embedded the photo-receptors. **1964** [see below]. **1969** F. E. ROUND *Introd. Lower Plants* ii. 14 The locomotory flagellum [of the alga *Euglena*]. It has a.. swelling, the 'photoreceptor', near its entry into the cell. **1974** *Photochem. & Photobiol.* XIX. 435/1 The question as to the identity of the photo-receptor pigment (carotenoids or flavins) for phototropism in higher plants has not been resolved.

So **'photoreception**, the process of absorption, and esp. of detection, of light by an animal or plant; **'photoreceptive** *a.*, able to respond to light; of or pertaining to photoreception.

1906 C. S. SHERRINGTON *Integrative Action Nervous Syst.* ix. 334 The elaborateness of the photo-receptive organs of the flying Insecta corresponds with the great power of these forms to traverse space. **1908** *Amer. Jrnl. Physiol.* XXI. 198 The immediate results following the destruction of photo-reception in one eye are: (1) The production of rapid rotations..on the longitudinal axis of the body, [etc.]. **1943** *Vitamins & Hormones* I. 211 Ordinarily these organisms contain a structure which appears to be specifically concerned with photoreception, the stigma or eye-spot. **1964** *Ann. N.Y. Acad. Sci.* CXVII. 211 Red rays can penetrate to the hypothalamus with a sufficient intensity to activate the deeper photo-receptive structures. **1964** *Oceanogr. & Marine Biol.* II. 403 The photoreceptor pigment is unknown... That in *Diadema*..has an absorption maximum in its acid form at 462/63 mμ, but whether it is involved in the photoreceptive process is as yet unknown. **1973** J. J. WOLKEN in L. P. Miller *Phytochem.* I. ii. 26 Experimental observations..indicated that the photosynthetic process was not a simple photoreception sensitized by chlorophyll.

photo-reconnaissance, -recovery: see PHOTO- 2, 1.

,photore'duction. Also with hyphen. [f. PHOTO- 3 + REDUCTION.] **1.** Chemical reduction effected by light; in *Bot.*, such a reduction of carbon dioxide in which water is formed (rather than oxygen, as in ordinary photosynthesis).

1888 MELDOLA *Chem. Photogr.* (1889) 24 Photo-reduction may mean either a liberation of oxygen or of some other negative element, such as chlorine. **1939** *Jrnl. Cellular & Compar. Physiol.* XIII. 333 For the photo-reduction of one mole of carbon dioxide in the photosynthetic purple bacteria Streptococcus varians at high light intensity 2·6 moles of gaseous hydrogen are used. **1940** H. GAFFRON in *Amer. Jrnl. Bot.* XXVII. 282/2 Such a..conception of photosynthesis in green plants and bacteria allows us to group the light metabolism of the bacteria and the 'anaerobic light respiration' of the plants under one term: 'anaerobic photosynthesis' or, shorter, 'photoreduction'. This leaves 'aerobic photosynthesis' or 'photosynthesis' proper for the assimilation of carbon dioxide with the liberation of molecular oxygen. **1957** *Jrnl. Amer. Chem. Soc.* LXXIX. 294/1 Acriflavine and fluorescein-type dyes in solution undergo photoreduction in the presence of mild reducing agents. **1970** C. A. PRICE *Molec. Approaches to Plant Physiol.* ii. 115 A number of algae show 'photoreduction',..in which no O_2 is evolved. **1972** DEPUY & CHAPMAN *Molec. Reactions & Photochem.* iv. 48 Photoreduction of ketones is one of the oldest and most thoroughly investigated photochemical processes.

2. Reduction in size effected photographically.

1967 E. R. LANNON in Cox & Grose *Organiz. Bibliogr. Rec. by Computer* IV. 95 This latter version is printed..on 17″ × 22″ pages, suitable for 50% photoreduction and subsequent publication by offset press. **1968** *Bodl. Libr. Rec.* VIII. 64 The flexowriter produced a text in double column..from which, after 30 per cent photo-reduction, offset-litho plates were made. **1972** *Sci. Amer.* Dec. 15/1 All the equipment for integrated-circuit work, including the photoreduction microscope and the ultrasonic bonder, was of Chinese manufacture.

So **photore'duce** *v. trans.*, to reduce photochemically; **photore'duced, -re'ducing** *ppl. adjs.*

1957 G. OSTER in H. Gaffron et al. *Res. Photosynthesis* I. 53 Acriflavine under conditions where it is not photoreduced in the unbound state, is readily photoreduced when bound to polymeric acids. **1959** —— in R. B. Withrow *Photoperiodism* I. 7 In my opinion..intermediate colored forms of photoreduced porphyrins are obtainable. **1965** *Biochim. & Biophys. Acta* XCIX. 159 The lost NADP photoreducing activities of the sonicated chloroplasts..are fully restored on addition of plasto-cyanin. **1968** *Plant Physiol.* XLIII. 606/1 All the mutants appeared to have the enzymes needed for the reduction of carbon dioxide..but..they photoreduced little or no CO_2.

photoregulate to **-repairable**: see PHOTO- 1.

photo-reportage, -reporting: see PHOTO- 2.

photoresist (fəʊtəʊrɪ'zɪst). Also **photo-resist.** [f. PHOTO- 1 + RESIST *sb.*] A photosensitive resist which when exposed to (usu. ultraviolet) light loses either its resistance or its susceptibility to attack by an etchant or solvent.

1953 *Printing Mag.* Oct. 56/1 The Kodak Photo-Resist, developed by Eastman Kodak Co., has great possibilities. It is the result of an extensive study and seems to possess ideal properties for a photoresist. **1960** *Times Rev. Industry* Aug. 46/1 The copper-clad phenolic panels..are sprayed with a photo-resist. **1965** D. I. GAFFEE in L. Holland *Thin Film Microelectronics* vi. 261 Kodak Photo-resist was originally designed for making letter-press printing plates and lithographic plates. **1969** *R. & E. Coordinator* (Res. & Engin. Council Graphic Arts Industry) Apr. 10/1 The new photoresist can be used in chemical milling of copper, copper alloys, and stainless steel, provided only acid solution etchants are used. **1972** *Daily Tel.* 23 Mar. 30 (Advt.), The Applications Laboratory requires a technologist to work on new and improved Kodak lithographic printing plates... The person filling the post will probably have had experience with similar plates.., including some knowledge of photo-resists. **1973** *Sci. Amer.* Apr. 70/1 (*caption*) High-performance MOSFET is made in these steps. Light admitted through a mask sensitizes a 'photoresist' protecting a silicon oxide layer grown on a silicon wafer... Unprotected silicon oxide is etched away and phosphorus atoms are diffused into them to produce 'source' and 'drain' areas.

photoresistance to **-resistor**: see PHOTO- 1.

,photorespi'ration. *Bot.* [f. PHOTO- 1 + RESPIRATION.] A respiratory process in many higher plants by which they take up oxygen in the light and given out some carbon dioxide, contrary to the general pattern of photosynthesis.

1945 E. I. RABINOWITCH *Photosynthesis* I. xx. 569 We now come to the problem of 'photorespiration' proper, that is, a direct photochemical acceleration of normal respiration which disappears in the dark as instantaneously as does photosynthesis. *Ibid.* 570 None of the experiments described above provides a final proof of the nonexistence of true 'photorespiration'. **1966** *Physiologia Plantarum* XIX. 732 Evolution of carbon dioxide in light, or photorespiration, was affected by oxygen... Oxygen had no effect on dark respiration. This discrepancy.. can best be explained by an assumption that photorespiration and dark respiration are two different processes. **1972** [see PEROXISOMAL *a.*]. **1977** I. M. CAMPBELL *Energy & Atmosphere* iv. 76 Plants with high rates of photorespiration such as wheat.

Hence **photore'spire** *v. intr.*, to carry out photorespiration; **photore'spired** *ppl. a.*, evolved by photorespiration; **photore'spiring** *ppl. a.*; **photore'spiratory** *a.*, of, pertaining to, or evolved by photorespiration.

1968 *Plant Physiol.* XLIII. 1840/1 Glycolate oxidation appears to be responsible for much of the photorespiratory CO_2. *Ibid.* 1843/2 At high concentrations of CO_2 the synthesis of the photorespiratory substrate, glycolate, is severely inhibited. **1969** *Proc. Nat. Acad. Sci.* LXIII. 668 Species of the first group also photorespire, evolving CO_2 into the atmosphere in light. **1970** *Nature* 14 Nov. 687/2 Such plants may not photorespire, or alternatively may be capable of refixing all the photorespired CO_2 by an unusually efficient photosynthetic mechanism. *Ibid.* 688/1 Glycollate seems to be the primary substrate for photorespiration, and it does not normally accumulate in photorespiring tissue. **1974** H. FOCK et al. in *Bull. R. Soc. N.Z.* XII. 235 (*heading*) Estimation of carbon fluxes through photosynthetic and photorespiratory pathways. *Ibid.* 237 At 400 ppm CO_2 most or all of the photorespired carbon dioxide from intact leaves.. may be derived from ^{14}C-labelled early products of photosynthesis.

photoresponse to **-reversible**: see PHOTO- 1.

photoscan to **-scanning**: see PHOTO- 2.

photoscope ('fəʊtəskəʊp). [f. PHOTO- + -SCOPE.] **a.** A means of examining light, e.g. for purposes of analysis. **b.** An instrument for measuring the intensity of light by means of the varying electrical resistance of some substance sensitive to light, such as selenium. **c.** (See quot. 1896.) **d.** [with *photo-* taken as = *photograph.*] A lens or apparatus with lenses, through which photographs are viewed.

1872 tr. *Schellen's Spectr. Anal.* xli. 230 The solar spectrum is the most perfect photoscope that in the present state of science can be imagined. **1875** KNIGHT *Dict. Mech.* 1690/1 *Photoscope*, an instrument or apparatus for exhibiting photographs. **1896** *Current Hist.* (Buffalo) VI. 16 An instrument called a 'photoscope'.. to examine certain internal parts of the human body.. with the aid of sunlight only.

photoscopic (-'skɒpɪk), *a.* [f. as prec. + -IC.] **a.** Pertaining to the examination of light. **b.** Belonging to a photoscope.

1872 tr. *Schellen's Spectr. Anal.* xli. 230, I.. recommend to the scientific investigator a camera obscura specially adapted to these photoscopic observations.

c. *Computing.* Applied to a photographic method of storing digital information.

1955 *Sci. Amer.* June 100/3 Gilbert W. King.. has undertaken to exploit the great density of information storage that is possible through the use of high-resolution photographic emulsions. With his 'photoscopic' technique information can be stored at densities more than a hundred times as great as those possible in magnetic media. **1970** O. DOPPING *Computers & Data Processing* x. 151 One example of photographic film memories is the photoscopic memory, which has been used for dictionaries in mechanical translation from one natural language to another. The medium is a continuously rotating disk of transparent plastic carrying a photographic layer upon which a pattern corresponding to zeroes and ones has been recorded.

photo-sculptural, -sculpture: see PHOTO- 2.

photosensitive (fəʊtəʊ'sɛnsɪtɪv), *a.* [f. PHOTO- 1 + SENSITIVE *a.* and *sb.*] Responding to light in some way (biologically, chemically, electrically, etc.).

1886 *Jrnl. R. Microsc. Soc.* VI. 596 [In the Elateridæ] the photosensitive reflex action has its seat in the cerebroid ganglia. **1918** *Science* 23 Aug. 199/2 Decomposition of the photosensitive material by light, presupposes the formation of this substance within the sense organ. **1925** *Jrnl. Chem. Soc.* CXXVII. 1. 787 (*heading*) The photosensitive formation of water from its elements in the presence of chlorine. **1957** G. E. HUTCHINSON *Treat. Limnol.* I. vi. 399 The study of the transmission of light by means of suitably photosensitive instruments. **1967** D. G. HAYS *Introd. Computational Linguistics* iv. 68 Another mirror is used to position the beam at the desired place on the photo-sensitive stock. **1977** 'E. TREVOR' *Theta Syndrome* v. 64 Mancini was lying down with dark glasses on... He was photo-sensitive.

Hence **photo'sensitiveness** (*rare*), **,photosensi'tivity.**

1889 R. MENDOLA *Chem. of Photography* i. 13 The photo-sensitiveness of ferric compounds has long been known. **1914** *Physical Rev.* IV. 228 The plan.. was to observe the time changes in contact potential differences and photosensitiveness of photo-electrically or mechanically treated surfaces. **1918** *Science* 23 Aug. 198/2 (*heading*) Adaptation in the photosensitivity of *Ciona intestinalis.* **1939** *Jrnl. Inst. Electr. Engin.* LXXXIV. 473/1 In the normal Emitron the photo-sensitivity is limited to about 12 μA/lumen. **1947** *New Biol.* III. 93 Many other urodeles, *i.e.*, tailed Amphibia, retain their photosensitivity and continue to move away from light after their eyes have been removed. **1961** *Lancet* 26 Aug. 450/2 His clinical photosensitivity showed fluctuations of intensity which corresponded with quantitative changes in his erythrocyte and fæcal porphyrins; hence it seems justifiable to conclude that the porphyrins produced in his body are responsible for his photosensitisation. **1970** R. A. & B. M. MAIER *Compar. Animal Behavior* xvii. 365 Photo-sensitivity seems to have evolved from a general sensitivity to chemical stimulation.

,photosensiti'zation. [f. PHOTO- 1 + SENSITIZATION.] **a.** *Chem.* The initiation of a reaction by light acting on a suitable photosensitizer.

1924 H. S. TAYLOR *Treat. Physical Chem.* II. xviii. 1241 Uranium salts are positive catalysts for the photoreaction, presumably by photo-sensitization. **1933** *Jrnl. Amer. Chem. Soc.* LV. 587 A maximum of twenty per cent. photosensitization to visible light was found for the polymerization among seventy organic substances tried. **1974** D. R. ARNOLD et al. *Photochem.* vi. 133 Photosensitization involves the absorption of radiation by a strongly absorbing substance, the photosensitizer and its collisional transfer to another substance which is non-absorbing at the same wavelength.

b. (The production of) a condition in which light of certain wavelengths is harmful to an individual, usu. owing to the presence in the body of a photodynamic substance.

1926 E. MAYER *Clin. Applic. Sunlight* v. 86 (*heading*) Photosensitization. **1927** K. M. L. GAMGEE *Artificial Light Treatm. Children* xii. 108 Experimental photosensitization in animals and human beings is known to follow the administration of certain substances, such as eosin and haematoporphyrin, and death may result on exposure to light. **1941** H. F. BLUM *Photodynamic Action* xv. 159 Mathews.. finds part of the symptoms which follow feeding on *Agave lechuguilla*, found in the arid regions of New Mexico, Mexico and Texas, to result from photosensitization. **1961** *Lancet* 26 Aug. 450/2 In cases of porphyria with photosensitization, it is often uroporphyrin which is present in greatest excess, and the response to irradiation is by erythema and itching followed by slowly developing œdema. **1973** STOUT & SCHULTES in L. P. Miller *Phytochem.* III. xiv. 384 These last [*sc.* photodynamic toxins] may act either by sensitizing the animal directly.. or by causing liver damage, which then leads to photosensitization as a secondary consequence.

photosensitize (fəʊtəʊ'sɛnsɪtaɪz), *v.* [f. PHOTO- 1 + SENSITIZE *v.*] *trans.* **a.** *Chem.* Of a substance: to initiate (a chemical change) by absorbing light energy and transferring it to a reactant.

1927 *Jrnl. Amer. Chem. Soc.* XLIX. 2763 (*heading*) Hydrogen peroxide formation photosensitized by mercury vapor. **1928** *Proc. R. Soc.* A. CXXI. 297 Uranyl ion has.. been found to photosensitize the decomposition of glucose in solution. **1951** *Symp. Soc. Exper. Biol.* V. 142 Photolysis of water can be accomplished with much less energy if the process is suitably 'photosensitized', for instance, if water is irradiated in the presence of suitable ions. **1966** GUCKER & SEIFERT *Physical Chem.* (1967) xxiii. 722 The dissociation of hydrogen molecules into atoms requires.. a quantum of wavelength 2770 Å. Hydrogen molecules do not absorb light of this wavelength, but mercury atoms, which absorb light at 2536·52 Å, have plenty of energy to photosensitize the formation of hydrogen atoms.

b. To make photosensitive.

1933 *Jrnl. Inst. Electr. Engin.* LXXIII. 441/2 The mosaic .. is composed of a very large number of minute silver globules, each of which is photo-sensitized by cæsium through utilization of a special process. **1941** *Nature* 10 May 581/2 Carcinogenic hydrocarbons in very low concentration are able to photosensitize Paramecia. **1977** J. L. HARPER *Population Biol. of Plants* xvii. 503 The plant is a serious weed.. because it photosensitizes the skin of white-skinned animals.

Hence **photo'sensitized** *ppl. a.*, **-'sensitizing** *vbl. sb.* and *ppl. a.*

1914 S. E. SHEPPARD *Photo-Chem.* xi. 435 The photochemical sensitiveness of dye-stuffs.. depends in part upon the formation of a specific adsorption-complex of the dye with the substance sensitized. This photosensitizing is of considerable interest. **1931** R. G. W. NORRISH in *Photochem. Processes* (Faraday Soc.) II. 461 (*heading*) The photosensitized formation of hydrogen peroxide in the system hydrogen-oxygen-chlorine. **1935** *Discovery* Sept. 278/1 The mosaic screen is made up of millions of isolated photo-sensitised elements upon a mica sheet. **1964** *Oceanogr. & Marine Biol.* II. 406 There are indications that urchins can be induced to cover by injecting photo-sensitizing dyes. **1974** *Photochem. & Photobiol.* XIX. 35/1 Some amino acids.. are sensitive to photosensitized oxidation.

photosensitizer (fəʊtəʊ'sɛnsɪtaɪzə(r)). [f. PHOTO- 1 + SENSITIZER.] **a.** *Chem.* A substance capable of photosensitizing a reaction.

1914 S. E. SHEPPARD *Photo-Chem.* vii. 293 Winther succeeded in showing that the chlorine water was not a true photo-sensitizer since it had the same effect in darkness upon the precipitation of calomel. **1928** *Proc. R. Soc.* A. CXXI. 296 It is not to be supposed that only fluorescent substances will act as photosentitizers; substances capable of absorbing radiation of the appropriate frequency may be effective, whether fluorescent or not. **1957** G. E. HUTCHINSON *Treat. Limnol.* I. xvi. 865 In addition to ultraviolet light certain oxides must be present as photosensitizers. **1974** *Photochem. & Photobiol.* XIX. 441/2 The versatility of flavins as photosensitizers in numerous photoprocesses.

b. A photodynamic substance.

1925 *Practitioner* Aug. 103 The visible rays, however, have this effect when the irradiated cells are incorporated with photosensitizers, such as eosin and hæmatoporphyrin. **1946** *Nature* 14 Dec. 877/2 They found that the cancerogenic substances had a stronger effect than the non-cancerogenic photosensitizers. **1967** M. E. HALE *Biol. Lichens* xi. 161 The possibilities that uric acid may be a photosensitizer and a cause of respiratory allergy are also being explored. **1975** *Sci. Amer.* July 72/3 A number of widely prescribed drugs (such as the tetracyclines) and constituents of foods (such as riboflavins) are potential photosensitizers.

photosensor(y): see PHOTO- 1.

photosetting ('fəʊtəʊ,sɛtɪŋ), *vbl. sb. Printing.* [f. PHOTO- 2 + SETTING *vbl. sb.*] = PHOTOCOMPOSING *vbl. sb.* 1. So **'photoset** *v. trans.*; **'photoset** *ppl. a.*; **'photo,setter**, a photocomposing machine.

1957 *Americana Ann.* 330/1 Tabular matter can be photoset in the same manner as ordinary typewriting. **1958** *Ibid.* 243/1 An electric combination photosetting and photocomposing machine was developed. **1959** *Times* 14 Jan. 12/4 Photosetting machines are unlikely to replace all these [hot-metal typesetting machines]. **1959** in E. Fitzgerald tr. *Hils's Toy* 4 Printed in England from photoset typematter. **1961** *Printing News* 30 Mar. 6/5 One American printer is currently producing upwards of 100 photoset books a year. **1968** A. BLUHM *Photosetting* i. 6 The beginning of the 'modern' period of photosetting may be conveniently dated at 1955, when prototypes.. of several current machines for text setting were shown at the IPEX exhibition in London. **1970** *Brit. Printer* Dec. 72/2 A new photosetter in what is described as the moderate price range has been introduced. **1974** *Times* 14 Oct. (Sheffield Suppl.) p. iv/8 Both papers.. have.. an ambitious reorganization scheme... It includes changing to photo-setting instead of the traditional typesetting.

photoshock: see PHOTO- 1.

photosphere ('fəʊtəsfɪə(r)). [f. PHOTO- + Gr. σφαῖρα ball, SPHERE.]

1. A sphere or orb of light, radiance, or glory. (In mod. use only as *fig.* from 2.)

1664 H. MORE *Myst. Iniq., Apol.* iii. §15. 503 Though.. Christ be surrounded with Gleams and Raies of inaccessible Light and Glory, which envelop his Body,.. yet if any mortal could get within this so refulgent Photosphere (as I may so call it) or Orb of glory and brightness [etc.]. **1878** SYMONDS *Shelley* v. 97 The central motive of *Laon and Cythna* is surrounded by so radiant a photosphere of imagery and eloquence that it is difficult to fix our gaze upon it. **1891** T. HARDY *Tess* II. xiv, Her hopes mingled with the sun-shine in an ideal photosphere which surrounded her as she bounded along the soft south wind.

2. *Astron.* The luminous envelope of the sun (or a star), from which its light and heat radiate.

1848 HERSCHEL *Ess.* (1857) 287 A self-luminous nebulous matter, of a vaporous or gaseous nature, of which these photospheres, and, perhaps, some entire nebulæ, may consist. **1861** W. FAIRBAIRN *Addr. Brit. Assoc.*, The remarkable discoveries of Kirchoff and Bunsen require us to believe that a solid or liquid photosphere is seen through an atmosphere containing iron, sodium, lithium, and other metals in a vaporous condition. **1893** SIR R. BALL *Story of Sun* 137 That envelope of glowing clouds surrounding the Sun which we call the photosphere.

photospheric (fəʊtəʊs'fɛrɪk), *a.* *Astron.* [f. prec. + -IC.] Of or pertaining to the photosphere.

1865 *Reader* 7 Jan. 16/3 Photospheric clouds affecting forms reminding one of the flocculent mass of an incandescent metal, in suspension in a liquid. **1878** NEWCOMB *Pop. Astron.* III. ii. 266 Above the photospheric layer [of the sun] lies an atmosphere of a very complex nature. **1893** SIR R. BALL *Story of Sun* 196 The selective absorption of photospheric light.

photo-stable: see PHOTO- 1.

Photostat ('fəʊtəʊstæt). orig. *U.S.* Also **photostat.** [f. PHOTO- 2 + -STAT.] **a.** The proprietary name of a kind of photocopying machine. **b.** A copy made on such a machine; *loosely*, any photocopy. Also *attrib.*

1911 *Trade Marks Jrnl.* 24 May 761 Photostat... Photographic cameras for making photographic copies of the pages of books, drawings, applications for life insurance and the like. Commercial Camera Company.., Providence,

Rhode Island, United States of America; manufacturers. **1912** *Chambers's Jrnl.* June 414/2 By means of the photostat a new filing method is possible. **1927** *Glasgow Herald* 26 May 9 The reference to a subterranean photostat room is quite in accord with the general cinematographic nature of the raid... Such photostats exist nowadays in most large commercial undertakings. **1928** P. S. ALLEN *Let.* 27 July (1939) 258, I should be glad to have the photostats (where does the word come from?) quickly. **1931** *Times Lit. Suppl.* 17 Dec. 1028/1 The number of manuscripts known has increased.. to eighty-four, of which photostats are now at the University of Chicago. **1932** [see *book-page* s.v. BOOK *sb.* 19]. **1940** *Chambers's Techn. Dict.* 639/1 *Photostat*, trade-name for photographic apparatus (also for any print made by it) designed for rapidly copying, to the required size, flat originals on sensitised paper, and giving a negative image. **1959** T. S. ELIOT *Elder Statesman* II. 57 I'm afraid I can't show you the originals; They're in my lawyer's safe. But I have photostats Which are quite as good, I'm told. **1961** T. LANDAU *Encycl. Librarianship* (ed. 2) 121/1 The 'Photostat' has after many years become a household word among librarians and readers, and is indiscriminately used in describing any photographic reproduction of a document. It is in fact a trade name, and a 'Photostat' copy of a document is one produced by the 'Photostat' apparatus. **1964** 'R. MACDONALD' in *Manhunt* May 142/1, I pulled out my photostat and slapped it down on the desk. **1975** *Guardian* 25 Feb. 5/7 Inside the envelope there were simply photostats of correspondence. **1976** *Gloss. Documentation Terms* (*B.S.I.*) 48 *Photostat*, a trade mark of Kodak Ltd. for photocopying cameras, chemicals and sensitive materials, the optical copies produced being right-reading.

Hence **'photostat** *v. trans.*, to photocopy; so **'photostat(t)ed** *ppl. a.*, **'photostat(t)ing** *vbl. sb.*; also **photo'static** *a.*, of, pertaining to, or produced by a Photostat or other photocopying machine.

1914 *Amer. Machinist* 9 Apr. 642/1 A prism is used to 'turn the corner', making it more convenient than if the book or other object being 'photostated' had to be set up on edge. **1925** M. R. RINEHART *Red Lamp* 139 One of the evening newspapers to-night prints a photostatic copy of the cipher found in our garage. **1932** *N. & Q.* 5 Nov. 328/1 In corresponding about having the letter photostated we were informed of still another letter. **1937** MRS. P. CAMPBELL *Let.* 25 Aug. in *B. Shaw & Mrs. Campbell* (1952) 314 He doesn't know I have had two photostated copies made of them. **1947** [see EAGER *a.* 6]. **1957** *Amer. Speech* XXXII. 57 Libraries quickly learned the uses they could make of photostatic machines. **1959** H. HAMILTON *Answer in Negative* i. 8 All our printing, and photo-statting of cuttings, is done by the *Echo's* dark-room. **1967** N. FREELING *Strike Out* 141 They weren't going to open an embassy safe and photostat the contents. **1973** R. HILL *Ruling Passion* III. iii. 179 He passed out some photostatted sheets. **1976** T. ALLBEURY *Only Good German* ix. 59 A photostated copy of an item in *The Times.* **1978** *Daily Tel.* 5 May 14/6 Some might feel that for a rather smaller price the 'Compact' DNB, the full work with minute, photostated text,.. might be a better buy.

photostationary to **-surface**: see PHOTO- 1.

photostereogram to **-story**: see PHOTO- 2.

photosynthate (fəʊtəʊˈsɪnθeɪt). *Bot.* [f. next + *-ate*, after *filtrate*, *precipitate*.] A substance formed by photosynthesis.

1913 W. F. GANONG *Living Plant* ii. 24 The process being one of formation, or synthesis, under action of light, is called scientifically photosynthesis, while the substance made is the photosynthate. **1938** WEAVER & CLEMENTS *Plant Ecol.* (ed. 2) xiv. 395 Many species of evergreens are known to make photosynthate in winter in sufficiently large amounts to balance that oxidized in respiration. **1978** *Nature* 5 Jan. 93/2 A conifer manufactures photosynthates at all times of the year except when climatic conditions are unsuitable, due for example to low temperatures or drought stress.

photosynthesis (fəʊtəʊˈsɪnθɪsɪs). *Bot.* [ad. G. *photosynthese*: see PHOTO- 1 + SYNTHESIS.] The process by which carbon dioxide is converted into organic matter in the presence of the chlorophyll of plants under the influence of light, which in all plants except some bacteria involves the production of oxygen from water; also, any photochemical synthesis of a chemical compound.

1898 *Botanisches Zentralblatt* LXXVI. 258 It is not important whether photosyntax or photosynthesis, or some other word, finally comes into general use to describe the manufacture of carbohydrates by green tissues under the action of light. **1902** *Encycl. Brit.* XXXI. 760/1 The course of photosynthesis has been with tolerable certainty found to lead to the construction of sugar. **1914** S. E. SHEPPARD *Photo-Chem.* vii. 295 The photo-synthesis of phosgene ($COCl_2$) from chlorine and carbon monoxide.. has been studied by several observers. **1924** *Industr. & Engin. Chem.* Oct. 1018/1 The optimum experimental conditions having been determined, it has been found possible to carry out the photosynthesis on a larger scale than in the test tube. **1927** *Proc. R. Soc.* A. CXVI. 203 The photosynthesis of complex organic substances takes place when carbonic acid in the presence of a surface is exposed to ultra-violet light. **1932** FULLER & CONARD tr. *Braun-Blanquet's Plant Sociol.* v. 97 There is a limited amount of photosynthesis in the invisible infra-red and ultra-violet. **1952** P. W. RICHARDS *Trop. Rain Forest* vii. 180 Even at the low light intensities found in the shade of the Tropical Rain forest, a high carbon dioxide concentration would probably allow a rate of photosynthesis considerably higher than at normal concentration. **1957** *Times* 11 Sept. 6/2 Recent studies using radiocarbon indicated that the yield of photosynthesis by the plankton of the oceans was at least equal to that of the land flora, and might be several times greater. **1958** R. Y. STANIER et al. *Gen. Microbiol.* xi. 213 In bacterial photosyntheses, there is also a light-driven reduction of CO_2 to cell material, but oxygen is never produced because water cannot serve as the ultimate hydrogen donor. Instead, the reduction of CO_2 is coupled with the oxidation of externally supplied organic or inorganic hydrogen donors. **1964** E. J. H. CORNER *Life of Plants* iii. 38 There are chromoplast colours that work together with chlorophyll in photosynthesis. **1975** H. SMITH *Photochrome & Photomorphogenesis* ii. 15 Photosynthesis presents an excellent example of light and dark reactions acting sequentially.

Hence **,photosyn'thetic** *a.*, of, pertaining to, produced by, or involved in photosynthesis; ***photosynthetic quotient*** or ***ratio***, the rate of evolution of oxygen by photosynthesizing tissue divided by its rate of consumption of carbon dioxide, or the reciprocal of this; **,photosyn'thetically** *adv.*

1900 A. J. EWART tr. *Pfeffer's Physiol. Plants* I. vii. 293 The photosynthetic assimilation in the chloroplastid only provides the organic food, which in green and non-green plants, and in animals also, has the same function to perform. *Ibid.* 326 With the exception of carbon dioxide, no carbon compounds are known which can be photosynthetically assimilated. **1913** W. F. GANONG *Living Plant* ii. 27 The photosynthetic sugar and starch which appear in lighted green leaves. **1926** H. A. SPOEHR *Photosynthesis* ii. 92 The photosynthetic quotient may yield some information relative to the first product formed in photosynthesis. **1931** E. C. MILLER *Plant Physiol.* viii. 431 The determination of the photosynthetic ratio is difficult, because the process of respiration is proceeding at the same time and in the opposite direction [to that of photosynthesis]. **1945** E. I. RABINOWITCH *Photosynthesis* I. iii. 31 The 'photosynthetic quotient', Q_p : Q_p = $\Delta O_2/-\Delta/CO_2$. (The term 'photosynthetic quotient' has been used by many authors.. to designate the inverse ratio, $-\Delta CO_2/\Delta O_2$; this difference calls for care in the quotation of numerical results.) **1962** *Listener* 3 May 768/2 Some scientists believe that free oxygen is entirely biological in origin and that it arose *after* the emergence of photosynthetic life. **1971** *Sci. Amer.* Sept. 92/3 Plants reflect about 8 percent of photosynthetically active wavelengths. **1971** I. ZELITCH *Photosynthesis* v. 129 At the high O_2 concentrations, *Amaranthus* leaves had a photosynthetic quotient of 0·50 and bean leaves 0·33. **1974** A. HUXLEY *Plant & Planet* iii. 22 It was probably not the seaweeds that gave rise to land plants but, from their similar photosynthetic pigments and photosynthetic mechanism, the green algae.

photosynthesize (fəʊtəʊˈsɪnθɪsaɪz), *v. Bot.* [f. prec. + -IZE.] **a.** *trans.* To create by photosynthesis. **b.** *intr.* To carry out photosynthesis.

1921 *Jrnl. Chem. Soc.* CXIX. 1029 Carbohydrates can be photosynthesised from carbon dioxide and water in two stages. **1927** *Proc. R. Soc.* A. CXVI. 212 These [results] convinced us that it is possible by the use of coloured powders to photosynthesise organic compounds from carbonic acid with the help of visible light. **1951** *Symp. Soc. Exper. Biol.* V. 300 When algae or barley leaves photosynthesize.. in $C^{14}O_2$ for 30 sec. [etc.]. **1974** A. HUXLEY *Plant & Planet* iii. 18 Some bacteria.. can either photosynthesize or, if in the dark, gain energy from decomposing organic matter.

Hence **photo'synthesized, photo'synthesizing** *ppl. adjs.*; also **photo'synthesizer**, an organism which carries out photosynthesis.

1910 F. KEEBLE *Plant-Animals* iii. 79 From the photosynthesised carbohydrate are derived the cellulose substances. **1927** *Proc. R. Soc.* A. CXVI. 213 The photosynthesised compounds are very similar in appearance to those described in the previous paper. **1937** *Enzymologia* IV. 254 (*heading*) On the fluorescence of photosynthesizing cells. **1958** *Sci. News* XLIX. 25 Animals, fungi, and most of the bacteria.. only shuffle.. the materials the photosynthesizers have made. **1970** L. MARGULIS *Origin of Eukaryotic Cells* iv. 94 This gas [*sc.* hydrogen sulphide] was utilized by anaerobic photosynthesizers as hydrogen donors in photosynthesis. **1973** *Sci. Amer.* Oct. 83/3 They supplied carbon dioxide labeled with carbon 14 to photosynthesizing sugarcane plants.

'photosystem. *Bot.* [f. PHOTO(SYNTHETIC *a.* + SYSTEM.] Either of the two biochemical mechanisms in plants by which light is converted into useful energy.

1965 *Biochim. & Biophys. Acta* CIX. 349 Photoreduction of substrate V by photosystem 1. **1973** J. J. WOLKEN in L. P. Miller *Phytochem.* I. ii. 26 This phenomenon termed the 'red drop' is interpreted, at present, as due to a special form of 'long wavelength absorbing' chlorophyll belonging to a Photosystem I. *Ibid.*, The low efficiency of the far-red (beyond 680 nm) would require another pigment-complex absorbing below 680 nm, which has been designated as Photosystem II. **1974** *Nature* 4 Jan. 4/1 There now seems to be no doubt that KCN inhibits photosynthesis by specifically blocking electron flow through photosystem one (S1).

phototactic (fəʊtəʊˈtæktɪk), *a. Biol.* [ad. G. *phototaktisch* (E. Strasburger 1878: see PHOTOTAXIS), f. Gr. φῶς light, PHOTO- 1 + τακτικ-ός fit for ordering or arranging.] Exhibiting or characterized by phototaxis.

1882 S. H. VINES tr. *F.G.J. von Sachs's Text-bk. Bot.* III. iii. 752 Zoogonidia which exhibit these phenomena are said, by Strasburger, to be phototactic. **1885** *Encycl. Brit.* XIX. 62/1 Protoplasmic masses which respond to the directive action of light are said to be 'phototactic'. **1901** G. N. CALKINS *Protozoa* 296 The most phototactic forms are the flagellated cells. **1907** *Jrnl. Exper. Zool.* V. 72 Any organism is said to be positively phototactic when it moves towards the source of light and negatively phototactic when it goes in the opposite direction. **1969** F. E. ROUND *Introd. Lower Plants* ii. 15 Euglenoids are positively phototactic. **1976** *Sci. Amer.* June 42/1, I had noticed a phototactic response in *H. halobium*; the cells reversed their direction of swimming when the intensity of illumination was decreased in the red part of the spectrum.

Hence **photo'tactically** *adv.*

1914 [see KINETIC *a.* 2 b].

phototaxis (fəʊtəʊˈtæksɪs). *Biol.* Pl. **-taxes** (-ˈtæksiːz). [mod.L., coined in Ger. (E. Strasburger 1878, in *Jenaische Zeitschr. f. Naturwissensch.* XII. 587): see PHOTO- 1 and TAXIS.] The innate movement in a definite direction of an organism or part of one in response to the stimulus of light; *esp.* the bodily movement or orientation of a freely motile organism (see quot. 1960 and cf. PHOTOTROPISM).

1893 *Athenæum* 16 Sept. 375/3 Phototaxis and chemiotaxis are the last instances of physiological adaptation cited [by J. S. B. Sanderson]. **1894** J. S. B. SANDERSON in *Rep. Brit. Assoc. Adv. Sci. 1893* 24 A single instance.. must suffice to illustrate the influence of light in directing the movements of freely moving cells, or, as it is termed, phototaxis. **1902** *Jrnl. R. Microsc. Soc.* 31 Phototaxis is the peculiarity displayed by free-swimming organisms of orienting the body so as to place its long axis in a definite relation to the direction of the rays. **1911** A. WILLEY *Convergence in Evolution* iii. 25 The vegetable kingdom as a whole exhibits positive phototaxis. **1954** *New Biol.* XVII. 49 Several workers have found negative phototaxis (movement away from light) in a number of species [of woodlice]. **1960** THIMANN & CURRY in Florkin & Mason *Compar. Biochem.* I. vi. 244 In all these organisms the response to light is a free movement of the whole body directed towards or away from the light, and this is defined as phototaxis. In fungi and higher plants, as also in the colonial hydroids, the body is anchored at one end and the response to light is shown by a curvature. It is this which is phototropism properly speaking... Zoologists have, it is true, used the term phototropism for free movements of animals, while botanists have been more precise in preserving the distinction, but the distinction is a valuable and even essential one to make... In Phototaxis the light influences the organs of movement,.. while in Phototropism it influences the growth of the organism. **1975** *Nature* 3 Jan. 43/2 It would seem that the light intensity dependent behaviour in these two examples could be divided into retinally evoked phototaxes and an extraretinally evoked kinesis which cannot be separated in sighted larvae. *Ibid.* 4 Sept. 44/2 The internal parts of the maze were of clear Perspex which allowed the flies to be attracted through the maze by phototaxis.

phototelegram to **-telegraphy**: see PHOTO- 1.

photo-timer: see PHOTO- 2.

‖**phototonus** (fəʊˈtɒtənəs). *Bot.* [mod.L., f. Gr. φῶς, φωτο- light (see PHOTO-) + τόνος tension, TONE.] Name given by Sachs to the normal condition of sensitiveness to light in leaves and other organs, maintained by continued exposure to light, as opposed to the rigidity induced by long exposure to darkness. Hence **phototonic** (fəʊtəʊˈtɒnɪk) *a.*, exhibiting phototonus; sensitive to light.

1875 BENNETT & DYER tr. *Sachs' Bot.* 678 The power of movement in plants is lost when they have remained in the dark for a considerable time..; in other words, they become rigid by long exposure to darkness..; the exposure to light must continue for a considerable time.. before the motile condition which I have termed 'Phototonus' is restored. *Ibid.* 790 Changes in the intensity of the light produce the same effect as irritants, but only on healthy phototonic plants; leaves which have become rigid from exposure to the dark show no irritability to variations in its intensity until they have again become phototonic from long-continued exposure to light.

,phototo'pography. Also with hyphen. [f. PHOTO- 2 + TOPOGRAPHY.] A system of surveying which employs photography as well as the usual methods.

The word has largely given way to *photogrammetry*.

1893 *Geogr. Jrnl.* I. 89 Photo-topography. **1895** *Rep. U.S. Coast & Geodetic Survey 1893* II. 42 During the Franco-Prussian war phototopography was called into service by the German army. **1922** *Geogr. Jrnl.* LIX. 274 The methods of Phototopography developed by Laussedat in France and by Deville in Canada.. depend on the measurement of identical points on pairs of plates taken on determined azimuths at trigonometrical points. **1970** *Canad. Cartographer* VII. 19/2 The ground photo-topography continued in the mountains of British Columbia.

Hence **,phototo'pographer**, one who is skilled in phototopography; **,phototopo'graphic, -ical** *adjs.*, of, pertaining to, or using phototopography; **,phototopo'graphically** *adv.*

1895 *Rep. U.S. Coast & Geodetic Survey 1893* II. 45 A phototopographic survey of the Oasis Gassr Dachel in the Libyan desert. **1902** *Encycl. Brit.* XXXIII. 95/2 The field work of a photo-topographic party consists primarily in execution of a triangulation by the usual methods. *Ibid.*, The photo-topographical survey. **1906** J. A. FLEMER *Elem. Treat. Phototopogr. Methods* xii. 387 The phototopographer .. can in a few good days, cover a larger territory than is possible with any other surveying method. *Ibid.* 390 A large territory may be reconnoitered phototopographically in a comparatively short time. **1926** A. L. HIGGINS *Phototopography* ii. 42 Phototopographical instruments. **1970** *Canad. Cartographer* VII. 18/1 During the development of the photo-topographic work it became the practice to rule a perspective grid onto the print of the photograph to assist.. in positioning horizontal detail.

phototoxic to **-transient**: see PHOTO- 1.

phototransistor (ˌfəʊtəʊtrɑːnˈzɪstə(r), -æ-). *Electronics.* Also with hyphen. [f. PHOTO- 1 +

TRANSISTOR.] A junction transistor which responds to incident light by generating and amplifying an electric current.

1950 J. N. SHIVE in *Bell Lab. Rec.* XXVIII. 337/2 Experiments have resulted in the production of a new photoconductivity cell, called the 'Phototransistor'. **1959** *Control* Feb. 95/2 It is a logical step from the photodiode to the *p-n-p* phototransistor, in which the amplifying action of the transistor is applied to the photocurrent. *Ibid.*, The Mullard OCP71 phototransistor is enclosed in a glass bulb 5·9 mm in diameter and 15 mm in length. **1959** *Electronic Engin.* XXXI. 36 The advent of the commercially produced junction photo-transistor has brought with it the possibility of operating a relay directly from the light sensitive element. **1962** P. M. WILLIAMS in G. A. T. Burdett *Automatic Control Handbk.* ix. 52 Photo-transistors can be made which are sensitive to X-rays, ultra violet and infra red. **1970** *New Scientist* 24 Dec. 554/1 The new reading head is only a few centimetres across and contains a matrix of 144 bipolar photo-transistors on a silicon chip 3 × 5 mm in size.

photo-trichro'matic, *a.* [f. PHOTO- 2 + TRICHROMATIC.] Of or pertaining to three colours used in colour-photography, or to colour-photography in which three colours are used.

1896 C. G. ZANDER (*title*) Photo-trichromatic printing. **1904** *Westm. Gaz.* 2 May 9/3 The photo-trichromatic inks of commerce are not optically the true complements of the red, violet, and green, which are the primary colour sensations.

phototroph to **-trophy**: see PHOTO- 1.

phototropic (ˌfəʊtəʊˈtrɒpɪk, -ˈtrəʊpɪk), *a. Biol.* [f. PHOTO- + Gr. -τρόπος turning + -IC: cf. Gr. τροπικός of or pertaining to turning.]

1. Exhibiting or characterized by phototropism. So **photo'tropically** *adv.*

1899 C. B. DAVENPORT *Exper. Morphol.* II. 438 Aquatic plants..are only very slightly phototropic. *Ibid.* 440 Etiolated willow shoots, upon which..the more strongly refractive rays only act phototropically. **1903** *Mark Anniversary Vol.* xxiii. 455 Loeb maintained that butterflies as well as moths are positively phototropic. *Ibid.* 457 When feeding or near food the butterflies do not respond phototropically. **1943** *Vitamins & Hormones* I. 211 In some structures also (*Avena, Pilobolus, Phycomyces*) carotenoid pigmentation has been shown to be concentrated in or restricted to the phototropically sensitive zones. **1972** *Plant Physiol.* XLIX. 993/1 Etiolated plants are known to be more sensitive phototropically than are green ones. **1976** BELL & COOMBE tr. *Strasburger's Textbk. Bot.* (rev. ed.) 350 Phototropic behaviour is not confined to the higher plants; it occurs also in fungi and algae.

2. = PHOTOCHROMIC *a.*

1900 *Jrnl. Chem. Soc.* LXXVIII. II. 125 Benzilosazone, salicylosazone, and vanillylosazone are, however, not phototropic. **1929** *Chem. Rev.* VI. 220 Most phototropic substances exhibit phototropy only in the solid state. **1960** *New Scientist* 2 June 1423/2 In the same family of substances some derivatives are phototropic while others, which resemble them closely, do not show the effect. **1971** *Materials & Technol.* II. vi. 410 Phototropic glass is made by melting an alkali-alumino-borosilicate glass containing some lead and small amounts of silver, chloride, bromide, and iodide, forming the glass in the normal way, and then submitting the article to a heat treatment for several hours.

phototropism (fəʊˈtɒtrəpɪz(ə)m, fəʊtəʊˈtrəʊpɪz(ə)m). [f. PHOTO- 1 + TROPISM.]

1. *Biol.* [ad. G. *phototropie* (F. Oltmanns 1892, in *Flora* LXXV. 214).] The innate movement in a definite direction of an organism or part of one in response to the stimulus of light; *esp.* the directional bending or growth of a plant or sessile animal (see quot. 1960 and cf. PHOTOTAXIS).

[**1892** *Jrnl. R. Microsc. Soc.* 513 The phenomena of phototropy—i.e. positive or negative heliotropic movements.] **1899** C. B. DAVENPORT *Exper. Morphol.* II. 437 Effect of Light upon the Direction of Growth—Phototropism. [*Note.*] On some accounts it is unfortunate to accept this word rather than the older, more familiar term 'heliotropism'; but..the latter is obviously unfitted to our broader view of the subject. **1900** *Nature* 4 Jan. 219/1 The comparative effects of flash light and steady light in producing phototropism in seedling plants. **1902** *Jrnl. R. Microsc. Soc.* 31 He [*sc.* W. A. Nagel] applies the term phototropism to the peculiarity displayed by many sedentary organisms or special organs, of taking up a fixed position in regard to light, by means of bending movements, movements of growth or of torsion. **1907** T. H. MORGAN *Exper. Zoöl.* xvi. 265 Growth toward the Light; Phototropism... Some animals that are fixed turn toward the light. **1924** R. M. OGDEN tr. *Koffka's Growth of Mind* iii. 111 A cockroach possesses a negative phototropism. **1947** *Biol. Bull.* XCII. 127 The terms, phototropism and phototaxis, will be used synonymously in this paper. **1960** [see PHOTOTAXIS]. **1965** B. E. FREEMAN tr. *Vandel's Biospeleol.* xxv. 400 Light very frequently attracts or repels animals and these conditions are given the names of positive and of negative phototropism. **1976** G. C. AINSWORTH *Introd. Hist. Mycol.* vii. 198 Phototropism has been much studied in the Mucorales.

fig. **1923** R. GRAVES *Whipperginny* 38 Watch the blind Phototropisms of my fluttering mind.

2. = PHOTOCHROMISM.

1921 *Jrnl. Amer. Chem. Soc.* XLIII. 333 (*heading*) Studies on phototropism in solution. **1952** K. VENKATARAMAN *Chem. Synthetic Dyes* II. xl. 1217 A review of phototropism in solution and on dyed textiles. **1962** J. T. MARSH *Self-Smoothing Fabrics* xviii. 298 Phototropism is the change in shade which occurs on exposure to strong light, followed by a gradual return to the original shade when the light is removed. **1974** RATTEE & BREUER *Physical Chem. of Dye Adsorption* vii. 229 Three dyes..were all found to exhibit phototropism on cellulose acetate film.

phototropy (fəʊˈtɒtrəpɪ). [ad. G. *phototropie* (W. Marckwald 1899, in *Zeitschr. f. physik. Chem.* XXX. 140), f. Gr. φωτο- (see PHOTO-) + -τροπία turning.] = PHOTOCHROMISM, PHOTOTROPISM 2.

1900 *Sci. Amer.* 24 Feb. 123/2 To these phenomena the experimenter gives the name of phototropy. **1929** [see PHOTOTROPIC *a.* 2]. **1949** *Thorpe's Dict. Appl. Chem.* (ed. 4) IX. 585/2 There is evidence..that phototropy is not a purely physical phenomenon. **1954** *Jrnl. Amer. Chem. Soc.* LXXVI. 3846/1 Observations on the phenomenon of phototropy in alkaline earth titanates. **1971** R. L. M. ALLEN *Colour Chem.* iii. 23 The stereoisomerism of azo dyes is of practical importance..in that it gives rise to the phenomenon of phototropy.

phototube (ˈfəʊtəʊtjuːb). [f. PHOTO- 1 + TUBE *sb.*] A photocell in the form of a vacuum tube or gas-filled tube with a photo-emissive cathode and an anode.

1930 *Electronics* I. 418/1 (*heading*) Phototube voltage supervisor. An aid to tube production. **1953** [see MARK *sb.*[1] 13 e]. **1964** *Oceanogr. & Marine Biol.* II. 358 It is only since the adoption by biologists of the multiplier phototube..that more precise measurements of the spectral composition of luminescence,..and rates of flashing, have become feasible. **1973** *Nature* 12 Jan. 132/2 The emission was observed at right angles..and detected photoelectrically with a '1P28' phototube.

phototype (ˈfəʊtətaɪp), *sb.* [f. Gr. φῶς light, PHOTO- + -TYPE.] A plate or block for printing from, produced by a photographic process, or by a combination of photography with etching or some mechanical process; also, the process by which such a plate is produced, or a picture, etc., printed from it. Formerly, name of a process of carbon printing invented by M. Joubert. Also *attrib.*

1859 *Sat. Rev.* 26 Feb. 242/1 The term Phototypes being reserved for such as yield impressions that may be taken off from a flat surface by a mechanical method of printing, analogous to that of the lithographer or of the anastatic printer. **1867** *Athenæum* 20 July 90/1 The process generally employed has been that of lithography from the phototype. **1881** *Nation* (N.Y.) XXXII. 441 A phototype portrait of the late Thomas A. Scott. **1888** *Academy* 16 June 405/1 The phototypes are frequently too dark and sombre. **1902** WALL *Dict. Photogr.* 503 *Phototype*, a mechanical printing process in which a gelatine film itself is used to print from.

Hence **'phototype** *v. trans.*, to reproduce (a picture, MS., etc.) by means of phototypy; **phototypic** (-ˈtɪpɪk) *a.*, pertaining to or of the nature of a phototype; **photo'typically** *adv.*, by means of a phototype; **'phototypist**, a maker of phototypes; **'phototypy**, the art or process of making phototypes.

1859 *Sat. Rev.* 22 Jan. 98/1 Each of the phototypic methods at present before the world..seeks to attain this object by acting upon one and the same fundamental chemical fact. *Ibid.*, Various processes of photoglyphy and phototypy. **1887** *Sci. Amer.* 17 Dec. 385/1 A combined albumen and asphalt process of phototypy. **1888** *Athenæum* 11 Aug. 198/3 May Prof. Brunn and his editor, his phototypist and his subscribers, live for ever. **1891** *Chicago Advance* 16 July, Phototypically. *Mod.* The MS. is being phototyped.

phototypesetting (fəʊtəʊˈtaɪpsetɪŋ), *vbl. sb. Printing.* [f. PHOTO- 2 + *type-setting* s.v. TYPE *sb.*[1] 10.] = PHOTOCOMPOSING *vbl. sb.* 1. Also *attrib.* So **photo'typeset** *ppl. a.*; **photo'typesetter**, a photocomposing machine.

1931 *A.S.M.E. News* 7 Apr. 3/3 Louis Flader..described the Uher photo-typesetting machine, having recently inspected it in Germany. **1949** E. THIRKETTLE in H. O. Smith *Rotophoto Process* 3 Technical improvements in lithographic printing presses are conveniently keeping in line with phototypesetting developments. **1955** *Times* 5 July 6/5 Outstanding among the advances of the last two decades has been the development known as phototypesetting. **1966** N. S. M. COX et al. *Computer & Library* v. 74 The phototypesetter can produce 'graphic arts quality' printing. **1970** *Brit. Printer* Dec. 43 Massive trade typesetting operations based on computers (the one in question was a Fototronic, the highest speed phototypesetter at present available) can be assimilated. **1971** *Penrose Ann.* LXIV. 176 Many more phototypesetting devices will come on to the market over the next few years. *Ibid.*, Throughout 1970, technical innovation flowed on unabated, with ten new phototypesetters announced. **1973** *Physics Bull.* Dec. 743/1 The World Patents Index..is computer generated and will publish the information in a phototypeset gazette. **1976** *Nature* 24 June 664/2 CSIRO's computer with its microfilm output equipment (a COMp 80 phototypesetter) is now being used to produce camera-ready copy.

phototypography (ˌfəʊtəʊtaɪˈpɒgrəfɪ). [f. PHOTO- + TYPOGRAPHY.] Printing from an engraving in relief produced by a photo-mechanical process. Hence **phototypographic** (fəʊtəʊtɪpəˈgræfɪk) *a.*, of, pertaining to, or of the nature of phototypography.

1890 *Cent. Dict.*, *Phototypographic.* **1892** WOODBURY *Encycl. Phot.* 540 Phototype..is now applied to a method of Collotype or Albertype printing and to blocks produced by any photo-typographic process. *Ibid.*, *Photo-typography*, a general term applied..to a large number of processes in which printing surfaces are made by the aid of light.

photovisual (fəʊtəʊˈvɪʒjuːəl), *a.* (*sb.*) Also **photo-visual.** [f. PHOTO- 2 + VISUAL *a.* and *sb.*]

1. Of a lens or an optical instrument: bringing both visible and actinic, non-visible rays to the same focus. Also as *sb.*, such a lens or telescope.

1909 in *Cent. Dict.* Suppl. **1922** L. BELL *Telescope* iv. 89 The..objective.. carries the name of 'photo-visual' since the exactness of corrections is carried well into the violet, so that one can see and photograph at the same focus. **1955** J. B. SIDGWICK *Amateur Astronomer's Hand-bk.* xxiii. 422 For photography a reflector is to be preferred, unless a photovisual is available. **1958** J. STRONG *Concepts of Classical Optics* xiv. 323 Three different glasses, properly chosen for their partial dispersions, can be combined in components to yield a composite lens... Fig. 14-14 gives a tabulation..for the three glasses used in the Cooke photo-visual triplet lens. **1964** *Yearbk. Astron. 1965* 191 The main instruments at present are a 13-inch reflector, a 10-inch refractor, a 6-inch photovisual refractor, a 16 centimetre transit telescope and various cameras. **1977** *Sci. Amer.* Sept. 29/2 (Advt.), Sixth, the design must be photovisual so that he could record on film whatever these superior optics would present to the eye.

2. *Astr.* Applied to stellar magnitudes determined in terms of the spectral response of the eye by photographic or photoelectric means.

1914 *Carnegie Inst. Yearbk. 1913* 214 The comparison of these 'photovisual' results with the ordinary photographic magnitudes shows an increase in the color index as the variable approaches its minimum. **1927** H. N. RUSSELL et al. *Astron.* II. xviii. 620 With isochromatic plates and a 'color filter' to cut off the blue and violet light and let through the green and yellow, magnitudes may be obtained which agree very closely with the visual scale. These are called photo-visual magnitudes. **1958** C. C. ADAMS et al. *Space Flight* 132 At this time it is expected to be of the fifth photovisual magnitude, which is about the same brightness as the faintest star that, under reasonably good observing conditions, can be seen with the naked eye. **1963** C. W. ALLEN *Astrophysical Quantities* (ed. 2) x. 195 The effective wavelengths of a colour index system change with the colour itself. The U.B.V. system..has replaced the international photographic and photovisual systems.

photovitrotype to **photovoltaic**: see PHOTO-.

photozinc (ˈfəʊtəʊzɪŋk), **photo'zinco**, abbrev. of PHOTOZINCOGRAPHIC *a.*

1884 *Athenæum* 19 Jan. 88/3 From the Ordnance Survey photozinc facsimile of the original charter. **1892** WOODBURY *Encycl. Phot.* 590 Photo-zinco Engraving = Photo-zincography.

photozincography (ˌfəʊtəʊzɪŋˈkɒgrəfɪ). [f. PHOTO- + ZINC + -GRAPHY.] The art or process of producing by photographic methods a design on a zinc plate from which prints can be taken (analogous to PHOTOLITHOGRAPHY). Hence **photo'zincograph** *sb.*, a plate, or a picture or facsimile, produced by photozincography; **photo'zincograph** *v. trans.*, to produce or copy by photozincography; **ˌphotozinco'graphic, -ical** *adjs.*, of or pertaining to, of the nature of, or produced by photozincography.

1860 (Feb. 4) SIR H. JAMES *Rep. Progr. Ordnance Survey* 6 (Parl. Papers XXIII. 400) We have also tried a method.. by which the reduced print is in a state to be at once transferred to stone or zinc, from which any number of copies can be taken, as in ordinary lithographic or zincographic printing... I have called this new method Photo-zincography. **1860** —— *Photo-zincography* 5 By the term Photo-Zincography is meant..the art of producing a photographic facsimile of any subject, such as a manuscript, a map, or line engraving, and transferring the photograph to zinc, thereby obtaining the power of multiplying copies in the same manner as is done from a drawing on a lithographic stone, or on a zinc plate. **1861** (*title*) Domesday Book: Cornwall. Photo-Zincographed..at the Ordnance Survey Office, Southampton. **1862** SCOTT & JAMES *Photo-zincography* Pref. 4 This was the first Photo-zincograph ever taken here or elsewhere. *Ibid.* 1 The Photo-zincographic and Analogous Processes practised at the Ordnance Survey Office, Southampton. **1865** *Pall Mall G.* 4 Aug. 11/1 With large photo-zincographical plates prepared at Southampton under the superintendence of Sir Henry James. **1866** *Contemp. Rev.* III. 520 The reproduction of facsimiles by the photozincographic process. **1877** *Reg. Privy Council Scot.* I. Introd. 50 The process of photozincography is available. **1895** *Q. Rev.* Jan. 56 The sheets..are photozincographed.

photo'zincotype. [f. PHOTO- + ZINCOTYPE.] A plate for printing from, produced by photozincography. So **photozincotypy** (-ˈzɪŋkəʊtaɪpɪ), printing from photozincotypes; photozincography.

1886 *Sci. Amer.* 24 July 49/2 (*heading*) Photo-zincotypy and other Photographic Printing Methods for the Printing Press... In place of wood cuts, photo-zincotypes are very often used.

Photronic (fəʊˈtrɒnɪk). Also **photronic.** [f. PHOT(O- 1 + ELEC)TRONIC *a.*] An American proprietary name for a kind of photovoltaic cell. Also *attrib.* or as *adj.*

The word is registered in the U.S. as a proprietary term for several other devices also.

1932 *Official Gaz.* (U.S. Patent Office) 15 Mar. 554/1 Weston Electrical Instrument Corporation, Newark, N.J. Filed Oct. 1, 1931. Photronic. For light sensitive cells. Claims use since Sept. 25, 1931. **1938** G. H. SEWELL *Amateur Film-Making* ii. 21 The light intensity is received by a photronic type of cell. **1948** *Electronic Engin.* XX. 136/2 A method is described by which it is possible to check the balance of the printer instantly by means of tricolour readings with a photronic cell.

‖**photuria** (fəʊ'tjʊərɪə) *Path.* [mod.L., f. Gr. φῶς, φωτ- light + οὖρον urine.] Phosphorescence of the urine (Dunglison *Med. Lex.* 1853).

‖**Photuris** (fəʊ'tjʊərɪs). *Entom.* [mod.L., f. Gr. φῶς, φωτ- light + οὐρά tail.] A genus of American coleopterous fire-flies of the *Lampyridæ* or glowworm family; *esp.* the common firefly or lightning-bug of the eastern United States (*P. pennsylvanica*).

1883 C. F. Holder in *Harper's Mag.* Jan. 190/2 In the foliage..the brilliant green light of the photuris appears.

photy ('fəʊtɪ). *colloq.* (chiefly *Sc.*). [f. PHOT(OGRAPH *sb.* + -Y[6].] A photograph.

1973 *Sunday Post* (Glasgow) 5 Aug. 17/3 *Wannysee wurphoties?*—Are you prepared for an hour of utter boredom?.. *Attaka noffiphoty*—Photographs never flatter me. **1974** *Weekly News* (Glasgow) 31 Aug. 11/5 'Maist o' yer photies seems tae be of Edwina,' Wee Sadie remarked.

‖**phragma** ('frægmə). *Nat. Hist.* Pl. **-ata.** Rarely anglicized as **phragm.** [mod.L., a. Gr. φράγμα, -ματ- fence; in mod.F. *phragme* (Littré).] A partition, septum: *spec.* **a.** *Entom.* A transverse partition separating the prothorax from the mesothorax, found in some insects, as the Mole-cricket.

1826 Kirby & Sp. *Entomol.* III. xxxiii 368 Phragma (the Phragm). The Septum that closes the posterior orifice of the Prothorax in Gryllotalpa. *Ibid.* xxxv. 582 The phragm, or septum of the prothorax is most conspicuous in the mole-cricket (Gryllotalpa), in which it is a hairy ligament attached to the inside of the upper and lateral margins of the base of that part: inclining inwards, it forms the cavity which receives the mesothorax.

b. *Bot.* See quot. 1866.

1830 Lindley *Nat. Syst. Bot.* 136 Tribulus has the fruit separating into spiny nuts, with transverse phragmata. **1863** J. H. Balfour *Man. Bot.* §447. **1866** *Treas. Bot., Phragma*, a spurious dissepiment in fruits, i.e. one which is not formed by the sides of carpels; a partition, of whatever kind.

Hence **phrag'matic** *a.* (see quot.).

1858 Mayne *Expos. Lex., Phragmaticus*,..applied to cattle, etc., which suffer from colic or obstruction of the bowels: phragmatic.

phragmites (fræg'maɪtiːz). [mod.L. (C. B. Trinius *Fundamenta Agrostographiæ* (1820) 134), f. Gr. φραγμίτης growing in hedges.] = REED *sb.*[1] 4. Also *attrib.*

1920 *Blackw. Mag.* May 650/1 It may be necessary to cleave a passage..—cutting through papyrus, tearing at the tangling *Phragmites*, severing the long stems of the water-convolvulus. **1946** F. E. Zeuner *Dating Post* iii. 56 Peats growing under or at the water level: *Phragmites* peat (peat formed by the Common Reed and similar plants growing in shallow water). **1957** E. E. Evans *Irish Folk Ways* xv. 217 Large lake rushes provided materials for caulking..and phragmites stems for winding yarn in the shuttle. **1959** J. D. Clark *Prehist. S. Afr.* viii. 201 Phragmites reeds cut transversely and possibly left over from making arrow shafts,..abound in the upper layers of the cave. **1965** P. Wayre *Wind in Reeds* xi. 156 Little pockets of phragmites had sprung up in the odd corners and shallow bays all round the main [gravel] pit. **1977** *New Yorker* 5 Sept. 23/2 An impenetrable marsh of phragmites..and other plants clogs the length of the channel.

'**phragmocone.** *Zool.* Also *erron.* **phragma-.** [f. Gr. φραγμό-ς fence (or φραγμο- = φραγματο-: see PHRAGMA, and cf. σπερμο-) + κῶνος CONE.] The conical chambered internal skeleton of a fossil belemnite; also, by extension, the corresponding spiral or otherwise-shaped part in other fossil cephalopods.

1847 *Nat. Encycl.* I. 141 (*Actinocamax*) The species..had no true alveolar cavity or phragmacone. **1851-6** Woodward *Mollusca* 48 Its phragmocone is but the representative of the calcareous axis (or splanchno-skeleton) of a coral. **1862** Dana *Man. Geol.* 451 [In Belemnites] a small chambered cone, called the phragmocone..which has a siphuncle. **1888** Rolleston & Jackson *Anim. Life* 457 The chambered shell ..known in *Belemnitidae* as 'phragmacone'.

Hence **phragmo'conic** *a.*, of, pertaining to, or of the nature of the phragmocone of a belemnite.

1890 in *Cent. Dict.*

phrag'mophorous, *a. Zool.* [ult. f. Gr. φραγμο- (see prec.) + -φόρος bearing + -OUS.] Having a phragmocone; belonging to the *Phragmophora*, a section of decacerous cephalopods, having a phragmocone.

1890 in *Cent. Dict.*

phragmoplast ('frægməʊplɑːst, -æ-). *Bot.* [a. G. *phragmoplast* (L. Errera 1888, in *Bot. Centralbl.* XXXIV. 397), f. Gr. φράγμ-α fence, screen: see -O and -PLAST.] A set of fibrils which appears during mitosis in some plant cells as a barrel-shaped structure joining the two sets of chromosomes after their separation to the poles and which lasts until the formation of the cell plate.

1912 W. H. Lang tr. *Strasburger's Text-bk. Bot.* (ed. 4) 89 A barrel-shaped figure, the phragmoplast, is formed, which either separates entirely from the developing daughter nuclei, or remains in connection with them by means of a peripheral sheath. **1941** *Amer. Jrnl. Bot.* XXVIII. 227/2 In late anaphase or during telophase the phragmoplast extends laterally and a cell plate is formed across the cell. **1976** A. W. Davidson in M. M. Yeoman *Cell Division in Higher Plants* xii. 419 The phragmoplast, which heralds cell plate formation, appears at the equator of the mitotic spindle and moves centrifugally outwards along the phragmosome.

Hence **phragmo'plastic** *a.*

1952 A. Hughes *Mitotic Cycle* iv. 147 This form of cytokinesis..is really a variety of the phragmoplastic method. **1953** K. Esau *Plant Anat.* iii. 62 Phragmoplastic fibers appearing at the margins of the cell plate.

phragmosome ('frægməʊsəʊm). *Bot.* [f. as prec. + -SOME[4].] **a.** A layer of darker cytoplasm which forms during mitosis in some plant cells at the site of the future cell plate. **b.** One of the large number of small particles that form this layer.

1940 Sinnott & Bloch in *Proc. Nat. Acad. Sci.* XXVI. 226 This cytoplasm..tends to become aggregated into a series of strands..which occupies the position of the future wall and which thus indicates..where the plane of the division is to be. For this plate of cytoplasm the writers propose the term phragmosome. **1960** *Proc. 4th Internat. Conf. Electron Microscopy* 505 Other structures of the cytoplasm are consistently associated with the plate... The more obvious of these bodies (phragmosomes) tend to be a uniform distance from the cell plate. *Ibid.*, How these phragmosomes contribute to plate formation is not very clear. **1965** Frey-Wyssling & Mühlethaler *Ultrastruct. Plant Cytol.* 279 During and after the formation of the cell plate osmiophilic particles become evident in the phragmoplast, which can reach light microscopic dimensions and which are known as phragmosomes. **1971** *Canad. Jrnl. Bot.* XLIX. 927 RNA was concentrated in phragmosomes and at the newly formed cell plates. **1976** A. W. Davidson in M. M. Yeoman *Cell Division in Higher Plants* xii. 414 It is changes that occur within this limiting membrane [*sc.* the plasmalemma] which determine the point at which the phragmosome is formed and hence the position of the new cell wall.

phraisse, var. PHAIRS, obs. Sc. f. FARCE *sb.*[2]

phrampell, obs. form of FRAMPOLD.

phrantic, -ick, obs. forms of FRANTIC.

phrasal ('freɪzəl), *a.* [f. PHRASE + -AL[1].]

a. Of the nature of or consisting of a phrase. Used in *Gram.* in collocations qualifying the name of a part of speech to denote phrases which have the function of that part of speech, esp. ***phrasal verb***, an idiomatic verbal phrase consisting of a verb and adverb or a verb and preposition.

1871 Earle *Philol. Eng. Tongue* §445 Often we see that we are obliged to translate a flexional Greek adverb by a phrasal English one. *Ibid.* §529 A third series..are the phrasal prepositions, consisting of more than one word. **1879** J. Earle *Philol. Eng. Tongue* (ed. 3) x. 553 Modern English has made a new phrasal verb, and one that yet waits for a name. In this new verb the pronoun *it*, referring to no noun, acts as an objective accompaniment, and runs next after the verb. **1925** L. P. Smith *Words & Idioms* v. 172 Even more numerous are the idiomatic collocations of verbs followed by prepositions, or by prepositions used as adverbs. Collocations of this kind, 'phrasal verbs' we may call them, like 'keep down', 'set up', 'put through', and thousands of others. [*Note*] The term 'phrasal verbs' was suggested to me by the late Dr. Bradley. **1954** E. Gowers *Compl. Plain Words* vi. 71 There is today a tendency to form phrasal verbs to express a meaning no different from that of the verb without the particle... *Drown out, sound out, lose out, rest up, miss out on*, are other examples of phrasal verbs which I am told are used in America in senses no different from that of the unadorned verb. **1959** M. Schlauch *Eng. Lang.* 310 (Index), Phrasal adjectives. **1961** R. B. Long *Sentence & its Parts* ix. 218 In units such as *three-year-old*, whether used as phrasal nouns (as in *the three-year-old next door*) or as prepositive modifiers (as in *any three-year-old child*), the construction is different but obviously related. *Ibid.* x. 235 Units such as *tomorrow afternoon*..are syntactically much like phrasal-proper-name units such as Earlham College. **1973** *Word 1970* XXVI. 116 The following contain phrasal verbs: *You will have to look out for yourself*; *He did away with himself.*

b. *Mus.* Of or belonging to a phrase (in sense 5 of the sb.).

1946 R. Blesh *Shining Trumpets* v. 106 This solo puts the semitonally flatted third and fifth in phrasal conjunction.

'**phrasally,** *adv.* [f. PHRASAL *a.* + -LY[2].] In or by phrases; as a phrase.

1934 in Webster. **1971** *Archivum Linguisticum* II. 61 The fact that *black bird* is labelled phrasally reflects, it seems, a combination of conventional practice, analytical convenience, and the ascribing of special semantic significance to this particular type of structural relationship. **1973** *Ibid.* IV. 47 A given 'place' may..be occupied by more than one phrasally contributing form.

phrase (freɪz), *sb.* Also 6 in form **phrasis**; 6 **phraze, phrais**; *Sc.* (chiefly in sense 4) 7–9 **frase,** 8–9 **fraise,** 8 **fraze.** [ad. late L. *phrasis*, a. Gr. φράσις speech, way of speaking, phraseology, f. φράζ-ειν to point out, indicate, declare, tell; possibly through F. *phrase* (which however is not cited before Montaigne *c* 1575), also *frase*; so It., Sp. *frase*, OSp., Pg. *phrase*; Du., Ger. *phrase.*]

1. Manner or style of expression, esp. that peculiar to a language, author, literary work, etc.; characteristic mode of expression; diction, phraseology, language.

1530 Palsgr. Introd. 39 Of the differences of phrasys betwene our tong and the frenche tong... The phrasys of our tong and theyrs differeth chefely in thre thynges. **1535** Joye *Apol. Tindale* (Arb.) 38 Yt is the comon phrase of scripture to saye *spiritus sanctificationis pro spiritu sancto* [etc.]. **1540-1** Elyot *Image Gov.* Pref. (1556) 3 Conforme the stile thereof with the Phrase of our Englishe. **1573** Tusser *Husb.* (1878) 207 From Paules I went, to Eaton sent, To learn streight waies the latin phraies. **1579** Lyly *Euphues* (Arb.) 137 So I would have abiect and base phrase eschewed. **1593** Drayton *Eclogues* iv. 19 These men..press into the learned troop With filed Phraze to dignifie their Name. *a* **1600** Montgomerie *Sonn.* xliv, 3it, as I dar, my deutie sall be done With more affectione nor with formall phrais. *a* **1654** Selden *Table-T.* (Arb.) 20 The Bible is rather translated into English Words, than into English Phrase. The Hebraisms are kept, and the Phrase of that Language is kept. **1774** Warton *Hist. Eng. Poetry* vi. (1840) II. 6 Adam Davie writes in a less intelligible phrase than many..antient bards. **1812** J. Wilson *Isle Palms* iv. 619 Her Mary tells in simple phrase Of wildest perils in former days. **1882** A. W. Ward *Dickens* vii. 205 The supreme felicity of phrase in which he has no equal.

2. a. A small group or collocation of words expressing a single notion, or entering with some degree of unity into the structure of a sentence; an expression; esp. one in some way peculiar to or characteristic of a language, dialect, author, book, etc.; an idiomatic expression.

1530 Palsgr. Introd. 42 The table of verbes where all suche phrasys be set out at the length. *Ibid.* 814/2 When all is doone and sayd, *pour tout potaige*, a phrasis. **1551** T. Wilson *Logike* (1580) 64 b, By the mistaking of wordes, or by false vnderstanding of phrases. **1613** Purchas *Pilgrimage* I. xi. (1614) 59 The liquid pitch floateth on the top of the water, like clouted creame, to vse his owne phrase. **1662** *Bk. Com. Prayer* Pref., Some words or phrases of ancient usage. **1697** W. Pope *Bp. S. Ward* 104 My lord, I might bear you in hand; a western frase, signifying to delay or keep in expectation. **1812** Southey *Omniana* II. 13 This phrase, *a priori*, is in common most grossly misunderstood. **1875** Helps *Ess., Advice* 50 'If I were you' is a phrase often on our lips. **1878** Bosw. Smith *Carthage* 334 The phrase 'it would have been', is a dangerous phrase to use in the study of history.

†**b.** Applied to a single word. *Obs.*

1597 Shaks. *2 Hen. IV*, III. ii. 79 Accommodated, it comes of *Accommodo*: very good, a good Phrase. **1598** Shaks. *Merry W.* I. iii. 33 Conuay: the wise it call: Steale? foh: a fico for the phrase. **1699** Cotes tr. *Dupin's Hist. O. & N. Test.* I. I. i. 3 St. Jerom is one of the first who absolutely us'd the Phrase of *Canon* to denote the Catalogue of the Sacred Books.

c. *Grammatical Analysis*: see quot. 1865.

1852 Morell *Anal. Sent.* §17 The predicate may be extended in various ways:—1. By an adverb, or an adverbial phrase. **1865** Dalgleish *Gram. Anal.* 15 A phrase is a combination of words without a predicate; a clause is a term of a sentence containing a predicate within itself, as *Phrase*, spring returning; *Clause*, when spring returns. **1904** C. T. Onions *Adv. Eng. Syntax* 13 Adverb-equivalents: (1) A Phrase formed with a Preposition—He hunts *in the woods*... (4) A Clause—*When you come*, I will tell you. *Ibid.* 15 Two or more Sentences, Clauses, Phrases, or Single Words, linked together by one of the Conjunctions *and, but, or, nor, for*, are called co-ordinate..[as] A youth *to fortune* and *to fame* unknown; *To be* or *not to be*—that is the question.

d. *transf.*

1908 G. Jekyll *Colour in Flower Garden* 15 While the wide-stretching shadow-lengths throw the woodland shades into woodland *phrases* of broadened mass. **1922** [see CHOREOGRAPHICALLY *adv.*].

3. A peculiar or characteristic combination of words used to express an idea, sentiment, or the like in an effective manner; a short, pithy, or telling expression; sometimes, a meaningless, trite, or high-sounding form of words.

1579 W. Wilkinson *Confut. Familye of Loue* 1 b, These be their sweete and amiable wordes, and lovely phrases. **1588** Shaks. *L.L.L.* I. i. 166 A man in all the worlds new fashion planted, That hath a mint of phrases in his braine. **1641** J. Jackson *True Evang. T.* I. 19 Thus man degrades himselfe, and (according to the phrase, *Apoc.* 19. 20) receives..the mark of the beast. **1780** Cowper *Let. to Hill* 16 Mar., To use the phrase of all who ever wrote upon the state of Europe, the political horizon is dark indeed. **1816** Scott *Bl. Dwarf* ii, Greyhounds..who were wont, in his own phrase, to fear neither dog nor devil. **1841** D'Israeli *Amen. Lit.* (1867) 578 The phrase was tossed about till it bore no certain meaning. **1879** Froude *Cæsar* xii. 164 He called him, in the Senate, 'the saviour of the world'. Cicero was delighted with the phrase. **1899** *Daily News* 20 July 6/4 Humanity is the slave of phrase, and the phrase, 'Integrity of the Turkish Empire', is as much a matter of course to the English as 'Britannia rules the waves'.

4. *Sc.* and *north. dial.* Exclamatory or exaggerated talk; an outburst of words, whether in wonder, admiration, boastfulness, praise, or flattery; 'gush'; esp. in ***to make (a) phrase***, to express one's feelings in an exclamatory way, to 'gush', to make much ado about a person or thing (sometimes implying mere talk); ***to make muckle*** or ***little phrase about***, to talk or express one's feelings much or little about.

1725 Ramsay *Gentle Sheph.* I. ii, He may indeed, for ten or fifteen days Mak muckle o' ye, with an unco fraise. *Ibid.* v. iii, I ne'er was good at speaking a' my days, Or ever lov'd to make o'er great a frase. **1768** Ross *Helenore* III. 105 Gin that's the gate, we need na mak gryte fraze. **1816** Scott *Antiq.* xxxiv, An honest lad that likit you weel, though he made little phrase about it. **1901** G. Douglas *House w. Green Shutters* 175 He made a great phrase with me.

5. *Mus.* Any (comparatively) short passage, forming a more or less independent member of a longer passage or 'sentence', or of a whole piece or movement.

1789 BURNEY *Hist. Mus.* IV. 27 More forms or phrases of musical recitation still in use, may be found in Peri and Caccini, than in Monteverde. **1866** ENGEL *Nat. Mus.* iii. 82 A phrase extends over about two bars, and usually contains two or more motives, but sometimes only one. **1871** B. TAYLOR *Faust* (1875) I. Notes 228 In the over-ture to *Don Giovanni* a certain musical phrase occurs which is not repeated till the finale. **1880** SIR C. H. PARRY in Grove *Dict. Mus.* II. 706/1 The complete divisions are generally called periods, and the lesser divisions phrases. The word is not and can hardly be used with much exactness and uniformity.

6. *Fencing.* A continuous passage in an assault without any cessation of attack and defence.

Common in mod.French, and occasionally used by recent Eng. writers on Fencing. (Sir F. Pollock.)

7. *attrib.* and *Comb.*, as *phrase-coiner*, *-composition*, *-compound*, *-family*, *-form*, *-formative*, *-Latin*, *-meaning*, *-repeater*, *-tag*, *-type*; *phrase-final*, *-internal* adjs.; **phrase-book**, a book containing a collection of idiomatic phrases used in a language, with their explanation or translation; also *attrib.*; also †**phrase-like** *adv.*, phrase by phrase; **phrase-maker**, a maker of telling or fine-sounding phrases; also, a composer of musical phrases; hence **phrase-making** *vbl. sb.* (also in literal sense); **phrase-mark**, a sign in musical notation to indicate the proper phrasing: see sense 5; **phrase-marker** *Linguistics*, a diagrammatic or formulaic representation of the constituent structure of a sentence; abbrev. *P-marker* s.v. P III 5; **phrase-monger**, one who deals in or is addicted to fine-sounding phrases; so **phrase-mongering**, **-mongery**; **phrase-structure**, a group of words that constitutes a phrase; in *Gram.*, the structure of a sentence in terms of its constituent phrases (also *attrib.*); hence *phrase-structurally* adv.; **phrase-word** (see quot. 1933). Also PHRASEMAN.

1594 NASHE *Unfortunate Traveller* sig. F 1, In emptying their *phrase bookes, the ayre emptied his intrailes. **1600** NASHE *Summer's last Will* Wks. (Grosart) VI. 149 Hang copies, flye out phrase books, let pennes be turnd to picktooths. **1723** [see *phrase-Latin*]. **1898** *Westm. Gaz.* 11 Oct. 2/1 You must have a phrase-book knowledge of the language. **1905** G. MEREDITH *Let.* 7 May (1970) III. 1522 A pocket Italian-English phrase-book should be taken. **1963** L. DEIGHTON *Horse under Water* xiv. 60 He had used pompous phrase-book Portuguese. **1968** *Listener* 27 June 827/3 Pack one of those old-fashioned and much-mocked phrase books. **1901** *Daily Chron.* 17 May 3/2 Professional *phrase-coiners. **1902** GREENOUGH & KITTREDGE *Words* 70 *Phrase-composition..is alike active in slang and in law-abiding speech. *Ibid.* 188 Native *phrase-compounds are *beside*,..*betimes*,..*undershot*, *overlord* [etc.]. **1907** 'MARK TWAIN' *Christian Sci.* II. vii. 163 These great officials are of the *phrase-family of the Church-Without-a-Creed..that is to say, of the family of Large-Names-Which-Mean-Nothing. **1949** E. A. NIDA *Morphol.* (ed. 2) v. 126 In *phrase-final position. **1968** *Language* XLIV. 80 The glide on the short nucleus may be phonetically long, particularly in phrase-final position. **1911** BRERETON & ROTHWELL tr. *Bergson's Laughter* ii. 114 Sometimes, too, the effect is a complicated one. Instead of one commonplace *phrase-form, there are two or three which are dovetailed into each other. **1926** L. BLOOMFIELD in *Language* II. 156 The possessive [z] in *the man I saw yesterday's daughter*... Such a bound form is a *phrase-formative. **1964** E. BACH *Introd. Transformational Gram.* vi. 137 The rules begin with a string of forms..which are bracketed by numbered boundaries of two kinds: *phrase-internal and compound-internal boundaries. **1723** S. MORLAND *Spec. Dict. Eng. & Lat.* 5 There have..been some Phrase Books put out into the World, and esteemed as a Supplement to Dictionarys ..'Twas my Father's Opinion, that to these we owe the Introductioin of a thing call'd *Phrase-Latin. **1549** W. BALDWIN (*title*) The Canticles or Balades of Salomon, *phraselyke declared in Englysh Metres. **1822** T. MITCHELL *Aristoph.* I. 291 This *phrase-maker Hath ta'en thy very senses. **1901** *Academy* 23 Mar. 247 All the characters are phrase-makers and epigrammatists. **1924** P. C. BUCK *Scope of Music* 39 There will come a time when the phrase-maker desires to extend his tune beyond the limits of one breath. **1967** *Listener* 22 June 835/3 Certainly 'the dramatization of the significant' (what phrasemakers these Americans are!) is a worthy aim. **1977** *Rolling Stone* 7 Apr. 63/1 He knows how to 'use' television, he's a phrasemaker, he's good-looking and has a deep voice. **1867** W. D. WHITNEY *Lang. & Stud. Lang.* 116 All word-making by combination..is closely analogous with *phrase-making. **1905** *Athenæum* 25 Nov. 717/3 Phrase-making is not style.., nor is rhetoric the sole canon of speech. **1926** V. WOOLF *Writer's Diary* (1953) 96 No power of phrase-making. Difficulty in writing. **1929** C. DAY LEWIS *Transitional Poem* I. 17 Phrase-making, dress-making—Distinction's hard to find; For thought must play the mannequin. **1963** CHOMSKY & MILLER in R. D. Luce et al. *Handbk. Math. Psychol.* II. 288 We assume that such a tree graph must be a part of the structural description of any sentence; we refer to it as a **phrase-marker* (P-marker). **1965** N. CHOMSKY *Aspects of Theory of Syntax* i. 17 The *base* of the syntactic component is a system of rules that generate a highly restricted (perhaps finite) set of *basic strings*, each with an associated structural description called a *base Phrase-marker*. These base Phrase-markers are the elementary units of which deep structures are constituted. **1968** J. LYONS *Introd. Theoret. Linguistics* vi. 259 A labelled-bracketing of a string is referred to, technically, as a *phrase-marker*. Phrase-markers may also be represented by means of a tree-diagram with labelled nodes. **1971** *Archivum Linguisticum* II. 129 Removing all sequences of morphemes which can be referred to embedded phrase-markers, we are still left with complicated strings which obviously demand an ingenious transformational explanation of a kind which has not yet been offered. **1973** *Studies in Eng. Lit.: Eng. Number* (Tokyo) 52 Irrelevant structural details will hereafter be omitted from our phrase markers. **1931** G. STERN *Meaning & Change of Meaning* 2 *Phrase-meanings and word-meanings. **1815** *Zeluca* III. 149 The ineffable little old *phrase-monger. **1877** MORLEY *Crit. Misc.* Ser. II. 122 If Robespierre had been a statesman instead of a phrase-monger, he had a clear course. **1879** F. HARRISON *Choice Bks.* iii. (1886) 73 The jackanapes *phrasemongering of some Osric of the day. **1830** *Examiner* 598/2 We have commenced with his *phrase-mongery, and from it we shall proceed to some specimens of his philosophy. **1965** *Language* XLI. 277 A constituent string, which is always marked *phrase-structurally for terminal fade. **1975** *Studies in Eng. Lit.: Eng. Number* (Tokyo) 69 They suggest..that *Jane* and *Bill* be generated phrase-structurally. **1957** N. CHOMSKY *Syntactic Struct.* iv. 28 The determination of the *phrase structure (constituent analysis) of the derived sentence. **1960** J. B. CARROLL in Saporta & Bastian *Psycholinguistics* (1961) 337/2 In the latter part of the babbling period..there are the *first* evidences of..phrase-structures on the part of the child. **1967** D. G. HAYS *Introd. Computational Linguistics* viii. 147 A comparatively simple phrase-structure grammar produces deep structures with associated terminal strings. **1976** *Word 1971* XXVII. 257 Phrase-structure rules generate the deep-structure b-sequence from which the well-formed a-sequence is derived by transformation rules. **1957** N. FRYE *Anat. Crit.* 103 The fixed epithets and *phrase-tags of medieval romance and ballad. **1933** L. BLOOMFIELD *Language* xi. 180 The forms of the type *devil-may-care* are classed as words (*phrase-words) because..as a phrase *devil-may-care* would be an actor-action form, but as a phrase-word it fills the position of an adjective. **1979** *Dictionaries* I. 78 Other phrase words were very late innovations, stemming mostly from New High German times.

phrase, *v.* Also 6-7 frase. [f. prec. sb. Cf. F. *phraser* (1755 in Hatz.-Darm.).]

1. *intr.* To employ a phrase or phrases.

a **1550** *Image Hypocr.* III. 475 in *Skelton's Wks.* (1843) II. 439 Thoughe ye glose and frase Till your eyes dase. **1888** [see PHRASING *ppl. a.*].

2. *trans.* To put into words; to find expression for; to express in words or a phrase, esp. in a peculiar, distinctive, or telling phraseology; to word, express. *to phrase it*, to express the thing, to 'put it'.

1570 FOXE *A. & M.* (ed. 2) 55/2 Clement..who..was adioyned with Paule..dyd phrase them ['Epistle to the Hebrues'] in his style, and maner. **1625** BP. MOUNTAGU *App. Caesar* 64 So Ezechial phraseth it. *a* **1652** J. SMITH *Sel. Disc.* vi. 295 The Seventy..have much varied the manner of phrasing things from the original. **1701** ROWE *Amb. Step-Moth.* III. ii, Nor can I phrase my speech in apt Expression, To tell how much I love and honour you. **1771** JOHNSON *Let. to Mrs. Thrale* 7 July, He has had, as he phrased it, 'a matter of four wives'. **1879** H. GEORGE *Progr. & Pov.* x. v. (1883) 388 The free spirit of the Mosaic law.. inspired their poets with strains that yet phrase the highest exaltations of thought.

3. To describe (a person or thing) by a name, designation, or descriptive phrase; to call, designate; †to signify.

1585-7 T. ROGERS *39 Art.* (Parker Soc.) 230 The papists ..phrase the preachers to be uncircumcised Philistines. **1613** SHAKS. *Hen. VIII*, I. i. 34 When these Sunnes (For so they phrase 'em). **1614** CAMDEN *Rem.* (ed. 2) 205 To poore man ne to priest the penny frases nothing. Men giue God aie the least, they feast him with a farthing. **1636** PRYNNE *Unbish. Tim.* 36 The Scripture..never phrasing him a Bishop, nor giving him that Title. **1858** BUSHNELL *Nat. & Supernat.* iv. (1864) 105 Phrasing the conduct and doings of men. **1902** KIPLING in Monkshood & Gamble *Life* 49 He is supremely original: which makes it quite difficult to phrase him comparatively.

4. with *adv.* To do (a thing) *away*, do (a person) *out of* etc., by phrases or talk.

a **1718** PENN *Tracts* Wks. 1726 I. 471 If People will be phrased out of their Religion they may. **1830** *Examiner* 81/1 The Monarch is not permitted to phrase away his people's troubles.

5. *intr. Sc.* To 'make a phrase' (prec. 4), to talk exaggeratedly or 'gushingly', esp. in appreciation or praise. Also *trans.* To make much of in words.

1786 BURNS *Ep. to G. Hamilton* 3 May, To phrase you and praise you, Ye ken your laureate scorns. **1808** J. MAYNE *Siller Gun* IV, In vain his heralds fleech'd and phrased.

6. **a.** *trans. Mus.* To divide or mark off into phrases, esp. in execution; to perform according to the phrases. Also *absol.* (See also PHRASING *vbl. sb.* 2.)

1796 BURNEY *Mem. Metastasio* II. 332 The air should be phrased and symmetric. **1876** STAINER & BARRETT *Dict. Mus. Terms* 348 s.v. *Phrasing*, A performer who brings into due prominence the grouping of sounds into figures, sentences, &c., is said to *phrase* well. **1877** G. B. SHAW *How to become Mus. Critic* (1960) 29 It is easy to say that a singer 'phrases' well, because so few know what phrasing means. **1896** *Peterson Mag.* VI. 279/1 She phrases naturally and her intonation is admirable. **1962** *Times* 15 June 13/7 All thrushes (not only those in this neck of the Glyndebourne woods) sooner or later sing the tune of the first subject of Mozart's G minor Symphony (K. 550)—and, what's more, phrase it a sight better than most conductors. **1976** *Gramophone* Oct. 611/1 He has rather a sour tone and does not phrase the music as elegantly as his rivals.

b. *Dance.* To link (movements) in a single choreographic sequence, or part of a sequence.

1959 *Times* 22 Jan. 3/4 Miss Georgina Parkinson, who phrases travelling movements with much smoothness.

phrased ('freɪzd), *a.* [f. PHRASE *sb.* or *v.* + -ED.] Expressed in phrases, worded; characterized by phrases (of a specified kind).

1557 NORTH *Gueuara's Diall Pr.* Prol. A ij b, Suche, so straunge, and high phrased was the matter whiche he talked of. **1886** A. W. TUER in *Pall Mall G.* 8 Oct. 2/2 The quaintly phrased advertisements are genuine.

'**phraseless**, *a.* [f. PHRASE *sb.* + -LESS.] Without a phrase or phrases; in quot. app. 'which there is no phrase to describe'; but cf. 'his speechless hand' in *Coriol.* v. i. 67 (Schmidt).

1597 SHAKS. *Lover's Compl.* 225 O, then, aduance of yours that phraseles hand, Whose white weighes downe the airy scale of praise.

phraselet ('freɪzlɪt). *rare.* [-LET.] A short phrase (in music).

1925 P. A. SCHOLES *Second Bk. Gramophone Rec.* 86 The Clarinet repeats its last phraselet.

phraseman ('freɪzmən). [f. PHRASE *sb.* + MAN.] A man successful in making or using telling phrases; a phrase-monger.

1798 COLERIDGE *Fears in Solitude* 111 The poor wretch.. Becomes a fluent phraseman. **1814** CARY *Dante, Paradise* VIII. 153 Ye..of the fluent phraseman make your King.

phraseogram ('freɪzɪːəgræm). [irreg. f. Gr. φράσις + -GRAM: see PHRASEOLOGY.] A written character or symbol representing a phrase; *spec.* in phonography or other shorthand system, a conventional combination of signs or letters standing for a phrase.

1847 I. PITMAN *Man. Phonogr.* (ed. 8) 63 An extensive list of phraseograms is given in the 'Reporter'. **1868** *Ibid.* 15 *Phraseogram*, a combination of shorthand letters representing a phrase or sentence. **1895** W. E. A. AXON in W. Andrews *Curious Ch. Customs* 251 There are phraseograms for 'in the name of the Lord', 'wherefore said the psalmist', etc.

phraseograph ('freɪzɪːəgrɑːf, -æ-). *Shorthand.* [f. as prec. + -GRAPH.] A phrase for which there is a phraseogram. So **phraseo'graphic** *a.*, of the nature of a phraseogram, written in phraseography. **phrase'ography** [see -GRAPHY], (*a*) the representation of phrases or sentences by abbreviated characters in writing, esp. in systems of shorthand; the use of phraseograms; (*b*) written phraseology.

1845 I. PITMAN *Man. Phonogr.* 52 Phraseography. To promote expedition..the advanced phonographer may join two or more words together, and thus sometimes express a phrase without removing the pen. **1847** *Ibid.* (ed. 8) 64 It is not safe to write the phrase, *I cannot*, as a phraseograph. **1881** —— *Phonographic Phrase Bk.* Pref., With very little practice..the phraseographic combinations are found to be quite as legible as the ordinary Phonography. **1888** —— *Man. Phonogr.* 11 *Phraseograph*, a phrase that is written without lifting the pen. **1899** *Pall Mall Mag.* Feb. 198 The ..task of rendering it [the chorography] into modern phraseography.

phraseo'logic, *a. rare.* [f. PHRASEOLOGY (or its mod.L. orig.) + -IC.] = next, 2.

1828-32 in WEBSTER.

phraseological (freɪzɪəʊ'lɒdʒɪkəl), *a.* Also 8 phrasio-. [f. as prec. + -AL[1].]

1. Using phrases or peculiar expressions; expressed in a special phrase or phrases.

1664 H. MORE *Myst. Iniq.* To Rdr., A Rude, uncivil, uncharitable, phraseological Form of railing against such Things or Persons as are..Sacred. **1748** RICHARDSON *Clarissa* (1811) VII. lxxxi. 344 He said, in his phraseological way, that one story was good till another was heard. **1877** BLACK *Green Past.* viii, Her father professed an elaborate phraseological love for her.

2. Of or pertaining to phraseology; dealing with phrases, or with the phraseology of a language, etc., or that peculiar to an author or work.

1664 GOULDMAN (*title*) A Copious Dictionary..With.. Etymological Derivations, Philological Observations, and Phraseological Explications. **1694** *Lond. Gaz.* No. 3037/4 Phraseological Books..published. **1716** M. DAVIES *Athen. Brit.* III. 3 Jacobus Billius's Greek Phrasiological Collection. **1860** ADLER *Fauriel's Prov. Poetry* viii. 157 The correction of a barbarism or phraseological vice. **1899** H. G. GRAHAM *Soc. Life Scot. in 18th C.* (1901) VIII. i. 26 *note*, A phraseological peculiarity of these tracts.

phraseo'logically, *adv.* [f. prec. + -LY[2].] In a phraseological way; with the use of a phrase.

1867 *Nation* (N.Y.) 3 Jan. 9/1 When the verb *faire* is used phraseologically with a substantive. **1884** *W. Chester* (Pa.) *Local News* XII. No. 44. 3 Phraseologically speaking, it is a 'cold day' when our Justices of the Peace don't have a scene at their offices.

phraseologist (freɪzɪ'ɒlədʒɪst). [f. next + -IST.] **a.** One who treats of phraseology. **b.** A maker or user of phrases; one who uses striking or sounding phrases, esp. in an indiscriminate manner; a phrase-monger.

1713 BERKELEY *Guardian* No. 39 ¶ 14 The author..is but a mere phraseologist. **1727** BAILEY vol. II, *Phraseologist*, an Explainer of elegant Expressions in a Language. **1809** W. IRVING *Knickerb.* IV. i. (1849) 201 To borrow a favorite.. appellation of modern phraseologists. **1899** in *Westm. Gaz.*

18 May 3/2 There is something.. which in time perverts its advocate into a mere phraseologist.

phraseology (freɪzɪˈɒlədʒɪ). [ad. mod.L. *phraseologia*, Gr. φρασεολογία, erroneously formed by M. Neander (see quot.) from Gr. φράσις + -λογια, -LOGY; the correct Gr. form (used in mod.Gr.) is φρασιολογία **phrasiology*: cf. φυσιολογία physiology, etc.

Neander appears to have had in his mind the genitive case φράσεως; and the erroneous form has perh. been perpetuated in Eng. under the influence of *phrase*.]

†**1.** A collection or handbook of the phrases or idioms of a language; a phrase-book. *Obs.*

[**1558** M. NEANDER (*title*) ΦΡΑΣΕΟΛΟΓΙΑ ΙΣΟΚΡΑΤΙΚΗ ΕΛΛΗΝΙΚΟΛΑΤΙΝΗ. Phraseologia Isocratis Græcolatina: id est, Phraseon siue locutionum, elegantiarumue Isocraticarum Loci, seu Indices. **1681** W. ROBERTSON (*title*) Phraseologia generalis... A Full, Large, and General Phrase Book.] **1776** BARETTI (*title*) Easy Phraseology, for the use of young Ladies who intend to learn the colloquial part of the Italian Language.

2. The choice or arrangement of words and phrases in the expression of ideas; manner or style of expression; the particular form of speech or diction which characterizes a writer, literary production, language, etc.

1664 H. MORE *Myst. Iniq.*, *Apol.* iv. §6 The Conclusions or Phraseologies of the School-Divines touching this Point. **1669** GALE *Crt. Gentiles* I. III. x. 96 Such is the incomparable Majestie of the Scripture stile, and Phraseologie. **1714** *Spectator* No. 616 ¶ 1 That ridiculous Phraseology, which is so much in Fashion among the Pretenders to Humour and Pleasantry. **1771** BURKE *Corr.* (1844) I. 254 Men, according to their habits and professions, have a phraseology of their own. **1857-8** SEARS *Athan.* 6 Religious phraseologies from which religious ideas have been expunged. **1875** JOWETT *Plato* IV. 130 Parmenides.. is the founder.. in modern phraseology, of metaphysics and logic.

†**3.** (See quots.) *Obs. rare*$^{-0}$.

1670 BLOUNT *Glossogr.* (ed. 3), *Phraseology*, a speaking of Phrases, or of the proper form of Speech. **1678** PHILLIPS (ed. 4), *Phraseology*, (Greek) a Discourse of Phrases, or an uttering of Phrases in common Speech.

†**4.** *Mus.* Arrangement of phrases. *Obs.*

1789 BURNEY *Hist. Mus.* IV. 571 The want of symmetry in the phraseology of his melodies.

phraser (ˈfreɪzə(r)). [f. PHRASE *v.* + -ER[1]. Cf. F. *phraseur* (18th c. in Hatz.-Darm.).] One who uses phrases, or expresses himself in a peculiar or striking manner; a phrase-monger.

1637 J. WILLIAMS *Holy Table* 212 According to this English Phraser. **1878** J. THOMSON *Plenip. Key* 19 And though he speaketh much,—beyond demur, No phraser, but a trusty messenger. **1879** G. MEREDITH *Egoist* v, Like all rapid phrasers, Mrs. Mountstuart detested the analysis of her sentence.

phrasial (ˈfreɪzɪəl), *a. rare.* [f. PHRAS(E *sb.* + -IAL.] Of or pertaining to (musical) phrases.

1918 *Proc. Musical Assoc.* Apr. 135 The phrasial formalities.. engender a monotony.

†ˈ**phrasical**, *a. Obs. rare*$^{-1}$. [f. Gr. φράσ-ις PHRASE *sb.* + -ICAL.] Of the nature of a phrase; idiomatic.

1615 T. ADAMS *Eng. Sickn.* Wks. 1861 I. 395 'Daughter of my people'.. This is an abstractive phrase.. Here it is phrasical, and therefore not to be forced.

†ˈ**phrasify**, *v. Obs.* [f. L. *phrasi-s* PHRASE *sb.*: see -FY.] *intr.* To use a phrase.

1633 AMES *Agst. Cerem.* II. 267 That which the Def. neglected, the Rejoynder taketh to supplie, *least we should bragge*, as it pleaseth him to phrasifie. **1674** HICKMAN *Hist. Quinquart.* (ed. 2) 191 To disgrace the Calvinists, by calling them Gospellers; For thus he phrasifieth.

ˈ**phrasiness.** *colloq.* [f. PHRASY + -NESS.] The quality of being of the nature of a phrase: see PHRASE *sb.* 3; proneness to use phrases.

1892 *Review of Rev.* 14 Apr. 376/1 The Germans are heartily sick of the phrasiness of their ruler. **1896** W. W. PEYTON in *Contemp. Rev.* June 837, I use the word 'communication' of design to release the idea of communion from religious phrasiness.

phrasing (ˈfreɪzɪŋ), *vbl. sb.* [f. PHRASE *v.* + -ING[1].]

1. The action of the vb. PHRASE; manner or style of verbal expression; phraseology, wording.

1611 BIBLE *Transl. Pref.* 11 Wee haue not tyed ourselues to an vniformitie of phrasing, or to an identity of words. **1741** RICHARDSON *Pamela* (1824) I. iv. 238 He says, in his usual way of phrasing, that he'll make it as easy to you as a glove. **1887** SAINTSBURY *Hist. Elizab. Lit.* ix. (1890) 325 Milton.. mixes the extremest vernacular with the most exquisite and scholarly phrasing.

2. a. *Mus.* The rendering of musical phrases. Also *attrib.* as *phrasing slur*, a slur indicating the proper phrasing.

1877 [see PHRASE *v.* 6 a]. **1880** SIR H. PARRY in Grove *Dict. Mus.* II. 706/2 Just as the intelligent reading of a literary composition depends upon two things, accentuation and punctuation, so does musical phrasing depend on the relative strength of the sounds, and upon their connection with or separation from each other. **1886** *Academy* 17 July 48/3 He aroused the sympathy and interest of his audience by his soft and liquid tone, his neat playing, and by his delicate and finished phrasing. **1898** *Westm. Gaz.* 29 Dec. 3/2 Where it has seemed desirable, phrasing slurs have been added. **1921** A. RIVARDE *Violin & its Technique* i. 11 Many violinists.. are constantly blustering with long bows, very often spoiling the phrasing and making violinistic rather than musical effects. **1966** *Crescendo* Feb. 35/3 To hear drum phrasing at its very best. **1976** *Gramophone* Apr. 1611/3 Though individual soloists are naturally as fine as one expects of the LSO, the style of phrasing in ensembles is stiffer than it might be.

b. in sense 6 b of the verb.

1978 *Daily Tel.* 22 Aug. 9/1 In the pas de trois,.. in spite of some uncertainty over supported pirouettes, there was splendidly crisp phrasing from Kenneth McCombe and his partners.

3. *transf.*

1949 M. MEAD *Male & Female* iii. 65 All these themes are present in every cultural phrasing of the mother-child relationship. **1967** W. W. NEWCOMBE in F. Kirkland *Rock Art of Texas Indians* iv. 40/2 Certainly the two cultural complexes are phrasings of a single basic culture.

ˈ**phrasing**, *ppl. a.* [f. as prec. + -ING[2].] That phrases; using phrases; in *Sc.*, loudly or exaggeratedly expressing one's feelings or sentiments.

1785 BURNS *To W. Simpson* ii, In sic phraisin terms ye've penn'd it, I scarce excuse ye. **1888** STEVENSON *Across the Plains*, *Beggars* iv. (1892) 268 A.. tale of some worthless, phrasing Frenchman.

phrasy (ˈfreɪzɪ), *a. colloq.* Also erron. **phrasey.** [f. PHRASE + -Y.] Abounding in phrases; characterized by great use of phrases.

1849 *Ecclesiologist* IX. 125 They resemble what is familiarly known as a piece of phrasy Latin. **1871** *Daily News* 11 Mar., The document smacks overmuch of the phrasey, and is less redolent of the vigorous than of the lachrymose.

phrator (ˈfreɪtɔː(r)). [a. Gr. φράτωρ, another form of φράτηρ clansman: cognate with Skr. *bhrātā*, Zend *bhrātar*, L. *frāter*, Goth. *brôþar* BROTHER.] A member of a Grecian phratry; also *transf.* a fellow-clansman.

1847 GROTE *Greece* II. x. III. 87 If a man was murdered, first his near relations, next his gennêtes and phrators, were both allowed and required to prosecute the crime at law. **1881** L. H. MORGAN *N. Amer. Ethnol.* IV. 11 To preserve some degree of equality in the number of phrators in each.

phratriac (ˈfreɪtrɪæk), *a. rare.* [ad. Gr. φρᾱτριακ-ός, f. φρᾱτρία PHRATRY: see -AC.] = next.

1884 *Athenæum* 21 June 795/3 In Attica there were also two great organizations, one based originally on locality, and another whose sole qualification was that of birth—the demotic and the phratriac.

phratric (ˈfreɪtrɪk), *a.* [ad. Gr. φρᾱτρικ-ός, f. φράτρ-α = φρᾱτρία PHRATRY + -IC.] Of or pertaining to a phratry or clan; consisting of phratries.

1847 GROTE *Greece* II. x. III. 75 The phratric union, binding together several gentes, was less intimate [than the gentile union]. **1881** L. H. MORGAN *Contrib. N. Amer. Ethnol.* IV. 11 The phratric organization has existed among the Iroquois from time immemorial.

phratry (ˈfreɪtrɪ). [ad. Gr. φρᾱτρία, f. φράτηρ: see PHRATOR. In F. *phratrie* (Littré).]

1. *Ancient Gr. Hist.* A politico-religious division of the people, which took its first rise from the ties of blood and kinship; in Athens, each of the three subdivisions into which the phyle was divided; a clan.

[**1753** CHAMBERS *Cycl. Supp.*, *Phratriarchus*, among the Athenians, a magistrate that presided over the phratria, or third part of a tribe. He had the same power over the phratria, that the phylarchus had over the tribe.] **1833** THIRLWALL in *Philol. Museum* II. 307 The desire of the higher classes to keep aloof from the rustics.., who had been admitted into the phratries. **1875** JOWETT *Plato* (ed. 2) I. 231 A family Zeus, and a Zeus guardian of the phratry. [**1884** *Athenæum* 21 June 795/3 No deme coincided with a phratria or with any subdivision of a phratria.]

2. *transf.* Applied to tribal or kinship divisions existing among primitive races, as the Indians of North America, aborigines of Australia, etc.

1876 L. H. MORGAN in *N. Amer. Rev.* CXXIII. 65 It is.. ..probable.. that the Mound-Builders were organized in gentes, phratries, and tribes. **1882** H. SPENCER *Pol. Inst.* 549 Not only where descent in the male line has been established, but also where the system of descent through females continues, this development of the family into *gens*, phratry, and tribe is found. **1891** WESTERMARCK *Hist. Hum. Marriage* (1894) 298 The Seneca tribe of the Iroquois was divided into two 'phratries', or divisions intermediate between the tribe and the clan.

†**phrayes**, obs. illit. form of FROISE, FRAISE.

1686 *Oldbury Parish Reg.* in *Blakeway MS.* (Bodl.) 3. 72, 2 gamon of Bacon and phrayes made of y[e] egges.

phreak (friːk), *sb.* and *v.* [Modified spelling of FREAK *sb.*[1], *v.*, under influence of PHONE *sb.*[2], *v.*]

A. *sb.* = PHONE PHREAK *sb.* **B.** *vb. trans.* and *intr.* To use an electronic device to obtain (a telephone call) without payment. So ˈ**phreaking** *vbl. sb.*

1972 *Daily Tel.* 15 Apr. 3/2 The craze started in America and there are said to be 150 'phreaks' in this country who swop information and have equipment and dialling codes which give them free use of the world's telephone system. **1972** *Oxford Times* 9 June 7/5 Used telephone codes and his expert knowledge to 'phreak' phone calls... 23 attempts at 'phreaking', of which seven were successful.

phreatic (frɪˈætɪk), *a.* [ad. F. *phréatique* (G. A. Daubrée *Les Eaux Souterraines* (1887) I. ii. 19), f. Gr. φρέαρ, φρέατ- well, cistern + -IC.] **1.** Of, pertaining to, or designating water below the water-table, esp. that which is capable of movement.

1891 R. J. HINTON *Irrigation in U.S.: Progress Rep. for 1890* (U.S. 51st Congress, 2nd Sess. Senate Ex. Doc. No. 53) 42 At the point at which most of them leave the mountain ranges there commences an enormous phreatic absorption of the volume of flow that has descended from the summit above. **1892** R. HAY *Final Geol. Rep.* (U.S. 52nd Congress, 1st Sess. Senate Ex. Doc. No. 41) III. 8 Prof. Hill has given definitions of the technical words used by him, and to his list may be added the new word *phreatic*, which is a very convenient term for underground waters which can be, or which it is hoped may be, reached by wells or other sub-ground works. [*Note*] This word was first used in American hydro-geologic investigation by the Artesian and Underflow Office in 1890. **1892-3** *14th Rep. U.S. Geol. Surv.* II. 16 'Phreatic water'. [*Note*] This term was coined by Hay, in the course of the recent artesian and underflow investigation.., as a convenient designation for 'underground waters which can be, or which it is hoped may be, reached by wells or other subground works'. **1917** *Econ. Geol.* XII. 494 Daubrée (1887, p. 19) invented 'phreatic' from a Greek expression for 'well'... Originally.. the word meant seepage water and particularly that below the water-table. It was so used by Hay (1892, p. 8) and McGee (1894, pp. 16, 42)... Suess (1909, p. 655) appears to have included in 'phreatic water' that of connate origin as well as seepage water... The writer believes that the history of the word and practical expediency should make 'phreatic' mean the infiltered waters which are bounded above by the water-table. **1954** *Times Lit. Suppl.* 5 Feb. 93/2 Theories of their [*sc.* caves'] formation are classed as 'vadose' or 'phreatic' according as it is held that caves are formed above the water-table or below it. **1966** DAVIS & DEWIEST *Hydrogeol.* ii. 42 The zone of phreatic water merges at depth into a zone of dense rock with some water in pores, although the pores are not interconnected so that water will not migrate. **1973** *Nature* 9 Nov. 77/2 After the solutional formation of a cavity beneath the water table, incision and reduction of local base level produced lowering of the phreatic surface. **1977** A. HALLAM *Planet Earth* 108 Where the top of the zone of saturation of an aquifer is a free-water surface it is known as the water table (or phreatic surface).

2. Of, pertaining to, or designating a volcanic explosion caused by the sudden heating and volatilization of underground water when it comes into contact with hot magma or rock.

1909 H. B. C. & W. J. SOLLAS tr. *Suess's Face of Earth* IV. xvi. 568 Phreatic explosions. When juvenile hydrogen encounters an unlimited quantity of vadose water, we witness a spectacle such as was presented by Krakatoa in 1883... In this case the effect may have been due to phreatic water in the neighbourhood of the sea, but when phreatic water is confined in the fissures of a limestone formation, the explosion shatters the limestone. **1926** R. A. DALY *Our Mobile Earth* iv. 158 Not all explosions are due to the pressure of magmatic gas... In the year 1888 the side of the Japanese cone, Bandai-San, was ripped out... The cavity, technically called a 'phreatic caldera', is about two miles long. *Ibid.*, The 1924 explosion at Kilauea was of phreatic character. **1964** *New Scientist* 5 Mar. 585/2 The co-existence and maintenance of such 'phreatic' activity (here ascribable to sea water suddenly flashed into steam by contact with hot lava in a vent) with the contrasting fire-fountains, characteristic of 'Strombolian' volcanic activity.., calls for somewhat unusual conditions. **1975** FIELDER & WILSON *Volcanoes of Earth, Moon & Mars* iv. 53/2 In a phreatic eruption, horizontal surges carry low density loads outwards from the eruptive centre. **1976** P. FRANCIS *Volcanoes* iv. 143 This steam sometimes blasts its way up to the surface through the lava, causing what is known as a phreatic explosion.

phreatophyte (friːˈætəʊfaɪt). [f. Gr. φρέαρ, φρεατ- tank, cistern + -PHYTE.] A plant with a deep root system that draws its water supply from near the water-table.

1920 *Bull. Geol. Soc. Amer.* XXXI. 333 In arid regions plants of certain species habitually utilize water from the zone of saturation. For such plants the name *phreatophyte* (meaning a well-plant) has been proposed... Willow trees are among the most common phreatophytes in the arid West. **1928** *Ecology* IX. 474 The phreatophytes or 'well plants' which derive their water supply from the ground water and are more or less independent of local rainfall. **1963** D. W. & E. E. HUMPHRIES tr. *Termier's Erosion & Sedimentation* vi. 136 Most other plants in dry regions need roots long enough to reach down to the water table, or at least to its capillary fringe; these are the phreatophytes. **1965** R. G. KAZMANN *Mod. Hydrol.* v. 144 The most widespread of the desert phreatophytes in the United States are salt grass, greasewood, mesquite, and salt cedar. **1974** *Internat. Gloss. Hydrol.* 171/2 *Phreatophytes*, water-loving plants that grow mainly along stream courses and/or where their roots reach the capillary fringe.

‖**phren** (friːn). Pl. phrenes (ˈfriːniːz). [mod.L., a. Gr. φρήν midriff, in pl. φρένες parts about the heart, breast; heart, mind, will.]

1. *Anat.* The diaphragm; the upper part of the abdomen: anciently supposed to be the seat of the mind.

1706 PHILLIPS, *Phrenes*,.. the Membranes about the Heart; also the Diaphragm or Midriff. **1893** *Syd. Soc. Lex.*, *Phren*,.. the diaphragm; also, the epigastrium.

2. *Philos.* The seat of the intellect, feelings, and will; the mind.

phrenalgia: see PHRENO-.

† **phre'nesiac**, *a. Obs.* [f. Gr. φρένησις (see next), taken as = φρενησία (cf. It. *frenesia*) + -AC.] = PHRENETIC *a.* 1.

1814 SCOTT *Wav.* xliii, Like an hypochondriac person, or, as Burton's Anatomia hath it, a phrenesiac or lethargic patient.

‖**phrenesis** (frɪ'niːsɪs). *Path.* [L. *phrenēsis* delirium, a. late Gr. φρένησις, f. φρήν, φρεν-: see next, and cf. FRENZY.] = PHRENITIS.

1547 BOORDE *Brev. Health* lvii. 26 In the head may be many infirmities, as the Apoplexie, the Scotomy, the Megrym, the Sood, the Phremyses [**1598** phrenises]. **1551** ASCHAM *Let.* 18 May, Wks. 1865 I. II. 288 The prince of Spain..is this day fallen sore sick of a phrenesis. **1561** HOLLYBUSH *Hom. Apothec.* 5 An apostemacion in the braynes of some litle skinnes, that enuiron the braynes, the same are called Phrenesis. **1800** LAMB *Let. to Manning* 27 Dec., At last George Dyer's phrenesis has come to a crisis; he is raging and furiously mad.

phrenetic (frɪ'nɛtɪk), *a.* (*sb.*) Forms: α. 4 frenetyk, 4-6 -ike; 5 frena-, 6 frenetyke, -ik, 6-7 -ick, 7 frenitick, 9 frenetic. β. 6 phrenetike, 6-7 -ique, 7 -icke, 7-8 -ick, 9 -itic, 7- phrenetic. [a. OF. *frenetike* (*Dial. S. Greg.* 12-13th c.), ad. L. *phrenēticus*, a. late Gr. φρενητικός (Epict.), for φρενιτικός afflicted with φρενῖτις delirium, f. φρήν, φρεν- heart, mind. Formerly stressed '*phrenetic*, whence PHRENTIC, FRANTIC.]

† **1.** Of persons: Delirious; mentally deranged; insane; crazy: = FRANTIC *a.* 1. *Obs.*

α. *c* **1374** CHAUCER *Troylus* v. 206 (Camps.) And in his þrowes frenetyk [*v.r.* frentyk] and madde He curssed Ioue, Appollo, and ek Cupide. **1377** LANGL. *P. Pl.* B. x. 6 To flatereres or to folis þat frantyk [*v.r.* frenetike] ben of wittes. **1483** CAXTON *Gold. Leg.* 193/1 Saynt marcial heled one that was frenatyke. **1596** DALRYMPLE tr. *Leslie's Hist. Scot.* VIII. 84 Donald and quha with him appeiret frenetik.

β. **1558** KNOX *First Blast* (Arb.) 11 The foolishe, madde and phrenetike shal gouerne the discrete. **1651** HOBBES *Leviath.* III. xxxiv. 215 Those that became Phrenetique, Lunatique, or Epileptique. **1751** LAVINGTON *Enthus. Meth. & Papists* III. (1754) 139 They [Persons bit by the Tarantula] are Phrenetic and delirious. **1778** *Phil. Trans.* LXVIII. 206 All that survived..were to the highest degree phrenetic and outrageous.

2. *transf.* Affected with excessive excitement or enthusiasm, esp. in religious matters; furious; frantic; fanatic. Cf. FRANTIC *a.* 2.

α. *c* **1540** tr. *Pol. Verg. Eng. Hist.* (Camden) I. 109 This..restrained the rude raginge of the frenetick Scotts. **1657** HAWKE *Killing is M.* 40 The foolish dictates of such frenetick Impostor. **1819** WIFFEN *Aonian Hours* (1820) 109 Frenetic zealots. **1882** *Pall Mall G.* 27 Oct. 1 Some of the more frenetic of the franc-tireurs of Liberalism.

fig. **1872** BROWNING *Fifine* v, How the pennon from its dome, Frenetic to be free, makes one red stretch for home!

β. **1565** CALFHILL *Answ. Treat. Crosse* 23 It is to be feared greately, least their arise some phrenetike persons, which will bragge and boast..that they be Prophetes. **1660** INGELO *Bentiv. & Ur.* v. 138 He esteems Prophetick Visions only as Dreams of phrenetick men. **1858** *Times* 4 Nov. 6/4 The chivalrous and phrenetic Montbar, whose name was a cry to hush infants. **1878** J. P. NEWMAN in *N. Amer. Rev.* CXXVII. 321 When inspired, their individuality was intact. They [sacred writers] were never..phrenetic.

3. † **a.** Of a disease: Consisting of or attended by delirium or temporary madness: = FRANTIC *a.* 3 a. *Obs.* **b.** Of actions, etc.: Insane; erratic; passionate: = FRANTIC *a.* 3 b.

α. *a* **1529** SKELTON *Agst. ven. Tongues* viii. 10 Ye are so full of vertibilite, And of frenetyke folabilite. **1641** MILTON *Ch. Govt.* II. iii. 50 Sometimes he shuts up [the man] as in frenetick, or infectious diseases. **1816** KEATINGE *Trav.* (1817) I. 198 [Of Mohammedanism] Its frenetic might, enthusiasm, too, evaporating in the diffusion of conquest. **1895** MARIE CORELLI *Sorrows Satan* 378 They run up the gamut of baffled passion to the pitch of frenetic hysteria.

β. **1595** DANIEL *Civ. Wars* IV. v, Impotent, By means of his Phreneticque maladie. **1615** H. CROOKE *Body of Man* 139 Rending the membranes, cause all our motions to be headstrong and giddy, our sensations phrenetick and mad. **1754** O. in *Connoisseur* No. 28. ⁋1 Tom Dare-Devil..was carried off last week by a phrenetic fever. **1815** MARY A. SCHIMMELPENNINCK *Demolit. Monast. Port Royal* III. 268 He struck every one who approached him, with the most phrenitic violence. **1860** T. MARTIN *Horace, Odes* I. xvi, Clashing again And again their wild cymbals, such fervour phrenetic.

¶ **4.** *Catachrestic* for PHRENIC *a.* 1.

1704 J. HARRIS *Lex. Techn.* I, *Phrenetick Nerves*, are those which are called also *Stomachick*..These descend between the Membranes of the *Mediastinum*, and send forth Branches into them. **1706** in PHILLIPS.

B. as *sb.* A madman: = FRANTIC *sb.*

α. **1693-4** MOLINEUX *Let.* 17 Feb. in *Locke's Lett.* (1708) 75 How comes it to pass that want of consciousness cannot be proved for a drunkard as well as for a frenitick? **1837** CARLYLE *Fr. Rev.* III. I. iv, All men's minds may go mad, and 'believe him', as the frenetic will do, 'because it is impossible'.

β. [**1607** MARSTON *What you will* II. i, A company of odd phrenetici Did eate my youth.] **1612** SELDEN *Illustr. Drayton's Poly-olb.* xvii, [They] made this poore King..euen as a Phrenetique, comit what posterity receiues now amongst the worst actions..of Princes. **1695** WOODWARD *Nat. Hist. Earth* II. (1723) 99 A common Fold of Phreneticks and Bedlams. **1881** W. R. SMITH *Old Test. in Jew. Ch.* x. 281 The visions of poor phrenetics.

Hence **phre'neticness**, madness (Bailey vol. II, 1727).

† **phre'netical**, *a. Obs.* Also 6 phræ-, 6-7 fre-. [f. as prec. + -AL[1].]

1. = PHRENETIC *a.* 1 and 2.

1588 J. HARVEY *Disc. Probl.* 34 Do they not..proceede from some odde vaine phantasticall, or phreneticall braines? **1663** BP. PATRICK *Parab. Pilgr.* (1673) 122 Dæmoniacks and phrenetical people. **1674** OWEN *Holy Spirit* (1693) 195 Some Persons Phrenetical and Enthusiastical, whose Madness is manifest to all.

2. = PHRENETIC *a.* 3.

a **1548** HALL *Chron., Hen. V* 65 b, Thether came Isabell, the Frenche Quene, because the kyng her husband was fallen into his old freneticall desease. **1602** T. FITZHERBERT *Apol.* 62 The phantastical or rather phrenetical opinions of these new fangled fellowes. **1696** BP. PATRICK *Comm. Exod.* x. 170 Another raving fit or phrenetical symptom.

phrenetically (frɪ'nɛtɪkəlɪ), *adv.* [f. prec. + -LY[2].] In a frenzy; frantically.

1837 CARLYLE *Fr. Rev.* II. II. ii, If all mobs are properly frenzies, and work frenetically with mad fits of hot and of cold. **1898** *Westm. Gaz.* 14 Jan. 3/1 We welcome his sober prose and phrenetically applaud his common sense.

phreniatric (frɛnaɪ'ætrɪk), *a.* [f. Gr. φρήν, φρεν- mind + IATRIC.] Of or pertaining to the treatment of mental disease.

In mod. Dicts.

phrenic ('frɛnɪk), *a.* (*sb.*) [ad. mod.L. *phrenicus* or a. F. *phrénique* (1690 in Hatz.-Darm.), f. Gr. φρήν, φρεν- diaphragm, mind: see -IC.]

1. *Anat.* and *Path.* Of, pertaining to, or affecting the diaphragm; diaphragmatic.

1704 J. HARRIS *Lex. Techn.* I, *Phrenick Vessels*, are the Veins and Arteries that run through the Diaphragm, Mediastinum, and Pericardium. **1741** MONRO *Anat. Nerves* (ed. 3) 19 Press one or both the phrenic Nerves. **1832** J. THOMSON *W. Cullen* I. 441 The Phrenic or Epigastric Centre. **1842** E. WILSON *Anat. Vade M.* 350 The Phrenic veins return the blood from the ramifications of the phrenic arteries. **1899** *Allbutt's Syst. Med.* VI. 649 Phrenic neuritis.

† **2.** Of or relating to the mind; mental. *Obs.*

1835-6 TODD *Cycl. Anat.* I. 126/2 The nerves of animal, or, better, of phrenic life. **1838** *Fraser's Mag.* XVII. 27 The Theosophs were right in separating entirely the mind from the soul, in considering them..as different principles, as the physic and the phrenic. **1847** MEDWIN *Shelley* I. 149 Two sorts of dreams, the Phrenic and the Psychic.

B. *sb.* (absolute use of A.)

1. *Anat.* Short for *phrenic nerve*.

1776 CRUIKSHANK in *Phil. Trans.* LXXXV. 187 The possibility of having divided only one of the phrenics. **1881** MIVART *Cat* 209 It gives off a long and very slender branch, called the superior phrenic.

2. *Med.* A remedy or medicine for mental disease.

1853 DUNGLISON *Med. Lex., Phrenica*, diseases affecting the intellect... Also remedies that affect the mental faculties—Phrenics.

3. *pl.* **phrenics**: That branch of science which relates to the mind; psychology.

1841 R. PARK *Pantology* II. iii. (1847) 82 We would apply the term Phrenics to Mental Philosophy; or to that branch of knowledge, which treats of the faculties of the human mind, and their laws of action. **1893** *Syd. Soc. Lex., Phrenics*..also metaphysics.

phrenicectomy (frɛnɪ'sɛktəmɪ). *Surg.* [f. as next + -ECTOMY.] Surgical removal or destruction of a section of a phrenic nerve, formerly carried out as an alternative to phrenicotomy.

1929 *Surg., Gynecol. & Obstetr.* XLVIII. 274/1 The indications for phrenicectomy are lesions which may be benefited by partial compression and immobilization of a lung. **1943** B. M. DICK in C. F. W. Illingworth *Textbk. Surg. Treatm.* xxviii. 381 Phrenicectomy is used as an adjuvant to other types of collapse therapy—as an independent measure where artificial pneumothorax has failed owing to adhesions, and as a palliative for hæmoptysis, harassing cough, vomiting, or pain due to diaphragmatic adhesions. **1957** E. H. HUDSON in F. R. G. Heaf *Symposium of Tuberculosis* vii. 381 Stuertz of Cologne is credited as the first to perform phrenicectomy as a therapeutic measure in the treatment of brochiectosis of the lower lobe of the lung in 1911.

phrenicotomy (frɛnɪ'kɒtəmɪ). *Surg.* [f. PHRENIC *a.* (*sb.*) + -O + -TOMY.] Surgical cutting of a phrenic nerve, so as to paralyse the diaphragm on the same side.

1913 *Internat. Abstr. Surg.* XVII. 417/2 Oehlecker..performed the phrenicostomy [*sic*] in three cases. **1926** *Encycl. Brit.* III. 691/1 Phrenicotomy (division of the phrenic nerve in the neck) is said to paralyse the corresponding half of the diaphragm; it is sometimes practised in conjunction with other means of putting one lung at rest. **1950** J. K. BERMAN *Princ. & Pract. Surg.* viii. 231 Compression of the lung is best secured by the subperiosteal resection of ribs over the affected side. Should symptoms persist after pneumothorax and phrenicotomy, thoracoplasty may be used. **1974** *Jrnl. Appl. Physiol.* XXXVII. 315/1 Tracings of pleural pressure on the intercostal and diaphragmatic surfaces under normal conditions and after complete bilateral phrenicotomy are shown in Fig. 5.

‖**phre'nicula.** *Path.* [mod.L., f. as PHRENIC *a.* (*sb.*) + dim. suffix: see -CULE.]

1799 M. UNDERWOOD *Dis. Children* (ed. 4) I. 282 What he [i.e. Dr. Paterson] calls a phrenicula, or diminutive species of phrenitis. **1893** *Syd. Soc. Lex., Phrenicula*, term used by Rust for Brain-fever.

phrenism ('frɛnɪz(ə)m). [f. Gr. φρήν, φρεν- mind + -ISM.] Thought-force: see quot.

1871 COPE *Origin of Fittest* v. (1887) 205, I discard the use of the term 'Vital Force', what was originally understood by that term being a complex of distinct ideas. The *Vital forces* are (nerve-force) *Neurism*, (growth-force) *Bathmism*, and (thought-force) *Phrenism*.

phrenitic (frɪ'nɪtɪk), *a. Path.* [ad. Gr. φρενῑτικός, f. φρενῖτ-ις PHRENITIS: see -IC.] Affected with or suffering from phrenitis; subject to fits of delirium or madness.

1771 T. PERCIVAL *Ess.* (1777) I. 24 He indulged his phrenitic patients in the use of wine. **1838** *Encycl. Brit.* (ed. 7) XVII. 453/2 *Phrenitic*, a term used to denote those who, without being absolutely mad, are subject to such strong sallies of imagination as in some measure pervert their judgment. **1893** *Syd. Soc. Lex., Phrenitic*, belonging to phrenitis.

† **phre'nition.** *Obs. rare.* [irreg. f. PHRENITIS.] Frenzy; rage.

1642 H. MORE *Song of Soul* I. III. viii, The fourth of furious fashion Phrenition hight, fraught with impatiencies.

‖**phrenitis** (frɪ'naɪtɪs). *Path.* [Late L. *phrenītis*, a. Gr. φρενῖτις delirium, f. φρήν, φρεν- mind + -ITIS. Cf. F. *phrénite.*] Inflammation of the brain or of its membranes, attended with delirium and fever; brain fever.

1621 BURTON *Anat. Mel.* I. i. I. iv, *Phrenitis*,..is a disease of the mind, with a continual madness or dotage,..or else an inflammation of the brain. **1684** BOYLE *Porousn. Anim. & Solid Bod.* iii. 28 Oftentimes the matter,..being discharged upon some internal parts of the Head, produces a Delirium or Phrenitis. **1841** BREWSTER *Mart. Sc.* III. ii. (1856) 187 His wife was seized with fever, epilepsy and phrenitis.

phreno-, before a vowel **phren-**, a. Gr. φρενο- (combining form of φρήν, stem φρεν-, midriff, mind), an element of Greek compounds, and of modern scientific and technical words, usually in sense of 'the mind, mental faculties'.

phre'nalgia [Gr. ἄλγος pain], acute mental distress; psychalgia; melancholia. **phreno'colic** *a.* [Gr. κόλον COLON[1]], pertaining to both the diaphragm and the colon, as in ***phrenocolic*** (also *pleurocolic*) ***ligament*** (*Syd. Soc. Lex.* 1893). **phreno'gastric** *a. Anat.* as in ***phrenogastric ligament***, = GASTROPHRENIC *a.* (Mayne *Expos. Lex.* 1858, *Syd. Soc. Lex.*). **'phrenogram**, the curve or tracing made by the phrenograph (Webster 1902). **'phrenograph**, (*a*) an instrument for recording the movements of the diaphragm in respiration; (*b*) a phrenological description or 'chart' of a person's mental characteristics. **phre'nography**, the observation and description of phenomena in comparative psychology. **phreno-'hypnotism** (see quot. and HYPNOTISM). **phreno-'magnetism**, the excitation of the phrenological organs by magnetic influence; hence **phreno-mag'netic** *a.* **phreno-'mesmerism**, the excitation of the powers of the brain by mesmeric influence. **phrenonar'cosis** [Gr. νάρκωσις a benumbing], Schultz's term for a dulling of the senses or intellect; a state of stupor (Mayne, *Syd. Soc. Lex.*) **phre'nonomy** [Gr. -νομια distribution, management], the deductive and predictive part of comparative psychology. **phrenopa'ralysis** = *phrenoplegy* (*Syd. Soc. Lex.*). **phre'nopathy** [-PATHY] disease of the mind; so **phreno'pathic** *a.* **phrenophysi'ognomist**, one skilled in phrenophysiognomy. **phrenophysi'ognomy**, a combination of phrenology and physiognomy. **'phrenoplegy** [Gr. φρενοπλήξ, -πληγ- stricken in mind, f. πληγή stroke], sudden failing of the mind; disturbance of mental balance (Mayne, *Syd. Soc. Lex.*). **phreno'splenic** *a. Anat.*, of or pertaining to the diaphragm and the spleen (Mayne, *Syd. Soc. Lex.*). **phreno'tropic** *a.* = PSYCHOTROPIC *a.*

1890 BILLINGS *Nat. Med. Dict.*, *Phrenalgia. **1899** *Allbutt's Syst. Med.* VIII. 361 Melancholia and Hypochondriasis, Syn[onyms]—In the older English writers Lypemania and Phrenalgia. **1893** *Syd. Soc. Lex.*, **Phrenograph*..Rosenthal's lever..he used it to demonstrate the stoppage of those movements produced by faradisation of the cut end of the vagus nerve. **1896** *Voice* (N.Y.) 13 Feb. 6/6 A phrenograph of a famous French actress, lately in this city. **1881** *Smithson. Inst. Rep.* 501 Observing and descriptive stage... *Phrenography... Inductive and classifying stage... Phrenology... Deductive and predictive stage... Phrenonomy. **1896** *Cosmopolitan* XX. 368/2 Adding to the magnetizer's equipment the extravagant doctrine of *phreno-hypnotism: the excitation of the phrenological organs by pressing various points on the heads of hypnotized subjects. **1845** G. MOORE *Power of Soul over Body* (1846) 161 Assuming all that is related of *phreno-magnetism and neurypnology to be true. **1854** HUXLEY *Lay Serm.* v. (1870) 99 The simple physiological phænomena known as spirit-rapping, table-turning, phreno-magnetism. **1855** SMEDLEY, etc. *Occult Sc.* 240 *note*, It was not necessary to resort to *phreno-mesmerism. **1858** MAYNE *Expos. Lex., Phreno-Magnetism, Phreno-Mesmerism*, terms for a combination of two assumed branches of science embracing the rationalities of Phrenology and more questionable pretensions of Mesmerism. **1881** *Phrenonomy [see *phrenography*]. **1858** MAYNE *Expos. Lex.*, *Phrenopathia*,..*phrenopathy. **1899** *Allbutt's Syst. Med.* VIII. 197 The various types and classes of the phrenopathies. **1892** MISS A. J. OPPENHEIM in *Daily News* 4 Aug. 6/6 A scientific *phreno-physiognomist... To explain *phreno-physiognomy from a scientific point of view. **1956** *Phrenotropic [see PSYCHOTROPIC *a.*]. **1957** *Ann. N.Y. Acad. Sci.* LXVI. 765 Ibogaine began to be of interest to us in connection with its possible phrenotropic activity.

†**phre'nologer.** *Obs.* [f. PHRENOLOG-Y + -ER[1].] One who practises phrenology, a phrenologist.

1846 in WORCESTER (citing *Phren. Jrnl.*). **1849** H. MILLER *Footpr. Creat.* xiv. (1874) 265 Low-minded materialists and shallow phrenologers.

phrenologic (frɛnəʊ'lɒdʒɪk), *a. rare.* [f. as prec. + -IC. In mod.F. *phrénologique*.] Of or belonging to phrenology.

1821 *Joseph the Book-Man* 12 For learned Phrenologic lore Were needful such a man t' explore. *a* **1845** HOOD *Craniology* iii, These men I say, make quick appliance And close, to phrenologic science.

phrenological (frɛnəʊ'lɒdʒɪkəl), *a.* [f. as prec. + -AL[1].] Of or pertaining to phrenology; connected with or relating to phrenology.

1823 (*title*) Phrenological Journal. **1836-7** SIR W. HAMILTON *Metaph.* I. App. ii, When I publish the results [of my enquiry] they will disprove a hundred times over all the phrenological assertions in regard to the cerebellum. **1870** DICKENS *E. Drood* xvii, As to the phrenological formation of the backs of their heads.

Hence **phreno'logically** *adv.*

1838 E. FITZGERALD *Lett.* (1889) I. 44 Phrenologically speaking, he must be fully and equally furnished with the bumps of ideality and causality. **1846** POE *G. Bush* Wks. 1864 III. 23 The forehead, phrenologically, indicates causality and comparison, with deficient ideality.

phrenologist (frɪ'nɒlədʒɪst). [f. PHRENOLOG-Y + -IST. In mod.F. *phrénologiste* (1875 in Littré).] One skilled in phrenology.

1815 T. FORSTER in *Pamphleteer* V. 222 The Phrenologist admits an arrangement of certain organs, which gives us free-will. **1850** KINGSLEY *Alt. Locke* i, Call it.. conformation of the brain..if you are..a phrenologist. **1876** C. M. DAVIES *Unorth. Lond.* 33 A collection of heads that would have delighted a phrenologist.

phrenologize (frɪ'nɒlədʒaɪz), *v.* [f. as prec. + -IZE.]

1. *trans.* To treat or locate phrenologically. **b.** *humorous.* To produce 'bumps' or protuberances (on the head) by blows.

1848 *Blackw. Mag.* LXIII. 262 You emerged with a broken hat, and a head phrenologised by a blacking bottle. **1858** J. W. DONALDSON *Lit. Greece* III. 13 He not only made the soul a mere function of the body, but even phrenologized it by placing it in the forehead.

2. To examine or analyse phrenologically.

1860 O. W. HOLMES *Prof. Breakf.-t.* viii, It only remained to be phrenologized. **1895** *Daily News* 22 Nov. 4/7 Burns's skull was phrenologised.

phrenology (frɪ'nɒlədʒɪ). [f. Gr. φρήν, φρεν- mind + -LOGY; lit. 'mental science'; in F. *phrénologie* (Gall 1818, Hatz.-Darm.), Ger. *phrenologie*.] The scientific study or theory of the mental faculties (quots. 1815, 1881); *spec.* (and in ordinary use), the theory originated by Gall and Spurzheim, that the mental powers of the individual consist of separate faculties, each of which has its organ and location in a definite region of the surface of the brain, the size or development of which is commensurate with the development of the particular faculty; hence, the study of the external conformation of the cranium as an index to the development and position of these organs, and thus of the degree of development of the various faculties.

1815 T. FORSTER (*title pamph.* in *Pamphleteer* V. 219), Sketch of the new Anatomy and Physiology of the Brain and Nervous System of Drs. Gall and Spurzheim, considered as comprehending a complete system of Phrenology. *Ibid.* 222 The objection therefore falls to the ground, which accuses the new Phrenology of supporting the doctrine of Fatalism. [When reprinted in the same year, 'Phrenology' was altered to 'Zoonomy'.] **1817** *Blackw. Mag.* I. 367 The word Craniology is an invention of Spurzheim's enemies. It is not of the bone he treats, but of the manifestations of the mind as dependent on organization. Phrenology would be a more appropriate word. **1819** G. COMBE *Ess. Phrenol.* Introd., The real subject of the system is the Human Mind: I have therefore adopted the term 'Phrenology'..as the most appropriate, and that which Dr. Spurzheim has for some years employed. **1841-4** EMERSON *Ess.*, *Nature* Wks. (Bohn) I. 228 Astronomy to the selfish becomes astrology;..and anatomy and physiology become phrenology and palmistry. **1866** BRANDE & COX *Dict. Sc.*, etc. II. 896/1 By forcing the inductive method of enquiry into mental philosophy, phrenology has laid the foundations of a true mental science. **1881** *Smithsonian Inst. Rep.* (1883) 499 Again, we find this being [man] endowed with a set of faculties called intellectual, allied in certain particulars to those of the lower animals, but so far transcending them as to form a separate branch of study, requiring totally diverse methods and machinery of observation, and enlisting an entirely different set of investigators. To all these studies we have given the name of Comparative Psychology or Phrenology.

'**phrenosin.** *Chem.* [f. Gr. φρήν, φρεν- mind + -OSE + -IN[1] (after *myosin*).] A substance ($C_{34}H_{67}NO_8$) obtained from the brain.

1878 KINGZETT *Anim. Chem.* xv. 305 To the first of these Thudichum reserves the name of cerebrine, the second he terms phrenosine, and the third kerasine.

phrensical, phrensy, -zy, etc., var. of FRENZICAL, FRENZY.

†**phrentic, -ick(e,** obs. syncopated f. PHRENETIC = FRANTIC *a.* and *sb.*

a. 1547-94 [see FRANTIC *a.*]. **1621** BRATHWAIT *Nat. Embassie* (1877) 121 To moue his phrenticke passions to remorse. **1702** FLOYER *Cold Bathing* I. iv. (1709) 143 A Phrentick Fever..cured by Bathing the Head with Cold Water. **1716** M. DAVIES *Athen. Brit.* III. *Arianism* 56 When this Phrentick Arian had published his Original Evidence.

b. 1565-1695 [see FRANTIC *sb.*]. **1707** FLOYER *Physic. Pulse-Watch* 109 The Pulse of the Phrentic is small.

‖**phronesis** (frəʊ'niːsɪs). [a. Gr. φρόνησις thinking, understanding, intelligence, perception, practical sense, etc., f. φρονεῖν to think, be in one's senses, etc., f. φρον-, ablaut of φρεν-, stem of φρήν mind.] Understanding, practical judgement.

1890 in *Cent. Dict.* **1893** in *Syd. Soc. Lex.*

phro'netal, *a. Biol.* [mod. f. Gr. type *φρονητής thinker (f. φρονεῖν to think: see prec.) + -AL[1].] (See quot.)

1904 J. MCCABE tr. *Haeckel's Wonders of Life* 14, I propose to call the sensory-cells or sense-centres *æsthetal cells*, and the thought-cells or thought-centres *phronetal cells*.

phrontist ('frɒntɪst). *rare.* [ad. Gr. φροντιστής a deep thinker (Aristoph. *Nub.* 267), f. φροντίζειν to be thoughtful, f. φροντίς thought.] One who is devoted to meditation and study; a deep thinker: by Aristophanes ironically applied to Socrates.

1822 T. MITCHELL *Comm. Aristoph.* II. 18 Wieland is led to conclude, that before Aristophanes applied the term *phrontist* to Socrates and his friends, the word itself was not in common use.

phrontistery ('frɒntɪstərɪ). Often in Gr. or Latinized forms **phronti'sterion, phronti'sterium** (7 **fron-**). [ad. Gr. φροντιστήριον, f. φροντιστής: see prec.] A place for thinking or studying; a 'thinking shop': a term applied by Aristophanes in ridicule to the school of Socrates; hence applied to modern educational institutions.

1614 TOMKIS *Albumazar* I. iii. Biij b, 'Tis the learn'd Phrontisterion Of most Divine Albumazar. **1624** BP. HALL *Gt. Impostor* Wks. 501, I know where I am; in one of the famous Phrontisteries of Law, and Iustice. *a* **1634** RANDOLPH *Muses' Looking-Gl.* III. i, 'Twill be the great Gymnasium of the realme, The Frontisterium of Great Britany. **1672** D. T. *Answ. Eachard's Cont. Clergy* 136 England's grand Phrontisteries, Seminaries and Seed-plots of Learning..Oxford and Cambridge. **1845** MAURICE *Mor. & Met. Philos.* in *Encycl. Metrop.* (1847) II. 583/1 The maps and geometrical instruments which the old Athenian found in the phrontisterium. **1881** CHURCH *MS. Let.* 12 May, In the first brilliant days of Oriel..it used to be called half in compliment and half in sneer the φροντιστήριον. **1888** *Amer. Jrnl. Philol.* IX. 344 As to the scenery [in the old Greek comedies], he holds that the inside of the phrontistery is never seen.

‖**Phryganea** (frɪ'geɪniːə). *Entom.* [mod.L., f. Gr. φρυγανίς or φρύγανον a dry stick, in reference to the stick-like appearance of the larva-cases.] A genus of neuropterous insects, typical of the family *Phryganeidæ* or caddis-flies.

1855 KINGSLEY *Glaucus* 159 As the caddis-baits appear at the top of the water as alder-flies and sedge-flies (*Phryganeæ*).

Hence **phryganeid** (frɪgə'niːɪd) *a.*, of or pertaining to the caddis-flies; *sb.*, any member of the *Phryganeidæ*; **phry'ganeoid** *a.*, resembling or akin to the *Phryganeidæ*.

Phrygian ('frɪdʒɪən), *a.* (*sb.*) [ad. L. *Phrygiānus*, f. *Phrygia*: see -AN.] **A.** *adj.* **a.** Of or pertaining to Phrygia, an ancient country of Asia Minor, or its inhabitants.

Phrygian mode (*Mus.*): (*a*) One of the ancient Greek modes, of a warlike character, supposed to have been derived from the ancient Phrygians; (*b*) The second of the 'authentic' ecclesiastical modes, having its 'final' on E and 'dominant' on C.

1579 E. K. *Gloss. Spenser's Sheph. Cal.* Oct. 27 The.. Musitian playd the Phrygian melodie. **1674** PLAYFORD *Skill Mus.* I. 59 The Phrygian Mood was a more warlike and couragious kind of Musick, expressing the Musick of Trumpets and other Instruments of old, exciting to Arms. **1807** ROBINSON *Archæol. Græca* V. xxiii. 534 In music.. there were four principal νόμοι or modes; the Phrygian, the Lydian, the Doric, and the Ionic... The Phrygian mode was religious. **1826** ELMES *Dict. Fine Arts*, *Phrygian Marble*, called likewise Synnadique, was either white or red. *Phrygian Stone*, a substance..employed..in the process of dyeing.

b. Applied to a conical cap or bonnet with the peak bent or turned over in front, worn by the ancient Phrygians, and in modern times identified with the 'cap of liberty'.

1796 STRUTT *Dresses & Habits of Eng.* I. I. i. 12 The cap, most commonly worn by the Saxons..bears no distant resemblance to the ancient Phrygian bonnet. **1846** FAIRHOLT *Costume* (1860) 50 Figure 2 gives us the Phrygian-shaped cap, borrowed from classic costume. *Ibid.* 482 A head of Paris in the Phrygian cap has been copied.

B. *sb.* **a.** A native or inhabitant of Phrygia. **b.** One of a Christian sect of the second century, a CATAPHRYGIAN.

a **1490** J. SKELTON tr. *Diodorus Siculus' Bibliotheca Historica* (1956) I. IV. 293 Than went she downe throughout by all the lande of the Phirigians vnto the grete see. **1585-7** T. ROGERS *39 Art.* (Parker Soc.) 158 This truth is gainsaid by the Phrygians. **1837** *Encycl. Brit.* (ed. 7) XV. 426/2 *Montanists*..are sometimes styled Phrygians and Cataphrygians. **1963** *Times* 12 Jan. 9/6 It sounded like an Aesop's fable (and it occurred suddenly to me that Aesop, a Phrygian, had lived near Sivrihisar). **1966** G. E. BEAN *Aegean Turkey* v. 125 This was a time of good relations between the Phrygians and the Greeks, when King Midas was the first barbarian to make an offering at Delphi.

c. The Indo-European language of the ancient Phrygians.

1791 W. JONES in *Asiatick Researches* (1792) III. 14 A drum is called *dindima* both in Sanscrit and Phrygian. **1888** J. WRIGHT tr. *Brugmann's Elem. Compar. Gram. Indo-Gmc. Lang.* I. 3 Of others we have only very scanty fragments left, ..as of Phrygian. **1933** C. D. BUCK *Compar. Gram. Greek & Latin* 13 Phrygian is known, apart from proper names and glosses, from a few old inscriptions in an archaic Greek alphabet and some others of Christian times. **1967** M. SCHLAUCH *Language* ii. 28 Among the Indo-European languages no longer spoken, some are known to us from inscriptions (for instance, Thracian and Phrygian). **1972** W. B. LOCKWOOD *Panorama Indo-European Lang.* 174 Early or Old Phrygian survives in nearly 25 short inscriptions of doubtful date (perhaps eighth to sixth centuries B.C.) written in an alphabet of an archaic Greek type. A more recent form of the language, Late or New Phrygian, is found in about a hundred inscriptions in the Greek alphabet dating from the first three centuries A.D.

Phrygianize ('frɪdʒ(ɪ)ənaɪz), *v.* [f. prec. + -IZE.]

1. *trans.* To make Phrygian in character.

1893 W. M. RAMSAY *Ch. Rom. Emp.* xvii. 438 The natural tendency of the Phrygians to Phrygianise their beliefs.

2. *fig.* To frizzle.

1836 LANDOR *Pericles & Aspasia* liii. Wks. 1846 II. 376/1 But whenever an obvious and natural thought presents itself, they either reject it for coming without imagination, or they *phrygianize* it with such biting and hot curling-irons, that it rolls itself up impenetrably. **1869** DOWDEN *Stud. Lit.* (1890) 182 He [Landor] never Phrygianized (to borrow his own word) an obvious and natural thought.

†'**Phrygic,** *a. Obs. rare.* [ad. assumed L. **Phrygic-us* for *Phrygius* PHRYGIAN.] = PHRYGIAN *a.*

1638 SIR T. HERBERT *Trav.* (ed. 2) 125 The Bells, brasse Cimbals, kettle musick and whistles, storming such a Phrygick discord.

phthalaldehyde (fθæ'lældɪhaɪd). *Chem.* [f. PHTHAL(IC *a.* + ALDEHYDE.] Any of three isomeric compounds of formula $C_8H_6O_2$ having two formyl groups bonded directly to a benzene ring; *spec.* the *ortho* isomer, a yellow crystalline solid.

1886 *Jrnl. Chem. Soc.* L. 455 By the oxidation of phthalic alcohol with chromic mixture, a thick, viscid oil is obtained containing phthalaldehyde, phthalide, and unaltered phthalic alcohol. All attempts to isolate phthalaldehyde from this mixture were fruitless. **1942** *Jrnl. Amer. Chem. Soc.* LXIV. 315 (*heading*) A new synthesis of phthalaldehydes. **1951** I. L. FINAR *Org. Chem.* I. xxix. 586 When treated with ozone, naphthalene forms the diozonide and this, on treatment with water, gives phthalaldehyde. **1967** L. F. & M. FIESER *Reagents for Org. Synthesis* I. 740, *o*-Phthalaldehyde reacts with nitromethane in alcoholic alkali to give, after acidification yellow 2-nitro-3-hydroxyindene.

phthalazine ('fθæləziːn). *Chem.* [ad. G. *phtalazin* (C. Liebermann 1886, in *Ber. d. Deut. Chem. Ges.* XIX. 766), f. *phtal-* (cf. *phthal-* s.v. PHTHALIC *a.*) + *azin* AZINE.] A colourless, crystalline, heterocyclic base, $C_8H_6N_2$; also, any derivative of this.

1893 *Jrnl. Chem. Soc.* LXIV. I. 347 The bye-product obtained in methylating phthalazine is very similar to the last compound. **1929** [see CINNOLINE]. **1947** *Nature* 11 Jan. 53/2 Phthalazine derivatives are formed by the action of excess sodium hydroxide on the diazosulphonate derived from diazotized *p*-nitro-aniline and *β*-naphthol-l-sulphonic acid. **1956** I. L. FINAR *Org. Chem.* II. xii. 468 Phthalazines are formed by heating the benzoyl derivative of benzaldehyde hydrazones. *Ibid.* xix. 706 Thus there are probably four $C_8H_4N_2$ units, each having an *iso*indole structure,..or a phthalazine structure. **1970** W. F. BEECH *Fibre-Reactive Dyes* v. 175 Phthalazines. In this series also only one compound has so far become of importance for making reactive dyes, viz. 1, 4-dichlorophthalazine-6-carbonyl chloride.

phthalic ('fθælɪk), *a. Chem.* [Abbreviated from NAPHTHALIC.] Of, pertaining to, or obtained from naphthalene, as *phthalic anhydride*, etc. ***phthalic acid***, a white crystalline compound ($C_8H_6O_4$) produced by the action of nitric acid on naphthalene, alizarin, purpurin, etc.; also called ALIZARIC *acid*. ***phthalic anhydride***, the anhydride of phthalic acid, a white crystalline solid, $C_8H_4O_3$, which is made industrially by the catalytic oxidation of naphthalene or *o*-xylene, and is widely used in the manufacture of plastics, resins, dyes, etc.

1855 W. ODLING tr. *Laurent's Chem. Method* 53 Thus we can obtain in a direct manner the..tartaric, camphoric, succinic, phthalic, &c., anhydrides. **1857** MILLER *Elem. Chem.* III. 575 Phthalic or Naphthalic Acid..is produced by the long-continued action of nitric acid upon naphthalin. **1859** H. WATTS tr. *Gmelin's Hand-bk. Chem.* XIII. 15 Phthalic anhydride forms long white needles having the lustre of silk and united in feathery groups. **1873** —— *Fownes' Chem.* (ed. 11) 766 The xylenes are converted into Phthalic acids. **1885** REMSEN *Org. Chem.* (1888) 244 We may select either the three xylenes or the three phthalic acids. **1913** THORPE *Dict. Appl. Chem.* (ed. 2) IV. 251/2 Owing to the extensive use of phthalic anhydride in the manufacture of synthetic indigo..a cheap technical process for its preparation in large quantities was essential. **1945** H. BARRON *Mod. Plastics* xxvii. 559 Glycerine and phthalic anhydride are the two most important constituents for alkyd resins. **1966** R. M. STEPHENSON *Introd. Chem. Process Industries* xvi. 329 About 459 million pounds of phthalic anhydride were produced in the United States in 1963.

So, from base **phthal-**: **phthalamic** (fθə'læmɪk) *a.* [see AMIC], derived from or containing phthalic acid and ammonia: in ***phthalamic acid***, a crystalline acid ($C_8H_7NO_3$) produced by the action of aqueous ammonia on phthalic anhydride. **'phthalate**, a salt of phthalic acid. **phthalein** ('fθælɪɪn) [see -IN[1]], one of a series of organic dyes produced by combining phthalic anhydride with the phenols, with elimination of water. **phthalide** ('fθælaɪd) [-IDE, here short for *anhydride*], the anhydrous form of phthalic acid, a white crystalline substance, $C_8H_4O_3$ = $C_6H_4(CO)_2O$, obtained by distilling the acid. **'phthalimide** [see IMIDE], a derivative of ammonia in which two atoms of hydrogen are replaced by phthalyl; a colourless crystalline inodorous and tasteless body, $C_8H_4O_2{\cdot}NH$. **phthalin** ('fθælɪn) [see -IN[1]], a colourless crystalline substance obtained from phthalein (see quot.). **phthalyl** ('fθælɪl) [see -YL], the radical of phthalic acid ($C_8H_4O_2$).

1857 MILLER *Elem. Chem.* III. 231 *Phthalamic acid (amidated phthalic acid). **1866** WATTS *Dict. Chem.* IV. 627 *Phthalamic acid*.. crystallizes in a mass of fine flexible needles, forming an acid solution with water. *Ibid.* 628 **Phthalates*, Phthalic acid is dibasic, forming acid salts, $C_8H_5MO_4$, and neutral salts, $C_8H_4M_2O_4$. **1875** *Ibid.* VII. 977 Potassium phthalate is easily decomposed [by an electric current]. **1877** WATTS *Fownes' Chem.* (ed. 12) II. 499 **Phthaleins*..compounds formed, with elimination of water, by the combination of phenols with phthalic anhydride. **1904** *Daily Chron.* 20 Jan. 3/6 Aniline blues and violets were followed by phthaleïne and the great group of azo and cotton dyes. **1857** MILLER *Elem. Chem.* III. 231 *Phthalimide, $HN.C_{16}H_4O_4$. **1875** WATTS *Dict. Chem.* VII. 977 By the action of nascent hydrogen the phthaleins are converted into colourless compounds called *phthalins, which by oxidation in the air, are reconverted into phthaleins. **1866** *Ibid.* IV. 633 Chloride of *phthalyl.

phthalocyanine (fθæləʊ'saɪəniːn). *Chem.* [f. PHTHAL(IC *a.* + -O + CYANINE.] **a.** A greenish-blue crystalline porphyrin, $C_{32}H_{18}N_8$, or any of its substituted derivatives. **b.** Any of the metal chelate complexes of these, which form a large and important class of pigments and dyes ranging in colour from green to blue.

1933 R. P. LINSTEAD in *Rep. Brit. Assoc. Adv. Sci.* 465 When phthalimide is heated with certain metals,..in a current of ammonia, a complex reaction occurs with the formation of highly coloured substances of a novel type. These have been named phthalocyanines from their origin and deep-blue colour,..The metal may be eliminated from the magnesium compound..to yield phthalocyanine, the parent substance of the group. **1942** *Endeavour* I. 80/2 Phthalocyanines, themselves entirely products of the chemist's skill, have resemblances to two important substances which occur abundantly in nature. **1961** COCKETT & HILTON *Dyeing of Cellulosic Fibres* v. 207 Copper phthalocyanine is the important pigment Monastral Blue BS, the lead compound being Monastral Green. **1972** RYS & ZOLLINGER *Fund. Chem. & Applic. Dyes* vii. 97 Because of their good fastness properties phthalocyanines are suitable for almost all processes in which pigments are used.

c. phthalocyanine blue (also with capital initials), copper phthalocyanine, an important blue pigment; **phthalocyanine green** (also with capital initials), a chlorinated (or brominated) derivative of copper phthalocyanine, important as a green pigment.

1942 E. R. ALLEN in J. J. Mattiello *Protective & Decorative Coatings* II. viii. 261 Likewise phthalocyanine green shows a somewhat similar relationship to orthodox pigments. **1947** L. S. PRATT *Chem. & Physics Org. Pigments* ii. 8 Other pigments which also contributed to this change were..very recently the benzidine yellows and phthalocyanine blues and greens. **1967** V. STRAUSS *Printing Industry* ix. 592/2 The development of phthalocyanine blue, perhaps better known under its duPont trade-mark as Monastral blue, was one of the greatest achievements in the field of pigments. **1968** KIRK & OTHMER *Encycl. Chem. Technol.* (ed. 2) XV. 491 Phthalocyanine green (Pigment Green 7, CI 74260) is a polychlorinated copper phthalocyanine containing about fourteen atoms of chlorine. The most usual shade is the G type although there are several shades in the G range, representing slight variations in degree of chlorination or particle size and shape. *Ibid.*, Two yellower shades of green are available as Phthalocyanine Green 27... In these types, part of the chlorine has been replaced by bromine. **1970** [see MONASTRAL]. **1972** *Materials & Technol.* V. xi. 359 Phthalocyanine blues are intense blues which are not used in full colour because bronzing develops... Two forms are used, beta phthalocyanine blue of relatively green shade,.. and the less stable alpha phthalocyanine blue, of a redder shade.

phthalylsulphathiazole (ˌfθælɪlsʌlfə'θaɪəzəʊl). *Pharm.* Also (*U.S.*) **-sulfa-**. [f. PHTHALYL + SULPHATHIAZOLE.] A sulphonamide drug, $HOOC{\cdot}C_6H_4{\cdot}CONH{\cdot}C_6H_4{\cdot}SO_2NH{\cdot}C_3H_2NS$, that is a whitish powder and is used to suppress bacteria in the gastro-intestinal tract.

1943 POTH & ROSS in *Federation Proc.* II. 89/2 An extension of the studies on acylated sulfonamides as intestinal antiseptics..has uncovered another effective derivative of this series of drugs, phthalylsulfathiazole. **1961** M. HYNES *Med. Bacteriol.* (ed. 7) x. 138 Inabsorbable compounds (e.g., phthalyl-sulphathiazole) are available for oral treatment of intestinal infections. **1970** PASSMORE & ROBSON *Compan. Med. Stud.* II. xx. 25/1 Succinylsulphathiazole and p[h]thalysulphathiazole are both poorly absorbed from the gastrointestinal tract and have been advocated for the treatment of intestinal infections and for prophylactic use in elective operations on the colon. **1977** *Proc. R. Soc. Med.* LXX. 482/1 The preliminary results of this study have shown that a combination of oral phthalylsulphathiazole and metronidazole for preparation of the bowel for surgery reduces the incidence of postoperative infection compared with phthalylsulphathiazole alone.

phthanite ('fθænaɪt). *Min.* [a. F. *phthanite*: named by Haüy 1822 (*phtanite*), f. Gr. φθάν-ειν to anticipate + -ITE[1], 'because its thick schistoid texture and argillaceous character seem to announce beforehand its passage into schist' (*Traité de Mineral* (ed. 2) IV. 546). Dana spells it *-yte*, as being the name not of a mineral but of a rock.] A hard compact rock, consisting essentially of cryptocrystalline silica.

1868 DANA *Min.* 195 Cryptocrystalline Varieties [of Quartz]..13. *Basanite, Lydian Stone* or *Touchstone*, a velvety black siliceous stone..passes into a compact fissile, siliceous, or flinty rock, of grayish and other colors, called siliceous slate, and also Phthanyte.

†**'phthartic**, *a.* *Med. Obs.* [ad. mod.L. *phthartic-us*, a. Gr. φθαρτικ-ός destructive, f. φθείρειν to destroy.] Destructive, deadly.

1858 in MAYNE *Expos. Lex.* **1893** *Syd. Soc. Lex.*, *Phthartic*, deadly, deleterious. Formerly applied to poisons.

phthinode ('fθɪnəʊd). *Path.* [ad. Gr. φθινώδης consumptive, f. φθινο- wasting, decaying; see -ODE[1].] One subject to or suffering from phthisis. So **'phthinoid** *a.*, of or pertaining to phthinodes.

1870 S. GEE *Auscult. & Percuss.* I. ii. 14 The thorax of phthinodes (persons predisposed to phthisis) is, as Galen says, narrow and shallow. *Ibid.* 16 The phthinoid chests are natural deformities.

phthinoplasm ('fθɪnəʊplæz(ə)m). *Path.* [f. Gr. φθινο- wasting, decaying + -PLASM.] (See quot.)

1871 C. J. WILLIAMS *Pulmon. Consumpt.* i. 6 All are due to the presence of various kinds of *phthinoplasm*, a withering or decaying modification of the proper plasma or formative material of the body. [*Note*] I have found it necessary to coin this word,..to give expression to one of the leading ideas of this book, and to avoid the common use of the word *tubercle*.

phthiocol ('fθaɪəkɒl). *Biochem.* [f. PHTHI(SIS + -O + *-col* (perh. f. al*col*ol).] A yellow crystalline pigment, 3-hydroxy-2-methyl-1,4-naphthoquinone, $C_{11}H_8O_3$, originally isolated from tubercle bacilli, which has the action of vitamin K.

1933 ANDERSON & NEWMAN in *Jrnl. Biol. Chem.* CIII. 197 In order to indicate its origin, we propose to designate the pigment by the name phthiocol. **1954** H. J. ALMQUIST in Sebrell & Harris *Vitamins* II. ix. 393 Synthetic phthiocol tested with vitamin K-deficient chicks was found to be distinctly active in restoring normal blood-clotting time and thus became the first completely identified form of vitamin K. **1960** A. E. BENDER *Dict. Nutrition* 133/2 Natural vitamin K chemically is a phylloquinone... The synthetic materials, menadione..and phthiocol (2-methyl-3-hydroxy-1:4-naphthoquinone), are more active than the naturally occurring vitamins. **1964** ASSELINEAU & LEDERER in V. C. Barry *Chemotherapy of Tuberculosis* i. 21 Phthiocol.. isolated..after saponification of mycobacterial fat, is an artefact, produced from a vitamin K-like polyisoprenoid naphthoquinone.

phthioic (fθaɪ'əʊɪk), *a.* *Biochem.* [f. PHTHI(SIS + -OIC.] ***phthioic acid***: a yellowish oil, now known to be a mixture of fatty acids, which was orig. obtained from tubercle bacilli and is capable of inducing the symptoms of tuberculosis; hence, any of these constituent acids or their synthetic derivatives.

1929 R. J. ANDERSON in *Jrnl. Biol. Chem.* LXXXIII. 171 In order to indicate the relation of this acid to tuberculosis we wish to designate it by the name phthioic acid. **1946** *Nature* 5 Oct. 489/1 Phthioic acid $C_{26}H_{52}O_2$, is a liquid saturated fatty acid isolated from the lipoids of tubercle bacilli. **1951** *Chem. & Industry* 11 Aug. 685/1 Recent work on the fatty acids of the lipins of tubercle bacilli has shown that Anderson's phthioic acid was a mixture. **1964** W. PAGEL et al. *Pulmonary Tuberculosis* (ed. 4) ii. 31 Phthioic acids synthetized [*sic*] by Robinson (1946) were shown to produce necrosis and granulomata in guinea-pigs.

‖**phthiriasis** (fθ-, θaɪərɪ'eɪsɪs). *Path.* Also 9 phtheir-. [L., a. Gr. φθειρίασις lousiness, morbus pedicularis, f. φθειριᾶν to be lousy.] A morbid condition of the body in which lice multiply excessively, causing extreme irritation; pediculosis.

1598 SYLVESTER *Du Bartas* II. i. III. *Furies* 507 But with the griefs that charge our outward places Shall I account the loathsome Phthiriasis? *a* **1656** USSHER *Ann.* (1658) 245 Calisthenes..fell there sick of the Phthiriasis, or lowsie disease. **1774** GOLDSM. *Nat. Hist.* (1862) II. I. iv. 458 The Phthiriasis... Herod, Antiochus Epiphanes,..Cassander, Callisthenes, and Sylla, all died of this disorder. **1861** HULME tr. *Moquin-Tandon* II. VI. i. 295 Lice of Sick Persons —Pediculus Tabescentium... This name has been proposed for a louse which gives rise to a disease termed Phthiriasis.

phthirophagous (fθ-, θaɪ'rɒfəgəs), *a.* Also phtheiro-, *erron.* phthirio-. [f. mod.L. *phthīrophagus* sb., f. Gr. φθείρ louse + -φάγος eating: see -PHAGOUS; in F. *phthirophage*.] Louse-eating.

1858 MAYNE *Expos. Lex.* 951/1 Phthiriophagous. **1886** GUILLEMARD *Cruise Marchesa* II. 263 These Alfuros were phtheirophagous, going over the dense mat adorning their heads with the most praiseworthy perseverance. **1899** *Brit. Med. Jrnl.* 4 Nov. 1278 Lice..caused little inconvenience and afforded employment to the phtheirophagous natives.

†**phthisiatry.** *Med. Obs. rare*[−1]. [f. PHTHISI(S + Gr. ἰατρεία healing, medical treatment, f. ἰατρός healer.] = PHTHISIOTHERAPY.

1928 *Amer. Rev. Tuberculosis* XVIII. 105 The method can give genuinely beneficial results, and its possibilities should always be valuable in phthisiatry.

phthisic ('tɪzɪk), *sb.* and *a.* Now *rare.* Forms: α. 4–5 tysyk, tisyk, -ik(e, 5 tyseke, -ik, 6 tysyc, -ike, tisicke, tissike, 7 tissick(e, -ique, tisick, tizzick, tysick(e, thisicke. β. 5 ptisike, 6 ptisique, ptysyke, 6–7 ptisicke, 7 ptysick, pthysic(k, -isicke, 7–8 ptisick, 8 ptysic. γ. 6 phthisik(e, -icke, 6–8 -ick, 7 -ysique, phtisique, -ick, 8 phthysick, 8– phthisic. [ME. *tisik(e* sb., a. OF. *tisike, -ique*, later *ptisique, thisique* = It., Sp. *tisica* consumption, phthisis, repr. a Romanic *phthisica, thisica* sb. fem., absolute use of *phthisic-us, -a, -um* adj., a. Gr. φθισικ-ός consumptive, f. φθίσις PHTHISIS. OF. had also the adj. *tisike, tesike* (11th c. in Littré, 13th c. in Hatz.-Darm.), *ptisique*, mod.F. *phtisique, phthisique*; the F. sb. is now *phthisie*. The current pronunciation has come down from the ME. *tisik*.]

A. *sb.* **1.** A wasting disease of the lungs; pulmonary consumption.

α. **1340** HAMPOLE *Pr. Consc.* 701 Many yvels..Als fevyr, dropsy, and launys, Tysyk, goute and other maladys. *c* **1400** *Lanfranc's Cirurg.* 164 Men þat ben hurt in þe lungis fallip in þe tisik. **1551** TURNER *Herbal* I. F iv b, It is also good for the tysyc. **1607** TOPSELL *Four-f. Beasts* (1658) 536 The milk of a sow..is also good against the bloudy flux and tissick. **1656** EARL MONM. tr. *Boccalini's Advts. fr. Parnass.* 41 Hectick Feavers and Tissicks. *a* **1683** OLDHAM *Poet. Wks.* (1686) 44 But count all Reprobate..Whom he, when Gout or Tissick Rage, shall curse.

β. *c* **1450** *Trevisa's Barth. De P.R.* VII. xxxi. (Bodl. MS.), Ptisike is consumcioun and wasting of kinde humours of þe bodie. Euerich þat haþ tisike haþ etike. **1572** J. JONES *Bathes of Bath* Pref. 2 Some with Ptisique, Stone, Strangurie [etc.]. **1669** WORLIDGE *Syst. Agric.* (1681) 297 The North-wind.. is injurious to the Cough, Ptisick, and Gout. **1762–71** H. WALPOLE *Vertue's Anecd. Paint.* (1786) III. 225 Being troubled with a ptysic, he retired to Marybone.

γ. **1576** BAKER *Jewell of Health* 58 The Phthisick or Sore in the Lunges with a Consumption of all the bodie. **1693** *Phil. Trans.* XVII. 1002 Of the various Kinds and Causes of the Phthisick. **1756** C. LUCAS *Ess. Waters* III. 367 A variety of pulmonic phthisics. **1844** *Blackw. Mag.* LVI. 199 If he left off without having thrown himself into a phthisic.

†**2.** Loosely applied to various lung or throat affections; a severe cough; asthma. *Obs.*

?*a* **1412** LYDG. *Two Merch.* 315 Drye tisyk is withal partable. *c* **1430** —— *Min. Poems* (Percy Soc.) 51 A drye tysik makith old men ful feynt. **1432–50** tr. *Higden* (Rolls) IV. 287 Herode Ascalonite..was vexede..with vermyn commenge from his secrete membres, with a stynche intollerable, and with a violente tisike. **1641** MILTON *Animadv.* 8 When liberty of speaking..was girded and straight lac't almost to a broken-winded tizzick. *a* **1741** CHALKLEY *Wks.* (1766) 286 A sore Fit of the Asthma or Phthysick.

B. *adj.* = PHTHISICAL *a.*

1398 TREVISA *Barth. De P.R.* V. xxii. (Bodl. MS.), Tisike men alwey cowȝeþ for þe boch of þe lunges. **1587** MASCALL *Govt. Cattle, Hogges* (1627) 263 They wil haue the disease of the lights, which is, to bee pursie and ptisicke. **1610** BARROUGH *Meth. Physick* II. xii. (1639) 90 You must prescribe to those that be ptisick, a convenient diet. **1694** *Phil. Trans.* XVIII. 280 In Hectick, Phthisick, and Asthmatick cases. **1859** SALA *Tw. round Clock* (1861) 372 His colleague's accordion is suspended in the midst of a phthisic wheeze.

phthisical ('tɪzɪkəl), *a.* Forms: 7 tizicall, ptisical(l, phthysical, 7–8 tissical, 7– phthisical, 8 pht-, pthisical. [f. prec. + -AL[1].] Of the nature of or pertaining to phthisis.

1611 COTGR., *Phtisique*, Tysicall. **1658** R. WHITE tr. *Digby's Powd. Symp.* (1660) 40 Half of them who dye in London, dye of phthisicall and pulmonicall distempers. **1659** T. PECKE *Parnassi Puerp.* 174 When Tissical distempers stopt my Breath. **1793** BEDDOES *Consumpt.* 135 The phthisical inflammation may so alter the structure of the lungs. **1839** RAMADGE *Curab. Consumpt.* (1861) 52 There was old phthisical disease in the summit of both lungs.

b. Of persons: Affected with or having a tendency to phthisis; consumptive. Of a house: where phthisis exists.

1651 FRENCH *Distill.* ii. 50 This Water..is very good for those that are ptisicall. **1709–10** ADDISON *Tatler* No. 121 ¶1 Poor Cupid..has always been Phtisical, and..we are afraid it will end in a Consumption. **1843** R. J. GRAVES *Syst. Clin. Med.* xxiii. 283 You will frequently find that he will die phthisical. **1899** *Times* 14 Jan. 8/6 The visitation of phthisical houses was not only practicable, but was of as great importance to the public weal as similar visits in houses where fever or enteric fever had occurred.

c. *fig.*

1642 MILTON *Apol. Smect.* iii. 28 He will bestow on us a pretty modell of himselfe: and sobs me out halfe a dozen tizicall mottoes where ever he had them. *a* **1849** H. COLERIDGE *Poems* (1850) II. 254 His wasp-stung wits were grown so quaint and phthisical. **1887** *Fortn. Rev.* Sept. 427 That phthisical Idealism which claimed the empire in despite of Nature.

phthisicky ('tɪzɪkɪ), *a.* [f. PHTHISIC + -Y.] Phthisical, consumptive; asthmatic; wheezy.

1697 *Lond. Gaz.* No. 3322/4 Stolen by a Ptisicky middle-sized Man. **1722** *Ibid.* No. 6119/3 He..has a Ptysicky Cough. **1777** LIGHTFOOT *Flora Scot.* I. 382 Found successful in pthisicky complaints. **1897** *Outing* (U.S.) XXIX. 594/1 Diminutive and phthisicky mules, wheezing for breath.

†**phthisiogenesis** (fθ-, θɪzɪəʊ'dʒɛnɪsɪs). *Med. Obs.* [f. PHTHISI(S + -O + GENESIS.] The causation and development of phthisis. Hence †,**phthisioge'netic** *a.*, causing or pertaining to the development of phthisis.

1904 C. BOLDUAN tr. *E. von Behring's Suppression of Tuberculosis* 45 Observations concerning the study of phthisiogenesis in man and animals. *Ibid.* 46 Improbability, so far as importance as a phthisiogenetic factor is concerned, of a primary bronchial..Tb infection. **1924** *Amer. Rev. Tuberculosis: Abstr. Tuberculosis* X. 24/2 Experimental studies on phthisiogenesis.—Inoculation of human tubercle bacilli into the tonsils or soft palate in rabbits of different ages resulted in a tuberculosis running the course of pulmonary phthisis. **1936** *Univ. Durham Coll. of Medicine Gaz.* XXXVI. 128 The study of phthisiogenesis involves the reconciliation of..much discordant data.

phthisiology (fθ-, θɪzɪ'ɒlədʒɪ). *Med.* [f. PHTHISI-S + -(O)LOGY.] The science or study of phthisis, or a treatise thereon. Hence **phthisio'logical** *a.*; **phthisi'ologist**, a specialist in phthisiology.

1842 DUNGLISON *Med. Lex.*, *Phthisiology*, a treatise on phthisis. **1858** in MAYNE *Expos. Lex.* **1893** *Syd. Soc. Lex.*, *Phthisiology*, the scientific study of Phthisis. **1913** *Q. Jrnl. Med.* VI. 259 Artificial pneumothorax has become the topic of the day in phthisiological literature. **1928** *Amer. Rev. Tuberculosis* XVIII. 110 The general conclusions..were not accepted at once by phthisiologists. **1946** H. T. HYMAN *Integrated Pract. Med.* III. civ. 2208 The indications for inducing an artificial pneumothorax are best discussed by the practitioner with the consultant phthisiologist. **1947** *Ibid.* IV. clxxxii. 3901 In the larger medical communities and fully staffed institutions, internal medicine is subdivided... Thus there are established departments of gastro-enterology, hematology,..phthisiology, metabolism, [etc.]. **1953** *Tubercle* XXXIV. 237/1 It is most deplorable that phthisiologists ever applied and accepted so wrong and unfitting a term [*sc.* therapeutic 'collapse'] to a condition which in fact is no 'collapse' at all. **1957** F. R. G. HEAF *Symposium of Tuberculosis* p. xv, The amount of disablement caused by bone and joint tuberculosis in overseas countries is very great, so the chapter dealing with this subject should be of value to the general physician and surgeon, as well as the specialist in phthisiology.

phthisiophobia (fθ-, θɪzɪəʊ'fəʊbɪə). *Med.* [f. as next + -PHOBIA.] An unjustified or exaggerated fear of tuberculosis.

1906 J. B. HUBER *Consumption* xi. 445 It is really deplorable to consider the degree of cruelty and selfishness to which this phthisiophobia has driven people. **1948** F. M. POTTENGER *Tuberculosis* xxxvi. 579 If we frighten people into believing that tuberculosis is a highly infectious disease.., we create an unnecessary and harmful phthisiophobia, which reacts against the patient.

†**phthisiotherapy** (fθ-, θɪzɪəʊ'θɛrəpɪ). *Med. Obs.* [f. PHTHISI(S + -O + THERAPY.] The medical treatment of phthisis. Also ,**phthisiothera'peutics** *sb. pl.*

1899 S. A. KNOPF *Pulmonary Tuberculosis* xix. 284 Modern phthisio-therapeutics, as carried out in well-equipped sanatoria, must be practically studied. **1900** DORLAND *Med. Dict.* 505/1 Phthisiotherapy. **1903** *Med. Rec.* (N.Y.) 2 May 719/1 There is abundant evidence..of his deep interest in phthisiotherapy. **1934** *Amer. Rev. Tuberculosis* XXX. 188 The maintenance by each sizeable sanatorium of a resident thoracic surgeon whose special training in phthisiotherapy can be relied upon to aid in careful selection of suitable cases for surgical collapse.

Hence ,**phthisiothera'peutist**, **phthisio'therapist**, a specialist in or practitioner of phthisiotherapy.

1899 S. A. KNOPF *Pulmonary Tuberculosis* xix. 285 The peculiar psychological state of nearly all phthisical patients ..makes it necessary for the true phthisiotherapeutist..to be..his best and most confidential friend. **1907** *Med. Rec.* (N.Y.) 9 Nov. 758/2 The pneumatic cabinet..although long since discarded by most phthisio-therapists, has been persistently used by a few. **1929** *Amer. Rev. Tuberculosis* XIX. 76 There are some phthisiotherapists..who advocate rib-resection in lieu of pneumothorax. **1933** *Jrnl. Amer. Med. Assoc.* 4 Feb. 313/1 Collapse therapy is considered by the majority of expert phthisiotherapists to have created a revolution in the treatment of pulmonary tuberculosis. **1939** *Amer. Rev. Tuberculosis* XXXIX. 162 The value of artificial pneumothorax in closing open cavities is admitted by every phthisiotherapeutist.

‖**phthisis** ('θaɪsɪs, 'fθɪsɪs). *Path.* Also 6 ptisys, -is, 7–8 pthisis, 8 phthysis. [L. (Celsus), a. Gr. φθίσις wasting, consumption, f. φθίνειν (root φθι-) to decay, waste away. In mod. F. *phthisie.*] A progressive wasting disease; *spec.* pulmonary consumption: see quot. 1873

[**1525** tr. *Brunswyke's Surg.* L iij b/2 Dothe the parsone falle in ptisym and to outdryeng of the naturall moystnes. **1527** ANDREW *Brunswyke's Distyll. Waters* D j. Ptisim, that is a brethe comynge of the longues.] **1543** TRAHERON *Vigo's Chirurg.* (1586) 448 Phthisis, in greke signifieth wasting..a consumption as we call it. **1616** SURFL. & MARKH. *Country Farme* 728 Another kind of disease with which birds are troubled, is called the subtle disease, Pthisis. **1793** BEDDOES *Consumption* 130 The inconsiderable number of sailors who die of phthisis. **1873** T. H. GREEN *Introd. Pathol.* (ed. 2) 300 By pulmonary phthisis is understood a disease of the lungs which is characterized by progressive consolidation of the pulmonary texture, and by the subsequent softening and disintegration of the consolidated tissue.

attrib. **1898** *Allbutt's Syst. Med.* V. 157 In several towns the phthisis death-rate had undergone a notable decrease since the introduction of an improved system of sewerage. **1901** *Westm. Gaz.* 6 Aug. 2/1 A number of phthisis patients.

b. With defining word, applied to tuberculosis of various organs.

1846 G. E. DAY tr. *Simon's Anim. Chem.* II. 92, I made an analysis of pus which was discharged with the urine in [a case of] phthisis vesicæ. **1893** *Syd. Soc. Lex.*, *Abdominal Phthisis*..1. Intestinal tuberculosis..2. Peritoneal tuberculosis. *Ibid.*, *Dust Phthisis*, a variety of fibroid phthisis set up by..dust..in certain industries.

c. *fig.*

1881 J. MARTINEAU *Ess.*, etc. (1891) IV. 302 The delirium of passion, the grasp of cupidity, the phthisis of romance.

phthisozoics (fθaɪsəʊ'zəʊɪks). *rare.* [erron. for *phthirozoics*, f. Gr. φθείρ-ειν to destroy + ζῷον animal.] The art of destroying noxious animals.

1816 BENTHAM *Chrestom.* 50 *Phthisozoics*,..the art of destroying such of the inferior animals, as, in the character of natural enemies, threaten destruction, or damage, to himself, or to animals [useful to him]. *a* **1843** SOUTHEY *Doctor* (1847) VII. ccxxviii. 325 A science which Jeremy the thrice illustrious Bentham calls Phthisozoics.

phthongal (fθ-, 'θɒŋgəl), *a. rare.* [f. Gr. φθόγγ-ος a sound, the voice + -AL[1].] Of or pertaining to a sound; consisting of a sound; vocal.

1875 WHITNEY *Life Lang.* iv. 62 These are their sonant (or vocal, phthongal, intonated) counterparts.

phthon'gometer. *rare.* [f. as prec. + -METER.] A measurer of the intensity of vowel sounds.

1837 WHEWELL *Hist. Induct. Sc.* (1857) II. 266 We may.. consider this instrument as a phthongometer, or measure of vowel quality. **1848** in SMART *Supp.*, and in later Dicts.

†**phthore.** *Obs. Chem.* [a. F. *phthore*, ad. Gr. φθορά destruction, f. φθείρ-ειν to destroy, corrupt.] Old name for the element FLUORINE, because of the corrosive action of hydrofluoric acid. Hence †'**phthoric** *a.*, fluoric; †'**phthorine**, fluorine.

1858 MAYNE *Expos. Lex.*, *Phthoricus*...applied by Guibourt to..binary compounds, in which..fluor, or fluorine, performs the part of a negative element: phthoric. *Ibid.*, *Phthorina*, *Chem.*, term for the presumed base of fluoric acid..: phthorine. **1895** *Funk's Stand. Dict.*, *Phtor.*

†**phu.** *Obs.* [a. F. *phu*, a. L. *phū* (Plin.), a. Gr. φοῦ valerian.] The Garden Valerian or Cretan Spikenard, *Valeriana Phu.*

1562 TURNER *Herbal* II. 86 Phu, which som call also wild Spiknard, groweth in Pontus, and it hath a lefe lyke vnto.. Alexander. **1607** TOPSELL *Four-f. Beasts* (1658) 81 The herb Valerian (commonly called Phu). *Ibid.* 532 Mingle..these hearbs following, Agrimony, Rue, Phu, Scabious, Betony. **1753** CHAMBERS *Cycl. Supp.*, *Phu*, in botany, a name by which some authors call the great garden valerian.

phugh, var. PHEW *int.*

phugoid ('fju:gɔɪd), *a.* and *sb.* [f. Gr. φυγή flight (*sb.*[2]: erron. taken for FLIGHT *sb.*[1]) + -OID.]

A. *adj.* Of or pertaining to the longitudinal stability of an aircraft flying a nominally horizontal course in a vertical plane; applied *spec.* to a slow fore-and-aft oscillation in which the flight path assumes the form of a series of shallow waves and the aircraft undergoes synchronous increases and decreases of speed.

1908 F. W. LANCHESTER *Aerodonetics* ii. 37 The Phugoid theory deals with the longitudinal stability, and the form and equations of the flight path of an aerodone. *Ibid.* 40 This is the general equation to the curves of flight or the phugoid equation. *Ibid.* iii. 59 The plotting of the phugoid curves forming a complete series, from the straight line representing the path of uniform gliding, to the tumbler type of curve with constants varying to any desired degree, may be termed a phugoid chart. **1920** *Flight* XII. 817/1 They would talk of bumps and pitching when, of course, they merely meant anabatics or katabatics, or peradventure nothing more serious than a phugoid oscillation. **1965** G. SUTTON *Mastery of Air* v. 125 The enhanced speed brings about an increase in lift, which ultimately stops the descent and causes the machine to climb again. At the top of the climb the machine has insufficient lift to maintain itself and if left alone will fall again and so on. This is the phugoid oscillation, consisting of a wave-like path or a series of loops. **1974** H. ASHLEY *Engin. Anal. Flight Vehicles* iii. 62 The latter situation arises..during the higher portion of the entry trajectory of a lifting glider. The long-period or phugoid longitudinal mode may then have a period as great as half the total interval required for entry.

B. *sb.* A phugoid oscillation.

1908 F. W. LANCHESTER *Aerodonetics* ii. 42 With these two equations we are in a position to investigate the general characteristics and particular forms of the curves of flight or Phugoids, as they may be appropriately termed. **1945** *Jrnl. R. Aeronaut. Soc.* XLIX. 346/1 He became so interested in a phugoid that he allowed it to develop beyond control, and he found himself spinning inverted at 33,000 feet. **1948** L. M. MILNE-THOMSON *Theoret. Aerodynamics* xvi. 309 A phugoid is the path of a particle which moves under gravity in a vertical plane and which is acted upon by a force L normal to the path and proportional to V^2, the square of the speed. **1975** L. J. CLANCY *Aerodynamics* xvi. 485 The consequence of the disturbance is an oscillation in which the aircraft successively gains and loses height, while losing and gaining forward speed. This oscillation is known as a phugoid.

‖**phulkari** ('p(h)u:lkari). *N. India* [a. Hindī *phūlkārī* a tissued flower on cloth, etc., f. *phūl* a flower + *-kār*, suffix of agent.] A kind of flower embroidery; a cloth or shawl so embroidered.

1872 B. H. BADEN-POWELL *Hand-bk. Econ. Products of Punjab* II. ix. 100/1 'Phúlkárí' (*lit.* 'flower work') scarf, value Rs. 11. *Ibid.* x. 106 Over the head is thrown a 'chádar' of coarse cloth, prettily embroidered in many colored silks, called 'phulkári'. **1887** H. G. H. BLACKWOOD *Jrnl.* 1 Dec. in *Our Viceregal Life in India* (1889) II. xiii. 224 They were collected in a small inner court, which was hung with the pretty phulcarries they make here. **1888** MRS. F. A. STEEL in *Jrnl. Indian Art* II. 72 Intending purchasers..should remember that *phulkari* work is a true art. *Ibid.*, *Phulkaris* are still a necessary part of a Hindu and Sikh bride's trousseau. **1890** in *Cent. Dict.* **1893** G. BIRDWOOD in *Catal. Loan Exhib. Embroidery by Indian Women* (Soc. Encouragement Indian Art) 15, I did not know of any needlework being produced by the women of India for sale, excepting the *phul-kāri* (*i.e.*, 'flower-work'). **1896** YOUNGSON *40 Yrs. Punjab Mission* ii. 11 Phulkaries, or shawls of coarse cloth tastefully adorned with silk by the women, are worn. **1969** *Eve's Weekly* (Bombay) 20 Dec. 43/1 Another in magenta white and saffron phulkari against brown is styled on the same lines. **1969** *Femina* (Bombay) 26 Dec. 8/4 She had revived an old art like the 'phulkari'... The applique work was bold and mirror work pretty. **1971** *Sunday Australian* 8 Aug. 46 Phulkari embroidery is the traditional work used on all the linen items in a girl's glory box.

phulwara: see FULWA.

Phurnacite ('fɜ:nəsaɪt). Also **phurnacite**. A proprietary name for a kind of smokeless fuel made by carbonizing briquettes at relatively low temperatures.

1937 *Trade Marks Jrnl.* 10 Feb. 150/1 Phurnacite... Powell Duffryn Associated Collieries, Limited,..London, ..colliery owners. **1951** *Good Housek. Home Encycl.* 32/1 Smokeless fuel, the bulk of which is known as Phurnacite. **1952** *Economist* 1 Nov. 332/2 The favourite small coals of the domestic consumer—anthracite and the best briquettes—remain scarce. The board [*sc.* the National Coal Board] still has only one—now considerably enlarged—plant making 'phurnacite', which is an excellent but expensive carbonised briquette. **1955** *Times* 4 July 5/5 Welsh coals..and 'Phurnacite', a member of the manufactured fuel group, are still restricted, but coke, 'Coalite', and 'Rexo' are said to be freely available. **1976** *Guardian* 10 Apr. 10/8 The coalman poured the sack of phurnacite into the bunker.

phusee, phusy, obs. erron. ff. FUSEE[2], wheel of a watch.

phut (fʌt), *int.* (*adv.*, *sb.*) Also fut. [Echoic, but cf. Hindi and Urdu *phatnā* to split or burst.] An imitation of a dull, abrupt sound, esp. that of a firearm. Phr. *to go phut*: to come to a sudden end; to break down, cease to function. Also as *sb.*, the sound of something 'going phut'.

1888 KIPLING *Story of Gadsbys* (1889) 55 The whole thing went *phut*. She wrote to say that there had been a mistake. **1892** —— & BALESTIER *Naulahka* 259 The hospital has all gone *phut*. **1898** STEEVENS *With Kitchener to Khartum* 143 Thud! went the first gun, and phutt! came faintly back, as its shell burst on the zariba. **1898** J. M. FALKNER *Moonfleet* ix. 125 There came a flash of fire..and a fut, fut, fut, of bullets in the turf. **1905** *Blackw. Mag.* July 57/2 **1908** A. S. M. HUTCHINSON *Once aboard Lugger* III. iii. 150 The plans.. have all gone fut. **1917** 'CONTACT' *Airman's Outings* 242 He will sometimes hear the rattle of a mysterious machine-gun, or even the phut of a bullet. **1917** W. J. LOCKE *Red Planet* xiii. 156 There's a limit to the power of bearing strain. As soon as you feel you're likely to go *fut*, throw it all up and come and see me. **1918** A. QUILLER-COUCH *Foe-Farrell* 47 'It's a lie!' Foe was on his legs, and he fairly shouted it. Shell-shock? Phut!—It exploded right at our feet below the platform. **1919** G. PAGE *Veldt Trail* i. 10 The carburetter went *fut* yesterday. **1921** *Punch* 30 Nov. 429/1 Send me a subject with a bit more pep in it or the Club will go phut. **1923** *Daily Mail* 22 Jan. 8 He stood to lose some enormous number of millions of marks if Germany went *phut*. **1926** S. HORLER *Order of Octopus* 238 Now that this pet stunt..had gone phut. **1931** E. F. Benson *Mapp & Lucia* x. 270 She'd still have been terribly interested in life till she went phut. **1972** *Daily Tel.* (Colour Suppl.) 24 Nov. 7/3 The kids had broken a window, and the colour television had gone phut. **1973** H. Carvic *Miss Seeton Sings* (1974) 72 The trigger pulled and—*phut*, the enemy dropped dead. *Ibid.* 83 Never before had this place been used for target practice, with things that went *phut*. **1978** D. Bloodworth *Crosstalk* xxi. 164 It was a bomb... But when it went off it was only like some kind of firecracker, just, you know—phut!—and that was it.

Hence **phut** *v. intr.*, to land with an abrupt sound; of a bullet: to land with a dull abrupt sound; to 'go phut', to cease to function.

1901 *Westm. Gaz.* 3 Jan. 2/1 The bullets..came more thickly now, squealing over our heads and futting on the ground between the horses' hoofs. **1916** G. Frankau *Guns* 26 Waking, they know the instant foe, the bullets phutting by. **1959** J. Verney *Friday's Tunnel* xxvii. 250 He and Robin ..got inside last night, only the torch phutted.

phut-phut, *sb.* and *v.* [Reduplication of prec.] = put-put *sb.*, *v.*

1951 M. R. Anand *Seven Summers* 78 The sahibs who came on bicycles or 'phut-phuties'. **1952** R. Finlayson *Schooner came to Atia* 144 Phut-phut goes the exhaust. **1956** 'J. Wyndham' *Seeds of Time* 39 He listened to the phut-phutting of the old engine. **1958** J. Carew *Black Midas* vi. 103 The motor sputtered, then settled down to a steady phut-phutting. **1958** *Spectator* 10 Oct. 479/2 People on the outskirts would receive less noise from a VTOL airliner than from a clip-on phut-phut passing along the road outside their houses. *a* **1966** M. Allingham *Cargo of Eagles* (1968) xi. 129, I dropped over on my phut-phut about half past eight. **1971** *Guardian* 14 May 11/1 Phutt-putting around London on her three-wheeled scooter. **1977** P. Harcourt *At High Risk* i. 93 The schoolkids were streaming out of the *lycée* and tearing up the street on their phut-phutting *quarante-neufs*.

† **phuz**, erron. f. fuzz, loose volatile matter.

1716 M. Davies *Athen. Brit.* III. *Arianism* 60 One continu'd Phuz of Canting Contradictions and sad Aspersions.

phwat, repr. an Ir. pronunc. of what *pron.*, etc.

1898 J. D. Brayshaw *Slum Silhouettes* ii. 12 Oh, murther aloive! Phwat did ye do that for? **1914** R. Brooke *Let.* Nov. (1968) 630 'How many handkerchiefs have you?'..'How many phwat, sorr?' **1920** 'Sapper' *Bull-Dog Drummond* vi. 154 And phwat the divil has that got to do with it, at all? **1936** M. Franklin *All that Swagger* xvii. 164 But seeing phwat has happened, I can do no other.

phy, obs. erron. form of fie *int.*

phy (faɪ), slang abbrev. of physeptone.

1971 *Guardian* 30 Mar. 11/6 There is thus now a completely new group [of drug addicts in Britain] on methadone, or 'phy' (physeptone is the British word for which the World Health Organisation title, methadone, is being substituted). **1973** *Times* 22 Mar. 6/2 She said to him: 'Do you want some phy (Physeptone)?' and made it quite clear that she meant the drug.

phycic ('faɪsɪk), *a. Chem.* [f. Gr. φῦκ-ος fucus, seaweed + -ic.] In *phycic acid*, a crystalline body extracted from *Protococcus vulgaris* by alcohol, colourless, somewhat unctuous to the touch, tasteless, inodorous, and permanent in the air.

1864-8 Watts *Dict. Chem.* II. 504 The mother-liquor of the phycic acid which is deposited on cooling, separates. **1866-8** *Ibid.* IV. 633 Phycic acid dissolves in strong sulphuric acid, and is reprecipitated by water.

phycite ('faɪsaɪt). *Chem.* [f. as prec. + -ite[1] 4.] A sweet-tasting crystalline substance ($C_4H_{10}O_4$) extracted from *Protococcus vulgaris*; also called *erythromannite*. Hence in extended sense (see quot. 1866-8).

1864-8 Watts *Dict. Chem.* II. 504 The substance from *Protococcus vulgaris* was originally called phycite. **1866-8** *Ibid.* IV. 633 The term phycite has lately been extended by Carius to the series of tetratomic alcohols..homologous with natural phycite.

phyco- ('faɪkəʊ), combining form of Gr. φῦκος (L. *fūcus*) seaweed, used in the formation of modern scientific terms relating to seaweeds or algæ.

phycochrom ('faɪkəkrɒm), a species or individual of the order *Phycochromaceæ* or *Cryptophyceæ* of *Algæ* or seaweeds; so **phycochro'maceous** *a.*, of or pertaining to this order. **phycochrome** ('faɪkəˌkrəʊm), the bluish-green colouring matter of some algæ, being chlorophyll modified by an admixture of phycocyanin. **phycocyan** (ˌfaɪkəʊ'saɪən), **phyco-'cyanin, phycocy'anogen**, the blue colouring matter which is combined with chlorophyll in certain algæ, as *Phycochromaceæ*, and gives to them their bluish-green colour. **ˌphyco-'erythrin**, the red colouring matter found similarly in *Florideæ*, and giving to them their reddish colour. **phy'cography** [-graphy], systematic description of seaweeds (*Cassell's Encycl. Dict.* 1886). **phyco'hæmatin** (see quot.). **phyco'logical** *a.*, of, pertaining to, or dealing with, phycology. **phy'cology** [-logy], the branch of botany treating of seaweeds or algæ; algology; so **phy'cologist**, a student of phycology; an algologist. **phycomater** (faɪkəʊ'meɪtə(r)): see quots. **phycomycetous** (ˌfaɪkəʊmaɪ'siːtəs) *a.*, of or pertaining to the *Phycomyceteæ*, a division of Fungi, mostly parasitic, of which the genus *Phycomyces* is the type. **phyco'phæin** [Gr. φαιός dusky], a reddish-brown pigment found in the olive-brown seaweeds, as the *Fucaceæ* and *Phæosporeæ*. **'phycoplast** *Cytology* [-plast], an array of microtubules found between pairs of nuclei in algal cells after mitosis (see quot. 1972). **phyco'xanthin** [xanthin], a yellow colouring-matter, = diatomin.

1888 *Amer. Naturalist* Aug. 671 The *Phycochroms never reach as great a size as do members of each of the other sections. **1873** *Q. Jrnl. Microsc. Sci.* 221 The cultivation of *phycochromaceous gonidia obtained from lichens of a different nature. **1880** *Nature* 26 Feb. 391/1 Desmideae, Diatomaceae, and phycochromaceous forms furnish no less than 600 out of the total 794 species. **1874** Cooke *Fungi* 12 The green matter originally arises within the primary chlorophyll- or *phycochrom-bearing cellule. **1875** Bennett & Dyer tr. *Sachs' Bot.* 273 Certain parasitic Ascomycetes penetrate them [certain Algæ]..and often form an intimate attachment with those..cells which contain phycochrome (as *Plectospora, Omphalaria*). **1866-8** Watts *Dict. Chem.* IV. 633 **Phycocyan*, and *Phycoerythrin*, these names are applied by Kützing to a blue and red colouring matter, apparently of the same composition, existing in several red sea-weeds. **1873** H. C. Sorby in *Proc. Roy. Soc.* XXI. 464 Phycocyan gives a spectrum with a well-marked absorption-band in the orange, and has a very intense red fluorescence. **1875** Bennett & Dyer tr. *Sachs' Bot.* 216 The *phycocyanine is diffused from dead or ruptured cells, and thus produces, for example, the blue stains on the paper round herbarium specimens of *Oscillatoriæ*. **1881** Watts *Dict. Chem.* VIII. 1637 *True *Phycocyanogen*, with a distinct absorption-band in the orange, and a narrow one in the red, imparting to the solution a very intense red fluorescence. **1873** H. C. Sorby in *Proc. Roy. Soc.* XXI. 464 **Phycoerythrine Group*... I.. call one pink phycoerythrine and the other red phycoerythrine. Neither are fluorescent, and both are soluble in water. **1866-8** Watts *Dict. Chem.* IV. 633 **Phycohæmatin*, a red colouring matter, obtained by Kützing from *Rytiplæa tinctoria*. It is extracted from the fresh alga. **1892** (*title*) *Phycological memoirs, being researches made in the Botanical Department of the British Museum. Edited by George Murray. **1895** J. D. Hooker *Let.* 9 June in L. Huxley *Life J. D. Hooker* (1918) II. xli. 294, I have this morning received..a notice published in the 'Phycological Memoirs' of *Pachytheca*, which is enough to turn your hair grey—if it were not so already! **1954** *Nature* 14 Aug. 294/1 The botanical world, and more especially the phycological section of it, has suffered grievous loss in the passing of Prof. Fritsch. **1973** J. R. Stein (*title*) Hand-book of phycological methods. **1890** *Cent. Dict.*, *Phycologist. **1901** *Nature* 14 Feb. 377/1 The great Swedish phycologist. **1951** G. W. Prescott in G. M. Smith *Man. Phycology* i. 4 The marine phycologist Harvey..established many genera. **1969** *Brit. Phycological Jrnl.* IV. 141 Virtually the whole of his [*sc.* Hustedt's] career as a phycologist was devoted to diatoms. **1847** J. Lindley *Elem. Bot.* (ed. 5) p. lxx/2 *Phycology. That part of Botany which treats of Sea-weeds. **1892** *Nation* (N.Y.) 10 Nov. 360/3 *Algology*, another hybrid, is honored with a definition..while *Phycology*, the preferable word linguistically, is given only as a synonym. **1935** J. E. Tilden *Algae* p. v, Phycology offers an enormously stimulating field for research. **1951** G. W. Prescott in G. M. Smith *Man. Phycology* i. 1 The history of phycology is as old as the history of botany. **1976** *Biol. Abstr.* LXI. 6112/1 The history of marine phycology in New England (USA) is summarized, followed by citations emphasizing recent research dealing with the local marine algal vegetation. **1842** Brande *Dict. Sci.*, etc., *Phycomater*, the gelatine in which the sporules of Algaceous plants first vegetate. **1858** Mayne *Expos. Lex.*, *Phycomater*, term for a single cell resting on semi-liquid substance, possessing the power of producing other cells similar to itself in form and composition out of the organic substances in which it grows. **1890** *Cent. Dict.*, *Phycomycetous. **1900** *Nature* 27 Sept. 540/1 The phycomycetous Fungi, and the siphonaceous Algæ..the vegetative body of which does not consist of cells. **1885** Goodale *Physiol. Bot.* (1892) 295 Analogous pigments extracted by water from algae of colors other than red have received the following names,—*phycophæine (brownish), phycocyanine (bluish), phycoxanthine (yellowish-brown). **1898** tr. *Strasburger's Bot.* 330 The cells of the Phæophyceæ..contain a brown pigment, phycophæin. **1972** J. D. Pickett-Heaps in *Cytobios* V. 63 Since this disposition of microtubules is so common in algae, I have coined the term '*phycoplast' to describe it. This implies that it can to some extent be considered an analogue of the higher plant cell phragmoplast, but its main distinguishing feature is the orientation of its constituent microtubules in the plane of cytoplasmic cleavage. **1975** *Nature* 6 Nov. 32/1 The unicellular condition, the possession of basal bodies, flagella, a closed centric spindle, a phycoplast and cell division by furrowing, are deemed to be primitive features. **1873** H. C. Sorby in *Proc. Roy. Soc.* XXI. 457 *Phycoxanthine. This name was first proposed by Kraus for a substance he obtained from *Oscillatoriæ*. **1875** Bennett & Dyer tr. *Sachs' Bot.* 216 The peculiar bluish- or brownish-green colour which the Nostocaceæ share with the Chroococcaceæ, is caused by a mixture of true chlorophyll with phycoxanthine and phycocyanine.

phycobilin (faɪkəʊ'baɪlɪn). *Bot.* [a. G. *phycobilin* (R. Lemberg 1929, in *Naturwissenschaften* XVII. 541/2): see phyco- and bilin.] **a.** Any of a group of compounds that are present in some algæ as prosthetic groups of chromoproteins such as phycocyanin and phycoerythrin. **b.** Also *phycobilin pigment*. Any of these chromoproteins.

1945 E. I. Rabinowitch *Photosynthesis* I. xv. 417 The separation of the chromophoric groups from the carrier protein was achieved by Lemberg (1929), who introduced the name 'phycobilins' because of the similarity between these chromophores and the bile pigments. **1950** *Jrnl. Gen. Physiol.* XXXIII. 418 Light absorbed by the phycobilin pigments (phycoerythrin and phycocyanin) is utilized with good efficiency. **1962** C. Ó hEocha in R. A. Lewin *Physiol. & Biochem. of Algae* xxv. 421 Photo-synthetically active red and blue biliproteins, called phycoerythrins and phycocyanins, respectively, have been isolated only from algae. Their prosthetic groups or chromophores are tetrapyrroles known as phycobilins. Unlike the chlorophylls, phycobilins are not readily released from associated proteins. **1965** Bell & Coombe tr. *Strasburger's Textbk. Bot.* 466 Rhodophyceae, red algae... Chlorophyll and the associated carotinoids..are masked by a red, strongly fluorescent, water-soluble pigment, phycoerythrin (a phycobilin..with absorption-bands differing from those in the Cyanophyceae). **1971** *Nature* 26 Nov. 232/1 One of the first obvious effects of nitrogen starvation in blue-green algae is the disappearance of phycobilin pigments, which normally constitute about 15% of the dry weight.

phycobiliprotein (ˌfaɪkəʊbaɪlɪ'prəʊtiːn). *Bot.* [f. prec. + protein.] Any chromoprotein having a phycobilin as the prosthetic group; a phycocyanin or a phycoerythrin.

1966 *Brookhaven Symp. Biol.* XIX. 402 The blue-green algae have predominantly phycocyanin as the major phycobiliprotein. **1975** *Nature* 24 Jan. 285/2 The chlorophylls, carotenoids and phycobiliproteins of the blue-green algae are particularly similar to those of the red algae.

phycobilisome (faɪkəʊ'baɪlɪsəʊm). *Bot.* [f. as prec. + -some[4].] In certain algæ, a photosynthetic granule containing phycobiliprotein.

1966 Gantt & Conti in *Brookhaven Symp. Biol.* XIX. 404 The following are the reasons for considering these chloroplast granules of *P[orphyridium] cruentum* as sites of phycobilin aggregation... For these granules we propose the name phycobilisomes. **1971** *Jrnl. Cell Biol.* XLVIII. 285/2 Whereas it is true that phycobilisomes have not yet been found in every species of red and blue-green algae, they are believed to exist in all photo-synthetic species of these two groups. **1976** *Nature* 24 June 697/2 Those [algal cells] from *Diplosoma virens*..show no evidence of phycobilisomes on the thylakoids.

phycobiont (faɪkəʊ'baɪɒnt). *Bot.* [f. phyco- + Gr. βιουντ-, pr. pple. stem of βιοῦν to live, f. βίος life.] The algal component of a lichen; any alga which is associated with a fungus to form a lichen.

1957 G. D. Scott in *Nature* 2 Mar. 486/2 Three new terms are here proposed... They are: (1) 'phycobiont', applicable to an alga in association with a fungus in the formation of a lichen; [etc.]. **1962** *New Scientist* 28 June 719/1 Efforts have previously been made to investigate the exact nature of the relationship between the algal partner (sometimes called the phycobiont) and the fungus. **1969**, **1973** [see mycobiont]. **1976** G. C. Ainsworth *Introd. Hist. Mycol.* iv. 98 The phycobiont frequently shows no apparent differences from its free-living counterpart.

phycomycete ('faɪkəʊmaɪsiːt). *Bot.* [sing. of mod.L. *Phycomycetes* (A. de Bary *Morphol. & Physiol. der Pilze* (1866) p. vi), f. phyco- + mycetes.] A fungus belonging to one of the primitive groups formerly included in the class Phycomycetes, nearly always characterized by a vegetative thallus without septa and either asexual reproduction by means of sporangiospores or conidia or sexual reproduction by means of oospores or zygospores. Also *attrib.* Cf. *phycomycetous* adj. s.v. phyco-.

[**1887** H. E. F. Garnsey tr. *A. de Bary's Compar. Morphol. & Biol. Fungi* iv. 132 Groups 1-4 [of the Ascomycete series] have been brought together under the name of Phycomycetes on account of their close approximation to the Algae.] **1932** *Bot. Gaz.* XCIII. 427 The attachment to the flagellum or flagella of the phycomycete zoospore is usually posterior or lateral. **1933** *Trans. Brit. Mycol. Soc.* XVIII. 199 (*heading*) *Azygozygum chlamydosporum* Nov. gen. et sp. A phycomycete associated with a diseased condition of *Antirrhinum majus*. *Ibid.* 201 The Phycomycete was isolated from several varieties of *Antirrhinum*. **1936** *Forestry* X. 14 All three species showed mycorrhizal infection of the well-known 'phycomycete type'. **1976** G. C. Ainsworth *Introd. Hist. Mycol.* ix. 236 The most important [aquatic fungi] taxonomically were the phycomycetes.

phycomycosis (ˌfaɪkəʊmaɪ'kəʊsɪs). *Path.* Pl. **-mycoses**. [f. phycomyc(ete + -osis.] Infection with or a disease caused by phycomycetes, esp. the genera *Mucor*, *Rhizopus*, or *Absidia*; mucormycosis.

1959 Lie-Kian-Joe et al. in *Amer. Jrnl. Clin. Path.* XXXII. 62/1 We use the name phycomycosis to designate a fungous infection caused by a member of the Phycomycetes. It is proposed in order to avoid the more restricted connotations of mucormycosis, and includes infections caused by Mucor, Absidia, Rhizopus, Mortierella, Basidiobolus, and similar Phycomycetes. The name is useful, too, for mycoses in which no culture was obtained but in which sections of involved tissues reveal the presence of a fungus with the morphology usually associated with a Phycomycete. **1965** [see mucormycosis]. **1972** *Radiology* CIII. 332/2 Craniofacial phycomycosis appears to originate by invasion of the nasal mucosa.

phygogalactic (ˌfɪgəʊgə'læktɪk), *a.* and *sb.* [f. Gr. φυγο- shunning (φεύγειν to flee, shun) + γαλακτ- milk: see galactic.] **a.** *adj.* Preventing

the secretion of milk, and promoting the reabsorption of milk already secreted. **b.** *sb.* A substance or drug having these qualities.
In mod. Dicts.

†**'phylacist.** *Obs. rare*⁻⁰. [ad. L. *phylacista* (Plaut.), ad. Gr. φυλακιστής jailer, f. φυλακή prison.]
1656 Blount *Glossogr.*, *Phylacist*, the keeper of a prison.

†**phy'lacter.** *Obs.* [a. Gr. φυλακτήρ guard: cf. F. *phylactère*: see next.] = PHYLACTERY.
1599 Sandys *Europæ Spec.* (1632) 225 Their Phylacters.. serving as Locall memories of the Law. **1604** Drayton *Owl* 621 Then of his knowledge in the cabalist,..Then of Philacters what their vertue be. **1647** Cleveland *Char. Lond. Diurn.* 44 Who place Religion in their Velam-eares; As in their Phylacters the Iewes did theirs. **1661** Morgan *Sph. Gentry* II. ii. 27 Ensigned with a Mytre,..and the Phylacters. [See PHYLACTERY 4.]
Hence †**phy'lactered** *ppl. a.*, furnished with a phylactery; in quot. *fig.*
1738 Matt. Green *Spleen* 19 Who for the spirit hug the spleen, Phylacter'd throughout all their mien.

phylacterian (fılæk'tɪərɪən). [f. L. *phylactēri-um*: see next + -AN.] (See quot.) So **phylacteric** (-'ɛrık), **-ical** *adjs.*, of or pertaining to phylacteries; **phy'lacterize** *v.* [ad. late Gr. φυλακτηρίζειν], *trans.* to guard or protect with a phylactery.
1616 T. Godwin *Moses & Aaron* I. x. (1625) 54 In the yeere of our Lord, 692. certaine Sorcerers were condemned for the like kind of Magick ['hanging the beginning of Saint Iohns Gospell about their necks'] by the name of φυλακτήριοι, that is, Phylacterians. **1698** L. Addison *Chr. Sacr.* 128 (R.) In their private or phylacterical prayers, it [Amen] was omitted. *a* **1641** Bp. Mountagu *Acts & Mon.* vii. (1642) 406 Εαυτους φυλακτηρίζουσιν, ἵνα τῶν δαιμόνων οὐδεὶς ἐφαψηται, They phylacterize, or blesse and defend themselves that no ill Spirit or Divell annoy them.

phylactery (fı'læktərı). Forms: 4 fil-, philaterie, 6 -eri, -ery, -ory, phylatorye, philacterie, 6–7 philactery, 7– phylactery (6–7 -ie). Also in med.L. forms philateria, -um, phil-, phylacterium. [ME. ad. L. *fyl-*, *phylactērium* (Vulg.), a. Gr. φυλακτήριον a watchman's post, a safeguard, an amulet, f. φυλακτήρ a guard, f. stem φυλακ- of φυλάσσειν to guard. Cf. OF. *filatiere* (12th c.), mod.F. *phylactère*.]
1. A small leathern box containing four texts of Scripture, Deut. vi. 4–9, xi. 13–21, Ex. xiii. 1–10, 11–16, written in Hebrew letters on vellum and, by a literal interpretation of the passages, worn by Jews during morning prayer on all days except the sabbath, as a reminder of the obligation to keep the law. Cf. Deut. xi. 18 'Ye shall bind them [my words] for a sign upon your hand, and they shall be for frontlets between your eyes.'
c **1380** Wyclif *Serm.* Sel. Wks. II. 61 In stede of philateries men maken gret volyms of newe lawes. **1382** —— *Matt.* xxiii. 5 Thei alargen her filateries [*gloss* that ben smale scrowis]. **1387** Trevisa *Higden* (Rolls) IV. 325 þey bere scrowes in her forhedes and in hir lift armes and cleped þe scrowes philateria; in þe scrowes were þe ten hestes. **1526** Tindale *Matt.* xxiii. 5 They sett abroade there philateris. **1548** Udall, etc. *Erasm. Par. Matt.* xxiii. 5 They walke vp and doune bearyng about brode Philacteries. **1581** Marbeck *Bk. Notes* 823 They ware in their foreheads scrowles of parchment, wherein were written the tenne commaundements giuen by God to Moses, which they called Philaterias. **1616** T. Godwin *Moses & Aaron* I. (1641) 42 There were..Phylacteries for the head, or frontlets, reaching from one ear to the other, and tied behind with a thong; and Phylacteries for the hand fastned upon the left arme above the elbow on the inside, that it might be neer the heart. **1821** Scott *Kenilw.* xxx, A broad girdle inscribed with characters like the phylacteries of the Hebrews. **1879** C. Geikie *Christ* xv. 156 Pharisees, with broad phylacteries.
b. *fig.* A reminder; a religious observance or profession of faith; an ostentatious or hypocritical display of piety or rectitude, a mark of Pharisaism; a burdensome traditional observance. Phrase: ***to make broad the phylactery*** (from Matt. xxiii. 5), to vaunt one's righteousness.
1645 Milton *Tetrach.* Introd. Addr. Parlt., I send him back again for a phylactery to stitch upon his arrogance. **1682** Sir T. Browne *Chr. Mor.* I. §21 Trust not to thy Remembrance in things which need Phylacteries. *Ibid.* III. §10 To thoughtful Observators the whole World is a Phylactery, and every thing we see an Item of the Wisdom ..of God. Happy are they who..make their Phylacteries speak in their Lives. **1687** Dryden *Hind & P.* I. 399 And Fathers, Counsels, Church, and Church's head, Were on her reverend Phylacteries read. **1847** Ld. Cockburn *Jrnl.* II. 189 Five statutes.., each of which tends in its way to disentangle us of the phylacteries of the feudal system. **1893** Morley in *Daily News* 3 Mar. 5/5 Mr. Russell..has worn his broadest phylacteries, used his most pharisaical language.
c. Erroneously applied to the fringe or the blue ribbon, which the Israelites were commanded to wear as a remembrancer (Num. xv. 38, 39); hence extended to a fringe or border generally.
1576 N. T. (Tomson) *Matt.* xxiii. 5 *note*, Phylacteries. —It was a thread, or ribband of blewe silke in the fringe of a corner, the beholding whereof made them to remember the Lawes and ordinances of God: and therefore was it called a phylacterie, as you would say, a keper. **1715** tr. *Pancirollus' Rerum Mem.* I. II. xiv. 97 The Flames had rambled to the Borders and the Phylacteries (as it were) of this Obelisk. **1878** B. Taylor *Deukalion* III. iii. 112 She walks, And droops her loosed phylacteries in the dust.
2. An amulet worn upon the person, as a preservative against disease, etc.; also *fig.* a charm, safeguard.
[**1693** tr. *Blancard's Phys. Dict.* (ed. 2), *Phylacterium*, a sort of Amulet, for the cure of Venomous Diseases.] **1809** Malkin *Gil Blas* x. vii. (Rtldg.) 355 Very good books,..a never-failing phylactery against the blue devils [F. *une ressource assurée contre l'ennui*]. **1850** Leitch tr. *C.O. Müller's Anc. Art* §436 (ed. 2) 628 The figure of Serapis was a customary phylacterion. **1852** Hook *Ch. Dict.* (1871) 585 Phylactery..properly denotes a preservative, such as pagans carried about to preserve them from evils, diseases, and dangers; for example, stones or pieces of metal engraved under certain aspects of the planets. **1860** —— *Lives Abps.* I. v. 223 The bishops..were required..to put down pagan observances, auguries, phylacteries, and incantations.
3. A vessel or case containing a holy relic.
1398 Trevisa *Barth. De P.R.* xix. cxxviii. (Add. MS. 27944) Philaterium is a litel vessel of glas oþer of Cristal in þe whiche holy relikes ben ikepte. **1520** in *Archæologia* LIII. 14 One phylatorye siluer and gylte..contenyng wᵗyn a bone of saynt Stephen. **1536** in *Antiq. Sarisb.* (1771) 194 One Philatory, long, ornate with silver,..standing on four feet, ..and containing a tooth of St. Macarius. **1869** Freeman *Norm. Conq.* III. App. 686 Harold is shown swearing between two chests or phylacteries.
4. In mediæval art, The inscribed scroll proceeding from a person's mouth or held by him, to indicate his words; *fig.* a record, a roll. Also, the label or infula of a mitre.
1855 tr. *Labarte's Arts Mid. Ages* ii. 74 The legends painted upon the phylacteries in painted glass. **1863** Cowden Clarke *Shaks. Char.* xvii. 423 Here is the phylactery of his vices—wily, wary, cold, calculating, indirect, faithless.
Hence **phy'lacteried** *a.*, furnished with phylacteries; also *fig.*
1841 *Tait's Mag.* VIII. 277 Without any phylacteried display of Independence and Non-intrusion oratory.

†**phy'lactic.** *Obs. rare.* [ad. Gr. φυλακτικός adj., having the quality of guarding, f. stem φυλακ- (see prec.).] A preservative; a prophylactic.
1706 Cary (*title*) A Physician's Phylactic, Against a Lawyer's Venefic: or, An Answer to a Book, abusively Entitled, *The Rights of the Christian Church, Asserted.*

phy'lactocarp. *Zool.* [f. Gr. φυλακτός, vbl. adj. f. φυλάσσειν to guard + καρπός fruit.] A 'fruit-case'; a receptacle in certain hydroids protecting the gonothecæ. Hence **phylacto'carpal** *a.*
1883 Allman in *Challenger Rep.* VII. III. 10 The term phylactocarp may be used as a..general expression for the various forms under which the apparatus destined for the protection of the gonangia shows itself in the phylactocarpal Plumularidæ... The commonest and longest known form of phylactocarp is the corbula of *Aglaophenia*. **1888** Rolleston & Jackson *Anim. Life* 759.

phylacto'læmatous, *a. Zool.* [f. mod.L. *Phylactolæmata* (f. Gr. φυλακτο-, f. φυλάσσειν to guard + λαιμός throat + L. *-āta* (pa. pple)) + -OUS.] Belonging to the *Phylactolæmata*, an order of Polyzoa, having the lophophore bilateral, and the mouth overhung by a small ciliated mobile lobe, the epistome.
1877 Huxley *Anat. Inv. Anim.* viii. 461 Between the bases of the arms there is a rounded or pentagonal disk with raised and ciliated edges, which occupies the place of the epistoma in the phylactolaematous Polyzoa.

phylactology (ˌfaılæk'tɒlədʒı). *nonce-wd.* [f. Gr. φυλακτ-ός or -ήριος vbl. adjs. f. φυλάσσειν to guard + -OLOGY.] The science or business of counter-espionage. Hence **phylacto'logical** *a.*; **phylac'tologist**.
1966 K. Amis *Anti-Death League* I. 18 Apparently what's called the philosophy of phylactology—spy-catching to you —has been transformed. *Ibid.* 108, I had no idea you were practised in phylactological thought. *Ibid.* III. 269 This mere technician, this electrical eavesdropper, seemed to imagine he was on a level with a qualified phylactologist like himself.

phylarch ('faılɑːk). Also 7–8 phil-. [ad. L. *phȳlarchus*, a. Gr. φύλαρχος chief of a tribe, f. φυλή tribe + -αρχος, f. ἄρχειν to rule. Cf. F. *phylarque*.]
1. The chief or ruler of a phyle or tribe in ancient Greece; hence, a tribal chief generally.
1656 J. Harrington *Oceana* (1658) 56 Moses chose able men.., and made them heads over the people; (Tribunes.. or Phylarches, that is) Princes of the Tribes. **1659** —— *Law-giving* II. ii. (1700) 400 These Degrees were of two sorts; first, Phylarchs or Princes of Tribes; and secondly, Patriarchs, or Princes of Familys. **1728** Morgan *Algiers* I. iii. 32 One of the Numidian petty Princes, called by Greek Authors Philarchs, and by the Arabs &c. Sheikhs. **1861** W. Muir *Mahomet* Introd. 183 The Romans recognized as kings or phylarchs of the Syrian Arabs the chiefs of the Bani Salih.
2. In ancient Attica, An officer elected to command the cavalry of each of the ten phylæ.
1830 tr. *Aristoph., Birds* 214 Diitrephes, with only wicker wings, was chosen Phylarch,—next, Hipparch. **1846** Grote *Greece* II. viii. II. 607 The tribe appears to have been the only military classification known to Athens, and the taxiarch the only tribe officer for infantry, as the phylarch was for cavalry, under the general-in-chief.
3. The title given to certain magistrates in the ideal commonwealths of Plato, More, etc.; in Harrington's *Oceana* given to the magisterial body.
1551 Robinson tr. *More's Utopia* II. iii. (1895) 135 Euerye thyrty families or fermes chewse them yearlye an offycer, whyche in their olde language is called the Syphograunte, and by a newer name the Phylarche [*phylarchum*]. **1656** J. Harrington *Oceana* (1658) 76 All and every one of these Magistrates, together with the Justices of Peace: and the Jury-men of the Hundreds,..are the Prerogative Troop or Phylarch of the Tribe. **1849** Macaulay *Hist. Eng.* iii. I. 407 During twenty years the chief employment of busy and ingenious men had been to frame constitutions..All the nomenclature..of the imaginary government was fully set forth,..Phylarchs, Tribes [etc.].
Hence **phy'larchic, -'archical** *adjs.*, of or pertaining to phylarchs or to tribal government; consisting in the rule of great families; **'phylarchy**, the office of a phylarch, tribal government.
1819 *Blackw. Mag.* V. 640 Feelings of decent reverence for the old *phylarchic aristocracies of England. **1861** W. Muir *Mahomet* I. Introd. 146 The national tradition and poetry of the Arabs,..with respect to genealogical and *phylarchical events. **1728** Earbery tr. *Burnet's St. Dead* II. 56 The twelve Apostles and the twelve patriarchs joined together, or the *phylarchies of the Jews. **1869** *Pall Mall G.* 9 July 11 A Bedawin phylarchy, in which the chief is the political and religious ruler of the nation.

†**phylaxis** (fı'læksıs). *Path. Obs.* [ad. Gr. φύλαξις watching, guarding; cf. ANAPHYLAXIS.] The protection of a cell or organism against the effects of a toxin, esp. a neurotoxin, by the action of an artificially introduced substance which prevents its uptake by cells. Hence **phy'lactic** *a.*
1913 [see ANAPHYLAXIS]. **1919** A. E. Wright in *Lancet* 29 Mar. 490/1 To combat bacterial infection the organism must have defensive powers. That power of guarding itself against infection we may—the suggestion is Lord Moulton's —call phylactic power. The leucocytes and the bacteriotropic substances in the blood fluid we may call phylactic agents. **1931** H. Gainsborough tr. *Billard's Phylaxis* i. 11 After a discussion with G. Ramon and in agreement with him..I adopted a new term—phylaxis. *Ibid.* iii. 29 (*heading*) Phylaxis by certain mineral waters against certain neurotoxins. *Ibid.* 40 As regards the phylactic action of sparteine I have insisted at some length on the particular affinity of the neurotoxins for the lipoids. **1931** *Times Lit. Suppl.* 3 Dec. 985/4 Phylaxis is a conception mainly due to Professor Billard's experiments.

‖**phyle** ('faıliː). *Ancient Gr. Hist.* Pl. -æ. [a. Gr. φυλή tribe.] In ancient Greece, a clan or tribe, based on supposed kinship; in Attica, after the reforms of Clisthenes, a political, administrative, and military unit, the division of the people into ten phylæ being mainly geographical; also the cavalry brigade furnished by an Attic tribe.
1863 *Blackw. Mag.* Sept. 290 The Greek Eupatrid or the Roman Patrician, who had to court the votes of his Phyle or of his clients. **1868** *Smith's Dict. Gr. & Rom. Antiq.* (ed. 7) 389 The tribes or phylæ [of Attica] were divided..each into three phratriæ. *Ibid.* 390 All foreigners admitted to the citizenship were registered in a phyle.

phylembryo (faı'lɛmbrıəʊ). *Biol.* [f. PHYL-UM + EMBRYO.] The ancestral embryo form of a race of animals or plants. Hence **phylem-bry'onic** *a.*
1899 *Pop. Sci. Monthly* 464 The ancestral form of this group, the phylembryo, has been found in Paterina, whose adult represents the youngest stage, the beak of the shell, of other Brachiopods. **1902** Webster *Suppl.* s.v. *Phylo-*, Phylembryonic.

phyletic (faı'lɛtık), *a. Biol.* [a. G. *phyletisch* (E. Haeckel *Generelle Morphologie der Organismen* (1866) II. xx. 299), ad. Gr. φυλετικός, f. φυλέτης a tribesman, f. φυλή a tribe.] Of or pertaining to the development of a species or other taxonomic group.
1881 *Science Gossip* No. 203. 249 Presenting a picture..of phyletic development (that is, the changes through which the species has passed in its development). **1892** Mivart *Ess. & Crit.* 457 The growth of the species, or phyletic growth. **1893** tr. *Weismann's Germ-Plasm* I. i. 56 The entire phyletic transformation of a species does not by any means alone depend on its intra-cellular variation. **1928** *Brit. Jrnl. Med. Psychol.* VIII. 59 It is my essential position that what we call mental is itself physiological when viewed in a social or phyletic as well as in an individual or ontogenetic sense. **1933** *Proc. Linn. Soc.* CXLV. 155 He does not claim that his analysis necessarily represents the true phyletic position of the various species. **1943** [see *group-analysis* s.v. GROUP *sb.* 6 b]. **1944** G. G. Simpson *Tempo & Mode in Evolution* vii. 205 Phyletic evolution goes on continuously..in populations of all sizes and kinds. **1951** G. H. M. Lawrence *Taxon. Vascular Plants* ii. 96 Some phylogenists have given too little attention to the phyletic significance of pollen grain and starch grain morphology. **1963** Davis & Heywood *Princ. Angiosperm Taxon.* ii. 44 Both *phyletic* and *phylogenetic* refer to the course of evolution and are virtually interchangeable. **1969** E. Mayr *Princ. Systematic Zool.* x. 251 Species living at the present time are the current end points of innumerable phyletic lines. **1972** *Sci. Amer.* Jan. 98/3 Individuals representing nothing more than successive stages of a single phyletic line have in a number of cases been assigned distinctive taxonomic names, as if they had actually

been contemporaries and neighbors. **1973** A. J. POMERANS tr. *Piaget & Inhelder's Memory & Intelligence* 2 Our first problem, then, is to distinguish between the acquired memory (or the memory proper) and the phyletic memory or conservation and utilization of hereditary information.

Hence **phy'letically** *adv.*, as regards the phylum, racially; regarding a common evolutionary descent.

1893 tr. *Weismann's Germ-Plasm* ii. 115 Salamanders.. are much younger phyletically, and much more highly organised. **1930** *Psyche* XI. II. 78 After all, the whole field of man's unconscious life..must be regarded phyletically as man's inattention in the immediate moment. **1933** *Proc. Linn. Soc.* CXLV. 162 A and B may be the nearest allies phyletically. **1950** [see *intention movement*]. **1951** G. H. M. LAWRENCE *Taxon. Vascular Plants* v. 99 The Magnoliales are phyletically old. **1965** ZUCKERKANDL & PAULING in Bryson & Vogel *Evolving Genes & Proteins* 111. 164 Any variants within a given type of tertiary structure and function seem to have a much greater chance to be phyletically related than unrelated. **1976** *Nature* 24 June 694/1 Many species will evolve phyletically with no change in size.

phyletism ('faɪlɪtɪz(ə)m, 'fiː-). Also erron. **philetism** (perh. infl. by PHILO-). [f. Gr. φυλέτ-ης fellow tribesman, f. φυλή tribe: see -ISM.] In the Orthodox Church, an excessive emphasis on the principle of nationalism in the organization of church affairs; a policy which attaches greater importance to ethnic identity than to bonds of faith and worship.

The term is applied chiefly in hist. use to the claim of the Bulgarian Church to jurisdiction over Bulgarian nationals in all parts of the world, leading in 1872 to the condemnation passed by the Synod of the Ecumenical Patriarchate in Constantinople and to a schism between the Greek-speaking Orthodox churches and the Bulgarian Church which lasted until 1945.

1900 'ODYSSEUS' *Turkey in Europe* 285 The Patriarchate.. stigmatised by the name of Phyletism the doctrine that persons of a particular race..are entitled to a separate ecclesiastical administration. **1907** A. FORTESCUE *Orthodox Eastern Church* IV. x. 278 He finds Philetism to be a deadly heresy. Poor Patriarch!.. Shall he denounce Philetism, stand out for the old rights of the hierarchy and of the chief sees, preach unity and ancient councils? **1923** R. L. LANGFORD-JAMES *Dict. Eastern Orthodox Church* 99/1 Phyletism is the error of the undue exaltation of the necessary independence of National Churches, so that Nationalism in religion overshadows Catholicism. **1927** B. J. KIDD *Churches of Eastern Christendom* xii. 301 This last phase of shrinkage and retreat, ending..in the emancipation of the Balkan nations, had encouraged Philetism and diminished the range of the Patriarch's authority by the creation of National Churches. **1957** tr. *V. Lossky's Mystical Theol. Eastern Church* i. 15 The view which would base the unity of a local church on a political, racial or cultural principle is considered by the Orthodox Church as a heresy, specially known by the name of *philetism*. **1961** D. ATTWATER *Christian Churches of East* II. 248 *Phyletism*.., the name by which the patriarch of Constantinople condemned a form of nationalism in the Orthodox Church in 1872. **1974** *Encycl. Brit. Macropædia* VI. 159/1 The council [of 1872] condemned 'phyletism'—the national or ethnic principle in church organization—and excommunicated the Bulgarians, who were certainly not alone guilty of 'phyletism'.

phylic ('faɪlɪk), *a.*[1] [f. Gr. φυλ-ή tribe + -IC.] Of or pertaining to a Greek phyle or tribe.

1891 *Jrnl. Hellenic Stud.* XII. 30 The increase of the *Phylae* involved changes in the institutions based upon the phylic system. **1908** J. L. MYRES in R. R. Marett *Anthropol. & Classics* 142 The solidarity of the Greek phylic institutions.

phylic ('faɪlɪk), *a.*[2] *Psychol.* [f. PHYL(UM + -IC.] Of or relating to the phylum (sense b). Also *absol.*

1949 T. BURROW *Neurosis of Man* vii. 169 As an outgrowth of this phylic principle of integration, the individual remains always an integral element within the organism of man as a unit. **1952** W. J. H. SPROTT *Social Psychol.* 246 The fault lies mainly in our individualism, or, rather, in our isolationism. We have over-developed the 'private' and lost touch with the 'phylic'. **1953** T. BURROW *Sci. & Man's Behavior* vi. 74 The term 'species'..has no adjectival form. In order to fill this breach, I adopted 'phylic', from *phylum*, which in its original Greek had the meaning of 'tribe'.

Phyllarea, -erea, obs. erron. ff. PHILLYREA.

phyllary ('fɪlərɪ). *Bot.* [ad. mod.L. *phyllārium*, a. Gr. φυλλάριον, dim. of φύλλον leaf.] Each of the small leaves or bracts constituting the involucre of a Composite flower.

1857 HENFREY *Bot.* §122 In the Compositae..the bracts form an involucre the parts of which are sometimes called phyllaries. **1861** BENTLEY *Man. Bot.* (1870) 182.

† **phyllet**, obs. erron. form of FILLET.

1426 LYDG. *De Guil. Pilgr.* 22339, I haue knyues, phyllettys, callys.

phyllidiobranchiate (fɪˌlɪdɪəʊ'bræŋkɪət), *a.* *Zool.* [f. next + L. *branchia*: see BRANCHIATE.] Belonging to or having the characters of the *Phyllidiobranchia*, a division of gastropod molluscs, in which the ctenidia are replaced by lamellæ (the *phyllidia*) within the fold of the mantle.

1883 LANKESTER in *Encycl. Brit.* XVI. 656/1 Dorsal and ventral view of *Pleurophyllidia lineata* (Otto), one of the Phyllidiobranchiate Palliate Opisthobranchs.

‖**phyllidium** (fɪ'lɪdɪəm). *Biol.* [mod.L., f. Gr. φύλλ-ον leaf + -ιδιον dim. suffix.] One of the rudimentary ctenidia or *lamellæ* of certain gastropod molluscs, called by E. R. Lankester *capitopedal bodies*.

phylliform ('fɪlɪfɔːm), *a. rare.* [irreg. f. Gr. φύλλον leaf + -FORM.] Leaf-shaped, leaf-like.

1848 E. FORBES *Naked-eyed Medusæ* 37 Four phylliform ovaries.

Phyllirea, obs. erron. variant of PHILLYREA.

‖**Phyllirhoe** (fɪ'lɪrəʊiː). *Zool.* [f. Gr. φυλλορρόος shedding leaves, f. φύλλ-ον leaf + -ροος, from ῥοή flow.] A genus of degenerate gastropod molluscs, having no cerata nor ctenidium, and of thin translucent body, without shell, gills, or foot, the general surface being respiratory in function; usually called from their appearance ocean-slugs.

The species *P. bucephalus* is highly phosphorescent.

1878 BELL tr. *Gegenbaur's Comp. Anat.* 339 These gills are atrophied in many Opisthobranchiata, when the whole of the integument takes on the respiratory function (Phyllirhoe).

Hence **phyllirhoid** ('fɪlɪrɔɪd) *a.* and *sb.* *Zool.*; (*a*) *adj.*, akin to the genus *Phyllirhoë*; having the characters of the family *Phyllirhoidæ*; (*b*) *sb.*, a mollusc of this family, an ocean-slug.

Phyllis: see PHILLIS.

phyllite ('fɪlaɪt). [f. Gr. φύλλον a leaf + -ITE[1].]
1. *Min.* **a.** A species of magnesia-mica, occurring in small scales in argillaceous schist or slate. **b.** A rock consisting of an argillaceous schist or slate containing scales or flakes of mica.

See A. R. Hunt *Notes on Petrolog. Nomencl.* in *Geol. Mag.* Jan. 1896, 31–35.

a. 1828 THOMSON in *Ann. N.Y. Lyceum Nat. Hist.* III. 47 Phyllite..will probably constitute a new species. **1862** DANA *Man. Geol.* vi. 77 The ottrelite has been called phyllite. **1892** —— *Min.* (ed. 6) 642.

b. 1881 *Rep. Geol. Expl. N. Zealand* 128 A series of less altered rocks (phyllites) form the northern part of the Eyrie Mountains. **1886** GEIKIE *Class-bk. Geol.* 223 By increase of its mica-flakes a clay-slate passes into a phyllite. **1892** TEALL in *Proc. Somerset Archæol. Soc.* 211 A schistose rock intermediate between a phyllite and a mica-schist.

2. *Geol.* A general name for a fossil leaf. ? *Obs.*

1843 HUMBLE *Dict. Geol. & Min.*, *Phyllite*, a pertrified leaf.

Hence **phyllitic** (fɪ'lɪtɪk) *a.*, consisting of or having the character of phyllite.

1888 *Nature* 8 Nov. 31/1 Generally the slates are schistose, phyllitic, and chiastolitic.

phyllo- (fɪləʊ-), repr. Gr. φυλλο-, combining form of φύλλον leaf, in various scientific terms.
phyllochromogen (-'krəʊmədʒɛn) *Chem.* [see CHROMOGEN], a constituent of chlorophyll, supposed by Liebermann to give rise, by oxidation or reduction, to the various colouring-matters of flowers. **phyllocyanic** (-saɪ'ænɪk) *a.* *Chem.* [see CYANIC 2], in ***phyllocyanic acid*** = next. **phyllocyanin** (-'saɪənɪn) *Chem.* [see CYANIN], a blue or bluish-green substance supposed by Frémy to be a constituent of chlorophyll (see *phylloxanthin* below). **'phyllocyst** (-sɪst) *Zool.*, a cyst or cavity in the hydrophyllium (see HYDRO-) of certain Hydrozoa; hence **phyllo'cystic** *a.*, pertaining to or of the nature of a phyllocyst. **phyllogen** ('fɪlədʒɛn) [-GEN] = *phyllophore*. **phyllogenetic** (-dʒɪ'nɛtɪk) *a.* [-GENETIC], pertaining to the production of leaves. **phyllogenous** (fɪ'lɒdʒɪnəs) *a.* [-GEN 2 + -OUS], growing upon leaves. ‖**phyllo'mania** *Bot.* [mod.L.: cf. Gr. φυλλομανεῖν to run wildly to leaf], an abnormal development of leaves. **'phyllomorph** [Gr. μορφή form], the representation of a plant in art. **phyllomorphic** (-'mɔːfɪk) *a.* [Gr. μορφή form], leaf-shaped; in quot., characterized by imitation of the forms of leaves; so **phyllo'morphous** *a.*, leaf-shaped. **'phyllomorphy**, metamorphosis of other organs into leaves (= PHYLLODY). **phyllophæin** (-'fiːɪn) *Chem.* [Gr. φαιός dusky: see -IN[1]] = PHÆOPHYLL. **'phyllophore** (-fɔə(r)) *Bot.* [Gr. φυλλοφόρος leaf-bearing], the growing-point or terminal bud from which the leaves arise, esp. in palms; so **phyllophorous** (-'lɒfərəs) *a.*, leaf-bearing; in *Zool.*, bearing parts resembling leaves, as the nose-leaf of certain bats. **phylloporphyrin** (-'pɔːfɪrɪn) *Chem.* [Gr. πορφύρα purple dye], a black substance obtained by decomposition of chlorophyll; its aqueous solution is purple (*Syd. Soc. Lex.*, citing Geissler and Möller). **'phyllosphere**, the surface area of the leaves, or, more generally, of all the parts of a plant above ground. **phylloxanthin** (fɪlɒk'sænθɪn) *Chem.* [a. F. *phylloxanthine* (Frémy), f. Gr. ξανθός yellow], a yellow constituent of chlorophyll, also called XANTHOPHYLL.

1879 WATTS *Dict. Chem.* VIII. 452 The basic component [of chlorophyll], *phyllochromogen, is capable of assuming the most various colours under the influence of oxidising and reducing agents. **1881** *Ibid.* 1637 Chlorophyll..When digested with hydrochloric acid..splits up into phylloxanthin, a brown substance,..and Frémy's *phyllocyanic acid, an olive-green substance. **1861** BENTLEY *Man. Bot.* 744 M. Frémy..has ascertained that it [chlorophyll] is composed of two colouring principles,—one a yellow, which he has termed *phylloxanthine*; and the other a blue, which he has called **phyllocyanine*. **1885** GOODALE *Physiol. Bot.* (1892) 291 Frémy's later researches have led him to regard the so-called phyllocyanin as really an acid (*phyllocyanic*). **1859** HUXLEY *Oceanic Hydrozoa* 14 They always contain a diverticulum of the somatic cavity, or *phyllocyst. **1877** —— *Anat. Inv. Anim.* iii. 139 Phyllocyst or cavity of hydrophyllium with its process. **1890** *Cent. Dict.*, **Phyllogen*. **1893** in *Syd. Soc. Lex.* **1898** *Nature* 26 May 74/2 Theories of *phyllogenetic development. **1858** MAYNE *Expos. Lex.*, *Phyllogenus*,..that which grows upon leaves..: *phyllogenous. **1670** E. TONGE in *Phil. Trans.* V. 2073 Whether the delay of Sap, staying Fruit and Blossoms, as is suppos'd, by tying, will cure the *Phyllo-mania, as Cross-hacking? **1856** GRINDON *Life* viii. (1875) 97 No plant can suffer from phyllomania and be fruitful at the same moment. **1889** *Trans. Lancs. & Cheshire Antiquarian Soc.* VII. 166 The forms of ornament demonstrably due to structure require a name... Those taken from animals are called zoomorphs, and those from plants *phyllomorphs. **1895** A. C. HADDON *Evol. Art* 126 The terms 'zoomorph' and 'phyllomorph' have been employed for the representation in art of plants and animals. **1882** *Academy* 4 Feb. 76 It [Celtic art] was zoomorphic, but not *phyllomorphic. **1849** *Fraser's Mag.* XXXIX. 669 Classified under the head of the Walking Leaf, or *Phyllomorphous insects. **1886** *Cassell's Encycl. Dict.*, **Phyllomorphy*, the same as *Phyllody*. **1858** MAYNE *Expos. Lex.* 954/1 The dusky or brown colouring matter of the leaves of plants: *phyllophein. **1893** *Syd. Soc. Lex.*, *Phæophyll*, the brown colouring-matter of the Fucoïdeæ; also called *Phyllophæin*. **1848** LINDLEY *Introd. Bot.* (ed. 4) I. 227 The growing point, or **phyllophore* [of Mirbel]. **1885** GOODALE *Physiol. Bot.* (1892) 132 That portion of a palm-stem which lies above the lowest active leaves..is of a conical shape..often much elongated, and carries all the new and forming leaves. It is known as the *Phyllophore*. **1828** WEBSTER, **Phyllophorous*. **1955** F. T. LAST in *Trans. Brit. Mycol. Soc.* XXXVIII. 221 It is suggested that, as with roots and the 'rhizosphere', leaves have a '*phyllosphere', with a characteristic micro-flora that may contain many species. **1956** J. RUINEN in *Nature* 4 Feb. 221/2 These observations suggested the existence of a characteristic milieu which is conditioned by the leaf, and may be called, in analogy with the rhizosphere, the 'phyllosphere'. **1972** J. G. CRUICKSHANK *Soil Geogr.* vi. 175 On the surface of living aerial parts of plants, particularly on the leaves—the phyllosphere. **1858** MAYNE *Expos. Lex.* 954/2 The yellow colouring matter of the leaf of a plant: *phylloxanthin. **1861** BENTLEY *Man. Bot.* 745 The experiments of M. Frémy show, that the yellow leaves of autumn contain no phyllocyanine, and hence that their colour is entirely due to the phylloxanthine, either in its original condition or in an altered state.

‖**phyllobranchia** (fɪləʊ'bræŋkɪə). *Zool.* Pl. -æ. [mod.L., f. Gr. φύλλον leaf + βράγχια gills.] Each of the leaf-like, foliaceous, or lamellar gills of certain crustaceans. Also **phyllo'branchial** *a.*, of or pertaining to a phyllobranchia; **phyllo'branchiate** *a.*, having phyllobranchiæ.

1878 HUXLEY in *Proc. Zool. Soc.* 4 June 782 The structure ..which obtains in *Gebia* and *Callianassa*, which are truly phyllobranchiate. **1880** —— *Crayfish* v. 271 The prawn's gills are..phyllobranchiæ;..the central stem of the branchia..bears only two rows of broad flat lamellæ. **1880** E. R. LANKESTER in *Nature* XXI. 355/2 Crayfishes..differ from prawns..in..being 'trichobranchiate' in place of 'phyllobranchiate'.

phyllocarid (fɪləʊ'kærɪd). *Zool.* [a. mod.L. name of division *Phyllocarida* (A. S. Packard 1879, in *Amer. Naturalist* XIII. 128), f. PHYLLO- + Gr. καρίς shrimp, prawn.] A crustacean belonging to a group of the subclass Branchiopoda, which includes those types distinguished by the broad, flat limbs known as phyllopodia. Also *attrib.* Hence **phyllo'caridan** *a.*

1882 A. S. PACKARD in *Amer. Naturalist* XVI. 870 He [*sc.* Claus] failed to appreciate the independent, synthetic nature of the Phyllocaridan type. **1896** *Proc. Geol. Soc.* LII. p. xcvi, We have here..a passage upward from the more ancient Phyllocarid type..to the more modern Cumacea. **1902** *54th Ann. Rep. N.Y. State Mus. Nat. Hist. 1900* I. 98 The museum record of localities now bears the following entries at which species of these phyllocarids have been obtained. **1911** *Geol. Mag.* VIII. 64 In the black shales we succeeded in finding organic remains, including..a bivalve phyllocarid crustacean. *Ibid.*, A few specimens of a bivalve phyllocarid allied to *Caryocaris* and *Lingulocaris*. **1935** TWENHOFEL & SHROCK *Inverteb. Paleontol.* x. 444 Nebaliacea—A heterogeneous group of living and fossil phyllocarids. **1973** P. TASCH *Paleobiol. of Invertebr.* xi. 600/2 There have been several finds of fossil phyllocarids with appendages preserved.

phylloclade ('fɪləʊkleɪd). *Bot.* [ad. mod.L. *phyllocladium* (fɪləʊ'kleɪdɪəm) (also in Eng. use), f. Gr. φύλλον leaf + κλάδος branch.] A branch of an enlarged or flattened form, resembling or performing the functions of a leaf, as in Butcher's Broom or the *Cactaceæ*.

1858 MAYNE *Expos. Lex.*, *Phyllocladium*,..a term proposed by Bischoff for the *Phyllodium*, produced by a branch enlarged and flattened in the form of a leaf. **1883**

Athenæum 3 Mar. 283/3 There is a curious *Exocarpus* with phyllocladia. **1884** Bower & Scott *De Bary's Phaner.* 301 This arrangement is found..also in the phylloclades of Ruscus and Myrsiphyllum. **1897** Willis *Flower. Pl.* I. 181 Stems..with long shoots transformed into flat green expansions, which act as leaves, whilst the true leaves are reduced to scales..are termed *phylloclades*.

Hence **phyllo'cladioid** *a.* [-OID], resembling a phylloclade (in quot. misused as if = having phylloclades); **phy'llocladous** *a.* [-OUS], having phylloclades.

1883 *Jrnl. Linn. Soc., Bot.* XX. 249 A phyllocladioid Exocarpus..an oblanceolate thick rigid phylloclade. **1895** Kerner & Oliver *Nat. Hist. Plants* I. 334 The most striking forms of phyllocladous plants.

phyllode ('fɪləʊd). Also in L. form **phy'llodium**. [a. F. *phyllode*, ad. mod.L. *phyllōdium* (fɪ'ləʊdɪəm), also in Eng. use, f. Gr. φυλλώδης leaf-like, f. φύλλον leaf: see -ODE[1].]

1. *Bot.* A petiole or leaf-stalk of an expanded and (usually) flattened form, resembling and having the functions of a leaf, the true leaf-blade being absent or much reduced in size, as in many Acacias.

1848 Lindley *Introd. Bot.* (ed. 4) I. 297 The curious transformation undergone by the petiole when it becomes a phyllode. **1861** Bentley *Man. Bot.* (1870) 175 To such a petiole the name of phyllodium or phyllode has been applied. **1885** Goodale *Physiol. Bot.* (1892) 347 All the eight species of this genus [Sarracenia] have hollowed *phyllodia*, which form slender pitchers or urns.

2. *Zool.* = PETAL *sb.* 2.

1888 Rolleston & Jackson *Anim. Life* 557 In the *Cassidulidae* the peristomial ends of the ambulacra dilate into petala or phyllodes, forming a figure known as *floscella*.

Hence **phy'llodial** *a.*, pertaining to or of the nature of a phyllode; **phyllo'dineous, phy'llodinous** *a.* [irreg.], bearing phyllodes; also = prec.; **phyllodini'ation**, formation of phyllodes.

1858 Mayne *Expos. Lex., Phyllodialis*, applied to the cup of an ascidiated leaf..when it is formed by the *phyllodium*, or the petiole enlarged in the form of a leaf, as in the *Saracenia purpurea*: *phyllodial. **1848** Lindley *Introd. Bot.* (ed. 4) II. 307 Among the *phyllodineous Acacias. **1880** A. R. Wallace *Isl. Life* 307 Australian affinities are shewn..by a *phyllodinous Acacia. *a* **1850** R. Brown cited in Cassell for **Phyllodiniation*.

phyllody ('fɪləʊdɪ). *Bot.* [f. prec. + -Y.] **a.** The condition in which certain organs, esp. parts of the flower, are metamorphosed into ordinary leaves. **b.** The condition in which the leaf-stalk is metamorphosed into a phyllode.

1888 Henslow *Orig. Floral Struct.* xxx. 302 Phyllody of the Carpels and Ovules.

phylloid ('fɪlɔɪd), *a.* and *sb.* [f. mod.L. *phylloīdēs*, f. Gr. φύλλ-ον leaf: see -OID.]

a. *adj.* Resembling a leaf; foliaceous. **b.** *sb.* A part in lower plants, analogous to or resembling a leaf.

1858 Mayne *Expos. Lex., Phylloides*,..applied by Mirbel to parts which have the form of leaves, that is, which are flattened and herbaceous, as the stem of the *Cactus phyllanthus*: phylloid. *Ibid.* s.v. *Phyllosoma*, A crustaceous animal with phylloid or bladder-like sacs attached to the hinder part of the body. **1875** Bennett & Dyer *Sachs' Bot.* 211 For the sake of finding an expression for these relationships in Algæ..the leaf-like appendages might be termed Phylloids, the root-like appendages Rhizoids.

So **phy'lloidal, phy'lloideous** *adjs.* = prec. a.

1866 *Treas. Bot., Phylloideous*, the same as Foliaceous. **1888** Henslow *Orig. Floral Struct.* xxx. 302 The ovules then undergo phylloidal changes of different degrees.

phyllome ('fɪləʊm). *Bot.* [ad. mod.L. *phyllōma*, f. Gr. φύλλωμα foliage, clothing of leaves, f. φυλλοῦν to clothe with leaves, f. φύλλον leaf. (But *-ome* has here rather the mod. sense of 'formation' as in *caulome, rhizome*.) So in mod.F.]

1. The general name for a leaf or any organ homologous with a leaf, or regarded as a modified leaf (as a sepal, petal, stamen, carpel, bract, etc.).

1875 Bennett & Dyer *Sachs' Bot.* 130 If now we accept ..Thallome, Stem (Caulome), Leaf (Phyllome), and Hair (Trichome), in the senses indicated. **1880** Gray *Struct. Bot.* 6 *note*, The German botanists use..*Phyllome* in this sense.

2. (See quot.) *rare*$^{-0}$.

1858 Mayne *Expos. Lex., Phylloma.* Herschel terms thus ..the whole of the germs destined to produce the leaves which come from the bud..when it is developed: a phyllome.

Hence **phyllomic** (fɪ'ləʊmɪk) *a.*, pertaining to or of the nature of a phyllome.

1886 *Nature* 6 May 17/2 Even on this explanation the true stamen is phyllomic.

phyllophagan (fɪ'lɒfəgən). *Zool.* [f. mod.L. *phyllophaga* pl., a. Gr. type *φυλλοφάγα, f. φύλλον leaf + φάγος eating.] A member of the *Phyllophaga*, a name applied in different classifications to various groups of animals which feed on leaves: viz. (*a*) a tribe of marsupials, including the phalangers; (*b*) a group of edentates, comprising the sloths; (*c*) a group of lamellicorn beetles, including the chafers; (*d*) of hymenopterous insects, including the saw-flies. So **phy'llophagous** *a.*, leaf-eating; belonging to the *Phyllophaga*.

1842 Brande *Dict. Sc.*, etc., **Phyllophagans, Phyllophaga*, the name of a tribe of Marsupials, including the Phalangers, Petaurists, and Koala; also of a tribe of beetles, including those which live by suction of the tender parts of vegetables, as the leaves and succulent sprouts. **1858** Mayne *Expos. Lex.*, s.v. **1868** Owen *Anat. Vertebr.* §332 III. 451 The thick epithelium continued over the inner surface of that part in the Phyllophagous species.

phyllopod ('fɪləpɒd), *sb.* and *a.* *Zool.* [f. mod.L. *Phyllopoda* pl., f. Gr. φύλλο-ν leaf + πούς, ποδ- foot.] **a.** *sb.* A member of the *Phyllopoda*, a group of entomostracous crustaceans, having lamellate or foliaceous swimming feet; a leaf-footed crustacean. **b.** *adj.* Belonging to the *Phyllopoda*; leaf-footed.

1863 Ramsay *Phys. Geog.* v. (1878) 63 Also a phyllopod crustacean. **1865** *Athenæum* No. 1983. 571/2 The little modest ostracods and phyllopods. **1878** Bell tr. *Gegenbaur's Comp. Anat.* 239 The form of the Phyllopod foot.

So **phyllopodal** (fɪ'lɒpədəl), **phy'llopodan, phy'llopodous** *adjs.* = prec. b; **phyllopodiform** (fɪləʊ'pɒdɪfɔːm) *a.*, having the form of a phyllopod.

1878 tr. Claus in *Encycl. Brit.* VI. 650/2 *note*, The maxilla of the Decapod larva is a sort of *Phyllopodal foot. **1869** W. S. Dallas tr. *F. Müller's Facts fr. Darwin* 84 A *Phyllopodiform Decapod. **1852** Dana *Crust.* I. 14 These *Phyllopodous species seem..to be recent representatives of ancient forms, the Trilobites.

phyllopode ('fɪləpəʊd). *Bot.* [mod. f. Gr. φύλλο-ν leaf + πούς, ποδ- foot.] Name for the dilated sheathing-base of the leaf in *Isoëtes*, analogous to a petiole in Phanerogams.

1875 Bennett & Dyer tr. *Sachs' Bot.* 420 The structure of the leaves of Isoëtes varies according as the species grow submerged in water, in marshes, or on dry ground... In the third case..the basal portions of the dead leaves (phyllopodes) form a firm black coat of mail round the stem.

phyllopodium (fɪləʊ'pəʊdɪəm). [f. PHYLLO- + PODIUM.] **1.** *Bot.* The base of a leaf stalk, or the main axis of a leaf.

1884 F. O. Bower in *Phil. Trans. R. Soc.* CLXXV. 569, I therefore propose the term phyllopodium to express the whole of the main axis of the leaf, exclusive of its branches. **1923** —— *Ferns* I. v. 82 The branches are then arranged in two longitudinal rows, one on either side of a central stalk or rachis, which is continuous below into the stipe or petiole, often of considerable length. The whole of this, including petiole and rachis, may be styled the Phyllopodium. **1951** McLean & Ivimey-Cook *Textbk. Theoret. Bot.* I. xvi. 653 Delpino..described the stem as a pseudaxis or phyllopodium. *Ibid.* xxii. 978 The mature leaf consists of three portions, the lamina, the petiole, and the leaf base or phyllopodium. *Ibid.* 979 (*caption*) Development of the phyllopodium as a leaf sheath.

2. *Zool.* (See quot. 1967.)

1926 L. A. Borradaile in *Ann. & Mag. Nat. Hist.* XVII. 194, I have..argued in support of the view that all the post-antennulary limbs of the primitive crustacean were alike, and that they were flat structures with endites and exites. It is convenient to call such appendages 'phyllopod limbs' or phyllopodia, whether they occur in the Phyllopoda (Branchiopoda) or elsewhere. *Ibid.*, The phyllopodium has all the essentials of a biramous limb. **1967** P. A. Meglitsch *Invertebr. Zool.* xviii. 755/1 An unusual feature of the branchiopods is the soft, flattened type of trunk appendage characteristic of most of the groups. Covered with a delicate cuticle, they are flexible enough to move freely without segmentation. This type of appendage is known as [a] phyllopodium.

phylloquinone (fɪləʊ'kwɪnəʊn). *Biochem.* [ad. G. *phyllochinon* (Karrer & Geiger, at the suggestion of H. Dam, in *Helv. Chim. Acta* (1939) XXII. 946), f. Gr. φύλλον leaf + G. *chinon* quinone (cf. CHINA[3] 2).] Vitamin K_1, a yellow, fat-soluble oil that is present in green leafy vegetables and is important in blood clotting; 2-methyl-3-phytyl-1,4-naphthoquinone, $C_{31}H_{46}O_2$.

1939 *Chem. Abstr.* XXXIII. 8191 The light yellow vitamin K_1 from alfalfa, named by Dam ..'α-phylloquinone', (I) crystallizes at low temp. **1953** Fruton & Simmonds *Gen. Biochem.* xxxviii. 908 Vitamin K_2 (2-methyl-3-difarnesyl-1,4-naphthoquinone), which is formed by some bacteria.., differs from phylloquinone only in the substituent in the 3 position of the naphthoquinone ring. **1970** R. W. McGilvery *Biochem.* xxvi. 651 (*caption*) Phylloquinones from plants are absorbed to some extent as such, and they have vitamin K activity. However, the side chain is removed from most of the ingested compounds by intestinal bacteria; the resultant menadione is absorbed and a new side chain is constructed to create menaquinone, the principal form of vitamin K found in animals. **1972** *Materials & Technol.* V. xix. 692 Menadione, phylloquinone and the menaquinones can all be obtained synthetically, but only menadione is produced in any quantity.

phyllorhine ('fɪləraɪn), *a.* and *sb.* *Zool.* [ad. mod.L. *Phyllorhīn-us*, f. Gr. φύλλο-ν leaf + ῥίς, ῥῑν- nose.] **a.** *adj.* Of a bat: Having a nose-leaf, or leaf-like appendage to the nose; leaf-nosed; *spec.* belonging to the *Phyllorhininæ*, a subfamily of the *Rhinolophidæ* or horseshoe-bats. **b.** *sb.* A leaf-nosed bat; *spec.* one of the *Phyllorhininæ*. Also **phyllo'rhinine** *a.* and *sb.*

phylloscopine (fɪ'lɒskəpaɪn), *a.* *Ornith.* [f. mod.L. *Phylloscop-us* (f. Gr. φύλλο-ν leaf + -σκοπός viewing) + -INE[1].] Of or related to the genus *Phylloscopus* containing the chiffchaff and warblers.

1890 *Cent. Dict.* cites H. Seebohm.

phyllosilicate (fɪləʊ'sɪlɪkeɪt). *Min.* [a. G. *phyllosilikat* (H. Strunz 1938, in *Zeitschr. für ges. Naturwiss.* IV. 185), f. as PHYLLO-: see SILICATE.] Any of the group of silicates characterized by SiO_4 tetrahedra linked in sheets of indefinite extent in which the ratio of silicon and aluminium to oxygen is 2:5.

1947 *Mineral. Abstr.* X. 52 The different types of SiO_4 bonding give at last a systematic classification of silicates into nesosilicates.., sorosilicates.., inosilicates.., phyllosilicates.., and tectosilicates. **1966** *McGraw-Hill Encycl. Sci. & Technol.* XII. 312/1 The phyllosilicates as a group typically have a platy crystal habit, with a cleavage parallel to the plane of layering of the structure, and are optically negative with rather high birefringence. **1972** *Nature* 1 Sept. 7/1 Phyllosilicates are the most common material in carbonaceous meteorites.

phyllosome ('fɪləsəʊm). *Zool.* [ad. mod.L. *Phyllosōma*, f. Gr. φύλλο-ν leaf + σῶμα body: see quot. 1858.] The larval form of certain macrurous crustaceans (formerly supposed to be adult forms constituting a separate group); a glass-crab.

1835 Kirby *Hab. & Inst. Anim.* II. xv. 59 The most remarkable animals belonging to the order [Stomapods] are the Phyllosomes of Dr. Leach. **1858** Mayne *Expos. Lex., Phyllosoma*, name of a crustaceous animal with phylloid or bladder-like sacs attached to the hinder part of the body: a phyllosome.

phyllostome ('fɪləʊstəʊm). *Zool.* [ad. mod.L. *Phyllostoma*, f. Gr. φύλλο-ν leaf + στόμα, στοματ- mouth.] A bat of the genus *Phyllostoma* or family *Phyllostomatidæ*, having a nose-leaf or other appendage of the snout. Also **phyllo'stomatid, phy'llostomid.** So **phyllo'stomatoid, phyllo'stomatous, phy'llostomine, phy'llostomoid, phy'llostomous** *adjs.*, belonging to or having the characters of the *Phyllostomatidæ*.

1858 Mayne *Expos. Lex., Phyllostomatus, Phyllostomus*, applied by Goldfuss, Gray [etc.] to a Family (*Phyllostomata*) of the *Cheiroptera*, having the nose or mouth encumbered with a simple leaf: phyllostomatous: phyllostomous. **1866** *Athenæum* No. 2002. 339/1 Genera of phyllostomine or leaf-nosed bats.

‖**phyllotaxis** (fɪləʊ'tæksɪs). *Bot.* [mod.L., f. Gr. φύλλο-ν leaf + τάξις arrangement.] The arrangement or order of leaves (or other lateral members, e.g. scales of a pine-cone, florets of a composite flower, etc.) upon an axis or stem; the geometrical principles of such arrangement. Also '**phyllotaxy**.

The principal kinds of phyllotaxis are (1) the *cyclical* or *verticillate*, in which a number of leaves (two or more) stand at the same level, forming a pair or whorl; and (2) the *spiral* or *alternate*, in which each leaf stands singly, their points of insertion forming a spiral (the *genetic spiral*) round the stem; in the latter case the phyllotaxis is expressed by a fraction denoting the angle (or portion of one turn of the spiral) between two successive leaves; thus in a $\frac{2}{5}$ phyllotaxis there are 5 leaves in every 2 turns of the spiral.

1857 Henfrey *Elem. Bot.* §60 A particular study of those laws has been pursued, under the name of Phyllotaxy. **1863** Darwin in *Life & Lett.* (1887) III. 51 Do you remember telling me that I ought to study Phyllotaxy? **1875** Bennett & Dyer *Sachs' Bot.* 173 In a $\frac{2}{5}$ phyllotaxis..the 6th member stands over the 1st, the 7th over the 2nd, and so on.

Hence **phyllo'tactic, phyllo'tactical** *adjs.*, belonging or relating to phyllotaxis.

1857 Henfrey *Elem. Bot.* §140 [In the Flower] the leaves, arranged according to the general phyllotactic laws, are more or less changed in form and texture. **1888** Henslow *Orig. Floral Struct.* xxxii. 339 From phyllotactical reasons, it is clear that the origin and arrangements of the floral members are entirely foliar.

‖**Phylloxera** (fɪlɒk'sɪərə). *Entom.* [mod.L., f. Gr. φύλλο-ν leaf + ξηρός dry.] A genus of *Aphididæ* or plant-lice; *esp.* the species *P. vastatrix*, also called *vine-pest*, which is very destructive to the European grape-vine, infesting the roots and leaves, and causing the death of the plant.

The genus *Phylloxera* was named in 1834 to include a plant-louse which was observed to dry up the leaves of the oak in Provence; in 1868 Planchon showed that the vine disease was caused by a new species, which was constantly found on the roots of affected vines, and which he named *P. vastatrix*. (See *Comptes Rendus* 1868 II. 588.)

1868 *Gard. Chron.* 31 Oct. 1138. **1869** *Ibid.* 30 Jan. 109 M. Signoret..considered that the insect belongs to the genus Phylloxera. **1880** *Athenæum* 11 Sept. 340/3 All the vineyards within reach flooded during winter, as a protection against the ravages of the phylloxera. **1886** *Edin. Rev.* Oct. 367 In 1865 the first appearance of the phylloxera in France occurred in the plateau of Pujant, near Roquemaure, on the right bank of the Rhone. **1888** A. E. Shipley in *Encycl. Brit.* XXIV. 239/1 The Phylloxera has spread to Corsica; it has

appeared here and there amongst the vineyards of the Rhine and Switzerland.
fig. **1897** *Westm. Gaz.* 7 May 1/3 Spite of his rosy cheeks, '*la maladie des désabusés*', that phylloxera of the mental vineyard, holds him in its deadly grip.

b. *attrib.* and *Comb.*, as ***phylloxera outbreak, visitation***; **phylloxera-mite**, a minute acarid, *Tyroglyphus phylloxeræ*, which infests the phylloxera.
1901 *Westm. Gaz.* 30 Jan. 8/1 The stocks..being larger than they have been at any time since the phylloxera visitation. **1902** *Ibid.* 7 Jan. 2/3 The failure of the vines, due to the phylloxera outbreak in the sixties.

Hence **phylloxeral** (-'ɪərəl), **phylloxeric** (-'ɛrɪk) *adjs.*, pertaining or relating to the phylloxera; **phy'lloxerated, phy'lloxerized** *ppl. adjs.*, infested with the phylloxera.
1881 *Nature* 6 Oct. 552/1 Treatment of phylloxerised vines by the use of sulphide of carbon and sulpho-carbonate of potassium. **1882** *St. James' Gaz.* 6 Apr. 4/2 Getting rid of the few phylloxerated spots which appeared there six years ago. **1886** *Edin. Rev.* Oct. 378 The inspector of the phylloxeric service reports that unless energetic measures are taken the vineyards of Portugal will be ruined. **1902** *Speaker* 20 Sept. 646/2 Thanks to the beneficent influence of the phylloxeral crisis.

‖**phyllula** (fɪ'l(j)uːlə). *Bot.* Also **phyllule.** [mod.L., f. Gr. φύλλ-ον leaf + οὐλή scar.] The scar left on a branch by the fall of a leaf.
1858 Mayne *Expos. Lex., Phyllula*,..term by Zuccarini for the cicatrix which, after its fall, each leaf leaves upon the bark at the place of its insertion: the phyllule. **1866** in *Treas. Bot.*

Phyllyræa, -rea, obs. erron. ff. Phillyrea.

phylo-, before a vowel **phyl-,** combining form of Gr. φῦλον, φυλή a tribe (see phyle, phylum), used in mod. scientific terms, mostly of biology. **phyloa'nalysis** *Psychol.*, analysis of an individual that takes account of him as part of a phylum (sense b); hence **phylo'analyst; phyloana'lytic** *a.* **'phylocycle,** the cycle or whole course of the development of a phylum; hence **phylo'cyclic** *a.* **phyloge'rontic** [gerontic] *a.*, of or pertaining to the old age or stage of decay of a race or type of organisms. **phyloge'rontism,** phylogerontic character or condition. **phylo-nepi'onic** *a.* [Gr. νήπιος infant], of or pertaining to the nepionic stage of phylogenesis, or that following the embryonic (cf. phylembryonic). **phy'lopterous** *a.* [Gr. πτερόν wing], of or pertaining to the *Phyloptera*, in some classifications a superorder of insects, containing the *Neuroptera, Pseudoneuroptera, Orthoptera*, and *Dermaptera*.
1930 T. Burrow in *Psyche* XI. ii. 67 (*heading*) Physiological behavior-reactions in the individual and the community: a study in *phyloanalysis. **1940** Hinsie & Shatzky *Psychiatric Dict.* 418/2 Phyloanalysis regards the symptoms of the individual and of society as but outer aspects of impaired tensional processes which affect the balance of the organism's internal reaction as a whole. **1949** T. Burrow *Neurosis of Man* vii. 168 Phyloanalysis set out with the attempt to analyse the affecto-symbolic 'I'-persona and its special prerogative as commonly assumed by social man; and it undertook to differentiate this pseudo-entity from the organism's biological basis of integration and behaviour. **1933** W. Galt *Phyloanalysis* ii. i. 113 The *phyloanalyst does not at all credit the obvious manifestation. **1932** T. Burrow *Struct. Insanity* vi. 66 The aim, therefore, of the *phyloanalytic method is the application of a technique that will enable the patient to acquire a facility for rendering his own physiological tensions objectively perceptible to him. **1893** *Proc. Boston Soc. Nat. Hist.* XXVI. 109 It is proposed to use ..*phylocycle or phylocyclon for [the cycle] of the phylum. *Ibid.* 124 Possibility of the simultaneous origin of phylocycles discussed. *Ibid.* 90 The oldest stages of different individuals of a species, and the corresponding *phylogerontic types of different groups arising from the same common ancestor, resemble each other. **1902** *Amer. Naturalist* XXXVI. 940 In the majority of specialized gastropods *phylogerontism is expressed, not in the non-coiling of the last portion of the spire, but in its expansion and wrapping about the earlier whorls. **1902** Webster *Suppl.* s.v. *Phylo-*, *Phylonepionic.

phy'logenal, *a. rare.* [irreg. f. phylogeny + -al[1].] = phylogenetic.
1890 *Nature* 6 Feb. 316/2 He has..confounded ontogenal steps of growth with phylogenal phases of plan.

phylogenesis (faɪləʊ'dʒɛnɪsɪs). *Biol.* [mod.L. f. phylo- + -genesis; coined in Ger. (E. Haeckel *Generelle Morphologie der Organismen* (1866) II. xx. 299).] The genesis or evolution of the tribe or race; the evolution of any organ or feature in the race; = phylogeny 1. Also *transf.*
1875 tr. *Schmidt's Desc. & Darw.* 217 The families within which we have as yet been able to compare Ontogenesis with Phylogenesis, constantly approximate in their origin. **1879** tr. *Haeckel's Evol. Man* I. i. 7 Phylogenesis is the mechanical cause of Ontogenesis: The Evolution of the Tribe..effects all the..Evolution of the Germ or Embryo. **1881** S. V. Clevenger in *Amer. Nat.* July 513 Certain aspects in the phylogenesis of the spinal cord. **1926** W. McDougall *Introd. Social Psychol.* (ed. 20) 402 The psychologist may legitimately speculate on the problems of phylogenesis; but he is under no obligation to offer any phylogenetic theory. **1940** Hinsie & Shatzky *Psychiatric Dict.* 418/2 The biological concept of phylogenesis has been used in different ways for analytical analogies in the psychological sphere, in order to emphasize the role of racial elements in the manifestations of the psyche. **1957** *Times Lit. Suppl.* 1 Nov. 659/1 He [*sc.* Jung] claimed that the doctrine which asserts that ontogenesis is a repetition of phylogenesis was also true of psychic life. **1966** Davis & Zangerl tr. *Hennig's Phylogenetic Systematics* iii. 199 Phylogenesis is the origin of groups of species from a stem species and its descendants by progressive splitting. **1977** P. Johnson *Enemies of Society* xvii. 226 Since the phylogenesis of music is communication, it must have a structure.

phylogenetic (ˌfaɪləʊdʒɪ'nɛtɪk), *a.* [f. as prec. + -genetic.] Of, pertaining to, or characteristic of phylogenesis or phylogeny; relating to the race history of an organism or organisms.
1877 Huxley *Anat. Inv. Anim.* Introd. 41 The validity of phylogenetic conclusions, deduced from the facts of embryology alone. **1885** W. A. Herdman (*title*) A Phylogenetic Classification of Animals (for the Use of Students). **1897** *19th Cent.* May 793 From these ontogenetic details to see what deductions may be drawn in regard to the phylogenetic origin of Languages.

So ˌ**phyloge'netical** *a. rare.* Hence ˌ**phyloge'netically** *adv.*, with reference to phylogenesis; in or as regards the evolution of the race.
1872 Elsberg in *Microsc. Jrnl.* July 185 A chain of gradations..through which higher organisms have passed phylogenetically, and do pass ontogenetically. **1878** Bell tr. *Gegenbaur's Comp. Anat.* 413 The earliest characters of the embryonic head, or of its equivalent in all Vertebrata, point to its being phylogenetically, the most ancient portion of the body. **1879** tr. *Haeckel's Evol. Man* I. vii. 150 First, observe the facts of Ontogeny and then attach their phylo-genetical significance to them. **1888** *Pop. Sci. Monthly* XXXIII. 479 The morphological and phylogenetical study of the higher plants.

phylogeneticist (ˌfaɪləʊdʒɪ'nɛtɪsɪst). [f. phylogenetic *a.* + -ist.] = phylogenist.
1968 R. D. Martin tr. *Wickler's Mimicry in Plants & Animals* iii. 39 The famous phylogeneticist George Gaylord Simpson called for a detailed investigation.

phylogenetics (ˌfaɪləʊdʒɪ'nɛtɪks), *sb. pl.* [f. phylogenetic *a.*: see -ic 2.] The study of phylogeny, esp. the factors influencing its course. (Usu. const. as *sing.*)
1937 K. Faegri in *Bot. Rev.* III. 400 (*heading*) Some fundamental problems of taxonomy and phylogenetics. *Ibid.* 422 Phylogenetics: the science of the tribal history and descent (phylogeny) of plants and animals. **1966** Davis & Zangerl tr. *Hennig's Phylogenetic Systematics* iii. 201 Determining the significance of individual factors in the total evolutionary process is the unique task of phylogenetics. **1975** *Nature* 18 Dec. 641/2 Palaeogenetics.. as well as protein phylogenetics..assume that comparative analyses of amino acid sequence data..yield a realistic image of evolution.

phylogenic (faɪləʊ'dʒɛnɪk), *a.* [f. as phylogenist + -ic.] Of or pertaining to phylogeny; phylogenetic.
1877 Huxley *Anat. Inv. Anim.* xii. 669 *note*, A great variety of surprising phylogenic speculations. **1878** Foster *Phys.* iv. v. 556 This..has a morphological or phylogenic, as well as a physiological or teleological, significance.

phylo'genically, *adv.* [f. phylogenic *a.*: see -ically.] = phylogenetically *adv.*
1975 *Nature* 5 June 483/1 So far the only studies on the teratogenic effects of this virus have been in the chick embryo and rodents, animals phylogenically distant from *Homo sapiens.*

phylogenist (faɪ'lɒdʒɪnɪst). [f. next + -ist.] One versed or skilled in phylogeny.
1881 *Gardeners' Chron.* 17 Sept. 364/3 Phylogenists have agreed on a few main points. **1885** *Athenæum* 18 Apr. 507/1 The principle of archaic forms..started by the father of phylogenists.

phylogeny (faɪ'lɒdʒɪnɪ). *Biol.* [ad. mod.Ger. *phylogenie* (E. Haeckel *Generelle Morphologie der Organismen* (1866) I. iii. 57), f. Gr. φῦλον race, phylum + -γένεια birth, origin.]
1. The genesis and evolution of the phylum, tribe, or species; ancestral or racial evolution of an animal or plant type, or of particular organs or other components of a plant or an animal (as distinguished from *ontogenesis*, the evolution of the individual).
1872 Darwin *Orig. Spec.* (ed. 5) xiv, Professor Häckel in his Generelle Morphologie..has recently brought his great knowledge and abilities to bear on what he calls Phylogeny, or the lines of descent of all organic beings. **1872** [see ontogeny]. **1878** Bell tr. *Gegenbaur's Comp. Anat.* 451 The phylogeny..of a few of the cephalic bones is as yet unknown. **1897** *Bot. Gaz.* XXIV. 172 We are warranted in strenuously urging a conformity of taxonomy with phylogeny. **1901** *Trans. Linn. Soc.* (*Zool.*) VIII. 270 The Plates attached to this paper represent with approximate accuracy the phylogeny of the intestinal tract in birds. **1903** C. W. Saleeby in *Academy* 13 June 594/1 Von Baer's law may be stated thus: 'Ontogeny is the recapitulation of phylogeny'. **1940** J. S. Huxley *New Systematics* 19 Phylogeny may be almost hopelessly obscured by parallel or convergent evolution. **1953** E. Mayr et al. *Methods & Princ. Systematic Zool.* iii. 42 It is the avowed aim of a modern classification to reflect phylogeny. **1971** J. Z. Young *Introd. Study Man* xxxv. 486 We cannot measure the development of the frontal lobes in phylogeny accurately.
2. The history or science of evolution or genealogical development in the phylum, tribe, or species; the race history of an animal or vegetable type; tribal history.
1872 [see bathmic *a.*]. **1875** Dawson *Dawn of Life* viii. 218 Science fails to inform us, but conjectural 'phylogeny' steps in. **1877** Huxley *Anat. Inv. Anim.* Introd. 41 A special branch of biological speculation termed phylogeny. **1894** Drummond *Ascent of Man* 77 Phylogeny—the history of the race.
3. A pedigree or genealogical table showing the racial evolution of a type of organisms.
1870 Rolleston *Anim. Life* p. xxv, 'Phylogenies', or hypothetical genealogical pedigrees, reaching far out of modern periods, are likely to remain in the very highest degree arbitrary and problematical. **1888** Dawson *Geol. Hist. Plants* 269 It is easy to construct a theoretical phylogeny of the derivation of the willows from a supposed ancestral source. **1892** *Nation* (N.Y.) 27 Oct. 325/3 The phylogenies given by the different authors are usually regarded by students as subjects for all sorts of changes and revisions.

phylological (faɪləʊ'lɒdʒɪkəl), *a. nonce-wd.* [f. phylo- + -logical: after *philological.*] Of or pertaining to the history of the evolution of races.
1891 G. J. Romanes in *Monist* Oct. 67 For, archaic though they be in a philological sense, in a phylological sense they are things of yesterday.

‖**phylum** ('faɪləm). *Biol.* Pl. **-la.** [mod.L., a. Gr. φῦλον race, stock.] **1. a.** A tribe or race of organisms, related by descent from a common ancestral form; a series of animals or plants genetically related; a primary division or subkingdom of animals or plants supposed to be so related. Also *transf.* and *fig.*
1876 tr. *Haeckel's Hist. Creation* II. xvi. 42 By *tribe*, or *phylum*, we understand all those organisms of whose blood-relationship and descent from a common primary form there can be no doubt, or whose relationship, at least, is most probable from anatomical reasons, as well as from reasons founded on historical development. **1878** Bell tr. *Gegenbaur's Comp. Anat.* p. xvii, I have arranged the chief phyla first of all in the form of a genealogical tree. **1888** Rolleston & Jackson *Anim. Life* 578 The classes.. collectively termed Vermes do not constitute a phylum.. comparable..to the phyla Mollusca or Echinodermata.
transf. and *fig.* **1945** Auden *Coll. Poetry* 162 Whole phyla of resentments every day Give status to the wild men of the world Who rule the absent-minded. **1971** *New Scientist* 25 Mar. 682/1 We have to regard science as a 'phylum' (as the term is used by Pierre Teilhard de Chardin)—that is, as an expanding movement within the four-dimensional spacetime continuum of the social system. **1973** *Sci. Amer.* Apr. 121/1 Computers are no longer individuals with names but a phylum of many species, rapidly evolving under selection pressures.
b. *Psychol.* The human race or group as it is relevant to the development of the individual.
1927 T. Burrow in *Brit. Jrnl. Med. Psychol.* VII. 199 The social group or phylum. *Ibid.* 202 In a comprehensive view of our human phylum there remains no other conclusion than that the social mind..comprises a systematization of social images. **1930** —— in *Psyche* XI. ii. 69 Medicine, then, became a science when the symptoms of the individual ceased to be the focus of interest and when interest became focussed instead upon the pathological germ or cause of definite alterations of tissue and their characteristic symptoms, as these..were observed within the organism of man..as a species or phylum. **1940** H. G. Baynes *Mythol. of Soul* i. xii. 460 The concept of individuality as a self-contained, self-regulating organism has no validity unless it also embraces this backward extension of the ancestral phylum. **1953** T. Burrow *Sci. & Man's Behavior* vi. 73 Some of my colleagues commented upon the unusual sense in which I use the term 'phylum'... By this term I do not mean to separate man from the rest of the vertebrates. I am merely trying to discuss man, with his social needs and interests, as a biological organism.
2. *Linguistics.* A group of languages related, or believed to be related, less closely than those of a family or stock.
1958 H. Hoijer in R. H. Thompson *Migrations in New World Culture Hist.* 59 There is no indication that the families of a phylum, or the phyla of a macro-phylum, need be connected by clearly statable phonetic correspondences. **1965** *Canad. Jrnl. Linguistics* X. 142 The reconstruction (by comparative method linguistics) is systematic... The reconstruction (in phylum linguistics) is illustrative and restricted to a relatively small set of cognates and typological samenesses which point to an earlier phylum parent language in the prehistoric era. **1973** A. P. Sorensen in D. R. Gross *Peoples & Cultures of Native S. Amer.* 333 Two of them represent the comparative method linguistics approach..; the other two represent the phylum linguistics approach. **1973** *Language* XLIX. 239 Tarascan, like Zuni, is a one-language phylum.

‖**phyma** ('faɪmə). *Path.* Pl. **-ata.** [L. *phȳma* (Cels.), a. Gr. φῦμα, φυματ- swelling, tumour.] An inflamed swelling, of various kinds; an external tubercle; in nosological systems variously applied to orders or genera of diseases.
1693 tr. *Blancard's Phys. Dict.* (ed. 2), *Phyma*, a Swelling: There are Five sorts. **1739** Huxham in *Phil. Trans.* XLI. 668 An exceeding painful Phyma near the Verge of the Anus. **1799** Hooper *Med. Dict., Phyma*, tubercles in any part of the body. **1858** in Mayne *Expos. Lex.* **1893** in *Syd. Soc. Lex.*

Hence **phy'matic** *a.*, of or pertaining to phyma; **'phymatoid** *a.*, resembling phyma.

ˈphymatin. *Chem.* [f. Gr. φῦμα, φῦματ-, PHYMA + -IN[1]. Cf. F. *phymatine.*] An organic substance obtained from tubercle.

1847–9 TODD *Cycl. Anat.* IV. 107/1 Phymatin is described as a peculiar extractive matter.

phymosis, erron. form of PHIMOSIS.

†**phynx.** *Obs. rare.* [var. of SPHINX: cf. Bœotian Φίξ *phix.*] = SPHINX.

1688 R. HOLME *Armoury* II. 9/1 Pallas [is drawn] with an Helmet.. and.. on her Helmet a Phynx or Cock. *Ibid.* 201/2 The Phynx, or Sphynga, or Sphynx.. are.. in the shape of Women.

‖**phyogemmarium** (ˌfaɪəʊdʒɛˈmɛərɪəm). *Zool.* Pl. -ia. [mod.L., f. Gr. φύ-ειν to produce + L. *gemmārius* adj., f. *gemma* a bud.] A small reproductive bud, in certain Hydrozoa.

1861 J. R. GREENE *Man. Anim. Kingd., Cœlent.* 105 Numerous small gonoblastidia, which resemble polypites, and are termed 'phyogemmaria'. **1870** NICHOLSON *Man. Zool.* 83 The limb is traversed by.. canals, which.. communicate with the cavities of the phyogemmaria.

-phyre (faɪə(r)), comb. form of PORPHYRY used in names of porphyritic rocks, as GRANOPHYRE, KERATOPHYRE.

‖**physa** (ˈfaɪsə). *Zool.* [mod.L., a. Gr. φῦσα bellows.] A small freshwater gastropod.

1842 BRANDE *Dict. Sci.* etc., *Physa,* a genus of freshwater snails; so called from the thinness and inflated appearance of the shell. **1855** LYELL *Elem. Geol.* xx, Freshwater strata.. filled.. with Valvata, Paludina, Planorbis, Limnæus, Physa, and Cyclas. **1902** CORNISH *Naturalist Thames* 16 Tiny physas and succineas, no larger than shot.

physagogue (ˈfaɪsəgɒg), *a.* (*sb.*) *Med.* [f. Gr. φῦσα flatulence + ἀγωγός drawing forth.] Expelling flatus. **b.** *sb.* A medicine having this effect.

1858 in MAYNE *Expos. Lex.* **1893** in *Syd. Soc. Lex.*

‖**Physalia** (faɪˈseɪlɪə). *Zool.* [mod.L., f. Gr. φυσαλέος inflated with wind, φυσαλλίς bladder, bubble.] A genus of oceanic hydrozoa; the Portuguese man-of-war: see MAN-OF-WAR 4. Hence **phyˈsalian** *a.*, belonging to this genus; also *sb.*, a species of Physalia.

1842 BRANDE *Dict. Sci.* etc., *Physalis,* or *Physalia,* the name of a hydrostatic Acalephan, commonly called the Portuguese man-of-war. **1855** H. SPENCER *Princ. Psychol.* (1872) I. v. iii. 521 Oceanic Hydrozoa which.. have long pendant tentacles, such as Physalia. **1861** HARTWIG *Sea & Wond.* xv, The *Physalia caravella* or Portuguese man-of-war, is the mariner's admiration. On a large float-bladder.. rises a vertical comb [etc.].

physaliferous (faɪsəˈlɪfərəs), *a.* *Biol.* [f. Gr. φυσαλλ-ίς bladder + -IFEROUS.] = PHYSALIPHOROUS *a.*

1954 G. L. FITE tr. R. Virchow in *Amer. Jrnl. Leprosy* XXII. 209 They [*sc.* the cells] have one characteristic that is especially noteworthy, i.e., their tendency to form a sort of vacuole, apparently from taking up water, so that under the circumstances they acquire a wholly physaliferous appearance. **1977** *Proc. R. Soc. Med.* LXX. 276/2 A large number of the cells had a vacuolated cytoplasm with hyperchromatic nuclei, the pattern being that of 'physaliferous' cells characteristic of a chordoma.

physalin (ˈfaɪsəlɪn). *Chem.* [f. mod.L. *Phȳsalis* (ad. Gr. φυσαλλίς bladder) + -IN[1].] A yellow bitter amorphous substance ($C_{14}H_6O_5$), the active principle of the winter cherry, *Physalis Alkekengi.*

1863 *N. Syd. Soc. Year-bk. Med.* 457 All parts of the plant [*Physalis Alkekengi*] possess a strong bitter taste which is probably due to a crystalline principle, named physaline. **1866** WATTS *Dict. Chem.* IV. 634.

physaliphore (faɪˈsælɪfɔə(r)). *Biol.* [ad. Ger. *physaliphor* (Virchow), f. Gr. φυσαλλίς a bladder + -φόρος bearing: see -PHORE.] A cell containing vesicles (*physalides*) which produce daughter-cells.

1860 F. CHANCE tr. *R. Virchow's Cellular Path.* xviii. 401 (*caption*) Endogenous new formation; cells containing vesicles (physaliphores). **1876** BRISTOWE *The. & Pract. Med.* (1878) 73 They not unfrequently become vacuolated, or hollowed out here and there into globular cavities, which are termed by Virchow 'physaliphores', and are regarded by him as reproductive cavities.

Hence **physaˈliphorous** *a.*, that contains vesicles; cf. PHYSALIFEROUS *a.*

1964 D. F. CAPPELL *Muir's Textbk. Path.* (ed. 8) xvii. 701/2 The tumour tissue [of a chordoma] consists of lobules of rounded or polyhedral cells arranged in alveoli or cords: some of these cells contain numerous intracytoplasmic vacuoles of mucin, 'physaliphorous cells'.

physalis (ˈfaɪsəlɪs, faɪˈseɪlɪs). [mod.L. (Linnæus *Hortus Cliffortianus* (1738) 62), f. Gr. φυσαλλίς bladder, in reference to the inflated calyx.] An annual or perennial herb of the genus so called, belonging to the family Solanaceæ, mostly native to North or Central America, and bearing white, yellow, or purple flowers and, in some species, edible red or purplish berries; cf. ALKEKENGI, *Cape gooseberry* s.v. CAPE *sb.*[3] 4, *Chinese lantern* (*plant*) s.v. CHINESE *a.* 2, *ground-cherry* b s.v. GROUND *sb.* 18 c, WINTER CHERRY 1 a.

1807 *Curtis's Bot. Mag.* XXVII. 1068 (*heading*) Eatable Physalis or Cape Gooseberry. **1907** T. W. SANDERS *Flower Garden* 196 The Physalises belong to the Nightshade order. **1930** *Times Educ. Suppl.* 18 Oct. 431/2 The windows of the florists are bright just now with the fruits of physalis, the winter cherry. **1961** *Amat. Gardening* 30 Sept. 7/2 'Lanterns' of physalis.. can be skeletonised. **1968** S. C. EMBERTON *Garden Foliage* ix. 219 Mustard yellow achillea and orange 'lanterns' of physalis teamed up with bulrushes.

physalite (ˈfɪsəlaɪt). *Min.* [ad. Ger. *physalith* (Werner 1817), shortened from *pyrophysalith* PYROPHYSALITE.] A variety of topaz: see quots.

1819 W. PHILLIPS *Min.* (ed. 2) 69 Pyrophysalite, physalite. **1821** R. JAMESON *Man. Min.* 190 Physalite, or Pyrophysalite... Colours greenish-white and mountain-green. **1868** DANA *Min.* (ed. 5) 377 Physalite or pyrophysalite is a coarse nearly opaque variety [of topaz] in yellowish-white large crystals from Finbo; it intumesces when heated, and hence its name.

†ˈ**physˌbuttocke.** [f. FISE, FIZZ + BUTTOCK: cf. FIZGIG.] A contemptuous term for a coxcomb.

1570 LEVINS *Manip.* 159/6 Physbuttocke, *trossulus.*

physcony (ˈfɪskəʊnɪ). *Path.* [ad. mod.L. *physconia,* f. Gr. φύσκων pot-belly, f. φύσκη sausage, f. φυσᾶν to blow up. Cf. F. *physconie.*] A tumour or swelling of the abdomen; parabysma.

1822–34 *Good's Study Med.* (ed. 4) II. 5 Those vast formations of pus which are sometimes found in parabysmic tumours or physconies. *Ibid.* IV. 53 A physcony of the abdomen, accompanied with peculiar feelings.

Hence **phyˈsconic** *a.* (Mayne *Expos. Lex.* 1858).

Phys. Ed., phys. ed., colloq. abbrev. of *physical education.* Also *attrib.*

1955 *Amer. Speech* XXX. 304 *Phys ed major,* mannish female. **1957** O. NASH *You can't get there from Here* 84 Get them interested in hotel management and phys. ed. **1968** A. HOLDEN *Death after School* iv. 31 There's the Phys Ed man. **1972** P. MARKS *Collector's Choice* ii. 82 A converted basement of the Phys Ed building. **1977** *Time* 9 May 50/3, I was very poor on the parallel bars, and my phys.-ed class came at the damn wrong hour.

physem (ˈfaɪsɛm). *Phonetics.* [ad. Gr. φύσημα the action or product of blowing, f. φυσᾶν to blow.] A name applied by A. J. Ellis to elements of speech produced by 'the bellows-action of the lungs'; comprehending the ordinary aspirate (*h*) in its varieties, and the 'wheeze', Arabic ح, 'arising from suddenly forcing breath through the cartilaginous glottis'.

1887 A. J. ELLIS in *Encycl. Brit.* XXII. 382/2. *Ibid.* 386/2 [In Palæotype] (h) when no letter, and, at most, some sign precedes, [is] used for the unanalysed physem.

physemarian (faɪsiːˈmɛərɪən), *a.* and *sb.* *Zool.* [f. mod.L. *Phȳsēmāria* pl., f. Gr. φύσημα bubble.] **a.** *adj.* Belonging to the *Physemaria,* a name applied by Haeckel to a group of Metazoa; now abandoned. **b.** *sb.* One of the *Physemaria.*

1877 HUXLEY *Anat. Inv. Anim.* xii. 678 The spheroidal, free-swimming monad aggregates.. are in many respects comparable to Physemarian or Poriferan embryos. *Ibid.* 681 That common form, when the special characters.. are eliminated.. would be exceedingly similar to a Physemarian.

Physeptone (faɪˈsɛptəʊn). *Pharm.* Also **physeptone.** A proprietary name for methadone hydrochloride. Cf. PHY.

1947 *Lancet* 6 Sept. 370/2 (*heading*) Miadone (Physeptone) in obstetrics. **1948** *Trade Marks Jrnl.* 15 Sept. 743/1 Physeptone... All goods included in class 5 [*sc.* pharmaceutical, veterinary and sanitary substances, etc.]. The Wellcome Foundation Limited,.. London,.. manufacturing chemists. **1951** *Pharmaceutical Jrnl.* CXII. 52/1 An inquest was held at Coventry on a three-year-old boy who died from an overdose of Physeptone linctus. **1969** *Daily Tel.* 3 Feb. 22/6 Physeptone, a narcotic drug first used in America for the gradual withdrawal of drug addicts from heroin, is proving successful in 'weaning' British addicts off hard drugs. **1971** [see PHY]. **1972** J. BROWN *Chancer* ii. 30 She was on 5 and 3 at the time—five one-sixth grains of heroin and three ten-milligram ampoules of physeptone. **1976** H. FERGUSON *Confessions Long Distance Acid Head* 7 Apart from cannabis, I have used barbiturates, amphetamines,.. the synthetic opiate physeptone, morphine, cocaine,.. even apomorphine once.

physeter (faɪˈsiːtə(r)). [a. L. *phȳsētēr* a cachalot (Plin.), a. Gr. φυσητήρ a blower, a whale, f. φυσᾶν to blow.]

†**1.** A large blowing whale. *Obs.*

1591 SYLVESTER *Du Bartas* I. v. 109 When on the surges I perceiue from far Th' Ork, Whirlpoole, Whale, or puffing Physeter. **1706** PHILLIPS, *Physeter,* the Whirl-pool, puffing or spouting Whale. **1786** *Phil. Trans.* LXXVI. 444 These bones belonged to physeteres or respiring fishes.

2. *Zool.* The generic name of the cachalots or larger sperm-whales.

1753 CHAMBERS *Cycl. Supp.* s.v., The physeter with the upper jaw longer than the under one.. The head of this fish is so large, that it is half as long as the body, and thicker than the thickest part of it. **1806** HOME in *Phil. Trans.* XCVII. 100 The oil of the physeter, which crystallizes into spermaceti. **1833** SIR C. BELL *Hand* (1834) 298 The Physeter or cachelot whale.. is remarkable for having teeth.

3. A filter acting by air-pressure.

1842 FRANCIS *Dict. Arts,* etc., *Physeter,* a filtering machine, consisting of a tub, with an air-tight perforated stage half-way up. The feculent liquid to be filtered is put above the stage, and a syringe, by withdrawing the air from below the stage, occasions the clear part of the liquid to pass through, owing to the pressure of the atmosphere above it.

Hence **phyˈseterine, phyˈseteroid** *adjs.*, of or pertaining to the sperm-whales; *sbs.* A member of this group.

1883 *Encycl. Brit.* XV. 393/2 Almost all the other members of the suborder range themselves under the two principal heads of Ziphioids (or Physeteroids) and Delphinoids.

physetoleic (faɪsiːtəʊˈliːɪk), *a.* *Chem.* [f. PHYSET-ER 2 + OLEIC.] In *physetoleic acid,* an unsaturated fatty acid ($C_{16}H_{30}O_2$), obtained by saponification of spermaceti; isomeric, if not identical, with hypogæic acid.

1857 MILLER *Elem. Chem.* III. 419 *Physetoleic acid* was obtained from the oil of the ordinary sperm whale (*Physeter macrocephalus*). **1866** WATTS *Dict. Chem.* IV. 635 Physetoleic acid crystallises in stellate groups of colourless needles.

phys-harmonica (faɪs-, fɪshɑːˈmɒnɪkə). [f. Gr. φῦσα bellows + HARMONICA.] A primitive form of harmonium, in which metal springs are set in vibration by a current of air; invented by Häckel of Vienna in 1818, and originally made to be attached to a piano. **b.** A kind of reed-stop on the organ, imitating the tone of this.

1838 *Encycl. Brit.* (ed. 7) XVII. 476/2 *Physharmonica,* a musical instrument, in which the immediate sonorous bodies are springs of steel or of brass, thrown into vibration by a current of air impelled against them. **1852** SEIDEL *Organ* 101 Phys-harmonica is a newly-invented reed-register, with a soft, agreeable tone. **1881** BROADHOUSE *Mus. Acoustics* 176 Musical tones of this description are those of.. phys-harmonica (harmonium, concertina, accordion) [etc.].

physiˈanthropy. [f. Gr. φύσις nature + -ανθρωπία, f. ἄνθρωπ-ος man.] (See quots.)

1828–32 WEBSTER, *Physianthropy,* the philosophy of human life, or the doctrine of the constitution and diseases of man, and the remedies. **1885** MRS. C. L. WALLACE (*title*) Physianthropy, or the Home Cure and Eradication of Disease.

physiatric (fɪzɪˈætrɪk). [a. Ger. *physiatrik,* f. Gr. φύσις nature + IATRIC.] The doctrine or system of nature-cure (Ger. *naturheilkunde*); the application of natural agencies in medicine. Also **physiˈatrics.** Hence **physiˈatrical** *a.*

1858 MAYNE *Expos. Lex.* 956/1 Physiatrics.. Physiatrical. **1901** BILZ *Nat. Meth. Healing* 5, I now come to speak of physiatric (Science of nature cure).

physic (ˈfɪzɪk), *sb.* Forms: α. 3–4 **fisyke, 4 fisyk, fizike, 4–5 fisik(e, fysik, fysyk(e, 5 fisykke, fesike, 5–6 fesyk.** β. **4 phisek, phesike, 4–6 phisik(e, -yk(e, 4–7 phisique, 5 phisikke, phesyk, 5–6 phisyque, physyk(e, 5–7 phisick(e, -ik(e, 6 -ycke, 6–7 physike, 6–8 -ick(e, 7 -iq(ue, 7– physic.** [ME. *fisike,* a. OF. *fisique* (12th c.), ad. L. *physica,* a. Gr. φυσική (ἐπιστήμη) the knowledge of nature: see PHYSIC *a.*]

1. Natural science, the knowledge of the phenomenal world; = PHYSICS 1. Now *rare.*

13.. *Seuyn Sag.* (W.) 186 And eke alle the seven ars. The first so was grammarie.. Rettorike, and ek fisike. **1390** GOWER *Conf.* III. 89 Phisique.. Thurgh which the philosophre hath founde To techen sondri knowlechinges Upon the bodiliche thinges, Of man, of beste, of herbe, of ston. **1477** NORTON *Ord. Alch.* v. in Ashm. *Theat. Chem. Brit.* (1652) 57 But it is not so in the Phisick of Mines. **1586** T. B. *La Primaud. Fr. Acad.* I. (1594) 72 Physike, which is the studie of naturall things: metaphysike, which is of supernaturall things. **1685** BAXTER *Paraphr. N.T.* 1 Cor. ii, True Physick is the Knowledge of the knowable Works of God, and God in them. **1742** POPE *Dunc.* IV. 645 Physic of Metaphysic begs defence, And Metaphysic calls for aid on Sense! **1883** A. BARRATT *Phys. Metempiric* 171 This is the only form in which the question of mind and matter has any meaning to Physic, for Physic knows nothing of either mind or matter except as objects and physical phenomena.

2. The knowledge of the human body; *esp.* the theory of diseases and their treatment; medical science, medicine. *arch.*

[**1125** W. MALMESB. *De Gestis Regum Angl.* II. Prol., Physicam quæ medetur corporis valetudini.] *c* **1386** CHAUCER *Prol.* 411 Wiþ vs ther was a Doctour of Phisik, In al this world ne was ther noon hym lik To speke of phisik and of Surgerye. **1390** GOWER *Conf.* III. 23 For in Phisique this I finde, Usage is the seconde kinde. **1509** HAWES *Past. Pleas.* xvi. (Percy Soc.) 62 Of phisike it is the properte To ayde the body in every sekenes. **1542** *Act 32 Hen. VIII,* c. 40 The science of phisicke dothe comprehend, include, and conteyne, the knowledge of surgery as a speciall membre and parte of the same. **1662–3** PEPYS *Diary* 27 Feb., To Chyrurgeon's Hall.. where.. we had a fine dinner and good learned company, many Doctors of Phisique. **1758** BLACKSTONE *Study of Law* I. in *Comm.* (1765) I. 14 The gentleman of the faculty of physic. **1808** *Med. Jrnl.* XIX. 468 To admit 'certificates from schools of physic may prevent the possibility of ascertaining a regular education'.

3. a. The art or practice of healing; the healing art; the medical profession.

1297 R. GLOUC. (Rolls) 3162 Suþ þe monekes abit on him he let do, And nom wiþ him spicerie þat to fisyke drou. **1340** *Ayenb.* 54 Hit iualþ ofte þet þe ilke þet be fisike leueþ be fizike sterfþ. **1481** CAXTON *Myrr.* I. xii. 38 Phisyke.. is a mestier or a crafte that entendeth to the helthe of mannes body. **1523** *Act 14 & 15 Hen. VIII*, c. 5 §3 Suffred to excercyse or practyse in Physyk. **1700** S. L. tr. *Fryke's Voy. E. Ind.* 4 Any service suitable to my profession, which was Physick. **1813** J. THOMSON *Lect. Inflam.* Introd., The practice of Medicine has long been divided into two departments, Physic and Surgery. **1871** SIR T. WATSON *Princ. & Pract. Physic* Introd. Lect., This art of Physic.. needs to be begun under the protecting eye..of a master in the craft.

b. The medical faculty personified; physicians.

1362 LANGL. *P. Pl.* A. VII. 256, I dar legge boþe myn Eres, þat Fisyk schal his Forred hod for his foode sulle. **1576** GASCOIGNE *Steele Gl.* 984 That Phisicke thriue not ouer fast by murder. **1672** SIR T. BROWNE *Let. Friend* §20 Amply satisfied that his Disease should dye with himself, nor revive in a Posterity to puzzle Physick. **1764** GRAY *The Candidate* 5 'Lord, sister', says Physic to Law, 'I declare [etc.]'.

†**c.** Medical treatment or regimen. *Obs.*

c **1386** CHAUCER *Knt.'s T.* 1902 Ffarewel Phisik; go ber the man to chirche. **1471** J. PASTON in *P. Lett.* III. 7 My leche crafte and fesyk..hathe cost me sythe Estern Day more then v *li.* **1503** *Act 19 Hen. VII*, c. 36 §1 The same Sir William.. lay both at Surgery and Fesyk..by the space of ii yeres and more. **1568** BIBLE (Bishops') *Ecclus.* xviii. 18 Goe to phisicke or euer thou be sicke. *a* **1674** CLARENDON *Hist. Reb.* IX. §83 The Lord Goring being not then well, but engaged in a course of Physick. **1700** PRIDEAUX *Lett.* (Camden) 194 An end will soon be made beyond yᵉ remedy of physic and repentance.

4. a. = MEDICINE *sb.*¹ 2. (Now chiefly *colloq.*)

1591 HARINGTON *Orl. Fur.* Pref., Tasso..likeneth Poetrie to the Phisicke that men giue vnto little children when they are sick. **1605** SHAKS. *Macb.* V. iii. 47 Throw Physicke to the Dogs, Ile none of it. **1696** TATE & BRADY *Ps.* civ. 14 Herbs, for Man's use, of various Pow'r, That either Food or Physick yield. **1730** WESLEY *Wks.* (1830) I. 11 A little money, food or physic. **1862** MRS. H. WOOD *Mrs. Hallib.* II. vi, And, Janey, you'll take the physic, like a precious lamb: and heaps of nice things you shall have after it, to drive the taste out. **1872** GEO. ELIOT *Middlem.* x, As bad as the wrong physic,—nasty to take, and sure to disagree.

b. *spec.* A cathartic or purge.

1617 ABP. ABBOT *Descr. World* (1634) 303 The people.. doe vse it [Tobacco] as Physicke to purge themselues of humours. **1624** DONNE *Serm.* xvii. (1640) 170 Affliction is my Physick; that purges, that cleanses me. **1831** YOUATT *Horse* iv. 56 The spring grass is the best physic that can possibly be administered to the horse. It carries off every humour which may be lurking about the animal.

†**5. a.** *fig.* Wholesome or curative regimen or habit.

c **1386** CHAUCER *Nun's Pr. T.* 18 Atempree diett was al hir phisik. **14..** in *Q. Eliz. Acad.* etc. 49 Erly to ryse is fysyke fyne. **1591** GREENE *Farew. to Follie* Wks. (Grosart) IX. 239 Dinner being done, counting it Phisicke to sit a while, the old Countesse [etc.]. **1699** DRYDEN *To J. Driden* 116 Who, nature to repair, Draws physic from the fields in draughts of vital air.

b. Mental, moral, or spiritual remedy. *Obs.*

1390 GOWER *Conf.* III. 349 The wofull peine of loves maladie, Ayein the which mai no phisique availe. *c* **1440** *Generydes* 6876 If I here kyssid, I think, so god me save, It were the best fisykke that I cowde haue. **1561** T. NORTON *Calvin's Inst.* II. vii. (1634) 160 To crave the Phisicke of grace that is in Christ. **1656** *Burton's Diary* 16 Dec. (1828) I. 150 He is a madman. It is good physic to whip him. *a* **1703** BURKITT *On N.T.* Matt. v. 4 Sorrow for sin is physick on earth, but it is food in hell.

6. *attrib.* and *Comb.*, as †*physic-craft*, †*-god*, †*-rack*, †*-word*; *physic-taking* adj.; **physic-ball**, medicine in the form of a ball or bolus for administration to a horse, dog, etc.; †**physic-bill**, a medical prescription; also a medical advertisement; **physic-box**, a medicine-chest; †**physic-finger** = PHYSICIAN *finger*; †**physic-school**, a medical school. Also PHYSIC GARDEN. (In some of these, *physic* may have originally been the adj.: see PHYSIC *a.* 2 for similar uses.)

1831 YOUATT *Horse* xxiii. 398 The most effectual and safest *physic ball. **1845** —— *Dog* vi. 118 A physic-ball was given him in the evening, and on the following morning. **1614** T. ADAMS *Divell's Banket* 19 It is..a *physick-bill of hell, that they must not wash till they have drunk. **1711** SHAFTESB. *Charac., Misc.* v. iii. (1737) III. 340 To..be scrupulous in our choice, and (as the current physick-bills admonish us) beware of counterfeits. *a* **1661** HOLYDAY *Juvenal* ii. 23 No babes they leave behind. Big Lyde's *physick-box can this ne're gain. **1900** H. LAWSON *On Track* 55 An' if yer don't get yer physic-box an' come wi' me, by the great God I'll—. **1756** C. LUCAS *Ess. Waters* II. 217 The incorporated bands of the *physic-craft that call themselves the college of physicians. **1621** MOLLE *Camerar. Liv. Libr.* v. ii. 321 The Ring-finger or *Physicke-finger. **1613** PURCHAS *Pilgrimage* (1614) 93 Hee was their Æsculapius or *Physicke-god. **1706** BAYNARD in Sir J. Floyer *Hot & Cold Bath.* II. 280 Brought to the *Physick-Rack, viz. Bleedings,..Diet-drinks, Oyntments. **1677–8** in Willis & Clark *Cambridge* (1886) III. 24 The *Physick schooles. **1767** GOOCH *Treat. Wounds* I. 371 A man, who was executed, and dissected in the physic-schools. **1823** J. BADCOCK *Dom. Amusem.* 165 The valetudinary, consumptive, and *physic-taking..fall victims of the ship's motion. **1843** MIALL in *Nonconf.* III. 637 That definition which makes man 'a physic-taking animal'. *a* **1658** CLEVELAND *Gen. Poems*, &c. (1677) 164 Ἐκλείπεσθαι is a *Physick-word, and signifies the Labour of a Disease.

Hence (*nonce-wds.*) †'**physiclike** *adv.*, medicinally; †'**physicship**, humorous title of a medical authority; †'**physicster**, contemptuous term for a medicinal practitioner.

1581 MULCASTER *Positions* xi. (1887) 60 Musick..was vsed in the olde time Physiclike, to stay mourning and greife. **1689** G. HARVEY *Curing Dis. by Expect.* xviii. 137 The description..ought to be razed by their Physickships out of their Pharmaceutic Records. *Ibid.* xvii. 128 If any young Physickster has an itch to experiment.

physic ('fɪzɪk), *a.* Now *rare.* [a. F. *physique*, ad. L. *physic-us*, a. Gr. φυσικός natural, f. φύσις nature, f. φύειν to produce.]

1. Physical, natural.

1563 HYLL *Art Garden.* (1593) 23 A phisicke experiment of Democritus. **1669** GALE *Crt. Gentiles* I. I. ii. 14 Some Physic Contemplations of Job. *Ibid.* II. viii. 99 There are three Kinds of Theologie; the first is called Mythic.. another Physic. **1807** J. BARLOW *Columb.* IV. 455 O'er great, o'er small extends his physic laws. *c* **1811** FUSELI in *Lect. Paint.* iv. (1848) 439 Invisible physic and metaphysic ideas.

b. Belonging to physics or natural philosophy.

1883 J. B. THOMAS in *Homilet. Monthly* (N.Y.) 8 Jan. 204 Sensitive, nutritive, physic, and chemic phenomena.

†**2.** Medical; medicinal. *Obs.* (= PHYSIC *sb. attrib.*, PHYSICAL *a.* 4, 5.)

1422 tr. *Secreta Secret., Priv. Priv.* 144 Libral Sciencis.. as gramer, arte fisike, astronomye, and otheris. *c* **1440** *Pol. Rel. & L. Poems* 217, I axst a mayster of fysyke lore, what wold hym drye and dryve away? **1551** ROBINSON tr. *More's Utop.* II. vi. (1895) 216 My companion..caried with him phisick bokes, certein smal woorkes of Hippocrates, and Galenes Microtechne. **1577** B. GOOGE *Heresbach's Husb.* (1586) 52b, When you haue seuered..your Physicke Hearbes by themselues, and your Potte hearbes and Sallets in another place. **1577** MOUNTAIN *Gardener's Labyrinth* Title-p., The physick benefit of each herb, plant, and flower. *a* **1617** HIERON *Wks.* I. 25 The physick potion..is cleane against the stomacke. **1620** VENNER *Via Recta* ii. 28 Red wine is..good for physicke vses, to stop cholericke vomitings. **1704** RAY *Creation* II. 252 The chief Physick Herbs. **1736** *N. Jersey Archives* XI. 446 A Root call'd Physick Root, filarie or five leaf'd Physick.

physic ('fɪzɪk), *v.* Inflexions **physicked**, **physicking**. [f. PHYSIC *sb.* 3–5.]

1. *trans.* To dose or treat with physic or medicine, esp. with a purgative. Now *colloq.*

1377 LANGL. *P. Pl.* B. xx. 321, I may wel suffre..That frere flaterer be fette and phisike [C. XXIII. 323 fysyke] ȝow syke. **1575** TURBERV. *Faulconrie* 279 The Italians order of phisicking his hawke. **1600** SHAKS. *A.Y.L.* I. i. 92, I will physicke your ranckenesse. **1733** CHEYNE *Eng. Malady* I. vi. §2 (1734) 50 The Animals..are physick'd almost out of their Lives. **1831** YOUATT *Horse* xxiii. 382 In physicking a horse, whatever is to be done, should be done at once. **1876** FOX BOURNE *Locke* II. xii. 258 Locke laid down the rule..that children ought to be physicked as little as possible.

b. *fig.* To treat with remedies, relieve, alleviate.

1589 NASHE *Pref. Greene's Menaphon* (Arb.) 7, I wold perswade them to phisicke their faculties of seeing and hearing. **1605** SHAKS. *Macb.* II. iii. 55 The labour we delight in, Physicks paine. **1641** MILTON *Reform.* I. (1851) 12 Then was the Liturgie given to a number of moderate Divines, and Sir Tho. Smith a Statesman to bee purg'd, and Physick't. **1763** CHURCHILL *Duellist* I. 34 Vice, within the guilty breast, Could not be physic'd into rest. **1819** BYRON *Juan* II. xix, A mind diseased no remedy can physic.

2. *slang.* To punish in purse or pocket.

1821 EGAN *Life Lond.* II. v. (Farmer), You may be most preciously physicked in your clie. **1823** BEE *Dict. Turf* 134 Winning a man's blunt at cards, or other wagers, is 'giving him a physicking'. 'The physicking system' was put in force at the Doncaster St. Leger, 1822.

3. *Metallurgy.* To treat (molten iron, etc.) with an oxidizing body, which combines with and eliminates phosphorus and sulphur.

1876 HEELEY in Ure *Dict. Arts* (1878) IV. 475 If with their present plants they could not effectually eliminate sulphur by puddling, ought they not to try to do so by physicking?

Hence '**physicking** *vbl. sb.*; also '**physicker**, one who administers physic.

1658 GURNALL *Chr. in Arm.* verse 16. ii. (1669) 187/1 He hath undertook the physicking of his Saints. **1826** MISS MITFORD *Village* Ser. II. (1863) 415 Dr. Tubb..bleeder, shaver, and physicker of man and beast. **1838** DICKENS *Nich. Nick.* viii, 'Now', said Squeers,..'is that physicking over?'

physical ('fɪzɪkəl), *a.* (and *sb.*) Also 5–7 phis-, 6 phus-; 5 -ycal, -ichal, 6–7 -icall. [ad. med.L. *physicālis*, f. *physica*, PHYSIC *sb.*: see -AL¹.]

I. 1. a. Of or pertaining to material nature, or to the phenomenal universe perceived by the senses; pertaining to or connected with matter; material; opposed to *psychical*, *mental*, *spiritual*.

Often in such collocations as ***physical cause***, ***energy***, ***power***; ***physical possibility***, ***impossibility***, etc.: see also 7.

1597 HOOKER *Eccl. Pol.* v. lvii. §4 Sacraments..are not physicall but morall instruments of saluation. **1604** E. G[RIMSTONE] *D' Acosta's Hist. Indies* II. viii. 99 In naturall and phisicall things, we must not seeke out infallible and mathematicall rules, but that which is ordinary and tried by experience. **1605** BACON *Adv. Learning* II. 29 For the handling of finall causes mixed with the rest in Phisicall enquiries, hath intercepted the seuere and diligent enquirie of all reall and phisicall causes. **1666** BOYLE *Orig. Formes & Qual.* (1667) 7 Whether or no the Shape can by Physicall Agents be altered. **1695** ALINGHAM *Geom. Epit.* 86 If..the line E..be moved parallel to it self, through every phisical point in the line A, it will produce the rectangle AE. **1752** HUME *Ess. & Treat.* (1777) I. xxi. 215 As to physical causes, I am inclined to doubt altogether of their operation in this particular. **1832–4** DE QUINCEY *Cæsars* Wks. 1859 X. 14 Everything physical is measurable by weight, motion, and resistance. *c* **1860** FARADAY *Forces Nat.* i. 16 Some of the more elementary, and, what we call, physical powers. **1880** HAUGHTON *Phys. Geog.* i. 2 The physical structure of the earth and stars. **1885** *Lyell's Elem. Geol.* 100 There may be a physical break—unconformity—and also a palæontological break, between two successive groups of strata.

absol. **1836** KINGSLEY *Lett.* (1878) I. 36 The dreamy days of boyhood, when I knew and worshipped nothing but the physical. **1883** EDERSHEIM *Life Jesus* II. 200 An attempt to shift the argument from the moral to the physical.

b. Belonging or relating to Natural Philosophy or Natural Science; of, pertaining or relating to, or in accordance with, the regular processes or laws of nature.

1580 G. HARVEY *Three Proper Lett.* Wks. (Grosart) I. 48 With great Physicall, and Naturall Reason. **1587** GREENE *Euphues to Philautus* Wks. (Grosart) VI. 204 Neyther can fishermen tell the Phusicall reasons of the motions of the Sea. **1796** H. HUNTER tr. *St.-Pierre's Stud. Nat.* (1799) I. 497 Of some general laws of nature... We shall divide these Laws into Laws physical and Laws moral. **1808** J. WEBSTER *Nat. Philos.* 7 It is an object worthy of attention to instruct the youthful mind in physical knowledge. **1830** HERSCHEL *Stud. Nat. Phil.* II. ii. 98 The law of gravitation is a physical axiom. **1841** W. SPALDING *Italy & It. Isl.* III. 304 The most interesting feature in the physical history of the Calabrias, is the frequency of their earthquakes. **1865** MOZLEY *Mirac.* (ed. 2) Pref. 11 None of them are or profess to be physical explanations of miracles, i.e. reductions of them to laws of nature in the scientific sense of that term.

c. Of persons: Dealing with or devoted to natural science (in quot. 1768, materialistic).

1678 CUDWORTH *Intell. Syst.* I. iv. 391 Out of whom, according to the Physical Empedocles, proceed all things that were, are, and shall be, viz. Plants, Men, Beasts and Gods. **1768** STERNE *Sent. Journ.* (1775) I. 5 (*Calais*) Every power which sustained life, perform'd it with so little friction, that 'twould have confounded the most Physical *precieuse* in France: with all her materialism, she could scarce have called me a machine. **1898** *Harper's Mag.* XCVI. 623 The foremost physical philosophers of the time came to the aid of the best opticians.

2. Belonging to the forces of nature and properties of bodies, other than chemical and vital; belonging to the science of physics: see PHYSICS 2.

1734 *Keill's Exam. The. Earth* 267 His excellent Observations, both Astronomical and Physical. **1805–17** R. JAMESON *Char. Min.* (ed. 3) 2 Physical characters are those physical phenomena which are exhibited by the mutual action of minerals and other bodies; such as magnetic properties [etc.]. **1813** BAKEWELL *Introd. Geol.* (1815) 47 The internal and external parts will vary both in their physical and chemical properties. **1878** HUXLEY *Physiogr.* 104 The physical properties of matter may be altered without affecting its deeper chemical constitution.

3. a. Of the body, and bodily members or faculties (as distinct from the mind); bodily, corporeal.

1780 BENTHAM *Princ. Legisl.* xiv. §3 Suppose for example the physical desire has for its object the satisfying of hunger. **1820** HAZLITT *Lect. Dram. Lit.* 259 Milton has got rid of the horns and tail, the vulgar and physical insignia of the devil. **1832** AUSTIN *Jurispr.* (1879) I. xii. 358 Physical or natural persons..In this instance 'physical' or 'natural'..denotes a person not fictitious or legal. **1860** TYNDALL *Glac.* I. xvi. 104 The man gave me the impression of physical strength. **1885** E. GARRETT *At any Cost* i. 10 Mrs. Sinclair..had long parted from the last bloom of physical youth. **1886** W. J. TUCKER *E. Europe* 108 We take no physical exercise, except riding. **1899** *Westm. Gaz.* 24 May 5/1 The lads..went through a course of physical drill with wonderful precision.

b. as *sb.* (*pl.*) = physical powers. *colloq. rare.*

1824 *Examiner* 26/2 He lacks physicals for swagger. **1842** G. A. MᶜCALL *Lett. fr. Frontiers* (1868) 394 Disease, and the wear and tear incidental to the exposure of the physicals in such a country as this.

c. as *sb.* A medical examination to determine physical fitness.

1934 N. SAINSBURY *Gridiron Grit* in *Stirring Football Stories* (1941) 77 He found that everybody had had the same idea about physicals and that there were at least forty candidates..ahead of him. **1944** H. MCCLOY *Panic* 131 If you imagine he didn't try to get in the Army, you're mistaken... I saw him each time he got back from his physical. **1968** *Guardian* 28 Dec. 1/5 A day of medical tests —which will go far beyond the 'complete physical' that an ordinary citizen knows. **1973** W. MCCARTHY *Detail* i. 66 Doctor Miller will see you..for a short physical. **1978** N. FREELING *Night Lords* xix. 89 No cop got sent to investigate his own apartment block... It was..like a doctor being asked to give his own wife a physical.

d. Characterized by or suggestive of bodily (as distinct from mental or psychological) activities or attributes. Of a person or activity: inclined to be bodily aggressive or violent.

1970 J. G. VERMANDEL *Dine with Devil* xii. 77 He's obviously one of these tremendously *magnetic* types. And you Scorpios are so *physical*, aren't you? **1972** J. MOSEDALE *Football* vii. 100 Facing the very physical Philadelphia team. **1974** 'J. LE CARRÉ' *Tinker, Tailor* viii. 59, I was feeling pretty physical. Frustrated, you could almost say. **1975** J. MITCHELL *Smear Job* xiii. 104 It's up to you. Either you belt up or I'll get physical. **1976** *Ilkeston Advertiser* 10 Dec. 16/3 Morton became involved and there was 'some physical horseplay'. **1978** *Rugby World* Apr. 8/3 Rugby is a physical game.

II. 4. a. Of or belonging to medicine; medical. Now *rare.* †***physical garden*** = PHYSIC GARDEN.

c **1450** LYDG. & BURGH *Secrees* 1803 Sleep..ffrom these seknessys the boody doth Recure, Which previd is by phisichal prudence. **1576** FLEMING *Panopl. Epist.* 225 He shall learne to be skilfull in the art Geometrical, Arithmeticall, Musicall, Cheyrurgicall, Physical. **1679** *Trials of Wakeman*, etc. 49 There is only that part of it which is the Physical Prescriptions. **1739** JOHNSON *L.P.*, *Boerhaave* Wks. IV. 343 His profession of botany made it part of his duty to superintend the physical garden. **1759** B. MARTIN *Nat. Hist. Eng.* II. *Cambr.* 94 Furnishing a Physical Hospital. **1799** (*title*) The Medical and Physical Journal. **1826** SOUTHEY in *Q. Rev.* XXXIV. 311 Physical books being the most dangerous that any person can take to perusing—except metaphysical ones.

†**b.** Of persons: Practising medicine; medical.
1748 RICHARDSON *Clarissa* (1811) IV. xlv. 296 These cursed physical folks can find out nothing to do us good, but what would poison the devil. **1749** SMOLLETT *Gil Bl.* II. iv. ¶2, I resumed my physical dress, and..visited several patients. **1757** W. THOMPSON *R.N. Advoc.* 44 Which their ..Friends, the top of the Physical Faculty can verify. **1796** CHARLOTTE SMITH *Marchmont* IV. 274 The physical men who attend her seem to think not.

†**c.** *physical finger* = PHYSICIAN *finger*. *Obs.*
1623 tr. *Favine's Theat. Hon.* I. v. 49 To this Physicall finger a veine answereth.

†**5. a.** Used in medicine, medicinal. *Obs.*
1579–80 NORTH *Plutarch, Demetrius* (1895) V. 391 Phisicall herbes, as Helleborum, Lingewort and Beares foote. **1613** MARKHAM *Eng. Husbandman* II. I. v. (1635) 22 The red Rose is not..so tender as the Damaske, yet it is much more Phisicall, and oftner used in medicine. **1658** J. JONES *Ovid's Ibis* 86 Medea was the first that invented Physical baths. **1692** TRYON *Good House-w.* xxvi. (ed. 2) 208 This sort of drink [coffee] ought not to be used, but in a Physical way. **1775** ADAIR *Amer. Ind.* 412 Angelica..is one of their physical greens. **1828** WALKER *Dict.*, *Guaiacum*, a physical wood.

b. Beneficial to health; curative, remedial; restorative to the body, good (*for* one's health). Also *fig.* *Obs.*
1447 BOKENHAM *Seyntys* (Roxb.) 13, I cowde as weel bothe forge and fyle As cowd Boyce in hys phisycal consolacyoun. **1601** SHAKS. *Jul. C.* II. i. 261 Is Brutus sicke? and is it Physicall To walke vnbraced, and sucke vp the humours Of the danke Morning? **1604** E. G[RIMSTONE] *D' Acosta's Hist. Indies* IV. xl. 318 They say moreover, that this wooll..is phisicall for other indispositions, as for the gowt. **1616** R. C. *Times' Whistle* v. 2212 With mediocrity..To take Tobacco thus were phisicall. *a* **1633** AUSTIN *Medit.* (1635) 113 A physicall Banket for our Soules.

c. Of the nature of or like medicine (in taste, smell, etc.); as bad as medicine. *Obs.*
a **1648** DIGBY *Closet Open.* (1677) 63 All other herbs..give it a physical taste. **1681** R. KNOX *Hist. Ceylon* 5 The Tree hath a pretty Physical smell like an Apothecaries Shop. **1706** T. BAKER *Tunbr. Walks* II. i, Wretched hatchet-fac'd things that are physical to look at 'em.

†**6.** In need of medical treatment, sick; under medical treatment. *Obs.*
1633 SHIRLEY *Witty Fair One* III. iv, What meanes this Apothecaries shop about thee, art Physicall? —— *Bird in Cage* III. ii, Thou lookst dull and Phisicall me thinkes. **1761** *Brit. Mag.* II. 388 In the latter [hospital] are near 300 physical patients, and about 60 chirurgical ones.

7. In special phrases and collocations.
physical anthropology, the study of the evolution of man and animals closely related to him, involving the observation or measurement of anatomical features, growth rates, genetic mechanisms, etc.; so **physical-anthropological** *a.*, **physical anthropologist**. **physical astronomy**, that branch of astronomy which treats of the motions, masses, positions, light, heat, etc. of the heavenly bodies. **physical atom**: see quot. **physical chemistry**, the application of the techniques and theories of physics to the study of chemical systems; the study of the interrelation of chemical and physical properties; so **physical-chemical** adj. (= physico-chemical), **physical chemist**. **physical culture**, the development of the body by exercise; hence **physical culturist**, an advocate or exponent of physical culture. **physical drill**, physical exercises. **physical education**, regular instruction in bodily exercise and games, esp. in schools. **physical force**, material as opposed to moral force; in politics, the use of armed power, to effect or repress political changes; also *attrib.* **physical geography**, that branch of geography which deals with the natural features of the earth's surface, as distinct from its political divisions, commercial or historical relations, etc. **physical geology**, the study of the formation and history of strata and eruptive rocks, apart from palæontology. **physical horizon**: see HORIZON 1. **physical jerks**: see JERK *sb.*[1] 2 d. **physical laboratory**, a laboratory for experiments in physical science. **physical metallurgy**, the science dealing with the structure and physical properties of metals. **physical mineralogy**, that which treats of the physical properties of minerals, apart from their chemical composition. **physical object** *Philos.*, an object that exists in space and time and that can be perceived; also *attrib.* **physical optics**, that branch of optics which deals with the properties of light itself (as distinguished from the function of sight); sometimes restricted to that part which relates to the undulatory theory and the phenomena specially explained by it, as interference, etc. **physical point**, a point conceived as infinitely small, and yet a portion of matter. **physical science** or **philosophy** = PHYSICS. **physical sciences**, the sciences that treat of inanimate matter, and of energy apart from vitality: opposed to the biological or to the moral sciences. **physical sign**, a symptom of health or disease ascertainable by bodily examination. **physical theology**: see THEOLOGY. **physical therapy** = PHYSIOTHERAPY; hence **physical therapist**, a physiotherapist. **physical torture** *slang*, physical training. **physical training**, the systematic use of exercises to promote physical fitness.
1958 G. DANIEL *Megalith Builders of W. Europe* i. 25 The word race is used..in its strict *physical-anthropological connotation of a group of people with heritable physical characteristics in common. **1878** *Jrnl. Anthrop. Inst.* VII. 540 The *physical anthropologist often regards the prehistoric worker as an antiquarian only, whilst the former is sometimes simply looked upon in the light of a demonstrative anatomist. **1936** R. LINTON *Study of Man* ii. 23 The first physical anthropologists..believed that every species and variety was the result of a separate act of creation and was therefore fixed and unchangeable. **1974** *Times* 8 Nov. 12/4 The leprous bones were identified by..a physical anthropologist (an expert with skeletons). **1873** A. L. FOX in *Jrnl. Anthrop. Inst.* II. 361 The two expeditions which have lately left this country for Central Africa..have been furnished with detailed notes and queries on general anthropology, *physical anthropology, religions, myths, customs, [etc.]. **1904** W. L. H. DUCKWORTH *Morphol. & Anthropol.* ii. 14 This application of the principles of Morphology to the special case of Man constitutes the essence of Physical Anthropology. **1923** A. L. KROEBER *Anthropol.* i. 5 Biological or physical anthropology—'Somatology' it is sometimes called in Anglo-Saxon countries, and simply 'anthropology' in continental Europe—has in part constituted a sort of specialization or sharpening of general biology. **1951** E. E. EVANS-PRITCHARD *Social Anthropol.* i. 3 Physical anthropology..is a branch of human biology and comprises such interests as heredity, nutrition, sex differences, the comparative anatomy and physiology of races, and the theory of human evolution. **1976** *Ann. Rev. Anthropol.* V. 5 Hrdlicka was the founding father of American Physical Anthropology. **1834** *Penny Cycl.* II. 529/2 The third department of astronomy..is that which goes under the name of **physical astronomy*, and consists in the combination of the various phenomena as actually observed, in order to find out what are their physical causes, and according to what laws those causes act. **1903** AGNES M. CLERKE *Astrophysics* 1 Kepler first speculated on the causes of celestial movements, and introduced the term 'physical astronomy'. **1850** DAUBENY *Atom. The.* v. (ed. 2) 147 [Dumas] proposes to designate that description of molecular groups into which bodies are resolved by heat, *physical atoms. **1964** *Economist* 29 Feb. 790/1 The Humboldt university, of whose *physical-chemical institute he is the director. **1967** *Oceanogr. & Marine Biol.* V. 63 It shows itself essentially in the form of a dome structure.. which can be detected in all the physical-chemical properties of the water. **1971** *Who's Who* 331/1 *Bowen*, Edmund John... Papers on physical chemical subjects in scientific journals. **1929** *Amer. Jrnl. Physiol.* LXXXIX. 171 *Physical chemists..have criticized methods which make use of tubes of small diameter. **1935** *Discovery* Apr. 98/2 A problem for a physical chemist, assisted by a bio-chemist. **1893** I. REMSEN *Princ. Theoret. Chem.* (ed. 4) p. v, I have been tempted to change the book fundamentally and give it a character more in keeping with the recent tendencies of work in the field of *Physical or General Chemistry. **1898** C. L. SPEYERS *Text-bk. Physical Chem.* i. 1 Physical Chemistry is the science which has for its object the investigation of chemical changes by physical methods. **1902** *Fortn. Rev.* June 1014 A mechanism of the atoms, or, as it has come to be called in Germany, a physical chemistry, was developing. **1940** GLASSTONE *Text-bk. Physical Chem.* p. xi, Obviously, atomic combination involves atomic forces, and it is one of the objects of physical chemistry to see how far the chemical interactions observed between atoms and molecules can be interpreted by means of the forces existing within and between atoms. **1966** *McGraw-Hill Encycl. Sci. & Technol.* X. 203/1 There are three different approaches to the study and use of physical chemistry: thermodynamics,..kinetics, ..and molecular structure. **1867** S. D. KEHOE *Indian Club Exercise* 18 Having discoursed..on the important benefits to be derived from *physical culture..we will now describe some of the special means of exercise. **1893** *Harper's Mag.* Apr. 668/2 In the high-school department,..further instruction is given in..physical culture. **1912** V. L. WHITECHURCH *Thrilling Stories of Railway* 11 He was a strong faddist on food and 'physical culture'. **1963** D. WEBSTER *Compl. Physique Bk.* ii. 9 In all the systems of physical culture existing throughout the world non-apparatus work plays a most important part. **1904** C. L. NEIL *Mod. Physical Culture* xviii. 115 (*heading*) The *physical culturist's library. **1936** *Discovery* Nov. 362/2 The concluding chapter deals with the athlete, and it is of great value to the physical trainer and culturist. **1960** J. HEWITT *Yoga* iii. 56 A large number of the exercises popular with physical-culturists in the West are taken from Yoga. **1915** W. OWEN *Let.* 30 Oct. (1967) 362 This morning we had '*Physical Drill' under a special Gymnastic Instructor. **1838** S. SMILES *Physical Education* 10 Here we may state what is the scope and object of a proper *physical education. **1858** *Southern Cultivator* XVI. 32/1 The subject of physical education is beginning to attract attention. **1895** W. MACLAREN in A. Maclaren *Physical Educ.* (rev. ed.) p. v, It is now more than thirty years since the demand for systematized Physical Education began to make itself heard in this country. **1926** *Encycl. Brit.* III. 141/2 Physical education..includes systematic and graded exercises chosen for their physiological and corrective results, folk-dancing, swimming, organized games and sports. **1960** *Where* No. 3. 16 *Physical Education (PE)*, the current term for what most parents remember as 'gym' or PT. **1977** E. W. HILDICK *Loop* ix. 54 A Physical Education teacher. **1817** COBBETT *Wks.* XXXII. 362 It was a combat of argument, and they have taken shelter under the shield of *physical force. **1840** HOOD *Up Rhine* 165, I do wish our physical-force men would hire a steamer and take a trip up the Rhine. **1897** J. MCCARTHY in *Daily News* 27 May 6/1 He was entirely opposed to any attempt at rebellion by physical force, because he held..that there was no chance for a physical-force struggle. [**1625** N. CARPENTER *Geog. Del.* I. i. (1635) 4 The obiect in Geographie is for the most part Physicall, consisting of the parts whereof the Spheare is composed.] **1808** J. PLAYFAIR *Syst. Geogr.* I. p. ccv, To narrate the appearances which nature exhibits to our view, and to give an idea of what is movable and immovable upon, and under the surface of the earth, is the province of **Physical Geography*. **1852** A. K. JOHNSTON (*title*) Atlas of Physical Geography. **1866** BRANDE & COX *Dict. Sc.*, etc. II. 898/1 Physical geography is the history of the earth in its material organisation. **1914** *Physical metallurgy [see METALLURGY]. **1935** WILLIAMS & HOMERBERG *Princ. Metallogr.* (ed. 3) i. 1 Metallography is commonly subdivided into..(1) production metallurgy..and (2) physical metallurgy. **1956** A. W. CHAPMAN in D. L. Linton *Sheffield* x. 212 The faculty includes a postgraduate School of Physical Metallurgy in which the teaching is specially adapted to provide men from industry with instruction. **1965** R. W. CAHN *Physical Metallurgy* p. v, Physical metallurgy..is the root from which the modern science of materials has principally sprung. **1897** *Daily News* 17 Feb. 2/5 To find funds for the foundation and maintenance of a national *physical laboratory. **1912** B. RUSSELL *Probl. Philos.* i. 18 The real table, if it exists, we will call a '*physical object'. Thus we have to consider the relation of sense-data to physical objects. **1952** *Mind* LXI. 505 His only irrefutable position is to reduce his physical object claim to an announcement concerning his own sensations. **1954** A. J. AYER *Philos. Ess.* iv. 88 This procedure..serves to clarify the meaning of statements about physical objects by relating them to statements of a different logical form. **1973** —— *Cent. Questions Philos.* iii. 62 What Hume calls the philosophical account of physical objects differs from the vulgar account in that it distinguishes them from perceptions. **1831** BREWSTER *Optics* vii. 66 *Physical Optics is that branch of the science which treats of the physical properties of light. **1857** BUCKLE *Civiliz.* I. vii. 343 The business of *physical philosophy is, to explain external phenomena with a view to their prediction. **1845** STODDART *Gram.* in *Encycl. Metrop.* (1847) I. 60/1 That part of Grammar..is evidently Physical, and of course follows the common laws of *Physical Science. *a* **1862** BUCKLE *Misc. Wks.* (1872) I. 212 In the course of a few years Sir Isaac Newton changed the surface of physical science. **1879** *St. George's Hosp. Rep.* IX. 107 The *physical signs pointed to fluid at the left base, and to enlargement of the right lobe of the liver. **1954** *Physical therapist [see CRASH *sb.*[1] 7 b]. **1922** *Lancet* 2 Dec. 1175/1 The first edition of this book appeared in 1910. Notable advances in *physical therapy have now necessitated the preparation of a second edition. **1973** R. KRAUS *Therapeutic Recreation Service* i. 19/1 In the fields of occupational therapy or physical therapy, professional training is carried on in close cooperation with medical authorities or educators. **1900** *Dialect Notes* II. 48 **Physical torture*, physical culture. **1920** *331st Field Artillery* (U.S.) 417 The officers,..knowing that boat drills were something of a bore, attempted to make them more interesting..by giving us 'physical torture' at these times. **1959** I. & P. OPIE *Lore & Lang. Schoolch.* ix. 173 One feels Lewis Carroll would have liked the current terms Physical Torture (for P.T.) and Religious Destruction or Ridiculous Kapers (for R.K.). **1968** W. C. ANDERSON *Gooney Bird* iii. 35 The physical torture program..started promptly at 0630 every morning at Eglin Air Force Base. **1889** *Infantry Drill* 11 **Physical training.* In order to expand his chest, and develop his muscles, the soldier will be practised in the following exercises. **1910** STREET & GOODERSON *Handbk. Physical Training* I. 12 Physical training at schools should provide for the stimulation of the physiologic functions of the body. **1926** *Encycl. Brit.* III. 141/2 The model course, which originally consisted largely of military drill, has developed into the present Syllabus of Physical Training, based on the Swedish system. **1974** *Oxf. Jun. Encycl.* (rev. ed.) IX. 270/2 In the forces and in club work the aim is to train performers in set exercises and vaults which..are the result of physical training as opposed to physical education.

Hence **'physicalness**, the quality of being physical.
1727 BAILEY vol. II, *Physicalness*, Naturalness, also Medicinalness. **1857** J. HINTON *Let.* in *Life* vii. (1878) 133 The inertness, the evil, that is added by our physicalness.

physicalism ('fɪzɪkəlɪz(ə)m). *Philos.* [f. PHYSICAL *a.* 2 + -ISM.] A term originally used by members of the Vienna Circle for the theory that all science must eventually be capable of being expressed in the language of physics.
1931 O. NEURATH in *Monist* XLI. 618 (*title*) Physicalism: the philosophy of the Viennese Circle. *Ibid.* 620 In a sense unified science is physics in its largest aspect, a tissue of laws expressing time-space linkages—let us call it: Physicalism. **1936** L. BLOOMFIELD in *Language* XII. 93 The testing of this hypothesis of *physicalism* will be a task of the next generations, and linguists will have to perform an important part of the work. **1940** B. RUSSELL *Inquiry into Meaning & Truth* 93 The thesis which Carnap calls 'physicalism', which maintains that all science can be expressed in the language of physics. **1965** *Language* XLI. 196 He [*sc.* Bloomfield].. recommended a policy known first as 'mechanism' or 'anti-mentalism', later as 'physicalism' which..amounted to the emancipation of linguistics from irrelevant psychologizing. ..Bloomfield himself was not able to pursue this policy with complete success. **1972** *Science* 16 June 1204/3 Science has been..historically associated with a philosophy of physicalism, the belief that reality is all reducible to certain kinds of physical entities. **1975** *Jrnl. Philos.* LXXII. 565 Physicalism does not entail reductionism, at least if we follow Hellman and Thompson in taking reductionism to mean explicit definability.

physicalist ('fɪzɪkəlɪst). [f. PHYSICAL *a.* (and *sb.*) + -IST.] **1.** *Philos.* (See quots.)
1858 BUSHNELL *Nat. & Supernat.* i. (1864) 23 Physicalists, who, without pretending to deny Christianity, value them-selves on finding all the laws of obligation..in the laws of the body and the world. **1864** WEBSTER, *Physicalist*, one who holds that human thoughts and acts are determined by the physical organization of man.

2. One who adheres to the theory of physicalism. Also as *adj.*, of or pertaining to such a theory.
1934 *Times Lit. Suppl.* 5 July 479/1 The paper now translated was first published in 1932..under the title of 'Physicalist language as the Universal Language of Science'. **1937** J. R. FIRTH *Tongues of Men* ix. 119 Let us turn to the 'physicalists' or 'methodical materialists' of the Vienna Circle. **1956** A. J. AYER *Probl. Knowl.* 214 To apply the physicalist thesis to one's own experiences, is, as it were, to pretend to be anaesthetized. **1959** H. KUHN in P. A. Schilpp *Philos. C. D. Broad* xx. 606 The German *Geisteswissenschaft* and Phenomenology..have labored to rouse modern thought from its dogmatic physicalist slumber. **1972** R. PLANT in Cox & Dyson *20th-Cent. Mind* III. iii. 69 The relationship [between behaviour and pain] is not an external, contingent one as the dualist would suggest, nor is it a necessary one as the behaviourist or physicalist would claim. **1973** A. J. AYER *Cent. Questions Philos.* vi. 126 Materialists, or physicalists as they are now more often called, who deny the existence of mental as opposed to physical events.

physicalistic (fɪzɪkə'lɪstɪk), *a.* [f. PHYSICALIST + -IC.] Pertaining to or characterized by physicalism. Hence **physica'listically** *adv.*
1934 M. BLACK tr. *Carnap's Unity of Sci.* 95 For the sake of precision we might supplement or replace 'physical language' by the term '*physicalistic language*'; denoting by the latter the universal language which contains not only physical terms (in the narrow sense) but also all the various special terminologies (of Biology,..etc.) understood as

reduced by definitions to their basis in physical determinations. **1949** M. Schlick in Feigl & Sellars *Readings in Philos. Analysis* 407 The validity of the physicalistic assertion would be ever more restricted. **1954** Webster Add., Physicalistically. **1956** A. J. Ayer *Probl. Knowl.* v. 210 It is only if such statements [about thoughts, feelings] are interpreted 'physicalistically' that they can convey any information from one person to another. **1972** *Science* 16 June 1204/3 To physicalistic philosophy they [*sc.* altered states of consciousness] are epiphenomena. **1978** P. Pettit in Hookway & Pettit *Action & Interpretation* 51 Something as deep as the physicalistic prejudices of natural science or the postulates of rational man theory.

physicality (fɪzɪˈkælɪtɪ). [f. physical *a.* (and *sb.*) + -ity.] **1.** Physical condition; also †*humorously* as a title for a medical man.

1593 Nashe *Four Lett. Confut.* Wks. (Grosart) II. 241 Receiue some notes as touching his phisicallity deceased. He had his Grace to be Doctor ere he died. **1660** tr. *Paracelsus' Archidoxis* i. ix. 131 When we followed that Medicinal way..we could never (by that kind of Physicallity)..perceive any thing well founded. **1944** M. Weitz in P. A. Schilpp *Philos. B. Russell* 73 Here Russell objects because..some entities, the unperceived entities of physics, even though they are neutral—i.e., have no first-order property of mentality or physicality—cannot be brought into psychological causal laws. **1948** *Mind* LVII. 8 Ayer chooses to call the commonly accepted criteria of physicality (the various meanings attached to the word 'physical world') 'assumptions'. **1953** *Mind* LXII. 26 Ontological assumptions concerning the nature of physicality.

2. The quality that pertains to physical sensation or to the body as distinct from the mind.

1849 J. S. Mill *Lett.* (1910) I. 143 Take again all the delicacies respecting bodily physicalities which savages have not a vestige of. **1930** E. Sitwell *Coll. Poems* 126 This bestial consciousness that is desire Is the hot muscles' vast fluidity, Muscular life, not physicality. **1964** *Listener* 27 Aug. 317/1 The climax is Thornhill's visit to a bullfight. The terse physicality of Mr Scott's style, his ability to evoke place and register action, avoids much suggestion of the derivative. **1972** C. L. Cooper in W. King *Black Short Story Anthol.* 218 The trunk of her, he saw self-consciously, with a tiny tickle of physicality, was full to bursting with youth under the plain dress. **1977** *N.Y. Rev. Bks.* 24 Nov. 42/4 Dancing, because of its immediate physicality, its shift in time and space, has a fluid plausibility which is apparently undemanding.

ˈphysicalize, *v.* [f. physical *a.* + -ize.] *trans.* To express or represent by physical means, *spec.* in the theatre, to represent (an idea) in physical terms, as the movements of the body of an actor. So **physicaliˈzation**, the representation of an idea by physical means.

1947 E. Kazan in Cole & Chinoy *Directing Play* (1953) 297 An effort to put poetic names on scenes to edge me into stylizations and physicalizations. Try to keep each scene in terms of Blanche. *Ibid.* 308 Stanley..is completely self-absorbed to the point of fascination. To physicalize this: he has a most annoying way of being preoccupied—or of busying himself with something else while people are talking with him. **1972** *Village Voice* (N.Y.) 1 June 54/4 Its publicized aim: 'to explore various means of physicalization to test the theory that theatre should be a hieroglyphic of speaking icons'. **1977** *Rolling Stone* 7 Apr. 14/3 Lily is particularly taken with Rick at the moment, partly because when she did him on the 'friends of Lily Tomlin' videotape, when she 'physicalized' him by wearing a moustache, sideburns and leather jacket, strutting and tugging at his/her crotch, hardly anyone recognized that the stud was her.

physically (ˈfɪzɪkəlɪ), *adv.* [f. physical *a.* + -ly².] In a physical manner or way.

1. According to nature or the material laws of nature; materially; according to physics or natural philosophy or science; not intellectually, morally, or spiritually. ***physically impossible***, impossible from the nature or laws of material things.

1581 E. Campion in *Confer.* iii. (1584) Y iv, You reason physically: but we must not be led by senses in these misteries. **1666** Boyle *Orig. Formes & Qual.* (1667) 7 It is Physically impossible that it [matter] should be devoid of some Bulk or other, and some determinate Shape or other. **1675** R. Burthogge *Causa Dei* 48 It is not deni'd Physically, but Morally. **1794** Sullivan *View Nat.* I. 417 The swelling of the ocean, by the joint attraction of the sun and the moon, is less physically intelligible, than the periodical effusions of the polar ices. **1855** Grove *Corr. Phys. Forces* (ed. 3) 182 An atom or molecule physically indivisible. **1855** Macaulay *Hist. Eng.* xii. III. 217 It would be physically impossible for many of them to surrender themselves in time. **1863** Fawcett *Pol. Econ.* ii. ix. 264 It is physically impossible that any permanent rise in wages should take place without a corresponding diminution of profits. **1870** Jevons *Elem. Logic* ii. 13 Nothing can physically exist corresponding to a general notion.

†**b.** Naturally, essentially, intrinsically. *Obs.*

1629 H. Burton *Truth's Triumph* 58 Justification..the forme whereof is relatiue and not physically inherent in vs. **1684** T. Hockin *God's Decrees* 200 The will is physically ours, and the deed is also ours, but 'tis morally Gods. **1793** D. Stewart *Outl. Mor. Philos.* ii. ii. i. §322 Not to demonstrate that the soul is physically and necessarily immortal.

†**c.** Practically. *Obs.*

1690 Leybourn *Curs. Math.* 450 It is a Body, though Physically Round, yet full of uneven Asperities. **1757** Akenside in *Phil. Trans.* L. 324 The velocity of the fluids, in the remoter series of vessels, will be, physically, nothing.

2. As regards the body; in body; in bodily constitution; corporeally.

c **1600** *Timon* v. iv. (Shaks. Soc.) 87 Hee's an asse logically and capitally, not phisikallie and animallie. **1651** Baxter *Inf. Bapt.* 179 It may be the child's Action Morally, and in Law-sence, when it is only the Father's Action Physically. **1846** J. E. Ryland in *J. Foster's Life & Corr.* (1846) II. 107 Unless physically disabled. **1877** A. B. Bruce *Training Twelve* xxv. 425 Not till I become invisible physically shall I be visible to you spiritually. **1882** Mrs. Pitman *Mission L. Greece & Pal.* 194 These fellaheen are physically adapted to the climate.

†**3.** Medically; medicinally; by medical rules.

1582 Hester *Secr. Phiorav.* iii. cxv. 139 Then shall be finished the solution of Iron Phisically, the whiche thou maiest giue safely. **1674** R. Godfrey *Inj. & Ab. Physic* 208 To make it a Proverb, *Qui Medicè vivit, miserè vivit*, (i.e.) He that lives Physically, lives miserably. **1712** M. Henry *Sober-mindedness* Wks. 1853 I. 70 Then it [mirth] must be used like a medicine,—must be taken physically.

†**ˈphysicary.** *Obs. rare.* [f. physic *sb.* + -ary B. 2.] Medicinal preparations; materia medica.

1620 tr. *Boccaccio's Decameron* 109 A Quacksalver..one that deales in drugges and physicarie.

†**physic garden.** *Obs.* [See physic *sb.* 6, *a.* 2: cf. F. *jardin de pharmacie*.] A garden for the cultivation of medicinal plants; hence, a botanic garden; also *physical garden*, physical 4.

1637 *Lease fr. Magd. Coll. to Univ. Oxford* 17 Apr., [Ground] for a Physicke Garden. [Referred to in a petition of 5 July 1626 as 'the Phisitions Garden'.] **1644** Evelyn *Diary* 20 Oct., Pisa.—We went to the Colledge... To this the Physiq Garden lyes. **1699** *Phil. Trans.* XXI. 63 Rare and non-descript Plants,..cultivated either in publick Physick-Gardens, or those of private curious Persons. **1796** Morse *Amer. Geog.* II. 314 A very curious physic-garden, which contains the choicest exotics. **1814** *Hist. Univ. Oxford* II. 241 In 1715, John Robinson..presented many curious exotic plants to the Physic Garden. **1879** *Handbk. Univ. Oxford* 59 The Botanic Garden, formerly known as the Physic Garden, was founded in the year 1622.

physician (fɪˈzɪʃən), *sb.* Forms: α. 3–5 **fisicien**, 4–5 **-ian(e**, 4 **fiscician**, **-en**, **fyciscien**, 5 **fis-**, **fic-**, **fys-**, **-isian**, **-issyan**, **-isyen**, **-esyen**, 5–6 **fysician**, **visicion**; β. 4–5 **fesician(e**, 5 **-isyan**, **(-en)**, **-essian**, 6 **-ycien**, **-ysyan**, 5 **phesicyen**, 6–7 **-ycion**, **-icion**; γ. 4–6 **phisicien(e**, 5 **-ycien**, 5– 7 **-ician**, 6 **-icyon**, 6–7 **-itian**, **(-on)**, **-icion**, 7 **phizitian**, 4–5 **physicyen**, 5 **-icien**, 5–6 **-icion**, 6 **-ycyen**, **(phycyssyon)**, 6–7 **physitian**, **-ycyan**, **(-on)**, 6– **physician**. [ME. *fisicien*, a. OF. *fisicien* (Wace 12th c.), f. L. *physic-a*, F. *physique*: see physic and -ician.]

†**1.** A student of natural science or of physics.

a **1400–50** *Alexander* 4363 Ne foloȝe we na ficesyens, ne philosophour scolis, As sophistri & slik thing, to sott with þe pepill. **1610** Willet *Hexapla Dan.* 30 Naturall and humane dreames, the interpretation whereof belongeth vnto physicians and philosophers. [**1833** J. Martineau *Misc.* (1852) 6 An analysis of Dr. Priestley's character as a theologian, a *physicien*, a metaphysician.]

2. One who practises the healing art, including medicine and surgery.

a **1225** *Ancr. R.* 370 Auh, monie ancren,..þet schulden one lecnen hore soule mid heorte bireousunge & flesshes pinunge, uorwurðeð fisiciens & licomes leches. **1297** R. Glouc. (Rolls) 1552 His fisicians he clupede & suor is oþ anon Bote hii made him mid childe he wolde hom sle echon. *c* **1380** Wyclif *Serm.* Sel. Wks. I. 60 Man may spende al þat he haþ aboute oþir fisicians. **1393** Langl. *P. Pl.* C. xxiii. 176 A fisician with a forrede hod. **1484** Caxton *Fables of Æsop* iii. ii, I am a leche, and with al a good phesycyen. **1526** Tindale *Luke* iv. 23 Visicion heale thy silfe. **1540** *Act 32 Hen. VIII*, c. 40 Forasmuche as the science of phisicke dothe comprehend..the knowledge of surgery as a speciall membre and parte of the same, therefore be it enacted that anny of the said company or felawship of Phisitions..may ..exercise the said science of Phisick in all and every his membres and partes. **1542** Udall *Erasm. Apoph.* 278 b, The physicians dooe not fall to cuttyng, except all other meanes and wayes afore proved. **1605** Shaks. *Macb.* v. i. 82 More needs she the Diuine, then the Physitian. **1758** Johnson *Idler* No. 17 ¶7 The anatomical novice..styles himself physician, prepares himself by familiar cruelty..to extend his arts of torture..which he has hitherto tried upon cats and dogs. **1809** Kendall *Trav.* III. lxxii. 128 Physician is the title of all medical practitioners in the United States. **1875** Jowett *Plato* (ed. 2) III. 28 Physicians to cure the disorders of which luxury is the source.

b. One legally qualified to practise the healing art as above; *esp.* as distinguished from one qualified as a surgeon only.

In the United Kingdom, every medical practitioner is now required to have a qualification as Physician and also as Surgeon; so that a general practitioner usually describes himself as 'Physician and Surgeon'. The use of 'Physician' or 'Surgeon' alone usually implies that the person so styled is in practice a specialist in that branch. So especially with the designation 'Consulting Physician'.

c **1400** *Lanfranc's Cirurg.* 298 O lord, whi is it so greet difference bitwixe a cirurgian & a phisician. **1508** Dunbar *Lament for Makaris* 42 In medicyne the most practicianis, Lechis, surrigianis & phisicianis. **1548** Udall *Erasm. Par. Luke* Pref. 9 The physicians of the bodyes haue practicioners and poticaries that dooe ministre their art vnder them. **1612** Woodall *Surg. Mate* Pref. (1639) Bj, The more learned sort are justly stiled by the title of Physicians, and the more experienced sort are called Chirurgions or Surgeons. *a* **1654** Selden *Table-T.* (Arb.) 27 Your President of the Colledge of Phisitians..himself is no more than a Doctor of Physick. **1707** Chamberlayne *St. Eng.* iii. 550 Physicians in Ordinary to her Majesty's Person ..Apothecaries..Chirurgeons. **1813** J. Thomson *Lect. Inflam.* Introd. 15 It is from the separation produced by these two decrees [issued by Pope Boniface the Sixth, and Clement the Fifth, at Avignon], that we ought, I conceive, to date the true origin of the distinction between physician and surgeon, such as it has existed in modern times; a distinction unknown in the practice of the ancients. **1872** Geo. Eliot *Middlem.* xviii, To obscure the limit between his own rank as a general practitioner, and that of the physicians, who, in the interest of the profession, felt bound to maintain its various grades. **1895** W. Munk *Life Sir H. Halford* 135 The appointment of physician-extraordinary to the king.

c. *Proverbs.*

1546 J. Heywood *Prov.* ii. vii. (1867) 67 Feed by measure, and defie the physicion. **1606** Holland *Sueton., Tiberius* lxviii. *Annot.*, Whereupon might arise our English proverbe, A foole or a physition. **1622** Malynes *Anc. Law-Merch.* 254 We see the Prouerbe to be true, That the vnknowne disease putteth out the Physitians eye. **1721** [see fool *sb.*¹ 1 d].

3. *transf.* and *fig.* A healer; one who cures moral, spiritual, or political maladies or infirmities.

c **1400** Maundev. (Roxb.) xiv. 61 Efterwardes he was a phisiciene of saules. **1548** Udall *Erasm. Par. Luke* Pref. 8 b, Woordes and talke is the physician of a mynde beeyng diseased and sicke. **1687** Norris *Hymn, 'Long have I viewed'* ii, I'll trust my great Physician's skill. **1805** Surr *Winter in Lond.* (1806) III. 262 Time must be her physician. **1868** Lynch *Rivulet* cxl. vi, That thorny cares may yield sweet fruits, And comforts be physicians.

4. *Comb.*, as ***physician-accoucheur***, ***-author***, ***-founder***; †**physician finger**, the third or ring-finger; = leech-finger: cf. finger 1.

1623 tr. *Favine's Theat. Hon.* i. v. 48 Rings of gold are worne by noble persons on the medicinall finger of the left hand called by the Latines *Digitus medicus*... Aulus Gellius, ..declareth, that a small and subtile arterie..proceedeth from the heart, to beate on this Physition finger. **1828** D. le Marchant *Rep. Claims to Barony of Gardner* 71, I have been physician-accoucheur since 1817. **1901** *Daily Chron.* 6 Dec. 4/4 The regulations which the physician-founder drew up.

Hence **phyˈsician** *v.*, *trans.* (*a*) to make into a physician; (*b*) to put under the care of a physician; **phyˈsicianary** *a.*, of or pertaining to a physician; **phyˈsiciancy**, the office or position of physician; **phyˈsicianed** *a.*, qualified or licensed to act as a physician; **phyˈsicianer** *dial.* = physician 2; **phyˈsicianess**, a female physician: also *fig.*; **phyˈsicianless** *a.*, without a physician; **phyˈsicianly** *a.*, befitting a physician; **phyˈsicianship** = *physiciancy*; also the personality of a physician.

1839 G. Wilson *Let.* in *Life* (1860) iv. 205 The mystic medicating cap has not yet *physicianed me. **1896** D. Sladen in *Dominion Illustr.* Christmas No., The travellers bestormed were straight put to bed and physicianed. **1889** J. K. Jerome *Three Men* i, He..has a somewhat family-*physicianary way of putting things. **1881** *Times* 13 Jan. 11/3 The *Physiciancy to the Queen in Ireland. **1891** N. Moore in *Dict. Nat. Biog.* XXV. 94/2 His assistant discharged the duties of the physiciancy till his formal election as physician..on..14 Oct. 1609. **1758** H. Walpole *Lett. to Mann* 10 Feb., Dr. Lucas, a *physicianed apothecary. **1815** Mrs. Pilkington *Celebrity* I. 78 *Physicioners were sent for. **1821** Scott *Kenilw.* xi, A man of much skill and little substance, who practised the trade of a physicianer. **1836–48** B. D. Walsh *Aristoph. Clouds* i. iv, Brave Thurian prophets, physicianers rare. **1662** J. Chandler *Van Helmont's Oriat.* 171 If nature the *Physitianesse of her self, can overcome diseases by her own goodnesse. **1786** H. Walpole *Let. to H. More* 9 Feb., I might send for you as my physicianess. **1888** Talmage in *Voice* (N.Y.) 6 Sept., He died *physicianless. **1888** J. Clifford in *Contemp. Rev.* Apr. 503 Real knowledge of man and of men,..is indescribably rich in *physicianly force. **1732** Fielding *Mock Doctor* viii, I shall bind his *physicianship over to his good behaviour. **1879** *Cassell's Techn. Educ.* IV. 251/2 A promise of succeeding on the first vacancy to the physicianship in ordinary. **1888** T. Watts in *Athenæum* 17 Mar. 340/2 Latham..was..elected to the physicianship of the St. George's and St. James's Dispensary.

physicism (ˈfɪzɪsɪz(ə)m). [f. physic *sb.* + -ism.] A doctrine of physical phenomena; *esp.* one which refers all the phenomena of the universe, including life itself, to physical or material forces; materialism.

1869 Huxley *Lay Serm., Sci. Aspects Positivism* (1877) 163 In the progress of the species from savagery to advanced civilization anthropomorphism grows into theology, and physicism (if I may so call it) develops into Science. **1879** Escott *England* II. 391 Physicism, in its present shape, can scarcely hope to supplant religion. **1880** Goldw. Smith in *Atlantic Monthly* No. 268. 204 A probability..which physicism, in its hour of triumph, will do well to take with it in its car.

physicist (ˈfɪzɪsɪst). [f. physic *sb.* + -ist.]

†**1.** One versed in medical science. *Obs. rare.*

1716 M. Davies *Athen. Brit.* III. *Diss. Physick* 12 Anatomists, Naturalists, Physicists, Medicinists.

2. A student of physics (physics 2).

1840 Whewell *Philos. Induct. Sci.* Pref. 71 We might perhaps still use physician as the equivalent of the French *physicien*..but probably it would be better to coin a new word. Thus we may say that..the Physicist proceeds upon the ideas of force, matter, and the properties of matter. **1843** *Blackw. Mag.* LIV. 524 The word *physicists*, where four sibilant consonants fizz like a squib. **1869** Phipson tr. *Guillemin's Sun* (1870) 146 The method known to physicists as 'spectral analysis'.

b. A student of nature or natural science in general (cf. physics 1).

1858 Kingsley *Lett.* 24 Dec., This Christmas night is the one of all the year which sets a physicist, as I am, on facing the fact of miracle. **1859** R. F. BURTON *Centr. Afr.* in *Jrnl. Geog. Soc.* XXIX. 23 There remained then for the English physicist the honour of depicting by an admirable generalization the true features of the African interior.

3. One who holds the theory of a purely physical or material origin of vital phenomena; a believer in physicism: opposed to *vitalist*.

1871 MORLEY *Crit. Misc.* Ser. I. 229 The excessive pretensions and unwarranted certitudes of the physicist. **1872** NICHOLSON *Introd. Study Biol.* i. 16 No physicist has hitherto succeeded in explaining any fundamental vital phenomenon upon purely physical and chemical principles.

physicky ('fɪzɪkɪ), *a.* [f. PHYSIC *sb.* 4 + -Y.] Having the taste, smell, or other qualities of physic or medicine; influenced by physic.

1764 GRAINGER *Sugar Cane* I. 520 *note*, The flowers have a physicky smell. **1849** GEO. ELIOT in Cross *Life* (1885) I. 242 Dear Sara's letter is very charming—not at all physicky. **1854** BADHAM *Halieut.* 533 The cheeses from France, in Pliny's day, had a physicky flavour. **1886** FENN *Devon Boys* xxx. 263 'I rather like it', said Bob, with a rather physicky face.

'physic-nut. [f. PHYSIC *sb.* 4 + NUT.] The fruit of the euphorbiaceous shrub *Jatropha Curcas* L. (*Curcas purgans*), of tropical America, used as a purgative; the Barbados- or purging-nut; also the plant itself, more fully ***physic-nut bush*** or ***tree***.

Sometimes applied to species of the allied genus *Croton*. *French physic-nut*, the species *Jatropha multifida*.

1657 R. LIGON *Barbados* 67 They gathered all the physick nuts they could. **1703** DAMPIER *Voy.* III. I. 71 *Physick-Nuts* as Seamen call them are called here *Pineon*. **1756** P. BROWNE *Jamaica* 348 French Physic Nut. The plant is much raised in Jamaica, and forms no small ornament of their flower-gardens. **1871** KINGSLEY *At Last* xvi, The French Physic-nut, with its hemp-like leaves, and a little bunch of red coral in the midst.

attrib. **1750** G. HUGHES *Barbadoes* 115 The physic-nut-tree. This is generally a knotty shrubby tree. **1792** MAR. RIDDELL *Voy. Madeira* 88 The *croton lacciferum*, or physic nut bush, bears a seed which..acts as a powerful emetic. **1865** F. SAYER in *Fortn. Rev.* No. 5. 617 Even the street lamps [in Madeira] are lighted with physic-nut oil.

physico- ('fɪzɪkəʊ), combining form of Gr. φυσικός natural, physical, used generally as an adverbial or adjectival qualification of the second element, 'physically', 'physical' (see -O 1); also, sometimes expressing any relation, as simple combination or contact of the things or notions named in the two elements (see -O 2). The following are among the less important combinations:

ˌphysico-astro'nomical *a.*, of or pertaining to physical astronomy: see PHYSICAL 7. **ˌphysico-geo'graphical** *a.*, of, pertaining to, or dealing with physical geography. **ˌphysico-inte'llectual** *a.*, combining the physical with the intellectual. **ˌphysico-'logic**, logic illustrated by physics; hence **ˌphysico-'logical** *a.* †**ˌphysico-'medical** *a.*, physical and medical. **ˌphysico-'mental** *a.*, pertaining to both body and mind, or physical and mental phenomena. **ˌphysico-mi'raculous** *a.*, of the nature of a natural miracle. **'physicomorph**, a representation in art of an inanimate object or phenomenon of the physical world. **ˌphysico-'morphic** *a.* (opposed to *anthropomorphic*), having the form of or embodied in material nature; so **ˌphysico-'morphism**. **ˌphysico-phi'losophy**, the philosophy of nature, natural philosophy; hence **ˌphysico-philo'sophical** *a.* **ˌphysico-physio'logical** *a.*, of or pertaining to the physics of physiology. **ˌphysico-'psychical** *a.*, combining or intermediate to the domain of psychology and of physics. **ˌphysico-psycho'logical** *a.*, pertaining both to the physical and the psychological. †**ˌphysico-theo'sophical** *a.*, belonging at once to natural science and to theosophy. Also PHYSICO-CHEMICAL, etc.

1834 *Nat. Philos.* III. *Hist. Astron.* xvi. 82/2 (Usef. Knowl. Soc.) The *physico-astronomical system of Descartes. **1865** *Nat. Hist. Rev.* 385 An excellent *physicogeographical monograph of the island of Cyprus. **1900** *Westm. Gaz.* 21 July 3/1 Long isolation..brought about partly by physico-geographical, partly by political causes. **1840** DE QUINCEY *Style* Wks. 1862 X. 162 At the head of the *physico-intellectual pleasures, we find a second reason for quarrelling with the civilisation of our country. **1704** SWIFT *T. Tub* Introd., Wks. 1760 I. 27 This *physico-logical scheme of oratorial receptacles or machines contains a great mystery. **1689** *Lond. Gaz.* No. 2468/4 A *Physico-medical Essay concerning the late frequency of Appoplexies. *a* **1849** POE *Cockton* Wks. 1864 III. 461 A tingling *physico-mental exhilaration. **1870–9** SIR R. CHRISTISON in *Life* (1885) I. 91 The physico-mental gratification experienced in piercing the thin clear air of a Highland mountain. **1839** DE QUINCEY *Mod. Superstit.* Wks. 1862 III. 295 The faith in this order of the *physico-miraculous is open alike to the sceptical and the non-sceptical. **1895** A. C. HADDON *Evol. Art* 118 Under the term of '*physicomorph' I propose to describe any representation of an object or operation in the physical world. **1886** A. B. BRUCE *Mirac. Elem. Gosp.* i. 29 The Agnostic..sets up in his room a *physico-morphic divinity. *Ibid.* 28 The charge of anthropomorphism is met by a counter-charge of *physico-morphism. **1906** *N.E.D.*, *Physicophilosophical. **1977** M. COHEN *Sensible Words* 145 The restrictiveness of Ong's view can be estimated by his determination to turn Swift into a stubborn, and unhappy, physicophilosophical writer. **1899** *Allbutt's Syst. Med.* VI. 511 In the pieces of neurons usually employed for *physico-physiological study, the wave of disturbance..is propagated without alteration in height, length and speed. **1816** BENTHAM *Chrestomathia* Wks. 1843 VIII. 144 Purely Psychical or Thelematic; and mixed *Physico-psychical, Anthropophysiurgic or Psychothelematic. Under one or other of these heads will all original sources of motion..be found to be comprehended. **1927** A. HUXLEY *Proper Stud.* 34 It is..only in the abstract that we can discuss the varieties of intelligence without considering the varieties in the other constituents of the *physico-psychological personality. **1668** H. MORE *Div. Dial., Schol.* (1713) 565 The Mercava of Ezekiel [bears a triple meaning], viz. Ethico-political, *Physico-theosophical, and Literal.

physico-chemical (ˌfɪzɪkəʊ'kɛmɪkəl), *a.* [See PHYSICO-.] Of or belonging to physical chemistry; of or pertaining to physics and chemistry. So **ˌphysico-'chemically** *adv.*

1664 POWER *Exp. Philos.* I. 65 These several Physico-Chymical operations. **1731** *Hist. Litteraria* III. 252 It appears with all the Parade of a Physico-Chemical Experiment. **1835–6** TODD *Cycl. Anat.* I. 124/1 The general physico-chemical laws that dominate the rest of the universe. **1851** *Penny Cycl.* Suppl. II. 420/2 Sir John Herschel proposed the epithet of Actino-Chemistry for this new branch of physico-chemical science. **1885** I. B. YEO tr. *Oertel's Respiratory Therapeutics* II. 731 It has been thought that the diminution of air pressure acts physico-chemically in another sense. **1958** *Times Lit. Suppl.* 10 Jan. 14/4 He looks forward to the day when psychological changes can be correlated convincingly with physico-chemical processes. **1969** *Listener* 20 Mar. 389/1 Goldmann believes that the social sciences cannot be conducted on the model of what he calls the 'physico-chemical' sciences. **1970** AMBROSE & EASTY *Cell Biol.* viii. 258 Studies of the permeability of membranes to gases, water, non-electrolytes, and ions were interpreted physico-chemically. **1971** I. G. GASS et al. *Understanding Earth* viii. 120/1 The physico-chemical conditions within the meteorite parent bodies. **1973** *Nature* 21–28 Dec. 528/1 The crystals were identified physico-chemically by their solubility in HCl, by the Meingen reaction, by infrared spectroscopy, and by petrographic microscopy. **1977** *Dædalus* Summer 66 The neurological and physicochemical bases of human behavior are clearly not exhausted by genetically fixed enduring neuronal pathways.

So **ˌphysico-'chemist**, one skilled in physics and chemistry, or in physical chemistry; **ˌphysico-'chemistry**.

1866 *Athenæum* No. 1999. 236/1 The physico-chemist with his prism. **1909** *Jrnl. Industr. & Engin. Chem.* Mar. 158/2 Unless my friends, the physico-chemists, will.. discover some way for establishing some optical properties or other physical constants, we are very much at a loss to establish the molecular size of my product. **1934** *Current Res. Anesthesia & Analgesia* XIII. 86 (*heading*) The physico-chemistry concerned in the action of anesthesia on blood colloids in relation to the safer handling of surgical and anesthetic risks. **1953** S. E. LURIA *Gen. Virol.* iv. 82 Their tendency to lengthwise and sidewise aggregation has rendered their study by hydro-dynamic methods a most perplexing problem for the physicochemist. **1966** *Mineral Abstr.* XVII. 739/2 The physico-chemistry and origin of the deposits are discussed. **1972** *Nature* 3 Mar. 44/1 The physico-chemistry of fibrous proteins.

ˌphysico-mathe'matical, *a.* [See PHYSICO-.] Of or pertaining to the application of mathematics to physics or mixed mathematics.

1671 *Phil. Trans.* VI. 3070 The Experiments and the Reasons thence deduced for the Substantiality of light, approach very near to a Physico-Mathematical evidence. **1802** HELLINS in *Phil. Trans.* XCII. 449 Mathematical and physico-mathematical problems. **1852** J. DAVIDSON *Pract. Math.* (ed. 5) Introd. 1 The Mixed [Mathematics] consist of physical subjects investigated and explained by mathematical reasoning, comprehend Mechanics, Astronomy, Optics, &c. These are sometimes styled the Physico-Mathematical sciences.

ˌphysico-me'chanical, *a.* [See PHYSICO-.] Of or pertaining to the dynamics of natural forces, or the mechanical branch of natural philosophy.

1661 BOYLE (*title*) New Experiments Physico-Mechanical, touching the Spring of the Air, and its effects. **1674** —— *Excell. Theol.* II. iv. 171 The physico-mechanical instruments of working on nature's and art's productions being happily invented. **1709** HAUKSBEE (*title*) Physico-Mechanical Experiments on various subjects, containing an account of surprizing Phenomena touching Light and Electricity. **1860** MAURY *Phys. Geog. Sea* (Low) v. §271 The immense physico-mechanical power of this agent called heat.

ˌphysico-the'ology. [See PHYSICO-.] A theology founded upon the facts of nature, and the evidences of design there found; natural theology.

1712 DERHAM (*title*) Physico-Theology: or, a Demonstration of the Being and Attributes of God from His Works of Creation. **1776** PENNANT *Zool.* (ed. 4) II. 603 This is a mixed species of study (when considered as physico-theology). **1825** COLERIDGE *Aids Refl.* (1848) I. 333, I more than fear the prevailing taste for books of natural theology, physico-theology, demonstrations of God from Nature, evidences of Christianity, and the like. **1855** BADEN POWELL *Ess.* 309 A physico-theology supplies no such idea of the Deity as can offer any antecedent contradiction to the representations of his nature and attributes.

So **ˌphysico-theo'logical** *a.*, of or pertaining to natural theology; **ˌphysico-the'ologist**, one versed in natural theology.

1675 BOYLE *Reconcileablen. Reason & Relig.* ii, Some Physico-Theological Considerations about the Possibility of the Resurrection. **1688** —— *Final Causes Nat. Things* iv. 111. **1825** COLERIDGE in *Rem.* (1836) II. 341 The Saturnian χρόνοι ὑπερχρόνιοι..to which the elder physico-theologists attributed a self-polarizing power. **1877** E. CAIRD *Philos. Kant* II. xviii. 633 The Physico-theological argument, the argument from design.

†physicotherapy (fɪzɪkəʊ'θɛrəpɪ). *Obs.* [f. PHYSICO- + THERAPY.] = PHYSIOTHERAPY.

1903 *Med. Rec.* (N.Y.) LXIII. 881/2 Dr. J. Riviere of Paris advocated the employment of physicotherapy, or the combined action of electricity, heat, and light, in the treatment of uterine fibromata.

Hence †**ˌphysicothera'peutic** *a.*, physiotherapeutic.

1904 *Nature* 21 Jan. 280/1 The results achieved..in the treatment of inoperable malignant growths by physicotherapeutic means.

'physics. [Plural of PHYSIC *a.* used *subst.*, rendering L. *physica* neut. pl., a. Gr. τὰ φυσικά lit. 'natural things', the collective title of Aristotle's physical treatises; as an Eng. word, plural in origin and form, but now construed as a singular: cf. *dynamics*, *mathematics*, etc.]

1. Natural science in general; in the older writers *esp.* the Aristotelian system of natural science; hence, natural philosophy in the wider sense. Also, a treatise on natural science, as *Aristotle's Physics*.

The application of the term has tended continually to be narrowed. It originally (from Arist.) included the study of the whole of nature (organic and inorganic); Locke even included spirits (God, angels, etc.) among its objects. In the course of the 18th cent. it became limited to inorganic nature, and then, by excluding chemistry, it acquired its present meaning: see 2.

1589 NASHE *Anat. Absurd.* Wks. (Grosart) I. 37 Neither is there almost any poeticall fygment wherein there is not some thing comprehended, taken out..of the Physicks or Ethicks. **1602** WARNER *Alb. Eng.* XII. lxxv. (1612) 313 Nor wanted thear..that did relye On Physickes and on Ethickes, and.. a God deny. **1620** T. GRANGER *Div. Logike* 56 Whereof some are contemplatiue, as Mathematikes, Physikes, Metaphysikes. **1656** tr. *Hobbes' Elem. Philos.* (1839) 388, I have given to this part the title of *Physics*, or the *Phenomena of Nature*. **1674** BOYLE *Excell. Theol.* II. iv. 170 That great Restorer of Physicks, the illustrious Verulam. **1704** J. HARRIS *Lex. Techn.* I, *Physicks*, or Natural Philosophy, is the Speculative Knowledge of all Natural Bodies (and Mr. Lock thinks, That God, Angels, Spirits &c. which usually are accounted as the Subject of Metaphysicks, should come into this Science), and of their proper Natures, Constitutions, Powers, and Operations. **1710** J. CLARKE *Rohault's Nat. Phil.* I. i. **1756–82** J. WARTON *Ess. Pope* iii. §38 [Aristotle's] Physicks contain many useful observations, particularly his history of animals. **1800** *Med. Jrnl.* III. 181 If we consider medicine as a science, or as a system of rules, it..forms a principal department of physics, or experimental philosophy. **1845** MAURICE *Mor. & Met. Philos.* in *Encycl. Metrop.* (1847) II. 645/1 Then arose.. Roger Bacon, and mathematics, chemistry, and physics generally became as much the studies of Christians as they had already been of the Mahometans. **1858** MAYNE *Expos. Lex.*, *Physics*, term for that science which treats of the nature of the qualities which beings derive from birth, in contradistinction to those acquired from art—of the whole mass of beings comprising the universe—and of the laws which govern those beings; natural philosophy.

2. In current usage, restricted to The science, or group of sciences, treating of the properties of matter and energy, or of the action of the different forms of energy on matter in general (excluding Chemistry, which deals specifically with the different forms of matter, and Biology, which deals with vital energy). See quots. 1900.

Physics is divided into ***general physics***, dealing with the general phenomena of inorganic nature (dynamics, molecular physics, physics of the ether, etc.), and ***applied physics***, dealing with special phenomena (astronomy, meteorology, terrestrial magnetism, etc.). There is a tendency now to restrict the word to the former group.

1715 tr. *Gregory's Astron.* I. Auth. Pref. 2 The Celestial Physics, or Physical Astronomy, hath..the preference in Dignity of all Enquiries into Nature whatever. **1834** MRS. SOMERVILLE *Connex. Phys. Sc.* xxxii. (1849) 361 These motions come under the same laws of dynamics and analysis as any other branch of physics. **1860** TYNDALL *Glac.* II. ix. 272 M. Agassiz is a naturalist, and he appears to have devoted but little attention to the study of physics. **1892** G. F. BARKER *Physics* i. §8. 6 Physics regards matter solely as the vehicle of energy..physics may be regarded as the science of energy, precisely as chemistry may be regarded as the science of matter. **1900** J. B. STALLO *Concepts & The. Mod. Physics* (ed. 4) 27 The science of physics, in addition to the general laws of dynamics and their application to the interaction of solid, liquid, and gaseous bodies, embraces the theory of those agents which were formerly designated as imponderables—light, heat, electricity, magnetism, etc.; and all these are now treated as forms of motion, as different manifestations of the same fundamental energy. **1900** W. WATSON *Textbk. Physics* 2 We are led to define Physics in its most general aspect as a discussion of the properties of matter and energy. It is, however, usual..to exclude the discussion of those properties of matter which depend simply on the nature of the different forms of matter (Chemistry), as also the properties of matter and energy as related to living things (Biology). The line of demarcation separating Physics and Chemistry has never been very clear, and of late years has practically vanished.

†**3.** The science of, or a treatise on, medicine. *Obs. rare.*

1626 R. HARRIS *Hezekiah's Recovery* (1630) 33 For the second, Health: great Salomon hath written a Physicks for us. **1785** JEFFERSON *Writ.* (1859) I. 467 When college education is done with . . he must cast his eyes (for America) either on Law or Physics.

physiform ('faɪsɪfɔːm), *a. Zool.* [f. PHYSA + -FORM.] Having the form of the gastropod PHYSA.

†**physiner**, a corrupt or erroneous form of PHYSICIANER: cf. PHYSION.

1616 SIR R. BOYLE in *Lismore Papers* (1886) I. 100 Lent Mr. Shea of Kilkenny the phisiner iiij[li] x[8].

physio ('fɪzɪəʊ). Colloq. abbrev. of PHYSIOTHERAPIST or PHYSIOTHERAPY.

1962 *Times* 3 July 5/3 They should, like the orthopaedic physiotherapists, also be nurses... I tell my physios: 'Keep your hands off, keep your minds on.' **1967** PARTRIDGE *Dict. Slang* Suppl. 1291 *Physio*, physiotherapy. **1968** M. WOODHOUSE *Rock Baby* iii. 21 Don't have him doing full knee bends... Reminds me, I must get in the physios chop-chop. **1971** 'J. BELL' *Hole in Ground* iv. 59 Dr. Colthorp wants her to have physio after the plaster comes off. **1973** *Times* 7 Feb. 15/3, I remember we didn't have a physio of our own, so we had to go to the athletics one. **1977** *Lancet* 5 Feb. 301/2 His details are entered in the book for the agreed date, with comments such as 'very fat' or 'needs pre-op physio'.

physio- ('fɪzɪəʊ), combining element, representing Gr. *φυσιο-*, f. *φύσις* nature, as in *φυσιογνώμων* 'judging of a man's nature', *φυσιολόγος* discoursing upon nature, *φυσιοσκοπεῖν* to observe nature; used as a formative with the sense 'nature' or 'natural', as in PHYSIOCRACY, PHYSIOGNOMY, PHYSIOGRAPHY, PHYSIOLOGY, etc.; also in the following less important compounds (in some of which it is treated as an abbreviation of *physiology* or *physiological*):

ˌ**physio-'chemical** *a.*, pertaining to physiological chemistry. †ˌ**physio'glyphic** [after *hieroglyphic*] (see quot.). ˌ**physio'gnostic**, **physi'ognosy** [Gr. *γνῶσις* knowledge] (see quots.). ˌ**physio'medicalism**, the system of 'natural' medicine which uses vegetable drugs, only discarding those which are poisonous (*Syd. Soc. Lex.*); so ˌ**physio'medical** *a.*; ˌ**physio'medicalist**. ˌ**physio'pathic** *a.*, of or pertaining to physiopathy. ˌ**physiopatho'logical** *a.*, of or pertaining to a pathological state influenced by physiology. **physi'opathy** [Gr. *-παθεια*, f. *πάθος* suffering] (see quot.). **physi'ophilist** [Gr. *φιλεῖν* to love], a lover or student of nature. '**physioˌphyly** [see PHYLUM] (see quot.). ˌ**physio'plastic** *a.*, formed by nature. ˌ**physio-psy'chology**, physiological psychology; so ˌ**physio-psycho'logic**, **-'logical** *adjs.* '**physioˌscope** [Gr. *-σκόπος* viewing] (see quot. 1846). **physi'oscopy**, the rendering of the physical appearances and conditions in a painting. **physio-socio'logical** *a.*, combining physiology and sociology. **physi'osophy** [Gr. *σοφία* wisdom], an assumption of knowledge of nature; hence ˌ**physio'sophic** *a.* '**physiotype**, a process for taking an impression direct from a flat object, on prepared paper; also an image made by such process. '**physioˌtypy**, printing from plates made by various processes direct from natural objects; nature-printing.

1887 A. M. BROWN *Anim. Alkal.* 5 The presence of the alkaloid might be owing to *physio-chemical action after death. **1844** UPTON *Physioglyphics* 101 In a literal hieroglyphic, therefore, or what I shall now more aptly term a *physioglyphic, no name must be involved. **1635** PERSON *Varieties* II. 60 The Meteorologians answer not so fully satisfactorie as theirs, who treate of spirits, whom I may well call *Physiognosticks. **1811–31** BENTHAM *Logic* App., Wks. 1843 VIII. 284 Natural History . . which . . may more aptly and expressively, it should seem, be designated by the term *Physiognosy. **1880** C. A. CUTTER *Classif. Nat. Sc.* in *Library Jrnl.* June, A similar word, Fysiognosy . . supplies a name which was wanted for the natural sciences collectively. **1885** *Proc. Boston Soc. Nat. Hist.* XXIII. 226 It should consist of three parts or sections, first Statical Geognosy or Physiognosy. **1800** COLERIDGE in C. K. Paul *W. Godwin* (1876) II. 3 Your poetic and *Physiopathic feelings. **1897** *Allbutt's Syst. Med.* III. 777 We cannot even say if it . . be of a *physio-pathological character, or a specific germ. **1898** P. MANSON *Trop. Dis.* xxvi. 413 Certain physio-pathological qualities predisposing to the disease may be inherited. **1797–1803** FOSTER in *Life & Corr.* (1846) I. 212 What may be called *physiopathy, a faculty of pervading all nature with one's own being. **1804** COLERIDGE *Lett., to R. Sharp* (1895) 448, I have met with several genuine Philologists, Philonoists, *Physiophilists, keen hunters after knowledge and science. **1879** tr. *Haeckel's Evol. Man* I. i. 24 *Physiophyly. The tribal history of the functions, or the history of the palæontological development of vital activities. **1811–31** BENTHAM *Logic* App., Wks. 1843 VIII. 284/1 In their *physioplastic state, in the state in which, fashioned by the hand of nature, they [bodies] are found in the bosom of nature. **1939** *Burlington Mag.* June 300/2 The familiar opposition between geometrical and 'vital' forms, impressionist and expressionist art, 'ideoplastic' and 'physioplastic', and so on, is shown to possess a concrete sanction in the aesthetic attitudes of blind artists. **1943** Physioplastic [see IDEOPLASTIC *a.*]. **1932** G. BLUMER in *Practitioners Libr. Med. & Surg.* I. ix. 698 Constitution, which includes *physiopsychologic factors, may change considerably during life. **1874** J. CUNNINGHAM *New Theory of Knowing* 155 Every one . . knows what is meant by getting a 'start', though the *physio-psychological explanation of it is not so clear. **1875** C. WRIGHT *Let.* 12 July in R. B. Perry *Tht. & Char. W. James* (1935) I. 530 The other is in a book-notice by him [*sc.* William James] . . of Wundt's *physio-psychology. **1903** *Amer. Anthropologist* V. 586 In a general way, comparative physio-psychology has aided us in the search for the key to this great problem [of various intellectual endowment]. **1846** JOYCE *Sci. Dial., Optics* xxii. 332 What is the opaque microscope? . . Very much the same sort of thing as the magic lantern; except that the light, instead of passing through the object, shines upon it, and is reflected off through the lenses, and so onward to the screen. . . The *physioscope is the same instrument, employed to depict 'the human face' . . in colossal dimensions upon the screen. *c* **1865** J. WYLDE in *Circ. Sc.* I. 64/2 The physioscope is a modification of the magic lantern. **1886–94** H. SPENCER *Autobiog.* II. xlvi. 193 *note*, Under '*physioscopy' I propose to include the rendering of the phenomena of linear perspective, of aerial perspective, of light and shade, and of colour in so far as it is determined not by artistic choice, but by natural conditions. **1904** *Westm. Gaz.* 29 June 2/1 The average medical man cannot afford the leisure for the systematic study of the *physio-sociological problems that lie in his path. **1886** GÜNTHER in *Encycl. Brit.* XX. 437/1 Morphological facts are entirely superseded by fanciful ideas of the vaguest kind of *physiosophy. **1904** *Daily News* 23 June 11 A remarkable invention is . . called 'The *Physiotype'. A leaf, piece of lace, or other flat object is pressed upon a piece of prepared paper, but there is no visible mark made; the paper then has a powder . . brushed over it, and the structure of the leaf or the pattern of the lace immediately appears in black.

physiocracy (fɪzɪ'ɒkrəsɪ). [ad. F. *physiocratie* (1767 in Hatz.-Darm.): see PHYSIO- and -CRACY.] Government according to natural order; *spec.* the doctrine of the physiocrats.

1875 *Contemp. Rev.* XXV. 882 The doctrine that all wealth is formed out of the materials of the globe may be called Physiocracy. **1895** L. F. WARD in *Forum* (N.Y.) Nov. 304 If we had a pure physiocracy or government of nature, such as prevails among wild animals.

physiocrat ('fɪzɪəʊkræt). Also in Fr. form **-crate**. [a. F. *physiocrate*, f. *physiocratie*: see prec. and -CRAT.] One of a school of political economists founded by François Quesnay in France in the 18th c.; they maintained that society should be governed according to an inherent natural order, that the soil is the sole source of wealth and the only proper object of taxation, and that security of property and freedom of industry and exchange are essential: = ECONOMIST 4 c.

1798 W. TAYLOR in *Monthly Mag.* V. 352 About the year 1774, the philosophic sect of Physiocrates was already organized into a political body. **1804** —— in *Crit. Rev.* Ser. III. I. 21 The only merit of the *economistes*, or physiocrates, consists in arguing well against legal interference, and legal restraint. **1896** *Athenæum* 19 Sept. 390 Questions . . as to the relation of Adam Smith to the physiocrats.

physiocratic (ˌfɪzɪəʊ'krætɪk), *a.* [f. as PHYSIOCRAT + -IC.] Of or pertaining to physiocracy or the physiocrats.

1804 W. TAYLOR in *Ann. Rev.* II. 324 Much is said of the theory of the physiocratic sect. **1888** W. L. COURTNEY *J. S. Mill* 96 The physiocratic theory begins with the idea of a *Jus Naturæ*, a simple . . and beneficial code established by Nature.

So †**physio'cratical** *a. Obs. rare*$^{-1}$.

1792 A. YOUNG *Trav. France* 141 The *œconomistes*, in their writings, speak much of an experiment he made in their Physiocratical rubbish.

physiocratism (fɪzɪ'ɒkrətɪz(ə)m). [f. as prec. + -ISM.] **1.** = PHYSIOCRACY.

1890 in *Cent. Dict.*

2. In Kant's use, The doctrine that all causality is dependent on nature.

physiog, humorous colloquial abbreviation of PHYSIOGNOMY (sense 3).

1865 E. C. CLAYTON *Cruel Fortune* I. 145 Glad to behold your distinguished physiog.

physio'genesis. *Biol.* [f. as next + Gr. *γένεσις* GENESIS.] = next, b.

1887 COPE *Primary Factors Org. Evol.* 488 Changes may be effected in the weight, colour, and in functional capacity by temperature, humidity, food, &c., thus exhibiting physiogenesis.

Hence ˌ**physioge'netic** *a.*, of or pertaining to physiogenesis.

physiogeny (fɪzɪ'ɒdʒɪnɪ). [ad. mod.L. *physiogenia*, f. Gr. *φυσιο-* PHYSIO- + *-γένεια* -GENY. Cf. Ger. *physiogenie*.] †**a.** The genesis of natural bodies. *Obs.* **b.** *Biol.* The genesis of vital functions; the development or evolution of the functions of living organisms, which are the province of physiology; the science or history of this.

1858 MAYNE *Expos. Lex.*, *Physiogenia*, term for the operations of nature, according to Rumpf, of the formation of bodies from original elements: physiogeny. **1879** tr. *Haeckel's Evol. Man* I. 24 *Physiogeny*, the germ-history of the functions, or the history of the development of vital activities in the individual. *Ibid.* II. 461 So will Physiogeny . . make a true recognition of functions possible, by discovering their historic evolution.

Hence **physiogenic** (-'dʒɛnɪk) *a.*, of the nature of physiogeny.

†**physi'ognomer**. *Obs.* Forms: 6 **fisnomier**, **phisnamour**, **phisiognomier**, **-yer**, 7– **physiognomer**. [f. PHYSIOGNOMY + -ER[1]: cf. *astronomy, astronomer*.] = PHYSIOGNOMIST.

a **1500** P. JOHNSTON *Thre Deid Pollis* 42 This questioun quha can obsolue, lat see, Quhat phisnamour, or perfyt palmester. **1519** HORMAN *Vulg.* 19, I beleue nat the reders of dremes and fisnomiers. **1542** UDALL *Erasm. Apoph.* Table X ij b, Arte and profession of Phisiognomyers. **1586** A. DAY *Eng. Secretary* II. (1625) 55 When a Phisiognomer by chance . . came into the forum of Athens, he declared by the view of diuers mens faces, the diuersity of their conditions. **1656** H. MORE *Enthus. Tri.* 35 That Sanguine was the Complexion of David George, the foregoing description of his person will probably intimate to any Physiognomer. **1706** PHILLIPS, *Physiognomer* or *Physiognomist*.

physiognomic (ˌfɪzɪəʊ'gnɒmɪk, ˌfɪzɪəʊ'nɒmɪk), *a.* (*sb.*) [ad. late L. *physiognōmic-us* (Fulgentius, *c* 550), corruption of Gr. *φυσιογνωμονικ-ός*, f. *φυσιογνωμονία*: see PHYSIOGNOMY and -IC. In OF. *physionomique* (15th c. in Godef. *Compl.*), in mod.F. *physiognomonique* (*Dict. Trévoux* 1732).]

A. *adj.* **1.** Of the nature of physiognomy; relating to the face or form as indicating character; characteristic.

1755 JOHNSON, *Physiognomic*, drawn from the contemplation of the face. **1817** COLERIDGE *Biog. Lit.* II. xxii. 166 The very spirit which gives the physiognomic expression to all the works of nature. **1856** KINGSLEY *Lett.* 26 Feb., It is sad to see how much faults of character seem to depend on physiognomic defects. **1868** *Contemp. Rev.* IX. 75 Currents of thought and feeling which are physiognomic of the atmosphere he lives in.

2. Of, pertaining to, or skilled in physiognomy; 'conversant in contemplation of the face' (J.).

1755 in JOHNSON. **1818** COLERIDGE in *Lit. Rem.* (1836) I. 146 There is great physiognomic tact in Sterne. **1885** COUPLAND *Spirit Goethe's Faust* i. 11 Such physiognomic science [is] lighter than a water-bug.

3. *Ecol.* Of or pertaining to the physiognomy of a plant community (PHYSIOGNOMY 4 b).

1911 BEVIS & JEFFERY *Brit. Plants* ii. 16 The physiognomic groups into which we have divided the vegetation (woodland, grassland, heath, etc.) are only in part associated with definite types of climate. **1926** TANSLEY & CHIPP *Study of Vegetation* x. 204 It is . . by the physio-gnomic characters of the vegetation, especially when correlated with some topographic feature, that the traveller will find it easiest to recognise and record the chief types of vegetation in the course of his journey. **1951** *Ecology* XXXII. 279/2 The practical aspects of the physiognomic method are reflected in its use by foresters. **1959** *New Scientist* 29 Oct. 803/2 When the change in climatic pattern is gradual, the change in physiognomic type is correspondingly slow and *vice versa*. **1971** *Nature* 18 June 430/1 The Radforth muskeg classification system . . is based on physiognomic characteristics.

B. *sb.* (in *pl.*) See quots.

[**1693** tr. *Blancard's Phys. Dict.* (ed. 2), *Physiognomica*, Signs whereby we conjecture something by the Countenance.] **1704** J. HARRIS *Lex. Techn.* I, *Physiognomicks*, . . a Term used by some Physicians and Naturalists for such Signs as are taken from the Countenance of Persons, to judge of their Dispositions and Temper. **1727–41** in CHAMBERS *Cycl.* **1828** in WEBSTER, and in later Dicts.

physio'gnomical, *a.* [f. as prec. + -AL[1].]

1. Pertaining to, dealing with, or skilled in physiognomy; indicative of character.

1588 FRAUNCE *Lawiers Log.* I. viii. 43 b, Divers physionomicall conjectures, as that of Martiall. *Crine ruber, niger ore, brevis pede.* **1644** BULWER *Chirol.* 72 Hence Physiognomicall Philosophers . . doe easily discerne the differences. **1830** D'ISRAELI *Chas. I*, III. vi. 113 Had the physiognomical predicter examined the two portraits . . he might have augured a happier fate. **1840** CARLYLE *Heroes* iii. (1858) 264 All that a man does is physiognomical of him.

2. Of or pertaining to the face or form (properly) as an index of character, but often used simply in reference to personal appearance. (In quot. 1815 earlier term for *phrenological*.)

1811 LAMB *Danger Confound. Mor. w. Personal Deformity*, To distinguish between that physiognomical deformity which I am willing to grant always accompanies crime, and mere physical ugliness. **1812** R. H. in *Examiner* 28 Dec. 828/1 The analogy . . that appears between the physiognomical and intellectual . . character. **1815** (*title*) The Physiognomical System of Drs. Gall and Spurzheim, founded on an . . Examination of the Nervous System in general, and of the Brain in particular. [transl. of French ed. 1810] **1861** *Times* 16 Oct., Certain original physiognomical types peculiar to himself.

Hence **physio'gnomically** *adv.*, in a physiognomical manner; according to the rules of physiognomy; as regards characteristic features.

1608 TOPSELL *Serpents* (1658) 640 The one and other are thus Physiognomically described by the Poet. **1797** COLERIDGE *Wks.* (1893) p. xxxiv. *note*, My eyes, eyebrows, and forehead are physiognomically good. **1854** *Blackw. Mag.* LXXVI. 521 County differed from county physiognomically. **1882** *Academy* 14 Jan. 24/3 A charmingly etched and evidently characteristic portrait . . confirms physiognomically the popular estimate of his character.

physiognomist (fɪzɪˈɒgnəmɪst, -ˈɒnəmɪst). [a. OF. *physionomiste* (1557 in Godef. *Compl.*), f. *physionomie*: see -IST.] One skilled in physiognomy; one who reads character or disposition (or, formerly, professed to foretell destiny) from the face.

1570 DEE *Math. Pref.* c iv, The Anatomistes will restore to you, some part: The Physiognomistes, some. **1601** HOLLAND *Pliny* XXXV. x. 539 A certaine Physiognomist or teller of fortune. **1788** REID *Active Powers* II. iii. 540 The physiognomist saw, in the features of Socrates, the signatures of many bad dispositions. **1802** MAR. EDGEWORTH *Moral T.* (1816) I. xv. 123 By no means a good physiognomist, much less a good judge of character. **1865** DICKENS *Mut. Fr.* I. ix, Her remarkable powers as a physiognomist.

Hence †**physiognoˈmistic, -ical** *adjs.*, of or pertaining to a physiognomist; †**physiˈognomistry**, the art or trade of the physiognomist.

1651 BIGGS *New Disp.* §98 To be seen with Physiognomisticall corporall eyes. **1708** *Brit. Apollo* No. 66. 2/1 We may include Palmistry, Physiognomistry, etc.

physiˈognomize, *v.* [f. PHYSIOGNOMY + -IZE.]

1. *trans.* To examine or study physiognomically; to deduce the character of from physiognomy.

1660 STANLEY *Hist. Philos.* IX. (1701) 372/1 Before he had physiognomized the man what he were. **1796** SOUTHEY *Let. to G. C. Bedford* 24 Feb. in *Life* (1849) I. 269, I defy you or Mr. Shandy to physiognomise that man's name rightly. **1809** —— *Lett.* (1856) II. 173 That good lady who, as you remember, physiognomised me so luckily for 'a man of sorrow and acquainted with woe'.

†**2.** To assume the physiognomy or characteristic appearance of. *Obs. rare.*

1653 R. SANDERS *Physiogn.* bjb, Archangel physiognomising the fingers. *Ibid.* bij, Divers plants physiognomize the horns of Beasts, as Cornop, Plaintain.

physiognomonic (fɪzɪˌɒgnəʊˈmɒnɪk), *a.* (*sb.*) *rare.* [ad. med.L. *physiognōmonic-us*, a. Gr. φυσιογνωμονικός adj., f. φυσιογνωμονία: see PHYSIOGNOMY and -IC. In F. *physiognomonique.*] The etymologically correct form for PHYSIOGNOMIC.

1755 JOHNSON, *Physiognomonick* adj. **1798** FERRIAR *Illustr. Sterne* iv. 118 The chapter is concluded by the physiognomonic doctrine of the nose. **1858** MAYNE *Expos. Lex.*, *Physiognōmonica*,.. physiognomonics. **1893** in *Syd. Soc. Lex.*

physiognomonical (fɪzɪˌɒgnəʊˈmɒnɪkəl), *a.* Now *rare* or *Obs.* [f. as prec. + -AL[1].] Etymological form for PHYSIOGNOMICAL.

1668 G. C. in *H. More's Div. Dial.* Pref. (1713) 6 In the Character of which Person the Dramatist seems to have been judicious even to Physiognomonical Curiosity. **1737** FIELDING *Tom Thumb* (ed. 3) Pref., Affirmed by our English Physiognominical writers. **1805** T. HOLCROFT *Bryan Perdue* II. 114 Not having yet completed my course of physiognomonical experiments. **1814** *Phil. Mag.* XLIV. 305 Demonstrative Course of Lectures on Drs. Gall and Spurzheim's Physiognomonical System.

physiognomy (fɪzɪˈɒgnəmɪ, -ˈɒnəmɪ). Forms: see below. [ME. *fisnomye, fis-, phisonomye*, etc., a. OF. (13th c.) *fiz-, phis-, phizonomie, -anomie*, in mod.F. *physionomie* = Pr. *phizonomia*, Sp. *fisonomía*, Pg. *physionomia*, It. *fisio-, fisonomia*, ad. med.L. *phisonomia, physionomia, *physiognōmia*, ad. Gr. φυσιογνωμονία the judging of a man's nature (by his features), f. φύσις nature (PHYSIO-) + γνώμων, γνωμον- judge, interpreter: wrongly written φυσιογνωμία in Stob. Ecl. (Liddell and Scott), whence the med.L. form. As will be seen, the word shows contraction in all the Romanic langs., and still more in Eng., where in vulgar use it has even been abridged to *physiog.*, *phizog.*, and *phiz.* The pronunciation (fɪzɪˈɒnəmɪ) which formerly prevailed (see A. γ, quots. 1783, 1840) is now somewhat old-fashioned.]

A. Illustration of Forms.

α. 4–5 **fysnomye, -namye, fyss-,** 5–6 **fisnamy, phis-, physnomie,** 5–7 **-nomy,** 6 **phis-, phys-, fis-, fys, fiz-, -nomy, -namy (-ye, -ie), phisnami, (-nom, physnome),** 6–7 (9) **visnomy, -ie,** 7 **fisnomie.**

? *a* **1400** *Morte Arth.* 1114 He feyed his fysnamye with his foule hondez. **1450–80** tr. *Secreta Secret.* 38 The mervelous science of ffysnomye. *c* **1470** HENRYSON *Mor. Fab.* xiii. (*Frog & Mouse*) viii, Ane thrawart will, ane thrawin phisnomy. **1513** BRADSHAW *St. Werburge* I. 2765 His fysnamy restaured to his kynde agayne. **1548** UDALL, etc. *Erasm. Par. Mark* ix. 3 His face, whiche before seemed not to diffre from the common phisnami of others, shone as brighte as the sunne. *a* **1585** MONTGOMERIE *Flyting w. Polwart* 490 With flirting and flyring, their physnome they flype. *a* **1652** BROME *Love-sick Court* v. i, I can read guilty lines Palpably on this villans visnomy. **1660** J. S. *Andromana* IV. v. in Hazl. *Dodsley* XIV. 253 If he have not rogue writ in great letters in's face, I have no physnomy. [**1822** LAMB *Elia* Ser. I. *Distant Corr.* (1823) 245 A pun is reflected from a friend's face as from a mirror. Who would consult his sweet visnomy, if the polished surface were two or three minutes.. in giving back its copy?]

β. 4–6 **phisonomie,** 5 **phiso-, phizo-, physonomye, (physynomye, fysenamye),** 6 **vysonamy, visenomy,** 6–7 **phisognomie, -y,** 7 **-gminy.**

1390 GOWER *Conf.* III. 5 Thou scholdest be Phisonomie Be schapen to that maladie Of lovedrunke. *c* **1425** *Seven Sag.* (P.) 1072 The childe couthe of fysenamye That he saw evyl with hys eye. **1489** CAXTON *Faytes of A.* I. x. 27 By the phizonomye of yᵉ yongmen.. they knowe whiche were moost able. **1532** TINDALE *Wks.* (Parker Soc.) II. 127 The false prophets do well to paint God after the likeness of their own visenomy. *a* **1562** G. CAVENDISH *Wolsey* (1893) 33 A dosyn of other maskers,.. with visors of good proporcion of vysonamy. **1642** S. W. *Parl. Vind. agst. Pr. Rupert* 3 Not new in Phisognomy. **1678** W. STROTHER in *Lauderdale Papers* (1885) III. xciii. 161 We think Welsh was amongst them, by the discription of his phisogminy.

γ. 6– **physiognomy,** (6 **phisionomie, visionogmi,** 6–7 **phisio-, physiognomie,** 6–8 **phisio-,** 7 **visiognomy).**

1569 J. SANFORD tr. *Agrippa's Van. Artes* 50b, Physiognomie.. doth presume that shee is able to finde out .. by vewing of the whole bodie, the dispositions of the minde and body. **1660** *A. Durer Revived* 2 The Visiognomy or Circumference of a Face. **1783** JOHNSON *Let. to Mrs. Thrale* 21 Oct., Physiognomy, as it is a Greek word, ought to sound the G; but.. G, I think, is sounded in formal, and sunk in familiar language. **1840** A. R. WEBSTER *Oxf. Songs, Town & Gown*, You'll find it bad economy To carry home a tattered gown and battered physiognomy.

B. Signification.

I. 1. a. The art of judging character and disposition from the features of the face or the form and lineaments of the body generally.

1390 [see A. β]. **1422** tr. *Secreta Secret., Priv. Priv.* 219 One lyght manere and general of Phisnomye is to deme vertues and maneris of man aftyr the conpleccion. *c* **1450** LYDG. & BURGH *Secrees* 2467 The excellent science.. I mene phisonomye, Be which thou shalt.. knowe disposicion in ech degree and signe, Of al thy peple. **1591** GREENE *Farew. Follie* Wks. (Grosart) IX. 327, I haue not.. such assured sight in Phisognomie, as I dare auouch it for truth. **1638** R. BAKER tr. *Balzac's Lett.* (vol. III) 19 The reputation of my skill in Physnomie and Prognosticating. *a* **1720** SHEFFIELD (Dk. Buckhm.) *Wks.* (1753) II. 60 An illustrious exception to all the common rules of Physiognomy. **1853** C. BRONTE *Villette* vii. (1876) 60, I want your opinion. We know your skill in physiognomy.... Read that countenance.

†**b.** *transf.* A judging of the form of a living body from the skeleton. *Obs.*

1658 SIR T. BROWNE *Hydriot.* ii. 30 Since Bones afford.. Figure unto the Body, it is no impossible Physiognomy to conjecture at Fleshy Appendencies.

†**2.** The foretelling of destiny or future fortune from the features and lines of the face, etc.; the fortune so foretold: *loosely*, fortune foretold (or character divined) by astrology. *Obs.*

1531 *Act 22 Hen. VIII*, c. 12 §4 Physyke, Physnamye, Palmestrye or other craftye scyences wherby they beare the people in hande that they can tell theire destenyes deceases & fortunes. **1577** HARRISON *England* II. x. (1877) I. 220 Roges.. practisers of physiognomie and palmestrie, tellers of fortunes [etc.]. **1589** NASHE *Martins Months Mind* Ep. Ded., Wks. (Grosart) I. 146 For that it seemeth you have some skill in Astrologie,.. let vs haue a glimpse at the least of the fooles phisnomies. **1651** BAXTER *Inf. Bapt.* 242 According to my little skill in Physiognomy, I hope he may live yet many a yeer.

II. 3. a. The face or countenance, especially viewed as an index to the mind and character; expression of face; also, the general cast of features, type of face (of a race); vulgarly, the face or countenance (formerly very common, esp. in the α form, now rare).

c **1400** *Beryn* 3196, I knowe wele by thy fisnamy, thy kynd it were to stele. **1555** W. WATREMAN *Fardle Facions* I. iv. 39 Dyuers peoples of sondry phisonomy and shape. **1575** G. HARVEY *Letter-bk.* (Camden) 98 Eies glauncinge, fisnamy smirkinge. **1621** BURTON *Anat. Mel.* III. iii. I. ii. (1651) 605 She did abhorre her husbands phisnomy. **1623–33** FLETCHER & SHIRLEY *Night-Walker* v. i, I haue seen that physiognomy: Were you never in prison? *a* **1718** ROWE *Biter* II. i, That Blow upon your Forehead has decompos'd your Phisiognomy strangely. **1754** RICHARDSON *Grandison* (1781) I. ii. 8 The grace which that people call *Physiognomy*, and we may call Expression. **1856** EMERSON *Eng. Traits, Race* Wks. (Bohn) II. 21 Each religious sect has its physiognomy. The Methodists have acquired a face; the Quakers, a face; the nuns, a face. **1869** TOZER *Highl. Turkey* II. 305 The distinctive Greek physiognomy was no longer to be found.

†**b.** A representation of a face; a portrait. *Obs.*

1483 CAXTON *Gold. Leg.* 339/2 Oure lord.. toke fro the payntour a lynnen clothe and set it upon his vysage and enprynted the very physonomye of his vysage therin. **1587** in Ellis *Orig. Lett.* Ser. I. III. 52 *note*, One little Flower of gold with a frogg thereon, and therein Mounsier his phisnamye. **1603** H. CROSSE *Vertues Commw.* (1878) 130 Apelles would not loose a day without shadowing a phisnomie.

4. a. *transf.* The general appearance or external features of anything material; e.g. the contour or configuration of a country.

1567 MAPLET *Gr. Forest* 7 Efestides [a kind of stone] is in colour and Phisiognomie verie shamefast and childish. **1819** SHELLEY *Let.* Pr. Wks. 1888 II. 294 Its physiognomy indicates it to be a city, which.. yet possesses most amiable qualities. **1830** LYELL *Princ. Geol.* I. 362 The most grand and original feature in the physiognomy of Etna. **1863** HAWTHORNE *Our Old Home* (1879) 159 The old highways.. adapted themselves.. to the physiognomy of the country.

b. *spec.* in *Ecol.* The general appearance, form, or characteristics of a community of plants.

1909 GROOM & BALFOUR tr. *Warming's Oecol. Plants* vi. 25 The temperature and length of the vegetative season affect the physiognomy of the individual plant and the whole vegetation. **1926** TANSLEY & CHIPP *Study of Vegetation* ii. 11 The physiognomy or 'look' of an association is primarily determined by the life form of its dominant species. **1951** *Ecology* XXXII. 278/2 Gillman.. produced an excellent map of the physiognomy of the vegetation of Tanganyika. **1973** W. B. CLAPHAM *Nat. Ecosystems* vii. 230 Many of the basic variables of the microhabitat, such as temperature, humidity, and the like, are functions of the physiognomy of the climax community.

5. *fig.* The ideal, mental, moral, or political aspect of anything as an indication of its character; characteristic aspect.

a **1680** BUTLER *Rem.* (1759) II. 494 There is a Kind of Physiognomy in the Titles of Books, no less than in the Faces of Men, by which a skilful Observer will as well know what to expect from the one as the other. *c* **1796** T. TWINING *Trav. Amer.* (1894) 91 The moral physiognomy of certain sections of the United States. *a* **1854** H. REED *Lect. Eng. Lit.* iii. (1878) 93 You may discover the physiognomy, that is in speech, as well as in face. **1879** *Echo* No. 3374. 2 The utter change in the political physiognomy of the new Landtag.

physiˈognotype. [f. PHYSIOGN(OMY + Gr. τύπος impress, print, model.] 'A machine for taking casts and imprints of human faces or countenances' (Worcester).

a **1846** WORCESTER cites *Observer.* **1878** BARTLEY tr. *Topinard's Anthrop.* II. iii. 296 A craniograph, which must have been suggested by the physio[g]notype of Huschke, and reminds one of the circular band used by hatters.

physiogony (fɪzɪˈɒgənɪ). [f. Gr. φύσις nature (see PHYSIO-) + -γονία begetting, production.] The generation or production of nature.

a **1834** COLERIDGE in *Lit. Rem.* (1838) III. 158 Their physiology imbrangled with an inapplicable logic and a misgrowth of.. substantiated abstractions; and their physiogony a blank or dream of tradition. **1840** J. H. GREEN *Vital Dynamics* 103 The distinctive.. aim.. of physiogony is to present the history of Nature as preface and portion of the history of man.

physiographer (fɪzɪˈɒgrəfə(r)). [f. PHYSIOGRAPH-Y + -ER[1].] One versed in physiography; a physical geographer.

1885 *Amer. Jrnl. Sc.* Ser. III. XXX. 261 The same eminent.. physiographer, in his paper on the Ocean, remarks [etc.]. **1902** C. LENNOX *J. Chalmers* vi, A belt of very shallow water suggesting to the physiographer that it had once formed part of the continent.

physiographic (ˌfɪzɪəʊˈgræfɪk), *a.* [f. mod.L. *physiographia* PHYSIOGRAPHY + -IC.] Of or belonging to physiography: cf. next. ***physiographic province***: see PROVINCE 6 c.

1840 J. H. GREEN *Vital Dynamics* 104 The physiographic details which form the main body of these lectures. **1863** DANA *Man. Geol.* 7 Physiographic Geology,—a general survey of the earth's surface-features.

physiographical (ˌfɪzɪəʊˈgræfɪkəl), *a.* [f. as prec. + -AL[1].] Dealing with or treating of physiography; pertaining to physiography.

1796 MORSE *Amer. Geog.* II. 56 Other literary societies are formed at Upsala, Gottenburg, &c., and a physiographical one at Lund. **1882** GEIKIE *Text-bk. Geol.* VII. 910 The branch of geological enquiry which deals with the evolution of the existing contours of the dry land is termed Physiographical Geology. **1890** *Q. Rev.* July 88 The Vosges interested him profoundly, but from a purely physiographical point of view.

physiographically (fɪzɪəʊˈgræfɪkəlɪ), *adv.* [f. PHYSIOGRAPHICAL *a.* + -LY[2].] From a physiographical point of view.

1902 in *Encycl. Dict.* Suppl. **1908** *Westm. Gaz.* 24 Mar. 12/1 This church stands nearly 1,450 feet above sea-level, and is considered the 'highest'—not ecclesiastically, but physiographically—in Great Britain. **1928** V. G. CHILDE *Most Anc. East* ii. 22 Physiographically the last-named chains constitute a more real dividing line than the inland sea. **1973** *Nature* 1 June 277/2 Somewhat older deltas exist which receive little or no drainage today and are therefore harder to distinguish physiographically.

physiography (fɪzɪˈɒgrəfɪ). [mod. f. Gr. φύσις nature + -γραφία description, -GRAPHY: cf. F. *physiographie* (1812).]

1. A description of nature, or of natural phenomena or productions generally.

1828–32 WEBSTER, *Physiography*, a description of nature, or the science of natural objects. *Journ. of Science.* *a* **1834** COLERIDGE in *Lit. Rem.* (1838) III. 158 The ignorance of natural science, their physiography scant in fact, and stuffed out with fables. **1840** J. H. GREEN *Vital Dynamics* 101 The office of.. Physiography is to enumerate and delineate the effects and products of nature as they appear. **1878** HUXLEY *Physiogr.* Pref. 6, I undertook to deliver twelve lectures on natural phenomena in general; and I borrowed the title of 'Physiography'.. for my subject, inasmuch as I wished to draw a clear line of demarcation, both as to matter and method, between it and what is commonly understood by Physical Geography. **1891** E. HULL (*title*) Physiography: an introduction to the Study of Nature.

2. A description of the nature of a particular class of objects (in quot., of minerals).

[**1873** ROSENBUSCH (*title*) Mikroskopische Physiographie der petrographisch wichtigen Mineralien.] **1888** J. P. IDDINGS (*title*) Microscopical Physiography of the Rock-making Minerals:.. By H. Rosenbusch. Translated and abridged.

3. Physical geography.

1873 J. GEIKIE *Gt. Ice Age* xiii. 176 To restore the physiography of the land during successive stages of the glacial epoch. **1877** —— *Elem. Lessons in Phys. Geog.* 3 *note*, This term [physical geography] as here used is synonymous with Physiography, which has been proposed in its stead. **1895** *Educat. Rev.* Nov. 353 Physiography on the other hand treats of the science of earth-sculpture, viewed in the light of systematic processes.

physiolater (fɪzɪˈɒlətə(r)). [f. as prec. + Gr. -λατρης worshipper.] A worshipper of nature. So **physiˈolatry** [-LATRY], nature-worship.

1860 MAX MÜLLER *Hist. Sanskrit Lit.* (ed. 2) Introd. 32 The primæval physiolatry which was common to all the members of the Aryan family. **1879** *Scribner's Mag.* May 145 Physiolatry, or the worship of natural objects of awe, such as rivers, mountains, etc. **1882** L. F. WARD in *Internat. Rev.* May, These modern physiolaters are among the most eminent teachers of science and philosophy.

physiologer (fɪzɪˈɒlədʒə(r)). Now *rare* or *Obs.* Also 7 phis-. [f. PHYSIOLOGY (or L. *physiolog-us*, a. Gr. φυσιολόγος, one who discourses on nature, f. φύσις nature + -λόγος -speaking) + -ER[1].]

1. A student or teacher of natural science; *spec.* a philosopher of the Ionic sect.

1598 R. HAYDOCKE tr. *Lomazzo* II. 199 Astrologers, Physiologers, Optickes, Paynters. **1656** BLOUNT *Glossogr.*, *Physiologer*, he that searcheth out, or disputes of Natural things, a Natural Philosopher. **1678** CUDWORTH *Intell. Syst.* 9 Democritus and most of the Physiologers here commit a very great Absurdity, in that they make all Sense to be Touch. *a* **1688** —— *Immut. Mor.* (1731) 105 The very same with that which Aristotle imputes to the antient Physiologers as a Paradox, that Black and White were not without the Sight. **1707** *Curios. in Husb. & Gard.* 145 The famous Bacon, and several Physiologers assure, that 'tis easy to have Roses so backward, as not to blow till towards the End of Autumn. **1867** MAURICE *Patriarchs & Lawg.* ii. (1877) 53 The belief which a very large body of physiologers, not believers in the Bible, resolutely maintain.

2. = PHYSIOLOGIST 2.

1680 J. AUBREY in *Lett. Eminent Persons* (1813) III. 620 His head was of a mallet forme, approved by the physiologers. **1831** W. GODWIN *Thoughts Man* 8 An important remark, suggested to me many years ago by an eminent physiologer and anatomist. **1838–9** HALLAM *Hist. Lit.* IV. viii. §36 Willis, a physician at Oxford,..his bold systems have given him a distinguished place among physiologers.

† **physiˈologet.** *Obs.* In 3 fisiologet. [dim. (perh. in OF.) f. PHYSIOLOG-US + -ET[1]. Cf. PAMPHLET.] A diminutive or pet appellation for a physiologus or book on natural history.

c **1220** *Bestiary* 307 Ðus it is on boke set ðat man clepeð fisiologet.

physiologian (ˌfɪzɪəʊˈləʊdʒ(ɪ)ən). *rare*$^{-1}$. [f. L. *physiologia* PHYSIOLOGY + -AN: cf. *theologian.*] = PHYSIOLOGIST 2.

1825 BEDDOES *Let.* Sept., Poems (1851) p. xlvii, Blumenbach,..is, I fancy, of the first rank as mineralogist, physiologian, geologist, botanist, natural-historian, and physician.

physiologic (ˌfɪzɪəʊˈlɒdʒɪk), *a.* [ad. L. *physiologic-us*, a. Gr. φυσιολογικός adj., f. φυσιολόγος: see PHYSIOLOGER and -IC. Cf. F. *physiologique* (G. Budé, 16th c.).]

† **1.** Of or belonging to natural science. *Obs. rare.*

1669 GALE *Crt. Gentiles* I. Introd. 3 Thales..informed himself touching..the Chaos, and other Physiologic Contemplations. **1677** *Ibid.* II. III. 32 Our Gospel..has availed more to the Knowledge of God than al their Physiologic Contemplations. **1736–44** H. COVENTRY *Lett. Phil. to Hyd.* v. (T.), It may ascertain the true era of physiologic allegory.

2. = PHYSIOLOGICAL 2.

1828 in WEBSTER. **1838** MILLIGEN *Curios. Med. Exp.* (1839) 565 To elucidate obscure parts of physiologic enquiry. **1878** *N. Amer. Rev.* CXXVI. 553 No method is more alluring, in physiologic studies, than this of accurate measurement and description. **1884** J. W. POWELL in *Science* IV. 472/2 In early society, incest laws do not recognize physiologic conditions, but only social conditions.

physiological (ˌfɪzɪəʊˈlɒdʒɪkəl), *a.* Also 7 phi-. [f. as prec. + -AL[1]: see -ICAL.]

† **1.** Relating to the material universe or to natural science, physical; belonging to the Physiologers as students of nature. *Obs.*

1610 HEALEY *Vives' Comm. St. Aug. Citie of God* v. ix. (1620) 196 This opinion is Physiologicall and imbraced by Alexander, one of Aristotles interpreters. **1662** H. MORE *Def. Philos. Cabbala* App. i. (1712) 114 The Mosaical Philosophy, in the Physiological part thereof, is the same with the Cartesian. **1673** RAY (*title*) Observations Topographical, Moral, and Phisiological, made in a Journey through part of the Low Countries, Germany, Italy, and France. **1768–74** TUCKER *Lt. Nat.* (1834) II. 348 The laws of gravitation, attraction, and impulse, and other objects of physiological science. **1809–10** COLERIDGE *Friend* II. x. (1818) III. 188 With these secret schools of physiological theology the mythical poets were doubtless in connection.

2. a. Pertaining or relating to physiology; relating to the functions and properties of living bodies. ***physiological psychologist***, a specialist in physiological psychology.

1814 D. STEWART *Philos. Mind* II. iv. VI. 465 One of the most noted physiological works which have lately appeared on the Continent. **1845** G. E. DAY tr. *Simon's Anim. Chem.* I. 100 The General Physiological Chemistry of the Blood. **1861** BENTLEY *Man. Bot.* (1870) 1 Physiological Botany treats of plants, and their organs, in a state of life or action. **1873** RALFE *Phys. Chem.* Introd. 13 The term Physiological Chemistry is generally limited to the study of the chemical phenomena attendant upon the life of Animals. **1875** G. H. LEWES *Probl. Life & Mind* (ser. 1) II. 482 The common error of mistaking ideal separations for real separations.. leads the physiological psychologist to the conclusion that the objective aspect of the phenomenon..is the cause of the subjective aspect. **1880** RICHARDSON in *Med. Temp. Jrnl.* 70 The physiological action of alcohol. **1899** W. JAMES *Talks to Teachers* xii. 119 If we remember because of our associations, and if these are (as the physiological psychologists believe) due to our organized brain-paths, we easily see how the law of recency and repetition should prevail. **1904** E. B. TITCHENER tr. *Wundt's Princ. Physiol. Psychol.* p. vi, I have here sought to give this important chapter of physiological psychology at any rate a tentative systematic setting. **1933** Physiological phonetics [see *acoustic phonetics*]. **1950** *Sci. News* XV. 9 These facts caused Thomas Young, who has since been called 'the father of physiological optics' to propose, a century and a half ago, the three-colour theory of vision which bears his name. **1960** C. WINICK *Dict. Anthropol.* 411/2 Physiological phonetics is part of laboratory or experimental phonetics. **1967** R. F. THOMPSON *Found. Physiol. Psychol.* p. xxvii, Physiological psychology is concerned with the physiological bases of behavior. In the last analysis this means the organization and functions of the brain. **1973** DEWSBURY & RETHLINGSHAFER *Compar. Psychol.* 10 Lashley was a teacher of several men who became outstanding in the revitalization of comparative and physiological psychology that occurred after World War II.

b. *Med.* = NORMAL *a.* 2 f.

1896 *Jrnl. Physiol.* XX. 145 (*heading*) On the initial rate of osmosis of blood-serum with reference to the composition of 'physiological saline solution' in mammals. **1923** P. H. MITCHELL *Text Bk. Gen. Physiol.* vi. 148 Physiological salt solutions do not have irritating effects when in contact with open wounds. **1952** *Sci. News* XXIV. 27 Minced animal tissues were extracted with physiological saline (0·85% NaCl). **1969** J. H. GREEN *Basic Clin. Physiol.* vi. 37/1 The sodium chloride is present in plasma to the extent of 0·9 g. per 100 ml. A solution containing this amount of sodium chloride in water is termed normal isotonic or physiological saline, and it has the same electrolyte strength as blood.

physiologically (ˌfɪzɪəʊˈlɒdʒɪkəlɪ), *adv.* [f. as prec. + -LY[2].] In a physiological manner; according to the principles of physiology; from a physiological point of view.

1610 HEALEY *St. Aug. Citie of God* VI. viii. 246 But these things, say they, are all to be interpreted naturally and Phisiologically..as though we..sought Nature, and set God aside. **1775** HUNTER in *Phil. Trans.* LXV. 395 This animal may be considered, both anatomically and physiologically, as divided into two parts. **1874** P. BAYNE in *Contemp. Rev.* Oct. 697 The child..was physiologically a wreck,—damaged irretrievably in body and mind.

physiologist (fɪzɪˈɒlədʒɪst). [f. PHYSIOLOGY + -IST. Cf. F. *physiologiste* (1757 in Hatz.-Darm.).]

† **1.** A natural philosopher; a naturalist; = PHYSIOLOGER 1. *Obs.*

1664 POWER *Exp. Philos.* I. 72 The Physiologist also may gather something from the former Observations, touching the nature of Colours. **1677** GALE *Crt. Gentiles* II. III. 31 Socrates..perceiving how much his Predecessors, Thales &c. (who were generally Physiologists) had abused Physics. **1797** *Monthly Mag.* III. 50 Priestley, Black, Cavendish, and Macbride, had opened to physiologists a sort of new creation. **1827** R. P. WARD *De Vere* viii. (ed. 2) 145 Questions..which as they seem to depend upon a particular sort of air, we must leave to physiologists.

2. One versed in animal (or vegetable) physiology; a student or teacher of the science of the functions and properties of organic bodies.

1778 A. REID *Inquiry Suppress. Urine* (M.), The most skilful anatomist and physiologist. **1843** R. J. GRAVES *Syst. Clin. Med.* xxv. 312 This distinguished surgeon and physiologist has done more than all who preceded him to illustrate his subject. **1881** BURDON-SANDERSON in *Nature* 8 Sept. 440/2 The subjects of experiment used by the two last-mentioned physiologists were themselves; the work done was the mountain ascent from Interlaken to the summit of the Faulhorn.

physiˈologize (-dʒaɪz), *v.* [f. as prec. + -IZE.]

† **1.** *intr.* To speculate or reason on nature: to inquire into natural causes and phenomena. *Obs.*

1678 CUDWORTH *Intell. Syst.* Pref. 7 Divers of the Italicks, and particularly Empedocles—before Democritus—physiologized atomically. *Ibid.* I. iii. 120 They who first theologized, did physiologize after this manner. **1730–6** BAILEY (folio) Pref., *Physiologize*, to Study, Discourse or Reason on the Nature of Things.

† **2.** *trans.* To explain in accordance with physical or natural science. *Obs.*

1678 CUDWORTH *Intell. Syst.* I. iv. 450 Unless we would rather with Macrobius, Physiologize them all Three, and make Minerva to be the Higher Heaven, Jupiter the Middle Ether, and Juno the Lower Air and Earth, all Animated; that is, One God, as acting differently in these Three Regions of the world. **1819** G. S. FABER *Dispensations* (1823) I. 234 Much the same remark is made by Eusebius on the humour of physiologising the religious system of the Egyptians.

3. *intr.* To act the physiologist; to form physiological conclusions or theories. *rare.*

1866 OWEN *Vertebr. Anim.* (L.), The somewhat capricious appearance of the gall-bladder in vegetarian mammals discourages such attempts to physiologize.

Hence **physiˈologizing** *vbl. sb.*

1669 GALE *Crt. Gentiles* I. III. i. 17 Al which Poetic Physiologisings were but corrupt imitations of..Moses's description of the Creation.

physiologue (ˈfɪzɪəʊlɒg). *rare.* [ad. L. *physiologus*: see PHYSIOLOGER.] = PHYSIOLOGIST.

1877 J. D. HOOKER in L. Huxley *Life J. D. Hooker* (1918) II. 236, I think *Gnetum* is quite overlooked by the Physiologues in removing Gymnosperms from Dicots. **1923** A. HUXLEY *Antic Hay* v. 70, I have with me..a physiologue, a pedagogue and a priapagogue.

‖ **physiologus** (fɪzɪˈɒləgəs). [L., a. Gr. φυσιολόγος, natural philosopher (see PHYSIOLOGER): used by Epiphanius as the name of his work on Natural History with moral and theological applications, whence the mediæval use.] A BESTIARY: see quot.

1898 STOPFORD BROOKE *Eng. Lit.* xiii. 203 The three first [Old Eng. poems, the *Whale*, the *Panther*, and the *Partridge*] must be taken together, and form part..of an English *Physiologus*. A *Physiologus* in the literature of the Middle Ages was a collection of descriptions of beasts, birds, or fishes, of their life and habits..each..followed by a religious or moral allegory based on this description.

physiology (fɪzɪˈɒlədʒɪ). Also 6–7 phi-. [ad. L. *physiologia*, a. Gr. φυσιολογία (Arist.), natural philosophy, natural science, f. φυσιολόγ-ος: see PHYSIOLOGER, and -LOGY; perh. immed. a. F. *physiologie* (1547 in Hatz.-Darm.).]

† **1.** The study and description of natural objects; natural science or natural philosophy; also, a particular system or doctrine of natural science. *Obs.*

1564 *Bauldwin's Mor. Philos.* (Palfr.) II. i. 73 That it may be knowen what they beleued of god, of themselues, and of his woorkes, all which they them selues call Phisiologie. **1603** HOLLAND *Plutarch's Mor.* 1346 Certeine Epicureans.. standing much upon this their goodly and beautifull Physiologie forsooth (as they terme it). **1662** H. MORE *Def. Philos. Cabbala* App. i. (1712) 113 Whence there must be no small affinity betwixt this ancient Moschical, or rather Mosaical Physiology, and the Cartesian Philosophy. **1704** J. HARRIS *Lex. Techn.* I, *Physiology*, *Physicks*, or Natural Philosophy, is the Science of Natural Bodies. **1797** *Encycl. Brit.* (ed. 3) XVI. 18/1 Re-action, in physiology, the resistance made by all bodies to the action or impulse of others that endeavour to change its state whether of motion or rest.

2. The science of the normal functions and phenomena of living things.

It comprises the two divisions of ***animal*** and ***vegetable physiology***; that part of the former which refers specially to the vital functions in man is called ***human physiology***.

[**1597** A. M. tr. *Guillemeau's Fr. Chirurg.* 1 b/1 *Physiologia* handelethe and threatethe of the structure and situatione of mans bodye. **1611** COTGR., *Physiologie*,..also..that part of Phisicke which treats of the composition, or structure of mans bodie.] **1615** CROOKE *Body of Man* 289 Amongst the new writers Fernelius the best learned Physitian of them all, in the 7. book of his Phisiologie, proueth that this bloud is not Alimentarie. **1704** J. HARRIS *Lex. Techn.* I, *Physiology*, is by some also accounted a Part of Physick, that teaches the Constitution of the Body so far as it is sound, or in its Natural State; and endeavours to find Reasons for its Functions and Operations, by the Help of Anatomy and Natural Philosophy. **1748** HARTLEY *Observ. Man* I. iv. Concl. 511, I..bring some Arguments from Physiology and Pathology. **1804** ABERNETHY *Surg. Obs.* 244 The anatomy and physiology of the nervous system. **1831** CARLYLE *Sart. Res.* III. vi, A Peasant unacquainted with botanical Physiology. **1831** BREWSTER *Optics* xxxv. 293 This important truth in the physiology of vision. **1860** HUXLEY *Lay Serm.* xii. 284 That part of biological science which deals with form and structure is called Morphology—that which concerns itself with function, Physiology. **1871** tr. *Pouchet's Universe* ix. 482 Hales, whose beautiful experiments laid the foundation of vegetable physiology. *fig.* **1876** LOWELL *Among my Bks.* Ser. II. 26 As a contribution to the physiology of genius no other book is to be compared with the *Vita Nuova*. **1903** *Westm. Gaz.* 24 June 3/2 The amateur statistician may know something of the anatomy of commerce, but he knows nothing of what I may call its physiology—its circulating..and..digestive system[s].

† **physion, phision,** corrupt or erron. forms of PHYSICIAN (perh. only typographical errors).

c **1580** LODGE *Repl. Gosson's Sch. Abuse* (Hunter. Cl.) 5 That they like good Phisions: should so frame their potions. **1611** BIBLE *Transl. Pref.* 3 The Scripture is..a Physions-shop (Saint Basill calleth it).

physionomy, obs. spelling of PHYSIOGNOMY.

physiopathological (ˌfɪzɪəʊpæθəʊˈlɒdʒɪkəl), *a. Med.* Also **physio-** (with hyphen). [f. PHYSIO- + PATHOLOGICAL *a.*] Of or pertaining to physiopathology. Also **ˌphysiopathoˈlogic** *a.*

1867 ROBERTSON & RUTHERFORD tr. *Griesinger's Mental Path. & Therapeutics* I. iii. 23 (*heading*) Preliminary physio-pathological observations on mental phenomena. **1930** *Brit. Med. Jrnl.* 8 Feb. 234/2 Endarteritis obliterans is a special localization of athero-sclerosis. In fact, in athero-sclerosis the same constellation of etiological factors, and the same physio-pathological conditions (proliferation of the intima, disturbances in cholesterol metabolism, etc.), are found. **1938** *Arch. Neurol. & Psychiatry* (Chicago) XL. 1126 (*heading*) Physiopathologic and pathoanatomic aspects of major trigeminal neuralgia. **1968** E. KELEMEN *Physiopath. & Therapy Human Blood Dis.* (1969) p. xv, Contemporary physiopathological research..is, at least to some extent, very liable..to lose sight of the ultimate aim of the project.

physiopathology (ˌfɪzɪəʊpəˈθɒlədʒɪ). *Med.* Also **physio-** (with hyphen). [f. PHYSIO- +

PATHOLOGY.] (See quot. 1904.) Also, the physiology of a diseased organism. So ˌ**physiopaˈthologist**.

1904 STEDMAN *Dunglison's Dict. Med. Sci.* (ed. 23) 875/2 *Physiopathology*, study of function as modified by disease. **1930** *Brit. Med. Jrnl.* 8 Feb. 234/1 The frequency of the occurrence of this morbid condition raises important problems as to its physio-pathology and its treatment. **1953** HOMBURGER & FISHMAN (*title*) The physiopathology of cancer. **1954** *Acta Physiol. Scand.* XXXI. 359 A study has been made of the physiopathology of the asphyxiated human fetus in order to improve the results of resuscitation. **1972** GALLO & SANTAMARIA *Res. Progress Org.-Biol. & Med. Chem.* III. I. p. vi, The discovery of the photodynamic phenomenon helps the physio-pathologists to characterize diseases which were once joined together under general terms of skin disorders. **1974** *Nature* 29 Mar. 371/2 Fifty laboratories provide facilities for basic and applied research into bacteriology, virology, physiopathology, [etc.].

ˌ**physiophiˈlosophy**. [transl. of Ger. *Naturphilosophie*, i.e. philosophy of nature, in the title of Oken's *Lehrbuch der Naturphilosophie* 1808–11, called in the Eng. transl. 'Elements of Physiophilosophy'.] A name for the philosophic system of nature of Oken, who 'aimed at constructing all knowledge *a priori*, and thus setting forth the system of nature in its universal relations'.

1847 TULK tr. *Oken* (*title*) Elements of Physiophilosophy. **1856** R. A. VAUGHAN *Mystics* (1860) II. 254 He [Oken] imagined that he wrote his *Physio-philosophy* in a kind of inspiration. **1887** COPE *Orig. Fittest* 8 The disfavour in which physiophilosophy was held secured to evolution a cold welcome.

Hence ˌ**physioˈphilosoph**, ˌ**physiophiˈlosopher** [= Ger. *Naturphilosoph*], an adherent of the system of Oken; ˈ**physiophiloˈsophic, -ical** *adjs.*, of or pertaining to this system.

1887 COPE *Orig. Fittest* 8 The *physiophilosophs became extravagant and mistook superficial appearances for realities. **1861** G. MOORE *Lost Tribes* 127 Here.. it is that the *physio-philosophers have supposed mankind to have originated. **1865** tr. *Strauss' Life Jesus* I. I. xxx. 247 The allegorical interpretation.. applied to Homer and Hesiod in order to extract *physiophilosophical ideas out of the Gods and their histories.

physiophonetics (ˌfɪzɪəʊfəˈnɛtɪks), *sb. pl.* (const. as *sing.*) *Linguistics.* [f. PHYSIO- + PHONETICS *sb. pl.*] (See quot. 1950.) Hence ˌ**physiophoˈnetic** *a.*

1936 J. R. KANTOR *Objective Psychol. Gram.* xii. 162 It was Baudouin de Courtenay, according to Troubetzkoy, who first made a genuine separation between physical and physiological sounds and psychological phonic images—in other words gave the term *phoneme* what Troubetzkoy calls its present meaning—namely, the element of psychological language—and placed it within the field of psychophonetics instead of physiophonetics. **1950** D. JONES *Phoneme* xxix. 213 Professor Baudouin de Courtenay.. defined phonemes as 'mental images', and accordingly distinguished two kinds of phonetics which he called 'physiophonetics' and 'psychophonetics' respectively. He applied the term 'physiophonetics' to the study of sounds actually uttered, and used the term 'psychophonetics' to denote the study of the 'mental images' which uttered sounds are intended to represent. **1956** Physiophonetic [see PSYCHOPHONETICS *sb. pl.*].

physiotherapist (fɪzɪəʊˈθɛrəpɪst). [f. next + -IST.] One skilled or trained in physiotherapy.

1923 C. M. SAMPSON *Physiotherapy Technic* xxvi. 409 Lucky is the physiotherapist who can plan his department in a new building. **1944** *Times* 24 Jan. 5/5 A Chartered Physiotherapist to-day is trained not only in massage and gymnastics but also in electrical and all forms of ray therapy. **1958** *Times* 7 July 22/4 The role of physiotherapy is still large, and the supply of physiotherapists on the whole well maintained. **1972** D. HASTON *In High Places* ii. 20 My physiotherapist was very sympathetic. I worked really hard on exercises, and the wasted arm became stronger.

physiotherapy (fɪzɪəʊˈθɛrəpɪ). [f. PHYSIO- + THERAPY.] The treatment of disease, injury, or deformity by physical methods, such as massage, exercise, and the application of heat, light, fresh air, and other external influences.

1905 *Brit. Med. Jrnl.* 15 July 126/2 The first congress of physiotherapy will be held at Liége on August 12th. **1928** *Sunday Dispatch* 16 Dec. 1/1 Two new specialists, both experts in radiology and massage, and in the treatment generally known as physio-therapy, were called to Buckingham Palace yesterday. **1958** *Times Lit. Suppl.* 4 Apr. 187/2 Full details are given of methods of physiotherapy that can be carried out in the home. **1958** [see PHYSIOTHERAPIST]. **1975** SCRUTTON & GILBERTSON *Physiotherapy in Paediatric Pract.* 1 Physiotherapy involves the modification of the patient's physical external environment, either generally or topically, so as to promote healing or otherwise improve the body's efficiency.

Hence ˌ**physiotheraˈpeutic** *a.*, of, pertaining to, or involving physiotherapy.

1905 *Brit. Med. Jrnl.* 15 July 126/2 The abuses caused by 'healers' who pretend to treat by physiotherapeutic procedures. **1926** *Encycl. Brit.* III. 686/1 As convalescence goes on, physiotherapeutic measures.. are employed to hasten recovery. **1957** M. SPARK *Comforters* viii. 196 He is receiving physiotherapeutic treatment. **1976** NICHOLS & HAMILTON *Rehabilitation Med.* ii. 21 There are innumerable reports in the medical and physio-therapeutic literature extolling the virtues of specific techniques.

physique (fɪˈziːk). [a. F. *physique* sb. masc., absolute use of *physique* physical, i.e. that which is physical.] The physical or bodily structure, organization, and development; the characteristic appearance or physical powers (of an individual or a race).

1826 LADY GRANVILLE *Lett.* (1894) I. 384 You must allow that this describes his physique admirably. **1856** EMERSON *Eng. Traits, Manners* Wks. (Bohn) II. 47 So much had the fine physique and the personal vigour of this robust race worked on my imagination. **1864** R. F. BURTON *Dahome* II. 64 The masculine physique of the women enabling them to compete with men in enduring toil, hardships, and privations. **1881** A. G. C. LIDDELL in *Macm. Mag.* XLIV. 478/2 They.. had tremendous physiques, though rather fleshy.

physique, obs. form of PHYSIC.

physiqued (fɪˈziːkt), *a.* [f. PHYSIQUE + -ED[1].] Having a physique of a specified character.

1926 *Contemp. Rev.* June 690 These ill-fed, ill-housed, wretchedly physiqued and noisy communist agitators.

physisorb (ˈfɪzɪsɔːb), *v. Chem.* [Back-formation from next.] *trans.* and *intr.* To collect by physisorption. So ˈ**physisorbed**, ˈ**physisorbing** *ppl. adjs.*

1966 *Surface Sci.* IV. 103 (*heading*) Ordered physisorbed layers on graphite. **1967** *Ibid.* VI. 1 It has been argued that due to the weakness of physisorbing forces, the electron beam of the instrument would disturb the molecules significantly. *Ibid.* 2 Materials highly volatile at room temperature could not be physisorbed to concentrations approaching a monolayer. *Ibid.*, A substance with a vapor pressure of 1×10^{-2} Torr or more will not physisorb on graphite in quantities approaching a monolayer if its ambient pressure over the graphite is 1×10^{-4} Torr or less. **1970** C. OKKERSE in B. G. Linsen *Physical & Chem. Aspects Adsorbents & Catalysts* v. 253 Wirzing suggested the use of the combination band of water at 5265 cm^{-1} for the quantitative determination of physisorbed water. **1971** *Sci. Amer.* Dec. 51/1 A physisorbed species retains substantially its original structure.

physisorption (fɪzɪˈsɔːpʃən). *Chem.* [f. PHYSI(CAL *a.* + AD)SORPTION.] Adsorption which does not involve the formation of chemical bonds. Cf. CHEMISORPTION.

1965 *Progress Solid State Chem.* II. 94 At higher pressures and lower temperatures (−78°C) physisorption without formation of ordered structures was observed. **1973** *Sci. Amer.* May 34/2 There have been several more recent electron-diffraction studies of physisorption with other gases and other substrates. **1976** *Physics Bull.* May 218 This book.. is extremely timely in marshalling ideas on physisorption because there is now an increasing interest in the more difficult process of chemisorption.

physitheism (ˈfɪzɪθiːˌɪz(ə)m). [f. Gr. φύσι-ς nature + θεός God + -ISM: cf. *polytheism*.] The deification of the powers or phenomena of nature. So ˌ**physitheˈistic** *a.*

1891 J. W. POWELL in *Chautauquan* Dec. 291 (Funk) Physitheism is the theology and religion of the barbaric world. In this religion the weather-producing agents and the phenomena of the weather are personified and deified. **1889** G. MALLERY in *Pop. Sci. Monthly* XXXVI. 208 The prophets tried to pull the Israelites too rapidly through the zoötheistic and physitheistic stages into monotheism.

ˈ**physitism**. *rare.* [f. Gr. φύσι-ς nature + -ITE + -ISM.] A system of nature-worship.

1885 DUNS in *Proc. Soc. Antiq. Scot.* XIX. 396.

physiurgic (fɪzɪˈɜːdʒɪk), *a. rare.* [f. Gr. φύσι-ς nature + ἔργον work + -IC: cf. *theurgic*.] Produced or acted upon solely by nature.

1816 BENTHAM *Chrestom.* 187 Applied to bodies.. in their natural, or say physiurgic, state—human art—or say elaboration by human art—has two distinguishable objects. **1843** BOWRING *Introd. Bentham's Wks.* i. 16/2 Natural History and Natural Philosophy are respectively represented by Physiurgic Somatology, and Anthropurgic Somatology.

So **physiurgoˈscopic** *a. rare.*

1816 BENTHAM *Chrestom.* Wks. 1843 VIII. 86 Division of Somatology, or Somatics at large, into *Physiurgic* (Physiurgoscopic) and *Anthropurgic* (Anthropurgoscopic).

physnamy, -nomy, obs. ff. PHYSIOGNOMY.

physo- (faɪsəʊ), repr. Gr. φυσο-, combining form of Gr. φῦσα bellows, bladder, bubble, in a few Gr. compounds, and in many modern scientific terms.

physoˈcarpous *a. Bot.* [Gr. καρπός fruit], having an inflated or bladder-like fruit (Mayne *Expos. Lex.* 1858). ˈ**physocele** (-siːl), *Path.* [Gr. κήλη tumour], a tumour or hernia distended with gas. **physograde** (ˈfaɪsəgreɪd), *Zool.* [ad. mod.L. *Physograda*, f. *-gradus* going], (*a*) *adj.* moving by means of a hollow vesicular float or buoy; of or pertaining to the *Physograda*, a group of oceanic hydrozoa furnished with such floating organs; (*b*) *sb.* a member of this group; hence **phyˈsogradous** *a.* ‖**physometra** (faɪsəʊˈmiːtrə), *Path.* [Gr. μήτρα womb], the presence of gas in the uterus, uterine tympanites. **physonect** (ˈfaɪsəʊnɛkt), *Zool.* [Gr. νήκτης a swimmer, f. νήχειν to swim], a member of the *Physonectæ*, a suborder of siphonanthous siphonophores; hence **physoˈnectous** *a.* **physopod** (ˈfaɪsəʊpɒd) [Gr. πούς, ποδ- foot], a mollusc of the section *Physopoda* or *Thysanoptera*, rhipidoglossate gastropods, with a sort of sucker on the foot.

1753 CHAMBERS *Cycl. Supp.*, **Physocele*, a word used by many authors to express a wind-rupture. **1811** HOOPER *Med. Dict.*, *Physocele*, a species of hernia, whose contents are distended with wind. **1898** in *Syd. Soc. Lex.* **1835–6** TODD *Cycl. Anat.* I. 37/1 The principal organ of locomotion in the *physograda is the air-filled vesicle or bladder. **1858** MAYNE *Expos. Lex.* 957/2 Animals.. characterized by their body being provided with an aëriform dilatation of the intestinal canal, serving for a swimming organ: *physo-gradous. **1822** GOOD *Study Med.* IV. 434 Emphysema uteri. Inflation of the Womb... This is the *physometra of Sauvages and later nosologists. **1875** JONES & SIEV. *Pathol. Anat.* (ed. 2) 759 Physometra is sometimes observed after severe labours. **1890** *Cent. Dict.*, *Physopod.

physoclist (ˈfaɪsəʊklɪst), *a.* and *sb. Ichthyol.* [f. mod.L. *Phȳsoclīstī* (pl.), f. Gr. φῦσα bladder + -κλειστ-ος shut, closed.] **a.** *adj.* Belonging to the *Physoclisti*, a group of teleost fishes having the duct between the air-bladder and the intestine closed: cf. PHYSOSTOME. **b.** *sb.* A member of this group. So **physoˈclistic**, **physoˈclistous** *adjs.*, having the air-bladder so closed or cut off.

1887 HEILPRIN *Distrib. Anim.* 303 Both the *physoclist and physostome types appear.. very nearly simultaneously in the same deposits. *Ibid.*, The severance of the bladder in the physoclists being the result of the disuse of parts. **1883** LANKESTER in *Encycl. Brit.* XVI. 671/1 The parallel cases [of the secretion of gas] ranging from the Protozoon Arcella to the *Physoclistic Fishes. **1887** COPE *Orig. Fittest* 327 The descent of the *Physoclystous fishes has probably been from Holostean ancestors, both with and without the intervention of Physostomous forms.

physodin (ˈfaɪsəʊdɪn). *Chem.* [f. specific name *phȳsōd-ēs* (cf. Gr. φυσοειδής bladder-like) + -IN[1].] A neutral substance ($C_{12}H_{12}O_8$), a white loosely-coherent mass, occurring in a lichen, *Parmelia ceratophylla* or *physodes*.

1866–8 WATTS *Dict. Chem.* IV. 635 Physodin behaves to water like a resin, not being wetted thereby.

physog, var. PHIZOG.

physogastrism (faɪsəʊˈgæstrɪz(ə)m). *Ent.* [ad. G. *physogastre* (E. Wasmann *Kritisches Verzeichniss d. Myrmekophilen u. Termitophilen Arthropoden* (1894) 87), f. PHYSO- + Gr. γαστ(ε)ρ-, γαστήρ, belly: see -ISM.] In certain insects, a condition in which the abdomen becomes distended by the growth of fat bodies or other organs. Also ˈ**physogastry** in the same sense. So **physoˈgastric** *a.*, exhibiting this condition.

1903 *Nature* 12 Feb. 351/1 They [*sc.* symphilous beetles] also show certain modifications of the mouth-organs.., as well as 'physogastrism', accompanied by excessive development of the fat-bodies, or sexual glands. **1914** *Ann. Natal Museum* III. 103 Dr. Trägårdh examined many nests of termites in Natal, but no other physogastric Staphylinids were discovered. **1920** *Ibid.* IV. 326 In the female there is no excessive amount of fat-body. The physogastrism is mainly due to the great bulk of the genital organs and of the mid-gut. **1922** W. M. WHEELER *Social Life Insects* vi. 273 Many [termitophiles].. have acquired peculiar characters, the most characteristic of which is physogastry, or excessive enlargement of the abdomen. *Ibid.* 277 Probably this is also the case with other physogastric termitophiles. **1952** ROTHSCHILD & CLAY *Fleas, Flukes & Cuckoos* xi. 222 The abdomen becomes enormously distended owing to the abnormal growth of the fatty tissues. This curious condition is known as physogastry and it is usually developed by flies or beetles which are parasitic or symbiotic in ants' or termites' nests. **1971** R. R. ASKEW *Parasitic Insects* v. 73 The abdomen [of *Ascodipteron*] becomes bloated (physogastric) as the fly takes in blood from the host. *Ibid.* 311/2 Physogastry.

‖**Physophora** (faɪˈsɒfərə). *Zool.* [mod.L., f. Gr. φῦσα bladder + -φορος bearing, borne.] A genus of oceanic hydrozoa, the species of which float by means of numerous vesicular organs. So ‖**Physophoræ** *pl.* (sometimes **Physophora**), a suborder or division of *Siphonophora* (an order of *Hydrozoa Craspedota*), having the proximal end modified into a pneumatophore or float; **phyˈsophoran** *a.*, of or pertaining to the *Physophoræ*; *sb.*, a member of this division; also **physophore** (ˈfaɪsəfɔə(r)). ‖**Physoˈphoridæ** *pl.*, the family containing the genus *Physophora*; **physophorous** (faɪˈsɒfərəs) *a.*, of the nature of the *Physophoræ*, having pneumatophores or swimming-bells (Mayne 1858).

1869 tr. *Pouchet's Universe* (1871) 13 At other times it is owing to.. the *Physophora, trailing their tresses all spangled with stars like those of Berenice in the firmament. **1870** HARTWIG *Sea & Wond.* xv, The Hydrostatic Acalephæ, or *Physophoræ.. were formerly supposed to be a special class of animals, but have been proved by Sars and other naturalists to be merely alternating generations of the bell-shaped Acalephæ. **1888** ROLLESTON & JACKSON *Anim. Life* 774 In the *Physophores *Forskalia* and *Agalma* the single ovum is arrested in the endoderm, and surrounded by the spadix. **1860** H. SPENCER in *Westm. Rev.* Jan. 103 In the *Physophoridæ, a variety of organs similarly arise by transformation of the budding polypes. **1878** tr. *Gegenbaur's Comp. Anat.* 97 The greater development of these bladders, which in most Physophoridæ are rather small.

physostegia (ˌfaɪsəʊˈstɛdʒɪə). [mod.L. (G. Bentham 1829, in *Bot. Reg.* XV. 1289), f. Gr. φῦσα bladder + στέγη roof + -IA[1], in reference to the inflated calyx.] A perennial herb of the genus so called, belonging to the family Labiatæ, native to North America, and bearing spikes of pink or white flowers; also called the obedient plant or false dragonhead.

1830 J. C. LOUDON *Hortus Britannicus* 483 *Physostegia* Berth. [English name] Physostegia. **1835** *Curtis's Bot. Mag.* LXII. 3386 (*heading*) Imbricated Physostegia. **1905** E. V. BOYCE in M. T. Earle et al. *Garden Colour* 70 The habit of the Physostegia's little pale pinkish flower to stay fixed and still in whatever position it may be turned, was thought to be caused by coma. **1962** *Amat. Gardening* 17 Mar. 4/1 Among a number of self-supporting plants may be included.. physostegias. **1971** J. RAVEN *Botanist's Garden* xi. 201 The typical form of the Physostegia.. is of my least favourite shade somewhere between pink and mauve.

‖**Physostigma** (faɪsəʊˈstɪgmə). *Bot.* [mod.L., f. Gr. φῦσα bladder + στίγμα STIGMA.] A genus of leguminous plants, the flower of which has a spiral keel, and a bent style continued into an oblique hood above the stigma; the only species is *P. venenosum*, producing the highly poisonous Calabar bean. Hence, The Calabar bean or its extract as a drug.

1864 *N. Syd. Soc. Year-bk. Med.* 428 Dr. Fraser has used the physostigma internally in cases of erysipelas. **1878** A. HAMILTON *Nerv. Dis.* 118 Physostigma, aconite, and other cardiac sedatives may be mentioned as other anæmiants. **1880** GARROD & BAXTER *Mat. Med.* 322 The.. administration of an appropriate dose of physostigma.

physostigmine (faɪsəʊˈstɪgmiːn). *Chem.* and *Pharm.* Also †-in. [ad. G. *physostigmin* (Jobst & Hesse 1864, in *Ann. d. Chem. u. Pharm.* CXXIX. 118): see PHYSOSTIGMA and -INE[5].] A colourless or pale yellow crystalline tricyclic alkaloid, $C_{15}H_{21}N_3O_2$, which is the active principle of the calabar bean and is used medicinally (esp. as a miotic) on account of its anticholinesterase activity.

1864 *Chem. News* 5 Mar. 109/1 The physiological properties of the Calabar bean have been well studied in this country, but the authors above named are.. the first who have isolated the alkaloid to which it owes its activity, and to which they have given the name Physostigmine. **1865** *N. Syd. Soc. Year-bk. Med.* 447 Jobst and Hesse.. have succeeded in isolating the active principle of the Calabar bean, to which they give the name physostigmin. **1896** *Allbutt's Syst. Med.* I. 228 It is in this way that strychnine and physostigmine respectively stimulate and depress the spinal cord. **1907** J. H. PARSONS *Dis. Eye* iv. 74 Eserin or physostigmin, the most powerful miotic we possess, acts by stimulating the third nerve endings in the sphincter and in the ciliary muscle. **1938** *Thorpe's Dict. Appl. Chem.* (ed. 4) II. 200/1 The physiological action of physostigmine depends on its inhibition of the hydrolysis of acetyl choline by choline-esterase. **1970** *Nature* 4 Apr. 21/2 Drugs which .. increase the concentration [in the brain] of acetylcholine (for example, physostigmine) exacerbate Parkinsonism. **1974** M. C. GERALD *Pharmacol.* vii. 128 Many very common drugs are alkaloids, some of which include.. physostigmine.

physostome (ˈfaɪsəstəʊm), *a.* and *sb. Ichthyol.* [f. mod.L. *Phȳsostomī*, f. Gr. φῦσα bladder + στόμα mouth, -στομος -mouthed.]

a. *adj.* Belonging to the *Physostomi*, a group of teleost fishes, in which the air-bladder is connected with the alimentary canal by an air-duct: cf. PHYSOCLIST. **b.** *sb.* A member of this group. So **physoˈstomatous, phyˈsostomous** *a.*, having the air-bladder opening into an air-duct.

1880 GÜNTHER *Fishes* 199 [In] the Cretaceous group.. Physostomes and Plectognaths are likewise well represented. **1887** Physostome, Physostomous [see PHYSOCLIST, PHYSOCLISTOUS].

†**physy**, obs. f. FUSEE[2], wheel of a watch.

1690 LOCKE *Hum. Und.* III. vi. §39 Some Watches.. are made with four Wheels.. some have Strings and Physies, and others none.

physyk, obs. form of PHYSIC.

phyt- (faɪt, fɪt), combining form used before a vowel for PHYTO-.

phytalˈbumin, vegetable albumin. **phyˈtalbumose**, a form of albumen occurring in plants. **phyteˈconomy**, vegetable economy. **phytœˈcology** [Gr. οἶκος abode: see -LOGY], the science which treats of plants in relation to their environment or habitat; so **phytœˈcologist**.

1899 CAGNEY tr. *Jaksch's Clin. Diagn.* viii. (ed. 4) 405 The products of bacterial life, toxines, and *phytalbumins appear also to play an important part in the process of suppuration. **1890** *Cent. Dict.*, *Phytalbumose. **1897** *Allbutt's Syst. Med.* IV. 520 Ricin and abrin, phytalbumoses obtained from the seed of the castor-oil plant. **1902** *Brit. Med. Jrnl.* No. 2154. 920 The action of some of the phytalbumoses. **1898** *Naturalist* 180 If soils are a factor in its *phyteconomy. **1899** *Pop. Sci. Monthly* Nov. 99 One of the general views of *phytoecology is that the forms of plants are modified to adapt them to the conditions under which they exist. *Ibid.* 104 The *phytoecologist to-day watches his subject as it grows.

phytal (ˈfaɪtəl), *a. Ecol.* [f. PHYT- + -AL.] Of, pertaining to, or designating those parts of a body of water which are shallow enough to permit the growth of rooted green plants.

1918 R. A. MUTTKOWSKI in *Trans. Wisconsin Acad. Sci., Arts & Lett.* XIX. 378 The lake as a whole may be divided into three general regions,—the littoral, or phytal region; the aphytal region; and pelagic region. **1926** A. S. PEARSE *Animal Ecol.* vi. 210 Muttkowski uses 'littoral' as synonymous with 'phytal'.., but in very turbid lakes the phytal zone may be thinner than that of wave action, and in clear, small lakes it may be thicker. **1958** W. D. R. HUNTER in Miller & Tivy *Glasgow Region* 107 (*caption*) Map of Loch Lomond showing the extent of water (less than 13 feet deep), which is shallow enough to permit the growth of rooted green plants, *i.e.* the potential phytal zone. **1973** *Nature* 8 June 342/1 Marine grasses would also have provided new sources of food for the macrofauna and microfauna and new means of dispersal for benthonic and phytal organisms.

phytane (ˈfaɪteɪn). *Chem.* [ad. G. *phytan* (Willstätter & Hocheder 1907, in *Ann. d. Chem.* CCCLIV. 208): see PHYT- and -ANE.] A colourless liquid hydrocarbon, 3,7,11,15-tetramethylhexadecane, $C_{20}H_{42}$, that is the paraffin corresponding to phytol.

1907 [see PHYTOL]. **1911** *Chem. Abstr.* V. 874 Phytane, $C_{20}H_{42}$, obtained by the reduction of phytol,.. crystallizes in liquid air. **1965** *New Scientist* 6 May 378/1 Certain hydrocarbons, such as the branched-chain compounds phytane and pristane, can if found [in rocks] be taken to be definite evidence of life. **1971** *Sci. Amer.* May 38/3 The chemical analysis of organic material from the Gunflint cherts in several laboratories reveals the presence of the hydrocarbons pristane and phytane: two 'chemical fossils' that can most reasonably be regarded as being breakdown products of chlorophyll.

phytase (ˈfaɪteɪz, -s). *Biol.* [a. G. *phytase* (U. Suzuki et al. 1907, in *Bull. College Agric.* (Tokyo Imperial Univ.) VII. 503): see PHYT- and -ASE.] Any of a class of enzymes found esp. in cereals and yeast which convert phytic acid to *myo*-inositol and phosphoric acid.

1908 *Jrnl. Chem. Soc.* XCIV. I. 236 The change is shown to be due, not to putrefaction, but to an enzyme, phytase, which was isolated from rice bran and wheat bran. **1931** E. C. MILLER *Plant Physiol.* xi. 632 The glucoside phytin is decomposed into phosphoric acid and inosite, $C_6H_{12}O_6$, by the action of the enzyme phytase. **1947** *Nature* 18 Jan. 99/2, 25 ml. of the solution correspond to the phytase activity of about 15gm. barley. **1966** NOWAKOWSKI & CLARKE tr. *Kretovich's Princ. Plant Biochem.* vi. 215 The phytases of yeasts and flour split much of the inositol-phosphoric acid during fermentation of dough. **1975** *Science* 7 Feb. 432/3 A phytase which we extracted and purified from wheat bran.

-phyte, a terminal element representing Gr. φυτόν a plant, and denoting a vegetable organism, as ***microphyte, protophyte, saprophyte***. See also ZOOPHYTE (= animal plant).

phytic (ˈfaɪtɪk), *a. Biochem.* [f. PHYT(IN + -IC.] ***phytic acid***: a phosphoric acid ester, $C_6H_6(OPO_3H_2)_6$, of *myo*-inositol which is found (often as salts) in plants, esp. in the seeds of cereals.

1908 *Jrnl. Biol. Chem.* IV. 497 Wheat bran, which contains 1½ per cent of phosphorus, was found to be essentially free from inorganic phosphates, the whole of the phosphorus being present as salts of phytic acid. **1943** *Endeavour* II. 75/2 One important dietary constituent, phytic acid (inositol hexaphosphoric acid),.. interferes with calcification by precipitating calcium in the gut and making it unavailable. **1966** *McGraw-Hill Encycl. Sci. & Technol.* VII. 121/2 The phytic acid of whole wheat is of nutritional importance because it combines with dietary calcium, decreasing its availability. **1978** R. MITCHISON *Life in Scotland* ii. 71 Recent work on nutrition has shown that.. some foodstuffs contain inhibitors.., for instance, phytic acid.

Hence **ˈphytate**, a salt, or the anion, of phytic acid.

1908 *Jrnl. Biol. Chem.* IV. 498 In all cases blank determinations were made on the tissue extract alone and on a solution of sodium phytate which were digested in a similar manner. **1961** *Lancet* 26 Aug. 483/1 In dietary deficiency of vitamin B_{12}, serum-iron has been found to fall. .. This is thought to be due to ingestion of excessive amounts of phytate in wholemeal flour and bread. **1968** *New Scientist* 28 Nov. 512/2 The staple article of the typical village diet [in Iran] is wheat bread, which contains a chemical called phytate. This chemical renders zinc and possibly iron unavailable. **1976** *Sci. Amer.* Sept. 57/1 Ferrous iron, however, is absorbed less efficiently when it is ingested in combination with phytates and oxalates, which are found in leafy green vegetables and the whole-grain, unleavened bread of North Africa and the Middle East.

phytiform (ˈfaɪtɪfɔːm, ˈfɪtɪ-), *a. rare.* [irreg. f. Gr. φυτόν plant + -FORM.] Plant-like, phytoid.

1890 in *Cent. Dict.* **1893** in *Syd. Soc. Lex.*

phytin (ˈfaɪtɪn). *Biol.* and *Med.* [a. G. *phytin* (S. Posternak 1904, in *Schweiz. Wochenschr. f. Chem. u. Pharm.* XLII. 405): see PHYT- and -IN[1].] **a.** An insoluble salt of phytic acid with calcium and magnesium, which is found in plants, esp. cereals; also, *loosely*, the acid itself. **b.** Also **Phytin**, † **-ine**. A proprietary name for tonic preparations containing this.

1905 *Brit. Med. Jrnl.* 14 Jan. 81/1 Phytin has hitherto been simply described as a compound prepared from various seeds which contain phosphorus in combination... Phytin is claimed to be of use in all cases where invigorating treatment is indicated and to possess a specific action against impotence. **1905** *Official Gaz.* (U.S. Patent Office) 28 Feb. 2375/2 Certain named pharmaceutical products. Society of Chemical Industry in Basle, Basle, Switzerland. Filed Nov. 29, 1904. Phytine... used since February, 1903. **1906** *Amer. Jrnl. Physiol.* XVII. 76 Commercial phytin has lately been introduced into medical practice with somewhat extravagant claims. **1934** *Brit. Pharmaceutical Codex* 1656 *Phytin*, calcium and magnesium salt of inositol hexaphosphoric acid. **1936** [see INOSITOL]. **1938** E. C. MILLER *Plant Physiol.* (ed. 2) viii. 545 When chlorophyll is treated with dilute acids, the magnesium is removed and replaced with two hydrogen ions without otherwise changing the molecule. A series of decomposition products result [*sic*] which are called 'phytins' and which correspond to the alkali decomposition products of chlorophyll, except that the magnesium is lacking. **1947** *Dispensatory U.S.A.* (ed. 24) 1489/1 The calcium-magnesium salt of inositol hexaphosphate is available under the name *Phytin* (Ciba) in tablets containing 0·25 gm. **1957** G. E. HUTCHINSON *Treat. Limnol.* I. xii. 735 Chu (1946) found that *Nitzschia palea* could use phytin (magnesium inositol hexaphosphate) and glycerophosphoric acid as phosphorus sources. **1969** N. W. PIRIE *Food Resources* vii. 164 The old-fashioned method of making porridge.. destroys phytin which would otherwise make the calcium in the food less easy to absorb.

phytiphagan, -ous, incorrect forms of PHYTOPHAGAN, -OUS.

phytivorous (faɪˈtɪvərəs, fɪt-), *a.* Now *rare* or *Obs.* [irreg. f. Gr. φυτόν plant + -VOROUS.] Feeding on plants or vegetable substances.

1668 WILKINS *Real Char.* II. v. §4. 144 Birds may be distinguished by.. their food.. into.. Carnivorous; feeding chiefly on Flesh. Phytivorous; feeding on Vegetables. **1693** *Phil. Trans* XVII. 851 All which last are Herbivorous or Phytivorous Animals. **1798** *Ibid.* LXXXVIII. 46, I have not found the uric oxide in the urinary concretions of any phytivorous animal. **1833** MANTELL *Geol. S.E. Eng.* 394 The teeth and jaws of two other phytivorous saurians.

phyto- (ˈfaɪtəʊ, ˈfɪtəʊ), combining form of Gr. φυτόν a plant, lit. that which has grown, f. φύειν to produce, pass. and intr. to grow; used in forming scientific words, chiefly botanical.

As the υ in Gr. φυτόν is a short vowel, the etymological pronunciation of *phyt-* in all the following words is (fɪt); but the general tendency in English to view *y* as a long *ī*, as in *my*, *cry*, etc., has made the (etymologically erroneous) pronunciation (faɪt) all but universal: it is adopted in all the pronouncing dictionaries from Walker onward.

phytoˈbenthos [BENTHOS], the aquatic flora of the region at or near the bottom of the sea. **phytobiˈology**, the biology of plants; hence **phytobioˈlogical** *a.* **phytobranchiate** (-ˈbræŋkɪət) *a. Zool.* [see BRANCHIATE], of a group of isopodous crustaceans: having leaf-like gills. **phytoˈchemistry**, the chemistry of plants; so **phytoˈchemical** *a.*, **phytoˈchemically** *adv.*; also **phytoˈchemist**, an expert or specialist in phytochemistry. †**phyˈtochimy** [F. *chimie* chemistry] = *phytochemistry* (Webster 1847). **ˈphytochlore** [Gr. χλωρός green] = CHLOROPHYLL. **phytoˈcollite** *Min.* [Gr. κόλλα glue + -ITE[1]], name proposed for certain jelly-like hydrocarbons found in peat. **phytoˈecdysone** *Biol.* [ECDYSONE; prob. first formed in Jap.], any substance that occurs in a plant and causes moulting in insects. **phytoˈflagellate** [FLAGELLATE *sb.*], a plant-like flagellate belonging to the sub-class Phytoflagellata or Phytomastigophore. **phytogelin** (-ˈdʒɛlɪn) [GEL(ATIN) + -IN[1]], the gelatinous matter of Algæ (*Treas. Bot.* 1866). **phytoglyphy** (faɪˈtɒglɪfɪ, fɪ-) [Gr. γλυφή: see GLYPH], nature-printing, as originally used for plants; hence **phytoˈglyphic** *a.* **phytoˈmania** *nonce-wd.*, a mania for collecting plants. **phytomelin** (-ˈmɛlɪn) [Gr. μέλι, L. *mel* honey (in reference to its colour and appearance)] = RUTIN. **phytoˈmitogen**, a mitogen derived from a plant. **phytoˈmonad** [a. mod.L. order name *Phytomonadina*, f. generic name *Phytomonas* (C. Donovan 1909, in *Lancet* 20 Nov. 1496/2) + MONAD 4], a phytoflagellate belonging to the order Phytomonadina. **phyˈtonomy** [see -NOMY], the science of the laws of plant-growth. **ˌphytopalæonˈtology**, vegetable palæontology, study of fossil plants; hence **ˌphytopalæonˈtologist**. **ˌphytopaˈthology**, the study of the pathology or diseases of plants; hence **ˌphytopathoˈlogical** *a.*; **phytopaˈthologist**, one versed in phytopathology. **phyˈtophilous** *a.* [Gr. φίλος friendly], plant-loving: esp. of insects. **phytophthirian** *Entom.* (-ˈfθaɪrɪən) [Gr. φθείρ louse] (*a*) *adj.*, pertaining to the *Phytophthiria* or plant-lice; (*b*) *sb.*, a member of this group, a plant-louse. **ˌphytophylogeˈnetic** *a.*, relating to the phylogeny of plants. **ˌphytophysiˈology**, vegetable physiology. **phytoˈscopic** *a.* [Gr. σκοπεῖν to view], caused by sight of plants: said of the effect of surrounding vegetation on the colour of a larva. †**phyˈtoscopy**: see quot.

phy'tosophy, knowledge of plants; botany (Oken). **phy'tosterin** [Gr. στερεός solid]: see quot. 1881. **'phytotaxy** [Gr. τάξις arrangement], systematic botany. **,phytotera'tology**, vegetable teratology. **,phytovi'tellin** [L. *vitell-us* yolk], a globulin occurring in many seeds, and agreeing in all its reactions with vitellin from egg-yolk.

1931 R. N. CHAPMAN *Animal Ecol.* xvi. 333 The *phytobenthos is along the shore or in the littoral region. **1964** *Oceanogr. & Marine Biol.* II. 127 (*caption*) Other organisms listed include zooplankton, phytobenthos, zoobenthos, and fishes. **1973** *Nature* 6 Apr. 415/2 The rates of..photosyntheses of phytoplankton and phytobenthos.. have been made [*sic*] using carbon-14. **1887** *Athenæum* 26 Feb. 292/3 Sir J. Lubbock read the second part of his *phytobiological observations. **1890** *Ibid.* 1 Mar. 278/3 There remains a large collection of memoirs on general botany and *phyto-biology. **1858** MAYNE *Expos. Lex.* 959/1 *Phytochemical. **1877** *Chem. News* 4 May 185/1 (*heading*) On phyto-chemical processes. **1921** *Experiment Station Rec.* XLIII. 820 (*heading*) Phytochemical investigations on indigenous and naturalized plants. **1972** *Nature* 21 Jan. 134/1 The joint meeting of the Phytochemical Society and the Pharmaceutical Society of Great Britain on plant constituents of pharmacological interest. **1972** *Science* 9 June 1131/2 Schultes has repeatedly suggested that these additional 'peyote' cacti be examined *phytochemically. **1969** H. ERDTMAN in Harborne & Swain *Perspectives in Phytochem.* v. 109 That symposium was important because it brought together scientists of different specializations, botanical taxonomists, *phytochemists and chemists interested in biosynthetic problems. **1972** *Nature* 28 Apr. 469/2 The contributors are leading specialists in umbellifer taxonomy..together with many other scarcely less eminent systematists and phytochemists. **1837** *Phil. Mag.* X. 247 (*heading*) A report of the progress of *phytochemistry in the year 1835. **1866** WATTS *Dict. Chem.* IV. 636 Phytochemistry, the Chemistry of Plants. The most comprehensive treatise on this subject is that of Rochleder, published at Leipzig in 1854. **1912** *Carnegie Inst. Year Bk.* 49 The chief problems of the Department have been taken to lie in the domain of phyto-chemistry, in the water-relations of plants, and in the environic reactions of organisms. **1968** *Jrnl. Chromatogr.* XXXVI. 22 Methods for the separation and identification of microquantities of phenolic glycosides are of great importance for work in phytochemistry, pharmacognosy and chemotaxonomy. **1866** *Treas. Bot.*, *Phytochlore, green colouring matter; chlorophyll. **1881** H. C. LEWIS in *Proc. Amer. Phil. Soc.* XX. 117 *Phytocollite. **1968** *Tetrahedron Lett.* July 3883 Four additional *phytoecdysones have now been isolated from the leaves [of *Podocarpus macrophyllus*]. Interestingly, these new phytoecdysones..have steroid skeletons with 28 and 29 carbon atoms. **1974** HIKINO & TAKEMOTO in W. J. Burdette *Invertebr. Endocrinol.* II. 187 The occurrence of phytoecdysones in plants raises the question whether they have any beneficial or adverse effects on the plants themselves or on the phytophagous animals in their natural habitat... The leaves of *Morus* species and *Podocarpus macrophyllus* which are known to contain considerable amounts of phytoecdysones, are food of the larvae of the moths, *Bombyx mori* and *Milionia vasalis pryeri*, respectively. **1978** *Nature* 9 Mar. 122/1 The generic term 'phytoecdysones' should be abandoned. **1947** *Palestine Jrnl. Bot.* IV. 14 *Prymnesium parvum* Carter is a *phytoflagellate belonging to the order of the Chrysomonadales, differing from other members of this order in the presence of an immobile spine-like third flagellum, a feature unique among phytoflagellates. **1951** HUTNER & PROVASOLI in A. Lwoff et al. *Biochem. & Physiol. Protozoa* I. 29 The phytoflagellates are a heterogeneous group occupying a systematic position at intersections of plant and animal lines of descent. **1957** *New Biol.* XXIII. 93 This phytoflagellate [sc. *Prymnesium parvum*] was first blamed for mass fish mortality in Holland and later in Denmark. **1973** M. A. SLEIGH *Biol. Protozoa* i. 2 The cell possesses the basic components of a phytoflagellate, including flagella, nucleus, plastid,..and other..inclusions. **1864** WEBSTER, *Phytoglyphic,..relating to phytoglyphy. *Phytoglyphy,.. the art of printing from nature, by taking impressions from plants, or other objects. **1855** E. R. LANKESTER *Macgillivray's Nat. Hist. Dee Side & Braemar* 63 This risk incurred for the mere chance of finding a few rare plants..one can hardly designate it by any other name than *Phytomania. **1866** WATTS *Dict. Chem.* IV. 636 *Phytomelin or *Plant-yellow.* A name proposed by W. Stein for rutin, on account of its wide diffusion in the vegetable kingdom. **1961** MARSHALL & CAPON in *Lancet* 8 July 104/1 We suggest that until more is known about their structure, factors extracted from plants which exhibit mitogenic activity, be referred to as *phytomitogens. **1964** *Ibid.* 21 Nov. 1101/1 These observations suggest that the distribution of 'phytomitogens' in the plant kingdom may be more widespread than is recognised. **1974** *Jrnl. Exper. Med.* CXXXIX. 1553 The lymphocyte response to phytomitogens is generally considered to be nonspecific. **1926** G. N. CALKINS *Biol. Protozoa* v. 279 *Phytomonads with a bivalve shell, or at least a membrane which splits easily to form two lens-like halves, as in *Phacotus lenticularis.* **1953** R. P. HALL *Protozool.* iv. 151 Lipids, although usually not abundant, are stored by many phytomonads. **1961** R. D. MANWELL *Introd. Protozool.* xiv. 174 Most of the phytomonads are rather small, roundish forms. **1864** WEBSTER, *Phytonomy. **1883** *Science* 6 Apr. 252 The nature of some impressions described by *phytopaleontologists as remains of fossil Algæ. *Ibid.* 253 The evidence..renders great service to *phytopaleontology. **1889** *Cent. Dict.*, *Phytopathological. **1909** B. M. DUGGAR *Fungous Dis. Plants* 4 The foundations were laid for a more careful study of the fungi from a phytopathological point of view. **1959** *Ann. Rev. Microbiol.* XIII. 224 The term 'toxin', in the phytopathological literature, is used in the general sense of a poisonous substance generated by the pathogen regardless of its chemical nature. **1962** W. CARTER *Insects in Relation to Plant Dis.* p. vii, There..has been a growing awareness of the toxicogenic insect as a phytopathological agent. **1886** *Cassell's Encycl. Dict.*, *Phytopathologist. **1893** ELEANOR ORMEROD in *Autobiog. & Corr.* xx. (1904) 218 One of our leading European Phytopathologists. **1917** J. W. HARSHBERGER *Text-bk. Mycol. & Plant Path.* xxiii. 271 A study of phytopathology..presupposes that the would-be phytopathologist is acquainted with plant morphology, systematic botany..histology, cytology, embryology, genetics, physiology, [etc.]. **1958** *Austral. Jrnl. Biol. Sci.* XI. 275 The problem of disease resistance in plants has exercised the minds of phytopathologists for more than half a century. **1864** WEBSTER, *Phytopathology,..an account of diseases to which plants are liable. **1891** *Vet. Jrnl.* XXXII. 253 Phytopathology afforded many instances of local death of a part produced by the parasite. **1911** *Encycl. Brit.* XXI. 754/2 'Phytopathology' or plant pathology..comprises our knowledge of the symptoms, course, causes and remedies of the maladies which threaten the life of plants, or which result in abnormalities of structure that are regarded, whether directly injurious or not to life, as unsightly or undesirable... As a branch of botanical study it is of recent date. **1976** *Nature* 12 Feb. 449/1 A large proportion of the money devoted to agricultural research in the UK is spent on phytopathology and crop protection and has enabled the production of virus-free and disease-resistant crops. **1880** *Nature* 12 Feb. 364/1 On the method and data of *phyto-phylogenetic research. **1854** H. SPENCER in *Brit. Q. Rev.* July 115 Biology, Organosophy, Phytogeny, *Phyto-physiology, Phytology. **1892** POULTON in *Trans. Entom. Soc.* X. 294 The effect cannot be phytophagic in the strict sense of the word, but rather *phytoscopic, inasmuch as the colour of the surface of the leaf rather than its substance acts as the stimulus. **1730–6** BAILEY (folio), *Phytoscopy,..a viewing and contemplating or considering plants. **1854** H. SPENCER in *Brit. Q. Rev.* July 115 He [Oken] says..'Biology, therefore, divides into Organogeny, *Phytosophy, Zoosophy'. **1881** WATTS *Dict. Chem.* VIII. II. 1624 *Phytosterin, $C_{26}H_4O$... A neutral substance, identical or homologous with cholesterin, obtained from Calabar beans by extraction with petroleum-ether. **1897** *Naturalist* 47 Various higher alcohols and phytosterin being present therein as bases. **1883** L. F. WARD *Dynamic Sociol.* I. 120 *Phytotaxy. **1898** tr. *Strasburger's Bot.* I. 154 The study of the abnormal development of plants is called *Phytoteratology.

phytoagglutinin (faɪtəʊə'gl(j)uːtɪnɪn). *Biochem.* [f. PHYTO- + *agglutinin* s.v. AGGLUTINATE *v.*] Any plant protein that is an agglutinin.

1959 *Archiwum Immunologii i Terapii Doświadczalnej* VII. 793, 214 plant species from various botanic families were examined for the presence of phytoagglutinins; they have been found in seed extracts of 50 plant species. **1971** *Proc. Nat. Acad. Sci.* LXVIII. 1818/2 The *C[olletotrichum] lindemuthianum* polygalacturonase inhibitor isolated from Red Kidney bean hypocotyls has several properties which suggest that it is one of the glycoproteins commonly referred to as phytoagglutinins. **1974** A. HUXLEY *Plant & Planet* xxv. 285 Many plants..contain antibiotic substances which help to repel fungus invasions... These substances, which are possibly based on proteins known as phytoagglutins [*sic*], remind one of antibodies in animals.

phytoalexin (,faɪtəʊə'lɛksɪn). *Bot.* [a. G. *phytoalexin* (Müller & Börger 1941, in *Arb. aus der biol. Reichsanstalt Land- und Forstwirtschaft* XXIII. 223): see PHYTO- and ALEXIN.] Any substance that is produced by plant tissues in response to contact with a parasite and specifically inhibits the growth of that parasite.

The term was orig. defined with regard to fungal parasites only, but in 1956 Müller extended the meaning to cover all parasites.

1949 *Nature* 26 Mar. 498/2 The necrosis of the affected tissues must be accompanied by the formation or activation of a principle ('phytoalexin') which exercises a retarding influence on the penetrating parasite. **1956** K. O. MÜLLER in *Phytopath. Zeitschr.* XXVII. 254 'Phytoalexines' [*sic*] are defined as antibiotics which are the result of an interaction of two different metabolic systems, the host and the parasite, and which inhibit the growth of microorganisms pathogenic to plants. **1964** CRUICKSHANK & PERRIN in J. B. Harborne *Biochem. Phenolic Compounds* xiii. 534 Susceptibility [to fungal attack] may be due to the inability of the infecting fungus to stimulate the formation of the phytoalexin or to its capacity to tolerate the phytoalexin produced. **1975** *Sci. Amer.* Jan. 88/3 Plants do not produce antibodies but some of them do produce phytoalexins. **1977** *Observer* 4 Sept. 4/2 Dr. David Smith..told a meeting of the British Association for the Advancement of Science last week that chemicals called phytoalexins—substances produced by plants when they are attacked by disease—merited a major investigation.

phytobiology to **-chlore**: see PHYTO-.

phytochrome ('faɪtəkrəʊm). [f. PHYTO- + CHROME *sb.*] **1.** (See quot.)

1893 *Syd. Soc. Lex.*, *Phytochrome*, a name for chlorophyll. **1902** WEBSTER Suppl., *Phytochrome*, yellow pigment of plants.

2. *Bot.* A blue-green chromoprotein which regulates many aspects of development in higher plants according to the nature and timing of the light which it absorbs.

1960 BORTHWICK & HENDRICKS in *Science* 28 Oct. 1223/1 This control of flowering..implies a time-measuring system that distinguishes between light and darkness through mediation of a pigment... The pigment, now called phytochrome, is a blue or a bluish-green protein that exists in two forms interconvertible by light,..with 660 and 730 mμ the absorption maxima of the two forms. **1962** *Amat. Gardening* 20 Jan. 12 Phytochrome has been isolated, and shown to be sensitive even to very short periods of light. **1971** *New Scientist* 18 Feb. 365/1 One of the 'states' of phytochrome is physiologically active and plays a part in controlling many processes ranging from seed germination ..to the onset of reproductive behaviour. **1977** J. L. HARPER *Population Biol. Plants* v. 144 The phytochrome system which controls the light sensitivity of germination in many species involves an interconversion of two forms of phytochrome.

phytocidal (faɪtəʊ'saɪdəl), *a.* [f. PHYTO- + -CIDE + -AL[1].] Lethal or injurious to plants.

1934 *Ann. Rep. East Malling Res. Station 1933* 157 The immediate problem to be solved by this field spraying trial was whether..lime-sulphur could be used in conjunction with nicotine or with derris with satisfactory fungicidal, insecticidal and phytocidal results. [*Note*] This term is now being used in reference to the effect of sprays on the tree. **1936** H. MARTIN *Sci. Princ. Plant Protection* (ed. 2) vi. 110 It is convenient in describing phytocidal activity to distinguish between acute injury, characterized by the localized killing of plant tissue (necrosis) and popularly termed 'scorch' or 'burn', and chronic injury which involves deep-seated physiological changes and causes, for example, the stunting and premature drop of fruit and leaves. **1946** *Nature* 21 Sept. 417/2 One other point regarding phytocidal action may be mentioned. Unnecessarily heavy dressings of B.H.C. do not appear to have a hurtful action on the carrot, whereas with the Brassicæ even moderate dressings may seriously affect the stem at the point where contact is made. **1970** *Weed Res.* X. 367 (*heading*) The correlation of the phytocidal effect of 3-amino-1,2,4-triazole with the growth stage of oat plants.

So **'phytocide**, a phytocidal agent.

1936 *Ann. Rep. East Malling Res. Station 1935* 198 Cuprous cyanide..[etc.] were retained for further phytocide tests. **1961** *New Scientist* 21 Dec. 724/3 Treatment with selective phytocides such as copper sulphate.

phytoclimate ('faɪtəʊklaɪmət). *Bot.* [ad. Da. *fanerofytklimaet*, *kryptofytklimaet* (C. Raunkiaer 1908, in *Bot. Tidsskr.* XXIX. 54): see PHYTO- and CLIMATE *sb.*] Local climate in its ecological aspects.

1950 *Bot. Rev.* XVI. 1 (*heading*) Life-forms and phytoclimate. *Ibid.* 16 We have here only a general correlation between Raunkiaer's hemicryptophytic phytoclimate and Köppen's C and D climates which are based on physical data. **1968** J. M. MACLENNAN tr. *Sukachev & Dylis's Fund. Forest Biogeocoenol.* i. 31 Inter-crown and intra-crown breaking of twigs.., by increasing the distance between trees and lessening the depth and density of the canopy, causes substantial changes in the phytoclimate, litter, and soil processes. **1975** *Lesovedenie* VI. 36 (*heading*) Alteration of phytoclimate in stem pests nidus.

So **phytocli'matic** *a.*, of or pertaining to phytoclimate.

1913 *Jrnl. Ecol.* I. 18 In Table I we give a few of Raunkiaer's analyses for various types of climate; the locality is indicated, also the total species actually analysed, while in the later columns the results are given as percentages according to the grouping given above. Such an analysis for any region is termed a biological or phyto-climatic spectrum. **1976** *Biol. Abstr.* LXI. 5689/1 The following parameters are given for each provenance:.., phytoclimatic zone according to Pavari and soil.

phytocœnose (faɪtəʊ'siːnəʊz). *Ecol.* [f. PHYTO- + Gr. κοίνωσις mingling.] A community of plants; all of the plant species found at a particular site.

1930 G. E. DU RIETZ in *Svensk Bot. Tidskr.* XXIV. 489 Only of the phytocoenoses, or 'complete plant-communities', all units of higher and lower rank have been included. **1955** *Jrnl. Ecol.* XLIII. 650 It is always possible to list the species in a phytocoenose (i.e. the vegetation occupying a definite area of ground). **1964** *Bot. Zhurnal* XLIX. 74 The study of the sward structure in a phytocoenose reveals the fact that the latter consists of layers.

phytoene ('faɪtəʊiːn). *Chem.* [f. PHYTO- + -ENE.] A colourless viscous liquid, $C_{40}H_{64}$, which is a polyunsaturated branched-chain hydrocarbon and a precursor in the biological synthesis of carotenoids.

1950 PORTER & LINCOLN in *Arch. Biochem.* XXVII. 391 The name phytoene is given to a compound reported by Porter and Zscheile... It has previously been called a colorless, nonfluorescent polyene. **1966** *McGraw-Hill Encycl. Sci. & Technol.* II. 54/2 The synthesis of carotenoids leads..to the colorless compound, phytoene, which has the branched, 40-carbon chain characteristic of the carotenoid skeleton. **1978** *Sci. Amer.* Sept. 94/1 Carotenoids are derived from the 40-carbon compound phytoene.

phytoflagellate to **-gelin**: see PHYTO-.

phytogenesis (faɪtəʊ'dʒɛnɪsɪs, fɪtəʊ-). [f. PHYTO- + -GENESIS.] The generation or evolution of plants. So **phytoge'netic**, **phytoge'netical** *adjs.*, of or pertaining to phytogenesis; **phytoge'netically** *adv.*; also **phy'togeny** = *phytogenesis.*

1858 MAYNE *Expos. Lex.*, *Phytogenesis, term by Dupetit-Thouars for germination..phytogenesy. **1882** VINES *Sachs' Bot.* 904 In the latter case we have the end, in the former the beginning of *phytogenetic series. **1881** WILLIAMSON in *Nature* 27 Oct. 607/1 Minute, but *phytogenetically important forms of plant-life. **1854** H. SPENCER in *Brit. Q. Rev.* July 115 Biology, Organosophy, *Phytogeny.

phytogenic (faɪtəʊ'dʒɛnɪk, fɪtəʊ-), *a. Geol.* and *Min. rare.* [f. Gr. φυτόν plant + -GEN 2 + -IC.] Of vegetable origin. So **phy'togenous** *a. rare.*

1858 MAYNE *Expos. Lex.* 959/2 Under the name of *phytogenous substances*, Haüy has formed an Appendix to the *Combustibilia*, comprehending those of which the origin is evidently vegetable. **1878** LAWRENCE tr. *Cotta's Rocks Class.* 352 Phytogenic deposits are such as consist chiefly of vegetable substances.

ˌphytogeˈography. [f. PHYTO- + GEOGRAPHY.] The geographical distribution of plants.

1847 H. C. WATSON *Cybele Britannica* I. 2 This study has been variously denominated 'Phyto-Geography', 'Botanical Geography', 'Geographical Botany', and 'Geographical Distribution of Plants'. **1859** *Ibid.* IV. x. 373 Phytogeography traces out the history and distribution of plants in connexion with the geographical position. **1881** *Nature* 13 Oct. 556/1 The numerous writings on phytogeography of the late Prof. A. Grisebach. **1896** J. THOMSON *African Explorer* xiv. 343 The phytogeography of Central Africa. **1933** *Geogr. Jrnl.* LXXXI. 462 A further problem remains, far more serious in the case of zoogeography than with phytogeography. Can the essentials be put..without assuming a knowledge of taxonomy beyond the reach of the average geographer? **1956** H. GODWIN (*title*) The history of the British flora: a factual basis for phytogeography. **1960** N. POLUNIN *Introd. Plant Geogr.* i. 2 Plant geography, also called phytogeography.. deals with the plant cover of the world—with its composition, its local productivity, and particularly its distribution. **1976** *Conservation News* Sept./Oct. 3/1 The Library is one of the richest of its kind in the world, being particularly strong in plant taxonomy, phytogeography and related fields.

Hence **ˌphytogeˈographer**, one who is versed in phytogeography; **ˌphytogeoˈgraphic, -ˈgraphical** *adjs.*, of or pertaining to phytogeography, dealing with the geographical distribution of plants.

1859 H. C. WATSON *Cybele Britannica* IV. x. 375 The ultimate objects to be sought by phyto-geographical investigations, are neither the countries of plants nor the plants of countries. *Ibid.* 441 A first call on the phytogeographer is to ascertain where the plants are now distributed. **1883** THISELTON DYER in *Nature* 4 Jan. 224/2 A right understanding of the phyto-geographical facts of the north temperate flora. **1885** W. B. HELMSLEY in *Challenger Rep., Bot.* I. 6 For phyto-geographical purposes Insular Floras may be divided into three categories based upon their endemic element. **1886** *Athenæum* 5 June 750/2 Phytogeographical Map of Europe. **1889** *Nature* 30 May 98/1 Apart from the value of the work to the systematist and phytogeographer, it possesses an interest for a wide circle. **1951** *Geografiska Annaler* XXXIII. 149 The vegetative highland areas consist mainly of bogs, mostly of the type which in Icelandic is called *flá*. Phytogeographers are using *flá* as a phytogeographical concept. **1977** *Jrnl. R. Soc. Arts* CXXV. 225/1 The Swiss phytogeographer Alphonse de Candolle.

phytoglyphic, -glyphy: see PHYTO-.

†phyˈtognomy. *Obs.* [Formed on the analogy of *physiognomy*, after the mod.L. *Phytognomonica* of J. Baptista Porta (1583): see PHYTO- and GNOMIC.] The alleged art of discovering the qualities of a plant from its appearance; vegetable physiognomy. Hence **†phytoˈgnomical** *a.*

[**1583** PORTA (*title*) Phytognomonica..in quibus nova facillimaque affertur methodus, qua plantarum..ex prima extimæ faciei inspectione quivis abditas vires assequatur.] **1643** SIR T. BROWNE *Relig. Med.* II. §2, I hold moreover that there is a Phytognomy, or Physiognomy, not onely of men, but of Plants, and Vegetables. **1646** —— *Pseud. Ep.* II. vi. 93 Whoever shall peruse the signatures of Crollius, or rather the Phytognomy of Porta. **1653** R. SANDERS *Physiogn.* b ij, In Phytognomical Physiognomie we may observe certain plants resembling the heads of Animals.

phytograph (ˈfaɪtəʊgrɑːf, -æ-). *Ecol.* [f. PHYTO- + Gr. -γραφ-ος: see -GRAPH.] A diagram showing several quantifiable criteria of the ecological status of a (usu. silvan) species within an association.

1930 H. J. LUTZ in *Ecology* XI. 9 The term phytograph is proposed to designate a chart of this kind when used to characterize plant relationships. **1950** *Forestry Abstr.* XI. 580/2 Jack pine stands of equal age subjected to different degrees of thinning might be represented for purposes of comparison by phytographs constructed on 5 axes on which are shown their respective:—(1) average spacing of stems, [etc.]. **1971** F. C. FORD-ROBERTSON *Terminol. Forest Sci.* 194/1 Phytograph... A polygonal figure depicting the role of a species in a plant community.

phytography (faɪˈtɒgrəfɪ, fɪt-). [ad. mod.L. *phytographia*: see PHYTO- and -GRAPHY.]

1. Description of plants; descriptive botany.

[**1691** PLUKENET (*title*) Phytographia, seu Stirpium illustrium et minus cognitarum Icones.] **1696** RAY in *Lett. Lit. Men* (Camden) 202, I shall..put down what I find in.. Plukenet's Phytography. **1730–6** BAILEY (folio) Pref., *Phytography*,..a Treatise or Physiological Description of Plants and Vegetables. **1836** HENSLOW *Phys. Bot.* Introd. 3 A third..department is styled 'Phytography', in which a full description of plants themselves is given. **1885** GOODALE *Physiol. Bot.* (1892) 3 Phytography or Descriptive Botany.

2. = PHYTOGLYPHY.

Hence **phyˈtographer**, an expert in or writer on phytography; **phytoˈgraphic, phytoˈgraphical** *adjs.*, pertaining to phytography.

1890 *Cent. Dict.*, *Phytographer. **1693** *Phil. Trans.* XVII. 618 A new Set of *Phytographic Tables. **1888** *Nature* 5 July 220/1 The introductory narrative..enables a phytographic botanist to apprehend the nature of the country [Afghanistan] and climate. **1828–32** WEBSTER, **Phytographical*, pertaining to the description of plants.

phytohæmagglutinin (ˌfaɪtəʊhiːməˈgl(j)uːtɪnɪn). *Hæmatol.* Also (chiefly *U.S.*) -hem-. [f. PHYTO- + HÆMAGGLUTININ, HEM-.] Any plant protein that is a hæmagglutinin.

1949 *Blood* IV. 673 We rediscovered this phytohemagglutinin accidentally and independently. **1951** *Amer. Jrnl. Med.* X. 776/2 The phytohemagglutinin of red beans (Phaseolus vulgaris) was recently isolated in pure form. **1955** *Jrnl. Biol. Chem.* CCXII. 615 This phytohemagglutinin, in either the mucoprotein or the protein form, is a non-toxic, powerful hemagglutinin of all types of human erythrocytes, and those of the horse, pig, [etc.]. **1960** *Cancer Res.* XX. 462 The mucoprotein plant extract, phytohemagglutinin (PHA), employed originally as a means of separating the leukocytes from whole blood in preparing the cultures, was found to be a specific initiator of mitotic activity: in its presence, cell division occurred; in its absence, no mitoses appeared. **1977** I. M. ROITT *Essent. Immunol.* (ed. 3) vi. 180 Comparable changes can be induced in lymphocytes by certain plant mitogens of which the best known are phytohaemagglutinin (PHA) and concanavalin A (conA). These..react with the cell surface non-specifically (i.e. not as an antigen) and produce the same series of cellular events as does antigen locking on to its specific surface receptor.

phytohormone (faɪtəʊˈhɔːməʊn). *Bot.* [ad. G. *phytohormon* (Kögl & Smit 1931, in *K. Akad. von Wetenschoppen te Amsterdam: Proc. Sect. Sci.* XXXIV. 1416): see PHYTO- and HORMONE.] Any substance which has a hormonal effect on a plant; = HORMONE 2.

1933 *Chem. Abstr.* XXVII. 1645 (*heading*) Vegetable growth substances... A phytohormone of cell extension. **1940** W. R FEARON *Introd. Biochem.* (ed. 2) xxiv. 446 The effect of the phytohormones is non-specific as regards species. **1952** [see HORMONE 2]. **1959** L. J. AUDUS *Plant Growth Substances* (ed. 2) i. 16 In the past a rigid distinction has been made between..'synthetic growth-regulating substances' and 'natural phytohormones'. **1971** *Nature* 4 June 332/1 Jump suggested that a phytohormone produced by *A[ureobasidium] pullulans* (*Dematium pullulans*) may have been responsible for forking in red pine.

phytoid (ˈfaɪtɔɪd, fɪt-), *a.* and *sb. rare.* [f. Gr. φυτ-όν plant + -OID. Cf. Gr. φυτώδ-ης plant-like.]

A. *adj.* Plant-like; esp. in *Zool.* of an animal.

1858 in MAYNE *Expos. Lex.*

B. *sb. Bot.* (See quot.)

1858 CARPENTER *Veg. Phys.* §397 In order to distinguish between the separated buds of plants and animals, those of the former have been called phytoids, and the latter zooids.

phytol (ˈfaɪtɒl). *Biochem.* [a. G. *phytol* (Willstätter & Hocheder 1907, in *Ann. d. Chem.* CCCLIV. 207): see PHYT- and -OL.] A colourless oil whose molecule forms part of that of chlorophyll and vitamins E and K, and which is an acyclic terpenoid alcohol; 3,7,11,15-tetramethyl-2-hexadecenol, $C_{20}H_{40}O$.

1907 *Jrnl. Chem. Soc.* XCII. I. 784 The authors have been able..to remove the magnesium quantitatively and to obtain for the first time an ashless compound closely related to chlorophyll. This derivative is an ester, termed phaeophytin, and is hydrolysed readily by alkalis, yielding an unsaturated alcohol, phytol, $C_{20}H_{40}O$, which is formed also by the action of alkalis on chlorophyll. For the hypothetical saturated hydrocarbon, corresponding with this alcohol, the authors propose the name phytane. **1911** [see PHYTANE]. **1950** [see PHÆOPHORBIDE]. **1974** *Sci. Amer.* Dec. 73/1 Attached to the porphyrin ring in chlorophyll is a long hydrocarbon 'tail', the phytol chain. It consists of carbon atoms linked together, but only one of the bonds is double. **1977** *Nature* 18 Aug. 621/2 The precursors of these hydrocarbons are unknown, but it is surmised that they result from the diagenesis of phytol, a moiety widely distributed among plant pigments.

Hence **ˈphytyl** (-ɪl, -aɪl), the univalent radical derived from phytol by the loss of a hydrogen atom.

1911 *Jrnl. Chem. Soc.* C. I. 145 Phytyl hydrogen phthalates, $CO_2H{\cdot}C_6H_4{\cdot}CO_2{\cdot}C_{20}H_{39}$, are formed when the phytol and phthalic anhydride are boiled for five hours with benzene. **1956** [see PHÆOPHORBIDE]. **1973** *Nature* 20 July 155/1 Although other contributors, such as vitamin K_1, α-tocopherol and phospholipids from..bacteria and algae which have been shown to possess a phytyl side chain, are also possible, the most obvious source for the ketone is phytol.

‖**Phytolacca** (faɪtəʊ-, fɪtəʊˈlækə). *Bot.* [mod.L. (Tournefort 1700), f. Gr. φυτόν plant + mod.L. *lacca* crimson lake.] The genus of plants including the Pocan, Virginian Poke, Pokeweed, or Red-ink plant (*P. decandra*), and several other tropical or sub-tropical species, chiefly American; also various preparations of the Poke used medicinally. Hence **phytolaccin** (-ˈlæksɪn) *Chem.*, a neutral crystalline compound obtained from the Virginian Poke.

1753 *Scots Mag.* June 283/2 Give purges..with the phytolacca decoction. **1882** *Garden* 18 Mar. 179/3 Several other Phytolaccas are widely distributed throughout the Tropics. **1864** *N. Syd. Soc. Year-bk. Med.* 441 The dose of the concentrated preparation (phytolaccin).

ˈphytolith (ˈfaɪtəlɪθ). In sense 1 †-lite. [f. PHYTO- + -LITE, -LITH. In F. *phytolithe.*]

†1. A fossil plant. *Obs.*

1794 SULLIVAN *View Nat.* II. 175 The former are called zoophytes; the latter phytolites. **1849** MURCHISON *Siluria* xvi. 402 The so-called 'transition' and 'grauwacke' phytolites described by various German authors.

2. A minute mineral particle formed inside a plant.

1958 *Jrnl. Soil Sci.* IX. 154 *Nardus stricta*..contains phytoliths which could not be mistaken for those from any other of the grasses encountered. **1960** *Proc. R. Soc. Victoria* LXXII. 21 Phytoliths are important, if not abundant, constituents of dust in Australia. The common varieties are opal-phytoliths, but calcite-phytoliths and quartz-phytoliths have also been detected. **1964** *Ann. Bot.* XXVIII. 181 In some grasses..the absence or almost complete absence of phytoliths may be a characteristic of the species. **1975** *Nature* 17 Apr. 588/2 The abundance of opal phytoliths in the midden further indicate that there was then no scarcity of grass and reeds in the immediate vicinity of the site.

Hence **†ˌphytoliˈthology**, vegetable palæontology; **†ˌphytoliˈthologist**, a writer on this subject.

1864 in WEBSTER.

phytological (faɪtəʊˈlɒdʒɪkəl, fɪtəʊ-), *a.* Now *rare.* [f. as PHYTOLOGY: see -LOGICAL. Cf. F. *phytologique.*] Relating to the study of plants; botanical.

1654 GAYTON *Pleas. Notes* III. iii. 79 Priapus..the greatest Herbalist in the World;..This Phutologicall Deitie. **1673** GREW *Anat. Roots* Ep. Ded., The promotion of Phytological Science is one Part of Your Work. **1673** —— (*title*) An Idea of a Phytological History propounded. **1833** LYELL *Princ. Geol.* III. 332 The zoological and phytological characters of the same formations were far more persistent than their mineral peculiarities.

phytologist (faɪˈtɒlədʒɪst, fɪt-). Now *rare.* [f. PHYTOLOGY + -IST.] One versed in phytology; a botanist.

1699 EVELYN *Acetaria* (1729) 138 Charles Hatton Esq. to whom all our Phytologists and Lovers of Horticulture are oblig'd. **1727** BAILEY vol. II, *Phytologist*, a Botanist, one who treats of Plants. **1827** STEUART *Planter's G.* Pref. (1828) 5 If he be a Phytologist of research, or, still more, a Planter of experience. **1881** ROUTLEDGE *Science* ii. 34 There was a botanical garden for the phytologist.

phytology (faɪˈtɒlədʒɪ, fɪt-). Now *rare.* [ad. mod.L. *phytologia*, f. Gr. φυτόν plant + -λογία: see -LOGY. Cf. F. *phytologie* (d'Holbach 1753).] The science of plants; botany.

[**1647** G. DUVAL (*title*) Phytologia; sive, Philosophia Plantarum.] **1658** SIR T. BROWNE *Hydriot.* Ep. Ded to N. Bacon, We pretend not to multiply vegetable divisions by Quincuncial and Reticulate plants; or erect a new Phytology. **1819** *Pantologia, Phytology*, that part of Natural History which treats on plants. **1849** H. MILLER *Footpr. Creat.* xiv. (1874) 264 He calls into court Astronomy, Geology, Phytology and Zoology.

phytomania, -melin: see PHYTO-.

phytomer (ˈfaɪtəʊmə(r), ˈfɪt-). *Bot.* [ad. mod.L. *phytomeron*, pl. *-a*, f. Gr. φυτό-ν plant + μέρος part.] = PHYTON.

1880 GRAY *Struct. Bot.* (ed. 6) 7 *Phytomera*,..equivalent to plant-parts... In English, the singular may be shortened to Phytomer. *Ibid.* 9 The plant begins as a single phytomer.

phytometer (faɪˈtɒmɪtə(r)). *Bot.* [f. PHYTO- + -METER.] A plant or group of plants used to indicate, by its health and rate of growth, the physical properties of its surroundings.

1919 F. E. CLEMENTS et al. in *Carnegie Inst. Year Bk. 1918* 288 An endeavor has been made to devise a biological method of measuring habitats by means of standard plants. Batteries of such plants, for which the term 'phytometer' is suggested, have been installed at the various factor stations, and three series have been measured during the summer. **1929** WEAVER & CLEMENTS *Plant Ecol.* xiv. 330 Since phytometers are often placed in habitats that make extreme demands upon the plants, it is best to use species that are as hardy and vigorous as possible. **1954** *Austral. Jrnl. Bot.* II. 322 There is much to be said for the view that the complexes of environmental factors determining plant distribution can be indicated and measured better indirectly, through the plants themselves, than by direct physical measurements; this is, of course, the idea behind the use of 'phytometers' in agricultural meteorology. **1977** J. L. HARPER *Population Biol. Plants* xi. 361 It would be of immense interest to use standard plant units (phytometers), either pots freely supplied with water and nutrients or small water culture vessels with a test plant in each, and to place these units in transects across vegetation through open land, grassland, scrub and woodland.

phyton (ˈfaɪtɒn, ˈfɪtɒn). *Bot.* [a. F. *phyton*, a. Gr. φυτόν a plant, f. φύειν to produce.] A plant-unit; = prec.: see quot. 1898.

1848 E. FORBES *Naked-eyed Medusæ* 88 The several phytons comprising the first bud or plumule. **1854** BALFOUR *Outl. Bot.* I. iii. 267 The dicotyledonous embryo then is composed of two leaves or two unifoliar phytons..united together so as to form one axis. **1880** GRAY *Struct. Bot.* (ed. 6) 7 These ultimate similar parts..which are endowed with or may produce all the fundamental organs of vegetation, were by Gaudichaud called *Phytons*. **1898** BAILEY *Plant Lessons* lxxiii. 380 The propagation-unit in vegetative multiplication is the smallest part of root, stem or leaf which will grow when severed from the parent (although this is not a morphological or structural unit in the plant-body); and, for the purpose of terminology, this part may be called a phyton.

phytonisse, obs. form of PYTHONESS.

phytonomy, -palæontology: see PHYTO-.

phytopathogen (ˌfaɪtəʊˈpæθəʊdʒən). *Biol.* [f. PHYTO- + PATHOGEN.] Any micro-organism which produces disease in plants.

1934 in WEBSTER. **1943** *Phytopathology* XXXIII. 314 Experiments were performed to determine for the growth of the bacterial phytopathogens the suitability of a medium containing asparagin as the sole source of both carbon and nitrogen. **1959** *Ann. Rev. Microbiol.* XIII. 225 Pectinolytic enzymes are commonly formed by bacterial phytopathogens. **1976** *Nature* 15 Apr. 604/1 The ecological success of bracken is partly a result of its extensive rhizome system, and because of its ability to synthesise various secondary compounds which deter predators and phytopathogens.

phytopathogenic (ˌfaɪtəʊpæθəʊˈdʒɛnɪk), *a.* *Biol.* [f. PHYTO- + PATHOGENIC *a.*] Producing disease in plants. Hence **ˌphytopathogeˈnicity**; the property of being phytopathogenic.

1925 *Jrnl. Path. & Bacteriol.* XXVIII. 203 (*heading*) The investigation of phytopathogenic bacteria by serological and biochemical methods. *Ibid.*, An extensive literature has developed..with regard to the morphology and pathogenicity of various organisms isolated from phytopathogenic lesions. **1959** *Ann. Rev. Microbiol.* XIII. 224 Considerable effort has been expended in recent years in relating phytopathogenicity to discrete bacterial substances ('toxins') which induce disease symptoms in the host plant. *Ibid.* 225 Certain polysaccharides produced by phytopathogenic bacteria *in vitro* possess wilt-inducing properties. **1973** *Nature* 9 Mar. 87/3 Previous studies.. postulated a symbiotic or parasitic relationship between phytopathogenic bacteria and insect 'hosts'.

phytopathology, etc.: see PHYTO-.

phyˈtophagan, *a.* and *sb.* [f. mod.L. *Phytophaga* (see PHYTOPHAGOUS) + -AN.]

a. *adj.* Of or belonging to the *Phytophaga* in any sense. **b.** *sb.* A member of the *Phytophaga*, a vegetable-feeding animal of any class or order.

1890 in *Cent. Dict.*

phytophagic (faɪtəʊˈfædʒɪk, fɪtəʊ-), *a.* *Zool.* [f. as next + -IC.] Of or pertaining to phytophagy; derived from or caused by phytophagy: said of variation of the colouring of insect larvæ attributed to the plants on which they feed.

1866 DARWIN *Orig. Spec.* ii. (ed. 4) 55 These cases he [B. D. Walsh] has fully described under the terms of Phytophagic varieties and Phytophagic species. **1885** POULTON in *Proc. Roy. Soc.* XXXVIII. 313 Such effects are entirely inexplicable by the simple theory of phytophagic influence,..it would be wiser to abandon the term 'phytophagic', at any rate in the sense of producing these changes. The term still holds good for the broad fact that pigments derived from the food-plant play a most important part in larval coloration. **1887** J. T. GULICK in *Linn. Soc. Jrnl., Zool.* (1890) XX. 226 The innumerable cases where phytophagic varieties..of insects exist.

phytophagous (faɪˈtɒfəgəs, fɪt-), *a.* *Zool.* [f. Gr. φυτό-ν plant + -φάγ-ος eating + -OUS (see -PHAGOUS): cf. mod.L. *Phytophaga*, *-phagi.*]

a. Feeding on plants or vegetable substances: chiefly said of insects, molluscs, and the like. **b.** Belonging to the *Phytophaga*, a name given to various groups and divisions of animals, e.g. (*a*) leaf-beetles and their allies, (*b*) sawflies and horntails, (*c*) certain cyprinoid fishes, (*d*) the plant-eating edentates, (*e*) the plant-eating placental mammals.

1826 KIRBY & SP. *Entomol.* xlix. IV. 479 Out of a list of.. 8000 British insects..3724 [might be called] phytiphagous. *Note.* We employ this term, because the more common one, 'herbivorous', does not properly include devourers of timber, fungi, etc. **1832** LYELL *Princ. Geol.* II 143 It may deprive a large number of phytophagous animals of their food. **1876** D. WILSON *Preh. Man* (ed. 3) I. xv. 374 This phytophagous cetacean [the Manatee]..is found only in tropical waters. **1895** *Edin. Rev.* Oct. 371 Some of the true slugs are carnivorous instead of phytophagous.

phytophagy (faɪˈtɒfədʒɪ, fɪt-). [f. Gr. φυτόν plant + -φαγία eating.] The habit of feeding on plants or vegetable matter.

1890 in *Cent. Dict.*

phytophilous to **-phthirian**: see PHYTO-.

phytophthora (faɪˈtɒfθərə). [mod.L., f. PHYTO- + Gr. φθορά destruction.] A fungus of the genus so called, belonging to the order Peronosporales and including several parasitic species which damage plants, esp. *Phytophthora infestans*, the cause of potato blight. Also *attrib.*

[**1876** A. DE BARY in *Jrnl. Bot.* XIV. 106 The characters.. divide the..*Peronosporeæ* generally into two, perhaps better into three, genera, *Cystopus*, *Peronospora*, and a third, which may be called *Phytophthera*.] *Ibid.* 109 Up to this time the sexual organs have not been observed in *Phytophthora*, the Potato-fungus. **1925** *Jrnl. Agric. Res.* XXX. 463/2 Practically all of the fruit on the ground showed the typical symptoms of Phytophthora rot. **1930** *Phytopathology* XX. 209 Oospores had been reported previously in these two Phytophthoras. **1961** A. SCHOENFELD tr. *Stapp's Bacterial Plant Pathogens* II. 127 Together with *phytophthora* rot and leaf curl disease, it [*sc.* bacterial ring-rot] is..one of the three most severe potato diseases in the U.S.A. **1969** HAWKES & HJARTING *Potatoes of Argentina, Brazil, Paraguay, & Uruguay* II. 266 It may therefore be possible to transfer valuable qualities of *Phytophthora* resistance from these Mexican series.

phytoplankter (ˈfaɪtəʊplæŋktə(r)). *Biol.* [f. PHYTO- + PLANKTER.] A phytoplanktonic individual or species.

1957 G. E. HUTCHINSON *Treat. Limnol.* I. xiv. 798 Apart from diatoms, a few phytoplankters use silica. **1960** N. POLUNIN *Introd. Plant Geogr.* xvi. 517 The rate of sinking of a body heavier than water, as most phytoplankters (phytoplanktonic individuals) are, depends upon the ratio of surplus weight to friction. **1967** *New Scientist* 2 Feb. 276/3 The zoologist studies the nutritional requirements and efficiencies of food conversion of marine animals (zooplankters) feeding on marine phytoplankters or other small animals. **1972** *Science* 5 May 535/1 These substances are rapidly absorbed from water by organisms, including phytoplankters. **1976** *Nature* 17 June 584/1 *Gonyaulax*, a marine phytoplankter, is normally grown in a medium of approximately 500 mM salt.

phytoplankton (ˈfaɪtəʊplæŋktən). *Biol.* [f. PHYTO- + PLANKTON.] The microscopic plants forming part of the plankton. Also *attrib.* So **phytoplankˈtonic** *a.*

1897 P. T. CLEVE (*title*) A treatise on the phytoplankton of the Atlantic. **1900** *Geogr. Jrnl.* XV. 336 In the spring months there is a great development of bacteria and other Phytoplankton, which render the water less transparent than at other times of the year. **1909** E. WARMING *Oecol. Plants* xxxvii. 155 Phytoplankton..always consists of minute plants. *Ibid.*, Phytoplankton-organisms are all minute. **1928** *Daily Express* 28 May 10/7 Miss S. M. Marshall..is described technically as the 'phytoplankton worker'. **1944** *Jrnl. Marine Biol. Assoc.* XXVI. 285 Phytoplanktonic diatoms may utilize ammonium nitrogen in preference to nitrate nitrogen. **1956** *Nature* 3 Mar. 438/1 Smaller phytoplankton elements which will pass through the finest nets are of great importance in the productivity of the oceans. **1957** G. E. HUTCHINSON *Treat. Limnol.* I. xi. 714 These forms of iron may be assimilable by diatoms and perhaps by other phytoplanktonic organisms. **1964** *Oceanogr. & Marine Biol.* II. 137 Possibly fallout from a phytoplankton bloom would sometimes cause the immediate surface organisms to multiply. *Ibid.* 149 The amino acid compositions of phytoplankton and pure cultures of phytoplanktonic species have been determined. **1973** *Nature* 3 Aug. 307/1 The crustaceans in turn feed at least partially on the phytoplankton. **1977** P. B. & J. S. MEDAWAR *Life Sci.* i. 17 The most important—because they are the most abundant—organisms involved in the capture of carbon dioxide and the liberation of oxygen are forest trees and minute plants carried in the surface layers of the sea—'phytoplankton'.

phytosanitary (ˌfaɪtəʊˈsænɪtərɪ), *a.* [f. PHYTO- + SANITARY *a.*] Pertaining to the health of plants; applied *spec.* to a certificate stating a plant is free from infectious diseases.

1949 L. LING *Digest of Plant Quarantine Regulations* (U.N. Food & Agric. Organization) July 5 Importation into Belgian Congo requires a special permit in accordance with the prescribed conditions: the presentation of a phytosanitary certificate of origin. *Ibid.* 35 Shipments of plant materials must be accompanied by certificates indicating origin and phyto-sanitary conditions. **1960** E. GRAM in Horsfall & Dimond *Plant Path.* III. ix. 332 Countries with no phytosanitary service..are the happy hunting grounds of botanists and geneticists. **1976** *Nature* 12 Feb. 449/2 Much of this material is accompanied by phytosanitary certificates of the exporting countries which are not necessarily the countries of origin.

phytoscopic: see PHYTO-.

phytosociology (ˌfaɪtəʊsəʊʃɪˈɒlədʒɪ, -səʊsɪˈɒl-). [ad. Russ. *fitosotsiologiya*: see PHYTO- and SOCIOLOGY.] The study of plant communities, their composition and structure. So **phytosocioˈlogical**, *a.*, **phytosocioˈlogically** *adv.*; **phytosociˈologist**, one engaged in this study.

1928 K. D. GLINKA in *Proc. & Papers 1st Internat. Congr. Soil Sci.* I. 129 These ideas of Dokuchaiev could not but have the greatest influence on Russian works referring to.. botanical geography, phytosociology, forestry. *Ibid.*, The present day phytosociologist begins to pay an increasing attention to the geography and topography of soils. **1928** *Jrnl. Ecol.* XVI. 18 The establishment of ecological series of spruce communities gives us a clear idea of the phytosociological and genetical relations between these communities. **1932** FULLER & CONARD tr. *Braun-Blanquet's Plant Sociol.* p. vii, Phytosociology, the study of vegetation, has had a very rapid development. **1955** *Jrnl. Ecol.* XLIII. 226 (*heading*) The use of phytosociological methods in ecological investigations. *Ibid.* 227 Plant sociology (or phytosociology) is defined as the discipline which concerns itself with the study of vegetation as such, with its floristic composition, structure, development and distribution. **1967** M. E. HALE *Biol. Lichens* vii. 87 Phytosociology is probably the most thoroughly investigated aspect of lichen biology. **1969** *Nature* 19 Apr. 242/2 Specialized communities..are phytosociologically distinct. **1970** *Watsonia* VIII. 172 The phytosociological classification of the vegetation of the limestone dales. **1973** *Nature* 30 Mar. 354/2 In the chapter dealing with the phytosociology of heathlands, the reader might be forgiven for gaining the impression that..the southern limit of heathland is France. *Ibid.* 21–28 Dec. 537/1 Continental phytosociologists may feel that some of their carefully defined association binomials have been applied a little loosely. **1974** *Ibid.* 24 May 307/3 Bushmeat species are remarkably resistant to infections that kill domestic stock, and they seldom destroy the phytosociological structure of their habitats. **1976** *Jrnl. R. Soc. Arts* CXXIV. 640/2 Between 1960 and 1973 botanical surveys and collections of plants were made throughout the maritime Antarctic and South Georgia. From these, descriptive floras together with ecological and phytosociological accounts have been produced. **1977** *Dædalus* Fall 130 In some of its branches, such as biogeography and phytosociology, the systems of classification and quantitative description reached phantasmagoric extremes.

phytosterol (faɪˈtɒstərɒl). *Biochem.* [f. PHYTO- + -STEROL.] Any of a large class of sterols which are found in plants; orig. *spec.* = *phytosterin* s.v. PHYTO-.

1898 *Jrnl. Chem. Soc.* LXXIV. I. 598 The soluble fat, which is dark green, consists principally of the ethereal salts of phytosterol, $C_{26}H_{44}O + H_2O$ (melting at 137°), and oleic and palmitic acids. **1906** *Ibid.* XC. II. 311 The author has submitted a number of cholesterols and phytosterols to Neuberg and Rauchwerger's colour test. **1915** J. LONDON *Jacket* v. 34 Professor Schleimer had similarly been collaborating with me in the detection of phytosterol in mixtures of animal and vegetable fats. **1939** MEYER & ANDERSON *Plant Physiol.* xxiii. 396 Cholesterol is not known to occur in the higher plants, but a number of similar compounds, known as the phytosterols, have been isolated from plant tissues. **1975** D. JARVIS tr. *Hess's Plant Physiol.* 108 The biosynthesis of the phytosterols..is not completely understood.

phytotaxy to **-teratology**: see PHYTO-.

phyˈtotomist. [f. PHYTOTOM-Y + -IST.] One who is versed in vegetable anatomy.

1848 LINDLEY *Introd. Bot.* (ed. 4) I. 16 This admirable phytotomist.

phyˈtotomous, *a. rare.* [f. Gr. φυτό-ν plant + -τόμος cutting + -OUS.] Plant-cutting, leaf-cutting, as an insect or bird.

1890 in *Cent. Dict.*

phytotomy (faɪˈtɒtəmɪ, fɪt-). [f. Gr. φυτό-ν plant + -τομία a cutting.] The dissection of plants; vegetable anatomy.

1844 DUNGLISON *Med. Lex.* s.v. *Anatomy*, *Phytotomy* is the anatomy of vegetables. **1875** SIR W. TURNER in *Encycl. Brit.* I. 799/1 Vegetable Anatomy or Phytotomy. **1880** GRAY *Struct. Bot.* (ed. 6) Introd. 2 *Phytotomy*, or *Vegetable Anatomy*, the study of the minute structure of vegetables as revealed by the microscope.

phytotoxic (faɪtəʊˈtɒksɪk), *a.* [f. PHYTO- + TOXIC *a.*] Poisonous or injurious to plants.

1933 *Proc. Nat. Acad. Sci.* XIX. 487 Macht showed that the blood of leprosy patients also gives a specific phytotoxic reaction. **1953** *Phytopathology* XLIII. 663/1 Ethylene.. arises from plant tissue injured by such phytotoxic compounds as endothal. **1963** *Ann. Rev. Microbiol.* XVII. 223 The injurious effects of phytotoxic materials traditionally have been treated as plant diseases. **1976** *Weed Abstr.* XXV. 108/1 No treatment was phytotoxic to the blueberries.

Hence ˌ**phytotoˈxicity**, the property of being phytotoxic.

1945 J. G. HORSFALL *Fungicides* xvi. 172 Phytotoxicity is a term to describe the injuriousness of fungicides to host plants. **1958** *Times* 4 Dec. 1/5 (Advt.), Agricultural Research Council require a Plant Physiologist..to work on fundamental aspects of phytotoxicity. **1974** *Nature* 8 Feb. 337/3 Fungicides..must be selected and timed so that disease control is achieved with minimal phytotoxicity.

phytotoxicant (faɪtəʊˈtɒksɪkənt). [f. PHYTO- + TOXICANT *a.* and *sb.*] A substance poisonous or injurious to plants; *esp.* one present in the air. Also *attrib.* or as *adj.*

1959 *Internat. Jrnl. Air Pollution* I. 160 The decreased damage at the higher olefin concentration can be explained by the more rapid consumption of ozone to form the phytotoxicant which then partly decomposes before reaching the plants. **1961** *Ann. Rev. Plant Physiol.* XII. 431 The principal phytotoxicants recognized several decades ago were fairly specific, simple molecules, such as ethylene, fluorides, hydrogen sulfide, and sulfur dioxide. **1971** *McGraw-Hill Yearbk. Sci. & Technol.* 91/2, O_3 has been recognized as a phytotoxicant for at least 100 years. **1977** I. M. CAMPBELL *Energy & Atmosphere* viii. 248 The level of sophistication which has now been attained has resulted in the identification of single phytotoxicant species, together with the development..of computer simulation procedures for photochemical smog formation.

phytotoxin (faɪtəʊˈtɒksɪn). [f. PHYTO- + TOXIN.] **1.** Any toxin derived from a plant.

1909 R. J. M. BUCHANAN *Blood in Health & Dis.* xii. 289 Of chemical agents causing hæmorrhage, bacterial products take a prominent place, but many poisons, phytotoxins (plant poisons), zootoxins (animal poisons)..are especially effective. **1924** *Chem. Abstr.* XVIII. 1857 (*heading*) The protein phytotoxins, with special reference to the new 'modeccin'. **1974** *Nature* 18 Oct. 628/1 Very low concentrations of phytotoxins can kill mammalian cells, and some of them..have been reported to suppress protein synthesis in cells and cell-free systems.

2. A substance poisonous or injurious to plants, esp. one produced by a parasite.

1962 *Phytopathology* LII. 586/1 (*heading*) Production of a phytotoxin by *Rhizoctonia solani*. **1963** *Ann. Rev. Microbiol.* XVII. 224 The term 'phytotoxin' will be used for all products of living organisms toxic to plants. The designation, phytotoxin, does not imply that such a material plays any role whatever in relation to any disease caused by a pathogen. **1970** STROBEL & MATHRE *Outl. Plant Path.* xxii. 318 Phytotoxins induce few or none of the symptoms usually caused by the pathogen from which they originate. Compounds such as lycomarasmin, altemaric acid, and numerous smaller molecular weight organic acids fall into this category.

phytotron (ˈfaɪtətrɒn). [f. PHYTO- + -TRON: see quot. 1949.] A laboratory where plants can be maintained and studied under a wide range of controlled conditions.

1949 *Plant Physiol.* XXIV. 553 The word phytotron was coined for the new laboratory by Dr. R. A. Millikan.. who feels that it will play the same role in plant physiology and the applied plant sciences.. as the cyclotron has already had in pure and applied physics. **1958** *Observer* 7 Sept. 8/4 The Australian Government is to spend £500,000 on a new type of phytotron. **1974** *Telegraph* (Brisbane) 23 Sept. 6/6 The phytotron would enable scientists to grow four crops of rice a year and thus speed up research. **1976** *Sci. Amer.* Mar. 129/2 A phytotron is a combination of temperature-controlled greenhouses and artificially lighted rooms; here temperature, light and humidity can be controlled at will for the purpose of studying the response of plants to their environment.

phytovitellin: see PHYTO-.

‖**phytozoon** (faɪtəʊˈzəʊən, fɪtəʊ-). Also phytoˈzoum. Pl. -ˈzoa. [f. Gr. φυτό-ν plant + ζῷον animal; lit. 'plant-animal'; cf. *zoophyte*.]

1. *Zool.* A plant-like animal or zoophyte; a single polyp in a zoophyte. (The pl. *Phytozoa* has been variously applied in different classifications to animals supposed to be plant-like in some way, but is not a term of modern Zoology.)

1842 BRANDE *Dict. Sc.*, etc., *Phytozoons, Phytozoa*,.. this term is applied by various naturalists to different sections of the sub-kingdom *Zoophyta* of Cuvier. **1846** DANA *Zooph.* i. (1848) 7 *note*, Ehrenberg has proposed to substitute *phytozoa*, derived from the same roots [as Zoophyte].. and phytozoum refers only to a single polyp. **1858** MAYNE *Expos. Lex.*, *Phytozoum*, applied by Eichwald to a type of the animal kingdom comprehending animals in which (*Polypi, Hydræ, Corallia*) the inorganic texture gives place to that of vegetables, the exterior only presenting the character of animality in the homogeneous mass which constitutes it. **1861** H. MACMILLAN *Footnotes fr. Nat.* 31 This granular matter.. is resolved into a mass of apparently living animalcules called *phytozoa*.

2. *Bot.* A male generative cell, a spermatozoid.

1861 BENTLEY *Man. Bot.* 370 Minute cells called sperm-cells,.. in which are developed spiral ciliated filaments,.. termed spermatozoids or phytozoa.

phytyl: see PHYTOL.

phyz, variant of PHIZ, face.

phyzog, var. PHIZOG.

pi (paɪ), *sb.*[1] The name of the Greek letter π (in Gr. πῖ, (piː)). **1.** Used in *Math.* to express the ratio of the circumference or periphery (περιφέρεια) of a circle to its diameter: see P (the letter) II.

[**1748** EULER *Introd. in Anal. Infinit.* I. viii. (1797) I. 93 Satis liquet Peripheriam hujus Circuli in numeris rationalibus exacte exprimi non posse, per approximationes autem inventa est.. esse = 3,14159 [etc., to 128 places], pro quo numero, brevitatis ergo, scribam π, ita ut sit π = Semicircumferentiæ Circuli, cujus Radius = 1, seu π erit longitudo Arcus 180 graduum. **1841** *Penny Cycl.* XIX. 186/1 This number π must be the same for all circles. *Ibid.* 186/2 This measure of Archimedes gives 3·14286 for the approximate value of π, the ratio of the circumference to the diameter.]

2. *Electr.* Applied to a four-terminal set of three circuit elements in which one element is in series between two in parallel. Usu. written as π or *Π*.

1924 K. S. JOHNSON *Transmission Circuits for Teleph. Communication* xi. 124 If the structure shown in Fig. 1 is considered to be made up of *Π* sections.., each section may be regarded as terminating in a mid-shunt iterative impedance. **1930** DANNATT & DALGLEISH *Electr. Power Transmission* v. 118 This network is frequently used as an equivalent circuit for a transmission line, and is referred to as a π-circuit. **1930** [see *ladder network* s.v. LADDER *sb.* 6]. **1950** [see LATTICE *sb.* 2 d]. **1961** *Amat. Radio Handbk.* (ed. 3) vi. 175/1 The pi-network coupler is often used for delivering power to an aerial feeder. **1972** R. H. WARRING *Ham Radio* v. 68 The adoption of a pi-network tank circuit does not automatically ensure that no harmonics are radiated which may show up.. on near-by television receivers, when a transmitter is being worked on the various amateur bands.

3. *Physics* and *Chem.* [After P III. 2.] Used to designate electrons, orbitals, molecular states, etc., possessing one unit of angular momentum about an internuclear axis; *pi-* (or π-) *bond*, a bond formed by a π-orbital.

Usu. written π when it refers to one electron or orbital and *Π* when it refers to a molecule as a whole.

1929 R. S. MULLIKEN in *Chem. Rev.* VI. 532 The molecule contains two $1s\sigma$ electrons ($1s\sigma^2$).. and two $3s\sigma$ electrons, and (in NO and O_2) one or two $3p\pi$ electrons... The second (Greek) letter gives the value of a quantum number λ which does not exist for the atom, (σ, π, δ, ... mean λ = 0, 1, 2, ...). *Ibid.* 534 Two σ electrons of any one kind.., or four π, or δ, electrons of any one kind.. constitute a closed shell for a diatomic molecule. **1930** —— in *Physical Rev.* XXXVI. 616 The use of the symbols *Σ, Π, Δ, Φ, Γ, H*,.. to indicate *Λ* = 0, 1, 2, 3, 4, 5,.. is recommended. **1939** J. W. T. SPINKS tr. *Herzberg's Molecular Spectra* I. v. 291 Examples of $^2\Sigma - {}^2\Pi$ transitions are the ultraviolet OH bands. **1947** *Q. Rev. Chem. Soc.* I. 157 A double bond is normally a σ-bond and a π-bond together. **1952** L. N. FERGUSON *Electron Struct. Org. Molecules* ii. 19 The π electrons are bound less firmly and can be more easily polarized (that is, attracted to either end of the molecular orbital) than σ electrons, so the former are commonly referred to as mobile electrons, whereas the σ electrons are said to be localized. **1954** G. I. BROWN *Introd. Electronic Theories Org. Chem.* iv. 49 Two atoms linked by a σ-bond can rotate freely about the bond, unless there is some steric interference.., but free rotation is prevented when two atoms are linked by a π-bond. **1964** D. F. EGGERS et al. *Physical Chem.* xvi. 630 Since many molecular properties seem to be governed largely by the pi electrons, most theoretical calculations for such molecules are carried out for the pi electrons only. **1966** *New Scientist* 29 Dec. 735/2 So-called pi-bonded systems containing alternating sequences of single and double bonds. **1972** J. C. SCHUG *Introd. Quantum Chem.* xi. 263 The remaining six valence electrons [in the benzene molecule] occupy the unhybridized *p* orbitals of the carbon atoms, which are perpendicular to the plane of the molecule... Each of these so-called pi electrons can be paired with a pi electron on a neighboring atom to form three additional pi-type bonds, as in ethylene. **1973** A. W. ADAMSON *Textbk. Physical Chem.* xvii. 838 Pi bonding is considered not so much as providing the primary bonding holding a molecule together as supplementing an already present sigma bond. **1975** H. W. KROTO *Molecular Rotation Spectra* x. 224 The $^2\Pi$ ground state of NO.. has both orbital and spin angular momentum.

pi (paɪ), *a.* (*sb.*[2]) *Public School* and *Univ. slang.* [abbrev. of PIOUS.] Pious, religious, sanctimonious. Also *absol.* = a pious person; and as *sb.* = pious exhortation, etc. See also PIE *a.*[1]

c **1870** [at Eton], 'What did your tutor say to you?' 'Oh, he gave me a pi; asked me how I could reconcile my behaviour with my duty to God and my parents'. **1891** WRENCH *Winchester Word-bk.*, *Pi*, virtuous, sanctimonious. He's very pi now, he mugs all day. **1897** *Westm. Gaz.* 1 Sept. 8/1 The man who regularly affects the 'pi' and who 'plays up', with ready catholicity of spirit, the 'special missions' of every religious denomination in turn. **1916** [see FIT *a.* 5 b]. **1968** J. R. ACKERLEY *My Father & Myself* viii. 79 He invited the two of us into the billiard-room.. for a 'jaw', which could hardly be called 'pi' and which he himself described as 'man to man'. **1972** *South China Morning Post* (Hong Kong) 20 Nov. 16/4 The subject emerges, I believe falsely, as a kind of overgrown school-prefect, bossy, frustrated and a bit pi. **1975** J. HITCHMAN *Such Strange Lady* ii. 27 'That were only sparrers... They aren't good for nothing.' 'God made them,' retorted the clergyman's daughter, 'so they must be good for something.' All very pi' of course. **1978** *Broadcast* 3 Apr. 42/2 'Blue Peter', though never pi or holier than thou, is always on the side of the.. decencies.

pi, variant of PIE *sb.*[4] and *v.*[2] (disordered type, etc.); also of PIE *sb.*[5] (Indian copper coin).

pia[1] (ˈpaɪə). *Anat.* Short for PIA MATER.

1889 *Buck's Handbk. Med. Sc.* VIII 111 The successive coverings of the brain, hairy scalp, periosteum, calva, dura (ental periosteum), arachnoid, and pia. *Ibid.*, The ental surface of the pia. **1901** W. OSLER *Princ. & Pract. Med.* (ed. 4) 28 The most intense congestion of the cerebral and spinal pia.

‖**pia**[2]. Also **pya**. A Polynesian name for species of the monocotyledonous genus *Tacca*, some of which, esp. *T. pinnatifida* and *T. maculata*, are cultivated for their tubers, from which South-sea or Tahiti arrowroot is produced.

1858 HOGG *Veg. Kingd.* 765 *Tacca oceanica*, a native of the Sandwich Islands, yields a similar product [arrowroot] and is there called pya. [**1884** MILLER *Plant-n.* 254/1 *Tacca pinnatifida*, Otaheita Salep-plant, Pi-plant, South-Sea-Arrow-root-plant.]

pia-aˈrachnoid, piaˈrachnoid. *Anat.* [f. PIA[1] + ARACHNOID.] The pia mater and the arachnoid, considered as one structure. Also *attrib.*

1889 *Buck's Handbk. Med. Sc.* VIII. 111 The presence on the ental surface of the piarachnoid of a pial fold, the *ruga*. **1896** *Allbutt's Syst. Med.* I. 662 Acute inflammation of the pia-arachnoid. **1904** *Brit. Med. Jrnl.* 20 Aug. 371 An increase of pia-arachnoid fluid.

‖**piaba** (piːˈɑːbə). [Tupi *piaba*, also *piav', piau.*] A small fresh-water fish of the size of a minnow, found in Brazilian rivers.

[**1648** MARCGRAVE *Hist. Nat. Brasil.* 170 Piaba Brasiliensibus; magnitudine nostratis Eldrize.. pisciculus 2 aut 3 digitos longus.] **1686** RAY & WILLOUGHBY *Hist. Pisc.* 269. **1753** CHAMBERS *Cycl. Supp.*, *Piaba*,.. the name of a small fresh-water fish.. in the Brasils.. a well-tasted fish, and much esteemed by the Natives. **1846** G. GARDNER *Trav. Brazil* 126. **1869** R. F. BURTON *Highl. Brazil* II. 13 They can catch half-a-dozen sprat-like 'piabas' or 'piaus' by heaving up a calabash full of water.

piaçaba: see PIASSABA.

‖**piache** (piˈatʃe). Also 6–7 piace. [Tamanac (on the Orinoco) *piache*, in Accaway *piatsan* = Carib *piai* PEAI; in Sp. *piache*.] A medicine-man or witch-doctor among the Indians of Central and South America; a PEAI-*man*.

1555 EDEN *Decades* 181 The professours of this secte were called Piaces. **1613** PURCHAS *Pilgrimage* (1614) 826 They call their Priests Piaces. **1852** TH. ROSS tr. *Humboldt's Trav.* I. vi. 248 A resin very much sought after by the Piaches, or Indian sorcerers. **1855** KINGSLEY *Westw. Ho* xxiv, The Piache from whines rose to screams and gesticulations, and then to violent convulsions.

piacle (ˈpaɪək(ə)l). Now *rare*. [a. OF. *piacle* or ad. L. *piaculum*, f. *piāre* to appease: see -CULE.]

†**1.** Expiation; expiatory offering. *Obs.*

1490 CAXTON *Eneydos* xxvii. 103 Telle her.. that she brynge wyth her.. the shepe.. wyth the other pynacles [F. orig. *pinacles*] dedycated to the sacryfice. **1533** BELLENDEN *Livy* II. xvi. (S.T.S.) I. 194 We.. mycht nocht haue purgit ws þarof bot alanerlie be þe sacrifice of piacle [orig. *piaculum*]. **1654** R. CODRINGTON tr. *Iustine* VIII. 126 A Piacle for the sin committed. **1711** G. HICKES *Two Treat. Chr. Priesth.* (1847) II. 164 The LXX.. called the scape-goat.. the piacular goat, because he was offered to be a piacle.

2. A wicked action which calls for expiation; a sin, crime, offence.

1644 HOWELL *Eng. Teares* 178 To glut themselves with one another's bloud.. can there be a greater piacle against nature? **1676** *Doctrine of Devils* 77 Any Crime, Villany, or Piacle whatever. **1880** F. HALL *Doctor Indoctus* 52 Talk of regicide, of cannibalism.. or any other patibulary piacle.

†**b.** Offence, guilt. *Obs.*

1619 BP. J. KING *Serm. 11 Apr.* 52 May I without piacle forget.. what hee then did? *a* **1657** LOVELACE *Poems* (1864) 213 One proclaims it piacle to be sad.

piacular (paɪˈækjʊlə(r)), *a.* [ad. L. *piāculār-is* expiatory, f. *piāculum* PIACLE: see -AR[1]. Cf. F. *piaculaire* (1752).]

1. Making expiation or atonement; expiatory.

1647 OWEN *Death of Death* Wks. 1852 X. 267 He made his Soul an offering for sin—a piacular sacrifice. *a* **1703** BURKITT *On N.T.* Matt. xx. 28 Their piacular victims were ransoms for the life of the offender. **1818** G. S. FABER *Horæ Mosaicæ* II. 239 *note*, [They] do not seem.. to have sufficiently attended to the distinction between *eucharistic* and *piacular* sacrifices. **1871** MACDUFF *Mem. Patmos* xi. 143 The great brazen altar of burnt-offering, where piacular or bloody offerings were alone presented.

2. Requiring or calling for expiation; sinful, wicked, culpable.

1610 BP. HALL *Apol. Brownists* 79 If it were not piacular for you to reade ought of his. **1657** W. MORICE *Coena quasi Κοινη* xx. 175 They held it piacular to eat with sinners. **1728** R. NORTH *Mem. Music* (1846) 16 To add to or alter the instruments or modes, was almost piacular. **1857** DE QUINCEY *Whiggism* Wks. VI. 53 He.. left no stone unturned to cleanse his little.. fold from its piacular pollution.

Hence **piacuˈlarity**, the quality of being piacular: (*a*) expiatory character, (*b*) criminality; **piˈacularly** *adv.*, as an expiatory or atoning sacrifice; **piˈacularness** = *piacularity*.

1702 H. DODWELL *Apol.* §16 in S. Parker *Cicero's De Finibus*, That Philosopher makes the Piacularness of a violent Death to consist in its being without the consent of the Guardian Genius. **1818** G. S. FABER *Horæ Mosaicæ* I. 260 The goat.. was devoted as a sin-offering.. by its being piacularly slain. *Ibid.* 268 The essence of its being a sacrifice does not consist in the outward act of burning; but in the piacularity of the intention. **1864** WEBSTER, *Piacularity*,.. criminality, badness. *De Quincey*.

†**piˈaculary**, *a.* and *sb.* *Obs.* [ad. L. *piāculāris*: see -ARY[2].] **a.** *adj.* = PIACULAR. **b.** *sb.* = PIACLE.

1654 H. L'ESTRANGE *Chas. I* (1655) 59 Enjoyning her Majesty.. to make a progresse to Tyburn, there to present her devotions: A most impious piaculary. *a* **1670** HACKET *Abp. Williams* I. (1693) 102 This was his Piaculary Heresie.

piaculative (paɪˈækjʊlətɪv), *a.* *rare.* [f. L. *piāculum* PIACLE + -ATIVE.] = PIACULAR *a.* 1.

1919 T. S. ELIOT *Poems*, The young are red and pustular Clutching piaculative pence.

†**piˈaculous**, *a.* *Obs.* [f. L. *piācul-um* PIACLE + -OUS.] = PIACULAR 2.

1646 SIR T. BROWNE *Pseud. Ep.* v. xxi. 266 For piaculous it was unto the Romanes to pare their nayles upon the nundinæ. **1658** *Ibid.* III. xxv. 211 Unto the ancient Britains it was piaculous to tast a Goose. **1661** GLANVILL *Van. Dogm.* xv. 139 We think it so piaculous, to go beyond the Ancients.

‖**piˈaculum.** *Obs.* [L. *piāculum*.] = PIACLE.

1601 A. COPLEY *Answ. Let. Jesuited Gent.* 107 Their martyrdomes being to them as a *præmium* for the one, and.. a sufficient *Piaculum* for the other. **1646** J. BENBRIGGE *Usura Accom.* 21 These.. count it a *Piaculum* to live in seiled houses of their owne, whilest the Lords house lies wast. **1678** WOOD *Life* (O.H.S.) II. 422 'Tis a grand piaculum not to beleive the worst of reports.

piaffe (pɪˈæf), *v.* *Horsemanship.* [a. F. *piaffer* (16th c.) to strut, make a show. Cf. *piaffe* sb., ostentation. Ulterior origin uncertain.] *intr.* To advance the diagonally opposite legs (e.g. the right fore leg and the left hind leg) simultaneously, placing them on the ground and resting momentarily while the other two legs are advanced with the same movement; to move with the same step as in the trot, but more slowly.

1761 EARL PEMBROKE *Equitation* (1778) 72 To piaffe in backing is rather too much to be expected in the hurry which [etc.]. **1814** SCOTT *Wav.* lviii, He *piaffed* away.. to the head of Fergus's regiment. **1820** —— *Monast.* xv, Pressing and checking his gay courser, forcing him to piaffe, to caracole, to passage. **1884** *Jaunt in a Junk* xi. 180 Our seafarers saw Neptune's white horses piaffing.. around them.

Hence **piˈaffe** *sb.*, an act of piaffing.

1899 P. ROBINSON in *Contemp. Rev.* Dec. 800 It [a rabbit] diverts itself with queer sidelong cavorts, piaffes, jinklings, and somersaults.

piaffer (pɪˈæfə(r)), *sb.* *Horsemanship.* [f. F. *piaffer* to piaffe, infin. taken sbst.] The action of piaffing; a movement in which the feet are lifted in the same succession as in the trot, but more slowly.

1862 K. GARRARD *Nolan's Syst. Train. Cav. Horses* 65 The slow 'piaffer' is obtained by the slow and alternate pressure of the rider's legs. The quick 'piaffer' by quickening the alternate pressure of the leg. **1884** E. L. ANDERSON *Mod. Horseman.* II. xvii. 147 In the piaffer the horse should move the diagonal legs together and in perfect unison. *Ibid.* 148 A very slow passage to the front, side, or rear is often called the piaffer; but if there is any movement out of place it is not the piaffer.

†**pi'affer**, *v. Obs.* [a. F. *piaffer* pres. inf.: see PIAFFE *v.*] *intr.* = PIAFFE *v.*

1761 EARL PEMBROKE *Equitation* (1778) 51 To piaffer.. advancing gently, and well into the corners, is a very good lesson. **1785** R. CUMBERLAND *Observer* No. 84 III. 232 Pacing and piaffering with every body's eyes upon him.

piage, variant of PEAGE *Obs.*, pedage.

Piagetian (pɪə'ʒiːʃən), *a.* [f. the name of Jean *Piaget* (1896–1980) + -IAN.] Of or pertaining to the theories or methods of Piaget, Swiss educational child psychologist. Also **Piagetan** (pɪ'ɑːʒeɪən).

1960 *Jrnl. Child Psychol.* I. 191 (*heading*) Some points of Piagetian theory in the light of experimental criticism. **1973** *Jrnl. Genetic Psychol.* CXXII. 27 This study has as its point of departure the Piagetan conceptions of the nature and development of logical structures. *Ibid.* CXXIII. 277 The large number of investigations that have tried to establish normative data in the area of Piagetian conservations. **1974** *Nature* 30 Aug. 713/2 The Piagetian tests, which are intended to reflect changes in mental maturity, are sensitive to age differences. **1977** *Language* LIII. 483 Arguing from a Piagetian perspective of cognitive development, B concludes that children know very little about syntax prior to the use of two-word utterances.

piai: see PEAI *sb.*

pial ('paɪəl), *a.* [f. PIA[1] (*pia mater*) + -AL[1].] Of or pertaining to the pia mater.

1889 *Buck's Handbk. Med. Sc.* VIII. 111/1 [see PIA-ARACHNOID]. *Ibid.* 524/1 In some cases also the appropriate adjectives are employed, e.g. pial, dural. **1899** *Allbutt's Syst. Med.* VI. 502 In general paralysis the invasion is always from the pial surface and vascular tracts. *Ibid.* VII. 246 Nerve-fibres ramifying over the pial vessels.

‖**pia mater** ('paɪə 'meɪtə(r)). *Anat.* [med.L.; a somewhat incorrect rendering of the Arabic name *umm raqīqah* 'thin or tender mother' (Ibn Duraid, A.D. 933): cf. names of other investing membranes in *umm* mother, esp. DURA MATER.

(Fanciful explanations of the name are frequent in western writers: cf. quot. 1548.)]

A delicate fibrous and very vascular membrane which forms the innermost of the three *meninges* enveloping the brain and spinal cord; the other two being the *arachnoid* and the *dura mater*. In quots. 1593, 1606 *transf.* = brain.

c **1400** *Lanfranc's Cirurg.* 112 Pia mater enuyrounneþ al þe brayn, & departiþ him into iij celoles þat ben chaumbris. **1525** [see DURA MATER]. **1548–77** VICARY *Anat.* iv, It is called Piamater.. for because it is so softe and tender ouer the brayne, that it nourisheth the brayne and feedeth it, as doth a louing mother vnto her tender childe. **1593** NASHE *Four Lett. Confut.* Wks. (Grosart) II. 272 Thou turmoilst thy pia mater to prove base births better than the ofspring of many discents. **1606** SHAKS. *Tr. & Cr.* II. i. 78 His Piamater is not worth the ninth part of a Sparrow. **1761** *Brit. Mag.* II. 116 An inflammation of the pia mater, which had produced a most furious delirium. **1854** JONES & SIEV. *Pathol. Anat.* (1875) 232 The arachnoid is entirely dependent for its supply of blood upon the pia mater.

fig. **1681** *Whole Duty Nations* 35 It becomes the very ligament and sinews of Government, a pia mater to the sacredness of Authority.

Hence **pia-'matral** *a.*, of or pertaining to the pia mater; = PIAL.

1887 *H. Gray's Anat.* (ed. 11) 805 Between the pia-matral and the arachnoid sheath.

pian (pɪ'æn, pjɑ̃), *sb.* Also **epian**, and in pl. **pians**. [= Sp., Pg. *epian* and *pian*, F. *pian*, a. Galibi (Rio de Janeiro) *pian* (Roulin in Littré, suppl.). Cf. Guarani *pia* 'bubas, granos' (Montoya). Cf. Jas. Platt in *N. & Q.* 10th Ser. I. 5.]

A contagious tropical skin disease, occurring among Negroes, the same as FRAMBŒSIA or YAWS, q.v. (The names *pians* and *yaws* have occasionally been applied to two alleged forms of *frambœsia*. See quots.) Hence **pi'anic** *a.*

[**1768** F. B. DE SAUVAGES *Nosol. Method.* II. 554 Frambæsia; Yaw Guineesium; Epian vel Pian Americanorum.] **1803** T. WINTERBOTTOM *Sierra Leone* II. viii. 139 The Yaws.. is called by the Portuguese on the Coast Boba and by the French Pianes. *Ibid.* 145 Professor Sprengel has.. made a similar division of this disease into Yaws and Pians. **1874** T. H. BURGESS *Man. Dis. Skin* 233 The American disease called *Pian* or *Epian* seems to be identical with that denominated yaws in New Guinea. **1828** *Lancet* 15 Mar. 876/1 The pianic ulcers.. furnish an acrid matter.

Pian ('paɪən), *a.* [f. L. *Pius* (see PIOUS *a.*), a name adopted by several Popes + -AN.] Of or pertaining to Pius; *spec.* of or pertaining to the pontificate or liturgical reforms of Pope Pius V or Pope Pius X.

1916 *Month* Sept. 258 The publication of the Pian Breviary in 1568. **1959** N. ABERCROMBIE *Life & Work Edmund Bishop* v. ix. 353 Converts of Leo XIII's time must learn to curb themselves, and accommodate themselves to 'Pian days'. **1960** *Duckett's Reg.* Mar. 32/2 It was surely the intention of these 'Neo-Gallicans' to rid themselves.. of all that savoured of Trent and the Pian liturgical revision. **1971** *Tablet* 16 Jan. 65/2 Paul VI.. explains.. why the Pian document and Missal of 1570 give way to the Pauline rite.

piane, obs. form of PEONY.

pianet, variant of PIANNET, magpie.

pianette (piːə'nɛt). Also **pianet**. [f. PIANO *sb.*[2] + -ETTE.] 'A very low pianino or upright pianoforte' (Grove); orig. applied to a form introduced into England in 1857; subsequently to other small forms.

1879 WEBSTER Suppl., *Pianette*, a small piano-forte. **1887** MISS E. MONEY *Dutch Maiden* (1888) 89 'I can play any accompaniment you like'—glancing at the piannette in the corner. **1894** FLORA A. STEEL *Potter's Thumb* I. 127 The pianette at which Rose sang her Scotch songs. **1894** G. B. SHAW *How to become Mus. Critic* (1960) 222 Excellent French pianets. **1897** A. BEARDSLEY *Let.* 7 Jan. (1971) 240 Don't feel bound in any way about the pianette. I'm afraid you expected a larger affair. Of course it is quite a small instrument. **1908** G. B. SHAW *Pen Portraits* (1932) 80 Has Chesterton ever spent his last half-crown on an opera by Meyerbeer or Verdi, and sat down at a crazy pianet to roar it and thrash it through?

pianino (piːə'niːnəʊ). [a. It. *pianino*, dim. of *piano*: see PIANO *sb.*[2].] A name originally given to an upright pianoforte, as being smaller than the grand; now esp. applied to a small upright or cottage piano.

1862 *Illustr. Catal. Intern. Exh.* II. 99 A Pianino, or Small Cottage Pianoforte.. an example of the cheapest upright instrument. **1880** MRS. RIDDELL *Myst. Palace Gard.* ii. (1881) 19 Get a little pianino and stand it against the wall.

pianism ('piːənɪz(ə)m). [f. PIANO *sb.*[2] + -ISM.] **a.** The art of pianoforte playing, especially in its technical aspect; execution on the piano. **b.** The art of composing for the piano, *spec.* the particular skill or characteristic style of a composer of music for the piano; the action or art of arranging a musical composition for performance on the piano.

1844 H. F. CHORLEY *Music & Manners* III. 52 Will M. Liszt found a college of poetical pianism? **1883** *American* VII. 158 The reverent student of Beethoven, who would never for a moment subordinate the musical idea to mere 'pianism'. **1889** *Athenæum* 26 Oct. 569/1 A link between the pianism of the Hummel school and that of Franz Liszt. **1889** *Cent. Dict.*, *Pianism*,.. the adaptation of a piece of music to effective performance on the pianoforte. **1892** G. B. SHAW *Music in London 1890–94* (1931) II. 37 Her fault now is that her pianism has outstripped her musicianship. **1934** S. R. NELSON *All about Jazz* ii. 41 The diatonic and chromatic figurations that occur.. in ordinary piano compositions.. have no counterpart in dance pianism. **1946** R. BLESH *Shining Trumpets* (1949) II. xiii. 299 George Zack is as successful at this underworld pianism as any. **1960** [see HAUTE ÉCOLE]. **1961** *Listener* 19 Oct. 627/1 Liszt's pianism (his writing for the instrument as well as the style of performance) is perhaps the least problematic. **1964** *Ibid.* 27 Feb. 373/1 It is worth noting that pure pianism as such came into its own in the Romantic age, and that mastery of the new technical resources of Chopin and Liszt does not necessarily benefit the performance of earlier music. **1971** *Daily Tel.* 8 Mar. 10/2 Mr Lill's pianism was admirable, but its very virtues underlined the absence of a lively interpreting personality. **1971** [see PIANISTICALLY *adv.*]. **1977** *Listener* 17 Nov. 655/1 Young Sorabji seems to have been a composer.. who thought in terms of the most stratospheric achievements of transcendental pianism.

‖**pianissimo** (pja'nissimo, piːə'nɪsɪməʊ), *a.* (*adv.*) *sb. Mus.* [It.:—L. *plānissim-us*, superl. of *plānus*: see PIANO.] **a.** *adj.* Very soft. **b.** *adv.* Very softly. **c.** *sb.* A very soft passage. Abbrev. *pp.* or *ppp.*

1724 *Short Explic. For. Wds. in Mus. Bks.*, *Pianissimo*, or *PPP*, is extream Soft or Low. **1771** P. PARSONS *Newmarket* I. 36 Suffer me with a voice (*piano*) of the gentlest humility, to beg your opinion—but for pity's sake (*pianissimo*) let it be compassionate. **1867** J. HATTON *Tallants of B.* vi, In *pianissimo* passages of solo or chorus. **1883** ANNA K. GREEN *Hand & Ring* x, The last note of the song was dying away in a quivering *pianissimo*. **1890** 'L. FALCONER' *Mlle. Ixe* i. (1891) 21 She played something which was rather monotonous, and never rose above pianissimo. **1901** *Scotsman* 8 Mar. 7/1 All gradations of tone from loudest forte to tenderest pianissimo.

pianist ('piːənɪst). [ad. F. *pianiste*, It. *pianista*: see PIANO *sb.*[2] and -IST.] **a.** A player on the pianoforte.

1839 LONGF. in *Life* (1891) I. 336 Hear that Schlesinger, the great pianist in New York, is dead. **1842** MRS. F. TROLLOPE *Vis. Italy* I. xx. 333 Talberg, the Paganini of pianists. **1887** *Academy* 7 May 333/3 The pianist.. proving himself a good executant and a sound musician.

b. ***pianist's cramp***, hyperkinesis of the forearm, due to excessive piano-playing.

1899 *Allbutt's Syst. Med.* VI. 539 The so-called 'Professional hyperkineses' (writer's cramp, histrionic spasm, pianist's cramp, telegraphist's cramp &c.) admit of a similar explanation.

c. in appositive *Combs.*, as ***pianist-arranger***, ***-composer***, ***-conductor***, ***-leader***.

1955 KEEPNEWS & GRAUER *Pict. Hist. Jazz* xx. 264 Pianist-arranger George Handy.. turned.. to the work of such as Bartok and Stravinsky. **1958** M. WHITE in P. Gammond *Decca Bk. Jazz* xviii. 220 Lew Stone.. had been working as pianist-arranger for Roy Fox's band. **1928** E. BLOM *Romance of Piano* 156 The most accomplished amongst the earliest pianist-composers. **1942** —— *Music in Eng.* vii. 116 Thus arose the new race of pianist-composers which so conspicuously helps to people the musical history of this period, and to which even Mozart and Beethoven in a sense belong. **1959** 'F. NEWTON' *Jazz Scene* ii. 34 A wayward and notable pianist-composer. **1960** *Times* 22 Sept. 16/4 Rachmaninov the pianist-composer. **1934** S. R. NELSON *All about Jazz* v. 105 Claude Lapham.. began his career as a pianist, and appeared as pianist-conductor at such well-known New York theatres as Ziegfeld's. **1955** L. FEATHER *Encycl. Jazz* 185 Rose to prominence as pianist leader of a band that made its bow.. in 1924. **1958** C. Fox in P. Gammond *Decca Bk. Jazz* vii. 97 Another pianist-leader, though not quite of Hines' calibre, was Claude Hopkins.

‖**pianiste** (pjanist). [Fr.] = prec.; but often used in Eng. as if the feminine form.

1841 LONGF. in *Life* (1891) I. xxii. 409 A delightful musician here,—a Miss Sloman,—a pianiste of great talent. **1883** *Daily Tel.* 16 Jan. 3/3 This gifted pianiste is never so happy as when interpreting the music of his famous compatriot. **1885** MISS BRADDON *Wyllard's Weird* III. 58 Improving herself as a singer and a pianiste. **1885** MABEL COLLINS *Prettiest Woman* xviii, I wish some pianiste of the thundering school would attack the piano now.

pianistic (piːə'nɪstɪk), *a.* and *sb. pl.* [f. PIANIST + -IC.] **A.** *adj.* Of, belonging to, or characteristic of, a pianist or pianism. Also, pertaining to or suitable for performance on the piano.

1881 *London Figaro* 2 July 7/2[She] has shared with M. Rubinstein the pianistic honors of this very prolific season. **1893** *Athenæum* 10 June 743/1 Scholastic contrapuntal devices.. combined with the most modern pianistic treatment. **1921** I. SCHARRER in L. Ronald *Music Lovers' Portfolio* III. p. ix/1, First of all, I would emphasise the fact that it is perfect piano music; nothing before or since has been more absolutely pianistic, more thoroughly suited to the instrument. **1931** G. JACOB *Orchestral Technique* v. 50 Note the way in which the pianistic idiom.. has been translated into its orchestral equivalent. **1942** E. PAUL *Narrow St.* xxiii. 203 Only one pupil.. had such pianistic genius. **1950** *Chambers's Encycl.* VIII. 67/1 The same 12-bar pattern.. serves as a basis for the 'Boogie Woogie', a typically pianistic species. **1955** *Times* 4 July 12/4 Two pieces by his mother, Teresa de Rogatis, demonstrated the pianistic fluency of both mother and son. **1958** *Listener* 21 Aug. 285/1 Leonard Borwick's exquisitely pianistic version of Debussy's 'L'Après midi d'un faune'. **1975** *Ibid.* 18 Sept. 378/1 The most outstanding pianistic feat.. Dmitry Alexeev's playing of Prokofiev.

B. *sb. pl.* The art of playing the piano, *spec.* skilful technique in piano-playing.

1950 BLESH & JANIS *They all played Ragtime* viii. 149 The formidable eight-to-the-bar pianistics of Meade Lux Lewis, Albert Ammons of Chicago, and Pete Johnson of Kansas City. **1958** P. GAMMOND *Decca Bk. Jazz* xv. 184 His dazzling and immensely skilful display of pianistics.

Hence **pia'nistically** *adv.*, in a pianistic manner; from a pianistic point of view.

1926 W. C. HANDY *Blues* 20 Instrumentally and in particular pianistically, the mode was backward. **1928** *Daily Tel.* 5 June 9/5 She would have approached nearer to the real Bach if she had thought less pianistically in the matter of tone-colour. **1946** R. BLESH *Shining Trumpets* (1949) xiii. 317 Pianistically, it has passages of great beauty but it is not completely Negroid. **1971** *Daily Tel.* 6 Apr. 12/7 The most remarkable work of the evening pianistically—and pianism was this programme's concern—was the Grand Concert Fantasy on Themes from Bellini's 'Sonnambula'. **1977** *Gramophone* June 63/1 Berman's playing here has a child-like directness allied to playing which is, pianistically, very complex with all manner of material in the inner parts coming interestingly and engagingly through.

piannet, pianet ('paɪənɛt). Now *dial.* Forms: 6–7 **pieannet, pi-, pyannet**, 6–9 **pianot**, 7 **pie-annit, py-annot, pye-annat, pyanit**; *dial.* 8 **pianet, pynot**, 9 **pie-annet, piannot, pianet, pianate, pienet**, etc. [The first element is PIE *sb.*[1]; the second, in early examples, appears to be treated as orig. a distinct word, as if *Annet* or *Annette*, dim. of *Ann*; cf. the dial. synonym *pie-nanny*, and the etym. of *maggot-pie*, *magpie*, also from female names; but in mod. dial. use it is reduced to a mere suffix ('paɪənɛt, 'paɪnɛt), with which cf. F. *pionet* the spotted woodpecker (where *-on-et* is double dim. suffix). See also PIENET.

(*Annet* alone occurs as a local name of the common gull, and of the kittiwake.)]

1. A local name of the magpie.

1599 CHAPMAN *Hum. Dayes Myrth* Plays 1873 I. 76 Nor would I haue.. men.. looke a snuffe like a piannets taile, for nothing but their tailes and formall lockes. **1601** HOLLAND *Pliny* I. 285 There haue been seen Pyannets with long tailes, party coloured and flacked. **1613** MARKHAM *Eng. Husbandman* I. II. v. (1635) 139 From the annoyance of Pye-annats, and such like great birds. **1618** LATHAM *2nd Bk. Falconry* (1633) 99 The Pie-annit, the brauing and chattering Iaye. **1688** R. HOLME *Armoury* II. 249/2 A Mag-Pye.. is termed a Pye and a Pye-Annat, from its cry or chattering note. *c* **1746** J. COLLIER (Tim Bobbin) *View Lanc. Dial.* Wks. (1862) 50, I know Pynots ar os cunning Eawls os wawk'n oth' Yeorth. **1766** PENNANT *Zool.* I. 171 Pianet. **1825** BROCKETT *N.C. Gloss.*, *Pyannet, Pynet*, a magpie. **1828** *Craven Gloss.* (ed. 2), *Pianot*, a magpie.

b. *fig.* Applied to a person: A chatterer.

1594 W. PERCY *Sonn. Coelia* v, Ho, Muses blab you? Not a word Pieannets, or I will gag you.

c. *Comb.*

1600 *Look About You* vi. in Hazl. *Dodsley* VII. 408 Your pianot-chattering humour.

†**2.** Applied to the lesser spotted woodpecker [F. *pionet*]. *Obs.* (Perh. an error of Phillips.)

1706 PHILLIPS, *Piannet*, the lesser Wood-pecker, a Bird speckled with Black and White on the Wings.

‖**piano** (ˈpjano), *a.* (*adv.*) *sb.*[1] [It. *piano*:—L. *plān-us* flat, in later L. of sound, soft, low.]

I. *Mus.* **1. a.** *adj.* Of the expression: Soft, low (also *fig.* gentle, mild, weak). **b.** *adv.* Softly, in a low tone or voice. Abbrev. *p.*

1683 PURCELL *Sonnatas in 3 Parts* Pref., The English Practitioner..will find a few terms of Art perhaps unusual to him, the chief of which are..*Piano*. **1724** *Short Explic. For. Wds. in Mus. Bks.*, *Piano*, or the Letter *P*, signifies Soft or Low. **1762** COLMAN *Musical Lady* I. 11 O Piano, my dear Lady Scrape, Piano. *a* **1817** JANE AUSTEN *Persuasion* (1818) IV. vi. 120 James Benwick is rather too piano for me. **1856** MRS. C. CLARKE tr. *Berlioz' Instrument.* 5 Chords of three or four notes..produce rather a bad effect when played *piano*. **1884** *Blackw. Mag.* Dec. 782/2 The cry for peace will probably become very piano. **1886** BYNNER *A. Surriage* xiv. 157 The music lapsed from *piano* to *pianissimo*. **1900** E. GLYN *Visits of Elizabeth* 188 The Marquis..looked thoroughly worn out and as *piano* as a beaten dog. **1922** A. HUXLEY *Let.* 9 Sept. (1969) 209 Aunt Nettie is with us: but happily she is in a very calm and piano mood so that she is quite an agreeable companion. **1941** [see EXALTÉ *a.*]. **1953** E. M. FORSTER *Hill of Devi* 138 Very piano and tired, poor dear.

2. *sb.* A passage or series of notes sung or played softly; a soft or gentle tone.

1730 in Rimbault *Hist. Pianoforte* (1860) 149 An harpsichord, on which..may be performed..either in the *forts* or *pianos*. **1759** STERNE *Tr. Shandy* I. xix, That soft and irresistible piano of voice. **1859** GEN. P. THOMPSON *Audi Alt.* II. xcvii. 83 A musical performer, who filled his composition with *pianos*.

II. 3. *sb.* A flat or floor in an Italian dwelling-house, hotel, etc.

1860 HAWTHORNE *Marb. Faun* v, He ascended from story to story,..until the glories of the first piano were exchanged ..for a sort of Alpine region. *Ibid.* vii, At the Palazzo Cenci, third piano.

piano (pɪˈænəʊ), *sb.*[2] [a. It. *piano*, shortened from PIANOFORTE or FORTEPIANO. So in Fr., Sp., Pg., Du., Da., and Sw.]

1. a. A musical instrument, the PIANOFORTE.

1803 E. S. BOWNE in *Scribner's Mag.* II. 175/2 There is scarcely a house..without a Piano-forte; the Post Master has an elegant grand Piano. **1807–8** W. IRVING *Salmag.* (1824) 172 To hear a lady give lectures on the piano. **1838** DICKENS *Nich. Nick.* ii, The notes of pianos and harps float in the evening time round the head of the mournful statue. **1880** A. J. HIPKINS in Grove *Dict. Mus.* II. 718/2 Erard..in 1796..accomplished the making of a grand piano. **1890** *Pall Mall G.* 20 Feb. 2/1 The first piano brought to England was made at Rome, and belonged to Fanny Burney's friend Samuel Crispe.

b. Piano-playing.

1946 J. CARY *Moonlight* viii. 55, I was looking forward to some real old romantic piano, with the genuine macassar flavour. **1950** BLESH & JANIS *They all played Ragtime* iii. 55 Turpin, who had pioneered syncopated piano in the Missouri metropolis. **1968** *Blues Unlimited* Sept. 10, I heard ..some straggling piano. **1975** *Listener* 11 Dec. 796/2 A boy with a musical ear, who had picked up piano from an old black man in a city dive. **1978** *Gramophone* July 178/1 He then went on to study piano and finally, almost by accident, conducting.

c. Chiefly *U.S. slang.* = SPARE-RIB.

1911 J. W. HORSLEY *I Remember* xi. 254 Ingenuity and humour are sometimes the parents of slang terms..I was reminded by..'piano' for ribs of beef. **1942** Z. N. HURSTON in *Amer. Mercury* July 96/1 *Piano*, spare ribs (white rib-bones suggest piano keys).

2. *attrib.* and *Comb.* **a.** simple attrib., as *piano bench*, *-case*, *concerto*, *-cover*, *-key*, *-keyboard*, *-lamp*, *-leg*, *-lesson*, *-master*, *-music*, *-packing-case*, *piece*, *-rack*, *recital*, *recording*, *rehearsal*, *solo*, *sonata*, *-stool*; **b.** objective and obj. genitive, as *piano-maker*, *-player* (person or instrument), *-pounder*, *-tuner*; *piano-buying*, *-playing*, *-strumming*, *-thumping*, *-tuning* vbl. sbs. and ppl. adjs.; **c.** instrumental, etc., as *piano-distracted*, *-practising* adjs.; **d.** special combs.: **piano-accordion** (see ACCORDION); **piano-action**, the mechanism by which the impulse of the fingers upon the keys is communicated to the strings; **piano-conductor**, a musician who conducts a band while playing the piano part; **piano-failure**, pianist's cramp; **piano-monitor**, a bar of metal placed a few inches above and before the keys of a piano, on which to rest the wrists of learners; **piano part**, the part assigned to the piano in concerted music; **piano quartet** = *pianoforte quartet* s.v. PIANOFORTE b; **piano quintet** = *pianoforte quintet* s.v. PIANOFORTE b; **piano rag**, a rag for performance on the piano (see RAG *sb.*[5] 2); **piano reduction**, an arrangement of orchestral music for performance on the piano (see REDUCTION 11 d); **piano roll** = *music-roll* (*b*) s.v. MUSIC *sb.* 13 d; also (with hyphen) *attrib.*; **piano-school**, a school for the teaching of piano-playing; also, a method of instruction on the piano; **piano score**, a pianoforte score, *spec.* a condensed version of a full score for performance on the piano; **piano trio** = *pianoforte trio* s.v. PIANOFORTE b; **piano wire**, a special kind of strong steel wire used for the strings of pianos (see quot. 1956); a length of this; cf. *pianoforte wire*; **piano-writing**, composing for the piano.

1914 G. B. SHAW *Pygmalion* (1916) II. 137 Higgins..takes refuge on the *piano bench. **1977** *New Yorker* 19 Sept. 62/3 She picked up the score from the piano bench. **1850** *Rep. Comm. Patents 1849* (U.S.) I. 300 What I claim..is a *piano case or trunk lock. **1876** J. S. INGRAM *Centenn. Exposition* x. 334 Another very creditable piece of work was a rosewood piano-case. **1908** *Sears, Roebuck Catal.* 210/2 Every Beckwith piano case..is double veneered inside and outside. **1879** GROVE *Dict. Mus.* I. 387/2 In the whole of his *piano concertos..we find an allegro, a slow movement, and a finale in quick time. **1934** A. L. BACHARACH *Mus. Compan.* iv. 598 There are far greater depths in the two piano concertos of Brahms. **1975** *Times* 22 Mar. 11/3 With 18 versions of Schumann's piano concerto already available, an immediate reaction to HMV's latest could well be 'why another?' **1934** S. R. NELSON *All about Jazz* ii. 43 The *piano-conductor part of a commercial orchestration is very similar. **1957** MANVELL & HUNTLEY *Technique Film Music* i. 21 A series of scenes involving Lynch and Colonel Cameron, occupying two pages of the piano-conductor score. **1903** *Westm. Gaz.* 31 Aug. 2/3 Probably more neighbours are *piano-distracted than annoyed by marital disagreements. **1899** *Allbutt's Syst. Med.* VIII. 12 In cases of *piano-failure, I always examine carefully the extensors of the wrist and fingers. **1863** *Jrnl. Soc. Arts* 16 Oct. 747/2 The mere motion of a *piano key, without any alteration in the touch required. **1883** 'ANNIE THOMAS' *Mod. Housewife* 151 Their hands have not lost their cunning on the piano-keys. **1898** *Daily News* 20 Dec. 3/1 Shooting rapidly from one end of the *piano-keyboard..to the other. **1896** *Whims* Apr. 72 Ushered in, he found Margaret doing fancy-work under a large *piano-lamp in the parlor. **1897** *McClure's Mag.* Nov. 57 The soft, yellow light from the shaded piano-lamp fell about her. **1909** *Cent. Dict.* Suppl. 996/3 *Piano-lamp*, a lamp intended for use with a piano: usually one with a firm tripod or other base and an adjustable standard by which it can be raised or lowered. **1849** THACKERAY *Pendennis* xvi, Devoted to her mamma and her *piano-lesson. **1842** FRANCIS *Dict. Arts*, etc., **Piano-Monitor*. **1934** A. L. BACHARACH *Mus. Compan.* v. 482 There are..modern chamber works weighted with *piano parts that make as heavy demands on virtuosity as any concerto. **1955** G. ABRAHAM in H. Van Thal *Fanfare for E. Newman* 26 Telling touches were added ..notably the sharpening of the D in the piano-part. **1969** *Listener* 2 Jan. 25/1 Another [friend] was forbidden to have his new work performed unless he omitted some offending clusters from the piano part. **1897** *Sears, Roebuck Catal.* 538/1 Easy and medium *piano pieces..just the collection for home. **1935** E. FARJEON *Nursery in Nineties* 283 We drew up a programme..a group of Harry's last piano-pieces, a Solo by Joe. **1977** K. O'HARA *Ghost of T. Penry* iv. 32 Faintly..came the sound of the same piano piece. **1899** *Allbutt's Syst. Med.* VIII. 12 Cases of break down in *piano-players. **1906** *Chambers's Jrnl.* 31 Mar. 286/2 Anything in the nature of a mechanical piano-player uncontrolled by the taste and discretion of some guiding mind..is naturally abhorrent. Yet the instrument under review is..absolutely automatic. **1907** *Westm. Gaz.* 17 Sept. 10/1 The most rapid growth has been in mechanical piano-players and piano-playing attachments. **1933** H. S. WALPOLE *Vanessa* III. iv. 558 A typist whom Alfred had engaged actually owned a mechanical piano-player, bought of course on hire-purchase. **1964** L. DEIGHTON *Funeral in Berlin* x. 64 The piano-player did a fancy cadenza. **1857** C. G. LELAND in *Graham's Illustr. Mag.* May 458/1 Hans Breitmann gife a barty—dey had *biano-blayin. **1859** GEO. ELIOT *Let.* 7 Oct. (1954) III. 172, I had abundant time and opportunity for hours of piano-playing. **1881** H. JAMES *Portr. Lady* xxi, Speaking of her piano-playing. **1899** *Allbutt's Syst. Med.* VIII. 6 Perfection in any complicated manipulations such as writing, knitting, or piano-playing. **1956** 'C. BLACKSTOCK' *Dewey Death* vii. 169 She persistently told the world about ..her piano playing and her temperament. **1977** *Times* 15 Nov. 17/5 The idiosyncrasy of his piano-playing. **1883** HOWELLS *Register* ii, Some *piano-pounder is there. **1934** A. L. BACHARACH *Mus. Compan.* viii. 488 During the same four years he wrote also a piano trio..and the first of his *piano quartets. **1975** *Radio Times* 15 May 32/3 Dvořák... Piano Quartet in D major, Op. 23: Beaux Arts Trio with Walter Trampler (viola). **1925** E. SACKVILLE-WEST *Piano Quintet* i. 1 A *piano quintet, they were to start in a month's time upon a professional tour on the Continent. **1934** A. L. BACHARACH *Mus. Compan.* viii. 488 There are many who regard this work as the direct ancestor of the great piano quintets of Schumann and Brahms. **1959** *Collins Mus. Encycl.* 525/2 The combination of piano with string quartet is called a piano quintet. **1881** *Scribner's Mag.* XXI. 273/1 On the *piano-rack stood the song she had taught him. **1972** *Jazz & Blues* Oct. 32/1 (Advt.), Joshua Rifkin's first Nonesuch album of piano rags. **1974** *Melody Maker* 20 Apr. 46 The first piano rag publication was 'Mississippi Rag' in 1897 by William H. Kvell. **1881** *Harper's Mag.* May 814/1 *Piano and organ recitals have long been fashionable. **1950** L. SALTER *Going to Concert* 99 At everything but piano recitals, there is a second person involved who has it..in his power to turn the whole affair into a success or a failure. **1972** E. GREENFIELD *Penguin Guide to Bargain Records* No. 3. 297 As a popular piano recital this seems wholly successful. **1962** *Piano recording [see *piano-stool* below]. **1975** *Hi-Fi News* Feb. 131/3 One of the most unspectacularly natural piano recordings I have heard for a long time. [**1944** W. APEL *Harvard Dict. Mus.* (1946) 631/2 *Réduction*, Fr., arrangement. *Piano réduction*, arrangement for piano.] **1966** *Listener* 29 Dec. 976/2 Autograph or copyist's manuscripts are still turning up. To mention one striking find of recent years, a copyist's manuscript of a *piano reduction of the second Prologue of *Romeo and Juliet*. **1979** E. WILKINS et al. tr. *Sel. Lett. Gustav Mahler* 209, I hope you have received the piano reduction. **1966** *Listener* 10 Nov. 704/3, I had coached most of the singers..and I also played for his *piano rehearsals. **1926** WHITEMAN & MCBRIDE *Jazz* viii. 170 The mechanical royalties arising from phonograph and *piano roll records are usually protected in the contract. **1956** M. STEARNS *Story of Jazz* (1957) xiii. 143 Most piano-roll companies employed a hack who could 'rag' any tune for issue on a piano roll. **1965** *Listener* 1 Apr. 501/2 They did make a considerable number of piano-rolls, but with the ascendancy of the gramophone in the twenties, these perforated screeds of paper were relegated to the lumber-room of the past. **1973** *Guardian* 7 Mar. 10 'Maple Leaf Rug' underwrote [Scott] Joplin's reputation... His own piano rolls, cut late in his career when his health was failing, hardly do him justice. **1929** H. CRANE *Let.* 26 Feb. (1965) 339 They've promised to publish *The Bridge*—on sheets as large as a *piano score. **1938** *Oxf. Compan. Mus.* 851/2 A Piano Score is the reduction of an orchestral score to a piano version. **1964** D. FRANCIS *Nerve* ii. 16 My mother's grand piano lay inches deep in piano scores. **1977** R. BARNARD *Death on High C's* xviii. 185 The piano score of *Rigoletto*. **1923** J. REITH *Diary* 19 Mar. (1975) 131 There was no *piano solo so I..got him to play Schubert's 'Marche Militaire'. **1943** L. ABBOTT *Approach to Music* iv. 74 Schubert composed his 'Serenade' as a song, but Liszt transcribed it for piano solo. **1977** *Listener* 17 Feb. 215/3 The atmospheric 'Slow Drag'..includes a delicate piano solo by Kenny Kersey. **1859** A. J. MUNBY *Diary* 25 May in D. Hudson *Munby* (1972) 33 Songs, serious & comic: *piano-sonatas, and duets and trios with violin and violoncello. **1924** M. KENNEDY *Constant Nymph* xvi. 214 A piano sonata which Sebastian was to play at a concert. **1975** *Gramophone* Mar. 1629/1 She could play a piano sonata by ear as a child. **1847** C. BRONTË *Jane Eyre* II. iii. 82 She turned round on the *piano-stool. **1877** E. S. WARD *Story of Avis* 335 Barbara Allen sat on the piano-stool. **1930** G. GREENE *Two Witnesses* 34 We would finish up the evening sitting on either side of him on the piano-stool while he played and sang, in his funny husky tenor voice. **1962** A. NISBETT *Technique Sound Studio* 38 A piano-stool squeak can spoil a piano recording. **1906** *Westm. Gaz.* 11 Aug. 4/3 In these days of universal *piano-thumping. *c* **1909** D. H. LAWRENCE *Collier's Friday Night* (1934) II. 30 I'll bet it was a thump! Pomp! Pomp! (*Makes a piano-thumping gesture.*) **1934** A. L. BACHARACH *Mus. Compan.* vii. 486 The majority of his numerous *piano trios belong to this early period. **1977** *Listener* 20 Jan. 94/2 Detailed analyses of the piano trios, piano sonatas, string quartets and symphonies. **1858** *Boyd's Philad. City Business Directory* 223 (*heading*) *Piano Tuners. **1900** H. A. JONES *Mrs. Dane's Defence* I. 17 A young piano-tuner. **1973** A. CHRISTIE *Postern of Fate* II. iii. 80 It's the gentleman what's come to do the piano... You said I'd have to get a piano tuner. **1897** *Sears, Roebuck Catal.* 538/1 **Piano tuning hammer*... Long Rosewood handle, double head with oblong holes, and single head with star hole. **1974** *Times* 21 Oct. 24/3 (Advt.), Piano tuning and repairs. **1975** *Times* 2 Jan. 3/4 Total of piano-tuning trainees trebled. **1870** *English Mechanic* XII. 215/3 *Piano wire..—What are the different sizes of wire as now used for a 7 octave cottage piano? **1938** J. WILLIAMSON *Surveying & Field Work* (ed. 2) xvii. 430 Two heavy weights are suspended by five piano wires from an overhead frame. **1955** W. GADDIS *Recognitions* I. iv. 161 All you got to do is get them dumb cops on their motorcycles, and string a good piece of piano wire across the road. **1956** A. K. OSBORNE *Encycl. Iron & Steel Industry* 317/1 *Piano wire*, wire made from the best-quality plain carbon steel, with a carbon content of about 0·80% to 0·95%. It is usually drawn to a tensile stress of more than 120 tons per sq. in. **1973** R. BUSBY *Pattern of Violence* viii. 122 Black hostile faces confronted him in an atmosphere as taut as a piano-wire. **1977** *Sci. Amer.* Oct. 74/3 These light-weight gliders gave MacCready the idea of using an aluminum-tube skeleton braced with piano wire. **1946** E. LOCKSPEISER in A. L. Bacharach *Brit. Music* xv. 196 There is often clumsiness in the *piano-writing, too monotonous an insistence on pattern, or a lack of finish in the way he handles a phrase. **1959** D. COOKE *Lang. Mus.* i. 6 Comparisons such as those of piano-writing with black-and-white drawing, of orchestration with colour.

Hence **piˈano** *v. nonce-wd.*, to play the piano.

1855 SMEDLEY *H. Coverdale* xli. 284 She pianos and I do a little in a mild way on the flute.

pianoforte (pɪˌænəʊˈfɔːteɪ, -ˈfɔːt). [a. It. *pianoforte*, earlier *piano e forte* (*pian e forte*) 'soft and strong', occurring in 1598 as the name of a musical instrument of unknown action, and afterwards used by Cristofori in the descriptive name '*gravecembalo col* (or *di*) *piano e forte*', i.e. harpsichord with soft and loud, expressing the gradation of tone which it enables the performer to produce, as contrasted with the unvarying tone of the ordinary harpsichord. So F. *pianoforte*. Formerly also called (in It., Fr., and Eng.) FORTEPIANO, and now generally PIANO *sb.*[2].]

a. A musical instrument producing tones by means of hammers, operated by levers from a keyboard, which strike metal strings, the vibrations being stopped by dampers; it is commonly furnished with pedals for regulating the volume of sound (see PEDAL *sb.* 1 b). The pianoforte (the invention of which is usually ascribed to B. Cristofori of Padua *c* 1710) is essentially a dulcimer provided with keys and dampers, but in other respects imitates the harpsichord and clavichord, of which it has taken the place.

grand pianoforte or *piano*, a large pianoforte, harp-shaped like the harpsichord, and having the strings horizontal and at right angles to the keyboard. *square p.*, rectangular like the clavichord, having the strings horizontal, but parallel to the keyboard. *upright* or *cabinet p.*, rectangular upon edge, having the strings vertical. *oblique*, *boudoir*, or *cottage p.*, upright but lower, having the strings ascending obliquely or diagonally.

1767 *Play-bill of Theatre Royal* Covt. Gard. 16 May, At the end of Act I., Miss Brickler will sing a favourite song from 'Judith', accompanied by Mr. Dibdin, on a new instrument, called Piano Forte. **1767** STERNE *Lett.* lxxxv. Wks. (1839) 770/1 Your pianoforte must be tuned from the brass middle string of your guitar, which is C. **1768** MME. D'ARBLAY *Early Diary* Aug., He asked papa if he play'd much on piano fortes. **1774** *Specif. Jo. Merlin's Patent* No. 1081 The kind of harpsicord called piano forte. **1799** YOUNG in *Phil. Trans.* XC. 135 Take one of the lowest strings of a square piano forte. **1802** ROFF in *Naval Chron.* VIII. 169 He had been employed..to make a grand piano forte. **1879** STAINER *Music of Bible* 73 When the hammers of a dulcimer are connected with levers called 'keys', we call it a pianoforte.

b. *attrib.* and *Comb.*, as ***pianoforte concerto, -maker, -making, -manufactory, -player, -playing, recital, solo, sonata, -tuner***; **pianoforte jump, obstacle**, a jump or obstacle in a steeplechase whose shape resembles that of a pianoforte; **pianoforte quartet**, a quartet for violin, viola, cello, and pianoforte; **pianoforte quintet**, a quintet for pianoforte and string quartet; **pianoforte score** (see quot. 1876); **pianoforte trio**, a trio for violin, cello, and pianoforte; † **pianoforte wire** = *piano wire* s.v. PIANO *sb.*² 2 d.

1932 *Radio Times* 29 July 269/2 Hilda Bor and orchestra —pianoforte concerto in D minor—*Mozart.* **1934** A. L. BACHARACH *Mus. Compan.* iv. 591 The pianoforte concertos of the modern repertory begin with J. S. Bach, who arranged sixteen violin concertos of Vivaldi for the clavier. **1962** G. MOORE *Am I too Loud?* v. 52 Many people in different parts of the world have given it as their opinion that he [*sc.* Solomon] is the finest player of a pianoforte concerto they have ever heard. **1862** *Illustr. Catal. Intern. Exh.* XVI. 89 Patent pianoforte hammer-rails, keys, actions, mouldings, fret carvings, etc. **1908** *Daily Chron.* 9 June 3/5 Some of the Italian officers will give a display of what is known as the Pianoforte jump. **1783** *Specif. J. Broadwood's Patent* No. 1379 John Broadwood, of Great Pulteney Street..piano forte maker. **1909** *Westm. Gaz.* 8 Mar. 6/4 The 'pianoforte' obstacle will consist of four feet of water, followed by a sloping bank of turf with a three-foot wall at the end of it. **1836** DICKENS *Sk. Boz* II. 271 The pianoforte player.. fainted away. **1849** MRS. GASKELL *Let.* 13 May (1966) 829 Benedict the great piano-forte player. **1876** tr. *H. von Ziemssen's Cycl. Med.* XI. 352 Piano-forte player's spasm is of no uncommon occurrence. **1887** C. H. H. PARRY *Stud. Gt. Composers* iv. 108 Haydn is said to have persisted in regarding Beethoven as a pianoforte player, and not as a composer. **1780** MME. D'ARBLAY *Diary* 13 Apr., A lady whose pianoforte-playing I have heard extolled by all here. *a* **1814** *Last Act* II. ii. in *New Brit. Theatre* II. 386 A pianoforte-playing lady. **1883** GROVE *Dict. Mus.* III. 58/2 Next to the string quartet ranks the pianoforte quartet, which, however, is built on quite a different principle. **1954** *Ibid.* (ed. 5) I. 878/1 There is a precedent in the slow movement of Schumann's pianoforte Quartet. **1828** E. HOLMES *Ramble among Musicians of Germany* 282 M. Herder played a pianoforte quintet in E flat of his composition. **1954** *Grove's Dict. Mus.* (ed. 5) I. 877/1 The pianoforte Quintet in F minor..was originally composed, but not published, as a string Quintet with two cellos. **1914** G. B. SHAW *Misalliance* 56 How many of them could be bribed to attend a pianoforte recital by a great player? **1876** STAINER & BARRETT *Dict. Mus. Terms* 353/2 *Pianoforte score*, a score of a vocal or instrumental composition, under which is written in two lines a condensed form of the harmonies for the use of a pianoforte. **1912** W. OWEN *Let.* 11 Jan. (1967) 108, I shall substitute for it a pianoforte solo. **1954** *Grove's Dict. Mus.* (ed. 5) V. 946/2 Of other works for pianoforte solo the Fantasy in C minor..is of special importance. **1883** *Ibid.* (ed. 1) III. 577/1 The slow movements of both are very well known; that of the Pianoforte Sonata being the Funeral March. **1954** *Ibid.* (ed. 5) V. 947/2 It was in fact Mozart's own work in that form and was intended to become part.. of a complete pianoforte sonata. **1889** *Ibid.* (ed. 1) IV. 172/1 Pianoforte trios, as they are called, caused all others to retire into the background. **1954** *Ibid.* (ed. 5) V. 947/2 The pianoforte trios were mainly written for performance at private music meetings. **1801** BUSBY *Dict. Mus.* s.v. *Tuning fork*. This instrument [*sc.* a tuning-fork] is chiefly used by harpischord and piano-forte tuners. **1861** DICKENS *Gt. Expect.* I. xi. 183 At the pianoforte-tuner's across the street. **1838** *Osborne's Guide Grand Junction Railway* (Advt. section) 113 Piano Forte Wires and Roman Strings. **1870** *English Mechanic* 30 Sept. 35/2 Pianoforte wire.—What weights it will support, etc. **1902** *Chambers's Jrnl.* June 413/2 This kite is of the box or Hargreave pattern... Its 'string' consists of four miles of pianoforte-wire.

Hence **piano'forting** *vbl. sb. nonce-wd.*, playing on the pianoforte.

1822 COLERIDGE *Lett.*. *Convers., &c.* II. 159 Piano-forting, which meets one now with Jack-o'-lantern ubiquity in every first and second story in every street.

piano'fortist. *rare.* [f. prec. + -IST.] One who plays on the pianoforte; a pianist.

1841 *Fraser's Mag.* XXV. 400 [This] prevented any debate on the part of the pianofortist. **1893** T. FOWLER in *Class. Rev.* VII. 371 He was an accomplished pianofortist and much interested in the history and theory of music.

pi'anograph. [f. PIANO *sb.*² + -GRAPH.] An instrument which automatically records the notes played on a piano; a form of melograph or music-recorder.

1864 in WEBSTER.

Pianola (piːəˈnəʊlə). Also **pianola.** [app. intended as a dim. of PIANO *sb.*²] Proprietary name of a mechanical contrivance which when attached to a piano can be made to play tunes upon it: see quot. 1901; also, a piano which incorporates such a mechanism, a player-piano. Also *attrib.*

1901 *Scotsman* 5 Mar. 7/1 The pianola..is..a mechanical attachment to the piano..a small cabinet..easily adjustable to the keyboard of the piano and, being fed by a perforated roll of paper, and furnished with wind-power by means of bellows, can play the most difficult music without the performer..touching the keyboard. **1904** *Daily Chron.* 11 Oct. 1/5 The word Pianola is a Registered Trade Mark. **1908** *Daily Chron.* 31 July 5/4 The ingenious contrivance of an Australian engineer who claims to have invented an accurate recording target... The figures are printed on paper, which runs at the required speed on two rollers on what may be described as the pianola principle. **1912** *Collier's* 26 Oct. 23/1 It's usually one of the White Light hits to begin with—and it's odd how exquisite they are on the Pianola. **1916** *Proc. Musical Assoc. 1915–16* 16 The Press have adopted the term 'Pianola' as a generic name for all mechanical piano-player devices. **1943** J. B. PRIESTLEY *Daylight on Saturday* xii. 78 We'll find out..we're not making planes any more but sewing machines and pianolas. **1947** *Sat. Rev. Lit.* (U.S.) 25 Oct. 65/2 Unlike vaudeville, the pianola is not dead. **1953** DYLAN THOMAS *Under Milk Wood* (1954) 10 He sold the pianola. **1962** *Trade Marks Jrnl.* 26 Sept. 1315/2 Pianola... Player-pianos. Aeolian American Corporation.., New York,..United States of America; manufacturers and merchants. **1978** F. WELDON *Praxis* xii. 82 Mrs. Allbright played the pianola with too many stops out. **1980** L. LEWIS *Private Life of Country House* iv. 47 A large walnut Steck piano with pianola player incorporated.

b. = *pianola hand* below.

1974 *Country Life* 9 May 1155/3 With everything right, the [bridge] contract is a pianola.

c. *Comb.*, as ***pianola-like*** adj.; **pianola hand** *Cards*, a hand that is easy to play; **pianola roll** = *music-roll* (*b*) s.v. MUSIC *sb.* 13 d.

1913 F. IRWIN *Auction High-Lights* ii. 22 Which do you like better, a 'pianola' hand or a hand where you have to tussle and fight for every point? **1945** E. BOWEN *Demon Lover* 134 The pianola-like play of the conversation did not drown the nervousness round the table. **1915** *Chicago Daily News Almanac 1916* 615/2 The Coe music collection ..[contains] 560 pianola rolls. **1959** 'F. NEWTON' *Jazz Scene* ii. 33 Old pianola rolls by the leading composer-players of this earliest jazz style.

pianolaed (piːəˈnəʊləd), *a.* [f. PIANOLA + -ED¹.] Rendered by a Pianola.

1926 A. B. SMITH *Studies & Caprices* 176 The pauses.. are not, as in the pianolaed performance, the mere passing of time.

pianoless (pɪˈænəʊlɪs), *a.* [f. PIANO *sb.*² + -LESS.] Without a piano, esp. designating an ensemble of musicians which does not include a pianist.

1955 L. FEATHER *Encycl. Jazz* 66 Gerry Mulligan and others experimented with pianoless units. **1956** M. STEARNS *Story of Jazz* (1957) xviii. 240 Pacific Jazz recorded the pianoless quartet of Chet Baker and Gerry Mulligan. **1973** *Black World* Oct. 48/1 His preferred instrumental format for his own recordings is with pianoless groups.

pianolist (piːəˈnəʊlɪst). [f. PIANOLA + -IST.] A person who plays a Pianola.

1908 G. KOBBÉ (*title*) The pianolist: a guide for pianola players. *Ibid.* 8 Another purpose..is to furnish pianolists with a guide to the music which they play, or might play. **1916** *Proc. Musical Assoc. 1915–16* 24 There are many pianolists so keen that they will cut their own music in unique single copies. **1927** *Observer* 23 Oct. 14 The player seems to have the same sort of relation to his instrument as the pianolist to his.

‖**piano nobile** (ˈpjano ˈnobile). *Archit.* [It., f. *piano* floor, storey + *nobile* noble, great.] The main storey of a large house, usually on the first floor, of lofty structure, and containing the principal apartments.

1909 in *Cent. Dict.* Suppl., s.v. *piano*³. **1910** *Encycl. Brit.* X. 527/1 The principal floor is the storey which contains the chief apartments whether on the ground- or first-floor; in Italy they are always on the latter and known as the 'piano nobile'. **1922** F. G. ELLERTON *Let.* 14 Apr. in J. Bailey *Lett. & Diaries* (1935) 216 The great windows of the *piano nobile* and the fine ones of the second floor where the Strozzi still live after *four hundred and fifty years!* **1928** A. HUXLEY *Point Counter Point* iii. 37 Two flights up, between the *piano nobile* and the servants' quarters under the roof. **1939** J. D. S. PENDLEBURY *Archaeol. Crete* iv. 186 The South Propylaeum, from which access was obtained to the 'piano nobile'. **1955** L. WOOLLEY *Alalakh* iii. 94 The upper floor, the *piano-nobile*, no longer exists, but its principal room, the *grand salon*, can safely be reconstructed. **1965** B. SWEET-ESCOTT *Baker St. Irreg.* vi. 180 On the *piano nobile* was a large room in which Mr Bertram Mills himself had sat. **1970** *Guardian* 16 Sept. 11/1 The 'piano nobile', entered through a colonnaded portico and up a curving flight of carpeted marble. **1974** K. CLARK *Another Part of Wood* vi. 238 The whole *piano nobile*, with beautiful 'Adam' rooms, marble chimney pieces and painted ceilings, was completely unnecessary. **1976** J. LEES-MILNE *W. Beckford* v. 70 The Octagon Cabinet..and the Crimson Breakfast Parlour.. bring the apartments of the *piano nobile* of the Abbey to an end.

pi'ano-'organ. A mechanical piano constructed in the manner of a barrel-organ. So **pi,ano-'organist.**

1844 ALB. SMITH *Adv. Mr. Ledbury* (1856) I. vi. 47 Jack had hired..a piano-organ. **1882** MRS. B. M. CROKER *Proper Pride* I. i. 2 The new piano-organs are grinding away mercilessly at the corner of every street. **1885** W. S. GILBERT *Mikado* I. 9 The piano organist—I've got him on the list! **1900** *Westm. Gaz.* 18 Oct. 8/2 The communal administration of Ixelles, near Brussels, has decided to lease the right of piano organ-grinding in the streets. **1955** L. FEATHER *Encycl. Jazz* 123 Her husband, piano-organist Jesse Crump, worked and recorded with her.

‖**pi'ano pi'ano, pianpiano,** *adv. Obs.* [It., softly, softly.] Softly, gently, in a quiet leisurely manner, little by little.

1601 A. COPLEY *Answ. Let. Jesuited Gent.* 116 Our good men must goe as they may, *pean, peano*, and beare their quips the while. **1687** A. LOVELL tr. *Bergerac's Com. Hist.* 39 That Tyger of a Man being come down *Pian Piano.* **1741–70** ELIZ. CARTER *Lett.* (1808) 5, I go on piano piano with my history of the Incas. **1925** D. H. LAWRENCE *Let.* 25 Nov. (1962) II. 867 But it's no good: we've got to go *piano-piano.*

pianot: see PIANNET, magpie.

‖**pi'ano-vio'lin.** [A combination in which the two elements are arranged in French order, *violin* qualifying *piano*.] A keyed instrument, like the harmonichord, producing tones resembling those of the violin: see quot.

1880 A. J. HIPKINS in Grove *Dict. Mus.* II. 746/1 Chladni much favoured the idea of a piano violin, and under his auspices one was made in 1795 by von Mayer of Görlitz... At last, in 1865, Hubert Cyrille Baudet introduced one in Paris capable of rapid articulation,..patenting it in England as 'Piano-Violin'... The strings are of wire..and attached to a nodal, or nearly nodal, point of each, is a piece of stiff catgut.

piarachnoid: see PIA-ARACHNOID.

Piarist (ˈpaɪərɪst). [f. mod.L. title *patres scholarum piarum* fathers of the religious schools, the Piarists being the regular clerks of the *Scuole Pie* or religious schools.] A member of a Roman Catholic secular order, founded at Rome by St. Joseph Calasanctius shortly before 1600. They devote themselves to the gratuitous instruction of the young.

1842 BRANDE *Dict. Sc.*, etc., *Piarists* (Patres Scholarum Piarum). They still continue to superintend a great number of schools in Hungary, Poland, Bohemia, etc. **1885** *Catholic Dict.* (ed. 3) 661 The Piarists appear to have never entered ..any country outside the limits of Europe. **1901** *N.Y. Even. Post* 7 May 4/3 One of the large religious communities in Hungary, the Piarists, has just refused to admit Jesuit teachers within any of its colleges.

‖**piarrhæmia** (paɪəˈriːmɪə). [mod.L., f. Gr. πῖαρ fat + αἷμα blood.] The presence of fat in the blood, as a normal or as a pathological condition.

1858 MAYNE *Expos. Lex.*, Piarhæmia. **1860** C. T. COOTE in *Lancet* 15 Sept. 259/2 Piarrhæmia consists in an excess of saponifiable fat in the blood, not in the mere liberation of fat from its combinations. **1875** T. H. TANNER *Pract. Med.* I. 24 Piarhæmia is also a physiological result of digestion, pregnancy, lactation, and hybernation.

‖**piassava** (piːəˈsɑːvə). Also **piassaba, piaçaba.** [a. Pg. *pia'ssaba, pia'ssava, piassá* (Michaelis *Pg. Dict.* 1893), a. Tupi *piaçába* (Martius *Dict. Tupi* 1867). (Wrongly stressed in many dictionaries as *pi'assaba*, which is impossible in Tupi.)] A stout woody fibre obtained from the leaf-stalks of two Brazilian palm-trees, *Attalea funifera* and *Leopoldinia Piassaba*, and imported for the manufacture of coarse brooms, brushes, etc.; (also ***piassava fibre***). Sometimes applied to the tree; also, the tropical African palm, *Raphia vinifera*, or the fibre obtained from it.

[**1835** *Penny Cycl.* III. 54/1 *Attalea funifera*, called by the natives piaçaba... The best cordage in America, for naval purposes, is manufactured from the fibres of the leaf-stalks and other parts.] **1857** HENFREY *Elem. Bot.* 394 The bristle-like Piassaba fibres, used for brooms, are from *Leopoldinia Piassaba.* **1858** HOGG *Veg. Kingd.* 759 That fibre, resembling whalebone,..called in commerce Piassaba fibre, Monkey Grass, or Para Grass. **1866** *Treas. Bot., Para piassaba*, a finer and more valuable kind of Piassaba, obtained from *Leopoldinia Piassaba.* **1889** G. S. BOULGER *Uses of Plants* VI. 171 Pará Piassaba, of which the ramenta are used for brushes. **1922** W. SCHLICH *Man. Forestry* (ed. 4) I. 309 The valuable 'piassava fibre' is prepared from the leaves of the bamboo palm. **1936** *Nature* 28 Mar. 528/1 The Hard Fibres Section of the British Empire Producers' Organisation has arranged a comprehensive group of exhibits of sisal and sisal manufacturers... Other stands display..West African piassava. **1957** M. BANTON *W. Afr. City* iii. 43 Kola-nuts are grown in the south,..piassava along the southern coast. **1964** J. P. CLARKE *Three Plays* 21 Let's Sing of souls tied down with ropes Of piassava so strong. *Ibid.* 74 What single harm Have I done that this poison more catching Than fruit from the piassava palm should..be bailed into the stream Of my blood. **1966** E. J. H. CORNER *Nat. Hist. Palms* iii. 65 The thick brown coating of leaf-base fibres of the piassába or chiquichiqui palm *Leopoldinia piassaba*..are made into ropes. *Ibid.* xiv. 331 Piassava, or African bass, is derived from the vascular bundles of the leaf-stalk and sheath [of *Raphia vinifera*]. **1969** E. H. PINTO *Treen* 194 Piassava fibre..has been used in bass brooms for many centuries.

‖**Piast** (pjɑːst, -æ-). [Polish, after *Piast*, the name of the good peasant (reputed to have lived in the 9th c.) from whom the Polish kings were said to be descended.] A native Pole of regal or ducal rank; hence, a man of genuine Polish descent.

[**1684** *Scanderbeg Rediv.* iv. 59 He Advised them rather wholly to lay aside those Foreign pretensions, and chuse a *Piasti*, that is, some Nobleman of their own Countrey.] **1781** JUSTAMOND *Priv. Life Lewis XV*, I. 2 None but Piasts, or Polish Noblemen, born of Catholic fathers and mothers, could pretend to the crown. *c* **1830** TENNYSON *Sonn.* in J. C. Collins *Early Poems* 307 O for those days of Piast, ere the Czar Grew to this strength among his deserts cold. **1847** MRS. A. KERR tr. *Ranke's Hist. Servia* i. 11 Poland had, under the last Piasts, allied itself more closely to the Western States, in order to obtain protection from a similar subjugation.

attrib. **1833** ALISON *Hist. Europe* xvii. (1847) V. 14 The kings of the Piast race made frequent and able efforts to create a gradation of rank in the midst of that democracy.

Piastraccia (pjaˈstratʃa). The name of a quarry near Seravezza, between Carrara and Lucca in

N. Italy, used to designate a variety of white marble with slender grey veins quarried there.

1909 *Westm. Gaz.* 9 June 11/3 The entrance hall and corridor walls are faced with polished Piastraccia and Swedish green marble. **1955** W. Gaddis *Recognitions* III. i. 726 In response to the darkening sky, the sea changed its surface from glass to marble, the Breche rose marble of Italy reflecting the broken color of the sun, and losing that, to the gray-white Piastraccia, reflecting light from nowhere, veined with shadows.

piastre, piaster (pɪˈæstə(r)). Forms: 7 (**piastra, -o**), **pyaster**, 7– **piaster, piastre**. [a. F. *piastre* (1611 Cotgr.), ad. It. *piastra* 'any kind of plate or leafe of mettall' (Florio); as applied to a coin, short for *piastra d'argento* 'plate of silver', applied to the Spanish silver *peso*, whence also to the Turkish coin derived from it.

Piastra represents a late Lat. or Romanic **plastra* for L. *emplastra* (Gell.), by-form of *emplastrum* plaster (cf. It. *piastro* plaster), a. Gr. ἔμπλαστρον (Galen), var. of ἔμπλαστον plaster, f. ἐμπλάσσειν to daub on.]

1. A name, of Italian origin, for the Spanish *peso duro*, piece of eight, or dollar, and its representatives in Spanish America and other countries.

[**1617** Moryson *Itin.* I. 291 At Venice..the Spanish piastro of siluer is giuen for sixe lires.] **1630** Capt. Smith *Trav. & Adv.* iii. 5 Pyasters, Chicqueenes and Sultanies, which is gold and silver. **1674** Blount *Glossogr.* (ed. 4), *Piaster*, a Coyn in Italy, about the value of our Crown. **1776** *Ann. Reg.* 119 At Lisbon..the king..immediately ordered her 20,000 piastres. **1796** H. Hunter tr. *St.-Pierre's Stud. Nat.* (1799) III. 650 The happiness of a people is not to be estimated by the piastres of their traders. **1882** Bithell *Counting-ho. Dict.* (1893) 227 The Spanish Piastre is synonymous with the dollar or duro, sterling value 49·478*d*. *Ibid.* 228 The Spanish Piastre for exchange purposes is an imaginary coin of 5 pesetas or francs = 47·578 pence. *Ibid.*, The Piastre or Mocha Dollar is the unit of value in Arabia, and is worth nearly 3*s* 5*d*.

2. The English (French, German, etc.) name (It., Sp. *piastra*) of a small Turkish coin, called in Turkish *ghūrūsh*, $\frac{1}{100}$ of a Turkish pound, having in Turkey, in 1900, a circulating value of about 2*d*., in Egypt about 2½*d*., and in Tunis about 6*d*.

Originally the Spanish dollar, introduced into the Levant by the Venetians, but rapidly depreciated, being worth in 1618, 5*s*; in 1775, 2*s*. 6*d*.; in 1818, 9½*d*.; in 1877, 2½*d*.; in 1903, 2*d*.

1611 Cotgr., *Piastre*, a Turkish Coyne worth about iiij*s*. sterl. **1617** Moryson *Itin.* I. 276 In Turkey..The coynes..most esteemed..are the siluer ryals of Spaine (which the Italians call *Pezzi d'otto*, and *Pezzi di quattro*, pieces of eight, and pieces of foure, and the Turks call piastri, and halfe piastri). **1775** R. Chandler *Trav. Asia Minor* v. 16 A piaster is about half a crown English. **1819** Byron *Juan* II. cxxv, The sole of many masters Of an ill-gotten million of piastres. **1877** A. B. Edwards *Up Nile* ix. 241 Two silver piastres, or about fivepence English. **1899** J. Aird in *Westm. Gaz.* 8 Mar. 7/2 At Assouan..They get between three and four piastres a day, amounting to about a penny an hour, or five shillings a week.

3. (In form *piastre*.) The name of a unit of currency introduced in Indo-China under French rule in 1885.

1908 *Whitaker's Almanack 1909* 618/1 The financial and political unity of Indo-China was finally established in 1898. .. The revenue, about 51,850,000 piastres, is derived mainly from customs, excise, and other indirect taxes. **1955** [see kip *sb.*[8]]. **1968** R. West *Sk. Vietnam* i. 22 The street hawkers who offer you two hundred and fifty piastres a dollar. **1970** *Daily Tel.* 22 July 14 In Saigon, prices are sky high. The piastre, officially worth 118 to the dollar, is traded by black marketeers at nearly 400 to the dollar. **1977** *Private Eye* 1 Apr. 20/2 (Advt.), 100 piastre (£70 face value) South Vietnamese note.

Piat (ˈpiːət). [Acronym f. the initials of *p*rojector *i*nfantry *a*nti-*t*ank.] A weapon used by infantry against tanks in the war of 1939–45.

1944 *Hutchinson's Pict. Hist. War* 27 Oct. 1943–11 Apr. 1944. 321 The powerful new P.I.A.T. (projector, infantry, anti-tank) loaded and in position for firing... In this demonstration test of the 'Piat', a German tank has received a direct hit. **1948** Partridge *Dict. Forces' Slang* 140 *Piat*, Projector Infantry Anti-Tank. A mortar type of projector designed to destroy tanks at close range... It had a complement of two men, but could be easily handled by one. **1964** A. McKee *Caen* vii. 101 Small parties of infantry, with Piats,..began to stalk the Tigers. **1974** C. Ryan *Bridge too Far* III. xiv. 206 Frost could hear the crash of Vlasto's Piat bombs smashing into the pillbox.

piat, variant spelling of piet, magpie.

piation (paɪˈeɪʃən). *rare*. [ad. L. *piātiōn-em*, n. of action from *piāre* to appease.] Expiation, atonement.

1623 Cockeram, *Piation*, a purging by sacrifice. **1656** Blount *Glossogr.*, *Piation*,..a sacrificing or purging by Sacrifice. **1824** J. Symmons tr. *Æschylus' Agam.* 22 The first piation of the wind-bound fleet.

piaya (piːˈɑːjə): see peai.

1777 Robertson *Hist. Amer.* IV. (1783) II. 180 The Piayas, the..diviners and charmers in other parts of America.

piazza (pɪˈætsə, -z-). Also 6–7 **piazzo**, 7 **piaza, piatza, piatzza, piatzo**, (8 **piadza**). Pl. **piazze** (-tseɪ). [a. It. *piazza* (ˈpjattsa) square, market-place (= Sp. *plaza*, Pg. *praça*, F. *place*, Eng. place):—Com. Rom. type **plattia*, for *platia*, L. *platea* broad street, later courtyard, a. Gr. πλατεῖα (ὁδός) broad street.]

1. A public square or market-place: originally, and still usually, one in an Italian town; but in 16th to 18th c. often applied more widely to any open space surrounded by buildings, as the parade ground in a fort or the like. Also in extended and *transf.* uses.

1583 Foxe *A. & M.* (ed. 4) 1786/2 Wolfe came to Chalenors chamber [at Ratisbon], and prayed him familiarly to go walke with him abroad to yͤ Piazza or marketstead: which he gladly graunting so did. **1591** *Garrard's Art Warre* 131 Place the Ensignes with their garde of Halberdes..in the Piazza or void place, where the Ensigne is to be managed. **1599** Sir J. Harington in *Nugæ Ant.* (1804) I. 284 For the syte, it is so overtopped by a imminent height, not distant from it more than 150 paces, that no mann can stande firme in the piazza of the forte. **1611** Coryat *Crudities* 246 There are two very faire and spacious Piazzaes or market places in the Citie. **1647** R. Stapylton *Juvenal* 218 Forum Romanum: the Roman piatza, where..they had their exchange, courts of justice [etc.]. **1697** Potter *Antiq. Greece* I. viii. (1715) 39 The *Περιστύλιον*, or Piazza, which was a large Place Square, or sometimes oblong in the middle of the Gymnasium. **1730** A. Gordon *Maffei's Amphith.* 202 The Length of the Area or Piazza taken within the Walls, which circumscribe it. **1860** Hawthorne *Marb. Faun* ii. (1883) 33 A figure such as may often be encountered in the streets and piazzas of Rome. **1866** Howells *Venet. Life* iv. 46 Of all the open spaces in the city, that before the Church of St. Mark alone bears the name of Piazza. **1875** H. James *R. Hudson* xi. 402 The Villa..stood directly upon a small grass-grown piazza, on the top of a hill. **1942** *Country Life* 9 Oct. 694/3 (*caption*) Piccadilly Circus..a new building repeats that at present facing down Lower Regent Street. Between them a 'piazza' for pedestrians is formed. **1959** *Listener* 3 Dec. 962/2 The idea of enlarging the present underground booking-hall to create a vast below-street-level shopping piazza. **1962** *Ibid.* 19 Apr. 689/3 Among the features of the scheme is a paved piazza. **1967** C. Seton-Watson *Italy from Liberalism to Fascism* xi. 425 Many were appalled by the irruption of the *piazza* and the press into delicate questions of international diplomacy. **1976** *Times* 20 Feb. 12/5 George Street [in Edinburgh] still has the Georgian Assembly Rooms midway between the two great *piazze* of St Andrew Square and Charlotte Square. **1977** *New Yorker* 26 Sept. 32/2 Moulmein was reading..on his piazza when I got home. **1978** J. McNeil *Consultant* i. 21 He could see the City [of London], far below..the small *piazza* he had crossed.

attrib. **1820** *Gentl. Mag.* XC. I. 161 But lurking guilt midst Rome's piazza gloom, Now lowers with death.

fig. **1644** Milton *Areop.* (Arb.) 40 Sometimes 5 Imprimaturs are seen together dialogue-wise in the Piatza of one Title page.

2. a. Erroneously applied to a colonnade or covered gallery or walk surrounding an open square or piazza proper, and hence to a single colonnade in front of a building; an ambulatory with a roof supported on the open side by pillars. Now *rare*.

This arose from the Italian custom of constructing colonnades round open squares or courts, and appears to have begun with the vulgar misapplication of the name to the arcade built after the designs of Inigo Jones on the north and east sides of Covent Garden, London, instead of to the open market-place or area.

[**1638** Sir T. Herbert *Trav.* (ed. 2) 127 The Buzzar is also a gallant fabrick;..tis cover'd atop, archt, and (in piazza sort) a kinde of Burse.] **1642** *London Apprentices Declar.* in *Harl. Misc.* (1746) VIII. 571/2 Desiring all the Subscribers to meet at the Piazza's in Covent-Garden. **1656** Blount *Glossogr.* s.v., The close walks in Covent-Garden are not so properly the Piazza, as the ground which is inclosed within the Rails. **1682** *Lond. Gaz.* No. 1777/4 Mr. Ralph Smith, Bookseller, at the Bible in the Piazza of the Royal-Exchange. **1686** Burnet *Trav.* iii. (1750) 163 The Houses are built as at Padua and Bern, so that one walks all the Town over cover'd under Piazzas. **1695** in *Miscellanea* (Surtees, No. 37) 54 They live in one of the Piazzas in Covent Garden. **1778** *Eng. Gazetteer* (ed. 2) s.v. *Nottingham*, The sessions and courts..are kept in the town-hall, which is a grand fabric on piazzas. **1861** Musgrave *By-roads* 201 All four sides of the area display continuous rows of open arcades; in England termed piazzas. **1864** Sala in *Daily Tel.* 21 Nov., You may ask why I do not at once call this colonnade by its universally recognised name of a 'piazza'. I humbly submit that the term 'piazza', as English people and Americans usually apply it, is entirely a misnomer.

fig. *a* **1657** Lovelace *To Chloris* v, Each humble princesse then did dwell In the Piazza of her hair.

b. (Chiefly in U.S.) The verandah of a house. Also *attrib.*

1724 H. Jones *Present State Virginia* 26 It is a lofty Pile of Brick Building adorn'd with a Cupola... There is a spacious Piazza on the West Side, from one Wing to the other. **1771** J. S. Copley *Let.* 3 Aug. (1914) 137 You see I have Drawn the Chinea Clossit Store Room in the east piaza. **1787** M. Cutler in *Life*, etc. (1888) I. 225 A large, well-built house, with a piazza extending the whole length of the front. **1796** Stedman *Surinam* II. xviii. 55 When he makes his appearance under the piazza of his house. **1820** W. Irving *Sketch Bk.*, *Leg. Sleepy Hollow* (1865) 429 One of those spacious farmhouses..the low projecting eaves forming a piazza along the front, capable of being closed up in bad weather. **1838–9** Fr. A. Kemble *Resid. in Georgia* (1863) 29, I was summoned into the wooden porch or piazza. **1867** Motley *Let. to Wife* 20 Aug., He has put a broad verandah (which we so comically call a piazza) all around the house. **1876** A. D. Whitney *Sights & Insights* I. 8 There were settees, and regular piazza chairs. **1884** H. P. Spofford in *Harper's Mag.* Jan. 187/2 He enjoys..resting on the piazza of the hotel. *a* **1916** H. James *Ivory Tower* (1917) I. ii. 18 Shaking his little foot from the depths of a piazza chair,..where..the cool spreading verandah, commanded the low green cliff. **1977** McDavid & O'Cain in S. Greenbaum *Acceptability in Lang.* viii. 112 The uncultivated almost unanimously characterize *porch* as modern and *piazza* as old-fashioned.

Hence **piˈazzaed** (-əd) *a.*, having a piazza or piazzas; **piˈazzaless** *a.*, having no piazza; ‖**piazzetta** (pjatˈtsɛtta) [It. dim.], a little piazza or square (in Italy); *spec.* (with cap. initial), the *Piazzetta di San Marco* in Venice; **piˈazzian** *a.*, of, pertaining to, or of the nature of a piazza.

1698 Fryer *Acc. E. India & P.* 74 Towards the Market appears a State-house *Piatzed, where the Governour convocates the Fidalgos. **1714** Macky *Journ. thro' Eng.* (1724) II. ii. 12 He..hath an open Gallery piazza'd from his House to the End of his Garden. **1775** Jekyll *Corr.* 12 Apr. (1894) 9 The Place Royal,..a square piazz'd all round, with an equestrian statue. **1835** *Fraser's Mag.* XII. 362 Bologna: a piazzaed town; cold, dull, and monastic. **1903** Mary E. Wilkins *Wind in Rose-bush* 9 Now the cottage was transformed by..a bay window on the *piazzaless side. **1820** Byron *Mar. Fal.* v. iv, The Piazza and *Piazzetta of Saint Mark's. **1824** W. Irving *Tales of Traveller* I. I. 106 They crossed the Piazzetta, but paused in the middle of it to enjoy the scene. **1869** Geo. Eliot *Jrnl.* in J. W. Cross *George Eliot's Life* (1885) III. 45 Even landing on the Piazzetta, one has a sense..of being in an entirely novel scene. **1888** H. James *Aspern Papers* I. v. 84 The sea-breeze passed between the twin columns of the Piazzetta. **1906** *Edin. Rev.* July 194 To cross its bridges and its piazzette and to pass under its gateways. **1910** H. G. Wells *New Machiavelli* (1911) II. iii. 246 We would stroll on the Piazzetta, or go out into the sunset in a gondola. **1931** C. Bax *Venetian* I. i. 5 The main part of the stage represents a piazzetta or flagged yard. **1942** A. L. Rowse *Cornish Childhood* i. 22 It played the part of the back-alley in East End life, if not of the piazzetta in a little Italian town. **1966** *Listener* 20 Jan. 105/2 In little back alleys and piazzettas water will pour from a spout into a marble basin or stone trough. **1977** P. D. James *Death of Expert Witness* I. vi. 28 To see..that incomparable view of San Marco from the western end of the Piazza... To stand together on the Piazzetta..and look across the shimmering water. **1819** Keats *Lam.* I. 212 Where in Pluto's gardens palatine Mulciber's columns gleam in far *piazzian line.

pibald, obs. variant of piebald.

pibbil, -ble, pible, obs. forms of pebble.

ˈpibble-ˌpabble, pibble-babble, alterations of bibble-babble.

1599 Shaks. *Hen. V* IV. i. 72 There is no tiddle tadle nor pibble bable in Pompeyes Campe. **1953** *Essays & Stud.* VI. 112 Our South Wales dialect in English, a pibble-pabble inadequate to the demands of a full and varied literature. **1959** *20th Cent.* June, He was the main topic of the pibble-pabble in the forum last month.

‖**ˈpibcorn.** *Obs.* exc. *Hist.* [app. for Welsh *pib gorn* horn-pipe (Owen Pugh), lit. 'pipe of horn'; but the compound *pibgorn* would mean 'horn with a pipe', pipe-horn. The name appears to be a rendering of Eng. *hornpipe*.] A form of the horn-pipe formerly used in Wales: see quots.

(Never really an Eng. word, but admitted into Dictionaries from Crabb.)

1770 Daines Barrington *Mus. Instrum. Wales* in *Archæol.* III. (1775) viii. 33 Another very rude musical instrument..scarcely used in any other part of North Wales, except the island of Anglesey, where it is called a Pib-corn, and where Mr. Wynn of Penhescedd gives an annual prize for the best performer... The name of it signifies the *hornpipe* (*Note.* Literally the *Pipe-horn*). **1794** E. Jones *Rel. Welsh Bards* 116 Pib-gorn[1]. **1815** Roberts *Cambrian Pop. Antiq.* 145, I suppose the Scotch Pipe, like the Welsh Pib-gorn, had but six finger-holes. **1823** Crabb *Technol. Dict.*, *Pib-corn*, (*Mus.*) the Hornpipe. **1852** W. Wickenden *Hunchback's Chest* 214 Here and there a shepherd was seated on a grassy knoll playing his pigborn [*error for* pibgorn]. **1870** *N. & Q.* 4th Ser. VI. 512. *a* **1953** [see crwth]. **1968** J. Arnold *Shell Bk. Country Crafts* 316 The Pibcorn, of Wales, dating from the eighteenth century, was a pastoral hornpipe.

[**pibling**, error in Nares for *pipling*: see pipple *v.*]

piblokto (pɪˈblɒktəʊ). Also **piblockto, pibloktoq**. [Eskimo.] **a.** = *Arctic hysteria* s.v. Arctic *a.* 1 c. **b.** A form of hysterical illness prevalent among Eskimo dogs.

1898 *Geogr. Jrnl.* XI. 228, I pushed on until the 'piblockto', or Greenland dog madness, induced by the continued exposure, got such a hold of my dogs as to make it absolutely impracticable for me to go further. **1910** R. E. Peary *North Pole* xviii. 156 The adults are subject to a peculiar nervous affection which they call *piblokto*... The attack usually ends in a fit of weeping; and when the patient quiets down, the eyes are bloodshot, the pulse high, and the whole body trembles for an hour or so afterward. **1921** A. B. Reader tr. *Tremblay's Cruise of Minnie Maud* vi. 125 The adult Eskimo are often subject to a peculiar nervous affection, a form of hysteria, which they call piblokto... Eskimo dogs and foxes suffer also from piblokto. **1945** C. L. B. Hubbard *Observer's Bk. Dogs* 207 The dread Arctic disease, piblockto (a devastating form of distemper). **1959** *Camsell Arrow* (C. Camsell Hospital, Edmonton, Alberta) Jan.–Feb. 74/1 There is a strange Eskimo madness—piblokto. Men and women are seized with uncontrollable frenzies during which they do all sorts of weird and violent things. **1969** *Daily Tel.* 8 Feb. 16/3 Eskimos have been known to have seizures of *Pibloktoq*, in which they undergo periods of depression followed by wild excitement, then convulsions and stupor, possibly due to the biological effects of the loss of a human time-structure.

pi-bond: see pi *sb.* 3.

pibroch ('piːbrɔx). Also 8–9 **pibrach**. [ad. Gael. *piobaireachd* the art of playing the bagpipe, f. *piobair* a piper (f. *piob* a pipe, a. E. *pipe*) + *-achd*, suffix of function, quality, etc.] In the Scotch Highlands, a series of variations for the bagpipe, founded on a theme called the *urlar*. They are generally of a martial character, but include dirges.

1719 *Hardyknute* in Maidment *Scott. Ball.* (1868) I. 19 While playand pibrochs, minstralls meit Afore him stately strade. **1771** SMOLLETT *Humph. Cl.* 3 Sept., The pipers playing a pibroch all the time. **1791** NEWTE *Tour Eng. & Scot.* 275 A certain species of this wind music, called pibrachs, rouzes the native Highlander in the same way that the sound of the trumpet does the war-horse. **1810** SCOTT *Lady of L.* II. xv, Some pipe of war Sends the bold pibroch from afar. **1862** BEVERIDGE *Hist. India* III. IX. iv. 636 They cheered and charged with the bayonet, the pipes sounding the pibroch.

fig. **1860** C. SANGSTER *Hesperus*, etc. 81 The storm.. shouts its mighty pibroch o'er some shipwrecked vessel's grave.

¶ It has been erroneously used as if = bagpipe.

‖**pic**¹. *Obs.* [= F. *pic* or ad. Sp. *pico* a peak. See PEAK *sb.*², PIKE *sb.*³] A peak. (Orig. in *Pic of Teneriffe*.)

a **1667** COWLEY *Ess., Greatness* Wks. (1688) 124 When it is got up to the very top of the Pic of Tenariff, it is in very great danger of breaking its neck downwards. **1669** BOYLE *New Exp. Spring Air* xxiii. App., Navigators and travellers.. do almost unanimously agree that the pic of Teneriff is the highest mountain hitherto known in the world. **1760–72** tr. *Juan & Ulloa's Voy.* (ed. 3) I. 229 The signal was at first erected on the highest summit of Pichincha; but afterwards removed to another station at the foot of the pic. **1784** COOK *Voy.* I. iii, The Pic of Teneriffe, one of the most noted points of land with Geographers. **1817** J. BRADBURY *Trav. Amer.* 133 Near the centre there rises a pic, very steep, which seems to be elevated at least 100 feet above the hill on which it stands.

‖**pic**², **pike** (piːk). Also 7 pick, 8 peek, 9 pik. [= F. *pic*, a. Turk. *pik*, ad. Gr. πῆχυς ell, cubit.] A measure of length, used for cloth, etc., in the (former) Turkish Empire and in the Levant generally, and varying from about 18 to 28 inches, there being a long and a short standard.

1599 HAKLUYT *Voy.* II. 249 Nineteene and a halfe pikes of cloth, which cost in London twenty shillings the pike. **1687** A. LOVELL tr. *Thevenot's Trav.* I. 158 The Pic is a Measure of six Hands breadth. **1687** B. RANDOLPH *Archipelago* 39 A pettycoat.. that had above 40 pikes of dimity, which is about 30 yards; some have above 60 pikes. **1753** CHAMBERS *Cycl. Supp.*, *Pike*, is also the name of an Ægyptian measure, of which there are two kinds, the large and the small. The larger pike, called also the pike of Constantinople, is 27·92 English inches. **1796** MORSE *Amer. Geog.* II. 602 The daily increase [of the Nile] continues to be proclaimed, till it has attained the height of 16 peeks. **1858** SIMMONDS *Dict. Trade*, *Pic, Pik*, a variable Turkish cloth-measure, ranging from twenty-eight inches the long pic, to eighteen inches the short pic. **1880** *Times* 21 Sept. 8/1 A full Nile is represented by from 23 to 24 pics. **1893** *Whitaker's Almanac* 674/2, 1 Pike Nili = 21·287 inches.

pic³ (pɪk), U.S. colloq. abbrev. of PICAYUNE *sb.*

1839 *Spirit of Times* 18 May 129/1 The gentleman of the bar.. set back the bottle and popped the 'pic' in the drawer. **1841** E. R. STEELE *Summer Journey in West* 159 In paying for them I found a new currency here, my shillings and sixpences being transformed into *bits* and *pics* or picayunes. **1846** E. W. FARNHAM *Life in Prairie Land* II. i. 291 'How much does the muskito-bar cost a yard?' 'Two bits and a pic, or three bits.' **1850** 'M. TENSAS' *Odd Leaves Life Louisiana Swamp Doctor* 51 The animal, didn't mind him a pic. **1855** 'Q. K. P. DOESTICKS' *Doesticks, What he Says* xxiii. 202 A stranger must disburse an avalanche of 'bits', 'pics', and 'levys', before he can get even a plate of cold victuals. **1859** P. H. GOSSE *Lett. from Alabama* 103 The negroes ferried me over the romantic river, for which I paid a '*pic*' (*i.e.* a picayune, the sixteenth of a dollar, or half a 'bit'), the smallest silver coin current.

pic⁴ (pɪk), colloq. abbrev. of PICTURE *sb.* Cf. PICCY. **a.** In sense 2 b.

1884 RUSKIN *Let.* 16 Nov. in S. Birkenhead *Illustrious Friends* (1965) xxxiii. 304, I am so very sorry I cant 'reprieve'—as you call it—the 'pics'. **1891** KIPLING *Light that Failed* v. 82, I must see your pics first. **1910** C. E. MONTAGUE *Hind let Loose* v. 81 He was sent off to see some pics; an'.. he saw ..just what the men were about that had painted them. **1948** L. DURRELL *Spirit of Place* (1969) 98 I've suggested to Tambi that *Runciman* might do a small Patmos book to go with your pics? **1952** M. ALLINGHAM *Tiger in Smoke* i. 17 The pics themselves are covered with fingerprints. **1971** *Petticoat* 17 July 3/2 They're sold with ready-cut pics. **1976** *Sunday Post* (Glasgow) 26 Dec. 13/3 I sent £7.22 to photographer in Wembley for two coloured photos of a show jumping event in Warwickshire. When no pics came I wrote.

b. In sense 2 i.

1936 *Esquire* Sept. 160/4 Raft's next pic is *Proud Rider*. **1970** Y. CARTER *Mr. Campion's Falcon* iii. 26 The Hag is out for the evening—gone off.. to the pics. **1973** 'A. BLAISDELL' *Crime by Chance* (1974) vii. 125 All of a sudden, Latin romances sort of passé... Everybody doing the big war pics.

pic⁵ (pɪk). *colloq.* [Abbrev. PICADOR or Sp. *pica* lance.] **a.** A picador. **b.** A picador's lance, or the thrust made by it. Also as *v. trans.* and *intr.*

1925–6 E. HEMINGWAY in *This Quarter* Autumn-Winter 206 'How about picadors?'.. 'I've got to have one good pic.' **1926** —— *Sun also Rises* II. xv. 173 Watching the picador place the point of his pic. **1927** [see CUT *v.* 54 h]. **1932** R. CAMPBELL *Taurine Provence* 38 From the beginning of the 18th century we know almost every pass, pic, or estocada that has been performed up to the present day. **1934** —— *Broken Record* 195, I pic'd better than any of the professionals. **1957** A. MACNAB *Bulls of Iberia* vi. 63 The picador rides slowly forward towards the bull, it charges, and just as it arrives he jabs the pic down on the top of its shoulders behind the neck muscle. *Ibid.* 65 The sight of a brave, powerful bull being pic'd honourably.. is a fine one. **1967** MCCORMICK & MASCAREÑAS *Compl. Aficionado* ii. 30 If the toro refuses to take the pic, he is supposed to be returned to the corrals. **1976** E. P. BENSON *Bulls of Ronda* iv. 26 The bull.. felt the picador plunge the steel pic into its tossing muscle... Navarro distracted the bull and prepared him for another picing. **1978** M. WALKER *Infiltrator* i. 11, I want to watch the pics.

pic, obs. form of PICK, PIKE, PITCH.

pica¹ ('paɪkə). [med. (Anglo-) L. *pica* (cf. *pīca* PIE, magpie), found in sense 1, beside the Eng. *pye*, PIE, from end of 15th c. It does not appear which of these was a rendering of the other; but the equation of *pica* with *pie* shows that the name was commonly identified with that of the bird. Sense 2 is generally supposed to have been derived from sense 1 (cf. *brevier*, *canon*), although no edition of the *pica* or *pie* in 'pica' type appears to be known.]

†**1.** A collection of rules showing how to deal with the concurrence of religious offices resulting from the variability of Easter and other movable feasts; = PIE *sb.*³ 1, q.v. *Obs.*

1497 PYNSON *Directorium Sacerdotum* (incipit), Liber presens, directorium sacerdotum, quem pica Sarum vulgo vocitat clerus. **1555** *Breviary of Sarum* in Rowe Meres *Eng. Founders* 23, Incipit ordo breviarij seu portiforij secundum morem & consuetudinem ecclesie Sarum Anglicane: vna cum ordinali suo quod vsitato vocabulo dicitur Pica sive directorium sacerdotum in tempore paschali.

†**b.** = PIE *sb.*³ 2. *Obs. rare.* (Only in Dicts.)

1847 WEBSTER, *Pica, pye,* or *pie*,.. also, an alphabetical catalogue of names and things in rolls and records. [Hence in later Dicts.]

2. *Typogr.* (Also 7 **pique**). A size of type, next below English, and between Cicéro and St. Augustin in French type sizes, of about 6 lines to the inch, or 12 American points = 11·33 Didot. Used also as a unit of measurement for large type, leads, borders, etc. ***small pica***, a size of about 11 points, between long primer and pica. Also *attrib.*

two-line pica, the size of type having a body equal to two lines of pica. ***double pica*** (prop. ***double small pica***), a size of type equal to two lines of small pica.

1588 in *Udall's St. Ch. Eng.* (Arb.) Introd. 13 A presse with twoo paire of cases, with certaine Pica Romane, and Pica Italian letters. **1612** STURTEVANT *Metallica* xiii. 89 The Long-primer, the Pica, the Italica. *a* **1625** FLETCHER *Nice Valour* IV. i, Let him put all the Thumps in Pica Roman And with great Tees. **1629** C. BUTLER *Oratoria* A iv b, Genera literarum varia sunt: quæ corporum proceritate distinguuntur: Primier, Pique, English: & supra hæc, Great Primier, Double Pique, Double English: atque quod omnium maximum est, Canon. **1678** PHILLIPS (ed. 4), *Pica Letter*, a term among Printers being the Sixth Character in order of magnitude from Pareil, Small Pica being a degree less, and Double Pica a third degree beyond it. **1683** MOXON *Mech. Exerc., Printing* ii. ⁋2 Most Printing-Houses have.. Pearl, Nomparel, Brevier, Long-Primmer, Pica, English, Great-Primmer, Double-Pica, Two-Lin'd-English. **1755** *Flyleaf* in *Whole Duty of Man*, A Large Quarto Bible, printed on a new Pica Letter and Royal Paper. **1771** LUCKOMBE *Hist. Printing* 226 The difference betwixt Two Lines Pica and Double Pica as well in Face, as Body, is but inconsiderable. **1824** J. JOHNSON *Typogr.* II. 26 The number of each sort cast to a bill of Pica, Roman and Italic. **1850** W. IRVING *Goldsmith* 232 Eight volumes, each containing upwards of four hundred pages, in pica. **1888** JACOBI *Printer's Vocab., Pica*,.. the body usually taken as a standard for leads, width of measures, etc.—it is equal to two Nonpareils in body.

‖**pica**² ('paɪkə). *Path.* [mod. or med.L. *pīca*, a. L. *pīca* magpie, probably rendering Gr. κίσσα, κίττα magpie, jay, also false appetite (the magpie being a miscellaneous feeder). So F. *pica* (Paré 16th c.).] A perverted craving for substances unfit for food, as chalk, etc., symptomatic of certain diseases, and also occurring during pregnancy.

1563 T. GALE *Treat. Gonneshotte* 4 That sickenesse whiche is called Pica. **1584** FENNER *Def. Ministers* (1587) 49 When one is oppressed with the disease Pica, so that hee can not eate anie thing but pitche. **1673** *Phil. Trans.* VIII. 6152 The cause of the pica or unnatural appetite in young women, and others. **1822–34** *Good's Study Med.* (ed. 4) I. 115. **1897** *Allbutt's Syst. Med.* II. 1043 Perverted appetite—pica or geophagy, as it is sometimes called—is a common occurrence in this as in other forms of intestinal helminthiasis.

fig. *a* **1670** HACKET *Abp. Williams* I. (1693) 218 Suppose then one that is sick, should have this Pica, and long to be Annoiled? Why might not a Lay-Friend Annoil, as well as Baptize?

Hence **'pical**, **'picary** *adjs.*, belonging to or of the nature of pica; depraved, vitiated (in appetite).

1620 VENNER *Via Recta* vii. 123 They helpe their picarie affections. **1660** HICKERINGILL *Jamaica* (1661) 40 Through the depravement of their canine and pical Appetites.

pica, variant of PIKA, a small rodent.

‖**picador** ('pɪkədɔː(r)). [Sp., lit. 'pricker', f. *picar* to prick, pierce.] In a bull-fight, A mounted man, who opens the game by provoking the bull with a lance.

1797 *Encycl. Brit.* (ed. 3) III. 771/2 The bull.. has to contend first against the picadores, combatants on horseback, who, dressed according to the ancient Spanish manner.. wait for him, each being armed with a long lance. **1865** F. SAYER in *Fortn. Rev.* No. 5. 616 Miserable hacks.. that a picador would be ashamed to ride in a bull ring. **1892** E. REEVES *Homeward Bound* 257 The picador prods the bull in the back to weaken him while he is goring the horse.

b. *fig.* An agile debater, one who engages in a skirmish of wit.

1876 J. WEISS *Wit, Hum. & Shaks.* iii. 86 Then there is that picador of a clown, who plants in Malvolio's thin skin a perfect quick-set of barbed quips. **1882** *Pall Mall G.* 22 Dec. 19/1 He steps hither and thither.. like a literary picador amid a troop of huge, blundering cattle.

picage, variant of PICKAGE.

pical: see PICA².

picamar ('pɪkəmɑː(r)). *Chem.* [mod. (Reichenbach) f. L. *pix, pic-em* pitch + *amārus* bitter.] An intensely bitter thick transparent oil, obtained in the distillation of wood-tar.

1836 J. M. GULLY *Magendie's Formul.* (ed. 2) 202 The last product is creosote unalloyed by eupione, picamare, water, or other matters. **1840** *Penny Cycl.* XVIII. 143/2 Picamar. *a* **1864** GESNER *Coal, Petrol.*, etc. (1865) 90 Picamar was discovered by Reichenbach, with creosote, in the heavy oil of tar.

pican, obs. form of PISANG.

picaninny: see PICCANINNY.

†**picard, pickard, piker.** *Obs.* Forms: 4 **pyker, pycar,** 4–6 **picarde,** 5 **piccarde, pycard, pykkert,** 6 **picarte, pickard(e, pyckarde, pekart, pycker,** (7 **piker**). [app. from Fr.: origin and etymological form unascertained.

The form agrees with *Picard*, a native of Picardy; also with OF. *picart, pik-, pick-, piccart, pikar, picquar, piccar*, sharp, pointed, *sb.* a kind of nail; but connexion with either of these is as yet unproved.]

A large sailing-boat or barge formerly used for coast or river traffic.

1357 *Act 31 Edw. III*, Stat. II. c. 2 Et qe nul vessel, appelle Pyker de Londres, ne de nulle part aillours, nentre deinz le dit haven [Jernemuth] pour encherer la feyre. **1483** *Cal. Anc. Rec. Dublin* (1889) I. 364 All manner of men that occupieth shippes, piccardes, scaffes, and lighteres, in and unto the haven of the cite of Dyvelyn. **1497** *Acc. Ld. High Treas. Scot.* I. 378 In the Towne of Air, giffin for vj dosan of burdis.. to be grath to the Lord Kennydeis pykkert. **1542–3** *Act 34 & 35 Hen. VIII*, c. 9 § 1 Picardes and other greate botes with fore mastes of the burden of xv. toon and so to xxxvj toonne. *Ibid.* § 2 That no persone or persones.. shall enbote or lade.. any Wheate.. in any picarde bote or other Vessell at any creke pille banke or elswhere upon the Severne streme betwene the Keye of the Citie of Gloucestre, and the saide Citie or Towne of Bristoll. *a* **1552** LELAND *Itin.* II. 105 Picartes and other smaul Vessels cum up by a Gut out of the Haven to the other Bridge on the Causey at Plymtun Townes Ende. **1565** in Picton *L'pool Munic. Rec.* (1883) I. 108 With the said Captain and his company many fine trim and tall pickards from Liverpool and the coast. **1571** *Act 13 Eliz.* c. 11 Uppon payne to forfaite theyr Catch Monger Pycker or Vessel, with the Tackle and al the Fysh in the same. **1599** in *Stirling Nat. Hist. & Arch. Soc. Trans.* (1902) 29 To ye pekart at ye controllar command 1 lib bouter.

Picard ('pɪkɑːd, ‖pikar), *sb.*² and *a.* Also 7 **Picardin**. [a. F. *picard* in the same sense.]

A. *sb.* **a.** A native or inhabitant of Picardy, a region and former province centred on Amiens in northern France, now the departments of Somme, Aisne, and Oise. **b.** The dialect of French spoken there.

a **1400** [see BRETON *sb.* and *a.*]. **1598** J. STOW *Survey of London* 116 Iohn Mutas (a Picarde) or Frenchman. *a* **1666** EVELYN *Diary* an. 1644 (1955) II. 138 The University [of Orleans] is.. divided now.. into that of 4 Nations French, High-dutch, Normans and Picardins. **1900** H. BELLOC *Paris* i. 6 Here Calvin the Picard preached his Batavian theory. **1903** *Knowledge* Dec. 267/2 The dialect of the Isle of France supplanted Picard, Burgundian, and Norman, and became the French language. **1924** G. B. SHAW *Saint Joan* iv. 40 Are these Burgundians and Bretons and Picards and Gascons beginning to call themselves Frenchmen? **1932** W. L. GRAFF *Lang.* 377 French group, with its subdivisions:.. Norman, Picard, [etc.]. **1968** E. HYAMS *Mischief Makers* ix. 165 His name was Waché and he was, I think, from the north, a Picard. **1976** N. ROBERTS *Face of France* iv. 49 There are usually witnesses who have seen 'a sallow man.. of North African type' near the scene of the crime, of which, later, a blond Norman or Picard may be convicted.

B. *adj.* Of or pertaining to Picardy or its inhabitants.

1650 J. HOWELL in *Cotgrave's Fr.-Eng. Dict.* sig. a4, The French toung hath divers dialects, the Picard, that of Iersey and Guernsay.. the Provensall, the Gascon. **1833** MACAULAY in *Friendship's Offering 1833* 17 On that famed Picard field, Bohemia's plume, and Genoa's bow, and Caesar's eagle shield. **1954** W. FAULKNER *Fable* 60 One of those sweating stone courtyards which for a thousand years the French have been dotting about the Picard and Artois and Flanders countryside. **1972** R. COBB *Reactions to French Revolution* iii. 93 The apprentice is set upon by a group of big Picard servants.

picaree, variant of PECCARY.

picarel (ˈpɪkərɛl). [Fr.: cf. PICKEREL[1].] A small marine fish belonging to the family Centracanthidæ (Mæna), found in the eastern Atlantic, the Mediterranean, and the Indian Ocean; esp. the Mediterranean species, *Mæna smaris*.

1905 D. S. JORDAN *Guide to Study of Fishes* II. xix. 347 The Mænidæ, or Picarels, are elongate, gracefully formed fishes. **1972** A. DAVIDSON *Mediterranean Seafood* 107 In Venice you could insult someone by calling him a picarel-eater; and at Port Vendres and some other places in France the fish is known as mata-soldat, or kill-soldier... The picarel can be quite good fried.

picaresque (pɪkəˈrɛsk), *a.* Also **pickaresque**. [ad. Sp. *picaresco* roguish, knavish, f. PICARO: see -ESQUE; so in mod.F. (Littré).] **a.** Belonging or relating to rogues or knaves: applied esp. to a style of literary fiction dealing with the adventures of rogues, chiefly of Spanish origin. Also in *transf.* and extended uses. Also as *sb.*

[**1810** J. BALLANTYNE *Life De Foe* in *De Foe's Wks.*, Works of fiction in the style termed by the Spaniards *Gusto Picaresco*]. *Ibid.*, We could select from these *picaresque* romances a good deal that is not a little amusing. **1829** SCOTT *Jrnl.* 28 Feb., *Memoirs of Vidocq*.. a pickaresque tale.. a romance of roguery. **1837–9** HALLAM *Hist. Lit.* I. viii. §48 This [the Lazarillo de Tormes by Mendoza] is the first known specimen in Spain of the picaresque, or rogue style. **1895** H. B. M. WATSON in *Bookman* Oct. 19/2 He exalts Disraeli... He loves a trickster; the picaresque amuses him. **1918** A. G. GARDINER *Leaves in Wind* 245 Near by lives a distinguished lady of romantic picaresque tastes, who dotes on street pianos. **1955** *Times* 9 Aug. 9/7 The Russians are paying a price for the energetic imposing of rigid form.. on a nation which is in character essentially picaresque. **1958** *Listener* 19 June 1011/1 The first of a trilogy, it is more accessible than its companions, and more lively; a kind of psychological picaresque. **1959** J. M. S. TOMPKINS *Art R. Kipling* i. 29 There is some likeness in the broad, general plan of the two stories [sc. *Kim* and *Huckleberry Finn*]. They are picaresque narratives, with boys as travellers. **1965** *Times Lit. Suppl.* 25 Nov. 1035/4 There is a strong school of black picaresque. **1976** *Ibid.* 23 Apr. 481/5 The central character of this contemporary picaresque of the mind [*sc.* a novel].

¶**b.** Of a situation: transitory, impermanent. Of a person: drifting, peregrinatory.

An erron. usage from an inference that the picaresque hero is a vagrant or wanderer.

1959 *Manch. Guardian* 28 July 6/5 The boys are attracted by the picaresque nature of working with a private building or decorating firm. **1960** *Observer* 17 Apr. 20/7 One is beginning to dread that word 'picaresque'... He dashes his suburban hero all over the place. **1978** *Country Life* 6 July 57/4 Kyril Bonfiglioli.. has now produced.. an historical picaresque—picaresque in both the popular sense of roaming far afield and in the strict sense of being.. about a rogue.

picarian (paɪˈkɛərɪən), *a.* *Ornith.* [f. mod.L. *Pīcări-æ* (C. L. Nitzsch 1820, in *Deutsches Archiv für Physiol.* VI. 255), f. *pīcus* woodpecker: see -AN.] Of, pertaining to, or resembling the *Picariæ*, an order of non-passerine land-birds, formed by Nitsch (1820) for the reception of the woodpeckers, cuckoos, parrots, etc., but now to a great extent discarded.

1908 E. J. BANFIELD *Confessions of Beachcomber* I. iii. 96 Picarian Birds. Large-tailed Nightjar... Blue King-fisher. .. Bronze Cuckoo. **1955** [see HONEY-GUIDE 1].

†**pica'rini.** *Obs.* A bird, the AVOCET.

1770 PENNANT *Zool.* IV. 69 Avosettas.. are found.. near Foss-dyke wash in Lincolnshire, called there Yelpers, on account of their noise; and sometimes Picarinis. [Hence **1833** *Montagu's Ornith. Dict.* (ed. Rennie), *Picarani*.]

‖**'picaro.** Now *arch.* [Sp. *picaro* roguish, knavish, a rogue, knave, sharper = It. '*piccaro* rascal, beggar: of doubtful etymology; perh. related to Sp. *picar*, It. *piccare* to prick: cf. It. *piccante* sharp. See Diez s.v. *Picco*.] A rogue, knave, vagabond.

1623 MIDDLETON *Span. Gipsy* II. i. (1653) C ij, Basenes! the arts of Cocoquismo, and Germania us'd by our Spanish Pickeroes (I meane Filching, Foysting, Niming, Jilting. *c* **1626** *Dick of Devon.* I. ii. in Bullen *O. Pl.* II. 12 That word heard By any lowsy Spanish Picardo [*sic*] Were worth our two neckes. **1626** SHIRLEY *Brothers* v. iii. (1652) 62, I am become the talk Of every Picaro and Ladron. **1719** D'URFEY *Pills* II. 227 Poets, Pimps, Prentices, and poor Piacros [*sic*]. **1749** SMOLLETT tr. *Le Sage's Gil Blas* IV. x. xii. 115 If Scipio in his childhood was a real Picaro, he has corrected his conduct so well since that time, that he is now the model of a perfect servant. **1966** *New Statesman* 21 Jan. 96/2 The rude and cynical picaro, the philandering gambling tailor or tailoring gambler, finds himself so deeply fascinated by a wealthy young American college girl that he puts on a black roll-neck jersey, poses as a writer, and hopefully takes her to Italy. **1972** M. BRADBURY in Cox & Dyson *20th-Cent. Mind* III. xii. 343 Jack Donaghue in [Iris Murdoch's] *Under the Net* may seem a typical fifties *picaro*; but he is a novelist, facing the problem of the possible collapse into contingency of language and the fascinations of silence. **1977** *Times Lit. Suppl.* 20 May 605/2 Picaresque grants an author licence to switch his tones about as the picaro speeds from adventure to adventure.

picaroon (pɪkəˈruːn), *sb.*[1] Also 7– pick-, 7 (pich-), picqu-, piqu-, 8– picc-; 7 -aroone, -aroune, -eroone, -eron, 7–8 -eroon. [a. Sp. *picaron*, augm. of PICARO, rogue.]

1. A rogue, a knave; a thief, a brigand.

(Sometimes playfully as a term of endearment: cf. *rogue*.)

1629 WADSWORTH *Pilgr.* viii. 85, I answered, that he looked like a Picheron. *c* **1645** HOWELL *Lett.* (1650) I. 164 Your diamond hat-band which the Picaroon snatched from you in the coach. **1684** OTWAY *Atheist* II. i, Are you there indeed, my little Picaroon? **1748** RICHARDSON *Clarissa* (1811) IV. xxiii. 127 Thou who art worse than a pickeroon in love. **1821** SCOTT *Kenilw.* xx, I see in thy countenance something of the pedlar—something of the picaroon. **1904** BURGESS & IRWIN (*title*) The picaroons, a San Francisco night's entertainment. **1924** H. LANDON (*title*) The elusive picaroon. **1935** A. J. POLLOCK *Underworld Speaks* 87/2 *Picaroon*, thief who preys on tourists.

2. A pirate, sea-robber, corsair. Also *fig.*

1624 CAPT. SMITH *Virginia* v. 184 Meeting a French Piccaroune.. hee.. tooke from them what hee liked. *c* **1681** HICKERINGILL *Trimmer* Wks. 1716 I. 355 A Letter of Mart against the Common-Piqueroon of all good Mens Reputations. **1700** tr. *Fryke's Voy. E. Ind.* 191 The Streight of Sunda was very much infested with Pickaroons. **1824** W. IRVING *T. Trav.* II. 242 Somewhat of a trader, something more of a smuggler, with a considerable dash of the pickaroon. **1881** W. WALLACE in *Academy* 15 Oct. 289 A crew of social picaroons.

3. a. A small pirate ship; a privateer or corsair.

1625 *Impeachm. Dk. Buckhm.* (Camden) 11 Theis Picaroones.. will ever lye hankering upon our coaste. **1658** R. HADDOCK in *Camden Soc. Misc.* (1881) 5 Heere escaped out a small pickeron of 4 or 6 guns. *a* **1700** B. E. *Dict. Cant. Crew*, *Pickaroon*, a very small Privateer. **1775** JEFFERSON *Let.* Writ. 1892 I. 496 Montgomery had proceeded in quest of Carleton and his small fleet of 11 pickeroons. **1885** *Daily Tel.* 21 May 5/3 Strong exception is taken by the advocates of privateering to such words as corsair, picaroon, and the like being applied to a vessel armed with the authority of a letter of marque.

b. (With reference to BARRACOON.) A slave-ship.

1893 KIPLING *Seven Seas* (1896) 23 Then said the souls of the slaves that men threw overboard: 'Kennelled in the picaroon a weary band were we.'

4. *attrib.* and *Comb.*

1667 PEPYS *Diary* 28 Dec., The very Ostend little pickaroon men-of-war do offer violence to our merchant-men. **1858** *Athenæum* 1 May 556 What was the end of this picaroon woman? **1889** DOYLE *Micah Clarke* 224 That lean, rakish, long-sparred, picaroon-like craft.

pica'roon, *sb.*[2] *N. Amer.* [? F. *piqueron* a little pike, a javelin, dart, prick, goad (Cotgr.), f. *pique* pike, *piquer* to prick.] A long pole fitted with a spike or hook, used in logging and fishing.

1837 *North Amer. Rev.* Apr. 354 The rafters.. [make] use of a picaroon, or pole with a spike in the end of it, which is .. driven into the boards, taking out perhaps a piece at each time. **1850** S. JUDD *R. Edney* 42 Richard, armed with a picaroon, descended the slip.. to the basin, where the logs lay in the water ready to be drawn in. **1890** in *Cent. Dict.* **1905** *Bull. Bureau of Forestry* (U.S. Dept. Agric.) No. 61, 43 *Pickaroon*, a piked pole fitted with a curved hook, used in holding boats to jams in driving, and for pulling logs from brush and eddies out into the current. **1949** N. C. BROWN *Logging* II. v. 101 Pickaroons are short poles 35" to 40" long with a recurved pike or hook used in drawing or pulling small products such as cross ties, 4' pulpwood, fuel wood, chemical wood, cooperage, and bolts down steep slopes. **1972** F. FORD *Atush Inlet* viii. 78 The crew worked with picaroons spiking the fish into the scow.

picaroon (pɪkəˈruːn), *v.* [f. PICAROON *sb.*[1]]

1. *intr.* To play the pirate or brigand; to cruise about, skirmish, or keep watch for a prize. Also *fig.*

1675 CROWNE *Country Wit* II. i, These Night-corsairs and Algerines call'd the Watch, that pickaroon up and down in the streets. **1730–6** BAILEY (folio), *Pickeroon*,.. to skirmish as light horsemen do, before the main battle begins. **1860** *All Year Round* No. 71. 492 The gates were strictly guarded, the spies picarooning at every corner. **1894** RALPH in *Harper's Mag.* Aug. 337 Some of these raiders called their peculiar work by the name of 'picarooning'.

2. *trans.* To act piratically towards; to prey upon, pillage; in quot. *fig.*

1681 HICKERINGILL *Char. Sham Plotter* Wks. 1716 I. 212 He is the Land-Pirate, that Pickaroons Men's Lives and Estates, by putting out false Colours.

Hence **pica'rooning** *vbl. sb.* and *ppl. a.*

1625 *Impeachm. Dk. Buckhm.* (Camden) 220 The Admirall of France.. is only ruld and led by these picqueroning Captaines. **1727** BAILEY vol. II, *Pickering, Pickerooning*,.. going a plundering; also Skirmishing. **1727–41** CHAMBERS *Cycl.*, *Picqueering, Pickeering*, or *Pickerooning*, a little flying war, or skirmish, which the soldiers make when detached from their bodies, for pillage, or before a main battle begins. **1903** *Blackw. Mag.* July 36/1 A summer's picarooning off Flores.

picary, *a.*: see PICA[2].

picary, picas(e, obs. ff. PECCARY, PICKAXE.

Picassian (pɪˈkæsɪən), *a.* [f. the maternal name of Pablo (Ruiz y) *Picasso* (1881–1973), Spanish painter: see -IAN.] Of, pertaining to, or characteristic of Picasso or his style of painting. Also **Picasso'esque**.

1940 L. ADAM *Primitive Art* xvii. 115 Picasso's primitiveness is quite definitely his own 'Picassian primitiveness'. **1959** *Times* 21 Sept. 5/6 They have none of the Parisian flair, except for Mr Roque A. Riera Rojas, whose shadowy 'Bullfighter' with the piquant, Picassian features and costume of silver grey looming from the shadows is a thoroughly suave, skilful performance. **1968** *Time* 27 Dec. 30/1 *Yellow Submarine* combines every trick and treat of film animation with a dazzle of takeoffs on schools and styles of art. Picassoesque monsters compete with gentle grotesques. **1972** Y. YADIN *Hazor* II. vii. 82 It depicts in a schematic manner the naked body of a woman. Only half of her features are accentuated: one eye, half the nose and mouth, one breast, and half of the vulva. This Picassoesque figurine seems to represent 'life and death' or the 'born and unborn'. **1978** *Listener* 13 July 56/3 The Picassoesque line.. is a reminder of something he [*sc.* Henry Moore] learned from both Picasso and Matisse.

picathartes (pɪkəˈθɑːtiːz). *Ornith.* [mod.L. (R. P. Lesson *Manuel d'Ornithologie* (1828) I. 374), f. L. *pīca* magpie + *Cathartes*, generic name of certain American vultures, f. Gr. καθαρτής cleanser (f. καθαίρειν to cleanse.).] A bare-headed West African bird of the genus so called, belonging to the babbler family or Timaliidæ; also called the bald crow or rock-fowl.

1931 *Discovery* May 140/1 Looking at this bird, named misleadingly the white-necked bald crow, one's mind instinctively reverts to prehistoric times, for.. the Picathartes is a most extraordinary looking object. **1938** *Ibis* II. 255 An investigation of the stomach-contents of the rare West African bird *Picathartes* reveals the fact that insect fragments predominate. **1960** G. DURRELL *Zoo in Luggage* ii. 57 The *Picathartes* was about the size of a jackdaw, but its body had the plump, sleek lines of a blackbird. **1972** *Daily Colonist* (Victoria, B.C.) 30 July 27/3 The picathartes, a rare bald-headed bird.. will fetch £100.

†**pi'cation.** *Med. Obs.* [ad. med. or mod.L. *pĭcātio*, n. of action f. L. *pĭcāre* to bedaub with pitch, f. *pic-em* pitch; cf. obs. F. *pication* 'a pitching, or bepitching' (Cotgr.).] The application of warm pitch to the skin.

1684 tr. *Bonet's Merc. Compit.* XIV. 473 If.. Sulphureous Bathes.. do not succeed, we must proceed to Pication.

picayune (pɪkəˈjuːn), *sb.* and *a.* *U.S.* Also **piccayune, picharoon, pickayune.** [In Louisiana, a. Pr. *picaioun*, mod.F. *picaillon* (1750 in Hatz.-Darm.), name of an old copper coin of Piedmont, now in Fr. 'halfpence, cash, money': of uncertain origin (Hatz.-Darm.).]

A. *sb.* The name formerly given in Louisiana, Florida, etc., to the Spanish half-real, value 6¼ cents or 3 pence; now to the U.S. 5-cent piece or other coin of small value; hence *colloq.*, a person or thing considered small, mean, or insignificant.

1804 J. F. WATSON *Jrnl.* 4 Nov. in *Amer. Pioneer* (1843) II. 228 One can't buy anything [at New Orleans] for less than a six cent piece, called a *picayune*. **1832** R. BAIRD *View of Valley of Mississippi* xxii. 264 [In Louisiana] the words 'piccayune' (6 1–4 cents) and bit—(12 1–2 cents) fall upon the ear at every step. **1839** J. K. TOWNSEND *Narr. Journey Rocky Mts.* i. 17 We gave him a *pickayune* for his trouble, and went on. **1852** MRS. STOWE *Uncle Tom's C.* xx, From him she got many a stray picayune, which she laid out in nuts and candies. *Ibid.* xxxix, Our chance wouldn't be worth a picayune. **1903** *Scribner's Mag.* XXXIII. 508 A pack of jealous picayunes, who bickered while the army starved. **1904** *N.Y. Even. Post* 25 Jan. 6 It doesn't matter a picayune whether the justices or the members of the diplomatic corps were presented first. **1948** *Reader's Digest* Dec. 148/1 Don't care a picayune how you waste that boy's time, do you? **1979** M. G. EBERHART *Bayou Road* xxi. 288 His life wouldn't be worth a picayune.

B. *adj.* Mean, contemptible, paltry. Also *absol.* *colloq.*

1813 *Cramer's Pittsburgh Almanac 1814* 60 The incessant hum of the blabbering (coloured) market women, seated on the ground.. by the side of their picharoon (six cent) piles of vegetables. **1837** *Congress. Globe* 25th Congress 2 Sess. App. 19 The hon. Senator from Kentucky.. by way of ridicule, calls this a 'picayune bill'. **1856** H. GREELEY in *Greeley or Lincoln* 127 The infernal picayune spirit in which it is published has broken my heart. *a* **1859** *New York Herald* (Bartlett), There is nothing picayune about the members of St. George's [Cricket] Club. **1892** *Boston* (Mass.) *Jrnl.* 8 Nov. 4/3 Do you want another picayune Congress with all its stupidity and folly? **1915** *New Republic* 31 July 336/1 They instinctively regard the critic as puny and picayune. **1936** *Delineator* Nov. 11/2 No picayune place like this could pay that man. **1955** E. POUND *Classic Anthol.* II. 104 Your picayune in-laws in fat government jobs. **1965** H. MITCHELL *Underground War against Revolutionary France* iv. 46 Overlooking the serious divisions between the pure and constitutional royalists, Grenville naïvely expected them to bury their picayune differences in a sudden glow of friendship. **1967–8** *Bahamas Handbk. & Businessmen's Ann.* (ed. 7) 77 A picayune mongrel comes from its midday torpor. **1973** *Listener* 20 Dec. 849/3 His projects at that point were getting picayune. He was no longer a great baseball-player. **1974** [see NITPICKER]. **1975** *Encounter* Feb. 44/2 Most of the snags and pratfalls he cites seem to me picayune matters.

picayunish (pɪkəˈjuːnɪʃ), *a.* *U.S. colloq.* [f. prec. + -ISH[1].] Of little value or account, insignificant, paltry, mean. Hence **pica'yunish-ness.**

a **1859** *Blackw. Mag.* (Notes on Canada) (in Bartlett), That boat.. belongs to that darn picayunish old coon, Jim Mason, and he'll run her till she sinks or busts up. **1887** *Springfield Republican* (U.S.) 14 Oct., A sad commentary on the political picayuneishness that allows [etc.]. **1889** *Chicago Advance* 4 Apr. 267 Mr. Jos. Chamberlain's turn came, and then the occasion became literally and truly picayunish.

picayunity (pɪkəˈjuːnɪtɪ). [f. PICAYUNE *sb.* and *a.* + -ITY.] Insignificance, triviality.
1948 O. NASH in *New Yorker* 13 Nov. 32 In this imponderable world I lose no opportunity To ponder on picayunity. **1977** *Ibid.* 2 May 54/1 To the point of picayunity the state's road system is limited.

† **ˈpiccadill, ˈpickadill.** *Obs.* Forms: *α.* 7 pickadel(l, picadell; picca-, pica-, pickadil, -dill(e; pickedaille; pecca-, pecadill, -dile; pacadile; pickar-, picardil(l). *β.* 7 picca-, picka-, peccadillo. *γ.* 7 picka-, picca-, pecca-, pickydilly. [a. F. *pica-, piccadilles* (*a* 1589 in Godef.) 'the seuerall diuisions or peeces fastened together about the brimme of the collar of a doublet' (Cotgr. 1611), app. answering to a Sp. **picadillo*, dim. of *picado* pricked, pierced, punctured, slashed, minced (cf. *picada* a puncture, *picadillo* minced meat, hash, *picadura* ornamental gusset); cf. Du. (with dim. *-ken*) *pickedillekens* 'laciniæ' (Kilian).
Generally understood to be the origin of the name (originally a popular nickname) 'Pickadilly Hall', given before 1622 to a house in the parish of St. Martin's in the Fields, London, and now perpetuated in the street called Piccadilly. As to the connexion of 'Pickadilly Hall' with this word, various conjectures were current already in the time of Blount, 1656, who mentions two: either 'because it was then the outmost or *skirt* house of the Suburbs that way', or 'from this, that one Higgins a Tailor, who built it, got most of his Estate by Pickadilles, which in the last age [= generation] were much worn in England'. See full account in *Athenæum*, 27 July 1901, pp. 125–7.]
1. a. A border of cut work or vandyking inserted on the edge of an article of dress, esp. on a collar or ruff. **b.** The name was app. transferred to the expansive collar fashionable in the early part of the 17th c., which usually had a broad laced or perforated border.
α. **1607** DEKKER *Northw. Hoe* III. i. Wks. 1873 III. 37 A short Dutch waist with a round Catherine-wheel fardingale, a close sleeue with a cartoose collour and a pickadell. *c* **1614** DRAYTON *Moon Calf* in *Agincourt*, etc. (1627) 165 In euery thing she must be monstrous: Her Picadell aboue her crowne vp-beares; Her Fardingale is set aboue her eares. **1614** in *Lismore Papers* Ser. II. (1887) I. 253 A pickadell of white Sattin xxxˢ. **1616** *Burgh Rec. Stirling* (1887) 144 Buittis, schone, pantenes, and pickedaillis. **16..** B. JONSON *Underwoods* xxxii. Wks. (Rtldg.) 698/2 Ready to cast at one whose band sits ill, And then leap mad on a neat picardill. **1656** BLOUNT *Glossogr.* [from Cotgr.], *Pickadil*, the round hem, or the several divisions set together about the skirt of a Garment, or other thing; also a kinde of stiff collar, made in fashion of a Band. **1658** PHILLIPS, *Pickadil*, (from the Dutch word Pickedillekens) the hem about the skirt of a garment, also the extremity or utmost part of any thing.
β. **1648–60** HEXHAM, *Pickedillekens*, Pickadilloes, or small Edges.
attrib. **1821** SCOTT *Kenilw.* xi, Wayland Smith's flesh would mind Pinniewinks's awl no more than a cambric ruff minds a hot piccadilloe needle.
γ. **1611** RICH *Honest. Age* (1615) 20 He that some forty or fifty yeares sithens, should haue asked after a Pickadilly, I wonder who could haue vnderstood him. **1653** A. WILSON *Jas. I* 59 Great Cutwork Bands and Piccadillies (a thing that hath since lost the name) crouded in and flourished among us. **1655** tr. *Com. Hist. Francion* VI. 15 Taking two Eggs.. which he did th[r]ow at his face, and spoiled his worshipfull Pickadilly, which was set forth like a Peacocks tail. **1695** THORESBY *Diary* (ed. Hunter) I. 289 To..view his.. curiosities; he presented me with his grandfather's pickadilly.
2. A stiff band or collar of linen-covered pasteboard or wire, worn in the 17th c. to support the wide collar or ruff. [Cf. obs. F. *piccadille* 'porterabat' (Godef.).]
1611 COTGR., *Carte*,..also, a Pickadill, or supporter, of Pasteboard couered with linnen. **1611** in Heath *Grocers' Comp.* (1869) 91 [No apprentice to wear] any piccadilly or other support in, with, about the collar of his doublett. **1619** PURCHAS *Microcosmus* xxvii. 265 Larger Fall's borne vp with a Pickadillo; or scarsly Peeping out ouer the Doublet Coller. **1670** LASSELS *Voy. Italy* II. 191 The other half [of his band] was made of coarse lawne startched blew and standing out upon a pickydilly of wyer. **1688** R. HOLME *Armoury* III. 95/2 A *Pacadile*, a thing put about Man or Womans Neck to support and bear up the Band, or Gorget. *Ibid.* 237/2 Their Gorget standing up being supported by Wyers and a kind of Roll which they called a Pecadile.
3. *transf.* Applied humorously to a halter, etc.
1615 SIR E. HOBY *Curry-Combe* v. 237 Wee must beleeue ..that Thomas Becket furnished our Kentishmen with the like Pickadillies, for cutting off his horse tail. **1630** J. TAYLOR (Water P.) *Wks.* 34/1 One that at the Gallowes made her will Late choaked with the Hangman's Pickadill. **1678** BUTLER *Hud.* III. i. 1454 Which when they're prov'd in open Court, Wear wooden Peccadillo's for't.

piccadillo, obs. f. PECCADILLO: see also prec.

Piccadilly (pɪkəˈdɪlɪ). The name of a street and circus (sense 7) in London (see note s.v. PICCADILL, PICKADILL), used *attrib.* in ***Piccadilly weeper(s)***, long drooping side whiskers, sometimes extending below the chin, worn without a beard; loosely = *Dundreary whiskers* s.v. DUNDREARY; ***Piccadilly window*** (slang), a monocle.
1874 HOTTEN *Slang Dict.* 252 *Piccadilly weepers*, long carefully combed-out whiskers of the Dundreary fashion. **1894** Piccadilly weeper [see DUNDREARY]. **1897** E. GRAHAM *Golden Dustman* (song), Nah I'm goin' to be a reg'lar toff... A Piccadilly winder in my eye. **1907** [see BURNSIDE, BURNSIDE]. **1909** J. R. WARE *Passing Eng.* 195/2 *Piccadilly window (street*, '90's), single eye-glass worn by some men of fashion—hence the Piccadilly. **1936** P. M. CLARK *Autobiogr. Old Drifter* xiii. 177 'It' was a regular Ha-ha Johnnie with a 'Piccadilly window' in his eye. **1960** C. W. CUNNINGTON et al. *Dict. Eng. Costume* 163/1 *Piccadilly weepers.* 1870's and 1880's. (M.) Long combed-out whiskers fashionable in those decades. **1973** J. FLEMING *You won't let me Finish* ii. 19 A fragile moustache that drooped right down past his mouth, the kind of moustache that used to be called a 'Piccadilly weeper'.

piccage, variant of PICKAGE.

piccalilli (ˈpɪkəlɪlɪ). In 8 piccalillo, pacolilla. [Origin unascertained; ? a trade term fancifully made on *pickle*.] A pickle composed of a mixture of chopped vegetables and hot spices; also formerly called *Indian pickle*.
1769 MRS. RAFFALD *Eng. Housekpr.* (1778) 357 To make Indian Pickle or Piccalillo. **1796** MRS. GLASSE *Cookery* xix. 307 To make Paco-lilla, or Indian Pickle. **1845** BREGION & MILLER *Pract. Cook* 285 Piccalilli consists of all kinds of pickles. **1902** *Westm. Gaz.* 26 Mar. 2/1 Because of our meagre liver-action, piccalilli and black walnuts are falling out of favour.

piccaninny, pickaninny (ˈpɪkəˌnɪnɪ), *sb.*, (*a.*) Also 7 pickaninnie, picko-, 8 pickaniny, piga-, 9 pica-, pickininny; picanini, piccaniny, piccin, piccinini, piccney, picken, pickini, pickinny, pickne, pickney, picknie, pickny, pick'ny, picny; (in S. Africa) piccanini, piccanin, picannin. [A West Indian Negro deriv. of Sp. *pequeño* or Pg. *pequeno* little, small (prob. a diminutive: cf. esp. Pg. *pequenino* very little, tiny), which was carried by Europeans to other parts of the world. See Note below.
A. *sb.* A little one, a child: the term (which now often gives offence when used by people of European extraction) refers in the West Indies and America to children of Black African ethnic origin; in South and Central Africa and in Australia to those of the aboriginal peoples; in the latter cases introduced by Europeans, but often adopted by the natives themselves. Also *attrib.* **a.** In the West Indies and America. In the speech of West Indian Blacks freq. with uninflected pl.
1657 R. LIGON *Barbadoes* 48 When the child is borne, (which she calls her Pickaninnie) she [a neighbour] helps to make a little fire nere her feet... In a fortnight, this woman is at worke with her Pickaninny at her back. **1681** *Will of Jas. Vaughan* (of Antigua) in *Misc. Gen. & Her.* Ser. II. IV. 255 To my sister Mrs. Hannah Bell, four negroes and one Pickoniny [*printed* Pickoning] boy. **1707** SLOANE *Jamaica* I. p. lii, Their children call'd *Piganinnies* or rather *Pequenos Ninnos*, go naked till they are fit to put to clean paths, bring firewood [etc.]. **1790** J. B. MORETON *Manners & Customs West India Islands* 152 The women..are obliged to ..take their pickinnies (*i.e.* children) on their backs, to which they are tied with handkerchiefs. **1828** *Life Planter Jamaica* 93 The pickeniny gang consisted of the children who were taken to the field. **1833** HOOD *Doves & Crows* iii, Bring all your woolly pickaninnies dear. **1847** *Knickerbocker* XXX. 216 It might be very pleasant to be surrounded by half-a-dozen negro waiting-women, with their picaninnies. **1867** LYDIA M. CHILD *Rom. Repub.* ii. 16 The negroes at their work, and their black picaninnies rolling about on the ground. **1868** T. RUSSELL *Etym. Jamaica Gram.* 2 Pickne. *Ibid.* 6 Pickini—A child. African. **1907** W. JEKYLL *Jamaican Song & Story* 40 Now Toad have twenty picny. **1937** R. MACAULAY *I would be Private* II. i. 147 That naked piccney. **1958** J. CAREW *Wild Coast* viii. 117 All you is, is a maugre, skin-and-bone pickny. **1969** S. M. SADEEK *Windswept & Other Stories* 37 'I was working for the estate, until..' 'Until alyou get busy making picknie.' **1974** *Practitioner* CCXIII. 845 To 'give pickney' or to 'breed' [in Jamaica] is to get a woman with child. **1977** *Westindian World* 3–9 June 4/1 It has been made very plain that quite a number of teachers in schools up and down de country are in many cases more dunce than de pickney dem teach themselves.
b. In Australia, and South and Central Africa. Also, the offspring of an animal.
1830 R. DAWSON *Australia* 12 (Morris) 'I tumble down pickaninny here',..meaning that he was born there. **1841** R. HOWITT *Impressions Australia Felix* (1845) 103 Two women, one with a piccaniny at her back. **1847** LEICHHARDT *Jrnl.* xv. 520 Bilge introduced several old warriors..adding always the number of piccaninies, that each of them had. **1855** in J. W. Colenso *Ten Weeks in Natal* Add. p. 3 What will the poor little piccaninnies do, Boy? **1889** MRS. C. PRAED *Rom. of Station* 16 Three or four half-naked gins, with their picaninnies slung on their tattooed backs. **1893** *Voice* (N.Y.) 14 Dec., Even the pickaninnies and pygmies of the Congo valley are..entitled to protection from drink. **1900** S. CHAMBERS *Rhodesians* 50 Attended by a sable piccanin. **1911** *East London* (Cape Province) *Dispatch* 24 Nov. 7 (Pettman), Mothers nursing their picaninies and maidens listening to lovers rude. **1925** *Brit. Weekly* 31 Dec. 340/2 A mother..crooned gently to her 'piccin' not more than a few weeks old. **1926** *Ibid.* 27 May 158/1 A mischievous picannin..was weeding the vegetable garden. **1936** I. L. IDRIESS *Cattle King* xxviii. 245 He met numerous blackfellow friends, they and their lubras and piccaninnies, all in fat good humour. **1953** G. DURRELL *Overloaded Ark* iii. 59 Na catar beef, sah, and 'e get picken for 'e back. **1961** G. GREENE *Burnt-Out Case* IV. i. 100 The piccin that stole sugar from the white man's cupboard. **1963** *Sydney Morning Herald* 19 Nov. 6/4 The use of such words as 'boy', 'lubra' and..'piccaninny' to describe aborigines has been banned to Northern Territory welfare officers. **1966** C. SWEENEY *Scurrying Bush* xiv. 199 He guided me about half a mile up the road, the rest of the piccannins scampering behind. **1979** P. NIESEWAND *Member of Club* ii. 21 The bantu we've chosen..is a piccanin called Elias.
c. *humorously.* A child, in general. (Also *fig.*)
1785 GROSE *Dict. Vulgar T.*, *Pickaniny*, a young child, an infant; negroe term. **1817** SCOTT *Fam. Lett.* May (1894) I. xiii. 425 The little pickaninny has my kindest wishes. **1859** THACKERAY *Virgin.* lxviii, A little box at Richmond or Kew, and a half-score of little picaninnies. **1899** *Westm. Gaz.* 15 Dec. 12/1 She's Britannia's Picaninny, If she isn't very big! She's a Daughter of the Empire,..Natal!
B. *adj.* Very small; tiny, baby. spec. ***piccaninny dawn, daylight*** (chiefly *Austral.*), earliest dawn, first light.
1707 H. SLOANE *Voy. Jamaica* I. p. lii, They have.. Christmas Holidays, Easter call'd little or Piganinny, Christmas, and some other great Feasts. [**1796** STEDMAN *Surinam* (1813) II. xxvi. 268 Small, *peekeen*—Very small, *peekeeneenee.* **1835** R. R. MADDEN *Twelvemonth's Residence W. Indies* II. 153 To..spend piccanini Christmas (Easter) dancing. **1848** W. WESTGARTH *Australia Felix* viii. 104 The hut would be attacked before 'piccinini sun'. **1849** PICHARDO *Diccion. Prov. Voces Cubanas, Piquinini*..una persona ó cosa pequeña. **1870** in 'Mark Twain' *Screamers* (1871) xxv. 132 A pickaninny,..mud-turtle-shaped craft of a schooner. **1896** J. T. BENT *Ruined Cities Mashonaland* 58 Anything small, whether it be a child, or to indicate that the price paid for anything is insufficient, they [Kaffirs] term *piccanini*.] **1876** J. R. GREEN *Lett.* (1901) 439 A series which begins in the thirteenth century is a very young and pickaninny series. **1896** *Cosmopolitan* XX. 353/1, I soon discovered a pickaninny, or baby walrus. **1903** R. BEDFORD *True Eyes* lxi, By pickaninny daylight the mounted men were in motion. **1910** ANDERSON & CUNDALL *Jamaica Anancy Stories* 37 Go a pickney mumma yard an' you sure fe get somet'ing. *a* **1912** 'T. COLLINS' *Buln-Buln & Brolga* (1948) 107 Blackfellers mostly goes in for a piccaninny fire —jist three sticks, with the ends kep' together. **1936** M. FRANKLIN *All that Swagger* xvi. 153 At piccaninny dawn, the billy with the lid off was found rolling on the floor. **1953** G. DURRELL *Overloaded Ark* iv. 78 'Eh..aehh!' he shouted, 'napicken bushcat here for inside.' **1970** 'E. LINDALL' *Gathering of Eagles* viii. 101 The piccaninny dawn, that false lightening of the sky that fades to darkness before the sun finally makes its presence known. **1971** *Courier-Mail* (Brisbane) 12 July 2/6 Before piccaninny daylight on June 14, Vernon Boundy..was standing on the southern bank of Tallebudgera's tidal estuary. **1974** *Sunday Mail Mag.* (Brisbane) 15 Sept. 3/3 In the chilly piccaninny dawn we drove out to the Wyloo strip with kangaroos bounding along beside and in front of the truck.
[*Note.* Our earliest examples (17th c.), being from the formerly Spanish West Indies, with the existing Cuban Spanish *piquinini* (Pichardo *Dicc. Voces Cubanas*, 1849), suggest Spanish derivation; on the other hand, the Surinam form is more naturally derived from Portuguese, which moreover has the recognized dim. *pequenino*, not used in Spanish. Stedman gives *peekeen, peckeeneenee* in Eng. phonetic spelling; the Dutch of Surinam is '*pikien*, klein, weinig, jong; kind, jong, kroost' (Focke, *Neger-Engelsch Wbk.* 1855). But, wherever first used, the word was prob. soon carried from one colony to another; it may even have arisen in the Portuguese possessions in Guinea, and have been carried by slaves to various parts of America; witness the readiness with which it has been adopted by natives in Africa and Australia, in the 19th c. The Cape Dutch form *pikanini* may have been brought from the Dutch West Indies, or acquired from English, or from Portuguese (to which also some attribute the Rhodesian use). Some have suggested that the word is not a dimin., but a combination, = Sp. *pequeño niño* little child, or Pg. *pequeno negro*, now in Surinam *pikien-ningre* 'negerkinderen, kreolen' (Focke). But the word is not confined to children, being essentially an adj. meaning 'very little, tiny'.]

piccant, obs. form of PIQUANT.

† **picche**, *v. Obs. rare.* App. a by-form of PICK *v.*[1]
1377 LANGL. *P. Pl.* B. VI. 105 My plow-fote shal be my pyk-staf [*A.* pyk, *B.* pikid staf], and picche atwo þe rotes [so 1393 C. IX. 64; A. VII. 96 and posshen atte [*v.rr.* putte at þe; picche vp þe; to posse at þe] Rootes]. **1387** TREVISA *Higden* (Rolls) I. 387 þey wolde somtyme wiþ scharpe egged tool picche and kerue here owne bodies, and make þeron dyuers figures and schappes.

picche, obs. form of PITCH *sb.*[1] and *v.*[1] and [2].

piccolo (ˈpɪkələʊ). [a. It. *piccolo* small; hence absol., a small flute.]
1. (orig. ***piccolo flute***.) A small flute, an octave higher in pitch than the ordinary flute; also called the *octave flute*.
1856 MRS. C. CLARKE tr. *Berlioz' Instrument.* 121 Piccolo flutes are strangely abused now-a-days. **1864** LEECH in J. Brown *Horæ Subsecivæ* (1882) 45 Thackeray..playing on the piccolo. **1900** *Chr. Progress* Mar. 44 When in the great orchestra the little piccolo did not do its part in the rehearsal.
2. An organ stop having the tone of the piccolo.
1875 STAINER & BARRETT *Dict. Mus. Terms* (1898) 360/2 *Piccolo*, an organ stop of 2 ft. length—the pipes are of wood, the tone bright and piercing.
3. (for *piccolo piano*.) A small upright pianoforte.
1858 SIMMONDS *Dict. Trade*, *Piccolo*, a small pianoforte. **1880** HIPKINS in Grove *Dict. Mus.* II. 751/1 The 'piccolo' was finished to stand out in the room away from the wall.
4. A boy who assists a waiter at a hotel, restaurant, etc.; a page at a hotel.
1910 'SAKI' *Reginald in Russia* 71 Watching the amount that I gave to the piccolo. **1926** R. HALL *Adam's Breed* I. x. 94 He had six enormous aprons... He had been very generously equipped for his duties as 'piccolo'. **1927** *Observer* 19 June 12 [German hotels] Head waiter..; elder page,..younger page,..'piccolo', or very small page,..still smaller 'piccolo', just beginning career. **1960** O. MANNING *Great Fortune* iii. 31 The piccolo arrived, a scrap of a boy, laden with bottles, glasses and plates. **1972** L. P. BACHMANN

ULTIMATE ACT i. 9 In his early teens he began work as a piccolo in hotels and restaurants.

5. = *juke-box. U.S. slang.*

1938 *N.Y. Amsterdam News* 12 Mar. 17 The Harlem Hamfats grind out the tune on myriad Harlem piccolos. **1946** E. BISHOP *North & South* 50 He's drinking in the warm pink glow To th' accompaniment of the piccolo. **1950** *Publ. Amer. Dial. Soc.* XIV. 52 [S. Carolina] *Piccolo*, an automatic music box, worked by a nickel slot machine. Origin undetermined. **1970** C. MAJOR *Dict. Afro-Amer. Slang* 91 *Piccolo*, . . juke box.

Hence **'piccoloist**, one who plays on the piccolo.

1881 *Pennsylv. Sch. Jrnl.* XXX. 125, I was his successor as picoloist.

Picco pipe ('pɪkəʊ). *Mus.* Also with lower-case initial. [f. the name of *Picco* or *Picchi*, 'the Sardinian minstrel', who performed on this instrument with great virtuosity and was heard in London in 1856.] (See quot. 1876.)

1876 STAINER & BARRETT *Dict. Mus. Terms* 354/1 *Picco pipe*, a small pipe having two ventages above and one below. It is blown by means of a mouthpiece like a *flûte à bec* or whistle; and in playing, the little finger is used for varying the pitch by being inserted in the end. **1920** U. DAUBENY *Orchestral Wind Instruments* iii. 27 An instrument . . was revived about the middle of last century by a blind Italian peasant named Picco, who gave remarkable performances on the 'Picco pipe'. **1939** A. CARSE *Mus. Wind Instruments* x. 119 Probably the smallest of all whistle-flutes is the Picco pipe, a tiny shrill whistle about 3½ inches long. **1960** L. G. LANGWILL *Index Wind-Instrument Makers* 90 A young blind Sardinian shepherd, Angelo Picchi appeared in . . London (1856), playing on a small pipe (Zuffolo) which was named after him, Picco Pipe. **1977** *Early Music* Oct. 555/2 Amongst woodwind were items such as a picco pipe (£165), . . and a two-keyed oboe.

piccy ('pɪkɪ). Also **picky**. Colloq. abbrev. of PICTURE *sb.* 2 b. Cf. PIC⁴, PICKY.

1889 KIPLING *Let.* in C. E. Carrington *Rudyard Kipling* (1955) vi. 143 It's mighty curious to see behind an R.A.'s piccy and note the bits of things it is made up of. **1931** E. F. BENSON *Mapp & Lucia* iii. 64 Go on with your picky, as if I was not here. How well you've got the perspective! **1968** A. DIMENT *Bang Bang Birds* I. v. 75 They popped my piccy into a dud passport. **1977** *Hot Car* Oct. 75/1 The end result of fitting these packages on your Ford can be, if the piccies are anything to go by, rather on the eye-catching side.

‖**pice** (paɪs). Also 7 *pise, peise, peyse*, 8 *pyce*, 9 *pyse*. [ad. Hindī *paisā* (in all the Gauḍian langs.), a copper coin, the fourth part of an *ānā*: supposed by some to be a deriv. of *pā'i* or *pa'ī*:—Skr. *pad, padī*, quarter. See also PIE *sb.*⁵] A small East Indian copper coin equal in value to one-fourth of an anna.

1615 W. PEYTON in Purchas *Pilgrims* I. 530 Pice, which is a Copper Coyne; twelve drammes make one Pice. **1616** TERRY *ibid.* II. 1471 Brasse money, which they call Pices, whereof three or thereabouts counteruaile a Peny. **1698** FRYER *Acc. E. India & P.* 205 The Company's Accounts are kept in Book-rate Pice, . . 80 Pice to the Rupee. *c* **1813** MRS. SHERWOOD *Stories Ch. Catech.* xv. 125 Every pice that I could lay hold of went for liquor. **1862** BEVERIDGE *Hist. India* II. IV. ii. 76 If by so doing they can gain a few pice.

Hence **'piceworth**, as much as a pice purchases.

1832 MORTON *Bengali & Sanscrit Prov.* 127 A thousand crows crowding about a pice-worth of sauce. **1904** *Nineteenth Cent.* Aug. 289 A piceworth of your horse's grain.

pice: see also PAISA.

†**pice'aster.** *Obs.* [a. obs. F. *piceastre* 'the wild Pitch tree' (Cotgr.), f. L. *picea* the pitch-pine: see -ASTER.] The pitch-pine.

1707 MORTIMER *Husb.* (1721) II. 55 The Piceaster (a wilder sort of Pine) out of which the Pitch is boil'd.

picein ('pɪ-, 'paɪsiːɪn). [f. L. *pice-us* pitchy (f. *pix* PITCH *sb.*¹) + -IN¹.] **1.** *Chem.* [ad. F. *picéine* (Ch. Tanret 1894, in *Compt. Rend.* CXIX. 80).] A glucoside present in various trees, notably willows and conifers; *p*-hydroxyacetophenone-*β*-glucoside, $CH_3{\cdot}CO{\cdot}C_6H_4{\cdot}O{\cdot}C_6H_{11}O_5$.

1894 *Jrnl. Chem. Soc.* LXVI. I. 616 Picein, $C_{14}H_{18}O_7$, whether anhydrous or hydrated, crystallises in silky, prismatic needles, with a bitter taste. **1934** C. C. STEELE *Introd. Plant Biochem.* xi. 118 Picein, $C_{14}H_{18}O_7$, salinigrin, or salicinerin, occurs in several species of *Salix* and *Populus*. **1968** *Jrnl. Chromatogr.* XXXVI. 28 The collected fraction of pure trimethylsilyl picein also gave a satisfactory infrared spectrum.

2. Also *picein wax*, and with capital initial. An inert thermoplastic substance composed of hydrocarbons from rubber, shellac, and bitumen and used for sealing joints against air.

1927 G. W. C. KAYE *High Vacua* v. 69 Khotinsky cement . . is widely used in the States for vacuum work, while Picein finds extensive application on the Continent. **1936** *Discovery* Sept. 286/1 A plug of picein wax in the capillary is thereby melted and seals up the tube. **1968** *Chem. Abstr.* LXIX. 6796/1 An elec.-insulating material was developed which permitted one to apply fields of up to 2 × 10⁶ w./cm. The material consisted of varying amts. of quartz powder in picein. **1974** L. HOLLAND et al. *Vacuum Manual* i. 65 Picein. This is a classical vacuum wax—sticks well to metal and glass, is resistant to dilute acid and alkalies, is thermoplastic and made from bituminous substances. **1975** *Sci. Amer.* Feb. 110/3 Only prices are missing from this admirable guide to a world of high-technology commerce. String and sealing wax are gone (although not picein wax, quite).

Picene ('paɪsiːn), *a.* and *sb.* [f. L. *Picen-us* Picene: see -IAN.] **A.** *adj.* Of or pertaining to ancient Picenum, a region in eastern central Italy, or the pre-Roman iron-age culture associated with it. **B.** *sb.* A native or inhabitant of Picenum; the pre-Sabellian language attested there. Also **Pi'cenian.**

1600 HOLLAND tr. *Livy's Romane Hist* XXII. 437 He [*sc.* Hannibal] turned another way into the Picene countrie. **1601** —— tr. *Pliny's Nat. Hist.* XVIII. xi. 567 The Picenes in times past invented a way by themselves of making bread. **1863** W. P. DICKSON tr. *Mommsen's Hist. Rome* III. IV. ix. 332 The corps of Picenian volunteers soon grew to three legions. **1924** D. RANDALL-MACIVER *Villanovans & Early Etruscans* ii. 5 The burial rite of the Villanovans . . opposes them to the Etruscans and the Picenes. *Ibid.* iv. 75 It is natural to suppose that *all* the inhumations in the Forum are of the Picene race. **1933** R. S. CONWAY et al. *Prae-Italic Dial. Italy* II. iv. 213 This Picene culture extends along the Adriatic coast southwards from Rimini at least as far as the river Sangro. **1939** L. H. GRAY *Foundations of Lang.* xi. 335 A language sometimes called Pre-Sabellian, Liburnian, or Picenian. **1948** D. DIRINGER *Alphabet* II. ix. 498 The Picenian alphabet is . . very old. **1949** L. R. TAYLOR *Party Politics in Age of Caesar* ii. 45 In the elder Pompey's bodyguard . . was a group of young Picene officers. **1959** *Chambers's Encycl.* V. 461/2 In the east the Fossa peoples were supplemented by another Illyrian-speaking group, known as Picene, between Rimini and the Abruzzi. **1974** E. S. GRUEN *Last Generation of Roman Republic* ii. 63 Pompey's following went beyond . . the old aristocracy. From his father he inherited . . a virtual barony in Picenum. Some of his adherents, from lesser families, seem to possess Picene origins. *Ibid.* iii. 118 Q. Numerius Rufus was probably a Picene.

Picentine (pɪ'kɛntaɪn, paɪs-), *a.* and *sb.* Also 8 **Pycentine.** [f. L. *Picentin-us* Picentine: see -INE¹.] **A.** *adj.* = PICENE *a.* ***Picentine bread***, a kind of bread made in ancient Picenum (with reference to Pliny, *Nat. Hist.* XVIII. xxvii: see quot. 1958). **B.** *sb.* = PICENE *sb.*

1708 W. KING *Art of Cookery* 147 The first Chapter contains the admirable Receipt of a Salacacaby of Apicus. Bruise in a Mortar Parsley Seed, dry'd Peneryal, . . Raisons ston'd, Honey, . . Oyl and Wine, put 'em into a Cacabulum, three crusts of Pycentine Bread, the Flesh of a Pullet, . . pour a soup over it, garnish it with Snow. **1855** BOSTOCK & RILEY tr. *Pliny's Nat. Hist.* I. III. xviii. 235 The fifth region is that of Picenum, once remarkable for the denseness of its population; 360,000 Picentines took the oaths of fidelity to the Roman people. **1863** W. P. DICKSON tr. *Mommsen's Hist. Rome* III. IV. vii. 228 The Latin could remind the Picentine that they were both in like manner 'subject to the fasces'. **1888** [see MARRUCINIAN *sb.* and *a.*]. **1933** R. S. CONWAY et al. *Prae-Italic Dial. Italy* II. iv. 209 The insc. on the Osimo statuette . . resembles more closely than any of the rest the Italic dialects proper . . whether its language be described as 'Picentine' or as 'Umbrian'. **1939** A. J. TOYNBEE *Study of Hist.* IV. 312 The new foundation was called into existence by the . . 'civilization' (in the literal sense) of the indigenous population, as when . . the Romans organized . . a Picentine village into a *forum* or *conciliabulum*. **1958** FLOWER & ROSENBAUM *Roman Cookery Bk.* IV. 93 Picentine bread. According to Pliny . . this bread—invented by the people of Picenum—was made of spelt-grits. The spelt-grits were left to soak for nine days, and on the tenth day were made into dough by mixing them with raisin juice. The dough was put into earthenware pots and baked hard in the oven. **1974** E. S. GRUEN *Last Generation of Roman Republic* iii. 110 The trustworthy Picentine L. Afranius.

piceo-, combining form of L. *piceus*, PICEOUS, pitchy, pitch-, as in **piceo-fe'rruginous** *a.*, of a colour between reddish-black and rust-coloured; **piceo-te'staceous** *a.*, of a colour between piceous and dull brick-red.

1847 HARDY in *Proc. Berw. Nat. Club* II. 239 Antennæ black, the apex piceo-ferruginous. *Ibid.* 243 The joints and tarsi piceo-testaceous, or . . tinged with yellow and piceous.

piceous ('pɪsiːəs), *a.* [f. L. *pice-us* pitchy (f. *pix, pic-em* PITCH *sb.*¹) + -OUS.] Of, pertaining to, or resembling pitch: **a.** Inflammable, combustible; **b.** Pitch-black; brownish or reddish black.

1646 J. HALL *Horæ Vac.* 100 Comets, which blaze as long as their piceous substance remaines, and then vanish. **1826** KIRBY & SP. *Entomol.* IV. xlvi. 282 *Piceous* . . shining reddish black. The colour of pitch. **1847** HARDY in *Proc. Berw. Nat. Club* II. 236 Antennæ black, piceous towards the apex.

picescent (pɪ'sɛsənt), *a. rare.* [f. as prec. + -ESCENT.] Approximating to piceous in colour.

1847 HARDY in *Proc. Berw. Nat. Club* II. 245 Anterior coxæ picescent.

picey ('paɪsɪ), *a. slang.* [Prob. f. PICE + -Y¹.] Mean, niggardly.

1937 PARTRIDGE *Dict. Slang* 624/1 *Picey*, adj., mean: Regular Army: late C. 19–20. **1965** P. ROBINSON *Pakistani Agent* v. 61 She deserved better than that, the miller would be too *picey*.

piche, obs. form of PITCH, PIKE, PYCHE.

picher, pichet, obs. forms of PITCHER, PIQUET.

‖**pichey** ('pɪtʃɪ). Also **pichiy, pichy.** [Local name in the Spanish of Argentina: app. the native name in Guarani.] The Little Armadillo, *Dasypus minutus*, of La Plata.

1827 GRIFFITH tr. *Cuvier's Anim. Kingd.* III. 293 The pichiy of D'Azara is more like the hairy armadillo than any other species. **1849** *Sk. Nat. Hist., Mammalia* IV. 196 The pichy . . often tries to escape notice by squatting close to the ground. **1864** WOOD *Nat. Hist.* I. 770 The little Pichey Armadillo is only fourteen inches in length.

‖**pichiciago** (pɪtʃɪ'sjeɪgəʊ). [ad. Sp. *pichiciego*, f. (?) Guarani *pichey* (see prec.) + Sp. *ciego* (:—L. *cæcus*) blind.] A small burrowing edentate animal of Chili, *Chlamyphorus truncatus*, allied to the Armadillos; its back and head are covered with a hard leather-like shell attached only along the spine, and dipping abruptly over the haunches.

1825 R. HARLAN in *Ann. Lyceum N. York* 235 The animal is a native of Mendoza, and in the Indian language is named Pichiciago. **1893** MIVART *Types Anim. Life* (1894) 259 A small, very rare, and peculiar kind is the pichiciago.

picht, obs. form of PICT, PIGHT, PITCHED, PITH.

pichuric (pɪ'tʃʊərɪk), *a. Chem.* [f. next + -IC.] Of, pertaining to, or derived from pichurim beans. ***pichuric acid***, a synonym of LAURIC *acid*.

1866 WATTS *Dict. Chem.* IV. 636 *Pichuric acid*, . . Lauric Acid. **1880** *Libr. Univ. Knowl.* (N.Y.) VIII. 716 Lauric acid, also called . . pichuric acid, . . first described by Maisson in 1842, . . in the solid fat and volatile oil of pichurim beans.

‖**pichurim** ('pɪtʃərɪm). The native name of a lauraceous South American tree, *Nectandra Puchury* (*Laurus Pichurim* of Richard).

Hence ***pichurim bean***, the aromatic cotyledon of the seed of this tree, used in cookery and medicinally; ***pichurim camphor***, see quot.; ***pichurim oil***, a yellowish-green odorous oil obtained from pichurim beans.

1842 BRANDE *Dict. Sc.*, etc., *Pichurim bean*, an oblong heavy seed brought from Brazil, and used medicinally in the cure of colic. **1866** WATTS *Dict. Chem.* IV. 636 *Pichurim-oil.* Pichurim beans, . . yield by distillation with water, a yellow oil, smelling like bay and sassafras oil. *Ibid.* 637 *Pichurim-camphor* . . Pichurim-oil is resolved by cold alcohol into a strong-smelling elæoptene and a nearly inodorous camphor.

piciform ('pɪsɪfɔːm), *a.*¹ *rare.* [ad. mod.L. type **piciformis*, f. *pix, pic-em* PITCH *sb.*¹: see -FORM.] Of the nature of or resembling pitch; pitchlike.

1876 PAGE *Adv. Text-bk. Geol.* xx. 423 According to its texture and composition as fibrous, papyraceous, earthy, and piciform.

piciform ('paɪsɪfɔːm), *a.*² [ad. mod. Ornith.L. *pīciformis*, f. *pīc-us* woodpecker: see -FORM.] Having the form or structure of, or resembling, a woodpecker; of or pertaining to the *Piciformes*, a group of picarian birds.

1884 COUES *Key N. Amer. Birds* 476 The nearest relatives of the Piciform Birds are the Capitonidæ or Scansorial Barbets.

picine ('paɪsaɪn), *a. Ornith.* [f. L. *pīc-us* woodpecker + -INE¹.] Of, pertaining to, or allied to the woodpeckers.

1890 *Ibis* Jan. 31 In comparison with the Galline arrangement of the plantars and its modifications, the Picine arrangement appears to be quite distinct.

pick (pɪk), *sb.*¹ Forms: 4 *pikk*, 4–6 *pyk(k*, 4–8 *pic*, 5 *pikke, pykke*, 6 *pict, pycke*, 6–7 *picke*, 7 *pik*, 6– *pick*. [app. a collateral form, with short vowel, of PIKE *sb.*¹ (Cf. the collateral forms *pick* and *pike* in PICK *v.*¹) *Pick* is the form in general English use in sense 1; in other senses it is either obs., or only in local use in names of tools or implements. In senses 1 a, 1 b, 4 a, a dial. variant is *peck* (PECK *sb.*²).]

I. 1. a. A tool consisting of an iron bar, usually curved, steel-tipped, tapering squarely to a point at one end, and a chisel-edge or point at the other (but sometimes blunt at one end), attached through an eye in the centre to a wooden handle placed perpendicularly to its concave side; a pickaxe, mandril, mattock, 'slitter': used for loosening and breaking up stiff or hard ground or gravel, splitting up compact masses of rock, and the like. The pick and spade are the ordinary excavating or mining tools.

(= PIKE *sb.*¹ 1, PECK *sb.*² 1, which still exist as dial. forms.)

1340 *Ayenb.* 108 þanne nymþ he his pic and his spade and beginþ to delue and to myny. **1375** BARBOUR *Bruce* II. 541 Then war the wiffys thyrland the wall With pikkis. **14..** *Nom.* in Wr.-Wülcker 726/30 *Hec liga, vel mera*, a pyk. **1496** *Nottingham Rec.* III. 291 For mendyng of ij. pykkes to digg down gravell. **1552–3** *Inv. Ch. Goods, Staffs.* in *Ann. Lichfield* (1863) IV. 45 A pick and a spade to make graves with. **1565** *Reg. Privy Council Scot.* I. 360 Ane hundrith schulis, xl pickis and mattokis. **1653** MANLOVE *Lead Mines* 207 (E.D.S.) No miners . . Pick . . May be removed from their ground. **1708** J. C. *Compl. Collier* (1845) 42 [It] would be Dangerous for two persons to Work together, least they should strike their Coal-Pics into one another. **1851** H. MELVILLE *Whale* xxvi. 128 The arm that wields a pick or drives a spike. **1903** *Eng. Dial. Dict.* s.v., In salt-mining the picks used are of a somewhat special construction, . . the head is straight but tapering at each end, with sharp steel points.

b. A pointed or edged hammer used for dressing millstones (also formerly stone shot); a mill-pick; also a pointed hammer for stone-cutting and for breaking coal.

(= PIKE *sb.*¹ 1, PECK *sb.*² 1, which occur as dial. forms.)

1483 *Cath. Angl.* 278/1 A Pykke of A Milnere. **1622** DRAYTON *Poly-olb.* xxvi. (1748) 372 The mill-stones from the quarr with sharpen'd picks could get. **1805** FORSYTH *Beauties Scotl.* (1806) IV. 407 [In splitting blocks of granite] they..dig a row of little oblong grooves..by means of a weighty tool like a hammer, drawn to a blunt point at both ends, and highly tempered at the point. This they call a pick. **1842** FRANCIS *Dict. Arts*, etc., *Pick*, a hammer for dressing the stones of a flour mill. **1869** *Lonsdale Gloss.*, *Pick*,..a sharp-pointed mason's tool for facing limestone. **1884** *Upton-on-Severn Gloss.*, *Pick*, or *Peck*,..a pointed hammer for breaking coal.

c. *Archæol.* A prehistoric implement used for breaking up rocks, soil, etc.

1949 W. F. ALBRIGHT *Archaeol. of Palestine* iii. 59 Among large flint artifacts the most noteworthy are sickle-blades and 'picks', which point to the agricultural character of Natufian culture... Some of the so-called picks are rather hoes, used to break up the ground before sowing grain. **1959** J. D. CLARK *Prehist. S. Afr.* vi. 157 Small, nearly parallel-sided picks.

II. †**2.** A spike, a sharp point, as the pointed or piked end of a staff, a hedgehog's prickle or spine, or the like; the spike in the middle of a buckler: = PIKE *sb.*[1] 2. *Obs.*

1495 *Trevisa's Barth. De P.R.* XVIII. lxii. The yrchyn..his skynne is closyd abowte wyth pickys [*MSS.* pikes] and pryckes. **1599** PORTER *Angry Wom. Abingd.* in Hazl. *Dodsley* VII. 318, I had..then come in with a cross blow, and over the pick of his buckler two ells long, it would have cried twang, twang, metal, metal. **1612** BEAUM. & FL. *Cupid's Rev.* IV. iii, Take down my Buckler, and sweep the Cobwebs off: and grind the pick ont. **1614–15** in Willis & Clark *Cambridge* (1886) III. 296 Item for guilding the Iron pickes in the greate posts xv[s]. **1630** LENNARD tr. *Charron's Wisd.* I. xiv. §10 (1670) 55 The reason of man hath many visages: it is a two-edged Sword, a Staff with two picks. **1688** R. HOLME *Armoury* III. 313/1 A strong thick Staff..Hooped with Iron at both ends; into one is fastned a long Pin or Iron pick.

†**3.** A pikestaff: = PIKE *sb.*[1] 3. *Obs. rare.*

13.. *Sir Beues* (A.) 2241 And to þe gate Beues ȝode..pyk and skrippe be is side. **1673** R. HEAD *Canting Acad.* 192 Though he tip them the piks, they nap him agen.

4. The name of various pointed or pronged instruments: †**a.** for cutting or gathering peas, beans, etc. = PECK *sb.*[2] (quots. 1784–1813). [Cf. obs. Du. *picke* falx frumentaria, messoria, falx qua frumentum inciditur (Kilian).] *Obs.*

1423 in Rogers *Agric. & Pr.* III. 548, 2 Pikkys for hacking peas.

b. A pitchfork, a hay-fork (= PIKE *sb.*[1] 3 b); a fork-rake for collecting sea-weed. *dial.*

[**1410, 1472**: see PIKE *sb.*[1] 3 b.] **1777** in *Horæ Subsec.* 325 (E.D.D.). **1794** T. DAVIS *Agric. Wilts* (1811) 263 *Prong or pick*, a fork for the stable, or for haymaking. **1863** MORTON *Cycl. Agric.* Gloss. (E.D.S.), *Pick* or *Pikle*, a hay-fork. **1895** *Longm. Mag.* Nov. 33 He [the kelper] is armed with a 'pick', an implement resembling a very strong hay fork, but with prongs set, like those of a rake, at right angles to the handle. With this pick..he grapples the tumbling sea-weed and drags it up to the beach.

c. 'A sort of Tool us'd by Carvers' (Phillips 1706). (See PIKE *sb.*[1] 2 c.)

d. *Fishing.* A kind of gaff; an eel-spear; an instrument for detaching limpets. *dial.*

1875 G. C. DAVIES *Rambles Sch. Field-Club* xxxv. 262 'Stand by with the pick, it is a big 'un', and a fine codling was hauled in. The 'pick' was a rude kind of gaff. **1883** —— *Norfolk Broads* xxxi. (1884) 244 The [eel-spear] in use on the Yare and Bure is the 'pick', formed of four broad serrated blades or tines, spread out like a fan; and the eels get wedged between these. **1898** *Shetland News* 22 Jan., He took his cuddie an' pick an' guid i' da lempit ebb.

5. a. An instrument for picking: chiefly in *Comb.*, as EAR-PICK, TOOTHPICK, etc. **b.** Also short for (*a*) TOOTHPICK; (*b*) PICKLOCK (*Cent. Dict.* 1890).

1619 FLETCHER *Mons. Thomas* I. ii, Undone without Redemption; he eats with picks. **1890** *Cent. Dict.*, *Pick*,..a toothpick. *colloq.*

c. *Mus.* A plectrum. Cf. PICK *v.*[1] 12. orig. *U.S.*

1895 *Montgomery Ward Catal.* Spring & Summer 243/2 Mandolin picks, made of celluloid, imitation tortoise shell, oval pattern. **1973** *Advocate-News* (Barbados) 24 Feb. 3/6 (Advt.), Attention all musicians... Just arrived:..Picks Finger Picks Thumb Picks. **1976** D. MUNROW *Instruments Middle Ages & Renaissance* 25/4 The long stem of the quill is shown held between the third and index finger (as a modern guitarist holds a flat pick).

III. †**6.** (See quot. 1688.) *Obs.* (= PIKE *sb.*[1] 5.)

1585 *Rec. Leicester* (1905) III. 217, xi lands viz. viii in the midle of the furlong, ii picks of the south side, and on hadland. [*Ibid.*, 4 lands 23 pikes lying south upon Knighton Mere.] **1688** R. HOLME *Armoury* III. 137/1 *Pick of land*, is a parcel of Land that runs into a corner. **1775** ASH, *Pick*,..a small parcel of land, an odd bit of land.

IV. 7. The diamond in playing-cards. Also *transf.*: see quot. 1828. Now *north. dial.*

1598 FLORIO, *Quadri*, squares, those that we call diamonds or picts vpon playing cardes. **1611** COTGR., *Quarreau*,..a Diamond, or Picke, at Cardes. **1648** HERRICK *Hesper.*, *Oberon's Palace* 48 Those picks or diamonds in the card, With peeps of harts, of club and spade. **1791** *Gentl. Mag.* Jan. 16 The common people, in a great part of Yorkshire, invariably call diamonds, *picks*. **1825** BROCKETT *N.C. Gloss.*, *Picks*, the suit of diamonds at cards. **1828** *Craven Gloss.* (ed. 2) s.v. *Pick*, 'Picks and hearts', red spots on the shins occasioned by sitting too near the fire.

V. 8. *attrib.* and *Comb.*, as ***pick-carrier***, ***-handle***, ***-shaft***, ***-sharpener***, ***-sharper***, ***-shop***, ***-work***; ***pick-bearing***, ***-nosed*** adjs.; **pick-dressing**, in masonry, a pitted facing produced by a pointed tool, broached hewn-work; **pick-hammer**, (*a*) 'a pointed hammer for dressing granite' (Simmonds *Dict. Trade* 1858); (*b*) 'a hammer with a point, used in cobbing' (Raymond *Mining Gloss.* 1881); **pick-hole**: see quot.; **pick-money, -pence**: see quot.; **pick-pole** *U.S.* = PICAROON *sb.*[2]

1891 KIPLING *City Dreadf. Nt.* 86 The grimy, sweating, cardigan-jacketed, ammunition-booted, *pick-bearing ruffian turns into a well-kept English gentleman. **1888** W. E. NICHOLSON *Gloss. Coal-Trade Terms Northumbld.*, *Pick-carrier. **1903** *Eng. Dial. Dict.* s.v. *Pick* sb.[1], *Pick-carrier*, a boy employed to carry the blunt 'picks' to the pick-shop to be sharpened. **1895** *Funk's Stand. Dict.*, **Pick-dressing*, a tooling of the face of a stone with a sharp pick or hammer. **1850** N. KINGSLEY *Diary* 1 Nov. (1914) 156 Tinkered a little at *Pick handles, putting door in the tent, [etc.]. **1873** J. MILLER *Life amongst Modocs* v. 64 A long white pole, perhaps a sort of pick-handle. **1908** *Sears, Roebuck Catal.* 522/2 Drifting pick handles, 34 inches long. **1979** D. LOWDEN *Boudapesti 3* xiii. 68 The man who'd hit him four times with the pickhandle. **1894** HESLOP *Northumbld. Wds.*, **Pick-hole*, a wound made by the point of a pick. A miner's term. *Ibid.*, **Pick-money, pick-pence*, the money paid by the hewer to the 'pick sharper'. **1888** W. E. NICHOLSON *Gloss. Coal-Trade Terms*, *Pick-pence. **1837** *North Amer. Rev.* Apr. 353 The persons who undertake it [*sc.* breaking a log-jam] must go on to the mass of logs, work some out with their *pickpoles, [etc.]. **1972** *Christian Science Monitor* 28 Sept. 16/3 The river-drivers could stay on a pitching, twisting log long log, keeping balance with a pick-pole. **1497** *Acc. Ld. High Treas. Scot.* I. 349 Item, giffin to ane hors to bere *pykschaftis, spadis, and sic stuf..vs. xj*d*. **1887** P. M'NEILL *Blawearie* 86 [He was] batted out by the men with their pickshafts. **1892** in A. E. Lee *Hist. Columbus* (Ohio) II. 825 He obtained employment..as a *pick-sharpener. **1888** GREENWELL *Coal Trade Gloss.* 61 The colliery smith (called the *pick sharper). **1799** J. ROBERTSON *Agric. Perth* 112 When the ground requires some *pick-work..it costs more. **1883** GRESLEY *Gloss. Terms Coal-mining*, *Pickwork*, cutting coal with a pick.

†**pick**, *sb.*[2] *Obs.* Also 6 picke, *pl.* **pykkis.** A collateral form, chiefly *Sc.*, of PIKE *sb.*[5], F. *pique*, the military weapon.

push and pick: hand to hand combat, hand-grips. ***to pass the picks*** = to pass the pikes: see PIKE *sb.*[5] 2.

1513 DOUGLAS *Æneis* XII. iii. 24 All the rowtis of Awsonyanis,..Furth thryngis at the portis full attonis, With lancis lang and pykkis for the nonis. **1515** *Acc. Ld. High Treas. Scot.* V. 12 The dichting and heding of my lord governouris speris and pikkis. **1560** DAUS tr. *Sleidane's Chron.* 220 b, Being kept backe with pickes and Iavelyns. **1577** tr. *Bullinger's Decades* (1592) 150 Offering their liues to the push and picke of present death. **1587** *Mirr. Mag.*, *Elstride* l, How I past the pickes of painfull woe. **1639** BAILLIE in *Z. Boyd's Zion's Flowers* (1855) Introd. 45, I furnished to half-a-dozen..fellows, musquets and picks.

pick, *sb.*[3] [f. PICK *v.*[1], in various detached uses.]

1. An act of picking; a stroke with something pointed.

1513 DOUGLAS *Æneis* II. ix. 64 The auld waiklie..A dart did cast, quhilk, with a pik, can stynt On his harnys. **1865** DICKENS *Mut. Fr.* I. i, I'll..take a pick at your head with the boat-hook. **1895** *E. Anglian Gloss.*, *Pick or Bang*, a way of deciding which side is to go in first in any game. A stick is thrown up, and if it falls upright it is *pick*, and *bang* if it falls flatling.

2. The picking *of* a quarrel.

a **1648** LD. HERBERT *Hen. VIII* (1683) 38 He understood this expostulation to be nothing but the pick of a Quarrel to assist the French.

3. An act of choosing or selecting; *transf.* that which is selected; the best or choicest portion or example of anything; the choicest product or contents.

1760–72 H. BROOKE *Fool of Qual.* (1809) II. 58, I might have my pick and choice of all the..dukes in the nation. **1826** D. ANDERSON *Poems* (ed. 2) 44 (E.D.D.) Purchase goods at Lon'on town Whare he wad get his pick an' wale. **1829** DARWIN in *Life* I. (1887) 177 Letting —— have first pick of the beetles. **1855** BROWNING *Up at a Villa* ix, You get the pick of the news. **1858** GLADSTONE *Homer* I. 421 The chiefs are the pick and flower of the whole Greek array. **1872** GEO. ELIOT *Middlem.* xi, Mamma—I wish you would not say 'the pick of them'..it is rather a vulgar expression. **1874** GREEN *Short Hist.* ii. §6. 90 Customers had to wait..till the buyers of the Abbot had had the pick of the market. **1874** [see BASKET *sb.* 1 d]. **1887** JESSOPP *Arcady* iv. 117 These young men..were the very pick of the parish. **1896** GRAHAM *Red Scaur* 23 The lad..he's the pick of the basket.

4. The taking of a bit or mouthful of food; a slender or sparing meal. Now *dial.*

1688 R. HOLME *Armoury* II. 253/1 He [the cock] is to be fed..Every meal having 12 picks, or Corns of Barley. *a* **1810** TANNAHILL *Poems* (1846) 30 See, here's my dish, come tak' a pick o't, But, deed, I fear there's scarce a lick o't. **1835** J. D. CARRICK *Laird of Logan* 275 (E.D.D.) There were few in our house could tak ony dinner that day; I took my ordinar pick. **1890** P. H. EMERSON *Wild Life* 96 (E.D.D.) I'm gettin' scrannish [hungry] and could do a pick. **1899** MACMANUS *Chimney Corners* 99 Won't ye sit down and have a pick of dinner with us?

5. The quantity or portion of any crop (as hops, peas, etc.) picked or gathered at one time or turn; a gathering.

1887 *Daily News* 13 Dec. 2/4 American and Californian hops are being gradually cleared off the market,..the second pick is now selling at proportionate value.

6. *Painting.* See quot. and PICK *v.*[1] 17 a.

1836 SMART, *Pick*,..that which is picked in, either by a point or by a pointed pencil. **1882** in OGILVIE; and in later Dicts.

7. *Printing.* **a.** A speck of hardened ink or dirt that gets into the hollows of types in forme and causes a blot on the printed page. **b.** An intrusive bit of metal on an electrotype or stereotype plate.

1683 MOXON *Mech. Exerc.*, *Printing* 387 When..pieces of the..Film that grows on Inck with standing by, or any dirt, get into the Hollows of the Face of the Letter, that Film or Dirt will fill or choak up the Face of the Letter, and Print Black; and is called a Pick; because the Press-man with the Point of a Needle, picks it out. **1731** BAILEY (ed. 5), *A Pick* (among Printers), a Blot occasioned by Dirt on the Letters. **1771** LUCKOMBE *Hist. Printing* 352 It will be a Pick, and print black, and deface the work. **1882** J. SOUTHWARD *Pract. Printing* (1884) 14 Foreign matter that adheres to the face of a type..causes a blotch in the impression. This is called pick. **1886** *Cassell's Encycl. Dict.*, *Pick*,..little drops of metal on stereotype plates.

†**8.** Each of the spots on dice; = PIP *sb.*[2] 1. *Obs. rare.*

1610 GUILLIM *Heraldry* IV. xii. 222 The square, which alwaies falleth right howsouer it be cast, is the Embleme of Constancy, but the vncertainety of the Picks, is the very Type of inconstancy, and mutability.

9. A local name of the bar-tailed godwit.

1885 SWAINSON *Prov. Names Brit. Birds* 198 Bar-tailed Godwit..Pick (Norfolk), Prine (Essex). From its habit of probing the mud for food.

10. In basketball, a permissible block (see quot. 1961).

1951 *Sun* (Baltimore) 24 Dec. 13/2 There is no consistency among officials on calling picks and screens. **1961** J. S. SALAK *Dict. Amer. Sports* 325 To set a pick, the offensive player is entitled to take up a position in front of a defensive opponent provided such maneuver does not hinder the 'normal movement' of the defensive man. **1976** A. CROSS *Question of Max* iv. 43 Kate..had become someting of a basketball aficionado... To her..regret, she could never recognize when someone had set a 'pick', and she tended to admire the wrong members of any team.

pick, *sb.*[4] *north. dial.* [f. PICK *v.*[2]]

1. An act of throwing or pitching, a cast, throw; a push or thrust; = PITCH *sb.*[2]

1627 HAKEWILL *Apol.* (1630) 423 He adventured four hundred thousand Sesterces upon every pick of the dice. **1876** *Mid-Yorks. Gloss.* s.v., He gave him a pick, and over he went..'Give him a pick-ower'. **1877** *Holderness Gloss.*, *Pick*, a sudden push.

2. *Weaving.* A cast or throw of the shuttle; the stroke that drives the shuttle: taken as a unit of measurement in reckoning the speed of the loom.

1851 L. D. B. GORDON in *Art Jrnl. Illustr. Catal.* p. viii**/2 The new looms can be driven at 220 picks per minute. **1875** KNIGHT *Dict. Mech.* 1696/2 The pick is the blow which drives the shuttle, and is delivered upon the armed head of the shuttle by the *picker-head* on the end of the oscillating *picker-staff*. **1894** *Contemp. Rev.* Feb. 194 Our Lancashire weaver attends on an average 3·9 looms running 240 picks a minute.

b. *transf.* In textiles, A single thread of the weft (produced by one pick of the shuttle): esp. used in reference to the number of threads in the inch, as determining the fineness of the fabric.

double pick loom, a loom in which two shots or picks of weft are inserted together into the shed or opening of the warp.

1860 BARTLETT *Dict. Amer.* (ed. 3) s.v., The relative quality of cotton cloth is denoted by the number of picks it has to the inch. **1876** HOLDSWORTH (*title*) Ready Reckoner for Hanks in Worsted Pieces, being Tables giving the net yarn in hanks required in pieces from five to fifty picks per quarter inch. **1878** A. BARLOW *Weaving* xxxi. 318 The warp is eight of black and four of white, the filling is pick and pick, black and white. **1898** *Daily News* 7 Mar. 2/1 Most classes of goods have hitherto been made with a change of shed for each pick of weft put in by the shuttle. The weft in this double Pick Loom is carried on two bobbins placed in a shuttle of the same length as the ordinary one, and such is the nature of the arrangement that the weft is carried through the shed, and one end laid behind the other with the greatest ease.

3. That which is pitched or thrown, as a flat stone in the game of PICKIE. *dial.*

1898 ALICE B. GOMME *Games* II. 451 The pick (small flat stone) is pitched into No. 1 bed..The player must hop and use the foot on the ground to strike 'pick'.

4. An emetic. *dial.*

1828 *Craven Gloss.* (ed. 2), *Pick*, an emetic. **1880** *N. & Q.* 6th Ser. I. 344 The doctor gave him a pick.

pick, *sb.*[5] *north. dial.* [ad. F. *pique* spade in cards, prop. 'pike'.] The spade in playing-cards.

1787 GROSE *Provinc. Gloss.*, *Picks*, spades; from piques, French. *N. Pick-Ace*, the ace of spades. *N.* **1819** J. BURNESS *Tales* 286 (Jam.) He then laid out the ace o' picks. **1825** JAMIESON, *Picks*, the suit of cards called spades. *Mearns, Aberd.*

pick, *sb.*[6], northern form of PITCH *sb.*[1]

pick, *sb.*[7], obs. form of PIKE, mountain peak.

pick, *sb.*[8], obs. and Sc. variant of PIQUE.

pick, *sb.*[9], obs. form of PIC[2], the measure.

pick, *a.* *colloq.* [attrib. use of PICK *sb.*[3] 3.] Picked, chosen, best.

1819 LADY MORGAN *Autobiog.* (1859) 302 We had the pick and choice singers of the two great operas. **1899** *Daily News* 2 Sept. 6/4 It is the pick week of the season.

pick (pɪk), *v.*[1] Forms: *α.* 1 ? pic(i)an, 4 pyken (5 -yn), piken, 4–9 *Sc.* and *north. dial.* **pike, pyke.** *β.*

(? 4–6 pik), 5–7 picke, 6 pycke, picque, *Sc.* pyk, pikk, 6– pick. [This vb. is found with long and short *i*, *pīken*, *pik(k)en*, *pike*, *pick*, of which the former is app. the earlier, but the latter the surviving form in Standard Eng., though *pike* (paɪk) survives in the same senses in northern and some midland dialects. The earliest known trace of the word is in the vbl. sb. *picung* (? (iː) or (ɪ)), a gloss on L. *stigmata*, in Corpus Gloss. *c* 725, implying a vb. *pician* ((iː) or (i)) or *pīcan* to puncture. MS. F. of the OE. Chronicle has, anno 796, a verb uncertainly read *pycan* or *pytan*, more prob. the latter. Otherwise no examples have yet been found before 1300. In sense 1 there is evident connexion with PICK *sb.*[1] 1, PIKE *sb.*[1] 1, and (esp. in 1 b) some agreement of sense with F. *piquer* (which is similarly related to *pic*); but the sense-development in Eng. is very different from that of F. *piquer* and the cognate Pr., Sp., Pg. *picar* and It. *piccare*, which adhere always more or less closely to the sense 'puncture, pierce, prick, sting', a notion which in Eng. barely enters into sense 2, and is entirely absent from the other senses. On the other hand, verbs akin in form and meaning occur in the Middle and Modern stages of the Teutonic langs.: cf. late ON. (13th c.) *pikka, pjakka* 'to peck, prick' (Vigf.), Norw. *pikka*, Sw. *picka*, Da. *pikke* to pick, peck, pierce with pointed tool, also to beat, palpitate, throb; MLG., LG., E.Fris. *pikken* to pick, peck, MDu. *picken* to pick, peck as a bird, pierce or strike with beak, cut with sickle or scythe (Kilian); Du. *pikken* to pick, peck; mod.Ger. (from LG.) *picken* to peck as a bird, pick or puncture with a sharp tool (also *pīken, pieken*). Compare also Welsh *pīgo*, Corn. *piga* 'to prick, sting, pick, peck' (said e.g. of a pin, a thorn, a bird), which goes with *pīg* sb. fem. 'anything pointed, sharp point, beak, bill, neb', with similar forms in Breton, and a large family of derivatives and connected words, from the root *pīk-*. All these words in the various languages go back to earlier forms in *pīk-*, *pik-*, *pikk-*; but the question of their ulterior history and relations is involved in obscurity and conflicting difficulties. The Romanic verbs point to an original form **pĭccāre*, related to **pīccus*, Sp. *pico*, F. *pic*, for conjectures as to the origin of which see PIKE *sb.*[1], note. In OE., *pīcung* is supported by the sb. *piic, pīc*, PIKE; but there are no cognate words in the other Teutonic languages in their early stage. In Welsh and Cornish, however, *pīgo, pīga*, appear to be native words; going back, with the cognate sb. *pīg*, to a Brythonic root *pīk-*, corresponding perhaps to a proto-Celtic **qīk-* (see PIKE *sb.*[1], note). The modern Irish and Gaelic *pic, pioc*, and their derivatives are, of course, from English.

The two forms *pick* and *pike* might have been treated as separate words, as in the sbs. PICK[1], PIKE[1]. But in the inflected forms of the vb. in early quots., the length of the *i* is often doubtful, so that the separation would be difficult; and in modern times, *pike* exists only as a dialect form of *pick*. It is therefore most convenient to combine the two under the current literary form *pick*, separating the examples, where possible, under α and β, and stating in what senses *pike* continues in dialect use. Sometimes there is differentiation: in S. E. Scotch, *pike* is distinct from *pick*, and used only in senses 2, 2 b, 3, b, c; but in other Sc. and Eng. dialects, and in earlier Sc., *pike* is used in other senses also.]

I. 1. a. *trans.* To pierce, penetrate, indent, dig into, or break the surface of (anything) by striking it with something sharp or pointed, as to break up (ground, a road, etc.) with a pick, to indent the surface of (a millstone); †rarely, to hoe. Also *absol.*, to ply the pick, mattock, pickaxe, etc.

α. *c* **1330** R. BRUNNE *Chron.* (1810) 272 Pikit him, & dikit him, on scorne said he, He pikes & dikes in length, as him likes, how best it may be. **1377** LANGL. *P. Pl.* B. XVI. 17 And . . hath þe londe to ferme . . to pyken it and to weden it. **1483** CAXTON *Gold. Leg.* 424/1 To whome the . . bysshop gafe of his wode as moche as he myght pyke & delue & throwe doun with hys owne handes.

β. *c* **1375** *Sc. Leg. Saints* vii. (*Jacobus minor*) 754 He saw a wal wes fow thyke; & his mynowris þare gert he pyke, In entent to caste it done [*for* thyk, pyk, *or* thykke, pykke]. **1513** DOUGLAS *Æneis* VIII. Prol. 168, I grapit graithly the gyll, Every modywart hyll, Bot I mycht pyk thair my fyll Or penny com out. *a* **1625** SIR H. FINCH *Law* (1636) 135 A Mill-stone, though it be lifted vp to be picked and beaten . . remaineth parcell of the Mill. **1756** J. LLOYD in W. Thompson *R.N. Advoc.* (1757) 51, I have often desired the Grinder not to pick his Mill so often with the sharp Pikes. **1874** RAYMOND *Statist. Mines & Mining* 369 There is an immense body of ore in sight which can be easily picked and shoveled up. **1883** GRESLEY *Gloss. Terms Coal-mining, Pick* . . , to dress with a pick the sides of a shaft or other excavation. **1895** *Funk's Stand. Dict., Pick the flint*, formerly, to freshen the striking surface of a gun-flint to insure ignition: now used figuratively; as, to pick one's flint and try again. **1898** MACMANUS *Bend of Road* 40 The same lad . . can see as far through a millstone as the man picked it. *Mod.* The ground is so hard, that it will be necessary to pick it.

†**b.** Of a bird: To pierce or strike with the bill, to peck; of an insect: to puncture. *Obs.*

1555 EDEN *Decades* Pref. (Arb.) 53 Isopes frogges to whom . . Iupiter sent a hearon to picke them in the hedes. **1585** T. WASHINGTON tr. *Nicholay's Voy.* II. viii. 41 b, Small . . wormes, which with their billes and stinges picking the other figs, sodaynely after they are picked, they come to . . perfect rypenesse. **1599** MINSHEU *Sp. Dict., Picar*, to picke or pecke . . Also to pricke or picke as with a pin or needle. **1604** DEKKER *Honest Wh.* Wks. 1873 II. 107 Shall a silly bird picke her owne brest to nourish her yong ones? **1645** G. DANIEL *Poems* Wks. 1878 II. 45 Or like the Falcon, knit Vnto the Perch . . I picke my Iesses; and assay For Libertie, in everie way.

c. To make or form by picking: in phrase ***to pick a hole*** or ***holes in*** something. ***to pick a hole in a person's coat***: see HOLE *sb.* 9.

1648–1898 [see HOLE *sb.* 9]. **1651** C. CARTWRIGHT *Cert. Relig.* I. 6 Saint Hierom was the first that ever pickt a hole in the Scriptures. **1681** FLAVEL *Meth. Grace* xxix. 503 The most envious and observing eyes . . could not pick a hole . . in any of his words or actions. **1768–74** TUCKER *Lt. Nat.* (1834) II. 314 We of the civilized countries have still so much of the savage left in us, that we fall . . picking holes in characters, manners, and sentiments. **1828** *Craven Gloss.* (ed. 2) s.v. *Pike*, Thou's ollas piking a hole i my cooat. **1849** THACKERAY *Pendennis* ix, Not being able to pick a hole in poor Miss Fotheringay's reputation.

2. a. To probe or penetrate with a pointed instrument, or the like (e.g. with the finger-nail, or a bird with its beak, etc.), so as to remove any extraneous matter: e.g. *to pick the teeth, the nose, the ear, the nails.*

α. *c* **1430** LYDG. *Stans Puer* 12 in *Babees Bk.* 27 Pike not þi nose; & moost in especial . . to-fore þi souereyn cratche ne picke þee nouȝt. *Ibid.* 42 þi teeþ also at þe table picke with no knyf [*v.r.* ne pike not with thi knyff]. *a* **1651** CALDERWOOD *Hist. Kirk* (1843) II. 204 Have yee not seene one . . sitting . . where yee sitt, pyke his nailes, and pull doun his bonnet over his eyes, when . . vices were rebooked?

β. *c* **1430** (see α). **1607** TOPSELL *Hist. Four-f. Beasts* (1658) 239 It is good toward night to pick, cleanse, and open his hoofs, with some artificial instrument. **1728** YOUNG *Love Fame* iii. 36 Like the bold bird upon the banks of Nile, That picks the teeth of the dire crocodile. **1768** LADY M. COKE *Jrnl.* 13 Aug. (1889) II. 336 He picked his Nose, which you know is neither graceful or royal. **1784** COWPER *Task* II. 627 He picks clean teeth, and, busy as he seems With an old tavern quill, is hungry yet. **1832** MARRYAT *N. Forster* xxxiv, The Portuguese picked their teeth with their forks.

b. Applied to using the finger-nails to remove or relieve a pimple, scab, or sore place.

1676 WISEMAN *Chirurg. Treat.* II. x. 193 An *Herpes exedens* . . being heated by scratching or picking with their Nails will terminate corrosive. **1854** *Hooper's Physician's Vade Mecum* (ed. 4) 590. **1899** *Allbutt's Syst. Med.* VIII. 837 An itching or tingling which induces the patient to pick or scratch the part.

II. 3. a. To clear or cleanse (a thing), with the fingers or the like, of any extraneous or refuse substance, as to pick a fowl (of its feathers), to pick fruit, as currants, strawberries, etc. (of their stalks, calyx leaves, etc.); to cleanse (anything) by removal of refuse, dirt, or unsuitable parts. ***a crow to pick*** (properly *pluck*): see CROW *sb.*[1] 3 b.

α. *c* **1325** *W. de Bibbesw.* in Wright *Voc.* 153 Eschuvet flatour [*gl.* losenjour] ke seet flater, Trop seet ben espeluker [*gloss* piken]. **1390** GOWER *Conf.* III. 162 He satte him thanne doun and pyketh, And wyssh his herbes in the flod. *c* **1440** *Promp. Parv.* 397/2 Pykyn, or clensyn, or cullyn owte the on-clene, *purgo*. *c* **1440** *Anc. Cookery* in *Househ. Ord.* (1790) 428 Take flesh of a Roo and pyke hit clene. **1530** PALSGR. 657/1, I pyke or make clene, *je nettoye* . . . I prye you, pyke my combe. *Ibid.*, I pyke saffrone or any floure or corne, whan I sorte one parte of them from another.

β. **1764** ELIZ. MOXON *Eng. Housew.* (ed. 9) 154 Gather your gooseberries . . pick and bottle them. **1806** A. HUNTER *Culina* (ed. 3) 226 Put in three sets of goose giblets well picked. **1865** *Sat. Rev.* 5 Aug. 179/1 To say nothing of all the crows which he finds to pick with his author on his own account. **1871** *Routledge's Ev. Boy's Ann.* May 273 There was only one thing he could really do properly, and that was, pick birds. **1883** GRESLEY *Gloss. Terms Coal-mining, Pick* . . 3. To remove shale, dirt, &c., from coals.

b. ***to pick a bone***, to clear it of all adherent flesh (which in this case is the valuable part); so ***to pick a carcass***, etc.: with various constructions. Hence, *fig.* to strip or rob ***a person*** of all he has, to reduce to starvation or indigence. ***to have a bone to pick with any one***: see BONE *sb.* 6 c.

α. **1483** *Cath. Angl.* 278/1 To Pike A bane, *opisare, opicare*. **1724** RAMSAY *Vision* xxiii, Sum thanes their tennants pykt and squeist. **1737** —— *Scot. Prov.* (1776) 33 He's unco fou in his ain house that canna pike a bane in his neighbour's. **1863** MRS. TOOGOOD *Yorks. Dial.*, You can pike that bone.

β. **1579** [see BONE *sb.* 6 c]. **1651** CLEVELAND *Poems* 37, I wrong the Devil, should I pick their bones. **1676** W. ROW *Contn. Blair's Autobiog.* xii. (1848) 462 Pick a bishop to the bones, he'll soon gather flesh and blood again. **1700** T. BROWN *Amusem. Ser. & Com.* 33 The Cannibal Man-catchers . . that . . pick the Bones of all the Paupers that fall into their Clutches. **1730** SWIFT *Death & Daphne* 34 Bare, like a carcase pickt by crows. **1774** GOLDSM. *Nat. Hist.* (1776) V. 110 [Vultures] pour down upon the carcass; and, in an instant, pick its bones as bare and clean as if they had been scraped by a knife. **1799** SOUTHEY *God's Judgem. Wicked Bishop* xix, They have whetted their teeth against the stones, And now they pick the Bishop's bones. **1840** THACKERAY *Catherine* i, He could pick the wing of a fowl. **1845** MRS. S. C. HALL *Whiteboy* iv. 35 A leg of mutton . . fit for the most delicate lady in Ireland 'to pick'. **1884** RIDER HAGGARD *Dawn* iv, I consider that I have got a bone to pick with Providence about that nose.

c. *intr. Sc.*

c **1550** R. BIESTON *Bayte Fortune* A ij, And cast thee forth a bone to pike vpon. **1565** [see BONE *sb.* 6 c]. **1794** BURNS *Amang the Trees* ii, The hungry bike did scrape and pike Til we were wae and weary, O.

†**4.** To cleanse, make trim or neat, trick out, prank; to deck, adorn; of a bird: to preen (its feathers). Also *absol.* *Obs.* (Cf. APYKE *v.*)

α. *c* **1330** R. BRUNNE *Chron. Wace* (Rolls) 11191 þenne come chamberleyns & squiers, Riche robes of mani maners, To folde, to presse, & to pyke [*rime* strike]. *c* **1386** CHAUCER *Merch. T.* 2011 He kembeth hym, he preyneth hym and pyketh. *c* **1440** *Gesta Rom.* lv. 237 (Harl. MS.), She lovide ande pikide, fedde, ande tawȝte this childe. **1483** CAXTON *Gold. Leg.* 189 b/2 Saynt loye . . made clene theyr heedes & wysshe them and them that were lowsy and ful of vermyne he hym self wold pyke and make them clene. **1486** *Bk. St. Albans* B vij b, Then after when she [an hawke] begynnyth to penne, and plumyth, and spalchith and pikith her selfe. **1549** COVERDALE, etc. *Erasm. Par. Eph.* v. 27 Though she was disteyned before tyme . . he clensed her, he pyked her, and made her perfectly trimme in euery poynt. **1552** ELYOT *Dict., Como*, to kembe or decke the busshe: . . to trymme, to attyre, to pyke.

arch. [*a* **1643** W. CARTWRIGHT *Ordinary* II. ii. (1651) B vij b, Cembeth thy self, and pyketh now thy self; Sleeketh thy self.]

β. *c* **1540** tr. *Pol. Verg. Eng. Hist.* (Camden) I. 243 But the woman . . decked and picked herselfe in the hartiest manner. **1611** MARKHAM *Countr. Content.* I. i. (1668) 12 Hounds love naturally to stretch them, and pick themselves in the Sun. **1657** J. WATTS *Dipper Sprinkled* 31 A common pond . . wherein . . Geese, Ducks, do daily duck and pick themselves. **1681** W. ROBERTSON *Phraseol. Gen.* (1693) 989 To pick or prain, as a bird doth herself. [*a* **1682** SIR T. BROWNE *Tracts* ii. *Garlands*, The Ægyptians . . beside the bravery of their garlands, had little birds to peck their heads and brows.]

III. 5. a. To detach and take, esp. with the fingers, (anything) from the place in which it grows or adheres, or from that which contains it; to pluck, gather, cull (growing flowers, fruit, etc.); said also of a bird, with its beak. See also 18, 19.

α. *c* **1325** *Gloss W. de Bibbesw.* in Wright *Voc.* 156 Autre foyȝe le lyn eslyseȝ flax [*gl.* pik thi flax]. *c* **1380** [see *pick away*, 16]. **1550** BALE *Eng. Votaries* II. A iv, Arnold bishop of Metis . . at layser made the king to go pike a salet. **1855** ROBINSON *Whitby Gloss.*, To *Pike*, to pick or take up, to gather.

β. **1523** FITZHERB. *Husb.* §23 That the moldywarpe-hilles be spredde, and the styckes cleane pycked out of the medowe. **1562** TURNER *Herbal* II. 89 b, Hole nuttes lately pikked from the trees. **1593** SHAKS. *2 Hen. VI*, IV. x. 9 Wherefore on a Bricke wall haue I climb'd into this Garden, to see if I can eate Grasse, or picke a Sallet another while. **1601** —— *All's Well* IV. v. 15 Wee may picke a thousand sallets ere wee light on such another hearbe. **1769** MRS. RAFFALD *Eng. Housekpr.* (1778) 229 Pick the female barberries clean from the stalks. **1859** TENNYSON *Guinevere* 33 As the gardener's hand Picks from the colewort a green caterpillar. **1863** KINGSLEY *Water Bab.* i. 12 Tom . . longed . . to get over a gate, and pick buttercups. **1875–81** To pick hops [see HOP[1] 1, HOP-PICKER]. **1896** H. FREDERIC *Illumination* 117 She picked some of these [pinks] for him.

fig. **1580** LYLY *Euphues* (Arb.) 246 The women there are wise, the men craftie: they will gather loue by thy lookes, and picke thy minde out of thy hands. **1596** SHAKS. *Merch. V.* II. ix. 48 And how much honor [would then be] Pickt from the chaffe and ruine of the times, To be new varnisht. **1603** KNOLLES *Hist. Turks* (J.), Hope, that he should out of these his enemies distresses pick some fit occasion of advantage. *a* **1613** OVERBURY *A Wife*, etc. (1638) 130 He picks a living out of others gaines. **1859** TENNYSON *Enid* 1751 Full seldom doth a man repent, or use Both grace and will to pick the vicious quitch Of blood and custom wholly out of him.

†**b.** *fig.* To 'gather' or 'draw' with the mind; to infer, deduce, make out. *Obs.*

1565 CALFHILL *Answ. Treat. Crosse* (Parker Soc.) 104 And truly, if we mark the place itself, much better doctrine may be pyked of it, than to prefigurate I wot not what manner of Cross unto us. **1590** SHAKS. *Mids. N.* V. i. 100 Trust me sweete, Out of this silence yet, I pickt a welcome. **1593** —— *Lucr.* 100 But she that never coped with stranger eyes, Could pick no meaning from their parling looks. **1621** QUARLES *Div. Poems, Esther* (1717) 104 'Twas not the sharpness of thy wandring eye, (Great King Assuerus) to pick Majesty From out the sadness of a Captive face.

c. Phr. ***pick your own***, used *attrib.* (usu. hyphened) and *absol.* of a marketing system at a farm, orchard, or the like, where customers gather the produce themselves instead of being served by the seller. Abbrev. *p-y-o*, *PYO* s.v. P III.

1969 *Agriculture* May 221 In Kent there is a growing tendency for strawberry growers with roadside plots to encourage 'pick your own' selling. **1969** *Farm Q.* Harvest 64/3 He sold wholesale strawberries for 16 years before deciding to go pick-your-own exclusively. **1970** *Globe & Mail* (Toronto) 28 Sept. 5/1 Chudleigh's is a 'pick your own' farm and hundreds of families jump into their cars every weekend in the fall to pick their own apples. **1987** *Daily Tel.* 21 Feb. 14/1 All manner of exotic crops . . and unlikely livestock . . have been proposed [as alternative land uses] as well as the more conventional: forestry, food processing and 'Pick Your Own'.

6. a. Of birds, and some beasts: To take up (grains or small bits of food) with bill or teeth; also, of persons, to bite or eat in small bits or delicately; *colloq.* to eat. Cf. PECK *v.*[1] 4.

1430–40 LYDG. *Bochas* IX. i. (1558) 20 b, Milke white doues which that piked greine. **1616** SURFL. & MARKH. *Country Farme* 717 Lay before her flies, or little wormes, which by their crauling will stir vp the bird to picke them. **1728** VANBR. & CIB. *Prov. Husb.* IV. iv, I'd fain pick a bit with you. **1786** Capt. T. Morris *Songs, Lyra Urban.* (1848) I. 80–2 (Farmer), I hope from their budget they'll pick out a song, While I'll pick a little more dinner. **1844** Dickens *Mart. Chuz.* xxv, 'I think, young woman', said Mrs. Gamp, ..'that I could pick a little bit of pickled salmon'. **1862** Borrow *Wild Wales* xlviii. (1901) 154/1 A few miserable sheep picking the wretched herbage. **1879** Stevenson *Trav. Cevennes* 167, I picked a meal in fear and trembling. **1893** —— *Catriona* 22 We'll pick a bit of dinner.

b. *intr.* To eat with pecking or small bites; of a person, 'to eat slowly and by small morsels' (J.), to eat fastidiously or daintily; *slang* or *colloq.* to take food, to eat. Cf. peck *v.*[1] 4.

1584 Cogan *Haven Health* ccxiii. (1636) 222 For (as it is said) children and chicken, would bee alwayes picking. **1648–78** Hexham, *Picken als de vogels*, to Pick as Birds doe. **1693** Dryden *Persius' Sat.* iii. 231 Why stand'st thou picking? Is thy Pallat sore? **1786** Capt. T. Morris *Songs, Lyra Urban.* (1848) I. 80–82 (Farmer) For me I protest, if it wasn't for shame, I could pick till to-morrow at dinner. **1800** Mrs. Hervey *Mourtray Fam.* I. 178 Rather picking than eating any thing, because she affected ill health. **1886** Stevenson *Kidnapped* iii 18, I could never do mair than pyke at food. **1895** Mrs. B. M. Croker *Village Tales* (1896) 74 The milch goats were browsing, and the poultry picking about.

IV. 7. a. To choose out, select carefully, cull; cf. *pick out*, 19 b; colloq. phr. ***to pick them***: in emphatic contexts, to make a wise choice, *spec.* in personal relationships (freq. *ironical*). Also in ***to pick one's men, one's words***, etc.

α. **1390** Gower *Conf.* I. 296 Rathere, if it mihte hir like, The beste wordes wolde I pike. *Ibid.* II. 90 Hou that men schal the wordes pike After the forme of eloquence. *a* **1586** Sidney *Arcadia* iii. (1622) 402 Let us pike our good from out much bad. **1709** Strype *Ann. Ref.* I. l. 505 He either wholly omitted Nowel's sayings..[or] here and there piked what he thought good. **1825** Brockett *N.C. Gloss.*, *Pike*, v., to pick, to select, to chuse. Dut. *picken*.

β. **1568** Grafton *Chron.* I. 188 [They] purged the olde and corrupt lawes, and picked out of them a certain..most profitable for the commons. **1634** W. Tirwhyt tr. *Balzac's Lett.* (vol. I.) 243 From thence the best Poets ordinarily pick their comparisons to pourtraite the rarest beauties. **1689** I. Mather in *Andros Tracts* II. 6 They have caused Juries to be pick'd of Men who are not of the Vicinity. **1735** Pope *Ep. Lady* 273 Heav'n..Picks from each sex, to make the Fav'rite blest, Your love of Pleasure, our desire of Rest. **1822** Hazlitt *Table-t.* Ser. ii. i. (1869) 29 You can pick your society no where but in London. **1859** Tennyson *Enid* 1028 Geraint, dismounting, pick'd the lance That pleased him best. **1897** *Evesham Jrnl.* 25 Sept. (E.D.D.), This player was not picked at the committee meeting. **1945** A. Marshall in *Coast to Coast 1944* 84 He greeted Olive cheerfully, then turned to me with simulated surprise. 'Well, you can certainly pick 'em,' he said. **1953** A. Christie *Pocket Full of Rye* x. 62 My stepmother was there... The old boy certainly knew how to pick them. **1966** H. Waugh *Pure Poison* (1967) ii. 11 Fred, glancing..to the young face of his daughter-in-law to be, had to admit that Larry could pick 'em. **1973** G. Scott *Water Horse* (1974) vii. 44 An art student, Polly? You do pick them, don't you. **1976** P. Henissart *Winter Quarry* xv. 150 'Christ, she really picks them,' muttered McGuire. 'Does she know who he is?' **1978** L. Meynell *Papersnake* iii. 53 Baa-Lamb came home..at the very agreeable odds of twelve to one... 'What did I tell you, cobber?.. If you can pick 'em, you can pick 'em.'

b. Phr. ***to pick one's way, steps***: to choose a way carefully through dirty or dangerous ground, in order to avoid its difficulties, etc.

1714 Gay *Trivia* i. 239 Deep through a miry lane she pick'd her way, Above her ancle rose the chalky clay. **1781** Crabbe *Library* 294 While judgment slowly picks his sober way. **1840** Dickens *Old C. Shop* lxii, A treacherous place to pick one's steps in. **1849** Clough *Dipsychus* ii. iv. 93 The dashing stream Stays not to pick his steps among the rocks. **1883** F. M. Peard *Contrad.* xxxii, She..picked her way between the heather and bracken.

†**c.** To search through (a place). *Obs. rare.*

1589 *Pappe w. Hatchet* (1844) 38, I picke hell, you shall not find such reasons.

d. *intr.* To search with some selection.

1824 Miss Ferrier *Inher.* xli, A vast collection of letters, ..amongst which she picked for some time..for the missive in question. **1897** *Daily News* 23 Dec. 7/1 A bran tub..from which they will pick for a present.

e. ***to pick and choose*** (or †***cull***), to select fastidiously or nicely. Often *absol.* or *intr.*

α. *c* **1407** Lydg. *Reson & Sens.* 6032 Noght but golde and stonys Chose and piked for the nonys.

β. **1585** T. Washington tr. *Nicholay's Voy.* iii. vii. 80 [They] are 300..chosen and picked out of the most.. excellent archers amongst the Ianissaries. **1665** Sir T. Herbert *Trav.* (1677) 37 So little was the resistance he found as he had the liberty to pick and choose. **1666** W. Boghurst *Loimographia* (1894) 90 Out of which you may pick and choose which you like best. **1705** Addison *Prol. to Steele's Tend. Husb.* 17 Our Modern Wits are forc'd to pick and cull, And here and there by Chance glean up a Fool. **1713** Steele *Guardian* No. 171 ¶3, I shall always pick and cull the Pantry for him. **1718** Hickes & Nelson *J. Kettlewell* iii. lxvi. 351 If Men were at Liberty to pick and chuse what they please in the Offices of the Church. **1862** Goulburn *Pers. Relig.* iv. v. (1873) 290 Picking and choosing the words which are used. *Mod.* Take them as they come: you must not pick and choose.

f. *ellipt.* for *to pick one's way*.

1865 R. D. Blackmore *Cradock Nowell* (1866) I. xvi. 153 Hogstaff tottered along before him, picking uneasily over the stones. **1878** Hardy *Ret. Native* I. iii. 66 The track is rough, but if you've got a light your horses may pick along wi' care. **1961** 'G. Holden' *Deadlier than Male* xiv. 102 This time the search took twice as long, cutting down on his extra reading, for he had to pick through several columns of one- and two-line social notes in each issue.

g. *trans.* To guess, deduce; to predict. *Austral.* and *N.Z. colloq.*

c **1926** 'Mixer' *Transport Workers' Song Bk.* 128 I'm picking we'll soon have a row. **1943** N. Marsh *Colour Scheme* vi. 100 There's a bit of a shelf above the cliff... I picked that was where he'd go. **1959** D. Niland *Big Smoke* vi. 145 He looked up at the boy with a pleased, questioning expression. 'I pick it right?'

8. a. To seek and find an occasion of; as ***to pick a quarrel with*** (†***against, at, to, unto***) a person, †also formerly ***to pick fault, to pick (an) occasion of*** (offence, etc.) or ***occasion to do*** (something), etc.

α. *c* **1449** *Paston Lett.* I. 87 The seyde parsone..hathe pekyd a qwarell to on Mastyr Recheforthe. *c* **1470** Henryson *Mor. Fab.* x. (*Fox & Wolf*) xxix, Ane wickit man ..pykis at thame all quarrellis that he can. **1513** More *Rich. III* (1883) 17 In his presence they piked a quarell to the Lorde Richard Graye. **1530** Palsgr. 657/1, I pyke a quarell, or fynde maters to fall out with one for. **1540** Hyrde tr. *Vives' Instr. Chr. Wom.* iii. vi. (1541) 138 b, They medle with other folkes busines..exhort and giue preceptes, rebuke and correcte, pyke fautes. **1581** J. Bell *Haddon's Answ. Osor.* 156 b, From whence doth he pike this quarell? **1584** Hudson *Du Bartas' Judith* iv, Yet some will quarrell pike, And common bruit will deem them all alike.

β. *a* **1529** Skelton *Bowge of Courte* 314 Fyrste pycke a quarell, and fall oute with hym then. **1530** Palsgr. 656/2, I pycke no mater, or I pycke no quarrell to one. *c* **1555** Harpsfield *Divorce Hen. VIII* (Camden) 270 Then is there a causeless quarrel picked against the Popes. **1568** Grafton *Chron.* II. 811 Neyther the Lion, nor the Bore shall picke any matter at anye thing here spoken. **1599** *Life Sir T. More* in Wordsw. *Eccl. Biog.* (1853) II. 132 Every day some quarrelling matter or other was pickt against him. **1599** Shaks. *Hen. V*, iii. ii. 111, I sall quit you with gud leue, as I may pick occasion. **1610** Willet *Hexapla Dan.* 182 They ..picke what matter they can against him. **1623** Laud in Ellis *Orig. Lett.* Ser. ii. III. 242 They..have picked all the occacions they could to detract from mee. **1674** Allen *Danger Enthusiasm* 29 [They] raised Cavils and pickt Quarrels against it. **1697** J. Sergeant *Solid Philos.* 367 He will..doubtless, pick new Quarrels at the Definition. **1709** Strype *Ann. Ref.* I. lvii. 581 These did too often (where they could pick occasion) use rigor towards such as more sincerely and earnestly served God. **1785** Jefferson *Corr.* Wks. 1859 I. 449 The question is..with whom the Emperor will pick the next quarrel. **1894** Hall Caine *Manxman* v. xiv. 325 Some of the men began to pick quarrels.

†**b.** Phrase. ***to pick a thank*** (***thanks***) ***of*** (***with***) (a person): to curry favour with, as by sycophancy or tale-bearing; also *absol.*, to play the sycophant or tale-bearer. Cf. pickthank.

α. *c* **1412** Hoccleve *De Reg. Princ.* 3048 A þank to pike, His lordys wil and witte he iustifieth. **1549** Coverdale, etc. *Erasm. Par. 2 Pet.* 17 False prophetes..whiche eyther to pyke a thanke at yͤ princes hande or elles..for hatred of other, prophecied the thinge, whiche the spirite of God spake not. **1560** Daus tr. *Sleidane's Comm.* Pref. 5 b, Manye of those wryters seke to pike a thanke.

β. **1560** Pilkington *Expos. Aggeus* (1562) 347 Thinkinge thereby too picke a thanke, and get a rewarde of David. **1579** Lyly *Euphues* (Arb.) 55 Least I should seeme either to picke a thanke with men, or a quarel with women. **1600** Holland *Livy* vi. xxvi. 235, I will not..pick my selfe a privat thanke for a publike benefit. **1611** Cotgr., *Escornifler*,..to pick a thanke or carry tales for victuals. **1627** Sanderson *Serm.*, *Ad Mag.* ii. (1657) 134 Doeg to pick a thank with his Master, ..told tales of David and Abimelech. *a* **1648** Ld. Herbert *Hen. VIII* (1683) 481 Some..that would now perchance pick them thank without desert. **1681** W. Robertson *Phraseol. Gen.* (1693) 989 To pick thanks, *sycophantari*.

†**c.** ***to pick*** (***acquaintance*** or ***chat with***): to seek occasion of, cultivate, make gradually. *Obs.*

1720 De Foe *Capt. Singleton* xviii, The doctor was made the first to pick acquaintance. **1770** J. Adams *Diary* 19 Aug., Mr. Royal Tyler began to pick chat with me.

V. 9. a. To rob, plunder (a person or place); to rifle the contents of (anything); †to take by robbery, to steal (goods, etc.). Now only in phr. ***to pick*** a person's ***pocket*** or ***purse***, also *fig.*, his ***brains***.

α. *c* **1300** *Song of Husbandman* 25 in *Pol. Songs* (Camden) 150 Thus me pileth the pore and pyketh ful clene. **1301** [see piker[1] 1]. *c* **1325** *Song of Yesterday* 178 He [Death] comeþ so baldely, to pike his pray. *c* **1385** Chaucer *L.G.W.* 2467 *Phillis*, [He] pikid of hire al the good he myghte. **1390** Gower *Conf.* II. 367 He..thoghte he wolde be som weie The tresor pyke and stele aweie. *c* **1400** *Destr. Troy* 1371 The Grekes..Prayen and pyken mony priuey chambur. **1401** *Pol. Poems* (Rolls) II. 66 Ther we piken but seely pans Thi secte pikith poundis. *c* **1460** *Towneley Myst.* xxviii. 335 Thi close [clothes] so can [= gan] thai fro the pyke. *a* **1476** *5th Rep. Hist. MSS. Comm.* 530/1 If ony be founde.. pikeyng purses or other smale thynges. **1530** Lyndesay *Test. Pap.* 678, I did persaue, quhen preuelye ȝe did pyke Ane chekin frome ane hen, vnder ane dyke. **1612** Jas. I in Ellis *Orig. Lett.* i. III. 106 To cause youre Officers..pyke shillings from poore Skottismen. [**1865** G. Macdonald *A. Forbes* 19 An' min' and no pyke the things i' the chop (= shop).]

β. **1531** Tindale *Expos. 1 John* (1537) 8 He were a foole which wolde trust hym..that hath pycked his purse before his face. **1555** W. Watreman *Fardle of Facions* App. 338 Lette him that shall haue picqued either Golde or Siluer paye the double. **1591** Greene *Maidens Dreame* x, Delaying law, that picks the client's purse. **1596** Shaks. *1 Hen. IV*, iii. iii. 94 Shall I not take mine ease at mine Inne, but I shall haue my Pocket pick'd? **1612** J. Taylor (Water P.) *Trav.* Wks. (1872) 35 One of them held the good wife with a tale, the whilst another was picking her chest. **1727** Gay *Begg. Op.* i. vi, He hath as fine a hand at picking a pocket as a woman. **1838** Lytton *Alice* vii. v, His success in picking the brain of Mr. Onslow of a secret encouraged him. **1879** Spurgeon *Serm.* XXV. 112 A person may very readily pick my pocket of my purse. **1885** T. A. Guthrie *Tinted Venus* 89 Want to pick my brains?

b. *intr.* or *absol.* In later use felt as a kind of euphemism for: To practise petty theft, to pick up 'unconsidered trifles', to appropriate small things or portions of things such as it is thought will not be noticed; to pilfer, to filch. Chiefly in phr. ***pick and steal***, familiar from the Church Catechism, and now app. associated with sense 5.

α. **1390** Gower *Conf.* II. 351 This proverbe is evere newe, That stronge lokes maken trewe Of hem that wolden stele and pyke [*v.r.* pile]. **1559** *Mirr. Mag.*, *Owen Glendour* iii, The suttle Fox doth pyke.

β. **1548–9** (Mar.) *Bk. Com. Prayer, Catech.*, To kepe my handes from picking and stealing. **1552** Latimer *Rem.* (Parker Soc.) 87 Many folks..exhort themselves to do wickedly, to steal, to pick, and to do all lewdness. **1552** Huloet, Picke craftelye, *Manticulor* [printed *Mantiscinor*]. [**1565–73** Cooper, *Mantiscinor, aris*, to steale craftily.]

10. To open (a lock) with a pointed instrument, a skeleton key, or the like; to open clandestinely. (Usually with implication of intended robbery.)

1546 J. Heywood *Prov.* (1867) 81 She mynded..To picke the..locke. **1592** Shaks. *Ven. & Ad.* 576 Were beauty under twenty locks kept fast, Yet love breaks through and picks them all at last. **1757** R. Lloyd *Ep.* Poet. Wks. 1774 I. 101 If chests he breaks, if locks he picks. **1833** Marryat *P. Simple* xxi, O'Brien pulled out his picklocks to pick it. **1853** C. Bronte *Villette* xiv, The lock of resolution which neither Time nor Temptation has..picked. **1881** Young *Every Man his own Mechanic* §1494 When a key is lost, and the door happens to be locked, a smith will pick it, as it is technically called, with a piece of bent wire.

transf. **1883** D. H. Wheeler *By-ways Lit.* viii. 150 (Funk) Cassius..picks Brutus open as easily as he would an oyster.

VI. 11. a. To separate by picking, to pull or comb asunder: usually with defining adv. or phrase: as ***pick to pieces*** (also *fig.*); but simply in ***pick oakum, pick cotton*** or ***wool***.

1536 [*implied in* wulpiker: see picker[1] 1 f]. **1538** Elyot *Lat. Dict.*, *Carminarii*, they that do pike [*ed.* 1545 picke] or make clene wulle, or carde. **1565–78** Cooper *Thesaurus*, *Carminatio*, the picking or carding of wull.. He or she that picketh or cardeth wull. **1683** in *New Mills Cloth Manuf.* (S.H.S.) 55 For piking scribbling and oyll. **1690** Child *Disc. Trade* (1694) 105 The girls may be employed in mending the clothes of the aged... The boys in picking okam. **1733** P. Lindsay *Interest Scot.* 23 Easy Labour at first, such as picking of Wool or Cotton, teasing of Ockam. **1859** Helps *Friends in C.* Ser. ii. II. iv. 83 Power of picking what I say to pieces. **1869** Trollope *He Knew*, etc. lxxxi. (1878) 449 They'll pick you to pieces a little among themselves. **1874** *Punch* 14 Mar. 110/1 Picking oakum in penal servitude.

b. *intr.* for *pass.* To admit of being picked.

1794 *Rigging & Seamanship* I. 62 The yarn..will pick into oakum.

12. To pluck the strings of a musical instrument, as the banjo. *U.S.*

1860 Bartlett *Dict. Amer.* (ed. 3) s.v., In the South, to pick the banjo or guitar, means to play upon these instruments. Comp. the French *pincer*. **1891** *Century Mag.* Nov. 52 He could pick the banjo in a way no one had ever heard it picked before. **1901** *Munsey's Mag.* XXIV. 485/1 The strings [of a Polynesian instrument] are strummed, rather than picked.

13. Short for *pick out*, 19 g.

1892 *Cath. News* 23 Jan. 3/2 Picturesque green sashes, picked with black crape.

VII. Intransitive uses with prepositions.

14. ***to pick at***——: **a.** To aim at picking, make a motion to pick (in various prec. senses).

1525 Ld. Berners *Froiss.* II. xlii. 131 This byrde sawe hymselfe so well fethered..he began to waxe prowde, and.. pycked and spurred at them. **1603** Harsnet *Pop. Impost.* 17 Some curious head..may pick at a Moate, and ask me two or three questions out of this Narration. **1897** *Allbutt's Syst. Med.* II. 143 Muscular tremors, picking at the bed-clothes ..appear in bad cases [of scarlatina].

b. *fig.* To find fault with, gird at, nag at; to carp or cavil at. Now only *dial.*, *U.S.*, and *Austral.*

a **1670** Hacket *Abp. Williams* i. (1692) 9 The second thing calld culpable in him, but was not, was pick'd at by the cross humours of some in the end of Q. Elizabeth's reign. **1786** Jefferson *Writ.* (1859) I. 605 The Emperor, the Empress, and the Venetians seem all to be picking at the Turks. **1822** Galt *Provost* xxiii, The rising generation began to pick and dab at him. **1876** *Whitby Gloss.*, *Pick at*, v. to quarrel with. 'They're always picking at teean t'other', at each other. **1884** Roe *Nat. Ser. Story* ii, When the papers have nothing else to find fault with, they pick at West Point. **1896** *Cosmopolitan* XX. 430/2 I'm always being picked at. I wish I was dead. **1916** C. J. Dennis *Songs Sentimental Bloke* 127 *Pick at*, to chaff; to annoy. **1941** Baker *Dict. Austral. Slang.* 54 *Pick at*, to blame, chaff, irritate.

15. ***to pick on, upon***——: = prec. b; also, to single out for attention or adverse criticism; to victimize.

c **1370** *Robert Cicyle* 269 in Horstm. *Altengl. Leg.* (1878) 215/2 Alle men on him gon pike, For he rod oþer vnlike. **1875** W. D. Parish *Dict. Sussex Dial.* 87 They always pick upon my boy coming home from school. **1888** in Farmer *Americanisms* (1889) 419/1 Joseph White..slept for five days and nights, and then jawed his wife for waking him up. He said she was always picking on him when she saw him taking comfort. **1890** Mary E. Wilkins *Mod. Dragon* in *Humble Romance*, etc. (1891) 100, I don't see..what makes you girls for ever pick on each other. **1899** B. W. Green *Virginia Word-bk.*, *Pick upon*, to annoy; the other boys always *pick upon* this one. *c* **1910** D. H. Lawrence *Phoenix II* (1968) 26 You always pick on the Gordons—you're always on to us—! **1919** Wodehouse *Coming of Bill* (1920) ii. iii. 141 That wouldn't make no difference.—She'd pick on me just the same. **1929** J. Buchan *Courts of Morning* iii. ii. 331 Looks as if you folk had been picking on my poor little country. **1930** J. B. Priestley *Angel Pavement* vi. 297 They begin picking on her and she stands up for herself. **1930** S. Jepson *I met Murder* ii. 27 Have you any idea why the

Inspector should have picked on you first? **1947** 'N. SHUTE' *Chequer Board* 73 Last night they was picking on the coloured boys—saying nasty things about niggers in their hearing. **1959** G. FREEMAN *Jack would be Gent.* 140 Don't keep picking on him, please, Mum. **1961** [see BACK *sb.*[1] 23 d]. **1975** *Times* 15/4 Why pick on the present Government? Has any government..in the past 30 years ever..done anything to encourage that aim?

VIII. In combination with adverbs.

16. pick away: see senses 1 and 5, and AWAY.
c **1380** WYCLIF *Serm.* Sel. Wks. I. 103 þe fendis may..pike awey þe seed. **1618** BRATHWAIT *Descr. Death* viii, Fleshie He was, but it is pickt away. **1899** *Allbutt's Syst. Med.* VII. 508 When the membrane had been picked away the optic thalami could be made out.

17. pick in. a. To work in or fill in, in a painting or drawing.
1836 [see PICK *sb.*[3] 6]. **1859** SALA *Gaslight & D.* ii. 24 Then the shadows are 'picked in' by assistants.

b. *dial.* To pick or take hold of and bring in.
1891 QUILLER COUCH *Noughts & Crosses* 251 My landlady was out in the garden, 'picking in' her week's washing from the thorn hedge. **1904** *Daily Chron.* 20 June 3/4 The man..who gets his boat broadside across the lock's entrance, and is superciliously 'picked' in by the..assistant.

18. pick off. a. See sense 5 and OFF.
13.. *E.E. Allit. P.* B. 1466 Þay prudly hade piked of pomgarnades. **1706** E. WARD *Wooden World Diss.* (1708) 19 These..just pick'd off from a Taylor's Shop-board. **1899** *Allbutt's Syst. Med.* VIII. 588 When the scales are picked off, the apertures of the hair-sacs are seen to be dilated.

b. To shoot with deliberate selection and aim, to shoot one by one. Also *fig.*
1810 *Vandeleur's Lett.* 1 Nov. (1894) 17 Our men are capital shots. I could see them pick the fellows off one at a time just as day began to appear. **1817** *Parl. Deb.* 316 The corps of political riflemen..employed in picking off place after place, however important or serviceable. **1885** *Scribner's Mag.* XXX. 396/1 Partisan rangers..picking off an English officer with as little ruth as they felt in shooting a stag.

c. *Baseball.* To put out (a runner) at a base.
1948 *Sun* (Baltimore) 1 Dec. 17/4 The play in question came when Bobby Feller, Cleveland pitcher, whirled and threw to Manager Lou Boudreau in an effort to pick off Masi, Boston catcher. **1974** *Spartanburg* (S. Carolina) *Herald* 23 Apr. A6/4 Dancy was picked off by catcher Luis Rosado as he inexcusably wandered too far off third.

19. pick out. a. To extract by picking (senses 1, 2, 5); to dig out, peck out. Also *fig.* In quot. 1843, to undo by extracting the stitches one by one.
α. *c* **1380** WYCLIF *Serm.* Sel. Wks. I. 401 3if þin i3e sclaundre þee, pyke it out. *c* **1420** *Pallad. on Husb.* III. 28 Ye must..diligently clodde it, pyke out stones. **1530** PALSGR. 657/1, I pyke out, as a ravyn dothe a deed beestes eye. **1591** HARINGTON *Orl. Fur.* Pref., The like..Allegories I could pike out of other Poeticall fictions. **1861** RAMSAY *Remin.* Ser. II. 74 Corbies winna pike out corbies' een.
β. **1388** WYCLIF *Prov.* xxx. 17 Crowis of the stronde picke [1382 pecken] out thilke i3e, that scorneth the fadir. **1601** SHAKS. *All's Well* II. iii. 276 Go too sir, you were beaten in Italy for picking a kernell out of a Pomgranat. **1613** PURCHAS *Pilgrimage* (1614) 824 They shewed them the vse..to pick out thornes in their feet. **1725** B. HIGGONS *Rem. Burnet* Hist. Wks. 1736 II. II. 120 To breed up young Presbyterians with the Money of the Church of England, to pick out her Eyes. *a* **1756** MRS. HAYWOOD *New Present* (1771) 64 Pick the mussels out from the shells. **1843** MRS. CARLYLE *Lett.* I. 246 Picking out her sewing has been such sorrowful work. **1899** *Allbutt's Syst. Med.* VIII. 555 Small plugs of horny epidermis can be picked out, leaving pits behind.

b. To select, to choose out with care or deliberation; in recent use said also of natural agents, as diseases.
1530 PALSGR. 657/1, I can pyke out the best and I were blyndefelde. **1538** STARKEY *England* I. iv. 122 The most general thyngys..wych among infynyte other, I haue pykyd out. **1596** SHAKS. *1 Hen. IV*, II. iv. 403 Could the World picke thee out three such Enemyes againe? **1712** ADDISON *Spect.* No. 291 ¶10 He then bid him pick out the Chaff from among the Corn. *a* **1758** RAMSAY *Fables* xvii. 20 Take the canniest gate to ease, And pike out joys by twas and threes. **1871** L. STEPHEN *Playgr. Eur.* (1894) iv. II. 316 A guide..can almost always pick out at a glance the most practicable line of assault. **1899** *Allbutt's Syst. Med.* VI. 710 These fibres in the peripheral nerves which when picked out by disease give rise to incoordination of movement.

†**c.** To extract or gain with effort, to acquire; = *pick up*, 21 c. *Obs.*
1577 B. GOOGE *Heresbach's Husb.* (1586) 174 The good husband by cherishing of them [Bees], picketh out many times a good peece of his liuing. **1607** DEKKER & WEBSTER *Westw. Hoe* II. Wks. 1873 II. 295, I picke out a poore liuing amongst em: and I am thankefull for it.

d. To distinguish from surrounding objects, etc., with the senses.
1552 LATIMER *Rem.* (Parker Soc.) 30 He will not forget us, for he seeth us in every corner; he can pick us out, when it is his will and pleasure. **1596** SHAKS. *Tam. Shr.* Ind. i. 24 Why Belman is as good as he my Lord, He..twice to day pick'd out the dullest sent. **1872** BLACK *Adv. Phaeton* xv, Now and then Bell picked out the call of a thrush or a blackbird. **1873** —— *Pr. Thule* i, An eye accustomed to pick out objects far at sea.

e. To make out or gather (sense or meaning); to piece out and ascertain (facts) by combining separate fragments or items of information.
1540 HYRDE tr. *Vives' Instr. Chr. Wom.* (1592) A iij, Because euerye body shall picke out the ways of liuing out of these mens authoritie. **1589** PUTTENHAM *Eng. Poesie* III. xviii. (Arb.) 198 We dissemble againe..when we speake by way of riddle (Enigma) of which the sence can hardly be picked out. **1607** BEAUMONT *Woman Hater* I. iii, He brings me informations, pick'd out of broken words, in men's common talk. **1678** (ed. 2) BUNYAN *Pilgr.* (1847) 129 Hopeful..called to Christian (for he was learned) to see if he could pick out the meaning..'Remember Lot's Wife.' **1882** M. ARNOLD *Speech at Eton* in *Irish Ess.* 185 Goethe..did not know Greek well and had to pick out its meaning by the help of a Latin translation.

f. To identify the notes of (a tune) and so play it by ear.
1893 STEVENSON *Catriona* v. 55 She picked it out upon the keyboard, and..enriched the same with well-sounding chords. **1901** H. HARLAND *Com. & Errors* 97 If I were to pick it out for you on the piano, you would scoff at it.

g. To deck out, to adorn; now *spec.* to lighten or relieve the ground colour of (anything) by lines or spots of a contrasted colour following the outlines, mouldings, etc.
c **1450** *Mirour Saluacioun* 621 Thay had graces of whilk thaire pride thai myght pike out. **1794** W. FELTON *Carriages* (1801) I. 193 The picking out to a carriage is the ornamenting the ground with various contrasted colours, which is to lighten the appearance, and shew the mouldings to advantage. **1844** DISRAELI *Coningsby* VIII. v, The ceiling..was richly gilt and picked out in violet. **1882** *Q. Rev.* Jan. 257 A few are 'picked out', as a coach painter might say, with bright scarlet. **1897** *Daily News* 7 Jan. 2/2 Every arch and capital..was outlined, and as the expression is 'picked out' by holly, ivy, laurustinus, &c.

20. pick over. To sort; to select the best from (a group or collection); to pick off dead flowers from.
1917 *Dialect Notes* IV. 397 She is picking over blackberries. **1924** A. D. SEDGWICK *Little French Girl* i. 6 She..picked over the herbs that were to be dried for *tisane.* **1946** D. C. PEATTIE *Road of Naturalist* iii. 40 The supplies were picked over and over. One necessity after another was thrown away, as the owner remembered that he might have to carry it, if the oxen died. **1971** *Vogue* Dec. 48/3 The geraniums had flowered once, and needed to be picked over to induce a second flowering. **1972** D. WESTHEIMER *Over Edge* (1974) ii. 20 Karen..could spend hours happily picking over rejects in a surplus store. **1973** E. PAGE *Fortnight by Sea* i. 8, I don't think there'll be any strawberries left... The beds were picked over pretty thoroughly a couple of days ago. **1978** *Lancashire Life* Apr. 78/2 Though the summer suns are not yet exactly at the glowing stage, wise girls will buy their summer clothes now, rather than wait till the best things have been picked over.

21. pick up.

a. To break up (ground) with a pick; to extract from the ground by picking; to take up.
1362 LANGL. *P. Pl.* A. VII. 104 And summe, to plese perkyn, pykeden [B. VI. 113 piked] vp þe weodes. **1573** TUSSER *Husb.* (1878) 37 A pike for to pike them [fitchis] vp handsom to drie. **1894** *Times* 21 May 4/4 A gang of men was sent..to pick up and relay the part of Onslow-gardens.

b. To take up with the fingers or beak; to lay hold of and take up (esp. a small object) from the ground or any low position; to lift lightly, smartly, or neatly; in *Knitting*, to take up (stitches) with a knitting-needle or wire. *to pick oneself up*, to recover oneself smartly from a fall, etc. Also *spec.* (*a*) *trans.* to gather (a shorn fleece) from the floor of the shearing shed, carry it to a table, and throw it out flat so that it can be skirted, rolled, and classed, also *absol.* (*Austral.* and *N.Z.*) (*b*) *absol.* in game-shooting, to make a retrieval, esp. to collect unretrieved game after a shooting party.
c **1325** *Poem Times Edw. II* 237 in *Pol. Songs* (Camden) 334 He doth the wif sethe a chapoun and piece beof,..The best he piketh up himself, and maketh his mawe touht. *a* **1704** LOCKE (J.), The acorns he picked up under an oak in the wood. **1711** BUDGELL *Spect.* No. 77 ¶1 Will. had picked up a small Pebble. **1774** GOLDSM. *Nat. Hist.* (1776) V. 338 Its common food should be mixed with ants, so that when the bird goes to pick the ants it may pick up some of that also. **1809** ROLAND *Fencing* 99 Pick up his foil and deliver it politely to him. **1861** HUGHES *Tom Brown at Oxf.* ii, Tom picked himself up, and settled himself on his bench again. **1880** MISS BRADDON *Just as I am* xxi, Picks up her feet nicely, doesn't she? **1880** *Plain Hints Needlework* 32 Pick up the side loops for right-hand gusset, cast on the same number of loops as were on the needle before the heel began to be turned (28), and pick up the loops for the left-hand gusset. **1898** *Spectator* 3 Dec. 837 The broken cable of 1865 was picked up and repaired.
(*a*) **1862** J. G. WALKER *Jrnl.* 10 Nov. (typescript) 24 My job at first was picking up fleeces. **1926** J. DEVANNY *Butcher Shop* 11 The naked feet of the brown women 'picking up' from the shining greasy floor. **1940** F. SARGESON *Man & Wife* (1944) 47 It was early summer, shearing time. Tom and me went into the country and we got a job picking up fleeces in a big shed. **1967** J. MORRISON in *Coast to Coast 1965–66* 157 He'd been away picking-up in the shearing sheds.
(*b*) **1888** W. B. LEFFINGWELL *Wild Fowl Shooting* xxxvi. 364 After the pup has gotten to understand your orders of picking up, and bringing the glove to you from short distances, throw it farther. **1897** *Encycl. Sport* I. 442/1 The keeper..must be careful to judge accurately when to start the next drive, after one is over, so as to give reasonable time for picking up. **1976** *Shooting Times & Country Mag.* 16–22 Dec. 20/2 My immediate neighbours..did help pick up and I am happy to say the count, if nothing else, was quite gratifying.

c. To acquire, attain, gain, earn, collect, gather, or get possession of as chance or opportunity offers; to come upon and possess oneself of; to make (a livelihood) by occasional opportunity.
1513 DOUGLAS *Æneis* III. Prol. 35 This text is full of storyis euery deill, Realmes and landis, quharof I haue na feill..To pike thame wp perchance 3our eene suld reill. **1608** SHAKS. *Per.* IV. ii. 36 If in our youths we could pick up some pretty estate, 'twere not amiss to keep our doors hatched. **1693** J. EDWARDS *Author. O. & N. Test.* 102 This ridiculous fable which Plato had pick'd up. **1699** DAMPIER *Voy.* II. I. 167 By this Trade the Freemen of Malacca pick up a good livelihood. **1711** ADDISON *Spect.* No. 159 ¶1 When I was at Grand Cairo, I picked up several Oriental Manuscripts. **1750** H. WALPOLE *Let. to Mann* 10 Jan., If you can pick me up any fragments of old painted glass..I shall be excessively obliged to you. **1788** FRANKLIN *Autobiog.* Wks. 1840 I. 209 Exhibiting them in every capital town, he picked up some money. **1843** PRESCOTT *Mexico* (1850) I. 227 During his residence in Cuba [he] had picked up some acquaintance with the Castilian. **1860** READE *Cloister & H.* lv, He spoke but little..but listened to pick up their characters. **1884** G. ALLEN *Philistia* I. 80, I picked it up for a song. **1886** J. R. REES *Pleas. Bk.-Worm* i, 'I picked it up' has become a recognised phrase in all kinds of collecting manias. **1889** JESSOPP *Coming of Friars* ii. 84 There were many ways of picking up a livelihood by these gentlemen. **1897** MARY KINGSLEY *W. Africa* 673 The white child..is not so quick in picking up parlour tricks.

d. To seize, snap up, capture (a vessel), as on a cruise; to capture in detail. Now *rare.*
1687 A. LOVELL tr. *Thevenot's Trav.* I. 110 The Christian Corsairs pick up several of them [vessels] now and then. **1779** F. HERVEY *Nav. Hist.* II. 148 Blake was very active in the Channel, in picking up their merchantmen. **1793** SMEATON *Edystone L.* §265 A fishing boat, which..had been picked up by the French for the sake of intelligence. **1885** U. S. GRANT *Personal Mem.* xxii. I. 309 He had..scattered the little army..so that the most of it could be picked up in detail.

e. To take (a person or thing overtaken or fallen in with) along with one, into one's company, or into a vessel or vehicle; also said of a vehicle, a ship, etc.; *spec.* to form an acquaintance with (a person) casually or informally, esp. with the intention of having a sexual relationship.
1698 VANBRUGH *Prov. Wife* IV. iii, So—now, Mr. Constable, shall you and I go pick up a whore together? **1698** J. COLLIER *Short View Immorality Eng. Stage* vi. 238 Nothing being more common than to see Beauty surpriz'd, Women debauch'd, and Wenches Pick'd up at these Diversions. **1716** *Lond. Gaz.* No. 5474/4 Whoever has pickt her [a lost bitch] up,..shall receive 10s. Reward. **1734** *Select Trials 1720–1724* 59/1 The Prosecutor pick'd me up and went with me to my Lodgings..where he would have lain with me. **1785** COWPER *Let.* 4 June in *Corr.* (1904) II. 325 He was seen by Mr. Shepherd..leading a female companion into a wood.., whom he saw him pick up as he went. **1812** J. H. VAUX *Vocab. Flash Lang.* in *Mem.* (1964) 257 To pick up a cull, is a term used by blowers in their vocation of street-walking. **1820** J. W. CROKER *Diary* 10 Mar., Lord Yarmouth..came over to pick me up on our way to town. **1834** PRINGLE *Afr. Sk.* vi. 200 Picked up in their boats by a vessel homeward bound. **1839** W. CHAMBERS *Tour Belgium* 73/1 One of the many omnibusses which drive round to pick up passengers from the hotels. **1840** MARRYAT *Poor Jack* xiii, He was picked up by a gentleman..in a wherry, holding on to the wool of a sheep which..was swimming. **1891** T. HARDY *Tess* (1900) 139/1 To walk to the first station onward, and let the train pick him up there. **1893** G. B. SHAW *Widowers' Houses* I. viii. 29 'I have made the acquaintance of'—or you may say 'picked up', or 'come across', if you think that would suit your friend's style better. **1921** *Sat. Even. Post* 1 Oct. 18/2 You are right in thinking there must be something wrong with girls who try to 'pick up' strange men as no girl with self respect would do such a thing. **1932** E. BOWEN *To North* iv. 34 She wished she had not picked Markie up in the train and given him her address. **1933** *Times Lit. Suppl.* 30 Mar. 223/3 One evening Sam 'picks up' a young woman at an open-air concert. **1942** E. PAUL *Narrow St.* xvii. 135 The wife of one of the officers..formed the habit of picking up rich gentlemen in department stores. **1961** J. DOS PASSOS *Midcentury* 94 Eileen got to dancing..and trying to pick up strange men. **1975** *Evening Standard* 14 May 5/3 It is not difficult to learn..that it is possible to obtain money, food or a bed for the night by being 'picked up'. **1976** D. MARLOWE *Nightshade* xii. 143 Who was that old man?.. He was trying to pick you up.

f. *trans.* and *intr.* To steal, rob, pilfer; to cheat, swindle. *slang.*
c **1770** R. KING *Frauds of London Detected* 39 [Highwaymen] have various schemes for carrying on their business, such as seeing ostlers, bribing landlords, on the road, for intelligence of *who is worth picking up.* **1829** H. WIDOWSON *Pres. State Van Diemen's Land* 73 There are always a number of loose characters lurking about, on the look-out for strangers, to 'pick them up', as they term it, which, in other words, means to rob them. *a* **1876** E. LEIGH *Gloss. Words Dial. Cheshire* (1877) 154 *Picking up*, a term for picking a pocket. **1903** *Mark of Broad Arrow* vii. 108 Within twenty-four hours of that man's release the three prison-made thieves were looking round the town to see what they could 'pick up'—in plain language, to see what they could thieve. **1928** *Detective Fiction Weekly* 8 Sept. 565/2 Gentleman George..would mark down his traveler, knowing him to be in possession of jewelry or other valuables, and tirelessly follow him until the opportunity arose to 'pick-up' his all-important bag.

g. *trans.* To find fault with, call to account; to detect (a person) in a mistake; to show up. *colloq.*
1846 S. F. SMITH *Theatr. Apprenticeship* 149 The bystanders..were crowding around the table in great numbers to see the fun—all considering me most undoubtedly 'picked up'. **1878** B. HARTE in *Scribner's Monthly* Dec. 184/1 When we were coming down the valley you picked me up twice..*contradicted* me, that's what I mean. **1922** *Daily Mail* 5 Dec. 11, I am picked up for saying that the initiative in the Steamer case should have come from the stewards.

h. In *Cricket*, to succeed in hitting (a ball, esp. one that pitches close to the ground).
1851 J. PYCROFT *Cricket Field* vii. 153 If you reach far enough, even a shooter may be picked up. **1862** —— *Cricket Tutor* 8 The old bat used to be heavy at the point—very requisite for picking up a Grounder. **1959** *Times* 29 May 4/1 He could not have picked up the ball off his legs so crisply.

i. To come upon, find (a path, etc.), *esp.* to recover, regain (a track, trail, etc. lost or departed from); to catch sight of (a light, signal, etc.); succeed in seeing, hearing, detecting, receiving, etc., by means of an appropriate instrument or apparatus. ***to pick up a wind***: see quot. 1867. ***to pick up the range*** (of a rifle or gun).

1857 DUFFERIN *Lett. High Lat.* (ed. 3) 210 It was now time to run down West and pick up the land. **1860** *Merc. Marine Mag.* VII. 30 No stranger should attempt to pick up the.. Light in thick weather, nor enter the port at night. **1867** SMYTH *Sailor's Word-bk.*, *Pick up a wind*,..to run from one trade or prevalent wind to another, with as little intervening calm as possible. **1876** G. F. CHAMBERS *Astron.* 658 Suppose that the observer suddenly picks up an unknown comet. **1879** *Cassell's Techn. Educ.* IV. 258/1 The condenser.. framed with the view of picking up the greatest number of rays from the source of light. **1880** SUTHERLAND *Tales Goldfields* 58 He was fortunate enough to pick up the track. **1888** *Electrician* 2 Nov. 833/1 For researches of this description it is necessary to employ as sensitive an instrument as it is possible to obtain, to pick up, so to speak, such minute currents. **1890** 'R. BOLDREWOOD' *Col. Reformer* (1891) 209 The advance guard could..pick up the trail on more favourable ground. **1900** *Westm. Gaz.* 29 June 10/1 If the fireman as well as the driver had been picking up the Slough signals there would have been no accident. **1901** *Scotsman* 28 Feb. 5/6 They considered that their system was just as useful, if not better, for picking up the range. **1908** *Rep. Brit. Assoc. Adv. Sci. 1907* 621 The receiving apparatus..would pick up a number of disturbances from other stations. **1908** *Westm. Gaz.* 23 Oct. 5/3 The following notes will enable it [*sc.* a comet] to be 'picked up' with the aid of an opera-glass and a star-map. **1913** *Pop. Mag.* 1 May 79/2 The only signals which it was picking up now were.. those of the enemy. **1921** [see GET *v.* 22 b]. **1922** *Encycl. Brit.* XXX. 88/2 Presently the airship was 'picked up', and immediately from all quarters of the defences searchlights could be seen moving across to get on to it. **1929** S. ERTZ *Galaxy* xvii. 365 She and the General thoroughly enjoyed their wireless in the evening, and it was amusing to pick up Paris or Berlin. **1941** [see ATMOSPHERE *sb.* 4 b]. **1948** F. P. SHEPARD *Submarine Geol.* ii. 16 The radar screen will pick up land objects and will show the position of islands, capes and mountain peaks, giving their direction and distance. **1960** *McGraw-Hill Encycl. Sci. & Technol.* XIII. 462/1 Television camera tubes are designed primarily to pick up live programs, indoors and outdoors, as well as to reproduce motion pictures. **1973** *Guardian* 20 June 13/1 BBC Monitoring Service reports that the only Moscow Radio commentaries on Watergate picked up so far in any language were in Quechua. **1977** *Lancet* 4 June 1187/2 Clinically, cerebral blood-flow is measured after intra-arterial injection of xenon-133; gamma radiation is picked up by two detectors and the scintillation-counts are fed into a laboratory digital computer. **1978** *Nature* 6 Apr. 481/2 This detection capability has improved roughly threefold; explosions of yields of 1 or 2 kilotons in hard rock in most parts of the Northern Hemisphere would now most likely be picked up.

j. *trans.* To cause (a person) to revive; to serve as a 'pick-me-up' for (someone).

1857 DICKENS & COLLINS *Lazy Tour* v, in *Househ. Words* 31 Oct. 412/1 Several..look in at the chemist's..to be 'picked up'. **1889** 'R. BOLDREWOOD' *Robbery under Arms* xlii, I suppose a decent dinner will pick me up. **1914** G. B. SHAW *Misalliance* 80 Have you had your tea?.. A cup of tea will pick you up. **1978** J. CARROLL *Mortal Friends* I. ii. 22 'You know me, Colman. Tea anytime.' 'Indeed, Father. It picks a body up.'

k. *trans.* and *intr.* To tidy or clean up; to put in order; ***to pick up a room***, see quot. 1889. *colloq.* (chiefly *U.S.*).

1861 *Trans. Illinois Agric. Soc.* IV. 204 We did not find 'things picked up in it'—no air of comfort about it. **1874** E. S. WARD *Trotty's Wedding Tour* 214 It had taken all day to 'pick up' after the departed travellers. **1888** N. PERRY *Flock of Girls* 81 She mends these little bits of things and 'picks up' after you, as you call it. **1889** FARMER *Dict. Amer.* s.v. *Pick*, *To pick up a room*, is a New England phrase for putting it in order. **1966** J. BALL *Cool Cottontail* (1967) v. 44 'The room isn't properly picked up yet,' the woman said. 'When you have five kids..you can't get everything done.' **1973** *Sunday Bull.* (Philadelphia) 7 Oct. (Parade Suppl.) F5/4 Ask your children for their ideas. It's the best way to enlist their help in keeping their rooms 'picked-up'.

l. *trans.* To arrest, apprehend. Cf. sense 21 d. *slang* (orig. *U.S.*).

1871 *Congress. Globe* 5 Jan. 317/2 They are picked up for taking horses or sheep or anything of that sort. **1887** *Lantern* (New Orleans) 11 June 2/2 I'll have the police pick him up for blackmail. **1934** J. T. FARRELL *Young Manhood* xii. 192 He gazed around the church to see if any of the boys were present. Seeing none of them, he guessed that they must all have been picked up, and were enjoying Christmas Day in the can. **1938** F. D. SHARPE *Sharpe of Flying-Squad* xiv. 157, I picked them up for stealing a man's wallet. *Ibid.* xvi. 183, I picked Billy up, knowing that he was 'wanted' for a job. **1946** F. SARGESON *That Summer* 102 We all had to stand there with a crowd of jacks in plain clothes standing round, and one in uniform called out our names and said what we'd been picked up for. **1956** H. GOLD *Man who was not with It* (1965) xxii. 202 You want to be able to tell the fuzz the truth if we're picked up? **1961** *Confidential* Jan. 39/2 When Farouk was overthrown, police picked up his personal pimp, Pulley Bey. **1976** 'TREVANIAN' *Main* x. 213 Things start to go badly for him. His boys..get picked up for every minor charge in the book. **1979** *Massachusetts Daily Collegian* 30 Apr. 14/4 He said he was not drunk when picked up on East Pleasant St. on March 29.

m. *trans.* To pay (a bill, account, etc.); esp. in phr. ***to pick up the bill, check, tab***, etc.; also *fig. colloq.* (orig. *U.S.*).

1945 *Sun* (Baltimore) 23 Oct. 4 (*heading*) 'Lobbyist' said to have picked up check for Truman outing. **1947** *Ibid.* 12 May 2/5 Some United States diplomats have entertained each other with the taxpayers picking up the check. **1956** S. BELLOW *Seize the Day* ii. 26 His father might have offered to pick up his hotel tab. **1956** B. HOLIDAY *Lady sings Blues* (1973) xxiii. 196 Americans used to make fun of the British health system, where sick people could go to doctors and hospitals for free and the government picked up the tab. **1961** R. BLOCH *Blood runs Cold* 215 I'm permitted to attend a party..when they go out to eat because I always pick up the check. **1964** WODEHOUSE *Frozen Assets* ii. 32 'Coffee's out, I'm afraid.' 'Nonsense. I'll pick up the tab.' **1966** M. BREWER *Man against Fear* vii. 77 Tonight we pick up her bill. **1967** *Canad. Ann. Rev. 1966* 65 Ottawa would pick up a $14 million tab for a system already in operation. **1976** *S. Wales Echo* 27 Nov. 2/2 Mr. Gray asked if the college should be expected to 'pick up the tab' for even greater expenditure if grants to the theatre were cut. **1978** *Daily Tel.* 13 Feb. 6/5 Ratepayers would have to pick up the bill if important jobs were transferred from the county councils to some of the larger districts.

n. Phrases: ***to pick up one's crumbs***: see CRUMB *sb.* 4; ***to pick up flesh***: to regain flesh, put on flesh again; ***to pick up (one's) spirit, courage***, etc.: to 'pluck up' heart; ***to pick up the pieces*** (fig.): to (try to) redeem some advantage or compensation from an apparently hopeless situation.

*c*1645–1888 [see CRUMB *sb.* 4]. **1730–6** BAILEY (folio), *To Pick up One's Crums*, to gather strength. **1749** *Phil. Trans.* XLVI. 79 He has pick'd up his Flesh, and promises to enjoy a good Habit of Body. **1790** J. BRUCE *Source of Nile* I. 195, I picked up courage, and..said..without trepidation, 'What men are these before?' **1872** BLACK *Adv. Phaeton* iii, She had so far picked up her spirits. **1872** *Punch* 29 June 269/1 The process of pulling myself together and picking myself up. **1912** KIPLING *Divers. Creatures* (1917) 17, I should have said it was half a night. Now, shall we go down and pick up the pieces? **1938** M. ALLINGHAM *Fashion in Shrouds* vi. 92 It'll come to a quiet, uncomfortable end and you'll have to stand by and pick up the pieces. **1951** J. C. FENNESSY *Sonnet in Bottle* v. iv. 163 Injy was very good at taking things as they came. But he generally found it was his job to pick up the pieces afterwards. **1970** A. TOFFLER *Future Shock* (1971) xvii. 391 By proliferating enclaves of the past, living museums as it were, we increase the chances that someone will be there to pick up the pieces in case of massive calamity. **1973** A. BROINOWSKI *Take One Ambassador* vii. 97 We could see them [*sc.* the Japanese] picking up the pieces in Indo-China after the Americans. **1977** R. PERRY *Dead End* i. 12 If anything does go wrong it'll be nice having you around to pick up the pieces.

o. *intr.* To recover health, strength, or energy after an illness; to grow well again; to recover, improve, 'look up', after any check or depression.

1741 RICHARDSON *Pamela* I. 237 Now this Woman sees me pick up so fast, she uses me worse. **1751** GRAY *Lett.*, *to Wharton* 10 Oct., His College, which had much declined for some time, is picking up again. **1804** SCOTT in Lockhart *Life* 21 Aug., He was sent down here..in a half-starved state, but begins to pick up a little. **1849** C. STURT *Exp. Centr. Australia* I. 262 The fact of the natives having crossed the plain confirmed my impression that the creek picked up [*i.e.* recovered itself] beyond it. **1864** GEO. ELIOT in Cross *Life* II. 389 He is wonderful for the rapidity with which he 'picks up' after looking alarmingly feeble. **1896** *Indianap. Typogr. Jrnl.* 16 Nov. 404 Business in our trade is rapidly picking up.

p. To enter into conversation, make acquaintance or companionship *with* (some one casually met).

1865 *Pall Mall G.* 7 Aug. 3 On the railway to Cologne he had picked up with Jones. **1884** G. ALLEN *Philistia* I. 13 Herbert..had picked up at once with a Polish exile in a corner. *Ibid.* 45 So you've let your Polly go and pick up with some young man from town.

q. *intr.* and *trans.* Of a vehicle, aircraft, etc.: to gain speed after being slow-moving or stationary; to recover (speed). Cf. sense 21 o.

1922 S. LEWIS *Babbitt* v. 53 He noted how quickly his car picked up. **1932** C. ISHERWOOD *Memorial* III. i. 181 'That's a damn fine bus,' said Farncombe earnestly. 'My Christ, Gerald, you should see the way she picks up.' **1939** *War Illustr.* 29 Dec. 539/3 However, as we got down to five hundred feet the engines began to pick up.

r. ***to pick up on***: (*a*) to draw near, begin to overtake (a person) in a race; (*b*) *U.S. slang*, to understand, appreciate, or obtain.

1908 *Daily Chron.* 27 Nov. 7/6 At the fifth lap..Dorando held him, and then began to pick up on him. **1944** D. BURLEY *Orig. Handbk. Harlem Jive* 15 Let me boot you to my play [*sc.* inform you of my plan] and, maybe, you can pick up on the issue. **1946** MEZZROW & WOLFE *Really Blues* 377 *Pick up on*, get, take, learn. *Ibid.*, *Pick up on what's going down*, understand what's happening. **1956** B. HOLIDAY *Lady sings Blues* (1973) i. 8 In Baltimore, places like Alice Dean's were the only joints fancy enough to have a victrola and for real enough to pick up on the best records. **1972** *Jazz & Blues* Feb. 19/1 They came to gig in their own clubs before white people picked up on them. **1977** MCKNIGHT & TOBLER *Bob Marley* iii. 46 Paul McCartney was noted as having 'picked up on reggae'.

pick (pɪk), *v.*[2] Now only *dial.* or *techn.* Also 4 pykke, pik(ke, 6–7 picke, 6 pycke. [A collateral form of PITCH *v.*[1]

In ME. known only in Petyt MS. of R. Brunne (exc. l. 9939, where *pykke* may be PICK *v.*[1]).]

†**1.** *trans.* To fix, stick, plant (something pointed) in the ground, etc.; to pitch (a tent or the like). *Obs. rare.*

*c*1330 R. BRUNNE *Chron. Wace* (Rolls) 4645–6 þey.. pyght [*Petyt MS.* piked] þeym pauylons & tente. Right als þey picched [*Petyt* piked] þer pauylons, Cam Cassibolan. [*Ibid.* 9939 He dide hewe tres & pykke, & palysed hit aboute ful þykke.] *Ibid.* 12512 His pauilons, his penceles, pykke Nought fer fro þenne had þey don wyk [*Petyt MS.* pikke]. *a*1548 HALL *Chron.*, *Hen. VI* 106 [They] picked stakes before every Archer, to breke the force of the horsemen. **1597–1602** *Transcr. W. Riding Sessions Rolls* (Yorks. Archæol. Assoc.) 118 Sett in the Stocks..with feathers picked in his apparaile.

2. To thrust, drive; to pitch, hurl; to throw. Now *dial.*

1523 LD. BERNERS *Froiss.* I. clxiii. 201 The frenche squyer dyd pycke his swerde at hym, and by happe strake hym through both the thyes. ?**15..** *Flodden F.* 316 in Furniv. *Percy Folio* I. 332 He..keped me within his woone till I was able of my selfe both to shoote & picke the stone. **1583** STUBBES *Anat. Abus.* I. (1879) 184 Seeking to ouer-throwe him & to picke him on his nose. *Ibid.*, To catch him vpon the hip, and to pick him on his neck. **1607** SHAKS. *Cor.* I. i. 204 As high As I could picke my Lance. **1681** W. ROBERTSON *Phraseol. Gen.* (1693) 989 To pick or throw, *projicere*. **1762** COMYNS *Digest Laws Eng.* (1780) I. 190 I'll have thee picked over the Bar [cf. BAR *sb.*[1] 24]. **1828** *Craven Gloss.* (ed. 2) s.v., He tried to pick me down. **1870** AXON *Folk Song Lanc.* 15 Hoo pick'd him o' th' hillock. [In many northern and north-midl. dial. glossaries.]

b. *spec.* To throw (hay or corn) with a pitchfork (upon a cart or stack). *dial.*

1880 *N.W. Linc. Gloss.*, *Pick*,..to lift up sheaves of corn to the stack.

3. *intr.* To throw, cast; *spec.* (also ***pick over***) to throw the shuttle across the loom. Cf. PICK *sb.*[4] 2.

1530 PALSGR. 657/2, I pycke with an arrowe, *je darde*... I holde a grote I pycke as farre with an arowe as you. **1570** LEVINS *Manip.* 120/28 To Pick, *iaculari*. **1573–80** BARET *Alv.* P 333 To Picke, or cast. **1848** MRS. GASKELL *M. Barton* iv, He ne'er picked ower i' his loife. **1883** *Almondbury & Huddersfield Gloss.* s.v., To pick also means to throw the shuttle, and the thread thus laid is called a 'pick'... 'To pick a pick' is to throw the shuttle once across.

4. *intr.* To pitch or fall forward, as in † ***to pick over the perch***: cf. PEAK *v.*[1] 1 b.

1591 in Nichols *Progr. Q. Eliz.* (1823) III. 95 If anie pearch higher than in dutie they ought, I would they might sodenly picke over the pearch for me. **1883** GRESLEY *Gloss. Terms Coal-mining*, *Pick away*, to *dip* rapidly.

5. *trans.* Of animals: To bring forth prematurely (= CAST *v.* 21). Common in *dial.* and rustic use.

1790 MRS. WHEELER *Westmld. Dial.* 55 We hed twoa Kaws pickt Coaf. **1810** *Sporting Mag.* XXXV. 191 Lord Strathmore's Heroine..picked twins by Remembrancer, a short time since. **1849** STEPHENS *Bk. Farm* (ed. 2) I. 221/2 Ewes in lamb..kept in a wet lair, will pick lamb, that is, suffer abortion. **1852** R. S. SURTEES *Sponge's Sp. Tour* (1893) 326 Two of my cows picked calf.

6. (Chiefly ***pick up***.) To vomit, 'cast up', 'throw up'; †formerly also *intr.* to come up, be vomited. Now only *north. dial.*

1563 FOXE *A. & M.* 1704/1 His meate woulde not go downe, but rise & picke vp agayne. **1566** DRANT *Wail. Hierim.* K iv, My lyver pyckte up, through great force, tremblyng on grounde dyd tumble. **1828** *Craven Gloss.* (ed. 2), *Pick*, to vomit. **1855** ROBINSON *Whitby Gloss.*, *To Pick up*, to vomit or pitch up.

7. ***pick on***, to pitch upon, fix upon, choose. *Sc.* and *north. dial.*

1824 MACTAGGART *Gallovid. Encycl.* (1876) 267 The first twa that he picked on War Rab and Jock the Tar. **1883** MRS. F. MANN *Parish of Hilby* xi. 135 She..picks upon the most beautiful thing she knows, and shapes her angels accordingly. **1894** W. G. STEVENSON *Puddin* iii. 52 He picked on one of the porters waiting at the gate for a job.

pick, *v.*[3], north. dial. form of PITCH *v.*[2]

pick, picke, obs. forms of PIQUE.

pick- in *Comb.* Mostly the stem or imperative of PICK *v.*[1] with an object, forming sbs.

pick-a-bud *dial.*, the bullfinch; **pick-and-gad** *a.* (see quot.); **pick-and-shovel** *a.*, that uses a pick and shovel; also *fig.*; **pickbrain** *a. poet.*, that picks one's brains; **pick-cheese** *dial.*, the great and blue tits; the fruit or cheese of the mallow; †**pick-fault** *sb.*, a fault-finder; *adj.* fault-finding; †**pick-harness**, one who strips the slain of their armour; †**pick-mote**, one who draws attention to trivial faults in others; †**pick-penny**, one who greedily collects or steals money; †**pick-point**, some obsolete game for children; **pick-proof** *a.*, secure against picking; **pick-shelf**, a pilferer of provisions; †**pick-straw**, a trifler: cf. *to pick straw* s.v. STRAW *sb.*; **pick-thong** *dial.*, a kind of apple. Also †**pick-free** *a.*, safe from picking or plundering. See also PICK-A-TREE, PICKLOCK, PICKPOCKET, PICKTHANK, etc.

1852 *P. Parley's Ann.* 182 The bullfinch has got a very bad character, and gardeners have a great dislike to what they call the '*Pick-a-bud'. **1883** *Encycl. Brit.* XVI. 444/2 The so-called '*pick and gad' work consists in breaking away the easy ground with the point of the pick, wedging off pieces with the gad, [etc.]. **1895** F. REMINGTON *Pony Tracks* 193 They are all cavalry..and are not hindered by..*pick-and-shovel work. **1907** *Westm. Gaz.* 11 Mar. 9/3 You don't look much like pick-and-shovel men. **1911** *Chambers's Jrnl.* Mar. 167/2 The ordinary pick-and-shovel man earns..one shilling and eightpence per day. **1930** BLUNDEN *De Bello Germanico* 42 Taking pick-and-shovel troops forward. **1953** *Sun* (Baltimore) 24 Nov. 40/1 Chief Magistrate Sherr yesterday called the search for motorists who have ignored a series of tickets a 'pick and shovel job', in contrast to the 'machine age system' he saw in action during a trip to New York city. **1977** H. GREENE *FSO-1* vii. 63 He had a love for the pick-and-shovel people, the working stiffs behind the men..who wielded power. **1934** DYLAN THOMAS *18 Poems* 25 My *pickbrain masters morsing on the stone Despair of blood, faith in the maiden's slime. *a* **1825** FORBY *Voc. E. Anglia*, *Pick-cheese, the tit-mouse. **1848** *Zoologist* VI. 2186 *Parus major* and *cæruleus* are both known by the name of 'pick-cheese'. **1863** ATKINSON *Stanton Grange* (1864) 229 They was mostlings thae blue-caps or pick-cheeses. **1895** EMERSON *Birds* 64 Tree-mallows or 'pick-cheese trees', as they are locally called. **1546** PHAER *Bk. Childr.* (1553) A ij, I neuer intended nor yet doo entende to satisfie yᵉ mindes of any suche *pikefautes. **1565** T. STAPLETON *Fortr. Faith* 120 The Manichees, busy pickefault heretikes of that age. *a* **1652** BROME *Court Beggar* Epil., You wil secure their Purses cut-free, and their pockts *pick-free. **1377** LANGL. *P. Pl.* B. xx. 261 Alle other in bataille ben yholde bribours, Pilours and *pykehernois [1393 C. XXIII. 263 pyke-herneys]. *c* **1460** *Towneley Myst.* II. 37 How! pike-harnes, how! com heder belife! **1549** LATIMER *3rd Serm. bef. Edw. VI* (Arb.) 80 Kinges haue clawe backes and docter *pyke mote and his fellowe aboute them. *c* **1440** *Promp. Parv.* 397/1 *Pyke-peny, *cupidinarius.* **1664** H. MORE *Myst. Iniq.* ix. 143 [The Pope] sending out..his hungry Pick-peny's throughout the whole Pastorage of the Empire. **1801** STRUTT *Sp. & Past.* IV. iv. §16 *Pick-point, Venter-point, Blow-point, and Gregory, occur in a description of the children's games in the sixteenth century. **1950** *Sun* (Baltimore) 4 Mar. 2/7 A new electric '*pickproof' motor car lock..is being manufactured. **1976** *National Observer* (U.S.) 29 May 9/2 Eastside tailor seeks design for pick-proof man's hip pocket. **1861** L. L. NOBLE *Icebergs* 295 The ship's cat..an incorrigible thief and *pick-shelf, and bent on making the most of us while we last. **1580** G. HARVEY *Let. Spenser* Wks. (Grosart) I. 72, I know what peace and quietnes hath done with some melancholy *pickstrawes in the world. **1871** T. HARDY *Desperate Remedies* I. viii. 274 We are only just grinden down the early *pick-thongs.

pick-a-back, var. of PIGGY-BACK.

'pickable, *a.* [f. PICK *v.*¹ + -ABLE.] Capable of being picked.

1895 *Naturalist Mag.* No. 241. 225 The Journal..furnishes the key to this lock hardly pickable by the general. **1966** C. SWEENEY *Scurrying Bush* x. 142 This little bird is supposed to enter the mouths of crocodiles to pick their teeth, but..the teeth of a crocodile..are widely spaced so that they are not really pickable—no particles of food being likely to remain. **1969** K. BENTON *24th Level* iv. 59 Black people..going downwards to the city and jobs and suckers with pickable pockets.

pick-a-cud: see PICK-.

pickadevant, -aunt, pick-a-divant, var. ff. PICKE-DEVANT *Obs.*

pickadil, -adilly, -ardil, var. ff. PICCADILL.

pickage, piccage ('pɪkɪdʒ). Forms: 4 pyk-, 5 pyck-, 7–8 pic-, 7– pick-, piccage. [f. PICK *v.*¹ + -AGE. In AF. *picage* (Calais 1376), med.(Anglo-)L. *picāgium* (Du Cange), f. F. *piquer*: cf. PICK *v.*¹] A toll paid for breaking the ground in setting up booths, stalls, tents, etc. at fairs.

1364 in *Cal. Letters City Lond.* (1885) 105 [They are and ought to be quit of] pykage. [**1376** *Rolls of Parlt.* II. 359/1 (Reply to Burgesses of Calais) Lastallage..et auxint le picage en la Marche.] *c* **1440** *Jacob's Well* 29 To paye toll, pyckage, murage, or grondage. **1610** W. FOLKINGHAM *Art of Survey* III. iv. 70 Immunities and Exemptions from..Pontage, Picage, Murage. **1627** F. LITTLE *Mon. Chr. Munif.* (1871) 31 The pickage, stallage and tolls usually paid by buyers and sellers to the lord of the fair. **1778** *Eng. Gazetteer* (ed. 2) s.v. *Hitchin*, Paying piccage and stallage to the lordship of the manor. **1864** *Leeds Mercury* 30 May, On Saturday, the pickage and stallage of the Wigan market were let by tender for twelve months, for the sum of £560. **1885** *Law Rep. 14 Q. Bench Div.* 246 All tolls, dues, piccage, stallage, and other profits..to such market..belonging.

pickande, -ant, -ante, obs. ff. PIQUANT.

pickaninny, variant of PICCANINNY.

†**'pickard.** *Obs.* [For *pick-card*, f. PICK *sb.*¹ 2 + CARD *sb.*¹] A card with iron spikes or teeth, for raising a nap on cloth, as distinguished from a green or thistle-card (of teasel).

1549 *Act 3 & 4 Edw. VI*, c. 2 §1 Noe person shall..occupye anye yeron cardes or pyckardes in rowninge of anye sett Clothe..upon payne to forfeyte..the saide Yeron cardes or pickardes. **1619** DALTON *Countrey Just.* xi. (1630) 43. **1801** *Chron.* in *Ann. Reg.* 456 For a machine..for dressing or dubbing cloths, either wet or dry, otherwise than by green cards and pickards.

pickard, pickaroon, var. PICARD, PICAROON.

pickaternie, var. PICTARNIE, the common tern.

pickatevant, var. PICKE-DEVANT *Obs.*

pick-a-tree, pickatree. Chiefly *north.* Also 7 picktree, pictree. [f. PICK- in comb. + TREE.] The great green woodpecker.

1615 BRATHWAIT *Strappado* (1878) 134 A nimble Squirrell or a picke-a-tree. **1647** J. HALL *Poems* I. *Satire* 62 Pictrees feed the devil nine times a day. **1688** R. HOLME *Armoury* II. 276/1 A Wood-pecker, or Wood-spite,..in the North of England Pickatrees. **1831** *G. Montagu's Ornith. Dict.* 372 *Pick-a-tree*, a name for the Popinjay. **1885** SWAINSON *Prov. Names Birds* 100.

pickaxe, pickax ('pɪkæks), *sb.* Forms: α. 4 pyk-, pycoys(e, pykois(e, 4–5 picois, pikoys, 5 pikoise, pic(k)oys, -oss, pycos(s, pykoys, pecoyse, pyquoys, pycows. β. 4–5 pykeys, 5 pikeys, pykeis, -as, picas, peyckes, 6 pykes. γ. 5 pek-ex, picaxse, 5–7 pykax, pykeaxe, 6 pikeax, 6–7 pickeax(e, 7– pickax, 8– pickaxe. [ME. *pikoys, picois*, a. OF. *picois* pickaxe (11th c.), med.L. *picosi-um*, connected with OF. *pic*: see PIKE *sb.*¹ The later form arose from confounding the suffix with AXE *sb. Pickis, peckis* survive in s.w. dial.]

A tool consisting of a curved iron bar with two sharp points at the ends and a handle set at right angles in the middle, used for digging or breaking up hard ground, stones, etc.; a miner's, quarryman's, or digger's pick: = PICK *sb.*¹ 1. In early use often identified with a mattock.

[**1157–8** *Grt. Rolls of Pipe 2–4 Hen. II* (1844) 168 In Picosiis .xiii.s. & .v.d. **1292** in J. Stevenson *Histor. Doc., Scotl.* (1870) 344, iiij testes de pykoys.]

α. **1329–30** *Durham Acc. Rolls* (Surtees) 17, j pykoys..emend. pykoss' molendini. **1377** LANGL. *P. Pl.* B. III. 307 Eche man to pleye with a plow, pykoys or spade. **1382** WYCLIF *Joel* iii. 10 Bete..3our plowis in to swerdis, and 3our pikoysis [*gloss* or mattokis] in to speris. *c* **1420** *Pallad. on Husb.* I. 1153 Yit toles moo The mattok, twyble, picoys forth to goo. **14..** *Metr. Voc.* in Wr.-Wülcker 627/20 *Ligo*, pycows. **1458** in Leland *Itin.* (1769) VII. 80 The peple preved her power with the pecoyse [*rime* noyse]. **1481** CAXTON *Godeffroy* xcii. 142 Grete plente of pyquoys. **1483** *Cath. Angl.* 31 A Byll or A pickoss, *fossorium, ligo.* **1489** CAXTON *Faytes of A.* I. xiv. 37 Pycosis, sawes, axes, nayles.

β. **1303** R. BRUNNE *Handl. Synne* 941 Mattok is a pykeys, Or a pyke, as sum men says. *c* **1400** *Sowdone Bab.* 387 Every man Shulde withe Pikeys or with bille The Wallis over throwe. *c* **1440** *Promp. Parv.* 397/1 Pykeys, mattokke, *ligo, marra.* **1491** CAXTON *Vitas Patr.* (W. de W. 1495) I. xxxv. 31 b/1 He founde neyther pykeys ne shouel for to make a pytt or graue. **1495** in I. S. Leadam *Star Chamb. Cases* 54 Item j peyckes iiij*d.* **1495** *Naval Acc. Hen. VII* (1896) 150 A pykas & ij pyles shoue weying xiij lb. **1497** *Ibid.* 84 Picases ..Shovills..Scopes. *a* **1529** SKELTON *Poems agst. Garnesche* Wks. 1843 I. 122 A pykes or a twybyll. **1842** PULMAN *Rustic Sketches, E. Devon* (1853) 18 (E.D.D.) Wi' shoulder'd shule and peckiss. **1887** DAWSON *Bp. Hannington* vi, At 7 a.m. we all turned out with pickisses, two-bills, crowbars and spades.

γ. *c* **1440** *Jacob's Well* 266 Of þe howe or a pek-ex wher-wyth 3e muste stubbe out þe grauel. *c* **1489** CAXTON *Sonnes of Aymon* xxviii. 581 We shall take eche of vs a pykeaxe. **1494** FABYAN *Chron.* IV. lxix. 48 With a Pykax or Mattoke, with his owne hande, breke the grounde. *Ibid.* VII. 497 With longe pycaxses and sharpe, approched them vnto the wallys. **1530** PALSGR. 254/1 Picke axe, *picq, hoiau, pique de fer.* **1578** T. N. *Conq. W. India* 332 Twelve labourers with pikeaxes and shovels. **1610** HOLLAND *Camden's Brit., Irel.* II. 151 An yron toole, to wit, a Pykax. **1611** COTGR., *Picquois*, a Pickax. **1750** JOHNSON *Rambler* No. 43 ¶10 A single stroke of the pick-ax. **1796** H. HUNTER tr. *St.-Pierre's Stud. Nat.* (1799) I. 138 Solid rock, so hard and so thick, as to bid defiance to the pick-axes and the mattocks of our labourers. **1855** MACAULAY *Hist. Eng.* xiii. III. 354 The weapons by which the Highlanders could be most effectually subdued were the pickaxe and the spade.

b. *attrib.* and *Comb.* **pickaxe team**, a pair of horses with a third horse in front, a unicorn team.

1878 in J. Philipson *Harness* (1882) 51, I have driven pick-axe teams..but although safer than a tandem, I cannot say I like that single leader. **1882** *Gard. Chron.* XVII. 25 The pickaxe-beaked starling. **1895** KIPLING *2nd Jungle Bk.* 108 The things his pick-axe beak might steal. **1899** *Daily News* 19 Oct. 7/1 Her jaw has a pickaxe-like motion.

'pickaxe, 'pickax, *v.* [f. prec. sb.] **a.** *trans.* To break with a pickaxe. **b.** *intr.* To work with or use a pickaxe.

1887 FRITH *Autobiog.* II. 83 The workmen..pickaxing away the lava and ashes. **1892** *Temple Bar Mag.* Nov. 417 The cliff has been blasted and pickaxed away.

pickback, variant of PIGGY-BACK, PICK-A-BACK.

pick-cheese: see PICK- in *Comb.*

picked ('pɪkɪd), *a.* [f. PICK *sb.*¹ 2 + -ED².]

1. Having a pike or sharp point; acuminated, pointed, spiked; = PEAKED *a.* 1, PIKED *a.*¹ 1. Now *arch.* or *dial.*

c **1430** *Hymns Virg.* 61 Harpe & giterne þere may y leere, And pickid staffe & buckelere, þere-wiþ to plawe. **1579–80** NORTH *Plutarch* (1676) 3 They have for the mark and stamp of their Money, the three picked Mace, which is the sign of Neptune. **1628** *World Encomp. by Sir F. Drake* 25 Picked rockes like towers. **1660** SHARROCK *Vegetables* 70 The shield is to be made picked at both ends. **1686** tr. *Livy* I. xliii. 25 But their Arms were changed..a Javelin, and a picked Dart like a Spit. **1709** HEARNE *Collect.* 30 Nov. (O.H.S.) II. 316 Twas triangular, but picked & sharp at top. **1763** GRAY *Let.* in W. Mason *Mem.* (1807) II. 184 The tall picked arches, the light clustered columns. *a* **1845** HOOD *Lost Heir* 84 To..be poked up behind with a picked pointed pole, when the soot has ketch'd, and the chimbly's red hot. **1863** PRIOR *Pop. Names Brit. Plants* (1879) 90 Gad is still used in our Western counties for a picked stick. **1863** J. R. WISE *New Forest* Gloss. 284 'A picked piece' means a field with one or more sharp angular corners. **1887** S. H. A. HERVEY *Wedmore Chron.* I. 327 (E.D.D.) Children still use 'picked' of a pencil with a good point to it.

b. In names of animals, etc.: Having prickles or spines, spiny; as ***picked dog-fish*** (*Spinax acanthius*): cf. PIKED *a.*¹ 1 b.

1758 *Descr. Thames* 235 Fins, on..which are placed two Spines or Thorns, from whence he is called the Picked Dog-Fish. **1848** *Zoologist* VI. 1975 Picked Dog, Spear Dog, *Spinax acanthius.* **1862** WOOD *Reptiles, Fishes*, etc. 74 The Picked Dog-fish derives its name from the powerful..weapons with which it is armed..the word Picked is a dissyllable, and must be pronounced Pick-ed.

†**2.** Peaked, tapering to a thin end. *Obs.*

1552 HULOET, Pycked head, whiche is sharpe about lyke a suger lofe, *argutum caput.* **1615** G. SANDYS *Trav.* 63 Yellow or red slip-shooes, picked at the toe. **1665** HOOKE *Microgr.* 156 Sorrel has a..three-square seed, which is picked at both ends. **1666** J. DAVIES *Hist. Caribby Isles* 25 The top of this Mountain seems to be very picked. **1683** EVELYN *Diary* 7 Dec., Dragoons..habited after the Polish manner, with long picked caps. **1696** *Lond. Gaz.* No. 3237/4 John Symons, Maltman.., with a picked Chin. **1762–71** H. WALPOLE *Vertue's Anecd. Paint.* (1786) I. 150 The head of a man, with a hat and picked beard.

picked (pɪkt, *formerly* and *poet.* 'pɪkɪd), *ppl. a.* Forms: α. 4, 6–7 **pyked**, 5 **i-pikid**, *Sc.* **pykit**, 5–7 **piked.** β. 5–6 **pycked**, 6– **picked**; 6–7 **pickt**, 7 **pict**, 7–8 **pick'd**; *Sc.* 6 **pickit**, 8 **-et.** [f. PICK *v.*¹ + -ED¹.]

1. Cleaned or cleared with a pick or toothpick; made bare or bald by picking; cleared of stalks, husks, or refuse parts. See PICK *v.*¹

a **1400** HYLTON *Scala Perf.* (W. de W. 1494) II. xliii, Hym nedeth to haue whyte teeth & sharpe & well pycked that sholde byte of this ghostly brede. **1508** KENNEDY *Flyting w. Dunbar* 548 Hangit, mangit, eddir-strangit, stryndie stultorum..Pickit, wickit, conuickit, lamp Lollardorum. **1637** HEYWOOD *Dialogues* ii. Wks. 1874 VI. 120 Thin his haire,..his crowne Picked. **1790** A. SHIRREFS *Poems* 358 Nae doubt his hoose is thacket, But..I think it unco poor and picket, And far frae bonny. **1799** *Hull Advertiser* 2 Nov. 1/1 For sale..Riga picked flax. **1806** A. HUNTER *Culina* (ed. 3) 178 A gill of picked shrimps.

†**2.** Adorned, ornate, trimmed; exquisitely fashioned or apparelled, spruce, refined, exquisite, nice, finical, particular, fastidious. *Obs.*

The exact sense is often doubtful.

α. **13..** *E.E. Allit. P.* A. 1035 Vch pane of þat place had þre 3atez,..þe portalez pyked of rych platez. *c* **1400** *Beryn* 1734 The Ches was al of yvery, the meyne fressh & newe I-pulsshid, & I-pikid, of white, asure, & blewe. **1423** JAS. I *Kingis Q.* vii, In his faire latyne tong, So full of fruyte, and rethorikly pykit. *c* **1570** *Pride & Lowl.* (1841) 19 Piked he was, and handsome in his weede. **1606** HOLLAND *Sueton.* 148 Contemning the milder and more piked kinde of writing. **1613** W. BROWNE *Sheph. Pipe* I. xviii, Gay, fresh and piked was she.

β. **1573–80** BARET *Alv.* P 349 A more curious and picked style, *accuratius & exquisitius dicendi genus.* **1592** GREENE *Def. Conny Catch.* (1859) 33 Certayne quaint, pickt, and neate companions, attyred..*alla mode de Fraunce.* **1602** SHAKS. *Ham.* v. i. 151 The Age is growne so picked, that the toe of the Pesant comes so neere the heeles of our Courtier, that hee galls his Kibe. **1605** CHAPMAN *All Fooles* v. iv, 'Tis such a picked fellow, not a haire About his whole Bulke, but it stands in print. **1635** LAUD in *Ussher's Lett.* (1686) 377 In this nice and picked Age, you have ended all things canonically. **1636** B. JONSON *Discov.* Wks. (Rtldg.) 759/1 When the words are proper and apt, their sound sweet, and the phrase neat and picked. [**1892** *Daily News* 7 Mar. 5/1 Words..somewhat blunter in expression than our 'picked' age..would care to entertain.]

3. a. Chosen out, selected, esp. for special excellence or efficiency, or for a definite purpose.

a **1548** HALL *Chron., Hen. VI* 89 b, For feare of hym, or his picked armie. **1565–73** COOPER *Thesaurus* s.v. *Corpus, Delecta Corpora*,..chosen and pyked men. **1570** FOXE *A. & M.* (ed. 2) 157/1 The best & pikedst thynges chosen out of many churches. **1610** SHAKS. *Temp.* v. i. 247 At pickt leisure ..I'le resolue you,..of euery These happend accidents. **1626** G. HAKEWILL *Comparison*, etc. 27 The pict choice men of the land. **1672** MARVELL *Reh. Transp.* I. 209 As pick'd a man as could have been..found out in a whole Kingdome. **1799** J. ROBERTSON *Agric. Perth* 538 Picked ewes from the Ochill flocks. **1873** M. ARNOLD *Lit. & Dogma* (1876) 8 Only a few picked craftsmen can manage it. **1877** RAYMOND *Statist. Mines & Mining* 250 The highest assay made from picked rock yielded $1,560.41 per ton.

†**b.** *Cricket.* Chosen from outside. *Obs.*

1772 in Waghorn *Cricket Scores* (1899) 88, Sept. 28 was played at Egerton, a match at wicket..Egerton had two picked men on their side. **1773** *Ibid.* 98 The gentlemen of that place and one picked man.

†**4.** Contrived, provoked, designedly brought about; as, ***a picked quarrel.*** *Obs.*

c **1470** HENRYSON *Mor. Fab.* XII. (*Wolf & Lamb*) xix, Syne vexis him..With pykit querrellis, for to mak him fane To flit. **1679** OATES *Narr. Popish Plot* 68 Poysoning and Assassinating by pickt Quarrels or otherwise.

5. With adv. *out, up*: see PICK *v.*¹ 19, 21. ***picked-over***, from which the best has already been selected.

1771 J. ADAMS *Diary* 9 June, We had a picked up dinner. **1839** *Congress. Globe* 25th Congr. 3 Sess. App. 47/2 All the emigrants went on to the new lands, where they could get first choices at $1.25 per acre, because they could not give that sum for picked-over lands in the old counties. **1886** N. SHEPPARD *Before Audience* viii. 124 Audiences in England outside of the Established Church are weeded. To an American lecturer or preacher they have a picked-over appearance. The church takes the cream, the chapel the milk of society. **1889** MIVART *Orig. Hum. Reason* 80 Groups of picked-up straws. **1896** *Daily Chron.* 22 Aug. 3/2 Native seamen yelling and singing..coiling the picked-up cable. **1979** A. PARKER *Country Recipe Notebk.* iii. 60 Fill up with well-picked-over berries.

Hence **'pickedly** *adv.* (also 6 **pykedly**), †neatly, trimly, elegantly, daintily, fastidiously (*obs.*); **'pickedness** (also 7 **pikednesse**), † adornment, elegance, trimness, spruceness (*obs.*).

1540 HYRDE tr. *Vives' Instr. Chr. Wom.* I. xvi. (1557) 57 b, Maids..goodly and *pykedly araied. **1565–73** COOPER *Thesaurus* s.v. *Cura, Curiose loqui*, to speake curiously, or pykedly. **1593** NASHE *Christ's T.* (1613) 154 Their houses, so pickedly and neately must be trickt vp,..as if..they were to receiue Angels. **1578** TIMME *Caluine on Gen.*, Heauenly and secret wisdom,.. which.. can[not] neede the *pickednes and entisement of wordes. **1606** HOLLAND *Sueton.* 74 Negligent though hee were in all manner of pikedness, for combing and trimming of his head so carelesse. **1630** LENNARD tr. *Charron's Wisd.* III. xl. §1 (1670) 517 Neither affected uncleannesse, nor exquisite pickednesse [in dress]. **1636** B. JONSON *Discov., De Mollibus* Wks. (1692) 706 Too much pickedness is not manly.

†picke-devant, pique devant. *Obs.* Forms: 6 pique de vant, pickede vaunt, pickerdevant, (pickenovant); 6–7 pike-devant, pickadevaunt, -devant, -ante, 7 picadevant, pick-a-divant, pickatevant, pickitiva(u)nt, pickydevant, peake devant, 7–8 picke-devant. [A phrase app. made up of Fr. words, but itself unknown in Fr., and found only in Eng. (from *c* 1587 to 1630 or later). App. either for *pique* (or ? *pic*) *devant*, meant for 'peak in front', or for *piqué devant*, 'peaked in front'. The various spellings *pickede, picka-, picker-, picki-, picky-, pick-a-* seem to suit the latter, though the forms in *pick, pike*, and *peake* app. imply the sb. (Cf. also F. *pique* a spade at cards.) *Pickenovant* might be meant for *pique en avant*.]

A short beard trimmed to a point; a peaked or Vandyke beard: fashionable in England in the latter part of the 16th and earlier part of the 17th c.

1587 HARRISON *England* II. vii. (1877) I. 169 Our varietie of beards, of which some are shauen from the chin..; some made round like a rubbing brush, other with a *pique de vant* (O fine fashion!), or now and then suffered to grow long. **1589** *Pappe w. Hatchet* (1844) 28 Take away this beard, and giue me a pickede vaunt. **1592** LYLY *Midas* v. ii, And here I vow by my conceald beard, if euer it chaunce to be discouered to the worlde, that it maye make a pike deuant. **1594** *Taming of Shrew* (1844) 22 You haue many boies with such Pickadeuantes. **1596** NASHE *Saffron Walden* 5 Twice double his patrimonie hath he spent in carefull cherishing and preseruing his pickerdeuant. **1609** HOLLAND *Amm. Marcell.* xxv. vi. 270 Wearing his beard.. with a sharpe peake devant. **1618** *Owles Almanacke* 49 The picky-deuant .. will be the cutt. **1621** BURTON *Anat. Mel.* III. ii. IV. i. 619 To turne vp his Munshato's, and curle his head, prune his Pickitivant. **1638** R. BAKER tr. *Balzac's Lett.* (vol. III.) 108 Hee consists wholly of a Pickedevant and two Mustachoes. [**1688** R. HOLME *Armoury* II. 391/1 The Pick-a-devant Beard.. ends in a point under the chin. **1709** *Poor Robin* (N.), Entreaties upon such an account, are as ridiculous as pickedevant beards, or trunck-breeches.]

β. **1594** *2nd Rep. Dr. Faustus* xvii. G iv, He takes the greate slaue by the tip of his pickenouant.

b. *transf.* A man with a picke-devant.

1636 HEYWOOD *Challenge* v. i. Wks. 1874 V. 68 Point me out the man. That Picke-devant that elbowes next the Queene.

Hence **†pickedevanted** *a. Obs.*, having a picke-devant.

1591 HARINGTON *Orl. Fur.* XLI. 349 *note*, Seldome goeth deuotion with youth, be it spoken without offence of our Peckedeuaunted Ministers. **1621** BURTON *Anat. Mel.* III. ii. II. iv. 578 A young pickitiuanted [*ed.* 1676 pittivanted], trim-bearded fellow saith Hierome, will come with a company of complements.

†picked-hatch. *Obs.* Also pickt-, pict-, pick-hatch. [f. PICKED *a.* + HATCH *sb.*[1]] *lit.* A hatch or half door, surmounted by a row of pikes or spikes, to prevent climbing over; *spec.* a brothel; as proper name, see quot. 1832.

[Cf. **1616** E. S. *Cupid's Whirligig* F iij, Set some pickes vpon your hatch, and I pray professe to keepe a Bawdy-house.]

1598 SHAKS. *Merry W.* II. ii. 19 Goe.. to your Mannor of Pickt-hatch. **1599** MARSTON *Sco. Villanie* III. xi, Did euer any man ere heare him talke But of Pick-hatch, or of some Shoreditch baulke? **1610** B. JONSON *Alch.* II. i, The decay'd Vestalls of Pickt-hatch.. That keepe the fire a-liue, there. **1616** —— *Ev. Man in Hum.* I. ii, From the Burdello it might come as well, The Spittle: or Pict-hatch. **1832** TOONE *Gloss.*, *Pickt hatch*, this was a cant word, in the time of Queen Elizabeth, for a part of the town, supposed to be Turnmill Street, Clerkenwell, then noted for houses of ill fame... The term was derived from the hatch or half door, in houses of this description, being guarded with iron spikes, as the houses of sheriffs officers are at this time.

attrib. **1598** MARSTON *Sco. Villanie* I. iii. C vj, His old Cynick Dad Hath forc'd him cleane forsake his Pickhatch drab. **1607** WALKINGTON *Opt. Glass* 89 These bee your picke-hatch curtesan wits. *a* **1634** RANDOLPH *Muses' Looking-gl.* IV. iii. (1638) 72 My Pick-hatch grange, And Shoreditch farme, and other premises Adjoyning.

pickeer (pɪˈkɪə(r)), *v. Obs.* or *arch.* Forms: α. 7–8 pi'ckere, pi'cqueer, (7 pi'ckeere, pi'quere, pi'ckqueer, pi'ckear, pe'keer), 7– pi'ckeer, (8 pi'quier, picku'eer, 8–9 piqueer; β. 7 pickquer, picquer, 7–8 picker. [Derivation obscure: perh. an unexplained alteration of F. *picorer* (16th c.) to forage, maraud, pillage, plunder, pilfer, f. *picorée* foraging, marauding; according to Hatz-Darm., ad. Sp. *pecoréa*, vbl. sb. from *pecorear* to steal or carry off cattle, f. L. *pecus*, pl. *pecora* cattle: cf. med. or mod.L. *pecorare*, pr. pple. *pecorantes* 'pillagers of cattle', cited by Littré, and *pecoria* ('duo prædia, quæ secundum linguæ suæ (Flandricæ) consuetudinem *pecorias* appellant' *Chron. Afflegemiense* c. xx), in Du Cange.

The chief difficulty in thus accounting for the word is the final stress, proved by rimes, and by the spellings *-eer, -eere, -ere, -ear, -ier*. The occasional later *picquer'd, pickering* suggest indeed the pronunciation '*picker*; but *pickering* in D'Urfey 1719 is *pi'ckering* from *pi'ckere*. Moreover, the Fr. word is not cited in the maritime sense; nor have we much evidence for the Eng. vb. in the sense 'to forage'.]

†1. *intr.* To maraud, pillage, plunder; to practise privateering or piracy. *Obs.*

[*c* **1645** T. TULLY *Siege of Carlisle* (1840) 12 The restlesse spirits, weary of rest, went out a pickquering every day, and seldome returned without pray or prisoner.] **1651** OGILBY *Æsop* (1665) 18 A rush Candle purchas'd by pickeering. *a* **1661** FULLER *Worthies, Hants.* II. (1662) 10 Our Coasts were much infested with French-piracies. There was a Knight of Malta.. who liv'd by pickeering, and undoing many English Merchants. **1678** E. SMITH in *12th Rep. Hist. MSS. Comm.* App. v. 51 The French Ambassador.. said they were a fine company of men for picqueering and forrageing. **1718** OZELL tr. *Tournefort's Voy.* I. 111 Your Lordship has forbid pickeering from island to island for plunder.

2. *trans.* To skirmish, reconnoitre, scout (in war); to bicker (*with* the enemy).

c **1645** T. TULLY *Siege of Carlisle* (1840) 6 The scot[c]h hors Picquering a while close by the wals on the east, drew of, after they had faild in snapping Col. Grayes small regement of hors at Stanwick. *Ibid.* 20 Ye Scots sent out 6 or 7 horse to pickere with the other three scouts. **1652** WADSWORTH tr. *Sandoval's Civ. Wars Spain* 290 The Garrison of Simancas,.. went almost every daie Pekeering to the gates of Valladolid. *a* **1657** LOVELACE *Lucasta* II. Poems (1864) 203 So within shot she doth pickear, Now galls the flank, and now the rear. **1658** PHILLIPS, To *Pickear* (French *piquer*), is when particular persons fight between two Armies before the main Battle is begun. **1674** BLOUNT *Glossogr.* (ed. 4), *Pickeer* (from the Ital. *Picare*), to skirmish, as Light-horsemen do. **1691** *Lond. Gaz.* No. 2686/3 Several of our young Gentlemen passed over towards the Enemies Camp, and picquer'd with some of the French. **1705** SIR E. WALKER *Hist. Disc.* i. 65 Every Day to see ours and their Parties piquier from their Guards. **1719** D'URFEY *Pills* (1872) I. 141 When bold Dragoons have been pickering there. **1728** GORDON *Tacitus, Annals* XIII. 335 Tiridates, on his side, pickeer'd about, yet never approach'd within the throw of a dart. **1862** CARLYLE *Fredk. Gt.* XIII. xii. (1872) V. 122 South of us.. are the Enemy, camped or pickeering about.

3. *fig.* **a.** To reconnoitre, to scout.

1649 G. DANIEL *Trinarch., Hen. IV* lvi, Soe.. may wee see A Flea pickeere vpon a Lady's hand. **1737** L. CLARKE *Hist. Bible* (1740) II. I. 82 The Pharisees who were always pickering for occasions of finding fault. **1878** STEVENSON *Edinburgh* (1889) 65 Slinking.. and pickeering among the closes. **1892** *Sat. Rev.* 26 Mar. 345/1 The Front Opposition Bench had sent out the Irresponsibles to 'piqueer', as an agreeable word in classical English has it.

†b. To skirmish playfully or amorously; to dally, flirt. *Obs.*

1651 CLEVELAND *Senses Festival* vi, Two souls pickearing in a kiss. **1676** SHADWELL *Virtuoso* v. Wks. 1720 I. 403 There's a Lady hovering about you, and longs to pickeer with you. **1685** CROWNE *Sir C. Nice* I. Dram. Wks. 1874 III. 272 There was never such an open and general war made on virtue; young ones at thirteen will pickeere at it. **1709** MRS. MANLEY *Secret Mem.* (1720) IV. 120 She at first designed Pickueering for Adoration, only to please her Lord.

†c. To wrangle; to bicker in verbal strife. *Obs.*

1678 BUTLER *Hud.* III. ii. 448 No sooner could a hint appear, But up he started to pickere [18th c. *edd.* piqueer, picqueer]. *a* **1715** BURNET *Own Time* (1823) II. 25 He said to me, he had often picqueered out (that was his word) on Sheldon and some other bishops. **1717** *Entertainer* No. 6. 32 Pamphlets pickering and pecking at one another from the Press.

Hence **†pi'ckeer** *sb.*, a military skirmish.

1668 WILKINS *Real Char.* II. xi. §3. 276 Skirmishing, Fray, Velitation, pickeer. **1688** R. HOLME *Armoury* III. xix. (Roxb.) 187/1 Pickeering or firing in Picceer: is a kind of fighting betweene small parties.. which is by fireing one at another in their galloping in and out.

pickeerer (pɪˈkɪərə(r)). *Obs.* or *arch.* [f. prec. vb. + -ER[1].] A skirmisher; *fig.* one who provokes assault; a contentious or cavilling person.

a **1658** CLEVELAND *London Lady* 20 The Club Pickeerer, the robust Church Warden Of Lincolne's Inn back-corner. **1673** *Lady's Call.* I. i. § 19 What the end will be of these piqueerers in impudence, who thus put their vertu on the forlorn hope. *a* **1734** NORTH *Exam.* II. v. §145 He is now a Picquerer, relates Nothing but by Way of Cavil.

pi'ckeering, *vbl. sb. Obs.* or *arch.* [-ING[1].]

1. Skirmishing: see quot. 1894.

1650 R. STAPYLTON *Strada's Low C. Warres* VII. 76 The Prince of Orange.. being entertained with some pickeering (for Alva was resolved not to venture a battaile). **1704** STEELE *Lying Lover* I. (1747) 15 Still running over.. Mines, Counter-mines, Pickeering, Pioneers, Centinels, Patrols, and others. **1864** CARLYLE *Fredk. Gt.* XVII. vi. IV. 579 All hitherto has been pickeering. [**1894** LD. WOLSELEY *Life Marlborough* II. lxx. 237 What our soldiers called 'pickeering'.. the practice common amongst the volunteers and other gentlemen who followed both head-quarters, of riding out in front to fire their pistols at one another.]

2. *fig.* Wordy, playful, or amorous skirmishing; wrangling, bickering, petty quarrelling.

1677 GILPIN *Demonol.* (1867) 137 His particular temptations to sin are but inconsiderable, less successful picqueerings in comparison. **1715** M. DAVIES *Athen. Brit.* I. Pref. 2 Salmon's Pickeerings with the Colledge of Physicians. **1737** L. CLARKE *Hist. Bible* (1740) II. v. 139 At last, after all their pickeering, Jesus was pleased to ask them a question. **1862** CARLYLE *Fredk. Gt.* XIII. ii. (1872) V. 30 Mere pickeerings and beatings about the bush.

So **pi'ckeering** *ppl. a.*

1661 OGILBY *Relat. Entertainm.* 18 Give Fire, Bounce, Bounce, Pickeering Villains trounce.

†pickehorn. *Obs. rare*[−1]. ? Corrupt form of BYCORNE.

c **1580** JEFFERIE *Bugbears* III. iii. 71 in *Archiv Stud. Neu. Spr.* (1897), Hermafrodites, pickehornes, and lestrigoni.

pickel, var. PIKEL.

‖pickelhaube (pɪkəlˈhaʊbə). Also pickel-haube (with hyphen) and with capital initial. Pl. pickelhauben, pickelhaubes. [G.] A German spiked helmet of a type worn esp. before and during the earlier part of the war of 1914–18. Also, by metonymy, a German soldier.

1875 *Encycl. Brit.* II. 596/2 The [Prussian] uniform is a dark blue tunic, grey trousers with red stripe, helmet of black leather with brass ornaments and spike (*Pickel-haube*). **1880** G. A. SALA *Amer. Revisited* 213/2 The brutal jest of the cynical master of so many thousands of stolid men with needle-guns and *pickelhaubes* [*sc.* Bismarck] could turn all into mockery and contempt! **1887** *Athenæum* 1 Jan. 16/1 Here is represented the old Empire with powder and wigs, while in Julius Grosse's novel.. we find the new Empire with its *Pickelhaube*. **1890** *Times* (Weekly ed.) 28 Feb. 16/1 A dragoon regiment with *pickelhaube* helmet. **1901** *Scotsman* 29 Nov. 5/4 Germany is defied in a manner fitted to stiffen the pickelhauben of the General Staff. **1927** *Bulletin* (Glasgow) 4 Oct. 12/2 A German officer's silver-plated pickel-haube. **1931** E. LINKLATER *Juan in Amer.* II. xvii. 181 Prussian wombs bore pickel-haubes. **1969** G. COPPARD *With Machine Gun to Cambrai* xxi. 89 A dozen Jerry soldiers... The *pickelhaubes* on their heads made them look a leering bunch of devils. **1972** M. GLENNY tr. *Solzhenitsyn's August 1914* xxv. 260 Even when the *Pickelhauben* were no more than a hundred yards away, the Russians showed no fear. **1976** *Leicester Chron.* 26 Nov. 14/5 The first distinctive German steel helmets were introduced in 1916 as a replacement for the pickelhaube, and other armies quickly followed suit.

pickell, obs. f. PICKLE, PIGHTLE.

pickenovant: see PICKE-DEVANT.

picker[1] (ˈpɪkə(r)). [f. PICK *v.*[1] + -ER[1].]

1. *generally.* A person who picks.

a. One who picks, plucks off, or gathers (fruit, flowers, roots, hops, cotton, potatoes, etc.); one who picks up or collects (rags, refuse, etc.). Also a second element in numerous combinations, as ***fruit-, hop-, potato-, rag-, rag-and-bone-picker***, etc.

1669 WORLIDGE *Syst. Agric.* (1681) 152 A Shed,.. which will both defend your Pickers from the Sun, and your Hops. **1763** *Museum Rust.* I. lx. 256 Pickers ready to gather up the roots as fast as they are thrown up by the spade. **1805** R. W. DICKSON *Pract. Agric.* II. 630 Such potatoes as may have escaped the pickers. **1861** *Illustr. Times* 5 Oct. 221 The festoons [of hops].. already destined to the picker's bin. **1884** *Cassell's Family Mag.* Feb. 156/2 The pickers, who are mostly Italians, gather £150,000 worth [of rags] yearly in the streets and roads. **1893** *Daily News* 5 Jan. 5/6 Forty-five thousand men and women.. subsisting on pickings from household rubbish... There are pickers and pickers, grades, aristocrats and plebeians in this profession as in every other.

b. One who steals, esp. small things that may be readily picked up. ***pickers and stealers*** (see PICK *v.*[1] 9 b, PICKING *vbl. sb.*[1] 2), *allusively*, hands.

[**1301–1549**: see PIKER[1].] **1526** TINDALE *Tit.* ii. 10 The servauntes exhorte to be obedient.. nether be pickers. **1549** CHEKE *Hurt Sedit.* (1641) 21 Shall we call you pickers or hid theeves? **1552** HULOET, Pycker or priuye stealer, *furax, cis.* **1580** *Orders for Orphanes* A iv, If any womanchilde.. be a common Picker. **1591** *Art. conc. Admiralty* 21 July §42 Petite transgressors, or pickers, which haue stollen.. Anchors, Cables,.. girdles, Shirts, Breeches, or other small things whatsoeuer. **1602** SHAKS. *Ham.* III. ii. 348 So I do still, by these pickers and stealers. **1775** S. J. PRATT *Liberal Opin.* x. I. 108 Their pickers and stealers were at liberty, to secrete certain portable moveables. **1822** SCOTT *Nigel* Introd. Epistle, These unhappy pickers and stealers.

c. One who seeks occasion, as ***a picker of quarrels***. **d.** One who chooses out or selects. **e.** One who picks a lock: see PICK *v.*[1] 10.

1530 in W. H. Turner *Select. Rec. Oxford* (1880) 92 He is a comyn pyker of quarrells. **1564** RASTELL *Confut. Jewell's Serm.* 107 b, Peekers of quarells are abrode. **1617** MINSHEU *Ductor*, A Picker of quarrels, *qui omnem captat litigandi ansam, & venatur.* **1825** *Gentl. Mag.* XCV. I. 216 It [the coffee-berry] is then winnoed, and goes into the hands of the pickers. **1830** CUNNINGHAM *Brit. Paint.* I. 64 One who was no picker of paths. **1870** SPURGEON *Treas. Dav.* Ps. l. 17 There are pickers and choosers of God's word. **1888** J. PAYN *Myst. Mirbridge* xxi, The law.. is, moreover, itself a picker of locks.

f. In various trades and occupations, a person who picks, in technical senses: e.g. (*a*) a wool-carder, a wool-picker; (*b*) one who touches up or removes slight defects in electrotypes; (*c*) a quarryman who uses a pick; (*d*) a fisherman who catches eels with a pick: see PICK *sb.*[1] 4 d.

(*a*) [**1536** *Act 28 Hen. VIII*, c. 4 §1 Weavers, tokers, spynners, diers, and wulpikers haue bene.. withoute worke.] **1552** HULOET, Pickers or toosars of wolle, *carminarij.*

(*b*) **1882** J. SOUTHWARD *Pract. Print.* (1884) 600 The pickers are those who have the work of touching up electros. **1885** C. G. W. LOCK *Workshop Receipts* Ser. IV. 216/2 The picker's first duty is to chip down the 'whites' of the plate, so that they shall not take the ink in printing.

(*c*) **1883** *Stonemason* Jan., The face of the rock is first disturbed by a 'picker' who, standing on a stage, clears away by blows from a pick delivered horizontally, a space .. about 5 feet through.
(*d*) **1885** *Sat. Rev.* 21 Nov. 673/1 The Norfolk-men mostly use 'picks' formed of four broad blades .. mounted on long slender poles to enable them to be thrust into the mud. The 'picker' notices the .. bubbles.

g. One who picks (PICK *v.*[1] 12) or plucks the strings of a musical instrument such as the banjo or guitar; usu. with the name of the instrument prefixed.

1923 in *John Edwards Mem. Foundation Q.* (1969) V. II. 62 Old fiddlers and banjo pickers. **1934** S. R. NELSON *All about Jazz* vi. 126 The modern method of picking and slapping on the bass was found to be much more rhythmic. So a race of pickers and slappers .. sprang into being. **1951, 1959** [see *guitar-picker* s.v. GUITAR *sb.* b]. **1964** *Amer. Folk Music Occasional* I. 43, I know a banjo picker who hasn't performed for anyone except his wife for the last three years. **1969** N. COHN *A Wop Bopa Loo Bop* (1970) viii. 77 A strange city, filled to overflowing with guitar pickers by the thousand. **1976** *National Observer* (U.S.) 23 Oct. 20/3 It's not a novel story. Country music is rife with legend about pickers hitting Lower Broad with a nickel and a song.

2. A tool or instrument for picking.

a. In agriculture: (*a*) A sort of mattock or pickax; (*b*) a tool for taking up turnips; (*c*) the part of a potato-digging and picking-machine which separates the potatoes from the soil; (*d*) a machine for gathering cotton in the field. Often in *Comb.* as ***potato-picker***, ***turnip-picker***.

1707 MORTIMER *Husb.* (1721) I. 192 Having with an Iron Picker cleared away all the Earth out of the Hills, so as to make the Stock bare to the principal Roots [of the hops]. **1805** R. W. DICKSON *Pract. Agric.* II. 750 A tool which has the title of a picker. **1884** *Cassell's Family Mag.* Feb. 189/2 The shaker or picker separates the tubers from the soil and delivers them to the rear of the machine. **1886** C. SCOTT *Sheep-Farming* 69 A handy turnip hoe or picker, for picking up the shells of the roots.

b. In the textile industries: (*a*) A machine for separating and cleaning the fibres of cotton, wool, and the like; (*b*) an implement for burling cloth.

1795 *Edin. Advert.* 6 Jan. 15/3 Five common carding engines, one waste engine, four pickers. **1825** J. NICHOLSON *Operat. Mechanic* 379 The first machine .. for the further clearing of the particles [of cotton] is called a picker. **1879** TIMBS in *Cassell's Techn. Educ.* VIII. 128/2 The separate materials are first passed through a machine called a picker and blower.

c. In *Mining* and *Metallurgy*: in Cornwall, a miner's hand-chisel; a miner's needle for picking out the tamping of an unexploded charge. In *Founding*, a light pointed steel rod, used for lifting small patterns from the sand into which they have been rammed; a tool for piercing a mould.

1874 J. H. COLLINS *Metal Mining* (1875) 62 The pickers used in the Western mines are longer and narrower. They are used, as the name implies, to pick out the small fragments of loose rock which wedge in larger portions in some situations. **1881** RAYMOND *Mining Gloss.*, *Picker* or *Poker*, a hand chisel for *dzhuing*, held in one hand and struck with a hammer.

d. The name of various tools: e.g.

A toothpick; a tool for picking stones from a horse's foot; a tool for clearing out small openings, as in a lamp or a powder-flask; a priming-wire for clearing the vent of a gun; a tool for scraping clod-salt from the bottom of a salt-pan; in brick-making, one of two spike-toothed horizontal shafts which revolve in opposite directions, and disintegrate the raw clay; a picklock; a needle for making anglers' flies; a tool, like a graver, used in touching up electrotypes.

1624 *Harington's Schoole Salerne* II. xi. 44 After meat taken .. clense the teeth either with Iuory .. or some picker of pure siluer or gold. **1649** G. DANIEL *Trinarch.* To Rdr. 208 Euery hand Of accident doth with a Picker stand, To scale the wards of Life. **1678** J. COLLINS in *Phil. Trans.* XII. 1063 Clod-Salt, which grows to the bottom of the Phats .. is digged up with a picker (.. made like a Masons Trowel, pointed with Steel and put upon a short staff). *c* **1785** in *Daily Chron.* 9 Dec. (1904) 4/6 Two of us .. when alone would with pickers pick the mortar out of the bricks till we had opened a hole big enough to go in. **1839** URE *Dict. Arts* 837 The rubbish is withdrawn as it accumulates, at the bottom of the hole, by means of a picker. **1859** F. A. GRIFFITHS *Artil. Man.* (1862) 221 Mane-comb, picker.

3. A young cod, too small to swallow bait. *Sc.* and local *U.S.*

1895 MRS. F. A. STEEL *Red Rowans* x. 153, I believe .. pickers or suckers is really only the local name [Sc.] for young codlings, lythe, or cuddies. In fact for all young fish.

4. a. With adv. as **picker-up**, one who picks up or gathers; a man employed to collect the game shot by a shooting party; in Australia and New Zealand, the man who gathers the fleece when it is shorn from a sheep.

1761 STERNE *Tr. Shandy* III. xxxiv. 159 Indissolubly annex'd by the picker up, to the thing pick'd up. **1857** BORROW *Rom. Rye* I. x. 140, I dislike a picker-up of old words worse than a picker-up of old rags. **1874** MOTLEY *Barneveld* II. xvi. 217 A mere picker-up of trifles. **1881** A. BATHGATE *Waitaruna* xii. 172 The 'pickers-up' were busy gathering the fleeces as they fell from the bereft sheep and carrying them to the sorting table. **1890** *Melbourne Argus* 20 Sept. 13/7 As the fleece drops off, a soft woolly whole, the 'picker up', of whom there is one to about eight shearers, .. gathers it up with the 'locks' and 'pieces'. **1913** A. BATHGATE *Sodger Sandy's Bairn* 57 The pickers-up gathered the fleeces as they fell intact from the shears and bore them to the sorting table, where they were quickly 'skirted' and 'classed'. **1940** *Essays & Stud.* XXV. 111 The picker-up of unconsidered historical trifles. **1956** S. HOPE *Diggers' Paradise* 99 A sixteen-year-old lad could earn £17 a week as a 'picker-up' in the wool-shed. **1959** H. P. TRITTON *Time means Tucker* iii. 26/2 Pickers-up took the fleece as it fell on the board and spread it skin-side down on the wool-tables. **1977** *Shooting Times & Country Mag.* 13–19 Jan. 22/1 There are plenty of pickers-up on this shoot, and little is lost.

b. picker-upper, one who, or that which, picks up.

1936 *Esquire* Sept. 162/2 *Variety* maintains a news staff —not a bunch of press-release picker-uppers. **1942** *Amer. Speech* XVII. 104/1 *Picker-upper*, service car with crane. **1944** *N.Y. Times* 3 Sept. S2/6 Her devoted spouse is an avid picker-upper of any hairpins he can find. **1947** *Philadelphia Bull.* 28 July 8 (Advt.), Energy picker-upper .. chocolate cookies. **1961** *Times* 19 Aug. 6/7 A mechanical means of gathering up lumps of oil .. has been built. It is described as a 'picker-upper', which might be drawn by a tractor.

5. *Comb.* **picker-bar**, a toothed bar for discharging the ashes and cinders from the grate in a mechanical stoker.

picker[2] ('pɪkə(r)). *Weaving.* [f. PICK *v.*[2] + -ER[1].] In a loom, the small instrument which travels backwards and forwards in the shuttle-box and drives the shuttle to and fro through the warp.

[**1831**: see PECKER 2 c.] **1841** *Encycl. Brit.* (ed. 7) XXI. 824/2 The two ends of this shuttle-race are closed up at the sides, so as to form short troughs, in which two moveable pieces of wood, called pickers, or peckers, traverse along pieces of wire. *Ibid.*, Formerly the shuttle was thrown by the hand, but about one hundred years ago, the picker, or fly-shuttle, was invented by one John Kay of Bury, in Lancashire. **1865** *Public Opinion* 4 Feb. 132 The principle upon which the new loom acts is that of discharging a jet of compressed air from the valves of the shuttle-box, upon the end of the shuttle, at each pick or stroke, and thus substituting for the imperfect motion of the 'picker' the pneumatic principle, simply applied. **1875** KNIGHT *Dict. Mech.* 1697 *Picker* .. the upper or striking portion of a picker-staff, which comes against the end of the shuttle and impels it through the shed of the warp. **1886** HARRIS *Techn. Dict. Fire Insurance*, *Pickers*, made of buffalo hide, and used for throwing the shuttles backwards and forwards in cotton-weaving.

b. *Comb.*, as ***picker-cord***, ***-maker***, ***-manufacturer***, ***-strap***; **picker-bend** (see quot. 1858); **picker-motion**, the mechanism involved in impelling the shuttle to and fro; **picker-staff**, the oscillating bar which imparts motion to the shuttle.

1858 SIMMONDS *Dict. Trade*, *Picker-bends*, pieces of buffalo hide .. imported for the use of power-loom weavers, who attach them to the shuttle. **1864** *Times* 12 Mar., O. & S., Halifax, picker makers. **1878** BARLOW *Weaving* v. 81 The two pickers are connected together by a slack cord to the centre of which the 'picking stick' is attached. Two short cords are connected to the picker cord to keep it suspended and free to work. *Ibid.* xxv. 271 The pickers are fixed upon the ends of the sticks. In this plan the picker straps and spindles are dispensed with.

picker[3], anglicized f. PIQUEUR, huntsman.

1863 LD. LYTTON *Ring Amasis* II. II. ii. viii. 100 He turned round to take the horn and the hunting-knife from the picker.

picker: see PICKEER *v.*

pickerdeuant, variant of PICKE-DEVANT *Obs.*

pickerel[1] ('pɪkərəl). Forms: 4–6 **pyk-**, 4–7 **pikerel(l(e**, 5 **pykrelle**, **pyckerylle**, 5–6 **pekerell(e**, 6 **pykarelle**, 6–7 **pikrel(l**, 6–8 **pickrel(l**, **-erell**, 6– **pickerel**, (7 **-il**, **pikrill**, 9 **pickarel**). [dim. of PIKE *sb.*[4], either of Anglo-Fr. origin, or formed in ME. on OF. analogies: cf. COCKEREL and -REL. (Fr. has *picarel*, 16th c. in Godef., as a local name for a salt-water fish on the Mediterranean coast.)] A young pike, especially at a certain stage of its growth: cf. quot. 1587.

1338 *Durham Acc. Rolls* (Surtees) 35 In quatuor pykerells empt. ixd. *c* **1386** CHAUCER *Merch. T.* 175 Bet is .. a pyk than a pykerel. *c* **1425** *Voc.* in Wr.-Wülcker 641/25 *Hic lucellus*, pyckerylle. **1462** *Mann. & Househ. Exp.* (Roxb.) 562 My master put in the said pond in smale pekerelles, xx. *c* **1483** CAXTON *Dialogues* 12 *Lu[c]es, becques, becquets*, luses, pikes, pikerellis. **1579** in W. H. Turner *Select. Rec. Oxford* (1880) 402 No pickerell is lawfull eyther to be taken or solde not beinge in length tenne ynches fishe. **1587** HARRISON *England* III. iii. (1878) II. 18 The pike as he ageth, receiueth diuerse names, as from a frie to a gilthed, from a gilthed to a pod, from a pod to a iacke, from a iacke to a pickerell, from a pickerell to a pike, and last of all to a luce. **1608** TOPSELL *Serpents* (1658) 671 To sundry fishes .. as to the Tench, Pike or Pikerel. **1767** *Phil. Trans.* LVII. 281 A small pickerel .. contained no fewer than 25,800 eggs. **1891** E. FIELD *West. Verse, Long Ago* 196, I knew the rushes near the mill Where pickerel lay that weighed a pound.

b. In U.S. and Canada, The name of several species of *Esox*, esp. the smaller species; about the Great Lakes, the true pike; also the pike-perch, wall-eye, or glass-eye (*Stizostedion vitreum*).

1765 T. HUTCHINSON *Hist. Mass.* I. v. 465 Pickrel, bream, pearch, and other freshwater fish. **1860** O. W. HOLMES *Elsie V.* 50 [They] used to go and fish through the ice for pickerel every winter. **1881** *Harper's Mag.* Sept. 512 The principal catch is pickerel, which can be taken even by an unskilful fisherman. **1897** *Outing* (U.S.) XXX. 435/2 What we termed 'pickerel' (wall-eyed pike) were better table-fish.

'**pickerel**[2]. [? dim. f. PICK. Cf. DOTTEREL.] A bird: the common name in Scotland of the dunlin (*Tringa alpina*).

1831 *Montagu's Ornith. Dict.* 144 Dunlin .. *Provincial.* Purre, Least Snipe .. Pickerel. **1885** SWAINSON *Prov. Names Birds* 193 Dunlin. .. Pickerel (Scotland generally). A name applied to all small waders.

pickerel frog. *U.S.* [PICKEREL[1].] A common North American frog, *Rana palustris*.

1839 D. H. STORER in Storer & Peabody *Rep. Fishes, Reptiles & Birds Mass.* 238 The pickerel frog .. is .. met with about the margins of fresh water brooks and ponds. **1906** M. C. DICKERSON *Frog Bk.* 189 The brook and the fields and meadows near make the home of the Pickerel Frogs. **1961** D. M. COCHRAN *Living Amphibians of World* 107/1 The entire skin of the North American pickerel frog, *Rana palustris*, secretes a substance which is lethal to frogs of other species.

'**pickerel-weed.** [f. PICKEREL[1] + WEED.]

1. A name locally applied to certain weeds, found in still waters, amongst which pikes breed, and which formerly were popularly supposed to breed them; most commonly to species of *Potamogeton* or Pondweed.

1653 WALTON *Angler* vii. 148 His feeding is .. sometime a weed of his owne, called *Pikrel-weed*, of which .. some think some Pikes are bred. **1823** E. MOOR *Suffolk Words*, *Pickarel-weed* is .. well known in Suffolk and Cambridge—and the idea that the sun's heat helps the breeding of pike in it, is common. **1853** G. JOHNSTON *Nat. Hist. E. Bord.* I. 250 The Pickerell-weeds throw out their oval or elliptical leaves that float so lightly on the surface.

2. In N. America, Any species of *Pontederia*, lacustrine plants, with sagittate leaves, and spikes of blue flowers. Also ***pickerel-flower***.

1836 EMERSON *Nature, Beauty* Wks. (Bohn) II. 146 In July, the blue pontederia or pickerel-weed blooms in large beds in the shallow parts of our pleasant river. **1867** —— *May-Day*, etc., ibid. III. 419 Through gold-moth-haunted beds of pickerel-flower. **1868** LOSSING *Hudson* 21 This in the books, is called Pickerel Weed (*Pontederia cordata* ..), but the guides call it moose-head.

pickeridge ('pɪkərɪdʒ). [f. PICK *v.*[1] + RIDGE, back.] 'One of the varieties of warbles; a swelling occurring on the backs of cattle' (*Syd. Soc. Lex.*).

1882 in OGILVIE; and in later Dicts.

pickering[1]. *Obs.* exc. *U.S.* = PICKEREL[1].

1528 in T. D. Whitaker *Hist. Craven* (1812) 307 Item, in great pike, & pickering, 6 score. 8. l.

Pickering[2] ('pɪkərɪŋ). *Physics.* The name of Edward Charles *Pickering* (1846–1919), U.S. astronomer, used, usu. *attrib.*, with reference to a series of lines in the spectrum of ionized helium with wave numbers represented by $4R(1/4^2 - 1/m^2)$ (where R is the Rydberg constant and $m = 5, 6, \ldots$), of which the first line has a wavelength of 1012 nanometres and the series limit is at 364 nanometres; (observed by Pickering in 1896 (*Astrophysical Jrnl.* IV. 369, V. 92)).

1922 A. D. UDDEN tr. *Bohr's Theory of Spectra* I. 3 Recently however the question has been reopened and Fowler (1912) has succeeded in observing the Pickering lines in ordinary laboratory experiments. **1923** H. L. BROSE tr. *Sommerfeld's Atomic Struct. & Spectral Lines* iv. 208 Pickering's series (7) includes only one-half of the lines represented by (7a), namely, those for which *k* is odd. *Ibid.*, It is .. unjustifiable and arbitrary to detach one-half as the Pickering series and to ascribe it to hydrogen. The other half was overlooked earlier only because it could not be separated from the neighbouring true hydrogen lines. **1942** J. D. STRANATHAN *'Particles' of Mod. Physics* vi. 222 Alternate lines of the Pickering series of helium coincide almost exactly with the Balmer lines of hydrogen. But .. the Pickering lines fall at slightly shorter wave lengths. **1967** W. R. HINDMARSH *Atomic Spectra* ii. 5 It was first believed that the Pickering series arose from a special form of hydrogen but it is now known to be due to ionized helium.

'**pickeringite.** *Min.* [Named 1844 after John Pickering, President of the American Academy: see -ITE[1].] A hydrous sulphate of aluminium and magnesium, found in Peru and Nova Scotia, in masses of silky white fibres, and as acicular crystals.

1844 *Amer. Jrnl. Sc.* XLVI. 360 Pickeringite a native magnesian alum.

pickeroon, variant of PICAROON.

pickery[1] ('pɪkərɪ). Also 6 **pikry**, **pikery**, **pykery**, **picory**, *Sc.* **pikary**, 6–7 **pykrie**, **-ry**. [f. PICKER[1], PIKER[1]: see -ERY.] Petty theft. Still a term of Scotch law.

1508 in Pitcairn *Crim. Trials* I. *53 [Convicted of common Theft and] Pikry. **1522** in Boys *Sandwich* (1792) 683 Prevy picory. **1536** BELLENDEN *Cron. Scot.* (1821) II. 107 He conquest his leving on thift and pikary. **1553** in *Hakluyt's Voy.* (1598) I. 266 For pickerie ducked at yardes arme, and so discharged. **1613–17** in R. M. Fergusson *Alex. Hume* (1899) 200 For .. preventing of the grite stewthe and pykrie that daylie incressis. *a* **1765** ERSKINE *Princ. Sc. Law* (1773) IV. iv. §59 The stealing of trifles, which in our law-language is styled *pickery*, has never been punished by the usage of Scotland, but with imprisonment, scourging, or other corporal punishment. **1815** SCOTT *Guy M.* xlii, A trifle stolen in the street is termed mere pickery. **1861** W. BELL *Dict. Law Scot.*, *Pickery*, is the stealing of trifles, which has never been punished in any other way than by an arbitrary punishment.

†**pickery**[2], obs. form of PECCARY.

1706 PHILLIPS, *Pickery*, an American Beast like a Hog.

picket ('pɪkɪt), *sb.*[1] Forms: *α.* 7 picquett, 8 piquett, 8– picquet, piquet; *β.* 7– picket. [a. F. *piquet* pointed stake, also in other senses, f. *piquer* to prick, pierce, with dim. suffix: see -ET[1].]

I. 1. A pointed stake, post, or peg, driven into the ground; used for various purposes, e.g.

a. in the construction of a stockade or fence (fence picket = pale); **b.** to hold in position gabions, fascines, and other means of fortification; **c.** to mark positions in surveying, etc.; also, a triangular or arrow-shaped mark cut in turf or placed on masonry, used in making measurements. **d.** to fasten a rope or string to, esp. in order to tether a horse or other animal, also to secure a tent; **e.** sharpened also at the upper end, as a defence against cavalry or other assailants.

1702 *Military Dict.*, *Picket*, or *Piquet*, is a Stake sharp at the end, which serves to mark out the Ground, and Angles of a Fortification, when the Ingenier is laying down the Plan. They are commonly pointed with Iron. There are also large *Piquets*, which are drove into the Earth, to hold together the Fascines, or Faggots, in any Work cast up in haste. *Pickets* are also Stakes drove into the Ground, by the Tents of the Horse in the Field to tye their Horses to. **1711** *Lond. Gaz.* No. 4871/2 Most of the Horses..breaking loose from their Pickets.., some were taken. **1762** STERNE *Tr. Shandy* VI. xxi. **1803** WELLINGTON in Gurw. *Desp.* I. 487 One end of the cable must be..fixed to a picket or to any thing firm. **1807** HUTTON *Course Math.* II. 57 Sometimes pickets, or staves with flags, are set up as marks or objects of direction. **1834–47** J. S. MACAULAY *Field Fortif.* (1851) 88 The small branches cut from an abatis may be rendered useful by making pickets of them. **1838** *Civ. Eng. & Arch. Jrnl.* I. 96/1 Marking the middle line, or axis of the road, by stakes or pickets, placed at equal intervals apart. *Ibid.* 98/1 The fascines are laid in alternate layers crosswise and lengthwise, and the layers..connected by pickets. **1859** F. A. GRIFFITHS *Artil. Man.* (1862) 218 Each horse standing at picket. **1869** PARKMAN *Discov. Gt. West* (1883) 20 A square fort of cedar pickets. **1873** TRISTRAM *Moab* iv. 63 A lurking thief had cut the pickets of the horses. **1883** E. INGERSOLL in *Harper's Mag.* Jan. 208/2 Fence posts are made..and after these the rough split fence pickets so commonly used in this part of the State.

f. A stockade. *rare.*

1841 CATLIN *N. Amer. Ind.* I. xi. 81 The piquet is composed of timbers..eighteen feet high set firmly in the ground at sufficient distances from each other to admit of guns and other missiles to be fired between them.

2. A stake with pointed top, used in a military punishment in vogue in the 17th and 18th c.: see quot. 1706. Hence, a name for this punishment, and for similar forms of torture.

1690 *Royal Proclam.* in Starke *Obs. Milit Punishm.* (1901) 5 If a trooper he shall stand three several times on the Picquett. **1702** *Military Dict.* s.v. **1706** PHILLIPS, *To Stand upon the Picket*, is when a Horseman for some Offence, is sentenc'd to have one Hand ty'd up as high as it can reach, and then to stand on the Point of a Stake with the Toe of his opposite Foot; so that he can neither stand, nor hang well, nor ease himself by changing Feet. **1806** MAR. EDGEWORTH *Leonora* xlv, If I put a poor fellow on the picket. **1843** R. R. MADDEN *United Irishmen* Ser. II. II. xvi. 353 The tortures of the lash, the picquet and the knotted cord. **1862** LD. STANHOPE *Pitt* III. 116 Many of these unhappy men underwent the military punishments of the lash and the picket—this last consisting in being made to stand with one foot upon a pointed stake.

†**3.** A peg, pin, plug. *Obs. rare.*

1868 *Rep. to Govt. U.S. on Munitions War* 14 (Boxer ammunition), The bullet has a picket of wood running through its centre half-way from the apex of the cone towards the base. *Ibid.* 16 The bullet, as in the Boxer, has the wooden picket through half its longer axis, and the clay plug in the base for expansion.

II. 4. a. *Mil.* A small detached body of troops, sent out to watch for the approach of the enemy or his scouts (*outlying picket*), or held in quarters in readiness for such service (*inlying picket*); also applied to a single soldier so employed. In the Army Regulations spelt *piquet.*

1761 *Brit. Mag.* II. 105 A vanguard, composed of the piquets, which were formed into battalions and squadrons, for securing the head of their cantonments. **1781** in Simes *Milit. Guide* (ed. 3) 8 [The Adjutant-general] may..visit them at their posts, and always see that the piquets are in good order. **1799** WELLINGTON in Gurw. *Desp.* I. 22 The advanced picquets of the British army were attacked by the enemy. **1844** *Regul. & Ord. Army* 1 If an Officer's Tour of Duty happen when he is on the Inlying Piquet,..his Tour upon the Piquet is to pass him. **1844** H. H. WILSON *Brit. India* II. 384 The village of Yuva..was guarded by a strong picquet of cavalry and infantry. **1861** MRS. E. BEERS *All Quiet along the Potomac*, Now and then a stray picket Is shot as he walks on his beat to and fro. **1884** *Sat. Rev.* 26 July 126/2, 600 Chasseurs of the Imperial Guard..attacked our picquets, but were repulsed.

b. A camp-guard, sent out to bring in men who have exceeded their leave.

1787 *Gentl. Mag.* LVII. II. 1199/2 The piquets and double patroles abandoned their officers, and joined their mutinous comrades. **1851** DIXON *W. Penn* iv. 135 A sergeant and piquet of soldiers entered the room. **1886** *Pall Mall G.* 7 Oct. 9/1 A serious military riot..occurred in the streets of Aldershot..last evening.. The military police and pickets had to be reinforced.

c. *transf.* and *fig.* A party of watchers or sentinels, an outpost; an outlying post.

1847–8 H. MILLER *First Impr.* xiv. (1857) 228 Two insulated outliers, that..form the outer piquets of the newer and higher system. **1860** G. H. K. in *Vac. Tour* 173 There, two miles off, are lying deer,..pickets of keen eyed and keener scented hinds thrown out in every direction. **1866** NEALE *Seq. & Hymns* 52 The picquets of the Spirit-host.

d. Short for *picket duty.*

1775 J. HALLAM *Let.* 10 Dec. in H. P. Johnston *Nathan Hale* (1901) 158 Your being on Picquet is a sufficient excuse that you wrote no more. **1834** *Chambers's Edin. Jrnl.* III. 167/2 For three weeks I have been on picquet every night. **1861** O. W. NORTON *Army Lett.* (1903) 34, I have just returned from picket. **1944** J. S. PENNELL *Hist. Rome Hanks* 41 You're on picket, aren't you?

5. (usually *pl.*) Applied to people acting in a body or singly who are stationed by a trades-union or the like, to watch people going to work during a strike or in non-union workshops, and to endeavour to dissuade or deter them. Similarly applied to a person or group conducting a demonstration at particular premises, a particular installation, etc. Also collective sing. Also, the conduct or activity of pickets; an instance of picketing.

1867 *Times* 22 Aug. 8/3 The pickets kept their places from early morning till night; they reviled the workmen who went in and out; they forced women to call upon the police for protection; they threatened that those who took work.. should have none when the Union was triumphant. **1869** *Pall Mall G.* 31 Aug. 1 We will assume..that they issue positive orders to the pickets to resort to nothing in the shape of coercion. **1885** *Even. Standard* 19 Dec., The strikers have posted pickets at all stations. **1886** *Globe* 2 Feb. 6/5 In connection with a strike, the defendant acting as a 'picket'. **1891** *Newcastle Even. Chron.* 17 Jan. 4/1 To.. prevent the pickets of the strikers from indulging in demonstrations against the loyal men. **1938** *Sun* (Baltimore) 7 Sept. 2/2 Patient parish pickets, determined to retain the Rev. Simon Borkowski as pastor of St. Barbara's Catholic Church, kept their vigil today as they have for more than three weeks to prevent him from fulfilling a transfer order. **1973** *Freedom* 12 May 4/4 (Advt.), Stop the French tests. Regular picket, and London-Paris walk 14th May–3rd June. **1977** *New Society* 30 June 657/2 The picket's mood turned restive, apprehensive. *Ibid.* 657/1 Comment on the picket has almost entirely missed the point by concentrating on how the law might be changed to reconcile heavy strike-breaking vehicles and mass pickets.

III. 6. An elongated rifle bullet, with a conoidal front; a cylindro-conoidal bullet.

(Said in E. S. Farrow, *American Small Arms* (1904) 56, to have been 'made for Col. Pickett, the well-known grizzly bear killer'.)

1858 DEANE *Hist. & Sc. Fire-arms* 263 A form of conical projectile used and called a 'picket' in the United States, and also used in several of the German states. **1859** J. SCOFFERN *Projectile Weapons* (ed. 4) 219 *note*, The Americans term the new elongated projectile conoids 'pickets'; and a very good term it is. **1874** KNIGHT *Dict. Mech.* 402/1. **1881** GREENER *Gun* 177 The regulation Martini-Henry rifling would send a long-range picket clean through an elephant. **1901** T. F. FREMANTLE *Bk. Rifle* 38 The pointed bullet with a flat base, known as a 'flat-ended picket'.

IV. 7. *attrib.* and *Comb.*, as (sense 1) ***picket-fence, fort, -gate, -machine, -pin, -rope, -strap, tent, work***; (senses 4, 5) ***picket duty, system, trench***; **picket-boat, -launch, -ship**, a vessel employed for reconnoitring, or scouting in advance of the fleet, or on a river in military operations; **picket-clamp**, a clamp for holding fence-pickets while being pointed; **picket-guard**, an inlying picket, also a picket protecting a position; **picket-header, -pointer**, a machine for pointing fence-pickets; **picket-house**, in a garrison, the building where a picket is stationed; **picket-launch**: see *picket-boat*; **picket line**, (*a*) a tether; (*b*) a line held by pickets; **picket-pin (gopher)** *U.S.*, a ground squirrel of the genus *Citellus*, esp. *C. richardsoni*, found in parts of western North America; **picket-pointer**: see *picket-header*; **picket-ship**: see *picket-boat.*

1866 *Oregon State Jrnl.* 13 Jan. 1/4 For the capture of the Albermarle [*sic*], by Lieu[t]. Cushing's *picket-boats, the crew netted $100 per man. **1885** *Daily News* 23 Jan. 6/2 He will have with him [on the Nile] the picket boats commanded by Lieutenants Montgomerie and Tyler. **1890** *Pall Mall G.* 2 June 2/1 The large steam-launches known in the navy as 'picket-boats' are perfectly adapted for the purpose. **1942** *R.A.F. Jrnl.* 13 June 28 On the far side of the harbour, was the dockyard, with its cranes and bustling tugs and picket boats. **1975** *Times Lit. Suppl.* 22 Aug. 936/2 As a fifteen-year-old midshipman in HMS Bacchante, he commanded a picket boat during and after the landings [at Gallipoli in 1915]. **1862** O. W. NORTON *Army Lett.* (1903) 112 Very little drill or other duty, no *picket duty or trenching. **1867** *Times* 23 Aug. 9/2 Flood and nearly all the rest of the prisoners did picket duty there. **1871** *Daily News* 18 Jan., This extra picket duty from other companies forms a separate roster. [**1800** *Carpenters' Rules of Work* (Boston) 32 Plain picket open fence.] **1817** S. R. BROWN *Western Gazetteer* 66 A garden..with high, substantial *picket fences to prevent the thefts of the Indians. **1857** R. TOMES *Amer. in Japan* ix. 207 Cottages..surrounded by either stone walls or bamboo picket fences. **1946** D. C. PEATTIE *Road of Naturalist* iii. 36 At home, in fertile Illinois, with the clean snow on the picket fences of Galena, they would be cooking goose. **1951** J. FRAME *Lagoon* 126 We were sitting in little brown summer-houses, and touching the brown picket-fences. **1972** *Evening Telegram* (St. John's, Newfoundland) 24 June 9/6 Grand Beach is..a clean place with picket fences. **1775** in *Mass. Hist. Soc. Coll.* (1814) 2nd Ser II. 230 This fort consists of two large block houses, and a large barrack, which is enclosed with a *picket fort. **1846** T. L. MCKENNEY *Mem.* I. vi. 127 The old picket fort standing on the plain..quite a ruin. **1857** R. TOMES *Amer. in Japan* xiv. 317 The streets of Hakodadi..are subdivided into various wards by means of *picket-gates. **1703** *Lond. Gaz.* No. 3923/2 Our *Piquet Guard was..ordered out to attack them. **1866** LONGF. *Killed at Ford* ii, As we rode along ..To visit the picket-guard at the ford. **1883** E. INGERSOLL in *Harper's Mag.* Jan. 208/2 Planers, shingle machines, *picket headers. **1901** *Westm. Gaz.* 14 Mar. 6/1 A draft of about fifty men..in Guernsey..attacked the *picquet house on the pier at St. Peter's Port. **1856** R. GLISAN *Jrnl. Army Life* (1874) xx. 277 Indians broke through the *picket line. **1867** LATHAM *Black & White* 105 The opposing lines were not more than two hundred yards apart, and between these were the picket lines, about one hundred yards from one another. **1899** *Scribner's Mag.* XXV. 19/1 It was no easy matter to handle them on the picket-lines, and to provide for feeding and watering. **1945** A. HUXLEY *Let.* 13 Oct. (1969) 536 Matthew was fortunately absent when the violence broke out on the picket line, but he got arrested. **1973** *Guardian* 11 June 13/8 The manual workers at Salford will hold a mass meeting to decide if they will cross the picket line. **1978** *Guardian Weekly* 29 Jan. 17/2 It violates the basic military axiom of not putting the main body of troops on the picket line. Crowding the bulk of NATO's troops along the front line shows the Soviets where the alliance is strong and where it is weak. **1867** *Times* 23 Aug. 9/2 Many of the *picket men had behaved illegally. **1851** MAYNE REID *Scalp Hunt.* iv. 28 The *picket-pins [were] driven home. **1859** MARCY *Prairie Trav.* iii. 91 The picket-pins, of iron, fifteen inches long, with ring and swivel at top. [**1893** V. BAILEY *Prairie Ground Squirrels* 32 Striped Prairie Spermophile... The little Striped Spermophile..is seen standing upright on its hind feet, straight and motionless as a stick... At a little distance it is impossible to distinguish it from an old picket pin or tent stake.] **1901** E. T. SETON *Lives of Hunted* 214 The darling ambition of his life..was to catch one of the *Picket-pin Gophers... These little animals have a trick of sitting bolt upright on their hind legs, with their paws held close in, so that at a distance they look exactly like picket-pins. **1936** *Univ. Arizona Gen. Bull.* III. 79 Last of the ground squirrels to be mentioned are the small ones.. variously known over the West as spermophiles, picket-pin gophers, or simply ground squirrels. **1947** V. H. CAHALANE *Mammals N. Amer.* 342 They spend a great deal of time sitting straight up on their haunches, their backs and necks as straight as ramrods. For this reason they are often called 'picket pins'. **1962** W. STEGNER *Wolf Willow* II. i. 41 The earth was densely peopled with small creatures as with large —prairie dogs, picket-pin gophers, field mice. **1967** D. L. ALLEN *Life of Prairies* 78 Overlapping the prairie country.. is the realm of a truly abundant grassland rodent, the Richardson's ground squirrel. Sometimes we count dozens or even hundreds to the acre as each squirrel stands high on its hind feet beside a mound of fresh earth. It is evident why this creature will be called 'picket pin'. **1834** in *New Mexico Hist. Rev.* (1927) II. 298 The Acting Asst. Qr Master will have prepared a suitable number of wooden posts for the support of the *Picket rope. **1946** *Sierra Club Bull.* (San Francisco) Dec. 4 We had carried with us all of our pack and picket ropes that could be spared. **1961** C. FARRELL *Trail of Tattered Star* xvi. 171 Mike ran down the line, slashing picket ropes with the bayonet. **1898** *Daily News* 9 May 6/3 It is supposed..that the Spanish fleet was probably following its *picket ship. **1872** BAKER *Nile Tribut.* x. 165 Each horse was furnished with..a long leathern thong as a *picket strap. **1866** *Sat. Rev.* 20 July 59 The victims of the *picket system are..men who are outside the pale of the Trades Unions. **1862** O. W. NORTON *Army Lett.* (1903) 59 We pitched our *picket tents..on the ground lately occupied by a *secesh* regiment. **1804** LEWIS & CLARK *Orig. Jrnls. Lewis & Clark Expedition* (1904) I. 208 The [Mandan] Village.. containes houses in a kind of *Picket work.

picket, *sb.*[2] A local name of the tern: cf. PICTARNE.

1831 *Montagu's Ornith. Dict.* 508 Tern..*Provincial.* Pirr. ..Kirmew. Picket.

picket ('pɪkɪt), *v.* [f. PICKET *sb.*[1]]

1. a. *trans.* To enclose or secure with pickets or stakes; to palisade; to fix *down* by means of pickets.

1745 *Jrnl. Siege Louisburg* in W. Shirley *Let.* (1746) 18 A Blockhouse..picketted without, and defended by eight Cannon. **1847** *Nation. Cycl.* I. 10 The trees are picketed to the ground. **1884** *Mil. Engineering* (ed. 3) I. II. 55 The hides are laid on the ground and picketed firmly down; the sandbags are then built up..to such a height as to allow each hide to be drawn well over the top row and round the ends, which are then picketed into the parapet.

b. To tether (a horse, etc.) to a picket or peg fixed in the ground.

1814 SCOTT *Wav.* xlvi, Their horses, saddled and picqueted behind them. **1857** LIVINGSTONE *Trav.* vii. 138 The goat is picketed to a stake in the bottom [of a pit]. **1868** *Regul. & Ord. Army* §872 The guards of the Cavalry will be mounted, and the horses picketed.

2. To punish or torture with the picket. *Obs.* exc. *Hist.*

1746–7 HERVEY *Medit.* (1818) 252 Others..act the part of their own tormentors: they even picquet themselves, and call it amusement. **1762** STERNE *Tr. Shandy* V. xxi, I would be picquetted to death, cried the corporal,..before I would suffer the woman to come to any harm. **1839–1860** [see PICKETING].

3. a. *Mil.* To post as a picket. **b.** *intr.* (for *refl.*) To post oneself as a picket; to act on picket duty.

1775 J. BROWN in Sparks *Corr. Amer. Rev.* (1853) I. 462 They have intrenched and picketed out some distance from their other works. **1859** F. A. GRIFFITHS *Artil. Man.* (1862) 154 To encamp and picket expeditiously. **1880** DIXON *Windsor* IV. xxii. 201 These men were picketed in the town.

4. In a labour dispute: **a.** *intr.* To act as a picket; **b.** *trans.* to beset or molest with pickets. See PICKET *sb.*[1] 5 and PICKETING b.

1867 *Times* 22 Aug. 11/1 His employer's shop was picketed by about two or three men in the morning. *Ibid.*, He recognized the defendants..in company with others, picketing daily. **1885** *Daily Tel.* 21 Oct. (Cassell), They picketed the men coming to and going from Mr. R.'s shops. **1941** B. SCHULBERG *What makes Sammy Run?* viii. 156 Wilson ought to picket in front of Sammy's office... Sammy Glick Is Unfair to Organized Double-Crossers! **1972** *Daily Tel.* 25 Jan. 6/2 The power station is being picketed by miners attempting to stop oil supplies used to ignite coal in its boilers. **1977** *Times* 27 June 2/5 Six strikers..were picketing near the main gates.

Hence ˈ**picketed** *ppl. a.*; ˈ**picketer**, a person engaged in picketing during a strike; also, one engaged in a demonstration at particular premises, etc.

1758 *Essex Inst. Hist. Coll.* (1881) XVIII. 102 Two *Piquitted Forts or Garisons and A Hospetle. **1817** S. R. BROWN *Western Gazetteer* 27 Almost every house has a spacious picketed garden in its rear. **1818** SCOTT *Rob R.* xxxii, The appearance of the picqueted horses, feeding in this little vale. **1870** EMERSON *Soc. & Solit.* vi. 121 There is a great deal of enchantment in a chestnut rail or picketed pine boards. **1885** *Even. Standard* 4 Nov. (Cassell), The old picketed and bastioned forts are disappearing. **1890** KIPLING *Barrack-Room Ballads* (1892) 97 The picketed ponies, shag and wild, Strained at their ropes as the feed was piled. **1905** H. COHEN *Law Strikes & Lock-Outs* 16 He was watching the employed coming from the picketed works. **1867** *Times* 23 Aug. 9/1 Even if all the gaols of the country were filled with *picketers the system must be continued. **1898** *Westm. Gaz.* 9 Sept. 4/1 A stronger contingent of picketers arrived on the spot to relieve the sandwich-men. **1930** *Times Educ. Suppl.* 19 July 325/4 The picketers broke a barrier on the stairway. **1972** W. P. McGIVERN *Caprifoil* (1973) i. 8 They are vocal liberals. Marchers, picketers, demonstrators. **1975** *Time Out* 17 Oct. 5/1 Many of the morning's picketers had lined up behind the main banners. **1978** S. BRILL *Teamsters* v. 181 The truck sped wildly toward the gate, with the picketers in full view.

picket, pickette, obs. forms of PIQUET.

†**picket-beard.** [See PICKED[1] 2, PIKED *a.*[1] 2.]

1670 G. H. *Hist. Cardinals* I. III. 73 A great dispute.. betwixt a certain Picket-beard (as they call them in Italy) or Protestant,..and a Catholick.

picketee, obs. form of PICOTEE.

picketing (ˈpɪkɪtɪŋ), *vbl. sb.* [See -ING[1].] The action of the vb. PICKET; **a.** see PICKET *v.* 2; *spec.* **b.** in a labour dispute, the posting of men to intercept non-strikers on their way to work and prevail upon them to desist. **secondary picketing**: see SECONDARY *a.*

a. 1753 MISS COLLIER *Art Torment.* 15 Punishments for faults, such as whipping and picketing amongst the soldiers. **1839** MARRYAT *Diary Amer.* Ser. I. II. 306 The commanding-officer..replied, that he would be hung up by his thumbs till he fainted—a variety of piquetting. **1842** R. R. MADDEN *United Irishmen* I. xi. 335 The pickettings and half-hangings, and other modes and instruments of torture. **1860** H. GOUGER *Imprisonment in Burmah* xiii. 141 On this button the culprit stood with bared foot at the manifest risk of being lamed for life. This torture was called picketting.

b. 1867 *Times* 22 Aug. 8/3 Baron Bramwell said..that if picketing were done in such a way as to excite no reasonable alarm or not to annoy or coerce those who were the subjects of it, it would be no offence in law... The picketing which Mr. Druitt and his friends organized..was intimidation, and nothing less. **1891** *Guardian* 11 Mar. 377/2 In theory picketing is merely the use of fair argument to dissuade men from becoming 'blacklegs'. In practice the force of the argument is found to depend very largely on the numbers and demeanour of those who employ it.

c. *concr.* A fence or palisade made of pickets; picket-work. *U.S.*

1755 in *New Hampsh. Hist. Soc. Coll.* (1837) V. 254 Seven men..who were out..getting a few poles to complete the new picketing of the fort. **1860** J. F. H. CLAIBORNE *Life & Times Gen. Sam. Dale* 25 These forts were merely a number of log cabins built round a small square,..the whole surrounded by a rough picketing.

pickey, var. PICKIE.

pick-fault: see PICK- in *Comb.*

Pickford (ˈpɪkfəd). The name of a firm engaged in the removal of furniture, used *ellipt.* or in the possessive to denote a van used by Pickfords to remove furniture, or the firm itself. Also *fig.* and *attrib.*

[**1833** C. MATHEWS *Let.* 8 Oct. in A. Mathews *Mem. Charles Mathews* (1839) IV. 205 It will be lighter for posting than any travelling carriage now in his yard. It cannot be called *a Pickford*, at any rate.] **1864** *Chambers's Jrnl.* 5 Mar. 152 The ubiquitous Pickford breaks the street-lamps, by going too near to the pavement. **1865** DICKENS *Mut. Fr.* II. IV. xii. 263 The sanctuary was..a kind of criminal Pickford's. The lower passions and vices were regularly ticked off in the books, warehoused in the cells, carted away. **1873** D. G. ROSSETTI *Let.* 18 Dec. (1967) III. 1250 Pickfords must be mad if they really took it to the wrong station. **1901** *Daily Tel.* 14 Nov. 4/5, I have seen a pair-horse Pickford tip coming up London Bridge. **1907** G. B. SHAW *John Bull's Other Island* p. xv, We cannot crush England as a Pickford's van might crush a perambulator. We are the perambulator and England the Pickford. **1975** J. HONE *Sixth Directorate* III. 94 What he isn't taking is being stored. Pickfords are coming tomorrow. **1980** R. McCRUM *In Strange State* ix. 74 'Keys to the boot, please, sir.'.. Another constable.. rummaged about among his books, papers and clothes. 'A regular Pickfords.'

ˈ**pickfork.** *Obs.* exc. *dial.* Forms: 3 pic-, 5 pykk-, pik-, pyke-, 5–6 pyk-, 6 picke-, 6 (9 *dial.*) pike-, pick-fork. [Origin of the first element obscure: occurring as *pic, pik, pyke*, it appears to be identical with PICK *sb.*[1], PIKE *sb.*[1], as if 'a fork with pikes or sharp points'; but the word, with its variant PITCHFORK, seems to have been at length associated with the vb. PICK[2], PITCH[1], from the use of the implement in pitching sheaves, etc.] = PITCHFORK. (The sense in the quot. from Layamon is doubtful.)

c **1205** LAY. 21597 Wið heore pic-forcken, Heo ualden heom to grunde. **1410** in Rogers *Agric. & Prices* III. 546/2, 3 pyk forkes. *c* **1440** *Promp. Parv.* 397/1 Pykkforke, *merga.* **1481** CAXTON *Reynard* (Arb.) 95 The men of the village cam out..with flaylis and pikforkes. **1485** *Nottingham Rec.* III. 246 Paid..to a smyth for makyng of a grete pykefork..þat was broken with þe ice. ij d. **1523** FITZHERB. *Husb.* §25 If the grasse be very thycke, it wolde be shaken with handes, or with a short pykforke. **1560** BIBLE (Genev.) *1 Sam.* xiii. 21 Yet they had a file for the shares, and for the mattockes, and for the pickeforkes [1535 COVERD. forckes, 1539 (Great) dong forckes] & for the axes. **1589** FLEMING *Virg. Georg.* II. 31 Clods must alwaies broken be with pick-forks turnd therein. *a* **1600** *Flodden F.* ii. (1664) 11 Some made long pikes and lances light, Some Pike-forks for to joyn and thrust. **1673** R. HEAD *Canting Acad.* K iij, One of the Horse-keepers..did..belabour him with a Pikefork. **1825** BROCKETT *N.C. Gloss., Pick-fork*, a hay fork. **1885** WESTALL *Old Factory* xxi. (E.D.D.), Chaps..as I wouldn't touch with a pikefork.

pick-goose, corrupt f. PEAK-GOOSE *Obs.*

pick-harness: see PICK-.

pickhill: see PIGHTLE.

pickie (ˈpɪkɪ). *Sc.* and *Ir. local.* Also **pickey.** [f. PICK *sb.*[4] + -Y[6], -IE.] Hopscotch. Also *pl.* (const. *sing.*). Also *Comb.*

1885 'J. STRATHESK' *More Bits from Blinkbonny* ii. 33 The 'pickies' (or the 'beds', or the 'Pall-all'), played with a flat stone on the pavement. **1906** *N.E.D.* s.v. PICK *sb.*[4] 3. **1922** JOYCE *Ulysses* 76 With careful tread he passed over a hopscotch court with its forgotten pickeystone.

†**pickieman.** *Sc. Obs.* Also 7 **peckcaman.** [f. PICK *v.*[1] + MAN.] A miller's assistant, whose duty was to pick the millstone: cf. PIKEMAN[2] 2.

1604 *Court Bk. Barony Urie* (1892) 3 Sum tennentis.. wald nocht content thame selffis with the serwice of the Peckcaman. **1808** JAMIESON, *Pickie-man*, the name formerly given to a miller's servant, from his work of keeping the mill in order. **1825** *Ibid., Pikman, Pikeman, Pikieman*, the same as *Pickie-man*, and pron. as three syllables.

pickietar, dial f. PICTARNE, the common tern.

pickill, obs. f. PICKLE *sb.*[2], a grain, corn.

picking (ˈpɪkɪŋ), *vbl. sb.*[1] Also **piking**, etc.: see PICK *v.*[1] [f. PICK *v.*[1] + -ING[1].]

1. a. The action of PICK *v.*[1] in various senses.

a. c **1330** R. BRUNNE *Chron.* (1810) 273, & þou has for þi pikyng, mykille ille likyng. *c* **1440** *Promp. Parv.* 397/2 Pykynge, or clensynge, *purgacio.* **1531** in W. H. Turner *Select. Rec. Oxford* (1880) 100 Conspiryces.., and pykyn of quarells day by day.

β. **1548** ELYOT *Lat. Dict., Carminatio*..the pickyng or cardynge of woull. **1672** WILKINS *Nat. Relig.* 234 Without any such picking and chusing amongst them, as may bend the laws to make them suitable to our own interests. **1693** EVELYN *De la Quint. Compl. Gard.* II. 80 Picking or culling of Fruits. **1844** G. DODD *Textile Manuf.* i. 25 This opening of the matted cotton is first partially effected by the process of 'picking'..Women and children partially disentangle the cotton. **1885** C. F. HOLDER *Marvels Anim. Life* 174 The inspiriting picking of the banjo. **1934** [see PICKER[1] 1 g]. **1956** [see *guitar-picking* s.v. GUITAR *sb.* b]. **1973** *Time Out* 2–8 Mar. 21/1 The audience whoop away like madmen, and there's some marvellous pickin' and fiddlin'.

b. With adverbs. Also *attrib.*

1618 H. WOTTON *Let.* in L. P. Smith *Life & Lett. Sir H. Wotton* (1907) II. 159 Remarkable how the divine justice, in a casual picking out of the foresaid number, from a 150 tumultuary men, did direct the man employed about this choice. **1825** J. NICHOLSON *Operat. Mechanic* 606 The stopping and picking-out tools are made of polished steel. **1846** G. DODD *Brit. Manuf.* 6th Ser. v. 131 The part of the coach-painter's work which requires the largest amount of care and neatness is that of 'picking-out', or painting fine lines, scrolls, &c. of one colour on a groundwork of a different colour. **1863** *Once a Week* 14 Nov. 569/2 There is one infamous method of thieving in the streets..which is called 'picking up'... This 'picking-up' system abounds in every large town... A woman is always the principal actor in these cases, and she is called the 'picking-up moll'. **1868** L. M. ALCOTT *Little Women* I. xi. 169 They [*sc.* plates of fruit] dwindled sadly after the picking over. **1869** F. HENDERSON *Six Yrs. in Prisons Eng.* vii. 76 'I heard a bloke talking about a "picking-up moll" he used to live with. What did he mean by that?' 'O! that's a very common racket. He meant a "flash-tail", or prostitute who goes about the streets at nights trying to pick up "toffs".' **1889** [see *cosher* s.v. COSH *sb.*[3]]. **1890** *Pall Mall G.* 4 Oct. 7/2 A grapnel was lowered over the bows by means of a long rope, the end of which was taken under the dynamometer to the picking-up drum. **1904** H. BLACK *Pract. Self Culture* iv. 105 The picking up of crumbs of knowledge is not in itself education. **1925** *Times* 23 May 9/3 The picking-up power of an aërial varies as the square of the effective height. **1976** *West Lancs. Evening Gaz.* 8 Dec. 8/3 If a train leaving Blackpool early on Saturday morning for London is full by the time it leaves its last picking-up point at Wigan, it will have 500 people aboard helping a scout effort. **1977** *Gay News* 24 Mar. 15/4 Glasgow SMG is still suffering from the bad image—'a closetted picking-up place'—of the early years. **1979** P. COSGRAVE *Three Colonels* 189 That greatest of vices of warriors after a battle, the picking over..of memories.

2. *spec.* **a.** Stealing, theft; in later use, petty theft, pilfering; esp. in ***picking and stealing***: see PICK *v.*[1] 9 b.

a. **1401** *Pol. Poems* (Rolls) II. 66 That almes is pykyng, y fynde it in thi boke. *c* **1470** HENRYSON *Mor. Fab.* III. (*Cock & Fox*) iv, In pyking of pultrie baith day and nycht. **1535** COVERDALE *Bible* Ded., His pestilent pykynge of Peter pens out of youre realme.

β. **1548–9** (Mar.) *Bk. Com. Prayer, Catech.*, To kepe my handes from picking and stealing. **1753** *Scots Mag.* May 260/2 He had been in a continual practice of picking and stealing. **1806** FORSYTH *Beauties Scotl.* III. 437 Sheep.. carried away, if above the number seven..[M'Gregor] styled lifting; if below seven, he only considered it as a picking.

b. *Weaving.* A finishing process of cloth-making: see quot. 1875. **c.** *Metallurgy.* Rough sorting of ores. **d.** The finishing of an electrotype plate by removing picks or defects. **e.** *Masonry.* Dabbing: see DAB *v.*[1] 1, quot. 1876. **f.** *Basket-weaving.* (See quot. 1912.)

1839 URE *Dict. Arts* 812 The mechanical preparation of ores, including picking, stamping, and different modes of washing. **1875** KNIGHT *Dict. Mech.* 1698/1 *Picking Cloth*... It is subjected to a strong light, and all blemishes removed from its surface by tweezers. Spots which have escaped the action of the dye are touched with dye by a camel's-hair brush. **1881** RAYMOND *Mining Gloss., Piking.* See *Cobbing.* **1890** *Cent. Dict., Picking*..6. Removing picks..in electrotype plates with the tools of an electrotype-finisher. **1912** T. OKEY *Introd. Art of Basket-Making* 153 Picking, cutting off the projecting ends of rods when the work is partially or wholly finished.

3. *concr.* †**a.** A mark produced by pricking; a prick. (Only OE.)

This is the earliest known trace of a verb corresp. to *pike* or *pick* in OE.; see etymology of PICK *v.*[1]

c **725** *Corpus Gloss.* (Hessels) S. 572 *Stigmata*, picung.

b. That which is or may be picked, or picked up; the produce of picking, the amount picked; a scraping, a scrap; *pl.* gleanings of fruit, remaining scraps of food, or portions of anything worth picking up or appropriating.

1642 MILTON *Apol. Smect.* xii. Wks. 1851 III. 321 The Vulturs had then but small pickings. **1768–74** TUCKER *Lt. Nat.* (1834) II. 531 Then reason began to open; and we gathered by little pickings the ideas of good and mischievous, of right and wrong. **1808** H. HOLLAND *Cheshire* 62 These pickings [from salt pans] were analysed. .. He found 480 parts..to contain 40 of muriate of soda, 60 of carbonate, and 380 of sulphate of lime. **1847** C. BRONTË *J. Eyre* xi, The scanty pickings I had now and then been able to glean at Lowood. **1892** WALSH *Tea* (Philad.) 115 At 4 o'clock each evening the day's 'picking' is carried to the factory. **1893** [see PICKER[1] 1 a]. *Mod.* (Kent) The boy was sent to jail for stealing apples, but they were only a few peekings.

c. Chiefly *pl.* Perquisites privately picked up, or dishonestly come by; pilferings.

1765 FOOTE *Commissary* I. Wks. 1799 II. 10 Rich as an Indian governor. Heaven knows how he came by it... Pretty pickings, I warrant, abroad. **1809** MALKIN *Gil Blas* V. i. ¶12 The pretty pickings to be made out of this juggle. **1866** GEO. ELIOT *F. Holt* Introd., But heir or no heir, Lawyer Jermyn had had his picking out of the estate. **1893** W. P. COURTNEY in *Academy* 13 May 413/1 It must be confessed that the pickings of the office [of Paymaster-General] were enormous.

4. a. (See quot.) **b.** *pl.* 'Pounded oyster shells for gravel walks' (Simmonds *Dict. Trade* 1858).

c **1858** *Archit. Publ. Soc. Dict.* II. 140/1 The same sort of brick if burnt a little harder, is called a *paver*, and if rather softer than it ought to be, and of pale colour, a *picking.*

5. *attrib.* and *Comb.*, as ***picking-season, -table, -time***, etc.; (sense 2 f) ***picking-knife***; **picking-bed**, a bed in a quarry that is picked away; **picking-bee** *N. Amer.* (see BEE[1] 4); **picking-belt**, a travelling belt on which coal is picked; **picking-ground**, ground capable of being picked; **picking salt**: see quot.

1883 *Stonemason* Jan., Of this the top 12 inches is used as a *picking-bed, so that blocks 6½ feet deep can always be obtained when required. **1828** in *Dict. Americanisms* (1951) s.v. *picking bee*, Mother went to a *picking Bee to pick wool. **1905** M. G. SHERK *Pen Pict. Early Pioneer Life Upper Canada* 177 The wool was then picked over by the women and girls, to get out any burs or lumps of dirt that might have adhered to it, 'pickin'' bees being frequently made for this purpose. **1943** S. MENEFEE *Assignment: U.S.A.* 48 In 1943 the townspeople were prepared to turn out for a picking-bee lasting most of the season, if necessary, to save the crop. **1901** *Chambers's Jrnl.* May 312/2 The excellent condition in which the coal was shipped,..was in great part due to the use of an appliance known as a '*picking' belt. **1921** *Spectator* 28 May 680/1 Girls on a picking-belt or in a colliery brick-works were earning similarly inflated wages. **1874** RAYMOND *Statist. Mines & Mining* 514 The removal in blasting-ground of 200 cubic feet, and in soft *picking-ground..of 800 cubic feet. **1912** T. OKEY *Introd. Art of Basket-Making* vi. 28 The ends of the bottom-sticks are now cut off by the shears and the projecting tops and butts neatly picked off with the *picking knife. **1960** E. LEGG *Country Baskets* 57 The last operation is the trimming off of all ends of canes and rods, 'picking the basket' as the craftsman calls it, for which he uses a special picking knife. **1884** *Chester Gloss.*, *Picking salt..*, the first salt made after a pan has been 'picked', that is, has had the scale taken off the bottom. **1874** *Chambers's Encycl.* s.v. *Cotton*, From the date of blooming to the close of the *picking season, warm dry weather is essential. **1901** *Scotsman* 15 Oct. 4/8 After being thoroughly screened, the lump coal is carried on to *picking tables. **1835** J. H. INGRAHAM *South-West* II. 285 '*Picking time'..continues where full crops are made until the first of December. **1848** [see KNOCK *v.* 8]. **1949** C. S. MURRAY *This our Land* 87 Picking time begins about August 20. **1682** DRYDEN *Abs. & Achit.* II. 418 He was too warm on *Picking-work to dwell.

'picking, *vbl. sb.*[2] [f. PICK *v.*[2] + -ING[1].] The action of PICK *v.*[2]

1. *Weaving.* The driving of the shuttle to and fro in a loom; esp. *attrib.* as in †*picking peg* (obs.) = PICKER[2]; *picking cord, lever, motion, shaft, staff, stick*, names of parts employed in this action: cf. PICKER[2] b.

1827 *Edin. Rev.* XLVI. 4 Mechanical contrivance technically denominated a picking peg. **1839** URE *Dict. Arts* 1285 He lays hold of the picking-peg in his right hand, and, with a smart jerk of his wrist, drives the fly-shuttle swiftly from one side of the loom to the other... The plan of throwing the shuttle by the picking peg and cord is a great improvement upon the old way of throwing it by hand. **1875** KNIGHT *Dict. Mech.* 1698/1 In one form of hand-loom, the picking-peg is drawn by a cord. In the power-loom the driver is on a vibrating staff. *Ibid.*, *Picking-stick* (*Weaving*), the picker-staff for driving the shuttle of a power-loom. **1878** BARLOW *Weaving* xxv. 269 (*heading*), Shuttles and picking motions. *Ibid.* 271 This plan was to affix inclined planes to the peripheries of fly-wheels—one at each end of the crank shaft, so as to strike against a stud fixed upon a picking-shaft connected to each picking-stick. **1897** *Westm. Gaz.* 22 Jan. 7/2 For shafts he has used a lot of the hickory picking staffs used in power looms.

2. *Spinning.* 'The travelling of the bobbin up and down the spindle in the process of being filled, so that it may be equally full all over' (McLaren).

1884 W. S. B. MCLAREN *Spinning* (ed. 2) 152 The spool.. requires a triple motion; a very short one at first filling the lower end, during which time the bobbin only moves a little way up and down, and then a longer 'picking'..up and down, with the constantly lowering motion the same as for the tube.

3. The action of pitching or throwing sheaves, etc. Also *attrib.*, as **picking-fork**, a hay-fork, pitchfork; **picking-hole**, a window or door aloft in a barn or hayloft, through which hay or sheaves are pitched; a pitch-hole. *north. dial.*

1847–78 HALLIWELL, *Picking-hole.* **1854** 'TOM TREDDLEHOYLE' *Bairnsla Foak's Ann.* 25 Made it into hay, an thrawn it throo t' pickin-hoyle. **1873** CORDEAUX *Birds of Humber* 14 One of the picking-holes at the north end of the barn.

picking ('pɪkɪŋ), *ppl. a.* Also 6 **pyking**, *Sc.* **-and**. [f. PICK *v.*[1] + -ING[2].]

1. That picks, in the senses of the verb; *spec.* thievish.

1535 LYNDESAY *Satyre* 2657 Sic pykand peggrall theifis ar hangit. **1550** LEVER *Serm.* (Arb.) 38 Pickinge theft, is lesse than murtheryng robrye. **1561** T. HOBY tr. *Castiglione's Courtyer* IV. (1577) T viij, The ouerwealthy..waxe stiffe necked and recklesse, the poore, desperate and pyking. **1565–73** COOPER *Thesaurus*, *Diætarij*, picking fellowes looking into chambers or parlours..onely of purpose to steale. **1894** KIPLING *Jungle Bk.* 52 Nothing but foolish words and little picking thievish hands.

†**2.** Dainty; fastidious; trifling, nice. *Obs.* Perh. *vbl. sb.* used *attrib.*

1589 R. HARVEY *Pl. Perc.* (1590) 3 If thy mill stones be not worne too blunt, for want of pecking, there is picking meat for thee. **1597** SHAKS. *2 Hen. IV*, IV. i. 198 The King is wearie Of daintie, and such picking Grieuances. **1678** BUNYAN *Pilgr.* Auth. Apol. (ed. 2) 227 Dost thou love picking meat?

pickitivant, corrupt f. PICKE-DEVANT, *Obs.*

pickle ('pɪk(ə)l), *sb.*[1] Forms: 5 **pekille, pykyl, pikkyll, pykulle**, 6 (**pegyll, pigell**), **pyccle, pikle, pykle**, 6–7 **pickel(l**, 6– **pickle**. [app. a. MDu. *pekel*(*e*, *peeckel* (*a* 1473 in *Teuthonista*) or MLG. *pēkel*, LG., Du. *pekel*, E.Fris. *pekel, päkel*, mod.Ger. *pökel* brine, pickle. Ulterior origin obscure.

(Verdam suggests that Du. *pekel* was a deriv. of verbal root *pik-*, *pek-*, in sense 'that which pricks or is piquant'.)]

1. a. A salt or acid liquor (usually brine or vinegar, sometimes with spices) in which flesh, vegetables, etc., are preserved. (In early use, also applied to certain sauces eaten with flesh as a relish.)

a **1440** *Morte Arth.* 1027 Sevene knave childre, Choppid in a chargour of chalke whytt sylver, With pekille and powdyre of precious spycez. *c* **1440** *Promp. Parv.* 397/2 Pykyl, sawce, *picula*. *c* **1450** *Two Cookery-bks.* 77 Pikkyll pour le Mallard. **1502** ARNOLDE *Chron.* (1811) 189 To make a Pigell to kepe freshe Sturgen in. **1530** PALSGR. 254/1 Pyccle sauce, *savlmure*. **1553** EDEN *Treat. Newe Ind.* (Arb.) 29 Keping it in a certayne pickle. **1600** SURFLET *Countrie Farme* II. li. 349 A pickle..made of two parts of vineger, and one of salt brine. **1606** SHAKS. *Ant. & Cl.* II. v. 66 Thou shalt be whipt with Wyer, and stew'd in brine, Smarting in lingring pickle. **1728** E. SMITH *Compl. Housew.* (ed. 2) 63 Make a Pickle of Vinegar, Salt, whole Pepper, Cloves, Mace, and boil it, and pour it on the Mangoes. **1809** KENDALL *Trav.* II. xlvi. 132 The strength of the water being now such as to constitute it a brine or pickle.

fig. **1649** *Woodstock Scuffle* xi. in Scott *Woodst.* App. 1, Nothing else is history But pickle of antiquity. **1675** HOBBES *Odyssey* (1677) 62 He was in the sea o'r head and ears: At last he rais'd his head above the pickle.

b. *in pickle* (*fig.*), kept in preparation for use; esp. in phr. *a rod in pickle*, a punishment in reserve, ready to be inflicted on occasion: see ROD.

1589 *Pappe w. Hatchet* E j b, I but he hath..arguments that haue been these twentie yeres in pickle. **1625** B. SPENSER *Vox Civitatis* 26, I feare God hath worse rods in pickell for you. **1828** *Craven Gloss.* (ed. 2) s.v., This is a threatening admonition for an idle or truant boy. 'There's a stick i pickle for thee my lad'. **1881** MRS. LYNN LINTON *Rebel of Family* II. vii, It was only after the last good word of glad tidings had been said that the rod was taken out of the pickle. **1885** *Daily News* 3 Nov. 5/2 He will return to the tranquil enjoyment of his 1,000,000 dollars now in pickle, it is said, in the English funds.

2. Some article of food preserved in pickle; usually (*pl.*), vegetables (as cabbage, cauliflower, onions, cucumbers, walnuts, mangoes, etc.) pickled, and eaten as a relish.

1707 MORTIMER *Husb.* (1721) II. 26 The Keys of the Ash are a good Pickle while young and tender; and when near ripe. **1710** ADDISON *Tatler* No. 255 ⁋2 Conserves [are] of a much colder Nature than your common Pickles. **1758** JOHNSON *Idler* No. 33 ⁋24 Received a present of pickles from Miss Pilcocks. **1853** SOYER *Pantroph.* 64 Mallows.. occupied one of the first ranks among pickles.

3. An acid solution, or other chemical preparation, used for cleansing metal or wood, or for other purposes.

1776 WITHERING *Brit. Plants* (1796) I. 38 Filtre it through paper; keep it in a bottle closely corked, and call it the pickle. **1839** URE *Dict. Arts* 860 These plates, while still warm, are rubbed over with a dilute acid or pickle. **1879** *Cassell's Techn. Educ.* IV. 299/2 A dipper had..left a quantity of work all night in the 'pickle' or cleansing solution.

4. *fig.* **a.** A condition or situation, usually disagreeable; a sorry plight or predicament. (Usually with defining word.) Now *colloq.*

[Cf. Du. *in de pekel zitten, iemand in de pekel laten zitten.*]

1562 J. HEYWOOD *Prov. & Epigr.* (1867) 157 Freilties pickell. **1573** TUSSER *Husb.* (1878) 125 Reape barlie with sickle, that lies in ill pickle. **1585** FOXE *Serm. on 2 Cor.* v. 21 In this pickle lyeth man by nature, that is, all wee that be Adams children. *a* **1620** J. DYKE *Worthy Commun.* (1645) 382 Who could have..embraced a person in so filthy a pickle? **1741** RICHARDSON *Pamela* (1824) I. 77, I warrant, added she, he was in a sweet pickle! **1823** BYRON *Juan* VIII. xliii, The Turkish batteries thrash'd them like a flail, Or a good boxer, into a sad pickle. **1893** STEVENSON *Catriona* 291, I could see no way out of the pickle I was in. **1926** H. CRANE *Let.* 29 Mar. (1965) 243 I'm in no particular pickle at present. **1943** E. CALDWELL *Georgia Boy* ii. 21 I've got that marriage ceremony to perform in less than half an hour. It's too late for me to hunt up anybody else to ring the bell, and if you don't ring it for me, I'll be in a pretty pickle. **1955** *Times* 24 May 4/7 Leicestershire would have been in a pretty pickle without their captain, C. H. Palmer, in their current match with Surrey at Leicester. **1960** M. SPARK *Bachelors* ii. 19 You're going to leave Alice in a nice pickle if the case goes against you. *Ibid.* viii. 115 You've got us in a pickle. **1961** B. FERGUSSON *Watery Maze* x. 245 This landing had got into a pickle partly because of the bad weather, which had impeded the rate of build-up. **1967** G. F. FIENNES *I tried to run Railway* iv. 40 In a matter of days we were in a rare pickle. **1977** *Jersey Even. Post* 26 July 8/6 Don't leave jobs unfinished in order to start on something new, or you'll end up in a right old pickle.

b. *gen.* Condition, trim, guise. *rare.*

1706 PHILLIPS, *Accoutrement*, Dress, Garb, Pickle. **1846** HAWTHORNE *Mosses* I. ix. 190 It is difficult to conceive how he keeps himself in any decent pickle.

c. *pl.* Nonsense, something worthless, an absurd statement. Also as *int. slang.* (No longer current.)

1846 *Swell's Night Guide* 34 'Pickles,' as the swell draper would say, 'but they frizzle and mangle music like bricks.' **1859** H. J. BYRON *Maid & Magpie* v. 31 If you and your minion Indulge that opinion, Ten pounds to an onion its pickles, I bet. **1889** J. HATTON *Reminisc. J. L. Toole* II. v. 150 Or, the advance being ordered, had he exclaimed, 'Oh, Pickles!' before seeking convenient shelter from the foe? **1898** L. MERRICK *Actor-Manager* v. 66 The rent they ask is a hundred and fifty, but that's all pickles!

5. a. A person, usually a boy, who is always causing trouble: cf. PICKLED[1] 2 b; a troublesome or mischievous child; †a wild young fellow. *colloq.*

1788 *Hist. Schoolboy* 72 He told Master Blotch he was a pickle, and dismissed him to his cricket. **1809** MALKIN *Gil Blas* I. xvii. ⁋6 If the little gentleman is a pickle, they will lay all the blame on your bad management. **1811** *Lex. Balatron.*, *Pickle*, an arch waggish fellow. **1828** J. W. CROKER *Diary* 23 Apr. in *C. Papers* (1884) I. 416 The Duke of Cumberland was there, and his son Prince George. This little pickle is about nine. **1837** MISS MITFORD *Country Stories* (1850) 55 Young Sam Tyler, Jem's eldest hope, a thorough Pickle. **1885** [see PICKLESOME].

†**b.** *attrib.* or as *adj.* = PICKLED *ppl. a.*[1] 2 b.

1797 MRS. A. M. BENNETT *Beggar Girl* (1813) III. 278 His son, a pickle young dog.

c. A woman with a sour disposition; an unattractive woman. *slang.*

1950 [see LEMON *sb.*[1] 1 b]. **1970** *Women Speaking* Apr. 5/1 If a man doesn't like a girl's looks or personality, she's a.. pickle, prune, [etc.].

6. *attrib.* and *Comb.*, as *pickle-barrel, -boiler, -bottle, -dealer, -farm, -jar, -pot, -room, -shop*; **pickle-cured** *a.*, cured or preserved in pickle; **pickle-leaf**, an ornamental dish, in the form of a leaf, for pickles, etc.; **pickleman**, one who makes or sells pickles; **pickle-worm** *U.S.*, the caterpillar of a moth (*Phacellura nitidalis*), which destroys young cucumbers, etc.; **pickle-yard**, the yard in which meat is pickled for the navy.

1757 W. THOMPSON *R.N. Advoc.* 14 A Cooper and a *Pickle-Boiler being two distinct Employments. **1852** DICKENS *Bleak Ho.* (1853) v. 35 *Pickle bottles, wine bottles, ink bottles. **1879** MRS. A. E. JAMES *Ind. Househ. Managem.* 21 A wide-mouthed pickle-bottle, with air-tight cork. **1945** *Coast to Coast 1944* 140 Davie always had a pickle bottle for staging heroic contests between red-joes and black-joes. **1791–3** in *Spirit Pub. Jrnls.* (1799) I. 116 A *Pickle-dealer and an Italian Fidler. **1890** *Daily News* 20 Sept. 3/1 A *pickle-farm at the present time of year, with its peeling and brining processes, is an interesting sight. **1836** DICKENS *Sk. Boz* 1st Ser. I. 237 Some *pickle-jars; some surgeons' ditto. **1899** *Allbutt's Syst. Med.* VIII. 13 A man whose work consisted of covering pickle-jars with bladder. **1952** *Coast to Coast 1951–52* 29 The farmer carried a glass pickle-jar with a screw-top lid. **1977** G. MARTON *Alarum* 49 The Russians re-ordered the smoked salmon—ate the garnish of pickles around the salmon and..wanted the whole pickle jar. **1859** SMILES *Self-Help* ii. (1860) 41 Melon table-plates, green *pickle-leaves, and such like articles. **1731** *Lond. Even. Post* 9 Nov., John Potts, *Pickleman in Gracious Street. **1769** MRS. RAFFALD *Eng. Housekpr.* (1778) 43 Put them into *pickle pots; when the liquor is cold pour it upon the oysters. **1903** *Nature* 19 Nov. 68/2 After Watt's patent, Newcomen engines were made with separate condensers without air-pumps, the air being discharged through a snifting-valve. Such condensers were known as 'pickle-pots'. **1809** KENDALL *Trav.* II. xlvi. 132 From the water-rooms, it is drawn into a second range of vats or rooms, called *pickle-rooms. **1773** GOLDSMITH 13 Apr. in Boswell *Johnson*, The very next shop to Northumberland-house is a *pickle-shop. **1757** W. THOMPSON *R.N. Advoc.* 22, I..was..made inspecting Cooper of the *Pickle-yard.

pickle ('pɪk(ə)l), *sb.*[2] *Sc.* and *north. dial.* [Origin unknown.

The two senses are not generally felt to be the same word in Scotch; but cf. the use of *grain* in 'I hae-na a grain o' saut i' the hoose'; 'A man without a grain o' sense'.]

1. A single grain or corn of wheat, barley, or oats, e.g. a *barley-pickle*, a barley-corn. **b.** Formerly, also, a single grain or particle (of sand, dust, etc.).

1552 ABP. HAMILTON *Catech.* (1884) 204 As breid is maid of mony pickillis of corne. **17..** *Song, O gin my Love* ii, O gin my love were a pickle of wheat, Awa' wi' that pickle o' wheat I wad flee. **1805** R. W. DICKSON *Pract. Agric.* I. 557 The ears are found to have alternately a plump well-filled *pickle* and an empty husk. **1868** ATKINSON *Cleveland Gloss.*, *Pickle*, a single grain or kernel; of corn, rice, or the like.

b. 1632 RUTHERFORD *Lett.* (1862) I. xxii. 87 Ye shall run out your glass even to the last pickle of sand. **1656** JEANES *Mixt. Schol. Div.* 150 Rotten, and dissolved into innumerable pickles of dust.

2. A small quantity or amount (of fluid, powder, or anything quantitative); a little. (Followed by sb. without *of*.)

a **1724** in *Ramsay's Tea-t. Misc.* (1733) I. 9 Sick's I ha'e ye's get a pickle. **1724** RAMSAY *I have a Green Purse* i, I have a green purse, and a wee pickle gowd. *a* **1810** TANNAHILL *Poems* (1846) 16 I've spun a pickle yarn. **1816** SCOTT *Old Mort.* xl, I wad get my pickle meal and my soup milk. **1822** GALT *Provost* xxxviii. (1868) 110 A pickle tea and sugar. **1893** STEVENSON *Catriona* 75 Ye'll have..to think a wee pickle less of your dainty self.

pickle ('pɪk(ə)l). *v.*[1] [f. PICKLE *sb.*[1] Cf. MDu. (*a* 1479), Du., MLG. *pekelen*, Ger. *pökeln*.]

1. a. *trans.* To put into or steep in pickle; to preserve in pickle. (Sometimes, To preserve with salt, to salt, as butter.)

1552 [see PICKLED[1] 1]. **1570** LEVINS *Manip.* 122/1 To Pickle flesh, *condire, salire*. **1599** HAKLUYT *Voy.* II. 110 They vse to pickle them with vineger and salt. **1661** LOVELL *Hist. Anim. & Min.* 220 Salmon... If pickled it's like Sturgian. **1732** BERKELEY *Alciphr.* VI. §14 A physician, who, having pickled half a dozen embryos [etc.]. **1768** COWPER *Let. to J. Hill* 3 May, Mrs. Rebecca Cowper's receipt to pickle cabbage. **1893** KATE SANBORN *Truthf. Wom. S. California* 28 The processes of pickling olives.

b. To fill (a vessel) with pickle or brine for preserving meat.

1757 WOOD in W. Thompson *R.N. Advoc.* 12 The Casks to be always drove and pickled in Time.

c. *intr.* To undergo the process of pickling.

1904 G. PARKER *Ladder of Swords* ix. 110 You have prepared your own brine, monsieur; in it you shall pickle.

2. *Naut.* To rub salt, or salt and vinegar, on the back after whipping or flogging: formerly practised as a punishment.

1706 *Inq. Naval Miscarriages* in *Harl. Misc.* (Park) I. 574 The whipping and pickling of seamen (a barbarous practice which has been much used of late) has likewise been a great hindrance to the manning of our fleet. **1725** DE FOE *Voy. round World* (1840) 90 Pickling, that is to say, throwing salt and vinegar on the back after the whipping. **1887** J. K. LAUGHTON in *Dict. Nat. Biog.* XII. 205/1 It was acknowledged that [in Corbet's ship, *c* 1808] the number of men flogged was very great;..and that the backs of the sufferers were habitually pickled.

3. a. To steep in or treat with some acid, or other chemical preparation, for cleansing or other purpose, in various manufactures, etc.

1844 STEPHENS *Bk. Farm* II. 503 Seed-wheat should be *pickled*, that is, subjected to a preparation in a certain kind of liquor, before it is sown. **1858** GREENER *Gunnery* 219 'Pickled' is the term also used to describe the process, which is simply eating away the softer metals from around the steel or harder material. **1868** JOYNSON *Metals* 103 The sheets to be galvanised are pickled, scoured, and cleaned. **1887** GUMMING *Electricity* 213 The objects are first 'pickled' in a bath of mixed dilute nitric and sulphuric acids. **1889** *Standard* 22 Oct. 2 The ordinary dressings with which seed-corn is 'pickled', to prevent bunt or smut.

b. 'To prepare, as an imitation, and sell as genuine; said of copies or imitations of paintings by the old masters. *Art Jour.*' (Webster 1864).

4. *transf.* and *fig.* in various applications.

c **1620** Z. BOYD *Zion's Flowers* (1855) 18 For this our eyes are pickled up with teares, That are most brinie. **1651** CLEVELAND *Elegy on Abp. Canterbury* 36 Not to repent, but pickle up their Sin. **1790** BURKE *Fr. Rev.* Wks. V. 47 A theory, pickled in the preserving juices of pulpit eloquence. **1904** *Daily Chron.* 1 Sept. 8/2, I think you are pickling a rod for your own back.

5. *trans.* (See quot. 1970.) *U.S.A.F. slang.*

1966 *Time* 20 May 36/3 'I broke to the right,' recalled Dudley after last week's action, 'and pickled (dropped) my fuel tanks.' **1970** *Word Watching* Apr. 7/1 *Pickle*, to drop extra fuel tanks or equipment: to drop bombs.

'pickle, *v.*² *Obs.* or *dial.* [dim. or freq. of PICK *v.*¹]

†**1.** (?) To pick clean, cleanse by minute picking.

c **1440** *Promp. Parv.* 397/1 Pykelynge, *purgulacio.* **1591** SYLVESTER *Du Bartas* I. vi. 286 The Wren.. Into his [the crocodile's] mouth he skips, his teeth he pickles Cleanseth his palate.

2. *trans.* and *intr.* To pick in a small way, or a little at a time; to peck, nibble; to eat sparingly or delicately. Also *fig.* Chiefly *Sc.* and *dial.*

1513 DOUGLAS *Æneis* XII. Prol. 158 Phebus red fowle.. Pykland his meyt in alleis quhar he went. **1570** LEVINS *Manip.* 122/2 To Pickle, eat nicely, *edere minutim.* **1583** GOLDING *Calvin on Deut.* i. 6 Whensoeuer we haue.. but pickled vpon the doctrine without suffering it to work any true liuelinesse in vs. *a* **1585** POLWART *Flyting w. Montgomerie* 727 Lick where I laid, and pickle of that pye. **1793** T. SCOTT *Poems* 325 (Jam.) Robin Routh and Marion Mickle, Wha baith contentitlie did pickle Out o' ae pocke. **1818** SCOTT *Hrt. Midl.* xxviii, Aweel, lass,.. then thou must pickle in thine ain poke-nook, and buckle thy girdle thine ain gate. **1855** ROBINSON *Whitby Gloss.*, *Pickle*,.. to eat or pick but a small quantity at a time, as sickly cattle are said only to pickle a bit out of the hand at once.

b. To deal with in a minute way, to PIDDLE (*obs.*); see also quot. *a* 1825.

a **1568** ASCHAM *Scholem.* (Arb.) 158 To busie my selfe in pickling about these small pointes of Grammer. *a* **1825** FORBY *Voc. E. Anglia*, *Pickle*, v. to glean a field a second time, when, of course, very little can be found.

pickle, obs. var. PIGHTLE; local var. of PIKEL.

pickled ('pɪk(ə)ld), *ppl. a.*¹ [f. PICKLE *v.*¹]

1. a. Preserved in pickle; steeped in some chemical preparation: see PICKLE *v.*¹ 1, 3.

1552 HULOET, Pykled or bryned, *muriaticus.* **1620** MIDDLETON *Chaste Maid* I. ii, My wife.. longs For nothing but pickled cucumbers. **1629** [see DAN(T)ZIG]. **1739** E. SMITH *Compl. House-wife* (ed. 9) 43 Strow upon your Cutlets pickled walnuts in quarters. **1747** H. GLASSE *Art of Cookery* ii. 22 Put to it some pickled Gerkins chopp'd and boil'd Chestnuts. **1757** W. THOMPSON *R.N. Advoc.* 9 Pickled, unpickled, and undrained Casks rolled away together. **1837** DICKENS *Pickw.* xlviii. 519 Demanding a mutton chop and a pickled walnut instantly. **1843** —— *Mart. Chuz.* (1844) vi. 66, I remember thinking.., in the days of my childhood, that pickled onions grew on trees. **1849** B. S. ELY *There she Blows* i. 9 An Irishman.. wanted some pork to make 'pickled oysters'. This dish was made by cutting raw pork up fine, and covering it with pepper sauce and black pepper. **1876** SCHULTZ *Leather Manuf.* 19 Pickled hides should be kept separate from Salted. **1877** E. S. DALLAS *Kettner's Bk. of Table* 423 *Shalot Sauce* is the same as what is called Sharp Sauce or Sauce Piquante, with this only difference—that to the latter there is added pickled gherkins. **1898** *Westm. Gaz.* 20 Jan. 7/2 The vessel was loaded with pickled sleepers. **1945** *Sun* (Baltimore) 22 Oct. 4/1 Hot-rolled pickled and cold rolled sheet deliveries run late into the second quarter next year. **1967** K. GILES *Death & Mr Prettyman* iv. 87, I put out a bit of ham.. and some pickled walnuts. **1969** T. C. THORSTENSEN *Pract. Leather Technol.* v. 76 In the manufacture of garment suede leather the raw materials are primarily the pickled sheep skins based on New Zealand lamb and sheep. **1970** C. KERSH *Aggravations M. Ashe* iii. 45, I have terrible dreams if I eat pickled cucumbers. **1974** J. STUBBS *Painted Face* i. 23 Trying.. to banish the cheese and pickled onions from the table. **1977** G. SCOTT *Hot Pursuit* iii. 25 Pickled eggs like lumps of coal.

b. *pickled herring*: see PICKLE-HERRING.

2. *fig.* **a.** See PICKLE *v.*¹ 4; *spec.* drunk. *slang.*

1633 P. FLETCHER *Purple Isl.* VI. lxiii, With lips confession and with pickled cries. **1635** QUARLES *Embl.* IV. xii, My pickled eyes did vent Full streames of briny teares. **1820** LAMB *Elia* Ser. I. *Christ's Hosp.*, In lieu of our half-pickled Sundays. **1842** S. LOVER *Handy Andy* xxv, The poor pickled electors were driven back to their inn in dudgeon. **1900** ADE *More Fables* 171 'It may be that I was a mite Polluted,' he suggested. 'You were a teeny bit Pickled about Two..,' said Mr. Byrd. **1919** WODEHOUSE *Damsel in Distress* xx. 236 On that occasion a most rummy and extraordinary thing happened. I got pickled to the eyebrows. **1926** WOOD & GODDARD *Dict. Amer. Slang* 20 *Gills, pickled to the*, soused; drunk. **1933** WODEHOUSE *Heavy Weather* vii. 95 The ink was still wet on a paragraph where, searching like some Flaubert for the *mot juste*, he had run his pen through the word 'intoxicated' and substituted for it the more colorful 'pickled to the gills'. **1939** [see BIRD *sb.* 1 e]. *a* **1953** DYLAN THOMAS *Prospect of Sea* (1955) 128 On Sundays, and when pickled, he sang high tenor, and had won many cups. **1959** P. MOYES *Dead Men don't Ski* vii. 86 He gets the most extraordinary ideas sometimes, and he's pretty pickled, anyhow.

†**b.** Of a person: Thoroughly 'imbued' with mischief; mischievous, roguish. *Obs.*

1691 tr. *Emilianne's Frauds Rom. Monks* (ed. 3) 343 Most impudent and pickel'd youths. **1706** FARQUHAR *Recruiting Officer* v. vii, His poor boy Jack was.. a pickled dog, I shall never forget him. **1804** COLLINS *Scrip-scrap, Epit. on Foote* 3 Here a pickled rogue lies, whom we could not preserve, Though his pickle was true Attic Salt.

†**'pickled,** *ppl. a.*² *Obs.* Also 5 pykeled. [? Early variant of PECKLED.] Variegated, speckled.

14.. *Voc.* in Wr.-Wülcker 593/15 *Liridus, i. diversi coloris*, pykeled. *Ibid.* 610/23 *Dicitur gallina lirida scou*, pykeled hen show. *c* **1620** W. LAUSON in Arb. *Garner* I. 194 Wings of a feather of a mallard, teal, or pickled hen's wing.

'pickle-,herring. Now *rare.* [Found first as *pickled herring*, f. PICKLED *ppl. a.*; somewhat later *pickle-herring*, after MD. or early mod.Du. *peeckel-harinck* (1567 Junius *Nomenclator*), MLG. *pekel-herink* (Lübben-Walther), both in sense 1, mod.Du. *pekel-haring*, mod.G. *pickelhäring.*]

†**1.** *lit.* A pickled herring. *Obs.*

α. *c* **1570** *Pride & Lowl.* (1841) 75 For feare of meeting with a pickled hearing And mountaynes made of matters frivolous. **1598** MERES *Pallad. Tamia* II. 286 b, Robert Greene died of a surfet taken at Pickeld Herrings, & Rhenish wine. **1796** H. HUNTER tr. *St.-Pierre's Stud. Nat.* (1799) I. 260 Those which are caught far to the North, known, in Holland, by the name of pickled herrings.

β. **1573–80** BARET *Alv.* H 405 A pickle Herring, *halec conditanea.* **1600** ROWLANDS *Lett. Humours Blood* vi. 77 Taken with a Pickle-herring or two, As Flemmings at Saint Katherines vse to do. **1607** DEKKER *Knts. Conjur.* (1842) 76 Hee had.. shortened his dayes by keeping company with pickle herrings.

2. A clown, a buffoon, a merry-andrew.

This application of the term originated in German. It appears in 1620 in *Engelische Comedien vnd Tragedien ..sampt dem Pickelhering*, where it is the name of a humorous character in one of the plays, and of the chief actor in a series of 'Pickelhärings-spiele' and 'Singspiele' (= JIG *sb.*¹ 4). One of the latter is a version of R. Cox's *Singing Simpkin*, and a Dutch version of this, from the German, as *Singende klucht van Pekelharingh in de Kist*, 1648, is the first known evidence of the use in Dutch, to which Addison attributed it in 1711—the first mention in English. (Grimm's Dictionary is in error in ascribing to it an English origin.)

α. **1711** ADDISON *Spect.* No. 47 ¶6 A Set of merry Drolls ..whom every Nation calls by the Name of that Dish of Meat which it loves best. In Holland they are termed Pickled Herrings; in France, Jean Pottages; in Italy, Maccaronies; and in Great Britain, Jack Puddings. **1726** ARBUTHNOT *Diss. Dumpling* (ed. 5) 8 Content your selves with being Zanies, Pickled-Herrings, Punchionellos.

β. **1716–20** *Lett. fr. Mist's Jrnl.* (1722) I. 81 Pickle-Herring was then in the Heighth of his Archness, Activity, and Grimaces. **1790** *Bystander* 134 Making a Merry-Andrew of himself, in imitation of the other Pickle-herring. **1849** tr. *Meinhold's Sidonia the Sorceress* II. 232 People think it must be pickelherring, or some such strolling mummers come to exhibit to the folk during the evening.

attrib. **1789** WOLCOTT (P. Pindar) *Ode to eight Cats* ix, She mounteth with a pickle-herring spring, Without th' assistance of a rope. **1831** CARLYLE *Sart. Res.* I. ix, Their high State Tragedy.. becomes a Pickleherring-Farce to weep at, which is the worst kind of Farce.

pickler¹ ('pɪklə(r)). ? *Obs.* [f. PICKLE *v.*² + -ER¹.]

a. One who picks a little at a time, or who eats sparingly. **b.** See quot. 1718.

1581 MULCASTER *Positions* vi. (1887) 46 The diet.. must be small, as nature is a pickler, and requires but small pittaunce. **1718** *Entertainer* No. 14. 90 A pernicious Sect of Animals called Picklers; who take upon themselves.. to ridicule every Thing that does not square with their own Humours.

'pickler². [f. PICKLE *v.*¹ + -ER¹.]

1. A vegetable (cucumber, onion, etc.) grown for pickling.

1763 MILLS *Pract. Husb.* IV. 166 The latter crop of cucumbers, commonly called picklers. **1846** J. BAXTER *Libr. Pract. Agric.* (ed. 4) II. 174 In Essex.. onions are grown largely in field culture.... Picklers are grown upon poor, light ground, to keep them small.

2. A person or thing that pickles (*lit.* and *fig.*).

1865 SIR P. WALLIS in Brighton *Life* (1892) 265 The Droitwich saline baths.. powerful picklers indeed they are. **1883** *Daily News* 29 May 8/3 To Picklers, Laundrymen, and Others.—Convenient Premises to Let.

3. A vessel in which vegetables can be pickled.

1862 *Illustr. Catal. Internat. Exhib., Industr. Dept., Brit. Div.* II. No. 6870, Bottles, filters, jars, foot-warmers, jugs, picklers, casks, jelly-cans.

picklesome ('pɪk(ə)lsəm), *a. nonce-wd.* [f. PICKLE *sb.*¹ + -SOME.] Of the character of a 'pickle' (PICKLE *sb.*¹ 5); inclined to mischief.

1885 *Century Mag.* XXX. 380/2 Violet Carmine was a pickle.... A residence of five months in.. New York had not by any means tended to make her less picklesome.

picklet, obs. variant of PIKELET 1.

'pickling, 'picklin, *sb. dial.* Also 6 pyglyng. [Origin doubtful.] See quots. 1825, 1868.

1545 *Rates of Customs* c j b, Pyglyng the C. elles contey. xii score elles xxs. **1583** *Ibid.* D vij, Pickling the c, contayning xii, xx. elles iii*l.* *a* **1825** FORBY *Voc. E. Anglia*, *Picklin*, a sort of very coarse linen, of which seedsmen make their bags, dairy maids their aprons, etc. **1868** ATKINSON *Cleveland Gloss.*, *Pickling*, a kind of fine canvas, used for covering meat-safes, and other like objects.

pickling ('pɪklɪŋ), *vbl. sb.*¹ [f. PICKLE *v.*¹]

a. The action of PICKLE *v.*¹, in various senses.

1691 T. H[ALE] *Acc. New Invent.* p. ix, The Dutch way of Pickling of Herrings. **1734** BERKELEY *Let. to T. Prior* 30 Apr., Wks. 1871 IV. 227 A good cook, and understands pickling and preserving. **1858** GLENNY *Gard. Every-day Bk.* 220/1 Cabbages for Pickling are now coming to heart. **1867** SMYTH *Sailor's Word-bk.*, *Pickling*, a mode of salting naval timber.. to insure its durability. **1881** RAYMOND *Mining Gloss.*, *Pickling*, cleaning sheet-iron or wire by immersion in acid.

b. *attrib.* Used for pickling; of vegetables, grown for pickling, intended to be pickled.

1812 SIR J. SINCLAIR *Syst. Husb. Scot.* I. 326 Wheat must have as much lime put upon it, as soon as it comes out of the pickling tub, as will dry it quickly. **1831** *Lincoln Herald* 23 Dec. 3/6 Half a dozen pickling-jars. **1855** DELAMER *Kitch. Gard.* 37 To obtain small pickling onions. **1906** *Daily Chron.* 31 Oct. 8/4 At Southwold the pickling-plots.. will be just at the back of the landing wharves. **1958** *Times Rev. Industry* June 50/3 To produce stainless [steel] strip.. required.. the installation of.. a pickling line.

pickling, *vbl. sb.*² *Obs.*: see PICKLE *v.*² 1.

picklock ('pɪklɒk), *sb.*¹ and *a.*¹ [f. PICK *v.*¹ + LOCK *sb.*²: see PICK-.]

A. *sb.* **1.** A person who picks a lock; *spec.* a thief who opens a door by picking the lock.

1553 T. WILSON *Rhet.* 76 b, I haue one.. to whom there is no cofer lockt, nor dore shut.., meanyng that he was a picklock, and a false verlet. **1651** CHARLETON *Ephes. & Cimm. Matrons* II. (1668) 9 Locking the door behind him, with as little noise as a Pick-lock. **1889** *Daily News* 3 Dec. 7/2 She called him a 'picklock' and a 'Paul Pry'.

fig. **1614** B. JONSON *Bart. Fair* III. v, Talke with some crafty fellow, some picklocke o' the Law! **1716** M. DAVIES *Athen. Brit.* II. 37 Sir Thomas Bolen.. was called the Pick-lock of Princes. **1929** R. BRIDGES *Testament of Beauty* I. 21 This picklock Reason is still a-fumbling at the wards.

2. An instrument for picking locks.

1591 PERCIVALL *Sp. Dict.*, *Ganzua*, a false keye, a picke-locke. **1603** SHAKS. *Meas. for M.* III. ii. 18 We take him to be a Theefe.. for wee haue found vpon him.. a strange Pick-lock. **1683** CROWNE *City Politiques* v. i, I have a picklock in my pocket. **1828** W. SEWELL *Oxf. Prize Ess.* 63 A vile Laconian lock, with three stout wards, Which no picklock or nail can reach to open. **1879** *Cassell's Techn. Educ.* IV. 244/1 The.. most ingenious picklock ever seen.

fig. **1581** J. BELL *Haddon's Answ. Osor.* 393 b, By which picklockes they locke fast the gates of hell, and open the gates of heaven to whom they list. **1702** *Eng. Theophrast.* 72 Money is the very pick-lock that opens the way into all Cabinets and Councils.

B. *adj.* Used for picking a lock; *esp.* in ***pick lock key*** = A. 2. Also *fig.*

1607 ROWLANDS *Guy Warw.* 75 Hell's picklock powder was unknown to men. **1670** *Lond. Gaz.* No. 446/4 A bunch of picklock keys. **1693** C. DRYDEN in *Dryden's Juvenal* vii. (1697) 174 The well-lung'd Civilian.. opens first the Cause, Then with a Pick-lock Tongue perverts the Laws. **1850** CHUBB *Locks & Keys* 32 He thought it would be impossible to pick them.. by any picklock keys.

picklock, *sb.*² and *a.*² *Wool Manuf.* [f. PICK *a.* or *v.*¹ 7 + LOCK *sb.*¹] Name for the highest quality of English wool.

1794 FOOT *Agric.* 61 (E.D.D.) The dearest class of wool, called 'picklock', is estimated at thirty-two pence a pound. **1842** BISCHOFF *Woollen Manuf.* II. 114, I have.. divided them [wools] into six classes,.. 1st class—the pick-lock and prime. 2nd class—the choice and super... 5th class—livery and short coarse. 6th class—pick-lock, grey, &c. &c. **1884** W. S. B. MCLAREN *Spinning* (ed. 2) 17 In the woollen trade the following names are common for English wool:—picklock, which, as the name implies, is the choicest of all; prime, which is very similar; choice, a very little stronger; super, from the shoulders [etc.].

pickman. [In sense 1, f. PICK *sb.*¹ + MAN.]

1. A labourer who works with a pick; e.g. a miner or collier who uses a pick, a hewer.

1856 *Househ. Words* XIII. 544 Miners from Cornwall,.. Muckshifters, Pickmen [etc.]. **1878** URE *Dict. Arts* IV. 631 (*Ozokerite*), Five or more gangs work at a time, each consisting of four or five men, one pickman cutting the ground, one for drawing stuff to the shaft bottom, two at the windlass.

2. A raker who rakes the hay into rows. *dial.*

1863 BARNES *Dorset Dial.* Gloss. s.v. *Haymeaken*, In raking grass into double rollers, or pushing hay up into weals, the fore raker or pickman is said to *rake in* or *push in*, or *row* or *roo*, and the other to *close.*

3. = PICKMAW. *dial.*

1899 PREVOST *Cumberland Gloss.*, *Pickman*, the tern.

pickman, obs. form of PIKEMAN¹.

pick'maw. *Sc.* and *north. dial.* Also 9 *Northumb.* picki-maw. [Second element MAW³, gull; first uncertain (some conjecture *pick*, PITCH).] A common name in Scotland of the Black-headed Gull, *Larus ridibundus*: see GULL *sb.*¹

c **1450** HOLLAND *Howlat* 183 Parfytlye thir Pikmawis, as for priouris, With thar party habitis present tham thar. **1805** A. SCOTT *Poems* (1808) 224 The lav'rock, the peasweep, an' skirlin pickmaw. **1818** SCOTT *Br. Lamm.* xxv, The very pick-maws and solan-geese out-by yonder at the Bass hae ten times their sense! **1894** *Northumbld. Gloss.* 529 Peewit Gull.. also called *sea crow*, and *pick-i'-ma* [on p. 533 erron. *picima*].

'pick-me-up. *colloq.* [A phrase used as *sb.*: see PICK *v.*¹ 21, and PICK-.] **1. a.** *orig.* A stimulating drink serving to restore vigour after exhaustion; extended to beverages, medicinal preparations, etc., supposed to have restorative and tonic qualities.

1867 LATHAM *Black & White* 80 Who could induce the American loafer to drink home-brewed ale.. instead of pick-me-ups. **1871** *Standard* 13 Feb., A good trade in 'foaming pick-me-ups',.. was done at the various American bars. **1884** *Pall Mall G.* 4 Apr. 4/1 The land of cocktails and pick-me-ups. **1900** *Westm. Gaz.* 5 Feb. 5/2 Incautious use of a pick-me-up in which strychnine was an ingredient.

b. *transf.* and *fig.* Anything serving to restore strength or vigour, or having a bracing effect.

1876 'OUIDA' *Winter City* vii. 217 To Society the Père Hilarion was only a sort of mental liqueur, as Jenny Léa was an American 'pick-me-up'. **1887** *Poor Nellie* (1888) 278 Dr. Doseman's lively wrath proved a pick-me-up to his. **1890** W. J. GORDON *Foundry* 102 The pick-me-up we saw administered was a small dose of spiegeleisen from a furnace close by. **1891** M. O'RELL *Frenchm. in Amer.* 43 This man is in constant need of moral support and pick-me-up.

2. A woman who readily allows herself to be picked up; a prostitute. Cf. PICK-UP *sb.* 3.

1922 JOYCE *Ulysses* 49 She lives in Leeson park, with a grief and kickshaws, a lady of letters. Talk that to some else, Stevie: a pickmeup. **1941** J. SMILEY *Hash House Lingo* 42 *Pick me up*, loose woman.

[**pickmire**, an erroneous book-name for the PICKMAW: prob. a copyist's or printer's error.

Appears in Bewick's *Brit. Birds*, 1808, vol. II (not by Bewick) 226, whence in Montagu *Ornith. Dict.* 1812, Swainson *Prov. Names Brit. Birds* (E.D.S.), who erroneously locates it in Roxburghshire (where *pick-maw* is the name).]

picknick, -er, -ing: see PICNIC, etc.

'**pick-off.** Also pickoff, pick off. [f. vbl. phr. *to pick off* s.v. PICK $v.^1$ 18.] **1.** Chiefly *Aeronaut.* In an automatic control or guidance system, any device which produces or alters a pneumatic or an electrical output in response to a change in motion.

1938 P. V. H. WEEMS *Air Navigation* (ed. 2) xiv. 243 If the aircraft changes attitude laterally, one of the ports..of the air pick off is opened fully and the other closed. **1938** A. JORDANOFF *Through Overcast* xiv. 180 Whenever you wish to fly in a certain direction under automatic control, you must be sure to set the air pick-offs at neutral at the same time your plane points in the direction which gives the desired reading on the directional gyro. **1940** E. MOLLOY *Aeroplane Maintenance & Operation* II. I. 12 In actual practice the air pick-off consists of a disc attached to the gyro element, with knife edges which intercept the air flow at two nozzles on the supporting frame. **1958** J. G. TRUXAL *Control Engineers' Handbk.* xvii. 49 The displacement gyro is continually being torqued by the coupling of the motion of the base through the gimbal gearing friction and pickoff loading to the wheel. **1962** F. I. ORDWAY et al. *Basic Astronautics* ix. 377 The precession..is sensed by a pickoff that sends a signal to the servo amplifier.

2. In baseball: the act of catching a runner off base by means of the pitcher or catcher suddenly throwing the ball at that base. Freq. *attrib.*

1939 G. S. COCHRANE *Baseball* iv. 76 The danger of a throw to first for the pickoff is that the runner has over-run first not only too far to get back but far enough to make a break for second. **1948** *Sun* (Baltimore) 19 July 12 (*caption*) Bill Martin gets back in time as Eddie Shokes..tries to complete pickoff attempt in opener. **1968** *Washington Post* 4 July C2/4 Wills moved to second when Ryan's attempted pickoff throw went wide. **1968** *Globe & Mail* (Toronto) 10 July 26/6 Killebrew..said Tiant's pickoff throw on Mays, which opened the gates for the winning run, was behind the runner. **1974** *Spartanburg* (S. Carolina) *Herald* 23 Apr. A6/4 Bill Dancy of Spartanburg singled with one out in the fourth, moved to second on an errant pickoff attempt and went to third on Mark Ammons' infield hit. **1976** *Washington Post* 19 April D2/2 Manning scored the only run Cleveland needed in the first inning when he..came home when Busby threw away a pickoff throw.

3. Used *attrib.* to designate auxiliary parts of a machine positioned so as to be easily selected or brought into use when required.

1949 *Tool Engineers Handbk.* (Amer. Soc. Tool Engineers) xxxv. 602 A secondary operation may be eliminated by the use of a pick-off attachment, which is an independently driven spindle and collet arrangement mounted in the cutoff position. **1950** J. A. OATES in A. W. Judge *Machine Tools & Operations* III. i. 30 These 'pick-off' gears are arranged under a cover..in some easily accessible position, and it is only a matter of two or three minutes to change over to a new speed or feed.

pickoss, -oys, obs. forms of PICKAXE.

pickpack: see PIGGY-BACK, PICK-A-BACK.

pickpenny, *Obs.*: see PICK-.

pickpocket ('pɪkpɒkɪt), *sb.* [f. PICK $v.^1$ 9 + POCKET: see PICK-.]

1. One who steals from or 'picks' pockets; a thief who follows the practice of stealing things from the pockets of others.

1591 GREENE *Disc. Coosnage* Pref. (1592) 2 The picke-pockets and cut-purses, are nothing so dangerous to meete, as these coosning Cunny-catchers. **1668** ROLLE *Abridgm.*, *Action sur Case* xx. 73 Si home dit de A. He was a Pick-pocket, and he picked my pocket, and took 12*s.* of money out of my pocket. Nul Action gist. **1711** STEELE *Spect.* No. 78 ¶4 It was only a Pickpocket, who during his Kissing her stole away all his Money. **1858** LYTTON *What will he do* I. iv, He did not wish to..turn shoeblack or pickpocket.

transf. and *fig.* **1593** G. HARVEY *Pierce's Super.* Wks. (Grosart) II. 272 The pickthanke of vanity, the pickpocket of foolery, the pickpurse of all the palteries, and knaueries in Print. **1823** LAMB *Elia* Ser. II. *Old Margate Hoy*, The nibbling pick-pockets of your patience.

attrib. *a* **1716** SOUTH *Serm.* (1744) XI. 29, I do not mean the auricular pick-pocket confession of the Papists. **1764** GRAY *Candidate* 6 Such a sheep-biting look, such a pick-pocket air! **1823** SYD. SMITH *Wks.* (1859) II. 12/2 His mission to the fifth or pickpocket quarter of the globe.

2. *dial.* Given as a name to various weeds which impoverish the land, as Shepherd's Purse, Corn Spurrey, etc.: cf. next 2 and see Eng. Dial. Dict.

1875 *Sussex Gloss.*, *Pickpockets*, Shepherd's purse.

Hence '**pick,pocket** *v.*, usually as *vbl. sb.*; **,pick-'pocketing**, stealing from pockets; **pick-'pocketism**, the practice of picking pockets; also *transf.*; **pick'pocketry** = prec.: in quot. 'plagiarism'.

1673 R. HEAD *Canting Acad.* 5 They will dextrously *pick pocket. **1789** G. PARKER *Life's Painter* xv. 176 Going upon the knuckle is going a thieving, *pickpocketing, &c. **1818** J. MILNER in F. C. Husenbeth *Life J. Milner* (1862) xx. 353 Not only an affront of a real diabolical nature, but also a serious pick-pocketing roguery. **1838** DICKENS *O. Twist* xliii, A pick-pocketing case, your worship. **1886** *Pall Mall G.* 17 Sept. 4/1 Pickpocketing is merely another form of gambling. **1957** MANVELL & HUNTLEY *Technique Film Music* 232 The 'Juggler's Waltz' is a period piece for a music-hall act which takes place in a Paris café during an incident in which the visiting Inspector of Police witnesses a pick-pocketing attempt. **1977** *New Society* 7 July 5/2 Their game has confused pickpocketing with bag snatching and mugging. **1830** *Examiner* 612/1 The *pick-pocketism above alluded to cannot be defended. **1803** SOUTHEY *Lett.* (1856) I. 238 The crime of pedantry, stupidity, jackassness, and *pickpocketry.

† '**pickpurse.** *Obs.* [See PICK-.]

1. One who steals purses or from purses; a pickpocket.

c **1386** CHAUCER *Knt.'s T.* 1140 Ther saugh I first... The pykepurs [*v.r.* pykpurs]. **1393** LANGL. *P. Pl.* C. VII. 370 A dosen harlotes Of portours and of pykeporses. **1542** UDALL *Erasm. Apoph.* 121 b, The pikepurses and stealers of apparell. **1543** in *Lett. & Papers Hen. VIII*, XVIII. II. 316 All pickpurses' ears are not set on the pillory as yet. **1615** T. ADAMS *White Devill* 47 The pick-purse..doth not so much hurt as this general robber. **1727** SWIFT *Dreams* Wks. 1755 III. II. 234 His fellow pick-purse..Fancies his fingers in the cully's fob.

b. *transf.* and *fig.*

a **1586** SIDNEY *Astr. & Stella* lxxiv, I am no pick-purse of anothers wit. *a* **1602** W. PERKINS *Cases Consc.* (1619) 332 Inordinate and affected care is commonly a great pickpurse. **1611** COTGR. s.v. *Argent*, Good cheape commodities are notable picke-purses.

c. *attrib.*

1508 DUNBAR *Flyting* 114 Pynit pykpuris pelour. *c* **1550** *Dice-Play* B v, Hyghe law [signifieth] robbery, Figginge lawe, picke purse crefte. **1612** *Pasquil's Night-Cap* (1877) 8 To see a pilfring and a pick-purse knaue,..Diue to the bottome of a true mans purse.

d. ***purgatory pickpurse, pickpurse purgatory***: a dyslogistic term of 16th c. controversy, used orig. app. by Latimer, in reference to the use made of the doctrine of purgatory to obtain payments for masses for departed souls, etc.

1537 tr. *Latimer's Serm. bef. Convoc.* D ij, They that begotte and brought forth, that one old ancient purgatorie pycke pourse. *c* **1550** BALE *K. Johan* (Camden) 63 Your pardons, your bulles, your purgatory pyckepurse. **1556** OLDE *Antichrist* 81 b, That most pestiferous fornace of the popes pikepurce Purgatorie. *a* **1591** H. SMITH *Arrow agst. Ath.* (1622) 60 It may be well and justly called Purgatorie Pick-purse; wealth and great riches of the clergy, was the only mark they aimed at. **1712** M. HENRY *Popery* Wks. 1853 II. 346/2 'Purgatory pick-purse', so it has been called.

2. A name of Shepherd's Purse, *Capsella Bursapastoris*, from its impoverishing the land. Also of Corn Spurrey, *Spergula arvensis*. Cf. prec. 2.

1597 GERARDE *Herbal* II. xxiii. §2. 215 Shepheardes purse is called..in the North part..Pickepurse, and Caseweede. **1617** MINSHEU *Ductor*, *Pickepurse* an hearbe so called... *Shepheards purse* or *Shepheards Pouch.* **1787** W. MARSHALL *E. Norfolk* Gloss., *Pickpurse*, or *Sandweed*, *spergula arvensis*, common spurrey.

† '**pick-,quarrel.** *Obs.* [See PICK-.]

1. One given to picking quarrels; a quarrelsome person.

1530 TINDALE *Pract. Prelates* Wks. (Parker Soc.) II. 264 He hath been all his life a pick-quarrel. **1532** *Ibid.* 27 Cursed be the peace-breakers, pick-quarrels, whisperers, backbiters. **1588** E. AGGAS tr. *Pres. Estate France* 56 All the pickquarrels, all the porters of Paris..are at thy becke.

2. An occasion of quarrel; a cause of dispute.

1611 SPEED *Hist. Gt. Brit.* IX. xxiv. §54 If all these pretences and demands were cancelled, and Callis forgotten, which hath beene the continuall picke-quarrell betwixt these two Realmes.

pickquet, pickrel, pickroon, obs. ff. PIQUET, PICKEREL, PICAROON.

Pick's disease ('pɪks dɪ'zi:z). **1.** [f. the name of Friedel *Pick* (1867–1926), Austrian physician.] A form of multiple serositis characterized by constrictive pericarditis, hepatomegaly, and ascites.

1900 DUNGLISON *Dict. Med. Sci.* (ed. 22) App. 1314/2 *Pick's disease*, pseudocirrhosis of the liver, sometimes accompanying adhesive pericarditis. **1935** *Lancet 14 Sept.* 602/1 The prognosis of Pick's disease without surgical treatment is unfavourable for health and in some cases for life. **1940** E. ROSENTHAL *Dis. Digestive Syst.* iii. 278 Such a perihepatitis may be the result of liver disease or may accompany 'pericarditic pseudocirrhosis' (Pick's disease). **1959** BAILEY & LOVE *Short Pract. Surg.* (ed. 11) xx. 376 The best example of perisplenitis occurs in association with multiple serositis (Pick's disease).

2. [f. the name of Arnold *Pick* (1851–1924), Austrian psychiatrist and neurologist.] A condition, chiefly afflicting persons in late middle age, which is characterized by deterioration of intellect and judgement, speech disturbance and eventual dementia, and is caused by progressive atrophy of the frontal and temporal lobes of the brain.

1931 *Lancet* 20 June 1331/2 Pick's disease is a slowly progressive dementia starting usually in the sixth decade and accompanied by focal manifestations. **1935** *Jrnl. Nervous & Mental Dis.* LXXXII. 71 High blood pressure and arteriosclerosis are peculiarly absent in Pick's disease. **1955** H. H. MERRITT *Textbk. Neurol.* vi. 417 The cardinal symptoms of both Pick's and Alzheimer's disease are progressive dementia and disturbances in the speech. **1974** PASSMORE & ROBSON *Compan. Med. Stud.* III. xxxv. 76/1 The underlying cerebral atrophy..is restricted to the frontal and temporal lobes in Pick's disease. **1976** SMYTHIES & CORBETT *Psychiatry* vii. 126 Pick's disease is marked by a rapid and profound blunting of social judgement.

picksome ('pɪksəm), *a.* [f. PICK $v.^1$ + -SOME.] Choice, fastidious, dainty; particular.

1867 F. FRANCIS *Angling* vi. (1880) 190 Trouts are picksome and hard to please. **1888** BESANT *Fifty Yrs. ago* viii. 136 We were not quite so picksome in the matter of company as we are now. **1899** *19th Cent.* 608 The Committee should be very picksome and particular. [Halliwell's sense 'Hungry, peckish' was app. a mistake.]

Hence '**picksomeness**, daintiness.

1881 BESANT & RICE *Captain's Room* i, Cucumber readily adapts itself to all palates save those set on edge with pick-someness.

pickstaff, obs. form of PIKESTAFF.

pickthank ('pɪkθæŋk), *sb.* and *a. arch.* and *dial.* [f. the phrase *to pick a thank* or *thanks*: see PICK $v.^1$ 8 b, and PICK-.]

A. *sb.* One who 'picks a thank', i.e. curries favour with another, esp. by informing against some one else; a flatterer, sycophant; a tale-bearer, tell-tale.

1500–20 DUNBAR *Poems* xxii. 43 To be a pykthank I wald preif. **1551** *Gray's N.-Y. Gift to Somerset* 86 in Furniv. *Ballads fr. MSS.* I. 423 Refuse those pikethanckes that Imagyn lyes! **1565–73** COOPER *Thesaurus*, *Delâtor*,..a secrete accusour or complayner: a tell tale: a picke thanke. **1596** SHAKS. *1 Hen. IV*, III. ii. 25. *a* **1641** BP. MOUNTAGU *Acts & Mon.* (1642) 289 These speeches that pick-thank reported to Antipater, with exaggerations of his own to make them more odious. **1710** L. MILBOURNE *Resist. Higher Powers* 24 When other pick-thanks might be ready to inform against them. **1820** SCOTT *Abbot* vi, I had been called *pickthank* and *tale-pyet*. **1879** SALA *Paris herself again* (1880) I. xvii. 279 What a pickthank..that simple party of English people might have thought me.

B. *adj.* (attrib. use of *sb.*) Given to 'picking thanks'; flattering, sycophantic; tale-bearing; basely officious.

1561 AWDELAY *Frat. Vacab.* 14 This is a pickthanke knaue, that would make his Maister beleue that the Cowe is woode. **1600** DEKKER *Gentle Craft* Wks. 1873 I. 15 He sets more discord in a noble house, By one daies broching of his pick-thanke tales, Than can be salved again in twentie yeares. **1692** R. L'ESTRANGE *Josephus, Antiq.* XVI. xvi. (1733) 446 He..never fail'd of some pick-thank Story or other to carry away with him. **1850** L. HUNT *Autobiog.* xii. (1860) 200 An effeminate parader of phrases of endearment and pickthank adulation.

Hence † '**pickthankly** *a.*, of the character of a pickthank; † '**pickthankness**, the quality or character of being a pickthank.

1702 C. MATHER *Magn. Chr.* III. II. xiii. (1852) 410 The Arch-Bishop, instead of being offended as the pick-thankly reporter hoped he would have been, fell a laughing heartily. **1672** MARVELL *Reh. Transp.* I. 284 But for the pickthankness of some of the Clergy, who will alwayes presume to have the thanks and honour of it.

'**pickthank,** *v. rare.* [f. prec. sb.] *intr.* To play the pickthank, curry favour *with* (a person); †*trans.* to obtain by sycophancy (*obs.*). Hence '**pickthanking** *vbl. sb.* and *ppl. a.*

Sometimes app. misused for to *pick faults*, *pick holes*.

1621 LADY M. WROTH *Urania* 43 While he did credit pickthanking Counsellors. **1642** ROGERS *Naaman* 308 Many there bee who..to flatter and pickethanke with their Masters..do great things. *a* **1734** NORTH *Exam.* II. iv. §95 (1740) 278 He did it to pick-thank an Opportunity of getting more Money. [**1830** *Examiner* 132/2 The most fastidious and pick-thanking critic. **1863** COWDEN CLARKE *Shaks. Char.* v. 131 How constantly Shakespeare releases himself from the pick-thanking of his critics.]

picktooth ('pɪktu:θ), *sb.* and *a.* Now *rare.* Pl. picktooths; sometimes erron. **pickteeth.** [f. PICK $v.^1$ 2 + TOOTH: see PICK-.]

A. *sb.* **1.** An instrument for picking the teeth; a toothpick.

1542 *Acc. Ld. High Treas. Scot.* in Pitcairn *Crim. Trials* I. *321 For ane Pennare of silver to keip Pyke-teithe in, to þe Kingis grace. **1572** GASCOIGNE *Wks.*, *Hearbes*, *Weedes*, etc. (1587) 154 As with a piketooth byting on your lippe. **1594** PLAT *Jewell-ho.* III. 73 Small Iuniper stickes, with sharpe points like picketoothes. **1685** LLOYD in *Lett. Eminent Persons* (1813) I. 29 Now he gave him his case of pick-teeth. **1755** H. WALPOLE *Let. to Montagu* 20 Dec., I was afraid you would think I had sent you a bundle of pick-tooths, insted of pines and firs. **1812** W. TENNANT *Anster F.* VI. xxxii, Guest and hostess backward leaning, all Their picktooths now were plying.

2. The umbelliferous plant *Ammi Visnaga*, also called Toothpick Bishopweed; so called from the use made of the dry stalks of the umbels.

1760 J. Lee *Introd. Bot.* App. 322 Pick-tooth, *Daucus.* **1866** *Treas. Bot.*, Picktooth, *Ammi Visnaga.* **1884** Miller *Plant-n.*, Pick-tooth, *Daucus Visnaga.*

3. *attrib.*, as ***picktooth case.***

1685 *Lond. Gaz.* No. 2068/4 A Pick-Tooth Case wrought. **1711** Puckle *Club* (1817) 74 Accoutred with a large muff..snuff-box, diamond ring, pick-tooth-case, silk handkerchief. **1807** Crabbe *Par. Reg.* ii. 237 His milk-white hand Could pick tooth case and box for snuff command.

B. *adj.* Idle, indolent, easy, leisurely (like a person resting and picking his teeth after a meal).

1728 Vanbr. & Cib. *Prov. Husb.* ii. i, My Lord and I, after ..dinner, sat down by the fire-side, in an idle, indolent, pick-tooth way. **1767** Mrs. S. Pennington *Lett.* III. 39 We breakfast..with Aristotle, and pass our pick-tooth hours with Orpheus. **1809** Malkin *Gil Blas* iv. ix. ¶3 The pick-tooth carelessness of a lounger. **1865** *Pall Mall G.* 29 May 1 That easy, picktooth air of fashion, with which the noble Marquis is good enough to transact the business of the nation.

pickueer, obs. form of PICKEER.

pick-up, *sb.* (*a.*) Also pickup. [f. the phr. *to pick up*: see PICK *v.*[1] 21.]

A. *sb.* **1.** The act of picking up; *spec.* **a.** in Cricket, the picking up of the ball, in order to return it.

1886 *Daily News* 27 July 3/2 [A cricketer] conspicuous for the quickness of his pick-up and the accuracy of his return. **1891** W. G. Grace *Cricket* 262 Pick-up and return must be one action, or the batsman will steal a sharp run.

b. [PICK *v.*[1] 21 b (*b*).] The collection of unretrieved game after a shooting party; the quantity of game so collected.

1897 *Encycl. Sport* I. 443/1 Too large a 'pick up' means that the work was not properly done on the day itself. **1939** *Country Life* 11 Feb. 153/1, I wish all hosts would provide themselves with those little cards that tell you the total bag together with the pick-up and the names of the guns. **1976** *Shooting Times & Country Mag.* 16-22 Dec. 16/2 At the end of the pick-up a smile at last creased the face of keeper Bunny Spicer for the total bag was 253 pheasants, a record!

c. [PICK *v.*[1] 21 l.] The act of apprehending or arresting. orig. *U.S.* Also, ***pick-up van*** (S. Afr.), a police van.

1908 J. M. Sullivan *Criminal Slang* 18 *Pickup*, an arrest followed by no charge of crime. **1934** L. Berg *Revelations Prison Doctor* viii. 109 Rao..called his arrests 'pickups' and inferred that the charges were too trivial to be worthy of notice. **1942** P. Abrahams *Dark Testament* i. xii. 63 They all turn, and see a group of policemen jumping out of the moving pick-up van and running towards them. **1946** *Sun* (Baltimore) 8 Nov. 6/2 The Kansas sheriff responded with a request for a 'pick-up' on another man in the case. **1948** O. Walker *Kaffirs are Lively* xi. 173 There comes the big van. .. They call it the *pick-up van.* **1953** P. Lanham *Blanket Boy's Moon* i. vi. 50 'Police! Police! The pick-up van's coming.' Even as he shouted the warning, the police arrived in their closed van with a squealing of brakes. **1970** G. Jackson *Let.* 10 June in *Soledad Brother* (1971) 34, I.. started getting 'picked up' by the pigs more often... These pick-ups were mainly for 'suspicion of' or because I was in the wrong part of town.

d. [PICK *v.*[1] 21 o.] Recovery, improvement.

*a***1916** H. James *Ivory Tower* (1917) i. iii. 69 'It's one of Mr. Betterman's [nurses] taking a joy-ride in honour of his recovery!'.. 'His pick-up *will* be a sell,' [Davey] ruefully added. **1922** H. Titus *Timber* xxxii. 279 During all those years there will be a steady pick-up in quality. **1933** *Sun* (Baltimore) 10 Nov. 14/1 It is idle to suggest..that this newest relief scheme will help to tide the jobless over until 'the spring pick-up begins'. **1958** *Times Rev. Industry* Sept. 50/2 Export orders continue to be small, and there is little hope, with the American recession affecting steel-using industries on the Continent, of any pick-up in the near future. **1961** *Wall St. Jrnl.* 4 Oct. 1 Farm machinery dealer Bob Houtz tilts back in a battered chair and tells of a sharp pickup in sales. **1970** *Daily Tel.* 3 Feb. 19/2 Car sales showed their expected pick-up last month.

e. [PICK *v.*[1] 21 i.] Reception of signals by electrical apparatus; *spec.* interference; also, a received radio or television programme.

1923 *Electrical Communication* I. iv. 25/1 A portable amplifier for use with the 'pick-up' microphones..made it possible to pick up speeches or music at any desired point.. and distribute the output to sound projectors. **1925** *Scribner's Mag.* Oct. 90 (Advt.), Low-loss doughnut coils.. conquer 'pick-up' of unwanted stations. **1937** *Discovery* Nov. 330/2 To provide the subject matter for transmission, direct pick-up, artists in the studio, or previously photographed sound-film may be used. **1943** *Electronic Engin.* XV. 521/3 Although the balanced input circuit minimises the pick-up it is sometimes essential to enclose the patient in a screened cubicle. **1948** *Sun* (Baltimore) 3 Jan. 2/2 It was a thirty-minute radio network program with pick-ups from scattered points in the United States and abroad. **1949** Frayne & Wolfe *Elem. Sound Recording* xxxii. 674 Microphone placement is less exacting in the stereophonic pickup of orchestral music. **1956** *Electronics* Feb. 170/2 A series of measurements was made on the cross pickup of pulses in a 100-foot length of..communication cable. **1965** *Wireless World* Aug. 383/2 When ferrite aerials are close to the inverter transformers, inductive pick-up can result. **1971** *Sci. Amer.* Oct. 28/1 With a community wired from one or more terminal points to individual homes the local pickup would not be limited to the channels of the commercial television networks; instead participants could receive through the satellite a number of services to meet individual tastes. **1976** *Broadcast* 29 Nov. 18/1 The camera has to be blimped to prevent noise pick-up from microphones.

f. [Cf. PICK *v.*[1] 21 f.] Robbery, theft. Freq. *attrib. slang.*

1928, etc. [see *pick-up man* (sense B. a)]. **1938** F. D. Sharpe *Sharpe of Flying Squad* i. 14 Lower down come the suit-case thieves, the pick-up merchants, small time smash-and-grabbers, [etc.]. *Ibid.* xxiii. 240 He had been persuaded to try his hand at 'the pick up' (stealing from unattended motor cars). **1962** *Gross's Criminal Investigation* (ed. 5) viii. 206 *At the pick-up*, suitcase stealing.

g. [Cf. PICK *v.*[1] 21 e.] Collection and transportation by means of an aircraft, motor vehicle, ship, etc. Freq. *attrib.*

1938 W. L. G. Cowan *Loud Report* iii. 220 We usually kip in the afternoon and push on at night. There's a better chance of a pick-up. **1940** *Mech. Engin.* Apr. 283/1 The record is not clear as to exactly when the first pickup in flight was made. *Ibid.* 285/2 The pickup system..makes possible the picking up of heavier loads. **1943** *Jrnl. R. Aeronaut. Soc.* XLVII. (Abstr. from Sci. & Techn. Press) 72 The Air Mail Pick-up service was started by the American Post Office Department in 1939. *Ibid.*, Since short hauls seem to offer the best field for cargo glider operation, a similar method of pick-up becomes most attractive. **1952** E. F. Davies *Illyrian Venture* iv. 68 The American pilot signalled Cairo that it was possible to rescue them by air pick-up from Gjinokaster airfield. **1960** R. Williams *Border Country* iv. 94 'Where's the pickup then?' 'Signalled now.'.. Rees..crossed the line and walked down..to the siding. **1960** R. W. Marks *Dymaxion World of B. Fuller* 22/1 Fuller's toilets.. consisted of a splashless hermetic and waterproof packaging system which mechanically packed, stored, and gross-cartoned wastes for eventual pickup for processing by chemical industries. **1971** P. O'Donnell *Impossible Virgin* xii. 238, I fixed for the 'copter to stand by for a pick-up at eighteen 'undred hours. *Ibid.* xiv. 275 They rested beside.. a triangle of flat stony ground... This was the pick-up area Willie had arranged. **1972** 'G. Black' *Bitter Tea* (1973) vii. 100 The *Kao Ming* hasn't been converted for carrying.. steel containers, serving out her now very limited time on the copra pick-up routes. **1974** L. Deighton *Spy Story* xix. 208 That radio signal obliges us to continue with the pick-up, even if we were certain it's phoney. **1976** *National Observer* (U.S.) 11 Dec. 4/3 Ankeny, Iowa, saved $9,000 by opening dump sites to the public for two weekend clean-ups a year and abolished curbside pickups. **1977** *Chicago Tribune* 2 Oct. xii. 2/2 The garbage just piled up all summer. No pickup. **1978** J. Krantz *Scruples* ix. 259 Billy also established a delivery service in a town where multimillionaire customers have to do their own pickups in every boutique.

h. *Nuclear Physics.* A reaction in which an incident particle such as a proton or deuteron captures one or more nucleons from an atomic nucleus. Usu. *attrib.*

1950 *Physical Rev.* LXXVII. 470 It is proposed that the fast deuterons observed among the products of high energy nuclear reactions are to be understood in terms of a 'pick-up' or sudden rearrangement process. *Ibid.*, The pick-up process must not be thought of as taking place within the nucleus. **1970** I. E. McCarthy *Nuclear Reactions* i. v. 95 If one of these interactions seems more plausible than the other to the reader, he need only consider the time-reversed situation (pick-up). **1971** W. M. Gibson *Nuclear Reactions* vii. 108 A pick-up reaction in a nucleus with an odd neutron outside a closed inner shell can provide useful information about the state of the odd neutron..which is directly relevant to the shell model of the nucleus. **1975** *Nature* 6 Mar. 19/3 The spectroscopic factors for stripping and pickup reactions on the same nucleus can be related to each other.

2. a. That which picks up, as a railway-train.

1877 *N.W. Linc. Gloss.* s.v., The last train at night which runs..from Sheffield to New Holland, is called the Pick up. **1891** *Pall Mall G.* 20 Oct. 6/2 The experiments for Mr. Edison's new electric tramcar were conducted at his laboratory at West Orange, New Jersey... Its chief feature is the 'pickups' which take the current from one line of rails. **1898** *Tit-Bits* 18 June 220/3 Those [lights] of slow goods trains and 'pick-ups' are distinguished by a single green light..placed over the left-hand buffer. **1972** M. Glenny tr. *Solzhenitsyn's August 1914* xlii. 419 Trams passed, clanging, their pick-ups hissing along the wires. **1974** *Physics Bull.* Apr. 154/3 The dangers caused by power failure in magnetic hoists are avoided in a new design from Mullard. For the pickup is a permanent magnet rather than the usual ferroelectric magnet.

b. (*a*) A sensor or transducer.

1943 D. G. Fink *Television Standards & Pract.* iv. 91 Specifications to be placed on the spectral response of each of the three color-sensitive elements of the pickup. **1957** R. A. Heinlein *Door into Summer* v. 79, I suppose it was a stethoscope he used although it looked like a miniaturized hearing aid... The pick-up he pushed against me was as cold and hard as ever. **1961** *Engineering* 8 Sept. 309/1 Phototransistor pickups, focused on rotating black and white discs, provide signals for the phase meter. **1962** F. I. Ordway et al. *Basic Astronautics* vii. 316 By placing temperature pickups at various points on the model flame deflector it was possible to determine the approximate temperatures encountered..in an actual firing. **1978** J. Gores *Gone* (1979) iii. 24 He was at the corner where he knew the concealed pickup was.

(*b*) *spec.* = CARTRIDGE 1 e, HEAD *sb.*[1] 11 g, *pick-up arm* in sense B. a below.

1926 *Glasgow Herald* 5 Oct. 5 Instead of the conventional sound-box an electrical device known as a magnetic 'pick-up' is guided over the record, converting the mechanical vibrations imparted to the needle into electrical vibrations. **1926** *Gramophone* Dec. 294/1 Instead of a sound-box there is what is known as a 'pick-up'. **1938** *Times* 25 Aug. 8/2 It has been specially designed as a supplementary unit for existing radio receivers having pick-up terminals. **1940** *Gramophone* Sept. 93/1 The output is very much less than that given by the average moving iron or piezo electric types of pick-up. **1941** [see CARTRIDGE 1 e]. **1946** *Newsweek* 13 May 23 (Advt.), Your Victrola's jewel-point pickup floats like a feather on water. **1951** [see HEAD *sb.*[1] 11 g]. **1959** *New Scientist* 31 July 517/2 The whole pick-up must be able to do the manœuvres required of it without giving rise to excessive pressures which would damage the record. **1963** *Which?* Jan. 8/2 The pick up is composed of two parts—an arm, and at the end of the arm..a head. **1975** G. J. King *Audio Handbk.* viii. 170 The modern pickup consists of an arm and a cartridge. **1976** 'J. Fraser' *Who steals my Name?* ix. 107 The needle on the pick-up of his record player..had a beard on it... His room was filthy.

(*c*) *spec.* A device that produces an electrical signal corresponding to the displacement, speed, or acceleration of a vibrating body.

1950 P. G. Andres *Survey Mod. Electronics* viii. 346 Electronic comparator gauges use a pickup that operates on the principle of displacing an armature..to generate a corresponding voltage. *Ibid.* 363 Since the pickup responds to the acceleration of the vibratory motion, integrating networks convert its output..into readings proportional to velocity or displacement. **1966** *McGraw-Hill Encycl. Sci. & Technol.* VIII. 667/1 A vibration pickup can be used to generate an electrical signal directly from the vibration of a string; this is the case in the electric guitar and electric piano. **1968** *Melody Maker* 6 Apr. 5 (Advt.), Take our pickups... To get sound from a metal guitar string, all you have to do is wind wire around a magnetic core and place it near that string. **1970** R. H. Wallace *Understanding & measuring Vibration* iv. 40 Because the aircraft structure is such that low frequencies under, say, 10 Hz are readily transmitted,.. it will be vital to use pickups and read-out equipment going down to zero frequency, or near. **1972** M. P. Blake in Blake & Mitchell *Vibration & Acoustic Measurement Handbk.* xx. 422 The proximity pickup is likely to become increasingly popular for monitoring the shafts of high-speed, large, powerful drives, such as turbines, reading directly in displacement which, in this application, is usually the parameter of most interest. *Ibid.*, A growing tendency among those who measure vibration favors the acceleration pickup.

c. In full, ***pick-up truck*** or ***van.*** A small truck or van used for carrying light loads (see also sense 1 c above). So ***pick-up body***, a small, detachable body for use on various types of light trucks.

1932 *Kansas City* (Missouri) *Times* 21 Jan. 22 There was a delivery car with a pick-up body on it in King City. **1939** *Sun* (Baltimore) 18 Jan. 7/2 Dairies' pickup trucks were subject to commission regulation. **1944** *Democrat* 29 June 1/4 This includes all operators of trucks and pickups whose gasoline rations are not controlled. **1948** *Southern Sierran* (Los Angeles) Apr. 4/1 The work will be made lighter if someone will provide the use of a pick-up truck for removing the dirt. **1959** F. Stark *Riding to Tigris* 96 A piece of the bull-dozer was extracted and loaded on the pick-up, which looked like a bright orange lorry. **1973** A. Ross *Dunfermline Affair* 45 He must be going out in the pick-up. *Ibid.* 48 There were still plenty of motor cars in the car park, but no small grey pick-up truck. **1977** *Cork Examiner* 8 June 14/3 (Advt.), 30 cwt. pick-up truck and driver available. **1977** *Western Morning News* 30 Aug. 2/2 (Advt.), J.4 Pick-up J registered..long M.O.T.

3. That which is picked up, as a pick-up meal (see B. b); one who is picked up, a chance passenger, acquaintance, etc.; *spec.* a person whose acquaintance is formed with the intention of having a sexual relationship; a prostitute or street-walker; also, the act of forming such an acquaintanceship.

1848 Trollope *Kellys & O'Kellys* III. xi. 269 The pick-up on the Derby is about four thousand. **1860** [see B]. **1871** L. H. Bagg *4 Years at Yale* 46 *Pick-up*,..a street-walker, of the less disreputable sort. **1890** W. A. Wallace *Only a Sister* 311 She..will be a grand pick-up for somebody when he goes. **1895** *Funk's Stand. Dict.* s.v. *Pick* vb., *Pick-up*, (Slang) a woman whose acquaintance is made on the street; especially, a street-walker. **1898** Wollocombe *Morn till Eve* ii. 15 Each driver was anxious to get the first chance of pick-ups on the road. **1927** Dunning & Abbott *Broadway* xvi. 158 'Dan McCorn out there?' enquired Porky. Steve nodded. 'He's talking to one of the pick-ups.' **1930** *San Antonio* (Texas) *Light* 31 Jan. 14/7 (Advt.), A real pickup for someone: 50 feet on Broadway... An exceptional site. **1930** J. B. Priestley *Angel Pavement* iv. 170 The big teashops.. were always crowded with girls and always offered a chance of a pick-up. **1935** G. Greene *England made Me* iv. 169 She might be meeting her lover and not a pick-up in Gothenburg. **1944** M. Laski *Love on Supertax* iv. 52 And what about you, Clarissa? Who's your latest pickup? **1957** 'M. Yourcenar' *Coup de Grâce* 66 She was fairly throbbing against me, and no previous feminine encounter, whether with a chance pick-up, or with an avowed prostitute, had prepared me for that sudden, terrifying sweetness. **1970** [see FILLE DE JOIE]. **1974** T. Allbeury *Snowball* ix. 48 The pick-up lacked grace and she made it clear she was bored. **1977** *New Yorker* 22 Aug. 66/3 Paolo..accedes with wearied eyelids to the blandishments of yet another of his pickups.

4. An informal game between sides picked on the spot.

1905 *Daily Chron.* 31 Aug. 3/1 If one accidentally pulled a ball in a school pick-up. **1917** A. Waugh *Loom of Youth* i. ii. 31 Even a desultory Pick-Up woke into excitement when the shrill, piping voice of a full-back came in with, 'The Bull's coming.'

5. *Printing.* 'Standing matter that comes into use and is counted as new matter'

6. = PICK-ME-UP.

1881 Hardy *Loadicean* III. v. iii. 36 Every sip you took of your pick-up as you sat there showed me something was wrong. **1921** D. Marquis *Old Soak* 10, I took mine straight for the most part, except when I needed some special kind of a pick-up in the morning. **1936** *N.Y. Herald-Tribune* 25 Aug. 8 Mix it with orange, lemon, grapefruit, pineapple juices or with ginger ale for a zesty pick-up. **1949** *Sun* (Baltimore) 9 Nov. 15/4 Investigation of methods to improve your morning pickup [*sc.* coffee].

7. [Cf. PICK *v.*[1] 21 q.] The capacity of an engine for recovering speed; acceleration.

1909 *Times* 27 Apr. 4/1 The flexibility and 'pick up' of the engine were such that the merest novice could handle the car with ease. **1923** *Daily Mail* 16 Mar. 10 (Advt.), An engine of great power, exceptional pick-up and flexibility, of notable smoothness and quietness. **1930** *Engineering* 12 Sept. 326/1 Apart from these factors, a smooth pick up, absence of vibration, and uniform torque are of great value. **1934** W. Nelson *Seaplane Design* vi. 53 The form of the underwater portion of the float must be such that water resistance does not hinder a quick pick-up to planing attitude. **1963** *Lebende Sprachen* VIII. 108/1 The car has good pick-up.

8. *Mus.* A series of introductory notes leading to the opening of a tune or portion of a tune.

1934 S. R. Nelson *All about Jazz* iii. 65 After a short passage of one or two bars, as a 'pick up', the ensemble will then take the last chorus and coda. **1949** L. Feather *Inside Be-Bop* 62 The last phrase starts with a three-beat pickup into an on-the-beat quarter note on the first beat of bar 7. **1956** O. Duke *Sideman* xii. 150 Bert played a piano intro and Bernie took pickups into *Laura* and then just sang it.

9. Tendency to pick up or absorb.

1938 *World Petroleum* Apr. 45/3 The flow through the main part of the furnace is in four parallel paths, each designed to have the same heat pick-up. **1955** Mondolfo & Zmeskal *Engineering Metall.* viii. 181 Pickup is the inclusion of foreign particles, especially scale, on the surface of the rolled product. **1955** *Jrnl. Soc. Dyers & Colourists* LXXI. 896/2 Although high pick-up is generally desirable, some fabrics need to be well squeezed. *Ibid.* 899/1 The padding temperature was 50°C. and the pick-up of the medium-weight rayon-staple fabric to be dyed was 100%. *a* **1977** *Harrison Mayer Ltd. Catal.* 67/1 The batts and props we supply are designed to have a low glaze pick up.

B. *attrib.* or as *adj.* **a.** = that picks up or is used in picking up, as in ***pick-up apparatus, circuit, water-trough***, etc.; **pick-up arm**, in a record-player or record deck, an arm carrying the stylus at one end and usu. counter-balanced at the other so as to be able to swing horizontally over the turntable and vertically; **pick-up baler**, a machine that picks up hay, etc., and bales it; **pick-up man** *colloq.*, (*a*) a thief, esp. of luggage; (*b*) *U.S.*, one who collects money wagered with bookmakers; (*c*) at a rodeo: see quot. 1961; **pick-up tube** *Television*, a vacuum tube that produces an electrical signal corresponding to an optical image formed in or on it; a camera tube. **b.** = picked up for the nonce, as in ***pick-up crew, dinner, game, team***.

a. **1889** G. Findlay *Eng. Railway* 106 The tenders attached to the engines have a 'pick up' apparatus, provided with a scoop, which can be lowered into the trough while the train is passing over it at full speed, and the trucks are filled with water in a few seconds. **1937** Pick-up arm [see overhang *sb.* d]. **1946** [see cartridge 1 e]. **1976** *Gramophone* July 237/2 Installing the QDC-1e cartridge in an SME 3009/II pickup arm with Thorens TD125/II turntable presented no problems. **1946** *Agricultural Progress* XXI. 1. 34 The increasing use of the one-man, twine tying, pick-up baler. **1951** *Engineering* 26 Jan. 92/1 Imports from the United Kingdom were to include 6,000 wheeled tractors..; imports from the United States..pick-up balers and combine harvesters. **1876** Preece & Sievewright *Telegraphy* 274 The faulty section of the through wire is thrown out until the fault is removed. In its place is substituted the section cd of the 'pick-up' circuit. Communication is thus preserved between a and e. **1894** *Westm. Gaz.* 29 Jan. 5/1 A pick-up goods train driver and fireman experienced a shock as if the locomotive had struck some hard substance lying on the rails. **1928** *Detective Fiction Weekly* 8 Sept. 564/2 (*heading*) International crooks I have known; No. 6—'Gentleman George', pick-up man. **1944** C. Himes *Black on Black* (1973) 244 The pickup man took his book one day, and he told Clara, 'We should have been on the other end.' **1961** *Times* 14 Nov. 12/7 From the moment that he leaves the chute, the cowboy must remain in the saddle for 10 seconds. Then, on a whistle signal, two mounted 'pick-up' men converge on the buckhorse and the cowboy dismounts as best he can. The 'pick-up' men gallop after the riderless horse. One of them grabs the rein or head collar, and forces him out of the arena through a gate into a collecting ring. This in itself is often a thrilling spectacle, as it is a point of honour for the 'pick-up' men to take out the bucking animal at full gallop. **1964** A. Wykes *Gambling* iv. 92 These agents are known as 'pickup men' or 'writers'; they collect and pay out on behalf of the bookmakers, who pay them 10 per cent of their net winnings. **1966** *Sunday Mail Mag.* (Brisbane) 9 Jan. 1/3 As soon as a gong had clanged the all-clear, pick-up men..tore after them on horses. **1933** *Jrnl. Inst. Electr. Engin.* LXXIII. 438/2 The development of the pick-up tube was pushed on, and the results..soon surpassed those of mechanical scanning. **1965** *Wireless World* Sept. 461/2 A small television camera which uses a solid-state image sensing panel in place of the conventional electron-beam pick-up tube. **1978** *Broadcast* 21 Aug. 12/3 An Ikegami CT2-2400 three-tube colour camera, with Saticon pick-up tubes, and synchronised to a broadcast sync pulse generator.

b. *a* **1859** *Maj. Downing in London* (Bartlett), They had only a pick-up dinner. **1860** Bartlett *Dict. Amer.* (ed. 3), A *pick-up dinner*, called also simply a *pick-up*, is a dinner made up of such fragments of cold meats as remain from former meals. **1909** *Q. Rev.* Oct. 618 The rest of the administration was arranged on the principle which governs 'pick-up' sides in a school-match. **1936** *Rhythm* Apr. 28/1 The ensemble is good, allowing for the difficulties surrounding the formation of a pick-up nine-piece band. **1938** D. Baker *Young Man with Horn* iv. iii. 220 He..made records with who knows how many pick-up bands. **1956** D. Flower tr. *Panassié & Gautier's Dict. Jazz* 197 *Pick-up band*, a band formed of musicians who regularly play elsewhere, but who come together for a special purpose, e.g. a recording date, a broadcast, a concert, a short nightclub engagement. **1959** 'F. Newton' *Jazz Scene* iv. 65 These were mostly small groups playing in odd night-clubs, or pick-up bands for recordings. **1962** *Sunday Times* (Colour Suppl.) 10 June 3 His strength is as the lead of pick-up groups of first-rate players. **1972** J. Mosedale *Football* iv. 47 He suffered a leg injury in a pick-up basketball game. **1977** *Gramophone* Apr. 1618/1 Lester headed a pick-up group containing trumpeter Billy Butterfield and pianist Johnny Guarnieri. **1977** *Tennis World* Sept. 17/3 A 'pick-up' doubles team is a scratch combination. **1977** *Transatlantic Rev.* lx. 120 Every Sunday morning he and his friends had a pick-up game over on Wentbridge Common.

c. **pick-up camper** (see quots.).

1973 *Country Life* 15 Nov. 1568/3 The 'pick-up' camper ..is the coachbuilt caravan in demountable form on a pick-up truck... On arrival on site, it is jacked clear of the vehicle. **1974** *Trailer Life* Nov. 92 Some trailerists, concluding it was easier to drive a truck than hitch and unhitch a trailer, had their trailers mounted on a truck bed. This was practical. But since the trailers had not been designed for their new purpose, it proved unattractive. And so the pickup camper came into being, followed by a more stable and spacious chassis-mount.

pickwick[1] ('pɪkwɪk). [See Pickwickian.] Trade name for a cheap kind of cigar.

1851 Mayhew *Lond. Labour* I. 441 The last time I sold Pickwicks and Cubers a penny apiece with lights for nothing, was at Greenwich Fair. **1865** *Sat. Rev.* 15 July 79/1 Smoking his pipe or his pickwick where he will. **1871** M. Collins *Mrq. & Merch.* I. ii. 92 By your Lordship's leave I'll smoke a pickwick.

'pickwick[2]. [See pick-.] A pointed instrument for pulling up the wick of an oil-lamp.

1864 in Webster.

Pickwickian (pɪk'wɪkɪən), *a.* and *sb.* [f. *Pickwick*, surname in Dickens's *Posthumous Papers of the Pickwick Club* (1837).]

A. *adj.* **1.** Of or pertaining to Mr. Pickwick, or the Pickwick Club; chiefly *humorous* in phr. ***in*** (*a*) ***Pickwickian sense, language***, in a technical, constructive, or conveniently idiosyncratic or esoteric sense; freq. in reference to language 'unparliamentary' or compromising in its natural sense.

1836 Dickens *Let.* 18 Feb. (1965) I. 132 Believe me (in Pickwickian haste) Faithfully Yours Charles Dickens. **1837** —— *Pickw.* i, The Chairman felt it his imperative duty to demand..whether he had used the expression..in a common sense. Mr. Blotton had no hesitation in saying that he had not—he had used the word in its Pickwickian sense. **1866** Felton *Anc. & Mod. Gr.* I. i. vi. 100 Out it comes.. with no mincing of phrase, and no Pickwickian or Congressional explanations afterwards. **1899** [see Prussian *a.* 2 b]. **1902** Chamberlain *Sp. B'ham* 17 Nov., In every case it had only a political, perhaps I might say a Pickwickian, meaning. **1953** 'N. Blake' *Dreadful Hollow* 147 Blount, whose Pickwickian exterior camouflaged a mind as ruthlessly purposeful as a guided missile. **1975** J. Symons *Three Pipe Problem* xvii. 173 Johnson's Pickwickian features were unusually solemn.

2. *Med.* Also **pickwickian**. [Named in allusion to the fat boy Joe in *Posthumous Papers of the Pickwick Club*.] Having or being a syndrome occurring in some obese adults (rarely in obese children) characterized by somnolence, respiratory abnormalities, and bulimia.

1956 C. S. Burwell et al. in *Amer. Jrnl. Med.* XXI. 812/1 Figure 1 represents Thomas Nast's drawing of Mr. Wardle's boy, Joe. This masterful description by Charles Dickens of a patient with marked obesity and somnolence is the first complete description of this syndrome that we have been able to find in the literature. For this reason we have called it the Pickwickian syndrome. **1965** *Progress Brain Res.* XVIII. 157 The short diurnal periods of light sleep (10–12 sec duration) in Pickwickian patients are characterized by apnea, increased cyanosis and muscular relaxation. **1977** *Lancet* 7 May 993/1 There are many other conditions, usually clinically obvious such as the pickwickian syndrome, in which there is both a respiratory and sleep abnormality.

B. *sb.* **1.** A member of the Pickwick Club.

1836 Dickens *Pickw.* (1837) i. 1 A proposal, emanating from the aforesaid Samuel Pickwick..and three other Pickwickians..for forming a new branch of United Pickwickians. *Ibid.* ii. 7 The intelligence of the Pickwickians being informers was spread among them. **1905** *Daily Graphic* 1 Feb. 9/4 The minds of many of the lovers of Dickens who were present at the Dickens Character Ball.. reverted to another ball-room—still in existence—where one of the most famous of the incidents in the 'Pickwick Papers' occurred—that of the Bull Inn at Rochester. And that ball, too, like this one, wherein not only the Pickwickians but many other characters which sprang from the brain of their creator were incarnated, was a charity ball. **1909** [see bathlessness].

2. *Med.* A person with the Pickwickian syndrome.

1965 *Progress Brain Res.* XVIII. 156 Most obese people.. present no diurnal sleeping syndrome, and so far as is known no nocturnal apnea, so that the Pickwickian should have some central disturbance of respiration and arousal. **1975** *Electroencephalogr. & Clin. Neurophysiol.* XXXIX. 579/2 The data obtained were compared with those observed in a group of 59 hypersomnolent patients aged between 19 and 83.., 18 of whom were Pickwickians.

Hence **Pickwicki'ana**, publications about the *Posthumous Papers of the Pickwick Club*; **Pick'wickianism**, a statement made in a Pickwickian sense; **Pick'wickianly** *adv.*, in a Pickwickian sense.

1887 *Chicago Advance* 14 Apr. 229/1 Dr. Arthur Little discussed almost convincingly, albeit somewhat pickwickianly, 'the Advantages of Presbyterianism'. **1894** *Ibid.* 28 June, This author does not mean his assertions to be taken as facts, but only as bits of critical pickwickianisms. **1899** J. Grego (*title*) Pictorial Pickwickiana.

picky ('pɪkɪ), *a.* [f. pick *v.*[1] + -y[1].] Fastidious, finicky, 'choosey' (see also quot. 1867). Hence **'pickiness**.

1867 W. Dickinson *Gloss. Words & Phrases Cumberland* (Suppl.) 28 *Picky*, of weak appetite. **1900** Dickinson & Prevost *Gloss. Dial. Cumberland* (rev. ed.) 243/1 T'barn's nut weel, it's too picky by far. **1917** in *Dialect Notes* (1918) V. 12 Not an ugly picky thing in all she has to say. **1932** *New Yorker* 11 June 50/2 People who are picky about their food on shipboard..will be glad to know that the Clyde-Mallory Lines now allow you to buy a ticket for transportation only and order meals à la carte. **1957** 'R. Traver' *Anat. Murder* (1958) i. xv. 101, I don't want to seem picky, Lieutenant, but I happen to consider your particular doctor professionally on a par with Amos Crocker. **1966** *New Statesman* 29 Apr. 618/2 A hesitant, picky account of Mississippi's economic and electoral..history. **1971** D. Bagley *Freedom Trap* iii. 62 This is a very exclusive mob; very picky and choosy. **1974** D. Scannell *Mother knew Best* iii. 27, I was always 'gastric' and Mother would get different meals for me as she thought me a 'picky' eater and needed tempting. **1977** *Sci. Amer.* Apr. 145/1 He was meticulous, even picky, about expense accounts. **1977** *Verbatim* May 6/1 And if you are willing to discard mere pickiness, you know what *taken for granite* and *scuenting* mean, too.

picky, Sc. and north. dial. var. pitchy.

picky, var. piccy.

pickydeuant, variant of picke-devant *Obs.*

pickydilly, picle: see piccadill, pightle.

picloram ('pɪklɔræm). [f. pic(oline + ch)lor-[2] + am(ine.] A white crystalline compound, 4-amino-3,5,6-trichloropicolinic acid, $C_6H_3Cl_3N_2O_2$, which is used as a herbicide and defoliant against deep-rooted weeds and woody plants.

1965 *Proc. Northeast. Weed Control Conf.* XIX. 140 Effective control [of mugwort]..was obtained with.. 4-amino-3,5,6-trichloropicolinic acid (picloram). **1965** *B.S.I. News* May 24 The following new names have been approved by the Pest Control Products Industry Standards Committee for eventual inclusion in B.S. 1831... picloram. .. 4-amino-3,5,6-trichloropicolinic acid. **1969** *Sci. Jrnl.* Feb. 10/1 According to one estimate, no less than 2250 tonnes of picloram have been dumped on South Vietnam in 1968. **1970** *Guardian Weekly* 21 Feb. 6/4 The recently introduced chemical, picloram, is one of the longest-lived pesticides. **1974** *Sci. Amer.* Apr. 49/2 The herbicides sprayed over Vietnam were chemicals that are routinely applied for weed control: 2,4-D and 2,4,5-T, picloram and cacodylic acid.

picnic ('pɪknɪk), *sb.* Also 8–9 **pique-nique, pick-nick, pic-nic, pic nic.** [Occurs (in reference to foreign countries) from 1748, but app. not before *c* 1800 as an English institution; ad. F. *pique-nique*, stated by Ménage *Dict. Etymol.* (1692) to be of recent introduction; in *Dict. Acad.* 1740. In use in Germany *a* 1748, in Sweden *a* 1788 (Widegren's *Dict.*). See Note below.]

1. a. Originally, A fashionable social entertainment in which each person present contributed a share of the provisions; now, A pleasure party including an excursion to some spot in the country where all partake of a repast out of doors: the participants may bring with them individually the viands and means of entertainment, or the whole may be provided by some one who 'gives the picnic'.

The intermediate stage is seen in quot. 1868. The essential feature was formerly the individual contribution; now, it is the *al fresco* form of the repast.

1748 Chesterf. *Let. to Son* (in Germany, app. Berlin) 29 Oct., I like the description of your *Pic-nic*; where, I take it for granted, that your cards are only to break the formality of a circle. **1763** Lady M. Coke *Lett., to Lady Strafford* 23 Sept. (1889) I. 7, I was last night at a Subscription Ball which is called here [Hanover] Picquenic. *c* **1800** Miss Knight *Autobiog.* I. 45 We stayed here [at Toulon] till the 17th [Feb. 1777] and on the previous day went to a 'pique-nique' at a little country house not far from the town. **1802** *Ann. Reg.* 169 The rich have their sports, their balls, their parties of pleasure, and their *pic nics*. **1806–7** J. Beresford *Miseries Hum. Life* (1826) xv. Introd., She's so full of Fête and Pic-nic and Opera. **1826** [J. R. Best] *Four Yrs. France* 289 Parties..establish a pic-nic, and pass the day together. **1826** Disraeli *Viv. Grey* iii. iv, Nature had intended the spot for pic-nics. **1866** Miss Braddon *Lady's Mile* iii. 35 They held impromptu pic-nics on breezy heights above the level of the sea. **1868** Latham *Johnson's Dict.*, *Picnic*, open air party, in which a meal, to which each guest contributes a portion of the viands, is the essential characteristic. **1873** *Hobgoblins* 39 After the picnic had been eaten, a dance was improvised. **1886** Mrs. Ewing *Mary's Meadow* 21 We had a most delightful picnic there.

†**b.** ***by picnic***: by contributions from each member. *Obs.* [Cf. F. 'l'ancienne tournure adverbiale *à pique-nique*' (Genin in Scheler).]

1832 *Examiner* 324/2 A sort of *pasticcio*, made up apparently by picnic from the portmanteaus of the performers.

c. *transf.* and *fig.* Now usu. something straightforward or agreeable; a lively time; a treat; ***no picnic, not a picnic***, not an easy task; a formidable undertaking.

1818 Keats *Let.* Dec. (1958) II. 13 Perhaps as you were fond of giving me sketches of character you may like a little pic nic of scandal. **1825** H. Wilson *Mem.* II. 248, I sate down to consider the plan of a book, in the style of the Spectator, a kind of pic nic, where every wiseacre might contribute his mite of knowledge. **1886** *Lantern* (New Orleans) 27 Oct. 6/1 Hanley sparred with a smile on his face much as to say, 'What a picnic I've got with this kid.' **1887** L. J. BEAUCHAMP in *Voice* (N.Y.) 28 Apr. 3/2 For that length of time the dogs had a picnic. **1888** KIPLING *Wee Willie Winkie* 84 'Taint no bloomin' picnic in those parts I can tell you. **1890** —— *Life's Handicap* (1891) 125 A knot of furious brother officers demanding the court-martial of Tommy Dodd for 'spoiling the picnic'. **1900** *Daily News* 20 Oct. 5/7 We go about and keep the Boers on the run..I think everything points to the end of this picnic. **1901** W. CHURCHILL *Crisis* II. iii. 136 This isn't any picnic. **1909** 'O. HENRY' *Roads of Destiny* xxii. 315 It was a picnic for the census takers. They just counted the marshal's posse that it took to subdue us, and there was your population. **1914** A. BENNETT *Price of Love* xii. 248 'But doesn't it *hurt*?' 'Depends what you call hurt. It ain't a picnic.' **1916** [see EMBUSQUÉ]. **1919** *Mr. Punch's Hist. Gt. War* 114 It is not a picnic for the men in our front line. **1926** GALSWORTHY *Escape* II. iv. 50 If you want to get thin. It's a top-hole cure for adipose. An escape's no picnic. **1947** *Richmond* (Virginia) *Times-Dispatch* 4 May 26/5 The war memorial.. was rejected as 'morbid': those who object to the ban on this work argue that the war was no picnic. **1961** B. FERGUSSON *Watery Maze* xvi. 394 It was going to be no picnic co-ordinating land, sea and air forces from so many different points of departure at so many different speeds. **1965** *Listener* 3 June 835/3 It can have been no picnic to be a poet in the age of Eliot. **1971** S. HILL *Strange Meeting* i. 10 Think yourself lucky you got off a bit early. It's no picnic now. **1974** J. STUBBS *Painted Face* xxiii. 286 What do *you* know of prison? This here's a picnic compared to what it will be.

d. *Austral.* and *N.Z.* Used ironically of an awkward situation or a difficult or unpleasant experience.

1896 in Morris *Austral Eng.* (1898) 351/1 If a man's horse is awkward and gives him trouble, he will say, 'I had a picnic with that horse,' and so of any misadventure or disagreeable experience in travelling. **1939** N. MARSH *Overture to Death* xiii. 125 I'm sorry to have neglected you like this; but we're in for a picnic, and no mistake, with this case up at Moorton Park. **1941** BAKER *Dict. Austral. Slang* 54 *Picnic*, any unpleasant experience, a disagreeable and complicated task. **1945** *Coast to Coast 1944* 125 What a mess, what a picnic! **1955** D. NILAND *Shiralee* 38 All I know is I'm going to have one helluva picnic if she doesn't find it. **1959** BAKER *Drum* (1960) 68 We call a wild confusion or a particularly difficult task a picnic.

e. *U.S.* = *picnic ham* below.

1910 L. D. HALL *Market Classes Meat* 281 *Picnics* or *calas* (formerly termed California hams) are cut 2-½ ribs wide... They..are sold almost entirely as sweet-pickled, smoked and boiled meats. **1949** *New Harmony* (Indiana) *Times* 5 Aug. 6/2 (Advt.), Smoked Picnics, 3 to 5 lb. average lb. 45c. **1974** *Columbia* (S. Carolina) *Record* 24 Apr. 21-B (Advt.), Sliced picnic 1.89. **1976** *Washington Post* 19 Apr. A19/1 (Advt.), Smoked picnics.

†**2.** A member of the Picnic Society: see 3. *Obs.*

1802 *Spirit Pub. Jrnls.* VI. 197 One famous *Pic-Nic* indeed..came forward and said, they were 'a harmless and inoffensive society of persons of fashion'. *Ibid.* 198 Nor was the public amazement lessened, when they were informed, that Pic-Nics were men who acted plays and wrote plays for their own amusement. **1830** H. ANGELO *Remin.* II. 5 General A...was the most prominent pic-nic of our dramatis personae. **1878** W. H. HUSK in Grove *Dict. Mus.* I. 82 A fashionable association termed the Pic-nics, who had burlettas, vaudevilles and ballets on a small scale performed there.

3. *attrib.* Pertaining to, or of the nature or character of, a picnic; in earlier use with reference to contributions made by each member of a party or company, as at a 'picnic' in the original sense.

† ***Picnic Society***, name of a society of people of fashion in London about the beginning of the 19th c., for social entertainments, private theatricals, etc., to which each member contibuted his share.

1802 Pic-nic Society [see PICNICKIAN]. **1802** *Spirit Pub. Jrnls.* VI. 200 Fat capons, prize-beef, ham and chickens,.. Ye Gods, what pretty Pic-Nic pickings! **1807** *Director* I. 267 A pic-nic conversation, where each contributes in his turn from his stores of reading and observation. **1815** MME. D'ARBLAY *Diary* (1876) IV. lxiv. 305 We boarded and lodged by pic-nic contract with the Princesse. **1818** BENTHAM *Ch. Eng., Catech. Exam.* 81 [The history] of the pic-nic formation of this Creed by its putative fathers the Apostles, may be found in their proper places. **1828** *Sporting Mag.* XXII. 225 A pack of hounds..got together.. in a sort of pick-nick manner by a few gentlemen in London. **1851** W. W. COLLINS *Rambles beyond Railw.* ix. (1852) 183 The girls and young men of the pic-nic party are dancing merrily.

b. ***picnic basket, hamper, pie, shelter, site, spot, stove, tea***; **picnic area**, a piece of ground designated as suitable for picnics; **picnic chair**, a (usu. collapsible) chair for use on a picnic; **picnic ground** = *picnic area*; **picnic ham** *U.S.*, a small cut of shoulder bacon in the form of a ham; **picnic lunch**, a packed lunch, *spec.* one provided by a hotel in place of a regular meal; **picnic meal**, a meal eaten as a picnic; also, a quick meal eaten indoors; **picnic plate**, a plastic or paper plate suitable for use on a picnic; **picnic race meeting, races** *Austral.* and *N.Z.*, a race meeting held in a country area, accompanied by other social events; **picnic supper** [cf. F. *souper à pique-nique* (Genin in Scheler)] (see quot. 1802); **picnic table**, a table suitable for use on a picnic; a small hinged table in a car.

1959 Picnic area [see PIPED *ppl. a.*[1] 3 c]. **1968** *Guardian* 5 July 3/2 The NCB will restore the landscape and provide access roads, car parks, picnic areas, a hard standing and slipway for boats. **1968** [see *camp-ground* s.v. CAMP *sb.*[2] VII. b]. **1973** V. CANNING *Flight of Grey Goose* i. 9 A large picnic area on the edge of a wood. **1885** *List of Subscribers, Classified* (United Telephone Co.) (ed. 6) 125 (*heading*) Luncheon and picnic basket manufacturers. **1931** *N. & Q.* 11 Apr. 258/2 The car was packed with bathing things, camp-stools and picnic basket. **1955** A. HUXLEY *Let.* 4 Apr. (1969) 739 Yes, by all means let us take a picnic basket so that we can be independent of restaurants. **1972** D. E. WESTLAKE *Cops & Robbers* (1973) xvi. 239 Macy's has a wicker picnic basket. It costs around eighteen bucks, with the tax. **1975** 'A. HALL' *Mandarin Cypher* xvii. 233 One narrow bunk..cheap cardtable and picnic chair. **1977** M. JANCATH *Seatag* I. vii. 41 Emrich was surprised to see a wooden picnic table and chairs. **1926** *Daily Colonist* (Victoria, B.C.) 2 July 5/3 The streets were almost deserted save for those hastening toward some of these attractive picnic grounds. **1947** E. S. GARDNER in *Amer. Mag.* Aug. 148/3 You can see the camp and the picnic grounds from here. **1969** H. MACINNES *Salzburg Connection* ii. 33 He began walking down towards the picnic ground. **1974** *Country Life* 3 Oct. 930/3 A 14-acre picnic ground has been cleared. **1897** *Sears, Roebuck Catal.* 13/3 Meats... Picnic Hams. **1944** *Chicago Daily News* 13 July 21/2 A picnic ham may be boned, rolled and tied before roasting to make carving easier. **1973** *Black Panther* 25 Aug. 3/3 Picnic ham at 97 cents or salt pork at 99 cents a pound? **1862** W. COLLINS *No Name* I. 332 We have a picnic hamper with us ..and away we drive on a pleasure trip. **1896** E. TURNER *Little Larrikin* xviii. 208 Several picnic hampers and a case of champagne. **1966** B. COOPER *Drown him Deep* vi. 52 He went to the back of the car, and began to pull out the picnic hamper. **1972** R. HILL *Fairly Dangerous Thing* II. vi. 179 We ..took our picnic-hamper with us into a wood. **1917** D. CANFIELD *Understood Betsy* (1922) x. 189 They were to meet the Wendells in the shadow of Industrial Hall and eat their picnic lunch together. **1933** E. O'NEILL *Ah, Wilderness!* (1934) I. 18 We're going to have a picnic lunch on Strawberry Island. **1971** J. TYNDALL *Death in Lebanon* vii. 105 Let's ask the hotel for a picnic lunch and get off as soon as we can. **1972** *Guardian* 22 July 7/3, I continued along the D94..but soon stopped for a picnic lunch. **1876** GEO. ELIOT *Dan. Der.* I. II. xiv. 264 The coachful of servants with provisions had to prepare the picnic meal. **1889** HENTY *With Lee in Virginia* (1890) 129 The whole party sat down to a picnic meal on the ground. **1911** A. BENNETT *Hilda Lessways* II. iii. 161 They had been very busy in Hilda's house..and had eaten only a picnic meal. **1929** S. ERTZ *Galaxy* xiii. 294 They had a picnic meal of bread and cheese and fruit and California wine. **1972** 'G. NORTH' *Sgt. Cluff rings True* x. 78 Discards from picnic meals defaced verges. **1849** H. C. ROBINSON *Diary* 22 June (1967) 255 A picnic party had been formed..to take tea on the top of the hill. **1977** R. BARNARD *Blood Brotherhood* vi. 61 The thought of some fearsome affray..came upon him with all the welcomeness of a thunderclap on a picnic party. **1865** TROLLOPE *Can you forgive Her?* II. xxx. 234 Cold chickens, picnic-pies, and the flying of champagne corks. **1911** G. STRATTON-PORTER *Harvester* xvi. 371 Big, fancy brick and frame things..gay as frosted picnic pie. **1926–7** *Army & Navy Stores Catal.* 378B/4 Picnic plates. **1933** E. A. ROBERTSON *Ordinary Families* i. 16 The boats were only old cardboard picnic plates. **1896** N. GOULD *Town & Bush* xiv. 225 The owners of the horses running at picnic races are generally men of means. **1911** C. E. W. BEAN '*Dreadnought' of Darling* xxxiv. 294 If a town has picnic races or a polo week, it is 'alive'. **1928** 'BRENT OF BIN BIN' *Up Country* xiii. 202 Here took place the first picnic races of the district, which affairs, so informally started among neighbours, in later days command special trains and viceregality. **1955** P. WHITE *Tree of Man* (1956) II. ix. 132 Always in demand,..and above all at picnic races. **1964** D. HORNE *Lucky Country* 52 One of the most rigid institutional manifestations of this difference [between landed family and town] appears at the annual picnic races. **1972** *Sunday Tel.* (Sydney) 15 Oct. 132 Everyone, but everyone, is getting ready for the Bong Bong Picnic Races next Saturday. **1978** O. WHITE *Silent Reach* xvi. 160 He's a pansy and goes for the public school jackeroos at the picnic races. *Ibid.* xxi. 219 The Fitzroy Crossing picnic race meeting. **1943** J. S. HUXLEY *TVA* ix. 61 Picnic shelters are included in the parks and campgrounds. **1959** *Canad. Geogr. Jrnl.* Feb. 55/1 Picnic shelters have been constructed for the convenience of picnickers during inclement weather and thirty-two of these are now in use. **1976** *Billings* (Montana) *Gaz.* 28 June 1-B/1 The state Board of Examiners this week approved expenditure of $398,565 for building of picnic shelters and other recreation facilities, landscaping and construction of restrooms at the park. **1971** P. GRESSWELL *Environment* 187 Picnic sites need to be considered in relation to planning policy. **1972** *Country Life* 7 Dec. 1581/1 Somerset County Council has decided to spend some money this year on..picnic sites. **1959** I. & P. OPIE *Lore & Lang. Schoolch.* xii. 253 On Easter Day we usually pack a picnic lunch, including a hard boiled egg. When we reach the picnic spot we sit down and play at games. **1977** B. PYM *Quartet in Autumn* v. 43 When they arrived at the picnic spot, Marjorie produced two folding canvas chairs from the boot of the car. **1963** *Which?* Mar. 89/2 A solid fuel for picnic stoves. **1974** *Janet Frazer Catal.* Spring/Summer 458/2 Camping Gaz International picnic stove... Boils water quickly. **1802** *Times* 16 Mar., A Pic-Nic Supper consists of a variety of dishes. The Subscribers to the entertainment have a bill of fare presented to them, with a number against each dish. The lot which he draws obliges him to furnish the dish marked against it, which he either takes with him in his carriage, or sends by a servant. **1802** *Ann. Reg.* 376 This season has been marked by a new species of entertainment, common to the fashionable world, called a Pic Nic supper. Of the derivation of the word, or who was the inventor, we profess ourselves ignorant, but the nature of it..is [etc.]. **1926–7** *Army & Navy Stores Catal.* 225/1 The 'picnic' table... Folds perfectly flat. **1963** 'H. CALVIN' *It's Different Abroad* ii. 16 Between them was a folding picnic-table. **1970** *Times* 16 Apr. 3/3 (Advt.), We don't forget power assisted steering, adjustable steering column, reclining seats and picnic tables. **1976** *Norwich Mercury* 17 Dec. 9/6 Two picnic tables with bench seats were officially handed over. **1976** N. THORNBURG *Cutter & Bone* ix. 219 It was a small park, not much more than a few acres of grass fringed with eucalyptus trees and three or four picnic tables. **1900** C. M. YONGE *Mod. Broods* xvi. 153 My mother wants you all to come up to picnic tea to see the foxgloves in the dell. **1907** R. FRY *Let.* 24 Sept. (1972) I. 291 This afternoon we are to drive out to a picnic tea at Blackwell. **1932** 'E. M. DELAFIELD' *Thank Heaven Fasting* III. ii. 262 Monica and the vistor set out..taking with them a picnic tea. **1955** A. SINCLAIR in *Granta* 26 Nov. 10/1 We'll say we want a picnic tea.

†**4.** as *adv.* In the way of a picnic; by contributions from each person. *Obs.*

1803 J. DAVIS *Trav. U.S.* 176 A sum that may enable him to ask a friend to dine with him pic nic.

[*Note.* The chronology of the word in French and English, with the fact that our earliest instances refer to the Continent, and are sometimes in the French form *pique-nique*, show that the word came from French (although some French scholars, in ignorance of these facts, have, in view of the obscurity of its derivation, conjectured that the French word was from Eng.). Hatzfeld-Darmesteter merely say 'Origin unknown: the Eng. *picnic* appears to be borrowed from French'. Scheler mentions several conjectures, amongst others that of Boniface (18..) 'repas où chacun *pique* au plat pour sa *nique* (*nique* taken in the sense of "small coin")'. Others think it merely a riming combination formed on one of its elements. In Foote's *Nabob* (1772) Act I, one of the characters uses *nick-nack* for *pick-nick*; intended perhaps to show that *pick-nick* was still a little-known word, liable to be confounded or associated with better known native words or combinations, such as *knick-knack*. But cf. PICNICKERY quot. 1803, 'pick-nickery and nick-nackery'.]

picnic ('pɪknɪk), *v.* Inflexions **picnicked, picnicking.** [f. prec.

(As to the spelling of the inflexions, and of the following words, see remarks under C and K.)]

1. *intr.* To hold, or take part in, a picnic.

1842 TENNYSON *Audley Court* 2 Let us picnic there At Audley Court. **1861** J. H. BENNET *Winter Medit.* I. viii. (1875) 212 Lay..musing on the beach, or pic-niced among the ruins of the Castle. **1861** THORNBURY *Turner* (1862) I. 371 He has drawn people riding and pic-nicking. **1871** L. STEPHEN *Playgr. Eur.* iv. III. 238 We picnicked on the grass outside the monastery.

†**2.** *trans.* To furnish (provisions) by contributions from each person, as at a picnic. *Obs.*

1821 MOORE *Mem.* (1853) III. 268 The Villamils and I picnicked our provender.

3. To entertain (a person) with picnics.

1884 H. COLLINGWOOD *Under Meteor Flag* 77 We were balled, fêted, picnicked, and generally made much of.

Hence '**picnicking** *vbl. sb.* and *ppl. a.*

1842 MRS. F. TROLLOPE *Visit Italy* I. xix. 312 The description of one of the pic-nicing days. **1864** *Daily Tel.* 6 Apr., Yet can green, picnicking Simla ever wrest the crown away from Calcutta? **1883** H. P. SPOFFORD in *Harper's Mag.* Mar. 578/2 Mr. Claxton suggested their picnicking. **1888** W. R. CARLES *Life in Corea* iii. 25 The hill is used as a lounge and picnicking place.

picnicker ('pɪknɪkə(r)). [f. PICNIC *v.* + -ER[1].] One who picnics, or takes part in a picnic.

1857 DE QUINCEY *R. Bentley* Wks. VII. 171 *note*, He will not be able without a glass to see the gay party of pic-nickers. **1865** MISS BRADDON *Sir Jasper* xxiv, The kind of day that all picnickers would demand of Providence. **1888** *Pall Mall G.* 19 July 7/1 The samovar (the tea-urn) enabled the picnicers to turn out a delicious cup of tea.

pic'nickery. [f. PICNIC *sb.* + -ERY.] †**a.** See quot. 1803: apparently alluding to the dramatic performances of the original Picnic Society: cf. quots. in PICNIC *sb.* 2. †**b.** A collection of things contributed from various sources, like the provisions at a picnic. **c.** *pl.* The requisites for a picnic.

1803 *Times* 4 Jan., We are induced to contend against any thing so contemptible as the pick-nickery and nick-nackery —the pert affectation, and subaltern vanity of rehearsing to an audience that cannot understand, in a language one cannot pronounce. **1822** MRS. E. NATHAN *Langreath* III. 66 The pick-nickery of sea stock brought on board by the different passengers. **1830** H. ANGELO *Remin.* I. 290 Gillray let fly..with his double-barrelled gun, charged at pic-nickery, with his crayon and etching tool. **1852** *Aquatic Notes Camb.* 4, 2 kettles, 9 plates, 4 dishes, a charcoal bag, with a host of other picniceries.

†**Pic'nickian.** *Obs.* [f. as prec. + -IAN.] †**a.** A member of the Picnic Society (see PICNIC 3). **b.** One who takes part in a picnic.

1802 CUTSPEAR *Dram. Rights*, etc. 45, I am not of the Pic-nic Society, therefore not a *Pic-nickian.* I only wish to prove that, if the Pic-nickians choose to have a Pic-nic supper, they have an undoubted right to do so. **1853** READE *Chr. Johnstone* 166 The other discontented Pic-nician was Christie Johnstone.

picnickish ('pɪknɪkɪʃ), *a. rare.* [f. PICNIC *sb.* + -ISH[1].] Suitable for or suggestive of picnics.

1852 'G. GREENWOOD' *Haps & Mishaps Tour in Europe* (1854) v. 101 It is a pretty, picturesque, and picnickish place.

picnicky ('pɪknɪkɪ), *a. colloq.* [f. as PICNIC *sb.* + -Y.] Belonging to or characteristic of a picnic.

1870 *Standard* 26 Nov., Occupied in a pleasant pic-nicky way in getting ready their breakfast before the start. **1885** *Fortnt. in Waggonette* 2 To do everything in such an entirely rustic and picnicky fashion.

picnid, picnometer, bad spellings of PYCN-.

‖**pico** ('piko). *Obs.* [Sp. *pico*: see PEAK *sb.*[2] II.] A peak, the pointed top of a mountain; a conical mountain. (Originally applied to the Peak of Teneriffe: see PEAK *sb.*[2] 5, PIC[1], PIKE *sb.*[3])

1665 SIR T. HERBERT *Trav.* (1677) 4 This high Pico rises from the middle part of the Isle [Teneriffe]. *a* **1691** BOYLE *Hist. Air* (1692) 171 An exact relation of the Pico Teneriff. *Ibid.*, These calcined rocks lie for three or four miles almost round the bottom of the Pico. **1692** BENTLEY *Boyle Lect.* viii. 290 As high as the Pico of Teneriff. **1742** *De Foe's Tour Gt. Brit.* (ed. 3) III. 206 Yet there is one of them [Cheviot Hills] a great deal higher than the rest, which, at a Distance, looks like the Pico-Teneriffe, in the Canaries.

pico, var. PIKAU *sb.*

pico- ('pi:kəʊ, 'paɪkəʊ), *prefix.* [f. Sp. *pico* beak, peak, (in phrases) little bit.] Prefixed to the names of units to form the names of units 10^{12} times smaller, i.e. one million-millionth part of them (symbol p), as ***picoamp*** (so ***picoammeter***), ***-curie***, ***-farad***, ***-gramme***, ***-litre***, ***-volt*** (so ***-voltmeter***), ***-watt***. Also PICOSECOND.

1915 W. H. ECCLES *Wireless Telegr.* 18 Symbols for multiples and sub-multiples... 10^{-12}... Pico-... p or $\mu\mu$. **1947** *Compt. Rend. de la 14me Conf.* (Union Internat. de Chimie) 115 The following prefixes to abbreviations for the names of units should be used to indicate the specified multiples or sub-multiples of these units:.. p pico- $10^{-12}\times$. **1952** *Wireless World* Jan. 19/2 The suggestions to adopt new prefixes, 'nano' and 'pico' for small capacitance values, would permit any value to be expressed as a whole number. **1952** [see NANO-]. **1975** *Physics Bull.* Feb. 67/1 A range of stabilized high voltage power supplies and picoammeters manufactured by V G Electronics Ltd will also be shown. *Ibid.* June 249/2 (Advt.), Sensitivities down to 1 microvolt, 10 picoamps, and 1 milliohm are founded on Keithley's lifetime of expertise in designing and building low-level instrumentation. **1963** *Times* 15 Feb. 8/1 The level of 150 picocuries over a three-month period is considered by scientists to be the tolerable limit for humanity. **1976** *Globe & Mail* (Toronto) 16 Jan. 1/3 The readings in 30 of these, however, are less than three picocuries of radon for each litre of air, the exposure level that Government standards allow the public. For workers in atomic plants, the standard is 30 picocuries a litre. **1926** *Gloss. Terms Electr. Engin.* (Brit. Engin. Stand. Assoc.) 26 *Picofarad*, a unit of electrostatic capacity equal to 10^{-12} farad. Symbol: $\mu\mu$F. **1945** *Electronic Engin.* XVII. 473/2 At a working frequency of ½ Mc/s., a difference of about 1/10 picofarad can be readily observed. **1976** *Gramophone* Jan. 1283/1 A slight platform rise of up to about 2 dB from 12 kHz upwards was measured which I take to be a result of the Dual's low capacitance cable, whereas Shure recommend 400 to 500 pico-farads per channel. **1951** Picogram [see *nanogramme* s.v. NANO-]. **1967** *Oceanogr. & Marine Biol.* V. 271 If carbon content is compared with the surface area of [plankton] cells, the range of variation is smaller, 0·11 to 0·66 picograms/μ^2. **1975** WILLIAMS & WILSON *Biologist's Guide to Princ. & Techniques Pract. Biochem.* iii. 72 It has very high sensitivity and can detect as little as one picogramme of these compounds. **1973** *Sci. Amer.* Sept. 160/2 (Advt.), For electron probe sampling, hundreds of picoliter fluid droplets are positioned automatically under an electron beam. **1971** *Physics Bull.* Nov. 678/2 The picovolt measuring system permits the detection of small voltages from sources at low temperatures which would be overwhelmed by thermal voltages in the leads to a room temperature instrument. *Ibid.* 678/3 The picovoltmeter will be useful for the measurement of low temperatures by means of thermocouples. **1967** D. H. HAMSHER *Communication Syst. Engin. Handbk.* xvi. 10 The noise power measurement without any weighting of the frequency response of the instrument is expressed usually in picowatts (10^{-12} watt = pw). **1977** *Sci. Amer.* Feb. 62/2 At the earth station the 30-metre dish antenna collects a scant three picowatts of energy and feeds it into a low-noise receiver.

picoid ('paɪkɔɪd), *a. Ornith.* [f. L. *pīcus* woodpecker + -OID.] Resembling the *Picidæ* or Woodpeckers in form.

picoideous (paɪ'kɔɪdɪəs), *a. Ornith.* [f. mod. L. *picoide-us* PICOID + -OUS.] Of, pertaining to, or characteristic of the *Picoideæ*, a suborder of birds including Woodpeckers, Honey-guides, Barbets, Toucans, Jacamars, and Puff-birds. So **pi'coidean**, a member of the *Picoideæ*.

picoise, obs. f. PICKAXE.

picol: see PICUL.

picoline ('pɪkəlaɪn). *Chem.* [mod. f. L. *pix, picem* pitch + *ol-eum* oil + -INE[5]: so in mod.F.] A colourless liquid compound (C_6H_7N) obtained from bone-oil, coal-naphtha, tar, peat, etc., having an intensely powerful smell.

1853 *Pharmac. Jrnl.* XIII. 134 The sulphates of.. picoline, petinine are.. insoluble. **1857** MILLER *Elem. Chem.* III. 260. **1865** MANSFIELD *Salts* 263 The double series of isomeric compounds, of which Aniline and Picoline are respectively members: both of these bodies have the composition $C_{12}H_7N$.

picolinic (pɪkə'li:nɪk), *a. Chem.* [f. PICOLIN(E + -IC.] ***picolinic acid***: a colourless crystalline acid, pyridine-2-carboxylic acid, $C_5H_4N(COOH)$, which is derived from picoline by oxidation of the methyl group.

1880 *Jrnl. Chem. Soc.* XXXVIII. 268 Picolinic Acid, $C_6H_5NO_2$.. Crystallises in prismatic needles.. which are easily soluble in alcohol and in water. **1946** A. A. MORTON *Chem. Heterocyclic Compounds* viii. 213 Picolinic acid.. is obtained in 50 to 51 percent yield from α-picolin. **1968** *Listener* 21 Mar. 376/1 A second class of compounds being used [as defoliants, etc.] are derivatives of picolinic acid.

Picon (pikɔ̃). [Fr., the name of *Picon* et Cie, the manufacturers.] In full, ***Amer Picon*** [Fr. *amer* bitter]. The proprietary name of an aperitif of bitters (see quot. 1967).

1914 [see PERNOD]. [**1917** *Bull. Offic. Marques de Fabrique* 25 Jan. 54/1 *Amer Picon.* M.p. désigner un amer, déposée.. par MM. Picon et Cie.] **1934** H. MILLER *Tropic of Cancer* (1961) 21 Paris.. shutters going up with a bang.. *Amer Picon* in huge scarlet letters. **1936** BENTLEY & ALLEN *Trent's Own Case* xi. 133 Sipping his Amer Picon—that formidable brown drink of which.. a single undiluted drop will burn a neat round hole in a shirt cuff. **1939** L. MACNEICE *Autumn Jrnl.* 22 Something out of the usual, a Pimm's Number One, a Picon. **1950** D. AMES *Corpse Diplomatique* i. 11 He ordered a *Pernod* and an *Amer Picon.* **1962** N. FREELING *Love in Amsterdam* I. 48 Herman had raw *schinken* with kümmel in it, and a bottle of Picon. **1967** A. LICHINE *Encycl. Wines* 71/1 *Amer Picon*, a proprietary French bitters used as an aperitif, made with a wine and brandy base to which has been added quinine (to impart a bitter taste), orange peel, and innumerable herbs. It is drunk with ice, diluted with water, and usually sweetened with grenadine or cassis.

picong ('pi:kɒŋ). [ad. Sp. *picón.*] In Trinidad and some other parts of the Caribbean: verbal insult or ridicule; facetious raillery; taunting; esp. in phr. ***to give picong***. Cf. *to play (the) dozens* s.v. PLAY *v.* 16e.

1956 *Caribbean Q.* IV. III–IV. 198 The Congos.. carried on 'picong' or 'fatigues', elaborate ribbing of each other and the bystanders. **1960** *Tamarack Rev.* XIV. 19 Then again, the boys might start to give Frederick picong, when Bat beg them to ease up. **1974** *Sunday Guardian* (Port-of-Spain) 28 July 8/2 They [*sc.* students] were screaming and laughing and giving picong to all kinds of rhythms, on the edge of Grand Etang. *Ibid.* 12/4 The humour here is not at all picong, but more humour for its own sake.

pico-passerine (paɪkəʊ'pæsəraɪn), *a. Ornith.* [f. L. *pīc-us* woodpecker + *passer* sparrow + -INE[1].] Of or belonging to the *Pici-* or *Pico-passeres*, an order proposed by Seebohm to include Picine and Passerine birds.

1890 *Ibis* Jan. 33 Each of these six characters appears in every Pico-Passerine bird.. but the combination of the six.. never.. outside the limits of the Pico-Passeres.

picornavirus (pɪ'kɔ:nə,vaɪərəs). *Microbiol.* [f. PICO-, taken to mean 'very small' + RNA + VIRUS.] Any of a group of very small animal viruses consisting of single-stranded RNA in an unenveloped icosahedral capsid, which includes enteroviruses, rhinoviruses, and the virus of foot-and-mouth disease.

1962 *Adv. Virus Res.* IX. 296 At a meeting of the Virus Subcommittee of the International Nomenclature Committee, held in Montreal in August 1962, the following decisions were made: (1) The proposed name nanivirus is to be replaced by Picornavirus. **1963** *Internat. Bull. Bacteriol. Nomencl. & Taxon.* XIII. 218 It was agreed that a name was needed for the small ether-resistant RNA viruses of which enteroviruses form an important part. The name 'Nanivirus'.. was discarded in favour of 'Picornavirus'. The prefix Pico- implies very small size, and RNA of course indicates nucleic-acid composition. (The initial letters of Picornavirus may be taken to refer to Poliomyelitis, insensitivity to ether, Coxsackie, orphan and Rhinovirus.) **1974** L. LEVINTOW in Fraenkel-Conrat & Wagner *Comprehensive Virology* II. iii. 154 Picornaviruses are the agents of a number of other important diseases of man and animals which remain to be controlled, including the common cold. **1976** FENNER & WHITE *Med. Virology* (ed. 2) xviii. 333 There are no antigenic relationships between most of the picornaviruses.

†**'picory.** *Obs.* Also -ie, -ee. [ad. F. *picorée* (16th c. in Littré) marauding, ad. Sp. *pecorea*: see PICKEER.] Plundering or pillage by armed force; foraging, marauding; looting.

[**1590** SIR J. SMYTH *Disc. Weapons* Ded. 9b, In stead of pay haue suffered them to goe *alla picoree*, that was, to robbe and spoyle the Boores their friends.] **1591** *Garrard's Art Warre* 13 If otherwise they be not prouided by forrage or Picorée. **1594** R. ASHLEY tr. *Loys le Roy* 45 He chastised such as failed, or were giuen to picory. **1596** RALEIGH *Discov. Guiana* Ep. Ded. 4 It became not the former fortune in which I once liued, to goe iourneys of picorie. [**1903** *Blackw. Mag.* July 29/1 Smith alone having saved by care in picory some moneys.]

picosecond ('pi:kəʊ-, 'paɪkəʊsɛkənd). [f. PICO- + SECOND *sb.*[1]] A unit of time equal to one million-millionth of a second.

1966 in *Random House Dict.* **1967** *Electronics* 6 Mar. 60/2 The.. circuits.. have switching speeds of 350 pico-seconds. **1972** *Sci. Amer.* Dec. 16/2 A sampling oscilloscope with a rise time.. of 44 picoseconds. **1974** *Nature* 15 Mar. 222/2 A complete formalism now exists to do the complete physics of the first picoseconds of the big-bang origin of the universe. **1975** *Daily Colonist* (Victoria, B.C.) 9 July 5/8 By using lasers capable of picosecond, or trillionth of a second, bursts of light and using ultra fast 'streak' cameras, researchers are now able to measure the conversion of light to other forms of energy in plants.

‖**picot** (piko), *sb.* [F. *picot*, dim. of *pic* peak, point, prick.] A small loop of twisted thread, larger than the pearl or purl, one of a series forming an ornamental edging to lace, ribbon, or braid; also, in embroidery, a raised knot similarly formed to represent a leaf, petal, ear of corn, etc.

1882 CAULFEILD & SAWARD *Dict. Needlework* 391/1 *Picots* .. are little Loops or Bobs that ornament Needle-made Laces of all kinds, and that are often introduced into Embroidery. **1891** *Weldon's Pract. Needlework* VI. No. 69. 14/1 The term 'worms'.. is.. not nearly so euphonious as the time-worn appellations of 'twisted stitch' or 'bullion', 'roll picot'.. all different names for the same stitch. **1893** *Ibid.* VIII. No. 90 11/1 The raised picots of which this leaf is composed are worked something after the manner of French knots.

b. *attrib.*, as ***picot-edge***, ***ribbon***, ***stitch***.

1886 *St. Stephen's Rev.* 13 Mar. 14/1 A bow of yellow picot ribbon. **1887** *Daily News* 11 Jan. 3/1 Some ingenious manufacturer conceived the happy idea of embellishing the edges of the ribbon with a small loop of silk. The idea was developed, and ribbons with a *picot* edge became the order of the day. **1891** *Weldon's Pract. Needlework* VI. No. 69. 3/1 The daisy loops—which also are known as leaf-stitch and picot stitch.

picot ('pi:kəʊ), *v.* [f. the sb.] *trans.* To ornament (cloth) with picots. So **picoted** ('pi:kəʊd) *ppl. a.*; **picoting** ('pi:kəʊɪŋ) *vbl. sb.*

1927 *Daily Express* 7 Mar. 5/5 Flowers were cut out of sheet metal.. even the picotted [*sic*] edges of certain varieties of carnation being faithfully rendered. **1928** *Ibid.* 11 May 5/3 Buy a square of plain or flowered.. georgette, and have it picoted all round by machine. The picoting is really machine hemstitching cut through the middle.

‖**picotah, picottah** (pɪ'kɒtə). Also pa-, picota, paecottah. [Hindī, etc., a. Pg. *picota* a pump-brake (in a ship).] The name applied in parts of India to a device for raising water, consisting of a beam, resting on an upright support, which is weighted at one end and has a bucket suspended from the other; the operator stands upon it and uses his own weight to dip and raise the bucket; the same as the SHADOOF of the Nile.

1807 F. BUCHANAN *Journ. Mysore* I. 15 In one place I saw people employed in watering a rice field with the *Yatam*, or *Pacota*, as it is called by the English. **1885** C. G. W. LOCK *Workshop Receipts* Ser. IV. 91/2 Termed a *paecottah* or *picota* in Bengal.

‖**picoté** (pikɔte), *a.* [F., pa. pple. of *picoter* to peck, etc.: see PICOTEE.] **a.** *Her.* Spotted, speckled. **b.** Furnished with picots: see PICOT *sb.*

c **1828** BERRY *Encycl. Herald.* I. Gloss., *Picoté*, a French term, which signifies speckled.

picotee (pɪkə'ti:), *sb.* (*a.*) Also 8 picketee, -ttee, -tty, 9 piquoté, piccotee. [a. F. *picoté, -ée*, pa. pple. of *picoter* to prick often, mark with pricks or points, f. *picot*: see PICOT *sb.*]

A. *sb.* A florists' variety of the carnation (*Dianthus Caryophyllus*), the flowers of which have a light ground, the petals being marked or edged with a darker colour.

The early variety had a white ground marked with specks of colour.

1727 BRADLEY *Fam. Dict.* s.v. *Carnation*, Each of those Tribes are very numerous, but chiefly the Picketees, of which, he says, he had seen above an hundred different Sorts in one Garden. **1808** SIR J. E. SMITH in *Mem.* (1832) I. 565 Your Piquoté (I never knew before how to spell that word, neither do I know its etymology now) pink is a curious plant. **1843** *Tait's Mag.* X. 617 By what process gooseberries may be made gigantic, and piccotees enriched with piedness. **1887** *G. Nicholson's Dict. Gardening* III. 123 Picotees are only distinguished from Carnations by the markings of their flowers. The petals of.. the Picotee have a ground colour, and are edged with a second colour.

B. *adj.* Applied to colours resembling those of the flowers or leaves of the picotee.

1899 *Daily News* 7 Oct. 8/6 Fine late tulips. Picotee, white, with picotee red edge. *c* **1900** *Needlecraft* Ser. I. No. 34. 9/2 The shading and grass upon the bank,.. work in dark picotee greens.

picotite ('pɪkətaɪt). *Min.* [a. mod.F., named 1812 after Picot, Baron de la Peyrouse (1744–1818), who described it: see -ITE[1].] A black variety of spinel containing chromium, occurring in minute grains and crystals in lherzolite.

1814 T. ALLAN *Min. Nomencl.* 37. **1832** C. U. SHEPARD *Min.* I. 246 Picotite. **1879** RUTLEY *Study Rocks* xiii. 264 The picotite appears, under the microscope, in very irregular brown, or.. deep olive-green, patches or grains. **1892** DANA *Min.* (ed. 6) 221 Picotite or chrom-spinel.

picoys, obs. f. PICKAXE.

picquancy, picquant, etc.: see PIQ-.

picque, obs. f. PICK *v.*[1]

picqué: see PIQUÉ.

picqueer, picquerer, picqueroon, picquet: see PICKEER, PICAROON, PICKET, PIQUET.

picqueter ('pɪkɪtə(r)). [f. F. *piquet* (*de fleurs*) bunch (of artificial flowers, for hats) + -ER[1].] One who arranges artificial flowers in bunches.

1898 *Daily Chron.* 24 Sept. 10/6 Artificial flower mounters, picqueters, jet hands, wanted. **1901** *Ibid.* 9 Apr. 10/4 Artificial Flower Picqueters.—Improvers wanted.

picquier, obs. form of PICKEER, PIQUIER.

picquois, obs. form of PICKAXE.

‖**picra** ('pɪkrə). *Pharmacy.* [Short for HIERA PICRA (Gr. πικρά bitter).] A bitter cathartic powder or paste: = HIERA PICRA.

1860 BUSHNELL in *Life* xxi. (1880) 439, I used to have a certain pride in taking picra without crying.

picral ('pɪkræl). *Metallurgy.* Also **Picral.** [f. PICR(IC *a.* + AL(COHOL.] An etchant consisting of about 2 to 5 per cent of picric acid in ethyl alcohol.

1928 WILLIAMS & HOMERBERG *Princ. Metallogr.* (ed. 2) 237 The term *picral* is frequently applied to any solution of picric acid in alcohol. **1936** [see NITAL]. **1963** C. H. SAMANS *Metallic Materials in Engin.* vi. 267 The action of picral is similar, except that it etches fine pearlite much more uniformly than nital does. However, it does not etch ferrite so rapidly as nital, and does not indicate the ferrite grain boundaries clearly.

picrate ('pɪkreɪt). *Chem.* [f. as PICRIC + -ATE[1].] A salt of picric acid: used as an explosive.

1866 WATTS *Dict. Chem.* IV. 403 The metallic picrates are mostly crystallisable, bitter, and of yellow colour. They explode when strongly heated. **1870** *Daily News* 27 July 6 The entrances east and west are closed by *torpilles* charged with picrate of potass.

Hence **pi'crated** *ppl. a.*, containing or partly composed of a picrate: applied to certain fireworks.

picric ('pɪkrɪk), *a. Chem.* [mod. f. Gr. πικρ-ός bitter + -IC.] In ***picric acid***, also called *trinitrocarbolic* or *carbazotic acid*, *artificial indigo-bitter*, a yellow intensely bitter substance ($C_6H_3N_3O_7 = C_6H_3(NO_2)_3O$), crystallizing in yellow shining prisms or laminæ, first observed by Hausmann in 1788, used in dyeing and more recently in the manufacture of explosives.

1852 *Chemical Gaz.* X. 137 Thus picric acid is phenylous acid..in which a substitution of 3 equivs. NO_4 for 3 equivs. H has taken place... Picric acid is consequently trinitrophenylous acid. **1860** O'NEILL *Chem. Calico Print.* 256 *Picric Acid.*—This is only lately introduced as a dyeing material for silks and woollens: it has no affinity for cotton. **1890** *Nature* 4 Sept. 444 The relative value of violent explosive agents, like picric acid or wet gun-cotton.

picrite ('pɪkraɪt). [f. Gr. πικρ-ός bitter: see -ITE[1].] †**1.** *Min.* [a. G. *picrite(s)* (J. F. Blumenbach *Handb. der Naturgeschichte* (ed. 5, 1797) xii. 584).] = DOLOMITE. *Obs. rare.*

1814 T. ALLEN *Min. Nomencl.* 9 Crystallized muricalcite, bitterspath, picrite. **1836** T. THOMSON *Outl. Min., Geol.* I. 181 Calcareo-carbonate of Magnesia. Dolomite—conite—..muricalcite—pearl spar—picrite [etc.]. **1896** CHESTER *Dict. Names Min., Picrite*, an obs. syn. of dolomite, bitter-spar.

2. *Petrogr.* Also 9 **picryte, pikrite.** [ad. G. *pikrit* (G. Tschermak 1866, in *Sitzungsber. der K. Akad. der Wissensch.* (*Math.-naturw. Classe*) LIII. 262).] A dark ultrabasic igneous rock, commmonly hypabyssal, containing a substantial amount of olivine together with augite and other ferromagnesian minerals and a small amount of plagioclase.

1868 J. D. DANA *Syst. Min.* (ed. 5) 258 A chrysolite rock occurring at L. Lherz, consisting largely of chrysolite, has been called Lherzolyte... Another similar rock from Moravia, called picryte, consists half of chrysolite, along with feldspar, diallage, hornblende, and magnetite. **1879** RUTLEY *Study Rocks* xiii. 265 Picrite is a blackish-green crystalline rock with a compact, black matrix, containing porphyritic crystals and grains of olivine. **1882** A. GEIKIE *Text-bk. Geol.* 151 Olivine Rocks... The following are the more important species:—Pikrite, a rock rich in olivine, usually more or less serpentinized, with augite, magnetite, or ilmenite, and a little brown biotite, hornblende, or apatite; [etc.]. **1931** S. J. SHAND *Study of Rocks* vii. 112 Picrites with forty to seventy-five per cent. of olivine have been described in Skye. The picrite of Tabankulu, South Africa, is composed to the extent of one-third to two-thirds of well-shaped crystals of olivine which are enclosed in larger crystals of pyroxene and felspar. **1976** *Mineral. Mag.* XL. 683 Exposures of baked siltstone occur on top of the ridge with picrite exposed only on the scarp face... The picrite averages 50% olivine, 35% plagioclase, and 15% pyroxene with a maximum grain size of 6 mm.

Hence **pi'critic** *a.*

1931 *Amer. Jrnl. Sci.* CCXXI. 403 Even a picritic sub-basalt..exhibits some interstitial quartz. **1958** *Trans. R. Soc. Edin.* LXIII. 459 In this paper it is proposed to use the term 'pictritic' to denote, in minor intrusions and lavas, an amount of forsteritic olivine considerably beyond that which normally crystallizes in basaltic magma. This amount of olivine varies between 25 and 60 per cent. **1965** *Carnegie Inst. Year Bk. 1964* 126/2 In general, picritic lavas and hypabyssal intrusives are few in number and restricted to the lower parts of both oceanic and continental volcanic columns. **1974** P. G. HARRIS in H. Sørensen *Alkaline Rocks* vi. 430/1 At pressures of about 30–40 kbar, i.e. depths below 90–100 km, the mantle mineralogy will be that of a garnet lherzolite, and there is a marked change in the first-formed liquid which is now picritic or ultrabasic.

picro- ('pɪkrəʊ), before a vowel sometimes **picr-**, combining form of Gr. πικρός bitter, used to form scientific terms, (*a*) in the sense 'having a bitter taste or smell', esp. in the names of magnesium minerals, because magnesium salts have often a bitter taste; (*b*) in names of derivatives of PICRIC acid, as ***picramic acid, picramine, picrammonium, picro-acetate of lead, picro-carbonate of ammonia.***

Among these are **picro'carmine**, a red staining fluid used in histologic microscopy; picro-carbonate of ammonia. **picro'chromite** *Min.*, a chromite of magnesium, $MgCr_2O_4$, which in its pure form is known only as an artificial product (see quots. 1939) and which in nature is a brittle black mineral that contains a substantial amount of ferrous iron replacing magnesium. **picroe'rythrin** *Chem.* [ERYTHRIN] (see quot. 1866). **picro'glycion** *Chem.* [Gr. γλυκύς sweet], a crystalline substance obtained from the bittersweet; = DULCAMARIN. **picroilmenite** (pɪkrəʊ'ɪlmənaɪt) *Min.* [ad. G. *pikroïlmenit* (P. Groth *Tabellarische Übersicht der Mineralien* (ed. 4, 1898) ix. 143)], a magnesian variety of ilmenite. **'picrolite** *Min.* [Gr. λίθος stone] (see quots.). **'picromel** [Gr. μέλι honey], a bitter-sweet substance obtained from bile. **pi'cromerite** *Min.* [Gr. μερίς, μεριδ- a part], sulphate of magnesium and potassium found in white crystals and crystalline crusts. **picro'nitrate** *Chem.* = PICRATE. **picro'pharma-colite** *Min.* (named by Stromeyer, 1819), a mineral resembling pharmacolite, but containing magnesium. **'picrophyll** *Min.* [Gr. φύλλον a leaf], a massive, fibrous, or foliated greenish-grey variety of pyroxene. **picro'phyllite** = prec. (Webster 1864). **pi'crosmine** *Min.* [Ger. *picrosmin*, named by Haidinger, 1824, f. Gr. ὀσμή odour], a greenish-white, dark-green, or greyish fibrous hydrous silicate of magnesium, which emits a bitter and argillaceous odour when moistened. **'picrotin** *Chem.* [f. *picrotoxin*], a bitter crystalline substance existing with picrotoxin in the *Cocculus indicus*. **picro'toxic** *a. Chem.* [f. next: see -IC], of, pertaining to, contained in, or derived from picrotoxin. **picro'toxin** *Chem.* [cf. TOXIN], formerly **picrotoxia**, the bitter poisonous principle ($C_{12}H_{14}O_5$) of the seeds of the *Cocculus indicus*.

1866 WATTS *Dict. Chem.* IV. 406 *Picramic [or] Dinitrophenamic..Acid..Produced by the action of sulphide of ammonium or of ferrous salts on picric acid. *Ibid.* 640 *Picramine, or hydrate of *picrammonium, cannot be isolated on account of its ready oxidability. *Ibid.* 404 A *picro-acetate of lead..is deposited..when a boiling mixture of potassic picrate and an excess of lead-acetate is left to cool. **1880** *Q. Jrnl. Microsc. Sc.* XX. 230 By using osmic acid, followed by *picrocarmine, it is easy to preserve the ectoderm with its clothing of cilia. **1899** *Allbutt's Syst. Med.* VI. 551 The picrocarmine reaction shows that decalcification is taking place. **1920** E. S. SIMPSON in *Mineral. Mag.* XIX. 100 Dealing with the minerals of the spinel-chromite series.., the four variables, which constitute two pairs, are MgO, FeO, Al_2O_3, Cr_2O_3. Four mineral species are possible, the pure forms of which are (1) $MgO.Al_2O_3$ spinel, (2) $MgO.Cr_2O_3$ *picrochromite, (3) $FeO.Al_2O_3$ hercynite, and (4) $FeO.Cr_2O_3$ chromite. [*Note*] New name required to complete the series and to designate already known minerals. *Ibid.* 104 At least three previously described minerals, viz. chrompicotite of Dun Mt., New Zealand; magnesiochromite of New Caledonia; and 'chromite' of Lake Memphremagog in Quebec, are members of a new species for which the author proposes the name picrochromite. **1939** *Special Rep. Iron & Steel Inst.* No. 26. 202 Picrochromite was prepared in a manner similar to that used for spinel but employing equivalent amounts of magnesia and chromic oxide. *Ibid.* 204 Picrochromite was green in daylight and reddish-grey in artificial light..when viewed in mass. It occurred as aggregates of minute crystals which were practically colourless and presented occasional octahedral faces. **1970** *Mineral. Abstr.* XXI. 314/2 (*heading*) Determination of the fusion temperature of picrochromite. **1857** MILLER *Elem. Chem.* III. 541 *Picro-erythrin..is a colourless substance... It has a very bitter taste. **1866** WATTS *Dict. Chem.* IV. 641 *Picroerythrin* ($C_{12}H_{16}O_7$), a body produced, together with orsellinic ether, by the action of boiling water on erythrin. **1858** MAYNE *Expos. Lex.*, **Picroglycion, Picroglycium*... Name by Pfaff for a particular substance first obtained by him from the *Solanum dulcamara*. **1866** WATTS *Dict. Chem.* IV. 642 *Picroglycion. Dulcamarin.* **1900** *Mineral. Mag.* XII. 389 *Picroilmenite... The same as picrotitanite, a variety of ilmenite rich in magnesium. **1906** *Ibid.* XIV. 166 It is advisable to divide the ferro-magnesian titanates into ilmenites and geikielites, and to regard picroilmenite as the middle member of the series. **1972** *Mineral. Abstr.* XXIII. 338/1 Picroilmenite occurs, associated with diamond, in the kimberlites and in the Carboniferous, Jurassic, and Cretaceous formations [in the Anabar area, western Yakutia]. Its hardness ranges from 450 to 750 kg/mm²; it is anisotropic, optically negative, and has a weak bireflectance. **1816** R. JAMESON *Min.* (ed. 2) I. 536 *Picrolite. **1866** WATTS *Dict. Chem.* IV. 642 *Picrolite*, a fibrous dark-geen variety of serpentine, somewhat resembling asbestos; found in Silesia [etc.]. **1896** CHESTER *Dict. Names Min., Picrolite*,..a fibrous or columnar var. of serpentine. **1815** HENRY *Elem. Chem.* (ed. 7) II. 332 *Picromel. **1819** J. G. CHILDREN *Chem. Anal.* 307 Picromel is obtained from bile. **1880** J. W. LEGG *Bile* 2 Thenard.. obtained a body which he named picromel from its taste. **1866** WATTS *Dict. Chem.* IV. 642 **Picromerite*, potassio-magnesic sulphate..crystallised from solutions of saline crusts. **1868** DANA *Min.* 642. **1875** *von Ziemssen's Cycl. Med.* III. 642 Picric acid in the form of *picronitrate of potassa and soda. **1823** W. PHILLIPS *Min.* (ed. 3) 178 The analysis ..of *picropharmacolite has been published. **1866** WATTS *Dict. Chem.* IV. 387 Picropharmacolite from Riechelsdorf.. is probably pharmacolite having the lime partly replaced by magnesia. *Ibid.* 643 **Picrophyll*,..from Sala in Sweden... It is perhaps an altered augite. **1868** DANA *Min.* (ed. 5) 406 Pyrallolite..Picrophyll... These are names of pyroxene in different stages of alteration, between true pyroxene and either serpentine or steatite. **1825** HAIDINGER tr. *Moh's Min.* III. 137 *Picrosmine. **1852** C. U. SHEPARD *Min.* (ed. 3) 148 Picrosmine..[occurs] at the Greiner in Tyrol. **1893** *Syd. Soc. Lex., Picrotoxin*..can be split up into the two bodies *Picrotoxinin* and **Picrotin*. **1826** HENRY *Elem. Chem.* II. 305 **Picrotoxia*,..name given to the acrid narcotic principle residing in the cocculus indicus. **1866** WATTS *Dict. Chem.* IV. 643 **Picrotoxic acid*, the name given by Pelletier and Couerbe to picrotoxin, because it unites with metallic oxides. **1815** HENRY *Elem. Chem.* (ed. 7) II. 254 *Picrotoxine. **1840** *Penny Cycl.* XVIII. 147/1 Picrotoxin.. is intensely bitter. **1878** tr. *von Ziemssen's Cycl. Med.* XVII. 813 The first and most important step in the treatment of picrotoxin-poisoning.

picrolichenic (pɪkrəʊlaɪ'kənɪk), *a. Biochem.* [f. next + -IC.] ***picrolichenic acid***: a very bitter, crystalline, polycyclic acid, $C_{25}H_{30}O_7$, isolated from the lichen *Pertusaria amara*; = next.

1902 *Jrnl. Chem. Soc.* LXXXII. I. 465 The name *picrolichenic acid* is suggested for picrolichenin. **1957** *Chem. & Industry* 27 July 1042/2 Picrolichenic acid, a constituent of the common crustose lichen *Pertusaria amara* Ach... is responsible for the well known, very bitter, quinine-like taste of this lichen. **1959** *New Biol.* XXIX. 86 Picrolichenic acid..is a previously undescribed type of lichen acid in which the ring structures in the molecule are joined by a direct carbon to carbon link rather than by an oxygen atom as is the case in depsidones. **1973** S. HUNECK in Ahmadjian & Hale *Lichens* xv. 511 The only hitherto known depsone from lichens is picrolichenic acid.

picrolichenin (pɪkrəʊ'laɪkənɪn). *Biochem.* [a. G. *picrolichenin* (A. Alms 1832, in *Ann. d. Pharm.* I. 62), f. *picro-* PICRO- + *lichenin* LICHENIN.] = PICROLICHENIC *acid*.

1862 H. WATTS tr. *Gmelin's Hand-bk. Chem.* XV. 56 A pound of the lichen yields half an ounce of picrolichenin. **1901** *Jrnl. Chem. Soc.* LXXX. I. 88 The author has isolated salazinic acid and picrolichenin from *Pertusaria amara*. **1958** *Svensk Kem. Tidskr.* LXX. 129 The bitter principle isolated by Alms from this lichen—'Picrolichenin'—was claimed to be useful as a remedy in the treatment of malaria, and this is now being checked.

picryl ('pɪkrɪl, 'pɪkraɪl). *Chem.* [f. Gr. πικρ-ός bitter, or immed. f. PICR-IC + -YL.] †**1.** Also **picril, picryle.** [a. F. *picryle* (A. Laurent 1844, in *Rev. sci. et industr.* XVIII. 201).] (See quot. 1866.) *Obs.*

1847 W. GREGORY *Outl. Chem.* (ed. 2) 546 *Picrine*, Syn. *Picryle*, $C_{42}H_{15}NO_4$, is formed when the mass produced by acting on oil of bitter almonds by sulphuret of ammonium is distilled. **1858** H. WATTS tr. *Gmelin's Hand-bk. Chem.* XII. 188 Picril dissolves very readily in ether. **1866** —— *Dict. Chem.* IV. 644 *Picryl* or *Cripin*, a substance formed, together with others, by submitting to dry distillation the crude product of the action of sulphydrate of ammonium on bitter-almond oil... Picryl is also used as synonymous with trinitrophenyl, $C_6H_2(NO_2)_3$, the radicle of picric acid.

2. The 2,4,6-trinitrophenyl group, $-C_6H_2(NO_2)_3$, contained in picric acid.

1866 [see sense 1]. **1875** *Jrnl. Chem. Soc.* XXVIII. 165 Metanitraniline and picryl chloride act on one another when dissolved in boiling absolute alcohol. **1877** *Ibid.* XXXII. 758 It is..very possible that in one of the resulting compounds the two picryl groups may be identical. **1889** G. M'GOWAN tr. *Bernthsen's Text-bk. Org. Chem.* xxiii. 385 Picryl chloride, $C_6H_2(NO_2)_3Cl$.., resembles the acid chlorides..in behaviour. **1937** F. C. WHITMORE *Org. Chem.* 737 Picryl iodide is a stable yellow crystalline product obtainable from the chloride and KI. **1964** J. W. LINNETT *Electronic Struct. Molecules* vii. 107 The reason why the diphenyl picryl compound is more stable than the triphenyl compound is presumably that the picryl group relieves the adjacent nitrogen atom of some of the negative charge. **1975** *Nature* 3 Jan. 72/2 The lymph node cells of mice rendered unresponsive by the injection of picryl sulphonic acid (PSA) depress the passive transfer of contact senstivity.

Pict (pɪkt), *sb.* Forms: α. 1 *pl.* **Peohtas, Pehtas, Pih-, Pyhtas,** 4 **Peghttes,** 5 *sing.* **Peght(e,** *pl.* (*Sc.*) **Peychtis, Pightis,** 6 *sing.* **Peight,** 6– **Pecht,** (8 **Peht,** 9 **Peght, Piht).** β. 4–6 *pl.* **Pictes, -is,** 5 **Pyctes,** 7– *sing.* **Pict.** [In late L. *Pictī*, identical in form with *pictī* painted or tattooed people, which may be the meaning; but the L. may be merely an assimilated form of a native name: cf. *Pictavi*, *Pictones* in Gaul. The OE. *Peohtas* represents an earlier *Pihtas*, which would answer to a foreign *Pict-* (cf. *Wiht* for L. *Vectis*); its direct descendant is the Scottish *Pecht*; *Pict* is from L.]

1. One of an ancient people of disputed origin and ethnological affinities, who formerly inhabited parts of north Britain. According to the chroniclers the Pictish kingdom was united with the Scottish under Kenneth MacAlpine in 843, and the name of the Picts as a distinct people gradually disappeared.

In Scottish folk-lore, the *Pechts* are often represented as a dark pygmy race, or an underground people; and sometimes identified with elves, brownies, or fairies.

Picts' houses, the name given to underground structures attributed to the Picts, found on the east coast of Scotland and in Orkney. *Picts' wall*: see quot. 1753 in β.

α. *a* **900** tr. *Bæda's Hist.* I. i. (1890) 28 Ða ferdon Peohtas in Breotone, & ongunnon eardiȝan þa norðdælas þyses ealondes... Mid þy Peohtas wif næfdon. *Ibid.*, þridde cynn Scotta Breotone onfeng on Pehta dæle. **a900** *O.E. Chron.* an. 449 (Parker MS.) Se cing het hi feohtan agien Pihtas, & hi swa dydan. **c1122** *Ibid.* (Laud MS.), Heo þa fuhton wið Pyhtas. ? **a1400** *Morte Arth.* 4126 Peghttes and paynymes.. disspoylles our knyghttes. **c1425** WYNTOUN *Cron.* IV. xix. 1757 A company Out of þe kynrik of Sithi Coyme of Peychtis [*Wemyss MS.* Pightis] in Irlande. **1483** *Cath. Angl.* 272/2 A Peghte (*A.* A Peght or Pigmei), *pigmeus.* **1566** T. STAPLETON *Ret. Untr. Jewel* iii. 129 The forrain inuasions of the Scottes and Peightes or Red-shankes. **1596** DALRYMPLE tr. *Leslie's Hist. Scot.* III. 198 The Pechtes.. called a counsel. **1789** PINKERTON *Enquiry* I. III. x. 367 The common denomination among the people of Scotland, from the Pehts Wall in Northumberland to the Pehts houses in Ross-shire, and up to the Orkneys, is Pehts. **1822** SCOTT *Pirate* ii. *note*, The ancient Picts, or, as [the inhabitants of the Orkneys] call them with the usual strong guttural, Peghts. **1834** *Penny Cycl.* II. 415/2 He [Arthur] received intelligence of the revolt of Modred, who had allied himself with the Saxons, Scots, and Pihts. **1881** *Blackw. Mag.* Sept. 398 A stranger.. whom the most knowing man.. pronounced to be a 'Pecht', for he was small and black and had all the characteristics of the traditional 'Pecht'.

β. **1387** TREVISA *Higden* II. 147 þei beeþ i-cleped Pictes by cause of peyntynge. **c1420** *Chron. Vilod.* 48 Pictis, and Scottys, and Hyrysshe also. **1753** J. WARBURTON (*title*) Vallum Romanum; or, the History and Antiquities of the Roman Wall, Commonly called the Picts Wall, in Cumberland and Northumberland, Built by Hadrian and Severus.. Seventy Miles in Length, to keep out the ..Picts and Scots. **1813** J. GRANT *Orig. Gael* (1814) 292 The Picts of Albinn.. inhabited the whole range of low country from the Frith of Forth, northward. **1822** SCOTT *Pirate* xxvii, One of those dens which are called Burghs and Picts-houses in Zetland. **1851** D. WILSON *Preh. Ann.* (1863) I. iv. 116 These structures, for which—we retain the popular name of Picts houses.. are erected on the natural surface of the soil and have been buried by an artificial mound heaped over them.

attrib. **a1856** in G. Henderson *Pop. Rhymes* 8 Grisly Drædan sat alane By the cairn and Pech stane. **1897** H. TENNYSON *Mem. Ld. Tennyson* II. xiv. 280 We had a drive of ten miles to Maeshowe, a Pict burial-mound.

†**2.** *humorous.* One who paints the face. *Obs.*

1711 STEELE *Spect.* No. 41 ¶4, I have.. distinguished those of our Women who wear their own, from those in borrowed Complexions, by the Picts and the British. **1892** *Daily News* 8 Dec. 5/1 Men must be tolerant of 'Picts', as the old 'Spectator' calls them, or Picts would not be so prevalent.

pict, *v. rare.* [f. L. *pict-*, ppl. stem of *ping-ĕre* to paint.] *trans.* To paint; to depict, represent. Hence **'picted** *ppl. a.*, painted.

1483 CAXTON *Gold. Leg.* 431 b/1 They ne shold fro thens forthon pourtrayne nor pycte the forme or fygure of the crosse. **1866** J. B. ROSE *Virg. Ecl. & Georg.* 79 Races.. From picted Gelon to Arabian. **1866** —— tr. *Ovid's Fasti* VI. 428 In picted vestments and in open hall.

pict, obs. f. PICK *sb.*[1] 7; obs. var. PICK *v.*[2]

pictareen, erroneous form of PISTAREEN.

pictarne. *Sc.* ? *Obs.* Also 9 pickietar. [Of uncertain origin: but cf. PICKMAW and TERN.] = next.

1710 SIBBALD *Hist. Fife* II. iii. 46 Hirundo Marina, *Sterna Turneri*: Our People call it the *Pictarne.* **1771** PENNANT *Tour Scotl. in 1769.* 65 Great Terns, called here *Pictarnes.* **1851** T. EDWARDS in *Zoologist* IX. 3080, I observed several parties of pickietars busily employed in fishing in the Firth.

pictarnie (pɪk'tɑːnɪ). *Sc.* Also 9 pic-, picketarney, pickaternie, (piccatarrie). [dim. of prec.: see -IE.] The common tern, *Sterna fluviatilis.* Also locally, the Arctic tern, *S. macrura.*

1802 G. MONTAGU *Ornith. Dict.* (1833) 508 Common Tern.. Provincial, Pirr.. Tarney or Pictarney. **1816** SCOTT *Antiq.* xxxix, 'It's but a sea-maw.' 'It's a pictarnie, sir', said Edie. **1835** D. SMITH *Emigrant's Farew.* 17 Wild ducks and pictarnies may play on the stream. **1899** *Shetl. News* 14 Jan. (E.D.D.), The graceful and elegant tern, the 'piccatarrie' of our beaches and lochs.

pictel, obs. form of PIGHTLE.

picthatch, variant of PICKED-HATCH.

Pictish ('pɪktɪʃ), *a.* and *sb.* [f. PICT *sb.* + -ISH.]

A. *adj.* Of or pertaining to the Picts or their language (or languages).

1710 R. SIBBALD *Hist. Fife & Kinross* I. ii. 3 Both in Bertius his excellent Edition and the late Map of Gale, it [*sc.* Votadini] is read Vacomagi, and the Greek in both these answer to Vacomagi, which by the by.. doth much confirm Mr. Robert Maule his Ratio nominis Veach, Pictus, since in Veach here, and in Wauchopdale in the South.. the Pictish Veach appears to be the rise of both these Words. **1762** BP. FORBES *Jrnl.* (1886) 140 Abernethie, where is a Church and Steeple, reckoned to be Pictish work. **1840** *Penny Cycl.* XVIII. 148/2 Their language appears to have nearly resembled the Welsh. One Pictish word only has been expressly mentioned by any old writer, *Peanvahel.* **1868** W. F. SKENE *Four Ancient Bks. of Wales* I. viii. 130 In the fifth, the Pictish *duiper* and the Gaelic *saoibher* are the same word. **1884** Q. VICTORIA *More Leaves* 274 The old fortress.. is supposed to have belonged to the Pictish Kings. **1892** J. RHYS in *Proc. Soc. Antiquaries Scotl.* XXVI. 310 Lastly, Pictish *enn* is to be found in some instances where the Celtic stem is usually made to end.. in *on.* **1946** T. F. O'RAHILLY *Early Irish Hist. & Mythol.* 369 Compare Celt. *vroiko-* giving Pictish **vrōg*, whence.. Sc. *frōg*, 'a fen'. **1955** K. H. JACKSON in F. T. Wainwright *Probl. Picts* vi. 142 *Forcus* at St Vigeans is the exact Gaelic equivalent of Pictish *Uurguist.*

B. *sb.* The language (or languages) of the Picts.

Pictish is evidenced only in a few proper names, inscriptions, and glosses, and its affliations have been much disputed. The view most widely accepted now is that expressed by K. H. Jackson in F. T. Wainwright *The Problem of the Picts* (1955) 152: 'There were at least two languages current in northern Scotland before the coming of the Irish Gaels in the fifth century. One of them was a Gallo-Brittonic dialect not identical with the British spoken south of the Antonine Wall, though related to it. The other was not Celtic at all, nor apparently even Indo-European, but was presumably the speech of some very early set of inhabitants of Scotland.'

1857 W. REEVES *Life St. Columba* 62/2 This case saves that recorded in ii. 32, *infra*, from being 'a solitary allusion to the diversity of Gaelic and Pictish'. **1868** W. F. SKENE *Four Ancient Bks. of Wales* I. viii. 138, I consider, therefore, that Pictish was a low Gaelic dialect... Old Scottish.. was the high Gaelic dialect, and Pictish the low Gaelic dialect. **1891** W. STOKES in *Trans. Philol. Soc. 1888–90* 417 The foregoing list of names and other words contains much that is still obscure; but on the whole it shows that Pictish, so far as regards its vocabulary, is an Indo-European and especially Celtic speech. Its phonetics, so far as we can ascertain them, resemble those of Welsh rather than of Irish. **1892** J. RHYS in *Proc. Soc. Antiquaries Scotl.* XXVI. 307 Pictish being, as I take it, a non-Aryan language. **1923** J. FRASER *Hist. & Etym.* 15 Rhys's view that Pictish was a non-Indogermanic language involves the same fallacy as the view that it was Goidelic or Brythonic. **1946** T. F. O'RAHILLY *Early Irish Hist. & Mythol.* 353 The preponderant opinion of modern scholarship is that Pictish was a Celtic language, different from both British and Goidelic, but decidedly more akin to the former than to the latter. **1955** K. H. JACKSON in F. T. Wainwright *Probl. Picts* vi. 134 We seem to find it implied or clearly stated by contemporary and almost contemporary writers that Pictish was a separate speech of its own, identical neither with the Gaelic of Scotland and Ireland nor with Brittonic. **1963** N. K. CHADWICK *Celtic Brit.* i. 20 In Scotland the royal Pictish families seem to have spoken Pictish as late as the ninth century. **1976** C. F. & F. M. VOEGELIN *Classification World's Lang.* (1977) 104 [Goidelic = Q-Celtic] Pictish. Formerly spoken in Scotland but not necessarily as a Celtic language.

Pictland ('pɪktlænd). [f. PICT + LAND.] The land of the Picts: a name for Scotland north of the Forth.

[**1701** J. BRAND (*title*) A Brief Description of Orkney, Zetland, Pightland-Frith, and Caithness.] **1846** MCCULLOCH *Acc. Brit. Empire* (1854) I. 225 The inhabitants of this district, the Caledonians of Tacitus, were afterwards known by the name of Picts; and from them the country was for some centuries called Pictland. *Ibid.* 425 In the third century, the terms Picts and Pictland began to be substituted for Caledonians and Caledonia. **1860** SHAIRP *Sk.* (1887) 36 To convert Pictland and plant the Church there.

pictogram ('pɪktəgræm). [f. L. *pict-us* painted + -GRAM.] = PICTOGRAPH.

1910 *Encycl. Relig. & Ethics* III. 549/2 The primitive characters or 'pictograms'.. afford unmistakable evidence as to the ideas which existed long anterior to the time of Confucius. **1936** V. G. CHILDE *Man makes Himself* viii. 208 Even the picture-signs, though much more realistic than Sumerian pictograms, conform to a social convention. **1939** *Trans. Philol. Soc.* 76 K. Haag.. worked out a scheme of pictograms, based partly on the fundamental space relations and supplemented by the use of symbols like the heart for emotion. **1952** G. SARTON *Hist. Sci.* I. ii. 20 We may assume that the Egyptians began by using pictograms (images) representing things or ideas rather than words. **1960** E. H. GOMBRICH *Art & Illusion* viii. 280 They see the picture still as a flat surface covered with a pictogram. **1965** H. K. COMPTON *Gloss. Purchasing & Supplies Managem. Terms* 101 *Pictogram*, diagrams drawn in different sizes more or less to scale to demonstrate relative sizes of statistical batches which are illustrated, often by pictures depicting the subject matter. **1970** *Which?* Nov. 352/2 The use of pictograms (eg '?' to show an information desk) is increasing. **1971** *Nature* 16 July 148/3 At the top there are pictograms of a sword, a shield and two crosses and a triangle. **1973** J. M. ANDERSON *Struct. Aspect Lang. Change* 14 Pictograms can be read.. with varying choice of words in any language. **1977** *New Yorker* 2 May 135/3 Occasionally he resorts to dance pictograms.

pictograph ('pɪktəgrɑːf, -æ-). [mod. f. L. *pict-us* painted + -GRAPH.] **a.** A pictorial symbol or sign; a writing or record consisting of pictorial symbols (the most primitive form of records). Also *attrib.*

1851 SCHOOLCRAFT *Ind. Tribes* I. 416 Plate 60 Pictograph A. Chippewa Petition to the President of the United States. **1871** TYLOR *Prim. Cult.* I. 277 We know enough of the Indian pictographs, to guess how a fancy.. came into the poor excited creature's mind. **1894** A. J. EVANS in *Academy* 25 Aug. 136/2 Some of them.. belonged to that interesting class of pictographs which is rooted in primitive gesture language. **1900** SAYCE *Babylonians & Assyrians* x. 209 In Egypt the hieratic or running-hand of the scribe developed out of the primitive pictographs. **1937** *Discovery* Aug. 249/1 The Lachish dagger with pictograph inscription. **1955** *Bull. Atomic Sci.* Mar. 91/2 An Indian pictograph enthusiast.. noticed carnotite stain on a cliff face in the Edgemont, S.D., area. **1955** *Sci. News Let.* 9 July 31/2 The crescent is not a common figure among petroglyphs and pictographs of northern Arizona. **1971** N. SMITH *Hist. Dams* i. 23 In ancient Egypt.. the hieroglyph for a 'province' is a pictograph of an irrigation system. **1973** *Nature* 26 Oct. 422/2 He sees close parallels with the Juxtlahuaca Cave paintings, as well as the earlier pictographs at Chalcacingo, and attempts to define the symbolic elements common to all of them. **1978** *New York* 3 Apr. 32/3 Pictographs from the Warlis, an East Indian tribe.

b. A pictorial representation of statistical data.

1937 R. MODLEY *How to use Pictorial Statistics* iii. 19 The chief variation is that the bar chart can indicate the diversity in subject only in its printed legend, while the pictograph expresses the subject by the character of the symbols which make up each 'bar'. In other words the bar chart is an abstract presentation of facts; the pictograph is concrete. **1954** D. HUFF *How to lie with Statistics* vi. 66 The daddy of the pictorial chart, or pictograph, is the ordinary bar chart.

Hence **picto'graphic** *a.*, of, belonging to, or of the nature of, picture-writing; **pic'tography**, picture-writing; the recording of ideas or events by pictorial symbols.

1851 SCHOOLCRAFT *Ind. Tribes* I. 333 Indian Pictography. *Ibid.*, The Pictographic Method of Communicating Ideas by Symbolic and Representative Devices of the North American Indians. **1862** MAX MÜLLER *Chips* (1880) I. xiv. 316 Genuine specimens of American pictography. **1895** [see ETEOCRETAN *a.* and *sb.*]. **1896** A. J. EVANS in *Academy* 18 July 53/3 A beautiful 'pictographic' seal of red cornelian. **1932** [see ACROPHONIC *a.*]. **1952** G. SARTON *Hist. Sci.* I. ii. 20 Words containing the same sounds, especially proper names or abstract words, which were not susceptible of pictographic representation. **1971** *Nature* 30 Apr. 552/1 The signs on these three small baked clay plaques were accepted.. as representing a script closely resembling the pictographic writing seen on the 'protoliterate' tablets from Uruk in Mesopotamia.

pictoresque, obs. form of PICTURESQUE.

pictorial (pɪk'tɔərɪəl), *a.* (*sb.*) [f. late L. *pictōri-us* (f. *pictor* a painter) + -AL[1]. (Used by Sir T. Browne (in sense 1), but not in general use before 1800.)]

A. *adj.* **1.** Of, belonging to, or produced by the painter; of or pertaining to painting or drawing. Now *rare.*

1646 SIR T. BROWNE *Pseud. Ep.* III. xxiv. 170 Sea-horses.. are but Crotesco deliniations which fill up empty spaces in Maps, and meere pictoriall inventions, not any Physicall shapes. **1755** JOHNSON, *Pictorial*, produced by a painter. [Quotes Browne, and remarks] 'A word not adopted by other writers, but elegant and useful.' **1810** in *Spirit Pub. Jrnls.* XIV. 205 Royal Academy Dinner. A pictorial vision. **1813** T. BUSBY *Lucretius* II. IV. Comm. p. xii, Attention to the laws of perspective, which is, in fact, but a pictorial optic, will instruct the reader. **1833** J. MARTINEAU *Misc.* (1852) 32 Conception.. is emphatically the pictorial faculty needed by the illustrating artist. **1855** THACKERAY *Newcomes* xii, 'Far be it from me to say that the pictorial calling is not honourable', says Uncle Charles.

2. Consisting of, expressed in, or of the nature of, a picture or pictures.

1807 ANNA SEWARD *Lett.* (1811) VI. 329 Not the wealthy.. who exhibit in their boudoirs and drawing rooms, new publications in the luxury of pictorial ornaments. **1861** STANLEY *East. Ch.* ix. (1869) 305 Pictorial communications are probably the chief sources of religious instruction imparted to the.. Russian peasantry. **1876** BIRCH *Egypt* 8 The hieroglyphs or pictorial forms were used.. above one thousand years after they ceased to represent the vernacular or spoken language of Egypt.

3. Containing or illustrated by a picture or pictures; illustrated. ***pictorial paper*** = sense B.

1826 DISRAELI *Viv. Grey* I. i, Taught at home on the new system, by a pictorial alphabet. **1840** HOOD *Up Rhine* 49 Its features being such as are common on the pictorial Dutch tiles. **1864** KNIGHT *Passages Work. Life* II. xii. 253 At the beginning of 1836, the first number of 'The Pictorial Bible' was issued. In hitting upon the word 'Pictorial' I felt that I was rather daring in the employment of a term which the Dictionaries pronounced as 'not in use'. **1873** 'MARK TWAIN' & WARNER *Gilded Age* xliii. 394 The pictorial papers caricatured its friends. **1897** *Pearson's Mag.* IV. 405 It is a wonderful invention—this pictorial postcard craze. **1933** *Burlington Mag.* Sept. 140/2 The student who has not an extensive library might like to have possessed a pictorial record. **1935** *Discovery* Dec. 365/2 Sets of pictorial postcards of the park and its inhabitants. **1937** J. R. HUNT (*title*) Pictorial journalism. **1948** C. ABEL *Business of Photogr.* v. 37 Another offshoot of commercial photography.. is the growing field of pictorial journalism. **1968** G. JONES *Hist. Vikings* III. ii. 188 From the Gotland pictorial stones it appears that sail could be effectively shortened by the use of reefing lines.

4. *fig.* Like a picture; representing as if by a picture; picturesque, graphic.

1829 LANDOR *Imag. Conv.*, *Marvel & Bp. Parker* Wks. 1853 II. 116/2 He has given us such a description of Eve's beauty as appears to me somewhat too pictorial, too luxuriant. **1841** D'ISRAELI *Amen. Lit.* (1867) 477 Of all poets Spenser excelled in the pictorial faculty. **1882** FARRAR *Early Chr.* I. 262 If God is spoken of as having hands, arms, feet, and so on, those, he says, must be simply looked upon as pictorial phrases.

B. as *sb.* **1.** A journal of which pictures are the main feature.

1844 *Knickerbocker* XXIII. 197 'The Columbian'.. is to run a brisk competition.. with the other pictorials. **1851** C. CIST *Sk. Cincinnati in 1851* iv. 77 Illustrated Western World... Oncken's Western Scenery... These two last are pictorials. **1880** (*title of periodical*) The Lady's Pictorial. **1904** *Westm. Gaz.* 17 Aug. 10/1 In the case of magazine articles, pamphlets, &c.,.. and of periodicals and 'pictorials'. **1934** G. B. SHAW *Too True to be Good* I. 43 In her lily hand was a copy of The Lady's Pictorial. It contained an illustrated account of your jewels.

2. A postage stamp on which a picture or scene is printed, usu. to commemorate a particular anniversary or event.

1934 in WEBSTER. **1939** P. HAMILTON *Hundred Years of Postage Stamps* v. 74 Pictorials are a characteristic feature of the second half of our hundred years of postage stamps. **1953** HARRISON & ARMSTRONG *New Approach to Stamp Collecting* xii. 173 The rocky finances of certain Central and South American states were the healthier for some really splendid 'pictorials'. **1973** *Daily Tel.* 8 Jan. 9/3 The islands' first pictorials, showing views of the various islands, were issued in 1942–43. **1974** W. FINLAY *Illustr. Hist. Stamp Design* ix. 119/1 The issues of the six Australian states.. included a fair number of pictorials.

Hence **pic'torialism**, the practice of a pictorial style (*lit.* and *fig.*), the use of pictorial representation; **pic'torialist**, one who practises a pictorial style; **pic'torialize** *v.*, to represent in, or as in, a picture; to illustrate with pictures; hence **pic,toriali'zation**; **pic'torialness**, pictorial quality, graphic character.

1869 *Pennsylv. School Jrnl.* Feb. 218 Sensationalism and *pictorialism, and the imaginings of sensuousness and sentimentality. **1885** *Manch. Exam.* 4 Feb. 3/5 Unfaithful to the traditions of pictorialism. **1839** *Blackw. Mag.* XLV. 530 Not by the minute pencilling of the *pictorialists. **1971** *Amat. Photographer* 3 Mar. 6/2 The panel..does not have the dynamic impact of new pictures or of the more forceful avant-garde work of some modern pictorialists. **1979** G. MACDONALD *Camera* xii. 169/1 The aping of the avant garde by some of the pictorialists. **1901** *Edin. Rev.* Jan. 36 The impulse towards the *pictorialisation of nature. **1870** *Daily News* 20 Dec., We have been eulogised and *pictorialised to an extent almost incredible. **1888** CAVE *Inspiration O. Test.* vi. 309 There is no pictorializing, there is no idolizing of deity. **1876** EDERSHEIM *Jew. Life Days Christ* vii. 103 The multiplicity and *pictorialness of the expressions. **1881** *Scribner's Mag.* XXII. 148 This group adds immensely to the pictorialness of the picture.

pictorially (pɪk'tɔərɪəlɪ), *adv.* [f. prec. + -LY².] In a pictorial manner.

1. By means of a picture or pictures.

1843 tr. *Custine's Empire of Czar* II. 257 Russia is less known than India: it has been less often described and pictorially illustrated. **1870** LUBBOCK *Orig. Civiliz.* ii. (1875) 44 It is indeed but a step to record pictorially some particular hunt.

2. In the manner of a picture; as a picture, or as the subject of a picture.

1860 HAWTHORNE *Marb. Faun* (1879) I. v. 50 That partial light which..is the just requisite towards seeing objects pictorially. **1883** T. HARDY in *Longm. Mag.* July 259 Like the men, the women are, pictorially, less interesting than they used to be.

pic'toric, *a. rare.* [f. L. *pictor* painter + -IC: cf. ORATORIC.] Of painting or drawing; pictorial.

1902 B. KIDD *Western Civiliz.* vi. 187 The standard of taste in the plastic and pictoric arts.

pic'torical, *a. rare.* [f. as prec. + -ICAL.] Concerned with painters or painting; pictorial. Hence **pic'torically** *adv.*, in the manner of a painter, from the point of view of painting.

1596 HARINGTON *Metam. Ajax* (1814) 20 Since this travel we have been both poetical and I musical and pictorical. **1656** [see PICTURAL]. **1761** STERNE *Tr. Shandy* III. v, He must have redden'd, pictorically and scientintically speaking, six whole tints and a half..above his natural colour. **1883** SCHAFF *Hist. Ch.* II. XII. lxxxi. 637 He is fond of the historical present..of pictorical participles and of affectionate diminutives.

pictour(e, obs. form of PICTURE.

||**pictura** (pɪk'tjʊərə). *Zool.* [L. *pictūra* painting.] The arrangement and effect of coloration of an animal.

1890 *Cent. Dict.* s.v., Pictura differs from coloration in noting the disposition and effect of coloring, not the color itself.

,pictura'bility. [f. PICTURABLE *a.*: see -ILITY.] The state or quality of being picturable; capacity for visual representation.

1934 in WEBSTER. **1957** R. W. BROWN in Saporta & Bastian *Psycholinguistics* (1961) 505/1 The concrete noun with the smaller denotation is likely to be more picturable than its superordinate, and picturability is another common sense of 'concrete'. **1968** M. JAMMER in R. Klibansky *Contemp. Philos.* II. 349 The shackles of intuitive picturability ('*Anschaulichkeit*').

picturable ('pɪktjʊərəb(ə)l, -tʃə-), *a.* [f. PICTURE *v.* + -ABLE.] Suitable for representation in a picture, capable of being painted or pictured.

1796 W. MARSHALL *W. England* II. 72 A fine..view of the Estuary and its banks: broad, but grand, and picturable. **1801** *Monthly Rev.* XXXV. 275 The rich..[might build] small picturable habitations for their labourers. **1890** CLARK RUSSELL *Ocean Trag.* I. iv. 79 He..stalked,..in the most melancholic manner picturable, to his cabin.

Hence **'picturableness**.

1883 MOMERIE *Personality* ii. (1886) 60 *Picturableness* is not necessary to the existence of a concept.

'pictural, *a.* (*sb.*) *rare.* [f. L. *pictūra* PICTURE + -AL¹.] **A.** *adj.* Of or pertaining to pictures; pictorial.

1656 BLOUNT *Glossogr.*, *Pictorical, Pictorian, Pictural*, of or belonging to a Picture; garnished, painted, gaily or trimly set forth. *Dr. Br.* **1799** T. GREEN *Diary Lover of Lit.* (1810) 177 Writing, he deduces, from pictural representations, through hieroglyphics..to arbitrary marks..like the Chinese characters and Arabic numerals. **1828** *Q. Rev.* XXXVII. 304 Horace Walpole..has traced the history of gardening, in a pictural sense, from the mere art of horticulture to the creation of scenery.

†**B.** *sb.* A picture, a pictorial representation. *Obs. rare.*

1590 SPENSER *F.Q.* II. ix. 53 Whose wals Were painted faire with memorable gestes Of famous Wisards; and with picturals Of Magistrates.

picture ('pɪktjʊə(r), -tʃə(r)), *sb.* Forms: 5–6 pict-, pyctour(e, pycture, 5– picture, (6 pyghtur, 6–7 pictor, -ur). [ad. L. *pictūra* painting, f. *pict-*, ppl. stem of *pingĕre* to paint. Cf. It. *pittura.*]

†**1.** The action or process of painting or drawing; the fact or condition of being painted or pictorially represented; the art of painting; pictorial representation. *Obs.*

c **1420** LYDG. *Assembly of Gods* 1767 The furst behynde the yn pycture ys prouydyd. *c* **1500** *Melusine* 352 There were the armes of Lusynen wel shewed and knowen in pycture. **1606** PEACHAM *Art of Drawing* 3 Certain Festival dayes were yearly appointed at Corinth for the exercise of Picture. **1636** B. JONSON *Discov.* Wks. (1692) 707 Picture took her feigning from Poetry. **1693** DRYDEN *To Sir G. Kneller* 36 By slow degrees the godlike art advanced; As man grew polished, picture was enhanced. **1744** COLLINS *Epist. to Sir T. Hanmer* 108 O might some verse with happiest skill persuade Expressive Picture to adopt thine aid! **1844** L. HUNT *Imag. & Fancy* (1846) 104 That subtler spirit of the art [poetry], which picture cannot express.

2. The concrete result of this process.

†**a.** Pictorial representations collectively; painting.

c **1420** LYDG. *Assembly of Gods* 1865 The pycture also yeueth clere intellygence Therof. *c* **1430** —— *Min. Poems* (Percy Soc.) 120 The riche is shitte withe colours and picture, To hide his careyne stuffid withe foule ardure. **1573–80** BARET *Alv.* P 338 Picture, worke of wood, stone, or mettall finelie set in diuers colours, as in chesse boords and tables.

b. An individual painting, drawing, or other representation on a surface, of an object or objects; *esp.* such a representation as a work of art. (Now the prevailing sense.)

1484 CAXTON *Fables of Æsop* IV. xv, A pyctour, where as a man had vyctory ouer a lyon. **1542** BOORDE *Dyetary* xl. (1870) 302 To holde a crosse or a pyctour of the passyon of Cryste before the eyes of the sycke person. **1598** E. GILPIN *Skial* (1878) 23 Pictures are curtaind from the vulgar eyes. **1653** WALTON *Angler* To Rdr. 2 He that likes not the discourse, should like the pictures of the Trout and other fish. **1705** ADDISON *Italy* Pref., Accounts of Pictures, Statues and Buildings. **1839** *Sat. Mag.* 13 Apr. 139/2 The photogenic picture being formed, requires fixing. **1852** RUSKIN *Arrows of Chace* (1880) I. 71 Every noble picture is a manuscript book, of which only one copy exists, or ever can exist. **1854** J. SCOFFERN in *Orr's Circ. Sc.* I. 88 This means of taking actinic pictures. **1893** *Westm. Gaz.* 16 June 3/2 A picture, using the word as language is ordinarily used, is a picture of something, and it is rather important to the artist that it should be a picture of something he can paint.

c. *spec.* The portrait or likeness of a person. Now *rare.*

1505 in *Mem. Hen. VII* (Rolls) 271 In case that the said yonge quyn were here ye shuld have the pictor of hir with yow. **1538** CROMWELL in Merriman *Life & Lett.* (1902) II. 120 To thentent he might..visite and see his daughter and also take her picture. **1601** SHAKS. *Twel. N.* III. iv. 228 Heere, weare this Iewell for me, tis my picture. **1662** PEPYS *Diary* 3 May, At the goldsmith's, took my picture in little..home with me. **1712** ADDISON *Spect.* No. 328* ¶1 She..draws all her Relations Pictures in Miniature. **1790** COWPER (*title*) On the receipt of my Mother's Picture out of Norfolk.

†**d.** By extension, An artistic (in quot. 1771 natural) representation in the solid, esp. a statue or a monumental effigy; an image. *Obs.*

c **1500** *Cov. Corpus Chr. Plays* 40/227 O Lorde! thogh that I be nothynge worthe To see the fassion of thi most presseose pyctore. **1509** HAWES *Past. Pleas.* i. (Percy Soc.) 6 This goodly picture was in altitude Nyne fote and more, of fayre marble stone. **1577** HELLOWES *Gueuara's Chron.* 49 He ..did erect vnto them pictures of Alabaster. **1590** in Pitcairn *Crim. Trials* I. ii. 192 Thow art accusit for the making of twa pictouris of clay. **1608** HEYWOOD *Rape Lucrece* V. vi, Thy noble picture shall be carv'd in brass, And fix'd..In our high Capitol. **1682** R. BURTON *Admirable Curios.* (1684) 132 But K. Henry 7. afterward caused a Tomb to be set over the Place, with his Picture in Alabaster. **1771** LANGHORNE *Fables of Flora* ix, I sought the living Bee to find, And found the picture of a Bee.

e. A group of persons, generally motionless, picturesquely arranged and posed, representing a scene, or mimicking an action; a tableau; *spec.* in the drama, at the end of an act or play. Also ***living picture*** (F. *tableau vivant*).

1802 T. HOLCROFT *Tale of Mystery* 30 Enter Malvoglio. He stops in the middle of the stage: the company start up... The peasants, alarmed and watching: the whole, during a short pause, forming a picture. *c* **1825** J. POOLE *Paul Pry* I. ii. 13 There is a general shout of '*Paul Pry*'. *Picture, and act closes.* **1865** TYLOR *Early Hist. Man.* iv. 59 Imitation of actions, or 'pictures in the air'. **1904** *Daily Chron.* 9 Dec. 8/5 The great excitement comes when four of the girls are called upon to practise the 'picture'. In this language of the dance a 'picture' means the moment when the dance is stopped, and the dancers get into a most uncomfortable attitude and pretend to enjoy it.

f. A visible image *of* something formed by physical means, as by a lens.

1668 HOOKE in *Phil. Trans.* II. 741 A Contrivance to make the Picture of any thing appear on a Wall,..or within a Picture-frame, &c. in the midst of a Light room. **1831** BREWSTER *Optics* ii. 15 The image of any object is a picture of it formed either in the air, or in the bottom of the eye, or upon a white ground, such as a sheet of paper. **1915** *Wireless World* June 193/1 A picture, constant as long as the cells are under the influence of the original picture, is thus obtained on the receiving screen. **1928**, etc. [see FRAME *sb.* 12c]. **1934** J. H. REYNER *Television* iii. 33 Fig. 14 shows the number of pictues per second at which flicker can just be detected, in terms of illumination. **1943**, etc. [see FIELD *sb.* 16d]. **1953** AMOS & BIRKINSHAW *Television Engin.* I. i. 14 This time must be short to enable pictures to be transmitted in quick succession, as in cinema film projection. **1956** *B.B.C. Handbk.* 1957 215 The television services of the two countries use different standards, the English system based on a 405-line picture and the French on one of 819 lines. **1960** J. STROUD *Shorn Lamb* xxii. 240 Some well-intentioned hostesses obligingly turned off the sound but not the picture. **1972** G. WHITE *Video Recording* iii. 17 The definition of the reproduced picture depends upon the frequency response of the signal system. **1976** *Daily Tel.* 30 June 2/6 Pictures sent back so far show that areas previously believed to be smooth channels..are pock marked with craters. **1977** J. FRENCH *Small Craft Radar* iii. 86 The radar picture is built up by displaying on a time-related sweep line the instantaneous point of arrival of the echo.

g. A person so strongly resembling another as to seem a likeness or imitation of him or her; = IMAGE *sb.* 4. Const. *of.*

1712 *Spect.* No. 520 ¶1 My daughter, who is the picture of what her mother was. **1715** DE FOE *Fam. Instruct.* I. v. (1841) I. 109 The sons are the very picture of their father. **1755** J. SHEBBEARE *Lydia* (1769) II. 258 'Lydy', says his lordship, 'it [a boy] is your picture to the utmost resemblance'. *a* **1817** JANE AUSTEN *Northanger Abbey* (1818) I. iv. 49 'How excessively like her brother Miss Morland is!' 'The very picture of him, indeed!' **1877** G. MACDONALD *Marquis of Lossie* III. iv. 81 Isna his mere 'at they ca' Kelpie jist the pictur' o' the deil's ain horse. **1896** P. A. GRAHAM *Red Scaur* 271 You're the verra pictur' o' awd Mr. Selwyn.

h. *fig. colloq.* A very beautiful or picturesque object. See also ***pretty as a picture*** s.v. PRETTY *a.* II. 4a.

1815 *Sporting Mag.* XLVII. 135/2 She looked a perfect picture. **1827** J. CONSTABLE *Let.* 4 Oct. in *Corr.* (1962) I. 234 Minna looks so nice in her pelisse—the blew band or what it is called was a picture. **1842** C. BRONTË *Let.* 20 Jan. in W. Gérin *C. Brontë* (1967) xii. 179 He sits opposite to Anne at Church sighing softly..and Anne is so quiet..they are a picture. **1848** DICKENS *Dombey* lvii. 575 He has been working..to make his cabin what the Captain calls 'a picter', to surprise his little wife. **1871** G. MEREDITH *Let.* 15 Feb. (1970) I. 439 The French..have many a noble turning, and are always a picture, good for study. **1937** A. CHRISTIE *Dumb Witness* vii. 65 The gardens are a picture. **1961** *Guardian* 9 June 12/1 The bride was, as they say, 'a picture'. **1977** *Daily News* (Perth, Austral.) 19 Jan. 50/5 The rain this week won't have hurt. All it has done is make the grass greener. The court looks a picture.

i. A representation (of a scene) on a cinematographic film; the film produced or its projection on a screen, = FILM *sb.* 3c. Freq. in *pl.*, (*a*) cinematographic productions collectively; (*b*) usu. with *the*, the showing of a film in a cinema, a picture-show.

1896 [see PROJECT *v.* 9d]. **1912** *Home Chat* 25 May 391/1 In order to get a picture of the sacking of a village, an actual village was some time ago purchased and fired. **1913** *Ibid.* 20 Sept. 530/1 The pictures one sees nowadays are..in much better taste than those of a few years ago. **1915** *Kinematograph & Lantern Weekly* 1 July 61/2 During his very successful career in 'pictures' he has appeared in some ..thrilling productions. **1915** T. BURKE *Nights in Town* 110 Mother and Father..go to the pictures at the Palladium near Balham Station. **1916** *Variety* 27 Oct. 12/2 His bride was in the Kellermann picture, 'A Daughter of the Gods'. **1923** WODEHOUSE *Inimitable Jeeves* xii. 129 Charlotte is coming to the Zoo with me this afternoon. Alone. And later on to the pictures. **1937** D. L. SAYERS *Busman's Honeymoon* x. 225 Off to them pictures again. **1947** A. HUXLEY *Let.* 27 July (1969) 573 The ticklish situation on the set made it impossible to come to New York for Claire's wedding. But we hope and intend to make the trip after the picture is finished. **1960** M. STARK *Ballad of Peckham Rye* viii. 187 They came out of the pictures at eight o'clock. **1974** *Sat. Rev. World* (U.S.) 19 Oct. 56/2 My son had gone to the movies... I asked him, 'How was the picture?' **1977** I. SHAW *Beggarman, Thief* III. xi. 354 The picture was not scheduled to start for another ten minutes. **1978** P. GRACE *Mutuwhenua* iii. 11, I went to the pictures or a social with my cousins.

j. Phr. ***every picture tells a story***, orig. popularized by an advertising slogan (see quot. 1927); also in extended uses.

[**1847** C. BRONTË *Jane Eyre* I. i. 5 The letter-press..I cared little for... Each picture told a story.] **1906** *S.A. News Weekly* 26 Sept. 23/3 (Advt.), Every picture tells a story... At the first sign of kidney disease..take Doan's Backache Kidney Pills. **1923** A. HUXLEY *Antic Hay* xxi. 290 'I'm very ill,' she went on expiringly. 'Look at me,' she pointed to herself, 'and me again.' She waved her hand towards the sizzling brilliance of the portrait. 'Before and after. Like the advertisements, you know. Every picture tells a story.' **1927** W. E. COLLINSON *Contemp. Eng.* 65 The wording accompanying..the distressing pictures of human suffering, amenable to treatment by Doan's Backache Kidney Pills, supplies us with the useful Every picture tells a story!—often used derisively of anecdotal paintings. **1976** *Radio Times* 25 Sept. 5 (*caption*) Every picture tells a story: Rod Stewart, the working-class boy who has become a working-class hero.

k. ***one picture is worth ten thousand words*** and varr.

[**1921** *Printer's Ink* 8 Dec. 96 (*heading*) One look is worth a thousand words.] **1927** *Ibid.* 10 Mar. 114 (*caption*) Chinese proverb. One picture is worth ten thousand words. **1954** R. HAYDN *Jrnl. Edwin Carp* 90 'One picture speaks louder than ten thousand words.' Mr. Bovey repeated the adage this morning when..he handed me my finished portrait. **1979** *Daily Tel.* 14 Aug. 11 If proof was ever needed that a few good pictures are worth more than a thousand statistics it came with bludgeoning force in last night's account of *The Voyage of Rainbow Warrior* (BBC-2) in the 'Inside Story' series.

3. *transf.* **a.** A scene; the total visual impression produced by something; hence extended to a vivid impression received by the other senses, or produced by intellectual perception; a mental image, a visualized conception: = IDEA 8.

clinical picture: the total impression or apprehension of a diseased condition, formed by the physician.

a **1547** Surrey *Æneid* iv. 6 In her brest Imprinted stack his wordes, a pictures forme. **1837** Syd. Smith *Ballot* Wks. 1859 II. 316/1, I have often drawn a picture in my own mind of a Balloto-Grotical family voting and promising under the new system. **1855** Bain *Senses & Int.* iii. iv. §12 (1864) 603 A botanist can readily form to himself the picture of a new plant from the botanical description. **1857** Dufferin *Lett. High Lat.* (ed. 3) 179 The vigorous imagination of the north ..creating a stately dreamland, where it strove to blend, in a grand world picture,..the influences which sustained both the physical and moral system of its universe.

b. *Med.* The sum of the clinical or histological features present in a particular state of the body.

1897 *Allbutt's Syst. Med.* II. 771 In such cases the disease of the liver may be dominant in the clinical picture. **1931** *Jrnl. Exper. Med.* LIV. 244 The clinical picture of 'mad itch' is very suggestive of pseudorabies. **1940** *Endocrinology* XXVII. 127 The histological pictures of the hypertrophied uteri after vitamin E administration and after mechanical stimulation of the cervix uteri were identical. **1966** Wright & Symmers *Systemic Path.* II. xxxix. 1475/1 The histological picture of psoriasis is distinctive but not pathognomic. **1977** *Lancet* 30 July 241/1 Another renal biopsy on March 31 revealed a hyperacute picture (diffuse small and medium arteriolar fibrin thrombi, infarction, and glomerular necrosis).

c. In extended uses, a set of circumstances or state of affairs, esp. in phrs. ***to be in the picture***, to understand or be involved in a particular situation or activity, to be in harmony with one's surroundings; similarly ***to be out of the picture***, to be uninvolved, inactive, or out of place; ***to get the picture***, to grasp or become aware of certain circumstances or facts; ***to put*** (someone) ***in the picture***, to inform (that person) of particular circumstances or facts.

1900 Beerbohm *Around Theatres* (1924) I. 165 His performance is, strictly, more 'in the picture' than was Mr. Robertson's. **1902** C. Morris *Stage Confidences* 202 Oh, well, I feel that I am in the picture, when I wear black during Lent. **1918** Ld. Derby in R. S. Churchill *Lord Derby* (1959) xv. 337 He [*sc.* a new ambassador in Paris]..would..by entertaining be able to bring the British Embassy more, what I may call, 'into the picture' than it is at the present moment. **1923** T. E. Lawrence *Let.* 19 Mar. (1938) 411, I said to one 'They're the sort who instinctively fling stones at cats'..and he said 'Why what do you throw?' You perceive that I'm not yet in the picture. **1923** Wodehouse *Good Morning, Bill!* i. 24 'And what's the matter with taking me along?' 'I don't think you would be quite in the picture.' **1926** Maines & Grant *Wise-Crack Dict.* 11/2 *Out of the picture*, in the wrong company. **1936** R. Lehmann *Weather in Streets* iii. iv. 320 Think of me as out of the picture..for ever. Unless, of course, you should wish to see me. **1937** L. Bromfield *Rains Came* i. xlv. 190 She should never have come out to India. She doesn't fit into the picture. **1938** [see chin *sb.*[1] 1 d]. **1939** L. M. Montgomery *Anne of Ingleside* xlii. 327 Christine took possession of the whole room... Anne felt as if she were not in the picture at all. **1942** E. Waugh *Put out More Flags* ii. 150 'Put these men in the picture, Smallwood,' he said, and there had followed a tedious and barely credible narrative about the unprovoked aggression of Southland against Northland. **1950** N. Streatfeild *Mothering Sunday* 144 You keep calling me a criminal, darling, but that's where you aren't in the picture. **1959** P. McCutchan *Storm South* xvii. 239, I would have to be kept right out of the picture so far as the Australian public eye and the police..are concerned. **1960** C. S. Lewis *Studies in Words* v. 128 The attitude of any slave-owning society is and ought to be repellent to us, but it is worth while suppressing that repulsion in order to get the picture as Aristotle saw it. **1961** T. Coffin *Not to the Swift* xviii. 201 Do you get the picture of the kind of fellow he was? **1963** A. Huxley *Let.* 17 Nov. (1969) 964 Under what conditions is this being done and where do I come into the picture? **1966** 'A. Hall' *9th Directive* i. 14 At this time..the South-east Asian picture is confused and threatening. **1970** G. Greer *Female Eunuch* 128 Nurses are skilled menials, and as such they fall into line with the dominant pattern of female employment. Salesgirls..waitresses..tea ladies, fill out the picture. **1971** K. Amis *Girl, 20* iv. 129 I'm sorry I've been out of the picture, but I've been up to my neck... Haven't had a bloody minute. **1973** A. Behrend *Samarai Affair* xiii. 136 Come over here soon as possible and I'll put you in the picture. **1975** N. Luard *Travelling Horseman* viii. 198, I explained all this... He seems to get the picture. **1977** *New Yorker* 15 Aug. 36/2, I suppose you were trying to make me jealous—jealous and not jealous. Tearing poor Ann down but letting me know she was in the picture.

4. a. *fig.* A graphic description, written or spoken, capable of suggesting a mental image, or of imparting a notion, of the object described; also *abstr.* word-painting, figurative language.

1588 Shaks. *L.L.L.* v. ii. 38, I am compar'd to twenty thousand fairs. O he hath drawne my picture in his letter. **1677** Lady Chaworth in *12th Rep. Hist. MSS. Comm.* App. v. 44 Two of your acquaintances have their picture drawne in it [*Hudibras*]..to the lyfe. **1736** Butler *Anal.* i. i. (1874) 31 To afford the poets very apt allusions to the flowers of the field in their pictures of the frailty of our present life. **1801** Strutt *Sports & Past.* Introd. §6 Chaucer says [etc.] The picture is perfect, when referred to his own time. **1819** Stark (*title*) The Picture of Edinburgh. **1867** Froude *Short Stud.* (1883) IV. i. xi. 139 The details of the miracles contain many interesting pictures of old English life.

b. *Philos.* In the study of meaning, the mental image that is assumed to correspond to a fact; also *attrib.*

1922 tr. *Wittgenstein's Tractatus* 39 We make to ourselves pictures of facts. *Ibid.*, The picture presents the facts in logical space, the existence and non-existence of atomic facts. **1940** B. Russell *Inquiry into Meaning & Truth* xiii. 230, I can make a picture of Brutus killing Caesar..but I cannot make a picture, either real or imagined, of quadruplicity killing procrastination. **1946** *Mind* LV. 47 With their use of 'the picture gallery method', and with their insistence on the marginal case, the W[ittgensteinia]ns should be the first persons to admit..this possiblity. **1956** J. O. Urmson *Philos. Analysis* v. 54 The relation of language and the world, or picture of fact and fact. **1970** D. M. Taylor *Explanation & Meaning* xi. 132 (*heading*) The picture theory of meaning. **1975** Hargreaves & White tr. *Wittgenstein's Philos. Remarks* iii. 63 The essential difference between the picture conception [of intention] and the conception of Russell, Ogden and Richards, is that it regards recognition as seeing an internal relation. *Ibid.*, The intention never resides in the picture itself. **1977** G. Hallett *Compan. to Wittgenstein's 'Philos. Investigations'* 41 The direction Wittgenstein's thinking took momentarily when he pondered the implications of the picture theory.

5. a. A symbol, type, figure; the concrete representation of an abstraction; an illustration.

1656 Jeanes *Mixt. Schol. Div.* 49 Mans soule is Gods temple, and picture. **1779–81** Johnson *L.P., Butler* Wks. II. 190 Of the ancient Puritans... Our grandfathers knew the picture from the life. **1792** Gouv. Morris in Sparks *Life & Writ.* (1832) II. 182 The best picture I can give of the French nation is that of cattle before a thunder storm. **1863** Mary Howitt *F. Bremer's Greece* I. vii. 246, I had before me daily..a beautiful picture of the life of the Greek grand seigneur on his native island.

b. With *of* and abstract sb.: An object, esp. a person, possessing a quality in so high a degree as to be a symbol or realization of that quality.

1580 Lyly *Euphues* (Arb.) 312 Behold England, wher Camilla was borne, the flower of courtesie, the picture of comelynesse. **1749** Fielding *Tom Jones* xviii. ii, Upon these words, Jones became in a moment a greater picture of horror than Partridge himself. **1871** *Punch* 15 July 17/2 He looks the picture of health. **1888** Burgon *Lives 12 Gd. Men* I. iii. 331 Those rooms were the very picture of disorder.

6. *attrib.* and *Comb.* **a.** attrib. Concerned in the painting, disposal, collection, etc. of pictures, as ***picture-art, -craft, -critic, -knowledge, library, -merchant, -ring, -shop***, etc.; consisting of or expressed in a picture or pictures, as ***picture-cycle, -dialect, -language, -poem, -puzzle, -story, -thought, -word***; adorned or illustrated with a picture or pictures, pictorial, as ***picture-cover, frock, gown, newspaper, -paper, -sheet, -sign, -strip, -table, -tile***; having a character resembling a picture or suitable for one, as ***picture dress, house, sleeve***; (in sense 2 i) ***picture-house, -palace, -play, -playhouse, theatre***. **b.** Objective and objective gen., as ***picture-borrowing, -buying, -cleaning, -dealing, -going, -hanging, -making, -painting, -taking, -viewing*** sbs. and adjs.; ***picture-cleaner, -dealer, -drawer, -framer, -gazer, -goer, -keeper, -maker, -restorer, -seller, -taker***, etc. **c.** Instrumental, as ***picture-broidered, -hung, -pasted*** adjs.; ***picture-lesson, -thinking***.

1879 N. Michell *Palenque* in *Poems Places, Br. Amer.*, etc. 149 Their gorgeous buildings.. Their *picture-art, and creeds of gloom and fear. **1904** T. S. Moore *Ode to Leda* etc. p. x, Thy *picture-broidered train might be a book. **1766** Goldsm. *Vic. W.* xx, To instruct you in the art of *picture-buying at Paris. **1763** H. Walpole *Let.* 1 July in *Corr.* (1941) X. 84 Gilders, carvers, upholsterers and *picture-cleaners are labouring at their several forges. **1812** J. Smyth *Pract. of Customs* (1821) 36 Canada Balsam..is much used by Picture-cleaners for their Varnishes. **1902** *Chambers's Jrnl.* July 433/2, I entrusted the panel to the most expert picture-cleaner of my acquaintance, from whose hands it came out perfect. **1978** *P.O. Telephone Directory: Yellow Pages Classified: London (North)* Apr. 294/3 Picture cleaners and restorers. **1871** D. G. Rossetti *Let.* 4 Aug. (1967) III. 966, I (like most artists) am quite ignorant about *picture cleaning. **1937** *Burlington Mag.* May p. xxxiv/1 The picture-cleaning controversy at the National Gallery. **1894** Eliz. L. Banks *Newspaper Girl* xii. (1902) 146 He won't get the colouring from the *picture-cover [of a book] in his mouth. **1762–71** H. Walpole *Vertue's Anecd. Paint.* (1786) II. 207 *note*, An adept in all the arts of *picture-craft. **1856** R. A. Vaughan *Mystics* (1860) I. 8 If the *picture-critics would only write their verdicts after dinner, many a poor victim would find his dinner prospects brighter. **1968** *Medium Ævum* XXXVII. 56 This *picture-cycle must have been in existence by 1215. **1971** *Amer. N. & Q.* Sept. 14/2 The whole vast field of early Biblical picture-cycles. **1824** Byron *Juan* xvi. lvi, There was a *picture-dealer. **1847** A. Brontë *Agnes Grey* i. 14 What do you say to doing a few more pictures..getting them framed..and trying to dispose of them to some liberal *picture-dealer? **1950** E. H. Gombrich *Story of Art* xx. 311 He had..to rely on middlemen, picture dealers. **1805** M. A. Shee *Rhymes Art* (1806) 83 And patronage in *picture-dealing dies! *Ibid.* 93 *note*, By some ingenious picture-dealing anecdote. **1901** *Daily Chron.* 14 Dec. 8/1 With this *picture-dialect at your command, why trouble to learn Sicilian? **1888** *Pall Mall G.* 20 Feb. 5/2 These are '*picture dresses', called so..on account of the fact that their salient features are copied from the paintings of Lawrence, Reynolds, Gainsborough, and other masters of the last century. **1598** E. Gilpin *Skial.* (1878) 24 Painted Nigrina with the *picture face. **1933** *New Yorker* 1 Apr. 37/3, I..hurried around to the nearest *picture-framer. **1972** *Times* 30 Sept. 11/1 Pass the picture framer's on the right. **1905** in C. W. Cunnington *Eng. Women's Clothing* (1952) ii. 67 The rage for the *picture frock for evening, of the Greuze or Romney style. **1930** *Daily Express* 8 Sept. 3/6 There must be curls..to harmonise with the long Victorian dresses and picture frocks. **1975** G. Howell *In Vogue* 92 (*caption*) This picture frock of pale blue taffeta. **1922** *Moving Picture Stories* 30 June 23/3 The millions who are regular *picture-goers. **1947** *Landfall* I. 294 The contemporary cinema, as it is seen by the New Zealand picture-goer. **1976** *Cumberland & Westmorland Herald* 4 Dec. 3/4 Picturegoers may remember the woman who used to turn and smile from the screen as the hallmark of Gainsborough productions. **1976** 'G. Black' *Moon for Killers* i. 19, I always watch the movie. I really catch up on my *picture-going in airplanes. **1922** *Liberty Dresses* (Catal.) Spring 25 *Picture gown, adapted from a 17th-Century design. **1949** A. Christie *Crooked House* xiv. 107 Magda, the Duchess of Three Gables, in a picture gown of taffetas. **1975** G. Howell *In Vogue* 147 (*caption*) Picture gown of black tulle. **1880** Carnegie *Pract. Trap.* 12 The nooses..should be made of *picture-hanging wire. **1896** Mrs. Caffyn *Quaker Grandmother* 72 What a dear old *picture house! **1908** *Variety* 23 May 12 Hundreds seated in a picture house who..watch with cooling brows the reels run off. **1913** *Punch* 31 Dec. 543/3 Scene outside an Islington Picture-house. **1939** [see fried *ppl. a.* b]. **1975** *Country Life* 6 Feb. 326/1 In 1928, the publisher..laid out £4,000 promoting a song..sending lantern slides..to every picture house in the country. **1684** E. Chamberlayne *Pres. St. Eng.* i. (ed. 15) 181 One *Picture-keeper, Mr. Henry Norris. **1887** Ruskin *Præterita* II. v. 180, I had advanced in *picture knowledge since the Roman days. **1855** Pusey *Doctr. Real Presence* Note E. 69 They are figures (as in what is plainly *picture-language). **1857–8** Sears *Athan.* iii. vi. 305 The natural world..is taken up and framed into a picture-language, and thus made to represent the things which are invisible. **1882** R. W. Dale in *Gd. Words* Apr. 262 It was the gospel..taught in *picture-lessons. **1958** *Times* 31 July 4/6 B.B.C. buy *picture library. The B.B.C. have bought the Hulton picture library from Hulton Press Ltd., it was announced yesterday. The library, which was originally called the Picture Post library..will be known as Radio Times Hulton picture library. **1975** N. Luard *Travelling Horseman* vi. 167, I got back..from the picture library about 5.30. **1589–90** *Rec. Borough Leicester* (1905) III. 263 Affabell Watson of Markefyld *picture maker. **1633** Ford *Love's Sacr.* ii. ii, Where dwells the picture-maker? **1755** Johnson, *Limner*, a painter; a picture-maker. **1894** A. Macdonell *Thomas Hardy* x. 232 Story-teller, picture-maker, humourist, it is entertainment he offers us. **1926** V. Woolf *Captain's Death Bed* (1950) 167 The picture-makers seem dissatisfied with such obvious sources of interest. **1889** *Anthony's Photogr. Bull.* II. 118 Any one who has a glimmering of the science of *picture-making. **1902** *Westm. Gaz.* 23 June 8/2 The value of bromide paper as a picture-making medium. **1926** V. Woolf *Captain's Death Bed* (1950) 169 The picture-making power. **1961** J. McCabe *Mr. Laurel & Mr. Hardy* (1962) viii. 159 The trouble with modern picture-making is the lack of time for preparation. **1760** D. Webb *Beauties of Painting* Pref. 11 An idle art more useful to a *picture-merchant, than becoming a man of taste. **1853** Dickens *Bleak Ho.* xxxiii. 329 There comes the artist of a *picture newspaper. **1979** G. Macdonald *Camera* x. 148/2 The development of picture magazines and newspapers. **1899** *Westm. Gaz.* 6 Apr. 3/2 It would be interesting to make..a *picture-painting artist out of a creative milliner or dress-maker. **1908** *Stage Year Bk.* 48 There are now indications that before long these *picture 'palaces' will be a feature of London and the larger provincial towns. **1937** D. L. Sayers *Busman's Honeymoon* iv. 85 The neighbourhood boasted a picture palace. **1973** *Listener* 26 July 124/3 A secure world of..visits to the pie-and-mash, and Tuesdays at the Carlton picture-palace. **1867** *Harper's Mag.* 2 Feb. 80/1 I'm sure, Dear, the *Picture Papers can not make Frights of us now! **1878** *N. Amer. Rev.* CXXVII. 9 Scandalous picture-papers. **1894** S. Fiske *Holiday Stories* (1900) 183 An artist of the picture-paper school. **1959** T. S. Eliot *Elder Statesman* ii. 43 I'll feel more confidence after a fortnight..Of people not staring Or offering picture papers. **1887** T. N. Page *Ole Virginia* (1893) 144 The *picture-pasted walls of her house. **1911** *Chambers's Jrnl.* Sept. 621/1 Many of the leading dramatists now devote their energies seriously to the elaboration of scenarios for *picture-plays. **1923** Picture play [see *picture magazine* in sense 6d below]. **1919** *Honey Pot* I. iv. 1 (Advt.), The New Gallery Kinema, Society's *Picture Playhouse. **1966** J. Derrick *Teaching Eng. to Immigrants* vii. 224 There are in fact several wall charts and picture-story picture sets especially printed for language teachers. **1893** W. B. Worsfold in *19th Cent.* Apr. 290 We have at least learnt to be grateful for Rossetti's *picture-poems and poem-pictures. **1898** *Daily News* 10 Dec. 6/3 We believe that this is the right word for this kind of *picture-puzzle. **1831** *Edin. Rev.* 166 The rude hands of *picture-restorers. **1885** H. Pearson *Browning* 13 Only the position of the *picture-rings determines whether the thing shall be hung upside, downside, or end-wise. **1666** Pepys *Diary* 20 June, Thence to Faythorne, the *picture-seller's. **1732** Savage *Author to be let* Wks. 1775 II. 268, I wish my portrait might shine in a mezzotinto through the glass windows of *picture-shops. **1899** *Daily News* 19 Aug. 7/7 On the other side of the high-way..is the *picture-sign of the house. **1894** *Westm. Gaz.* 6 Oct. 5/3 *Picture sleeves, finished with a flounce of silk and chiffon. **1895** Kipling *2nd Jungle Bk.* (Tauchn.) 208 He left the *picture-story with Kadlu, who lost it in the shingle. **1968** *Tamarack Rev.* Spring 18 Somebody passed Jake the issue of *Life* magazine with the lead *picture story on Israel. **1949** Koestler *Insight & Outlook* xxiv. 345 Transitions from primitive *picture-strip language to more abstract forms of expression. **1959** I. & P. Opie *Lore & Lang. Schoolch.* ix. 172 Few people now are nicknamed 'Giglamps'.., although derivatives persist in the picture strips. **1966** J. Derrick *Teaching Eng. to Immigrants* v. 183 Picture-strip stories, in which a little episode is told in pictures as in comic strips. **1979** 'S. Kemp' *Goodbye, Pussy* ix. 115 Just like a picture-strip, isn't it? **1629** H. Burton *Truth's Triumph* 10 An artificiall indented *picture-table. **1909** *Westm. Gaz.* 10 July 14/2 Two out of three men.. neglect their apparatus and drift out of the ranks of the *picture-takers. **1969** *Amat. Photographer* 28 May 53 (Advt.), The sort of picture-taker who winds the film on the wrong way. **1976** *Daily Progress* (Charlottesville, Va.) 27 Apr. (Advt.), CB spoken here.. *Picture taker*, radar unit. **1908** *Variety* 16 May 11 A new *picture theatre will be opened at 276 State Street. **1970** *Southerly* XXX. 124 The town which could offer them a pub, picture theatre, souvenir shops, milk bars. **1976** *Times* 13 Mar. 9/1 All the Continental towns they visited had moving picture theatres while Ireland had none. **1874** W. Wallace tr. *Hegel's Logic* 30 Conception or *picture-thinking works with materials from the same sensuous source. **1879** A. B. Bruce in *Expositor* X. 143 We have before us..picture-thinking in which these nations are used symbolically. **1945** R. A. Knox *God & Atom* vii. 90 One will depend more on picture-thinking, on crude, unanalysed notions, than another. *a* **1963** C. S. Lewis *Poems* (1964) 78 Film, broadcast, propaganda, picture-thinking. **1874** W. Wallace tr. *Hegel's*

Logic 53 The predicates by which the object is to be determined are supplied from the resources of *picture-thought. **1896** *Daily News* 30 July 2/3 Furnishing and decorating with *picture tiles a ward which is now being added to this hospital. **1855** PUSEY *Doctr. Real Presence* Note F. 63 Passages..in which the words 'Door' and 'Husbandman' are figurative, metaphorical, *picture-words.

d. Special combs.: **picture black** *Television*, the light level of the darkest element of a television picture, or the picture signal voltage corresponding to this; **picture-board**, a decoration consisting of a plank shaped and painted to resemble some object; employed especially in the 18th c.; **picture-book**, a book consisting wholly or partly of pictures, esp. for children; also *attrib.* or as *adj.*, characteristic or suggestive of a picture-book; excessively or sentimentally pretty; **picture-card**, any card bearing a picture; *spec.* (*a*) a court-card in a pack of cards (see also PICTURED 2 b); (*b*) short for *picture postcard*; also *fig.*; **picture-coffin**, a name suggested for leaden coffins of early 17th c. date, somewhat resembling in shape the outer case of an Egyptian mummy, and bearing a mask of the deceased; **picture-documents** *Anthrop.*, records wholly or (in later times) partly in picture-writing, such as were used by the ancient Mexicans, and continued in use for certain purposes long after the Spanish conquest; **picture element** *Television*, any of the minute areas of uniform illumination of which a television image is composed and which are produced successively by the scanning beam; **picture-frame**, a frame (see FRAME *sb.* 12), often of an ornamental character, forming a border round a picture; also *attrib.*; also *Theatr.*, used *attrib.* and *absol.* to designate the stage or stage setting regarded as a picture enclosed by a frame; also *transf.*; **picture frequency** *Television*, † (*a*) (the frequency of) the picture signal; (*b*) the number of times per second a complete television image is scanned or transmitted; **picture-frustration** *Psychol.*, used *attrib.* to designate personality tests that aim to assess a subject's prejudices or personality traits through his reactions to pictures that show potentially frustrating incidents; **picture gallery**, a hall or building containing a collection of pictures; the collection itself; also *fig.*; **picture hat**, a lady's wide-brimmed hat, generally black and adorned with ostrich-feathers, after a fashion celebrated in the paintings of Reynolds and Gainsborough; hence **picture-hatted** *a.*; **picture-lens**, a large double-convex lens of long focus, mounted in a frame, and used for viewing pictures; **picture magazine**, an illustrated magazine; **picture-miniature**, a miniature the subject of which is other than a portrait, e.g. genre; **picture monitor** *Television*, a television screen which is used to provide an immediate display of the image being received by a television camera; **picture-mosaic**, mosaic consisting of pictures instead of geometrical designs, as Roman mosaic and the styles derived from it; **picture-moulding**, a horizontal wooden moulding, parallel to the ceiling of a room, for hanging pictures; **picture-nail**, a strong nail for picture-hanging, having an ornamental head, which is attached after the nail is in position; **picture-plane**, an imaginary plane on which the perspective of a painting or the like meets the eye of the viewer; **picture postcard**, a postcard having on the back a picture (esp. a view) printed, photographed, or otherwise produced; also *fig.*, a scene, etc., reminiscent of or suitable for a picture postcard; freq. *attrib.* or as *adj.*, conventionally attractive or pretty, in the manner of a picture postcard; so **picture-postcardish** *a.*; **picture-rail, -rod**, a rod occupying the position and serving the purpose of a *picture-moulding*; **picture show**, (*a*) an exhibition of pictures; (*b*) a cinema performance, a film show; **picture signal** *Television*, the component of the video signal which carries the information relating to the brightness of the picture elements; **picture-space**, a painted canvas considered as a whole in relation to parts of the painting; **picture stage**, a picture-frame stage; **picture telegraphy**, the telegraphic transmission of still pictures, now usu. called *facsimile telegraphy*; cf. *phototelegraphy* s.v. PHOTO- 1; **picture-telephone** = VIDEOPHONE; **picture tie**, a neck-tie with a representational design; **picture-tree**: see quot.; **picture tube** *Television*, a cathode-ray tube of the kind used for forming the picture in a television set; **picture window**, a large window consisting of a single pane of glass; also *transf.* and *fig.*; hence **picture-windowed** *a.*; **picture-wire**, wire of the kind used for hanging pictures. Also PICTURE-DRAWER, -WRITING

1938 *Jrnl. Inst. Electr. Engin.* LXXXIII. 770/1 The insertion of the d.c. component into a train of picture signals implies that the signal corresponding to *picture black is established at a definite potential. **1961** G. MILLERSON *Technique Television Production* iii. 51 Picture black may not be constant. The darkness of the blackest tones in the picture may vary from shot to shot, with picture content. **1972** G. J. KING *Beginner's Guide Television* (ed. 5) ii. 43 In television parlance, below-picture black level is called blacker than black. **1847** THACKERAY *Van. Fair* (1848) xxxvii. 338 Rawdon bought the boy plenty of *picture-books, and crammed his nursery with toys. **1854** (*title*) Picture Book for a Noah's Ark: Description of 200 Animals. **1854** EMERSON *Lett. & Soc. Aims, Poet. & Imag.* Wks. (Bohn) III. 148 A man's action is only a picture-book of his creed. **1922** A. HUXLEY *Mortal Coils* 201 It's one of those picture-book German towns. **1926** T. E. LAWRENCE *Seven Pillars* (1935) xxxiv. 199 A tiny, picture-book train rolled slowly into view across the hollow sounding bridge. **1965** *Eng. Stud.* XLVI. 370 A..human figure which looks half like..a picture-book goddess. **1974** *Sat. Rev. World* (U.S.) 2 Nov. 9/3 Kyrenia..gave promise..of a picture-book port. **1976** H. KEMELMAN *Wednesday the Rabbi got Wet* xlix. 272 A lovely sunny day with a blue sky and picture-book clouds. **1979** *Jrnl. R. Soc. Arts* CXXVII. 662/2 The book succeeds in being an attractive picture book. **1837** DICKENS *Pickw.* xliv. 479 Keep quiet, do,..there never vos such a old *picter-card born. **1838** —— *O. Twist* xxv, He..offered to cut any gentleman..for the first picture-card, at a shilling a time. **1908** R. FRY *Let.* 11 July (1972) I. 304 I've sent picture cards to the dear ones. **1932** H. CRANE *Let.* 13 Aug. (1965) 409, I must write him a picture card at least in answer; but I'm damned if I want to continue any correspondence of that kind. **1959** I. & P. OPIE *Lore & Lang. Schoolch.* ix. 166 Bubble gum,..with its tempting picture card in each packet, is known as 'beetle fat'. **1966** J. DERRICK *Teaching Eng. to Immigrants* 239 The work cards, picture-cards, wall pictures and flashcards which accompany the course, are also recommended. **1884** E. PEACOCK in *N. & Q.* 6th Ser. IX. 218/2, I suggested at the time, and still think, that it may have been part of a *picture-coffin. **1865** TYLOR *Early Hist. Man.* v. 96 It is to this transition-period that we owe many ..of the *picture-documents still preserved. **1927** *Wireless World* 1 June 684/2 The mosaic of dots, or *picture elements, would be a jumble..if there was an error of 1-90,000th part of a second in the synchronisation between the sending and receiving apparatus. **1940** D. G. FINK *Princ. Television Engin.* ii. 25 The transmission of television images..is accomplished by analyzing the scene into its picture elements, which are selected from the picture area in the orderly sequence of scanning and transmitted one after the other. **1976** *Science* 27 Aug. 792 (*caption*) At this resolution an object 6 m in size subtends one picture element at the nominal horizon. **1668** *Picture-frame [see PICTURE *sb.* 2 f]. *a* **1790** POTTER *New Dict. Cant.*, *Picture frame*, the gallows, or pillory. **1804** *Europ. Mag.* XLV. 16/2 In a.. picture-frame waistcoat, i.e...trimmed with broad gold lace. **1817** LADY MORGAN *France* v. 29 Arranged along their walls in their perriwigs and picture-frames. **1928** J. DOLMAN *Art of Play Production* iii. 43 There are many who are ruthlessly condemning the modern theatre for its illusion, its 'peep-hole' realism, its 'picture-frame' stage. **1936** P. ROTHA *Documentary Film* II. i. 76 Guidance of the actors in speech and gesture, composition of the separate scenes within the picture-frame. **1959** *News Chron.* 29 Dec. 4/2 By the late 'sixties the flat 30 in. picture-frame sets hanging discreetly on our walls, masked during non-viewing periods by..a Constable or a Breughel, will be giving us a reasonably good colour picture. **1966** J. R. TAYLOR *Penguin Dict. Theatre* 254 By the middle of the nineteenth century the picture-frame stage, in which the whole stage was framed by the proscenium with virtually no forestage at all, had become general. **1978** *Listener* 8 June 740/3 The cast.. will be holding their breaths to squeeze on to the little picture-frame stage. **1926** *Wireless World* 5 May 645/1 The same wavelength carries both the *picture frequency, from which the received photograph is built up, and the synchronism frequency which controls the motors. **1930** *Electronics* Aug. 236/2 The Bell 50-line system, 17·7 repetition rate and theoretical maximum picture frequency of 22,125 cycles. **1935** *Discovery* Sept. 277/2 They [*sc.* T.V. pictures] are bright, steady (having regard to picture frequency). **1953** AMOS & BIRKINSHAW *Television Engin.* I. i. 15 The number of complete pictures transmitted per second is known as the picture frequency and must be high enough to give the impression of natural movement and to minimise flicker. **1967** H. A. COLE *Basic Television* I. 32 The number of complete pictures presented in every second is called the picture frequency. **1945** *Jrnl. Abnormal Psychol.* XL. 200/1 The *Picture-Frustration Study is a limited projective technique for assessing an individual's characteristic modes of reaction. **1949** S. ROSENZWEIG *Psychodiagnosis* vii. 167 The Picture-Frustration (P-F) Study, or—by its full name—the Picture-Association Study for Assessing Reactions to Frustration, is a limited projective procedure for disclosing patterns of response to everyday stress. **1968** *Jrnl. Abnormal Psychol.* LXXIII. 381 (*heading*) Coronary artery disease and response to the Rosenzweig picture-frustration study. **1761** WESLEY *Jrnl.* 11 May, One side of it is a *picture gallery. **1842** W. P. HAWES *Sporting Scenes* I. 178 [Wild geese are] willing to wait for the wooden devices which we have anchored in the shallow feeding-grounds, as a picture-gallery of their uncles, cousins, and sweet-hearts. **1850** C. FOX *Jrnl.* 1 Apr. (1972) 196 This evening Clara Balfour's picture-gallery included Christina of Sweden, Anne of England [etc.]. **1856** EMERSON *Eng. Traits, Aristocr.* Wks. (Bohn) II. 85 At this moment, almost every great house has its sumptuous picture-gallery. **1931** *Amer. Mercury* Nov. 353/2 *Picture gallery*, the tattooed man. **1941** F. THOMPSON *Over to Candleford* x. 152 One of these new fancy bazaars..was to be held in the picture gallery. **1979** R. COX *Auction* i. 23 The museum's picture gallery. **1887** *Daily News* 20 July 6/1 A large '*picture' hat in black velvet is to be worn with an all-white dress and black gloves. **1900** *Westm. Gaz.* 4 June 3 It seems not improbable that the wearing of picture hats with evening frocks..may get its chance. **1928** MRS. BELLOC LOWNDES *Diary* 20 Feb. (1971) 112 A black lace frock with a large picture hat trimmed with roses. **1958** L. DURRELL *Balthazar* ix. 178 Inside the cupboard I found an immense, old-fashioned picture-hat of the 1912 variety. **1975** G. HOWELL *In Vogue* 112/2 Dressed by Norman Hartnell, she wore..a picture hat and a long full dress for receptions. **1977** *Jersey Even. Post.* 26 July 10/1 Her matching picture hat was decorated with white tulle and flowers. **1922** W. J. LOCKE *Tale of Triona* vii. 71 Her exquisitely *picture-hatted head. **1959** Picture-hatted [see *goose pimples* s.v. GOOSE *sb.* 8]. **1923** ADE *Let.* 26 Jan. (1973) 91 Two or three weeks ago I picked up a *picture magazine and read the outline of the new picture play called 'Fury'. **1967** G. STEINER *Lang. & Silence* 417 He is as remote, or more so, than is the modern picture-magazine and paper-back from the chained, leather-bound folio of the late medieval scholar. **1979** J. SCOTT *Clutch of Vipers* vii. 120 She was..reading a picture magazine designed for semi-literate young ladies. **1903** *Westm. Gaz.* 16 Apr. 10/2 A private view of *picture-miniatures painted by Mr. Charles Sainton. **1933** *Proc. IRE* XXI. 1690 The *picture monitor may be connected to either the output of the picture amplifier or to a radio receiver, which makes possible the monitoring of the radiated signals. **1961** G. MILLERSON *Technique Television Production* i. 15 The [production control] room's dominating feature is the row of picture monitors. **1975** A. BERMINGHAM et al. *Small Television Studio* 60 A picture monitor is, to all appearances, a high grade TV set without sound. **1797** *Encycl. Brit.* XIV. 182/1 If BA be drawn in the ground plan, and EV be drawn parallel to it, meeting the *picture-plane or perspective-plane in V, [etc.]. **1934** *Burlington Mag.* Aug. 91/2 The projection of the three dimensions of nature on to the two dimensions of the picture-plane. **1959** P. & L. MURRAY *Dict. Art & Artists* 240 *Picture plane*, the extreme front edge of the imaginary space in the picture. It lies immediately behind the glass of the frame and is the plane at which the world of the spectator and of the picture make contact. **1972** E. LUCIE-SMITH *Eroticism in Western Art* iii. 63 Her hips seem to swell towards us out of the picture-plane. **1899** *Daily News* 18 July 5/1 Every method has been placed in the service of the *picture post-card industry, and much has been produced which in its artistic execution may lay claim to lasting value. **1900** *Westm. Gaz.* 24 Sept. 10/1 The exhibition of picture postcards..opened in the Rue Bonaparte at Paris contains no fewer than 150,000 examples from all parts of the world. **1904** *Daily Chron.* 15 Apr. 4/7 There has been some discussion of late as to who invented the picture postcard, and the fad has been traced back to a German..it is said, in 1872. **1907** R. BROOKE *Let.* 23 Aug. (1968) 100, I shall be looking at them [*sc.* antiquities] when you & Arthur Watts are staring at picture-postcard skies & snow. *a* **1930** D. H. LAWRENCE *Phoenix II* (1968) 285 As a picture of Sicily in the middle of the last century, it is marvellous. But it is a picture done from the inside. There are no picture-postcard effects... There is nothing showy. **1936** A. HUXLEY *Eyeless in Gaza* xli. 491 Against a picture postcard of sunset the immoderately tall thin palms were the emblems of a resigned hopelessness. **1957** J. BRAINE *Room at Top* xi. 113 Her picture-postcard face with the dyed red bubble-curls and the Lily Langtry nose and chin. **1959** *Sunday Express* 22 Mar. 9/8 The picture-postcard village of Finchingfield. **1973** V. CANNING *Flight of Grey Goose* v. 90 You're like all summer tourists. All you see is a nice picture-postcard sort of place. **1977** *Time* 24 Oct. 55/2 Bibi Andersson is pallid by comparison, a picture-postcard beauty. **1969** *Daily Tel.* 14 Mar. 16/4 Bavaria and the Vorarlberg, through which they travel in spring-time, look very *picture-postcardish in Robert Paynter's colour photography. **1869** D. G. ROSSETTI *Let.* 24 Dec. (1965) II. 781 Nor indeed do I ever go to any *picture shows whatever now. **1912** *Home Chat* 20 Apr. 148/1 She takes me to theatres and picture shows. **1921** R. MACAULAY *Dangerous Ages* ii. 47 I'll go to theatres and picture shows and concerts and meetings. **1940** R. CHANDLER *Farewell, My Lovely* xxx. 227 Folks took me to the picture show. **1948** E. POUND *Pisan Cantos* (1949) lxxx. 94 And he said to Yeats at a vorticist picture show: 'You also of the brotherhood?' **1976** J. M. BROWNJOHN tr. *Kirst's Time for Payment* vi. 137 Let's inspect the results of our picture show. **1927** SECOR & KRAUS *Television* iii. 15 As the incoming *picture signals are passed through an electromagnet or solenoid, it is caused to open and close a light shutter made of a small piece of aluminum and a spring. **1953** AMOS & BIRKINSHAW *Television Engin.* I. i. 17 The picture signal voltage at any point in a television system varies between two limits, one representing the maximum brightness it is intended to transmit and known as white level and the other representing zero tonal value or black and known as black level. **1972** G. J. KING *Beginner's Guide Television* (ed. 5) ii. 43 The picture signal controls the brightness of the scanning spot. **1925** *Picture-space [see IMAGINALLY *adv.*]. **1937** *Burlington Mag.* Apr. 183/1 The balance between the figures and the picture-space as a whole is roughly identical. **1959** H. READ *Conc. Hist. Mod. Painting* v. 156 The arrangement of the elements within the picture-space remains intuitive. **1951** C. B. PURDOM *Producing Plays* (ed. 3) viii. 113 There can be no doubt that the *picture stage is doomed and that stages in new theatres should not be constructed on that principle. **1961** R. WILLIAMS *Long Revolution* II. vi. 254 The modern picture-stage. **1913** *Wireless World* Sept. 354/2 Just as with *picture-telegraphy with conductors, we can distinguish between a black and white method..and a half-tone method. **1934** *Discovery* Dec. 336/2 Partly owing to..the.. lack of general realisation of the existence of picture telegraphy services, these have not yet been nearly as freely used as they might be. **1976** Picture telegraphy [see PRIVATE *a.* 4 d (i)]. **1968** *Listener* 1 Aug. 155/3 *Picture-telephones are not only going to be embarrassing to live with, they are going to drain a lot more magic out of life. **1969** *Sci. Jrnl.* May 36/3 This summer the Swedish L. M. Ericsson concern..is to install and test a picture-telephone connection between Stockholm and Gothenburg. **1969** P. WEST *Words for Deaf Daughter* vi. 151 Will you zoom off into a future which..brings shopping by picture-telephone? **1957** R. MASON *World of Suzie Wong* II. iv. 151, I thought how quietly dressed you were for an American. I mean, you weren't wearing a *picture-tie, or anything like that. **1963** 'D. RUTHERFORD' *Creeping Flesh* i. 63 That black man with the blue suit and silk picture tie. **1885** LADY BRASSEY *The Trades* 145 One variety [of Euphorbiaceæ] which bears green leaves, and yellow and white markings, is called the 'geographical-tree', or sometimes the '*picture-tree'. **1940** D. G. FINK *Princ. Television Engin.* i. 19 The image-reproducing tube ('*picture' tube)..is a funnel-shaped glass structure in the narrow end of which is contained an electrode structure capable of producing a narrow beam of electrons. **1966** H. NIELSEN *After Midnight* (1967) v. 77 My picture tube blew at ten-thirty and I went straight to bed. **1976** *Guardian* 21 Apr. 19/1 Picture tubes account for 40 per cent of the cost of the components in a set. **1938** *Amer. Home* Nov. 20/2 If you have a large *picture window, we suggest sill-length casement drawn curtains. **1942** *Pencil Points* Nov. 65/1 Extensive fenestration makes it possible to bring the outdoors into the house (note the plate glass, stationary picture windows). **1945** NELSON & WRIGHT *Tomorrow's House* vi. 75/2 Storage cupboards have been grouped in such a way that picture windows could be used. **1958** J. CANNAN *And be a Villain* iv. 79 It was a fairly recent erection with 'picture' windows. **1960** *Chicago Rev.* Autumn-Winter 117 Everett Knight is all for bringing intellectuals down from their tower. The question is whether he himself has actually come out of it or simply ordered some picture windows installed. **1969** *New Yorker* 12 Apr. 90/3 For twenty-one days, the astronauts may look out of a huge picture window, tinted brown against the Texas sun. **1972** J. MANN *Mrs. Knox's Profession* x. 78 The local style was for picture windows..affording a good view of the modern furniture drawn up around the television set. **1977** *Time* 25 July 9/2 He staked out the eighth-floor penthouse, with picture windows offering a panoramic view of Lake Geneva and the Alps, as his personal pad. **1969** R. BLYTHE *Akenfield* 16 The 'young marrieds' go less and less for the converted cottage and more for *picture-windowed bungalows. **1978** G. MITCHELL *Mingled with Venom* vi. 63 Dame Beatrice..took him into the dimly-lit lounge, out through the picture-windowed bar. **1895** *Montgomery Ward Catal.* Spring & Summer 352/3 Braided *picture wire..2¼ yards. **1923** KIPLING *Land & Sea Tales* 88 Carpenter was off in pursuit of rabbits, with a pocket full of fine picture-wire. **1973** R. HAYES *Hungarian Game* ii. 22 He took the guy out with a two-foot length of picture wire and sweet *Jesus* it was great.

Hence **'pictureful** *a.*, full of pictures; **'pictureless** *a.*, without a picture or pictures; **'picturely** *a.*, like a picture; so **'pictury** *a.* (depreciative).

1861 *Temple Bar Mag.* II. 255 My recollections seem to take very *pictureful forms. **1821** LAMB *Elia* Ser. I. *Mrs. Battle on Whist*, With their naked names upon the drab pasteboard, the game might go on very well, *picture-less. **1881** *Sat. Rev.* 3 Sept. 293/1 Empty niches are as meaningless decorations as pictureless frames. **1832** W. BARNES in *Gentl. Mag.* CII. 216/2 To preserve so interesting and *picturely an object. **1819** *Blackw. Mag.* VI. 175 That *pictury-looking glare and freshness which distinguishes the scenery at our theatres.

picture ('pɪktjʊə(r), -tʃə(r)), *v.* [f. prec. sb.: cf. It. *pitturare.*]

1. a. *trans.* To represent in a picture, or in pictorial form; to draw, paint, depict; *transf.* to reflect as a mirror. Also with *out*.

c **1489** CAXTON *Sonnes of Aymon* xxv. 512 Margarys..bare in his armes a dragon pyctured wyth an horryble figure. **1495** *Trevisa's Barth. De P.R.* XIX. xxxvii. JJ v/2 He that pictureth ymages and lyknesse of thynges is callyd a payntour. **1600** HAKLUYT *Voy.* III. 274 We haue seene and eaten of many more [fowl], which for want of leasure..could not be pictured. **1608** D. T[UVIL] *Ess. Pol. & Mor.* 23 b, Hee was pictur'd out in the religious garment of a Monke. **1632** MASSINGER *Emperor East* I. ii, A cunning painter thus.. would picture Justice. **1762–71** H. WALPOLE *Vertue's Anecd. Paint.* (1786) III. 61 On the ceiling..he has pictured Antony earl of Shaftsbury, in the character of Faction, dispersing libels. **1836** J. H. NEWMAN in *Lyra Apost.* (1849) 64 Its pure, still glass Pictures all earth-scenes as they pass.

b. To figure, to represent symbolically or by sensible signs.

1526 *Pilgr. Perf.* (W. de W. 1531) 49 b, What these graces be, it is more playnly pictured & set forth in this tree folowyng. **1782** MISS BURNEY *Cecilia* VII. vi, The anxiety of his mind was strongly pictured upon his face. **1857** PUSEY *Real Presence* ii. (1869) 232 When the people were so much taught by the eye, it pictured to them the mysteries of the Redemption.

2. To describe graphically, depict in words. Also with *out*, *forth*.

1585 FERNE *Blaz. Gentrie* To Gent. of Inner Temple, She pictureth out their base and seruile conditions. **1621** T. WILLIAMSON tr. *Goulart's Wise Vieillard* 98 Horace in his art of Poetrie doth pensill and picture out an old man in this manner. **1787** MME. D'ARBLAY *Diary* 26 Feb., I think this last sentence pictures him exactly. **1838** CARLYLE *Misc.*, *Scott* (1869) V. 217 To picture-forth the life of Scott. **1894** BESANT *Equal Woman* 122 Such a woman as you have pictured is rare indeed.

3. To resemble as a picture or image.

1850 MRS. F. TROLLOPE *Petticoat Govt.* 138 Never, perhaps, did a child more accurately picture a parent, than Judith did her mother.

4. To form a mental picture of, to imagine. Often ***to picture to one's self***.

1738 GLOVER *Leonidas* II. 182 Imagination pictures all the scenes. **1832** HT. MARTINEAU *Life in Wilds* viii. 101 He had pictured to himself the settlement. **1835** JAMES *Gipsy* i, He seemed to doubt the very love, the happiness of which he pictured so brightly. **1869** HUXLEY in *Sci. Opinion* 28 Apr. 487/1 Kant pictures to himself the universe as once an infinite expansion of formless and diffused matter. **1874** GREEN *Short Hist.* viii. §1. 449 We must not..picture the early Puritan as a gloomy fanatic. *a* **1906** *Mod.* Picture to yourself the predicament in which I found myself. **1923** *Mind* XXXII. 467 It is not asserted that the picture must have the same logical form as what it pictures, but that all pictures must have *the* logical form.

pictured ('pɪktjʊəd, -tʃəd), *ppl. a.* [f. prec. + -ED[1].]

1. Represented or depicted in or as in a picture; painted, drawn.

1738 GRAY *Propertius* ii. 50 Pictured horrour and poëtic woes. **1854** MARION HARLAND *Alone* xii, The examination of the artist's pictured treasures. **1894** F. N. RAGG *Quorsum* xiii. 139 They downwards gazed to see the pictured heaven, And pictured light, which dark-hued waters hold.

2. Adorned or illustrated with a picture or pictures, or *fig.* with word-painting.

1608 WILLET *Hexapla Exod.* 866 A pictured and wrought coate. **1754** GRAY *Progr. Poesy* 109 Bright ey'd Fancy, hovering o'er, Scatters from her pictured urn Thoughts that breathe, and words that burn. **1813** BYRON *Br. Abydos* I. x, The pictured roof and marble floor. **1818** —— *Ch. Har.* IV. lxxxii, Alas for Tully's voice, and Virgil's lay, And Livy's pictur'd page!

b. ***pictured card***, a card bearing a picture, a court-card or picture-card; the king, queen, or knave. ***devil's pictured books***, a hostile name for playing-cards.

1786 BURNS *Twa Dogs* 226 They..Pore owre the devil's pictur'd beuks. **1812** BUCHAN in Singer *Hist. Cards* (1816) 361 Each honour, or pictured card, is considered as equivalent in value to ten. **1864** BOWEN *Logic* xiii. 442 A pack contains 52 cards, divided into four equal suits, into 12 pictured and 40 plain cards.

picturedom ('pɪktjʊədəm, -tʃə-). [f. PICTURE *sb.* + -DOM.] Pictures or moving pictures collectively.

1902 *Strand Mag.* Apr. 440/1 One who knows him says that 'Zim' is the 'Mark Twain' of picturedom. **1920** *Chambers's Jrnl.* 21 Feb. 188/1 It was at the same ranch [near Los Angeles] that many of the most terrible battles in picturedom were fought and filmed. **1945** *Sun* (Baltimore) 2 Oct. 5/7 (Advt.), True antiques of picturedom.

'picture-,drawer. One who draws a picture; in 17th and early 18th c., the regular word for *portrait-painter*.

1586–7 in Jeaffreson *Middlesex County Rec.* (1886) I. 173 Edmund Barton picture drawer. **1635** J. HAYWARD tr. *Biondi's Banish'd Virg.* 115 The Philosophers (humanities picture-drawers) have indeede drawne many pictures. *a* **1715** BURNET *Own Time* (1766) I. 24 Sir Anthony Vandike, the famous picture drawer. *a* **1734** NORTH *Lives* (1826) III. 280 One Mr. Blemwell, a picture-drawer.

So **picture-drawing**.

1625 in Rymer *Foedera* (1726) XVIII. 111 Wee, haveing experience of the Facultie and Skill of Daniel Mittens in the Art of Picture draweing, of Our especiall Grace..have given [etc.].

picturedrome ('pɪktjʊədrəʊm, -tʃə-). [f. PICTURE *sb.* 2 i + -DROME, after HIPPODROME *sb.* 3.] A building intended for picture shows; a cinema.

1914 *Durham Advertiser* 19 June 8 Arrangements are being made..for the 'Varsity students' 'rag'..to be shown at the Assembly Rooms Picturedrome. **1918** A. QUILLER-COUCH *Foe Farrell* 116, I dragged him and Petunia back into the shadow under the side-wall of the Picturedrome. **1927** *Punch* 27 July 97/3 Give us more dance saloons, More epileptic tunes, More syncopating coons, More Picture-dromes. **1933** P. MACDONALD *Mystery of Dead Police* i. 2 The colossal Pantheon Picturedrome—all Ionic pillars and organ solo. **1945** *Gen* 5 May 24/2 A cinema owner can extol the modernity of his 'Picturedrome'.

picturegraph ('pɪktjʊəgrɑːf, -tʃə-, -græf). [f. PICTURE *sb.* + -GRAPH.] A symbol representing a picture or image; a pictograph. Also *fig.*

1926 G. MURRAY in *Pioneer of Reformed Spelling* Apr. 2 You could communicate ideas by making certain signs or marks on some material—from that you get, first picturegraphs, and eventually alphabetical writing. *a* **1930** D. H. LAWRENCE *Apocalypse* (1931) ix. 127 Every image fulfils its own little circle of action and meaning, then is superseded by another image... Every image is a picturegraph, and the connection between the images will be made..differently by every reader. **1962** *Punch* 11 Apr. 570/2 There was..Diplodocus Carnegii,..alive, in his own era—a rare picturegraph in those days.

Picturephone ('pɪktjʊəfəʊn, -tʃə-). Also with lower-case initial. [f. PICTURE *sb.* + PHONE *sb.*[2]] A videophone. Cf. *picture-telephone* s.v. PICTURE *sb.* 6 d.

A proprietary name in the U.S.

1964 *N.Y. Times* 21 Apr. 31/2 The Picturephone was demonstrated yesterday with a see-as-you-talk call between the World's Fair and Anaheim, Calif. **1965** *Punch* 23 June 912 The picturephone is not yet domesticated. There is an experimental commercial hook-up between New York, Chicago and Washington. **1966** *Official Gaz.* (U.S. Patent Office) 27 Sept. TM192/2 American Telephone and Telegraph Co., New York. Filed April 13, 1965. Picturephone. For: See-while-you-talk, sometimes known as visual telephone, services. First use at least as early as April 20, 1964. **1970** *Nature* 25 July 331/1 The first commercial picturephone service was opened recently by the Bell Telephone Service. **1970** *New Scientist* 24 Dec. 565 As befits an executive in a communications company,.. Thomas has a Picturephone on his desk, and takes part in conferences by TV. **1974** *Times Lit. Suppl.* 1 Nov. 1216/1 Set in the near future (though the only concession to documentary detail is the picturephone over which leading political figures are apt to receive 'blank-screen calls').

'picturer. Now *rare*. [f. PICTURE *v.* + -ER[1].] One who pictures; a painter of pictures; a painter.

1608–9 in *Eng. Hist. Rev.* (1897) XII. 446 Benedickt Horsley, a pictorer and painter. **1646** SIR T. BROWNE *Pseud. Ep.* V. iv. (1650) 200 Not meerly a pictoriall contrivance or invention of the Picturer, but an ancient tradition and conceived reality. **1690** WOOD *Life* 30 Jan. III. 323 'An illustrator', or 'picturer of great letters in books'.

picturesque (pɪktjʊə'rɛsk, -tʃə-), *a.* and *sb.* Also 8 pittor-, pictoresque, picturesk. [ad. F. *pittoresque*, ad. It. *pittoresco* (F. Redi *a* 1664), f. *pittore*:—L. *pictōr-em* painter: see -ESQUE; prop. 'in the style of a painter' (cf. quot. 1810 in sense 1); but in Eng. assimilated to *picture*, giving the sense 'in the style of a picture'.

Pittoresque appears to have been in French early in 18th c. (cf. quot. 1712 from Pope), but the earliest evidence in Hatzfeld-Darmesteter is for *pittoresquement* in 1732.]

A. *adj.* **1. a.** Like or having the elements of a picture; fit to be the subject of a striking or effective picture; possessing pleasing and interesting qualities of form and colour (but not implying the highest beauty or sublimity): said of landscape, buildings, costume, scenes of diversified action, etc., also of circumstances, situations, fancies, ideas, and the like.

1703 STEELE *Tender Husb.* IV. (1723) 141 That Circumstance may be very Picturesque. **1712** POPE *Let. to Caryll*, Mr. Philips has two lines, which seem to me what the French call very *picturesque*. **1717** —— *Iliad* x. Note liv, The marshy Spot of Ground,..the Tamarisk.., the Reeds that are heap'd together to mark the Place, are Circumstances the most Picturesque imaginable. **1749** U. RHYS *Tour Spain & Port.* 86 The Ends of their Veils..tied in so pretty a Manner, as to render their Figures extremely pittoresque. **1768** W. GILPIN (*title*) An Essay upon Prints: containing remarks upon the principles of picturesque beauty. **1773** LADY MARY COKE *Jrnl.* 8 July (1896) IV. 186 The *Cours* was a very picturesk scene. **1810** D. STEWART *Philos. Ess.* II. I. v. 273 Picturesque properly means what is done in the style, and with the spirit of a painter. **1864** BAGEHOT *Lit. Studies* (1879) II. 341 Susceptible observers..say of a scene 'How picturesque'—meaning by this a quality distinct from that of beauty, or sublimity, or grandeur; meaning to speak..of its fitness for imitation by art. **1877** BLACK *Green Past.* ii, Most girls become acquainted at some time or other with a little picturesque misery.

b. ***picturesque gardening***, the arrangement of a garden so as to make it a pretty picture; the romantic style of gardening, aiming at irregular and rugged beauty.

a **1763** [see *landscape-gardening* s.v. LANDSCAPE *sb.* 5]. **1783** W. BURGH in W. Mason *Eng. Garden* 236 There is nothing in picturesque Gardening which should not have its archetype in unadorned Nature. **1816** T. L. PEACOCK *Headlong Hall* iii, Mr. Milestone was a picturesque landscape gardener of the first celebrity. **1843** *Gray's Corr.* 101 *note*, That Johnson should have no conception of the value or merit of what is now called picturesque gardening we cannot wonder, as he was so extremely short-sighted, that he never saw a rural landscape in his life.

2. Of language, narrative, etc.: Strikingly graphic or vivid; sometimes implying disregard of fact in the effort for effect.

a **1734** NORTH *Exam.* Pref. (1740) 7 He goes on in the same pittoresque Vein. **1758** JORTIN *Erasm.* I. 483 An account of a conversation with Longolius, which is picturesque. **1864** BURTON *Scot Abr.* I. iii. 128 Picturesque accounts have often been repeated of a scene where Douglas..brought the Admiral to an elevated spot. **1868** J. H. BLUNT *Ref. Ch. Eng.* I. 401 Picturesque history is seldom to be trusted. **1874** BANCROFT *Footpr. Time* i. 63 The highly picturesque language of the primitive Aryan people.

†**3.** Marked as if with pictures. *Obs. rare.*

1762 tr. *Busching's Syst. Geog.* I. 41 Others [marbles].. are Picturesque, or marked with all manner of figures, &c. *Ibid.* 42 *Oculus mundi*..by polishing receives a beautiful lustre, and is partly spotted or striped, partly picturesque.

†**4.** Having a perception of or taste for picturesqueness. *Obs.*

1789 W. GILPIN *Observations Rel. Picturesque Beauty* I. viii. 72 Let the picturesque traveller watch for these effects. *Ibid.* xiv. 139 The picturesque eye regrets the loss of it's towers. **1795** R. ANDERSON *Johnson* 7 Had he not possessed a very picturesque imagination. **1818** RHODES *Peak Scen.* I. 5 To the picturesque traveller they are therefore comparatively of but little value. **1831** T. L. PEACOCK *Crotchet Castle* iii. (1887) 39 They came round to the side of the camp where the picturesque gentleman was sketching.

B. *absol.* as *sb.* **1.** ***the picturesque***, that which is picturesque; the picturesque principle, element, or quality; picturesqueness.

1749 D. HARTLEY *Observations on Man* I. 427 The Nature of the Caricatura, Burlesque, Grotesque, Picturesque, &c. may be understood from what is delivered..concerning Laughter, Wit, Humour, the Marvellous, Absurd, &c. to which they correspond. **1782** W. GILPIN *Observations on River Wye* 93 Col. Mitford..is well-versed in the theory of the picturesque. **1794** U. PRICE (*title*) An Essay on the Picturesque, as compared with the Sublime and the Beautiful. **1796** JANE AUSTEN *Pride & Prej.* x, No, no; stay where you are. You are charmingly grouped... The picturesque would be spoilt by admitting a fourth. **1812** COMBE (*title*) Dr. Syntax's Tour in Search of the Picturesque. **1832–4** DE QUINCEY *Cæsars* Wks. 1859 X. 79 The ancients, whether Greeks or Romans, had no eye for the picturesque. **1927** C. HUSSEY *Picturesque* iii. 66 The Picturesque was to be a practical aesthetic for gardeners, tourists, and sketchers. **1955** N. NICHOLSON *Lakers* iii. 46 In the Picturesque, the only creative act is that of man himself, a small, mean, self-satisfied manipulation of an abstract landscape. **1961** *Amer. Q.* Winter 529 The outlook for the amateur..is usually dependent on his fondness for local history or for the picturesque.

2. A picturesque landscape. *rare.*

1889 G. MEREDITH *Let.* 20 May (1970) II. 959 We had here a young and promising Bostonian..fresh from a ride over the picturesques of Greece.

Hence **pictu'resquish** *a.*, somewhat picturesque; also (rare and jocular nonce-words) **picturesqui'escity**, growing picturesqueness; **picturesquifi'cation**, a making picturesque; **pictu'resquize** *v.*, to 'do' or pursue the picturesque.

1812 COMBE *Picturesque* XVI. 176 Nor had the way one object brought That wak'd a picturesquish thought. **1815** W. TAYLOR in Robberds *Mem.* II. 455 The engineer..is not to lose his time in zoologizing, entomologizing, botanizing and picturesquizing. **1828** ELMES *Metrop. Improv.* 89 The master mark of currency among the people of picturesquiescity. **1834** *Tait's Mag.* I. 233 From the pages of Rousseau..Leman, Uri, and Zurich have undergone their sentence of picturesquification.

pictu'resque, *v. rare.* [f. prec.] **a.** *trans.* To make or render picturesque. **b.** *intr.* To pose picturesquely. **c.** *to picturesque it*, to practise or pursue the picturesque.

1795 C. MARSHALL *Review Landscape* 45 If he plant trees of size round the building to be picturesked. **1812** COMBE *Picturesque* I. 130 I'll prose it here, I'll verse it there, And picturesque it ev'ry where. **1834** *Tait's Mag.* I. 733/1 His parents..sometimes dream of Dick as standing behind my lady's chair, in the suit of blue and silver, &c., picturesquing. **1892** *Punch* 6 Aug. 49/1 With out-of-fashion toilet sets..She picturesques her cabinet's Quaint heterodoxies.

pictu'resquely, *adv.* [f. as prec. + -LY[2].] In a picturesque manner.

1796 MARY WOLLSTONECR. *Lett.*, etc. 139 In a recess of the rocks was a clump of pines, amongst which a steeple rose picturesquely beautiful. **1859** JEPHSON *Brittany* iv. 41 Alive with the picturesquely attired peasantry. **1881** MISS BRADDON *Asph.* II. 86 The shallow streamlet came tumbling picturesquely over gray stones.

picturesqueness (pɪktjʊə'rɛsknɪs, -tʃə-). [f. as prec. + -NESS.] The quality of being picturesque. Also *transf.* and *fig.*

1794 U. PRICE *Ess. Picturesque* I. 38 Grandeur and beauty have been pointed out and illustrated by painting as well as picturesqueness. [*Note*] I have ventured to make use of this word, which I believe does not occur in any writer. **1827** HARE *Guesses* (1859) 13 Picturesqueness is that quality in objects which fits them for making a good picture. **1861** CRAIK *Hist. Eng. Lit.* II. 64 There is little or nothing, however, of poetry or picturesqueness in Feltham's writing. **1867** [see FEATURELINESS]. **1894** BARING-GOULD *Deserts S. France* I. 136 A bridge that surpasses even that of Prague in picturesqueness. **1907** 'MARK TWAIN' *Christian Sci.* II. iii. 130 Repetition of pet poetic picturesquenesses.

picturesquerie (pɪktjʊə'rɛskərɪ, -tʃə-). [f. PICTURESQUE *a.*, after GROTESQUERIE.] The picturesque; picturesqueness.

1962 *Punch* 12 Sept. 392/3 Miscegenation and picturesquerie on beaches. **1963** *Punch* 20 Mar. 396/2 An endless stream of..picturesquerie, from Maundy Money to the Royal Enclosure. **1968** *Listener* 12 Sept. 322/1 Soon, we were back with French TV's old faults of inconsequential folklore and half-conscious chauvinism. Shock and protest gave place to a routine rag-bag of patriotic picturesquerie. **1978** 'M. DELVING' *No Sign of Life* i. 5, I hadn't much time for prettiness and picturesquerie.

'picture-,writing.

1. The method of recording events or expressing ideas by pictures or drawings which literally or figuratively represent the things and actions; *concr.* a writing or inscription consisting of pictorial symbols.

Such were the picture-writing of the Mexicans and the hieroglyphs of the Egyptians in their earliest form.

1741 WARBURTON *Div. Legat.* IV. iv. II. 67 The first Essay towards Writing was a mere Picture. We see this remarkably verified in the Case of the Mexicans, whose only Method of recording their Laws and History, was by this Picture-Writing. **1748** HARTLEY *Observ. Man* I. iii. 300 If we suppose Picture-writing to be of divine Original. **1862** MAX MÜLLER *Chips* (1880) I. xiv. 316 The little that is known of the picture-writing of the Indian tribes. **1894** H. DRUMMOND *Ascent Man* 232 Chinese writing is picture-writing, with the pictures degenerated into dashes.

2. *transf.* Any expression of notions by pictures, as in a comic or satirical paper.

1896 *Daily News* 17 Oct. 4/7 Forain is the jester of a society in its old age... His work is the picture-writing of sordid cynicism, and it robs life of all joy by robbing it of all ideal.

3. Language or writing that is graphic or vivid. *rare.*

1942 BLUNDEN *Romantic Poetry & Fine Arts* 19 Such picture-writing as Tennyson's 'Palace of Art'; of which I remember my old headmaster saying..'very much like paintings'.

'picturing, *vbl. sb.* [f. PICTURE *v.* + -ING[1].]

a. The making of a picture; depicting; also *concr.* a pictorial representation, a picture.

1559 ABP. SANDYS *Serm.* (Parker Soc.) 66 They labour.. by incantation, magic, sorcery and witchcraft, to consume, kill, and destroy the Lord's anointed by picturing, &c. **1638** CHILLINGW. *Relig. Prot.* I. iii. §90. 184 Things.., which Christians in S. Austins time held abominable, (as the picturing of God). **1656** *Artif. Handsom.* 185 They can be friends with..picturings by pencill, or embroyderies. **1836** F. MAHONY *Rel. Father Prout, Songs France* iii. (1859) 270 The painter David..whose glorious picturings of 'The Passage of the Alps by Bonaparte' [etc.] shed such radiance on his native land.

b. Picturesque description in words; formation or expression of a mental picture; imagining to oneself or describing to others.

1837 W. IRVING *Capt. Bonneville* xlix. III. 262 We here close our picturings of the Rocky mountains and their wild inhabitants. **1876** GEO. ELIOT *Dan. Der.* xxxviii, It was akin to the boy's and girl's picturing of the future beloved. **1956** J. O. URMSON *Philos. Analysis* v. 76 By no means all the atomists used the terminology of 'picturing'. **1963** W. SELLARS *Sci., Perception & Reality* vi. 211 But what if, instead of construing 'picturing' as a relationship between *facts*, we construe it as a relationship between linguistic and nonlinguistic *objects*? **1970** R. RHEES *Discussions of Wittgenstein* i. 5 Well, how do you know? How do you know there is any such picturing? **1971** F. W. GARFORTH *Scope of Philos.* xii. 237 Nor is 'picturing' an adequate account of what language is and does.

'picturing, *ppl. a.* [f. as prec. + -ING[2].] That pictures (in any sense of the verb).

1841 D'ISRAELI *Amen. Lit.* (1867) 503 The grave melodious stanza and the picturing invention of Spenser.

picturization (,pɪktjʊəraɪ'zeɪʃən, -tʃə-). [f. next.] Representation by means of a picture or pictures (in the various senses of the sb.).

1917 *N.Y. Times* 12 Mar. 9/2 A picturization of 'A Tale of Two Cities' was the new offering at the Academy of Music. **1918** *Dialect Notes* V. 9 'The Little American' is a stirring picturization of events in France during the great war. **1920** [see CINEMATOGRAPH *sb.*]. **1925** *Lit. Digest* 4 July 30/2 The public does not demand picturizations which truly mirror American life. **1938** I. KUHN *Assigned to Adventure* vi. 71 He made the stories inspirational and romantic by vivid picturization of human beings at a dramatic time in their lives. **1951** G. HUMPHREY *Thinking* ix. 286 The hindrance to thought that comes from..picturization or fitting the images into a consistent picture. **1957** V. J. KEHOE *Technique Film & Television Make-Up* viii. 97 There are a number of differences between film and television picturizations.

picturize ('pɪktjʊəraɪz, -tʃə-), *v.* [f. PICTURE *sb.* + -IZE.] *trans.* To represent by or adorn with a picture or pictures (in the various senses of the sb.). Hence **'picturized** *ppl. a.*; **'picturizing** *vbl. sb.*

1846 in J. E. Worcester *Universal & Crit. Dict. Eng. Lang.* **1918** *Dialect Notes* V. 13 The Common Law, by R. W. Chambers, is soon to be picturized by one of the leading film companies. **1918** *N.Y. Times* 11 Nov. 13/3 William A. Brady as producer, Harley Knowles as director, and all others concerned have done a good piece of work in the so-called 'picturizing' of 'Little Women', which was shown yesterday at the Strand Theatre. **1920** *Ibid.* 24 May 20 The photoplay, however, remains simply a picturized reproduction of the stage play. **1923** *Westm. Gaz.* 26 July 8/6 It is..not an attempt..to picturise the whole of scientific theory on the subject. **1930** *Publishers' Weekly* 1 Mar. 1127 (Advt.), The new Encyclopædia Britannica humanized and picturized. **1952** N. V. PEALE *Power of Positive Thinking* iv. 49 When either failure or success is picturized it strongly tends to actualize in terms equivalent to the mental image pictured. **1967** SINGHA & MASSEY *Indian Dances* iii. 46 The really expert dancer appears to picturize the music with her arms and body.

picucule ('pɪkju:kju:l). *Ornith.* Also erron. piculule. [a. F. *picucule* (D'Aubenton, *a* 1780, Plate 621 in Buffon (etc.) *Oiseaux*), name given to a bird of the genus *Dendrocolaptes*, f. L. *pīcus* woodpecker + *cuculus* cuckoo.] (See quots.)

1829 GRIFFITHS *Cuvier's Anim. Kingd., Aves* II. 350 Picucule Creeper, Climbing Grackle. *Lath.* **1875** NEWTON in *Encycl. Brit.* III. 743/2 The Picucules [*misspelt* Piculules] (*Dendrocolaptidæ*) with as many genera, and over 200 species. **1894** NEWTON *Dict. Birds*, *Picucule*, a name.. adopted for want of a better, as that of the large Family of *Tracheophonæ*, *Dendrocolaptidæ*, which is so highly characteristic of the Neotropical Region.

picuda (pɪ'ku:də). [Amer. Sp., f. Sp. *picudo*, *-a* pointed, sharp.] The great barracuda, *Sphyræna barracuda*, of the family Sphyrænidæ, a large marine fish found in oceans bordering eastern central America, from Florida to Brazil.

1931 B. MIALL tr. *Guenther's Naturalist in Brazil* ii. 48 There is also, on the coast of north-eastern Brazil, a fish of the Mullet family, the Picuda, which is sometimes as much as six feet in length. **1963** H. ULRICH *America's Best Deep-Sea Fishing* II. 102 Barracuda... Other Names: Great barracuda, common barracuda, picuda, sea tiger, cuda. **1975** FELTON & FOWLER *Best, Worst & most Unusual* 234 The men work two or three short days a week fishing for picuda.

‖**picul** ('pɪkʌl). Forms: 6 pyco, 6–7 pico, 7 picull, peecull, 7–8 pecul, 7–9 picul, picol, 8–9 **pekul**, 9 **pikul**. [Malay-Javanese *pikul* a man's load (Yule); in Sp. *pico*.] A measure of weight used in China and the East generally, equal to 100 catties, i.e. about 133⅓ lbs. avoirdupois.

1588 PARKE tr. *Mendoza's Hist. China* 367 One pyco of rice. **1598** W. PHILLIP *Linschoten* I. (Hakl. Soc.) I. 149 Every Pico is 66⅔ Caetes. **1618** R. COCKS *Diary* (Hakl. Soc.) II. 3, 30 pico silk..30 picull of silk. **1625** PURCHAS *Pilgrims* I. 369 The Peecull, which is one hundred Cattees, making one hundred thirtie pound English subtill. *Ibid.* 390 Foure Peeculls. **1662** J. DAVIES tr. *Mandelslo's Trav.* II. (1669) 106 A hundred Picols of black Lacque, at ten Thails the Picol. **1771** J. R. FORSTER tr. *Osbeck's Voy.* I. 262 A Pekul or Idaam as the Chinese call it. **1838** CAPT. P. P. KING in *Penny Cycl.* XII. 271/1 If each vessel returns with 100 picols of trepang, her cargo will be worth 5000 dollars. **1862** ST. JOHN *Forests Far East* II. 31 Obtained two pikuls more of sago. **1888** LITTLE *Yangtse Gorges* 279 The coal is sold for 130 cash.. per picul of 133 pounds.

picule ('pɪkju:l). *rare*⁻⁰. [dim. f. L. *pīcus* woodpecker.] = next.

1890 in *Cent. Dict.*

piculet ('pɪkjʊlɪt). *Ornith.* [f. as prec. + -ET[1] dim.] A bird of the subfamily *Picumninæ*; a small soft-tailed woodpecker.

1849 G. R. GRAY *Genera Birds* II. 432 *Picumninæ* or *Piculets* have the Bill short, straight; the sides compressed towards the tip [etc.]. **1894** NEWTON *Dict. Birds* 720.

[**'picy** (in *Piquet*): see PIQUE *sb.*[2]]

piddle ('pɪd(ə)l), *v.* [Origin obscure. The form is that of a dim. or freq. vb. Cf. the synonymous PEDDLE *v.* 3, PADDLE *v.*[1] 2, 3, PITTLE *v.* Of these the first two seem to be corruptions of *piddle*, erroneously confused with *peddle*, *paddle* in their proper senses. *Pittle* was an inconsiderable variant. (It is questionable if sense 2 here and in PITTLE *v.* are the same word as 1.)

Words corresponding in form and sense are used in some German dial.: viz. Hessian *piddeln* (v. Pfister *Nachtr. z. Vilmar's Idiotikon v. Hessen*, 1886, p. 204); Westerwald *pitteln*, *pütteln* (Schmidt *Westerwäld. Idiot.* 1800, p. 138); Jülich and Berg *pötteln* (*ibid.*). The first two, if old may go back to an orig. **puddlian* or **puddilôn*, which would also give an OE. **pyddlian* and Eng. *piddle*; but the late appearance of the Eng. word, with absence of evidence as to the age of the Ger. dial. forms, leaves their relation doubtful. Even if related, the ulterior etymology (of root **pudd-*) is unknown.]

1. a. *intr.* To work or act in a trifling, paltry, petty, or insignificant way; to trifle, toy, dally; = PEDDLE *v.* 3. (Always depreciatory.) Now freq. with *about*, *around*.

1545 ASCHAM *Toxoph.* (Arb.) 117 Neuer ceasynge piddelynge about your bowe and shaftes whan they be well. **1594** CAREW *Huarte's Exam. Wits* (1616) 182 Such as I haue marked to be good practitioners, do all piddle somewhat in the art of versifying, and raise not vp their contemplation verie high. **1602** —— *Cornwall* 65 b, Very few among them make use of that opportunity..for building of shipping, and trafficking in grosse: yet some of the Eastern townes piddle that way. **1606** *Sir G. Goosecappe* II. i. (Bullen *O. Pl.*), My head must devise something, while my feet are pidling thus. *a* **1619** FLETCHER *Wit without M.* I. ii, She..begins to piddle with Philosophie. **1752** H. WALPOLE *Lett. Mann* (1834) III. 15, I am always piddling about ornaments and improvements for Strawberry-Hill. **1754** *Connoisseur* No. 7 ¶2 During our conversation he was..piddling with her fingers, tapping her cheek, or playing with her hair. **1776** ADAM SMITH *W.N.* IV. vii. (1869) II. 205 Instead of piddling for the little prizes..they might then hope..to draw some of the great prizes. **1828** *Craven Gloss.* (ed. 2), *Piddle*, to be employed in trifles or to do things ineffectually; to take short steps in walking. **1878** BROWNING *Poets Croisic* lxxxviii, Fussily feeble, harmless..Piddling at so-called satire. **1938** M. K. RAWLINGS *Yearling* iii. 25 Don't you and your Pa be gone too long now, follerin' that fool hound. I'm o' no mind to set around waitin' breakfast and you two piddlin' around in the woods. **1957** R. A. HEINLEIN *Door into Summer* (1960) ii. 32, I piddled along with the help of the shop mechanics until I had *Frank* looking less like a three-car crash. **1961** I. JEFFERIES *It wasn't Me!* iv. 56 We piddled about with ballistics too, but mostly talk. **1973** *N.Y. Times* 10 June VII. 22/3 Since the whole family piddled with archery, we had our gear with us. **1977** *Sounds* 9 July 22/3 He returned to New York and 'piddled around' doing Public Relations.

b. Said of a bird: To move the bill about, feeling for food in a hole, heap of refuse, etc.

1598 BARCKLEY *Felic. Man* (1631) 225 As he [Mahomet] was preaching..there commeth a Dove flying towards him, and alighteth upon his shoulder, and pidleth in his eare looking for meate, having used her before to feede in his eare for the same purpose. **1651** OGILBY *Æsop* (1665) 63 This [Stork] piddles with his bill While young Sir Reynard did whole Rivers swill. **1799** J. STRUTHERS *To Blackbird* vii, Beware in that caff heap to piddle.

c. To trifle or toy with one's food; to pick at one's food instead of eating heartily.

a **1620** J. DYKE *Sel. Serm.* (1640) 292 Diseases..that make them eate nothing at all, or else they doe but piddle and trifle. **1660** SWINNOCK *Door Salv. Op.* 177 If thou shouldst sit at table and see a man pidling at his meat, picking and chusing. *a* **1761** CAWTHORN *Poems* (1771) 112 Is there a saint that would not laugh to see The good man pidling with his fricassee? **1785** MRS. MONTAGU in Doran *Lady of last Cent.* xiii. (1873) 330 The lovers sigh'd and look'd..and piddled a little on a gooseberry tart. **1824** BYRON *Juan* XV. lxvi, And 'entremets' to piddle with at hand.

d. *trans.* *piddle away*, to trifle away.

1760 C. JOHNSTON *Chrysal* (1822) I. 143 A house where she used to piddle away her leisure hours. **1942** BERREY & VAN DEN BARK *Amer. Thes. Slang* §239/3 *Waste*,..piddle away. **1958** 'E. MCBAIN' *Killer's Payoff* (1960) xvii. 160 Ruther had inherited money which..he'd piddled away. **1965** [see INTERFACE 2 a]. **1978** D. A. STANWOOD *Memory of Eva Ryker* ii. 15, I was patrolling Kapiolani Boulevard, piddling away the final moments of my ungodly long shift.

2. *intr.* To make water, urinate. *colloq.* or in childish use.

1796 *Grose's Dict. Vulg. T.* (ed. 3), *To Piddle*, to make water: a childish expression. **1836** SMART *Walker's Dict.* (ed. 3), *Piddle*,..this word is now scarcely used except as a child's word in the sense of to make water. **1931** R. CAMPBELL *Georgiad* II. 21 Across the lawn they [*sc.* dogs] shank it on all fours, To argue, fight, and copulate, and piddle Around the sacred lamp-post in the middle. **1947** M. LOWRY *Let.* May (1967) 142 Meantime we have been here quietly piddling in our pants with suspense. **1974** R. ADAMS

Shardik xxv. 205, I have no idea what portents he employs —possibly the bear piddles on the floor and he observes portents in the steaming what-not. **1976** *Listener* 15 July 55/3 To greet the crowd meeting him, he openly piddles on the platform.

fig. **1814** W. SCOTT *Let.* 10 Nov. (1932) III. 515 The last act is ill contrived. He piddles (so to speak) through a cullender, and divides the whole horrors of the catastrophe ..into a kind of drippity-droppity of four or five scenes. **1871** B. TAYLOR *Faust* (1875) II. IV. i. 232 Fountain jets.. There grandly shooting upwards from the middle, While round the sides a thousand spirt and piddle. **1951** H. BENNETT *We never called him Henry* iii. 18 Mr. Ford..would tell me, 'So-and-so was piddling in my ear'. That was a favourite expression of his.

piddle ('pɪd(ə)l), *sb. colloq.* [f. the vb.] **1.** Urine; an act of urinating. Also *fig.*

1901 in Farmer & Henley *Slang* V. 191/1. **1937** PARTRIDGE *Dict. Slang* 625/2 *Piddle*, urine; occ. the act of making water. **1959** E. BURGESS *Divided we Fall* x. 115 Take the poodle for its piddle. **1962** M. DUFFY *That's how it Was* xii. 105, I envied him his ability to tie his little soft winkle into a knot at the end and blow it out like a balloon with unshed piddle. **1972** D. BLOODWORTH *Any Number can Play* x. 77 How could these red-haired brutes eat that filthy muck, not to mention the piddle and milk they called tea?

2. A trifle; nonsense.

1910 R. BROOKE *Let.* 2 Mar. (1968) 223 It's the alteration of the little words that makes all the difference between Poetry & piddle.

piddle, variant of PIGHTLE.

piddler ('pɪdlə(r)). [f. PIDDLE *v.* + -ER[1].] One who piddles; a poor ineffectual worker; a dabbler, toyer, trifler: see the verb.

1602 MIDDLETON *Blurt, Master-Constable* II. ii. 129 These flaxen-haired men are such pulers, and such piddlers. *a* **1625** FLETCHER & MASSINGER *Elder Bro.* IV. iv, I'm but a pidler, A little will serve my turn. **1646** N. B[ARNET] *Regenerate Man's Growth Grace* 42 We are but Pidlers in his service, we can do nothing to any purpose. **1779** J. LOVELL in *J. Adams's Wks.* (1854) IX. 490 If this was not the piddler, it might be the oddity of Virginia. **1800** in *Spirit Pub. Jrnls.* IV. 360 He was a mere piddler compared to me. **1911** R. D. SAUNDERS *Col. Todhunter* ii. 25, I ain't never seen no piddler at meal times that was fit to do a man's work.

piddling ('pɪdlɪŋ), *vbl. sb.* [f. as prec. + -ING[1].] The action of PIDDLE *v.*; trifling, toying, etc.

1573 TUSSER *Husb.* (1878) 127 If hops looke browne, go gather them downe. But not in the deaw, for piddling with feaw. **1655** *Clarke Papers* (Camden) III. 37 The French Ambassadour makes a pidling still. **1760** C. JOHNSTON *Chrysal* (1822) I. 87 This dissipated pidling soon gave way to the serious business of the evening. **1816** SCOTT *Old Mort.* xii, No piddling..but that steady and persevering exercise of the jaws which is best learnt by early morning hours.

'piddling, *ppl. a.* [f. as prec. + -ING[2].]

1. Trifling, insignificant, petty, paltry.

1559 AYLMER *Harborowe* Q ij b, You haue the pidlyng Scottes, whiche are alwayes Frenche for their lyues. **1593** G. HARVEY *Pierce's Super.* 14 Pidlinge and driblinge Confuters, that sitt all day buzzing vpon a blunt point, or two. **1675** PRIDEAUX *Lett.* (Camd.) 41 We have two or three small pidleing things printeing here. **1735** POPE *Prol. Sat.* 164 Yet ne'er one sprig of laurel grac'd these ribalds, From slashing Bently down to pidling Tibalds. **1768–74** TUCKER *Lt. Nat.* (1834) II. 342 The man of business has not time for such piddling work. **1827** SCOTT *Chron. Canongate* Introd. i, For the piddling concern of a few shillings. **1866** A. L. PERRY *Elem. Pol. Econ.* (1873) 524 The country is too large for the petty, piddling processes of 'protection'. **1902** W. E. HENLEY *Views & Reviews: Art* 10 *The Castle of Otranto* is a piddling piece of super-nature. **1936** [see DOLESS *a.*]. **1948** [see GOUGER c]. **1966** *Electronics* 31 Oct. 149 The European market for IC's is still piddling. **1971** *Maclean's Mag.* Sept. 4/1 In plain words, I found out what my job was. No piddling assignment either. What it amounted to was saving the country. **1972** V. CANNING *Rainbird Pattern* i. 2 Use other people's..piddling fears about their own status, and the world is at your feet. **1976** 'D. FLETCHER' *Don't whistle 'Macbeth'* 47 You'd never drown... Not in that piddling little stream.

2. Making water, urinating.

1968 *Listener* 2 May 579/3 Far and away the best..is *Thinking Girl.* Some may be inclined to poke fun by retitling Miss Meacock's book *Piddling Girl*, after counting the number of times the characters are glimpsed in lavatories.

piddly ('pɪdlɪ), *a.* [f. PIDDLE *sb.* + -LY[1].] = PIDDLING *ppl. a.* 1.

1946 B. MARSHALL *George Brown's Schooldays* xv. 72 Filthy little funks, skittering away down a piddly little track like that.

piddock ('pɪdək). Also piddick. [Origin unascertained. It has the form of a dim. in *-ock.*] A bivalve mollusc of the genus *Pholas* or family *Pholadidæ*, which burrow in soft rock, wood, etc.; *esp.* one of the common species, such as *P. dactylus*, with a long ovate shell, which are used for bait.

1851 *Zoologist* IX. 3175 Notes on the Pholas dactylus, or Sussex Piddick. **1868** WOOD *Homes without H.* v. 99 Our next example of the burrowing molluscs is the well known Pholas, popularly called the piddock (*Pholas dactylus*).

pide, pidgeon, obs. forms of PIED, PIGEON.

pidgin, pigeon ('pɪdʒɪn, -ən). Also pidjin, pidjun, pidgeon.

a. A Chinese corruption of Eng. *business*, used widely for any action, occupation, or affair. Hence **pidgin-English**, the jargon, consisting chiefly of English words, often corrupted in pronunciation, and arranged according to Chinese idiom, orig. used for inter-communication between the Chinese and Europeans at seaports, etc. in China, the Straits Settlements, etc.; also *transf.* (quot. 1891).

1826 B. HALL *Acct. Voy. Corea* (rev. ed.) vi. 287, I come to see about your pigeon. *Ibid.* 288, I afterwards learned that ..'pigeon', in the strange jargon spoken at Canton by way of English, means business. **1845** J. R. PETERS *Misc. Remarks upon Chinese* vii. 73 Pidgeon, is the common Chinese pronunciation of business. **1850** BERNCASTLE *Voy. China* II. 65 The Chinese not being able to pronounce the word 'business', called it 'bigeon', which has degenerated into 'pigeon', so that this word is in constant use. **1859** *All Year Round* I. 20 *'Piece of China'*, A-tye will row you out, because she can speak pigeon English. **1872** A. D. CARLISLE *Round World* x. 106 The dialect..current between Englishmen and Chinamen..goes by the name of Pigeon-English. **1873** *Macm. Mag.* Nov. 45 [Article]. **1876** LELAND *Pidgin English Sing Song* 3 Pidgin is with great ingenuity made expressive of every variety of calling, occupation, or affair. **1876** BESANT & RICE *Gold. Butterfly* xlv. He had a ghost story of his own—an original one in pigeon English. **1901** A. LANG *Magic & Relig.* 37 His rude *lingua franca*, or pidgin English. (See also *N. & Q.* 10th s. V. 90/2.)

b. A language as spoken in a simplified or altered form by non-natives, *spec.* as a means of communication between people not sharing a common language. Freq. *attrib.* or in *Comb.* Also *fig.*

1891 *Argus* (Melbourne) 7 Nov. 13/4 That ridiculous pigeon-English which the whites have used..throughout Queensland..as their medium of communication with the blacks. **1921** H. E. PALMER *Princ. Language-Study* 107 Pidgin or pidgin-speech may be defined as that variety of a language which is used exclusively by foreigners. **1943** R. A. HALL *Melanesian Pidgin Eng.* 8 The phonetics of Melanesian Pidgin are basically those of a slightly sub-standard English. *Ibid.* 9 In the absence of native speakers, Pidgin does not present the same constant features of pronunciation and grammatical usage as do major languages. **1955** P. STREVENS *Papers in Lang.* (1965) ix. 120 Esperanto is, in fact, a kind of glorified Pidgin Indo-European. **1962** *Listener* 27 Sept. 467/2 Pidgin exists in India and Africa as well—but the context is very different from that of Pidgin in New Guinea. **1964** *Ibid.* 5 Mar. 388/2 At Layer Marney the old is all. The Renaissance motifs are handled awkwardly. This is trying to speak Italian without command of grammar, syntax, or vocabulary... It is the pidgin-Italian spoken by the sturdy Englishman of the Perpendicular. **1968** W. J. SAMARIN in J. A. Fishman *Readings Sociol. of Lang.* 667 In the fifteenth century there developed a pidgin Portuguese which may have originated in the first contacts with the Africans, but ultimately spread to the ports of the Far East. *Ibid.* 671 The ease with which Korean Bamboo English developed leads one to imagine the inevitability of pidgins in the world. **1968** *Economist* 14 Dec. 4/1 The Soviet graduates, to whom you refer, are as little satisfied with pidgin marxism as young opinion in the British 1930s was with Mr. Neville Chamberlain. **1974** *Florida FL Reporter* XIII. 17/1 While agreeing with Nida and Fehderau that pidgin-using and koine-forming situations are strongly analogous, I cannot agree that the 'Sabir Pidgins'..at least are special formations. **1975** *Language* LI. 684 The use of morphemes borrowed by a pidgin or creole language..from a European language often diverges widely from the use of the source morpheme in the source language. **1978** *Verbatim* Feb. 10/1 Both authors hold to..the Creolist theory, which traces the present-day Black English vernacular to a Plantation Creole, to a plantation-maritime pidgin, to an African origin.

c. Phr. *(to be) someone's pigeon*: to be (that person's) concern, affair, etc.

1904 KIPLING *Traffics & Discov.* 293 'What about their musketry average?' I went on. 'Not my pidgin,' said Bayley. **1919** B. RUCK *Disturbing Charm* II. x. 248 It was not Jack's pidgin to do anything until then. **1924** G. L. MALLORY *Let.* 11 May in E. F. Norton *Fight for Everest: 1924* (1925) II. 233 Geoffrey Bruce whose 'pigeon' it is to deal with the porters. **1929** C. MACKENZIE *Gallipoli Memories* xiii. 237 'Nothing known of this man here.' 'Pass to N.T.O. K beach.' 'From M.L.O. Lancashire Landing to A.P.M. K beach. This is your pigeon, I think.' **1929** J. MASEFIELD *Hawbucks* 164 This is my pidgin; none of yours at all. **1935** *Punch* 30 Jan. 136/1 'There's trouble in Paraguay,' said the man from Geneva. 'Then leave it there,' said I. 'It's not my pigeon.' **1957** 'J. WYNDHAM' *Midwich Cuckoos* iii. 26 'Not our kind of job,' he said, with the air of one recalling a useful Union decision. 'More like the fire chaps' pigeon, I'd say.' **1959** *Times* 6 Mar. 11/7 If it is the fur (not our pigeon) that makes Mr. Page furious, maybe the answer is mothballs. **1961** L. P. HARTLEY *Two for River* 45 Well, you do something, Thomas Henry, it's your pigeon. **1977** B. PYM *Quartet in Autumn* xviii. 160 Janice wondered whether anyone else had been to see Marcia... She was Janice's special pigeon, if you could put it like that.

pidginize ('pɪdʒɪnaɪz), *v.* [f. PIDGIN b. + -IZE.] To produce a simplified or pidgin form of (a language). So **pidgini'zation**, the fact or process of pidginizing; a pidginized language; **'pidginized** *ppl. a.*

1934 PRIEBSCH & COLLINSON *German Lang.* I. ii. 35 This 'pidginization' [in Afrikaans] is thought to be due to sudden contact with a Creolized language, in this case a blend called Malayo-Portuguese. **1937** J. R. FIRTH *Tongues of Men* vi. 80 If English were to be pidginized the simplification of pronunciation would have to be based on those differences between sounds which most men could hear..without expert tuition. **1949** [see CREOLIZED *ppl. a.* 2]. **1956** J. LOTZ in Saporta & Bastian *Psycholinguistics* (1961) 14/1 Various attempts at an international language like Esperanto or Basic English either end up as incomplete replicas of natural languages or as primitive pidginizations. **1962** *Listener* 27 Sept. 467/1 The more pidginised the language becomes, obviously the less useful English can be as a world language. **1972** J. L. DILLARD *Black English* iii. 135 Theoretically, any language can be pidginized, although historically not all have been. **1974** L. TODD *Pidgins & Creoles* i. 5 Pidginization and creolization may have been much more prevalent in language change than linguists have hitherto acknowledged. **1977** *Language* LIII. 495/1 First he discusses borrowings from American Indian languages, particularly the pidginized forms that underwent various semantic shifts and are still current, such as *bury the hatchet* and *Great White Father.*

pi-dog, var. PYE-DOG.

pid-pad. [Echoic: cf. PAD *sb.*[5]; the two different vowels suggesting alternation, as in *zigzag.* Cf. PIT-PAT.] Imitation of the dull sound of footsteps.

1900 'HEADON HILL' *Plunder Ship* iii. 31, I..heard the pid-pad of bare feet. *Ibid.* xxiii. 214 There was..a pid-pad of sandals on the deck.

pidrero, variant of PEDRERO, a small gun.

pie (paɪ), *sb.*[1] Also 4–8 pye, 5–6 py, (6 pee). [a. OF. *pie* (13th c. in Littré) = Pr. *piga*, It. *pica*:—L. *pica* magpie.]

1. The bird now more usually called MAGPIE.

a **1250** *Owl & Night.* 126 Þat pie and crowe hit todrowe. **1303** R. BRUNNE *Handl. Synne* 355 Beleue nouȝt yn þe pyys cheteryng. *c* **1380** WYCLIF *Serm.* Sel. Wks. I. 165 It is a foul þing þat prestis speken as pies. **1398** TREVISA *Barth. De P.R.* XII. i. (Bodl. MS.), Alle foules of rauen kinde as chogghes crowes rokes rauens and pies. *a* **1450** *Knt. de la Tour* (1868) 22 Ther was a woman that had a pie in a cage. ? *c* **1475** *Sqr. lowe Degre* 47 (text of Copland *c* 1550), The woodwale, The pee, and the Popiniaye. *a* **1548** HALL *Chron., Hen. VI* 85 Pies will chatter and Mice will pepe. **1559** *Mirr. Mag.* (1563) N iv, The Fox descrye the crowes and chateryng Pyen. **1646** J. HALL *Poems* 4 Pies Do ever love to pick at witches eyes. **1713** SWIFT *Salamander* Wks. 1755 III. II. 75 Pyes and daws are often stil'd With christian nick-names like a child. **1774** GOLDSM. *Nat. Hist.* (1776) V. 219 Birds of the Pie Kind. **1853** C. BRONTE *Villette* xiii, Chattering like a pie to the best gentleman in Christendom.

2. *fig.* Applied to †**a.** a cunning or wily person: esp. in phr. *wily pie* (*obs.*); **b.** a chattering or saucy person, a 'chatter-pie' (= MAGPIE 2).

[*c* **1374** CHAUCER *Troylus* III. 478 (527) Dredles it clere was in the wynd From euery pye and euery lette game.] **1542** UDALL *Erasm. Apoph.* 321 b, One Accius..a wylie pye, and a feloe full of shiftes. *c* **1554** *Interlude of Youth* in Hazl. *Dodsley* II. 22 Ye be a little pretty pye! i-wis, ye go full gingerly. **1563** B. GOOGE *Eglogs* vii. (Arb.) 60 Than cownt you them for chatring Pies Whose tongs must alwayes walke. **1579** FULKE *Heskins's Parl.* 47 Maister Heskins like a wilie Pye, obiecteth this article of the resurrection. **1692** WASHINGTON tr. *Milton's Def. Pop.* M.'s Wks. 1738 I. 523 Salmasius, that French chattering Pye. **1886** MRS. LYNN LINTON *P. Carew* xl, 'She was no more a hussy than you, you bold pie!' said Patty in a fume.

3. With defining words, applied locally to various other birds, usually having black-and-white ('pied') plumage: see quots. (See also SEA-PIE.)

1883 *List Anim. Zool. Soc.* (ed. 8) 283 *Dendrocitta vagabunda*, Wandering Tree-Pie... *D. sinensis*, Chinese Tree-Pie. **1885** SWAINSON *Prov. Names Brit. Birds* 30 Dipper... The white breast and blackish upper plumage have caused it to be called..River pie (Ireland). *Ibid.* 31 British Long-tailed Titmouse..Long-tailed pie. *Ibid.* 47 Great Grey Shrike..Murdering pie. *Ibid.* 209 Black-headed Gull..Scoulton pie, or Scoulton peewit. **1890** *Cent. Dict.* s.v., The smoky pie, *Psilorhinus morio.*

b. *French pie, rain-pie, wood-pie*: applied to various species of woodpecker. [Here perh. = OF. *pi* (mod.F. *pic*, but *pivert, pi vert* great green woodpecker):—L. *pic-us* woodpecker; if so, really a distinct word. But *French pie* in quot. 1677 may be the shrike or butcher-bird, F. *pie cruelle, pie grièche grise*; cf. *murdering pie* above.]

1677 N. COX *Gentl. Recreat.* II. (ed. 2) 161 Of the Short-winged Hawks there are these:..The Sparrow-hawk and Musket, Two sorts of the French Pie. **1783** AINSWORTH *Lat. Dict.* (ed. Morell) II, *Picus*,..a woodpecker, a speckt, a hickway, or heighhould; a French pie, a whitwall. **1837–40** MACGILLIVRAY *Hist. Brit. Birds* III. 80 Greater spotted woodpecker..wood-pie, French-pie. **1885** SWAINSON *Prov. Names Brit. Birds* 98 Great Spotted Woodpecker..Wood pie (Staffordshire; Hants)... Lesser Spotted Woodpecker.. Little wood pie (Hants). *Ibid.* 99 Green Woodpecker.. Wood pie (Somerset). *Ibid.* 100 The constant iteration of its cry before rain..gives it the names Rain bird; Rain pie.

4. Applied to a pied or parti-coloured animal (cf. F. *pie* = *cheval pie*, Littré): in quot. to a pied hound. Cf. 5 b.

1869 *Daily News* 7 Aug., A couple of those beautiful lemon pyes, Nosegay and Novelty..just beat the flower of the Brocklesby 'lady pack'.

5. *attrib.* and *Comb.* **a.** In compounds relating to the bird, as *pie-pecked* adj.; †**pie-maggot**, a magpie (= MAGGOT[2]).

1597 J. KING *On Jonas* Ep. Ded. (1618) ¶ iij b, We all write, learned and vnlearned, crow-poets and py-poetesses. **1601** HOLLAND *Pliny* II. 296 *margin*, The Deuill take thee, or, the Rauens peck out thine eies, or I had rather see thee Pie pekt. **1602** *Contention Liberality & Prodigality* IV. iv. in Hazl. *Dodsley* VIII. 366 O thou vile, ill-favoured, crow-trodden, pye-pecked rout! **1628** LAYTON *Syons Plea* (ed. 2) 21 [The bishops are] Rauens and Pye-Maggots to prey upon the State. *a* **1652** BROME *Queenes Exchange* V. i. Wks. 1873 III. 537 What are thou..thus Piepickt, Crow-trod, or Sparrow blasted?

b. In compounds denoting 'parti-coloured', 'of various colours' (like the black-and-white plumage of the magpie: cf. PIED 1), as ***pie-coated, -coloured*** adjs. See also PIEBALD.

1630 BRATHWAIT *Eng. Gentlem.* (1641) 11 To display thy pie-coloured flag of vanity. **1813** HOGG *Queen's Wake* 291 The pye-duck sought the depth of the main. **1848** THACKERAY *Bk. Snobs* ii, The liveries of these pie-coated retainers.

c. *Friars of the Pie*: see *Pied friars*, PIED *a.*

pie (paɪ), *sb.*[2] Also 4–9 pye, 6 py, (7 paye). [Occurs (in Latin context) in 1303; evidently a well-known popular word in 1362. No related word known outside Eng. (exc. Gaelic *pighe*, from Eng. or Lowland Sc.). Being in form identical with PIE *sb.*[1] (known half a century earlier), it is held by many to have been in some way derived from or connected with that word. See Note below.]

1. a. A dish composed of meat, fowl, fish, fruit, or vegetables, etc., enclosed in or covered with a layer of paste and baked.

The *pie* appears to have been (*a*) at first of meat or fish; doubtful or undefined uses (*b*) appear in 16th c.; *fruit pies* (also called, esp. in the north of England and Ireland, in Scotland, and often in U.S., *tarts*) appear (*c*) before 1600, the earliest being APPLE-PIE, q.v.

(*a*) **1303** *Bolton Priory Compotus* lf. 68b, Frumentum expenditum..In pane..pro Priore Celerario et aliis..et in pyis et pastellis per annum 9 qr. 1 bus. di. **1304** *Ibid.* lf. 82 In pane furnato..et in pyes et pastellis, 33 qr. 2 bus. di. **1362** LANGL. *P. Pl.* A. Prol. 104 Cookes and heore knaues cryen 'hote pies, hote! Goode gees and grys, Gowe dyne, Gowe!' *c* **1386** CHAUCER *Prol.* 384 He koude rooste and sethe and boille [*v.r.* broille] and frye, Maken Mortreux and wel bake a pye. *c* **1425** *Voc.* in Wr.-Wülcker 662/26 *Hec artocria* [Gr. ἀρτόκρεας bread and meat], a pie *de pundio*. *c* **1430** *Two Cookery-bks.* 53 Pyez de parez [p. 75 of Parys].—Take and smyte fayre buttys of Porke, and buttys of Vele, to-gederys [etc.]..; þan caste þer-to ȝolkys of Eyroun [etc.]..; þen make fayre past, and cofynnys, & do þer-on; kyuer it, & let bake, & serue forth. *c* **1440** *Promp. Parv.* 395/2 Pye, pasty, *artocrea, pastillulus.* **1511** FABYAN *Will* in *Chron.* (1811) Pref. 9 If it happen the saide obite to fall in Lent, than..for the peces of beeff abovesaid..be ordeyned pyes of elys, or som other goode fysh mete. *a* **1568** *Nyne Ordour of Knavis* 66 in *Bannatyne Poems* (Hunter. Cl.) 448 He thrawis and he puttis fast at his vly pyiss. **1624** HEYWOOD *Gunaik.* IX. 444 Burnt alive, for killing young infants and salting their flesh and putting them into pyes. **1784** COOK *Third Voy.* IV. xi. II. 495 A pye made in the form of a loaf..inclosed some salmon, highly seasoned with pepper. **1838** DICKENS *Nich. Nick.* vii, It's a pity to cut the pie if you're not hungry..Will you try a bit of the beef?

(*b*) **1530** PALSGR. 254/1 Pye a pasty, *pasté*. *a* **1568** '*In somer quhen flouris will smell*' 35 in *Bannatyne Poems* (Hunter. Cl.) 400 It is lyk that ye had eitin pyiss, Ye are so sweit. **1577** WHETSTONE *Life Gascoigne* xviii, Spight foule Enuies poysoned pye. **1694** CROWNE *Regulus* II. 12 A man all vertue, like a pye all spice, will not please. *c* **1710** CELIA FIENNES *Diary* (1888) 242 He weares a great Velvet cap..like a Turbant or great bowle in forme of a great open pye. **1765** GRAY *Shakespeare* 24 Glorious puddings and immortal pies. *a* **1839** PRAED *Poems* (1864) II. 58 And lords made love,—and ladies, pies. **1853** SOYER *Pantroph.* 284 All pass away whether they be temples, columns, pyramids, or pies.

(*c*) **1590–1861** [see APPLE-PIE]. **1706** PHILLIPS, *Pie*, a well known Dish of Meat, or Fruit bak'd in Paste. **1864** SALA in *Daily Tel.* 18 Aug., There it is; pumpkin pie, blackberry pie, whortleberry pie, huckleberry pie—pie of all kinds.

b. With defining word, usually denoting the essential ingredient, as ***apple-pie, eel-pie, game-pie, meat-pie, mince-pie, pigeon-pie, plum-pie, pork-pie, rhubarb-pie, venison-pie***, etc. (see these words); also ***Christmas pie*** (see CHRISTMAS 4), ***French pie*** (see quot. 1611), ***Périgord pie*** (see PÉRIGORD).

1602 *2nd Pt. Ret. fr. Parnass.* v. ii. (Arb.) 66 A black Iack of Beere, and a Christmas Pye. **1611** FLORIO, *Carne ne tegami*, meate stewed between two dishes, which some call a French pie. **1698** in Warrender *Marchmont* (1894) 184 Could pigeon paye. *a* **1700** B. E. *Dict. Cant. Crew*, *Superstitious-Pies*, Minc'd, or Christmas-Pies, so Nick-nam'd by the Puritans, or Precisians. **1769** MRS. RAFFALD *Eng. Housekpr.* (1778) 155 Send it up hot without a lid, the same way as the French pye. **1798** FRERE & CANNING in *Anti-Jacobin* No. 23. 120 Youthful Horner..Cull'd the dark plum from out his Christmas pye. **1834** SOUTHEY *Doctor* cix. (1848) 266/2 The great goose-pye, which in the Christmas week was always dispatched by the York coach to Bishopsgate Street. **1872** CALVERLEY *Fly Leaves* (1881) 21 But I shrink from thee Arab! Thou eat'st eel-pie.

c. In more general allusive use, an affair, concern, etc., regarded in terms of one's possible involvement in it: ***to have a finger*** **(†*hand*)** ***in the pie***: to have a part or share in the doing of something (often implying officious intermeddling); ***to put a finger into*** **(*another's*)** ***pie*** (and variants), to meddle in (someone else's) business; ***to cut a pie*** (*U.S.*), to become involved in a particular matter; ***cold pie***: see COLD *a.* 19. See also HUMBLE PIE.

1553 *Respublica* (Brandl) I. iii. 105 Bring me in credyte, that my hande be in the pye. **1604** DEKKER *Honest Wh.* Wks. 1873 II. 171 My hand was in the Pye, my Lord, I confesse it. **1613** SHAKS. *Hen. VIII*, I. i. 52 The diuill speed him: No mans Pye is freed From his Ambitious finger. **1649** *Man in Moon* No. 33. 262 We heare Jermyn and the Lord Culpepper had a finger in the pye. **1843** T. C. HALIBURTON *Attaché* 1st Ser. I. xi. 180 By gosh Aunty,..you had better not cut that pie: you will find it rather sour in the apple sarse, and tough in the paste. **1868** 'MARK TWAIN' *Let.* 6 Feb. (1920) 85 They want to send me abroad, as a Consul or a Minister. I said I didn't want any of the pie. **1871** J. O. BROOKFIELD *Influence* II. 12, I don't see what excuse she has for putting her finger into everybody's pie as she does. **1879** *London Society* Christmas Number 87/2 If you keep straight yourself you'll have quite enough to do, without putting your fingers into other folks' pies. **1659, 1886** [see FINGER *sb.* 3c]. *a* **1845** MOORE *Fragm. Character* xi, Whatever was the best pye going, In that Ned..had his finger. **1921** L. STRACHEY *Queen Victoria* iii. 93 Her uncle Leopold had apparently determined..that her cousin Albert ought to be her husband. That was very like her uncle Leopold, who wanted to have a finger in every pie. **1924** A. CHRISTIE *Poirot Investigates* i. 19 What I do now is for my own satisfaction—the satisfaction of Hercule Poirot! Decidedly, I must have a finger in this pie. **1940** N. MITFORD *Pigeon Pie* iii. 57 Aristocrats are inclined to prefer Nazis while Jews prefer Bolshies. An old bourgeois like yourself..should keep your fingers out of both their pies. **1970** G. JACKSON *Let.* 17 Apr. in *Soledad Brother* (1971) 224 We don't want their culture. We *don't* want a piece of that pie. **1979** *Homes & Gardens* June 90/2 One of the many pies he keeps a finger in is the Color Association of the USA.

d. Assets, proceeds, wealth, etc., considered as something to be apportioned or shared out (cf. CAKE *sb.* 7b).

1967 *Boston Sunday Herald* 7 May III. 14/4 The result of an Appellate Court victory..which cut Weymouth's total property valuation by $40 million to give the town a bigger slice of the sales tax pie. **1971** *Ink* 12 June 7/4 The thousands of workers..are searching for ways to fight not only for a bigger portion of the capitalist pie but for a freer and more dignified life. **1978** *Washington Post* 29 July D30/2 Although more than 50 million watches will be sold in the United States this year, there is no consensus on what piece of the pie digitals will get.

2. Applied to something resembling a pie. ***bran-pie***, a tub full of bran with small articles hidden in it to be drawn out at random, at Christmas festivities, etc. See also CLAY-*pie*, DIRT-PIE, MUD-*pie*.

1842 ORDERSON *Creol.* ii. 14 The Jews..still withheld their unleavened pie..a simple crust covering a pretty round sum. **1873** GARDNER *Hist. Jamaica* 199 The governor's purse was called a pie. **1877** *Cassell's Family Mag.* May 377/1 In the last division of the tent we had..a bran-pie... The bran-pie was an oblong washing-tub..filled with bran, in which were hidden..small articles. **1889** *Peel City Guardian* 28 Dec. 7/4 Sometimes what is termed a 'bran pie' is employed..for storing the presents in. **1902** *Little Folks* Jan. 54/2 Every single thing was bought, including the packets in the bran-pie. **1904** *Daily Chron.* 27 Feb. 3/2 The bran-pie..is the receptacle of second-rate presents: gifts not quite showy enough to be displayed upon a Christmas tree. **1916** *Daily Colonist* (Victoria, B.C.) 4 July 4/4 All sorts of seasonable refreshments will be served and the blue ribbon girls will have an attraction in the form of a bran pie. **1931** V. WOOLF *Waves* 236, I think more disinterestedly than I could when I was young and must dig furiously like a child rummaging in a bran-pie to discover myself.

3. a. Applied to a collection of things made up into a heap; *spec.* a shallow pit, or heap of potatoes or other roots, covered with straw, earth, etc. for storing and protection from frost; also, a heap of manure stacked for maturing. *local.*

1526 in *Househ. Ord.* (1790) 227 Item, that the Pye of Coales be abridged to the one halfe that theretofore had been served. **1791** *Trans. Soc. Arts* IX. 42 [The potatoes] were taken up, and a large pye made of them, which is laying them in a heap and covering them with straw. **1848** *Jrnl. R. Agric. Soc.* IX. II. 514 Mangolds..stored 'in pies' on the level surface. **1886** *S.W. Linc. Gloss.* s.v., Potatoes or other roots placed in a hole,..against the winter,..are said to be 'pied down' or..'in pie'. **1887** *Daily Tel.* 4 Apr. 2 Making 'pies' of the green fodder just as dung pies are made.

b. *Austral.* (See quot. 1960[1].)

1960 *Times Rev. Industry* Jan. 103/1 A pie is a combination of wool buyers who do not bid against one another at wool sales, then divide the wool purchased by members of the group. **1960** *Sydney Morning Herald* 25 Mar. 7 He said he had known since 1945 that 'pies' were operating. **1966** BAKER *Austral. Lang.* (ed. 2) iii. 58 The Australian public became aware in 1958 that wool-buying was not always a straightforward operation... Some buyers were combining into *pies* (also called *rings*) to bid and then share purchases, so that competition was reduced.

4. *fig.* **a.** Something to be eagerly appropriated; a prize, a treat; a bribe. Also used in comparative phrases: ***(as) good (nice, sweet,*** etc.) ***as pie.*** *slang* (orig. *U.S.*).

1857 'DOW JR.' *Dow's Patent Sermons* 1st Ser. 21 Let her alone and in five minutes the storm will be over, and she as good as pie again. **1884** 'MARK TWAIN' *Huck. Finn* ii. 15 You're always as polite as pie to them. *Ibid.* v. 34 So he took him to his own house, and dressed him up clean and nice,..and was just old pie to him, so to speak. **1887** R. T. COOKE *Happy Dodd* xvii. 178 We've been awful good; good as pie, hain't we? **1888** W. F. CODY *Story of Wild West* 531, I wanted to reach Fort Larned before daylight, in order to avoid if possible the Indians, to whom it would have been 'pie' to have caught me there on foot. **1891** *Harper's Mag.* Sept. 579/1 Ain't he as polite as pie to her? **1895** *Outing* (U.S.) XXVI. 436/1 Green dogs are pie for him [the racoon]. **1902** *Westm. Gaz.* 16 June 3/1 Sometimes he is 'pie' for the cartoonist to an unfortunate extent. **1922** JOYCE *Ulysses* 309 See him of a Sunday with his little concubine of a wife, and she wagging her tail up the aisle of the chapel,..nice as pie, doing the little lady. **1933** E. O'NEILL *Ah, Wilderness!* IV. iii. 151, I ran into him upstreet this afternoon and he was meek as pie. **1939** J. STEINBECK *Grapes of Wrath* vi. 65 Well, the guy that come aroun' talked nice as pie. **1952** M. LASKI *Village* vi. 109 She was as sweet as pie, said she was awfully sorry. **1958** *Listener* 11 Sept. 388/3 When foreign dignitaries come from all corners of the world to pay their respects to me..I am as nice as pie. **1974** P. DE VRIES *Glory of Hummingbird* (1975) xviii. 265 People were wonderful, nice as pie, glad to see me fallen. **1978** F. WELDON *Praxis* xxiv. 256 She's very stubborn. Sweet as pie just so long as she's doing exactly what she wants.

b. Political favour or patronage. *U.S. slang.*

1910 *Richmond* (Virginia) *Weekly Times-Dispatch* 17 Aug. 10 Representative Slemp was looked upon as the dispenser of the patronage in Virginia because of the promise of the President that he would allow the pie to be handed out by the men who did the fighting. **1916** *N.Y. Times* 12 May 10/4 Take your tribute, but buy national defense with it, don't waste it in 'pork' and 'pie' and Populist lunacies!

c. Something easily accomplished or dealt with, a 'cinch'; *spec.* in phr. ***easy (simple,*** etc.) ***as pie.*** *slang* (orig. *U.S.*). Cf. PIE IN THE SKY.

In some uses not clearly distinguishable from sense 4a.

1889 *Outing* Nov. 151/2, I thought it would just be pie for me to buy him, and take him through the 'bushes'... (The 'bushes', you know, means the country fairs.) **1905** N. DAVIS *Northerner* 93 It will be just—what was it you said—pie?—pie for them, won't it. **1919** WODEHOUSE *Coming of Bill* (1920) I. v. 54 This Kid Mitchell was looked on as a coming champ in those days... I guess I looked pie to him. **1923** E. WALLACE *Missing Million* xx. 161 Murder was cream pie to Tod. **1925** WODEHOUSE *Sam the Sudden* xix. 156 'How do you propose to make your entry?'..'Easy as pie. Odd-job man... They always want odd-job men.' **1937** D. L. SAYERS *Busman's Honeymoon* xii. 210 He's knocked out... Simple as pie. No cutting or stealing keys or hiding blunt instruments or telling lies. **1948** J. B. PRIESTLEY *Linden Tree* I. 39 It's as simple as pie. **1959** C. BUSH *Case of Careless Thief* vii. 87 It's in the bag... Everything we wanted and easy as pie. **1967** G. F. FIENNES *I tried to run a Railway* iii. 26 In the current work York was pie compared with Cambridge. **1972** WODEHOUSE *Pearls, Girls & Monty Bodkin* iv. 53 Interesting Llewellyn in Silver River would be pie, but I'd also have to interest her, and she's not the right woman for that.

5. *attrib.* and *Comb.*, as ***pie-baker, -eater, -feast, -fork, -gaudy*** (GAUDY *sb.* 5), ***-knife, -maker, -meat, -pan, -paste, -plate, shell, -shop, -tin***; **pie-biter**, (*a*) *U.S.*, one who has a fondness for pies; *fig.* (in sense 4b), one who takes part in political patronage; (*b*) *Austral. slang* = *pie-eater* (*b*); **pie-board**, a board on which pies are made, baked, or carried; **pie-card** *U.S. slang*, (*a*) a meal ticket; one who begs for a meal; (*b*) a union-card; the holder of a union-card; also *attrib.*; **pie-cart** *N.Z.* (see quot. 1922); **pie chart** = *pie diagram*; **pie-counter** *U.S.*, a counter at which pies are sold; *fig.*, a source of grants or favours (see sense 4b); **pie diagram**, a circle divided by radii into sectors whose areas are proportional to the relative magnitudes or frequencies of a set of items; **pie-dish**, the deep dish in which a pie is made; **pie-eater**, (*a*) someone who eats pies; (*b*) *Austral. slang*, someone of no importance, a 'small-timer'; also, a fool or simpleton; so ***pie-eating*** ppl. adj.; **pie-funnel**, a support for a pie-crust during cooking; **pie-house**, a house at which pies are sold, a pie-shop; **pie-lass**, a girl who sells pies; **pie-melon**, †(*a*) *U.S.*, a melon used for pies (*obs.*); (*b*) *Austral.*, a variety of watermelon, *Citrullus lanatus*; **pie-plant**, any plant yielding fruit, etc. used for pies; *spec.* (*U.S.*) garden rhubarb; also locally applied to the wild *Rumex hymenosepalus*, which is similarly used (*Cent. Dict.*); also *attrib.*; **pie-wagon** *U.S. slang* (see quot. 1960); †**pie-wife, pie-woman**, a woman who sells pies. See also PIE-CRUST, PIEMAN.

1379 in Riley *Memorials* (1868) 432 *Pie bakere. *c* **1440** *Promp. Parv.* 395/2 Pye baker, *cereagius*. **1594** R. ASHLEY tr. *Loys le Roy* 28b, Prepared and dressed by Cookes and pybakers. **1868** *Daily Territorial Enterprise* (Virginia City, Nevada) 2 Apr. 3/1 Through these same [April fool] doughnuts many a lunch-eater and *pie-biter came to grief. **1902** O. WISTER *Virginian* ix. 104 He held out to his pony a slice of bread matted with sardines, which the pony expertly accepted. 'You're a plumb pie-biter, you Monte,' he continued. **1908** in W. R. HUNT *North of 53°* (1974) xxvi. 225 Persons interested in other points, and paid knockers and piebiters may pound and hammer until their auditors are deafened. **1911** E. DYSON *Benno* 144 He was that angry with the South pie-biters, he didn't care what 'appened to 'em. **1938** K. DOUTHITT *Romance & Dim Trails* 106 [He was] better known over the northwest and in camp life as Pie Biter, because he was very fond of pie. **1709** *Brit. Apollo* II. No. 70. 3/2 The Puny Author who supplies still The Cooks, and on their *Pye-boards lies still. **1844** DICKENS *Mart. Chuz.* xxxix, She tripped downstairs into the kitchen for the flour, then for the pie-board. **1909** W. G. DAVENPORT *Butte & Montana beneath X-Ray* 56 Say, on the dead level, Andy, couldn't you let me have a lonely ten spot?.. Say, Andy, you've just got to jar loose with five bucks for my *pie card is so full of holes it looks like a piece of mosquito bar. **1929** *Amer. Speech* IV. 343 *Pie card*, a union card used to obtain food or lodging. **1931** 'D. STIFF' *Milk & Honey Route* 211 *Pie card*, one who hangs around and lives on a remittance man or some other person with money. **1945** *Seafarers' Log* 25 May 2/1 The Commie stooges and pie-cards kick us around. **1948** MENCKEN *Amer. Lang.* Suppl. II. 678 *Pie-card*, a union card used as a credential in begging. **1960** *New Left Rev.* 26 Sept. 41/1 The retired..comfortably fixed pie-card artists of every lost..cause of the labour and radical movements. **1973** C. RUBIN *Log* 64 All of them phony, pie-card officials who sit on their big fat asses and twiddle their thumbs. **1922** C. G. TURNER *Happy Wanderer* 37 We drifted down..to the *pie-cart (coffee-stall, in your speech). **1949** D. M. DAVIN *Roads from Home* 70 Somebody having a feed at the pie-cart. **1954** *Numbers* Nov. 23 A poky..kind of joint, just one degree better than a pie-cart. **1963** *Weekly*

News (Auckland) 5 June 37/2 The Mussons..were many years in the piecart business in Christchurch. **1973** A. Holden *Girl on Beach* 160 We went down town to the all-night pie-cart and bought masses of pies and chips..and drove up to the top of Mount Victoria. **1922** A. C. Haskell *Graphic Charts in Business* xiv. 75 Because the circle, divided..into sections, resembles a pie which has been cut in the usual manner, the Circular Percentage Chart is sometimes referred to as the '*pie chart'. **1972** Pie chart [see *line graph* s.v. line *sb.*^{2} 32]. **1977** *Lancet* 17 Dec. 1264/2 There is neither graph nor histogram nor pie chart to help the reader. **1903** *N.Y. Times* 16 Dec. 3 When his constituents asked him why he could not secure more routes [for free postal delivery] the only reply he could make was that he could not get up to the *pie counter. **1912** M. Nicholson *Hoosier Chron.* 470 I'm in the ranks of the patriots and not looking for the pie counter. **1921** H. Secrist *Statistics in Business* v. 65 *Pie-diagram showing the distribution of the total stock of hams, bacon and shoulders, reported August 31, 1917. **1954** *Brit. Jrnl. Psychol.* XLV. 149 The book is..well produced with numerous pie-diagrams, bar diagrams and other pictographic devices. **1979** *Jrnl. R. Soc. Arts* July 493/2 Whether they be dancers, writers, poets, actresses, painters or musicians they are largely unproductive of material which can be categorized, computed, stored, programmed, evaluated or turned into pie diagrams. **1859** Jephson *Brittany* iv. 38 Scanty ablutions of the morning in my *pie-dish. **1864** *Soc. Science Rev.* 37 A pie-dish and decanter take the place of jug and bason at the washing stand. **1904** *Daily Chron.* 12 Sept. 4/6 New Englanders, those champion *pie-eaters of the world. **1953** Baker *Australia Speaks* 134 *Pie-eater*.., a small-time crook. **1953** K. Tennant *Joyful Condemned* xviii. 166 He's one of those big he-men that go sneaking around the park waiting to snitch some chromo's handbag. Just a pie-eater. **1966** *Sunday Tel.* (Sydney) 22 May 25/2 The Australian appetite for pies has even added to our slang with the term 'pie eater'. Once meaning a small time crook, it is now used as a derogatory expression, close in meaning to 'a dill'. **1975** *Sun* (Sydney) 10 Jan. 52/7 A bunch of pie-eaters. Excuse me if I find an expression from my old mate, the late Siddie Barnes, but that's what the English team has turned out to be. **1949** L. Glassop *Lucky Palmer* 96 The trouble is, Mr. Hughes, you're too good for the *pie-eating bookmakers round these parts. You bet too well for them, Mr. Hughes. *c* **1550** *Lusty Juventus* in Hazl. *Dodsley* II. 78 Will you go to the *pie-feast? **1887** C. B. George *40 Yrs. on Rail* ix. 187 An exquisite set of *pie forks, of English make, and valued at seventy-five dollars. **1910–11** *Junior Army & Navy Stores' Catal.* 1304 *Pie funnel. **1926** S. E. Nash *Cooking Craft* xx. 186 Pile [meat] up in the centre to support the pastry, if there is not sufficient meat use an egg cup or pie funnel. **1960** *Woman* 23 Apr. 3/3 Use an empty salt cellar... It works as well as a proper pie funnel. **1659** Heylin *Certamen Epist.* 136 The suppressing of so many Gaudies, and *Pie-Gaudies, to the destruction of the hospitality and charity of the noble foundation. **1589** Rider *Bibl. Schol.* 1087 A *pie house, *artocrearium*. **1875** Mrs. Stowe *We & our Neighbors* liii. 474 Of course the reader knows that there were the usual amount of berry-spoons, and *pie-knives, and crumb-scrapers. **1836–48** B. D. Walsh *Aristoph., Knights* iii. i, Why, that he'll seize on the *pie-lass, And rob her and render her pieless. *c* **1450** *Dict. Garlande* in Wright *Voc.* 127 *Pastillarii* [gloss] *pye-makyers. **1598** *Epulario* C ij b, Mince it..like *Pie meat. **1860** *Trans. Mich. Agric. Soc. 1859* X. 623 Best *pie melon, H. J. Young..$0.50. **1882** W. D. Hay *Brighter Britain!* I. vii. 223 We grow large quantities of melons—..rock-melons, Spanish melons, pie-melons and so on. **1945** [see choko]. **1965** *Austral. Encycl.* III. 140/1 Some introduced cucurbits have become troublesome weeds, notably the..pie melon (*Citrullus vulgaris*); colocynth..and squirting cucumber. **1978** J. A. Michener *Chesapeake* 833 A pie-melon was a kind of gourd raised along the edges of cornfields, and..it produced one of the world's great pies. **1838** *Youth's Mag.* (N.Y.) July 91 Half a dozen roots of the *pie-plant (rhubarb) will furnish abundant materials for pies and tarts. **1847** Webster, *Pie-plant, Pie-rhubarb*, the garden rhubarb, used as a substitute for apples in making pies. **1864** Lowell *Fireside Trav., Cambridge*, His pie plants..blanched under barrels, each in his little hermitage, a vegetable Certosa. **1884** E. W. Nye *Baled Hay* 207 Afterward pulverize and spread over the pie plant bed. **1894** *Harper's Mag.* May 931/2 There is one old soul who especially loves rhubarb pies,..and it is she who remembers me and my row of pie-plant. **1952** J. Steinbeck *East of Eden* xvii. 159 He..chatted about the pieplant roots. **1976** *Hortus Third* (L. H. Bailey Hortorium) 967/2 Rhubarb is a strong, hardy, Old World perennial grown for the thick leaf stalks, which are cooked fresh in early spring for their agreeable acid flavor. It is also known as pie plant. **1598** Florio *Worlde of Wordes* 394/2 *Statccia* [sic], a cake, a tarte. Also any flat thing or *pye plate. **1653** R. Verney *Let.* May in M. M. Verney *Mem.* (1894) III. iv. 113, I presume there are dishes, pyplates, candlesticks. **1741** *Compl. Fam.-Piece* i. ii. (ed. 3) 105 Cover your Bason with a Pye-plate. **1895** *Montgomery Ward & Co. Catal.* Spring & Summer 431/3, Agate iron pie plates. **1948** *Good Housek. Cookery Bk.* 410 Place the round of pastry neatly and evenly on a flat pie plate. **1978** E. Tidyman *Table Stakes* ii. iii. 187 A broad Irish face as open as a pie plate. **1935** *Motion Picture* Nov. 79/2 Pour into baked *pie shell. **1976** Turgeon & Birmingham *All Amer. Cookbk.* (1977) 206/2 Put the pie shell in the refrigerator while rolling out the top crust. **1898** *Pie-wagon [see *moving-van* s.v. moving *vbl. sb.* 5]. **1904** 'No. 1500' *Life in Sing Sing* 257/1 *Pie wagon*, patrol wagon. **1960** Wentworth & Flexner *Dict. Amer. Slang* 388/2 *Pie wagon*, a police truck used to transport arrested persons to jail; a Black Maria. **1593** Nashe *Four Lett. Confut.* Wks. (Grosart) II. 283 To..cosen poore victuallers and *pie-wiues of Doctours cheese and puddinges. **1817** J. Evans *Excurs. Windsor*, etc. 343 An old *Pie-woman carried them provisions, but never saw them.

[*Note.* Prof. Skeat suggests 'from the miscellaneous nature of its (i.e. the dish's) contents' which might recall the black and white or piebald appearance of the bird; others have thought of the habit which the magpie has of picking up and forming accumulations of miscellaneous articles. In this connexion, the similarity between the forms of the words haggis and haggess (F. *agace, agasse*) magpie, has also been pointed out. The quotations for the word afford no light, exc. that in one place in a late 14th c. L. poem *Modus cenandi* (Furnivall, *Babees Book*, ii. 36) l. 51, 'sint inter fercula pice, Pastilli cum fartulis', appears to mean, 'let there be served between the dishes, pies, pasties' as if the writer identified *pie*, the dish, with *pica* the *pie* or magpie. On the other hand, in two early 14th c. quotations the Eng. word is used in Latin context, as if not identified with *pica*.]

pie, pye, *sb.*^{3} Now only *Hist.* [The Eng. word answering to med.L. *pica*; thus both in L. and Eng. identical in form with the name of the bird: see pie^1, and pica^1.]

1. A collection of rules, adopted in the pre-Reformation Church, to show how to deal (under each of the 35 possible variations in the date of Easter) with the concurrence of more than one office on the same day, accurately indicating the manner of commemorating, or of putting off till another time, the Saints' days, etc., occurring in the ever-changing times of Lent, Easter, Whitsuntide, and the Octave of the Trinity. (Cf. Blades *Caxton*, 1882, 240.)

c **1477** Caxton *Advertisement* (*Broadside*), If it plese ony man spirituel or temporel to bye ony pyes of two and thre comemoracions of salisburi vse enpryntid after the forme of this present lettre whiche ben wel and truly correct, late hym come to westmonester in to the almonesrye at the reed pale and he shal haue them good chepe. **1498** *Will of Thomson* (Somerset Ho.), My boke callid a pie. **1507** *Yatton Churchw. Acc.* (Som. Rec. Soc.) 129 Payd for a Masboke and a pye.. xj^s. vi^d. **1548–9** (Mar.) *Bk. Com. Prayer* Pref., The nombre and hardnes of the rules called the pie, and the manifolde chaunginges of the seruice, was the cause, y^t to turne the boke onlye, was so hard and intricate a matter, that many times, there was more busines to fynd out what should be read, then to read it when it was founde out. **1549** *Act 3 & 4 Edw. VI*, c. 10 §1 All Books called..Manuals, Legends, Pies, Portuasses, Primers..shall be..abolished. *a* **1568** Ascham *Scholem.* ii. (Arb.) 136 If he..could turne his Portresse and pie readilie. **1852** Hook *Ch. Dict.* (1871) 585 The pie was the table used before the Reformation to find out the service for the day. It may be referred to the Greek πίναξ or πινακίδιον. But the Latin word is *pica*, which perhaps came from the ignorance of the friars, who have thrust many barbarous words into the liturgies. **1879** Marquis of Bute tr. *Roman Breviary* I. p. xii, As to anything else, see the Chapters of the Pye treating specially of each detail.

b. Hence app. cock and pie, q.v.

†**2.** (Usually **pye book.**) An alphabetical index to rolls and records. *Obs.*

There are 'Pye Books' to Indictments extending as far back as 1660; but there is nothing to show when the term first came into use. It was in use in the Court of King's Bench early in the 18th century. It was also pretty generally used in the Courts of the Palatinate of Lancaster, the Indexes to the Affidavits, Declarations, and Sessional Papers being each styled 'Pye Books' (J. J. Cartwright, Sec. Publ. Rec. Office).

1788 *Chambers' Cycl.* (ed. Rees) s.v., In much the same sense the term was used by officers of civil courts, who called the calendars or alphabetical catalogues directing to the names and things contained in the rolls and records of their courts the Pyes.

pie (paɪ), *sb.*^{4} *Printing.* Also 7 **py**, 7–9 **pye**, (*U.S.*) **pi.** [Origin obscure: supposed by some to be a transferred use of pie *sb.*^{2}, in reference to its miscellaneous contents; others think of pie *sb.*^{3}, and the unreadable aspect of a page of the pie.]

A mass of type mingled indiscriminately or in confusion, such as results from the breaking down of a forme of type.

1659 Howell *Vocab.* li. (Printing terms), A Corrector, a proof, a revise,..pye all sorts of letter mixed, *Correctore*, &c. **1683** Moxon *Mech. Exerc., Printing* 370 Breaking the orderly Succession the Letters stood in, in a Line, Page, or Form, &c. and mingling the Letters together, which mingled Letters is called *Py*. **1771** Franklin *Autobiog.* Wks. 1887 I. 144 Having impos'd my forms..one of them by accident broke, and two pages reduced to pi, I immediately distributed and compos'd it over again before I went to bed. **1845** Carlyle *Cromwell* I. Introd. ii. 12 This same Dictionary..gone to pie, as we may call it. **1847** Webster, *Pi* [app. after Franklin]. **1882** J. Southward *Pract. Print.* (1884) 80 If composed matter gets..into a state of confusion, it is 'pie'.

b. *transf.* A disintegrated and confused mass; a jumble, medley, confusion, chaos; a 'mess'.

1837 Carlyle *Fr. Rev.* II. ii. iv, Your.. Arrangement going all (as the Typographers say of set types, in a similar case) rapidly to pie! **1841** Catlin *N. Amer. Ind.* II. xli. 53 We were thrown into 'pie' (as printers would say) in an instant of the most appalling alarm. **1870** *Daily News* 30 Nov., It was the merest luck..that the bones of the kings were not made inextricable 'pie' of. **1888** Mrs. Lynn Linton in *Fortn. Rev.* Oct. 532 Witness the 'pie' he made of his finances. **1897** *Spectator* 30 Jan. 162/2 To make pie of the European arrangements for securing peace.

‖**pie** (paɪ), *sb.*^{5} Also **pai, pi.** [a. Hindī, Marāṭhī, etc. *pā'ī*, from Skr. *pad, padī*, quarter, being 'originally, it would seem, the fourth part of an anna, and in fact identical with *pice*' (Yule).] The smallest Anglo-Indian copper coin, the twelfth part of an anna; before the depreciation of the rupee in 1899, about one-eighth of a penny.

1859 Lang *Wand. India* 69 He would tell you the interest due on such sums as three rupees, five annas, and seven pie, for twenty-one days, at forty-one three-fourth per cent. **1879** Mrs. A. E. James *Ind. Househ. Managem.* 49 The copper coins—1 anna = 4 pice. 1 pice = 3 pie. **1883** F. M. Crawford *Mr. Isaacs* xii. 261 Several coins, both rupees and pais. **1904** *Mission Field* June 64 The charge of a small fee, six pies (one cent) for the first prescription.

pie, variant of pee *Obs.*, kind of coat or jacket.

pie, *a.*^{1} [a. F. *pie*, fem. of OF. *pi, pis, piu, pif*:—L. *pi-us* pious.] Pious.

In occasional use as a variant of pi *a.*

c **1450** *Mirour Saluacioun* 786 Sho was ouer craft to telle humble pie [*v.r.* mercifull] and devoute. **1932** C. S. Lewis in *Essays & Stud.* XVII. 71 She is an admirable person. The only trouble is that she is rather *pie*. **1957** M. A. Jeeves *St. Thomas Becket* i. 13 Some of the more lugubrious sects' offsprings from the Reformation are also responsible for the eulogizing of 'pie' types of people.

pie (paɪ), *a.*^{2} *N.Z. slang.* [ad. Maori *pai* good.] (See quots.) Cf. half-pie *a.*

1941 Baker *N.Z. Slang* vi. 56 *To be pie at* (or *on*), to be expert or efficient at something, is another phrase of wide use in this country. It has been derived from the Maori *pai*, good. **1943** *Amer. Speech* XVIII. 93 'To be pie on' (= to be very good at) seems to be derived from the Maori *pai ana*.

†**pie,** *v.*^{1} *Obs. nonce-wd.* [f. pie *sb.*^{1}] *trans.* To repeat like a magpie.

1657 J. Watts *Dipper Sprinkled* 74 Yea, to Pie and Parrat out our Tongues, Degrees, and Learning of the University.

pie, *v.*^{2} *local.* Also **pye**; *vbl. sb.* **pying.** [f. pie *sb.*^{2} 3.] *trans.* To put (potatoes, etc.) in a pit or heap and cover them with straw and earth, for storing and protection from frost.

1791 *Trans. Soc. Arts* IX. 44 Weeding potatoes, getting them up, and pyeing them. **1817–18** Cobbett *Resid. U.S.* (1822) 164 He may pie them [potatoes] in the garden..but he must not open the pie in frosty weather. **1845** *Jrnl. R. Agric. Soc.* V. ii. 326 This system of pyeing turnips is a very common one in Norfolk. **1886** [see pie *sb.*^{2} 3].

pie, *v.*^{3} *Printing.* [f. pie *sb.*^{4}] *trans.* To make (type) into 'pie'; to mix or jumble up indiscriminately.

1870 [see pied^2]. **1889** *Daily News* 17 June 7 (Advt.), The ..delay..in printing offices, caused by what is technically called 'pyeing'. **1893** *Linotype Company's Prospectus*, In the economy of this machine... To pye matter is impossible. **1903** *Brit. & Col. Printer* 19 Nov. 15/4 Nearly all the cases are empty and those that have anything in are pied.

pie-annet: see piannet.

piebald (ˈpaɪbɔːld), *a.* (*sb.*) Forms: 6 **pibald, pibauld,** 6–7 **py(-)bald,** 6– **pie(-)bald,** 7 **pye(-)bald, pyedball,** 7–8 **pye-balled (-ball'd),** 8– **pye(-)ball.** [f. pie *sb.*^{1} + bald *a.* 5: cf. ball *sb.*^{3}]

A. *adj.* Of two different colours, esp. white and black or other dark colour (like the plumage of a magpie), usually arranged in more or less irregular patches; pied: usually of animals, esp. horses. Loosely used of other colours (cf. skewbald) or of three or more colours; parti-coloured.

1594 Barnfield *Aff. Sheph.* i. xxviii, I haue a pie-bald Curre to hunt the Hare. **1610** Markham *Masterp.* i. x. 26 His colour is either a milke white, a yellow dun, a kiteglewd or a pyedball. **1622** Malynes *Anc. Law-Merch.* 328 Signified by the Pybald horse whereon hee was mounted. **1626** *Faithful Friends* i. i, Millions..lavished in excessive sports, And piebald pageantry. **1676** *Lond. Gaz.* No. 1135/4 A white Gelding..having pye-bald marks on both flanks of bluish colour. **1789** Mrs. Piozzi *Journ. France* II. 20 [At Naples]. Yesterday..shewed me what I knew not had existed—a skew-ball or pyeballed ass. **1802** *Med. Jrnl.* VIII. 97 There are Negroes, (Albinoes) born white, some are party coloured or pie-bald. **1822–34** *Good's Study Med.* (ed. 4) IV. 542 Individuals thus motley coloured are commonly called piebald negroes, or are said to have piebald skins. **1845** Darwin *Voy. Nat.* xi. (1852) 233 Dusky woods, piebald with snow. **1871** —— *Desc. Man* II. xvi. 230 Piebald birds..for instance, the black-necked swan, certain terns, and the common magpie.

b. *fig.* Composed of parts or elements of dissimilar or incongruous kinds; of mixed characters or qualities (always in bad sense); motley, mongrel.

1589 R. Harvey *Pl. Perc.* (1590) 13 Leaue thrumming thy Pibauld Iestes with Scripture. **1663** Butler *Hud.* i. i. 96 A Babylonish Dialect, Which learned Pedants much affect. It was a Parti-colour'd Dress Of patch'd and Pye-ball'd Languages. **1763–5** Churchill *Candidate* 716 Shall hurl his piebald Latin at thy head. **1815** W. H. Ireland *Scribbleomania* 58 note, To produce such a pyebald style of composition. **1878** Bayne *Purit. Rev.* ii. 27 In the piebald character of the man.

B. *sb.* A piebald animal, esp. a horse. **b.** *fig.* A person or thing of mixed character, a 'mongrel'.

1765 Foote *Commissary* ii. Wks. 1799 II. 26 The right honourable Peer..calls me..Plebeian, and says if we have any children, they will turn out very little better than pye-balls. **1842** Tennyson *Walking to Mail* 104 As quaint a four-in-hand As you shall see—three pyebalds and a roan. **1845** Ford *Handbk. Spain* i. 53 Strabo..had an idea that Spanish piebalds..changed colour if taken out of Spain.

Hence ˈ**piebalding,** becoming piebald, development of patches of different colours; ˈ**piebaldism,** ˈ**piebaldness,** the quality of being piebald; ˈ**piebaldly** *adv.*, in a piebald manner, with patches of different colours.

1886 Romanes in *Life & Lett.* (1896) III. 175 The young ones show no signs of *piebalding. **1881** *Standard* 8 Sept. 5/3 Domestication tends to produce irregular colour, or what is commonly called *piebaldism. **1613** Campion *Relat. Entertainm. Ld. Knowles*, A strawn hat, *piebaldly drest with flowers. **1893** *Sat. Rev.* 8 Apr. 375/2 Glaring *piebaldness. **1899** E. Phillpotts *Human Boy* 120 The piebaldness of the rat was the great feature.

piece (piːs), *sb.* Forms: 3–7 pece (3–5 pees, 4 pise, 4–5 pice, peis, 5 pes, peyce, peese, 5–6 pes(s, pesse); 5– piece, (5 pyece, 5–8 peace, 6 pease, peise, peyss, (*Sc.* peax), pysse, 6–7 peece, 6–8 peice). Plural in ME. sometimes the same as the sing. [ME. *pece*, in 15th c. *piece*, a. OF. *pece* (1241 in Godef.), *piece* (Roland, 11th c.), mod.F. *pièce* = Pr. *peza*, *pessa*, Sp. *pieza*, Pg. *peça*, It. *pezza* piece of cloth, rag, beside *pezzo* 'piece' in other senses. The Romanic forms point to late L. types **pettia*, **pettium*: cf. early med.L. *pecia*, *petia*, also *pecium*, *petium*, 'broken piece, fragment', also 'piece of land'. Ulterior origin obscure: see Note below. The sense-development is in many points uncertain, though most of the senses occur also in French: the following arrangement is to a great extent provisional.]

I. In general sense; or followed by *of*.

1. a. A separate or detached portion, part, bit, or fragment of anything; one of the distinct portions of which anything is composed; now *spec.* one of the irregular sections of a jig-saw puzzle. Freq. *fig.*

a **1225** *St. Marher.* 122 þe scourgen [were] smerte & kene; Bi peces þe flesch orn adoun, þe bones were isene. *c* **1320** *Sir Tristr.* 1086 His swerd brak in þe fiȝt And in morauntes brain Bileued a pece briȝt. *a* **1450** *Voc.* in Wr.-Wülcker 601/11 *Pecia*, a pece, or lytyl part of a thyng. **1560** Daus tr. *Sleidane's Comm.* 25 That day..is roosted a whole Oxe..a piece whereof is serued to the Emperours table. **1570** Levins *Manip.* 48/15 A Peece, *pars, partis.* **1605** Camden *Rem.* 189 In delivering of livery and seisin a peece of the earth is taken. **1653** Walton *Angler* iv. 108, I think the best [rods] are of two pieces. **1713** M. Henry *Catech. Youth* Wks. 1853 II. 169/1 Gave them a piece of a honeycomb to eat. **1847** Carpenter *Zool.* §603 The tegumentary skeleton of Insects, that is to say, the hard skin of these animals... We see in it a great number of pieces, which are sometimes soldered (as it were) together; whilst in other instances they are united by soft portions of the skin. *Ibid.* §605 The head is formed only by a single piece. **1911** *Encycl. Brit.* XXII. 675/1 The commonest of all puzzles are coloured maps, pictures ('jig-saw') or designs, dissected into numerous variously shaped pieces, to be fitted together to form the complete design. **1925** E. Wallace *Fellowship of Frog* xix. 144 She's only another little bit of the jigsaw puzzle that will fall into place when we fix the piece that's shaped like a Frog. **1935**, etc. [see jig-saw *sb.* b].

fig. **1821** Lamb *Elia* Ser. i. *Imperfect Sympathies*, They are content with fragments and scattered pieces of Truth. **1935** W. G. Hardy *Father Abraham* 140 Quite suddenly the pieces seemed to fit together. **1955** H. Kurnitz *Invasion of Privacy* (1956) ix. 67 Mr. Fenn think[s] that there might be something about this case he doesn't understand, a missing piece somewhere. It spoils the picture for him. **1963** A. Heron *Towards Quaker View of Sex* i. 5 The study of homosexuality and its moral problems could not be divorced from a survey of the whole field of sexual activity: a few pieces of the jigsaw-puzzle could not be identified without the whole picture. **1973** G. Scott *Water Horse* (1974) xxii. 152 If Oliver were really involved in this organization, then certain jigsaw pieces could fall more satisfactorily into place. **1977** P. Cosgrave *Cheyney's Law* vii. 65 He had a name... If pieces were not exactly falling into place, there was at least movement.

b. ***in pieces***: broken, divided, disintegrated, in fragments: *fig.* divided, at variance. ***in, into,*** †***on,*** †***a pieces***: into fragments, asunder. ***to take in pieces***: to separate the parts of, to analyse.

1297 R. Glouc. (Rolls) 375 Is scolle to brec in peces manion. *c* **1320** *Sir Tristr.* 1456 Eft þat spere tok he;..It brast on peces þre. **13..** *K. Alis.* 2999 A-two peces he hadde him gurd. *c* **1380** *Sir Ferumb.* 5591 þe stede ful doun on peces tweye. **1390** Gower *Conf.* III. 244 He kut it into pieces twelve. **1393** Langl. *P. Pl.* C. xxi. 62 *note*, The wal of þe temple to-cleef euene a two peces. *c* **1400** *Laud Troy Bk.* 10305 Hir heer was rent & torne In pes. *c* **1400** Maundev. (Roxb.) x. 38 Men..paynd þam to breke þe stane in pecez. **1470–85** Malory *Arthur* i. xxiii. 71 But the swerd of the knyght smote kyng arthurs swerd in two pyeces. **1480** Caxton *Chron. Eng.* ccxxiv. 227 Ther man myght see hir baners displayed hakked in to pyeces. **1562** Pilkington *Expos. Abdias* Pref. 9 The forther that the bowe is drawen, the sooner it flies in pieces. **1600** J. Pory tr. *Leo's Africa* iii. 133 The butchers cut their flesh a peeces, and sell it by weight. **1659** *Burton's Diary* (1828) IV. 480 This takes in pieces your whole form. *c* **1680** Hickeringill *Hist. Whiggism* Wks. 1716 I. ii. 154 If we offer to tear them apieces. **1687** A. Lovell tr. *Thevenot's Trav.* i. 169 A fair large Church..where..the Body of St. Catherine is in pieces. **1754** Richardson *Grandison* IV. iv. 21 We are all in pieces: we were in the midst of a feud, when you arrived. **1761–2** Hume *Hist. Eng.* (1806) IV. lxi. 566 The instrument of government was taken in pieces, and examined, article by article. **1843** Macaulay *Lays Anc. Rome, Virginia* 264 Must I be torn in pieces? **1876** Freeman *Norm. Conq.* IV. xviii. 193 When they submitted, their army..at once fell in pieces.

c. ***to pieces***: into fragments, asunder; also *fig.* ***to go*** or ***come to pieces***: to break up, dissolve, lose cohesion. ***to take to pieces***: to separate into its parts. ***to hit, huff, puzzle, vex***, etc., ***to pieces***: to bring by such action to a state of distraction, disorganization, confusion, or rout.

By omission of *come, gone, torn*, or other pple., *to pieces* is sometimes = 'in pieces': see quots. 1622, 1690.

c **1290** *S. Eng. Leg.* I. 46/24 And to-brak it al to smale peces. **13..** *Cursor M.* 6542 (Cott.) To pees [*Gött. etc.* in pecis] he þam brak right þar. *c* **1400** *Laud Troy Bk.* 8386, I schal ȝow hewe al to pece. *a* **1533** Ld. Berners *Huon* cxvii. 419 Our shyp brast all to pecys. **1622** Massinger & Dekker *Virgin Martyr* ii. iii, The smock of her charity is now all to pieces. **1661** Boyle *Exam.* ii. (1682) 6, I thus take Mr. Hobbs his Argument to pieces. **1667** Pepys *Diary* 29 Aug. (1974) VIII. 406 The Court is at this day all to pieces, every man of a faction of one sort or another. **1690** J. Wilson *Belphegor* iv. i, They [friends] 're all to pieces. **1700** Congreve *Way of World* i. 6 She once us'd me with that Insolence, that in Revenge I took her to pieces. **1703** Moxon *Mech. Exerc.* 253 Pulling the Building to pieces after it is begun. **1727** *Philip Quarll* (1816) 73 The flat-bottomed boat ..he had taken to-pieces. **1741** Richardson *Pamela* I. 144 She has huffed poor Mr. Williams all to-pieces. **1765** Cowper *Wks.* (1837) XV. 1, I am puzzled to pieces about it. **1832** Fr. A. Kemble *Jrnl.* in *Rec. of Girlhood* (1878) III. 215, I thought I should have come to pieces in his hands, as the housemaids say of what they break. **1883** R. Buchanan *Love me for Ever* i. ii. 28 A large ship had gone to pieces on the Wantle reef. **1890** *Daily News* 11 July 3/6 The Oxonians went all to pieces after passing the post. **1892** 'Mark Twain' *Amer. Claimant* xvii. 173 The hackman will just go all to pieces when he sees that. **1902** *Daily Chron.* 7 Aug. 3/6 To analyse anything implies..the taking it to pieces in a chemical sense. **1923** H. Crane *Let.* 21 July (1965) 140 The center of such pain as would tear me to pieces to tell you about. **1925** W. S. Maugham *Painted Veil* xiv. 47 When he has bad cards he goes all to pieces. **1933** J. Hilton *Lost Horizon* ix. 196 You were so damned good in that Baskul affair that I can hardly believe you're the same man. You seem to have gone all to pieces. **1957** A. MacNab *Bulls of Iberia* ii. 26 Once a grand herd under the old Duke, now gone all to pieces. **1976** *Daily Record* (Glasgow) 22 Nov. 27/1 How can a team perform so well, score a goal, then go to pieces?

d. ***all to pieces***: completely, through and through, from beginning to end. *dial.* and *U.S.*

1839 C. F. Briggs *Adventures H. Franco* I. iv. 27 'Do you know the name of that individual who helped you to steak?' 'I know him all to pieces,' replied the gentleman. **1840** C. F. Hoffman *Greyslaer* I. i. x. 114, I know the ground here all to pieces. **1892** W. G. Lyttle in *Eng. Dial. Dict.* (1903) IV. 491/2 She wud a pleesed ye a' tae pieces, an' wud a been charmed tae a haen a minister fur a son-in-law. **1925** *Dialect Notes* V. 325, I knows un all to pieces.

e. ***to fall to pieces*** (*fig.*): to give birth to a child. *dial.* and *Austral. slang.*

1881 S. Evans *Evans's Leicestershire Words* (new ed.) 212 Anybody can say what's the matter wi' yew wi' 'af a oy. Ye'r a-gooin' to fall to paces. **1941** Baker *Dict. Austral. Slang* 28 *Fall to pieces*,..to undergo confinement, to give birth to a child.

f. ***to pick up the pieces***: see pick *v.*[1] 21 n.

†**2. a.** A part *of* a whole, marked off, ideally separated, or considered as distinct; a portion *of* an immaterial thing. (Now superseded by *part*, *portion*.)

1377 Langl. *P. Pl.* B. xiv. 48 þanne was it a pece of þe pater-noster, fiat voluntas tua. **1534** More *Passion* Wks. 1303/1 That he might steale a peece of the pryce. **1535** Joye *Apol. Tindale* (Arb.) 24 In the fourthe peise [= paragraph] of his pistle. **1562** *Child-Marriages* 116 Roberte Rile the younger neuer promysid her any pease of the lease of the house where her husband nowe dwellis, nor nothinge els. *a* **1639** Wotton in *Reliq.* (1651) 438 One of the most fastidious pieces of my life, as I account,..the week of our Annuall Election of Scholers. **1642** Rogers *Naaman* 182 Now in a word, for the other peece of the question. **1699** Wanley in *Lett. Lit. Men* (Camden) 292 For other Saxon books, I have copied large pieces of them. **1755** Washington *Lett.* Writ. 1889 I. 161 After waiting a day and piece in Winchester.

b. A limited portion *of* land, enclosed, marked off by bounds, or viewed as distinct. (An early sense of med.L. *petia*, *petium*.)

a **1450** *Knt. de la Tour* (1868) 88 A man that was called Nabot, the whiche had a good pece of wyne. **1463** in *Bury Wills* (Camden) 31 There is vij acres lond lying..not ferre from Herdwyk wich vij acres lieth in ij pecys. **1535** Coverdale *Josh.* xxiv. 32 The bones of Ioseph..buried they at Sichem, in the pece of the londe, yᵗ Iacob boughte of the children of Hemor. **1611** Bible *Luke* xiv. 18, I haue bought a piece of ground. **1772** *MS. Award, Winterton, Lincs.*, All that other peice or parcel of Ground. **1796** Stedman *Surinam* (1813) II. xxix. 367 The planting ground..is divided into large square pieces. **1808** Col. Hawker *Diary* (1893) I. 13, I went into a piece of potatoes..without a dog. **1897** J. W. Clark *Barnwell* Introd. 10 A list of the different pieces of property, with their yearly values.

c. A portion *of* a road, rope, line, linear distance.

1561 T. Hoby tr. *Castiglione's Courtyer* i. Kijb, Accompaninge the Pope a peece of the way. *Mod.* A weak piece in a rope. A piece of the road is now under repair.

d. Phrase. ***a piece of one's mind***: something of what one thinks; one's candid opinion; a rebuke, scolding. Cf. bit *sb.*[2] 4.

1572 Sandys in Ellis *Orig. Lett.* Ser. ii. III. 24 Thus am I bolde to unfolde a peece of my mynde. **1667** Dryden *Maiden Queen* ii. i, I have told her a piece of my mind already. **1838** Dickens *Let.* 25 Oct. (1965) I. 445 Kate boasts..of having told you 'a piece of her mind'. **1861** Mrs. H. Wood *East Lynne* ii. xiii. (1888) 233 The justice was giving her a 'piece of his mind'. **1914** W. Owen *Let.* 24 May (1967) 256 Now it is Wednes. and I have had with delight your news. I shall hope to have an important piece of your mind on Sunday. **1930** G. B. Shaw *Apple Cart* i. 5 He is coming here today to give the King a piece of his mind.. about the crisis. **1946** E. S. Gardner *Case of Borrowed Brunette* (1951) ii. 21 He said I could wear what I had on, no matter where I went. And I certainly gave him a piece of my mind about that. **1956** E. Wilson (*title*) A piece of my mind: reflections at sixty. **1979** D. Sanders *Queen sends for Mrs. Chadwick* 14 I'm going to give a few people a piece of my mind.

†**e.** *fig.* ***a piece of*** (***a scholar, logician, surgeon, philosopher***, etc.): somewhat of; 'a bit' of; one who partakes to some extent of the character mentioned. *Obs.* Cf. bit *sb.*[2] 4.

[**1552** Elyot *Dict.*, *Frustum hominis*, a litle pretie felow, that semeth to be but a peece of a man. Plaut. *Petit bout d'homme: moitié de homme.*] **1581** Sidney *Apol. Poetrie* (Arb.) 19 If I had not beene a peece of a Logician before I came to him. **1633** J. Clarke *Second Praxis* 12 Hoo! would you faine be thought a peece of an Astronomer now? *a* **1635** Naunton *Fragm. Reg.* (Arb.) 57 Being a good peece of a Schollar. **1743** in Howell *State Trials* (1813) XVII. 1172 He is a piece of a surgeon. **1768** Sterne *Sent. Journ.* (1778) I. 101 If I am a piece of a philosopher.

3. a. A portion or quantity *of* any substance or kind of matter, forming a single (usually small) body or mass; a bit; as 'a piece of lead, granite, ice, bread, dough, cloth, paper'; also, ***piece of water***, a small detached sheet of water, a small lake.

Such a 'piece' is, in fact, often a portion of a larger mass, but this is not thought of in the use of the word, the notion being rather that of so much of the substance or material in question forming one body of finite dimensions, which may be either a small or a large piece. It is a separate part or portion of the whole existing stock of the substance.

1362 Langl. *P. Pl.* A. vii. 297 Mai no peny Ale hem paye, ne no pece of Bacun. **1483** *Cath. Angl.* 272/2 A Pece of leder ..or of clathe. **1530** Palsgr. 252/2 Pece of steele. **1535** Coverdale *1 Sam.* ii. 36 For a syluer peny and for a pece of bred. *c* **1595** Capt. Wyatt *R. Dudley's Voy. W. Ind.* (Hakl. Soc.) 26 Our Generall caused our Queenes armes to be drawne on a peece of lead. **1657** Austen *Fruit Trees* i. 43 A hard peece of wood. **1698** Norris *Pract. Disc.* (1707) IV. 224 Like a red-hot piece of Iron upon an Anvil. **1769** Wesley *Jrnl.* 24 Aug., Pieces of water that surround it. **1831** Macaulay *Civ. Disabilities Jews* Ess. 146 The scrawl of the Jew on the back of a piece of paper.

b. In this sense *piece* is commonly used in *Sc.* without *of* (cf. Ger. *ein Stück Brod*). Cf. bit *sb.*[2] 9.

1580 J. Haye in *Cath. Tract.* (S.T.S.) 59 That we adore ane peace bread for God. **1681** Colvil *Whigs Supplic.* (1751) 106 There a piece of beef, there a piece cheese lyes. **1787** [Beattie] *Scoticisms* 73 A piece cheese, bread, &c. **1876** Whitehead *Daft Davie* (1894) 205 (E.D.D.) She had a piece bread and cheese in her pouch. *a* **1906** *Mod.* Give me a small piece paper.

c. ***piece of money, of gold, of silver***: A coin.

1526 Tindale *Matt.* xxvi. 15 And they apoynted vnto hym [Judas] thyrty peces of syluer [Wyclif 1382 thritti platis of seluer, 1388 thretti pans of siluer]. *a* **1533** Ld. Berners *Huon* xliii. 143 To pay these .iiii. peses of golde yerly. **1540** *Act 32 Hen. VIII*, c. 14 A piece of flemmishe money called an Englyshe. **1560** Daus tr. *Sleidane's Comm.* 57 b, His Purse..chatcheth vp the other thinkyng to haue a pece of money. **1675** Brooks *Gold. Key* 302 Look, as the worth and value of many pieces of Silver, is to be found in one piece of Gold. **1726** Swift *Gulliver* i. ii, My purse with nine large pieces of gold. **1841** Lane *Arab. Nts.* III. 6, I.. amassed three thousand pieces of silver.

d. ***piece of flesh***, applied to a living person, a human being; ***piece of goods***, applied humorously or contemptuously to a woman or child; now *dial.* Also ***piece of ass, tail***, etc. (*U.S.* coarse slang), a person, esp. a woman, regarded as an object of sexual gratification; hence, sexual intercourse; also *ellipt.* as ***piece***.

1593 *Tell-Troth's N.Y. Gift* (1876) 30 Oh, she is a tall peece of flesh. **1611** Shaks. *Cymb.* iv. ii. 127 Why should we be tender, To let an arrogant peece of flesh threat vs? *a* **1759** Sir C. H. Williams *Song* vii. in Locker *Lyra Eleg.* (1867) 163 This beautiful piece Of Eve's flesh is my niece. **1809** Malkin *Gil Blas* i. ii. ¶6 She seemed a pretty piece of goods enough. **1895** Pinnock *Black Country Ann.* (E.D.D.), Her's a nice piece o' goods to be a skule guvness. **1922** Joyce *Ulysses* 66 A wild piece of goods. Her slim legs running up the staircase. **1942** Berrey & Van den Bark *Amer. Thes. Slang* §362/1 *Copulation*,..piece, piece *or* hunk of tail, -skirt, -ass *or* butt. **1950** 'D. Divine' *King of Fassarai* xxviii. 252 Them guys from the merchant ships will do anything for a piece of tail. **1953** T. Morrison *Stones of House* v. iii. 243 You couldn't put up a memorial to a boy whose younger brother had just given the family and the college a bad name, not even sneaking off to a house somewhere if he wanted a piece. **1957** G. Greene *Quiet American* (new ed.) i. iii. 28 Get me another drink. And then let's go and find a girl. You've got a piece of tail. I want a piece of tail too. **1968** E. Lovelace *Schoolmaster* xii. 191 Boy, go and getta pieca ass, then go in your bed. **1972** G. V. Higgins *Friends E. Coyle* xix. 119 Him and four buddies want a little dough to get a high class piece of tail. **1972** *Screw* 12 June 21/2 Several revolutionary leaders and a host of government figures all stop by for a piece of ass. **1974** H. L. Foster *Ribbin'* v. 208 He said he fucked your baby sister and poked your baby niece And when he sees your little brother he's going to ask him for a piece. **1978** J. Krantz *Scruples* ii. 21 He..thought she was a flaming, fabulous piece of ass.

e. Of something non-material, as ***a piece of poetry, of prose, of music***.

1601 Shaks. *Twel. N.* ii. iv. 2 Giue me some Musick.. that peece of song, That old and Anticke song we heard last night. **1616** B. Jonson *Epigr.* xlv, Here doth lye Ben Ionson his best piece of poetrie. **1852** Mrs. Stowe *Uncle Tom's C.* xvi, He sat down to the piano, and rattled a lively piece of music. *Mod.* A piece of nervous prose.

f. With *of*. A share in; a financial interest in (a business, project, etc.); freq. in phr. ***a piece of the action***. (*U.S. slang.*)

1929 *Theatre Mag.* June 33/3 *Piece*, share. As 'A piece of the show', a financial share in the production. **1930** *Amer. Mercury* Dec. 457/1 He muscles in for a piece of the cleaners' racket. **1940** J. O'Hara *Pal Joey* 66 He owns a piece of the room [*sc.* nightclub] where I sing in. **1950** *Democrat & Chron.* (Rochester, N.Y.) 13 Jan. 22/1 Offered to let me buy a small piece of 'As You Like It'. **1972** 'E. Lathen' *Murder without Icing* ii. 18 'I've had a piece of the Huskies for a long time now.'..'I figure your interest is worth twice what you paid.' *Ibid.* 21 What's it got to do with her if you sell your piece of action? **1973** C. Alverson

Fighting Back (1978) i. 2 This is a very pretty little bar you've got here... I want a piece of it. I think you could use a partner. **1976** C. Frick in *6,000 Words* 156 They were.. managers and agents and producers and all the others that had a piece of the action. **1978** R. Lewis *Uncertain Sound* iii. 78 Manson would be wanting a 'piece of the action'.

g. ***a piece of cake***: see cake *sb.* 7c.

4. A (more or less) definite quantity in which various industrial products are made or put up for sale or use.

a. A length (varying according to the material) in which cloth or other textile fabric is woven; also, a length *of* wall-paper as made (in England, generally 12 yards). Often used *absolutely*: cf. 15 c.

A *piece* of muslin is 10 yards; of calico, 28 yards; of Irish linen, 25 yards; of Hanoverian linen, 100 double ells, or 128 yards. (Simmonds *Dict. Trade* 1858.)

1523 *Act 14 & 15 Hen. VIII*, c. 3 §7 Every peace of Worstede Sayes or Stamyns to be made withyn any of the said Townes. **1588** *Acc. Bk. W. Wray* in *Antiquary* XXXII. 54 Item j peace tawnye buffing xxs. Item ij pece blacke buffing, xxiiijs. **1622** E. Misselden *Free Trade* (ed. 2) 9 Ther they goe at Twelve Gilders eight stivers the piece. **1706** Phillips (ed. Kersey), *Piece*,.. a certain Number of Ells or Yards of Cloth, Stuff, Silk, etc. **1711** Shaftesb. *Charact.* (1737) II. 200 Some of those rich stuffs.. with such irregular work, and contrary colours, as look'd ill in the pattern, but mighty natural and well in the piece. **1810** J. T. in *Risdon's Surv. Devon* p. xxvi, The.. trade took off.. about 35,000 pieces, each piece containing 26 yards. **1844** G. Dodd *Textile Manuf.* ii. 48 A 'piece' of cotton cloth varies from twenty-four to forty-seven yards in length, and from twenty-eight to forty inches in width. **1881** Young *Every Man his own Mechanic* §1639 A 'piece' of English paper is 12 yards long and a piece of French paper about 9½ yards.

b. A half-pig *of* lead.

1773 *Gentl. Mag.* XLIII. 63 Blocks of lead.. called pigs.. being found too heavy to be easily managed, as they weighed three hundred weight.. are now commonly made in Derbyshire into two pieces. **1829** *Glover's Hist. Derby* I. 81 The pieces, or half-pigs of lead are not of any certain weight, though the smelter endeavours.. to approach as near to 176½ lbs. as he can.

5. A cask *of* wine or brandy, varying in capacity according to the locality, but generally equivalent to the butt, or to two hogsheads. [Fr. *pièce.*]

c **1490** *Paston Lett.* III. 364, I sen my lady a lytyll pes of Renysch wyne of the best, of x. gallons. **1523** Ld. Berners *Froiss.* I. ccii. 238 They wanne the good town of Athyen.. and there they founde mo than a hundred peces of wyne. **1619** Fletcher *Mons. Thomas* viii. x, Home, Launce, and strike a fresh piece of wine; the town's ours. **1687** *Lond. Gaz.* No. 2223/4, 76 Pieces of Conyack Brandy in 32 Lotts. **1705** *Ibid.* No. 4089/3 One hundred and eighty Pipes or Pieces, of double Spanish Brandy. **1839** Ure *Dict. Arts* 4 There are tuns which can contain from 12 to 15 pieces of wine. **1840** T. A. Trollope *Summer in Brittany* II. 281 A 'piece'.. of the best brandy, consisting of four hundred bottles, may be purchased at Bordeaux for two hundred and fifty francs. **1895** *Westm. Gaz.* 8 Apr. 3/2 Forty to fifty basketfuls [of grapes] are put upon the press at one time, and yield from ten to twelve pieces of wine.

¶For the sense 'cup, wine-cup', see pece *Obs.*

6. a. A single object or individual forming a unit of a class or collective group, as ***a piece of furniture, of plate, of artillery*** or ***ordnance, of luggage***; †a head of cattle or game (*Sc. obs.*). See also 18.

c **1400** *Destr. Troy* 9504 Syluer and Sarrigold sadly þai grippet,.. Pesis of plates plentius mekyll. **1473** Sir J. Paston in *P. Lett.* III. 102, I most have myn instrumentes hydder, whyche.. I praye yow and Berney.. to trusse in a pedde. and sende them me hyddre in hast, and a byll ther in how many peces. **1523** Earl Surrey in Ellis *Orig. Lett.* Ser. I. I. 216 Dyvers other good peces of ordynaunce for the feld. **1563** *Reg. Privy Council Scot.* I. 237 Ane brasin pece of artailyerie, ten irn pecis. **1715** *Lond. Gaz.* No. 5336/2 A Piece of Plate of the value of 100 Ducats. **1792** *Gentl. Mag.* 12/2 A statue or a piece of plate require inscriptions very different from a monument. **1832** Southey *Hist. Penins. War* III. 319 A regiment.. succeeded in taking two pieces of cannon. **1837** Goring & Pritchard *Microgr.* 62, I can almost always see the shot of a piece of ordnance when I fire it myself. **1886** Mary Linskill *Haven under Hill* I. xv. 201 It was a handsome piece of furniture. **1899** *Westm. Gaz.* 15 May 10/1 It handled last year 6,214,447,000 pieces of mail matter. **1899** *Daily News* 12 Sept. 7/5 It had at our ports been deemed sufficient to take about one 'piece' of luggage in five for examination. But when the dynamiters came.. the inexorable order went forth that every 'piece' was to be searched.

b. A member of an orchestra or band. In isolation usu. pl. Freq. (sing.) with prefixed numeral forming an attrib. phrase (see sense 24b); also *absol.*

1912 J. Webster in *Ladies' Home Jrnl.* May 70/2 We had.. a band consisting of fourteen pieces (three mouth organs and eleven combs). **1922** S. Lewis *Babbitt* xii. 156 Their favorite motion-picture theater.. had an orchestra of fifty pieces. **1925** F. Scott Fitzgerald *Great Gatsby* (1926) iii. 48 The orchestra has arrived, no thin five-piece affair, but a whole pitful of oboes and trombones and saxophones. **1938** *Melody Maker* 27 Aug. 11/4 Billy will use his 14-piece stage band. **1959** P. Capon *Amongst those Missing* 221 It was like shouting against a ninety-piece orchestra. **1965** *New Yorker* 2 Jan. 40/1 The only band we had trouble with.. was the Savoy Sultans, the house group at the Savoy Ballroom in Harlem. They only had eight pieces, but they could swing you into bad health. **1966** *Crescendo* Apr. 12/1 A Saturday night last August. A ten-piece required a little way out of town. **1975** *New Yorker* 21 Apr. 7/3 On Monday: Dave Matthews' twelve-piece band, made up of studio musicians.

7. ***piece of work***: **a.** A product of work, a production, a (concrete) work.

c **1540** Heywood *Four P.P.* in Hazl. *Dodsley* I. 363 Here is an eye-tooth of the Great Turk. Whose eyes be once set on this piece of work, May happily lese part of his eyesight. **1568** Grafton *Chron.* II. 941 The Kings Chapell at Westminster,.. one of the most excellent peeces of worke, wrought in stone, that is in Christendome. **1602** Shaks. *Ham.* II. ii. 315 What a piece of worke is a man! how Noble in Reason! how infinite in faculty! in forme and mouing how expresse and admirable! **1638** Ussher *Incarnation* (1649) 2 Most admirable peeces of work.

b. A task, difficult business; *fig.* a commotion, ado (*colloq.*).

1594 Carew *Huarte's Exam. Wits* (1616) 103 It were an infinit peece of worke. **1715** tr. *Gregory's Astron.* I. 462 It would be a tedious Piece of Work to take out the two component Parts with their Signs. **1724** De Foe *Mem. Cavalier* (1840) 76 It would be a long piece of work. **1810** *Sporting Mag.* XXXVI. 262 He kept jawing us, and making a piece of work all the time. **1844** Dickens *Mart. Chuz.* xxx, What are you making all this piece of work for? **1872** 'Ouida' *Fitz's Election* (ed. Tauchn.) 194 How do you expect to get along.. when it's such a piece of work to make you shake hands?

c. Applied, usu. contemptuously, to a person.

1928, etc. [see nasty *a.* 7]. **1936** 'N. Blake' *Thou Shell of Death* vii. 122 She.. had been Fergus's mistress. She *is* a pretty grand piece of work. **1965** A. Nicol *Truly Married Woman* 109 Jolson.. looking at Newi's heavy square mahogany face.. thought what an obstinate and unpleasant piece of work the fellow was.

8. An individual instance, exemplification, specimen, or example, *of* any form of action or activity, function, abstract quality, etc.

a. Applied to a concrete thing.

a **1568** Ascham *Scholem.* (Arb.) 104 The conference of these two places, conteinyng so excellent a peece of learning, as this is. **1657** Sir W. Mure *Hist.* Wks. (S.T.S.) II. 235, I have adventured to offer this small peace of labour to posteritie. **1664** Power *Exp. Philos.* I. 58 These puny automata, and exsanguineous pieces of Nature. **1686** tr. *Chardin's Trav. Persia* 398 A.. delicate Piece of Architecture. **1705** J. Taylor *Journ. Edinb.* (1903) 71 A noble Monument of its former Grandeur, being one of the finest pieces of ruin in the Kingdom. **1723** T. Thomas in *Portland Papers* VI. (Hist. MSS. Comm.) 74, I think it is the worst piece of portrait that ever in my life I saw. **1869** Goulburn *Purs. Holiness* Pref. 7 A piece of religious literature.

b. Applied to an abstract thing.

1570 Foxe *A. & M.* (ed. 2) 2279/1 What a peece of Gods tender prouidence was shewed of late vpon our English brethren and countrey men. *a* **1586** Sidney *Arcadia* I. (1622) 51 Making a peece of reverence unto him. **1601** R. Johnson *Kingd. & Commw.* (1603) 211 They want the use of footmen, to whom these peeces of service doe properly belong. **1656** Earl Monm. tr. *Boccalini's Advts. fr. Parnass.* I. lxv. (1674) 84 It being an hateful piece of petulancy to envy great Princes. **1691** Ray *Creation* I. (1692) 112 Eminent pieces of Self-denial. **1748** *Anson's Voy.* III. x. 407 It would have been a piece of imprudence. **1832** Ht. Martineau *Hill & Valley* xiii. 123 Some fresh piece of bad news. **1876** Trevelyan *Macaulay* I. iii. 139 A rare piece of luck. **1884** Sir F. North in *Law Times Rep.* 22 Mar. 122/2 Another piece of carelessness on the part of the auctioneer.

†**c.** Applied to a person in whom some quality is exemplified or realized. *Obs.*

1623 Fletcher *Rule a Wife* III. v, The master of this little piece of mischief. *a* **1635** Naunton *Fragm. Reg.* (Arb.) 38 Sir Nicholas Bacon, An arch-piece of Wit and Wisdom. **1648** Goodwin in Jenkyn *Blind Guide* i. 6 Green-head, young peece of presumption, Prelaticall peece of Presbytery,.. swelling peece of vanity. **1712** Arbuthnot *John Bull* III. i, One of your affected curt'sying pieces of formality. **1778** Miss Burney *Evelina* (1791) II. xxx. 182 As to the little Louisa, tis such a pretty piece of languor.

II. Absolute uses (elliptical, contextual, or conventional), without *of* and specification of the substance, etc.

9. A person, a personage, an individual.

a. Applied to a man. *arch.* and *dial.*

In early use often = One of a multitude, army, or company; in 17th c. tending to be dyslogistic: cf. b.

1297 R. Glouc. (Rolls) 7314 He at stod vpe þe brugge mid an ax alone,.. A stalwarde pece þat was, nou god cupe is soule loue. *a* **1300** *Cursor M.* 11058 Til Ion were born, a wel god pece. *c* **1330** R. Brunne *Chron. Wace* (Rolls) 156 In his buke has Dares demed, Both of Troie & of Grece, whatkyns schappe was ilka pece. *c* **1400** *Laud Troy Bk.* 4446 That fel faire for men of Grece, Thei hadde elles dyed euery pece. **1614** B. Jonson *Bart. Fair* I. iv, Hee is another manner of peece then you think for. **1651** Isaackson in *Fuller's Abel Rediv., Andrewes* (1867) II. 161 King James.. selecting him as his choicest piece, to vindicate his regality. **1673** Kirkman *Unlucky Citizen* 171 She having so untoward a piece to her Husband, was undone by him. **1691** Wood *Ath. Oxon.* II. 179 Say & Sele was a seriously subtil piece. **1736** Chandler *Hist. Persec.* 346 Bancroft.. was, as the historian calls him, a sturdy Piece. **1746** in *Leisure Hour* (1880) 117 An old nasty grunting bishop.. who plagues me out of my life, he is such a formal piece. **1918** L. Strachey *Eminent Victorians* 63, I hate that man, he is such a forward piece.

b. Applied to a woman or girl.

In recent use, mostly depreciatory, of a woman or girl regarded as a sexual object.

13.. *E. E. Allit. P.* A. 192 A precios pyece in perlez py3t. **1567** Turberv. *Ovid's Epist.* 157b, Faire Helena, that passing peece. **1576** Fleming *Panopl. Epist.* 441 Stately, proude, and disdainefull peeces. **1613** Shaks. *Hen. VIII*, v. v. 27 All Princely Graces That mould vp such a mighty Piece as this is [Queen Elizabeth]. **1621** Burton *Anat. Mel.* I. ii. IV. i. (1651) 143 A waspish cholerick slut, a crazed peece. **1668** Sedley *Mulb. Gard.* III. ii, She is a tender Piece. **1694** R. L'Estrange *Fables, Life Æsop* 5 Xanthus having a kind of a Nice froward Piece to his wife. **1783** Wolcott (P. Pindar) *Odes to Roy. Acad.* vi, Think of the Sage, who wanted a fine piece. **1846** *Swell's Night Guide* 86 She is a charming piece. **1854** M. J. Holmes *Tempest & Sunshine* iv. 57 Dr. Lacey laughed heartily at this speech and called her an 'original little piece'. **1873** J. Miller *Life amongst Modocs* xv. 194 Rather a good-looking piece you got here now, ain't she? *a* **1906** *Mod. dial.* She is a forward piece. **1908** Z. Gale *Friendship Village* 251 [When] Zorah had took sick.. this little piece here had up an' offered [to dance in the carnival]. **1939** W. Faulkner *Wild Palms* 334 'Woman. It was a fellow's wife.' 'You mean you had been toting one piece up and down the country day and night for over a month and now.. you got to get in trouble over another one?' **1946** K. Tennant *Lost Haven* (1947) x. 160 You speak to him, Alec... Gallivanting around with that peroxided piece. **1966** K. Amis *Anti-Death League* 329 Those two pieces in leather who served you your coffee. **1972** F. van W. Mason *Roads to Liberty* 18 Katie wouldn't be a bad-looking piece,.. if she'd half take care of her appearance. **1978** I. B. Singer *Shosha* xiii. 232 He was allegedly going to divorce his wife, who was a common piece.

10. a. A piece of armour; †esp. in the phrase ***armed at (of) all pieces***, at all points, completely [F. *armé de toutes pièces*] (*obs.*). Also in *Comb.*, as ***head-piece, shoulder-piece, thigh-piece***, etc.

c **1400** *Destr. Troy* 181 Knightes, Armyt at all peses, able to were. *Ibid.* 12878 Armet at all pes. *c* **1500** *Melusine* 248 Thenne toke he his armures & armed hym of al pieces. **1600** Holland *Livy* XXXI. 799 The regiment of the footmen.. came but slowly forward, by reason they were heauily armed at all peeces. **1635** J. Hayward tr. *Biondi's Banish'd Virg.* 157 Deadora.. arming herself at all peics, ranne to the prore.

†**b.** A fortified place, fortress, stronghold. *Obs.*

1525 *St. Papers Hen. VIII*, I. 160 The demaundes made by Mons[r]. de Buren for the Duchie of Burgon, and diverse other gret peaces in Fraunce. **1527** *Ibid.* 187 With the revocacion of tharmye, and rendicion of Genes, and other peces, whiche the Frenche King shulde rendre. **1568** Grafton *Chron.* II. 83 He receyued againe all the holdes and peeces which his father had lost. **1570–6** Lambarde *Peramb. Kent* (1826) 136 They set wide open their gates, and made a sudden salie out of the peece. **1602** Warner *Alb. Eng.* x. lviii. (1612) 254 This Guise bereft vs Calice, and in France our Peeces all. **1673** Ray *Journ. Low C.* 3 Ostend.. is most regularly and exactly fortified, so that it seemed to us one of the strongest Pieces in all the Low-Countries. **1721** Strype *Eccl. Mem.* II. II. v. 288 A commission.. to repair.. to the town of Calais and to certain other pieces on that side of the seas.

†**c.** A sailing or rowing vessel. *Obs.*

1545 *St. Papers Hen. VIII*, I. 809 Capitaynes and leaders of His Highnes rowyng peces. **1675** *Lond. Gaz.* No. 1004/1 To go and see the Royal James,.. and several other pieces built by Commissioner Deane.

11. A weapon for shooting, fire-arm. **a.** A piece of artillery; a cannon, gun.

a **1550** *Sir A. Barton* in *Surtees Misc.* (1888) 68 He hath three-score peece on ether side. **1565** *Reg. Privy Council Scot.* I. 360 To mak bullettis for small pecis. **1585** T. Washington tr. *Nicholay's Voy.* II. xxiv. 65b, Diuers great and little peeces aswell of brasse as of yron. **1600** Fairfax *Tasso* IX. liv, So from a piece two chained bullets flie. **1669** Sturmy *Mariner's Mag.* v. xii. 67 To know what Shot and Powder is meet for every Piece. **1706** Phillips, *Pieces*, (in Warlike Affairs) signify Cannon or great Guns, as Battering-Pieces which are us'd at Sieges..: Field-pieces. **1875** Clery *Min. Tactics* x. (1877) 123 Part of the attacking force should be directed against the covering party and part against the pieces.

b. A portable fire-arm, hand-gun; as a musket, carbine, pistol, fowling-piece. Now chiefly *U.S. slang.*

1581 Styward *Mart. Discip.* I. 44 Such must haue.. a good and sufficient peece, flaske, touch bore, pouder, shot, &c. **1590** Sir J. Smith *Disc. Weapons* 42 *margin*, The inuention of artillery, powder, shot, and small peeces of fire was not first in Germanie. **1591** G. Fletcher *Russe Commw.* (Hakl. Soc.) 76 The stocke of his piece is not made caliever wise but.. somewhat like a fowling piece. **1603** Knolles *Hist. Turks* (1621) 332 Taught to handle all manner of weapons, but especially the bow, the peece, and the Scimetar. **1704** *Lond. Gaz.* No. 4044/3 Our Grenadiers.. put their Bayonets in the Muzzles of their Pieces. **1788** Priestley *Lect. Hist.* v. lx. 475 Considering how many arrows might be drawn before one piece could have been loaded and discharged. **1855** Macaulay *Hist. Eng.* xvi. III. 674 Five hundred grenadiers rushed.. to the counterscarp, fired their pieces, and threw their grenades. **1870** E. Peacock *Ralph Skirl.* III. 254 He knelt on one knee, and levelled his piece direct at William's head. **1930** *Amer. Speech* V. 392 *Piece*, a firearm of any kind, including a pistol. **1956** 'E. McBain' *Cop Hater* (1958) x. 91 In this neighbourhood, you don't carry a knife or a piece, you're dead. **1970** L. Sanders *Anderson Tapes* xxxi. 82 You're a good shot... But you've never carried a piece on a job... If this campaign goes through, you'll have to pack a piece. **1973** *Black World* July 55/2, I slid the piece from under my shirt. **1976** *Times Lit. Suppl.* 6 Aug. 998/2 A high-class, good burglar.. who has never carried a piece in his life.

†**c.** A crossbow. *Obs.*

1590 *Nottingham Rec.* IV. 60 Quod dictus Fabianus non sagittabit in aliquo le peece ad aliquam rem vivam. **1598** Dallington *Meth. Trav.* (1606) T iv b, The Crossebowe. .. Once in a yere, there is in each city a shooting with the Peeces at a Popingay of wood. *Ibid.* T v, By this practise.. he groweth more ready and perfit in the vse of his Peece.

12. Each of the pieces of wood, ivory, etc., also called 'men', with which chess is played; technically restricted to the superior 'men' ('pieces of honour', 'dignified pieces'), as distinguished from the pawns. Also extended to those with which draughts, backgammon, etc., are played. [So It. *pezzo*, Sp. *pieza*, F. *pièce.*]

In the Continental use of the word, traces of its restriction in chess to the eight superior 'men' are found already in the 16th c.

[1497 Lucena *Arte de Axedres* A j b, Sabiendo como juega cada pieza. *c* 1570 *B.M. Add. MS.* 28710 lf. 360 a, Todas las pieças y peones salvo el Rey.] 1562 Rowbothum *Play Cheasts* A iv, The principle is to knowe the pieces, to wit, the name, the number, and the seat of euery one. As for the fashion of the pieces, that is according to the fantasie of the workman. 1591 Florio *Sec. Fruites* 262 *A.* Doth it pleese you then to play at the chesse..? *S.* Order your peeces. *a* 1649 Drumm. of Hawth. *Fam. Epist.* Wks. (1711) 146 In this case they [pawns] are surrogated in those void rooms of the pieces of honour, which, because they suffered themselves to be taken, were removed off the board. 1688 R. Holme *Armoury* III. xvi. (Roxb.) 67/1 What peice or man soeuer of your owne you touch or lift from its place, you must play it for that draught where you can. 1778 C. Jones *Hoyle's Games Impr.* 139 If..you find a Prospect of Success, rush on boldly and sacrifice a Piece or two. 1788 *Chambers' Cycl.* (ed. Rees) s.v. *Chess*, In this game each player had eight dignified pieces..and also eight pawns... These pieces are distinguished by being painted in white and black colours. 1797 *Encycl. Brit.* (ed. 3) s.v. *Chess*, In order to begin the game, the pawns must be moved before the pieces. 1870 Hardy & Ware *Mod. Hoyle, Chess* 37 Eight pieces of different denominations and powers, and eight Pawns, are allotted to each competitor... The pieces are named.. King, Queen, Bishop, Knight, Rook. *Ibid., Draughts* 139 The antagonist can insist on this being done or huff the piece. 1898 Culin *Chess & Playing Cards* 836 Set of thirty-two domino pieces of teak wood. *Ibid.* 841 *Jeu de l'Oie*.. the pieces are moved according to the throw.

13. a. A piece of money (see 3 c); a coin. Often with defining word, as ***seven-shilling piece***, ***crown piece***, ***threepenny piece***, ***twopenny piece***, ***penny piece***, ***five-franc piece***, etc.

1575 *Reg. Privy Council Scot.* II. 455 To be payit all in half merk pecis. 1617 Moryson *Itin.* I. 289 They coyne any peece, of which they can make gayne. 1642 Rogers *Naaman* 106 He must be a foole who really can satisfie himselfe in counters as if they were peeces. 1658 Wood *Life* (O.H.S.) I. 241 A piece of p(ope) Jo(hn) the 23, and also a French peice. 1710 *Lond. Gaz.* No. 4748/4 A Queen Elizabeth Piece of 35*s.* 1711 Hearne *Collect.* (O.H.S.) III. 102 The Gold Piece found in St. Gyles's Field. 1788 Priestley *Lect. Hist.* III. xvi. 134 These pieces were not called *farthings*, but *farthing tokens*. 1845 Ford *Handbk. Spain* I. 5 The value..of any individual piece is very uncertain.

†**b.** *spec.* Popularly applied to an English gold coin; orig. to the *unite* of James I, and afterwards to the sovereign, and guinea, as the one or other was the current coin. Hence ***half-piece***. *Obs.*

The *Unite* was issued in 1604 as = 20 shillings; but was raised in 1612 to 22 shillings.

1616 B. Jonson *Devil an Ass* I. i. 5 I'll warrant you for halfe a piece. *Ibid.* III. iii. 83 What is't? a hundred pound? ..No, th' Harpey, now, stands on a hundred pieces. 1618 Featly *Clavis Myst.* xxxii. (1636) 426 All our crownes and soveraines, and pieces, and halfe pieces, and duckatts and double duckatts are currant but to the brim of the grave. 1659–60 Pepys *Diary* 14 Mar., Here I got half-a-piece of a person of Mr. Wright's recommending to my Lord to be Preacher of the Speaker frigate. *a* 1700 B. E. *Dict. Cant. Crew*, *Job*, a Guinea, Twenty Shillings, or a Piece. 1706 Estcourt *Fair Examp.* III. i. 34 Fifty Pieces are 50 Pound, 50 Shillings, and 50 Six-pences: I know what they are well enough, and you too. 1727–41 Chambers *Cycl.* s.v. *Coin*, Guinea, or piece.

c. ***piece of eight***, the Spanish dollar, or *peso*, of the value of 8 *reals*, or (in 1906) about 4*s.* 6*d.* It was marked with the figure 8.

1610 B. Jonson *Alch.* III. iii. 15 Round trunkes, Furnish'd with pistolets, and pieces of eight. 1670 Narborough *Jrnl.* in *Acc. Sev. Late Voy.* I. (1694) 97 The Spaniards..paid for what things they bought in good Pillar pieces of Eight. 1679 Oldham *Sat. upon Jesuits* ii, Strange!.. What charity pieces of eight produce. 1706 Phillips, *Piece of Eight* or *Piece of eight Ryals*, a Spanish Coin; of which there are several sorts. 1748 *Earthquake of Peru* i. 9 His annual Allowance is 7,000 Pieces of Eight. 1882 Arber *Garner* V. 227 *note*, *Peso*..was the monetary Unit of Central America; afterwards known as the Piece of Eight, and is the Mexican dollar of the present day.

14. A portion of time or space. Now *dial.*

a. A portion or space of time; *esp.* a short space of time; a while.

(Occurs in OF. in 13th c., and in AF. in Britton II. iii. §12 Cum il avera esté graunt pece en seisine.)

a 1300 *Cursor M.* 7063 Þe wer lasted sa lang a pece. 14.. in *Pol. Rel. & L. Poems* (1866) 245 About þis a pece I wyl spede, þat I myth þis lettrys rede. 1825 Brockett *N.C. Gloss.*, *Piece*, a little while. 'Stay a piece and then aw will'. *c* 1825 in *N. & Q.* 9th Ser. III. 330 A piece back, three tides came up the Trent on one day. 1897 Kipling *Capt. Cour.* viii. 165 We'll fish a piece till the thing lifts. 1937 G. Heyer *They found him Dead* iv. 68, I wouldn't run the risk of bumping off an old man who had a valvular disease of the heart. Guess I'd wait a piece for Nature to do its work.

†**b.** Here probably belongs *o pece*, *opece*, *opese* (*a peace*), in ***still opece*** (erron. ***still a peace***), continually, continuously, constantly: see still *adv.* *Obs.*

c 1440 *Generydes* 1385 He wold not leve, butt stille alway opece Dede all that he cowde to hurt Generydes. *Ibid.* 3391 And euer more in prayours still opese, Vnto the tyme she knew it shuld goo. *Ibid.* 5254 Haue here a ryng and kepe it still opece, To the tyme that ye come onto Clarionas. 1555 W. Watreman *Fardle Facions* II. xii. 294 How she from thre yeres of age..remained ther [in the temple] seruing God stil a peace.

c. A portion of the way or distance between two points; a short distance. Chiefly *dial.*

1612 Brinsley *Lud. Lit.* 230 By practice, euery day going a piece, and oft reading ouer and ouer, they will grow very much, to your great ioy. *c* 1730 Burt *Lett. N. Scotl.* (1818) I. 151 He told us we must go west a piece..and then incline to the north. 1760–72 H. Brooke *Fool of Qual.* (1809) III. 59 Then I would run a piece off,..and again I would delay, and stop. *c* 1817 Hogg *Tales & Sk.* V. 231 I'll make my brother Adam carry it piece about with you. 1852 Mrs. Stowe *Uncle Tom's C.* vii, I've walked quite a piece to-day, in hopes to get to the ferry. 1873 E. B. Tuttle *Boy's Bk. Indians* 134 Major Gordon descended the ridge..and carrying the body of Stambaugh a piece, hid it away in some bushes. 1908 L. M. Montgomery *Anne of Green Gables* ii. 18 We've got to drive a long piece, haven't we? Mrs. Spencer said it was eight miles. 1931 *Amer. Speech* VII. 20 *Piece*, a short walk. 'I will go a piece with you.' 1940 Bryant & Aiken *Psychol. of Eng.* 84 Come and walk a piece with me. 1956 B. Holiday *Lady sings Blues* (1973) x. 98, I thought we were stranded until I saw a car down the road a piece. 1971 *Sunday Express* (Johannesburg) 28 Mar. (Home-finder section) 3/3 (Advt.), Fabulous fishing, Superb surfing. Nearby golf courses, Not forgetting swinging Margate.. just up the road a piece. 1978 G. Mitchell *Wraiths & Changelings* i. 11 He's in a bad way..on the floor of my cottage. It's just a piece down the road.

15. A (small) portion of some specific substance.

a. A small portion, scrap, or cutting, of cloth, leather, or the like; esp. as used to repair a hole or tear: a patch. Cf. piece *v.* 1.

c 1380 Wyclif *Wks.* (1880) 41 þei may pese hem [cloþis] aȝen or cloute hem of sacchis & oþere pecis. 1433 *Rolls of Parlt.* IV. 452/1 The same Clothe to be sold for a remenaunt, or for a pece and nat for a Clothe. [1526 Tindale *Matt.* ix. 16 Noo man peceth an olde garment with a pece [ἐπίβλημα, *commissuram*, Wycl. medlynge, clout] off newe clothe.]

b. Short for 'piece of bread' (with or without butter, etc.); *spec.* such a piece eaten by itself, not as part of a regular meal. *Sc.* and *Eng. dial.* (Northumb. to Shropsh., and Cornwall). Also used sporadically elsewhere.

1787 A. Shirrefs *Bess & Jamie* IV. i, Neither tak' her siller nor a piece. 1834 *Chambers's Edin. Jrnl.* III. 254/2 Receiving each a piece and jelly on't from granny, because they were guid bairns. 1878 C. Hallock *Sportsman's Gazetteer* (ed. 4) 696 *Piece*, a lunch, a snack (Pennsylvania). 1881 Gregor *Folk-Lore* 93 Pieces, however, were ordinarily given. 1883 *Daily News* 12 Dec. 2/6 On one occasion defendant gave her a bit of bridescake, on another a jelly piece. 1893 Stevenson *Catriona* xvi. 185, I..took the road again on foot, with the piece in my hand and munching as I went. 1898 *Westm. Gaz.* 14 Dec. 2/1 When they get off at mid-day to eat their 'piece', there is talking and laughing among the field workers. 1903 *Eng. Dial. Dict.* (Wigtown), A dry piece is plain loaf bread or oat cake, without butter, jam, or treacle. *Ibid.* (Cornwall), If a child tells you she had 'nothing but a piece all day', you know she means bread and butter. 1911 E. M. Clowes *On Wallaby* vi. 164 The children..wander..in and out of the kitchen, with incessant demands for what is known as 'a piece'—a liberal slice of bread, butter, and jam. 1949 'J. Tey' *Brat Farrar* xix. 175 Saturday afternoon was a holiday for the Ashby children and they were accustomed..to take a 'piece' with them and pursue their various interests in the countryside until it was time to come home to their evening meal. 1962 M. Duffy *That's how it Was* x. 85 'Gi's a piece, our mam,' and they would run off with a doorstep of bread and jam. 1973 'J. Patrick' *Glasgow Gang Observed* 234 *Piece*, sandwich. 1978 *Jrnl. Lancs. Dial. Soc.* Jan. 15/2 [Edinburgh] *Piece*, sandwich. E.g. *jeely piece* (one containing cheap jam).

c. A length of cloth, wall-paper, etc.: see 4 a.

d. *Whaling.* A section or chunk of blubber, more fully called ***blanket-piece***.

e. *Bookbinding.* A tablet of leather which fills a panel on the back of a book, and receives the title (***lettering-piece***).

f. *Malting.* A quantity of grain steeped and spread out at one time: = floor *sb.*[1] 6 b.

1832 W. Champion *Maltster's Guide* 43 The turning of his floors or pieces. 1876 Wyllie in *Encycl. Brit.* IV. 268/2 It is of importance to the maltster that the law allows him to sprinkle water over the 'pieces' on the floor.

g. pl. *pieces.* An inferior quality of crystallized sugar obtained in the manufacture of crystals and crushed sugar.

1867 *Produce Markets Rev.* 13 July 161/1 The character of the Pieces Sugar made in London retrogrades rather than improves as a whole. 1875 *Ure's Dict. Arts* III. 948 The first crystallisation is called 'crushed' and the second 'pieces', the drainage from which goes by the name of 'syrup'. 1884 *West. Morn. News* 4 Sept. 6/5 Sugar..London pieces, rather quiet, steady.

h. pl. *pieces.* The oddments of wool which are detached from the skirtings of a fleece; also, the skirtings themselves. Chiefly *Austral.* and *N.Z.*

1881 A. Bathgate *Waitaruna* 173 The 'pickers up' were ..carrying [the fleeces] to the sorting table, where they were stripped of the 'pieces', which were thrown aside. 1891 R. Wallace *Rural Econ. Austral. & N.Z.* xxix. 384 The washing of wool, either before or after shearing, is, with the exception of locks and pieces, which are generally scoured, almost entirely given up. 1951 [see *fleece-wool* s.v. fleece *sb.* 6]. 1965 [see *piece picker*, sense 23]. 1971 J. S. Gunn *Distrib. Shearing Terms N.S.W.* 20 The south was the only area where..there was a preference for *pieces* rather than *skirtings*.

i. A quantity of a drug (esp. morphine or heroin) approximately equal to one ounce. *U.S. slang.*

1935 A. J. Pollock *Underworld Speaks* 2/2 *Piece, a*, an ounce of morphine, cocaine or heroin. 1945 W. J. Spillard *Needle in Haystack* viii. 77 'I hava da pieces—pure stuff.' Pieces was an underworld term for ounces. 1963 *U.S. Supreme Court Reports* 371 U.S. 474 Johnny kept about a piece of heroin. [*Note*] A 'piece' is approximately one ounce. 1965 *Reader's Digest* June 228 He buys heroin in 'pieces' (ounces) cuts it, and bags it.

16. A separate article or item of baggage or property in transit; *spec.* (*Hist.*) in the N. Amer. fur trade, a package of goods or furs weighing about ninety pounds. (Chiefly *U.S.*)

The exact weight of the pound referred to is not certain.

1774 [see pack *sb.*[1] 2]. 1809 A. Henry *Trav. & Adventures Canada* II. ii. 15 The freight of a canoe..consists in sixty pieces, or packages, of merchandize, of the weight of from ninety to a hundred pounds each. *Ibid.* 24 The method of carrying the packages, or pieces, as they are called, is the same with that of the Indian women. 1836 G. Back *Narr. Arctic Land Expedition* i. 32 Every package had been reduced or augmented to a 'piece' of 90 lbs. weight. 1890 Cooley, etc. *Railways Amer.* 253 The cases in which pieces go astray are astonishingly rare. 1899 *Westm. Gaz.* 15 May 10/1 The postal establishment of the United States.. handles more pieces, employs more men, spends more money..than any other human organisation, public or private. 1931 G. L. Nute *Voyageur* 38 Each package, or piece, was made up to weigh ninety pounds, and two ears were left at the top by which the voyageur could lift it easily in the manner of a modern flour bag. 1949 *World-Herald* (Omaha) 19 June III. 5/2 In the north, 80 pounds is considered a 'piece'... In the days of the early fur traders that was considered a proper load of skins for a man. 1972 T. McHugh *Time of Buffalo* viii. 89 A single sack, weighing about ninety pounds, was known as a 'piece' of pemmican, and made a convenient parcel for back-packing or portaging.

17. a. A production, specimen of handicraft, work of art; a contrivance; = *piece of work* (7 a). See also masterpiece.

1604 E. G[rimstone] *D'Acosta's Hist. Indies* v. viii. 349 They buried with them much wealth, as golde, silver, stones,..bracelets of gold, and other rich peeces. 1626 B. Jonson *Staple of N.* v. i, It were a piece Worthy my night-cap, and the Gowne I weare, A Picklockes name in Law. 1643 Sir T. Browne *Relig. Med.* I. §15 Ruder heads stand amazed at those prodigious pieces of Nature, Whales, Elephants, Dromidaries and Camels. 1650 Baxter *Saints' R.* I. vii. (1662) 121 Surely were it not for Eternity, I should think man a silly piece. 1697 Dampier *Voy.* (1729) I. 517 He busied himself in making a Chest..he was as proud of it as if it had been the rarest piece in the World. 1698 A. Brand *Emb. Muscovy to China* 71 Several rare pieces made at Augsburgh, that moved by the help of Clock-work. 1904 H. James *Golden Bowl* I. vii. 141 Representative precious objects, great ancient pictures..fine eminent 'pieces' in gold, in silver..had for a number of years..multiplied themselves round him. 1976 *National Observer* (U.S.) 6 Nov., 'Orders are pouring in like gang-busters,' says Bob Koppang, a Hopkins, Minn., novelty dealer. 'Last week alone we sold nearly 29,000 pieces.' 1978 I. Murdoch *Sea* 31 The big oval mirror in the hall..is perhaps the best 'piece' in the house. 1979 *Country Life* 12 Apr. 1142/1 Special-occasion pieces..help these self-supporting artists. .. A piece of jewellery by a contemporary artist is a wonderfully exciting thing to own.

b. A painting, a picture; †a portrait.

1574 *Appius & Virginia* in Hazl. *Dodsley* IV. 125 O fond Apelles, prattling fool, why boasteth thou so much, The famous't piece thou mad'st in Greece? 1594 Plat *Jewell-Ho.* III. 51 To refresh the colours of olde peeces that bee wrought in oyle. 1662–3 Pepys *Diary* 27 Feb., There is also a very excellent piece of the King, done by Holbein. 1697 tr. *C'tess D'Aunoy's Trav.* (1706) 173, I was all alone in my apartment, busie in painting a small Piece. 1770 Langhorne *Plutarch* (1879) I. 183/1 The painter valued himself upon the celerity and ease with which he dispatched his pieces. 1853 Lytton *My Novel* I. xii, The walls..were thickly covered, chiefly with family pictures:..now and then some Dutch fair, or battle-piece. 1861 M. Pattison *Ess.* (1889) I. 45 Among the portraits which hung above were two allegorical pieces by Master Hans Holbein.

c. A piece of statuary or sculpture.

1579 Fulke *Confut. Sanders* 634, I do so honour auncient images, that I make as great account of a peece of Nero,..as I do of Constantius. 1629 Maxwell tr. *Herodian* (1635) 61 Most of the fairest Peeces in all the Citie, perish in these flames. 1950 D. Gascoyne *Vagrant* 13 A hand-high Rodin piece. 1961 C. P. Fitzgerald in *Webster* s.v., Images of the Buddha are made to certain conventional patterns and there is often great difficulty in determining the origin of any piece on stylistic grounds. 1979 *Country Life* 12 Apr. 1142/1 Sculptor Peter Lyon['s] pendant..is very reminiscent of his full-scale work..for example..a piece in the central gardens of Park Town, Oxford.

d. A literary composition, in prose or verse, generally short. Also, an article for a newspaper, journal, or other publication.

1533 More *Debell. Salem* Pref., Wks. 930/1 Vnto one little piece, one greate cunning man had made a long aunswere, of twelue whole shetes of paper. 1643 Sir T. Browne *Relig. Med.* I. §20 That Villain and Secretary of Hell, that composed that miscreant piece *Of the Three Impostors*. 1691 Ray *Creation* I. (1692) 32 There is a Posthumous piece extant, imputed to Cartes. 1710 Shaftesb. *Advice Author* iii, That exteriour Proportion and Symmetry of Composition, which constitutes a legitimate Piece. 1775 Johnson *Let. to Mrs. Thrale* 22 May, I am not sorry that you read Boswell's journal. Is it not a merry piece? 1824 J. Johnson *Typogr.* I. 529 He printed most of Archbishop Cranmer's pieces. 1878 Browning *Poets Croisic* xxix, A poet also, author of a piece Printed and published. 1936 D. Powell *Turn, Magic Wheel* I. 36 That..fellow who was always after him to write a 'piece' for the weekly he ran. 1961 *Noble Savage* Oct. 10 A period in which he..had a small piece in *Partisan Review*. 1974 'D. Craig' *Dead Liberty* xxi. 124 Dravier worked on two features for the paper,..a piece about price stability in East Germany..and..a Youth article. 1976 *Gramophone* June 32/3 In the same month came Beethoven's Symphony No. 9 on seventeen sides, to which WRA [*sc.* the reviewer] devoted a page and a half..; one of WRA's most perceptive pieces.

e. A drama, a play.

1643 Sir T. Browne *Relig. Med.* I. §47 In the last scene, all the Actors must enter to compleat and make up the Catastrophe of this great peece. 1779 Sheridan *Critic* I. i, On the first night of a new piece they always fill the house with orders to support it. 1851 Thackeray *Eng. Hum.* v. (1876) 315 To supply himself with [money]..he began to write theatrical pieces. **1867** FREEMAN *Norm. Conq.* I. iv. 252 Arnulf, as usual, appears as the villain of the piece. **1885** *Bath Herald* 17 Jan. 3/2 The usage was to engage stars for the run of the piece.

f. A musical composition, usually short, either independent or forming an individual part of a larger work.

1825 J. NEAL *Bro. Jonathan* I. 95 Nobody can bear to hear ..a favourite piece over and over again the same night. **1856** *Amy Carlton* 208 Amy..played the piece that she was learning. **1880** in Grove *Dict. Mus.* II. 751 *Piece.* This word ..has since the end of the last century been applied to instrumental musical compositions as a general and untechnical term.

g. A short discourse; a passage for recitation (*dial.* and *U.S.*). Also colloq. phr. ***to say*** (or ***speak***) ***one's piece***: to express one's opinion or judgement on a subject or question; to have one's say.

1845 C. M. KIRKLAND *Western Clearings* 158 Some of the best speakers mount the platform, and 'speak a piece'. **1865** C. F. BROWNE *A. Ward: his Travels* II. i. 128, I have spoken my piece about the Ariel. **1879** *Congress. Rec.* 16 May 1380/2, I expect to read tomorrow [in the papers] that I spoke a piece, that is the way they print it sometimes, in favor of slavery. **1882** NODAL & MILNER *Gloss. Lancs. Dial.* 212 We're gooin' a-sayin' pieces at schoo'. **1886** R. HOLLAND *Gloss. Words County of Chester* 258 In the country schools when children recite poetry it is always called 'saying their pieces'. **1890** *Harper's Mag.* Dec. 139/2 Don't you want to hear me speak my piece? **1895** 'ROSEMARY' *Under Chilterns* 83 All the 'pieces' that the children learnt to repeat at school they taught to her. **1896** *Leeds Mercury Suppl.* 26 May, Ahr Louisa wor allus a gooid un at sayin pieces. Hes ta le'nt that piece yut? **1902** MRS. G. M. MARTIN *Emmy Lou* 115 Emmy Lou had to learn a piece for Friday. It was poetry, but you called it a piece. **1941** U. ORANGE *Tom Tiddler's Ground* vi. 117 Lady Cameron was simply furious with me after that concert-party episode, when I just flatly refused to say my piece. **1942** [see DRIFT *v.* 1 c]. **1949** *North Dakota Hist.* Jan. 23 He didn't like recitations, and would rather hunt rabbits than speak pieces. **1949** G. B. SHAW *Buoyant Billions* IV. 54 Dick, I will say that you are wonderful when you speak your piece, though I never understand a word. **1973** J. PORTER *It's Murder with Dover* xi. 115 'You didn't speak to Marsh again?' 'No. I'd said my piece.' **1976** A. MILLER *Inside Outside* xi. 181 A structured or unstructured group where all were free to say their piece.

III. Phrases. (See also 1 b, c, 2 d, 10 a, 14 b.)

18. ***a piece, the piece, each*** (Sc. ***ilk***) or ***every piece***: each piece of a number of pieces; each unit of a number, set, or company; each of them or these: esp. in stating the share or price of each unit or individual member (see sense 6). Hence, *adverbially*, APIECE, q.v., ***the piece, per piece.*** [F. *la pièce.*]

Apiece can still be said of persons as well as things (so *the piece* in Sc. and north dial.).

a **1400-50** *Alexander* 5474 Lamprays of weȝt Twa hundreth pond ay a pece. *c* **1483** CAXTON *Dialogues* 47 The good candelmaker Gyueth foure talow candellis For one peny the pece [F. *le piece*]. **1489** *Acta Audit.* (1839) 131/1, xiij. horss and meris, price of þe pece xl.*s.* **1529** in *Wills Doctors Commons* (Camden) 18, xiij^xx peerles at iij*d.* the peace. **1530** TINDALE *Answ. More* Wks. (1573) 267/1 The Pope..set vp in Rome a stewes of xx. or xxx. thousand whores, taking of euery pece tribute yearly. **1533** *Test. Ebor.* (Surtees) VI. 35, xij*d.* a peice. **1553** *Reg. Privy Council Scot.* I. 150 Thai had payit ane grott for the heid off ilk peax [of cattle] for thair poindlaw. **1566** *Ibid.* 493 The soum of ten markis for ilk pece of xxv. oxin. **1600** J. PORY tr. *Leo's Africa* VII. 289 Horses..sold againe for fortie and sometimes for fiftie ducates a piece. **1637** in *Bury Wills* (Camden) 169, I giue..John Mount and John Muske *xs.* peece, Margaret Texall xxs. **1660** *Act 12 Chas. II*, c. 4 Sched. s.v. *Bowes*, Bowes, vocat. stone-bowes of steel, the piece *x.s.* *a* **1670** SPALDING *Troub. Chas. I.* (1850) I. 81 The bischopis had causit imprint thir bookis..and sould haue gottin fra ilk minister four pundis for the peice. **1686** tr. *Chardin's Trav. Persia* 355 Sold for five hunder'd Crowns a piece. *a* **1692** POLLEXFEN *Disc. Trade* (1697) A vij b, Fat Oxen were often sold at 6*s.* per piece. **1797** *Statist. Acc. Scot.* XIX. 48 A fine of a cow the piece [= each person]. *a* **1906** *Mod. Sc.* He gae them twa shillin' the piece for helpin' him.

19. ***by the piece***: at a rate of so much for a definite amount or quantity; according to the amount done. ***on (the) piece***: at piece-work.

1703 T. N. *City & C. Purchaser* 23 These Posts are.. made by the Piece, viz. 1*d.*..per Post. **1807** SOUTHEY in Robberds *Mem. W. Taylor* II. 209, I think such work is good enough to be paid by the piece. **1859** JEPHSON *Brittany* iii. 23, I could not ascertain whether they worked by the day or by the piece. **1879** *Print. Trades Jrnl.* XXIX. 40 An employer is not bound to provide constant work for a man on the piece. **1885** *Times* (weekly ed.) 9 Oct. 4/2 Most pottery workers are paid by 'piece'. **1903** [see LINOTYPE]. **1911** *Rep. Labour & Social Conditions in Germany* (Tariff Reform League) III. 96 Those on 'piece' earn from 49s. to 58s. 9d. per week. All the men are on 'piece', and work 53 hours per week.

20. ***in*** or ***of one piece***: consisting of a single or undivided piece or mass. Also *fig.*, whole, without injury or loss.

[**1535** COVERDALE *Exod.* xxxvii. 22 The knoppes & braunches..were all one pece of fyne beaten golde.] **1585** T. WASHINGTON tr. *Nicholay's Voy.* II. xvi. 50 [An] obelisque of coloured stone all of one peece 50. cubits high. **1825** J. NICHOLSON *Operat. Mechanic* 317 The whole is cast in one piece in bell-metal. **1864** LONGF. in *Life* (1891) III. 32 Finished to-day the revision and copying..the translation of the *Purgatorio*, so as to have it all of one piece with the rest. **1885** BIBLE (R.V.) *Exod.* xxxvii. 8 Of one piece with the mercy-seat made he the cherubim at the two ends thereof. **1929** D. HAMMETT *Dain Curse* (1930) xiii. 141, I returned to the ravine..reaching the bottom all in one piece with nothing more serious the matter with me than torn fingers. **1968** W. GARNER *Deep, Deep Freeze* xxxi. 256 My orders are just to get him to London in one piece. After that, he's someone else's worry. **1973** 'D. JORDAN' *Nile Green* vi. 29, I thought I'd come and see you through Customs in one piece. **1976** P. & W. PROCTOR *Women in Pulpit* v. 88 When I arrived at a church, I was glad to be there in one piece, and the people were just as glad to see me.

21. a. ***of a piece***: of one piece, in one mass (= 20); often *fig.* of one and the same kind or quality; uniform, consistent; in agreement, harmony, or keeping. [F. *tout d'une pièce.*] Also ***all-of-a-piece*** attrib. phr.; hence ***all-of-a-pieceness.***

1612 CHAPMAN *Widow's Tears* sig. I, O happy starres. And now pardon, Ladie; me thinks these [kisses] are all of a peece. **1632** MASSINGER *City Madam* I. iii, I have seen and heard all..and wish heartily You were all of a piece. **1639** N. N. tr. *Du Bosq's Compl. Wom.* II. 23 Those Nations who make their Doublet and Shirt all of a peece. **1644** DIGBY *Nat. Bodies* xii. §3. 102 To moue all of a peice. **1663** BUTLER *Hud.* I. ii. 448 He and his Horse were of a Piece, One Spirit did inform them both. **1700** DRYDEN *Pref. Fables* Wks. (Globe) 503 He writes not always of a piece, but sometimes mingles trivial things with those of greater moment. **1726** SWIFT *Gulliver* I. ii, One of them was covered, and seemed all of a-piece. **1809** MAR. EDGEWORTH *Absentee* vi, After all, things were not of a piece. **1812** COL. HAWKER *Diary* (1893) I. 51 The harness..second-hand, one horse in plated, another in brass harness, and, in short, all of a piece. **1912** GALSWORTHY *Sheaf* (1916) 21 Odd how all of a piece taste is! **1914** G. B. SHAW *Misalliance* 71 It's all of a piece here. The men effeminate, the women unsexed. **1924** GALSWORTHY *Forest* II. i. 35 An expedition like this has to be all of a piece, in the leader's hand. **1938** W. S. MAUGHAN *Summing Up* xvii. 58, I think what has chiefly struck me in beings is their lack of consistency. I have never seen people all of a piece. **1956** A. WILSON *Anglo-Saxon Att.* II. ii. 318 Goodness isn't all of a piece..any more than badness. **1958** *New Statesman* 20 Dec. 88/1 What is remarkable about this remarkable musical is its all-of-a-pieceness. **1960** *Times* 1 Nov. 16/1 He is a convincing all-of-a-piece characterization. **1962** *Times* 6 Apr. 20/1 A corresponding all-of-a-piece protein.

b. ***of a piece with.***

1665 BOYLE *Occas. Refl.* IV. ii. (1848) 176 None appear'd more of a piece with the Earth than he. **1711** ADDISON *Spect.* No. 256 ⁋3 It is not of a Piece with the rest of his Character. **1849** MACAULAY *Hist. Eng.* ii. I. 233 All their proceedings were of a piece with this demand. **1916** GALSWORTHY *Caravan* (1925) 579 Mr. Bosengate looked at this peach with sorrow rather than disgust. The perfection of it was of a piece with all that had gone before this new and sudden feeling. **1957** G. RYLE in C. A. Mace *Brit. Philos. in Mid-Cent.* 258 The assumption that doing philosophy..is of a piece with doing natural science. **1977** G. BUTLER *Brides of Friedberg* iii. 59 How like the innocent Empress Frederick to lease such a place for me. But it was entirely of a piece with all one knew of her.

†**c.** ***o pece, opece, opese***: see 14 b.

22. ***piece by piece*** (†***piece and piece***, Sc. obs.): one piece or part after another in succession; a piece at a time, piecemeal, little by little, gradually. [F. *pièce à pièce.*]

1560 BIBLE (Genev.) *Ezek.* xxiv. 6 Bring it out piece by piece. **1621** QUARLES *Argalus & P.* (1678) 115 Peece by peece they dropt upon the ground. **1719** DE FOE *Crusoe* I. 65 Had the calm Weather held I should have brought away the whole Ship Piece by Piece. **1877** SPURGEON *Serm.* XXIII. 208 The great architect unrolls his drawings piece by piece.

1533 BELLENDEN *Livy* III. iii. (S.T.S.) I. 252 Fra thens þe pepill began Ilk day pece & pece to convalesce in þare bodyis fra all maledyis. *a* **1584** MONTGOMERIE *Cherrie & Slae* 273, I felt My hart within my bosome melt, And pece and pece decay. **1681** COLVIL *Whigs Supplic.* (1751) 121 Then piece and piece they dropt away, As ripe plumbs in a rainy day. **1721** *Wodrow Corr.* (1843) II. 550 Piece and piece as your leisure allows, pray send me what hath been remarkable as to religion and learning this last year.

IV. 23. *attrib.* and *Comb.*: **piece-bag, box** *U.S.*, a bag or box for holding pieces of cloth; **piece-bright** *a.* (*poet. nonce-use*), ? bright here and there; **piece-compositor**, a compositor who is paid by the piece; **piece-dye** *v. trans.*, to dye (cloth) after it is woven; **piece-dyed** *a.*, of cloth, dyed after it is woven; so **piece-dyeing**; **piece-fraction**, in *Typog.* (see quot.); **piece-hall**, an exchange where cloth is sold by the piece; **piece hand** = *piece-compositor*; **piece-knife** (see quot.); **piece-labour**, labour paid by the piece; **piece-looker**, an inspector of cloth woven in definite lengths; **piece-maker, -man** = PIECE-WORKER; **piece-market**, the market for cloth sold by the piece; **piece-master**, a middleman who acts between the employer and the employed in the giving out of piece-work; †**piece-money**, money distributed to recipients at so much apiece; **piece-mould**, in *Sculpture*, a plaster-of-Paris mould, removed in pieces, and then fitted together; also, a mould consisting of separate pieces of metal, etc., which are fitted and beaten together upon the model; **piece-patch**, a piece inserted as a patch; **piece-patched** *a.*, patched up; **piece-payment**, payment by the piece; **piece picker** = *fleece picker* s.v. FLEECE *sb.* 6; **piece-price**, a price paid for piece-work; **piece-rate**, rate of payment for piece-work; also *attrib.*; **piece-stuff**, lumber or timber in pieces; **piece-trade**, the trade in pieces of cloth; **piece-velvet**, velvet made in the piece of various widths (as distinguished from narrow ribbon-velvet, etc.); **piece-wage**, a wage paid by the piece of work; **pieceways** *U.S. dial.* = PIECE *sb.* 14 c. See also PIECE-BROKER, -GOODS, etc.

1869 L. M. ALCOTT *Little Women* II. i. 11 So rich a supply of dusters, holders, and *piece-bags. **1900** E. A. DIX *Deacon Bradbury* 251 Mr. Bradbury..sought his wife, who was upstairs sorting over her piece-bag. **1898** M. DELAND *Old Chester Tales* 272 It has been lying there in my *piece-box for six years. **1877** G. M. HOPKINS *Poems* (1967) 67 This *piece-bright paling shuts the spouse Christ home. **1897** *Westm. Gaz.* 6 July 10/1 It took time, and time to the *piece compositor..means bread. **1931** E. MIDGLEY *Technical Terms Textile Trade* I. 10 The cloth is woven in a white or undyed condition and *piece-dyed black for wool, so that the cotton fibres remain their natural colour. **1962** W. J. ONIONS *Wool* xi. 253 Interesting coloured effects may also be obtained by piece-dyeing cloth already made up of white and coloured yarn. **1978** *Country Life* 9 Nov. 1494/2 The fabric..is now finished and piece-dyed in Huddersfield. **1844** G. DODD *Textile Manuf.* iii. 97 The wool being always dyed either in the state of wool, before spinning, or after being woven. This gives rise to the distinction between 'wool-dyed' cloth and '*piece-dyed' cloth. **1898** *Westm. Gaz.* 13 Dec. 8/1 The Bradford *piece-dyeing trade. **1900** DE VINNE *Pract. Typogr.* 174 *Piece fractions, or split fractions in two pieces, or on two bodies, are not proper parts of the font, and are sold in separate fonts at higher rates. **1844** G. DODD *Textile Manuf.* iv. 119 Instead of having a cloth-hall or a *piece-hall of its own, its productions are sent to one or other of those two towns for sale at the piece-halls. **1849** C. BRONTË *Shirley* iv, The tradesman in the Piece Hall, i.e. the Cloth Exchange. **1890** in E. Howe *London Compositor* (1947) 316 The rapid growth of the 'stab system has rendered the condition of the *piece hand in many instances almost unbearable. **1947** E. HOWE *Ibid.* 60 The piece-hand could reckon to earn more [than the establishment wage], by the exercise of both energy and skill. **1965** J. S. GUNN *Terminol. Shearing Industry* II. 8 *Piece picker*, sometimes called the 'fleece picker' or 'fleecy', his main job is to take the skirting from the roller and to divide it into lines defined by the classer, for example 'broken wool', 'first pieces'..and 'pieces'. **1833** J. HOLLAND *Manuf. Metal* II. 17 The *piece-knives, or sportsmans' knives, as those complex articles containing saws, lancets, phlemes, gun-screw, punches, large and small blades, &c. used to be called. **1866** ROGERS *Agric. & Prices* I. xv. 252 For the most part day labour. The other two are *piece labour. **1867** *Address to J. Bright* in *Morn. Star* 28 Jan., J. Moloney, *piece looker. **1895** *Daily News* 13 Mar. 3/1 To obtain a piecework statement to be based upon a *piecemaker's average. *Ibid.* 11 Mar. 3/3 The Union notice to the *piece-men being circulated. **1883** *Ibid.* 28 Sept. 2/7 The *piece market is without material alteration. **1851** MAYHEW *Lond. Labour* II. 256 The abolition of the middleman, whether 'sweater', '*piece master', 'lumper' or what not, coming between the employer and employed. **1890** *Pall Mall G.* 11 Mar. 7/1 The present sweating piece-master system. **1610** *MS. Acc. St. John's Hosp., Canterb.*, Item payd in *pesse mony xvijs. vj*d.* **1642** *Ibid.*, Payed to 38 brothers and sisters for peesmoney xixs. **1895** *Daily News* 20 June 6/3 A *piece-mould is made upon the statue itself, and from this a hollow wax statue is cast. **1880** *Plain Hints Needlework* 27 A straight stitch 6 or 8 threads deep on each *piece-patch and material. *a* **1625** FLETCHER *Bloody Bro.* II. i, This *piece-patcht friendship, This rear'd-up reconcilement on a billow. **1903** *Daily Chron.* 11 July 3/7 London daily newspapers are.. produced on a *piece payment system. **1895** *Westm. Gaz.* 21 Mar. 2/2 The question which underlies all surface disputes is that of fixing *piece-prices for the new machinery which is being introduced into the trade. **1892** *Pall Mall G.* 27 July 1/2 A reduction in the *piece-rates per ton at certain furnaces. **1954** J. A. C. BROWN *Social Psychol. of Industry* vi. 181 Workers..who are paid on an individual piece-rate basis. **1955** *Times* 3 May 10/1 The men allege that the piece-rate schedules are out of date and demand a revision. **1976** *Ilkeston Advertiser* 10 Dec. 2/2 Why is a factory worker who fiddles a 25p piece-rate coupon sacked on the spot, whereas his factory manager who fiddles his expense accounts to the tune of several pounds each week gets away with it? **1881** *Chicago Times* 14 May, The cargo..consisting of short length *piece-stuff. **1891** *Times* 5 Oct. 4/3 There is no change to note in the *piece trade. **1872** HOWELLS *Wedd. Journ.* (1892) 246 The *piece-velvets and the linens smote her to the heart. **1879** MRS. A. E. JAMES *Ind. Househ. Managem.* 17 Buy also some piece-velvet, silk, ribbon, flowers, feathers, net,..bonnet and cap wire. **1900** *Fabian News* Sept. 28/2 This 'log'..is 'a remarkable effort to adjust a *piece-wage rate on a time-wage basis'. **1932** W. FAULKNER *Light in August* i. 9, I was trying to get up the road a *pieceways before dark.

24. a. *Piece* is often the second element in a combination, in various senses, e.g. *back-piece, base-piece, bodice-piece, breech-piece, catch-piece, ear-piece, eye-piece, franc-piece, head-piece, penny-piece*, etc. See the first element.

b. With prefixed numeral, forming attributive phrases, as *one-piece, three-piece*, etc.: see the first element.

Hence (*rare* or *nonce-wds.*) **'pieceless** *a.*, without pieces or parts; **'piecely** *adv.*, in pieces.

a **1631** DONNE *To C'tess Bedford* Poems (1650) 181 In those poore types of God (round circles) so Religions types the peecelesse centers flow. **1552** HULOET, Piecelye, or in pieces, *concise, frustatim.*

[*Note.* L. *Pecia*, in sense of 'fragment', occurs in the Salic Law (*a* 596, MSS. 5 and 6, *c* 800) lx, (Ibi iiii Fustes alninos super caput suum frangere debet et illos in quattuor pecias [*earlier and later recensions* partes] per quattuor angulos iactare debet); *petia, petium*, in sense 'piece of land', appear in Muratori *Ant. Ital.* A.D. 730 'et alia petia', 757 'uno petio de terra' (Diez); see also many later med.L. instances in Du Cange. The ulterior source has been the subject of much research: see Diez s.v. *Pezza*; Scheler, Littré, Hatz-Darm. s.v. *Pièce*; Körting s.v. *pett-* (7106); Thurneysen s.v. *Pezza*. The prevalent opinion is that late pop.L. **pettia, -ium*, were derived from a Brythonic stem *pett(i-*, represented by Breton *pez* a piece, Welsh and Cornish *peth* a part, cognate with proto-Celtic *quett(i-, whence *cotti-, in OIr. cuit, genitive cota, mod. Gaelic cuid part, share; but there are many difficulties. A very frequent early sense in OF. was that of 'portion or space of time' (see Godef.) = 14 above. The sense 'person', found so early in Eng., is not met with in French till late in 16th c.]

piece (pi:s), *v.* [f. prec. sb.]

I. 1. a. *trans.* To mend, repair, make whole, or complete by adding a piece or pieces; to patch.

c **1380** WYCLIF *Wks.* (1880) 41 þei may pese hem aȝen or cloute hem of sacchis & oþere pecis. *c* **1440** *Promp. Parv.* 388/2 Pecyn, or set pecys to a thynge, or clowtyn, *repecio*, .. *sarcio, reficio*. **1530** PALSGR. 655/1, I pece a thyng, I sette on a pece... If it be broken it muste be peced, *sil est rompu il le fault piecer*. **1596** SHAKS. *Tam. Shr.* III. ii. 63 Petruchio is comming..with..one girth sixe times peec'd, and a womans Crupper..heere and there peec'd with pack-thred. **1601** *Vestry Bks.* (Surtees) 135 For picing a bell clapper that brake when Andrew Hawkins was buried, xij*d*. **1775** MME. D'ARBLAY *Early Diary* 28 Feb., She was piecing a blue and white tissue with a large patch of black silk! **1884** *Harper's Mag.* July 306 It's nothin' but play, piecin' quilts.

b. *fig.*

1606 SHAKS. *Ant. & Cl.* I. v. 45, I will peece Her opulent Throne, with Kingdomes. **1633** P. FLETCHER *Purple Isl.* I. i, To paint the world, and piece the length'ning day.

2. a. To join, unite or put together, so as to form one piece; to mend (something broken) by joining the pieces; also *absol.* in spinning, to join or piece up threads, to work as a PIECER.

1483 *Cath. Angl.* 272/2 To Pece, *assuere*. **1559** *Ludlow Churchw. Acc.* (Camden) 90 Payd for a rope to pysse the lyttelle belle rope. **1637** SUCKLING *Aglaura* V. i, There is no piecing Tulips to their stalks When they are once divorc'd by a rude hand. **1793** SMEATON *Edystone L.* §138, I found the seamen..employed in piecing the ground cable, which ..had again parted. **1819** *Evidence fr. Rep. Committee Ho. Lords*, 'How do they get their breakfast and afternoon meal?' '..When the machinery is moving, they eat it as they are piecing'. **1859** MRS. GASKELL *Round the Sofa* 35, I cannot piece the leg as the doctor can.

b. *fig.* To put together, join, unite; *refl.* to join oneself *to*, unite *with*.

1579 W. WILKINSON *Confut. Familye of Loue* Ep. Ded. *iij b, To peece vnto themselues this their broken Religion. **1632** B. JONSON *Magn. Lady* III. i, *Item.* I heard they were out. *Nee.* But they are pieced, and put together again. **1652–62** HEYLIN *Cosmogr.* III. (1673) 5/2 This Prusias, when the Romans became so considerable..pieced himself with them. **1656** —— *Surv. France* 214 She hath peeced her self to the strongest side of the State. **1681** DRYDEN *Abs. & Achit.* I. 661 His judgment yet his memory did excel, Which pieced his wondrous evidence so well. **1879** G. MEREDITH *Egoist* xxiv, Piecing fragments of empty signification.

† 3. *intr.* To unite, come together, assemble; to come to an agreement, agree; to join on. *Obs.*

1622 BACON *Hen. VII* 23 It pieced better and followed more close and handsomely vpon the bruit of Plantagenet's escape. **1625** —— *Ess., Innovations* (Arb.) 526 New Things peece not so well. **1636** SIR H. WOTTON in *Lismore Papers* Ser. II. (1888) III. 260 Owre Schoole Annually breaketh vp two weekes before Whitsontyde and peeceth agayne a fortnight after. **1692** R. L'ESTRANGE *Josephus, Antiq.* XVI. viii. (1733) 434 Telling him..that things would mend in Time, and Friends piece again, if they could but come to.. a fair Understanding.

II. In combination with adverbs.

4. piece down. *trans.* and *intr.* To increase the length or width of (a garment) by the insertion of a piece of material.

1870 J. P. SMITH *Widow Goldsmith's Daughter* vi. 80 Mrs. Goldsmith's economy would not permit her to cast aside any garment that could be pieced down. **1903** K. D. WIGGIN *Rebecca* xvii. 176 The limit of letting down and piecing down was reached.

5. piece in. a. *trans.* To join in, add by insertion; **† b.** *intr.* To join in (in action), unite (*obs.*).

a **1656** HALES *Gold. Rem.* I. (1673) 247 He that can comply, and peice in with all occasions, and make an easie forfeiture of his honesty. **1724** DE FOE *Mem. Cavalier* II. 187 The..Officers..pieced in some Troops with those Regiments.

6. piece on. *trans.* and *intr.* To fit on (as the corresponding piece).

1849 H. MILLER *Footpr. Creat.* iv. (1874) 45 The super-occipital bone..pieces on to the superior frontal. **1869** FREEMAN *Norm. Conq.* III. xii. 218 It is so hard to fix the date of the event, or to piece it on in any way to the undoubted facts of the history, that [etc.].

7. piece out. *trans.* To complete, eke out, extend, or enlarge by the addition of a piece.

1589 PUTTENHAM *Eng. Poesie* II. xiv. (Arb.) 138 Ye may note..how much better some bissillable becommeth to peece out an other longer foote then another word doth. **1639** FULLER *Holy War* IV. xxix. (1840) 232 Like a cordial given to a dying man, which doth piece out his life. **1643** SIR T. BROWNE *Relig. Med.* I. §18 He..pieces out the defect of one by the excess of the other. **1728** YOUNG *Love Fame* v. 436 The motion of her lips, and meaning eye, Piece out the idea her faint words deny. **1858** HAWTHORNE *Fr. & It. Note-Bks.* I. 133 The old Pons Æmilius..has recently been pieced out by connecting a suspension bridge with the old piers.

8. piece together. *trans.* To join together, combine (pieces or fragments) into a whole; to make up of pieces so combined.

1589 PUTTENHAM *Eng. Poesie* III. ix. (Arb.) 168 To peece many words together to make of them one entire, much more significatiue than the single word. **1618** BOLTON *Florus* (1636) 235 Himselfe..peeceth together no lesse an army than the former mad-man. **1687** A. LOVELL tr. *Thevenot's Trav.* I. 134 Cut out of the natural Rock..though it seem to be of five Stones pieced together one upon another. **1865** MERIVALE *Rom. Emp.* VIII. lxiii. 65 Our account of his exploits..must be..pieced imperfectly together.

9. a. piece up. *trans.* To make up (esp. that which is broken); to repair by uniting the pieces, parts, or parties; to patch up.

1586 A. DAY *Eng. Secretary* I. (1625) 75 Let these.. constraine thee..whilst there is yet but one craze..in the touch-stone of thy reputation, piece it vp & new flourish again by a great excellency. **1625** BACON *Ess., Unity Relig.* (Arb.) 429 When it is peeced vp, vpon a direct Admission of Contraries. **1630** *R. Johnson's Kingd. & Commw.* 368 All being now piec't up betweene them. *c* **1645** HOWELL *Lett.* I. IV. xx. (1650) 124 'Tis thought the French King will peece him up again with new recruits. **1794** BURKE *Corr.* (1844) IV. 213 They will of course endeavour to piece up their own broken connexions in England. **1884** *Pall Mall G.* 20 Nov. 3/2 Arranging, disposing, and piecing up these fragments.

b. *intr.* To make up matters, come to an arrangement.

1654 EARL MONM. tr. *Bentivoglio's Warrs Flanders* 212 By all means it was necessary to piece up with Alanson.

‖**pièce** (pjɛs). The French for 'piece'; occurring in French phrases, more or less in current Eng. use.

a. A document used as evidence; esp. in ***pièce justificative***, a document serving as proof of an allegation; a justification of an assertion.

1789 HAN. MORE in W. Roberts *Mem.* (1834) II. III. iv. 160 You will think me a great brute and savage..till you have read my *pièce justificative*. **1882** A. J. MUNBY *Diary* 5 Apr. in D. Hudson *Munby* (1972) 405 Some day I may publish some of these—*piéces* [sic] *justificatives*, as the phrase is. **1917** N. DOUGLAS *South Wind* xxxiv. 412 The various *pièces justificatives* were lying in their sealed envelopes. **1954** W. K. HANCOCK *Country & Calling* viii. 227 The historian, although he may employ analysis and its technical language in his preliminary studies or his *pièces justificatives*, remains just as deeply committed as Herodotus and Thucydides were to narrative and the language of narrative. **1975** *Listener* 7 Aug. 186/1 Laud wanted to publish the Greek and oriental manuscripts which..were *pièces justificatives* of the continuous, independent Church of England.

b. ***pièce de résistance*** (pjɛs də rezistɑ̃s): the most substantial dish in a repast; also *fig.* the chief item in a collection, group, or series; in quot. 1860, used for 'a means of resistance'.

[**1797** BURKE *Regic. Peace* iv. Wks. IX. 7 Our appetite demands a *piece of resistance*.] **1839** LOCKHART *Scott* xix. III. 214 *note*, In answer to her host's apology for his *piece de resistance*. **1840** THACKERAY *Misc. Ess., Pict. Rhapsody* (1885) 184 To supply the picture-lover with the *pièces de résistance* of the feast. **1860** JOWETT in *Essays & Reviews* 335 This authorized text is a *pièce de résistance* against innovation. **1893** *Outing* (U.S.) XXII. 149/2 The *pièce de résistance* of the entire ride lies between Poughkeepsie and Yonkers.

c. ***pièce de conviction*** (pjɛs də kɔ̃viksjɔ̃): an object produced as evidence in a criminal case, an exhibit; also *fig.*, the conclusive argument which decides a question.

1877 [see *Black Museum* s.v. BLACK *a.* 19]. **1894** G. B. SHAW *Let.* 6 Dec. (1965) I. 469 Perhaps it may a little disappoint you, after the fantastic solution of Peer Gynt, and the no-solution of Rosmersholm, that a real solution is only found in something that brings the great Ibsen into line with Monsieur Tout-le-monde; but that, in my view, is the final *pièce de conviction*.

d. ***pièce d'occasion*** (pjɛs dokazjɔ̃): a play or other literary work, or a musical composition, written for a special occasion.

1883 E. B. BAX *Kant's Prolegomena & Metaphysical Found. Nat. Sci.* p. xxvii, Kant believed himself to have no special bent for the professorate in question, which would have involved the criticism of all *pièces d'occasion*, as well as the composition of such on academic festivals. **1891** G. B. SHAW *Quintessence of Ibsenism* p. vi, I had laid it aside as a *pièce d'occasion* which had served its turn. **1914** —— *Dark Lady of Sonnets* 103 This little *pièce d'occasion*, written for a performance in aid of the funds of the project for establishing a National Theatre as a memorial to Shakespear. **1934** C. LAMBERT *Music Ho!* II. 63 These mild pièces d'occasion no more affected the main course of music than an Olde Worlde Bunne Shoppe affects..architectural experiments. **1955** *Times* 29 Aug. 10/6 The result may not be homogeneous enough in style to ensure the work a place in the regular orchestral repertory, but it is certainly a splendid *pièce d'occasion* for this orchestra, who played it with tremendous verve and finish [at their Prom début]. **1971** *Nature* 25 June 537/1 His Presidential Address of 1951 ..is..an attempt to condense the history of chemistry in a single *pièce d'occasion*. **1979** *Jrnl. R. Soc. Arts* CXXVII. 181/2 This book is a *pièce d'occasion*—a collection of essays published to coincide with the exhibition of Cézanne's late work, held in New York and Houston in 1977 and in Paris in 1978.

e. ***pièce de circonstance*** (pjɛs də sirkɔ̃stɑ̃s): a literary composition, theory, etc., having its genesis in a particular situation.

1926 R. H. TAWNEY *Relig. & Rise of Capitalism* ii. 89 His sermons and pamphlets..were *pièces de circonstance*, thrown off in the storm of a revolution. **1972** R. PLANT in Cox & Dyson *20th-Cent. Mind* II. iv. 68 The fact that the historical circumstances which gave rise to [social] theories no longer obtain does not thereby entail that they have become outmoded. Such theories, far from being mere *pièces de circonstance*, rather embody an element which transcends the particular problems which generated them.

f. ***pièce noire*** (pjɛs nwar): a play or a film with a tragic or macabre theme.

1958 *Times* 17 Apr. 3/4 *Payment Deferred* or *The Postman Always Rings Twice* are good *pièces noirs* [sic] because their characters are motivated by passions so intensely conveyed that the subsequent developments are inescapable. **1959** *Oxf. Compan. French Lit.* 22/2 [Anouilh's] *Pièces roses*..and *Pièces noires*..like Shaw's *Plays Pleasant and Unpleasant*.. deal with the lighter or the darker side of life. **1963** *Punch* 20 Nov. 754/3 As black a *pièce noire* as can be.

g. ***pièce rose*** (pjɛs roz): a play or a film having a theme which is pleasantly entertaining; a comedy.

1959 [see *pièce noire* above]. **1963** *Times* 18 May 5/1 It is, what Anouilh calls a *pièce rose* and lightly tosses around such ideas familiar to the playwright as innocence and faith, illusion and reality. **1968** *Punch* 6 Nov. 668/3 Eighteen years (and *Look Back in Anger*) later Anouilh's *pièce rose* seems pathetically pale and withered around the edges.

h. ***pièce à thèse*** (pjɛs a tɛz): = *thesis-play* s.v. THESIS 6.

1961 *Times* 17 Oct. 16/5 In most hands this [television play] could turn into a mechanical *pièce à thèse*. **1974** *Independent Broadcasting* Aug. 5/2 How far the *pièce à thèse*, the play with a social or political message, is permissible within the impartiality rule.

piece-broker. (See quot. 1756.)

1697 *Lond Gaz.* No. 3304/3 One Gawen Hardy.., Piece-Broker, was..Indicted for Felony.., for paying and putting off Counterfeit Milled Money. **1720** STRYPE *Stow's Surv.* II. IV. vii. 118/2 Hollowel Street..a Place inhabited by divers Salesmen and Piece-Brokers. **1756** ROLT *Dict. Trade*, *Piece-broker*, is a shopkeeper in London, who buys the shreds and remnants of all materials that go through the hands of the taylor, and sells them again to such persons as want them for mending cloaths; being generally decayed taylors, or some cunning men who have crept into the secrets of the trade. **1770** *Chron.* in *Ann. Reg.* 143/2 Mr. Muzere, aged 90, many years an eminent piece-broker, who never trusted any money out at interest, but put it into an iron chest. **1858** SIMMONDS *Dict. Trade*, *Piece-broker* [as in Rolt].

pieced (pi:st), *ppl. a.* [f. PIECE *v.* + -ED[1].]

1. Composed or made up of pieces joined together.

1420 in *E.E. Wills* (1882) 42 To Robard Leget my pesid Bowe. [*Ibid.*, A Bowe wyth-owte pecis.] **1569** *Wills & Inv. N.C.* (Surtees) I. 305 Also I gyue to ffrancis walker my peaced bowe. **1601** SIR W. CORNWALLIS *Ess.* II. xxvii. (1631) 21 A pieced stuffe of divers colours of divers ragges. **1785** SARAH FIELDING *Ophelia* II. vi, To descend..down a pieced ladder, appeared..terrible. **1851** RUSKIN *Stones Ven.* I. viii. §11 A larger number of solid and perfect small shafts, or a less number of pieced and cemented large ones.

2. Mended, patched, made up. Also *fig.*

1542–5 BRINKLOW *Lament.* 6 b, Is Christ a peced God, or a patched Redeamer? **1609** B. JONSON *Sil. Wom.* I. i, A poxe of her autumnall face, her peec'd beautie. **1617** MORYSON *Itin.* I. 4 Three Marble pillars..one of them is peeced for one foot.

3. With adverbs: see PIECE *v.* II.

1635–56 COWLEY *Davideis* I. 313 The infected King.. started back at piec'd up shapes, which fear And his distracted Fancy painted there. **1901** *Daily Chron.* 16 Oct. 3/3 A mere pieced-together book.

piece-goods, *sb. pl.* Textile fabrics, such as calico, shirtings, mull, etc., woven in recognized lengths (see PIECE *sb.* 4 a) for sale; a term formerly applied to Indian and other Oriental fabrics exported to Europe, but subsequently chiefly applied to Lancashire cotton goods exported to the East.

1665 *Lond. Gaz.* No. 12/1 A Fregat of the Eastern Squadron, hath sent in a Vessel laden with Wax, Pitch, Tar, and Piece-goods. **1722** *Ibid.* No. 6045/9 All Piece Goods, as Bays, Cloaths, Stuffs, or any other Manufactury. **1785** in Seton-Karr *Select. Calcutta Gaz.* (1864) I. 82 That the Captains and Officers of all ships that shall sail from any part of India, after receiving notice hereof, shall be allowed to bring eight thousand pieces of piece-goods, and no more. **1817** JAS. MILL *Brit. India* I. I. iii 45 *note*, Piece goods is the term..chiefly employed by the Company and their agents to denote the muslins and wove goods of India and China in general. **1844** G. DODD *Textile Manuf.* i. 36 The cotton yarn is woven into piece-goods either by the hand-loom or the power-loom. **1886** YULE & BURNELL *Anglo-Ind. Gloss.* s.v., Lancashire..has recently procured the abolition of the small import duty on English piece-goods in India. **1898** *Westm. Gaz.* 8 Oct. 6/3 Combination of the worsted piece-goods dyers.

'piece-lace. Lace made in broad pieces, which can be cut and used like cloth.

1702 *Lond. Gaz.* No. 3806/8 A new Piece-Lace Head.., and a loop'd Flanders Lace Head. **1899** *Westm. Gaz.* 16 Mar. 3/1 Some amazingly good imitations of Irish lace—.. being but a few shillings per yard—for piece lace, that is. **1901** *Ibid.* 12 July 3/1 These coats are made mainly from piece laces with lace flouncing rippling round the edge.

piecemeal ('pi:smi:l), *adv.* (*sb.*, *a.*) Forms: see PIECE *sb.* and MEAL *sb.*[2] [ME. f. *pece*, PIECE + *-mêle*, -MEAL. Taking the place of OE. *styccemælum*; *pece-mêle* being a later word has not the OE. form in *-mælum*, nor an early ME. in *-mêlen*. The later amplification *by pece-mele* follows other words in *-mele* with *be, by* (e.g. DROPMEAL, FLOCKMEAL, FOOTMEAL, HEAPMEAL), and introduces the quasi-sb. use B. The example in *-s* (1 β) was prob. due to the plural notion rather than an instance of the adverbial genitive.]

A. *adv.* **1.** One part or piece at a time; piece by piece, gradually, by degrees; separately, by pieces.

1297 R. GLOUC. (Rolls) 5624 þat folc to drou þat traytour, ech lime pece mele. *c* **1440** *Jacob's Well* 151 þei etyn a man no3t al hole, but pece-mele. **1513** More *Rich. III* (1883) 85 Miles Forest at sainct Martens pecemele [*a* **1548** Hall *Chron., Rich. III* 28 by pece meale] rotted awaye. **1579** Tomson *Calvin's Serm. Tim.* 125/1 Now it remaineth that we looke peecemeale vnto these wordes. **1617** Moryson *Itin.* I. 5 The stone couering him is compassed with a grate, least it should bee broken and carried away peece-meale by Passengers. **1773** Burke *Corr.* (1844) I. 423 The business will be done covertly and piecemeal. **1865** Kingsley *Herew.* xvii, He means to conquer England piece-meal. **1885** Sir J. Pearson in *Law Rep. 29 Ch. Div.* 453 A party is not allowed to bring his case before the Court piecemeal.

β. **1698** Norris *Pract. Disc.* IV. 424 To have taken him Piecemeals, Paragraph by Paragraph, and to have consider'd every single Objection distinctly.

b. With *by* (rarely *in*). (Transitional to B.)

1545 Raynold *Byrth Mankynde* 100 Lette it be cut out by pese mele. **1566** Drant *Horace* To Rdr. 3, I..haue dispatched it by piece meale, or inche meale. **1692** Washington tr. *Milton's Def. Pop.* Pref., Wks. 1851 VIII. 5, I am forced to write by piece-meal, and break off almost every hour. **1693** W. Freke *Sel. Ess.* xix. 114 They that can bear Pedantry in Piece-meal, will be even sick when they peruse his Masse of it. **1796** Jefferson *Writ.* (1859) IV. 130 It is better to do the whole work once for all, than to be recurring to it by piece-meal. **1868** E. Edwards *Ralegh* I. viii. 129 After previous alienations by piecemeal.

†**c.** ***in piecemeal***: piece by piece, in detail. (Cf. B.) *Obs.*

1561 T. Hoby tr *Castiglione's Courtyer* III. (1577) R v, To reason thus in peecemeale of these rules.. were a taking of an infinite matter in hand. *Ibid.* IV. V iij b, [To] vnderstand in peecemeale whatsoeuer belongeth to hys people.

2. Piece from piece; into or in pieces or fragments: with *break, tear, cut*, etc.

1570 Googe *Pop. Kingd.* I. (1880) 7 Who rather will be peecemeale torne than once their prince forsake. *c* **1580** Sidney *Ps.* II. 21 Bruse Thou shalt and peecemeale breake These men like potshards weake. **1664** Butler *Hud.* II. i. 751 I'll be torn piece-meal by a Horse, E'er I'll take you for better or worse. **1712** E. Cooke *Voy. S. Sea* 75 Hewing them Piece-meal, and delighting in their Blood. **1826** Scott *Woodst.* viii, To be now pulled asunder, broken piecemeal and reduced.

†**b.** With *in*. *Obs.* (Cf. B.)

1577 Stanyhurst *Descr. Irel.* in *Holinshed* (1808) VI. 40 The fishmongers were forced to hacke it in gobbets, and so to carrie it in peecemeale throughout the countrie. *c* **1590** Marlowe *Faust.* xiii. 69 Revolt, or I'll in piece-meal tear thy flesh. **1704** Swift *T. Tub* ix. 178 Is any Student tearing his Straw in piece-meal, Swearing and Blaspheming?

†**B.** quasi-*sb.* (with *pl.*) A small piece, portion, or fragment; chiefly in phrase ***by piecemeals***, also ***at, in, into piecemeals***. *Obs.*

1577 Whetstone *Life Gascoigne* xxviii, By peece meales care so wrought me vnder foot. **1612** Woodall *Surg. Mate* Wks. (1653) 268 *Buccellatio* is dividing into gobbets, or by peece-meals. **1616** J. Maitland in *Scot. Hist. Soc. Misc.* (1904) 171 He choosit rather to blame, tax and charge my father..in hidlings and at peece-male. **1642** T. Goodwin *Zerubbabels Enc.* 17 That..perfection of light which the Apostolicall times had..by piece-meals and degrees. **1651** R. Vaughan in *Ussher's Lett.* (1686) 562 To register any thing to the purpose..that I could come by, (some few piecemeals excepted). **1657** W. Rand tr. *Gassendi's Life Peiresc* II. 294 Being torn into piece-meales. **1762** Sterne *Tr. Shandy* V. iii, Those are falling..by piece-meals to decay.

C. *adj.* (*attrib.* use of the adv.). Consisting or done in pieces or by instalments; done bit by bit.

1600 Rowlands *Lett. Humours Blood* vi. 75 A pox of peecemeale drinking. **1713** Derham *Phys. Theol.* To Rdr., None..have done it otherwise than in a transient, piece-meal Manner. **1768–74** Tucker *Lt. Nat.* (1834) I. 640 What tortures and piecemeal executions have not been practised by tyrants and persecutors. **1831** J. W. Croker in *Croker Papers* 9 Oct., Giving no opinion on piecemeal reform. **1871** Freeman *Norm. Conq.* IV. xviii. 184 Our history just at this time has to be put together in so piecemeal a way.

ˈ**piecemeal**, *v.* Now *rare.* [f. prec.] *trans.* To divide or distribute piecemeal; to dismember. Also const. *out*. Hence ˈ**piecemealing** *vbl. sb.*

1611 Cotgr., *Emmenuiser*, to make small, to peecemeale, to reduce into little parcels, or peeces. *Ibid.*, *Parcelé*, peecemealed; cut, or made, into parcels. **1632** Heywood *1st Pt. Iron Age* v. i. Wks. 1874 III. 338 My seuen-fold Targe With thousand gashes peece-meald from mine arme. **1655** Gurnall *Chr. in Arm.* I. 20 The glory of the work shall not be crumbled, and piece-mealed out, some to God, and some to the Creature. *a* **1700** *Oxford Laureat* in Johnson *L. P., Yalden*, Had he ta'en the whole ode, as he took it piece-mealing, They had fin'd him but ten-pence at most. **1718** *Entertainer* No. 21. 144 The Piece-meal'd Quarters.. exposed to the four Corners of the Earth. **1749** Fielding *Tom Jones* XIII. i, The heavy, unread, folio lump, which long had dozed on the dusty shelf, piece-mealed into numbers, runs nimbly through the nation. **1853** *Tait's Mag.* XX. 259 The division, the piece-mealing of Germany, is the strength of Russia. **1975** *Washington Post* 6 Sept. A2/4 To announce even the topic of the hearings would result in 'prematurely piecemealing the information out',—he said.

†ˈ**piecemealwise**, *adv.* *Obs.* *rare*$^{-1}$. [See -wise.] = piecemeal 1.

1594 Carew *Tasso* (1881) 78 The Christians force peecemale-wise to impair.

piecen (ˈpiːs(ə)n), *v. local* or *techn.* [f. piece *sb.* + -en[5] 2.] *trans.* To join, to piece; chiefly, to join broken threads or ends in spinning.

1835 Ure *Philos. Manuf.* 180 The children have..to piecen their slubbing ends with double rapidity. *Ibid.* 223 With the covers has been also introduced a new method of piecening or joining on any end.., namely, by splicing it to the adjoining roving. **1844** G. Dodd *Textile Manuf.* i. 18 The plan of 'piecening', by which time is saved in spinning cotton. **1887** *19th Cent.* Dec. 820 The building..has been piecened and enlarged from time to time.

piecener (ˈpiːs(ə)nə(r)). [f. prec. + -er[1].] One who pieces or piecens; a piecer; *spec.*, a child or young person employed in a spinning-mill to keep the frames filled with rovings, and to join together the ends of threads which break while being spun or wound; formerly, also, to join the cardings or slivers for the slubber, a work now done by machinery: see piecer 2.

1835 Ure *Philos. Manuf.* 178 The cardings..are taken up by the children, called pieceners, from the nature of their work, being to piece or join those porous rolls together, to fit them for being drawn into a continuous thread. **1839** Mrs. F. Trollope *M. Armstrong* I. viii. 191 *note*, The children whose duty it is to walk backwards and forwards before the reels, on which the cotton, silk, or worsted is wound, for the purpose of joining the threads when they break, are called piecers, or pieceners. **1843** *Penny Cycl.* XXVII. 552/1 A child, called a 'piecener', takes the cardings from the carding machine... The pieceners are employed and paid by the slubber.

piecer (ˈpiːsə(r)). [f. piece *v.* + -er[1].]

1. *generally.* One who pieces; a patcher.

1836 L. Hunt in *New Monthly Mag.* XLVIII. 70 Fancy's the wealth of wealth, the toiler's hope, The poor man's piecer-out. **1841** *Blackw. Mag.* L. 155 The English are blunderers here, piecers and patch-workers. **1858** Gladstone *Homer* I. 46 The piecers, who say that there were originally a number of Iliadic or Odyssean songs, afterwards made up into the poems such as we now have them.

2. *spec.* In a spinning-mill: see piecener.

1825 J. Nicholson *Operat. Mechanic* 384 The pieces are joined by children, called piecers, who are in attendance on each mule, to join any yarn that may be broken in the act of stretching or twisting. **1833** Ht. Martineau *Manch. Strike* i. 3 You earn as much as a piecer as some do at a hand-loom. **1857** Livingstone *Trav.* Introd. 3, I was put into the factory as a 'piecer'. **1891** *Labour Commission* Gloss., *Piecers*, assistants to the mule spinner or minder, with the special duty of keeping the frames filled with 'rovings'. They derive their name from their work of piecing up the broken threads.

ˈ**piece-wise**, *adv.* Also **piecewise**. By pieces; *spec.* in *Math.*, throughout each of a finite number of separate parts or regions but not necessarily throughout the whole.

1674 N. Fairfax *Bulk & Selv.* 107 Whether wholewise or piece-wise? **1933** H. B. Phillips *Vector Anal.* v. 101 Vectors which are only piecewise differentiable. **1939** *Mind* XLVIII. 366 They have to proceed piece-wise, measuring every little line and bend. **1953** L. V. Ahlfors *Complex Anal.* ii. 65 We shall say that the arc is differentiable if $z'(t)$ exists and is continuous... An arc is piecewise differentiable ..if the same conditions hold except for a finite number of values t. **1962** Alley & Atwood *Electronic Engin.* xvi. 546 This method is known as the piecewise-linear method, since the tube or transistor is assumed to be linear over certain regions of operation. **1966** Scott & Tims *Math. Anal.* vi. 209 It is useful also to consider functions which, while not continuous in a whole interval, are nevertheless made up of a *finite* number of continuous pieces. Such functions are called piecewise continuous. **1979** *Nature* 12 Apr. 623/1 Their major effect is to re-order, piecewise, the fibre map of the eye circumference laid out across the t axis of the ribbon.

piece-work (ˈpiːswɜːk). Also **piecework**.

1. Work done and paid for by the piece: see piece *sb.* 19.

1549 *Coventry Leet Bk.* (1909) III. 792 No persone of the Craft of Cappers shall put owt eny pece-woork, but to suche of the same Craft as the maisters..shall agree & consent vnto. **1770** J. Wedgwood *Let.* 12 May (1965) 91 You will certainly do right in bringing the painting to piece work. **1795** Washington *Let.* Writ. 1892 XIII. 58 The new have gone more into the execution of it by contracts, and piece work. **1817** H. L. Piozzi *Let.* 14 Apr. in A. Hayward *Autobiogr. Mrs. Piozzi* (1861) II. 200 A gentleman..called fifteen of his principal people..and told them he was no longer able to give them piece-work. **1830** *Cumb. Farm Rep.* 60 in *Libr. Usef. Knowl., Husb.* III, Labourers are easily obtained here, either for piece-work or by the day. **1878** Jevons *Prim. Pol. Econ.* viii. 74 Some trades-unions endeavour to prevent their members from earning wages by piece-work. **1885** G. B. Shaw *Let.* 29 Dec. (1965) I. 149 Paquito has not the remotest idea of what it is to be exploited on the piece-work system by newspapers. **1894** [see feller[1] 4]. **1911** *Rep. Labour & Social Conditions in Germany* (Tariff Reform League) III. 31 He also informed us that most of the joiners worked piecework. *Ibid.* 186 There was a lock-out in the building trade, owing to a grievance in the piecework system. **1967** M. Argyle *Psychol. Interpersonal Behaviour* iv. 73 Under competition hostile attitudes will develop; an example of this is the payment of salesgirls by individual piece-work, leading to their fighting over the more desirable customers. **1970** T. Lupton *Managem. & Social Sci.* (ed. 2) iii. 63 Pitting wits against management on piecework rates.

attrib. **1890** *Daily News* 1 Nov. 3/2 This is one of the last of the piece-work jobs in Victoria Dock under the agreement of last November.

2. = patchwork 4 b.

1842 C. M. Kirkland *Forest Life* I. 90 No gorgeous piece-work bed-quilts exhibiting stars of all magnitudes and moons in all quarters. **1935** M. M. Atwater *Murder in Midsummer* viii. 71 You'll find a piecework spread in the bottom drawer.

Hence ˈ**piece-ˌworker**, a workman who does piece-work, or is paid according to the amount done.

1884 *Harper's Mag.* Sept. 625/1 With a piece-worker, time is literally money. **1891** *Times* 7 Oct. 4/6 Piece-workers are supposed to earn, on the average, from one-fourth to one-third more than their rating.

piecing (ˈpiːsɪŋ), *vbl. sb.* [f. piece *v.* + -ing[1].] The action of the verb piece; patching, mending or completing by joining pieces.

1399 Langl. *Rich. Redeles* III. 168 Ffor þei ffor þe pesinge paieth pens ten duble That þe cloþe costened. **1545** Ascham *Toxoph.* (Arb.) 127 Peecynge of a shafte with brasell and holie..is to make the ende compasse heauy. **1649** Bp. Hall *Cases Consc.* IV. ii. Wks. 1863 VII. 374 The piecing up of these domestick breaches betwixt husband and wife. *a* **1680** Butler *Rem.* (1759) II. 303 Rhime is like Lace, that serves excellently well to hide the Piecing and Coarsness of a bad Stuff. **1771** Luckombe *Hist. Print.* 281 Piecing of Rules is often attended with considerable trouble. **1835** Ure *Philos. Manuf.* 312 The pieceing is soon over, as the carriage does not stop an instant at the frame. **1884** *Athenæum* 1 Nov. 562/3 An infinite piecing of minute facts.

b. *attrib.* and *Comb.*

1545 *Rates of Customs* c iij, Pesing threde the dossen pound xii*s.* iiii*d.* **1594** *Acc.-Bk. W. Wray* in *Antiquary* XXXII. 347, i *li.* pecinge thred, ii*s.* vj*d.* **1640** in Entick *London* (1766) II. 170 Whited brown or pieceing thread. **1881** Jacobi *Printer's Vocab.* 100 *Piecing leads*, in wide measures of type the leads required are usually pieced.

piecrust (ˈpaɪkrʌst). [f. pie *sb.*[2] + crust.]

a. The baked paste forming the crust of a pie.

1582 Hester *Secr. Phiorav.* III. liii. 75 Ye shall not eate.. Butter, Milke, Cheese, or Pie crustes, or suche like thynges. **1626** B. Jonson *Staple of N.* II. i, One that..preserues himselfe, Like an old hoary Rat, with mouldy pye-crust. **1817** Scott in Lockhart *Life* (1837) IV. 98 The posts, which are as cross as pye-crust, have occasioned some delay. **1869** *Hazlitt's Eng. Prov.* 320 Promises are like pie-crust, made to be broken.

b. *fig.* (in reference to hardness or dryness).

1869 Blackmore *Lorna D.* xlii, I will work it out by myself, you pie-crusts. **1872** Baker *Nile Tribut.* xviii. 322 The dry season baked it into a pie-crust.

c. *attrib.*; proverbially and humorously of promises lightly broken (see quot. 1869 above), as ***piecrust pledge, promise***; of the colour of piecrust, as ***piecrust hair, straw***; applied to a table having an ornamental edge suggestive of the crust of a pie, as ***pie-crust table, top***.

1739 'R. Bull' tr. *Dedekindus' Grobianus* 162 Then all the Vengeance of the Gods invoke, In Case this Pye-crust Promise should be broke. **1888** *Pall Mall G.* 7 Dec. 11/1 Having laid to Mr. Smith's charges another piecrust pledge. **1889** W. S. Gilbert *Foggerty's Fairy*, etc. (1892) 98 The pie-crust hair had not been placed in mourning. **1902** L. V. Lockwood *Colonial Furnit. Amer.* 232 The handsomest of the Dutch tea-tables were what are popularly known as 'pie-crust tables'. **1914** R. & E. Shackleton *Charm of Antique* iii. 49 The most sought-for and rarest of little tables is the 'pie-crust' tip-table, so named from its apparently finger-dented pie-crust-like margin of regular irregularity. **1923** W. Deeping *Secret Sanct.* xx. 210 She had closed the lid of her work-basket and placed it on the 'pie-crust' table by the window. **1951** *Good Housek. Home Encycl.* 106/1 Tri-pod tables..with 'piecrust' tops. **1969** A. Negus *Going for Song* 120 So on original pie-crust tables there are no joins at all round the pie-crust edge. **1973** A. Behrend *Samarai Affair* iv. 53 The glossy telephone on the antique piecrust table.

pied (paɪd), *ppl. a.*[1] Also 6–7 **pide**, 6–8 **pyed**, 7 **py'd, pyde**, (6 *Sc.* **pyet**). [As if pa. pple. of a verb *pie*, f. pie *sb.*[1]: see -ed.]

a. Parti-coloured; originally, black and white like a magpie; hence, of any two colours, esp. of white blotched with another colour; also of three or more colours in patches or blotches. Also, wearing a parti-coloured dress.

1382 [see c]. **1509** Hawes *Past. Pleas.* xxix. (Percy Soc.) 134 With a hood, a bell,..and a bagge; In a pyed cote he rode brygge a bragge. **1575** *Brieff Disc. Troubles Franckford* (1846) 203 To weare the pied coate off a foole. **1588** Shaks. *L.L.L.* v. ii. 904 Dasies pied, and Violets blew, And Cuckow-buds of yellow hew. **1596** —— *Merch. V.* I. iii. 80 That all the eanelings which were Streakt and pied Should fall as Iacobs hier. **1611** Cotgr., *Pecile*, a pide, or skude colour of a horse. **1627** Drayton *Nymphidia* xviii, The wing of a pyde Butterflee. **1652** Gaule *Magastrom.* 366 In a town within the territories of Brunswick, they had hired a pyed piper to conjure away all the rats and mice, that much infested him. [Cf. quot. *c* 1645 in f.] **1665** Sir T. Herbert *Trav.* (1677) 16 Zebræ or Pide-horses. **1774** Lambert in *Phil. Trans.* LXVI. 493 The bullock is pyed, white and red. **1839** Youatt *Horse* 376 The pied horse is one that has distinct spots or patches of different colours, but almost invariably of white with some other colour. **1841** Catlin *N. Amer. Ind.* II. xli. 58 Others [horses] were pied, containing a variety of colours on the same animal.

b. Construed as *pa. pple.* = variegated.

1632 Milton *L'Allegro* 75 Meadows trim with Daisies pide, Shallow Brooks, and Rivers wide. **1671** Marten in *Acc. Sev. late Voy.* II. (1694) 79 In the middle, they are white pyed with black. **1853** G. Johnston *Nat. Hist. E. Bord.* I. 122 A garment pied with daisies, and buttercups, and dandelions. **1887** Bowen *Virg. Æneid* v. 566 A Thracian courser with white all dappled and pied.

†**c.** ***Pied Friars, Friars of the Pie***: orig. name of a small order of friars: see quot. 1904; in *P. Pl. Crede* app. applied to the Carmelites or White Friars (whose dress was a brown tunic and a white cloak): see Skeat *Student's Pastime* §53. ***Pied Monk***, a Bernardine or Cistercian, from their white tunic and large black scapular. *Obs.* exc. *Hist.*

1382 in *Pol. Poems* (Rolls) I. 262 With an O and an I, fuerunt pyed freres; Quomodo mutati sunt rogo dicat Pers. [*c* **1394** *P. Pl. Crede* 65 Sikerli y can nou3t fynden, who hem first founded, But þe foles foundeden hem-self, freres of the Pye. *c* **1440** Walsingham *Hist. Angl.* (Rolls) I. 182 Cadaver ..in quodam veteri cœmeterio, quod fuerat quondam

Fratrum quos 'Freres Pyes' veteres appellabant,.. projecerunt.] **1530** PALSGR. 254/1 Pyed monke, *barnardin*. **1537** WRIOTHESLEY *Chron.* (Camden) I. 63 An Abbott condam of Fountens, of the order of pyed monkes. **1904** GASQUET *Eng. Monast. Life* xi. 242 Pied Friars, or Fratres de Pica,.. had but one house in England, at Norwich, and.. were obliged by the Council of Lyons [1245] to join one or other of the four great mendicant Orders.

d. In the specific names of many birds and other animals characterized by variegated colouring; as **pied antelope** = BONTEBOK; **pied blackbird**, any Asiatic thrush of the genus *Turdulus* (Webster 1890); **pied brant** = HARLEQUIN *brant*; **pied crow**, the black and white crow, *Corvus albus*, found in most parts of Africa south of the Sahara; **pied duck**, the extinct *Somateria labradoria*; **pied finch**, the chaffinch, *Fringilla cœlebs*: cf. PIEFINCH; **pied flycatcher** a black and white flycatcher, *Muscicapa* (or *Ficedula*) *hypoleuca*, found in Europe and north and west Africa; **pied goose** = MAGPIE *goose*; **pied grallina**, the Magpie Lark of Australia (*Grallina australis* or *picata*); **pied hyena**, the spotted hyena (*H. crocuta*); **pied hornbill**, species of *Anthracoceros*; **pied kingfisher**, *Ceryle rudis*, a native of India and Africa; **pied seal**, the Mediterranean Seal (*Monachus albiventer*); **pied starling**, an extinct starling of Réunion (*Fregilupus varius*); **pied wagtail**, a western European wagtail, *Motacilla alba yarrelli*; **pied wigeon**, (*a*) the Garganey (*Anas querquedula*); (*b*) the Golden-eye (*Clangula glaucion*); (*c*) the Goosander (*Mergus merganser*) (Swainson *Prov. Names Birds* 1885); **pied wolf**, a pied variety of the American wolf.

1930 W. L. SCLATER *Systema Avium Ethiopicarum* II. 650 *Pied Crow... Throughout the Ethiopian Region. **1958** G. DURRELL *Encounters with Animals* III. 109 A pied crow from West Africa.. suddenly decided that I was the only person in the world for him. **1967** W. CONDRY *Birds & Wild Afr.* iv. 65 In one palm a pair of pied crows were courting. **1899** *Cambr. Nat. Hist.* IX. 119 The extinct '*Pied Duck'.. was black, with white head, neck, chest [etc.]. **1776** T. PENNANT *Brit. Zool.* (ed. 4) I. 351 (*heading*) *Pied fly-catcher. **1843** W. YARRELL *Hist. Brit. Birds* I. 169 The Pied Flycatcher.. is a rare bird in England. **1882** [see FLY-CATCHER 2]. **1894** C. DIXON *Nests & Eggs Brit. Birds* 157 The Pied Flycatcher arrives in our islands during the latter half of April. **1971** *Country Life* 25 Mar. 705/2 Other garden birds [in West Berlin] include redstarts and pied flycatchers. **1898** MORRIS *Austral Eng.*, *Magpie-Goose*.. called also *Swan-goose*, and *Pied-goose. **1865** W. BOYD *Swartzen* 72 Robes of striped or *pied hyena. **1865** *Ibis* 2nd Ser. I. 408 *Pied Kingfisher. Appears to be the common species of Lower Bengal. **1924** W. L. SCLATER *Systema Avium Æthiopicarum* I. 211 Pied Kingfisher... The Greek Islands, Cyprus, Asia Minor and Egypt to the Persian Gulf. **1953** G. DURRELL *Overloaded Ark* xiii. 221 There were Pied kingfishers, vivid black and white. **1971** *Country Life* 28 Oct. 1127/2 The much larger pied kingfishers hovered like kestrels, then plunged into the water from a height. **1901** *Nature* 10 Jan. 254/2 A notable loss is the handsome crested *pied starling.. which is believed to have become extinct about the middle of the [19th] century. **1837** GOULD in *Mag. Nat. Hist.* N.S. I. 460, I was.. surprised to find that the sprightly and *pied wagtail.. could not be referred to any described species. **1894** C. DIXON *Nests & Eggs Brit. Birds* 64 The White Wagtail does not differ in its habits.. from the Pied Wagtail. **1964** G. B. SCHALLER *Year of Gorilla* (1965) i. 39 Pied wagtails flitted around the huts. **1975** E. SIMMS *Birds of Town & Suburb* i. 25 The trodden grass swards may be visited by an occasional pied wagtail.

e. *fig.*

1600 B. JONSON *Underwoods*, *Misc. P.* xxiii, Not wearing moods, as gallants do a fashion, In these pied times. **1635** [GLAPTHORNE] *Lady Mother* I. iii. in Bullen *O. Pl.* II. 120 Noe speckd serpent weares More spotts than her pide honor. **1658** OSBORN *Adv. Son* II. Pref. (1673) K v, Py'd and contaminated constructions. *Ibid.* 166 This pied Goddess [Fortune].

f. *Pied Piper*: in a German legend (the subject of Browning's poem *The Pied Piper of Hamelin* (1845)), a piper in parti-colour dress who rid the town of Hameln (Hamelin) of a plague of rats by charming them to follow him into the river Weser, and who, on being refused the promised reward, led away the children of the town: used allusively.

1942 'N. SHUTE' (*title*) Pied piper. **1946** KOESTLER *Thieves in Night* 154 There was a horra in the Square with Mendl doing his Pied Piper act. **1966** *Listener* 27 Oct. 631/3 There was something very unpleasant about this Pied Piper of adolescent religious feelings [*sc.* David Wilkerson, an American evangelist]. **1972** T. P. MCMAHON *Issue of Bishop's Blood* (1973) i. 15 The pathetic thousands who trek endlessly after the Pied Pipers of the cancer cures. **1976** *Western Producer* (Saskatoon, Saskatchewan) 24 June 7/4 In Ottawa.. Bobby Gimby, Canada's pied piper, will sail along Rideau Canal followed by a flotilla of canoes filled with youngsters singing his pop Canadian hit 'Canada'. **1977** S. BRETT *Star Trap* xiii. 144 Charles could not help admiring the Pied Piper strength of the man's personality. The company was carried along on the wave of his vitality. **1979** *Guardian* 2 May 10/7 I'm the Pied Piper and every toddler is.. singing 'Vote vote vote for Mr Ashton'.

g. *Comb.* (parasynthetic), as *pied-billed*, *-coated*, *-coloured*, *-faced*, *-winged*, etc.

1595 CHAPMAN *Coronet Mistr. Philos.* vi, The Protean rages Of pied-faced fashion. **1653** S. R. *Noble Soldier* II. i. in Bullen *O. Pl.* I. 276 These pide-winged Butterflyes. *c* **1645** HOWELL *Lett.* I. VI. xlix. (1650) 241 The said Town of Hamelen was annoyed with Rats and Mice; and it chanc'd, that a Pied-coated Piper came thither. **1709** STRYPE *Ann. Ref.* I. xxiii. 236 Eighteen great horses, all of them pyed coloured. **1888** TRUMBULL *Bird Names* 82 *note*, The Pied-billed Grebe.. familiar to us all.

pied (paɪd), *ppl. a.*² *rare.* [f. PIE *v.*³ + -ED¹.] Converted into printers' pie; mixed up, confused.

1870 *Daily News* 2 Oct., Since then matters stand as above described, in a curiously pied condition. **1904** 'MARK TWAIN' in *Harper's Weekly* 10 Dec. 12/2 A thing that gets pied is dead,.. its chance of seeing print is gone. **1956** J. WHATMOUGH *Language* i. 9 A haphazard jumble of symbols, say a pied text, is a.. nightmare.

‖**pied à terre** (pjedatɛr). Pl. pieds à terre. [Fr., lit. 'foot on the ground'.] A small town house, flat, or room used for short periods of residence; a 'home base'.

1829 CARLYLE in *Foreign Rev.* III. VI. 445 She is perpetually travelling: a peaceful philosopher is lugged over the world, to Cirey, to Lunéville, to that *pied à terre* in Paris. **1838** J. PARDOE *Beauties of Bosphorus* 20 The Greek emperor .. acceded to the desire of Mahomet to possess a *pied-à-terre* on the European edge of the channel. **1870** D. G. ROSSETTI *Let.* 15 Mar. (1965) II. 815, I have not yet written to thank you for a much more independent and promising *pied-à-terre* than I could have found in the tents of the stranger. **1901** 'L. MALET' *Hist. R. Calmady* v. i. 383 Richard Calmady had taken her husband's villa at Naples on lease, it offering, as he said, a convenient *pied à terre* to him while yachting along the adjacent coasts. **1926** [see METROLAND]. **1927** C. CONNOLLY *Let.* Dec. in *Romantic Friendship* (1975) 316 It might help you to have a *pied-à-terre*. **1936** F. CLUNE *Roaming round Darling* i. 7 Australia is still a land of change and Australians, generally, are a restless race, preferring a mere *pied-à-terre* before a taxable home-fire. **1958** [see *accommodation address* s.v. ACCOMMODATION 6b]. **1964** C. WILLOCK *Enormous Zoo* vii. 114 They had given us a room in their own house which we were free to use as a *pied-à-terre*. **1977** *Wandsworth Borough News* 7 Oct. 23/2 (Advt.), Ideal pied-a-terre—very reasonably priced studio flat in a detached Victorian property.

‖**pied d'éléphant** (pje delefɑ̃). [Fr., lit. 'elephant's foot'.] A padded sack used to protect the lower part of the body on a bivouac in mountaineering and rock climbing.

1956 C. EVANS *On Climbing* viii. 120 For alpine bivouacs, it is customary to make the sleeping bag as it were a part of your clothing using.. a sawn-off sleeping-bag, the 'pied d'elephant', to cover the legs. **1963** P. NOCK *Rock Climbing* ix. 81 One addition which is sometimes carried is a 'pied d'elephant'. This is like the bottom half of a sleeping bag of minumum weight. **1966** C. BONINGTON *I chose to Climb* xvi. 188, I was once again fully equipped with borrowed duvet, pied d'éléphant, [etc]. **1968** P. CREW *Encycl. Dict. Mountaineering* 91/1 *Pied d'Elephant*,.. a waist length bag for protecting the lower part of the body on bivouacs. **1973** C. BONINGTON *Next Horizon* x. 149, I managed to pull my boots off, slipped them in my rucksack and them pulled the pied d'éléphant over my legs, ending up with my feet in my rucksack.

piedestal(l, **-istal**, **piedstal**, **-stoole**, obs. ff. PEDESTAL.

piedly ('paɪdlɪ), *adv. rare.* [f. PIED *a.*¹ + -LY².] In a pied manner; in clothes of divers colours.

1545 BRINKLOW *Compl.* xxiv. (1874) 70 How pyedly goo thei lyke mommers, disgysed from the common peple.

piedment, obs. form of PEDIMENT.

piedmont ('pi:dmɒnt), *sb.* (*a.*) [Orig. (in sense 1) *Piemont*, after It. *Piemonte*, lit. 'mountain foot', name of a region of N. Italy, f. *piede* foot (:—L. *ped-*, *pēs*) + *monte* mountain (:—L. *mont-*, *mons*).] **1.** Also **Piedmont**. The name of a fertile upland region of the U.S. between the Blue Ridge and Appalachian Mountains to the west and the Atlantic coastal plain to the east, and extending from near New York to Alabama. Freq. *attrib.*

1755 L. EVANS *Geogr. Ess.* 7 Between the South Mountain and the hither Chain of the Endless Mountains.. is the most considerable Quantity of valuable Land that the English are possest of; and runs through New-Jersey, Pensilvania, Mariland and Virginia. It has yet obtained no general Name, but may properly be called Piemont, from its Situation. **1855** *Southern Lit. Messenger* XXI. 672/2 The next breadth of country known in several of the States as the Piedmont district, was more salubrious in its atmosphere. **1857** 'PORTE CRAYON' *Virginia Illustr.* 235 The soil of this [*sc.* Amherst Co., Va.], in common with many other of the piedmont counties, is of a bright red in many places. **1905** W. H. NORTON *Elem. Geol.* iii. 87 The surface of the Piedmont is gently rolling. **1927** H. C. GROOME *Fauquier during Proprietorship* i. 1 A contour line through the falls of these rivers marks the boundary between Tidewater Virginia and that region which rolling upward to the foothills of the Appalachians is today known as the Piedmont Plateau. **1929** J. BUCHAN *Courts of Morning* II. xi. 257 A rambling country-house high up in the South Carolina piedmont, with the blue, forested hills behind. **1951** TRAGER & SMITH *Outl. Eng. Struct.* I. 25 In the Southeast of the United States, in both the Coastal and Piedmont speech. **1968** R. W. FAIRBRIDGE *Encycl. Geomorphol.* 844/2 The Piedmont Province.. is the older part of the Appalachians... Rocks of the piedmont.. are of early Paleozoic to Precambrian age. **1972** H. KURATH *Stud. Area Linguistics* viii. 128 From 1790 to 1860 Negro slaves outnumbered the Whites in the piedmont of Virginia. **1976** *Scottish Rev.* Summer 5 After the failure of the Forty-Five, many Highland families moved to the pine barrens and hills of piedmont North Carolina.

2. Any region or area at the foot of a mountain or mountain range.

1860 MAYNE REID *Odd People* 430 Having reached the *piedmont* of the Andes, you still find yourself on a plain, but one which is elevated 3,000 feet above the point from which you started. **1944** A. HOLMES *Princ. Physical Geol.* xi. 201 Where closely spaced streams discharge from a mountainous area across a piedmont (a mountainfoot lowland), their deposits coalesce to form a piedmont alluvial plain. **1960** [see BAJADA]. **1962** *Times* 2 June 11/6 Those along the northern piedmont consider themselves Bughtis and owe their allegiance to the Nawab in the remote tribal capital of Dera Bughti. **1974** *Encycl. Brit. Micropædia* I. 741/3 A bajada is usually composed of gravelly alluvium... In humid climates, landforms of this nature are usually referred to as piedmonts.

3. (See quot. 1905¹.)

1905 H. T. FERRAR in R. F. Scott *Voy. 'Discovery'* II. 461 Large areas of ice which lie at the foot of high land and which have no obvious single source may be described as 'piedmonts'. *Ibid.*, Piedmonts afloat are by far the most important. **1914** [see *ice-shelf* s.v. ICE *sb.* 8].

4. *attrib.* or as *adj.* Situated or occurring at the foot of a mountain or mountain range.

1891 I. C. RUSSELL in *Nat. Geogr. Mag.* May 122 The Malaspina glacier belongs to a class of ice bodies not previously recognized, which are formed at the bases of mountains by the union of several glaciers from above. Their position suggests the name of *Piedmont glaciers* for the type. **1905** W. H. NORTON *Elem. Geol.* iv. 99 Mountain streams may build their confluent fans into widespread piedmont (foot of the mountain) alluvial plains. **1907** *Bull. Geol. Soc. Amer.* XVIII. 355 On leaving the mountains the Tarim river enters the great plain which forms the floor of the Lop, or Tarim basin... At the lower ends of many small streams which now wither to nothing in the piedmont gravel or sand of the basin floor, there are old channels and strips of vegetation. **1936** P. FLEMING *News from Tartary* 334 It brought us to Igiz Yar, a little oasis on a rolling slope of piedmont gravel. **1942** [see PEDIPLANE]. **1957** G. E. HUTCHINSON *Treat. Limnol.* I. i. 57 The numerous and remarkable large lakes produced in piedmont regions. **1962** *Times* 2 June 11/6 The piedmont zone of hill slopes has long formed the ethnic frontier between the plundering hill men and the peaceful Sindhi cultivators. **1965** [see OUED]. **1974** *Nature* 29 Nov. 373/1 The United States Range where piedmont glaciers descend southwards along the northern edge of the Hazen Plateau. **1976** R. C. SELLEY *Introd. Sedimentol.* viii. 257 Between mountains and adjacent lowlands it is often possible to define a distinct belt known as the piedmont zone.

Piedmontese (pi:dmɒn'ti:z), *sb.* and *a.* Also 7 **Piemontese**. [f. *Piedmont* (see prec.) + -ESE.]

A. *sb.* **a.** The dialect of Piedmont in Italy. **b.** A native or inhabitant of Piedmont. **B.** *adj.* Of or pertaining to Piedmont, its inhabitants, or the dialect spoken by them.

1642 [see MILANESE *sb.* 3]. **1655** MILTON *Poems* (1925) I. 236 Slain by the bloody Piemontese. **1673** J. RAY *Observations Journey Low-Countries* 249 The Piemontese are generally well to live. **1768** STERNE *Sentimental Journey* II. 200 The lady was a Piedmontese of about thirty. **1770** [see COURIER 3]. **1776** LADY A. MILLER *Lett. from Italy* I. 90 The Spanish army.. had not failed to guard all the passes they knew of, in order that no communication should be kept up between the Savoyards, the Piedmontese, and Swiss army. **1846** DICKENS *Let.* 22 June (1977) IV. 568 It [*sc.* Lausanne] contains only one Roman Catholic church, which is mainly for the use of the Savoyards and Piedmontese. **1858** A. GALLENGA *Country Life in Piedmont* 31 There is hardly an instance of a Piedmontese mountaineer settling permanently abroad. *Ibid.* 128, I have tried to convince the Piedmontese Press that [etc.]. **1878**, **1880** [see EMILIAN *a.* and *sb.*]. **1902** *Encycl. Brit.* XXXI. 769/2 The Piedmontese dialect has been rather strongly influenced by French. **1927**, etc. [see LIGURIAN *sb.*]. **1931** *Times Lit. Suppl.* 15 Oct. 787/2 The young Prince.. was made commandant of the Piedmontese artillery. **1932** G. F.-H. BERKELEY *Italy in Making* I. xi. 160 Of course Gioberti was a Piedmontese, and in Piedmont the people were satisfied. **1968** D. M. SMITH *Mod. Sicily* xlviii. 446 Observers remarked on a tremendous feeling against everything which smacked of Piedmontese. **1974** *Times* 1 Feb. 18/4 After his death the secretaryship passed on [to] Luigi Longo, a dour Piedmontese. **1977** *Canad. Jrnl. Linguistics* XXII. I. 17 *The Sermoni Subalpini*.. is the first extant Piedmontese document.

piedmontite ('pi:dmɒntaɪt, 'pje:m-). *Min.* [Alteration (by J. D. Dana) of G. *piemontit*: see PIEMONTITE.] = PIEMONTITE.

1854 DANA *Min.* Index, Piedmontite. **1894** *Min. Mag.* X. 261 In the rhyolites the manganese-epidote, Piedmontite, is widely distributed. **1933** *Mineral. Mag.* XXIII. 417 The pleochroic colours shown by the mineral in thin section closely resemble those of piedmontite from Japan and from South Mountain, Pennsylvania. **1961** *Current Sci.* XXX. 223/1 (*heading*) Some observations on piedmontite from Goldongri Manganese Mine.

piedness ('paɪdnɪs). [f. PIED *a.* + -NESS.] The quality of being pied; or parti-coloured.

1600 HAKLUYT *Voy.* III. 269 For their likenesse and vniformity in roundnesse, orientnesse, and pidenesse of many excellent colours. **1635** HEYWOOD *Hierarch.* III. 142 Superfluous Fare and Pydenesse in Attyre. **1843** *Tait's Mag.* X. 617 By what process goose-berries may be made gigantic, and piccotees enriched with piedness.

‖**pied noir** (pje nwar). Pl. pieds noirs. [Fr., = black foot.] A name given to people of French origin living in Algeria during French rule, and to those who returned to Europe after the granting of independence to Algeria in 1962.

The name was applied formerly to Algerian stokers who worked bare-footed on French cargo-boats, and by extension, to Algerians generally.

1961 *Times* 6 May 9/6 They are the *pieds noirs*, fiercely proud of this pejorative nickname given them by the metropolitan French. **1962** *Economist* 28 Apr. 344/3 Returned conscripts [from Algeria] and vacationing *pieds noirs*..played an important part in informing the public. **1963** *Times Lit. Suppl.* 31 May 384/3 These two large monographs are devoted to painters—both dead—..the one Flemish, the other a *pied noir* from Constantine. **1965** *Economist* 27 Mar. 1365/1 Marseilles, a sprawling city with an ethnically mixed-up population—Greek, Armenian, Italian, Corsican, and now *pied-noir* from North Africa—has a certain charm. **1969** *Listener* 27 Mar. 417/2 M. Fabre was an elderly colon, one of the original French families in Algeria—a *pied noir*, as they like to be called. **1972** D. Lees *Zodiac* 9 This one..was called Daria-Daria Massenet, which made her a Pied Noir. **1977** *Time* 21 Nov. 12/1 Unlike the white settlers of Rhodesia or the French *pieds-noirs* of Algeria, the Afrikaners have no ties to a European motherland.

pie-dog: see PYE-DOG.

‖**piedouche** (pjeduʃ). [F. *piédouche*, ad. It. *pieduccio*, dim. of *piede* foot.] A small pedestal.

1704 J. Harris *Lex. Techn.* I, *Piedouche*, in Architecture, is a little Square Base smoothed, and wrought with Mouldings, which serves to support a Bust or Statue drawn half way, or any small Figure in Relief. **1727–41** in Chambers *Cycl.*, and in mod. Dicts.

‖**piedra** (ˈpjɛdrə). *Path.* [Sp. *piedra* stone:—L. *petra*.] An epiphytic affection of the hair, prevalent in certain parts of Colombia, in S. America.

1895 *Westm. Gaz.* 20 May 8/1 Dr. Unna recognised the disease as 'piedra', which is chiefly met with in Colombia. **1898** P. Manson *Trop. Diseases* xxxvii. 587 Piedra is supposed by some to be induced by the mucilaginous hair applications in vogue among the Colombians.

‖**piedroit** (pjedrwa). *Arch.* [F. *pied droit*, lit. 'straight foot', the vertical wall supporting an arch, also as below.] A square pier or pillar attached to a wall, which differs from a pilaster in having neither base nor capital.

1696 Phillips (ed. 5), *Piedroit* [*ed.* **1706** *Pied-droit*], a square Pillar, that is partly within the Wall. **1704** J. Harris *Lex. Techn.* I, *Pied-droit*, in Architecture, is a Square Pillar, differing from a Pillaster in this respect, that it hath no Base nor Capital: It is taken also for part of the Jaumbs of a Door or Window. **1723** Chambers tr. *Le Clerc's Treat. Archit.* I. 38 Cornices which terminate the Piedroits of Portico's.

pie-eyed (paɪˈaɪd), *a. slang* (orig. *U.S.*). [f. PIE *sb.*[2] + EYED *ppl. a.*] Intoxicated to such an extent that vision is affected; drunk.

1904 Ade *True Bills* 41 They put him down at a Table and sat around him and inhaled the Scotch until they were all Pie-Eyed. **1910** S. E. White *Rules of Game* I. xvii. 103 'Oh, *he's* in town..' 'Drunk, eh?' 'Spifflicated, pie-eyed, loaded, soshed.' **1924** *T.P.'s & Cassell's Weekly* 6 Sept. 631/1 He is partial to a 'shot of gin', and on occasion will drink till he is 'pie-eyed'. **1924** Wodehouse *Ukridge* x. 256 What they put in that stuff..I don't know, but the fact remains that the bird almost instantly became perfectly pie-eyed. **1932** —— *Hot Water* iii. 89 It is our great fancy costume carnival... Everybody puts on funny clothes and becomes pie-eyed. **1937** *Daily Express* 27 Jan. 19/1 Personally I didn't care if the whole band was pie-eyed, I wanted them to be busy playing good dance music. **1946** E. O'Neill *Iceman Cometh* IV. 225 Why the hell don't you get pie-eyed and celebrate? **1957** J. Braine *Room at Top* xxx. 255 'You are pie-eyed, aren't you?' Eva said. **1959** 'J. Christopher' *Scent of White Poppies* iii. 43 He was utterly pie-eyed. He could scarcely talk straight. **1970** *New Yorker* 8 Aug. 34/2 Piet, who is pie-eyed drunk and needs to be helped homeward. **1974** N. Freeling *Dressing of Diamond* 32 You shouldn't be driving at all, you're pie-eyed.

pie-face (ˈpaɪfeɪs). [f. PIE *sb.*[2] + FACE *sb.* I.] A person of round or blank countenance; a stupid person. (In quot. 1922 used of an effeminate man.)

1922 S. Lewis *Babbitt* vii. 99 Oh, there's a swell bunch of Lizzie boys and lemon-suckers and pie-faces. **1930** *Amer. Speech* VI. 92 The following expressions belong to colloquialisms and slang, including movie and radio neologisms... *Pie-face*. **1960** Wentworth & Flexner *Dict. Amer. Slang* 388/2 *Pie-face*, a person with a round face and a blank, funny, or homely expression; a stupid person.

pie-faced, *a.* [f. PIE *sb.*[2] + FACED *ppl. a.*[2]] Of a person, having a round countenance or a blank or solemn facial expression; stupid. Now commonly used as a general term of mild abuse (see also quot. 1939). Also *transf.*

Quot. 1955 may represent PIE *a.*[1] rather than PIE *sb.*[2]

1912 *Dialect Notes* III. 585 *Pie-faced*,..round-faced; flat-faced. **1923** Wodehouse *Inimitable Jeeves* x. 112 Did you put that pie-faced infant up to bally-ragging Mr. Bassington-Bassington? **1935** —— *Luck of Bodkins* xiv. 147 You don't suppose I care what old pie-faced Gertrude thinks of me, do you? **1938** G. Heyer *Blunt Instrument* x. 183 'Pie-faced creature, with a nasty, sly smile.' 'The Mona Lisa!' **1939** J. B. Priestley *Let People Sing* i. 17 He was disturbed again, this time by..a messy, dribbling, pie-faced urchin. **1955** *Times* 29 Aug. 10/7 They spare us those moments of pie-faced solemnity with which comic dramatists here are wont to becloud their activities.

piefinch (ˈpaɪfɪnʃ). [f. PIE *sb.*[1] 5 b + FINCH.] A local name of the chaffinch.

1848 *Zoologist* VI. 2191 In Warwickshire, as elsewhere,.. the chaffinch [is] a 'piefinch'.

pie-gow, var. PAI KAU.

pie in the sky. *colloq.* (orig. *U.S.*). [see PIE *sb.*[2] 4.] A prospect, often illusory, of future happiness, esp. as a reward in heaven for virtue or suffering on earth; an extravagant promise that is unlikely to be fulfulled. Also (with hyphens) *attrib.* Hence **pie-in-the-skyer**, one who puts forward a prospect or promise of this kind.

1911 J. Hill in G. M. Smith *Joe Hill* (1969) i. 20 You'll get pie in the sky when you die. **1926** *Amer. Mercury* Jan. 65/1 *Pie in the sky* is a somewhat cynical reference to the bourgeois heaven. **1939** N. Monsarrat *This is Schoolroom* IV. xviii. 426 Christianity..would end by backing the guns, blessing the flags, and preaching pie-in-the-sky-when-you-die. **1941** *Archit. Rev.* LXXXIX. 117/1 Utopianism, or wishful-thinking, or pie-in-the-sky, or whatever we care to call it. **1951** [see JAM *sb.*[2] b]. **1951** R. Hoggart *Auden* vi. 190 He is afraid that God will be just a woozy dream, pie-in-the-sky, to his subjects. **1958** *Times Lit. Suppl.* 26 Dec. 750/4 Rightly mistrusting the idea of 'pie in the sky', he [*sc.* the American] expects to have his reward here. **1959** *Sunday Express* 30 Aug. 12/7 With the election moving remorselessly nearer, pie-in-the-sky days are here again. Everything our hearts could desire is promised us by politicians. **1960** O. Manning *Great Fortune* vi. 79 Pie in the sky. Accept the condition it has pleased God to put you in. **1962** *Times* 11 Oct. 10/5 General Eisenhower has attacked the Kennedy Administration as a 'pie-in-the-sky' Government. **1971** *Physics Bull.* June 322/1 Is this just pie-in-the-sky dreaming about some utopian future where there will be no more pollution, poverty, malnutrition and similar afflictions? **1973** *Time* 25 June 4/2 Exposing shenanigans, militants, self-servers and pie-in-the-skyers must be done, no matter how or by whom. **1975** *Listener* 16 Jan. 89/1 Pie-in-the-sky wage claims. **1976** E. Maclaren *Nature of Belief* iv. 34 The point is obvious when the argument for belief is as crude as some traditional pie-in-the-sky promises. **1977** *Undercurrents* June-July 12/1 To expert the NHS to encompass all sorts of fringe or alternative practices whilst even the level of basic medical care that people want is unobtainable in some areas (abortion) is pie in the sky.

piejamah, variant of PYJAMA.

pie-jim-jams (paɪˈdʒɪmdʒæmz). A child's name for 'pyjamas'.

1902 *Little Folks* Apr. 265/2 'Why! I'm in my pie-jimjams!' he murmured..with a doubtful look at his bare feet and his pyjamas. **1964** M. Laski in S. Nowell-Smith *Edwardian England* iv. 204 For bedwear, pyjamas—'pie-jim-jams'—were recommended for boys and girls alike.

piel (piːl). *Sc.* 'An iron wedge for boring stones' (Jamieson, 1808). (North of Scotl.)

1858 in Simmonds *Dict. Trade*. Hence **1864** in Webster, etc.

piel, pielage, pieled, pieler, pieller, obs. ff. PEEL, PILLAGE, PILED, PEELED, PEELER[1].

pi electron: see PI *sb.* 3.

pieless (ˈpaɪlɪs), *a.* [f. PIE *sb.*[2] + -LESS.] Without a pie; having no pies.

1836–48 Walsh *Aristoph., Knights* III. i, Why, that he'll seize on the pie-lass, And rob her and render her pieless. **1901** *Daily News* 9 Mar. 5/1 We think we would sooner pay our money..and go pieless.

pielet (ˈpaɪlɪt). [See -LET.] A small pie.

1881 Wilmington in *Delaware Morn. News* IV. No. 44. 2 It..was too much like a dinner in tarts and pielets. **1896** *Westm. Gaz.* 24 Dec. 2/3 Extend to it the caution you bestow on pielets of mince and puddings of plums.

†**pielf**, variant of PELF *v. Obs.*, to pilfer.

1542 Udall *Erasm. Apoph.* 105 A poore sely folle that hath percase pielfed away tenne grotes. *Ibid.* 126 The one partie had pielfed, or embesleed awaye a thyng of the others.

piemag (ˈpaɪmæg). [f. PIE *sb.*[1] + MAG *sb.*[2]] A local name of the Magpie.

1885 Swainson *Prov. Names Birds* 75–6 Magpie..Pye Mag (Hundred of Lonsdale). Pie nanny, do.

pieman (ˈpaɪmən). A man who makes pies for sale; a vendor of pies.

c **1820** *Nursery Rime*, Simple Simon Met a Pyeman, Going to the Fair; Says Simple Simon To the Pyeman, Let me taste your ware. **1823** *Blackw. Mag.* XIV. 508 The flying pieman ceases his call. **1865** *Sat. Rev.* 12 Aug. 204/2 Beware of cheap cook-shops and itinerant piemen.

piement, -mento, var. of PIMENT, PIMENTO.

piemontite (ˈpiːmɒntaɪt). *Min.* [ad. G. *piemontit* (G. A. Kenngott *Das Mohs'sche Mineralsystem* (1853) 75), f. *Piedmont* (It. *Piemonte*, lit. Mount-foot), its locality + -ITE 2 b.] A brownish red or reddish black silicate of aluminium, iron, manganese, and calcium, resembling epidote; often called manganese epidote. Also called PIEDMONTITE.

Adopted in place of PIEDMONTITE as more in accord with the original Ger. spelling and with European practice.

1892 E. S. Dana *Dana's Syst. Min.* (ed. 6) 1125/3 (Index), Piedmontite 521. Piemontite, 521. **1950** *Arsbok Sveriges Geologiska Undersökning* XLIV. II. 15 In some parts of the limestone,..crystalline masses of piemontite appear in zones measuring many meters in thickness. **1956** *Mineral Mag.* XXXI. 241 The piemontite from the schist is granular in form, ruby red, and has pearly lustre. **1971** *Ibid.* XXXVIII. 104 Recommendations of the Commission [on New Minerals and Mineral Names of the International Mineralogical Association] on minerals for which more than one name is in common use... Piemontite, not piedmontite. **1973** *Canad. Jrnl. Earth Sci.* X. 1401/1 Most piemontites are the product of metasomatic or low-grade regional metamorphism of manganiferous rocks.

piend (piːnd). *Arch. local.* [Origin unascertained.] The edge or angle formed by the meeting of two surfaces. Also *attrib.*, as ***piend check, joint, rafter, stone, tree***.

1842–76 Gwilt *Archit.* Gloss., *Piend*, an arris; a salient angle; a hip. It is a northern appellation. *Ibid.*, *Piend Check*, the rebate formed on the piend or angle at the bottom of the riser of a stone step of a stair, to catch upon the angle formed at the top of the under step. **1881** *Archit. Publ. Soc. Dict.*, *Pien*, *Peind* or *Piend*, a term used in the south-west districts of Scotland, being the hip rafter of a roof. It is sometimes called 'pien-tree'. *Pien stone*, the stone covering the rafter in continuation of the ridge stones.

piend, dial. form of PEIN *sb.*

1882 in Ogilvie.

pienet (ˈpaɪnɪt). *local.* [A deriv. of PIE *sb.*[1]: perh. the same as PIANNET.]

1. A name of the sea-pie or oyster-catcher.

1833 *G. Montagu's Ornith. Dict.* 351 Oyster-catcher.. provincial, Pienet, Olive. **1885** Swainson *Prov. Names Birds* 188 Pienet.

2. A local form of Piannet, the magpie.

1900 in *Eng. Dial. Dict.* s.v. *Pianet*, Pienet, *W. Yorksh.*

piep, obs. form of PEEP *v.*[1]

piepowder (ˈpaɪpaʊdə(r)), *a.* and *sb.* Forms: 3 (*adj.*) pepoudrous, -rus, *Sc.* piepowdrous, pipouderous, -rus, pipuderous, 5 pypoudrus; (*sb.*) 4 pipoudre, 5–6 pepowder, 5–9 pipowder, 6 pipoulder, 6–8 pye(-)powder, 7 pye-poulder, -pouldre, pi-, pie-, pypouder, pypoudre, 7–8 py(-)powder, 7– pie(-)powder, 8– pie(-)poudre. [Anglo-Fr. had in 13th c. *piepuldrus*, *-pouldrous*, *-poudrous* = F. *pied-poudreux* adj., sing. and pl., = med.(Anglo-)L. *pede-pulverōsus* dusty of foot, dusty-footed, also as sb., a dusty-footed man, a DUSTYFOOT, a wayfarer, itinerant merchant, etc.; found also in 15th c. English, and in 15–16th c. Scottish versions of the Burgh Laws. ME. had *pie-poudres*, *pie-powders* sb. pl., wayfarers, esp. in the designation *Court of Piepowders* = Court of wayfarers or travelling traders, whence through the attrib. use in *Piepowder Court* came the less correct *Court of Piepowder*.]

†**1.** (*piepoudrous*, etc.) *adj.* 'Dusty-footed'; wayfaring, itinerant; *absol.* as *sb. sing.* and *pl.* = 2. *Obs.*

1220–1 *Liber Albus* (Rolls) I. 67 Terminare querelas transeuntium per villam qui moram non poterunt facere, qui dicuntur *pepoudrous*. *a* **1267** Bracton V. I. vi. §6 (Rolls) 126–7 Propter personas qui celerem habere debent justitiam, sicut sunt mercatores quibus exibetur justitia pepoudrous [*v.r.* pepoudrus]. *a* **1300** *Leges Burg.* xxix. in *Stat. Scotl.* I. App. v. 361 De placito inter piepoudrous [*Skene*, pede pulverosum et alios]. Si quis extraneus mercator..vagans qui vocatur piepowdrous [*Skene*, piepouldreux] hoc est anglice dustifute [tr. *a* **1500** Ony stranger man merchand..beand vagabund in þe contre þe quhilk is callit pipouderus]. *Ibid.* xxxi. *ibid.* 362 Burgensses qui sunt mercatores et pedepuluerosi [*tr.* Burges or merchandis or pipouderous]. *a* **1436** *Domesday Ipswich* in *Black Bk. Admir.* (Rolls) II. 23 The plees be twixe straunge folk that men clepeth pypoudrus, shuldene ben pleted from day to day. **1609** Skene *Reg. Maj., Burrow Lawes* 136 Ane stranger merchand..vaigand fra ane place to ane other, quha therefore is called *pied-puldreux*, or dustifute.

2. (*piepowder*) *sb.* †**a.** A travelling man, a wayfarer, *esp.* an itinerant merchant or trader. Chiefly used in ***Court of Piepowders***, a summary court formerly held at fairs and markets to administer justice among itinerant dealers and others temporarily present.

1399 Langl. *Rich. Redeles* III. 319 To ben of conceill ffor causis þat in þe court hangid, And pledid pipoudris alle manere pleyntis. **1477** *Rolls of Parlt.* VI. 187 To iche of the same Feyres is of right perteynyng a Court of Pepowders. **1531** *Dial. on Laws Eng.* I. vii. (1638) 13 To every fair and market is incident..a Court of Pipowders. **1614** B. Jonson *Bart. Fair* II. i, Many are the yeerely enormities of this Fayre, in whose Courts of Pye-pouldres I haue had the honour during the three dayes sometimes to sit as Iudge. **1658** Phillips, *Piepouders Court* [*ed.* **1678** *Pie-Powders* Court; **1706** *Pie-Powder Court*]. *a* **1735** Arbuthnot *John Bull* II. xvi, Dost think, that John Bull will be tried by Piepowders?

b. *attrib.* and *sb. sing.* esp. in ***Piepowder Court, Court of Piepowder*** = *Court of Piepowders* (in a).

1574 in *10th Rep. Hist. MSS. Comm.* App. v. 335 That the citie, by auncient usage have a Pipoulder Courte, commonly called the Courte of Delyverannce, for thexpedition of strangers. **1631** Brathwait *Whimzies, Pedlar* 138 His pypouder court is his onely terror. **1664** Butler *Hud.* II. II. 306 To..Have its Proceedings disallow'd, or Allow'd, at fancy of Py-powder. **1671** F. Phillips *Reg. Necess.* 180 The Steward of the Sheriffs Turn, or a Leet, or of a Court of Piepowder. **1768** Blackstone *Comm.* III. iv. 32 The lowest, and at the same time the most expeditious, court of justice known to the law of England is the court of *piepoudre, curia pedis pulverizati*. *a* **1797** H. WALPOLE *Geo. II* (1847) II. iii. 113 Such poor little shifts and evasions might do in a pie-poudre court. **1881** *Newcastle Proclam. of Fair* in *Antiquary* Oct. 180/2 Notice is Hereby Further Given, That a Court of Piepowder will be holden during the time of this Fair, that is to say, one in the forenoon, another in the afternoon. **1896** *Daily News* 21 July 8/3 The government of the town [Hemel Hempstead] at present ostensibly rests in a Bailiff, Bailiff's Committee, and Court of Pie Poudre, though in reality in the Parish and District Councils.

†**pier**, *sb.*¹ *Obs. rare.* [a. OF. *piere, pierre* stone:—L. *petra*, Gr. πέτρα rock.] A stone: in *fraunche pier*, F. *franche pierre*, FREESTONE; *precious pier*, F. *pierre précieuse*, precious stone.

a **1400–50** *Alexander* 4356 Ne nouthire housing we haue, ay quils we here duell Bot at is fetid of flesch & of na fraunche piers. *Ibid.* 5270 Onycles & orfrays & orient perles ..with þire precious piers of paradise stremes.

pier (pɪə(r)), *sb.*² Forms: 2–4 per, 4–8 pere, 5–8 peer, (6 piere, pyre, pyerre), 6–7 peere, peir, pire, (8 peor), 6– pier. [In 12th c. *per*, rendering med.L. *pera* (prob. *pēra*), of unknown origin.

It was suggested by Lambard, Spelman, and Du Cange, that *pera* was derived from OF. *piere* or L. *petra* stone, but this satisfies neither the phonetics nor the signification. There is an OF. (Picard and Flamand) word *pire* (rarely *piere* Godef.), meaning a breakwater or barricade of piles, a weir on a river, a boom defending a harbour, which might perh. have given the sense, but it is difficult to equate the form with *pēra* and *pēr*.]

1. One of the supports of the spans of a bridge, whether arched or otherwise formed.

(Appears in 12th c. and then not till end of 14th; examples not numerous till 17th c.)

c **1150** *Rochester Bridge-bote Charter* in Birch *Cart. Sax.* III. 657 Primum ejusdem civitatis episcopus incipit operari in orientali brachio [pontis] primam peram de terra: deinde tres virgatas planeas ponere, & tres sulinas .i. tres magnas trabes supponere... Secunda pera pertinet ad gillingeham & de cætham [etc.]. *Ibid.* 659 [*OE. version*] Ærest þære burȝe biscop fæhð on þone earm to wercene þa land peran & þreo ȝyrda to þillianne, & iii sylla to lyccanne... Ðonne seo oþer per ȝebyrað to gyllingeham & to Cætham [etc.; nine examples of *per*]. *c* **1380** *Sir Ferumb.* 1682 Sixty pers [*error for* arches, F. *xxx ars*] þar buþ þar-on þat buth grete & rounde. *Ibid.* 1684 Oppon ech pere þar stent a tour [F. *x breteques y a, chascune sor piler*] enbataild wyþ queynte engynne. *c* **1440** *Promp. Parv.* 394/1 Pere, or pyle of a brygge, or other fundament, *pila*. **1624** WOTTON *Archit.* in *Reliq.* (1651) 238 Pilasters must not be..too Dwarfish and grosse, lest they imitate the Piles and Peers of Bridges. **1718** ROWE tr. *Lucan* IV. 24 A stable Bridge runs cross from Side to Side,..And jutting Peers the wint'ry Floods abide. **1756–7** tr. *Keysler's Trav.* (1760) III. 133 The harbour of Puzzuolo..is formed by fourteen piers, or pilasters, rising above the surface of the water, which were anciently joined together by arches. **1761** *Brit. Mag.* II. 333 Tuesday, June 23. The first stone of the first pier of Black-Friars bridge, was laid. *a* **1842** ARNOLD *Later Hist. Rome* (1846) II. xii. 419 The emperor Hadrianus..took away all the upper part of the bridge, and left merely the piers standing. **1866** BRANDE & Cox *Dict. Sc.* II. 902/2 An abutment pier in a bridge is that next the shore; and, generally, this is made of a greater mass than the intermediate piers.

2. a. A solid structure of stone, or of earth faced with piles, extending into the sea or a tidal river to protect or partially enclose a harbour and form a landing-place for vessels; a breakwater, a mole; in modern times, also of iron or wood, open beneath and supported on columns or piles, forming a pleasure promenade and place of resort, or combining this purpose with that of a landing-place; also, a projecting landing-stage or jetty on the bank of a river or lake, as the piers on the Thames in London.

[**1390** *Pat. Roll 14 Rich. II*, II. m. 44 Concessimus vobis in auxilium construccionis cuiusdam pere per vos iam nouiter pro saluacione et defensione nauium et batellorum in Conuerso vocato Crowemere.] **1453** in W. Rye *Cromer* (1889) 56 *note*, [Will of John Bound, leaving] sustentacioni fretisfragii alias vocati le pere viij.s. **1487** *Ibid.*, [Will of Rich. Fenne] emend' le peer [3s 4d]. **1511** *Regist. Mag. Sig. Reg. Scot.* (1882) 764/1 Rex..concessit preposito [etc.] burgi de Edinburgh..le Newhavin..libertate, et spatio, ad edificandum et prolungandum munitionem, viz. le pere et bulwark ejusdem. **1515** *Aberdeen Regr.* (1844) 94 To the reparatioun and biggin of thar common peir and key. **1530** *Test. Ebor.* (Surtees) V. 300 (*Will of J. Ledum, Whitby*) Also to the peir, if it go furthwardes, xls. **1530–1** in *Chron. Calais* (Camden) 123 Also the pere that standeth in the Fishers gapp, must be new made. **1545** *Act 37 Hen. VIII*, c. 14 (Preamble) Shippes Bootes and Vesselles..within the Key or Peere in the Haven of Scardburghe. **1546** *Reg. Privy Council Scot.* I. 39 To pass to the mercat croces of Edinburgh..Quenisferrie, pere and schore of Leith, Dunde,..and uthair places neidfull. **1551** in W. Rye *Cromer* (1889) 57 The same Inhabytantes hathe..defended the same by makyng of grete peeres. **1559** *Acts Privy Council* (1893) VII. 82 Sent to Dovour to vieu..the state of the blacke Bulwerke and pyerre there. **1559** *Contn. Fabyan's Chron.* VII. 706 The toune of Lithe also, and the hauen and pire destroied. **1572** BOSSEWELL *Armorie* II. 65 The mole or pere whiche Alexander the great had caused to bee made agaynste the citie of Tyre. **1582** N. LICHEFIELD tr. *Castanheda's Conq. E. Ind.* I. x. 26 b, There is a certain Piere or recife wheron the sea doth beat. **1610** B. JONSON *Alch.* III. iii, Our Castle, our cinque-Port, Our Douer pire. **1626** BACON *Sylva* §658 Timber..some are best for..Peers, that are sometimes Wet and some-times dry. **1656** BLOUNT *Glossogr.*, *Peere*,..seems properly to be a Fortress made against the Force of the Sea. **1677** OTWAY *Cheats of Scapin* II. i, We went to walk upon the Pier. **1708** J. C. *Compl. Collier* (1845) 52 There wants a Peor, as at Whitby and Burlington. **1721** PERRY *Daggenh. Breach* 33 He then resolv'd to square and compleat his Jetties, or Peers. **1726** LEONI *Alberti's Archit.* II. 121 To carry out a Pier into the Sea in order to fortifie a Port. **1823** LADY GRANVILLE *Lett.* (1894) I. 239, I have been all the morning on the Chain Pier [Brighton], which is delicious. **1852** MRS. CARLYLE *Lett.* II. 160 They..offered to land us at any pier we liked. **1884** PAE *Eustace* 119 The boats to be at the pier at noon.

transf. **1774** GOLDSM. *Nat. Hist.* (1776) IV. 161 This [beaver] dam, or pier, is often four score or an hundred feet long, and ten or twelve feet thick at the base. **1853** PHILLIPS *Rivers Yorks.* iv. 143 Nature has run out immoveable piers of hard lias shale with a long deep channel between them.

†**b.** *transf.* A haven. *Obs.*

a **1552** LELAND *Itin.* (1711) II. 60 [This] makith the Fascion of an Havenet, or Pere, whither Shippelettes sumtime resorte for socour. *Ibid.* III. 9 The Pere [at Pendinas] is sore chokid with Sande. **1600** HOLLAND *Livy* XXVIII. vi. 671 It maketh a shew of a double peere or haven [*portus*], opening upon two divers mouths, but in very truth, ther is not..a worse harborogh, & a more daungerous rode for ships. **1622** R. HAWKINS *Voy. S. Sea* (1847) 239 The cittie..hath also a pere in itselfe for small barkes; at full sea it may have some sixe or seaven foote water, but at low water it is drie. **1721** PERRY *Daggenh. Breach* 110 Preventing the rolling of the Beach from choaking up the Entrance into the Peer. *Ibid.* 114 Scowering away the Beach from the Mouth of the Peer.

3. *Arch.* and *Building.* A solid support of masonry or the like designed to sustain vertical pressure: **a.** A square pillar or pilaster; **b.** The solid masonry between doors, windows, or other openings in a wall; **c.** Each of the pillars from which an arch springs; **d.** Each of the pillars or posts of a gate or door; **e.** A solid structure of masonry or ironwork supporting a telescope or other large instrument.

1663 GERBIER *Counsel* 44 So must well proportioned window-cases be,..that the peeres of Brick or Stone between them, will fall to be of a fit width. **1666** *Act 18 & 19 Chas. II*, c. 8 §6 That there shall be Partie walls and Partie peeres sett out equally on each Builders ground. **1706** PHILLIPS (ed. Kersey), *Peer*..also a solid Wall between two Doors or Windows; also a sort of square Pillar. **1710** J. HARRIS *Lex. Techn.* II, *Peers*, in Architecture, are a kind of Pilasters or Buttresses for Support, Strength, and sometimes Ornament. **1727** BRADLEY *Fam. Dict.* s.v. *Greenhouse*, The Front [of a greenhouse] towards the South should be all of Glass,..there ought to be no Peers of Brick-work, or Timber in the glaz'd Part, for they cast more Shade into the House. **1823** P. NICHOLSON *Pract. Build.* 291 The mode, now commonly adopted, of constructing arches between piers of stone. **1836** PARKER *Gloss. Archit.* (1845) I. 283 *Pier*,..this name is often given to the pillars in Norman and Gothic architecture, but not very correctly. **1842–76** GWILT *Archit.* §2734 The composition..of gates and their piers. **1870** F. R. WILSON *Ch. Lindisf.* 140 The Saxon [tower] lay in ruins, save the piers. **1879** SIR G. G. SCOTT *Lect. Archit.* I. iii. 135 The piers destined to bear several arches divide themselves into as many columns as there are arches. **1883** *Knowledge* 15 June 357/2 To mount to the top of the pier and lubricate..the joints of the giant [telescope].

f. *transf.* and *fig.*

1611 in Gutch *Coll. Cur.* I. 113 By the King's summons to the parliament..as piers and strong rocks in the common-wealth. **1889** J. M. DUNCAN *Clin. Lect. Dis. Women* xxii. (ed. 4) 188 It lies between the posterior pier of a labium and the adjoining tuber ischii.

†**4.** Short for PIER-GLASS. *Obs. rare.*

1760–72 H. BROOKE *Fool of Qual.* (1809) II. 49, I dashed the piers and jars to shivers.

5. *attrib.* and *Comb.*, as (in sense 2) ***pier-crane, -fishing, -man, -master, -shed, -warden***; (in sense 3) ***pier-mullion, -order, -stone***; ***pier-supported*** adj.; **pier-arch**, an arch springing from piers; so **pier-arcade**; **pier-cap**, the cap of a gate-pier; **pier-looking-glass, -mirror** = PIER-GLASS; †**pier-reeve**, the officer in charge of a pier, a pier-master; **pier-stake**, one of the columns or piles on which a pier is supported; **pier-table**, a low table or bracket occupying the space between two windows, often under a pier-glass.

1879 SIR G. G. SCOTT *Lect. Archit.* I. 117 The triforium was united with the *pier-arcade. **1842–76** GWILT *Archit.* Gloss., **Pier Arch*, an arch springing from a pier. **1843** *Ecclesiologist* II. 51 A single arch of the same breadth as the pier-arch. **1897** *Daily News* 3 June 3/3 Charged..with wilfully damaging a *pier-cap. **1894** *Westm. Gaz.* 22 Oct. 5/3 At South Shields the *pier-crane was washed away. **1745** *De Foe's Eng. Tradesman* xxii. (1841) I. 207 Two large *pier looking-glasses, and one chimney-glass are in the shop. **1897** *Westm. Gaz.* 30 Nov. 5/2 One *pierman..declared..that last night was the highest tide he had known. **1936** J. GRIERSON *High Failure* ii. 27, I slept in the *piermaster's cottage in order to be as near my machine as possible. **1971** *Daily Tel.* 16 July 7/1, I liked the pier-master, pompous but human in nautical beard and gold braid. **1976** *Southern Even. Echo* (Southampton) 11 Nov. (Advt. Suppl.) 12/7 Fairey Yacht Harbours Pier Master required for yacht harbour. **1863** O. W. NORTON *Army Lett.* (1903) 185 *Pier mirrors twenty feet high on three sides of the room. **1969** *Sears Catal.* Spring/Summer 1295, 2-piece pier table and mirror set. **1901** P. M. JOHNSON in *Archæol. Jrnl.* Mar. 64 The east window consists of two broad lancets divided by a wide *pier-mullion. **1879** SIR G. G. SCOTT *Lect. Archit.* II. 76 An arch-order may be moulded or otherwise decorated, while the corresponding *pier-order may remain square. **1591** *Replication* in Rye *Cromer* (1889) p. lviii, He was lately *Pereive of the said Peire. *Ibid.* p. lix, Perereves. **1927** JOYCE *On Beach at Fontana* in *Pomes Penyeach*, Wind whines and whines the shingle, The crazy *pierstakes groan. **1955** A. ROSS *Australia 55* ix. 122 Watching schools of parrot fish and pike twist among the pier-stakes. **1667** PRIMATT *City & C. Build.* 68 *Peer-stones on both sides the Building, fronting high and principal Streets. **1803** M. WILMOT *Let.* 25 July in *Russ. Jrnls.* (1934) I. 24 A *pier table furnish'd with splendid Gilt China cups and saucers 'wisely kept for shew'. **1856** MRS. HAWTHORNE in *N. Hawthorne & Wife* (1885) II. 90 In front of a golden pier-table over which hung a vast mirror. **1952** J. GLOAG *Short Dict. Furnit.* 361 (*caption*) Pier glass and pier table, designed as a decorative unit. **1979** W. J. BURLEY *Charles & Elizabeth* v. 81 A pair of carved and gilded pier tables with mirrors above. **1657** in *Sussex Archæol. Coll.* (1862) XIV. 96 That all persons..bring the same [timbers, etc.] unto the *Peere Wardens.

pier (pɪə(r)), *v. rare.* [f. PIER *sb.*²] **a.** *trans.* To provide with a pier. **b.** *intr.* To reach *out* like a pier.

1857 *Trans. Mich. Agric. Soc.* VIII. 731 If they can coax Uncle Sam to pier the outlet of that Lake and make it a splendid harbor for navigable purposes. **1951** W. SANSOM *Face of Innocence* iii. 25 Above them the curved glass cupola ..that goes piering out over the garden.

pierage ('pɪərɪdʒ). [f. PIER *sb.*² + -AGE.] †**a.** The use of, or privilege of using, a pier or wharf (*obs.*). **b.** The toll or fee paid for this; wharfage.

c **1599** in J. J. Cartwright *Chapters Hist. Yorks.* (1872) 273 The fees due for anchorage and perage. **1656** BLOUNT *Glossogr.*, *Peerage*, which word may also signifie an Imposition for maintenance of a Sea-peer. **1809** R. LANGFORD *Introd. Trade* 134 *Pierage*, money paid for the use of a pier or wharf. **1894** *Manch. Even. News* 7 Nov. 2/7 Vessels entering the port..will only be charged a moderate pierage.

pierce (pɪəs), *v.* Forms: α. 3–6 perce, (4 parse), 4–6 perse, *Sc.* perss(e, 5 peerce, peerse, 6 *Sc.* peirs(e, pers, pairse, 6–7 pearce, pearse, pierse, 6–8 peirce, 6– pierce. β. 4–5 persche, persshe, perisse, -ische, perisshe, -issche, 4–6 perch(e, perish(e, 5 pershe, peresche, 5–6 perysshe, 6–7 (9 *dial.*) pearch. [a. OF. *percer*, earlier *percier* (11–12th c., also *persier* 13th c.), ONF. *perchier*, mod. Picard *percher*; ulterior etymology uncertain.

Ménage, Diez, Burguy, Hatz.-Darm. take *percer* as:—L. type **pertusiāre*, deriv. of L. *pertundĕre* to thrust or bore through (pa. pple. *pertūsus*, n. of action *pertūsio*), although the contraction *pertusier, pert'sier, percier* is violent, and there are the full forms F. *pertuiser*, Pr. *pertusar*, It. *pertugiare*. For other conjectures see Littré and Scheler. The β-forms appear to have been confused with those of *perish* v.]

1. *trans.* To penetrate, or run through or into (a substance), as a sharp-pointed instrument does; of an agent: to thrust (anything) through *with* such an instrument; to stab, prick, puncture.

1297 R. GLOUC. (Rolls) 9019 Þei it ne percede noȝt þat yre þat blod vaste adoun drou. *c* **1315** SHOREHAM *Poems* (E.E.T.S.) i. 2209 Þo hand and fet and al hys lymes I-persed were ine payne. **1375** BARBOUR *Bruce* XIV. 292 Scottis men.. perssit thar armyng. **1470–85** MALORY *Arthur* XVI. viii. 675 Thenne they came to gyders with suche a raundon that they perced their sheldes and their hauberkes. **1526** TINDALE *John* xix. 37 They shall loke on hym, whom they pearsed. **1590** SPENSER *F.Q.* I. vi. 43 They perst both plate and maile. **1596** SHAKS. *1 Hen. IV*, V. iii. 59 If Percy be aliue, Ile pierce him: if he do come in my way. **1727–41** CHAMBERS *Cycl.*, *Piercing*, among farriers.—*To pierce a horse's shoe lean*, is to pierce it too near the edge of the iron.—*To pierce it fat* is to pierce it further in. **1784** COWPER *Task* III. 201 Pierce my vein, Take of the crimson stream meand'ring there, And catechise it well. **1860** TYNDALL *Glac.* I. ix. 62 The mighty Aiguilles piercing the sea of air. *Ibid.* II. xi. 290, I pierced the ice with the auger, drove in the stake, and descended.

β. **1377** LANGL. *P. Pl.* B. XVII. 189 Were þe myddel of myn honde ymaymed or ypersshed [*v.rr.* ypersed, I-perisshed]. *c* **1380** *Sir Ferumb.* 5301 Þe nayles three, & þe croune, þat perschede cryst on ys passyoune. *c* **1400** MAUNDEV. (Roxb.) xxi. 94 So þat þe bark be perched; and þan commez oute a licour thikk. *c* **1500** *Joseph Arim.* (W. de W.) 31 His..handes & feet perysshed with the spere & nayles.

absol. *c* **1380** WYCLIF *Wks.* (1880) 288 Men stable in bileue ben a þick walle to turnen aȝen þis þondir þat it persiþ noȝt. **1576** FLEMING *Panopl. Epist.* 118 It is..as commendable to pearce to the bone, as to pare the skinne.

fig. **1526** *Pilgr. Perf.* (W. de W. 1531) 256 b, It myght not swage the malyce of the iewes, ne..pearse theyr pryde. **1557** N. T. (Genev.) *1 Tim.* vi. 10 They erred from the faith, and perced them selues throwe with many sorowes.

b. *transf.* and *fig.*; *spec.* said of the penetrating action of cold, etc.

1390 GOWER *Conf.* I. 294, I telle him schent, If he mai perce him with his tunge. **1563** *Mirr. Mag.*, *Induct.* 4 With chilling cold had pearst the tender green. **1697** DRYDEN *Virg. Georg.* III. 673 A scabby Tetter on their Pelts will stick, When the raw Rain has pierc'd them to the quick. **1832** HT. MARTINEAU *Ireland* iii. 44 Gusts of wind..piercing her with cold through her scanty raiment.

absol. **1562** BULLEYN *Bulwark*, *Dial. Soarnes & Chir.* 2 Colde weather draweth nere,..Borias perseth.

c. With various constructions and extensions.

a **1400–50** *Alexander* 3675 Þe thinnest was a nynche thicke quen þai ware þurȝe persed. *c* **1400** *Destr. Troy* 9477 Paris.. Waited the wegh in his wit ouer, In what plase of his person to perse of his wede. *c* **1485** *Digby Myst.* (1882) I. 99 I shall not spare..with sharpe sword to perse them all bare. **1535** COVERDALE *2 Kings* xviii. 21 This broken staffe of rede.. which who leaneth vpon, it shall go in to his hande, & pearse it thorow. **1781** GIBBON *Decl. & F.* xix. II. 153 His only son ..was pierced through the heart by a javelin. **1840** THIRLWALL *Greece* VII. lvii. 216 Neoptolemus..pierced him in the groin. **1859** TENNYSON *Geraint & Enid* 104 Could I so stand by And see my dear lord..pierced to death?

2. To make a hole, opening, or tunnel into or through (something); to bore through, perforate; to broach (a cask, etc.).

13.. *Seuyn Sag.* (W.) 1148 In a thousand stede he let the tonne perce. *c* **1391** CHAUCER *Astrol.* I. §3 The moder of thin Astrelabie is þe thikkeste plate, perced with a large hole. *c* **1420** *Pallad. on Husb.* IX. 160 This must be doon by persyng the mountayn The water so to lede into the playn. **1432–50** tr. *Higden* (Rolls) I. 231 Marcus pereschenge the walle of the cite [TREVISA, made an hole þorwe þ e wal]. **1579** in *10th Rep. Hist. MSS. Comm.* App. v. 429 Any suche butte or hogsed..pearched or drauin. **1656** STANLEY *Hist. Philos.* v. (1701) 211/2 Whensoever he pierced a Vessel of Wine, it was sowred before he spent it. **1687** A. LOVELL tr. *Thevenot's Trav.* I. 200 A neat Brazen Door..pierced through to let in light from above. **1798** *Hull Advertiser* 14 Apr. 2/4 Le Ceres, French ship privateer pierced for 14 guns. **1849** CURZON *Visits Monast.* (1897) 140 The mountain of Quarantina..is pierced all over with the caves excavated by the ancient anchorites. **1853** HOBBS & TOMLINSON *Locks* xi. 159 The process of piercing the key consists in making the pipe or barrel.

b. To make (a hole, etc.) by piercing.
c **1412** HOCCLEVE *De Reg. Princ.* 127 Yitte may we, by the persed holes well,..Behalde and see, that [etc.]. **1538** ELYOT, *Foro*..to perce or boore a hole. **1703** [see PIERCER 4]. **1859** HAWTHORNE *Fr. & It. Note-Bks.* II. 281 Narrow loopholes, pierced through the immensely thick wall. **1884** BAGSHAWE in *Law Times* 14 June 120/2 Valliant..pierced a doorway between the forge and the adjacent cottage.

3. To force one's way through or into; to succeed in penetrating; to break through or into; to break (an enemy's line). Also *fig.*
1297 R. GLOUC. (Rolls) 391 Corineus..made is wey bi eiþer side & percede þe route. **1362** LANGL. *P. Pl.* A. XI. 302 Suche lewide iottis Percen wiþ a pater noster þe paleis of heuene. **1432–50** tr. *Higden* (Rolls) V. 95 Alexander persynge the costes of Ynde in xij. yere. **1545** ASCHAM *Toxoph.* II. (Arb.) 136 Nature..made the rayne droppes rounde for quicke percynge the ayer. *Ibid.* 138 These [arrow] heades be good..to perche a wynde wythal. **1555** EDEN *Decades* To Rdr. (Arb.) 51 Neyther dydde any of his shyppes..perce the Ocean. **1599** SHAKS. *Hen. V*, IV. Prol. 11 Steed threatens Steed, in high and boastfull Neighs Piercing the Nights dull Eare. **1639** S. DU VERGER tr. *Camus' Admir. Events* 84 His magnificence and liberality..pierced the eyes of the people, and made him commendable. **1667** MILTON *P.L.* VI. 356 Where the might of Gabriel fought, And with fierce Ensignes pierc'd the deep array Of Moloc furious King. **1731** MEDLEY *Kolben's Cape G. Hope* I. 83 Some of them..had pierc'd the country several ways by command. **1878** H. M. STANLEY *Dark Cont.* II. xii. 334 The wide wild land which, by means of the greatest river of Africa, we have pierced.

4. To reach or penetrate with the sight or the mind; to see thoroughly into, discern. (Not now used with a personal or concrete obj. as in quot. 1640.)
a **1400–50** *Alexander* 5537 Þat he mi3t..with his se3t persee Ane & othire & all þing. *c* **1450** HOLLAND *Howlat* 318 Ernes..Quhilk in the firmament..Perses the sone, with thar sicht selcouth to herd. **1563** T. GALE *Antidot.* Pref. 2 The hard names of medicines by oft reding will be persed. **1614** RALEIGH *Hist. World* II. (1634) 374 [This] is wide of Saint Paul's meaning, so farre as my weak understanding can pierce it. **1640** *Prerog. Parl. in Eng.* in *Select. fr. Harl. Misc.* (1793) 244 My lord, learn of me, that there is none of you all, that can pierce the king. **1748** JOHNSON *Van. Hum. Wishes* 64 Attentive..to..pierce each scene with philosophick eye! **1814** CARY *Dante, Paradise* XXVIII. liii, Contemplating, I fail to pierce the cause. **1850** ROBERTSON *Serm.* Ser. III. iii. (1872) 36 He pierced the mysteries of nature.

†**b.** To 'go into' (a matter), to examine. *Obs.*
1640 YORKE *Union Hon., Battels* 12 Presently a Parliament was called at London, where matters being pierced againe, the King's side grew stronger dayly.

5. To penetrate with pain, grief, or other emotion; to wound or affect keenly; to touch or move deeply. In ***pierce the heart***, the notion is often more or less physical.
1387–8 T. USK *Test. Love* Prol. 8 Rude wordes and boystous percen the herte of the herer to the inrest point. *a* **1400–50** *Alexander* 5158 It mi3t a persid any hert to here how scho wepid. **1509** HAWES *Past. Pleas.* xix. (Percy Soc.) 88 O lady clere! that perste me at the rote. **1596** SHAKS. *Merch. V.* IV. i. 126 Can no prayers pierce thee? **1614** RALEIGH *Hist. World* III. (1634) 27 Cyrus being pierc't with Crœsus answer. **1715–20** POPE *Iliad* XI. 323 While pierc'd with grief the much-lov'd youth he view'd. **1833** TENNYSON *Fatima* v, My heart, pierced thro' with fierce delight.

6. *intr.* To enter, penetrate, or pass, as something sharp-pointed, *into* or *through*; †to make one's (or its) way *into, to, through*; *transf.* to project or jut sharply, have direction. Also *fig.*
1387 TREVISA *Higden* (Rolls) VIII. 85 Som of þe Iewes parsed among oþere and come with ynne þe paleys gate. *c* **1440** *Generydes* 2965 Thorough owt ye harnes persid ye spere. **1557** N. T. (Genev.) *Luke* ii. 35 Yea and a sword shal pearce through thy soule. **1600** E. BLOUNT tr. *Conestaggio* 9 They haue not pearst into the maine lande. **1610** SHAKS. *Temp.* II. i. 242 So high a hope, that euen Ambition cannot pierce a winke beyond. **1629** R. HILL *Pathw. Piety* (ed. Pickering) I. Pref. 4 True prayer..pierceth thither, whither flesh cannot come. **1639** FULLER *Holy War* III. xiii. (1840) 137 King Richard..intended to pierce through Germany by land, the nearest way home. **1667** MILTON *P.L.* IV. 99 Where wounds of deadly hate have peirc'd so deep. **1698** KEILL *Exam. The. Earth* (1734) 241 It is suppos'd..that..the heat of the Sun must have peirced thro' the Crust of the Earth, and reached the Abyss. **1724** DE FOE *Mem. Cavalier* (1840) 89 My lord Craven..pierced in with us, fighting gallantly in the breach. **1872** BLACK *Adv. Phaeton* xxi, Narrow promontories, piercing out into the water.

b. *transf.* and *fig.* To penetrate with the mind or the sight *into* (anything); to see *into*.
1549 COVERDALE, etc. *Erasm. Par. Gal.* 15 Ye cleaue to the litterall meanyng onely, and pearce not to the spiritual sence therof. **1576** FLEMING *Panopl. Epist.* 242 So farre foorth as my dimme and darke eyesight is able to pearce into the view of his vertues. **1613** SHAKS. *Hen. VIII*, I. i. 68, I cannot tell What Heauen hath giuen him: let some Grauer eye Pierce into that. **1719** DE FOE *Crusoe* (1840) II. iii. 66 There was no piercing with the eye..into the plantation. **1850** ROBERTSON *Serm.* Ser. I. xvi. (1866) 269 It was reserved for One to pierce with the glance of intuition.

pierce, *sb. rare.* [f. prec.] The act or process of piercing; a hole made by piercing.
1613 R. CAWDREY *Table Alph.* (ed. 3), *Perforation*, hole, or pierce through. **1688** R. HOLME *Armoury* III. iii. 89/2 *Pearses*.., the holes in the [horse] shooe. **1819** KEATS *Isabella* xxxiv, Like a lance, Waking an Indian from his cloudy hall With cruel pierce.

†**pierce**, *a. Obs. nonce-wd.* [f. PIERCE *v.*; in quot. perh. with punning allusion to the name *Percy*.] Piercing, sharp, keen, fierce.
1593 B. BARNES *Parthenophil & Parthenophe* Sonn. xliv. in Arb. *Eng. Garner* V. 365 That Saints divine, are known Saints by their mercy! And Saint-like beauty should not rage with pierce eye! *Ibid.* xlvi. *ibid.* 366 Ah, pierce-eye piercing eye, and blazing light!

pierce-, the verb-stem or sb. in comb., as in **pierce-free** *a.*, free from perforations, or wounds made by piercing; **pierce-work**, work (in metal, etc.) done by piercing or perforation.
1628 GAULE *Pract. The.* (1629) 176 Men neyther shrinke, nor shrike, that their Cloathes are beaten, or rent, when they perceiue their Bodies pierce-free, or paine-free. **1833** J. HOLLAND *Manuf. Metal* II. 195 In the production of ordinary pierce-work.

pierceable ('pɪəsəb(ə)l), *a.* [f. PIERCE *v.* + -ABLE.] That may be pierced; penetrable.
1552 HULOET, Perceable or penetrable, or whyche may be perced, *penetra[bi]lis.* **1590** SPENSER *F.Q.* I. i. 7 Loftie trees ..Not perceable with power of any starr. **1615** DANIEL *Hymen's Tri.* IV. iii. 58 The woman..hauing veynes of nature, could not bee But peircible. **1859** LEWES in *Cornh. Mag.* I. 72 Between the segments of the insect's armour, a soft and pierceable spot is found.

pierced (pɪəst, *poet.* 'pɪəsɪd), *ppl. a.* Forms: see PIERCE *v.* [f. PIERCE *v.* + -ED[1].] **1. a.** Punctured, perforated, penetrated, etc.: see the verb.
c **1400** *Sege Jerusalem* 703 So was he pyned fram prime with persched sides, Tolle þe sonne doun sou3t. **1552** HULOET, Perced, *fossus, foratus.* **1693** in *Dryden's Juvenal* IV. (1697) 87 Mark the pointed Spears That from thy Hand on his pierc'd Back he wears! **1835** J. COLDSTREAM in J. H. Balfour *Biog.* III. (1865) 103 Soothing and cheering the agitated and pierced mind. **1848** RICKMAN *Archit.* App. 43 Plain parapets are common, and perhaps pierced parapets.. still more so. **1858** C. F. ALEXANDER *Hymn, 'When wounded sore'* i, One only hand, a pierced hand, Can salve the sinner's wound.

b. *spec.* in *Her.* (*a*) Said of a charge represented as perforated with a hole (of different shape from the charge itself: cf. VOIDED), so that the tincture of the field appears through. (*b*) Said of an animal used as a charge, represented as having an arrow, spear, etc., fixed in its body but not passing through it (cf. TRANSFIXED).
1610 GUILLIM *Heraldry* II. vii. 70 He beareth Sable, a Crosse couped, Pierced, by the name of Grill. **1658** PHILLIPS, *Pierced*,..in Heraldry, as a crosse pierced, i.e. bored in the middle. **1725** COATS *New Dict. Her.* s.v., If a Cross have a square Hole, or Perforation in the Center, it is blazon'd, *Square pierced*... When the Hole, or Perforation is round, it must be express'd, *Round pierced.* **1823** RUTTER *Fonthill* p. xxi, Three Cinque-foils, Ermine, pierced of the field. **1882** CUSSANS *Her.* iv. 63 If only that part [of a cross] where the limbs are conjoined be removed, it is termed Quarterly-pierced... A Cross with a square aperture in its centre, smaller than the last, is Quarter-pierced.

c. Of silver, plate, china, porcelain, etc.: ornamented with perforations.
1756 in R. W. Read *Reprint of Orig. Catal. Chelsea Porcelain Manuf.* (1880) 6 Four round pierced baskets enamel'd in flowers. *Ibid.* 7 A fine perfume pot pierced, chased and gilt, and enamel'd in birds. **1785** *Daily Universal Reg.* 1 Jan. 3/2 Pierced and engraved oval salts... Pierced and solid headed mustard pots. **1875** E. METEYARD *Wedgwood Handbk.* 338 The high fluted pillar candle-stick, the pierced fruit basket,..and various other articles, all show an infinite variety, beauty, and fitness of outline. **1931** E. WENHAM *Domestic Silver* v. 88 Pierced baskets for bread were also made in the Early Stuart period and..are the prototypes of the baskets popular in the eighteenth century. **1956** [see *cake-basket* s.v. CAKE *sb.* 9 a]. **1970** G. SAVAGE *Dict. Antiques* 319/2 In more recent times George Owen (d. 1917) made elaborately pierced or reticulated porcelain for the Royal Worcester Porcelain Company. **1974** A. GRIMWADE *Rococo Silver* iv. 45 An exceptional set of twelve [salt-cellars] by Emick Romer, about 1760, have glass bowls enclosed in pierced cagework on *chinoiserie* motifs.

2. Special collocations, as **pierced earring** *U.S.*, an earring designed to be worn in a pierced ear; **Pierced-nose** = NEZ PERCÉ, NEZ PERCE.
1965 *Time* 15 Oct. 70/3 Pierced earrings are by far the most attractive ones available. **1966** *N.Y. Times* 6 June 53 Variation on the pierced earring theme. **1971** *Tuscaloosa* (Alabama) *News* 31 Dec. 8 The package deal includes the purchase of a $6 pair of pierced earrings... The customer may..have her (or his) ears pierced free of charge. **1805** W. CLARK in Lewis & Clark *Orig. Jrnls. Lewis & Clark Expedition* (1905) III. 78 They call themselves the *Cho pun-nish* or Pierced noses. **1831** R. COX *Adventures Columbia River* II. vi. 122 We had many reasons to suspect that the Pierced-noses..were actuated by feelings of hostility. **1837** W. IRVING *Rocky Mountains* I. xviii. 183 A Pierced-nose chief, named Blue John by the whites. **1908** H. J. SPINDEN in *Mem. Amer. Anthropol. Assoc.* II. III. 172 Ross says the people are called Pierced Noses from the custom 'of having their noses bored to hold a certain white shell like the fluke of an anchor'.

piercel ('pɪəsəl). *dial. rare*[−0]. [f. PIERCE *v.* + -EL[2].] = PIERCER 2.
1858 SIMMONDS *Dict. Trade Prod.*, *Piercel, Piercer*, a kind of awl or gimlet for giving vent to casks of liquor.

pierceless ('pɪəslɪs), *a. rare.* [f. PIERCE *v.* + -LESS; cf. *dauntless, quenchless*, etc.] Incapable of being pierced; impenetrable. So **'pierceless-ness**, impenetrability.
1674 N. FAIRFAX *Bulk & Selv.* 108 We cannot tear from it piercelessness or impenetrability, which is the closest sticker to a body. **1755** J. G. COOPER *Tomb Shakspeare* Sel. Poems (1762) 149 Sharp spears in pierceless phalanx reared.

piercement ('pɪəsmənt). *Geol.* [f. PIERCE *v.* + -MENT, tr. G. *durchspiessungs(falten).*] The penetration of overlying strata by a mobile rock core, often of salt. Usu. *attrib.* Cf. DIAPIR.
1925 D. C. BARTON in *Bull. Amer. Assoc. Petroleum Geologists* IX. 1239 The salt is merely part of the peculiar type of fold called by Mrazec 'diapir' fold, or by Krejci 'piercement' folds (*Durchspiessungsfalten*). **1942** M. P. BILLINGS *Structural Geol.* xiv. 254 Salt domes are classified by some geologists into piercement domes and non-piercement domes, the former being discordant, the latter concordant. **1965** A. HOLMES *Princ. Physical Geol.* (ed. 2) ix. 206 Diapiric folds (also known as piercement folds). **1965** E. LEHNER et al. in G. J. Williams *Econ. Geol. N.Z.* xix. 337/2 It seems improbable that the Tertiary anticlinal structure[s] without piercement cores, or at a long strike distance away from them, could owe their shape solely to hidden diapirism (e.g., upward movement of the clay core without a breakthrough to surface), without at least some help from tangential forces. **1975** *Nature* 29 May 393/2 Because of the circular exposure of evaporite surrounded by younger disturbed rocks, Haughton Dome has been considered a piercement dome.

'piercent, *a. rare.* = PERCEANT.
1829 *Examiner* 470/2 The spiked gauntlet of indignation, and the piercent spear of invective are both seen and felt.

piercer ('pɪəsə(r)). Forms: 5–6 persour, percer, (5 persor, -ore, -owre, -owyr, -ure, -ere, parsoure, perescher), 6 perser, -ar, parser, pearser, pierser, 6–7 pearcer, 7– piercer. [Orig. a. Anglo-F. *perceour, persour* = F. *perceur*, f. *percer* to pierce: see -ER[1] 2.]
1. *gen.* One who or that which pierces. Also *fig.*
1432–50 tr. *Higden* (Rolls) II. 357 This my3hty Hercules was the tamer of the worlde, the victor of þe Amazones, the perescher of Ynde [HIGDEN *Indiæ penetrator*]. **1568** GRAFTON *Chron.* II. 578 Vnneth any creature..could holde either hand close, or purse shut, such a strong percer is monie. *a* **1586** SIDNEY *Arcadia* II. xxvii. (1590) 223 b, Basilius,..not the sharpest pearcer into masked minds. **1777** PENNANT *Zool.* (ed. 4) IV. 128 Teredo. Piercer.. Penetrates into the stoutest oak plant, and effects their destruction. **1838** DICKENS *O. Twist* xix, 'It must be a piercer, if it finds its way through your heart', said Mr. Sikes.

b. *colloq.* or *slang.* Applied to an eye having a keen, piercing, or penetrating glance.
1752 FOOTE *Taste* I. Wks. 1799 I. 11 She had but one eye, indeed, but that was a piercer. ? **1782** H. WALPOLE *Lett., to Mason* (1846) VI. 164 How much more execution a fine woman could do with two pair of piercers! **1834** *Blackw. Mag.* XXXV. 743 Her eyes were piercers.

2. An instrument or tool for piercing or boring holes, as an auger, awl, gimlet, stiletto, etc.
1404 *Durham Acc. Rolls* (Surtees) 399, j persour. *c* **1440** *Promp. Parv.* 395/1 Persowre (or wymbyl), *terebellum.* ? *a* **1500** *Chester Pl.* vi. 120 With this axe that I beare, This percer, and this nawger,..I haue wonne my meate. **1533** *MS. Acc. St. John's Hosp., Canterb.*, For persars iijd. ob. **1541** *St. Papers Hen. VIII*, I. 687 Such tooles as persers, augers, sawes, and suche other. **1573–80** BARET *Alv.* P 213 Pearcer; 310 Pierser. **1602** R. T. 5 *Godlie Serm.* 185 Except the Lord boare our eares with the piercer of his spirit. **1616** SURFLET & MARKH. *Country Farme* 610 Hee must pearce it ..with a pearcer. **1776** G. SEMPLE *Building in Water* 19 The Sand will set upon your Piercer or Augre. **1886** C. SCOTT *Sheep-Farming* 48 The man..provided with a 'gavelock' or 'piercer'—a strong iron bar rounded and sharpened at the heavy end—makes holes at intervals of eight or ten feet for the reception of the stakes.

b. A bodily organ (in an insect, or the like) used in piercing, as a sting or an ovipositor.
1691 RAY *Creation* II. (1692) 78 The hollow Instrument (*terebra*, he calls it, and we may English it piercer) wherewith many Flies are provided. **1861** HULME tr. *Moquin-Tandon* II. vi. i. 294 Rostrum [of the Head-louse] ..c, piercer, formed of four capillary threads.

3. A person employed or skilled in perforated wood or metal work.
1736 BYROM *Jrnl. & Lit. Rem.* (1856) II. I. 43 Went to Mr. Joyce's the piercer..he had made a specimen or two of etching and piercing. **1898** *Daily Chron.* 24 Sept. 10/6 Saw Piercer wanted, one used to leaf work. **1902** *Ibid.* 20 Feb. 8/7 Silver Piercer.—Young lady requires Situation.

4. *attrib.* or *Comb.* (in sense 2), as ***piercer-bit***, ***-blade***, ***-iron***.
1421–2 *Durham Acc. Rolls* (Surtees) 228 Et in persouryrnes et ij fenestris vitreis pro parvo celario de Wytton, xij d. **1530** PALSGR. 253/2 Percerblade, *estoc.* **1703** MOXON *Mech. Exerc.* 155 They Pierce holes, with a Piercer-Bit.

†**'pierce-stone.** *Obs.* [f. PIERCE *v.* + STONE *sb.*] A name for the herb Samphire.
1600 SURFLET *Countrey Farme* I. xvi. 223 (*heading*) Of.. pearcestone [Fr. *perce-pierre ou christe-marine*]. (*margin*)

Pearce stone or sampier [Fr. *Christe-marine*]. **1688** R. HOLME *Armory* II. vi. 100/1 *Sampire*, or *Rock-Sampire*, the stalk is tender and green... It is called *Pearceston*.

piercing ('pɪəsɪŋ), *vbl. sb.* [f. PIERCE *v.* + -ING[1].] The action of the verb PIERCE; perforation, boring, penetration, etc.: see the verb.

c **1386** CHAUCER *Sir Thopas* 151 Ouer that an haubergeon ffor percynge of his herte. *c* **1440** *Promp. Parv.* 393/2 Peercynge, or borynge, ..*perforacio*. **1610** GUILLIM *Heraldry* II. vii. 70 Piercing is a Penetration or Perforation of things that are of solid substance: and it is threefold: That is to say Round, Losengwaies, Quadrate. **1611** BIBLE *Prov.* xii. 18 There is that speaketh like the pearcings of a sword. **1685** DRYDEN *Hor. Odes* III. xxix. 4 Make haste to meet the generous wine, Whose piercing is for thee delay'd. **1776** G. SEMPLE *Building in Water* 17 Borings or Piercings into the Bed of the River. **1897** *Daily News* 23 Apr. 3/3 The piercing of the bed of coal at the Shirebrook Colliery.

b. A hole or perforation.

1887 E. PEACOCK in *Athenæum* 9 July 54/2 These ornamental piercings.. were like church windows. **1894** BLACKMORE *Perlycross* 4 The tower was famous.. for.. height, and proportion, and piercings.

c. *attrib.* and *Comb.*

1792 OSBALDISTONE *Brit. Sportsm., Farriery* 255 Make the nails.. answerable to the piercing-holes. **1833** J. HOLLAND *Manuf. Metal* II. 195 The plate.. having been prepared by rolling and planishing.. is brought to the piercing-shop. **1875** KNIGHT *Dict. Mech.* 1699/2 *Piercing-file*, a sharp and narrow file to enlarge a narrow drilled hole. *Piercing-saw*, a thin blade fastened by screw-clamps in a light frame, and used for piercing gold and silver smiths' works.

piercing ('pɪəsɪŋ), *ppl. a.* [f. as prec. + -ING[2].] That pierces in various senses: see the verb.

1. Perforating, penetrating, as a sharp-pointed instrument or weapon.

1412–20 LYDG. *Chron. Troy* I. vi. (MS. Digby 230) lf. 42/2 Harded with stele trenchaunt or percinge. **1607** TOPSELL *Four-f. Beasts* (1658) 157 Their Armour made full of sharp pricks or piercing piked Nailes. **1742** GRAY *Eton* 70 Sorrow's piercing dart.

b. Having a physical effect resembling or suggesting the action of a pointed instrument; sharp, keen and penetrating; *esp.* of cold and sound.

1423 JAS. I *Kingis Q.* ciii, With the stremes of ȝour percyng lyght. **1593** G. HARVEY *Pierce's Super.* 12 Not with ..the trickling water of Helicon, but with piercing Aqua fortis. **1615** W. LAWSON *Country Housew. Gard.* (1626) 21 There is nothing more hurtfull for yong trees than piercing drought. **1767** SIR W. JONES *Sev. Fountains* Poems (1777) 34 Ten comely striplings.. Blew piercing flutes. **1855** ROBINSON *Whitby Gloss., Pearching*, cold to a degree of intensity. **1884** PAE *Eustace* 8 A piercing shriek rang through the silent.. air.

c. Having an analogous effect on the feelings or mind; penetrating; keenly or painfully affecting; deeply distressing.

1509 HAWES *Past. Pleas.* xxvii. (Percy Soc.) 132, I made mine othe with percing influence, Unto them all for to remayne full true. *c* **1586** C'TESS PEMBROKE *Ps.* (1823) LXIX. iv, The shott of piercing spight. **1657** SPARROW *Bk. Com. Prayer* (1661) 71 This most humble and piercing Supplication. **1791** MRS. INCHBALD *Simp. Story* IV. 142 A state of the most piercing inquietude. **1832** J. HODGSON in J. Raine *Mem.* II. 283 Piercing misfortunes and troubles.

2. Able to 'see into' a thing; having penetration; sharp, keen. Said of the eyes, sight, or mind (formerly also of a person or animal); also of the appearance or expression of the eyes.

1423 JAS. I *Kingis Q.* clv, The percyng lynx. **1583** BABINGTON *Commandm.* iv. (1637) 31 If the pearcing eyes of the living God should prie into us. *a* **1586** SIDNEY *Arcadia* (1622) 243 Wherein he sharpned his wits to the piercingest point. **1603** KNOLLES *Hist. Turks* (1621) 12 A most subtil sharp and pearching wit. **1704** S. SLATER in Spurgeon *Treas. Dav.* Ps. xcvii. 2 Men of the largest and most piercing intellectuals. **1779** J. MOORE *View Soc. Fr.* (1789) I. xxix. 242 The most piercing eyes I ever beheld are those of Voltaire. **1805** FOSTER *Ess.* I. v. 60 The piercing and immense intelligence that can know, or.. assume, that there is no God. **1885** G. ALLEN *Babylon* x, Piercing black eyes as bright as diamonds.

3. *Comb.*, as ***piercing-sighted*** adj.

1768–74 TUCKER *Lt. Nat.* (1834) I. 667 There is none so piercing-sighted as to see to the very end of the line.

piercingly ('pɪəsɪŋlɪ), *adv.* [f. prec. + -LY[2].] In a piercing manner or degree; penetratingly, keenly (*lit.* and *fig.*).

c **1410** *Master of Game* (MS. Digby 182) v, An olde boore ..smyteth gret strokes but not so persynglich as a yonge boore. **1593** NASHE *Christ's T.* (1613) 96 [They] sing sweetly, glance piercingly, play on Lutes rauishingly. **1781** H. DOWNMAM tr. *Voltaire's Dram. Wks.* I. 81 Doubt is a torment piercingly severe. **1834** PRINGLE *Afr. Sk.* ix. 309 A piercingly cold night.

piercingness ('pɪəsɪŋnɪs). [See -NESS.] Piercing quality; penetrativeness, keenness.

1638 MAYNE *Lucian* (1664) 254 The edge, and piercingnesse of her judgment. *a* **1697** AUBREY *Brief Lives* (1898) I. 220 His eie.. had a strange piercingness. **1713** DERHAM *Phys.-Theol.* v. i. 303 The prodigious Quickness and Piercingness of its Thought. **1888** B. W. RICHARDSON *Son of Star* III. xiii. 231 A voice.. deadly in its piercingness.

† **'piercive**, *a. Obs. rare.* Also 6 persiue. [f. PIERCE *v.* + -IVE: cf. *coercive*.] Having the quality of piercing; penetrative.

1567 MAPLET *Gr. Forest* 68 b, The fift or odde Crane in maner of a persiue sterne.. flieth all alone before. **1615** BRATHWAIT *Strappado*, etc. (1878) 257 Two sparkling eyes piercive as Diamond. **1631** —— *Eng. Gentlew.* (1641) Ded., Upon approvement of his more piercive judgement.

piere, obs. form of PEER *sb.*

pierelle (pɪə'rɛl). [app. ad. F. *pierraille* a shapeless heap of stones, f. *pierre* stone + pejorative suffix *-aille*.] (See quot.)

1875 KNIGHT *Dict. Mech.* 1699/2 *Pierelle*, a mass of stones filling a ditch and covered with clay.

pier-glass ('pɪəglɑːs, -æ-). [f. PIER *sb.*[2] 3 + GLASS *sb.* 8.] A large tall mirror; orig. one fitted to fill up the pier or space between two windows, or over a chimney-piece.

1703 *Lond. Gaz.* No. 3889/4 Lost.. 7 Peer Glasses, 2 in black Frames, and 5 in Japan'd Frames with cross Bars. **1713** STEELE *Guard.* No. 95 ¶9 The room above stairs is.. furnished with large peer-glasses for persons to view themselves in. **1805** W. TAYLOR in *Ann. Rev.* III. 655 It begins to be fashionable to place in front of every pier-glass a marble guardian. **1875** KNIGHT *Dict. Mech.* 1699/2 *Pier-glass*, a large looking-glass between windows, frequently standing on a pier-table.

pier-head. [f. PIER *sb.*[2] 2 + HEAD *sb.*[1] 18 b.]

1. The outward or seaward end of a pier.

a **1682** SIR T. BROWNE *Wks.* (1836) I. 346 At a competent distance from the peere head. **1779** G. KEATE *Sk. fr. Nat.* (ed. 2) II. 199 Half Margate thronged the Pier-Head. **1853** KANE *Grinnell Exp.* l. (1856) 487 Our noble friend Henry Grinnell was the first to welcome us on the pier-head.

2. *attrib.* and *Comb.* **a. pier-head jump**, (*a*) (see quot. 1892); (*b*) an act of leaving a ship as it is about to sail; (*c*) a person who joins a ship as it is leaving the dock; hence ***pier-head jumper***.

1892 *Labour Commission* Gloss., *Pier-head Jump*, the act of joining a ship as she is leaving the dock, owing to some of the (signed) crew not fulfilling their engagements. **1899** *Daily News* 11 Sept. 7/5 A pier-head man.. hearing a crash through the pier, hastily dressed, and.. rowed to the spot. **1927** F. SHAW *Knocking Around* 65 One man was short: he'd done a pierhead jump. **1928** F. P. HARLOW *Making of Sailor* 229 All the other members of the crew had made a pier-head jump during the night. **1931** S. W. RYDER *Blue Water Ventures* iii. 40 At the last minute the scallywags who could not get a ship in the ordinary way had to be accepted; these 'pier-head jumpers' being pushed on board by the boarding-house runners as the steamer was moving out of dock. **1936** B. ADAMS *Ships & Women* xi. 238 Often among pierhead jumps were rattling good sailors. **1938** E. LINKLATER *Child under Sail* 169 There were no pier-head jumpers to be found, and we had to sail a man short. **1945** *Seafarers' Log* 13 July 6/4 Fred took a few minutes to call his family, and then made the tanker on a pierhead jump. **1967** S. WATERS *Indentures Indorsed* 117 He had not passed the doctor, but was a pier-head jump. **1978** *Navy News* Dec. 6/1 The cartoon on page 14 reminded me of a pierhead jump I had from the Defiance in 1940.

b. Designating a type of variety entertainment traditionally associated with summer shows on piers in seaside resorts.

1932 *Statesman* (Calcutta) 2 Aug., There is always a public, and not only a pierhead public, for a thoroughly good pierrot show. **1960** *Times* 2 Mar. 13/2 Here was good old bandsman's pier-head stuff. **1963** *Times* 8 Feb. 14/5 Some ambiguous remarks..—in the best early pierhead manner—suggesting that he is either describing the chassis of a car technically or that of a young woman vulgarly.

Pierian (paɪ'ɪərɪən), *a.* [f. L. *Pīerius* adj. (cf. *Pīeria*, a. Gr. Πιερία) + -AN. So F. *Piérien*.]

1. Belonging to Pieria, a district in N. Thessaly, the reputed home of the Muses; *spec.* an epithet of the Muses; hence allusively in reference to poetry or learning.

1591 SPENSER *Ruins of Time* 394 Whom the Pierian sacred sisters loue. **1617** MORYSON *Itin.* III. 119 Of old a people called Pieres.. dwelt vnder Parnassus, of whom it was called the Pierian Mountaine, and the Muses were called Pierides. **1623** COCKERAM, *Pierean maids*, the Muses nine. **1709** POPE *Ess. Crit.* 216 A little learning is a dang'rous thing; Drink deep, or taste not the Pierian spring. **1873** SYMONDS *Grk. Poets* iii. 75 Pierian Muses! hear my prayer.

2. *Entom.* = PIERIDINE *a.*

pierid ('paɪərɪd), *sb.* and *a. Ent.* Also Pierid, †-ide. [f. mod.L. family name *Pieridæ*, f. the generic name *Pieris* (see PIERIS) + -ID[3].] **A.** *sb.* A white or yellow butterfly belonging to the family Pieridæ. **B.** *adj.* Of or pertaining to this family.

1885 W. F. KIRBY *Elem. Text-bk. Entomol.* 155 A white, black-bordered species.. could hardly be mistaken for anything but a Pieride. **1905** V. L. KELLOGG *Amer. Insects* xiv. 445 The males of many Pierids give off a pleasing aromatic odor. **1926** *Contemp. Rev.* Sept. 370 Pierids are essentially creatures of the open country. **1932** METCALF & FLINT *Fund. Insect Life* viii. 291 (*caption*) Three common pierid butterflies. **1954** BORROR & DELONG *Introd. Study Insects* xxvi. 494 The pierids are medium-sized to small butterflies, usually white or yellowish in color. **1963** V. NABOKOV *Gift* ii. 109 The long cloud consisting of myriads of white pierids.. moves through the sky. **1973** *Nature* 9 Feb. 408/2 Mating behaviour in pierid butterflies is affected by light intensity.

pieridine (paɪ'ɛrɪdaɪn), *a. Entom.* [ad. mod.L. *Pīeridīn-æ*, f. *Pieris*, name of the typical genus.] Belonging to the family *Pieridæ*, or subfamily *Pieridinæ* of *Papilionidæ*, typified by the genus *Pieris*, containing the cabbage butterflies.

pierie, var. PERRIE *Obs.*, jewellery; obs. f. PIRRIE, a squall.

Pierine ('paɪəriːn, -aɪn), *sb.* and *a. Ent.* [f. mod.L. subfamily name *Pierinæ*, f. next + -INE[1].] **A.** *sb.* A white butterfly belonging to the subfamily Pierinæ, which includes the common cabbage white. **B.** *adj.* Of or pertaining to this subfamily.

1898 *Rep. Brit. Assoc. Adv. Sci. 1897* 691 A white butterfly with such a border becomes an extremely conspicuous object, and this appearance of *Mylothris* is mimicked.. by species from a number of Pierine genera. **1930** *Proc. Entomol. Soc. London* V. 66 (*heading*) Attacks by a sparrow upon the Pierine butterfly *Aporia bieti*, Oberth., at Tachienlu, Tibet. **1934** *Discovery* July 195/2 It seemed unlikely that certain features in which the Pierines resembled the supposed models were simply adopted from the latter. *Ibid.*, The similar features.. were on the whole most distinct and most Pierine-like in those forms that were locally associated with the Pierine *Pereutes* and *Euterpes*.

pieris ('paɪərɪs). [mod.L., f. L. *Pīeris* a Muse, f. *Pīeria* (see PIERIAN *a.*).] **1.** [Adopted by D. Don 1834, in *Edin. New Philos. Jrnl.* XVII. 159.] An evergreen shrub of the genus so called, belonging to the family Ericaceæ, native to the southern United States, China, and Japan, and bearing panicles of small, bell-shaped white flowers.

1838 J. C. LOUDON *Arboretum* II. 1115 The oval-leaved Pieris.. was introduced in 1825. **1909** *Curtis's Bot. Mag.* CXXXV. 8283 The introduction into European gardens of this handsome *Pieris* appears to have taken place upwards of half a century ago. **1935** A. J. SWEET *Trees & Shrubs* xi. 82 Andromeda can be increased by division and cuttings.. and Pieris by layering. **1962** R. PAGE *Educ. Gardener* ix. 260 Evergreens, such as rhododendrons, skimmias, pieris, aucuba. **1975** *Country Life* 10 Apr. 891/3 Other ericaceous plants inclue pieris with its splendid spring leaf colours.

2. [Adopted by F. von P. Schrank 1801, in *Fauna Boica* II. 152.] A white butterfly of the genus so called, which includes the common cabbage whites.

1863 H. W. BATES *Naturalist on River Amazons* I. i. 22 Numbers of fine showy butterflies were seen... A white Pieris (P. Monuste), and two or three species of brimstone and orange-coloured butterflies. **1969** R. F. CHAPMAN *Insects* xvii. 330 Female *Pieris* ready to oviposit are attracted to green surfaces.

pierk, obs. f. PERK *v.*[1]

pierless ('pɪəlɪs), *a.* Having no pier.

1861 SMILES *Engineers* II. 378 Wretched pierless ferries, let to poor cottars, who rowed, or hauled, or pushed a crazy boat across. **1893** *Daily News* 23 May 2/3 Dover.. the chief of the Cinque Ports has hitherto remained in the ordinary sense pierless... The something wanting was a promenade pier with pavilion and band.

pierpoint, corruption of PARPEN.

1891 H. FISHWICK *Hist. St. Michaels-on-Wyre* 91 The church was built of brick, but afterwards faced with pier-points.

† **'pierrerie.** *Obs.* In 5 perrierie, 5–6 pyerrerye. [a. F. *pierrerie* (pjɛrəri), in 14th c. *perrerie*, f. *pierre* stone: see PIER *sb.*[1] and -ERY.] Jewellery; = PERRIE.

c **1400** *Destr. Troy* 1670 A sete rioll, Pight full of perrieris & of proude gemys. **1491** CAXTON *Vitas Patr.* (W. de W. 1495) I. xli. 62 b/1 Vppon her was seen noo thynge but golde and syluer and ryche pyerrerye. *c* **1503** *Marriage Jas. IV & Marg.* in Leland *Collect.* (1770) IV. 300 She.. had on a ryche Coller of Pyerrery... Hys churte was bordered of fyne Pierrery and Pearles.

‖**pierrette** (pɪə'rɛt, pjɛ'rɛt). [F., fem. dim. of *Pierre* Peter, corresponding to PIERROT.] A female member of a company of pierrots.

1888 *Pall Mall G.* 9 Mar. 6/1 His pierrettes, his ballet-girls, and his eighteenth-century Sir Roger-de-Coverley dancers. **1889** *Ibid.* 7 Mar. 3/1 (*Carnival at Nice*) Mysterious dominoes and masks, excited pierrots and pierrettes, pretty figures, short skirts.. have been the order of the day.

pierrie, -rye: see PERRIE, jewellery; PIRRIE, a squall.

‖**Pierrot** ('pɪərəʊ, 'pjɛro). In senses 1 and 3 also pierrot. [F. *pierrot*, dim. of *Pierre*, a peasant's name, applied to a 'clown' or buffoon:—L. *Petrum*, nom. *Petrus* PETER.]

1. A typical character in French pantomime: now, in English, applied to a buffoon or itinerant minstrel having, like the stage *Pierrot*, a whitened face, and loose white fancy dress.

1741–70 ELIZ. CARTER *Lett.* (1808) 61 He was one of the oddest fellows I ever saw.. and in all his gestures extremely like a *pierrot*. **1838** THOMS in *Bentley's Misc.* III. 620 The more immediate relative.. of the modern clown, is the Pierrot,.. now very rarely introduced upon the stage. **1889** *Sat. Rev.* 16 Mar. 309/2 [An etching of] a little boy, dressed as a white Pierrot. **1904** *Daily News* 12 July 6 Niggers at the seaside have.. given place to pierrots.

2. A kind of sleeved basque (see BASQUE 4) with a low neck, worn by women late in the 18th c.

1794 *Residence in France* (1797) II. 329 The lady of the house in a nankeen pierrot.

3. *attrib.* and *Comb.*, as (sense 1) ***Pierrot costume, doll, show***; ***Pierrot-like*** adj.; **Pierrot collar** (see quot. 1957).

1957 M. B. Picken *Fashion Dict.* 250/2 Pierrot collar, ruff like that worn by French pantomime character. **1977** *Time* 8 Aug. 38/1 Pierrot collars and flounces adorned many of Bohan's dresses, capes and blouses. **1893** A. Beardsley *Let.* c. 15 Feb. (1971) 43 Strange hermaphroditic creatures wandering about in Pierrot costumes or modern dress; quite a new world of my own creation. **1960** Pierrot costume [see *concert-party*]. **1935** A. Christie *Three Act Tragedy* iii. ix. 188 A ridiculously elongated pierrot doll [was] lying across the sofa. **1967** A. Wilson *No Laughing Matter* ii. 39 Rupert lolling on cushions.. aimlessly waving the limp Pierrot doll beside him. **1979** A. Buchan *Scrap Screen* viii. 132 Emancipated girls.. moved into bedsitters.. and filled them with black and orange cushions and Pierrot dolls. **1977** *Rolling Stone* 19 May 73/1, I hadn't quite expected the faultless intonation.. of that shining, graceful, Pierrot-like figure. **1951** J. Fleming *Man who looked Back* i. 14 They saw the pierrot show from comfortable deck-chairs. **1978** M. Gilbert *Empty House* xiii. 107 There's.. a pierrot show in the Palais de Dance [*sic*].

Hence **'pierrotism**, the action of a pierrot.

1734 *Prompter* 20 Dec. 2/2 The graceful Motion of fine Dancers, and mute Harlequinery, and Pierrotism.

Pierrotic (pɪə'rɒtɪk), *a.* [f. pierrot + -ic.] Of, belonging, or pertaining to pierrots.

1927 *Observer* 16 Oct. 15/3 The delightful tenor raptures of Mr. Georges Metaxa are in the best Pierrotic tradition. **1931** *Times Lit. Suppl.* 13 Aug. 614/1 Mr. Nicoll seems to pass lightly over his [*sc.* Punch's] white-bloused, Pierrotic, Neapolitan avatar.

piert, obs. or dial. form of pert.

pies, var. pize *sb. Obs.*, a form of imprecation.

piet, pyet, pyot ('paɪət). Chiefly (now only) *Sc.* and *north. dial.* Forms: 3, 6–7 piot, 5–9 pyot, (6 -ott), 6–9 pyet, pyat, (9 -att), (8 peyet), 9 piet, (piat). [In ME. *piot*, f. pie *sb.*[1] + -ot[1], in later use written with better known suffix -et[1]: cf. F. *piette* the dipper, dim. of *pie* magpie.]

1. The magpie: = pie *sb.*[1] 1.

a **1225** *Ancr. R.* 88 Ane kikelot [*MS. C.* piot] þet cakeleð hire al þat heo isihð, oðer ihereð. *c* **1450** Holland *Howlat* 176 Thar was Pyotis and Partrikis and Pluwaris. **1500–20** Dunbar *Poems* xxii. 16 The pyet.. Fenȝeis to sing the nychtingalis not. **1536** Bellenden *Cron. Scot.* (1821) II. 89 The piottis and nicht-crawis faucht with the ravinnis. *a* **1600** Montgomerie *Sonn.* v, The pratling pyet matchis with the Musis. **1601** Holland *Pliny* I. 301 The Piot ordinarily brings forth nine Piannets. **1819** Scott *Ivanhoe* xxxii, Here cometh the worthy prelate, as pert as a pyet. **1829** Cunningham *Magic Bridle* in *Anniversary* 138 Words specked and spotted like a pyat.

b. The dipper or water-ouzel. Also ***water-piet***.

1839 Jardine *Brit. Birds* II. 67 The common Water Crow, or Pyet, as it is familiarly termed in Scotland. **1885** Swainson *Prov. Names Brit. Birds* 30 Dipper (*Cinclus aquaticus*)... The white breast and blackish upper plumage have caused it to be called Piet... Water piet (Scotland).

2. A piebald horse.

1756 Mrs. Calderwood *Jrnl.* (1884) 27 The Duke of Marlborough had a sett of peyets, very prettily marked.

3. *fig.* (from 1). Applied to a talkative or saucy person. Cf. *tale-piet*, tattler, tell-tale. (*Sc.*)

1574 *Reg. Privy Council Scot.* II. 372 Archie Crosar callit the Pyott. **1814** Chalmers *Let.* in Hanna *Mem.* I. 340 From the great officers of State at St. James's,.. down to the little female piets who were taught to squall what they did not understand, 'No fanatics!' **1855** Robinson *Whitby Gloss.* s.v., 'A pawky young pyet', a saucy young person.

4. *attrib.* **a.** Resembling a magpie in appearance; pied, piebald.

1508 *Acc. Ld. High Treas. Scot.* IV. 114 Ane pyot hors giffin to the King. *c* **1843** Carlyle *Hist. Sk.* (1898) 256 Thirteen score of volunteer guards-royal.. all in.. beautiful pyet plumage.

b. Like a magpie; chattering.

1573 *Satir. Poems Reform.* xlii. 82 Quhen ȝe ȝourselfis ar daft and ȝoung, And hes nocht but ane Pyat toung.

Hence **'piety, 'piotie, 'pyoty** *a. Sc.*, piebald.

1811 W. Aiton *Agric. Surv. Ayrs.* 462 (Jam.) The butter will acquire a freckled or cloudy appearance, or in the language of the district, become *pyotty*. **1825** Jamieson, *Pyat, Pyatie, Pyotie, Pyotty*.., variegated like a magpie,.. as, 'a *pyatie* horse', one whose skin has large spots of white, completely separated from those of black, brown, etc.

‖**Pietà** (pje'ta). [It.:—L. *pietāt-em* piety.] A representation, in painting or sculpture, of the Virgin Mary holding the dead body of Christ on her lap.

1644 Evelyn *Diary* 21 Apr., On one side, is the statue of the Virgin Mary or Pieta, with the dead Christ in her lap. **1715** J. Richardson *The Painting* 85 In a *Pietà* of Van-Dyck. **1859** Mrs. Jameson *Early Ital. Paint.* 187 In 1500,.. he [Angelo] produced the famous group of the dead Christ on the knees of his Virgin Mother (called the Pietà). **1881** Miss Braddon *Asph.* xxvii, The fifteenth-century stained glass, the sculptured Pietas, and the choir stalls.

‖**pietas** (piː'eɪtɑːs). [L.] An attitude of respect towards an ancestor, scholarship, an institution, a country, etc.

1924 J. Bailey *Let.* 27 Apr. (1935) 244 Both Llanthony, to which, of course, *pietas* specially draws me, and Llangammarch look very attractive. **1930** *N. & Q.* 22 Feb. 143/1 Yet another Early English Text appears under the editorship of an American scholar, a new proof of *pietas*. **1944** *Horizon* Sept. 188 And yet, with all his *pietas*, when Joyce died.. he had not set foot in his native city for over thirty years. **1960** C. Day Lewis *Buried Day* i. 26 *Pietas*—a habit of respect for gods, ancestors, parents, country, institutions. **1961** *Times* 30 Nov. 16/2 *Pietas* is the curse of the commissioned biographer. **1965** N. St. John-Stevas in *Bagehot's Coll. Wks.* I. 11 The *Economist*.. has supported this undertaking, as.. an act of *pietas* to its.. most famous editor. **1976** *Church Times* 16 Jan. 15/5 A requiem will be sung for him in St. Oswald's, Durham, with his music—not just as an act of *pietas*, but in gratitude to God for one who, although a man of his age, yet reminds us of several needs in today's Church.

pieteous, pietious, var. pietous *Obs.*

pietic (paɪ'ɛtɪk), *a. rare*[−1]. [irreg. f. piety: see -ic.] Characterized by piety or pietism; pious; pietistic. So **pi'etical** *a.*

1782 Eliz. Blower *Geo. Bateman* II. 175 Her father has imbued a heap of his parsonical, pietical notions into her head. **1865** in *Pall Mall G.* No. 166. 11/1 The sober or pietic side of the jubilee.

pietifull, obs. form of pitiful.

pietism ('paɪɪtɪz(ə)m). [ad. Ger. (mod.L.) *Pietismus*, formed after pietist: see -ism.]

1. *Ch. Hist.* (Often with a capital initial.) Name for the movement (originated by Spener late in the 17th century) for the revival and advancement of piety in the Lutheran church (see next, 1); the principles or practices of the German Pietists.

1697 *State Philadelph. Soc.* 11 The first Motion or Eruption of it may be said to have been in Germany, where it has spread it self.. under the Name of *pietism*. **1705** *A. H. Franck's Pietas Hallensis* Introd. 21 Dr. Spener.. Wrote and Published a Book, long before the name of Pietism was brought into use... Among which.. he caused to appear again such Mystical and Spiritual Books of the best note. **1716** C. Mather *Let.* 6 June in *Harvard Stud.* (1897) V. 63 I believe yᵉ American puritanism to be much of a piece with Frederician pietism. **1877** E. Caird *Philos. Kant* i. 123 Say what you will of Pietism, no one can deny the real worth of the characters which it formed.

b. Also in extended use, any similar movement within Protestantism.

1900 tr. *A. Ritschl's Christian Doctrine of Justification & Reconciliation* i. 84 It is.. an inversion of the Reformation point of view when Pietism makes the moral power of faith the object which God invests with the value which moral conduct would possess when carried out. **1934** R. N. Flew *Idea of Perfection in Christian Theol.* xvi. 275 The essential mark of Pietism is its quest for individual holiness. **1958** E. L. Mascall *Recovery of Unity* i. 9 The word 'pietism'. By this I mean an attitude to Christianity.. which, in contrast to the corporate, objective, liturgical and theocentric religion of the primitive Church, is individualistic, subjective, pietistic and Christocentric. **1967** D. T. Kauffman *Dict. Relig. Terms* 354/1 *Pietism*, protestant religious current emphasizing personal devotions, Bible study, evangelism, and the like. **1967** M. J. Heinecken in J. Macquarrie *Dict. Christian Ethics* 257/1 Pietism has been and continues to be a valid protest against sterile orthodoxism and false sacramentalism.

2. Devotion to religious feeling, or to strictness of religious practice; pious sentiment; often implying an affectation or exaggeration of piety.

1829 I. Taylor *Enthus.* ii. (1867) 30 Genuine humility would shake the towering structure of this enthusiastic pietism. **1861** Tulloch *Eng. Purit.* ii. 227 The attempt.. to cover Charles' delinquencies by an appeal to his.. diligent pietisms. **1889** Jessopp *Coming of Friars* vi. 272 The stimulators of an emotional pietism.

pietist ('paɪɪtɪst). [a. Ger. *Pietist*, f. L. *pietās* piety + -ist. Applied in derision to the followers of Spener, in reference to the *collegia pietatis*, or unions for mutual religious edification, formed by them, and adopted at Leipsic, *c* 1690, by some of Francke's congregation.]

1. *Ch. Hist.* A member of the party of reformers in the Lutheran church which originated from a movement begun by Philipp Jakob Spener at Frankfort about 1670 for the deepening of piety and the reform of religious education.

1697 C. Leslie *Snake in Grass* (ed. 2) 185 There is a Sect like unto these [Quietists] rose up in Germany, call'd Pietists. **1705** *A. H. Franck's Pietas Hallensis* Introd. 25 Dr. Spener's Work.. for which he was also by the Adversaries in way of Derision called, *The Patriarch of the Pietists*. *Ibid.* 27 The Professors of Divinity there, by the World called Pietists. **1733** *Oxf. Methodists* 19 He compares them to the Pietists in Saxony and Switzerland. **1877** E. Caird *Philos. Kant* i. 123 A clergyman who was a leader among the pietists.

2. A person characterized by or professing special piety; one who cultivates, or lays stress on, depth of religious feeling or strictness of religious practice, esp. as distinct from intellectual belief; one who is emotionally, mystically, or exaggeratedly pious.

1767 R. Dean *Future Life Brute Creatures* 72 Numbers of them [dumb creatures] make as great a Point of attending at Church on public Service Days, as the most rigid Pietists do. **1827** G. Higgins *Celtic Druids* 136 The ultra pietists make a terrible outcry. **1861** Thackeray *Four Georges* iii. (1862) 161 William Cowper, that delicate wit, that trembling pietist, that refined gentleman. **1882** Farrar *Early Chr.* II. 142 St. John.. was wholly unlike the effeminate pietist of Titian's or of Raphael's pictures.

3. *attrib.* (in sense 1 or 2). That is a pietist; pertaining to or characteristic of pietists; pietistic.

1705 *A. H. Franck's Pietas Hallensis* Introd. 41 The Industrious Zeal of the (so called) *Pietist-Divines*. **1855** Miss Cobbe *Intuit. Mor.* 133 Religious writers of Pietist tendencies. **1861** *Sat. Rev.* 21 Dec. 648 The celebrated Pietist leader [Spener] so completely drew around himself all that there was of religious movement in his generation, that his life is a history of the Lutheran Church during the latter half of the seventeenth century.

pietistic (paɪɪ'tɪstɪk), *a.* [f. prec. + -ic.] Pertaining to pietists or pietism (in either sense of these words); characterized by pietism; emotionally or affectedly pious.

1830 Pusey *Hist. Enq.* ii. 293 The Ordinance, with regard to Pietistic books, was enacted also in the same year. **1856** Miss Winkworth *Tauler's Life & Serm.* (1857) 110 The Pietistic movement of Spener and Franke. **1884** Seeley in *Contemp. Rev.* Nov. 665 The 'Beautiful Soul' represents the pietistic view of life.

So **pie'tistical** *a.*; hence **pie'tistically** *adv.*

1800 W. Taylor in *Monthly Mag.* X. 319 The multiplicity of the pietistical rhapsodies would weary even Saint Theresa. **1884** Vern. Lee *Euphorion* II. 17 A great art cannot.. be pietistically self-humiliating.

piet-my-vrou ('pɪtmeɪfrəʊ). *S. Afr.* Also piet-myn-vrouw. [Afrikaans, lit. 'Peter my wife', echoic, f. the bird's call.] The red-chested cuckoo, *Notococcyx* (or *Cuculus*) *solitarius*; also, occasionally used as a name for the noisy robin-chat, *Cossypha bicolor*, which imitates the call of the red-chested cuckoo.

[**1790** E. Helme tr. *Le Vaillant's Trav. Afr.* II. xviii. 367 One of them [*sc.* the Hottentots] named *Pit*, was the first who brought me this bird... He had no sooner shot the hen, than the cock flew after him, repeating several times *Pit me frow*; it must be observed, it is the usual cry of this bird, as I was afterwards convinced, on shooting some of the same kind.] **1835** A. Steedman *Wanderings S. Afr.* I. v. 189 The 'Piet myn vrouw', a bird of which the Hottentots relate many amusing stories. **1923** F. W. Fitzsimons *Nat. Hist. S. Afr.: Birds* II. 31 (*caption*) Noisy Robin Chat, or Piet-myn-vrouw (*Cossypha bicolor*). An active and efficient policeman of the forests and dense scrub on the eastern side of South Africa. **1937** M. Alston *Wanderings of Bird-Lover in Afr.* viii. 50 The Dutch call him [*sc.* the noisy robin-chat] the piet-myn-vrouw because of his imitating the red-chested cuckoo. **1949** *Cape Argus Mag.* 5 Nov. 7/6 The piet-my-vrou and turtle doves make the afternoon drowsy with their calls. **1966** E. Palmer *Plains of Camdeboo* xii. 216 Sometimes in the bush we hear.. the Piet-my-vrou, and its call is unmistakable. **1971** *Stand. Encycl. S. Afr.* III. 517/1 The piet-my-vrou or red-chested cuckoo (*Cuculus solitarius*) is a fairly large, brownish cuckoo.

‖**pieton**. *Obs.* [OF. *pieton* (F. *piéton*) foot-soldier, f. L. type **peditō-nem*.] A foot-soldier.

1474 Caxton *Chesse* iii. i. E j b, I shal begynne first at the first pawn,.. they be al named *pietons* that is as moche to say as footmen. **1550** J. Coke *Eng. & Fr. Heralds* §91 (1877) 85, .iiiiᵐ. men of armes, and a great nombre of pietons.

pietose ('paɪɪtəʊs), *a. rare.* [ad. late L. *pietōs-us* (It. *pietoso*) full of piety, f. *pietās* piety: see -ose.] Marked by affectation of piety; pietistic.

1893 *Nat. Observ.* 15 Apr. 542/1 Certain verbose and pietose lines of lamentation.

†**pietous**, *a. Obs.* Also 5 pyetous, 6 *Sc.* pietuous, -ious, -eous. [a. OF. *pietous*, *piteus*:—late L. *pietōs-us*, f. *pietās* piety: see -ous, -itous.] An early form of piteous, q.v.

(In Chaucer and Gower, of three syllables *pi-et-ous*, but in 16th c. Sc. writers pronounced *pit-ous* or *piet-e-ous*, and so passing into piteous.)

c **1374** Chaucer *Troylus* iii. 1395 (1444) (Corpus) As thoughte him tho, for pietous [*v.rr.* piteous, pitous] distresse. **1390** Gower *Conf.* III. 193 Bot wher a king is Pietous [*v.rr.* pitous, -eous, -euous], He is the more gracious. *Ibid.* 202 Fro which he hath with strengthe prived The pietous [*v.rr.* pitous, piteuous] Justinian. **1489** Caxton *Faytes of A.* i. vii. 17 Fiers to his enemyes, pyetous to them that be vainquisshed. **1490** —— *Eneydos* ii. 15 It were a thynge inhumayne to beholde theym wythoute pyte, but yet more pyetous to telle it lyke as it was doon in dede. **1513** Douglas *Æneis* ix. viii. 49 Wyth hyr peteus [*ed.* **1553** pietuous] reuthfull complayntes sayr The hevynnis all scho fillit and the ayr. **1567** *Gude & Godlie B.* (S.T.S.) 36 With voice full pietious. **1571** *Satir. Poems Reform.* xxviii. 14 Ane pieteous spreit appeirit to my thocht.

Hence †**pietously** *adv. Obs.*, piteously.

1474 Caxton *Chesse* ii. v. D v, Thou emperour gouerne the peple pyetously. *c* **1489** —— *Sonnes of Aymon* xxii. 473 The four sones of aymon.. that so many tymes have praied for it humbly & full pyetously.

‖**pietra** (pi'ɛtra). Pl. pietre (-e). The Italian for 'stone'; occurring in Italian phrases, more or less in current use in the terminology of art, etc.

a. pietra commessa (kom'mɛssa), pl. **commesse** (-e) [fem. of *commesso*, pa. pple. of *commettere* to fit together]: mosaic work; an example of this.

a **1666** Evelyn *Diary* an. 1644 (1955) II. 191 Here were divers incomparable tables of Pietra Commessa, which is a marble ground inlayd with severall sorts of marbles & stones of divers colours, in the shapes of flowers, trees, beasts, birds & Landskips like the natural. *a* **1668** R. Lassels *Voy. Italy* (1670) II. 220 A curious table of *pietre commesse* about 12 foot long & 5 wide. **1766** Smollett *Trav.* II. xxviii. 70 These *pietre commesse* are better calculated for cabinets, than for ornaments to great buildings. **1848** H. R. Forster *Stowe Catal.* 287 A box, with slabs of pietre commesse, of birds, fruits, and flowers.

b. pietra dura ('dura), pl. **dure** (-e) [fem. of *duro* hard]: (see quot. 1962); also (sing. and pl.) mosaic work of such stones; also *attrib.*

1805 P. BECKFORD *Familiar Lett. from Italy* I. 148 The best part of the furniture is the inlaid tables in Pietra Dura, a work of great labour and great expence. **1845** R. FORD *Hand-bk. for Travellers Spain* II. 580/2 Observe the Florentine pulpit of *Pietre dure.* **1901** 'L. MALET' *Hist. R. Calmady* III. v. 199 Certain treasures, unique in historic worth, locked in the glass tables and fine Florentine and *piétra dura* cabinets of the Long Gallery. **1942** *Burlington Mag.* Apr. 87/1 The chief piece of furniture mentioned is the enormous cabinet of *pietra dura* that now stands in the ballroom at Badminton. **1961** *Connoisseur* Dec. p. xxxiii, Louis XVI cabinets..inset with panels of pietre dure in the form of flat mosaics of different birds. **1962** R. G. HAGGAR *Dict. Art Terms* 259/1 *Pietra dura*,..those stones which, mainly composed of silicates, are in English generally described as semiprecious stones. *Pietra dura* were much used for altar frontals, table-tops, and the like in the sixteenth century. **1970** *Oxf. Compan. Art* 871/1 *Pietre dure.* .. A term applied to a particular kind of mosaic work in which coloured stones..are used to imitate as far as possible the effect of painting. **1976** *Country Life* 27 May (Suppl.) 47 A Florentine pietra dura casket with ormolu mounts.

c. pietra serena (se'rena) [fem. of *sereno* clear]: a bluish sandstone much used for building in Florence and throughout Tuscany; also *attrib.*

1873 S. & J. HORNER *Walks in Florence* II. xxii. 296 The aisles are carried round the nave and transepts by a line of handsome columns, of pietra-serena, with Corinthian capitals. **1888** G. J. OAKESHOTT *Detail & Ornament of Ital. Renaissance* Pl. 37 Examples of Corbels from Florence, Siena etc..in pietra serena by Donatello in the Bargello. **1927** E. W. ANTHONY *Early Florentine Archit. & Decoration* x. 69 The sculpture of the Gothic period, in general, gives up the decorated backgrounds of the older school, and the reliefs are executed in white marble or *pietra serena.* **1931** R. FRY *Let.* 22 July (1972) II. 661 It's odd that Florence.. couldn't make a city and these rather second-rate Bolognese could—it's true they had brick instead of that abominable *pietra-serena.* **1971** F. M. GODFREY *Ital. Archit. up to 1750* iv. 198 The interior differs from the Cappella Pazzi by the stressed corner pilasters in dark *pietra serena*, supporting the arches at the joints. **1975** *Ashmolean Mus. Rep. Visitors 1973–74* 34 The present building with its *pietra serena* pilasters and window frames, so characteristic of Renaissance architecture in Tuscany.

†**pietranel.** *Obs.* [ad. It. *pietranello* PETRONEL.] = PETRONEL b, PETRONELLIER.

1598 BARRET *Theor. Warres* Table Y iv b, *Pistollier*, a French word; and is the souldier on horse backe, armed as the Pietranell, weaponed with a pistoll.

piety ('paɪɪtɪ). Forms: 4 (6 *Sc.*) piete, 5–7 pietie, 7– piety. [a. OF. *piete* (12th cent.), ad. L. *pietās* dutifulness, piety, f. *pius* PIOUS. (The popular form in Fr. was *pité* PITY.)]

I. † **1.** An early form of PITY, in various senses.

a **1310** in Wright *Lyric P.* xxx. 89 For he that dude is body on tre, Of oure sunnes have piete. **1393** LANGL. *P. Pl.* C. XII. 268 Paul þe apostel, þat no pite [*MS. I* piete] hadde cristene peuple to culle. **1533** BELLENDEN *Livy* III. xix. (S.T.S.) II. 26 Virgineus petuislie praying þame to haue piete erare of him and his dochter, þan to haue ony piete of þe Claudianis. **1548–9** (Mar.) *Bk. Com. Prayer, Commination*, Thou art a mercifull God..and of a great pietie. **1606** HOLLAND *Sueton.* 266 Of your gracious Piety (which I know I shall hardly obtaine).

II. The quality or character of being pious.

2. Habitual reverence and obedience to God (or the gods); devotion to religious duties and observances; godliness, devoutness, religiousness.

1604 R. CAWDREY *Table Alph.*, Pietie, godlinesse, holines. **1605** CAMDEN *Rem., Epigr.* 10 A woman of rare pietie. **1696** PHILLIPS (ed. 5), *Piety*, a Moral vertue which causes us to have an affection and esteem for God and Holy Things. **1742** YOUNG *Nt. Th.* VIII. 691 'Is virtue, then, and piety the same?'—No; piety is more; 'tis virtue's source. **1781** COWPER *Truth* 176 True piety is cheerful as the day. **1875** MANNING *Mission H. Ghost* xi. 295 Piety is the filial affection of the sons of God. **1877** E. R. CONDER *Bas. Faith* i. 19 'Piety', says Cicero, 'is justice towards the gods'.

3. Faithfulness to the duties naturally owed to parents and relatives, superiors, etc.; dutifulness; affectionate loyalty and respect, esp. to parents.

1579 LYLY *Euphues* (Arb.) 103 Ah Lucilla, thou knowest not the care of a father, nor the duetie of a childe, and as farre art thou from pietie as I from crueltie. **1580** *Ibid.* 338 If she be voyd of pitie, why shoulde I not be voyde of pietie? **1611** BIBLE *1 Tim.* v. 4 Let them learne first to shew pietie at home, and to requite their parents. *a* **1634** CHAPMAN *Revenge for Hon.* Plays 1873 III. 309 Though he could put off paternal pietie, 't gives no priviledg for us to wander from our filial dutie. **1656** STANLEY *Hist. Philos.* VI. (1701) 228/1 Her Picture, Aristotle, in piety to her [his mother's] Memory, caused to be made by Protogenes. **1729** SWIFT *Libel on Dr. Delany* 77 Pope..Whose filial piety excels Whatever Grecian story tells. **1857** [see FILIAL 1 a]. **1875** MANNING *Mission H. Ghost* ix. 230 The word piety in its original meaning signifies the natural affection which parents have for their children and children for their parents.

†**b.** ***Our Lady* (*of*) *Piety***: the Virgin Mary represented with the dead body of Christ on her lap: cf. PIETÀ. *Obs.*

1542 *Inv. R. Wardrobe* (1815) 58 Ane antepend of blak velvot broderrit with ane image of our Lady pietie upoun the samyne. *c* **1600** *Rites of Durham* (Surtees) 38 Yᵉ piller next adioyning to yᵉ Lady of Pieties alter.

c. ***mount, mountain of piety***: see MOUNT *sb.*, MOUNTAIN. ***pelican in her piety***: see PELICAN *sb.*

4. with *a* and *pl.* (in sense 2 or 3). An instance of religious devotion or affectionate loyalty; a pious act, observance, or characteristic.

1652 SPARKE *Prim. Devot.* (1673) 617 The pieties of the church and laws of the land. **1682** SIR T. BROWNE *Chr. Mor.* II. §12 Persons..more ready to be advanced by impressions from above, and christianized unto pieties. **1860** HAWTHORNE *Marb. Faun* (1879) I. xiii. 134 This great burden of stony memories which the ages have deemed it a piety to heap upon its back. **1895** ZANGWILL *Master* 431 Inextricably woven with all the pieties of childhood.

5. *attrib.* and *Comb.*

1830 in *W. Cobbett's Rur. Rides* (1885) II. 317 St. Botolph ..must lament that the piety-inspiring mass has been.. supplanted by the monotonous hummings of an oaken hutch. **1893** E. BELLASIS *Mem. Serjt. Bellasis* 158 A complete *razzia* was made upon the piety shops for rosaries, medals, &c.

pievish, pievit, obs. ff. PEEVISH, PEWIT.

piewe, obs. form of PEW.

piewipe: see PEEWEEP.

†**pieze**, obs. form of PEISE *v.*, to weigh out.

1634 PEACHAM *Gentlem. Exerc.* II. vii. 125 An indifferent arbiter betweene the day and night, piezing to each his equall houres.

piezo (paɪ'iːzəʊ), *a.* = PIEZOELECTRIC *a.*

1922 GLAZEBROOK *Dict. Appl. Physics* II. 600/1 To demonstrate the piezo effect it is convenient to place a sheet of tinfoil on a slab of tourmaline and connect the foil to an electrometer. **1930** *Proc. IRE* XVIII. 491 A piezo oscillator is the most suitable frequency standard thus far devised. **1946** W. G. CADY *Piezoelectricity* i. 6 Piezo resonators and oscillators have proved useful in many kinds of electrical measurement. **1970** J. EARL *Tuners & Amplifiers* i. 27 Some of the inexpensive systems use a piezo cartridge (crystal or ceramic). **1975** G. J. KING *Audio Handbk.* viii. 174 Early piezo pickups used a natural crystal element..as the signal generator.

piezo- (paɪ'iːzəʊ, 'paɪɪzəʊ), used as a combining form from Gr. πιέζειν to press, squeeze; as in **piezo-crystal**, a piezo-electric crystal used in an electrical circuit; **piezo-crystalli'zation** *Geol.* [ad. G. *piezokrystallisation* (E. Weinschenk 1895, in *Abhandl. d. Bayerischen Akad. d. Wissensch.* (*Math.-phys. Klasse*) XVIII. 741)], crystallization of a magma, usu. in a distinctive or abnormal manner, under conditions of mechanical stress; (? *obs.*); **piezo'magnetism** [ad. G. *piezomagnetismus* (W. Voigt 1901, in *Nachrichten v. d. K. Ges. d. Wissensch. zu Göttingen* (*Math.-phys. Klasse*) I. 1)], magnetism induced in a crystal by the application of mechanical stress; hence **piezomag'netic** *a.*, of, pertaining to, or exhibiting piezomagnetism; **piezore'sistance, -resi'stivity**, change in the electrical resistance or resistivity of a solid when subjected to mechanical stress; freq. *attrib.*; so **piezore'sistive** *a.*, of, pertaining to, or utilizing this effect.

1928 *Exper. Wireless* July 414/2 (*caption*) Mounting piezo crystals. **1936** *Amer. Speech* XI. 95/2 A piezo-crystal cutter for aluminum discs with which frequencies from 40 to 10,000 cycles can be recorded. **1958** *Engineering* 31 Jan. 160/3 An alternative type of drum is the large sheet of steel with a piezo-crystal fixed to a particular part of it. **1903** A. GEIKIE *Text-bk. Geol.* (ed. 4) II. 718 He [*sc.* Weinschenk] believes that rock to have been part of a normal granitic magma which crystallized under abnormal conditions, and that it owes its mineralogical composition and characteristic foliated structure..to the peculiar relations of tension accompanying the plication of the mountains. To these relations he has given the name of 'piezocrystallization'. **1938** A. JOHANNSEN *Descr. Petrogr. Igneous Rocks* IV. 79 The parallel texture is seen in dynamometamorphosed rocks or in border facies. In the latter case it may be due to piezocrystallization, for the feldspars also are often more or less parallel. **1954** R. L. PARKER tr. *Niggli's Rocks & Min. Deposits* xiv. 523 Effects of stress on partly solidified material. Such effects leave their impression on stuctures and textures and are responsible for the piezo-crystallization of magmas. **1901** *Sci. Abstr.* A. IV. 1043 The recorded observations determine, for the pyro- and piezo-magnetic excitement, only superior limiting values. **1959** *Physics & Chem. of Solids* XI. 77/2 The piezomagnetic moment will be reversed in sign when the antiferromagnetic sublattice magnetizations are reversed in sign. **1972** *Nature* 8 Dec. 348/2 Both volcanic eruptions and the San Andreas creep increments are very imperfectly understood so that a large scale control experiment which demonstrates quantitatively the role of the piezomagnetic effect in producing local magnetic anomalies is very desirable. **1978** *Ibid.* 9 Mar. 130/1 When a stress is applied to, or removed from, a rock there is a distortion of crystal structure which often gives rise to a small change in the rock's remanent magnetisation. This is known as the piezomagnetic effect and has an obvious application to the prediction of earthquakes. **1901** *Sci. Abstr.* A. IV. 1043 (*heading*) Pyro- and piezo-magnetism of crystals. **1931** S. R. WILLIAMS *Magn. Phenomena* v. 164 With the advent of the electron theory of matter,..physicists began to inquire as to the possibility of the phenomena of pyro- and piezo-magnetism. **1967** CONDON & ODISHAW *Handbk. Physics* (ed. 2) IV. viii. 143/1 In antiferromagnetic crystals of sufficiently low symmetry, such as CoF_2 and MnF_2, the magnetic analogue of piezoelectricity, piezomagnetism, can occur. **1978** *Nature* 9 Mar. 130/1 In practice, piezomagnetism has been of little use in earthquake prediction. **1954** *Physical Rev.* XCIV. 42/2 The piezoresistance results for germanium and silicon ..have been expressed in terms of the pressure coefficient of resistivity and two simple shear coefficients. **1970** *Jrnl. Appl. Physics* XLI. 811/2 (*heading*) Piezo-resistance in SnTe. *Ibid.*, The piezoresistance effect has been used in the past with success in determining the symmetry of the bands in various semiconductors. **1935** J. W. COOKSON in *Physical Rev.* XLVII. 194/2 It is herein meant by the piezo-resistive effect that change in electrical resistance which a homogeneous body undergoes when subjected to mechanical stress. **1963** *Jrnl. Appl. Physics* XXXIV. 684/2 The piezoresistive effect in semiconductors..is generally a result of the dependence of the electronic energy levels of a crystal on the state of strain in the crystal. **1973** *Physics Bull.* Dec. 743/3 The cartridge consists of an elastic stainless steel cantilever on to which a pair of silicon piezoresistive strain gauges have been fused. **1958** *Solid State Physics* VI. 232 The most important examples of unsymmetrical fourth rank properties and the classical piezooptic effect (photoelasticity) and the piezoresistivity effect. **1965** *Wireless World* Aug. 380/2 Although carbon has been used as the sensitive element in pressure transducers, piezoresistivity in ordinary carbon composition resistors appears to have attracted little attention.

piezoelectric (paɪ,iːzəʊɪ'lɛktrɪk, ,paɪɪ-), *a.* and *sb.* Also piezo-electric. [f. PIEZO- + ELECTRIC *a.* and *sb.*]

A. *adj.* Of, pertaining to, exhibiting, or utilizing piezoelectricity.

1883 *Jrnl. Chem. Soc.* XLIV. 412 (*heading*) Actinoelectric and piezoelectric properties of quartz. **1921** *Physical Rev.* XVII. 531 The possibility is discussed of using the piezo-electric resonator for a standard of high frequency. **1947** CROWTHER & WHIDDINGTON *Science at War* iv. 175 Modified quartz piezo-electric hydrophones were used to measure vibrations as low as 1 cycle per second. **1958** N. CUSACK *Electr. & Magn. Prop. Solids* xviii. 410 The piezoelectric properties of Rochelle salt have been widely used in gramophone pick-ups, microphones, loudspeakers, surface roughness analysers, and other electromechanical devices. **1972** *Last Whole Earth Catalog* (Portola Inst.) 88/2 The piezoelectric effect has been observed in a number of organic materials, among them wood, bone, tendon and skin. **1973** M. WOODHOUSE *Blue Bone* xvii. 190 He was talking about some kind of reversed piezoelectric effect. **1977** *Rolling Stone* 7 Apr. 88/1 (Advt.), But only Ovation's six-element piezo-electric pickup captures both top *and* individual string vibration.

B. *sb.* A piezoelectric substance or body.

1913 *Phil. Mag.* XXVI. 1053 These high resistances..are both cheaper and easier to use than either standard capacities or quartz piezoelectrics. **1971** B. JAFFE et al. *Piezoelectric Ceramics* i. 1 The creation of useful piezo-electrics by treatment of a polycrystalline material depends on ferroelectricity. **1975** *Physics Bull.* May 212/3 For economic and technical reasons the piezoelectrics most commonly used for SAW generation are lithium niobate and quartz.

Hence **piezoe'lectrical** *a.* = PIEZOELECTRIC *a.*; **piezoe'lectrically** *adv.*, as regards, or by means of, piezoelectricity.

1923 *Physical Rev.* XXI. 350 Quartz, another piezo-electrically active substance. **1937** *Discovery* Jan. 22/1 One method of producing them [*sc.* ultra-sounds]..is to employ the piezo-electrical effect in quartz. **1969** *Sci. Jrnl.* Aug. 21/2 Current from the voltage source is fed through a superconductive coil which is vibrated by a piezoelectrically driven metal tuning fork. **1976** *Physics Bull.* Feb. 61/3 New techniques include..very high frequency phonon generation..using a far infrared laser on a piezoelectrical crystal.

piezoelectricity (paɪ,iːzəʊɪlɛk'trɪsɪtɪ, ,paɪɪ-). Also **piezo-electricity**. [ad. G. *piezoelectricität* (W. G. Hankel 1881, in *Ber. d. K. Sächsischen Ges. d. Wissensch. zu Leipzig* XXXIII. 52).] Electric polarization in a substance resulting from the application of mechanical stress, esp. in certain crystals.

1883 *Jrnl. Chem. Soc.* XLIV. 412 This phenomenon the author proposes to call piezoelectricity. **1895** STORY-MASKELYNE *Crystallogr.* i. §13 Compression of a crystal of tourmaline along its morphological axis also produces electrification (*piezo-electricity*). **1929** J. A. RATCLIFFE *Physical Princ. Wireless* i. 2 The facts of piezo-electricity have been applied in the quartz oscillator. **1956** *Nature* 17 Mar. 537/2 Tests for pyroelectricity and piezoelectricity were negative. **1974** J. KYLE *Electronics Unravelled* (1975) ii. 45 Piezoelectricity is due to an unusual crystal structure found in several materials.

piezometer (paɪ,iː'zɒmɪtə(r), ,paɪɪ-). [mod. (J. Perkins 1820) f. Gr. πιέζ-ειν to press + -(O)METER. So F. *piézomètre.*] An instrument for measuring pressure (or something connected with pressure).

An instrument **a.** for measuring the compressibility of water or other liquid under varying pressures; **b.** for measuring the pressure of water at any point in a water-main or an aquifer; **c.** for measuring the pressure of gas in the bore of a gun; **d.** for measuring the sense of pressure on different parts of the surface of the body. **e.** A sounding apparatus for measuring the depth of water by means of the compression of air in a tube.

1820 J. PERKINS in *Phil. Trans.* 324 Having believed for many years, that water was an elastic fluid, I was induced to ..ascertain the fact..by constructing an instrument which I call a piezometer. **1842** BRANDE *Dict. Sci.*, etc., *Piezometer*, an instrument for ascertaining the compressibility of liquids. **1882** OGILVIE, *Piezometer*... 2. An instrument consisting essentially of a vertical tube inserted into a water-main, to show the pressure of the fluid at that point, by the height to which it ascends in the tube of the piezometer. **1884** KNIGHT *Dict. Mech.* Supp. 678/2 *Piezometer*.., an instrument to measure the sense of pressure... The sense of pressure is strongest on the forehead, tongue, and cheek... An instrument to ascertain the pressure set up in the bore of a gun when a charge of powder is fired. **1884** *Health Exhib. Catal.* 132/1 Thermometer..Piezometer..Hygrometers.

1904 *Johns Hopkins Hosp. Bull.* XV. 293 (*heading*) The piezometer, an instrument for measuring resistances. *Ibid.* 293/2 There are two ways of using the piezometer for the purpose of outlining an abdominal tumor. **1954** ROE & AYRES *Engin. Agric. Drainage* x. 266 The piezometer is a length of ¼- or ⅜-inch iron pipe driven into the soil so that there is no leakage into or out from the sides. **1970** *Nature* 4 July 11/1 Piezometers were used to measure water pressures in the rock joints.

Hence **piezo'metric** *a.*; *spec.* in *Hydrology*, of or pertaining to the measurement of hydrostatic pressure in an aquifer; ***piezometric surface*** (see quot. 1923[2]).

1923 O. E. MEINZER in *Water-Supply Papers U.S. Geol. Survey* No. 494. 6 The expression piezometric surface is obtained from the French. *Ibid.* 38 The piezometric surface of an aquifer is an imaginary surface that everywhere coincides with the static level of the water in the aquifer. It is the surface to which the water from a given aquifer will rise under its full head. **1966** DAVIS & DEWIEST *Hydrogeol.* ii. 48 The elevation to which water will rise in artesian wells, or wells penetrating confined aquifers, defines the piezometric surfaces. *Ibid.* 49 The general direction of ground-water flow can be shown.. on piezometric maps. **1973** GREGORY & WALLING *Drainage Basin Form & Process* iii. 113 This data is used to plot lines of equal piezometric head or equipotentials on a vertical cross section of the aquifer... Similarly, equipotentials or piezometric surfaces could be plotted for several horizontal planes at different depths.

piff (pɪf), *int.* An imitation of various sounds, as of that made by the swift motion of a bullet through the air. Cf. PHIT, PHUT. So ***piff-paff***.

1775 GARRICK *Bon Ton* 8 Present, fire, piff-pauff—'tis done. **1901** *Westm. Gaz.* 16 Dec. 2/1 Some of them think we're only a part of his dream, and that we shall all go 'piff' when he wakes up. **1902** *Words Eyewitness* 190 Piff, piff, piff, skip the little projectiles amongst the naval guns.

Piffer ('pɪfə(r)). *slang.* [From the initials of the name of the force + -ER[1].] A member of the Punjab Frontier Force (a military unit raised in 1849 and employed esp. to police the North-West Frontier of India during British rule) or of one of the regiments that succeeded it. Also (*attrib.*), the force itself.

1892 *Pall Mall Gaz.* 24 Oct. 3/1 The Punjab Frontier Force is known in India as 'The Piffers'. **1901** *Blackw. Mag.* June 780/1 A strong garrison of the three arms, all Piffers. *Ibid.* 788/2 One regiment of Piffer infantry could move anywhere in the hills. **1922** *19th Cent.* Jan. 48 The establishment of a British observation corps, similar to the 'Piffers' of later times. **1958** O. CAROE *Pathans* xx. 345 For many years the Piffers served under the Panjab Lieutenant-Governor. **1970** A. J. SMITHERS *Man who Disobeyed* x. 100 The Guides, the Punjab Frontier Force (Piffers), the Sikhs and the Gurkhas, would have allowed no affectations of superiority from any British regiment, household or line.

‖**pifferaro** (piffe'raro). Pl. **pifferari**. [It.] A performer on the *piffero*.

1854 THACKERAY *Newcomes* I. xxii. 212 A Contadina and a Trasteverino dancing at the door of a Locanda to the music of a Pifferaro. **1860** *Once a Week* 14 July 71/2 Three of the *pifferari* whom you find at Christmas time in such numbers in the Piazza di Spagna at Rome. **1870** QUEEN VICTORIA *Let.* 6 June in R. Fulford *Your Dear Letter* (1971) 281 Imagine our astonishment at seeing in the village [*sc.* Balmoral] this morning an Italian pifferaro.. and two boys dancing. **1920** *Punch* 30 June 510/3 The local condettieri, pifferari, banditti and lazzaroni. **1974** *Times Lit. Suppl.* 8 Mar. 228/4 The charming shepherds who came to the cities from the Abruzzi to play their bagpipes in front of the wayside shrines—the pifferari. **1977** *Gramophone* June 41/3 He also draws a marvellously keen, edgy sound from piccolo and oboe in the Serenade, for all the world like a *pifferaro* squealing on the Abruzzi air.

‖**piffero** ('piffero). Also 8 **-aro**. [It. *piffero* = Sp. *pifaro*, F. *fifre*, a fife or pipe, ad. OHG. *pfîfari* piper, f. *pfîfa* PIPE, FIFE.] (See quots.)

1724 *Short Explic. For. Wds. in Mus. Bks.*, *Piffaro*, is an Instrument somewhat like a Hautboy. *Ibid.*, *Piffero*, is a small Flute or Flagelet. **1880** W. H. STONE in Grove *Dict. Mus.* II. 753 *Piffero*.. in the *Dizionario della Musica*, is described as a small flute with six finger-holes and no keys. But the term is also commonly used to denote a rude kind of oboe, or a bagpipe with an inflated sheepskin for reservoir, common in Italy.. the players being termed *Pifferari*.

'**piffing**, *vbl. sb. slang.* [Cf. PIFF *int.*] (See quots.)

1928 *Daily Tel.* 10 Jan. 11/5 Gunnery training is confined for the most part to sub-calibre firing—'piffing', as it is known in service parlance. **1962** GRANVILLE *Dict. Sailors' Slang* 88/1 *Piffing*, sub-calibre firing. Echoic of the sound. (Gunnery term.)

piffle ('pɪf(ə)l), *v. dial.* and *slang*. Also 9 *dial.* **pifle**, **pyfle**. [? Onomatopœic, with dim. ending: cf. also Sc. *pifer*, *pyfer*, in cognate sense.] *intr.* To talk or act in a feeble, trifling, or ineffective way.

1847-78 HALLIWELL, *Pifle*, to be squeamish or delicate. **1896** KIPLING *Seven Seas, Mary Gloster* (1897) 146 They piddled and piffled with iron; I'd given my orders for steel! **1897** *Sunday Times* 2 Jan. 6/7 Their defence is sound, and their attack altogether good, save a tendency to 'piffle' in front of goal at times.

Hence '**piffle** *sb.*, foolish or formal nonsense; twaddle; trash; also used as a derisive retort; '**piffler**, a trifler, a twaddler; '**piffling** *vbl. sb.* and *ppl. a.*

1890 *Sat. Rev.* 1 Feb. 152/2 If there is.. a certain amount of the 'piffle' (to use a University phrase) thought to be incumbent on earnest young princes in our century, there is a complete absence of insincerity. **1900** O. ONIONS *Compl. Bachelor* ii. 18 He'd talk a lot of piffle, wouldn't he? **1914** 'HIGH JINKS, JR.' *Choice Slang* 16 *Oh piffle*, an exclamation denoting inconsequence of the subject in question. **1920** 'B. L. STANDISH' *Man on First* xviii. 127 'The Hawks have the lead on us, still.' 'Piffle!' said Cady. 'We'll even things up to-morrow.' **1959** *Elizabethan* Apr. 10/1, I gave you a bar of chocolate on the train from London. So piffle! **1892** *Star* 14 July 1 The nervousness of the other juvenile and titled piffler. **1896** *Westm. Gaz.* 4 Dec. 2/1 Lord; but this chap is dull... Dull! he's a perfect piffler. **1864** MRS. E. LYNN LINTON *Lake Country* 309 Pyklin an' pyflin, thoo gits nowt doon. **1894** *Westm. Gaz.* 21 May 2/3 He seems.. to have convinced himself that he is an old man, and settled down to a piffling eld. **1916** 'BOYD CABLE' *Action Front* 17 You don't think a pifflin' little Pip-Squeak shell could go through *his* head? **1927** *Daily Express* 26 July 3/4 The Bench consider that this is a piffling offence, and.. that a warning would have been sufficient. **1927** *Observer* 13 Nov. 10/4 The mechanical parts of the moving-pictures are superb, but the imaginative and intellectual parts are piffling. **1963** *Times* 12 June 8/7 The sum involved was piffling compared with the firm's £25m. a year turnover. **1973** J. WAINWRIGHT *Pride of Pigs* 56 The lesser hooks being pulled in for the piffling crimes, while the big boys work the blinders.

pifflicated ('pɪflɪkeɪtɪd), *ppl. a. U.S. slang.* [A fanciful formation of PIFFLE *v.*, infl. by SPIFLICATE *v.*] Drunk, intoxicated.

1905 TAYLOR & GIBSON *Log of Water Wagon* 50 (*caption*) Professor Bunn's patent plugs for pifflicated people. **1934** S. ROBERTSON *Devel. Mod. Eng.* (1936) xi. 465 English (chiefly American) terms for the idea of 'drunk' or 'intoxicated' ... *shellacked, soused, piffled, pifflicated, blotto, stinko.*

pig (pɪg), *sb.*[1] Forms: 3-7 **pigge**, 4-6 **pygge**, 5 **pygg**, 5-8 **pigg**, 6 **pyg**, (7 **bigg**), 6- **pig**. [Early ME. *pigge*:—prob. OE. **picga*, **pigga*. Etymology obscure.

In formation, **picga* wk. masc. corresponds to other animal names, *docga*, ME. *dogge* dog, *frocga*, *frogga*, ME. *frogge* frog, *hogga*, ME. *hogge* hog. The word is perh. found in *picbred*, ? for **picg-bréad*; for the shortening cf. *gum-cynn*, *sunn-béam*, etc.; for *pic-* instead of *picg-*, cf. *bric-bot* = *brycg-bot* (Laws of Æthelred, 11th c.), *wic-cræft* = *wicg-cræft*, etc. *Pigman* is cited by Bardsley as a name *temp.* Richard I, 1189-99. Low G. and early mod.Du. have, in same sense, *bigge*, Du. *big* a young pig; MDu. *vigghe*; but the phonology is difficult: see Franck.]

I. 1. a. The young of swine; 'a young sow or boar' (J.).

a **1225** *Ancr. R.* 204 þe Suwe of ȝiuernesse, þet is, Glutunie, haueð pigges þus inemned. *Ibid.*, þus beoð þeos pigges ieruwed. *c* **1386** CHAUCER *Reeve's T.* 358 And in the floor with nose and mouth to-broke They walwe as doon two pigges in a poke. **1387** TREVISA *Higden* (Rolls) I. 237 A white sowe wiþ þritty pigges [*triginta porcellis*]. *c* **1400** MAUNDEV. (1839) vi. 71 The Sarazines bryngen forth no Pigges, nor thei eten no Swynes Flessche. *c* **1440** *Promp. Parv.* 395/2 Pygge, gryce, *porcellus*. **1523** FITZHERB. *Husb.* §121 And if thy sowe haue moo pygges than thou wilt rere, sel them, or eate them. **1577** B. GOOGE *Heresbach's Husb.* III. (1586) 149 Euery Pigge doth know his owne Pappe. **1607** TOPSELL *Four-f. Beasts* (1658) 512 As in English we call a young Swine a Pig. **1688** R. HOLME *Armoury* II. 180/1 In English we call a young Swine a Bigg; a sucking or weaning Bigg. **1719** DE FOE *Crusoe* (1840) II. ix. 196 Three sows big with pig. **1828** WEBSTER, *Pig*, the young of swine, male or female. **1869** BLACKMORE *Lorna D.* xvii, Two farrows of pigs ready for the chapman.

b. Phr. ***in pig***, of a sow: pregnant; also *transf.* of a girl or woman (*slang*).

1886 J. LONG *Bk. Pig* iv. 59 They [*sc.* gilts] are less costly than if either tolerably fat or, as it is called, 'in pig', or in farrow. **1905** J. P. STILWELL in *N. & Q.* 10th s. IV. 512 About here [in Hants] a pig is a pig from birth till six or eight months old, when it becomes a boar, a hog, or a sow. **1917** W. POWELL-OWEN *Pig-Keeping* v. 59 Sows that are in-pig do best when given their liberty. **1937** H. M. RIKARD-BELL *Handk. Mod. Pig Farming* ii. 33 Watch carefully after three weeks have elapsed for fear that the recurrence of their oestrum periods will prove them [*sc.* gilts] to be not in-pig. **1945** N. MITFORD *Pursuit of Love* x. 83, I am in pig, what d'you think of that? **1950**, etc. [see IN-PIG *a.*]. **1976** 'D. HALLIDAY' *Dolly & Nanny Bird* vii. 86 Since when had her mother paid the slightest attention to anything her darling daughter said or did, except to do her level best to keep her from marrying anything less than a duke, until she had to get herself in pig.

†**c.** Applied to the young of the badger. *Obs.*

1575 TURBERV. *Venerie* 183 There are foxes and theyr cubbes, and badgerdes and theyr Pigges.

2. a. By extension: A swine of any age; a hog. (Clear examples of this use are rare before the 19th c.) [**1526** *Pilgr. Perf.* (W. de W. 1531) 158b, Let vs syng or say our seruice distinctly.. not syngynge in yᵉ nose as pygges. **1596** SHAKS. *Merch. V.* IV. i. 47 Some men there are loue not a gaping Pigge.] **1663** BUTLER *Hud.* I. ii. 472 Not onely Horse, but Cows, Nay Pigs, were of the elder house. **1784** in *Boswell's Johnson* (1887) VI. 373, I told him (says Miss Seward).. of a wonderful learned pig. *Ibid.* 374 'Certainly (said the Doctor): but how old is your pig?' I told him, three years old. **18..** SOUTHEY *Ode to a Pig*, And when, at last, the closing hour of life Arrives (for pigs must die as well as men). **1820** SHELLEY *Œdip. Tyrann.* I. *Chorus of Swine* 3 Under your mighty ancestors, we pigs Were blessed as nightingales on myrtle sprigs. *Ibid.*, *Semichorus* iii, Happier swine were they than we, Drowned in the Gadarean sea.. Alas! the Pigs are an unhappy nation! **1863** LYELL *Antiq. Man* 23 The domesticated species comprise the dog, horse, ass, pig, goat, sheep, and several bovine races. **1867** D. G. MITCHELL *Rur. Stud.* 63 The pig can hardly be regarded as a classic animal.

b. Applied to a wild swine or hog; also used *collectively* = wild swine in the mass.

1889 R. S. S. BADEN-POWELL *Pigsticking* 67, I have even seen a pig break its leg in.. the act of jumping down a small bank. **1901** *Munsey's Mag.* (U.S.) XXV. 328/2 There is much to be seen—deer in herds, a sounder of pig, perchance, scurrying away.

c. The figure of the animal used as an ornament, etc. ***Sussex pig***, a drinking vessel in the form of a pig.

1884 *Mag. Art* Jan. 102 A popular vessel is the 'Sussex pig'. When filled, this quaint, uncouth utensil is.. set upright on the brute's tail; empty, it stands on all-fours. In Sussex these 'pigs' were, and still are, brought into use at weddings.

3. The animal or its flesh as an article of food. Usually referring to a young or sucking pig; otherwise only *humorous*, the regular name for the meat being *pork*, dial. also *pig-meat*; cf. also *bacon*, *ham*, *griskin*, etc.

c **1430** *Two Cookery-bks.* 40 Broche þin Pygge; þen farce hym, & sewe þe hole, & lat hym roste. **1477** NORTON *Ord. Alch.* vii. in Ashm. *Theat. Chem. Brit.* (1652) 103 Heate wherewith Pigg or Goose is Scalded. **1549** COVERDALE, etc. *Erasm. Par. Tit.* 28 They feare to be contaminate yf they eate eyther porke or pigge. **1590** SHAKS. *Com. Err.* II. i. 66 The Pigge quoth I, is burn'd. **1684** BUNYAN *Pilgr.* II. Introd. 161 Some start at Pigg, slight Chicken, love not Fowl. **1822** LAMB *Elia* Ser. I., A Dissertation upon Roast Pig.

4. Applied with distinguishing epithet to various species of the family *Suidæ*, as ***bush-pig***, ***wood-pig***; also extended to include animals in some way resembling the pig, as **sea-pig**, (*a*) the porpoise; (*b*) the tunny. See also GUINEA-PIG.

1664 [see GUINEA-PIG]. **1785** G. FORSTER tr. *Sparrman's Voy. Cape G. H.* II. 279 We had the good luck to catch a young wood-pig. **1826** MISS MITFORD *Village* Ser. II. (1863) 387 Driving about an unhappy porpoise in a wheel-barrow, and showing it at two-pence a head, under the name of a sea pig. **1896** KIRBY (*title*) In Haunts of Wild Game,.. Reedbuck and Small Game, Bush-pigs, Leopards. **1897** MARY KINGSLEY *W. Africa* 613, I deeply regret not having been able to bring home a Bobia pig... These.. are black in colour, as indeed is common in African pigs, two-thirds head, and after a very small and very flat bit of body, end in an inordinately long tail.

5. a. Applied, usually contemptuously or opprobriously, to a person, or to another animal. (Cf. F. *cochon*.)

1546 J. HEYWOOD *Prov.* (1867) 65 What, byd me welcome pyg. *a* **1586** SIDNEY *Arcadia* III. (1629) 360 The pretie pigge, laying her sweet burden about his necke. **1885** G. ALLEN *Babylon* xv, Knew him well, the selfish old pig. **1891** H. S. CONSTABLE *Horses, Sport & War* 46 He is usually called a sulky pig of a horse. **1927** *Dialect Notes* V. 458 *Pig*, a woman—sottish, surly, disgruntled, stinking—who has sunk to the lowest level of prostitution. The bum who *keeps a pig* rents her out to others. **1931** E. O'NEILL *The Hunted* IV, in *Mourning becomes Electra* 155 That yaller-haired pig with the pink dress on! **1932** J. T. FARRELL in *Story* Mar.-Apr. 47 Jack told of an anecdote about a pig he had picked up once. She was too lousy and scummy to take a chance on. **1960** I. JEFFERIES *Dignity & Purity* v. 83 I'm having a golf lesson from the Advertising pig tomorrow. **1966** *Sunday Times* (Colour Suppl.) 13 Feb. 35/4 *Pig*, an unattractive girl. **1968-70** *Current Slang* (Univ. S. Dakota) III-IV. 91 *Pig*, a girl who is both promiscuous and drunken. **1973** *Daily Californian* 1 Feb. 1/4 The Pentagon Papers.. 'provide evidence of pig foreign policy. A pig is someone who attacks you and at the same time claims he is the victim', he said. **1976** *National Observer* (U.S.) 21 Feb. 14/6 The quick resort to the phrase 'pig' for the blue-collar, lower-class people who were doing the job they thought they were supposed to do. **1977** P. G. WINSLOW *Witch Hill Murder* II. 227, I had some beautiful birds in London, but I had to stay on the good side of that pig, or she might have noticed more than was good for her. **1979** R. RENDELL *Make Death love Me* i. 16 I'm not demeaning myself to reply to you, pig.

b. Colloq. phr. ***to make a pig of oneself***, to gluttonize.

1942 BERREY & VAN DEN BARK *Amer. Thes. Slang* §272/3 *Be greedy or selfish*,.. make a pig.. of oneself. **1961** F. S. ANTHONY in *Webster* s.v., Not make such a gorging pig of himself. **1979** *Guardian* 22 June 9/5 We had made pigs of ourselves on the bread.

c. Applied contemptuously or opprobriously to a thing.

1975 'W. HAGGARD' *Scorpion's Tail* i. 2 What a summer, he thought—what a perfect pig. The rain and the cold. **1978** *Times* 15 Feb. 8/1 Miller was out in Collinge's second over to a pig of a ball. **1978** F. MULLALLY *Deadly Payoff* xi. 154 Watch for the potholes. It's a pig of a road. **1978** *Hot Car* June 93/4 The car became a pig to start.

6. *slang.* †**a.** A sixpence (*obs.*). **b.** A police officer. Now usu. disparaging. **c.** A pressman in a printing-office.

1622 FLETCHER *Beggars Bush* III. i, Fill till't be sixpence, And there's my pig. *a* **1700** B. E. *Dict. Cant. Crew*, *Pig*, Sixpence. **1811** *Lexicon Balatronicum*, s.v. *Pig*, a China street pig; a Bow-street officer. **1812** J. H. VAUX *Flash Dict.*, *Pigs* or *Grunters*, police runners. **1821** EGAN *Life in London* I. i. (Farmer), Do not frown upon me,.. thou bashaw of the pigs, and all but beak! **1841** SAVAGE *Art Printing* s.v., Pressmen are called pigs by compositors, sometimes by way of sport, and sometimes of irritation. **1857** *N. & Q.* 2nd Ser. IV. 192/1 Compositors are jocosely called mokes or donkeys, and pressmen pigs. These nicknames.. were well understood in the early part of the last century. **1874** HOTTEN *Slang Dict.* 253 *Pig*, a policeman; an informer. The word is now almost exclusively applied by London thieves to a plain-clothes man, or a 'nose'. **1967** C. DRUMMOND *Death at Furlong Post* v. 63, I had to give the local P.C. a lift. I dropped the pig at Packenham. **1970** *Times* 7 Aug. 4/7 'Pig' is slang for a policeman—and the defence says that the word 'pig' was scrawled over the doors of the house after the killings. **1973** *Black World* July 56/1 The pigs swooped by, going west, the emergency light blinking green. **1975** D. LODGE *Changing Places* v. 170 Any pig roughs you up, make sure you get his number. **1975** N. LUARD *Travelling Horseman* vi. 146 The police Rover and some motorcycle pigs providing escort. **1977** 'E. CRISPIN' *Glimpses of Moon* xi. 217 'My God, it's the pigs,' said the hunt saboteuse disgustedly.

d. An informer. ? *Obs.*

1874 [see 6b above]. **1904** 'No. 1500' *Life in Sing Sing* 251/1 *Pig*, prisoner who reports another; stool-pigeon. **1918** *Amer. Law Rev.* LII. 891 A 'prison stool pigeon' is a 'trusty', 'psalm singer' or 'pig'.

e. Any of various forms of transport (see quots.).

1898 *North Amer. Rev.* June 723 Whalebacks, or 'pigs', as the lake sailors call them. **1938** L. BEEBE *High Iron* 223/2 (Gloss.), *Pig*, locomotive. **1946** *Jrnl. R. Aeronaut. Soc.* L. 85 He had made no great contribution publicly to aeronautical science, but the fact that he had taken the first 'pig' (the name sometimes applied to early biplanes—Ed.) into the air. **1961** *Amer. Speech* XXXVI. 273 *Pig, n.*, an old truck. **1967** *Evening Standard* 26 July 13/3 'We'll hop in my pig, catch the rays and have a boss time.'.. The latest in American teenage talk.. 'The pig' is a car which looks powerful but has a small engine; 'catching the rays' is getting a sun tan; and 'boss' is the same as great. **1971** *Guardian* 27 Aug. 11/7 He did indeed ride with Melbourne's Hell's Angels.. garaging his extremely powerful pig (bike) beside his Porsche. *Ibid.*, 22 Nov. 6/1 The soldiers were in a convoy of 'pigs'—armoured personnel carriers, trucks, and Land-Rovers. **1972** *Times* 8 June 16/2 It was only a patrol of one armoured personnel carrier, a great heavy green vehicle, which everyone calls a 'pig' because of its snout shaped bonnet. **1973** *Amer. Speech 1969* XLIV. 207 *Pig*, 1. Trailer transported on a flat car. 2. Tractor with little power. **1978** *Times* 19 Jan. 29/3 The Pig, the armoured vehicle most used in Belfast.

f. *pl.* Used as a derisive retort. Also const. *to*. *Austral. slang.*

1906 E. DYSON *Fact'ry 'Ands* i. 5 'Pigs to you!' said Benno, with incredible scorn. **1933** N. LINDSAY *Saturdee* ix. 165 Peter had to cover his confusion by saying 'Pigs to you' as he went out kicking the door. **1957** 'N. CULOTTA' *They're a Weird Mob* (1958) iv. 47 'She's worn out.' 'Pigs she is. There's a lot of life in 'er yet.' **1975** L. RYAN *Shearers* 119 'Ar, pigs to you!' 'In your dinger, too!'

g. ***blind pig***: see BLIND *a.* (and *adv.*) 16.

II. Technical uses.

7. An oblong mass of metal, as obtained from the smelting-furnace; an ingot.

In this connexion *sow* is found earlier: viz. of lead 1481, of silver 1590, of iron 1612; *sow-iron* 1608, *sow-metal* 1674. The original differentiation of *sow* and *pig* (if there was any) was prob. in the size, the smaller masses being called *pigs*. The modern explanation, i.e. that the *sow* comes from the main channel, and the *pigs* from derivative channels into which the liquid metal is run from the furnace (applicable only to iron) is a later adaptation of the terms to the development of the iron-industry, of which the earliest indication is in quot. 1686 in d, where however 'sow' and 'piggs' may in themselves refer merely to size.

a. Generally. (Not now of gold or silver.)

1630 J. TAYLOR (Water P.) *Praise of Hempseed* Wks. III. 65/1 Ships.. That bring gold, siluer, many a Sow and Pig. **1683** *Lond. Gaz.* No. 1873/3, 150 Piggs of Silver. **1726** SHELVOCKE *Voy. round World* 312 We return'd for what we had of him some bales of coarse broad cloth,.. some piggs of copper. **1836–41** BRANDE *Chem.* (ed. 5) 820 Cast into oblong pieces called pigs, which are broken up, roasted, and melted with a portion of charcoal... Malleability is here conferred upon the copper.. by stirring [etc.]. **1868** G. STEPHENS *Runic Mon.* I. 372 This Pig of Tin is well known and has often been engraved. **1894** *Times* 16 Aug. 6/4 Zinc in blocks or pigs, one cent per pound.

b. Of lead (the earliest use): now usually of a definite weight; see quot. 1823.

1589 J. WHITE in Capt. Smith *Virginia* (1624) 15 We found.. many barres of Iron, two pigs of Lead,.. and such like heauie things throwne here and there. *a* **1616** BEAUM. & FL. *Scornful Lady* v. ii, Lusty Boys to throw the Sledge, and lift at Pigs of Lead. **1688** R. HOLME *Armoury* III. 260/2 A Pig or Sow of Lead, is generally about three hundred Pounds apiece. **1747** HOOSON *Miner's Dict.* I iv, Amongst Lead Merchants it [a Fodder] is nine Pieces or Piggs of Lead. **1823** P. NICHOLSON *Pract. Build* 405 The moulds.. take a charge of metal equal to one hundred and fifty-four pounds; these are called in commerce, pigs, or pigs of lead. **1865** MERIVALE *Rom. Emp.* VIII. lxvi. 206 Inscriptions on pigs of lead, &c. refer to the reigns of Claudius.

c. Of iron (now the chief use): see quots. Also, in mod. use (without *a* or plural), short for *pig-iron*. ***pig of ballast***, a pig of iron (rarely of lead) used as ballast.

1674 RAY *Words, Iron Work* 126 The lesser pieces of 1000 pound or under they call Pigs. **1678** *Phil. Trans.* XII. 934 From these Furnaces, they bring their Sows and Pigs of Iron (as they call them) to their Forges. **1769** GRAY *Let. to Nicholls* 24 June, The iron is brought in pigs to Milthrop by sea from Scotland, &c. **1789** *Trans. Soc. Arts* VII. 218 Pigs of ballast, to sink the lower part. **1829** *Glover's Hist. Derby* I. 82 A pig of iron is three feet and a half in length, and of one hundred pounds weight. **1837** MARRYAT *Dog-fiend* liv, Get up a pig of ballast. **1866** *Reader* 8 Sept. 778 The changes which have to be effected in the crude cast-iron, called pig, in order to convert it into malleable or bar-iron. **1871** *Trans. Amer. Inst. Mining Eng.* I. 149 White pig is made with a slag ranging from 40 to 48 per cent. **1883** *Daily News* 1 Sept. 2/6 Metals... Scotch pigs quiet, closing at 47*s.* for m.n. warrants.

d. Applied to the moulds or channels in the pig-bed.

[**1686** PLOT *Staffordsh.* 162 They make one larger furrow than the rest,.. which is for the Sow, from whence they draw two or three and twenty others (like the labells of a file in Heraldry) for the piggs.] **1805** [see PIG-IRON 1]. **1856** RICHARDSON *Suppl.* s.v., When the lead is tapped from the smelting furnace, it runs down a straight channel, technically called the *sow*, from which branch off on each side some smaller channels, called *pigs*. **1868** JOYNSON *Metals* 23 The iron.. is.. run into rough moulds or channels made in sand, and to which the name of 'pig' is given.

8. In various technical and local uses: **a.** A bundle of hemp-fibre of about $2\frac{1}{2}$ lb. weight. **b.** A block or cube of salt. **c.** A segment of an orange or apple. **d.** See quots. *a* 1843, 1902, 1926, 1941.

c **1825** CHOYCE *Log Jack Tar* (1891) 33 This [rock salt] they cut out into square pigs weighing about sixty pounds which they send to Guacho on mules. *a* **1843** in Southey *Comm.-pl. Bk.* (1851) IV. 417 Your man beat his antagonist by a pig and an apple-pie. *Note.* A pig is still a provincial term for an apple puff. *c* **1860** H. STUART *Seaman's Catech.* 57 It [hemp] is then weighed into small parcels called 'pigs', weighing about $2\frac{1}{2}$ lbs. each. **1870** VERNEY *Lettice Lisle* vi. 75 'What beautiful fruit', said he, beginning to eat the 'pigs' into which she was cutting it [an apple]. **1877** *N. & Q.* 5th Ser. VII. 134/1. **1902** *Daily Chron.* 11 Oct. 8/4 'Pigs in Blankets' the Americans call oysters wrapped in bacon. We .. term them 'Angels on Horseback'. **1926** MAINES & GRANT *Wise-Crack Dict.* 12/2 *Pig in a blanket*, sausage in a roll. **1941** J. SMILEY *Hash House Lingo* 43 *Pig in a blanket*, frankfurter sandwich. **1943** E. M. ALMEDINGEN *Frossia* vi. 240 Some people are like oranges.. all divided into neatly separated pigs. **1961** I. FLEMING *Thunderball* iv. 38 The orange, carefully sliced into symmetrical pigs. **1973** *Observer* (Colour Suppl.) 16 Sept. 83/2 The famous savoury angels on horseback. (The Americans call it pigs in blankets.) **1974** P. DICKINSON *Poison Oracle* v. 133 They were sharing a second orange, putting it pig by pig into each other's mouths.

9. A device that fits snugly inside an oil or gas pipeline and can be sent through it, e.g. to clean the inside or to act as a barrier between fluids either side of it.

1949 *Amer. Speech* XXIV. 33 A few field workers apply the term [*sc.* 'rabbit'] to scrapers used in pipelines to remove paraffin, but the most common name for this device is *pig*, because of the grunting noise it makes as it is forced through the line. **1949** *Sun* (Baltimore) 30 Nov. 13/1 In order to make sure that the pipe had no leaks and was free of all foreign matter, a 'pig'—a rubber object headed by a washer the same diameter as the pipe—was sent through by air pressure. **1956** *Ibid.* (B ed.) 27 Oct. 11/6 A 'pig' is a contraption consisting of blades, wheels, and brushes that runs through a pipeline to clean it. **1970** W. G. ROBERTS *Quest for Oil* xii. 126 (*caption*) Plastic pig used to clean a 30-inch diameter pipeline in Libya. *Ibid.*, A third way of checking what is going on in a pipeline is to insert some solid separator at the interface [between different products], fitting closely enough in the pipe to make sure that it will be pushed along at the same rate as the oil. Such devices are known as 'batching pigs'. **1977** *Time* 27 June 37/1 The moving oil will push the pig through the 48-in.-diameter steel pipe at 1 m.p.h. As it goes, the cylinder will shove out of the pipe any refuse that may be contained (for example, tools left behind by forgetful workmen) and emit beeps indicating its location.

10. In the names of various games.

pigs in clover, a game which consists in rolling a number of marbles into a recess or pocket in a board by tilting the board itself. ***pig*** (also ***piggy***) ***in the middle***, (*a*) a game in which one child is encircled by others and must escape by any of a number of (usu. vigorous) means; (*b*) a chasing game in which players must cross from one side of an open space to the other without being stopped by a child (or children) in the middle; (*c*) a ball game, usu. for three, in which the middle child tries to intercept the ball as it passes between the other two; also, the player in the middle in any of these games; also *transf.* and *fig.* ***placing*** (or ***chalking***) ***the pig's eye, putting on the pig's tail***: see quot. 1903.

1887 *Folk-Lore Jrnl.* V. 50 Some of the games were much rougher such as 'Pig in the middle and can't get out'. **1889** *Amer. Stationer* 14 Feb. 355/3 'Pigs in Clover' is the taking name of a new game which has just been placed upon the market by the toy house of Selchow & Righter. **1892** 'MARK TWAIN' *Amer. Claimant* xxiv. 250 A toy puzzle called Pigs in Clover, had come into sudden favor. **1898** *Daily News* 3 May 6/2 Those games and pastimes by which the patrons of the Peninsular and Oriental Company are wont to beguile time. Of such are the 'Game of Buckets', 'Playing Bull', 'Placing the Pig's Eye', and the 'Cigarette Race'. **1900** *Westm. Gaz.* 6 June 2/2 All those who have played 'Pigs in Clover' will know the exasperating way in which, when you have safely wriggled one pig into position another immediately wriggles itself out. **1903** *Daily Chron.* 4 Feb. 5/1 'Putting on the pig's tail' is a familiar game on board ship. A tailless pig is drawn in chalk upon the deck. Each passenger is blindfolded, turned round three times, and then proceeds to put the tail on the pig—usually yards away from the animal. **1915** W. S. MAUGHAM *Of Human Bondage* xi. 39 The new boys were told to go into the middle, while the others stationed themselves along opposite walls. They began to play *Pig in the Middle.* The old boys ran from wall to wall while the new boys tried to catch them: when one was seized and the mystic words said—one, two, three, and a pig for me—he became a prisoner and, turning sides, helped to catch those who were still free. **1962** *Guardian* 3 Aug. 4/5 He was.. pig-in-the-middle between his sweet, faint, pietistic mother and his impossibly stiff-necked father. **1962** C. STORR *Robin* viii. 37 You're blue with cold... You *will* have to play pig-in-the-middle. **1969** I. & P. OPIE *Children's Games* viii. 238 This game (Bull in the ring) seems to be less played today than in the nineteenth century, when it was frequently recorded.. 'Pig in the Middle and Can't Get Out'. **1970** *Times* (Saturday Rev.) 28 Feb. p. i/6 Dr. Robinson has thus been rudely abused from all sides of the shrinking Kingdom, piggy-in-the-middle of a debate which .. is.. fought with.. bitterness. **1970** N. FISHER *Walk at Steady Pace* IV. 231 They all knew more.. than I did. All three were able to use me as pig in the middle. **1973** M. AMIS *Rachel Papers* 125 Four boys.. stood in a semicircle round a fifth... Having looked round for encouragement or approval, one of the boys leaned over and slapped the piggy in the middle quite hard on the face. **1977** W. MCILVANNEY *Laidlaw* xii. 51 He's not a good *polis*-man... He doesn't know which side he's on. He's pig in the middle. **1977** *Times* 1 Sept. 5/2 You have to take the decisions, and often you are the piggy in the middle; in our case, for example, between pilots and shipowners.

III. Proverbial phrases.

11. † **a.** ***when the pig is offered, to hold open the poke***: to seize upon one's opportunities. (And variants of this.) **b.** ***to buy*** (or ***sell***) ***a pig in a poke*** (or ***bag***): to buy anything without seeing it or knowing its value. † **c.** ***to give any one a pig of his own*** (or ***another's***) ***sow***: (*a*) to give any one a part of his own (or another's) property; (*b*) to pay any one back in his own coin, treat him as he has treated others. **d.** ***please the pigs***: please the fates; if circumstances permit; if all's well. [Here some have suggested a corruption of *pyx* or of *pixies*, but without any historical evidence.] **e.** ***to carry pigs to market***: to try to do business or attain to results. ***to drive*** (or ***bring***) ***one's pigs to a fine, pretty,*** etc. ***market***: (usually ironical) to be disappointed or unsuccessful in a venture. **f.** ***to draw pig on*** (or ***upon***) ***pork*** (or ***bacon***) (Commercial slang): (see quots.); hence ***pig-on-bacon***, a bill drawn in this way. **g.** ***in a pig's eye, ear, arse***: used as a derisive retort; freq. as a strong negative or an emphatic. (Most of the examples are *U.S.* or *Austral.*) **h.** ***on the pig's back*** (occas. ***the pig's ear***): in a fortunate position; on top of the world; riding high. **i.** ***to make a pig's ear*** (***out***) ***of***: to make a mess of; to bungle.

a. *c* **1530** R. HILLES *Common-pl. Bk.* (1858) 140 When ye proffer the pigge open the poke. **1616** *Withals' Dict.* 579 *Quod datur accipe*, when the pig is offered, hold ope the poake. *a* **1620** SIR T. THROCKMORTON *Life & Death Sir N. Throckmorton* xci, To profferd Pig each man doth ope his Poke.

b. **1562** J. HEYWOOD *Prov. & Epigr.* (1867) 139, I will neuer bye the pyg in the poke. **1679** G. R. tr. *Boaystuau's Theat. World* 201 Buying, as they say, a Pig in a Bag. **1785** *Rolliad* 74 Except, indeed, when he essays to joke; And then his wit is truly pig-in-poke. **1860** GEN. P. THOMPSON *Audi Alt.* III. cxxxvi. 108 The reason the parliamentary jobber hates the Ballot, is because he does not like buying a pig in a poke.

c. **1553** BALE *Gardiner's De vera Obed.* G iij, I thought it not mete.. to make men thinke I had geuen them a pigge of another mannes sowe. **1562** J. HEYWOOD *Prov. & Epigr.* (1867) 155 Syr ye gyue me a pyg of myne owne sowe. **1611** COTGR. s.v. *Chemise*, To giue one a pig of his owne sow; to affoord him helpe out of his owne meanes. **1731** FIELDING *Grub St. Op.* III. xiv, If you come to my house I will treat you With a pig of your own sow.

d. **1702** T. BROWN *Lett. fr. Dead* Wks. 1760 II. 198 I'll have one of the wigs to carry into the country with me, an't [*printed* and] please the pigs. **1755** *Gentl. Mag.* XXV. 115 The expression I mean is, *An't please the pigs*, in which .. *pigs* is most assuredly a corruption of *Pyx*. **1800** SOUTHEY *Let. to Lieut. Southey* 15 June in *Life* (1850) II. 83. **1825** T. HOOK *Say. & Doings* Ser. II. I. 183, I know what I will do, and that is, please the Pix, I'll marry Louisa to her cousin George. **1891** *Blackw. Mag.* June 819/1 There I'll be, please the pigs, on Thursday night.

e. **1748** SMOLLETT *Rod. Rand.* xv, Strap.. observed that we had brought our pigs to a fine market. **1771** —— *Humph. Cl.* 19 May, Let. ii, Roger may carry his pigs to another market. **1873** *Punch* 21 June 262/2 Government finds that in producing the competition Wallah, it has driven its pigs to a pretty market.

f. **1849** J. W. *Perils Emigrant* ii. 84, I.. had exhausted every means of renewal, borrowing, exchanging cheques, drawing 'pig on pork', as it is technically called. **1872** *Porcupine* 16 Nov. 515/2 In Liverpool.. issuing a bill on their London branch establishment.. in commercial phraseology, is termed drawing 'pig upon bacon'. **1911** W. THOMSON *Dict. Banking* 397/1 '*Pig upon bacon.*' In the case of an accommodation bill, where e.g., Brown accepts merely to oblige the drawer, Jones, Brown has no intention of meeting the bill at maturity. He expects that Jones will himself provide the funds necessary to pay the bill when it is due. As Jones in his own mind considers himself practically the acceptor as well as the drawer, Jones on Brown is therefore likened to a bill drawn by 'Pig on Pork' or 'Pig upon Bacon'. **1920** A. C. PIGOU *Econ. of Welfare* II. v. 144 The variety of accommodation bills known as 'pig-on-bacon', where the acceptor is a branch of the drawing house under an *alias*, is.. different. **1930** W. THOMSON *Dict. Banking* (ed. 7) 548/2 When the drawers and drawees of a bill are the same, as when a foreign branch of a firm draws on its London office, and there are no documents for goods attached to the bill, the firm is said to be drawing 'Pig on Pork'.

g. **1872** 'P. V. NASBY' *Struggles* cxiii. 315 A poetickal cotashun.. which.. wuz,—'Kum wun, kim all, this rock shel fly From its firm base—in a pig's eye.' **1919** W. H. DOWNING *Digger Dial.* 38 *Pig's ear*, a contemptuous ejaculation. **1932** O. R. COHEN *Star of Earth* xxv. 270 'Here I am,' he says: 'I did it.. and that means Mary didn't!'.. 'In a pig's eye it does!' **1942** BERREY & VAN DEN BARK *Amer. Thes. Slang* §166/7 *I don't believe it!*.. It is in a pig's eye or arse! *Ibid.* §170/8 *You are mistaken*... It is in a pig's eye! or arse! *Ibid.* §229/5 *You will not!*.. In a pig's eye or arse you will! **1951** E. LAMBERT *Twenty Thousand Thieves* 322 'Pig's arse to that!' another voice cried. 'A jack-up—that's the shot.' **1957** J. BLISH *Fallen Star* v. 70 'You'll have to.' 'In a pig's eye,' she said. **1962** *Observer* 21 Jan. 11/7 Immigration from Ireland, said the Prime Minister.., will be included in the general controls. In a pig's eye it will. **1968** W. GARNER *Deep, Deep Freeze* ix. 110 'One stops short of probing the private lives of people for whom one has a regard.' 'In a pig's ear!' she said vulgarly. 'If duty called you'd have a man under the bed on my honeymoon.' **1968** H. WAUGH *Con Game* v. 53 'He claimed he didn't want to—.' Mrs. Fogarty said, 'In a pig's eye he didn't want to.' **1969** G. JOHNSTON *Clean Straw for Nothing* 307 'That's because she won't face realities.' 'Pig's arse. And anyway who are you to talk?' **1973** J. WAINWRIGHT *Pride of Pigs* 83 'Preston,' suggested Harris. 'In a pig's eye!' growled Ripley. **1974** P. LARKIN *High Windows* 35 My wife and I have asked a crowd of craps To come and waste their time and ours: perhaps You'd care to join us? In a pig's arse, friend. **1976** *Time* 5 Apr. 23/2 Attorney General Edward Levi let it be known that he considered the matter 'extremely serious'. To officials of the

Federal Bureau of Investigation, Levi's comment was a monumental understatement. 'Extremely serious in a pig's eye,' said one. 'It's a disaster.'

h. **1900** *19th Cent.* July 81 [Ireland] 'You're on the pig's back' means prosperity. 'The pig is on your back' indicates misfortune. **1922** JOYCE *Ulysses* 177 That'll be two pounds ten... Three Hynes owes me... Five guineas about. On the pig's back. **1930** [see HOME *adv.* 2 b]. **1946** C. MANN in *Coast to Coast 1945* 27 We always were lucky. He's home on the pig's ear. **1949** H. WADMAN *Life Sentence* I. i. 10 Could anything be nicer? Basil is on the pig's back. **1958** J. LODWICK *Bid Soldiers Shoot* viii. 277 Nixon, who in Crete had suffered horribly from solitude, was now a happy man—on the pig's back, one might say, and the image is appropriate since the grunting of the corralled porkers never ceased. **1962** R. WALLIS *Point of Origin* 11 Then aerial topdressing came in and they were on the pig's back. **1966** 'L. LANE' *ABZ of Scouse* II. 78 *On ther pig's back*, lucky; doing well; in the money.

i. **1954** E. HARGREAVES *Handful of Silver* xii. 183 'I've made a real pig's ear of it, haven't I?' said Basil, with an attempt at lightness. **1973** *Observer* 29 July 14/5 If you are doing something wrong, you will..make a pig's ear of its execution.

12. In various other phrases and locutions.

1546 J. HEYWOOD *Prov.* (1867) 84 Who that hath either of these pygs in vre, He hath a pyg of the woorse panier sure. **1670** RAY *Prov.* 209 Like Goodyers pig, never well but when he is doing mischief. *Chesh.* **1709** *Brit. Apollo* II. No. 62. 3/2 Whom all the Town follow, Like so many St. Anthony's Pigs. **1761** *Brit. Mag.* II. 440 You'd have sworn he had got the wrong pig by the ear. **1808** SCOTT *Let. to Ellis* 23 Dec. in *Lockhart*, I believe.., that when he [Sir A. Wellesley] found himself superseded [after Vimeiro], he suffered the pigs to run through the business. **1823** BYRON *Juan* VII. lxxxv, Ask the pig who sees the wind! **1828** *Craven Gloss.* (ed. 2) s.v., 'To drive pigs', to snore. **1837** DISRAELI *Corr. w. Sister* 21 Nov., Gibson Craig..rose, stared like a stuck pig, and said nothing. **1845** MRS. CARLYLE *New Lett., to Carlyle* 20 Aug., I 'did intend' that you should have had plenty of Letter to-day, but the pigs have run through it—and be hanged to them. **1903** S. HEDIN *Centr. Asia* II. 318 The sleeping men..went on driving their pigs to market for all they were worth.

b. In various phrases and locutions connected with the idea of pigs flying, freq. as a type of the unlikely or untrue.

1616 W. CLERK *Withals's Dict. Eng. & Lat.* (rev. ed.) 583 Pigs fly in the ayre with their tayles forward. **1639** J. CLARKE *Paroemiologia Anglo-Latina* 147/1 Pigs fly in the aire with their tailes forward. **1670** J. RAY *Coll. Eng. Proverbs* 189 Pigs fly in the air with their tails forward. *c* **1860** *Proverb*, Pigs may fly; but they are very unlikely birds. **1865** 'L. CARROLL' *Alice's Adventures in Wonderland* ix. 155 'I've a right to think,' said Alice sharply... 'Just about as much right,' said the Duchess, 'as pigs have to fly.' *a* **1871** A. DE MORGAN *Budget of Paradoxes* (1872) 275 There is a proverb which says, A pig may fly, but it isn't a likely bird. [**1871** 'L. CARROLL' *Through Looking-Glass* iv. 76 'The time has come,' the Walrus said, 'To talk of many things: Of shoes—and ships—and sealing-wax—Of cabbages—and kings—And why the sea is boiling hot—And whether pigs have wings.'] **1880** C. H. SPURGEON *John Ploughman's Pictures* 32 They say that if pigs fly they always go with their tails forward. **1913** *Punch* 13 Aug. 156/1 'If pigs could fly...' The clumsy brutes can't, of course, while we flies *can* pig—see us in a confectioner's shop. **1937** PARTRIDGE *Dict. Slang* 628/2 *Pigs fly, when*, never. **1949** 'J. TEY' *Brat Farrar* x. 81 'I may, some day. I may.' 'Pigs may fly.' **1952** WODEHOUSE (*title*) Pigs have wings. **1972** 'J. QUARTERMAIN' *Rock of Diamond* xxvii. 176 'I'll wait... Perhaps he'll have news...' 'Maybe... And maybe pigs have wings.' **1973** 'J. HIGGINS' *Prayer for Dying* xii. 165 'Something could come out of that line of enquiry.' 'I know... Pigs might also fly.'

IV. *attrib.* and *Comb.* (Cf. those in HOG *sb.*[1] VI.)

13. a. attributive, as ***pig-belly***, ***bin*** (also *fig.*), ***-boy***, ***-broth***, ***-butcher***, ***-byre***, ***-eye***, ***-feast***, ***house*** (also *fig.*), ***-hutch***, ***-leather***, ***-life***, ***-man*** (also *fig.*), ***manure***, ***-meat*** (also *fig.*), ***-merchant***, ***-pail***, ***-pen*** (also *fig.*), ***-philosophy***, ***-swill***, ***-trough***, ***-tub***, ***-wire***, ***-yard***; (sense 6 b) ***pig car***, ***station***; from sense 7, ***pig ballast***, ***trade***, etc.

1797 S. JAMES *Voy. Arabia* 201 The boat..full of *pig ballast..was always half full of water. **1622** FLETCHER & MASSINGER *Span. Curate* II. i, No man would think a stranger such as I am Should reap any great commodity from his *pigbelly. **1959** I. & P. OPIE *Lore & Lang. Schoolch.* ix. 167 They call him [*sc.* a greedy-guts]: dustbin, ..*pig-bin, [etc.]. **1972** P. BLACK *Biggest Aspidistra* II. iv. 124 Outside the houses stood a row of huge bins, one for collecting paper, one for tins, one for bottles, one for kitchen waste. They were known as pigbins, though..the pigs ate only the waste. **1979** 'M. HEBDEN' *Death set to Music* iii. 29 Pel sniffed at his stew. 'I think they took it from the pig bin,' he observed coldly. **1614** B. JONSON *Barth. Fair* Induct., The language some where sauours of Smithfield, the Booth, and the *Pigbroath, or of prophaneness. **1906** *19th Cent.* June 967 Already half the cottage *pig-byres stand empty in our lanes. **1970** G. JACKSON *Let.* 10 June in *Soledad Brother* (1971) 36, I sat in the back of the pig car and bled for two hours. **1714** *Lond. Gaz.* No. 5274/11 A little swarthy Woman, hath small *Pig Eyes. **1823** *Blackw. Mag.* XIV. 520 The mallet-pate, pig-eye Chinese. **1845** C. CIST *Cincinnati Misc.* I. 186 A stout looking fellow set his gun leaning on a *pig house, and jumped in to catch some fowls. **1950** *N.Z. Jrnl. Agric.* Apr. 369/1 In considering the design of pig houses there are two main factors. **1960** *Farmer & Stockbreeder* 9 Feb. 76/2 The value of..good pighouse insulation. **1963** *Amer. Speech* XXXVIII. 173 [Kansas University] A sorority known for its unprepossessing members..*campus pig house..pig house.* **1839** CARLYLE *Chartism* iv. 127 He lodges to his mind in any *pighutch or doghutch. **1886** W. J. TUCKER *E. Europe* 304 His legs..in strong *pig-leather boots. **1825** *Whole Proc. Old Bailey* 15 Jan. 116/2, I..saw the prisoner in the kitchen—he said, if I came with any **pigman* he would knock my head off. **1898** *Blackw. Mag.* Nov. 666/1 The pigman..had caught the five piglings. **1971** *Farmers Weekly* 19 Mar. 75/3 Continental pigmen want hybrid boars. *a* **1975** WODEHOUSE *Sunset at Blandings* (1977) vii. 52 Clarence's pig man claims to have seen the White Lady of Blandings one Saturday night. **1976** *Eastern Daily Press* (Norwich) 19 Nov. 11/1 (Advt.), Assistant pigman/woman required..to join staff of five, on 500-sow herd. **1960** *Farmer & Stockbreeder* 1 Mar. 107/1 Future developments include a *pig-manure spreading service which will give back to the members the pig manure they would have had if they had reared their pigs on their farms. **1975** J. WYLLIE *Butterfly Flood* (1977) xxiii. 105 The compost heap was..activated by pig manure. **1798** J. WOODFORDE *Diary* 2 July (1931) V. 125 *Pig Meat now is but of little value to what it has been. **1817** *Parl. Deb.* 743 It prevented the preservation of meat, and especially of pig meat. **1895** *N. & Q.* 10th Ser. IV. 512 [In Hants] The spare-rib and griskin of a bacon hog or sow are called pig-meat, whether large or small. **1897** *Allbutt's Syst. Med.* II. 790 In most cases the infected food has been pig meat. **1942** Z. N. HURSTON in *Amer. Mercury* July 96/1 *Pig meat*, young girl. **1970** G. GREER *Female Eunuch* 265 Perhaps words like *pig*, *pig-meat* or *dog* are inspired by the sadness which follows unsatisfactory sex. **1971** *Farmers Weekly* (Extra) 19 Mar. 12/2 High beef prices have pushed up demand for fresh pigmeat. **1977** *Times* 8 Feb. 17/3 We break the [EEC] rules by subsidizing pigmeat. **1853** HICKIE tr. *Aristoph.* (1887) I. 33 A *pig-merchant of Megara. **1908** *Westm. Gaz.* 18 Jan. 2/3 The cricket climbed the side of the..*pig-pail. **1833** MARRYAT *P. Simple* xxvii, There are two cow-pens between the main-deck guns..converted into *pig-pens. **1872** *Harper's Mag.* Apr. 690/2 A one-story wooden structure.. became the rallying-place of the tribes. This [room], by reason of its general unsightliness, was denominated by Tammany's political adversaries the 'Pig-Pen'. **1907** J. LONDON *Let.* 25 July (1966) 247 He left his stateroom the filthiest pig-pen I ever saw. **1952** R. P. BISSELL *Monongahela* i. 5, I took my paper suitcase out of the pigpen and up to the mates' room, and one thing sure, that mates' room smelled better than the deckhands' bunkroom, and even had a light in the bunk to read by, and a clean blanket with no fuel oil or coal ground into it. **1960** T. HUGHES *Lupercal* 38 Toward the pig-pens on his right. **1971** M. TAK *Truck Talk* 118 *Pigpen*, a sloppy, ill-run truck stop. **1978** J. WAINWRIGHT *Jury People* xxxv. 106 They carried him to the pig-pens. **1979** R. GILLESPIE *Crossword Mystery* v. 116 'Did you search his place?' 'Yeah. A pigpen.' **1874** LISLE CARR *Jud. Gwynne* I. i. 8 The *pig-philosophy of 'rest and be thankful'. **1970** G. JACKSON *Let.* 10 June in *Soledad Brother* (1971) 34, I stopped attending school regularly, and started getting 'picked up' by the pigs more often. The *pig station, a lecture, and oak-stick therapeutics. **1975** P. MOYES *Black Widower* i. 13 Assemble..outside the Georgetown Pig Station..for a protest march. **1889** A. SIDGWICK in *Jrnl. Educ.* Feb. 117 We began with Delectus—an awful institution, no more reading than a *pigtub is food. **1964** *Listener* 19 Mar. 458/1 Scrapping the hedges, replacing them with concrete posts and *pigwire. **1971** *Ideal Home* Apr. 119 To restrain dogs and children the cheapest and strongest I know is Smith's (of Bristol) Bulwark fencing—what my father calls pig-wire—a heavy galvanised mesh varying from 6 in. square at the top to 6 in. by 3 in. at the bottom, 32 in. high.

b. objective and obj. genitive, as ***pig-buyer***, ***-dealer***, ***-driver***, ***-eater***, ***-feeder***, ***-jobber***, ***-keeper***, ***-killer***, ***-netter***, ***-stalker***, ***-stealer***, ***-taker***; ***pig-breeding***, ***-dealing***, ***-driving***, ***-eating***, ***-feeding***, ***-keeping***, ***-rearing***, ***-stalking***, sbs. and adjs. (sense 7) ***pig-breaking***.

1902 *Encycl. Brit.* XXIX. 578/1 A great saving of labour was effected by the introduction of '*pig-breaking' machines. **1891** *Pall Mall G.* 23 Dec. 2/1 Ballybricken is.. chiefly remarkable as the place of residence of the *pig-buyers. **1851** MAYHEW *Lond. Labour* I. 359/2, I also entered into the *pig-dealing line. **1654** GAYTON *Pleas. Notes* II. v. 57 Like Bartholemew Faire *pig-dressers. **1687** *Lond. Gaz.* No. 2234/4 John Williams a Welshman, a *Pig driver. **1608** MIDDLETON *Trick to Catch Old One* IV. i, Convey my little *pig-eater out. **1810** *Splendid Follies* I. 109 Industrious peasants pursuing their morning labours—some milking—some *pig-feeding. **1906** *Westm. Gaz.* 20 Aug. 10/1 The fact, too, that acorns are a heavy crop will gladden the hearts of *pig-keepers. **1971** *Farmers Weekly* (Extra) 19 Mar. 33/2 The slump has hit heavy hog producers hardest of all pig-keepers. **1923** *Blackw. Mag.* Dec. 768/1 They concocted a plan by which the boar should be netted... Professional *pig-netters were summoned. **1907** *Westm. Gaz.* 31 July 12/2 *Pig-rearing..is on the downward grade. **1960** *Farmer & Stockbreeder* 29 Mar. 88/3 The most important ingredient of pig-rearing success is undoubtedly hard work. **1978** *Dumfries Courier* 13 Oct. 20/1 A sow and seven piglets died early yesterday afternoon when fire raged through a pig-rearing building at Laghall Farm, New Abbey Road, Dumfries. **1908** *Westm. Gaz.* 2 Mar. 5/2 'The indiscriminate offer of rewards in no way tends to the destruction of the real man-eater,' says Mr. Rees, 'while it ensures the extermination of the useful..deer and *pig-stalker.' **1867** M. A. BARKER *Station Life N.Z.* (1870) xv. 109 We go over the hills *pig-stalking. **1828** P. CUNNINGHAM *N.S. Wales* (ed. 3) II. 250 Breadman had been a great *pig-stealer in his day.

c. instrumental, parasynthetic, etc., as ***pig-bribed***, ***-haunted***, ***-ploughed***; ***pig-backed***, ***-chested***, ***-eyed***, ***-footed***, ***-haired***, ***jawed***, ***-snouted***; ***pig-fat***, ***-ignorant*** (hence ***pig-ignorance***), ***-lucky***, ***-proof***, ***-sick***, ***-sober***, ***-sticky***, ***-stupid***, ***-tight***, adjs.

In the last type of use, often merely with the force of an intensifier: extreme(ly), thorough(ly).

1880 ZAEHNSDORF *Bookbinding* xi. 42 Nothing can be more annoying than to see books lop-sided, *pig-backed. **1880** *Daily News* 17 Sept. 16/2 The latter animal [a goat] is slightly pig-backed. **1613** BEAUM. & FL. *Coxcomb* V. iii, Why kneel you to such a *pig-bribed fellow? **1895** *Review of Rev.* Aug. 162 A sickly boy, '*pig-chested'. **1835** BOOTH *Analyt. Dict.* 228 **Pig-eyed* is a rude epithet when speaking of eyes that are small and deeply seated in the head. **1864** KINGSLEY *Rom. & Teut.* iii. 74 Pig-eyed hideous beings. **1897** *Cavalry Tactics* ii. 8 Not..that the troop horse is useless if he is not *pig fat. **1884** *Cassell's Fam. Mag.* Apr. 272/1 The *pig-footed bandicot is another curious variety seen here. **1973** H. MILLER *Open City* xvii. 187 Boorishness and Glasgow-bred *pig-ignorance. **1972** J. WAINWRIGHT *Requiem for Loser* iv. 82 I'm not *pig-ignorant... But you're pig-*stupid.* **1973** A. PRICE *October Men* vi. 84 [He] was clearly pig-ignorant of everything that did not concern him. **1976** T. HEALD *Let Sleeping Dogs Die* vii. 132 Those press johnnies ..would never twig. Too gullible and too pig ignorant. **1942** 'M. INNES' *Daffodil Affair* I. v. 30 'A nice dog,' Appleby said... Mr Gee swung round. 'Dish-faced,' he said... 'And undershot... *Pig-jawed, in fact.' **1939** J. STEINBECK *Grapes of Wrath* xvi. 253 'Get her fixed?' 'We was *pig lucky,' said Tom. 'Got a part 'fore dark.' **1921** H. GUTHRIE-SMITH *Tutira* xix. 165 These *pig-ploughed shreds [of land]. **1883** *Pall Mall G.* 21 Sept. 12/2 The immense number of wild pigs makes cultivation impracticable without *pig-proof fences. **1948** A. BARON *From City from Plough* i. 9 Wha's up, Sergeant?.. You look *pigsick. **1965** A. PRIOR *Interrogators* xiii. 244 He was pig-sick of talking to the old bastard. **1977** J. WAINWRIGHT *Nest of Rats* I. vii. 51, I was pig-sick of Rawle and his devious ways. **1923** E. SITWELL *Bucolic Comedies* 9 And old *pig-snouted Darkness grunts and roots in the hovels. **1960** *Times* 29 Sept. (Nigeria Suppl.) p. xxi/5 The weighty pig-snouted aardvark. **1945** KOESTLER *Twilight Bar* III. 62, I thought so. *Pig-sober. **1922** JOYCE *Ulysses* 445 Eat it and get all *pigsticky. **1972** *Pig-stupid [see *pig-ignorant* adj.]. **1859** *Pig-tight [see *bull-strong* s.v. BULL *sb.*[1] 11]. *a* **1930** Pig-tight [see *horse-high* adj. s.v. HORSE *sb.* 28 a].

14. a. Special Comb. (cf. HOG *sb.*[1] 13): **pig board** *Surfing* (see quots.); **pig-boat** *U.S. slang*, a submarine; **pig-boiling** *Metallurgy*, the puddling of unrefined pig-iron, which is characterized by a period of rapid bubbling of gas from the molten metal; **pig brass**, brass as it is cast after the first fusion; **pig-cheer**, viands made from the flesh or viscera of swine; **pig-dog**, (*a*) a dog used in hunting wild pigs in Australia and New Zealand; (*b*) used as a term of abuse; **pig-hole**, an aperture in a steel furnace through which fresh supplies of pig-iron may be introduced; **pig-hull** *dial.* = PIGSTY; **pig-lifter**, one employed in moving pig-iron: see quot.; **pig-louse**, the wood-louse or HOG-LOUSE, *Oniscus*; **pig-maker**, a manufacturer of pig-iron; **pig-market**, (*a*) a market held for the purchase and sale of swine; (*b*) a name vulgarly given to the Proscholium or antechamber of the Divinity School at Oxford: see quot. 1681; **pig-mould**, one of the channels in a pig-bed; **pig net**, a type of strong net; **pig-plate** = PIG-IRON 2; **pig-potato**, a small potato used to feed swine; = *hog-potato* (HOG *sb.*[1] 13); also *fig.*; **pig-ring**, a ring or strip of metal fixed in the snout of a hog to prevent it from grubbing, a hog-ring; **pig-root** *v.*, (*a*) to root or grub in the earth like swine; (*b*) *Austral.*, of a horse or other animal, to kick upwards with the hind legs, the forelegs remaining rigid; **pig-rooting** *vbl. sb.*, (*a*) *N.Z.*, a patch of ground grubbed or rooted up by wild pigs; (*b*) the action of *pig-root* vb. (b); **pig-run**, a tract of land used by (wild) pigs; also, a track made or used by wild pigs in a forest; **pig-sign** *N.Z.*, the droppings of wild pig(s); **pig-stone**, a concretion occurring in the intestines of the wild boar; **pig-trotter**, the foot of a pig, as an article of food; **pig-washing** *Metallurgy*, the refining of molten pig-iron by treatment with molten iron oxide; †**pig-woman**, a woman who sold roast pig at fairs, etc.; **pig-wool**, the finer hair of the swine, used in making flies for anglers; **pig-yoke**, (*a*) = HOG-YOKE; (*b*) a sextant or quadrant (*slang*). See also PIG-BED, etc.

1965 J. POLLARD *Surfrider* ii. 18 Your board can be a '*pigboard'—wide at the stern and tapered to a point at the nose. **1970** *Studies in English* (Univ. Cape Town) I. 28 Older designs include the *pig board*, that is, a board characterized by a narrow nose and a broad tail. **1921** *Periscope* (U.S. Submarine Base, San Pedro, Calif.) Apr. 21/1 The dukes what passes the exam..finally goes to the subs..and they career as a *pig bout [*sic*] sailor is started. This of course, means a sub, witch they is also called sea pigs. **1939** *Newsweek* 9 Jan. 20/1 Presumably Germany will now build up to this by constructing ocean-going pigboats. **1974** G. JENKINS *Bridge & Magpies* xiv. 218, I understand now what the pig-boat saying means—'by guess and by God'. **1975** *Redbook* Aug. 118/3 What do you think about Pearl Harbor? The newer boats are there. I'd like to get one of them and avoid the old pig-boats if I can. **1856** J. HALL in *Birmingham Jrnl.* 26 Sept. Suppl. 3/5 As regards the improved apparatus for the refinery, my principle is the *doing away* with the *refinery process* by *pig boiling. **1882** [see WET *a.* 17]. **1928** H. M. BOYLSTON *Introd. Metallurgy Iron & Steel* vi. 187 Hall's process was also known as the 'pig-boiling process' because of the vigorous boiling or bubbling of the molten metal. **1958** A. D. MERRIMAN *Dict. Metallurgy* 244/1 *Pig boiling*, the name used in reference to that stage in the puddling process..when the original pig iron is melted and thoroughly mixed with the oxidising substances... The whole mass..becomes agitated with the escape of carbon monoxide giving the impression of 'boiling'. **1897** *Allbutt's Syst. Med.* II. 938 Those who remelt the *pig brass, and are called 'founders'. **1871** *Archæologia* (1873) XLIV. 208 Christmas was formerly, as now, the principal season for '*pig-cheer'. **1845** E. J. WAKEFIELD *Adv. in N. Zealand* II. i. 6 The *pig-dogs are of rather a mongrel breed. **1877** GILLIES in *Trans. N.Z. Inst.* X. 321 A pig-dog of the bull-terrier breed. **1922** JOYCE *Ulysses* 460 Pig dog and always was ever since he was pupped! **1961** B. CRUMP *Hang on a Minute* 18 My mate reckoned he'd never laughed so much since his brother's pig-dogs got loose and followed him into the Waitawheta dance hall! **1977** *N.Z. Herald* 8 Jan. 4–9/6 (Advt.), Pig dog pups, boxer blue merle pointer cross. **1828** *Craven Gloss.* (ed. 2), **Pighul*, a pig cote or stye. **1892** *Labour Commission Gloss.*, **Pig-lifters*, also called 'metal-carriers'.. those who take the pig-iron out of the troughs of sand into which it has been placed to cool, and stack it on the trucks used in conveying it away for sale. **1819** G. Samouelle *Entomol. Compend.* 111 It is commonly called *Pig-louse, Wood-louse, Millepede. **1891** *Daily News* 12 Jan. 2/7 *Pigmakers are complaining of the exceedingly high prices of coke. **1681** Wood *Life* 11 Feb. (O.H.S.) II. 517 Note that the Divinity Schoole hath been seldome used since altered and changed (but before 'twas a *pig-market). **1853** E. Bradley *Verd. Green* v, They made their way to the classic 'Pig-market', to wait the arrival of the Vice-Chancellor. **1839** Ure *Dict. Arts* 754 The smelter runs off the lead into the *pig-moulds. **1907** *Yesterday's Shopping* (1969) Index p. xlvi/3 Nets... *Pig. **1966** D. Francis *Flying Finish* v. 54 A cart with a pig-net over it. **1971** *Country Life* 11 Mar. 533/1 Some chaps got a tiddler [*sc.* a sturgeon], weighed a hunderd pound, in a pig net. **1787** J. Farley *Lond. Art Cookery* (ed. 4) 35 Having spitted your pig, sew it up, and lay it down to a brisk, clear fire, with a *pig-plate hung in the middle of it. **1796** Stedman *Surinam* II. xxvi. 244 These roots are tuberous, flattish, small,.. not unlike *pig-potatoes. **1866** Geo. Eliot *F. Holt* xxviii, Not very big or fine, but a second size—a pig-potato, like. **1862** Wilde *Catal. Antiq. in R. Irish Acad.* 18 A small portion had been cut out.. to make a *pig-ring. **1890** 'R. Boldrewood' *Miner's Right* xix, *Pig-rooting a man's very prospecting claim, as if it was 'old ground'. **1913** W. K. Harris *Outback in Australia* 27 We had a second horse afflicted with a tendency to buck, and this one could be depended upon to 'pig-root' for at least half a mile as soon as we made a start. **1957** P. White *Voss* x. 276 This caused Turner to curse and kick, and his nag in consequence to sidle and pigroot. **1921** H. Guthrie-Smith *Tutira* xix. 169 It [*sc.* manuka] now began to colonise the paddock.. appearing about *pig-rootings, along sheep-tracks. **1966** 'J. Hackston' *Father clears Out* 168 Bucking, backbending, side-jumping, leaping, and pig-rooting. **1848** T. Chapman *Jrnl.* 3 Dec. II. 381 (typescript), Thousands of Acres on all sides of you... Here and there little patches are under cultivation—the rest are '*pig-runs'. **1900** *Geogr. Jrnl.* XVI. 174 In dense forest where the pig-runs are the only means of passage. **1950** *N.Z. Jrnl. Agric.* 346/3 This type of utilisation.. at the same time allows some rejuvenation of the pasture in the permanent pig runs. **1960** B. Crump *Good Keen Man* 57, I was thoroughly interrogated every evening as to the whereabouts of any fresh pig-sign I had seen that day [in the bush]. **1851** Mayhew *Lond. Labour* I. 18/2 The.. *pig-trotter women will give you notice when the time is come. **1887** Phillips & Bauerman *Elem. Metallurgy* (ed. 2) 280 A similar process, used for some time by Krupp, was described by the late Mr. A. L. Holley under the name of '*pig-washing'. **1910** *Encycl. Brit.* XIV. 824/2 In the Bell-Krupp or 'pig-washing' process.. advantage is taken of the fact that.. the phosphorus and silicon of molten cast iron are quickly oxidized and removed by contact with molten iron oxide. **1958** A. D. Merriman *Dict. Metallurgy* 244/2 *Pig-washing process*, a term used in reference to those methods of refining molten pig iron by oxidising treatment at relatively low temperatures. **1614** B. Jonson *Barth. Fair* II. vi, Smoak'd like the back-side of the *Pig-woman's Booth, here. **1892** *Gentlewomen's Bk. Sports* I. 20 His fly-book of silk-bodied, *pig-wool, red or orange feathered flies. **1836** Marryat *Midsh. Easy* xiv, Old Smallsole could not do better with his '*pig-yoke' and compasses. **1845** *Knickerbocker* XXV. 424 Yellow buttons.. 'and geese', as he said, 'sittin' on a pig-yoke, printed on to 'em.' **1885** *Athenæum* 10 Oct. 468 The pig yoke was a wooden frame which was fastened around the necks of pigs to hinder them from forcing a way through hedges.

b. In names of animals and plants: as **pig-cony**, the guinea-pig; **pig-deer**, the Babiroussa; **pig-face, pig's face** *Austral.*, a succulent plant belonging to the family Aizoaceæ, esp. *Disphyma* (formerly *Mesembryanthemum*) *australe*, bearing pink or purplish-red flowers and edible fleshy berries; also, the berries themselves; also *attrib.*; **pig-fern** *N.Z.* the hard fern, *Paesia scaberula*, of the family Polypodiaceæ; also called lace-fern, ring-fern, and scented fern; **pig-fish**, a popular name in America and Australia of various fishes; **pig-lily**, a popular name in S. Africa of the Arum lily, *Zantedeschia æthiopica*, the root of which is eaten by porcupines; **pig-mouse**, the water-shrew; **pig-pea**, a variety of field pea. (Cf. hog *sb.*[1] 13 c, d.)

1607 Topsell *Four-f. Beasts* (1658) 88 Indian little *Pig-cony. I received the picture of this beast from a certain Noble-man. **1834** Ross *Van Diemen's Land Ann.* 133 (Morris) *Pig faces; called by the aborigines.. canagong. **1846** Lindley *Veg. Kingd.* 526 The natives of Australia eat the fruit of *M[esembryanthemum] æquilaterale* (Pig-faces, or Canagong). **1889** J. H. Maiden *Useful Native Plants Austral.* i. 44 'Pig Faces'... The fleshy fruit is eaten raw by the aborigines. The leaves are eaten baked. **1898** Morris *Austral Eng.*, Pig-face, Pig-faces, and Pig's face, or Pig's-faces. **1920** B. Cronin *Timber Wolves* 69 On the crest of a knoll, Heritage paused a moment to admire the royal purple of the pig-face bloom. **1933** *Bulletin* (Sydney) 29 Nov. 21/3 The fleshy leaves of the pigface plant, which grows along the sandy seashores. **1944** [see ice-plant]. **1963** Moore & Adams *Plants N.Z. Coast* 59 *Disphyma australe*.. ice-plant, pig-face. **1977** J. Galbraith *Field Guide Wild Flowers S.E. Austral.* 114 'Pigface' with large pink flowers. **1926** F. W. Hilgendorf *Weeds N.Z.* ii. 19 Hard fern (*Paesia scaberula*), called also *pig fern and silver fern, is abundant in both islands. **1929** W. Martin *N.Z. Nature Bk.* (1930) II. iv. 44 Pig-fern and Lace-fern are local names given to a dwarf species (*Paesia scaberula*), with finely divided leaflets. **1952** G. R. Gilbert *Glass* 59 Struggling through the thick scrub and tangled pig-fern, the brother and sister tramped on towards the mountains. **1860** Bartlett *Dict. Amer.* (ed. 3) s.v. *Sea-robin*, From the croaking or grunting noise it makes when caught, it is sometimes called *Pig-Fish. **1898** Morris *Austral Eng.*, *Pig-fish*, name given to the fish *Agriopus leucopœcilus*,.. in Dunedin; called also the Leather-jacket... In Sydney it is *Cossyphus unimaculatus*,.. a Wrasse, closely related to the Blue-groper. In Victoria, *Heterodontus phillipi*,.. the Port Jackson Shark. **1848** C. J. F. Bunbury *Jrnl. Residence Cape of Good Hope* viii. 188 *Calla* (*Zantedeschia*) *Æthiopica*... Commonly called at the Cape the *Pig Lily. **1870** *Cape Monthly Mag.* Aug. 104 The 'arum'.. grows in all the ditches under the title of 'pig-lily'. **1880** *Silver & Co.'s S. Africa* (ed. 3) 148 Associated by name with the Lilies is what is known as the Pig Lily. **1887** Rider Haggard *Jess* 44 Thousands of white arum lilies,—pig-lilies they call them there. **1971** U. van der Spuy *Wild Flowers S. Afr. for Garden* 229/2 It [*sc. Zantedeschia æthiopica*] is said to have been given the common name of 'pig-lily' because in the south-western Cape, where it grows prolifically, pigs are said to relish the rootstock. **1905** *Standard* 8 Feb. 2/5 The '*pig mouse' of the cress farmer is the water shrew. **1766** *Complete Farmer* s.v. *Pease*, The common white pea, the gray pea, the *pig pea, and some other large winter peas.

c. Combinations with *pig's*: as ***pig's cheek, cote, eye, fry, hair***; **pig's breakfast**, used as a type of the unappetizing or unattractive; **pig's ear** *Rhyming slang*, beer; **pig's face**: see *pig-face* in b; **pig's foot**, †(*a*) a dipping-pail used in brewing, and also for carrying dry articles; (*b*) a kind of crow-bar; (*c*) = *pig-trotter* (chiefly *pl.*); **pig's meat**, food for swine; also *fig.*; **pig's whisper**, (*a*) a very brief space of time (*slang*); (*b*) a low whisper (*dial.*); **pig's whistle** *U.S. slang* = *pig's whisper* (*a*). Also pig's-wash. Many of the combinations with *pig's* also occur in phrases (see 11).

1933 L. G. D. Acland in *Press* (Christchurch, N.Z.) 9 Sept. 15/7 Two may possibly be Canterbury expressions.. (1) As rough as a bag. (2) As rough as a *pig's breakfast. **1948** K. M. Wells *Owl Pen Reader* (1969) I. 45 Lucy and I looked unbelievingly at the mess in the kettles. Bits of charred wood, charcoal, old leaves and wood ash floated there in the midst of an uninviting white scum. It looked like poor porridge, a pig's breakfast to us. **1844** Stephens *Bk. Farm* II. 242 The heads should be cut off one after the other, and eaten as green *pig's-cheek. **1880** D. W. Barrett *Life & Work among Navvies* (ed. 2) ii. 40 'Now, Jack, I'm goin' to get a tiddley wink of *pig's ear..'. A tiddley wink of pig's ear!.. What does it mean? Simply this... a workman.. goes to get a drink of beer. Had our friend wished for something more potent than the pig's ear aforesaid, he would have substituted the phrase.. 'Tommy get out, and let your father in', meaning thereby *gin*. **1936** J. Curtis *Gilt Kid* xx. 199 But the most of the fiver would go in the old pig's ear. **1974** P. Wright *Lang. Brit. Industry* x. 88 In the pub you can ask for a pint of *pig's ear* (beer). **1853** Kingsley *Hypatia* xix, With a sleek pale face, small *pig's eyes, and an enormous turban. **1848** Westgarth *Australia Felix* ix. 132 The *pig's face is an extremely common production of the Australian soil. **1929** 'M. B. Eldershaw' *House is Built* III. ix. 217 Nothing but a few clumps of pig's face throve in the pockets of earth it provided. **1467** *Yatton Churchw. Acc.* (Som. Rec. Soc.) 120 Payd for a *pyggsfote to bare cols, j[d]. **1790** Pennant *London* (1813) 322 That resistless species of crow, well known to housebreakers by the name of the Pig's-foot. **1922** H. Crane *Let.* 23 Jan. (1965) 78 We begin with pigs' feet and sauerkraut. **1968** C. Brown in *Esquire* Apr. 88/1 Certain foods.. are associated almost solely with the nigger: collard greens.. hog maws, black-eyed peas, pigs' feet. **1788** J. Woodforde *Diary* 7 Nov. (1927) III. 63 We had for Dinner, Some Fish.. Giblets, *Piggs Fry. **1939** F. Thompson *Lark Rise* i. 13 The first delicious dish of pig's fry sizzling in the frying-pan. **1970** G. E. Evans *Where Beards wag All* xxv. 264, I had a fancy for something tasty, and one night I gave her a pig's fry and asked her to cook it for us for next day. **1894** Du Maurier *Trilby* (1895) 105 His twiddling little footle *pig's-hair brush. **1896** Crockett *Grey Man* xxxv. 233 A pail of *pigs' meat in her hand. **1821** P. Egan *Real Life in London* I. xi. 189 The lad *nibbled the bait*, and was off in a **pig's whisper*. [Note] *Pig's Whisper*—A very common term for speed. **1837** Dickens *Pickw.* xxxii, You'll find yourself in bed, in something less than a pig's whisper. **1883** *Gd. Words* 84 He confided his secret, wrapped up in a pig's whisper to the earth. **1963** *Times* 11 Mar. 1/7 If you are unfortunate enough to snore, you are said 'to drive pigs', or perhaps you may do something in a very short time, in which case it is said that you have done it 'in a pig's whisper'. **1860** Bartlett *Dict. Amer.* (ed. 3) s.v., 'I'll do so in less than a *pig's whistle'.

pig (pɪg), *sb.*[2] Now *Sc.* and *Northumbld.* Forms: 5 pygg, 6 pyg, pigge, 9 pigg, 6– pig. [Origin unknown; see also piggin.]

1. An earthenware pot, pitcher, jar, or other vessel; especially one that has no specific name; a crock. Rarely a vessel of tin or wood (*obs.*).

c **1440** *Alphabet of Tales* 340 Euerilk day.. was broght vnto hym a lofe of bread and a pygg with wyne & a light candyll. **1488** *Acc. Ld. High Treas. Scot.* I. 79 Deliuerit be Dene Robert Hog, channoune of Halirudhous, to the Thesaurare, tauld in presens of the Chancellare, Lord Lile.. in a pyne pig of tyn. **1513** Douglas *Æneis* vii. xiv. 25 Furth of ane payntit pyg, quhair as he stude, A gret river defundand or a flude. **1588** *Wills & Inv. N.C.* (Surtees) II. 312, j litle wood coup, j paer of muster quernes of wood, j litle wood pigge, iiij wood dishes, j earthen panne. **1673** *Wedderburn's Vocab.* 13 (Jam.) *Urna*, a pitcher or pig. **1724** in Ramsay *Tea-t. Misc.* (1733) II. 181 A pig, a pot, and a kirn there ben. **1818** Miss Ferrier *Marriage* II. 187, I would send him one of our hams, and a nice little pig of butter. **1818** Scott *Hrt. Midl.* xlix, It wad be better laid out on yon bonny grass-holms, than lying useless here in this auld pigg. **1862** Hislop *Prov. Scot.* 170 She that gangs to the well wi' an ill-will, either the pig breaks or the water will spill.

†**b.** Applied to a cinerary urn. *Obs.*

1535 Stewart *Cron. Scot.* (Rolls) I. 244 Syne all his bodie brint wes untill ass.. Syne in ane pig wounderfullie wes wrocht, Tha war put in and to the tempill brocht. **1536** Bellenden *Cron. Scot.* (1821) II. 346 Ane pig craftely ingravin, in quhilk was found certane bonis wound in silk.

c. A chimney-pot (of earthenware). *rare.*

1822 Galt *Provost* xxiv. 177 Pigs from the lum-heads came rattling down like thunder-claps.

d. Earthenware as a material; also, a pot-sherd or fragment of earthenware such as children use in some games. *Sc. dial.*

1808–18 in Jamieson. *Mod. Sc.* Made o' common pig, not o' cheenie. The wee lassie was playan' wi' her pigs on the grund.

e. ***pigs and whistles***, fragments; trivialities; ***to go to pigs and whistles***, to be ruined.

1681 Colvil *Whigs Supplic.* (1751) 161 Discoursing of their Pigs and whistles, And strange experiments of Muscles [*note*, Pigs and whistles, *Gimcraks*]. **1786** *Har'st Rig* xlviii. (1801) 18 So he to pigs and whistles went And left the land. **1862** Mrs. Carlyle *Lett.* III. 125 Curious what a curative effect a railway journey has on me always, while you it makes pigs and whistles of!

2. *Comb.* (all *Sc.*): **pig-ass**, an ass which draws a **pig-cart**, a cart filled with crockery for sale, a mugger's cart; **pig-man**, a seller of crockery, a mugger; **pig-shop**, a crockery shop; **pig-wife**, a female vendor of crockery.

1787 W. Taylor *Poems* 79 Frae Phoebus' beams ye apes retire, Wi' your *Pig-asses. **1898** *Westm. Gaz.* 25 Oct. 2/1 Sometimes the clanging of a '*pig-cart' bell is heard far down the street. **1681** Colvil *Whigs Supplic.* (1751) 120 Wallace, Who in a *pig-man's weed, at Bigger Espied all the English leaguer. **1896** 'Ian Maclaren' *Kate Carnegie* 226 His father keepit a *pig chop [= shop]. **1787** W. Taylor *Poems* 79 *note*, Some ape Poets may be said rather to lead *Pig Wives' cripple Asses. **1821** *Blackw. Mag.* Jan. 423 Already has the 'Pig Wife's' early care Mark'd out a station, for her crockery ware.

pig (pɪg), *v.* [f. pig *sb.*[1]]

1. Of a sow: To bring forth pigs; to farrow. (Cf. *to child, kid, lamb, foal*, etc.) Also *transf.* and *fig.* **a.** *intr.*

c **1532** Du Wes *Introd. Fr.* in Palsgr. 952 To pygge as a sowe, *pourceler*. **1607** Topsell *Four-f. Beasts* (1658) 532 A Sow which hath once pigged. **1660** *Peters Last Will* in *Harl. Misc.* (Park) VII. 135 The bed that Pope Joan pigged in. **1844** Stephens *Bk. Farm* II. 698 A sow.. about to pig.. will carry straw in her mouth, and collect it in a heap in some retired corner of a shed.

b. *trans.*

1575 Turberv. *Venerie* 150 When his dame dothe pigge him, [the bore] hath as many teeth as euer he will haue whyles he liueth. **1593** Nashe *Four Lett. Confut.* Wks. (Grosart) II. 199 This is not halfe the littour of inckehornisme, that those foure pages haue pigd. **1699** E. Tyson in *Phil. Trans.* XXI. 432 This Monster was pigged alive. **1760** *Chron.* in *Ann. Reg.* 117/1 A large sow.. has pigged 21 pigs at one litter. **1805** R. W. Dickson *Pract. Agric.* II. 1194 The litters which are pigged in June.. should always be reared.

2. a. *intr.* To huddle together in a disorderly, dirty, or irregular manner; to herd, lodge, or sleep together, like pigs; to sleep in a place like a pigsty; also *to pig it.* Also const. *along*, to live from day to day like an animal.

1675 Cotton *Scoffer Scoft* 52 When I pig'd with mine own Dad. **1697** Vanbrugh *Provok'd Wife* v. ii. 65 So, now you being as dirty and as nasty as myself, we may go pig together. **1806–7** J. Beresford *Miseries Hum. Life* (1826) xiv. i, The only hole in which you can pig for the night. **1828** *Craven Gloss.* (ed. 2), 'To *pig* together', to lie, like pigs, two or three together. **1857** *Ecclesiologist* XVIII. 312 The six-and-thirty Irish families who pig in the adjoining alley. **1889** G. Allen *Tents of Shem* ii, You'd have to pig it with the goats and the cattle. **1896** *Pall Mall Gaz.* Sept. 70 She isn't fit to pig along in the way we have to here. **1909** [see master-mind *sb.* a]. **1930** J. Buchan *Castle Gay* ix. 145 They would have to pig it in a moorland inn. **1931** *Times Lit. Suppl.* 19 Feb. 131/3 It was not enough for Arthur Phelps 'just to pig along', working to live and living to work. **1939** G. B. Shaw *In Good King Charles's Golden Days* II. 112 Give me a skilled trade and eight or ten shillings a week, and you and I, beloved, would pig along more happily than we have ever been able to do as our majesties. **1964** 'M. Innes' *Money from Holme* xxvi. 171 'Dear me,' Binchy said. 'If it isn't friend Cheel.' He turned to Braunkopf. 'Cheel and I pig together, more or less.' **1977** —— *Honeybath's Haven* iii. 34 He didn't approve of the proposal to pig it in the studio.

b. *trans.* To crowd (persons) together like pigs.

1882 Schouler *Hist. U.S.* II. 276 Pigging travellers together in the same chamber if not in the same bed. **1882** *Daily News* 20 May 2/2 Women and children were often found in them 'pigged' into small rooms.

†**3.** *Glove-making.* To hang many skins together.

1688 R. Holme *Armoury* III. 86/2 *Pigging* is hanging of many skins together. **1726** *Dict. Rust.* s.v. *Wet-glover.*

pigage, erron. obs. form of pygarg.

pig-back, dial. form of piggy-back, pick-a-back.

'pig-bed. [f. pig *sb.*[1] + bed *sb.*]

1. A place where a pig lies, a pigsty, a pig's lair.

1821 in Cobbett *Rur. Rides* (1825) 17 Their dwellings are little better than pig-beds.

2. The bed of sand in which pigs of iron are cast.

1884 Lock *Workshop Rec.* Ser. III. 254/2 The first 2 or 3 cwt. of iron.. sometimes will have to be poured into a pig-bed. **1890** W. J. Gordon *Foundry* 99 On another pig-bed we see the next operation in progress; the men are with sledge-hammers breaking apart the pigs from the sows, and knocking them into separate existence.

3. *Comb.*, as **pig-bedman**: see quot.

1892 *Labour Commission* Gloss., *Pig-bedmen*, term synonymous with 'pig-lifters'.

pig-bel (ˌpɪgˈbɛl). *Med.* Also pigbel. [See quot. 1966.] A severe necrotizing enterocolitis found in Papua New Guinea, caused by *Clostridium welchii* and associated with feasts of pork.

1966 T. G. C. Murrell et al. in *Lancet* 29 Jan. 217/2 It was felt that the syndrome in New Guinea, being ætiologically related to pig-feasting, should be designated by a specific name. 'Pig-bel' has been proposed because this is the 'pidgin English' name used by medical orderlies to describe the abdominal discomfort which follows a large pork meal. **1969** Edington & Gilles *Path. in Tropics* vi. 273 A diffuse sloughing enteritis of the jejunum, ileum, and colon (enteritis necroticans, 'pigbel') has been described in Germany and New Guinea... It is the commonest acute abdominal condition requiring laparotomy in hospital practice in the highlands of New Guinea. The disease in this area, in both epidemic and sporadic forms, is related to pig feasting. **1977** *Lancet* 17 Sept. 617/2 The epidemic forms of necrotising enteritis ('pig-bel' and *Darmbrand* enteritis) have been consistently associated with strains of *C. welchi* producing mainly b [*recte* β] toxin.

ˈ**pig-cote.** Also pigs-cote. [f. pig *sb.*^{1} + cote *sb.*^{1}] A pig's house or pigsty.

1600 Heywood *2nd Pt. Edw. IV*, Wks. 1874 I. 94, I will not leaue S. Paul or Burgundy A bare pigs-cote to shroud them in. **1605** in Halliwell *Shaks.* (1887) II. 142 Warning to Henry Smyth to plucke downe his pigges-cote which is built nere the chapple wall. **1810** *Hull Improv. Act* 53 Any hogstie or pigscote. **1888** C. Kerry in *Jrnl. Derby Archæol. Soc.* X. 20 A stone from this wall formerly decorated the gable-end of a pig-cote.
attrib. **1865** B. Brierley *Irkdale* I. 144 Throwing his arms upon the pig-cote wall.

pigdom (ˈpɪgdəm). *nonce-wd.* [f. pig *sb.*^{1} + -dom.] The condition of a pig; the realm of pigs.
1879 Sala *Paris Herself Again* I. iii. 41 Every phase of human hoggishness developed by excess into an unmitigated pigdom is there illustrated. **1884** G. Allen *Philistia* I. 301 No doubt a very refined and cultivated specimen of pigdom.

pigell, obs. form of pickle.

pigeon (ˈpɪdʒən), *sb.* Forms: 4-5 pejon, 5 -oun, pegion, -geon, -gon, pyjon, 5-6 pygeon, (6 pegyn, -gyon, 6 pigin, -gen, -gion, pygion, -gon), 7 pidgion, pydgion, (pigeing), 7-9 pidgeon, 5- pigeon. [ME. *pyjon*, *pejon*, a. OF. *pijon* (13th c.), *pyjoun* young bird, esp. young dove, dove, mod.F. *pigeon* (whence the mod.Eng. spelling), = Pr. *pijon*, Sp. *pichon*, It. *piccione*:—late L. (3rd c.) *pīpiōn-em* (*pīpio*) a young cheeping bird, squab, f. *pīpīre* to chirp, cheep.]

A. Illustration of Forms.
?*c*1390 *Form of Cury* xlviii. (1780) 29 Peions ystewed. Take peions and stop hem with garlec ypylled and with gode erbes ihewe. *c*1430 *Two Cookery-bks.* (E.E.T.S.) 58 Pyionys. *Ibid.* 109 Mynce þe rostid peiouns. *c*1450 *Ibid.* 68 Peions rosted. **1467** *Mann. & Househ. Exp.* (Roxb.) 399 Item, [my mastyr spent] in vij.^{xx} peyre pegones, xj.*s.* viij.*d.* **1483** *Cath. Angl.* 277/2 A Pigeon, *pipio*. **1486** *Bk. St. Albans* A iv, The mawe of a pegeon. *Ibid.* C viij, The gut of a pegion. **1502** *Will of Moore* (Somerset Ho.), A Welsh pygon. *c*1532 Du Wes *Introd. Fr.* in *Palsgr.* 911 The pygions, *les pigeons*. **1533** Elyot *Cast. Helthe* II. xli. (1541) 31 Pygeons be easily digested. **1556** *Chron. Gr. Friars* (Camden) 68 For kecheynge of pegyns in the nyght. **1577** B. Googe *Heresbach's Husb.* IV. (1586) 168 For breeding of Pigions. **1587** Mascall *Govt. Cattle* (1627) 273 Pigins dung, and hennes or poultry dung. **1596** Shaks. *Merch. V.* II. vi. 5 O ten times faster Venus Pidgions flye. **1663** Pidgeon [see B. 2]. **1808** A. Parsons *Trav.* v. 137 In shooting wild pidgeons.

B. Signification.

I. † **1.** A young dove. *Obs.*
(Cf. Suff. dial. *pigeon-gull* = a young gull.)
*c*1440 *Promp. Parv.* 396/1 Pyione, yonge dove, *columbella*. **14..** in *Tundale's Vis.* (1843) 128 A pejon as law doth devyse Sche schuld eke offur as for hur trespace. **1481** Caxton *Reynard* (Arb.) 58 Had goten two pygeons [Flemish orig. *twee ionghe duuen*] as they cam first out of her neste. **1530** Palsgr. 254/1 Pygion a byrde, *pigon, colombette*. **1570** Levins *Manip.* 165/34 A Pigion, *pipio*. **1577** B. Googe *Heresbach's Husb.* IV. (1586) 171 Turtle Doues.. the olde ones be not so good, as neither the Pigion is. **1601** Holland *Pliny* x. xxxiv. 290 As well the male as the female be carefull of their young pigeons and love them alike.

2. a. A bird of the family *Columbidæ*, a dove, either wild or domesticated.
1494 Fabyan *Chron.* VII. 445, vi. peions for a peny, a fatte goos for .ii.*d.*, a pygge for a peny. **1526** Tindale *Luke* ii. 24 A payre off turtle doues or ij yonge pigions [νεοσσοὺς περιστερῶν, pullos columbarum, Wyclif twey culuere briddis]. **1570** B. Googe *Pop. Kingd.* IV. (1880) 53 b, On Whitsunday, whyte Pigeons tame, in strings from heauen flie. **1592** Davies *Immort. Soul* XXXII. xlvii, As Noah's Pigeon, which returned no more. **1663** Pepys *Diary* 19 Oct., The Queene.. was so ill as to be shaved, and pidgeons put to her feet, and to have the extreme unction given her by the priests. **1756-7** tr. *Keysler's Trav.* (1760) III. 306 At Modena.. pigeons are taught to carry letters to a place appointed, and bring back answers. **1790** *Bystander* 376 The doctor was putting the pigeons to the feet of an old miser. **1857** Buckle *Civiliz.* (1858) I. ix. 578 No Frenchman.. could keep pigeons, unless he were a noble.

b. Many varieties and breeds are distinguished, the pigeon being a noted object of fancy breeding; as *Barb* or *Barbary pigeon*, carrier-pigeon, *homing pigeon, nun pigeon, pouter pigeon, tumbler pigeon*, etc.: among the distinct species are the **bronze-, bronzed-,** or **gold-winged p., crown, crowned,** or **goura p., fruit p., ground p., nutmeg p., partridge p.,** passenger-p., **rock p., tooth-billed p., wild p., wood-pigeon**: for the more important of which see the qualifying word; cf. also dove *sb.* 1. Applied also with defining word to other birds, as **Cape, hill,** or **mountain pigeon**, a small species of petrel, *Procellaria* or *Daption capensis*, abundant at the Cape of Good Hope; **diving** or **sea pigeon**, the black guillemot or dovekie.

1694 *Acc. Sev. Late Voy.* II. (1711) 84 The first Diving Pigeon I got.. at Spitzbergen. **1707** Mortimer *Husb.* I. 261 Pigeons or Doves are of several sorts,.. as Wood-pigeons, Rock-pigeons, Stock or Ring-doves, Turtle-doves, Dovecoat-pigeons. **1719** De Foe *Crusoe* I. 89, I found a kind of wild Pidgeons, who built not as Wood Pidgeons in a Tree, but rather as House Pidgeons, in the Holes of the Rocks. **1731** Medley *Kolben's C.G. Hope* II. 158 Call'd at the Cape the Hill or Mount Pigeon. **1819** Shaw *Gen. Zool.* XI. I. 11 Red-Crowned Pigeon (*Columba rubricapilla*).. Native of Antiqua in the Isle of Panay. **1832** J. Bischoff *Van Diemen's Land* II. 31 By far the most beautiful birds in the island.. are called bronze-winged pigeons. **1884** 'R. Boldrewood' *Melb. Mem.* 11 The lovely bronze-wing pigeons were plentiful then amid the wild forest tracks of Newtown. **1898** *Daily News* 5 Jan. 2 Chequered blue dragon pigeons.

3. *fig.* **a.** A young woman, a girl; a sweetheart; also, † a coward. *Obs.*
1586 A. Day *Eng. Secretary* II. (1625) 80 *Antaphrasis*, when a word scornefully deliuered, is vnderstood by his contrary, as.. of a blacke Moore woman to say: Will yee see a faire pigeon? **1592** Greene *Disput.* Wks. (Grosart) X. 223 [When] they had spent vpon her what they had.. then forsooth, she and her yoong Pigion [her daughter] turne them out of doores like prodigall children. **1604** Dekker *Honest Wh.* I. i. Wks. 1873 II. 20 Sure hee's a pigeon, for he has no gall. **1682** N. O. *Boileau's Lutrin* II. 13 He had left her in the Lurch.. And under colour of Religion Courted another pretty Pigeon. **1916** Joyce *Portrait of Artist* iii. 116 Is that you, pigeon? **1940** *Music Makers* May 37/3 *Pigeon*, a young girl. **1970** G. Greer *Female Eunuch* 265 The basic imagery behind terms like.. *pigeon* is the imagery of food. **1977** J. Wambaugh *Black Marble* (1978) viii. 125 She accepted it graciously, thinking she must remember to give Philo a bonus for finding a little pigeon with tits big enough to bring old Landon McWhorter back to life.

b. *slang.* One who lets himself be swindled, esp. in gaming; a simpleton, dupe, gull; esp. in phrase ***to pluck a pigeon***, to 'fleece' a person. Also in extended use. [= F. *pigeon* in same sense, in allusion to its harmlessness, and to pigeon-catching.]
1593 G. Harvey *Pierce's Super.* Wks. (Grosart) II. 245 As wily a pigeon, as the cunning Goldsmith, that accused his neighbour, and condemned himselfe. **1639** S. Du Verger tr. *Camus' Admir. Events* 112 This pigeon being not of full age, could not contract it without the consent of his mother. **1654** Gayton *Pleas. Notes* 187 Nor is Sancho behind him for a Pigeon; both deluded commit equall errors. **1794** *Sporting Mag.* IV. 47, I was instantly looked up to as an impending pigeon.. and every preparation was made for the plucking. **1809** Malkin *Gil Blas* IV. vii. ¶4 A flatterer may play what game he likes against the pigeons of high life! **1862** Thackeray *Four Georges* iv, He was a famous pigeon for the play-men; they lived upon him. **1941** *Sun* (Baltimore) 14 Aug. 13/7 These amateur gamblers are the greatest pigeons I ever knew. **1956** B. Holiday *Lady sings Blues* (1973) xvii. 136 So they handed me a white paper to sign... I signed... The rest was up to them. I was just a pigeon. **1959** [see Murphy^2 4]. **1962** J. D. MacDonald *Girl* xi. 150 Anybody steals that much, they're a pigeon for the first people that get to him. **1977** *Tennis World* Sept. 17/3 A 'pigeon' is a frequent victim—that is, until he plays out of his tree. **1978** G. A. Sheehan *Running & Being* xii. 165 Whatever your game, you can always spot a pigeon. When I warm up for a road race I can usually tell at a glance the newcomers to the sport.

† **c.** A sharper of a particular kind: see quot. *Obs.* [Allusion to *carrier-pigeon*.]
1801 *Sporting Mag.* XVIII. 101 *Pigeons.*—Sharpers who, during the drawing of the lottery, wait ready mounted, near Guildhall, and as soon as the first two or three numbers are drawn, which they receive from a confederate.. ride with them.. to some distant insurance office.. where there is another of the gang, commonly a decent looking woman.. to her he secretly gives the numbers, which she insures for a considerable sum.

d. = *stool-pigeon* s.v. stool *sb.* 19 b.
1849 *National Police Gaz.* (U.S.) 12 May 2/7 The Mayor of Philadelphia having discovered that an old pigeon known as Bill Forebaugh was accustomed to point out his officers to the different knucks who arrived in the city, determined to put a stop to this new lay. **1859** G. W. Matsell *Vocabulum* 66 *Pigeon*, a thief that joins in with other thieves to commit a crime, and then informs the officer, who he pigeons for, and for this service the officer is supposed to be *occasionally* both deaf and blind. **1934** R. Chandler in *Black Mask* Oct. 14/2 Don't come here again—.. I don't like—pigeons. **1966** *Sunday Tel.* (Brisbane) 15 May 15/1 In the underworld, this is the mark of the 'copper', 'grass', 'nark', 'pigeon', or 'squealer'. **1971** 'D. Shannon' *Ringer* (1972) ix. 154 A lot of our pigeons offer the info to the other side too. **1976** R. Rosenblum *Sweetheart Deal* i. 11 For years guarding witnesses remained a.. shoestring operation. Rent a hotel room and keep the pigeon under wraps.

4. a. A flying target, used as a substitute for a real pigeon; also, a toy consisting of an imitation propeller which is made to fly in the air.
clay pigeon, a saucer of baked clay thrown into the air from a trap, as a mark at shooting-matches.

b. ***to fly the blue pigeon*** (*Naut. slang*): to heave the deep-sea lead.
1897 Kipling *Captains Courageous* 77 'I'll learn you how to fly the Blue Pigeon. Shooo!'.. The lead sang a deep droning song as Tom Platt whirled it round and round.

II. *attrib.* and *Comb.* **5. a.** attributive, in sense 'of a pigeon', 'of pigeons', as ***pigeon-dung, -egg, -gun, -louse, -racing***; 'for, used by, or inhabited by pigeons', as ***pigeon-basket, -box, -cote, -hutch, -loft*** (also fig.), ***-room, -roost, -tower***; 'containing or made of pigeons', as ***pigeon-pie***; **b.** objective and obj. gen., as ***pigeon-eating, -feeder, -keeper, -killer, -shooter, -shooting***; **c.** instrumental, as ***pigeon-haunted*** adj.; **d.** similative, as ***pigeon-tailed, -tinted*** adjs.
1750 Franklin *Let.* Wks. 1887 II. 206, I had.. nailed against the wall of my house a *pigeon-box that would hold six pair. **1626** Bacon *Sylva* §402 There was Wheat, steeped in Water.. mixed with *Pigeon-Dung. **1588** Shaks. *L.L.L.* v. i. 77 Thou halfpenny purse of wit, thou *Pidgeon-egge of discretion. **1898** *Allbutt's Syst. Med.* V. 258 The *pigeon-feeder fills his own mouth with a watery mixture of canary-seeds and vetch seeds. **1892** Greener *Breech-Loader* 131 Nor is it assumed that they alone can make good shooting *pigeon-guns. **1842** Sir A. de Vere *Song of Faith* 207 *Pigeon-haunted chestnuts musical. **1844** *Zoologist* II. 453 A *pigeon-hutch fastened against one of the walls. **1879** L. Wright (*title*) Practical *Pigeon Keeper. *c*1611 Chapman *Iliad* xv. 220 Thus from th' Idæan height, Like air's swift *pigeon-killer, stoop'd the far-shot God of light. **1735** J. Moore *Columbarium* 3 A *Pigeon Loft ought to be built to the South or South-west. **1891** Kipling *City of Dreadful Night* v. 34 Do you mean that you can from this absurd pigeon-loft locate the wards in the night-time! **1969** *Times* 4 Sept. 3/1 The difference between the sun's time at the pigeon loft, given by the pigeons' internal sense of time, and the time registered by the sun's position at the release site, gives a measure of the difference in longitude between the two points. **1977** *Evening Post* (Nottingham) 27 Jan. 7/7 They also admitted two accusations of jointly entering two pigeons lofts as trespassers. **1655** in M. M. Verney *Mem.* (1894) III. iv. 129 Madcap.. brags.. that she hath jeer'd you into good *pidgeon pies. These were soe good that there is not one left of them. **1721** Amherst *Terræ Fil.* No. 41 (1754) 217 Built in the form of pidgeon-pye, A house there is for rooks to lie And roost in. **1779** J. Woodforde *Diary* 15 Apr. (1924) I. 249 We had for dinner.. a Pidgeon Pye. **1843** *Ainsworth's Mag.* IV. 13 Swallowing a morsel of *foie gras* as uncognizantly as though it had been pigeon-pie. **1937** *Daily Herald* 8 Feb. 7/4 Pigeon-pie parties, an old-fashioned country custom, will be renewed this week in England and Wales. **1978** K. Bonfiglioli *All Tea in China* xx. 248 The black puddings, râgout of kidneys and pigeon pie.. were barely touched. **1899** *Westm. Gaz.* 3 May 10/1 We gather that *pigeon-racing is now almost a national sport. **1651** Cleveland *Poems* 29 Like to a martyr'd Abbeys courser doom, Devoutly alter'd to a *Pigeon room. **1793** *Sporting Mag.* Feb. 251 *Pigeon-shooting. Embellished with a beautiful Representation of a Pigeon Shooting Match. **1892** Greener *Breech-Loader* ix. 234 Pigeon-shooting, against the practice of which many sportsmen protest.. is of lowly origin. **1901** W. Churchill *Crisis* II. ix. 202 The red *pigeon-tailed coat. **1957** W. Faulkner *Town* iv. 83 Come in a Pullman in striped britches and gold watch chain big enough to boom logs with and gold eyeglasses and even a gold toothpick and the pigeon-tailed coat. **1883** V. Stuart *Egypt* 269 Dechney.. abounds in *pigeon-towers.

6. a. Special Combs.: **pigeon-cherry** = *pin-cherry* (pin *sb.* 13); † **pigeon-diver**, the black guillemot or dovekie; **pigeon drop** *U.S. criminals' slang*, (*a*) a form of confidence trick which begins with the dropping of a wallet before the victim or 'pigeon'; (*b*) (see quot. 1959); so **pigeon dropper; pigeon dropping** = *pigeon drop* (*a*); **pigeon-express** = *pigeon-post*; **pigeon-fancier**, one who keeps and breeds fancy pigeons; so **pigeon-fancy, -fancying; pigeon-fieldfare**, the fieldfare, *Turdus pilaris*, or a variety of it; **pigeon-flyer**, one who lets homing pigeons fly, or takes part in pigeon-races; so **pigeon-flying;** † **pigeon-foot** = *pigeon's foot*: see b; **pigeon-goose**, an Australian goose, *Cereopsis novæ hollandiæ*, having a remarkably large cere; the Cape-Barren goose; **pigeon grass**, (*U.S.*) a grass of the genus *Setaria*, esp. *S. glauca* or *S. viridis*; **pigeon-guillemot**, *Cepphus columba*, a sea-fowl of the North Pacific; **pigeon-hearted** *a.*, faint-hearted, timid, chicken-hearted; † **pigeon-livered** *a.*, meek, gentle; **pigeon man**, see quot.; **pigeon marl**, dove-coloured marl, columbine marl; **pigeon-match**, a match at shooting pigeons released from traps at a fixed distance from the competitors; **pigeon millet** = *pigeon grass*; **pigeon-pair**, boy and girl twins; also, a family consisting of a son and daughter only; so called from a pigeon's brood, which usually consists of a male and female; also *transf.*; **pigeon-post**, the conveyance of letters or dispatches by homing pigeons; **pigeon-poult**, the young of a pigeon; **pigeon ruby** = *pigeon's blood* (see b); **pigeon salt**, see quot.; **pigeon-shot**, one skilled in pigeon-shooting; **pigeon-tail**, an American name of the pintail duck (*Dafila acuta*); **pigeon-tick**, see quot.; **pigeon-weed** *U.S.*, the corn gromwell, *Lithospermum arvense*, or the spikenard, *Aralia racemosa*; **pigeon-woodpecker**, (*U.S.*) a flicker, *Colaptes aureus*, found in eastern North America.
1694 *Acc. Sev. Late Voy.* II. (1711) 83 The *Pigeon-diver .. one of the beautifullest birds of Spitzbergen. **1937** E. H. Sutherland *Professional Thief* iii. 67 Among the short-con rackets, dropping the poke (also known as the *pigeon-drop) is frequently used. **1959** *Washington Post* 18 Mar. A3/1 In

the pigeon drop a confidence man tells his victim he has found a large amount of money and will share it if the victim will kick in some money as a show of good faith. **1961** HARNEY & CROSS *Narcotic Officer's Notebk.* vi. 118 Sometimes it was the 'pigeon-drop'. A purse or billfold containing a considerable amount of money was dropped. The 'sucker' was allowed to find it right along with a member of the mob. **1979** *Monitor* (McAllen, Texas) 22 July 2F/5 A Houston woman held on attempted theft charges claims to be part of a national 'pigeon drop' confidence ring. **1961** WEBSTER, Pigeon-dropper. **1977** J. WAMBAUGH *Black Marble* (1978) vi. 76 *Pigeon droppers, pursepicks, muggers. Don't walk the Boulevard at night. **1850** *Green's St. Louis Directory for 1851* p. xviii, Such practice is immensely more disrespectable than procuring money under false pretenses—no more honorable than veritable *pigeon-dropping. **1955** K. SULLIVAN *Girls who go Wrong* (1956) xii. 128 Elmira became the more proficient of the pair at the badger game—flim flam and pigeon dropping. **1970** C. MAJOR *Dict. Afro-Amer. Slang* 91 *Pigeon dropping*, confidence game-playing. **1807** SOUTHEY *Lett. from Eng.* I. xxi. 233 The Columbarians or *pigeon-fanciers. **1822** M. EDGEWORTH *Let.* 19 Jan. (1971) 326 He explained to me what is meant by being *in the fancy*—pigeon fanciers—rabbit fanciers &c. **1861** DICKENS *Gt. Expect.* xxxii, You were quite a pigeon-fancier. **1899** *Westm. Gaz.* 20 Sept. 7/3 A well-known homer pigeon-fancier. **1941** [see DART *sb.* 1 d]. **1976** *Deeside Advertiser* 9 Dec. 2/3 He was employed at the C.E.G.B. Power Station and a keen pigeon fancier. **1879** L. WRIGHT *Pract. Pigeon Keeper* v, It is almost impossible to make any real mark in the *pigeon-fancy without exhibiting in some form. *Ibid.* ix, The almond Tumbler..has done more to raise the tone of pigeon-fancy than any other breed. *a* **1845** BARHAM *Cousin Nicholas* xxiv, A flight of *pigeon-fieldfares..alighted among the berries of the shrubbery. **1879** FARRAR *St. Paul* (1883) 124 For membership of the Sanhedrim..a man must not be a dicer, usurer, *pigeon-flyer, or dealer in the produce of the Sabbatical year. **1898** *Westm. Gaz.* 19 Apr. 2/3 [Places] in which *pigeon-flying is a sport more honoured in the breach than the observance. **1736** AINSWORTH *Lat. Dict.*, *Pigeon foot (an herb), *Geranium, pes columbinus*. **1890** *Cent. Dict.* s.v. *Cereopsis*, There is but one species..called the *pigeon-goose. **1838** H. COLMAN *1st Rep. Agric. Mass.* (Mass. Agric. Survey) 128 There were several patches of black or *pigeon grass when the dyke was built. **1901** C. T. MOHR *Plant Life Alabama* 358 Chactochloa glauca... Pigeon Grass. **1926** F. W. HILGENDORF *Weeds N.Z.* facing p. 17 (*caption*) Pigeon grass (*Setaria glauca*). **1621** FLETCHER *Pilgrim* III. iv, I never saw such *pigeon-hearted people! **1840** DICKENS *Old C. Shop* lxii, This fellow is pigeon-hearted, and light-headed. **1602** SHAKS. *Ham.* II. ii. 603 But I am *Pigeon-Liuer'd, and lacke Gall To make oppression bitter. **1903** *Westm. Gaz.* 2 Dec. 12/2 Those London Stock Exchange celebrities of the thirties, the '*pigeon men'. They established a service of pigeons between London and Paris. **1601** *Pigeon marle [see COLUMBINE *a.* 3]. **1610** W. FOLKINGHAM *Art of Survey* I. x. 32 Columbine or Pidgeon Marle lies in lumpes and cloddes. **1764** *Museum Rust.* II. 377 The auger brought up marle..some of it mixed with blue veins (which I will here call pigeon marle). **1810** *Sporting Mag.* XXXV. 140 A *pigeon match for a stake of 200 guineas. **1948** A. L. BLOMQUIST *Grasses N. Carolina* 186 One species (*S[etaria] viridis*) known as '*pigeon millet' or 'foxtail' is an obnoxious weed in cultivated ground in some of the Northern states. **1847–78** HALLIWELL, *Pigeon-pair. **1878** HARDY *Ret. Native* I. II. i. 240 She and Clym Yeobright would make a very pretty pigeon pair—hey? **1900** in *Eng. Dial. Dict.* **1954** *Publ. Amer. Dial. Soc.* XXI. 34 *Pigeon pair*, a boy and girl, usually brother and sister, close enough in age to be congenial playmates. **1960** *Woman* 23 Apr. 5/2 A mother there had twins—boy and girl—on February 29, brother and sister for her pigeon pair born on the *previous* Leap Year Day. **1964** D. VARADAY *Gara-Yaka* xx. 178, I recognized Moll [*sc.* a lion] in the harem-nursery with three lively youngsters, while the two older females both appeared to have chipped in with a pigeon-pair each. **1873** LYTTON *Parisians* XII. xv, We learnt that through a *pigeon-post. **1892** *Daily News* 5 Nov. 5/5 The Caliphs made the pigeon post a regular institution in the Nile delta. *Ibid.*, There were six pigeon-posts between Cairo and Damascus, and ten between the latter city and Behnessa. **1899** *Westm. Gaz.* 7 Nov. 7/2 In the pigeon-post message of Friday no reference to the use of infantry is made. **1909** *Chambers's Jrnl.* Oct. 661/2 Extensive practice is carried out in..photographing forts and positions of troops, and sending the films by means of pigeon-post to be developed and printed at headquarters. **1963** *Times* 3 May 13/7 It also became, thanks to Julius Reuter and his pigeon post of 1850, a vital link in the network of telegraphic communications. **1975** *Times* 15 Mar. 14/7 It will cost 7p to have a first-class letter delivered. .. To set up a pigeon post is remarkably cheap and easy. **1885** BURTON *Arab. Nts.* II. 50 On the night of the consummation they cut the throat of a *pigeon-poult. **1897** *Daily News* 23 Feb. 6/2 Colour shades ranging from..pale rose to intense *pigeon ruby red. **1678** *Phil. Trans.* XII. 1063 A fift sort is *Pigeon Salt, which is nothing but the Brine running out through the crack of a Phat, and hardens to a clod on the outside over the fire. **1894** *Westm. Gaz.* 24 Nov. 3/1 A sportsman of renown in many branches, especially as a '*pigeon-shot'. **1902** WEBSTER Suppl., **Pigeon-tick*, (*a*) A parasitic mite (*Argas reflexus*) found on pigeons. (*b*) The common bird mite. **1785** *Mem. Amer. Acad. Arts & Sci.* I. 431 *Aralia... Berry-Bearing Angelica.* Shot Bush. *Pigeon Weed. Blossoms white. Berries black. Common in new plantations. **1851** J. F. W. JOHNSTON *Notes on N. Amer.* I. 305 Richer clover also had come up on another drained spot, and less of the pigeon-weed..with which this clay land is infested. **1889** G. VASEY *Agric. Grasses U.S.* (new ed.) 103 Pigeon-Weed..grows chiefly in cultivated grounds. **1844** J. E. DEKAY *Zool. N.Y.* II. 192 This species..is called Highhole, Yucker, Flicker, Wake-up and *Pigeon Woodpecker..in this State. **1847** THOREAU *Let.* 15 Feb. in *Corr.* (1958) 175, I remember a pigeon-woodpecker's nest in the grove on the east side of the yard. **1870** [see FLICKER *sb.*[4]]. **1917** T. G. PEARSON *Birds Amer.* II. 163 Flicker. *Colaptes auratus auratus*... Clape; Pigeon Woodpecker; Yellowhammer. **1955** *Amer. Speech* XXX. 181 Of bird names given for size, consider:..pigeon woodpecker.

b. Combs. with *pigeon's*: **pigeon's blood**, *attrib.* (of a ruby) dark red, rather lighter than beef's blood; **pigeon's egg**, a bead of Venetian glass, of the shape and size of the egg of a pigeon; **pigeon's-foot** (= F. *pied de pigeon*), dove's-foot (*Geranium columbinum, G. molle*); **pigeon's grass** [cf. Gr. περιστερεών, a kind of verbena, f. περιστερά dove], the common vervain; **pigeon's throat**, see quot.; **pigeon's wing**, (*a*) see quot. 1884; (*b*) = PIGEON-WING 3 (q.v. for quot.); (*c*) a type of wig worn in the 18th century; also *attrib.*

1894 *Daily News* 13 Apr. 6/6 If this were a real *pigeon's blood ruby it might command a price of £700 a carat. **1894** *Times* 14 Apr. 15/5 The stone..was made up to resemble a pigeon's blood stone. **1597** GERARDE *Herbal* II. cccxli. 793 Commonly called in Latin *Pes Columbinus*:..it may be called..in English Doues foote, and *Pigeons foote. **1706** PHILLIPS, *Pigeon's-Foot.* **1884** MILLER *Plant-n.* 199 *Geranium columbinum*, Pigeon's-foot Crane's-bill. **1597** GERARDE *Herbal* II. ccxxxv. 581 Veruain is called..in English..of some *Pigeons grasse, or Columbine, because Pigeons are delighted to be amongst it, as also to eate thereof, as Apuleius writeth. **1884** in MILLER *Plant-n.* **1883** *Cassell's Fam. Mag.* Oct. 698/2 The newest colour for this purpose is '*pigeon's throat', a pretty blue-green shade. **1753** *Pigeon's wing [see NEGLIGENT *sb.* 2]. **1884** *Cassell's Fam. Mag.* Apr. 312/1 Such delicate mixtures as pigeon's-wing—blue, grey, and pink blended—will be used in some of the best dresses. **1966** J. S. COX *Illustr. Dict. Hairdressing* 113/1 *Pigeon's wing periwig*, a man's wig dressed with two horizontal rolls above the ears. The top, sides and back being dressed smooth and plain. This style was worn with different styles of queue.

pigeon, *v.* [f. PIGEON *sb.*]

1. *trans.* To treat as a pigeon, make a pigeon of (see PIGEON *sb.* 3 b); to gull, cheat, delude, swindle; esp. at cards or any kind of gaming.

1675 COTTON *Scoffer Scoft* 2 Of Lies, and Fables, which did Pigeon The Rabble into false Religion. **1785** G. A. BELLAMY *Apology* VI. 69 They have pigeoned me out of my money. **1805** SURR *Winter in Lond.* (1806) II. 252 They mean to pigeon him, as their phrase is. **1807** E. S. BARRETT *Rising Sun* II. 60 Having one night been pigeoned of a vast property. **1859** THACKERAY *Virgin.* xlvi, You sit down with him in private to cards, and pigeon him.

2. To send (a message) by a pigeon.

1870 *Pall Mall G.* 25 Nov. 5 Gambetta has 'pigeoned' a message to-day..that ought to be very reassuring.

Hence **'pigeoned** *ppl. a.*, **'pigeoning** *vbl. sb.* (in quot. 1873 = subsisting on pigeons). Also **'pigeonable** *a.*, easily cheated, gullible; **'pigeoner**, a swindler, a sharper.

1844 TUPPER *Heart* vi. 58 Patron of two or three *pigeonable city sparks. **1853** *Blackw. Mag.* Oct. 450 A knowledge of human nature under its more credulous and pigeonable aspect. **1777** *Gamblers* 45 *Pigeon'd Jockies curse thy deeper wit. **1849** ALB. SMITH *Pottleton Leg.* 110 You might divide them into two parties—the *pigeoners and the pigeoned. **1808** ELEANOR SLEATH *Bristol Heiress* III. 222 She was not worth *pigeoning. **1873** LELAND *Egypt. Sk. Bk.* 70 He married the lady who put him up to pigeoning.

pigeon: see PIDGIN

'pigeon-berry. [f. PIGEON *sb.* + BERRY *sb.*[1]]

1. One of several plants whose fruit is attractive to birds, esp. in North America, the pokeweed, *Phytolacca americana*, or a dogwood, *Cornus canadensis* or *C. alternifolia*, and, in the West Indies, *Duranta repens*; also, the fruit of these plants.

1775 A. BURNABY *Trav.* 7 The pigeon-berry and rattle-snake-root, so esteemed in all ulcerous and pleuretical complaints. **1792** BELKNAP *Hist. New Hampsh.* III. 134 About the second or third year, another weed, called pigeon-berry, succeeds the fireweed. **1856** W. E. CORMACK *Narr. Journey across Newfoundland* iii. 13 The surface [of the ground] is bespangled..by..*Cornus canadensis*, bearing a cluster of wholesome red berries, sometimes called pigeon berries. **1868** *Canad. Naturalist* III. 409 Among the most common plants which overspread the burned ground..are ..the pigeonberry (*Cornus canadensis*); and the red strawberry. **1885** LADY BRASSEY *The Trades* 425. **1885** A. BRASSEY *In Trades, Tropics, & Roaring Forties* xviii. 425 A pretty tree with a large lavender flower, and great orange-coloured clusters of what are called 'pigeon-berries'. **1920** BRITTON & MILLSPAUGH *Bahama Flora* 372 *Duranta repens*. .. Bermuda; Florida; West Indies and Mexico to northern South America. Pigeon-berry. **1942** W. R. VAN DERSAL *Ornamental Amer. Shrubs* xii. 183 The plant [*sc. Cornus alternifolia*] has a number of common names, including.. purple dogwood, pigeon-berry, umbrella tree, and pagoda cornel. **1958** J. G. MACGREGOR *North-West of 16* v. 62 The bright red pigeon-berries, and the piles of spruce cones shelled out by the squirrels. **1971** H. M. S. LEWIN in E. L. Wardman *Bermuda Jubilee Garden* v. 90/2 *D[uranta] repens*. Pigeon-berry, Sky-flower, Golden dewdrop. A slender evergreen shrub with drooping sprays of lilac-blue flowers that are followed by clusters of golden yellow berries. **1973** HITCHCOCK & CRONQUIST *Flora Pacific Northwest* 104 *P[hytolacca] americana* L. Pokeberry, pokeweed, pigeon-berry.

2. pigeon-berry ash *Austral.*, an evergreen tree of the genus *Elæocarpus* or *Cryptocarya*; **pigeon-berry bush** = sense 1 above; **pigeon-berry tree** *Austral.*, the native mulberry, *Litsea dealbata*; also = *pigeon-berry ash*.

1785 *Mem. Amer. Acad. Arts & Sci.* I. 411 *Pigeon-Berry Bush*... Pigeons feed on the berries, which has been the occasion of its trivial name. **1832** W. D. WILLIAMSON *Hist. State Maine* I. 115 The pigeon-berry bush is as tall as that of a blackberry, bears an abundance of small purple berries, the chief food of pigeons. **1884** A. NILSON *Timber Trees New South Wales* 55 *E[læocarpus] obovatus*.— Ash; Pigeon-berry Tree.—A noble tree, attaining sometimes a height of 130 feet. **1889** J. H. MAIDEN *Useful Native Plants Austral.* 563 *Litsea dealbata*... 'Pigeon-berry Tree.' 'Native Mulberry.' 'Black Ash.' **1936** J. W. AUDAS *Native Trees Austral.* 190 Elaeocarpus Baurleni..grows in New South Wales to the Queensland border, known popularly as Pigeon-Berry Ash. *Ibid.* 192 Elaeocarpus obovatus..is known as Pigeon-berry Ash. *Ibid.* 229 Litsea dealbata... A well-known tree of Queensland and New South Wales called Native Mulberry or Pigeon-Berry Tree. **1965** *Austral. Encycl.* III. 137/1 The rose maple or rose walnut..is most generally known to timber-getters as pigeon-berry ash.

'pigeon-breast. *Path.* A deformed human chest, laterally constricted, so that the sternum is thrust forward, as in a pigeon.

1842 DICKENS *Let.* 3 Apr. (1974) III. 180 That valiant general..is an old, old man with..the remains of a pigeon-breast in his military surtout. **1849–52** *Todd's Cycl. Anat.* IV. 1039/2 It was observed that he had the 'pigeon breast' form of chest. **1879** KHORY *Princ. Med.* 46 The pigeon-breast is produced by pressure on their ribs at their angles when they are young and yielding.

So **'pigeon-ˌbreasted** *a.*, having a breast narrow and projecting like a pigeon's.

1815 SOUTHEY in *Q. Rev.* July 509 The French cuirass is made pigeon-breasted, so that unless a musket ball be fired very near it is turned off. **1826** MISS MITFORD *Village* Ser. II. (1863) 300 Madame la duchesse, in her..long-waisted, pigeon-breasted gown. **1840** DICKENS *Old C. Shop* xxviii, All the [waxwork] gentlemen were very pigeon-breasted. **1872** T. G. THOMAS *Dis. Women* 67 Of rather lanky appearance and pigeon-breasted.

pigeoneer (pɪdʒəˈnɪə(r)). *U.S.* [f. PIGEON *sb.* + -EER.] **a.** A person who trains or breeds homing pigeons, formerly esp. in the U.S. Army Signal Corps. **b.** (See quot. 1944[1].)

1918 *Boston Evening Rec.* 11 Jan. 9/2 A pigeoneer is an expert handler of homing pigeons. **1918** *Personnel Specifications* (U.S. Signal Corps) 21 Chief Pigeoneer:.. homing pigeon expert..in charge of the training and instruction of the men as pigeoneers. **1940** *Amer. Pigeon Jrnl.* Dec. 420/1 We have hundreds of young men of military age who have had the advantage of the experience and training of the pigeoneers of 1917–1918. **1944** *Sunday Jrnl. & Star* (Lincoln, Nebraska) 30 Apr. 8 Frank Robbins receives calls daily from people who wish pigeons to be exterminated around their homes... Assistant 'pigeoneer' at different times is Detective Captain Eugene Masters who is also an expert shot. **1944** M. B. COTHREN *Pigeon Heroes* i. 7 [The pigeon] dropped abruptly down on the landing board of its loft and walked through the trap door... In a jiffy a pigeoneer pulled out the message.

pigeon (English): see PIDGIN.

'pigeongram. [f. PIGEON *sb.*, after *telegram*.] A message transmitted by a homing pigeon.

1885 *Times* 7 Apr. 4 On Sunday a message was sent by pigeons from Brighton to Dover..A telegram in reply said —'Your pigeongram..caused much rejoicing.' **1887** *Ibid.* 11 Apr. 11/2 Pigeongrams were freely used in the course of Saturday, and with success. **1899** *Westm. Gaz.* 16 Nov. 12/1 The need is being supplied by the Great Barrier Pigeongram Agency of Picton-street, Auckland. *Ibid.*, The edges are fastened by sticking on a pigeongram postage stamp, a copy of which we reproduce.

'pigeon-ˌhawk. A hawk that preys on pigeons: a name given in England to the sparrow-hawk, and sometimes to the goshawk; in U.S. to the American merlin (*Falco columbarius*) and related species, also sometimes to the sharp-shinned hawk (*Accipiter velox*).

1731 M. CATESBY *Nat. Hist. Carolina* I. 3 The Pigeon-Hawk..is a very swift and bold Hawk, preying on Pigeons and wild Turkeys while they are young. **1772** J. RUTTY *Ess. Nat. Hist. Co. Dublin* I. 297 The Pigeon Hawk or Goshawk ..is said to breed in Ireland's Eye. **1831** J. J. AUDUBON *Ornith. Biogr.* I. 467 The Pigeon Hawk does not, I believe, raise its young within the United States, but somewhere farther to the north. **1871** J. BURROUGHS *Wake-Robin, Adirondac* (1884) 106 A pigeon-hawk came prowling by our camp. **1884** COUES *Key N. Amer. Birds* 528 *Accipiter fuscus*, Sharp-shinned Hawk, 'Pigeon' Hawk, so-called, but not to be confounded with *Falco columbarius*. **1885** SWAINSON *Prov. Names Birds* 136 Sparrow-Hawk..also called.. Pigeon hawk. **1913** H. K. SWANN *Dict. Eng. & Folk-Names Brit. Birds* 181 Pigeon Hawk: The Goshawk.... also the Sparrow-hawk. **1958** E. T. GILLIARD *Living Birds of World* 111/2 A well-known small species of the Northern Hemisphere, the Pigeon Hawk or Merlin (*Falco columbarius*), is very similar to the Peregrine in general shape and color.

'pigeon-hole, *sb.* [f. PIGEON *sb.* + HOLE *sb.*]

1. A hole (usually one of several) in a wall or door for the passage of pigeons; hence *transf.*, *esp.* one of a series of holes for the passage of liquids, escape of gases, etc.

1683 SALMON *Doron Med.* II. 569 Two doors, the one at the bottom with a 'Pidgeon' hole in it. **1858** DICKENS *Lett.* 25 Aug., To see him and John sitting in pay-boxes, and surveying Ireland out of pigeon-holes. **1890** *Cent. Dict.*, *Pigeon-hole*,..one of a series of holes in an arch of a furnace through which the gases of combustion pass... One of a series of holes in the block at the bottom of a keir through which its liquid contents can be discharged.

2. A small recess or hole (usually one of a series) for domestic pigeons to nest in. Hence any small hole, recess, or room for sitting or staying in; also, a small flat.

[**1577** B. GOOGE *Heresbach's Husb.* IV. (1586) 171 To feede and fatte them [turtle doves] in little darke roomes like Pigions holes.] **1622** *Chapel Warden's Acc. Bks.* in D.

Lysons *Environs Lond.* (1795) II. 221 Paid for making a new payre of pigeing-holes, 2s. 6d. **1777** P. THICKNESSE *Year's Journey* II. li. 151 All the rest of the apartments are pidgeon-holes, filled with fleas, bugs, and dirt. **1820** SCOTT *Fam. Lett.* July (1894) II. xvi. 89 We have plenty of little pigeon holes of bedrooms. **1852** MUNDY *Antipodes* (1857) 212 There was..a single dormitory for four hundred men!.. Each pigeon-hole is six feet and a half long, by two feet in width. **1869** 'MARK TWAIN' *Innoc. Abr.* viii. 80 You can rent a whole block of these pigeon-holes for fifty dollars a month.

†**3.** A cant name for the stocks; also for the similar instrument in which the hands of culprits were confined, when being flogged. *Obs.*

1592 GREENE *Disput.* Wks. (Grosart) X. 233, I dare scarce speake of Bridewell because my shoulders tremble at the name of it,..yet looke but in there, and you shall heare poore men with their handes in their Piggen hoales crye, Oh fie vpon whoores, when Fouler giues them the terrible lash. **1614** B. JONSON *Barth. Fair* IV. iv, Downe with him, and carry him away, to the pigeon-holes. **1694** ECHARD *Plautus* 193 He'll be stock'd into the Pigeon Holes, where I'm afraid the poor Devil must make his Nest tonight.

†**4.** *pl.* An old out-door game, the particulars of which are doubtful: cf. quot. 1847–78. *Obs.*

1608 *Great Frost* in Arb. *Garner* I. 97 Then had they other games of 'nine holes' and 'pigeon holes' in great numbers. **1632** ROWLEY *New Wonder* II. i. 17 What were deale you in? Cards, Dice, Bowls, or Pigeon-holes? **1684** *Ballads illustr. Gt. Frost* (Percy Soc.) 7 In several places there was nine-pins plaid, And pidgeon holes for to beget a trade. **1699** *Poor Robin* (N.), The boys are by themselves in shoiles, At nine-pins or at pigeon-holes. [**1847–78** HALLIWELL, *Pigeon-holes*, a game like our modern bagatelle, where there was a machine with arches for the balls to run through, resembling the cavities made for pigeons in a dove-house.]

5. *Printing.* An excessively wide space between two words. Now not common.

1683 MOXON *Mech. Exerc., Printing* xxii. ¶4 These wide Whites are by Compositers (in way of Scandal) call'd Pigeon-holes. **1771** LUCKOMBE *Hist. Print.* 396 [Too] many Blanks of m-quadrats will be contemptuously called *Pigeon-holes*. *Ibid.* 398 Doubles..are conspicuous by the Pigeon-holes which are made to drive out what was doubled. **1825** HONE *Every-day Bk.* I. 1140. **1841** SAVAGE *Dict. Printing* 590. **1900** POWELL *Practical Printing* 174.

†**6.** A seat in the top row of the gallery of a theatre. *Obs.*

1747 *Gentl. Mag.* XVII. 22/1 All tickets to be stampt *pro rata*..; a first gallery ticket for the play, one six-penny stamp: an upper gallery, or pigeon hole, or upper seat ticket for the play, to have one three penny stamp. **1828** *Lights & Shades* I. 254 On his benefit-night Brandon may be seen in one of the pigeon-holes, counting the house. *Ibid.* II. 104 But in the pigeon-holes!..you lean over—you hear the undistinguishable joke that sets every body else laughing.

7. a. One of a series of compartments or cells, in a cabinet, writing-table, or range of shelves, open in front, and used for the keeping (with ready accessibility) of documents or papers of any kind, also of wares in a shop.

1688 LOCKE *Let.* 6 Feb. in B. Rand *Corr. J. Locke & E. Clarke* (1927) 245 Another way may be with pigeon-holes as they call them: at these twenty-four holes, over the first paste an *A*, over the second a *B*, [etc.]. **1789** *Trans. Soc. Arts* (ed. 2) II. 156, I put the papers..into a pigeon hole in a cabinet. **1796** BURKE *Let. to Noble Ld.* Wks. VIII. 58 Abbé Sieyes has whole nests of pigeon-holes full of constitutions ready made, ticketed, sorted, and numbered. **1862** SALA *Ship-Chandler* iii. 48 Pigeon-holes full of samples of sugar, of rice, tobacco, coffee, and the like. **1879** J. A. H. MURRAY *Addr. Philol. Soc.* 8 This has been fitted with blocks of pigeon-holes, 1029 in number, for the reception of the alphabetically arranged slips. **1972** C. ACHEBE *Girls at War* 99 'Can I see your pigeon-hole?'.. 'That's the glove-box. Nothing there.' **1978** *Lancashire Life* Nov. 151/1 Some find it possible to envy those who sit on the official side of counter or pigeonhole.

b. *fig.* One of a series of ideal 'compartments' for the classification of facts or objects of thought, or of persons, as by occupations.

[**1847** FR. A. KEMBLE *Later Life* III. 305 People whose minds are parcelled out into distinct divisions—pigeon-holes, as it were.] **1879** FARRAR *St. Paul* II. 189 Without attempting to arrange in the pigeon-holes of our logical formulæ the incomprehensible mysteries encircling that part of it. **1902** L. STEPHEN *Stud. Biog.* III. iii. 90 He was incapable of arranging his thoughts in orderly symmetrical pigeon-holes. **1938** [see ALL-ROUNDER]. **1957** [see DEFERRAL].

8. *attrib.* Consisting of, like, or having pigeon-holes or small apertures.

1685 LOCKE *Jrnl.* 28 Aug. in P. King *Life Locke* (1829) 167, I saw a boor's house a mile or more from Amsterdam. .. There were three pigeon-hole beds, after the Dutch fashion. **1874** RAYMOND *Statist. Mines & Mining* 403 When the fire-place is separated from the ore compartment by pigeon-hole walls. **1875** W. MCILWRAITH *Guide Wigtownshire* 31 Large fronts pierced by small pigeon-hole windows. **1899** *Academy* 30 Sept. 329/1 Mr. Saintsbury has the pigeon-hole form of mind..collecting any quantity of conclusions and facts, and after tying them up and labelling them, putting them away for future use in the pigeon-holes of memory. **1968** R. A. LYTTLETON *Mysteries Solar Syst.* iv. 137 On a simple pigeon-hole argument, the probability of the distribution being due to pure chance turns out to be less than 1 in 1000.

'pigeon-hole, *v.* [f. prec. sb.]

1. *trans.* To deposit in a pigeon-hole (7); to put away in the proper place for later reference; hence, to put aside (a matter) for (or on pretence of) future consideration, to shelve for the present.

1840 C. CAMPBELL in T. Bland *Bland Papers* I. p. v, The lady..reached down a bundle of letters..from the interstices of the eaves of the porch, where they were nicely pigeon-holed. **1855** *Knickerbocker* XLVI. 95 The bill of the gentlemanly proprietor..was deliberately met by a bill for 'damages to cow-catcher', and pigeon-holed. **1861** *Sat. Rev.* 20 July 67 We do not doubt that Lord Lyveden, by duly pigeon-holing the complaint, added another to the long list of his public services in that line. **1872** H. SPENCER *Princ. Psychol.* (ed. 2) II. VII. xviii. 485 Duly arranged and, as it were, pigeon-holed for future use. **1889** PEMBERTON *E. A. Sothern* 69 Robertson's original adaptation..was, for a period of eight years, 'pigeon-holed'. **1940** WODEHOUSE *Eggs, Beans & Crumpets* 154 Putting the prophet Hosea to one side for the moment and temporarily pigeon-holing the children of Adullam. **1949** *Jrnl. R. Aeronaut. Soc.* LIII. 410/2 Although the flying bomb project was pigeon-holed, out of this early work the Mark 1A Auto-pilot and the Queen Bee target aeroplane emerged. **1955** *Times* 15 June 3/3 Why had the Minister pigeon-holed the Phillips report? **1963** *Ann. Reg. 1962* 205 Tentative plans for an exchange of television appearances by the Soviet and American leaders were also pigeon-holed. **1976** *Milton Keynes Express* 16 July 2/5 One plan that seems to have been pigeon-holed for the time being is the idea of finding another site for the College of Further Education.

2. To assign to a definite place in the memory, or in an ordered group of ideas; to place or label mentally; to classify or analyse exhaustively.

1870 H. STEVENS *Bibl. Geogr. & Historica* Introd. 4 The writer has thought it well to pigeon-hole the facts. **1880** *Times* 2 Oct. 11/3 Text-books should be merely used as means for..pigeon-holing knowledge previously acquired. **1889** *Athenæum* 16 Mar. 338/1 [Bacon admonishes] against ..wilful rejection of facts that we are unable to pigeon-hole. **1950** D. GASCOYNE *Vagrant* 59 Keep your labels for people who need them; I cannot be pigeonholed neatly. **1978** J. B. HILTON *Some run Crooked* v. 41 Why? 'To avoid Cantrell.. having already pigeon-holed him as a kerb-crawler.'

3. To furnish with or divide into a set of pigeon-holes; also *fig.*

1848 [see PIGEON-HOLED below]. **1879** J. A. H. MURRAY *Addr. Philol. Soc.*, I had proposed to pigeon-hole the walls of the drawing-room for the reception of the dictionary material. **1883** J. PAYN *Thicker than Water* xiii, A huge sandbank..pigeonholed by sand-martins. **1895** *Amer. Ann. of Deaf* Apr. 132 The mind will have been pigeon-holed, and the knowledge classified. **1940** [see DING AN SICH, DING-AN-SICH].

4. To deposit (a corpse) in a columbarium. *rare.*

1858 HAWTHORNE *Fr. & It. Note-Bks.* I. 117 Decently pigeon-holed in a Roman tomb.

Hence **'pigeon-holed** *ppl. a.*, **'pigeon-holing** *vbl. sb.* Also **'pigeon-holer.**

1848 *Bachelor of Albany* 192 It was a pigeon-holed, alphabeted mind. **1878** *N. Amer. Rev.* CXXVII. 63 He obtained a formal list of the 'pigeon-holed' treaties. **1884** *Q. Rev.* July 23 The lover of uniformity and pigeon-holed schemes. **1886** W. J. TUCKER *E. Europe* 120 A dozen large, clumsy-looking desks, with a variety of pigeon-holed shelves. **1890** *Cent. Dict.*, *Pigeon-holed*, formed with pigeonholes for the escape of gases of combustion..or for the discharge of liquids. **1895** *Pop. Sci. Monthly* Apr. 754 That terrible pigeonholer of freight schedules at Washington. **1904** G. MEREDITH in *Daily Chron.* 5 July 3/2 Most women have a special talent for pigeon-holing.

'pigeon-house. A building or structure in which pigeons are kept; a columbarium, dovecote.

1537–8 in Willis & Clark *Cambridge* (1886) III. 592 The windows of the pigeon-house. **1644** SIR E. NICHOLAS in *N. Papers* (Camden) 63 They sought everye place in my howse for me, and my pydgion howse and all my out-howses. **1766** *Complete Farmer* s.v. *Pigeon*, Any lord of a manor may build a pigeon-house on his land, but a tenant cannot do it without the lord's licence. **1840** *Cottager's Man.* 26 in *Libr. Usef. Knowl., Husb.* III, The perspective elevation shows the bee-house, with pigeon-house over.

transf. **1599** NASHE *Lenten Stuffe* Wks. (Grosart) V. 263 A cage or pigeon house, romthsome enough to comprehend her and..her nurse.

pigeonite ('pɪdʒənaɪt). *Min.* [f. the name of *Pigeon* Point in NE. Minnesota + -ITE[1].] A silicate of magnesium, ferrous iron, and calcium, $(Mg,Fe^{II},Ca)(Mg,Fe^{II})Si_2O_6$, that is a monoclinic calcium-poor pyroxene substantially free of aluminium and ferric iron, and that is found chiefly in basic igneous, esp. volcanic, rocks.

1900 A. N. WINCHELL in *Amer. Geol.* XXVI. 204 Since the anomalous condition was first discovered in the rocks from Pigeon point, it would be appropriate to call pyroxene thus optically abnormal pigeonite. **1931** *Amer. Jrnl. Sci.* CCXXI. 405 The clino-pyroxenes.. form a continuous series of mix crystals, from diopside-rich (the phenocrysts are always diopsidic augites) to clino-enstatite- and hypersthene-rich (pigeonites). **1951** *Jrnl. Geol.* LIX. 480/1 Pigeonites under plutonic conditions invert with cooling to orthopyroxenes. **1970** *Nature* 25 Apr. 334/2 Interstitial pigeonite and augite in the lunar gabbroic anorthosite have Cr contents of 0·6 and 6·0 per cent respectively. **1975** J. W. FRONDEL *Lunar Mineral.* ix. 217 Because of their chemical variability, exsolution textures, epitaxy with augite and orthopyroxene,..and relative abundance, lunar pigeonites have played a significant role in a reconstruction of the crystallization histories of mare basalts.

Hence **pigeo'nitic** *a.*

1931 *Amer. Mineralogist* XVI. 207 The groundmass pyroxene is often said to be of the pigeonitic variety (Holmatindur, Eskifjord; Vágsfjord, Faeroes; etc.). **1957** *Mineral. Mag.* XXXI. 540 It is evident that the degree of inversion of the pigeonitic pyroxenes..must, in general, be correlated with the composition of the minerals as well as with their cooling history. **1972** *Contrib. Mineral. & Petrol.* XXXV. 235 (*heading*) Variation of rare earth concentrations in pigeonitic and hypersthenic rock series from Izu-Hakone region, Japan.

'pigeon-pea. [= F. *pois-pigeon*, in sense 1.]

1. A leguminous shrub, *Cajanus cajan*, probably native to Africa, but widely cultivated in tropical and subtropical regions; = CAJAN, DAL.

1725 SLOANE *Jamaica* II. 31 Pigeon-pease..their chief use is to feed pigeons, whence the name. **1756** P. BROWNE *Jamaica* 196 Pigeon or Angola Peas. **1760** J. LEE *Introd. Bot.* App. 322 Pigeon Pea, *Cytisus*. **1858** HOGG *Veg. Kingd.* 279 In Jamaica..the plant has been called *Pigeon Pea*. **1866** *Treas. Bot.* 189 In the West Indies they [the two varieties of *Cajanus indicus*] are called Pigeon peas. **1907** FREEMAN & CHANDLER *World's Commercial Products* 260 Pigeon Pea or Dhol of commerce..is an erect sub-shrubby plant..widely cultivated in the tropics and sub-tropics of both hemispheres. **1952** S. SELVON *Brighter Sun* v. 85 Is just dat yuh must love de tomatoes and lettuce and pigeon peas. **1969** *Oxf. Bk. Food Plants* 34/1 In the West Indies..pigeon peas provide a useful part of the protein supply in the diet of the poorer people, and a canning industry has been developed. **1972** I. ARNON *Crop Production in Dry Regions* II. vi. 255 The Pigeon-pea (*Cajanus cajan*) is a tropical legume of very ancient cultivation that is grown in tropical and sub-tropical regions of Asia and Africa. **1975** *Sunday Advocate-News* (Barbados) 15 June 8/1 Pigeon peas, rice,.. bread and cream of wheat are fairly good nutritional buys.

2. The black bitter-vetch, *Ervum Ervilia*.

1884 in MILLER *Plant-n.*

'pigeon-plum.

1. A tree of the W. Indies and Florida, *Coccoloba Floridana*, N.O. *Polygonaceæ*, the wood of which is used in cabinet-making; also, its edible grape-like fruit.

1747 CATESBY in *Phil. Trans.* XLIV. 604 *Cerasus latiore folio*... The Pidgeon-Plum. The Fruit is ripe in December, is pleasant-tasted, and is the Food of Pidgeons, and many wild Animals. **1884** in MILLER *Plant-n.*

2. A West African tree of the genus *Chrysobalanus*, N.O. *Rosaceæ*; also, its succulent edible fruit.

1884 MILLER *Plant-n.*, Pigeon Plum-tree, Sierra Leone. *Chrysobalanus ellipticus* and *C. luteus*.

'pigeonry. [f. PIGEON *sb.* + -RY.] A place where pigeons are kept; a pigeon-house.

1840 *Cottager's Man.* 24 in *Libr. Usef. Knowl., Husb.* III, The pigeonry over the porch. **1894** BARING-GOULD *Deserts S. France* I. 21 Well-built farmhouses, with their pigeonries like towers.

pigeon's milk. Also pigeon milk.

1. The partly-digested food with which pigeons feed their young.

1888 ROLLESTON & JACKSON *Anim. Life* 53 The young [of the pigeon]..are fed with the so-called 'pigeon's milk' regurgitated by the parent bird into the mouth of the young. **1891** R. WOODS *Pract. Guide Successful Pigeon-Culture* vii. 73 The parent birds..are also provided with an ample supply of veritable pigeon's milk. **1897** PARKER & HASWELL *Text-bk. Zool.* II. xiii. 380 It [*sc.* the young pigeon] is at first covered with fine down, and is fed by the parents with a secretion from the crop, the so-called 'Pigeon's milk'. **1943** T. I. STORER *Gen. Zool.* xxxi. 659 In adult pigeons, while rearing young, the epithelial lining sloughs off as 'pigeon milk' used to nourish squabs in the nest. **1967** D. GOODWIN *Pigeons & Doves of World* 45 The parent takes the squab's soft bill..into his, or her, own mouth and regurgitates pigeon's milk. **1973** *Sci. Amer.* Dec. 142/2 They [*sc.* pigeons] breed fast, and they..feed the young ones in the nest from the protein-rich 'pigeon milk', a curd formed in the parent bird's gut.

2. An imaginary article for which children are sent on a fool's errand.

1777 BRAND *Antiq.* 398 Sending Persons on what are called sleeveless Errands..for Pigeon Milk, with similar ridiculous Absurdities. **1811** *Lex. Balatr.* s.v., Boys and novices are frequently sent on the first of April to buy pigeons milk. **1828** in *Craven Gloss.* **1872** *Punch* 3 Feb. 46/2.

'pigeon-,toed, *a.*

1. *Ornith.* Having the toes arranged on a level as in pigeons; peristeropod.

1890 *Cent. Dict.* s.v., The pigeon-toed fowl are the mound-birds or *Megapodidæ* of the Old World and the curassows or *Cracidæ* of America.

2. Of persons or horses: Turning the toes or feet inwards; in-toed.

1801 *Sporting Mag.* XVII. 119 When the horse is pigeon-toed, that is turns his toes inwards. **1805** T. HARRAL *Scenes of Life* III. 66 She stooped, and was pigeon-toed. **1842** BARHAM *Ingol. Leg.* Ser. II. *Dead Drummer*, The pigeon-toed step, and the rollicking motion Bespoke them two genuine sons of the Ocean. **1887** *Harper's Mag.* Dec. 71/2 One would have imagined that he would deem it meet that a Kittredge should be pigeon-toed. **1976** A. WHITE *Long Silence* i. 6 It does my heart good to see these lads come here pigeon-toed and flat-chested and go out..holding themselves upright.

So **'pigeon-'toes** *sb. pl.*, feet which turn inwards.

1886 ELWORTHY *W. Somerset Word-bk.* s.v. *Pigeon-toed*, Bow-legs and pigeon-toes usually go together.

'pigeon-wing, *sb.*

1. A wing belonging to, or like that of, a pigeon.

1781 COWPER *Conversation* 576 Like angel heads in stone with pigeon-wings.

2. A mode of dressing the side hair, fashionable with men towards the end of the 18th c.; also, a wig of the same form.
1889 G. W. CABLE *Stories of Louisiana* xiii. 94 It was impossible for us to work up a [hair] club and pigeon wings like those I saw on the two young Du Clozels.

3. A particular fancy step in dancing; also, a dance; the music for such a dance or dance-step. Also, a fancy figure in skating. *U.S.*
1807–8 W. IRVING *Salmag.* (1824) 78 [He] is famous at the *pirouet* and the pigeon-wing. [**1849** J. P. MORIER *M. Toutrond* 166 Camille was very skilful at cutting capers.. I shone in making pigeon's wings, and I made plenty of room for myself among the islanders.] **1854** W. IRVING in *Life* 6 Apr., The scene brought my old dancing-school days back again, and I felt very much like cutting a pigeon-wing. **1873** B. HARTE *Mrs. Skaggs's Husbands* 166 A light figure.. cut a pigeon-wing,.. and then advanced to the footlights. **1889** *Century Mag.* Apr. 858/2 A row of cavaliers.. cut the pigeon wing in square-toed pumps. **1935** Z. N. HURSTON *Mules & Men* (1970) I. v. 117 Jack was justa dancin' fallin' off de log and cuttin' de pigeon wing—(diddle dip, diddle dip—diddle dip) 'from pine to pine Mr. Pinkney'. **1947** E. H. PAUL *Linden on Saugus Branch* 50 He had.. a Chickering grand piano on which he played.. all the reels, jigs, pigeon-wings, moriscos, sarabands, [etc.]. **1954** *Publ. Amer. Dial. Soc.* XXI. 34 *Pigeonwing*, a type of dance involving the use of the arms.

Hence **'pigeon-wing** *v.*, (*a*) *trans.* (see 3 above); (*b*) *refl.*, to convey or transport (oneself) by or in the manner of one dancing or cutting pigeon-wings.
1826 F. COOPER *Mohicans* (1829) II. iv. 59 The toes are squared, as though one of the French dancers had been in, pigeon-winging his tribe! **1839** POE *Devil in Belfry* in *Tales of Grotesque* (1840) 166 The rascal.. pigeon-winged himself right up into the belfry of the House of the Town Council.

pigeon-wood ('pɪdʒənwʊd). A name given to the wood of various tropical or sub-tropical trees or shrubs, mostly used in cabinet-work, so called from the marking or colouring; also, the trees themselves. Among these are
a. *Connarus guianensis*, the zebra-wood of S. America and the W. Indies; **b.** *Diospyros tetrasperma*, a W. Indian ebony shrub; **c.** *Dipholis salicifolia*, a large fragrant W. Indian tree, of the star-apple kind; **d.** *Guettarda speciosa*, a small evergreen, growing in the tropics of both hemispheres; **e.** *Pisonia obtusata*, the beefwood, corkwood, or porkwood of the W. Indies and Florida; **f.** species of *Coccoloba* (PIGEON-PLUM): *long-leaved p.*, *C. diversifolia*; *small-leaved p.*, *C. punctata*, *C. leoganensis*.
1745 H. WALPOLE *Let. to G. Montagu* 13 July, My lady Hervey.. is charmed with the hopes of these new shoes, and has already bespoke herself a pair of pigeon wood. **1756** P. BROWNE *Jamaica* 368 Pigeon Wood. This shrubby tree is greatly esteemed on account of its wood. **1866** *Treas. Bot.* 887 Pigeon-wood, Zebra-wood, of which there are several kinds. Jamaica P., *Guettarda speciosa*.

'pig-faced, *a.* Having a face resembling that of a pig.
pig-faced lady or ***woman*** (earlier *hog-faced gentlewoman*), a reputed woman of rank or wealth, with a pig's face, for whom a husband was supposed to be wanted; the subject of much delusion among the credulous, from the 17th c. onwards. See Chambers' *Book of Days* II. 255.
[Cf. 1640 *hog-faced*: HOG *sb.*^{1} 12 c.]
1815 *Chron.* in *Ann. Reg.* 17/1 The original invention of the pig-faced woman, about the year 1764. **1858** LYTTON *What will he do* I. i. 1 Farther on.. rose the more pretending fabrics which lodged the attractive forms of the Mermaid, the Norfolk Giant, the Pig-faced Lady, the Spotted Boy, and the Calf with Two Heads. **1864** R. CHAMBERS *Bk. Days* II. 255/1 There can be few that have not heard of the celebrated pig-faced lady, whose mythical story is common to several European languages. *Ibid.* 257/2 The 'pig-faced lady' is not unfrequently exhibited.. by showmen at fairs, etc... represented by a bear having its head carefully shaved, and adorned with cap, bonnet, ringlets, etc.

'pigful. [f. PIG *sb.*^{2} + -FUL.] As much as fills a pig or earthen pot.
1590 in *Law's Memorials* (1818) Pref. 28 Sending a pigfull of poyson to the house where young Foullis was. **1665** LD. FOUNTAINHALL *Jrnl.* (1900) 92 A pigful of holy water w^t a spung in it.

'pigfully, *adv. humorous nonce-wd.* [After *manfully*.] In a manner befitting a pig.
1891 ATKINSON *Last Giant Killers* 68 And.. didn't the two little pigs concerned play their parts pigfully!

piggard: see PIG-HERD.

piggeis: see PEGGY-MAST.

piggen, obs. form of PIGGIN.

piggery^1 ('pɪgərɪ). [f. PIG *sb.*^{1} + -ERY.]
1. A place where pigs are kept; a pig-breeding establishment; a pigsty. Also *fig.*
1781 R. F. GREVILLE *Diary* 9 Aug. (1930) 20 Returned to The Grove after viewing The Farm & well kept Piggery. **1799** *Times* 1 June 4/3 Stabling for 3 horses, chaise-house, piggery, and out-buildings. **1804–6** SYD. SMITH *Mor. Philos.* (1850) 195 Go to the Duke of Bedford's piggery at Woburn. **1841–54** J. L. STEPHENS *Centr. Amer.* 110 The interior was a perfect piggery full of fleas and children. **1867** J. HATTON *Tallants of B.* iii, There were model cow-houses, cattle-sheds, piggeries. **1868** RUSKIN *Time & Tide* (1872) 193 Here we are in a piggery, mainly by our own fault, hungry enough, and for ourselves, anything but respectable. **1936** *Times Lit. Suppl.* 29 Feb. 182/3 She contrasts the spoilt young things in luxurious homes with the free young things in Chelsea piggeries. **1971** *Farmers Weekly* (Extra) 19 Mar. 5/1 For cleaning and sterilising piggeries, equipment, troughs and machinery, etc. **1972** T. A. BULMAN *Kamloops Cattlemen* xiv. 80 One part of the Grande Prairie layout was designated as the piggery.

2. Piggish condition; piggishness.
1867 MACGREGOR *Voy. Alone* ii. (1868) 65 Is the positive piggery of the lowest stratum of our fellows part of the price we pay for glorious freedom? **1885** *Sat. Rev.* 21 Feb. 238/1 They prefer piggery to decency. **1972** *Daily Tel.* 10 Nov. 15/2 The pin-up is just male chauvinist piggery. **1977** H. GREENE *FSO-1* i. 4 A black citadel of male-chauvinist piggery.

3. Pigs collectively.
1888 *Harper's Mag.* Mar. 633 That sackful of rebellious piggery heaving and struggling.

'piggery^2. *Sc.* [f. PIG *sb.*^{2} + -ERY.] A place where pots and vessels of earthenware are made or sold; a pottery; a crockery-shop; also, earthenware, crockery.
1825 in JAMIESON.

piggicide ('pɪgɪsaɪd). *nonce-wd.* [f. PIG *sb.*^{1} + -CIDE 1.] One who kills pigs.
1834–5 S. R. MAITLAND *Voluntary Syst.* (1837) 345 Of course these piggicides were as much obliged to pay [etc.].

piggin ('pɪgɪn). Chiefly *dial.* Also 7 -an, 7–9 -en, -on, 9 -ing; β. 6 pickein. [perh. a deriv. of PIG *sb.*^{2}; but the history is obscure. The Gaelic *pigean* is dim. of *pige*, *pigeadh*, app. ad. Lowl. Sc. *pig*. Ir. *pigin* and W. *picyn* are app. from Eng.] A small pail or cylindrical vessel, esp. a wooden one with one stave longer than the rest serving as a handle; a milking pail; a vessel to drink out of.
The word is recorded in the *Eng. Dial. Dict.* from Northumberland to Hampshire, also from Shetland; but it is not prevalent in Scotland. It is applied very variously in different localities; in Northumberland it may denote an earthenware pitcher, and sometimes, a small iron kailpot (Heslop); in W. Yorksh. 'a tin receptacle, a deep tin tureen' (E.D.D.); but it is generally described as of wood. Its size varies according to purpose: it is described as 'holding near a pint', 'containing about a quart', 'holding from one to two gallons' (Eng. Dial. Dict.).
1554 *Lanc. Wills* (1857) 113, ij butter trowghis xiij^d.—iiij piggins iiij^d. **1572** *Richmond Wills* (Surtees) 152, xiij stannis and barels vj^s viij^d, iij skelis, ij collockis, ij. pickeins, ij^s. **1611** COTGR., *Traïot*, a milking Pale, or Piggin. **1647** HERRICK *Noble Numbers, His Wish to God*, A little piggin and a pipkin by, To hold things fitting my necessity. **1659–60** *Knaresb. Wills* (Surtees) II. 245, 1 wooden piggon. **1674** RAY *N.C. Words* 37 *A Piggin*, a little pail or tub with an erect handle. **1764** HARMER *Observ.* xiv. ii. 71 Three or four piggins, or great wooden bowls. **1803** R. ANDERSON *Cumberld. Ball.* 74 A three-quart piggen full o' keale, He'll sup, the greedy sinner. **1827** *Chron.* in *Ann. Reg.* 177/2 A piggin, or small pail, out of which the animal fed. **1841** S. C. HALL *Ireland* I. 83 The usual drink is buttermilk..; which drink goes round in a small piggin, a sort of miniature of the English pail. **1863** FR. A. KEMBLE *Resid. in Georgia* 52 A very small cedar pail—a piggin as they termed it. **1887** *Strathearn Mag.* Feb. 15 So cease your useless jigging, And bring the can and pigging, To hold the luscious buttermilk That will be ready soon.

pigging ('pɪgɪŋ), *vbl. sb.*^{1} [f. PIG *v.*^{1} + -ING^1.]
1. Farrowing; huddling.
1607 TOPSELL *Four-f. Beasts* (1658) 518 An easie and safe pigging. **1898** B. BURLEIGH *Sirdar & Khalifa* xii. 191 The 'pigging' in Soudan dirt and heat.

2. **pigging back** *Metallurgy*, the addition of more pig-iron to the charge in an open-hearth furnace in order to raise its carbon content when this has fallen too much during boiling.
1900 *Jrnl. West of Scotland Iron & Steel Inst.* VII. 128 For quick working, plenty of carbon in the pig in proportion to phosphorus is desirable,.. otherwise there is delay by the addition of grey pig for 'pigging back' or.. prolonging the boil. **1951** G. R. BASHFORTH *Manuf. Iron & Steel* II. vii. 174 The 'pigging back' of a large furnace to the extent of 20 points of carbon gave very beneficial results.

3. The use of pigs (PIG *sb.*^{1} 9); cleaning by means of a pig.
1972 L. M. HARRIS *Introd. Deepwater Floating Drilling Operations* xix. 208 A system that permits: pump-down tools; pigging of lines; [etc.]. **1976** *Offshore Engineer* Mar. 52/3 Production manifold, the third subsystem, gives gathering, gas-lift, testing, pigging and through flowline capability.

pigging ('pɪgɪŋ), *vbl. sb.*^{2} *Sc.* [f. PIG *sb.*^{2}] The purchasing of pigs or crockery.
1821 *Blackw. Mag.* VIII. 432 Around this gay temptation, wives are prigging, And even maidens go sometimes 'a pigging'.

'pigging, *vbl. sb.*^{3} *U.S.* [f. PIG *sb.*^{1}] Hog-tying; only *attrib.* in **pigging string**, a short cord or rope used for hog-tying.
1926 R. SANTEE *Men & Horses* 4 On came the roper.. his 'piggin' string between his teeth. **1971** H. A. SMITH *View from Chivo* ii. 28 He stood for a moment looking at the rope in his hand, reflecting on the fact that it was known as a piggin' string. **1976** 'D. HALLIDAY' *Dolly & Nanny Bird* vii. 98 Hog-tie it! Get the crittur! Where's your pigging-string? Get him down, boys! Throw him!

piggish ('pɪgɪʃ), *a.* [f. PIG *sb.*^{1} + -ISH^1.] Of, pertaining to, or characteristic of a pig; piglike; hoggish; stubborn; selfish, mean; unclean, vile.
1792 [implied in PIGGISHLY]. **1820** W. IRVING *Sketch Bk., Rip Van Winkle* §18 One had.. small piggish eyes. **1829** SOUTHEY *O. Newman* II. 124 He hath not left His native country in that piggish mood Which neither will be led nor driven. **1873** J. R. GREEN *Lett.* (1901) 364, I don't like to be piggish and cantankerous. **1891** *N. & Q.* 7th Ser. XII. 511/2 He did not mean they were piggish or coarse.

Hence **'piggishly** *adv.*; **'piggishness.**
1792 COLERIDGE *Lett., to Mrs. Evans* (1895) 38 Mr. Hague who played on the violin most piggishly. **1804** CHARLOTTE SMITH *Conversations*, etc. I. 86 She is very piggishly brought up, indeed. **1858** MAYHEW *Upper Rhine* v. §3 (1860) 277 Our friend.. was fairly taken aback by the piggishness.

'piggism. *rare.* [f. PIG *sb.*^{1} + -ISM.] Piggish behaviour.
1852 MRS. GASKELL *Schah's Eng. Gardener* in *Househ. Words* V. 321/1 They ate their peas and beans unshelled.. a piece of piggism which especially scandalised him. **1979** *Daily Tel.* 10 Feb. 20 Women's Lib and male chauvinist piggism are both based upon the false premise that people are merely bodies instead of free spirits temporarily housed in flesh.

piggle ('pɪg(ə)l), *sb. dial.* [f. next.] (See quot. 1889.)
1889 *Cent. Dict.*, *Piggle*.., a many-pronged hook, with a handle like that of a hoe, used in digging potatoes, and in mixing various materials, as clay, mortar, compost, etc. **1922** C. SIDGWICK *Victorian* xxxvii. 278 Impident toad! Comes up to me and sez we aren't agoin' to build this hedge with a foundation! Oh! aren't we? sez I. You get to yer work, my lad, and do a bit with that piggle.

'piggle, *v. dial.* [Origin obscure: cf. PIDDLE *v.* 1.] **a.** *trans.* To uproot; to pick at, to pick out. **b.** *intr.* To trifle or toy *with*. So **'piggling** *ppl. a.*, petty, paltry, niggling.
1847 J. O. HALLIWELL *Dict. Archaic & Provinc. Words* II. 622/2 *Piggle*, to root up potatoes with the hand. **1877** F. Ross et al. *Gloss. Words Holderness* 107/1 *Piggle*.., to pick out with a pointed instrument. **1911** D. H. LAWRENCE *White Peacock* II. iii. 265 Don't be piggling and mean and Grundyish. **1923** —— *Kangaroo* i. 7 Awful piggling suburban place. *Ibid.* iii. 40, I can't piggle with those draughtsmen dodges. **1976** SCOLLINS & TITFORD *Ey up, mi Duck!* I. 59 *Piggle*, to work away at something with the fingers. A certain spreader of acne.

Piggly-Wiggly (ˌpɪglɪ'wɪglɪ). *U.S.* [Fanciful.] A type of self-service store (see quots. 1928, 1953). Also *attrib.* or as *adj.*
'Piggly Wiggly' is a registered service mark in the United States.
1917 *Printer's Ink* 20 Dec. 17/1 Perhaps no chain of stores that has been organized in recent years has been the object of so much curiosity and speculation as the Piggly Wiggly stores, which were started in Memphis, Tenn., in 1916. *Ibid.* 20/1 As an experiment in distribution, Piggly Wiggly is interesting and is worth watching. **1928** *Publishers' Weekly* 10 Nov. 1972/2 The obvious objection to the idea of a Piggly-Wiggly bookshop is that few book stores are adapted to the customary Piggly-Wiggly pattern, with the turn-stile entrances and exits, and all the merchandise set out onto tables in a U-shaped semi-circle. **1953** *Sun* (Baltimore) 17 Oct. 8/1 News comes of the death.. of Clarence Saunders, founder of the Piggly Wiggly stores. It is probable that few members of the younger generation know what a Piggly Wiggly was. Certainly they would not regard it as the novelty it was at the time of its creation 36 years ago. For the Piggly Wiggly.. was nothing more than a clerkless grocery store in which a customer helped himself to goods off the shelves and paid at the door as he went out. In short, save perhaps for minor details.., the Piggly Wiggly represented a system that since has become standard as the super-market. **1955** 'P. QUENTIN' *Man with Two Wives* xxii. 246 He used to work in the Piggly-Wiggly. That's a kind of store they have out there [in California] like the A. and P. **1971** 'S. WOODS' *Knavish Crows* v. 55 There were houses.. a do-it-yourself laundry—a Piggly Wiggly supermarket. **1973** *Guardian* 2 June 11/5 Grants, New Mexico.. has 56 garages, 421 motel rooms, a Piggly Wiggly Supermarket.

piggy, piggie ('pɪgɪ), *sb.*^{1} [f. PIG *sb.*^{1} + -Y.]
1. A little pig, or animal so called; also playfully applied, with various connotations, to a child.
1799 in *Spirit Pub. Jrnls.* III. 25 Go to the forest, piggy, and deplore The miserable lot of savage swine. **1890** *Spectator* 10 May, If the worm objected to come out of the hole, 'piggy' [a hedgehog], with his head on one side, gently scratched away the grass with his right fore-paw and extracted him.

2. The game of tip-cat; the 'cat' or piece of wood used in this game. Also *attrib.*
1862 C. C. ROBINSON *Dial. Leeds* 384 *Piggy*, a game played by boys with sticks, and a piece of rounded wood, pointed at each end, called the 'piggy', which, when struck at either end, rebounds, similar to the game of 'cat' elsewhere. **1867** *Standard* 11 June, The game which is played by the street boys of London under the name of 'tip-cat'.. is, it appears, called 'piggie' in the north. **1884** *Manch. Guard.* 22 Sept. 8/4 'Piggy' (which some members.. recognise under the name of 'tip-cat') [was] among the features he described as objectionable in our street life. **1909** *Westm. Gaz.* 10 May 12/1 About 300 spectators attended the Barnsley Queen's Grounds.. on the occasion of a long knock piggy match for £50 and the championship of Yorkshire. **1971** C. BONINGTON *Annapurna South Face* iv. 49 We have.. a game of 'Piggy', where you throw a small peg into the air, strike it as far as you can with a stick, and nominate the number of strides a member of the opposing team must take to reach the peg; he can challenge you to meet the nominated number of strides.

3. Special Combs., as **piggy-and-stick** = sense 2; **piggy bank**, a pig-shaped money-box, often made of pottery (see also quot. 1976); also (with hyphen) *attrib.*; **piggy-in-the-middle**: see PIG *sb.*^{1} 10; **piggy-stick**, (*a*) *Mil. slang*, the wooden handle of a soldier's entrenching tool; (*b*) = sense 2.

1932 L. Golding *Magnolia St.* i. ix. 159 The little Jewboys..started playing ball or piggy-and-stick. 1941 *Butler Brothers Dry Goods, Home Goods, Toys Catal.* Spring 312B/2 Piggy Banks..flesh colored composition. 1951 Wodehouse *Old Reliable* x. 129 'Listen, I've busted banks.' 'You mean piggy banks?' 1955 A. Huxley *Genius & Goddess* 51 Ruth broke her piggy bank and squandered a year's accumulated savings on a make-up kit and a bottle of cheap perfume. 1972 *Daily Colonist* (Victoria, B.C.) 12 Jan. 28/1 Police said a piggy bank thief entered the house through an unlocked window. 1976 Lieberman & Rhodes *Compl. CB Handbk.* i. 20 To identify your own location.. look for the nearest landmark. A few examples: the 'piggy bank' (toll booth) you just went through, a milepost, [etc.]. 1977 *New Yorker* 29 Aug. 69/2 The passengers who rode American trams were so honest that they didn't even use tickets—they just dropped the fare in a piggy bank for the driver to collect when he was ready. 1930 Brophy & Partridge *Songs and Slang 1914–18* 149 *Piggy-stick*, the wooden helve for the entrenching tool which the infantryman carried next his bayonet... From a child's game, tip-cat. 1968 P. Jennings *Living Village* 179 The game which we knew in Coventry as *tip-cap*..was called in Yorkshire *Knur and spel*, in Cumberland *piggy-stick*.

'piggy, *sb.*[2] *dial.* [dim. of PIG *sb.*[2]] A little pot.
16.. *Country Lass* in Whitelaw *Bk. Scot. Song* (1844) 304/1 My Paisley piggy, corked with sage Contains my drink but thin, O.

'piggy, *a.* [f. PIG *sb.*[1] + -Y.] Piglike; resembling that of a pig. Also, suggestive of pigs; *loosely*, unpleasant, unreasonable. Also *comb.*
*a*1845 Hood *Literary & Literal* xii, Miss Ikey, Whose whole pronunciation was so piggy. 1874 Burnand *My time* xxii. 198 He was fresh-coloured, with little piggy eyes. 1927 J. Masefield *Midnight Folk* 24 There were seven old witches..at a very good supper... They were very piggy in their eating (picking the bones with their fingers, etc.). 1942 [see GRABBY *a.*]. 1957 'N. Shute' *On Beach* viii. 264 'Getting a bit piggy, isn't it?'.. 'Everything shut up, and dirty, and stinking.' 1958 —— *Rainbow & Rose* iv. 159, I started back and it began to rain and it got very piggy. *a*1963 S. Plath *Crossing Water* (1971) 35 They have a piggy and a fishy air. 1970 *New Yorker* 26 Sept. 39/2 'I don't want you to make love to anyone but me.' 'That's being piggy.' 1976 P. Hill *Hunters* xi. 158 Did she know her husband had lied to cover for Gatwood? Fat piggy-eyed Gatwood.

'piggy-back, 'pick-a-back, *adv. phr.* (*a.*, *sb.*, *v.*) Forms: α. 6–7 **a pick back**, 6–9 **pickback**, 8– **a pick-a-back, pick-a-back** (*dial.* 9 **pack-a-back, picki-, picky-back**). β. 6–7 **on pick-pack(e**, 7 **a pick-pack, a pick-a-pack**, 7–9 *dial.* **pick-pack, pick-a-pack**. γ. 8 **on pig back**, 9 *dial.* **pig-aback, pigga-back, pig-back**, 9–**piggy-back**. [Origin and form uncertain; the earliest examples have *back*, but the usual 17th c. forms had *pack*, which still occurs in some dialects; the primitive form was perh. either *a pick back* or *a pick pack*, whence, by dropping *a*, the later *pick-*, *pick-a-*, *pig-*, *pig-a-*, etc.
The evidence does not show whether the expression originally referred to a *pack picked* (pitched) on the back or shoulders, or to the *back* on which it is pitched; nor does it appear whether *a pick* answered to the F. *à pic* 'vertically, perpendicularly', was due to reduplication as in *tip-top*, etc., or had some other source. Cf. Ger. *hucke-pack* in same sense, found in Low and Middle Ger. from 18th c., which Schambach refers to *pack* the bundle carried (see Grimm s.v.). Whatever the origin, it is evident that popular etymology analysed it in various ways from a very early date.]
a. On the shoulders or back like a pack or bundle: said in reference to a person (or animal) carried in this way.
α. 1565 Calfhill *Answ. Treat. Crosse* 42b, To easy..is that way to heauen, whereto we may be caried a pickbacke on a Roode. 1570 Foxe *A. & M.* (ed. 2) 12/1 [The pope] being caried pickbacke on mens shoulders. 1663 Butler *Hud.* i. ii. 72 For as our modern Wits behold, Mounted a Pick-back on the Old. 1825 Hone *Every-day Bk.* I. 1185 One of the leopards was carried by his keeper a pick-a-back. 1837 Dickens *Pickw.* xxxviii, If I find it necessary to carry you away, pick-a-back. 1884 M. G. Humphreys in *Harper's Mag.* Nov. 842/2 They..bring the men pick-back triumphantly to shore. 1896 E. A. King *Ital. Highways* 114 Pulcinello..travels pick-a-back on the shoulders of a lean old woman.
β. 1591 Harington *Orl. Fur.* xxxix. xlvii, Now Brandimart..leaps behind, a pick pack, on his backe, And holds his armes. 1614 B. Jonson *Barth. Fair* ii. vi, By this light, I'le carry you away o' my backe [*Stage-direction.* He gets him vp on pick-packe]. 1655 *Verney Mem.* (1894) III. 222 'Tis now the new fashion for Maydens in toun to ride a Pick Pack. 1677 W. Hughes *Man of Sin* iii. iii. 75 St. Christopher carried Christ a Pick-pack over an Arm of the Sea. 1682 tr. *Selden's Eng. Janus* Auth. Pref., Such creatures as carry the Goddess Nemesis on pickpack. 1694 R. L'Estrange *Fables* ccxlviii. (1714) 263 Ina Hurry..carries the Other a Pick-a-Pack upon her Shoulders. 1858 Mayhew *Upper Rhine* iv. §2 (1860) 205 Like a cottage perched pick-a-pack on a church roof. 1894 *Outing* (U.S.) XXIV. 438/2 [In China] we overtook a beggar and his wife traveling pick-a-pack along the stone road.
γ. 1783 Ainsworth *Lat. Dict.* (ed. Morell) s.v. *Back*, To carry on pig back, *humeris..ferre*. *a*1825 Forby *Voc. E. Anglia*, *Pig-back*, on the back. 1888 *Voice* (N.Y.) 31 May, To see us perched 'piggy-back' crossing the stream.
b. quasi-*adj.* and *sb.* Also in reference to a thing; *spec.* (*a*) an aircraft, rocket, or the like, to which is attached another aircraft, etc., usu. for launching in mid-air; (*b*) a flat railway car on which a truck, container, or the like is carried.
(With quot. *c* 1590 cf. BACK *sb.* 23d.)
*c*1590 Greene *Fr. Bacon* ii. 89 Mary sir, hee'le straight bee on your pickpacke to know whether the feminine or the masculine gender be most worthy. 1823 Lamb *Elia* Ser. ii. *New Year's Coming of Age*, E'en whipt him over his shoulders pick-a-back fashion. 1864 Knight *Passages Work. Life* I. ii. 89 A pickaback ride through the surf in a dirty fellow's grasp. 1901 *Punch* 2 Oct. 247/1 Oh, Mr. Green,..Effie..is so miserable because she hasn't had her donkey ride. Would you mind giving her a pick-a-back? 1931 R. Campbell *Georgiad* i. 21 The garden path—a sort of Rotten Row Where oft a merry pick-a-back they go. 1936 [see *mother plane* s.v. MOTHER *sb.*[1] 17a]. 1936 L. A. G. Strong *Last Enemy* iii. 203 Ann came up. 'Piggy-back, please,' she said. 'You mustn't worry poor Mr. Boyle. It's too hot.'.. Ann, hoisted on Denis's back, turned to her. 1944 *Sun* (Baltimore) 13 July 9/2 Two Liberator crewmen with only one parachute between them made a 'piggyback' leap recently from a burning bomber. 1946 L. E. O. Charlton *Britain at War: R.A.F. & U.S.A.A.F., July 1943–Sept. 1944* 306 The 'pick-a-back' consisting of an Me 109 fighter mounted on the back of a Ju 88... When approaching its target the Ju 88 was released and guided by remote control towards its objective. 1953 *Evening Jrnl.* (Lincoln, Nebraska) 3 Nov. 6 No sooner had 'piggy back railroading' (hauling truck trailers on flat cars) been hailed by various railroads and one automotive manufacturer as a strikingly simple idea for abating highway congestion and cutting the high price of trucking, than the organized truck operators rose to denounce it. 1954 *Economist* 13 Mar. 779/1 These 'piggy-backs' or 'trailers-on-flat-cars (TOFC)'.. have now become a major preoccupation of the railways. 1954 *Railway Age* 26 July 3/2 Further expansion of piggyback by the Chicago & North Western took effect on July 15. 1954 *Times* (Seattle) 21 Sept. 16/1 Railroads throughout the country are studying or instituting limited pickaback service. 1956 *Sun* (Baltimore) 29 Feb. 7/3 A 'piggyback' experiment in which vacationists' automobiles will accompany them on train trips in Germany is planned for next summer. 1959 H. Pinter *Birthday Party* ii. 37 Maybe I played piggy-back with you. 1960 *Daily Tel.* 23 June 1/4 (*heading*) U.S. 'pick-a-back' spheres over Russia every 101 min. *Ibid.*, Two 'pick-a-back' satellites were launched by the same rocket from Cape Canaveral, Florida, early today. 1961 *Flight* LXXIX. 827/1 Under the heading 'aerodynamic efficiency' an interesting 'piggyback' vehicle was exhibited. 1965 *Listener* 1 July 6/1 A series of pick-a-back rockets called the Precious Stones are the most important outcome. 1969 [see MANIFEST *sb.* 3]. 1969 I. & P. Opie *Children's Games* vi. 185 Riding on people's backs ('Horse Race', 'Piggyback Race'). *Ibid.* vii. 217 The craze at our school is piggy-back fighting. 1969 *Sat. Rev.* (U.S.) 28 June 18/3 Railways are currently taking pride in their new innovation, 'piggy-back' service, in which highway trailers ..can travel across long distances hitching rides on various railroads. 1973 *Kingston* (Ontario) *Whig-Standard* 21 Sept. 9/6 The CPR diesels still thunder through the hamlet with their cargoes of 'piggy backs', but the little station has been gone for many years now. 1974 W. Foley *Child in Forest* i. 25 Our usual practice of running to meet him for pick-a-backs up the garden path. 1977 *Time* 14 Feb. 54/3 The orbiter will be 'mated' to a carrier plane, a Boeing 747 with special mounts on top... The piggyback pair will first run up and down the Edwards runway to test for vibration and stability.
c. *Comb.*, as **piggy-back plant**, a perennial herb, *Tolmiea menziesii*, of the family Saxifragaceæ, native to western North America and distinguished by cordate leaves that appear to grow one on top of another.
1946 M. Free *All about House Plants* xviii. 275 The Picka-back Plant has come very much to the fore as a house plant. 1973 J. L. Faust *N.Y. Times Bk. House Plants* 135 Piggyback plant (*Tolmiea menziesii*) has somewhat fuzzy leaves. 1973 Hitchcock & Cronquist *Flora Pacific Northwest* 199 *Tolmiea*... Youth-on-Age; Pig-a-Back-Plant; Thousand Mothers.
d. as *v. intr.* and *trans.* To ride piggy-back; to attach on the back of; to carry or transport by means of a piggy-back method. Also *fig.* So **'piggy-backing** *vbl. sb.*
1959 *Wall St. Jrnl.* 29 Jan. 1/1 A number of railroad and truck equipment makers have jumped into the manufacture of rail cars and trailers especially designed for piggybacking. 1960 *Economist* 3 Sept. 894/2 The haulage industry is threatened by the rapid spread of the practice of 'piggy-backing'—transporting a loaded lorry or trailer on a railway wagon. 1967 *Freight Management* Jan. 48/2 Piggybacking must not be left out of any argument about future inter-modal methods of transportation. 1968 *Wall St. Jrnl.* 25 Mar. 14/3 To the degree heroin does piggyback on marijuana, it seems more due to the law than to the pushers. 1968 A. Diment *Gt. Spy Race* iv. 56 Mr Spont would have to piggy-back me all the way to get a commission. 1973 T. H. White *Making of President 1972* (1974) v. 123 They're tired of Humphrey, he's been around too long... But we have to piggyback him on local campaigns. Wherever we back a local candidate in the primary, we'll pack Hubert in on top. 1975 C. Beeck in *Proc. 25th Electronic Components Conf.* 158/1 Selecting a shaft diameter which would accommodate a coaxial shaft inside it in case another control had to be piggy-backed to the knob. 1975 *Time* (Canada ed.) 17 Mar. 7/1 Arctic Gas argues that the only economical way to bring Canadian gas south is by 'piggybacking' on a line largely given over, at first, to carrying more abundant Alaskan gas. 1976 *Billings* (Montana) *Gaz.* 7 July 4-B/1 The women are content to let the men set the standards and then piggy-back on our efforts. 1977 *Offshore Engineer* May 97/3 A free-standing well-protector jacket platform is attached or 'piggybacked' to the mobile platform at the dock before tow-out. 1977 C. McCullough *Thorn Birds* ii. 21 Come on, Meggy, I'll piggyback you the rest of the way. 1979 *Economist* 17 Nov. 79/2 Why not piggy-back a federal sales tax on to the levies which people are used to paying and collecting?

'piggy-'wiggy. Also **piggy-wig**. A childish riming extension of *piggy*, little pig; also applied playfully to a child.
1862 Miss Yonge *Stokesley Secret* i. (ed. 2) 15 There's plenty for piggy-wiggy. 1865 Dickens *Mut. Fr.* i. iv, 'Well, Piggywiggies', said R. W., 'how de do to-night.' 1870 Lear *Nonsense Songs, The Owl and the Pussy-cat* ii, And there in a wood a Piggy-wig stood, With a ring at the end of his nose. 1879 [see PITTY[2]]. 1929 E. Bowen *Last Sept.* vi. 62 Your scrumptious Irish teas make a perfect piggy-wig of me. 1957 [see *nursery word* s.v. NURSERY 8a].

pig-head ('pɪghɛd). [f. PIG *sb.*[1] + HEAD *sb.*[1], after next.] An obstinate stupid head.
1889 *Daily News* 12 Dec. 3/1 It took..years to drive the notion of a steam roller into the pig-heads of our vestries.

pigheaded ('pɪgˌhɛdɪd), *a.* [Parasynthetic deriv. of PIG *sb.*[1] + HEAD *sb.*[1] + -ED[2].] Having a head like that of a pig; usually *fig.*, having the mental qualities ascribed to a pig; obstinate; stupid; perverse.
1620 B. Jonson *News fr. New World*, You should be some dull tradesman by your pig-headed sconce now. 1774 Goldsm. *Nat. Hist.* (1862) I. vi. iii. 471 The pig-headed Armadillo, with nine bands. 1811 *Lex. Balatron.*, *Pig-headed*, obstinate. 1838 Dickens *Nich. Nick.* xiii, A nasty, ungrateful, pig-headed,..obstinate, sneaking dog. 1881 Besant & Rice *Chapl. of Fleet* III. 99 My brother Will is as obstinate as he is pigheaded.
Hence **'pigˌheadedly** *adv.*; **'pigˌheadedness**.
1886 *Pall Mall G.* 2 July 6/1 To the credit of his instructors..he has learned his lesson pigheadedly and well. 1803 Mar. Edgeworth *Belinda* I. iv. 79 With true English pigheadedness..they went and polled for an independent candidate of their own choosing. 1865 Masson *Rec. Brit. Philos.* iii. 225 A kind of pigheadedness, or indifference to ideas.

pig-herd ('pɪghɜːd). Also 7 ? **piggard**. [f. PIG *sb.*[1] + HERD *sb.*[2] The form *piggard* prob. belongs here, but may be:—*pigward*.] A keeper of a herd of pigs: cf. HOGHERD, SWINEHERD.
1591 Percivall *Sp. Dict.*, *Porquero*, a pigheard. *a*1697 Aubrey *Brief Lives* (1898) II. 304 He sent for all his servants, even the piggard-boy, to come and heare his palinode. 1820 Shelley *Œdipus Tyr.* ii. i. 136 Squabbling makes pig-herds hungry, and they dine On bacon, and whip sucking-pigs the more. 1886 W. J. Tucker *E. Europe* 213 Magyar..cattle-drivers, Bulgarian pig-herds,..Wallachian shepherds.

pighill, obs. var. PIGHTLE.

pig-hole: see PIG.

pight, arch. pa. t. and pa. pple. of PITCH *v.*[1]: see also PITCHED *pp. a.*[1]

pight (paɪt), *v.* [The pa. t. and pa. pple. of PITCH *v.*[1] erroneously used as a present tense.] *trans.* To pitch.
[1459 *Rolls of Parlt.* V. 348/2 It was nyghe evynne or ye.. raungede youre Batailles, pightede youre tentes.] 1586 Warner *Alb. Eng.* ii. vii. (1589) 23 And hauing in their sight The threatned Citie of the Foe, his Tents did Affer pight. 1594 *2nd Rep. Doctor Faustus* in Thoms *E.E. Prose Rom.* (1858) III. 348 Two most beautiful places to pight tapers on. 1866 J. B. Rose *tr. Ovid's Met.* 48 There doth he pight his net and pitch his snare. 1867 —— tr. *Virgil's Æneid* 325 Behold the pighted foe and battle-field.

pightle ('paɪt(ə)l). *local.* Forms: α. 3 **pichtel, pichtil, pictel, pigtel**, 5 **pyghtell**, 5–6 **pytell**, 6–7 **pightell, putell**, 6–9 **pightel, pitle**, 8 **pightal**, 7– **pightle**, (8–9 *corruptly* **pigtail**). Also β. 3 **pichel, pychel, pychil, pughull**, 6–8 **pighill**, 7–8 **peighill**; 6 **pykkyll**, 7 **pickhill, pickell**, 7–8 **pickle**. γ. 7–9 **picle**. δ. 7–8 **piddle**. See also PINGLE *sb.*[2] [Origin obscure; the form seems to be diminutive.
The two types *pightel* and *pighel* (*pichel*) are both found soon after 1200; the former was midl. and southern; in E. Anglia and Essex it became before 1500 *pitel*; *pichel* was northern, and appears to have given the hardened form *pickel*; *picle* was app. a phonetic variant of *pitle*, whence perh. also *piddle* through **pittle*. Cf. also PINGLE *sb.*[2]]
A small field or enclosure; a close or croft.
α. 1210 *Fines in Cur. Dom. Reg., Bucks* (1835) I. 247 Croftam..que vocatur Leuernues pigtel. 12.. *Deed* in *N. & Q.* 10th ser. V. 26/2 Totam croftam illam que vocatur Wlstones pictel que jacet sub Bosco. 1250–60 *Furness Coucher* (Chetham Soc., new ser. XI. 444), Totam terram.. in loco qui vocatur Pichtil cum una acra ad caput Pichil. 1403 *Court-roll Gt. Waltham Manor, Essex*, Idem dominus habet unum fossatum non scuratum erga Chalf-pyghtell. 1494 in T. Gardner *Hist. Dunwich* (1754) 52 My Pytell lyinge in the Parische of All Seints within the said Town. 1541 in Wigram *Elstow* (1885) 161 One messuage, and one pightell, with appurtenances. 1562 in Glasscock *Rec. St. Michael's, Bp. Stortford* (1882) 55 Wood of ye pytell called thorley wyk. 1650 *Brasenose Coll. Doc.* E[2] 19 A little close or pasture called Pightle about 1 rood in area. 1730 in *Rep. Comm. Inq. Charities* (1837) XXXI. 141 (Cambs.) Two pightals in Bottisham, and a dolver in Braddyls. 1819 Rees *Cycl.*, *Pig-Tail*,..a provincial term sometimes applied to a small strip of ground generally in the state of grass. 1826 Miss Mitford *Village* Ser. ii. 53 Never had that novelty in manure whitened the crofts and pightles of Court-Farm. *a*1843 Southey *Comm.-pl. Bk.* (1851) IV. 430 The pigtail of the field, a small strip in grass. 1854 Knight *Once upon a Time* II. 117 There was one meadow..called the Pitle (still a Norfolk word). 1893 J. C. Jeaffreson *Bk. Recollect.* (1894) I. i. 15 The paddocks and pightels about the town of my birth.
β. *c*1220 *Selby Chartul.* II. 15 Unum essartum..quod vocatur Pichel. 1254–80 *Ibid.* 81 Cum uno pychel prati in

Ower Seleby. *c* **1275** *Whalley Coucher* (Chetham Soc., Old Ser. XVI. 688), Partem cujusdam terræ..quod vocatur Mikel pughull et Litel pughull. **1503** *Will of Wyne* (Somerset Ho.), Pykkyll otherwise called crofte. **1651** *MS. Indenture* (co. Derby), One land called the Pickell land. **1688** *MS. Indenture*, Close called..the Peighill. **1699** *MS. Indenture*, Also the Pickhills [*elsewhere* Pickills] in Brampton [co. York]. **1711** in *Rep. Comm. Inq. Charities* (1822) VIII. 721 (Yorks.) [J. S. charged] a pighill next but three to his close [with 5*s.* yearly to the poor]. **1737** *Court Roll, Wakefield*, Close called..Peighill. **1737** *MS. Indenture* (Rolleston, co. Stafford), A piece of meadow..lying near to an inclosure called Pickle Meer.

γ. **1641** *Termes de la Ley* 219 *Picle* or *pitle*..signifies with us a little small close or inclosure. *a* **1825** FORBY *Voc. E. Anglia*, *Pitle*, *Picle*, a small piece of inclosed ground, generally pronounced in the first, but not unfrequently in the second form.

δ. **1638** *Brasenose Coll. Mun.*, *Covt. Burwaldescote*, A piddle of pasture grownde of half an acre. *a* **1693** ASHMOLE *Antiq. Berks.* (1723) I. Introd. 39 Two Houses, and a Piddle of Land belonging to them.

pig-hull, -hutch, etc.: see PIG *sb.*[1] IV.

'pig-hunting, *vbl. sb.* Chiefly *N.Z. Hist.* [f. PIG *sb.*[1] + HUNTING *vbl. sb.*] Hunting for wild pigs. Hence **'pig-hunt** *v.*; **'pig-hunter**. Also **'pig-hunt** *sb.*

In quot. 1614 a humorous exaggeration.

1614 JONSON *Barth. Fair* (1631) III. ii. 34 These are Banbury-bloods, o' the sincere stud, come a pigge-hunting. **1845** R. BURROWS *Diary* 1 May (1886) 24 They..went off to pig-hunt. **1850** C. O. TORLESSE *Torlesse Papers* (1958) vii. 132 We have to cater for ourselves in the way of meat, which involves some pig hunting. **1851** J. R. CLOUGH *Jrnl.* 19 May in J. Deans *Pioneers of Canterbury* (1937) 293 Four pig-hunters came here; stopped all night. **1880** J. C. CRAWFORD *Recoll. Trav. N.Z. & Austral.* 163 Just below Puketapu we met a canoe laden with dogs going on a pig-hunting expedition. *a* **1948** L. G. D. ACLAND *Early Canterbury Runs* (1951) x. 262 In 1878..one of the shepherds, took a pig-hunting contract. **1961** J. REID *Kiwi Laughs* 9 The misfortunes of that pig-hunt which is an almost indispensable episode in fiction or memoirs.

pig-iron. [f. PIG *sb.*[1] 7: cf. SOW-IRON.]

1. Cast iron in pigs or ingots, as first reduced from the ore.

1665 D. DUDLEY *Mettallum Martis* (1851) 49 Some Furnaces make Twenty Tuns of Pig Iron *per* Week. **1805** FORSYTH *Beauties Scotl.* (1806) III. 104 The lateral moulds or channels are called pigs, and hence cast-iron receives the appellation of pig-iron. **1872** YEATS *Techn. Hist. Comm.* 325 The finest English pig-iron is from Cumberland hæmatite. **1881** RAYMOND *Mining Gloss.* s.v., Mine-pig is pig-iron made from ores only; cinder-pig, from ores with admixture of some forge or mill-cinder.

attrib. **1882** *Pall Mall G.* 31 May 9/2 The pig-iron market opened with little doing at 47*s.* 2½*d.* cash.

2. *Cookery.* An iron plate hung between the meat and the fire when the latter is too hot.

a **1756** MRS. HAYWOOD *New Present* (1771) 105 If it [the fire] should be too fierce in the middle, you must make use of a pig-iron. **1847–78** in HALLIWELL.

Pig Island. *Austral.* and *N.Z. slang.* Also with lower-case initials and in *pl.* [PIG *sb.*[1]] New Zealand, so called because of the introduction of pigs (which then went wild) by Captain Cook. Also *attrib.* So **Pig Islander**, a native or inhabitant of New Zealand.

1917 [see HOOT *sb.*[3]]. **1917** E. MILLER *Camps, Tramps & Trenches* (1939) 65 We Pig Islanders are not nearly so hot-blooded in our manner of speaking [as Australians]. **1927** J. DEVANNY *Old Savage* 278 I'll back one pig island miner against three of the best that ever came out of England. **1933** *Bulletin* (Sydney) 13 Sept. 29/4 The Pig Islanders are due in Britain in 1936. **1938** 'R. HYDE' *Nor Years Condemn* 164 They call us Homies... A lot of people called the New Zealanders Pig Islanders, and the Australians the Aussies. **1945** J. HENDERSON *Gunner Inglorious* 149 Back home in old Pig Island. **1946** L. R. C. MACFARLANE *Amuri* III. 117 *He* returned to the Pig Islands. **1948** in J. Reid *Kiwi Laughs* (1961) 161 The hell with all those soft-brained pig-islanders. They remind me of yahoos. **1952** *Landfall* VI. 262 It [*sc.* his voice] reverts to a rough pig-island twang. **1960** I. CROSS *Backward Sex* v. 103, I felt it, and was made easier by it, being a pig islander. **1967** F. SARGESON *Hangover* vii. 48 'Young man,' he said, 'it is my advice that you get off back to England... Pig Island is no place for the likes of you.' **1970** *N.Z. Listener* 21 Dec. 8/4 Another guy got blackmailed into taking a shelia half-way around Pig Island.

'pig-jump, *v.* app. orig. *Australian slang.* [f. PIG *sb.*[1] + JUMP *v.*] *intr.* To jump in a frolicsome way from all four legs, without bringing them together as in buck-jumping. Hence **'pig-jump** *sb.*, a jump from all four legs without bringing them together; **'pig-jumper**, a horse which pig-jumps.

1892 *Daily News* 7 May 5/4 The vice of some of these pig-jumpers and buckers in the arena is very directly a matter of original sin. **1893** MRS. C. PRAED *Outlaw & Lawm.* I. xi. 241, I don't mind what I sit, short of a regular buck-jumper. I can even manage a little mild pig-jumping. *Ibid.* 242 This horse won't even pig-jump. **1928** *Funk's Stand. Dict.* s.v. *Pig n.*, Pig-jump, n. **1929** K. S. PRICHARD *Coonardoo* 51 Up and down it the colt went, slewing, rooting, pig-jumping. **1943** 'W. HATFIELD' *I find Austral.* iv. 52 Sending it [*sc.* a mule] away in a series of flying pig-jumps while Tim felt for his off stirrup. *Ibid.* xvi. 213 We'll see what you can do on this pig-jumper of ours.

pig Latin. Also pig latin. [f. PIG *sb.*[1] + LATIN *sb.*] An invented language formed by systematic distortion of the source language; *spec.* one in which the initial consonant or consonant cluster of each word is transferred to the end of that word and a vocalic syllable (usually (eɪ)) added. Also *transf.* and *attrib.*

1937 R. CHANDLER in *Dime Detective Mag.* Nov. 50/1 'Big white father say come now.'.. 'Don't give me any more of that pig Latin.' **1937** E. LYONS *Assignment in Utopia* (1938) III. xii. 402 Ideological hair-splitting and proletarian pig-Latin. **1938** F. SCOTT FITZGERALD *Let.* Feb. (1964) 22 But when anything, Latin or pig latin, was ever put up to me.. I could always rise to meet that. **1944** [see JIVE *sb.* 3]. **1956** B. CLEARY *Fifteen* (1962) i. 16 *Utpay atthay ownday*..the boy was saying, 'Put that down,' in pig Latin. **1959** 'F. NEWTON' *Jazz Scene* v. 89 The whites, whose slang name, *ofays*—from the pig latin for 'foe'—sufficiently indicates the tension between the races. **1959** I. & P. OPIE *Lore & Lang. Schoolch.* xiv. 321 'Pig Latin'..thus: 'Unejay ithsmay isay igpay' (June Smith is a pig)..has been spoken by children since before the First World War. **1960** C. GEERTZ in J. A. Fishman *Readings Sociol. of Lang.* (1968) 294 A kind of 'pig-latin' form in the higher term involving..various forms of medial or final nasalization. **1965** *Language* XLI. 219 Pig Latin would have infixes where English has suffixes. **1978** R. MOORE *Big Paddle* i. 7 'Fee-a-zuck yee-a-zoo, I'm wee-a-zith ee-a-zit!' Cliff remembered his father's warning about obscenities, but in carney pig-latin it didn't sound too bad.

†**'pigle.** *Obs.* [According to *Alphita*, = med.L. *pigula*, F. *pigle*, of which nothing further is known. It was perh. another form of the word PAIGLE, though in ME. applied to an entirely different plant, and app. only in 16th c. identified with *paigle* the cowslip. (In the *Supplement* to Gerarde, 1597, *Pagle* is given as '*stichwort*'.)]

1. The Stitchwort, *Stellaria Holostea* (apparently).

a **1387** *Sinon. Barthol.* (Anecd. Oxon.) 27 *Lingua avis*, i. stichewort i. pigle. *Ibid.* 34 *Pigle*, i. stichewort. *c* **1450** *Alphita* (ibid.) 103 *Lingua auis*, pigula idem, florem habet album. *gallice* pigule. *anglice* sticheuurt. *Ibid.* 146 *Pigula*, lingua avis. [Cf. *Brit. Mus. Add. MSS.* 15236, '*Lingua avis*, gallice pigle, latine vero pigla'.]

2. = PAIGLE, the cowslip (apparently).

1570 LEVINS *Manip.* 129/35 Note, that ofttimes *ble* is written for *bil*, ..*gle* for *gil* [etc.]... Pigle [*mispr.* Pigil], for pigil, *verbasculum*.

pig-lead. Lead in the form of pigs, as it comes from the smelting-furnace.

1825 J. NICHOLSON *Operat. Mechanic* 360 The methods by which pig-lead is manufactured into sheet-lead. **1832** BABBAGE *Econ. Manuf.* xviii. (ed. 3) 166 The price of Pig-Lead was £1 1*s.* per cwt. **1903** J. MASEFIELD *Ballads* 19 With a cargo of Tyne coal, Road-rails, pig-lead.

'pigless, *a.* [f. PIG *sb.*[1] + -LESS.] Without a pig or pigs; having no pigs.

1895 *Daily News* 28 June 2/4 The National Pig Breeders met at a pigless show for the second time.

piglet ('pɪglɪt). [f. PIG *sb.*[1] + -LET.] A little pig.

1883 MISS BROUGHTON *Belinda* I. I. iv. 66 The little piglets..toddle sweetly about. **1895** C. SCOTT *Apple Orchards* 73 The black and white piglets, not yet weaned.

piglike ('pɪglaɪk), *a.* and *adv.* [f. as prec. + -LIKE 1.] Like, or like that of, a pig.

1612 *Two Noble K.* v. iv, Pig-like he [a restive horse] whines At the sharp rowel. **1849** *Sk. Nat. Hist.*, *Mammalia* IV. 138 Their voice, a pig-like grunt. **1897** MARY KINGSLEY *W. Africa* 195, I can see the pink, pig-like hippo, whose colour has been soaked out by the water, lying on the lower deck.

pig-lily: see PIG *sb.*[1] 14 b.

pigling ('pɪglɪŋ). In 8 **piglin**. [f. as prec. + -LING[1].] A little or young pig; a sucking-pig.

1713 C'TESS WINCHELSEA *Misc. Poems* 212 Then every Piglin she commends, And likens them to all their swinish Friends. **1833** SIR F. B. HEAD *Bubbles of Brunnen* (1834) 96 Tiny, light-hearted, brisk, petulant piglings. **1887** JESSOPP *Arcady* vii. 218 She tends the poultry,..she looks after the piglings [etc.].

Hence **'piglinghood**, the condition of a pigling.

1885 A. STEWART *Twixt Ben Nevis & Glencoe* 153 The stye which from early piglinghood had been its home.

'pigly, *a. nonce-wd.* [f. PIG *sb.*[1] + -LY[1].] Of, pertaining to, or befitting a pig.

1859 TROLLOPE *W. Indies* ii. (1860) 19, I believe that pigly grace consists in plumpness and comparative shortness.

pigmæan, pigmean, variants of PYGMÆAN.

pig-maker, -market: see PIG *sb.*[1] IV.

pigmeater ('pɪgmiːtə(r)). *Australian slang.* [f. PIG *sb.*[1] + MEAT *sb.* 1 + -ER[1].] A bullock which does not fatten; a beast only fit for pigs' food.

1884 'R. BOLDREWOOD' *Melb. Mem.* xiv. 105 Bullocks, which declined with fiendish obstinacy to fatten. They were what are known by the stock-riders as 'ragers' or 'pigmeaters'. **1890** —— *Col. Reformer* xvi. (1891) 195 The last camp..contained an unusual number of 'pigmeaters'.

pigmen, erron. variant of PYGMY.

pigment ('pɪgmənt), *sb.* [ad. L. *pigmentum*, f. *pig-*, *ping-ĕre* to paint. So OF. *pigment* (12–13th c.). *Pyhment* occurs in late OE. in sense 2. Cf. PIMENT.]

1. A colouring matter or substance.

a. Any substance (usually artificially prepared) used for colouring or painting; a paint, dye, 'colour'; in technical use, a dry substance, usually in the form of powder or easily pulverized, which, when mixed with oil, water, or other liquid vehicle, constitutes a 'paint'.

1398 TREVISA *Barth. De P.R.* XIX. xxvi. (Bodl. MS.), Minium is a red coloure..: In Spayne is more suche pigment þan in oþer londes. **1616** BULLOKAR *Eng. Expos.*, *Pigment*, a painting. **1621** BURTON *Anat. Mel.* III. ii. III. iii. (1651) 469 Artificial inticements and provocations of Gestures, Cloaths, Jewels, Pigments. **1663** BOYLE *Exp. Hist. Colours* III. xii. Wks. 1772 I. 735 Allow me,..for the avoiding of ambiguity, to employ the word pigments to signify such prepared materials (as cochineal, vermilion, orpiment) as painters, dyers, and other artificers make use of. **1684–5** —— *Min. Waters* iv. Wks. IV. 806 *Balaustium*, logwood, brasil, and other astringent vegetable pigments. **1799** G. SMITH *Laboratory* I. 312 A beautiful white pigment called ceruse. **1883** RUSKIN *Art Eng.* 11 The harmonies possible with material pigments.

b. *Nat. Hist.*, etc. Any organic substance occurring in and colouring any part of an animal or plant; the natural colouring-matter of a tissue.

[**1835–6** TODD *Cycl. Anat.* I. 3*/1 During pregnancy an increased secretion of pigmentum is said to take place.] **1842** PRICHARD *Nat. Hist. Man* (ed. 2) 89 The discoloration depended on the presence of cells filled with pigment. **1884** BOWER & SCOTT *De Bary's Phaner.* 68 Grains of chlorophyll and allied pigments.

†**2.** = PIMENT 1. *Obs.* (in Scott, *arch.*)

[**1150–1200** in *Sax. Leechd.* III. 136 Nim hwyt cudu & gyngyfere & recels..of oþþrum pyhmentum ane sticcan fulne. **1398** TREVISA *Barth. De P.R.* XIX. lix. (Bodl. MS.), *Pigmentum* haþ þat name as it were pilis mentum, quod scilicet in pila est contumsum [sic] þat is ibete in a morter: of þe whiche spicery by pigmentary crafte he makeþ likinge drinke and electuaries.] *c* **1420** *Pallad. on Husb.* VI. 167 To sauour..with puttyng to pygment, Or pepur, or sum other condyment. **1471** RIPLEY *Comp. Alch.* XI. ii. in Ashm. *Theat. Chem. Brit.* (1652) 181 As musk in Pygments. **1819** SCOTT *Ivanhoe* iii, Place the best mead,..the most odoriferous pigments, upon the board.

3. a. *attrib.* and *Comb.* (usually in sense 1 b), as ***pigment-cell***, ***-grain***, ***-granule***, ***-molecule***, ***-particle***, ***-speck***, ***-spot***; ***pigment-bearing***, ***-forming***, ***-laden*** adjs.

1842 PRICHARD *Nat. Hist. Man* (ed. 2) 89 Description of the pigment-cells in the negro. **1859** J. R. GREENE *Protozoa* 65 A bright coloured particle (usually red), termed the ..'pigment spot', is found in the bodies of many *Infusoria*. **1875** tr. *von Ziemssen's Cycl. Med.* I. 248 The pigment bacteria, which cannot be distinguished from one another microscopically. *Ibid.* II. 625 Cells and flakes containing pigment granules. **1879** HARLAN *Eyesight* ii. 14 A layer of flat, dark brown, or nearly black, pigment cells..also covers the posterior surface of the iris. **1898** P. MANSON *Trop. Diseases* iii. 73 For the most part these pigment grains are enclosed in leucocyte-like bodies. *Ibid.* 81 The tendency the pigment-laden leucocytes exhibit to carry their burden to the spleen. **1899** *Allbutt's Syst. Med.* VIII. 916 The etiology of pigment-bearing new growth.

b. Special combs.: **pigment colour** (see quot.); **pigment epithelium** or **layer** *Ophthalm.*, the layer of the retina next to the underlying choroid, which consists of a single layer of pigmented cells having processes that extend between the rods and cones of the adjacent layer, and which continues forwards over the posterior surfaces of the ciliary processes and the iris; **pigment-printing**, (*a*) a method of printing calicoes, etc. with pigments attached to the cloth by an albuminous substance; (*b*) the printing of permanent photographs with carbon or other pigments.

1873 tr. M. Schultze in *Stricker's Man. Human & Compar. Histol.* III. xxxvi. 269 Although..not directly continuous with the nerve fibres, the layer of pigment cells, ordinarily termed the pigment epithelium of the choroid, still belongs, both physiologically and morphologically, to the retina. **1862** O'NEILL *Dict. Calico Printing & Dyeing* 168 *Pigment colours*, this name has been given to those colours which are in the state of powder, and insoluble in the vehicle by which they are applied to the fabric. **1892** A. DUANE tr. *Fuchs's Text-bk. Ophthalm.* iv. 247 The inner surface of the uvea is everywhere coated with a layer of pigmented cells, belonging to the retina and having the character of epithelial cells (pigment-epithelium). **1971** T. L. LENTZ *Cell Fine Struct.* 386 The pigment epithelium has traditionally been considered as a layer of the retina. It may more logically, however, belong to the choroid, because the basement lamina..of the pigment epithelium is part of the glassy or Bruch's membrane of the choroid. **1889** J. LEIDY *Elem. Treat. Human Anat.* (ed. 2) xvi. 875 Pigment-layer of the choroidea. **1974** D. SHEPRO et al. *Human Anat. & Physiol.* ix. 251 The pigment layer absorbs extraneous light that might randomly stimulate receptor cells and create a poorer image. **1883** *Hardwich's Photogr. Chem.* (ed. Taylor) 339 Carbon, or pigment printing [in Photography]. **1897** J. NICOL in *Outing* (U.S.) XXX. 496/2 The carbon or pigment printing method gives the very highest class of positives.

pigment ('pɪgmənt), *v.* [f. the sb.] *trans.* To colour with or as with a pigment.

1900 *Nature* 1 Mar. 416/1 To pigment the image, a piece of carbon tissue is soaked in a weak solution containing acetic acid, hydroquinone, and ferrous sulphate, squeezed on to the print and allowed to dry. **1908** A. S. M. HUTCHINSON *Once aboard Lugger* v. i. 285 The stain enters the blood and, thence oozing, pigments every part of the being. **1979** G. MACDONALD *Camera* xii. 175 Robert Demachy experimented skilfully with gum prints which allowed him to pigment and work the coatings until the images looked more like drawings than photographs.

Hence **'pigmenting** *ppl. a.*

1906 *Westm. Gaz.* 1 Dec. 18/2 The effect of the silver image in the bromide print, in conjunction with the 'pigmenting' solution taken up by the plaster, is to render the pigmented compound forming the plaster..insoluble. **1958** *Engineering* 21 Mar. 384/1 The material is a blend of polymeric materials, solvents, stabilisers, and pigmenting compounds. **1971** *Brit. Poultry Sci.* XII. 206 The purpose ..was to evaluate the efficacy of canthaxanthin for the augmentation of naturally occurring pigmenting compounds found in yellow corn and alfalfa for the pigmentation of broilers.

pigmental (pɪg'mɛntəl), *a.* [f. L. *pigmentum* (see PIGMENT *sb.*) + -AL[1].] = PIGMENTARY *a.* 2. Hence **pig'mentally** *adv.*

1842 PRICHARD *Nat. Hist. Man* (ed. 2) 83 The mucous or pigmental membrane. **1886** *Belgravia Mag.* LIX. 353 Over-coloured, pigmentally and orally. **1896** *Allbutt's Syst. Med.* I. 114 Atrophy and pigmental degeneration (as apart from pigmental infiltration).

pigmentary ('pɪgməntərɪ), *sb.* and *a.* Also 4 pymentarie, -ye, 5 **pygmentarie.** [ad. L. *pigmentāri-us* adj., of or belonging to paints or unguents; sb. a dealer in these, in med.L. esp. in scents, spices, and aromatic confections, f. *pigment-um*: see PIGMENT *sb.* and -ARY[1].]

†**A.** *sb.* **a.** A maker or seller of ointments, drugs, etc.; an apothecary. **b.** (In quot. 1474) app. an aromatic confection. *Obs.*

1382 WYCLIF *Exod.* xxxvii. 29 Ensence of moost clene swete smellynge spices, with the werk of pymentarye [*Vulg.* opere pigmentarii; 1388 a makere of oynement; 1609 BIBLE (Douay) pigmentarie]. —— *Song Sol.* v. 13 The chekes of hym as litle flores of swote spicis, plaunted of pymentaries. **1474** CAXTON *Chesse* III. v. 101 Makers of pygmentaries, spicers and apotiquaries.

B. *adj.* †**1.** Pertaining to an apothecary or maker of aromatic confections. *Obs.*

1382 WYCLIF *Song Sol.* iii. 6 Smoke of the swote spices, of myrre, and of encens, and of alle pymentarie poudre [1388 al poudur of an oynement makere]. **1398** [see PIGMENT *sb.* 2].

2. Of, pertaining or belonging to, or consisting of pigment; producing or containing pigment or colouring-matter; in *Path.* characterized by the formation or presence of pigment.

1851 CARPENTER *Man. Phys.* (ed. 2) 590 To reflect the light that reaches the interior of the eye, when..not prevented from doing so by the interposition of the pigmentary layer. **1851** WRIGHT *Richardson's Introd. Geol.* xii. 385 The ink, though fossilised, retaining its pigmentary property. **1860** O. W. HOLMES *Prof. Breakf.-t.* iv, The purple-black of the..whiskers is constitutional and not pigmentary. **1876** BRISTOWE *The. & Pract. Med.* (1878) 84 The deposition of yellow, red, and brown pigmentary granules.

pigmentation (pɪgmən'teɪʃən). *Biol., Nat. Hist.*, and *Path.* [mod. f. L. *pigmentātus* painted (f. *pigmentum* paint) + -ION[1]: see -ATION. So F. *pigmentation.*] Coloration or discoloration by formation or deposition of pigment in the tissues.

1866 A. FLINT *Princ. Med.* (1880) 59 Pigmentation is not in itself a morbid process of much importance. **1876** tr. *Wagner's Gen. Pathol.* (ed. 6) 315 Pigmentation of the skin affects either the rete Malpighii or the corium.

pigmented ('pɪgməntɪd), *a.* [f. PIGMENT *sb.* + -ED[2].] Charged or coloured with pigment.

1866 A. FLINT *Princ. Med.* (1880) 246 These atrophic lungs are usually deeply pigmented. **1883** *Hardwich's Photogr. Chem.* (ed. Taylor) 347 The pigmented tissue should be of that kind which has a minimum of Gelatine and a maximum of colouring matter.

'pigmentless, *a.* [f. as prec. + -LESS.] Destitute of pigment.

1890 in *Cent. Dict.*

pigmentocracy (pɪgmən'tɒkrəsɪ). [f. PIGMENT + -OCRACY.] A ruling class made up of people of one skin-colour (usu. white); a country or state with such a ruling class.

1952 *Economist* 6 Dec. 702/2 A natural white aristocracy, with aristocratic virtues as well as vices, was already becoming merely a pigmentocracy. **1956** A. SAMPSON *Drum* xv. 210 In the 'pigmentocracy' of South Africa, skin colour was firmly linked with money and success. **1959** *New Statesman* 19 Dec. 874/3 South Africa is a pigmentocracy, dedicated before God and the whole world to the proposition that 'South Africa is the white man's country: it shall never be ruled by Kaffirs, Hottentots and Coolies.'

'pigmentose, *a.* [f. as next + -OSE.] = next.

pigmentous (pɪg'mɛntəs), *a.* [f. L. *pigment-um* PIGMENT *sb.* + -OUS.] Characterized by the presence of pigment; pigmentary.

1836-9 *Todd's Cycl. Anat.* II. 961/1 The exterior surface of the retina being covered by a dark pigmentous membrane.

'pig-,metal. [f. PIG *sb.*[1] 7 + METAL: cf. SOW-METAL.] Metal, usually iron, in the form of pigs.

1731 *Gentl. Mag.* I. 167 [He] proposes with Pit-coal Fire to make Bar Iron from Pig-metal. **1761** *Chron.* in *Ann. Reg.* 73/1 His new invented method of making malleable iron from pig or sow metal. **1831** J. HOLLAND *Manuf. Metal* I. 27 *Sow metal*, or *pig metal*, epithets..referring to the blocks as they may have been run in the main or the collateral gutters, the former being called *sows*, and the latter *pigs*, respectively.

pigmy: see PYGMY.

pigne, obs. form of PINE.

pignerate, -ation: see PIGNORATE, -ATION.

†**'pignolate, 'piniolate.** *Obs.* [a. F. *pignolat*, 'the preserued kernell of a Pine-apple, or conserue of Pine-kernells' (Cotgr.); cf. It. *pignolo* 'a kinde of meate of pine-apples' (Florio 1598), also PIGNON[1], and -ATE[1].] A conserve or confection made of pignons or pine-kernels.

1544 PHAER *Regim. Life* (1560) D j, All swete thynges are verye good as apples sodden with suger..pignolate, penedies, whyte pylles, suger candy, and the iuice of likorice. *Ibid.* (1553) D iv b, Pignolate, and swete almondes. **1657** TOMLINSON *Renou's Disp.* 171 Another kind of paste.. which the Neotericks call Piniolate or Pignolate because its made of Pine kernells.

‖**pignon**[1]. ? *Obs.* [F. *pignon* (piɲɔ̃) a pine-kernel = Sp. *piñon*, Pg. *pinhão*:—late L. type **pīniōn-em*, f. *pīnea* pine-cone. Cf. PINION *sb.*[5], PIÑON.]

1. A pine-kernel; the edible seed of the stone-pine (*Pinus Pinea*) of the south of Europe, or of other species of pine.

1604 E. G[RIMSTONE] *D'Acosta's Hist. Indies* IV. xxx. 292 There are great pine trees in New Spaine, though..they beare no pignons or kernells, but empty apples. **1866** *Treas. Bot.*, *Pignon*, or *Pinone*, the edible seed of the cones of various pines, as those of *Pinus Pinea*,..eaten in Italy.

†**2.** The physic-nut of S. America: = Pg. *pinhão*, PINION *sb.*[5] 1. *Obs.*

1604 E. G[RIMSTONE] *D'Acosta's Hist. Indies* IV. xxix. 289 There are a thousand of these simples fit to purge, as.. pignons of Punua..and many other things.

‖**pignon**[2] (piɲɔ̃). *Arch.* [F. *pignon* a gable-end = It. *pignone* (Littré), Romanic augmentative of L. *pinna* pinnacle; see PINION *sb.*[2]] A gable.

1875 F. I. SCUDAMORE *Day Dreams* 38 Rich in houses with gables and pignons.

pignorate ('pɪgnərət), *ppl. a.* [ad. L. *pignerāt-us*, pa. pple. of *pignerāre*: see next.] **a.** Given or taken in pledge; pledged, pawned. **b.** Relating to things pledged, pigneratitious.

16.. *Corshill Baron-Court Bk.* in *Ayr & Wigton Arch. Coll.* IV. 115 The said William Glen pursued the said Robert for the said pistoll for what the same wes pignorat. **1886** MUIRHEAD in *Encycl. Brit.* XX. 690/2 Pignorate and hypothecary rights were unknown as rights protected by action at the time now being dealt with.

pignorate ('pɪgnəreɪt), *v.* Also **pignerate.** [ad. L. *pignerāre* (in med. spelling *pignorāre*) to give as a pledge, f. *pignus* (*pigner-*, *-or-*) pledge: see -ATE[3].] *trans.* To give or take as a pledge; to pledge, pawn. Hence **'pignorated** *ppl. a.*

1623 COCKERAM, *Pignerate*, to pawne. **1656** BLOUNT *Glossogr.*, *Pignerate*, to lay a gage, or mortgage; also to take in pawn. **1842** *W. Smith's Dict. Grk. & Rom. Antiq.* 760/1 If the pledger sold a movable thing that was pignerated. **1878** *Ibid.* 1037/1 A man could not acquire possession by means of a pignorated slave.

pignoration (pɪgnə'reɪʃən). Also **pigner-.** [ad. L. *pignorātiōn-em* pledging, f. *pignerāre*: see prec.] The action of pledging or pawning.

1623 COCKERAM, *Pigneration*, a pawning or morgaging. **1658** PHILLIPS, *Pigneration* [*ed.* **1678** *Pignoration*], a gaging or laying to pawn. **1875** MAINE *Hist. Inst.* ix. 270 The Pignoration of the Continental Teutonic Law is more archaic than the Distress with which we are familiar in England.

pignoratitious (,pɪgnərə'tɪʃəs), *a. rare.* Also **pigner-.** [f. L. *pignerātīcius* adj., belonging to a pledge: see PIGNORATE *ppl. a.* and -ITIOUS.] Relating to things given in pledge or pawned.

1656 BLOUNT *Glossogr.*, *Pigneratitious*, that which is laid in pledge, or pertaining to gage. **1795** WYTHE *Decis. Virginia* 57 Questions arising on pigneratitious contracts.

'pignorative, *a.* [ad. F. *pignoratif* (1567), f. L. *pignorāre*: see PIGNORATE and -ATIVE.] That gives in pledge; pledging, pawning.

1611 COTGR., *Pignoratif*, pignoratiue, impledging, ingaging by suretiship, or with a pawne. Hence **1616-63** BULLOKAR *Expositor*, *Pignorative*, impledging, ingaging by suretiship, or with a pawne. **1818** in TODD. **1848** in WHARTON *Law Dict.*

'pig-nut. [f. PIG *sb.*[1] + NUT.]

1. The tuber of *Bunium flexuosum*; = EARTH-NUT 1.

1610 SHAKS. *Temp.* II. ii. 172, I with my long nayles will digge thee pig-nuts. **1693** ROBINSON in *Phil. Trans.* XVII. 826 The Roots..commonly call'd Kepper-Nuts, Pignuts and Gernuts in the North, lie very deep, and fatten Hogs. **1711** ADDISON *Spect.* No. 69 ¶5 No Fruit grows Originally among us, besides Hips and Haws, Acorns and Pig-Nutts. **1883** STEVENSON *Treas. Isl.* (1886) 277 Dig away, boys,.. you'll find some pig-nuts.

†**2.** Applied to an acorn (with reference to *Don Quixote* ch. xi). *Obs. nonce-use.*

1711 E. WARD *Quix.* I. 373 At length the Don in Pensive Mood His Golden Pignuts [*i.e.* acorns, as eaten in the Golden Age] gravely view'd.

3. *N. Amer.* The small pear-shaped nut of the broom hickory, *Carya glabra*, or the closely related species, *Carya ovalis*; also, the trees themselves, which belong to the family Juglandaceæ; = HOG-NUT 1. Also *attrib.*

1666 *Early Rec. Warwick, Rhode Island* (1926) 323 Upon a straight lyne from the pond to a pignut tree standing upon a hill. **1705** R. BEVERLEY *Hist. Virginia* II. iv. 16 There are also several Sorts of Hickories, call'd Pig-nuts. **1760** J. LEE *Introd. Bot.* App. 322 Pig Nut, *Juglans*. **1785** H. MARSHALL *Arbustrum Amer.* 68 White, or Pig-nut Hickery [*sic*]... generally grows pretty large. **1829** [see HOG-NUT 1]. **1832** D. J. BROWNE *Sylva Amer.* 183 The pignut hickory is one of the largest trees of the American forest. **1866** [see HOG-NUT 1]. **1884** MILLER *Plant-n.*, Pig-nut, American, *Carya porcina*. **1908** N. L. BRITTON *N. Amer. Trees* 237 Pignut hickory... A tree of drier ground than that in which most other hickories grow. **1969** T. H. EVERETT *Living Trees of World* 98/2 The pignut..occurs as a native in dryish soils from New York to Missouri and Florida. *Ibid.*, The closely related sweet pignut..differs in that its leaves have seven leaflets rather than the usual five.

'pig-rat. [transl. of Telugu *pandikokku*, BANDICOOT.] The large bandicoot rat of India.

1859 TENNENT *Ceylon* (1860) I. 150 Another favourite article of food with the coolies is the pig-rat or Bandicoot. **1865** *Reader* 14 Jan. 43/3 Bandicoot is..intended to represent the Telugu *pandi-kokku*, literally, '*pig-rat*'.

‖**pi'gritia.** *Obs.* [L., = sloth, slothfulness.] A former name of the sloths of South America.

[**1642** FULLER *Holy & Prof. St.* IV. iv. 256 The beast in Brasil, which the Spaniards call *Pigritia*, which goes no farther in a fortnight then a man will cast a stone.] **1706** PHILLIPS, *Pigritia*, Slothfulness... Also an American Beast call'd a Sloth. **1775** ADAIR *Amer. Ind.* 417 Nearly related to the South-American animal *Pigritia*, that makes two or three days journey in going up a tree.

†**pi'gritious,** *a. Obs. rare*[−1]. [f. L. *pigritia* sloth (f. *piger* slothful) + -OUS.] Slothful. So †**'pigritude** [f. L. type **pigritūdo*], †**'pigrity** [ad. L. *pigritās*], slothfulness (*obs. rare*[−0]).

1623 COCKERAM, *Pigritie*, *Pigritude*, slothfulnes. **1638** T. WHITAKER *Blood of Grape* Pref. 8 Pigritious and impudent persons. **1656** BLOUNT *Glossogr.*, *Pigritude*.

pig's in *Comb.*: see PIG[1] 14 c.

pig-sconce ('pɪgskɒns). [See SCONCE.] A pig-headed fellow; a pig-head.

1632 MASSINGER *City Madam* III. i, *Ding.* He is No pig-sconce, mistress. *Secret.* He has an excellent head-piece. **1879** G. MEREDITH *Egoist* III. 78 These representatives of the pig-sconces of the population judged by circumstances.

'pigskin. [f. PIG *sb.*[1] + SKIN.] **1. a.** The skin of the pig or hog (called in 18th c. HOGSKIN); leather made of this. Hence in *Sporting slang*, (*a*) a saddle; also *attrib.*; (*b*) *U.S.*, a football; also *attrib.*

1855 *Athenæum* 29 Dec. 1531 The Major..sees more things in pigskin and whipcord than are found in most men's philosophy. **1876** BESANT & RICE *Gold. Butterfly* ii, The best servant who ever put his leg across pig-skin. **1894** J. K. FOWLER *Recollect. O. Country Life* vi. 44 He was not particularly noted in the pigskin. **1894** *University of Chicago Weekly* 11 Oct. 8/2 Roby put the pigskin over the line. **1898** *Sporting Times* 26 Nov. 3/3 He..has again electrified English turf followers by riding rings around their crack knights of the pigskin. **1899** MACKAIL *Life Morris* II. 326 The white pigskin binding with silver clasps. **1928** GALSWORTHY *Swan Song* II. i. 105 Val..had picked him up on his retirement from the pig-skin in 1921. **1941** BAKER *Dict. Austral. Slang* 54 *Pigskin artist*, a jockey. **1945** *Richmond* (Virginia) *Times-Dispatch* 25 Oct. 10/6 Our football prophets are unfortunate fellows... I was told by the prophets of the pigskin that Ohio State would romp over poor Purdue. **1970** *New Yorker* 3 Oct. 34/3 A quick-thinking distaff pigskin zealot. **1974** *Anderson* (S. Carolina) *Independent* 24 Apr. 5B/1 He carried the pigskin on the end around 11 times for 73 yards, or an average of 6.6 yards per carry. **1977** *Time* 14 Nov. 49/2 The British-born geologist.. may not help his school's pigskin standings, but no matter.

b. The skin of a hog used as a bottle.

1883 V. STUART *Egypt* 37 Water-carriers loaded with pig-skins were conspicuous among the throng.

2. *Med.* = PEAU D'ORANGE.

1898 [see PEAU D'ORANGE]. **1943** C. F. GESCHICKTER *Dis. Breast* xx. 480 There is no sharp dividing line between the inflammatory change in the skin observed in acute carcinoma and the more common pigskin or lenticular dermatitis observed late in the disease in cases of large infiltrating mammary cancer. **1966** WRIGHT & SYMMERS *Systemic Path.* I. xxviii. 1010/2 Other cutaneous changes are local oedema ('pigskin', *peau d'orange*..) due to tumour cells growing in and blocking the lumen of the lymphatics in the superficial tissue of the breast, [etc.].

pigsney, -ny. *arch.* and *dial.* Forms: α. 4 piggesneyȝe, 4-6 piggesnye, 6 pyggysny, pygges nye, pigges-ny, pygs(-)nie, pygsnye, pigesnie, 6-8 pigs(-)nye, 7 pigsneye, pignie, 8 pig-nye, 6- pigsny, pigs(-)nie, pigs(-)ney; β. 6 pigseie, 9 (*dial.*) pigsy. [ME. f. *pigges* pig's + *neyȝe*, var. of *eyȝe*, *eye* with prosthetic *n*, app. derived from *an eye*, *min eye*; prob. originating in children's talk and the fond prattle of nurses.

The eye of the pig (as that of a bird in BIRD'S-NIE) is taken as a familiar type of a small eye; the expression is thus equivalent to *pinke* or *pinkie nye*, PINKENY, 'tiny eye', which was used in the same way as a term of endearment; but early examples showing *pigges nye* applied to the eye itself (sense 2) have not yet been found.]

1. One specially cherished; a darling, pet; commonly used as an endearing form of address. **a.** Chiefly applied to a girl or woman; in *mod. dial.* often opprobrious.

α. *c* **1386** CHAUCER *Miller's T.* 82 She was a prymerole a piggesnye ffor any lord to leggen in his bedde. *a* **1529** SKELTON *Womanhod*, etc. 20 What prate ye, praty pyggysny? **1549** CHALONER *Erasm. on Folly* F ij, Another fall in love with some yonge pygsnie. *a* **1553** UDALL *Royster D.* I. iv. (Arb.) 27 Then ist mine owne pygs nie, and blessing on my hart. **1589** *Triumphs Love & Fort.* F ij b, Then will I make my loving song upon mine owne pigsnye. **1629** MASSINGER *Picture* II. i, If thou art, As I believe, the pigsney of his heart, Know he's in health. **1667** DRYDEN *Tempest* IV. iii, How does my Pigs-nye? **1698** FARQUHAR *Love & Bottle* I. i, And the little pigsny has mamma's mouth. **1784** R. BAGE *Barham Downs* I. 11 Never think I shall long survive thee, pigsnye. **1834** SOUTHEY *Doctor* liv. (1848) 121/2 When pigsnie arrives and the purchaser opens the close sedan chair in which she has been conveyed to his house. **1876** MADOX-BROWN *Dwale Bluth* I. v. 102 She began to pour forth.. insinuations relative to a certain 'Trapseing, hautecking, kerping, pigsnie'.

β. **1553** BALE tr. *Gardiner's De vera Obed.* K j b, How doth my sweteheart, what saith now pigges eye? **1869** J. P. MORRIS *Gloss. Words Furness* 71 *Pigsy*, a term of endearment, as 'Thow lile pigsy'.

†**b.** More rarely applied to a man or boy. *Obs.*

1581 J. BELL *Haddon's Answ. Osor.* 68 b, And your sweet piggesnye Emanuel will smoyle close in his sleave. *a* **1588** TARLTON *Jests* (1844) Introd. 21 The player fooles deare darling pigsnie He calles himselfe his brother. **1708** *Brit. Apollo* No. 68. 2/2 You, ven once they have your Money, No more their Pigsnies are nor Honey.

†**2.** An eye; a 'dear little eye'. *Obs.*

1663 BUTLER *Hud.* II. i. 560 And shine upon me but benignly, With that one, and that other Pigsneye. **1709** *Brit. Apollo* II. No. 11. 3/1, I rise, And rub my Pigs Nyes. *a* **1774** GOLDSM. tr. *Scarron's Com. Romance* (1775) II. 10 The hostess received such a blow on her little pig-nyes, that she saw a hundred thousand lights at the same time.

pig-stick ('pɪgstɪk), *sb.* [f. PIG-STICKING.] A wild-boar hunt; a pig-sticking. Also *fig.*

1906 *Westm. Gaz.* 13 July 2/1 Pickle meanwhile was having a pig-stick on the sands, with Floss in the rôle of pig. **1906** *Daily Chron.* 26 Oct. 3/4 His book..is just a simple account of his every-day life in Algeria, including a bath and a shave, a 'pig-stick', and a visit to a café.

pigsticker ('pɪgˌstɪkə(r)). [f. PIGSTICKING: see -ER[1].] **a.** One who follows the sport of pigsticking.

1866 TREVELYAN in *Fraser's Mag.* LXXIII. 387, I may be a young pig-sticker, but I am too old a sports-man to make such a mistake as that. **1889** *Athenæum* 24 Aug. 255/1 The courage, horsemanship, and skill with his spear required in the pigsticker.

b. A horse trained to pigsticking.

1900 SIR J. FAYRER *Recollect.* iii. 62, I bought a horse, a well-known pig-sticker.

c. A sharp implement or weapon, as a lance, bayonet, knife, etc. *slang.*

1890 BARRÈRE & LELAND *Dict. Slang* II. 129/1 *Pigsticker* (army), sabre. **1895** *Funk's Stand. Dict.*, *Pigsticker*..3. A boar-spear. 4. (Slang.) A large pocket-knife. **1902** FARMER & HENLEY *Slang* V. 198/2 *Pig-sticker*... 2. (common).—A long-bladed pocket-knife; and (3) a sword. **1918** C. J. SWAN *My Company* viii. 129 All this time the steel pigsticker was resting on his rotund stomach with the rifle behind it cocked. **1941** J. SMILEY *Hash House Lingo* 43 *Pig sticker*, carving knife. **1964** G. L. COON *Short End* 242, I had awful visions of somebody clinging to the business end of that pig sticker of mine. **1978** A. MELVILLE-ROSS *Blindfold* xxx. 191 Trelawney crossed to the far wall, yanked the knife from it. .. 'You'll hand over that pig-sticker and come home with uncle.'

d. A butcher of swine (cf. PIGSTICKING 2). *dial.* and *slang.*

1886 H. BAUMANN *Londinismen* 138/1 *Pig-sticker*.. scherzhaft: Schweineschlächter. **1895** in *Funk's Stand. Dict.* **1939** F. THOMPSON *Lark Rise* i. 12 The travelling pork butcher, or pig-sticker. **1948** *Amer. Speech* XXIII. 317/2 *Pig sticker*, man who bleeds hogs.

pigsticking ('pɪgˌstɪkɪŋ). [f. PIG *sb.*[1] + STICKING *vbl. sb.*]

1. The hunting of the wild boar with a spear. Also *attrib.*

1848 THACKERAY *Van. Fair* lx, Describing the sport of pigsticking..with great humour and eloquence. **1881** J. GRANT *Cameronians* I. iii. 32 The dinner-gong..recalled his thoughts from pig-sticking and Central India. **1907** *Yesterday's Shopping* (1969) 666/2 The usual length for pig-sticking lances is:—For use in Bengal Presidency, 6 ft. 6 in. to 7 ft. **1910** *Blackw. Mag.* Apr. 559/1 The Ganges Cup was first run for in 1869 after the pig-sticking season. **1972** *Shooting Times & Country Mag.* 1 July 21/2, I now treat you to a potted picture of a typical pig-sticking run.

2. The butchering of swine by sticking a knife into the heart or aorta.

1884 M. ARNOLD in *Harper's Mag.* Oct. 797/2, I would not go to see the pig-sticking at the stock-yards.

Hence **'pigstick** *v. intr.*, to hunt the wild boar.

1891 KIPLING *City Dreadf. Nt.* 74 Animals who stand on one hind leg and beckon with all the rest, or try to pigstick in harness.

pig-stone, -swill, etc.: see PIG *sb.*[1] IV.

pigsty ('pɪgstaɪ). A sty or pen for pigs, including a shed or covered enclosure.

1591 PERCIVALL *Sp. Dict.*, *Çahorda*, a pigges stie, *Hara.* **1629** MASSINGER *Picture* IV. ii, 'Slight! 'tis a prison, or a pig-sty! **1710** STEELE *Tatler* No. 169 ¶ 1 What Wash is drank up in so many Hours in the Parlour and the Pigsty. **1853** H. WHARTON *Digest Cases Pennsylv.* 473 A pigstye in a city is per se a nuisance.

b. *transf.* Applied to a dwelling only fit for a pig; a miserable or dirty hovel.

1820 SYD. SMITH *Wks.* (1867) I. 311 All degrees of all nations begin with living in pigstyes. **1884** LABOUCHERE in *Fortn. Rev.* Feb. 219 The poor in our great towns are condemned to live in pig-styes, and to pay excessive rents for this accommodation.

'pig's wash, pigwash. The swill of a brewery or kitchen given to pigs; = HOGWASH. Also applied contemptuously to weak inferior liquor, and in other abusive senses.

1630 *Tinker of Turvey* A iij, These comming as farre short of his, as Bragget goes beyond the Pigs wash or small Beere. **1850** CARLYLE *Latter-d. Pamph.*, *Jesuitism* 29 Moral evil is unattainability of Pig's Wash. **1866** GEO. ELIOT *F. Holt* v, If I had not seen that..pig-wash, even if I could have got plenty of it, was a poor sort of thing, I should never have looked life fairly in the face. **1887** RUSKIN *Præterita* II. 284 [I was] content in my dog's chain, and with my pig's-wash, in spite of Carlyle.

'pigtail. [So called from resemblance to the tail of a pig.]

1. a. Tobacco twisted into a thin rope or roll.

1688 R. HOLME *Armoury* III. xxii. (Roxb.) 274/1 Pig taile, is a very small wreath or roll tobacco. **1740** SWIFT *Will* Wks. 1745 VIII. 384, I bequeath to Mr. John Grattan..my silver box..in which I desire the said John to keep the tobacco he usually cheweth, called pigtail. **1760** H. WALPOLE *Lett. to Mann* 7 May, He..took some pigtail tobacco out of his pocket. **1839** 'J. FUME' *Paper on Tobacco* 120 Pig-tail when smoked is equally as strong as shag.

b. A farthing candle. *dial.*

1828 *Craven Gloss.* (ed. 2) s.v., The watching of the pig-tail was a superstitious ceremony observed in Craven..on the Eve of St. Mark. On that evening, a party of males or females..place on the floor a lighted pig-tail, for so a small or farthing candle is denominated. **1867** HARLAND & W. *Lanc. Folk-lore* 140 On the fast of St. Agnes she watches a small candle called a 'pig-tail', to see the passing image of her future husband.

c. *Naut.* A short length of rope; a rope's end.

1894 *Daily Tel.* 18 Oct. 6/5 Hit..with a 'pigtail', a piece of thick rope.

d. *Electr.* A short length of flexible conductor; *spec.* one in an electrical machine connecting a brush to its brush-holder; (see also quot. 1971).

1903 HAWKINS & WALLIS *Dynamo* (ed. 3) xix. 606 The flexible copper conductor..forms a twisted pig-tail with enough slack to allow of the normal amount of brush movement. **1949** *Jrnl. Appl. Physics* XX. 805/2 Some cartridges..were fitted with pigtails for convenience in wiring. **1962** C. O. SWANSON in Roberson & Farrior *Guidance & Control* 400 The pigtails, which pass power to and from the floated assembly, are very small in size. **1963** ROSENBLATT & FRIEDMAN *Direct & Alternating Current Machinery* ii. 15 Except in small dynamos, the current is taken from the brush by means of a flexible copper wire embedded in the brush, called the pigtail. **1964** R. F. FICCHI *Electr. Interference* ix. 166 The conductor may be buried in the concrete slab under the equipment with pigtail conductors protruding above the concrete for equipment grounds. **1971** M. TAK *Truck Talk* 118 *Pigtail*, the cable that transmits electricity to the trailer from the tractor.

2. a. A plait or queue of hair hanging down from the back of the head; applied *spec.* to that worn by soldiers and sailors in the latter part of the 18th and beginning of the 19th century, and still frequently by young girls, and *esp.* to that customary among the Chinese under the Manchus.

1753 HANWAY *Trav.* (1762) I. VII. xciii. 428 They observe an uniformity about their heads by wearing pigtails. **1768–74** TUCKER *Lt. Nat.* (1834) II. 595 The French carpenter can-not saw his boards, without a long pig-tail and ruffled shirt. **1822** W. IRVING *Braceb. Hall* (1849) 52 A soldier of the old school, with powdered head, side locks, and pigtail. **1830** *Examiner* 801/1 Trousers came in with the French Revolution, pigtails went out with Lord Liverpool. **1838** DICKENS *Nich. Nick.* xiv, [Mrs. Kenwigs' girls] had flaxen hair, tied with blue ribbons, hanging in luxuriant pigtails down their backs. **1874** LADY HERBERT tr. *Hübner's Ramble* I. xii. 193 Chinamen..with their black caps, and equally black pig-tails. **1885** FAIRHOLT *Costume in Eng.* (ed. 3) II. 321 Pig-tails in the army were reduced in 1804 to seven inches in length and in 1808 cut off. *c* **1890** *F. Wilson's Fate* 76 He..wiped his grizzled moustache and twisted its extremities into pig-tails. **1895** MRS. B. M. CROKER *Village Tales* (1896) 66, I was still a rather troublesome schoolgirl in short frocks and a pig-tail.

b. *transf.* The wearer of a pigtail; a Chinese.

1886 *Cornh. Mag.* July 55 Sweetmeats..being great favourites with the 'pigtails'.

†**3.** A pigtailed monkey. *Obs.*

1774 GOLDSM. *Nat. Hist.* IV. 215 The Maimon of Buffon, which Edwards calls the Pigtail, is the last of the baboons, and..no larger than a cat. [Cf. PIGTAILED *a.* 1.]

4. *attrib.* and *Comb.* (chiefly from 2). **a.** in sense 'of, pertaining to, wearing a pigtail'; *colloq.* Chinese: as ***pigtail brigade, land, party***; **b.** in sense 'characteristic of the period when pigtails were worn', old-fashioned, pedantic, absurdly formal (cf. Ger. *zopf*), as ***pigtail drill, period, professor, tory***; **c.** = PIGTAILED 1, as ***pigtail macaque***; also ***pigtail tobacco*** (see 1 a); ***pigtailwise*** adv.

1817 COBBETT *Wks.* XXXII. 114 Do the Pig tail Order suppose, that such means will be resorted to now? **1859** SALA *Tw. round Clock* (1861) 186 How I should have liked to witness the old pigtail operas and ballets performed at the Pantheon. **1865** M. PATTISON *Ess.* (1889) I. 348 Heyne was essentially a dull, wooden man,—a pigtail professor after all. **1867** WOOD *Pop. Nat. Hist.*, *Mammalia* 16 Bruh or Pig-tail Macaque.—*Macacus nemestrinus.* **1885** *Leisure Hour* Jan. 32/1 Emancipation from the 'pigtail drill'. **1887** ASHBY-STERRY *Lazy Minstrel* (1892) 199 Her ample tresses one descries Are closely plaited, pig-tail-wise. **1890** *Pall Mall G.* 10 Feb. 7/2 These same monkeys, the so called pig-tail variety, are taught by the Malays to pick fruit for them in the forests. **1898** *Athenæum* 19 Mar. 366/1 He was a typical 'pigtail Tory'. **1899** *Daily News* 25 Oct. 2/1 Mr. Yerburgh, the leader of what was known last Session as 'the Pigtail Party' in the House of Commons, is contemplating a journey to China.

pigtail, corrupt form of PIGHTLE.

pigtailed ('pɪgteɪld), *a.* [f. prec. + -ED[2].]

1. Having a tail like a pig's; *spec.* in ***pigtailed macaque*** or ***monkey***, ***Macaca nemestrina***, native to southern Asia, Sumatra, and Borneo.

1758 EDWARDS *Glean. Nat. Hist.* I. 8 The Pig-tailed Monkey, from the Island of Sumatra, in the Indian Sea. **1864** ATKINSON *List Provinc. Names Birds*, Pig-tailed Winder, Prov. name for Pintail Duck. **1896** *List Anim. Zool. Soc.* (ed. 9) 24 *Macacus nemestrinus*..Pig-tailed Monkey... East Indies. **1932** S. ZUCKERMAN *Social Life Monkeys* vi. 90 The cycle in the pig-tailed macaque varies roughly from thirty to forty days. *Ibid.* xi. 188 The pig-tailed monkeys that live on the Island of Singapore are believed to be escaped captives. **1969** *Daily Tel.* 22 Aug. 19/8 A pig-tailed monkey was born at London Zoo on Sunday. The species.. is named because of its ability to curl its tail like a pig's. **1977** ROONWAL & MOHNOT *Primates of S. Asia* 177 Owing to the local demand for pig-tailed macaques for food..its numbers are rapidly declining all over its range.

2. Having a pigtail; tied up or plaited into a pigtail.

1754 SHEBBEARE *Matrimony* (1766) I. 189 Hair.. powder'd and pig-tail'd. **1775** SHERIDAN *St. Patr. Day* II. iv, All the pigtailed lawyers and bagwigged attorneys. **1791–3** in *Spirit Pub. Jrnls.* (1799) I. 67 A pig-tailed periwig. **1892** *Spectator* 27 Feb. 305/1 To wonder at pig-tailed China.

'pigtaily, *a. nonce-wd.* Of or pertaining to the pigtail period; old-fashioned.

1859 SALA *Tw. round Clock* (1861) 300 Old fashioned, out of date, rococo, and pigtaily.

†**'pig-taker.** *Obs.* A purveyor of pigs: formerly an office in the Royal Household.

1455 in *Househ. Ord.* (1790) *21 Th' office of the Catery.. 1 Grome Piggetaker. **1538** *Ibid.* 218 Allowance to be given ..unto Thomas Playfoote, Yeoman-Pigtaker for every Veale, being fatt and good,..that he shall send into the Larder.

pig-trotter, -trough, -tub, etc.: see PIG *sb*[1].

'pigweed. A name given to many plants used as animal fodder or potherbs, esp. goosefoots belonging to the genus *Chenopodium* and amaranths, esp. *Amaranthus retroflexus*; in Australia, a name for purslane, *Portulaca oleracea*.

1806 T. G. FESSENDEN *Orig. Poems* (rev. ed.) 17 The hyacinth and daffodil, With now and then a big weed Of purslain and of pig weed. **1835** J. H. INGRAHAM *South-West* II. 110 A weed not unlike the common pig-weed. **1844** H. HUTCHINSON *Pract. Drainage Land* 159 The roots of a weed called pig weed. **1850** [see *apple-peru*]. **1854** THOREAU *Walden* vii. (1886) 159 That's Roman wormwood,—that's pigweed,—that's sorrel,—that's piper-grass. **1864** R. HENNING *Let.* 4 Mar. (1966) 157 The Irish family..were so alarmed at the idea of getting scurvy also..that the two little girls..devoted their leisure to picking 'pigweed', rather a nasty wild plant, but supposed to be exceedingly wholesome, either chopped up with vinegar or boiled. **1865** *Daily Tel.* 7 Nov. 5/1 The tiny islets being covered with pig-weed, large earwigs, and land crabs. **1884** *Harper's Mag.* Mar. 601/2 Here we find..pig-weed six inches in stem, and wearing a huge flower like a hat. **1892** *Ch. Times* 15 Jan. 43/1 [Famine in Russia] Those who have bread are compelled to adulterate it with pigweed [*Chenopodium rubrum*], which, taken in quantities, is a bitter emetic. **1893** J. A. BARRY *S. Brown's Bunyip*, etc. 146 We..lived for months at a time on damper, bullock and pigweed in a bark humpy. **1909** L. M. MONTGOMERY *Anne of Avonlea* xxvii. 319 I've begun to grow like pigweed in the night. **1911** W. R. GUILFOYLE *Austral. Plants* 298 Portulaca oleracea. 'Common Purslane' or 'Pigweed'. **1927** M. M. BENNETT *Christison* xi. 116 It's a hungry place, Lammermoor! Nothing to eat but pigweed and mutton. **1941** I. L. IDRIESS *Great Boomerang* vii. 55 There were creepers too, crowfoot and pigweed, parakelia and geranium. **1943** FERNALD & KINSEY *Edible Wild Plants Eastern N. Amer.* 177 Pigweed, Goosefoot, Lamb's-Quarters, *Chenopodium album* and 14 other species... The common Pigweed, so familiar in rich garden soil, in barnyards, and similar habitats, has always been a popular potherb. **1945** J. M. FOGG *Weeds of Lawn & Garden* 75 The Green Amaranth or Pigweed is the most common species of the genus found as a garden weed. **1965** *Austral. Encycl.* VII. 232/1 The almost cosmopolitan *P[ortulaca] oleracea* (..purslane or pigweed) is used as a green food by Indonesian and Polynesian peoples. **1966** L. J. KING *Weeds of World* i. 12 The grain amaranths are inextricably involved in any history of the non-cultivated or weedy amaranths or 'pigweeds'. **1975** D. MCCLINTOCK *Wild Flowers of Guernsey* 86 Pigweeds [*sc.* species of *Amaranthus*] are unexpectedly rare in Guernsey.

†**pig'widgin, -'widgeon.** *Obs.* Also pig wigeon. Of obscure origin and meaning: see quots. 1730–1785.

Some have identified it with *Pigwiggen*, *-wiggin*, used by Greene and Nashe as a *quasi*-proper name, and by Drayton as the name of a fairy knight favoured by Queen Mab the wife of Oberon, also by Davenant. In Cotton it is apparently a term of contempt, and rimes with *biggin*, cap or hood. *Pig-*

widgin (-widʒin) appears in Cleveland *attrib.* as a contemptuous or hostile epithet for the Scotch; spelt by Bailey *-wigeon*, by Johnson *-widgeon*, app. after the name of the bird. Its connexion with *Pigwiggin* is not proved.

[*a* **1592** GREENE *Selimus* 1909 Now will I be as stately to them as if I were maister Pigwiggen our constable. **1596** NASHE *Saffron-Walden* Wks. (Grosart) III. 191 No more will I of his calling me Captaine of the boyes, and Sir Kilprick; which is a name fitter for his Piggen de wiggen, or gentlewoman. **1599** —— *Lenten Stuffe* To Rdr., If it were so, goodman Pig-wiggen, were not that honest dealing? **1627** DRAYTON *Nymphidia* xii, Pigwiggen was this Fairy Knight, One wond'rous gracious in the sight Of fair Queen Mab, which day and night He amorously observed. **1629** DAVENANT *Albovine* II. i. Dij, *Albo.* Is not your name Pigwiggin? *Cuny.* Pigwiggin! your Grace was wont to call me Cunymond: I am no Faery. **1675** COTTON *Scoffer Scofft* 68 What such a nazardly Pigwiggin, A little Hang-strings in a Biggin?]

1687 *Cleveland's Wks., Rebel Scot* 12 To see his Country sick of Pym's disease; By Scotch Invasion to be made a prey To such Pig-Widgin Myrmidons as they. **1730–6** BAILEY (folio), *Pig Wigeon* (*with the Vulgar*) a silly fellow. **1755** JOHNSON, *Pigwidgeon*..is a kind of cant word for any-thing petty or small. [Quotes Cleveland.] **1785** GROSE *Dict. Vulg. T.* s.v. *Pig, Pig-widgeon*, a simpleton.

Hence **pig'widgin, -'widgeon** *v.*

1852 M. W. SAVAGE *Reuben Medlicott* I. III. Argt. 214 In short the Medlicotts were Pigwidgeoned, and we are not to pity them, for they brought the Pigwidgeoning on themselves. Pigwidgeoning will prove to be a social usage, nearly akin to spunging.

pig-woman, -wool, etc.: see PIG[1] 14.

†**'pigwort.** *Herb. Obs.* = PIGWEED.

1575 TURBERV. *Venerie* 73 Pigwort, woodbynd, birche and such like, whereof they croppe the toppes.

pi-jaw ('paɪdʒɔː), *sb. slang* (now *arch.*). [f. PI *a.* (*sb.*) + JAW *sb.*[1]] A pious lecture or exhortation, esp. one addressed to schoolboys or young persons by their teachers or parents. Hence **'pi-jaw** *v. trans.*, to lecture or exhort; **'pi-jawing** *vbl. sb.*

1891 R. G. K. WRENCH *Winchester Word-bk.* 31 He pi-jawed me for thoking. **1912** G. W. E. RUSSELL *One Look Back* ii. 25 It was his custom..to call us all together.., and give us what we called a 'Pi-jaw'. **1913** *Pearson's Mag.* June 606/2 There is no suspicion of 'pi-jaw' about it. **1922** A. S. M. HUTCHINSON *This Freedom* IV. iv. 303 You..get me here to pijaw me about my duty to my pretty young wife. **1923** *Blackw. Mag.* Jan. 56/1 He..treated me to the Persian equivalent of a 'pi-jaw'. **1925** M. I. ROGERS in *Inner Life* (ser. 2) xiii. 257 Older children..are more interested in ideas and the way in which things happen. They dislike 'pi-jaw'. **1930** J. DOUGLAS *Down Shoe Lane* 210 It may be that they yawn over pompous pi-jawing and middle-aged platitudinarianism. **1937** G. FRANKAU *More of Us* xi. 121 The tortures of a miserable Upper Pi-jawed beyond the sacred hour of supper. **1945** G. B. GRUNDY 55 *Yrs. at Oxf.* 38 What a boy or young man loathes above all is pi-jaw.

pik, obs. form of PICK *v.*[1], PIKE *sb.*[1], PITCH.

‖**pika** ('paɪkə). Also pica. [ad. *piika*, native name in Tunguse of Siberia (Pallas *a* 1800).]

a. A small herbivorous quadruped belonging to the genus *Ochotona*, closely related to hares and rabbits, distinguished by short, rounded ears, reddish-brown or grey fur, and the lack of a tail, and found in mountainous regions of western North America and north-east and central Asia.

1827 GRIFFITH *Cuvier's Anim. K.* III. 223 The pika is an inhabitant of the highest mountains of the extreme North of Europe and Asia. **1849** *Sk. Nat. Hist., Mammalia* IV. 163 The most obvious peculiarity of these pikas is their voice, from which they have acquired their trivial name. **1851** J. RICHARDSON *Arctic Searching Exped.* I. v. 178 The little Pika, or tail-less hare, occupies the grassy eminences, and lays up a stock of hay for winter use. **1858** J. PALLISER *Jrnl.* 16 Aug. in I. M. Spry *Papers of Palliser Exped. 1857–1860* (1968) 294, I also heard the squeaking note of the little Pica or tailless hare... It is about the size of a small rat, but made exactly like any other rabbit, excepting that it has round open ears. **1925** E. F. NORTON *Fight for Everest: 1924* 173 Our ponies were off after them in a mad gallop down the nullah side, heedless of rocks and pika burrows. **1936** D. MCCOWAN *Animals Canad. Rockies* iv. 36 Pikas feed on grass and the many varieties of small Alpine plants. **1958** L. WHISHAW *As far as You'll take Me* xi. 176, I had the impression that a pika had spotted us. **1964** L. S. CRANDALL *Managem. Wild Mammals in Captivity* 201 The round-eared, nearly tailless pikas (*Ochotona*) are found in rock areas or 'slides', generally at high altitudes. **1971** L. H. MATTHEWS *Life of Mammals* II. v. 138 The genus *Ochotona*, the only one in the Ochotonidæ, contains about twelve species of whistling hares or rock rabbits, generally known as pikas. **1973** P. GEDDES *Ottawa Allegation* vi. 83 A pika is a bunny... When the sun shines he..cuts all the grass he wants for winter and lays it out to dry.

b. *Comb.* **pika-squirrel**, a name suggested by Coues for the chinchilla.

1885 *Stand. Nat. Hist.* V. 86.

†**pika'nier.** *Obs. rare.* [a. Ger. *piekenier*, f. *pieke, pike* PIKE *sb.*[5]: cf. OF. *piquenaire* pikeman.] A soldier armed with a pike; a pikeman.

1816 *Gentl. Mag.* LXXXVI. I. 213/1 They were first raised as pikaniers, and behaved gallantly in the Turkish campaigns.

pikar, obs. Sc. f. PIKER, thief.

pikary, obs. f. PICKERY.

pikau ('piːkaʊ), *sb. N.Z.* Also peko, pico. [Maori.] A pack for carrying on the back, a knapsack, a swag. Also *attrib.* Hence **'pikau** *v. trans.*, to carry (a pack) on the back.

1836 J. A. WILSON *Jrnl.* 23 Aug. in *Missionary Life & Work N.Z.* (1889) III. 48 Our natives weary with their *pikaus*. **1847** G. F. ANGAS *Savage Life* II. i. 3 [The natives] severally carried [our baggage] in their *pikau* or knapsacks, strapped over their shoulders with the leaves of flax. **1848** *McLean Papers* V. 265 (MS.) One of the natives left us at Woons..so we had to put the *pico* on the mule and trudge along. **1851** J. C. RICHMOND *Let.* 25 Mar. in *Richmond-Atkinson Papers* (1960) I. ii. 79 We were 6 in party, ourselves, young Stark & 3 Maoris with 'pikau' burdens. **1874** W. M. BAINES *Narr. E. Crewe* iii. 49 [The pig's] legs [were] tied together so as to make him a handy 'pikau'. **1882** W. D. HAY *Brighter Britain!* II. 94 Both men and women [*sc.* Maoris] are able to pikau (hump, or carry on the back and shoulders) great weights. **1882** T. H. POTTS *Out in Open* 24 A line of women and girls..have just brought away from the potato pits their heavily-laden kits, carried pikau fashion. **1892** E. S. BROOKES *Frontier Life* 148 Most of us were now loaded with heavy pekoes or swags on our backs. **1902** W. SATCHELL *Land of Lost* vii. 50 He..commenced to fill his *pikau*. **1911** *Chambers's Jrnl.* 4 Mar. 223/2 We succeeded almost noiselessly in doing to death a fine young sow, and, having cut up the carcass, started for camp with the meat 'pikaued' (carried as in a knapsack) in sugar-bags on our shoulders. **1950** F. SARGESON in *Landfall* IV. 285 The rest of his [*sc.* a farmer's] luggage would be a *peko* slung on his shoulders. **1958** *Tararua* XII. 27 The gumdiggers used a *pikau*, a bag with shoulder straps, a good deal smaller than the usual tramper's pack. **1960** B. CRUMP *Good Keen Man* 123 To ensure [my dog] Flynn's co-operation I tied him to my belt with the rope off my pikau.

pikaxe, obs. f. PICKAXE.

pike (paɪk), *sb.*[1] Forms: 1 piic, 1, 3 pic, 3–4 pike, 3–6 pyk, 4–7 (9) pyke, 4– pike. [Found in OE. as *piic* (8th c.), *píc*, in ME. *pīk* (pl. *pīkes*), later *pȳke*, *pīke*; beside which there existed from 14th c., in same senses, a collateral form with short vowel, *pic, pik, pykk*, now PICK *sb.*[1] Cf. PICK *v.*[1], with its collateral form *pike*. In mod.Eng., in sense 1, *pike* is now local or dial., *pick* being in general use; but senses 2 and 3 are in general Eng. *pike*, while *pick* is obs. or dial.; sense 4 is now generally *peak*; sense 5 is dial. or local. OE. and ME. *píc, pic* agree in form and sense with F. *pic* (of which, however, examples are known only from the 12th c.). In the earliest instances, both in OE. and OF., *pic* was applied to a pick, pickaxe, or pick-hammer, with handle at right angles to the head; but, in both, the word was soon applied to a straight instrument or tool pointed at one end, or to the sharp point of such (cf. OE. *hornpíc* a pinnacle, in *Lindisf. Gosp.* Matt. iv. 5), as in Fr. to a poker, a glass-blower's tool, the end of a ship's yard, etc. The Eng. uses are not the same, but the development is on the whole parallel. See Note below.]

I. 1. A pickaxe; a pick used in digging, breaking up ground, etc., also for picking a millstone. *Obs.* except as *dial.* form of PICK *sb.*[1]

(It seems certain that the OE. examples belong here. In Goetz *Corpus Gloss. Lat.* VI. 17, *Acisculum* is glossed as 'σκάφιον ἤτοι δρὺξ κηπουρική; malliolum structorium; quod habent structores, quasi malleolus est ad cædendos lapides; μυλοκόπον'.)

c **725** *Corpus Gloss.* (O.E.T.) 49 *Acisculum*, piic. *c* **1000** *Ælfric's Voc.* in Wr.-Wülcker 109/4 *Acisculum*, pic. **1303** R. BRUNNE *Handl. Synne* 941 Mattok is a pykeys, Or a pyke, as sum men seys. **13..** *Seuyn Sag.* (W.) 1253 'Tak a pike, To-night thou schalt with me strike'..An hole thai bregen, all with ginne [etc.]. **1756** LLOYD in W. Thompson *R.N. Advoc.* (1757) 51, I have.. desired the Grinder not to pick his Mill so often with the sharp Pikes, or to keep it so rough. **1877** E. LEIGH *Gloss. Dial. Chesh., Pike*, an iron instrument sharp on the one side and like a hammer on the other, used for splitting and breaking coals. **1879** MISS JACKSON *Shropsh. Word-bk.* 323 *Pike*..3. A pick. [E.D.D. has it also from S. Staffordsh.] **1881** RAYMOND *Mining Gloss., Pike.* See *Pick*.

II. 2. a. A sharp point, the pointed tip of anything, a spike; as the pointed metal tip of a staff or of an arrow or spear, the spike in the centre of a buckler: = PICK *sb.*[1] 2.

a **1225** *Leg. Kath.* 1923 Swa þet te pikes & te irnene preones se scharpe & se starke borien þurh & beoren forð feor on þet oðer half. *c* **1275** *XI Pains of Hell* 70 in *O.E. Misc.* 149 A hwel of stele is furþer mo... A þusend spoken beoþ þer-on, And pykes ouer al idon. *c* **1290** *S. Eng. Leg.* I. 205/170 Þis kniȝt heo bounden honden and fet and a-midde þe fuyre him caste, With Irene Ovles and pikes heo to-drowen him wel faste. *c* **1320** *Sir Beues* 3856 Here bordones were imaked wel Wiþ longe pikes of wel gode stel. **1362** LANGL. *P. Pl.* A. IX. 88 Dobest..Bereþ a Busschopes cros, Is hoket atte ende,..to holden hem in good lyf. A pyk is in þe potent to punge adoun þe wikkede [**1393** C. XI. 94 With þe pyk putte adoune *preuaricatores legis*]. *c* **1380** *Sir Ferumb.* 4648 And þe walles were of Marbreston. Wyþ pykes of yre y-set þer-on, Oppon þe crest ful þykke. *c* **1440** *Promp. Parv.* 396/2 Pyke, of a staffe, or oþer lyke, *cuspis, stiga. Ibid.*, Pyke, or tyynde of yryne (or prekyl), *carnica*. **1480** CAXTON *Chron. Eng.* ccxxiii. 220 He fonde in a chambre aboute v honderd of grete staues of fyne oke with longe pykes of yren and of stele. *a* **1548** HALL *Chron., Edw. IV* 197 b, The lord Scales had a gray courser, on whose schaffron was a long and a sharpe pyke of stele. **1565–6** *Roy. Proclam. as to Apparel* 12 Feb., Any buckler with any poynt or pyke aboue two ynches in length. **1598** GRENEWEY *Tacitus' Ann.* IV. xi. (1622) 107 Contrarily the Romaine souldier..thrust them backe with the pikes of their bucklers. **1651** BIGGS *New Disp.* §80 All ice beginning, maketh jagged pikes, after the fashion of a Nettle-leafe. **1825** SCOTT *Talism.* i, The front-stall of the bridle was a steel plate,..having in the midst a short, sharp pike. *Ibid.* vi, In the tilt-yard..spears are tipped with trenchers of wood, instead of steel pikes. *a* **1906** *Mod. Sc.* The pike has come out of the peery (= peg-top). **1976** *New Yorker* 9 Feb. 32/3 Her sleeve catches in the metal pike of the turnstile and Jane picks it out, in the nick of time.

†**b.** A prickle, a thorn; a hedgehog's prickle or spine; = PICK *sb.*[1] 2. Chiefly *Sc. Obs.* or *dial.*

c **1305** *St. Edmund King* 47 in *E.E.P.* (1862) 88 As ful as an illespyl is of pikes al aboute As ful he stikede of arewen wiþ-inne & wiþoute. **1398** TREVISA *Barth. De P.R.* XVIII. lxii, Herenacius is an Irchoun..& his skyn is closid all a boute with pykes and prickis. *c* **1470** HENRYSON *Orpheus & Eurydice* 292 (Bann. MS.), Syne our a mvre, with thornis thik and scherp,..he went, And had nocht bene throw suffrage of his harp, With fell pikis he had bene schorne and schent. **1500–20** DUNBAR *Poems* lxii. 23 [The] Thirsill..Quhois pykis throw me so reuthles ran. **1508** —— *Tua Mariit Wemen* 15 Throw pykis of the plet thorne I presandlie luikit. **1549** *Compl. Scot.* xvii. 148 He vas crounit vitht ane palme of gold, be rason that the palme tre hes schearp broddis and pikis. **1570** LEVINS *Manip.* 122/23 A pike, pricke, *aculeus*. **1572** BOSSEWELL *Armorie* II. 61 So is the little Hiricion with his sharpe pykes almoste the leaste of all other beastes. *a* **1600** MONTGOMERIE *Misc. Poems* (S.T.S.) xl. 46 Sen peircing pyks ar kyndlie with the rose. **1789** ROSS *Helenore* 26 A hail hauf mile she had at least to gang, Thro' birns and pikes [*ed.* 1768 pits] and scrabs, and heather lang.

c. *Turning.* The spike or pin in a lathe upon which one end of the object to be turned is fixed.

1680 MOXON *Mech. Exerc.* x. 180 Upon the points of this Screw and Pike the Centers of the Work are pitcht. *Ibid.* XIII. 220 Having prepared the Work fit for the Lathe..they pitch it between the Pikes.

†**d.** *fig.* A horn of a dilemma: = HORN *sb.* 27.

1548 UDALL, etc. *Erasm. Par. Matt.* xix. 94 They propose a question with two pykes. *Ibid.* xxi. 102 A question with two pikes.

†**e.** An ear-pick; = PICK *sb.*[1] 5. *Obs.*

1570 LEVINS *Manip.* 122/26 A Pike, for the ear, *scalprum*.

3. a. A staff having an iron point or spike, a pikestaff (now *dial.*); †*spec.* a pilgrim's staff (*obs.*): = PICK *sb.*[1] 3.

to tip (a person) ***the pikes***, to give (him) the slip: cf. PICK *sb.*[1] 3, quot. 1673.

c **1205** LAY. 30731 Þa imette he enne pilegrim pic bar an honde [Wace *bordon à pélerin*]. *Ibid.* 30745 Brien..saide þat he wes pelegrim ah pic nefden he nan mid him. *Ibid.* 30848 His pic he nom an honden & helede hine under capen. **13..** *Coer de L.* 611 They were redy for to wende, With pyke and with sclavyn, As palmers were in Paynym. **1362** LANGL. *P. Pl.* A. v. 257 (MS. T) Þat Penitencia his pike [**1377** B. v. 482 pyke] he shulde pulsshe newe. *Ibid.* VI. 26 Sauh I neuere Palmere with pyk [**1377** B. v. 542 pike] ne with scrippe. **1724** J. SHIRLEY *Triumph Wit* (ed. 8) 171 Tho' he tips [*printed* rips] them the Pikes they nig him again. **1869** G. TICKELL *Life Marg. Mary Hallahan* (1870) 165 Mother Margaret could not venture as far as the post-office without the aid of a pike.

b. A pitchfork, a hay-fork: = PICK *sb.*[1] 4 b. Now *dial.*

1410 in Rogers *Agric. & Pr.* III. 546/2, 3 dung pykes. **1472** *Durham Acc. Rolls* (Surtees) 245 Item j Pyke pro feno extrahendo. **1573** TUSSER *Husb.* (1878) 37 A rake for to hale vp the fitchis that lie, A pike for to pike them vp handsom to drie. **1706** PHILLIPS, *Pike*..In Husbandry, a Prong, or Iron-fork. **1766** *Compl. Farmer, Pike*, a name given in some counties to what is generally called a fork, used for carrying straw, &c. **1825** in HONE *Every-day Bk.* I. 854 Pitchforks, or *pikes*, as in Cornwall they are..called. **1870** *Auct. Catal.* [Shropshire] (E.D.D.), Pikes and rakes.

c. In *Salt-making.* (See quot.)

1884 R. HOLLAND *Chesh. Gloss., Pike, s.* salt-making term; a one-pronged instrument (one can hardly call it a fork, seeing it has but one prong) used for lifting and handling lumps of salt.

d. Applied to a tent-pole or its pointed end.

1827 *Perils & Captivity* (Constable's Misc.) 303 It is the women..who lift the pikes of the tents, when their husbands are resolved to move their camp.

III. 4. An extremity tapering to a point; a PEAK.

a. The long point or peak of a shoe, such as was fashionable in 14th–15th c.; a poulaine. *Obs.* exc. *Hist.*

c **1380** WYCLIF *Sel. Wks.* III. 124 Men deformen hor body by hor foule atyre, as pikes of schoone. **1432–50** tr. *Higden, Harl. Contin.* (Rolls) VIII. 497 But mony abusions comme from Boemia into Englonde with this qwene, and specially schoone with longe pykes. **1463–4** *Rolls of Parlt.* V. 505/1 Eny shoes or Boteux, havyng pykes passyng the length of ii ynches. *a* **1548** HALL *Chron., Hen. VIII* 6 b, Bootes with pykes turned vp. **1611** SPEED *Hist. Gt. Brit.* IX. xvii. (1623) 870 The pikes in the Toes were turned vpward and with siluer chaines, or silke laces tied to the knee. [**1723** THORESBY in *Phil. Trans.* XXXII. 345 In Stow's Chronicle, *ad An.* 1465, we read of a Proclamation against the Beaks or Pikes of Shoone, or Boots, that they should not pass two Inches. **1834** PLANCHÉ *Brit. Costume* 202 No one under the estate of a lord was permitted to wear pikes or poleines to his shoes..exceeding two inches in length.]

b. The pointed end, 'beak', or 'horn' of an anvil. *Obs.* or *dial.*

1677 MOXON *Mech. Exerc.* I. 3 A Black Smiths Anvil..is sometimes made with a Pike, or Bickern, or Beak-iron at one end of it. **1680** *Ibid.* x. 179 A strong Iron Pike, but its point is made of tempered Steel. **1688** R. HOLME *Armoury* III. 300/2 *Pike*..that as comes out of one end of [an Anvil]. **1957** [see BICK].

5. *dial.* A narrow pointed piece of land at the side of a field of irregular shape; = GORE *sb.*[2] 1 b, PICK *sb.*[1] 6.

1585 *Rec. Leicester* (1905) III. 217, 4 lands, 23 pikes, lying south upon Knighton Mere. **1724** *MS. Indenture* (co. Derby), Together with all mounds, fences,..pikes, balkes, land ends. **1737** *MS. Indenture, Estate at Rolleston, Stafford.*, Pikes selions or butts of arable land in a field called Crowthorn field. **1847–78** HALLIWELL, *Pikes*, short butts which fill up the irregularity caused by hedges not running parallel. **1898** *N. & Q.* 9th Ser. I. 454/1 Hereabouts [Worcestershire] 'pikes' [of ploughed land] are the 'peaked' bits.

IV. 6. *attrib.* and *Comb.*: † **pike-bolt**, a sharp-pointed bolt; **pike-pole**, *U.S.*, a pole provided with a spike and a hook, used by lumbermen in driving logs, also as a boat-hook; **piketail** *U.S.*, the pintail duck; **pike-wall** *dial.*, a gable-wall; **pike-wise** *adv.*, in peaked or cuneiform formation.

1622 R. HAWKINS *Voy. S. Sea* (1847) 206 Many..have left the use of them and of sundry other preventions as of shere-hookes,..*pike bolts in their wales and divers other engines of antiquitie. *c* **1440** *Promp. Parv.* 397/1 *Pykewalle ..*murus conalis, piramis, vel piramidalis.* **1556–7** in Willis & Clark *Cambridge* (1886) II. 455 The pyke wall in tholde Hall. **1513** in *Three 15th Cent. Chron.* (Camden) 87 The Kyng of Scottes armye was devyded in to fyue batelles,.. part of them were quadrant, some *pykewyse.

[*Note.* The etymology of *pike*, with the related PICK *sb.*[1], PEAK *sb.*[1], and the vbs. PIKE[1], PICK[1], PECK, presents many difficulties. OE. *píc*, ME. *pic*, seem to be the same word as OF. and mod.F. *pic*, corresp. to Prov. *pic*, Sp., Pg. *pico*, all applied to something sharp-pointed, and having a cognate vb., F. *piquer*, Pr., Sp., Pg. *picar*, It. *piccare*, to pierce, prick, sting, etc. The origin of this Romanic family is disputed. Diez referred it to L. *pīc-us* the woodpecker, in reference to the action of the long and powerful beak with which that bird hammers, picks, and pierces the bark of trees. The phonetic difficulty that the *c* of L. *pīc-us* and a derived **pīcā-re* would not remain in the mod. langs., but be lost in F. (*pi*, **pier*), and elsewhere become *g*, has been met by the suggestion that the group, being of echoic origin, retained the *c* or *k* unchanged, or that late L. had, beside *pīc-us*, the popular forms **pīcc-us* and **pīcc-āre* (perh. due to echoic modification), which would phonetically give the modern forms. Celtic origin or influence has also been suggested. Welsh *pīg* anything pointed, pointed end, point, pike, beak, bill, with its cognate vb. *pīgo*, Cornish *pīga* to prick, sting, pick, peck (said of a thorn, a bird, etc.), and a large group of connected words in Welsh, Cornish, and Breton, point to an original *pīk-*, the Brythonic cognate of OIr. *cīch* (Proto-Celtic **qīk-*), found on the OIr. gloss *cich* i. *ger* (i.e. 'sharp') from the *Book of Lecan*, printed by Stokes in *Archiv für Celtische Lexicographie* I. 59 (note on 73). In the Teutonic langs. OE. *pīc* appears to stand alone in the early period. ON. had *pík*, app. as a personal nickname (*Hakon pík*) in 12th c., and as a common noun *pík* a pikestaff *c* 1330; in same sense MSw. had *piik*, and 13th c. Norw. had *píkstafr*; mod.Sw. and Norw. *pīk*, M.Da. *piig*, Da. *pig* pike, point, prickle. The probability appears to be that these were adopted from the same source as Eng. *pike*. See also PICK *v.*[1]]

pike (paɪk), *sb.*[2] *north. Eng.* Also 3, 7 **pik**, 6 **pyke**. [app. either a local application of PIKE *sb.*[1], or of Norse origin: cf. West Norw. dial. *pîk* a pointed mountain, *pîktind* a peaked summit.]

1. A northern English name for a pointed or peaked summit, or a mountain or hill with a pointed summit; entering extensively into the nomenclature of mountains and hills in and around the English Lake district.

The names in *Pike* have their centre in Cumbria and Lancashire-above-the-sands, where are Scawfell Pike, Langdale Pikes, Pike o' Stickle, Causey Pike, Grisedale Pike, Red Pike, White Pike, Wansfell Pike, etc.; they gradually thin off in the surrounding counties, examples being Rivington Pike in mid-Lancashire; Backden Pike, Pinnar Pike, Haw Pike, in Yorkshire; Pontop Pike, West Pike, in Durham; Glanton Pike, East Pike, West Pike, Three Pikes, in Northumberland; Hartshorn Pike, The Pike in Roxburghshire, The Pike in Selkirkshire, etc. It is notable that the *pikes* are localized in the district of England characterized by Norse topographical names, the country of the *becks*, *fells*, *forces*, *ghylls*, *hows*, *riggs*, *scaurs*, *screes*, *thwaites*, and *tarns*, that the name is ancient, as old as sense 2 of PIKE *sb.*[1], and that *pîk* is used in precisely the same way in West Norwegian dialect.

c **1250** *Lanc. Charters* No. 1974 (Brit. Mus. MS. Add. 32107 lf. 280 b), Et sic sequendo dictum diuisum forrestæ et metæ de Rothington se diuidunt vsque ad Winterhold pike et sic sequendo altitudinem del Egges vsque in Romesclogh heued. **1277–90** *Grant by Cecilia widow of Wm. of Rivington* (MSS. of W. H. Lever), Et sic sequendo altam viam ultra Roinpik [= Rivington Pike] vsque Stondandestan. **1322** *Close Roll* 15 Edw. II., memb. 2 *dorso* (P.R.O.), Et sic vsque ad altum de Yowberg et sic vsque le Mikeldor de Yowberg, et exinde vsque le Rede Pike [Wast Water]. *a* **1400–50** *Alexander* 4818 þai labourde vp agayn þe lift an elleuen dais, & quen þai couert to þe crest, þen clerid þe welkyn..þan past þai doun fra þat pike in-to a playn launde. *a* **1552** LELAND *Itin.* (1744) V. 90 But communely the People therabout caullith hit Riven-pike. **1588** in E. Baines *Hist. Lancs.* (1889) III. 229 *note*, The hundreth of Sallford is to paie for the watchinge of [the] Beacon of Rivington Pyke [from 10 July to 30 September]. **1604** *Surv. Debat. Lands, Bound. Eng. & Scot.*, From the head of Blakeup the boundes extendeth to Bell's Rigg, and so to Blakeley Pike. **1664** *Acc. Bk. D. Fleming, Rydal Hall, Westmld.* 26 Sept., It. for walling one day at yᵉ Low-pike. **1673** BLOME *Britanniæ* 132 Amongst which Hills these are of chief note, viz. Furness Fells, Riving Pike, and Pendle Hill. **1738** S. FEARON & J. EYES *Sea Coast Eng. & Wales* 18 Keep away about S.S.E. 'til the Westermost of the two fair Houses at Banks be in a line with Rivington Pike. *Ibid.*, Keep so' til Wharton Chappel comes in a line with Porlock Pike. **1793** WORDSW. *Descript. Sk.* 482 Pikes, of darkness named and fears and storms, Uplift in quiet their illumined forms. **1819** SHELLEY *Peter Bell the Third* I. xii, Then there came down from Langdale Pike A cloud, with lightning, wind, and hail. **1865** BELLEW *Blount Tempest* I. 70 On the East, the moors and pikes of Yorkshire..descend and slope towards the sea. **1872** JENKINSON *Guide Eng. Lakes* (1879) 73 Pike O'Stickle ..looks like a huge petrified haycock. **1888** MRS. H. WARD *R. Elsmere* I. vii, Masses of broken crag rising at the very head of the valley into a fine pike.

b. A cairn or pillar of stones erected on the highest point of a mountain or hill; also, a beacon, tower, or pile on an eminence.

Many of the natural pikes (e.g. Rivington Pike) were beacon hills; hence the name appears to have been sometimes associated with a beacon.

1751 in E. Baines *Hist. Lancs.* (1888) II. 333 [Inscription on a conical pillar on the summit of Hartshead Hill, 8 miles ENE. of Manchester.] This Pike was rebuilt by Publick Contributions, Anno Do. 1751. *a* **1815** in *Pennecuik's Wks.* (1815) 49 *note*, These piles of stones are often termed Cairn, Pike, Currough, Cross, &c. **1856** T. T. WILKINSON in *Lanc. & Chesh. Hist. Soc. Trans.* 4 Dec., Pikelaw [near Burnley, Lancs.] has much the appearance of a large tumulus, but as its name indicates, it has long been used for the purposes of a beacon.

2. A pointed or peaked stack of hay, made up (of a number of hay-cocks) temporarily in the hayfield, until it can be carted to the farm-yard; also, a stack of corn, circular in form, pointed, and of no great size. (*Eng. Dial. Dict.*)

1641 BEST *Farm. Bks.* (Surtees) 37 A sacke is made allwayes after the manner of a longe square, having a ridge like the ridge of an howse; and a pyke, rownde, and sharpe att the toppe. **1796** *Trans. Soc. Arts* XIV. 193 Employing every hand in making it into large cocks (or pikes). **1832** *Scoreby Farm Rep.* 12 in *Libr. Usef. Knowl., Husb.* III, Ten or twelve cocks may be formed into a 'pike', containing about a ton of hay. **1886** *Pall Mall G.* 8 Nov. 3/1 The habit of allowing hay to remain in the fields in 'pikes', as they are called in the north,..is one of the customs of the country.

† **pike** (paɪk), *sb.*[3] *Obs.* Also 6–7 **pick(e**, 7 **pique**: see also PIC[1], PICO. [ad. Sp. *pico* beak, bill, nib, peak, Pg. *pico* summit, top; cf. also mod.F. *pic* in same sense. Distinct from PIKE *sb.*[2], as being of much later introduction, and of general, not local, use, and as having at length passed into *peak*, while the northern Eng. word remains *pike*.]

1. The earlier form of PEAK *sb.*[2] (sense 5), the conical summit of a mountain; hence in the name of certain mountains of conical form. Used first in the name ***Pike*** (***Picke***) ***of Teneriffe***; also in other geographical names, as ***Adam's Pike***, ***Pike of Daman***, etc., in all of which PEAK has now taken its place.

The name *Pike of Teneriffe* appears in Eden 1555 (as *picke*), and was prevalent during 16–17th c.; the modern equivalent PEAK appears in 1634, and prevailed after 1700, though the older *pike* occurs as late as 1776. In French, Thevenot used in 1663 the Spanish form *pico* (see PEAK *sb.*[2] 5, quot. 1687). *Pic* occurs first in 1690 in Furetière, 'mot.. qui se dit en cette phrase, Pic de Teneriffe..ce mot vient de l'espagnol *pico*, qui signifie montagne'; it is not in Richelet 1680, but appears in ed. 1693; it was admitted into the Dict. Acad. in 1740, with the instances 'pic de Teneriffe, pic d'Adam, pic du Midi'. But locally, *pic* was used in the Pyrenees, and is found in Provençal in 14th c.

1555 EDEN *Decades* 351 Teneriffa is a hygh lande and a greate hyghe picke like a suger lofe... By reason of that picke, it may be knowen aboue all other Ilandes. **1613** W. BROWNE *Brit. Past.* II. v, That sky-scaling Pike of Tenerife. **1622** R. HAWKINS *Voy. S. Sea* (Hakl. Soc.) xii, The pike of Tenerifa..is the highest land..that I haue seene... Going up to the pike, the cold is so great that it is insufferable. **1652** BENLOWES *Theoph.* I. viii, Higher than Ten'riff's Pique he flies. **1660** BOYLE *New Exp. Phys.-Mech., Digress.* 358 The top of the Pike of Tenariff. **1697** DAMPIER *Voy. round World* (1699) 42, I am of opinion that it is higher than the Pike of Tenariff. **1715** J. EDENS in *Phil. Trans.* XXIX. 317 We saw the Pike with a white Cloud covering the Top of it like a Cap. *c* **1765** T. FLLOYD *Tartar. T.* (1785) 14 A mountain.. was called Adam's Pike. **1776** R. TWISS *Tour Irel.* 118 The Pike of Teneriffe.

b. By extension, Any mountain peak; *esp.* a volcanic cone.

Quot. *a* 1697 is placed here, as not belonging to PIKE *sb.*[2] (*Abergavenny's Pike* and *Cam's Pike* (in *Eng. Dial. Dict.*) are not local names, the former being called *the Sugar Loaf* and the latter *Cam Peak* or locally *Cam Pick*.)

1604 E. G[RIMSTONE] tr. *D'Acosta's Hist. Indies* III. xxiv. 193 Ordinarily these Volcans be rockes or pikes of most high mountaines. **1676** F. VERNON in *Phil. Trans.* XI. 581 The Pique of Parnassus. **1692** RAY *Disc.* II. ii. (1732) 104 The highest Pikes and Summits of those Mountains. *a* **1697** AUBREY *Wilts.* (Roy. Soc. MS.) 71 (Halliw.) Not far from Warminster is Clay-hill, and Coprip..; they are pikes or vulcanos. **1775** R. CHANDLER *Trav. Asia M.* (1825) I. 29 The pikes both of Athos and of Tenedos suggest the idea that their mountains have burned. **1796** MORSE *Amer. Geog.* II. 311 Snow..of a dazzling whiteness..on the highest pikes.

2. In the nautical phrase ***on*** (***the***) ***pike***, in a vertical position, vertically, straight up and down: see the later form APEAK, and PEAK *v.*[3]

[French has also *à pic* in the same sense, cited before 1600, and it is a question in which language the phrase arose. But it is probable that in the phrases *on the pike*, *on pike*, *a-pike*, later *a-peak*, we have the same word as in sense 1, with its later form PEAK *sb.*[2] 5, the connexion between *pike* = summit, and *a-pike*, being analogous to that between *vertex* and *vertical*, *-ally*.]

1594 GREENE & LODGE *Looking-glass* Wks. (Rtldg.) 129/2 Our yards across, our anchors on the pike, What, shall we hence, and take this merry gale? **1628** LE GRYS tr. *Barclay's Argenis* 306 Setting their Oares on pike expected what those which were coming would command.

pike (paɪk), *sb.*[4] Also 4 **pik**, 4–5 **pyk**, 5–8 **pyke**, 6 **pycke**, (7 **pick**). [app. short for *pike-fish*, from PIKE *sb.*[1], in reference to its pointed beak; cf. GED[1], and F. *brochet* pike (fish), f. *broche* a spit.]

1. A large, extremely voracious, freshwater fish of the northern temperate zone, *Esox lucius*, with a long slender snout; a jack, luce; among anglers the name is sometimes restricted to a specimen of a particular age or size (see quot. 1840–70, and PICKEREL[1] quot. 1587). Hence, by extension, any fish of the genus *Esox* or of the family *Esocidæ*.

Among N. American species are the federation pike, *Esox americanus*, great pike, *E. nobilior*, hump-backed pike, *E. cypho*.

1314 in *Wardr. Acc. Edw. II* 21/12 Dars roches et pik. **1337–8** *Durham Acc. Rolls* (Surtees) 33, j pyk. **1347–8** *Ibid.* 546 Willelmo..piscando in Mordon Kerr pro pikes capiend. xx*d.* *c* **1430** *Two Cookery-bks.* 10 On a fyssday take Pyke or Elys, Codlyng or Haddok. *c* **1440** *Promp. Parv.* 396/1 Pyke, fysche, *dentrix*,..*lucius*,..*lupus*. **1532** MORE *Confut. Tindale* Wks. 395/2 As lollardes dyd of late, that put a pygge into yᵉ water on good fryday, & sayd goe in pygge, and come oute pyke. **1655** MOUFET & BENNET *Health's Impr.* (1746) 279 Pikes or River-wolves are greatly commended by Gesner and divers learned Authors for a wholesome Meat. **1806** *Gazetteer Scot.* (ed. 2) 334/2 It [Water of Leith] abounds with trout, and contains a few pike. **1807** CRABBE *Par. Reg.* III. 100 What ponds he empty'd and what pikes he sold. **1840–70** BLAINE *Encycl. Rur. Sports* 1101 When the fish does not exceed 4 lbs. or 5 lbs. in weight it is called in England 'a jack', and above that weight 'a pike'. **1855** LONGF. *Hiaw.* v. 49 He..Saw the pike, the Maskenozha. **1870** MORRIS *Earthly Par.* I. I. 167 And watch the long pike basking lie Outside the shadow of the weed.

2. Applied in U.S. and the colonies to various fishes resembling, in their slender body or sharp snout, the pikes proper: e.g. two cyprinoid fishes, *Ptychochilus lucius* and *Gila grandis*, of California, and species of *Sphyræna* of Australia.

1871 KINGSLEY *At Last* vi, These barracoutas—Sphyrænas as the learned, or 'pike' as the sailors, call them, though they are no kin to our pike at home. **1880** *Rep. Fish. N.S. Wales* 21 (Fish. Exhib. Publ.), *Sphyræna novæ hollandiæ* and *obtusata* and *Neosphyræna multiradiata*, all of them named, from the elongate muzzle and strong teeth, 'pike', though in no way related to the well-known European fish of that name.

b. With distinctive adjuncts:

bald p., a ganoid fish of N. America, *Amia calva*; **blue, grey, green, yellow p.**, names of a species of the pike-perch, *Stizostedion vitreum*; **bony p.**, a gar-fish of the family *Lepidosteidæ*; **Brazilian p.**, a fish of the genus *Hemirhamphus* (Pennant); **glass-eyed, goggle-eyed, wall-eyed p.**, the pike-perch, *Stizostedion americanum* (or *S. vitreum*); **ground-p.**, **mud-p.**, **sand-p.**, the sauger (*S. canadense*); **sand-p.**, also the lizard-fish, *Synodus fœtens*; **sea p.**, the common gar-fish or gar-pike, *Belone vulgaris*: see also GAR-PIKE.

1810 P. NEILL *List of Fishes* 16, *Esox Lucius*, Sea-pike; Gar-pike. **1847** ANSTED *Anc. World* iv. 61 The sturgeon, the *Siluridæ* or Cat-fish, the bony pike of the North American Lakes.

3. *attrib.* and *Comb.*, as ***pike-fish***, ***-fisher***, ***-fishing***, ***-haunt***, ***-leister***, ***-monger***, ***-pool***, ***-slayer***, ***-trap***, ***-trolling***; ***pike-eyed***, ***-grey***, ***-snouted*** adjs.; † **pike-monger**, a dealer in pike and other freshwater fish; **pike-perch**, a percoid fish of the genus *Stizostedion*, with jaws like those of a pike, species of which are found in European and N. American rivers; esp. *S. americanum* and *S. vitreum*; **pike-sucker**, a fish of the family *Gobiesocidæ*, characterized by a long snout like that of a pike and a ventral sucker like that of a goby; **pike-whale** = *piked whale*: see PIKED *a.*[1] 2 b.

1897 RHOSCOMYL *White Rose Arno* 60 By getting out here I shall avoid that *pike-eyed porter at the entrance. **1494** *Nottingham Rec.* III. 280 In *pykeffyssh xs. ijd.* **1633** *Naworth Househ. Bks.* (Surtees) 306, 5 pick fishes, xvᵈ. **1871** *Routledge's Ev. Boy's Ann.* Aug. 478 With this tackle the *pike-fisher can go forth. **1862** CARLYLE *Fredk. Gt.* VIII. vi. (1872) III. 57 He..puts-off the *pike-gray coat. **1895** SUFFLING *Land of Broads* 61 The reaches about Bramerton are noted *pike haunts. **1464** *Mann. & Househ. Exp.* 252 Payd for a pyke and an ele that my mastyr owt the *pykemonger before, xx*d.* *c* **1610** in Gutch *Coll. Cur.* II. 15 Every Pikemonger, that bringeth fresh fish to this Fair to sell, as Pike, Tench, Roche, Perch, Eel. **1854** BADHAM *Halieut.* 114 The German sandre, *pike perch, one of the best flavored of the family. **1883** *Fisheries Exhib. Catal.* (ed. 4) 104 Stuffed Specimen of a 'Pike-Perch'..from the Danube. **1884** MATHER in *Cent. Mag.* Apr. 908/1 The pike-perch becomes a 'salmon' in the Susquehanna, Ohio, and Mississippi rivers. **1884** HARRIS in *Littell's Living Age* CLXI. 90 Your..*pike-snouted Chinese porker. **1883** *Fisheries Exhib. Catal.* 366 *Pike Trap with funnel-shaped inlet. *Ibid.* 375 The *Pike Whale..from the coast of Bohuslän.

pike (paɪk), *sb.*[5] Also 6 **pique**, **pyke**; and see PICK *sb.*[2] [Found first in 16th c.: a. F. *pique* sb. fem. (in Flanders 1376, Hatz.-Darm.), a military term = Pr. *piqua*, Sp., Pg. *pica*, It. *picca* (with doubled *c*); from the same root as F. *piquer* to pierce, puncture, and F. *pic*, PIKE *sb.*[1] (Ger. *Pike*, Du. *piek*, Da. and Sw. *pik*, are all from F. *pique*.)]

1. A weapon consisting of a long wooden shaft with a pointed head of iron or steel; formerly the chief weapon of a large part of the infantry; in the 18th c. superseded by the bayonet. † (*to sell*) ***under the pike*** (L. *sub hasta*), by auction; cf. SPEAR. ***to trail a pike***: see TRAIL *v.*

In later times the simple form of the pike was sometimes modified, as by the addition of a lateral hook; and the name has been also loosely applied to forms of the halberd and to the half-pike or spontoon, formerly carried by infantry officers.

c **1511** *1st Eng. Bk. Amer.* (Arb.) Introd. 28/1 There wepyns is lange pykes & stones. **1579–80** NORTH *Plutarch* (1676) 96 He stood at pike against the greatest and mightiest persons that bare the sway and government. **1590** SIR J. SMYTH *Disc. Weapons* 12 b, With piques, and half piques, swords and targets. **1594** KYD *Cornelia* v. 444 See the wealth that Pompey gain'd in warre, Sold at a pike. **1598** BARRET *Theor. Warres* I. i. 4 For the plaine field, neither.. Halbard, nor Partizan comparable to the Pike. **1599** SHAKS. *Hen. V*, IV. i. 40 Trayl'st thou the puissant Pyke? **1626** GOUGE *Serm. Dignity Chivalry* §11 Such men are more fit.. to lift a pitchforke then to tosse a pike. **1706** PHILLIPS, *Pike*,.. a Weapon for a Foot-Soldier, from 14 to 16 Foot long, arm'd at the end with a sharp Iron-spear. **1727–41** CHAMBERS *Cycl.* s.v., The pike continues the weapon of foot-officers, who fight pike in hand, salute with the pike. **1832** HT. MARTINEAU *Ireland* v. 85 The searchers reappeared, bringing with them a dozen pikes, a blunderbuss, and three braces of pistols. **1849** MACAULAY *Hist. Eng.* v. I. 610 He had been seen on foot, pike in hand, encouraging his infantry by voice and by example.

†**2.** Phrases. **a.** ***to pass*** (***pass through***) ***the pikes*** [= F. *passer par les piques*, *passer les piques*, It. *passar per le picche*], in quot. 1654 *lit.* to run the gauntlet; but usually *fig.* to pass through difficulties or dangers, *esp.* to come through successfully; to run the gauntlet *of*. Similarly ***to run through***, (***to be***) ***past, the pikes***, etc. *Obs.*

1555 BRADFORD in Coverdale *Lett. Mart.* (1564) 289 Of al temptations this is the greatest, that god hath forgotten or will not helpe vs throughe the pykes, as they say. **1573** G. HARVEY *Letter-bk.* (Camden) 20 So mutch the harder it is like to go with me when.. I must run thorouh the pikes. **1579** LYLY *Euphues* (Arb.) 39 Thou arte heere amiddest the pykes betweene Scylla and Carybdis. **1621** SANDERSON *Serm.* I. 24 Neither Johns mourning, nor Christs piping can pass the pikes: but the one hath a devil, the other is a glutton and a wine-bibber. **1654** EARL MONM. tr. *Bentivoglio's Warrs Flanders* 121 It [the squadron].. making those who according to their laws have deserved it, sometimes pass the pikes [*passar per le picche*], and sometimes be shot to death. **1688** R. HOLME *Armoury* III. xix. (Roxb.) 218/2 To run the pikes (of some termed running the gauntlett), that is to be slashed and whipt throwe two files of men, 60 or 100 deepe. **1712** M. HENRY *Life P. Henry* Wks. 1857 II. 720/1 None of them [had] past the pikes of that perilous distemper. **1785** COWPER *Let. to Lady Hesketh* 30 Nov., Wks. 1836 V. 187 So far, therefore, I have passed the pikes. The Monthly Critics have not yet noticed me.

†**b.** ***to run*** (***push, cast oneself***, etc.) ***upon the pikes***: (*fig.*) to expose oneself to peril, rush to destruction. *Obs.*

a **1555** PHILPOT *Exam. & Writ.* (Parker Soc.) 16 But now I can not shew you my mind, but I must run upon the pikes, in danger of my life therefor. **1576** FLEMING *Panopl. Epist.* 390 Of a couragious harted man, of his owne accorde, to pushe vpon the pykes of death. **1611** BIBLE *Transl. Pref.* 2 He casteth himselfe headlong vpon pikes, to be gored by euery sharp tongue. **1671** CROWNE *Juliana* III. 23 For this I .. run on the pikes of my great Father's anger.

†**c.** ***push of pike***, close combat, fighting at close quarters; also *fig. Obs.*

1596 NASHE *Saffron-Walden* Wks. (Grosart) III. 154 To trie it out at the push of the pike. **1598** BARRET *Theor. Warres* 167 Nor so easie to come to the push of the pike, as to pen out a Lawing plea. [**1682** BUNYAN *Holy War* 54 Half afraid that when they and we shall come to push a pike, I shall find you want courage to stand it out any longer.] **1699** in Somers *Tracts* Ser. IV. (1751) III. 157 *By that Time the Blue Regiment was got within Push of Pike. **1707** [N. WARD] *Hudibras Rediv.* II. VII. VII. 10 But when at Push a Pike we play With Beauty, who shall win the Day? **1852** THACKERAY *Esmond* II. xii. The French battalions never waiting to exchange push of pike or bayonet with ours.

†**3.** *transf.* = PIKEMAN[1]. *Obs.*

1557 Q. MARY in *Buccleuch MSS.* (Hist. MSS. Comm.) I. 222 One fourth parte to be argabusiers or archers, one oother fourth parte pikes, and the rest billes. **1590** SIR J. SMYTH *Disc. Weapons* 13 b, Backed with some squadrons of Piques. **1633** T. STAFFORD *Pac. Hib.* II. xv. (1821) 381 Sent some three-score Shott and Pike to the foot of the hill. *a* **1649** DRUMM. OF HAWTH. *Hist. Jas. V*, Wks. (1711) 91 The French could not spare so many men.. but they gave him three thousand pikes, and one thousand launces.

4. *attrib.* and *Comb.*, as ***pike-handle***, ***-length***, ***-point***; **pike-hammer** = *hammer-pike*: see HAMMER *sb.* 7. See also PIKE-HEAD, PIKEMAN[1], etc.

1585–6 EARL LEYCESTER *Corr.* (Camden) 428 First clime the brech, a pike-length before and aboue anie person that followed him. **1799** *Hull Advertiser* 23 Feb. 3/1 One fine young wood.. had been cut down for pike-handles. **1834** T. SINGLETON in J. Raine *Mem. J. Hodgson* (1858) II. 350 Before this parish had a hearse.. the bodies of deceased parishioners were carried to the grave on poles resting on men's shoulders; these poles were the perquisite of the rector, and were called 'pikehandles', a custom rising rather from the nature of his residence in a fortalice in an unquiet country than from any ecclesiastical claim. **1891** ATKINSON *Last Giant Killers* 128 That some among those.. pike-points might penetrate between his rings.

pike, *sb.*[6] *dial.* or *local colloq.* and *U.S.* [Short for TURNPIKE: first prob. in combinations: see 3.]

1. a. A bar or gate on a road at which toll is collected; a toll-bar or toll-gate.

1837 DICKENS *Pickw.* xxii. *Ibid.* lvi, I dewote the remainder of my days to a pike. **1840** HALIBURTON *Clockm.* Ser. III. xi. 145 S'pose any gentleman that keeps a pike was to give you a bad shillin' in change. **1896** *Longm. Mag.* Nov. 66 The man at the pike.. ran to open the gate.

b. *transf.* The toll paid at a turnpike-gate.

1837 DICKENS *Pickw.* lii, She [Mrs. Weller] paid the last pike [*i.e.* died] at twenty minutes afore six o'clock yesterday evenin. **1852** R. S. SURTEES *Sponge's Sp. Tour* lvii. 323 He wouldn't haggle about the pikes. **1894** BLACKMORE *Perlycross* 330 Oh, you have paid the pike for me.

2. a. A turnpike road, 'turnpike', highway. Also *fig.* Freq. in phr. (N. Amer. colloq.) ***to come down the pike***: to appear on the scene; to come to notice. ***to hit the pike***: see HIT *v.* 11 a.

1812 M. EDGEWORTH *Absentee* in *Tales Fashionable Life* VI. xvi. 377 Keep the *pike* till you come to the turn at Rotherford, and then you strike off into the by-road to the left. **1852** MRS. STOWE *Uncle Tom's C.* vii, The road.. had formerly been a thoroughfare to the river, but abandoned for many years after the laying of the new pike. **1897** *Outing* (U.S.) XXX. 385/1 There were ruts and gulleys in it.., and yet they called it a pike and collected toll. **1899** B. TARKINGTON *Gentleman from Indiana* iv. 44 The roans setting a sharp pace as they turned eastward on the pike toward home and supper. **1903** [see FLOSSY *a.*]. **1904** [see HIT *v.* 11 a]. **1907** 'E. C. HALL' *Aunt Jane of Kentucky* v. 107 Horseback riders had been pouring into town over the smooth, graveled pike. **1910** W. M. RAINE *Bucky O'Connor* 73 Cut loose and hit the pike for yourself. **1912** [see *duck soup* s.v. DUCK *sb.*[1] 12]. **1926** *Flynn's* 16 Jan. 640/2, I also got cases on a couple of flivvers for a getaway, as we were about fourteen kilos from the main pike. **1934** E. LINKLATER *Magnus Merriman* 82 Then I hit the pike for home. **1949** *Sun* (Baltimore) 12 Oct. 12/1 Unfortunately, the State cannot control roadside development on the sections of the pike completed thus far. **1956** E. O'CONNOR *Last Hurrah* v. 101 Your uncle's the ablest politician to come down the pike in these parts in the last fifty years. **1963** [see *defenceman, defenseman* s.v. DEFENCE *sb.* 9]. **1966** R. S. RUDNER *Philos. Social Sci.* 2 'Normative' itself is not the clearest term to come to us down the philosophical pike. **1968** *Down Beat* 7 Mar. 19/2 Jack thought that Jimmy was just about the greatest 'bone that had ever come down the pike, and Jimmy felt the same way about Jack, putting him above Miff Mole, who also was a tremendous trombone on that scene. **1970** *New Yorker* 28 Feb. 41/1 A big truck went by way up on the pike. **1974** *Anderson* (S. Carolina) *Independent* 24 Apr. 2A/1 The plan is 'halfway down the pike' but much more effort is needed to make its redevelopment a reality. **1976** *New Yorker* 26 Apr. 59/3 You could see how tired she was after a few hours of 'being presentable to every Tom, Dick, and Harry who comes down the pike'.

b. A railway line or system (real or model). *U.S.*

1940 *Railroad Mag.* XXVII. VI. 69/1 Lake Erie & International.. recently highballed its first Limited around the newly completed circuit of main line. The pike boasts one Diesel-electric and one steam loco.., and its rolling stock is steadily growing. *Ibid.*, Metropolitan Society of Model Engineers... tackled three layouts at one time. The first, a small HO pike was recently presented to the Union Station. **1945** F. H. HUBBARD *Railroad Avenue* ii. 9 They knew he [*sc.* Casey Jones] never dawdled at coal chutes, water cranes, or cinder-pit tracks or wasted time along the pike. **1945** *Railroad Mag.* XXXVII. II. 13 The financing of this little pike was an epic in itself... People along the route were so eager to see the rails laid that they donated labor.

3. *Comb.*, as ***pike-keeper***, ***-road***. Also PIKEMAN[3].

1827 HONE *Every-day Bk.* II. 1372 Sellers of cattle.., with the *pike* tickets in their hats. **1837** DICKENS *Pickw.* xxii, 'What do you mean by a pike-keeper?' inquired Mr. Peter Magnus. 'The old 'un means a turnpike keeper, gen'lm'n', observed Mr. Weller, in explanation. **1838** 'J. PUNKIN' *Downfall of Freemasonry* II. 115 This threw everything into commotion, and as the teamsters say of a drove of cattle on a dirty pike road, 'kicked up a dust'. **1897** *Outing* (U.S.) XXX. 132/2 We found greater comfort in the well-kept pike-road, with ridable grades, and lined in places with pleasant shade trees.

pike, *sb.*[7], obs. variant of PIQUE, grudge.

pike, *sb.*[8], obs. form of PITCH *sb.*[1]

pike, *sb.*[9], variant of PIC[2], measure of cloth.

Pike (paɪk), *sb.*[10] *N. Amer. dial.* [f. *Pike* County, Missouri, whence the first of these persons are said to have come to California.] Term of contempt on the Pacific coast for a person of no means or of migratory habits; a poor white; a thief. Cf. PIKER[4]. Also as *adj.*

1854 G. H. DERBY in *Pioneer* (San Francisco) June 379 A tall yellow-haired, sun-burned Pike, in the butternut-colored hat, coat and so forths 'of the period'. **1860** C. W. WILSON *Mapping Frontier* (1970) II. 126 There are about 350 inhabitants, miners, gamblers, sharpers, Jews, Pikes, Yankees, loafers & *hoc genus omne*. **1863** *Harper's Mag.* June 25/2 Society in San José is decidedly 'Pike' in its character. **1872** C. NORDHOFF *California* xi. 138 The true Pike, however, in the Californian sense of the word, is the wandering, gipsy-like southern poor white. **1928** R. W. RITCHIE *Hell Roarin' Forty-Niners* xv. 234 This Pike had an imagination and a devilishly sly humor which would qualify him to-day for one of our highly specialized lines of salesmanship. **1946** *St. Louis* (Missouri) *Globe-Democrat* 17 Nov. E 2/6 The term 'Pike' or 'piker', in the sense of a worthless, lazy, good-for-nothing person arose first in California in the days of the Forty-Niners.

pike (paɪk), *sb.*[11] [Origin obscure.] A position of the body in diving (see quot. 1928); cf. JACK-KNIFE *sb.* 3. Also, a similar body position in gymnastics. Also *attrib.*

1928 *Daily Express* 13 July 4/4 For a pike dive spring up as for a header, then bend sharply at the waist and touch the toes without bending knees or ankles, then straighten again and enter head first. **1931** *Morning Post* 21 Aug. 14/5 The pike reverse is a combination of the front pike and reverse. **1956** KUNZLE & THOMAS *Freestanding* v. 60 Aim for a rhythmic drop and beat without any intermediate pause, but make sure that the pike is a full one. **1964** *Trampolining* ('Know the Game' Ser.) 11/2 Piked straddle jumping. Similar to the Pike Jump. **1974** *Rules of Game* 203 In pike dives with twist, the twist must follow the pike.

†**pike**, *a. Obs.* [Origin and meaning obscure: ? related to F. *piqué* turned sour (of wine), *piquant* pungent, spiced (of sauce, etc.).] (?) Hot, biting, seasoned, spiced: esp. in ***pike sauce***, also *fig.* sarcasm, pungent wit.

1519 HORMAN *Vulg.* 160 Let us haue chekyns in pyke sauce [*in oxigaro*]. **1589** *Pappe w. Hatchet* E b, I but he hath sillogismes in pike sauce, and arguments that haue been these twentie yeres in pickle. **1593** G. HARVEY *Pierce's Super.* Wks. (Grosart) II. 228 Now the fiercest Gunpouder, and the rankest pike sawce, are the brauest figures of Rhetorique *in esse*. **1727** BRADLEY *Fam. Dict.* s.v. *Egg*, Bread 'em [eggs] with Crums.. cover 'em with a Pike-hash and some scraped Cheese, and bring them to a fine Colour.

pike, *v.*[1] Collateral form of PICK *v.*[1] (q.v. for examples), still in dialectal use in various senses. To this app. belongs the obs. expression ***to pike*** or ***pick a bow***, the exact meaning of which is uncertain: ? to trim: = PICK *v.*[1] 4 (or ? to point; cf. PIKE *v.*[2]).

1463 *Mann. & Househ. Exp.* (Roxb.) 235 Item, payd for pesynge off bowys and ovyr-drawynge off bowis, and ffor pykynge off bowys, xxj.*d.* **1545** ASCHAM *Toxoph.* (Arb.) 116 In dressing and pikyng it [the stave] vp for a bow. *Ibid.* 120 For thys purpose must your bowe be well trymmed and piked of a conning man that it may come rounde in trew compasse euery where. *Ibid.* 120–1 Pike the places about the pinches, to make them somewhat weker, and as well commynge as where it pinched, and so the pinches shall dye. **1579** in W. H. Turner *Select. Rec. Oxford* (1880) 403 Hit ys also agreed.. that Nicholas Gosson [Bowmaker] shall frome henceforth be free of this Cytie, ffor the wch he shall.. [*inter alia*] newe scoure and fether all suche arrowes as the twone howsse nowe hathe, and newe pycke all theire bowes wch have nede to be done.

pike (paɪk), *v.*[2] Now *rare*. Also 5–6 pyke, 6 pycke, 6–7 pick. [f. PIKE *sb.*[1] 2.] *trans.* To furnish with a pike, spike, or (iron) point.

1387 TREVISA *Higden* (Rolls) IV. 45 þere þe Affres closed hym in a streiȝt tree þat was þicke pikede wiþ ynne wiþ longe and scharpe nayles. *c* **1440** *Promp. Parv.* 397/2 Pykynge, of a staffe, or oþer lyke *cuspidacio*. **1530** PALSGR. 657/1, I pycke a staff with pykes of yron, *je enquantelle*. **1611** COTGR. s.v. *Enquantellé, Baston bien enquantellé de fer*, a staffe well piked, or well grained, with yron.

pike, *v.*[3] Also 5–6 pyke, 6 picke, pycke. [Orig. refl. *to pike oneself*, perh. = to furnish oneself with a pike or pilgrim's staff (cf. *to cut one's stick*): see PIKE *sb.*[1] 3. Cf. Old Da. *pikke*, Da. *pigge af* to hasten off, Sw. dial. *pikka åstad* to make off. Another conjectural derivation is from F. *piquer* to spur.]

†**1.** *refl.* To make off with oneself, go away quickly, be off. Also with *away*. *Obs.*

c **1420** LYDG. *Assembly of Gods* 1348 Then Reson hym commaundyd pyke hym thens lyghtly. **1470–85** MALORY *Arthur* IX. xliv. 411 And thenne anone that damoysel pyked her away pryuely. *a* **1530** *Parl. Byrdes* 254 in Hazl. *E.P.P.* III. 180 When his fethers are pluked he may him go pike. **1530** PALSGR. 656/2, I pycke me forth out of a place, or I pycke me hence, *je me tyre auant*.. Come of, pycke you hence and your heles hytherwarde. *Ibid.* 770/2 Walke, pyke you hence, *tire avant*. **1535** COVERDALE *2 Sam.* xix. 3 A people that is put to shame, pycketh them selues awaye. *a* **1553** UDALL *Royster D.* IV. iii. (Arb.) 64 Auaunt lozell, picke thee hence. **1562** J. HEYWOOD *Prov. & Epigr.* (1867) 111 Into what place so euer H. may pike him, Where euer thou finde ache, thou shalt not like him. *c* **1570** *Ane Ballat of Matrymonie* 71 in Laing *Pop. Poet. Scot.* II. 77 He bad them then go pyke them home.

2. *intr.* To depart; to proceed or go; *fig.* to die. Also ***to pike it***, and with adverbs. Now *slang* or *colloq.*

1526 SKELTON *Magnyf.* 957, I bade hym pyke out of the gate. **15..** *Jack Juggler* (Roxb.) 16 Pike and walke, a knaue, here a waye is no passage. **1697** DAMPIER *Voy. round World* (1699) 526 When.. forced to lye down, they made their Wills, and piked off in 2 or 3 Days. *a* **1700** B. E. *Dict. Cant. Crew*, *Pike*, to run away, flee, quit.. the Place; also to Die. **1724** SHIRLEY *Triumph Wit* (ed. 8) 154 We file off with his Cole, as he pikes along the Street. **1753** [see LUMBER *sb.*[2] 3]. *c* **1789** PARKER *Sandman's Wedding* in Farmer *Musa Pedestris* (1896) 65 Into a booze-ken they pike it. *a* **1825** FORBY *Voc. E. Anglia*, *Pike off!* begone! **1846** *Swell's Night Guide* 127/2 *Pike off*, run away. **1864** 'E. KIRKE' *Down in Tennessee* xiii. 162, I piked off for the ruin. **1886** *Outing* IX. 49/2 Tell ye what, jist climb onto my pony, an' we'll pike fer the spring. **1893** H. FREDERIC *Copperhead* (1894) 191 It looked kind o' curious to me, your pikin off like that. **1900** ADE *More Fables* (1902) 106 When all the Smart Set get ready to pike away for the Heated Term.. she would remain at Home. **1902** H. L. WILSON *Spenders* iv. 44 Do me a last favour before you pike off East. **1904** S. E. WHITE *Silent Places* vi. 50 'We'd better pike out, if we don't want to get back with th' squaws,' suggested Dick. **1909** R. A. WASON

Happy Hawkins xvii. 207, I piked on over to Danders thinkin' I'd get on a train an' go somewhere. **1924** P. MARKS *Plastic Age* 18 Say, I've got to pike along; I've got a date with my faculty adviser. **1927** H. CRANE *Let.* 4 July (1965) 303 My old jack tar friend.. was back from his long trip.. so I just piked in and saw him.

3. *intr.* To shirk; to hold back; to back *out*; (see also quot. 1889).

1889 FARMER *Americanisms* 420/1 *To pike* (Cant), to play cautiously and for small amounts, never advancing the value of the stake... Those who gamble in this fashion are called *pikers*. **1954** A. FULLERTON *Bury Past* I. iii. 47 Queer fellow —he worked like hell at the office stuff, the routine, the paper-work, and then suddenly when it came to the push, he'd pike, like he'd done tonight. **1959** *Numbers* Feb. 13/1 'No dogs', said Mr Reginald. 'You wouldn't be piking, would you?' Sonny murmured. **1969** *Southerly* XXIX. 287 Ann's heart began to thump with her secret fear. She waited for someone to veto the idea, not daring herself. But no one did. She could not 'pike' out.

†**pike**, *v.*^{4} *Obs. rare.* App. ad. F. *piquer*, in phrase *to pike on the wind* = F. *piquer au vent*, to sail close to the wind, to hug the wind.

1584 JAMES MELVILL *Autobiog. & Diary* (Wodrow Soc. 1842) 169 Finding us contrare our course.. he cust about and pykit on the wind, halding bathe the helme and scheit.

b. *to pike up*: (*trans.*), ? to sail close to.

1513 DOUGLAS *Æneis* III. v. 18 And wp we pike the coist of Epirus, And landit thair at port Chaonyus. *Ibid.* x. 99 The dangerus schaldis and coist vp pykit we.

pike (paɪk), *v.*^{5} [f. PIKE *sb.*^{5}] *trans.* To thrust through or kill with a pike.

1798 *Hull Advertiser* 22 Sept. 4/2 Many prisoners were taken out.. and being carried to the camp were piked. The manner of piking was by two of the rebels pushing their pikes into the front of the victim. **1803** WELLINGTON *Let.* in Gurw. *Desp.* II. 327, I lost two horses, one shot and the other piked. **1874** FROUDE *English in Irel.* III. x. i. 433 The day after the battle of New Ross a batch of [Protestant] prisoners was carried out from Wexford Gaol to Vinegar Hill, and piked in front of the windmill.

fig. **1866** FITZ-PATRICK *Sham Sqr.* 243 Giffard sought to stab with his pen, and pike with his tongue every friend to national progress.

pike, *v.*^{6} [f. PIKE *sb.*^{1}] *trans.* To lift with a pike.

1850 SCORESBY *Cheever's Whalem. Adv.* xii. 162 Others piking the pieces from one tub to another.

pike, *v.*^{7} *dial.* [f. PIKE *sb.*^{2} 2.] *trans.* To heap or pile up (hay) into pikes.

1844 STEPHENS *Bk. Farm* III. 970 The reason that hay should be piked if stacked all in one day. **1896** P. A. GRAHAM *Red Scaur* v. 80 Tumbling among the cocks when hay was being 'piked'. **1896** *Longm. Mag.* Oct. 575 Come, let's be off; they'll be done piking directly.

pike (paɪk), *v.*^{8} *Diving* and *Gymnastics.* [f. PIKE *sb.*^{11}] **a.** *intr.* To adopt a pike position. **b.** *trans.* To move (a part of the body) as for adopting a pike position. Cf. PIKED *a.*^{2}

1956 KUNZLE & THOMAS *Freestanding* iii. 36 When falling backwards with straight legs, first pike, then drop backwards. *Ibid.* 41 Roll over one shoulder with a half turn, tucking in the head and piking at the hips. **1964** G. C. KUNZLE *Parallel Bars* ii. 45 Pike the hips sharply.. and press off the bar strongly with the arms.

pike, obs. form of PEEK *v.*^{1}, to pry; PEAK *v.*^{3}, to top a yard, etc.

piked (ˈpaɪkɪd, paɪkt), *a.*^{1} Also 4–6 **pyked**, 5 **pykyd, -id**, 6 *Sc.* **pykit, pikit**: see also PICKED *a.* [f. PIKE *sb.*^{1} or *v.*^{2} + -ED.]

1. Furnished with a pike, spike, or sharp point; fashioned with a sharp point (or points); sharp-pointed; = PICKED *a.* 1.

c **1330** R. BRUNNE *Chron.* (1810) 328 With piked staues grete, beten salle he be. **13..** *Gaw. & Gr. Knt.* 769 A park al aboute, With a pyked palays, pyned ful þik. *c* **1447** in *Jarrow & Wearm.* (Surtees) 241 He and his fellows.. wt lang pykid staves and lang dagers mad a asawtte to ye said kepper. **1513** DOUGLAS *Æneis* VII. xiii. 62 Casting dartis or macis wyth pykyt heidis. **1561** DAUS tr. *Bullinger on Apoc.* (1573) 83 b, He put me as a piked Arrow, he hydde mee in hys quever. **1609** HOLLAND *Amm. Marcell.* 298 The enemies ships armed with piked beake-heads. **1670** MILTON *Hist. Eng.* II. Wks. 1851 V. 70 The Batavians.. running in upon them.. with their piked Targets bearing them down. **1695** J. EDWARDS *Perfect. Script.* 211 Some of them [spears] were piked or pointed at both ends. **1805** DICKSON *Pract. Agric.* I. 7 Perhaps the Hertfordshire wheel-plough, which has a piked share, may be the most suitable implement. **1814** SCOTT *Ld. of Isles* v. v, The good old priest.. Took his piked staff and sandall'd shoon.

b. Of animals, plants, etc.: Furnished with a pike or sharp point, or with spines or prickles, as in *piked dogfish*; = PICKED *a.* 1 b.

1621 G. SANDYS *Ovid's Met.* IV. (1626) 73 Inuiron'd with no marish-louing Reeds, Nor piked Bull-rushes. **1875** *Trans. Devon Assoc.* VII. 145 Piked Dog-fish. **1896** J. H. CAMPBELL *Wild Life Scot.* 99 The piked dog-fish owes his common name to the pikes or spikes, standing up like detached rays, in front of the dorsal fins.

2. Tapering to a point or peak; pointed, peaked.

1538 ELYOT *Lat. Dict.* Addit. Gg vj b, *Argutum caput*, a sharpe or pikyd hedde lyke a sugar lofe. **1565–73** COOPER *Thesaurus* s.v. *Compono*, *Aciem per cuneos componere*, to set in pyked fronts. **1577** B. GOOGE *Heresbach's Husb.* (1586) 45 b, When it [hay] is dryed, we.. make it vp in Cockes, and after that in Moowes, which must be sharp and piked in the toppe. **1610** HOLLAND *Camden's Brit.* I. 515 A little piked hill cast up. **1615** G. SANDYS *Trav.* 42 Messapus for his high steepe piked rocks to be wondred at. **1775** R. CHANDLER *Trav. Asia M.* (1825) I. 11 The cape named Tænarum, now Matapan, which is the extremity of a mountain sloping to a point, having before it a piked rock. **1800** D. LYSONS *Environs London* Suppl. 159 Sir Edward is represented in armour, with piked beard and whiskers.

b. piked horn, a tall conical headdress worn by ladies in the 14th and 15th c.; **piked shoe**, a shoe with a long peak at the toes, as was the fashion towards the end of the 14th c., and later; a crakow, poulaine; **piked whale**, the lesser rorqual, or pike headed whale, *Balænoptera rostrata*.

1377 LANGL. *P. Pl.* B. xx. 218 Proude prestes come with hym moo þan a thousand In paltokes and pyked shoes. *a* **1450** MYRC 43 Cuttede clothes and pyked schone. **1580** STOW *Annals* (1601) 471 Noble women vsed high attire on their heads, piked like hornes. **1587** HARRISON *England* II. i. (1877) I. 33 They went.. with their shooes piked. **1698** J. CRULL *Muscovy* 137 Their Boots.. are piked towards the Toes. **1747** VERTUE in *Phil. Trans.* XLIV. 575 Piked Shoes appear in several Reigns from Ed. III. to Rich. III. in England. **1748** H. WALPOLE *Let. to G. Montagu* 11 Aug., Anne of Bohemia.. introduced the fashion of *piked horns*, or high heads. **1787** HUNTER in *Phil. Trans.* LXXVII. 418 The *Balæna rostrata* of Fabricius or Piked Whale. **1835–6** *Todd's Cycl. Anat.* I. 577/2 The subclavian artery in the Piked Whale. **1892** C. R. B. BARRETT *Essex Highways*, etc. 71 The curious headdress of piked-horns.

piked (paɪkt), *a.*^{2} *Diving* and *Gymnastics.* [f. PIKE *sb.*^{11} or *v.*^{8}] In a pike position; with the body in a pike position.

1951 *Swimming* (Eng. Schools Swimming Assoc.) v. 71 There are three recognized positions in which the body may be held during the execution of a dive... *Piked.* The body is bent forward at the hips, but the legs must remain straight at the knees with toes pointed. **1956** KUNZLE & THOMAS *Freestanding* iii. 34 If it is properly timed, the roll will finish in piked stand... Loose hamstrings are essential to allow sufficient pike at the hips. **1964** *Trampolining* ('Know the Game' Ser.) 11/1 Piked jumping. Keep trunk as erect as possible... Point toes and touch upper insteps. **1974** *Rules of Game* 36 Two or three running steps into forward piked salto, land on one leg. *Ibid.* 38 Swing forward over bar with legs piked.

piked, obs. variant of PICKED *ppl. a.*

pike-devant, variant of PICKE-DEVANT.

pikefork, obs. and dial. variant of PICKFORK.

pike-head (ˈpaɪkhɛd). [f. PIKE *sb.*^{4}, ^{5} + HEAD.]

1. The metal head of a PIKE (*sb.*^{5}).

1596 SPENSER *F.Q.* IV. vii. 27 He.. therein left the pike-head of his speare. **1659** RUSHW. *Hist. Coll.* I. 464 The Enemy holds upon their Pike-heads mutton, capons, turkies, &c. to let the English see they had no want. **1841** LEVER *C. O'Malley* lxxxi, The Cossacks with the red beards.. and long poles with pike-heads on them.

2. A fish of the family *Luciocephalidæ*.

So **pike-headed** *a.*, having a head with long snout and jaws, like those of the PIKE (*sb.*^{4}); as ***pike-headed alligator, anolis***; ***pike-headed whale***, the piked whale: see PIKED 2 b.

1769 PENNANT *Zool.* III. 40 Pike-headed whale.. this species takes its name from the shape of its nose, which is narrower and sharper pointed than that of other whales. **1774** GOLDSM. *Nat. Hist.* VI. 193 The Pike-headed Whale. **1890** *Cent. Dict.* s.v., *Pike-headed alligator*, the common Mississippi alligator.. *Alligator lucius*.

pikeir, variant of PIQUIER *Obs.*, a pikeman.

pikel, pikle (ˈpaɪk(ə)l). *dial.* Also locally **pickel, pickle, pikehil, poikel, -kle.** [f. PIKE *sb.*^{1} 3 b; prob. with *-el, -le*, instrumental, as in *handle, spindle, shovel*.] A hay-fork, pitchfork. (Common in local use, in the Midland and Western Counties from Lancashire southwards.)

1602 J. BRUEN in Hinde *Life* xlvi. (1641) 147 One casting a pikell.. one being behind him, the two greins of the pikell ran on both sides of his leg, and hurt him not. **1681** P. HENRY *Diaries & Lett.* (1882) 307 From ye lower Hay-bay.. they pitcht it and carry'd it on Pikehils to ye Carts. **1688** R. HOLME *Armoury* III. 73/1 Take.. a Pikell of Hay, as much as hangs together on the points or grains of a Pikell. *a* **1874** 'B. CORNWALL' *Manch. Streets* 87 Her Majesty.. had seen the threatening clouds 'rain poikels' as Lancashire alone can rain them. **1879** *Eddowes' Shrewsbury Jrnl.* 3 Sept., Charge of stabbing with a pikel.

pikelet^{1} (ˈpaɪklɪt). *local.* Forms: 8 **pyclet**, 8– **pikelet, picklet** (*dial.* **piklet, pyklet, piclate, pifelet, pyflet**, etc.). [Shortened from BARA-PICKLET.]

a. A Western and Midland name for a small round tea-cake, made of fine flour; a crumpet, or, in some districts, a muffin.

1790 *Bystander* 382 They were not muffins the chevalier hawked about, when a boy, but pyclets. **1797** ANNA SEWARD *Lett.* (1811) V. 15 That doughty son of Themis.. crumpled up his broad face like an half-toasted pikelet. **1825** BROCKETT *N.C. Gloss.*, *Picklet*, or *Pikelet*, a small round light cake—a sort of muffin. **1862** MRS. H. WOOD *Mrs. Hallib.* II. i. 152 Janey.. revelled in an early tea and pikelets. **1904** *Windsor Mag.* Jan. 260/1 A silver-covered dish containing hot pikelets. [Mod. dial. forms: see *Eng. Dial. Dict.*] **1974** P. WRIGHT *Lang. Brit. Industry* iv. 43 *Pikelet* is used in the West and Midlands for a round teacake with small holes, to be buttered and toasted; but in other districts it seems to be a sticky unsweetened crumpet or else a muffin.

b. Chiefly *Austral.* and *N.Z.* A drop-scone.

Known personally to me in N.Z. in the 1920s.—R.W.B. **1943** A. L. SIMON *Conc. Encycl. Gastron.* IV. 97/2 *Welsh Pikelets*.. flour.. sugar.. salt.. bicarbonate of soda.. buttermilk.. Take a tablespoon of this batter and fry in a little hot lard.. turn when half cooked. **1952** B. NILSON *Penguin Cookery Bk.* xviii. 332 Drop Scones, Pikelets.. or Scotch Pancakes. Cooking time 3–4 minutes each batch. **1963** *Moderna Språk* LVII. I. 4 *Pikelets*,.. This is the name of the most popular teacake in Australia, yet most Englishmen from South England at least, have never heard of it. **1965** S. T. OLLIVIER *Petticoat Farm* vi. 83 'I've brought some pikelets,' she said. **1970** D. M. DAVIN *Not Here, Not Now* II. ix. 119 Then she made pikelets for tea. **1977** *N.Z. Woman's Weekly* 10 Jan. 54/1 It is then easy to slip the ice in sheets from the sides by using the spatula normally used for turning girdle scones or pikelets.

pikelet^{2} (ˈpaɪklɪt). [f. PIKE *sb.*^{4} + -LET.] A small or young pike.

1892 *Illustr. Sporting & Dram. News* 2 July 604/1 A diminutive pikelet. **1896** GEDNEY *Angling Holidays* 83 When killed, this hungry pikelet had in his pouch a trout nearly one quarter of a pound weight!

pikeman^{1} (ˈpaɪkmən). *Obs.* exc. *Hist.* [f. PIKE *sb.*^{5} + MAN *sb.*^{1}] A soldier armed with a pike.

15.. *Sir A. Barton* in *Surtees Misc.* (1888) 66 Yea, pick-men more, and bowmen both, This worthye Howard tooke to the sea. **1566** PARTRIDGE *Plasidas* 993 The pike-men, they on walles doe stande their towne for to defende. **1627** *Maldon, Essex, Documents* (Bundle 201 No. 40), Further that every pickman come full armed. **1647** CLARENDON *Hist. Reb.* IV. §199 The Pikemen had fasten'd to the tops of their pikes.. printed Papers of the Protestation. **1885** *Spectator* 30 May 715/2 The Swiss pikemen at Morgarten.. brought this ascendency to the ground.

pikeman^{2} (ˈpaɪkmən). Also (in sense 1) **pikesman.** [f. PIKE *sb.*^{1} + MAN *sb.*^{1}]

1. A man who wields a pick; a pickman; a miner; one who hews the coal with a pickaxe.

1845 DISRAELI *Sybil* VI. vi, 'My missus told it me at the pit-head when she brought me my breakfast', said a pike-man. **1864** *Daily Tel.* 26 Oct., It is stated the best miners, known as pikesmen, can hew a stent and a half in a day. **1880** *Ibid.* 28 Oct., The pikeman's recumbent position and the easy strokes he appears to take at the coal.

2. A man who picks the mill-stones and keeps them in order; hence, the tenant or man in charge of a thirlage, baronial, or burghal mill. (*Sc.*)

15.. *Aberdeen Regr.* (Jam.), Pikeman of the townis millis. **1576** *Rec. Sheriff Crt. Aberdeensh.* (1904) 242 Alex. Williamsone.. pikeman of the Miln.. and uptaker of the multur and knaifschipe of the tounes and lands of the Miltoun of Auchnagat. **1877** G. FRASER *Wigtown* 60 The Clerk.. and Jamie the Pikeman [had] a mutual dislike and dread of each other.

ˈ**pikeman**^{3}. [f. PIKE *sb.*^{6} + MAN *sb.*^{1}] The keeper of a turnpike.

1857 HUGHES *Tom Brown* I. iv, The cheery toot of the guard's horn, to warn some drowsy pikeman or the ostler at the next change. **1865** *Daily Tel.* 1 Nov. 4/6 On certain roads you may travel for leagues without being interrupted by the 'pike-man'.

ˈ**pike-pole.** *N. Amer.* [PIKE *sb.*^{1} 2.] **a.** A lumberer's tool; a pole having a spike at the end and a hook near it, used for driving and guiding floating logs.

1850 N. KINGSLEY *Diary* (1914) 139 The weeds are put down with a pike pole and the pressure of the water keeps them to their place. **1878** *Scribner's Mag.* XV. 147 The running and rafting implements, pike-poles, etc., are made ready. **1891** C. ROBERTS *Adrift Amer.* 206, I.. was at once put to work pushing logs down a long channel with a pike pole. **1926** *Daily Colonist* (Victoria, B.C.) 5 Jan. 1/3 Mattatall sighted it [*sc.* a bag] and hauled it up with a pike pole. **1945** D. D. CALVIN *Saga of St. Lawrence* 68 Men.. sorted out with their long pike-poles (which were like twenty-foot boat-hooks with a sharp point and hook) the longer, thinner pieces. **1964** *Daily Colonist* (Victoria, B.C.) 27 Sept. 36/2 A powered boom scooter rides herd on logs in the water where the timber used to be shoved around by a man with caulk boots, a pike pole and the agility of a cougar. **1968** R. M. PATTERSON *Finlay's River* 103 Careering downstream, steering their heavy craft by means of long pike-poles, they crashed into one driftpile, sheered out and spun end for end three times.

b. A long pole having a fire-hook at one end.

1949 *Chicago Daily News* 17 Sept. 1/7 Firemen worked with pike pole and shovel in the wreckage. **1969** *Publ. Amer. Dial. Soc.* LII. 34 *Pike pole*, a rake-like device used to pull plaster loose or to clear an area. 'Clear it out with the pike pole.'

ˈ**piker**^{1}. Now *dial.* Also 4–6 **pyker**, 5–6 **-ar.** [f. *pike*, var. of PICK *v.*^{1} + -ER^{1}: see PICKER^{1}.]

†**1.** A robber, a thief; in later use, a petty thief, pilferer; = PICKER^{1} 1 b. *Obs.*

1301 *Pol. Poems* (Rolls) II. 66 But if alwey pikers, Iak, thou wolt us maken, ther we piken but seely pans, the secte pikith poundis. **1393** LANGL. *P. Pl.* C. VI. 17 Kepe my corn in my croft fro pykers and þeues. *c* **1440** *Promp. Parv.* 395/2 Pykare, lytylle theef, *furculus*. **1503** *Act 19 Hen. VII*, c. 6 §1 Knowyng theves and other pikars. **1549** COVERDALE, etc. *Erasm. Par. Philem.* 31 He reconsileth vnto the Maister [Philemon] his seruaunt that had bene both a runneagate and a piker. **1549** *Records of Elgin* I. 98 Blasfemyng of Jhone Gadderar, eldar.. calland him auld pikar theyf carll.

2. An instrument to 'pike' or pick out dust, dirt, or obstructions; a picker. *Sc.*

1828 MOIR *Mansie Wauch* xii, The piker for clearing the motion-hole.

†**piker**[2], **piquer.** *Obs.* [f. *pique*, PIKE *sb.*[5] + -ER[1], or ad. F. *piquier*: see PIQUIER.] A soldier armed with a pike, a pikeman.

1590 SIR J. SMYTH *Disc. Weapons* Ded. 7b, Their old soldiers Piquers with their piques. *Ibid.* 2b, Their footmen piquers, they doo allowe for verie well armed. **1598** BARRET *Theor. Warres* III. i. 35 The piker his armings and weapon.

ˈ**piker**[3]. *slang* or *dial.* [app. f. PIKE *sb.*[6] turnpike: cf. also dial. *pikey* in same sense.] **1.** A vagrant, a tramp; a gipsy.

1838 HOLLOWAY *Dict. Provinc.* 23/2 Cadgers and pikers are tramps. *E. Suss.* **1874** BORROW *Wordbk. Eng. Gypsy Lang.* 215 The people called in Acts of Parliament sturdy beggars and vagrants, in the old cant language Abraham men, and in the modern *Pikers.*

2. *Austral.* A wild ox living in the bush. Also *transf.*

1887 *All Year Round* 30 July 67 'Pikers' are wild cattle. **1893** K. MACKAY *Out Back* (ed. 2) III. vi. 265 Blowed if this cask ain't harder to round up nor a mallee piker. **1904** 'G. B. LANCASTER' *Sons o' Men* 22 The grunt of broken-winded pikers came clear above the sharp crackle of undergrowth where the boys rode. **1936** I. L. IDRIESS *Cattle King* vii. 62 The boy bought a teamster's cast-off bullock for two pounds. It was an old piker, worked to the very bone. **1941** —— *Great Boomerang* vii. 51 Fine upstanding beasts, the pick of a dozen stations. No old 'pikers' these.

ˈ**Piker**[4]. [f. PIKE *sb.*[10] + -ER[1].] = PIKE *sb.*[10]

1859 in L. Hafen *Colorado Gold Rush* (1941) 318 An extra train of [returning] 'Pikers' came in [to Hannibal] about 2 o'clock yesterday afternoon. **1869** R. KEELER *Gloverson & his Silent Partners* 92 He is what we call a 'Piker', you see,.. and he stole some of our sheep. **1873** J. H. BEADLE *Undevel. West* xxxv. 763 These old Pikers don't want the country fenced up and the game scared off. **1907** W. E. CONNELLEY *Doniphan's Exped.* 9 Mr. Moore says that in California in the early days Missourians were called 'Pikers' indiscriminately and generally.

piker[5]. *slang* (orig. *U.S.*). [Cf. PIKE *v.*[3] 3.]

a. A cautious or timid gambler who makes only small bets; a person who takes no chances; a 'poor sport' or 'poor thing'; a shirker; a lounger. Also *attrib.*

[**1872** E. CRAPSEY *Nether Side N.Y.* 98 A 'piker' is a tolerated collapse who makes a stray bet when he can borrow a 'check'.] **1889** [see PIKE *v.*[3] 3]. **1901** 'H. MCHUGH' *John Henry* 92 She put us wise to the fact that.. Edgar Allen Poe was a piker compared with her. **1910** W. M. RAINE *Bucky O'Connor* 233 Do you think I'm a cheap piker? **1912** R. W. SERVICE *Rhymes of Rolling Stone* (1913) 96 It's the plugging away that will win you the day, So don't be a piker, old pard. **1919** H. L. WILSON *Ma Pettengill* vii. 216 'I says to myself the other day: "I'll bet a cookie he'd like to be like me!"' Homer was a piker, even when he made bets with himself. **1929** J. BUCHAN *Courts of Morning* I. xii. 138, I don't say there mayn't be some pikers at Headquarters. **1935** Z. N. HURSTON *Mules & Men* (1970) 308 The pikers choose a card each from among those turned off to bet on. **1947** *Sat. Even. Post* 15 Mar. 111/3 It is natural that I should have gone far beyond the sort of piker activities which characterize the average soldier. **1947** D. M. DAVIN *Gorse blooms Pale* 207 'Don't be a piker, Mick,' he said. **1957** 'N. CULOTTA' *They're a Weird Mob* (1958) xiii. 203 It [*sc.* bludger] means that you are criminally lazy.. that you are a 'piker'—a mean, contemptible, miserable individual. **1968** M. RICHLER in R. Weaver *Canad. Short Stories* 2nd Ser. 156 The dirty piker he asked her to marry him he hasn't even got a job. **1969** *Southerly* XXIX. 308 Mat saw me coming. He said: 'We've got a piker on our hands. He reckons he hasn't got enough for a feed at La Roma. Pulling out on us he is.' **1971** H. W. TILMAN *In Mischief's Wake* III. x. 112 He is definitely no piker and although only 22 is one of the old school and believes in discipline. **1973** K. GILES *File on Death* ii. 43 'You have that much authority?' 'He is no piker. I run the place... I can roughly do what I like on the business side.'

b. A person who speculates in stocks, esp. with only small sums.

1898 *N.Y. Jrnl.* 12 Aug. 1/7 John Pettit started in as a 'piker'. That's what the downtown brokers call a man who speculates with a few hundreds at a time instead of with thousands. **1901** *McClure's Mag.* June 159/1 In the absence of complaisant lambs, the financial cannibals known as 'room traders' and 'pikers' tried to 'scalp eighths' out of each other for weeks. **1902** H. L. WILSON *Spenders* xxxi. 360 They're used to those fifty and a hundred thousand dollar pikers down in that neighbourhood. *Ibid.* 365 We'll make those Federal Oil pikers think we've gnawed a corner off the subtreasury. **1942** BERREY & VAN DEN BARK *Amer. Thes. Slang* §563/1 *Piker*, a speculator on a small scale.

piker[6]. [Etym. unknown.] Also **pika.** In Guyana, a plover.

1936 J. BOND *Birds W. Indies* 101 South American Ring Plover (*Charadrius collaris*)... Little Ploward; Nit; Pika; Snipe. *Ibid.* 102 Wilson's Plover (*Charadrius wilsonia*)... Snipe; Little Ploward; Nit; Pika. **1958** J. CAREW *Black Midas* x. 200, I saw curlews and pikers.. flying low over a rim of amber foam.

piker, var. PICARD *Obs.*, large sailing-boat.

pikerel, pikery, obs. ff. PICKEREL, PICKERY.

ˈ**pikess.** *nonce-wd.* A female pike (fish).

1854 BADHAM *Halieut.* 302 The spawning season occupies from two to three months; the young pikesses of three years taking the lead.

pikestaff (ˈpaɪkstɑːf, -æf). [In senses 1 and 2, f. PIKE *sb.*[1] 1, 2 + STAFF: cf. ON. *píkstafr* (13th c.), mod.Norw. *pikstav*, MSw. *pikstaff*; in sense 3, f. PIKE *sb.*[5] Hence two distinct words, but often not capable of separation, esp. in the phrases in 4.]

1. A staff or walking-stick with a metal point at the lower end like an alpenstock. Now only *Sc.* Sometimes app. the wooden handle of a pick.

1356 in Riley *Mem. Lond.* (1868) 284 (Lett.-Bk. G. lf. 45), Pikstef. **1377** LANGL. *P. Pl.* B. VI. 105 My plow-fote shal be my pyk-staf [*MS. B* pikid staf; A. VII. 96 pyk, *MS. U* pykstaf, *MS. H* pilgrimstaf] and picche atwo þe rotes. **1393** *Ibid.* C. VII. 329 Penaunce hus pyk-staf [A. v. 257 pike, piked staf] he wolde polische newe. *c* **1470** HENRYSON *Mor. Fab.* XI (*Wolf & Sheep*) iii, With pykestaff and with scrip to fair of toun. **1592** GREENE *Upst. Courtier* Wks. (Grosart) XI. 212 He stands sollemnlie leaning on his pike staffe. *a* **1642** SIR W. MONSON *Naval Tracts* I. (1704) 228/1 The Weapon is a Pike-Staff, such as Keepers and Warreners use for the guard of the Game. *a* **1776** in Herd *Scot. Songs* (1902) 109 Fare ye weel, my pyke-staff. **1816** SCOTT *Antiq.* iv, Setting his pike-staff before him.

†**2.** Part of a wagon or cart: app. the same as PIKESTOWER. *Obs.*

1523 FITZHERB. *Husb.* §5 The crosse somer, the keys and pikstaues.

3. The wooden shaft of a pike (the weapon).

1580 HOLLYBAND *Treas. Fr. Tong, Zagaye*, is a staffe longer and more slender than a pike staffe, otherwise called *Azagaye.* **1642** CHAS. I *Answ. Declar. Both Houses* 1 July 24 Gisarms (which were Pikestaves). **1904** SIR H. MAXWELL in *Blackw. Mag.* June 754/2 Ash was the proper wood for pike-staves.

4. In proverbial phrases. ***as plain as a pikestaff***, an alteration of the earlier phrase *as plain as a* PACKSTAFF (in reference to its plain surface). Also ***as stiff as a pikestaff. to call a pikestaff a pikestaff*** = to call a spade a spade.

1591 GREENE *Disc. Coosnage* (1592) 4 A new game.. that hath no policie nor knauerie, but plaine as a pikestaffe. **1719** D'URFEY *Pills* III. 22 When a Reason's as plain as a Pike-staff. **1848** THACKERAY *Bk. Snobs* xvii, When will you acknowledge that two and two make four, and call a pikestaff a pikestaff? **1851** H. MELVILLE *Whale* iv. 30 Sat up in bed stiff as a pike-staff. **1867** TROLLOPE *Chron. Barset* I. xlii. 367 The evidence against him was as plain as a pike-staff.

†ˈ**pikestower.** *Obs.* [f. PIKE *sb.*[1] + *stower* dial. stake, post, rung.] Part of a wagon or cart; explained as 'The iron bar or standard fixed in the "ear-breed" of a cart, strengthening the sides'.

1641 BEST *Farm. Bks.* (Surtees) 48 The foreman is to bee forewarned that he seeke out three or fower pikestowers aforehande, and some keyes and false shelvinges.

pikey (ˈpaɪkɪ). *dial.* or *slang.* Also **piky.** [f. PIKE *sb.*[6] turnpike] = PIKER[3].

1847 J. O. HALLIWELL *Dict. Archaic & Provinc. Words* 623/2 *Piky*, a gipsey. *Kent.* **1874** HOTTEN *Slang Dict.* 253 *Pikey*, a tramp or gipsy. **1887** PARISH & SHAW *Dict. Kentish Dial.* 116 *Piky*,.. a turnpike traveller; a vagabond; and so generally a low fellow. **1955** P. WILDEBLOOD *Against Law* 125 My family's all Pikeys, but we ain't on the road no more!

pikeys, pikfault, obs. ff. PICKAXE, PICKFAULT.

piki (ˈpiːkɪ). [Hopi.] Bread made from maize-meal, baked in very thin sheets on heated stones by the Hopi Indians of the south western U.S. Also *attrib.*

1889 in *Cent. Dict.* s.v. *peekee, piki.* **1893** T. DONALDSON *Moqui Pueblo Indians* 72 Piki, or corn bread of many colors, is plentiful, and the evidences of a feast are on every hand. **1922** E. S. CURTIS *N. Amer. Indian* XII. 43 The commonest food derived from corn is piki. **1936** A. M. STEPHEN *Hopi Jrnl.* II. 1197 The men quarry out and roughly dress the piki stone to required dimensions, but the women finish and smooth it by rubbing. **1948** *Southwestern Jrnl. Anthropol.* Winter 376 Corn, flour, breadstuffs—especially piki (wafer bread)—melons, chili, and dried fruit were most sought after. **1959** E. TUNIS *Indians* 119/2 The [Hopi] Pueblos knew fifty-two ways of cooking corn. Most of them weren't unlike the ways other Indians cooked it, but the 'paper bread', called piki, belonged to them alone. It was made from a thin batter and was cooked on a flat stone placed over the fire.

piking (ˈpaɪkɪŋ), *vbl. sb.* and *ppl. a. dial.* and *slang.* [?f. *pike*, var. PICK *v.*[1]: cf. PIKER[1].] Cheating; using sharp practices.

1884 in *Western Pennsylvania Hist. Mag.* (1918) I. 97 After considerable deliberation I concluded to try a little 'piking', and had Leslie sell five thousand barrels 'short' at 64. **1955** W. GADDIS *Recognitions* II. v. 490 The Father of His Country was crumpled, folded, and offered in the most piking and meretricious traffic millions of times a day. **1972** *Daily Tel.* 1 Nov. 2/6 An East End publican who referred in his bar to the Tibbs family as 'dirty piking bastards' was attacked in the street by four men with knives and an axe.

pikipiki (ˈpikipiki). [Mbuti.] A whistle used by the Mbuti pygmies of Zaïre (see quot. 1933). Also *attrib.*

1933 G. GRIFFIN tr. *Schebesta's Among Congo Pygmies* iii. 78 The pikipiki is.. a kind of whistle, about the thickness of a man's finger, and is cut out of a round piece of wood. In both ends holes are.. burned, with a red-hot spike. It can then be used as a whistle like a hollow key. Pikipikis often have one hole only, and may be decorated with spiral metal ornamentations... The pikipiki is used for making magic, not only by the huntsmen, but by every member of the pygmy community. **1936** —— tr. *Schebesta's My Pygmy & Negro Hosts* vi. 114 It seems that all the negro tribes believe in the supernatural powers of the 'pikipiki whistle'. **1958** *Listener* 2 Oct. 508/1 The production of shrill notes from their whistles called pikipikis. **1960** *New Scientist* 6 Oct. 903/1 The songs which they sing nightly to the accompaniment of pikipiki whistles all reflect their belief that.. the forest is the great provider and eternal refuge of the chosen people, the Ba'mbuti.

ˈ**pikish,** *a. nonce-wd.* [f. PIKE *sb.*[4], [5] + -ISH[1].]

a. ? Of or pertaining to pikes (weapons). **b.** Of or proper to pike (fish); voracious.

1799 in *Spirit Pub. Jrnls.* III. 163 Liberty.. in pikish majesty she'll rise. **1890** *Pall Mall G.* 19 May 5/2 An undoubted instance of pikeish voracity.

pikit, obs. Sc. form of PIKED, PITCHED.

pikk, obs. variant of PICK, PIKE, PITCH.

pikke, pikky, obs. forms of PITCH, PITCHY.

pikle, variant of PIKEL, pitchfork.

†**pik-moyane.** *Sc. Obs.* [f. *pik*, of uncertain meaning + F. *moyen* middle, middle-sized. Cf. *culverin moyen* in CULVERIN.] A kind of culverin: explained as 'one of the smallest size'.

1513 *Acc. Ld. High Treas. Scot.* IV. 517 Item, the first culvering pikmoyane drawin with xvj oxin of the kingis.

pikoise, obs. form of PICKAXE.

pikrolite, variant of PICROLITE.

piky (ˈpaɪkɪ), *a.*[1] *rare.* [f. PIKE *sb.*[1] + -Y.] Having pikes or sharp points; spiky; pointed.

1744-50 W. ELLIS *Mod. Husbandm.* III. I. 87 (E.D.S.) Long piky roots.

piky, *a.*[2] erron. pikey. [f. PIKE *sb.*[4] + -Y.] Of, of the nature of, or abounding in pike (fish).

1877 G. MACDONALD *Marquis of Lossie* II. xi. 120 A lake of deep fresh water,.. the pikey multitude within. **1902** B. GRUNDY *Thames Camp* 90 He is a long way from other gudgeon, in a deep pikey hole.

piky, obs. form of PITCHY.

piky, var. PIKEY.

piladex (ˈpɪlədɛks). Also **pilla-.** [f. L. *pila* ball + *dex-* in L. *dextra*, Gr. δεξιά right hand.] The name of a parlour game consisting in keeping an inflated ball or bag in the air by striking it to and fro over a line on a table with the back of the hand. (Formerly proprietary.)

1897 in *Army & Navy Stores List* 1658. **1901** *Speaker* 9 Feb. 505/2 That rather unmeaning phrase.. will be thrown into the political air and buffeted like a pilladex by the fists of opposing champions. **1901** *Daily News* 27 July 8/6 Parlour Games... Blowing Games, such as puff billiards, piladex, and a feather on a sheet.

pilaf, -aff, variants of PILAU.

pilage (ˈpaɪlɪdʒ). Also 9 **pileage.** [f. PILE *sb.*[5] 1 + -AGE.] The hair, wool, or especially fur, with which an animal is covered; = PELAGE.

a **1825** tr. *Bacon's De Calore et Frigore* in Wks. (1825) I. 334 Cold maketh the pilage of beasts more thick and long. **1867** A. L. ADAMS *Wand. Nat. India* 214 In winter.. the fur becomes dense from the woolly pileage, which gives a lighter color to the coat than during midsummer and autumn, when .. the fur is short and brown. *Ibid.* 234 During Winter the ibex is thickly clad with hair and woolly pileage.

pilao, variant of PILAU.

pilar (ˈpaɪlə(r)), *a. rare.* [f. mod.L. *pilār-is*, f. *pilus* hair: see -AR[1].]

1. Of or pertaining to hair.

1858 MAYNE *Expos. Lex.*, *Pilāris*,.. Zool. pertaining to hair; hairy; pilar. **1893** *Syd. Soc. Lex.*, Pilar muscles, *arrectores pilorum* [muscles that cause the hair to bristle].

2. Downy. *rare.*

1859 R. F. BURTON *Centr. Afr.* in *Jrnl. Geog. Soc.* XXIX. 196 Most of the men and almost all the women remove the eyelashes, and pilar hair rarely appears to grow.

So **pilary** (ˈpaɪlərɪ), *a.* = PILAR 1.

1888 *Med. News* LIII. 411 She had never suffered from any pilary loss [or] cutaneous affection. **1893** *Syd. Soc. L.*

pilaster (pɪˈlæstə(r)). *Arch.* Also 6–7 **pillastre, -ter,** 7 **pyl(l-, (pilley-stair).** [a. F. *pilastre* (1545 in Hatz.-Darm.), a. It. *pilastro*, in med.L. *pīlastrum* (1341), f. *pīla* a pillar: see -ASTER.]

1. A square or rectangular column or pillar; *spec.* such a pillar engaged in a wall, from which it projects with its capital and base a third, fourth, or other portion of its breadth; an engaged pillar; an anta; formerly applied also to the square pier of an arch, abutment of a bridge, or similar structure.

1575 LANEHAM *Let.* (1871) 50 Vpon a base a too foot square,.. a square pilaster rizing pyramidally, of a fyfteen foote hy. **1598** FLORIO, *Pilastro*, any kinde of piller or pilaster. **1603** DRAYTON *Bar. Wars* VI. xxxi, A Roome prepar'd with Pilasters,.. That to the Roofe their slender Poynts did reare. **16..** *Lindesay's Chron. Scot., Contin.* (1728) 233 A square low Gallery, some four Foot from the Ground, set round about with Pilley-stairs. **1613–39** I. JONES in Leoni *Palladio's Archit.* (1742) I. 103 The Pilaster is the Basement against the Bank of the River. **1624** WOTTON *Archit.* in *Reliq.* (1651) 238 Pylasters must not be too tall and slender, lest they resemble Pillars, nor too Dwarfish and grosse, lest they imitate the Piles or Peeres of Bridges. **1670** *Moral State Eng.* 87 An house adorned without with various Pillars, and Pillasters of several Orders. **1715** LEONI *Palladio's Archit.* (1742) II. 36 The Jambs or Pilasters of the Doors. **1776** G. SEMPLE *Building in Water* 11 The Piles or Pilasters, which are fixed in the River; the Arches which these Pilasters support. **1860** EMERSON *Cond. Life, Beauty* Wks. (Bohn) II. 433 Our taste in building..refuses pilasters and columns that support nothing.

transf. **1875** *Wonders Phys. World* I. i. 39 Piles or pilasters of ground ice which supported the superficial crust.

†**2.** A pillar-like or cylindrical shape or figure.

1589 PUTTENHAM *Eng. Poesie* II. xi. (Arb.) 110 The Piller, Pillaster or Cillinder. **1601** HOLLAND *Pliny* II. 613 They delight to cut their Berils into long rolls or pillastres in manner of cylindres [L. *cylindros ex eis malunt facere*].

3. *attrib.* and *Comb.*, as *pilaster block, buttress, capital, pier, pinnacle*; *pilaster-like* adj.; *pilaster-fashion, -wise* adv.; **pilaster-strip**: see quot. 1874.

1616 SURFL. & MARKH. *Country Farme* 277 Fashion your battlements of what shape soeuer you please to haue them; whether made plaine, or pyllaster-wise [etc.]. **1703** T. N. *City & C. Purchaser* 224 Revailed or Pilaster-peers, from 10 to 14 Pounds a pair. **1727–51** CHAMBERS *Cycl.* s.v. *Brick*, *Pilaster, or buttress bricks*,.. are of the same dimensions with the great bricks, only they have a notch at one end, half the breadth of the brick; their use is to bind the work at the pilasters of fence-walls, which are built of great bricks. **1773** NOORTHOUCK *Hist. Lond.* 599 These buttresses run up pilaster fashion. **1874** PARKER *Goth. Archit.* Gloss. 326 *Pilaster Strips*, a term used to describe the vertical projecting parts of the towers supposed to be Saxon. **1879** SIR G. G. SCOTT *Lect. Archit.* I. 49 Flat, pilaster-like buttresses.

pilastered (pɪˈlæstəd), *a.* [f. prec. + -ED².] Furnished with or supported on pilasters.

a **1687** COTTON *Entertainm. to Phillis* 16 The polish'd Walls of Marble be Pillaster'd round with porphyry. *a* **1774** W. HARTE *Charitable Mason* Poems (1810) 383/1 Pilaster'd jas mines 'twixt the windows grew. **1838** *Fraser's Mag.* XVIII. 706 Pilastered galleries.

pilastrade (pɪlæˈstreɪd). *Arch.* [ad. It. *pilastrata* (f. *pilastrare* to adorn with pilasters): see -ADE.] A row or range of pilasters.

[**1730** A. GORDON *Maffei's Amphith.* 222 The Pilastrata or Range of Pilasters, which support the Arch.] **1812** *Examiner* 5 Oct. 635/1 A pilastrade of two columns. **1886** WILLIS & CLARK *Cambridge* I. 103 A regular Ionic pilastrade.

Hence **pilaˈstraded** *a.*, having a pilastrade.

1847 *Nat. Encycl.* I. 644 A pilastraded ordinance, forming a species of attic.

†**ˈpilastrel.** *Obs. rare*⁻¹. [ad. It. *pilastrello*, dim. of *pilastro* PILASTER.] A small pilaster.

c **1620** ROBINSON *Mary Magd.* 351 The leauy pillastrells were neatly shorne; The grassy seats, yᵉ eyes to slumber wed.

pilat, -e, obs. forms of PILOT.

Pilate (ˈpaɪlət). [a. F. *Pilate*, ad. L. *Pilātus*, proper name.] The name (Pontius Pilate) of the Roman procurator of Judæa concerned in the crucifixion of Jesus Christ; hence allusively as a term of reproach. Also, the character of Pilate in the mystery plays; hence † *Pilate's voice*, a loud magisterial voice (*obs.*).

c **1400** *Apol. Loll.* 56 Prelats not preching are raþer pilats þan prelatis. **1530** PALSGR. 837 In a pylates voyce, *a haulte voyx.* **1542** UDALL *Erasm. Apoph.* (1877) 382 He heard a certain oratour speaking out of measure loude and high, and altogether in Pilate's voice. **1604** HIERON *Wks.* I. 559 Indeed in Rome there diuers be, That beare the name of prelacie: Better we Pilates may them call, Seeking the churches funerall. **1888** *Pall Mall G.* 29 Oct. 7/2 Pontius Pilates, who washed their hands of what might happen to France provided they could continue to exploit her.

‖**pilau, pilaw** (pɪˈlaʊ, pɪˈlɔː, pɪˈləʊ), **pilaff** (pɪˈlɑːf, -æf). Forms: 7– pilau, pillau, pilaw, pillaw, pilao, pelaw; also 7 pilo, -oe, pillow(e, peloe, palau, pullow, 7–8 pelo (pleo), 8 pillou, pilloe, pellow, pilow, 9 pillao, pulao, pullao, pi(l)laf(f. [a. Pers. *pilāw* (in Turkish *pilāw, pilāv* (or *pilāf*), Urdū *pilāo, palāo*) boiled rice and meat (occurs in Bus-ḥaq of Shíráz, ob. 1426). So F. *pilau*, It. *pilao*, mod.Gr. πιλάφι, Russ. *pilavŭ* (= *pilaff*). Appears in Eng. in many forms, according to the language or locality whence the writer has adopted it; the earlier examples, from 17th c. Turkish, are identical with Persian. *Pilaff* represents modern Turkish pronunciation.]

An Oriental dish, consisting of rice (or, in certain areas, wheat) boiled with fowl, meat, or fish, and spices, raisins, etc.

Spelt in many different ways in various regions.

1612 *Trav. Four Englishm.* 55 The most common dish [amongst the Turks] is Pilaw..made of Rice and small morsels of Mutton boiled therein. **1612** CORYAT *Jrnl.* in Purchas *Pilgrims* x. xii. (1625) 1828 The vse of this Butter is verie frequent, by reason of the abundance of *Pillaue* that is eaten in Constantinople. **1634** SIR T. HERBERT *Trav.* 97 (Persia) A dish of Pelo, which is Rice boyled with Hens, Mutton, Butter, Almonds and Turmerack. *Ibid.* 173 Boyld Rice, *Peloe. c* **1645** HOWELL *Lett.* (1650) I. 367 The Turk when he hath his tripe full of pelaw, or of mutton and rice, will go to nature's cellar. **1687** A. LOVELL tr. *Thevenot's Trav.* II. 95 Their boiled meat consists in *Pilao* or *Schilao.* **1696** OVINGTON *Voy. Suratt* 397 Palau, that is Rice boil'd..with Spices intermixt, and a boil'd Fowl in the middle. **1698** FRYER *Acc. E. India & P.* 399 The most admired Dainty, wherewith they stuff themselves, is Pullow. **1711** C. LOCKYER *Trade India* viii. 231 They cannot often go to the Price of a Pilloe, or boil'd Fowl and Rice. **1782** COLMAN *Prose on Sev. Occas.* (1787) III. 235 Methinks I hear some Alderman, all hurry, Cry, where's the Pellow? Bring me out the Curry! **1811** KIRKPATRICK tr. *Sel. Lett. Tippoo Sultan* App. p. xlii, All the Musulman officers..shall be entertained..with a public repast, to consist of *Pullâo* of the first sort. **1813** BYRON *Corsair* II. ii, Removed the banquet, and the last pilaff—Forbidden draughts, 'tis said, he dared to quaff. **1821** —— *Juan* v. xlvii, A genial savour Of certain stews, and roast meats, and pilaus,.. Made Juan in his harsh intentions pause. **1849** THACKERAY *Pendennis* xlii, The Colonel was famous for pillaus and curries. **1860** R. F. BURTON *Centr. Afr.* I. 393 The plat de resistance was, as usual, the pillaw, or, as it is here called, pulao. **1877** A. B. EDWARDS *Up Nile* xxi. 666 The pilaff which followed is always the last dish served at an Egyptian or Turkish dinner. **1883** ALIPH CHEEM *Lays of Ind* (ed. 7) 2 From rice and pillaos To truffles and grouse. **1930** W. J. LOCKE *Town of Tombarel* iv. 114 A pilaff of sea-fruits is a succulent dish, composed of rice and as many fruits of the sea as you can imagine. **1935** H. EDIB *Clown & his Daughter* xxiv. 130 Who would believe that any city under the sun could produce such crowds, such colour..and above all such colossal quantities of roast lamb and pilaff! **1936** P. FLEMING *News from Tartary* 288 We lunched off pilaffe and sour milk. **1938** M. K. RAWLINGS *Yearling* xxxi. 392 Ma Baxter made a pilau of the squirrels for supper. **1949** B. A. BOTKIN *Treas. S. Folklore* IV. i. 552 Marylanders grow lyrical over Brunswick stew..South Carolinians, over rice, calibash, and pilaus (pronounced pé-los, púr-loos). **1956** R. MACAULAY *Towers of Trebizond* xv. 182 He did not mind me lying on his floor, he fed me with yoghourt and coffee and offered me some rice pilav. **1959** F. MACLEAN *Back to Bokhara* ii. 88 A veritable mountain of pilav or *plov*—rice cooked in mutton fat. **1967** *Punch* 12 Apr. 543/1 The lobster pilaf, *côtelettes à la Kiev* and *pommes Anna* with which Carlos Lacerda entertained the Gunthers when he was governor of Guanabara. **1971** *Carry Singapore in your Pocket* (Singapore Tourist Promotion Board) (ed. 3) 31 One first-class Kashmiri restaurant..serves..a wide variety of naan and pilau prepared in Kashmiri style. **1971** *Hindustan Times Weekly* (New Delhi) (Suppl.) 4 Apr. p. iv/5 Just heat up some *ghee*, fry the rice as for a *pullao.* **1971** *Illustr. Weekly India* 25 Apr. 57/2 We will have a proper lunch. Pulao, Chapattis, Shreekand, the lot. **1971** R. RUSSELL tr. *Ahmad's Shore & Wave* ix. 118 'Can I get you anything?' he asked. 'Chicken? Pulao?' **1978** *Detroit Free Press* 16 Apr. 6c/1 (Advt.), This Sunday, Monday or Tuesday you can order our thick and juicy prime rib (served with our special rice pilaf).

Hence **pilaued** (pɪˈlaʊd) *a.*, made into pilau.

1897 LD. ROBERTS *41 Yrs. in India* xlvi. (1898) 353, I took my first lesson in eating roast kid and pillaued chicken.

pilch (pɪltʃ), *sb.* Forms: 1 pyl(e)ce, 3–6 pilche, 4 pilchche, 4–6 pylche, 6– pilch. [OE. *pylece*, ad. med.L. *pellicea* a furred garment, fem. of L. *pelliceus* adj., made of skins, f. *pellis* a skin. Cf. PELISSE.]

†**1.** An outer garment made of skin dressed with the hair; in later use, a leathern or coarse woollen outer garment. *Obs.* exc. *Hist.*

c **1000** ÆLFRIC *Alcuin's Interrog. Segewulfi* in *Anglia* (1883) VII. 30 Hwi worhte god pylcan adame & euan æfter þam gylte? *a* **1100** *Voc.* in Wr.-Wülcker 328/11 *Pellicie*, pylece. *a* **1225** *Ancr. R.* 362 He is of þe te-tore uolke, þet to-tereð his olde kurtel, & to-rendeð þe olde pilche of his deadliche uelle. *c* **1250** *Gen. & Ex.* 377 Two pilches weren ður3 engeles wro3t, And to adam and to eue bro3t. *a* **1300** *Siriz* 225 Warme pilce and warme shon, With that min hernde be wel don. *c* **1390** CHAUCER *Proverbs* 4 Affter heet komeþe colde, No man caste his pilchche away. **1416** *Will of Holt* (Somerset Ho.), Pelche de foxe. *c* **1440** LYDG. *Hors, Shepe & G.* 366 Ther is also made of sheepis skyn, Pilchis & glovis to dryve awey the cold. *c* **1440** *Promp. Parv.* 397/2 Pylche, *pellicium, pellicia.* **1548** UDALL *Erasm. Par. Luke* vii. 85 Clothed in a pilche of a camels hyde. **1563–87** FOXE *A. & M.* (1596) 1613/1 Some wandred to and fro in sheepes pilches, in goates pilches, forsaken, oppressed, afflicted. **1602** DEKKER *Satiromastix* Wks. 1873 I. 231 Ile beate five pound out of his leather pilch. **1674** BLOUNT *Glossogr.* (ed. 4), *Pilch*.., a woollen or fur garment [*obs.*]. **1853** STEVENSON *Anglo-Sax. Chron.* 127 Of costly pilches, and of grey skins. **1901** *Archæol. Jrnl.* Mar. 4 Every canon had..a pilch or cassock (*pellicea*).

2. †**a.** A rug or pad laid over a saddle. *Obs.* **b.** A light frameless saddle for children: = PAD *sb.*³ 2.

1552 HULOET, Pilche for a saddle, *instratum.* **1684** *Lond. Gaz.* No. 1895/4 Taken away.., a Pye-bald Gelding,.. with a Pannel and Pilch on his Back. *a* **1728** KENNETT *Lansd. MS.* 1033 lf. 297 A course shagged piece of rug laid over a Saddle for Ease of a Rider is in our midland parts calld a *pilch.* **1863** BARING-GOULD *Iceland* 397 Take also with you a light saddle without a tree, commonly called a pilch. **1900** *List Civil Serv. Supply Assoc.*, Saddles..Child's Pilch, all over quilted hogskin, for boy or girl.

3. A triangular flannel wrapper for an infant, worn over the diaper or napkin.

1674 BLOUNT *Glossogr.* (ed. 4), *Pilch*..now used for a flannel cloth to wrap about the lower part of young children. *a* **1728** KENNETT *Lansd. MS.* 1033 lf. 297 A piece of flannel or other woolen put under a child next the clout is in Kent calld a *Pilch.* **1799** M. UNDERWOOD *Treat. Dis. Childr.* III. 91 *note*, An error worthy of remark.., is, that of wearing a pilch (as it is called), an old fashion still too much in use. *a* **1825** FORBY *Voc. E. Anglia, Pilch*, a flannel wrapper for an infant. **1861–80** MRS. BEETON *Bk. Househ. Managem.* §2626 Baby-linen..4 pilches,..2 waterproof pilches,..4 dozen napkins.

4. *attrib.* and *Comb.*, as *pilch-clout, -maker.*

a **1225** *Ancr. R.* 212 Þe deoflen schulen pleien mid ham ..& dvsten ase enne pilcheclut, euchon touward oðer. **13..** *Coer de L.* 6736 Here armure no more I ne doute, Thenne I doo a pylche-cloute. *c* **1483** CAXTON *Dialogues* 14 Wauburge the pilchemaker Formaketh a pylche well.

pilch (pɪltʃ), *v.* Now *dial.* Forms: 3 pileken, pilken, 6– pilch, 9 *Sc.* pilk. [Origin uncertain. Cf. LGer. *pül(e)ken, pölken* to pick (*up den knaken pülken* to pick a bone); Norw. and Færöese *pilka* to pick, scrape, prick. Cf. also OF. *peluchier*, OPicard *pelukier, plusquier* (mod.Picard *pluquer*) to pick, clean, peck: see PLUCK *v.*] *intr.* To pick, pluck; to pilfer; to rob.

a **1225** *Ancr. R.* 84 3et wolde he teteren & pileken [*v.rr.* pilewin, picken], mid his bile, roted stinkinde fleshs, as is reafnes kunde. *Ibid.* 86 Uor euere me schal þene cheorl pilken [*v.r.* plokin] & peolien, uor he is ase þe wiði þet sprutteð ut þe betere þet me hine ofte croppeð. **1570** LEVINS *Manip.* 130/10 Pilch, miche, *suffurari.* **1573** TUSSER *Husb.* (1878) 33 Some steale, some pilch, some all away filch. **1665** JAS. FRASER *Polichronicon* (S.H.S. 1905) 163 The country was free from all manner of thift and pilching. **1808** JAMIESON, *To Pilk*,.. I. To shell peas,..also, to pick periwinkles out of the shell;..2. To pilfer..as 'She has pilkit his pouch'. **1900** *Eng. Dial. Dict.*, *Pilch*, to pilfer, filch (S. Worcester, Glouc.).

pilchard (ˈpɪltʃəd). Forms: α. 6–8 pilcher, (6 piltcher, 6–7 pilchar(e, pylcher); β. 6– pilchard, (6 pycherd(e, pilcharde, 7 -erd). [Origin obscure. The *d* is excrescent. (Cf. Ir. *pilseir* from Eng.)

Skeat compares Norw. *pilk* an artificial bait, whence Dan. dial. *pilke*, Swed. dial. *pilka* to fish in a particular manner. Cf. also Sc. dial *pilch* a short fat person, anything thick or gross, a tough skinny piece of meat.]

A small sea fish, *Clupea pilchardus*, closely allied to the herring, but smaller, and rounder in form; it is taken in large numbers on the coasts of Cornwall and Devon, and forms a considerable article of trade; in U.S. and Eng. Colonies locally applied to other fishes of the herring kind, e.g. the *C. sagax* of the Pacific, the *Harengula macrophthalma* of Bermuda; also to the young menhaden.

† *to take sturgeons with pilchards*, to get large returns from a small outlay (*obs.*).

1530 PALSGR. 254/1 Pylcher a fysshe, *sardine.* **1542** BOORDE *Dyetary* xxx. (1870) 293 He must not eate..fresshe heryng, pylcherdes, etc. **1570** LEVINS *Manip.* 30/35 Pilcharde, *gerres, halecula. Ibid.* 74/37 Pylcher, fish, *mena, æ. c* **1600** NORDEN *Spec. Brit., Cornw.* (1728) 22 The..recheste fishing is of the leaste fishe which is called a pilcharde. **1601** SHAKS. *Twel. N.* III. i. 39 Fooles are as like husbands, as Pilchers are to Herrings. **1656** EARL MONM. tr. *Boccalini's Advts. fr. Parnass.* I. xlviii. (1674) 63 They have built commodious Inns to take Sturgeons with Pilcherds. **1711** *Lond. Gaz.* No. 4941/2 Pilchers for the Streights. **1796** H. HUNTER tr. *St.-Pierre's Stud. Nat.* (1799) I. 263 The continuation and direction of these two bands, the pilchers of the South, and the herrings of the North, are nearly of the same length. **1813** SIR H. DAVY *Agric. Chem.* (1814) 288 The refuse pilchards in Cornwall are used..as a Manure. **1865** KINGSLEY *Herew.* v, Savoury was the smell of fried pilchard.

attrib. **1685** PETTY *Last Will* p. vi, I set up iron-works and pilchard-fishing in Kerry. **1824** HITCHINS & DREW *Cornwall* II. 471 The pilchard fishery furnishes the staple commodity of the place.

†**pilcher**¹. *Obs.* A term of abuse, frequent at the beginning of the 17th c. It has been conjecturally explained as meaning 'One who wears a pilch or leathern jerkin or doublet', or 'One who pilches, a thief'; in two instances it is either fig. from *pilcher*, PILCHARD, the fish, or punningly associated with that word.

1601 B. JONSON *Poetaster* III. iv, Whither doe you dragge the gent'man? you mungrels, you curres, you ban-dogs, wee are Captaine Tucca, that talke to you, you inhumane pilchers. **1602** MIDDLETON *Blurt, Master-Constable* I. ii, Pilcher, thou'rt a most pitiful dried one. *a* **1619** FLETCHER *Wit without M.* III. iv, Upbraid me with your benefits, you pilchers. *a* **1625** —— *Women Pleas'd* II. iv, Hang him, Pilcher, There's nothing loves him: his owne Cat cannot endure him. *a* **1640** DAY *Parl. Bees* iv, Smoaked Pilcher vanish!

†**pilcher**². *Obs. rare.* [? Extended from PILCH.]

1. = PILCH *sb.* 1.

1635 EARL OF CORK *Diary* in *Lismore Papers* Ser. I. (1886) IV. 104, I haue..written to Mʳ Ned Boyle to furnish him with pilchers.

2. A scabbard. (Apparently *contemptuous.*)

1592 SHAKS. *Rom. & Jul.* III. i. 84 Will you pluck your Sword out of his Pilcher by the eares?

ˈpilcorn. [For *pildcorn*, f. PILLED *ppl. a.* 1 b + CORN.] A variety of the cultivated Oat, considered by Linnæus a species (*Avena nuda*), in which the glumes or husks do not adhere to the grain, but leave it bare. Also called *pilled oats*, †*pillotes*.

1578 LYTE *Dodoens* IV. xiii. 467 There is an other kinde of Otes, whiche is not so inclosed in his huskes as yᵉ other is, but is bare, and without huske whan it is threshed... The seconde kinde may be called in Englishe, Pilcorne, or pylde Otes. *c* **1640** J. SMYTH *Lives Berkeleys* (1883) I. 155 And had also Drage, pilcorne, mixtilion, brotcorne..words I professe, not well to vnderstand. **1832** *Veg. Subst. Food* iii. 71 The *Avena sativa*..has several varieties. The most remarkable..are the black or long-bearded oat..and the naked oat, or pilcorn. **1866** *Treas. Bot.*, Pillcorn, or Pilcorn.

pilcrow ('pɪlkrəʊ). *arch.* Forms: 5 pylcraft(e, pilecrafte, 6 pilcrowe, (7 pilkrow, pill-crow, peelcrow, pilgrow), 6– pilcrow. [App. for *pilled crow*: cf. *pilcorn*, *pilgarlic*, etc. The application of the word, with the form *pylcraft*, has suggested that it originated in a perversion of PARAGRAPH, through *pargrafte*, **parcrafte*, etc.: cf. quots. *c* 1460 and 1617. But the history of the word is obscure, and evidence is wanting.] = PARAGRAPH *sb.* 1.

[**1500** *Ortus Voc.*, *Paragraphus*, Anglice, a pargrafte in writing.] *c* **1440** *Promp. Parv.* 398/1 Pylcrafte, yn a booke ..*asteriscus, paragraphus*. *c* **1460** *Medulla* in Way *Promp. Parv.* 398 *note*, *Paragrapha*, pylcraft in wry[t]ynge. **1573** TUSSER *Husb.* (1878) 2 In husbandrie matters, where Pilcrowe ye finde That verse appertaineth to Huswiferie Kinde. **1602** R. T. *Five Godlie Serm.* 18 To stand as a Cypher in Augrim, or as a pilcrow in a latine Primmer. **1617** MINSHEU *Ductor*, *Pilkrow*, contractum videtur corruptumque ex paragrapho. *a* **1625** FLETCHER *Nice Valour* IV. i, But why a Peel-crow here?.. A Scar-crow had been better. **1706** PHILLIPS, *Pilcrow*, an old Word for a Paragraph. **1897** S. S. SPRIGGE *T. Wakley* xv. 141 The leading article..calling attention to them with interjections ..and all sorts of verbal pilcrows.

pild, obs. form of *pilled*: see PILL *v.*[1]

pile (paɪl), *sb.*[1] Forms: 1 pil, 4– pile, (4–8 pyle, 6 pyll, 7 peil). [OE. *pîl* masc. = OLG. **pîl* (MLG., MDu. *pîl*, Du. *pijl* dart, arrow, also ON. *píla* fem., arrow, Da., Sw. *pil*, from LG.), OHG., MHG. *pfîl*, Ger. *pfeil* dart, arrow, shaft, West Ger. *pîl*, a. L. *pīl-um* the heavy javelin of the Roman foot-soldier, orig. 'pestle'.

The L. *pīlum* was no doubt adopted by the Germans in the L. sense 'javelin', which passed on the continent into that of 'dart', and hence 'arrow', in which latter sense it superseded the native word. In OE. the sense 'javelin' passed into those of 'dart' and 'pointed stake' (= L. *sudis*): but the former is known only in a few poetic compounds, *flīȝe-pīl* flying-dart, *hylde-pīl* battle dart, and the earliest examples of the simple word in this sense are ME.; if applied to an arrow, it was only as subsidiary to native names.]

1. †**a.** A dart; a shaft; (?) an arrow. *Obs.*

a **1000** *Be Mannes Mod* 26 Bið þæt æfþonca eal ȝefylled feondes fliȝepilum. —— *Riddles* xviii. 6 Frea þæt bihealdeð hu me of hrife fleoȝað hyldepilas. **13..** *Guy Warw.* (A.) 3490 Schetep wiþ piles & ȝif hem deþ wounde. *c* **1400** *Destr. Troy* 6976 þen Paris..with a pile sharp, Rut hym in thurgh þe rybbis with a roid wond.

b. The pointed head of a dart, lance, or arrow.

1592 CONSTABLE *Sonn.* I. v, Thine eye the pyle is of a murdring dart. *c* **1611** CHAPMAN *Iliad* IV. 545 Through both his temples struck the dart, the wood of one side show'd, The pile out of the other look'd. **1627** DRAYTON *Court of Fairy* Wks. (1748) 166 His spear—a bent both stiff and strong,..The pile was of a horse-fly's tongue. **1639** FULLER *Holy War* II. x. (1840) 63 Like an arrow well feathered, but with a blunt pile; he flew swift, but did not sink deep. **1700** HICKES *Let.* in *Pepys' Corr.* 19 June, Elf arrows..are of a triangular form, somewhat like the beard or pile of our old English arrows of war. [**1796** PEGGE *Anonym.* (1809) 103 Fletcher, he that trimmed arrows by adding the feathers; Arrowsmith, he that made the piles.] **1875** *Encycl. Brit.* II. 376/1 Arrows are manufactured generally of red-pine timber,..glued on one end, upon the point of which the iron pile is fixed. **1894** H. WALROND in Longman & Walrond *Archery* xviii. 304 Arrows are..called 'self' or 'footed' according as to whether they are footed or not with hard wood at the pile end. **1939** P. H. GORDON *New Archery* II. vi. 67 The solid-tipped 'parallel pile' is preferable to hollow-point 'bullet ferrules'. **1958** WISEMAN & BRUNDLE *Archery* 83 The piles or tips of arrows are made of brass, steel, aluminium, horn or plastic. **1972** T. FOY *Beginner's Guide Archery* xvi. 124 In the eighteenth-century the Turks were superb Flight Shots, and they invented 'barrelled' arrows which were thicker at the centre than at the nock and pile. **1979** R. LAIDLAW *Lion is Rampant* xiii. 104 They were target arrows with conical piles.

c. Used to render L. *pīlum*, the heavy javelin of the ancient Roman foot-soldier.

c **1620** FLETCHER & MASS. *False One* I. i, How the Roman Peils..drew Roman blood. **1627** MAY *Lucan* I. 8 Knowne Ensignes Ensignes doe defie, Piles against Piles, 'gainst Eagles Eagles fly. (*Note.* If any man quarrell at the word *Pile*, as thinking it scarse English, I desire them to give a better word.) **1687** DRYDEN *Hind & P.* II. 161 That was but civil war, an equal set, Where piles with piles, and eagles eagles met. **1688** R. HOLME *Armoury* III. xvi. (Roxb.) 89/1 The Germans came so violently vpon the Romans that the souldiers cast away their piles, and betooke them to their swords. **1718** ROWE tr. *Lucan* I. 7 Piles against piles oppos'd in impious fight, And Eagles against Eagles bending flight. **1850** MERIVALE *Rom. Emp.* (1865) I. vi. 273 The Romans threw their piles, and rushed headlong upon the unwieldy mass.

2. †**a.** A spike, a nail; a spine (of a prickly plant, in ME. of a hedgehog); the pointer of a sun-dial.

c **1000** ÆLFRIC *Saint's Lives* v. 388 He ȝehæfte [hi] on anum micclum stocce, and mid isenum pilum heora ilas ȝefæstnode and cwæð þæt hi sceoldon swa standan on þam pilum. *c* **1000** *Sax. Leechd.* I. 304 Heo [sea-holly] hafað stelan hwitne..on ðæs heahnysse ufeweardre beoð acennede scearpe and þyrnyhte pilas. *a* **1100** *O.E. Gloss.* in Wr.-Wülcker 337/6 *Gnomon* dægmæles pil. *a* **1200** *Fragm. Ælfric's Gram.* (ed. Phillips 1838), Prikiende so piles on ile. *c* **1225**, **1387** [see *ilespiles* s.v. IL]. *c* **1290** *S. Eng. Leg.* I. 179/50 Heo stikeden al-so þicke on him, so yrichon deth of piles. *Ibid.* 298/49 Ase ful ase is an Irchepil of piles al-aboute.

b. A (pointed) blade (of grass). [Cf. Da. dial. *pile*, *græspile*, Fl. *pijl*, *graspijl*.]

1513 DOUGLAS *Æneis* XIII. Prol. 25 At euery pilis point and cornis croppis The techrys stude, as lemand beriall droppis. **1607** HIERON *Wks.* I. 153 More sinnes then there bee grasse piles vpon the earth. **1687** A. LOVELL tr. *Thevenot's Trav.* I. 291 There shall not a pile of Grass be left within his Kingdom. **1765** *Museum Rust.* IV. xxviii. 122 Appearance of red clover, where not a pile of this grass had before been known. **1812** SIR J. SINCLAIR *Syst. Husb. Scot.* I. 372 The grass was..smaller in the pile, and more luxuriant in its growth. **1895** CROCKETT *Men of Moss-Hags* xxi, Every pile of the grass that springs so sweetly in the meadows.

c. A single glume or pale (of chaff). *Sc.*

1786 BURNS *Address to Unco Guid* heading, The cleanest corn..May hae some pyles o' caff in.

3. a. A pointed stake or post; *spec.* in later use, a large and heavy beam of timber or trunk of a tree, usually sharpened at the lower end, of which a number are driven into the bed of a river, or into marshy or uncertain ground for the support of some superstructure, as a bridge, pier, quay, wall, the foundation of a house, etc. Also extended to cylindrical or other hollow iron pillars, used for the same purposes.

In prehistoric times villages or settlements were built upon wooden piles in lakes: see *pile-dwelling*, etc. in 5.

? *a* **1100** *O.E. Chron.* (Laud MS.) Introd. (from Bæda), Ða ȝenamon þa Walas, and adrifon sumre ea ford ealne mid scearpum pilum [BÆDA sudibus, *D.* stængum: cf. Wr.-Wülcker 509/14 *sudibus* stengum] greatum innan þam welere sy ea hatte Temese. *c* **1330** R. BRUNNE *Chron. Wace* (Rolls) 4611 Longe pyles & grete dide þey [Britons] make; Faste yn Temese dide þey hem stake. **1377** LANGL. *P. Pl.* B. XVI. 23 þe tree..With þre pyles was it vnder-piȝte. **1387–8** T. USK *Test. Love* II. v. (Skeat) l. 116 If the pyles ben trewe, the gravel and sand wol abyde. **1480** CAXTON *Chron. Eng.* ccxlviii. (1482) 316 The duk hym self with ij or thre lepe vpon the pyles, and so were saued with helpe of men that were aboue the bridge. **1497** *Naval Acc. Hen. VII* (1896) 171 The brekyng vp of the dokke hede at Portesmouth weyng vt of the piles & shorys. **1530** PALSGR. 254/1 Pyle to be set in a fauty grounde, *pilot.* **1555** EDEN *Decades* 226 Theyr houses..are..buylded aboue the grownde vppon proppes & pyles. **1602** WARNER *Alb. Eng.* Epit. (1612) 356 Two walles, the one of Turffe, and the other of Pyles and Tymber strongly and artificially interposed. **1768–74** TUCKER *Lt. Nat.* (1834) II. 405 Like the houses of Amsterdam. which are reported to stand upon piles driven deep into the quagmire. **1863** LYELL *Antiq. Man* ii. (ed. 3) 17 Habitations..constructed on platforms raised above the lake, and resting on piles.

fig. **1886** RUSKIN *Præterita* I. xii. 416 Drive down the oaken pile of a principle.

b. With various qualifications expressing purpose or nature: e.g.

bearing p., *bridge p.*, *foundation p.*, *guide p.*, *hollow p.*, *sheathing p.*, *short p.*, *weir p.*, etc. *close pile*, a timber pile forming one of many set close together; *false pile*, a pile to which additional length is given after driving; *filling pile*, one of those filling up the space between gauge piles; *hydraulic pile*, a pile sunk in sand by means of a powerful jet of water led either inside or outside of it. Also FENDER *p.*, GAUGE *p.*, GUARD *p.*, GUIDE *p.*, PNEUMATIC *p.*, SCREW *p.*, SHEET or SHEETING *p.*, STAY *p.*, for which see these words.

1859 G. MEREDITH *R. Feverel* I. xvii. 266 The Magnetic Youth leaned round to note his proximity to the weir-piles. **1875** KNIGHT *Dict. Mech.* II. 1700/2 A hollow pile is a cylinder which is sunk by excavation proceeding inside. **1877** *Ibid.* III, *Short-pile*..driven as closely as possible without causing the driving of one pile to raise the adjacent ones. They are used to compress and consolidate ground for foundations.

†**c.** A stake or post fixed in the ground, at which swordsmen practised their strokes. *Obs. rare.*

c **1480** *Knyghthode & Batayle* (MS. Cott. Titus A. xxiii. lf. 6 b), Nooman..is seyn prevayle, In feeld..That with the pile, nathe firste grete exercise.

4. *Her.* A charge, regarded by some as an ordinary, by others as a sub-ordinary, consisting of a figure formed by two lines meeting in an acute angle (generally assumed to represent an arrow-head), issuing, when not otherwise stated, from the chief or top of the escutcheon, with the point downwards. *in pile*: arranged in the form of a pile. *party per pile*: divided by lines in the form of a pile.

[App. a special use of sense 1 b, or directly from L. *pīlum*. Not known in OF.: Littré has it as a neologism, *pile* masc., and refers it to L. *pīlum*; but it may have been taken directly from Eng. heraldry.]

1486 *Bk. St. Albans*, *Her.* E v b, Certan armys in the wich iij. pilis mete to gedyr in oon coone... He berith golde iij. pilis of sable. **1523** LD. BERNERS *Froiss.* I. ccxxxvii. 337 The baner..was of syluer a sharpe pyle goules. **1562** LEIGH *Armorie* 46 The eight particion, which is to be blased on thys sorte. Party per pile in pointe, Or and Sable. *Ibid.* 143 He beareth Ermin, a Pile in pointe Gueules. **1610** GUILLIM *Heraldry* II. vi. (1611) 62 He beareth Argent a Triple Pile, Flory on the tops, issuing out of the Sinister base, in Bend towards the Dexter corner, Sable. This sort of bearing of the Pile, hath a resemblance of so many Piles driuen into some water-worke, and..incorporated at their heads. *Ibid.* II. vi. (1660) 73 A Pile is an Ordinary consisting of a two-fold line formed after the manner of a Wedge; that is to say broad at the upper end, and..meeting together at the lower end in an Acute-angle. **1704** J. HARRIS *Lex. Techn.* I, *Pile*, in Heraldry,..probably something like the Figure of the Roman *Pilum*, which was a tapering Dart, about five Foot long, and sharpened at the Point with Steel. **1766–87** PORNY *Heraldry* (ed. 4) 135 The sixteenth is Argent, three piles meeting near the point of the base Azure. *c* **1828** BERRY *Encycl. Her.* I. Gloss., *Pile*, triple, or triple-pointed, in base, bendwise,..by Ferne, termed a pile, naisant, in bend, triple-flory. **1864** BOUTELL *Her. Hist. & Pop.* ix. (ed. 3) 50 Sa., three Swords in pile arg. **1872** RUSKIN *Eagle's N.* §235 The Pile, a wedge-shaped space of colour with the point downwards, represents what we still call a pile; a piece of timber driven into moist ground.

5. *attrib.* and *Comb.* (from 3). **a.** attrib. Of a pile, as *pile-head*, *-wood*; formed of piles, as *pile-breakwater*, *-dam*, *-planking*, *-structure*; supported on piles, as *pile-bridge*, *-habitation*, *-lighthouse*, *-pier*, *-road*, *-settlement*, *-village*; used as a pile, as *pile-plank*. **b.** obj. and obj. gen., as *pile-fixer*, *guide*, *-screwing*. **c.** instrumental, as *pile-supported* adj. **d.** Special Comb.: **pile-building**, a building erected on piles, esp. one of such dwellings of certain prehistoric and primitive peoples; so also **pile-builder**, **pile-built** *a.*; **pile-cap**, a cap or plate for the head of a pile; also, a beam connecting the heads of piles; **pile-drawer**, a machine for extracting piles; **pile-dwelling**, a dwelling built on piles, especially in shallow water, as a lake, but sometimes on dry ground; hence **pile-dweller**; **pile-engine** = PILE-DRIVER; **pile-hoop**, a hoop or band round the head of a pile to keep it from splitting; **pile-house**, a house built on piles, a pile-dwelling; **pile-saw**, a saw for cutting off piles below the surface of the water; hence **pile-sawing**; **pile-shoe**, an iron point fixed to the lower end of a pile; **pile-worm**, the teredo, or other worm or animal which bores into piles. See also PILE-DRIVER, PILEWAYS, PILE-WORK.

1895 *Outing* (U.S.) XXVI. 445/1 Under the protection of two huge *pile-breakwaters. **1899** *Westm. Gaz.* 9 Dec. 5/3 The scarcity of timber or other material suitable for the erection of a trestle or *pile bridge. **1940** *Chambers's Techn. Dict.* 643/1 *Pile bridge*, a bridge whose superstructure is carried on piles. **1884** *Nature* 19 June 169/1 There are good reasons for believing these *pile-builders are the direct descendants of the pre-Aryan aboriginals. **1865** LUBBOCK *Preh. Times* v. 127 The Lake-dwellers followed two different systems..which he distinguishes as..*Pile-buildings, and..Crannoges. **1886** *Athenæum* 24 Apr. 556/1 The pile-buildings of the Swiss lakes. **1851** A. O. HALL *Manhattaner* 5 It was a modest commercial plain; *pile-built, and earth filled. **1898** C. E. FOWLER *Coffer-dam Process for Piers* iv. 49 The small hammer..is used for sheet pile work by inserting a 'follower' of oak which fits the base or pile cap, and which has a slit in the lower end to fit the sheet pile. **1903** KIPLING *5 Nations* 41 Do you know the pile-built village where the sago-dealers trade? **1944** [see PILING *vbl. sb.*[1] 2]. **1975** R. HOLMES *Introd. Civil Engin. Construction* iv. 166 Pile caps are usually constructed of concrete to such a depth as will ensure full transfer of load to the piles and, at the same time, resist punching shear. **1800** *Hull Advertiser* 5 Apr. 1/3 The constructing of a *pile dam opposite to the clough. **1880** DAWKINS *Early Man* 302 The *pile-dwellers possessed vegetables not traceable to wild stocks now growing in Switzerland. **1863** LYELL *Antiq. Man* 29 It relates to the earliest age of *pile-dwelling. **1874** SAYCE *Compar. Philol.* iii. 114 Their [the Etruscans'] predecessors of the Neolithic age whose pile-dwellings..have yielded wheat and coral, evidences of Eastern intercourse. **1776** G. SEMPLE *Building in Water* 36 The Platform of the *Pile-engine. **1853** SIR H. DOUGLAS *Milit. Bridges* (ed. 3) 154 The piles were driven by pile-engines..constructed on the boats of the country. **1974** *People's Jrnl.* (Inverness & Northern Counties ed.) 29 June 22 (*caption*) In one of the biggest lifts ever in the off-shore oil industry a 940-ton *pile guide cluster is lifted into position to be fixed to the base of the huge oil rig jacket now being finished at Nigg. **1975** *Offshore* Sept. 11/1 The 'Heerema Steel Structure' consists essentially of a jacket made up of four steel towers which fit into a steel base frame incorporating pile guides. **1886** A. WINCHELL *Walks Geol. Field* 283 Jars of dried apples and wheat..have been yielded from the *pile-habitations. **1875** W. MCILWRAITH *Guide Wigtownshire* 45 Dowalton Loch.. celebrated by the discovery there of *pile-houses. **1884** *Nature* 19 June 169/2 The races who now build these pile-houses, often on hill-tops. **1895** *Daily News* 27 Sept. 5/4 Unlike the old *pile piers, it is a substantial structure of masonry. **1823** P. NICHOLSON *Pract. Builder* 590 **Pile-planks*, planks of which the ends are sharpened, so as to enter into the bottom of a canal. **1838** *Civ. Eng. & Archit. Jrnl.* I. 150/1 A scaffold was erected, upon which the pile drivers were placed for driving the sheet piles (pile planks)..of the best North Carolina heart pine. **1793** R. MYLNE *Rep. Thames* 24 A Jettee of *Pile-planking..should be run a little way down from the Point. **1860** WEALE *Dict. Terms* s.v., As a considerable length of the Utica and Syracuse railroad passes through a deep swamp, a foundation of great permanency was required: this gave rise to a modification of the superstructure, and formed that which is known as *pile-road. **1875** KNIGHT *Dict. Mech.* 1703/1 Vogler's *pile-sawing attachment for boats. **1897** R. MUNRO *Preh. Problems* 304 A *pile-settlement of the Bronze Age. **1495** *Naval Acc. Hen. VII* (1896) 150 A pykas and ij *pyles shone. **1844** *Mech. Mag.* XL. 54 Improvement in the formation of pile-shoes. **1887** *Westm. Rev.* June 340 Along this line [Barmston and Skipsea Drain] five or six other *pile-structures have been found. **1869** *Routledge's Ev. Boy's Ann.* 389 An old *pile-supported pier. **1879** *Athenæum* 6 Sept. 312/1 *Pile-villages have been found on the shores of Gmunden. **1894** C. WELCH *Tower Bridge* 133 Snuff-boxes and other memorials..turned from the *pile wood. **1733** tr.

Rousset (*title*) Observations on the Sea or *Pile Worms discover'd in Pile or Woodworks in Holland.

†**pile**, *sb.*[2] *Obs.* Forms: 4–6 **pyle**, 5 **pyl**, **pyll**, **pylle**, 5–8 **pile**. [Of doubtful origin.

Evidently distinct historically from PILE *sb.*[3], sense 4. It may, however, be an earlier adoption of the same Fr. word. In sense it agrees exactly with PEEL *sb.*[1], senses 3 and 4; and in the 16th c. the Border *peels* usually appear in the English State papers as *pyles* or *piles*. Yet the words cannot be doublets, for in *pile* the final *e* is evidently original.]

A small castle, tower, or stronghold; = PEEL *sb.*[1] 3.

13.. *E.E. Allit. P.* A. 685 Þe ryȝtwys man also sertayn Aproche he schal þat proper pyle [*rime* gyle]. **1377** LANGL. *P. Pl.* B. XIX. 360 That holy-cherche stode in vnite As it a pyle were. **1393** *Ibid.* C. XXII. 366 Holy churche stod in holynesse as hit were a pile. *c* **1430** *Hymns Virg.* (1867) 45 Þanne y councellid euoul with-inne a while.. þat alle men children in towne & pile To slee þem, þat ihesus myght with hem die. *c* **1435** *Torr. Portugal* 573 Yf I dwelle in my pylle of ston. *c* **1450** LONELICH *Grail* xii. 349 It [Castle of Valachim] was On of the Strengest pyl, That Euere Man Sawgh in Ony Exyl. **14..** *Coventry Corp. Chr. Pl.* (E.E.T.S.) 16 Yett do I marvell In whatt pyle or castell These herdmen dyd hym see. **1542** UDALL *Erasm. Apoph.* 222 b, The grekes wer besieged in a litle preatie pyle or castle. **1568** GRAFTON *Chron.* II. 866 They sayled into Englande.., and landed..at the pyle of Fowdrey within lytle of Lancaster [called in 1423 *Act 2 Hen. VI*, c. 5 le Peele de Foddray en le Counte de Lancastre]. **1602** in Moryson *Itin.* II. III. i. (1617) 270 To build little piles of Stone in such Garrisons [in Ireland] as shall be thought fittest to be continuall bridles vpon the people. **1609** HOLLAND *Amm. Marcell.* XIV. viii. 18 Arabia,..a rich land,..replenished also with strong castles and piles [*castris oppleta ualidis et castellis*]. [**1679** BLOUNT *Anc. Tenures* 20 *Pele* or *Pile*, is a Fort built for defence of any place. **1727–41** CHAMBERS *Cycl.*, *Pille of Foddray*, or *Pile of Fouldrey*,..called *pille*, by the idiom of the county, for a *pile*, or fort.]

b. *spec.* Applied to the Peels on the Scottish border: = PEEL *sb.*[1] 4.

1494 FABYAN *Chron.* VII. 512 The which..threwe downe certayne pylys and other strengthis, and a parte of the Castell of Beawmount. *a* **1548** HALL *Chron.*, *Hen. VIII* 203 The kyng entended..to make new diuers Pyles and stoppes to let the Scottysh men from their inuasions. **1577–87** HOLINSHED *Chron.* III. 881/1 He ouerthrew certeine castels, piles, and small holds, till he came through the dales to Iedworth. *a* **1649** DRUMM. OF HAWTH. *Hist. Jas. V*, Wks. (1711) 91 Thomas earl of Surrey,..had burnt many towns, and overthrown castles and piles. **1774** LAMBE *Battle of Flodden* cxliv, Where piles be pulled down apace.

pile (paɪl), *sb.*[3] Forms: 5– **pile**, (5–7 **pyle**, 6 **pyele**). [a. F. *pile* heap, pyramid, mass of masonry, pier of a bridge (1340 in Godef.) = It. *pila* mole, pier, pillar, Sp. *pila*, Pg. *pilha* pile, heap:—L. *pīla* pillar, pier, or mole of stone.]

†**1. a.** A pillar; a pier, esp. of a bridge. *Obs.*

(Not to be confused with PILE *sb.*[1] 3.)

c **1420** *Pallad. on Husb.* I. 1089 Pilis maad of tilis must ascende Too feet and half. *c* **1440** *Promp. Parv.* 398/1 Pyle, of a bryggys fote, or oþer byggynge.., *pila*. *a* **1577** GASCOIGNE *Flowers* Wks. (1587) 59 Then waues of euil doe worke so fast my piles are ouerrun. **1617** MORYSON *Itin.* I. 115 Of this Bridge thirteene piles of bricke may bee seene neere the shore at Pozzoli. **1702** ECHARD *Eccl. Hist.* (1710) 434 This bridge consisted of twenty piles, each 60 foot in thickness, and 150 in height, besides the foundation. **1730** A. GORDON *Maffei's Amphith.* 219 Of the Stones.., one of them is still seen in the middle Pile of the Bridge *delle Navi*.

†**b.** *fig.* Applied to the neck, leg, etc.

1584 LODGE *Alarum agst. Usurers* (Hunter. Cl.) 72 Her stately necke where nature did acquite Her selfe so well,.. For in this pile was fancie painted faire. *Ibid.* 73 The stately thies, Like two faire compast marble pillers rise..Next which the knees..This stately pyles with gladsome honour greete. **1589** —— *Scillaes Met.* (Hunter. Cl.) 41 Now Nature stands amazd her selfe to looke on Beauties feete,..So small a pile so great a weight, like Atlas to vphold The bodie.

†**2.** A mole or pier in the sea. *Obs.*

c **1630** RISDON *Surv. Devon* §334 (1810) 345 There is a harbour for ships, by means of a pile built. **1652** NEEDHAM tr. *Selden's Mare Cl.* 87 But if no man sustain damage, hee is to bee defended who build's upon the shore, or cast's a Pile into the Sea.

3. a. A heap of things (of some height) laid or lying one upon another in a more or less regular manner; also *fig.*

c **1440** *Promp. Parv.* 398/1 Pyle, or heep, where of hyt be, *cumulus*. *Ibid.*, Pyle of clothys..on a presse, *panniplicium*. **1530** PALSGR. 254/1 Pyle of clothes or any other heape, *pille*. **1653** MILTON *Hirelings* Wks. 1738 I. 579 To how little purpose are all those piles of Sermons, Notes, and Comments on all parts of the Bible. *a* **1656** BP. HALL *Rem. Wks.* (1660) 53 You are called out to see piles of dead carcasses. **1703** MAUNDRELL *Journ. Jerus.* (1707) 15 A rude pile of Stones erected..for an Altar. **1744** BERKELEY *Siris* §13 Such heaps or piles of wood were sometimes a hundred and eighty cubits round. **1812** J. WILSON *Isle of Palms* II. 363 Behold yon pile of clouds, Like a city, round the sun. **1833** J. HOLLAND *Manuf. Metal* II. 231 The sheet printed on both sides is delivered upon the board,..and laid upon the pile. **1891** E. PEACOCK *N. Brendon* I. 310 A large pile of letters and packages.

b. A series of weights fitting one within or upon another, so as to form a solid cone or other figure. (So F. *pile*.)

This sense is certain for quots. 1611, 1690; but quot. 1440 is doubtful. The attrib. use in *pile weight* apparently belongs here.

c **1440** *Promp. Parv.* 398/1 Pyle, of weyynge, *libramentum, libra*. **1585** SIR F. KNOLLYS *Abstr. syzinge Troye weyghte* (MS. Rawl. D. 23 lf. 18), They argve that the gowlde smythes pyle weyghte is muche tooe heavy, to be the trewe Troy weyghte. **1611** COTGR., *Pile*,..also, the pile, or whole masse, of weights vsed by Goldsmithes, etc. **1647** in Cochran-Patrick *Rec. Coinage Scotl.* (1876) I. Introd. 80 Compared the forsaid round brasse stone weight..with a new brasse stone pyle weight in the coinyehouse, and I found the said new pyle weight havier by almost halfe one oz. *Ibid.*, The new 4 lb pyle marked with a fleure de lyce boght from J. Falconar Warden from Holland. *Ibid.* 81 Having examined the French pyle marked with the fleure de lyce amongst the weights now used. **1660** *Act 12 Chas. II*, c. 4 Sched. s.v. *Brass*, Brass of Pile weights the pound, j.s. **1690** BOYLE *Medicina Hydrostat.* Wks. 1772 V. (Plate at end), The Explication of the Figure..*q*. the Pile of Weights.

†**c.** A large group, clump, or collection of things, without reference to height; a 'lot'. *Obs.*

1622 R. HAWKINS *Voy. S. Sea* (1847) 47 Of these ilands are two pyles: the one of them..little frequented; the other ..containeth six in number, to wit: Saint Iago, Fuego, Mayo, Bonavisto, Sal, and Bravo. **1864** EMILY DICKINSON *Lett.* (1894) II. 253 Father has built a new road round the pile of trees between our house and Mr. S——'s.

d. *spec.* A heap of combustibles on which a dead body is burnt (*funeral pile*).

1615 G. SANDYS *Trav.* I. 83 Laying them vpon their backs on beds, they conueyed them vnto the funerall pile..on beares. **1699** GARTH *Dispens.* III. 30 And with Prescriptions lights the solemn Pyle. **1700** DRYDEN *Palamon & Arc.* III. 990 Full bowls of wine, of honey, milk, and blood, Were poured upon the pile of burning wood. **1878** MACLEAR *Celts* ii. (1879) 19 Some even voluntarily came forward to share the pile with an honoured person deceased. **1879** FROUDE *Cæsar* xviii. 305 Made a pile of chairs and benches and tables, and burnt all that remained of Clodius.

e. A heap of wood or faggots on which a sacrifice or a person is burnt.

1577 tr. *Bullinger's Decades* (1592) 64 Isaac was layde on the pile of wood to bee offered up in sacrifice. *a* **1618** SYLVESTER *Maidens Blush* 1783 The Father makes the Pile: Hereon he layes His bond-led, blind-led Son. **1848** MRS. JAMESON *Sacr. & Leg. Art* (1850) 331 Then the people kindled the pile; but though the flame was exceedingly large it did not touch her. **1902** *Westm. Gaz.* 12 July 1/3 'It is disgraceful', said the curate, who was all for the pile of faggots.

f. *Mil.* A stack of arms regularly built up.

1608 D. T[UVIL] *Ess. Pol. & Mor.* 122 b, Germanicus.. caused a pyle of weapons to be raised. **1887** BOWEN *Æneid* I. 296 Sinful Rebellion..Piling her fiendish weapons, shall sit firm bound on the pile.

g. An oblong rectangular mass of cut lengths of puddled iron-bars, laid upon each other in rows, for the purpose of being rolled after being raised to a welding temperature in a reheating furnace; a 'faggot'.

1839 URE *Dict. Arts* 707 Four rows of these [iron bars] are usually laid over each other into a heap or pile which is placed in the re-heating furnace..and exposed to a free circulation of heat, one pile being set crosswise over another. **1881** RAYMOND *Mining Gloss.*, *Pile*, the fagot or bundle of flat pieces of iron prepared to be heated to welding-heat and then rolled.

h. *ellipt.* (for *pile of wealth*, *money*, *dollars*, etc.) A heap of money; a fortune accumulated or heaped up. Chiefly in colloq. phr. *to make one's pile*; also *to go one's pile*, to stake all one's money on a single chance, to 'go the whole hog'.

[**1613** SHAKS. *Hen. VIII*, III. ii. 107 What piles of wealth hath he accumulated To his owne portion? **1839** THIRLWALL *Greece* VI. 233 It seems to have been one of the state maxims..to draw as little as possible from this pile of wealth. **1876** HOLLAND *Sev. Oaks* xxiii. 324 Yes, and I've made piles of money on them.]

1741 FRANKLIN in *Poor Rich. Alm.* Apr. (Bartlett), Rash mortals, ere you take a wife, Contrive your pile to last for life. **1839** *Picayune* (New Orleans) 29 Mar. 2/2 Friends of the Lubber, becoming excited at the unexpected termination of the first heat, were willing to go a 'small pile' somewhere in the neighborhood of even. **1840** *Spirit of Times* X. 498 Considerable sums were laid out..the Georgians 'going their pile' on the Andrew filly. **1852** F. MARRYAT *Gold Quartz Mining* 8 On the old Californian principle of 'making a "pile" and vamosing the ranché'. **1862** *Fraser's Mag.* July 27 Every partisan blackleg bets his 'pile' upon his favourite. **1864** ELIZ. A. MURRAY *E. Norman* III. 182 The hope which cheers..so many [Australian diggers]..'We may make our pile yet, and go home'. **1865** 'MARK TWAIN' *Celebr. Jumping Frog* (1867) 37 His last acts was to go his pile..when there was a 'flush' out agin him. **1887** JESSOPP *Arcady* vii. 196 Capitalists who had made their pile were consumed by a desire to walk over their own broad acres. **1915** J. BUCHAN *39 Steps* i. 10, I had got my pile—not one of the big ones, but good enough for me. **1915** WODEHOUSE *Psmith Journalist* xxii. 166 He made a bit of a pile out of the job, and could afford to lie low for a year or two. **1969** *Listener* 24 July 103/2 So many Poles or Ukrainians..had spent part of their life in the United States, and returned home after making a decent pile. **1973** *Times* 22 Mar. 25/1 This is tough talk from a man who first made his pile as an investment banker. **1977** MCKNIGHT & TOBLER *Bob Marley* i. 17 The only way to get ahead, make your pile and escape from the overwhelming oppression and depression of poverty.

i. A nuclear reactor.

1942 H. L. ANDERSON et al. in E. Fermi *Coll. Papers* (1965) II. 129 At the end of September, 1941, a new and taller exponential pile was set up and the accuracy was further increased by using a 2 gram Ra + Be source instead of the original source of about 600 mg. **1945** H. D. SMYTH *Gen. Acct. Devel. Atomic Energy Mil. Purposes* v. 48 In a memorandum written to Bush on May 14, 1942.., Conant estimated that there were five separation or production methods that were..likely to succeed: the centrifuge, diffusion, and electromagnetic methods of separating U-235; the uranium-graphite pile and the uranium-heavy-water pile methods of producing plutonium. **1945** *War Illustr.* 9 Nov. 439/1 The natural uranium (U238) is in the shape of rods embedded in a graphite block and contained in an atomic 'pile'. **1945** *Nature* 29 Dec. 768/2 They give.. brief accounts..of the construction and testing of the first self-sustaining chain-reacting pile. **1946** *Ann. Reg. 1945* 354 A pile, containing 12,400 lb. of uranium in lumps separated by graphite, set up in Chicago under the direction of Prof. E. Fermi, was first operated on December 2, 1942. **1948** K. K. DARROW *Atomic Energy* iv. 66 When I heard the name in its new meaning and knew that Fermi an Italian had invented the new pile, I took it for granted that he had intentionally chosen the appellation of Volta. Great was my surprise when I learned from Fermi that it was a mere coincidence. He had conferred the name on his device because it was 'such a big pile of graphite and uranium'. **1952** *Nucleonics* Mar. 11/1 In later developments, most of the assemblies bear no resemblance to piles so that the expression nuclear reactor is to be preferred. Some British writers make the distinction that piles imply the use of natural uranium, and reactors, the use of enriched uranium. **1954** C. P. SNOW *New Men* vi. 100 'If the pile gets too hot, then they automatically shut the whole thing off,' said Luke. **1955** *Sci. News Let.* 26 Mar. 201/2 Fissionable material to fuel the pile will be obtained from the AEC on an extended loan basis. **1957** *Times* 12 Oct. 6/1 The danger of radioactivity being disseminated from the pile chimney in steam. **1964** M. GOWING *Britain & Atomic Energy, 1939–1945* x. 284 The theoretical physicists also contributed greatly to a whole range of pile theory and pile design problems. **1976** *Sci. Amer.* Dec. 32/2 Barely two and a half years elapsed between the initial chain-reacting pile on December 2, 1942, and the explosion of the first plutonium bomb on July 16, 1945.

4. a. A lofty mass of buildings; a large building or edifice.

1607 J. NORDEN *Surv. Dial.* III. 84 If this loftie Pyle bee not equalized by the estate and reuenewes of the builder, it is as if Paules steeple should serue Pancras Church for a Belfry. **1663** COWLEY *Verses Sev. Occas.*, *Queen's Repairing Somerset-Ho.*, Two of the best and stateliest Piles which e're Man's liberal Piety of old did rear. **1687** A. LOVELL tr. *Thevenot's Trav.* II. 28 Over against the middle of the Bridge,..there is a great square pile of building in the Water. **1791** BOSWELL *Johnson* 21 Sept. an. 1773, There is a very large unfinished pile, four stories high. **1823** SCOTT *Peveril* xxx, This antiquated and almost ruinous pile occupied a part of the site of the public offices in the Strand ..commonly called Somerset House. **1855** PRESCOTT *Philip II*, I. I. vii. 102 Philip testified his joy..by raising the magnificent pile of the Escorial. **1870** H. SMART *Race for Wife* ii, Glinn was a large pile of brickwork.

b. *fig.*

1671 MILTON *Samson* 1069 His look Haughty as is his pile high-built and proud. **1770** LANGHORNE *Plutarch* (1879) I. 89/2 The beautiful pile of justice which he had reared presently fell to the ground. **1835** THIRLWALL *Greece* I. 39 Afraid of raising a great pile of conjecture on a very slender basis of facts.

5. A series of plates of two dissimilar metals, such as copper and zinc, laid one above the other alternately, with cloth or paper moistened with an acid solution placed between each pair, for producing an electric current (*galvanic* or *voltaic pile*). Also extended to other arrangements of such plates: cf. BATTERY.

dry pile, a voltaic pile in which no liquid is used, and which generates a feeble but very permanent current.

1800 *Med. Jrnl.* IV. 119 When they used the order of silver, card, zinc, &c... This pile gave us the shock as before described. *Ibid.*, The plate A was connected with the top of the electrometer and the silver end of the pile. **1849** NOAD *Electricity* 198 The chemical power of the voltaic pile was discovered and described by Messrs. Nicholson and Carlisle, in the year 1800. **1871** TYNDALL *Fragm. Sc.* (1879) I. xiv. 381 Behind the screen..was an excellent thermo-electric pile. **1894** BOTTONE *Electr. Instr. Making* (ed. 6) 146 This pile was used with a large paraffin burner having an iron chimney nearly touching the interior ends of elements. [*Ibid.*, Fig. 56 is reproduced from a photograph of the identical thermopile.]

pile (paɪl), *sb.*[4] *arch.* Also 4 **pyl**, 6 **pyle**, **pyll**, **pyell**. [a. OF. *pile* (12th c. in Littré), also in med.L. *pīla*. In Fr. opposed to *croix*, as in Eng. to 'cross', also in mod.F. to *face*, in *à pile ou face*.

F. *pile*, L. *pīla*, in this sense was app. the same word as in prec., the *pile* or under iron of the *coin* (COIN *sb.* 4) being a small upright iron pillar, on the flat top of which the piece of metal was laid to be stamped: see sense 1.]

†**1.** The under iron of the minting apparatus with which money was struck; its surface bore the die of which the impression was made on the reverse or pile side of the piece. Opposed to *trussell* or *tursall*, F. *trousseau* (Cotgr.): see quot. 1876. *Obs.*

[**1293** *Memoranda K.R.* 20 & 21 Edw. I, m. 35 b *cedule*, Inuente sunt inter bona illa due pecie quarum vna vocatur pila et alia crosse que vocantur cuneus ad monetam Regis cudendam. **1300** (Nov. 10) *Ibid.* 28 & 29 Edw. I. 61 De cuneis Cambii Dunelmensis... Vous enueyames del dit Eschekier..deux peire de Cuyns noueaux en .vj. peces. E puis..vne peire noue en treis peces, cest a sauoir a chescone peire vne pile e ij Trusseux.]

1562–3 *Reg. Privy Council Scot.* I. 227 Ane pile and ane tursall maid for cunyeing of certane pecis of gold and silvir, the pile havand sunkin thairin foure lettris. **1587–8** *Ibid.* IV. 265 To grave, sink and mak countaris of lattoun, with sic pyles and tursallis as may serve to that effect. **1605** *Ibid.* VII. 54 To ressave the pyllis and tursellis laitlie send hame from England, and the puncheons for making of ma pyllis and tursellis. **1611** COTGR., *Pile*.., also, the pile, or under-yron of the stampe wherein money is stamped. **1876** COCHRAN-PATRICK *Rec. Coinage Scotl.* I. Introd. 49 Each moneyer had two irons or puncheons, one of which was called the 'pile', and the other the 'trussell'. The 'pile' was from seven to eight inches long, and was firmly fixed in a block of wood (called '*ceppeau*' in the French Ordonnances). On the 'pile' was engraved one side of the coin, and on the 'trussell' the other.

2. Hence, The side of a coin opposite to the 'cross' or face; the reverse. *arch.* ***cross and*** (***or***) ***pile***, in phrases: see CROSS *sb.* 21 b-e.

1390 GOWER *Conf.* I. 172 Whos tunge neither pyl ne crouche Mai hyre. *c* **1430** LYDG. *Min. Poems* (Percy Soc.) 51 Of crosse nor pile there is no recluse, Prynte nor impressioun in all thy seyntwarye. **1523** LD. BERNERS *Froiss.* I. cliv. 185 The frenche kyng made newe money of fyne golde, called florence of yᵉ lambe, for in the pyell there was grauyn a lambe. [Cf. *Chron. de S. Den.*, B.N. 2813, lf. 396 Appellez florins a l'aignel pour ce que en la pile avoit un aignel.] **1530** PALSGR. 254/1 Pyle of a coyne, the syde havyng no crosse, *pile*. **1678** BUTLER *Hud.* III. iii 688 That you as sure, may Pick and Choose, As Cross I win, and Pile you lose. **1706** PHILLIPS, *Pile*,..the backside of a piece of Money. **1843** MILL *Logic* III. xviii. §1 Why, in tossing up a halfpenny, do we reckon it equally probable that we shall throw cross or pile?

pile (paɪl), *sb.*⁵ Also 5-6 pyle. [ad. L. *pĭlus* hair. (Not through OF., which had *peil, poil.*)]

1. a. Hair, *esp.* fine soft hair, down; *rarely*, a single hair of this kind; the fine short hair of cattle, deer, etc.; the wool of sheep; the fine undercoat of certain rough-coated dogs, esp. the Old English sheep-dog; in *Entom.* fine hairs on an insect.

1486 *Bk. St. Albans* E iij b, All that berith greece and piles ther vppon Euer shalle be strypte when thay be vndoon. **1513** DOUGLAS *Æneis* VI. iv. 16 Four ȝoung stottis..blak of pyle. *Ibid.* VIII. iii. 150 My grene ȝouth that tym, wyth pylis ȝing, Fyrst cleyd my chyn, or beird begouth to spring. **1762** STERNE *Tr. Shandy* V. i, He has no whiskers,..not a pile. **1805** LUCCOCK *Nat. Wool* 18 The native..wraps himself in sheep skins, and blesses that hand which made their pile thick, warm and ponderous. **1826** KIRBY & SP. *Entomol.* III. 306 Some Hymenoptera..have the upper lip of the male clothed with silver pile. **1859** R. F. BURTON *Centr. Afr.* in *Jrnl. Geog. Soc.* XXIX. 318 The East African is by no means a hairy man. Little pile appears upon the body. **1893** LYDEKKER *Horns & Hoofs* 159 In order to withstand the intense cold of a Tibetan winter, the chiru is clothed with a thick and close woolly pile. **1905** J. WATSON *Dog Bk.* v. 386 The under coat [of the bob-tailed sheep dog] should be a waterproof pile. **1938** E. C. ASH *New Bk. Dog.* x. 395 Coat [of Old English sheep-dog].—Profuse, and of good hard texture... The undercoat a pile when not removed by grooming. **1971** DANGERFIELD & HOWELL *Internat. Encycl. Dogs* 348/1 Pile. Dense undercoat.

b. *transf.* Applied to the downy plumage of a bird, or the downy part of a feather.

1340-70 *Alisaunder* 814 Of his grounden gras, þe wus can hee take, þeron hee brynges þe brid, & bathes his pilus. **1847** *Whistlebinkie* (1890) II. 147, I can my falcon bring Without a pile of feather wrong on body, breast or wing.

c. Red or yellowish markings on white or pale-coloured fowls; a fowl with this coloration. Also *attrib.*

1854 *Poultry Chron.* I. 289 The 'white or pile game'.. were withheld from prizes altogether. **1913** W. BATESON *Mendel's Princ. Heredity* (rev. ed.) 120 The coloration known as 'Pile' in fowls is seldom bred for exhibition from two pile kinds. **1929** E. BROWN *Poultry* I. iii. 62 Pile Leghorns were produced by Mr. George Payne, of Woking. *Ibid.* 69 Pile.—This is purely exhibition fowl, so named from its having the markings of the old variety of Game fowl with the same designation.

2. a. A nap upon cloth; now *esp.* the downy nap or shag of velvet, plush, and similar fabrics, produced by an accessory or secondary warp the loops of which are cut so as to form a nap; also, loops in a carpet similarly produced and forming a nap.

double pile, pile upon pile, two-pile, three-pile, attrib. phr.: having the pile of double or treble closeness: see *pile-warp* in 3.

1568 R. SEMPILL *Ballads* (1872) xxxviii. 238 With the sleik stanis..for the nanis They raise the pyle I mak ȝow plane. **1591** GREENE *Art Conny Catch.* II. (1592) 22 He cals to see a boul of Saten, veluet,..and not liking the pile, culler, or bracke, he cals for more. **1605** ROWLANDS *Hell's Broke Loose* 39 Rich Taffata and Veluet of three pile, Must serue our vse to swagger in a while. **1611** COTGR. s.v. *Poil*, *Velours à deux poils*, two-pile Veluet. **1784** COWPER *Task* I. 11 Satin smooth, Or velvet soft, or plush with shaggy pile. **1875** KNIGHT *Dict. Mech.* 1701/2 In Brussels carpet..the wires are simply withdrawn and the loops left standing..In the Imperial Brussels the figure is raised above the ground and its pile is cut, but the ground is uncut. In the Royal Wilton the pile is raised higher than in the common Wilton, and is also cut. **1884** *Nonconf. & Indep.* 17 Jan. 59/1 Persian carpets..take front rank..for general excellence, softness of pile, and harmony of colouring.

b. Each of the fine hair-like fibres of velvet, flannel, wool, or cotton.

1787 HUNTER in *Phil. Trans.* LXXVII. 395 Like coarse velvet, each pile standing firm in its place. **1802** BEDDOES *Hygëia* v. 84 Flannel..is more likely to be hurtful..by the stimulating effect of its piles. **1805** LUCCOCK *Nat. Wool* 13 The 'hair' of this wool, i.e. the fineness or coarseness of the pile, the first object of a stapler's concern.

c. A fabric with a pile or nap, *esp.* velvet.

1843 LYTTON *Last Bar.* IV. v, It is not often that these roads witness riders in silk and pile.

d. *transf.* The burr on a plate in etching.

1883 S. HADEN in *Harper's Mag.* Jan. 233/2 Rembrandt employed the etching-needle..in such a way as to throw up with its point as much of the pile, or 'burr', as he required.

3. *attrib.* and *Comb.* (from sense 2). Having a pile, as ***pile-carpet***, ***-fabric***: belonging to or forming the pile, as ***pile-thread***; **pile-beam**, a separate warp-beam, upon which the pile-warp is wound and carried; **pile-warp**, the secondary warp, which furnishes the substance of the pile, also called *nap-warp*; it may consist of one, two, or three threads in the loop, producing ***single-***, ***double-***, or ***three-pile*** velvet; **pile-weaving**, the weaving of fabrics with a pile or nap, by means of the pile-warp, which, by being passed over the pile-wires, forms loops, which are afterwards cut, or, in some cases, left standing; **pile-wire**, one of a number of wires used in pile-weaving; in the case of cut-pile fabrics, grooved on the upper side to facilitate cutting.

1844 G. DODD *Textile Manuf.* vi. 204 Striped velvets.. owe their peculiar appearance to some of the *pile-threads being left uncut. **1875** KNIGHT *Dict. Mech.*, **Pile-warp*, a warp which is woven in loops on the face to form a nap. *Ibid.* 1701/2 In *pile-weaving, in addition to the usual warp and weft threads, a third thread is introduced.., and is thrown into loops by being woven over wires of the breadth of the cloth. *Ibid.*, **Pile-wire*, the wire around which the warp-threads are looped to make a pile-fabric.

pile (paɪl), *sb.*⁶ *Path.* Usually *pl.* **piles**. Also 5-6 pyle, (6 pylle). A disease characterized by tumours of the veins of the lower rectum; hæmorrhoids. Rarely *sing.*, a hæmorrhoid.

a **1400-50** *Stockh. Med. MS.* 15 A good medic[i]ne for the pylys & for the emerawdys. **1527** ANDREW *Brunswyke's Distyll. Waters* B iv, Sores and pyles on the fondament lyke wrattes. **1533** ELYOT *Cast. Helthe* (1541) 61 b, Of hemoroides or pylles. **1608** MIDDLETON *Fam. Love* IV. iv, A pile on ye, won't you! **1715** S. SEWALL *Diary* 29 Sept., Mr. Pemberton was very sick of the Piles. **1811** HOOPER *Med. Dict.* s.v. *Hæmorrhois*, A small pile, that has been painful for some days, may cease to be so, and dry up. **1869** CLARIDGE *Cold Water Cure* 176 Persons subject to piles should especially avoid all heating and stimulating drinks.

b. *Comb.*, as ***pile-clamp***, ***-supporter***.

1875 KNIGHT *Dict. Mech.*, *Pile-clamp*, an instrument for removing hemorrhoids. *Ibid.*, *Pile-supporter*, a suppository for preventing protrusion of the rectum. **1893** *Syd. Soc. Lex.*, *Pile-clamp*, an instrument..for crushing the base of the pile before cutting off, or for holding and compressing the pile.

pile, *sb.*⁷, obs. form of PILLOW.

pile (paɪl), *v.*¹ [f. PILE *sb.*¹ in sense 3.]

1. *trans.* To furnish, strengthen, or support with piles (esp. of timber); to drive piles into.

c **1440** [see PILING *vbl. sb.*¹ 1]. *a* **1552** LELAND *Itin.* II. 31 Toward the North End of this Bridge stondith a fair old Chapelle of Stone.., pilid in the Foundation for the rage of the Streame of the Tamise. **1661** *Brasenose Coll. Mun.* 30. 20 They had in some cases to pile an arch to build on. **1716-17** E. RUD in Willis & Clark *Cambridge* (1886) II. 646 Part of the north ditch piled and planked. **1747** *Gentl. Mag.*, *Hist. Chron.* Sept. 445 Mr. King first carpenter to the [Westminster] Bridge protested against it without piling the foundation. **1790** *Trans. Soc. Arts* VIII. 96 It [a wall] was planked and piled internally. **1881** *Chicago Times* 14 May, Heavy oak pieces, twenty-five feet in length, will be used for piling the 'coolies' on Yellowstone division.

†**2.** To fix, drive in (as a stake or pile). *Obs.*

1523 LD. BERNERS *Froiss.* I. cccciii. 701 The flemynges had pyled in the ryuer of Lescalt great pyles of great tymbre, so that no shyppe coulde come fro Tourney to Andewarpe. **1613** PURCHAS *Pilgrimage* (1614) 695 These were piled in the earth, and vpon them were set the skulls of dead men, which they had slaine in the warres.

pile, *v.*² [f. PILE *sb.*³]

1. a. *trans.* To form into a pile or heap; to heap up. Often with *up*, *on*.

c **1358** [see PILING *vbl. sb.*²]. *c* **1400** *Destr. Troy* 903 The ȝepe knight..Pight hom into ploghe, pilde vp the vrthe, Braid vp bygly all a brode feld. **1576** FLEMING *Panopl. Epist.* 372 What enormities be there, but ignoraunce, doth (as it were) pile them vp one vpon another. **1607** ROWLANDS *Diog. Lanth.* 6 He..got wealth, and pylde vp golde euen as they pyle vp stockfish in Island. **1638** SIR T. HERBERT *Trav.* (ed. 2) 135 Upon many of these Mosques the Storks have pyld their nests. **1663** GERBIER *Counsel* 46 The Labourers.. ought to take the bricks out of the Carts and pile them. **1711** ADDISON *Spect.* No. 3 ¶5 A prodigious Heap of Bags of Mony,..piled upon one another. **1794** SULLIVAN *View Nat.* II. 17 Like Pelion and Ossa piled one upon the other. **1832** TENNYSON *Lady of Shalott* I. iv, The reaper weary, Piling sheaves in uplands airy. **1871** R. ELLIS *Catullus* lxiv. 304 Many a feast high-pil'd, did load each table about them. **1891** E. PEACOCK *N. Brendon* I. 341 The refuse was piled in heaps.

b. *Mil.* ***to pile arms***: to place muskets or rifles (usually three) in a position in which their butts rest on the ground and their muzzles come together, so as to form a pyramidal figure: a mode of disposing of them so as to be readily available when wanted, practised by soldiers, etc., while resting during a march or other military operation; to stack arms. Also *fig.*

c **1778** *Conquerors* 65 Thus each griev'd soldier pil'd his arms and wept. **1862** BEVERIDGE *Hist. India* III. IX. ii. 573 The sepoys..at once obeyed the order to pile their arms. **1865** T. HUGHES in *Morn. Star* 5 Dec., The states-men of our own country had piled arms with the view of seeing how liberal institutions would succeed in America. **1879** *Martini-Henry Rifle Exerc.* 37 The squad will be taught to pile arms as follows.

c. *Metall.* = FAGGOT *v.* 2: cf. PILE *sb.*³ 3 g.

1839 *Civil Engin. & Arch. Jrnl.* II. 17/2 A reverberatory furnace of the common construction employed in 'puddling', 'balling', or 'piling' iron. **1891** R. R. GUBBINS (*title*) A New System of Hot-Charging and Hot-Piling Puddle Bars.

d. *Leather-making.* See PILING *vbl. sb.*¹ 1 b.

e. ***to pile up***: to wreck (a ship); to crash (an aircraft, vehicle, etc.).

1899 C. J. C. HYNE *Further Adventures Capt. Kettle* vi. 137 If the bar had shifted, he himself could have put this steamer on the ground as handily as the other man had piled up the branch boat. **1923** *Times Lit. Suppl.* 29 Mar. 218/2 An old battle-cruiser which gets adrift in a gale..[and] is piled up on the rocks. **1925** FRASER & GIBBONS *Soldier & Sailor Words* 223 *Pile up one's bus, to*, an airman's expression for coming a 'crash'. **1930** KIPLING *Limits & Renewals* (1932) 230 We had a passenger..who wanted to see Caesar. It cost us our ship... He piled up the *Eirene* on his way. **1932** 'N. SHUTE' *Lonely Road* ix. 196 The fellow was so drunk that he'd probably have piled his car up anyway. **1942** N. STREATFEILD *I ordered Table for Six* 236 Andrew cautiously steered Claire to the centre of the floor... He was afraid if he talked he might pile her up. **1959** G. JENKINS *Twist of Sand* iv. 78, I hope to God they don't pile that monster up on my runways. **1971** M. TAK *Truck Talk* 119 *Pile up*, to wreck a truck.

2. a. *transf.* and *fig.* To amass, accumulate.

1844 MRS. BROWNING *Drama of Exile* Poems 1850 I. 19 Shall I..here assume To mend the justice of the perfect God, By piling up a curse upon His curse Against thee. **1860** *Baily's Mag.* Sept. 429 The Kent innings was piled up the next day to 152. **1870** *Athenæum* 15 Oct. 489 Cowley often excels in piling his effects. **1873** *Baily's Mag.* Dec. 287 We fancy there are some batsmen who would pile up the runs rapidly off his leg balls. **1886** W. HOOPER *Sk. fr. Academic Life* 49 A man who on every occasion piles up the titles which he possesses..sins against good taste. **1889** JESSOPP *Coming of Friars* ii. 54 Included in the estate slowly piled up by the Yelvertons. **1898** J. A. GIBBS *Cotswold Village* xi. 246 Once fairly started on a sequence of big scores, the cricketer goes on day by day piling up runs. **1948** 'N. SHUTE' *No Highway* i. 25 The Reindeers were flying over the Atlantic piling up the hours faster than Mr. Honey's test.

b. ***to pile up*** (or ***on***) ***the agony*** (*colloq.*), to prolong and intensify to a climax the effect of anything painful by adding fresh elements or details. Also *to pile it on*.

1835-40 HALIBURTON *Clockm.* (1862) 444, I was actilly in a piled-up-agony. **1839** MARRYAT *Diary Amer.* Ser. I. II. 235. I do think he piled the agony up a little too high in that last scene. **1852** C. BRONTE in Mrs. Gaskell *Life* (1857) II. xi. 267, I doubt whether the regular novel-reader will consider the 'agony piled sufficiently high' (as the Americans say). **1852** *Star* (Los Angeles) 3 Apr. 1/5 The wags observed that Caleb was getting exceedingly uneasy, and 'piled it on'. **1876** 'MARK TWAIN' *Old Times Mississippi* viii. 43 'Now I don't want to discourage you, but—' 'Well, pile it on me; I might as well have it now.' **1892** *Even. Echo* 23 Jan. 2/2 Airing their eloquence and piling up the agonies on their respective opponents. **1943** J. B. PRIESTLEY *Daylight on Saturday* xxxviii. 297, I fancy you're piling it on too much. There are lots of things you can enjoy, if you set about it properly. **1969** E. GÉBLER *Shall I eat you Now?* 56 But that was piling it on a bit; she wasn't that daft. *a* **1974** R. CROSSMAN *Diaries* (1976) II. 601, I suppose he will get what he wants at Cabinet but he's piling it on a bit thick. **1976** *West Lancs. Evening Gaz.* 15 Dec. 8/2 And now they want to pile on the agony with rip-roaring monsters going round and round.

3. a. *intr.* for *refl.* or *pass.*

1613-16 W. BROWNE *Brit. Past.* II. iv, The hart-like leaves oft each with other pyle As doe the hard scales of the Crocodyle. **1785** BURNS *Winter Night* 80 Chill o'er his slumbers, piles the drifty heap! **1860** SIR W. E. LOGAN in *Borthwick's Brit. Amer. Rdr.* 149 The ice in the St. Lawrence piles up over every obstacle. **1897** *Bookman* Jan. 125/1 Money..continues to pile up and up at the bankers of a good lady. **1926** *Scribner's Mag.* Sept. 266/1 'How things did pile up!'.. Almost every person Peter particularly dislikes came in for tea and..Feinberg showed up with Sally. **1930** *Morning Post* 14 July 6/7 Vehicles crossing the circus diagonally had to 'pile up' in the centre. **1942** *We speak from Air* 39 Whether you get the Hun or miss him, he frequently piles up on the ground through making his landing in fright. **1947** *John o' London's Weekly* 25 July 502/3 In referring to the traffic 'piling up', did he mean that motor-cars, lorries, bicycles were stacked up in neat heaps on the roadway? **1956** 'C. BLACKSTOCK' *Dewey Death* vii. 160 The work is just piling up. **1975** *Times* 18 Mar. (Greece Suppl.) 1/4 It is not just the old problems. Each day new ones pile up.

b. To climb *on* or go *into* (a vehicle, building, etc.) so as to form a pile; hence, to enter (a place) in crowds; and simply, to mount, enter, etc. orig. *U.S.*

1841 L. B. SWAN *Jrnl. of Trip to Michigan* (1904) 30 Brooks brought up his lumber wagon and we all 'piled in'. **1854** M. J. HOLMES *Tempest & Sunshine* iii. 44 Fanny with half a dozen other girls..began piling on to Bill's old sled. **1879** J. BURROUGHS *Locusts & Wild Honey* (1884) 38 They [*sc.* bees] come piling in till the rain is upon them. **1884** 'MARK TWAIN' *Huck. Finn* xxxvi. 345 Here comes a couple of the hounds in from under Jim's bed; and they kept on piling in till there was eleven of them. **1923** R. D. PAINE *Comrades of Rolling Ocean* vii. 114 Judson introduced his four shipmates who piled into the automobile. **1929** R. GRAVES *Good-Bye to all That* x. 103 There were about three thousand prisoners already there and more piled in every day. **1943** N. COWARD *Middle East Diary* (1944) 100 We flagged a passing lorry.., piled into it bag and baggage and whirled off to the airport. **1956** B. HOLIDAY *Lady sings Blues* (1973) viii. 72 We piled into his car and were off. **1972** J. WAMBAUGH *Blue Knight* (1973) xiii. 231 We jawed..and finally piled into the cars.

c. Hence used of the reverse processes: to climb *down from*, or *off* (a vehicle); to come *out of* (a place), etc., in crowds. orig. *U.S.*

1884 'MARK TWAIN' *Huck. Finn* xxii. 205 A lot of men begun to pile down off of the benches and swarm toward the ring. **1896** ADE *Artie* xi. 100 We stopped in front of the church and piled out. **1902** S. E. WHITE *Blazed Trail* xx. 150 Then they piled out for the boss. **1908** —— *Riverman* xxii. 195 They piled off the train at Sawyer's. **1921** C. E.

MULFORD *Bar-20 Three* xvii. 224 Six sleeping men piled from their bunks and..chased the cursing trail-boss. **1972** *Times* 20 Nov. 8/6 Hundreds more piling off every train.

d. *to pile on to* (N. Amer.), to attack vigorously, to assail.

1894 *Outing* XXIV. 417/1 The dog..[will] never 'pile onto' any more bears. **1906** U. SINCLAIR *Jungle* xvi. 183 Like as not a dozen [policemen] would pile on to him at once, and pound his face into a pulp. **1970** *Globe & Mail* (Toronto) 25 Sept. 30/1 The Australian tub, Gretel, hit the American scow, Intrepid, below the gunwale the other day, or tugged its saddle blanket, or piled on with unnecessary roughness.

e. To move or advance in a throng.

1925 H. L. FOSTER *Trop. Tramp with Tourists* 102 The tourists piled towards the exits.

f. *to pile in*: to crash.

1944 G. NETHERWOOD *Desert Squadron* ii. 21 So low did Pilot Officer Weeks fly as he did the Victory Roll, that those watching him made certain that he would 'pile in'.

4. *trans.* To cover or load *with* things heaped on.

1667 MILTON *P.L.* v. 632 Tables are set, and on a sudden pil'd With Angels Food. **1809** W. IRVING *Knickerb.* II. vii. (1849) 120 By degrees a fleet of boats and canoes were piled up with all kinds of household articles. **1817** COLERIDGE *Sibyl. Leaves* Poems (1862) 268 Gay thy grassy altar piled with fruits. **1878** BROWNING *La Saisiaz* 552 Its floor Piled with provender for cattle.

pile, obs. f. PILL *sb.*[1], and PILL *v.*[1], to rob, etc.

pilea (ˈpaɪlɪə). [mod.L. (J. Lindley *Collectanea Botanica* (1821) 4), f. L. *pileus* cap.] An annual or perennial herb of the genus so called, belonging to the family Urticaceæ, native to many tropical regions, and cultivated elsewhere as a house plant; esp. *Pilea muscosa*, the artillery or gunpowder plant, which discharges clouds of pollen when it is touched.

1918 N. L. BRITTON *Flora of Bermuda* 105 Large-leaved Pilea, Jamaican, seen in the garden at Mt. Hope in 1914. **1958** *Times* 29 Nov. 9/5 We have the pileas, the tradescantias, and..all the various forms of *Begonia rex*. **1971** *Country Life* 25 Nov. 1443/1 Among the most interesting recent introductions are three pileas. **1974** W. DAVIDSON *All about House Plants* 156/1 On the whole pileas are small, compact plants.

pileage: see PILAGE.

pileate (ˈpaɪliːət), *a. Nat. Hist.* [ad. L. *pīleāt-us* (better *pilleatus*) capped, f. *pīl(l)eus*: see PILEUS.] Having a pileus or cap.

1828–32 in WEBSTER. **1858** MAYNE *Expos. Lex.*, *Pileatus*, *Bot.* applied by Fries to an Order..of the *Hymenomycetes*.. pileate. **1866** *Treas. Bot.* [see PILEIFORM]. **1874** COOKE *Fungi* 56 The Discomycetes are of two kinds, the pileate and the cup-shaped.

pileated (ˈpaɪlɪeɪtɪd), *a.* [f. as prec. + -ED.]

1. *Nat. Hist.* = prec.; *spec.* applied to certain Echini or sea-urchins; also, to certain birds having the feathers of the pileum very conspicuous, as the ***pileated woodpecker*** (*Dryocopus pileatus*) of N. America, the male of which has a scarlet pileum.

a **1728** WOODWARD *Fossils* II. (1729) 70 A pileated Echinus, taken up, with different Shells of several kinds. **1749** *Phil. Trans.* XLVI. 146, I have seen some Specimens of the common pileated and galeated Echinites. **1782** LATHAM *Gen. Synop. Birds* I. 554 Pileated Woodpecker. **1884** J. BURROUGHS in *Century Mag.* Dec. 222/2 The log-cock, or pileated woodpecker..I have never heard drum. **1928** G. M. SUTTON *Introd. Birds Pennsylvania* 81 The call of the Pileated is a high, irregular cackle. *Ibid.*, The food of the Pileated Woodpecker is chiefly grubs. **1956** G. DURRELL *Drunken Forest* ix. 169 Pileated jays have long, magpie-like tails of black and white... The feathers on the forehead were black, short, and plushy, and stuck up straight. **1969** R. LOWELL *Notebk. 1967–68* 57 A large pileated bird flies up. **1971** W. HILLEN *Blackwater River* ix. 80 A pileated woodpecker gave his jungle-like call and flashed his scarlet crest through the trees.

2. Wearing the *pileus* (see PILEUS 1).

1856 W. H. SMYTH *Catal. Coins Dk. Northumbld.* 233 Two pileated but otherwise naked men standing with spears.

piled (paɪld), *ppl. a.*[1] [f. PILE *sb.*[1] or *v.*[1]]

†**1.** *Her.* Of arms: Charged with piles: see PILE *sb.*[1] 4. *Obs.*

1486 *Bk. St. Albans, Her.* E v b, Off pilit armys now here it shall be shewyt.

†**2.** Of a javelin or lance: Having a pile or head: see PILE *sb.*[1] 1 b. *Obs.*

c **1611** CHAPMAN *Iliad* xv. 211 At Dolops, Meges threw A speare well pilde. **1615** —— *Odyss.* xx. 201 Took to his hand his sharp-piled lance.

3. Built on piles.

1905 *Blackw. Mag.* Mar. 340/2 To pole up stream past piled village and fertile rice-flats.

piled, *ppl. a.*[2] [f. PILE *v.*[2] + -ED[1].] **a.** Laid or reared in a pile or piles, heaped. Also with *up*.

1613 W. BROWNE *Brit. Past.* I. v. (1616) 98 While the piled stones Re-eccoed her lamentable grones. **1630** MILTON *On Shaks.*, What needs my Shakspear for his honour'd Bones, The labour of an age in piled Stones? **1715–20** POPE *Iliad* XXIII. 207 Achilles cover'd with their fat the dead, And the pil'd victims round the body spread. **1791** CHARLOTTE SMITH *Celestina* (ed. 2) III. 64 Behind those piled-up stones against which you leaned. **1848** C. A. JOHNS *Week at Lizard* 264 The piled appearance of the rocks. **1880** BROWNING *Dram. Idylls, Pan & Luna* 37. **1898** P. GEDDES *Let.* Feb. in P. Boardman *Worlds of Patrick Geddes* (1978) vi. 167 The piled-up picturesqueness of Old Edinburgh. **1935** C. S. FORESTER *African Queen* vi. 109 The *African Queen*..reared up as she hit the piled-up water. **1948** H. INNES *Blue Ice* vii. 191 Mile on ghastly mile of piled-up snow-capped peaks. **1978** 'L. BLACK' *Foursome* i. 7 The piled-up dishes, bowls, plates.

b. With all sails set.

1851 H. MELVILLE *Moby Dick* II. ix. 62 With every mast-head manned, the piled-up craft rolled down before the wind.

c. Crashed, wrecked.

1939 J. STEINBECK *Grapes of Wrath* vi. 61 They ain't whole, out lonely on the road in a piled-up car. They ain't alive no more. **1943** C. H. WARD-JACKSON *Piece of Cake* 48 *Piled in* or *up*, crashed.

piled, *ppl. a.*[3] [f. PILE *sb.*[5] + -ED[2].]

1. Covered with pile, hair, or fur.

1426 LYDG. *De Guil. Pilgr.* 13703 Off look and cher ryht monstrous, Pyled and seynt as any kaat, And moosy-heryd as a raat.

2. Having a pile or long nap, as velvet.

double-piled, three-piled, etc.; see PILE *sb.*[5] 2.

1589 R. HARVEY *Pl. Perc.* (1860) 20 My plain speeches may haue as much wooll..as is in your double pild veluet. **1603** SHAKS. *Meas. for M.* I. ii. 33–5 Thour't a three pild-piece I warrant thee; I had as liefe be a Lyst of an English Kersey, as be pil'd, as thou art pil'd, for a French Veluet. **1808** SCOTT *Marm.* v. viii, His cloak, of crimson velvet piled, Trimmed with the fur of marten wild. **1881** MORRIS in Mackail *Life* (1899) II. 55, I don't say that any flat-woven stuff can stand sunlight as well as a piled material.

ˈpile-ˌdrive, *v.* [Back-formation from PILE-DRIVER.] **a.** *trans.* To construct (something) using a pile-driver; to act as or like a pile-driver on (something).

1809, etc. [implied at *pile-driven, pile-driving* below]. **1894** KIPLING in *Century Mag.* Dec. 295/1 I'll catch 'em by the back o' the neck, an' pile-drive 'em a piece. **1932** *Daily Express* 27 June 9/4 Trotsky may not convince the world that the revolution in which he and Lenin were the giants was a splendid thing, but he pile-drives the contention that it was inevitable in Russia. **1971** 'D. HALLIDAY' *Dolly & Doctor Bird* vii. 94 They're still pile-driving the quayside. **1972** D. HASTON *In High Places* vii. 91 Chris was falling every second turn, pack pile-driving his head into the snow.

b. *intr.* (See quot. 1929.)

1898 *Nautical Mag.* LXVII. 355 After pile-driving off Cape Horn for some days, she squared away..and eventually reached San Francisco. **1929** F. BOWEN *Sea Slang* 103 *Pile Driving*, steaming or sailing into a heavy head sea. **1937** G. S. DOORLY *In Wake* viii. 127 We had been 'pile-driving' heavily through the night.

So **ˈpile-ˌdriven** *a.*, **ˈpile-ˌdriving** *vbl. sb.* and *ppl. a.* (also *fig.*).

1809 *Phil. Trans.* Abr. XIV. 498 On the Theory of Pile-Driving. **1818** *Gentl. Mag.* LXXXVIII. II. 398 Built on what the Dutch call pile-driven bases, on a marshy and unstable soil. **1823** P. NICHOLSON *Pract. Build.* 305 Requiring no machine beyond a pile-driving engine. **1894** 'MARK TWAIN' in *Century Mag.* Jan. 335/1 The title came upon them as a kind of pile-driving surprise. **1942** PARTRIDGE *Usage & Abusage* (1947) 126/2 If the point is still not made, let us take a few more of Jespersen's pile-driving examples. **1960** *Farmer & Stockbreeder* 15 Mar. 46/2 This simple pile-driving machine, easily attached to any tractor fitted with P.T.O. and hydraulic lift will reduce fencing costs to a minimum.

ˈpile-ˌdriver. **1. a.** A machine for driving piles (PILE *sb.*[1] 3) into the ground, usually consisting of a heavy block of iron, suspended in a frame between two vertical guide-posts, and alternately let fall upon the pile-head, and raised by steam, manual, or other power; some, working with steam, act on the principle of the steam-hammer.

1772 HUTTON *Bridges* 99 *Pile Driver*, an engine for driving down the piles. **1862** SMILES *Engineers* III. 412 In the case of the steam pile-driver..the whole weight of a heavy mass is delivered rapidly upon a driving-block of several tons weight placed directly over the head of the pile. **1879** *Cassell's Techn. Educ.* II. 80 A pile-driver consists of vertical guide-bars, between which a weight called the 'monkey' is drawn up..and is suddenly released.

b. A man who drives piles into the ground.

1882 in OGILVIE (Annandale)

2. *transf.* A very strong or powerful hit, stroke, kick, etc., in various games; something of great strength or power.

1858 A. MAYHEW *Paved with Gold* II. xii. 189 After some sparring, Jack threw out his 'pile-drivers' and caught Ned on the 'sniffer', but the nose didn't suffer much. **1929** *Star* 21 Aug. 17/1 Hammond was let off when 59 from a pile-driver to third man. **1929** *Daily Express* 7 Nov. 19/1 Their inside right put in a couple of pile-drivers that missed the target by inches only. **1952** M. ALLINGHAM *Tiger in Smoke* i. 18 His piledriver personality forced home the suggestion. **1962** [see *back-breaker* s.v. BACK- B]. **1964** *Guardian* 2 Mar. 7/6 He's using pile-drivers (dropping on the head). **1968** R. WEST *Sk. Vietnam* ii. 60 'The noise of these pile-drivers,' he said with great satisfaction, 'was heard as far as Saigon.' **1973** *Sunday Tel.* 4 Mar. 38/8 Jones picked up a loose clearance from Feltwell, and her pile-driver took the paint off the post. **1973** D. LEES *Rape of Quiet Town* vi. 93 The big boys were dishing out pile-drivers and body-slams, cracking heads and snapping spines.

pileiform (ˈpaɪliːɪfɔːm), *a. Bot.* [ad. mod.L. *pileiformis*: see PILEUS and -FORM.] Having the form of a pileus or cap.

1858 MAYNE *Expos. Lex.*, *Pileiformis*,..pileiform. **1866** *Treas. Bot.*, *Pileate*, *Pileiform*, having the form of a cap; or having a pileus.

†**ˈpilement.** *Obs. rare*[−1]. [f. PILE *v.*[2] + -MENT.] The action or product of piling; a piled heap.

1597–8 BP. HALL *Sat.* III. ii. 16 Costly pilements of some curious stone.

Pilentum (pɪˈlɛntəm). *Hist.* Also **pilentum.** [f. L. *pilentum* an easy chariot used by ladies or for carrying the vessels, etc., for sacred rites.] A type of carriage (see quot. 1961).

1837 W. B. ADAMS *Eng. Pleasure Carriages* xvii. 278 The next attempt in the 'service of the public', was the introduction of a vehicle with the..title of a Four-wheeled Cabriolet. This is a modification of..a Pilentum. **1843** *Ainsworth's Mag.* IV. 100 If I could have built a mother for myself, as one does a Brougham or pilentum. **1849** E. RUSKIN *Let.* 30 Sept. in M. Lutyens *Effie in Venice* (1965) I. 41 We concluded by fixing to take two [carriages], one for John..and an elegant *Pilentum* for Charlotte and me. It is an open carriage but shuts very easily... It is rather heavy ..and will require three horses. **1961** M. WATNEY *Elegant Carriage* 60 The Pilentum..was an open carriage with the doorway very near the ground, the driving seat was also low, but it was built in different sizes to carry four or six people, and to be drawn by one or two horses. In appearance, the Pilentum was not unlike a Victoria, although it had doors at the sides. **1974** F. SELWYN *Cracksman on Velvet* II. 76 On its indiarubber bearings..the swan's neck Pilentum seemed to roll in air above the glittering spokes of its wheels.

pileole (ˈpaɪliːəʊl). *Bot.* [ad. L. *pīleolus*: see next. Cf. F. *piléole*.] = next; *spec.* in grasses, etc. (see quots.).

1858 MAYNE *Expos. Lex.*, *Pileola*... name given by Mirbel to a perfectly close primordial leaf, having the form of a funnel, and which covers and hides the other leaves of the gemmule, as in the *Scirpus*: a pileole. **1880** C. & F. DARWIN *Movem. Pl.* 62 With the Gramineæ the part which first rises above the ground has been called by some the pileole.

‖**pileolus** (pɪˈliːələs). *Bot.* [L. *pīleolus* (better *pill-*), dim. of PILEUS.] A little pileus; as the small cap-like receptacle of certain fungi.

1858 in MAYNE *Expos. Lex.* **1866** *Treas. Bot.*, *Pileolus*, a little cap or cap-like body..; the receptacle of certain fungals.

‖**pileorhiza** (paɪliːəʊˈraɪzə). *Bot.* Also **pileorrhiza**; and in anglicized form **ˈpileoˌrhize.** [mod.L., f. L. *pīleus* cap + Gr. ῥίζα root. Cf. COLEORHIZA.] The mass of tissue which covers and protects the growing-point of a root; the root-cap.

1857 HENFREY *Bot.* §771 The conical hood upon the apex of the root, called the *pileorrhiza*. *Ibid.*, The focus of development of the root is within the *pileorrhiza*, which is pushed forward by the continual development of cells just behind the apex. **1857** BERKELEY *Cryptog. Bot.* §49 There is the same highly developed pileorhize, which is no special organ, but the same thing with the pileorhize in more complicated plants. **1870** BENTLEY *Man. Bot.* (ed. 2) 113.

pileous (ˈpaɪliːəs), *a. rare.* [f. L. type **pile-us* (f. *pil-us* hair) + -OUS: cf. *osseous*, *carneous*.] Pertaining to or consisting of hair, hairy.

1842 DUNGLISON *Med. Lex.*, *Pileous*, that which relates to the hair. **1872** T. G. THOMAS *Dis. Women* (ed. 3) 700 When the predominating element of the mass is hair, these tumors are called pileous or piliferous. **1893** *Syd. Soc. Lex.*, *Pileous system*, Bichat's term for the arrangement of hair on the body.

ˈpiler. [f. PILE *v.*[2] + -ER[1].] One who piles.

1611 COTGR., *Accumulateur*,..a heaper, or piler; a hoorder. **1835** BROWNING *Paracelsus* v. 292 The sacred fire may flicker..And die, for want of a wood-piler's help.

piler, pilery, obs. forms of PILLAR, PILLORY.

piles, hæmorrhoids: see PILE *sb.*[6]

pilet, variant of PELLET *sb.*[2] 2, *Obs.*, pelt.

‖**pileum** (ˈpaɪlɪəm). *Ornith.* [L. *pīleum* (better *pilleum*), collat. form of *pīleus* (*pilleus*): see PILEUS] The whole of the top of the head of a bird, comprising the *frons*, *corona* or *vertex*, and *occiput*.

1874 COUES *Birds N.W.* 457 A broad, transverse, coronal, black bar of varying width (sometimes occupying half the pileum, sometimes a mere line). *Ibid.* 665 Crown and long occipital crest deep glossy greenish-black. This pileum extends..to a level with the lower border of the eye.

ˈpile-up. [f. vbl. phr. *to pile up*: see PILE *v.*[2] 1 a, e] **1.** A crash or collision, often involving several vehicles; a vehicle that has been involved in a crash. Also *fig.*

1929 *Papers Mich. Acad. Sci., Arts & Lett.* X. 314 *Pile-up*, a crash; a smash. **1945** *Richmond* (Virginia) *Times-Dispatch* 18 Sept. 15/2 (*heading*) Five harness racers injured in pile-up. **1951** W. SANSOM *Face of Innocence* x. 138 We passed one pile-up with its dead-slumped radiator and its ragged little crowd. **1954** L. KLEMANTASKI tr. *Fraichard's Le Mans Story* v. 46 A tremendous multiple pile-up, which was visible from the grandstands, had eliminated six of the competing cars. **1957** S. MOSS *In Track of Speed* iii. 34 Both of us had escaped a pile-up of about half a dozen cars early in the race. **1968** *New Scientist* 3 Oct. 38/2 A recent pile-up on the M1 in Bedfordshire involving 30 cars has apparently moved the Ministry of Transport to do some thinking. **1973** *Black Panther* 31 Mar. 8/1 When the sky rocketing demands for human rights and the technology of the super-industrial state (U.S.A.) clash head on, there is a bloody social pile-up. **1973** *Times* 1 Aug. 2/8 Three people were killed and three seriously injured in a pile-up involving three lorries and a car on the A17. **1977** *Belfast Tel.* 27 Jan. 1/3 A woman and her nine-year-old son were killed in a traffic pile-up in Dublin today.

2. a. An accumulation; an amassing of tasks, papers, etc. Also *attrib.*

1945 *Sun* (Baltimore) 14 Feb. 6/7 The Marshalls, the mid-Pacific cluster of coral pileups just above the equator. **1946** *Ibid.* 26 Apr. 10/3 Rain slowed air traffic in and around Washington, causing a 'pile-up' of planes over the Washington airport. **1948** M. LASKI *Tory Heaven* viii. 119 Unless one can get each crop of débutantes married off as it comes out, we're only going to get the same pile-up all over again. **1951** C. W. MILLS *White Collar* I. iii. 39 A tangled pile-up of restrictive legislation. **1963** *Times* 5 Feb. 13/3 More people might well be laid off in spite of the pile-up of work waiting for them. **1964** *Amer. Folk Music Occasional* I. 88 An endless 'pile-up song' which begins: I had a hen, and the hen pleased me. **1964** V. J. CHAPMAN *Coastal Vegetation* viii. 194 The 'pile-up' to form our shingle beaches is due to the action of direct onshore waves. **1966** *Word Study* Dec. 2/2 Sentences were talk-built, producing both fragments and pileups. **1968** C. HELMERICKS *Down Wild River North* II. xxiii. 368 We jumped out into the water and struggled to thrust the boat up onto a pileup of logs which was wedged there.

b. *Electronics.* A lack of linearity or resolution in a pulse circuit caused by the pulses arriving too rapidly.

1962 C. SUSSKIND *Encycl. Electronics* 18/2 Pile-up is not necessarily an excursion into a nonlinear region but the result of coupling capacitances not fully discharging after each pulse. **1973** *Nature* 23 Mar. 270/2 This potential source of electronic pile-up background was eliminated by anti-pile-up circuitry allowing detection of the desired gamma rays in the presence of counting rates up to 10^5 s^{-1} below 1 MeV.

‖**pileus** ('paɪli:əs). Pl. pilei ('paɪlɪaɪ). [L. *pīleus* (better *pilleus*, but *pīleus* is the form in late MSS.) a felt cap. Cf. Gr. πῖλος in same sense.]

1. *Antiq.* A felt cap without a brim, worn by the ancient Greeks and Romans. (Cf. PETASUS.)

1776 J. ADAMS *Fam. Lett.* (1876) 210 For the seal, he proposes..on one side..Liberty with her pileus. **1850** LEITCH tr. *C. O. Müller's Anc. Art* §404 (ed. 2) 542 On coins of Nicaea Pan stands with a pileus. **1879** *Cassell's Techn. Educ.* IV. 134/1 The pileus of the former [the most ancient Greeks] being nearly the same as the modern fez.

2. *Bot.* A cap-like formation in various fungi; *esp.* the cap-like or umbrella-like structure at the top of the stipes, bearing the hymenium on its under surface, in the *Hymenomycetes* (mushrooms, etc.); also called *cap* (see CAP *sb.*[1] 10 a).

1760 J. LEE *Introd. Bot.* II. xxxi. (1765) 154 *Agaricus*, with the Pileus on a Stipes. **1776** WITHERING *Brit. Plants* (1796) I. 376 The Gills are the flat, thin substances, found underneath the Pileus. **1875** BENNETT & DYER *Sachs' Bot.* 249 The naked pilei are originally gymnocarpous.

3. *Ornith.* = PILEUM.

pilew(e, obs. form of PILLOW.

†'**pileways**, *adv. Her. Obs. rare.* [f. PILE *sb.*[1] 4 + -WAYS.] In the manner of a pile or piles.

1572 BOSSEWELL *Arm.* II. 122 The Arrowes standing pilewaies in poincte, is one of ye honorable ordinaries general.

†**pilewhey.** *Obs.* [Obscure: the second element appears to be *whey*: see Skeat *Gloss.* to *P. Pl.*] ? Some kind of whey, or ? perry.

1362 LANGL. *P. Pl.* A. v. 134 Peni Ale and piriwhit [*v. rr.* pile-whey; pilewhew; pilwhay; *B* and *C* podyng ale] heo pourede to-gedere.

'**pile-work.** [f. PILE *sb.*[1] 3 + WORK *sb.*]

1. Work constructed or consisting of piles.

1702 *Lond. Gaz.* No. 3781/3 A new Pile-work is run out about 80 Foot from the Peer-head of Minehead. **1726** LEONI *Alberti's Archit.* I. 72/2 Make the pile-work deep and broad every way. **1896** *Daily News* 26 Sept. 2/2 In its fall it smashed the wooden pile work.

2. A prehistoric structure of piles in a lake.

1863 LYELL *Antiq. Man* 28 The pile-works of Chamblon, which are of the bronze period, must be at the least 3300 years old. **1865** LUBBOCK *Preh. Times* v. 169 The age of the Swiss Pileworks was at an end.

[**pile-worn**, in Jodrell and some later Dicts., erroneous alteration of *plimworth*, PLYMOUTH, in Massinger.]

pilewort ('paɪlwɜ:t). [f. PILE *sb.*[6] + WORT, from its reputed efficacy against piles, after the med.L. name *ficaria*: cf. FIGWORT.] The Lesser Celandine or Figwort (*Ranunculus Ficaria* or *Ficaria verna*), an early spring-flowering plant allied to the buttercups, with bright yellow starry flowers. Also extended to the whole genus or sub-genus *Ficaria*.

1578 LYTE *Dodoens* I. xx. 31 The lesser [Celandine] is called..in English Pyle worte, or Figworte. **1597** GERARDE *Herbal* II. cclxxix. 669. **1741** *Compl. Fam.-Piece* II. iii. 363 Violets, Dazies, double Pilewort. **1832** *Veg. Subst. Food* 186 The young leaves of Pilewort..are boiled and used as an edible by the Swedish peasantry.

†**b.** Formerly applied with qualifications to species of *Scrophularia*: cf. FIGWORT b.

1640 PARKINSON *Theatr. Bot.* 612 *Scrophularia major*..we in English [call it] great Figgewort, and great Pilewort. *Ibid.* 1616 *Guacatane*, Indian Pilewort.

pilfer ('pɪlfə(r)), *sb.* Now *rare.* Forms: 5 pilfre, pelfyr, -fere, 5–6 pylfre, 7– pilfer. [In earlier form app. a. OF. *pelfre* spoil (11th c. in Godef.): see PELF *sb.* In 17th c. use, perh. viewed as formed immediately on PILFER *v.*] **1.** That which is pilfered or plundered; spoil, plunder, booty; in early use also = PILFERY 1.

c **1400** *Mandeville's Brut* (E.E.T.S.) 13 All þat other pylfre he ȝaf vn-to other folk of þe ost. **1412–20** LYDG. *Chron. Troy* III. xxvii. (MS. Digby 230 lf. 133/2), Nor swiche pilfre spoilinge nor roberie Appartene nat to worthy chiualrie. *c* **1440** *Promp. Parv.* 391/1 Pelfyr, *spolium.* **1496** *Dives & Pauper* VII. i. 277/1 Open theft is whan the theef is taken with his pelfere. **1539** *St. Papers Hen. VIII*, III. 155 The..Scottys fled, and left mych corne, butters, and other pylfre. **1607** R. C[AREW] tr. *Estienne's World of Wonders* 85 Peaceably to enjoy their pilfer and pray. **1791** W. GILPIN *Forest Scenery* II. 40 Too many..depend on the precarious supply of forest pilfer.

2. *Comb.*, as ***pilfer-proof*** adj.

1959 *Light Metals* Jan. 18/3 Specially designed extrusions ..provide a weather- and pilfer-proof seal where the two pivoting roof sections meet axially. **1965** *Economist* 3 July 35/4 Weld mesh cages, fitted to the decks, can be locked before being stowed, thus becoming pilfer-proof. **1969** *Jane's Freight Containers 1968–69* (Advt. section) 21 Because the Freightank is pilferproof insurance premiums are reduced.

pilfer ('pɪlfə(r)), *v.* Also 6 pelfer, pylfer. [app. a. OF. or AF. *pelfre-r* to pillage, rob (11th c. in Godef.): see PELF *v.*; but (from its late appearance) perh. an Eng. formation on *pelfer*, PILFER *sb.*]

1. *trans.* To plunder, steal; *spec.* (in later use), to steal in small quantities, to filch, peculate.

1550 BALE *Eng. Votaries* II. 28 He taught hym how to recouer agayne the possessyons and landes pelfered awaye by the kynges from hys archebyshopryck. **1577** NORTHBROOKE *Dicing* (1843) 135 If during the time of their play, any thing be pilfered or stollen out of his house, hee shall haue no lawe at all for it. **1633** G. HERBERT *Temple, Submission* iii, Pilfring what I once did give. **1756** MITCHELL in Ellis *Orig. Lett.* Ser. II. IV. 376 Happening to meet a waggon..he thought there might be something to pilfer. **1836–9** DICKENS *Sk. Boz, Black Veil*, Old palings..mended with stakes pilfered from the neighbouring hedges.

fig. **1625** BACON *Ess., Greatness of Kingd.* (Arb.) 473 The Commanders..wisht him, to set vpon them by Night; But hee answered, He would not pilfer the Victory. **1784** COWPER *Task* I. 131 And not a year but pilfers as he goes Some youthful grace that age would gladly keep. **1807–8** W. IRVING *Salmag.* xix. (1860) 441 Old time..is a knave who..From the fairest of beauties will pilfer their youth.

b. To plunder or rob (a person or place). *rare.*

1838 PRESCOTT *Ferd. & Is.* (1846) I. vii. 314 The Egyptians, whom it was a merit to deceive and pilfer. **1888** BRYCE *Amer. Commw.* II. lxvii. 520 In some States the treasury was pilfered.

2. *intr.* or *absol.* To pillage, plunder; *spec.* (in later use), to commit petty theft.

a **1548** HALL *Chron., Hen. VIII* 204 b, And when the Turkes saw the Cristen men styll pylfer (as the vsage of Souldiers is) they issued out of their holde. *a* **1618** RALEIGH *Rem.* (1664) 90 As many of your Lordships as have pilfered from the Crown. **1726–31** TINDAL *Rapin's Hist. Eng.* XVII. (1743) II. 121 An Englishman being taken pilfering raised a quarrel. **1879** H. SPENCER *Data of Ethics* xv. §102. 264 A servant who..pilfers, may have to suffer pain from being discharged.

Hence '**pilfered**, '**pilfering** *ppl. adjs.*; also '**pilferingly** *adv.*

1599 SHAKS. *Hen. V*, I. ii. 142 To defend Our in-land from the pilfering Borderers. **1611** COTGR., *Subreptivement*, pilferingly, by stealth, by false meanes. **1821** CLARE *Vill. Minstr.* I. 73 Mistaking me for pilfering boy. **1878** B. TAYLOR *Deukalion* I. v, My pilfered strength shall of itself return.

pilferage ('pɪlfərɪdʒ). [f. prec. + -AGE.] The action or practice of pilfering; petty theft; in first quot., the product of pilfering, stolen goods. Also *Comb.*

c **1626** *Dick of Devon.* II. iv. in Bullen *O. Pl.* II. 40 Your horse and weapons I will take, but no pilferage. **1811** in J. Smyth *Pract. Customs* (1812) 271 If any pilferage, or other misdemeanor, be detected at the said wharf, whereby the revenue may be prejudiced. **1862** SMILES *Engineers* I. v. viii. 426 Conveyed..at great risk of breakage and pilferage. **1964** *Spectator* 13 Mar. 337/2 An installation with a primary mission of production control can simultaneously be used to promote safety and prevent pilferage. **1969** *Daily Tel.* 22 July 17 (Advt.), We have the only through-pallet service between here and the Far East via the U.S.A...which means much less chance of loss, pilferage, and damage. **1969** *Jane's Freight Containers 1968–69* 482/3 In the side walls there are pilferage-proof ventilation openings. **1971** *Daily Mail* 6 May 24/4 Pilferage last year totalled half of 1p.c. of the..turnover. **1974** *Islander* (Victoria, B.C.) 1 Sept. 11/2 When visitors leave, all their baggage is inspected by police to forestall pilferage.

pilferer ('pɪlfərə(r)). [f. as prec. + -ER[1].] One who pilfers; a petty thief.

1580 HOLLYBAND *Treas. Fr. Tong, Desrobbeur & pilleur*, a theef, a robber, a picker, a pilferer. **1587** HARRISON *England* III. xv. (1878) II. 101 [Small fairs] are oft preiudiciall to such as dwell neere hand..by pilferers that resort vnto the same. **1634** WITHER *Emblemes* 167 The poore and petty pilferers you see On wheeles, on gibbets and the gallow tree. **1728** YOUNG *Love Fame* III. 90 Thieves of renown, and pilferers of fame. **1840** MACAULAY *Ess., Clive* (1854) 533/2 The whole crew of pilferers and oppressors from whom he had rescued Bengal.

'**pilfering**, *vbl. sb.* [f. as prec. + -ING[1].] The action of the vb. PILFER. †**a.** Pillaging, plundering, robbery (*obs.*). **b.** Stealing or thieving in small quantities; petty theft.

a **1548** HALL *Chron., Hen. V* 66 b, The Englishmen durst not..ones deuide them selues or fal to pilfryng. *Ibid., Hen. VII* 57 b, The people..cryed to God dayly for an ende of their pilfrynge. **1583** STUBBES *Anat. Abus.* II. (1882) 38 Licentious persons..liuing vpon pilfering and stealing. **1596** BACON *Max. & Use Com. Law* I. (1635) 17 Some whose offences are pilfring under twelve pence value, they judge to be whipped. **1849** MACAULAY *Hist. Eng.* ix. II. 464 There had..been..much less waste and pilfering in the dockyards than formerly.

attrib. **1624** CAPT. J. SMITH *Virginia* III. vii. 70 This businesse..thus abused by such pilfring occasions. **1865** DICKENS *Mut. Fr.* I. xiv, Sneaking in and out among the shipping..in a pilfering way.

'**pilferment.** *rare*[−1]. [f. as prec. + -MENT.] Pilfering, petty theft; something pilfered.

1823 CHALMERS *Serm.* I. 174 [They] number such pilferments as can pass unnoticed among the perquisites of their office.

†'**pilfery.** *Obs.* Forms: 5 pylfry, 6–7 pilfry, -rie, pilfery, -erie, 7 pilfrey. [app. in origin a variant of *pelferie*, PELFRY (a. OF. **pelferie*, *peuferie*); but from the first denoting the action of F. *pelfrer* 'to pillage, plunder, rob', rather than the concrete 'booty, spoil', and afterwards associated with the special sense of PILFER *v.*]

1. The action of plundering or pillaging; robbery.

1494 FABYAN *Chron.* VII. 630 To vacabondys..that lokyd for pylfry & ryfflynge. **1577** HARRISON *England* II. x. (1877) I. 219 What notable roberies, pilferies [etc.] I need not to rehearse.

2. Petty theft, pilfering, peculation.

1573 TUSSER *Husb.* (1878) 17 To folow profit earnestlie but meddle not with pilferie. **1579–80** NORTH *Plutarch* (1595) 1069 Lucius Pella..was accused and conuicted of robbery, and pilferie in his office. **1628** LE GRYS tr. *Barclay's Argenis* 148 A seruant had done a pilfery; he fled and was pursued by his master. **1720** STRYPE *Stow's Surv.* I. II. ii. 10/1 For the restraining of which Naughtiness and Pilferies, the said John had again purchased it.

attrib. **1589** PUTTENHAM *Eng. Poesie* III. xix. (Arb.) 228 To excuse a fault..as to say of a great robbery, that it was but a pilfry matter.

3. The produce of plundering or pilfering; stolen or pilfered property.

1592 NASHE *P. Penilesse* (ed. 2) 17 b, You slowe spirited Saturnists, that haue nothing but the pilfries of your penne. **1626** T. H[AWKINS] *Caussin's Holy Crt.* 301 As one should pull a pilfry out of a theeues coffer.

pilgarlic (pɪl'gɑ:lɪk). Also 6 pyllyd, 7 pild-, peeled garlic(k; 7–9 peel-garlic. [f. PILLED, PEELED *ppl. a.*[1] + GARLIC *sb.*; cf. PILCORN, PILLEDOW, PILPATE.] An appellation given first to a 'pilled' or bald head, ludicrously likened to a peeled head of garlic (see *garlic-head*, GARLIC *sb.* 3), and then to a bald-headed man, sometimes with insinuation as to an alleged cause (quots. 1619, 1671); from the 17th c. applied in a ludicrously contemptuous or mock-pitiful way: 'poor creature'. Now *dial.* in various shades of meaning. Also *attrib.*

α. *a* **1529** SKELTON *Poems agst. Garnesche* Wks. 1843 I. 122 Ye loste hyr fauyr quyt; Your pyllyd garleke hed Cowde hocupy there no stede; She callyd yow Syr Gy of Gaunt. ? *a* **1605** (?) STOW (Farmer), He will soon be a peeled garlic like myself. **1619** J. T. (*title*) The Hunting of the Pox: a pleasant Discourse betweene the Authour and Pild-Garlike, wherein is declared the Nature of the Disease, how it came, and how it may be cured. *Ibid.* i, I ouertooke Pild-Garlike on the way. *Ibid.* ii, He had of Spanish Buttons store vpon his forehead mixt; And where that they were falne away, there Stooles in place were fixt. **1671** SKINNER *Etymol. Ling. Angl.*, *Pill'd* or *Peel'd Garlick*, cui Cutis (hoc est Pellis) vel Pili omnes ex morbo aliquo, præsertim Lue Venerea, defluxerunt.

β. *a* **1625** FLETCHER *Hum. Lieut.* II. ii, And there got he a knocke and down goes pilgarlike, Commends his soule to his she-saint and exit. **1667** DENHAM *Direct. Painter* II. viii. 28 Poor Peel-Garlick George. **1699** BOYER *Dict. Franc. Ang.* I. s.v. *Sangler*, The poor pilgarlick was soundly horsewhipped. **1824** CARLYLE in Froude *Life* (1882) I. xiv. 247 The strange pilgarlic figures that I saw breakfasting over a few expiring embers on roasted apples. **1843** J. BALLANTINE *Gaberl. W., Wee Raggit Laddie* iv, Our gentry's wee peel-garlic getts Feed on bear meal an' sma' ale swats. **1880** *Antrim & Down Gloss.*, *Peel garlick*, a yellow person; a person dressed shabbily or fantastically. **1888–90** *Sheffield Gloss.*, *Pillgarlic*, *sb.* a poor, ill-dressed person; an object of pity or contempt. **1894** *Punch* 21 Apr. 186 No! 'tis Bull is pilgarlic and martyr.

b. Used by the speaker of himself as a *quasi*-proper name; commonly ***poor Pilgarlic*** = poor I, poor me. *dial.* and *U.S. colloq.* or *slang.*

1694 ECHARD *Plautus* 116 They cou'dn't save poor Pilgarlick from going to Pot. **1738** SWIFT *Pol. Conversat.* 75 They went all to the opera; and so poor Pilgarlick came home alone. **1793** BURNS *Lett., to G. Thomson* Sept., A ballad is my hobby-horse,..that..is sure to run poor pilgarlick, the bedlam jockey, quite beyond any useful point or post in the common race of men. **1884** H. COLLINGWOOD

Under Meteor Flag 173 Little Summers and I—poor Pilgarlic—were so entirely consumed with disgust. **1889** FARMER *Dict. Amer., Pilgarlic*.., one's self. Thus a thief will inform a pal that pilgarlic was engaged in any given undertaking.

Hence **pil'garlicky** *a.*, pitiable, poor-spirited.
1893 E. GOSSE *Crit. Kit-Kats* (1896) 96 It is a pilgarlicky mind that is satisfied with saying, 'I like you, Dr. Fell, the reason why I cannot tell'.

† **pilgate, pilget, pilȝet.** *Sc. Obs.* app. = PILLION *sb.*[1]

1511 *Acc. Ld. High Treas. Scot.* IV. 221 Item, to Robert Spetele, for reformyng and lyning of ane pilȝet to hir. **1537** *Ibid.* VI. 356 Deliverit be the said Patrik ane pair of girthis to ane pilgate..ijs. **1619** in *14th Rep. Hist. MSS. Comm.* App. III. 46 For blak clothe..to the Lady Dudope hir womans pilget, and for making it.

'**pilger**, *sb.*[1] *dial.* [perh. f. PILE *sb.*[1] + *gar*, GARE *sb.*[1]: cf. ELGER.] A fish- or eel-spear.

a **1825** FORBY *Voc. E. Anglia, Pilger*, a fish-spear. **1877** *Holderness Gloss., Pilger*, a three-pronged eel-spear. **1899** *Westm. Gaz.* 22 Feb. 5/2 He was using a pilger, and brought up an eel 6lb. 2oz., and measuring 4ft. 4in.

pilger ('pɪlgə(r)), *sb.*[2] and *v. Metallurgy.* Also **Pilger.** [a. G. *pilger* pilgrim, in allusion to the alternate feeding in and partial withdrawal of the billet during the operation of the mill, which is said to resemble the steps of pilgrims approaching a shrine.] Used *attrib.* (in ***pilger mill, process, roll***, etc.) with reference to a rolling mill for reducing the outside diameter of a tube without changing the inside diameter, its two rollers each having a semicircular groove of decreasing diameter passing round the circumference, so that in conjunction they form a circular hole through which the tube can be forced on cylindrical mandrel and which decreases gradually and increases suddenly in size during each revolution of the rollers.

1902 *Proc. S. Wales Inst. Engineers* XXII. 351 One of the most interesting..devices is the machine named the Pilger carriage, to which the hollow billet is attached previous to being operated upon in the pilgrim mill. **1905** *Min. Proc. Inst. Civil Engineers* CLIX. 335 A tube produced by means of pilger-rolls frequently possesses a rippled or undulating surface. **1922** *Iron & Coal Trades Rev.* 9 June 849/1 The Pilger mill consists of two..'cam' rolls, fixed in housings, and driven through two-high pinions in practically the same manner as a two-high merchant bar mill, except that the Pilger rolls rotate in an opposite direction. **1954** A. R. BAILEY *Text-bk. Metallurgy* xii. 419 (*caption*) Diagram showing the step-by-step method of rolling in the Pilger process. **1968** R. N. PARKINS *Mech. Treatm. Metals* iv. 263 In the Pilger mill, the tube is deformed over a mandrel between rolls that work the tube during only part of each revolution. **1973** [see below].

So '**pilger** *v. trans.*, to make in a pilger mill; '**pilgering** *vbl. sb.*

1902 *Proc. S. Wales Inst. Engineers* XXII. 350 Pilgering or pilgrim mill. This mill derives its name from its peculiar intermittent action upon the hollow billet. **1923** HARBORD & HALL *Metallurgy of Steel* (ed. 7) II. xxiii. 467 Tubes are not usually made by pilgering with walls less than 9 or 10 gauge in thickness. **1945** *Metallurgia* XXXIII. 61/1 If the partly pilgered tube is withdrawn, the shape of the cone between bloom and tube will thus be a projection of the groove that varies around the roll. *Ibid.* 61/3 One company once pilgered a tube 10½ in. outside diameter × $\frac{3}{16}$ in. thick by no less than 135 ft. 8 in. long. **1973** J. G. TWEEDDALE *Materials Technol.* II. iv. 95 Pilgering is the name given to the second tube-forge-rolling system, which is done in a pilger mill.

pilgrim ('pɪlgrɪm), *sb.* Forms: 2–4 **pilegrim**, 3 **pele-, pillegrim**, 4 **pylegrym, pylgrime, pilgerim**, *Sc.* **pilgram, pilgerame**, 4–6 **pilgrym(e, -grame, pylgrim**, 4–7 **pilgrime**, 5–6 **pylgreme, -grym(e**, 6 **pyl-, pilgrem, pilgrum**, 4– **pilgrim**. *β.* 4 **pilegrin**, 6 **pilgrin**, *Sc.* **-gren**. [Early ME. *pelegrim, pilegrim*, repr. OF. **pelegrin*, antecedent form to *pèlerin* (11th c. in Littré) = Pr. *pelegrin*, Cat. *pelegri, peregri*, It. *pellegrino*, Sp. *peregrino*:—L. *peregrin-um* one that comes from foreign parts, a stranger, f. *peregrē* adv., from abroad, abroad, *pereger* that is abroad or on a journey, f. *per* through + *ager* field, country, land: see PEREGRINE. In Romanic, *peregrino* became, by dissimilation of *r...r*, *pelegrino, pelegrin*, whence F. *pèlerin*. In Eng. (rarely in OF.), final *n* became *m*, making *pelegrim, pilegrim, pilgrim* (cf. OHG. *piligrīm*), also *pelrimage*: see PILGRIMAGE. (Gower has also the later Fr. form, PELERIN.)]

A. Illustration of Forms.

α. *c* **1200** Pilegrim [see B. 1]. *c* **1205** LAY. 30736 Þe pillegrim hine talde Al þat he wolde. *Ibid.* 30744 Brien.. saide þet he wes pelegrim Ah pic nefden he nan mid him. **13** .. *Cursor M.* 17288 + 339 (Cott.) Art þou not a pilgrim þat walkes here in land? *c* **1375** *Sc. Leg. Saints* iii. (*Andreas*) 1001 Thane come a pylgrime sodanly. —— 1056 Quhen þe pilgram had herd þis. *Ibid.* xxvii. (*Machor*) 1218 He as pilgerame thocht at Rome to be. **1382** WYCLIF *Heb.* xi. 13 For thei ben pilgrymes [**1388** pilgryms], and herborid men vpon the erthe. —— *1 Pet.* ii. 11, I beseche you, as comelynges and pilgrimes [**1388** pilgrymys]. *c* **1440** *Promp. Parv.* 398/2 Pylgreme..*peregrinus*. **1500–20** DUNBAR *Poems* lxxiii. 9 Walk furth, pilgrame. **1530** PALSGR. 254/1 Pylgryme, *pellerin*. **1535** COVERDALE *2 Esdras* xvi. 40 Be euen as pylgrems vpon earth. **1563** WINȜET *Wks.* (S.T.S.) II. 16 It apperis to me, the Pilgrum.

β. **1390** GOWER *Conf.* I. 110 Two pilegrins of so gret age. *a* **1600** BUREL *Pilgr.* in J. Watson *Collect.* (1709) II. 22 Bot I who wes ane pure Pilgren And half an Stronimeir.

B. Signification.

1. One who travels from place to place; a person on a journey; a wayfarer, a traveller; a wanderer; a sojourner. (Now *poet.* or *rhet.* in general sense.)

c **1200** *Vices & Virtues* 35 Swa doð pilegrimes ðe lateþ her awen eard, and fareð in to oðre lande. *a* **1300** *Cursor M.* 6835 (Cott.) To pilgrime and to vncuth þou ber þe wit þi dedis cuth. *c* **1330** R. BRUNNE *Chron. Wace* (Rolls) 15066 Ȝe are of so fer contre, And als pylegryms. **1382** WYCLIF *Luke* xxiv. 18 Thou aloone ert a pilgrym of Jerusalem. **1483** *Cath. Angl.* 278/1 A Pilgrame, *peregrinus*, ..*extraneus, exoticus*. **1582** STANYHURST *Æneis* I. (Arb.) 17 Lyke wandring pilgrim too famosed Italie trudging. **1727–46** THOMSON *Summer* 964 A suffocating wind the pilgrim smites With instant death. **1764** GOLDSM. *Trav.* 197 And haply too some pilgrim, thither led, With many a tale repays the nightly bed. **1840** DICKENS *Old C. Shop* xv, The two pilgrims..pursued their way in silence. *a* **1850** ROSSETTI *Dante & Circle* I. (1874) 106 Any man may be called a pilgrim who leaveth the place of his birth.

2. *spec.* One who journeys (usually a long distance) to some sacred place, as an act of religious devotion; one who makes a pilgrimage. (The prevailing sense.)

a **1225** *Ancr. R.* 350 Oðre pilegrimes goð mid swinke uorte sechen one holie monnes bones, ase Sein James oðer Sein Giles. **1362** LANGL. *P. Pl.* A. Prol. 46 Pilgrimes and Palmers ..For to seche Seint Ieme and seintes at Roome; Wenten forþ in heore wey. *c* **1386** CHAUCER *Prol.* 26 Pilgrimes were they alle That toward Caunterbury wolden ryde. **1456** SIR G. HAYE *Law Arms* (S.T.S.) 238 All pilgrymes to quhat voyage that ever thai pas in the service of God and his sanctis, thay ar all in the protectioun and salvegarde of the pape. **1560** DAUS tr. *Sleidane's Comm.* 341 b, At the same time were very manye Pilgrimes at Rome,..to thentent they might..receiue cleane remission and forgeuenes of theyr sinnes. **1596** SHAKS. *1 Hen. IV*, I. ii. 140 There are Pilgrimes going to Canterbury with rich Offerings, and Traders riding to London with fat Purses. **1764** BURN *Poor Laws* 205 Pilgrims were licensed to wander, and beg by the way, to render their devotions at the shrines of dead men. **1841** LANE *Arab. Nts.* I. 26 Pilgrims returning from the holy places bring water of Zemzem, dust from the Prophet's tomb.

3. *fig.* (chiefly in allegorical religious use: cf. PILGRIMAGE *sb.* 1 c).

a **1225** *Ancr. R.* 350 Þeo pilegrimes þet goð touward heouene, heo goð forte beon isonted, & forte iuinden God sulf. **1340–70** *Alex. & Dind.* 983 For erþe is nouht our eritage..But we ben pore pilegrimus put in þis worde. **1382** [see A. α] . *c* **1430** LYDG. *Min. Poems* (Percy Soc.) 122 To erthely pilgrymes that passen to and froo, Fortune shewithe ..How this world is a thurghefare ful of woo. **1526** TINDALE *Heb.* xi. 13 They..confessed that they were straungers and pilgrems [WYCLIF pilgrymes and herborid men] on the erthe. **1678** BUNYAN (*title*) The Pilgrim's Progress from this World to That which is to come. *Ibid.* I. 90, I was a Pilgrim, going to the Cœlestial City. **1732** LAW *Serious C.* i. (ed. 2) 8 To live as Pilgrims in Spiritual Watching. **1838** EMERSON *Addr., Lit. Ethics* Wks. (Bohn) II. 206 A divine pilgrim in nature, all things attend his steps.

4. *Amer. Hist.* Name given in later times to those English Puritans who founded the colony of Plymouth, Massachusetts, in 1620. Now usually **Pilgrim Fathers**.

Governor Bradford in 1630 wrote of his company as 'pilgrims' in the spiritual sense (sense 3) referring to Heb. xi. 13. The same phraseology was repeated by Cotton Mather and others, and became familiar in New England. In 1798 a Feast of the 'Sons' or 'Heirs of the Pilgrims' was held at Boston on 22 Dec., at which the memory of 'the Fathers' was celebrated. With the frequent juxtaposition of the names *Pilgrims, Fathers, Heirs* or *Sons of the Pilgrims*, and the like, at these anniversary feasts, 'Pilgrim Fathers' naturally arose as a rhetorical phrase, and gradually grew to be a historical designation.

[**1630** BRADFORD *Hist. Plymouth Colony* 36 They knew they were but pilgrimes, & looked not much on those things; but lift vp their eyes to yᵉ heauens, their dearest cuntrie. **1654** E. JOHNSON *Wond.-w. Prov.* 216 Yet were these pilgrim people minded of the suddain forgetfulness of those worthies that died not long before. **1702** C. MATHER *Magn. Chr.* I. i. §4 They took their leave of the pleasant City [Leyden], where they had been Pilgrims and Strangers now for Eleven Years. *Ibid.* II. i. §1 They found..a New World ..in which they found that they must live like Strangers and Pilgrims. **1793** C. ROBBINS *Serm.* 29 But they knew they were pilgrimes.] **1798** *Columbian Centinel* 26 Dec. 2/4 The Feast of the 'Sons of the Pilgrims'. *Ibid.* 29 Dec. 2/4 'The Heirs of the Pilgrims' Celebrated on Saturday Dec. 22, the 177th Anniversary of the landing of their Forefathers at Plymouth Rock..the day of the nativity of New-England. **1892** *Nation* (N.Y.) 21 Apr., What shall we say to the descendants of the Pilgrims, and the Signers,..who are happy and content under his [Croker's] sway?

1799 *Columbian Centinel* 25 Dec. 3 An Ode [by Samuel Davis], in honor of the Fathers, was sung..by the company to the tune of Old Hundred... It concluded with the following verse:—Hail Pilgrim Fathers of our race, With grateful hearts your toils we trace, Oft as this votive Day returns, We'll pay due honors to your urns. **1801** *Ibid.* 23 Dec. 2/4 'Sons of the Pilgrims.' Yesterday, the anniversary of the landing of our Pilgrim Fathers, at Plymouth, in 1620, was celebrated. **1813** J. DAVIS *Disc.* 3 To look back to the origin of our state, and to revive..the transactions and the toils of our pilgrim fathers, who, at such a season, first landed on these shores. **1820** J. THACHER *Hist. Plymouth* (1832) 246 The present year closes the second century since the pilgrim fathers first landed on our shores. **1828** MRS. HEMANS (*title*) The Landing of the Pilgrim Fathers in New England. **1841** ALEX. YOUNG (*title*) Chronicles of the Pilgrim Fathers of the Colony of Plymouth, from 1602 to 1625. **1853** MARSDEN *Early Purit.* 295 The May-flower and the Speedwell..in which the exiles of Leyden, the pilgrim fathers, embarked upon their voyage.

5. *U.S.* and *Colonial.* An original settler; a new-comer, a recent immigrant (also said of animals).

1841 W. L. MACCALLA *Adventures in Texas* 46 After such an address from a citizen of that calumniated country Texas to a shattered old pilgrim, I took the liberty of withdrawing to another apartment. **1851** in W. Pratt *Colonial Experiences* 234 (Morris) [In the 'Dream of a Shagroon', which bore the date..April 1851,..the term] 'pilgrim' [was first applied to the settlers]. **1865** LADY BARKER *Station Life N. Zealand* iii. (1874) 20 Fifteen years ago a few sheds received the 'Pilgrims', as the first comers are always called. **1867** J. F. MELINE *Two Thousand Miles on Horseback* 22 The term Pilgrims for emigrants first came into use at the period of the heavy Mormon travel—the Mormons styling themselves 'Pilgrims to the promised land of Utah'. **1885** *Rep. Indian Affairs* (U.S.) 120 This, we think, is a very fair crop of calves considering the fact that the cattle were what is called 'pilgrim' cattle (cattle for the States that had never passed through a winter before without being housed and fed). **1887** L. SWINBURNE in *Scribner's Mag.* II. 508/1 'Pilgrim' and 'tenderfoot' were formerly applied almost exclusively to newly imported cattle,..they are usually used to designate all new-comers, tourists, and business-men. **1888** *Century Mag.* Feb. 509/1 Those herds consisting of pilgrims,.. animals driven up on to the range from the South, and therefore in poor condition. **1903** *Daily Chron.* 30 Mar. 5/2 Sir John Hall..was one of the original 'Canterbury pilgrims', as the first settlers in the New Zealand province founded under the auspices of the Church of England were styled. **1942** E. E. DALE *Cow Country* 194 They mingled with 'drift cattle' from Kansas or with the trail herds of 'pilgrim cattle' from Texas. **1943** J. K. HOWARD *Montana* 139 They were for the most part 'pilgrims' who remained and were 'made into hands'.

6. A peregrine falcon: see PEREGRINE A. 4.

1866 *Morn. Star* 4 Aug., Sparrow hawks, gerfalcons, hobbies, pilgrims, vultures, and merlins.

7. 'A term given about 1765 to an appendage of silk, fixed to the back of a lady's bonnet, by way of covering the neck, when walking' (Fairholt *Costume in Eng.* (1860) Gloss.): cf. PELERINE.

8. *attrib.* and *Comb.*

a. *attrib.* (sometimes quasi-*adj.*) That is a pilgrim; going on pilgrimage; consisting of pilgrims; of, pertaining or relating to a pilgrim or pilgrims: as ***pilgrim chief, city, foot, garland, life, man, monk, poet, sheet, soul, spirit, state, step, throng, trade, traffic, train, warrior, weed; pilgrim-cloak, -staff (-stave), -tax***. Also ***pilgrim-like*** adj. and adv., ***pilgrim-monger, pilgrim-wise*** adv., ***pilgrim-worn*** adj.

1805 SCOTT *Last Minstr.* VI. xxviii, When *pilgrim-chiefs, in sad array, Sought Melrose' holy shrine. **1823** MRS. HEMANS *Vespers Palermo* I. i, He folds around him His *pilgrim-cloak. **1382** WYCLIF *Zeph.* i. 8 Clothid with *pilgrim [*gloss* or straunge] clothing [L. *veste peregrina*]. **1878** BROWNING *La Saisiaz* 325 Sward my *pilgrim-foot can prize. **1860** PUSEY *Min. Proph.* 591 Their *pilgrim-life from the passage of the Red Sea. **1574** NEWTON *Health Mag.* Epist. 7 Dwelling (*Pylgrymlike) in the bodies of all men, women, and fourfooted beastes. **1715** M. DAVIES *Athen. Brit.* I. 284 As the *Pilgrim-Monger Mr. Medcalf undauntedly own'd it in 1712. **1844** MRS. BROWNING *Vis. Poets* ccxxvii, He our *pilgrim-poet. **1618** BRATHWAIT *Descr. Death* xvi, *Pilgrim-remouer that depriues vs sence. **1768** BARETTI *Acc. Italy* I. 25 That he might not lie..in beggarly *pilgrim sheets. **1850** MRS. BROWNING *Runaway Slave at Pilgrim's Point* ii, O *pilgrim-souls, I speak to you! **1812** S. ROGERS *Columbus* Poems (1839) 41 Oh, had ye vowed with *pilgrim-staff to roam. **1671** MILTON *P.R.* IV. 427 Till morning fair Came forth with *Pilgrim steps in amice gray. **1839** *Lett. fr. Madras* (1843) 252 Do you know that Government has abolished the *pilgrim-tax? **1824** MONTGOMERY *Hymn, 'Sing we the song of those who stand'* iii, Toil, trial, suffering, still await On earth, the *pilgrim-throng. **1700** DRYDEN *Charac. Good Parson* 1 A parish-priest was of the *pilgrim-train. *c* **1610** *Pilgrim's Song* in Farr *S.P. Jas. I* (1848) 110, I am a *pilgrim-warriour bound to fight Under the red crosse, 'gainst my rebell will. *c* **1470** HENRY *Wallace* I. 277 His modyr graithit hir in *pilgrame weid. *a* **1591** H. SMITH *Wks.* (1867) II. 485 In earth, man wanders, *pilgrim-wise. **1899** *Academy* 15 July 56/2 Thine [Shakspere's] the shrine more *pilgrim-worn than all The shrines of singers.

b. Special Comb. (often with the possessive *pilgrim's*): **pilgrim-bottle, pilgrim's bottle**, a flat bottle with a ring on each side of the neck for the insertion of cords by which it may be hung and carried (= COSTREL[1]); **Pilgrim Fathers** (*Amer. Hist.*): see sense 4; hence **pilgrim-fatherly** *a. nonce-wd.* (after *fatherly*), characteristic of the Pilgrim Fathers; **pilgrim's pouch**, a variety of *pilgrim's sign* (q.v.), consisting of a piece of lead or other material in the form of a small pouch; **pilgrim's ring, pilgrim-ring** (see quot.); † **pilgrim-salve, pilgrim's salve**, 'an old ointment, made chiefly of swine's grease and isinglass' (Halliw.); in quot. 1670 euphemism for 'ordure, filth'; **pilgrim's shell**, a cockle- or scallop-shell carried by a pilgrim as a sign of having visited the shrine of St. James of Compostella or some sacred place; also an artificial carved imitation of such a shell; **pilgrim's sign**, a medal or other small object presented to a pilgrim at a shrine or other sacred place as a sign of his having visited it; **pilgrim's vase**, a flat vase made in imitation of a *pilgrim's bottle*.

1874 *Archæol. Jrnl.* Dec. 431 Mrs. Baily sent for exhibition two costrels, or *pilgrims' bottles. **1905** H. D. Rolleston *Dis. Liver* 27 This grooved condition.. has been spoken of as the 'pilgrim's bottle liver'. **1883** Freeman *Impress. U.S.* vii. 64 It sounds, so to speak, '*pilgrim-fatherly'. **1877** W. Jones *Finger-ring* 181 The '*pilgrim-ring' of Edward the Confessor.. was in after times preserved with great care. *Ibid.* 266 One of the rings given to tourists to the holy city, as a certificate of their visit, and called.. pilgrims' rings. *c* **1580** Jefferie *Bugbears* I. iii. 90 in *Archiv Stud. Neu. Spr.* (1897) XCVIII. 313 A drane of *pylgrim salve to clap to hiss nosse. **1670** *Mod. Acc. Scot.* in *Harl. Misc.* (Park) VI. 137 The whole pavement is pilgrim-salve. **1672** [H. Stubbe] *Rosemary & Bayes* 18 Cutaneous pustules, for which the pilgrims salve will be necessary.

'pilgrim, *v.* [f. prec. sb. Cf. OF. *peleriner*, Ger. *pilgern*.] *intr.* To be, or act as becomes, a pilgrim; to make a pilgrimage, go on pilgrimage; to travel or wander like a pilgrim. Also *to pilgrim it*. Hence **'pilgriming** *vbl. sb.* and *ppl. a.*

[**1561** *Chaucer's Wks.* 285 b (*Test. Love* I. Prol.), When I pilgramed [*ed.* 1532 pilgrymaged] out of my kithe in wintere.] **1681** Grew *Musæum* I. 176 The Palmer-worm, *Ambulo*.. pilgrims up and down every where, feeding upon all sorts of Plants. **1827** Carlyle *Germ. Rom.* III. 154 He pilgrimed to his old sporting-places. **1831** —— *Sart. Res.* II. vii, His mad Pilgrimings, and general solution into aimless Discontinuity. **1864** Burton *Scot Abr.* II. ii. 184 With my staff in my hand I pilgrim'd it away all alone.

pilgrimage ('pɪlgrɪmɪdʒ), *sb.* Forms: 3 **pelrimage, pilegrim-**, 4 **pilgrin-, pylgryn-**, 4- **pilgrimage**, (4-6 **pylgrym-, pylgrim-, pilgrym-, pilgrem-, pylgrem-, pelgrymage**, 5-6 **pil-, pylgramage**). [ME. *pelrim-* (rarely *pelrin-*)*age*, a. OF. *pelrim-, pelryn-, pelerinage*, also *pel(l)egrin-, peligrinage* (Godef.), f. *peleriner* (etc.) vb., to go as a pilgrim: see PILGRIM *v.* and -AGE. In ME. nearly always with *m* for original *n*, and conformed to the contemporary spelling of *pilgrim*. But Gower has the French form *pelrinage* (see PELERINAGE), and MSS. of *c* 1400 have *pilgrin-, pylgrynage*, with *n*.]

1. a. A journey made by a pilgrim; a journey (usually of considerable duration) made to some sacred place, as an act of religious devotion; the action of taking such a journey. Phr. *to go on* (†*in*, †*a*) *pilgrimage*.

c **1250** *O. Kent. Serm.* in *O.E. Misc.* 28 Si Mirre signefiet[h] uastinge for þo luue of gode.. go ine pelrimage.. and to do alle þe gode þet me may do for godes luue. *c* **1290** *S. Eng. Leg.* I. 40/200 A gret pilegrimage it is i-holde.. To sechen þat ilke holie stude þare seint Iemes bones beothþ. *Ibid.* 473/391 To don þis pelrimage ȝwy raddest thou me? *c* **1315** Shoreham I. 1028 Pelgrymage and beddyng hard, Flesch fram lykynge to arere. *c* **1325** *Metr. Hom.* 54, I mac mi vaiage Til sain Jam in pilgrimage. *c* **1386** Chaucer *Prol.* 21 In Southwerk at the Tabard as I lay, Redy to wenden on my pilgrymage To Caunterbury with ful deuout corage. *c* **1400** *Titus & Vespasian* (Roxb.) 837 Þus bygan her pilgrinage [*v.r.* pylgrynage]. *c* **1400** *Destr. Troy* 2022 When þai hade.. Perfourmet þere pilgramage, prayers and all. *c* **1450** tr. *De Imitatione* I. xxiii. 31 þey þat gon muche a pilgrymage are but seldom þe holier. **1553** T. Wilson *Rhet.* (1580) 177 All Englande reioyseth that Pilgrimage is banished, and Idolatrie for euer abolished. **1631** Weever *Anc. Fun. Mon.* 202 To this new shrined Martyr, people.. flocked in pilgrimage. **1703** Maundrell *Journ. Jerus.* (1732) 1 It was to my purpose to undertake this Pilgrimage. **1844** H. H. Wilson *Brit. India* III. III. v. 215 After a visit to Calcutta, and a pilgrimage to Mecca,.. Syed Ahmed returned.. to the Upper Provinces.

b. *transf.* or *gen.* A journey; a travelling about, peregrination; sojourning. Now with allusion to prec. sense: A journey undertaken for some pious purpose, or to visit a place held in honour from association with some person or event.

13.. *Cursor M.* 2659 (Cott.) Þat þou has had in pelrimage [*Fairf.* pilgrimage] þine sal it haue in heritage, Al þe kyngrike o þis land. **1387** Trevisa *Higden* (Rolls) III. 287 Oon axede of Socrates why pilgremages [L. *perigrinationes*] stood hym to no profit. **1483** Caxton (*title*) The Pylgremage of the sowle. (*Colophon*) Here endeth the dreme of pylgremage of the soule. **1582** Stanyhurst *Æneis* II. (Arb.) 68 Thow must with surges bee banged and pilgrimage yrcksoom. **1596** Shaks. *Merch. V.* I. i. 120 Tel me now, what Lady is the same To whom you swore a secret Pilgrimage. **1694** Scottow *Plant. Mass. Col.* Mass. Hist. Coll. (1858) IV. 306 Thus far of the Light and white side of the Pillar, which attended us in this our Wilderness Pilgrimage. **1797** Mrs. Radcliffe *Italian* xii, Theirs seem a pilgrimage of pleasure. **1849** Macaulay *Hist. Eng.* iii. I. 337 The library, the museum, the aviary, and the botanical garden of Sir Thomas Browne, were thought by Fellows of the Royal Society well worthy of a long pilgrimage.

c. *fig.* The course of mortal life figured as a journey, or a 'sojourn in the flesh', esp. as a journey to a future state of rest or blessedness.

a **1340** Hampole *Psalter* lxiv. 1 Haly saules þat turnys fra pilgrymage of þis life til endles gladnes. **1340** —— *Pr. Consc.* 1395 Þis world es þe way and passage, Þurgh whilk lyes our pilgrimage. *c* **1430** Lydg. *Min. Poems* (Percy Soc.) 101 Gyven to man here in oure pilgremage. **1526** *Pilgr. Perf.* (W. de W. 1531) 1 This treatyse called the pilgrymage of perfeccion, is.. diuyded in to thre bokes. **1526** Tindale *1 Pet.* i. 17 Se that ye passe the tyme off your pilgremage [παροικίας, Wycl. pilgrimage, *Geneva* dwelling, *Rhem.* peregrination, 1611 soiourning] in feare. **1736-7** Doddridge *Hymn*, '*Oh God of Bethel*' i, Who thro' this weary Pilgrimage Hast all our Fathers led. **1859** Geo. Eliot *A. Bede* iv, That his mother might be.. comforted by his presence all the days of her pilgrimage.

d. *Pilgrimage of* (†*for*) *Grace*, in *Eng. Hist.*, the name assumed for their movement by those who rose in the North of England in 1536 in opposition to the dissolution of the monasteries and other features of the Reformation.

1536 *Lett. & Papers Hen. VIII*, XI. 304 By all the whole consent of the herdmen of this our pilgrimage for grace. [*Ibid.* 305 Crist crucifyid, For thy woundes wide, Us commons guyde, Which pilgrimes be Thrughe Godes grace.] *a* **1548** Hall *Chron.*, *Hen. VIII* 230 b, They named this there sedicious and traiterous voiage, an holye and blessed Pilgrimage. **1601** Stow *Ann.* 967 (*marg.* Oth of the rebels in Yorke-shire.) Yee shall not enter into this your pilgrimage of grace for the common wealth onely, but for the loue that you do beare to Gods faith and the church militant [etc.]. **1823** Lingard *Hist. Eng.* VI. 331 Their enterprise was quaintly termed the pilgrimage of grace: on their banners were painted the image of Christ crucified, and the chalice and host.

2. *transf.* A place to which a pilgrimage is made.

1517 Torkington *Pilgr.* (1884) 56 Som visited pylgrymages. **1529** More *Dyaloge* I. Wks. 145/1 To.. doo honour to their reliques, & visit pilgrimages. **1680** Morden *Geog. Rect., Germany* (1685) 125 Seckavar.. a Bishops See and Cell are of the greatest Pilgrimages in the Austrian Territory. **1864** Neale in *Ecclesiologist* XXV. 102 The chapel of S. Odele in Auvergne, a great pilgrimage.

3. *attrib.* **pilgrimage church, town, village**, etc., a church, town, village, etc., to which pilgrimages are made.

1719 J. T. Philipps tr. *Thirty-four Confer.* 92 How long they had lead that Pilgrimage State of Life? **1773** J. Conder *Let.* in *Evang. Mag.* (1813) XXI. 92 In your pilgrimage-course live above, and live on Him who lives above. **1889** L. T. Smith tr. *Jusserand's Eng. Wayfaring Life in Middle Ages* III. iii. 348 It was.. a town of inns and churches, as pilgrimage towns have generally been. **1897** *Daily News* 30 Sept. 6/2 It [Kano] is on the pilgrimage route. **1908** *Westm. Gaz.* 28 July 8/2 [They] paid a visit to the picturesque pilgrimage village of Sainte Anne de Beaupré. *Ibid.*, His Royal Highness alighted and proceeded to enter the Pilgrimage Church, the steps of which were crowded with cripples and pilgrims. **1935** *Burlington Mag.* Oct. 183/1 The great aisled transept [of Laon cathedral], she derives from the so-called 'pilgrimage churches' of which much has been written in recent years.

'pilgrimage, *v.* [f. prec. sb.]

† **1.** *intr.* To sojourn, to live among strangers.

1382 Wyclif *2 Kings* viii. 2 And gooynge with hyre hous [she] pylgrymagid in the lond of Phylisteis many dayes. —— *Jer.* xxxv. 7 That ȝee lyue manye daȝes vpon the face of the lond, in which ȝee pilgrimagen. **1387-8** T. Usk *Test. Love* I. Prol., in *Chaucer's Wks.* (1532), As they me betiden whan I pilgrymaged out of my kyth in wynter. **1669** Penn *No Cross* Wks. 1782 II. 356 [Moses] chuses rather to sojourn and pilgrimage with the despised afflicted, tormented Israelites in the wilderness.

2. *intr.* To make a pilgrimage; to go on pilgrimage. Also *to pilgrimage it*.

1621 Bp. Mountagu *Diatribæ* 496 It is arbitrary.. vnto what Shrine.. they will giue: vnto whom they will pilgrimage it. **1647** R. Stapylton *Juvenal* VI. 555 T' Egypt she'll pilgrimage, at Meroe fill Warme drops to sprinkle Isis Temple. **1829** Lamb *Let. to B. Barton* 25 Mar., Who.. of us that never pilgrimaged to Rome? **1883** G. Stephens *Bugge's Stud. N. Mythol.* 56 Christians in the West early pilgrimaged to the Holy Land.

Hence **'pilgrimaging** *vbl. sb.* and *ppl. a.*; also **'pilgrimager**, one who pilgrimages, a pilgrim.

c **1449** Pecock *Repr.* II. xiv. 195 The seid pilgrimaging. **1591** in Row *Hist. Kirk* (Wodrow Soc.) 142 Sayers and hearers of mass, pilgrimagers, papisticall magistrats. **1693** tr. *Emilianne's Hist. Monast. Ord.* III. 274 The Women who went thither a Pilgrimaging. **1731** *Gentl. Mag.* I. 321 A late Edict of the French King to forbid Pilgrimaging. *a* **1819** Wolcott (P. Pindar) *Wks.* (1830) 186 (D.) Like pilgrimaging rats, Unawed by mortals, and unscared by cats. **1898** M. P. Shiel *Yellow Danger* 266 Each of these pilgrimaging masses of men was in itself a nation.

pilgri'matic, -'atical, *adjs. nonce-wds.* Of or proper to a pilgrim or pilgrims. **'pilgrimdom**. *nonce-wd.* Pilgrim state or domain.

1772 *Birmingham Counterfeit* I. xviii. 257 We sat out, in order to make the usual pilgrimatical tour. **1838** Struthers *Poetic Tales* 25 On its pilgrimatic way.

1887 *Home Missionary* (N.Y.) Oct. 252 Soon Arkansas will be annexed to Pilgrimdom, fully under the dominion of the Lord Christ's regnant will.

'pilgrimer. *rare.* Also 6 *Sc.* -ar, 7 *Sc.* **pilgramer**. [f. PILGRIM *v.* (or *sb.*) + -ER¹.] One who 'pilgrims' or goes on pilgrimage; a pilgrim.

a **1581** in *Wodrow Soc. Misc.* 297 In this lyfe we are but travellauris, pilgrimaris and strangearis. **1609** Skene *Reg. Maj.*, *Stat. Dav. II* 39 All pilgrameris, quha for salvation of their saules, will visie the places of halie Saints. **1820** Scott *Abbot* xv, I was.. a matron of no vulgar name; now I am Magdalen, a poor pilgrimer, for the sake of Holy Kirk. **1827** Carlyle *Germ. Rom.* IV. 290 The quaint, fitful, and most dainty story of *The Foolish Pilgrimers.*

'pilgrimess. *rare.* A female pilgrim.

1611 Cotgr., *Pelerine*, a pilgrimesse; a woman that goes on Pilgrimage. **1696** (*title*) The Light of the World: A most True Relation of a Pilgrimess, M. Antonia Bourignon, Travelling towards Eternity. **1841** *Fraser's Mag.* XXIII. 475 The young pilgrimesses.. glided gently to the table.

'pilgrimism. *rare.* Pilgrim condition or practice.

1886 *Amer. Missionary* Dec. 360 The A.M.A. has reproduced in the South the pilgrimism of colonial life.

pilgrimize ('pɪlgrɪmaɪz), *v.* [See -IZE.]

1. *intr.* To play the pilgrim, travel as a pilgrim, go on pilgrimage. Also *to pilgrimize it*.

1598-9 B. Jonson *Case is Altered* II. iv, I'll bear thy charges, an thou wilt but pilgrimize it along with me to the land of Utopia. **1789** Coxe *Trav. Switz.* I. vii. 56 All the world pilgrimises to his bones. **1835** R. Chambers in *Blackw. Mag.* XXXVIII. 70 Thou shalt pilgrimize through life, unfriended and alone. **1891** Besant *London* (1894) 43 Rahere.. pilgrimised to Rome.

2. *trans.* To make into a pilgrim.

1755 Smollett *Quix.* (1803) IV. 140 Tell me who has pilgrimised thee; and wherefore hast thou dared to return to Spain?

Hence **'pilgrimizing** *vbl. sb.*

1818 C. Mills *Crusades* (1822) I. i. 15 No causes.. gave such strength to the spirit of pilgrimising as the opinion.. that the reign of Christ, or the Millennium was at hand. **1858** R. Chambers *Dom. Ann. Scot.* I. 3 The king himself sought for his highest religious comfort in pilgrimising to St. Duthac's shrine in Ross-shire.

pili ('pi:lɪ). [Hawaiian.] A Hawaiian name for the perennial grass, *Heteropgon contortus*, formerly used as a thatching material. Also *attrib.*

1888 W. Hillebrand *Flora Hawaiian Islands* 508 Common on all islands, the 'Pili' of the natives, very troublesome on account of its awns, which get entangled in the wool of sheep. **1915** W. A. Bryan *Nat. Hist. Hawaii* v. 59 Should a chief order a house built, certain men would cut the timbers, others gather the pili grass. **1917** *Nature* 20 Sept. 57/2 The grass used for this purpose [*sc.* thatching] is usually pili.., an indigenous grass. **1934** M. D. Frear *Lowell & Abigail* ii. 94 It was easy to accept the Hawaiian roof of thatch, using.. *ti* leaf where *pili* grass was not to be had. **1949** P. H. Buck *Coming of Maori* II. ii. 119 The Hawaiians used a similar [thatching] technique with *pili* grass. **1965** M. C. Neal *In Gardens of Hawaii* 80 In Hawaii, *pili* was preferred to other thatch material because of its pleasant odor, brown color, and neat appearance.

pili, pl. of PILUS, hair, down.

piliated ('pɪ-, 'paɪlɪˌeɪtɪd), *a. Bacteriol.* [f. *pili-*, taken as comb. form of PILUS + -ATE² + -ED¹, or directly f. PILUS + *-iated* after *fimbriated*.] Bearing pili.

1960 *Biochim. & Biophys. Acta* XLII. 298 Many piliated strains of bacteria can exist in two forms, the completely piliated.. or the completely non-piliated. **1973** Doetsch & Cook *Introd. Bacteria* ii. 28 Bacteria capable of producing pili, when freshy isolated from natural sources, are usually 'piliated'.

pilicock, variant of PILLICOCK *Obs.*

‖**pilidium** (paɪ'lɪdɪəm). *Nat. Hist.* [mod.L., a. Gr. πιλίδιον little cap, dim. of πῖλος a felt cap.]

1. *Zool.* A name given to the cap-shaped larvæ of some species of Nemertean worms, formerly considered as a distinct genus.

1877 Huxley *Anat. Inv. Anim.* xi. 651 The production of the Nemertid larva within its pilidium. **1888** Rolleston & Jackson *Anim. Life* 640 *note*, The *larva of Desor* is probably not so primitive a form as the *Pilidium*.

b. A genus of limpets of the family *Acmeidæ*.

2. *Bot.* The hemispherical apothecium of certain lichens.

1842 in Brande *Dict. Sc.* etc.

†**pilidod**, obs. variant of *peridod*, PERIDOT.

1404 *Durham Acc. Rolls* (Surtees) 394, j annulus Pontificalis cum j pilidod.

piliferous (paɪ'lɪfərəs), *a.* [f. L. *pilus* hair + -FEROUS] Bearing or having hair; *spec.* in *Bot.*, bearing hairs or tipped with a hair.

a **1846** Loudon is cited by Worcester. **1852** Dana *Crust.* I. 307 The oblique piliferous crest. **1857** Bullock *Cazeaux' Midwif.* 45 The sebaceous and piliferous follicles are exceedingly numerous. **1885** Goodale *Physiol. Bot.* (1892) 108 The piliferous layer has no intercellular spaces.

piliform ('paɪlɪfɔːm), *a.* [ad. mod.L. *piliform-is*, f. *pilus* hair: see -FORM.] Having the form of a hair; hair-like.

1826 Kirby & Sp. *Entomol.* III. xxxv. 649 In most of them the scales of the primary wings are piliform. **1828** Stark *Elem. Nat. Hist.* II. 44 Two long tentacula, covered with piliform filaments.

piligerous (paɪ'lɪdʒərəs), *a.* [f. L. *pilus* hair + -GEROUS.] Bearing hair, clothed with hair.

1835 Kirby *Hab. & Inst. Anim.* (1852) II. 112 The various piligerous, plumigerous, pennigerous, and squamigerous animals. **1893** *Syd. Soc. Lex.*, *Piligerous*, piliferous.

pilimiction (paɪlɪ'mɪkʃən). [ad. mod.L. *pilimictio*, f. *pilus* hair + late L. *mictio*, f. *mingĕre* to make water.] A diseased state in which piliform or hair-like bodies are passed in the urine.

1847-9 *Todd's Cycl. Anat.* IV. 142/2 Cases of.. pilimiction are.. to be received with distrust. **1874** Van Buren *Dis. Genit. Org.* 255 Cysts sometimes.. constitute nuclei for stone, or give rise to pilimiction.

piline ('paɪlɪn), *sb.* Short for SPONGIOPILINE.

1874 Garrod & Baxter *Mat. Med.* (1880) 209 Spirits of Camphor.. lightly sprinkled on impermeable piline.

piline (ˈpaɪlaɪn), *a.* [f. L. *pil-us* hair + -INE[1].] Of the nature of hair, hairy.

1887 *Pall Mall G.* 12 July 13/2 Darwin tells us we have shed the piline pelt which was the clothing of that ancestral ape.

piling (ˈpaɪlɪŋ), *vbl. sb.*[1] [f. PILE *v.*[1] + -ING[1].]

1. The action of PILE *v.*[1]; the driving of piles; the forming of a foundation or defence with piles.

c **1440** *Durham Acc. Rolls* (Surtees) 143 In mundacione de langmerdyk cum le pylyng ibidem fact. *c* **1582** T. DIGGES in *Archæol.* XI. 226 Yt is..doubtfull..whether they shall euer with any pyling reach so deepe as to make a sure foundation. **1739** LABELYE *Acc. Piers Westm. Bridge* 55 The Grounds which most require piling are a loose Sand, soft Clays, and ..fenny Places. **1793** SMEATON *Edystone L.* §336 The piling of this foundation was finished. **1973** *Daily Tel.* 3 Apr. 21 (Advt.), Piling has also been completed on the Hutchison House site and construction of the foundation is well in hand. **1975** *BP Shield Internat.* May 2 (*caption*) Piling into sea bed after removal of flotation tanks. **1977** *Daily Times* (Lagos) 25 Feb. 3/4 Mr. Ogundiya recalled that during the initial piling on the site, the management of Leventis wrote to his ministry threatening to claim ₦6 million if there was any damage to their building.

2. A mass of piles; a structure composed of piles; pilework; wood for piles.

1488 *Maldon, Essex, Liber B.* lf. 39 (MS.) The Brygge in Maldon..was so in decaye bothe in stone werke and also in wodyng and pylyng. **1580** HOLLYBAND *Treas. Fr. Tong, Pilotis*, a pyling with timber in water workes. **1772** HUTTON *Bridges* 99 A border of piling to secure the foundation. **1883** *Century Mag.* XXVI. 422 Seven hundred feet of piling were driven. **1939** A. RANSOME *Secret Water* xiv. 170 The wood of the quay was rotting, and water was working in and out through gaps in the piling. **1944** *Sun* (Baltimore) 18 Mar. 6/2 It is claimed that the timber piling is not sufficiently strong to support the structure and the loads it carries; the pile caps and stringers are in poor condition. **1975** *Lamp* (Exxon Corporation) Winter 11/2 When the platform's steel jacket was being emplaced this spring, the pilings struck a patch of sand in the bottom clay and couldn't be driven until larger and more powerful pile-driving equipment was moved to the site. **1977** *New Yorker* 9 May 118/2 They should see Prudhoe Bay. It's so damned clean and neat and sterile—with refrigerated pilings, so the tundra won't melt.

3. *attrib.*, as ***piling engine***.

1863 *Daily Tel.* 6 Apr., Instructed to collect timber, piling engines, staff, &c. **1898** *Engineering Mag.* XVI. 91 The timber..is chiefly for piling purposes and spars.

piling (ˈpaɪlɪŋ), *vbl. sb.*[2] [f. PILE *v.*[2] + -ING[1].]

1. The action of forming into a pile or piles; heaping up, building up in a regular pile.

c **1358** *Durham Acc. Rolls* (Surtees) 561 Will'o Randman pro pilyng et sortyng lane. **1435-6** in Heath *Grocers' Comp.* (1869) 418 Paid for costis, ffreight, cariage, wharvage, & pilyng up of ii shippes of waloill. **1580** HOLLYBAND *Treas. Fr. Tong, Entassement*, heaping, a piling. **1807** HUTTON *Course Math.* II. 262 Of the Piling of Balls and Shells. **1867** BARRY *Sir C. Barry* ii. 50 This piling of house upon house. **1875** KNIGHT *Dict. Mech.*, *Piling* (*Metallurgy*), building up pieces of sheared or scrap iron into a pack suitable for heating in a balling or reheating furnace. **1884** PHIN *Dict. Apiculture, Piling*, placing hives one above the other; storyfying.

b. *Leather-making.* The putting of hides in a pile or heap in order to sweat them and cause the hair to come off; also including other processes (such as hanging them up in a stove) by which the result is expedited. *U.S.*

1875 KNIGHT *Dict. Mech.* II. 1703/2 *Piling*,..(Leather) unhairing hides by piling [i.e. heaping] or hanging up in a stove, so called. **1885** C. T. DAVIS *Leather* vii. (1897) 126 Piling is nothing more nor less than a slow inward sweating.

2. *attrib.* and *Comb.*, as ***piling furnace***, ***swivel***.

1853 KANE *Grinnell Exp.* xxii. (1856) 176 The piling action of storms. **1861** FAIRBAIRN *Iron* 121 The pieces [of scrap iron]..being piled or faggotted into convenient sized masses..are placed in a reheating or piling furnace. **1904** *Westm. Gaz.* 9 Dec. 7/2 A cut-off..—with a piling swivel subsequently asked for—is fitted to all naval rifles.

piliol, penny-royal, etc.: see PULIOL.

pilion, pilioun, obs. forms of PILLION.

Pilipino (pɪlɪˈpiːnəʊ), *sb.* (and *a.*) [a. Tagalog, ad. Sp. *Filipino*: see FILIPINO *sb.* and *a.*] The national language of the Republic of the Philippines. Also *attrib.* or as *adj.*

1936 *Michigan Alumnus* Summer 216/1 The movement.. aroused only academic interest and the use of the 'Pilipino' language was not essayed by writers. **1961** *Comment* (Manila) XIII. 80 Filipino nationalists believe that addition would be better: Pilipino *plus* English. *Ibid.* 81 The Pilipino language program. **1964** *Whitaker's Almanack 1965* 907/2 Pilipino, the national language, is based on Tagalog. **1975** *Congress. Q.* 25 Apr. 309 The official language is Pilipino.., but English is widely spoken. **1984** *N.Y. Times* 29 Jan. 3/1 In the Pilipino language, balik bayan means return to the country.

pilk, pilken: see PILCH *v.*

pilkins (ˈpɪlkɪnz), *sb. pl. local.* [Perh. f. PILCH *v.*: see *N. & Q.* Aug. 1979, p. 305.] = TAILING *vbl. sb.*[1] 2 a.

1859 G. MEREDITH *Ordeal R. Feverel* I. vi. 101 He swears soam o' our chaps steals pilkins. *Ibid.* xii. 177 The Bantam said he had seen Tom secreting pilkins in a sack.

pilkoc, variant of PILLICOCK *Obs.*

pill (pɪl), *sb.*[1] Now *dial.* Forms: 4 **pile**, 5 **pylle**, 6 **pille, pyl(l**, 6–7 **pil**, 6–8 (9 *dial.*) **pill**. See also PEEL *sb.*[3] [app. related to PILL *v.*[1] as the collateral form PEEL *sb.*[3] is to PEEL *v.*[1]]

The covering or integument of a fruit; the shell, husk, rind, or skin; the bark, or any layer of the bark, of wood; the epiderm of hemp or flax; *esp.* the thin rind or peel of fruits, tuberous or bulbous roots, and the like; = PEEL *sb.*[3]

1388 WYCLIF *2 Sam.* xvii. 19 As dryynge barli with the pile takun a wey [1382 as dryynge pild barli, *Vulg.* siccans ptisanas]. **1491** CAXTON *Vitas Patr.* (W. de W. 1495) II. 218 By me I do ley a quantyte of small palmes of the whiche I pare the pylles & therof I make mattes. **1530** PALSGR. 254/1 Pyll of fruyte, *pellevre*. *Ibid.*, Pyll of hempe, *til* [mod.F. *tille*]. **1541** R. COPLAND *Galyen's Terapeut.* 2 H ij, The huske or pyl of the pomgarnet. **1558-68** WARDE tr. *Alexis' Secr.* 42 Take..a piece of the pille of a Citron confiete. **1565-73** COOPER *Thesaurus, Calyx*,..the pill of a nutte or almon. **1573-80** BARET *Alv.* P 360 The pill of wood betweene the barke and tree. **1613** PURCHAS *Pilgrimage* IX. iv. 841 Boughes tied together with the pills of trees. **1653** H. COGAN tr. *Pinto's Trav.* xxxi. (1663) 123 Boats likewise laden with dried orange pils. **1658** tr. *Porta's Nat. Magic* III. x. 80 You must set the bud of a Rose into the bark or pill thereof. **1716** M. DAVIES *Athen. Brit.* II. 350 An Onion with many Pills or Skins. ? **18..** *Harvest Song* (L.), Broom..bears a little yellow flower, Just like the lemon pill. **1896** *Warwicks. Gloss.*, Orange-pill, tater-pill. **1898** G. MILLER *Gloss. Warwicks.*, Taking the pill off the oziers. [In E.D.D. cited from Midland Counties.]

†**b.** The shell of crustaceans; the hard integument of other invertebrates. *Obs.*

1565-73 COOPER *Thesaurus, Crusta*.., pilles of certaine fishes, as of crauishes, &c. **1601** HOLLAND *Pliny* I. 242 Some be couered ouer with crusts or hard pills, as the locusts: others haue..sharpe prickles, as the vrchins. **1608** TOPSELL *Serpents* (1658) 784 Aristotle is of opinion that the matter is outward, as it were a certain shell or pill.

†**c.** The skin and other refuse of a hawk's prey: cf. PELT *sb.*[1] 6. *Obs.*

1615 LATHAM *Falconry* (1633) Words Art expl., *Pill*, and pelfe of a fowle, is that refuse and broken remains which are left after the Hawke hath been relieued. **1678** PHILLIPS, *Pelf*, or *Pill* of a Fowl.

†**d.** Used for PELL, *sb.* 1 b: see quot. 1575, s.v.

1727 BRADLEY *Fam. Dict.*, *Fraying*,..[of] Deer,..their rubbing and pushing their Horns against Trees, to cause the Pills of their new Horns to come off.

pill (pɪl), *sb.*[2] Forms: 5–7 **pylle, pille**, 6 **pyll**, 6–7 **pil**, 7 **piele**, 6– **pill**. [Formerly also *pil.* in 15–17th c. *pille*: cf. Du. *pil*, formerly *pille* (Hexham 1678), MDu., MLG. *pille*, Ger. *pille*, MHG. *pillele*, F. *pilule* (in 1507 *pillule*, Hatz.-Darm.), It. *pillola*, also (Florio) *pillula*, ad. L. *pilula*. dim. of *pila* ball. Franck refers to a med.L. *pilla* (? syncopated from *pilula*, or from the mod. langs.) which might be the direct source of *pille*; but cf. OF. *pile* (13th c.) in same sense, app. ad. L. *pila*.]

1. a. A small ball or globular mass of medicinal substance, made up of a size convenient to be swallowed whole.

1484 CAXTON *Fables of Poge* x, A phisycyen..had a seruaunt..whiche made pylles. **1570** LEVINS *Manip.* 123/22 A Pil,..*catapotium, i.* **1607** TOPSELL *Four-f. Beasts* (1658) 292 If it be in Winter, purge him with these pils. *c* **1696** PRIOR *Remedy Worse than Disease* i, He felt my pulse, prescrib'd his pill. **1763** *Brit. Mag.* IV. 436 The cannon-shot, and doctor's pill With equal aim are sure to kill. **1789** W. BUCHAN *Dom. Med.* (1790) 685 The ingredients which enter the composition of pills are generally so contrived, that one pill of an ordinary size may contain about five grains of the compound. **1838** T. THOMSON *Chem. Org. Bodies* 580 Aloes..is usually administered in pills.

b. In figurative expressions; esp. something disagreeable that has to be 'swallowed' or endured.

1548 UDALL *Erasm. Par. Luke* iv. 47 Yet cannot they abide to swallowe down the holsome pille of the veritie beeyng bittur in their mouthes. **1595** GOODWINE *Blanchardine* II. I iv b, Learne by me to disgest the hard and harsh pilles of vnhappie fortune. **1625** K. LONG tr. *Barclay's Argenis* II. i. 70 Selenissa had privately guilded those pills of suspicion, which shee gave the King against Timoclea. **1674-1857** [see GILD *v.*[1] 1 b]. **1779** H. WALPOLE *Last Jrnls.* (1859) II. 338 It was a bitter pill for the King and Lord Mansfield to swallow. **1893** *Times* 30 May 9/3 He must make up his mind to swallow the bitter pill without delay. **1928** L. NORTH *Parasites* 87 There are lots of folks to give you a lift down in the morning... It's getting up that hill at night is the pill. **1931** R. CAMPBELL *Georgiad* II. 38 He..takes his pleasures as a bitter pill Or social duty, much against his will. **1943** J. B. PRIESTLEY *Daylight on Saturday* xxv. 195 Fincham [*sc.* a factory] especially is a pill. We never ought to have allowed ourselves to have been persuaded into using that old mill. **1961** B. FERGUSSON *Watery Maze* ii. 68 Dakar was indeed a bitter pill, both professionally and politically. **1977** *Times* 9 Nov. 15/3 Mrs Williams is well aware of this and her decision to champion parental choice is sugar on the pill of her pledge to support local authorities in the matter of school closures. **1978** P. BAILEY *Leisure & Class in Victorian Eng.* ii. 54 The entertainments..were devised to sugar the pill of instruction.

c. ***the pill*** or ***Pill***: a contraceptive pill.

1957 'C. H. ROLPH' *Human Sum* 6 He gives a modestly exciting account of the quest now going on..for what laymen like myself insist on calling 'the Pill'; and by this phrase..I mean the simple and completely reliable contraceptive taken by the mouth. **1958** A. HUXLEY *Brave New World Revisited* (1959) xii. 156 'The Pill' has not yet been perfected. **1960** *Economist* 22 Oct. 335/1 For about thirty years a campaign has been carried on for the reform of Britain's abortion law... It..looks as if the search for the 'Pill'—a simple, safe contraceptive—may be rewarded first. **1964** 'J. MELVILLE' *Murderers' Houses* vii. 116 Emily knew all about the Bomb and the Pill. **1969** *New Scientist* 22 May 415/2 As contraceptives, IUDs are not as effective as the pill. **1970** *Daily Tel.* 17 July 2/8 Investigations showed that the increased risk of thrombo-embolism declined rapidly after the patient stopped taking the pill. **1975** D. LODGE *Changing Places* i. 20 They went on the Pill and suffered side-effects. **1975** *Woman's Jrnl.* Sept. 110/1 Emma's burgeoning again. .. It seems she can't remember to take the pill. **1976** [see ON *prep.* 1 k].

d. A pill or tablet of a barbiturate or amphetamine. *slang.*

1963 [see *pill popper* below]. **1967** *Trans-Action* Apr. 7/1 Pills are 'reds' and 'whites'—barbiturates and benzedrine or dexedrine. **1970** *New Statesman* 16 Jan. 90/1 The police were not too hip on drugs, and pills used to be passed out at clubs like ordinary cigarettes. **1972** *Guardian* 5 Dec. 15/3 It's impossible to discover how many adolescents use the more common illicit soft drugs—cannabis, LSD, 'pills' (amphetamines, barbiturates or mixtures of both). **1976** DEAKIN & WILLIS *Johnny go Home* ii. 38 The suburban kids' drugs: pills, uppers and downers, bennies and blueies.

2. a. Any small globular or pill-like body; a pellet.

1575 TURBERV. *Falconrie* 228 Giue her..a pyll as bygge as a nut of Butter washt seuen or eyght tymes in freshe water. **1601** HOLLAND *Pliny* I. 511 After that the little balls or pills (which be the fruit thereof) be gathered, they are laid in the Sun to dry. **1735** *Dict. Polygraph.* I. S vij, Mix these two powders well,..make little pills of them with common water [in diamond-making]. **1875** *Ure's Dict. Arts* III. 1059 Let the mixture boil, until..it will roll into hard pills.

b. A cannon-ball; a bullet. Also, a shell, bomb, or hand grenade; *spec.*, the atom bomb. Hence in *pl.*, ammunition. *humorous.*

c **1626** *Dick of Devon* II. i. in Bullen *O. Pl.* II. 26, I have halfe a score pills for my Spanyards—better then purging comfitts. **1758** CAPT. TYRREL in *Naval Chron.* X. 359, I gave him a few of my lower-deck pills. **1823** BYRON *Juan* VIII. xii, Thirty thousand muskets flung their pills Like hail. **1841** H. J. MERCIER *Life in Man of War* 234 A dose of Yankee *pills*.. would take her some time to digest. **1883** *United Service* June 652 That serpent was rather hard on the pills... How do you account for that fellow's swallowing those shells so easily? **1888** *Times* (weekly ed.) 2 Nov. 15/4 They will commit suicide without the pills. **1917** P. S. ALLEN *Let.* 24 Mar. (1939) 137 The submarine proceeded to lie on the bottom..but one day they realized they were spotted. 'Pills' kept dropping close to them, and sending the water a-swish all round. **1919** V. VIGORITO in Hamilton & Corbin *Echoes from Over There* III. xi. 203 A sergeant..counts out the required number of pills (H.E. grenades). **1921** *Amer. Legion Weekly* 15 Apr. 22 Damn the Boche that threw the pill. **1921** *Flight* XIII. 618/2 Another range-finding bomb was dropped by the next Martin, and then the following machine scored the first hit with its 2,000-lb. 'pill', which struck the deck in the bow. **1927** L. H. NASON *Three Lights from Match* 220 What do they use those pills in? **1939** P. G. HART *Hist. 135th Aero Squadron* 135 When I got over the town I let my pills go. **1948** PARTRIDGE *Dict. Forces' Slang* 142 *Pills*, ammunition. (Army; especially among gunners.) **1957** *Daily News* (N.Y.) 7 Aug. 7 A Jesuit priest who was a survivor of the A-bombing of Hiroshima 12 years ago..said he was drinking coffee when the big pill came down. **1969** M. PEI *Words in Sheep's Clothing* (1970) vi. 51 Interestingly, 'the Pill' was used around 1957 with reference to the Hiroshima atom bomb.

c. in *pl.* = BILLIARDS. Also in *sing.*, = BALL *sb.*[1] 4 a. *slang.*

1896 *Westm. Gaz.* 28 Oct. 1/3 We can play pills then till lunch, you know. **1905** *Athenæum* 18 Feb. 202/1 After 'hall' (*i.e.*, dinner) the blood will perhaps play 'pills', which are billiards, for a while. **1908** *Atlantic Monthly* Aug. 224/2 Mr. O'Hooligan, steeped in the lore of the 'spitball',..and aware that the finger-tips, as the 'pill' leaves the hand, endow it with its rotary genius, pays this wizard [*sc.* the pitcher] the homage of a somewhat more enlightened reverence. **1909** P. A. VAILE *Mod. Golf* viii. 110 The ball is microscopic—a veritable, as it is sometimes slangily called, 'pill'. **1916** *Dialect Notes* IV. 279 *Pill*,..golf ball. 'Curses on that *pill*. It won't get off the ground.' **1922** WODEHOUSE *Clicking of Cuthbert* ix. 203 'I don't mind her missing the pill,' said the young man. 'But I think her attitude toward the game is too light-hearted.' **1946** B. MARSHALL *George Brown's Schooldays* 6 As a matter of fact, I think that's the dirty cad hacking that footer pill over there. **1977** SCOLLINS & TITFORD *Ey up, mi Duck!* II. 50 *Pill*, ball: usually a football.

d. A pellet of opium prepared for smoking.

1887 *Lantern* (New Orleans) 21 May 4/2 The longer end of the stem is handed the person opposite and so the pill is consumed by the party drawing in their breath, which some call the 'long draw'. **1926** J. BLACK *You can't Win* xvii. 238 He feverishly rolled the first 'pill'... Each succeeding pill is smaller, more carefully browned over the lamp, and smoked with increased pleasure. **1935** A. J. POLLOCK *Underworld Speaks* 88/1 *Pill*, after opium has been cooked for smoking, it takes the form of a round pill, which is placed in the pipe and smoked. **1948** [see COOK *v.*[1] 2 d]. **1948** *Amer. Speech* XXIII. 247/1 *Pill*, the pellet of opium which has been prepared for smoking. **1955** *U.S. Senate Hearings* (1956) VIII. 4162 The opium pill must be brought to a flaming heat before being placed in position over a hole in the center of the well-heated bowl of the pipe. *Ibid.*, 'Cook a pill', heat opium for smoking.

e. *slang.* A cigarette.

1914 'HIGH JINKS, JR.' *Choice Slang* 16 *Pill*, a cigarette. **1927** *Amer. Speech* II. 281/2 *Pill*,..cigarette. **1927** D. HAMMETT in *Black Mask* Feb. 31/2 Those pills you smoke are terrible. **1934** *Amer. Ballads & Folk Songs* 135 Then we rode down the hill, each a-puffin' a pill. **1966** 'L. LANE' *ABZ of Scouse* 82 *Pill*, a cigarette.

f. An animal's dropping. Usu. *pl.*

1926 D. H. LAWRENCE *David* xii. 89 They have passed, letting fall promises as the goat droppeth pills. *a* **1930** —— *Phoenix* (1936) 10 So we had him [*sc.* a pet rabbit] upstairs, and he dropped his tiny pills on the bed.

g. in *pl. slang.* The testicles; *fig.* nonsense (cf. BALL *sb.*[1] 15 b).

1935 I. MILLER *School Tie* xi. 158, I explained to him about the prayers... 'Awful pills,' I whispered; 'but it can't be helped.' *Ibid.* xiv. 270 'No, it really is true. Not doing much good here, you know.' 'Pills! Bags of pills!' **1937** PARTRIDGE *Dict. Slang* 630/2 *Pills*,..testicles. **1968** A. DIMENT *Gt. Spy Race* vi. 77, I..wished I had followed up my elbow in the throat with a hefty boot in his peasant pills. One in the balls is worth two in the teeth—a motto of unarmed combat instructors.

h. A small ball of fluff found on the surface of a fabric (see PILL *v.*[1] 6 c, PILLING *vbl. sb.* 2 b).

1958 *New Scientist* 3 Apr. 17/2 The 'pills' are the little balls of fibre which, in the course of wear, form on the surface of cardigans, jerseys and similar articles. **1963** A. J. HALL *Textile Sci.* v. 273 The formation of a pill is primarily due to a rubbing of the fabric surface to cause a number of fibre ends to protrude and then become entangled. **1969** —— *Stand. Handbk. Textiles* (ed. 7) v. 336 The presence of these pills gives the fabric a highly objectionable appearance... As the material is further worn so do the anchoring fibres gradually wear and weaken until they break and the pill falls off. **1970** [see PILL *v.*[1] 6 c].

3. An objectionable person; a bore. *slang.*

1871 L. H. BAGG *4 Years at Yale* 141 The name 'Delta Phi man' is fast becoming a synonym for 'scrub', and 'pill', and even the neutrals regard its members with a sort of pitying contempt. **1880** A. A. HAYES *New Colorado* (1881) v. 64 He was the worst-looking pill you ever saw. **1886** *Galaxy* 1 Oct. 272 Various sorts of contemptible young men are designated as..'pills', 'squirts', [etc.]. **1897** MAUGHAM *'Liza of Lambeth* iii. 41 Well, you are a pill! **1897** FLANDRAU *Harvard Episodes* 98 In the patois of her locality, she was called a 'pill'; a girl whom Harvard men carefully avoid until it is rumoured that her family shortly intends to 'give something' in the paternal pill-box. **1925** WODEHOUSE *Carry on, Jeeves!* iii. 61 What's to be done?.. That pill is coming to stay here. **1939** L. M. MONTGOMERY *Anne of Ingleside* xxxiii. 242 That kid is a pill. My, doesn't she think it smart to fool people! **1970** *Women Speaking* Apr. 5/1 If a man doesn't like a girl's looks or personality, she's a..pill. **1977** B. GARFIELD *Recoil* xi. 120 'Do you love your wife?' ..'You're a pill. Yes, I love her.'

4. (Also *Pills*.) Nickname for a physician; *spec.*, (a member of) the Royal Army Medical Corps; a medical officer or his orderly. *slang.*

1860 *Slang Dict.*, *Pill*, a doctor— *Military.* **1866** *Harper's Mag.* July 268/1 One day..the two young 'pills' were arguing some case. **1890** M. WILLIAMS *Leaves of a Life* I. iii. 30 The 'pill' of the regiment..had come out to inspect the men. **1899** MARY KINGSLEY *W. Afr. Stud.* iii. 86 Pills, are they all mad on board that vessel or merely drunk as usual? **1915** 'BARTIMEUS' *Tall Ship* ix. 159 They seized the Young Doctor, who was a small man, and deposited him on the deck. 'Couldn't you see I was asleep, Pills?' demanded the other. **1924** 'NAUTICUS' *Sea Ways & Wangles* ix. 57 In some ships the sick list is so small that one of the young doctors —or 'Pills' as a Surgeon Lieutenant is sometimes called in order to distinguish him from his more venerable senior the P.M.O.—has even found time to take on the keeping of the ward-room wine accounts. *Ibid.* 58 Then again at a ward-room sing-song after dinner 'Pills' will often help matters along by playing the piano. **1925** FRASER & GIBBONS *Soldier & Sailor Words* 223 *Pills*,..a nickname for a Medical Officer's orderly. **1929** *Papers Mich. Acad. Sci., Arts & Lett.* X. 314 *Pills*.., the surgeon.

5. *attrib.* and *Comb.*, as *pill-gilder*, *-maker*, *-man*, *-monger*, *-roller*; *pill-boasting*, *-dispensing*, *-gilding*, *-rolling*, *-shaped*, *-taking* adjs.; **pill-bag**, a bag in which pills are carried; **pill-beetle**, a small beetle of the genus *Byrrhus*, which, when it feigns death, contracts itself into a ball; **pill-bug**, a woodlouse of the genus *Armadillidium*, able to roll itself into a ball; **pill-chafer**, a pilulary or tumble-dung beetle, *Ateuchus pilularius*, which forms pills of dung about its eggs, and rolls these into a hole; **pill-coater**: see quot.; **pill cooker** *slang* (see quot.); **pill-crab** = *pea-crab*: see PEA *sb.*[1] 7; **pill-gilded** *a.*, *fig.* gilded like a pill; **pill head** *slang*, a drug addict; **pill-machine**: see quot.; **pill-masser**, a machine for compounding the mass out of which pills are made; **pill-millipede**, a millipede belonging to the order Oniscomorpha, esp. the genus *Glomeris*; in quot. 1868 = *pill-bug*; **pill-nettle**, the Roman nettle (*Urtica pilulifera*); **pill peddler**, **pusher**, **roller** *slang*, a doctor or pharmacist; **pill popper** *slang*, one who takes barbiturate or amphetamine pills freely; a barbiturate or amphetamine addict; hence ***pill-popping*** vbl. sb.; **pill-rolling** *vbl. sb.*, the action of making into pills by rolling (also *fig.*); **pill shooter** *slang*, a doctor; **pill slab**, **pill-tile**: see quots.; **pill-woodlouse** = *pill-bug*; **pill-worm**, a pill-milleped or the like. See also PILL-BOX, etc.

1852 *Knickerbocker* XL. 470 After procuring his degree, he had not the wherewithal to buy him *pill-bags. **1874** E. EGGLESTON *Circuit Rider* xx. 189 'And you want me to see him,' said the doctor,..seizing his 'pill-bags' and donning his hat. **1930** J. F. DOBIE *Coronado's Children* i. 43 James had been educated to medicine in Kentucky..and riding with his 'pill bags' over the far-stretched hills of the Colorado River satisfied his ambition. **1816** KIRBY & SP. *Entomol.* xxi. (1818) II. 234 Another genus of insects..the *pill-beetles (*Byrrhus*..), have recourse to a method the reverse of this. **1628** VENNER *Baths of Bathe* in *Harl. Misc.* (Malh.) IV. 119 A *pill-boasting surgeon. **1884** J. S. KINGSLEY *Stand. Nat. Hist.* II. 72 In common parlance these forms [of terrestrial isopod] are known as 'sow-bugs', '*pill-bugs', and 'wood-lice'. **1915** W. A. BRYAN *Nat. Hist. Hawaii* xxxi. 408 The curious oval little silver-gray creature found in large numbers in damp places, under boards and stones, is usually an introduced species known to many as the pill-bug, slater, sow-bug or wood-louse. **1954** *New Biol.* XVII. 41 *Porcellio* and *Armadillidium* (the pill-bug) appear to be able to withstand drier conditions than the rest [of the woodlice]. **1971** E. S. BAKKER *Island called California* xii. 191 If you examine such a decaying log, you are likely to find centipedes and pill bugs curled in the dirt. **1804** BINGLEY *Anim. Biog.* 245 In its habits of life the *Pill Chafer is one of the most remarkable of the Beetle tribe. **1884** KNIGHT *Dict. Mech.* Suppl., **Pill-coater*, a machine..in which pills are coated with sugar. **1929** M. A. GILL *Underworld Slang*, **Pill cooker*, opium smoker. **1872** *Daily News* 23 Aug., All flotsam and jetsam in connection with the sprat, the mussel, or the soft *pill-crab is welcome to the hungry gull. **1809** MALKIN *Gil Blas* VII. xvi. (Rtldg.) 7, I had taken..a dislike..to the *pill-dispensing tribe. **1822** T. MITCHELL *Aristoph.* II. 237 Such *pill-gilded superfine speeches. **1828** SCOTT *F.M. Perth* xxxii, To tell how the poor mediciner, the *pill-gilder, the mortar-pounder, the poison-vender, met his fate. **1764** FOOTE *Mayor of G.* I. i. 6 *Pill-gilding puppy! **1965** *Maclean's Mag.* 4 Sept. 31/1 The population totalled.. fourteen narcotic addicts, two marijuana smokers and two '*pillheads', including me. **1969** *Courier-Mail* (Brisbane) 2 July B/1 He was all boy, and a drug taker—'A Pill Head' in his own words. **1971** S. HOUGHTON *Current Prison Slang* (MS.) 23 *Pill head*, amphetamine addict. **1973** *Times Lit. Suppl.* 16 Mar. 299/4 (Advt.), His experiences with junkies, pillheads, homosexuals and drop-outs in Soho. **1976** N. THORNBURG *Cutter & Bone* x. 244 Oh, she was a pillhead, yeah. And maybe the world's worst housekeeper too. **1893** *Syd. Soc. Lex.*, **Pill machine*,..an instrument used for rolling and cutting up a pill mass. **1904** *Daily Chron.* 26 Feb. 4/5 The *pill-maker has a morbid secretiveness as to the soap and bread wherewith he binds his wares. **1884** *Health Exhib. Catal.* 112/2 *Pill Massers [and] Powder Mixers for druggists. **1868** BATE & WESTWOOD *Hist. Brit. Sessile-Eyed Crustacea* II. 494 It [sc. *Armadillo vulgaris*]..is often seen running about foot-paths, rolling itself up into a ball at the least alarm. This has gained for it the name of *Pill millepede [*sic*]. **1899** W. T. FERNIE *Animal Simples* 236 Hoglouse, or Pill Millipede... This Hoglouse, or Millipede, was the primitive medicinal pill. **1958** J. L. CLOUDSLEY-THOMPSON *Spiders, Scorpions, Centipedes & Mites* xi. 17 The family Glomeridae contains the common British pill-millipede. **1967** P. A. MEGLITSCH *Invertebr. Zool.* xix. 839/1 Order Oniscomorpha. Pill millipedes. Mostly tropical millipedes..; body can be rolled into a ball. **1706** BAYNARD in Sir J. Floyer *Hot & Cold Bath.* II. 392 This Pulp-pated *Pill-monger. **1764** FOOTE *Mayor of G.* I. i. 7 An impudent pill-monger, who has dar'd to scandalize the whole body of the bench. **1713** J. PETIVER in *Phil. Trans.* XXVIII. 35 Roman or *Pill Nettle. **1857** M. J. HOLMES *Meadow Brook* v. 78 Why, he's a young *pill-peddler, who's taken a shine to Rosa. **1925** S. LEWIS *Arrowsmith* xiii. 137 How could old Max have gone over to that damned pill-pedler? **1931** [see CROAKER 4]. **1941** J. SMILEY *Hash House Lingo* 43 *Pill peddler*, druggist. **1963** *Time* 1 Nov. 74 Can a lonely New Jersey *pill popper who sleeps on a board find enduring happiness with an ebullient Hungarian gourmet who sleeps on a rug? **1975** *Publishers Weekly* 27 Jan. 286/3 The author, then a sophomore at a Wisconsin law school, was a pill popper—amphetamine to get her through the days, phenobarbital to get her through the nights. **1972** *Jrnl. Social Psychol.* LXXXVII. 121 The film illustrates the dangerous psychological and physiological effects of *pill-popping. **1977** J. WAMBAUGH *Black Marble* (1978) xii. 304 They have a pill-popping party and she..dies of an overdose. **1909** J. R. WARE *Passing Eng.* 196/2 **Pill-pusher* .., doctor. Fine example of the graphic in phraseology. **1919** H. S. WARREN *Ninth Company* 34 *Pill pusher*, member of the medical corps. **1935** A. J. POLLOCK *Underworld Speaks* 88/1 *Pill pusher*, a doctor. **1961** *Amer. Speech* XXXVI. 147 *Pill pusher*, a specialist in internal medicine, as contrasted with a practitioner of the surgical specialties. Loosely, any M.D. **1969** LINN & PEARL *Masque of Honor* 66 Hell, I'm only a pill-pusher, Lieutenant. **1917** *Editor* 13 Jan. 33 **Pill rollers*, Hospital Corps. **1918** *Yank Talk* 21 'Why?' asked the pill roller. **1930** J. W. BARKLEY *No Hard Feelings!* 268 He told me to get it on record with the pill-rollers. **1936** J. CURTIS *Gilt Kid* viii. 87 He was damned if he let a lousy pill-roller know just how bad he felt. **1942** FRENCH & SLIPER *Army-Navy Guide* 181 *Pill roller*, an enlisted member of the medical corps. **1968** R. HOOKER *MASH* (1969) 175 Let the pill rollers..do it. **1961** R. D. BAKER *Essent. Path.* xxii. 597 Parkinsonism..is a chronic disorder usually of elderly persons characterized by '*pill-rolling' rhythmic movements of the hands. **1972** *Country Life* 9 Mar. 572/3 Such things [*sc.* pill-slabs or -tiles] were used for pill-rolling and also, as in the more elaborate slabs..for hanging up as a sign of the owner's profession. **1825** *Greenhouse Comp.* I. 56 *Erica laxa*, *pill-shaped purple flowers. **1928** L. H. NASON *Sergeant Eadie* 337 The gallant *pill-shooters won't let us stay in these nice soft beds any longer than they can help. **1938** PARTRIDGE *World of Words* III. vii. 196 *Doctor* becomes..slang *the vet* or..*pill-shooter*. **1941** J. SMILEY *Hash House Lingo* 43 *Pill shooter*, physician. **1966** H. MARRIOTT *Cariboo Cowboy* ix. 89 In those years, an average fellow was darn near down-and-out before he headed out to see a pill-shooter. **1893** *Syd. Soc. Lex.*, **Pill slab*, a slab for rolling pills upon. **1960** H. HAYWARD *Antique Coll.* 218/2 Apothecaries' pill-slabs were made in tin-glazed earthenware at Lambeth. **1972** *Daily Tel.* 19 Jan. 9 A polychrome Delft heart-shaped pill-slab, which was used for rolling pills, was bought by Tilley for £2,800 at Sotheby's yesterday. **1972** *Country Life* 9 Mar. 572/3 The plaque..which was in the same sale is a pill slab of 1664, also English Delft, and an exceptional rarity. **1875** KNIGHT *Dict. Mech.*, **Pill-tile*, a corrugated metallic slip for rolling pills on. **1863** *Pill-woodlouse [see WOOD-LOUSE 2]. **1906** *Essex Naturalist* XIV. 53 'The common armadillo'..is the old name for the pill-woodlice now known as *Armadillidium*. **1931** W. T. CALMAN in W. P. Pycraft *Standard Nat. Hist.* ix. 169 The common Pill Woodlouse, *Armadillidium*, may often be seen crawling actively about on rocks in hot sunshine.

pill (pɪl), *sb.*[3] Forms: 1 pyll, 6 pille, 7 pile, 6- pill, (9 pyll). [In 16th c. *pille*, *pill*, app.:—OE. *pyll*, var. of *pull*, *pul* 'pool, creek' (Bosw.-Toller): cf. OE. *pól*, Welsh *pwll* pool.] **1.** A local name, on both sides of the Bristol Channel, on the lower course of the Severn, and in Cornwall, for a tidal creek on the coast, or a pool in a creek or at the confluence of a tributary stream.

All the examples of *pull* and *pyll* in the charters in Kemble's *Cod. Dipl.*, refer to the Severn estuary or valley; so that, although no ME. instances have yet been found, the identity of the OE. and 16th c. word seems certain.

a **1000** in Kemble *Cod. Dipl.* III. 449 [Rodden and Langley, Somerset] Andlang dice west on pull; of pylle on ford..eft on ȝerihte innan mycela pyll; andlang pylles. *Ibid.*, On ða dic innan holapyll; andlang holapylles. **1542-3** *Act 34 & 35 Hen. VIII*, c. 9 §1 Dwellers next vnto the streme of Seuerne, & vnto the crikes & pilles of the same. *a* **1552** LELAND *Itin.* III. 34 From Fowey Townend by North in the Haven is Chagha Mille Pille a litle uppeward on the same side. *Ibid.*, From Lantiant Pille to Bloughan Pille or Creke nere a Mile, it crekith up but a litle. **1577-87** HARRISON *England* I. xii. in *Holinshed*, In like maner from Saint Justes pill or créeke (for both signifie the same thing). **1603** OWEN *Pembrokeshire* (1892) 66 At the Mouthe of Millford havon.. at a place called west pill: where the one side of the pill you shall perceave the lyme-stone. *c* **1630** RISDON *Surv. Devon* §272 (1810) 282 Whereby the sea shooteth up with many branches, men call them piles, very commodious for mills. **1832** *Act 2 & 3 Will. IV*, c. 64 Sched. O. 23 Along the river Usk to the point at which the same is joined by a pill opposite the castle. **1840** *Archæol.* XXVIII. 19 The term Pyll is still used, and means a Creek subject to the tide. The *pylls* are the channels through which the drainings of the marshes enter the river. **1880** *E. Cornwall Gloss.*, *Pill*, a pool in a creek.

2. *Comb.*, as **pill yawl**, a sprit-rigged, three-masted boat used in the Bristol Channel.

1883 *Boats of World* 30 The Bristol Channel, where the Pill Yawls, large or small, decked or undecked, hold their own with any craft of their size. **1929** F. C. BOWEN *Sea Slang* 103 *Pill Yawl*, a Bristol Channel pilot boat.

pill (pɪl), *v.*[1] Forms: *α.* 2 pylian, 3 pilien, 3-5 pile(n, 4-5 pyle. *β.* 4-6 pille, pylle, 4-7 pil, (6 pyl, pyll), 4- pill. [Found in late OE. (12th c. MS.) in inflected form *pyleð*, in early 13th c. as *peolien*, *pilien*, 1300-1450 *pilen*, forms which point to an OE. **pilian*, *pylian*, varying with **piolian*, *peolian*: cf. *clipian*, *clyp-*, *cliop-*, *cleop-*. *Pile*, with single *l* (usually *pīle*), is found down to *c* 1450, when it was displaced by *pill* and *pele*, both of which had appeared in R. Brunne (1303-30). *Pill* and *pele* (now PEEL *v.*[1]) continued as synonyms in all senses down to 17th c., when *peel* became the general Eng. form in branch II, *pill* now surviving only as a literary archaism, chiefly in sense 1; but, in the dialects, *pill* is widely used in the sense 'peel' (decorticate). No cognate words are found in Teutonic. OE. *pilian* was prob. ad. L. *pilāre* to make bare of hair, and (prob.) of skin: cf. the compound *depilāre* to make bald of hair or feathers, also to strip of the skin, to peel (Vulg., Ezek. xxix. 18), fig. to pluck, plunder, fleece, cheat; also OF. *peler* to make bald, to peel or skin (the latter sense now usually referred to OF. *pel*, L. *pellem*), It. *pelare* to make bald, skin, fleece, flay. With OE. *pilian*, from L. *pilāre*, cf. OE. *plantian* from L. *plantāre*, etc.

The early ME. *pile* (usually *pīle*, but R. Brunne rimes *begīled*, *pīled*) regularly represented OE. *pilian*, but *peolian* naturally gave *pele* (cf. *cleopian*, CLEPE), which was probably identified with F. *peler*. The later *pill* (for *pīle*) was prob. influenced by F. *piller* (= Pr., Sp. *pillar*, Pg. *pilhar*):—late L. *pillāre*, found in med.L. (Du Cange) for L. *pīlāre* to pillage, plunder. But no differentiation of sense between *pile*, *pill*, *pele*, is found in ME., nor between *pill* and *peel* in early mod. Eng. and existing Eng. dialects. It is possible however that the influence of F. *piller* and *peler* is to be seen in the tendency since 17th c. to differentiate *pill* and *peel* (so far as *pill* has survived) in literary use.]

I. To pillage, rob: = PEEL *v.*[1] I.

1. a. *trans.* To plunder, rifle, pillage, spoil; to commit depredation or extortion upon; to despoil (a person or country) *of* (anything). Now *arch.*

α. *a* **1225** *Ancr. R.* 86 Uor euere me schal þene cheorl pilken & peolien [*MS. C.* plokin & pilien]. *c* **1300** *Song Husbandman* 19 in *Pol. Songs* (Camden) 150 Thus me pileth the pore that is of lute pris. *Ibid.* 25. *c* **1325** *Poem Times Edw. II* 320 ibid. 338 Ac were the king wel avised, and wolde worche bi skile, Litel nede sholde he have swiche pore to pile. *c* **1330** R. BRUNNE *Chron.* (1810) 42 þat non in alle þe cuntre more suld be piled Bot euer was Eilred fouly begiled. **13..** *E.E. Allit. P.* B. 1282 Nabuzardan..pyled þat precious place & pakked þose godes. *c* **1386** CHAUCER *Friar's T.* 64 He wolde..somne hem to the chapitre bothe two And pile [*v.rr.* pil, pille] the man and lete the wenche go. **1387** TREVISA *Higden* (Rolls) VIII. 301 Spiritualte and temporalte was alway i-pyled. **1390** GOWER *Conf.* II. 202 For thanne schal the king be piled [*rime* his londes tiled]. *c* **1450** *Merlin* xxvii. 556 Thei cessed neuer to robbe and pile oure londes.

β. **1303** R. BRUNNE *Handl. Synne* 5450 þat he shulde haue on hem mercy, And pylle hem nat but mesurly. *a* **1340** HAMPOLE *Psalter* ii. 9 þou sall noght be tyraunt til þaim to pil þaim & spoile þaim. **1382** WYCLIF *1 Esdras* i. 36 He pilde the folc of an hundrid talentus of siluer. *c* **1425** *Castell Persev.* 450 þis man, with woo schal be pylt..for hys folye schal make hym spylt. *c* **1450** *St. Cuthbert* (Surtees) 7717 Many pepill þai robbid and pild [*rime* kyld]. **1523** LD. BERNERS *Froiss.* I. xviii. 19 The Scottis had brent and wasted, and pilled the countrey about. **1530** PALSGR. 657/2, I pyll, I robbe, *je pille*... He hath pylled me of all that ever I have. **1593** SHAKS. *Rich. II*, II. i. 246 The Commons hath he pil'd with greeuous taxes. **1616** B. JONSON *Epigr.* I. liii, Having pill'd a book which no man buyes Thou wert content the authors name to lose. **1722** WOLLASTON *Relig. Nat.* vii. 149 Unless to be unjustly treated, pilled, and abused can be happiness. **1867** J. B. ROSE tr. *Virgil's Æneid* 250 The fields Ausonian they have held and pilled.

†**b.** To exhaust, impoverish (soil); = PEEL *v.*[1] 1 b. *Obs.*

1594 PLAT *Jewell-ho.* I. 51 Flax, whose seede..doth most burne, and pill the ground. **1610** W. FOLKINGHAM *Art of Survey* I. ix. 23 Wilde Oates pestering and pilling of Tilthes.

†**2.** *absol.* To commit depredation, rapine, pillage, or extortion; to rob, plunder. *Obs.*

α. *c* **1330** R. BRUNNE *Chron. Wace* (Rolls) 6282 þey.. pylede & robbed at ilka cost. *c* **1386** CHAUCER *Pars. T.* ¶695 They ne stynte neuere to pile. *c* **1450** *Merlin* 191 For thei hadde so piled and robbed thourgh the contrey and the portes where the shippes were a-ryved.

β. **1513** MORE *Rich. III* (1883) 6 For whiche hee was fain to pil and spoyle in other places. *a* **1548** HALL *Chron., Hen. IV* 7 He..suffered them to robbe and pill without correction or reprefe. **1607** SHAKS. *Timon* IV. i. 12 Large-handed Robbers your graue Masters are, And pill by Law. **1678** SHADWELL *Timon* IV. ii, They govern for themselves and not the people, They rob and pill from them.

†**3.** *trans.* To take by violence, force, or extortion; to make a prey of. *Obs.*

α. **13..** *E.E. Allit. P.* B. 1270 þenne ran þay to þe relykes as robbers wylde, & pyled alle þe apparement þat pented to þe kyrke. **1390** GOWER *Conf.* I. 17 What Schep that is full of wulle Upon his back, thei tiose and pulle, Whil ther is eny thing to pile [*rime* skile].

β. *c* **1400** *Destr. Troy* 2282 In enpayryng of our persons, & pyllyng our goodes. **1513** MORE *Rich. III*, Wks. 62/1 So that there was dayly pilled fro good men & honest, gret substaunce of goodes. **1594** SHAKS. *Rich. III*, I. iii. 159 You wrangling Pyrates, that fall out, In sharing that which you haue pill'd from me. **1618** WITHER *Motto, Nec Habeo* Juvenilia (1633) 521, I have no Lands that from the Church were pild.

†**4.** To pluck, pull, tear. *Obs.*

c **1533** LATIMER *Let. to Morice* in Foxe *A. & M.* (1570) 1911/2 Who can pill Pilgrimages from Idolatry? **1566** T. STAPLETON *Ret. Untr. to Jewel* Epist., Your Borrowed Fethers pilled awaye. **1599** NASHE *Lenten Stuffe* Wks. (Grosart) V. 261 In spite of his hairie tuft or loue-locke, he leaues on the top of his crowne, to be pilld vp, or pullied vp to heauen by. **1605** CAMDEN *Rem.* 235 Such which in Ordinaries..will pill and pull them by their wordes..as it were by the beards.

II. To decorticate: = PEEL *v.*[1] II.

5. a. *trans.* To strip of the skin, rind, or integument, as an orange, apple, potato, garlic, etc., a tree of its bark, etc.; to remove the peel of. Rarely const. *of* (that which is stript off): = PEEL *v.*[1] 3. Now *arch.* (in Bible of 1611), and *dial.*

α. [*a* **1225** *Ancr. R.* 150 þeonne is þe figer bipiled, & te rinde irend of.] **1382** WYCLIF *Gen.* xxx. 37 And riendis drawun awey; in thilke that weren pilde semede whytnes [1388 and whanne the ryndis weren drawun awei, whitnesse apperide in these that weren maad bare]. **1393** LANGL. *P. Pl.* C. x. 81 To rubbe and to rely russhes to pilie [*v.r.* pil].

β. *c* **1420** [see PILLED 1]. *c* **1440** *Promp. Parv.* 399/1 Pyllyn, or schalyn nottys, or garlyk, *vellifico.* **1523** FITZHERB. *Husb.* §134 Yf there be any okes..fell them and pyll them and sell the barke. **1530** PALSGR. 657/2 Pyll these oignons whyle I skumme the potte. **1535** COVERDALE *Gen.* xxx. 38 The staues that he had pilled [**1611** *ibid.* the rods which he had pilled, 1885 *R.V.* peeled]. **1596** SHAKS. *Merch. V.* I. iii. 85 The skilfull shepheard pil'd me certaine wands, And..stucke them vp before the fulsome Ewes. **1653** H. COGAN tr. *Pinto's Trav.* xxvi. 101 We met with three men that were pilling flax. **1678** RAY *Prov.* (ed. 2) 53 Pill a fig for your friend, and a peach for your enemy. **1721** BAILEY, To *peel*, to pill or take off the rind. **1745** *MS. Indenture* (Sheffield), The burgesses may pill and fell timber trees. **1865** T. F. KNOX tr. *Suso's Life* 226 The sisters went..to pill the flax which they had gathered. **1879** MISS JACKSON *Shropsh. Word-bk.* s.v., They'n al'ays got a stick to pill. [In E.D.D. from Yorksh. to Somerset.]

b. To strip off (bark, skin, etc.); to pare off: = PEEL *v.*[1] 3 b. Often with *off*. Also *fig.*

c **1440** *Promp. Parv.* 399/1 Pyllyn, or pulle bark, or oþer lyke, *decortico.* *c* **1440** *Anc. Cookery* in *Househ. Ord.* (1790) 436 Take hom [chickens] up and pylle of the skynne. **1542** BOORDE *Dyetary* xxi. (1870) 283 If the pyth or skyn be pylled of. **1593** SHAKS. *Lucr.* 1167 Ay me, the Barke pild from the loftie Pine, His leaues will wither. **1599** HAKLUYT *Voy.* II. 264 Cinamon..is pilled from fine young trees. **1604** E. G[RIMSTONE] *D'Acosta's Hist. Indies* IV. xxiv. 278 This fruite is most vsuall in Mexico, having a thinne skinne, which may be pilled like an apple. *a* **1680** BUTLER *Rem.* (1759) II. 81 If you do but pill the Bark off him he deceases immediately. [**1887** *N.W. Linc. Gloss.* 405, I seed 'em pillin' bark e' Mr. Nelthorpe woods..to daay.]

†**c.** To make or form by peeling. *Obs. rare.*

1535 COVERDALE *Gen.* xxx. 37 But Iacob toke staues of grene wyllies,..and pylled [**1611** pilled, **1885** *R.V.* peeled] whyte strekes in them.

6. a. *intr.* Of skin, bark, etc.: To become detached, come off, scale or peel *off*. (The earliest recorded sense.) **b.** Of animal bodies, trees, etc.: To become bare of skin or bark; also, to admit of being peeled or barked. = PEEL *v.*[1] 4. Now *dial.*

c **1100** (MS. *a* 1200) *Sax. Leechd* III. 114 þis lace cræft sceal to þan handan þe þæt fell of pyleþ. *c* **1400** *Lanfranc's Cirurg.* 199 Al his fleisch wole pile & alle hise heeris wolen falle awei. **1523** FITZHERB. *Husb.* §134 To fall..all okes as sone as they wyll pyll. **1545** RAYNOLD *Byrth Mankynde* I. ii. (1634) 19 The which thin skin..skaleth or pilleth off the hands. **1611** BIBLE *Tobit* xi. 13 The whitenesse pilled away from..his eyes. *a* **1631** DONNE *Serm.* xcv. IV. 238, I have seen Marble buildings, and..a face of Marble pill off and I see brick bowels within. **1631** R. H. *Arraignm. Whole Creature* vi. 46 Neither doth the Tree wither so long as the sap is found at the roote, though the barke pill, the flowers fall. **1886** *S.W. Linc. Gloss.* s.v., They'll not cut them [oaks] while [till] the bark'll pill.

c. To gather into small balls of fluff on the surface of a fabric (said of the fibre, and of the fabric as a whole). Hence **pilled** *ppl. a.*, of or pertaining to fibres that have gathered in this way.

1962 *Which?* Aug. 240/1 One [Orlon cardigan]..was starting to pill after 10 washes. **1970** *Cabinet Maker & Retail Furnisher* 23 Oct. 173/2 Cloth so blended 'pilled'—fluffed, if you prefer it—very badly. *Ibid.*, While most worsted and woollen cloths, like a woollen carpet, tend to pill in the beginning, these pills wear off quickly and never recur. **1970** *Which?* Oct. 301/3 Trousers didn't pill, but as they were knitted some snagged. **1971** *Daily Tel.* 19 Apr. 12/4 That curious pilled wool we wore a few years ago, bumpy as if the wool had come out in a rash. **1971** *New Yorker* 21 Aug. 46/2 (Advt.), An exclusive Hathaway process that keeps the collar from pilling (i.e., fuzzing) throughout the life of the shirt.

7. a. *trans.* To make bare of hair, remove the hair from, make bald; to remove (hair). *Obs.* [Cf. F. *peler* 'to bauld or pull the haire off' (Cotgr.).]

c **1400** *Lanfranc's Cirurg.* 186 þou schalt anoynte his heed wiþ þe oynement þat wole pile awei þe heeris. *c* **1410** *Master of Game* (MS. Digby 182) xii, þat one is cleped quyc maniewes, þe whiche pileth [*Douce MS.* pilleth, *Royal MS.* pelyth] þe houndes and breketh hyr skynnes in many places. **1591** PERCIVAL *Sp. Dict.*, *Pelar*, to pill, to make balde, to make bare, *depilare, deglabrare.* **1612** tr. *Benvenuto's Passenger* I. iv. §16. 265 Tell him that I will pill his beard, hair by hair. **1648** HERRICK *Hesper.*, *Duty to Tyrants*, Doe they first pill thee, next pluck off thy skin?

†**b.** *intr.* To lose hair, become bald. *Obs.*

c **1386**- [see PILLED *ppl. a.* 2]. **1523** FITZHERB. *Surv.* xli. (1539) 58 b, Those beastis in the house haue short here and thynne, and towarde Marche they wyll pylle and be bare. **1614** MARKHAM *Cheap. Husb.* II. vii. (1668) 75 The Closh or Clowse which causeth a Beast to pill and loose the hair from his Neck.

8. *trans.* To bare (land) by eating or shaving off, or cutting down crops, etc., close to the ground. [Cf. F. *peler la terre*, 'enlever le gazon' (Littré).]

1555 W. WATREMAN *Fardle Facions* App. 347 Pille ye not the countrie, cutting doune the trees. **1615** W. LAWSON *Orch. & Gard.* (1623) 12 Whosoeuer makes such Walls, must not pill the ground in the Orchard, for getting earth. **1903** *Eng. Dial. Dict.*, *Pill*..2 To graze land very closely. *Som.* I put some sheep in to pill the field.

III. 9. Phrase. *to pill (peel) and poll*, also *poll and pill* (*lit.* to make bare of hair and skin too): to ruin by depredations or extortions; to rifle, strip bare, pillage; also *absol.*; rarely, to plunder or rob *of* something. *Obs.* or *arch.* (Common in 16–17th c. See also POLL *v.*)

1528 TINDALE *Obed. Chr. Man* Prol., Wks. (1573) 105 They haue no such authoritie of God so to pylle and polle as they do. **1545** BRINKLOW *Compl.* ii. (1874) 14 The officers robbe his grace, and polle and pylle his leage subiectys in his name. **1550** CROWLEY *Epigr.* 278 Thus pore men are pold and pyld to the bare. *c* **1557** ABP. PARKER *Ps.* liv, They have no God before theyr eyes, they me both pill and powle. **1583** STUBBES *Anat. Abus.* II. (1882) 30 No man ought to poole and pill his brother. *a* **1652** BROME *City Wit* IV. i, Churches poule the People, Princes pill the Church. **1675** CROWNE *Country Wit* II. i, 'Tis a rare thing to be an absolute prince, and have rich subjects; Oh, how one may pill 'em and poll 'em. **1844** BROWNING *Colombe's Birthday* I, We tax and tithe them, pill and poll, They wince and fret enough, but pay they must.

a **1635** NAUNTON *Fragm. Reg.* (Arb.) 27 His Father dying in ignominie, and at the Gallows, his Estate confiscate, and that for peeling and polling. **1687** tr. *Sallust, Life* 3 By Peeling and Polling the Country, he so well lin'd his Coffers. **1865** KINGSLEY *Herew.* xxx, Us..whom he hath polled and peeled till we are [etc.].

pill (pɪl), *v.*[2] [f. PILL *sb.*[2] Cf. *to dose.*]

1. a. *trans.* To dose with pills.

1736 FIELDING *Pasquin* IV. i, Handle her pulse, potion and pill her well. **1775** J. ADAMS in *Fam. Lett.* (1876) 58, I found Dr. Young here, who..has pilled and electuaried me into pretty good order. **1850** *Fraser's Mag.* XLII. 345 The.. patient is again pilled and purged.

b. *fig.* (see PILL *sb.*[2] 2 b).

1900 *Daily News* 14 May 3/2 Our fellows will probably pill you with their rifle fire.

2. To make or form into pills. *rare.*

1882 in OGILVIE (Annandale).

3. a. To reject by ballot; to blackball. *slang.*

1855 THACKERAY *Newcomes* xxx, He was coming on for election at Bays', and was as nearly pilled as any man I ever knew in my life. **1883** *Cornh. Mag.* Oct. 412 (*Heading*) On being 'Pilled'. **1894** SALA *London up to Date* v. 68 A practically accurate opinion as to how many candidates will be elected..and how many will be 'pilled'.

b. To fail (a candidate) in an examination. *slang.*

1908 A. S. M. HUTCHINSON *Once aboard Lugger* I. i. 15 'Your examination?' George half turned away. The bitterest moment of a sad day had come. He growled: 'Pipped.' 'Pipped?' 'Pilled.' 'Pilled?' 'Spun... I failed. I was referred for three months.' **1925** W. DEEPING *Sorrell & Son* xxii. 208 Gorringe had a sick face... 'Pilled,' thought Kit, and was not sorry, for Gorringe needed a course of pilling.

Hence **'pilling** *vbl. sb.*

1882 *Sat. Rev.* 18 Mar. 324 The pastime of 'pilling' seems to have begun at a large non-political club. **1883** *Cornh. Mag.* Oct. 412 The 'pilling'..is the delicate expression in club circles for black-balling.

pilla, obs. f. PILLOW.

pillaf(f, var. PILAU.

pillage ('pɪlɪdʒ), *sb.* Forms: 4-5 **pilage**, 5 **pyl-**, **pel-**, **peilage** (*Sc.*), 5-6 **pyllage**, 6 **pielage**, **pilladge**, 5- **pillage**. [a. F. *pillage* (14th c. in Hatz.-Darm.), f. *piller* to plunder (PILL *v.*[1]).]

1. The action of plundering or taking as spoil; spoliation, plunder: chiefly that practised in war; but also in extended sense, extensive or wholesale robbery or extortion. Also *fig.*

1390 GOWER *Conf.* III. 153 Thilke folk, that were unsauhte Toward here king for his pilage. **1494** FABYAN *Chron.* v. lxxxvii. 64 [He] shall sette his mynde all to Pyllage and Rauyne. **1560** DAUS tr. *Sleidane's Comm.* 48 They desyre to be deliuered from the pillage..of the Bishoppe of Rome. **1581** J. BELL *Haddon's Answ. Osor.* 278 With such furious outrage..pilladge & polladge. **1639** S. DU VERGER tr. *Camus' Admir. Events* 87 Exposing his reputation to the pillage of every mans tongue. **1781** GIBBON *Decl. & F.* xxxvi. (1869) II. 313 The pillage lasted fourteen days and nights. **1798** FERRIAR *Illustr. Sterne* ii. 34 Beroalde has furnished subjects of pillage to a great number of authors. **1800** COLQUHOUN *Comm. Thames* Introd. 27 Pecuniary losses suffered by pillage and embezzlements. **1838** *Murray's Hand-bk. N. Germ.* 176 He gave it up to pillage for three days, and then set fire to it. **1844** H. H. WILSON *Brit. India* II. 190 The object of the incursion being pillage, not fighting.

†**2.** Goods forcibly taken from another, esp. from an enemy in war; booty, spoil, plunder. *Obs.*

a **1400** *Prymer* (1891) 102 (Ps. cxix. 162) He þat fyndeth manye pilages. **1456** SIR G. HAYE *Law Arms* (S.T.S.) 121 All suld be at his will—prisonaris and pillagis, to part at his will. **1494** FABYAN *Chron.* VI. cxlvii. 133 He commandyd all the pyllage to be brought to one place. **1596** SPENSER *F.Q.* v. ix. 4 That robbed all the countrie there about, And brought the pillage home, whence none could get it out. **1623-33** FLETCHER & SHIRLEY *Night-Walker* I. ii, I know this wedding Will yield me lusty pillage. **1750** BEAWES *Lex Mercat.* (1752) 7 Nations greedy of blood and pillage.

†**3.** Some kind of impost or tax; cf. PEAGE, PEDAGE, PICKAGE. *Obs.*

1513 BRADSHAW *St. Werburge* II. 1782 All theyr tenauntes and seruauntes haue fre passage Within all chesshire without tolle and pillage. **1591** *Canterbury Cath. MS.*, All the other profits..of all the Pillage, Stallage, Toll and other advantages belonging unto the said Dean and Chapter within the said market and fair.

pillage ('pɪlɪdʒ), *v.* [f. PILLAGE *sb.*]

1. *trans.* To rob, plunder, sack (a person, place, etc.): esp. as practised in war; to rifle.

c **1592** MARLOWE *Jew of Malta* v. iv, To feast my train Within a town of war so lately pillaged, Will be too costly, and too troublesome. **1634** MASSINGER *Very Woman* v. v, We were boarded, pillaged to the skin, and after Twice sold for slaves. **1642** FULLER *Holy & Prof. St.* II. xxi. 136 He pillaged many Spanish towns, and took rich prizes. **1765** GOLDSM. *Ess.* Pref., Our modern compilers..think it their undoubted right to pillage the dead. **1790** BURKE *Fr. Rev.* (Walter Scott Libr.) 292 They pillaged the crown of its ornaments, the churches of their plate, and the people of their personal decorations. **1874** GREEN *Short Hist.* iii. §5. 140 His armed retainers pillaged the markets.

2. To take possession of or carry off as booty; to make a spoil of; to appropriate wrongfully.

1600 HAKLUYT *Voy.* III. 196, I..tooke away from our men whatsoeuer they had pillaged, and gaue it..to the owners. **1670** W. SIMPSON *Hydrol. Ess.* 11 Those four wayes of imbibitions..are pillag'd out of Dr. French his book. **1789** JEFFERSON *Writ.* (1859) III. 98 Hoping to pillage something in the wreck of their country. **1855** MACAULAY *Hist. Eng.* xvii. IV. 55 Every thing that was given to others seemed to him to be pillaged from himself.

3. *absol.* or *intr.* To take booty; to plunder; to rob with open violence.

1593 NASHE *Christ's T.* Wks. (Grosart) IV. 140 Eyther to hang at Tyborne, or pillage and reprizall where he may. **1811** WELLINGTON in Gurw. *Desp.* VIII. 7, I will not allow the soldiers to pillage. **1855** MACAULAY *Hist. Eng.* xiv. III. 417 They were suffered to pillage wherever they went.

Hence **'pillaged** *ppl. a.*, **'pillaging** *vbl. sb.* and *ppl. a.*; also **'pillageable** *a.*, that may be pillaged; **pilla'gee** [see -EE], one who is pillaged.

1895 SAINTSBURY *Corrected Impress.* xvii. 188 Authorities quotable and *pillageable. **1711** STEELE *Spect.* No. 152 ¶3 The Devastation of Countries, the Misery of Inhabitants, the Cries of the *Pillaged. **1800** *Miscell. Tracts in Asiat. Ann. Reg.* 150/2 A man who had come to his pillaged hut. **1856** DE QUINCEY in *Titan Mag.* July 93/2 He urged his friend by marrying to enrol himself as a *pillagee elect. **1629** WADSWORTH *Pilgr.* 8 For feare hee should loose the *pillaging of the other. **1870** *Daily News* 3 Sept. 5 The pillaging of provision waggons by MacMahon's own troops. *c* **1670** WOOD *Life* Apr. an. 1645, This is that captaine Bunce, who shot the *pillaging Scot cal'd major Jecamiah Abercromy. **1875** C. GORDON *Let.* 1 Nov. in *More about G.* (1894) 152 A pillaging horde of brigands.

pillager ('pɪlɪdʒə(r)). [f. PILLAGE *v.* + -ER[1].] One who pillages; a plunderer.

c **1611** CHAPMAN *Iliad* IV. 146 Joves seed the pillager, Stood close before, and slackt the force the arrow did confer. **1715** POPE *Iliad* x. 408 Some..nightly pillager that strips the slain. **1809-10** COLERIDGE *Friend* (1818) I. 122 The power of transporting mediately the pillagers of his hedges and copses. **1882** SERJT. BALLANTINE *Exper.* iii. 37 These pillagers of the public had to submit to be pillaged themselves.

pillaloo ('pɪləlu:, -lju:), *sb.* (*int.*) *dial.* Also **pillilew**, **pilliloo**, etc. [Imit.] **a.** A cry expressing grief or anger. **b.** A name for such a cry; a noise, disturbance, or outcry; a fierce argument. Hence **pilla'looing** *vbl. sb.*

1796 *Hull Advertiser* 23 July 4/2 The woman, having prostrated herself on the grave of the deceased, continued some time in silent meditation or prayer; then crying *Pillilew*! after the manner of the Irish at funerals, she sorrowfully departed with her husband. **1811** *Lexicon Balatronicum*, *Pillaloo*, the Irish cry or howl at funerals. **1829** G. GRIFFIN *Collegians* I. v. 101 She got a stitch an' died ..an'.. Dan made a *pilliloo* an' a *lavo* over her, as if he lost all belongen' to him. *Ibid.* xiv. 303 Jug.. began bawling.. the mother joined her, and such a pillilu as they raised between 'em was never known. **1847** *Paddiana* I. 100 Divle such a pillalooing as Lanty made out o' the windy ye never heerd! **1851** H. NEWLAND *Erne* xiii. 385 Such a combination of huzzaing and pillalooing as never English ears had heard. **1888** 'Q.' *Troy Town* xi. 120 What wi' the rumpus an' her singin' out 'Pillaloo!'.. the Lawyer's sarmon ..was clean sp'iled. **1899** S. MACMANUS *In Chimney Corners* 189 Nanny sitting in the chimney corner whillilewing and pillilew-ing, crying the very eyes out of her head. **1900** *N. & Q.* 12 May 373/1 To have 'a pillilew' it is not always necessary that there should be a fight, as a wrangle in which a number take part is 'a pillilew'. **1900** *Yorks. Weekly Post* 22 Sept. 11/1 We ran after him wol we collared him, en then then we made him sing pillilew.

pillao, variant of PILAU.

pillar ('pɪlə(r)), *sb.* Forms: α. 3-6 piler, (3-5 -ere, 4 pelyr, -ar, 4-5 -er, pylere, 4-6 pyler, pylar, 5 pelare, -ere, -our, pylour, -eer, 6 pylard). β. 4-5 pillare, (4 -yre), 4-6 pyllar, (5 pillere, pyllare), 5-6 pyller, (pillour, peller), 5-7 piller, (6 -or), 6- pillar. [a. OF. *piler* (mod.F. *pilier*) = Pr., Sp. *pilar*:—late pop.L. *pīlāre* (in med.L. also *pīlārium*, *-us*), deriv. of L. *pīla* pillar, pier, mass.]

1. a. *Arch.* A detached vertical structure of stone, brick, wood, metal, or other solid material, slender or narrow in proportion to its height, and of any shape in section, used either as a vertical support of some superstructure, as a stable point of attachment for something heavy and oscillatory, or standing alone as a conspicuous monument or ornament; also, a natural pillar-shaped stone, etc. A word of wider application than COLUMN (which is properly a pillar of particular shape and proportions), and applicable to a structure composed of several columns or shafts, engaged in a central core.

pillar of flagellation, that to which Christ was supposed to have been bound when scourged; hence, 'the pillar' was one of the Symbols of the Passion. Cf. FLAGELLATION, PASSION-FLOWER.

a **1225** *Ancr. R.* 188 His swete bodi ibunden naked to þe herde pilere. **13..** *Coer de L.* 2600 A gret cheyne.. Ovyr the havene.. festnyd to two pelers. **1340-70** *Alex. & Dind.* 1140 A pelyr of marbyl. *c* **1375** *Sc. Leg. Saints* xxi. (*Clement*) 206 þare of glas twa mykil pelaris ware. *Ibid.* xxxvi. (*Baptista*) 779 In myddis wes a pillare, þat þe charge of þe kirk suld bere. **1398** TREVISA *Barth. De P.R.* XVII. clxiii. (1495) 710 To vndersette bemes and gyestys wyth postes or pylars. *a* **1400** in *Rel. Ant.* I. 6 *Torques*, a pillyre. *c* **1400** *Destr. Troy* 310 Tow pyllers he [Hercules] pight.. Vppon Gades groundes. *c* **1420** *Sir Amadace* (Camden) xxvi, The marchand wente tille one pillere. **14..** *Nom.* in Wr.-Wülcker 722/3 *Hic stilus*, a peller. **14..** *Sir Beues* 1133 (MS. M.) Pelouris and durris were all of brasse. *c* **1440** *Promp. Parv.* 398/2 Pylere, *columpna*. *a* **1450** *Cursor M.* 16433 (Laud MS.) To a pillour [*Trin.* piler] they hym bond. *c* **1450** LYDG. *Secrees* 705 Reysed in a pyleer. **1483** *Cath. Angl.* 278/1 A Pyllare, *columpna*. **1500-20** DUNBAR *Poems* lxxii. 34 Till ane pillar thai him band. *c* **1532** DU WES *Introd. Fr.* in *Palsgr.* 1068 His precious body was tyed to the pylar by Pilate. *Ibid.*, The pylard and the crosse. **1535** COVERDALE *Gen.* xix. 26 His wife.. was turned in to a pillar of salt. —— *Judg.* xvi. 26 They set him betwene two pilers. **1570** LEVINS *Manip.* 76/2 A Pillor, *columna*. **1579** *Nottingham Rec.* IV. 189 Posterne Brygg.. in decay for wante of a pillar. **1590** SPENSER *F.Q.* II. iii. 28 Like two faire marble pillours.. Which doe the temple of the Gods support. **1644** EVELYN *Diary* 12 Nov., [In the Church of S. Praxedeis, Rome] is the Pillar or Stump at which they relate our Bl. Saviour was scourged. **1774** GOLDSM. *Nat. Hist.* (1776) II. 112 All the bones.. may be compared to a pillar supporting a building. **1780** VON TROIL *Iceland* 20 The most remarkable are Oransay and Columskill, on account of their antiquities;.. and Staffa, on account of its natural pillars. **1851** RUSKIN *Stones Ven.* (1874) I. vii. 71 All good architecture adapted to vertical support is made up of pillars. **1860** TYNDALL *Glac.* II. viii. 265 As the surface [of the glacier] sinks, it leaves behind a pillar of ice, on which the block is elevated.

†**b.** A whipping-post. †**c.** A platform or stand on which women publicly appeared as a penance.

1530 PALSGR. 254/1 Pyller to do justyce, *estache*. **1556** *Chron. Gr. Friars* (Camden) 78 Was sett up at the standerde in Cheppe a pyller new made of a good lengthe from the grownde, and too yonge servanddes tayed un-to yt.. and to bettyn with roddes soore on their backes. *Ibid.* 95 The same man.. was betten with whyppes at the peller in Chepe at the standert. *c* **1580** in *Jyl of Brentford's Test.*, etc. (1871) 40 Ye vold taiken it ill to me.. and mad me sit on the pillar of repentance. **1646** in Z. Boyd *Zion's Flowers* (1855) App. 42/1 That women who appear on the pillar with plaids, and holds not down their plaids from their heads, it shall not be esteemed a day of their appearance. **1647** *Ibid.*, Pillars and a place of public repentance to be made in the New Kirk and Blackfriars.

d. *Manège.* (See quot.)

1727-41 CHAMBERS *Cycl.*, *Pillar*, in the manage, signifies the centre of the volta, ring, or manage-ground, round which a horse turns; whether there be a wooden pillar placed therein, or not. **1819** *Pantologia* s.v., Most.. riding-schools have pillars fixed in the middle of the manage ground.

e. = PILLAR-BOX.

1865 MRS. CARLYLE *Lett.* III. 255 Should it [the letter] be put in the pillar to-night? **1884** EDNA LYALL *We Two* xxxvii, Just drop that in the pillar on your way home.

2. a. In wider sense: Any plain or ornamental vertical support to any structure; a post, a pedestal; e.g., one of the four posts of a bedstead; one of the posts in a framed truss in a roof; a vertical post of timber or iron supporting a horizontal deck-beam; the single central support or pedestal of a table, a machine, etc.; also *attrib.*, as ***pillar (and claw) table, stand***, etc., having a pillar (and claws: see CLAW *sb.* 5).

1360-1 *Durham Acc. Rolls* (Surtees) 384 Rogero Turnour pro pylers pro eisdem lectis. *c* **1400** MAUNDEV. (Roxb.) xxx. 136 þe pilers þat beres þe tablez er of þe same maner of precious stanes. *c* **1485** *E.E. Misc.* (Warton Club) 24 Fyrst take the pylere out of thyne ye, Or one me thou put anny defaute. **1607** in W. H. Hale *Prec. in Causes of Office* (1841) 7 To provide a new comunion table with turned pillers before Easter. **1657** WOOD *Life* 14 Aug. (O.H.S.) I. 225 All curiously cut in stone in the pillars of the window. **1715** LEONI *Palladio's Archit.* (1742) I. 88 Making every brace bear up its pillar, and every pillar the cross beam. **1744** WARRICK in *Phil. Trans.* XLIX. 487 A middle sized pillar and claw tea-table. **1774** M. MACKENZIE *Maritime Surv.* 42 How to adjust Bird's twelve-inch Quadrant... The Pillar is to be set perpendicular to the Horizon. **1823** CRABB *Technol. Dict.*, Pillars (Mar.), pieces of wood or iron fitted under the beams of the decks, in order to support them. **1833** J. HOLLAND *Manuf. Metal* II. 302 The lever.. is ten feet long, nine feet from the smaller end to the axis of suspension in the pillar M, and one foot from the latter point to the eye of the descending rod. *c* **1850** *Rudim. Navig.* (Weale) 137 *Pillars*, the square or turned pieces of timber erected perpendicularly under the middle of the beams for the support of the decks. **1867-77** G. F. CHAMBERS *Astron.* VII. ii. 637 Telescope mounted on a Pillar-and-Claw Stand. **1881** YOUNG *Every Man his own Mechanic* §768 A round table is generally described as having 'pillars and claws'.

b. The upright post in the frame of a harp.

1838 *Penny Cycl.* XII. 52/2 Its form [Irish harp] is not unlike that of the modern instrument, but the pillar is curved outwards. **1880** A. J. HIPKINS in Grove *Dict. Mus.* I. 685/1 The pillar is hollow to include the rods working the mechanism.

c. A metal column in the bodywork of a vehicle separating the front and rear doors, or the front door and wind-screen. Also, a thin metal strip dividing the windscreen into two parts.

1907 *Car* 25 Sept. 261/1 The hind pillars were painted white from top to bottom. **1926** *Motor* 26 Oct. 637/1 The roof.. slides back as far as the pillars in front of the rear doors. **1937** *Motor* 9 Mar. 219/3 A point.. noticeable when sitting in the car is the wide range of vision made possible by extremely narrow pillars. **1938** *Times* 13 Oct. 8/1 Designers are.. taking.. pains to reduce the width of pillars. **1964** *Which? Car Suppl.* Apr. 47/2 The VW Devonette had its windscreen divided by a pillar which did not help forward vision. **1971** *Sci. Amer.* Oct. 11/3 (Advt.), Deflector fins on the front pillars keep the side windows free from dirt. **1977** *Custom Car* Nov. 19/2 The new Granada shape is clean and very smart, though it has lost the rather pleasant kink by the rear pillar.

3. *fig.* **a.** An imaginary or ideal prop or support on which the heavens or the earth is poetically represented as resting.

1340 HAMPOLE *Pr. Consc.* 5388 þe pylers of heven bright. **1382** WYCLIF *Job* xxvi. 11 The pileris of heuene togidere quaken. **1535** COVERDALE *Ps.* lxxiv. [lxxv.] 3 The earth is weake & all that is therein, but I beare vp hir pilers. **1707** WATTS *Hymn*, *'Praise, everlasting praise'* vii, Then, should the earth's old pillars shake [etc.].

b. A person who is a main supporter of a church, state, institution, or principle; in phr. ***pillar of society, of the establishment*** (see also 3 c below).

c **1325** *Poem Times Edw. II* 39 in *Pol. Songs* (Camden) 325 Seint Thomas.. a piler ariht to holden up holi churche. **1382** WYCLIF *Gal.* ii. 9 James, and Cephas or Petre, and John, the whiche weren seyn to be pileris. **1485** CAXTON *Charles the Grete* 31 The patryarke of Iherusalem.. sente to hym [Charles] the standart of the fayth as to the pyler of crystente. **1590** SPENSER *To Ld. Grey of Wilton*, Most Noble Lord, the pillor of my life. **1592** NASHE *P. Penilesse* D iij b, What age will not praise immortal Sir Philip Sidney.. Sir Nicholas Bacon.. and merry sir Thomas Moore, for the chiefe pillers of our Eenglish speeche. **1594** *Contention* I. i. 75 Braue Peeres of England, pillers of the State. *a* **1674** CLARENDON *Hist. Reb.* x. §110 The Earl of Manchester, and the Earl of Warwick, were the two Pillars of the Presbyterian Party. **1781** GIBBON *Decl. & F.* xxvii. III. 22 The scourge of Arianism, and the pillar of the orthodox faith. **1850** TENNYSON *In Mem.* lxiv, Some divinely gifted man.. The pillar of a people's hope. **1961** *Ann. Reg. 1960* 445 The melodramas and crime dramas included.. *Never Take Sweets from a Stranger*, with Felix Aylmer as a small-town pillar of society responsible for the seduction of small girls. **1961** NEW ENG. BIBLE *Gal.* ii. 9 Those reputed pillars of our society, James, Cephas, and John, accepted Barnabas and myself as partners. **1964** *Ann. Reg. 1963* 32 One by one the pillars of the establishment—Lord Salisbury, Lord Stuart of Findhorn, Lord Eccles among them—deserted a baffled and pleading Lord Chancellor. **1970** *Nature* 26 Sept. 1371/1 Those pillars of the establishment of the 1920s, such as Nancy Astor, Lord Haldane and the editors of *The Times* and *The Observer*. **1979** D. CLARKE *Heberden's Seat* iii. 48 Heberden! A pillar of society locally.

c. A fact or principle which is a main support or stay of something.

1578 TIMME *Caluine on Gen.* 324 To the end the new promise may lean upon a better piller. **1640** QUARLES *Enchirid.* I. xlvi, A Kingdome.. whose two maine Supporters are the Government of the State, and the Government of the Church: It is the part of a wise Master to keepe those Pillars in their first posture. **1654** JER. TAYLOR *Real Pres.* 67 The pillar and ground of Transubstantiation is supplanted. *a* **1720** SEWEL *Hist. Quakers* (1795) I. 30 The church was the pillar and ground of truth, made up of living stones. **1888** W. ARCHER tr. H. Ibsen (*title*) The pillars of society and other plays. **1900** MORLEY *Cromwell* 46 Free Inquiry and Free Conscience, the twin pillars of Protestantism. **1902** G. B. SHAW *Mrs. Warren's Profession* Pref. p. vii, Dearer still.. is that sense of the sudden earthquake shock to the foundations of morality which sends a pallid crowd of critics into the street shrieking that the pillars of society are cracking and the ruin of the State at hand.

4. a. *transf.* An upright pillar-like mass or 'column' of air, vapour, water, sand, etc.

c **1250** *Gen. & Ex.* 3293 A fair piler son hem on o niȝt, And a skie euere on daiȝes liȝt. **1382** WYCLIF *Exod.* xiii. 21 The Lord.. wente beforn hem.. bi day in the pilere of a clowde, and bi nyȝt in a piler of fier. *c* **1586** C'TESS PEMBROKE *Ps.* LXXVIII. vi, A flaming piller glitt'ring in the skies. **1611** BIBLE *Joel* ii. 30 Blood, and fire, and pillars of smoke. **1702** SAVERY *Miner's Friend* 62 Such an immense Weight as a Pillar of Water a thousand foot high. **1755** YOUNG *Centaur* i. Wks. 1757 IV. 125 The Scripture, like the cloudy pillar.. is light to the true Israelite, but darkness to the Egyptians. **1815** J. SMITH *Panorama Sc. & Art* II. 50 The same appearance of moving pillars of sand again presented themselves.

b. *transf.* Pressure resulting from or indicated by a column of liquid.

1843 *Budd's Patent Specif.* No. 9495 A blast of atmospheric air.. maintained at a pressure or pillar of upwards of 2½ lbs. on the square inch. **1857** S. B. ROGERS *Iron Metall.* 94.

†**5.** A portable pillar borne as an ensign of dignity or office. *Obs.* exc. *Hist.*

Two of these, of silver gilt, were borne by pillar-bearers before Cardinal Wolsey and Cardinal Pole. They are not recorded otherwise, and appear to have been substituted by Wolsey for the silver mace or stick with a silver (or gold) head, to which a cardinal had a right, and to have been retained by Pole. Representations of Wolsey's pillars, sometimes borne by griffins, sometimes crossed in saltire with an archbishop's cross between, occur in the decorations of Christ Church, Oxford. Those of Pole are represented in the illumination on the first page of his Register of Wills at Somerset House; they are figured as Corinthian columns with capital and base, about the size of Roman fasces, 3½ to 4 ft. long.

1518 WRIOTHESLEY *Chron.* (Camden) I. 12 He havinge borne before him 2 pillers of sylver and guylt. *c* **1525** BARNES *Cause of Condemnation* Wks. (1572) 215/1 Then sayd hee [Wolsey],.. were it better for me.. to coyne my pyllers, and pollaxes, and to geue the money to .v. or vj. beggers?.. To this I did aunswere, that.. the pyllers and pollaxes came with him, and should also goe away with him. *c* **1525** SKELTON *Speke Parrot* 510 Suche pollaxis and pyllers, suche mvlys trapte with gold. **1528** *Rede me* (Arb.) 56 After theym folowe two laye men secular, And eache of theym holdynge a pillar In their hondes, steade of a mace. *a* **1548** HALL *Chron., Hen. VIII* 57 b. He [Wolsey] receaued the habite, hat and piller and other vaynglorious tryfles, apperteygnyng to the ordre of a Cardinall. **1599** THYNNE *Animadv.* 63 Euery Cardinall had, for parte of his honorable ensignes borne before hym, certeine siluer pillers; as had cardinall Wolsey.. and Cardinall Poole, in my memory. **1613** SHAKS. *Hen. VIII*, II. iv. (*Stage direct.*).

†**6.** A column of letterpress or figures; = COLUMN *sb.* 4. *Obs.*

1557 RECORDE *Whetst.* Kj, A table.. where in the firste columpne you se the rootes set, and in the seconde piller, right against eche roote, there is set his square. **1577** HANMER *Anc. Eccl. Hist.* (1619) 104 The pages divided into pillars and columns.

7. *Mining.* A solid mass of coal or other mineral, of rectangular area and varying extent, left to support the roof of the working.

pillar and stall, also ***pillar and room, board and pillar***, a method of working coal and other minerals in which pillars are left during the first stage of excavation; ***rib and pillar***, a modification of this system.

1708 J. C. *Compl. Collier* (1845) 43 The Remainder of four Yards is left for a Pillar to support the Roof and Weight of the Earth above. **1839** URE *Dict. Arts* 975 Working coal-mines.. with pillars and rooms, styled post and stall. **1851** GREENWELL *Coal-trade Terms Northumb. & Durh.* 38 Pillars vary from 20 to 40 yards in length, and from 2 to 20 yards in thickness. **1883** GRESLEY *Gloss. Coal Mining*, *Rib and Pillar* .., a system upon which the Thick coal seam was formerly ..mined. **1904** *Daily Chron.* 24 Sept. 8/4 Most of the coal in America is mined on what is called the pillar-and-stall system.

8. In various technical uses in particular trades; e.g. in *Watch-making* (see quots.).

1684 *Lond. Gaz.* No. 1991/4 Another Watch a Spelter Box and Case all in one.. with a round Pillar going 18 hours. **1875** KNIGHT *Dict. Mech.* 1703/2 *Pillar*.. [*inter alia*] The nipple of a fire-arm. A frame on which the tobacco-pipes rest in a kiln. **1884** F. J. BRITTEN *Watch & Clockm.* 193 The pillars of a watch are the three or four short pieces of brass which serve to keep the two plates of the movements in their proper relative positions.

9. *Anat.* and *Phys.* Applied to certain bodily structures in reference to their form or function: as ***pillars of the abdominal ring, of the brain, of the fauces, of the diaphragm***: see quots.

1807-26 S. COOPER *First Lines Surg.* (ed. 5) 463 The abdominal ring.. which is rather of a triangular shape, the os pubis forming the base of the triangle; the two fasciculi, or, as they are termed, pillars, its sides. **1876** *Trans. Clinical Soc.* IX. 81 The pillars of the fauces were immovable. **1893** *Syd. Soc. Lex.*, *Pillars of external abdominal ring*, the free borders of the divided aponeurosis of the external oblique muscle, which bound the external abdominal ring. *Ibid.*, *Pillars of fauces*, two arching folds of mucous membrance containing muscular fibres, which pass from the base of the uvula outwards and downwards, on either side. **1899** *Allbutt's Syst. Med.* VI. 74 The posterior mediastinum between the pillars of the diaphragm.

10. *Conch.* The central axis of a spiral shell; the modiolus or columella.

1841 JOHNSON in *Proc. Berw. Nat. Club* I. 269 Throat of the aperture brown, the pillar pale. **1843** HUMBLE *Dict. Geol. & Min.*, *Pillar*, in Conchology, the columella, or perpendicular centre, which extends from the base to the apex, in most of the spiral shells.

11. Phrase. ***from pillar to post***, originally ***from post to pillar***: from one party or place of appeal or resource to another; hither and thither, to and fro: implying repulse and harassment. Orig. a figure drawn from the real-tennis court, and used chiefly with *toss*; also with *bang*, *bounce*, *bandy*, *drive*; later with *chase*, *hunt*, *drag*, *flee*, *run*, etc.

The later order appears to have been first used to rime with *tost, tossed*.

a. *c* **1420** LYDG. *Assembly of Gods* 1147 Thus fro poost to pylour he was made to daunce. **1514** BARCLAY *Cyt. & Uplondyshm.* (Percy) 67 From poste unto piller tossed shalt thou be. **1549** LATIMER *7th Serm. bef. Edw. VI* (Arber) 199 He was tost from post to piller, one whyle to hys father.. anothe whyle, to hys frendes, and founde no comfort at them. *a* **1569** KINGESMYLL *Comf. Afflict.* (1585) E ij, The prophet Ely, being persecuted.. fledde from post to pillar. **1582** STANYHURST *Æneis* IV. (Arber) 104 From thee poast toe piler with thoght his rackt wyt he tosseth. **1631** HEYWOOD *Eng. Eliz.* (1641) 79 Hurried from one place to an other, from post to pillar. **1694** MOTTEUX *Rabelais* IV. xv. (1737) 63 They had been.. toss'd about from Post to Pillar. **1859** JEPHSON *Brittany* iv. 37 Dragged about from post to pillar.

b. *a* **1550** *Vox Populi* 185 in Hazl. *E.P.P.* III. 274 From piller vnto post The powr man he was tost. **1598** TOFTE *Alba* (1880) 70 And though from piller tost he be to poste. *a* **1602** *Liberality & Prodigality* II. iv. in Hazl. *Dodsley* VIII. 349 Every minute tost, Like to a tennis-ball, from pillar to post. *a* **1624** BRETON *Charac. Eliz.* Wks. (Grosart) 5/1 In the tyme of her sister Queene Maries raigne, how was shee handled? tost from piller to post, imprisoned, sought to be put to death. **1664** COTTON *Scarron.* I. 6 A Trojan true.. Who.. Was packt, and wrackt, and lost, and tost, And bounc'd from Pillar unto Post. **1807** JEFFERSON *Writ.* (1830) IV. 91 If the several courts could bandy him from pillar to post. **1832** HT. MARTINEAU *Homes Abr.* v. 63 We could not have borne to be.. driven from pillar to post. **1891** T. HARDY *Tess* i, Here I have been knocking about.. from pillar to post.

attrib. **1886** SAINTSBURY *Ess. Eng. Lit.* (1891) 241 The inveterate habit of pillar-to-post joking. **1887** *Pall Mall G.* 31 Aug. 2/2 The pillar-to-post travels from one official to another.

12. *attrib.* and *Comb.*, as ***pillar-bearer*** (sense 5), ***-cap***, ***-head***, ***-orphrey***, ***-pin*** (sense 8), ***-punishment***, ***-row***; ***pillar-shaped***, ***-strong***, ***-wise*** adjs.; ***pillar-like*** adj. and adv.; **pillar (and) scroll (top) clock** (see quot. 1960); **pillar apostle**, a chief apostle (a name given to Peter, James, and John, in allusion to Gal. ii. 9); **pillar bracket** *Mech.*, a support for a bearing raised on a pedestal or pillar: opposed to *pendent bracket*; **pillar-brick**, one of the bricks placed on end in building a clamp; **pillar-buoy**, ? a cylindrical or pillar-shaped buoy; **pillar clock** (see quot. 1962); **pillar-compass**: see quot.; **pillar-cross**, a pillar with cruciform summit; **pillar-deity**, a deity worshipped under the symbol of a phallic pillar; **pillar-dollar**: see DOLLAR 5; **pillar drill** or **drilling machine** *Engin.*, a drilling machine incorporating a work-table supported on a column attached to the base of the machine; **pillar-file**: see quots.; **pillar-hermit** = PILLARIST 1; **pillar letter-box** = PILLAR-BOX; **pillar-lip** *Conch.*, the inner lip of a spiral shell; **pillar-monk**, **-percher** = PILLARIST 1; **pillar-plait** *Conch.*, a columellar fold; **pillar plate**, the plate of a watch movement next below the dial; **pillar-post** = PILLAR-BOX; **pillar-road** *Coal-mining*: see quot.; **pillar rose**, a climbing rose suitable for training on a pillar; **pillar-saint** = PILLARIST 1; **pillar-stone**, (*a*) a stone set up as a monument; (*b*) a foundation-stone, corner-stone; **pillar-symbol**, a pillar erected in honour of a phallic deity, or with some kindred signification; **pillar-wall** *Coal-mining* = sense 7; **pillar-working**, driving a working through the pillars: see sense 7.

1882–3 *Schaff's Encycl. Relig. Knowl.* III. 1814 Later he [Peter] was one of the three *pillar-apostles. **1886** *Pall Mall G.* 26 Apr. 4/2 St. Paul had seen two of those called the pillar Apostles shortly after the Master's death. *a* **1562** CAVENDISH *Wolsey* (1893) 25 He had ii crosberers & ii *piller berers. **1887** LOW *Machine Draw.* 34 End elevation of a *pillar bracket for carrying a pillow block. **1858** *Merc. Marine Mag.* V. 285 A Black *Pillar Buoy bearing a bell, with perch and ball. **1933** *Burlington Mag.* Aug. p. xvi/1 Mr. Mody.. retains the useful terms 'Lantern, Bracket, and *Pillar Clocks' to describe the main types. **1962** E. BRUTON *Dict. Clocks & Watches* 131 *Pillar clock*, French drum clock with round movement and dial on four vertical pillars standing on a round base. The pendulum hangs in the middle of the pillars... Also a special form of Japanese clock showing time by a pointer moving along a linear scale, or any clock on a pillar. **1875** KNIGHT *Dict. Mech.*, **Pillar-compass*, a pair of dividers, the legs of which are so arranged that the lower part may be taken out, forming, respectively, a bow-pen and bow-pencil. **1849** J. D. CHAMBERS in *Ecclesiologist* IX. 89 The Scotch *pillar-crosses we must assign to Danish times. **1874** WESTROPP & WAKE *Anc. Symbol Worship* 61 The peculiar titles given to these *pillar-deities.. led to their original phallic character being somewhat overlooked. **1881** E. MATHESON *Aid Bk. Engin. Enterprise* II. xxiii. 313 The self-contained *Pillar drill is useful, as there is more room around the machine within which to move the article. **1942** W. STEEDS *Engin. Materials* xiii. 204 The sensitive drilling machines taking drills up to about $\frac{1}{2}$ or $\frac{5}{8}$ in. diameter and the pillar drill up to as much as 2 in. diameter, according to size. **1964** S. CRAWFORD *Basic Engin. Processes* ix. 224 The multi-spindle machines consist of a series of pillar drills mounted over a common table, thus eliminating the constant tool change associated with the single-spindle machine. **1873** C. P. B. SHELLEY *Workshop Appliances* vii. 214 (*heading*) Double-geared *pillar drilling machine. **1975** BRAM & DOWNS *Manuf. Technol.* vii. 198 The pillar drilling-machine.. is similar in general design to the sensitive drill. **1683** MOXON *Mech. Exerc.*, *Printing* xiii. ¶3 A small Flat-File, called a *Pillar-File. **1884** F. J. BRITTEN *Watch & Clockm.* 193 A pillar file is generally understood to mean one three inches and a half long from the point to the end of the cut. **1483** *Cath. Angl.* 278/1 A *Pillare hede.., *abacus, epistilium*. **1879** TROLLOPE *Duke's Children* (1880) I. xxiv. 284 'Has it gone?' asked the Countess. 'I put it myself into the *pillar letter-box.' **1682** CREECH *Lucretius* (1683) 199 Dark and heavy Clouds.. *Pillar-like descend and reach the Seas. **1776** WITHERING *Brit. Plants* (1796) I. 304 Placed in a whirl round the pillar-like receptacle. **1776** DA COSTA *Conchol.* x. 218 Umbilicated Whelks, or those that have a perpendicular hollow or navel aside the columella or *pillar-lip. **1843** HUMBLE *Dict. Geol. & Min.*, Pillar-lip,.. a continuation of the glossy process with which the aperture of shells is lined, expanded on the columella. *a* **1638** MEDE *Apostasy Later Times* 150 Peter à Metra, a famous Stylite, or *Pillar-Monk. **1888** F. G. LEE in *Archæol.* LI. 362 An inscription runs down the *pillar-orphrey of the chasuble. **1791** G. WAKEFIELD *Enquiry* 15 The perseverance of Simeon the *pillar-percher. **1885** C. G. W. LOCK *Workshop Receipts* Ser. IV. 327/1 Push out the *pillar pins, and remove the top plate. **1825** J. NICHOLSON *Operat. Mechanic* 504 This pinion drives the wheel *x* round a stud on the *pillar-plate. **1884** F. J. BRITTEN *Watch & Clockm.* 199 The chief plate called the pillar plate lies underneath the dial. **1881** H. JAMES *Portr. Lady* xv, The big red *pillar-post on the south-east corner. **1842** TENNYSON *St. Sim. Styl.* 59 Not alone this *pillar-punishment. **1883** GRESLEY *Gloss. Coal-mining*, **Pillar Roads*, working-roads or inclines in pillars having a range of long-wall faces on either side. **1837** T. RIVERS *Rose Amateur's Guide* 81 Clarissa Harlowe is a *pillar-rose, of first-rate excellence. **1856** MRS. STOWE *Dred* II. 129 She was sitting.. under the shadow of one of the pillar-roses. **1869** S. R. HOLE *Bk. about Roses* ix. 128 These Pillar Roses are beautiful additions to the Rosarium. **1882** *Garden* 27 May 368/3 Pillar Roses.. are often overlooked as regards watering. **1965** G. S. THOMAS *Climbing Roses* xii. 176 Isolated pillars to take 'pillar' roses can be connected with a wooden beam. **1974** *News & Press* (Darlington, S. Carolina) 25 Apr. 7/4 Pillar roses at the lantern post are not only beautiful by day but have an accent of beauty when the light is turned on at night. **1860** C. JEROME *Hist. Amer. Clock Business* iii. 44, I took about one dozen of the *Pillar Scroll Top Clocks, and went to.. Wethersfield to sell them. **1912** N. H. MOORE *Old Clock Bk.* caption facing p. 113 Pillar and scroll top clock. **1929** G. H. BAILLIE *Watchmakers & Clockmakers of World* 349/2 They were at first wall clocks, but from 1814 brackets or shelf clocks known as Pillar Scroll Top clocks. **1950** B. PALMER *Bk. Amer. Clocks* 10 The Pillar and Scroll Clock remained the most popular Shelf Clock until about 1825 and survived well into the 1830's. **1960** H. HAYWARD *Antiq. Coll.* 218/2 *Pillar and scroll clock*, an American shelf or mantel clock... The wooden works are housed in a vertical rectangular case with a scrolled-arch top, small, round pillars at the sides, and delicately small feet. **1970** K. D. ROBERTS *Contrib. of Joseph Ives to Connecticut Clock Technol. 1810–1862* iv. 64 (*caption*) Pillar and scroll shelf clock with looking glass by Ives and Lewis. **1776** J. LEE *Introd. Bot.* Explan. Terms 392 *Cylindrica*, *pillar-shaped. **1827** G. HIGGINS *Celtic Druids* 218 *note*, Our columns and *pillar-stones. **1832** G. DOWNES *Lett. Cont. Countries* I. 164 A rude pillar-stone here marks the spot where, in 1444, the burgomaster Stussi fell. **1854** *Ecclesiologist* XV. 361 A word that has lately become popular in the *Ecclesiastical Gazette* and elsewhere—for what we used to know as the 'first' or corner stone of a church—I mean '*pillar stone*'. **1657** R. CARPENTER *Astrology* 1 The Reason is *Pillar-strong. **1874** WESTROPP & WAKE *Anc. Symbol Worship* 51 Another instance of the use of the *pillar-symbol. **1839** URE *Dict. Arts* 980 Taking out all the coal, either on the Shropshire system, or with *pillar-walls and rooms. **1857** DUFFERIN *Lett. High Lat.* vii. 160 The brass carronades set on end, *pillar-wise. **1882** *Standard* 19 Aug. 3/5 Constituting 'an especial danger' in *pillar working or in the long-wall face.

pillar ('pɪlə(r)), *v.* [f. prec. sb.]

1. *trans.* To support, buttress, or strengthen with or as with pillars. Also *fig.*

1607 [see *pillaring* below]. **1711** W. SUTHERLAND *Shipbuild. Assist.* 40 Pillaring of Beams is to a Ship as Bracing to a Drum. **1839** J. ROGERS *Antipopopr.* XVI. iv. 333 Five particular plans for pillaring up the priesthood. **1880** *Mem. J. Legge* iv. 46 It needs the props of truth to pillar it.

b. *intr.* To rest on or be supported by a pillar.

1711 W. SUTHERLAND *Shipbuild. Assist.* 36 So order the Beams, that they may pillar on the Floor-riders.

2. *trans.* To embody in the form of a pillar; to display in the figure of a pillar. *rare.*

1812 BYRON *Ch. Har.* I. vii, Yet strength was pillared in each massy aisle. **1846** TENNYSON in Ld. Tennyson *Mem.* (1897) I. xi. 231 Hotel full of light.., pillaring its lights in the quiet water. **1890** H. HAYMAN in *Dublin Rev.* Oct. 424 The inward and outward wholeness of sincerity.. pillars itself aloft over their heads.

3. ***to pillar and post*** (*nonce-phr.*), to drive from pillar to post: see PILLAR *sb.* 11.

1901 GWENDOLINE KEATS *Tales Dunstable Weir* 62 He must have been pillared and posted a deal in his bit of life.

Hence **'pillaring** *vbl. sb.*

1607 *Schol. Disc. agst. Antichr.* I. ii. 66 Scarce any thing else is thought on, then the pillering vp of ceremonies. **1874** THEARLE *Naval Archit.* 116 The pillaring of a frame adds.. to its strength, by acting both as a strut and a tie.

pillar, variant of PILLOR *v. Obs.*, to pillory.

pillar-block, a corruption of PILLOW-*block* (Knight *Dict. Mech.* 1875).

'pillar-box. a. A hollow pillar about five feet high, erected in a public place, containing a letter-box or receptacle for posting letters.

1858 *Brit. Postal Guide* 146 A collection is made from the Pillar Boxes at 5 A.M. for the morning mails. **1871** M. COLLINS *Mrq. & Merch.* I. ix. 300 I've a.. letter to write, which you must send to a pillar-box. **1939** 'J. STRUTHER' *Mrs. Miniver* 173 She put on a mackintosh and struggled up the square to the pillar-box. **1978** L. DAVIDSON *Chelsea Murders* xix. 106 This one had been posted in a street pillar box.

b. In full, ***pillar-box red***: a shade of red, that of a pillar-box.

1916 *Sphere* 1 July p. iv/1 Some charming *chapeaux* of the new pillar-box red. **1926** *Daily Colonist* (Victoria, B.C.) 21 July 16/4 (Advt.), Attractive Dresses of silk crepe, spun silk and silk broadcloth... Shades include black and white, blue.. pillar-box red. **1934** *Archit. Rev.* LXXV. 108/1 It [*sc.* a built-in gramophone fitment].. is made entirely of laminated boarding painted white on the outside and pillar box red on the inside. **1950** 'E. CRISPIN' *Frequent Hearses* i. 44 A wind-machine, painted a minatory pillar-box red. **1959** J. BRAINE *Vodi* i. 16 Dick thought of the shop... It had been redecorated in pillar-box red and white. **1963** *Listener* 10 Jan. 84/2, I don't like the colours, especially the Ribena, pillarbox, scrofula, and sulphur. **1970** *Vogue* Jan. 37/1 (Advt.), Pillar box cotton jersey for the jeans.. and cropped T-shirt. **1973** P. EVANS *Bodyguard Man* vi. 50 A small Fiat in pillar-box red swirling round the corner fifty metres away and out of sight.

†'pillard. *Obs. rare.* Also 5 pillyarde. [a. F. *pillard* (in 14th c. *pillart*), f. *piller* to rob, pillage: see -ARD.] A plunderer, a robber.

1456 SIR G. HAYE *Law Arms* (S.T.S.) 233[They] suld be erar callit cruell and pillarde, no worthy men of armes. *Ibid.* 243 Pillardis that never wald have pes na concorde in this warlde amang cristyn folk. **1489** CAXTON *Faytes of A.* I. v. 10 Grete foyson of theues and pillyardes.

Hence **†'pillardise** [f. F. type **pillardise*: see -ICE[1]], robbery, extortion.

1598 FLORIO *Ital. Dict.* To Rdr. a vj b, Men.. whose communication is Atheisme, contention, detraction, or pillardise.

pillared ('pɪləd), *ppl. a.* [f. PILLAR + -ED.]

1. a. Having, supported on or by, or furnished with a pillar or pillars. Also *fig.*

c **1394** *P. Pl. Crede* 192 Þanne kam I to þat cloister & gaped abouten Whouȝ it was pilered and peynt & portred well clene. **1634** MILTON *Comus* 598 If this fail, The pillar'd firmament is rott'nness, And earths base built on stubble. **1726** POPE *Odyss.* XVII. 36 He props his spear against the pillar'd wall. **1814** WORDSW. *Excursion* VIII. 471 The pillared porch, elaborately embossed. **1924** R. CAMPBELL *Flaming Terrapin* i. 16 In that pillared temple grew a heart. **1924** E. SITWELL *Sleeping Beauty* iii. 21 That pillared avenue Of tall clear-fruited ripe trees. **1953** E. M. FORSTER *Hill of Devi* 129 One passes through a pillared hall on to a terrace. **1961** *N.Y. Times* 3 July 13 The many country mansions.. that dot the environs of Vicenza. How far that pedimented and pillared style has shed its influence Mr. Sansom reminds us. **1978** *Morecambe Guardian* 14 Mar. 23/1 (Advt.), The accommodation provides: pillared porch, hall, lounge, [etc.].

b. Borne on stalks, stalked.

1871 DARWIN *Desc. Man* I. x. 341 In one of the Ephemerae, namely Chloëon, the male has great pillared eyes.

2. Fashioned into or like a pillar or pillars. Also *fig.*

1698 MOLYNEUX in *Phil. Trans.* XX. 221 A sort of Pillard Stone in Misnia near Dresden. **1727** THOMSON *Summer* 60 Of growling Hills, that shoot the pillar'd Flame. **1738** H. BROOKE *Tasso's Jerus. Del.* III. 16 Where the fair Head and pillar'd Neck were knit. **1808** SCOTT *Marm.* V. xxv, Dun-Edin's cross, a pillar'd stone, Rose on a turret octagon. **1864** TENNYSON *Voyage* in *Enoch Arden* 145 How oft we saw the Sun retire, And burn the threshold of the night, Fall from his Ocean-lane of fire, And sleep beneath his pillar'd light! **1887** *Times* (weekly ed.) 21 Oct. 3/3 A background of.. pillared basalt. **1924** R. CAMPBELL *Flaming Terrapin* iii. 45 Thick mælstroms propped the dense and sagging shades With pillared thunder. **1929** R. GRAVES *Poems* 20 True to the eagle nose, the pillared neck, (Missed by the intervening generation).

pillaret ('pɪlərɛt). [f. PILLAR *sb.* + -ET[1]. Cf. OF. *pileret*, dim. of *piler*.] A small pillar.

a **1661** FULLER *Worthies, Wilts.* (1662) 144 The Pillars and Pillarets of Fusill Marble. **1790** *Archæol.* (1792) X. 188 [A font] at Ancaster with interlaced arches on long pillarets. **1871** B. TAYLOR *Faust* (1875) II. III. 186 There you see pillars, pillarets, arches great and small.

pillarie, -ary, obs. forms of PILLORY.

pillarist ('pɪlərɪst). [f. PILLAR *sb.* + -IST.]

1. An ascetic who passes his life on a pillar; a pillar-saint, a stylite.

a **1638** MEDE *Apostasy Later Times* (1641) 109 Holy Simeon, surnamed Stylita or the Pillarist. **1871** R. B. VAUGHAN *Life S. Tho. of Aquin* II. 265 *note*, The *Stylitæ* or Pillarists, lived on pillars.

2. One who is in favour of a pillar (e.g. as a monument). *nonce-use.*

1814 J. W. CROKER in *C. Papers* (1884) I. iii. 58, I quite agree with the Committee in its predilection for a pillar [as a monument to Wellington]. I was one of the pillarists in the Nelson case.

pillarize ('pɪləraɪz), *v. nonce-wd.* [f. PILLAR *sb.* + -IZE, after *penalize*.] *trans.* To inscribe on or commemorate by a pillar.

1827 LAMB *Lett.* (1837) II. xvi. 218 To pillarize a man's good feelings in his lifetime is not to my taste.

pillarless ('pɪləlɪs), *a.* [f. PILLAR *sb.* + -LESS.] Lacking or without pillars.

1889 W. B. YEATS *Wanderings of Oisin* II. 28 And the dome Windowless, pillarless, multitudinous home Of faces, watched me. **1922** *Glasgow Herald* 7 June, The experimental work on 'pillarless' electric safety lamps.. has been conducted by the Miners' Lamps Committee. **1977** *Custom Car* Nov. 50/3 And there it sits, in all its glory; four-door pillarless body skulking over a mill of 390 cubic inch displacement.

'pillarlet. *rare.* [see -LET.] = PILLARET.

1828 CARLYLE *Misc.* (1872) I. 155 Ye arches, archlets, pillars, pillarlets.

'pillary, *a. nonce-wd.* [f. PILLAR *sb.* + -Y.] Of the nature of a pillar. (*Pillary cloud* put for *cloudy pillar.*)

1864 NEALE *Seaton. Poems* 109 The pillary cloud went on.

pillas ('pɪləs). *Cornish dial.* Also **pilez, pillez, pillis, -us, peallas.** The Naked Oat or PILCORN.

(In quot. 1837 applied to the Naked or Pilled Barley.)

1815 G. B. WORGAN *View Agric. Cornwall* 66 The *Avena Nuda*, provincially called Pilez, or Pillas... One gallon of Pilez. **1837** *Penny Cycl.* VIII. 31/2 Amongst the varieties of grain raised in Cornwall, we may notice the naked barley, which is there called *Pillez*. **1846** in *Eng. Dial. Dict.* s.v. *Pellas*. **1847–78** HALLIWELL, *Pelles*, a kind of oats. *Cornw.* **1882** JAGO *Cornw. Gloss.*, *Pillas, Pillis*, or *Pellas*, naked oats, bald, bare, or naked oats without husks.

pillaster, -trell, obs. ff. PILASTER, -TREL.

pill-box ('pɪlbɒks). [f. PILL *sb.*[2] + BOX *sb.*[2]] **a.** A box for holding pills; a shallow cylindrical box of cardboard for this purpose.

1730 *Maryland Hist. Mag.* (1924) XIX. 182 From Eyre & Beecher (Druggists)... 12 Papers pill boxes. **1737** KNIGHT in *Phil. Trans.* XLI. 706 The hairy Substance, or fine *Capillamenta*, inclosed in the Pill-box, were discharged. **1741** RICHARDSON *Pamela* I. 3, I seal it up in one of the little Pill boxes which my Lady had. **1872** RUSKIN *Fors Clavig.* II. xxiv. 4 The first shilling I ever got in my life I put in a pill-box and put it under my pillow, and couldn't sleep all night for satisfaction. **1934** G. B. SHAW *Too True to be Good* I. 27 A measuring glass, a pill box, a clinical thermometer in a glass of water. **1977** *Halcyon Days Catal.* 8 A new range of small pill-boxes with snap-on enamelled lids.

b. Ludicrously applied to various boxes, closed vehicles, or enclosures of narrow dimensions; *spec.* a small round concrete emplacement used for housing a machine-gun or similar weapon; also *transf.* and *fig.* Also, short for *pill-box cap, hat.*

1835–40 HALIBURTON *Clockm.* (1862) 402 Packed up in a snug pill-box in the same grave-yard. **1855** DICKENS *Dorrit* I. xxxiii, A one-horse carriage, irreverently called, at that period of English history, a pill-box. **1871** KINGSLEY *At Last* x, Getting up to preach in a sort of pill-box on a long stalk. **1883** *Congregationalist* May 374 'Pill-boxes', as pulpits are sometimes appropriately called. **1887** R. D. BLUMENFELD *Diary* 27 June (1930) 17 The pill-box.. protects only a small portion of the head and forehead from the sun. **1893** VIZETELLY *Glances Back* I. xxi. 410 The select assemblage, crammed into the little pill-box called a town-hall. **1903** *Longm. Mag.* Aug. 289 The 'pill-box', as Lady Mary irreverently named the vicar's covered waggonette. **1917** *Scotsman* 13 Sept. 6/4 The strength of these concreted farm cellars and individual pillboxes is amazing. **1923** *Daily Mail* 26 Feb. 7 On reaching shore again he [*sc.* a fox] made for the cliffs and hid in a concrete pill-box, where he was caught and killed. **1929** *Papers Mich. Acad. Sci., Arts & Lett.* X. 314/2 *Pill-boxes*, concrete structures or blockhouses developed by the Germans for use in their 'elastic' defense. They were employed as machine-gun nests. **1930** H. A. TAYLOR *Good-Bye to Battlefields* 136 The Germans, by means of their almost indestructible pill-boxes, have taught the inhabitants the virtues of concrete. **1935** A. J. POLLOCK *Underworld Speaks* 88/1 *Pill box*, enclosure of machine gun on prison wall. **1944** *Daily Progress* (Charlottesville, Va.) 2 Oct. 1/8 The planes dropped hundreds of tons of explosives on Nazi pillboxes and gunposts. **1958** L. DURRELL *Mountolive* viii. 166 Red pill-boxes mounted upon cancelled faces. **1958** *Listener* 4 Dec. 933/2 Is it another pill-box attempt to debunk the shameful Victorians of the middle and upper classes because the contemplation of the shameless purity and austerity of their private lives is galling to the rebellious youth of today? **1968** T. PARKER *People of Streets* 27, I was the lift boy and I had one of those round hats, pill-boxes they used to call them. **1973** *Guardian* 6 Mar. 6 The pillbox on the left is in yellow straw with a white daisy. **1974** *Times* 16 Jan. 2/4 He had led Mr Brook across the fields... They rested in a wartime pillbox and then got a lift to the outskirts of Chelmsford. **1978** J. KRANTZ *Scruples* iv. 99 Billy, about to go for job interviews, took herself to the custom-order millinery salon.. in order to have Halston, then Jackie Kennedy's favorite hat designer, make her one perfect pillbox.

c. *attrib.* and *Comb.* Like a pill-box in shape or size, as ***pill-box cap, hat, house***; also ***pill-box maker***; **pill-box hydatid** (see quot. 1893).

1836–9 *Todd's Cycl. Anat.* II. 117/2 Pill-box Hydatid of Hunter. **1851** in *Illustr. Lond. News* 5 Aug. (1854) 119/3 (Occupations of People) Pill-box maker. **1862** *Macm. Mag.* Aug. 284/1 One of those little wooden pill-box houses you see about seaport towns. **1893** *Syd. Soc. Lex.*, *P[ill-box] hydatid*, a sterile hydatid or *Acephalocyst*. **1902** *Daily Chron.* 29 Nov. 8/4 The sketch suggests the round pill-box hat. **1910** *Daily Chron.* 18 Apr. 1/7 It is much greater fun to wear the B.-P. hat of the scout than the neat 'pill-box' cap of the Church Lads' Brigade. **1964** MRS. L. B. JOHNSON *White House Diary* 10 Mar. (1970) 82 Archbishop Iakovos.. dressed in long, black clerical garb.. and the black pillbox hat from which flowed long black veils. **1974** *Country Life* 3–10 Jan. 54/3 That badge of 1960s elegance, the Jackie Kennedy pillbox hat.

pill-crow, variant of PILCROW *Obs.*

pille, obs. form of PILLOW.

pilled (pɪld), *ppl. a. arch.* and *dial.* Forms: α. 4–5 **piled, pyled.** β. 4–7 **pild,** 5 **pyllyd, pillid,** 5– **pilled,** (6 **pyld(e, pylled, pield,** 6–7 **pilde, pilld**). [f. PILL *v.*[1] + -ED[1].]

1. Stripped of skin, bark, rind, etc.; decorticated, excoriated: = PEELED 4. *Obs.* or *dial.*

pilled barley, decorticated, hulled, or pot barley (quot. 1382); but see another sense in b.

1382 WYCLIF *2 Sam.* xvii. 19 Dryynge pild barli [Vulg. *quasi siccans ptisanas*; 1388 with the pile takun a-wey]. *c* **1420** *Liber Cocorum* (1862) 14 Take pilled garlek and herbys anon. **1573–80** BARET *Alv.* P 360 Pilled, *decorticatus*. **1634** CANNE *Necess. Separ.* (1849) 21 Some there are that beg more craftily.. and.. offer pilled rods to passengers, to get a piece of money therewith. **1778** *Eng. Gazetteer* s.v. *Okeley*, The poor people.. draw pill'd rushes thro' melted grease, to save the expence of candles. **1828** *Craven Gloss.* (ed. 2), *Pilled*, pared, stripped.

b. ***pilled barley, pilled oats***, varieties of these cereals in which the grain is free from the husk or glumes; naked barley, naked oats: cf. PILCORN.

1578 LYTE *Dodoens* IV. xiii. 467 The seconde kinde may be called in Englishe Pilcorne, or pylde Otes. **1616** SURFL. & MARKH. *Country Farme* 565 Mixt prouander.. will be verie good if it be sowne with pilde barley.

2. Deprived or bereft of hair, feathers, etc.; bald, shaven, tonsured: = PEELED 2. *Obs.* or *dial.*

c **1386** CHAUCER *Reeve's T.* 15 As piled as an Ape was his skulle. *Ibid.* 386 She.. smoot the Millere on the pyled skulle [*v.rr.* piled, pylede, pilede, pilled]. *a* **1450** *Knt. de la Tour* (1868) 22 Euer after, whanne the pie sawe a balled or a pilled man. **1533** J. HEYWOOD *Merry Play* (1830) 15 A very myschyefe Lyght on the pylde preest. **1611** CORYAT *Crudities* 41 The ostriches.. their.. legs.. are pilled and bare. **1611** COTGR., *Pelé*, pild, hairelesss, bauld. **1650** BULWER *Anthropomet.* 88 A round white pil'd or smooth Chin. **1665** BRATHWAIT *Comment Two Tales* 13 His eyes so effeminately pilled, his shooes artifically carved. **1681** W. ROBERTSON *Phraseol. Gen.* (1693) 198 To make bald or pilled, *depilare*. **1828** *Craven Gloss.* (ed. 2), *Pilled*, to be made bald.

b. Of fibres or fabric: see PILL *v.* 6 c.

†**3.** Bare; bare of nap, threadbare; bare of pasture; poor; miserable: = PEELED 3. *Obs.*

1362 LANGL. *P. Pl.* A. VII. 143 One.. bad go pisse him with his plouh, pillede [*B.* for-pyned] screwe! *a* **1548** HALL *Chron., Rich. III* 40 Appareled in a pilled blacke cloke. **1556** WITHALS *Dict.* (1568) 10 b/2 Pilled or bare (grounde), as vnfertile grounde. **1613** PURCHAS *Pilgrimage* (1614) 631 Bloud is a slippery foundation, and pillage a pill'd wall.

†**b.** *fig.* Beggarly, meagre, bald. *Obs.*

1526 TINDALE *Parable Wicked Mammon* (1528) Hiij b, The vayne disputyng of them that ascrybe so hye a place in heuen vnto theyr pylde merytes. **1553** BECON *Reliques of Rome* (1563) 163 A pylde and beggarly ceremony. **1599** B. JONSON *Ev. Man out of Hum.* I. i, I am no such pild Cinike to beleeue, That beggery is the onely happinesse. **1605** M. SUTCLIFFE *Brief Exam.* 58 *note*, They laugh at this pild prologue that would threape kindnesse upon them.

4. [f. PILL *v.*[1] 1.] Plundered, robbed, pillaged: = PEELED 1. *arch.* or *dial.*

1514 BARCLAY *Cyt. & Uplondyshm.* (Percy Soc.) 34 The temples pylled dothe bytterly complayne. **1535** COVERDALE *Isa.* xviii. 2 To a fearful people,.. to a desperate and pylled folke. [Cf. PEELED 5.] **1611** COTGR., *Pillé*, pilled, rauaged, ransacked, robbed, despoyled, or bereaued of all. **1828** *Craven Gloss.* (ed. 2), *Pilled*, robbed.

5. *Comb.* (from 2), as ***pilled-pated, -skinned,*** etc.

1542 UDALL *Erasm. Apoph.* 227 b, The pield pated Theodore of Tharsus was a briber and a theefe. **1563** BECON *Displ. Popish Mass* Wks. III. 44 That thing which yͤ pildepate Priest holdeth vp in his handes. **1576** NEWTON *Lemnie's Complex.* (1633) 232 For these.. persons are of body ill-favoured, leane, dry, lanke, pilde-skinned, and without haire.

Hence **'pilledness,** baldness, bareness, threadbareness.

1398 TREVISA *Barth. De P.R.* VII. iii. (Bodl. MS.) lf. 48/2 But somme for oþer skalldenes oþer pilledness leue and beþ isene alwaye þerafter. **1578** LYTE *Dodoens* II. cxvi. 310 Euphorbium.. cureth.. pyldenesse, causing the heare to renewe and growe againe. **1600** HAKLUYT *Voy.* (1810) III. 211 Some scorned the pildnesse of his [Columbus's] garments. **1656** W. D. tr. *Comenius' Gate Lat. Unl.* ¶ 304. 83 Pilledness, baldness, hoaryness, arise from the want of radical moisture.

†**'pilledow.** *Sc. Obs.* [For *pilled daw*: see PILLED, and cf. CADDOW.] A plucked or bald daw; *fig.* a tonsured priest.

1603 *Proph. of Merlin* (Bannatyne Cl.) 12 Their shal a Galyart gayt with a gilten horne A Pilledow with a tode, sic a prime holde. **1603** *Proph. of Waldhaue* (ibid.) 33 A proude powne in a preis Lordly shal light With Piotes and Pilliedowes pulled [= pilled] in the crowne.

pilleis, obs. Sc. pl. of *pillie*, PULLEY.

pillen, obs. form of PILLION *sb.*[1]

piller ('pɪlə(r)). *Obs.* or *dial.* Forms: α. 4–6 **pylour,** 4–5 **piloure,** 4–7 **-our.** β. 4–6 **pillour,** 5 **pylowre,** 5–7 **piller,** (5–6 **pyllar,** 6 **-er**). See also PEELER[1]. [ME. *pilour*, f. PILL *v.*[1], prob. after OF. *pilleur* (1345 in Hatz.-Darm.) in same sense (f. *piller* to plunder), with later suffix-change: see -ER[2] 3.]

†**1.** A robber, despoiler, plunderer; a thief; = PEELER[1] 1. *Obs.*

α. *c* **1330** R. BRUNNE *Chron. Wace* (Rolls) 6682 Ffor ay þey [Britons] lyue wyþ pylours in drede. *c* **1386** CHAUCER *Knight's T.* 149 To ransake in the taas of the bodyes dede.. The pilours diden bisynesse and cure. **1433** *Rolls of Parlt.* IV. 422/1 Pilours, Robbours, Oppressours. *c* **1440** *Promp. Parv.* 399/1 Pylowre, or he þat pelythe oþer menne, as catchepollys, & oþer lyke, *pilator*. **1496** *Dives & Paup.* (W. de W.) VIII. xvii. 344/2 Theues, pylours, extorcyoners.

β. **1399** LANGL. *Rich. Redeles* III. 303 To preson þe pillourz þat ouere þe pore renneth. **1470–85** MALORY *Arthur* XXI. iv, Pyllars and robbers were comen in to the felde. **1475** *Bk. Noblesse* (Roxb.) 31 Suche.. oughte rather be clepid pilleris, robberis,.. than men of armes chevalerous. **1581** J. BELL *Haddon's Answ. Osor.* 219 Pillers and pollers of all commonweales. **1596** Z. I. tr. *Lavardin's Hist. Scanderbeg* VIII. 324 Two most notable pillers and not pillours of the common wealth. *a* **1661** FULLER *Worthies* I. (1662) 42 The Land then swarmed with Pilours, Robbers, Oppressors of the People. **1674** STAVELEY *Rom. Horseleach* (1769) 164 That pillar and poller and filcher of our money.

b. Applied to a plant that exhausts the soil.

1615 W. LAWSON *Country Housew. Gard.* (1623) 8 Trees are the greatest suckers and pillers of earth.

2. One who peels; an instrument for peeling; = PEELER[1] 2. Now *dial.*

1483 *Cath. Angl.* 279/1 A Pillar (*A.* A Pyllare), *vellicator*. **1828** *Craven Gloss.* (ed. 2), *Pillers*, persons, also instruments, for peeling oak trees, &c.

piller, obs. f. PILLAR; var. PILLOR *v. Obs.*

pillerie, -ery, obs. forms of PILLORY.

†**'pillery.** *Obs.* [a. F. *pillerie* (1345 in Hatz.-Darm.), f. *piller* to pillage, *pilleur* pillager: see -ERY.] The action of plundering; plunder, pillage, robbery; an instance of this.

1449 *Rolls of Parlt.* V. 147/2 Open Robberyes, Oppressions and Pilleries withoute nombre. **1502** *Ord. Crysten Men* (W. de W. 1506) IV. xxi. 268 False pletynges, exaccyons, pylleryes, and other dyuers inuencyons. **1609** DANIEL *Civ. Wars* IV. lxxv, And then concussion, rapine, pilleries. *a* **1627** HAYWARD *Edw. VI* (1630) 66 They did palliat these pillaries with the faire pretence of authority and of law.

†**pillet,** obs. form of PELLET *sb.*[1]

a **1400–50** *Stockh. Med. MS.* 113 For to makyn pillettis. **1561** HOLLYBUSH *Hom. Apoth.* 3 Seth the same together and make pillets thereof the bignesse of a haselnut or filberte.

pilletorie, obs. f. PELLITORY.

pillew, obs. f. PILLOW.

pillez, var. PILLAS.

pillfer, obs. f. PILFER.

pilliall, obs. f. PULIOL, pennyroyal.

†**'pillicock.** *Obs.* Forms: 4 **pilkoc,** 6 **pilicock,** 6– **pillicock,** (7 **peli-**). Cf. also PILLOCK[2]. [f. *pill*, also *pillie* and *pilluck*, all north. dial., = Norw. dial. *pill* (Aasen) penis: cf. COCK *sb.*[1] 20.]

1. The penis (*vulgar*).

1300–25 in *Rel. Ant.* II. 211 Mi pilkoc pisseth on mi schone. **1598** FLORIO, *Dolcemelle*.. also pilicock. [See also s.vv. *Pinco, Pinchino, Rozzone*.] **1605** SHAKS. *Lear* III. iv. 78. **1719** D'URFEY *Wit & Mirth* Song, Pillicock.

2. 'A flattering word for a young boy'; = 'my pretty knave' (Cotgr.).

1598 FLORIO, *Zugo*,.. a pillicocke, a darling, or a wanton, or a minion. **1611** COTGR., *Mistigouri*, my pillicocke, my prettie rogue. **1653** URQUHART *Rabelais* I. xli, By my faith.. I cannot tell (my Pillicock), but thou art more worth then gold.

pillie, pl. **pilleis,** obs. Sc. form of PULLEY.

pilliewinkes: see PILLIWINKS.

'pilling, *vbl. sb.* [f. PILL *v.*[1] + -ING[1].] The action of PILL *v.*[1] in its various senses.

1. †**a.** Plundering, robbing, spoliation; extortion.

α. *c* **1380** WYCLIF *Wks.* (1880) 417 A prest shulde raþere.. suffere deþ or he assentide.. to siche piling of pore men. **1387** TREVISA *Higden* (Rolls) VII. 369 Þat hopede to blende his pylyng and hys robborie by þe sympilnesse of Wolston.

β. **1399** LANGL. *Rich. Redeles* I. 13 By pillynge of ȝoure peple ȝoure prynces to plese. **1496** *Dives & Paup.* (W. de W.) V. viii. 206/1 They be.. full of crueltee in pyllynge of the poore people. **1556** OLDE *Antichrist* 73 b, The pilling and rauine, that they vse openly. **1603** KNOLLES *Hist. Turks* (1621) 990 All began prowdly to plot unto themselves nothing but sackings, pillings, taking of prisoners. **1627** SPEED *England*, etc. *Irel.* iv. §7 Certaine.. oppressed the poore people a long time with extorting, pilling, and spoiling.

b. *arch.* or *dial.* ***pilling (peeling) and polling***: see PILL *v.*[1] 9.

1547 *Homilies* I. *Agst. Adultery* II. (1859) 125 Doth not the adulterer give his mind.. to polling and pilling of other? **1607** DEKKER *Knts. Conjur.* (1842) 58 Heers worse pilling and polling then amongst my countrey-men the vsurers.

1658 J. HARRINGTON *Prerog. Pop. Govt.* II. ii. (1700) 332 The pilling and polling of her Provinces, which happen'd through the Avarice, and Luxury of her Nobility. *a* **1661** FULLER *Worthies, Berks.* (1662) 90 Vexed at his polling and peeling of the English people.

2. †The removal or falling off of hair; depilation.

1561 T. HOBY tr. *Castiglione's Courtyer* I. H, The pilling of the browes and forehead. **1597** GERARDE *Herbal* I. lxv. 90 The ashes of this Bulbe..cureth the pilling or falling of the haire in spots. **1611** COTGR., *Pelement*, a pilling; a pulling off the haire. **1635** SWAN *Spec. M.* vi. §4 (1643) 248 The ashes ..cure the pilling of the hair from the head.

b. The gathering of fibres into small balls of fluff on the surface of a fabric (see PILL *v.*[1] 6 c).

1958 *New Scientist* 3 Apr. 17/2 In a test cardigan..the treated sleeve showed a remarkable resistence to pilling. **1959** A. J. HALL *Stand. Handbk. Textiles* (ed. 5) v. 314 Pilling has become especially noticeable since the introduction of the synthetic fibres. **1965** *New Scientist* 8 Apr. 95/1 Synthetic fabrics have one common short-coming: they are hightly susceptible to what is known as 'pilling', a tendency to form small tangled knots of fibres. **1968** J. IRONSIDE *Fashion Alphabet* 244 *Pilling*,..the term used when fibres gather into a ball on the surface. **1970** *Cabinet Maker & Retail Furnisher* 23 Oct. 173/2 The inclusion of nylon in the blend..aggravated the pilling. **1970** *Which?* Oct. 300/2 A few brands suffered slightly from pilling (little balls of fibre on the surface). **1972** *Times* 28 Nov. 19/8 E. Gomme..has encountered problems of 'pilling' in the fabric. **1974** *Amer. Speech 1970* XLV. 179 An antistatic pilling-resistant (resistant to gathering small 'pills' of fuzz) finish.

3. Removal of the skin, bark, etc.: = PEELING *vbl. sb.* 1 b. Now *dial.*

1580 HOLLYBAND *Treas. Fr. Tong*, *Escorcement*, a barking of trees, a pilling, a rinding. **1618** in *N. Riding Rec. Soc.* (1884) II. 175 A Gillinge man for pilling of the barke. **1742** *MS. Agreement* (co. Derby), [Lessee to have] authority for pilling, cutting down..wood. **1794** *Trans. Soc. Arts* XII. 138 Pilling [of osiers], per load.

†**b.** The coming off of bark, skin, etc.: = PEELING *vbl. sb.* 1 c. *Obs.*

1601 HOLLAND *Pliny* II. 141 A faire medicine to cure..the scailing and pilling of the face. **1661** LOVELL *Hist. Anim. & Min.* 113 It helps the pilling of the skin about the nails.

4. *concr.* That which is peeled or peels off: = PEELING *vbl. sb.* 2. Now *dial.*

c **1400** *Rowland & O.* 1265 He sett þe lawes of Cristyantee Nott at a pillynge of a tree. **1418** PAGE *Siege of Rouen* in *Hist. Coll. Citizen Lond.* (Camden) 18 Oynonnys, lykys, bothe in fere Was to hem a mete fulle dere;..Welle was hym that myght gete a pyllynge. **1523** FITZHERB. *Husb.* §136 Bastes or pyllynge of wythy or elme to bynde them with. **1601** HOLLAND *Pliny* II. 31 That part of the Hempe which is next to the rind or pilling..is worst. **1671** GREW *Anat. Plants* vi. §2 The Pilling [of an Apple] is but the Continuation of the utmost part of the Barque. **1828** *Craven Gloss.* (ed. 2) s.v., Potatoe pillings. **1877** *Holderness Gloss.*, *Pillins*, sb. pl., the skins of onions, potatoes, &c., after removal. [So in many dialects: see Eng. Dial. Dict.]

5. *attrib.*, as ***pilling-knife***, ***-iron***.

1688 R. HOLME *Armoury* III. 350/2 The Pilling Knife, of some called a Pilling Iron,..takes off all the Hair of the Hide; being a four square Iron set in two Handles, Hooped.

'pilling, *ppl. a.* [f. PILL *v.*[1] + -ING[2].] That pills.

a. Plundering, rifling, thieving. *arch.*

1586 MARLOWE *1st Pt. Tamburl.* III. iii. 250 The galleys and those pilling brigandines, That..hover in the Straits for Christians' wrack. *a* **1618** SYLVESTER *Paradox* Wks. (Grosart) II. 56 To guard from souldiers pilling hands. **1692** R. L'ESTRANGE *Fables* ccliv. (1714) 271 Suppose Pilling and Polling Officers, as Busie upon the People as these Flies were upon the Fox.

b. That peels. Now *dial.*

[**1483** *Cath. Angl.* 279/1 Pillynge..Pyllynge, *vellicans*.] **1681** COTTON *Wond. Peak* (ed. 4) 42 Neighbours..Must needs perceive the pilling Cliff retire.

pillion ('pɪljən), *sb.*[1] Also 6 *Sc.* pilȝane, pyllyon, pyllen, 7 pillen, -ian, 8 pilion. Cf. also PILGATE. [app. of Celtic origin: in Irish *pillín*, Gaelic *pillin*, *-ean*, in same sense, dim. of *pell* (*peall*), gen. sing. and nom. pl. *pill*, couch, pallet, cushion (a. L. *pellis* skin, pelt, felt).

Pill occurs in the *Boramha* of the Bk. of Leinster, *c* 1160–1170 (*pill cuilcthe cluimhe* 'pallet with downy coverlet'). *Pillin* was prob. adopted in Lowl. Sc. from Gaelic, in Eng. from Irish: cf. quot. *a* 1620. The Guernsey *pillon* cited by Moisy *Anglo-Normand* from Métivier, may be from English, no such word occurring in French.]

a. A kind of saddle, *esp.* a woman's light saddle. Also, a pad or cushion attached to the hinder part of an ordinary saddle, on which a second person (usually a woman) may ride; also used for resting a mail or piece of luggage in transport: see *mail pillion*, s.v. MAIL *sb.*[3] 4. *Obs.* exc. *Hist.* In modern use, a seat located behind the saddle of a motor cycle, on which a second person may ride. Hence *to go*, *ride* (cf. RIDE *v.* 1 d), *sit pillion*, to travel on this seat. Also *transf.*

The application in quot. 1878 is unusual, but anticipates use in the modern sense.

1503 *Acc. Ld. High Treas. Scot.* II. 214 Item, for v elne claith of gold to be ane pilȝane to the Quene, quhen hir aun wes brint in Dalketh. **1530** PALSGR. 254/1 Pyllyon for a woman to ryde on, *hovsse à femme*. **1571** *Wills & Inv. N.C.* (Surtees) I. 361, ij owld chystes ij[s]. vj[d].—j bodgett, on capcase & ij male piniors [? pillions] xij[d].—ij armones j[s]. *a* **1620** MORYSON *Itin.* IV. II. v. (1903) 235 The Irish..vse no sadles, but either long narrow pillions bumbasted, or bare boardes of that fashion. **1628** WITHER *Brit. Rememb.* II. 1774 To get her neighbors footstoole, and her pillian. **1688** R. HOLME *Armoury* III. 397/2 In former times the Side sadle had only a Pillen fastned upon the Tree of the Sadle..over which Pillen and Tree was cast a Sadle-cloth. **1766** GOLDSM. *Vic. W.* x, Next, the straps of my wife's pillion broke down. **1820** W. IRVING *Sketch Bk.*, *Leg. Sleepy Hollow* §54 Some of the damsels mounted on pillions behind their favourite swains. **1867** SMILES *Huguenots Fr.* xii. (1880) 207 De Bostaquet rode first, with his sister behind him on a pillion. **1878** *Design & Work* IV. 215/1 To use the electric light on a bicycle is very easy, if you can arrange to place upon a pillion behind you a large steam engine and boiler and a Gramme machine, the whole weighing only about 3 tons. **1911** *Motor Cycle* 27 Apr. 481/1 The pillion or tandem seat is likely to become increasingly popular. **1923** *Weekly Dispatch* 13 May 9 Riding his motor-cycle..with Miss Esther Gwyther, a nurse, on the pillion, he collided [etc.]. **1926** T. E. LAWRENCE *Seven Pillars* (1935) IV. xliv. 255 He stopped babbling, and began to wail out his sorrows. I sat him, pillion, on the camel's rump; then stirred her up and mounted. **1927** *Glasgow Herald* 31 Aug. 10 A clerk..on whose machine Miss Paterson was riding pillion. **1934** T. S. ELIOT *Rock* i. 21 But every son would have his motor cycle, And daughters ride away on casual pillions. **1958** J. BETJEMAN *Coll. Poems*, And country girls with lips and nails vermilion Wait, nylon-legged, to straddle on the pillion. **1965** *Listener* 27 May 785/1 They [*sc.* Vietnamese girls] ride bicycles, sit pillion on motor-bicycles, and manage their delightful floating garments with elegance and dignity at all times. **1973** J. WAINWRIGHT *Pride of Pigs* 142, I got rid of my scooter, and started going pillion with Lance. **1979** R. RENDELL *Make Death love Me* iii. 30 Alan had once seen her get off the pillion of a boy's motor-bike.

b. *attrib.*, as ***pillion gelding***, ***mail***, ***passenger***, ***ride***, ***rider***, ***-riding*** vbl. sb. and ppl. adj., ***seat***; **pillion cloth**, a cloth placed under a pillion; **pillion stick**, a stick fastened in a pillion to hold luggage in place; **pillion stone**, a stone used to facilitate mounting to a pillion seat.

1648 *Public Rec. Colony of Connecticut* (1850) I. 508, 1 sidesaddle and pillion cloath. **1684** *Essex Inst. Hist. Coll.* (1888) XXV. 155 In the Kitchine..a sadle, pillyon and pillyon cloath. **1929** J. DE F. SHELTON *Salt-Box House* iv. 34 Cuffee busied himself making sure that the dark blue pillion-cloth protected her dress from the horse's flank. **1539–40** *Rutland MSS.* (1905) IV. 289 To Poppes man for bryngyng of on pyllen gyldyng for my Lady, xx *d.* **1818** SCOTT *Hrt. Midl.* xli, That trunk is mine, and that there band-box, and that pillion mail, and those seven bundles, and the paper bag. **1973** J. WAINWRIGHT *Pride of Pigs* 92 The pillion-passenger was thrown clear, but the motor-cyclist was pinned under his machine. **1976** *Deeside Advertiser* 9 Dec. 24/3 A teenage motor cyclist died and his pillion passenger was injured in an accident on a sharp bend on the main Corwen-Chester Road at Treuddyn. **1935** T. E. LAWRENCE *Let.* 31 Jan. (1938) 845 It was a good idea, that pillion ride. **1963** L. DEIGHTON *Horse under Water* xxiv. 107 Giorgio had got a pillion ride..with a two-stroke motor bike. **1920** *Motor Cycle* 24 June 714/2 Motor-cyclists are summoned for having their number plates obscured by any part of a pillion-rider's dress. *a* **1974** R. CROSSMAN *Diaries* (1975) I. 40 We had the most amiable cup of tea before driving home to Prescote through the fog, where I found that another pillion rider had come down with my third red box. **1920** *Motor Cycle* 8 July 45/1 The local authorities have threatened a campaign against pillion riding. **1927** W. E. COLLINSON *Contemp. Eng.* 35 Probably pillion-riding..will also be prohibited and dazzle head lights have to be dimmed. **1932** H. S. WALPOLE *Fortress* I. 83 Many came in pillion-riding as for hundreds of years they had done, while the grander farmers were proud in the 'shandy-carts'. **1970** *R.A.C. Guide & Handbk.* 59/1 Pillion Riding. Only one passenger may be carried on a solo motor cycle, and..must be seated astride behind the driver on a proper pillion seat. **1878** *Cumberland Gloss.*, *Pillion seat*, a seat to fix behind the saddle for a female to ride on. Out of use since about 1830. **1911** *Motor Cycle* 27 Apr. 418/2 A pillion seat, if not very sociable, certainly has some advantages. **1973** J. WAINWRIGHT *Pride of Pigs* 88 The youth astride the Road Rocket kicked the starter... His companion settled himself on the pillion-seat. **1784** J. F. D. SMYTH *Tour U.S.A.* II. 248 All these papers were concealed in the mail pillion-sticks on which the servant carried his portmanteau. **1907** *Manch. Guardian* 20 July 7/7 On one side of the porch is a horsing or pillion stone.

†**pillion**, *sb.*[2] *Obs.* Forms: 4 pylion, 4–6 pilioun, 5 pylioun, pelyone, pillyon, 5–6 pillion(e, pyllyon. [app. a derivative of L. *pīleus*, *pilleus* cap (see PILEUS), which word it was used by Trevisa to render. No corresponding form has been found in other langs.] A hat or cap, esp. of a priest or doctor of divinity.

1387 TREVISA *Higden* (Rolls) I. 217 Þei myȝte nouȝt in þe holy day suffre on hire piliouns and here cappes for hete [*L.* Quando non poterant præ calvitate diebus festivis pileum deferre]. *c* **1420** LYDG. *Assembly of Gods* 1577 Gregory and Ierome, Austyn and Ambrose, With pylyons on her hedys, stood lyke doctours. *c* **1449** PECOCK *Repr.* I. xvi. 88 Summe wereres of piliouns in scole of dyuynyte han scantli be worthi for to be in the same scole a good scoler. *c* **1500** in Peacock *Stat. Cambridge* App. A. p. lii, The Bedell shall gether of every Doctour Comensar..a Grote for hys Pylyon. **1515** BARCLAY *Egloges* iv. (1570) C iv b/1 Mercury shall giue thee giftes manyfolde, His pillion, scepter, his winges and his harpe. *a* **1562** CAVENDISH *Wolsey* (1893) 30 Uppon hys [Wolsey's] hed a round pyllion with a nekke of blake velvett set to the same in the inner side.

attrib. ? *a* **1400** *Morte Arth.* 3461 Thane rysez the riche kynge... And one he henttis..A pavys pillione hatt, þat pighte was fulle faire With perry of þe oryent.

Hence †**'pillioned** *a.*, wearing a pillion. *Obs.*

1553 BALE *Vacacyon* 10 No mete mynisters..though they be neuer so gorgyously mytered, coped, and typpeted, or neuer so fynely forced, pylyoned and scarletted.

†**pillion**, *sb.*[3] *Obs.* (See quots.)

1778 PRYCE *Min. Cornub.* v. iii. 283 The pillion in the first and second of the stampings is separated from the scoria in the same manner as Copper Ore from its waste. *Ibid.* Gloss. 325 *Pillion*, the Tin which remains in the scoria or slags after it is first smelted, which must be separated and remelted. **1882** JAGO *Cornish Dial.* [from Pryce].

pillion ('pɪljən), *v.* [f. PILLION *sb.*[1]] **1.** *trans.* To equip (a horse or saddle) with a pillion. Chiefly in pa. pple. or ppl. adj.

1843 *Knickerbocker* XXII. 431 The cozy couple..ride..side by side upon the pillioned saddle. **1929** J. D. SHELTON *Salt-Box House* iv. 33 Thaddeus's best pacing-mare being duly saddled and pillioned. **1935** W. FORTESCUE *Perfume from Provence* 234 They rode upon pillioned horses decorated with favours.

2. *trans.* To place on a pillion. Chiefly as *ppl. adj.*

1906 A. NOYES *Drake* I. II. 59 Little the boy remembered of that flight, Pillioned behind his father. **1910** W. DE MORGAN *Affair of Dishonour* iv. 46 A horseman here and there, alone or with a wench pillioned behind. **1958** P. MORTIMER *Daddy's gone a-Hunting* i. 8 A motor cycle turned into the road... She caught sight of..a pillioned girl with hair streaming.

3. *intr.* To ride on the pillion of a motor cycle. *rare.*

1935 T. E. LAWRENCE *Let.* 31 Jan. (1938) 845 Pretty awful pillioning with a suitcase and masterpiece in one's arms!

pillionaire (pɪljə'nɛə(r)). Now *rare* or *Obs.* [f. PILLION *sb.*[1] after MILLIONAIRE.] One, usu. female, who rides on the pillion of a motor cycle or on a seat at the back of a bicycle.

1931 *Newark Advertiser* 26 Aug. 7/2 'What is a proper pillion seat?' was the question for the wisdom of the Bench at Newark Borough Police Court. Apparently it is a seat occupied by a pillionaire. **1931** *Times* 4 Sept. 6/5 On the back of his bike the defendant had a pillionaire—a female. **1937** PARTRIDGE *Dict. Slang* 630/1 *Pillionaire*, a female occupant of a 'peach-perch' or 'flapper-bracket'.

pillionist ('pɪljənɪst). *rare.* [f. PILLION *sb.*[1] + -IST.] One who rides on the pillion of a motor cycle.

The more usual term is *pillion rider*.

1923 *Motor Cyclist* 26 Sept. 643/1 As a confirmed pillionist I do not add my voice to those who are clamouring for legal abolition of this form of passenger riding.

pillitore, obs. form of PELLITORY.

'pilliver. Now *north. dial.* Forms: 1 pylewer, 2 pulewar, 4 peloware, pylwere, 6–7 (9 *dial.*) pilliver, 7 pillover. [app. f. OE. *pyle*, PILLOW + ON. *ver* case, cover: cf. ON. *koddaver* pillow-case = CODWARE[2]. (But the element *-war*, *-ware* may have a different origin; with the forms in *-ver* cf. *pillowber*, PILLOW-BERE.)]

A pillow-case. (In the early quots., down to 1440, the meaning seems to be 'pillow'.)

a **1100** in Napier *O.E. Glosses* 222/16 *Ceruical*, pylewer. *a* **1200** in *MS. Bodley* 730 lf. 144 b, Hoc auriculare et hic pulvillus idem sunt .s. oreiler .i. pulewar. et hoc cervical. **14..** *Nom.* in Wr.-Wülcker 742/24 *Hoc cervical*, a peloware. *c* **1440** *Jacob's Well* 243 Sche..leyde hym in here bed, & a softe pylwere vnder his heuyd. **1581–2** in Best *Rur. Econ.* (Surtees) 172, 5 pillivers of lininge. **1599** in *Antiquary* XXXII. 243 Item iiij pillivers & one table clothe, iijs. viijd. **1611** *Knaresb. Wills* (Surtees) II. 20, iij pillovers. **1655** *Ibid.* 207, 3 pillovers. **1869** GIBSON *Folk-speech Cumberland* 31 He laid back on his pilliver. **1898** B. KIRKBY *Lakeland Words* (E.D.D.), An' a pilliver tuck't inta t' sma' ov his back.

pilliwinks ('pɪlɪwɪŋks). *Obs.* exc. *Hist.* Forms: 4 pyrwykes, 5 pyrewinkes; *Sc.* 6–7 pilli(e)winkes, -is, 8 -winks, -wincks, 6 pinniwinkis, 8 pinniewinks; 8–9 pilni(e)winks. (Also 9 (erroneously) pilliwinkies, pennywinkis, pinnywinkles, pilniwinky, pilni(e)winkies, pirliewinkles.) [In English use, *c* 1400, *pyrwykes*, *pyrewinkes*. In Scottish use, *c* 1600, *pilliwinkes* and *pinniwinkis*; corrupted by later historical or antiquarian writers, novelists, journalists, etc. to *pilniewinks*, *pinnywinkles*, *pirliewinkles*, etc. Origin unknown: the 15th c. Eng. *pyrewinkes* coincides with a contemporary spelling of *periwinkle* (the flower); but there is no obvious connexion of sense. The early forms do not agree (as has sometimes been thought) with those of *periwinkle* the shell-fish, the forms in *-winkle* being merely later corruptions after the word had become obsolete soon after 1600.] An instrument of torture for squeezing the fingers; supposed to resemble the thumbkins of thumb-screw.

1397 in W. P. Baildon *Sel. Cas. Chanc.* (1896) 30 Johan Skypwyth..adonqes esteant viscont de Nicole [= Lincoln], par colour de son office aresta le dit Johan..et lui mist en ceppes..et sur sez mayns vne paire de pyrwykes. ? **1401** *Cartular. Abbatiæ S. Edmundi* (MS.) lf. 341 (in Cowell's Interpr. (1701) Ss ij b), Quendam Robertum Smyth de Bury ..Ceperunt..et ipsum..in ferro posuerunt—et cum cordis ligaverunt, et super pollices ipsius Roberti quoddam instrumentum vocatum *Pyrewinkes* ita strictè et durè posuerunt, quod sanguis exivit de digitis illius. **1591** *Newes from Scotland* (in Pitcairn *Crim. Trials* I. II. 215), Her maister..did with the help of others torment her with the torture of the pilliwinkes vpon her fingers. **1596** *Ibid.* 376 The dochter, being sewin yeir auld, but in the pinniwinkis [*so MS. Record*; in Maclaurin, 1774, pilniewinks]. *Ibid.* 377 Hir sone tortourit in þe Buitis, and hir dochtir put in þe Pilliewinkis. **1680–1700** in *Maclaurin's Crim. Cases* Introd.

37 Lord Roystoun observes:..'Anciently I find other torturing instruments were used, as pinniewinks or pilliwinks, and caspitaws or caspicaws [*misreading of* cashilaws; in Pitcairn I. 275, caschielawis], in the Master of Orkney's case, 24th June 1596... But what these instruments were, I know not'. **1774** *Ibid.* 36 It was pleaded for Alaster Grant, who was indicted for theft and robbery 3rd August 1632, that he cannot pass to the knowledge of an assize, in respect he was twice put to the torture, first in the boots, and next in the pilliewinks or pinniewinks. [**1818** SCOTT *Br. Lamm.* xxiii, They prick us and they pine us, and they pit us on the pinnywinkles for witches. **1830** —— *Demonol.* ix. 310 His finger bones were slintered in the pilniewinks. **1865** LECKY *Ration.* I. i. 142 The three principal [tortures]..were the pennywinkis, the boots, and the caschielawis. **1890** *Spectator* 31 May 768 The 'pirliewinkles', a form of thumb-screw ingeniously constructed for the express purpose of crushing all the fingers of one hand.]

pill-machine, pill-nettle, etc.: see PILL[2] 4.

pillo, obs. form of PILLOW.

†**pillock**[1]. *Obs.* [See -OCK.] A small pill.
1570 LEVINS *Manip.* 159/11 Pillocke, *pilula.*

pillock[2] ('pɪlək). *north. dial.* and *slang.* Also †**pillok, pilloch, pilluck.** [Variant of PILLICOCK.]

1. = PILLICOCK 1.

1535 LYNDESAY *Satyre* 4410 My pillok. **1903** *Eng. Dial. Dict.* IV. 503/1 *Pill,..pilluck* Wm. Yks..., the male organ, the penis.

2. *transf.* A fool, a stupid person; also in weakened sense, a fellow, bloke.

1967 J. BURKE *Till Death do us Part* viii. 135 What are you talking about, you great hairy pilloch? **1968** J. WAINWRIGHT *Darkening Glass* viii. 70 She..glared across the room and said: 'Where's that pilluck with the drinks?' **1976** —— *Bastard* vii. 93 'You always were a pillock,' he says, with feeling. **1978** 'J. GASH' *Gold from Gemini* vii. 70 The pillock mistook my astonishment for awe.

pilloe, obs. variant of PILAU.

†'**pillor,** *v. Obs.* Also 7 **-owr, -ar,** 8 **-er.** [app. a back-formation from PILLORY *sb.* (OF. had *piloreme*nt, as if from a vb. *pilorer*, instead of *pilorier*.)] *trans.* = PILLORY *v.*

1638 *Div. & Politike Observ.* 8 In pillaring, or putting to death such as refuse to doe any worship. **1651** FULLER *Abel Rediv.* 436 So justly pillored for cheaters to all posterity. **1706** HEARNE *Collect.* 30 Apr. I. 238 De-Foe..was pillor'd for it. **1715** *Exeter Mercury* 1 Apr. 8 Lists..containing the Names of such as they would have Beheaded,..Piller'd. **1819** *Metropolis* III. 170 Pillored in capes and cravats.

pillorize ('pɪləraɪz), *v.* [f. PILLORY *sb.* + -IZE: or a. OF. *pil-, pilloriser* (14–16th c. in Godef.), f. *pilori.*] *trans.* To put in the pillory; = PILLORY *v.*

1646 J. HALL *Poems* 66 Defect of Organs may me cause By chance to pillorize an Asse. **1691** WOOD *Ath. Oxon.* I. 814 Henry Burton..was..degraded, deprived of his benefice, pillorized with Prynne and Bastwicke. **1721** STRYPE *Eccl. Mem.* III. i. 14 One had been pillorized for speaking some words for Queen Mary, on the 11th of this month. **1837** *Fraser's Mag.* XV. 237 Being thus pillorized, he was fit for nothing until he was released.

Hence '**pillorized** *ppl. a.*, '**pillorizing** *vbl. sb.* and *ppl. a.*; also **pillori'zation.**

1656 S. HOLLAND *Zara* (1719) 68 A Pilloriz'd Factionist. **1688** in Ld. Campbell *Chancellors* (1857) IV. cii. 412 High commissions, *quo warrantos*, dispensations, pillorizations. **1720** STRYPE *Stow's Surv.* (1754) II. VI. iii. 630/1 The punishment of Pillorising inflicted for this crime by the Star Chamber. **1890** MISS R. H. BUSK in *N. & Q.* 7th ser. IX. 150/1 *Dandin* has become a pillorizing name adopted (probably from folk-speech) by many French authors..for types of various forms of folly they have undertaken to scathe.

pillory ('pɪlərɪ), *sb.* Forms: 3–4 **pillori,** 3–7 **pyllory,** 4–7 **pilory,** 5 **pilery, pullery, pull-, pyllorie, pelory,** 5–6 **pillery, -ie, pyllere, -ery, pylery, pillorye,** 5–7 **pillorie,** 6 **pyllary, pillarie,** 7 **pillary,** 3– **pillory.** [ME. *pillori, pilory*, etc., a. OF. *pellori* (1168), *pilorit, pilori* (13th c., Godef.), also *pillori, peulauri, pellerich*, of uncertain origin: see Note below.]

A contrivance for the punishment of offenders, consisting usually of a wooden framework erected on a post or pillar, and formed, like the stocks, of two movable boards which, when brought together at their edges, leave holes through which the head and hands of an offender were thrust, in which state he was exposed to public ridicule, insult, and molestation. In other forms, the culprit was fastened to a stake by a ring round his neck and wrists. (In quot. *a* 1380, the name is applied to the cross.) The Chinese *cangue* is a species of portable pillory.

In Great Britain the punishment of the pillory was abolished, except for perjury, in 1815, and totally in 1837. In Delaware, U.S., it was not abolished till 1905.

[*a* **1189** *Charter of Hen. II* in *Dugdale's Monast.* (1819) II. 351/1 Monachi de Middeltone habeant..omnes terras.. cum..assisa panis et cervisie, cum furcis, pilloriis et cum omnibus aliis pertinentiis.] **1274–5** *Rot. Hundred.* (1818) II. 194/1 (MS. m. 33), Abbas Sancti Edmundi habet..Pyllory et Trebuchet in Mercato de Bocholnesdal. **1275** [see PIT *sb.*[1] 2 b]. *a* **1300** *Sat. People Kildare* xvi. in *E.E.P.* (1862) 155 ȝe [bakers] pincheþ on þe riȝt white aȝen goddes law To þe fair pillori ich rede ȝe tak hede. *c* **1325** *Poem Times Edw. II* 477 in *Pol. Songs* (Camden) 345 The pilory and the cucking-stol beth i-mad for noht. **1362** LANGL. *P. Pl.* A. III. 69 To punisschen on pillories or on pynnyng stoles Brewesters, Bakers, Bochers and Cookes. **1393** *Ibid.* C. III. 216 Let hym nat a-skapie Er he be put on þe pullery. *a* **1380** *Minor Poems fr. Vernon MS.* lii. 15 Chyld, whi artou not a-schamed On a pillori to ben I-piled? [See also PIN *v.*[1] 1.] **14..** in *Surtees Misc.* (1888) 60 Þe sayd Burgese sall.. ordan a pelory and a thew, lawfull and strang. **1444** *Maldon, Essex Liber A.* lf. 32 b (MS.), If eny baker or brewer be ateynt of fals weght or of fals mesure, he shall be twyes amerced and at the thirde tyme he shall be sette in the pilery. **1511–12** *Act 3 Hen. VIII*, c. 6 §1 Upon payn to be sett upon the pillorie or the Cukkyngstole, Man or Woman as the case shall requyre. **1530** PALSGR. 254/1 Pyllary to punysshe men at, *pilory.* **1556** *Chron. Gr. Friars* (Camden) 49 Another prest this yere was sett on the pyllere in Chepe. **1575** *Nottingham Rec.* IV. 157 The rog that was set on the pylery. **1628** MEADE in Ellis *Orig. Lett.* Ser. I. III. 276 Being whipt from the Fleet to Westminster palace, where he stood in the pillory, had one ear nailed and cutt of close to his head and..his nostrils also slit. **1678** MARVELL *Def. J. Howe* Wks. 1875 IV. 236 [He] erects another pair of columns..betwixt which Mr. Howe is to look as through a pillary. **1703** *Lond. Gaz.* No. 3936/3 London, July 31. On the 29th Instant Daniel Foe, alias de Foe, stood in the Pillory before the Royal Exchange in Cornhill. **1778** JOHNSON 18 Apr. in *Boswell*, They should set him in the pillory, that he may be punished in a way that would disgrace him. **1837** *Act 7 Will. IV, & 1 Vict.* c. 23 (*title*) An Act to abolish the Punishment of the Pillory. **1877** BLACK *Green Past.* xliii, Then your reward would be the pillory for every coward..to have his fling at you.

fig. **1838** DISRAELI *Corr. w. Sister* 1 Mar., Standing like a culprit before several hundred individuals sitting. After all, it is a moral pillory. **1876** 'OUIDA' *Winter City* iv. 82 What Molière would have fastened for all time in his pillory.

b. *finger-pillory*: a similar contrivance by which the fingers were held with the first joint bent to a right angle.

1851 *N. & Q.* 25 Oct., Amongst the old-time relics at Littlecote Hall, an ancient Wiltshire mansion, may still be seen a finger-pillory. **1899** W. ANDREWS *Bygone Punishments* 171 Finger pillories or stocks..were probably frequently employed in the old manorial halls of England.

c. *attrib.* and *Comb.*, as *pillory-bird* (cf. GALLOWS-BIRD), *-hole, -house*; *pillory-faced, -like* adjs.

c **1420** LYDG. *Assembly of Gods* 698 Tyburne coloppys, and pursekytters, Pylary knyghtes, double tollyng myllers. **1526** SKELTON *Magnyf.* 361 Boyes..wolde haue made me Freer Tucke, To preche out of the pylery hole. **1562** *Jack Juggler* (Roxb.) 23 Wine shakin, pilorye peepours, of lice not without a pecke. **1599** HAKLUYT *Voy.* II. II. 75 Two boords, amid them both a pillery-like hole for the prisoners necke. **1656** EARL MONM. tr. *Boccalini's Advts. fr. Parnass.* II. lxxviii. (1674) 230 Danger of being discovered to be a Pillory-bird. **1796** CHARLOTTE SMITH *Marchmont* III. 45 That old pillory faced blood-hound. **1884** *St. James's Gaz.* 5 Apr. 6/2 They had not, as before the Revolution, the pillory-house to live in.

[*Note.* Numerous forms of this word occur in med.L. (of France): Du Cange has *pilorium, pillaurium, spilorium* (Bordeaux), *pellerinum*, also *pilaricum, pil-, pill-, pelloricum, pellericum* (Aragon), most of which, if not all, appear to be formed on French or other vernacular forms. The forms in *pil-* suggest derivation from L. *pīla*, or its deriv. *pīlāre*, F. *piler, pilier*, pillar; but for those in *pill-, pell-*, this is phonologically unsuitable. The F. *pilori* is identified through Gascon *espilori* (*Coutumes de Gontaud* xlvii, *a* 1305) with Pr. *espitlori* 'pillory', which some connect with Cat. *espitllera* 'little window, peep-hole', with supposed reference to the hole through which the head was thrust in the pillory.]

'**pillory,** *v.* [f. prec. sb.; cf. F. *pilorier* (15th c. in Hatz.-Darm.).] *trans.* To set in the pillory; to punish by exposure in the pillory.

? *a* **1600** *Collier of Croydon* II. i. in Hazl. *Dodsley* VIII. 409, I have been five times pilloried, my coals given to the poor, and my sacks burnt before my face. **1685** EVELYN *Mem.* 16 May, Titus Oates was sentenced to be whipped and pilloried with the utmost severity. **1714** B. MANDEVILLE *Fab. Bees* (1733) I. 8 Tho' some, first pillory'd for cheating, Were hang'd in hemp of their own beating. **1849** MACAULAY *Hist. Eng.* i. I. 89 The government was able, through their instrumentality, to fine, imprison, pillory and mutilate without restraint.

transf. **1863** HAWTHORNE *Our Old Home* (1879) 15 A.. bust of General Jackson, pilloried in a military collar which rose above his ears.

b. *fig.* To expose to public ridicule or abuse.

1699 BENTLEY *Phal.* Pref. 18 He has Pilloried himself for't in Print, as long as that Book shall last. **1863** EMERSON *Misc. Papers, Thoreau* Wks. (Bohn) III. 326 He wanted a fallacy to expose, a blunder to pillory.

Hence '**pilloried** *ppl. a.*, '**pillorying** *vbl. sb.*

1671 F. PHILLIPS *Reg. Necess.* 167 A worse than Pilloried note of Ingratitude. **1705** HICKERINGILL *Priest-cr.* IV. (1721) 224 Cropping of Ears, Pillorying, Gaoling. **1893** VIZETELLY *Glances Back* I. i. 10 The rough handling that usually befel pilloried culprits.

†**pillotes.** *Obs.* = *pill oats, pilled oats*: see PILLED *ppl. a.* 1 b: cf. PILCORN.

1551 TURNER *Herbal* I. E vj, Ther is an other kinde of otes, called pillotes, which growe in Sussex: it hath no husk abydyng vpon it, after that it is threshed, & is lyke otemele.

pillou, obs. var. PILAU.

pillour, var. PELURE *Obs.*; obs. f. PILLER.

pillover, obs. f. PILLIVER.

pillow ('pɪləʊ), *sb.* Forms: see below. [OE. *pyle, pylu*:—**pulwi* = MDu. *pöluwe* (*puluwe*), *pēluwe* neut., ? fem., Du. *peluw, peuluw* fem.; MLG. *pöle*, LG. *pöl* masc.; OHG. *pfuliwi* neut., *pfulwo* masc., MHG. *pfülwe* neut., *pfulwe* masc., Oberd. *pfulbe, pfulwe*, Ger. *pfühl* masc., neut. These forms represent a WG. **pulwî(n*, a. L. *pulvīn-us* cushion, which, from the phonology, must have been adopted by the Germani as early as the 2nd or 3rd c.

The normal development in OE. would be nom. **pulwi, puli, pyle*, gen. **pulwes, pylwes.* Form-levelling gave from *pylwes* a new nom. *pylu*, whence ME. *pilwe*, mod. *pillow*; *pyle* was inflected *pyles*, and remained as ME. *pyle, pile, pele*, mod. dial. *pill, peel.* (See Napier in *Mod. Lang. Quarterly* 1897 Nov. 52.)]

A. Illustration of Forms.

α. 1–6 **pyle,** 4–5 **pile, pule,** 9 *dial.* **pill.**

c **893** K. ÆLFRED *Oros.* v. xi. §1 Mon..dyde ælces consules setl ane pyle hierre þonne hit ær wæs. *c* **1000** ÆLFRIC *Gram.* ix. (Z.) 38 *Cervical*, pyle. **1387** TREVISA *Higden* (Rolls) VII. 421 Under his pelewe [*MS. β.* pile; *γ.* pule; *Caxton* pyle]. **1502** *Privy Purse Exp. Eliz. of York* (1830) 65 For making of a pyle cloth. **1886** ELWORTHY *W. Som. Word-bk.* s.v. *Pill*, I never can't zlape way a soft pill.

β. 4 **pele,** 6 **pelle,** 8–9 **peel.**

13.. *S. Eng. Leg.* (MS. Bodl. 779) in Herrig *Archiv* LXXXII. 318/454 Nold he non oþer pele to legge his heued vppon. **1553** *Inv. Ch. Goods Staffs.* in *Ann. Lichfield* (1863) IV. 45 Itm. ij stolles, v fannes, xij pelles, ij chesables. **1746** *Exmoor Courtship* 428 (E.D.S.) Darning up of old blonkets, and rearting tha Peels. **1825** JENNINGS *Obs. Dial. W. Eng.* 170 Tha..gee me stra vor bed an peel!

γ. 1 **pylu,** 4–5 **pilewe, pilwe,** 5 **pylwe, pilowe, -ow,** (**pilwo, pilve, pyliwe, pilou, pilu**), 5–6 **pylow(e, pyllow(e, pillowe,** (**pillo(e, pilo,** 6–7 **pilla**), 6– **pillow.**

a **1100** in Napier *O.E. Glosses* 198/4 *Ceruical*, pylu. *c* **1374** CHAUCER *Troylus* III. 395 (444), He tornede on his pylwes [*v.rr.* pilwis, pilous] ofte. *Ibid.* v. 224 Saue a pilwe [*v.r.* pilwo] I fynde nought tenbrace. **1382** WYCLIF *Mark* iv. 38 He was..slepynge on a pilewe. *c* **1386** CHAUCER *Merch. T.* 760 Vnder his pilwe [*v.rr.* pilowe, pylow]. *c* **1420** LYDG. *Assembly of Gods* 12 To rowne with a pylow me semyd best tryacle. *c* **1440** *Promp. Parv.* 399/1 Pylwe (*P.* pyllowe), *pulvinar. c* **1460** *Towneley Myst.* xxx. 290 On sich pilus I me set. **1463** *Bury Wills* (Camden) 23 A greet pilve and a small pilve. **1482** *Nottingham Rec.* II. 322, v. pillois cum uno bolster. **1500** *Ibid.* III. 74, iij pillowes valent vj*d.* **1541** R. COPLAND *Guydon's Quest. Chirurg.* L iv, Called plumeceaulx or pylowes of fethers in frenche. **1573** etc. Pillow [see B. 1 b].

δ. 4–5 **pelewe,** 5 **pelouhe,** 5–6 **pelowe, pelow, pelloe,** 6 **pellow, pelo.**

c **1369** CHAUCER *Dethe Blaunche* 254 (MS. Fairf.) Many a pelowe [*v.r.* pilow] and euery bere Of clothe of raynes. **1387** TREVISA *Higden* (Rolls) VII. 421 Under his pelewe [**1432–50** tr. *Higden* pelowe]. *c* **1400** *Destr. Troy* 12613 Pres it to þe pelow. *c* **1430** LYDG. *Min. Poems* (Percy Soc.) 29 Thus may thi man at thi pelouhe appere. *c* **1485** *E.E. Misc.* (Warton Cl.) 18 Thy lusty pellois. **1526** TINDALE *Mark* iv. 38 A slepe on a pelowe. **1532** *Test. Ebor.* (Surtees) VI. 34 A blankett, a boulster, a pellow. **1536** in W. H. Turner *Select. Rec. Oxford* (1880) 135 A coverlet, pelloe, and tester. *a* **1544** *Lanc. Wills* (1860) II. 152, ij pelo berys. **1561** HOLLYBUSH *Hom. Apoth.* 14 b, Take a heade pelow.

B. Signification.

1. a. A support for the head in sleeping or reclining; *spec.* a cushion or case made of linen or the like, stuffed with feathers, down, or other soft material; especially as forming part of a bed.

Also applied to the bamboo or rattan frame, the block of wood with a concave or crescent-shaped top, etc., used by the natives of various countries, and to any object improvised for the same purpose.

c **897** K. ÆLFRED *Gregory's Past. C.* xix. 143 Wa ðæm þe willað under ælcne elnboȝan lecgean pyle & bolster under ælcne hneccan. *c* **1000** *Sax. Leechd.* I. 226 Leȝe him, nytendum, under his pyle. **1390** GOWER *Conf.* II. 103 Upon a fethrebed alofte He lith with many a pilwe of doun. **1474** CAXTON *Chesse* 21 She put in a pelowe of fethers a serteyn somme of money. **1480** —— *Chron. Eng.* v. (1520) 67/1 They put on his mouth a pilowe and stopped his breth. *a* **1548** HALL *Chron., Edw. V* 2 b, He caused hym self to bee raised vp with pillowes. **1605** SHAKS. *Lear* III. iv. 55 That hath laid Kniues vnder his Pillow. **1611** BIBLE *Gen.* xxviii. 18 And Iacob..tooke the stone that hee had put for his pillowes [COVERD. that he had layed vnder his heade] and set it vp for a pillar. **1762** GOLDSM. *Cit. W.* xiii, In that chair the Kings of England were crowned; you see also a stone underneath, and that stone is Jacob's pillow. **1765** H. WALPOLE *Let. to Earl of Hertford* 7 Apr., They flung pillows upon the question, and stifled it. **1768–74** TUCKER *Lt. Nat.* (1834) II. 619 It will be very difficult to get a man from his pillow..if he has nothing to do when he is up. **1809** *Med. Jrnl.* XXI. 318 The limb being supported by pillows in a relaxed position. **1860** TYNDALL *Glac.* I. xi. 71 Placing my bag for a pillow, he lay down. **1866** J. MARTINEAU *Ess.* I. 64 Coleridge ..slept with the *Observations on Man* under his pillow. **1884** SIR H. JOHNSTON *River Congo* xvi. 432 Many pretty little things are carved in wood:—pillows or head-rests are made, much like those used by the ancient Egyptians.

b. Phrase. *to take counsel of,* or *consult with, one's pillow*, etc.: to take a night to consider a matter of importance; to 'sleep upon' it.

1573 G. HARVEY *Letter-bk.* (Camden) 21 You counsel me to take counsel of mi pillow. **1633** *Battle of Lutzen* in *Harl. Misc.* (Malh.) IV. 197 [The Polonians] took counsel of the pillow, and..concluded to come to a treaty. **1709** STEELE *Tatler* No. 60 ¶1 [He] frequently consulted his Pillow to know how to behave himself on such important Occasions. **1800** *Proc. E. Ind. Ho.* in *Asiat. Ann. Reg.* 68/2 They contained surmises and circumstances of such a nature, that he should carry it with him to his pillow.

c. In various figurative uses.

c **1440** *Jacob's Well* 114 Slowthe makyth þe þe restyng place of þe deuyl, for þou art þe feendys pylwe. **1588** SHAKS. *Tit. A.* v. iii. 163 [He] Sung thee asleepe, his Louing Brest, thy Pillow. **1667** Flavel *Saint Indeed* (1754) 38 That soft pillow of creature-delights on which thou restedst before. **1771** *Junius Lett.* l. (1820) 261 You are the pillow upon which I am determined to rest all my resentments. **1817** Wolfe *Burial Sir J. Moore* v, As we..smoothed down his lonely pillow. **1889** *Sat. Rev.* 6 Apr. 414/2 He took it for granted that nobles and gentlemen who lived about the Court should one day lay their heads upon a bloody pillow.

d. Phrase. ***to sew pillows under people's elbows*** (etc.): to give a sense of false security.

1382 Wyclif *Ezek.* xiii. 18 Woo to hem that sewen to gidre cusshens vndir eche cubit of hoond, and maken pilewis vnder the heed of eche age, for to take soulis. **1560** Bible (Genev.) *ibid.*, Woe vnto the women that sowe pillowes vnder all arme holes. **1572** in Neal *Hist. Purit.* (1732) I. 285 'Tis no time to blanch or sew pillars under mens elbows. **1620** J. King *Serm. 24 Mar.* 45 When I come to reprove sinne, I shall sowe no pillowes. **1672** Wycherley *Love in Wood* I. i, No, Mrs. Joyner, you cannot sew pillows under folks' elbows;..you cannot tickle a trout to take him.

†**2.** A cushion. *Obs.*

c **1440** [see A. *y*]. **1466** in *Archæologia* (1887) L. I. 42 Item j pyllow of rede whyte and yollowe clothe of sylke wᵗ ymages and birdes. **1522** *Bury Wills* (Camden) 115 To the chyrche of Pakenham a pelow of blew sylke. **1566** *Eng. Ch. Furniture* (1866) 118 Item one litle pillowe which was accustomed to be laid vpon the altare. **1573–80** Baret *Alv.* P 374 A pillowe, or cushin, *puluinar*.

3. Applied to something padded; a pad.

a. The pad of a saddle; a pillion.

1607 Markham *Caval.* II. (1617) 258 When you haue placed..both your knees hard and firme vnder each of the fore-Pillowes of the Saddle. **1651** *Miller of Mansf.* 15 With pillows and Pannells. **1895** *Wales* Apr. 179/1 Went to yearly meeting at Hereford with a few others, Molly Lloyd riding on pillow behind him.

b. A padded or stuffed support or ground upon which bone-lace is made.

1781 Cowper *Truth* 318 Yon cottager, who weaves at her own door, Pillow and bobbins all her little store. **1864** *Spectator* 1446 The manner of making pillow lace... The 'pillow' is a round or oval board, stuffed so as to form a cushion, and placed upon the knees of the workwoman.

c. *U.S. slang.* A boxing-glove.

1894 *Outing* (U.S.) XXIV. 443/1 Piled on a little table were four as dirty and badly-stained 'pillows' as I had ever set eyes on.

4. In various technical applications: A block or support resembling a pillow in form or use: *spec.* **a.** *Naut.* The block of timber on which the inner end of a bowsprit rests. **b.** The 'truck' or circular piece of wood or metal fixed on the head of a pole or mast. **c.** *Arch.* (See quots.) **d.** A cross-piece of wood which supports the beam of a plough or the bed of a wagon: cf. bolster *sb.*¹ 3 a, e. **e.** *Mech.* A bearing of brass or bronze for the journal of a shaft. **f.** The socket of a pivot (Knight *Dict. Mech.* 1875).

1446 *Yatton Churchw. Acc.* (Som. Rec. Soc.) 84 It. payd for fellyng of a brasen pelewe for worspryng. **1474–5** in Swayne *Sarum Churchw. Acc.* (1896) 20 It' in castynge of pelewes for the iij grettyst bellys xis.

a. 1626 Capt. Smith *Accid. Yng. Seamen* 12 The boule spret, the pillow, the sturrop, the spret sayle. **1627** —— *Seaman's Gram.* iii. 16. **1688** R. Holme *Armoury* III. xv. (Roxb.) 36/2 The Pillow is that tymber on which the bolt-sprit beares at the coming out of the hull called the pillow of the bolt-sprit. **1769** Falconer *Dict. Marine* (1789), *Couche*, the pillow of a stay, or the piece of wood upon which it rests.

b. 1632 Lithgow *Trav.* IV. 154 Then hoysing him vp to the pillow or top of the tree, they let the rope flee loose, whence downe he falles.

c. 1664 Evelyn tr. *Freart's Archit.* 128 The Return [of the Volute] or Pillow betwixt the Abacus and Echinus resembles the side-plaited tresses of Women's haire. **1704** J. Harris *Lex. Techn.* I. s.v. *Voluta*, These Voluta's are more especially remarkable in the Ionick Capital, representing a kind of Pillow or Cushion laid between the Abacus and the Echinus. **1842–76** Gwilt *Archit.* Gloss., *Volute*, a spiral scroll which forms the principal feature of the capital of the Ionic order... The returns or sides are called *pulvinata* or pillows.

d. 1733 Tull *Horse-Hoeing Husb.* xxi. 301 Two Rows of Holes, whereby to raise or sink the Beam, by pinning up or down the Pillow..to increase or diminish the Depth of the Furrow. **1764** *Museum Rust.* I. cxiii. 479 A pin..through the fore bed, about one foot behind the upper pillow,..the other through the under pillow. **1813** T. Davis *Agric. Wilts* Gloss. 263 Parts of a Waggon..; Peel, the pillow over the axle.

e. 1814 R. Buchanan *Millwork* (1823) 547 The bearings on which gudgeons and journals rest and revolve, are sometimes termed pillows and frequently brasses.

5. A kind of plain fustian.

1839 Ure *Dict. Arts* 537 The common fustian..is known by the name of pillow. **1875** Knight *Dict. Mech.*, *Pillow*,.. a kind of fustian having a four-leaved twill.

6. *Geol.* A body of rock, esp. lava, likened to a pillow or filled sack in shape and usu. occurring with other similar bodies. Cf. *pillow lava, structure* below.

[**1890** *Q. Jrnl. Geol. Soc.* XLVI. 312 The structure is more commonly irregular, the masses resembling pillows or soft cushions pressed upon and against one another.] **1899** *Summary of Progress Geol. Survey U.K. 1898* 108 It shows the 'pillow' structure already referred to, some of the 'pillows' being a yard or more in diameter. **1944** C. A. Cotton *Volcanoes* xv. 290 Lava pillows are commonly three to four feet in diameter. **1955** Longwell & Flint *Introd. Physical Geol.* v. 72 We conclude that pillows result from immersion of hot lava in water. **1962** E. A. Vincent tr. *Rittmann's Volcanoes* ii. 71 The freshly formed pillows are in effect bladders filled with still-fluid lava, which roll down.. and pile up one above the other. **1971** I. G. Gass et al. *Understanding Earth* xxi. 302/2 Being erupted under water, the lava flows tend to segregate and to form accumulations of sub-cylindrical bodies called pillows.

7. *attrib.* and *Comb.*, as *pillow-habit, -linen, -making, -rest; pillow-nestling* adj.; **pillow-bar**: see quot.; **pillow-block**, a cradle or bearing to hold the boxes or brasses forming the journal-bearing of a shaft or roller; **pillow-book**, (*a*) a book suitable for reading in bed; freq. an erotic book; (occas. used as the title of such a book); (*b*) in Japan, a type of private journal or diary; **pillow coat, -cote** = pillow-case; **pillow-counsel**: cf. 1 b; **pillow cover** = pillow-case; **pillow-cup**, a cup or drink taken before going to bed, a 'night-cap'; **pillow-fight**, a fight with pillows (in a bedroom); also as *vb.*; **pillow-lace**, lace worked on a pillow (sense 3 b); **pillow lava** *Geol.*, lava exhibiting pillow structure; **pillow mound** *Archæol.* (see quots.); **pillow muff** = muff *sb.*² 1 a; **pillow-pipe**, a pipe smoked before going to bed; **pillow-sham**: see quot. 1879; **pillow-slip, -tie** = pillow-case; **pillow structure** *Geol.*, a rock structure in which numerous closely fitting 'pillows' are fused together, found in some lavas and attributed to eruption under water; (cf. sense 6 above); **pillow talk**, conversation, usu. of an intimate kind, held in bed; also as *vb.*; **pillow tank**, a collapsible rubber container used for storing large quantities of liquid; **pillow-word** (in Japanese verse): see quot. 1880.

1890 *Cent. Dict.*, **Pillow-bar*, the ground or filling of pillow-lace, consisting of irregular threads or groups of threads drawn from one part of the pattern to another. These bars may either be plain or have a minute pearl-edge. **1844** Stephens *Bk. Farm* II. 534 The axle of these wheels is 1¼ inch diameter,..and is in two lengths supported in *pillow-blocks bolted to the lower edge of the bars. **1882** *Rep. to Ho. Repr. Prec. Met. U.S.* 586 Pillow blocks for mining machinery shafts. **1906** N. G. R. Smith (*title*) The *Pillow-Book. *Ibid.* Pref., The pillow reader will surely find passages taken and left from the pillow books of his own election. **1907** *Daily Chron.* 5 July 3/4 When one thinks of it, Scott in verse is certainly a good pillow book. **1928** A. Waley *Pillow-Bk. of Sei Shōnagon* 21 The *Pillow-Book*.. consists partly of reminiscences, partly of entries in diary-form. *Ibid.* 24 Shōnagon protests, as do most diarists and makers of journals, that the *Pillow-Book* was intended for herself alone. **1960** *Ibid.* (rev. ed.) 16 To keep some kind of journal was a common practice of the day [*sc.* the 10th century]. The name Pillow-Book, *Makura no Sōshi*, was given at the time to notebooks in which stray impressions were recorded. **1963** 'Han Suyin' *Four Faces* 33 'Your blonde..is she a writer?' 'Pillow books.' **1967** *Spectator* 22 Dec. 782/3 Presumably one tries to write as well in a pillow-book as in a novel. **1968** *Guardian* 7 May 6/1 Around the walls were eleventh-century Indian temple sculptures, pillow books from Japan..and too many modern works. **1977** E. J. Trimmer et al. *Visual Dict. Sex* (1978) xxi. 222 Any erotic books can be pillow books if they have the right effect on the reader. **1534** *Inv.* in *Lett. & Pap. Hen. VIII*, LXXXIII. lf. 117b (P.R.O.), A bedstedyll' with a Fetherbed:..One pillowe with a *pillocote. **1600** in W. F. Shaw *Mem. Eastry* (1870) 226 Forty payer of sheetes..viij payer of pillow coates six payer of pillowes. **1651** in *Mayflower Descendant* (1908) X. 39, I give her the bed.. with two paire of sheets two pillows two paire of pillow coates. **1727** in *Ibid.* 15, I Give to my Granddaughter Mary Bangs A pillow-coat. **1573** G. Harvey *Letter-bk.* (Camden) 21, I am aferd al the *pillow counsel in Walden is scarc able to counsel to so hard a case. [**1644** in *Essex County, Mass. Probate Rec.* (1916) I. 41 Two Pilcovrs and two Payer of course sheets, 10s.] **1912** N. L. McClung *Black Creek Stopping-House* 113 There disappeared at the same time towels, *pillow-covers, and a few small tools. **1969** Widdowson & Halpert in Halpert & Story *Christmas Mumming in Newfoundland* 151 Pillowcovers were also worn, or a large sheet might be draped over the head, with holes cut for eyes, nose, and mouth. **1829** Scott *Anne of G.* xix, To hand round to the company a sleeping-drink or *pillow-cup, of distilled water, mingled with spices. **1871** L. M. Alcott *Little Men* i. 16 We always allow one *pillow-fight Saturday night. **1892** 'Mark Twain' *Amer. Claimant* xiii. 119 They generally wound up with a pillow fight, in which they banged each other over the head, and threw the pillows in all directions. **1903** T. Roosevelt *Lett. to his Children* (1919) 69 The pillow fight raged up and down the hall. **1904** Lloyd George in *Westm. Gaz.* 8 Jan. 9/2 It was too much of a pillow-fight... There was a great show of effort and of striking without very much damage done. **1939** C. Isherwood *Goodbye to Berlin* 268 Two young men were pillow-fighting with cushions. *a* **1953** E. O'Neill *More Stately Mansions* (1965) I. iii. 52 We had a pillow fight. **1960** L. Hellman *Toys in Attic* III. 66 Shall we have a pillow fight or make fudge? **1976** *Ulverston* (Cumbria) *News* 3 Dec. 4/4 Gary White, of the Barrow Sailing Club was the winner of the pillow fight on the pole. **1858** Simmonds *Dict. Trade*, **Pillow-lace*, lace worked by hand on a small cushion or pillow. **1869** Mrs. Palliser *Lace* vii. (ed. 2) 87 That pillow lace was first made in the Low Countries, we have the evidence of contemporary paintings. **1903** *Amer. Geologist* XXXII. 67 Immediately above the lava sheet is the *pillow lava, proved to be about 60 meters in thickness. **1971** I. G. Gass et al. *Understanding Earth* xxi. 302/2 The presence of such pillow lavas in ancient rock sequences..is unequivocal evidence of sub-aqueous eruption. **1977** A. Hallam *Planet Earth* 96 Ridges or cones of granular glassy rocks and pillow lavas result from the subglacial eruption through fissures or vents respectively. **1928** Crawford & Keiller *Wessex from Air* 23 At High Beech the rabbits use the *pillow-mounds very extensively. **1932** *Field Archæol.* (Ordnance Survey) 5 Low, flat mounds of earth have been noticed. They are called Pillow-mounds, and appear to be of a much later date [than long barrows]. **1963** E. S. Wood *Collins Field Guide Archæol.* II. ii. 233 *Pillow mounds*, these are low, oblong mounds..2 to 3 ft. high; most have a shallow ditch round them. **1908** *Westm. Gaz.* 24 Dec. 15/2 Her furs were cinnamon fox with a bunch of violets in the *pillow muff. **1832** L. Hunt *Ariadne Waking* 8 Her *pillow-nestling cheek. **1752** Fielding *Amelia* III. ii, I sat with him, whilst he smoaked his *pillow pipe, as the phrase is. **1871** Napheys *Prev. & Cure Dis.* II. ii. 429 There should be in every sick-room two *pillow-rests. **1871** 'S. May' *Prudy keeping House* 43 As she had decided to call herself Mother Hubbard, she made an ample cap, by folding a '*pillow-sham', and putting two of its ruffled edges around her face for a double border. **1879** Webster Suppl., *Pillow-sham*, a covering, usually of embroidered linen, laid over the pillow of a bed when it is not in use. **1889** *Century Mag.* XXXVII. 786 Pillow-shams ..neatly folded out of the way. **1914** Kipling *Lett. Travel* (1920) 244 Our great National Policy of co-educational housekeeping! Ham-frills and pillow-shams. **1926** *Chicago Tribune* 11 Sept. 2/2 Then there was the pillow-sham holder. **1947** *Christian Sci. Monitor* 15 Jan. 6/5 And pillow shams! Like the splashes, they were painstakingly worked in red outline. **1963** G. H. Thomson *Crocus Country* xvi. 100 The pillow-shams or covers..were all crisp and white. **1975** *New Yorker* 17 Nov. 134/2 To bring a woman's brass bed into line with her nightshirt, there are antique pillow-shams, often copiously trimmed with lace, eyelet, and tucks. **1828** *Craven Gloss.* (ed. 2), **Pillow-slip*, *Pillow-bear*, the cover or case of a pillow. **1874** J. A. Mair *Handbk. Proverbs* 461 *Pillow-slip*, pillow-case. **1883** *Longm. Mag.* Apr. 648 The wife will rise..and with pillow-slip in hand will gather the mushrooms that have grown with the night. **1920** T. S. Eliot *Ara Vos Prec* 22 Pushing the framework of the bed And clawing at the pillow slip. [**1897** A. Geikie *Anc. Vocanoes G.B.* I. iii. 26 Some basic lavas on flowing into water or into a watery silt have assumed a remarkable spheroidal sack-like or pillow-like structure.] *Ibid.* xiv. 244 Some of the diabase-masses display the *pillow-structure and amygdaloidal texture. **1930** Peach & Horne *Geol. Scotl.* 142 Pillow-structure is well developed in some of the volcanic rocks, the chilled margins of the pillows and the concentric arrangement of the vesicles being marked features. **1971** I. G. Gass et al. *Understanding Earth* xiii. 165/1 There may be some instances (e.g. pillow structures in lavas) when igneous and metamorphic rocks yield important information. **1977** A. Hallam *Planet Earth* 188 Similar pillow structures characterize basaltic lavas erupted on the present ocean floors. **1939** Joyce *Finnegans Wake* I. 57 Mid *pillow talk and chithouse chat, on Marlborough Green as through Molesworth Fields. **1971** *Femina* (Bombay) 16 Apr. 7/2 Is your husband out pillow-talking with some bright young doll? **1971** *Daily Tel.* 17 Dec. 9/6 Thanks to a bug under the bed, a man down in the basement..is putting on tape all Ingrid's pillow talk, not to mention her sighs and squeals. **1973** R. Thomas *If you can't be Good* (1974) xii. 109 She told the senator. Pillow talk, I would think. **1975** *Times* 23 Aug. 4/7 Mrs Ford..makes it plain she gets her views across to Mr Ford in what she calls 'Pillow talk'. **1951** *Sci. News Let.* 10 Feb. 93/1 A new synthetic rubber-nylon '*pillow' tank for gasoline that lies flat on the ground and provides 10,000 gallons of storage in ten minutes will soon be servicing U.S. fighting tanks and trucks at the front. **1959** *Post & Times Herald* (Washington) 5 Aug. B7 (*caption*) The pillow tanks can be used to transport virtually all types of liquid on trucks, railroad cars and barges. When not in use, the collapsible containers can be rolled up and packed in a box. **1962** *Engineering* 26 Jan. 144 An example of the collapsible pillow tank principle, in the transport of water. **1847–78** Halliwell, *Pillowbere*, a pillow-case... Also called a pillow-slip or *pillow-tie. **1877** B. H. Chamberlain in *Trans. Asiat. Soc. Japan* V. 80 A '*Pillow-Word'. **1880** —— *Classic. Poetry Japanese* Introd. 5 There are..some usual additions to the means at the Japanese versifier's command. They are three in number, and altogether original, viz., what are styled 'Pillow-words', 'Prefaces', and 'Pivots'. The 'Pillow words' are meaningless expressions which are prefixed to other words merely for the sake of euphony. Almost every word of note has some 'Pillow-word' on which it may, so to speak, rest its head. **1899** *Eng. Hist. Rev.* Apr. 225 The rhymeless metre..is eked out by pillow-words.

'pillow, *v.* [f. prec. sb.]

1. *trans.* To rest or place (the head, etc.) on or as on a pillow; to lay down on a pillow. Also *fig.*

1629 Milton *On Nativity* 231 So when the Sun in bed,.. Pillows his chin upon an Orient wave. **1796** Southey *Rudiger* xxii, And Rudiger upon his arm Pillow'd the little child. *c* **1830** E. Irving in *Gd. Words* Jan. (1884) 46/2 Pillowing their hopes upon something else than the sanctification..which the Gospel hath wrought. **1832** R. & J. Lander *Exped. Niger* I. i. 7 He appeared in deep reflection,..pillowing his head on his hand.

b. Of a thing: To serve as a pillow for.

1801 Southey *Thalaba* IV. xii, Wrapt in his mantle Thalaba reposed, His loose right arm pillowing his easy head. **1819** Byron *Juan* II. cxiv, And her transparent cheek, all pale and warm, Pillow'd his death-like forehead.

c. In *pa. pple.* Laid on, or as on, a pillow.

1794 Coleridge *Lines on Friend who died of Frenzy Fever* 50 'Mid fitful starts I nod, And fain would sleep, though pillowed on a clod! **1818** Mrs. Iliff *Poems Sev. Occas.* (ed. 2) 29 Languor and pain confess thy charm, When pillow'd on thy friendly arm.

2. *intr.* To rest the head on or as on a pillow.

1800 W. Taylor in *Monthly Mag.* VIII. 890 Like him, I pillow on the cheek, And nestle near the languid eye. *a* **1820** J. R. Drake *Culprit Fay* 55 Thou shalt pillow on my breast While heavenly breathings float around.

3. *trans.* To support or prop *up* with pillows.

1839 Sir J. Paget in *Mem. & Lett.* v. 106 On my arm he came, and breakfasted with me in his sitting-room, blanketted and pillowed. **1850** *Life H. Heugh* xxvii. (1852) 486 He wished to be pillowed-up more.

Hence **'pillowed** (-əʊd) *ppl. a.* (also in *Arch.* [f. pillow *sb.*] = cushioned 3); **'pillowing** *ppl. a.*

1832 L. Hunt *To T. L. H.* 9 Thy sidelong pillowed meekness. *a* **1851** Moir *Unknown Grave* x, With pillowing daisies for his bed. **1861** Geo. Eliot *Silas M.* xii, An effort to regain the pillowing arm. **1882** Ogilvie (Annandale), *Pillowed*..2. In *arch.* a term applied to a rounded frieze. Called also *Pulvinated.*

pillow, -e, obs. variants of pilau.

pillow-bere (ˈpɪləʊbɪə(r)). *arch.* Forms: first element: see PILLOW; second, 4- -beer, 6–8 bear, (6–7 -beare), 6- -ber, -bier, (6 -beier), 5- -bere: see BEAR *sb.*[4] (Also 7 phillaber, 8 pillyber.) [f. PILLOW *sb.* + BEAR *sb.*[4]] = PILLOW-CASE.

c **1386** CHAUCER *Prol.* 694 Ne was ther swich another Pardoner For in his male he hadde a pilwe beer, Which þat he seyde, was oure lady veyl. **1480** *Wardr. Acc. Edw. IV* (1830) 131 Pilowe beres off fustian unstuffed iiij. **1503** in *Calr. Doc. rel. Scotl.* (1888) IV. 341 [For the Queen of Scots ..] 2 'pilloberes' [of an ell long, at 2 s. an ell]. **1519** *Maldon, Essex, Liber B.* lf. 160 (MS.), iiii pillows, iiii pillow-bers, ii coverletts. **1558** *Lanc. Wills* (1857) I. 176 Sixteyne pillew beares. **1561** HOLLYBUSH *Hom. Apoth.* 25 Putte thys into a softe sack or pilow bier. **1564** *Wills & Inv. N.C.* (Surtees) II. 219 A pilleber having Iesus sued vpon ytt. **1566** *Eng. Ch. Furniture* (1866) 81 A crosse crosse (*sic*) clothe, a pillowe beier, were sold the yeare 1560. **1598** MARSTON *Pygmal.* viii. 125 And makes him wish for such a Pillow-beare [*rime* appear]. **1640** in MCDOWALL *Hist. Dumfries* (1867) 405 Holland shirts and phillabers..damask table-cloths. **1683** in *Bedfordshire N. & Q.* (1889) II. 236, I giue to my goddaughter a pair of fine pillowbears. **1743** *Phil. Trans.* XLII. 366 Numbers of Pillows, each with its Pillow-bier. **1771** SMOLLETT *Humph. Cl.* 2 Apr. Let. iii, Take care of.. the pillyber. **1776** ANSTEY *Election Ball* Wks. (1808) 222 An obstinate bolster Which I think I have seen you attempting, my dear, In vain to cram into a small pillowbeer. **1885** EDNA LYALL *In Golden Days* II. x. 211 A pillow-beer—friend of many a weary journey—lay hard by.

'pillow-case. The washable case or covering, usually of white linen or cotton cloth, which is drawn over a pillow.

a **1745** SWIFT *Direct. Servants* viii, When you put a clean pillow-case on your lady's pillow. **1857** WOOD *Com. Obj. Sea Shore* 57 The general shape of the egg [of the dog-fish] has been aptly compared to a pillow-case, with strings tied to the corners. **1869** E. A. PARKES *Pract. Hygiene* (ed. 3) 496 The use of bedding (pillows and pillow-cases).

pillowing (ˈpɪləʊɪŋ), *a. rare.* [f. PILLOW *sb.* + -ING[2].] Pillow-making.

1924 *Times Trade & Engin. Suppl.* 29 Nov. 247/2 Bleaching fabrics such as pillowing, art, or handkerchief linens.

'pillowless, *a.* [See -LESS.] Without a pillow.

a **1847** ELIZA COOK *Song of Beggars* vi, We On our pillowless couch sleep as soundly as he.

pillowy (ˈpɪləʊɪ), *a.* [f. PILLOW *sb.* + -Y.] Having the quality of, or resembling, a pillow; soft; yielding. Also *fig.*

1798 SOTHEBY tr. *Wieland's Oberon* (1826) I. 181 Soft on the pillowy moss he seats his bride. **1805–6** WORDSWORTH *Prelude* (1959) III. 99 From these I turned to travel with the shoal Of more unthinking natures, easy minds And pillowy. **1821** SOUTHEY *Vis. Judgem.* i. 12 The clouds had gather'd above them High in the middle air, huge, purple, pillowy masses. **1871** R. ELLIS *Catullus* lxiv. 88 Pure from a maiden's couch, from a mother's pillowy bosom.

pilluck, var. PILLOCK.

pillulary, pillule: see PILULARY, PILULE.

pillwort (ˈpɪlwɜːt). [f. PILL *sb.*[2] + WORT: so called from its small globular involucres.] Any plant of the cryptogamous genus *Pilularia*, esp. the British species *P. globulifera*.

1861 MISS PRATT *Flower. Pl.* VI. 156 Pill-wort. Capsules globular, 4-celled, each cell containing two different kinds of bodies. **1864** T. MOORE *Brit. Ferns*, etc. 105 The pillwort or pepper-grass..is a small creeping plant with grassy leaves, growing usually in the shallow margins of lakes and pools where it is occasionally overflowed; but sometimes occurring entirely submerged.

pillyber, pillycane, pillyon, obs. forms of PILLOW-BERE, PELICAN *sb.*, PILLION *sb.*[2]

† **pilmall,** obs. (erroneous) var. of PALL-MALL.

1672 W. RAMSEY *Gentlem. Comp.* IV. 133 Exercises which are used abroad that may befit a Gentleman..are Pilmall, Gauff, these by striking the Ball exercise the whole Man.

pilo, obs. form of PILLOW.

pilo, piloe, obs. variants of PILAU.

pilo- (ˈpaɪləʊ), combining form of L. *pilus* hair, as in **pilo'cystic** *a.*: see quot.; **'piloerection,** the erection or bristling of hair or fur; **'piloerector,** an agent that causes piloerection; **pilo-'fatty** *a.*, in *pilo-fatty cyst* = pilocystic tumour; **pilo'motor** *a.*, applied to those nerves which produce movement of the hairs; more widely, involved in or pertaining to the movement of hair by bodily processes; also as *sb.*, a pilomotor nerve or muscle; **pilo'nidal** *a.* [L. *nīd-us* nest]: see quot.; **pilo-se'baceous** *a.*, applied to sebaceous glands that open into hair-follicles.

1893 *Syd. Soc. Lex.*, **Pilocystic tumour*, a dermoid cyst, so called because of its often containing hairs. **1938** J. F. FULTON *Physiol. Nervous Syst.* xiii. 248 The most important mechanisms of heat production and preservation are shivering, mobilization of carbohydrate reserve, vasoconstriction, *piloerection, increase in heart rate, and elevation of metabolic activity. **1958** *Jrnl. Investigative Dermatol.* XXX. 107/2 Injection of..epinephrine regularly produced 'goose-flesh' and piloerection. **1974** CARLSON & HSIEH in N. B. Slonim *Environmental Physiol.* iv. 67/2 Fur-bearing animals can greatly increase the insulation of their outer coat by piloerection. **1977** RUMBAUGH & GILL in D. M. Rumbaugh *Language Learning by Chimpanzee* ix. 175 Lana's response was to hoot with apparent agitation; she also displayed piloerection and a furrowed brow. **1946** A. KUNTZ *Autonomic Nervous Syst.* (ed. 3) xv. 327 Intracutaneous administration of acetylcholine..elicits strong fleeting *pilo-erector activity. **1965** *Jrnl. Investigative Dermatol.* LXIV. 86/1 The vasoconstrictor and pilo-erector effect in man of noradrenaline was compared with those of ..dopamine. **1847–9** *Todd's Cycl. Anat.* IV. 142/2 Teeth are frequently found in *pilo-fatty cysts. **1891** LANGLEY & SHERRINGTON in *Jrnl. Physiol.* XII. 278 It will be convenient to have a short name for the nerve- fibres, stimulation of which causes contraction of the erectores pilorum. We shall call them '*pilo-motor' fibres on the analogy of 'vaso-motor' fibres. **1892** *Ibid.* XIII. 701 This class of fibres consists of the eye-fibres of the sympathetic. Langley has shewn this for cat and rabbit, and they often in monkey extend a segment higher than do the pilo-motors for the scalp. **1893** *Athenæum* 18 Feb. 223/2 Observations upon Pilomotor Nerves. **1899** *Allbutt's Syst. Med.* VIII. 86 There are the waves of goose-skin passing over the body due to stimulation of the pilo-motor nerves. **1909** *Ibid.* XXXVIII. 174 The paralysis of the pilo-motor mechanism is one of the ..results of nerve section. **1927** *Ibid.* LXIV. 98 Shallow incisions..through the layers which contain the insertions of the pilomotor muscles into the hair roots. **1932** *Amer. Jrnl. Physiol.* CII. 30 The pilomotors reacted..to single shocks. **1948** A. BRODAL *Neurol. Anat.* xi. 394 The hypothalamus is probably concerned in integrating the activity of the pilomotors with other autonomic functions. **1880** R. M. HODGES in *Boston Med. & Surg. Jrnl.* CIII. 486/1 For the development of this rather singular lesion, to which..I venture to give the name of *pilo-nidal (*pilus*, a hair, *nidus*, a nest) sinus, the following elements are necessary:—(1.) The presence of a congenital coccygeal dimple. (2.) Abundant pilous development...(3.) Insufficient attention to cleanliness. **1893** *Syd. Soc. Lex.*, *Pilonidal sinus*, a sinus occasionally found in the human subject as an abnormality, opening near the tip of the coccyx, and containing hair. **1956** *Lancet* 15 Dec. 1244 An interdigital sinus behaves like a fistula-in-ano or a pilonidal sinus elsewhere... These pilonidal sinuses appear to be acquired and may be caused by loose hairs, foreign bodies, or inspissated secretions being drawn into small abrasions or acne pits in the skin. **1957** S. L. ROBBINS *Textbk. Path.* xxx. 1186/2 Anatomically, these lesions consist sometimes of sinus tracts, pilonidal sinus, communicating with the surface through minute (probe diameter) pores; at other times well developed epidermal-lined cysts, pilonidal cyst, that may or may not communicate with the surface. **1964** D. E. SMITH in L. V. Ackerman *Surg. Path.* xxvi. 1063 In their simplest form pilonidal sinuses or cysts are tracts lined by epidermis that extend beneath the skin toward the dura. **1899** *Allbutt's Syst. Med.* VIII. 880 The orifices of the *pilo-sebaceous glands.

pilocarpine (paɪləʊˈkɑːpaɪn). *Chem.* [f. mod.L. *Pilocarpus*, generic name in Bot. (f. Gr. πῖλος wool, felt + καρπ-ός fruit) + -INE[5].] A white crystalline or amorphous alkaloid, $C_{11}H_{16}N_2O_2$, obtained from the leaves of Jaborandi, *Pilocarpus pinnatifolius* (or other species), used in pharmacy. So **pilo'carpene**, a volatile oil, and **pilo'carpidine**, an alkaloid, from the same source.

1875 H. C. WOOD *Therap.* (1879) 517 Pilocarpin is superior to jaborandi in the certainty of its action. **1880** *Libr. Univ. Knowl.* (N.Y.) VIII. 201 According to Hardy the oil consists of a hydrocarbon, *pilocarpene*. **1881** WATTS *Dict. Chem.* 3rd Suppl. s.v. *Jaborandi*. **1887** *Athenæum* 8 Oct. 473/2 The synthetical pilocarpidine thus obtained..is converted into pilocarpine. **1893** *Syd. Soc. Lex.* s.v. *Pilocarpus*, The leaflets contain a volatile oil, and the alkaloids, pilocarpine, jaborine, pilocarpidine, and jaboridine.

† **'pilole.** *Obs. rare.* [f. PILL *sb.*[2] + *-ole*, dim. suff. Cf. F. *pilule*, It. *pillola*.] A small ball, a pill.

14.. *Noble Bk. Cookry* (Napier 1882) 25 Mele it well and mak ther of small piloles.

pilolite (ˈpaɪləʊlaɪt). *Min.* [f. Gr. πῖλος felt + -LITE.] A name under which Heddle has included much of the Mountain-leather and Mountain-cork formerly referred to asbestos.

1878 M.F.HEDDLE in *Min. Mag.* II. 206.

pilón (piːˈləʊn). *South-western U.S.* Also **pilon.** [Mexican Sp., a. Sp. *pilón* sugar-loaf, mortar.] A free gift given when a purchase is made or an account paid; = LAGNIAPPE. Also *fig.*

1892 *Dialect Notes* I. 251 *Pilón*.., the gratuity given by merchants to customers, whenever accounts are settled. **1932** H. W. BENTLEY *Dict. Spanish Terms in Eng.* 180 *Pilon*, ..a favor; a gratuity. Literally the word signifies a small cone-shaped cake of sugar. It may be conjectured that a small *dulce* of this sort constituted the *pilon* originally. **1947** R. BEDICHEK *Adventures with Texas Naturalist* vii. 75 It [*sc.* yaupon]..stands drought, resents coddling, and throws in, as a *pilon* to its domesticator, decorative red berries in the fall and winter. **1962** E. B. ATWOOD *Regional Vocab. Texas* iii. 68 The custom of giving something extra with a purchase (or when a bill is paid) is firmly established in the United States. .. Most areas lack a specific word for this sort of gift. In the Southwest, the West, and part of Central Texas *pilón* is very well known and widely used. *Ibid.* vii. 124 (*heading*) Lexicographical pilón. *Ibid.* 128 Modern stores are becoming less and less inclined to give pilón.

‖ **pilori** (pɪˈlɔːrɪ). [Abbreviation of the specific name.] More fully *pilori-rat*, the Cuban hutiaconga, *Capromys pilorides*.

1774 GOLDSM. *Nat. Hist.* (1862) I. VI. i. 454 The Pilori is a native of the West India Islands: and has a short tail, as thick at one end as the other. **1836** *Encycl. Brit.* (ed. 7) XIV. 133/1 One of the largest and most destructive rats..is the *pilori*, or musk-rat of the Antilles (*Mus pilorides*).

pilory, obs. form of PILLORY.

pilose (ˈpaɪləʊs), *a.* [ad. L. *pilōs-us* hairy, f. *pilus* hair.] Covered with hair, esp. with soft flexible hair; hairy; pilous.

1753 CHAMBERS *Cycl. Supp.* s.v. *Leaf*, *Pilose Leaf*, one whose surface is furnished with hairs so large and long, as to be distinguishable by the eye separately. **1819** G. SAMOUELLE *Entomol. Compend.* 150 Pilose antennæ. **1826** KIRBY & SP. *Entomol.* III. xxx. 175 Of the pilose larvæ some ..have a few scattered hairs. **1877** COUES & ALLEN *N. Amer. Rod.* 865 The soles..in some specimens densely pilose, and in others nearly naked.

b. *Comb.* **pilose-hispid** *a.*, rough with hairs; **pilose-setaceous** *a.*, having pilose setæ.

1847 W. E. STEELE *Field Bot.* 129 *Echium violaceum.* Stem erect, branched, diffuse, pilose-hispid. *Ibid.* 13 *Centauridæ.* .. Pappus..; second row longest, pilose-setaceous.

‖ **pilo'sella.** *Obs.* [mod. or med.L., dim. of *pilōsa*, fem. of *pilōsus* hairy.] A name given by the herbalists to two Composite plants with pilose or woolly leaves, viz. Great Pilosella, the Mouse-ear Hawkweed, *Hieracium Pilosella*, and Small Pilosella, *Gnaphalium dioicum*.

1578 LYTE *Dodoens* I. lx. 87 The great is now called in Latine *Pilosella maior*: in English also Great Pilosella. **1640** BP. HALL *Chr. Moder.* II. xvi. 170 It is not for Christians to be like unto Thistles, or Teazels, which a man cannot touch without pricking his fingers; but rather to Pitosella [*sic*], or Mouse-eare,..which is soft and silken.

pilosity (paɪˈlɒsɪtɪ). [f. L. type **pilōsitās*, f. *pilōsus* hairy, PILOSE: see -ITY.] The quality or state of being pilose; hairiness.

1605 BACON *Adv. Learn.* II. vii. §7 That pilositie is incident to orifices of moisture. **1626** —— *Sylva* §680 Beasts are more Hairie than Men;..And the Plumage of Birds exceedeth the Pilositie of Beasts. **1830** *Blackw. Mag.* XXVIII. 466, I allude to the pilosity of chin. **1871** DARWIN *Desc. Man* II. II. xx. 378 *note*, Observations were..made on the pilosity of 2129 black and coloured soldiers, whilst they were bathing.

pi'loso-, used as combining form of L. *pilōsus* hairy, PILOSE, as in **piloso-'fimbriate** *a.*, fringed with soft hairs; **piloso-'hispid** *a.*, having somewhat stiff hairs.

1806 GALPINE *Brit. Bot.* 17 Viola, L[eaves] cordate, piloso-hispid. **1887** W. PHILLIPS *Brit. Discomycetes* 252 *Lachnella acutipila*... Margin piloso-fimbriate.

pilot (ˈpaɪlət), *sb.* Also 6 pilotte, pylotte, -lett, -late, 6–7 pilote, pylot(e, 6–8 pilate, 7 pilat. [a. early mod.F. *pillotte* (1529 in Hatz.-Darm.), *pillot, pilot* (1530), mod.F. *pilote*, ad. It. *pilota*, *-to* (so Sp., Pg. *piloto* med.L. *pilōtus*, 1486 in Rymer XII. 300), supposed to be altered, perh. by popular etymology, from It. *pedota* (Florio), *pedotta* (Du Cange), in OF. *pedot* (*Geste des Chiprois* c 1500). Cf. It. *pedoto, pedotto* rudder, steersman, beacon. (Breusing (*Niederdeutsches Jahrb.* V.) suggests ad. late Gr. *πηδώτης steersman, f. πηδόν an oar, in pl. rudder.)

Du. *piloot*, in 16–17th c. *pijlloot* (Kilian), *pijloot* (Hexham), mod.Ger. *pilot*, are from Fr.]

1. a. One who steers or directs the course of a ship; a steersman, helmsman; *spec.* a person duly qualified to steer ships into and out of a harbour, or wherever the navigation requires local knowledge.

1530 PALSGR. 254/1 Pylotte that governeth a shippe, *pilot*. **1549** THOMAS *Hist. Italie* 74 When any shippe cometh in, she taketh fyrst pilottes to sounde the waie. *a* **1568** *Satir. Poems Reform.* xlvi. 3 Quhat pylett takis my schip in chairge. **1578** T. N. tr. *Conq. W. India* 4 His pilote was not expert in that nauigation. **1581** W. STAFFORD *Exam. Compl.* i. (1876) 26 What Ship can bee longe safe from wracke, where euery man will take vpon him to bee a Pylate? **1624** CAPT. SMITH *Virginia* I. 1 King Henry the eight..made him [S. Cabot] grand Pilate of England. *c* **1645** HOWELL *Lett.* I. xxvii. (1650) 44 Ther are Pylots, that in small Shallops, are ready to steer all ships that passe. *a* **1694** TILLOTSON *Serm.* lii. (1742) IV. 490 An experienced pilate and seaman. **1719** DE FOE *Crusoe* (1840) II. i. 8, I was like a ship without a pilot, that could only run before the wind. **1847** JAMES *Convict* ii, A large shaggy great coat commonly at that time used by pilots.

b. *transf.* and *fig.* One who or that which serves as a guide through some unknown place or through a dangerous or difficult course of affairs; a guide; a leader in the hunting-field; esp. a skilled guide employed on land.

1593 SHAKS. *Lucr.* 279 Desire my Pilot is, Beautie my prise. **1653** A. WILSON *Jas. I* 161 The Pilots of the Commonwealth had an eye to the dangers that lay in the way. **1672** J. PAINE *Jrnl.* in *Publ. Colonial Soc. Mass.* (1917) XVIII. 189 Wee mett with ye Riuor Hosick wch wee Set or corse for by Direction of or Indian Pilate and ther..wee dismounted. **1710** T. BUCKINGHAM in S. Knight *Jrnls.* (1825) 94 Mr. Christophers and myself, having provided horses and a pilot, set out for Boston. **1800–24** CAMPBELL *To Sir F. Burdett* i, For forty years the pilot of reform! **1802** G. CANNING *Song* in *Lyra Elegant.* (1867) No. 199 Here's to the pilot [i.e. Pitt] that weather'd the storm! **1847** J. PALMER *Jrnl. Trav. Rocky Mts.* 15 In case the company would elect him pilot, and pay him five hundred dollars, *in advance*, he would bind himself to pilot them to fort Vancouver. **1883** MRS. KENNARD *Right Sort* ix, To take compassion upon an unprotected female, and constitute himself her pilot for a few days. **1887** MISS BRADDON *Like & Unlike* xi, He was my pilot through some of our best runs. **1927** *Dialect Notes* V.

459 *Pilot*, the boy who accompanies a blind beggar. The American 'Lazarillo'. **1936** I. L. Idriess *Cattle King* vii. 63 A squatter was overlanding with a big mob of stock, his wagons loaded with a year's supplies. He had taken up country on the 'blind', without ever having seen it... He needed a pilot to show him the waterholes on his own country.

c. Short for *pilot boat, car, engine, light*.

1883 F. M. A. Roe *Army Lett.* (1909) 313 It requires two engines to pull even the passenger trains up, and when the divide is reached the 'pilot' is uncoupled and run down ahead. **1896** *Daily News* 16 Nov. 4/3 It was..ten minutes past one when Mr. Lawson, in his pilot, came in, having repaired on the way. **1904** *Westm. Gaz.* 1 Sept. 3/1 Uncertainty..as to whether the pilot was going through with the train or intending to pass to the siding. **1964** E. Berckman *Simple Case of Ill-Will* x. 98, I smelled *gas*!.. There's a pilot on your cooker, an open flame. **1973** R. L. Simon *Big Fix* (1974) vi. 48 All the lights were out except for a couple of pilots beneath the tape decks.

d. One who controls an aircraft, balloon, spacecraft, or the like during flight, usu. a person duly qualified to do so. ***automatic pilot***: see automatic *a.* 2.

1848 *Sporting Life* 12 Aug. 289/1 The aëronautic race was conducted by Lieutenant Gale and Professor Gypson,..the latter acting as the pilot of the Royal Albion. **1851** *Illustr. London News* 13 Sept. 330/2 We..threw out more ballast.., and descended..in a..field. I fell.., and the car over us all; while 'the pilot who had weathered the storm' was thrown with..violence from among the cordage. **1852** *Ibid.* 18 Sept. 224/3 'Sit still, all of you, I say!' roared our pilot, as he saw some one endeavouring to leave the car. *Ibid.*, Indeed, long shall we all remember the pleasant night we passed with the old ethereal pilot on his 500th ascent with the Royal Nassau Balloon. **1899** *English Mechanic* 14 July 480/3 The new machine..is said to be able to carry in its car as many as six men and travel easily at a rate of 100 miles an hour under the absolute mastery of its engineer and pilot. **1907** *Navigating the Air* (Aero Club Amer.) 247 In order to qualify as a pilot one must make ten ascensions, one of which must be made at night, and two of which must be made alone. **1913**, etc. [see *air pilot* s.v. air *sb.*[1] B. III. 4]. **1916**, etc. [see fly *v.*[1] 1 g]. **1936**, etc. [see *bush pilot* s.v. bush *sb.*[1] 11]. **1953** 'N. Shute' *In Wet* v. 136 This was the first Ceres that had visited Edmonton, and a small crowd of pilots and R.C.A.F. officers gathered around it on the tarmac. **1962** *Into Orbit* 243 *Backup pilot*, an Astronaut who..may go on the mission himself if the Astronaut named as pilot is unable to make the flight at the last minute. **1974** *Daily Tel.* 14 June 8/4 Among the pilots flying this weekend will be Charles Dollfus, 83-year-old leading French balloonist who has been flying since 1911. **1978** *Dumfries Courier* 13 Oct. 9/1 He..would like other hang-glider 'pilots' in the area to contact him with a view to starting a Dumfriesshire Hang-Gliding Club.

e. ***to drop the pilot***: to abandon a trustworthy adviser.

After a cartoon by J. Tenniel in *Punch*, 20 Mar., 1890 depicting the recent dismissal of Bismarck from the Chancellorship of Germany by William II.

1926 G. M. Trevelyan *Hist. Eng.* iv. vi. 456 In face of these signs Charles decided to 'drop the pilot'. It was indeed tempting to make a scapegoat of Clarendon. **1958** J. Raymond *England's on Anvil!* 149 The Kaiser is aged thirty. He has been on the throne a year and is already preparing to 'drop the pilot', get rid of Bismarck. **1979** D. Gurr *Troika* vi. 32 Khruschev'll be dropping that pilot before they clear the river.

f. Short for *pilot film, plant, programme*, etc.: see sense 8 b below.

1962 *Listener* 18 Oct. 633/2 A little tighter and tauter and the production would have looked for all the world like a pilot for a new series. **1971** M. Babson *Cover-up Story* xiv. 153, I came by..to talk over a few points before we started filming the pilot tomorrow. **1971** *Guardian* 26 Feb. 13/4 Sir Lew Grade..gave an uncharacteristically terse 'no comment' when asked if he had made any pilots in the recent past. **1971** *Inside Kenya Today* Mar. 9/1 If this pilot is successful an important export oriented mining enterprise will be established. **1973** *Nation* (Barbados) 16 Dec. 2/2 He has recently signed to be..a star in a pilot for a television series which is being written by Everett Chambers. **1975** *Radio Times* 30 Aug.–5 Sept. 14/3 It was only a pilot which would not be seen by the general public. **1977** *Time Out* 17–23 June 16/2 Thames' fourth telefilm in three days. Repeat of the pilot for a never-made series about a big city newspaper.

g. A jockey.

1976 *Horse & Hound* 10 Dec. 41/1 He was to underline his Epsom misfortune by streaking home in the Irish Sweeps Derby, when his French pilot was replaced by Geoff Lewis. **1976** M. Maguire *Scratchproof* iv. 54 Will Highwayman jump the fence without a pilot?

2. = *pilot-cloth* (see sense 8).

1844 G. Dodd *Textile Manuf.* iii. 110 Each buyer is invited..to look at some 'olives', or 'browns', or 'pilots'. **1887** *Daily News* 23 Feb. 2/6 Heavy tweeds, unions, meltons, pilots, and other cheap fabrics.

3. = cow-catcher. *U.S.*

1864 Webster, *Pilot*...3. The cow-catcher of a locomotive. (*U.S.*) **1883** E. Ingersoll in *Harper's Mag.* Jan. 198/2 There is no cab,..no pilot, head-light, or any other appurtenances of an ordinary locomotive. **1891** C. Roberts *Adrift Amer.* 247 Most English people know the wedge-shaped pilot in front of the American engine well enough by repute to recognise it.

4. a. The copperhead = *pilot-snake* (*c*). **b.** = pilot-fish 1. **c.** The black-bellied plover, *Squatarola helvetica*.

1782 Crevecoeur *Lett.* 236 The most dangerous one is the pilot, or copperhead:..it bears the first name because it always precedes the rattle-snake; that is, quits its state of torpidity in the spring a week before the other. **1835** *Encycl. Brit.* (ed. 7) XII. 185 *note*, The pilot swims constantly in front of the shark... When the sea-angel neared the ship, the pilot swam close to the snout, or near one of the breast fins of the animal. **1888** G. Trumbull *Names & Portr. Birds* 192 On the coast of Virginia..the name of Pilot has been given, as it is always seen leading the large flights of birds which the rising tides drive from the shoals and oyster rocks.

5. An instrument for correcting the error of a compass.

1892 in Webster.

6. *Telecommunications.* An unmodulated signal transmitted with another signal for purposes of reference or control. Freq. *attrib.*, as ***pilot carrier***, ***tone***, etc.

1935 *Proc. IRE* XXIII. 702 The high degree of frequency stability required for single side-band suppressed-carrier transmissions can be dispensed with by transmitting a pilot frequency over the channel. **1957** D. G. Fink *Television Engin. Handbk.* xviii. 31 The L3 system makes use of six pilots for dynamic regulating and equalizing purposes. These are 308, 556, 2,064, 3,096, 7,266, and 8,320 kc. *Ibid.* xvi. 249 Oscillator-frequency drift causes picture-hue shift by changing the signal location on the phase characteristics of the pilot carrier and sideband circuits. **1962** C. F. Boyce *Open-Wire Carrier Telephone Transmission* vii. 95 Over the 3-channel carrier range a single pilot can regulate for changes in flat and slope loss... In a 12-channel system two pilots, one at each end of the band, are required. **1966** M. Schwartz et al. *Communication Syst. & Techniques* xi. 492 One technique for monitoring the channel state in a digital signaling system would be to transmit a pilot tone (unmodulated tone) along with the information-bearing waveforms. **1974** H. Burstein *Q. & A. about Tape Recording* (1975) xv. 194 The FM stereo broadcast contains a 19 kHz pilot signal. **1974** Harvey & Bohlman *Stereo F.M. Radio Handbk.* ii. 23 The reason for using a 19 kHz oscillator in the signal encoder now becomes clearer, since the oscillator provides a reference between the transmitted 19 kHz pilot tone and the 38 kHz subcarrier feed to the balanced modulator. **1975** *Which?* Sept. 278/3 An FM stereo radio signal has three parts. The main one is a mono signal... The extra information the tuner needs to produce stereo is in the other two parts—a sub-carrier and a pilot tone.

7. *Elect.* = *pilot wire* in 8.

1940 *Chambers's Techn. Dict.* 644/1 *Pilot*, in power systems, a conductor used for auxiliary purposes, not for the transmission of energy. **1957** M. D. Kippen in E. O. Taylor *Power Syst. Communications* i. 6 It has been the policy of many city undertakings when laying power cables to lay protection pilots and, in some cases, telephone pilots in the same trench. **1966** W. J. Cheetham in Taylor & Boal *Electr. Power Distribution 415V–33kV* iii. 125 Post-office pilots are much more prone to interference during maintenance work on adjacent communication circuits.

8. a. *attrib.* and *Comb.*, Of or pertaining to a pilot or pilots, as ***pilot-brig***, ***-coble***, ***-craft***, ***-cutter***, ***error***, ***-ground***, ***-launch***, ***-schooner***, ***-sloop***, ***-tower***, ***-vessel***; that acts as a pilot or in any way as a guide, as ***pilot-balloon***, ***-engine***, ***-locomotive***, ***-star***, ***-train***, ***-tunnel***, ***-wheel***; **pilot biscuit** *U.S.*, ship's biscuit; **pilot-bread**, (see quot. 1858); **pilot cable** *Electr.* = *pilot wire* below; **pilot chute** or **'chute** (see quot. 1925); **pilot-cloth**, (see quot. 1858); **pilot-coat** = pea-jacket; **pilot driver**, an engine-driver who accompanies another over a route with which the latter is unfamiliar; **pilot-flag** = *pilot-jack*; **pilot-flame** = *pilot-light*; **pilot-frame**, a low truck supporting the fore-part of a locomotive engine: = bogie 2; **pilot guard** (see quot. 1921); **pilot-house**, an enclosed place on the deck of a ship, sheltering the steering-gear and the helmsman; the wheel-house; also (*U.S.*), a house on land in which a pilot lives or stays; **pilot-jack**: see quots.; **pilot-jacket** = pea-jacket; **pilot lamp** = *pilot light* (*c*); **pilot light**, (*a*) a minute gas-light kept burning beside a large burner, so as automatically to light the latter when the flow through is turned on; †(*b*) a small light left permanently on to provide illumination; (*c*) a small electric light used to give an indication or warning rather than illumination; † **pilot-major**, a chief pilot; also, an honorary title conferred on distinguished discoverers and sailors; **pilot-man**, a railway official who directs the movement of trains over a section of track being temporarily used as a single line; also, a pilot driver; **pilot officer**, a commissioned rank in the Royal Air Force, equivalent to a second lieutenant in the Army; **pilot parachute** = *pilot chute*; **pilot's anchor**: see quot.; **pilot-snake**, (*a*) a large N. American snake, *Coluber obsoletus*; (*b*) the pine-snake, *Pituophis melanoleucus*; (*c*) the copperhead; **pilot valve** *Engin.*, a small auxiliary valve that is operated in association with a larger valve; **pilot-water** (also **pilot's water**), a piece of water in which the service of a pilot is obligatory; **pilot-weed**, the compass-plant, *Silphium laciniatum*; **pilot-whale**, the round-headed porpoise or ca'ing whale; **pilot wire** *Electr.*, an auxiliary wire or cable for conveying information about an associated power line or telegraph line or for operating apparatus connected with one. Also pilot-bird, -boat, -fish.

1802 *Sporting Mag.* XX. 295/1 A *Pilot Balloon, as it is called, was first launched. **1846** Mrs. Gore *Sk. Eng. Char.* (1852) 155 To..send up..such a pilot-balloon as might fore-arm and forewarn his patron of the object of their mission. **1858** Simmonds *Dict. Trade, Pilot-balloon*, a small balloon sent up to try the wind. **1924** Pilot balloon [see ballon-sonde]. **1942** *Endeavour* I. 118/2 The information on temperature is obtained from pilot-balloons—small balloons carrying a cage of instruments to read temperature, ..at the altitude at which the balloon is set to burst, the cage then falling safely to earth. **1836** T. Power *Impressions Amer.* I. 21 Lift a piece of *pilot biscuit, request some kind soul to shave the under side of the corned round for you, then..fly the place and seek the deck. **1944** *Chicago Daily News* 11 Oct. 25/1 The pilot biscuit—great flat round crackers that may be purchased at the grocer's—were toasted and lightly spread with butter. **1788** *Maryland Jrnl.* 7 Mar. 4/2 (Advt.), The subscriber..has just begun to bake Ship, *Pilot, and Cag Bread. **1831** [see *navy bread*]. **1858** Simmonds *Dict. Trade, Pilot-bread*, a name in the West Indies for hard or ship biscuit. **1868** Lossing *Hudson* 28 A sufficient stock of Boston crackers, pilot-bread, or common loaf bread. **1894** *Outing* XXIV. 252/2 He quickly wrapped up some pilot-bread. **1977** *New Yorker* 9 May 112/2 With.. six pieces of pilot bread, he got into his single Klepper and bobbed down the river. **1844** J. Tomlin *Mission. Jrnls.* 368 We met with another *pilot brig going up to Calcutta. **1937** H. Cotton *Transmission & Distribution of Electr. Energy* xv. 349 The pilot wires are usually in the form of a three-core cable, which can be buried in the ground in the case of an insulated cable system, or slung from the towers in the case of an overhead system. Apart from the high cost of these *pilot cables, [etc.]. **1967** M. F. Buchan *Electr. Supply* x. 296 As the two ends of the system may be some distance apart, an information link is required, and this may be a pilot cable, a radio link, or carrier currents superimposed on the system itself. **1925** *Sci. Amer.* Mar. 203/2 The majority of parachutes are equipped with a '*pilot chute' which is a miniature structure made with ribs and spring in umbrella fashion. When the pilot pulls the 'rip cord'..the 'pilot chute' springs out, catches the air and helps to lead out the main parachute. **1973** 'A. Hall' *Tango Briefing* x. 118 Free fall... Seven, eight, nine. Pull it. Crack of the pilot 'chute. Then the jerk and the drag. **1834** W. F. Tolmie *Jrnls.* (1963) 262 Have donned *pilot cloth vest. **1840** *Knickerbocker* XV. 140 His winter clothing is usually a peet jacket and trowsers, of strong pilot cloth. **1851** H. Melville *Whale* xvi. 78 Rolled up in blue pilot-cloth. **1858** Simmonds *Dict. Trade, Pilot-cloth*, an indigo blue woollen cloth, used for great coats, and for the clothing of mariners and others. **1836** Dickens *Sk. Boz.* (1837) 2nd Ser. 96 *Pilot great coats with wooden buttons, have usurped the place of the ponderous laced coats with full skirts. **1840** *Spirit of Times* 9 May 116/2 A young man attired in a pilot coat and velvet stock. **1842** Dickens *Amer. Notes* I. ii. 41 The captain comes down again, in a sou'-wester hat..and a pilot-coat. **1858** Trollope *Three Clerks* I. ii. 29 A short bargee's pilot-coat, and a pipe of tobacco, were soon familiar to him. **1884** F. M. Crawford *Amer. Politician* II. ii. 30 Enormous Irishmen in pilot coats..were struggling to keep the drifts from the pavement. **1867** Smyth *Sailor's Word-bk.*, *Pilot cutter, a very handy sharp built sea-boat used by pilots. **1907** *Westm. Gaz.* 15 Feb. 7/1 Drivers should not be allowed to drive an engine over a road that they were not acquainted with without a *pilot driver. **1838** *Chr.* in *Ann. Reg.* 40/1 His engine came into collision with another *pilot engine. **1955** *Railway Mag.* May 302/1 A halt was made at Blarney, to detach the pilot engine. **1975** *Times* 3 Sept. 1/2 Last year the International Air Transport Association said that half of all air accidents were caused by *pilot error. **1978** J. Gardner *Dancing Dodo* xxxii. 252 The thing went wrong... If they wanted accuracy, they needed men to ensure it. What they got was..pilot error, or malfunction. **1895** *Funk's Stand. Dict.*, *Pilot-light*..called also *pilot-flame. **1843** J. Weale *Ensamples Railway Making* p. xx, Engines having..what is termed a truck or *pilot frame. **1854** J. L. Stephens *Centr. Amer.* 1 Avoiding altogether the regular *pilot-ground, at midnight [we] reached St. George's Bay. **1881** *Instructions to Census Clerks* (1885) 33, 78 Railway Guard... *Pilot Guard. **1921** *Dict. Occup. Terms* (1927) §702 *Pilot guard*, a guard..who pilots trains over portion of line where single line working is necessitated, or over bridges under repair. **1812** A. Stoddard *Sk. Louisiana* 160 On the south side of the east pass, about three miles from the bar, is the *pilot house. **1827** J. L. Williams *View of West Florida* 18 A small fort and pilot house formerly stood near the west end of the island. **1846** *Spirit of Times* 16 May 133/1 He placed his hand upon a small brass knob at the back of the pilot house. **1863** 'G. Hamilton' *Gala-Days* 120 An Indian pilot comes on board, and mounts to the pilot-house. **1883** *American* VI. 40 A seaman might rise from the forward deck to the pilot-house and the master's quarters. **1897** W. B. Yeats *Secret Rose* 207 The disused pilot-house looks out to sea. **1900** *Everbody's Mag.* III. 529 The pilot-house, a wrought-iron structure situated well forward near the bow, and projecting 4 ft. above the deck. **1967** *Jane's Surface Skimmer Systems 1967–68* 34/2 Forward of the well..is the pilothouse. **1977** I. Shaw *Beggarman, Thief* I. i. 7 Alone in the pilothouse.. stood Wesley Jordache. **1977** *Washington Post* 4 Sept. A12/1 The top tier of this floating cake is the 'pilot house'—what a seagoing sailor would call the 'bridge'. **1858** Simmonds *Dict. Trade*, **Pilot-jack*. **1894** C. N. Robinson *Brit. Fleet* 96 When surrounded by a white border it [the 'jack']..is a signal for a pilot, and..it is known as a 'Pilot jack'. **1840** Marryat *Poor Jack* xxxviii, The..men..had lain down in their gregos and *pilot-jackets. **1884** *Jrnl. Soc. Telegr. Engin.* XIII. 515 As the speed began to increase, the lamp lit up intermittently, but in a few seconds more the machines dropped into step together, and the *pilot lamp lit up to full brightness and became perfectly steady. **1906** J. Poole *Pract. Telephone Handbk.* (ed. 3) xvii. 220 Whenever a call is made on any one of these lines the pilot relay is operated, and causes a specially large lamp, called the 'pilot lamp', to glow. **1918** R. Knox *Radiogr. & Radio-Therapeutics* II. 437 There is nearly always a pilot lamp on the switchboard by which the tints may be accurately gauged. **1977** 'E. Trevor' *Theta Syndrome* i. 14 In the main laboratory there were only the pilot lamps going. **1890** *Cent. Dict.*, *Pilot-light. *a* **1906** *Mod.* The gas lamps in the streets of Oxford are now furnished with incandescent burners and pilot-lights. **1906** *Daily Colonist* (Victoria, B.C.) 26 Jan. 10/1 *Pilot lights have also been placed in all the hallways and dark passages of the building. **1907** *Daily Chron.* 16 Apr. 6/7 This is the 'pilot' light, which is never extinguished, which burns night and day from the time a theatre is opened throughout the whole of its existence. **1939** I. Baird *Waste Heritage* x. 130 The radio man clicked on the pilot light and grunts and squeals began to come from the little machine. **1964** J. Cheever *Wapshot Scandal* vi. 58 The pilot light on the gas range isn't working and the cook has to keep lighting the range with matches. **1970** *Which?* Nov. 332/2 A pilot light goes on while the iron is heating. **1972** *Guardian* 2 Dec. 8/8 People were asked to turn their gas taps to 'off' so that unlit pilot lights ..would not allow gas to seep into their homes when the supply was restored. **1907** *Westm. Gaz.* 21 Sept. 12/2 An antique *pilot-locomotive slouched out and stopped. **1604** E. G[rimstone] *D'Acosta's Hist. Indies* iii. xi. 155 Cape de Vert, from whence the *Pilote maior returned to Peru. **1820** W. Scoresby *Acc. Arctic Reg.* I. 72 Richard Chancellor, pilot-major of the fleet. **1894** *Daily News* 18 Sept. 6/1 Vespucci..was finally appointed Pilot-Major to the King of Spain. **1881** *Instructions to Census Clerks* (1885) 33, 77 Railway Engine Driver... Pilot, *Pilot-man. **1921** *Dict. Occup. Terms* (1927) §701 *Pilotman*.., a guard..who accompanies a train between given points on single line, other line being temporarily out of use, to advise driver of difficulties of road, special signalling arrangements, etc. **1971** D. J. Smith *Discovering Railwayana* x. 58 *Pilotman*, driver taking charge of single-line workings, especially when one line of a double track is under repair. **1919** *Monthly Air Force List* Aug. 15 Air Ministry... Directorate of Personnel. .. Staff Officers, 3rd Class... Dawes, *Pilot Officer H., Gunn, Pilot Officer D.B. **1935** T. S. Sprigg *Royal Air Force* xii. 91 Accepted candidates who have not had previous experience in the Air Force are entered in the Special Reserve with the rank of Pilot Officer on probation. **1965** W. M. W. Fowler *Countryman's Cooking* p. x, Where the fault lay was obvious even to a very young Pilot Officer. **1975** *Sunday Times* 23 Feb. 19/7 In May, 1943, I was a lowly WAAF serving on a station in Hampshire... My fiancé, Ken, was a pilot officer. **1926** *Pilot parachute [see pack *sb.*¹ 1 g]. **1942** A. M. Low *Parachutes* 41 The effect of pulling the rip-cord was first of all to release the pilot parachute packed on the outside of the pack so that this in turn may draw out the main parachute. **1867** Smyth *Sailor's Word-bk.*, **Pilot's anchor*, a kedge used for dropping a vessel in a stream or tide-way. **1896** *Daily News* 5 Dec. 5/7 The *pilot-sloop, with half a dozen Exmouth pilots, put off to assist the vessel and get her off. **1853** R. B. Marcy *Explor. Red River* (1854) 196 The names of Bull, Pine, and *Pilot snake are commonly given to different species of this genus [sc. *Pituophis*]. **1890** *Cent. Dict.*, **Pilot-snake*, a harmless snake of the United States, *Coluber obsoletus*. **1890** *Century Mag.* Aug. 615/2, I killed two large snakes called the 'pilot-snake', from the fact that they are generally found in the vicinity of rattlesnakes. **1946** G. Stimpson *Bk. about Thousand Things* 480 The pilot snake..gets its name from the curious belief that it precedes rattlesnakes and warns them of the approach of danger. **1956** L. M. Klauber *Rattlesnakes* II. xviii. 1244 Another phase of the myth is that pilot snakes are crosses between rattlesnakes and bull snakes. **1791** E. Darwin *Bot. Gard.* ii. 156 High in air..Shone the bright lamp, the *pilot star of Love. **1859** Tennyson *Enid* 1155 Enid, the pilot star of my lone life, Enid, my early and my only love. **1900** *Daily News* 19 May 2/1 The shelling of the armoured *pilot-train on its return journey. **1891** *Cent. Dict.* (s.v. *tunnel*), **Pilot tunnel*, a device for directing a tunnel in the prescribed grade, consisting of a flanged tube made up of interchangeable plates, which can be bolted to the shield and forced concentrically into the silt in advance of the face of the heading. **1906** *Chambers's Jrnl.* 29 Sept. 701/1 Within the small pilot-tunnel a large number of refrigerating tubes is placed. **1958** *Engineering* 18 Apr. 502/1 Short pilot tunnels were driven out from the shore on both sides of the Channel. **1902** *Internat. Library of Technol.* VII. B. §39. 13 For high-speed hydraulic elevators..the relief valve is not sufficient to guard against shocks..nor is it possible to regulate the speed readily... This has led to the introduction of the auxiliary, or *pilot, valve. *Ibid.* 18 The pilot valve allows a perfect regulation of the speed of the [elevator] car. **1953** E. Molloy *Maintenance Engineers' Pocket Bk.* ii. 67 In large boilers..pilot valves are often fitted to the main stop valves, and the pilot valve should be opened to warm up the steam main before the main stop valve is opened, thus avoiding the danger of water hammer. **1971** H. C. Town *Design & Construction of Machine Tools* ix. 194 If the reversing valve has to handle large volumes of oil..the reverse valve is better operated by a pilot valve which may be trip operated. **1825** *Act 6 Geo. IV*, c. 125 §3 An Apprenticeship of Five Years to some *Pilot Vessel. **1788** *Chambers' Cycl.* (ed. Rees) s.v. *Pilot*, A pilot, when conducting one of his majesty's ships in *pilot-water, shall have the sole charge and command of the ship. **1867** Smyth *Sailor's Word-bk.*, *Pilot's Fairway*, or *Pilot's Water*, a channel wherein, according to usage, a pilot must be employed. **1848** W. H. Emory *Notes Mil. Reconn.* 11 In the uplands..occasionally is found the wild tea,..and *pilot weed. **1885** *Girl's Own Paper* Jan. 171/1 The compass plant—variously known, also, as the pilot weed, polar plant, and turpentine weed—is a vigorous perennial. **1951** *Dict. Gardening* (R. Hort. Soc.) III. 1957/1 Compass Plant, Pilot Weed, Polar Plant. **1867** *Athenæum* 21 Sept. 373/1 The *pilot whale, *Globiocephalus Svinevaly*. **1901** Shipley & MacBride *Zool.* xix. 527 The Ca'ing or Pilot Whale.., which also feeds chiefly on cuttle-fish, has teeth in both upper and lower jaws. **1921** J. T. Jenkins *Hist. Whale Fisheries* viii. 268 A third whale fishery practised in northern waters..was that for the Grindhval or Pilot Whale. **1962** E. Lucia *Klondike Kate* ii. 40 At times schools of happy pilot whales followed the vessel. **1974** G. B. Corbet in D. L. Hawksworth *Changing Flora & Fauna of Brit.* xi. 199 Species that are more frequent in the recent period are pilot whale (*Globicephala melaena*) with 46 strandings between 1948 and 1966. **1890** J. W. Urquhart *Electric Light* (ed. 3) x. 321 It is far more important to be informed as to the actual potential of the mains at the various points of consumption. For low tension constant current systems this is usually accomplished by the use of '*pilot wires'. **1930** *Engineering* 12 Sept. 347/1 An examination of the available protective schemes not involving the use of pilot wires had shown that a close approximation to the performance of pilot protective gear could be obtained by the use of distance relays. **1968** P. J. Freeman *Electr. Power Transmission & Distribution* x. 275 On long sections the capacitance currents between the pilot wires may be high enough to operate the relay, causing instability.

b. Used *attrib.* or as *adj.* to denote something that serves as a prototype or experimental undertaking prior to full-scale operation, activity, or use; experimental, initial; as ***pilot film, plant, programme, project, scheme, study, survey, trial***; so **pilot-scale** *a.*, done on the scale of a pilot scheme. Cf. *pilot-tunnel* above.

1928 *Daily Mail* 13 Aug. 18/2 This company produced 40 tons of tin concentrates with its small pilot mill in the June quarter. **1934** *Planning* I. xvii. 9 Actually research has become specialised not only by subjects but by processes and each process—background, basic, *ad hoc* and pilot, or whatever else they may be termed—is inseparable from the one before it and from the one after it. **1936** *Economist* 1 Feb. 275/1 The dry crushing and roasting plant treated 186,422 tons [of ore] and the pilot flotation plant 5,688 tons. **1938** *Rep. R. Comm. Oil from Coal* §27 in *Parl. Papers 1937–38* (Cmd. 5665) XII. 439 Experimental work started at Billingham early in 1927, and in 1929 it was decided to build a pilot plant there to treat 10 tons of coal per day. **1939** *Nature* 12 Aug. 279/2 The Department of Biochemistry ..[has conducted] pilot scale tannery operations to improve the vegetable chrome process. **1944** *Times* 18 Mar. 2/3 The Ministry of Food has recently installed a pilot plant for drying meat near Belfast. **1947** *Yale Law Jrnl.* Dec. 197 They had an opportunity to build a 'pilot model', a spacious though inexpensive cooperative in..a Warsaw suburb. **1951** (*title*) The Haiti Pilot Project: Phase One (UNESCO). **1951** *Chambers's Jrnl.* Oct. 638/1 Two recent American developments, both at present in the pilot or experimental stage, may widen the already verstile uses of glass. **1952** Pilot reactor [see criticality 2]. **1952** W. H. J. Sprott *Social Psychol.* vi. 102 The 'open-end' question may be used in a pilot survey, which helps to determine the multiple-answer question. **1952** *Times* 25 Jan. 3/4 The corporation stated that it did not propose to proceed with a large-scale irrigation scheme for rice cultivation until results on a pilot area had shown this to be economically possible. **1953** *Britannica Bk. of Year* 638/2 *Pilot scheme* (a preliminary to a full scale agricultural or industrial project). **1953** *Ann. Reg. 1952* 416 A new vaccine selected from pilot trials of the previous winter. **1954** A. Huxley *Let.* 12 Dec. (1969) 718 The TV decision would not be made until after the production of a pilot film. **1956** *Planning* XXII. 19 In 1954 the Nottingham Book Festival was organised by a committee of the Booksellers Association as a pilot scheme for a national publicity campaign. **1957** *Ann. Reg. 1956* 348 In Russia it appeared that underground gasification of coal was passing from the pilot stage to industrial operation... In Britain..the Coal Board and the Central Electricity Authority decided to proceed with pilot plant for producing electricity from gas made underground from inferior coal. **1957** R. K. Merton *Social Theory* (rev. ed.) ii. x. 387 The initial substantive aim of this pilot study was fourfold. **1959** *Listener* 22 Jan. 173/1 We hoped to do a pilot survey on the reactions of individuals to television programmes. **1961** *Technology* Feb. 34/4 The scheme will start in three pilot areas. **1961** *Harper's Bazaar* Feb. 23 The trend-setters.., the 'pilot' clothes that look ahead. **1964** M. Gowing *Britain & Atomic Energy, 1939–1945* v. 150 The Chicago pilot-scale graphite pile. **1966** T. Pynchon *Crying of Lot 49* ii. 33 They've done the pilot film of a TV series, in fact, based loosely on my career. **1969** N. W. Pirie *Food Resources* 13 With less initial obstruction, and a steady increase in the scale of pilot projects, the ultimate acreage aimed at would probably have been reached earlier. **1971** *Brit. Med. Bull.* XXVII. 6/2 Sensitivity and specificity may be assessed from the results of a pilot trial undertaken on a group of individuals similar to those who are to be screened. **1971** *Guardian* 26 Feb. 13/3 US networks are no longer so keen to buy British programmes without seeing a pilot episode. **1971** *Jrnl. Gen. Psychol.* Apr. 191 On the basis of a pilot study..it was predicted that..total list acquisition would not differ as a function of stimulus clustering. **1974** *Nature* 1 Feb. 248/3 Pilot plants started within the next year or two could be working productively within the next five years. **1975** *Radio Times* 30 Aug. 14/2, I saw a pilot programme for the new series. **1975** *Daily Tel.* 3 Oct. 7/2 A pilot plan to 'lock' radioactive wastes inside solid glass is now being commissioned. **1976** *Leicester Chron.* 26 Nov. 2/3 Leslie Crowther presented the pilot show but future commitments prevented him taking it on permanently. **1978** *Jrnl. R. Soc. Arts* Dec. 8/2 Examinations in Communication were offered ..on a pilot basis.

Hence **ˈpilotess**, a female pilot.

1834 *New Monthly Mag.* XLII. 108 Our fair pilotess has not suffered shipwreck.

ˈpilot, *v.* [f. pilot *sb.*, or a. F. *pilote-r* (1530 in Palsgr.); cf. *pilotier* 'to play the Pilot' (Cotgr.).]

1. a. *trans.* To conduct as a pilot; to direct the course of (a vessel) through difficult or dangerous waters; to steer, guide.

1693 Luttrell *Brief Rel.* (1857) III. 152 One Chetworth ..piloted in the French privateers that burnt the lord Widdringtons house 2 years since. **1727–41** Chambers *Cycl.* s.v. *Pilot*, Pilots..having done their parts in piloting the vessel, return to shoar where they reside. **1805** Nelson in Nicolas *Disp.* (1846) VI. 471 [He] very cheerfully offered his services to pilot the Fleet. **1879** H. George *Progr. & Pov.* v. ii. 256 He..can pilot himself by the sun or the stars.

b. To act as pilot on (an aeroplane or other aircraft) in the air; to fly (passengers) in an aircraft. Also *absol.*

1852 *Illustr. London News* 18 Sept. 224/3 The veteran aëronaut who had successfully piloted them and some hundred others through the air. **1911** *Daily News* 20 July 2/4 The Dutch aviator has decided to pilot a..monoplane.. instead of a..biplane. **1931** F. L. Allen *Only Yesterday* viii. 222 If you did not know how to pilot a plane you could still be a passenger. **1946** *Happy Landings* (Air Ministry) July 6/3 These considerations led to me to select a Mosquito ..and to pilot myself. **1955** *Times* 22 Aug. 5/4 The crowd saw a fly-past of aircraft piloted by men of the R.A.F. **1958** 'Castle' & 'Hailey' *Flight into Danger* viii. 113 The first officer, then the captain were taken sick. Luckily there was a passenger on board who had piloted before and he took over the controls. **1977** *Daily Tel.* 7 Apr. 7/3 An attempt.. to become the first woman to pilot a hot air balloon across the English Channel.

2. *transf.* and *fig.* **a.** To guide or conduct through unknown, intricate, or dangerous paths or places, or through a difficult course of affairs; to conduct as a 'pilot' in the hunting-field.

1649 J. Eliot in *Early Rec. Lancaster, Mass.* (1884) 16, I therefore hired a..man of Nashaway..to mark trees so that he may Pilot me thither in the spring. **1761** Wesley *Jrnl.* 18 Apr., He piloted us over the next mountain. **1838** Dickens *Nich. Nick.* xxi, The big footman..piloted them in perfect safety to the street-door. **1877** Tennyson *Harold* i. i. 148 Go—the Saints Pilot and prosper all thy wandering out And homeward. **1881** Mrs. Power O'Donoghue *Ladies on Horseback* iii. vi. 94 Any man who will not take this trouble is unfit to pilot a lady.

b. To secure the passage of (a bill) *through* a legislative assembly; to carry. orig. *U.S.*

1929 *Randolph Enterprise* (Elkins, W. Virginia) 21 Mar. 1/4 The bill..piloted..thru the House by Representative Karl Kyle. **1974** *Lebende Sprachen* XIX. 39/2 He piloted through the House the government's elaborate education bill. **1976** *Leicester Mercury* 16 July 4 It now goes to the Lords. It is likely to be piloted there by Liberal Lord Avebury.

c. To use experimentally; to try out, test.

1960 *Sunday Times* 10 Jan. 14/6 Practically all these devices for saving time and labour have been piloted in the fifties. The sixties should see them put into commercial production in sufficient quantity to make them financially feasible. **1965** *New Society* 23 Dec. 15/3 The Rowntree survey (piloted in Harrow, and subsequently carried out in York). **1967** G. Wills in Wills & Yearsley *Handbk. Managem. Technol.* 186 Always, but always, *pilot* a questionnaire before sending it out into the field. Never try and scorn the researcher who asks for time and money to pilot his work. **1977** *Jrnl. R. Soc. Arts* CXXV. 308/2 Not only does he [*sc.* the skilled question designer] pilot his questionnaire, but periodically he tests his questions to find out how they are actually understood.

3. To act as pilot on (a course or way), in or over (an extent of water, etc.).

1725 Pope *Odyss.* iv. 880 Mentor, Captain of the lordly crew, Safe from the secret rock and adverse storm Pilots the course. **1846** *Mech. Mag.* July 20 [They] piloted the way with the Number 1 engine of the Stockton and Darlington Railway Company. **1871** Browning *Hervé Riel* vi, Morn and eve, night and day, Have I piloted your bay.

Hence **ˈpiloting** *vbl. sb.*

1716 B. Church *Hist. Philip's War* (1865) I. 126 By their Piloting, he soon came..to the top of the great Tree which the Enemy had fallen a-cross the River. **1766** J. S. Speer (*title*) The West India Pilot, containing Piloting Directions for Port Royal Harbour in Jamaica. **1891** S. Mostyn *Curatica* 148 Never mind, I'll do the piloting. **1900** *Blackw. Mag.* May 655/2 Piloting, that is the placing of two engines ..at the head of a train, is common upon almost all our lines. **1919** W. H. Berry *New Traffic (Aircraft)* i. 5 Good piloting does not depend on cleverness in tinkering with the engine. **1922** *Encycl. Brit.* XXX. 14/1 Aerial navigation, as distinct from piloting with the ground in view, developed tardily everywhere. **1959** *Manch. Guardian* 6 July 2/4 The hour's piloting round a town that makes up most [driving] lessons. **1977** *Belfast Tel.* 28 Feb. 9/2 (*caption*) Too old for piloting in 1939 he became an air gunner with 235 Squadron Coastal Command.

pilotage (ˈpaɪlətɪdʒ). [a. F. *pilotage* (1540 in Hatz.-Darm.), f. *piloter*: see prec. and -age.]

1. a. The action or practice of piloting; the function or office of a pilot; pilotship.

compulsory pilotage, compulsory employment of a pilot within certain limits, according to local law.

a **1618** Raleigh *Apol.* 55 Otherwise we must for ever abandon the Indies, and loose all our knowledge, and our Pylotage of that part of the world. **1633** T. Stafford *Pac. Hib.* iii. x. 325 At the other end of this Iland [Innisherkan] (with good pilotage) a ship of two hundred Tunne by day may safely come in. **1656** Blount *Glossogr.*, *Pilotage* or *Pilotism*, the office or art of a Pilot. **1786–7** Bonnycastle *Astron.* i. 14 They have paid the utmost attention to pilotage. **1819** Scott *Leg. Montrose* xiv, I shall never save the ship by my own pilotage. **1868** *Morn. Star* 28 Mar., Mr. Candlish did good service..by proposing the abolition of compulsory pilotage. **1922** *Encycl. Brit.* XXX. 13/2 Then came pilotage and the elements of commercial flying. **1924** *Air Pilot: Gt. Britain* ii. iv. 19 (*heading*) Pilotage Directions. **1932** *Flight* 6 Oct. 949/1 The Air Council have had under consideration the policy regarding training in air pilotage. **1946** *Happy Landings* (Air Ministry) July (verso front cover), The various sciences which together contribute to our present day knowledge of practical pilotage. **1969** *Daily Mail* 16 Jan. 5/6 We had some difficulty on Apollo 8, with 'pilotage', that is, trying to plot our path on the map of the back side of the Moon.

b. *transf.* and *fig.* (cf. pilot *v.* 2).

1726 S. Sewall *Diary* 16 May, By the pilotage of the Lt. Governour's Servant..Went the way by Mr. Prescott's Meetinghouse. **1848** Dickens *Dombey* vi, He left the room under the pilotage of Mrs. Chick. **1887** Sir R. H. Roberts *In the Shires* ii. 22 A chosen lot..look to him for pilotage through the line of gates.

2. The cost or charge for piloting; pilotage dues.

1622 Malynes *Anc. Law Merch.* 141 The Merchant like-wise doth couenant to pay Pilotage, if a Pilot be vsed to bring the ship into the harbor. **1825** *Act 6 Geo. IV*, c. 125 §38 Every Pilot so taken to Sea..shall, over and above his pilotage, have and receive Ten Shillings and Sixpence *per Diem*. **1840** Marryat *Poor Jack* xxviii, I've got all my pilotage too, so I'm a rich man.

3. An association, authority, or establishment for supervising a body of pilots.

1881 *Times* 17 Jan. 12/4 If frost persists and ice increases, the pilotage will probably refuse pilots to sailing vessels, unless they are assisted by tugs.

4. *attrib.*, as ***pilotage certificate, dues, signal***, etc.

1830 LYELL *Princ. Geol.* I. 230 Many Swedish officers of the pilotage establishment declared..in favour of this opinion. **1873** in Bedford *Sailor's Pocket Bk.* iii. (1875) 68 The International Code Pilotage Signal indicated by P.T. **1905** *Westm. Gaz.* 27 Apr. 7/2 At the time of the accident the ship was in pilotage waters.

pilotaxitic (ˌpaɪləʊtæk'sɪtɪk), *a. Min.* [As if f. **pilotaxite* (f. Gr. πῖλο-ς felt + τάξις arrangement + -ITE) + -IC.] (See quot.)

1888 F. H. HATCH in Teall *Brit. Petrogr.* Gloss., *Pilotaxitic*, the name given by Rosenbusch..to a holocrystalline structure especially characteristic of certain porphyrites and basalts. The groundmass of these rocks consists essentially of slender laths and microlites of felspar in felted aggregation, and often presents fluxion phenomena.

'pilot-bird. [f. PILOT *sb.* + BIRD *sb.*] A name applied to various birds; †**a.** A sea-bird of the W. Indies (*obs.*); **b.** An Australian bird, *Pycnoptilus floccosus*; **c.** ? An albatross (quot. 1888).

1678 PHILLIPS (ed. 4), The *Pilot Bird*, a certain Bird about the Caribe Islands, which gives notice to Ships that sail that way, when they come near any of those Islands. [Hence in BAILEY, CRABBE *Technol. Dict.*, and later Dicts.] **1888** R. L. STEVENSON *Diary* in G. Balfour *Life* (1901) II. 43 Some attendant pilot birds, silent, brown-suited, quakerish fellows, infinitely graceful on the wing. **1893** *Argus* (Melbourne) 25 Mar. 4/6 (Morris) Here, close together, are eggs of the lyre-bird and the pilot-bird—the last very rare, and only found quite lately in the Dandenong Ranges. **1903** NORTH (of Sydney, N.S.W.) *Let. to Prof. A. Newton*, Relative to the name of 'Pilot-bird' for *Pycnoptilus floccosus*, this species has been so labelled in the National Museum, Melbourne, for the past twenty-five years. The name is probably derived from its loud and distinct notes quite unlike those of any other species.

'pilot-boat. A boat in which pilots cruise off shore in order to meet incoming vessels.

1588 T. HICKOCK tr. *Frederick's Voy.* 14 Like to our little pilot boats. **1710** *Lond. Gaz.* No. 4682/3 He came not to Anchor, only spoke with a Pilot-Boat. **1832** MARRYAT *N. Forster* li, A..note sent on shore by a pilot-boat.

piloted ('paɪlətɪd), *ppl. a.* [f. PILOT *v.* + -ED[1].] Controlled or guided by a pilot.

1945 C. MILBURN *Diary* 18 Mar. (1979) 278 Last night piloted enemy planes were over northern England and.. casualties also occurred from V bombs in the south. **1946** *Jrnl. R. Aeronaut. Soc.* July 508/1 The other piloted rocket aircraft was intended to be catapulted at an angle of 75°. **1952** *Ann. Reg. 1951* 411 The next stage [in space travel] would be piloted rockets designed as space stations. **1961** *Shell Aviation News* Dec. 4/1 Already, in certain circumstances 'the one who controls the aeroplane' can equally well be in another aircraft or on the ground. In this new situation the terms 'piloted' and 'pilotless' become confusing anomalies.

pilotee (paɪlə'tiː). [f. PILOT *v.* + -EE.] A person who is piloted, e.g. in the hunting-field.

1883 MRS. KENNARD *Right Sort* ix, The pilotee can always see what he [the 'pilot'] is doing, how hard he rides, how well he goes.

†**pilo'teer.** *Obs.* [f. PILOT *v.* + -EER[1].] One who pilots (a ship); a pilot or steersman.

c **1645** HOWELL *Lett.* (1650) III. 8 As to the Pole the lilly bends In a sea-compas..Wherby the wandring piloteer His cours in gloomy nights doth steer.

'pilot-fish. [f. PILOT *sb.* + FISH *sb.*[1]]

1. A small carangoid fish of warm seas, *Naucrates ductor*, reputed to act as a pilot or guide to the shark; it is of a silvery blue colour, with dark vertical bars upon the back.

1634 SIR T. HERBERT *Trav.* 5 Sharkes..are alwayes directed by a little specled fish, called a pilot fish, by guiding their Monster-masters to a prey. **1712** E. COOKE *Voy. S. Sea* 27 Pilot-Fishes, which the Shark, tho' never so hungry, does not devour. **1833** MARRYAT *P. Simple* xli, When you meet the pilot-fish, the shark arn't far off, you know. **1835** *Encycl. Brit.* (ed. 7) XII. 185/1 *Naucrates ductor*, the famous pilot-fish of navigators.., so named from its habit of keeping company with ships at sea, and frequently swimming beneath their bows.

2. Applied to other fishes: **a.** A general term for the *Carangidæ*, as the amber-fish (*Seriola dorsalis*), or the rudder-fish (*Seriola zonata*); **b.** The remora or sucking-fish (*Echeneis*); **c.** The round-fish (*Coregonus quadrilateralis*).

1792 MAR. RIDDELL *Voy. Madeira* 69 The pilot or rudder fish. [**1835** *Encycl. Brit.* (ed. 7) XII. 186/1 The name of *pilot* has been bestowed on various other fishes, and the genus Naucrates itself contains several species.]

‖**pilotis** (pilɔti). [Fr.] A series of columns or piles, esp. used to raise the base of a building above ground-level.

1947 *Archit. Rev.* CI. 172/1 Low-growing palms make patterns against the pale pink granite pilotis. **1957** *New Yorker* 5 Oct. 166/2 The most striking feature of the building [*sc.* Le Corbusier's Unity House] is that it is raised twenty-four feet aboveground on a double row of cyclopean, wedge-shaped concrete columns, or *pilotis*, which uphold the hollow canopy of concrete that forms the basement of the building proper. **1971** *Country Life* 25 Nov. 1444/3 The studio stood on *pilotis*, but..it has been converted into a house. **1972** E. LUCIE-SMITH in Cox & Dyson *20th-Cent. Mind* II. xiv. 492 Pure forms achieved by the use of continuous window-strips, glass walls, flat roofs; the lightness which came from raising the structure on *pilotis*.

pilotism ('paɪlətɪz(ə)m). [f. PILOT *sb.* + -ISM.] The practice of a pilot; pilotage.

1611 COTGR., *Pilotage*, Pilotisme; th'office, or Art of a Pilot. **1652–62** HEYLIN *Cosmogr.* Introd. (1674) 24/1 Petrus de Medina..and Johannes Aurigarius..chief Writers in the Art of Pilotism. **1776** S. J. PRATT *Pupil of Pleas.* II. 32, I am between a Scylla and a Charybdis, and uncommonly skilful must be my pilotism, or I must split upon the rocks.

pilotless ('paɪlətlɪs), *a.* [f. PILOT *sb.* + -LESS.] Without a pilot; now esp. of aircraft.

1605 SYLVESTER *Du Bartas* II. iii. III. *Law* 168 Though Rudder-lesse, not Pilot-lesse this Boat. **1806** SCOTT *Let.* 20 Sept. (1932) I. 317 The pilot-less state in which the political vessel has remained since his [*sc.* Pitt's] death. **1883** *Harper's Mag.* Aug. 441/2 The pilotless narrows which lead to Fiddler's Green, where all good sailors go. **1909** *Westm. Gaz.* 22 Oct. 7/2 We only just missed the new spectacle of a pilotless aeroplane. **1922** *Glasgow Herald* 15 Nov. 9 The Army Air Service [U.S.A.] announces that successful tests have been made with automatically controlled pilotless aeroplanes. **1937** *Aeroplane* 16 June 3 (Advt.), A pilotless flyaway plane. **1943** R. V. JONES *Most Secret War* (1978) xxxix. 356 The Germans are installing..a large and important ground organization in Belgium-N. France which is probably concerned with directing an attack on England by rocket-driven pilotless aircraft. **1944** [see *buzz-bomb* s.v. BUZZ *sb.*[1] 5]. **1945** H. KNIGHT in *Penguin New Writing* XXIII. 47 Pilotless men whose personalities have been disintegrated by concussion and too many action stations. **1961** [see PILOTED *ppl. a.*]. **1966** M. WOODHOUSE *Tree Frog* v. 35 The curious blind look of all pilotless aircraft which stems from having no cockpit. **1974** *Guardian* 18 Mar. 5/4 The pilotless planes, named Falcons, are designed for taking aerial photographs.

'pilotry. *rare.* [f. PILOT *sb.* + -RY.] = PILOTAGE.

1744 HARRIS *Three Treat.* Notes (1765) 278 As a Ship is the End of Ship-building, or Navigating the End of Pilotry. **1842** *Blackw. Mag.* LI. 318 Under such skilful pilotry did I pass days and nights in the prosecution of my one great purpose.

'pilotship. *rare.* [f. PILOT *sb.* + -SHIP.] The discharge of the office or function of a pilot.

1664 in Brand *Hist. Newcastle* (1789) II. 705 The pylottship..bringing up and carrying down, and in and out, of all such ships. **1692** *Lond. Gaz.* No. 2814/3 They committed the Pilotship to the 5 Dutch Men. **1711** SHAFTESB. *Charact.* (1737) III. 158 Whither bound? On what business? Under whose pilotship, government, or protection?

†**pi'lotte,** obs. form of PELLET *sb.*[1]

14.. *Noble Bk. Cookry* (Napier 1882) 92 Mak it in pilottes as gret as plomes.

†**pilotty, piloty.** *Obs.* [ad. F. *pilotis*, f. *piloter* to drive piles, f. *pilot* a pile, augm. of *pile* pile.] A foundation of piles driven into the sea, upon which a building is erected.

1688 BURNET *Lett.* (1708) 129 To see so vast a City [Venice] situated thus in the Sea..the Pilotty supplying the want of Earth to build on. *Ibid.* 299 Unless the Foundation go very Deep, or that it be laid upon Piloty.

pilou, pilour(e, obs. ff. PILLOW, PILLER.

pilous ('paɪləs), *a.* [ad. L. *pilōsus* hairy (in F. *pileux*): see -OUS, and cf. PILOSE.] Characterized by or abounding in hair; of the nature or consisting of hair; hairy, pilose, pileous.

1658 J. ROBINSON *Endoxa*, etc. 124 The excrements of voracious doggs, which is seen to be very pilous. **1661** LOVELL *Hist. Anim. & Min.* Introd., The eares are..pilous in the rat. **1776** J. LEE *Introd. Bot.* Explan. Terms 385 *Pilosum*, pilous, covered with long Hairs that appear distinctly. **1836–9** *Todd's Cycl. Anat.* II. 380/1 No pilous system..exists in any of the Gasteropods. **1842** MONTAGU in *Proc. Berw. Nat. Club* II. No. 10. 33 It is covered with a rough pilous epidermis. **1874** COUES *Birds N.W.* 291 The face lacking the crimson velvety pilous area.

pilow(e, obs. form of PILLOW.

†**pilpate.** *Obs. rare.* Also pyl-. Short for *pilled pate* tonsured head, i.e. priest (with allusion to *prelate*): see PILLED 2.

1530 TINDALE *Pract. Prelates* I vij, If it had bene as greatlye vnto the profyte of the pope and his pilpates, I wold saye prelates, as it were to the honoure of god. **1560** BECON *New Catech.* Wks. (1564) 496 These smeared Pylpates, I would saye, Prelates, first of all accused hym.

pilpul ('pɪlpəl). *Rabbinism.* [a. Heb. *pilpul* (f. *pilpēl* to debate hotly, referred by some to *pilpel* pepper).] Subtle or keen rabbinical investigation or argumentation; an instance of this. Also *transf.*, hair-splitting and unprofitable disputation.

1894 tr. *Graetz's Hist. Jews* IV. xiii. 418 The astonishing facility of ingenious disquisition on the basis of the Talmud (Pilpul), attributed to Polak, which attained its highest perfection in Poland, proceeded from a native of Poland. **1905** J. Z. LAUTERBACH in *Jewish Encycl.* X. 39/2 (*heading*) Pilpul. A method of Talmudic study. The word is derived from the verb 'pilpel' (lit. 'to spice', 'to season', and in a metaphorical sense, 'to dispute violently'..or 'cleverly'..). Since by such disputation the subject is in a way spiced and seasoned, the word has come to mean penetrating investigation, disputation, and drawing of conclusions, and is used especially to designate a method of studying the Law. .. The essential characteristic of pilpul is that it leads to a clear comprehension of the subject under discussion by penetrating into its essence and by adopting clear distinctions and a strict differentiation of the concepts. **1920** OESTERLY & BOX *Short Survey Lit. of Rabbinical & Mediæval Judaism* IV. ii. 228 So far from destroying *pilpul*—casuistical discussion—the *Code* or *Mishneh Torah* itself became the object of pilpulistic comment. **1964** H. KEMELMAN *Friday the Rabbi slept Late* (1965) xxi. 156 We read a passage..of the Law... We were adding our own arguments..and twists of logic, the so-called pilpul. **1966** —— *Saturday the Rabbi went Hungry* i. 10 The cantor's chuckle told him he was won over. The rabbi returned to the table. His wife shook her head with a smile. 'That was a terrible pilpul.' **1967** C. POTOK *Chosen* II. v. 107 Pilpul, these discussions are called—empty, nonsensical arguments over minute points of the Talmud. **1968** L. ROSTEN *Joys of Yiddish* 287 *Pilpul*,..unproductive hair-splitting that is employed not so much to advance clarity or reveal meaning as to display one's own cleverness. **1976** *Brit. Jrnl. Sociol.* XXVII. 41 A key difficulty in the concept of alienation is that many of the succeeding theoretical discussions of the idea have taken off from the false leads in Marx, and the Talmudic *pilpul* over dissecting his text has only produced further confusion.

'pilpulist. *Rabbinism.* [f. PILPUL + -IST.] A subtle or keen disputant, esp. in rabbinical argumentation. Hence **pilpu'listic** *a.*

1859 P. BEATON *Jews in East* II. iii. 93 There is not among them a talmudist or pilpulist of any reputation. **1878** *N. Amer. Rev.* CXXVII. 90 To exercise the understanding in pilpulistic tournaments. **1898** ZANGWILL *Dreamers Ghetto* 237 We passed by the village Beth-Hamidrash, whence loud sounds of 'pilpulistic' (wire-drawn) argument issued.

Pils (pɪlz, pɪls). [Abbrev. PILSENER, PILSNER.] A type of beer similar to Pilsener.

1961 *Dude* Sept., I had part of a bottle of French beer called Panther Pils (so help me) then switched to Tuborg. **1962** [see EXPORT *sb.* 3 b]. **1971** M. SINCLAIR *Sonntag* iii. 22 In..the scruffy *Bierstube* he sat scowling with a thin glass of *Pils*. **1972** P. CLEIFE *Slick & Dead* xx. 157 Normally I never drink when I'm flying but thought..that a light Belgian Pils would be harmless. **1977** *Grimsby Even. Tel.* 24 May 10/2 (Advt.), Large Quantity of beers... Newcastle Brown, Prize Medal, Carlsberg, Pils in bottles, etc.

Pilsen ('pɪlz-, 'pɪlsən). Also with lower-case initial. [See next.] = next.

It is not certain that quot. 1939 belongs here.

1939 JOYCE *Finnegans Wake* (1964) III. 492 My dodear devere revered mainhirr was confined to guardroom, I hindustand, by my pint of his Filthered pilsens bottle. **1964** L. DEIGHTON *Funeral in Berlin* xxxi. 162 The waiter had brought two tall, ice-cold Pilsen lagers. **1968** *Listener* 25 July 103/3 One continually meets these ironies in Bohemia. Over stew and dumplings and draught Pilsen, he boasted that his son had actually been named in the Moscow press as a dangerous deviationist. **1977** P. SOMERVILLE-LARGE *Eagles near Carcase* iv. 61 The barman..had some tall cold bottles of Pilsen.

Pilsener, Pilsner ('pɪlz-, 'pɪls(ə)nə(r)). [G., f. *Pilsen* (Czech. *Plzeň*), a province and city in W. Bohemia, Czechoslovakia.] In full ***Pils(e)ner beer.*** A pale-coloured lager beer with a strong hop flavour. Also *attrib.*

The name now designates type rather than origin. Beer from Plzeň itself is known as *Pils(e)ner Urquell* (G., primary source).

1877 C. SCHREIBER *Jrnl.* 3 Aug. (1911) II. 49 Much rain—no breakfasts in the garden and Pilsner beer luncheons this year! **1890** KIPLING *Life's Handicap* (1891) 161 'Pilsener?'..'Beer's out, I'm sorry to say.' **1894** *Clarion* 3 Nov. 2/4 The elder waiter sent my empty bottle of Pilsener flying. **1909** M. DIVER *Candles in Wind* iii. 35 A glass of Pilsener to ward off regrets next morning. **1920** E. SITWELL *Wooden Pegasus* 67 And sat and drank our Pilsener beer. **1933** *Sun* (Baltimore) 6 Dec. 18/5 (Advt.), Light Pilsner style or dark kulmbacher—as you prefer it. **1964** L. DEIGHTON *Funeral in Berlin* xxxi. 161 Groups of men shouted for slivovice, borovicka or Pilsner Urquell. **1980** *Brit. Med. Jrnl.* 29 Mar. 916/1 It [*sc.* class 2 beer] was available in two strengths—a middle European Pilsner beer ..and a somewhat stronger English lager type.

b. Special Combs., as **Pils(e)ner glass, pils(e)ner glass,** a tall beer glass tapered at the bottom.

1966 'E. LATHEN' *Murder makes Wheels go Round* xvi. 130 Waymark pushed his pilsener glass to one side. **1971** J. BALL *First Team* (1972) xxvi. 406 Zalinsky poured out the two drinks in pilsner glasses. **1975** *Times* 18 Jan. 12/1 A..sight of the world..through the bottom of a Pilsner glass.

†**'pilsenite.** *Min. Obs.* [a. Ger. *pilsenit* (Kenngott, 1853), f. Deutsch-Pilsen, Hungary, where found.] An obsolete synonym of WEHRLITE.

1868 DANA *Min.* (ed. 5) Index.

†**pilser.** *Obs. rare*⁻⁰. (See quots.)

1736 AINSWORTH, A pilser, *musca luminibus advolitans.* **1755** JOHNSON, *Pilser*, the moth or fly that runs into a candle flame. *Ainsworth.* [Hence in mod. Dicts.]

†**pilt, pult,** *v. Obs.* Forms: α. 2–4 pulte(n; β. 2–5 pilte(n, 3–4 pylte; γ. 4–5 pelte. *Pa. t.* α. 3–4 pulte, 4–5 pult; β. 3–4 pylte, pilte, 5 pylt; γ. 4–5 pelt(e. *Pa. pple.* α. 2–3 i-, y-pult, 3–4 pult; β. 3–5 pilt, 4 pylt, 4–5 pylte; γ. 5 pelt. [ME. *pülten, pylten, pilten*, repr. an unrecorded OE. **pyltan*.

App. ad. L. *pultare* to beat, strike, knock; cf. OE. *tyrnan*, ad. L. *tornare*. No examples of *pult, pylt, pilt*, in sense 1 or 2, are known after 1400, nor of sense 3 after *c* 1430 (when *pult* in this sense was generally succeeded by *put*). Instances of *pelt* occur somewhat later in a Northern text; but it is doubtful whether this is the mod.Eng. verb PELT.]

1. *trans.* To thrust, push; to thrust away or out.

α. *c* **1175** *Lamb. Hom.* 129 Heo weren ipult ut of paradise. *c* **1275** LAY. 7527 Nemnius pulte vp [*c* 1205 hæf vp] his scelde. *Ibid.* 10839 Bruttes þane broc Galli cleopede, For þat Liuius Gallus was þar on i-pult þus. *c* **1290** *S. Eng. Leg.* I. 56/78 Huy harleden him wel faste, And smiten and pulten here and þere. *Ibid.* 328/189 Darstþov þine moder pulte? **1297** R. GLOUC. (Rolls) App. EE. 22 Hit was þe spere..þat was ypult to his herte. *c* **1305** *St. Andrew* 72 in *E.E.P.* (1862) 100 In to þe vrþe hi pulte faste þe tuei endes of þe Rode. *c* **1320** *Cast. Love* 207 Out of his heritage he is pult For synne and for his owne gult. **1377** LANGL. *P. Pl.* B. VIII. 96 A pyke is on þat potente to pulte [*v.rr.* pelte, pilte, putte; *A.* punge, *C.* pulte, putte] adown þe wikked. *a* **1380** *Minor Poems fr. Vernon MS.* lii. 92 Mi mouþ I pulte, my sweore I streiȝt To cusse his feet. *c* **1380** *Sir Ferumb.* 774 [He] pulte is bowels in ageyn.

β. *c* **1200** *Trin. Coll. Hom.* 197 þe neddre..hire oðer eare pilteð hire tail þer inne. **1303** R. BRUNNE *Handl. Synne* 1296 Ho-so curseþ wiþoutyn gylt Hyt shal on hys hede be pylt. ? **1370** *Robt. Cicyle* §89 And so hath he done for my gylte: Now am y of my lande pylte.

γ. **13..** *Guy Warw.* (A.) 4086 þat heued þai han on a spere y-sett:..Mani on pelt her finger þer-to. *a* **1400** *Octavian* 595 The lyonesse..on the schyp sche gan to clym..The schypmen..ofte her pelte ynto the see. *c* **1460** *Towneley Myst.* xxi. 284 Yit wold I gif of my gold yond tratoure to pelt [*rimes* swelt, belt, felt] ffor euer.

b. *fig.* To impel, drive, force.

a **1250** *Owl & Night.* 871 Mid mine songe ich hine pulte þat he groni for his gulte.

2. To put forcibly. ***pilt out***, to put or take out by force.

α. **1297** R. GLOUC. (Rolls) 7713 Wo so..slou hert oþer hind. Me ssolde pulte [*v.r.* putte] out boþe is eye & makye him pur blind. **13..** *Verses for Palm Sunday* xxii. in *Rel. Ant.* II. 244 To dethe a wolde hym pulte.

β. *a* **1300** *Fall & Passion* 56 in *E.E.P.* (1862) 14 Fort godis sone in rode was pilt. *a* **1300** *Ten Commandm.* 12 *Ibid.* 16 Whan ȝe sweriþ gret oþis in rode þou piltist him apan. *c* **1350** *Will. Palerne* 4219 Neuer-more for no man mowe [þei] be deliuered, ne pult out [of] prison. *Ibid.* 4593 He bar doun vs alle, & pult vs in prison.

γ. *c* **1450** *St. Cuthbert* (Surtees) 4550 þe paynyms to dede war pelt..whils þai [cristen men] dede dyntes delt.

3. To put, place, set; to apply. ***pilt out***, to put forth, publish, exhibit, display.

α. **1297** R. GLOUC. (Rolls) 9550 So þat it was uorþ ipult þat þe king and heo So sibbe were þat hii ne miȝte leng to gadere beo. *c* **1300** *Beket* 1316 He nele bileve nevere mo, Bote ȝe pulte ȝoure hond therto to bringe ous out of wo. **1377** LANGL. *P. Pl.* B. I. 125 Ac lucifer lowest lith of hem alle; For pryde þat he pult [*v.rr.* pelt, putte, put, puttede] out.

β. *c* **1250** *Gen. & Ex.* 2214 Ðo breðere seckes hauen he filt, And in euerilc ðe siluer pilt. *a* **1300** *Fall & Passion* 29 in *E.E.P.* (1862) 13 Womman mai turne man-is wille whare ȝho wol pilt hir to. *c* **1325** *Lai le Freine* 136 With a lace of silke therm pilt. *c* **1400** *Gamelyn* 894 Sitthen in gode office þe kyng hath alle them pilt. *c* **1430** *Two Cookery-bks.* 21 Take þin þombe & pylt þer-on, & ȝif it cleuey, let it boyle.

γ. *c* **1320** *Sir Tristr.* 1520 His mouþe opened þai And pelt treacle in þat man.

4. *intr.* To thrust oneself, push; to impinge with force; ***pulten aȝean***, to rebound.

α. *a* **1225** *Ancr. R.* 366 Hwar se muchel dunt is, hit pulteð up aȝean o þeo þet þer neih stondeð. Sikerliche, hwose is neih him þet ikepte þe heuie duntes, hit wule pulten [*v.r.* butten, bulen] on him.

β, γ. *a* **1300** *K. Horn* (Harl.) 1433 Ffykenild aȝeyn hire pylte [*Laud* 1415 pulte, *Camb.* 1470 pelte] mid his suerdes hylte.

Hence †**pilting**, **pulting** *vbl. sb.*, pushing, thrusting, impact.

a **1225** *Ancr. R.* 366 þe pultunge is ful liht to þolien uor his luue þet underueng so heuie duntes. **1297** R. GLOUC. (Rolls) 4313 þer was pultinge & ssouinge & stroc monyon.

†**pilt, pult,** *sb. Obs. rare.* [f. prec. vb.] A thrust; a push.

13.. *Sir Beues* (A.) 3466 Damme, for-ȝeue me þis gilt, I ne ȝaf þe noþer dent ne pilt! *a* **1350** *Childh. Jesus* 422 He ful a doun ded for is gult. Ne hadde he noþur dunt ne pult.

Piltdown ('pɪltdaʊn). The name of a village in Sussex, England, used *attrib.* esp. in **Piltdown jaw, man, skull,** with reference to the fossil remains of a skull found there, or the primitive hominid described as *Eoanthropus dawsoni*, to which these remains were attributed; the skull was proved fraudulent in 1953 by J. S. Weiner and K. P. Oakley. Also *absol.*

1912 *Times* 19 Dec. 4/5 He [*sc.* A. S. Woodward] inclined ..to the theory that..surviving modern man might have arisen directly from the primitive source of which the Piltdown skull provided the first discovered evidence. **1913** *Q. Jrnl. Geol. Soc.* LXIX. 139 It seems reasonable to interpret the Piltdown skull as exhibiting a closer resemblance to the skulls of the truly ancestral mid-tertiary apes than any fossil human skull hitherto found. **1931** *Times Lit. Suppl.* 23 Apr. 317/1 On comparing her [*sc.* a female hominid] with the Piltdown man he [*sc.* Sir A. Keith] makes amends by describing her as Piltdown refined. **1933** A. S. ROMER *Man & Vertebrates* xi. 246 Can it be that the Piltdown jaw does not belong with the skull? **1953** WEINER & OAKLEY in *Bull. Brit. Mus.* (*Nat. Hist.*), *Geol.* II. III. 145 The iron and chromate staining of the Piltdown jaw seems to us to be explicable only as a necessary part of the deliberate matching of the jaw of a modern ape with the mineralized cranial fragments. **1955** *Bull. Brit. Mus.* (*Nat. Hist.*), *Geol.* III. VI. 228 We are now in a position to give an account of the full extent of the Piltdown hoax... Not one of the Piltdown finds genuinely came from Piltdown. **1955** J. S. WEINER *Piltdown Forgery* 204 The end of Piltdown man is the end of the most troubled chapter in human palaeontology. **1956** *Proc. R. Inst. Gt. Brit.* XXXVI. 150 The Piltdown forgery was the greatest archaeological hoax of its kind ever perpetrated. **1957** T. STEELE in *Time* 30 Dec. 48/1 Rock with caveman Roll with caveman... Piltdown poppa sings this song Archaeologist done me wrong The British Museum's got my head Most unfortunate 'cause I ain't dead. **1970** R. LOWELL *Notebk.* 98 The Piltdown Man, first carnivore to laugh. **1973** *Listener* 10 May 605/3 Man.. was not put together from the cranium of one primate and the jaw of another—that misconception..only makes a fake like the Piltdown skull.

2. *transf.* and *fig.*

1956 A. WILSON *Anglo-Saxon Att.* I. i. 27 Alas, we historians have so little scandal. We are not palaeontologists to display our Piltdowns. **1961** *Times* 9 Nov. 17/1 We must always be beholden to Evans over whom suspicions of a Piltdown sort hang, darkened now by Professor Palmer's discoveries in the Ashmolean. **1971** N. FLEMING *Hash* i. 12 So there is a brain underneath that thatch-covered Piltdown skull of yours. **1976** *Spectator* 2 Oct. 7/3 Ford..is waiting to be shot full of holes, not only because of his Piltdown Man performance as a congressman, but as the head of a government which is clearly out of administrative control.

So **'Piltdowner** = *Piltdown man* (lit. and fig.).

1954 A. HUXLEY in *Encounter* Feb. 11/1 In the tiny Natural History Museum at Idaho Falls, we found ourselves talking to two people from a far remote past... These were Piltdowners whose reaction to the stuffed grizzly was a remark about sizzling steaks of bear-meat. **1961** C. WILLOCK *Death in Covert* i. 6 A big-boned, shambling man ..with the stance of a Piltdowner. **1978** 'J. GASH' *Gold from Gemini* v. 37 He really talks like this, the Piltdowner. No wonder he's thick.

piltock ('pɪltək). *dial.* Also 9 piltack, -tik. [Of unascertained etymology; app. a diminutive.] The name in Shetland, Orkney, and Caithness of the coal-fish, *Merlangus carbonarius*, in its second year.

1793 *Statist. Acc. Scot.* V. 190 Piltocks, sillocks, haddocks, mackarels, and flounders, are got immediately upon the shore. **1822** HIBBERT *Descr. Shetl. Isl.* 119 About the month of May ensuing, they are found to have grown from 8 to 15 inches, acquiring during this period of their growth the name of Piltocks. **1883** J. SANDS in *Standard* 12 Oct. 6/5 A boat that was fishing for piltocks, or saithe.

attrib. **1883** *Chamb. Jrnl.* 211 Blue-eyed fishermen with their circular piltock nets over their shoulders.

pilu, obs. form of PILLOW.

pilular ('pɪljʊlə(r)), *a.* [f. L. type **pilulār-is*, f. *pilula* PILL *sb.*²: see -AR.] Of, pertaining to, or characteristic of a pill; of the nature of a pill or pills.

1802 *Med. Jrnl.* VIII. 48 This preparation..may be exhibited in a pilular form. **1822** *Blackw. Mag.* XI. 16 Pilular productions of the pestle. **1883** R. HALDANE *Workshop Receipts* Ser. II. 281/1 Evaporate the alcoholic tincture to a pilular consistence.

†**'pilulary**, *a. Obs. rare.* [ad. mod.L. *pilulāri-us*, f. *pilula* PILL *sb.*²: see -ARY¹. Cf. F. *pilulaire*.] Applied to a beetle which rolls up dung into small balls: cf. *dung-beetle* (DUNG *sb.* 5 c).

1661 LOVELL *Hist. Anim. & Min.* Introd., The pilularie beetle and spanish flies. **1765** *Universal Mag.* XXXVII. 130/1 The worm that is transformed into the pillulary and stercorary beetle.

pilule ('pɪlju:l). Also 6–9 pillule. [a. F. *pilule*, ad. L. *pilula*: see PILL *sb.*²] A pill; a small pill. Also (*pl.*) as an exclamation of outrage or exasperation (*rare*). Also *fig.*

1543 TRAHERON tr. *Vigo's Chirurg.* xv. 25 b/2 The dose or geuynge of these pillules is [etc.] according to yᵉ strength of yᵉ patient. **1580** HOLLYBAND *Treas. Fr. Tong*, *Pilules*, pillules, or as we call them pilles. **1889** E. DOWSON *Let.* c. 10 May (1967) 77 Pilules! What in Heaven's name do they mean! **1890** *Ibid.* 12 Jan. 131 Excuse these pilules—but I warned you that I had absolutely nothing to say. **1891** *Pall Mall G.* 24 Dec. 3/1 The Bible..is apt to pall when served up, as Mr. Ruskin says, in pilules. **1907** [see DROSERA]. **1960** L. P. HARTLEY *Facial Justice* xxx. 250 At the thought of 'then' her throat contracted and would hardly let the pilule pass.

Hence **'pilulist**, a dealer in pills.

1807 *Edin. Rev.* XI. 66 Is he refreshed by immediate fees like the accomplished pillulist?

pilu'liferous, *a.* [f. L. *pilula* PILL *sb.*² + -FEROUS.] Pill-bearing, bearing globular bodies.

1730–6 BAILEY (folio), *Piluliferous*, bearing or producing round berries or fruit like pills. **1858** MAYNE *Expos. Lex.*, *Urtica pilulifera* is so named because of its fruits, which, by their union, form a globulous mass: piluliferous.

pilulous ('pɪljʊləs), *a.* [f. as prec. + -OUS.] Resembling a pill; pill-like in size, minute.

1872 GEO. ELIOT *Middlem.* ii, Has any one ever pinched into its pilulous smallness the cobweb of pre-matrimonial acquaintanceship? **1905** *Athenæum* 1 July 7/2 Literature is made to descend on them in a gracious rain of pilulous duodecimos.

pilus ('paɪləs). *Bacteriol.* Pl. pili. [L. *pilus* hair.] Any of the several types of filamentous appendages, other than flagella, that are facultatively produced by some bacterial cells.

1959 C. C. BRINTON in *Nature* 21 Mar. 782/2 Pili have been called by several different names: 'fine threads', 'bristles', 'fimbriæ', and 'filaments'. It is felt that the word 'pilus' is the most descriptive term, since the pili usually cover most of the bacterial surface and are continually growing out in a manner quite analogous to hair or fur. **1969** A. M. CAMPBELL *Episomes* iii. 36 Of the various types of pili formed by enteric bacteria, F-pili are distinguishable by the specific adsorption of male-specific bacteriophages to their surfaces. **1975** *Ann. Rev. Microbiol.* XXIX. 104 Once mating pairs were formed, phage f1 failed to interfere with the conjugation event, suggesting the involvement of the pilus..in the transfer of bacterial DNA. **1976** P. COLLARD *Devel. Microbiol.* viii. 108 A number of pilus-specific phages have been discovered.

pilve, pilwe, pilwo, obs. forms of PILLOW.

†**'pilwater.** *Obs. rare.* The Manx shearwater.

1603 OWEN *Pembrokeshire* (1892) 131 The Countrie yeeldeth allso diuerse other fowle, as wild geese,..both sorts of dyvers or dippers, the pilwater, the Wigion.

pily ('paɪlɪ), *a.*¹ *Her.* [f. PILE *sb.*¹ 4 + -Y: cf. PALY, etc.] Divided into a number of piles, the number and direction being usually indicated.

1638 GUILLIM *Heraldry* v. iv. (ed. 3) 376 He beareth Barry pily of eight peeces, Gules and Or. *c* **1828** BERRY *Encycl. Herald.* I. Gloss., *Pily of eight*, traverse in point to the sinister fesse. *Ibid.*, *Pily bendy* merely differs from *pily barry* by throwing the piles bendways..instead of barways.

pily ('paɪlɪ), *a.*² [f. PILE *sb.*⁵ 2 + -Y.] Having a pile or nap (as velvet); of the nature of a pile; esp., in reference to the coat of certain dogs, containing a mixture of short, soft hairs and longer, harder ones.

1533 *Acc. Ld. High Treas. Scot.* (1905) VI. 80 To be the King ane ryding galcoit, vj quarteris pylie franche gray. **1878** *Scribner's Mag.* XVI. 101/1 The coat should be what is called 'pily',—a mixture of hard and soft hair. **1889** 'G. STABLES' *Dog Owners' Kennel Comp.* v. §4. 54 The coat [of the Dandie Dinmont] is pily, or mixture of about two-thirds hardish hair and one-third linty—i.e. soft, but not silky. **1894** M. H. HAYES *Men & Horses* xiii. (ed. 2) 190 That few, if any,..knew much about the virtues of thick 'pily' coir matting and strait-jackets for horses. **1922** R. LEIGHTON *Compl. Bk. Dog* p. xiv, Pily.—A peculiar quality of coat consisting of two kinds of hair, the one soft and woolly, the other long and wiry. **1942** [see FEATHER *sb.* 11 b]. **1963** S. M. LAMPSON *Country Life Bk. Dogs* 123/2 The coat [of the Dandie Dinmont terrier]..is a mixture of hardish and soft hair, which gives it a pily feeling.

†**'pilyie**, *v. Sc. Obs.* Also pilȝie. [ad. F. *piller* = Pr. *pilhar*, Sp. *pillar*, Pg. *pilhar* to pillage, It. *pigliare* (to take): repr. a late L. type **piliāre*, **pileāre*, for L. *pilāre* to deprive of hair, make bare, f. *pilus* hair.] *trans.* To pillage, plunder.

15.. *Aberdeen Regr.* XV. (Jam.), Pilyeit in the streme be menn of wair or serevaris, or ony guddis cassin be storme of wedder. *c* **1575** in *Balfour's Practicks* (1754) 635 To tak and pilȝie that quhilk thay may of the said prize. **1598** *Sc. Acts Jas. VI* (1816) IV. 190/2 Samekle of the said armour as salbe pilleit or lost by sey.

Pima ('pi:mə). Also 9 Pimo. ['Said to be from a native word meaning "no" incorrectly understood and applied by missionaries. The term prob. was brought into American use from Spanish.' (*D.A.*)] **1.** A North American Indian people living chiefly along the Gila and Salt rivers in Arizona; a member of this people. Also, the Uto-Aztecan language of the Pima and Papago, especially the dialect of the Pima. Also *attrib.* See also PAPAGO *sb.* and *a.*

[**1775** P. FONT *Diary* 29 Oct. (1913) 16 Muy de mañana se despacharon unos Yndios, â dar aviso de nuestra venida â los Pimas del rio Gila.] **1850** *California Courier* (San Francisco) 3 July 2/3 From the Pecos river in Texas to the Pimos villages on the Gila, roving bands of Apaches are hovering around the emigrants, stealing their animals. **1864** *Harper's Mag.* Dec. 23/2 It was gratifying..to know that the Pimos were rapidly becoming a civilized people. **1884, 1912** [see HOHOKAM *sb.* and *a.*]. **1918** A. A. BRILL tr. *Freud's Totem & Taboo* (1919) ii. 68 After a Pima Indian had killed an Apache he had to submit himself to severe ceremonies of purification and expiation. **1932** W. L. GRAFF *Lang.* 430 The Uto-Aztec group comprises the three branches of Shoshonean, Pima-Sonoran, and Nahuatl. **1959** C. OGBURN *Marauders* vi. 189 Herman Manuel was a swarthy, squat Pima Indian from Arizona. **1960** C. WINICK *Dict. Anthropol.* 414/2 *Pima-Papago*, a general term used to describe the art of the south-west Indians of the United States. It includes the techniques of several crafts. **1962** D. H. HYMES in J. A. Fishman *Readings Sociol. of Lang.* (1968) 118 The functional load of /p/ in a community cannot be analyzed apart from the nature and use of various channels, as when among the Pima the functional load of /p/ differs between singing and recitation. **1964** S. M. LAMB in *Univ. Calif. Publ. Linguistics* XXXIV. 110 The Papagos speak Pima. **1965** *Canad. Jrnl. Linguistics* X. 141 Daughter languages of the Uto-Aztecan family..(Hopi, Pima-Papago, [etc.]). **1974** *Encycl. Brit. Micropædia* VII. 1009/3 *Piman languages*, Uto-Aztecan language group.., including Papago, Pima, [etc.]. **1979** *Tucson Mag.* Apr. 26/1 Ask a Pima or a Papago Indian— these are people who have been here for hundreds of years.

2. [f. *Pima* County, S. Arizona.] In full ***Pima cotton.*** A fine quality cotton developed from Egyptian cotton. Also *attrib.*

1936 *Sears Catal.* (ed. 173) 469 Pima is the finest of all American cotton. **1953** *New Biol.* XIV. 59 In Arizona a local selection of Egyptian origin, known as Pima, proved to be long but relatively weak. **1962** A. HUXLEY *Island* ix. 134 A Whisper-Pink Bra in Dacron and Pima Cotton. **1965** J. M. CAIN *Magician's Wife* (1966) xii. 86 She met him downstairs ..in dark blue pima suit. **1976** *National Observer* (U.S.) 23 Oct. 9/6 (Advt.), Nothing compares to our handsome, pure pima cotton broadcloth plain collar shirts.

Piman ('pi:mən), *a.* and *sb.* [f. prec. + -AN.]

A. *adj.* Of or pertaining to the Pima and Papago Indians or their language. Also, of or pertaining to any of several ethnic and linguistic groupings of Indians of varying extent, comprising the Pimas, the Papagos, and certain other related peoples. **B.** *sb.* **a.** A Pima or Papago Indian; *pl.* the Pima and Papago Indians considered as a single ethnic and linguistic group. **b.** The Uto-Aztecan language of the Pima and Papago; also called *Papago*, *Pima*, *Pima-Papago*, and *Papago-Pima*. Also used of any of several wider groupings (see the adj.).

1891 J. W. Powell in *7th Ann. Rep. U.S. Bureau Amer. Ethnol. 1885–86* 98 (*heading*) Piman family. **1933** L. Bloomfield *Language* iv. 72 The Piman family (east of the Gulf of California). **1936** B. L. Whorf in *Ess. in Anthropol. presented to A. L. Kroeber* 198 Piman,..one of the groups most unlike the groups with which we began the classification. **1942** Castetter & Bell *Pima & Papago Indian Agric.* 1 The Pimans, a name applied to the whole group of Pima-Papago in both Mexico and the United States, anciently extended in irregular distribution from southern Sonora to the Gila River. **1950** J. H. Steward *Handbk. S. Amer. Indians* VI. 501 Its major use has been by the *Cáhita* and *Piman* tribes and their neighbors, that is, in the area adjacent to the upper Gulf of California. **1965** *Canad. Jrnl. Linguistics* X. 79 He also includes Nahuatl and Sonoran (Piman). **1969** K. L. Hale in D. & L. Saxton *Dict. Papago & Pima* Introd., The Piman languages, of which Papago-Pima is the northernmost, are of considerable interest for the fact that they constitute a close-knit, well defined subfamily within Uto-Aztecan. **1973** B. L. Fontana in —— *Legends & Lore Papago & Pima Indians* p. xi, This volume of Papago and Pima literature makes available to readers of both Piman and English an important collection of heretofore widely scattered materials, much of it provided by Piman spokesmen many years ago. **1975** D. M. Bahr *Pima & Papago Ritual Oratory* 1 The hero of Piman (Pima-Papago) ritual oratory is a medicine man. [*Note*] The Pima and Papagos today are separate tribes. This study includes texts from each and considers ideas they have in common. I use the word 'Piman' to represent this common culture. *Ibid.*, Oratory..must have afforded the Pimans a means of harmonizing these various activities. *Ibid.* 3 A second group interested in this poetry is of course the native speakers of Piman, Pima and Papago Indians of southern Arizona.

pimaric (pɪˈmærɪk, paɪ-), *a. Chem.* [mod. f. *Pī(nus) mar(itima)* + -ic; in F. *pimarique*.] In ***pimaric acid***, 'an acid resin ($C_{20}H_{30}O_2$) occurring in the turpentine of *Pinus maritima*' (Watts).

1857 Miller *Elem. Chem.* III. 502 White resin or *galipot* is obtained from Bordeaux turpentine, furnished by the *Pinus maritima*, and consists almost entirely of an acid resin, the *pimaric*. **1880** Garrod & Baxter *Mat. Med.* 364 The Resin consists of three isomeric acids, Pimaric, Pinic, and Sylvic, differing in their solubility in alcohol. Pinic acid is soluble in cold alcohol; sylvic in warm alcohol; pimaric requires boiling spirit; the formula..is $C_{20}H_{30}O_2$.

†**pimble-stone, pimple-stone**, obs. nasalized var. of pebble-stone.

1577 Frampton *Joyful News* ii. (1596) 73 Pure Pimple stones of a brooke or Riuer. **1622** Malynes *Anc. Law-Merch.* 491 To lay little pimble stones vnder their tongue, to eleuate the same.

†**pime.** *Obs. rare*$^{-1}$. [? Imitative.] A plaintive cry, a wail or whine.

c **1470** Henryson *Mor. Fab.* viii. (*Preach. Swallow*) xxiv, The swallow swyth put furth ane pietious pyme, Said, 'Wo is him can not be war in tyme'.

pimelea (pɪˈmiːlɪə). Also (erron.) **-ia.** [mod.L. (D. Solander in J. Gaertner *De Fructibus et Seminibus Plantarum* (1788) I. 186), f. Gr. πῑμελή fat, in allusion to the oily seeds.] An evergreen shrub of the genus so called, belonging to the family Thymelaeaceæ, native to Australasia, and bearing small terminal clusters of white, pink, or yellow flowers.

[**1793** J. E. Smith *Specimen Bot. New Holland* 32 Gaertner..adopted the name of *Pimelea* from the manuscripts of Dr. Solander.] **1810** W. Aiton *Hortus Kewensis* (ed. 2) I. 25 Flax-leaved Pimelea. Nat[ive] of New South Wales. **1842** W. Colenso *Let.* 1 Sept. in *Lond. Jrnl. Bot.* (1844) III. 8, I found a handsome *Pimelea* in flower, a shrub of 2–3 feet in height. **1885** T. Baines *Greenhouse & Stove Plants* 281/1 All the kinds of Pimelea strike readily from cuttings made of the points of the young shoots. **1951** *Dict. Gardening* (R. Hort. Soc.) III. 1572/1 Pimeleas are compact, free-growing plants needing greenhouse conditions. **1966** H. E. & J. Bawden *Making Shrub Garden* 216 Some of the pimelias are greenhouse shrubs... There are other pimelias which grow high up in the mountains.

pimelic (pɪˈmɛlɪk), *a. Chem.* [f. Gr. πῑμελή fat + -ic.] In ***pimelic acid***, an acid ($C_7H_{12}O_4$) obtained in small crystalline grains by the action of nitric acid on various fatty substances. Hence **pimelate** (ˈpɪmələt), a salt of pimelic acid.

1838 R. D. Thomson in *Brit. Ann.* 349 Pimelic acid..was obtained by Laurent from the mother liquor. **1857** Miller *Elem. Chem.* III. 422 Pimelic acid. **1866** Watts *Dict. Chem.* IV. 646 Pimelate of methyl.

pimelite (ˈpɪməlaɪt). *Min.* [Named by Karsten, 1800, f. Gr. πῑμελή fat: see -ite[1].] A hydrous silicate of aluminium, iron, nickel, and magnesium, of apple-green colour, greasy in appearance and to the touch.

1808 T. Allan *Names Min.* 49 The name of pimelite has been given by Karsten. **1868** Dana *Min.* (ed. 5) 510 Pimelite gives water in the closed tube.

pimelode (ˈpɪmələʊd). *Ichthyol.* [ad. mod.L. *Pīmelōdus*, a generic name, f. Gr. πῑμελώδης like fat, fatty, f. πῑμελή fat: see -ode[1].] A cat-fish of the genus *Pimelodus*. So ˈ**pimelodine** *a.*, belonging to the *Pīmelōdīnæ*, a subfamily of cat-fishes of the family *Siluridæ*, typified by the genus *Pimelodus*; *sb.* a cat-fish of this subfamily.

†**piˈment.** *Obs.* Also 3–5 (8) **piement**, 4 **pimente**, 4–6 **pyement**, 4–6 (8) **pyment**, 5–6 **pymente**. [a. OF. *piment*, earlier *piument* (12th c. in Hatz.-Darm.) = Pr. *piment*, *pigment*, Sp. *pimiento*:—L. *pigmentum*, orig. pigment, paint, also (scented) unguent; in med.L. scented or spiced confection, spiced drink (Du Cange). See also next.]

1. A drink composed of wine sweetened with honey and flavoured with spices.

a **1225** *Ancr. R.* 404 Loke hwu heo ȝulden him! uor piment of swete huni luue, eisil of sur nið. *c* **1300** *Havelok* 1728 Pyment to drinke, and god clare. *c* **1374** Chaucer *Boeth.* ii. met. v. 35 (Camb. MS.), They cowde make no pyment nor clarree. **1390** Gower *Conf.* III. 12 That on [tonne] is full of such piment Which passeth all entendement. ? *c* **1475** *Sqr. Lowe Degre* 760 Wyne of Greke, & muscadell, Both clare, pyment, and rochell. **1530** Palsgr. 254/1 Pyment, *piment*. **1725** C. W. Forbes *Let.* 6 Apr. in Burton *Life*, Drink pyment to your meat dashed with strong wine. **1824** Henderson in *Blackw. Mag.* XVI. 16 The varieties of piment most frequently mentioned are the Hippocras and Clarry.

2. A scented or perfumed unguent.

c **1290** *S. Eng. Leg.* I. 466/130 Min heued..with no-manere Oynement Ne smeordest, with none salue ne with no piement. *a* **1300** *Cursor M.* 3702 (Cott.) þe odor o þi uestement It smelles als o piement. **1382** Wyclif *Esther* ii. 12 Sixe monethis..thei shulden vse maner pimentis and swote spice. —— *Isa.* lvii. 9 Thou..enournedest thee with kingus oynement, and multepliedest thi pymentus.

3. = pimento 1, Cayenne pepper. (F. *piment*.)

1705 tr. *Bosman's Guinea* xvi. 305 The last sort of Pepper called here Piement, and in Europe Spanish Pepper, grows here in abundance.

pimento (pɪˈmɛntəʊ). [ad. Sp. *pimienta*, Pg. *pimenta* pepper (generally), repr. L. *pigmentum*, in med.L. spiced drink, hence spice, pepper (generally). Sp. *pimiento*, F. *piment* are applied to Cayenne or Guinea pepper, capsicum; in Eng. the name has passed to allspice or Jamaica pepper, Pg. *pimenta da Jamaica*, F. *piment de Jamaïque*.]

†**1.** Formerly, Cayenne or Guinea pepper. *Obs.*

[**1673** Ray *Journ. Low C.* 494 They [Spaniards] delight much in *Pimentone*, i.e. Guiny pepper.] **1697** tr. *C'tess D'Aunoy's Trav.* (1706) 241 They perswade me to eat some of a Fruit they call Pimento, which is as long as ones Finger, but as hot as Pepper.

2. a. Now, The dried aromatic berries of the tree *Pimenta dioica* (see 3); also called *Jamaica pepper* or *allspice* (F. *piment de Jamaïque*, Pg. *pimenta da Jamaica*).

1690 *Hist. Acc. W. Indies* in *Harl. Misc.* (ed. Park) II. 371 Piemento is another natural production of..Jamaica; from whence many call it Jamaica pepper. **1718** Quincy *Compl. Disp.* 84 Pimento, is call'd by the common People All-Spice. **1783** Justamond tr. *Raynal's Hist. Indies* VI. 332 These berries..turn brown and acquire a spicy smell, which in England hath given the name of all spice to this pimento. **1832** *Veg. Subst. Food* 364 Pimento combines the flavour and properties of many of the oriental spices. **1889** G. S. Boulger *Uses of Plants* i. 66 Allspice, or Pimento, is the dry berry of *Pimenta officinalis* Lindl...a West Indian evergreen-tree. **1969** *Oxf. Bk. Food Plants* 132/2 Allspice (*Pimenta dioica*) is a small tropical tree whose unripe dried berries provide the spice called allspice... It is also known as 'pimenta' and 'pimento'.

b. = pimiento, paprika 2.

1918 A. Quiller-Couch *Foe-Farrell* 94 What do you say now..to a pig's trotter farced with pimento. **1943** D. Welch *Maiden Voy.* xvi. 132 The soup..was delicious; pieces of pimento swam about in it like goldfish. **1950** E. David *Bk. Mediterranean Food* 132 Mixed red, green, and yellow pimentos, cooked a few minutes in boiling water, then peeled and sautéd in butter. **1978** *Nagel's Encycl.-Guide: China* 375 *Hu nan* and *Hu bei* are both known for chicken and pimento (*la zi ji*), soy-bean omelettes (*dou pi*) and bread with stuffing.

c. = *pimento red*.

1976 *Northumberland Gaz.* 26 Nov. 16 (Advt.), Triumph Dolomite. Pimento, tan fabric trim. **1977** *Time* 21 Feb. 43/1 A pimento handkerchief-style dress.

3. The tree which yields this spice, *Pimenta dioica* or *Pimenta officinalis* (N.O. *Myrtaceæ*), an evergreen, native of the West Indies, and much cultivated in Jamaica; also, the wood of this tree.

1756 P. Browne *Jamaica* (1789) 247 Pimento, or All-spice... The berries of this tree have an agreeable aromatic and sub-astringent taste. **1777** Robertson *Hist. Amer.* (1783) II. 104 Pimento, a small tree, yielding a strong aromatic spice. **1892** *Joseph Gardner & Sons' Monthly Circular* 1 Oct., Pimento, £5 per ton. **1893** McCarthy *Red Diamonds* II. 43 The dried seeds of pimento. **1950** P. Bottome *Under Skin* x. 95 You had better stop here under this pimento. *Ibid.* xvi. 137 Pimento trees with their greenish bark and dark glossy leaves. **1958** D. P. Storer *Familiar Trees & Cultivated Plants of Jamaica* 69 The Pimento grows to about 30 ft. in height.

4. *attrib.*, as **pimento berry** = sense 2 a; **pimento cheese**, soft cheese flavoured with chopped sweet peppers; **pimento dram**, a Jamaican liqueur made with pimento berries; **pimento myrtle, tree, wood** = 3; **pimento red**, an orange-red colour; also *attrib.* or as *adj.*; **pimento walk**, a plantation of pimento trees; **pimento water**, a cordial made from pimento.

1893 C. Sullivan *Jamaica Cookery Bk.* 104 Pimento Dram... Put four quarts of ripe pimento berries into a jar, and boil till the berries burst... Add two bottles of brandy or good old rum... Then add a thick syrup of loaf sugar. **1907** *Daily Consular & Trade Rep.* (U.S. State Dept.) 5 Oct. 11 Ripe pimento berries are used to make pimento dram, a native drink. **1970** *Nature* 8 Aug. 556/2 Pimento berries are gathered while still green. **1916** *Daily Colonist* (Victoria, B.C.) 1 July 6/5 (Advt.), Cream or Pimento Cheese, each 10¢. **1967** Mrs. L. B. Johnson *White House Diary* 23 Apr. (1970) 510, I had had a platter of sandwiches put in the refrigerator—roast beef and pimento cheese. **1893**, **1907** Pimento dram [see *pimento berry* above]. **1958** D. P. Storer *Familiar Trees & Cultivated Plants of Jamaica* 70 'Pimento-dram' is a delicious Jamaican liqueur made, essentially, by soaking the ripe berries in rum. **1836** Macgillivray tr. *Humboldt's Trav.* xxiv. 371 The pimento-myrtle is produced in the woods. **1975** *Vogue* Dec. 107 Pimento red Hurel jersey. **1979** U. Curtiss *Menace Within* ix. 90 An abstract painting in pink and pimento red. **1847** E. J. Seymour *Severe Dis.* I. 2 Rhubarb and peppermint, or nitre and soda in pimento water enable the stomach to bear its load. **1712** W. Rogers *Voy.* (1718) 126 He built two Hutts with Piemento trees. **1825** *Gentl. Mag.* XCV. i. 216 The Pimento-tree grows to the height of 30 or 40 feet, with a very straight trunk. **1825** *Gentl. Mag.* XCV. i. 216 A Pimento walk, when in full blossom, is a very delightful object. **1712** W. Rogers *Voy.* (1718) 126 The Piemento Wood..served him both for Firing and Candle, and refresh'd him with its fragrant Smell.

pi-meson (ˌpaɪˈmiːzɒn, -ˈmɛzɒn). *Nuclear Physics.* Also **pi meson, pimeson.** [f. pi *sb.* + meson[3].] The original name for the pion. (Freq. written *π-meson*.)

[**1947** Lattes, Occhialini, & Powell in *Nature* 4 Oct. 455/1 It is convenient to refer to this process..as the μ-decay. We represent the primary mesons by the symbol π, and the secondary by μ.] *Ibid.* 456/1 The restricted range of the π-mesons in the emulsion. **1950** D. Halliday *Introd. Nucl. Physics* xii. 455 When negative pi-mesons are absorbed in matter,..there is a major nuclear disruption. **1953** *Jrnl. Brit. Interplanetary Soc.* XII. 203 The neutral pi-meson dissociates almost immediately into two high energy gamma rays (photons), which inititate the photon-electron cascades that are frequently observed in cosmic ray processes. **1968** *Times* 19 Jan. 13/8 The object..is to see how frequently an electron and a positive electron (or positron) would be converted..into the radio-actively unstable particles of matter called pimesons (or pions). **1972** *Daily Colonist* (Victoria, B.C.) 3 Mar. 16/8 The new technique involves a radioactive beam of sub-atomic particles called pimesons. **1978** *Sci. Amer.* Mar. 57/1 The mass of the muon (106 MeV) is quite close to the mass of the pi meson, or pion (140 MeV).

Hence **pi-ˈmesic, -meˈsonic** *adjs.* = pionic *a.*

1952 *Physical Rev.* LXXXVIII. 134/1 We have found direct evidence for π-mesic atom formation with the nuclei of carbon, oxygen, and beryllium. **1953** *Ibid.* XCII. 789/2 Experimental studies of π-mesonic x-rays in light elements have been made. **1954** *Ibid.* XCVI. 774 (*heading*) Energy level displacements in pi-mesonic atoms. **1970** Lock & Measday *Intermediate Energy Nucl. Physics* xi. 276 Because of the mass of the π^- (139·6 MeV) is greater than that of the μ^- (105·7 MeV), the energies of the pi-mesonic x-rays are about 30% higher than those of the equivalent mu-mesic x-rays.

†**pimˈgenet.** *slang* or *dial. Obs.* Forms: 7 **pimpgenet, pimginnit**, 7–8 **-ginit**, 8 **-ginet, -gennet**, 9 **pimgenet**. [Origin unknown. For Forby's conjecture in quot. *a* 1825, evidence is wanting; the alleged sense 'pomegranate' is not recorded in Eng. Dial. Dict.] A pimple: see quots.

1693 tr. *Cowley's Plants* i. in *C.'s Wks.* 22 My conquering hand Pimpgenets cannot shun, Nor blackish, yellow spots the Face o'er-run. **1694** *Dunton's Ladies Dict.* (N.), To stand ..parching his pimginits, carbuncles, and buboes. *a* **1700** B. E. *Dict. Cant. Crew*, *Pimginnit*, a large, red, angry Pimple. **1719** D'Urfey *Pills* V. 314 The Lass with a Wainscot Face, and from Pim-ginets free. *a* **1825** Forby *Voc. E. Anglia*, *Pimegenet*. 1. A very delicate and mincing diminutive of *piemgenet* for *pomegranate*. 2. A small red pimple. Possibly a hyperbolically figurative application of the first sense. **1847–78** Halliwell, *Pimgenet*, a small red pimple. 'Nine pimgenets make a pock royal', Old Saying.

pimiento (pɪmɪˈɛntəʊ). Also (*rare*) **pimienta**. [Sp.] = paprika 2.

1845 [see gazpacho]. **1846** R. Ford *Gatherings from Spain* xi. 131 Add a bit of bacon, onions, garlic, salt, pepper, *pimientos*, a bunch of thyme. **1901** *Daily Colonist* (Victoria, B.C.) 15 Oct. 6/6 (Advt.), Glass Jars Olives (with Pimientos). **1937** A. F. Hill *Econ. Bot.* xx. 476 The paprikas are European varieties [of sweet pepper] with large mild fruits. Spanish paprika..is better known as pimiento. **1960**, **1969** [see paprika 2]. **1979** L. Kallen *Introducing C. B. Greenfield* xii. 144 My grocery bag of chicken, shrimp, olives, pimentos.

b. = pimento 2 c.

1972 J. Potts *Trouble-Maker* iii. 18 Her living-room—avocado and chocolate brown, pimiento accents.

2. *attrib.* **pimiento cheese** = *pimento cheese* s.v. pimento 4; **pimiento(-stuffed) olive**, an olive with its stone replaced by a piece of red sweet pepper.

1922 *Hotel World* 15 Apr. 15/1 American or Pimiento cheese. **1972** *Harrod's Christmas Catal.* 60/2 Jar Harrods Pimiento Olives. **1974** *Ibid.* 40/1 Jar Pimiento Stuffed Olives.

piminy ('pɪmɪnɪ). *nonce-wd.* [? Shortened f. MIMINY-PIMINY *a.* and *sb.*, NIMINY-PIMINY *a.*] ? Something expressive of affectation.

1819 KEATS *Let.* 22 Sept. (1958) II. 175 Poor thing she little thinks how she is.. making her nose quite a piminy.

†'**Pimlico**¹. *Obs.* [app. a place-name or personal surname.]

1. Name of a place of resort (perh. from the name of its proprietor) at Hogsdon (now Hoxton), a suburb of London, formerly celebrated for its ale, cakes, etc.; also, ale named after this place.

[**1598** *Newes from Hogsdon* (N.), Hey for old Ben Pimlico's nut-browne.] **1609** (*title*) Pimlyco, or Runne Red Cap. 'Tis a Mad World at Hogsdon. **1610** B. JONSON *Alch.* v. ii, Gallants.. seene to flock here.. as to a second Hogs-den, In dayes of Pimlico and Eye-bright! **1614** J. COOKE *Greene's Tu Quoque* in Hazl. *Dodsley* XI. 233, I have sent my daughter this morning as far as Pimlico, to fetch a draught of Derby ale. **1670** in J. Nichols *Coll. Poems* (1780) III. 263 Or stout March-beer, or Windsor-ale,.. Or Pimlico, whose too great sale Did marr it.

2. A drinking-vessel of some kind.

1654 GAYTON *Pleas. Notes* III. vi. 103 No small service nor miser glasses will doe the businesse here, nor Pimlicos discharg'd to the round in the middle.

3. Some white dress fabric.

1687 *Hist. Sir J. Hawkwood* ii. 23 The laughing Fellow, dressed up in Pimlico, as Painters.. Picture.. the shadow of a Ghost. **1760** *Life Cotton* in *Walton's Angler* II. p. xx, To bedizen them out in Pimlico, or bloat them up with turgid bombast.

pimlico² ('pɪmlɪkəʊ). [Echoic, from the cry of the bird.] †**a.** Variant of PEMBLICO. *Obs.* **b.** The Australian friar-bird: see FRIAR *sb.* 6.

1848 J. GOULD *Birds Australia* IV. pl. 58 From the fancied resemblance of its notes to these words, it has obtained from the Colonists the various names of 'Poor Soldier', 'Pimlico', 'Four o'clock', etc.

Pimm's (pɪmz). Also **Pimms**, (*erron.*) **Pim**. [Proprietary term, f. the name of the proprietor of the restaurant where these drinks were created.] Used to designate any of four spirit-based mixed drinks ('cups'), taken neat or used as a basis for long drinks; also, a drink of one of these. Also *ellipt.*

Where no number is specified, the reference is usually understood to be to *Pimm's Number One Cup*, which is gin-based.

[**1888** *Trade Marks Jrnl.* 20 June 817 Pimms. Poultry. London. Pimms & Co.,.. Poultry, London; restaurant proprietors... Wines and spirits, excepting brandy.] **1912** *Ibid.* 27 Nov. 1782 Pimm's No. 1 Cup... An Alcoholic beverage. H. D. Davies & Co., Limited,.. London,.. wine merchants. **1931** R. H. HEATON *Perfect Hostess* 56 Pim Cup. One wineglass of No. 1 Pim cup mixture [etc.]. **1939** L. MACNEICE *Autumn Jrnl.* v. 22 And this, we say, is on me; Something out of the usual, a Pimm's Number One. **1957** J. BRAINE *Room at Top* xxv. 202 The de-luxe bar and the iced Pimm's. **1960** *20th Cent.* July 73 Exams are over for ever, Pimm's is flowing. **1966** 'K. NICHOLSON' *Hook, Line & Sinker* v. 66 Mrs. Fairchild created a diversion by mixing everyone a Pimms. **1967** A. LICHINE *Encycl. Wines* 404/1 There are four Pimm's Cups, and it is said that they were originated by a bartender at Pimm's Restaurant in London and so delighted the customers that the staff was continually being asked to put some up for people to take home. As a result, they begun to be made commercially. **1972** F. WARNER *Lying Figures* I. 6 Barman! Make it a double Pimms!

Pimo, var. PIMA.

pimozide ('pɪməʊzaɪd). *Pharm.* [f. PI(PERIDINE + elements in *benzimidazolin*, part of the systematic name of the compound (see IMIDE and AZO-).] A derivative of piperidine that is a colourless powder used as a tranquillizer in the treatment of schizophrenia and anxiety states.

1968 *Arzneimittel-Forschung* XVIII. 261 (*heading*) Pimozide, a chemically novel, highly potent and orally long-acting neuroleptic drug. **1976** SMYTHIES & CORBETT *Psychiatry* iii. 27 Other effective anti-psychotics.. include the butyrophenones and pimozide. **1977** *Lancet* 21 May 1105/1, I have treated a boy of 17.. for anorexia nervosa... He received pimozide 4 mg three times a day for a month.

pimp (pɪmp), *sb.*¹ [Origin obscure.

Generally thought to be in some way related to 16th c. F. *pimper* vb., pr. pple. *pimpant* alluring or seducing in outward appearance or dress, *pimpesouée* a pretentious woman (Hatz.-Darm.). F. *pimper* is taken as = Pr. *pimpar*, *pipar* to render elegant (Littré). But these leave much to be explained in the history of the word before 1600.]

a. One who provides means and opportunities for unlawful sexual intercourse; a pander, procurer.

1607 MIDDLETON *Five Gallants* II. i. 36 *First Courtesan.*—Our pimp's grown proud. **1666** PEPYS *Diary* 10 June, The Duke of York is wholly given up to his new mistress... Mr. Brouncker, it seems, was the pimp to bring it about. **1711** STEELE *Spect.* No. 51 ¶6 He has been used as a Pimp to ravishing Tyrants, or successful Rakes. **1860** MOTLEY *Netherl.* (1868) I. ii. 51 The honest soldier had refused to become his pimp. **1932** *Evening Sun* (Baltimore) 9 Dec. 31/5 *Pimp*, man who is supported by women. **1961** J. DOS PASSOS *Mid-century* I. vii. 96 I'd thought him a pimp or procurer but he didn't seem to be. **1968–70** *Current Slang* (Univ. S. Dakota) III-IV. 92 *Pimp*, one who solicits women and girls to sell themselves and turn all the money over to him. He, in turn, gives them their salary. **1972** T. KOCHMAN *Rappin' & Stylin' Out* 243 The 'pimp'.. a person of considerable status in the street hierarchy.. has acquired a stable of girls to hustle for him and give him money. **1976** *Toronto Star* 21 Aug. B1/2 It's getting busier partly because so many black American hookers and their pimps come and check into a hotel here for the weekend and compete for our territory.

attrib. **1871** B. TAYLOR *Faust* (1875) I. xi. 135 A fitter woman ne'er was made To ply the pimp and gypsey trade.

b. *transf.* and *fig.* One who ministers to anything evil, esp. to base appetites or vices.

a **1704** T. BROWN *Sat. on Quack* Wks. 1730 I. 63 Thou churchyard pimp, and pander to the grave. **1789** WOLCOTT (P. Pindar) *Imit. Hor.* I. xii. 8 That sends to counties, borough-towns, his crimps, Alias his vote-seducing pimps. **1843** MIALL in *Nonconf.* III. 441 The most abandoned pimp of the literary world. **1866** FELTON *Anc. & Mod. Greece* II. I. ii. 32 [The slave] is the pimp and pander to all the vices of the young. **1962** S. E. FINER *Man on Horseback* xii. 241 Mill recognized the 'necessity' of some despotic régimes; but he saw them.. as a *pis aller*. He did not, like today's pimps of tyranny, pretend that the despotism was superior to the system of representative government. **1968** *Listener* 22 Aug. 252/1 Of course, it's cheaper to take on men trained in Fleet Street than to train them yourself, but the BBC should be the custodian of, not the pimp for, popular forms.

c. In various other uses: (*a*) *Austral.* and *N.Z. slang*, an informer, a tell-tale; (*b*) *Welsh dial.*, one who spies on lovers, a peeping Tom; (*c*) *U.S. slang*, a male prostitute.

a **1885** *Penguin Bk. Austral. Ballads* (1964) 74 Blue-coat imps, Who were laid on to where he slept, By informing peeler's pimps. **1938** X. HERBERT *Capricornia* 567 'I'm not a pimp.' 'What you mean pimp?' 'I'm not a police-informer.' **1940** DYLAN THOMAS *Portrait of Artist as Young Dog* 126, I lay like a pimp in a bush by Tom's side and squinted through to see him round his hands on Norma's breast. **1942** G. CASEY *It's Harder for Girls* 51 'I just say I'm not a pimp,' Brownie insisted, beginning to blubber. **1942** Z. N. HURSTON in A. Dundes *Mother Wit* (1973) 223 In Harlemese, *pimp* has a different meaning than its ordinary definition as a procurer for immoral purposes. The Harlem pimp is a man whose amatory talents are for sale to any woman who will support him... He is actually a male prostitute. **1969** D. NILAND *Dead Men Running* 290 'There's a pimp at work.'.. 'The same pimp is it, that potted Shannessy and Halloran?' **1974** *Age* (Melbourne) 12 Oct. 12/1 You fat pimp! The standard response to 'I'm going to tell on you'.

d. *attrib.* and *Comb.*, as ***pimp-errant***, ***-master***, ***-tenure***; ***pimp-like*** adj.; †**pimp-whisk**, **-whiskin (-ing)** *obs. slang* = PIMP.

1614 B. JONSON *Barth. Fair* III. v, I neuer saw a young *Pimpe errant, and his Squire better match'd. **1681** OTWAY *Soldiers Fort.* IV. i, His undoubted Right to be *Pimp-Master-General of London and Middlesex. **1684** SOUTHERNE *Disappointment* II. i, Now thou art Pimp-master in Ordinary to my family. **1701** *Cowell's Interpr.* (White Kennett) N ij/2 [quotes *Assize Roll, No.* 48, m. 28ᵈ, of 12 Edw. I (1284), 'Willelmus Hoppeshort, tenet dimidiam virgatam terre [in Bokhampton] de domino rege, per servitium custodiendi domino regi sex damisellas, scil. meretrices ad custum domini regis', and adds] *i.e.* by *Pimp Tenure. **1874** HAZLITT *Tenures of Land*, etc. 30. **1707** J. STEVENS tr. *Quevedo's Com. Wks.* (1709) 350 Such.. Sayings are a Discredit to your self.. As for Instance... a *Pimp whisk; a Tatterdemallion; Tittle tattle. **1638** FORD *Fancies* I. ii, 'Tis a gallant life to be an old lord's *pimp-whiskin.

pimp, *sb.*² *local.* [Origin uncertain. Cf. PIMPING *a.*] A name in London and the southern counties for a small faggot or bundle of firewood.

1742 *De Foe's Tour Gt. Brit.* (ed. 3) I. 129 Those small light Bavins which are used in Taverns in London to light their Faggots, and are called in the Taverns a Brush, and by the Wood-men Pimps. **1785** GROSE *Dict. Vulg. T.*, *Pimp*,.. also a small faggot used about London for lighting fires, named from introducing the fire to the coals. **1862** MRS. GROTE *Collected Papers* 157 Buying wood in the copses.. and cutting it up at home in little faggots, called 'pimps'. **1889** *Official Advertisement* 17 Jan., The Commissioners of H.M. Works &c. are prepared to receive tenders for the supply of brushwood fagots (pimps) to the royal palaces, government offices, &c.

pimp, *v.* [f. PIMP *sb.*¹]

1. a. *intr.* To act as pimp or pander; to pander.

1636 MASSINGER *Bashf. Lover* v. i, Hence, and pimp To your rams and ewes. **1671** DRYDEN *Evening's Love* Pref., His friend, Mr. Truewit.. is not ashamed to pimp for him. **1728** POPE *Dunc.* II. 213 *note*, A creature unletter'd, who.. pimpeth to the pleasures of such vain, braggart, puft Nobility. **1751** SMOLLETT *Per. Pic.* lxxx, He was well known to have pimped for three generations of the nobility. **1975** *New Yorker* 26 May 18/2 His father (Jack Warden) pimps to add to his income as a taxi-driver. **1976** *Ibid.* 1 Mar. 79/1, I also especially enjoyed Roscoe Onman as Pretty Eddie, the 'happy dust' addict who pimps for his girl.

b. *fig.* or in generalized sense.

1681 DRYDEN *Abs. & Achit.* 81 The careful Devil.. providently pimps for ill desires. **1733** CHEYNE *Eng. Malady* II. iv. (1734) 331, I had never pimp'd to the Vices or Infidelity of any. **1813** SHELLEY *Notes to Q. Mab* Poet. Wks. (1891) 66/2 How much longer will man continue to pimp for the gluttony of Death?

c. ***to pimp on***: to scrounge off; to take advantage of. *U.S. slang.*

1942 Z. N. HURSTON in A. Dundes *Mother Wit* (1973) 226/1 'You got any money?' the girl asked... 'Nobody ain't pimping on me. You dig me?'

2. *trans.* To bring *together* as a pimp. *nonce-use.*

1672 CROWNE *City Politiques* v. (1683) 72 Sirrah.. where ha' you pimp'd this couple together?

3. *intr.* To tell tales; to inform *on* someone. *Austral.* and *N.Z. slang.*

1941 BAKER *Dict. Austral. Slang* 54 *Pimp*,.. to inform on. **1945** G. CASEY *Downhill is Easier* 109 This dago bastard pimped on him to Hayes, an' lost him his job. **1949** *Landfall* Mar. 30 He would grope out, head down, afraid to meet someone who would pimp on him. **1957** J. WATEN *Shares in Murder* 155 You made up to me so you could get me to pimp on Charlie for you. **1960** N. HILLIARD *Maori Girl* 229 She's bound to pimp and make trouble.

4. *intr.* To spy on lovers. *Welsh dial.*

1976 R. LEWIS *Witness my Death* i. 13 Dai—Pimping again then, is it?

Hence '**pimping** *vbl. sb.*¹ and *ppl. a.*

1640 H. MILL *Nights Search* 27 A pimping theife, his life and death. **1668** R. L'ESTRANGE *Vis. Quev.* (1708) 5 The Poets do us many a good turn, both by Pimping and otherwise. **1682** *Roxb. Bail.* (1882) IV. 269 What Pimping Whig shall dare controule, or check the Lawful Heir [James Duke of York]? *a* **1704** T. BROWN *Pleas. Love* Wks. 1730 I. 111 And pimping darkness shut out day. **1849** MACAULAY *Hist. Eng.* vi. II. 50 He succeeded in acquiring.. partly by gambling, and partly by pimping, an estate of three thousand pounds a year. **1957** C. MACINNES *City of Spades* II. ix. 165 Ite.. put on his tailored duffel coat, and said, 'Now I must get out in the cold and do me pimpin'... A little coloured lady for you?' **1967** *Trans-Action* Apr. 8/2 The degree of organization in hustling depends frequently on the kind of hustling. Regular pimping and pushing require many trusted contacts and organization.

pimpel, variant of PIPPLE *v.*

†'**pimper**, *v.*¹ *Obs.* or *dial.* In 6 pym-. [Attenuated from *pamper.*] *trans.* To pamper, coddle.

1537 LATIMER *Let. Cromwell* 8 Nov. in *Lett. Suppress. Monast.* (Camden) 148 Butt I have a good nursshe.. wych.. hath fachyd me hoom to here owne howsse, and doth pymper me upe with all dylygence. [Cf. *Eng. Dial. Dict.* s.v. *Pimper* 2. To bring up children over-delicately; to over-indulge them in the matter of food, nw. Derby.]

†'**pimper**, *v.*² *Obs. rare.* [Cf. early mod.Du. *pimp-ooghen* to blink, look through half-shut eyes (Kilian).] *intr.* (?) To blink.

1600 J. LANE *Tom Tel-troth* 620 But when the drinke doth worke within her head, She rowles and reekes, and pimpers with the eyes.

pimpernel ('pɪmpənɛl). Forms: α. 5 pimpernelle, -nolle, 5–6 pymper- (-ir-, -yr-), -nol, -nel, -nele, -nell(e, -nyll, 6–7 pimpernell, 6– pimpernel, (6–8 pempernell, 7 pimpernill). β. 6 (in senses 1, 2) pimpinell, 9 -el. [a. OF. *pimprenele*, *pimpernelle*, earlier *piprenelle* (12th c.), also *pimpi-*, *pimpenelle* (Godef.), mod.F. *pimprenelle* = It., Pg. *pimpinella*, Sp. *pimpinela*, med.L. *pipinella* (12th c. in Hatz.-Darm.), all in our sense 1. Diez concludes that *pipinella* was a corruption of *bipinnella*, dim. of *bipinnula*, dim. deriv. of *bipennis* 'two-winged' (perhaps referring to the pinnate or bipinnatifid leaves); and, in fact, the Burnet appears in the herbals and vocabularies of the 16th c. generally, as *bipinnella* or *bipenella*, sometimes *bipennula*. Cf. also Ger. *bibernelle*, MHG. *bibenelle*. The word has undergone much change of form, app. under the influence of 'popular etymology', as well as change of sense.

Before 1500, the L. name *Pimpinella* was transferred on the Continent, by 'the Poticaries', to an umbelliferous plant resembling the Burnets in its leaves, and hence called Burnet Saxifrage, to which also in 1763 Adanson appropriated the botanical name *Pimpinella Saxifraga*. In Eng. this appears in the *Great Herball* of 1516 as *pimpernel*, and in Turner as *pimpinell* after the L., while he gives *pympernell* for *Anagallis*, to which it had already been applied in 15th c. vocabularies. No explanation of this last transference of the name appears.]

†**1.** Originally (as still in the Romanic languages) applied to Great Burnet, *Sanguisorba officinalis*, and Salad Burnet, *Poterium Sanguisorba*. (According to some, properly to the latter.) *Obs.*

The first quot. is doubtful; but Godefroy identifies F. *pimpre* with *pimprenelle*, which in Fr. has only this sense.

[*c* **1265** *Voc. Names Plants* in Wr.-Wülcker 557/35 *Pinpernele, i.* pinpre, *i.* briddestunge.] **14..** *Lat.-Eng. Voc.* ibid. 603/7 *Piponella* anglice Pympernele. *c* **1450** *Alphita* (Anecd. Oxon.) 146 Pimpinella assimilatur saxifrag[i]e in foliis et in stipite. sed differunt in radicibus.. gᵉ. et aᵉ. pympernele [*v.r.* pimpernelle]. **1545** ELYOT, *Bipennella*, an herbe callyd Pympernell. **1548** *Ibid.*, *Bipinnella*, called commonly *Pympinella*, of some *Pampinula*, and *Bipennula*, an herbe called Pimpernell. **1548** TURNER *Names of Herbes* Hj b, Bipennella or bipennula Italica is called English Burnet. The Poticaries cal it Pimpinellam. **1570** LEVINS *Manip.* 57/27 Pimpernel, *bipenella.* **1578** LYTE *Dodoens* I. xcvi. 137 Of Burnet, or Pimpinell. Pimpinell is of two sortes, the great and wilde; and the small garden Pimpinell. [Figs. of Sanguisorba officinalis and Poterium Sanguisorba.] *Ibid.* 138 Pimpinell is.. in Latine *Pimpinella*, *Bipennula*, *Pampinula*, and of some *Sanguisorba*,.. in English Burnet, and Pimpinell. **1855** MAYNE *Expos. Lex.*, *Italian pimpinel*, common name for *Sanguisorba officinalis*.

†**2.** Burnet Saxifrage (*Pimpinella Saxifraga*, N.O. *Umbelliferæ*). *Obs.*

1516 *Grete Herball* ccclv, The pimpinella. Self heale or pympyrnell. Pimpernel is an herbe that groweth in sandy places at yᵉ fote of hylles. It is good to resowdre woundes yf the powder.. be often layde therto. **1548** TURNER *Names of Herbes* Hj b, Bipennula Germanica, is Saxifragia Italorum, and it is called in englishe Pimpinel, the duche cal it Bibinellen. **1551** —— *Herbal* I. O iv, Pimpinell doth.. agre wyth the secunde kynde of daucus in descryptyon, and also in vertues. **1587** *In Commend. Gascoigne* in *G.'s Wks.*, *Herbs*, etc., Pinks please some, and pempernell doth serve to stanch the blood.

3. a. Now, The common name of *Anagallis arvensis* (N.O. *Primulaceæ*), a small decumbent annual found in cornfields and waste ground, with smooth ovate opposite leaves, and bright scarlet flowers (varying with blue, and, more rarely, flesh-coloured or white) which close in cloudy or rainy weather (whence its rustic names *poor man's weatherglass, shepherd's glass,* etc.): distinctively called ***field*** or ***scarlet pimpernel***. Hence extended to the whole genus.

male pimpernel, an old distinctive name for the common red-flowered variety; the blue-flowered, by some considered a distinct species (*A. cærulea*), being called ***female pimpernel***.

?**14..** *Lat.-Eng. Voc.* in Wr.-Wülcker 563/43 *Anagallus*, pympernele. **1538** Turner *Libellus*, *Anagallis*..dicitur anglice Pympernell. **1551** —— *Herbal* I. C iij b, Pympernell is of ij kyndes: it that hath the blewe floure, is called the female, but it that hath ye cremesine is called ye male. **1578** Lyte *Dodoens* I. xxxvii. 54. **1601** Holland *Pliny* II. 234 The herbe Pimpernell, some call Anagallis, others Corchoros. Of it be found two kindes; the male with a red floure, the female with a blew. **1744** J. Claridge *Sheph. Banbury's Rules* 38 The pimpernel..shuts itself up..close against rainy weather. **1865** Gosse *Land & Sea* (1874) 115 Whole patches are radiant with the pimpernel. Except the corn poppy, this is said to be the only scarlet flower we have. **1865** Thoreau *Cape Cod* viii. 154 Prettiest of all, the scarlet pimpernel, or poor-man's weather-glass.

b. With defining words, applied to other species of *Anagallis*, consisting of small trailing herbs with rotate flowers of various colours, chiefly red or blue; also to plants naturally allied

bastard or **false pimpernel**, (*a*) Chaffweed, *Centunculus minimus*; (*b*) 'an American name for *Ilysanthes gratioloides*' (*Treas. Bot.* 1866, Miller *Plant-n.* 1884). **bog pimpernel**, *Anagallis tenella*, a creeping plant with delicate pink flowers. †**female pimpernel** (see 3). **Italian pimpernel**, (*a*) *Anagallis Monelli*, a species with large blue flowers; (*b*) *Sanguisorba officinalis* (see 1). †**male, red, scarlet pimpernel** (see 3). **round(-leaved) pimpernel**, Brookweed. **sea** or **seaside pimpernel**, *Honkenya peploides*. **water pimpernel**, (*a*) the greater and lesser Brooklime, *Veronica Beccabunga* and *V. Anagallis*, called by the herbalists *Anagallis aquatica*; (*b*) Brookweed, *Samolus Valerandi* or other species. **wood** or **yellow pimpernel**, *Lysimachia nemorum*.

1597 Gerarde *Herbal* II. clxxxiv. 495 Of Brookelyme, or water Pimpernell... There be fower sorts of Water herbes comprehended vnder the name *Anagallis aquatica*, or water Pimpernell, or water Chicken weede. **1633** *Ibid.* cxcvi. 622 Anthyllis lentifolia, siue Alsine cruciata marina... I haue Englished it Sea Pimpernell, because the leaues in shape are as like those of Pimpernel as of any other Plant. **1756** J. Hill *Brit. Herb.* 66 Genus VII. Round Pimpernell, *Samolus.* **1760** J. Lee *Introd. Bot.* App. 322 Pimpernel, Yellow of the Woods, *Lysimachia*. *Ibid.*, Round-leaved Water Pimpernel, *Samolus.* **1861** Miss Pratt *Flower. Pl.* IV. 245 Small Chaffweed, or Bastard Pimpernel. **1865** Gosse *Land & Sea* (1874) 47 The bog-pimpernel..was profusely strewn over the spongy moors. **1866** *Treas. Bot.* 59 *Anagallis*,.. Pimpernels, by which name the species are popularly known... Every one is familiar with the common red Pimpernel (*A. arvensis*). The *A. indica*, with blue flowers, scarcely differs from it, except in colour and the larger size of its blossoms... The Italian Pimpernel (*A. Monelli*), with still larger flowers. *Ibid.* 704 *L[ysimachia] nemorum*.. approaches in size and habit the scarlet pimpernel, but has bright yellow flowers; from this resemblance it is often called Wood Pimpernel.

4. (Chiefly with capital initial.) [The name given to Sir Percy Blakeney, hero of Baroness Orczy's novel *The Scarlet Pimpernel* (1905), who rescues victims of the Terror and smuggles them out of France, characterized (ch. xii) as 'that demmed, elusive Pimpernel'.]

a. Something elusive or much sought after. **b.** Someone whose exploits are comparable to those of 'The Scarlet Pimpernel'. See also *Scarlet Pimpernel* s.v. scarlet *a.* 4 a, and 3 a above.

1955 *Times* 10 May 14/1 The elusive pimpernel, the Liberal vote, is being eagerly sought by the two main parties in the Peterborough division. **1961** *House & Garden* Oct. 112/3 Highlanders soon became a band of Pimpernels smuggling their aristocratic whiskies to the Lowlands. **1962** *Guardian* 9 Aug. 7/6 The man who has become known as the 'Black Pimpernel of South Africa'. **1963** *Times Lit. Suppl.* 18 Jan. 40/5 In the hope of being able to function like a modern-day Pimpernel. **1974** 'D. Craig' *Dead Liberty* xvii. 81 Hans Lenzlinger, the greatest Pimpernel between East and West ever known.

5. *attrib.*, as *pimpernel chaffweed, pimpernel rose, pimpernel water*: see quots.

1776–96 Withering *Brit. Plants* (ed. 3) II. 199 Bastard Pimpernel. Pimpernel Chaffweed. **1886** Britten & Holland *Eng. Plant-n.*, *Pimpernel Rose*, a book-name for *Rosa spinosissima*, suggested by its synonym, *R. pimpinellifolia*, and referring, like *Burnet Rose*, to the form of its leaves. **1837** E. Howard *Old Commodore* ii. 43 If she'd only..use my pimpernel water, for she has one monstrous freckle on her forehead.

†**pimpernol.** *Obs.* [= OF. *pimpernel*, *-neau*, 'a broad-nosed variety of the common eel' (G. A. Boulanger), 'a grig, scaffling, spitchcocke, fowson Eele' (Cotgr.).] A small kind of eel.

1251 *Liberate Roll 35 Hen. III*, 15 Sept. (P.R.O.), Rex vicecomiti Cantebrigie salutem. Precipimus tibi quod in balliva tua emas ad opus nostrum x milia anguillarum que vocantur Pimpernoll. **1392–3** *Earl Derby's Exp.* (Camden) 215 Pro piscibus recentibus..item pro xxvj pimpernol, xvjs.

pimpillo, -owe, var. pinpillow *Obs.*, pincushion, also prickly pear.

pimpinel(l, obs. form of pimpernel.

ˈ**pimping**, *a.* [Of uncertain origin; dialectally *pimpy* is found in same sense. Cf. pimp *sb.*[2], and Cornish dial. *pimpey* weak watery cider; also Du. *pimpel* weak little man, Ger. *pimpelig* effeminate, sickly, puling, which imply a stem *pimp*.] Small, trifling, insignificant, peddling, paltry, petty, mean; in poor health or condition, sickly.

1687 T. Brown *Saints in Uproar* Wks. 1730 I. 77 Out of a little pimping corner of Britain. *a* **1704** —— *Charac. Dutch Women* Wks. 1711 IV. 315, I am quarter'd in a little pimping Village on the Frontier of Flanders. **1762** Sterne *Tr. Shandy* v. i, To go sneaking on at this pitiful,—pimping,—pettifogging rate. **1778** [W. Marshall] *Minutes Agric.* 27 Apr. an. 1775 This pimping patch of two acres and a quarter. **1824** Lamb *Lett.* (1837) II. 166 She writes such a pimping, mean, detestable hand. **1845** S. Judd *Margaret* iv, 'Was I so little?' asked Margaret. 'Yes, and pimpin' enough.' **1878** *Print. Trades Jrnl.* xxv. 23 If the narrow, pimping fractions in general use had been retained. [See also Eng. Dial. Dict.]

pimping, *vbl. sb.*[1] and *ppl. a.*: see pimp *v.*

pimping, *vbl. sb.*[2] *local.* [f. pimp *sb.*[2] + -ing[1].] The preparation of bundles of firewood. (In quot. comb.)

1930 V. Sackville-West *Edwardians* vi. 251 He looked into the pimping-shed, where old Turnour was chopping faggots.

pimpish (ˈpɪmpɪʃ), *a.* [f. pimp *sb.*[1] + -ish[1].] Resembling or characteristic of a pimp.

1935 W. Empson *Some Versions of Pastoral* 47 The comic characters' experimental wish to satisfy all parties..has a certain pimpish complacence. **1971** W. Burroughs *Wild Boys* 11 Six pimpish young men burst through the door in a reek of brilliantine. **1976** *Daily Tel.* 19 Aug. 11/7 A horde of football fans attempt to lure into their bedrooms a pair of tarts by arrangement with the pimpish day porter.

pimple (ˈpɪmp(ə)l), *sb.* Also 5 pinple, 6 pymple, pimpel, 6–7 (9 *dial.*) pumple. [Origin unknown: connexion with L. *papula* or *papilla* has been conjectured; but evidence is wanting. Cf. OE. *pipliȝende* shingly, affected with herpes, in *Sax. Leechd.* I. 266.]

1. A small solid rounded tumour of the skin, usually inflammatory, without, or rarely with, suppuration; a papule or pustule.

c **1400** *Lanfranc's Cirurg.* 248 Scabies is whanne þe iȝe liddis ben reed & to-swolle, & ful of reed pinplis. **1523** Fitzherb. *Husb.* §49 The pockes appere..lyke reed pymples, as brode as a farthynge. **1578** Lyte *Dodoens* I. lix. 86 The distilled water..is good against the freckles, spottes, and pimpels of the face. **1633** T. James *Voy.* 87 Our faces were swolne hard out in pumples. *a* **1704** T. Brown *Sat. Fr. King* Wks. 1730 I. 60 My very pimples bilk my face. **1876** Bristowe *The. & Pract. Med.* (1878) 253 The pimple which results from syphilitic inoculation.

2. *fig.* A small rounded swelling, as a bud, etc.

1582 Stanyhurst *Æneis* Ded. (Arb.) 6, I should bee thoght ouer curious, by prying owt a pimple in a bent. **1784** Cowper *Task* III. 528 He pinches from the second stalk A pimple, that portends a future sprout. **1855** Delamer *Kitch. Gard.* (1861) 103 The pimples daily grow bigger and bigger. .. They grow into buttons, which spread into mushrooms. **1881** Darwin *Veg. Mould* vi. 286 On poor pasture land,.. the whole surface is sometimes dotted with little pimples,.. and these pimples consist of old worm-castings.

b. *slang.* The head.

1818 *Sporting Mag.* I. 298 Scroggins..planted many clumsy hits upon his adversary's pimple. *a* **1825** Forby *Voc. E. Anglia*, *Pimple*, the head. It must be a diminutive as well as a feeble head which is denominated. **18..** *Racing Song* in Baumann *Londinismen* (1887) 138/1 Sharp brains in my noble pimple.

†**3.** 'A boon companion' (Farmer). *Obs. slang.*

1700 Congreve *Way of World* IV. x, The sun's a good Pimple, an honest Soaker.

4. *attrib.* and *Comb.*, as ***pimple eruption, face, spot***; ***pimple-faced, -like, -nosed, -spangled*** adjs.; **pimple copper, pimple metal**, the product of one of the successive operations in copper-smelting, containing about 75 per cent. or more of copper, and having pimples on the surface from the escape of bubbles of sulphurous acid; **pimple-mite**, a minute acarid (*Demodex folliculorum*) which infests the sebaceous follicles of the face (*Syd. Soc. Lex.*).

1607 Topsell *Four-f. Beasts* (1658) 104 The same.. taketh away pimple-spots out of the face. **1632** J. Hayward tr. *Biondi's Eromena* 16 Of a crabbed nature, pimple faced, and a creple. **1758–65** Goldsm. *Ess.* i, The pimple-nosed Spirit at the president's right elbow. **1868** Joynson *Metals* 98 The copper—in its form known..as 'pimple' copper—is put into the furnace. **1877** Raymond *Statist. Mines & Mining* 380 Treatment of the pimple metal. **1898** P. Manson *Trop. Diseases* xviii. 298 Minute pimple-like abscesses.

ˈ**pimple**, *v.* [f. prec. sb.]

a. *trans.* To raise pimples upon; to spot or deface with pimples (in quot. *fig.*). Also, to cover as with pimples. **b.** *intr.* To become pimply. Also *transf.*, to develop small bulges. Hence ˈ**pimpling** *vbl. sb.* and *ppl. a.*

1604 T. M. *Black Bk.* in *Middleton's Wks.* (Bullen) VIII. 40 You will pimple your souls with oaths, till you make them as well-favoured as your faces. **1638** Venner *Via Recta, A Censure* (1650) 379 Such as have..red pimpling Faces, and adusted Humours. **1666** Pepys *Diary* 12 July, A rose touching his skin..would make it rise and pimple. **1909** 'O. Henry' *Roads of Destiny* xix. 311 The levee where his freight-car stood was pimpled with dark bulks of merchandise. **1940** [implied in pimpling *vbl. sb.* 2]. **1940** L. MacNeice *Last Ditch* 14 The rain of London pimples The ebony street with white. **1961** *Daily Tel.* 29 Aug. 18/4 Caravans and tents pimpling remote villages and hillsides are causing concern to planning authorities. **1970** *Motoring Which?* July 93/2 On all three cars, the rear light surrounds were pimpling and the bumpers had begun rusting. **1972** K. Bonfiglioli *Don't point that Thing at Me* xix. 167 Lurid tents and tasteful pastel caravans pimple the landscape. **1974** P. Dickinson *Poison Oracle* iv. 98 The dunes along the marsh were pimpled with their tents.

pimpled (ˈpɪmp(ə)ld), *a.* [f. prec. sb. or vb. + -ed.] Having, or characterized by, pimples.

1622 Massinger & Dekker *Virgin Mart.* II. i, The Armado of pimpled, deep scarletted, rubified, and carbuncled faces. *a* **1697** Aubrey *Brief Lives* (1898) I. 141 A gentleman with red, ugly, pumpled face. **1747** tr. *Astruc's Fevers* 317 It is called pimpled measles, when the pustules are big and elevated. **1870** J. Roskell in *Eng. Mech.* 18 Feb. 547/2 This copper is termed 'blistered' or 'pimpled' copper, according to its quality.

Comb. **1840** Dickens *Old C. Shop* xlix, Men..of a red-nosed, pimpled-faced, convivial look.

pimple-stone: see pimble-.

pimpling (ˈpɪmplɪŋ) *vbl. sb.* [f. pimple *sb.*, *v.* + -ing[1].] **1.** The presence of pimples; the fact of being covered with pimples.

1599 A. M. tr. *Gabelhouer's Bk. Physicke* 253/1 An excellent oyle of Tartar, agaynste all pimplinge of the Face.

2. The presence of small bulges on the surface of metal.

1940 J. D. Jevons *Metall. Deep Drawing & Pressing* viii. 293 A troublesome defect, which is sometimes encountered, particularly when the carbon content is rather high, is that known in the shops as 'pimpling'. **1962** J. C. Wright *Metall. in Nucl. Power Technol.* vi. 106 Examples of workable solutions to pimpling are the use of an aluminium-silicon brazed bond which does not spread significantly with time in the neighbourhood of 300°C, and the provision of anodic coating on the inside of the aluminium tubing.

†**pimpling**: see pippling *ppl. a.*

pimploe: see pinpillow.

pimplous (ˈpɪmpləs), *a. rare.* [f. pimple *sb.* + -ous.] Characterized by pimples; pimply.

1906 W. J. Locke *Beloved Vagabond* xii. 152 Cooling medicaments wherewith to mitigate a certain pimplous condition of cheek.

pimply (ˈpɪmplɪ), *a.* [f. pimple *sb.* + -y.] Full of pimples; covered or spotted with pimples. Also *fig.*

1748 Richardson *Clarissa* (1811) I. xxxi. 227 Belton's [face] so pert and so pimply. **1769** Pennant *Zool.* III. 7 The Toad,..the back flat, and covered with a pimply dusky hide. **1838** Dickens *Nich. Nick.* xxx, A handsome face, only a little pimply as though with drinking. **1958** *Spectator* 22 Aug. 260/1 The man-eating British lion By a pimply age brought down. **1973** M. Amis *Rachel Papers* 17 It was a month I always think of with a certain pimply lyricism.

Comb. **1873** *Routledge's Yng. Gentl. Mag.* Feb. 174/2 A short..pimply-faced youth.

Hence ˈ**pimpliness**.

1893 *Strand Mag.* VII. 35 A pimpliness of countenance.

pimpmobile (ˈpɪmpməʊbiːl). *U.S. slang.* [f. pimp *sb.*[1] + auto)mobile *sb.*] A large, flashy car used by a pimp.

1973 *Washington Post* 21 Apr. D7/1 Features of the luxury pimpmobile—glittering striping, dual spares, elaborate scrollwork and amber sunroofs—are showing up, somewhat toned-down, in stylized automobiles, according to car customizers. **1975** *Daily Mail* 13 Sept. 2/5 The pimpmobiles—the long, long Cadillacs with a Rolls front—no longer cruise everywhere. They are finding it less profitable to keep girls here. **1977** *Rolling Stone* 24 Mar. 71/1 'Norman', the story of a gambler who rides around in a Rambler (a secondhand pimpmobile?), is introduced by a melancholy horn riff with the drummer loping along like a dragging muffler, while Romeo's voice is high and airy.

[**pimprint**, error for primprint, privet.]

pimpship (ˈpɪmpʃɪp). [f. pimp *sb.* + -ship.] The personality of a pimp: used as a mock title.

1682 Oldham *Juvenal's Sat.* iii. Poems (1684) 203 Saving your reverend Pimpship, where'd ye ply? **1693** *Bacchan. Sess.* 14 What precious intreigues could my Pimpship discover.

pin (pɪn), *sb.*[1] Forms: 1 pinn, 4–7 pynne, pinne, 5–6 pyn, (5 pene, pyne, 6 pynn, pine), 6–8 pinn, 6– pin. [Late OE. *pinn*, a common Low Ger. word: MLG., LG. *pinne*, *pin*, LG. also *penne*, *pen* (*Brem. Wbch.*), MDu. *pinne* ('pinna, spiculum, cuspis, veruculum, aculeus, scopus, clavus ligneus' Kilian), Du. *pin* pin, peg (in Hexham *pinne*, 'also the pinnacle of a steeple'); MHG. (rare) *phinne* nail, plug, Ger. *pinne* and *pin*: late ON. *pinni* (14th c.), Norw., Sw. *pinne*, Da. *pind*;

generally held to be ad. L. *pinna*, in the Vulgate, Luke iv. 9 = 'pinnacle', 'applied to points of various kinds, battlements, cutting edge of an ax' (Walde *Lat. Etym. Wbch.*, where it is distinguished from *penna* feather, also often spelt *pinna*).]

I. Primary sense: = *peg*.

1. a. A small piece of wood, metal, or other solid substance, of cylindrical or similar shape, often tapering or pointed, used for some one of various purposes, as to fasten or hold together parts of a structure, to hang something upon, to stop up a hole, or as a part of mechanism to convey or check motion; a peg, a bolt.

a **1100** *Gerefa* in *Anglia* (1886) IX. 265 Ne sceolde he nan þing forȝyman..ne musfellan, ne, þæt ȝit læsse is, to hæpsan pinn. *c* **1325** *Gloss. W. de Bibbesw.* in Wright *Voc.* 167 E par deuz hietes [*gloss* the ax-tre pinnes] se tenent owel. *Ibid.* 168 Devaunt les braceroles sount biletz [*gloss* pinnes]. [**1329** *Wardr. Acc.* (*Acc. Exch. K.R.* Bd. 383. No. 9) m. 1 Pro..pynnis ac cathenis pro leporariis ligandis.] *c* **1386** CHAUCER *Sqr.'s T.* 119 And turne ayeyn with writhyng of a pyn. *c* **1412** HOCCLEVE *De Reg. Princ.* 1104 And vp is broken, lok, hasp, barre & pyn. *c* **1440** *Promp. Parv.* 399/2 Pynne, of tymbyr (or pegge..), *cavilla*. *Ibid.*, Pynne, of metalle, as yryne,..*spintrum*. **1484** CAXTON *Fables of Æsop* VI. vii, [The kat] hynge hym self by his two feet behynd at a pynne of yron which was styked at a balke. **1489** —— *Faytes of A.* II. xxiv. 138 Pinnes of wode to ioine the palys. **1527** *Churchw. Acc. St. Giles, Reading* 31 For lathes, nayles,..tile pynnes for the new hous. **1575** LANEHAM *Let.* (1871) 56 This tent had seauen cart lode of pynz perteining too it. **1607** NORDEN *Surv. Dial.* III. 125 As if a man should build a house, without pinne or nayle. **1632** SANDERSON *Serm.* 427 Not the least wheele or pinne or notch. **1664** EVELYN *Sylva* (1679) 27 Oak is excellent for..pinns and peggs for tyling, &c. *a* **1713** ELLWOOD *Autobiog.* (1765) 98 The Keys were hung upon a Pin in the Hall. **1825** J. NICHOLSON *Operat. Mechanic* 158 The lower frame-work..is connected by means of the pins or wedges. **1875** KNIGHT *Dict. Mech.*, *Pin*... 3. The axis of a sheave. An axis of a joint, as of the gimbal or compass-joint. **1884** F. J. BRITTEN *Watch & Clockm.* 51 A..cylinder studded with pins for lifting the hammers is a chiming train. **1885** *Law Rep.* 15 Q. Bench Div. 316 A catch..at the end of an iron pin, which prevented the pin, when passed through a slit, from repassing.

fig. **1637** RUTHERFORD *Let. to J. Gordon* 16 June, See that there be not a loose pin in the work of your salvation. **1711** *Countrey-Man's Let. to Curat* 34 The old Politick, that 'tis Dangerous to innovate or loose a Pinn.

b. An indicator of a long or pointed shape: as †the hand of a clock; †the gnomon of a sun-dial; †the index or tongue of a balance (*obs.*).

c **1440** *Promp. Parv.* 399/2 Pynne, of an orlage,..schowynge þe owrys of the day. **1639** G. DANIEL *Vervic.* 568 Number will prevaile, And turne the pin of bright Astrea's Skale. **1669** STURMY *Mariner's Mag.* VI. iii. 123 The Pin or Gnomon..being 37 parts, and the shadow..28.

†**c.** A peg, nail, or stud fixed in the centre of a target. *Obs.*

c **1450** *Cov. Myst.* (Shaks. Soc.) 138 Now be my trowthe ȝe hitte the pynne. **1584** W. ELDERTON in Halliw. *Yorks. Anthol.* (1851) 6 Walmsley did the vpshot win, With both his shafts so near the pin. **1592** SHAKS. *Rom. & Jul.* II. iv. 15 The very pinne of his heart, cleft with the blind Bowe-boyes but-shaft. **1642** FULLER *Holy & Prof. St.* V. xvii. 426 To cleave the pinne and do the deed.

d. In a stringed musical instrument: Each of the pegs round which the strings are fastened at one end, and by turning which they are tuned; a tuning-pin, tuning-peg: = PEG *sb.*[1] 2 a. Also *fig.*: cf. 16.

1587 GREENE *Tritameron* II. Wks. (Grosart) III. 121 Fearing if he wrested not the pin to a right key, his melody would be marred. **1592** —— *Philomela* ibid. XI. 126 Giouanni hearing hir harpe on that string [love] strained it a pin higher thus. **1594** LYLY *Moth. Bomb.* V. iii, He looses his rosen, that his fiddle goes cush, cush..his mouth so drie that he hath not spittle for his pinne. **1607–12** BACON *Ess.*, *Empire* (Arb.) 298 Nero could touch and tune the Harp well, But in gouernement sometymes he vsed to wynd the pynnes to highe, sometymes to let them downe to lowe. *a* **1800** *Bonny Bows o' London* in *Buchan's Ballads* (1828) II. 130 Ye'll take a lith o' my little finger bane, And ye'll make a pin to your fiddle then. **1885** C. G. W. LOCK *Workshop Receipts* Ser. IV. 285/2 As the pins and wires of pianos become worn, it is necessary to renew them.

†**e.** A peg, nail, etc. fixed in a surface, to mark a place, or for ornament or other purpose. *Obs.*

1648–78 HEXHAM, *Pen of de Trock-Tafel*, the Pin upon a Billyard table. *c* **1650** *Robin Hood his death* 44 in Furniv. *Percy Folio* I. 53 When they came to Merry church lees they knoc[k]ed vpon a pin. **1689** *Lond. Gaz.* No. 2429/4 A Silver Box and a pinn'd Case, many of the Pins being come out, so that the Brass was seen.

f. One of a set of pegs fixed on the inside of a large drinking-vessel, dividing it into equal parts, said by some to indicate the limit of each drinker's draught: = PEG *sb.*[1] 2 b.

1592 NASHE *P. Penilesse* 23 King Edgar..caused certaine iron cups to be chained..at euery Vintners doore, with iron pins in them, to stint euery man how much he should drinke: and he that went beyond one of those pins forfeited a penny for euery draught. **1655** FULLER *Ch. Hist.* III. ii. §3 That Priests should not go to Publick Drinkings, *nec ad pinnas bibant*, nor drink at Pins. This was a Dutch trick..of Artificial Drunkenness, out of a Cup marked with certain Pins, and he accounted the Man, who could nick the Pin, drinking even unto it. **1673** *Holborn Drollery* 76 Edgar away with pins i' th' Cup To spoil our drinking whole ones up. *a* **1700** B. E. *Dict. Cant. Crew*, *Nick it*,..to Drink to the pin or button. **1850** LONGF. *Gold. Leg.* I. *Court-yard of Castle* 17 No jovial din Of drinking wassail to the pin.

g. The cylindrical part in a lock on which the pipe or hollow stem of the key fits. Also, that part of a key which enters the lock (esp. if solid instead of hollow).

1703 MOXON *Mech. Exerc.* 25 If you have a Pin to the Lock,..the Pin is rivetted into the Plate. **1875** KNIGHT *Dict. Mech.*, *Pin*... 9. The part of a key-stem which enters the lock.

h. *Naut.* (*a*) A peg fixed in the side of a rowing-boat as a fulcrum for the oar; a thole-pin. (*b*) Applied to various pegs or bolts used in a ship, e.g. to make fast the rigging (BELAYING-*pins*), to keep the capstan-bars in place, etc.

1832 HT. MARTINEAU *Ella of Gar.* ii. 32 How are you to row? The pins are out that should fix your oars. **1836** MARRYAT *Midsh. Easy* xxvi, Holding on by the belaying pin. *c* **1850** *Rudim. Navig.* (Weale) 137 *Pins*, short iron rods fixed occasionally in the drum-heads of capstans, and through the ends of the bars, to prevent their unshipping. *Ibid.*, *Pins of boats*, pins of iron or wood fixed along the gunwales of some boats (instead of rowlocks) whose oars are confined by grommets. **1867** SMYTH *Sailor's Word-bk.* 161 *Capstan-bars*..are..held in their places in the drumhead holes, by little iron bolts called capstan or safety pins.

i. *Carpentry.* The projecting part or 'tenon' of a dovetail joint, which fits into the 'mortise'.

1847 SMEATON *Builder's Man.* 88 The projecting piece..is called the pin of the dovetail; and the aperture into which it is fitted..is called the socket. **1875** *Carpentry & Join.* 64 Cabinet-makers..do not often make broad dovetails, as they make the pins narrower and further apart in general than joiners.

j. *Quoits.* The peg or 'hob' at which the quoit is aimed.

[**1801** STRUTT *Sports & Past.* II. ii. §9 Quoits... To play at this game, an iron pin, called a hob, is driven into the ground [etc.].] **1857** *Chambers' Inform. People* II. 704/2 The quoit being delivered..with a steady aim at the pin. **1897** CROCKETT *Lad's Love* xviii, His first quoit fell within three inches of the pin.

k. *Golf.* An iron rod bearing a small flag, used to mark the position of a hole.

1901 SCOTSMAN 5 Sept. 7/3 His magnificent approach to within a yard of the pin. **1905** *Westm. Gaz.* 23 Aug. 5/1 Had a perfect mashie shot and lay three yards off the pin.

l. ? The latch or handle of a door: see Eng. Dial. Dict. s.v. *Pin* 4 and *Tirl* 2. *dial.*

?**17..** *Clerk Saunders* iv. in Scott *Minstr. Scot. Bord.* (1869) 377 Then take the sword from my scabbard, And slowly lift the pin; And you may swear, and safe your aith, Ye never let Clerk Saunders in. —— *Prince Robert* ix. *ibid.* 381 O he has run to Darlinton, And tirled at the pin. **1804** R. COUPER *Poetry* I. 232 (E.D.D.) Your fingers numb Will hardly turn the pin. **1816** SCOTT *Antiq.* xl, Murder tirl'd at the door-pin. **1870** MORRIS *Earthly Par.* III. IV. 39 There knocking, was he bidden in, And heedfully he raised the pin, And entering stood.

m. One of the metal projections of a plug, which make the electrical connection when it is inserted into a socket.

1888 [see PLUG *sb.* 1 c]. **1902** W. C. CLINTON *Electric Wiring* iv. 85 The flexible..terminates in two split pins, which are a spring fit into two tubular sockets. **1945** F. WISEMAN *Penguin Handyman* i. 19 One end is connected to the earth pin in the three-pin plug, whilst the other end is connected to the metal housing or frame of the fire. **1963** *House & Garden* Feb. 8/3 Replace those old-fashioned two-pin plugs with a three-pin, and check the fuse-box. **1972** *Electricity Supply & Safety* (Consumers' Assoc.) 49 You can connect an old type of plug with round pins to a rectangular hole socket with the right adaptor.

n. A metal peg which prevents a hand-grenade from exploding by holding down the activating lever.

1917 C. R. GIBSON *War Inventions* vi. 95 Until the soldier was ready to throw the bomb the little lever was held down by a metal pin. When the soldier withdrew this pin, the lever was still held down by the hand with which he threw the bomb, and not until it left his hand did the fuse begin to burn. **1920** A. R. BOND *Inventions of Gt. War* ii. 29 The Mills hand-grenade..was provided with a lever which was normally strapped down and held by means of a safety-pin. **1952** G. E. THORNTON *Handbk. Weapon Training* ix. 101 With a hand grenade these [techniques] include..the method of removing the safety pin or cap. **1972** 'H. CALVIN' *Take Two Popes* xv. 182 Soldiers..ready to pull out grenade pins with their teeth. **1977** C. FORBES *Avalanche Express* viii. 85 The grenade he would have withdrawn the pin from..if..faced with imminent arrest.

o. A coupling-pin. Used esp. in phr. ***to pull the pin***: to uncouple; also *fig.* (see quots.). *N. Amer. slang.*

1927 *Amer. Speech* II. 391/2 To *bunch*, or to *drag it*, means to quit. To *pull the pin* has the same meaning. This is a railroad term and means to uncouple. **1947** R. O. BOYER *Dark Ship* II. xvii. 227 The teamsters had pulled the pin too early. The strike is being lost. **1955** *Amer. Speech* XXX. 92 *Pull the pin*, to release the pin that connects a semitrailer to a fifth wheel. **1968** *Ibid.* XLIII. 289 *Pull the pin*, to resign, quit, or be fired from a job: 'They pulled the pin on him.' Relates to the switching function in the days of the link-and-pin coupler (long since replaced by the safer automatic coupler) by which a car was uncoupled and released. **1972** J. WAMBAUGH *Blue Knight* (1973) x. 161 An old man that should've pulled the pin years ago. Now he'd been here too long. He couldn't leave or he'd die. **1977** —— *Black Marble* (1978) ix. 168 Twenty-six years on the job when he pulled the pin and went to Arizona.

p. A support of an arch.

1928 *Daily Tel.* 7 Feb. 14/1 The arch is a two 'pin' crescent structure, and the distance from 'pin' to 'pin'..is 531 ft.

†**2.** *fig.* (from 1). That on which something 'hangs' or depends. *Obs.* (Cf. PEG *sb.*[1] 5.)

c **1407** LYDG. *Reson & Sens.* 2952 They hangen by another pyn. **1538** STARKEY *England* II. i. 164 A grete parte of thys mater hangyth apon one pine. **1648** *Eikon Bas.* xxiv. 236 A great part of whose piety hung upon that popular pin of rayling against, and contemning the Government and Liturgy of this Church. **1748** HARTLEY *Observ. Man* II. ii. 116 That Point, being settled, becomes a capital Pin, upon which all the Pagan Chronology depends.

II. = ME. and Sc. PREEN, F. *épingle*.

3. a. A slender piece of wire (now usually of brass or iron, tinned), formed with a sharp tapered point at one end and a flattened round head at the other, commonly used to fasten together parts of dress, loose papers, etc., for mounting entomological specimens, and for various purposes. Also applied to larger articles of the same kind made of steel, gold, silver, etc., often more or less ornamental, and used for securing the hair, a hat, shawl, scarf, etc., or merely for ornament. See also DRAWING-*pin*, HAIRPIN, HAT-*pin*, SAFETY *pin*, SCARF *pin*, etc. (The most frequent use.) Also (*U.S.*), a badge indicating membership of a university or college fraternity, or similar society, etc.

c **1380** WYCLIF *Wks.* (1880) 12 þei becomen pedderis berynge knyues, pursis, pynnys and girdlis [etc.] for wymmen. *a* **1450** *Knt. de la Tour* (1868) 64 She was atyred with highe longe pynnes lyke a iebet, and so..[they] saide she bare a galous on her hede. **1480** *Maldon, Essex, Crt. Rolls* Bundle 51 No. 3, xvi nedeles, xii dressyng pynnes. **1496** *Dives & Paup.* (W. de W.) VII. vii. 285 Yf children in ther youth stele pynnes or apples or ony other smale thynges. *Ibid.* xii. 295 A lady..can pynne her hode ayenst the wynde with a smale pynne of laton .xii. for a peny. **1545** *Rates of Customs* c ij, Pynnes the dossen thousande iis. **1632** MASSINGER *City Madam* IV. iv, A silver pin Headed with a pearl worth three-pence. **1668** PEPYS *Diary* 2 Jan., He that will not stoop for a pin will never be worth a pound. **1712** ADDISON *Spect.* No. 295 ¶4 A Pin a Day, says our frugal Proverb, is a Groat a Year. **1801** BLOOMFIELD *Rural T.*, *Rich. & Kate* xxi, As like him, ay, as pin to pin. **1851** D. WILSON *Preh. Ann.* (1863) I. II. vi. 475 The contents of the tumuli include bone pins, needles [etc.]. **1871** L. H. BAGG *4 Years at Yale* 144 Its original badge was a rectangular gold plate, about the size and shape of the present Beta Xi pin. **1893** W. K. POST *Harvard Stories* 216 Freddy..asked me one day why Sheffield wore that funny little pin all the time. **1910** J. HART *Vigilante Girl* 19 My dear fellow, you may cast aside your Eastern frigidity—in fact, I will call it your Cambridge frigidity, for I see you wear a Harvard pin. **1928** *Amer. Speech* III. 220 *Put out one's pin*, v. phr., to become engaged, to promise marriage. 'Scoop didn't have his pin on Dorothy very long, did he?' **1943** *Ibid.* XVIII. 154/2 *Plant a pin*, the process by which a fraternity man signifies his willingness to wait in the hall for the same girl every time. It consists of presenting her with his pin to wear. **1974** *Marlboro Herald-Advocate* (Bennettsville, S. Carolina) 18 Apr. 7/1 Rupert Kiker, president presented John L. Hargrave with a 20 year membership pin in the Lions International. Roy Easterling, Sr., was presented a 15 year pin. **1977** C. MCFADDEN *Serial* (1978) xviii. 43/2 He still wear his Key Club pin?

b. As a type of something very small, or of very slight value or significance: esp. in phr. ***not worth a pin*** (or ***two pins***), ***not to care a pin*** (or ***two pins***), etc. Also, ***a row of pins*** (in quot. 1896 as a type of similarity).

13.. *K. Alis.* 6146 (Bodl. MS.) He nolde ȝiue a pynne Bot he miȝth þise wynne. *c* **1460** *Towneley Myst.* III. 364 Thi felowship set I not at a pyn. *a* **1529** SKELTON *Magnif.* 1028 With a pere my loue you may wynne, And ye may lese it for a pynne. *c* **1530** H. RHODES *Bk. Nurture* 420 in *Babees Bk.* 93 Yet he is not worth a pin. **1579** FULKE *Confut. Sanders* 634, I would so esteeme them,..but not a pinne the more. **1590** SPENSER *F.Q.* I. v. 4 Who not a pin Does care for looke of living creatures eye. **1602** *Narcissus* (1893) 31 A pinne for povertye! **1628** EARLE *Microcosm.*, *Sceptic in Relig.* (Arb.) 67 He chuses this, not as better, but because there is not a pin to choose. **1777** SHERIDAN *Sch. Scand* III. i, 'Tis evident you never cared a pin for me. **1785** *European Mag.* VIII. 96 Your robe is not a pin the worse. **1887** [see CHOOSE *v.* 12]. **1891** [see FOR *prep.* 9]. **1896** KIPLING *Seven Seas* 193 When you get to a man in the case, They're like as a row of pins —For the Colonel's Lady an' Judy O'Grady Are sisters under their skins! **1900** POLLOK & THOM *Sports Burma* II. 43 One of my elephants..did not care two pins for a tiger. **1914** W. W. JACOBS *Night Watches* i. 25 'For two pins—' he began. 'For two pins I'll go back 'ome and stay there,' said Mr. Flynn. **1918** A. G. GARDINER *Leaves in Wind* 162 John Burns..does not care two pins who sees him or talks about him. **1920** W. J. LOCKE *House of Baltazar* i. 16 It doesn't seem to amount to a row of pins compared with my meeting you. **1947** [see HIDE *sb.*[1] 2 c]. **1973** J. PORTER *It's Murder with Dover* vii. 64 Her unsupported word isn't worth a row of pins. **1979** *Country Life* 16 Aug. 489/2 This Lord Hertford cared not two pins for society... His single passion was collecting.

c. ***pin's head***, ***pin's point***: in literal sense, or allusive as in b; also *attrib.* (cf. *pin matter* in 18).

1415–40 DK. OF ORLEANS *Poems* (1827) 8 And if she wolde ..But graunt me loo liche to a pynnys hed Part of hiris. **1526** *Pilgr. Perf.* (W. de W. 1531) 7 It is not so moche as a pynnes poynt, compared to yᵉ hole erth. **1622** MABBE tr. *Aleman's Guzman d'Alf.* I. 63 It had not beene a Pins-poynt matter; I should haue set light by it. **1698** *Christ Exalted* §78. 61 Man's Law will not hang a Man for stealing a Pins head. **1774** GOLDSM. *Nat. Hist.* (1776) VII. 301 The eggs are no larger than pins points. **1879** MRS. A. E. JAMES *Ind. Househ. Managem.* 76 We did not lose the value of a pin's head. **1879** *St. George's Hosp. Rep.* IX. 5 A pin's-head perforation in the sigmoid flexure.

d. ***pins and needles***: popular name for a pricking or tingling sensation, as that which accompanies the recovery of feeling in a limb after numbness. ***on pins and needles***: in a state of excessive uneasiness.

1810 J. POOLE *Hamlet Travestie* 8 Would it were supper-time... Till then I'm sitting upon pins and needles. **1813** W. DUNLAP *Mem. G. F. Cooke* II. xxx. 265 As it was—it was bad enough—my voice—haw!—there are pins and needles —I must send for a physician. **1844** J. T. HEWLETT *Parsons & W.* vi, The pins and needles sensations which followed. **1858** QUEEN VICTORIA *Let.* 8 Mar. in R. Fulford *Dearest Child* (1964) 72 All you say..reminds me of what I was always used to a child. Always on pins and needles, with the whole family hardly on speaking terms. **1869** *Routledge's Ev. Boy's Ann.* 640 He had enough pins and needles in his feet to stock a haberdasher's shop. **1885** T. A. GUTHRIE *Tinted Venus* 40 The shock ran up to his elbow and gave him acute 'pins and needles'. **1897** *Pall Mall Mag.* Aug. 530 He was plainly on pins and needles, did not know whether to take or to refuse a cigar. **1899** *Allbutt's Syst. Med.* VIII. 64 Subjective sensations such as heat and cold, pins and needles,..may persist during the intervals. **1944** W. S. MAUGHAM *Razor's Edge* iii. 112 The bishop had been a cavalry officer..and his austere, cadaverous vicar general was always on pins and needles lest he should say something scandalous. **1951** E. PAUL *Springtime in Paris* xv. 283 Dr. Thiouville was on pins and needles. **1979** *Country Life* 16 Aug. 489/4 The French were waiting on pins and needles to hear that the great [Wallace] collection would be theirs.

e. ***as neat as a (new) pin.***

1787 *Columbian Mag.* I. 636 [He was] neat as a new pin. **1801** J. WOLCOT *Wks.* (1812) V. 35 How neat was Ellen in her dress! As neat as a new pin! **1849** THACKERAY *Pendennis* I. xiii. 118 Major Pendennis, whom Miss Costigan declared to be a proper gentleman entirely,..and as neat as a pin. **1933** L. A. G. STRONG *Sea Wall* 245 Sheehan's pride was to have his cottage as neat as a new pin. **1961** *Dog World* Apr. 30 In the morning we leave the room looking as neat as a pin!

f. ***to be able to hear a pin drop*** (or ***fall***), etc.: used to suggest absolute silence or stillness.

[**1775** F. BURNEY *Diary* 11 June (1907) II. 81 Had a *pin* fallen, I suppose we should have taken it at least for a *thunder-clap*.] **1814** M. B. SMITH *Let.* Aug. in G. Hunt *40 Yrs. Washington Society* (1906) 113 It was so still you might have heard a pin drop on the pavement. **1824** S. FERRIER *Inheritance* II. xiv. 156 You might have heard a pin drop in the house while that was going on. **1831** MACAULAY *Let.* 30 Mar. (1974) II. 10 You might have heard a pin drop as Duncannon read the numbers. Then again the shouts broke out. **1870** MISS MULOCK *Fair France* IV. (1871) 145 As the phrase is, 'you might have heard a pin fall'. **1890** [see DROP *v.* 3]. **1914** *Maclean's Mag.* May 9/2 We could have heard a pin drop. **1934** A. CHRISTIE *Murder on Orient Express* III. ix. 246 Every eye was fixed upon him. In the stillness you could have heard a pin drop. **1959** I. & P. OPIE *Lore & Lang. Schoolch.* x. 193 'Let's 'ave a bit of shush', 'Let's hear this pin drop',..'Pipe down'. **1977** *Daily Mirror* 15 Mar. 3/3 They screamed, yelled and clapped between numbers, but while he sang you could have heard a pin drop.

g. ***to stick pins into*** (a person): to incite to action; to irritate or annoy.

1903 A. H. LEWIS *Boss* 184 This ain't meant to stick pins into you.

h. A gramophone needle.

1914 KIPLING *Lett. of Travel* (1920) 215 They slipped in pin and record.

4. *transf.* †**a.** A thorn or prickle. *Obs.* **b.** The incipient bur or blossom of the hop.

1643 TRAPP *Comm. Gen.* xiii. 6 There are pins in all the worlds roses. **1900** *Daily News* 23 July 2/4 The hop plant has grown well this week, and the bine is already putting out pin for burr.

III. (Cf. med.L. *pinna*, Du. *pinne* pinnacle.)

†**5.** A point, peak, apex. *Obs.* exc. *dial.*

c **1450** *Cov. Myst.* (Shaks. Soc.) 208 Up to this pynnacle now go we, I xal the sett on the hyȝest pynne. **1819** W. TENNANT *Papistry Storm'd* VI. (1827) 184 The sun was cockin' now upon The vera pin o' Mid-day's cone. **1838** *Penny Cycl.* XI. 57/2 The most prominent object [in Connamara] is a group of conical mountains called the Twelve Pins. **1892** JANE BARLOW *Irish Idylls* i. 2 Those twelve towering Connemarese peaks, which in Saxon speech have dwindled into Pins.

6. The projecting bone of the hip, esp. in horses and cattle: cf. *pin-bone, -buttock* in 18. Now *dial.*

1703 *Lond. Gaz.* No. 3886/4 A grey Nag,..gall'd upon the near Pin. **1726** *Brice's Weekly Jrnl.* 25 Mar. 3 A Brown Bay Nag..thin behind, the Pins standing a little out. **1807** VANCOUVER *Agric. Devon* (1813) 327 Line of the back straight..lying completely on a level with the pin or huckles. **1903** *Eng. Dial. Dict.* s.v., A cow 'high in the pins'.

IV. Transferred uses (chiefly from I).

7. A leg; usually in *pl.* Also *fig. colloq.* or *dial.*

c **1530** *Hickscorner* D iij, Than wolde I renne thyder on my pynnes As fast as I might go. **1628** EARLE *Microcosm., Downe-r. Scholar* (Arb.) 41 His body is not set vpon nice Pinnes. **1781** BURGOYNE *Ld. of Manor* III. iv, I never saw a fellow better set upon his pins. **1829** P. EGAN *Boxiana* 2nd Ser. II. 10 With all his struggling to right himself, he could not recover the use of his pins. *a* **1845** BARHAM *Ingol. Leg.* Ser. III. *Ld. Thoulouse* 275 Who ventures this road need be firm on his pins! **1880** 'MARK TWAIN' *Lett. to Publishers* (1967) 125. It saved the company's life and set them high on their pins and free of debt. **1883** *Standard* 8 Jan. 2/4 Iroquois [a race-horse] has been very 'dickey' on his pins. **1888** 'R. BOLDREWOOD' *Robbery under Arms* i, Wonderfully strong and quick on his pins. **1890** *Harper's Mag.* LXXX. 269/2 Glad to hear that he is on his pins yet; he might have pegged out in ten years, you know. **1917** 'H. H. RICHARDSON' *Fortunes R. Mahony* IV. viii. 355 Give your old pin here, and let me poultice it. **1960** [see FEW *a.* 2 f]. **1971** *Petticoat* 17 July 32/1 You need to be healthy too because you're likely to find yourself standing on your two pins all day and every day. **1976** *Daily Mirror* 11 Mar. 24/2 You look a bit wobbly on your pins, pet.

8. A skittle; also, a skittle or pin knocked down, as a scoring point. In *pl.* the game of skittles. See also NINEPINS, TENPINS.

1580 HOLLYBAND *Treas. Fr. Tong, Quilles*, as *iouër aux quilles*, to play at nine pins. **1600** ROWLANDS *Lett. Humours Blood* IV. 64 To play at..nine holes, or ten pinnes. **1694** S. JOHNSON *Notes Past. Let. Bp. Burnet* I. 39 A cleaverer Tip ..than taking out the Middle Pin and throwing down none of the rest. **1869** *Routledge's Ev. Boy's Ann.* 516 When all the pins [in American bowls] are knocked down by one ball. **1881** YOUNG *Every Man his own Mechanic* §86 The large pins used in skittle playing. **1974** *Cleveland* (Ohio) *Plain Dealer* 13 Oct. 8-C/3 Anthony..missed a perfect game by a single pin in the..finals. *Ibid.* 26 Oct. 5-D/4 A bowling ball can mean the difference of up to 20 pins in a game depending on the surface and balance of the ball. **1976** *Burnham-on-Sea Gaz.* 20 Apr. 21/5 Thatchers Arms A, the North Petherton Summer Skittles League champions, lost their first home match of the new season by six pins when Clarence Hotel A came from behind on the last hand. **1976** *Bridgwater Mercury* 21 Dec. 18/2 Brent Knoll Inn put an end to the last 100 per cent record in the first division of the Burnham, Highbridge and District Ladies' Skittles League by gaining a seven-pin away win at White Hart Hotel.

9. †**a.** A knot in wood (looking like a peg driven in). *Obs.*

1545 ASCHAM *Toxoph.* (Arb.) 115 The boughe commonlye is verye knotty, and full of pinnes. **1585** HIGINS tr. *Junius' Nomenclator* 144/1 The pinne or hard corne of a knot in timber, which hurteth sawes.

b. A hard spot occurring in steel during the process of manufacture.

1831 BREWSTER *Nat. Magic* v. (1833) 116 When the steel has hard portions called *pins* by the workmen. **1884** C. G. W. LOCK *Workshop Receipts* Ser. III. 279/2 Free from those hard bright spots which workmen call 'pins'.

†**10. a.** A hard swelling on the sole of a hawk's foot; a disease characterized by such swellings (also called *pin-gout*: see 18). *Obs.*

1575 TURBERV. *Falconrie* 260 Of the Pin in the Hawkes foote, a disease much like the corne in the foote of a man. *Ibid.*, The Pynne is a swelling disease, that doth resemble sharpe nayles, rysing vp in the bottome or palme of the Hawkes foote. **1615** LATHAM *Falconry* (1633) 134 With a sharpe knife search and pare out the pinne, or core, or corne. **1688** R. HOLME *Armoury* II. 237/2 The Pynne.

†**b.** A corn on the toe or foot. *Obs.*

1611 COTGR., *Frouelle*, an agnell, pinne, or warnell in the toe.

†**11.** ***pin and web***: name for a disease of the eye (? characterized by a spot or excrescence like a pin's head, and a film covering the general surface: according to Dr. S. B. Atkinson, 'phlyctenular ulcer with conjunctivitis'). *Obs.*

1533 ELYOT *Cast. Helthe* (1541) 79 By these destillations or reumes hapneth many diseases..as..pynne and webe in the eyes. **1575** TURBERV. *Falconrie* 300 This disease of the Pinne & webbe, is of some men called the Veroll. **1605** SHAKS. *Lear* III. iv. 122 This is the foule Flibbertigibbet;.. Hee giues the Web and the Pin, squints the eye, and makes the Hare-lippe. **1672** JOSSELYN *New Eng. Rarities* 96 To take off a Pin and Web, or any kind of Filme growing over the Eye. **1725** BRADLEY *Fam. Dict.*, *Pearl*, a Disease in an Horse's Eye, under which Head we shall comprehend Pins, Spots, Webs, &c. **1858** MAYNE *Expos. Lex.*, *Pin and Web*, an old popular name for an opacity of the cornea.

12. A small cask or keg holding half a firkin, or 4½ gallons.

1570 *Wills & Inv. N.C.* (Surtees) I. 341, iij pynnes for caryage of drenk a feld. *a* **1700** B. E. *Dict. Cant. Crew*, *Pin*, a small Vessel containing Four Gallons and a half, or the Eighth part of a Barrel. **1743** *Lond. & Country Brew.* IV. (ed. 2) 293 Powder one of the Balls and put it into a Pin or Half a Firkin. **1814** *Sporting Mag.* XLIII. 112 He used to have a pin of beer. *c* **1900** *Advertisement*, Beer in Cask. Discount for Cash on or before Delivery; 3d. Pin; 6d. Firkin; 1s. Kilderkin.

†**13.** A piece at chess; also, at the game of merels. In the latter referring app. to actual pegs; in chess extended either from these, or from the shape of Tudor chessmen, which were not unlike ninepins. *Obs.*

1688 R. HOLME *Armoury* III. xvi. (Roxb.) 66/1 The King is the first and highest of all the chesse pins. *Ibid.*, The Queene is the next pin in height to the King. **1784** COWPER *Task* VI. 271 At the chequer'd board..with a hand Trembling, as if eternity were hung In balance on his conduct of a pin.

14. a. *Cookery.* Short for ROLLING-PIN.

1894 *Cassell's Univ. Cookery Bk.* 740 Keep the board and pin well floured.

b. Short for KNITTING-*pin*, knitting-needle.

1897 *Tit Bits* 4 Dec. 175/3 As the old lady put down her pins, the Princess took them up, and finished the stocking-heel.

V. Phraseological uses.

15. In the phrase ***on*** or ***upon a merry pin***, esp. ***to set the heart on a merry pin, to have the heart hanging on a jolly pin***, whence also ***upon the peevish pin, on another pin***, etc.; later, ***in a merry pin***, in a merry humour, disposition, or frame of mind. *arch.* or *dial.*

The origin is obscure. In later use sometimes (cf. quot. 1658) associated with the musical tuning-peg, as in next.

c **1386** CHAUCER *Merch. T.* 272 By my fader kyn Youre herte hangeth on a ioly pyn. *c* **1440** *Partonope* 5552 Youre hert ys on another pynne. *c* **1485** *Digby Myst.* v. 492, I wyll sett my soule on a mery pynne. **1530** PALSGR. 844/1 Upon a mery pynne, *de hayt.* **1568** GRAFTON *Chron.* II. 578 King Charles heart by gettyng of Paris, was set vpon a mery Pinne. **1587** FLEMING *Contn. Holinshed* III. 1015/2 The commons hauing now their willes, were set vpon a pin, that the game was theirs. **1658** OSBORN *Adv. Son* i. (1896) 24 Success doth often wind him up to a jovial pin. **1666** J. SERGEANT *Let. Thanks* 42 You cannot for your heart yet wean your self of that merry pin of Fancy. **1676** SHADWELL *Virtuoso* I. i, I never was on a better pin in my life. **1694** L'ESTRANGE *Fables* cccii. (1714) 316 The Woman was One day upon the Peevish Pin. **1770** *Gentl. Mag.* XL. 559 To express the Condition of an Honest Fellow and no Flincher under the Effects of Good Fellowship, he is said to be..On a merry pin. **1779** T. HUTCHINSON *Diary* 6 Oct., Dined at Amen Corner..Sir John upon a merry pin. *Intended 18th c. lang.* [**1855** ANNE MANNING *O. Chelsea Bun-ho.* iv. 64 As for the Doctor, he was quite on the merry Pin.]

1661 BLOUNT *Glossogr.* (ed. 2) s.v., He is in a merry Pin. **1782** COWPER *Gilpin* 178 Right glad to find His friend in merry pin. **1818** *Blackw. Mag.* III. 407 Were I in the pin. **1887** A. RILEY *Athos* 210 Our prelate was in merry pin.

†**16.** Pitch; degree; step: esp. with ***higher, lower, utmost, raise, take down***. *Obs.* (Cf. PEG *sb.*[1] 3.)

Originally, a figure taken from a musical tuning-peg (see 1 d); in quot. 1617 perh. referring to the rack.

1584 GREENE *Myrr. Modestie* Wks. (Grosart) III. 24 The Iudges..seeing she had infringed their reasons, by the power of the law thought to wrest hir vpon a higher pin. **1617** HIERON *Wks.* II. 141 The prodigal sonne..sets his course euen vpon the racke, and stretcheth it out to the vtmost pinne. *a* **1624** BP. M. SMITH *Serm.* (1632) 188 They ..went more roundly and roughly to worke with them, taking them downe a pinne or two lower. *a* **1643** W. CARTWRIGHT *Ordinary* II. iii, He's but one pin above a natural. **1651** N. BACON *Disc. Govt. Eng.* II. vii. (1739) 41 To raise the price of their Cloaths to their own covetous pin. **1669** R. MONTAGU in *Buccleuch MSS.* (Hist. MSS. Comm.) I. 452, I am confident we shall bring them a pin lower. **1731** W. BOWMAN *Serm.* xxix, To set our selves on the same pin With Paul and Peter. **1776** C. KEITH *Farmer's Ha'*, They mak a loud and joyfu' din, For ilka heart is raised a pin.

17. Phrase. ***to put in the pin*** (*colloq.* or *slang*), to put a check or stop to some course; to call a halt; *esp.* to give up drinking. So ***to keep in the pin***, to keep from drinking; ***to let loose a pin***. (Eng. Dial. Dict.)

Supposed by some to have reference to the pins in a drinking-cup (1 f); but it may refer more generally to the use of a pin or peg in stopping motion or making fast, and of letting loose by taking out the pin.

1832-53 *Whistle-binkie* (Scot. Songs) Ser. III. 112, I ance was persuaded to 'put in the pin', But foul fa' the bit o't ava wad bide in, For whisky's a thing so bewitchingly stout, The first time I smelt it, the pin it lap out. **1835** J. MONTEATH *Dunblane Tradit.* (1887) 89 (E.D.D.) He had religiously abstained from drinking during the twelve months he had himself determined to keep in the pin. **1851** MAYHEW *Lond. Labour* I. 345/1 He had two or three times resolved to better himself, and had 'put in the pin', meaning he had made a vow to refrain from drinking. **1856** *Deil's Hallowe'en* 14 (E.D.D.) The Deil that e'en was ettlin' to let loose a pin.

VI. 18. *attrib.* and *Comb.*, as ***pin-box, -flag, -heel*** (so ***-heeled*** adj.), ***-hook, -manufactory, -mark, -seller, -snatcher, -sticking, -thrusting***; ***pin-sharp*** adj.; † **pin-auger**, an auger for boring holes for pins or pegs; **pin-bit** = *pin-drill*; **pin-block,** (*a*) a block of wood in which pins or pegs are fixed; (*b*) a block of wood to be shaped into a pin or peg (*Cent. Dict.*); **pinboard**, a panel having an array of identical sockets each connected to some of a set of wires, so that inserting a conducting pin into any of the sockets makes an electrical connection between some of the wires; † **pin-bole, pinboll**, ? some contrivance for floating a fishing-net; **pin-bone**, (*a*) the hip-bone, esp. of a horse (see 6); (*b*) (see quot. 1936); **pin-borer**, a Canadian beetle (*Xyleborus dispar*) which makes small round punctures like pinholes in the bark of pear-trees; † **pin-bouke** [see BOWK], some kind of vessel for liquids; **pin-boy** (see quots.); **pin-brained** *a.*, foolish, stupid; **pin-bush**, 'a fine reaming- or polishing-tool for delicate metal-work' (*Cent. Dict.*); **pin-buttock**, a narrow or sharp buttock; hence **pin-buttocked** *a.*; **pin-cherry**, the N. American wild red cherry (*Prunus pennsylvanica*); **pin-cloth**, a pinafore (? *obs.*); **pin clover**, name in California (from the shape of the seed-vessel) for the European stork's-bill (*Erodium cicutarium*), widely naturalized there; also, = ALFILARIA; **pin connexion**, a connexion of the parts of an iron or steel bridge by pins (instead of rivets, etc.; cf. *pin-joint*); so **pin-connected** *a.* (cf. *pin-jointed* adj.); **pin-cop** [COP *sb.*[2] 3], a pear-shaped 'cop' or roll of yarn, used for the weft in a power-loom; also *attrib.*; **pincord** = *needlecord* s.v. NEEDLE sb. 14; **pin-curl**, (*a*) an artificial curl of hair held in place by a hairpin; (*b*) a curl held in position during setting by a hairpin or other clip; **pin curler**, a pin or clip for securing pin-curls; **pin dot**, a tiny dot; *spec.* (see quot. 1957); **pin-drill**, a drill with a projecting central pin surrounded by a cutting face, used for countersinking, etc.; **pin-drop** *a.* (of silence) in which one could 'hear a pin drop'; **pin-dropping** *a.* = *pin-drop a.*; also as adv.; **pin-fall**, (*a*) the fall of a pin; a trifling incident; (*b*) the number of pins knocked down in a tenpin bowling game; a score in tenpin bowling; **pin-fish**, name for two N. American elongated sparoid fishes (*Lagodon rhomboides*, *Diplodus holbrooki*); also a small sun-fish, *Lepomis pallidus*; **pin-fit** *v. trans.* and *intr.*, in *Sewing*, to pin into position during fitting; **pin-flat**, a flat pin-cushion formed of two disks of cardboard lined and covered with some textile material, so that pins can be stuck into the edge (*U.S.*); **pin-footed** *a.* = *fin-footed*: see FIN *sb.*[1] 6; † **pin-gout**, a disease in a hawk's foot (see 10); **pin-grass** = *pin-clover*; **pin ground**, a *pin-spot* ground upon a textile; **pin hinge**, a hinge in which the two leaves are pivoted on a pin passing through a sheath in each; **pin-hold**, 'a place at which a pin holds or makes fast' (Smart, 1836); † **pin-hood**, 'the hood attached to a cloak, and fitted to be drawn over the hat or bonnet of the wearer' (Jam.); **pin-hooker** *U.S.* (see quot. 1944); **pin joint**, a form of joint in which two parts are connected by a pin passing through an eye in each; so **pin-jointed** *a.*; **pin-leg**, (*a*) a wooden leg; (*b*) a narrow, spindly leg; hence **pin-legged** *a.*; **pin lever**, used *attrib.* and *absol.* to denote a pin-pallet watch or escapement; **pin-machine**, a machine for making pins; **pin-man**, (*a*) a man who sells, or manipulates, pins; (*b*) a figure of a man appearing as composed of lines without breadth, esp. in a drawing; **pin-mandrel** (see quot.); **pin-mark**, a circular impression on the side of a piece of type, made by part of the mould used in casting; † **pin matter**, the matter of a pin, that which matters a pin; ***not a pin matter***, something that matters not a pin: cf. MATTER *sb.* 18; **pin-mill** = PIN-WHEEL 3; **pin-necked** *a.*, having tufts of feathers on the neck, as the pinnated grouse or prairie-hen; **pin-new** *a.*, brand-new; **pin oak**, a species of oak (*Quercus palustris*) found in swampy places in N. America; so called from the persistent dead branches, which resemble pins or pegs fixed in the trunk; also *attrib.*; **pin pallet** (see quot.); in an escapement, a pallet in the form of a metal pin or a semi-circular jewel (now used chiefly in cheap escapements); **pin-paper**, a paper of pins (PAPER *sb.* 6 b); *fig.* a collection of samples; **pin party** *Naut. slang* (see quot. 1946); **pin-patch** (*dial.*), a periwinkle (? because extracted from its shell with a pin); **pin plate**, *Engin.*, a plate with a hole for the pin that is riveted to a member at the site of a pin joint; **pin-pool**, 'a game played on a billiard-table with three balls, and five small pins' (*Century Dict.* 1889), or any of various related games; **pin-poppet** (*dial.*), a cylindrical case for pins; † **pin-powder** = PIN-DUST; **pin-prod** = PIN-PRICK; † **pin-purse**, ? a pin-case, or a pin-cushion; **pin-rack** *Naut.*, a rack or frame on the deck of a ship, in which belaying-pins are fixed; **pin-rail**, a rail or bar in which pins or pegs are fixed; **pin-rib**, 'a delicate cord or rib woven in the substance of fine muslin' (*Cent. Dict.*); **pin-rod**, 'in a locomotive, a tie-rod connecting the brake-shoes on opposite sides' (*Cent. Dict.*); **pin screen** *Cinematogr.* (see quot. 1976); also *attrib.*; **pin seal**, the treated skin of young seals; also *attrib.*; **pin-setter**, in tenpin bowling, a person who, or a machine that, rearranges fallen skittles; = *pin-boy*; hence **pin-setting** *vbl. sb.*; freq. *attrib.*; **pin-splitter** *Golfing slang*, (*a*) a crack golfer; (*b*) an accurate shot to the pin or a club which is supposed to aid such a shot; **pin-spot**, (*a*) each of a number of small round spots like pins' heads forming a pattern upon a textile fabric; (*b*) *Theatr.* (see quots.); hence **pin-spotted** *a.*; **pin spotter** = *pin-setter*; **pin stenter**, a stenter in which cloth is held by means of two rows of pins, one along each edge; **pin-stitch** (see quot. 1936); hence **pin-stitched** *a.*, **pin-stitching**; **pin switch** (*Telegr.*), a switch in which electric connexion is made by pins passing through holes in metal plates; **pin's-worth**, the worth of a pin, an extremely small amount; **pin-table** = *pin-ball machine* s.v. PIN-BALL 3; **pin-tongs** *sb. pl.*, a kind of tongs or pliers for holding pins or other small objects; **pin-tool**, a tubular cutting-tool for making cylindrical wooden pins (Knight *Dict. Mech.* 1875); **pin-tooth**, (*a*) each of the (sharp-pointed) teeth of the escapement-wheel in a clock or watch; (*b*) a canine tooth; † **pin-trace**, some part of horse-harness; **pin valve** = *needle valve* s.v. NEEDLE *sb.* 14; **pin-vice** (see quots.); **pin-weed**, a plant of the N. American genus *Lechea* (N.O. *Cistaceæ*); **pin-winged** *a.*, having the first primary feather of the wing attenuated, as in some American *Columbidæ*; **pin-wire**, wire of which pins are made; **pin-wood**, wood fit for pins or pegs; **pin-worm**, a parasitic nematode worm of the order Oxyuroidea; also = *tomato pinworm*. See also PIN-BASKET, PIN-CASE, PINCUSHION, etc. and *Eng. Dial. Dict.*

1523 FITZHERB. *Husb.* §5 An axe, a hachet, a hedgyngebyll, a *pyn awgur, a rest awgur, a flayle. **1873** E. SPON *Workshop Receipts* Ser. I. 134/2 With a..*pin-bit, bore a hole about a ½ of an inch deep. **1880** A. J. HIPKINS in Grove *Dict. Mus.* II. 722/1 The tuning-pin screws..into the thick metal wrestpin-piece, and through it into the wooden wrestplank or *pinblock. **1957** *Electronic Engin.* XXIX. 30 Problems are programmed by plugging step by step operations in columns on the *pinboards, a column for each operation, and when a pin is inserted into a hole, connexions are automatically made to carry out the instruction. **1966** R. K. RICHARDS *Electronic Digital Syst.* ix. 553 Like a plugboard, a complete pinboard assembly with its pins can be removed from a system and saved for re-use while other pinboards..are used for the solution of other problems. **1969** P. B. JORDAIN *Condensed Computer Encycl.* 383 A 10 × 10 pinboard with 100 holes can connect any of 10 incoming signals (horizontal) to any of 10 outgoing paths (vertical). **1615** E. S. *Britain's Buss* in Arb. *Garner* III. 625 Cork *pynboles or buyes belonging to those nets. *Ibid.* 631 For every two nets, there must be a Pynboll or Bwy hooped... Each Pynboll or Bwy must have a rope of a yard long, to fasten it to the War-rope. **1640** CAREW in *Doidge's W. Country Ann.* (1882) 211 It..strake Roger Nise on the *pinbone. **1711** *Lond. Gaz.* No. 4849/4 The Hair rubb'd off the near Pinbone. **1805** *Sporting Mag.* XXV. 226 Joint steaks, pinbone-steaks, sausages. **1936** *Discovery* Oct. 321/1 Pins had been made by individual craftsmen using a small bone implement, on the flat surface of which was a series of inch-long grooves, deep at one end but tapering at the other. This tool served to file the pins to a point, its formation making it possible to shape several at one time from lengths of wire. Many of these 'pin-bones' still exist. **1945** *ABC of Cookery* (Ministry of Food) ix. 29 Hip or pin bone steak. **1973** R. D. SYMONS *Where Wagon Led* p. xiii, I learned the cowboy's names, and could speak of pinbones and stifles and croups. **1978** *Sunday Tel.* 17 Sept. 11/3 Do you know, for example, what is called Pope's eye or heuk bone in Scotland, hip bone in the Midlands or pin bone in Wales? It's what many of us call rump. **1593** DRAYTON *Moses* III. Wks. (1748) 480/2 Pails, kits, dishes, basons, *pinboukes, bowls. **1858** SIMMONDS *Dict. Trade Products*, **Pin-box*, *Pin-case*, a small fancy box for holding pins. **1892** A. E. VOGELL *Bowling* 8 **Pin boy*, boy who returns the balls cast and resets the pins. **1958** *Wall St. Jrnl.* 9 Dec. 1/4 Automatic pinboys..have played a major role in the bowling boom. **1959** *Listener* 19 Mar. 501/1 The latest development is an automatic pin-boy. .. An ingenious electrical device will set up the pins and return the balls. **1975** *Oxf. Compan. Sports & Games* 92/1 In the earlier years of the game pin-boys were employed to re-set the pins after each frame. **1964** *Listener* 20 Feb. 313/1 A smug biologist and his *pin-brained wife. **1966** B. KIMENYE *Kalasanda Revisited* 31 His successor was flirting madly with some pin-brained girl. **1884** KNIGHT *Dict. Mech.* Suppl., **Pin Bush*, a reaming or polishing tool for pin holes. **1601** SHAKS. *All's Well* II. ii. 18 It is like a Barbers chaire that fits all buttockes, the *pin buttocke, the quatch-buttocke, the brawn buttocke, or any buttocke. **1725** BRADLEY *Fam. Dict.* s.v. *Rules buying horse*, The narrow pin Buttock, the Hog or Swine-Rump,..are full of Deformity. **1977** 'E. CRISPIN' *Glimpses of Moon* i. 11 There were several such benches in the bar-room—memorials to a centuries-extinct clientèle of pin-buttocks—but otherwise the furniture was all modern. **1601** HOLLAND *Pliny* II. 370 They are sharp rumped and *pin buttockt. **1683** *Lond. Gaz.* No. 1810/4 A Gelding,..Pin-Buttockt or narrow. **1791** *Gentl. Mag.* LXI. II. 964 One of the..children..approached so near the fire that the flames caught his *pin-cloth. **1846**, **1854** [see PINNER[2] 2]. **1884** MILLER *Plant-n.*, Pin-grass, or *Pin-clover, of California, *Erodium cicutarium*. **1913** W. C. BARNES *Western Grazing Grounds* 39 Alfileria is also known as 'heron's bill' and 'pin clover'. **1925** W. L. JEPSON *Man. Flowering Plants Calif.* 592 The term filaree..is, like the names Pin Clover or Pin Grass, indifferently applied to either this species [sc. *Erodium moschatum*] or to no. 5 [sc. *E. cicutarium*]. **1878** *Min. Proc. Inst. Civil Engin.* LIV. 179 All these American bridges are '*pin connected', this style of construction being preferred by American engineers for spans exceeding 100 feet, on account of the mathematical certainty with which the strains can be calculated. **1968** E. H. & C. N. GAYLORD *Struct. Engin. Handbk.* VI. 71 The AISC Specification requires that the allowable tensile stress on the net section transverse to the axis of the member be reduced 25 percent at pinholes in pin-connected plates. **1969** *Civil Engin.* (Easton, Pa.) June 45/1 Columns were pin-connected top and bottom to prevent any supplementary stress from differential settlement or rotation of the foundations. **1878** *Min. Proc. Inst. Civil Engin.* LIV. 214 There was undoubtedly a considerable difference in the use of what the Author [*sc.* T. C. Clarke] called *pin-connections as compared with rivet-connections. **1974** *Encycl. Brit. Macropædia* III. 177/2 The first major iron-truss bridge, with pin connections, was built in the United States in 1851. **1839** URE *Dict. Arts* 503 Yarns ..wound upon what is called a '*pin cop bobbin'. **1977** *New Yorker* 8 Aug. 72/1 (Advt.), Our handsome, lightweight hobby pants in no-iron Dacron/cotton *pincord, ideal for travel and leisure. **1979** A. SCHOLEFIELD *Point of Honour* 142 White pincord slacks. **1896** *Daily News* 27 Nov. 5/2 Our English great-grandmothers called 'coques' 'comb-curls' or '*pin-curls', because they were..stiffly arranged and held in their place with small side combs or hairpins. **1904** *Daily Chron.* 7 Oct. 8/5 She buys a 'pin-curl' and attaches it to her cycling hat! **1931** G. A. FOAN *Art & Craft of Hairdressing* 28/1 Pin-curls..may be used as side-pieces to be worn in front of the ears. **1950** E. HEMINGWAY *Across River* xix. 152 You ought to have to sleep in a bed with a girl who has put her hair up in pin curls to be beautiful tomorrow. **1963** D. B. HUGHES *Expendable Man* (1964) i. 10 'Don't you need a mirror?'.. But she could wind the pin curls without it. *Ibid.* 18 Her hair done up in *pin curlers under the dirty scarf. **1891** KIPLING *Light that Failed* (1900) 172 There were only weaving circles and floating *pin-dots before his eyes. **1957** M. B. PICKEN *Fashion Dict.* 252/2 *Pin dot*, smallest dot used as fabric design. **1978** *N.Y. Times* 30 Mar. A4/1 (Advt.), A pin-dot tie. **1875** KNIGHT *Dict. Mech.*, **Pin-drill*, a drill for countersinking. **1816** L. HUNT *Rimini* I. 244 A *pin-drop silence strikes o'er all the place. **1971** D. FRANCIS *Bonecrack* i. 9 There was a long *pin-dropping silence. **1973** *Advocate-News* (Barbados) 29 June 6/6 The lighting..succeeded in transforming the massive stadium through moods of harried excitement to 'pin-dropping' silence. **1977** *New Yorker* 19 Sept. 50/1 The hall was pin-dropping quiet. **1912** W. DEEPING *Sincerity* vii. 56 A good lady whose troubles had been so many *pinfalls in the closeted selfishness of her little life. **1974** *Cleveland* (Ohio) *Plain Dealer* 27 Oct. 1-C/4 Colwell began the first day of competition in this inaugural event with a 1363 pinfall. **1976** *Billings* (Montana) *Gaz.* 30 June 4-E/2 Here are the top 10 bowlers and their total pinfall after four rounds (26 games) of the $60,000 Portland Open Bowling Tournament. **1964** *McCall's Sewing* ii. 31/1 **Pin-fit*, to pin and adjust the garment to your figure before permanent stitching. *Ibid.* vi. 93/1 When you try on the garment, it is very easy to pin-fit and taper the legs to a becoming width. **1973** *Washington Post* 5 Jan. B5/4 (Advt.), Price includes fabric and labor with choice of skirt, self-cording and pin-fitting in your home. *a* **1916** 'SAKI' *Toys of Peace* (1919) 290 To-day we are putting little *pin-flags again into maps of the Balkan region. **1957** M. BANTON *W. Afr. City* ix. 176, 4,000 pin-flags were brought out of concealment and fastened in the clothing of their comrades. **1864** WEBSTER, **Pin-footed*, having the toes bordered by a skin. **1575** TURBERV. *Falconrie* 346 Of the swelling in a Hawkes foote, which we tearme the pin, or *pin Goute. *Ibid.* 346 Make plaisters thereof, and bestowe them on the pinnegoute. **1847** *Californian* (San Francisco) 10 July 3/1 Quality of Pasture—Bunch Grass; Clover; Wild Oats and *Pin Grass, all in abundance. **1888** [see ALFILARIA]. **1914** C. F. SAUNDERS *With Flowers & Trees in Calif.* iii. 55 Still another wild pasture-plant..is the stork's-bill.., commonly known as pingrass or filaree. **1949** E. L. PALMER *Fieldbk. Nat. Hist.* 241/3 Common names [of *Erodium cicutarium*] include wild musk, pin clover, pin grass, pinweed and heron's bill, mostly based on character of fruit. **1958** R. C. ROLLINS *Fernald & Kinsey's Edible Wild Plants Eastern N. Amer.* (ed. 2) 259 Storksbill, Pin-grass, *Erodium cicutarium*. **1825** COBDEN in Morley *Life* i. (1903) 8 Black and purple and *pin grounds. **1961** R. LONGRIGG *Daughters of Mulberry* i. 8 Giggles Ballantyne..teetered unhappily on tall *pin heels. **1960** C. STORR *Marianne & Mark* iv. 54 A pair of tight *pinheeled patent-leather shoes. **1963** *Times* 20 Feb. 14/7 We were joined by a girl in pointed pin-heeled shoes which soon put an end to her enthusiasm. **1940** *Chambers's Techn. Dict.* 644/2 *Pin hinge. **1964** W. L. GOODMAN *Hist. Woodworking Tools* ii. 53 This cupboard door, in a light-brown hardwood, appears to have been the right-hand leaf of a pair, as the pin hinge is slightly longer at the top. **1491** *Acc. Ld. High Treas. Scot.* I. 187 Item, ij elne sattin to lyne the cap of that cloyke, and to be a *pyn hwd. **1834** D. CROCKETT *Narr. Life* 207 In this hunt every..little *pin-hook lawyer was engaged. **1840** *Southern Lit. Messenger* VI. 386/2 Ellen used to fish there for minnoes with a pin-hook. **1897** *Outing* (U.S.) XXX. 439 This fish ranks among the first victims of pin-hook wiles. **1970** *Country Life* 17–24 Dec. 1199/1 Losing..a string of sausages to..a pin-hook on a piece of string. **1942** *Sun* (Baltimore) 23 Sept. 7/2 '*Pin hookers', who make small purchases in auction markets and then resell them in the same markets also are exempt from price control. **1944** *Richmond* (Virginia) *Times-Dispatch* 5 Oct. 18 The fixation of prices this year is bad business for the time honored 'pinhooker', the man with relatively small operating capital who, during the more spacious days of tobacco selling when the auctioneer got the green light for a sale from wall to wall, bought tobacco when the market was low and held it until it was high, pocketing the difference. The prices this year are so narrow that the pinhooker's business has been practically squeezed out. **1949** L. RAPPORT in B. A. Botkin *Treas. S. Folklore* IV. iii. 652 There's Carroll, Jones, and Mallory for the Big Three..buyers from the four large independents who are on this market, and seven or eight pinhookers. **1966** *Publ. Amer. Dial. Soc.* XLV. 19 The pinhooker will attach his sales tag to a lot of tobacco waiting to be received by the warehouse workers. **1886** A. B. W. KENNEDY *Mech. of Machinery* xii. 586 The efficiency of a *pin joint, or turning pair, is generally very much greater than that of a sliding pair. **1919** PIPPARD & PRITCHARD *Aeroplane Struct.* x. 122 An important case occurs when..a pin-joint is made in an aeroplane spar at any place other than near one of the positions of the points of inflection. **1978** J. E. GORDON *Structures* x. 205 The concentration of stress at the pin joints calls for a tough and ductile material, such as wrought iron. **1882** *Min. Proc. Inst. Civil Engin.* LXIX. 111 Of a well-designed *pin-jointed structure, all the principal members must be connected directly with the pin. **1908** E. S. ANDREWS *Theory & Design of Struct.* xvii. 508 Pin-jointed eye bars are not much used in this country for bridge work, and for roof work they are going out of use. **1974** *Nature* 4 Jan. 77/2 It covers the treatment of pin-jointed frameworks, beams, circular sandwich plates, Michell's structural continua and plates loaded in their planes. **1862** *Illustr. Catal. Internat. Exhib., Industr. Dept., Brit. Div.* II. No. 3600 A case with jointed *pin-leg, artificial human leg, and others. **1960** S. PLATH *Colossus* (1967) 39 The oracular ghost who dwindles on pin-legs. **1936** DYLAN THOMAS *Twenty-Five Poems* 44 *Pin-legged on pole-hills with a black medusa By waste seas where the white bear quoted Virgil. **1939** —— *Let.* Mar. (1966) 226 The English poets now are such a pinlegged..crowd. **1946** in D. de Carle *Pract. Watch Repairing* (prelim. advt.) The new *pin lever—seven jewels. **1962** *Which?* June 165/1 In many cheaper watches, there is a pin-pallet (or pin lever) type of escapement, in which the pallets are hardened steel pins instead of jewels. **1976** M. CUTMORE *Watch Collector's Handbk.* ii. 70 In the pin-lever design the impulse pallets on the lever are replaced by steel pins... The escape-wheel teeth supply most of the lift and have steeply sloped faces. **1884** KNIGHT *Dict. Mech.* Suppl., **Pin Machine*. *c* **1680** *Crys of London* 36 in *Bagford Ball.* I. 116 Here's your old *Pin Man, a coming agen. **1878** J. INGLIS *Sport & W.* iv. 34 The pinmen are busy sorting their pins. **1934** DYLAN THOMAS *Let.* 2 May (1966) 114 And I have, too, a violent desire to draw pin-men. **1953** J. MASTERS *Lotus & Wind* i. 8 The engineer was little more than a pin man in the distance. **1965** J. WADE *Boy with Sling* I. i. 11 He flicked at the ground..with a switch, drawing an elongated pinman. **1975** *Times Lit. Suppl.* 7 Feb. 129/3 The movement of the train, and the view through its windows, reduce what Rhoda sees to a scene of pin-men moving awkwardly and senselessly through an unwelcoming landscape. **1703** MOXON *Mech. Exerc.* 189 *Pin-Mandrels ..are made with a..Shank, to fit stiff into a round hole that is made in the Work that is to be Turned. **1835** URE *Philos. Manuf.* 304 The hardships which children have to endure in *pin-manufactories. [**1887** T. B. Reed *Hist. Old Eng. Letter Foundries* 26 A more probable explanation seems to be that the head of a small screw or pin, used to fix the side-piece of the mould, . . left its mark on the side of the types as they were cast.] **1888** C. T. Jacobi *Printers' Vocab.* 100 *Pin mark.—This is the slight mark in the side of a type near the top of the shank made in casting by machinery. **1916** Legros & Grant *Typogr. Printing-Surfaces* iii. 14 The pin-mark, or drag, . . only occurs in certain machine-made type. **1922** D. B. Updike *Printing Types* I. ii. 16 The pin-mark is an indentation on the upper part of the body, made by the pin in casting. **1951** S. Jennett *Making of Bks.* ii. 34 The other [side], in foundry type, bears the pin-mark, or occasionally two pin-marks... The pin-mark is formed by the mechanism that ejects the type from the mould when it is cast. **1611** Cotgr. s.v. *Passer, Passe sans flux*, not a *pinne matter. **1679** *Trails of White*, etc. 36 Is it a pin matter whether there was such a Bill or no? **1766** *Complete Farmer* s.v. *Surveying*, It is not a pin matter how rude or false the lines or angles be. **1885** C. T. Davis *Leather* xxiii. (1897) 331 From the 'soaks' the skins are removed, . . and placed . . in the '*pin-mill'. **1967** T. Keneally *Bring Larks* xxviii. 222 By the time he sighted the *pin-new East Indiaman, it had already ripped through the oyster-shell horizon far out to the south-east. **1976** *New Society* 19 Feb. 373/1 A dozen girls sit in the toy department of a pin-new department store. **1813** H. Muhlenberg *Catal. Plantarum Americæ Septentrionalis* 87 Swamp or *Pin Oak, (*Quercus palustris*). **1847** D. Coyner *Lost Trappers* I. 23 The young trapper was relieved by the arrival of two of the company, one of whom climbed a pin-oak tree. **1857** *Yale Lit. Mag.* XXII. 284 His head is as obtuse and spongy as the butt-end of a pin-oak rail. **1874** J. W. Long *Amer. Wild-fowl* xvi. 197 Pin-oaks, whose tiny acorns are greedily sought for by mallards and sprig-tails. **1897** *Outing* (U.S.) XXIX. 516/1 [Mallards] gather in the timbered sloughs and low swales bordering on the Mississippi, where the pin-oak and willow abound. **1941** P. P. Pirone *Maintenance of Shade & Ornamental Trees* iv. 45 Pin oaks in alkaline soils often develop yellow or chlorotic leaves. **1975** *Country Life* 16 Jan. 148/3 American woodland in the east . . is composed largely of oak, not our oak, but the slim and lofty red oak, white oak, pin oak and chestnut oak. **1860** E. Beckett *Rudimentary Treat. Clocks* (ed. 4) 103 *Pin Pallets. **1884** F. J. Britten *Watch & Clockm.* 194 [The] Pin Pallet Escapement . . used mostly in French Clocks, in which it is often placed in front of the dial. The pallets are formed of semi-circular jewels. **1903** F. J. Garrard *Watch Repairing* x. 101 The 'pin-pallet' escapement . . has round pins for pallets, and the inclines are on the scape teeth. **1946** D. de Carle *Pract. Watch Repairing* vi. 55 Some designs of pin pallets are so made that the arms carrying the pallet pins can be bent quite easily. **1976** M. Cutmore *Watch Collector's Handbk.* i. 47 The cheap watch had developed independently in Switzerland in the form which was eventually to become world-wide. Roscopf designed and produced a pin-pallet lever watch in 1867. **1673** Marvell *Reh. Transp.* II. 170 His Sermon is extant . . some Heads and Points of it I gave you . . as a *Pinne-paper of your modern Orthodoxy. **1817** Coleridge *Biog. Lit.* 209 The pin-papers, and stay-tapes, which might have been among the wares of his pack. **1942** *Ark Royal* (Ministry of Information) 18/2 When a squadron is preparing for a reconnaissance, the ground staff bring the aircraft from the hangar to the flight deck... The ranging party . . then take over and push the aircraft aft, assisted by a small '*pin party' to spread and secure the wings. **1946** J. Irving *Royal Navalese* 135 *Pin party*, . . the working party, in a Carrier, which prepares aircraft on the flying deck for taking off. **1694** Echard *Plautus* 164 Whole beds o' crabs, lobsters, oysters, *pinpatches, coral, muscles, and cockles. *a* **1825** Forby *Voc. E. Anglia*, *Pin-patches, Pin-paunches*, the small shell fish called periwinkles... They are commonly drawn out of their shells with a pin. **1893** J. B. Johnson et al. *Theory & Pract. Mod. Framed Struct.* xxi. 338 The Lengths of Bearing or *Pin Plates are determined by the following considerations. **1968** E. H. & C. N. Gaylord *Struct. Engin. Handbk.* vi. 71 Usually, a pin plate is assumed to transmit a fraction of the main member force proportional to its thickness. *c* **1866** W. B. Dick *Amer. Hoyle* (ed. 3) 428 The game of *Pin Pool is played with two white balls and one red, together with five small wooden pins. **1900** Ade *Fables in Slang* 16 The Local Editor . . was playing Pin-Pool with the Superintendent. **1915** B. Edwards in H. Dempsey *Best of Bob Edwards* (1975) v. 107 Men who blew all their money on whisky and pin pool. **1959** in Halas & Manvell *Technique Film Animation* xxvi. 304 (*heading*) Pin screen animation. *Ibid.*, The pin screen is designed for black-and-white films. **1976** *Oxf. Compan. Film* 11/2 After watching *L'Idée* (1934) in production in 1932 he [*sc.* Alexandre Alexeïeff] experimented with animation techniques and invented the pin screen, a metal surface pierced by about five million tiny holes through which he pressed metal pins which, obliquely lit, created shadows with all possible gradations from black to white according to the length of pin protruding from the screen. **1866** *Routledge's Ev. Boy's Ann.* 642 Driven into the '*pin-poppet', the old name by which these curious cases were best known. **1502** *Privy Purse Exp. Eliz. of York* (1830) 27 Item for *pyn powdre xij d. **1893** E. Crowe *With Thackeray in Amer.* i. 11 Reflection made him think the onslaught harmless, and the sting in it only of the *pin-prod order. **1608** T. Cocks *Diary* (1901) 35 Payde for a *pynne purse for my va[lentine] vs. **1875** Knight *Dict. Mech.*, **Pin-rack*, . . a frame placed on the deck of a vessel, and containing sheaves around which ropes may be worked, and belaying-pins around which they may be secured. **1877** Stainer *Organ* ii. §24 Under the keys a series of pins are arranged on a piece of wood forming a *pin-rail. These pins fit easily into holes in the keys and prevent them from oscillating. **1926–7** *Army & Navy Stores Catal.* 408B/3 *Pochettes*... *Pin seal leather, lined silk. **1934** *Times* 29 Nov. 19/3 In black pinseal with the new short handles there is a useful bag with a triple frame. **1961** [see *billfold(er* s.v. bill *sb.*[3] 11]. **1972** J. Mosher *Some would call it Adultery* iii. xv. 139 Then he took a change purse from an inside pocket. It was black pinseal leather, opening with a snap. **1974** *Country Life* 21 Nov. (Suppl.) 45 Pin seal wallet £30. **1608** H. Clapham *Errour Right Hand* 39 Tom Lace-seller and Abraham *Pin-seller. **1916** H. M. Rideout *Far Cry* xi. 150 Like a *pin-setter in a bowling alley, Mace carefully planted his bottles upright on the floor. **1958** *Economist* 20 Dec. 1085/1 In 1954 the American Machine & Foundry Company began large-scale production of an electronic automatic pin-setter, or pin spotter as it is also called. **1958** *Wall St. Jrnl.* 9 Dec. 1/4 In the past seven years they've [*sc.* automatic pinboys have] taken over the pinsetting chores on all but a small minority of the existing lanes. **1964** *Economist* 30 May 1024/3 The introduction of pin-setting machines that speeded the game. **1972** *Mainichi Daily News* (Japan) 7 Nov. 6/4 The company signed a contract with Yungtay Engineering Co. of Taichung to export pin-setting machines for 100 bowling lanes. **1947** W. de la Mare *Coll. Stories for Children* 60 He crinkled up his *pin-sharp eyes. **1978** *SLR Camera* Aug. 4/1 (Advt.), Pinsharp projection from corner to corner. **1900** *Echo* 12 June 3/4 Pick pockets and *pin-snatchers reaped a rich harvest. **1926** *Glasgow Herald* 26 June 8 Their prowess as 'par-beaters' and '*pin-splitters'. **1961** Partridge *Dict. Slang* Suppl. 1222/1 *Pin-splitter*... Since ca. 1935, predominantly a golf-shot dead on the pin. **1973** *Country Gentlemen's Mag.* Mar. 181/1 Gents Pinsplitter Golf Clubs. **1894** *Daily News* 28 Apr. 6/5 Single flowers scattered over a '*pin-spot' ground. **1903** *Westm. Gaz.* 12 Feb. 4/2 Many of them spotted, but with a regular pin-spot. **1947** *Gloss. Technical Theatr. Terms* (Strand Electr. & Engin. Co.) 22 *Pin spot*, any spot lantern so adjusted that its maximum light is focussed into the smallest possible area. **1961** A. Berkman *Singers' Gloss. Show Business* 7 *Baby spot*. . ., a small spotlight used for illuminating any small object on stage; often used for lighting just the face of the performer. (Also called *pin-spot*.) **1900** *Daily News* 14 July 4/7 The little bolero coat is faced with white linen, *pin-spotted with cornflower blue. **1958** *Pin-spotter [see *pin-setter*]. **1975** *Oxf. Compan. Sports & Games* 90/2 Modern bowling centres, with automatic pin-spotters and score-indicators, have replaced the rough, tough alleys lit by kerosene lamps, which catered for saloon crowds in the early days of the twentieth century. **1947** J. T. Marsh *Introd. Textile Finishing* i. 20 The beater untangles the matted pile, and the fabric then passes into the *pin stenter which is equipped with from eight to sixteen rotating cards. **1962** —— *Self-Smoothing Fabrics* xi. 171 Since the advent of the crease-resisting process, with its earlier emphasis on rayon fabric production, there has been a corresponding emphasis on pin stenters compared with the clip stenter. **1884** *Health Exhib. Catal.* 118/1 A *Pin-sticking Machine, for sticking pins on paper. **1936** A. M. Miall *Everyday Embroidery Bk.* viii. 74 *Punch, Lace, *Pin or Turkey-stitch* (it has all these names) is an open-work stitch which is sometimes used in rather elaborate *broderie anglaise*, or in cut-work . . as an open-work filling for a flower or motif. **1948** C. Christopher *Compl. Bk. Embroidery* viii. 185 Pin Stitch is used to applique motifs of self material on either wrong or right side of fabric. **1972** B. Snook *Creative Art of Embroidery* 92 *Pin stitch*. This is used along a hem edge. **1960** S. Plath *Colossus* (1967) 48 At the price of a *pin-stitched skin Fish-tailed girls purchase each white leg. **1935** G. W. Fry *Embroidery & Needlework* viii. 188 As with hemstitching so with *pin stitching, the decorative effect may be obtained with nothing more than outlines. **1884** Knight *Dict. Mech.* Suppl., **Pin Switch*... The connections are made with pins or plugs, which give a rubbing or frictional contact when thrust into the holes on the board. **1562** Bulleyn *Bulwark Sicke Men* 70 b, Did me neuer a *pinsworthe of pleasure. **1936** *Archit. Rev.* LXXIX. 135/1 Under one of these, however, peeps out a gay little shop in bright green paint, full of *pin-tables, where one can lose one's money in proper Strand fashion. **1957** *Observer* 20 Oct. 16/3 Entirely devoted to a single situation—pin-table saloon proprietors versus local councillor. **1973** 'M. Underwood' *Reward for Defector* ii. 13 Questions . . were flashing through his mind like lights on a pin-table. **1977** *Irish Press* 29 Sept. 16/1 (Advt.), Pool tables, pin tables, fruit machines, etc., on sharing basis. **1853** Byrne *Artisan's Handbk.* 81 For cutting the facets, they are held in small hand-vises or *pin-tongs. **1825** J. Nicholson *Operat. Mechanic* 521 That part of the stone pallets upon which the *pin teeth act. **1886** *Standard* 15 Jan. 2/5 Its 'pin', or pointed, teeth had not developed. **1440–41** *Durham Acc. Rolls* (Surtees) 627 Pro j *pyntrase. **1536–7** *Ibid.* 697, iij par. pyntracez. **1903** *Electr. World & Engin.* 18 July 115 The pressure is admitted to or withdrawn from the piston by means of a *pin-valve. **1875** Knight *Dict. Mech.*, **Pin-vise*, . . a hand-vise for grasping small arbors and pins. **1884** F. J. Britten *Watch & Clockm.* 196 Pin Vice . . chiefly used as a holder for pins and small pieces of work while they are being filed. **1854** Thoreau *Walden* xvii. (1886) 307 Golden-rods, *pinweeds, and graceful wild grasses. **1890** *Cent. Dict.*, The *pin-winged doves are pigeons of the genus *Æchmoptila* . . of Texas and Mexico. **1896** A. Morrison *Child of the Jago* 165 Her wedding-ring, worn to *pin-wire. **1573** Tusser *Husb.* xvii. (1878) 38 And seasoned timber for *pinwood to haue. **1910** K. Winslow *Prevention & Treatm. Dis. Domestic Animals* 191 Oxyuris, Whip, Thread or *Pin Worm. **1933** *Jrnl. Econ. Entomol.* XXVI. 138 In California, the Pin Worm [*sc.* an insect larva] has done much damage to tomatoes. **1961** E. R. & G. A. Noble *Parasitol.* vi. 312 *Oxyuris equi* is the common pinworm in the cecum and colon of horses. *Ibid.* 317 *Enterobius vermicularis* is the pinworm or seat-worm of man. **1974** M. C. Gerald *Pharmacol.* ii. 35 Piperazine (Antepar) and chloroquine . . have been quite effective in the cure of . . pinworm, and malaria, respectively.

pin, *sb.*[2] *local.* [Origin obscure: perh. connected with pin *v.* II.] The middle place in a tandem team of three horses. Hence **pin-bullock** *Austral.*, one of the pair of bullocks in a team nearest the wagon; **pin-horse**: see quots.

1877 *N.W. Linc. Gloss.*, *Pin-horse*, the middle horse in a team. **1881** Miss Jackson *Shropsh. Word-bk.*, *Pin*, the middle place for a horse, between the shafter and the leader in a team of three. *Pin-horse*. **1886** Elworthy *W. Som. Word-bk.*, Pin, Pin-horse. [Widely prevalent in rural use. In E.D.D. from N. Yorksh. to Somerset.] **1936** I. L. Idriess *Cattle King* viii. 68 They call the two polers the pin bullocks, because they swing the turntable of the wagon! **1959** H. P. Tritton *Time means Tucker* 36 A bullock-team is made up in four parts: polers, pin, body and leaders... The pin-bullocks take the pull.

pin, *sb.*[3] [f. pin *v.*[1] 5.] **1.** *Chess.* The act of pinning, the fact of being pinned.

1868 Selkirk *Bk. Chess* 72 Removing his Queen to obviate the 'pin'. **1911** A. C. White *First Steps Classification Two-Movers* 73 The Black King moves into a triple pin, which is the feature of the problem. **1932** *Times Lit. Suppl.* 8 Dec. 948/3 Forcing the king where he wanted it, and then releasing the 'pin' paved the way for the threatened 26. **1976** *Daily Tel.* 4 Dec. 11/6 Black thinks it time to bring his queen into play and finds an unexpectedly troublesome pin.

2. pin-fall *Wrestling*, a fall in which a wrestler must hold an opponent down for a specified length of time.

1907 *Daily Chron.* 21 Dec. 9/5 These two . . wrestlers having agreed to contest the best of three pin falls in the catch-as-catch-can style. **1976** K. Bonfiglioli *Something Nasty in Woodshed* iv. 41 He helps the other chap back into the ring . . then administers a fearsome forearm smash and the winning pinfall.

pin (pɪn), *v.*[1] Forms: see the sb. [In branch I., f. pin *sb.*[1] In branch II., perh. worn down from pind *v.*, but blending with I. in the sense 'fasten': cf also pen *v.*[1] 1 and 2.]

I. To transfix, fix, attach, confine, with a pin.

1. *trans.* To fasten (things or parts of a thing *together*, or one thing *to* another) with one or more pins, pegs, or bolts (see pin *sb.*[1] 1); to construct or repair by thus fastening the parts together; to make fast with a bolt, to bolt (a door, etc.). † ***to pin the basket***: see basket *sb.* 1 d.

13.. *Gaw. & Gr. Knt.* 769 With a pyked palays, pyned ful þik. **1377** Langl. *P. Pl.* B. xx. 296 Conscience . . made pees porter to pynne [*MS. B.* penne] þe ȝates Of alle tale-tellers and tyterers in ydel. *a* **1380** *Minor Poems fr. Vernon MS.* lii. 6 Cros, þou dost no trouþe, On a pillori my fruit to pinne. *c* **1440** *Gesta Rom.* lxxxvii. 409 (Add. MS.), I shall haspe the dore, and pynne it with a pynne. *a* **1533** Ld. Berners *Huon* cxvi. 411 No shyppe can depart hens without it be pynnyd with nayles of woode and not of Iron. **1579–80** North *Plutarch* (1595) 750 Rafters or great peeces of tymber pinned together. **1663** Gerbier *Counsel* 43 They pin down a planck. **1703** Moxon *Mech. Exerc.* 123 They pin it up with wooden Pins. **1875** *Carpentry & Join.* 104 The mortices cut quite through and pinned with oak or ash pins. **1883** Gilmour *Mongols* xxv. 301 The long rope, which is pinned down to the ground. **1884** F. J. Britten *Watch & Clockm.* 143 The lever is pinned to the pallets.

fig. **1727** Swift *State Irel.* Wks. 1755 V. ii. 164 An act of navigation, to which we never consented, pinned down upon us. **1820** Hazlitt *Lect. Dram. Lit.* 317 He is pinned down in more than one Review . . as an exemplary warning.

2. a. To fasten with a pin (see pin *sb.*[1] 3), or with a brooch, hairpin, or hat-pin; to attach with a pin or similar sharp-pointed instrument; to transfix with a pin; also with a lance or the like.

1423 Jas. I *Kingis Q.* clxxx, At my beddis hed... I haue it faire pynnit vp. *c* **1480** Henryson *Test. Cres.* 423 Thy plesand lawn pinnit with goldin prene. **1530** Palsgr. 658/1 Pynne your jacket togyther for taking of colde. **1590** Spenser *F.Q.* i. ix. 36 His garment, nought but many ragged clouts, With thornes together pind and patched was. **1594** *Contention* viii. Stage direction, Enter Dame Elnor Cobham bare-foote, . . with a waxe candle in her hand, and verses written on her backe and pind on. **1617** Moryson *Itin.* iii. 168 Gownes made with long traines, which are pinned vp in the house. **1701** *Lond. Gaz.* No. 3725/4 Lost . . , 3 Sheets of Paper made up in 3 Books, and pin'd in the middle. **1787** Mme. D'Arblay *Diary* 8 Nov., The wardrobe woman was pinning up the Queen's hair. **1838** James *Robber* vi, She had a shawl of fine white lace pinned across her shoulders. **1852** Stainton *Entom. Comp.* 74 The first object is to pin the insect. **1893** Earl Dunmore *Pamirs* II. 1 Pinning out his entomological specimens.

b. Used with a person as object, in respect of clothes. Chiefly *pass.*

1483 Caxton *G. de la Tour* C vij, Shall not this lady this day be pynned. **1610** B. Jonson *Alch.* i. i, You went pinn'd vp. *Mod.* Come and I'll pin you.

c. To spread *out* (dough or paste) with a rolling-pin.

1889 R. Wells *Pastrycook & Confect. Guide* 39 Pin them out not too thick, and cut them into four.

d. *Austral. slang.* To 'do down', to cause trouble for (someone). (See also quot. 1941.)

1934 C. Stead *Seven Poor Men of Sydney* iv. 122 A poor man . . never 'as anything but a poor, miserable, wretched, untidy, un'appy life. They don't let 'im even be honest or 'ave a friend, if some one wants to pin 'im. **1941** Baker *Dict. Austral. Slang* 54 *To pin someone*, to have someone 'set', to have a grudge against a person.

e. In phrases ***to pin someone's ears back*** (orig. *U.S.*), to chastise, to rebuke; ***to pin one's ears back***, to listen attentively.

In quot. 1977 'lugholes' is colloquially substituted for 'ears'.

1941 H. L. Ickes *Diary* 22 June (1954) III. 546 It certainly was intended to pin my ears back. **1949** Wodehouse *Uncle Dynamite* ix. 160 His manner that of a man who has had his ears pinned back. **1961** Partridge *Dict. Slang* Suppl. 1222/1 *Pin back your ears* or *pin your ears back*, listen carefully. **1962** N. Streatfeild *Apple Bough* xi. 146 I'd get my ears pinned back if I tried to cut down his practice time. **1966** 'L. Black' *Bait* iii. 33, I shall keep eyes open. And ears pinned back. **1977** D. Francis *Risk* xvi. 12 Well, mate, pin back your lugholes. That boat you were on was built at Lymington.

3. *Building.* †**a.** Formerly sometimes = underpin. †**b.** To face with stone, marble, etc. **c.** To fill in the joints of masonry with chips of stone; to fill up the interstices with small stones: cf. pinning *vbl. sb.* 2 a.

1427 *Rec. St. Mary at Hill* 65, ij masouns to pynne þe same hous. **1499–1500** *Durham Acc. Rolls* (Surtees) 656 *Reparaciones*. In pynnyng, Rakyng, et poyntyng. **1546** Langley *Pol. Verg. De Invent.* iii. v. 71 Mamurra a Knight that was Master of July Caesar's woorkes in Fraunce pinned first the Walles of his house wyth broken marble. **1589** Rider *Bibl. Schol.*, To Pin an house under the grounsile, *substruo.* **1824** MACTAGGART *Gallovid. Encycl.* (1876) 191 He didna batter, line, and pin, To please the e'e.

4. *fig.* **a.** To attach firmly *to* a person, or ostentatiously *to* or *on* his SLEEVE: to make absolutely dependent or contingent *on* a person or thing; now *rare*. Also, to fasten or fix (anything objectionable) *on* a person or thing; to append, affix, tack on.

1579 LYLY *Euphues* (Arb.) 109 Alas, fond-foole, art thou so pinned to their sleeues, yat thou regardest more their babble then thine owne blisse? **1583** GOLDING *Calvin on Deut.* cxxxi. 803 Was God pinned on Balaams sleeue? Was he bounde to him? **1588** SHAKS. *L.L.L.* v. ii. 321 This Gallant pins his Wenches on his sleeue. **1590** GREENE *Mourn. Garm.* (1616) 33 What is it for mee to pinne a fayre meacocke and a witty milkesop on my sleeue? **1626** MIDDLETON *Women Beware Wom.* III. i. 297 You were pleas'd of late to pin an error on me. **1627** E. F. *Hist. Edw. II* (1680) 35 Pinn'd to the mutability of popular Faction. **1639** FULLER *Holy War* II. xxv. (1840) 81 He made himself absolute master of all orders, pinning them on himself by an immediate dependence. **1660** F. BROOKE tr. *Le Blanc's Trav.* 97 They wholly pin themselves upon the advice of those Magitians. **1710** *Tatler* No. 219 ¶ 1 A Couple of professed Wits, who.. had thought fit to pin themselves upon a Gentleman. **1819** SHELLEY *Cenci* I. iii. 16 You seem too light of heart.. To act the deeds that rumour pins on you. **1841** LYTTON *Nt. & Morn.* II. iv, I might pin my fate to yours. **1924** 'W. FABIAN' *Sailors' Wives* 34 Dorrisdale credits me with at least three [lovers], but they've never been able to pin it on me with anyone. **1942** E. PAUL *Narrow St.* xxi. 169 As usual, when anything sinister happened, his enemies tried to pin everything on Caillaux, who cleared himself promptly. **1966** *Listener* 3 Nov. 652/3 Medical research workers have been suspicious that some difficult and resistant diseases.. are associated with these same PPLO or mycoplasma, but nobody has been able to pin it on them. **1970** N. FLEMING *Czech Point* ii. 39 No doubt up till now he had never had to cope with a crime more heinous than skiing without due care and attention. He could have pinned that rap on the Australian girl in the PVC outfit any day he cared. **1977** L. MEYNELL *Hooky gets Wooden Spoon* xii. 150 'Can the Law connect her with you?' '.. No, they couldn't pin anything on me.'

b. In phrases ***to pin one's salvation, soul, hope, knowledge, reputation***, or the like, ***upon, on, to*** (a thing or person); now esp. ***to pin one's faith upon, on*** (a thing, or person, or his SLEEVE), to place entire or openly professed trust or belief in.

1583 BABINGTON *Commandm.* iv. (1637) 35, I would.. never pin my everlasting estate in paine and blisse, upon so slender.. perswasions. **1599** *Life Sir T. More* in Wordsw. *Eccl. Biog.* (1853) II. 149, I never intended to pinne my soule to another mans sleeve. **1615** CROOKE *Body of Man* 318 It is not good.. to pin a mans knowledge vpon any particular mans sleeue. **1649** BP. REYNOLDS *Hosea* vii. 139 No man is to pinne his own soule and salvation.. upon the words of a man who may mislead him. **1651** CLEVELAND *Poems* 44 I'le pin my faith on the Diurnalls sleeve. **1665** J. WEBB *Stone-Heng* (1725) 22 Mr. Jones.. much less expected, that any Man should pin his Belief upon his [Jones's] Shoulders. **1677** W. HUGHES *Man of Sin* II. i. 11 Tradition.. deserveth rather nailing to the Pillory, than pinning Faith upon it. *a* **1700** B. E. *Dict. Cant. Crew, To pin one's Faith on another's Sleeve*, or to take all upon Trust, for Gospel that he saies. **1712, 1812, 1885** [see FAITH *sb.* 2]. **1828** LADY GRANVILLE *Lett.* (1894) II. 19, I now pin my hopes on a meeting at Dieppe. **1857** MRS. MATHEWS *Tea-Table Talk* I. 92 She pinned her faith upon a horseshoe nailed upon the outer gate. **1885** S. COX *Expositions* I. 4 Men who think for themselves, and pin their faith to no neighbour's sleeve.

5. *transf.* **a.** To hold fast (a man or animal) in a spot so that he cannot get away; to hold *down* or *against* something by force; to seize and hold fast.

1740 FIELDING in *Champion* 1 Apr., When he is pinned down,.. particularly by one large Mastiff, I do not perceive that Readiness to relieve him which hath been formerly shewn. **1814** COL. HAWKER *Diary* (1893) I. 95 [The buck] could only reach the third field, where Tiger pinned him in the hedgerow. **1816** SCOTT *Antiq.* xliii, Forth bolts the operative brother to pin like a bull-dog. **1840–70** BLAINE *Encycl. Rur. Sports* §437 The dog will not only seize him [a bull] by the nose, but will cling to his hold till the bull stands still; and this is termed *pinning the bull*. **1859** REEVE *Brittany* 238 While I pinned his arms from behind, Mr. Taylor seized his whip. **1888** BURGON *Lives 12 Gd. Men* II. v. 66 He caught me by my elbows, and pinned me up against the wall .. so that I could not stir. **1945** *Sun* (Baltimore) 21 Feb. 1/7 (*heading*) 4th Division pinned down by mortar fire 17 hours. **1970** *Globe & Mail* (Toronto) 25 Sept. 8/9 The Ambassador and 24 members of his staff.. were pinned down in the Embassy since the fighting started. **1977** *Times* 17 Jan. 7/1 Underwood did his usual job pinning the batsmen down with geometrical control.

b. *Chess.* To confine a piece to a spot, to prevent it from being moved, absolutely, or without serious loss of material.

1745 STAMMA *Chess* 112 Look first whether your Adversary cannot pin that Piece down. **1841** WALKER *Chess* 15 The Bishop is able in certain cases to confine and pin the Knight, until the King or some other piece comes up and takes him. **1868** SELKIRK *Bk. Chess* 73 White would then pin the Rook by Queen to Queen's 3rd.

c. *slang.* To seize.

1768 EARL OF CARLISLE in Jesse *Selwyn & Contemp.* (1843) II. 340, I am sure they intended to pin my money.

6. *fig.* **a.** To hold or bind (a person) strictly *to* a promise, course of action, etc.: often with *down*.

1710 PRIDEAUX *Orig. Tithes* ii. 74 The Law of God.. doth not absolutely pin us down to the manner of doing it. **1822** W. IRVING *Braceb. Hall* xxvi, One of those pestilent fellows that pin a man down to facts. **1894** TYNDALL in *Pop. Sci. Monthly* XLIV. 507, I am pinned this year by the meeting of the British Association at Liverpool.

b. With *down*. To manœuvre (a person) into a position where evasion is impossible.

1904 ADE *True Bills* 40 Horace tried to side-step the Questions about Drinking and Smoking, but Uncle pinned him down. **1914** 'HIGH JINKS, JR.' *Choice Slang* 16 (*To*) *pin down*, to corner.

c. With *down*. To define, evaluate, isolate; to restrict *to*.

1951 M. MCLUHAN *Mech. Bride* (1967) 137/1 The kind of spectator participation in baseball.. would be hard to pin down. **1955** *Times* 26 July 8/3 It would never be possible to pin down the cause of death to radiation, he added. **1963** T. PARKER *Unknown Citizen* v. 139 There was obviously a good deal more to it underneath, which you could never pin down. **1965** *Listener* 2 Dec. 920/2 This symbolism is far more difficult to pin down than Rublowsky seems to suppose. **1973** *Times* 27 Apr. 1/8 Attempts to pin down the origin of the disease were inconclusive.

7. To set or stud with pins for ornament.

1688 [see PINNED *ppl. a.* 2]. **1713** *Lond. Gaz.* No. 5155/4 The out-side Case Shagreen,.. pinn'd with Gold Pins.

8. To make a small hole as with a pin. **a.** *Sc.* To break (a pane of glass) by throwing a stone so as to make a small hole. **b.** To drill (a hole).

1824 SCOTT *Redgauntlet* let. i, And who taught me to smoke a cobbler, pin a losen, head a bicker..? **1897** *Daily News* 7 June 2/3 Drills shrieking shrill accompaniment to the hum of whirring machinery as they pinned rivet-holes in metal plates.

9. To clog (a file): said of particles adhering so firmly to the teeth of a file that they have to be picked out with a piece of steel wire.

1890 in *Cent. Dict.*

II. To confine within bounds: cf. PIND *v.*

10. a. To enclose by or as by means of bolts or bars; to confine within a space or enclosure; to hem in, to shut *up*; *spec.* to put in a pinfold, impound (a beast).

1362 LANGL. *P. Pl.* A. v. 127, I.. Putte hem in a pressour and pinnede hem þer-Inne. **1423** *Coventry Leet-bk.* 43 þer schall noo beestys be pynnyd at the comen pynfold by the comien seriante. *c* **1440** *Promp. Parv.* 400/1 Pynnyn, or put yn a pynfold, *intrudo*. **1513** BRADSHAW *St. Werburge* I. 2632 To be pynned and punysshed for theyr trespace. **1590** WEBBE *Trav.* (Arb.) 27, I found two thousand Christians pind vp in ston wals lockt fast in yron chaines. **1630** L. ROWZEE *Queenes Welles* iii. (1632) 16 To contract and pin up the Sea into narrower limits, by.. dikes [etc.]. **1674–91** RAY *Collect. Words* 17 A *Coop* is generally used for a Vessel or place to pin up or enclose any thing. **1824** BYRON *Juan* xv. xxvi, Pinn'd like a flock, and fleeced too in their fold.

b. *Draughts* (and similar games). See quots.

1688 R. HOLME *Armoury* III. xvi. (Roxb.) 68/1 The play is, by so many geese to pinne the fox, that he cannot stirre one hole further. **1870** HARDY *Mod. Hoyle, Draughts* 107 The object.. is to capture all your adversary's men, or to 'pin' them, or hem them in so that they cannot be moved.

†**11.** *fig.* To 'shut *up*', confine, restrict. *Obs.*

?a **1400** LYDG. *Chorle & Birde* 89 To be shette vp and pynned vnder drede, No thyng acordeth vnto my nature. **1584** FENNER *Def. Ministers* (1587) 9 Howe hath he.. pinned vp her authoritie, when he sought to enlarge it? **1638** JUNIUS *Paint. Ancients* 314 To have his phantasie pinned up within the narrow compass of a poor.. invention.

III. 12. *Comb.*, as **pin-faith** *a.*, that 'pins one's faith' on something (see 4 b), implicitly believing or credulous.

1800 ANNA SEWARD *Lett.* (1811) V. 316 The pin-faith multitude, which never thinks for itself.

pin, *v.*[2] (U.S.), variant form of PEEN *v.*

1875 KNIGHT *Dict. Mech., Pin*... 11. To swage by striking with the peen of a hammer; as splaying an edge of an iron hoop to give it the flare corresponding to that of the cask.

‖**piña** ('piːnja). Also 6 pinna, 6– pina. [S. Amer. Sp. *piña* (formerly *pinna*), Pg. *pinha* pine-apple, orig. pine-cone, pine-nut (ad. L. *pinea*).]

†**1.** (Spelt *pina, pinna, pinia*.) The pine-apple.

1577 FRAMPTON *Joyfull Newes* 90 The Pinnas are a fruite whiche bee moste sette of in all the Indias. **1596** RALEIGH *Discov. Gviana* 61 Great abundance of Pinas, the princesse of fruits that grow under the sun. **1621** BURTON *Anat. Mel.* I. ii. II. iii. (1676) 46 In America.. their meat Palmitos, Pinas, Potatos, &c., and such fruits. **1622** R. HAWKINS *Voy. S. Sea* (1847) 93 Our boats returned loaden with plantynes, pinias, potatoes, sugar-canes.

2. Pine-apple leaf fibres (Simmonds *Dict. Trade* 1858); a fine fabric made of these, more fully called **piña-cloth, piña-muslin**, *pine-apple cloth*.

1858 HOGG *Veg. Kingd.* 765 Pine-apple cloth,.. sometimes known by the name of Pina Muslin. **1858** SIMMONDS *Dict. Trade, Pina-cloth*, an expensive fabric made by the natives of the Philippines from the fibres of the pine-apple leaf. **1890** *Cent. Dict.*, Piña, Piña-cloth.

3. The spongy cone of amalgam left behind after part of the mercury has been eliminated: also anglicized **pinne**. (See also quot. 1875.)

1604 E. G[RIMSTONE] *D'Acosta's Hist. Indies* IV. xii. 245 They put all the mettall into a cloth, which they straine out very forcibly, so as all the quicke-silver passeth out.. and the rest remaines as a loafe of silver, like to a marrow of almonds pressed to draw oyle. And being thus pressed, the remainder containes but the sixt part in silver, and five in mercurie... Of these markes they makes pinnes, (as they call them,) like pine apples, or sugar loaves, hollow within, the which they commonly make of a hundred pound weight. **1858** SIMMONDS *Dict. Trade, Pina* (*Spanish*), amalgamated silver. **1875** KNIGHT *Dict. Mech., Pina* (Spanish), the pile of wedges or bricks of hard silver amalgam placed under a *capellina* and subjected to heat, for the expulsion of the mercury. **1890** *Cent. Dict.*, Piña.

4. piña colada (kəʊ'lɑːdə) [Sp., lit. 'strained pineapple'], a long drink made with pineapple juice, rum, and coconut.

1975 P. MOYES *Black Widower* xiii. 159 In the bar itself, ice tinkled merrily into tall glasses of rum punch and *pina colada*, and smooth, sun-tanned men and women sipped and chatted. **1977** *N.Y. Times Mag.* 4 Dec. 42/1 She is wearing a long, batik-printed dress and bearing two piña coladas on a tray. **1978** *Chicago* June 172/3 There was gin and piña coladas and talk about Estée Lauder.. and money.. and clothes.

pinace, obs. form of PINNACE.

pinaceous (paɪ'neɪʃəs). *a. rare.* [f. mod.Bot. L. *Pināceæ* the pine family (f. L. *pin-us* pine): see -ACEOUS.] Of or pertaining to the pine tribe.

1874 SIR R. CHRISTISON in *Trans. Bot. Soc. Edin.* (1876) XII. 167 A Pinaceous Fossil.. found in Redhall Quarry.

†**pi'nache.** *Obs. rare*[−1]. [Derivation unknown: the quot. corresponds notably with the first under PIQUET *sb.*[1]] Some game at cards.

1641 BRATHWAIT *Eng. Gentlem.* 126 In games at Cards, the Maw requires a quicke conceit.. the Cribbage a recollected fancy; the Pinache quick and vn-enforced dexterity. [Not in ed. 1630.]

†**pinacle,** *v. Obs.* Also **pinn-**. [Origin obscure: cf. *pinion* vb. and *manacle*.] *trans.* To pinion.

1614 BUDDEN tr. *Aerodius' Disc. Parents Hon.* (1616) 22 Like a prisoner with his armes fast pinacled. **1660** F. BROOKE tr. *Le Blanc's Trav.* 98 They pinnacle them, and deliver them up to the fury of the children.

pinacle, obs. form of PINNACLE.

pinacocyte ('pɪnəkəʊsaɪt). *Zool.* [f. Gr. πίναξ, πινακ- tablet + -CYTE.] Each of the flat plate-like cells (constituting *pavement-epithelium*) forming the ectoderm and part of the endoderm in sponges.

1887 SOLLAS in *Encycl. Brit.* XXII. 418/2 The ectoderm usually consists of simple pavement epithelial cells (*pinnacocytes*). **1900** E. R. LANKESTER *Zool.* II. *Sponges* 44.

Hence ,**pinaco'cytal** *a.*

1887 SOLLAS in *Encycl. Brit.* XXII. 427/1 The pinnacocytal layer.

pinacoid, pinakoid ('pɪnəkɔɪd), *a.* and *sb.* *Cryst.* [f. Gr. πίναξ, πινακ- slab: see -OID.]

A. *adj.* Applied to any plane, in a crystallographic system, intersecting one of the axes of co-ordinates and parallel to the other two. Opposed to *octahedrid* and *prismatoid*.

1895 STORY-MASKELYNE *Crystallogr.* ii. §18.

B. *sb.* A pinacoid plane, or a group of such planes constituting a 'form'.

1876 *Catal. Sci. App. S. Kens.* §3470 A Polyhedron of Calcite, cut.. so as to represent the optical characters.. in directions perpendicular 1. To the pinakoid. **1881** BAUERMAN *Text-bk. Syst. Min.* 198 The octahedron, or unit pyramid, is always the largest, and the cube rectangular prism, or pinakoid, the smallest of the constituent forms. **1895** STORY-MASKELYNE *Crystallogr.* vii. §303 The poles of the pinakoids form the angular points of the systematic triangles.

Hence **pina'coidal** *a.*, of the nature of or characteristic of a pinacoid.

1879 RUTLEY *Study Rocks* xiii. 245 A structural condition of pinakoidal separation.

pinacol ('pɪnəkɒl). *Chem.* [f. PINAC(ONE + -OL.] = PINACONE; **pinacol rearrangement**, a reaction typified by the conversion of pinacol into pinacolone, in which a 1,2-glycol loses water on heating with acid to form a ketone.

1911 *Chem. Abstr.* V. 3561 The solid pinacols have normal mol. wts. in dil. C_6H_6. **1912** *Ibid.* VI. 82 The fraction b. 214° of the products of hydrolysis of crude pinacol by H_2SO_4. **1936** L. J. DESHA *Org. Chem.* 538 The pinacol rearrangement is irreversible in the sense that pinacolins do not change into pinacols. **1938** E. S. WALLIS in H. Gilman *Org. Chem.* I. 723 Numerous examples of this reaction, now known as the pinacol rearrangement, have been found since the time of Fittig's discovery [in 1859]. **1964** N. G. CLARK *Mod. Org. Chem.* x. 180 Acetone is reduced with amalgamated magnesium to pinacol. **1966** *McGraw-Hill Encycl. Sci. & Technol.* III. 375/2 Ketones are converted to tetrasubstituted ethylene glycols (called pinacols) by certain reducing agents. **1966** SMITH & CRISTOL *Org. Chem.* xiii. 289 The pinacol rearrangement is quite general for glycols in which all four groups.. are alkyl or aryl groups.

pinacolin (pɪ'nækəlɪn). *Chem.* Also **-ine.** [a. G. *pinacolin* (R. Fittig 1860, in *Ann. d. Chem. u. Pharm.* CXIV. 58): see PINACONE, -OL, -IN[1].] A colourless oily liquid ($C_6H_{12}O$), having an odour of peppermint, variously produced from pinacone. Also, any other ketone in which the carbonyl group is bonded to at least one tertiary carbon atom. Now usu. called PINACOLONE. Hence **pina'colic** *a.*

1866 WATTS *Dict. Chem.* IV. 647 *Pinacolin*,.. an oily body produced by the dehydration of pinacone. **1875** *Ibid.* VII. 982 *Pinacolic alcohol*, $C_6H_{14}O$.. is produced by treating pinacolin with sodium in presence of water. **1884** [see PINACONE]. **1913** T. H. POPE tr. *Molinari's Treat. Org. Chem.* II. 183 When distilled with dilute sulphuric acid, it [*sc.* pinacone] is transformed into pinacoline, $(CH_3)_3C.CO.CH_3$. **1936** [see PINACOL]. **1973** B. J. HAZZARD tr. *Organicum* 587 In textbooks, the dihydric alcohol here termed pinacol is often called pinacone and the ketone produced by the rearrangement pinacoline.

pinacolone (ˈpɪnəkəˌləʊn). *Chem.* [f. PINACOL + -ONE.] = PINACOLIN.

1925 *Org. Syntheses* V. 91 The combined pinacolone fraction is dried over calcium chloride, filtered, and fractionally distilled. **1932** *Jrnl. Amer. Chem. Soc.* LIV. 825 Because of the need of large amounts of pinacolone for investigations in progress in this Laboratory, methods for its preparation have been studied. **1940** S. MIALL *New Dict. Chem.* 400/1 When heated with mineral or organic acids, pinacols undergo a molecular rearrangement with loss of water to give ketones known as pinacolones. **1944** *Jrnl. Amer. Chem. Soc.* LXVI. 634/2 It was anticipated that this pinacolone should be 3,3-dianisyl-2-butanone. **1967** L. F. & M. A. FIESER *Reagents for Org. Synthesis* I. 772 On brief exposure to moist air the fluorohydrin is rearranged to pinacolone..and hydrogen fluoride.

pinacone (ˈpɪnəkəʊn). *Chem.* [a. G. *pinakon* (G. Städeler 1859, in *Ann. d. Chem. u. Pharm.* CXI. 279), f. Gr. πίναξ tablet + -ONE.] A white crystalline substance ($C_6H_{14}O_2$), crystallizing in large tablets, produced by the action of sodium or sodium-amalgam on aqueous acetone. Also, any other alcohol having two hydroxyl groups which are bonded to adjacent tertiary carbon atoms. Now usu. called PINACOL.

1866 WATTS *Dict. Chem.* IV. 648 Liquid pinacone is a colourless syrup. **1877** —— *Fownes' Chem.* II. 177 Pinacone, when heated with acids, is converted into pinacolin. **1884** ROSCOE & SCHORLEMMER *Treat. Chem.* III. II. 12 The pinacones decompose very readily into water and the ketones, to which the name of pinacolines is given. **1913** T. H. POPE tr. *Molinari's Treat. Org. Chem.* II. 182 A special group of glycols, the pinacones, containing two adjacent tertiary alcohol groups. **1973** [see PINACOLIN].

‖**pinacotheca** (ˈpɪnəkəʊˈθiːkə). Also anglicized as ˈ**pinacoˌthek** (-θɛk). [L. *pinacothēca* (Varro), a. Gr. πινακοθήκη a picture-gallery (Strabo), f. πίναξ, πινακ- tablet, picture + θήκη repository. So It. *pinacotèca*, F. *pinacothèque*, Ger. *pinakothek*.] A place for the keeping and exhibition of pictures and other works of art.

[**1592** R. D. *Hypnerotomachia* 63 The..parlours, bathes, librarie and pinacloth, where coat Armors escuchions, painted tables, and counterfeates of strangers were kept.] **1624** WOTTON *Archit.* in *Reliq.* (1651) 207 Pinacothecia..by which he intendeth..certain Repositories for Works of Rarity in Picture or other Arts. **1766** SMOLLETT *Trav.* 288 The pinacotheca of this building was a complete Museum of all the Curiosities of Art and Nature. **1834** LYTTON *Pompeii* I. iii, A picture-saloon, or *pinacotheca*. **1844** *Fraser's Mag.* XXX. 315/1 Our walks through halls of art and pinacothecks.

pinafore (ˈpɪnəfɔə(r)), *sb.* [f. PIN *v.*[1] + AFORE, because originally pinned upon the dress in front.] **a.** A covering of washable material worn by children, and by factory girls or others, over the frock or gown, to protect it from being soiled. Also, a low-necked, sleeveless fashion garment worn by women and girls, usu. over a blouse or jumper.

The article so called was prob. originally a piece of washing material pinned on for the occasion; in Webster, 1847, it is defined as 'an apron for the front part of the body', in Latham's Johnson, 1868, as 'a small apron or bib for children'; as now used, it differs from an apron in meeting and being fastened at the back above the waist, and in having armholes; a little girl's pinafore is often an article of ordinary house dress, and may be more ornamental than the frock which it covers. See also BRAT, OVERALL.

1782 MISS BURNEY *Cecilia* VI. viii, A pin-a-fore for Master Mortimer Delvile, lest he should daub his pappy when he is feeding him. **1824** MISS MITFORD *Village* Ser. I. (1863) 234 She is still pretty, but not so elegant as when she wore frocks and pin-a-fores. **1863** MISS BRADDON *J. Marchmont* I. i. 7 To teach children their A B C, and mend their frocks and make their pinafores. **1882** —— *Mt. Royal* II. iv. 80 When you were in pinafores. [**1907**: see *pinafore-frock* below.] **1960** *Vogue Pattern Bk.* Autumn 46 Dark grey pinafore tops a gay printed blouse. **1974** *Country Life* 21 Feb. 398/1 Dark brown pinafore in fine corduroy worn with white cotton shirt. **1976** *Vogue* Jan. 44/2 Low-slung pinafore.

fig. **1845** *Athenæum* 4 Jan. 17 Exhibiting perhaps a smart architectural 'pinafore' in front, which turns out to be a mere 'coverslut' intended to hide meanness and deformity. **1849** D. J. BROWNE *Amer. Poultry Yard* (1855) 28 The chicks are large,..entirely shining black, except a pinafore of white on the breast.

b. *transf.* The wearer of a pinafore; *esp.* a child or little girl.

1836 T. HOOK *G. Gurney* III. 153 The pinafores were gone to bed.

c. *attrib.* and *Comb.*, esp. ***pinafore dress, frock, gown.***

1871 M. COLLINS *Mrq. & Merch.* I. x. 307 Younger folk ..in the pinafore stage of existence. **1894** ELIZ. L. BANKS *Camp. Curiosity* 181 Skill in pinafore-ironing. **1898** *Westm. Gaz.* 28 Apr. 3/2 A navy blue serge frock..one of the pinafore build to slip over shirts. **1907** *Westm. Gaz.* 8 Apr. 13/1 Our grown-up pinafore-frock must confess itself borrowed from the nursery. *c* **1909** D. H. LAWRENCE *Collier's Friday Night* (1934) ii. 35 She is wearing a dark blue cloth 'pinafore-dress'. **1932** *Mod. Weekly* 30 Apr. 118 Her adorable, black velvet, pinafore gown. The tiny puff-sleeves are of silver tissue. **1952** C. W. CUNNINGTON *Eng. Women's Clothing* ii. 71 *The Pinafore Gown* [in 1906] 'is often allied to the frock with brace over a lace blouse'. *Ibid.* iii. 91 The Pinafore frock is revived [in 1909], worn over a tucked chemisette. **1973** *Times* 15 Nov. 6/3 The bridesmaid, Lady Sarah Armstrong-Jones, wore a pinafore dress.

ˈ**pinafore,** *v.* [f. prec. sb.]

1. *trans.* To attire in a pinafore.

1857 GEO. ELIOT *Sc. Cler. Life, Janet's Repent.* viii, She was duly bonneted and pinafored, and then they turned out.

2. To put into the skirt of one's pinafore (cf. *to pocket*). *nonce-use.*

1893 *Daily News* 11 Jan. 2/2 There were hundreds.. feeding as one, and pinaforing the fragments that remained.

pinafored (ˈpɪnəfɔəd), *a.* [f. prec. sb. or vb. + -ED.] Attired in a pinafore.

1847 MRS. GORE *Castles* xxvii, The smallest dame-school that turns out its pinafored urchins on a village green. **1859** SALA *Gas-light & D.* xv. 167 Pinafored children..playing in the gutters.

pinakiolite (pɪˈnækɪəʊlaɪt). *Min.* [mod. (Flink, 1890) f. Gr. πινάκιον, dim. of πίναξ tablet + -LITE.] Borate of manganese and magnesium, found in brilliant black tabular crystals.

1891 *Amer. Jrnl. Sc.* Ser. III. XLI. 251 Pinakiolite is a new borate of manganese and magnesium.

pinakoid, -al, variants of PINACOID, -AL.

†ˈ**pinal,** *a. Obs. rare.* [f. L. *pīn-us* pine-tree + -AL[1].] Of the nature of or allied to the pine.

1791 NEWTE *Tour Eng. & Scot.* 150 Oaks, and other trees ..more difficult to be raised in northern and alpine climates than their pinal predecessors.

pinalic (pɪˈnælɪk), *a. Chem.* [f. PINA(CO)L-IN + -IC.] Derived from or contained in pinacolin, as *pinalic acid*, $C_5H_{10}O_2$.

1886 in *Cassell's Encycl. Dict.*

‖**pinang** (pɪˈnæŋ). Also 7 **-e**, 9 **penang**. [Malay *pinang* betel nut, areca. Also in Du., etc.] The areca tree (*Areca Catechu*), or its fruit, the areca nut (***pinang nut***): see ARECA.

1662 J. DAVIES tr. *Mandelslo's Trav.* 148 The Portuguez call the tree that bears it *Arre quero*..and the Malayans *Pinang*. **1665** SIR T. HERBERT *Trav.* (1677) 365 Their ordinary food..is Rice, Wheat, Pinange, Betele. **1771** J. R. FORSTER tr. *Osbeck's Voy.* I. 257 Pinang..is a fruit which looks like a nutmeg in the inside. **1883** MRS. BISHOP in *Leisure Ho.* 202/2 Pinang (from the *pinang*, or areca-palm) is the proper name of the island.

‖**pinard** (pinar). Also **Pinard.** [Fr.] Coarse red wine (orig. that issued to French troops), vin ordinaire; *loosely*, any wine; a glass of this wine.

1922 E. E. CUMMINGS *Enormous Room* iv. 85 A glass apiece of red acrid *pinard*. **1924** *Blackw. Mag.* Oct. 556/2 Some of the adversaries are toasting each other in pinard. **1928** R. HALL *Well of Loneliness* xxxvi. 335 The Unit's rations—cold meat, sardines, bread and sour red Pinard. **1937** PARTRIDGE *Dict. Slang* 631/1 *Pinard*, liquor; wine: Soho (-1935). **1947** M. LOWRY *Let.* Nov. (1967) 160 Wonderful skipper on this ship, engineers, seamen, cats, stewards, pinard. **1950** E. HEMINGWAY *Across River* xii. 112 In a Great Hotel, wine must cost money. You cannot get Pinard at the Ritz. **1969** B. WEIL *Dossier IX* iii. 23 He..drank a *pinard* as if the rough red wine would take away the taste of a probable duplicity.

pinarette (pɪnəˈrɛt). [f. PINA(FO)RE *sb.* + -ETTE.] A short pinafore (in the senses).

1951 *Sunday Pictorial* 21 Jan. 15/6 (Advt.), Pinarette, exclusive design in cotton print. Stock size. Fully cut with perfect finish. **1959** 'H. CARMICHAEL' *Stranglehold* xii. 102 A nondescript girl..wearing a pinarette and a maid's cap. **1962** J. CANNAN *All is Discovered* ii. 30 The gaudy cotton dress, the strong bare legs, the black felt slippers, the homely 'pinarette'. **1966** 'K. NICHOLSON' *Hook, Line & Sinker* ii. 27 She was wearing a floral pinarette over a pink satin blouse.

pinary, pinasse, obs. ff. PINERY, PINNACE.

pinaster (paɪˈnæstə(r)). *Bot.* [a. L. *pīnaster* (Plin.) wild pine, f. *pīnus* pine: see -ASTER. So F. *pinastre*, It., Sp. *pinastro*.] A species of pine (*Pinus Pinaster*) indigenous to south-western Europe; also called *cluster-* or *star-pine*.

(The *Pinaster* or Wild Pine of the ancients is thought by Daubeny to have been *P. maritima* of modern botanists.)

1562 TURNER *Herbal* II. 88 Pinaster is nothyng ellis but a wilde pyne tre of a meruelus hyght. **1601** HOLLAND *Pliny* I. 462 The Pine and the Pinaster cary leaues thin and slender ..long also and sharp pointed. **1731–3** MILLER *Gard. Dict.* s.v. *Pinus*, *Pinus sylvestris*..the Pinaster or wild Pine. **1770–4** A. HUNTER *Georg. Ess.* (1804) II. 21 The Pinaster is a variety of the Scotch Fir. **1842** SELBY *Brit. Forest Trees* 437 The introduction of the Pinaster into England by Gerard..A.D. 1596. **1887** MOLONEY *Forestry W. Afr.* 6 The principal timber tree of [St. Helena] is the pinaster.

‖**piñata, pinata** (pɪˈnjɑːtə, pɪˈnɑːtə). Also 9 **piñate.** [Sp., jug, pot.] In Mexico and Mexican-influenced areas of the U.S.A., a decorated container (orig. a pottery bowl), filled with sweets or other gifts which is broken by a blindfolded person or otherwise opened at Christmas and on other festive occasions.

1887 F. C. GOOCH *Face to Face with Mexicans* viii. 264 The breaking of the *piñate* is the chief sport of the *posada*. The *piñate* is an oval-shaped earthen jar, handsomely decorated and covered with bright ornaments... There are turkeys, horses, birds, monkeys, [etc.]. *Ibid.* 265 The fun of breaking the *piñate* begins. It is suspended from the ceiling, and each person..blindfolded..proceeds to strike the swinging *piñate*. **1934** E. FERGUSSON *Fiesta in Mexico* xiv. 254 There is a party, with..sweets and paper toys in a huge pottery ball decorated with paper to look like a turkey, Charlie Chaplin,..anything. The littlest child or favored guest pulls the string which releases the shower of candies. This is the piñata, which is in season anytime from the first posada to *Diá de los Reyes*, Twelfth Night. **1947** C. U. STOKER *Under Mexican Skies* 169 The *patio* looked very pretty with its gardens all in bloom. The children had hung a *piñata*, representing the Christmas Star, in the center of the *patio* with room enough for all to strike at it. **1959** C. RAMSDELL *San Antonio* IV. xv. 262/1 The *piñata*, in Texas at least, is now made in a charming variety of shapes. *Ibid.* 262/2 At Christmas or birthday parties the *piñata* is always the climax. Child after child, blindfolded, is whirled about, and turned loose to bat wildly in the supposed direction of the piñata, which dangles at the end of a rope. **1976** *Examiner* (Coolidge, Arizona) 13 May 10 (*heading*) Second graders celebrate Cinco de Mayo... The children learned some Spanish words..and made *piñatas*.

pinate (ˈpaɪnət). *Chem.* [f. PIN-IC + -ATE[4].] A salt of pinic acid.

1838 T. THOMSON *Chem. Org. Bodies* 506 The pinates.. may be obtained by digesting an ethereal solution of pinic acid over the alkaline carbonates. **1840** *Penny Cycl.* XVIII. 166/1 The pinates of ammonia, potash, and soda are soluble in water, but those of other bases are mostly insoluble in it.

‖**pinax** (ˈpɪnæks). Pl. **pinaces** (ˈpɪnəsiːz); also 9 **pinakes.** [L. *pinax*, a. Gr. πίναξ board, plank, tablet, picture.]

1. A tablet; hence a list, register, or the like inscribed on a tablet; a catalogue, index. ? *Obs.*

1682 SIR T. BROWNE *Chr. Mor.* I. §1 Consider whereabout thou art in Cebes's Fable, or that old Philosophical *Pinax* of the Life of Man. **1697** *Phil. Trans.* XIX. 434 This..may.. serve instead of a Pinax, or General *Index Plantarum*. **1785** MARTYN *Rousseau's Bot.* Introd. (1794) 7 This pinax..is still the guide to all those who study this subject.

2. *Antiq.* A plate, platter, or dish; *esp.* one with anything painted or engraved on it.

1857 BIRCH *Anc. Pottery* (1858) I. 286 The pinax or dish with a tall foot. *Ibid.* 296 Pinakes or plates, are also found at this period.

pin-ball (ˈpɪnbɔːl). orig. *U.S.* [f. PIN *sb.*[1] + BALL *sb.*[1]]

1. A pincushion.

1803 E. BOWNE *Girl's Life* (1887) 175 We went to a room where they keep their work for sale,—pocket-books, pin balls, [etc.]. **1870** L. M. ALCOTT *Old-Fashioned Girl* vi. 76 Her scissors and pin-ball at her side, and her thimble on. **1894** SARAH M. H. GARDNER *Quaker Idyls* vi, I gave him the pinball. **1963** *Times* 9 Mar. 11/5 Silver-banded pin-balls were then made to hang from the girdle and even Queen Elizabeth herself deigned to accept a New Year gift of a 'pin pillow embrodred'.

2. ***pinball-sight*** = bead-sight: see BEAD *sb.* 5 d.

1884 KNIGHT *Dict. Mech.* Suppl., *Pin-ball Sight*, (*Rifle*), another name for the *bead-sight*; also called pin-head sight.

3. A game resembling bagatelle, in which small balls are propelled across a sloping surface towards targets which indicate the score when they are hit. Freq. *attrib.*, as ***pin-ball arcade, game, machine, table.***

1911 *R. Bliss Illustr. Catal.* in B. Whitton *Bliss Toys & Dollhouses* (1979) 27 Pin ball game... One of our popular marble games. **1935** *Sun* (Baltimore) 2 Apr. 1/7 One of the bills would allow the State..to license claw machine and pinball games. **1936** *N.Y. Times* 5 Feb. 40/3 Justice Rosenman said he was surprised that the pin-ball machines had been licensed in the first place. **1937** *Pop. Mechanics* Feb. 278 (*heading*) Trip 'em; home pin-ball game. **1946** *Sun* (Baltimore) 30 Dec. 2/3 This ordinance also imposes a license fee on claw machines or pinball machines or similar devices for public amusement, operated through the insertion of a coin or token. **1951** J. D. SALINGER *Catcher in Rye* v. 46 We just had..hamburgers and played the pinball machine for a little while. **1959** *Times* 12 Feb. 10/7 To-day the senators were ringed with juke-boxes, pinball tables, 'one-armed bandits', and other coin-operated devices. **1969** N. COHN *Pop from Beginning* xix. 170 Kids..like myself, gave their lives to pinball. **1973** M. AMIS *Rachel Papers* 17 It was a month of plonk and coffee-bars, pinball arcades and party-hunts. **1975** R. L. SIMON *Wild Turkey* (1976) i. 4 Gunther lit up like a pinball machine on twenty replays. **1976** DEAKIN & WILLIS *Johnny go Home* iii. 57 Ernie showed Johnny how to fix the machines in the Amusement Arcades, and together they played the pin-ball tables.

pinbank, variant form of PINEBANK *Obs.*

ˈ**pin-ˌbasket.** *local.* A large ornamental pincushion, with pins of various lengths artistically inserted, so as to resemble a basket; formerly, in some places, presented to the mother of a family on the birth of each child. Hence, the youngest child in a family (in quot. 1794 of an animal).

1730–6 BAILEY (folio), *Pin-basket*, the last child a woman bears. **17..** SIR J. MARRIOT in Dodsley *Coll. Poems* (1782) IV. 304 Oft be your second race survey'd And oft a new pin-basket made. **1780** *Gentl. Mag.* L. 77 No less natural is it that the pin-basket of the lawful wife should have the greatest share of the father's affections. **1794** J. WILLIAMS *Shrove Tuesday*, etc. 4 My gay Chanticleer..The pin-basket of my Sultana hen. *a* **1825** FORBY *Voc. E. Anglia*, *Pin-basket*, the youngest child in a family.

pin-before (ˈpɪnbɪfɔə(r)). *rare.* [f. PIN *v.*[1] + BEFORE.] = PINAFORE.

1824 SOUTHEY in *Corr. w. C. Bowles* (1881) 71 During dinner he lifts up his pin-before to look at the buttons. **1830** *Examiner* 801/1 Young gentlemen in pinbefores. **1863** MRS. MARSH *Heathside Farm* II. 33 Her stiff black silk protected by an ample holland pinbefore, she was engaged in superintending hot cakes and pikelets.

'pin-case. A case for holding pins; also, a pincushion (? *obs.* exc. *dial.*).

1515 *Will of R. Symson* (Somerset Ho.), A pyncase of tysyn saten. **1530** PALSGR. 254/2 Pyncase, *esplinguette, esplinguiere.* **1614** B. JONSON *Barth. Fair* III. i, What do you lack, gentlemen? fine purses, pouches, pin-cases, pipes? **1828** *Craven Gloss.* (ed. 2), *Pin-cass*, a pin cushion, a corruption of *pin-case.*

†pince. *Obs.* [Variant of PINCH *sb.*; perh. immed. a. F. *pince.*] A galled or sore place on a horse.

1610 MARKHAM *Masterp.* II. xli. 281 The swelling, pince, wringing or gall, either vpon the withers or any parte of the backe of a horse.

pince, obs. occasional variant of PINCH *sb.* and *v.*

pincel, -eller, obs. ff. PENCIL, PENCILLER.

‖**pince-nez** (pɛ̃sne). Also pincenez. [F. *pince-nez*, lit. pinch-nose, nip-nose.] A pair of eyeglasses kept in position by a spring which clips the nose. Also *attrib.*

1876 GEO. ELIOT *Let.* 3 Feb. (1956) VI. 220 Our young Charles.. was slightly short-sighted and used only occasionally a pince-nez. **1880** *Sat. Rev.* 21 Aug. 235 It is amusing to meet a person whom one has been accustomed to see in regular spectacles wearing a *pince-nez* for the first time. **1888** J. PAYN *Myst. Mirbridge* vii, The lady, putting up her pince-nez, with a show of interest. **1894** H. DRUMMOND *Ascent of Man* 132 Man, when he sees with difficulty, does not now improve his Eye; he puts on a pince-nez. **1904** JOYCE *Let.* 28 Dec. (1966) II. 75, I shall go to an oculist.. to get pincenez glasses. **1927** F. B. YOUNG *Portrait of Clare* 26 She brushed the dust from her skirt.. her grey eyes swimming behind the lenses of her pincenez. **1941** *Punch* 13 Aug. 148/2 There was a frail creature in pince-nez at the other end of the table. **1974** *Oxf. Jun. Encycl.* (rev. ed.) XI. 422/2 The portrait of Cardinal Ugone in the church of San Nicolo at Treviso shows spectacles in which the two lenses are held together by a joint or hinge which fitted on the nose (an early form of pince-nez).

Hence **pince-nezed, -nez'd** [-ED²] *a.*, wearing a pince-nez.

1919 J. C. SNAITH *Love Lane* xi. 51 An important, pince-nezed gentleman. **1922** W. J. LOCKE *Tale of Triona* xv. 170 Mrs. Rowington, thin, angular, pince-nez'd. **1958** B. HAMILTON *Too Much of Water* i. 18 A spare pince-nez'd man with sandy-red hair. **1976** J. CROSBY *Snake* (1977) xxxviii. 232 The doctor was a precise, pince-nezed Spaniard.

pinceoun, variant of PINSON¹ *Obs.*

pincer ('pɪnsə(r)), *v.* [f. PINCERS.] *trans.* To compress with or as with pincers; to torture or wring with or as with pincers.

1703 PARKER *Eusebius* VIII. 147 The Judge.. gave in Order that she should be Pincer'd worse than ever any Body yet had been. **1864** CARLYLE *Fredk. Gt.* XVI. i, Face, not pincered together. **1897** RHOSCOMYL *White Rose Arno* 188 The pain of his wound racked and pincered his nerves.

†pincern. *Obs. rare*⁻¹. [ad. late and med.L. *pincerna*, a. late Gr. πιγκέρνης cup-bearer, prop. a wine-mixer, f. πίνειν to drink + κεράννυναι to mix: cf. OF. *pincerne* a butler.] A cup-bearer.

1611 SPEED *Hist. Gt. Brit.* IX. xiii. (1623) 729 [The] Lord Maior in his office of chiefe Pincern or Cup-waiter. [**1848** LYTTON *Harold* III. iii, There were to be seen [by the throne] *camerarius* and *pincerna*, chamberlain and cupbearer.]

pincers ('pɪnsəz), *sb. pl.* Rarely (exc. in comb.) in sing. form pincer. Forms: 4 pynceours, 4–5 pinsours, 4–7 -sers, 5 pynsors, -sours, 6 -cors, -sores, pinsars, 6–7 -sors, 6– pincers. [In ME. *pinsour(s, pynsour(s, -or(s, pynceour(s*, app. AF. agent-n. from *pincer* vb.: see PINCH; cf. OF. *pinchure* pincers, tongs, *pinçoir* a clip used as a book-mark; mod.F. *pince* (Cotgr. *pinces*) pincers. See also PINSON¹.]

1. a. A tool for tightly grasping or nipping anything, consisting of two limbs pivoted together, forming a pair of jaws with a pair of handles or levers by which they can be pressed tightly together. (Commonly ***a pair of pincers***; rarely ***a pincers.***)

1338 *Durham Acc. Rolls* (Surtees) 376, j par de Pynceours de ferro. **1371** *Ibid.* 129, j par de pinsers. *c* **1410** *Master of Game* (MS. Digby 182) xii, Kut ye a litell of her clees with pynsors. **1555** EDEN *Decades* 187 Two mouthes lyke vnto a paire of smaule pinsers. **1584** R. SCOT *Discov. Witchcr.* v. viii. (1886) 86 S. Dunstan lead the divell about the house by the nose with a paire of pinsors or tongs. **1590** SPENSER *F.Q.* III. xii. 16 A paire of Pincers in his hand he had, With which he pinched people to the hart. **1664** POWER *Exp. Philos.* I. 11 A Wood-Louse.. hath two pointers also before, like a pair of pincers. **1719** YOUNG *Revenge* v. ii, The flesh will quiver, where the pincers tear. **1796** SOUTHEY *Lett. fr. Spain* (1799) 201 A pointed instrument to raise the wick, a small pincers to prune it. **1873** E. SPON *Workshop Receipts* Ser. I. 188/2 The flask is then removed from the fire by wooden pincers.

sing. **14..** *Voc.* in Wr.-Wülcker 570/18 *Capana*, a pynsour. **1483** *Cath. Angl.* 280/2 A paire of Pynsours (*A.* A Pynsoure). **1570** LEVINS *Manip.* 76/3 Pincer, *forpeculæ.*

fig. **1855** BAIN *Senses & Int.* III. ii. §33 (1864) 524 He [Newton] has always his mind ready to seize it with the mathematical pincers.

b. *Mil.* = *pincer(s) movement* in sense 3 b below.

1942 T. RATTIGAN *Flare Path* II. i. 38 There wasn't anything fresh, I suppose. No pincers on anything anywhere? **1969** G. MACBETH *War Quartet* 73 Firing turn by turn, Encircling him with pincers.. At last.. we killed him. **1978** J. A. MICHENER *Chesapeake* 638 [In 1863] southern armies were involved in a stupendous march north in an effort to create a pincers which would curl back to engulf Philadelphia, Baltimore and Washington itself. The end of the war seemed at hand.

2. An organ (or pair of organs), in various animals, resembling pincers, and used for grasping or tearing; as the chelæ of crustaceans, the incisor teeth of a horse, etc.

1658 ROWLAND *Moufet's Theat. Ins.* Ep. Ded., Their [green locusts'] pincers.. are as sharp as keen rasors. **1713** ADDISON *Guardian* No. 156 ¶7 Every Ant brings a small particle of that earth in her pincers. **1796** H. HUNTER tr. *St.-Pierre's Stud. Nat.* (1799) I. 554 The feet of animals which scramble among rocks are provided with pincers. **1880** HUXLEY *Crayfish* iii. 95 A living crayfish is able to perform very varied movements with its pincers.

3. a. *Comb.*, as ***pincer-grip***; ***pincer-like*** adj.; **pincer-leg** = sense 2.

1611 COTGR., *Louve de fer*.. the (pinser-like) hooke of a Crane, &c. **1860** CARLYLE *Let. to Ruskin* 29 Oct., in *Eng. Illustr. Mag.* Nov. 105, I marvel in parts.. at the pincer-grip .. you take of certain bloated cheeks and blown-up bellies. **1870** ROLLESTON *Anim. Life* 142 Two terminal processes which make up a pincer-like organ. **1909** *Daily Chron.* 20 Aug. 4/4 Note the disparity in the size of the two large pincer-legs. **1941** H. G. WELLS *You can't be too Careful* v. iii. 249 When confronted by a pincer-like movement, a soldier and a gentleman abandons his men and material and bolts home. **1962** D. NICHOLS *Echinoderms* viii. 101 The two living classes with relatively non-flexible exterior surfaces, the echinoids and asteroids, are provided with almost unique pincer-like organs, the pedicellariae.

b. *Mil.* Used *attrib.*, esp. in ***pincer(s) movement***, to designate an operation involving the convergence of two forces on an enemy position like the jaws of a pair of pincers; a double envelopment; also *transf.* and *fig.*

1929 *Papers Mich. Acad. Sci., Arts & Lett.* X. 314/2 *Pincer drive*, an enveloping drive launched from two sides of an objective. **1939** AUDEN & ISHERWOOD *Journey to War* ix. 225 The Japs were to be.. destroyed by the time-honoured pincer-movement. **1944** S. PUTNAM tr. *E. da Cunha's Rebellion in Backlands* x. 458 As may be seen, it was a vigorous pincers movement which was thus planned. **1954** T. GUNN *Fighting Terms* 34 Planning when you have least supplies or clothing A pincer-move to end in an embrace. **1959** *Listener* 28 May 919/2 At one end of the barrier the Soviet Union is conducting a pincer movement on Persia, from Transcaucasia and Iraq. **1968** *Times* 8 Oct. 7/7 Hardened layers of sediment which accumulated on the bottom of the Tethys Sea and were later thrust up to the surface by the pincer movement of the two continental masses. **1973** *Times* 9 Aug. 17/1 The pincer movement against Unilever—soaring commodity prices.. on the one hand, and selling price controls.. on the other—is beginning to bite. **1975** D. BAGLEY *Snow Tiger* xiv. 120 Rickman and Lyall are cooking up something... It'll be a pincer movement.

‖**pincette** (pɛ̃sɛt) Also 6 pyncet(te, 6–7 pincet. [F. *pincette* small pincers, dim. of *pince* a pair of pincers.] A small pair of pincers; tweezers, forceps. (Also in *pl.*)

c **1532** DU WES *Introd. Fr.* in *Palsgr.* 908 The pyncettes, *les tenailles.* **1597** A. M. tr. *Guillemeau's Fr. Chirurg.* lf. xvi b/2 Purify the wounde internallye with the pincet. **1597** LOWE *Chirurg.* (1634) 9 Some to draw away, as tenals incisiue, pincets, tirbals. **1879** RUTLEY *Study Rocks* ix. 75 Various instruments, such as the tourmaline pincette, the dichroscope. **1899** *Westm. Gaz.* 20 Dec. 10/2 The piece of lead was at last extracted by a pincette expressly constructed for the purpose.

pinch (pɪn(t)ʃ), *sb.* Forms: see next. [f. PINCH *v.*]

I. 1. a. An act of pinching; a firm compression between the finger and thumb or any two opposing surfaces; a nip, a squeeze; †a seizure with the teeth, a bite (*obs.*).

1591 SHAKS. *1 Hen. VI*, IV. ii. 49 If we be English Deere be then in blood, Not Rascall-like to fall downe with a pinch. **1600** ROWLANDS *Lett. Humours Blood* vi. 75 He will never flinch, To giue a full quart pot the empty pinch. **1606** SHAKS. *Ant. & Cl.* v. ii. 298 If thou, and Nature can so gently part, The stroke of death is as a Louers pinch. **1738** SWIFT *Pol. Conversat.* 118 Mr. Neverout's Wit begins to run low, for I vow, he said this before: Pray, Colonel, give him a Pinch. **1836** I. TAYLOR *Phys. The. Another Life* 238 Feeling the pinch of a tight shoe,.. the pinch of a tight hat.

†b. *fig.* An ill-natured thrust; stricture, censure.

1581 MULCASTER *Positions* xliii. (1887) 271 Those generall pinches, which repining people do vse then most, when they are best vsed.

c. A theft; an act of stealing or plagiarism; something stolen or plagiarized. *slang.*

1757 *London Chron.* 15–17 Mar. 258/1 They have almost reduced Cheating to a Science; and have affixed technical Terms to each Species; three of which are the Pinch, the Turn, and the Mace. **1812** J. H. VAUX *Vocab. Flash Lang.* in *Mem.* (1964) 258 This game is called *the pinch.* **1903** 'J. FLYNT' *Rise of R. Clowd* (1904) i. 64 That was just a pinch that I took. *Ibid.* 66 One night.. on his way home.. Ruderick.. took a 'pinch' too large. **1931** G. IRWIN *Amer. Tramp & Underworld Slang* 146 *Pinch*,.. a small theft. **1965** *New Statesman* 19 Mar. 430/2 The 10-point charter drawn up hurriedly by its 'brains trust' during the much publicised Brighton weekend was almost a complete 'pinch' of the charter circulated in January by the Medical Practitioners' Union. **1966** *Melody Maker* 7 May 13/4 A pleasant selection of Italian-sung numbers—including what sounds like a Latin pinch from Presley.

d. An arrest or charge; imprisonment. Also *transf. slang* (orig. *U.S.*).

1900 'FLYNT' & 'WALTON' *Powers that Prey* 81 Told me to tell you't he'd have to make a pinch if you give the wheel another turn. **1906** E. DYSON *Fact'ry 'Ands* viii. 101 Ther Elder was back in er hour, 'n' had me outer pinch ez quick ez could be. **1926** [see CAPER *sb.*² 1 c]. **1939** J. STEINBECK *Grapes of Wrath* xx. 371 Sheriff gets seventy-five cents a day for each prisoner, an' he feeds 'em for a quarter. If he ain't got prisoners, he don't make no profit... This fella today sure looks like he's out to make a pinch one way or another. **1948** *Sun* (Baltimore) 7 Jan. 13/1 If an official sees a violation, he is duty-bound to make the pinch, you might say. There is no compromise. Either it is a foul or it isn't. **1960** 'H. CARMICHAEL' *Seeds of Hate* xix. 164 Before I make a pinch I like to be reasonably sure that the charge will stick. **1970** E. R. JOHNSON *God Keepers* (1971) ii. 20 Right now you got a goof-ball pinch... Get your coat on. **1978** P. G. WINSLOW *Coppergold* 24 More worried about his clobber than the pinch.

2. *fig.* Pressure, stress (usually of want, misfortune, or the like); difficulty, hardship. Esp. in phr. ***to feel the pinch.***

1605 SHAKS. *Lear* II. iv. 214 Necessities sharpe pinch. **1678** TEMPLE *Let. to Ld. Treasurer* Wks. 1731 II. 469, I am so tired out with this cruel Pinch of Business. **1688** MORE in Norris *Theory Love* 176 This pinch of time that I am in, has made me but huddle up things together. **1861** *Times* 22 Aug., So much money having been spent... All classes felt the pinch. **1878** BOSW. SMITH *Carthage* 279 Those who were rendered keener by the pinch of hunger. **1892** JESSOPP *Studies Recluse* Pref. (1893) 17 He never knew what the pinch of poverty was. **1961** NEW ENG. BIBLE *Luke* xv. 14 He had spent it all, when a severe famine fell upon that country and he began to feel the pinch. **1974** *Nature* 11 Jan. 79/1 The industrialised nations are the first to feel the pinch. **1977** *World of Cricket Monthly* June 46/1 Otago are really feeling the pinch.

†3. The pain or pang caused by the grip of death, or of remorse, shame, etc. *Obs.*

1567 R. EDWARDS *Damon & Pithias* in Hazl. *Dodsley* IV. 93 Ne at this present pinch of death am I dismay'd. **1610** SHAKS. *Temp.* v. i. 77 Sebastian (Whose inward pinches therefore are most strong) Would heere haue kill'd your King. **1642** ROGERS *Naaman* 608 No pinch of penalty is comparable to pinch of conscience. **1681** FLAVEL *Meth. Grace* xxvi. 451 Have these convictions.. brought you to a great pinch, and inward distress of soul?

4. a. A case, occasion, or time of special stress or need; a critical juncture; a strait, exigency, extremity. Now, usually, in phr. ***at (in, on) a pinch.***

1489 CAXTON *Faytes of A.* I. xviii. 53 Corageously at a pynche [he] shal renne vpon hem. **1529** MORE *Dyaloge* I. Wks. 164/2 What would ye than haue done? Quod he ye put me nowe to a pynche. **1574** J. DEE in *Lett. Lit. Men* (Camden) 39 Any notable benefit.. bestowed uppon me now in the very pynch and opportunytie. **1589** *Marprel. Epit.* B iij b, If I had thought they would driue me to suche pinches, I would not haue medled with them. *a* **1659** BP. BROWNRIG *Serm.* (1674) I. iii. 40 The Israelites.. send to hire the King of Egypt.. to help at a pinch. **1681** NEVILE *Plato Rediv.* 264 But that Apprehension appeared Groundless when it came to the pinch. **1789** BURKE *Corr.* (1844) III. 89 [We are] without our cook, but the dairy-maid is not a bad hand at a pinch. **1821** M. EDGEWORTH *Let.* 9 Nov. (1971) 259 Even her humor would *on a pinch* submit to her sense of duty. **1847** LD. G. BENTINCK in *Croker Papers* (1884) III. xxv. 146, I think on a pinch my father could still walk ten miles in a day. **1856** EMERSON *Eng. Traits, Ability* 56 Each of them could at a pinch stand in the shoes of the other. **1865** CARLYLE *Fredk. Gt.* XIX. v. (1872) VIII. 183 Fighting fellows all,.. but uncertain as to loyalty in a case of pinch. **1890** 'R. BOLDREWOOD' *Col. Reformer* (1891) 339 She could.. drive a team on a pinch. **1903** *Booklovers' Mag.* Dec. 582, I have seen her tend bar in a pinch. **1936** C. SANDBURG *People, Yes* 67 People lie in a pinch, hating to do it. **1943** H. READ *Politics of Unpolitical* i. 6 It has always been recognized that a king might easily degenerate into a tyrant, but his natural life is limited and can at a pinch be artificially shortened. **1966** M. R. D. FOOT *SOE in France* iv. 88 It could carry two passengers easily, three at a pinch, or four in a crisis. **1977** *Belfast Tel.* 17 Jan. 13/1 The Beetle cabriolet is a four-seater which can take five at a pinch.

b. The critical or crucial point of a matter.

1639 FULLER *Holy War* II. v. (1840) 54 The chief pinch of the cause lieth on the patriarch's proof, that the lands.. formerly belonged to his predecessors. **1720** WATERLAND *Eight Serm.* Pref. 40 Here indeed lies the very Pinch of the Argument. **1846** GROTE *Greece* II. vi. II. 457 Those two attributes which form the real mark and pinch of Spartan legislation, viz., the military discipline and the rigorous private training.

5. The critical (highest or lowest) point of the tide, the turn of the tide. Cf. PINCH *v.* 13, and *pinch-water* in PINCH-. ? *Obs. rare.*

1793 SMEATON *Edystone L.* §260, I took an opportunity at pinch of low water to view the works upon the rock.

6. *local.* The game of hustle-cap: see quots.

1828 *Craven Gloss.* (ed. 2), *Pinch*, the game of pitch-halfpenny or pitch and hustle. It is played by two or more antagonists, who pitch or cast a halfpenny each, at a mark. .. When they hustle, all the half-pence.. are thrown into a hat held by the player who claims the first chance. After shaking them together, he hits the crown of the hat a smart blow with his fist, which causes them to jerk out, and as many as lie with the.. head upwards belong to him. **1888** *Sheffield Gloss.* s.v., Some colliers were lately fined.. for playing at pinch on Sunday.

7. *slang.* Something easy to accomplish or attain; a certainty.

1886–96 in Farmer & Henley *Slang* (1902) V. 205/2 The race would be a pinch, Sir, barring accident or spill. **1899** 'G. G.' *Winkles* vi. 72 Harkaway for the Scurry Handicap at Landown, good, a 'pinch'; go nap on it! **1903** A. M.

BINSTEAD *Pitcher in Paradise* xii. 280 Sustained by the conviction that he had made his match a 'pinch' indeed.

II. A place or part at which something is (or appears to be) pinched.

†**8.** *Archery.* A weakened place in a bow or stick at which it tends to bend in an angle as if pinched at this point. (See PINCH *v.* 1 c.) *Obs.*

1545 ASCHAM *Toxoph.* (Arb.) 114 If you..fynde a bowe that is..not marred with..freate or pynche, bye that bowe. *Ibid.* 120 Freates be fyrst little pinchese, the whych when you perceaue, pike the places about the pinches, to make them somewhat weker, and as well commynge as where it pinched.

†**9. a.** A pleat or gather, in a skirt, etc.; an accordion-pleat. **b.** A bend or fold in the brim of a hat; a cock. (See COCK *sb.*[6] 3.) *Obs.*

1593 NASHE *Christ's T.* (1613) 146 It is not your pinches, your purles, your floury iaggings, superfluous enterlacings, and puffings vp, that can any way offend God. **1595** GOSSON *Pl. Quippes* 87 in Hazl. *E.P.P.* IV. 254 This cloth of price, all cut in ragges,..These buttons, pinches, fringes, jagges. **1712** STEELE *Spect.* No. 432 ¶2 Hats moulded into different Cocks and Pinches. **1860** J. P. KENNEDY *W. Wirt.* I. i. 20 This picture may remind us of Hogarth's 'Politician', with 'the pinch' so far projecting that the candle burns a hole through it.

10. A steep or difficult part of a road. Also, a steep hill. Now chiefly *dial.*, *Austral.*, and *N.Z.*

1754 WASHINGTON *Let.* Writ. 1889 I. 63 Wagons may travel now with 1500 or 1800 weight on them, by doubling the teams at one or two pinches only. **1759** FRANKLIN *Ess.* Wks. 1840 III. 401 Making the road thirty feet wide, and the principal pinches twenty. **1848** H. W. HAYGARTH *Recoll. Bush Life Austral.* xii. 126 As we approached the end of our journey we came to one or two 'pinches', which is the colonial term for steep hills. **1862** J. S. DOBIE *S. Afr. Jrnl.* (1945) 30 At an ugly pinch of boulders we had another stick up. **1893** MRS. C. PRAED *Outlaw & Lawmaker* II. 4 Stony pinches and deep gulleys. **1898** *Longman's Mag.* Nov. 51 Shepherd Robbins shambling slowly down the steep 'pinch' of road that led to the farm gate. **1901** M. FRANKLIN *My Brilliant Career* xxvi. 220 Don't push him too quickly up that pinch by Flea Creek, or he might drop dead with you. **1928** 'BRENT OF BIN BIN' *Up Country* xv. 253 She..could carry him up pinches so steep that no amateur could have sat on at such an angle. **1950** *N.Z. Jrnl. Agric.* Aug. 162 [inset] The steep pinches and faces take their toll of injuries and deaths.

11. *Mining.* A point at which a mineral vein is narrowed in or compressed by the walls of rock. Also, in *Geol.*, a similar narrowing of any stratum; freq. in phr. ***pinch and swell.*** Cf. PINCH-OUT.

1873 J. H. BEADLE *Undevel. West* 333 All the strange terms in mining parlance: 'true lodes, fissure-veins, pinches,.. variations and sinuosities'. **1877** RAYMOND *Statist. Mines & Mining* 234 The north shoot seems to be divided by a vertical pinch. **1916** F. H. LAHEE *Field Geol.* vi. 140 That the country rock was warm and plastic enough to be deformed by the force of intrusion is suggested by the pinch-and-swell form of many pegmatite dikes in schists. **1955** *Jrnl. Geol.* LXIII. 520/1 The pinch-and-swell structure so commonly developed in conformable pegmatites and quartz veins. **1972** L. E. WEISS *Minor Struct. Deformed Rocks* 15 Structures closely related to boudins also formed in progressively extended layers are..'pinch and swell' structures or 'necks'.

12. *Electronics.* (See quot. 1973.)

1941 A. V. EASTMAN *Fund. Vacuum Tubes* (ed. 2) ii. 22 All the electrodes are supported by wires held in a glass 'pinch' at the base of the tube and by a mica disk at the top. **1954** *Electronic Engin.* XXVI. 16/1 Electrical leakage may be due to..getter on the pinch and micas of the valve. **1973** *Gloss. Electrotechnical, Power Terms (B.S.I.)* I. vi. 19 *Pinch*, a flat fused glass seal forming part of the foot through which pass the leads from the electrodes to the pins in the base.

13. *Physics.* A cylindrical or toroidal plasma confined by the pinch effect.

1951 *Proc. Physical Soc.* B. LXIV. 161 The discharge becomes brighter when it is contracted, and the brightness and sharpness of the 'pinch' increase with decrease in pressure. **1966** F. I. BOLEY *Plasmas* ii. 38 The kink instability of the plasma pinch..is an example of a large class of instability phenomena that is important to the dynamics of plasma. **1971** *Nature* 16 July 152/2 Research on high beta toroidal confinement is still in an early stage as groups previously working on linear theta pinches move into the field.

14. ***with a pinch of salt*** (fig.): see SALT *sb.*[1] 2 d.

III. 15. As much of something (esp. snuff) as may be taken up with the tips of the finger and thumb; hence *fig.* a very small quantity.

1583 GREENE *Mamilla* Wks. (Grosart) II. 81 For a pince of pleasure we receiue a gallon of sorow. **1712** STEELE *Spect.* No. 344 ¶2 Flavilla..asked the Churchwarden if he would take a Pinch [of Snuff]. **1724** THOMSON *Let.* 11 Dec. (in *Sotheby's Catal.* 19–22 Feb. (1896) 86), Had I been taught to cut a caper, to hum a tune, to take a pinch and lisp nonsense with all the grace of fashionable stupidity. **1725** BRADLEY *Fam. Dict.* s.v. *Old Age*, Two Pinches of the Tops of Rosemary, a Pinch of Laurel Leaves, two Pinches of Hysop. **1833** HT. MARTINEAU *Manch. Strike* v. 61 Rowe took a long pinch of snuff. **1840** DICKENS *Old C. Shop* xxvi, A little more hot water, and a pinch of fresh tea.

IV. 16. An iron lever with a beak or point, used for moving heavy bodies, loosening coal, etc., by leverage or prizing; a crow-bar; a pinch-bar.

1816 SCOTT *Bl. Dwarf* ix, Pinches or forehammers will never pick upon't,..ye might as weel batter at it wi' pipe-staples. **1819** W. TENNANT *Papistry Storm'd* (1827) 190 Here scores their pinches and their picks Atween the ashlar stanes did fix. **1883** GRESLEY *Gloss. Coal-mining*, *Pinch*, a kind of crowbar used in breaking down coal.

17. *dial.* A close-fisted person; a 'screw'.

a **1825** FORBY *Voc. E. Anglia*, *Pinch*, a very parsimonious economist.

pinch (pɪn(t)ʃ), *v.* Forms: 4–6 pinche(n, pynche(n, (4–5 pinnche, 6 pyntche, pynshe, pench(e, *Sc.* pinsche), 6–7 pynch, 6– pinch. *β.* (*rarely*) 6 pinse, 7–8 pince. [a. ONF. *pinchier (in mod.Normand *pincher*), 3 sing. pr. *pinche*, = OF. *pincier*, mod.F. *pincer*; ulterior origin obscure.

The Fr. vb. was perh. nasalized from an earlier form repr. by Walloon *pissî*: cf. obs. It. *picciare*, Venet. dial. *pizzare*, mod.It. *pizzicare* to pinch, Sp. *pizca* a pinch; also early mod.Du. *pitsen*, Flem. *pinssen* (Kilian), Ger. *pfetzen* to pinch.]

I. In literal and closely connected senses.

1. a. *trans.* To compress between the tips of the finger and thumb, with the teeth, etc., or with any instrument having two jaws or parts between which something may be grasped; to nip, squeeze. (The principal literal sense.) Also *absol.* or *intr.*

1340–70 *Alex. & Dind.* 751 But bochours ben þei echon, ȝour body to dismembre, & euerich pinchen his part. **1495** *Trevisa's Barth. De P.R.* v. xxxviii. (W. de W.) 153 Yf the mete pytchyth and pryckyth, the stomake is pynchyd and prycked and compellyth it to passe out. **1530** PALSGR. 657/2, I pynche a thynge with my fyngar and my thombe. **1581** MULCASTER *Positions* xliii. (1887) 272 To pinch the heele where they pricke at the head. *a* **1628** PRESTON *Saint's Daily Exerc.* (1629) 119 A swine that is pinched..will cry exceeding loud. **1750** GRAY *Long Story* 59 They.. Rummage his Mother, pinch his Aunt. **1803** *Med. Jrnl.* IX. 44 The creature was scarcely able to withdraw its legs when the toes were pinched. **1856** SIR B. BRODIE *Psychol. Inq.* I. iv. 115 If the legs be pinched..the muscles are made to contract.

β. **1799** W. TAYLOR *Hist. Surv. Germ. Poetry* (1830) II. 65 That blacksmith, Who on his wall had drawn the arch-devil's picture, And us'd to pince at it with glowing tongs.

b. Said of a tight shoe, etc. which presses painfully upon the part which it covers; esp. in the proverbial phrase ***to know where the shoe pinches***, i.e. to know (by direct experience) the disadvantages of any situation, or the cause of a trouble or difficulty. (Usually *absol.* or *intr.*)

1426 LYDG. *De Guil. Pilgr.* 8253 Thys glouys byndë me so sore, That I may weryn hem no more, With her pynchyng to be bounde, Myn handys ben so tendre. **1573–80** BARET *Alv.* P 377 My shooe..pincheth my foote. *a* **1580** G. HARVEY *Letter-bk.* (Camden) 85 Subtle enemyes, that knowe..where the shooe pinchith us most. **1637** HEYWOOD *Dialogues* ii. Wks. 1874 VI. 121 When you pull on your shoo you best may tel In what part it doth chiefely pinch you. **1658** A. FOX *Würtz' Surg.* II. xxv. 163 Fit the splinters well ..that they pinch not the Patient any where. *c* **1720** PRIOR *Phillis's Age* ii, Stiff in brocade, and pinch'd in stays. **1856** READE *Never too late* lv, Oh, is that where the shoe pinches?

†**c.** *intr.* for *refl.* Of a bow: To receive a pinch: see PINCH *sb.* 8 *Obs.*

1545 ASCHAM *Toxoph.* (Arb.) 116 Take your bow in to the feeld,..looke where he commethe moost, prouyde for that place betymes, leste it pinche and so freate. *Ibid.* 121.

d. *pass.* To be jammed or compressed forcibly between two solid objects so as to be crushed.

1896 J. E. JEAFFRESON in *Westm. Gaz.* 4 Aug. 5/1 We have lost our walrus boat... She was pinched on shore in the land water on July 16,..by the heavy pack ice. **1899** *Ibid.* 29 Mar. 5/3 The chap that had it before me got pinched between the coupling hooks..he only lived a few hours. **1899** *Daily News* 11 Oct. 8/5 He was pinched between the train and the platform.

2. a. With *adv.* or *compl.* To bring or get into some state or position by pinching (in first two quots., by squeezing or pressing).

13.. *S. Erkenwolde* 70 in Horstm. *Altengl. Leg.* (1881) 267 Wyȝt werkemen..Putten prises þer to, pinchid one vnder. *a* **1425** *Langland's P. Pl.* A. IX. 88 A pyk is in þe potent to punge [*Univ. Coll. MS.* pynche] a-doun þe wikkede. **1579** TOMSON *Calvin's Serm. Tim.* 241/1 Let them keepe straite, and pinch in their shoulders. **1590** SHAKS. *Com. Err.* II. ii. 194 They'll sucke our breath, or pinch vs blacke and blew. **1645** FULLER *Good Th. in Bad T.* (1841) 23 Pinch me into the remembrance of my promises. **1799** G. SMITH *Laboratory* (ed. 6) I. 28 Pinch their ends close. **1899** *Allbutt's Syst. Med.* VIII. 676 The skin cannot now be pinched up.

b. *Hort.* To nip off part of (a shoot). Also to nip *out*; to shorten *back* or *down* by nipping.

1693 EVELYN *De la Quint. Compl. Gard.* I. 16 When the Branch so Pinch'd proves obstinate in shooting thick again, the same Operation of Pinching must be perform'd again. **1850** *Beck's Florist* May 129 When the shoots have grown three or four inches..I again pinch out their tops, in order to make them bushy. **1862** ANSTED *Channel Isl.* IV. xxi. (ed. 2) 490 As soon as six leaves were developed on any shoot they were pinched down to three. **1890** *Farmer's Gaz.* 4 Jan. 7/1 When [the shoots] are three or four inches long they are pinched back to three buds.

c. To force out by compression, squeeze out; in quots. *fig.* to extract, extort, wring, 'squeeze' (money) *from* or *out of* a person.

1770 MASSIE *Reas. agst. Tax on Malt* 10 The Money.. must be pinched from the bellies and backs of labouring Families. **1822** COBBETT *Weekly Reg.* 13 Apr. 69 The immense sums, thus pinched from the millions, and put into the hands of thousands. **1865** DICKENS *Mut. Fr.* III. xiii, He had always pinched the full interest out of himself with punctual pinches.

d. To put in or add by pinches (PINCH *sb.* 11); ***pinch empty***, to empty by removing the contents by pinches.

1821 CLARE *Vill. Minstr.* II. 84 The old dames..pinch the snuff-box empty by degrees. **1859** TENNYSON *Vivien* 608 Pinch a murderous dust into her drink.

e. ***to pinch off***: *intr.*, to undergo a localized constriction that progresses until separation into two portions occurs; to become separate in this way; also *trans.*, to detach in this way.

1687 A. LOVELL tr. *Thevenot's Trav.* II. 106 The ordinary Rack..is for men to pinch off the Flesh with hot Pinsers. **1910** *Jrnl. Morphol.* XXI. 278 (*caption*) Megakaryocyte showing a platelet in process of pinching off from a pseudopod. *Ibid.*, Various phases are shown in the process of pinching off portions of the cytoplasm of the thrombocytes to form blood platelet-like corpuscles. **1952** [see PINCH-OFF]. **1956** *Essays in Crit.* VI. 10 Science begins to appear in the odd role of being pinched off and occupying the lonely end of a polar opposition to religion. **1956** L. P. HUNTER *Handbk. Semiconductor Electronics* IV. 29 If the bias on the gate is high enough, the depletion region of the encircling PN junction becomes thick enough to 'pinch off' the channel through which the working current flows. **1956** *Jrnl. Biophysical & Biochem. Cytol.* II. Suppl. 107 The invaginated membrane is pinched off, resulting in the formation of an intracellular vacuole. **1959** *Bell Syst. Techn. Jrnl.* XXXVIII. 777 If sufficiently high voltage is applied, the channel will 'pinch off' and its current will essentially saturate. **1962** *Science Survey* III. 170 The living endothelial cell has almost nothing in its cytoplasm but masses of tiny smooth vesicles pinching-off and opening at the cell surfaces. **1966** *McGraw-Hill Encycl. Sci. & Technol.* X. 233/1 Once the process starts, the pressure at a narrow neck in the ring of fused metal is able to squeeze out the fluid metal until the neck pinches off completely, cutting off the current. **1979** *Nature* 11 Jan. 91/1 One suggestion has been made that the clathrin physically pinches off a membrane vesicle.

†**3.** *trans.* To pleat, gather in, or flute the surface of (a garment, etc.); to crimp or crinkle the edge of (a pie-crust). *Obs.*

c **1386** CHAUCER *Prol.* 151 Ful semyly hir wympul pynched was. *c* **1412** HOCCLEVE *De Reg. Princ.* 410 So wyde a gowne..as is pin, So smal I-pynchid. *c* **1420** *Liber Cocorum* (1862) 41 Kover hit [the chopped-up pork, etc.] with lyddes, and pynche hit fayre, Korven in þe myddes two loyseyns a payr. **1509–10** [see PINCHED *ppl. a.* 3].

†**4.** To seize, compress, or snap with the teeth. Often *absol.* *Obs.*

c **1410** *Master of Game* (MS. Digby 182) xxxv, Who pyncheth firste and goth þerwith to þe deth, he shall haue þe skynne. **1593** SHAKS. *3 Hen. VI*, II. i. 16 As a Beare, encompass'd round with Dogges: Who hauing pincht a few, and made them cry, The rest stand all aloofe. *c* **1611** CHAPMAN *Iliad* v. 462 Like a sort of dogs that at a lion bay, And entertain no spirit to pinch. **1700** DRYDEN *Theodore & Hon.* 115 Two mastiffs..came up and pinch'd her tender side.

†**5.** Said of actions causing a painful bodily sensation: To hurt, pain, torture, torment. (In first two quots. applied to the torture of the rack.) *Obs.*

1536 CROMWELL in Merriman *Life & Lett.* (1902) II. 30 Not sparing for the knowleage hereof to pynche him with paynes to the declaracion of it. **1587** FLEMING *Contn. Holished* III. 1371/1 They were constreined to commit him to such as are vsuallie appointed in the Tower to handle the racke, by whome he was laied vpon the same, and somewhat pinched, although not much. **1597** J. T. *Serm. Paules C.* 11 Which pincheth man with three great wounds. **1607** TOPSELL *Four-f. Beasts* (1658) 364 If it [a Dart] pinch them further, and draw bloud, they increase their punishment.

6. Said of the painful action of cold, hunger, exhaustion, or wasting disease: including the physical effects (to contract, make thin or shrunken), the painful physical sensations, and often the mental affliction or social injury. Also, in reference to plants: to nip, to cause to shrivel or wither up.

a **1548** HALL *Chron., Hen. V* 48 If famine had not pinched them, or colde wether had not nipped them. **1577** *St. Aug. Manual* (Longman) 30 Let fastynges forepine the body,.. let labour pinche it. **1581** MARBECK *Bk. of Notes* 913 If he be a little pinched with pouertie & aduersitie. **1591** SHAKS. *Two Gent.* IV. iv. 160 The ayre hath..pinch'd the lilly-tincture of her face. **1652** A. ROSS *Hist. World* I. iii. 13 His army being pinched with thirst. *a* **1661** FULLER *Worthies, Glouc.* (1662) 349 The most generous and vigorous land will..be imbarrened, when always pinched with the Plough. **1725** DE FOE *Voy. round World* (1840) 22 A most severe cold which pinched our men exceedingly. **1772** FOOTE *Nabob* II. Wks. 1799 II. 303 The polyanthuses were a little pinched by the easterly winds. **1884** *Fortn. Rev.* Jan. 2 The labouring classes..have been pinched..by hard times, by increased expenses, and by loss of wages.

absol. **1631** GOUGE *God's Arrows* III. §43. 260 When a famine begins to pinch. **1725** POPE *Odyss.* XIV. 548 The winter pinches, and with cold I die.

II. In non-physical and figurative senses.

7. a. To press upon, straiten, reduce to straits or distress; to bring into difficulties or trouble; to afflict, harass. *Obs.* exc. as consciously *fig.* from 1 or 6.

1548 UDALL *Erasm. Par. Luke* xiv. 127 To the ende they myght bee worse pynched at the herte roote. **1577** *F. de L'isle's Legendarie* H ij, The proposition of the lord Bretagne ..did chiefly pinch them. **1664** H. MORE *Myst. Iniq.*, *Apol.* 515 That no consciencious man may be pinched thereby. **1724** DE FOE *Mem. Cavalier* (1840) 215 The king finding his affairs pinch him at home. **1800** COLERIDGE *Piccolom.* I. xii, His compact with me pinches The Emperor. **1862** MRS. H. WOOD *Mrs. Hallib.* II. ix, Debt pinches the mind, more than hunger pinches the body.

β. **1630** M. GODWYN tr. *Bp. Hereford's Ann. Eng.* I. 49 Need began at length to pince him.

b. *intr.* or *absol.*

c **1611** CHAPMAN *Iliad* VIII. 278 Huge grief, for Hector's slaughter'd friend, pinch'd in his mighty mind. **1657** CROMWELL *Sp.* 20 Apr. in *Carlyle*, Another thing which doth a little pinch upon me. **1712** ARBUTHNOT *John Bull* II. iii, *Don Diego*. Pray tell me, how you came to employ this Sir Roger..and not think of your old friend Diego? *Mrs. Bull*. So, so, there it pinches!

†**8.** *intr.* To press narrowly or closely *on*: **a.** to encroach *on*; **b.** to put stress *upon*. *Obs.*

a **1300** *Sat. People Kildare* xvi. in *E.E.P.* (1862) 155 Hail be ȝe bakers wiþ ȝur louis smale..ȝe pincheþ on þe riȝt white aȝen goddes law. **1377** LANGL. *P. Pl.* B. XIII. 371 ȝif I ȝede to þe plow, I pynched so narwe [*C.* on hus half acre] þat a fote londe or a forwe, fecchen I wolde, Of my nexte neighbore. **1563** *Homilies* II. *Rogation Week* IV. (1859) 498 It is a shame to behold..how men pinch at such bierbalks, which by long use and custom ought to be inviolably kept. **1685** H. MORE *Paralip. Prophet.* xliv. 375 The Visions indeed at last pinch closest upon the Roman Hierarchy. *a* **1734** NORTH *Exam.* III. vi. §47 (1740) 457, I should haue pinched hard upon this Practice, if it had not been a Push-pin Game.

†**9. a.** *intr.* To carp or cavil *at*; to find fault, object. *Obs.*

c **1380** WYCLIF *Sel. Wks.* III. 347 We mai not pynche at þis lawe. *c* **1386** CHAUCER *Prol.* 326 Ther koude no wight pynchen at his writyng. **1430–40** LYDG. *Bochas* III. v. (1554) 74 b, If any man pyntche at their outrage. **1549** LATIMER *5th Serm. bef. Edw. VI* (Arb.) 140 Euerye waye thys offyce of preachynge is pyncht at.

†**b.** *trans.* To find fault with, blame, reproach, reprove. *Obs.*

1570 T. NORTON tr. *Nowel's Catech.* (1853) 218 So as he ..blot them [not] with stain or infamy, but pinch them and reprove them only with suspicion of their own conscience. **1594** HOOKER *Eccl. Pol.* IV. xiii. §9 The Corinthians hee pincheth with this demand.

10. †**a.** *intr.* To give or spend very sparingly and narrowly; to be close-fisted, meanly parsimonious, or miserly; to drive hard bargains. *Obs.*

13.. *Seuyn Sag.* (W.) 1243 That on was..Lef to give, an lef to spende; And that other lef to pinche. Bothe he was scars, and chinche. **1406** HOCCLEVE *Misrule* 181, I pynchid nat at hem in myn acate, But paied hem as þat they axe wolde. **1530** PALSGR. 657/2 He pyncheth as though he were nat worthe a grote. *a* **1578** LINDESAY (Pitscottie) *Chron. Scot.* (S.T.S.) I. 3 Ane hes that micht ane hundreith weill susteine and livis in vo and pinschis at his tabill. *a* **1617** HIERON *Wks.* I. 217 They pinch with the Lord, as Ananias.

b. *trans.* To limit or restrict narrowly the supply of (anything); to stint, to give barely or with short measure or weight; to give sparingly or grudgingly. Now *dial.*, exc. in phr. ***to pinch pennies*** (or ***a penny***): to be penny-pinching or parsimonious.

1530 *Proper Dyaloge* in *Rede me*, etc. (Arb.) 169 Let him ones begynne to pynche Or withdrawe their tithinge an ynche. **1561** NORTON & SACKV. *Gorboduc* II. i, If nature and the Goddes had pinched so Their flowing bountie and their noble giftes..from you. **1642** FULLER *Holy & Prof. St.* IV. xiii. 305 If ever she affordeth fine ware, she alwayes pincheth it in the measure. **1675** HOBBES *Odyssey* XI. 332 Do not pinch your Gift. **1695** in Picton *L'pool Munic. Rec.* (1883) I. 320 They are not to pinch the water from the faw-well. *a* **1906** *Mod. Sc.* Ye needna hae pincht the water; it's cheap aneuch ony way. Dinna pinch the elbow-grease. **1942** E. PAUL *Narrow St.* xix. 152 The surly Monsieur Salmon.. complaining and pinching pennies as he made his purchases. **1962** J. D. MACDONALD *Key to Suite* (1968) iii. 40 I'm not about to pinch a penny on a thing like this. **1973** J. CLEARY *Ransom* xi. 255 'This city is too expensive for a cop on my pay. Especially when it almost cost me my wife, too.' 'He's always pinching pennies,' said Lisa.

c. To straiten or stint (a person, etc.) *in*, in respect *of*, *for* (something), or in means generally; to subject (any one) to short measure.

1580 LYLY *Euphues* (Arb.) 220 Yet will I not pinch you of that pastime. **1591** GREENE *Disc. Coosnage* (1592) 25 She cald in her neighbors..that..had also been pincht in their coles, and shewed them the cosenage. **1596** BP. W. BARLOW *Three Serm.* ii. 78 Couetouslie pinching their Tables and almes. **1600** HAKLUYT *Voy.* (1810) III. 199 Those in the Frigat were already pinched with spare allowance. **1657** R. LIGON *Barbadoes* (1673) 121 Either pinch them of a great part, or give them that which is nastie. **1676** MOXON *Print Lett.* 10 You are pinched for room. **1732** BERKELEY *Alciphr.* I. §8 Was I not pinched in Time, the regular way would be to have begun with the Circumstantials of Religion. **1766** GOLDSM. *Vic. W.* vii, My wife..insisted on entertaining them all; for which..our family was pinched for three weeks after. **1784** COWPER *Let. to J. Newton* Feb., I am at this moment pinched for time. **1789** W. BUCHAN *Dom. Med.* (1790) 19 The error of pinching children in their food is more hurtful than the other extreme. **1876** F. E. TROLLOPE *Charming Fellow* II. xiv. 223 She wasn't used to be pinched for money herself. **1884** W. C. SMITH *Kildrostan* I. ii. 211 Some debts..he had to pay, Which pinched us for a while.

d. *intr.* in *refl.* or *pass.* sense. To pinch oneself or be pinched; to be straitened in means; to suffer from penury.

1549 CHEKE *Hurt Sedit.* (1641) 35 When yee see decay of victuals, the rich pinch, the poore famish. **1634** HEYWOOD *Maidenhead Lost* II. i. Wks. 1874 IV. 121, I told you, you were so prodigall we should pinch for't. **1738** SWIFT *Pol. Conversat.* 184 I'm forc'd to pinch, for the Times are hard. **1879** *Cassell's Techn. Educ.* IV. 11/2 Made merry..the whole week through, to pinch for it a fortnight after.

11. a. *trans.* To compress, confine, or restrict narrowly. Now *rare* or *Obs.*

1570 DEE *Math. Pref.* d iv b, No more than we may pinche in the Definitions of Wisedome or Honestie. **1633** G. HERBERT *Temple, Decay* iii, Thou dost thy self immure..In some one corner of a feeble heart: Where yet both Sinne and Satan..Do pinch and straiten thee. *a* **1677** BARROW *Serm.* Wks. 1716 II. 23 That doctrine which pincheth our liberty within so narrow bounds. **1856** EMERSON *Eng. Traits, Cockayne* Wks. (Bohn) II. 65 The same insular limitation pinches his foreign politics.

b. To reduce to straits (in argument, etc.); to bring into a difficulty or 'fix'; to 'put in a tight place'. Now *rare*.

1692 RAY *Disc.* I. iv. (1693) 59 When we are at a loss, and pinch't with an Argument. **1752** G. BROWN in *Scots Mag.* Nov. (1753) 559/2 The prosecutors are pinched in point of argument. *a* **1832** SCOTT in Smiles *Self-Help* iii. (1860) 60, I have felt pinched and hampered by my own ignorance.

c. ***to pinch courtesy***: see COURTESY 1 c.

III. In technical and slang uses.

12. a. *Racing.* To urge or press (a horse); to exhaust by urging.

1737 BRACKEN *Farriery Impr.* (1757) II. 148 It is the vulgar Opinion, that a Horse has not been pinch'd, or pinn'd down, in a Heat when he does not sweat out. *Ibid.* 149 If a Horse's Tail shake and tremble after any Heat, it is a Sign he is hard pinch'd. **1864** *Daily Tel.* 10 June, He declined to make an effort when 'pinched' by his jockey.

b. *Naut.* To sail (a vessel) close-hauled.

1895 *Daily News* 11 Sept. 5/5 Defender had to be pinched to make the mark before she started on the stern chase. *Ibid.*, Captain Cranfield was pinching Valkyrie hard, but she ..was..unable to keep as close into the wind as her rival. **1898** *Ibid.* 19 Sept. 3/5 While the Maid was pinched right through Irex had to make no less than three boards.

13. *intr.* Of the tide: To pass its highest or lowest level. (Cf. PINCH *sb.* 5.) *rare.* ? *Obs.*

1756 *Phil. Trans.* XLIX. 532 As soon as the tide pinched, the ebb came down at once.

14. *intr. Mining.* Of a vein or deposit of ore: To contract in volume, become narrow or thin; with *out*, to come to an end, 'run out'. Also, in *Geol.*, said of strata generally; also with *down*. Cf. LENS *v.*

1867 J. A. PHILLIPS *Mining & Metallurgy Gold & Silver* iv. 56 The lode, which is eight feet wide on the north side of the Eureka, pinches out very rapidly in that direction. **1872** RAYMOND *Statist. Mines & Mining* 307 The vein is 5 or 6 feet wide, on an average, but expanding sometimes to 15 or 20 feet, and pinching up in places to a few inches. *Ibid.*, The body of rich ore worked last year..was exhausted, the ledge pinching out. **1890** *Goldfields Victoria* 27 The characteristic of this district..is for the auriferous surface quartz to pinch or run out. **1891** M. COLE *Cy Ross* 93 The vein began suddenly to pinch last week..the vein is steadily pinching narrower and narrower as we advance. **1916** F. H. LAHEE *Field Geol.* ix. 240 Sometimes strata are irregularly thinned and thickened so that they 'pinch and swell', as seen in cross section. **1923** *Ibid.* (ed. 2) v. 88 If a stratum continues to thin out in a certain direction,..it may finally 'pinch out' or 'lens out' altogether. **1928** W. A. CHALFONT *Outposts of Civilization* 82 High-grade veins were followed as they pinched down, even to half inch seams which were profitably 'spooned out'. **1945** *Bull. Amer. Assoc. Petroleum Geologists* XXIX. 1563 The reservoir bed must pinch out in all updip directions. **1961** *Jrnl. Geol.* LXIX. 339/1 The layered marine sediments pinch out to the south.

15. *trans.* **a.** To steal, to purloin (a thing); to rob (a person). *slang.*

1656 *Witty Rogue Arraigned* xxi. 30 Pinch'd the Cully of a Casket of Jewels. **1673** R. HEAD *Canting Acad.* 191 The fifth is a Glasier, who when he creeps in: To pinch all the Lurry, he thinks it no sin. *a* **1700** B. E. *Dict. Cant. Crew*, *Pinch*, to Steal, or Slily convey any thing away. **1812** J. H. VAUX *Flash Dict.* s.v., I pinch'd him for a fawney, signifies I purloined a ring from him; Did you pinch anything in that crib? did you succeed in secreting any thing in that shop? **1869** *Daily News* 10 Aug., Brown was..alleged, in sporting phrase, to have 'pinched' the defendant out of 6*l.* 10*s.* **1900** [see COMMANDEER *v.* c]. **1930** J. B. PRIESTLEY *Angel Pavement* ix. 474 Buying cars that have been pinched like that is a mug's game. **1936** [see FAT *sb.*[2] 2 d]. **1969** *Listener* 24 July 103/2 'This was by car I take it—was there petrol?' 'Well, we somehow managed to pick it up.' 'You mean pinch it?' **1979** 'C. BRAND' *Rose in Darkness* xiii. 189 You simply pinched it from a shop.

b. To arrest, take into custody. [So F. *pincer* 'arrêter, saisir' (Littré).]

1837 *Sessions Papers Cent. Criminal Court* 4 Dec. 157 D—— d if I'm not *pinched* for housebreaking at last. **1860** *Slang Dict.*, *Pinch*..to catch, or apprehend. **1862** MAYHEW *Lond. Labour* (1865) III. 397 He got acquitted for that there note after he had me 'pinched'. **1882** *Five Yrs.' Penal Servitude* iii. 109 The blooming crushers were precious glad when they 'pinched' him. **1925** H. L. FOSTER *Trop. Tramp with Tourists* 41 A traffic policeman had stopped us. But not to pinch us for speeding. **1932** T. S. ELIOT *Sweeney Agonistes* 28 These fellows always get pinched in the end. **1938** [see GUY *v.*[4]]. **1955** *Times* 12 Aug. 5/4 He explained that Heard gave him the tobacco and then put in another officer to 'pinch' him. **1979** N. HYND *Fake Flags* iv. 25 Nobody knew what night Vasiliev was going to be pinched.

16. To move (a heavy body, as a loaded truck, a large cask) by a succession of small heaves with a pointed iron bar or 'pinch': see PINCH *sb.* 16.

1859 [see PINCHING *vbl. sb.* 5]. **1888** *Whitby Gaz.* 28 Apr. 4/4, I was engaged in pinching a bogie which was loaded with a ball of slag. **1895** T. PINNOCK *Black Country Ann.* (E.D.D.), Gie me the bar, I'll pinch it forrat a bit while yo' restin'.

pinch- in Comb.: [chiefly the imperative or verb-stem with the second element in objective relation to it; sometimes the sb.]

pinch-back, one who pinches his own or another's back, by stinting it of proper clothing; also *attrib.*; **pinch-bar** = PINCH *sb.* 16: see quot.; **pinch-batter** = *pinch-hitter*; **pinch-belly**, one who denies himself or others sufficient food; also *attrib.*; **pinch-bottle** *U.S.*, a bottle with indented sides, *spec.* a whisky bottle; so, by metonymy, whisky; **pinch-cock** *Mech.*, a clamp used to compress a flexible or elastic tube so as to regulate the flow of liquid, etc.; **pinch-commons**, one who stints the supply of food for himself or others; †**pinch-crust** = prec.; **pinch-eyed** *a.* (see quot.); **pinch-face**, a pinch-faced person; **pinch-faced** *a.*, having the features pinched or emaciated; †**pinch-fart**, a niggard, miser (in quot. *attrib.*); **pinch-fist**, a 'close-fisted' person, a niggard, miser; so **pinchfisted** *a.*, mean, miserly; **pinch-hit** *v. intr.* (orig. *U.S.*), in baseball, to bat as a substitute for another batter, esp. at a critical point in the game; freq. *transf.*, to act as a substitute, esp. in an emergency; to stand in *for* someone; also as *sb.*, a hit made by a substitute batter; so **pinch-hitter, -hitting**; **pinch-plane** *Math.* (see quot.); **pinch-pleat**, one of a cluster of small pleats, used esp. in curtains; hence **pinch-pleated** *a.*; **pinch-plum**, one who would divide a plum; a close, grasping person; **pinch-point**, (*a*) *Math.* (see quot.); (*b*) a point of congestion, confusion, or difficulty; **pinch roll**, (*a*) each of a pair of rolls, usu. hydraulically controlled, which grip the material passing between them; (*b*) = *pinch roller*; **pinch roller**, in a tape recorder or tape deck, a spring-loaded roller which presses the tape against the capstan; **pinch-runner** *N. Amer.* (see quot. 1961); **pinch-spotted** *a.*, discoloured with marks of pinches; **pinch-waist**, a tightly-fitted waist; also *attrib.*; hence **pinch-waisted** *a.*; **pinch-water**, high or low water; **pinch-weed**, dial. name for *Polygonum Persicaria* (see quot.); **pinch wheel** = *pinch roller*. Also PINCH-GUT, PINCHPENNY.

1600 NASHE *Summer's Last Will* in Hazl. *Dodsley* VIII. 76 Christmas,..a *pinchback, cutthroat churl. **1837** *Civ. Eng. & Arch. Jrnl.* I. 74/1 The application of a lever or *pinch-bar. **1875** KNIGHT *Dict. Mech.*, *Pinch-bar*, a lever with a fulcrum-foot and projecting snout: applied beneath a heavy body to move it by successive small raisings and shiftings. **1928** *Chicago Tribune* 5 Oct. 26/1 The *pinch batter exercised rare judgment and drew a pass. **1974** *Spartanburg* (S. Carolina) *Herald* 22 Apr. B1/2 Franklin walloped five home runs in the six-day series. He started five of the games and was a pinch-batter in the other two. **1648–60** HEXHAM, *Een Spaer-back*,..a Sparer,..or a *Pinch-belly. **1721** AMHERST *Terræ Fil.* App. (1754) 318, I am against all extremes, and especially on the pinch-belly side. **1939** C. MORLEY *Kitty Foyle* x. 103 Mr Rittenhouse gave him a lift to the bootlegger's, ordered a whole case of *pinchbottle on Pop's recommendation..and invited us down to..dinner. **1940** E. HEMINGWAY *For whom Bell Tolls* xvi. 204 'When we have electricity again, what a lamp we can make out of this bottle.' She looked at the pinch-bottle admiringly. **1963** *New Yorker* 8 June 57 We made it [*sc.* men's toiletry] clean-smelling and gutsy and put it up in hefty glass pinch bottles. **1873** RALFE *Phys. Chem.* 103 This flask is fitted with a bulb tube, filled with dilute nitric acid, which is prevented from flowing into the mixture by means of a *pinchcock. **1881** TYNDALL *Floating Matter of Air* 171 A pinchcock nipped the india-rubber tube at its centre. **1822** SCOTT *Pirate* vi, The crazed projector and the niggardly *pinch-commons by which it is inhabited. **1602** ROWLANDS *Greene's Ghost* (Hunter. Cl.) 9 A young Gentleman, Merchant, or old *pinchcrust. **1765** *Treat. Dom. Pigeons, Carrier* 83 The eye ..ought to be broad, round, and of an equal thickness; for if one part of the eye be thinner than the rest, it is said to be *pinch-ey'd, which is deemed a very great imperfection. **1917** W. OWEN *Let.* 27 Sept. (1967) 497, I called for the poet —a wizened little *pinch-face, about two feet high! **1863** G. M. HOPKINS *Let.* 22 Apr. (1956) 73 Woolcomb,..a *pinch-faced old man, whom everybody likes as much as they yawn over his divinity lectures. **1943** *Gen* 10 Apr. 23/1 Pinch-faced, thin-limbed, he seemed to be needing a good dinner. **1592** NASHE *P. Penilesse* Wks. (Grosart) II. 25 My *pinch-fart penie-father. *c* **1580** JEFFERIE *Bugbears* I. ii. 61 in *Archiv Stud. Neu. Spr.* (1897) XCVIII. 308 Our *pinchefist the old vecchio. **1681** W. ROBERTSON *Phraseol. Gen.* (1693) 990 A pinch-fist, *avarus*. **1917** 'H. H. RICHARDSON' *Fortunes R. Mahony* I. ix. 84 They were pinchfists when it came to parting with their money. **1978** *Verbatim* May 1/1 One incurs hostile mutters of *sparethrift* or *sparegood, scrapepelf* or *scrapegood, pinchfist* or *skinflint*. **1867** *Routledge's Ev. Boy's Ann.* Oct. 636 As hearty and liberal as they were once cold and *pinchfisted. **1931** *Kansas City* (Missouri) *Star* 17 Dec. 24 John Neilson gave the talk,..but I thought they were just using him to *pinch-hit for Bo McMillin. **1948** *Capital-Democrat* (Tishomingo, Okla.) 17 June 5/5 Duggan Smith, *pinch hitting for W. C. Whiteley, had sent a high drive out to center. **1957** R. LONGRIGG *Switchboard* iv. 59 'I wonder if you can help me out of a jam?.. I'm supposed to be lunching with a man called Robinson... I now find I can't do it. I've made some kind of nonsense with the dates —' 'Shall I pinch-hit?' **1966** *N.Y. Times* (Internat. ed.) 22 Apr. 12/1 California's Joe Adcock hit a pinch-hit single in the bottom of the eleventh inning. **1973** E. TAYLOR *Serpent under It* (1974) x. 156 'With no secretary, how do we find out where they are?' 'They've got some old girl from the History Department pinch-hitting.' **1974** *Cleveland* (Ohio) *Plain Dealer* 13 Oct. 14-C/4 If we were ahead by only one run, I would have pinch hit for Rollie in the top of the ninth because Catfish was ready. **1976** *Billings* (Montana) *Gaz.* 24 June 1-D/3. With one out, Kautzmann delivered a pinch-hit single to left field to drive in Art LaGaly with the lead run. **1912** *Lit. Digest* 10 Aug. 238/2 Things did not run very smoothly the famous 'Cub' *pinch hitter himself tells us. **1939** ADE *Let.* 7 June (1973) 210, I have tried to get either 'Chick' Evans or 'Red' Grange for the June party but without success. We don't want to miss a month and so..I am offering myself as a pinch-hitter. **1970** *Globe & Mail*

(Toronto) 26 Sept. 39/8 Singles, by pinch-hitter Mack Jones, Bob Bailey and pinch-hitter Jim Fairey in the bottom of the ninth produced one run. **1976** *Washington Post* 19 Apr. D4/1 Major league baseball has designated ABC as its pinch hitter for NBC on Monday night television this season. **1931** M. Loeb *Please stand By* I. x. 118 Just because Will Rogers did some *pinch-hitting for Fred Stone and got away with it is no reason why you should send some college cub-reporter up here to cover the greatest discovery on the air. **1947** *Los Angeles Times* 6 Oct. 11/7 Brown..kept up his red-hot pinch-hitting when he singled for Phillips in the third. **1974** *Anderson* (S. Carolina) *Independent* 23 Apr. 3A/5 At present, the recreational program is being operated by Assistant Director Benny Burrell, 'who is doing a good job of pinch hitting,' said Evatt. **1869** Cayley *Coll. Math. Papers* VI. 336 The *pinch-plane, or reciprocal singularity j' = l, is in fact a torsal plane touching the surface along a line, or meeting it in the line twice and in a residual curve. .. Considering..the reciprocal figure, the reciprocal of the pinch-plane is..a point of the nodal curve, and is a pinch-point. **1958** *Times* 23 June 11/3 For long windows the *pinch-pleat treatment in the last small sketch is very effective. **1973** *Guardian* 29 Mar. 13/3 The curtains are backed by Sekers's own make-up service which can provide pinch or pencil pleated or gathered curtains to the customer's own specifications. **1892** *Daily News* 25 April 5/7 The most beggarly-spirited *pinch-plum economy. **1868** Cayley *Coll. Math. Papers* VI. 123 A surface having a nodal line has in general on this nodal line points where the two tangent planes coincide, or as I propose to term them '*pinch-points'. **1961** *Times* 15 Aug. 10/3 No loading or unloading at all will be permitted at important intersections and other 'pinch points'. **1965** *New Society* 11 Nov. 10/3 Oliver Cox considers heating one of the major 'pinch-points' in building today. **1973** *Country Life* 31 May 1527/3 The bridge is a pinch-point and congestion soon builds up. **1953** *Engineer* 23 Oct. 526/2 The slabs have to be pressure fed into the rolls at a constant rate by *pinch or feed rolls. **1958** H. G. M. Spratt *Magnetic Tape Recording* vii. 202 The tape..is held in tight contact with it [*sc.* a roller] by means of a spring-loaded, free-running, rubber or rubber-covered roll generally referred to as the pinch roll. **1960** A. R. Bailey *Text-bk. Metall.* (ed. 2) 402 The steel slabs pass directly from the reheating furnace to a pair of pinch rolls that grip the metal and force it into the mill. **1964** A. A. McWilliams *Tape Recording* viii. 160 The tape is held in firm contact—with a rotating spindle—the capstan—by means of a rubber-tyred pressure roller, or pinch roll. **1969** W. R. R. Park *Plastics Film Technol.* ii. 41 At the same time, the pinch rolls are pulling the film away. **1949** S. J. Begun *Magnetic Recording* vi. 174 An interesting feature of this equipment is the..spindle which acts as a capstan as soon as a rubber-tyred *pinch roller sandwiches the tape against it. **1961** G. L. Davies *Magnetic Tape Instrumentation* iv. 79 The pinch roller..is operated by a solenoid. **1974** *Physics Bull.* Apr. 151/1 Another feature is the vacuum buffered, low tension drive which eliminates pinch-rollers and associated mechanical problems. **1961** J. S. Salak *Dict. Amer. Sports* 328 *Pinch runner* (baseball, softball), a substitute runner for a teammate who has reached a base, the original runner being out of the game from that time on. **1970** *Toronto Daily Star* 24 Sept. 17/1 Cash wound up at second and pinch-runner Freddie Patek at third. **1976** *Billings* (Montana) *Gaz.* 20 June 4-E/4 Tim Foli singled off starter Tommy John to open the inning and was replaced by pinch-runner Jim Lyttle. **1611** Shaks. *Temp.* iv. i. 261 Shorten vp their sinewes With aged Cramps, & more *pinch-spotted make them, Then Pard, or Cat o'Mountaine. **1969** *Times* 31 Jan. 55 Among the customers for his men's clothes—distinguishable by their long jackets and *pinch waists—are movie stars, [etc.]. **1975** M. Bradbury *Hist. Man* i. 11 She wears a white pinch-waist, full-length raincoat. **1977** *Times* 5 Oct. (Fashion Suppl.) p. i/7 The lavishly lapelled, *pinch-waisted..caricature..of the Italian style. **1681** *Phil. Trans.* XII. 103 After great Rains,..or strong westerly Winds,..then the *Pinch-water will be found earlier..by about half an hour. **1883** *Academy* 11 Aug. 92 Every leaf has a dark spot in the centre, just as though it had been pinched, on which account it goes by the name of *pinch-weed. **1962** H. B. Hadden *High-Quality Sound Production & Reproduction* x. 160 The tape is held in contact with the capstan by the *pinch wheel. **1968** C. N. G. Matthews *Tape Recording* iv. 36 The capstan and pinch wheel are disengaged.

ˈpinchable, *a.* [f. pinch *v.* + -able.] That may be pinched; that invites pinching. Hence **ˈpinchably** *adv.*

1921 *Public Opinion* 15 July 56/1 The greater the pinchable surface, the sharper the tweak that you will get. **1939** Joyce *Finnegans Wake* (1964) III. 417 As entomate as intimate could pinchably be. **1977** P. Ustinov *Dear Me* ix. 120 This volatile hedonist, with his unending stream of pinchable starlets.

†**ˈpinchbeck, -beke**, *sb.*[1] *Obs. rare.* [f. pinch- + ? beak.] A miserly, close-fisted person.

1545 Elyot *Dict.*, *Aridus homo*, a drye felowe, of whom nothyng may be gotten, som do call hym a pelt, or a pynchebeke. **1552** Huloet, Pynchebecke.

pinchbeck (ˈpɪn(t)ʃbɛk), *sb.*[2] (*a.*) [Named after the inventor Christopher Pinchbeck, a watch- and toy-maker in Fleet Street, London (died 1732); orig. a place-name; there is a village so named near Spalding. Hence F. *peinchebec* (Littré).

1732 *Daily Post* 27 Nov. (*Advt.*), That the toys made of the late ingenious Mr. Pinchbeck's curious metal..are now sold only by his son and sole executor, Mr. Edward Pinchbeck. **1755** Lady M. W. Montagu *Let. to C'tess Bute* 22 Sept., In the next box, put up..three of Pinchbec's watches, shagrine cases, and enamelled dial-plates. **1776** 'M. Mac-Gregor' [W. Mason] *Ode to C. Pinchbeck* (the Younger), For thy sake Of Pinchbeck's own mixt-metal make A huge Extinguisher.]

1. An alloy of about five parts of copper with one of zinc, resembling gold: used in clock-making, cheap jewellery, etc.

1734 Fielding *Intrig. Chamberm.* I. vii, He said,..that the nobility and gentry run so much into Pinchbeck, that he had not dispos'd of two gold watches this month. **1812** Sir H. Davy *Chem. Philos.* 419 United to zinc, copper produced Dutch gold, Rupert's metal and pinchbeck—from a third to a twelfth of zinc is used, the paler the alloy required the larger the quantity of zinc. **1825** J. Nicholson *Operat. Mechanic* 708 *Pinchbeck.*—No. 1. 5 oz. of pure copper, and 1 oz. of zinc... Some use only half this quantity of zinc, in which proportion the alloy is more easily worked, especially in the making of jewellery. **1885** R. Buchanan *Annan Water* xxv, He wore a massive chain of gold or pinchbeck.

2. *fig.* Contemptuously, as a type of what is counterfeit or spurious.

1859 Thackeray *Virgin.* xxii, Those golden locks were only pinchbeck. **1887** Lowell *Old Eng. Dram.* (1892) 128 The greater part of what I once took on trust as precious is really paste and pinchbeck. **1890** *Spectator* 24 May, Is it necessary..that the pinchbeck as well as the gold left behind him by this voluminous writer, should be preserved?

3. *attrib.* or as *adj.* **a.** Made of pinchbeck.

1746 Cooke in Hanway *Trav.* (1762) I. iv. liv. 248 Gold, silver and pinchbeck snuff-boxes. **1849** C. Bronte *Shirley* ii, He has a sort of pinchbeck watch; ditto, ring.

b. Of deceptive appearance and small value; spurious; simulating the genuine article; sham.

1850 Carlyle *Latter-d. Pamph.* iv. (1872) 113 Eloquent high-lacquered pinchbeck specimens. **1877** Symonds *Renaiss. Italy, Reviv. Learn.* viii. 505 A pinchbeck age of poetry. **1883** *Fortn. Rev.* Feb. 304 Overt State action against this pinch-beck Pretender may be..defended.

4. *Comb.*

1879 Rutley *Study Rocks* x. 119 The colour is..brownish-green, or pinchbeck-brown.

pinch-bug. *U.S.* A stag-beetle belonging to the family Lucanidæ.

1856 'Mark Twain' *Let.* 25 May in *Iowa Jrnl. Hist.* (1929) XXVII. 423 A tenor and bass duet by thirty-two thousand locusts and ninety-seven thousand pinch-bugs was sung. **1870** E. Eggleston *Bk. Queer Stories* ix. 74 We came to a log on which two of that sort of beetles that children call 'pinch-bugs', were fighting. **1876** 'Mark Twain' *Tom Sawyer* v. 47 It was a large black beetle with formidable jaws—a 'pinch-bug' he called it. **1915** W. A. Bryan *Nat. Hist. Hawaii* xxxi. 417 The stag-beetles or pinch bugs, so called on account of their large mandibles. **1959** A. B. & E. B. Klots *Living Insects of World* 132/2 There is little doubt that the 'pinch bug' Tom Sawyer took to church was a stag beetle.

pinche (pɪn(t)ʃ). Also 8 pinch. [a. F. *pinche*, ad. Sp. *pincho* (also in Eng. use).] A South American species of marmoset (*Midas œdipus*). Also *attrib.*

[**1745** La Condamine *Relat. Voy. Amer. Mérid.* 165 On les nomme Pinchés à Maynas, & à Cayenne, Tamarins.] **1774** Goldsm. *Nat. Hist.* IV. 237 The fifth is called the Pinch; with the face of a beautiful black, and white hair that descends on each side of the face, like that of man. **1780** Smellie tr. *Buffon's Nat. Hist.* (1791) VIII. 211 The Pinche, or Red-tailed Monkey,..though very small, is larger than either the ouistiti or the tamarin. **1890** *Cent. Dict.*, Pincho. **1896** *List Anim. Zool. Soc. Lond.* (ed. 9) 45 *Midas œdipus* (Linn.) Pinche Monkey. Hab. Colombia.

pinched (pɪn(t)ʃt), *ppl. a.* [f. pinch *v.* + -ed[1].]

1. a. Compressed between the finger and thumb, or two opposing bodies; nipped, squeezed; shaped as if compressed; contracted at one part. Also with *in*, *up*.

c **1530** L. Cox *Rhet.* (1899) 53 Thersites, with croked and penched shulders. **1610** B. Jonson *Alch.* I. i, Like the father of hunger,..with your pinch'd-horne-nose. **1611** Shaks. *Wint. T.* II. i. 51 He ha's discouer'd my Designe, and I Remaine a pinch'd Thing; yea, a very Trick For them to play at will. **1675** *Lond. Gaz.* No. 955/4 A Black Gelding,..a shorn Mane, pinch'd Buttock. **1836–9** Dickens *Sk. Boz, Th. about People*, Scanty grey trousers, little pinched-up gaiters. **1920** [see *dock-glass* s.v. dock *sb.*[3] 7]. **1941** *Amer. Speech* XVI. 67/1 Avoid pinched-in-waistlines for teen ages.

b. ? Castrated by ligature.

1514 *Will of Busby* (Somerset Ho.), A pynched oxe.

c. Of a ship: Much curved inward above the line of her extreme breadth; also ***pinched-in***.

1704 J. Harris *Lex. Techn.* I. s.v. *Housed*, She is Housed-in, or Pinched-in too much. **1867** Smyth *Sailor's Word-bk.* s.v. *Housing in*, She is said to be housed in, or pinched.

d. Of oysters: Long and narrow in form.

1890 in *Cent. Dict.*

e. *Physics.* Confined by the pinch effect.

1907 *Trans. Amer. Electrochem. Soc.* XI. 331, *C* is the column of liquid conductor,..and *P* is one of these pinched contractions. **1951** *Proc. Physical Soc.* B. LXIV. 161 Just after the breakdown the discharge..is observed to contract into a narrow filament; the discharge does not stay 'pinched' but immediately expands again, and proceeds to oscillate. **1959** *Daily Tel.* 23 July 7/8 But, unlike Zeta, the pinched gas will be stable. **1962** *Times* 28 Apr. 8/4 The first photograph of a 'pinched' lightning discharge has been obtained. **1973** Kettani & Hoyaux *Plasma Engin.* vii. 206 Consider a pinched column of fully ionised plasma.

2. Said in reference to the physical effects of cold, hunger, pain, or old age. Also with *up*, and parasynthetic, as ***pinched faced***, etc.

1614 D. Dyke *Myst. Self-Deceiuing* (1630) 83 Pinched with famine. **1807** Crabbe *Par. Reg.* II. 193 Pinched are her looks, as one who pines for bread. **1838** Dickens *Nich. Nick.* xxxii, Pale and pinched-up faces hovered about the windows. **1904** *Daily Chron.* 22 Oct. 4/5 Pinched-faced children whose under-feeding is caused by this kind of malnutrition.

†**3.** Gathered, pleated (cf. pinch *v.* 3). *Obs.*

1509–10 *Act 1 Hen. VIII*, c. 14 §1 No manne undre the degree of a Knyght [shall] were any garded or pynshed Sherte or pynched partelet of Lynnen clothe.

4. Straitened in extent; small, narrow, scanty.

1649 G. Daniel *Trinarch., Hen. V*, cclxi, Narrower Fames In a pinch't Canvace. **1691** tr. *Emilianne's Frauds Romish Monks* (ed. 3) 34 Their Cells..being too mean and ..too much pinch'd of room. **1894** N. Brooks *Tales Maine Coast* 94 A little pinched-up flower-garden lay between the house and the..river.

5. Straitened in means or circumstances.

1716 Hearne *Collect.* (O.H.S.) V. 159 Yet he is not pinch'd, being very rich as well as very stingy. **1840** Dickens *Barn. Rudge* xlv, Do you know how pinched and destitute I am? **1891** Baring-Gould *In Troubadour-Land* xx, They lived..in very pinched circumstances.

6. Suffering from a pang, distressed.

1900 Mrs. Craigie *R. Orange* xxii, With a pinched heart she went up the great staircase.

7. Of paper: slightly smaller than the normal size (see quots.).

1893 J. Kay *Paper* 100 Sizes of Papers... Demy..Post.. Pinched Post..Foolscap. **1894** G. Clapperton *Pract. Paper-Making* 193 Sizes of Lined Papers. Pinched for 8vo Expansion by 14½ in. **1926** *Paper Terminol.* (Spalding & Hodge) 20 *Pinched post*, a standard size of writing paper measuring 14½ × 18½ in. **1952** E. J. Labarre *Dict. Paper* (ed. 2) 199/1 *Pinched post*, a size of writing paper standardized at 18½" × 14½", but with variants still in use, also for drawings. .. For 'pinched' the same word is used in Dutch: *geknepen*, when a sheet is slightly reduced from the standard or normal dimensions for that size. **1962** F. T. Day *Introd. to Paper* vii. 70 An even greater variety of sizes is covered by these names by the addition of qualifying words—Single or Half, Double or Quad, Small or Large, Extra or Super, Pinched or Reduced. *Ibid.*, Pinched Post..14½ × 18½ in. Pinched Post (Double)..18½ × 29 in.

Hence **ˈpinchedly** *adv.*; **ˈpinchedness.**

1883 Miss Broughton *Belinda* I. ii, The pear-tree..was pinchedly struggling into flower. **1871** *Daily News* 11 Apr. 6, I saw both boaters and bathers..and the like for pinchedness, blueness, and overwhelming miser, may I never see again. **1877** Morley *Crit. Misc.* Ser. II. 276 The pinchedness of the real world about them.

pinch effect. [f. pinch *sb.* + effect *sb.*]

1. *Physics.* The constriction exhibited by a fluid through which a large electric current is flowing, caused by the attractive force produced by the interaction of the current with its own magnetic field.

[**1907** E. F. Northrup in *Physical Rev.* June 474 Some months ago, my friend, Carl Hering, described to me a surprising and apparently new phenomenon which he had observed. He found, in passing a relatively large alternating current through a non-electrolytic, liquid conductor contained in a trough, that the liquid contracted in cross-section and flowed up hill lengthwise of the trough... Mr. Hering suggested the idea that this contraction was probably due to the elastic action of the lines of magnetic force which encircle the conductor... As the action of the forces on the conductor is to squeeze or pinch it, he jocosely called it the 'pinch phenomenon'. **1907** C. Hering in *Trans. Amer. Electrochem. Soc.* Sept. 331 As the column of liquid looks as though it were being pinched by some mysterious and invisible force, the writer termed it the 'pinch phenomenon'. *Ibid.* 337 If to this field there is added another one, I see no reason why it should not add to the pinching effect.] **1911** G. H. Clamer in *Ibid.* XIX. 264 The heavy current..rapidly brings these columns of metal to the liquid condition, and produces therein the 'pinch' effect. **1956** *Sci. News Let.* 15 Sept. 174/1 Generating the high heat ..requires containers that will not melt or be otherwise affected. Using the 'pinch effect' would seem to eliminate the container problem, since the reacting gas column would contract to contain itself, thus not touch any walls. **1958** *Listener* 25 Sept. 454/2 The Americans and Russians independently have developed a principle different from Zeta, although both are working on the Zeta principle of what is known as the pinch effect. **1966** *McGraw-Hill Encycl. Sci. & Technol.* X. 233/1 The force of the pinch effect has..been known to manifest itself by a crushing of tubular conductors exposed to large impulsive currents such as occur in lightning strokes or high-power short circuits. **1972** *Physics Bull.* Feb. 83/2 Flash photolysis features in the Exhibition. Chelsea Instruments is showing its apparatus (based on its Garton flash tube) which utilizes the pinch effect (as in some thermonuclear apparatus) to produce high intensity.

2. The slight narrowing of a record groove caused by the transverse movement of the cutting stylus, resulting in a vertical movement of the stylus at that point during playing.

1935 H. C. Bryson *Gramophone Record* x. 271 Hill and Dale cut records possess great advantages... There is no pinch effect. **1965** J. Walton *Pick-Ups* iii. 40 A mono pick-up (as well as of course the stereo pick-up) should have some vertical compliance and low vertical mass if pinch effect is not to cause damage and excessive 'needle talk'. **1975** G. J. King *Audio Handbk.* viii. 192 Because the groove is cut by a chisel-shaped tool whose face is at right-angles to the motion of the record, the groove width decreases along the sloping sides of the waveform... This, called 'pinch effect', results in vertical oscillation of the replay stylus at a frequency twice that of the modulation and hence in second-harmonic distortion.

pinchem (ˈpɪn(t)ʃəm). [Echoic: from the bird's note.] A local name of the Blue Titmouse.

1809 T. Batchelor *Anal. Eng. Lang.* 140 *Pinchem*, a tom-tit, whose note resembles this name. **1885** in Swainson *Prov. Names Brit. Birds* 34.

pincher (ˈpɪn(t)ʃə(r)). [f. pinch *v.* + -er[1].]

1. One who or that which pinches; *fig.* one who saves in a miserly manner; a miser; a haggler.

c **1440** *Promp. Parv.* 399/2 Pynchar, or nyggarde. **1591** Percivall *Sp. Dict.*, *Regaton*, a pedler, a broker, a pincher in buying, a hucster. **1887** Gissing *Thyrza* III. iii. 62 Cold-blooded pinchers and parers.

2. One who uses a pinch or crow-bar.

1882 in OGILVIE.

3. An instrument for pinching or grasping something; in pl. ***pinchers*** often = PINCERS (for which it is widely used in the dialects).

1575 TURBERV. *Venerie* 182 Take out the Foxe or Badgerde with the clampes or pinchers. **1589** NASHE *Pasquil's Ret.* Wks. (Grosart) I. 115 They take the word by the nose with a paire of Pinchers. **1655** GOUGE *Comm. Heb.* xi. 37 The..persecutors..plucked off..his flesh with red hot pinchers. **1709** *Brit. Apollo* II. Supernum. No. 2.2/2 [A tooth] which I can't pull out with a Pincher. **1868** KEY *Philol. Ess.* 191 Thus *forcipes*, as 'a pair of pinchers' for the extraction of teeth, is used by Lucilius. **1884** KNIGHT *Dict. Mech.* Suppl., *Pincher*,..a nipping tool fitting the inside and outside of a bottle, in order to shape the mouth.

pinch-eyed to **pinch-fisted**: see PINCH-.

'pinch-gut, *sb.* (*a.*) Now *Obs.* or *vulgar.* [f. PINCH- + GUT.]

1. One who stints himself or others of food: = *pinch-belly* (PINCH-).

a **1659** *Lady Alimony* II. ii, A Mundungo's Monopolist, a paltry-penurious-pecking pinchgut. **1699** T. BROWN in R. L'Estrange *Erasm. Colloq.* (1711) 356 Did old Pinch-gut devour all his grey-pease by himself? **1828** *Craven Gloss.* (ed. 2), *Pinch-gut*, a covetous person, who will neither fill his own belly nor suffer his dependants to do so. **1867** SMYTH *Sailor's Word-bk.*, *Pinch-gut*, a miserly purser.

2. *attrib.* or *adj.* **a.** That pinches the stomach; niggardly or scanty in respect of food; in quot. 1682, characterized by scarcity of food. **b.** ***pinch-gut money*** (*Naut. slang*): money allowed to sailors in compensation for short allowance of food.

1615 BRATHWAIT *Strappado* (1878) 35 A pinch-gut Miser fell extreamely sicke. **1660** in *7th Rep. Hist. MSS. Comm.* 141 John Price..complains that Richard Hutchinson has wronged him by paying £16, besides Pinchgutt mony, to a wrong person. **1682** T. FLATMAN *Heraclitus Ridens* No. 65 (1713) II. 156 'Twas..promised, that the poor Prisoners should have Amends..for that pinch-gut Year they had. *a* **1700** B. E. *Dict. Cant. Crew*, *Pinch-gut-money*, allow'd by the King to the Seamen,..on Bord the Navy.., when their Provision falls Short. **1867** SMYTH *Sailor's Word-bk.*, *Pinch-gut pay*, the short allowance money.

So † **'pinch-gutted** *a.*, pinched in the stomach, famished.

1704 N. N. tr. *Boccalini's Advts. fr. Parnass.* III. 349 To satisfie so many hungry, ravenous,..pinch-gutted Fellows.

pinching ('pɪn(t)ʃɪŋ), *vbl. sb.* [f. PINCH *v.* + -ING[1].] The action of the verb, in various senses.

1. a. Compression between the tips of the finger and thumb or other opposing surfaces; nipping, squeezing, pressing; *spec.* in the manège (see quot. 1727–41); in *Hort*, (see PINCH *v.* 2 b).

1693 EVELYN *De la Quint. Compl. Gard.* I. 10 Besides the Pruning..we sometimes perform another Operation which we call Pinching or Breaking..: The Effect of this Pinching is to hinder the Branches from growing too thick..as also from growing too long. **1706** LONDON & WISE *Retir'd Gard.* I. II. v, The pinching of Peach-trees is a sort of Pruning, which is done by the Nails to Three or Four Eyes upon a new tender Shoot. **1727–41** CHAMBERS *Cycl.*, *Pinching*, in the manage, is when, the horse standing, the rider holds him fast with the bridle-hand, and applies the spurs just to the hairs of his sides, without pricking him. **1823** J. BADCOCK *Dom. Amusem.* 113 Repeated pinchings, left the patient in comparative ease. **1899** *Westm. Gaz.* 29 Mar. 5/3 They [railway employés]..were..disposed to make light of risks .. invariably referred to the horrible death between the buffers as 'pinching'.

b. *concr. pl.* What is pinched or nipped *off*.

1688 R. HOLME *Armoury* III. 89/2 Twitchings, ends of Horse-shooe Nails cut off. Pinchings, because pinched and writhen off from the out side of the hoof with the Pincers.

2. The sensation caused by pinching or gripping; the pressure of pain. Also *fig.*

1495 *Trevisa's Barth. De P.R.* v. xxxiii. (W. de W.) iv b/2 A lityl pryckyng other pinching in þe brest within is more sore than a grete wounde in þe arme. **1587** FLEMING *Contn. Holinshed* III. 1588/2 That other needfull vittels shall..grow to excessiue prices, to the pinching of the poorer sort. **1790** J. C. SMYTH in *Med. Commun.* II. 518 Patients have complained of slight griping, or pinching in their bowels.

†**3.** The action of cavilling or finding fault. *Obs.*

c **1530** L. COX *Rhet.* (1899) 51 By pynchynge and blamynge of our aduersarie.

4. Stinting as from straitened means; parsimony.

c **1440** *Promp. Parv.* 400/1 Pynchynge (or nyggardshepe). **1531** ELYOT *Gov.* III. xxii, Moche pinchyng and nygardshyppe of meate and drinke. **1653** URQUHART *Rabelais* I. iv. 23 There should be no want nor pinching for any thing. **1863** MISS YONGE *C'tess Kate* ii, There would not be so much pinching in the housekeeping.

5. In various other senses: see the verb.

1859 F. A. GRIFFITHS *Artil. Man.* (1862) 110 Pinching is the operation of moving a gun or mortar by small heaves of the handspike. **1903** *Westm. Gaz.* 17 June 9/1 The pinching out of the reef in the Chicago level.

6. *Comb.*: **pinching-bar** = *pinch-bar* (PINCH-); **pinching bug** = PINCH-BUG; † **pinching-iron**, (*a*) *sing.* and *pl.*, pincers, tweezers; (*b*) *pl.* curling-tongs; **pinching-nut** = *jam nut* (JAM *sb.*[1]); **pinching-pin**, in the steam-engine, a pin which keeps the slide-valve tightened on its seating; † **pinching-post**, in coursing deer in a paddock, the post marking the point which the deer had to pass before a victory could be claimed for either dog; **pinching-screw**, a screw which adjusts or fixes parts of a mechanism by compression; **pinching-tongs** (see quot.).

1850 L. H. GARRARD *Wah-to-Yah* xix. 253 Noah was so hurried to git the yelaphants, *pinchin bugs, an' sich varment aboard. **1877** R. J. BURDETTE *Rise & Fall of Mustache* 77 That Bilderback boy..put a pinching-bug as big as a postage-stamp down a boy's back. **1928** METCALF & FLINT *Destructive & Useful Insects* i. 16 A certain amount of pain may result from mere mechanical injury by insects as when a boy finds a 'pinching bug' for the first time. **1954** BORROR & DELONG *Introd. Study Insects* xxii. 381 These large brownish beetles [*sc.* stag beetles] are sometimes called pinchingbugs because of the large mandibles of the male. **1519** HORMAN *Vulg.* 169 b, They..plucke out theyr hearis with *pynchynge yrons. **1789** MRS. PIOZZI *Journ. France* I. 277 Heating the pinching-irons to curl my hair. **1875** KNIGHT *Dict. Mech.*, **Pinching-nut*, a jam-nut screwed down upon another nut, to hold it in position. **1839** R. S. ROBINSON *Naut. Steam Eng.* 105 The cap and *pinching pin, by which the clutch is secured to it. **1741** *Compl. Fam. Piece* II. i. 309 The third the Half Mile Post: The fourth the *Pinching Post. **1840** BLAINE *Encycl. Rur. Sports* (1870) §1953 If the deer swerved before he got to the pinching-post ..it was deemed no match. **1837** GORING & PRITCHARD *Microgr.* 9 A spring tube travelling on a slide, with a *pinching screw underneath, by which it is adjusted at a proper distance from the object. **1884** C. G. W. LOCK *Workshop Receipts* Ser. III 89/2 Nickel-plated caps, split and held by pinching screws to the carbon and zinc rods. **1875** KNIGHT *Dict. Mech.*, **Pinching-tongs* (Glass making), used for making chandelier drops, etc. Each jaw of the tongs carries a die, between which a lump of glass heated to plasticity is compressed.

pinching ('pɪn(t)ʃɪŋ), *ppl. a.* (*adv.*) [f. PINCH *v.* + -ING[2].] That pinches, in senses of the verb.

1. Compressing between two surfaces; squeezing.

1883 *Daily News* 10 May 5/1 Their narrow waists, their pinching shoes.

2. Causing pain or distress, physical or mental (likened to the effect of pressure); pressing severely or painfully; reducing to straits; distressing.

1565 COOPER *Thesaurus* s.v. *Aculeus*, The pinchyng cares and griefe of minde. **1579** SPENSER *Sheph. Cal.* Apr. 18 Ys loue such pinching payne? **1583** STUBBES *Anat. Abus.* II. (1882) 52 They applie..gnawing corrosiues, and pinching plaistures. **1667** MILTON *P.L.* x. 691 Pinching cold and scorching heate. **1753** *Stewart's Trial* 222 These circumstances are so pinching against the pannel, upon the capital point now in issue. **1822–34** *Good's Study Med.* (ed. 4) III. 276 Severe and pinching hunger. **1883** STEVENSON *Treas. Isl.* I. ii, One January morning,..a pinching, frosty morning.

3. Characterized by or involving stinting or parsimony, straitened; niggardly, parsimonious, grudging; restrained, very sparing.

1576 FLEMING *Panopl. Epist.* 49, I was more pinching and sparing in my writing concerning them. **1583** BABINGTON *Commandm.* viii. (1637) 80 Of malice and spite, or by a pinching minde. **1621** T. WILLIAMSON tr. *Goulart's Wise Vieillard* 73 Sometimes shee is all for belly cheare and banquettings,..then shee is niggardly and pinching againe. **1724** SWIFT *Reas. agst. Exam. Drugs* ¶6 Persons in pinching circumstances with numerous families of children. **1807** CRABBE *Par. Reg.* I. 447 Sparing, not pinching, mindful, though not mean.

4. Contracted, compressed, narrow; *spec.* in *Mining* (see PINCH *v.* 14).

a **1617** HIERON *Wks.* I. 7 It is a great eye-sore, to see a little, low, and pinching entry to a large and spacious dwelling. **1793** WOLLASTON in *Phil. Trans.* LXXXIII. 146 To..make the angle less pinching. **1898** M. DAVITT *Life & Progr. Australia* I. iii. 13 That these fields were of the 'pocket' and pinching-out character.

†**5.** *Mus.* ? Applied to higher notes (harmonics) produced on a wind instrument by stronger pressure of breath. *Obs. rare.*

1688 R. HOLME *Armoury* III. 161/1 Wind Musick *Pinching Notes* or *higher Notes*, are sounds that ascend 8 Notes higher than the plain notes.

B. as *adv.* = PINCHINGLY.

1620 VENNER *Via Recta* (1650) 225 When the weather is pinching cold. **1698** FRYER *Acc. E. India & P.* 295 It is pinching Cold, from January to the middle of February.

Hence **'pinchingly** *adv.*, in a pinching manner.

1574 T. CARTWRIGHT *Full Declar.* 113 We ought not to deale with them sparingly, couetouslye, and pinchingly. **1690** SHARPE *Wks.* (1754) I. Serm. vii. 190 Giving stingily and pinchingly, now and then a little pocket-money or so. **1825** R. WARD *Tremaine* III. xiii. 233, I have felt that case.. as pinchingly as..you would have me. **1859** RUSKIN *Arrows of Chace* I. 202 Our colleges..are..richly built, never pinchingly.

pinch-off. *Electronics.* Also pinch off. [f. vbl. phr. *to pinch off* s.v. PINCH *v.* 2 e.] In a field-effect transistor, the meeting of the two non-conducting depletion layers that border the channel, such that little further increase in current is achieved by increasing the drain voltage. Freq. *attrib.*, esp. in **pinch-off voltage**, the reverse bias that must be applied to the gate to achieve pinch-off and prevent the flow of current through the channel (equal to the drain voltage at which the current saturates when there is no bias applied to the gate).

1952 W. SHOCKLEY in *Proc. IRE* XL. 1367/1 W_0 is the magnitude of reverse bias required to make the space charge penetrate the entire *p*-region. We shall refer to it as the 'pinch-off voltage' since it is the voltage that will reduce the channel to zero and pinch off the conducting path. *Ibid.* 1374/1 We shall consider a structure operated with the drain beyond pinch-off. **1956** L. P. HUNTER *Handbk. Semiconductor Electronics* IV. 31 For the depletion region to fill the entire channel b = 0 and V(b) = V_0... V_0 is called the pinch-off voltage. *Ibid.* 32 As the bias..at the drain end is increased beyond V_0, the pinch-off condition moves toward the source. The field between the drain end and the point along the channel where pinch off is effectively reached must be large enough to maintain the current I flowing in the open part of the channel. **1962** J. EVANS *Fund. Princ. Transistors* x. 228 If V_G is large enough, pinch-off occurs at all values of V_D—the situation when $V_G = W_0$. **1972** *Field-Effect Transistors* (Mullard Ltd., London) ii. 8 The line joining the various drain-source voltages $V_{DS(p)}$ at which this pinch-off occurs (the pinch-off limit) is shown as a broken line in Fig. 7... To the right of the pinch-off limit —in the pinch-off region—the drain current only increases very slightly. **1974** HARVEY & BOHLMAN *Stereo F.M. Radio Handbk.* v. 88 The voltage corresponding to zero I_d is called the pinch-off voltage.

pinch-out. *Geol.* [f. vbl. phr. *to pinch out* s.v. PINCH *v.* 14.] A narrowing of a stratum, vein, or other body of rock to the point of extinction.

1928 in *Funk's Stand. Dict.* **1941** *Bull. Amer. Assoc. Petroleum Geologists* XXV. 1258 A pinch-out of a reservoir sand on a structural nose would..be considered a stratigraphic trap of a less perfect type. **1962** *Courier-Mail* (Brisbane) 15 Dec. 9/3 Seismic surveys had outlined a large closed structure which also had good stratigraphic pinch-out possibilities. **1974** P. L. MOORE et al. *Drilling Practices Manual* xii. 300 These permeability barriers may be faults, folds, salt domes, or permeability pinchouts.

'pinchpenny ('pɪn(t)ʃ,pɛnɪ). Pl. **-pennies**, also 6 **-pence**. [f. PINCH- + PENNY.] A niggardly person; a skinflint, a miser. Also *attrib.*

c **1412** HOCCLEVE *De Reg. Princ.* 4095 (MS. Reg. 17 D vi) Thou pynchepeny, there ay mote thou slepe. **1569** NEWTON *Cicero's Olde Age* 48 Myserable nygardes and penchpenies. **1577** tr. *Bullinger's Decades* (1592) 288 Let our wealthie pinchpence..leaue their..insatiable couetousnesse. **1582** STANYHURST *Æneis* I. (Arb.) 29 Pigmalions riches was shipt, that pinchepeny boucher. **1644** BULWER *Chirol.* 179 A close-fisted niggard,..an old pinch-penny. *a* **1693** *Urquhart's Rabelais* III. iv. 45 None will be..a Pinch-penny. **1931** 'D. STIFF' *Milk & Honey Route* viii. 85 You can always tell the home of the pinchpenny by the narrowness of the eaves. **1948** *Sun* (Baltimore) 8 Apr. 1/7 Lee M. Wiggins, Under Secretary of the Treasury, today warned Congress that a pinchpenny policy toward the Bureau of Internal Revenue will cost the nation billions in evaded taxes. **1955** T. STERLING *Evil of Day* i. 13 No pinchpenny ever knew anything about pennies. You have to spend them to know. **1977** *New Yorker* 25 July 36/2 In contrast to pinchpenny P.R. routine of the environmentalist groups..the Dow P.R. material is handsomely bound, with expensive paper, elegant design, and, sometimes, four-color illustrations. **1978** 'F. PARRISH' *Sting of Honeybee* iii. 39 The fences were a weird, pinchpenny patchwork, but they kept the ponies in.

pinch-plane to **pinch-point**: see PINCH-.

pinck: see PINK.

pincon, var. PINSON[1] *Obs.*

pinc-pinc ('pɪŋkpɪŋk). [Echoic, from the bird's note.] A name given to a South-African warbler (*Drymœca* or *Cisticola textrix*), to which has been erroneously attributed the building of the remarkable double nest of the Cotton-bird (*Ægithalus capensis*).

1868 WOOD *Homes without H.* xii. 217 The Pinc-pinc of Africa..has a similar custom, constructing a supplementary roosting-place upon the nest. **1894** NEWTON *Dict. Birds*, *Pinc-pinc* (or rather 'Tinc-tinc'), the name which a South-African bird..has given itself from its ringing metallic cry.

pincushion ('pɪn,kʊʃən).

1. A small cushion used for sticking pins in, to keep them ready for use.

1632 SHERWOOD, A pinne-case, pinne-pillow, or pinne-cushion. **1658** A. FOX *Würtz' Surg.* II. xv. 121 One leaning on a Pin-cushion, a needle run into his Finger, and a piece of it broke off. **1729** MRS. DELANY in *Life & Corr.* (1861) I. 209, I have got her pincushion to stick for her. **1865** DICKENS *Mut. Fr.* II. i, A little pincushion, a little housewife, a little book, a little workbox.

2. Local name for plants of the genus *Scabiosa*; also for the Guelder Rose and other plants: from the appearance of the flower-heads.

1886 in BRITTEN & HOLLAND *Eng. Plant-n.* **1898** BRITTON & BROWN *Illustr. Flora Northern U.S.* III. 290 Field Scabious..[is also called] blue caps, gypsy- or egyptian-rose, pincushion. **1965** *Austral. Encycl.* VII. 118/2 Pincushion, Australian, or blue pincushion, the popular name for *Brunonia*,..low herbaceous perennials, bearing blue flowers in very effective long-stalked heads; the projecting styles resemble pins sticking in a cushion.

3. ***sea pincushion***: a large kind of starfish.

1863 G. S. BRADY in *Intell. Observ.* IV. 253 *Goniaster equestris*, the Sea-pincushion, as it is called by our northern fishermen..the large fleshy mass of the animal is covered thickly with round bosses or tubercles of the size of a large pin's head.

4. a. *attrib.* and *Comb.*, as ***pincushion-box***, ***-flower*** (= sense 2), ***-maker***.

1706 *Lond. Gaz.* No. 4206/4 Stolen.., a Pincushion-Box. **1758–65** GOLDSM. *Ess.*, *Adv. Strolling Player*, He to sell his puppets to the pincusion-makers in Rosemary Lane. **1856** DELAMER *Fl. Gard.* (1861) 103 *Scabiosa atro-purpurea*... Pincushion Flower. **1911** W. R. GUILFOYLE *Austral. Plants* 201 *Hakea laurina* 'Pin Cushion Flower' (evergreen shrub or tree, 10 to 30 ft.), f[lowers] crimson—W. Aust. **1917** L. H. BAILEY *Stand. Cycl. Hort.* VI. 3106/1 *(caption) Scabiosa atropurpurea*.—The mourning bride or pin-cushion flower. **1938** T. Y. HARRIS *Wild Flowers Austral.* 25 Pincushion Flower (*Hakea laurina*)... Pink blossoms with cream stigmas projecting for some distance and the flowers in globular heads have earned the name for this most attractive plant. **1967** A. M. BLOMBERY *Guide Native Austral. Plants* III. 265 *H[akea] laurina*. Pincushion Hakea. A large bushy shrub with flat, lanceolate, greenish-red leaves and pink pincushion-like flowers. **1972** F. PERRY *Flowers of World* 101/1 *S[cabiosa] caucasica*, the Pincushion Flower, was introduced to Britain in 1591 and has become a favourite for border and cut-flower work.

b. pincushion distortion, a form of optical distortion in which a square is reproduced with sides curved inwards.

[**1886** J. H. DALLMEYER *Choice & Use Photogr. Lenses* 22 If the stop is placed at the same distance *behind* the lens.. the result is the opposite kind, or 'pincushion'-shaped distortion.] **1892** A. BROTHERS *Photography* I. iii. 48 The effect consists.. in the curvature of the images of straight lines produced by marginal rays causing barrel-shaped or 'pincushion distortion'. **1903, 1953** [see *barrel distortion* s.v. BARREL *sb.* 11]. **1965** *Wireless World* July 58 (Advt.), No oscilloscope is better than its tube. Build in all the circuit refinements you like, if the tube suffers from.. pin-cushion distortion.. your efforts are in vain. **1972** WILLIAMS & BECKLUND *Optics* viii. 188 An aperture stop located between a positive lens and the image increases pincushion distortion.

Hence (*nonce-wds.*) **'pin͵cushioned** *a.* or *pa. pple.*, pierced, like a pincushion with pins; **'pin͵cushiony** *a.*, resembling a pincushion.

1860 THACKERAY *Lovel the Widower* iv, Her heart was pincushioned with his filial crimes. **1852** MRS. STOWE *Uncle Tom's C.* xiii, A little, short, round, pincushiony woman stood at the door.

pind, *v. Obs.* exc. *dial.* Forms: 1 (ȝe)pyndan, 3 punde (ü), puinde, 5–6 pynd(e, 5, 9 *dial.* pind. [OE. (*ȝe*)*pyndan* (cf. also *forpyndan* to exclude, bar), f. **pund*: see POUND *sb.*², POND. Cf. ON. *pynda* to extort, torment (considered by Vigf. to be from OE.).]

†**1.** *trans.* To shut up, enclose; to dam up (water). *Obs.* in *gen.* sense.

c **897** K. ÆLFRED *Gregory's Past. C.* xxxviii. 276 Ðæt wæter, ðonne hit bið ȝepynd, hit miclað & uppað... Ac ȝif sio pynding wierð onpennad.. ðonne toflewð hit eall. [*a* **900** CYNEWULF *Crist* 97 þæt is euan scyld eal for-pynded.] *a* **1225** *Ancr. R.* 72 þe water, hwon me punt [*T.* puindes] hit, & stoppeð. *Ibid.* 128 Nout ase swin ipünd ine sti uorte uetten. *a* **1400–50** *Alexander* 5487 Gogg and magogg þe grete he with þir gomes pyndis. **1483** *Cath. Angl.* 280/1 To Pynde, *jncludere, trudere.*

b. *spec.* To put (beasts) in a pound, to impound.

c **1290** *St. Eustas* 214 in Horstm. *Altengl. Leg.* (1881) 215 Weddes nimen and orf to puinde. **1441–2** in *Finchale Priory* (Surtees) 120 Ughtred.. pynded the catell. *c* **1450** HOLLAND *Howlat* 783 The pundar.. Had pyndit all his pryss horss. **1533** *Presentm. Juries* in *Surtees Misc.* (1888) 34 To pynd no mans cattell frome hensfurth.

†**2.** To distrain: = POIND *v. Sc. Obs.*

1478 *Acta Audit.* (1839) 59/2 þ^t^ he sall.. desist fra pinding of his said landis in tyme to cum. **1480** *Acta Dom. Conc.* (1839) 60/2 þe saide Johne maxwell grantis þ^t^ þe said horse was Ridden efter he was pyndit. **1587** *Reg. Privy Council Scot.* IV. 162 Like as the personis foirsaidis.. pyndis thair bestiall and guidis by all ordour of law.

Hence **'pinded** *ppl. a.*, **'pinding** *vbl. sb.* (*spec.* in local use, in reference to sucking lambs: see quot. 1641).

c **897** Pynding [see sense 1]. **1596** DALRYMPLE tr. *Leslie's Hist. Scot.* I. 123 *marg.*, Pinding. **1641** BEST *Farm. Bks.* (Surtees) 11 Theire excremente.. berke together theire tayles and hinder partes, and soe stoppe theire fundament; the sheapheardes phraise is that such lambes are pinded, and that they must bee sette att liberty. **1804** in *Trans. Highl. Soc. Scotl.* (1807) III. 350 Pinding is another disease exclusively confined to sucking lambs.

pind, obs. pa. t. and pple. of PIN *v.*, PINE *v.*

‖**pinda**¹, **'pindar, pinder.** Also pindal. [ad. Pg. *pinda*, in Du. *piendel*, ad. Congo *mpinda*, Mpongwe *mbenda*: carried by Negroes to America.] Name in the West Indies and Southern U.S. for the ground-nut or pea-nut (*Arachis hypogæa*).

1696 J. OVINGTON *Voy. to Suratt* 77 Sometimes they feast with a little Fish, and that with a few Pindars is esteemed a splendid banquet. These Pindars are sown under ground, and grow there without sprouting above the surface. **1707** SLOANE *Jamaica* I. p. lxxiii, I was assured that the Negroes feed on Pindals or Indian Earth-nuts, a sort of pea or bean producing its pods under ground. **1756** P. BROWNE *Jamaica* 295 Pindars or Ground Nuts. **1796** STEDMAN *Surinam* II. xx. 115 The pistachio or pinda nuts they also convert into butter. **1814** tr. *Proyart's Loango* in Pinkerton *Voy.* XVI. 551 There is nothing which the Negroes cultivate with more care than the Pinda. **1875** R. F. BURTON *Gorilla L.* (1876) I. 158 The ground-nut or pea-nut,.. the Pindar of the United States,.. is eaten roasted. **1926** J. K. STRECKER in J. F. Dobie *Rainbow in Morning* (1965) 56 In the valleys of the Red River of Louisiana and the Sabine River of Louisiana and Texas, are to be found negroes who use many African words, the inheritance of their ancestors. A white man is a 'buckra'... A ground-nut (peanut) is a 'pinda'. **1938** M. K. RAWLINGS *Yearling* xviii. 214 The field of pindars was not doing so well. **1977** McDAVID & O'CAIN in S. Greenbaum *Acceptability in Lang.* viii. 115 The majority of the uncultured judge.. *groundnut* and *pindar* as old.

attrib. **1879** *Louisville* (U.S.) *Home & Farm* 15 Apr., My hogs.. had.. the run of potato, pinder and pea fields.

‖**pinda**² ('pi:ndə). *India.* Also 8 peenda, 9 pindee. [Skr. *piṇḍa* lump.] (See quots.)

1785 C. WILKINS *Bhāgvāt-Gēētā* 139 The Hindoos are enjoined by the *Vēds* to offer a cake, which is called *Pēēndā*, to the ghosts of their ancestors, as far back as the third generation. **1796** W. JONES tr. *Inst. Hindu Law* iii. 67 Sages have distinguished the monthly *sráddha* by the title of *anwáhárya*, or *after eaten*, that is, eaten after the *pinda* or ball of rice. **1811** W. WARD *Acct. Writings, Relig. & Manners Hindoos* II. v. 550 The place where the fire was kindled is plentifully washed with water, after which the son of the deceased performs pindee, viz. he makes two balls of boiled rice, and, repeating a mŭntrŭ, offers them to, or in the name of his father and mother, and lays them on the spot where they were burnt. **1877** M. MONIER-WILLIAMS *Hinduism* v. 68 The offering of the Piṇḍa, or ball or rice, &c., to deceased fathers at a S'rāddha is of great importance in regard to the Hindū law of inheritance. **1901** *Westm. Gaz.* 14 Nov. 9/2 The 'pindas' offered to their deceased ancestors were placed on plantain or 'jack fruit' leaves. **1909** *Encycl. Relig. & Ethics* II. 27/1 How closely this [Lithuanian cake for the dead] corresponds to the Indian *piṇḍa*, which is so characteristic of the Indian worship of the dead. **1964** R. ANTOINE in De Smet & Neuner *Religious Hinduism* xv. 166 *Piṇḍas* (rice balls) are then smeared with ghee, collyrium and oil, and dressed with a tuft of wool, so as to represent the ancestors. **1968** B. WALKER *Hindu World* II. 149 On the first day after death a round ball of rice or flour moistened with milk and water and known as the *piṇḍa* is offered to the preta.

pindan ('pɪndæn). *Austral.* [Aboriginal.] The type of vegetation characteristic of arid areas of Western Australia; hence, the region itself. Also *attrib.*

1934 T. WOOD *Cobbers* iv. 46 His black trackers were making boomerangs... Pindam [*sic*] gum: hard red wood, shaped from a knee in the timber. **1937** W. HATFIELD *I find Australia* xxiv. 315 Pindan is not really the name of the type of tree, but merely the native name for 'dry country', though general usage adopts the word as a description of the thin growth of whipstick saplings of the bloodwood and box type of eucalypt. **1945** BAKER *Austral. Lang.* xiii. 224 *Pindan* is the blacks' name for the desert country inland from Broome, W.A., so the whites call the Kimberley natives *pindan blacks*. To *live on the pindan* is to wander aimlessly in the Westralian outback. **1955** J. CLEARY *Justin Bayard* xi. 153 They would be out in the pindan watching the homestead. **1959** *Observer* 17 May 8/3 From the pindan scrub.. these ancient monuments [*sc.* mountains] rise. **1978** O. WHITE *Silent Reach* ii. 22 Half a million acres of pindan country.. carried two thousand head of merino sheep in a good season.

‖**Pindari** (pɪn'dɑːriː), *sb.* (*a.*) [a. Hindustānī *pinḍārī*, *pinḍārā*, for Marāthī *penḍhārī*, a member of a band of plunderers called *pendhār* or *pendhārā*, of disputed origin: perh. from a place-name *Panḍhār*: see *Indian Antiquary* XXIX. 140, May 1900.]

1. One of a body of mounted marauders who appear to have arisen in Central India in the 17th c., and in the 18th c. were frequently employed by contending princes as irregular cavalry to pillage the country and massacre the subjects of their enemies. They were crushed in 1817 by the Marquess of Hastings, when Governor-General of India. Also as *adj.*

1788 *Indian Voc.* 19 *Bindarra*,.. who receive no pay, but .. give a certain monthly sum to the commander in chief, for permission to maraud or plunder under the sanction of his banners. *Ibid.* 104 *Pindarries*, a set of plunderers who accompany a Maratta army. **1794** SCOTT tr. *Firishta's Ho. Deccan* II. 122 (Y.) The Pinderrehs took Velore. **1803** WELLINGTON in Gurw. *Desp.* (1844) I. 369 He has had 3000 pindarries in his service, to whom he gave no pay, and who subsisted by plundering the Rajah of Kolapoor. **1856** J. W. KAYE *Sir J. Malcolm* I. vi. 102 Some band of Pindarees. **1889** G. SMITH *Stephen Hislop* ii. 33 Central India was overrun by Pindari brigands.

2. The dialect of these and their descendants.

1901 *Census India, Classified List of Lang.* No. 81 Pendhārī or Kākarī a jargon based on Dakhinī, which is used by Musalman Pendhārās and Kākars in Dharwar (Bombay).

Pindaric (pɪn'dærɪk), *a.* and *sb.* [ad. L. *Pindaricus*, a. Gr. Πινδαρικός, f. Πίνδαρος, name of a famous ancient Greek lyric poet. Cf. F. *Pindarique*.]

A. *adj.* Of or pertaining to the poet Pindar; written, writing, etc. in a style resembling or supposed to resemble that of Pindar.

1640 *Ben Jonson's Execration agst. Vulcan* D ij b (*title*), Ode Pindarick On the Death of Sir Hen. Morison. **1656** COWLEY (*title*) Pindarique Odes. **1668** DRYDEN *Dram. Poesie* Ess. (Ker) I. 97 We may use the benefit of the Pindaric way.. where the numbers vary, and the rhyme is disposed carelessly. **1711** ADDISON *Spect.* No. 58 ⁋13 Those admirable English Authors who call themselves Pindarick Writers. **1765** BEATTIE *To Churchill* 34 He soars Pindaric heights. **1869** ROGERS *Hist. Gleanings* I. 19 He.. built up Pindaric odes to the day of his death.

B. *sb.* An ode or other poem, or a metre or form of verse, in imitation or supposed imitation of Pindar. (Formerly sometimes applied to an Alexandrine: see quot. 1697.) Chiefly in *pl.*

1685 MRS. BEHN (*title*) A Pindarick on the Death of Our Late Sovereign. **1697** DRYDEN *Æneis* Ded., Ess. (Ker) II. 218 His Alexandrine line, which we call, though improperly, the Pindaric, because Mr. Cowley has often employed it in his Odes. *Ibid.* 229, I generally.. make the last verse of the triplet a Pindaric. **1706** CONGREVE *Disc. Pindarique Ode* A j, The Character of these late Pindariques, is a Bundle of rambling incoherent Thoughts, express'd in a like parcel of irregular Stanza's. **1876** L. STEPHEN *Eng. Th. in 18th C.* I. 131 Wollaston.. had turned the Book of Ecclesiastes into 'Pindarics' in order to give vent to his feelings.

So †**Pin'darical** *a. Obs.* = PINDARIC A.; **'Pindarism** [cf. F. *pindarisme*], Pindaric style, imitation or supposed imitation of Pindar; **'Pindarist**, an imitator of Pindar, a writer of Pindaric verses; **'Pindarize** *v.* [ad. F. *pindariser* (O. de St. Gelais, *c* 1500)] *intr.* (or with *it*), to imitate Pindar, to write in Pindaric style; *trans.*, to make Pindaric.

1656 COWLEY *Pindar. Odes, Resurrection* (*Note*), This Ode is truly *Pindarical, falling from one thing into another, after his Enthusiastical manner. **1697** WATTS *Horæ Lyr.* II. *Freedom* iii, Thus my bold harp profusely play'd Pindarical. **1713** STEELE *Guardian* No. 141 ⁋6 Sometimes she made me foam at the mouth.. and act a sort of madness which the Athenians call the *Pindarism. **1867** M. ARNOLD *Celtic Lit.* 144 [Celtic poetry] has all through it a sort of intoxication of style,—a Pindarism, to use a word formed on the name of the poet, on whom, above all other poets, the power of style seems to have exercised an inspiring and intoxicating effect. **1779–81** JOHNSON *L.P.*, *Pope* Wks. IV. 117 Perhaps the like return might properly be made to a modern *Pindarist. **1607** R. C[AREW] tr. *Estienne's World of Wonders* 43 To vse the phrase of our descanting and *Pindarizing Poets. **1694** MOTTEUX *Rabelais* v. xviii. (1737) 81 Water's good, saith a Poet, let 'em Pindarise upon it.

pinde, obs. pa. t. and pple. of PINE *v.*

pinder ('pɪndə(r)). Forms: 5 pyndere, -are, 5–6 pynder, (7–8 pindar), 7– pinder. [f. PIND *v.* + -ER¹.] An officer of a manor, having the duty of impounding stray beasts. (See also PINNER².)

14.. *Nom.* in Wr.-Wülcker 688/25 *Inclusor*, a pynder. *c* **1440** *Promp. Parv.* 400/1 Pyndare of beestys (*Pynson* pynnar), *inclusor*. **1523** FITZHERB. *Husb.* §148 Than cometh the pynder & taketh hym & putteth hym in the pynfolde. **1632** (*title*) The Pinder of Wakefield: Being the merry History of George a Greene the lusty Pinder of the North. **1769** *De Foe's Tour Gt. Brit.* III. 63 [At Nottingham] they have.. two more [officers] called Pinders, one for the Fields, and the other for the Meadows. **1821** CLARE *Vill. Minstr.* I. 88 While pinders, that such chances look, Drive his rambling cows to pound. **1890** *Herts Mercury* 4 Jan., To continue the directions to the pinder not to allow any cattle beyond those belonging to the inhabitants of the old prescriptive borough to be depastured in Hartham.

pinder: see PINDA¹.

†**'pindfool.** *Obs.* Sarcastic perversion of PINFOLD, with play on *fool*.

1550 HOOPER *Serm. on Jonas* v. 132 Then beganne the pyndfooles and cloisters to be made in the churches.

'pindling, *a. dial.* and *U.S.* [? for *pingling*, or *piddling*.]

a. *dial.* Fretful, out of humour. **b.** *U.S.* Sickly, puny, delicate.

1861 MRS. STOWE *Pearl Orr's Isl.* iv. 25 I'm a-thinkin'.. whether or no cows' milk an't goin' to be too hearty for it, it's such a pindling little thing. **1890** MARY E. WILKINS *Humble Rom., Brakes & White Vi'lets* (1891) 169 Leviny's lookin' kinder pindlin', ain't she? **1895** *Cassell's Fam. Mag.* Apr. 333/2, I niver seed sech peevish, pindlin, fractious ways.

pindolol ('pɪndəlɒl). *Pharm.* [f. the initial letter of PROPANE, PROPYL + INDOL(E *sb.* + -OL.] The compound 1-indol-4-yloxy-3-isopropyl-amino-propan-2-ol, $C_{14}H_{20}N_2O_2$, which is an adrenergic blocking agent with uses similar to those of propranolol.

1971 *Biochem. Pharmacol.* XX. 2749 (*heading*) Influence of INPEA, Pindolol and Propanolol on the chronotropic and metabolic responses to β-adrenergic stimulation in intact rats. **1976** *Lancet* 11 Dec. 1298/1 Concomitant treatment of hypertension was started with 15 mg pindolol, 5 mg amiloride hydrochloride, and 50 mg hydrochlorothiazide daily. **1979** *Experientia* XXXV. 250/1 Pindolol is one of the beta-adrenoceptor blockers now widely used all over the world.

pin-drill, pin-drop: see PIN *sb.*¹ 18.

'pin-dust. Dust formed of filings of brass or other metal produced in the manufacture of pins.

1552 HULOET, Pynne dust, *peripsema, psegma*. **1593** G. HARVEY *Pierce's Super.* Wks. (Grosart) II. 239 Him that can bray the Asse-drumme in a morter; and stampe his Iewes-trumpe to Pindust. **1624** CAPT. SMITH *Virginia* 58 A claie sand so mingled with yeallow spangles as it had beene halfe pindust. **1668** H. MORE *Div. Dial.* III. xxxiii. (1713) 268 Those little fix'd Stars that shew but as scattered Pin-dust in a frosty night. **1827** HOR. SMITH *Tor Hill* (1838) II. 283 Pindust, and fine gilt paper.

pine (paɪn), *sb.*¹ *Obs.* or *arch.* Forms: 2– pine; also 3–5 pyn, 3–6 pyne, 4 pin. [Early ME. *pīne*:—OE. **pīn*, a. L. *pœna* punishment, pain (see Pogatscher §130–134). Cf. OS. *pīna*, (MD. *pīne*, Du. *pijne*, *pijn*), OHG. *pīna* (MHG. *pīne*, *pīn*, Ger. *pein*), ON. *pína* (Sw. *pina*, Da. *pine*); also OIr. *pian* (Ir. Gael. *pian*): all from Latin. App. introduced into Teut. and Celtic with Christianity, and in Eng. applied first to the pains of hell. It is notable that the sb. has not yet been found in OE., where the derived vb. *pínian* was common from an early period.]

†1. Punishment; suffering inflicted as punishment, torment, torture; *spec.* the penal sufferings of hell or of purgatory; = PAIN *sb.*[1] 1, 2 b. *Obs.*

c1160 *Hatton Gosp.* Matt. xxv. 46 And þanne fareð hyo on ece pine [*Ags. Gosp.* susle, *Lindisf.* tintergo]. c1175 *Lamb. Hom.* 43 Heo bið wuniende inne þisse pine. c1200 *Vices & Virtues* 7 Ðe pine of helle. c1300 *Cursor M.* 497 Þar pin [*v. rr.* pyne, pine] þai bere opon þam ai. 1362 LANGL. *P. Pl.* A. v. 29 To take twey staues, And fette hom Felice from wyuene pyne [i.e. the cucking-stool]. c1375 *Lay Folks Mass Bk.* (MS. B.) 472 Alle in purgatory pyne. c1384 CHAUCER *Ho. Fame* III. 422 Of Proserpyne That quene ys of the derke pyne. c1425 WYNTOUN *Cron.* VI. xii. 132 Þire Tyrandis tuk þis haly man, And held him lang in-til herd pyne. 1596 DALRYMPLE tr. *Leslie's Hist. Scot.* VII. 54 To stire vp..ill men to flie vice throuch the pines that thay see Ill men pinet with. 1600 FAIRFAX *Tasso* XVI. lvii. 4 The victor..pardons her, that merits death and pine.

†2. Suffering, affliction, distress, trouble.

a. Physical suffering; = PAIN *sb.*[1] 3. (In ME. often applied to the passion of Christ.) *Obs.*

1154 *O.E. Chron.* an. 1137, I ne can..tellen..alle þe pines ðæt hi diden wrecce men on þis land. a1225 *St. Marher.* 1 Efter ure lauerdes pine ant his passiun ant his deð on rode. c1275 *Orison of our Lord* 20 in *O.E. Misc.* 139 Cryst..þat for vs þoledest so swiþe muchel pyn. 1303 R. BRUNNE *Handl. Synne* 723 Þe pyne, he suffred for þy gode. 1480 *Robt. Devyll* 820 in Hazl. *E.P.P.* I. 251 God wotte hys belly [had] greate pyne. c1600 MONTGOMERIE *Cherrie & Slae* 1350 Be mediciner to the man, And schaw sic cunning as ȝe can, To put him out of pyne.

b. Mental suffering; grief, sorrow, trouble or distress of mind; anguish; = PAIN *sb.*[1] 4. (In quot. a1600, Grievous or intense longing *for* something: cf. PINE *v.* 6.) *Obs.* or *arch.*

c1205 LAY. 2515 Ofte heo hæfde seorwe & pine. 13.. *E.E. Allit. P.* A. 330 My precios perle dotz me gret pyne. 1461 *Paston Lett.* II. 13 And it lyke you to take the worchip uppon you..to the pyne and dyscomfort of all your ille wyllers. 1568 T. HOWELL *Arb. Amitie* (1879) 57 My pleasure, pine, and pain. a1600 MONTGOMERIE *Misc. P.* xxxvii. 6 Sen nane bot I hes for thy persone pyne. 1600 FAIRFAX *Tasso* XIX. civ, That high crie..Pierst through her hart with sorrow, griefe, and pine. 1721 RAMSAY *Richy & Sandy* 30 [He] sung on aeten reed the lover's pine. 1868 ISA CRAIG-KNOX *Ballad of Brides of Quair* ix, More than one hath lived in pine, And more than one hath died of care.

†3. Trouble taken or undergone in accomplishing anything; labour, toil, exertion, effort, pains; difficulty: = PAIN *sb.*[1] 5, 6. *Obs.*

a1300 *Cursor M.* 1136 Wit pine it sal þe ȝeild þi fode. c1330 R. BRUNNE *Chron. Wace* (Rolls) 1994 Þey ascaped wiþ mykel pyn. a1400–50 *Alexander* 1206 Þus ȝede þai furthe.. And slike a prai þam apreued as pyne were to reken. 1533 BELLENDEN *Livy* IV. xi. (S.T.S.) II. 84, I will tak pyne..to do sic thingis for defence of public liberte. 1674 RAY *N.C. Words* 37 It's Pine to tell; it is difficult to tell.

†4. Suffering caused by hunger or want of food; the condition of pining for food; famine; want; starvation. (Cf. PINE *v.* 4, 5.) Also *fig. Obs.*

1567 DRANT *Horace, Epist.* xviii. F iv, Greedie thirst and knawinge pyne of siluer, and of goulde. 1596 SPENSER *F.Q.* V. v. 22 Forst, through penurie and pyne,..For nought was given them to sup or dyne. 1725 POPE *Odyss.* XV. 367 On all their weary ways wait care and pain, And pine and penury.

b. A disease of sheep: = PINING *vbl. sb.* 2 b.

1804 in *Trans. Highl. Soc. Scot.* (1807) III. 405 In the pine,..the condition of the animal is too high, its blood too thick, and its pasture too arid.

5. Complaint, repining. *rare*$^{-1}$.

1804 *Something Odd* III. 179 To give way to unavailing pines.

6. *Comb.*, as †*pine-stall* (*pynstal*), place of punishment. See also PINEBANK.

c1420 *Lay Folks Mass Bk., York Hours* 43 Þai..gerte hym bere on his bak þe cros to þe pynstal.

pine (paın), *sb.*[2] Forms: 1 pīn, 4– pine; also 4 pigne, 4–5 pyne, 5 (7 *Sc.*) pyn. [OE. *pín*, ad. L. *pīnus* a pine-tree, in ME. a. F. *pin*:—L. *pīn-us*. Gower's form *pigne*, is not easy to explain: F. *pigne* = It. *pigna*, L. *pīnea* is cited only of 1528 in Godef.]

1. a. A tree of the genus *Pinus*, or of various allied coniferous genera; comprising trees, mostly of large size, with evergreen needle-shaped leaves, of which many species afford valuable timber, tar, and turpentine, and some have edible seeds.

c1000 ÆLFRIC *Hom.* (Th.) II. 508 Se halȝa..wolde aheawan ænne heahne pin-beam. a1300 *Cursor M.* 1377 Þai sal be cedre, ciprese, and pine. *Ibid.* 1384 Þe pine [*v.r.* pyne]. c1350 *Leg. Rood* (1871) 70 Þe secund [wand] sal be of cypres, And þe thrid of pine sal be. 1390 GOWER *Conf.* II. 161 Enclosed with the tres of Pigne [*rime* Nonarcigne]. 1483 CAXTON *Gold. Leg.* 357 b/1 Ther was a tree of a pyn which was dedyed to the deuylle. 1593 SHAKS. *Rich. II*, III. ii. 42 He [the sun] fires the prowd tops of the Easterne Pines. 1667 MILTON *P.L.* I. 292 His Spear, to equal which the tallest Pine, Hewn on Norwegian hills,..were but a wand. 1794 MRS. RADCLIFFE *Myst. Udolpho* iv, Mountains covered.. nearly to their summits with forests of gloomy pine. 1860 RUSKIN *Mod. Paint.* V. VI. ix. §4 Let the pine find only a ledge of vertical precipice to cling to, it will nevertheless grow straight.

b. The wood of these trees: = PINE-WOOD 1.

c1400 *Lanfranc's Cirurg.* 118 (Add. MS.) Ȝif þe hed be smyten with a lyȝt dreyȝe staff, as of salwe oþere ellys pyne [*Ashm. MS.* pinee]. 1847 EMERSON *Poems, House*, Rafters of immortal pine. 1870 F. R. WILSON *Ch. Lindisf.* 79 The stalls are oaken, the sittings generally being of pine.

2. a. With qualifying words, applied to various species of *Pinus* or other coniferous genera (or to their wood): as

Aleppo pine, *Pinus Halepensis*; **Amboyna pine** = *dammar-pine*; **Austrian pine**, *Pinus austriaca*; **Baltic pine**, a variety of the timber of *Pinus sylvestris*; **Bhotan pine**, *Pinus excelsa* (*Treas. Bot.* 1866); **bishop's pine**, *P. muricata*; **black pine**, *Pinus austriaca*; also *P. Murrayana* and *P. Jeffreyi* of N. America, and species of *Podocarpus* of New Zealand and *Frenela* of Australia; **Brazilian pine**, *Araucaria brasiliensis*; **broom-pine** = *long-leaved pine*; **bull-pine**, *Pinus Jeffreyi*, *P. Sabiniana*, *P. mitis*, and *P. ponderosa*, all of N. America; **candlewood pine**, the Mexican pitch-pine or torch-pine, *Pinus Zeocote*; **cedar-pine**, *Pinus glabra*, of Southern U.S.; **celery pine** (also *celery-leaved p.*, *celery-top(ped) p.*), the genus *Phyllocladus*, of Australia, New Zealand, etc. (Miller *Plant-names*); **cembra pine**, the Italian Stone-pine; **Chilean pine**, *Araucaria imbricata*; **cluster-pine** (see CLUSTER *sb.* 4); **Corsican pine** = *larch-pine*; **cypress pine**, species of *Frenela* (Morris *Austral Eng.*); **dammar-pine**, *Dammara orientalis* of the Moluccas, which yields the resin called DAMMAR (Henfrey *Elem. Bot.* (1857) §600); **digger-pine** (see DIGGER 6); **dwarf pine**, *Pinus Mughus* of S. Europe, and *P. Pumilio* of Austria, etc.; **dye-pine** = *king-pine*; **foxtail-pine**, *Pinus Balfouriana* and *P. serotina*; **frankincense-pine** (see FRANKINCENSE 3); **giant pine** = *sugar-pine*; **ginger-pine**, the Port Orford White Cedar, a species of cypress, *Chamæcyparis Lawsoniana*; **golden pine**, *Pinus Kæmpferi* (Miller *Plant-names* 1884); **grey pine**, *Pinus Banksiana*, of the northern parts of N. America; **hard pine** = *long-leaved pine*; **heavy pine** (see HEAVY *a.* 30); **hickory pine** (see HICKORY 4 b); **highland pine**, a variety of the Scotch pine with horizontal branches; **Himalayan pine** (see HIMALAYAN 1); **hoop-pine** (see HOOP *sb.*[1] 13 b); **Hudson's Bay pine** = *grey pine*; **Huon pine** (see HUON PINE); **Jersey pine**, *Pinus inops*, a small species of the eastern U.S.; **kauri pine** (see KAURI b); **king-pine** (see KING *sb.* 13 c); **knee-pine** (see KNEE *sb.* 13); **Labrador pine** = *grey pine*; **lace-bark pine**, *Pinus Bungeana* of China, which sheds its outer bark every year (Nicholson *Dict. Gard.* 1887); **larch pine**, *Pinus Laricio* of S. Europe; **loblolly pine** (see LOBLOLLY 4); **lodge-pole pine** (U.S.) = *ridge-pole pine*; **long-leaved pine**, *Pinus australis* (*P. palustris*), the pitch-pine of the Southern U.S.; **mahogany pine**, *Podocarpus Totara* of New Zealand; **maritime pine** = *sea-pine*; **meadow-pine**, *P. cubensis* of the southern U.S.; **mountain pine**, (*a*) *Pinus monticola* of the western U.S.; (*b*) = *dwarf pine*; **Norfolk Island pine**, *Araucaria excelsa*; **Norway pine**, (*a*) the spruce fir, *Abies* (*Picea*) *excelsa*; (*b*) (in U.S.) the N. American red pine, *Pinus resinosa*; (*c*) a variety of the timber of *Pinus sylvestris*; **nut-pine** (see NUT); **old-field pine** (see OLD FIELD b); **Oyster Bay pine**, *Callitris* (*Frenela*) *australis*, of Australia (Henfrey *Elem. Bot.* 1857); **parasol-pine** (see PARASOL *sb.* 3); **pitch pine** (see PITCH PINE); **pond pine**, *Pinus serotina*; **prince's pine** (see PRINCE); **red pine**, (*a*) *P. resinosa* of N. America; (*b*) (of Australia) *Frenela Endlicheri*; (*c*) (of New Zealand) *Dacrydium cupressinum*; also the timber = *Riga pine*; (see RED *a.* and *sb.*[1] 17 d); **ridge-pole pine** (U.S.), *Pinus Murrayana*; **Riga pine**, a variety of the timber of *Pinus sylvestris*; **rosemary-pine** = *frankincense-pine*; **sap-pine**, *Pinus rigida*; **Scotch pine**, *Pinus sylvestris*, commonly called *Scotch* FIR; **scrub pine**, (in U.S.) (*a*) = *grey pine*; (*b*) = *Jersey pine*; (*c*) (of Australia) = *red pine* b; **sea-pine, seaside pine**, *Pinus Pinaster* or *P. maritima*; **short-leaved pine**, *Pinus mitis* of N. America; **silver pine**, (*a*) = *heavy pine*; (*b*) *Pinus Picea*; (*c*) the silver FIR, *Abies* (*Picea*) *pectinata*; (*d*) (in New Zealand) *Dacrydium colensoi* (Morris *Austral Eng.*); **spruce-pine** (see SPRUCE *sb.*); **star-pine** = *cluster-pine*; **stone-pine** (see STONE-PINE); **sugar-pine**, *Pinus Lambertiana* of California, which yields a sweet resin used for sugar; **swamp-pine**, (*a*) = *frankincense-pine*; (*b*) = *long-leaved pine*; **torch-pine** = *candlewood-pine*; **umbrella-pine** = PARASOL-*fir*; **Virginian pine** = *long-leaved pine*; **water-pine**, *Glyptostrobus heterophyllus* (*Taxodium heterophyllum*) of China; **wax-pine**, the genus *Dammara*; **Weymouth pine**, the common American white pine, *Pinus Strobus*, largely planted by Lord Weymouth when introduced into England; **wild pine** = *Scotch pine* (see also 5 b); **yellow pine**, various species with yellow or yellowish wood, as the *long-leaved pine*, the *short-leaved pine*, the *heavy pine*, etc.

1866 *Treas. Bot.* 382 D[*ammara*] *orientalis*, the *Amboyna Pine, is a tree of the Moluccas, 100 feet high. *Ibid.* 891 *Baltic, Riga, Norway, Red, or Memel Pine is the timber of *Pinus sylvestris* as grown in the north of Europe. 1843 MARRYAT *M. Violet* xliv, The pine, both *black and white. 1866 *Treas. Bot.* 890 Black Pine, *Pinus austriaca*.—, of New Zealand, *Podocarpus ferrugineus*. 1827 in Bischoff *Van Diemen's Land* (1832) 180 The Green Forest..comprises myrtle, sassafras, *celery-top pine. 1866 *Treas. Bot.* 881 P[*hyllocladus*] *rhomboidalis*, the Celery-topped Pine, is in cultivation as an ornamental tree. 1785 MARTYN *Rousseau's Bot.* xxviii. (1794) 444 The *Cembra Pine has five leaves in a sheath. 1857 HENFREY *Elem. Bot.* §600 *Araucaria* includes the enormous *Chilian Pine, *A. imbricata*. *Ibid.*, P[*inus*] *Pinaster*, the *Cluster-pine. 1785 MARTYN *Rousseau's Bot.* xxviii. (1794) 444 *Frankincense Pine has three leaves coming out of the same sheath. 1890 *Boston* (Mass.) *Jrnl.* 3 Nov. (*Advt.*), A valuable tract of *hard-pine timber-land. 1848 *Jersey Pine [see *scrub pine*]. 1847 ANSTED *Anc. World* v. 89 Resembling the Altingia, or *Norfolk Island pine. a1817 T. DWIGHT *Trav. New Eng.* etc. (1821) II. 158 Here, for the first time, we saw the *Norway pine. 1866 [see *Baltic Pine*]. 1861 MRS. MEREDITH *Over the Straits* i. 16 Groups of our beautiful *Oyster Bay Pine. 1785 MARTYN *Rousseau's Bot.* xxviii. (1794) 443 The most known [pine] among us is the *Scotch Pine, or, as it is vulgarly called, Scotch Fir: this has two leaves in a sheath. 1848 GRAY *Bot. U.S.* 439 Jersey or *Scrub Pine..Barrens and sterile hills, New Jersey and southward. 1866 *Treas. Bot.* 891 Scrub Pine, *Pinus Banksiana*. 1884 MILLER *Plant-n.*, *Pinus Banksiana*, Gray, or Northern, Scrub-Pine-tree...—*inops*, New Jersey Scrub Pine. 1865 *Daily Tel.* 26 Oct. 4/4 He drained the soil,..and planted bent and the *sea-pine over sixteen hundred acres of windy sand. 1881 STEVENSON *Virg. Puerisque, Ordered South*, The troubled, busy-looking groups of sea-pines. 1887 *Nicholson's Dict. Gard.* s.v. *Pinus*, *P. Lambertiana*. *Sugar Pine... California, etc. 1827. This, one of the tallest of all Pines, has an enormous girth. 1857 HENFREY *Elem. Bot.* §600 P[*inus*] *palustris*, the *Swamp-pine of Virginia. 1866 *Treas. Bot.* 537 G[*lyptostrobus*] *heterophyllus*, a small tree eight to ten feet high, is the Chinese *Water Pine, planted along the margins of rice-fields near Canton. 1755 H. WALPOLE *Let. to Montagu* 8 Nov., A dozen of the New England, or Lord *Weymouth's pine. 1811 A. T. THOMSON *Lond. Disp.* (1818) 298 The *Wild Pine, or Scotch Fir. 1822 J. FLINT *Lett. Amer.* 229 White and *yellow pines, similar to those of Canada, are brought from Allegany river.

b. Also applied to plants of other orders, resembling the true pines in foliage or some other respect: e.g. certain species of *Lycopodium* or club-moss (*festoon pine*, *L. rupestre*; *moon-fruit pine*, *L. lucidulum*; *running pine*, *L. clavatum*) see also GROUND-PINE, PRINCE'S *pine*, SCREW-PINE, and senses 5, 5 b.

1760 J. LEE *Introd. Bot.* App. 323 Stinking Ground Pine, *Camphorosma*.

3. *transf.* Something made of pine-wood: e.g. a torch, a ship, a mast. Chiefly *poet.*

1586 A. DAY *Eng. Secretary* II. (1625) 78 *Synecdoche*..as to say, the lofty Pine did scowre the Seas; for the Shippe made of the Pine tree. 1640 GLAPTHORNE *Ladies Priviledge* IV. Plays 1874 II. 148 Hymen light thy Pine. a1704 T. BROWN *On Dk. Ormond's Recov.* Wks. 1730 I. 50 E'er.. floating pines were steered by daring man. 1762–9 FALCONER *Shipwr.* II. 917 Fast by the fated pine bold Rodmond stands.

†4. *pl.* The edible seeds of the stone-pine (*Pinus Pinea*) or other species. *Obs.* [app. from L. *pinea*.]

1335–6 *Durham Acc. Rolls* (Surtees) 527, j li. et di. de pynes. 1340 *Ibid.* 37 Maces, pynes, et galanga. c1430 *Two Cookery-bks.* 15 Mynced Datys, Pynys and Roysonys of Corauns. c1450 *Ibid.* 95 Resons of corance, Pynes, Clowes, Maces. 1583 *Rates of Customs* D vij, Pine the pound, vjd.

5. a. = PINEAPPLE 2: cf. PIÑA 1.

1657 *Bk. of Continuation of Forreign Passages* 46 Fruits.. Pyne, the best that ever was eat, in season almost all the year long. 1661 EVELYN *Diary* 9 Aug., The famous Queen Pine brought from Barbados..; the first that were ever seen in England were those sent to Cromwell foure years since. a1683 —— *Hist. Relig.* (1850) I. 29 The royal pine—a compendium of all that is delicious to the taste and smell. 1764 *Museum Rust.* III. xxxi. 142 It will produce about one hundred and fifty pines a year. 1833 *Penny Cycl.* I. 490/1 In the island of Penang..there is a sort [of pine-apple] all the flowers of which always change into branches, each of which bears a pine, terminated by a crown, so that a great cluster of pine-apples is produced by a single stem; specimens of this sort are called double pines. 1879 F. W. ROBINSON *Coward Conscience* II. xv, Two of the choicest pines had been cut for dessert. 1920 'K. MANSFIELD' *Bliss* 35 He bought a pineapple... The oysters and the pine he stowed away.. under the front seat. 1954 *Farmer's Guide* (Jamaica Agric. Soc.) 392 The Sugar Loaf is only of importance as a fresh fruit. It is not a suitable pine for canning.

b. *wild pine*: name in the West Indies, etc. for species of *Tillandsia* (allied to *Ananassa*), epiphytes growing upon trees.

1707 SLOANE *Jamaica* I. 189 The Wild Pine is a plant so called because it somewhat resembles the bush that bears the pine [i.e. pine-apple]. 1829 *Nat. Phil., Prelim. Treat.* 39 (Usef. Knowl. Soc.) In the West Indies..a kind of plant called the *Wild-pine* grows upon the branches of the trees.

c. A liqueur made from the pine-apple fruit.

1818 *Sporting Mag.* II. 285 Three glasses of pine and one of Curaçoa.

6. A figure of a pine-apple or a pine-cone.

1790 W. WRIGHTE *Grotesque Archit.* 13 On the top is a pine, which should be double gilt.

7. a. *attrib.* and *Comb.*, as *pine bark*, *board*, *bough*, *box*, *fire*, *forest*, *grove*, *hill*, *-log*, *plain*, *plantation*, *splint*, *stem*, *stump*, *thicket*, *timber*, *tract*, etc.; (sense 5) *pine frame*, *-pit*, *-plant*; *pine-bearing*, *-bordered*, *-built*, *-capt*, *-clad*, *-covered*, *-creeping*, *-crested*, *-crowned*, *-dotted*, *-encircled*, *-fringed*, *-grown*, *-panelled*, *-scented*, *-shaded*, etc. adjs.; **pine-beauty**, a moth, *Trachea piniperda*, whose larva feeds on pine-trees; **pine-beetle** (also *pine-bark beetle*), any one of various small beetles destructive to the bark or wood of pines; **pine bird's-nest** = *pine-sap*; **pine-blight**, a blight or disease of pine-bark caused by an aphis, as *Chermes pinicorticis*, which secretes a coating of white filaments; also the insect itself; **pine-blister(-rust)**, a fungus disease of pine trees, caused by species of *Cronartium* (*Peridermium*) characterized by yellowish swellings on the bark; formerly also applied to needle rust caused by *Coleosporium* species; **pine-bluff**, a bluff or precipitous cliff crowned with pine-trees; **pine-borer**, a longicorn beetle, whose larvæ live in pine trees; **pine-bud moth**, the Tortricine, *Orthotænia turionana*; **pine-bullfinch** = *pine-grosbeak*; **pine carpet**, a species of carpet-moth, as *Thera firmata*, whose larva feeds on pine-trees; **pine-chafer**, a N. American beetle, *Anomala oblivia*, which feeds on pine-leaves; **pine-cloth** = PINEAPPLE *cloth*; **pine-cone**, the cone or fruit of the pine-tree; **pine-creeper**, **-creeping warbler** = *pine warbler*; **pine drape** *U.S. slang* = *pine overcoat*; **pine-drops**, the N. American plant *Pterospora andromedea* (N.O. *Monotropaceæ*), parasitic on the roots of pine-trees (cf. *beech drops*); **pine finch**, (*a*) = *pine-grosbeak*; (*b*) = *pine-siskin*; †**pine-glandule** = PINEAL *gland*;

pine goldfinch = *pine-siskin*; **pine green**, the colour of pine needles; **pine grosbeak**, a large finch, *Pinicola enucleator*, inhabiting pine-woods in Europe and North America; **pine grouse** = *dusky grouse* (see GROUSE *sb.*[1] 1); **pine gum**, *U.S.*, the resin or turpentine obtained from several species of pine, esp. the slash pine, *Pinus caribæa*, and the southern pine, *P. echinata*; **pine hawk-moth**, a species of hawk-moth, *Sphinx pinastri*, whose larva feeds on the pine-tree; **pine-house** = PINERY 1; **pine-kernel**, (*a*) the seed of any pine-tree, esp. when edible; †(*b*) the pineal gland; **pine lappet (moth)**, a large brown European moth, *Dendrolimus pini*, whose larvæ feed on pines; also called the pine tree lappet; **pine-linnet** = *pine siskin*; **pine-lizard**, the common brown lizard of N. America, *Sceloporus undulatus*; **pine-marten** (see MARTEN 2); **pine-mast**, pine-cones collectively (see MAST *sb.*[2]); **pine-mouse**, a N. American meadow-mouse, *Arvicola* (*Pitymys*) *pinetorum*, usually inhabiting pine-barrens; **pine-needle**, the needle-shaped leaf of the pine (hence *pine-needle wool* = *pine-wool*); **pine-oil**, name for various oils obtained from the leaves, twigs, wood, or resin of pine-trees; **pine overcoat** *U.S. slang*, a coffin; †**pine-ploughed** *a.*, ploughed by 'pines', i.e. ships (cf. 3); **pine rust**, a disease of pine trees caused by a rust fungus, e.g. *pine blister*; **pine-sap**, a reddish fleshy plant, *Monotropa Hypopitys* (*Hypopitys multiflora*), formerly supposed to be parasitic on the roots of pine-trees; also, the allied *Schweinitzia odorata* (*sweet pine-sap*); **pine savanna(h)** *U.S.*, a savannah in which pines are the prevailing trees; **pine saw-fly**, any sawfly whose larvæ feed on pine-trees, esp. species of *Diprion* or *Gilpinia*; **pine siskin**, a small N. American siskin or finch, *Spinus pinus*, found in pine-woods; **pine-snake**, a large harmless snake of the N. American genus *Pituophis*, found in pine-woods; also *attrib.*; **pine-stove** = PINERY 1; **pine straw** *U.S.*, (esp. dried) pine needles; **pine-strawberry** (see STRAWBERRY); **pine swamp** *U.S.*, a low-lying or marshy piece of ground on which pine-trees grow; **pine tags** *U.S.*, pine needles; so *pine-tag* attrib.; **pine-thistle**, a species of thistle, *Atractylis* (*Carlina*) *gummifera*, the root of which contains a gummy substance; **pine-torch**, a torch made of pine-wood; **pine warbler**, a small N. American warbler, *Dendrœca pinus*, inhabiting pine-woods; **pine-weed**, a small N. American plant, *Hypericum gentianoides*, with wiry branches and small scale-like leaves; also called orange-grass (*Treas. Bot.* 1866); = NIT-WEED; **pine-weevil**, any weevil which infests pine-trees, as *Hylobius abietis* and species of *Pissodes* (*Nicholson's Dict. Gard.* 1887); **pine-wool**, a wool-like material made from the spun fibres of pine-leaves, used in some countries for garments (Miss Pratt *Flower. Pl.* (1861) 166); **pine-worm**, the larva of the *pine-sawfly*. See also PINEAPPLE, PINE-BARREN, etc.

1709 J. LAWSON *New Voy. to Carolina* 177 They make use of *pine bark. *a* **1816** B. HAWKINS *Sk. Creek Country* (1848) 71 They are covered with clay and that with pine bark. **1973** R. LOCKRIDGE *Not I, said Sparrow* (1974) x. 153 Bisecting the tracks were traces of pine bark... The pine bark—what's left of a bridle path. **1978** *Country Life* 12 Oct. 1094/1 Pine bark was found to be one of the most important foods [of beavers]. **1887** *Nicholson's Dict. Gard.*, *Pine Bark Beetles, numerous species of small beetles..live below the bark of Fir-trees and other Conifers. *c* **1614** SIR W. MURE *Dido & Æneas* II. 475 Aged Atlas, whose *pyn-bearing browes.. Nor haile..nor wind..eschewes. **1887** *Nicholson's Dict. Gard.* s.v. *Pinus*, The *Pine Beauty, *Trachea piniperda*. **1892** *Garden* 27 Aug. 200 The Scotch Fir shoots..have been tunnelled by the *Pine beetle. **1889** H. M. WARD *Timber & Dis.* xii. 259 It is thus seen that the fungus *Peridermium Pini* was regarded as a parasite of pines, and that it possessed two varieties, one inhabiting the leaves and the other the cortex. .. The disease may be popularly denoted '*Pine-blister'. **1894** W. SOMERVILLE tr. *Hartig's Textbk. Dis. Trees* I. 175 Three species of pine-blister-rust are to be distinguished in the cortex of trees. **1907** W. R. FISHER *Schlich's Man. Forestry* (ed. 2) IV. 441 Scots pines infected with this disease, which is very common in the British Isles and called pine-blister, are termed foxy trees by English foresters. **1929** T. THOMSON tr. *Büsgen's Struct. & Life Forest Trees* xiv. 411 Individual stems of the pine and their descendants are especially prone to the pine blister. **1766** J. BARTRAM *Jrnl.* 18 Jan. in W. Stork *Acc. E. Florida* 41 We rowed..by some oak and *pine-bluffs. **1637** *Early Rec. Dedham, Mass.* (1892) III. 39 To alowe for saweing *Pyne board 5s. **1728** *New Hampsh. Probate Rec.* (1914) II. 344 Eight thousand feet of good and merchantable pine boards every year. **1825** *Gentl. Mag.* XCV. I. 6 Lumber, such as pine-boards and scantling. **1870** DE B. R. KEIM *Sheridan's Troopers on Borders* xix. 125 A neat coffin had been made of pine boards. **1938** L. BEMELMANS *Life Class* III. v. 245 Their flooring was of scrubbed pine boards. **1890** 'R. BOLDREWOOD' *Col. Reformer* (1891) 292 Vast plains and *pine-bordered sandhills. **1862** *Rep. Comm. Patents 1861: Agric.* (U.S.) 614 The larvæ [*sic*] of this insect is evidently a *pine-borer, for I have found it about saw-mills. **1884** *Rep. Comm. Agric.* (U.S. Dept. Agric.) 379 The Common Longicorn Pine-Borer..is destructive to the white pine. **1977** *Listener* 20 Oct. 503/3 Only when he discovered a small collection of New Zealand insects..did he trace it to a specimen of the New Zealand pine-borer; *Prinoplus reticularis*. **1657** THORNLEY tr. *Longus' Daphnis & Chloe* 29 She crowned her head with *pine-boughes. **1819** SHELLEY *Prometh. Unb.* IV. 48 The pine boughs are singing Old songs with new gladness. **1847** W. T. PORTER *Quarter Race Kentucky* 86 Ar you a goin to tum-tum all nite on that pot-gutted old *pine box of a fiddle? **1867** O. W. HOLMES *Guardian Angel* 406 The long pine boxes came by almost every train,—no need of asking what they held! **1890** N. P. LANGFORD *Vigilante Days* II. xxv. 441 A company of twenty or more men approaching the station, bearing in their midst a long pine box. **1881** MISS ORMEROD *Injur. Insects* (1890) 246 The caterpillars of the *Pine-bud Moth are injurious to the Scotch Fir, Silver Fir, and various species of Pine. **1808** SCOTT *Marm.* VI. Introd. 10 His low and *pine-built hall. *a* **1811** R. CUMBERLAND in T. Mitchell *Aristoph.* (1822) II. 42 O'er the mountain's *pine-capt brow. **1885** *Encycl. Brit.* XIX. 103/2 The *pine-chafer..is destructive in some places. **1972** SWAN & PAPP *Common Insects N. Amer.* 435 The Pine Chafer, A[*nomala*] *oblivia*, is very similar [to the Oriental Beetle]..; it infests red, jack, and Scotch pines. **1786** R. P. JODRELL *Pers. Heroine* II. ix. 23 His *pine-clad head Old Athos bow'd. **1860** TYNDALL *Glac.* I. xii. 90 At the other side was the pine-clad slope. **1695** WOODWARD *Nat. Hist. Earth* II. (1723) 81 Nuts, *Pine-Cones, and the like. **1866** W. M. ROSSETTI in *Pol. Rel. & L. Poems* p. xlii, A gilt bronze pine-cone, hollowed, and 11 feet in height, used once to be at the summit of the Sepulchre or Mole of Hadrian. **1870** EMERSON *Soc. & Solit.*, *Farming* Wks. (Bohn) III. 60 Nature drops a pine-cone in Mariposa, and it lives fifteen centuries. **1820** M. EDGEWORTH *Let.* 5 Aug. (1979) 199 High *pine covered mountains. **1884** G. A. TOWNSEND in *Century Mag.* XXVII. 824 Pine-covered hills. **1955** E. POUND *Classic Anthol.* III. 184 High, pine-covered peak full of echos. **1731** M. CATESBY *Nat. Hist. Carolina* I. 61 The *Pine-creeper... They creep about Trees; particularly the Pine- and Fir-trees; from which they peck Insects. **1811** A. WILSON *Amer. Ornith.* III. 25 Pine-Creeping Warbler.. inhabits the pine woods of the Southern states. **1868** WOOD *Homes without H.* xiii. 248 The *Pine-Creeping Warbler (*Sylvia pinus*). **1917** T. G. PEARSON *Birds Amer.* III. 148 Pine Warbler. *Dendroica vigorsi*... Pine-creeping Warbler; Pine Creeper. **1777** ELIZ. RYVES *Poems* 36 Up the *pine-crown'd hill. **1871** PALGRAVE *Lyr. Poems* 141 Neath the *pine-dotted slopes of Tivoli. **1945** L. SHELLY *Jive Talk Dict.* 31 **Pine drape*, coffin. **1970** C. MAJOR *Dict. Afro-Amer. Slang* 91 *Pine drape*, coffin. **1866** *Treas. Bot.*, **Pine-drops*, an American name for *Pterospora*. **1810** A. WILSON *Amer. Ornith.* II. 133 *Pine Finch..seeks the seeds of the black alder. **1871** J. BURROUGHS *Wake-Robin* 78, I observed several pine finches a dark brown or brindlish bird. **1894** R. B. SHARPE *Handbk. Birds Gt. Brit.* I. 61 The Pine-finch, *Pinicola enucleator*. **1860** TYNDALL *Glac.* I. xii. 86 After dinner we gathered round the *pine-fire. **1799** C. B. BROWN *Arthur Mervyn* I. ii. 15 Betty Lawrence was a wild girl from the *pine forests of New-Jersey. **1822** SHELLEY *To Jane—the Recollect.* 1 We wandered to the Pine Forest. **1913** J. LONDON *Valley of Moon* 472 Vainly Saxon's eye roved the pine forest in search of her beloved redwoods. **1973** M. MONSARRAT *Bk. of Europe* 118/2 Värmland, a gentle place of rolling farmland, pine forests and grand manor houses. **1978** D. KYLE *Black Camelot* xviii. 273 Sheltering in the Bavarian pine forests. **1657** THORNLEY tr. *Longus' Daphnis & Chloe* 92 They crowned him [a goat] with *pine-garlands. **1615** CROOKE *Body of Man* 468 The backeside of the *Pine-glandule. **1970** *Globe & Mail* (Toronto) 28 Sept. 28/1 (Advt.), Reconditioned Alfa Romeo Sale..*pine green. **1974** *Simpson (Piccadilly) Christmas Catal.* 12 Jacquard patterned cashmere sweater. Light brown/white, pine green/white. **1772** FORSTER in *Phil. Trans.* LXII. 402 *Pine Grosbeak. **1884** *Harper's Mag.* Mar. 619/1 One of our most beautiful and interesting winter visitants is the pine grosbeak. **1880** 'MARK TWAIN' *Tramp Abroad* xxxv. 397 Some *pine-grown summits behind the town. **1915** R. LANKESTER *Diversions of Naturalist* 4 That pine-grown land. **1855** W. G. SIMMS *Forayers* 434 A leetle *pine-gum plaister on that head of yourn will stop up the sore places. **1921** *Frontier* (Missoula, Montana) May 5 The Sheep Eaters lived in tepees made of cedar thatched with moss and cemented by pine gum. **1938** M. K. RAWLINGS *Yearling* iv. 41 He sewed the two deepest cuts and rubbed pine gum into all of them. **1859** W. S. COLEMAN *Woodlands* (1862) 36 It will change first into a brown chrysalis, then into a large and pretty moth—the *Pine-hawk Moth. *a* **1652** *Rec. Early Hist. Boston* (1881) VI. 16 The land running northward upon a straite line untill it cometh to range even with north side of the shop..and foure accres more or lesse upon *pine hill south. **1773** J. MCAFEE *Jrnl.* in N. M. Woods *Woods-McAfee Memorial* (1905) 436/1 We..crossed Cantucky river within 8 miles of pine hills and broken mountains. **1947** DYLAN THOMAS *Let.* 20 May (1966) 307 The pinehills are endless. **1887** *Nicholson's Dict. Gard.* s.v. *Pine-apple*, Provision should be made, in *Pine-houses or pits, for applying a thin shading for a few hours on bright summer days. **1598** *Epulario* H iv b, Some dry Figges, and two ounces of *Pine kernels. **1653** H. MORE *Antid. Ath.* I. xi. (1712) 33 That particular piece of the Brain they call the *Conarion* or Pine-kernel. **1712** tr. *Pomet's Hist. Drugs* I. 144 The Indian Pine Kernels are little Almonds of a yellowish white Colour. [*c* **1760** B. WILKES *Eng. Moths & Butterflies* I. i. 29 The Wild Pine-tree Lappit-moth.] **1824** J. CURTIS *Brit. Entomol.* I. 7 (*heading*) *Pine lappet. **1907** R. SOUTH *Moths Brit. Isles*, 1st Ser. 106 This is..the 'Wild Pine tree Lappet Moth' and 'Pine Tree Lappet' of the more ancient authors. **1966** O. KUTHANOVÁ tr. *Moucha's Beautiful Moths* 106 Pine Lappet Moth... This moth is one of Central Europe's notorious pine forest pests. **1885** *Riverside Nat. Hist.* (1888) III. 421 *S*[*celoporus*] *undulatus*..prefers the more sandy localities covered with pine, and is often called the '*pine lizard'. **1895** *Outing* (U.S.) XXVI. 34/2 A pine lizard ran up the trunk of a cedar tree. **1694** *Mass. Hist. Soc. Coll.* (1852) 4th Ser. I. 105 Ye town is incompass'd with a fortification, consisting of *pine-logs. **1853** J. M. NEALE in *Oxf. Bk. Carols* (1928) 271 Bring me flesh, and bring me wine, Bring me pine-logs hither. **1902** S. E. WHITE *Blazed Trail* 266 The instant necessity was to get thirty millions of pine logs down the river. **1938** E. AMBLER *Cause for Alarm* xvii. 281 We stood in front of the fire... There were two half-consumed pine logs hissing..on the top. **1978** *Country Life* 12 Oct. 1096/4 The pine logs are first debarked and then loaded into the kilns and burnt [for charcoal]. **1772** FORSTER in *Phil. Trans.* LXII. 372 *Pine Marten. **1884** JEFFERIES *Red Deer* ix. 169 A reddish-brown marten-cat, or pine-marten. **1936** D. MCCOWAN *Animals Canad. Rockies* xxvi. 230 The Pine marten may long continue to frequent the green solitudes. **1964** H. N. SOUTHERN *Handbk. Brit. Mammals* II. 358 Pine Marten (*M*[*artes*] *martes*), the only one occurring in British Isles, distributed in Europe down to Mediterranean. **1866** in *Higginson's Harvard Mem. Biog.*, *Whittemore* I. 410 The dry leaves and *pine-needles are as luxurious to lie on. **1866** WATTS *Dict. Chem.* IV. 649 **Pine-oil* or *Fir-oil*,..names..applied to certain oils resembling oil of turpentine, obtained in various ways from pine and fir-trees. **1896** *Congress. Rec.* 20 Jan. 796/2 The bill provides that the Committee shall..get as cheap a coffin as it can bargain for..perhaps what they call in the army a pine overcoat. **1929** E. LINKLATER *Poet's Pub* xxiv. 259 The room ..was..*pine-panelled. **1952** M. LASKI *Village* vi. 106 Delicate satinwood furniture against the pine-panelled walls. **1968** J. SANGSTER *Touchfeather* xiv. 150 One of the main rooms..was about sixty feet long, pine panelled and cool. **1974** *Country Life* 21 Mar. 695/3 Specialists in carved or plain pine panelled Rooms. **1810** *Splendid Follies* I. 39 Scrambling over the *pine-pit, he sheered off. **1837** *Civ. Eng. & Arch. Jrnl.* I. 24/2 The iron-roofed vinery..with a pine pit in the middle. **1665** *Early Rec. Lancaster, Mass.* (1884) 79 A slipe of medow ground Runing through the most part of a great *pine plaine. **1779** *Proc. Mass. Hist. Soc.* (1886) 2nd Ser. II. 464 [We] encampt on a pine plain by the side of a Large flatt. *a* **1817** T. DWIGHT *Trav. New Eng.*, etc. (1821) II. 158 The lands..are either pine-plains, or intervals. **1935** *Ecol. Monogr.* Jan. 66 The sandy, so-called 'Pine plains' were pitch pine. **1766** *Compl. Farmer* s.v. *Pine-apple*, Generally..*pine plants..brought from the West-Indies, have a white insect adhering to them. **1775** G. WHITE *Selborne* xlii. 108 The *pine-plantations of that nobleman are very grand. **1598** SYLVESTER *Du Bartas* II. i. III. *Colonies* 186 The *Pine-plough'd Sea. **1890** 'R. BOLDREWOOD' *Col. Reformer* (1891) 185 The unbarked *pine-posts of the rude verandah. **1913** *Phytopathol.* III. 306 (*heading*) The introduction of a European *pine rust into Wisconsin. **1951** *Dict. Gardening* (R. Hort. Soc.) III. 1580/1 Weymouth Pine Rust is a disease of 5-needled pines caused by the aecidial stage of the rust fungus *Cronartium ribicola*. **1960** C. WESTCOTT *Plant Disease Handbk.* (ed. 2) iv. 355 (*caption*) Pine rusts. **1857** GRAY *First Lessons Bot.* (1866) 35 Other parasitic plants, like the Beech drops and *Pine-sap, fasten their roots under ground upon the roots of neighboring plants. **1735** *New Voy. to Georgia* 13 We rode about two Miles farther, where we came to a large *Pine Savannat [*sic, bis*]. **1791** W. BARTRAM *Trav. N. & S. Carolina* 208 The cattle which only feed and range in the high forests and Pine savannas are clear of this disorder. **1827** [see SAVANNAH 2]. **1976** WEST & AUGELLI *Middle Amer.* (ed. 2) ii. 47/2 The chief reason for the Nicaraguan pine-savanna is probably the porous, gravelly soil, which will support only drought-tolerant plants. **1840** J. & M. LOUDON tr. *Köllar's Treat. Insects* III. 345 The means devised by man for guarding against and destroying the *pine saw-fly are as follows. **1887** *Nicholson's Dict. Gardening* s.v., *Lophyrus Pini* is the one generally denoted by the name of Pine Sawfly. **1972** *Times* 10 June 1/7 The limited experimental evidence ..demonstrated an effective defence against the potato moth and the pine sawfly. **1891** O. WILDE *Pict. Dorian Gray* xviii. 299 The clear, *pine-scented air. **1937** M. SHARP *Nutmeg Tree* iv. 51 A gust of sweet pine-scented air. **1972** D. ANTHONY *Blood on Harvest Moon* ii. 19 The cabin reeked from the pine-scented disinfectant they used to clean the bathroom. **1885** LADY BRASSEY *The Trades* 344 The *pine-shipping season is..a period of great activity in the Bahamas. **1887** R. RIDGWAY *Man. N. Amer. Birds* 400 Northern North America, breeding from northern United States north-ward... *Pine Siskin. **1947** *Chicago Tribune* 28 Dec. VI. 1/1 Some pine siskins..were found munching on birch cones and pods. **1971** *Islander* (Victoria, B.C.) 13 June 13/1 A flock of pine siskins, flashing their yellow-banded wings in darting flight. **1791** *Pine-snake [see *bull-snake* s.v. BULL *sb.*[1] 11]. **1823** E. JAMES *Acct. Expedition Rocky Mts.* I. 131 A serpent..which has considerable affinity with the pine-snake of the southern states. **1880** *Libr. Univ. Knowl.* (N.Y.) XI. 720 Pine snake, *Pituophis melanoleucus*. **1895** *Outing* (U.S.) XXVI. 39/2 A pine snake, bloated and glistening, wriggles across the road. **1941** M. LYON *Take to Hills* 192 Inside that bird nest was a small piece of discarded pine snakeskin, the original bands still faintly visible. **1956** L. M. KLAUBER *Rattlesnakes* I. ix. 585 A timber rattler..had eaten a pine snake. *a* **1843** SOUTHEY *Comm.-pl. Bk.* Ser. II. (1849) 660/1 Candles made of the *Pine-splints. **1832** J. P. KENNEDY *Swallow Barn* I. xxviii. 295 The ground was strewed with a thick coat of *pine-straw,—as the yellow sheddings of this tree are called. **1884** G. W. CABLE *Dr. Sevier* lvii. 435 Here stood Mary Richling. She still had on the pine-straw hat. **1939** *These are our Lives* (Federal Writers' Project, U.S.) 51 The pen was grounded with pine straw as was the shelter. **1976** *National Observer* (U.S.) 15 May 18/3 Our toys were found or made on the farm. We rolled steel barrel hoops with a heavy wire pusher, slid down pine-straw hills on old disc-plow blades. **1659** *Rec. Watertown, Mass.* (1894) I. I. 65 Abram Brownes Land.. begins ten rod from Rich. Bloyse his lott, & soe apon a straite line to a *pine stump. **1816** *Niles' Reg.* IX. Suppl. 178/1 Many a farmer who heretofore dreaded the pine stump.. now swings his undisturbed scythe. **1894** *Home Missionary* (N.Y.) Oct. 328 This pine-stump land..is proving to be the best potato land in the world. **1635** *Cambridge* (Mass.) *Proprietors' Rec.* (1896) 6 More by the *pine swampe about six acers. **1705** *Early Rec. Providence, Rhode Island* (1903) XVII. 201 At the South End of a Piece of Meadow & a Pine Swampe. **1862** O. W. NORTON *Army Lett.* (1903) 62 We are bivouacked in a pine swamp. **1851** *Southern Lit. Messenger* XVII. 226/2 We made [a bonfire] of dead boughs and '*pine-tags'. **1881** *Harper's Mag.* Nov. 868/2 At night they [*sc.* the mountain people]..lie down on their pine-tag beds. **1947** *Richmond* (Virginia) *Times-Dispatch* 13 Oct. 10/3 Oat straw,..pine tags,..and lawn clippings and leaves also could be used [for a mulch]. **1836** in *Jrnl. Southern Hist.* (1935) I. 367, I have been lost nearly all day.., wandering about in *pine thickets. **1867** H. LATHAM *Black & White* 38 They always had to ride off at night six or seven miles, up into the pine-thickets, to sleep. **1671** *South Carolina Hist.*

Soc. Coll. (1897) V. 298, I have..dispatched the Carolina laden with *Pine timber. **1842** P. J. Selby *Brit. Forest Trees* 410 The durability of Pine timber..is considered to be scarcely inferior to that of the oak. **1866** *Rep. Indian Affairs* (U.S.) 288 There is much of their territory valuable for the pine timber upon it. **1857** Mayne *Exp. Lex.*, *Pine-thistle. **1832** G. Downes *Lett. Cont. Countries* I. 99 The Valley of Grindelwald, interspersed with verdant lawns and sable *pine-tracts. **1884** *Health Exhib. Catal.* 42/2 *Pine Wool Anti-rheumatic Underclothing. **1839** W. B. O. Peabody in Storer & Peabody *Rep. Fishes, Reptiles & Birds Mass.* 310 The *Pine Warbler..is not much known, because it resides in deep, evergreen forests. **1868** *Amer. Naturalist* II. 171 Soon after the pine-warbler has arrived..the Yellow Red-polled Warbler..makes his appearance. **1917** T. G. Pearson *Birds Amer.* III. 149/1 The Pine Warbler is a well-named bird, because its nesting sites are always in pine trees. **1961** O. L. Austin *Birds of World* 285/2 The well-named Pine Warbler..almost invariably nests in a clump of pine needles. **1814** J. Bigelow *Florula Bostoniensis* 73 *Sarothra gentianoides* *Pine weed... A small, erect branching plant. **1843**, **1907** Pine-weed [see nit-weed]. **1862** *Rep. Comm. Patents 1861: Agric.* (U.S.) 605 *Hylobius pales*..is the common '*pine weevil' of the north and the south. **1867** *Amer. Naturalist* I. 110 Many other weevils and boring-beetles, especially..the Pine Weevil (*Pissodes strobi*)..now abound. **1936** *Discovery* Feb. 47/2 Extensive planting of conifers since the War has raised the problem of undue increase of the damaging Pine Weevils. **1972** Swan & Papp *Common Insects N. Amer.* 486 Pine Weevil: *Hylobius congener*... Range: Massachusetts to Alaska.

b. *attrib.* passing into *adj.* Designating preparations having the aroma of pine-needles.

1890 T. H. Dean *How to be Beautiful* ii. 23 Pine bath. This is a bath much prized by a beautiful Russian lady. **1926-7** *Army & Navy Stores Catal.* 472/1 Klenitas Pine Bath—bot. 2/6. **1931** S. Jameson *Richer Dust* xiv. 420 Put some pine salts in my bath. **1939-40** *Army & Navy Stores Catal.* 404/3 Pine odour disinfectant powder. **1972** J. Aiken *Butterfly Picnic* x. 175 [A] powerful effusion of pine bath essence. **1976** J. Wilson *Let's Pretend* xvii. 179 A bottle of pine disinfectant.

pine (paɪn), *v.* Forms: 1-2 **pinian**, 3-7 **pyne**, 3- **pine**. [OE. *pínian*, f. *pín*, pine *sb.*[1]: cf. MDu., MLG. *pînen*, Du. *pijnen*, OHG. *pînôn* (MHG. *pînen*, Ger. *peinen*), ON. *pína* to torment, punish (Sw. *pina*, Da. *pine* to torment); cf. also OIr., Ir., Gael. *pian* to torment, f. *pian* sb. Cf. later Eng. *peine-n*, pain, from OF.]

† **1.** *trans.* To afflict with pain or suffering; to cause to suffer; to torment, trouble, distress. Also *absol. Obs.* (Cf. pain *v.* 2.)

c **893** K. Ælfred *Oros* ii. iii. §4 Ða pineden hie hiene mid ðæm ðæt hie his hand forbærndon. *c* **950** *Lindisf. Gosp.* Matt. viii. 29 Ða cuome hider ær tid to pinenne [*Ags. G.* þreaȝenne] usih. **1154** *O.E. Chron.* an. 1137 [Hi] pineden him alle þe ilce pining ðat ure Drihten was pined. *c* **1175** *Lamb. Hom.* 17 He was ipinet ermiliche to deðe. *a* **1225** *Ancr. R.* 404 Neuer er nu nes ich ful pined. *a* **1340** Hampole *Psalter* iv. 5 Doand penaunce & pynand ȝow for ȝowre synnes. **1494** Fabyan *Chron.* i. cxxii. 99 He was taken in suspeccion, and so turmentyd and pyned y[t] he confessyd. **1569** T. Underdown *Ovid agst. Ibis* K vj b, Aristophanes was by publike authoritie pyned to death. **1635** Quarles *Embl.* v. i. iii. 246 O tell him..how my soule is pin'd. **1724** Ramsay *Tea-t. Misc.*, *Scots Cantata*, Hence frae my breast, contentious care, Ye've tint the power to pine. [**1876** Freeman *Norm. Conq.* V. xxiii. 285 Truly might the Chronicler say..that never were martyrs so pined as they were.]

† **2.** *intr.* To suffer, to undergo pain. *Obs. rare.* (In later use merged in 5.)

c **1175** *Lamb. Hom.* 35 Ic walde fein pinian and sitten on forste and on snawe. *c* **1386** Chaucer *Pars. T.* ¶ 773 (Harl. MS.) To synne and to pyne of þe deþ þat is pardurable.

† **3.** *trans.* To put to labour; *refl.* to take pains, exert oneself, labour, toil (= pain *v.* 4). *Obs.*

13.. *K. Alis.* 5914 Mychel he hym pyned er al þis londe He hauep ywonne. *c* **1380** Wyclif *Serm.* Sel. Wks. I. 150 A bole þat shal be kild..is not pyned ne traveilid wiþ oþer beestis. *c* **1400** tr. *Secreta Secret.*, *Gov. Lordsh.* xcvii. 100 His fadyr and his modir pyned hem to lere hym som craft. *c* **1400** *Destr. Troy* 11558 All grauntid the gome to þe gay qwene, For to proker hir pes, & pyne hym perfore.

4. To exhaust or consume (a person, animal, etc.) by suffering of body or mind, esp. by want of food or by wasting disease; to cause to languish; to wear out, waste away, reduce to leanness, emaciate; to deprive or stint of food, to starve. Also with *away*, *to death*, etc. Now *rare* exc. *dial.*

1297 R. Glouc. (Rolls) 9230 Þis bissop was ney to grounde ibroȝt Mid honger..He wep & cride on is men þat hii ssolde on him rewe þat he nere to deþe ipined. *c* **1380** Wyclif *Serm.* Sel. Wks. II. 155 Þei pynen hem bi þe worste hungir. **1549** Cheke *Hurt Sedit.* (1641) 23 Seeing yee so unpittifully vex men,..pine them with famine. **1563** Ld. J. Gray in Ellis *Orig. Lett.* Ser. ii. II. 279 The thought and care she takethe..pines her awaye. **1596** Barrough *Meth. Physick* (ed. 3) 372 Phisitions keepe their patients in darkenes, pining them euen vnto bones. **1606** Holland *Sueton.* 111 When as shee was fully determined to pine her selfe to death: hee caused her mouth perforce to bee opened, and meate to be crammed into her throate. *c* **1646** in *Glover's Hist. Derby* i. (1829) App. 67 [Wingfield Manor] was a place that could not be otherwise taken, without they were pined out. **1731-3** Miller *Gard. Dict.* (ed. 2) s.v. *Crocus*, The Bulb seem'd..to be pin'd and emaciated. **1759** Sarah Fielding *C'tess of Dellwyn* I. 223 He fattened on Flattery, and pined himself away. *a* **1845** Hood *Lamia* iv, I'd pine him to a ghost for want of rest. **1848** Buckley *Iliad* 17 But he pined away his great heart, remaining there. **1881** *Leicestersh. Gloss.*, *Pine*, to starve, kill by starvation. 'They besieged the town in hope to pine 'em'. **1885-94** R. Bridges *Eros & Psyche* June iii, If she there had died of hunger pined.

absol. *c* **1613** Rowlands *Paire of Spy-Knaves* 19 Thou do'st onely pinch, and pine, and spare, To hord vp money.

5. a. *intr.* To become wasted or feeble, from suffering (bodily or mental), esp. from intense grief, etc., wasting disease, or want of sustenance; to lose vitality or vigour; to languish, waste away.

c **1440** *Boctus* (Laud MS. 559 lf. 10b), That he shulde other dayes nyne In prison leve and there pyne. *c* **1440** *Promp. Parv.* 400/1 Pynyn, or languryn in sekenesse, ..*langueo, elangueo.* **1548** Latimer *Ploughers* (Arb.) 25 So doeth the soule pyne a way for default of gostly meate. **1560** Daus tr. *Sleidane's Comm.* 392 His wife, whiche pined to deathe for sorowe. **1593** Shaks. *Lucr.* 1115 He ten times pines, that pines beholding food. *c* **1665** Mrs. Hutchinson *Mem. Col. Hutchinson* (1846) 266 Pining with spite and envy. **1774** Goldsm. *Nat. Hist.* (1776) VI. 18 They generally pine away..and die in a short time. **1782** Johnson *Let. to Boswell* 28 Mar. in *Life*, You must get a place, or pine in penury. **1871** R. Ellis *Catullus* viii. 14 But thou'lt be mourning thus to pine unask'd alway.

b. *transf.* Of things: To lose bulk, vigour, or intensity; to languish.

1727 Pope, etc. *Art of Sinking* 112 The sparkling flames raise water to a smile, Yet the pleas'd liquor pines, and lessens all the while. **1844** Mrs. Browning *Lay Brown Rosary* ii. 107 Ah me, the sun! the dreamlight 'gins to pine. **1887** Moloney *Forestry W. Afr.* 173 In the Canary Islands, where the tobacco industry had to be resorted to after the cochineal pined.

c. *trans.* with *away* or *out*: To consume or spend (life, health, etc.) in pining.

1725 Pope *Odyss.* xv. 383 She..for Ulysses lost Pined out her bloom, and vanish'd to a ghost. **1775** S. J. Pratt *Liberal Opin.* xxxiv. (1783) I. 208 Many..pining away existence under the lashes..of reproach. **1851** Thackeray *Eng. Hum.* vi, Barristers pining a hungry life out in chambers.

d. Of timber: to shrink.

1833 J. C. Loudon *Encycl. Cottage, Farm, & Villa Archit.* ii. ii. 492 The granary floor to be laid with inch-and-quarter white-wood battens, dressed and jointed: the battens to be laid loose, so as to take up and relay after pining (shrinking).

6. *intr.* To be consumed with longing; to languish with intense desire, to hunger after something; to long eagerly. Const. *for*, *after*, or *inf.*

1592 Shaks. *Rom. & Jul.* v. iii. 236 The new-made Bride-groome..For whom (and not for Tybalt) Iuliet pinde. **1696** Tate & Brady *Ps.* xlii. 2 For thee, my God,..My thirsty Soul doth pine. **1748** *Anson's Voy.* iii. ii. 312 Who died there pining for their native home. **1829** Lytton *Devereux* ii. vii, We pine for sympathy. **1881** Besant & Rice *Chapl. of Fleet* III. 258 Harry Temple was wise enough to give up pining after what he could not get.

7. a. *intr.* To repine, complain, fret.

1687 Norris *Hymn*, '*Long have I view'd*' ii, No longer will I grieve or pine. **1838** Lytton *Leila* ii. ii, The eager and ardent spirits that pined at the..inactivity of Ferdinand's.. campaign. **1840** Barham *Ingol. Leg.* Ser. i. *Bagman's Dog*, Scratching and whining, And moaning and pining.

b. *trans.* To repine at, lament, mourn. *arch.*

1667 Milton *P.L.* iv. 848 Abasht the Devil stood..and saw Vertue in her shape how lovly, saw, and pin'd His loss. **1872** Swinburne *Under Microscope* 8 We..see, and pine our loss.

8. a. *trans.* To cause (fish) to shrink, in the process of curing; to dry by exposure to the weather.

1560 *Aberdeen Regr.* XXIV. (Jam.), The fische wes nocht pynit nor rypit aneucht. **1641** S. Smith *Herring Buss Trade* 10 The Pickle..doth so pine and overcome the nature of the Herring, that it makes it stiffe. **1705** *Sc. Acts Anne* (1824) XI. 293/1 That all the herring or white fish..shall be pined cured and packed from the bottom to the top with forreign salt allennarly. **1814** Shirreff *Agric. Surv. Shetl.* 91 When the body of the fish is all equally dried, here called *pined*, which is known by the salt appearing on the surface in a white efflorescence, here called *bloom.*

b. *intr.* Of fish: To shrink or 'render', as in the process of curing.

1681 Chetham *Angler's Vade-m.* iv. §21 (1689) 53 Some expert Anglers preserve Salmon Spawn, from pining, with Salt.

pineal ('pɪniːəl, 'paɪniːəl), *a.* and *sb. Anat.* [a. F. *pinéal*, f. L. *pinea* a pine-cone: see -al[1].]

A. *adj.* **a.** Resembling a pine-cone in shape: applied to a small somewhat conical body (the ***pineal body*** or ***pineal gland***), situated behind the third ventricle of the brain, and containing sand-like particles, which secretes melatonin in various mammals and is concerned with photo-periodicity and circadian rhythms.

1681 tr. *Willis' Rem. Med. Wks.* Vocab., Pineal kirnel in the brain, in form of a pine-apple, called also *conarium.* **1696** Phillips (ed. 5), *Pineal Kernel*, is a Glandule seated between the Two Beds of the Optick Nerves, and the Prominencies which grow to the upper part of the Marrowy substance. **1712** Addison *Spect.* No. 275 ¶4 The Pineal Gland, which many of our Modern Philosophers suppose to be the Seat of the Soul. **1785** Reid *Intell. Powers* ii. iv. 99 Des Cartes, observing that the pineal gland is the only part of the brain that is single, was determined by this to make that gland the soul's habitation. **1831** Carlyle *Sart. Res.* i. x, How, without Clothes, could we possess the master-organ, soul's seat, and true pineal gland of the Body Social: I mean, a Purse? **1840** G. V. Ellis *Anat.* 44 The upper part of each lateral boundary is the optic thalamus, with the peduncles of the pineal body extending along it. **1888** Rolleston & Jackson *Anim. Life* 343 The pineal gland.. has been supposed to represent either the region of closure of the neural folds, or else, an unpaired eye. **1958** [see melatonin]. **1970** T. Hughes *Crow* 23 Crow split his enemy's skull to the pineal gland. **1971** J. A. Kappers in Wolstenholme & Knight *Pineal Gland* 22 The mammalian pineal gland is an end organ of the peripheral sympathetic system conveying photic and other stimuli to it. **1978** Lee & Laycock *Essent. Endocrinol.* v. 103 The relationship between the pineal gland and the development of puberty in man is still undecided.

b. Pertaining to or connected with the pineal body, as ***pineal eye***, ***peduncle***, ***ventricle***: see quots.

1888 Rolleston & Jackson *Anim. Life* Index, Pineal eye. [*Ibid.* 343 *note*, Recent researches have shown that in *Lacertilia* the apex of the pineal gland is transformed into an azygos eye.] **1893** *Syd. Soc. Lex.*, *Pineal peduncles*, the peduncles of the pineal gland... *P. ventricle*, a hollow in the pineal gland, a fœtal survival. **1974** D. P. Cardinali in James & Martini *Current Topics Exper. Endocrinol.* II. 113 The pineal capacity to take up and retain estradiol and testosterone resembles that observed in the uterus and the prostate, suggesting that specific receptors for sex steroids may be present in the pinealocytes. **1979** *McGraw-Hill Yearbk. Sci. & Technol.* 288/2 A pineal role in the photoperiodic control of reproduction in hamsters has been established.

B. *sb.* The pineal body.

1911 *Arch. Internal Med.* VIII. 854 In enlargements of the pineal, circulatory disturbances will develop first. **1963** A. Gorbman in Euler & Heller *Compar. Endocrinol.* I. viii. 303 Pflugfelder removed or destroyed the epiphysis (pineal) of the guppy (*Lebistes*) and found that the thyroid became greatly hypertrophied. **1966** Wright & Symmers *Systemic Path.* II. xxxiii. 1134/1 The pineal has another endocrine role, that of secreting the melanophore-contracting hormone, melatonin.., and this has been regarded as related to the original photo-receptor function of the gland. **1968**, **1974** [see melatonin]. **1974** D. P. Cardinali in James & Martini *Current Topics Exper. Endocrinol.* II. 115 The pineal is involved in the regulation of pituitary, gonadal, adrenal, and thyroid functions.

pinealectomy (pɪniːə'lɛktəmɪ, paɪniːə-). *Surg.* [f. pineal *a.* + -ectomy.] Excision of the pineal body.

1915 *Jrnl. Exper. Med.* XXII. 240 The purpose of this paper is to report briefly the results of pinealectomy in a series of young puppies and to describe the method which has been evolved for extirpation of the pineal body. **1941** *Endocrinol.* XXVIII. 837 All pinealectomies were performed at the age of 20 to 21 days under ether anesthesia. **1976** *Nature* 5 Feb. 431/2 An experiment showing that pinealectomy somewhat reduced maternal behaviour.

So **pinea'lectomize** *v. trans.*, to deprive of the pineal body; **pinea'lectomized** *ppl. a.*

1912 *Rev. Neurol. & Psychiatry* X. 477 When pinealectomised pullets, who had already begun to lay, were isolated with pinealectomised cockerels, their eggs proved fertile on artificial incubation. **1933** *Proc. Soc. Exper. Biol. & Med.* XXX. 766 Sixteen albino rats..were pinealectomized at about 26 days of age. **1970** *Sci. Amer.* Feb. 44/3 Seven out of 12 pinealectomized rats treated with PCPA displayed sexual excitement. **1972** *Science* 27 Oct. 421/3 At 6 weeks of age, half of the birds in each chamber were pinealectomized.

pinealoma (pɪniːə'ləʊmə). *Path.* [f. pineal *a.* + -oma.] A tumour of the pineal gland thought to arise from the parenchymal cells.

1923 K. H. Krabbe in *Endocrinol.* VII. 391 In none of the cases has the tumor been an adenoma or, more exactly, 'pinealoma', but always a teratoma. **1948** R. A. Willis *Path. of Tumours* lii. 820 Pineal tumours, either pinealomas or teratomas, occurring in young children have often been accompanied by precocious bodily, mental or sexual development. **1966** Wright & Symmers *Systemic Path.* II. xxxiii. 1134/2 Teratomas, pinealomas and gliomas are the usual neoplasms of the pineal gland, although collectively even these tumours are rare. **1974** J. M. R. Edwards in T. J. Deeley *Central Nervous Syst. Tumours* iv. 99 Some of the tumours occurring in the pineal gland are undoubtedly teratomas but there is controversy concerning the pathological nature of the 'pinealoma'.

pineapple, pine-apple ('paɪn,æp(ə)l). Forms: see pine *sb.*[2] and apple *sb.*; also 6 **pineable, pyneable.** [f. pine *sb.*[2] + apple *sb.*]

1. a. The fruit of the pine-tree; a pine-cone. *Obs.* exc. *dial.* Formerly also applied to the edible seeds or 'kernels' (*pine-nuts*).

1398 Trevisa *Barth. De P.R.* xvii. cxxii. (Tollem. MS.), Pinea, þe pinappel, is þe frute of þe pine tre..þe pinappel is þe moste gret note and conteyneþ in it selfe many curneles, closid in ful harde schales. *a* **1400** *Pistill of Susan* 82 On peren and pynappel þei ioyken in pees. **1548-77** Vicary *Anat.* vii. (1888) 57 The Harte hath the shape and forme of a Pyneapple. **1577** B. Googe *Heresbach's Husb.* (1586) 63 The Hartichoch..the fruit of it something resembleth the Pineable. **1665** G. Havers *P. della Valle's Trav. E. India* 69 To outward view it [Ananas] seems, when it is whole, to resemble our Pine-Apple. **1712** J. James *tr. Le Blond's Gardening* 147 The Pine is a Tree very different from the Fir ..Its Fruit is call'd the Pine-Apple.

b. A figure or image of a pine-cone, used as an ornament or decoration.

1483 *Wardr. Acc.* in Grose *Antiq. Rep.* I. 29 Blue clothe of gold, wroght with nett and pyne appels. **1661** Morgan *Sph. Gentry* iii. vii. 77 [Some] take the leaves of this coat to be pine-apples. **1779** Swinburne *Trav. Spain* xliv. 417 A slender square minaret terminating in a ball or pine-apple.

2. a. The juicy edible fruit of the Ananas, *Ananassa sativa*, a large collective fruit developed from a conical spike of flowers, and surmounted by a crown of small leaves; so called from its resemblance to a pine-cone: see quot. 1665 in 1; = pine *sb.*[2] 5. **b.** The plant which bears this, *Ananassa sativa* (N.O. *Bromeliaceæ*), a native of tropical South America, widely cultivated in tropical countries generally, and in hot-houses also in temperate climates.

1664 EVELYN *Kal. Hort.* 83 Pine-apples, Moly, Persian Jasmine. **1666** J. DAVIES *Hist. Caribby Isles* 58 The Ananas or Pine-Apple is accounted the most delicious fruit..of all America. **1694** *Phil. Trans.* XVIII. 277 The *Kapa-Tsiakka* or *Ananas*, called by our American planters, The *Pine-Apple*. **1746** H. WALPOLE *Lett.* (1846) II. 188, I had..given a guinea for two pine-apples. **1870** YEATS *Nat. Hist. Comm.* 186 Vessels can now bring ripe pine-apples from the West Indies to England in pretty good condition.

c. A bomb; a hand grenade or light trench mortar. *slang.*

[**1916**: see *pineapple bomb* below]. **1918** R. H. KNYVETT *Over There* 193 But Fritz can be very obstinate on occasions, and all our teasing with rifle-grenades failed to make him retaliate with anything larger than 'pineapples' (light trench-mortars). **1920** W. B. ELLINGTON *Company 'A' 23rd Engineers* 113 *Pineapple*, French hand grenade. **1928** [see GANGLAND]. **1932** E. WALLACE *When Gangs came to London* xv. 118 'By "pineapple" I mean "bomb",' said Jiggs gravely. 'It's part of the racketeer's equipment.' **1944** *Sun* (Baltimore) 2 Aug. 2/3 There was a crossfire of ten grenades before one of his pineapples destroyed a position with four enemy soldiers in it. **1972** J. QUARTERMAIN *Rock of Diamond* v. 28 'You..don't want that old-time pineapple lobbed through your store window. You know what a pineapple is, Raven?' 'A hand grenade.' 'Right.' **1976** 'B. SHELBY' *Great Pebble Affair* III. 143 He was Wild Wally of ice-pick, pineapple and machine-gun fame.

d. *the pineapple* (slang), unemployment benefit, 'the dole'.

1937 PARTRIDGE *Dict. Slang* 632/1 *Pine-apple, on the*, on parish relief. **1971** *Observer* 23 May 7 'There were just too many people on the pineapple.' The 'pineapple' is slang for the dole.

3. *attrib.* and *Comb.* †**a.** in sense 1, as **pine-apple kernel, seed,** a seed of the pine-cone, esp. as used for food; **pine-apple nut,** a pine-cone; **pine-apple tree,** a pine-tree, esp. *Pinus Pinea* (all *obs.*).

1576 BAKER *Jewell of Health* 93 b, *Pyne apple kirnels. **1725** BRADLEY *Family Dict.* s.v. *Syrup*, Add the Pine-Apple Kernel, Pistachees, and bruised Seeds. **1568** TURNER *Herbal* III. Pref., The kernelles of the *Pineaple nut. *c* **1420** *Pallad. on Husb.* IV. 686 *Pynappul seed is sow. **1398** TREVISA *Barth. De P.R.* XVII. cxx. (Tollem. MS.), The *pinapel tree is calde boþe 'pinus' and 'pinea'. **1667** PRIMATT *City & C. Build.* 153 Things which are green all Winter; As Juniper..Pine-Apple-trees, Eugh.

b. in sense 2, as *pine-apple culture, garden, juice, plant*; **pineapple bomb** *slang* = sense 2 c above; **pineapple chunks,** tinned pineapple cut into small cubes; also *fig.*; **pine-apple cloth,** a thin translucent cloth made from pine-apple fibre; = PIÑA 2; **pine-apple fibre,** the fibre of the leaves of the pine-apple; **pine-apple flower,** a flower, or plant, of the S. African genus *Eucomis* (N.O. *Liliaceæ*), in which the cluster of flowers is surmounted by a tuft of bracts like that of the pine-apple; **pineapple jelly,** jelly flavoured with pineapple; **pine-apple potato** (see quot.); **pineapple rum,** rum flavoured with pine-apple; **pine-apple shawl,** a shawl made of pine-apple cloth; **pine-apple strawberry** = *pine-strawberry* (see STRAWBERRY); **pineapple weed,** a small, aromatic, annual herb, *Matricaria matricarioides*, belonging to the family Compositæ and bearing yellow flower-heads smelling like pineapple when crushed.

1916 'BOYD CABLE' *Doing their Bit* iii. 45 We saw '*pineapple bombs' or hand grenades being made—'pineapple' being a neat description of the shape and crisscross pattern of lines marking the segments into which the grenade bursts. **1952** WODEHOUSE *Pigs have Wings* i. 9 You watch that pig of yours like a hawk, Clarence, or before you know where you are, this fiend in human shape will be slipping pineapple bombs into her bran mash. **1972** *Daily Tel.* (Colour Suppl.) 1 Sept. 19/1 The 'pineapple' bomb ploughs a furrow through the undergrowth with steel pellets. **1903** ATKINSON & HOLROYD *Pract. Cookery* (ed. 3) 113, 1 tin of *pineapple chunks. **1926** WODEHOUSE *Heart of Gold* ix. 300 Anastatia [*sic*] ordered pineapple chunks with whipped cream. **1963** R. CARRIER *Great Dishes of World* 175 Drain the pineapple chunks. Reserve juice. **1977** D. BEATY *Excellency* i. 15 A DC 6 was leaving, its propellers chopping a long shaft of light into pineapple chunks. **1858** HOGG *Veg. Kingd.* 765 *Bromelia pigna*, a native of Manilla, yields fine hair-like fibres, with which the celebrated *pine-apple cloth of the Philippines is made. **1875** *Ure's Dict. Arts* (ed. 7) III. 578 Pine-apple yarn and cloth. **1883** MOLONEY *W. African Fisheries* 24 (Fish. Exhib. Publ.) Dragnets..made of *pineapple or other fibre. **1897** MARY KINGSLEY *W. Africa* 266 The same pine-apple-fibre bag which he wore slung across his shoulder. **1884** MILLER *Plant-n., Eucomis*, *Pine-apple-flower. **1845** THACKERAY *Pimlico Pavilion* iii, The *pine-apple gardens of sweet Pimlico. **1841** THACKERAY in *Fraser's Mag.* June 723/1 They..served us..*pine-apple jelly. **1907** R. M. F. BERRY *Fruit Recipes* xix. 245 Pineapple jelly (without gelatine). **1958** W. BICKEL tr. *Hering's Dict. Cookery* 723 Fancy mould lined with pineapple jelly. **1904** MRS. H. M. YOUNG *Home-Made Cakes & Sweets* 33 Add..2 tablespoonfuls *pineapple juice. **1957** E. CRAIG *Collins Family Cookery* 392 Heat in pineapple juice. **1972** J. POTTER *Going West* 171 Ashley bought pineapple juices from a café. **1977** F. WEBB *Go far Out* viii. 144 The attendant..brought him a large glass of pineapple juice. **1779** COWPER *Let. to J. Hill* 2 Oct., Arrival of the Jamaica fleet. I hope it imports some *pine-apple plants for me. **1835** HENSLOW *Phys. Bot.* §64 In one peculiar variety of this tuber, termed the '*pine-apple potato'..each [bud] is subtended by a swollen projection which represents the base of the leaf-stalk, in whose axil we may consider it to have been formed. **1765** A. STUART *Let.* 25 July in Duke of Argyll *Intimate Society Lett. 18th Cent.* (1910) I. 111 Ye Greatest part of your *Pine aple rum went, as you desired in return for his many feasts, To Baron Dolbach. **1837** DICKENS *Pickw.* xxvii. 276 A glass of reeking hot pine-apple rum and water, with a slice of lemon in it. **1967–8** *Bahamas Handbk. & Businessmen's Ann.* (ed. 7) 56, I poured a double pineapple rum on the rocks. **1883** G. MACDONALD *Donal Grant* I. 102 A waistcoat of *pine-apple shawl stuff. **1860** *All Year Round* No. 63. 307 A dish of the light-red *pine-apple strawberries. **1908** ROBINSON & FERNALD *Gray's New Man. Bot.* 847 *Pineapple-weed... Odor of the bruised plant suggesting pineapple. **1945** J. M. FOGG *Weeds of Lawn & Garden* 168 Pineapple-weed provides an interesting example of a species which is indigenous to the far western states and has become naturalized not only in eastern North America but also in Europe. **1978** *Country Life* 22 June 1797/1 Pineapple weed, a coloniser of disturbed ground..assisted to and from a site on the tyres of wheel-barrows.

†**'pineate,** *a. Obs. rare.* [ad. med.L. *pīneātus*, f. L. *pīnea* pine-cone: see -ATE².] Of the shape of a pine-cone, conical. (Cf. PINEAL.)

c **1400** *Lanfranc's Cirurg.* 113 Þe myddel part of þe brayn ys lasse þen eny..oþere..& here forme ys pyneat, brod towarde þe furþere syde of þe hed and scharpere towarde þe hyndor syde.

‖**Pineau** (pino). Also with lower-case initial. Pl. **-eaux.** [Fr., f. *pin* pine (tree) + dim. suffix *-eau*: so called because of the form of the grape cluster.] **1.** = PINOT (which is now the usual form).

1763 [see TRESSEAU]. **1833** C. REDDING *Hist. Mod. Wines* v. 76 In all the distinguished vineyards of Champagne..they cultivate only the black grape.., being a variety of the vine called *pinet* and red and white *pineau*. **1845** *Encycl. Metrop.* XXV. 1275/1 The fine wines of Burgundy, and the best Champagne, come from the *pineau*, a black grape. **1888** *Encycl. Brit.* XXIV. 606/1 The white grapes employed are the *Pineau blanc*, which are vintaged a full fortnight later than the red grapes. **1911** *Ibid.* XXVIII. 727/2 Practically all the important wines of Germany are white, although there are a few red growths of some quality, for instance that of Assmannshausen in the Rheingau. The latter is produced from the black Burgundy vine, the Pineau. **1967** A. LICHINE *Encycl. Wines* 404/1 *Pinot, Pineau.* One of the most distinguished families of wine grapes.

2. More fully *Pineau des Charentes* (de ʃarɑ̃t). An aperitif made from unfermented grape juice and brandy.

1940 C. MORGAN *Voyage* III. iv. 260 Barbet came from the house carrying a tray on which were plums preserved in cognac and a bottle of pineau. Thérèse disliked pineau; the mixture of cognac and unfermented wine was too sweet for her taste. **1951** R. POSTGATE *Plain Man's Guide to Wine* iii. 60 There is a pleasant, not very distinctive drink called Pineau or Plessis, which is made from the must of wine in Charente (where cognac come from) and served in quantities in railway trains. **1959** *Listener* 15 Jan. 125/1 Mr. Root has too low an opinion of Pineau des Charentes as an apéritif. **1959** A. WAUGH *In Praise of Wine* xii. 162 The grapes of the Charente are poor to eat and little wine is made there now... But there is a local *apéritif* called Pineau, made in the same way as Port, the fermentation being stopped by alcohol. **1961** *Listener* 12 Oct. 574/1 A humdrum café-life among taxi-drivers and porters who also drank their *pineau* at the counter. **1968** A. LASKI *Keeper* ii. 21 You shall have an aperitif on the house. Gui! Bring the Pineau for Colin. **1973** C. RAY *Cognac* x. 127 For centuries past, certainly since the sixteenth century, the peasants of the Charentes..have made an aperitif drink for themselves by 'muting' (checking the fermentation of) fresh grape juice by the addition of brandy. The ratafia of Champagne, the pineau of the Charentes, are sweet, strong, and tasty. *Ibid.*, The best pineaux I drank in Cognac..were the Plessis of Camus and the Reynac of UNICOOP.

†**'pinebank.** *Obs.* Also 6 pyne-bank(e, pin-. [= MDu. *pijnbanck*, MHG., Ger. *peinbank*: cf. PINE *sb.*¹, and BANK².] An old name of the rack.

(Sometimes erroneously explained as 'a bank or row of *pins* or spikes'. Also often erroneously printed *-bauk.*)

1534 MORE *Comf. agst. Trib.* I. xviii. Wks. 1162/1 Than must he leaue his outwarde worship..and lye pantyng in his bedde as it were on a pine bank. **1542** *Sc. Acts Mary* (1814) II. 422/2 Seand vþeris of perfite aige and stark of persoune put on þe said pynebankis [*printed*-baukis]. **1550** J. COKE *Eng. & Fr. Heralds* (1877) 123 Seven dayes stretched on a pyne bank. **1570** FOXE *A. & M.* (ed. 2) 1028/1 Then was he thrise put to the pyne-banke, tormented most miserably, to vtter his setters on. **1580** HOLLYBAND *Treas. Fr. Tong, Bailler la question*.., to put one on the racke or pinbanke. [**1828–40** TYTLER *Hist. Scot.* (1864) II. 406 The witnesses [were], as was usual in this cruel age [1537]..examined under the rack, or pynebaukis.]

'pine-,barren. *U.S.* [f. PINE *sb.*² + BARREN *sb.*³] **a.** A level sandy tract of land, covered scantily with pine-trees: chiefly in the Southern States.

1731 *Pennsylvania Gaz.* 29 Apr.–6 May 1/2 We had a sandy Pine Barren to walk in, which was covered pretty thick with large Pine Trees. **1737** WESLEY *Jrnl.* 2 Dec. (1872) I. 62 (*Georgia*) The land is of four sorts,—pine-barren, oak-land, swamp, and marsh. **1743** M. CATESBY *Nat. Hist. Carolina* II. p. iv/1 The third and worst Kind of Land is the *Pine barren Land.* **1765** J. BARTRAM *Jrnl.* 27 Dec. in W. Stork *Acc. E. Florida* (1766) 10 At Johnson's Bluff..for a mile the sandy pine-barren comes close or near the shore. **1883** J. FISKE in *Harper's Mag.* Feb. 418/2 Huge pine-barrens near the coast hindered the first efforts of the planter. **1901** C. T. MOHR *Plant Life Alabama* 125 The pine-barren streams overflow their low banks of shifting sands and gravel. **1916** J. W. HARSHBERGER *(title)* Vegetation of the New Jersey pine-barrens. **1952** *Guardian* 3 Mar. 4/6 This long peninsula, traded back and forth for two centuries between Spain, France and Britain, was not much more than a pine-barren, pocketed with swamps, till the late nineteenth century. **1976** *Hortus Third* (L. H. Bailey Hortorium) 932/2 *Pyxidanthera*... Creeping, evergreen shrublets, forming cushionlike masses, native to pine barrens from N[ew] J[ersey] to S[outh] C[arolina].

b. *attrib.*, as **pine-barren beauty,** a small creeping evergreen, *Pyxidanthera barbulata* (N.O. *Diapensiaceæ*); **pine-barren scorpion,** a large scorpion found in pine-barrens; **pine-barren terrapin,** the box tortoise, *Terrapene carolina.*

1883 W. ROBINSON *Eng. Flower Garden* 237/2 Pine Barren Beauty..is an evergreen shrub, yet smaller than many Mosses. **1901** L. H. BAILEY *Cycl. Amer. Hort.* III. 1475/2 The Pyxie, Flowering Moss or Pine-barren Beauty is a pretty little creeping plant, native only to New Jersey and North Carolina. **1951** *Dict. Gardening* (R. Hort. Soc.) IV. 1722/2 P[*yxidanthera*] *barbulata.* Pyxie, Pine-barren Beauty, Flowering Moss. **1782** CREVECOEUR *Lett.* 236 Scorpions, from the smallest size, up to the pine barren, the largest species known here. **1884** G. B. GOODE *Fisheries U.S.: Nat. Hist. Aquatic Animals* 158 The Carolina Box Turtle... In the Southern States it is known as the 'Pine-barren Terrapin'.

pine-beauty to **pine bird's-nest:** see PINE *sb.*²

pine-blank ('paɪnblæŋk), U.S. dial. var. POINT-BLANK *a., sb.*, and *adv.*

1886 *Century Mag.* Jan. 433/2, I oughter 'a' said it then, but I'll say it now, right pine-blank. **1896** 'MARK TWAIN' in *Harper's Mag.* Aug. 345/1 They told him pine blank and once for all, he *couldn't*. **1937** *Frontier & Midland* Autumn 13 His eyes standin pine-blank open. **1954** *Publ. Amer. Dial. Soc.* XXI. 34 A *pine blank* lie. *Ibid.*, I swear *pine blank.*

pine-blight to **pine-cone:** see PINE *sb.*²

pined (paɪnd), *ppl. a.* [f. PINE *v.* + -ED¹.] Exhausted or wasted by suffering or hunger.

1508 DUNBAR *Flyting* 170 Thy lang lene craig, Thy pure pynit thrott. **1586** A. DAY *Eng. Secretary* I. (1625) 139 Stifned limmes become vnweldie supporters of his pined corps. **1658** COKAINE *Obstinate Lady* I. ii, The pin'd man Whom Poets phantasies have plac'd in Hell With fruit before him. **1765** STERNE *Tr. Shandy* VIII. v, A man with a pined leg (..from some ailment in the foot). **1897** *Allbutt's Syst. Med.* II. 897 The stress lies heavy upon the pined body.

†**'pineful,** *a. Obs.* [f. PINE *sb.*¹ + -FUL.] Full of 'pine' or suffering; painful, distressing.

a **1225** *St. Marher.* 2 Al hire passiun ant hire pinful deð. *a* **1300** *Cursor M.* 18223 Sathan, þat pinful prince, he laght And vnder might of hell him taght. *c* **1450** *Lay Folks Mass Bk.* (MS. F.) 214 A pyneful dede. **1562** WINȜET *Cert. Tract.* iii. Wks. (S.T.S.) I. 23 The..office..is to thaim..wonderous pynefull and almaist importable. **1597–8** BP. HALL *Sat.* v. ii. 82 With long constraint of pinefull penurie.

pine knot. *U.S.* [PINE *sb.*² 7.] A knot of pine-wood, usu. burned as a fuel or for illumination, and adduced as a symbol of hardness, toughness, etc. Also *fig.* and *attrib.*

c **1670** *Plymouth* (Mass.) *Rec.* (1889) I. 119 There shalbe noe pyne knot picked. **1791** W. BARTRAM *Carolina* 387 To collect a great quantity of wood and Pine knots to feed our fires. **1808** J. N. BARKER *Indian Princess* III. i. 47 [She] lit me with her pine-knot torch to bedward. **1835** 'H. BULL-US' *Diverting Hist. John Bull & Bro. Jonathan* (new ed.) i. 8 Jonathan, though as hard as a pine knot,..could bear it no longer. **1850** H. C. WATSON *Camp-Fires of Revolution* 31 We stuck to them as close as pine-knots. **1853** 'P. PAXTON' *Stray Yankee in Texas* 310 We stood..with the bright light of a pineknot fire shining full upon us. **1856** X. D. MACLEOD *Biogr. F. Wood* 48 The human pine-knot John C. Calhoun. **1876** S. & A. WARNER *Gold of Chickaree* 360 You know as well as I do, that you are a pine knot for endurance. **1897** *Outing* XXX. 69/2, I held a pine-knot for him to make the entry in our log-book. **1904** G. STRATTON-PORTER *Freckles* 95 He was as tough as a pine-knot and as agile as a panther. **1945** B. A. BOTKIN *Lay my Burden Down* 62 When the boys would start to the quarters from the field, they would get a turn of lider [*sc.* lightwood] knots. I 'specks you knows 'em as pine knots. **1961** B. PALMER *Many are Hearts* 137 The dark night flecked with pine-knot torches. **1979** M. G. EBERHART *Bayou Road* xvii. 175 There was the red, smokey flare of lighted pine knots ahead.

pine land. *U.S.* [PINE *sb.*² 7.] Land on which pine trees are the characteristic growth. Also *attrib.* Hence **'pine-lander,** one who lives on and derives a living from such land.

c **1658** [see OAK LAND]. **1665–70** *Early Rec. Lancaster, Mass.* (1884) 271 There is another piece of upland..Sum part pine Land & partly oak Land. **1735** *Georgia Hist. Soc. Coll.* (1842) II. 45 We encamped there, and found..the pine land very valuable. **1765** J. BARTRAM *Jrnl.* 26 Dec. in W. Stork *Acc. E. Florida* (1766) 8 We encamped on a bluff in the pine-land. **1789** J. MORSE *Amer. Geogr.* 446 They are often to be found in pine lands in the southern states. **1838** C. GILMAN *Recoll. Southern Matron* xxiii. 157 There is something picturesque in the evening hour at a pine-land village. **1839** F. A. KEMBLE *Jrnl. Residence Georgian Plantation* (1863) 75 He gave me a..description of the Yeomanry of Georgia, more properly termed pine-landers. **1890** *Harper's Mag.* Apr. 790/1 Quaint and indolent pine-landers and degraded swamp-dwellers, have all supplied our literary comedians with unique characters. **1903** 'P. PENNINGTON' *Woman Rice Planter* (1913) i. 53 Drove S—— to church in our little pine-land village; she seemed to enjoy the very simple service. **1922** H. KEPHART *Our Southern Highlanders* (new ed.) 433 These freedman were pushed further and further back upon more and more sterile soil They became 'pine-landers' or 'piney-woods-people'..or 'crackers'. **1948** *Sat. Even. Post* 4 Sept. 30/1 There was a stillness here in the flat lonesome pinelands. **1977** D. CLARK *Gimmel Flask* v. 95 A..voice broke into song. 'Tina, soon the leaves will be falling, From the pine-lands I'm calling, Won't you come back to me-e?'

‖**pinenchyma** (pɪˈnɛŋkɪmə). *Bot.* [mod.L. (contracted) f. Gr. πίναξ tablet + ἔγχυμα infusion, after PARENCHYMA.] Tissue consisting of thin flat cells; tabular parenchyma. Hence **pinenchymatous** (pɪnɛŋˈkɪmətəs), *a.*, belonging to or of the nature of pinenchyma.

1840 *Ann. Nat. Hist.* IV. 392 A cuticle with pinenchymatous cells, that is to say tabular-shaped.

pinene (ˈpaɪniːn). *Chem.* [ad. G. *pinen* (O. Wallach 1885, in *Ann. d. Chem. u. Pharm.* CCXXVII. 300), f. L. *pīn-us* PINE *sb.*[2] + G. *-en* -ENE.] Either or both of two isomeric liquid terpenes, $C_{10}H_{16}$, which are the major constituents of turpentine and differ in the position of the double bond.

1885 *Jrnl. Chem. Soc.* XLVIII. 551 The author proposes to classify the terpenes as follows:..B. True Terpenes, $C_{10}H_{16}$, divided into the following groups: 1. Pinenes (boiling point 160°). [Etc.] **1886** *Ibid.* L. 71 Terpine is formed by the inversion of pinenen with alcoholic sulphuric acid. **1922** *Nature* 16 Feb. 226/2 The yield of oil from leaves of the New South Wales sassafras tree was about 1 per cent. .. The principal constituents identified are safrol, camphor, pinene, sesquiterpenes, eugenol, and alcoholic bodies. **1960** A. R. PINDER *Chem. of Terpenes* v. 93, α-Pinene is of great importance commercially in the synthesis of camphor and related terpenes... β-Pinene, which is isomeric with α-pinene, accompanies the latter in most sources of the hydrocarbon. **1971** *Daily Tel.* 12 June 6/3 The leaf is pinched to break specialised cells containing these elements of geraniol, citral, eucalyptal, borneol, pinene and others.

ˈ**pine-nut.** Forms: 1 pinhnytu, 4 pinnote, 5 pynote, 6– pine-nut. [f. PINE *sb.*[2] + NUT.] A pine-cone, esp. one containing edible seeds; also, the edible seeds of several pines, esp. the European stone pine, *Pinus cembra*, and the Mexican stone pine, *P. cembroides*.

c **1000** *Sax. Leechd.* II. 180 ȝenim of pinhnyte .xx. ȝeclænsodra cyrnela. *Ibid.* III. 258 Seo eorðe stent on ȝelicnysse anre pinnhnyte. *c* **1430** *Two Cookery-bks.* 34 Take kyrnelys of Pynotys. *c* **1440** *Promp. Parv.* 400/2 Pynote, frute, *Pinum.* **1600** HAKLUYT *Voy.* III. 422 In the cottages .. we found many pine-nuts opened. **1772** NUGENT tr. *Hist. Fr. Gerund* II. 354 Dividing amongst them some .. filberds, and pine-nuts. **1821** BYRON *Sardan.* v. i. 276 Faggots, pine-nuts, and wither'd leaves. **1845** J. C. FRÉMONT *Rep. Exploring Exped.* 222 A party of twelve Indians came down from the mountains to trade pine nuts. **1869** *Harper's Mag.* Sept. 473/1 The pine-nut is one of the principal articles used as food by these Pintes. **1937** A. F. HILL *Econ. Bot.* xvi. 371 The pine nuts or piñons are the edible seeds of several species of *Pinus* that are native to the Rocky Mountain and Pacific Coast region. **1947** *Sierra Club Bull.* (San Francisco) Mar. 4/1 It is far too late now to advocate .. the Indian's custom of living on the income of natural resources, the replenishable deer, pine nuts and grasshoppers. **1954** E. DAVID *Italian Food* 32 Pine nuts or pine kernels .. come from the cones of the stone pine. **1977** *Homes & Gardens* Sept. 104/2 Toss pine nuts in a little butter until crisp and golden.

attrib. **13..** *Seuyn Sag.* (W.) 544 Als dede the pinnote tre Of his ympe. **1601** HOLLAND *Pliny* II. 131 With Cucumber seed and Pine-nut kernils.

piner[1]. *Obs.* exc. *dial.* Forms: 5–6 pynour, 6 pinor, poyner, pyner, -ir, -or, -owr, 6– piner, 6–9 poiner, 7 pynnour. [= MDu. *piner*, *pijner* (13th c.), f. *pinen*, *pijnen* to labour, toil: cf. PINE *v.* 3, *sb.*[1] 3.]

1. A labourer; now in N.E. Scottish dialects applied to a man who cuts peat, turf, etc.

c **1420** WYNTOUN *Cron.* II. 559 Þe Egiptis for invy Anoyit þaim [Israelites] dispitously, And in all werkis þaim pynouris maid. *Ibid.* 1154 And mak þai men þar lauboraris, Masons, wrychtis and pynowraris. **1497** *Acc. Ld. High Treas. Scot.* I. 348 Giffin to pynouris to bere the treis to be Mons new cradil to hir. **1503** *Ibid.* II. 392 Payit to .. James to cartaris and pynouris, for carying of beddis, clathes .. fra the Castell to the Abbay. **1543** *Aberdeen Regr.* XVIII. (Jam.), The pynouris to help to dycht & cleynge the calsais, euery pynour his day abowtt. *a* **1572** KNOX *Hist. Ref.* Wks. 1848 II. 160 Sa scho wes lappit in a cope of leid, and keipit .. unto the nyntene of October, quhen scho by pynouris wes caryed to a schip, and sa caryed to France. **1601** J. MELVILL *Diary* (Wodrow Soc.) 493, I ley down at your feit my Commission as the pynnour does his burding. **1759** *Fountainhall's Decisions* I. 236 Forcing them to employ the common Piners in the Town, and exacting money for it. **1806** *Case, Duff of Muirtown*, &c. (Jam.), The people she saw .. were poiners or carters from Inverness, who used to come there for materials. **1887** BULLOCH *Pynours* v. 41 The pynour-fishermen pursuing their proper calling on the vasty deep.

2. = PIONEER 1, 2.

1587 *Mirr. Mag., Aurel. Anton.* xxv, My piners eke were prest with showle and spade T' interre the dead. *Ibid., Sir N. Burdet* lxx, Hee pyners set to trenche, and vnder mine amayne. **1581** STYWARD *Mart. Discipl.* II. 122 There are to be placed thy piners who are to be garded with .500. shot of each wing.

piner[2] (ˈpaɪnə(r)). [f. PINE *v.* + -ER[1].]

†**1.** A tormentor. *Obs.*

c **950** *Lindisf. Gosp.* Matt. xviii. 34 Hlaferd his ȝesalde hine ðæm pinerum. **1596** DALRYMPLE tr. *Leslie's Hist. Scot.* VII. 46 The rest of his body, .. the pynouris raue with an yrne tangs, meruellous artificiouslie, to his dolour and langsum pane.

2. One who or that which pines; *spec.* an animal suffering from a wasting disease.

1882 *Pall Mall G.* 26 July 4/2 A large proportion of the grouse have the appearance of having died from starvation. .. The keepers .. call the emaciated birds 'piners'. **1893** *Westm. Gaz.* 11 Feb. 10/2 It seemed as if the bull would have to be killed as a 'piner'.

piner[3]. *local.* [f. PINE *sb.*[2] + -ER[1].]

a. *Tasmania.* A man employed in hewing pine-trees. **b.** *U.S. local.* An inhabitant of a region where pine-trees abound.

1891 W. TILLEY *Wild West Tasmania* 43 (Morris) The King River is only navigable for small craft... Piners' boats sometimes get in. **1894** RALPH in *Harper's Mag.* Aug. 337 The term 'piners' is synonymous with the term 'poor whites' in the South.

Pinerotic (pɪnəˈrɒtɪk), *a.* [f. the name *Pinero* (see below) + -OTIC.] Pertaining to or characteristic of the dramatist Sir Arthur Wing Pinero (1855–1934), or his plays.

1895 G. B. SHAW *Let.* 18 Mar. (1965) I. 501 It would appear so very easy to give my subjects the Pinerotic effect. **1896** *Sat. Rev.* 29 Feb. 223/1 It contains not a word about Mr. Pinero himself.., his hopes and fears for the drama, or anything else distinctively Pinerotic. **1938** C. MORGAN *Flashing Stream* p. xvi, The Pinerotic theory that a woman, to be entitled to our respect in the theatre, must, if she shares a man's bed, do so with a self-sacrificial reluctance.

pinery (ˈpaɪnərɪ). [f. PINE *sb.*[2] + -ERY.]

1. A place in which pine-apples are grown.

1758 J. RALPH *Authors by Profession* 41 All must have their Fooleries as well as their Pinaries. **1787** *Olla Podrida* No. 42 (1788) 425 The Pleasure of seeing Green-houses and Pineries arise. **1858** GLENNY *Gard. Every-day Bk.* 207/1 Separate vineries, forcing-houses, pineries, and hot-pits.

2. A plantation or grove of pine-trees. Also *attrib.* Chiefly *N. Amer.*

1783 *Rep. Bureau Arch. Ontario* (1906) III. p. cxx, There are fine pineries two or three miles from the water's edge where large masts may be procured. **1822** *Massachusetts Spy* 6 Feb. (Th.), There are also a few pineries, but of small extent. **1831** JANE PORTER *Sir E. Seaward's Narr.* II. 160 Our pines in the dell formed an infant pinery. **1882** *Harper's Mag.* Dec. 12/1 When the timber shall have been stripped from the pineries of Maine. **1926** *Amer. Speech* II. 100/2 The lumberjacks have found anthologists who appreciate better than did the singers themselves the charm of the pinery songs. **1952** D. F. PUTNAM *Canad. Regions* 138/1 Its 'pineries' formed the source of much of the timber which came down the Ottawa River.

pine-sap to **pine timber**: see PINE *sb.*[2]

ˈ**pine-top.** [f. PINE *sb.*[2] + TOP *sb.*[1]] **a.** The top of a pine-tree. **b.** *U.S. slang.* Cheap or illicit whisky.

1858 *Southern Lit. Messenger* XXVII. 463/2 A rough, but hearty frolic .. with profusion of 'pine-top' succeeded. **1878** O. WILDE *Ravenna* v. 10 The pine-tops rocked before the evening breeze. **1931** *Amer. Speech* VII. 50 The 'drinks' are 'pine-top', 'white mule', [etc.]. **1942** BERREY & VAN DEN BARK *Amer. Thes. Slang* §99/7 *Illicit whiskey*, .. pine-top. **1946** J. W. DAY *Harvest Adventure* xiii. 214 At the report the second, larger still, swung over a gap in the pine-tops and the next barrel knocked him sideways and sent him spinning in a long dive into the snipe marsh below the wood.

pine-torch, tract: see PINE *sb.*[2]

pine-tree. = PINE *sb.*[2] 1.

c **1000** *Sax. Leechd.* II. 216 Pintreowes þa grenan twigu ufeweard ȝegnid. *a* **1300** *Cursor M.* 6326 Þar sagh he stand Wexen o cipres, a wand; .. An-oþer he sagh o cedre tre; .. O pine tre þe thrid he fand. **1483** *Cath. Angl.* 279/2 A Pyne tre (*A.* A Pyne Appyltre), *pinus.* *c* **1489** CAXTON *Sonnes of Aymon* xvii. 390 He toke on his waye for to goo to the pintre of mountalban. **1562** TURNER *Herbal* II. 87 The Pyne tre bryngeth furth very litle rosin. **1710** LUTTRELL *Brief Rel.* (1857) VI. 669 The bill for preserving white pyne trees in our plantations for ships masts. **1837** W. IRVING *Capt. Bonneville* II. 168 Barricaded by fallen pine-trees and tremendous precipices.

b. *attrib.*, as *pine-tree bole*, etc.; **pine-tree money**, name for the silver coins (shilling, six-pence, and threepence) bearing the figure of a pine-tree, struck in Massachusetts in the latter half of the 17th century, being the first money coined in a British colony; **pine-tree State**, Maine, U.S., so called from its extensive pine-forests.

a **1848** CLOUGH *Early Poems* xvi. 88 The pine-tree boles are dimmer, And the stars bedimmed above. **1864** WEBSTER *Dict., Names Fiction*, Pine-Tree State. **1870** *Eng. Mechanic* 7 Jan. 416/1 These coins, now very rare.., are called 'Pine Tree Money'. **1888** *Boston Transcript* (Farmer), The good old Pine-tree State is pretty well represented in this locality. **1893** ELIZ. B. CUSTER *Tenting* 88 The most venomous of snakes, called the pine-tree rattlesnake. **1893** GOLDW. SMITH *United States* 28 She [Massachusetts] coined her own money, the pine-tree shilling. **1896** *Peterson's Mag.* (U.S.) VI. 288/2 These vessels all sailed under the pine-tree flag. This flag was of white bunting, on which was painted a green pine-tree, and upon the reverse..: 'Appeal to Heaven'.

‖**pinetum** (paɪˈniːtəm). Pl. -a, -ums. [L. *pīnētum* pine-grove, f. *pīnus* PINE *sb.*[2]] A plantation or collection of pine-trees of various species, for scientific or ornamental purposes.

1842 P. J. SELBY *Brit. Forest Trees* 392 In Northumberland, the first established and richest Pinetum is that of Sir C. L. M. Monck. **1881** VEITCH *Coniferæ* III. 320 The Pinetum, in its comprehensive sense, is a complete collection of living specimens of all the Coniferous trees and shrubs known. *Ibid.* 321 The planting of Pineta originated in the beginning of the present century.

ˈ**pine-wood.** [f. PINE *sb.*[2] + WOOD *sb.*]

1. The wood of the pine-tree. Also *attrib.*

1815 *Tweddell's Rem.* lxx. 315 *note*, A small bundle of splinters of pine-wood. **1850** LYELL *2nd Visit U.S.* II. 32 Holding .. large blazing torches of pine-wood. **1869** TOZER *Highl. Turkey* II. 164 The smoke of pinewood fires.

2. A wood or forest of pines.

1673 J. RAY *Observations Journey Low-Countries* 80 After one half-hours riding we entred into Pine-Woods, the first we met withal: They reach'd almost to our Lodging. **1790** *Pennsylvania Packet* 11 Oct. 3/4 A ganninipper is a kind of large horse-fly frequent in pine woods. **1813** W. S. WALKER *Poems* 144 (Jod.) No breezes waved the pine-wood tall. **1855** KINGSLEY *Heroes, Theseus* II. 215 All cold above the black pine-woods. **1867** H. MACMILLAN *Bible Teach.* iv. (1870) 70 The destruction of the grand pine-woods that once clothed the Apennines. **1872** R. G. MCCLELLAN *Golden State* xvii. 204 These hogs .. are somewhat like the North Carolina pine-woods hogs. **1917** D. H. LAWRENCE *Look! We have come Through!* 40 The jade-green river Goes between the pine-woods. **1939** E. E. MURPHEY *Wings at Dusk* 13 Whenever I see one Flushing befoh me Histing his flag, like a buck in de pine-wood [etc.]. **1978** 'I. DRUMMOND' *Stench of Poppies* xi. 167 In the foothills of the Taurus .. among superb pinewoods.

Hence ˈ**pine-woody** *a.* (*rare*), suggestive of pine-woods.

1945 J. BETJEMAN *New Bats in Old Belfries* 6 Mushroomy, pinewoody evergreen smells.

piney (ˈpaɪnɪ), **pinnay** (ˈpɪneɪ). Also piny. [ad. Tamil *pinnai* or *punnai*, in Skr. *punnāga*.] The name of two East Indian resinous trees, *Calophyllum inophyllum* (N.O. *Clusiaceæ*), called also **piney-tree**, and *Vateria indica* (N.O. *Dipteraceæ*); used *attrib.*, as in **piney dammar, resin, varnish**, the resin obtained from *Vateria indica*, also called *white dammar*, *Indian* or *Malabar copal*, or *gum animé*; **piney oil, piney tallow** (Tamil *punnaitailam*), a fatty or waxy substance from the fruit of the same tree, used for making candles.

1857 HENFREY *Elem. Bot.* §424 *Vateria indica* affords the Piney resin or Piney Dammar of India, sometimes called Indian Copal or gum Animi. *c* **1865** LETHEBY in *Circ. Sc.* I. 95/1 An oil named *Piney tallow* is expressed from the fruit of the panoe tree. **1866** *Treas. Bot.* 891 *Piney-varnish*, the resin or dammar obtained from *Vateria indica*. *Piney-tree*, *Calophyllum angustifolium*.

piney, erron. form of PINY *a.*

pin-eyed (ˈpɪnˌaɪd), *a.* [f. PIN *sb.*[1] + EYED *ppl. a.*] Having an 'eye' with a 'pin'; applied by florists to the long styled form of a flower (esp. *Primula*), which shows the stigma, resembling a pin's head, at the top of the corolla-tube (opp. to *thrum-eyed* or *rose-eyed*, applied to the short-styled form, which shows the anthers at the top).

1810 CRABBE *Borough* VIII, This is no shaded, run-off, pin-eyed thing, A king of flowers. **1861** DARWIN in *Jrnl. Linn. Soc.* VI. 77 Florists who cultivate the Polyanthus and Auricula .. call those which display the globular stigma at the mouth of the corolla 'pin headed' or 'pin-eyed'. **1877** —— in *Life & Lett.* (1887) III. 295 Some plants yield nothing but pin-eyed flowers in which the style .. is long.

piney wood. *U.S.* Also piny wood. [*piney* var. PINY *a.*] **a.** A pine-wood; a region of pine-woods; *spec.* (pl.) regions of poor land in the Southern United States of which pine-trees are the characteristic growth. Also *attrib.*

1809 M. L. WEEMS *Life Gen. F. Marion* xiv. 122 Had this savage spirit appeared among a few poor British *cadets*, or *piney wood* tories, it would not have been so lamentable. *a* **1816** B. HAWKINS *Sk. Creek Country* (1848) 29 Broken piny woods and reedy branches on its right side. **1860** BARTLETT *Dict. Amer.* (ed. 3) 321 *Piney woods*, the name given at the South to a large tract covered with pines, especially in the low country. **1863** LONGF. *Birds Killingw.* xiii, The green steeples of the piny wood. **1887** *Century Mag.* Aug. 544/1 Azalia, the little piney-woods village which Dr. Buxton had recommended as a sanitarium. **1946** *Sun* (Baltimore) 26 July 16/3 The ponies .. roam wild in the piney woods. **1963** *Social Problems* X. 365/1 Lest such piney-woods practices be thought beneath the sophistication of the urban Negro. **1973** *Daily Colonist* (Victoria, B.C.) 14 Aug. 2/3 Otter said that the twenty-seven victims found buried at the beach, in an east Texas piney wood and in a Houston boat shed, might be all the police will recover. **1976** J. CROSBY *Snake* (1977) xiii. 70 She found herself deep in piny woods and she could see nothing.

b. Special Combs., as **piney-woods cracker**, a poor Southern white; **piney-wood(s) tacky**, (*a*) a scrub pony; (*b*) = prec.

1872 *Kansas Mag.* Mar. 238/1 Who that has seen the 'clay-eater', the 'sandhiller', or the 'piney woods cracker' of the South, does not know that it is impossible to exaggerate the sinfulness which looks out through the loop-holes of his red apologies for eyes? **1935** Z. N. HURSTON *Mules & Men* (1970) I. v. 113 'Bout this time John seen a white couple come in but they looked so trashy he figgered they was piney woods crackers. **1846** *Spirit of Times* 11 July 234/3 Mac mounted a piney-woods-tacky .. and hied him off to Charleston. **1888** *Century Mag.* XXXVI. 799/2 If Mr. Catlett will come to Georgia and go among the 'po' whites' and 'piney-wood tackeys', he will hear the terms 'we-uns' and 'you-uns' in everyday use. **1944** B. A. BOTKIN *Treas. Amer. Folklore* II. 322 Such derogatory nicknames as .. sand-hillers, pineywoods tackies, hill-billies.

ˈpin-ˌfallow, *sb. Agric.* [f. (?) PIN *sb.* + FALLOW *sb.*] 'Winter-fallow; a fallow in which no crop is lost' (*Eng. Dial. Dict.*). Hence **pin-fallow** *v.*, to winter-fallow: see quots.

1668 R. HOLME *Armoury* III. 334/1 Pin Fallow is a Plowing twice for Peas, first in Christmas, then in March. **1790** W. MARSHALL *Midl. Counties* (1796) I. 191 Pin fallow ..the origin of this term I have not learnt; it appears to be synonymous with winter fallow or barley fallow. **1794** BILLINGSLEY *Agric. Survey Som.* 159 Pin fallow..ploughing after vetches, clover, or beans, two or three times, to prepare for a succeeding crop of wheat. **1881** *Leicestersh. Gloss.* s.v., When lea-land is fallowed about July or August, ready to be ploughed again for the crop, it is said to be pin-fallowed.

pin-feather (ˈpɪnˌfɛðə(r)), *sb.* [f. PIN *sb.*[1] + FEATHER.] An ungrown feather, before the vanes have expanded, and while the barrel is full of a dark serous fluid; any young feather from the time that it first pierces the skin, much in the form of a pin, until it bursts its confining sheath and expands its vanes: = PEN-FEATHER 2.

1775 ASH, *Pinfeather*, a feather just as it begins to shoot. **1839** AUDUBON *Ornith. Biog.* V. 520 The nest..still contained three young Cuckoos, all of different sizes,..the largest, covered with pin-feathers, would have been able to leave the nest in about a week. **1852** MRS. STOWE *Uncle Tom's C.* xviii, Shelling peas, peeling potatoes, picking pin-feathers out of fowls. **1879** J. BURROUGHS *Locusts & Wild Honey* (1884) 59 When nearly grown they [cuckoos] are covered with long blue pin-feathers.., without a bit of plumage on them.

attrib. **1901** *Longm. Mag.* May 21 The young birds were in the early pinfeather stage.

Hence ˈ**pin-ˌfeather** *v. trans.*, to pluck out the pin-feathers from; whence **pin-ˌfeatherer** [see -ER[1]]; ˈ**pin-ˌfeathery** *a.*, full of or abounding in pin-feathers.

1874 J. W. LONG *Amer. Wildfowl* xxii. 231 Skins of birds killed in spring are more valuable than those of fall birds, which are usually 'pin-feathery'. **1893** MRS. CARTWRIGHT in *Voice* (N.Y.) 30 Nov., Mrs. Piper was pin-feathering the noble bird. **18..** J. S. JOHNSON *Poultry Raising Guide* (Boston U.S.) 38 Pass her over to the pin-featherers, keeping three or four of these busy removing pin-feathers [etc.].

pin-feathered (ˈpɪnˌfɛðəd), *a.* [f. prec. + -ED[2], or f. PIN *sb.*[1] + FEATHERED.] Having immature feathers, half-fledged (as a young bird, or an adult bird when moulting); also *fig.*: = PEN-FEATHERED 1.

1641 BRATHWAIT *Mercurius Brit.* II. Bij, Thou beganst to flutter with the lapwing before thou wert pinfeathered. **1647** CLEVELAND *Char. Lond. Diurn.* 1 A Diurnall is a puny Chronicle, scarce pin-feather'd with the Wings of time. **1693** DRYDEN *Persius' Sat.* i. (1697) 411 Hourly we see, some raw pin-feather'd thing Attempt to mount, and Fights and Heroes sing.

ˈ**pin-fire**, *a.*[1] (*sb.*[1]) [f. PIN *sb.*[1] + FIRE *v.*]

A. *adj.* Applied to a form of cartridge for breech-loading guns, invented by Lefaucheux in 1836, fitted with a pin which, on being struck by the hammer of the lock, is thrust into the fulminate and explodes it. Also applied to a gun in which such a cartridge is used. **B.** *sb.* (or *ellipt.*) A pin-fire cartridge or gun.

[**1854** *Restell's Patent Specif.* No. 2530. 8–9 The hammer in this gun strikes downwards on a loose stud or pin inserted on the edge of the cartridge rim.] **1870** *U.S. Patent Specif.* No. 99721 A cross-section of an ordinary 'pin-fire cartridge'. **1875** GREENER *Breech-loaders* (ed. 2) 27 We.. make a hundred central-fire guns to one pin-fire. **1885** *Bazaar* 30 Mar. 1274/1, 6 chamber self action pinfire revolver. **1886** *Pall Mall G.* 24 Aug. 4/1 About that date [1866] breech-loaders began to make their appearance—all pin-fires and on the Lefaucheux principle. **1888** *Daily News* 18 Oct. 7/1 A revolver... The weapon is a pin-fire, and has six chambers.

ˈ**pin-fire**, *a.*[2] (*sb.*[2]) Also pinfire. [f. PIN *sb.*[1] + FIRE *sb.*] Used *attrib.* and *absol.* to designate precious opal characterized by closely spaced specks of colour.

1902 *Blackw. Mag.* Feb. 254/1 Two men found a large piece of 'pin-fire', or the best opal. **1902** [see ORANGE *a.* 1 b]. **1908** A. J. DAWSON *Finn* xxxi. 464 Sixty-six solid pounds o' best pin-fire—and us dyin' for want of a crust. **1964** W. C. EYLES *Bk. Opals* i. 25 Pin-fire opal is a type in which the main body of the stone is usually white and shows a myriad of small pinlike colors all through the surface and the body of the stone. **1971** R. PURVIS *Treasure Hunting* i. 27/2 In pin-fire opals, the colour play is in small pinlike dots thickly scattered through the mass. **1976** *Sci. Amer.* Apr. 84/3 In 'pinfire' varieties of opal the grains are up to a millimeter across, but in the more typical varieties they are several millimeters across.

pin-fish to **pin-footed**: see PIN *sb.*[1] 18.

pinfold (ˈpɪnfəʊld), *sb.* Forms: α. 2 pund fald, (3 *L.* punfaudum), 4 ponfold(e, pondfolde, poundfalde, 5 pundfald *Sc.*, 6 punfolde, pundfauld *Sc.*, 9 (*dial.*) punfaud. β. 4–7 pynfold, 5 -fald, pynd(e)fold(e, 5–6 pynfolde, 6 pinnefolde, pynfoalde, 6–7 pinfolde, -fould, 8 (*dial.*) pinfald, pindfold, 9 (*dial.*) pinfaud, pinfowd, -fowt, 6– pinfold. [Late OE. *pundfald* (in 12th c. MS., but doubtless earlier), f. **pund*, POUND *sb.*[2] + *fald*, FOLD *sb.*[2]; thence the ME. forms in *pun(d-*, *pound-*, *pond-*, retained in Sc. to 16th c. and in north Eng. dial. to 19th c. But from *c* 1400 the first element was associated with the verb *pyndan*, PIND, and perhaps with PIN *v.* Cf. also PENFOLD.]

1. A place for confining stray or distrained cattle, horses, sheep, etc.; a pound; in later use, sometimes, a fold for sheep, cattle, etc.

α. ? *a* **1200** *Spurious Charter of Edgar* (dated 961) in Birch *Cart. Sax.* III. 309 Of þam putte on hacan pund fold, of hacan pund falde oþ eft on þæt efer fearn. **1235–52** *Rentalia Glaston.* (Som. Rec. Soc.) 191 Et facit punfaudum. *c* **1450** HOLLAND *Howlat* 783 The pundar..Had pyndit all his pryss horss in a pundfald. **1574** *Reg. Privy Council Scot.* II. 417 Putting of the saidis gudis in ane unlauchfull punfauld. **1579** *Mem. St. Giles, Durham* (Surtees) 1 Payde to Rycharde Robinson one day for maykyn clene the punfolde. **1825** BROCKETT *N.C. Gloss.*, *Pun-faud* or *pin-faud*.

β. **1408** *Nottingham Rec.* II. 64 Willelmus Whytehals pro fractione pyndfold. **14..** *Voc.* in Wr.-Wülcker 590/12 *Interclusorium*, a pyndefolde. **1523** FITZHERB. *Husb.* §148 Yf thy horse breake his tedure..than cometh the pynder & taketh hym & putteth hym in the pynfolde. **1589** *Pappe w. Hatchet* E j b, I thinke them woorth..for their scabbednes to bee thrust from the pinfolde. **1628** COKE *On Litt.* 47 b, He that distraines anything that hath life, must impound them ..in a pinfold. **1664** BUTLER *Hud.* II. II. 200 But to confine the Bad and Sinful, Like Moral Cattle, in a Pinfold. **1796** MORSE *Amer. Geog.* II. 439 They resort to the caves..where they sleep in crowds like sheep in a pinfold. **1899** A. WHITE *Mod. Jew* Introd. 10 In the..ten provinces of Poland..the Jews are confined as in a pinfold. **1903** *Eng. Dial. Dict.*, *Pinfold*..2. An enclosure for sheep, a sheepfold. [Leicester to Suffolk.]

2. *transf.* and *fig.* A place of confinement; a pen; a trap; a spiritual 'fold'.

1377 LANGL. *P. Pl.* B. v. 633 Heo hath hulpe a þousande oute of þe deueles ponfolde [*v.rr.* pond-, pun-, pounfolde, pynfold]. *Ibid.* XVI. 264 Oute of þe poukes pondfolde [*v.rr.* ponfold, pynfold; *C.* poundfalde, pynfold] no meynprise may vs fecche. **1549** *Compl. Scot.* xi. 99 Thai hed the romans in that pundfald, quhar thai culd nothir fecht nor fle. **1634** MILTON *Comus* 7 Confin'd, and pester'd in this pin-fold here. *c* **1750** J. NELSON *Jrnl.* 41 You are gone out of the highway of holiness, and have now got into the devil's pinfold. **1863** COWDEN CLARKE *Shaks. Char.* viii. 211 The restraining of all dissentients within their own pinfold.

pinfold (ˈpɪnfəʊld), *v.* [f. prec. sb.] *trans.* To shut up or enclose in a pinfold; to pound; hence *fig.* to confine within narrow limits.

1605 T. HUTTON *Reasons for Refusal* 61 Take heede, howe they pinfold the worde (*faith*) in this or that sense after their owne private imagination. **1673** [R. LEIGH] *Transp. Reh.* 124 They exercise a petty royalty in pinfolding cattle. **1785** [W. HUTTON] *Bran New Wark* 38 If our nebbour's stot or stirk break into'th fog, let us net pinfald it. **1836** LANDOR *Pericles & Asp.* Wks. 1846 II. 394/2 My name..is a difficult ..one to pinfold in a tombstone.

ping (pɪŋ), *sb.* Also reduplicated. [Echoic.]

a. An abrupt ringing sound, such as that made by a rifle bullet in flying through the air, by a mosquito, the ringing of an electric bell, etc.

1835 J. E. ALEXANDER *Sk. Portugal* xi. 262 If a button was shown, 'ping' went a bullet at it immediately. **1856** *Sebastopol* I. xi. 132 The sharp 'ping' of a Minié bullet. **1861** W. B. BROOKE *Out w. Garibaldi* iii. 24 The 'ping, ping' of rifle bullets whizzing over one's head. **1880** GILL *River Gold. S.* II. vii. 258 The ping of the mosquitoes which was heard for the first time for many a long day. **1897** MARY KINGSLEY *W. Africa* 132 Mosquitoes..With a wild ping of joy..made for me. **1909** KIPLING *Rewards & Fairies* (1910) 272 *Ping-ping-ping* went the bicycle bell round the corner. **1921** D. H. LAWRENCE in *Hutchinson's Mag.* Nov. 463/1 They were interrupted by the ping of the shop-bell. **1930** J. B. PRIESTLEY *Angel Pavement* v. 263 She sent the typewriter carriage flying along. It gave a sharp ping. **1957** H. NICOLSON *Diary* 5 Oct. (1968) 339 The Russians have released a satellite... The B.B.C. have managed to record the signals, and play them over to us—just ping, ping, ping, ping. **1960** N. HILLIARD in C. K. Stead *N.Z. Short Stories* (1966) 235 They rested..listening to the..ping-ping-ping of crossing bells. **1977** *New Yorker* 20 June 94/3 Everyone assembled for an ostinato unison figure, and the music subsided with a string of tinkles and hums and pings.

b. A very short pulse of high-pitched, usu. ultrasonic, sound such as is emitted by sonar; also, a pulse of audible sound by which this is represented to a user of such equipment.

1943 *Penguin New Writing* XVIII. 27 'Daisy had a ping about an hour ago... We're doing an Asdic sweep.'.. A 'ping' is the slang term for an echo. **1946** *Sci. Illustr.* May 83/1 The sounds, or 'pings', sonar sends out are not at all like sounds to you and me. They are supersonic. **1956** *Deep-Sea Res.* III. 267 The system had a repetition rate of about 10 pings per second and a ping length of about two milliseconds. **1960** [see PINGER 1 a]. **1966** *McGraw-Hill Encycl. Sci. & Technol.* IX. 252/2 The Swallow-type neutrally buoyant float is a mid-depth current meter.. which..can float at a predetermined depth... It emits acoustic pings which can be heard for several miles from a quiet ship equipped with appropriate sound gear. **1967** J. B. HERSEY *Deep-Sea Photogr.* iv. 59/1 It was possible to obtain the height of camera above bottom simply by measuring the time interval between the arrival at the ship of the sound pulse, or ping, and its bottom echo.

c. Also *ping-man*. (See quots.) *slang.*

1946 J. IRVING *Royal Navalese* 135 *Ping-man*, an Asdic operator. **1948** PARTRIDGE *Dict. Forces' Slang* 142 *Ping*, an Asdic officer or rating.

d. = PINK *sb.*[6] 3.

More usual than *pink* in the U.S. and Australia.

1927 *Dyke's Automobile & Gasoline Engine Encycl.* Suppl. 1313/1 Engineers began an investigation as to the causes of pre-ignition and ping in an engine burning the present-day gasoline. **1942** *Pop. Sci.* Mar. 137/2 A slight ping when you step on the gas hard does not always mean trouble. **1953** H. R. RICARDO *High-Speed Internal-Combustion Engine* ii. 27 The mechanism of detonation is the setting-up within the cylinder of a pressure wave travelling at so high a velocity as, by its impact against the cylinder walls, to set them in vibration and thus give rise to a high-pitched 'ping'. **1958** *S.A.E. Jrnl.* Sept. 73/1 Rumble..is distinct from the high frequency spark knock or wild ping most people have heard. **1977** *Pop. Mechanics* May 49/2 My 1976 Ford Pinto with a 2.3-liter, four-cylinder engine has had a bad ping almost from day one.

ping (pɪŋ), *v.*[1] *Obs.* exc. *dial.* Forms: 1 pyngan, pingan, 3 pungen (ü), (pa. t. puinde), 4 punge, pyngen, pingen, 9 *dial.* ping. [OE. *pyngan* :—**pungian*, ad. L. *pungĕre* to prick.

(The mod. dial. vb. has strong and mixed forms of pa. t. and pa. pple. *pung*, *pung'd*.)]

trans. and *intr.* To prick; to poke, push, urge.

c **897** K. ÆLFRED *Gregory's Past. C.* xl. 297 He wærlice hine pynge mid sumum wordum ðæt he on ðæm ongietan mæge [etc.]. *c* **1205** LAY. 23933 Arður ut mid his sweorde.. and puinden [*c* **1275** pungde] uppen Frolle. *a* **1330** *Otuel* 779 He pingde his stede wiþ spores kene. **1362** LANGL. *P. Pl.* A. IX. 88 A pyk is in þe potent to punge a-doun þe wikkede. *c* **1380** *Sir Ferumb.* 1248 þe prisoun dore than wend heo ner & putte hure staf an vnder As sche wolde þe dore to-breke sche gan þo hebbe & pynge. **1382** WYCLIF *Prov.* xii. 18 Ther is that behoteth, and as with a swerd is pungid to the conscience. **1746** *Exmoor Scold.* 255 (E.D.S.) Tha wud'st ha' borst en to Shivers, nif chad net a vung en, and pung'd en back agen. **1787** GROSE *Provinc. Gloss.*, *Ping*, to push. **1876** MADOX-BROWN *Dwale Bluth* II. iii, I wish they'd gie thy cat ter th' butcher, ter naup and ping loose ower the moor-yavils out there.

ping (pɪŋ), *v.*[2] [Echoic: cf. PING *sb.*]

1. a. *intr.* To make an abrupt ringing sound like that of a rifle bullet; to fly with such a sound. Also const. *out* and *fig.*

1855 *Illustr. Lond. News* 15 Sept. 326/1 Rifle-bullets ..'pinging' over their heads. **1878** W. C. SMITH *Hilda among Broken Gods* (1879) 242 Balls from the rifle-pits ping about. **1924** GALSWORTHY *White Monkey* II. ix. 195 A footman..stood..waiting for an order to ping out, staccato, through the hum. **1930** J. B. PRIESTLEY *Angel Pavement* iii. 96 The typewriters rattled and *pinged*, the telephone bell rang. *a* **1963** S. PLATH *Crossing Water* (1971) 53 The glass.. will ping like a Chinese chime. **1967** *Listener* 16 Nov. 647/3 Words and concepts heard nowhere else pinged out on Third Programme drama. **1974** W. J. BURLEY *Death in Stanley St.* v. 90 He went in, the door bell pinged. **1978** T. WILLIS *Buckingham Palace Connection* viii. 151 A bullet pinged against the plating.

b. = PINK *v.*[3] 2.

1942 *Pop. Sci.* Mar. 136/1 Let's assume it is a couple of months from now, and that best available gas makes your car engine ping—or worse, knock—on a pick-up or a hard pull.

2. a. *trans.* To cause to make such a sound. Also *fig.*

1746 *Exmoor Scolding* (1879) 52 Tha wud'st ha' borst en to Shivers, nif chad net a vung en, and pung'd en back agen. **1902** *Westm. Gaz.* 10 Apr. 2/1 Automobiles that pinged their warning gongs. **1921** D. H. LAWRENCE in *Hutchinson's Mag.* Nov. 462/2 They 'pinged' the door-bell, and her aunt came running forward out of the kitchen. **1957** J. KEROUAC *On Road* (1958) 32 The air grew ice-cold and pinged our ears. **1961** J. H. FORD *Mountains of Gilead* v. 128 A room complete with moths pinging the light. **1974** 'P. B. YUILL' *Bornless Keeper* vii. 64 There was nobody at the little alcove marked Reception. Victoria pinged the bell.

b. To fire or discharge (a missile) with a pinging sound. Also *transf.*

1959 I. & P. OPIE *Lore & Lang. Schoolch.* xiii. 297 We.. ping pellets in class. **1977** A. C. H. SMITH *Jericho Gun* xiii. 171 He was able to ping off three one-shots.

Hence ˈ**pinging** *ppl. a.*

1865 *Daily Tel.* 29 May, The visit of pinging balls and cracking shells.

‖**pinga** (ˈpiŋa). [Pg., lit. 'drop (of water)'.] A raw white rum distilled from sugar-cane in Brazil.

1933 P. FLEMING *Brazilian Adventure* I. xii. 98 You drank black coffee with *pinga* in it. **1960** *Guardian* 14 June 9/6 Her breath reeked of pinga (a cheap drink made from sugar cane). **1974** *Country Life* 31 Oct. 1314/3 Sugar-cane spirit (or *pinga*). **1977** *Lancet* 24–31 Dec. 1365/2 We have studied 61 alcoholic patients with pellagra aged 23–49, most of them drinking more than 800 ml of *pinga* (a Brazilian alcoholic beverage similar to white rum) containing about 300 ml of pure ethanol.

pingao (ˈpiːŋaʊ). Also pingau. [Maori.] A New Zealand sedge, *Desmoschœnus spiralis*, with creeping underground stems which help to stabilize sand-dunes.

1855 J. D. HOOKER *Flora Novæ-Zelandiæ* I. 272 *Desmoschœnus spiralis*... Nat[ive] name, 'Pingao'. **1905** W. B. *Where White Man Treads* 2 White seashore sandhills.. for..the wind..to pile into hillocks, until the wily pingau (native sand grass), creeping snakelike along,.. bound [them] into masses. **1936** [see KAKAHO]. **1949** P. H. BUCK *Coming of Maori* II. iv. 156 The only other native colour to black, used in plaiting, was yellow obtained by using wefts of *pingao*, the leaves of which are a natural yellow. **1970** MOORE & EDGAR *Flora N.Z.* II. 171 Pingao... This is a well-known plant because it is an effective sand-binder and also because the Maoris used the dried golden leaves to give colour to articles woven from *Phormium*.

pinge (pɪndʒ), *sb.* and *v.* [Echoic: cf. PING *sb.*] A variant of PING *sb.* and *v.*[2]

1860 TRISTRAM *Gt. Sahara* ix. 138, I felt the pinge of a ball past my eyes. **1888** *Pall Mall G.* 18 Sept. 11/1 With bullets pingeing and singing close over his head.

pinger (ˈpɪŋə(r)). [f. PING *v.*[2] + -ER[1].] **1. a.** A device that transmits pings (PING *sb.* 1 b) at short intervals for purposes of detection, measurement, or identification.

1957 *Deep-Sea Res.* IV. 120 The three principal units which comprise the camera are the photographic unit, the electronic flash light and the acoustic signal generator or 'pinger'. **1960** *Electronics* 24 June 95/3 The detailed contour of the bottom with respect to the pinger can be determined by recording the direct and bottom-reflected pings. **1969** J. MAVOR *Voy. Atlantis* II. iv. 124 It was the shallowness of the water that made examination with Doc's pinger feasible. **1975** *Offshore Engineer* Nov. 51/1 The pinger receiver audibly indicates the direction to a pinger using a manually operated sensitivity control located on the end of the receiver and an earphone.

b. (See quot.)

1961 PARTRIDGE *Dict. Slang* (ed. 5) II. 1222/1 *Pinger*, the Asdic officer: Naval: since ca. 1936.

2. A timer that makes a ringing or pinging sound after a pre-set number of minutes.

1968 J. BINGHAM *I love, I Kill* vi. 72, I heard the old vibrant tinkling, like those kitchen ping-ers which tell you when the cabbage is ready cooked. **1973** *Times* 30 July 11/2 Many new cookers have automatic timing, with both a time of day clock for cooking while you are out and a 60-minute pinger for reminding you when you are in that a dish is cooked. **1976** P. DICKINSON *King & Joker* i. 10 Two eggs.. boiled for two minutes... The pinger pinged.

ˈpinging, *vbl. sb.* [f. PING *v.*[2] + -ING[1].]

a. The process of making an abrupt ringing sound or 'ping'; the sound itself; *spec.* = PINKING *vbl. sb.*[3]

More usual than *pinking* in the U.S. and Australia.

1898 *Daily News* 10 Dec. 6/5 Pinging of harps, tootling of flutes. **1955** *Pop. Mechanics* Nov. 203/2 Retard the spark a little at a time..until no pinging is heard. **1967** *Boston Sunday Herald* 28 May I. 2/6 'Pinging'..results from carbon deposits or fuel not high enough in octane rating. **1969** *Telegraph* (Brisbane) 1 Feb. 13/4 Tetra-ethyl lead is used to raise octane ratings, reduce engine knock or pinging and minimise engine misfires.

b. The production or emission of pings by sonar or similar equipment (see PING *sb.* 1 b).

1956 *Deep-Sea Res.* IV. 39 The pinging circuit of the echo sounder. **1959** H. BARNES *Oceanogr. & Marine Biol.* 203 New cameras have been described and in one contact with the bottom is indicated by a change of the 'pinging' rate of a small sound source attached to the unit. **1973** *Times* 27 Dec. 3/2 Teams of 71 Squadron split into two daily shifts, poring over the sands between tides to the 'pinging' of mine detectors. **1974** 'M. HEBDEN' *Pride of Dolphins* III. iii. 232 The relentless pinging of the asdic beam.

pingle (ˈpɪŋg(ə)l), *sb.*[1] *Sc.* [f. PINGLE *v.*]

1. A keen contest or struggle.

1543 *St. Papers Hen. VIII*, V. 237 *note*, [They made at each other, so that] with long pyngle with dagger [Somerset was slain]. **1719** HAMILTON in *Ramsay's Fam. Epist.* I. iv, 'Twad be a pingle, Whilk o' you three wad gar words sound And best to jingle. **1816** SIR A. BOSWELL *Skeldon Haughs* Wks. (1871) 167 Now is the pingle, hand to hand. **1819** W. TENNANT *Papistry Storm'd* (1827) 153 Papists and faes in dreidfu' pingle.

2. Struggle with difficulties; strenuous exertion.

1728 RAMSAY *To R. Yarde* 9 Skelping o'er frozen hags with pingle. **1786** *Har'st Rig* lxx, He's in a pingle. **1871** P. H. WADDELL *Ps. in Scottis* xxxiii. 16 Nae mighty man [is] redd by his mighty pingle.

pingle (ˈpɪŋg(ə)l), *sb.*[2] *Obs.* exc. *dial.* [Of uncertain origin: cf. PIGHTLE.] A small enclosed piece of land; a paddock, a close.

1546 *Yorks. Chantry Surv.* (Surtees) I. 154 Roger Blythe for one pyngle with..a gate thrugh the same. **1603** HOLLAND *Plutarch's Mor.* 275 The Academie, a little pingle or plot of ground,..was the habitation of Plato, Xenocrates, and Polemon. **1633** SANDERSON *Serm.* II. 43 They thrust and pen up the whole flock of Christ in a far narrower pingle than ever the Donatists did. **1674** RAY *N.C. Words* 37 A *Pingle*, a small croft or Picle. *a* **1864** J. CLARE *MS. Poems* (E.D.D.), Meadow and close, and pingle: where suns cling And shine on earliest flowers.

pingle (ˈpɪŋg(ə)l), *sb.*[3] *Sc.* [Origin unknown.] A small pan or cooking-pot of tinned iron, having a long handle. Also *pingle-pan.*

1789 D. DAVIDSON *Seasons* 6 The pingle-pan Is on the ingle set. **1821** *Blackw. Mag.* VIII. 429 You want a pingle, lassie [*note*, A small tin-made goblet, used in Scotland for preparing children's food]. **1858** SIMMONDS *Dict. Trade*, *Pingle-pan*, in Scotland, a small tin goblet with a long handle. **1863** J. L. W. *By-gone Days* 192 Supplying the 'gudewife' with pitchers, or repairing her 'pingle pans'.

pingle (ˈpɪŋg(ə)l, *north. dial.* ˈpɪŋ(ə)l), *v.* Also 6 pingil(l, pingyl, pyngle. [Origin obscure. Perhaps branches I and II are different words, I being only Sc. With II cf. Sw. dial. *pyngla* to be busy about small matters, to work in a trifling way (Rietz).]

I. †**1.** *intr.* To strive, contend, vie. *Sc. Obs.*

1508 DUNBAR *Flyting* 114 Bettir thow ganis to leid ane doig to skomer.. than with thy maister pingill. **1513** DOUGLAS *Æneis* I. iv. 14 To se the hewis on ather hand is wondir, For hicht that semis pingill with the hevin. **1635** D. DICKSON *Pract. Wks.* (1845) I. 27 They stood out long, pingling with God. **1789** D. DAVIDSON *Seasons* 36 How brithers pingled at their brochan, And made a din.

2. *trans.* †**a.** To press hard in a contest, to run (any one) hard, to vie with (*obs.*). **b.** To trouble, worry. *Sc.*

1513 DOUGLAS *Æneis* V. iv. 122 Quhan finally to pursew he adrest, And pinglis hir [the ship] onto the vtirmest. *c* **1587** MONTGOMERIE *Sonn.* xv. 14, I pingle thame all perfytlie in that parte [poverty]. *a* **1600** *Ibid.* xliv. 12 Let Mercure language to me len,..To pingill Apelles pynsell with my pen. **1814** SCOTT *Wav.* xxiv, To be pingled wi' mickle speaking.

3. *intr.* To struggle against difficulties; to work hard, labour, toil, exert oneself; to struggle or toil for a livelihood. *Sc.*

1513 DOUGLAS *Æneis* III. v. 14 Beselie our folkis gan to pingill and strife. *Ibid.* v. iv. 75 With all thar force than at the vterance, Thai pinglit ayris [= oars] wp to bend, and haill. *a* **1598** ROLLOCK *Lect. Passion* ix. Wks. (Wodrow Soc.) II. 109 To get that spirit to pingle out, and get the victory against this canker in the heart. **1836** M. MACKINTOSH *Cottager's Dau.* 66 She'll hae to pingle through the hard.

II. 4. *intr.* To work in a trifling or ineffectual way; to meddle or have to do *with* in a petty way; to piddle or peddle; to trifle or dally. Now *Sc.* and *north. dial.*

1574 R. SCOT *Hop Gard.* (1578) 35 Suffer them not to pyngle in pycking [hops] one by one, but let them speedily strip them into Baskets. **1579** J. STUBBES *Gaping Gulf* C vij, King Phillip, for al those dominions & mines of treasures, was content to be pingling with our purses: made Queene Mary to aske..frequent subsides. *a* **1598** ROLLOCK *Lect. Passion* xxxii. Wks. (Wodrow Soc.) II. 392 We may pingle with them a while here, but we remit them to that great day that the Judge appear. **1632** I. L. *Women's Rights* 152 If he doe but pingle, as suffer himselfe to be outlawed..this was neuer any forfeiture of franke tenement. **1871** P. H. WADDELL *Ps. in Scottis* xxxviii. 12 Wha ettle me ill speak a' mischieff an' pingle on lies the hail day.

5. *intr.* To pick at or trifle with food; to eat with little appetite, nibble. Now *dial.*

1600 NASHE *Summer's Last Will & Test.* in Hazl. *Dodsley* VIII. 27 Neither did he pingle, when it was set on the board. **1641** BEST *Farm. Bks.* (Surtees) 75 If wee knewe of any banke-sides that lay against the sunne.. wee tooke them [the hoggs]..to them, and lette pingle aboute. **1670** RAY *Prov.* 33 Great drinkers..do (as we say) but pingle at their meat and eat little. *a* **1825** FORBY *Voc. E. Anglia*, *Pingle*, *v.* to pick one's food; to eat squeamishly. [In *Eng. Dial. Dict.*, from Yorksh. to Herts and Essex.]

b. *trans. dial.*

1903 *Eng. Dial. Dict.* s.v., (Herts.) She just sits and pingles her victuals. (Essex) The child is not well, she pingles her food.

Hence **ˈpingling** *vbl. sb.*, (*a*) struggling, striving, exertion; (*b*) trifling with food or drink; **ˈpingling** *ppl. a.*, whence **ˈpinglingly** *adv.*, in a pingling way, with little appetite.

a **1578** LINDESAY *Chron. Scot.* XXI. xxxviii, They were all Borderers and could ryde and prick well, and held the Scottishmen in pingling [*so 2 MSS.*] be their pricking and skirmishing. **1768** ROSS *Helenore* 43 Wi' my teeth I gnew the raips in twa, And wi' sair pingling wan at last awa'.

(*b*) **1594** NASHE *Unfort. Trav.* 79 As long as they haue eyther oyle or wine, this plague feeds but pinglingly vpon them. **1602** ROWLANDS *Tis Merrie when Gossips meete* 17 Nay fill your Cup, Wee'le haue no pingling now we are alone.

ˈpingler. *Obs.* or *dial.* [f. prec. II + -ER[1].]

1. A trifler, dallier, dabbler. (In quot. opposed to *courser*, runner, one who runs in a race.)

[Conjectured by Nares to mean 'a labouring horse kept by a farmer in his homestead', from PINGLE *sb.*[2] Hence Ogilvie (and *Century Dict.*) 'a cart-horse, a workhorse'.]

1579 LYLY *Euphues* (Arb.) 109 Judging all to be clownes which be no courtiers, and al to be pinglers that be not coursers.

2. One who 'pingles' with food or drink.

1599 PORTER *Angry Wom. Abingd.* (Percy Soc.) 48 If I cannot drinke it downe..let me be counted nobody, a pingler. **1607** TOPSELL *Four-f. Beasts* (1658) 412 He filleth his mouth well, and is no pingler at his meat. **1657** M. LAWRENCE *Use & Pract. Faith* 206 Men that are..declining ..are but pinglers at their meat.

pingo (ˈpɪŋgəʊ). *Geomorphol.* Pl. pingos, less commonly pingoes. [Eskimo (see quot. 1928[1]).] A perennial conical or dome-shaped mound (often with a crater on top) found in regions with thin or discontinuous permafrost and consisting of a layer of soil over a large core of ice, the width being much greater than the height; also, a round depression or rampart in temperate regions thought to be the remains of such a mound formed when the climate was colder.

The word is applied rather differently in quots. 1928. The current techn. use derives from that of Porsild.

[**1928** L. KOCH in *Meddelelser om Grønland* LXV. 196 To denote a mountain entirely or partly covered with ice but whose form is still distinguishable, the Polar-Eskimos use the name 'Pingo', a term which in these regions corresponds to the name 'Nunatak'. The best example of a Pingo is Mt. Haffner, Pingorsoak, i.e. the great Pingo. *Ibid.* 197 We need no name for rounded nunataks. I have, however, introduced the name Pingo..to designate a mountain entirely submerged by the Inland Ice, but setting its mark upon the surface of the ice. *Ibid.* 203 The easternmost of these ranges consists of a series of high and precipitous nunataks and Pingos.] **1938** A. E. PORSILD in *Geogr. Rev.* XXVIII. 46 In literature the name 'gravel or earth mound' seems to be fairly well established. The Eskimo name *pingo*, meaning conical hill, which has come into universal use in the north, is here introduced as an alternative. *Ibid.* 54 (*caption*) Pingo near Tuktuayaktok on the Arctic Sea coast east of the Mackenzie delta showing the irregular rupture of the summit. This pingo is 134 feet high. **1961**, **1968** [see *hydrolaccolith* s.v. HYDRO-]. **1968** R. W. FAIRBRIDGE *Encycl. Geomorphol.* 848/2 The pingos of Wales seem to belong to the open system, the water having flowed down the slope between a thin permafrost and an impervious bedrock. **1972** *Nature* 14 Apr. 344/1 The pingos of Cardiganshire are not sparse in distribution but occur in a number of localities. **1974** *N.Y. Times* 26 May I. 34/4 There was little but ice and snow..occasional ice-cored hillocks called pingoes, and the prominent ribbons of the winter ice road.

pin-gout, etc.: see PIN *sb.*[1] 18.

ping-pong (ˈpɪŋˈpɒŋ), *sb.* [Echoic. Cf. PING *sb.*]

1. a. A parlour game resembling lawn-tennis, played on a table with bats, formerly of parchment stretched on a wooden frame, now usu. with a wooden blade covered with pimpled rubber and celluloid balls; so called from the sharp 'ping' emitted by the bat when striking; table-tennis. Also *attrib.*

Ping-pong is a proprietary name in the U.S.

1900 *Daily Chron.* 8 May 6/6 Our correspondent seems to hope that the unclean, playing Ping-Pong with the clean, will become unpleasantly conscious of his uncleanness and reform. **1901** *Ibid.* 2 May 3/2 The inventor of Ping-Pong has been discovered, it was Mr. James Gibb, an old Cambridge athlete, now living at Croydon. *Ibid.* 31 Dec. 5/1 Playtime's too short for us, bedtime too long, Since we have taken to playing Ping Pong. **1901** [see *table-tennis* s.v. TABLE *sb.* 22]. **1902** *Harper's Weekly* 7 June 739 To have your squash-court this summer, if you have any pretensions to style, is as necessary as to have your ping-pong table or your automobile. **1904** 'H. FOULIS' *Erchie* xiv. 90 The grocer in there wad be thinkin' I was awa' on the ping-pong if he didna ken I was a beadle. **1907** *Westm. Gaz.* 12 Oct. 3/2 A set of 'ping-pong' materials. **1949** *Official Gaz.* (U.S. Patent Office) 4 Oct. 40/2 Parker Brothers, Inc., Salem, Mass. ..*Ping-pong*... For game played with rackets and balls. Claims use since Aug. 1, 1900. **1958** R. LIDDELL *Morea* II. i. 47 Nick..had been playing ping-pong outside the hotel. **1968** *Listener* 13 June 783/2 No character ever entirely subsides: they are like those ping-pong balls at a fair that rise and fall on spurts of water. **1977** E. AMBLER *Send no more Roses* x. 231, I used the handle of a ping-pong bat to keep it [*sc.* a door] open.

b. *fig.* A series of (usu. verbal) exchanges between two parties. Also *attrib.*

1917 E. POUND *Let.* 11 Apr. in T. S. Eliot *Waste Land Drafts* (1971) p. xii, I want to boom Eliot and one cant have too obvious a ping-pong match at that sort of thing. **1934** L. B. LYON *White Hare* 50 After him came two high-brows playing a wordy ping-pong. **1955** *Times* 18 July 9/2 Coal is one industry that has escaped the political ping-pong which threatens steel. **1966** J. CLEARY *High Commissioner* iii. 51 Two hours of diplomatic ping-pong hadn't touched her; she looked..poised and unmarked. **1974** 'M. ALLEN' *Super Tour* (1975) v. 203 It was impossible to beat Mama in the game of verbal Ping-Pong. **1976** N. POSTMAN *Crazy Talk* 8 In the Ping-Pong ball theory, communication is conceived of as a discrete, quantifiable piece of stuff that will move from one source to another and then back. **1977** *Times* 5 Dec. 54/1 The French political journals, center and right, ravaged Courbet for years, and beside their vilifications the attacks on impressionism and cubism were mere Ping Pong.

2. A type of drum in a West Indian steel band (see quots.). Also, a melody played on such a drum.

1955 *New Commonwealth* 28 Nov. (Suppl.) p. xix/1 In the orchestra the pans are grouped into Ping Pongs, Alto Pans, Tenor Kittles, Kittle Booms, Tune Booms and Bass Booms. **1956** L. HUGHES *First Bk. of W. Indies* 42 Discarded oil drums are cut, heated, and hammered in such a way that each has its own pitch and tone. Those that carry the melody are called 'ping pongs'. **1959** W. A. SIMMONDS *'Pan'-Story of Steelband* 9 By the end of 1945, different bands had developed different 'beats'. The initiated could, by the rhythm and 'Ping-Pong', distinguish what band 'was beating pan'. *Ibid.* 12 The queen of them all—the sweet Ping-Pong. This is a steel drum cut to about six or seven inches from the top. After these are stretched, and tempered, between twenty-six and thiry-two notes are marked and tuned.

Hence **ˈping-ˈpongist**, a ping-pong player or enthusiast.

1901 *Daily Chron.* 27 Dec. 6/3 The competitors were presumably the pick of 'Ping-Pongists' in London.

ˈping-ˈpong, *v.* [f. the sb.] **a.** *intr.* To play ping-pong. Also, to move back and forth in the manner of a ping-pong ball. Also *fig.* **b.** *trans.* To send back and forth, to pass around aimlessly.

1901 *Times* 1 June 8/5 [He] is only required to be agreeable and to ping-pong. **1952** *Jackson* (Tennessee) *Sun* 1/1 (*heading*) Question of Margaret's guards ping-pongs across Atlantic. **1960** in Cassidy & Le Page *Dict. Jamaican Eng.* (1967) 351/2 A common Jamaican expression, if you say 'he ping-pongs at it' it means he doesn't do it very well —like me typing: I just ping-pong at it. **1970** *Washington Post* 22 Nov. B6 The administration 'ping-ponged' the proposal back and forth. **1971** *Daily Colonist* (Victoria, B.C.) 2 Sept. 13/7 It was 'unfortunate for this accused that he has been, if I may coin a phrase, pingponged from one court to another'. **1972** *Daily Tel.* 11 Mar. 11/2 He can time funny lines so that they ping-pong back and forth in long sustained volleys with the audience's laughter. **1974** *Times Lit. Suppl.* 27 Sept. 1033/2 They ping-pong helplessly between sea and sheets, between pub and plough. **1976** *Times* 31 Aug. 5/2 The report [of a Senate committee] states that 'investigators were repeatedly "ping-ponged" to neurologists, gynaecologists, internists, [etc.]'.

Hence **ˈping-ponger** = PING-PONGIST; **ˈping-ponging** *vbl. sb.*, playing ping-pong; also *fig.*; *spec.* (see quots.).

1901 *Morn. Leader* 18 Dec. 3/3 The ping-ponging, however, has not yet started. **1933** *Times* 14 Nov. 15/4 It cannot be, and is not, good for anyone to enjoy the high moments or ecstasies of lawn tennis without sharing its physical dangers; yet that is what the ping ponger is trying to do. **1962** G. COMPTON *Too Many Murderers* xvii. 144 She sidled round the ping-pongers. **1972** *Daily Colonist* (Victoria, B.C.) 6 Jan. 1/8 Medical groups..engaged in 'ping-ponging'—sending patients from one medicaid provider to another for services they did not need. **1972** *National Observer* (U.S.) 18 Mar. 16/1 The chief resident and Ping-ponger extraordinaire is one Dal-Joon Lee. **1975** *Time* 26 May 55/2 Many of the 'Medicaid mills' of clinics set up to handle poor patients in the nation's urban ghettos reap enormous profits by such practices as 'Ping Ponging' (passing a patient along to all the other doctors in the clinic). **1976** *Discursive Dict. Health Care* (U.S.) 122 *Ping-ponging*, the practice of passing a patient from one physician to another in a health program for unnecessary cursory examinations so that the program can charge the patient's third-party for a physical visit to each physician.

pin-grass, -ground: see PIN *sb.*[1] 18.

pingster: see PINKSTER.

pinguecula, var. PINGUICULA (in sense 2).

pinguedinous (pɪŋ'gwɛdɪnəs), *a.* Also 9 erron. -idinous. [f. L. *pinguēdin-em* fatness (f. *pingui-s* fat) + -OUS.] Of the nature of or resembling fat; fatty, greasy.

1599 A. M. tr. *Gabelhouer's Bk. Physicke* 65/1 Take an inveterate Oyle canne, which as yet is pinguedinous internallye. **1740** MALFALGUERAT in *Phil. Trans.* XLI. 366 This Excrescence..was for the most part of a pinguedinous Substance. **1826** H. N. COLERIDGE *West Indies* (1832) 161, I have..found a crassitude, a pinguedinous gravity in the meat.

So †**pin'guedinize** *v. Obs. rare*—0. = PINGUEFY.

1656 BLOUNT *Glossogr.*, *Pinguefie*..to make fat or gross; some have used Pinguedinize in the same sense.

†**pingue'faction.** *Obs. rare*—1. [n. of action f. L. *pinguefac-ĕre* to fatten: see PINGUEFY and -TION.] The action of pinguefying; *concr.* an application for this purpose.

1597 A. M. tr. *Guillemeau's Fr. Chirurg.* 36/1 We must then, with warme infusions and pingvefactions, soften..and make supple the same.

pinguefy ('pɪŋgwɪfaɪ), *v.* Now *rare.* Also 6–9 erron. pinguify. [ad. L. *pinguefacĕre* to fatten, f. stem of **pinguēre*, *pinguēscĕre* to grow fat + *facĕre* to make: see PINGUESCENT and -FY.]

1. *trans.* To cause to become fat; to fatten; to make greasy; to saturate with grease; also, to make (soil) rich or fertile.

1599 A. M. tr. *Gabelhouer's Bk. Physicke* 41/2 Pinguefye heerin a little linnen cloute, and applye the same on the Foreheade. **1603** HOLLAND *Plutarch's Mor.* 1158 The oile or ointment wherewith women..annoint the haire of their head..hath a certaine propertie in it to pinguifie withall. **1610** W. FOLKINGHAM *Art of Survey* I. x. 24 It pinguifies the soyle. **1678** CUDWORTH *Intell. Syst.* I. v. 810 The..Fumes, and Nidours of Sacrifices; wherewith their Corporeal and Spirituous Part, is as it were Pinguified. **1893** *Syd. Soc. Lex.*, *Pinguefy*,..to make fat.

2. *intr.* To become fat. ? *Obs.*

1597 A. M. tr. *Guillemeau's Fr. Chirurg.* 52b/2 Those partes doe increace and pingvifye. **1655** in *Narr. Gen. Venables* (1900) 141, I need not dr. Amie to keep me from pinguifying. **1825** *Blackw. Mag.* XVII. 72 Buttocks pinguifying on their own steaks.

Hence '**pinguefying** *ppl. a.*, fattening.

1733 TULL *Horse-Hoeing Husb.* xv. 201 The Pinguifying Virtue of this Medica Hay. **1828** *Blackw. Mag.* XXIII. 375 His object being to restrain the pinguifying impulses of hunger. **1857** MUSGRAVE *Pilgr. Dauphiné* I. xi. 245 The graziers' pinguifying processes.

pinguescence (pɪŋ'gwɛsəns). *rare.* [f. as next: see -ENCE.] The process of becoming or growing fat: *loosely*, fatness, obesity.

1822–34 *Good's Study Med.* (ed. 4) IV. 222 A standard weight of healthy pinguescence. **1897** *Allbutt's Syst. Med.* IV. 607 The sexual relations of pinguescence.

pinguescent (pɪŋ'gwɛsənt), *a.* [ad. L. *pinguēscent-em*, pr. pple. of *pinguēscĕre* to grow fat, f. *pinguis* fat: see -ESCE.] Becoming or growing fat, fattening; flourishing.

1797 SOUTHEY in Cottle *Remin.* 211 A very brown-looking man, of most pinguescent, and fullmoon cheeks. **1832** *Fraser's Mag.* VI. 716 Haggis..is unctuously pinguescent. **1852** *Tait's Mag.* XIX. 622 There are hundreds of noble and self-denying men in the ranks of the Church Pinguescent.

pinguetude, -tudinous, erron. ff. PINGUI-.

‖**Pinguicula** (pɪŋ'gwɪkjʊlə). Also 9- (the usual form in sense 2) pinguecula, and in anglicized form pinguecule. [L. fem. (sc. *planta*) of *pinguicul-us* fattish, dim. f. *pingui-s* fat. Introduced as a botanical name by Gesner, 1541, to represent Ger. *fettkraut* or *butterwurz* butterwort.]

1. *Bot.* A genus of small stemless insectivorous bog plants (N.O. *Lentibulariaceæ*) characterized by thick yellowish-green greasy leaves and slender single-flowered scapes; butterwort.

1597 [see BUTTERWORT]. **1753** CHAMBERS *Cycl. Supp.*, *Pinguicula*, butterwort..the name of a genus of plants..: the flower consists of one leaf. **1885** *St. James' Gaz.* 17 Aug. 6/2 On its slopes grow the insect-capturing pinguicula [etc.].

2. *Path.* A small blotch or growth of the conjunctiva, usually situated near the edge of the cornea.

1850 H. HOWARD *Anat. Eye* xvi. 230 Pinguecula.—This is a little yellowish colored tumour, situated partly in the conjunctiva, and partly in its cellular membrane. **1858** MAYNE *Expos. Lex.*, *Pinguecula*,..a pinguecule. **1878** T. BRYANT *Pract. Surg.* I. 351 Pinguiculæ are small yellowish growths situated beneath the conjunctiva, generally, near the outer and inner margins of the cornea. **1934** [see *interpalpebral* s.v. INTER- 6]. **1937** E. WOLFF *Dis. Eye* i. 12 Pingueculæ require no treatment. **1965** F. W. NEWELL *Ophthalm.* viii. 180/2 Rarely a pinguecula becomes inflamed, causing a foreign body sensation.

pinguid ('pɪŋgwɪd), *a.* Now usually *humorous* or *affected.* Also 8 pingued. [f. L. *pingui-s* adj., fat, or stem of **pinguē-re* (whence *pinguēsc-ĕre*: see PINGUESCENT) + -ID: cf. *gravid, languid, torpid*, etc.).] Of the nature of, resembling, or abounding in fat; unctuous, greasy, oily; of soil: rich, fertile.

1635 SWAN *Spec. M.* v. §2 (1643) 168 Hot and drie exhalations void of pinguid matter. **1769** R. GRAVES *Euphrosyne* (1776) I. 119 [He] snuffs the pinguid haunch's sav'ry steam. **1867** HOWELLS *Ital. Journ.* 111 A mighty mass of pinguid bronze, with a fat lisp.

b. *transf.* and *fig.*

1768–74 TUCKER *Lt. Nat.* (1834) I. 643 A pinguid, turgid style, as Tully calls the Asiatic rhetoric. **1893** J. W. PALMER in *Century Mag.* Dec. 258/1 The eyes of the Talbot swine stuck out with pinguid complacency.

pinguidity (pɪŋ'gwɪdɪtɪ). Also 6 erron. -edity. [f. prec. + -ITY.] Fatness; fatty matter.

1597 A. M. tr. *Guillemeau's Fr. Chirurg.* 23/1 Without applyinge any pinguiditye or oyles. **1599** —— tr. *Gabelhouer's Bk. Physick* 28/2 Take a good Capone,..discide therof all his pinguedity. **1630** J. TAYLOR (Water P.) *Taylor's Goose* Wks. I. 103 The pinguidity or fecundious fat of the Gooses axungia (vulgarly called greace). **1858** *Chamb. Jrnl.* X. 235/1 His cheeks!—I never saw such bags of pinguidity.

†**pinguie**, *a. Obs. rare*—1. [ad. L. *pingui-s* fat.] Of the nature of fat, fatty.

1637 VENNER *Via Recta*, etc., *Tobacco* 355 It eliquateth the pinguie substance of the kidnies.

pinguiferous (pɪŋ'gwɪfərəs), *a. humorous nonce-wd.* [f. L. *pingui-s* fat + -FEROUS.] Bearing or producing fat.

1855 *Tait's Mag.* XXII. 145 The pinguiferous slice from the salted swine.

pinguify, erron. form of PINGUEFY.

pinguin ('pɪŋgwɪn). Also penguin, penquin (pinquin). [Origin unascertained.] A West Indian plant (*Bromelia Pinguin*) allied to the pine-apple, or its fruit; used in fevers and as an anthelmintic.

It is not clear that Dampier's *penguin* was a Bromelia.

1696 PLUKENET *Almagesta* II. 29 Ananas Americana sylvestris altera minor Barbados et Insulæ Jamaica nostratibus colonis *Pinguin* dicta. **1697** DAMPIER *Voy.* I. 263 There is a sort of fruit growing on these Islands [Chametly], called Penguins: and 'tis all the fruit they have. The Penguin fruit is of two sorts, the yellow and the red. **1711** in A. Duncan *Mariner's Chron.* (1803) III. 316 We..then attempted to get over the hill, but found it impossible to force a way through the penguins, bryars, and other prickly plants which grew there. **1792** MAR. RIDDELL *Voy. Madeira* 85 The *bromelia karatas*, or *pinguin*, is a fruit resembling a small cucumber in shape. **1871** KINGSLEY *At Last* i, On one side of the path a hedge of Penguin.

attrib. **1756** P. BROWNE *Jamaica* 147 This plant..found climbing upon all the pinguin fences. **1894** ALICE SPINNER *Study in Colour* 16 On the other side of the red pinquin spears she saw a flash of crimson.

pinguin, erron. form of PENGUIN.

pingui-nitescent (ˌpɪŋgwɪnaɪ'tɛsənt), *a. nonce-wd.* [f. L. *pingui-s* fat + NITESCENT.] Having a greasy lustre; shining with grease.

1817 COLERIDGE *Biog. Lit.* x. (1882) 82 The lank, black, twine-like hair, pingui-nitescent.

†'**pinguious**, *a. Obs.* [f. L. *pingui-s* fat + -OUS.] Of the nature of fat; fatty, oily.

1747 tr. *Astruc's Fevers* 104 These glands being compressed, emit a pinguious substance. **1748** *Phil. Trans.* XLV. 558 Oil, or other pinguious Substances. **1764** *Projects* in *Ann. Reg.* 145/1 Heat sufficient for sending off the pinguious [*printed* pinguinous] and alkaline parts.

pinguipedine (pɪŋ'gwɪpɪdaɪn), *a.* (*sb.*) *Ichth.* [f. mod.L. *Pinguipedinæ*, f. *Pinguipēs*, f. *pingui-s* fat + *pēs*, *ped-* foot: see -INE[1].] Of or pertaining to the *Pinguipedinæ*, a subfamily of spiny-finned tropical fishes of which the genus *Pinguipes* is the type. **b.** *sb.* A fish of this family.

pinguite ('pɪŋgwaɪt). *Min.* [Named (Ger. *pinguit*) by A. Breithaupt, 1829, f. L. *pinguis* fat: see -ITE[1].] An oil-green hydrated silicate of iron, of a soapy consistency; a variety of CHLOROPAL.

1831 *Amer. Jrnl. Sci.* XX. 197 Pinguite, a new argillaceous mineral. **1837** DANA *Min.* 224 Closely allied to this species [Nontronite], is the Pinguite of Leonhard... Color siskin and oil-green... Extremely soft, resembling new-made soap. **1850** DAUBENY *Atom. The.* xii. (ed. 2) 410 Silicates that contain water..in which the water is simply united to the silicic combination... Example: Pinguite.

pinguitude ('pɪŋgwɪtju:d). *rare.* [ad. L. *pinguitūdo* fatness, f. *pinguis* adj., fat.] Fatness. Also *fig.* Openness or wideness of a sound.

1623 COCKERAM II, Fatnes, *pinguitude.* **1657** TOMLINSON *Renou's Disp.* 676 Juniper..will demit its oleaginous pinguetude. **1822** LAMB *Gentle Giantess* Misc. Wks. (1871) 363 To her mighty bone, she hath a pinguitude withal. **1871** R. ELLIS in *Academy* 1 Apr. 208 The pinguitude of the first letter will be found..to stand in the way of refining the second.

Hence **pingui'tudinous** *a. rare*—0.

1870 C. J. SMITH *Syn. & Antonyms* s.v. *Adipose*, Sebaceous. Pinguetudinous.

†'**pinguity.** *Obs. rare*—0. [f. L. type **pinguitās*, f. *pingui-s* fat: see -TY.] Fatness.

1623 COCKERAM, *Pinguitie*, fatnesse.

pin-head ('pɪnhɛd). Also pinhead. [f. PIN *sb.* + HEAD *sb.*[1]]

1. a. The head of a pin, a pin's head. Used as a type of something of very small size or value; and applied to things resembling a pin's head, as small grains, etc.

1662 R. MATHEW *Unl. Alch.* §86. 116 No more then a pin-head, and not a great one neither, but about one quarter of a grain. **1828** *Craven Gloss.* (ed. 2) s.v., It is not worth a pin-head. **1876** tr. *Wagner's Gen. Pathol.* (ed. 6) 99 Round spots of the size of a pin-head or lentil. **1892** WALSH *Tea* (Philad.) 74 The product of the first crop [of Gunpowder tea] is sometimes known as 'Pinhead', from its extremely small, globular and granulated appearance. **1894** *Daily News* 11 June 6/2 To the majority..it matters not a pin-head whether the Poems were the work of Ossian, the son of Fingal,..or of a James MacPherson. **1904** *Longm. Mag.* Dec. 185 There can be no joy in always making the same pinhead by machinery. **1951** J. CLEARY in Murdoch & Drake-Brockman *Austral. Short Stories* 439 The street lights are on, yellow pin-heads climbing the hill from the bay road. **1976** E. WARD *Hanged Man* xxvii. 168 Pubs known as 'happy', where a development of lysergic acid..is on sale as purple pinheads—a microdot of LSD embedded in plastic, sold for £1.

b. *attrib.* Resembling a pin's head; very small and of rounded form; also *fig.*

1835 URE *Philos. Manuf.* 23 The other seldom knows anything beyond the pin-head sphere of his daily task. **1872** O. W. HOLMES *Poet Breakf.-t.* iii. (1885) 77 His sharp-nose and pin-head eyes. **1880** *Bookseller* 3 Feb. 236 Most of the covers so much admired for the 'pin-head' grain were really seal-skin and not morocco. **1963** *Times* 30 Apr. 13/4 The many heavy lorries which, even though they may use their headlamps in the country, only have one pin-head size nearside sidelamp in the town, or perhaps a single flickering tail lamp. **1971** *Brit. Med. Bull.* XXVII. 55/2 In cases of the 'pin head' type of opacity there may be a slight drop in the transfer factor of the lung. **1974** D. SEAMAN *Bomb that could Lip-Read* xvii. 168 The pinhead microphone is set into the head of the explosive.

c. Applied to a pattern of small dots on cloth, or to the cloth itself. Also *ellipt.*, a garment having such a pattern.

1897 *Sears, Roebuck Catal.* 220/1 *French Sanitary Suspenders*...cream, blue, green, etc., with very fine pinhead dots of contrasting colors. **1923** *Daily Mail* 12 June 3 (Advt.), Greys are both light and dark, and include pinhead designs, herring-bones and stripes. **1935** L. A. G. STRONG *Tuesday Afternoon* i. 11 Those chaps in the city had so successfully turned his blue pinhead that several people had..thought it was brand new. **1964** L. DEIGHTON *Funeral in Berlin* iv. 27 He wore a well-cut Berlin suit of English pinhead worsted.

2. A part of a plough: see quot., and cf. quot. 1727 s.v. PIN-HOLE I.

1805 DICKSON *Pract. Agric.* I. Plate vii. 40 Pin head for regulating share, so as to form drains at different depths.

3. The top of the pin or peg at quoits.

1897 CROCKETT *Lad's Love* xviii, Shouts of triumph as the guide-paper was snatched from the pin-head and buried deep in the clay.

4. A small minnow.

1845 S. JUDD *Margaret* I. iv. 18 Minnows and pinheads were flashing and skirting through the clear bright stream.

5. A person with a small head; chiefly *fig.*, a person of little intelligence, a fool. Also *attrib.* or as *adj.*

1896 ADE *Artie* i. 3 I've got as much right to go out and do the heavy as any o' you pin-heads. **1909** *N.Y. Even. Post* (semi-weekly ed.) 22 Feb. 6 An innovation in dress that was ..said to indicate that the wearer was a 'pin head'. **1923** [see BONE *sb.* 3 b]. **1933** E. SEAGO *Circus Company* 295 *Pinheads*, freaks in a side-show. **1940** *Horizon* Apr. 236 An opponent particularly dangerous in these times is the near-artist, or Pinhead. **1947** H. S. TRUMAN in M. Truman *Harry S. Truman* (1973) xvii. 349, I am of the opinion that the country has had enough of their pinhead antics. **1973** 'M. YORKE' *Grave Matters* VII. iii. 118 She's no pin-head—she'd be a match for him intellectually. **1976** *New Yorker* 15 Nov. 23/2 It uses images of physical deformity for their enormous potential of horror, and at the end, when the pinheads and the armless and legless creatures scurry about to revenge themselves on a normal woman.., the film becomes a true nightmare.

Hence '**pin-ˌheading**, the occupation of fitting the heads on pins (as formerly done, when the heads were made separately).

1835 URE *Philos. Manuf.* 361 Three trades..pin-heading, fustian-cutting, and factory work.

'**pin-'headed**, *a.* [f. PIN-HEAD + -ED[2].]

a. Having a head like that of a pin; *spec.* of a flower = PIN-EYED.

1861 Pin-headed [see PIN-EYED].

b. Of a person: having a small head like that of a pin; *fig.* stupid. So **pin-'headedness.**

1901 ADE *Forty Mod. Fables* 67 Is it not Sad to see a pin-headed Rake dissipating a Large Fortune? **1927** *Scribner's Mag.* Feb. 209/1 He is living in parochial, hide-bound, pin-headed stupidity. **1928** WODEHOUSE in *Strand Mag.* Aug. 107 People..were accustomed to set him down as just an ordinary pinheaded young man. *Ibid.* 108 Then they realized that his pin-headedness, so far from being ordinary, was quite exceptional. **1954** 'N. BLAKE' *Whisper in Gloom* xiii. 178 A pin-headed, slick-haired man. **1960** *Sunday Express* 3 July 15/6 The 'pin-headed' look is on its way in.. shorter and still shorter hair. **1969** [see MILLE MIGLIA].

pinhoen: see PINION *sb.*[5]

pin-hold: see PIN *sb.*[1] 18.

'pinholder. [f. PIN *sb.*[1] + HOLDER[1].] A holder for cut flowers, etc., comprising a mounting or base and projecting pins.

1956 D. BEBB *Flowers for You* 24 Place the prepared branches firmly on a pin-holder, with some pieces of bright green moss covering it. **1960** *Woman* 23 Apr. 61/1 Any large-headed flowers should be arranged this way, in a pinholder in a very shallow dish. **1967** *Times* 22 Mar. 11 Most of them, like the pink daisies in *Through the Looking Glass* who turned white with shock when Alice threatened to pick them would..faint at the sight of a pin-holder. **1977** *Lancashire Life* Feb. 9/2 The design is held in a tall black well pin-holder within a rough glazed ivory-coloured ceramic container. **1979** I. WEBB *Compl. Guide Flower & Foliage Arrangem.* iv. 58/1 All three branches must emerge from the point on the pinholder where Branch 1 is placed.

pin-hole ('pɪnhəʊl). Also **pinhole.**

1. A hole into which a pin or peg fits.

1677 MOXON *Mech. Exerc.* II. 19 The inside of the Hinge below the Pin-hole of the Joynt. *Ibid.* 26 If your Key is to have a Pin-hole, drill the hole in the middle of the end of the shank. **1727** BRADLEY *Compl. Body Husb.* 43 The pin-holes in the beam, the use of which is to make this plough cut more or less deep, by fixing the wheels nearer to or farther from the paring-plate. **1880** A. J. HIPKINS in Grove *Dict. Mus.* I. 721/2 Single plates of metal, allowing room for the pin-holes [for the tuning-pins in a pianoforte] in the wooden block. **1891** P. G. STONE *Archit. Antiq. Isle of Wight* 112 The slates ..were thick, and still retained the original pin-holes.

2. a. A hole made by a pin; any very small aperture or perforation resembling a pin-prick.

1676 WISEMAN *Chirurg. Treat.* I. iv. 28 The Breast had at first broke..in a small pin-hole. **1822** IMISON *Sc. & Art* I. 233 We can easily see through a small pin-hole in a piece of paper. **1889** *Anthony's Photogr. Bull.* II. 330 The sensitizing solution should be constantly watched to avoid pinholes, surface markings, *et le reste.* **1897** *Allbutt's Syst. Med.* III. 880 The orifice of the appendix..may be a mere pinhole.

b. A small hole in timber caused by a wood-boring beetle or its larva.

1894 A. D. HOPKINS in *Bull. West Virginia Agric. Exper. Station* Jan. 291 In order that we may refer to the different kinds of defects caused by insects, by some simple, descriptive names, I will present the following, provisional classification and popular names. Pin Holes. Small, round holes, one-hundredth of an inch to one-fourth of an inch in diameter. **1907** *Circ. Bureau Entomol., U.S. Dept. Agric.* No. 82. 1 The principal injury to the wood of standing girdled cypress was found to consist of pinholes in the sapwood and heartwood. **1938** HUNT & GARRATT *Wood Preservation* iii. 53 The insect defects produced in wood before it is placed in service may be classified as pinholes or grub holes, the distinction being principally a matter of size. **1968** *Gloss. Terms Timber Preservation* (*B.S.I.*) 15 *Pinhole*, a worm hole not more than 1·5 mm in diameter.

c. A very small cavity in a solid, esp. a casting.

1906 H. ADAMS *Cassell's Engineers' Hand-bk.* IV. 174 Pin-holes, or blow-holes in brass castings are produced by overheating the metal. **1925** *Jrnl. Inst. Metals* XXXIII. 227 The 'pin-holes' are small cavities more or less spherical in shape, fairly uniformly disseminated through the body of the casting. **1947** J. C. RICH *Materials & Methods Sculpture* iv. 70 The most common surface blemishes that may mar an otherwise perfect cast are caused by pinholes resulting from air bubbles imprisoned in the plaster mix. **1968** D. R. CLIFFE *Technical Metall.* xi. 268 'Gas holes' (or 'pin-holes') are small, evenly distributed rounded cavities with bright walls caused by the release of dissolved gases during freezing.

d. A very small area from which a coating is absent.

1909 *Jrnl. Industr. & Engin. Chem.* May 295/1 Dealers who were previously large importers of tin plate..are willing to admit that even in the 'good old times' they were greatly annoyed by the so-called 'pin holes' in their goods. **1932** E. S. HEDGES *Protective Films on Metals* vii. 212 The examination of perforated cans has shown that the holes may occur..at pinholes in the tin coating. **1970** J. A. SCARLETT *Printed Circuit Boards* iv. 53 Most firms use Beta-ray backscatter tests to check thicknesses of gold plating, together with an electrograph porosity test against pinholes.

e. Ellipt. for *pin-hole camera.*

1976 *Broadcast* 29 Nov. 18/1 The camera is a box— be it a still camera, a film camera, a television camera, a Polaroid, a pinhole.

3. *attrib.* **a.** (In sense 2). Pertaining to, involving, or of the nature of a pinhole or very small aperture; of the size of a pin-prick.

a **1853** PEREIRA *Polarised Light* (1854) 296 If we look at a pin or needle through a pin-hole aperture in a card. **1879** *St. George's Hosp. Rep.* IX. 288 'Pinhole' wound leading to fracture on tibia. *Ibid.* 419 A pinhole perforation was found in the sigmoid flexure. **1946** C. W. BRIGGS *Metall. of Steel Castings* iii. 136 (*heading*) Pinhole porosity. **1962** F. I. ORDWAY et al. *Basic Astronautics* vi. 275 (*caption*) Pinhole insert to control rate of gas intake. **1973** G. J. DAVIES *Solidification & Casting* ix. 172 (*heading*) Pinhole cavities in a sand-cast aluminium alloy, the result of hydrogen evolution on cooling.

b. *Photogr.* Having or pertaining to the use of a pin-hole in place of a lens, as ***pin-hole camera, photography, picture, work.***

1891 *Phil. Mag.* Feb. 89 As the focal length increases, the brightness (B) in the image of a properly proportioned pin-hole camera diminishes. **1902** A. WATKINS *Photogr.* 56 Pinhole pictures..have a tendency to require longer exposures than the mathematically calculated ones. **1940** *Chambers's Techn. Dict.* 644/2 *Pinhole photography*, photography involving the use of a pinhole instead of a lens to form an image on a camera plate. **1948** A. L. M. SOWERBY *Dict. Photogr.* (ed. 17) 509 A recent article by L. A. Turner ..contains an improved theoretical treatment of pinhole work. **1962** M. L. HASELGROVE *Photographers' Dict.* 162 *Pinhole* (*camera*). Replacing the camera lens with a panel in which a small pinhole has been made will result in an image being formed on the milk.

c. Comb. **pinhole borer**, a small brown or black beetle or its larva belonging to the families Scolytidæ or Platypodidæ, which damages trees or felled timber by boring tunnels into the wood.

1916 *Indian Forester* XLII. 217 (*heading*) Ambrosia beetles or pin-hole and shot-hole borers. **1928** *Forestry Comm. Bull.* No. 9. 12 The pin-hole borers, poorly represented in Europe, are more numerous in the Southern States of North America, and are especially abundant in the tropics. **1946** CARTWRIGHT & FINDLAY *Decay of Timber* xiv. 276 The constant presence of staining around the tunnels of the pinhole borers..is usually due to growth of dark-coloured moulds in the wood surrounding the tunnels. **1963** N. E. HICKIN *Insect Factor in Wood Decay* viii. 256 Ambrosia beetles are also called Pinhole Borers. **1975** G. EVANS *Life of Beetles* iv. 92 Pin-hole borers, or 'ambrosia beetles'..are small beetles which bore very narrow tunnels of about the diameter of a thick pin.

Hence **pin-holed** ('pɪnhəʊld) *a.* or *pa. pple.*, perforated with or as with pin-prick.

1873 BROWNING *Red Cott. Nt.-cap* 69 Palace-panes Pin-holed athwart their windowed filagree By twinklings sobered from the sun outside. **1928** *Forestry Comm. Bull.* No. 9. 13 Apart from the tunnels cut by the beetles, secondary damage is found in pin-holed timber. This consists in a staining of the wood in a longitudinal direction on each side of the pin-hole.

'pinholing, *vbl. sb.* [f. PIN-HOLE + -ING[1].] The presence or production of pin-holes.

1925 *Jrnl. Inst. Metals.* XXXIII. 228 These facts..led to the conclusion that the cause of 'pinholing' [in castings] is occluded gas. **1941** *Light Metals* IV. 133/1 The foundry-man..has to produce castings free from serious pinholing. **1947** J. C. RICH *Materials & Methods Sculpture* ii. 51 Pinholing is frequently caused by firing the ceramic body and the glaze at the same time, although air that has been incorporated in the clay mass, dirt, and quick kiln cooling may also cause pinholing.

pin-hood, -hook, etc.: see PIN *sb.*[1] 18.

pinia: see PIÑA 1, pine-apple.

pinic ('paɪnɪk), *a. Chem.* [ad. F. *pinique*, f. L. *pīnus* PINE *sb.*[2]: see -IC.] Of, pertaining to, or derived from the pine-tree; spec. in ***pinic acid***, an acid ($C_9H_{14}O_4$) obtained from pine resin.

1831 T. THOMSON *Chem. Inorg. Bodies* II. 145 In the year 1826 M. Baup inserted a notice in a periodical work that he had discovered *pinic acid* in the resin called *colophon.* **1840** *Penny Cycl.* XVIII. 166/1 When pinic acid is washed and boiled in water, it forms on cooling a hard brittle substance, which becomes brown by fusing. **1866** WATTS *Dict. Chem.* IV. 650 Pinic acid is an amorphous resin, exactly like colophony.

pinicill, obs. variant of PENCIL.

pinicoline (paɪ'nɪkəlaɪn, -lɪn), *a. Zool. rare.* [f. L. type **pinicola* (f. *pīn-us* pine + *-cola* inhabitant) + -INE[1].] That inhabits pine-woods.

1884 COUES *Key N. Amer. Birds* 418 Habits..alpine and subboreal, pinicoline and pinivorous.

pinicolous (paɪ'nɪkələs), *a. Nat. Hist. rare.* [f. as prec. + -OUS.] Living or growing on pine-trees, or in pine-woods.

1858 MAYNE *Expos. Lex., Pinicolus*,..that which lives or grows on the pine,..pinicolous.

†pi'niferous, *a. Obs. rare*$^{-0}$. [f. L. *pīnifer*, f. *pīn-us* pine: see -FEROUS.] Bearing or producing pine-trees.

1656 in BLOUNT *Glossogr.*

piniform ('paɪnɪfɔːm), *a.* [f. L. type **pīniform-is*, f. *pīn-us* pine: see -FORM.] Having the form or shape of a pine-cone. ***piniform decussation***: see quots.

1890 BILLINGS *Nat. Med. Dict., Piniform decussation*, decussation of the pyramids, superior; interolivary layer. **1893** *Syd. Soc. Lex., P*[*iniform*] *decussation*, name for the decussation of the superior pyramids of the medulla oblongata.

pining ('paɪnɪŋ), *vbl. sb.* [f. PINE *v.* + -ING[1].] The action of the verb PINE.

†1. The infliction or undergoing of pain (bodily or mental); torment, torture; affliction, suffering.

c **1175** *Lamb. Hom.* 97 Hi neren aferede of nane licamliche pinunge. *c* **1315** SHOREHAM *Poems* I. 1110 3yf hys saule after hys deþe Soffrey harde pynynge. *c* **1460** *Towneley Myst.* xx. 499 My sawll is heuy agans the deth and the sore pynyng. **1530** PALSGR. 254/2 Pynyng of a man in prisone to confesse the trouthe, *torture.*

2. Exhaustion or wasting away by suffering, disease, or want of food; starvation; languishing; intense longing (*for* something).

a **1400** *Sir Beues* 86/1645 + 8 (MS. E.) Sende me mete & drynk..þou woost alle þyng, Al my nede and my pynyng. **1579** SPENSER *Sheph. Cal.* Jan. 48 With mourning pyne I, you with pyning mourne. **1621** T. WILLIAMSON tr. *Goulart's Wise Vieillard* 99 Consumptions, or pynings away of the bodie. *a* **1656** HALES *Gold. Rem.* I. (1673) 245 One of them ..resolved to die, by pining and abstaining from.. sustenance. **1847** BUSHNELL *Chr. Nurt.* II. iii. (1861) 286 The bitter pains and pinings of unsatisfied hunger. **1898** *Allbutt's Syst. Med.* V. 479 In pining..we note loss of water, loss of plasma, and loss of red corpuscles.

b. *spec.* A disease of sheep, characterized by a wasting away of the body.

1804 in *Trans. Highl. Soc. Scot.* (1807) III. 404 Pining.. is..most severe upon young sheep. **1846** J. BAXTER *Libr. Pract. Agric.* (ed. 4) II. 372 Two exterminating diseases, the pining and the foot-rot, neither of which was known in that district till the extermination of the moles.

c. *concr. pl.* Results of pining or withering (in quot., withered or withering leaves).

1849 M. ARNOLD *Dream*, On the wet umbrage of their glossy tops On the red pinings of their forest floor. [Cf. WORDSW. *Yew-Trees* (1803) 22 A pillared shade, Upon whose grassless floor of red-brown hue, By sheddings from the pining umbrage tinged Perennially.]

3. *attrib.* **†pining-stool**, a stool for punishment, a cucking-stool; **'pining-house, -lair**, a place where animals for slaughter are previously shut up to fast; = *hunger-house* (HUNGER *sb.* 4 e).

c **1230** *Hali Meid.* 35 þe care ayain þi pinunge þrahen binimeð þe nihtes slepes. *c* **1315** SHOREHAM *Poems* I. 2202 He by-held hyne þer a set, Ryȝt atte hys pynyng stake. **1362** LANGL. *P. Pl.* A. III. 69 To punisschen on pillories or on pynnyng stoles [B. III. 78 pynynge stoles] Brewesters, Bakers, Bochers and Cookes. **1802** *Hull Advertiser* 4 Dec. 2/2 Pining-house. **1875** *Gainsburgh News* 25 Sept., To be let ..butcher's shop, with slaughter-house, pining-house, and every convenience. **1893** *Whitby Gaz.* 3 Nov. 3/6 In two instances the pining-lairs or hunger-houses are within the [butchers'] shops or open directly into them.

'pining, *ppl. a.* [f. as prec. + -ING[2].] That pines (see the verb); †tormenting, afflicting (*obs.*); consuming, wasting; languishing.

a **1240** *Wohunge* in *Cott. Hom.* 269 Al þat pinende pik ne walde ham þunche bote a softe bekinde bað. **1387–8** T. USK *Test. Love* I. vi. (Skeat) I. 77 To dwelle in this pynande prison. **1583** *Middlesex County Rec.* I. 137 [Visitation of a certain infirmity called] the pining siknes. **1611** BIBLE *Isa.* xxxviii. 12 He will cut mee off with pining sickenesse. **1742** GRAY *Eton* 65 Pining Love shall waste their youth. **1817** COLERIDGE *Sibyll. Leaves, On revisiting Seashore* iii, Fashion's pining Sons and Daughters.

Hence **'piningly** *adv.*

1561 T. NORTON *Calvin's Inst.* I. 3 When the dull hardnesse, which yͤ wicked do desirously labor to get to despise God withal, doth lie piningly in their hartes. **1821** CLARE *Vill. Minstr.* I. 56 Small the wage he gains That many a child most piningly maintains.

piniolate, variant of PIGNOLATE *Obs.*

pinion ('pɪnjən), *sb.*[1] Forms: 5 **pynyon**, 6 **pynnyon, -nion, pinnyan,** 6–7 **pynion, pin(n)eon, (-oun), -nion,** 7 **pyneon,** 6– **pinion.** [a. OF. *pignon*, in Froissart *c* 1400 in pl. 'wing-feathers, wings, pinions', a collateral form of OF. *penon, pennon* (also 'feather of an arrow', and 'streamer, pennon') = It. *pennone*, orig. plume (cf. *pennoncello* little plume or feather), also streamer, pennon; a Romanic augmentative of L. *penna* (also written *pinna*) feather, wing-feather, wing (PEN *sb.*[2]). (See Godef. *pennon*[2], the same word as his *penon.*) *Pinion* thus preserves the lit. sense of Romanic *pennōne*, while PENNON has the transferred sense of 'streamer'.]

1. The distal or terminal segment of a bird's wing; hence (chiefly *poet.* or *rhet.*), a wing, esp. of a bird (always with reference to its use for flight).

c **1440** *Promp. Parv.* 400/2 Pynyon, of a wynge, *pennula.* **1530** PALSGR. 254/2 Pynnyon of a wyng, *bout de lesle.* **1538** ELYOT, *Armus*,..the pynion of a fowle. **1593** DRAYTON *Ecolgues* v. 58 With nimble Pineons shall direct her flight. **1594** —— *Idea* 780 To prove the Pynions, it ascends the Skyes. *a* **1633** AUSTIN *Medit.* (1635) 255 How oft do they [Angels] with golden Pinions cleave The flitting skies like flying Pursevant? **1755** GRAY *Progr. Poesy* III. iii, Nor the pride, nor ample pinion, That the Theban Eagle bear Sailing with supreme dominion Thro' the azure deep of air. **1821** MONTGOMERY *Hymn*, '*Hail to the Lord's Anointed*', Far as the eagle's pinion Or dove's light wing can soar. **1855** LONGF. *Hiaw.* XIX, First a speck, and then a vulture, Till the air is dark with pinions. **1865** LIVINGSTONE *Zambesi* xxi. 426 One [weaver-bird] glides with quivering pinions to the centre of the open space.

b. In carving, The part of a wing corresponding to the fore-arm. Formerly applied to the wing as a whole.

1655 MOUFET & BENNET *Health's Impr.* (1746) 203 The Pinions of Geese, Hens, Capons and Chickens, are of good Nourishment. **1741** RICHARDSON *Pamela* (1824) I. 180, I will help thee to a pinion, or breast, or anything. **1875**

Beeton's Everyday Cookery 507 Run a skewer through the pinion and thigh into the body to the pinion and thigh on the other side. *Mod.* 'Shall I give you a wing?' 'Yes: but take off the pinion.'

†**c.** The shoulder-blade of a quadruped. *Obs.*

1545 ELYOT, *Ala* is also the pinion of the shulder of a beast.

d. The human arm. (*humorous.*)

1848 THACKERAY *Bk. Snobs, Club Snobs* i, The *Standard* under his left arm, the *Globe* under the other pinion.

2. *fig.* (In reference to things poetically represented as having wings.)

1602 MARSTON *Antonio's Rev.* IV. v, The gloomie wing of night begins to stretch His lasie pinion over all the ayre. **1638** DRUMM. OF HAWTH. *Irene* Wks. (1711) 166 To league is imperiously to command their king and sovereign to cut short his pinions, and strive to be more than his equal. **1732** POPE *Ess. Man* I. 91 Hope humbly then; with trembling pinions soar. **1791** E. DARWIN *Bot. Gard.* I. 110 When light clouds on airy pinions sail. **1850** NEALE *Hymn*, '*The strain upraise of joy and praise*', Ye winds on pinions light!

3. The outermost feather, or any flight-feather, of a bird's wing; a pinion-feather.

1545 ASCHAM *Toxoph.* (Arb.) 131 The seconde fether in some place is better than the pinion in other some. **1606** SHAKS. *Ant. & Cl.* III. xii. 4 An argument that he is pluckt, when hither He sends so poore a Pinnion of his Wing. **1858** SIMMONDS *Dict. Trade, Pinion*,..the quills from the joint farthest from the body of the wing of the goose or swan, used for making pens.

†**b.** The shaft of a feather; a quill. *Obs.* *rare*$^{-1}$.

1697 tr. *C'tess D'Aunoy's Trav.* (1706) 4 Our Beds..being stuck with Feathers whose Pinions ran into our sides.

†**4.** Applied to some kind of embellishment worn on the shoulders or sleeves of women's dresses in the 16th and 17th c. Cf. PINIONING *sb.*

1583 STUBBES *Anat. Abus.* I. (1879) 73 The Women.. haue dublets and Ierkins,..made with wings, welts, and pinions on the shoulder points. **1650** R. STAPYLTON *Strada's Low C. Warres* IV. 78 The pinnions of their sleeves, which they call wings, are laid with silk fringe of divers colours.

5. The anterior border of an insect's wing; esp. in *Comb.* in collectors' names of moths, e.g. ***pinion-spotted pug*** (*Eupithecia consignata*), ***pinion-spotted yellow*** (*Venilia quadrimaculata*).

1720 ALBIN *Nat. Hist. Eng. Insects* Pl. XCV. *text*, A yellowish moth with brown clouds towards the pinions of the upper wings. **1775** MOSES HARRIS *Engl. Lepidoptera* 39 No. 275 Pinion, white spotted,..on elm trees in hanging wood. No. 276 Pinion, double spotted,..brown, having two white spots on the sector edge. **1832** RENNIE *Butterflies & Moths* 135, 145. **1869** E. NEWMAN *Brit. Moths.* 118/2 The Pinion-spotted Pug.

†**6.** *Her.* Applied to the saltire and the chevron.

1486 *Bk. St. Albans, Her.* B v b, Ther be in armys calde ij. pynyonys, Oon is Whan the feeld his a sawtri... The secunde pynyon is called cheffrounce.

†**7.** See quot. *Obs.* (? error, from PINION *v.*)

1736 AINSWORTH *Lat. Dict.*, Pinions, or manicles for the hands, *manicæ*. Pinions, or fetters for the feet, *compedes*. [Whence **1755** in JOHNSON.]

8. *attrib.* and *Comb.*, as ***pinion-feather***; **pinion-bones**, the bones of the manus or distal joint of a wing; **pinion-claw**, a horny claw borne by the index or pollex of certain birds.

1486 *Bk. St. Albans* B j, The federis that sum call the pynyon feder. **1601** HOLLAND *Pliny* I. 300 The pinion feathers blacke, the vpper plume reddish. **1678** RAY *Willughby's Ornith.* 300 The Sarcel is the extreme pinion feather in a Hawk's wing. **1880** BROWNING *Dram. Idylls, Pietro* 156 The eaglet callow Needs a parent's pinion-push to quit the eyrie's edge. **1884** G. ALLEN in *Longm. Mag.* Jan. 295 The Australian bush-turkeys have also the rudiment or last relic of a primitive pinion-claw.

pinion ('pɪnjən), *sb.*[2] *Obs.* exc. *dial.* Also 3 pynun, 4 pynoun. [a. OF. *penon, pinun* (Godef.), mod.F. *pignon* in same sense, Romanic augmentative of L. *pinna* battlement, pinnacle.] A battlement, pinnacle, or gable; = PIGNON[2]. ***pinion-end***, dial. *pinning-end*, a gable-end.

[**1278** *Bursar's Rolls, Merton* in *Archæol. Jrnl.* II. 142 Item ijs. vd. liberat. predicto Nicholao pro xiij pedibus de pynun table.] *a* **1300** *Cursor M.* 12958 (Cott.) þe warlau..sett him on þe hei pinion [*Gött.* pingnion, *Fairf.* pynoun] O þe temple o þe tun. **1882** T. HARDY *Two on a Tower* II. ii. 23 The wind have blown down the chimley..and the pinning-end with it. **1888** E. LAWS *Little Eng. beyond Wales* 421 *Pinion* or *Pine-end*, the gable end of a house; French *pignon*, a gable.

pinion ('pɪnjən), *sb.*[3] *Mech.* [ad. mod.F. *pignon* in same sense (Paré 16th c.), Sp. *piñon* tooth of a wheel, pinion, a spec. application of OF. *pignon* battlement (see prec.), the teeth of a wheel being compared to the crenellations of battlements.] A small cog-wheel the teeth of which engage with those of a larger one; also a spindle, arbor, or axle, having cogs or teeth which engage with the teeth of a wheel. (The teeth or cogs of a pinion are distinctively called *leaves.*) ***pinion and rack***, also ***rack and pinion***: see RACK *sb.*[2] 6.

1659 LEAK *Waterwks.* 9 If the Wheel A be turned by the Pinion C of 10. Teeth. **1704** J. HARRIS *Lex. Techn.* I, *Pinion of Report*, is that Pinion in a Watch which is commonly fixed on the Arbor of the Great Wheel..; it driveth the Dial Wheel, and carrieth about the Hand. **1815** J. SMITH *Panorama Sc. & Art* I. 358 If the teeth of wheels and the leaves of pinions consisted of materials perfectly hard, and were accurately formed..they would act on each other not only with uniform force, but also without friction. **1867** J. HOGG *Microsc.* I. i. 9 Capable of various adjustments, and regulated by a pinion and rack.

b. *attrib.* and *Comb.*, as ***pinion-flank, -shaft, -work***; **pinion-bottoming-file, pinion-file**, fine knife-edged files used in watch-making; **pinion-gauge**, fine callipers used by watch-makers; **pinion-jack** (see quot.); **pinion-leaf**, each of the cogs or teeth of a pinion (LEAF *sb.*[1] 13); **pinion-wire**: see quot. 1884.

1884 F. J. BRITTEN *Watch & Clockm.* 242 A file cutting only on the edge is more generally called a safe sided lever notch file, or a *pinion bottoming file. **1875** KNIGHT *Dict. Mech.*, **Pinion-file* (Watch-making), a knife-file employed by watchmakers. **1884** F. J. BRITTEN *Watch & Clockm.* 288 The *pinion flanks should be hypocycloidal in form. **1875** KNIGHT *Dict. Mech.*, **Pinion-gage.* **1884** F. J. BRITTEN *Watch & Clockm.* 193 [A] Pinion Guage..[is] a guage used by watchmakers for taking the height of pinion shoulders and other measurements. **1884** KNIGHT *Dict. Mech.* Suppl., **Pinion Jack* (*Milling*), a jack for raising the stone pinion out of gear. **1884** F. J. BRITTEN *Watch & Clockm.* 37 The tendency of *pinion leaves to butt the wheel teeth. **1844** STEPHENS *Bk. Farm* II. 137 These plummer-blocks are bolted down to the top-rails of the frame, to which also the separate bearings of the *pinion-shafts are..bolted. **1795** J. AIKIN *Manchester* 311 The drawing of *pinion wire originated here. **1884** F. J. BRITTEN *Watch & Clockm.* 194 Pinion wire..steel wire drawn with corrugations resembling pinion leaves, from which pinions are made. **1829** *Nat. Philos.* I. *Mechanics* II. vii. 28 (U. Kn. Soc.), A system of tooth and *pinion-work.

†**'pinion**, *sb.*[4] *Obs.* [Perh. a use of PINION *sb.*[1]] Name of an obsolete card-game.

c **1554** *Interlude of Youth* (1849) 38 At the cardes I can teche you to play, At the..Post, pinion, and also aumsase.

pinion, *sb.*[5]

1. Anglicized form of Sp. *piñon*, Pg. *pinhão*, pl. *pinhões* (sometimes written *pinhoens*), in full *pinhões do Brasil*, kernels of Brazil, the seed of *Jatropha Curcas*, the physic-nut of South America. See also PIGNON[1] 2.

1577 FRAMPTON *Joyful News* I. (1596) 22 They doe bryng from the newe Spayne certeyne Pinions or Carnels, wherwith the Indians dyd purge themselues: they bee like to our Pinions, which do growe out of our Trees. [**1648** W. PISO *Hist. Nat. Brasil.* IV. xl. 83 De *Munduy-guacu*, Lusitanis *Pinhoes do Brasil*, ejusque usu in Medicina. **1648** MARCGRAVE *Hist. Rerum Nat. Brasil.* III. iii. 96 *Mvndvbigvacv* Brasiliensibus, *Pinhones* Lusitanis, mihi *Nux cathartica.* **1822** SARA H. COLERIDGE tr. *Acc. Abipones* II. 261 In the Northern part of Paraguay there grows a nut called *Piñon del Paraguay* by the Spaniards, and by physicians *nux Cathartica*. **1884** DYMOCK *Mat. Med. W. India* IV. 573 *Jatropha multifida*... The seeds are powerfully purgative and emetic. In Brazil an oil called 'Pinhoen' is extracted from them and is used as an emetic.]

2. Anglicized spelling of PIÑON, the American Nut-pine. Also *attrib.* in ***pinion nut, pine***.

1831 J. O. PATTIE *Pers. Narr.* 43 A nut..which grows on a tree resembling the pine, called by the Spanish, pinion. **1846** R. B. SAGE *Scenes Rocky Mts.* xxi. 172 The hills enclosing the valley..are high and precipitous,—affording numerous groves of pine, pinion and cedar. *Ibid.*, Wild turkeys..will thrive in an extraordinary manner upon pinion-nuts. **1860** BARTLETT *Dict. Amer.* (ed. 3), *Pinion* (Span. *piñon*), a species of pine-tree, growing on the head waters of the Arkansas. **1878** J. H. BEADLE *Western Wilds* xi. 173 On many of the hills grows the pinion pine. **1960** 'I. DEVI' *Yoga for You* 189 Sunflower seeds or pinion nuts to taste. **1970** *People* (Austral.) 26 Aug. 44/4 Pinion nuts from the cones of introduced pines are a tasty novelty. **1979** *Yale* Apr. 39/2 (Advt.), 40 beautiful acres high ground with pinion, mountain views near mining town between Santa Fe & Albuquerque.

'pinion, *sb.*[6] *Woollen Manuf.* [erron. ad. F. *peignon* combings, f. *peigner* to comb.] (*pl.*) The short refuse wool remaining after the combing process; 'noils'.

1780 A. YOUNG *Tour Irel.* II. 18 To each stone there is one pound and three quarters of pinions of short wool that comes out in the combing. **1847–78** HALLIWELL, *Pinions*, refuse wool. *Somerset.* **1886** ELWORTHY *W. Somerset Word-bk.*, *Pinions*... This word..is thoroughly West Country. In other parts this regular article of commerce is called 'noils'.

pinion ('pɪnjən), *v.* [f. PINION *sb.*[1]]

1. *trans.* To cut off the pinion of one wing, or otherwise disable or bind the wings, in order to prevent a bird from flying. (With the bird, or the wing, as obj.)

1577 B. GOOGE *Heresbach's Husb.* IV. (1586) 169 They that meane to fatte Pigions..some..do softly tie their Legges:.. some vse onely to pinion them. **1641** BEST *Farm. Bks.* (Surtees) 123 The swanners gette up the young swannes about Midsummer..and then doe they allsoe pinnion them, cuttinge a joynte of theire right winges. *a* **1667** COWLEY *Ess. Verse & Prose, Shortness of Life*, Suppose, thou Fortune couldst to Tameness bring, And clip or pinion her wing. **1727** *Philip Quarll* (1816) 67 The two old ducks..being pinioned, could not fly away. **1849** D. J. BROWNE *Amer. Poultry Yd.* (1855) 242 They..should have been pinioned at the first joint of the wing.

2. To bind the arms of any one, so as to deprive him of their use; to disable by so binding; to shackle. (With the person, or the arms, as obj.)

1558 PHAER *Æneid* II. C iv, The shepeherdes..a yongman haue ycaught, And pynyond with his handes behind onto the kyng him brought. *c* **1611** CHAPMAN *Iliad* XXI. 31 All their hands he pinnioned behinde With their owne girdles. *a* **1680** BUTLER *Rem.* (1759) II. 84 He carries his elbows backward, as if he were pinioned like a trust-up Fowl. **1726** SWIFT *Gulliver* III. i, Finding us all prostrate upon our faces ..they pinioned us with strong ropes. **1851** *Wilson's Tales Borders* XX. 54 The sailors attempted to pinion Peter's arms.

b. *transf.* and *fig.*

1621 T. WILLIAMSON tr. *Goulart's Wise Vieillard* 70 Feare inuades them, and pynions them vp. **1641** MILTON *Animadv.* iii. Wks. 1851 III. 210 Laying before us universall propositions, and then thinks..to pinion them with a limitation. **1781** COWPER *Truth* 133 Yon ancient prude.. Her elbows pinioned close upon her hips.

c. To bind fast *to* something, or together.

a **1652** J. SMITH *Sel. Disc.* v. 135 Those dismal apprehensions which pinion the souls of men to mortality. *a* **1690** RUSHW. *Hist. Coll.* (1721) V. 131 The Prisoners.. being pinion'd two and two together by the Arms. **1742** POPE *Dunc.* IV. 134 And while on Fame's triumphal Car they ride, Some Slave of mine be pinion'd to their side. **1764** CHURCHILL *Gotham* II. 164 Let me..praise their heav'n, tho' pinion'd down to earth. **1831** T. L. PEACOCK *Crotchet Castle* xviii, Mr. Toogood..contrived to slip a ponderous coat of mail over his shoulders, which pinioned his arms to his sides.

Hence **'pinioning** *vbl. sb.*

1828 in P. L. Sclater *Rec. Progr. Zool. Soc.* (1901) 150, 11 wild ducks..caught for the purpose of pinioning.

attrib. **1864** SALA in *Daily Tel.* 21 Sept., Calcraft with his pinioning straps. **1894** *Westm. Gaz.* 12 Dec. 7/2 The convict ..quietly submitted to the pinioning operations.

†**pinio'nade.** *Obs.* In 4 pynyon-, pyn(n)on-, 4–5 pynenade. [app. f. some form of Romanic *pinion* (cf. PIGNON[1], PINION *sb.*[5]), f. L. *pīnea* pine-nut + -ADE. (Prob. in OF. or AF.)] A comfit or conserve of which pine-nuts formed a characteristic ingredient.

1329 *Acc. Exch. K.R.* Bd. 383 No. 9 m. 4 Pro..ccclxxxj lb. qr. gingebr'et Pynonad. v. lb. gariofilorum. **1353–4** *Durham Acc. Rolls* (Surtees) 554 In duabus copulis de Pynyonade et de Gyngebrede, cum duabus libris de anys confyt xviiis. viiid. *c* **1390** *Form of Cury* li. (1780) 31 Pynnonade. Take Almandes iblanched and drawe hem sumdell thicke with gode broth..set on the fire and seeþ it,..take Pynes yfryed in oyle oþer in greece and þerto white Powdour douce. **1390–1** *Earl Derby's Exp.* (Camden) 19 Pro iiij lb. pynenade ad xiiij d., iiij s. viij d. *c* **1440** *Anc. Cookery* in *Househ. Ord.* (1790) 450 At the seconde course jussett, pynenade to potage.

pinioned ('pɪnjənd), *a.* [f. PINION *sb.*[1] + -ED[2].] Having pinions or wings; winged. Also in parasynthetic comb., as ***strong-pinioned, swift-pinioned***.

c **1440** *Promp. Parv.* 400/2 Pynyonyd, *pennulatus*. **1552** HULOET, Pynnioned, *armatus, pennulatus*. **1697** DRYDEN *Virg. Past.* IX. 36 Thy Name, O Varus..The Wings of Swans, and stronger pinion'd Rhyme, Shall raise aloft. **1765** J. BROWN *Chr. Jrnl.* (1814) 204 What pinioned notions come and go! **1792** SOUTHEY *Lett.* (1856) I. 12 The cherub choir..bend their pinioned heads to hear.

'pinioned, *ppl. a.* [f. PINION *v.* + -ED[1].] In senses of the verb. **a.** Of a bird: Having the wings maimed or confined. **b.** Having the arms bound so as not to be moved; shackled.

1567 DRANT *Horace, Epist.* II. i. G vj, Captiue kinges.. with pinnyand armes behinde. **1647** R. STAPYLTON *Juvenal* 181 Least on us they fall, And to the barre their pinneon'd masters call. **1742** RICHARDSON *Pamela* IV. 319 A miserable little pinion'd Captive. **1892** *Daily News* 28 Jan. 5/1 A pair of pinioned wild duck..that is, whose wings had been so cut that they were unable to fly.

†**'pinioning**, *sb. Obs.* [f. PINION *sb.*[1] + -ING[1].] = PINION *sb.*[1] 4.

1597–8 BP. HALL *Sat.* III. vii. 41 His sleeues halfe hid with elbow-pineonings, As if he ment to flie with linnen wings.

†**'pinionist.** *Obs. nonce-wd.* [f. PINION *sb.*[1] + -IST.] A winged creature.

1613 W. BROWNE *Brit. Past.* I. iv, The flitting pinnionists of ayre.

'pinionless, *a. rare.* [f. as prec. + -LESS.] Without pinions; wingless.

1894 *Temple Bar Mag.* CI. 514 The pinionless fosterer of one's immaturity.

pinipicrin (paɪnɪ'pɪkrɪn). *Chem.* [f. L. *pīn-us* pine + Gr. πικρ-ός bitter + -IN.] A bitter substance ($C_{22}H_{36}O_{11}$) obtained from the needles and bark of Scotch fir (*Pinus sylvestris*), and the leaves of the American Arbor-vitæ (*Thuja occidentalis*).

1866 WATTS *Dict. Chem.* IV. 651 The needles, after exhaustion with alcohol, still retain a little pinipicrin... Pinipicrin is a bright yellow powder, which..becomes.. transparent and mobile at 100°, and solidifies on cooling to a brownish-yellow..mass. **1893** *Syd. Soc. Lex.*, *Pinipicrin*, ..a brown, bitter, amorphous glucoside.

pinite[1] ('pɪn-, 'paɪnaɪt). *Min.* [ad. Ger. *pinit* (Karsten, 1800), from its locality, the Pini mine, Schneeberg, Saxony: see -ITE[1] 2 b.] A hydrous silicate of aluminium and potassium, occurring in various crystalline forms.

1805 R. JAMESON *Syst. Min.* II. 552 Pinite..occurs seldom massive. **1811** PINKERTON *Petralogy* I. 217 Pinite, with gold pyrites and native gold. **1859** PAGE *Geol. Terms* (1865) 360 *Pinite*, a variety or sub-species of iolite.

pinite[2] ('paınaıt). *Chem.* [a. F. *pinite*, f. L. *pīnus* PINE *sb.*[2]: see -ITE[1] 4.] A crystallizable saccharine substance ($C_6H_{12}O_{10}$) obtained from the sap of two species of pine-tree, *Pinus lambertiana* and *P. sabiniana*.

1857 MILLER *Elem. Chem.* III. 70 A modification of mannite ($C_6H_6O_5$), to which the name of *pinite* has been given, has been found by Berthelot in the juice of the *Pinus Lambertiana*. **1873** WATTS *Fownes' Chem.* (ed. 11) 629.

pinivorous (paı'nıvərəs), *a.* [f. L. *pīn-us* pine + -VOROUS.] That feeds on pine-kernels.

1884 [see PINICOLINE].

‖**pinjane** ('pındʒeın). Also **pinjeen**. [Manx = Gael. *binndean*, Ir. *binidean* rennet.] 'Curds and whey' (E.D.D.).

1887 T. E. BROWN *Doctor*, etc. 152 A man can't live upon pin-jane. **1894** HALL CAINE *Manxman* 306 A spoonful of cold pinjane, Nancy.

‖**pinjrapol** ('pındʒrəpəʊl). Also **panjrapol**, **panjrapor**, **pinjrapole**, etc. [ad. Gujarati *pāṅjrāpol*, f. *panjra* (Skr. *panjara*, *pinjara*) a cage + *pol* an enclosed yard.] In India, an enclosure, reserve, etc., where old or sick animals are kept.

1808 R. DRUMMOND *Illustr. Gram. Parts Guzerattee* s.v. *Pinjrapole* or *Pânjrapôl*. Every marriage and mercantile transaction amongst them is taxed with a contribution for the *Pinjrapole* ostensibly. **1832** C. COLEMAN *Mythol. Hindus* xiii. 222 These hospitals are called *pinjra-pul*, and contain animals of various descriptions. **1855** H. H. WILSON *Gloss. Judicial & Revenue Terms* 418/2 *Pinjrâpor*, or *-pol*, also read *Pânjrâpor*, or *pol*, Guz..., an hospital for animals, kept up by the Jains of Guzerat in various places, out of small fees levied at marriages and on mercantile transactions. **1873** E. BALFOUR *Cycl. India* (ed. 2) IV. s.v. *Pinjrapol*. The Bombay Pinjrapol owes its origin as much to the Parsee worship of sacred dogs as to the superstitions of the Jains. **1929** H. G. RAWLINSON *Ovington's Voy. to Surat* 178 These animal hospitals or *pinjrapols* date back to the days of Asoka. **1960** *Guardian* 21 Apr. 12/5 A pinjrapole is a 'Cheshire home' for cows. **1968** B. WALKER *Hindu World* I. 16 The early Buddhists and Jains built hospitals for the care of animals, birds and even insects. Such institutions have survived through the centuries and are today known as *piñjrapol*.

pink (pıŋk), *sb.*[1] Now chiefly *Hist.* Forms: 5-7 **pinck**, 6 **pyncke**, 6-7 **pin(c)ke**, 7 **pynke**, 6- **pink**. [app. a. MDu. *pincke*, *pinke*, name of a small sea-going ship, also a fishing-boat (1477-8 in Verw. & Verdam), in Kilian *pinck*, mod.Du. *pink*; in MLG., LG., and mod.Ger. *pinke*; also F. *pinque* (1690 in Furetière, *pinquet* 1634 in Hatz.-Darm.), It. *pinco*: ulterior origin unknown (Jal).] A sailing vessel; orig. one of small size used for coasting and fishing, described as flat-bottomed and having bulging sides; in the 17th and 18th c. applied to ships of considerable size, esp. war-ships; see also quot. 1794. A common characteristic in later times appears to have been a narrow stern: cf. *pink-stern*, *-sterned* in b.

The description of the Dutch pinks and that of the pinks of the Mediterranean differ considerably: see the quots.

† *sword pink*, one provided with lee-boards [Du. *zwaard* (*sweerd* Kilian) a lee-board].

1471 *Sc. Acts Jas. III* (1814) II. 100/2 þat certain lordes .. & burowis ger mak or get Schippis buschis & vþer gret pynk botes witht nettes & al abilʒementes ganing þarfor for fysching. **1545** *St. Papers Hen. VIII*, I. 792 They mete also three Flemishe pynckes, laden with pouderd codde. **1545** ASCHAM *Toxoph.* (Arb.) 153 In Winter and rough wether, small bootes and lytle pinkes forsake the seas. **1573-80** BARET *Alv.* P 380 A Pinke, a little ship. **1601** J. REYMOR *Obs. Dutch Fishing* in *Phenix* (1721) I. 228 Above 1000 Sail of Pinks, Welboats, Dogger boats take Cod, Ling, and other Fish there. **1616** CAPT. SMITH *Descr. New Eng.* 12 The poore Hollanders .. hauing 2 or 3000 Busses, Flat bottomes, Sword pinks, Todes, and such like. **1688** *Lond. Gaz.* No. 2352/3 The Pink lost her Top-mast and Sprit-sail, had her Main-Yard broke, and her Hull and Rigging very much torn. **1710** J. HARRIS *Lex. Techn.* II. s.v., The Bends and Ribs compassing so as that her Sides bulge out very much; wherefore these Pinks are difficult to be boarded. They are often used for Store-Ships, and Hospital-Ships, in the Fleet. **1742** FIELDING *Jos. Andrews* II. xvii, The villains .. put me, a man, and a boy, into a little bad pink, in which .. we at last made Falmouth. **1748** *Anson's Voy.* I. ii. 14 The two Victuallers were Pinks, .. of about four hundred, and .. two hundred tons burthen. **1769** FALCONER *Dict. Marine* (1789), *Pink*, a name given to a ship with a very narrow stern; whence all vessels .. whose sterns are fashioned in this manner, are called *pink-sterned*. **1787** EARL MALMESBURY *Diaries & Corr.* II. 367, I have determined to dispatch a pink from Scheveling. **1794** *Rigging & Seamanship* I. 236 *Pinks* are mediterranean-vessels, and differ from the Xebec only in being more lofty, and not sharp in the bottom, as they are vessels of burthen. They have long narrow sterns, and three masts, carrying latteen-sails. **1823** SCOTT *Peveril* xviii, Suppose me .. detained in harbour by a revenue pink. **1867** SMYTH *Sailor's Word-bk.*, *Pink*, a ship with a very narrow stern, having a small square part above. The shape is of old date, but continued, esp. by the Danes, for the advantage of the quarter-guns, by the ship's being contracted abaft.

fig. *a* **1625** FLETCHER *Woman's Prize* II. vi, This pinck, this painted foist, this cockle-boat, To hang her fights out, and defie me, friends, A well known man of war.

b. *attrib.* and *Comb.*, as *pink-boat* (see quot. 1471 above), *pink-rigged* adj.; **pink-snow**, a snow resembling a pink in build; **pink-stern**, a stern like that of a pink; hence, a small vessel having a narrow stern; so **pink-sterned** *a.* (cf. 1769 above).

1711 W. SUTHERLAND *Shipbuild. Assist.* 60 For round or pink-stern'd Ships. **1722** FORSTER in *Phil. Trans.* XXXII. 100 A small Pink-Snow, called the *Richard and Elizabeth*. **1759** *Ann. Reg.* 64/2 A French privateer .. fell in with an English brig, pink-stern about 100 tons burthen. **1808** A. PARSONS *Trav.* viii. 169 The galliote which the Eagle had taken .. is built forward like a London wherry, with a pink or lute stern. **1861** L. L. NOBLE *Icebergs* 77 A pink-sterned schooner, of only sixty-five tons. *Ibid.* 89 At eight o'clock, our brave little pink-stern was lying at anchor in her haven. **1867** SMYTH *Sailor's Word-bk.*, *Flute*, or *Fluyt*, a pink-rigged fly-boat. *Ibid.*, *Pinkstern*, a very narrow boat on the Severn. **1890** in Haswell *Maister* (1895) 112 In 1833 .. I sailed in the well-known old *Liberty and Property*—a collier with 'pink' stern; the last of her race, I believe.

pink (pıŋk), *sb.*[2], **penk** (peŋk). Forms: *α.* 5- penk, 7 penck, penke; also 8-9 pank. *β.* 7 pinck, 7- pink. [Origin obscure: cf. dial. Ger. *pink(e* fem., (1) minnow, (2) small salmon, (3) a kind of eel. The historical Eng. form was *penk*, for which *pink* began to appear in 17th c., and has been adopted in fishery statutes in sense 2.

It has no connexion with *pink* the flower, nor with *pink* the colour, as erroneously assumed by some.]

1. A minnow. Now *dial.*

α. *a* **1490** BOTONER *Itin.* (1778) 358 Yn Wye-water sunt .. penkys. **1651-3** T. BARKER *Art of Angling* 4 The angling with a Menow, called in some places Pencks [*ed.* **1820**, Pincks]. **1653** WALTON *Angler* iv. 93 With a Worm, or a Minnow (which some call a Penke). **1787** GROSE *Provinc. Gloss.*, *Pank*, or *Pink*, a minnow. N. **1828** C. CROKER *Fairy Leg.* II. 57 Penk or Pink [is] the name of the little fish more commonly called in England minnow. **1891** A. LANG in *Longm. Mag.* Aug. 446 An artificial penk.

β. *a* **1687** COTTON *Angler's Ballad* ii. Poems (1689) 76 And full well you may think, If you troll with a Pink, One [fishing-rod] too weak will be apt to miscarry. **1755** JOHNSON, *Pink* .. 6. A fish; the minnow. **1787**, **1828** [see *α*]. **1879** MISS JACKSON *Shropsh. Word-bk.*, *Pink*, .. the Minnow. [E.D.D. cites it also from Sheffield, Derbysh., Leicester, Notts, Cheshire, & Warwicksh.]

2. a. A young salmon before it becomes a smolt; a samlet, parr.

1828 *Sporting Mag.* XXII. 26 There are a great number of samlets or pinks. **1861** *Act. 24 & 25 Vict.* c. 109 §4 All migratory fish of the genus salmon, whether known by the names .. salmon .. parr, spawn, pink, last spring, hepper, last-brood, .. or by any other local name. **1886** *St. Nicholas* Aug. 740/2 Presently the alevin grows into the fry, or pink, which is an absurd little fish about an inch long, goggle-eyed, and with dark bars on its sides.

b. A young grayling.

1901 H. A. ROLT *Grayling Fishing in S. Country Streams* i. 12 A one-year-old grayling is called a 'pink', and has neither spots nor lateral lines which can be observed. **1939** W. C. PLATTS *Grayling Fishing* vi. 60 Rolt says that a one-year-old grayling is called a 'pink', and a two-year-old a 'shut' or 'shote' grayling ... I have rarely come across these terms in general use. **1952** F. WHITE *Good Eng. Food* I. iv. 55 The principal grayling rivers .. are .. the Teme (where yearling fish are termed 'pinks' and second year fish 'shutts' or 'shots' or 'sheets') [etc.].

c. = *pink salmon* s.v. PINK *sb.*[4] and *a.*[1] C. c.

1921 *Daily Colonist* (Victoria, B.C.) 11 Mar. 19/41 The canneries announced their intention of packing practically no pinks or chums this season. **1935** W. M. HALLIDAY *Potlatch & Totem* 155 After the close of the sockeye season, what are commonly known as humpback salmon were caught; these are the fish which are now classed under the technical name of 'pinks'. **1965** A. J. MCCLANE *Standard Fishing Encycl.* 681/2 The ocean and Puget Sound sport fisheries take many pinks, but it is the commercial effort that accounts for the greatest take.

pink (pıŋk), *sb.*[3] [f. PINK *v.*[1], q.v. for Forms.]

†**1.** A hole or eyelet punched in a garment for decorative purposes; also, scalloping done for the same purpose: cf. PINKING *vbl. sb.*[1], *pinking-iron*.

1512 *Acc. Ld. High Treas. Scot.* IV. 215 Item, .. for iiij[c] powdringis and pinkis to the sam goune, .. xij s. **1598** FLORIO, *Tagliuzzi*, small pinks, cuts or iagges in clothes. **1599** B. JONSON *Cynthia's Rev.* v. iv, Is this pinke of equall proportion to this cut? **1632** —— *Magn. Lady* III. iv, You had rather have An ulcer in your body, than a pink More in your clothes.

†**2.** A stab with a poniard, rapier, etc. *Obs.*

1601 WEEVER *Mirr. Mart.* C j, At a great word she will her poynard draw, Looke for the pincke if once thou giue the lye. **1638** FORD *Lady's Trial* III. i, The fellow's a shrewd fellow at a pink.

b. A shot-wound.

1885 *Pall Mall G.* 13 May 4/1 He is spotted with marks of stabs and revolver 'pinks', and he takes all his wounds quite as matter of course.

pink, *sb.*[4] and *a.*[1] Forms: 6 **pynke**, 6-7 **pinck(e**, **pinke**, 7- **pink**. [Etymology obscure. By some conjectured to be named from its 'pinked' or jagged petals; but there is no evidence that PINK *v.* had the sense 'to cut or scallop the edges (of garments)' in the 16th c., or indeed before the 19th c. Others would connect the name with *pink eye*, small eye, comparing the Fr. name *œillet*, dim. of *œil* eye, and med.L. *Ocellus*, dim. of *oculus* eye.]

A. *sb.* **I. 1. a.** The general name of various species of *Dianthus* (N.O. *Caryophyllaceæ*), esp. of *D. plumarius*, a favourite garden plant, a native of Eastern Europe, with very numerous varieties having pure white, pink, crimson, and variegated sweet-smelling flowers.

1573 TUSSER *Husb.* (1878) 96 Herbes, branches, and flowers, .. Pinkes of all sorts. **1578** LYTE *Dodoens* II. vii. 155 The Pynkes, and small feathered Gillofers, are like to the double or cloaue Gillofers, .. sauing they be single and a great deale smaller. *Ibid.* 156 Called in Englishe by diuers names, as Pynkes, Soppes in wine, feathered Gillofers, and small Honesties. **1601** ? MARSTON *Pasquil & Kath.* I. 272 I'le lay me downe vpon a banke of Pinkes. **1662** PEPYS *Diary* 29 May, To the old Spring Garden, .. the wenches gathered pinks. **1779** SHERIDAN *Critic* II. ii, Sweet-william and sweet marjoram—and all The tribe of single and of double pinks. **1847** L. HUNT *Men, Women, & B.* I. ix. 159 A highly respectable individual .. clean as a pink, and dull as a pike-staff. **1870** MORRIS *Earthly Par.* I. II. 559 Starry pinks for garlands meet.

transf. **1885** T. MOZLEY *Remin. Towns*, etc. II. 339 Those blue eyes and that mixture of pinks and lilies that men, and women too, admire or quiz, as they are disposed.

b. Applied with qualifying words to other species of *Dianthus*, and to other plants allied to or resembling the pink; e.g.

Carolina pink = PINKROOT: cf. CAROLINA; **China** or **Chinese pink**, *Dianthus chinensis*: see CHINA *sb.*[1] 2 b; **clove pink**, *D. Caryophyllus*: see CLOVE *sb.*[2] 6; **Deptford pink**, *D. Armeria*; **fire** or **ground pink**, *Silene virginica*; see FIRE *sb.* II. 5 b; **Indian pink** = *China pink*; also applied to some West Indian and N. American species of *Ipomœa*; also = PINKROOT; †**jagged pink**, Ragged Robin, *Lychnis Flos-cuculi*; **maiden, maidenly**, or **meadow pink**, *Dianthus deltoides*: see MAIDEN *sb.* 10 b; **Maryland pink** = *Carolina pink*; **old maid's pink**, Soapwort, *Saponaria officinalis* (*Cent. Dict.* 1890); **pheasant's eye pink** = PHEASANT'S EYE 3; **sea-pink**, (*a*) Thrift, *Statice Armeria*; † (*b*) *Cerastium repens*; **Spanish pink**, *D. hispanicus*; **swamp pink**, *Azalea viscosa*; **wild pink**, any wild species of *Dianthus*; in U.S. applied to *Silene pennsylvanica* and *S. virginica* (= *ground pink*).

1860 BARTLETT *Dict. Amer.* (ed. 3), *Pink Root*, .. also known as the *Carolina Pink. **1741** *Compl. Fam.-Piece* II. iii. 361 The little Blue, the *China or Indian Pink. **1797** *Encycl. Brit.* (ed. 3) VI. 9/1 The Chinensis, *Chinese, or Indian pink. **1837** *Penny Cycl.* VIII. 475/2 D[*ianthus*] *Caryophyllus*, or the *Clove Pink. **1866** MOORE in Brande & Cox *Dict. Sc.*, etc. II. 906/2 What is called a Clove Pink is *Dianthus caryophyllus*, the source of the Carnation and Picotee. [**1597** GERARDE *Herbal* II. clxxiii. 476 A Wilde creeping Pinke, which groweth in our pastures neere about London .. but especially in the great field next to Detford, by the path side as you go from Redriffe to Greenewich.] **1664** EVELYN *Kal. Hort.* (1729) 205 *May*... Span. Pinks, *Deptford Pinks. **1831** J. DAVIES *Manual Mat. Med.* 447 *Ground pink. *Silene virginiana*. **1664** EVELYN *Kal. Hort.* (1729) 219 *September*... *Indian Pinks, Æthiopick Apples. **1741-97** [see *China, Chinese pink* above]. **1866** *Treas. Bot.* s.v. *Spigelia*, The Pink-root, Worm-grass, or Indian-pink of the shops is the produce of *S. marilandica*. **1573** BARET *Alv.* P 349 The *iagged Pinkes, *Vetonica Altilis minor* .. Dodon. **1753** CHAMBERS *Cycl. Supp.* s.v., The little creeping pink, with one flower on every stalk, called by many the *maiden-pink. **1597** GERARDE *Herbal* II. clxxiii. 477 *Caryophyllus Virgineus*, *Maidenly Pinkes. **1866** *Treas. Bot.* 891 Maiden or *Meadow Pink. **1733** MILLER *Gard. Dict.*, *Statice*, Thrift or *Sea Pink. **1759** *Ibid.* s.v. *Cerastium*, Hoary creeping Mouse-ear, by some called Sea Pink. **1854** H. MILLER *Sch. & Schm.* xviii. (1858) 397 Beds of thrift, with its gay flowers the sea-pinks. **1892** H. HUTCHINSON *Fairway Isl.* 97 Here and there a bunch of dead sea-pink. **1664** *Spanish Pink [see *Deptford Pink* above]. **1884** MILLER *Plant-n.*, Spanish Pink, *Dianthus hispanicus*. **1898** *Atlantic Monthly* LXXXII. 499/1 The familiar sweet-scented white azalea ..., the '*swamp pink' of my boyhood. **1753** CHAMBERS *Cycl. Supp.* s.v., The wild sweet-william, or common *wild pink. **1814** WORDSW. *Excursion* VI. Poems (1888) 497/2 The wild pink crowns the garden-wall. **1882** *Garden* 28 Oct. 375/2 S. pennsylvanica, or Wild Pink, as it is popularly called, with pink flowers.

c. Locally applied to the Cuckoo-flower or Lady's Smock, *Cardamine pratensis*.

1818 HOGG *Brownie of B.* xi, Enough to make the pinks an' ewe gowan blush to the very lip.

2. *fig.* **a.** The 'flower', or finest example of excellence; the embodied perfection (*of* some good quality).

1592 SHAKS. *Rom. & Jul.* II. iv. 61 *Mer.* Nay, I am the very pinck of curtesie. *Rom.* Pinke for flower. **1621** FLETCHER *Pilgrim* I. ii, This is the prettiest pilgrim—The pinck of pilgrims. **1711** STEELE *Spect.* No. 140 ¶10 Ladies, .. the very Pinks of Good-breeding. **1773** GOLDSM. *Stoops to Conq.* I. i, Setting off her pretty monster as the very pink of perfection. **1813** MOORE *Post-bag* viii. 4 Come to our Fête, and show again That pea-green coat, thou pink of men! **1825-9** MRS. SHERWOOD *Lady of Manor* III. xxii. 398, I have been admiring your cupboards; they are the very pink of elegance. **1893** BARING-GOULD *Cheap Jack Z.* i. 20 The pink and paragon of propriety.

b. The most perfect condition or degree *of* something; the height, extreme. Also freq. with ellipse of *of condition*, *of health*, etc. *colloq.*

1767 G. S. CAREY *Hills of Hybla* 20 Behold her sailing in the pink of taste, Trump'd up with powder, frippery and paste. *a* **1821** KEATS *Castle Builder* in *Poetical Wks.* (1907) 298 Let me think About my room,—I'll have it in the pink; It should be rich and sombre. **1840** THACKERAY *Paris Sk.-bk.* (1872) 173 In the very pink of the mode. **1845** DICKENS *Let.* 18 Mar. (1977) IV. 282 Of all the picturesque abominations in the World, commend me to Fondi. It is the very pink of hideousness and squalid misery. **1893** VIZETELLY *Glances Back* I. xiii. 255 [He] got himself up in the very pink of fashion. **1905** *Kynoch Jrnl.* Oct.-Dec. 201 Makers may despatch explosives from the factory in the pink of condition. **1914** *Isle of Man Weekly Times* 21 Nov. 7/5 He says that he is 'in the pink'. **1916** C. WINCHESTER *Flying Men* 193, I saw a couple of R.F.C. officers .. the other day. They looked 'in the pink'. **1923** WODEHOUSE *Inimitable Jeeves* xi. 115 'Oh, hallo!' I said. 'Going strong?' 'I am in excellent health, I thank you. And you?' 'In the pink. Just been over to America.' **1929** J. B. PRIESTLEY *Good Companions* II. vii. 453, I am writing these lines to say I am still in the pink and hoping you are the same. **1937** A. HUXLEY *Let.* 25 Feb. (1969) 415 Quant à moi, I was in the pink until about a week ago. **1950** [see COIN *v.*[1] 5 d]. **1973** 'P. MALLOCH' *Kick-back* vi. 37 Gilchrist shook hands. 'O.K. How about you?' 'In the pink,' Campbell said. **1976** DEXTER & MAKINS *Testkill* 129 A young Alsatian in the pink of condition.

c. A beauty; an exquisite, a smart person, one of the élite. ? *Obs.*

1602 BRETON *Merry Wonders* B iij, He had a pretty pincke to his own wedded wife. **1821** *Sporting Mag.* IX. 27 A new white upper tog, that would have given a sporting appearance to a pink of Regent-street. **1827** FONBLANQUE *Eng. under 7 Administr.* (1837) I. 55 His Vice runs into the contrary extreme. He is a Pink, an Exquisite.

3. *attrib.* or as *adj.* Exquisite; smart, 'swell'. Now only *U.S. colloq.* or *slang.*

1598 MARSTON *Pygmal.* iii. 149 For to perfume her rare perfection With some sweet-smelling pinck Epitheton. **1818** LADY MORGAN *Autobiog.* (1859) 42 It was Lady Cork's 'Pink night', the rendezvous of the fashionable exclusives.

4. *Comb.* (in sense 1), as ***pink growing*** sb., ***pink-like*** adj.; **pink-coloured** *a.*, of the colour of the pink; having a pink colour.

1681 T. JORDAN *London's Joy* B iv, A Mantle of pink colour'd sarsnet, fringed with Gold. **17..** MOORE *Trav.* II. xc. (Jod.), The dancers.. were dressed in white silk flounced with pink-coloured ribbands. **1807** J. E. SMITH *Phys. Bot.* 412 Little pink-like plants. **1826** MISS MITFORD *Village* Ser. II. (1863) 244 Lending his willing aid in waiting and entertaining on fair-days and market-days, at pink-feasts and melon-feasts. **1845** *Florist's Jrnl.* Sept. 186 The reminiscences of pink-growing are always most interesting to us.

II. sb. use of B.

5. a. A light or pale red colour with a slight purple tinge. (See also PINK *sb.*[5])

[**1828** WEBSTER, *Pink*, a color used by painters; from the color of the flower.] **1846** WORCESTER, *Pink*,.. the usual color of the flower; a light crimson. **1874** A. O'SHAUGHNESSY *Music & Moonlight, Ode to New Age* 183 Nay, by yon pink of slowly parting lips, A long rim near the dawn. **1892** *Speaker* 3 Sept. 289/2 Wild rose.. falling in close exquisite veils of pink and green down to the daisied grass.

b. With defining word prefixed to denote a particular shade: see B. 1 b.

1893 F. F. MOORE *I Forbid Banns* (1899) 88 The mellow crimson faded into shell-pink. **1900** *Daily News* 28 Apr. 6/6 A little prawn-pink is introduced under the embroidery. **1900** G. SWIFT *Somerley* 101 Soft cheeks with a sort of sunrise-pink on them—not that unhealthy, doll-like shell-pink.

c. As a colour commonly used on maps to indicate a British colony or dominion. Cf. RED *sb.*[1] 1 e.

1913 C. MACKENZIE *Sinister St.* I. II. xv. 407 She said half the world was composed of fools which accounted for the preponderation—I mean preponderance—of pink on the map.

6. a. Scarlet when worn by fox-hunters; a scarlet hunting-coat, or the cloth of which it is made.

1834 DISRAELI *Corr. w. Sister* 15 Feb., Although not in pink, [I] was the best mounted man in the field. **1860** R. E. WARBURTON *Hunt. Songs* l. (1883) 143 A sect.. Who blindly follow, clad in coats of pink, A beast whose nature is to run and stink. **1861** HUGHES *Tom Brown at Oxf.* i, They are the hunting set, and come in with pea-coats over their pinks. **1889** *Daily News* 12 Nov. 5/2 Scarlet, conventionally known as 'pink', will, he trusts, last as long as fox-hunting. **1900** *Ibid.* 24 Feb. 6/7 A short coat in hunting pink.

b. *transf.* A man in 'pink'; a fox-hunter.

1828 *Sporting Mag.* XXI. 323 Even in the strictest College a pink could unmolested walk across the Court. **1840** SHAIRP in W. Knight *Shairp & Friends* (1888) 44, I see the pinks flocking out to the 'meets'. **1869** E. FARMER *Scrap Bk.* (ed. 6) 91 Pinks call for their second [horse] to finish the run.

7. As the name of varieties of the potato. Cf. PINK-EYE 1.

1853 *Trans. Mich. Agric. Soc.* V. 208 Some of the more approved kinds are.. the White, Red, and Strawberry Pinks. **1861** MRS. BEETON *Bk. Househ. Managem.* 589 The Lancashire Pink is also a good potato, and is much cultivated in the neighbourhood of Liverpool.

8. A pink ball in snooker and some related games.

1910 *Encycl. Brit.* III. 938/2 It is also permitted in some rooms to take blacks and pinks alternately without pocketing a coloured ball between the strokes. **1935** *Encycl. Sports* 570/1 Black is on the billiard spot: pink on the centre line of the table, touching the apex ball of the pyramid. **1976** *Milton Keynes Express* 28 May 55/4 He played the cue ball the full length of the table, swerving past the green, back up the table, not only to hit the red but to pot it, plus the black, yellow, green, brown, blue and but for a miss on the pink would have cleared the table to win the frame. **1978** *Guardian* 7 Feb. 20/6 Pulman twice missed eminently possible pinks, with position on the black there for the taking.

9. *U.S. Blacks' slang.* A white-skinned person. Also *Comb.*, as **pink-chaser** (see quot. 1970).

1926 C. VAN VECHTEN *Nigger Heaven* I. ix. 157 Funny thing about those pink-chasers the ofays never seem to have any use for them. **1945** L. SHELLY *Jive Talk Dict.* 16/1 *Pink*, pretty white girl. **1970** C. MAJOR *Dict. Afro-Amer. Slang* 91 *Pink chasers*, black people who deliberately cultivate friendships with white people. **1973** 'TREVANIAN' *Loo Sanction* (1974) 159 P'tit Noel shrugged. 'All pinks sound alike.'

10. A person whose politics are left of centre, but closer to the centre than those of a 'red'; a radical; a liberal socialist. *colloq.* Cf. *parlour pink* s.v. PARLOUR 2 f.

1927 U. SINCLAIR *Oil!* xiii. 313 He's nuts on this red-hunting business, and the pinks are worse than the reds, he says. **1943** K. TENNANT *Ride on Stranger* xx. 225 Wilmot electorate covered an area of residential water-side suburbs inhabited less by Reds than by Pinks of all shades and hues. **1956** A. WILSON *Anglo-Saxon Att.* I. iv. 115 Less-informed business friends spoke to Robin of intellectuals as communists or pinks. **1968** *Punch* 17 July 95/3 The Tory Party.. now clutches pinks, finks and crumb-bums to its shrivelled teats. **1976** SCOTT & KOSKI *Walk-In* (1977) xxi. 140 His college professors.. thought that the boy was perhaps slightly leftish but no more so than most of the Pinks over at State. **1978** 'R. CASSILIS' *Winding Sheet* II. xii. 109 One of those old-fashioned egalitarians, like the pompous Pinks who had once been the backbone of the.. Labour Party.

11. A pink gin; the bitters in this drink.

1942 G. HACKFORTH-JONES *One-One-One* xxii. 203 'Eeyore' Smith absent-mindedly added a dash of 'pink' to his evening aperitif. **1969** G. GREENE *Trav. with my Aunt* I. xx. 213 'Another double', 'Pint of best bitter', 'Double pink'. **1976** 'F. CLIFFORD' *Drummer in Dark* iv. 15 'What'll it be?' 'A pink, please.'

B. *adj.* [orig. attrib. use of sense 1 of the sb.]

1. a. Of the colour of the pink (sense 1) in its single natural state; of a pale or light red colour, slightly inclining towards purple; of a pale rose-colour.

1720 MRS. MANLEY *Power of Love* (1741) I. 16 A Veil of Pink Colour. **1733-4** MRS. DELANY in *Life & Corr.* 431 Lady Dysart's clothes were pink armazine trimmed with silver. **1806** *Med. Jrnl.* XV. 58 The pustule was small... Its base was of a light red or pink colour. **1821-30** LD. COCKBURN *Mem.* vii. (1874) 350 He.. could not be looked at without his face becoming pink. **1875** PRINCESS ALICE in *Mem.* 14 Feb. (1884) 336 She looks pink and smiling.

b. With prefixed word expressing the particular shade, as *light, deep, dull, pale pink*; *arbutus-, coral-, currant-, old-, orange-, prawn-, purple-, raspberry-, shell pink*, etc. See also ROSE-*pink*, SALMON-*pink*.

1882 *Garden* 14 Oct. 347/1 A small flower with pale pink florets. **1887** *Daily News* 20 July 6/1 A coral-pink embroidered dress. **1888** *Lady* 25 Oct. 374/3 Some old pink rosebuds near the face. **1901** *Daily News* 19 Jan. 6/7 A band of prawn-pink velvet.

c. Of the coloration of a newspaper: indicating a sporting edition.

1887, etc. [see *Pink 'Un* (a), sense C c]. **1922** JOYCE *Ulysses* 659 The Gold Cup flat handicap, the official and definitive result of which he had read in the *Evening Telegraph*, late pink edition.

d. Of the coloration on a map: indicating a British colony or dominion. Cf. PINK *sb.*[4] 5 c.

1960 N. MITFORD *Don't tell Alfred* vii. 74 It was bad luck for Alfred that the government.. should be determined to paint the Minquiers pink on the map. **1973** *Listener* 20 Dec. 857/2 Industrialisation played a big part in the drive to paint the map pink. British industries needed raw materials. **1976** C. BERMANT *Coming Home* I. vi. 88, I took it that the great green-coloured mass of the Sahara would pass to Britain... Gradually the whole of Africa glowed pink before my eyes. **1979** *Listener* 26 July 112/3, I was drilled in geography... Most areas, I remember, were coloured pink on the map.

2. Applied to the colour of a hunting-coat: see A. 6.

1857 TROLLOPE *Barchester T.* xxii, He.. could not be persuaded to take his pink coat out of the press, or his hunters out of his stable.

3. Politically left of centre, progressive; applied to socialism of a less extreme character than that denoted by 'red'; loosely, Communist. Also *absol.* Cf. PINK *sb.*[4] 10.

1837 DE QUINCEY in *Tait's Mag.* Feb. 71/1 Amusing it is to look back upon any political work of Mr Shepherd's.. and to know that the pale pink of his Radicalism was then accounted deep, deep scarlet. **1859** LYTTON *What will he do with It?* I. I. i. 9 Young 'un, I'm a Tory—that's blue; and Spruce is a Rad—that's pink! **1920** MRS. P. SNOWDEN *Through Bolshevik Russia* 180 The people's flag is palest pink, It's not so red as you might think. **1924** *Scribner's Mag.* Oct. 441/1 The Middle West is becoming pink. But it is genuine American pink. Not Moscow Red! **1939** A. THIRKELL *Before Lunch* iv. 84, I wouldn't mind her trying to run her pink politics down my throat.. though I never see why being a Communist should make one abhor washing. **1973** *Listener* 28 June 864/1 'I am not Communist, but.. I am a little pink.' Thus spake King Sihanouk of Cambodia. **1979** 'S. WOODS' *This Fatal Writ* 81 The description 'pale pink intellectual' is far too tame for Susan... And he's just the opposite, a true blue Tory.

4. Violent, extreme; utter, absolute (see also quot. 1896). *slang.*

1896 W. C. GORE in *Inlander* Jan. 149 *Pink*, used to intensify the negative. 'He didn't know a pink thing about the lesson.' **1901** *Daily Express* 28 Aug. 4/3 The master of the house flies into a pink rage because his chop is not done. **1946** B. MARSHALL *George Brown's Schooldays* 145 These rotten new kids really are the pink limit.

5. Slightly indecent, violent, or vulgar; mildly 'blue' (see BLUE *a.* 9).

1898 R. HICHENS *Londoners* xvi. 280 Lovely needle-work! That's a funny beginning for a Pink un. **1900** *Daily News* 28 May 3/1 Most of their adjectives have a decidedly pink tinge. **1979** J. MELVILLE *Wages of Zen* xi. 117 One cinema showing 'pink films'.. and one strip show.

6. Of a plan, process, etc.: that must be kept secret.

1924 *Discovery* June 83/1 Little was said about it [*sc.* wireless direction for boats and torpedoes] and in navy parlance it is a subject which is still slightly 'pink', a cryptic term indicating that even if we do happen to know something, we are not prepared to make a song about it. **1925** FRASER & GIBBONS *Soldier & Sailor Words* 224 *Pink*, secret. An expression in some Government Offices during the war for secret telegrams. **1962** GRANVILLE *Dict. Sailors' Slang* 88/2 *Pink*... 2. Secret, hush-hush, from the pink (confidential) signal pads used in the Navy.

7. Of a person: white-skinned. Cf. PINK *sb.*[4] 9.

1936 G. B. SHAW *Millionairess* Pref. 121 Even in Africa, where pink emigrants struggle with brown and black natives for possession of the land, and our Jamaican miscegenation shocks public sentiment, the sun sterilizes the pinks to such an extent that Cabinet ministers call for more emigration to maintain the pink population. **1971** *Rand Daily Mail* 3 Apr. 5/8 We Pink South Africans are in danger of being cut off from the world. **1977** P. USTINOV *Dear Me* iii. 26 On my first application to enter the United States.. I described my colour as pink. I was told sternly that I was white, a fact which I denied, relying upon an Embassy mirror for evidence. A great deal of time was wasted, more especially since I failed to realize the subliminal implication of the word 'pink' in those days.

8. Phrases. ***strike me pink!*** (slang): an exclamation of astonishment or indignation; ***to paint the town pink***: to go on a spree (after *to paint the town red* s.v. PAINT *v.*[1] 10); ***to swear pink*** (colloq.): to make vehement protestations; to 'swear blind'; ***to tickle pink***: see TICKLE *v.*

1902 E. NESBIT *Five Children & It* viii. 218 When he beheld the magnificent proportions of Robert he said.. 'Strike me pink!' **1922** JOYCE *Ulysses* 623 And there he was at the end of his tether after having often painted the town tolerably pink. **1931** A. P. HERBERT *Derby Day* III. 115 Ten thousand serpents! Strike me pink! Where's that girl? She'll go to clink! **1956** E. POUND tr. *Sophocles' Women of Trachis* 20 And you swore pink they were bringing her to be Heracles' wife. **1969** *Sunday Mail Mag.* (Brisbane) 7 Sept. 10/1 He was further reported as commenting on certain African members of the Commonwealth in the words: 'Strike me pink, they'll do me for bloody butchers.'

C. Combinations (chiefly of the adj.).

a. Qualifying other adjs. of colour, as ***pink-brown, -pearl, -violet, -white***; also ***pink-and-white***, etc.

1845 D. JERROLD *Time Works Wonders* I. 2 *Jug.* I've some beautiful bacon, sir, Such pink and white! Streaked, sir, like a carnation. **1853** C. BRONTË *Villette* I. xiv. 292 Your pink and white complexion. **1860** GEO. ELIOT *Jrnl.* in J. W. Cross *George Eliot's Life* (1885) II. x. 169 The Churches.. with their wealth of gilding and rich pink-brown marbles. **1895** W. B. YEATS *Poems* 148 But all the little pink-white nails have grown To be great talons. **1897** HALL CAINE *Christian* x, The pretty dark girl with the pink and white cheeks like a doll. **1897** MARY KINGSLEY *W. Africa* 389 Some zoophyte of an exquisite bright mauve or pink-violet colour. **1900** *Daily News* 3 July 3/4 The crowds that give life to these wide pink-white streets present a bewildering display of colour. **1965** A. CHRISTIE *At Bertram's Hotel* ii. 22 It made her come to life again—Jane Marple, that pink and white eager young girl. **1979** P. MASON *Skinner* xiv. 96 We shall be junior to pink-and-white boys of eighteen straight from England.

b. Parasynthetic and instrumental, as ***pink-blossomed, -bound, -breasted, -checked, -cheeked, -coated, -complexioned, -faced, -flowered, -frilled, -haired, -handed, -leaved, -lipped, -ribbed, -scrolled, -shaded, -striped, -tinted, -veined, -vested*** adjs. ***pink-coloured***: see A. 4.

1805-6 WORDSWORTH *Prelude* (1959) VII. 260 Equestrians, Tumblers, Women, Girls, and Boys, Blue-breech'd, pink-vested. **1826** MISS MITFORD *Village* Ser. II. (1863) 373 The baby, adorned in a pink-checked frock, a blue spotted pinafore, and a little white cap. **1840** MRS. NORTON *Dream* 29 And pink-lipp'd shells and many-colour'd weeds. **1844** THACKERAY *Box of Novels* Wks. 1900 XIII. 403 Those pink-bound volumes are to be found in every garrison. **1873** MORRIS in Mackail *Life* (1899) I. 293 Abundance of pink-blossomed leafless peach and almond trees. **1890** 'R. BOLDREWOOD' *Miner's Right* (1899) 156/2 Built of pale, pink-veined, creamy free-stone. **1892** GREENER *Breech-Loader* 174 Pink-edged, pink-faced,.. and thick cardboard wads, cloth wads, and black wads, are used for special purposes. **1906** *Daily Chron.* 23 Aug. 5/6 A white gown and blue picture hat and pink-frilled parasol. **1940** E. POUND *Cantos* lxix. 174 Squad of the pink-haired snot. **1946** S. SPENDER *European Witness* ix. 46 A pink-complexioned mild-mannered man. **1955** D. DAVIE *Brides of Reason* 8 The nausea that struggles to despatch Pink-handed horror in a craggy room. **1962** I. MURDOCH *Unofficial Rose* iv. 41 She thrust a white-quartered green-eyed Madame Hardy in between two lilac-shaded pink-scrolled Louise Odiers. **1967** A. WEST in *Coast to Coast 1965-66* 219 It was a soft, pink-cheeked face. **1978** T. GIFFORD *Glendower Legacy* 264 She ..had a succulent moist look, freshly showered, pink-cheeked.

c. Special combinations and collocations: **pink-ash** (see quot.); **pink bed**, one of the beds of sandstone in the Swanage quarries; **pink bollworm**, the pinkish larva of a small brown moth, *Pectinophora gossypiella*, of the family Gelechiidæ, which feeds on the lint or seeds of cotton bolls; **pink button** *Stock Exchange*, a jobber's clerk; **pink champagne**, rosé champagne; champagne to which a small quantity of still red wine has been added; **pink-cheek**, a fish of New South Wales, *Upeneichthys porosus* (*Cent. Dict.* 1890); **pink disease**, a disease of children caused by mercury poisoning, characterized by pinkness of parts of the body, restlessness, and photophobia; **pink elephant**, used as a type of the extraordinary or impossible; also (chiefly pl.), a characteristic apparition seen by someone drunk or delirious; cf. *pink rat(s)*; **pink-fever** = PINK-EYE[1] 2 (*Syd. Soc. Lex.* 1893); **pink-fish**, a S. Californian pinkish-coloured gobioid fish, *Typhlogobius californensis*, which lives attached to the underside of stones (Webster 1902); **pink-foot** *a. poet.* = PINK-FOOTED *a.*; *sb.* the Pink-footed goose *sb.* (also *attrib.*); **pink-footed** *a.*, having pink feet: *spec.* applied to the Pink-footed Goose (*Anser fabalis brachyrhynchus*); **pink gilding, pink gold**, gilding having a pink tinge resulting from a combination of gold, silver, and copper; **pink gin**, gin-and-bitters; **pink-grass**, an agricultural name for species of sedge, esp. *Carex glauca* and *C. præcox*, found in pastures; **pink lady** *U.S.*, (*a*) a cocktail comprising gin, egg white, grenadine, and other ingredients; (*b*) (see quot. 1968–70); **pink madder**: see MADDER *sb.*[1] 3; **pink noise** *Physics*, random noise having equal energy per octave, and so differing from white noise in having a greater proportion of low-frequency components; **pink paper**, a parliamentary paper containing the information specified in quot. 1894; **pink pine** *N.Z.*, a small forest tree, *Dacrydium biforme*, of the family Podocarpaceæ, bearing linear juvenile leaves and scale-like adult ones, and yielding a resin from which manool is manufactured; **pink rat(s)**, a characteristic apparition seen by someone drunk or delirious; cf. *pink elephant*; **pink salmon**, the humpback salmon, *Oxyrhynchus gorbuscha*; **pink salt**, the ammonium salt of tetrachloride of tin, 2 $NH_4Cl.SnCl_4$, used in calico-printing; **pink saucer**, a saucer containing a pigment used to give a pink tint to the skin, or to garments; *transf.* the pigment itself; **pink slip** *U.S.*, a notice of dismissal from employment; also *transf.* and *fig.*; hence **pink-slip** *v. trans.*, to dismiss, to fire; **pink spot**, used to designate a substance of uncertain composition found in the urine of some schizophrenics, observed as a pink spot on a chromatogram of it; **pink tea** *N. Amer.*, a formal tea party or other social engagement; an exclusive gathering; also used as a type of the polite or genteel; also *attrib.*; **pink thorn**, a pink-flowered variety of the hawthorn, *Cratægus monogyna*; **pink toe(s)** *U.S. Blacks' slang*, a light-skinned black woman; a white girl; **Pink 'Un** [UN, 'UN[2]], a nickname for a newspaper printed on pink paper, *spec.* (*a*) *The Sporting Times*; also, a reporter for this newspaper; (*b*) *The Financial Times*; **pinkwash**, a composition used for rendering walls, etc., pink; so **pink-washed** adj.; **pink wine**, (*a*) *slang*, champagne; (*b*) vin rosé.

1881 RAYMOND *Mining Gloss.* s.v. *Coal*, Anthracite is divided in the United States according to the color of the ash after burning, into *white-ash*, *red-ash*, and **pink-ash coal*. **1858** A. C. RAMSAY, etc. *Rock Spec.* (1862) 142 (E.D.D.) The '*Pink Bed', which forms a part of the Freestone Series. **1906** H. MAXWELL-LEFROY *Indian Insect Pests* III. viii. 94 The *pink boll-worms are most abundant when the cotton forms bolls. **1917** *Jrnl. Agric. Res.* IX. 343 The pink bollworm..is one of the most destructive cotton insects known. **1932** [see *grain-moth* s.v. GRAIN *sb.*[1] 19]. **1955** *Sci. News Let.* 23 July 56/2 The preferred food of the pink bollworm larva is the kernel of the cotton seed. **1972** SWAN & PAPP *Common Insects N. Amer.* 325 Larvae of the Cotton Steam Moth..resemble pink bollworms. **1973** *Times* 16 June 18/2 *Pink buttons are not..the female equivalents of blue buttons. **1974** *Sunday Tel.* 7 Apr. 29/3 As 'pink buttons', they look after all the firm's communications, both between the floor of the House and the offices, and between the brokers and country exchanges. **1838** J. KENYON *Poems* 88 Lily on liquid roses floating—So floats yon foam o'er *pink champagne. **1940** N. MITFORD *Pigeon Pie* vi. 105 Oysters and pink champagne. **1974** P. ERDMAN *Silver Bears* v. 63 Sorbet flavoured with pink champagne. **1921** *Med. Jrnl. Austral.* 19 Feb. 146/1 When the rash is marked it is common to find the glands in the axillæ and groins enlarged. It is this pink rash, that leads to the name '*pink disease'. **1921** *Trans. 11th Sess. Australasian Med. Congr. 1920* 444 In Sydney the entity of this illness has long been recognized, and it is usually spoken of by Dr. Clubbe and others as 'the pink disease'. **1959** D. STOWENS *Pediatric Path.* x. 127/2 Acrodynia (Pink disease, Swift's disease, Feer's disease, Erythredema polyneuropathy). This bizarre condition is a manifestation either of poisoning by or hypersensitivity to, mercury. **1974** PASSMORE & ROBSON *Compan. Med. Stud.* III. xvii. 28/1 Pink disease earns its name from the colour of the hands and feet and not from an imaginary Dr Pink to whom many students credit its discovery. **1940** *This Week* 5 Oct. 2 *Pink elephants. **1943** F. BROWN *Angels & Spaceships* (1954) 88 You mean if I saw a pink elephant I wouldn't believe it? **1946** P. LARKIN *Jill* 77 Whiskey? Would it make him drunk, would he stagger about and see pink elephants? **1960** E. W. HILDICK *Boy at Window* v. 45 It's like pink elephants. Folk 'ud think you'd been drinking if you went round saying you'd seen white mice running about wild! **1973** L. COOPER *Tea on Sunday* xxxiv. 246 'I heard somebody.' He'd be seeing pink elephants next. **1870** MORRIS *Earthly Par.* I. I. 404 The *pink-foot doves Still told their weary tale unto their loves. **1931** H. J. MASSINGHAM *Birds of Seashore* 38 Individual birds do not conform to pink-foot pattern. **1956** C. WILLOCK *Death at Flight* iii. 31 At least a thousand pinkfeet. Gone out on the muds for the night. **1957** D. A. BANNERMAN *Birds Brit. Isles* VI. 239 In 1951 pink-foots arrived in Britain unusually late. **1972** *Shooting Times & Country Mag.* 4 Mar. 7/1 Three-quarters of the pinkfeet that winter in Britain come from Iceland. **1839** A. D. BARTLETT in *Proc. Zool. Soc.* VII. 7 On a new British species of the genus *Anser*... *Pink-footed Goose... Legs and feet, of a reddish flesh colour or pink. **1843** W. YARRELL *Hist. Brit. Birds* III. 66 The voice of the Pink-footed Goose differs from that of the Bean Goose in being sharper in tone. **1882** HEPBURN in *Proc. Berw. Nat. Club* IX. No. 3. 505 The Bean and the Pinkfooted Goose, almost daily visitors..during spring. **1932** *Discovery* Aug. 244/2 White-fronted and pink-footed geese..are supposed to be nesting at the sources of the rivers running northwards from the ice-cap [in Iceland]. **1976** G. EVANS in R. Durman *Bird Observatories in Brit. & Ireland* vii. 140 The Pink-footed Goose is now far from abundant. **1873** E. SPON *Workshop Receipts* Ser. I. 197/1 *Pink gilding,..should present at the same time, the red, yellow, and white shades, in such a manner that a practised eye will distinguish them. **1930** H. CRADDOCK *Savoy Cocktail Bk.* 1. 124 **Pink gin cocktail.* 1 Dash Angostura Bitters. 1 Glass Gin. **1952** E. GRIERSON *Reputation for Song* xxii. 178 She knew the type: a big car, and pink gins, and wine for dinner. **1974** J. MITCHELL *Death & Bright Water* xix. 230 'Pink gin, please,' he said, and she mixed it efficiently. **1873** E. SPON *Workshop Receipts* Ser. I. 196/2 *Pink gold [results] from the combination of gold, silver, and copper. **1944** S. BELLOW *Dangling Man* 149 She had been drinking *Pink Ladies, and she was running over. **1946** C. HIMES *Black on Black* (1973) 264 'Anything to drink?' the waiter asked. 'I think I should like a pink lady.' **1968–70** *Current Slang* (Univ. S. Dakota) III–IV. 92 *Pink ladies, n.* Barbiturates. (Drug users' jargon). **1972** M. J. BOSSE *Incident at Naha* II. 99 There they were, the little pills, the Red Devils, Yellow Jackets, Christmas Trees, and Pink Ladies. **1975** J. WAMBAUGH *Choirboys* (1976) i. 6 Now drink your Pink Lady. **1961** G. A. BRIGGS *A to Z in Audio* 151 *Pink noise is derived from white noise by applying a rising bass characteristic through the range. **1962** A. NISBETT *Technique Sound Studio* xii. 220 White noise with bass tip-up is 'pink' noise. **1976** *Gramophone* Apr. 1690/1 Measurements were made of the response of my lounge, using pink noise derived from a Rogers noise generator. [**1894** *1st Rep. Sel. Comm. Parl. Papers Distribution* p. iii. in *Parl. Papers* XIV. 497 A Schedule shall be circulated daily, weekly, or otherwise, as may be found most convenient, giving reference number, title, and short note of contents of all Papers presented to Parliament by Command of Her Majesty, or printed by Order of either House, since the date of the Schedule last issued. This Schedule shall be sent to each Member in the shape of a demand form, printed on pink paper, and returnable post free.] **1906** *Rep. Sel. Comm. Offic. Publ.* 43 in *Parl. Papers* XI. 95 The *pink paper was started in 1889 as an experiment, and it was ratified in 1894 by the Committee. **1908** *Rep. Sel. Comm. Publ.* 111 in *Parl. Papers* X. 849 The first Regulation directed the issue of what we all know as the 'pink paper'. **1928** COCKAYNE & TURNER *Trees N.Z.* ii. 43 *Pink-pine. A small tree, 15–40 ft. high, or a shrub, with the juvenile leaves distinct from the adult. **1958** *N.Z. Timber Jrnl.* Jan. 46/2 Pink pine... Small tree of sub-alpine forest of New Zealand. Often a shrub. **1969** *N.Z. News* 23 July 4/3 Pink pine..is so slow growing that 18 in diameter trees on the West Coast are believed to be 800 years old. **1914** C. D. BROAD *Perception* iv. 266 The *pink rats that can only be seen by those who habitually take excess of alcohol. **1925** —— *Mind & its Place* iv. 142 Some bright spirit will at once complain that the pink-rat situation has no object. **1932** H. H. PRICE *Perception* vi. 147 The celebrated case of the delirious man who 'sees a pink rat'. **1905** D. S. JORDAN *Guide to Study of Fishes* II. iv. 71 The humpback salmon, or *pink salmon..is the smallest of the American species. **1952** D. F. PUTNAM *Canad. Regions* 447/1 The humpback or pink salmon weighs, on the average, four pounds. **1976** J. S. NELSON *Fishes of World* 100 Pink salmon have a rigid two-year life span. **1856** MILLER *Elem. Chem.* II. 936 A similar constitution holds in the corresponding ammoniacal salt NH_4Cl, $SnCl_2$, which is the *pink salt of the dyer. **1868** WATTS *Dict. Chem.* V. 810 It is used in calico-printing under the name of *pink salt*, for the production of red colours. **1864** WEBSTER, **Pink-saucer*. **1888** *New York World* 22 July (Farmer *Amer.*), Flesh tights..colored with what we call pink saucer in the profession, a kind of stuff you buy at the druggists. **1915** 'B. L. STANDISH' *Covering Look-In Corner* ix. 100 And have Murphy hand me the *pink slip tonight! **1923** *N.Y. Times* 7 Oct. 2/1 *Getting the pink slip*, being canceled, which notice comes on pink paper. **1951** *Sat. Rev. Lit.* (U.S.) 23 June 7/1 In small colleges and large universities hundreds of instructors and professors are getting 'pink slips' after the diplomas have been handed out. **1953** BERREY & VAN DEN BARK *Amer. Thes. Slang* (1954) §67/4 Pink-slip, give the blue envelope *or* pink slip,..to give notice of discharge. **1963** WODEHOUSE *Stiff Upper Lip, Jeeves* ix. 71 You mean that if Madeleine hands Gussie the pink slip, she'll marry you? **1966** T. PYNCHON *Crying of Lot 49* v. 114 His wife had..left him the day after he was pink-slipped. **1975** *New Yorker* 8 Sept. 115/1 Patrolmen on the beat, for example—got their pink slips because firing them was a dramatic way of demonstrating that the city was taking the crisis seriously. [**1962** *Nature* 2 June 898/1 The application of a modified Ehrlich's reagent..resulted in a..pink spot.] **1966** *Listener* 14 July 48/1 This '*pink spot' substance, so called from how it appears in chemical analysis, has not yet shown hallucinogenic activity when swallowed by volunteers. **1973** T. A. BAN *Recent Adv. Biol. Schizophrenia* iv. 30 Papers..some confirming but many more challenging the association of 'pink spot' with schizophrenia... Counterclaims have been advanced that the 'pink spot' is not 3,4-dimethoxyphenylethylamine. **1886** *Weekly Manitoba Liberal* 26 Nov. 8/3 The *Pink Tea held under the auspices of the Women's Christian Temperance Union... The ladies in charge were all fittingly attired with pink caps and aprons and some of the gentleman patrons wore pink ties. **1887** *Harper's Mag.* Jan. 204/1 A Protestant good cause is to be furthered by a bazar or a 'pink tea'. **1905** J. LONDON *Let.* 15 Sept. (1966) 184 Do you remember how Bessie dragged Anna Strunsky's name through the mire? Through all the..pink-tea councils? **1906** *N.Y. Even. Post* 17 Nov. 1 From all accounts these [football] battles of the early eighties and late seventies were no 'pink tea' affairs. **1918** [see BOLSHEVISM]. **1934** N. SAINSBURY *Gridiron Grit* in *Stirring Football Stories* (1941) 55 What do you think football is, a pink tea? **1945** *Boulder* (Colorado) *Daily Camera* 2 Nov. 7/4 Yes, the war was no pink tea. **1952** *North Star* (Yellowknife, Northwest Territories) Dec. 2/1 We were only a name mentioned disparagingly at the clique's pink teas. **1852** C. M. YONGE *Two Guardians* x. 165 The *pinkthorn, dressed in all its garlands, before her window. **1892** —— *Old Woman's Outlook* xi. 263 There stood on the lawn..a pink thorn. **1942** Z. N. HURSTON in *Amer. Mercury* July 96/1 **Pink toes*, yellow girl. **1965** C. HIMES (*title*) Pinktoes. *Ibid.* 216 When *Word* whispered it about that even the great Mamie Mason had lost her own black Joe to a young Pinktoe, the same panic prevailed among the black ladies of Harlem as had previously struck the white ladies downtown. **1970** C. MAJOR *Dict. Afro-Amer. Slang* 91 *Pinktoes*, a black man's white girl friend; a white girl. **1887** *Referee* 31 July 2/1 Before doing so, I took the advice of one John Corlett, who propriets a paper called the **Pink 'Un*. **1898** A. M. BINSTEAD (*title*) A Pink 'Un and a Pelican. **1902** G. CALDERON *Downy V. Green* xii. 75 Downy amused himself with the only two weeklies that were in evidence, the 'Pink 'Un' and the 'Church Times'. **1930** W. S. MAUGHAM *Cakes & Ale* ix. 107 He gave me the *Pink 'Un* every week and I..read it in my bedroom. **1955** [see MAN *sb.*[1] 22 c]. **1970** PARTRIDGE *Dict. Slang* Suppl. 1330/1 *Pink 'Un..The Financial Times*, founded in 1913. **1975** *Blackw. Mag.* CCCXVIII. 126/1 A Pink 'Un was a member of the staff of the *Sporting Times* or one of its close associates. **1979** *Guardian* 2 Jan. 24/4 Today..the first Financial Times will hit Wall Street... But for all the..computer setting..the new international Pink 'un depends very much for its birth on the weather. **1953** DYLAN THOMAS *Under Milk Wood* (1954) 23 The main street, Coronation Street, consists, for the most part, of humble, two-storied houses many of which attempt to achieve some measure of gaiety by prinking themselves out..by the liberal use of *pinkwash. **1926** W. J. LOCKE *Stories Near & Far* 74 A long, two-storied, *pink-washed dwelling. **1936** M. ALLIS *Eng. Prelude* xxxiii. 253 Lavenham, with its pink-washed houses. **1976** *Eastern Even. News* (Norwich) 27 Aug., The track..passes closely to the right of a pinkwashed farmhouse. **1909** J. R. WARE *Passing Eng.* 197/1 **Pink wine* (*Military*), champagne. **1946** A. L. SIMON *Let Wine be Wine* 10 *Rosé* or pink wine is made in a number of different ways, either from grapes with a light red or pinkish skin; or from black grapes the skins of which are not left in the fermenting vat for more than a short while; or from red and white wines mixed together. **1972** *Times* 16 Sept. 11/1 Pink wines from southern European vineyards tend to be dark in hue.

pink, *sb.*[5] [Origin unknown: it appears to be a distinct word from prec.] A yellowish or greenish-yellow pigment or 'lake' obtained by the combination of a vegetable colouring matter with some white base, as a metallic oxide. Also ***pink-yellow*** = yellow lake.

brown pink and ***French pink*** are derived from Persian or Avignon berries (*Rhamnus infectoria*); ***Dutch, English***, and ***Italian pink*** from quercitron bark (*Quercus tinctoria*).

1634 PEACHAM *Gentl. Exerc.* I. xxiii. 75 Your principall yellow be these— Orpiment, Masticot, Saffron, Pinke Yellow, Oker de Luce, Umber. *Ibid.* xxvi. 90 For yellowish garments, thinne Pinke, and deepned with pinke and greene. **1658** PHILLIPS, *Pink*, a kinde of yellow colour used in painting. **1676** BEALE in H. Walpole *Vertue's Anecd. Paint.* (1765) III. i. 78, I gave Mr. Manby two ounces of very good lake of my making, and one ounce and half of pink. **1688** R. HOLME *Armoury* III. 148/2 Pinke, a kind of yellowish green. **1703** T. S. *Art's Improv.* I. 39 English Pink, grind it with common Size. **1758** *Ann. Reg.* 111/1 The colouring used..is supposed to be Dutch pink, which will make bohea tee of a fine green. **1823** CRABB *Technol. Dict.*, *Pink*,..a sort of yellow colour. **1861** MISS PRATT *Flower. Pl.* I. 67 To the juices of this yellow weed [*Reseda luteola*] the artist owes the colour called Dutch pink. **1862** *Archit. Publ. Soc. Dict.*, *French pink*, a pigment made of Troyes (i.e. Spanish) white with Avignon or French berries. **1875** *Ure's Dict. Arts* I. 895 Brown-pink, and others of the same class are also evanescent in their layers.

pink (pɪŋk), *sb.*[6] [Echoic.]

1. An imitation of the note of the chaffinch (often reduplicated, ***pink-pink***); hence *transf.*, a local name of the bird itself.

[**1809** BATCHELOR *Anal. Eng. Lang.* 140 *Pint*, a chaffinch (a Nottinghamshire word).] **1829** J. L. KNAPP *Jrnl. Nat.* 165 In Gloucestershire..from the constant repetition of one note, when alarmed or in danger, they have acquired the name of 'twinks', and 'pinks'. **1831** HOWITT *Seasons* (1837) 106 The weet-weet and pink-pink of the chaffinch. **1864** R. CHAMBERS *Bk. of Days* II. 4/2. **1894** R. B. SHARPE *Handbk. Birds Gt. Brit.* I. 36 The Chaffinch..Its familiar note, 'pink, pink', is heard everywhere in the spring.

†**2.** A sea-bird of some kind. *Obs.*

1670 NARBOROUGH *Jrnl.* in *Acc. Sev. Late Voy.* I. (1694) 81 Other such Sea-Fowls, as Pinks and Sea-mews.

3. = PINKING *vbl. sb.*[3]; a metallic rattle.

1927 *Fuel in Sci. & Pract.* VI. 121/1 Ricardo attributed the 'pink' to the sudden inflammation of residual unburnt charge owing to its compression by the expanding burnt and burning portion. **1934** *Automobile Engineer* XXIV. 346/1 'Detonation' or 'pink' might occur in any class of engine. **1946** [see KNOCKING *vbl. sb.* 1].

pink, *sb.*[7]: see PINK, *a.*[2]

pink, *sb.*[8]: see PINK, *v.*[3]

Pink, *sb.*[9], slang abbrev. of PINKERTON.

1904 'No. 1500' *Life in Sing Sing* i. 6 Don't you know me? I'm one of the Pinks. *Ibid.* xxiii. 263 Pink had me framed and it was like finding rags to the pusher... The cashier..picked my picture from the 'Rogues' gallery, where Pinkerton placed it some time ago. **1955** D. W. MAURER in *Publ. Amer. Dial. Soc.* XXIV. 141 The agency is called *the eye*..and its operators are sometimes called *pinks*. **1975** J. GORES *Hammett* (1976) i. 16, I was a Pink... A detective for the Pinkerton Agency.

pink, *a.*[1]: see PINK *sb.*[4] A. 3, B.

pink, *a.*[2] and *sb.*[7] *Obs.* or *dial.* [Of obscure history; as adj. used chiefly in *pink eye*, †*pink nye*, where it seems to be related to Du. *pink ooghen*: see PINK *v.*[2]; the sb. is used more widely in Sc.: cf. Du. *pink* the little finger, also a young bullock, a steer; pointing to an original sense 'something small'.]

A. *adj.* Small, contracted, diminutive; in the obs. or arch. phrase ***pink eye***, † ***pink nye***, a small eye, a winking or half-shut eye: see PINKENY.

1575 [see PINKENY 1]. **1606** SHAKS. *Ant. & Cl.* II. vii. 121 Come thou Monarch of the Vine, Plumpie Bacchus, with pinke eyne. **1608** TOPSELL *Serpents* (1658) 661 The third sort [of Cantharides]..are of a rusty colour, and their small pink eyes as black as Jet. **1825** BROCKETT *N.C. Gloss.*, *Pink*, small. 'Aw never saw sic a Pink-eed body'.

B. *sb. Sc.* Something very small: †**a.** A diminutive specimen or creature; brat, elf (*obs.*); **b.** A very small hole or spot, a small peep of light.

a **1585** MONTGOMERIE *Flyting* 119 On sike as thysell, little pratling pinke, Could thou not ware inke, thy tratling to tell? **1824** MACTAGGART *Gallovid. Encycl.* (1876) 382 A small mind, with only a pink, or small gleam of light in it. **1866** GREGOR *Banffsh. Gloss.* 126 *Pink*, a very small hole; a very small spot.

pink (pɪŋk), *v.*[1] Forms: 4–6 pynke, 6 pynk, pyncke, 6–7 pinke, pincke, 6–8 pinck, 6– pink. [Cf. LG. *pinken* to strike, peck ('schlagen, picken', Doornk.-Koolman s.v. *pinke*), suggested to be a nasalized modification of *picken*, PICK *v.*[1] The sense is more or less that of F. *piquer*, Pr., Sp. *picar*. (Some evidence (from Sp., Pg., Cat.) is adduced by Körting, No. 7163, for a Romanic stem *pinc-* prick, sting.) Cf. also the OE. Gloss *on pincan* = L. *in puncto* (Napier *OE. Glosses* No. 3683), which is however perh. a scribal error.]

1. *intr.* To make holes; to prick, thrust, stab. Now *rare* (or only as absol. use of 2 or 3).

The meaning of the first quot. is uncertain.

a **1307** *Sat. Consistory Courts* in *Pol. Songs* (Camden) 156 Heo pynkes with heore penne on heore parchemyn. **1530** PALSGR. 658/1, I pynke. [No Fr.] **1867** SMYTH *Sailor's Word-bk.*, To *Pink*,..to stab, as, between casks, to detect men stowed away.

2. *trans.* To pierce, prick, or stab with any pointed weapon or instrument. Also *fig.*

1598 B. JONSON *Ev. Man in Hum.* IV. ii, By my hand, I will pinck your flesh, full of holes, with my rapier for this. **1671** FOULIS *Hist. of Rom. Treas.* (1681) 281 Cutting and pinking his Body with their Swords. **1716** ADDISON *Drummer* IV. i, One of them pink'd the other in a duel. **1823** SCOTT *Peveril* xlii, I would I had pinked one of the knaves at least. **1893** VIZETELLY *Glances Back* II. xxxi. 190 [He] pinked his sarcastic adversary in the arm.

†**b.** To pierce with a bullet. Also, to nick or wound slightly with a bullet.

1661 OGILBY *King's Coronation* 19 With Bullets pink Their Quarters untill they sink. **1931** R. CAMPBELL *Georgiad* I. 14 'Onoto'—guns, As sported by Chicago's crooked sons, Able, at once, to..pink a stray policeman in the neck. **1950** *N.Y. Times* 30 Dec. 27/1 Wall has been the victim of three attempted assassinations, in two of which he was 'pinked', as he expressed it.

c. *fig.* (with play on sense 3). ***to pink one's jacket or doublet***, to pierce, hit, 'pepper', 'dress'.

1684 *Voy. Capt. Sharp* 45 But as soon as we began to pink some of their Jackets for them with our Fuzees, they got out of our reach. **1724** SWIFT *Wood's Exec.* Wks. 1814 VII. 297, *3rd Taylor.* I'll pink his doublet.

d. *Pugilistic slang.* To strike with the fist with visible effect.

1810 *Sporting Mag.* XXXVI. 44 Hall was without science, and Ballard pinked his head. **1816** *Ibid.* XLVIII. 180 The face of his opponent seemed a little pinked. **1821** *Ibid.* N.S. VII. 274 Hudson was pinked all over. **1963** *Times* 7 Feb. 3/5 At the end of the round Aldridge's left eye was looking 'pinked'.

3. To ornament (cloth, leather, or the like) by cutting or punching eyelet-holes, figures, letters, etc. (usually in order to display a rich lining or under-garment of contrasting colour); to perforate; also, in modern use, to decorate the raw edge of silk, etc., by scalloping and punching out a pattern on it. Also ***to pink out***.

1503 *Acc. Ld. High Treas. Scot.* II. 221 Item, for making of the said goun..xxs. Item, for pynking of the sleffis of it ..vs. xd. **1583** STUBBES *Anat. Abus.* II. (1882) 37 They [skins of leather] must be stitched finelie, pincked, cutte, karued. **1596** NASHE *Saffron-Walden* Wks. (Grosart) III. 141 A sute made of..white canuas pinkt vpon cotton. **1600** DEKKER *Gentle Craft* Wks. 1873 I. 16 Here take this paire of Shooes cut out by Hodge,..seem'd by my selfe, Made up and pinckt, with letters for thy name. **1642** FULLER *Holy & Prof. St.* III. xx. 207 The Turks did use to wonder much at our English men for pinking or cutting their clothes, counting them little better then mad for their pains to make holes in whole cloth. **1666** PEPYS *Diary* 15 Oct., A long cassocke..of black cloth, and pinked with white silke under it. **1719** D'URFEY *Pills* (1872) IV. 5 His skin did look like Satin pinck'd, With Gashes many a score. **1768** J. BYRON *Narr. Patagonia* (ed. 2) 225 Their shoes are pinked and cut. *c* **1800** MISS KNIGHT *Autobiog.* I. 16 His father kept a shop, and he was obliged to pink shrouds. **1893** *Lady* 17 Aug. 172/3 The edge may be pinked-out in the simple notches known as the 'saw' pattern. **1903** *Daily Chron.* 30 May 8/4 Such silk can be bought ready 'pinked' at the edges.

fig. **1576** NEWTON *Lemnie's Complex.* (1633) 43 Their bodies pinked full of scabs.

†**4.** To cut or puncture the skin as an adornment; to tattoo. Also *intr. Obs.*

1611 SPEED *Hist. Gt. Brit.* V. vii. 38 Their cutting, pinking, and pouncing of their flesh with garnishments..of sundry shapes and fashions. **1650** BULWER *Anthropomet.* 236 They of Sierra Leona..both men and women, race and pink over all their bodies. **1741** tr. *D'Argens' Chinese Lett.* xxx. 221 The Tunguses have the Skin of their Foreheads and Cheeks pink'd in the manner of Embroidery. **1781** [see PINKED 1].

5. To adorn, beautify, deck.

1558 PHAER *Æneid.* IV. I iv b, This pranking Paris fyne with mates of beardles kynde..With grekishe wymple pynkyd womanlyke. **1577** HANMER *Anc. Eccl. Hist.* (1650) 89 Is it seemly for a prophet to pinck and gingerly to set forth him-self? **1725** BRADLEY *Fam. Dict.* s.v. *Lily*, The Flowers..are..crooked, purpled, and pink'd with certain red Spots, they smell sweatly and please the Sight. **1892** *Temple Bar Mag.* Apr. 539 April..pink'd the earth with flowers. **1896** [C. ROGERS] *Bairnsla' Foak's Ann.* 20 (E.D.D.) T' windas wor pinked aht wi a touch a gas leet inside.

pink (pɪŋk), *v.*[2] *Obs.* exc. *dial.* Forms: 6 pynke, 6–7 pinck, pinke, 7– pink. [= Du. *pinken* to shut the eyes (Hexham, 1678), to wink, to leer, MDu. *pincken*, Du. *pinken* to blink, to glimmer, MHG. *pinken*. Kilian has also *pinck ooghen* 'connivere, nictare, oculis semiclausis intueri, oculos contrahere et aliquo modo claudere' (cf. mod.Du. *knipoogen* to blink, leer); also *pincke* sb. '(*vetus*) lumen, oculus'. History unknown.]

1. *intr.* **a.** Of the eyes: To be half shut, to blink; to peer, peep. Now *dial.* **b.** Of a person: To peep or peer with half-closed eyes; to blink or wink in a sleepy or sly manner; to look slyly. Now *dial.* †**c.** *transf.* Of a candle, etc.: To shine with a peep of light, to peep; to twinkle, to shine faintly (*obs.*).

a. *c* **1540** J. HEYWOOD *Four P.P.* B ij, And vpon drinkyng, myne eyes wyll be pinkynge. [Cf. *c* **1554** *Interl. of Youth* C iij, Yet I can tel you more and ye wyll con me thanke Pinke and drinke and also at the blanke And many sportes mo.] **1556** J. HEYWOOD *Spider & F.* lxix. 55 Though his iye on vs therat pleasantlie pinke, Yet will he thinke, that we saie not as we thinke. **1681** *Roxb. Ball.* V. 86 When our senses are drown'd, and our eyes they do pink. **1733–4** MRS. DELANY in *Life & Corr.* I. 426, I can't brag much of my eye. I find it still weak..though it went pinking and blinking to court last night.

b. **1587** HARRISON *England* II. vi. (1877) I. 160 They..sit still pinking with their narrow eies as halfe sleeping. *a* **1591** H. SMITH *Serm.* (1866) I. 395 They stand aloof from religion, pinking and winking. **1602** *Narcissus* (1893) 711 Thou dost pinke vpon mee with thine eyen. **1748** RICHARDSON *Clarissa* (1811) V. xix. 211 Mrs. Bevis presently returned with an answer (winking and pinking at me) that the lady would follow her down. **1806–7** J. BERESFORD *Miseries Hum. Life* (1826) *Post. Groans* xxxv, Pinking and blinking with his up-and-down-goggles full at me.

c. **1589** *Pappe w. Hatchet* D iv b, Martin with a wit worn into the socket, twinkling and pinking like the snuffe of a candle. **1616** BRETON *Good & Badde* 38 He is but the snuffe of a Candle, that pinke it never so long, 'it will out at last'. *a* **1674** HERRICK *Epithalamium* Poems (1869) 454 You starres, Begin to pinke.

2. ***pink in*** (of daylight, etc.): To close in, diminish, 'draw in'. *dial.*

1886 T. HARDY *Mayor of Casterbridge* II. vi. 87 It being now what the people called the 'pinking in' of the day, that is, the quarter-hour just before dusk. **1888** —— *Wessex Tales* (1889) 36 The evening is pinking in a'ready.

pink (pɪŋk), *v.*[3] [app. echoic.] **1.** *intr.* To trickle, drip; also, to make a tinkling sound in dripping. Hence **pink** *sb.*[8], a drop, also the sound made by a drop (*Jamieson's Dict.* 1880). *Sc.*

1768 ROSS *Helenore* 23 An' a' the time the tears ran down her cheek, An' pinked o'er her chin upon her keek. *a* **1812** W. INGRAM *Dream* in Walker *Bards Bon-Accord* (1887) 368 The soot draps pinkin frae the riggin'. **1815** *West Briton* 14 Apr. (Jam.), O'er crystall'd roof and sparry wall, Where pinking drops perpetual fall.

2. *intr.* Of an internal-combustion engine: to exhibit pinking (PINKING *vbl. sb.*[3]). Of a fuel: to cause pinking Also *fig.*

1904 KIPLING *Muse among Motors*, That cursed left-hand cylinder the doctors call my heart Is pinking past redemption—I am done! **1925** A. W. JUDGE *Carburettors & Carburation* ii. 19 The principal advantage of benzole is its higher detonating compression value; this enables it to be used in high compression petrol engines liable to 'pink' or knock, without experiencing these effects. **1933** *Petroleum Handbk.* (Shell Internat. Petroleum Co.) viii. 145 The tendency of a fuel to pink or detonate is its most important property in use. **1955** *Times* 12 July 12 The car tested was inclined..to pink slightly in accelerating from a low engine speed. **1970** 'D. HALLIDAY' *Dolly & Cookie Bird* vi. 78 My brain was pinking like the old Morris. **1972** *Drive* New Year 122/2 Such driving on the recommended 2-star petrol caused the engine to 'pink' noisily.

pink (pɪŋk), *v.*[4] [f. PINK *a.*[1]] **a.** *intr.* To become pink. Also with *up*.

1854 A. E. BAKER *Gloss. Northamptonshire Words* II. 116 *Pink*, to blush. 'How she *pinks* up!' **1909** R. A. WASON *Happy Hawkins* 136, I hadn't never seen those cheeks pink up for anything but fun or anger before. **1927** P. MARKS *Lord of Himself* 32 Mrs. Peter's eyes were sparkling again, and her cheeks pinked with happy colour.

b. *trans.* To shear (a sheep) closely so that the colour of the skin shows through; esp. in phr. ***to pink 'em***. (*Austral.* and *N.Z. colloq.*)

1898 *Bulletin* (Sydney) 17 Dec. 15 Another term for *fine-cut* is *pinkin' 'em*—showing the pink flesh. **1899** W. T. GOODGE *Hits! Skits! & Jingles!* 155 And he 'pinked' him like a leather-neck when squatters paid a pound! **1900** H. LAWSON *Verses, Pop. & Humorous* 168 Get the bell-sheep out;..But 'pink' 'em nice and pretty when you see the Boss's boots. **1933** *Bulletin* (Sydney) 15 Nov. 28/1 Instead of being 'pinked', there was sufficient wool left on as weather protection. **1956** G. BOWEN *Wool Away!* (ed. 2) 156 *Pink 'em*, to make a very good or better than average job of a sheep. Shearers sometimes call this a 'special cut'.

c. *trans.* To make pink (in various senses of the adj.).

1927 W. DEEPING *Kitty* xxvi. 330 You've more idea of colour than I have. I'm too fond of pinking things. **1929** D. H. LAWRENCE *Pansies* 22 The pretty pretty bourgeois pinks his language just as pink If not pinker.

†**pinkaninny.** *Obs.* ? A variant of PINKENY assimilated in the ending to *piccaninny*.

1696 D'URFEY *Quix.* III. IV. 41 Dear Pinkaninny, If half a Guiny, To love will win ye, I lay it here down.

†'**pinkardine.** *Obs.* Some precious stone.

13.. *E.E. Allit. P.* B. 1472 Penitotes, & pynkardines, ay perles bitwene.

pink bed to **pink-cheek**: see PINK *sb.*[4] C.

pinked (pɪŋkt), *ppl. a.* [f. PINK *v.*[1] + -ED[1].]

1. Pierced, pricked, wounded; also, tattooed.

1608 DAY *Hum. out of Br.* IV. iii, I like a whole skinne better then a pinkt one. **1781** COWPER *Expostulation* 486 Taught thee to clothe thy pinked and painted hide. **1929** *Papers Mich. Acad. Sci., Arts & Lett.* X. 314/2 *Pinked*, struck by bullets.

2. a. Of cloth, leather, etc.: Ornamented with perforations, or (later) cut edges; slashed, scalloped.

1598 FLORIO, *Trine*, cuts, iags, snips, or such cutting or pinching, pinckt worke in garments. **1613** SHAKS. *Hen. VIII*, V. iv. 50 There was a Habberdashers Wife..that rail'd vpon me, till her pinck'd porrenger fell off her head. **1688** R. HOLME *Armoury* III. 14/2 Pinked or raised Shooes, have the over leathers grain part cut into Roses, or other devices. **1693** SHADWELL *Volunteers* IV. Wks. 1720 IV. 462 I'll make thee fuller of Holes, then e'er pink't Satin was. **1807** CRABBE *Par. Reg.* III. 347 Verses fine Round the pink'd rims of crisped Valentine. **1849** JAMES *Woodman* ii, A sorry-coloured, pinked doublet.

b. Of flounces, frills, ribbons, etc.: Having the raw edge of the material stamped or cut into scallops, jags, or narrow points. Often ***pinked out***.

1862 MRS. J. B. SPEID *Our Last Yrs. in India* xi. 273 A black satin polka jacket with 'pinked' flouncing. **1884** *Daily News* 23 Sept. 6/1 The skirt..edged with a very thick ruche of pinked-out silk in the two colours. **1888** *Lady* 25 Oct. 378/2 A most becoming little bonnet in pinked-out cloth and velvet. **1893** *Ibid.* 17 Aug. 172/3 The bretelle frill is straight at the pinked edge.

pinkeen (pɪŋ'kiːn). *Anglo-Irish.* [f. PINK *sb.*[2] + *-een*, Ir. *-in*, dim. suffix.] A little minnow; *fig.* a very diminutive or insignificant person.

1831 S. LOVER *Leg. Irel.* iv. 39 I'll turn you into a pinkeen. **1892** JANE BARLOW *Irish Idylls* 169 Fishing for pinkeens along by the river. **1892** EMILY LAWLESS *Grania* II. III. vi. 89 Just a poor little pinkeen of a fellow.

pinken ('pɪŋkən), *v.* [f. PINK *a.*[1] + -EN[5].]

1. *intr.* To become pink.

1890 *Harper's Mag.* Nov. 867/2 Its spotless tip first pinkening like the point of some wondrous bud. **1936** WODEHOUSE *Laughing Gas* vii. 76 It caused Miss Brinkmeyer to pinken and breathe heavily. **1954** D. AMES *Crime, Gentlemen, Please* xxii. 130 Jack, too, was aware of the chill. He pinkened. **1976** *Listener* 15 Apr. 465/2 As the sky pinkened, we turned up a narrow tributary.

2. *trans.* To make pink.

1968 C. NICOLE *Self Lovers* i. 8 Her tan was pinkened by a liquor flush.

†'**pinkeny, 'pinkany.** *Obs.* (exc. *dial.* in sense 3). Forms: 6 pink nye, pinky ney, pinckeny, -anie, -any, pinkany, 7 pink-aneye, pinken eye. See also PINK *a.*[2], PINKIE *a.* [orig. *pink nye* (pl. *nyes, neyne*), i.e. PINK *a.*[2] small, narrow + *nye* = *ye*, EYE, with prosthetic *n* (cf. PIGSNEY). Cf. early mod.Du. *pinck ooghen* vb., *pincke* sb. (Kilian 1599: see PINK *v.*[2]). Prob. *pink nye, pinkie nye*, was orig. child's language, fondly imitated by nurses, and so became an expression of endearment.]

1. A small, narrow, blinking, or peering eye; a tiny or dear little eye.

1575 LANEHAM *Let.* (1871) 17 To see the bear with hiz pink nyez leering after hiz enmiez approch. **1593** RICH *Greenes Newes* D iv, The one of her eyes was bleard..the other was a pretty narrowe pinckeny, looking euer as though she smylde. **1594** LODGE *Wounds Civ. War* (Hunter. Cl.) 54 O most surpassing wine..Thou makest some to stumble, and many mo to fumble: And me haue pinkie nine. **1612** N. FIELD *Woman a Weathercock* IV. ii. H j, Those Pinkanies of thine, For I shall ne're be blest to call them mine.

2. *transf.* Applied to a person, usually as a term of endearment: Darling, pet; = PIGSNEY.

1599 NASHE *Lenten Stuffe* 42 The other..was Hero,..she was a pretty pinckany and Venus priest. **1599** PORTER *Angry Wom. Abingd.* (Percy Soc.) 68 *Mal.* Tis I! who I?..A Christ crosse rowe I? *Phil.* No, sweete pinckanie. **1622** MASSINGER & DEKKER *Virg. Mart.* II. i. Wks. 1873 IV. 23 That pink-an-eye jack-an-apes boy, her page.

3. ***pinkeny John***, also ***pinken-eyed John*** (corr. ***pink-o'-my-John***), a popular name of the pansy or heart's-ease, widely current in the midland counties of England.

1879 PRIOR *Brit. Plants* s.v. *Pansy*, Pink of my John. **1886** BRITTEN & HOLLAND *Eng. Plant-n.*, Pink-o'-my-John, *Viola tricolor*... Other forms of the name are Pinken-eyed John.. and Pink-eyed John..: also Pinkenny-John.

pinker (ˈpɪŋkə(r)), *sb.* [f. PINK *v.*^{1} + -ER^1.] One who pinks. **a.** One who stabs; a stabber.

a **1529** SKELTON *Mann. World* 113 So many pinkers.. Sawe I neuer.

b. One who punches designs in cloth, leather, etc.

1598 FLORIO, *Tagliuzzatore*, a slicer, a cutter, a pinker or iagger. **1611** COTGR., *Eschiffeur*, a Cutter or Pinker. **1858** SIMMONDS *Dict. Trade*, *Pinker*, one who stabs or cuts out flounces and borders, &c. with a machine, for ladies' dresses.

pinker (ˈpɪŋkə(r)), *v. dial.* [freq. of PINK *v.*^{2}: see -ER^5.] *intr.* To peer with half-shut eyes.

1754 W. WHITEHEAD in *World* No. 58 ¶6 They cannot even see with their eyes, but at most pinker through the lashes of them. **1903** *Eng. Dial. Dict.*, *Pinker*, v. with *about*: to go about with half-shut eyes; to potter. (Worc.)

Pinkerton (ˈpɪŋkətən). [From the name of Allan Pinkerton, who organized a body of detectives in the U.S. in 1850.] **a.** *attrib.* Applied to the semi-official detective force originally organized and controlled by Allan Pinkerton; as ***Pinkerton agency, man, method.*** **b.** *sb.* An officer or member of this force; an officer employed by any similar detective agency; an armed detective.

1888 *Philadelphia Inquirer* 22 Feb. (Farmer), Employed under the protection of Pinkerton men and special policemen. **1889** FARMER *Dict. Amer.*, *Pinkerton agency*, a well-known semi-official detective agency. **1892** *Daily News* 16 Aug. 5/2 We have seen what evil may come from the employment of Pinkertons and similar arguments for law and order. **1915** A. CONAN DOYLE *Valley of Fear* II. vi. 274 'The police?' 'Well, a Pinkerton.' **1955** D. W. MAURER in *Publ. Amer. Dial. Soc.* XXIV. 33 I'd say that better than fifty per cent of Pinkertons are ex-cons. *Ibid.* 38 One.. pickpocket, so popular that when he killed a Pinkerton detective more than a hundred thieves.. poured in to testify successfully in his defense. **1967** N. MAILER *Cannibals & Christians* I. 22 There were tough dull Pinkertons with a tendency to lean on a new visitor. *a* **1971** G. JACKSON *Blood in my Eye* (1972) 188 Every time I hear the word 'law' I visualize gangs of militiamen or Pinkertons busting strikes. **1973** L. HELLMAN *Pentimento* (1974) 177 Hammett.. didn't much like to be around people who took dope, in his Pinkerton days he had been more afraid of them than of murderers. **1978** J. CARROLL *Mortal Friends* II. iii. 168 Just hope to high heavens.. they keep their Pinkertons out.

So **Pinker'tonian** *a.*, of, pertaining to, or characteristic of Pinkerton or his men; **'Pinkertonism**, the employment of Pinkertons.

1891 *Voice* (N.Y.) 26 Feb., You can't make men moral by law and Pinkertonism. **1908** *Athenæum* 11 Apr. 442/2 While an article in the ensuing number entitled 'The Art of Advertising Made Easy', in which Colburn's Pinkertonian methods are held up to ridicule, is shown to be Hood's.

pink-eye^1. [f. PINK *a.*^{1} + EYE *sb.*^{1}]

1. (Also ***pink eye potato.***) A variety of potato having pink eyes or buds.

1795 W. MACRITCHIE *Diary Tour Eng.* in *Antiquary* Apr. (1896) 111/2 The Pink-eye potatoe, as it is here called, is becoming the fashionable potatoe of this country. **1805** R. W. DICKSON *Pract. Agric.* II. 602 The pink-eyes and copper-plates are of a hardy nature. **1828** *Craven Gloss.* (ed. 2), *Pinkneys*, pink-eyes, a particular species of potatoe with red eyes or ends. **1877** *N.W. Linc. Gloss.* **1886** ELWORTHY *W. Somerset Word-bk.*

2. a. A contagious fever or influenza in the horse, so called from the colour of the inflamed conjunctiva. **b.** A contagious form of ophthalmia in man (and in some likestock), marked by redness of the eyeball.

1882 *Field* 28 Jan. 130/3 The American term, 'pink-eye', .. is commonly given to the disease. **1883** *Times* 21 Feb. 8/4 Pink-eye is excessively prevalent among all classes of horses, particularly work horses in Sheffield. **1886** *Arch. Ophthalm.* XV. 451 This form of conjunctivitis is contagious and epidemic; it appears most plentifully in the spring and fall months... From the peculiar congestion of the ocular conjunctiva it has become popularly known as 'pink eye'. **1897** *Allbutt's Syst. Med.* II. 120 Clement Dukes believes that suffusion of the conjunctiva—pink-eye—may be the only symptom of an attack of rubella. **1933** [see *bung-eye* s.v. BUNG *sb.*^{1} 6]. **1938** S. DUKE-ELDER *Text-bk. Ophthalm.* II. xxxii. 1541 The intensity of the hyperæmia, sometimes associated with petechiæ, is characteristic, giving it [*sc.* Koch-Weeks' conjunctivitis] the popular name of 'pink-eye'. **1951** R. SEIDEN *Livestock Health Encycl.* 376 Pinkeye or specific ophthalmia.. is an inflammatory condition of the eyes of cattle and sheep]. **1974** [see KOCH-WEEKS BACILLUS].

3. An Australian species of duck (see quot.).

1896 NEWTON *Dict. Birds* 842 Apparently allied to the genus *Spatula* is *Malacorhynchus membranaceus*, the 'Pink-eye' of Australians, so called from a spot of that colour.. just behind the eye in the drakes.

4. *slang.* (chiefly *Austral.* and *Canad.*). Cheap whisky or red wine. (See also quot. 1945.) Cf. PINKIE, PINKY *sb.*^{3} 1 and RED-EYE 4.

1900 *Cornhill Mag.* June 778 His capital consisted of a yoke of oxen, a waggon, six four-gallon kegs of pink-eye and a Winchester rifle. **1941** *Coast to Coast* 23 Better put that bottle away... If the trooper comes round somebody'll be getting into trouble for selling Charley pinkeye again. **1941** [see PINKIE, PINKY *sb.*^{3} 1]. **1945** BAKER *Austral. Lang.* ix. 166 Recipes as published by an outback newspaper in 1936... Methylated spirits and Condy's crystals. (*Pinky.*).. Addicts of these noxious drinks are known as *meths*..and *pinkeyes*. **1953** W. B. MOWERY *Sagas of Mounted Police* 125 At Benders' joint, the price of a pint of pink-eye was a day's hard labor in a mine-head.

pink-eye^2 (ˈpɪŋkaɪ). *Austral.* Also pink-hi, pinkie. [Aboriginal name.] A festival or holiday.

1924 LAWRENCE & SKINNER *Boy in Bush* viii. 110 It was holiday—*pinkie*, the natives called it. **1929** K. S. PRICHARD *Coonardoo* 18 The tribes for a hundred miles about had gathered for pink-eye on Wytaliba. **1936** H. DRAKE-BROCKMAN *Sheba Lane* xi. 131 He found his natives in good tucker and clothes and gave the faithful Jimmy.. a horse and cart for the yearly pinkhi, when he visited his tribe. **1969** O. WHITE *Under Iron Rainbow* 139 This year Nolan's Ford Picnic Races and Rodeo.. was obviously going to be a successful pink-eye.

pink-eyed (ˈpɪŋkaɪd), *a.*^{1} *Obs.* exc. *dial.* Forms: 6 pinkyied, pynk iyde, pinke-eyed, pinky-ey'd, 7 pin(c)k-ey'd, 6- pink-eyed. [Parasynthetic f. *pink* or *pinkie eye* + -ED^2.]

1. Having small, narrow, or half-closed eyes; also, squint-eyed.

1519 HORMAN *Vulg.* 30b, Some haue mighty yies, and some be pinkyied [*quidam peti*]. **1523** SKELTON *Garl. Laurel* 626 Sum were made peuysshe, porisshly pynk iyde, That euer more after by it they were aspyid. **1601** HOLLAND *Pliny* XI. 335 [Maids] that were pinke-eied and had verie small eies, they tearmed *Ocellæ*. **1675** DUFFETT *Mock Tempest* I. ii, I see thou grow'st pinck-ey'd, go in and let the Nurse lay thee to sleep. **1867** *Country Words* 26 Jan. 208/2 *Pink-eyed* is small-eyed.

2. ***pink-eyed John***, a popular name of the pansy.

1877 *N.W. Linc. Gloss.* **1886** [see PINKENY 3].

pink-eyed, *a.*^{2} [f. PINK *a.*^{1} + EYE *sb.*^{1} + -ED^2.] Having a pink or light red eye or eyes.

1830 JENNER *Signs of Rain* 10 Closed is the pink-eyed pimpernel.

pink-fever to **pink-grass**: see PINK *sb.*^{4} C.

pinkie, pinky (ˈpɪŋkɪ), *sb.*^{1} Also pinkey. [f. PINK *sb.*^{1} + -IE, -Y, dim. suffix; or ? ad. MDu. *pinke.*] A narrow-sterned fishing-boat; = PINK *sb.*^{1}. Also *attrib.* and *Comb.*, as ***pinkie-stern schooner.***

1843 *Knickerbocker* XXII. 187 The 'pinkie' is a schooner rigged craft,.. sharp at both ends, a short peak running up aft, and designed for a chasing sea. **1873** G. H. PROCTER *Fisherman's Memorial* 72 Uncle Charlie's first remembrance was of the pinkey fleet. **1874** MOTLEY *Barneveld* I. viii. 339 The Scheveningen fisherman.. forgot the cracks of his pinkie. **1882** *Century Mag.* XXIV. 350 These pinkies are highly picturesque and seaworthy. **1882** *Fisherman's Own Bk.* 40 They were the old style of pinkey, without bowsprit or shrouds, with two masts and hempen sails. **1884** KNIGHT *Dict. Mech.* Suppl., *Pinkie*, a fishing vessel with a high, narrow-pointed stern. Used in the cod and coast fisheries. **1886** [see CHEBACCO]. **1897** KIPLING *Capt. Cour.* vi. 136 My father he run his packet, an' she was a kind a' pinkey, about fifty ton, I guess. **1903** *N. Y. Tribune* 25 Oct. 14 On another occasion the Houghton ran into a pinkey-stern schooner. **1950** R. MOORE *Candlemas Bay* 7 Capt. Malcolm Ellis.. had gone from a rowboat to a pinky to a mackerel schooner, and finally to a fleet of mackerel schooners. **1972** *Daily Colonist* (Victoria, B.C.) 19 May 1/5 Illusion of jetliner perched atop twin masts of reproduction of old pinky schooner was created this week.. as jets broke through low overcast.

pinkie, pinky (ˈpɪŋkɪ), *a.* and *sb.*^{2} Also pinkey. [Either f. PINK *a.*^{2}, or the orig. form of that word.]

A. *adj.* Small, diminutive, tiny: in general sense, a childish word. *Sc.* ***pinkie een***, 'eyes that are narrow and long, and that seem half-closed' (Jam.). Cf. PINK *a.*^{2}, PINKENY 1. Chiefly *Sc.*

1594 [see PINKENY 1]. **1715** RAMSAY *Christ's Kirk Gr.* II. vii, Meg Wallet wi' her pinky een Gart Lawrie's heart-strings dirle. **1808** JAMIESON, *Pinkie*, small in a general sense: 'There's a wee pinkie hole in that stocking'. **1818** W. MIDFORD *Collect. Songs* 31 A bussy-tailed pinkey wee Frenchman. **1896** BARRIE *Sent. Tommy* ii. 16 Never again should his pinkie finger go through that warm hole.

b. Comb. ***pinkie-eyed, pinky-eyed***, having small eyes. ***pinky-eyed John*** = ***pinkeny John***, the pansy.

1824 MISS FERRIER *Inher.* viii, A long-chinned pinky-eyed female.

B. *sb.* Anything small; *spec.* the little finger (Du. *pink*). Also *attrib.*

Orig. Sc., but now also quite common in certain areas of the U.S.

1808 JAMIESON, *Pinkie*, the little finger; a term mostly used by children, or in talking to them. **1828** MOIR *Mansie Wauch* i. 12 His pinkie was hacked off by a dragoon. **1860** BARTLETT *Dict. Amer.*, *Pinky* (Dutch *pink*), the little finger. **1898** J. PATON *Castlebraes* ix. 297 Raither.. than lift yae wee pinkie tae save that Deevilish man. **1931** A. J. CRONIN *Hatter's Castle* I. iii. 51 'I just flicked him with my pinkie,' declared Brodie complacently. **1941** *Sun* (Baltimore) 13 Oct. 8 (*caption*) Pinkey straight up, that's the class way to drink tea, pal! **1948** *Richmond* (Va.) *Times-Dispatch* 15 Mar. 17/4, I grip the ball with my thumb and pinky. **1950** J. DEMPSEY *Championship Fighting* 34 You might call that pinky knuckle the exit of your power line. **1958** P. DE VRIES *Mackerel Plaza* 155 My eye met Mrs. Spensible's across the room, and I thrust out my pinkie, smiling innocently. **1962** AUDEN *Shepherd's Carol* in *Musical Times* Oct. (Suppl.) 1 O lift your lit-tle pin-kie, and touch the win-ter sky. **1965** E. TUNIS *Colonial Craftsmen* vi. 140 Even the most elegant lady poured tea or coffee from her cup into her saucer to cool and then, with delicately extended pinkie, drank it from the saucer. **1970** S. ELLIN *Bind* lix. 299 Gela stared at him, gnawing at a hangnail on his pinkie. **1971** G. M. BROWN *Fishermen with Ploughs* 21 Fish as small as your pinkie. **1973** 'J. MARKS' *Mick Jagger* (1974) 11 As for Mick, he splashes on some fragrance and checks his eyeliner with his pinkie. **1975** *New Yorker* 1 Dec. 48/1 Seemed like his arm was *always* around somebody, and always there was the smell of his rich wool suit, the flash of a pinkie ring, a cloud of Havana, and Houtek's barony voice saying you and him were friends. **1976** *Scottish Rev.* Spring 3 Are ye still eatin' vinegar with a fork and holdin' out yer pinkie when ye sup yer tea? **1977** *New Yorker* 24 Oct. 122/2 Pagano had two pinky rings with nice stones.

pinkie, pinky (ˈpɪŋkɪ), *sb.*^{3} [f. PINK *sb.*^{4} and *a.*^{1} + -IE, -Y^6.] **1.** Cheap red wine; (see also quot. 1941). *slang* (chiefly *Austral.*).

1897 *Session Paper Cent. Criminal Court* 10 & 11 Mar. 417, I know I have done wrong; it is all through the drink; I have been having a drop of *pinkie*, and I am sorry for it. **1935** K. TENNANT *Tiburon* 93 Staines, nodding his fat, puffy face into his cup of pinkie.. hadn't a very good head for the cheap raw wine he was drinking. **1936** A. RUSSELL *Gone Nomad* vii. 55 Beer, whisky, 'pinky', delirium tremens, sore heads, and sandy blight were the chief.. maladies of the field. **1941** BAKER *Dict. Austral. Slang* 54 *Pink-eye*,.. an addict of the noxious drink called 'pinky', the constituents of which are either red wine and methylated spirits or methylated spirits and Condy's crystals. **1958** *Maclean's Mag.* 27 Sept. 63/3 Pinkie [in St. John's, Newfoundland] is a cheap wine highly regarded by waterfront connoisseurs, a chaser for screech. **1959** D. HEWETT *Bobbin Up* (1961) vii. 93 He'd drink anything they reckoned, plonk, pinkie, straight metho.

2. A white person (see also quot. 1970). *slang.*

1967 *Observer* 10 Sept. 17/2 The racial discrimination that black school-leavers find when they look for jobs is not a surprise: it is a confirmation. By the time they leave school, whites have become 'pinky', 'the grey man' or.. 'Mr. Charlie'. *Ibid.* 17/3 I've got a white friend I've known from school... No, I'm not a pinky-lover! He's learned to think black and think white and I can trust him. **1970** C. MAJOR *Dict. Afro-Amer. Slang* 91 *Pinky*.., Afro-American girl who looks white. **1972** K. JOHNSON in T. Kochman *Rappin' & Stylin' Out* 145 *Pinkie*, refers to the skin color of white women.

3. = PINK *sb.*^{4} 10. Cf. PINKO *sb.*

1973 *Nation Rev.* (Melbourne) 31 Aug. 1442/3 He called for a Liberal party 'crusade' to defeat the 'reds, the pinkies and the socialists' who are responsible for inflation. **1978** R. BARNARD *Unruly Son* xv. 166 He was always a drawing-room pinkie... As far as contact with the working-class movement was concerned, he hadn't any.

pinkie, pinky (ˈpɪŋkɪ), *sb.*^{4} [f. PINK *sb.*^{2} + -IE, -Y^6.] **1.** *S. Afr.* A small marine fish, either the rock grunter, *Pomadasys olivaceum*, of the family Pomadasyidæ, which is only a few inches long and is often used as live bait, or the red grunter, *Pagellus natalensis*, of the family Sparidæ, which is a food fish that may grow to about twelve inches.

1948 *Cape Times* 19 July 1/4 The fish was brought in and gaffed... The bait taken was 'live pinkie'. **1953** J. L. B. SMITH *Sea Fishes S. Afr.* 257 *Pomadasys olivaceum*... Rock-Grunter. Pinky (Natal). *Ibid.* 273 *Pagellus natalensis*... Red Grunter. Pinky. **1966** K. T. LILLIECRONA *Salt-Water Fish & Fishing in S. Afr.* i. 21 In deepish water next to the rocks, all one has to do is cast in this multi-hook trace among the fish, count twenty slowly and then retrieve to find every hook with a pinky on it.

2. The larva of a greenbottle fly of the genus *Lucilia*, used as a live bait in some fresh-water fishing.

1958 F. OATES *Coarse Fishing Baits* i. 23 'Pinkies' are well suited for the smaller fry which inhabit lakes and wide sluggish rivers, because being fairly heavy they can be thrown much farther than squats. **1971** *Angling Times* 10 June 12/2 (Advt.), Wholesalers of maggots, pinkies, squats, anattoes, brandlings. **1974** C. C. TRENCH *Hist. Angling* viii. 234 'Pinkies' are the larvae of greenbottles, rather smaller than other maggots, pinkish in colour and used generally for small roach and dace. **1979** *Guardian* 13 June 9/3 If you have got a box of pinkies in your fridge.. you are probably.. pre-occupied right now... For next Saturday is the opening day of the coarse fishing season.

pinkified (ˈpɪŋkɪfaɪd), *ppl. a.* [f. PINK *a.*^{1} + -IFY + -ED^1.] Made pink in colour.

1886 R. BROWN *Spunyarn & Spindrift* xxix. 351 The light of the sun came streaming across it, making our sails all pinkified.

pinkily (ˈpɪŋkɪlɪ), *adv.* [f. PINKY *a.* + -LY^2.] In a 'pinky' way; with a tinge of pink. So **'pinkiness**, the quality of being 'pinky'; a slight degree of pinkness.

1828 *Blackw. Mag.* XXIII. 99 A clear-skinned complexion of face, inclining to pinkiness. **1882** G. ALLEN *Col. Clout's Cal.* viii, The almost accidental pinkiness of the rays in a daisy. **1890** *Daily News* 15 Aug. 5/4 A variety of white raspberry, large, conical, and pinkily cream-coloured in tint.

pinking (ˈpɪŋkɪŋ), *vbl. sb.*^{1} [f. PINK *v.*^{1} + -ING^1.] **a.** The action of PINK *v.*^{1}; the operation of decorating cloth, leather, etc., with holes, or (later) scalloped edges; *concr.* work so treated.

1503 [see PINK *v.*^{1} 3]. **1611** COTGR., *Deschiquetement*,.. a iagging,.. a pinking, or small, and thicke cutting. **1666** PEPYS *Diary* 17 Oct., The King says the pinking upon whites makes them look too much like magpyes, and therefore hath bespoke one [vest] of plain velvet. **1688** R. HOLME *Armoury* III. 350/1 The Pinking of a Shooe, when the grain of the Leather is raised by a sharp pointed Tool, that the inner part is seen. **1766** GOLDSM. *Vic. W.* iv, These rufflings, and pinkings, will only make us hated by all the wives of our neighbours. **1860** FAIRHOLT *Costume in Eng.* (ed. 2) Gloss., *Pinking*, an ornamental edging cut to silk dresses by a machine that makes a semicircular jagged indent, something after the fashion of the ancient leaf-borders. **1883** *Daily News* 22 Sept. 3/3 The mode of finishing the edges..known as 'pinking-out', continues to be followed. **1884** *Girl's Own Mag.* 29 Mar. 409/1 Undertakers are the people who advertise to perform pinking.

b. *Comb.*, as ***pinking machine, scissors, shears***; **pinking-iron**, a sharp instrument for cutting out pinked borders; also *humorously*, a sword.

1761 in E. Singleton *Social N.Y. under Georges* (1902) 242 [I] have ever since been so scrupulous an observer of it [*sc.* taste] that I never was the mark of a pinking-iron behind it. **1780** *Chron.* in *Ann. Reg.* 227/2 The lightning had perforated a round hole in the lower part of his wig behind, which..looked as if it had been cut with a pinking iron. **1858** SIMMONDS *Dict. Trade, Pinking-iron*, a cutting instrument for scolloping the edges of ribbons, flounces, paper for coffin trimmings, &c. **1884** *Girl's Own Mag.* 29 Mar. 409/1 The shape of the pinking-irons used are more elaborate than they formerly were. *a* **1865** MRS. GASKELL *Lett.* (1966) 816 Dear Miss Watkins, Thank you very much for the use of the Pinking Machine. **1951** *Catal. of Exhibits, South Bank Exhib., Festival of Britain* 60/1 Pinking scissors. **1979** E. TAYLOR in I. Webb *Compl. Guide Flower & Foliage Arrangem.* viii. 103/1 Pinking scissors will avoid having to hem the edges. **1962** *House & Garden* Dec. 55/2 Pair of pinking shears. **1976** *Evening Post* (Nottingham) 15 Dec. 21 (Advt.), Dress-making scissors, pinking shears, nail scissors, [etc.].

pinking ('pɪŋkɪŋ), *vbl. sb.*[2] *Obs.* or *dial.* [f. PINK *v.*[2] + -ING[1].] The action of PINK *v.*[2]

1667 DRYDEN *Sir M. Mar-all* IV. i, Leave off your winking and your pinking.

pinking ('pɪŋkɪŋ), *vbl. sb.*[3] [f. PINK *v.*[3] + -ING[1].] (The production of) a metallic rattling sound in an internal-combustion engine as a result of the too rapid combustion of the mixture in the cylinder.

1913 ROGERS & WATSON *Motor Mechanics' Hand-bk.* i. 9 If the compression exceed 90 lb., there is great danger of frequent pre-ignition, and consequent knocking or 'pinking' in the cylinders. **1930** *Flight* 11 July 787 A further change was made to a poor grade spirit, and the symptoms of pinking combined with loss of efficiency were much exaggerated. **1937** [see DETONATION 1 b]. **1959** *Motor* 19 Aug. 6/2 Full throttle was avoided to prevent pinking. **1968** [see DETONATION 1 b]. **1970** M. SMITH *Aviation Fuels* vii. 35 High pressure waves..strike the walls of the combustion chamber with a hammer-like blow, producing a knocking noise. The high pitched, metallic sound known as 'pinking' is due to the vibratory nature of those waves. **1973** *Times* 19 Apr. 35/1 Lead..is added to petrol to raise octane ratings and prevent 'pinking'.

pinking ('pɪŋkɪŋ), *ppl. a.*[1] [f. PINK *v.*[1] + -ING[2].] That pinks; stabbing, murderous.

1644 LAUD *Wks.* (1854) IV. 343 His fellow, Wadsworth,.. called him pinking knave.

pinking ('pɪŋkɪŋ), *ppl. a.*[2] *Obs.* exc. *dial.* [f. PINK *v.*[2] + -ING[2].] Of the eye: That pinks; small, narrow; peering; blinking.

1566 DRANT *Horace, Sat.* iii. B iv b, The sonne he squynts, the father saythe he hath a pincking eye. **1597** LOWE *Chirurg.* (1634) 145 The littlenes of the Eye called *Atrophia* or *Macies oculi* commeth by nature, and is called the pigs Eye, or pincking-Eye. **1601** HOLLAND *Pliny* XI. xxxvii. I. 334 Some have great glaring eies; others againe as little and as pinking. *a* **1722** MRS. CENTLIVRE *Love at Venture* IV, Those pinking ogles of thine. **1826** *Ass* 1 Apr. 2 You there with the pinking eyes and the fish-knife nose.

pinkish ('pɪŋkɪʃ), *a.* [f. PINK *a.*[1] + -ISH[1].]

1. a. Somewhat pink; having a tinge of pink. Also in Comb. as ***pinkish-brown, -grey, -mauve, -purple, -red, -silver, -white, -yellowing.***

1784 HOME in *Phil. Trans.* LXXV. 338 Its outer surface is of a darkish brown colour; its inner of a pinkish white. **1843** PORTLOCK *Geol.* 92 The chalk is of a pinkish hue. **1857** GEO. ELIOT in J. W. Cross *George Eliot's Life* (1885) I. vii. 360 The castle is built of stone which has a beautiful pinkish-grey tint. **1870** HOOKER *Stud. Flora* 439 Panicle pale green or pinkish. **1894** R. B. SHARPE *Handbk. Birds Gt. Brit.* I. 105 The series..varies between a purplish- or pinkish-red, and stone-grey ground-colour. **1952** A. G. L. HELLYER *Sanders' Encycl. Gardening* (ed. 22) 59 Spathe yellowish-green and pinkish-brown. *Ibid.* 118 [*Clinopodium*] *georgianum*.., white to pinkish-purple, to 2 ft. *Ibid.* 276 [*Lilium*] *Kelloggii*, pinkish-mauve, July. **1952** S. SPENDER *Learning Laughter* i. 5 A tall stucco pinkish-yellowing house. **1959** E. H. CLEMENTS *High Tension* vi. 111 Sgurr Dhubh, pinkish-silver in the morning sun. **1961** R. L. GOURSE *With Gall & Honey* xviii. 272 He had a pinkish-white complexion, a small straight nose, [etc.]. **1973** POLUNIN & SMYTHES *Flowers S.W. Europe* iii. 384 A robust plant to 1m or more, distinguished by its large, very dense, globular head of numerous pinkish-purple flowers.

b. Politically somewhat left of centre.

1949 N. MARSH *Swing, Brother, Swing* ix. 206 Sallis's pinkish, facile..observations. **1968** W. ASH *Ride Paper Tiger* vii. 108 Certain pinkish professors back home are making rather a lot of the fact that Ortiz is a political martyr. **1977** *Time* 5 Dec. 67/2 He was born in New York City and spent his early childhood in Bayside, a pinkish nook of Queens.

2. [PINK *sb.*[4] 2 b.] Fit, 'in the pink'.

1949 J. CORRIE in J. Marriott *Best One-Act Plays 1948–49* 112 'You are looking very well.' 'I'm feeling very pinkish... Very pinkish, indeed, thank you.'

pinkishness ('pɪŋkɪʃnɪs). [f. PINKISH *a.* + -NESS.] Pinkish appearance; a suggestion of pinkness.

1909 M. B. SAUNDERS *Litany Lane* v. 60 With a pinkishness about his eyes not becoming to his blonde good looks.

pinkly ('pɪŋklɪ), *adv.* [f. PINK *a.*[1] + -LY[2].] With a pink hue. Also *fig.*, embarrassedly.

1836 FABER in *Blackw. Mag.* XL. 662 From its pinkly-clustered boughs A fragrance mild the hawthorn throws. **1866** NEALE *Sequences & Hymns* 176 Pinkly and faintly the sun..Fell upon cornice and frieze. **1923** H. C. BAILEY *Mr. Fortune's Practice* i. 2 He is plump and pinkly healthy. **1953** G. DURRELL *Overloaded Ark* viii. 156 We both looked at the almost sheer cliffs of N' da Ali gleaming pinkly in the evening sun. **1960** M. SPARK *Ballad of Peckham Rye* vii. 141 Mr. Willis pinkly took Merle's hand and glanced towards the shop door. **1973** 'D. HALLIDAY' *Dolly & Starry Bird* ii. 24 'You do such lovely parties, Timothy.' 'Oh, well,' he said pinkly. **1974** *Times* 30 Nov. 9/5 The pinkly roasted grouse. **1975** J. MCCLURE *Snake* xi. 148 Kramer watched the dawn of his insight spread pinkly up from Marais' collar. **1978** *Daily Tel.* 8 July 9/2 A garden where Dorothy Perkins rambles pinkly round the door.

†**'pink-needle.** *Herb. Obs.* [f. PINK *v.*[1] + NEEDLE.] A name given to the Stork's-bill (*Erodium moschatum*, or *E. cicutarium*), from the long tapering beaks of the seed-vessels.

(Erroneously taken as a name of *Scandix Pecten* by Halliwell, etc., through misunderstanding quot. 1562.)

1548 TURNER *Names Herbes* (E.D.S.) 39 Geranium..one kynde is called Pinke nedle or Cranes byl. **1562** —— *Herbal* II. 130 Scandix is supposed of som to be yᵉ herbe which is called in English Pinke nedle, or Storkes bill. **1578** LYTE *Dodoens* I. xxxii. 47 The first kinde [of Geranium] is called ..in English Storkesbyll, Pinkeneedell. **1611** COTGR., *Aiguille musquée*, musked Pinkneedle..or Cranes-bill. *Ibid.*, *Teste de grue*, Pinkneedle, Shepheards bodkin, Storks bill.

pinkness ('pɪŋknɪs). [f. PINK *a.*[1] + -NESS.]

a. The quality or state of being pink; pink colour.

1883 G. ALLEN in *Gentl. Mag.* Oct. 322 It [honeysuckle] still retains some memory of its original pinkness. **1894** *Daily News* 8 June 7/1 Glad to step down from the carriages and restore pinkness to their pretty cheeks.

b. The quality or state of being politically pink (cf. PINK *a.*[1] 3).

1931 F. L. ALLEN *Only Yesterday* iv. 76 The Fighting Quaker's inquisitorial methods..had at least the practical effect of scaring many Reds into a pale pinkness. **1940** R. S. LAMBERT *Ariel & all his Quality* iii. 76 Attacks upon the BBC for the 'redness' or 'pinkness' of broadcast talks.

pinkney, pink nye: see PINKENY.

pinko ('pɪŋkəʊ), *a.* and *sb. slang.* [f. PINK *sb.*[4] or *a.*[1] + -O[2].] **A.** *adj.* **1.** (See quots.)

1925 FRASER & GIBBONS *Soldier & Sailor Words* 224 *Pinko*, drunk. **1941** BAKER *Dict. Austral. Slang* 54 *Pinko*, drunk, esp. on methylated spirits.

2. = PINK *a.*[1] 3. Chiefly *U.S.*

1957 [see LONG-HAIR *sb.* 2 a]. **1959** C. MACINNES *Absolute Beginners* 38 Your pinko pals did what they wanted to when they got power. **1972** D. LEES *Zodiac* 65 He made Ronald Reagan look like a pinko liberal. **1976** N. THORNBURG *Cutter & Bone* xii. 284 That look and attitude..proclaimed them goddamn ready and eager for any commie revolution the pinko nigger-loving government might be cooking up. **1977** *Transatlantic Rev.* LX. 121 It's the number three song in China, sir. Saw it in one of those magazines my pinko parents subscribe to.

B. *sb.* = PINK *sb.*[4] 10. Chiefly *U.S.*

1936 J. G. COZZENS *Men & Brethren* 104 She's a good girl. .. Now only a healthy pinko. I've snatched her like a brand from the Young Communist League burning. **1948** 'B. ROSE' *Wine, Women & Words* 105, I wouldn't call him a Commie, but if he doesn't get a check from Moscow every week, he's being robbed... Unfortunately the pinko didn't drinko. **1959** *Times Lit. Suppl.* 25 Dec. 753/1 To save his family from being 'smeared' by 'left-wingers and pinkoes' he decides to use the pseudonym Victor J. Fox. **1971** *New Society* 7 Jan. 25/3 The new American jingoism wherein the enemy is not the enemy but all those disloyal pinkos at home. **1976** *Spectator* 14 Feb. 13/3 The statement 'we are all guilty'..is enough in itself to identify the speaker as a trendy pinko.

pinko- ('pɪŋkəʊ). [See -O.] Used as a combining form of PINK *sb.*[4] and *a.*[1] in **pinko-grey** *a.*, of a pinkish-grey colour; *spec.* = WHITE *a.* 4; hence as *sb.*, a 'white' person.

1924 E. M. FORSTER *Passage to India* vii. 62 The remark that did him most harm at the club was a silly aside to the effect that the so-called white races are really pinko-grey. **1953** W. G. WALTER *Living Brain* i. 1 By brain is meant.. something more than the pinko-grey jelly of the anatomist. **1961** P. MASON *Common Sense about Race* I. iii. 49 A pinko-grey man is rather more likely than a Negro to have traces of the ridges above the eyes..so prominent in the gorilla. **1964** 'M. INNES' *Money from Holme* x. 68 The pinko-greys out there [*sc.* in Africa] aren't exactly aesthetes. **1973** J. MANN *Only Security* xi. 142 A pinko-grey lib-lab, that's you. **1974** *Times* 5 June 16/5 The pinko-grays, to use E. M. Forster's accurate description, were entirely safe... Britain was about to quit India. **1977** T. HEALD *Just Desserts* iii. 47 His usual pinko-grey complexion.

pinkroot ('pɪŋkruːt). [f. PINK *sb.*[4] + ROOT.]

a. The root of *Spigelia marilandica*, or of *S. Anthelmia*, used as vermifuges and purgatives. **b.** The herb *Spigelia marilandica* (N.O. *Loganiaceæ*), a native of the Southern U.S., having showy funnel-shaped flowers, red outside and yellow within, called *Carolina pink*, *Indian pink*, or *worm-grass*; also, the allied species *S. Anthelmia*, of the W. Indies and S. America (***Demerara pinkroot***).

1763 *Ann. Reg.* 54/1 Produce of South Carolina..Pink-root, 1 cask. **1796** MORSE *Amer. Geog.* I. 681 Snakeroot, pink-root, and a variety of medicinal herbs grow spontaneously. **1875** H. C. WOOD *Therap.* (1879) 600 Pinkroot possesses decided narcotic powers. **1889** FARMER *Dict. Amer.* s.v. *Carolina pink*, The Pink Root of Maryland which, further South, is popularly known as the Carolina pink..bears beautiful flowers.

pink-salt, -saucer: see PINK *sb.*[4] C.

‖**pinkster** ('pɪŋkstə(r)). *U.S.* (N.Y.) Also pingster, pinxter. [Du. *pinkster* (now *pinxteren* dat. pl.) = OS *pincostôn*, MHG., Ger. *pfingsten*:—OHG. **pfinkustin* (dat. pl.), all prob. through Gothic *paintêkustê*, a. Gr. πεντηκοστή Pentecost.] Whitsuntide; usually in *attrib.* use: see quots.

1821 J. F. COOPER *Spy* (1823) III. v. 127 Upon my word you'd pass well at a pinkster frolic. **1845** —— *Satanstoe* I. vi. 162 Pinkster fields, and Pinkster frolicks, are no novelties to us, sir, as they occur every season. **1860** BARTLETT *Dict. Amer.* s.v., On Pinxter Monday the Dutch negroes.. consider themselves especially privileged to get as drunk as they can. **1866** *Treas. Bot.*, *Pinxter-flower*, an American name for *Azalea nudiflora*.

pink-stern, -sterned: see PINK *sb.*[1] b.

pink-weed. ? *Obs.* [f. PINK *sb.*[4] or *a.*[1] + WEED *sb.*] Knotgrass, *Polygonum aviculare*.

1657 W. COLES *Adam in Eden* ccxxi. 348 It is called..in English *Knot-Grasse*..: some also call it *Pink-Weed*, and some *Nine Joynts* of its great number of Joynts. **1866** *Treas. Bot.*, Pink-weed, *Polygonum aviculare*.

pinkwood ('pɪŋkwʊd). [f. PINK *sb.*[4] or *a.*[1] + WOOD *sb.*] Name for the ornamental wood of various trees, or for the trees themselves:

a. *Dicypellium caryophyllatum* (*Persea caryophyllata*), N.O. *Lauraceæ*, of Brazil, having a scent like that of carnations; **b.** *Physocalymma floribundum*, N.O. *Lythraceæ*, also of Brazil, having striped rose-coloured wood, also called Tulip-wood; **c.** *Beyeria viscosa*, N.O. *Euphorbiaceæ*, the Wallaby-bush, of Australia; **d.** *Eucryphia billardieri*, N.O. *Hypericaceæ*, of Tasmania.

1884 MILLER *Plant-n.*, Pink-wood-tree, *Persea caryophyllata*.—Brazilian, *Physocalymma floridum*. **1893** *Spon's Mechanic's Own Bk.* (ed. 4) 166 Pinkwood (*Beyeria viscosa*)... Used for sheaves of blocks and for turnery. **1898** MORRIS *Austral Eng.*, *Pinkwood*, a name for a Tasmanian wood of a pale reddish mahogany colour, *Eucryphia billardieri*,..and for the Wallaby bush, *Beyera viscosa*, Miq., N.O. *Euphorbiaceæ*, common to all the colonies of Australasia.

pinky ('pɪŋkɪ), *a.*[1] [f. PINK *sb.*[4] or *a.*[1] + -Y: cf. *rosy, creamy*, etc.] Tinged with or inclining to pink. **a.** Qualifying other adjs. or sbs. of colour.

1776–96 WITHERING *Brit. Plants* (ed. 3) IV. 225 Pileus and stem pinky white. **1817** COLERIDGE *Picture* Poems 1829 I. 177 Sketched on a strip of pinky-silver skin. **1901** G. DOUGLAS *Ho.w. Green Shutters* 101 A piece of pinkey-brown paper in his hand..was the first telegram ever seen in Barbie. **1907** *Westm. Gaz.* 2 Mar. 17/1 The little habit coats ..are generally faced with..emerald-green, or blue, or even pinky-red. **1927** D. H. LAWRENCE *Mornings in Mexico* 29 Pale belly, and soft, pinky-fawn claws. **1946** G. MILLAR *Horned Pigeon* vii. 78 The pinky-red pantiles of the terraced village. **1974** *Country Life* 2 May 1055/2 Raised panels.. painted in imitation of pinky-grey marble. **1975** C. FREMLIN *Long Shadow* x. 77 Myrtle's pinky-orangey lighting. **1977** *Vogue* Feb. 94 Pinky blonde, double-faced wool shirtjacket.

b. Qualifying sbs. in gen. Chiefly *poet.* or *rhet.*

1821 CLARE *Vill. Minstr.* I. 208 The wild-thyme's pinky bells. **1822–34** *Good's Study Med.* (ed. 4) I. 340 The urine ..sometimes deposits a pinky sediment. **1872** CALVERLEY *Fly Leaves, Lovers & a Reflection*, Or rosy as pinks, or as roses pinky.

c. Comb., as ***pinky-coloured*** adj. Also ***pinky-faded*** adj.

1817 COLERIDGE *Biog. Lit.* xvi. (1882) 160 *note*, Two engravings, the one a pinky-coloured plate of the day, the other a masterly etching by Salvator Rosa. **1926** D. H. LAWRENCE *Glad Ghosts* 23 A big pinky-faded carpet.

pinky, *a.*[2] and *sb.*: see PINKIE.

pinlay ('pɪnleɪ). *Dentistry.* [Blend of PIN *sb.*[1] + INLAY *sb.*] An inlay or onlay which is held in place partly by a pin or pins inserted in the tooth.

1915 J. K. BURGESS in *Dental Cosmos* LVII. 1338/2 The attachment..is a modified inlay and contour with pins, which I have chosen to call the 'pinlay' attachment. **1946** *Brit. Dental Jrnl.* LXXX. 14 (*caption*) Spring bridge carrying central incisor on pinlay abutment in canine. **1952**, **1973** [see next].

pinledge ('pɪnlɛdʒ). *Dentistry.* [f. PIN *sb.*[1] + LEDGE *sb.*; cf. prec.] A pinlay, esp. one covering the lingual surface of a tooth and dependent on pins inserted in ledges cut in the tooth for retention and stability.

1915 J. K. BURGESS in *Dental Cosmos* LVII. 1342/1 (*heading*) 'Pinledge' bridge attachment for anterior teeth. *Ibid.*, The anterior attachment is an outgrowth of the pinlay, being constructed on the same principle. I have chosen to call it the 'pinledge'. **1952** *Dental Practitioner* II. 328/1 The pinlay, or pinledge preparation as it is often called, for incisor or canine bridge abutment, has been known in one form or another for many years. **1973** D. H. ROBERTS *Fixed Bridge Prostheses* vii. 125 The pinledge preparation. This differs from the three-quarter pinlay in that the incisal edge of the tooth is not involved and so no gold is displayed labially. **1975** G. T. CHARBENEAU et al. *Princ. & Pract. Operative Dentistry* xiv. 387/1 The pinledge design may be used on incisor and cuspid teeth with conservative loss of tooth tissue.

'pinless, *a.* [-LESS.] Without a pin or pins.

1881 E. J. WORBOISE *Sissie* xxii, There was the tawdry pincushion—quite pinless now, however—which she had left behind her. **1892** LD. LYTTON *King Poppy* xii. 12 My lady's pincushion .. pinless proves.

† **'pinlock**[1]. *Obs.* [app. for *pindlock, f. PIND *v.* + LOCK *sb.*[2]] A poundmaster's fee for pinding or impounding beasts.

c **1700** KENNETT *MS. Lansd.* 1033 lf. 307 b/1 In these midland parts the money .. given to the Hayward or to any Person who locks and unlocks the pound gate is called *Pinne-Lock, Pyn-Lock.* **1884** REDSTONE in *N. & Q.* 6th Ser. (1884) X. 197/2 The pinlock, or pinder's fee, is regulated by an Act of Philip and Mary at fourpence for any number of cattle impounded, which custom has made into one of fourpence for each head.

'pin-,lock[2]. [f. PIN *sb.*[1] 1 g + LOCK *sb.*[2]] A lock having a pin, upon which the pipe of the key fits.

1884 *Athenæum* 16 Aug. 216/1 It is doubtful if the so-called 'pin-lock' was used by the very ancient Egyptians.

pin-machine to **pin-mill**: see PIN *sb.*[1] 18.

pinmaker ('pɪn,meɪkə(r)). One whose business or work is to make pins.

1530 PALSGR. 254/2 Pynne maker, *esplinguier.* **1644** *Canterbury Marr. Licences* (MS.), Thomas Lashford, pinmaker. **1764** FOOTE *Mayor of G.* I. Wks. 1799 I. 170 A paltry, praying, pitiful pin-maker! **1883** GOLDW. SMITH in *Contemp. Rev.* Dec. 807 Poet and pinmaker alike may aspire to the Christian Ideal.

So **'pin-,making** *sb.*; also *attrib.* or *adj.*

1835 URE *Philos. Manuf.* 288 Trades in which young persons are engaged in numbers, such as sewing, pin-making, or coal-mining. **1890** W. J. GORDON *Foundry* 184 Doctor Kinsley .. invented a pin-making machine.

pin-money ('pɪn,mʌnɪ). [f. PIN *sb.*[1] sense 3 + MONEY: see sense a, quots. 1542–1640. (Cf. F. *épingles*, in Littré, sense 4.)] **a.** An annual sum allotted to a woman for personal expenses in dress, etc.; *esp.* such an allowance settled upon a wife for her private expenditure. Also *transf.*, spending money; money for incidental expenses; a trivial sum of money.

[**1542** *Test. Ebor.* (Surtees) VI. 160, I give my said doughter Margarett my lease of the parsonadge of Kirkdall Churche .. to by her pynnes withal. **1621** BURTON *Anat. Mel.* III. ii. IV. i. (1651) 540 Caligula gave an 100000 sesterces to his Curtisan .. to buy her pins. **1640** EARL OF CORK in *Lismore Papers* Ser. I. (1886) V. 160 Which Rent I haue bestowed on my daughter Mary to buy her pins.] **1697** VANBRUGH *Relapse* v. v, *Hoyden*... He told me I should have two hundred a year to buy pins... *Nurse.* Ah, my dearest, .. These Londoners have got a gibberidge with 'em would confound a gipsy. That which they call pin-money is to buy their wives everything in the varsal world. **1712** ADDISON *Spect.* No. 295 ¶2 The Doctrine of Pin-money is of a very late Date, unknown to our Great Grandmothers, and not yet received by many of our Modern Ladies. **1766** BLACKSTONE *Comm.* II. xxxii. 498 If she has any pinmoney or separate maintenance, it is said she may dispose of her savings thereout by testament, without the control of her husband. **1809** MAR. EDGEWORTH *Manœuvering* ix, The point was, whether a wife should or should not have pin-money. **1892** *Munsey's Mag.* Oct. 112/1 The late Rose Terry Cooke, popular as her writings were, never made more than pin money with her pen. **1897** *Tit-Bits* 16 Oct. 48/1 A wealthy man .. who allows her £50 a year for pin money. **1926** H. CRANE *Let.* 1 June (1965) 256, I don't think you'll get pin money for the sale of the place. **1957** *Economist* 26 Oct. 291/1 A much better system than relying solely on attendance pin money for all peers would be to pay a full MP's salary to .. a score of 'nominated' peers on either side. **1971** *Farmers Weekly* 19 Mar. 94/2 In farming, we tend to use straw liberally and an odd wedge for a child to bed the rabbit hutch seems insignificant. But .. you could .. start a sideline enterprise. Good pin money? **1978** S. ALLAN *Inside Job* i. 17 If you did find yourself short of pin money you .. could get yourself a job.

b. *attrib.*

1837 T. BACON *First Impr. Hindostan* I. vi. 171 Marriage is .. out of the question .. unless .. the young lady .. have .. a small pin-money purse of her own. **1908** *Daily Chron.* 5 Oct. 5/6 This meeting .. protests against the employment of the 'pin-money clerk', who is a menace to the clerks of both sexes. **1961** PARTRIDGE *Dict. Slang* Suppl. 1222/1 *Pin-money spoof*, vague, pointless amateurish writing: journalistic: since ca. 1910. **1977** in *Centuryan* (Office Cleaning Services) Christmas 4/1 Six 'pin-money' schoolgirls whose journey home in a mini-bus ended in tragedy were being employed illegally.

‖**Pinna**[1] ('pɪnə). *Zool.* [L. *pinna*, variant of *pīna* (Cic., Plin.), a. Gr. πῖνα (also πίννα, πίννη), in same sense.] A genus of bivalve molluscs, having a large silky byssus or 'beard'.

c **1520** ANDREW *Noble Lyfe* lxx, Pinna is a fisshe that layeth alwaye in the mudde, .. & it is in a shell lyke a muscle. **1651** *Raleigh's Ghost* 113 The shelfish called *Pinna* is ever ingendred in muddy waters. **1759** B. STILLINGFL. tr. *Biberg's Econ. Nat.* in *Misc. Tracts* (1762) 111 There is a very large shell-fish in the Mediterranean called the *pinna*, .. furnished with very strong calcareous valves. **1851** WOODWARD *Mollusca* 11 The mussel and *pinna* spin a byssus.

b. *attrib.*, as *pinna shell*; **pinna-guardian**, rendering of *Pinnoteres*: see PINNOTHERE; **pinna-wool**, the byssus of the pinna as a textile.

1854 WOODWARD *Mollusca* II. 264 A little crab which nestles in the mantle and gills of the Pinna, .. received the name of Pinna-guardian (*Pinnoteres*) from Aristotle. **1884** J. T. BENT in *Macm. Mag.* Oct. 427/1 Bright red pinna shells. **1890** *Cent. Dict.*, Pinna wool.

‖**pinna**[2]. Pl. -æ (formerly also -as). [mod.L. uses of L. *pinna* = *penna*, in senses feather, wing, fin.]

1. *Anat.* The 'wing' of the ear, the broad upper part of the external ear; also applied to the whole external ear. (Cf. CONCHA 4 a.)

[**1693** *Blancard's Phys. Dict.* (ed. 2), *Pinna Auris*, the upper and broader part of the Ear, called the Wing.] **1840** G. V. ELLIS *Anat.* 194 The nerve .. gives branches to supply the anterior part of the tragus and the pinna above the meatus. **1872** MIVART *Elem. Anat.* ix. (1873) 396 The external ear, or pinna, may be entirely wanting, as in the whales and crocodiles.

b. Each lateral cartilage of the nose; = ALA I.

1668 CULPEPPER & COLE *Barthol. Anat.* III. x. 150 The lateral .. parts are termed *Pterugia Alæ, Pinnæ.* **1858** MAYNE *Expos. Lex., Pinna*, .. another term for the *ala*, or lower cartilage of either side of the nose.

2. *Bot.* Each primary division (leaflet, petiole with leaflets, or lobe) of a pinnate or pinnatifid leaf, esp. in ferns.

1785 MARTYN *Rousseau's Bot.* xxxii. (1794) 490 Common Polypody has pinnatifid fronds, the pinnas or lobes oblong. **1851** MOORE *Brit. Ferns & Allies* (1864) 10 The fronds are sometimes divided down to the rachis, .. when this occurs, the frond is said to be pinnate; and in this case, each of the distinct leaf-like divisions is called a *pinna.* **1880** GRAY *Struct. Bot.* iii. §4 (ed. 6) 104 *Pinnæ* is a convenient name for the partial petioles of a bipinnate leaf, taken together with the leaflets that belong to them.

3. *Zool.* **a.** The fin of a fish; any fin-like structure, as the flipper of a seal or cetacean. **b.** A wing-like expansion or branch in certain polyps or other invertebrates. **c.** *Entom.* A small oblique ridge forming one of the parallel lines of a pinnate surface, as in the leg of a grasshopper: see PINNATE *a.* 1 b.

1846 PATTERSON *Zool.* 21 If one of the wing-like expansions or pinnæ of the Virgularia is injured, the rest shrink as if all were hurt. **1858** MAYNE *Expos. Lex., Pinna.* .. *Ichthyol.* a fin. **1861** J. R. GREENE *Man. Anim. Kingd., Cœlent.* 149 The pinnæ are very contractile, so as to vary in form from mere lobes or tubercles to long filiform fringes.

pinna, early spelling of PIÑA, pine-apple.

pinnace ('pɪnəs). Forms: 6 **pennis, pinase, -esse, pinnes, pynice, -asse, pynneis, -esse,** 6–7 **pynn-, pinace, pinnesse, -is(e, -as(e, -ass(e,** 7 **pinise, pinnaisse, pynnis, pynace, -esse,** 6– **pinnace**; (*Sc.* 6 **pinag, pynnage, pynnege,** 6–7 **pinnage**). [a. F. *pinasse, pinace* = Sp. *pinaça* (1252–84 in Jal), Pg. *pinaça* (1326 in Jal), It. *pinaccia, -azza* (Florio). The earlier form in Eng. and Fr. was ME. 15th c. SPINACE, *spinas, spynes*, OF. *espinace* (1451), *espinasse* = med. (Anglo-) L. *spinachium* (1338 Knighton).

F. *pinasse* and its Romanic cognates are by Diez and others taken as derived from *pin-us, pino, pin* pine-tree (cf. Cotgrave '*pinasse* the Pitch tree; also a Pinnace'), L. type **pinācea*. But this leaves the form in *esp-, sp-*, unexplained.]

1. A small light vessel, generally two-masted, and schooner-rigged; often in attendance on a larger vessel as a tender, scout, etc., whence probably the use in 2. Since *c* 1700 only *Hist.* and *poet.*

[**1321–7** *Anc. Corr.* (P.R.O.) LVIII. 8 Kaunt ioe departi de Portismuth oue le espynasse le vent fust en countre.] **1546** in R. G. Marsden *Sel. Pl. Crt. Adm.* (1894) I. 138 In dictis navibus vocatis pynneis. *c* **1550** *Sir A. Barton* in *Surtees Misc.* (1888) 68 His pennis hath ninescorre men and more. *a* **1552** LELAND *Itin.* IV. 23 The old Toun was brent by the Pinesses of the Spaniardes. **1559** W. CUNNINGHAM *Cosmogr. Glasse* 143 Pincke, Pynice, Gally, or what so euer name they haue. **1565–73** COOPER *Thesaurus, Catascopium*, a spiall ship: a brigantine or pinneise [1548–52 spinner]. **1569** STOCKER tr. *Diod. Sicul.* III. xi. 120 The Shippes .. were haled out by the Gallies and other small pynnaces rowed with ores. **1591** in Heath *Grocers' Comp.* (1869) 85 That six shippes of war and one pynasse should be furnyshed and set forth by the Cittie. **1598** SYLVESTER *Du Bartas* II. i. *Eden* 27 Thou canst safely steer My ventrous Pinnasse to her wished Peer. **1600** HOLLAND *Livy* x. ii. 352 The soldiers were transported in lighter barkes and small pinnaces. **1612** S. MOUNTAGU in *Buccleuch MSS.* (Hist. MSS. Comm.) I. 243 This afternoon hath been the sea fight with some 15 or 16 pynesses and half a score galleys. **1622** R. HAWKINS *Voy. S. Sea* (1847) 170 We .. gave the bigger shippe to the Spaniards againe, and the lesser wee kept, with purpose to make her our pinnas. **1624** CAPT. SMITH *Virginia* I. 5 Full of flats and shoulds that our Pinnasse could not passe. **1650** S. CLARKE *Eccl. Hist.* I. (1654) 83 He entered into a Pinnace, and went up the River Nilus. **1666** *Despaut. Gram. Inst.* (Jam.), *Phaselus*, a Barge or Pinnage. **1710** J. HARRIS *Lex. Techn.* II, *Pinnace*, .. a small Vessel, with a Square Stern, going with Sails and Oars, and carrying three Masts; .. used as a Scout for Intelligence, and for Landing of Men. **1725** POPE *Odyss.* XIII. 187 The winged Pinnace shot along the sea. **1842** J. WILSON *Chr. North* (1857) I. 247 A fair pinnace to glide and float for aye!

fig. **1589** WARNER *Alb. Eng.* VI. xxix. (1612) 144, I will .. tough the Pinnesse of my thoughts to kenning of your Eyes. **1610** BOYS *Exp. Epist. & Gosp.* Wks. (1629) 165 First, we must be shipt with Christ in baptisme; After saile with him in the Pinnesse of the Church.

2. A double-banked boat (usually eight-oared) forming part of the equipment of a man-of-war; also applied to other small boats.

1685 *Lond. Gaz.* No. 2054/3 The *Larks* Boat being Commanded by Captain Leightons Brother, the *Bonadventures* Pinnace by Mr. Harrises, .. and the Yaule by Mr. Brisbane. **1745** P. THOMAS *Jrnl. Anson's Voy.* 55 We mann'd and arm'd our Barge, Pinnace, and the *Trial's* Pinnace. **1769** FALCONER *Dict. Marine* (1789) F iv, Pinnaces exactly resemble barges, only that they are somewhat smaller, and never row more than eight oars. **1840** R. H. DANA *Bef. Mast* xxiii. 68 There were five boats belonging to the ship—launch, pinnace, jolly-boat, larboard quarter-boat, and gig.

†**3.** Applied in figurative context to a woman; also *spec.* a mistress; a prostitute. *Obs.*

a **1568** in *Bannatyne Poems* (Hunter. Cl.) 1080 Now, gossop, I must neidis be gon, And leive my prettie pinnage to your guyde. **1568** SEMPILL *Margret Fleming* viii, Now is my pretty pynnege reddy. **1607** DEKKER & WEBSTER *Northw. Hoe* v. D.'s Wks. 1873 III. 78 If I like her personage .. Ile stand thrumming of Caps no longer, but board your Pynnis whilst 'tis hotte. **1614** B. JONSON *Bart. Fair* II. ii, Shee hath beene before mee, Punke, Pinnace and Bawd any time these two and twenty yeeres. **1693** CONGREVE *Old Bachelor* v. vii, A goodly pinnace, richly laden .. Twelve thousand pounds, and all her rigging.

†**pi'nnaceous**, *a.* *Obs. rare.* [f. PINNA[1] + -ACEOUS.] Related to the pinna (bivalve).

1684 *Phil. Trans.* XIV. 702 Some large fish of the pinnacious kind.

pinnach, obs. form of PANACHE.

pinnacle ('pɪnək(ə)l), *sb.* Forms: 4–6 **pynakle**, 4–7 **pynacle**, 4–8 **pinacle**, 5–6 **pynnacle**, 4– **pinnacle** (also 5 **penakull, pinnakyl, pynakell, -kill, pynnakel, -kylle,** 6 **pinakle, pinnakil, pynne-, pynnokill,** 7 **penacle,** 7–8 **pinnicle**). [ME. *pinacle*, a. OF. *pinacle* (1261), *pinnacle*, F. *pinacle*, ad. late L. *pinnāculum* (Tertull., Vulg. Matt. iv. 5), dim. of *pinna* wing, pinnacle, point.

In the Vulgate, Matt. iv. 5, *pinnāculum* renders Gr. πτερύγιον, dim. of πτέρυξ wing, and was thus evidently meant as a dim. of *pinna* in sense 'wing': cf. the parallel *pinna* in Luke iv. 9. But in later times *pinnāculum* appears to have been viewed as belonging to L. *pinna* in the sense 'point, edge, battlement', which Walde separates from *pinna*, variant of *penna* feather: see PIN *sb.*[1] The Old Latin version in its earliest form had in Matt. iv. 5 and Luke iv. 9 *fastigium* top or apex of a gable.]

1. a. A small ornamental turret, usually terminating in a pyramid or cone, crowning a buttress, or rising above the roof or coping of a building. (In early use sometimes applied to a battlement.)

c **1330** *Owayn Miles* 38 Arches y-bent with charbukel ston Knottes of rede gold .. And pinacles of cristal. *c* **1380** WYCLIF *Serm.* Sel. Wks. I. 110 þe fend .. putte him above þe pynacle of þe temple: þat sum men seyen weren þe aleis. **1382** —— *Matt.* iv. 5 Thanne the deuyl .. sette hym on the pynacle of the temple. **1387** TREVISA *Higden* (Rolls) VI. 369 þey took oure lady wib .. and sette þe smok uppon þe pinacles [*super propugnacula sua exposuerunt*] as it were a baner. **1448** HEN. VI *Will* in Willis & Clark *Cambridge* (1886) I. 355 A grete square Tour .. in .. height with the batelment and the pynacles .C.xl. fete. *a* **1548** HALL *Chron., Hen. VII* 59 The violence of the wynde had blowen doune an Egle of brasse .. from a pynnacle or spire of Paules Church. **1600** J. PORY tr. *Leo's Africa* II. 69 Upon the top of this turret is built a certaine spire or pinnacle rising sharpe in forme of a sugar-loafe. **1665** SIR T. HERBERT *Trav.* (1677) 75 He .. slew .. their Ring-leader, whose head he sent to Amadabat, and .. commanded that it should be set upon a Pinacle. **1696** PHILLIPS (ed. 5), *Pinnacle*, the highest Top of any Spire. **1777** ROBERTSON *Hist. Amer.* (1778) I. III. 241 They fancied these to be cities adorned with towers and pinacles. **1845** PARKER *Gloss. Archit.* s.v., Pinnacle .. consists of a shaft and top; this last is generally in the form of a small spire, surmounted with a finial and often crocketed at the angles, and is sometimes called a finial. **1851** RUSKIN *Stones Ven.* (1874) I. xv. 165 If there had been no other place for pinnacles, the Gothic builders would have put them on the tops of their arches .. rather than not have had them.

†**b.** *transf.* A vertical pointed structure resembling the above; a pyramid. *Obs.*

13.. *E.E. Allit. P.* B. 1463 þe coperounes of þe canacles þat on þe cuppe reres, Wer fetysely formed out in fylyoles longe; Pinnacles pyȝt þer apert þat profert bitwene. ? *a* **1400** LYDG. *Chorle & Birde* in *Min. Poems* (Percy Soc.) 183 Thowe my cage forged were with golde, And the pynacles of birrale and cristale. *c* **1530** in Gutch *Coll. Cur.* II. 328 Item vj Sponnes gilte withe Pynnacles of thends. **1535** *Aberdeen Regr.* XV. 587 (Jam.) Twa pynnokillis of skynnis. **15..** *Ibid.* XVI. 524 Ane pynnekill of skynnis, contenand ix score and six. **1632** LITHGOW *Trav.* III. 104 There was a Pinacle reared vpon the Walles of the Fort with their bare sculs. *a* **1674** MILTON *Moscovia* v, At Dinner he sat bare-headed, his Crown and rich Cap standing on a Pinacle by. **1703** T. N. *City & C. Purchaser* 2 Pedestals upon .. a Pediment to support Statues .. may properly be called Pinacles.

2. Any natural peaked formation; *esp.* a lofty rock or stone pointed at the top; a peak. Also, a rock projecting out of the sea. (In first two quots. perh. applied to a point projecting into the sea.)

13.. *Guy Warw.* (A.) 1719 At a pinacle bi þe se Gij seye a man of rewly ble Go in pilgrims wede. **14..** *Sir Beues* 1283

+ 94 (MS.C.) He kepeth him in a castel.. Closed with þe salt flood, In a penakull of the see. **1582** STANYHURST *Æneis* I. (Arb.) 19 Shee.. his carcasse on rockish pinnacle hanged. *c* **1611** CHAPMAN *Iliad* VIII. 115 The brows Of all steepe hils and pinnacles. **1795** ANDERSON *Brit. Embassy China* xv. 167 An immense pillar, or column of solid rock.. situated on the pinnacle of a large mountain. **1878** H. S. WILSON *Alp. Ascents* i. 7 The pure-white pinnacle of the.. Weisshorn. **1949** *Sun* (Baltimore) 5 Nov. 3/4 The big Panamanian freighter was listing badly and threatening 'to slip off at any minute'. It was described as being caught on a 'pinnacle' with water of 36 to 60 feet depth around it.

3. *fig.* A high or lofty place or situation; the highest point or pitch; the culmination or point of perfection; the acme, climax. (Sometimes applied to a person.)

14.. in *Tundale's Vis.* (1843) 141 Seyde tho virgyn withowttyn vice.. That holy pynakell preued of price. *c* **1485** *Digby Myst.* (1882) II. 240 He ys a chosen wessell,.. A very pynacle of the fayth. **1621** T. WILLIAMSON tr. *Goulart's Wise Vieillard* 92 Being ascended to the top and pynacle of true knowledge. *a* **1659** OSBORN *Charac.*, etc. Wks. (1673) 634 The highest Pinnacle of my Ambition. **1752** HUME *Ess. & Treat.* (1777) I. 254 To have reached the pinnacle of perfection. **1869** W. P. MACKAY *Grace & Truth* (1875) 167 How can I reach the pinnacle of earthly fame? **1878** BOSW. SMITH *Carthage* 267 This was the pinnacle of Hannibal's success, and a pinnacle indeed it was.

4. *attrib.* and *Comb.*

1594 NASHE *Terrors of Night* Wks. (Grosart) III. 263 Nere those pinacle rocks called the Needles. **1837** *Civ. Eng. & Arch. Jrnl.* I. 57/2 The archway.. is flanked with columns, niches, pediments, and crocketed pinnacle finials. **1890** *Cent. Dict.*, *Pinnacle work*, in *arch.* and *decoration*, ornamental projections, especially at the top of any object. **1901** *Wide World Mag.* VIII. 132/1 Jagged, pinnacle-like rocks. **1916** *Daily Colonist* (Victoria, B.C.) 14 July 11/3 On her last voyage in the westward route the Dora struck a pinnacle rock and developed a serious leak.

'pinnacle, *v.* [f. prec. sb.]

1. *trans.* To set on or as on a pinnacle; in quot. 1816, to rear as a pinnacle.

1656 S. H. *Gold. Law* 15 To stand.. pinacled on the highest point of the Temple, ready for precipitation. **1816** BYRON *Ch. Har.* III. lxii, The Alps, The palaces of Nature, whose vast walls Have pinnacled in clouds their snowy scalps. **1878** BROWNING *Poets Croisic* xxiii, Such a mighty moment of success As pinnacled him.. in full display, For the whole world to worship.

2. To form the pinnacle of, to crown. Also *fig.*

1818 BYRON *Ch. Har.* IV. cix, This mountain, whose obliterated plan The pyramid of empires pinnacled. **1840** R. C. HORNE *Gregory VII*, I. i. (ed. 2) 6 It pinnacles all crimes.. Touching God's footstool with a sharp assault!

pinnacled ('pɪnək(ə)ld), *ppl. a.* [f. PINNACLE *sb.* and *v.* + -ED.]

1. Having a pinnacle or pinnacles; furnished with pinnacles or peaks.

13.. *E.E. Allit. P.* A. 207 A pyȝt coroune.. Hiȝe pynakled of cler quyt perle. *c* **1503** in *Chron. Lond.* (ed. Kingsford, 1905) 250 The coveryng [of a Chapell].. paynted wᵗ Azur, and pynacled wᵗ Corven werk paynted and gilt. **1782** WARTON *Hist. Kiddington* 8 The pediment of the southern Transept is pinnacled.. with a flourished Cross. **1829** D. CONWAY *Norway* 61 The rocks rose in pinnacled confusion. **1849** FREEMAN *Archit.* II. I. xii. 239 The use of the embattled and pinnacled tower is.. one of our many insular peculiarities.

2. Elevated on or as on a pinnacle.

1863 W. M. ROSSETTI in *Reader*, His pinnacled supremacy as the poet and autocrat of landscape-painting. **1897** *Westm. Gaz.* 19 Oct. 2/1 Because of this pinnacled position, they assimilate like lightning.

'pinnaclet. *rare*$^{-1}$. [See -ET[1].] A small pinnacle.

1905 *Archæol. Jrnl.* LXII. 111 The pinnaclets supported on brackets thrown outward from the angles.

pinnacocytal, -cyte: see PINACOCYTAL, etc.

pinnadiform (pɪ'nædɪfɔːm), *a. Ichth.* [irreg. f. L. *pinna* in sense 'fin' + -FORM.] (See quot.)

1884 T. N. GILL in *Proc. U.S. Nat. Mus.* VII. 357 In the Chætodontids, an apparent expansion is manifested by the encroachment of the skin and scales on the soft dorsal and anal fins, and they may be distinguished as *pinnadiform.*

pinnæ, plural of PINNA.

†**'pinnage.** *Obs.* [f. PIN *v.* (in a = PIND) + -AGE.]

a. The action of impounding cattle. **b.** The action of fastening with a pin or peg.

1552 HULOET, Pynnage of cattell or powndage, *inclusio.* **1611** COTGR., *Chevillage*, a pegging, or pinning; peggage, pinnage.

pinnage, obs. Sc. form of PINNACE.

pinnal ('pɪnəl), *a. Anat.* [f. PINNA[2] + -AL[1].] Pertaining to the pinna of the ear or nose.

1896 *Allbutt's Syst. Med.* I. 202 Cartilage (Meckel's or pinnal).

pinnaped, variant of PINNIPED.

pinnate ('pɪnət), *a.* [ad. L. *pinnāt-us* feathered, winged, f. *pinna* feather, wing: see PINNA[2] and -ATE[2].]

1. *Nat. Hist.* Resembling a feather; having lateral parts or branches on each side of a common axis, like the vanes of a feather.

a. *Bot.* Applied to a compound leaf having a series of (sessile or stalked) leaflets arranged on each side of a common petiole, the leaflets being usually opposite, sometimes alternate (***alternipinnate***); also to more complex leaves of the same kind, in which the leaflets, thus arranged, are borne on secondary, tertiary, etc. petioles which are themselves similarly arranged (***bipinnate, tripinnate***, etc.).

interruptedly pinnate: see quot. 1861.

[**1704** J. HARRIS *Lex. Techn.* I, *Pinnata Folia*, in Botany.] **1727** BAILEY vol. II, *Pinnate*, deeply jagged or indented (spoken of the Leaves of Plants) resembling Feathers. **1760** J. LEE *Introd. Bot.* II. xxxi. (1765) 152 *Asplenium*, with pinnate Leaves. **1861** BENTLEY *Man. Bot.* 169 It is interruptedly pinnate.. when the leaflets are of different sizes, so that small pinnæ are.. intermixed with larger ones, as in the Potato and Silver Weed. **1872** OLIVER *Elem. Bot.* I. vii. 77 Compound leaves are either of the *pinnate* type, as Rose, or of the *digitate* type, as Horse Chestnut.

b. *Zool.* Having branches, tentacles, or other lateral parts arranged on each side of an axis; in *Entom.* applied to a surface (as in the legs of grasshoppers) marked with minute parallel lines on each side of a central ridge.

1846 DANA *Zooph.* iv. (1848) 73 The budding polyps are sometimes confined to two opposite sides of a branch, and pinnate forms result. **1854** WOODWARD *Mollusca* II. 191 Gills pinnate, placed round the dorsal vent. **1858** LEWES *Sea-side Stud.* 87 The tentacular filaments.. are numerous, each forming a little tree with pinnate branches. **1875** C. C. BLAKE *Zool.* 200 The tail is pinnate at the point.

c. *Physical Geogr.* Of a drainage pattern: resembling a feather in plan.

1932 E. R. ZERNITZ in *Jrnl. Geol.* XL. 512 These acute-angled joinings with the rather evenly spaced and parallel tributaries form a pattern so much like that of a feather that it might appropriately be called 'pinnate'... Figure 8 is an example of pinnate drainage. **1942** O. D. VON ENGELN *Geomorphol.* xi. 215 All the other recognized types of drainage pattern: rectangular, trellis, annular, pinnate, contorted, are responses to structure. **1968** R. W. FAIRBRIDGE *Encycl. Geomorphol.* 287/2 Modified dendritic drainage may be described as pinnate, sub-parallel or anastomatic.

2. *Zool.* Having feathers, wings, fins, or similar parts. *rare*$^{-0}$. (Cf. next, 2.)

1890 in *Cent. Dict.*

pinnated ('pɪneɪtɪd), *a.* [f. as prec. + -ED[1].]

1. = prec. 1. Chiefly *Bot.* and *Zool.*

1753 CHAMBERS *Cycl. Supp.* s.v. *Leaf*, *Pinnated*, or *pennated Leaf*.. composed of two ranges or series of folioles, annexed to the two sides of one common oblong petiole. **1777** LIGHTFOOT *Flora Scot.* I. 327 The leaves are pinnated with about 20 pair of long *Pinnæ*, which are again semi-pinnate with short indented *Pinnulæ*. **1815** KIRBY & SP. *Entomol.* viii. (1818) I. 235 [They] prey upon timber, feeding between the bark and the wood, and.. excavating curious pinnated labyrinths. **1846** PATTERSON *Zool.* 47 The species.. has five pair of beautifully pinnated arms.

2. *Zool.* Having parts like wings, or like fins. ***pinnated grouse***, any bird of the genus *Cupidonia*, having wing-like tufts of feathers on the neck, as the prairie-hen of N. America, *C. cupido*.

1776 PENNANT *Zool.* (ed. 4) I. 119 Pinnated Quadrupeds, With fin-like feet. **1831** A. WILSON & BONAPARTE *Amer. Ornith.* II. 322 Pinnated Grouse. **1874** COUES *Birds N.W.* 158 There is a stray pinnated Grouse now and then.

Hence **'pinnatedly** *adv.* = next.

pinnately ('pɪnətlɪ), *adv.* [f. PINNATE + -LY[2].] In a pinnate manner or form: see PINNATE 1.

1861 BENTLEY *Man. Bot.* 159 Feather-veined or pinnately veined leaves. **1883** [see PINNATI-].

pinnati- (pɪ'neɪtɪ, pɪ'nætɪ), combining form of L. *pinnātus* PINNATE: chiefly in botanical terms relating to leaves (cf. PINNATIFID): **pi,nnati'lobate, pi'nnatilobed** (-eɪtɪ-) *adjs.*, pinnately divided with rounded divisions or lobes; **pi,nnati'partite** (-eɪtɪ-) *a.* [L. *partītus* divided: see PARTITE], pinnately divided nearly to the midrib; **pi'nnatisect, pi,nnati'sected** (-eɪtɪ-) *adjs.* [L. *sectus* cut: see -SECT], pinnately divided quite to the midrib, but not articulated so as to form separate leaflets. See also PINNATIPED.

1857 HENFREY *Bot.* §93 We.. take the prefix *pinnati-*.. and subjoin to this a word indicating the degree or kind of division, thus: *pinnatifid*.. if the broad notches between the lobes extend from the margin to about half-way between this and the midrib; *pinnatisect*, if the notches extend on nearly to the midrib; *pinnatipartite*, if the separate lobes are almost free, and merely connected by a narrow strip of parenchyma. **1861** BENTLEY *Man. Bot.* (1870) 153 [Leaves] pinnatipartite, or pinnatisected, according to their depth. **1866** *Treas. Bot.*, *Pinnatilobed, Pinnatilobate*, when the lobes of a pinnatifid leaf are divided to an uncertain depth. **1883** G. ALLEN in *Nature* 8 Mar. 441 Steps by which a regularly pinnately-veined leaf, such as that of the common olive, may pass into a pinnatifid and pinnatisect form by non-development of the mainly cellular tracts.

pinnatifid (pɪ'nætɪfɪd), *a. Nat. Hist.* (chiefly *Bot.*) [ad. mod.L. *pinnātifidus*, f. *pinnāt-us* PINNATE + *findere*, *fid-* to cleave, split. So F. *pinnatifide*, *pennatifide*.] Of a leaf, etc.: Pinnately cleft or divided at least half-way to the middle.

[**1751** LINNÆUS *Philos. Bot.* 43 Folium.. pinnatifidum est transversim divisum laciniis horizontalibus oblongis.] **1753** CHAMBERS *Cycl. Supp.* s.v. *Leaf*, *Pinnatifid Leaf* expresses one divided into several parts in form of alæ. **1777** LIGHTFOOT *Flora Scot.* I. 500 *Centaurea scabiosa*... Great Knapweed or Matfellon.. the leaves are.. all pinnatifid. **1857**, **1883** [see PINNATI-]. **1877–84** F. E. HULME *Wild Fl.* p. viii.

Hence **pi'nnatifidly** *adv.*, in a pinnatifid manner.

1870 HOOKER *Stud. Flora* 16 Leaves entire, pinnate, or pinnatifidly lobed. **1881** HORNE *Fiji* 86 The leaf.. is handsome and pinnatifidly divided.

pinnation (pɪ'neɪʃən). *Nat. Hist.* [f. L. *pinnāt-us* PINNATE: see -ATION.] Pinnate condition or formation; division into pinnæ (PINNA[2]).

1875 BENNETT & DYER *Sachs' Bot.* 350 When the pinnation is compound. **1882** VINES *Sachs' Bot.* 212 The pinnation, like the formation of lobes, may be repeated.

pinnatiped (pɪ'nætɪpɛd), *a.* and *sb. Ornith.* [f. mod.L. *pinnātipēs*, *-pedem*, f. *pinnātus* winged + *pēs* foot.] **a.** *adj.* Having the toes furnished with lobes; lobiped, fin-footed. **b.** *sb.* A pinnatiped bird; a bird of the group *Pinnatipedes*, having this character.

1828 WEBSTER, *Pinnatiped*, fin-footed; having the toes bordered by membranes. **1842** BRANDE *Dict. Sci.*, etc., *Pinnatipeds*, a term applied by Temminck to an order of birds comprehending those which have the digits bordered by membranes. **1858** MAYNE *Expos. Lex.*, *Pinnatipes*... applied by Schæffer and Temminck to an Order (*Pinnatipedes*); by C. Bonaparte to a Family..: pinnatipede.

pinnato- (pɪ'neɪtəʊ), occasional advb. combining form of L. *pinnātus* PINNATE (cf. PINNATI-). **pi,nnato-'dentate** *a.* [DENTATE], pinnate, with toothed leaflets; **pi,nnato-'pectinate** *a.* [PECTINATE], having lateral projections like the teeth of a comb, arranged pinnately.

1806 GALPINE *Brit. Bot.* 58 L[eaf] linear, pinnato-dentate. **1846** DANA *Zooph.* (1848) 578 Branches pinnato-pectinate.

pinnatulate (pɪ'nætjʊlət), *a. Bot.* [f. L. *pinnāt-us* pinnate + *-ul-* dim. + -ATE.] = PINNULATE.

1882 in OGILVIE.

†**pinned,** *a. Obs.* [Variant of PENNED *a.*] Of a feather: **a.** Grown, formed. **b.** Undeveloped, rudimentary: see PIN-FEATHERED.

1399 LANGL. *Rich. Redeles* II. 148 Tyll her ffre ffedris be ffulliche y-pynned, þat þey heue wynge. **1665** HOOKE *Microgr.* xxxv. 165 An unripe or pinn'd Feather.

pinned (pɪnd), *ppl. a.* [f. PIN *sb.*[1] and *v.*[1] + -ED.]

†**1.** Enclosed, confined, shut up. *Obs.*

c **1412** HOCCLEVE *De Reg. Princ.* 4543 O, þy bagges vnsele; Opne hem;.. Thy pyned stuf many a man destroyeth.

2. Furnished, fitted, or adorned with pins; †*spec.* covered or studded with pins: cf. PIN *v.*[1] 7 (*obs.*).

1688 *Lond. Gaz.* No. 2408/4 A Silver Minute Pendulum Clock, in a pinn'd Case, the Shagreen a very fine grain. **1689** [see PIN *sb.*[1] 1 e]. **1871** SALA in *Belgravia* XIV. 430 [He] was highly.. chained, pinned, and locketed.

3. Fastened with a pin or pins.

1901 *J. Black's Illustr. Carp. & Build.*, *Scaffolding* 35 We have never seen a pinned ladder come apart.

4. = *pinded* (see PIND *v.*).

1802 C. FINDLATER *Agric. Surv. Peebles* 389 *note*, When the mothers have little milk, the lambs are rarely pinned.

5. In ***pinned straits*** and ***pinned whites***, names of some kind of cloth. (Meaning unascertained.)

1552–3 *Act 7 Edw. VI*, c. 9 §1 Euery piece of the sayd Clothes called whyte pynned Streightes.. being readye dressed to put to sale shall conteine in Lengthe xj Yardes at the least. **1584–5** *Act 27 Eliz.* c. 18 §2. *a* **1600** T. SMITH *Let. to Ld. Treasurer* in Strype *Stow's Surv.* (1754) II. v. xix. 401/2 Also of Pyndewhites and Playnes, made in the West Country. [**1642** *Rates of Merchandize* 133 Dorset and Somerset dozens rudge washt, Cardinals, Pinwhites, Straites.. shall goe and be accompted for a short cloth.]

6. ***pinned eye*** (see quot. and cf. PIN-EYED *a.*).

1842 *Florist's Jrnl.* III. 29 The style or stigma [of an auricula] ought not to rise higher than the stamens, forming what is called a pinned eye, which is reckoned a great deformity.

pinnel ('pɪnəl). *local.* [? Connected with PIN *v.*[1] 3 c, as if stuff useful for pinning.]

1. Coarse gravel; sandstone conglomerate.

1766 *Museum Rust.* VI. 153 If I find.. any gravel, sand, soft rock, pinnel, or other porous substance, I begin the good work immediately. **1774** PENNANT *Tour Scot.* (1790) II. 30 Two strata, one of pinnel or coarse gravel.

2. *Geol.* (See quot.)

1876 H. B. WOODWARD *Geol. Eng. & Wales* Gloss. 440 *Pinnel*, local name given to the Lower Boulder Drift in the north-west of England and Wales. Rammel and Sammel are local names similarly applied.

†**pinner**[1] ('pɪnə(r)). *Obs.* Also 5–7 pynner, (5 -ar). [f. PIN *sb.*[1] + -ER[1].] A pinmaker.

c **1400** *Destr. Troy* 1591 Parnters, painters, pynners also. **1483** *Act 1 Rich. III*, c. 12 §1 Artificers of the said Realm.. Pointmakers, Pinners, Pursers, Glovers. *c* **1515** *Cocke Lorell's B.* 9 Pynners, nedelers, and glasyers. **1611** FLORIO, *Agucchiarúolo*,.. a pinner or pinmaker. **1720** STRYPE *Stow's*

Surv. II. v. xv. 241/1 Pinners and Needlers. Foreign Pins and Needles being brought in about the Year 1597, did much prejudice these Callings. [**1890** GROSS *Gild Merch.* II. 209 Pewterers, smiths, pinners, barbers.]

pinner[2]. Now *local.* [Another form of PINDER, f. PIN *v.*[1] 10 = PIND *v.*] An officer whose duty it is to impound stray beasts: = PINDER.

1499 *Promp. Parv.* (ed. Pynson), Pynnar of beestys. **1552** HULOET, Pynner or empounder of cattell, *inclusor.* *a* **1592** GREENE *George-a-Greene* Wks. (Rtldg.) 255/1 George-a-Greene Hight Pinner of merry Wakefield town. **1664** GOULDMAN *Dict.*, A pinner or pounder of cattel, *inclusor.* **1871** *Standard* 4 Oct. 3 The town pinner,.. [of] Stafford, left the town on Saturday afternoon to serve an execution for debt at a small farm near Stamdon Bridge.

pinner[3]. [f. PIN *v.*[1] + -ER[1].] One who or that which pins.

1. A coif with two long flaps, one on each side, pinned on and hanging down, and sometimes fastened at the breast; worn by women, esp. of rank, in the 17th and 18th centuries. Sometimes applied to the flaps as an adjunct of the coif. Now only *Hist.*

1652 *N. Riding Rec.* V. 103 [Bill ignored against a woman for stealing a] pynner. **1664** PEPYS *Diary* 18 Apr., I saw.. my Lady Castlemaine in a coach by herself, in yellow satin and a pinner on. **1688** R. HOLME *Armoury* II. 465/1 Some term this sort of long eared Quoif by the name of a Pinner, or Laced Pinner. **1701** FARQUHAR *Sir H. Wildair* I. i, The pinners are double ruffled with twelve plaits of a side. **1710** STEELE *Tatler* No. 212 ¶3 A Treatise concerning Pinners, which I have some Hopes will contribute to the Amendment of the present Head-dresses. *c* **1720** DK. OF MONTAGU in *Buccleuch MSS.* (Hist. MSS. Comm.) I. 367 The women.. wear four pinners with great ribbons between, and eight lappets hanging down behind. **1751** JOHNSON *Rambler* No. 128 ¶9 A pinner, the pride of Brussels, may be torn by a careless washer. **1816** SCOTT *Bl. Dwarf* iii, The venerable old dame,.. dressed in her coif and pinners.

2. *dial.* A pinafore or apron with a bib.

[Perh. erroneous spelling of *pinna*, short for *pinafore.*]

1846 FAIRHOLT *Costume in Eng.* Gloss. 582 *Pinner*, an apron with a bib pinned in front of the dress. Its more modern name is pincloth and pinafore. **1854** MISS BAKER *Northampt. Gloss.* II. 116 *Pinner*, a pinafore. *Pincloth*, a child's pinafore. Called also Pintidy and Pinner. **1876** T. HARDY *Ethelberta* (1890) 363 Honest travelling have been so rascally abused since I was a boy in pinners. **1891** —— *Tess* xvii, He wore the ordinary white pinner.. of a dairy-farmer when milking.

3. One who pins, fastens, or transfixes with a pin.

1828 in WEBSTER. **1845** MRS. BROWNING *Lett.* (1899) I. 137 All that roughness and rudeness of the sin of the boar-pinner. **1851** MAYHEW *Lond. Labour* I. 272/1 The 'pinners-up'.. are the men and women.. who sell songs which they have 'pinned' to a sort of screen or large board, or.. to a blank wall.

4. The workman who inserts the pins in the revolving cylinder of a barrel organ.

1896 *Pall Mall Mag.* Nov. 336 To completely 'set' a cylinder takes an expert workman three days; then it is given to the 'pinner' who carefully hammers the pins into the places designated by the 'setter'. **1921** *Dict. Occup. Terms* (1927) §648 *Pinner*.. inserts, with pliers and pressing machine worked by treadle, steel pins in positions marked by music marker on revolving cylinder or roller of barrel organ. **1960** *Classification of Occupations* (General Register Office) 84/2 *Pinner*.., barrel organ mfr.

pinnet ('pɪnɪt). ? *Sc. rare.* [In sense 2, app. a corruption of *pennant*, with which it agrees in sense; in sense 1, perh. a mistaken use of the same, associated with med.L. *pinna* in sense 'pinnacle', or ? an independent dim. formation from the latter.]

1. A pinnacle. *rare*$^{-1}$.

1805 SCOTT *Last Minstr.* VI. xxiii, Blazed battlement and pinnet high, Blazed every rose-carved buttress fair.

2. A streamer, pennant.

1822 GALT *Provost* xviii, Laces and ribands of all colours, hanging down in front [of the booths], and twirling like pinnets in the wind. **1834** H. MILLER *Scenes & Leg.* xxviii. (1857) 422 A miniature mast.. bearing atop a gaudy pinnet.

pinni- ('pɪnɪ), combining form of L. *pinna*, *penna* wing, fin (cf. ancient L. *pennifer*, *penniger*, etc.). Hence **pi'nniferous** [-FEROUS], **pi'nnigerous** [-GEROUS] *adjs.*, bearing or having fins. (Cf. PENNIFEROUS, PENNIGEROUS.) **pinni'nervate, pinninerved** *adjs. Bot.*, pinnately veined (= PENNINERVATE). **pinni'sected** *a. Bot.* = PINNATIFID, or ? *pinnatisect* (see PINNATI-). **pinni'tarsal** *a.* [TARSAL], 'having pinnate feet, as a swimming-crab'. **pinniten'taculate** *a.* [TENTACULATE], 'having pinnate tentacles, as a polyp'. See also PINNIFORM, -GRADE, -PED.

1858 MAYNE *Expos. Lex.*, *Pinniferus*, having or bearing fins: *pinniferous. **1656** BLOUNT *Glossogr.*, **Pinnigerous*,.. that hath fins; finned like a fish. **1893** *Syd. Soc. Lex.*, **Pinninervate*, see *Penninervate*. *Ibid.*, **Pinnisected*, the same as *Pinnatifid.*

pinniewinks: see PILLIWINKS.

pinniform ('pɪnɪfɔːm), *a.* Also incorrectly **pinnæform.** [f. PINNI- + -FORM, where see note.]

a. Having the form of, or resembling, a fin. **b.** Having the form of, or resembling, a feather: = PENNIFORM. **c.** Of a pinnate form. **d.** Resembling the mollusc called *Pinna* (PINNA[1]).

1752 J. HILL *Hist. Anim.* 313 The Balæna, with.. a pinniform tuberosity on the back. **1821** W. P. C. BARTON *Flora N. Amer.* I. 43 Leaves.. often inclining to be pinnatifid; the pinnæform segments arcuate. **1858** MAYNE *Expos. Lex.*, *Pinniformis*, *Ornithol.*, applied to wings in the form of fins that are covered by thickly laid up feathers,.. and which serve only as organs of natation: pinniform.

pinnigrade ('pɪnɪgreɪd), *a.* and *sb.* *Zool.* [f. PINNI- + L. *-gradus* walking.] **a.** *adj.* Walking by means of fin-like organs or flippers, as the pinniped Carnivora. **b.** *sb.* A pinnigrade animal.

1849–52 *Todd's Cycl. Anat.* IV. 914/2 **1854** OWEN *Skel. & Teeth* in *Circ. Sc.* I. *Org. Nat.* 297 In the pinnigrade.. family of carnivores, we find the teeth.. more numerous. **1880** *Libr. Univ. Knowl.* (N.Y.) XI. 723 The pinnigrades include three families, the earless seals,.. the eared seals,.. and the walruses.

pinning ('pɪnɪŋ), *vbl. sb.* [f. PIN *v.*[1] + -ING[1].]

1. The action of the verb PIN.

a. The action of fastening, constructing, or repairing with pins; the supporting of a wall or foundation with pins or wedges; cf. *under-pinning.*

1427–8 *Rec. St. Mary at Hill* 67 For ij masons ij dayes for pynnynge of þe new pewes & leyeng of þe same tyle. **1533** *MS. Acc. St. John's Hosp., Canterb.*, To John Bryght for tyllyng and dabyng & outher pynyng xs. **1552** HULOET, Pynnynge of houses, *substructio.* *a* **1633** AUSTIN *Medit.* (1635) 279 Like a Shepheards Tent that falls to the ground for want of pinning, cording, and sowing. **1655** FULLER *Ch. Hist.* II. v. §37 Some Devise used by him about pinning and propping of the Room. **1727–41** CHAMBERS *Cycl.*, *Pinning*, in building, the fastening of tyles together, with pins of heart of oak; for the covering of a house, etc. **1842–76** GWILT *Archit.* Gloss., *Pinning up*, in underpinning, the driving the wedges under the upper work so as to bring it fully to bear upon the work below.

b. The action of fastening (dress, etc.) with a (brass) pin or pins. Also with adv. as ***pinning-out, up*** (in quot. 1676 *attrib.* = for pinning up).

1549 SIR T. HOBY *Trav.* (1902) 23 By the pinninge uppe of the hanging. **1593** NASHE *Christ's T.* 71 b, How you [Ladies] torture poore olde Time with spunging, pynning and pounsing. **1601** DENT *Pathw. Heaven* (1831) 35 They haue spent a good part of the day in.. pricking and pinning. **1676** *Lond. Gaz.* No. 1106/4 Two black pinning-up Petticoats, one being of Sarcenet, the other of Alamode. **1767** GOOCH *Treat. Wounds* I. 381 To be fixed by pinning or lacing, on the side opposite to the wound. **1905** *Sci. Amer.* 30 Sept. 262/1 The second-sizing and pinning-out is done by hand at so-called batteries.

c. The action of shutting up, inclosing or hemming in; also impounding (see PIND 1 b).

1573–80 BARET *Alv.* P 385 A Pinning, or pounding of cattell. Vide Pownde. **1900** *Westm. Gaz.* 26 May 3/3, I have composed for your irresistible museum of chess freaks an example of pinning *ad absurdum.*

d. = *pinding* (see under PIND *v.*).

1802 C. FINDLATER *Agric. Surv. Peebles* 389 Diarrhœa, or Looseness. This disorder is commonly called, by the shepherds, pinning.

e. An indication of a relationship, falling short of a formal engagement, between two young people through an exchange of fraternity or sorority pins; the exchange of such pins for that purpose. *U.S. University slang.*

1961 *Ann. Amer. Acad. Pol. & Social Sci.* Nov. 85/1 There are boxed proclamations in the newspaper [of Brooklyn College] of watchings, pinnings, ringings, engagements and marriages. **1964** *Amer. Speech* XXXIX. 194 That peculiar institution, the 'pinning' of quasi-engaged girls. **1967** *Punch* 13 Sept. 378/1 Most fraternities and sororities sustained this perfumed atmosphere of competition by requiring their members to date a different person every date night... I attribute the popularity of pinning—a kind of informal engagement to be engaged, signified by the exchange of fraternity and sorority pins—to the desire to escape from that pattern; certainly people got pinned and unpinned all the time.

2. *concr.* **a.** *pl.* Small stones used for filling the interstices of masonry (cf. PIN *v.*[1] 3 c). **b.** A pin, peg, or bolt, used for fastening.

1663 BLAIR *Autobiog.* ii. (1848) 50 As pinnings laid in to be foundations. **1742** J. WILLISON *Balm of Gilead* xii. (1800) 136 Not a stone moved, nor a pinning in it moved. **1799** J. ROBERTSON *Agric. Perth* 114 Persons who understand the building of dry stone-walls properly, find a bed for the larger stones, not by means of pinnings.. but by resting them firmly upon one another; and afterwards they close up the interstices with pinnings to ornament the wall. No part of the weight lies on the smaller stones. *a* **1825** FORBY *Voc. E. Anglia*, *Pinning*, the low masonry which supports a frame of stud-work.

c. A fastening with pins (cf. 1 b).

1882 ROSA MULHOLLAND *Four Little Mischiefs* viii, 'We must stand with our faces to the people always, or they might see the pinning', said Kitty.

3. *attrib.*, as ***pinning iron, stone, -fee.***

1688 R. HOLME *Armoury* III. 265/2 *Pinning Iron*, to widen the hole in the Slate to put the Pin in. **1708** S. MOLYNEUX in *Phil. Trans.* XXVI. 37 Part of the Plaister and Pinning Stones of the adjoyning Wall, was also broken off and loosened. **1892** J. S. FLETCHER *When Chas. I was K.* (1896) 55 The pinder.. made answer.. that the horses.. should not go thence until the pinning-fee were paid.

pinning-end = *pinion-end*: see PINION *sb.*[2]

pinnion, obs. form of PINION.

pinniped ('pɪnɪpɛd), *a.* and *sb.* *Zool.* Also **pinnipede, pinnaped.** [ad. mod.L. *Pinnipēs* (neut. pl. *Pinnipedia*), L. *pinnapēs*, *pennipēs* wing-footed (of Perseus), but used in Zool. in the sense 'fin-footed'; f. L. *pinna* in sense 'fin' + *pes*, *ped-* foot.] **a.** *adj.* Having feet resembling fins, fin-footed; *spec.* belonging to a suborder (*Pinnipedia*) of *Carnivora*, comprising the seals and walruses, which have fin-like limbs or flippers; also, belonging to other divisions of animals having limbs or organs resembling fins and adapted for swimming, e.g. the fin-footed or lobe-footed birds (cf. PINNATIPED), certain decapod crustaceans or crabs, the pteropod molluscs, etc. **b.** *sb.* A pinniped mammal; a seal or walrus.

1842 BRANDE *Dict. Sci.*, etc., *Pinnipeds*, the name of a section of crabs.. that have the last pair of feet.. terminated by a flattend joint fitted for swimming. **1858** MAYNE *Expos. Lex.*, *Pinnipes*, adj. *Zool.*.. pinnipede. **1866** T. N. GILL (*title*) Prodrome of a Monograph of Pinnipeds. **1881** *Athenæum* 17 Dec. 807/3 The various species of Hæmatopinus with which the seals, like the other pinnipeds, are annoyed. **1883** *Fisheries Exhib. Catal.* 194 Charts shewing distribution of the pinnapeds of the world.

So **pinnipedian** (-'piːdɪən) *a.* = prec. a.

1880 *Standard* 20 May 3 It is doubtful whether the close-time agreement.. will have any great effect on the longevity of the pinnipedian race.

pinnisected to **pinnitentaculate**: see PINNI-.

†**pinno**, *v.* *Obs. rare*$^{-1}$. = PINION *v.* 2.

1596 SPENSER *F.Q.* v. iv. 22 He saw a Knight, With both his hands behinde him pinnoed hard.

pinnock[1] ('pɪnək). Now *local.* Forms: 3 **pynnuc, pinnuc,** 5 **pynok,** 6 **pynnock,** 6–7 **pinnocke,** 8– **pinnock.** [prob. echoic, from the bird's note; but the ending simulates -OCK, dim. suffix.] A name for the hedge-sparrow or dunnock; also for the blue titmouse, and, locally, for some other birds: cf. DUNNOCK, and *Pinnick*[2] in *Eng. Dial. Dict.*

a **1250** *Owl & Night.* 1130 Pynnuc [*v.r.* pinnuc] goldfynch rok ne crowe Ne dar neuer cumen ihende. **14..** *Metr. Voc.* in Wr.-Wülcker 625/3 *Lirifa*, pynok. **1570** LEVINS *Manip.* 158/46 A Pinnocke, hedge sparrow. **1706** PHILLIPS, *Pinnock*, a sort of Bird. **1833** *G. Montagu's Ornith. Dict.*, *Pinnock*, a name for the Tomtit. **1885** SWAINSON *Prov. Names Brit. Birds* 29 Hedge Sparrow (*Accentor modularis*)... From its short piping note it is called Titlene (North), Pinnock.

pinnock[2]. *local.* Also **pennock, pinnold.** [Derivation unascertained; the ending seems to be -OCK, dim suffix.] A small bridge over a ditch or runnel; a brick or wooden drain under a road or across a gateway, a culvert; also, a structure composed of three boards in which a hare when hard-pressed in coursing can take refuge as in a small drain or culvert: used in Romney Marshes.

1838 HOLLOWAY *Dict. Provincialisms*, *Pinnold*, a small bridge. *Sussex.* **1846** WORCESTER, *Pinnock*.. a tunnel under a road to carry off the water; a culvert.. (Local, Eng.). **1847–78** HALLIWELL, *Pennock*, a little bridge over a water-course. *Sussex.* **1875** *Sussex Gloss.*, *Pennock*, a little bridge over a water course; a brick or wooden tunnel under a road to carry off the water. **1887** *Kent. Gloss.*, *Pinnock*, a wooden drain through a gateway.

pinnock[3]. *local.* [Origin obscure. Cf. PINNY *a.*] In Kent, a name for a particular kind of land: see quot. Hence **'pinnocky** *a.*

1796 J. BOYS *Agric. Kent* 78 *Pinnock*.. is a sticky red clay, mixed with small stones, but although it is deemed poor for cultivation of grain, &c. yet it produces very fine chestnut wood; and filberts likewise grow well upon it. **1881** WHITEHEAD *Hops* 52 The planter notices.. a small patch of yellowing plants in pinnocky or unkindly soil.

pinnoite ('pɪnəʊaɪt). *Min.* [a. Ger. *pinnoit*, named by Staute 1884 in honour of Oberbergrath Pinno: see -ITE[1].] A hydrous borate of magnesium, occurring in yellow or greenish fibrous masses or tetragonal crystals.

1885 *Amer. Nat.* 708 Pinnoite. **1892** DANA *Min.* (ed. 6) 885 Pinnoite [occurs] in the upper kainite layers.

pinnote, obs. form of PINE-NUT.

pinnothere ('pɪnəʊθɪə(r)), **pinnotere** ('pɪnəʊtɪə(r)). Also 7 **-ter,** 9 **-teer.** [ad. L. *pinno-*, *pīnotērēs* (*-thērēs*), a. Gr. πιννοτήρης (Aristoph. *Wasps* 1510), f. πῖνα, πίννα PINNA[1] + τηρεῖν to guard. The L. variant *pīnothērēs*, as if f. Gr. θηρᾶν to hunt, was adopted as the generic name by Latreille 1807, whence F. *pinnotère*, *pinnothère.*] Any of the small crabs of the genus *Pinnotheres*, which commensally inhabit the shells of various bivalves, as oysters and mussels; a pea-crab.

1601 HOLLAND *Pliny* I. 252 The least of all these kind of Crabs is called Pinnotheres (or Pinnoteres) and for his smalnesse most subiect and exposed to iniurie. **1651** *Raleigh's Ghost* 113 The Pinnoter.. giving him notice there-of by a little touch, the Pinna doth kill al the fishes with a hard and violent compression of them; so feeding himself.. and giving part of them to his fellow. **1822** T. MITCHELL *Aristoph.* II. 317 Nay, pinnoteer (I think) might better suit him—'Tis a most dwarfish breed. (*Note*) The pinnoteer is the smallest of crabs, and here serves to designate Xenocles, the tragedian. [**1835** KIRBY *Hab. & Inst. Anim.* I. viii. 253 Pliny says it [the Pinna] is always accompanied by a companion, the *Pinnotheres*.]

So **pinno'therian** *a.*, of the genus *Pinnotheres* or family *Pinnotheriidæ*; *sb.* a pinnothere.

pinnule ('pɪnjuːl). Also (in sense 1) 6–8 pinule; (in senses 2 and 3) in Lat. form pinnula (pl. -æ). [ad. L. *pinnula*, dim. of *pinna* plume, wing: see PINNA[2].]

1. Each of the two sights (consisting of a small square metal plate, pierced with holes, and turning on a hinge) at the ends of the 'alidade' or index of an astrolabe, quadrant, or similar instrument.

1594 BLUNDEVIL *Exerc.* VI. Introd. (1636) 608 Which Diopter is made with two Pinules or square Tablets. **1656** W. D. tr. *Comenius' Gate Lat. Unl.* §528 Out of two stations by the pinnules of the radius..they collect the quantity of the lines of a greater triangle, which is made between the two stations and the thing seen. **1773** *Gentl. Mag.* XLIII. 171 He has joined pinules to his barometer, which by this means furnishes him with an instrument for levelling. **1834** *Nat. Philos.* III. *Hist. Astron.* xiii. 67/1 (Usef. Knowl. Soc.) A radius, moveable on the centre of the circle, carried the pinnules, and traced out with its extremity..the arc it was wished to measure. **1879** NEWCOMB & HOLDEN *Astron.* 59.

2. *Bot.* Each of the secondary or ultimate divisions of a pinnate leaf; a subdivision of a pinna (branchlet, leaflet, or lobe): esp. in ferns.

1776–96 WITHERING *Brit. Plants* (ed. 3) III. 873 Distinct from *J. trilobata*, the pinnules of which are eared and the leafits smaller. **1857** HENFREY *Bot.* §95 In the Ferns..the primary divisions of the leaf are called *pinnæ*, the secondary pinnules, and the tertiary lobes or segments. **1877** *Academy* 3 Nov. 434/1 A long central rachis, carrying sub-sessile pinnules.

3. *Zool.* A part or organ resembling a small wing or fin, or a barb of a feather; *spec.* **a.** A small fin-like appendage, or short detached fin-ray, in certain fishes, as the mackerel. **b.** Each of the lateral branches of the arms in crinoids.

1748 HARTLEY *Observ. Man* I. i. 89 The rhomboidal Pinnulae in the abdominal Muscles of a living Frog, when under Contraction. **1752** J. HILL *Hist. Anim.* 244 The Scomber, with five pinnules at the extremity of the back. **1877** W. THOMSON *Voy. Challenger* II. ii. 97 The pinnules arising from either side of the arm alternately.

Hence **'pinnular** *a.*, of or pertaining to a pinnule; **'pinnulate, 'pinnulated** *adjs.*, having pinnules; **'pinnulet** [-ET], a small or subordinate pinnule; ‖**'pinnulus**, a form of 6-rayed spicule in sponges.

1828–32 WEBSTER, A *Pinnulate* leaf is one in which each pinna is subdivided. **1877** HUXLEY *Anat. Inv. Anim.* ix. 582 Pedicels..continued throughout the brachial and pinnular grooves. **1881** *Gard. Chron.* XVI. 685 The pinnæ, pinnules, and alternate pinnulets are all stalked. **1887** SOLLAS in *Encycl. Brit.* XXII. 417/1 The suppression of the proximal ray and the development of spines projecting forwards on the distal ray produce the *pinnulus*. **1890** *Cent. Dict.*, Pinnulated.

pinny ('pɪnɪ), *sb.* Nursery and colloquial name for PINAFORE. Also *attrib.* and *fig.*

1851 H. MELVILLE *Moby Dick* II. xxix. 203 A woman's pinny hand,—the man's wife, I'll wager. **1858** J. A. SYMONDS *Let.* 1 Nov. (1967) I. 170 Lady Young..engaged in the construction of *pinnies* for poor children. **1859** GEO. ELIOT *A. Bede* xx, Now, then, Totty, hold out your pinny. **1884** BLACKMORE *Tommy Upm.* II. 240 All the children.. with their pinnies full of sugar-plums. **1889** E. DOWSON *Let.* c 21 Oct. (1967) 111 She was disporting herself in a superb way in Gt Russell St—hatless & in a 'pinny'. **1939** A. THIRKELL *Brandons* i. 18 'If we had known mummie was coming, we'd have had our clean pinny on,' said Nurse. **1962** J. BRAINE *Life at Top* xvii. 198 'Get me a bloody pinny,' I said, 'and you can go out to work.' **1974** *Times* 15 Oct. 12/7 A new pinny idea of long skirt, chemise to the knee over a skinny sweater. **1975** *Country Life* 11 Dec. 1710/1 A practical and pretty pinny to tie round the waist.

Hence **pinnyed** ('pɪnɪd) *a.*, clad in a pinafore.

1963 *Guardian* 20 Feb. 7/2 The pinny-ed skivvy.

pinny ('pɪnɪ), *a. dial.* and *techn.* [? f. PIN *sb.* or *v.* + -Y.] Applied in various ways: e.g. **a.** to soil that is rough, hard, or stiff, and so not easily worked (cf. PINNOCKY); **b.** to steel full of rough hard spots (cf. PIN *sb.*[1] 9b); **c.** to wool that is clogged or matted together; **d.** to a file that is clogged or choked with small particles (cf. PIN *v.*[1] 9).

1692 RAY *Disc.* II. iv. (1732) 131 A Bed of a bluish sort of Clay very hard brittle and rugged: they call it a pinny Clay. **1795** PEARSON in *Phil. Trans.* LXXXV. 324 Notwithstanding this uneven and pinny appearance of the filed surface, a polish was produced. **1831** *Sutherland Farm Rep.* 81 in *Libr. Usef. Knowl., Husb.* III, What is open in the staple, or inclined to be pinny in the fleece, are haifed below the double shepherd's house. **1831** J. HOLLAND *Manuf. Metal* I. 261 He used the technical term already quoted from Dr. Pearson, observing that it was *pinny*. **1890** *Cent. Dict.*, *Pinny*, pinned, clogged, choked, as, a pinny file. **1893** *Wiltshire Gloss.*, *Pinny-land*, arable land where the chalk comes close to the surface, as opposed to the deeper clay land.

pinnywinkles: see PILLIWINKS.

pinocle ('pɪnəʊk(ə)l). *U.S.* Also penuchle, penuckle, pinochle, binocle. [Origin unascertained.] A game of cards resembling bezique; also, the occurrence of the queen of spades and knave of diamonds together in this game (cf. BEZIQUE).

1864 W. B. DICK *Amer. Hoyle* 127 Bézique is fast becoming popular in the United States... It is known among our German brethren as *Peanukle*. *Ibid.*, The game [*sc.* Bézique] became very popular in Sweden, and was finally introduced into Germany, changed in some respects, and called Penuchle. **1892** *Pall Mall Gaz.* 26 Sept. 3/2 He likes to play poker and pinochle, but never for high stakes. **1894** S. FISKE *Holiday Stories* (1900) 37 Let's get up a game of pinocle. *Ibid.* 38 'Oh, don't bother!' cried the pinocle players. **1897** *Foster's Compl. Hoyle* 363 A player has melded and scored four kings, and on winning another trick he melds binocle.

pinocytized (ˌpaɪnəʊ'saɪtaɪzd), *ppl. a. Biol.* [f. PINOCYT(OSIS + -IZE + -ED[1].] Taken into a cell by pinocytosis.

1970 *Amer. Jrnl. Anat.* CXXIX. 142/1 The nature of the intracellular hydrolysis of phagocytized or pinocytized substances has been established. **1970** *Nature* 26 Dec. 1284/1 Digestion of pinocytized materials should be impaired.

pinocytose (pɪn-, paɪnəʊ'saɪtəʊz), *v. Biol.* [Back-formation from next.] *trans.* To absorb by pinocytosis. Freq. *absol.*, to carry out pinocytosis.

1960 E. N. WILLMER *Cytol. & Evolution* vii. 118 Epitheliocytes... Can pinocytose. **1962** *New Scientist* 13 Dec. 620/1 A cell may pinocytose for a certain time and then stop. **1967** JAHN & BOVEE in Tze Juan Chen *Res. in Protozool.* I. 114 The effects of inducers which stimulate ingestion of *Tetrahymena* by a starved ameba are reduced if the starved ameba is first allowed to pinocytose for 20 min, before being fed *Tetrahymena*. **1971** *Nature* 19 Mar. 148/1 The two cells pinocytose projections from each other's sarcolemmas.

pinocytosis (ˌpɪnəʊ-, ˌpaɪnəʊsaɪ'təʊsɪs). *Biol.* [f. Gr. πίν-ειν to drink + -CYT(E + -OSIS, after PHAGOCYTOSIS.] A process by which liquid is taken into a cell as a result of the invagination and pinching off of the cell surface so as to form small vesicles.

The word was first coined as F. *pinocytose* (G. Gabritschewsky 1894, in *Ann. de l'Inst. Pasteur* VIII. 682) in a more specialized sense (see quot. 1895). It was not widely used until after it was coined again in 1931, in the present sense.

1895 *Jrnl. R. Microsc. Soc.* 216 The author [*sc.* G. Gabritschewsky]..suggests the probability that phagocytes are not only capable of seizing and assimilating solid bodies, but of imbibing and absorbing liquid substances, and of rendering them harmless to the organism. For this action the term *pinocytosis* is suggested. **1931** W. H. LEWIS in *Bull. Johns Hopkins Hosp.* XLIX. 17 Pinocytosis, drinking by cells; phagocytosis, eating by cells. .. The word 'pinocytosis', suggested by my colleague Prof. David M. Robinson, is derived from the Greek... By pinocytosis the cells are able to take in substances which cannot diffuse into them or be taken in by ordinary phagocytosis of semisolid particles. **1937** —— in *Amer. Jrnl. Cancer* XXIX. 666 Pinocytosis (drinking) by macrophages in tissue cultures is common. **1960** *Jrnl. Protozool.* VII. 184/2 Pinocytosis is a very demanding process in terms of membrane formation. **1969** [see *endocytosis* s.v. ENDO-]. **1977** P. B. & J. S. MEDAWAR *Life Sci.* xv. 124 Fibroblasts.. have the power..to imbibe tiny little droplets of whatever medium they may be living in, known as pinocytosis.

Hence **pino'cytic, ˌpinocy'totic** *adjs.*, of, pertaining to, or formed by pinocytosis.

1955 *Texas Rep. Biol. & Med.* XIII. 475 This cell..has been termed a variant pinocytic cell. **1959** *Exper. Cell Res.* XVIII. 71 The pinocytotic vacuole..was 7μ in diameter. **1964** N. S. COHN *Elem. Cytol.* iv. 68 The movement of fat particles in the intestinal villi appears to occur by pinocytic activity. **1974** *Jrnl. Cell Biol.* LXIII 998/2 Modification of macromolecules by enhancing their positive charges..leads to a preferential pinocytic uptake. **1975** *Nature* 17 Apr. 612/2 Each perineural epithelial cell contained numerous pinocytotic vesicles.

pinol ('paɪnɒl). *Chem.* [f. L. *pīnus* PINE *sb.*[2] + -OL[3].]

1893 *Syd. Soc. Lex.*, *Pinol*, a name for *Oleum pini pumilionis*. **1898** *Allbutt's Syst. Med.* V. 45 Members of the turpentine group—terebene, pinol, cresol, eucalyptol, creosote tar, carbolic acid, iodine and the like.

pinole (piː'nəʊleɪ). *U.S.* Also pi'nola, pinol (pɪ'nəʊl). [a. Amer. Sp. *pinole*, ad. Aztec *pinolli*.]

a. A meal made from parched corn-flour (more rarely wheat-flour) usually mixed with the sweet flour of mesquit-beans or sometimes with sugar and spice; a common article of food on the borders of Mexico and California.

1842 A. GANILH *Ambrosio de Letinez* I. vii. 91 Pinole is made with fine corn meal, pounded almonds, sugar and various spices. **1844** J. GREGG *Commerce Prairies* I. vii. 159 This pod..the Apaches and other tribes of Indians grind into flour to make their favourite *pinole*. **1853** COL. BENTON *Sp.* 7 May (Farmer *Amer.*), It is a small party..and goes unencumbered with superfluites: no wheels, two or three mules apiece, and pinole, pemmican, and beef-dodgers for their principal support. **1854** BARTLETT *Mex. Boundary* I. xi. 269 The daily ration consisting of two pounds of pinole [etc.]. **1856** *Rep. Explor. & Surveys U.S.A.* III. 115 (Stanf.) Its flavor is similar to that of pinole. **1893** KATE SANBORN *Truthf. Wom. S. California* 125 Pinola is parched corn ground fine between stones, eaten with milk. **1894** *Outing* (U.S.) XXIII. 355/1 Tortillas of pinol are far better than the best hoecakes of the Southern States. **1942** CASTETTER & BELL *Pima & Papago Indian Agric.* 38 In 1862 they sold the War Department more than one million pounds of wheat, as well as pinole, chickens, green peas, [etc.]. **1977** *New Yorker* 20 June 49/1 He carries dried chum salmon for his dogs, and his own food is dried moose or bear meat and pinole—ground parched corn, to which he adds brown sugar.

b. A mixture of vanilla and other aromatic powders used to flavour chocolate.

1858 SIMMONDS *Dict. Trade*.

pinoleum (pɪ'nəʊliːəm). [f. L. *pīnus* PINE *sb.*[2] + *oleum* OIL *sb.*] A material for sun-blinds, composed of very slender slips or rods of pine-wood coated with oil-paint and threaded close to each other so as to form a flexible sheet which can be rolled up.

1878 F. S. WILLIAMS *Midl. Railw.* 348 The Brussells carpets, the massive silken or woollen curtains, and the pinoleum blinds. **1905** *Civ. Serv. Supply Catal.* 432 Pinoleum or Tropical Sun Blinds, in a variety of new patterns.

‖**piñon** (pɪ'njɒn, 'pɪnjən). Also pinion, (pinon), pinone, pinyon. [Sp. (pi'ɲon): etymologically the same as PIGNON[1], q.v.] One of a group of small pines native to southwestern North America, esp. *Pinus edulis*, *P. monophylla*, and *P. quadrifolia*, which yield edible seeds; also, the nuts or the wood produced by these trees. Also *attrib.* See also PINION *sb.*[5]

α. **1839** Z. LEONARD *Narr. Adventures* 35/1 Its top is covered with the pinone tree. **1839** J. FORBES *Pinetum Woburnense* 49 This [*sc.* *Pinus Llaveana*] is the only Mexican species that bears edible fruit, and is called in that country 'piñones'. **1851** MAYNE REID *Scalp Hunt.* xxvi, Our faces partially screened by the foliage of the piñon trees. **1874** RAYMOND *Statist. Mines & Mining* 333 The only woods worth mentioning are piñon and cedar. **1882** C. M. CHASE *Editor's Run in New Mexico* 206 The common fuel is pinon, the best fire-place wood in the world. **1897** *Outing* (U.S.) XXX. 455/1 The background of spruce and piñon. **1936** *Nature* 22 Aug. 315/2 The woods which have been found best for the purpose of the investigation [into dendrochronology] are the western yellow pine..and the Douglas fir.., while the next best is the pinyon (*Pinus edulis*). **1945** *Antiquity* XIX. 219 Vegetable foods of which there is evidence include maize, kidney beans and pinyon nuts. **1946** D. C. PEATTIE *Road of Naturalist* iii. 37 Up there the Piutes were feasting on piñon nuts and mountain sheep. **1955** J. HAWKES *Journey down Rainbow* i. 10 The surface of the desert..is..often..boldly spotted with the compact, dark shapes of pinyon and juniper. **1967** N. T. MIROV *Genus Pinus* iii. 150 Piñons form a well-defined group... Their habitat extends to the southwestern Pacific Coastal Ranges, the Colorado Plateau, and the Mexican Volcanic Plateau. **1972** *Sci. Amer.* May 97/1 The growth of the pinyon pine..is affected more by winter climate. **1973** A. H. WHITEFORD *N. Amer. Indian Arts* 53 Bottles are waterproofed with piñon gum. **1976** *Hortus Third* (L. H. Bailey Hortorium) 875/2 Pinyon, pinyon p[ine] nut p[ine]. .. A source of edible piñon nuts. **1976** *New Yorker* 26 Apr. 125/3 People in that part of the San Luis Valley..gather piñon wood for their fires.

β. **1860** BARTLETT *Dict. Amer.* (ed. 3). *Pinion* (Span., *piñon*), a species of pine-tree, growing on the head waters of the Arkansas... Wild turkeys frequent groves of these trees for the sake of their nuts, which are sweet and palatable. **189.** H. TALLICHET *Span. & Mexican Wds. used in Texas*, *Piñón*, a species of pine tree, also the fruit or nuts of the tree... This is the Texas form of Spanish *piñon*.

pinosylvin (paɪnəʊ'sɪlvɪn). *Biol.* Formerly also -sylvine. [a. G. *pinosylvin* (H. Erdtman 1939, in *Naturwiss.* XXVII. 130), f. mod.L. *Pinus sylvestris*, taxonomic name of Scots pine (f. L. *pīnus* PINE *sb.*[2] + *syl-*, *silvestris* of a wood (f. *silva* a wood)): see -IN[1].] **a.** A colourless, toxic, crystalline compound, 3,5-dihydroxystilbene, $C_{14}H_{12}O_2$, which occurs in the heartwood of the Scots pine, where it confers resistance to fungal and insect attack. **b.** Any of the related antifungal compounds that occur in pines.

1939 *Chem. Abstr.* XXXIII. 4776 Pinosylvine is poisonous, fishes die in 0·002% soln. **1945** *Svensk Bot. Tidskr.* XXXIX. 312 In order to get an idea of the relative toxicity of the pinosylvin compounds experiments were made at the same time in solutions containing phenol. **1955** *Ibid.* XLIX. 421 The heartwoods of trees belonging to the *Pinaceae* family contain a number of peculiar phenolic constituents,..of which only the hydroxystilbenes (pinosylvins) show high fungicidal activity. **1968** *New Scientist* 11 Jan. 68/2 The natural resistance of certain types of wood to termite attack has been attributed to the presence of specific repellent chemicals such as..pinosylvin. **1973** *Ann. Rev. Phytopathol.* XI. 204 The formation of pinosylvins in *P. resinosa* cultures..may have been caused directly by ethylene.

‖**Pinot** (pino). Also with lower-case initial. [Fr.: see PINEAU.] Any of a family of vines yielding grapes used in wine-making; the grape of these vines. Also, wine made from Pinot grapes.

The principal varieties are the ***Pinot Noir*** (nwar) (black), used chiefly in making red Burgundy and Champagne, the white-wine-producing ***Pinot Blanc*** (blɑ̃) (white) or *Chardonnay* (ʃardɔne), and the ***Pinot Gris*** (gri) (grey), a black grape from which white wine is made.

1912 [see ALIGOTÉ]. **1959** W. JAMES *Word-Bk. Wine* 144 *Pinot*... There are both red and white varieties and a 'grey' variety grown in Alsace. **1962** *Economist* 29 Dec. 1283/1 A good Pinot Noir..from the Valais or Vaud cantons. **1965** A. SICHEL *Penguin Bk. Wines* III. 233 These four cantons, known as La Suisse Romande, produce 90 per cent of the total crop, the white wines from the Chasselas grape, the

Pinot Gris, Marsanne.., the Riesling, Sylvaner and Traminer, and the red wines from the Burgundian grapes Gamay and Pinot. **1967** A. LICHINE *Encycl. Wines* 404/2 Pinot Gris and Pinot Blanc, eminently noble vines, contribute to white burgundies. All Pinots abound also in the finer Champagne vineyards. **1968** J. M. WHITE *Nightclimber* ix. 65, I drained my Pinot. **1972** *National Observer* (U.S.) 27 May 4/1 The huge price increases are coming in the premium wines—Cabernet Sauvignon, Pinot Noir and Pinot Chardonnay. **1972** D. E. WESTLAKE *Bank Shot* ix. 66 A side dish of black rice, washed down with a good Pinot Noir. **1974** N. FREELING *Dressing of Diamond* 81 A nice bottle, a rosé Pinot, beautifully dry and flinty. **1976** N. ROBERTS *Face of France* ii. 24 The so-called Tokay d'Alsace, or *pinot gris*, is made from black grapes, whereas ..*pinot blanc* and sylvaner are made from white.

†**pinous**, *a. Obs.* By-form of PAINOUS. Hence †**pinously, pynously** *adv. Obs.*, painfully, in a painful manner.

c **1450** *Mirour Saluacioun* 2884 Whilk soeffred his oone son for oure lufe to dye thus pynously.

pin-pallet to **pin-patch**: see PIN *sb.*[1] 18.

pinpillow. Also 6 pynpyllowe, 7 pimpillowe, 8 pimpillo, pimploe, 9 pimplo. [f. PIN *sb.*[1] 3 + PILLOW: cf. the synon. *pin-bolster.*]

†**1.** A pincushion. *Obs.*

1530 PALSGR. 254/2 Pynpyllowe to stycke pynnes on. **1583** *Rates of Customs* D vij, Pinpillowes of cloth for Children. **1622** MABBE tr. *Aleman's Guzman d'Alf.* II. 131 We made thereof..purses, pimpillowes, sleeues for little children. **1650** BULWER *Anthropomet.* vii. 91 They of S. Christophers stick Pins on their Noses, making their Noses serve for Pinpillows.

2. The Prickly Pear: so called from its thick stems beset with spines.

1750 G. HUGHES *Barbadoes* 26 By the force of the wind.. thrown into a prickly Pimploe hedge. **1760** J. LEE *Introd. Bot.* App. 322 Pimpillo, *Cactus.* **1866** *Treas. Bot.*, Pinpillow, *Opuntia curassavica.* **1889** FARMER *Dict. Amer.*, Pimplo, a Barbadian term for the prickly pear..a corruption of 'pin-pililow'.

pin-point, *sb.* (and *a.*) Also pinpoint, pin point.

A. *sb.* **1.** The point of a pin: usually *fig.* as a type of something extremely small or sharp (cf. PIN *sb.*[1] 3 c). Also *attrib.*

1849 HARE *Par. Serm.* II. 234 At this very moment..even at this one little pinpoint of time. **1879** MISS BIRD *Rocky Mount.* 267 Snow as stinging as pinpoints beating on my hand. **1890** KIPLING in *Macmillan's Mag.* Sept. 323/2 Their blue eyes, driven into pin-points by th' wind. **1904** M. HEWLETT *Queen's Quair* III. i. 359 She was on pin-points till she saw her lover. **1926** E. GLYN *Love's Blindness* ii. 24 The centres of her light hazel eyes went to pin points. The dress did not deceive *her*! **1931** C. DAY LEWIS *From Feathers to Iron* xii. 25 Nightmare nags at his elbow and narrows Horizon to pinpoint, hope to hand's breadth. **1952** R. NEILL *Moon in Scorpio* xxviii. 247 His eyes were pin-points now, but their gaze was steady. **1959** E. H. CLEMENTS *High Tension* vi. 99 He let it [*sc.* a car] get well ahead and watched the pin-points of red disappear into the darkness. **1961** D. J. PLANTZ *Sweeney Squadron* x. 151 The Rising Suns were showing up, slightly brighter pinpoints in the gray gloom.

2. *Aeronautics.* A place seen and identified from an aircraft; hence, the ground position of an aircraft as found from such a sighting.

1942 *R.A.F. Jrnl.* 27 June 7 No pin-point was obtained on leaving the British shore. **1942** *Tee Emm* (Air Ministry) II. 81 It's up to you to verify all pinpoints. **1943** [see *astro-sight* s.v. ASTRO-]. **1944** *Air Navigation* I. i. 20 A Pin Point is a landmark recognised from the aircraft but which is not necessarily underneath the aircraft. A Fix is the ground position of the aircraft, found by direct observation of the ground or by employing wireless or astronomical methods. **1950** D. C. T. BENNETT *Compl. Air Navigator* (ed. 5) xi. 374 A Fix..is the position obtained by a Visual Pin-Point or by the intersection of two or more Posn. Lines. **1970** TAYLOR & PARMAR *Ground Stud. for Pilots* II. 14 Flying this Heading, we pass over Peterborough (5235N 0015W) at 1230 hrs precisely. Plot the position, as a small circled dot; it is a Pinpoint, the name given to a Fix obtained by visual observation of the ground. **1971** *Hindustan Times Weekly* (New Delhi) (Suppl.) 4 Apr. p. iii/2 He's been flying here for only six months and is still in the process of discovering new features and pinpoints.

3. (See quot. 1948[1].)

1943 H. T. U. SMITH *Aerial Photographs* xiii. 339 Vertical photography may involve the making of one or more flight strips, or of only isolated stereo pairs, known as 'pinpoints'. **1948** S. H. SPURR *Aerial Photographs in Forestry* ii. 13 A pin-point is an isolated pair of photographs taken so as to give stereoscopic coverage of a specific place on the ground. *Ibid.* 16 Specially designed instruments manufactured by the makers of mapping cameras are particularly well adapted for taking pin-points.

B. *attrib.* or as *adj.* **1.** Seeming as small or as sharp as the point of a pin.

1850 BROWNING *Chr. Eve* v, Man, therefore, stands on his own stock Of love and power as a pin-point rock. **1899** *Allbutt's Syst. Med.* VII. 114 The pupils..so small as to deserve the name of 'pin-point pupils'. **1907** J. H. PARSONS *Dis. Eye* iv. 67 In old people it is smaller than in the young, sometimes to so great an extent that the pupils are almost 'pin-point'. **1928** D. H. LAWRENCE *Woman who rode Away* 198 He never liked looking anything in the very pin-point middle of the eye. **1933** W. DE LA MARE *Fleeting* 95 With pin-point bill, and tail a-cock. **1936** W. HOLTBY *South Riding* I. vii. 72 Those trodden-down pin-point heels. **1944** *Times* 18 Mar. 4/4 Marauders attacked pin-point targets at Piedmonte. **1959** *Times* 23 Sept. 3/7 The stage effect of overhead lights, the surrounding darkness, and the pinpoint area of operations. **1961** R. B. LONG *Sentence & its Parts* vii. 153 In the narrowest sense the present time is a point so minute that it is already a part of the past before we can finish the sentence. But the present with which verbs are concerned is not this uncomfortable pin-point present. **1974** M. C. GERALD *Pharmacol.* xiii. 244 The pinpoint pupil is one of the cardinal signs of morphine poisoning. **1976** *Sat. Rev.* (U.S.) 30 Oct. 10/1 Bell scientists and engineers..have already developed pinpoint light sources—light-emitting diodes.

2. Very fine in texture or structure; characterized by very small points.

1899 *Daily News* 29 July 8/5 A clear Swiss muslin of very fine make, with a pin-point embroidery on it. **1942** *Oxoniensia* VII. 42 Deeply incised 'pinpoint' decoration.. varying a little and reverting to a plain chevron pattern. **1957** J. KEROUAC *On Road* (1958) 156 A misty pinpoint darkness. **1962** *Guardian* 23 Feb. 8/4 A seam-free, pin-point mesh stocking. **1969** *Sears Catal.* Spring/Summer 20 Full fashioned plus the extra elasticity of a pinpoint stitch.

3. Performed with or exhibiting great positional accuracy.

1944 *Manch. Guardian* 14 Dec. 3/2 Fighter Command's activities included thirty missions against V2 targets in Holland, where pin-point power-dive attacks resulted in direct hits on erection and launching installations. **1945** *Times* 27 June 3/4 Their pin-point bombing was on the biggest scale that Japan has yet experienced. **1949** *Sun* (Baltimore) 3 Oct. 2/7 'Kickless' guns, capable of pinpoint accuracy. **1958** J. R. BIGGS *Woodcuts* 81 If the design demands precise 'pin point' register, then a precise method must be used. **1958** *Listener* 21 Aug. 259/1 It is the ground controllers' job to see that collisions do not happen. With the equipment they have today this can be done with almost pin-point accuracy. **1973** *Times* 9 Aug. 5/5 He said he was aiming his balloon for France, 'but I would consider anything from Finland to Italy a pinpoint landing'. **1976** *Gramophone* Aug. 370 (Advt.), Dramatically improved solid stereo image and rear pin-point localisation. **1976** *Southern Even. Echo* (Southampton) 3 Nov., Clive Green almost snatched a second ten minutes later with a flying header from a pin-point cross by left-winger Mickey Mellows.

4. Highly detailed or specific.

1960 V. JENKINS *Lions Down Under* p. xv, Secretaries.. looked after our internal comfort with pin-point efficiency. **1971** *Morning Star* 1 July 4/1 This 'simple way' is, of course, the result of pin-point organisation and the working out of schedules.

pin-point, *v.* Also pinpoint. [f. the sb.]

I. *trans.* **1. a.** To locate with high precision.

1917 'CONTACT' *Airman's Outings* II. iv. 280 Meanwhile an exact position has been pin-pointed. **1936** J. GRIERSON *High Failure* v. 102 The next thing was to 'pin-point' myself: that is to find the exact spot on the map at which I had made a landfall. **1946** D. HAMSON *We fell among Greeks* iv. 46 The enemy was trying to pinpoint our position. **1955** C. S. FORESTER *Good Shepherd* 72 The fewer people who were aware how accurately the Admiralty was able to pin-point U-boat concentrations the better. **1955** *Times* 6 Aug. 8/4 Not only can the exact position of a find be pin-pointed ..but the possibility of future researches and future discoveries is preserved. **1977** *Daily Tel.* 18 Nov. 8/8 Amateur archaeologists believe they have pinpointed the site of a large Roman forum..under central Chichester.

b. To identify (an objective) as a target for pin-point bombing.

1940 *Times* 2 Nov. 4/1 Over Naples itself the aircraft crews were able to 'pin-point' the targets without great difficulty. **1941** *Times* 30 Sept. 4/7 The pilot managed to pin-point the factory. **1946** *R.A.F. Jrnl.* May 169 Lancasters equipped with 'H2S'..thundered through the night to pinpoint their objectives.

2. a. To cause to be conspicuous against a large or complex background; to bring into prominence, emphasize.

1943 *Penguin New Writing* XVI. 27 A solitary searchlight would come on suddenly. And, if it pin-pointed you, how you would writhe about the sky trying to shake it off before the endless beams of all the others caught up on you. **1956** [see PIN-POINTING *vbl. sb.*]. **1957** *Economist* 2 Nov. 420/1 Subsequent speakers from Asia, Latin America and Europe took up these themes, each country pinpointing its own problems. **1958** P. MORTIMER *Daddy's gone A-Hunting* xli. 239 The world was empty. But tiny, minutely raging, the figure of Rex was pin-pointed, the sole survivor. **1974** F. WARNER *Meeting Ends* I. v. 24 Lights down to pinpoint Shango in wheel, still spreadeagled, back to audience.

b. To identify precisely; to determine the exact nature of.

1946 *Birmingham* (Alabama) *News* 5 Jan. 1/6 The Pearl Harbor committee called for photographs of the Navy's ship location board today to pinpoint movements of the Pacific Fleet in the days just before the Japanese attack. **1950** *Sport* 22–28 Sept. 18/1 Johnny..would find it difficult to pinpoint the happiest day of his soccer life to date. **1955** *Sci. News Let.* 23 July 51/1 Tonsils, long under suspicion, have at last been pin-pointed as the primary site of polio infection. **1958** *Ann. Reg.* 1957 186 The House of Representatives asked the President to pin-point where substantial cuts could be made. **1960** *Analog Sci. Fact & Fiction* Nov. 13/1 The only actual trouble we can pin-point is that there seem to be a great many errors occurring in the paper-work. **1971** J. Z. YOUNG *Introd. Study Man* i. 9 There have been many attempts to pin-point the particular environmental or other features responsible for the appearance of man. **1977** L. GORDON *Eliot's Early Years* iii. 63 It is difficult to pin-point the sensibility that moves through Eliot's poems.

II. *intr.* **3.** To dwindle to the size of a pin-point (and disappear).

1957 J. KEROUAC *On Road* (1958) II. vii. 159 They pinpointed out of sight.

Hence **'pin-pointing** *vbl. sb.*; also **'pin-pointable** *a.*, capable of being pin-pointed.

1920 *Flight* XII. 374/2 Practical demonstration of principles learnt in Ground work:—(1) Flight by map alone; (2) Flight by compass alone on pre-determined course and time, turning point to be indicated—pin pointing. **1955** D. BARTON *Glorious Life* 71 Here, under his eyes, pinpointable, was the Fall. **1956** *Essays in Crit.* VI. 123 If we pinpoint the personal origin, certainly when the pinpointing is so merely speculative as it seems to be here, we leave out too much. **1962** *Listener* 27 Dec. 1086/1 Current technology, gossip column hearts and flowers..have no direct pin-pointable relation to my work of the moment, but they are not alien worlds. **1967** A. L. LLOYD *Folk Song in Eng.* iii. 150 Even such an apparently pinpointable ballad as 'Edom o' Gordon' has an English, a Lanarkshire and an Aberdeen setting. **1970** TAYLOR & PARMAR *Ground Stud. for Pilots* II. 15 While the pinpointing, plotting and wind finding was going on, so was the aircraft. **1978** J. WAINWRIGHT *Ripple of Murders* 53 It was..necessary to..let him *know* that he could be pin-pointed in King Street..if such pin-pointing became necessary.

'pin-pointed, *a.* [f. PIN-POINT *sb.* + -ED[2].] Having a fine or sharp point. Also *fig.*

1909 *Daily Chron.* 18 Sept. 10/6 The tiny pin-pointed mapping pen. **1931** E. S. GARDNER *Vanishing Corpse* in *Detective Fiction Weekly* 15 Aug. 19/1 His eyes..gazed at Sidney Zoom with pin-pointed intensity. *a* **1936** KIPLING *Something of Myself* (1937) viii. 230, I then abandoned hand-dipped Waverleys..and for years wallowed in the pin-pointed 'stylo'. **1976** J. WAINWRIGHT *Bastard* ix. 122, I check the time... They'll demand pin-pointed answers to their nit-picking questions.

'pin-pointed, *ppl. a.* [f. PIN-POINT *v.* + -ED[1].] That has been pin-pointed.

1944 *Hutchinson's Pict. Hist. War* 12 Apr.–26 Sept. 60 (*caption*) An attack by Mosquito aircraft..on what was probably the most pin-pointed objective which has ever been marked out as a target.

'pin-prick, *sb.* [f. PIN *sb.*[1] 3 + PRICK *sb.*]

1. The prick of a pin; a minute puncture such as that made by a pin-point. Also *fig.*

1862 *John & I*, II. 70, I would never move..to cause you the pain of a pin prick. **1899** *Allbutt's Syst. Med.* VI. 520 When ankle-clonus has disappeared..a pin-prick of the plantar skin will restore it. **1900** J. HUTCHINSON in *Arch. Surg.* XI. No. 41. 33 The nails themselves showed.. numerous minute pin-pricks. **1927** *New Republic* 12 Oct. 216/2 His pen is so subject to his moods that it can make a pin-prick read like a lightning bolt. **1949** E. COXHEAD *Wind in West* vii. 195 At the far end of the stifling tunnel, in which he was condemned to grope for ever, he seemed to see a pin-prick of light. **1978** *Times* 22 July 9/2 Beware of sea urchins and the pinpricks of coral.

2. *fig.* A petty annoyance, a minute irritation. Also *attrib.*, esp. as ***pin-prick raid.***

policy of pin-pricks, a course of petty hostile acts maintained as a national or party policy: applied first in Nov. 1898 to the policy attributed to France in reference to the conflicting colonial interests of France and Great Britain.

The French use of a corresponding phrase *coup d'épingle*, 'pin-stroke', goes back some centuries; in Eng. 'pin-pricks' is found in political use in 1885. On 8 Nov. 1898 the French journal *Le Matin* deprecated a 'politique des niches à l'Angleterre', and 'de continuelles piqûres d'épingle'; on 16 Nov. *The Times*, referring to this article, used the words 'a policy of "pinpricks"'; *Le Temps* of 19 Nov. (publ. evening of 18th) had an article denying on the part of France the existence of a 'politique de *coups d'épingle*', *The Times* of 19 Nov. quoted this as a 'policy of pin-pricks' (see quot.), which forthwith became a political phrase.

1885 *Public Opinion* 9 Jan. 29/2 Petty pin-pricks on the coast of Africa had rather irritated than roused public opinion. **1887** ROSA N. CAREY *Uncle Max* xxviii, It is strange how painfully these little pin-pricks to our vanity affect us. **1887** *Spectator* 16 Apr. 518/1 Wherever the French Government can give the British Government a sharp pin-prick, it gives it. **1898** *Times* 16 Nov. 9/3 Such a policy of 'pinpricks' is beginning to be recognized by sensible Frenchmen as a grievous error. *Ibid.* 19 Nov. 7/2 The *Temps* to-night contains a long article, entitled 'The Policy of Pin-pricks'. *Ibid.* 11/3 According to the *Temps* there has never been any policy of pin-pricks. **1898** *Globe* 6 Dec. 1/2 Disposed to bring the pin-prick policy to bear upon British interests in the Far East. **1901** *Daily Tel.* 22 Mar. 9/5 Russian provocation is at present but a policy of pin-pricks. **1902** *Westm. Gaz.* 28 Apr. 2/3 The extra penny stamp on cheques..may be a pin-prick, but the prospect is causing a good deal of irritation. **1926** T. E. LAWRENCE *Seven Pillars* (1935) I. xv. 104 The tribesmen..hindered and distracted the Turks by their pin-prick raids. **1976** A. WHITE *Long Silence* vi. 49 Sooner or later, the Germans were going to.. suspect..the source of the many pinprick raids. **1977** *Time* 4 Apr. 23/2 After launching a few pinprick air raids, Mobutu's Army Chief of Staff..claimed that the intruders were in retreat.

3. **pinprick picture**, a coloured print pierced with pin-holes to create an illusion of illumination.

1960 H. HAYWARD *Antique Coll.* 286/2 Pinprick pictures were a more simple form of transformation, since a coloured print was perforated with a number of small holes and, hence, when held to the light would appear to be illuminated. Coloured paper would sometimes be fastened behind the print. **1968** *Canad. Antiques Collector* Oct. 22/1 Pinprick pictures of ancient oriental origin are probably a branch of decoupage.

So **'pin-prick** *v.*, (quot. 1945 is in sense of PIN-POINT *v.* 1 b); **'pin-pricked** *ppl. a.*, pricked with a pin; spec. ***pin-pricked picture*** = ***pin-prick picture***; **pin-'pricking** *vbl. sb.* and *ppl. a.*

1755 SMOLLETT *Quix.* (1803) IV. 272 A dish of twitches, pinches, and pin-prickings. **1881** MRS. C. PRAED *Policy & P.* II. 270 Small slight, pinpricking insults. **1898** J. HUTCHINSON in *Arch. Surg.* IX. No. 36. 374 Dry and cracked finger-ends, with pin-pricked finger-nails. **1899** *Ibid.* X. No. 38. 147 A peculiar form of local erosion..in which little pits form as if the nail had been pinched..'the pin-pricked nail'. **1899** *Westm. Gaz.* 6 Feb. 2/3 A Committee to pin-prick them on the subject. **1909** *Daily Chron.* 15 July 4/4 Every book for the blind is carefully pin-pricked by voluntary workers who can see. **1912** J. BAILEY *Let.* 13 Aug. (1935) 132 You shall certainly pin-prick if you will when you come to London, if you don't find anything more amusing to do—and I will listen respectfully and gratefully. **1927** *Daily Express* 5 Dec. 1/4 The move is interpreted..as a step forward to stop the 'pin-pricking' that has been going on between the two countries. **1936** *Discovery* Oct. 321/2 That was a tragic pin which pricked out one of the last letters written by Marie Antoinette in the prison of the Conciergerie... The pin-pricked note miscarried. *Ibid.* 322/2 Some surviving specimens of these pin-pricked pictures date back two hundred years. *Ibid.* Pin-pricking with them was a fine art. **1945** R. A. KNOX *God & Atom* v. 71 Other men's lives are at stake; those..of British or American airmen who might be shot down in trying to pin-prick the targets of Hiroshima one by one, instead of devoting it to a general holocaust. **1950** *Times* 24 Jan. 3/5 We must bring home to the British Government that although most of us are loyal, we will not tolerate the pinpricking of loyalty. **1952** C. DAY LEWIS tr. *Virgil's Aeneid* XI. 245 Drances, hostile as ever to Turnus, whose high renown Pin-pricked him with sour envy to intrigue against him. **1958** B. HAMILTON *Too Much of Water* v. 119 He had..continued, in a small pin-pricking way, to belittle and snub Patricia Odell. **1958** R. GODDEN *Greengage Summer* iv. 38 Pinpricked all over with fear, I tiptoed away. **1961** M. CONWAY in *Conc. Encycl. Antiques* V. 231/2 The art of pin-pricking or 'Piercing Costumes on Paper' became a young ladies' amusement. *Ibid.*, Extremely attractive pin-pricking effects were achieved by outlining from the front with a fine pin—actually needles were used—the remainder being thickly pierced from the back. **1961** *Times* 1 July 11/1 One variety of pin-prickt picture deals with religious subjects. **1966** D. FRANCIS *Flying Finish* xi. 136 'There are some holes in the paper.' 'Where he put the pin.'..Simon had pinpricked four letters. **1972** *Times* 26 June 8/5 Much authentic [A.J.P.] Taylor—pinpricking, bubble-bursting. **1973** *Times* (Nepal Suppl.) 14 Apr. p. i/4 Nepal retaliates by such pinpricking gestures as refusing to cooperate wholeheartedly in the extradition of Naxalite terrorists who flee across the border from West Bengal. **1979** G. MACDONALD *Camera* Plate 4 A paper print of Venice, garishly coloured by hand then pin-pricked for back-lighting in a viewer.

pin-prod to **pin-rod**: see PIN *sb.*[1] 18.

pinsal(l, pinsell(e: see PENCEL, PENCIL.

pinsapo (pɪnˈsæpəʊ). [Sp.] The Spanish fir, *Abies pinsapo*, belonging to the family Pinaceæ, and native to mountainous regions of southern Spain. Also *attrib.*

1839 *Gardener's Mag.* XV. 109 He [*sc.* E. Boissier] first observed the Pinsapo at an altitude of about 4,000 feet. **1852** STANDISH & NOBLE *Pract. Hints Planting Ornamental Trees* 47 *Abies Pinsapo.*—Boissier. (Pinsapo Silver Fir.)... A very beautiful tree..indigenous to the mountains of Grenada. **1877** DISRAELI *Let.* 29 July in Monypenny & Buckle *Life Disraeli* (1920) VI. 171 Yesterday..I had to plant a tree—a pinsapo. **1887** *Encycl. Brit.* XXII. 297/1 Among other characteristic trees [in Spain] are the Spanish pine (*Pinus hispanica*), the Corsican pine (*P. Laricio*), the Pinsapo fir (*Abies Pinsapo*), and the *Quercus Tozza*.

pinsche, obs. form of PINCH.

pinscher (ˈpɪnʃə(r)). [Ger.] A short-coated, often dark-coloured terrier of the breed so called, usually having pricked ears and a docked tail; also, a smaller terrier with either pricked or drop ears, belonging to the miniature breed so called. Cf. DOBERMANN.

1926 W. S. SCHMIDT *Doberman Pinscher* i. 10 The ancestors of the doberman were the old German shepherd dog and the large variety of the black-and-tan, smooth-haired German pinscher. **1929** *Pure-Bred Dogs* (Amer. Kennel Club) 203 Miniature Pinschers are natives of Germany. **1935** *Toy Dogs* (Amer. Kennel Club) 55 If you like a small 'Pinscher'..see them trotting around and 'showing off' in some of the dog shows. **1954** M. K. WILSON tr. *Lorenz's Man meets Dog* v. 62 The small daughter of the house received..a charming little dwarf Pinscher. **1957** *New Yorker* 21 Sept. 46/2 Zoltan acquired a miniature pinscher. **1968** R. & A. FIENNES *Nat. Hist. Dog* vi. 77 Among the continental terriers with toy varieties are the schnauzers and pinschers. **1973** *Country Life* 15 Feb. 385/2 The toy group... The Yorkshire terrier, the miniature pinscher, the Italian greyhound. **1978** D. A. STANWOOD *Memory of E. Ryker* xii. 112 Dogs snarled behind me... Two pinschers hit the door.

†**pinse**, *v. Obs. rare.* [Etymology obscure: seems to be distinct from PINCH *v.*; in Ancr. R. varies with PINE *v.* to torment, torture, of which it may be a derived form: cf. *clean, cleanse.*] *trans.* To pain, put to pain or suffering, torture.

a **1225** *Ancr. R.* 368 Þet..bitocneð bittre swinkes, & flesches pinunge [T. pinsinge, Ca., Cl., Cp. pinsunge]. *a* **1300** *Fall & Passion* 89 in *E.E.P.* (1862) 15 In þis manere he was ipinsed as his swet wil hit was: an deþ for mankyn suffred, þe þrid dai vp he ros. *c* **1425** *Eng. Conq. Irel.* 89 Wanhoply shal hys pynsynge be.

†**pinsnet**. *Obs. rare.* [f. PINSON[2] + -ET[1].] = PINSON[2]. Cf. PISNET, PUISNET.

†ˈ**pinson**[1]. *Obs.* In use always in pl. **pinsons.** Forms: 4 **pinceoun**, 4–5 **pynsoun**, 4–6 **pynson(e**, 6 **pynsen, pincon, pyncheon.** 6–7 **pinson.** [a. OF. *pinçon* (Picard *pinchons* 1423) deriv. of *pince* pincers.] (*pl.*) Pincers, forceps.

1356 in Riley *Mem. Lond.* (1868) 283–4 (Lett.-Bk. G. lf. 45) Pynsouns, pynsons. ? *c* **1357** *Durham Acc. Rolls* (Surtees) 560 Stanaxes, Hakkes, pikkes, chesels, et pinceouns. **1426** LYDG. *De Guil. Pilgr.* 15827 In the tother hand she held A peyre off pynsouns. *c* **1440** *Promp. Parv.* 400/2 Pynsone, to drawe owt tethe, *dentaria*. **1493** *Festivall* (W. de W. 1515) 4 All the instrumentes of [Christ's] passyon, the spere, crowne, scourges, nayles, hamer, pynsons and the garlonde of thornes. **1563–87** FOXE *A. & M.* (1684) II. 85/1 His Nose with sharp Pinsons was violently pluckt from his Face. **1595** *Alcilia* (1879) 34 Sometime with pincons of despaire to wring it [the heart]. **1597** J. PAYNE *Royal Exch.* 23 His fleshe by gobbets was nipt of with burnynge pyncheons. **1610** MARKHAM *Masterp.* II. xcvi. 383 Grope the hoofe with a pair of pinsons.

†**pinson**[2]. *Obs.* Forms: 4–6 **pynson,** (5 **-one, pyncon**), 5–7 **pinson,** (6 **-one,** 7 **pinsen**). [app. related in some way to prec. or to F. *pincer* to pinch: cf. OF. *pinchon* (1423), F. *pinçon* toe-piece of a horse-shoe, f. *pince* toe of a hoof.] A thin shoe of some kind; a slipper or pump.

The *pinsons* appear to have become obsolete soon after 1600. No contemporary description of them is known: Kersey (Phillips) in 1706 suggested 'a sort of shoe without heels'; Halliwell has 'thin-soled shoes'; Way *Promp. Parv.* (note) suggests 'possibly, high and unsoled shoes of thin leather, worn with pattens'.

1390–1 *Earl Derby's Exped.* (Camden) 91 Pro furracione j pair pynsons. **1440** J. SHIRLEY *Dethe K. James* (1818) 15 His furrid pynsons. **1503** in *Calr. Doc. rel. Scotl.* (1888) 341 [Six pair of slippers with] pynsons [to same]. **1565–73** COOPER *Thesaurus* s.v. *Calx, Calceo*, to put on shoes, sockes or pynsons. **1599** MINSHEU, *Xervilla*, a pumpe or pinsen to weare in pantofles. **1606** HOLLAND *Sueton.* 147 Now and then was he also seene shod with womens pumps [*margin*] or pinsones. **1706** PHILLIPS, *Pinson* or *Pump*, or a sort of Shoe without Heels. [**1901** *Westm. Gaz.* 22 Feb. 10/1 A Regent Master..was bound..to wear heelless shoes, called 'pynsons'.]

pin-spot to **pin's-worth**: see PIN *sb.*[1] 18.

†**pinstocke**, obs. form of PENSTOCK[1].

1587 FLEMING *Contn. Holinshed* III. 1543/2 Herin..was laid first a pinstocke, and afterwards a sluse of great charge, the streame whereof meeting with the course of the great sluse increaseth the force thereof.

pin-stripe. [f. PIN *sb.*[1] 18 + STRIPE *sb.*[3]] A fine broken or continuous stripe, esp. one repeated as a pattern on cloth. Also *attrib.*, designating cloth with a pattern of such stripes or garments made of pin-stripe cloth. So *ellipt.* as *sb.*, a pin-stripe suit, conventionally worn by business men.

1897 *Sears, Roebuck Catal.* 183/1 *Extra good value, heavy pin-stripe*, with fancy navy blue square sailor collar. *Ibid.* 183/2 This suit is made of a fine brown pin stripe cassimere. **1906** *Westm. Gaz.* 2 June 16/3 The particular cloth I have in mind has a pin stripe in brown. **1922** JOYCE *Ulysses* 321 A dainty *motif* of plume rose being worked into the pleats in a pinstripe. **1935** WODEHOUSE *Luck of Bodkins* iv. 42 A pin-stripe flannel suit. **1942** S. SPENDER *Life & Poet* v. 84 The black-coated, pinstripe-trousered man. **1958** *Spectator* 15 Aug. 214/1 A suit that fits him rather less snugly than his usual pin-stripe. **1972** P. CLEIFE *Slick & Dead* I. i. 15 The usual aleatory fall-out of face fungus and brothel creepers mixing it with the pinstripes and the *Financial Times*. **1973** M. AMIS *Rachel Papers* 50 As I watched, there was a stir in the classroom; a cruel-faced bearded man in a pinstripe suit strode into camera. **1973** *Times* 15 Nov. 18/4, I wore my midnight blue suit with a wide pin stripe. **1975** 'D. JORDAN' *Black Account* iii. 23 This afternoon Magnus was..in a blue-chalk pinstripe, a heavy blue shirt..a near-black tie. **1977** *Hot Car* Oct. 50/3 Apply ⅛ in. or ¼ in. masking tape into the positions required for the pin stripe, then spray the complete panel in the required car colour.

So ˈ**pin-striped** *a.*, ornamented with narrow stripes; wearing clothes of pin-stripe cloth, conventionally dressed; also *fig.*, characteristic of the business man.

1896 *Westm. Gaz.* 18 Sept. 3/2 Pin-striped serge, a material that in navy blue with a white line makes a very smart costume. **1909** *Westm. Gaz.* 4 Sept. 15/1 A gown carried out on a khaki-coloured foundation has a decoration of a pin-striped black and gold collar. **1932** *Daily Tel.* 25 Apr. 4/4 A little tuck-in blouse of red and white pin-striped silk. **1958** *New Statesman* 3 May 562/3 Small wonder we..are unhappy with the pin-striped Executive of the Labour Party, stinking as it does with the air of neat suburban houses and well mannered conversation over garden fences. **1967** *Listener* 31 Aug. 263/2 The citizen everywhere, pin-striped or dungaree'd, puts his own interests before those of society as a whole. **1970** 'D. HALLIDAY' *Dolly & Cookie Bird* iii. 31 Big silver fish pinstriped in yellow. **1973** M. WOODHOUSE *Blue Bone* xiii. 148 A stuffy, pin-striped wheeler and dealer. **1975** *Radio Times* 13 Sept. 4/2 Pin-striped anonymity in the City once seemed a more likely destination.

pinswell (ˈpɪnzwɪl). Now *dial.* Also 8 **pinswill,** 9 *dial.* **penswell, -swoll, pinsweal, -swil, -sole, pinsel, -zel, pensil.** [Origin uncertain.] 'A boil, an abscess, ulcer; a pimple; a large blister'. Now only *s.w. dial.*: see *Eng. Dial. Dict.*

1591 PERCIVALL *Sp. Dict.* s.v. *Venenos*, Pinswels in the handes, *pustulæ*. *c* **1730** J. HAYNES *Dorset Vocab.* in *N. & Q.* 6th ser. VIII. 45/1 A pinswill, a boil. **1878** *Trans. Dev. Assoc.* IX. 96 Creeping under an Arched Bramble..To cure blackheads, or pinsoles.

pint[1] (paɪnt). Forms: 4–6 **pynt(e,** 5 **pintte, pyynte,** 5–7 **pinte,** 6 *Sc.* **point, poynt(t,** 7 *Sc.* **pinct,** 6– **pint.** [ME. *pynte*, a. F. *pinte* a liquid measure (13th c.) = It., Sp., Pg. *pinta*; so OFries. *pint*, MDu., MLG., MHG. *pinte*. Ulterior source uncertain. Diez inclined to think it the same word as Sp. *pinta* spot, coloured mark:—late L. *pincta* for *picta*, something painted or coloured. If so, the Fr. *pinte* must have been adopted from Sp. (or It.) *pinta*, since the native Fr. repr. of L. *pincta* is *peinte*; but the early history of the measure is as yet unknown. Med.L. *pinta* found in 14th c. is from the mod. langs.]

a. A measure of capacity for liquids (also for corn and other dry substances of powdery or granular nature), equal to half a quart or ⅛ of a gallon; of varying content at different times and places.

The imperial pint, since 1826 the legal measure in Britain, is equal to 34·66 cubic inches, or ·57 of a litre; in U.S. the standard pint is that of the old wine measure, equal to 28⅞ cubic inches, or ·47 of a litre. The old Scotch pint was equal to about 3 imperial pints (104·2 cubic inches). In local use also a weight, e.g. of butter in East Anglia = 1¼lb.

1384 *Exch. Rolls Scotl.* III. 107 De..iiij^c v^xx iij lagenis et j pynt vini. **1432** in *Muniment. Magd. Coll. Oxf.* (1882) 11, ij botelles de corio, unde j de quarte et j de pynte. **14..** *Voc.* in Wr.-Wülcker 611/15 *Semiquarta*, a pynte. *c* **1450** *M.E. Med. Bk.* (Heinrich) 201 A pinte of red swynes grece. **1523** FITZHERB. *Husb.* §58 Let hym blede the mountenaunce of a pynte. **1543** *Aberdeen Regr.* XVIII. (Jam.), Was sald..in Dundy for viij.d. the poyntt. **1598** BARCKLEY *Felic. Man* (1631) 628 Spare at the brimme, lest whilest thou shouldest poure out a pint, there run forth a pottle. **1599** NASHE *Lenten Stuffe* Wks. (Grosart) V. 207 The rate of no kinde of food is raised, nor the plenty of their markets one pinte of butter rebated. **1618** *Sc. Acts Jas. VI* (1816) 586/1 Twentie ane pincts and ane mutchkin of just Sterline Jug and measure. **1672** PETTY *Pol. Anat.* (1691) 64, I suppose a pint of Oatmeal equal to half a pint of Rice. **1829** *Glover's Hist. Derby* I. 229 The pint [of lead ore] contains forty-eight cubic inches. **1840** DICKENS *Old C. Shop* xviii, Fetch me a pint of warm ale.

b. A vessel containing a pint; a pint-pot.

c **1483** CAXTON *Dialogues* 7 Cannes of two stope Pintes and half-pintes. **1599** A. M. tr. *Gabelhouer's Bk. Physicke* 264/1 Put them in a pinte till it be fulle..then close the mouth of the pinte with a cloth verye close. **1649** G. DANIEL *Trinarch., Rich. II* xli, The Rebells enter, and the Apron Men Bid welcome, with their Pints. **1872** J. HARTLEY *Yorksh. Ditties* Ser. II. 133 It's time for sombdy to stand summat, for all th' pints is empty. **1901** M. FRANKLIN *My Brilliant Career* xxii. 194 'Good gracious, Julius!' exclaimed grannie, as he offered the governess a pot full of beer, 'Miss Craddock can't drink out of that pint.' 'Those who don't approve of my pints, let 'em bring their own.' **1961** H. C. DODGE *My Childhood Canad. Wilderness* i. 11 We had our meals from tin pints and tin plates, as we never took our china to the woods. **1968** K. WEATHERLY *Roo Shooter* 10 He ..filled a tin mug with tea from a fire-blackened oil tin that served as his billy. With the pint in his hand he sat down again.

c. *ellipt.* A pint of ale or beer, or other liquor.

1742 FIELDING *J. Andrews* I. II. ii. 142 He wished to find a house of publick Entertainment where he might have dried his clothes and refresh himself with a Pint. *Ibid.* iii. 144 He had just entered the House, had called for his Pint. **1767** S. PATERSON *Another Trav.* II. 209 'Ere I had finished my pint. **1861** GEO. ELIOT *Silas Marner* i. 7 He never strolled into the village to drink a pint at the Rainbow. **1922** JOYCE *Ulysses* 20 The sacred pint alone can unbind the tongue of Dedalus. **1952** 'J. TEY' *Singing Sands* xii. 205 Eventually he had Richards to himself in a corner with a pint. **1965** V. CANNING *Whip Hand* i. 10, I had a pint with him. **1976** W. J. BURLEY *Wycliffe & Schoolgirls* iv. 86 Middle-aged men whose wildest excess was a couple of pints at the local.

d. *attrib.* and *Comb.*, as ***pint-bottle, -cup, -glass, -measure, mug, -stoup, -vessel.*** See also PINT-POT.

1502 *Acc. Ld. High Treas. Scot.* II. 295 For ane tyn quart and ane poynt stopes. **1633** *Fife Witch Trial* in *Statist. Acc. Scot.* (1796) XVIII. App. 660 His hand swelled as great as a pint-stoup. **1713** T. CAVE *Let.* 16 Jan. in M. M. Verney *Verney Lett.* (1930) I. xiii. 244 The London Postmaster, who yet swallow'd down a pint glass of Ale to the poor Boy's health. **1771** SMOLLETT *Humph Cl.* 8 Aug. Let. i, Mr. Fraser called for pint-glasses. **1800** J. WOODFORDE *Diary* 19 Oct. (1931) V. 279 Miss Emeris sent us a Pint Bottle of Mushrooms. **1827** CLARE *Sheph. Cal.* 56 Clouded pint-horn with its copper rim. **1838** LYTTON *Alice* III. ix, I have no sympathy left for those who creep into the pint-bottle, or swallow the naked sword. **1847** DICKENS *Dombey & Son* (1848) xxxviii. 380 This profound reflection Mr. Toodle washed down with a pint mug of tea. **1856** —— in *Househ. Words* 28 June 554/2 Drinking beer out of thick pint crockery mugs. **1858** LARDNER *Hand-bk. Nat. Phil.* 54 If a pint vessel be exactly filled with boiling water, it will be something less than full when it becomes cold. **1871** KINGSLEY *At Last* xi, We sat beneath the shade of a huge Bamboo clump, cut ourselves pint-stoups out of the joints. **1922** JOYCE *Ulysses* 301 The memory of the dead, says the citizen taking up his pintglass and glaring at Bloom. **1968** M. WOODHOUSE *Rock Baby* vi. 51 Binnie gave me coffee in a pint mug. **1976** *Southern Even. Echo* (Southampton) 1 Nov. 9/4 By the end they were glad they had not started with pint glasses. **1978** R. BARNARD *Unruly Son* i. 7 At the end of the bar..was one solitary young man, his eyes concentrated on his pint mug.

pint[2] (paɪnt). Also **p'int.** Repr. a vulg. and dial. (esp. U.S.) pronunc. POINT *sb.*[1]

1837 DICKENS *Pickw.* xxiii. 238 Upon all little pints o' breedin', I know I may trust you as vell as if it was my own self. **1887** *Scribner's Mag.* Oct. 476/2 Jeff looked..p'int blank gashly. **1893** H. A. SHANDS *Some Peculiarities of Speech in Mississippi* 50 *Pint*.., Negro and illiterate white for *point*. **1901** M. FRANKLIN *My Brilliant Career* xxxii. 274 The pens had not enough 'pint'. **1943** J. STUART *Taps for Private Tussie* xiii. 149 'It's wonderful, Uncle George,' I said. 'It's pint-blank right,' Grandma said. **1946** *Richmond* (Va.) *Times-Dispatch* 10 Feb. 8-B/7 The natural sequence of racing between the flags starts with the hunting field, then to point-to-points (gleefully termed 'pint-to-pints' by some), continues to the hunt meetings, and finally ends with steeplechasing.

‖**pinta**[1] (ˈpɪntə). [a. Sp. *pinta*, prop. coloured spot, a. late L. *pincta* for *picta* sb. from fem. pa. pple. of *pingĕre* to paint.] A skin-disease prevalent in Mexico, caused by *Treponema carateum*, a spirochete related to those which cause syphilis and yaws, and characterized by roughness, blotches, and ulceration of the skin.

1825 *Amer. Med. Rev.* II. 164 (*heading*) An account of the pinta, or blue-stain, a singular cutaneous disease prevailing in Mexico. **1898** P. MANSON *Trop. Diseases* xxxvii. 586 Pinta is contagious and attacks both sexes and any age. **1899** *Allbutt's Syst. Med.* VIII. 853 *Pinta*..the spotted sicknesss of tropical America. **1942** *Arch. Dermatol. & Syphilol.* XLV. 858 The discovery of a spirochete in a Cuban case of pinta by Grau Triana and Alfonso Armenteros, of Habana, Cuba, on Aug. 3, 1938 definitely settled the discussions on the causation of pinta (mal del pinto or carate). **1971** *Nature* 5 Feb. 409/2 The oldest treponemal disease known at present is pinta..which dates back 15,000 years.

pinta[2] ('paɪntə). Repr. colloq. pronunc. of *pint o'* (*of*), introduced in a National Dairy Council advertising slogan. Freq. used *ellipt.* for *pint o' milk*; also *transf.* Cf. CUPPA.

1959 *Times* 30 May 10/1 Referring in his opening speech to the 'Drinka pinta milka-day' campaign, Mr. Amory said: ..'I drink a pint and a half a day.' **1960** *Harper's Bazaar* July 16 Your daily pinta is the best glamour food there is. **1965** *Observer* (Colour Suppl.) 18 Apr. 29/3 The Lamb tavern..worth stopping at for a pinta. **1967** J. PORTER *Chinks in Curtain* i. 17 Pity they don't supply the milk of human kindness by the pinta. **1970** A. JENKINS *Drinka Pinta* xii. 129 March 1958 saw the birth of one of the most famous advertising slogans of all time: 'Drinka Pinta Milka Day'. **1971** 'H. CARMICHAEL' *Quiet Woman* x. 106 Some milkman's leaving a pinta on her doorstep every day. **1973** *Observer* (Colour Suppl.) 25 Nov. 41/2 (*caption*) The blue tit ..pierces the metal cap to get at the milk in a pinta from a Welsh dairy.

‖**pintadera** (pɪntə'dɛərə). *Archæol.* [Sp.] An instrument for painting patterns on the body.

1910 A. MOSSO *Dawn of Mediterranean Civilization* xvi. 257 The great *tholos* of Haghia Triada contains rich material for the study of *pintaderas* of the copper age. **1929** V. G. CHILDE *Danube in Prehist.* vi. 103 Painting of the person is indicated both by the figurines, ornamented in Cucuteni style, and the occurrence of clay stamps or *pintaderas*, sometimes bearing traces of red colour. **1938** *Nature* 1 Oct. 602/1 Seals that could serve as models for Danubian II 'pintaderas' were current in Crete and Asia Minor throughout the third millennium. **1970** BRAY & TRUMP *Dict. Archaeol.* 180/1 Pintaderas of both stamp and roller types occur in many American cultures.

pintado (pɪn'tɑːdəʊ). Also 7 pinthado, payntatha, pentado, pintade, (pantado), 8–9 pintada. [a. Pg. (and Sp.) *pintado* literally 'painted', also (in Pg.) a guinea-fowl, pa. pple. of *pintar* to paint:—late L. *pinctare, frequent. of *pingere* to paint, from late pa. pple. *pinct-us for *pictus*.]

†**1.** A kind of Eastern cotton cloth painted or printed in colours: chintz. Also *attrib. Obs.*

1602 in Birdwood *First Lett. Bk. E. Ind. Co.* (1893) 34, 60 ffardells.. of blewes and checkered stuffes, some fine Pinthadoes. *c* **1605** SCOT *Disc. Java* in Purchas *Pilgrims* (1625) I. 165 About their loynes a faire Pintadoe. **1628** *World Encomp. by Sir F. Drake* 90 With cloth of diuerse colours, not much vnlike our vsuall pentadoes. **1638** SIR T. HERBERT *Trav.* (ed. 2) 138 Upon the carpets were spread fine coloured pintado Table cloaths. **1665** EVELYN *Diary* 30 Dec., I supped at my lady Mordaunt's..where was a roome hung with Pintado, full of figures..prettily representing sundry trades and occupations of the Indians. **1727** W. MATHER *Yng. Man's Comp.* 409 They Import..Cotton, Yarn, Callicoes, Pintadoes.

2. A species of petrel, *Daption capensis*, also called Cape Pigeon. Now ***pintado bird, petrel.***

1611 in Purchas *Pilgrims* (1625) I. 275 Sea-fowles, to wit Penguins, Guls, Pentados, which are spotted blacke and white. **1614** *Ibid.* 528 Wee saw many Pintados, Mangareludas and other fowles. **1634** SIR T. HERBERT *Trav.* 19 The Pantado birds (like Iayes in colours) who about these remote seas are ever flying. **1703** DAMPIER *Voy.* III. I. 95 Pintado Birds, as big as Ducks. **1767** *Byron's Voy. round World* in *Hawkesworth's Voy.* I. 9 Large flocks of pintadoes, which are somewhat larger than a pigeon, and spotted with black and white. **1844** J. TOMLIN *Missionary Jrnls.* 3 A few of the pintado birds, or Cape pigeons, joined us. **1894** Pintado petrel [see PETREL].

3. The Guinea-fowl.

1666 J. DAVIES *Hist. Caribby Isles* 89 A kind of Pheasants, which are called Pintadoes, because they are as it were painted in colours. **1698** FROGER *Voy.* 10 The Island [Gorea] affords great variety of Game: Turtle-Doves, Pintades, Pigeons and Patridges. **1774** GOLDSM. *Nat. Hist.* V. 192 The Pintada [*ed.* 1862 pintado] or Guinea-Hen:..in some measure unites the characteristics of the pheasant and the turkey. **1802** BINGLEY *Anim. Biog.* (1813) II. 249 The four species of Pintado hitherto known are all natives of Africa. **1824** BURCHELL *Trav.* I. 364 The missionaries have a few domestic fowls, ducks, geese, and Guinea hens or Pintadoes.

4. 'The West Indian mackerel, *Scomberomorus regalis*' (*Cent. Dict.*).

pintail ('pɪnteɪl). [f. PIN *sb.*[1] + TAIL.]

†**1.** An alleged name of the hare. *Obs. rare*$^{-1}$.

a **1325** *Names of Hare* in *Rel. Ant.* I. 134 In the worship of the hare..The go-bi-grounde, the sittest-ille [sic: sittestille], The pintail, the toure-hohulle.

2. (In full ***pintail duck.***) A widely-distributed species of duck (*Dafila acuta*), of which the male has the tail of a pointed shape, the two middle feathers being longer than the rest. (Also applied locally in U.S. to the ruddy duck, *Erismatura rubida*, which has stiff narrow pointed tail-feathers.)

1768 PENNANT *Zool.* II. 468 Pintail duck..Mr. Hartlib.. tells us that those birds are found in great abundance in Connaught in Ireland, in the month of February only. **1774** GOLDSM. *Nat. Hist.* VI. 130 The Pintail, with the two middle feathers of the tail three inches longer than the rest. **1871** DARWIN *Desc. Man* II. xiii. 84 The male pintail-duck.. loses his plumage for..six weeks or two months. **1873** TRISTRAM *Moab* xii. 217 Flocks of mallard and pin-tail feeding among the stunted scrub.

3. A species of grouse having a pointed tail, as the pintailed sand-grouse (*Pterocles setarius*) of the Old World, and the pintailed or sharp-tailed grouse (*Pediœcetes phasianellus*) of N. America (also called ***pintail chicken***).

1879 CONDER *Tentwork Pal.* II. 99 We also saw large coveys of the sand-grouse or pintail. **1894** J. S. CRANE in *Outing* (U.S.) XXIV. 385/2 We found the pin-tails more frequently on the sides of hills, about the coolies in the rolling prairie.

4. Ironically applied to a woman.

1792 *Elvina* II. 135 They are powdered, painted, and perfumed.—I wish I could catch such a pin-tail in my house. **1882** JAGO *Cornw. Gloss.*, *Pin-tail*, a person who is very small and narrow in the hips. **1897** PHILLPOTTS *Lying Prophets* 271 (E.D.D.) A pin-tail built lass.

5. (In full ***pintail surfboard.***) A surfboard the back of which tapers to a point.

1967 J. SEVERSON *Great Surfing* Gloss., *Pintail*, a surfboard with a long, drawn-out, pointed tail. **1969** *Sunday Truth* (Brisbane) 12 Jan. 61/1 The Gold Coast City Council is 'extremely concerned' about the growing number of 'pintail' surfboards appearing on local beaches. The surfboard, with a pointed tail and a razor sharp, scythe-shaped fin, appeared as a new design this summer. **1970** *Surf International* (Austral.) I. x. 9/2 The Hawaiian pintails have flow, but that means you're tied to the wave's tempo.

So '**pintailed** *a.*, having a pointed tail; also = PIN-BUTTOCKED *a.*: see PIN *sb.*[1] 18.

1875 'STONEHENGE' *Brit. Sports* I. I. viii. §1. 111 The pin-tailed duck is also occasionally found. **1900** PHILLPOTTS *Sons Morning* 105 (E.D.D.) A poor pin-tailed wench.

pintail, erron. variant of PINTLE 2 b.

Pinteresque (pɪntə'rɛsk), *a.* [f. the name *Pinter* (see below) + -ESQUE.] Of, pertaining to, or characteristic of the British playwright Harold Pinter (b. 1930) or his works. Also *absol.* as *sb.*

1960 *Times* 28 Sept. 15/4 Mr Adrian writes with a cruel mastery of our slipshod, contemporary idioms, and the long drunken coda to his play is a comic achievement none the less impressive for its Pinteresque overtones. **1965** *Punch* 6 Oct. 507/1 The sort of everyday absurdity, in speech or action, that can now be most easily described as 'Pinteresque'. **1969** *Observer* 8 June 26/3 Jonathan..was an excellently conceived character: a psychiatric worker.., rather prissy, sweetly reasonable on the surface but with a constant hint of query—queer malice showing through... This was a potentially Pinteresque situation. **1970** *Guardian* 7 Aug. 8/4 The Pinteresque as comedy. **1974** *Listener* 13 June 754/1 Suddenly everyone..talked like overheard conversations on buses. They invented a word for it—Pinteresque.

So also **Pinterian** (pɪn'tɪərɪən) *a.*, characteristic of Pinter or his works; '**Pinterish** [-ISH[1]] *a.*, characteristic or suggestive of Pinter or his works; hence '**Pinterishness**; '**Pinterism**, Pinterish style or an instance of this.

1960 *Times* 7 Oct. 4/7 Miss Quayle as a Pinterish woman on top of a bus. **1963** *Observer* 13 Oct. 23/3 Dave Freeman's script was ingeniously Pinterish. **1967** *Listener* 1 June 727/1 *The Dick Emery Show*..contained a sketch by Harold Pinter... The sketch..was a small master-piece, quintessentially Pinterian. Two aging women have tea together, and the conversation..is about a friend who used to go to the butcher's regularly on Wednesdays but now, since she's moved, doesn't go quite so much. **1970** *Guardian* 16 Dec. 8/1 Even on a straightforward social level, I am told, events assume a Pinteresque flavour when the Pinters arrive. What is this pervasive Pinterishness? **1971** *Ibid.* 24 Sept. 10/2 A precisely structured script, only very occasionally dropping into those meaningless meanings now known as Pinterisms. **1975** *Broadcast* 3 Nov. 14/3 Old Times by Harold Pinter..seems to epitomize 'Pinterism'—relaxed circumambient dialogue with lots of significant spaces between the words.

pintid ('pɪntɪd). Also pintide. [ad. Sp. *pintide* (F. Leon y Blanco 1940, in *Méd. Revista Mexicana* XX. 240), f. *mal del pint-o* PINTA[1] + *sifil-ide* SYPHILIDE.] A lesion of the skin of the type characteristic of pinta.

1940 *Q. Cumulative Index Medicus* XXVII. 886/2 Pinta —constant presence of Treponema herrejoni in cutaneous lesions of dyschronic period of mal del pinto and in 'pintides'. **1942** *Arch. Dermatol. & Syphilol.* XLV. 849 (*caption*) Trichophytoid pintid in Cuban pinta. **1965** HARGREAVES & MORRISON *Pract. Trop. Med.* iv. 161 A secondary stage..consists of a symmetrical eruption.., consisting of macules, and miliary papules or pintids. **1973** A. WISDOM *Colour Atlas of Venereol.* 150 The primary pintide appears, usually on exposed skin surfaces, after an average incubation period of six to eight weeks.

pintle ('pɪnt(ə)l). Forms: 1–7 pintel, 4–5 pyntyl, 5– ell(e, pentill, 5–6 pyntil, -ill, -yll, pintil, 6–7 -ill, 7–8 -ell, (7–9 pintail); 6– pintle. [OE. *pintel* (*-el* perh. dim.: see -LE). Cf. OFris. *pint*, *penth*, Dan. dial. *pint*, *pintel*, LGer., Du., Ger. *pint* penis; also CUCKOO-PINT. Ulterior history uncertain. (Kilian has †*Pint. j. punt.* Punctus, cuspis: & Mentula.)]

1. The penis. Now *dial.* or *vulgar*.

a **1100** *Ags. Voc.* in Wr.-Wülcker 292/16 *Uirilius*, pintel. **1398** TREVISA *Barth. De P.R.* v. xlviii. (Bodl. MS.), Amonge þe genitals oone hatte þe pintel. *c* **1410** *Master of Game* (MS. Digby 182) xiii, A litell pyntell and a litell hangynge, smale ballokes [etc.]. ? *a* **1500** *Chester Pl.* x. 363 Dame, shew me the child here, He must hopp upon my spere, And if it any pintle beare, I must teach him a play. **1541** R. COPLAND *Guydon's Quest. Chirurg.* Kj, Questyons vpon the Anathomy of the pyntyll. *c* **1550** LLOYD *Treas. Health* B iij, The pintle and splene of an Asse.

2. A pin or bolt, in various mechanical contrivances; *esp.* one on which some other part turns, as in a hinge. Among these are:

a. *Naut.* A pin forming part of the hinge of a rudder, usually fixed on the rudder and fitting into a ring on the stern-post. **b.** *Gunnery.* (*a*) An iron pin to prevent the recoil of a cannon; (*b*) the bolt on which a chassis oscillates in traversing; (*c*) 'the iron pin in the axletree of a limber, to which the trail-eye of the gun-carriage is attached for travel' (Knight *Dict. Mech.*); (also corruptly *pin-tail*). **c.** The king-bolt upon which the axle of a carriage turns in rounding a curve.

1486 *Naval Acc. Hen. VII* (1896) 15 A pyntell & a gogeon for the Rother. **1611** COTGR., *Masles*, the pintles of a sterne; the yron pinnes that enter into the rings, or gudgeons thereof. **1627** CAPT. SMITH *Seaman's Gram.* ii. 11 The holes wherein the pintels of the murderers or fowlers goe into. **1704** J. HARRIS *Lex. Techn.* I, *Pintles* in a Ship, are those Hooks by which the Rudder hangs to the Stern-post. **1706** PHILLIPS, *Pintel* or *Pintle*, (in Gunnery) an Iron-pin that serves to keep the Gun from recoiling. **1769** FALCONER *Dict. Marine* (1789) Cc iv, The pintle..serves as an axis to the bed; so that the mortar may be turned about horizontally. **1828** J. M. SPEARMAN *Brit. Gunner* (ed. 2) 177 Number 1 orders 'Halt Limber Up':..2, 3, and 6 lift the trail and place it on the pintail. **1843** *Chamb. Jrnl.* 17 June 176/3 The pintle upon which a looking-glass swings is commonly a piece of iron wire, having a screw-thread turned at each end. **1859** F. A. GRIFFITHS *Artil. Man.* (1862) 112 The pintail of the dismounted limber. **1869** SIR E. J. REED *Shipbuild.* iv. 60 The rudder post, with its lugs for the pintles.

3. *attrib.* and *Comb.*, as ***pintle end***; †**pintle-fish**, some kind of edible fish, so called from its shape (according to Jamieson, app. either a pipe-fish or the launce or sand-eel); **pintle-hook**, the hook on the pintle of a limber to which the eye of the gun-carriage is attached (see 2 b (*c*)).

1483 *Cath. Angl.* 281/1 A Pyntelle ende, *prepucium*. *c* **1549** D. MONROE *W. Isles Scot.* (1774) 34 In this ile [Eriskeray] ther is daylie gottin aboundance of verey grate pintill fishe at ebbe seas. **1655** MOUFET & BENNET *Health's Impr.* xviii. 174 Dr. Wotton termeth it grosly the *Pintle fish*.

‖**pinto** ('pɪntəʊ), *a.* and *sb.* orig. *S. Western U.S.* [Sp. *pinto* painted, mottled:—late L. *pinctus for *pictus*, pa. pple. of *pingĕre* to paint.] **A.** *adj.* **1.** Of a horse, etc.: Mottled, piebald. Also in Comb., as ***pinto-coloured*** adj.

1865 B. HARTE in *Californian* 15 Apr. 4/1 The devil in the shape of a fleet pinto colt. **1885** B. HARTE *Maruja* iii, It was you, Pereo, who took me before you on your pinto horse. **1902** R. CONNOR *Sky Pilot* ix, A most beautiful pinto pony. **1936** D. MCCOWAN *Animals Canad. Rockies* xvi. 141 An Indian boy on a pinto pony had chased him to cover. **1966** H. MARRIOTT *Cariboo Cowboy* iii. 39, I had two saddle horses... One was a pinto-coloured gelding.

2. pinto bean, the mottled seed of a variety of the kidney bean, *Phaseolus vulgaris*, which is widely cultivated in the southwestern United States and Central America; also, the plant itself. Also *ellipt.*

1916 'B. M. BOWER' *Phantom Herd* iii. 46 A girl gave me a handful of pinto beans. **1924** W. M. RAINE *Troubled Waters* xxvii. 269 Pinto beans..were no sooner out and stacked than the men were hard at it putting in winter wheat. **1941** J. A. & A. LOMAX *Our Singing Country* III. vi. 292 When you get through, you've not got a cent To buy fat-back meat, pinto beans. **1942** [see LIMA b]. **1963** MRS. L. B. JOHNSON *White House Diary* 29 Dec. (1970) 26 There were beans (pinto beans, always), delicious barbecued spare ribs. **1969** *New Yorker* 17 May 115/1 (Advt.), Subsisting day after day on a few greens around noon..and some pinto beans in the evening. **1973** *Black Panther* 5 May 7/2 Existence has become a diet of pinto beans and rice. **1977** *New Yorker* 20 June 49/1 From a supplier in Seattle he orders hundred-pound sacks of corn, pinto beans, unground wheat.

B. *sb.* A piebald horse.

1902 R. CONNOR *Sky Pilot* ix, She sprung upon her pinto and set off down the trail.

pin-tongs to **pin-truce**: see PIN *sb.*[1] 18.

pintoresque (pɪntə'rɛsk), *a. rare.* [ad. Sp. *pintoresco* picturesque: see -ESQUE.] Picturesque, forming a suitable subject for a painting.

1969 *Daily Tel.* (Colour Suppl.) 17 Jan. 29/4 Artists abound, since the Mediterranean is almost embarrassingly *pintoresque* wherever you may decide to go.

pint-pot. A pot containing a pint; *esp.* a pewter pot of this size for beer.

[**1552** in *Bury Wills* (Camden) 115 A thre pynt pott of pewter.] **1622** ROWLANDS *Good Newes & Bad N.* 45 Tom Tempest..fel'd him with a pintpot from a forme. **1840** DICKENS *Old C. Shop* lxi, Another officer..came up with a pint-pot of porter.

b. As a nickname for a seller of beer.

1563 BECON *Display. Popish Mass* Wks. II. III. 47 b, Ye praye for..the soules of good man Rynse-pytcher and good wyfe Pyntepot. **1596** SHAKS. *1 Hen. IV*, II. iv. 438 Peace good Pint-pot, peace good Tickle-braine.

pintre, obs. form of PINE-TREE.

†**pin-tree.** *Obs.* [f. PIN *sb.*[1] or *v.*[1] + TREE, wood.] A wooden bar or barrier; ? a pinfold.
1530 PALSGR. 254/2 Pynne tree, *parquet.*

'pint-size, *a.* [SIZE *sb.*[1]] Small; also quasi-*sb.*, as a nickname for a child or small person. So **pint-sized** *a.* in same sense; also *absol.* as *sb.*; also, having a capacity of one pint.
1938 *Sun* (Baltimore) 22 Apr. 3/2 The [air] ship, just a pint-sized affair compared to the giant Hindenburg, carried only three persons. **1939** R. CHANDLER *Trouble is my Business* (1950) 17 It was large enough for a pint-sized desk. **1949** *Sun* (Baltimore) 9 Apr. 6/1 (*heading*) Opportunity for cattle breeders: the pint-size cow. **1952** B. MALAMUD *Natural* 182 A brisk, pint-size chef with a tall puffed cap on. **1955** *Granta* 26 Nov. 11/2 Gorgeous Gloria, The Pint-sized Poppet. **1959** [see NIPPER *sb.*[1] 3 b]. **1961** M. BEADLE *These Ruins are Inhabited* iii. 36 Choristers, in pint-sized caps and gowns, trotting across the bridge for Evensong. **1971** *Times* 8 Sept. 21/4 (*heading*) Merits of the pint-sized company. Next week, the Bolton Committee of Inquiry on Small Firms plans to publish the results of a survey. **1972** WODEHOUSE *Pearls, Girls & Monty Bodkin* ix. 158 Where young pint size is at a disadvantage is in never having seen Grayce when she was really rolling. **1973** M. AMIS *Rachel Papers* 20 He read with concentration, his nose perhaps six inches above the page, mouthwashing with tea from a pint-sized mug which Jenny had time and again to refill. **1973** *Guardian* 22 May 13/2 Long double-breasted riding macs for the pint-sized. **1977** *Time* 8 Aug. 28/2 Andrea McArdle, 13, star of the Broadway musical *Annie*, led her pint-size cast onto the softball diamond against the peewees of Paramount Pictures's forthcoming kiddy sequel, *The Bad News Bears in Breaking Training.*

'pin-tuck. [PIN *sb.*[1] 18.] In *Sewing*, a narrow, chiefly ornamental, tuck. Also *attrib.* So **'pin-tucked** *a.*; **'pin-tucking.**
1903 K. D. WIGGIN *Rebecca* xxvii. 285 Costumes that included..drawing of threads,..hemstitching and pin-tucking. **1906** *Times* 4 May 10/2 The fulness of the skirt closely pin-tucked to the figure in sets of three. **1921** *Daily Colonist* (Victoria, B.C.) 13 Oct. 20/1 (Advt.), Flannelette Gowns, with high or 'V' -neck..trimmed with embroidery or pin-tucks. **1932** *Daily Tel.* 23 May 6 (Advt.), Pin tucks trim the small over-sleeve. **1964** *McCall's Sewing* xv. 270/1 If a slip needs to be shortened only a slight amount, you can do it by taking several small pin tucks around the lower edge. **1973** *Times* 15 Nov. 6/1 The tailored torso..made to fit even more rigidly by vertical rows of pin tucks. **1975** *Times* 7 Oct. 11/1 Jersey long dresses with pin tucking. **1975** *New Yorker* 15 Dec. 74/2 A zip-fronted aviator jacket with pin-tuck detailing on back and sleeves. **1976** *Daily Mail* (Hull) 30 Sept. 13/8 (Advt.), Suede and Leather Pin Tuck Jackets.. From £19·95. **1976** *Ilkeston Advertiser* 10 Dec. 14/2 The bridesmaids wore Victorian style pin-tucked beige dresses.

pinule, obs. form of PINNULE.

'pin-up, *a.* and *sb.* [f. vbl. phr. *to pin up*: see PIN *v.*[1]] **A.** *adj.* **1.** Adapted for being pinned up.
1677 *Lond. Gaz.* No. 1245/4 One black Sarsenet Pin-up-Petticoat.

2. Of a photograph or other picture, designed to be fixed to a wall, etc. Also applied to a favourite or sexually attractive young person, the typical subject of such a photograph; also in extended use. Also, pertaining to or characteristic of such a picture or person.
1941 *Life* 7 July 34 Dorothy Lamour is No. 1 pin-up girl of the U.S. Army. **1943** *Sun* (Baltimore) 8 Oct. 22/6 Bob Hope, radio and film comedian, today emerged victorious as the official pin-up boy of the WAC contingents here. **1944** *Richmond* (Virginia) *Times-Dispatch* 19 May 11/5 The ex-GI's who threw away all their pin-up pictures when they came home from the war are tacking pretty photos up on their bedroom walls again. **1946** *News Chron.* 27 Feb. 1/8 The honourable lady must not take advantage of the fact that she is my pin-up girl. **1948** 'E. CRISPIN' *Buried for Pleasure* iii. 19 She had a figure like the quintessence of all pin-up girls. **1948** M. A. MICHAEL tr. *Mielche's From Santos to Bahia* vi. 142 The hard, cold eyes of the American girls, ..calculation behind their vulgar 'pin-up' smile. **1953** *Encounter* Nov. 30/1 Women's locks, or corsets, or riding boots, and even pin-up portraits, may become the object of fetishist worship. **1958** E. H. CLEMENTS *Uncommon Cold* i. 69 That pin-up girl I talked to on the pier. **1960** *News Chron.* 13 July 3/1 Gillies Pelletier,..Gillies is the pin-up boy of practically every French-Canadian female who watches television. **1963** *Times* 22 Jan. 3/4 He is the 'pin-up' cricketer of the layman as much as of the connoisseur and he will be remembered always as a player who never grew old. **1969** *New Statesman* 18 July 71/1 Aubrey Jones, when I first knew him, was the pin-up boy of the modern Tory party. **1976** T. STOPPARD *Dirty Linen* 11 The man reacting to the pin-up photograph..*Maddie* in a pin-up pose.

B. *sb.* A pin-up photograph; the subject of such a photograph; also *transf.*
1943 *Yank* 30 Apr. 17/1 The yeoman who did all the worrying about this week's Coast Guard issue roared quite emphatically that this week's pin up would have to have his approval. **1945** *Times* 4 Jan. 5/4 There is always room for a 'pin-up' or a photograph. **1951** J. B. PRIESTLEY *Festival at Farbridge* II. ii. 281 I'll bring the two winsome pin-ups with me and we'll all have lunch. **1957** R. HOGGART *Uses of Literacy* vii. 175 Pin-ups used to be, and still are, standard decoration for servicemen's billets and the cabs of lorries. *Ibid.* 178 Sometimes a male pin-up for the ladies is produced. **1970** *Daily Tel.* 13 Jan. 14/6 He has since become the leading figure—the political pin-up—of the new régime. **1971** B. W. ALDISS *Soldier Erect* 61 Next morning before parade, I stuck the crumpled picture of the monkey god on the wall beside the bed, next to the pin-ups of Ida Lupino and Jinx Falkenberg. **1972** J. MCCLURE *Caterpillar Cop* ii. 15 The hundreds of murders committed for profit by writers ..kept things going, just like those pin-ups in Antarctic weather stations. **1979** 'M. YORKE' *Death on Account* xiii. 129 No pin-ups of nudes. It's like a monk's cell.

pin-vice, -weed, -wire, etc.: see PIN *sb.*[1] 18.

pin-wheel, *sb.* [f. PIN *sb.*[1] + WHEEL.]
1. a. 'A wheel in the striking train of a clock in which pins are fixed to lift the hammer' (F. J. Britten *Watch & Clockmakers' Handbk.* 196). **b.** 'A contrate wheel in which the cogs are pins set into the disk' (Knight *Dict. Mech.*).
1704 J. HARRIS *Lex. Techn.* I. s.v. *Striking-wheel*, In 16 Days Clocks, the first or great Wheel is usually the Pin-wheel; but in Pieces that go 8 Days, the second Wheel is the Pin-wheel or Striking-wheel. *c* **1790** IMISON *Sch. Art* I. 276 This wheel, thus with pins, is called the striking-wheel, or pin-wheel. **1825** J. NICHOLSON *Operat. Mechanic* 496 This single wheel serves the purpose of count-wheel, pin-wheel, detent-wheel, and the fly-wheel. **1884** F. J. BRITTEN *Watch & Clockm.* 196 The escape wheel of a Pin Wheel Escapement.

2. A firework in which the composition is contained in a long case wound spirally about a disk, which is supported upon a pin, and revolves like a wheel on being ignited; a small catherine-wheel.
1869 *Routledge's Ev. Boy's Ann.* 629 The pretty little catherine-wheel, or pin-wheel. **1869** ALDRICH *Story of Bad Boy* 92 The smaller sort of fireworks, such as pin-wheels, serpents, double headers.

3. A revolving circular wooden box or drum, with wooden pins projecting from the inner surface, in which hides are washed or softened in warm water or other liquid; also called *pin-mill.*
1885 NEWHALL in *Harper's Mag.* Jan. 275/2 The hides next pass into a queer-looking contrivance known as a 'pin-wheel', a stout circular wooden box, in which they are churned about in warmish water, dropping upon stout wooden pins attached to the circumference.

Hence **'pin-wheel** *v.*, (*a*) *trans.*, to subject (hides) to the action of a pin-wheel (sense 3); (*b*) *intr.*, to rotate in the manner of a pin-wheel (sense 2); also *fig.*
1885 NEWHALL in *Harper's Mag.* Jan. 276/2 Hides.., after having been..pin-wheeled,..are put under a 'scourer'. **1942** W. FAULKNER *Go down, Moses* 149 The shrill, frantically pinwheeling little dog. **1951** J. STEINBECK *Burning Bright* I. 12 The shrill band played the march of elephants and white horses, giraffes and hippopotamuses and pin-wheeling clowns. **1952** *Chambers's Jrnl.* Apr. 235/1 So he let fly at the nearer of them, and saw her tumble in the air, then pinwheel earthwards. **1976** W. GREATOREX *Crossover* 188 Memories pin-wheeled through Pavel's mind. **1977** D. BENNETT *Jigsaw Man* xii. 225 Strangely unrelated incidents pinwheeled through Farquar's mind.

pinwhites: see PINNED *ppl. a.* 5.

pin-winged to **pinnworm:** see PIN *sb.*[1] 18.

'pin-work, *sb.* [f. PIN + WORK.] The small fine raised parts of a design in needle-point lace.

'pin-work, *v.* [f. PIN *sb.*[1] + WORK *v.*] *trans.* To work (flax-yarn) on a stout wooden pin, by jerking and twisting, so as to make it supple.
1875 *Ure's Dict. Arts* II. 450 In order to give the yarns that soft and mellow feel so agreeable and characteristic of flax yarns, the hanks when brought from the drying are what is called slaken down and pin-worked.

pinxter, variant of PINKSTER.

Pinxton ('pɪŋkstən). The name of a town in Derbyshire used *attrib.* to designate a soft-paste porcelain made there from 1796 to 1813. Also quasi-*adj.*
1802 in C. L. Exley *Pinxton China Factory* (1963) 60 To be Sold by Auction, by Blackwell & Co. At their Auction Rooms, Long Row, Nottingham. Six Crates of Pinxton China and Earthenware. **1876** J. HASLEM *Old Derby China Factory* 244 In the general run of Pinxton patterns gold was rarely used, the edging being usually in blue. **1928** W. B. HONEY *Old Eng. Porc.* xi. 201 Some cups and saucers at South Kensington..were 'authenticated' as Pinxton by John Haslem. *Ibid.*, The later Pinxton porcelain may be well studied in Mr. Herbert Allen's collection. **1963** C. L. EXLEY *Pinxton China Factory* iii. 18 It is..likely that the elaborate gilding, so characteristic of the finest Pinxton ware, must have been reduced to a minimum during the last twelve months of Billingsley's connection with the factory. **1966** G. A. GODDEN *Illustr. Encycl. Brit. Pott. & Porc.* 257 Typical Pinxton porcelain is similar to puce-marked Derby porcelain of the 1790–1800 period. **1974** —— *Brit. Porc.* 351 Several examples featured as Pinxton in various books have every appearance of being of Coalport manufacture. **1976** *Times* 26 Oct. 16/4 A pair of Pinxton tapering beakers.

piny, U.S. and dial. variant of PEONY.

piny ('paɪnɪ), *a.* Also **piney.** [f. PINE *sb.*[2] + -Y. Cf. *briny, spiny.*] Abounding in, covered with, or consisting of pine-trees; of or pertaining to a pine-tree.
1627 MAY *Lucan* I. 419 The loud blast of Thracian Boreas On piny Ossa. *a* **1700** DRYDEN *Ovid's Met.* I. 282, I..Then cross'd Cyllene, and the piny shade. **1727–46** THOMSON *Summer* 1304 The piny top Of Ida. **1751** J. BARTRAM *Observ. Trav. Pennsylv.*, etc. 72 We rode over some stony poor land, then piney, white oak, and some middling land. **1809**, etc. [see PINEY WOOD]. **1849** RUSKIN *Sev. Lamps* vi. §1. 162 The rise of the long low lines of piny hills. **1863** LONGF. *Birds Killingw.* xiii, The green steeples of the piny wood. **1882** MRS. B. M. CROKER *Proper Pride* II. v. 88 She liked their aromatic piny smell. **1931** S. JAMESON *Richer Dust* xiv. 421 The water in the bath was faintly brown. The warm piney water soothed her. **1959** C. OGBURN *Marauders* ii. 37 Meredith had been at Fort Benning,..and his class..'had had an exercise in weapons placement out in some ol' piney hills'.

Pinyin (pɪn'jɪn). Also **Pin-yin, Pin-Yin.** [a. Chinese *pin-yin*, lit. 'spell sound'.] A system of Romanized spelling for the Chinese language, adopted officially by the People's Republic of China in stages since 1958. Also *attrib.*
[**1959** W. SIMON *Chinese Radicals & Phonetics* (rev. ed.) 432 A further Scheme, apparently to be regarded as final,.. on 11th February 1958 was approved by the Fifth Session of the First National People's Congress. Its Chinese name is Hanyu-Pinyin-Fang'an..(Chinese Language Spelling Scheme).] **1963** *McGraw-Hill Mod. Chinese-Eng. Dict.* p. iii/2 The Pinyin romanization, or 'phonetic construction', using the Roman alphabet, is very similar to the Wade-Giles system which has been standard in the Western world till very recently. **1972** *Computers & Humanities* VII. 262 The romanization system used in this article is Pinyin, adopted by the People's Republic of China as its official transcription system. **1974** *Encycl. Brit. Macropædia* XVI. 801/1 The Pin-yin system indicates unaspirated stops and affricatives by means of traditionally voiced consonants. **1977** *Daily Tel.* 10 Jan. 4/5 Primary school children are taught the 'Pin-Yin' system of writing the Peking dialect in the Roman alphabet before they tackle the more difficult system of Chinese characters. *Ibid.*, Most Chinese adults cannot read 'Pin-Yin' on its own. **1979** *China Now* Jan.–Feb. 9/1 The State Council has issued a document stipulating that *pinyin* romanization is 'suited to all languages using the Roman alphabet'.

pinyon, var. PIÑON.

piny resin, etc.: see PINEY.

‖**piob mhor** (piːp 'vɔər, ˌpiːəb voːr). [Gael., lit. 'big pipe'.] The Highland pipes, the bag of which is blown by a long pipe with a mouthpiece (see quot. 1954).
1838 A. MACKAY *Coll. Anc. Piobaireachd or Highland Pipe Music* 5 When the infirmities accompanying a protracted life, prevented him handling his favourite *Piob-mhor*, he would sit on the sunny braes, and run over the notes on the staff. **1845** *New Statistical Acct. Scotl.* XIV. 339 The names of some of the caves and knolls in the vicinity still point out the spots where the scholars used to practise, respectively on the chanter, the small pipe, and the *Piob mhor*, or large bagpipe. **1901** W. L. MANSON *Highland Bagpipe* i. 10 The *Piob Mohr* is not now an agency to be reckoned with by any one who wishes to explore the hills and glens... As a Highland war spirit, its glory has departed. **1920** *Glasgow Herald* 1 May 6 The clan is no more..; but the piobmohr [*sic*] remains.., and in its music there may be heard..the romance, and the tragedy, and the beauty of the story of the Scottish Highlands. **1954** *Grove's Dict. Mus.* (ed. 5) I. 345/2 The Highland pipe (*piob mohr*) is pre-eminently the martial instrument... The oldest known existing instrument is dated 1409... It now consists of a sheepskin bag into which are tied five stocks, which accommodate the three drones and the chanter with their reeds, and the blow-pipe. **1968** J. ARNOLD *Shell Bk. Country Crafts* 316 At this juncture it is convenient to define the features which distinguish the various pipes to be heard in Britain. They are the Great Pipes, or Piob Mhor, the Reel Pipes, [etc.]. *c* **1970** A. MACPHEE *Story of Scottish Highland Bagpipe* (An Comunn Gaidhealach) 5 The renaissance of interest over the past century in the 'piob-mhor' is in great measure due to the interest of the Army. **1975** F. COLLINSON *Bagpipe* 114 The contrast between the pastoral English bagpipe and the war-like Highland *piob-mhór.*

‖**piolet** (pjɔlɛ). [F., prop. Savoy dial. *piolet*, dim. of *piolo*, app. cognate with F. *pioche, pic.* Cf. med.L. *piola*, rabot, plane, scraper; also a kind of sword (Du Cange).] An ice-axe used by Alpine climbers.
1868 T. G. BONNEY *Alpine Regions* xii 323 If you intend to wander much on the glaciers without guides,..a *piolet* is preferable [to the alpenstock]. **1887** *Pall Mall G.* 3 Sept. 11/2 The old guides..stood at ease leaning on their piolets. **1902** *Daily Chron.* 19 Aug. 5/7 All three..had barely time to plant their piolets in the ice and fasten the cord before they were carried to the brink of a precipice.

pion ('paɪɒn). *Nuclear Physics.* [f. PI(-MESON + -ON[1].] Any of a group of mesons that have masses of approximately 140 MeV (270 times that of the electron), zero spin, zero hypercharge, and isospin of 1, and on decaying usually produce a muon and a neutrino (in the case of charged pions) or two photons (in the case of the neutral pion); a pi-meson.
1951 *Sci. News* XXI. 21 The mass of π-mesons, or pions as they are called in short,..appears to be in the neighbourhood of 276 times that of the electron. **1958** *Spectator* 13 June 778/3 The Japanese physicist Yukawa has shown that what causes the neutrons and the protons of the atomic nucleus to cling together with such tenacity are the revolving pions that link them. **1968** M. S. LIVINGSTON *Particle Physics* vi. 124 The neutral pion π^0 can be formed through the charge-exchange process $\pi^- + p \rightarrow n + \pi^0$ following capture of the π^- in a Bohr orbit (i.e., in liquid hydrogen). The π^0 decays promptly (10^{-16} sec) into two photons. **1971** P. E. HODGSON *Nucl. Reactions* ii. 37 The interaction of fast pions with nuclei can also give information on the relative extent of the neutron and proton distributions in matter. **1975** *Daily Colonist* (Victoria, B.C.) 26 Jan. 14/2 The new 17-foot-long generator shoots out

pions or sub-atomic particles generated by a high-energy accelerator.

Hence **pi'onic** *a.*, of, pertaining to, or involving a pion, or an atom having a negative pion orbiting the nucleus.

1960 P. ROMAN *Theory Elem. Particles* v. 511 All pionic interactions are of the same strength. **1967** J. C. SENS in G. Alexander *High Energy Physics & Nucl. Struct.* II. 117 In muonic atoms, the muon samples the distribution of *charge* in the nucleus; in pionic atoms the pions form in addition a probe for the nuclear *mass* distribution, through the strong interactions. **1970** D. F. JACKSON *Nucl. Reactions* x. 230 Additional information about the pion-nucleus interaction can be obtained from studies of pionic atoms and pionic x-rays.

†**'pion,** *v. Obs.* [a. OF. *pion-er, piouner* intr. to pick, dig, trench, excavate (1469 in Godef.), f. *pion* a foot-soldier: see PEON, PIONEER.] *trans.* and *intr.* To dig, trench, excavate; to do the work of a pioneer. Hence **'pioning** *vbl. sb.*

1590 SPENSER *F.Q.* II. x. 63 With painefull pyonings From sea to sea he heapt a mightie mound. **1609** BP. W. BARLOW *Answ. Nameless Cath.* 13 To remooue the Crime from the Iesuites, the Principall Instigators of the Pioning Traitors to the Act. **1643** T. GOODWIN *Van. Thoughts* 27 He'll digge and fall a pioning, with his thoughts, his engins, in the night. **1656** SIR T. BROWNE *Let. to Dugdale* 10 Nov., Wks. (Bohn) III. 405 The clearing of woods and making of passages, [and] all kind of pyoning and slavish labour.

pion, obs. form of PEON.

†**pionade.** *Obs.* Forms: 4 pionad, pyonad. [? f. ME. *pione*, PEONY + -ADE.] Some kind of confection. (Perh. containing or flavoured with peony-seeds: see PEONY.)

1302-3 *Durham Acc. Rolls* (Surtees) 504 In iiij pixidibus de pionad, xij s. **1310** *Acc. Exors. T. Bp. of Exeter* (Camden) 9 De iij pixidibus de gengebrad et pyonad venditis.

pione, pionee, obs. forms of PEONY.

†**'pioned,** *ppl. a. Obs.* [? f. PION *v.*] ? Dug, excavated, trenched.

The meaning of *pioned* in the Shaks. passage has been much disputed: see Aldis Wright in Clarendon Pr. ed. 'Tempest'. (The conjecture 'overgrown with marsh-marigold', offered in *Edin. Rev.* Oct. 1872, 363, and adopted by Schmidt, etc., is not supported by any sense of *peony*, known to Britten and Holland *Eng. Plant names*, or to *Eng. Dial. Dict.*) Bulwer's fig. use in quot. 1650, rendering *demissos* 'sloping down, low', is also obscure.

1610 SHAKS. *Temp.* IV. i. 64 Thy bankes with pioned, and twilled brims Which spungie Aprill at thy hest betrims. **1650** BULWER *Anthropomet.* 163 Terence in the description of a handsome slender woman, makes her to have *demissos humeros*, as it were Pion'd shoulders.

pioneer (paɪə'nɪə(r)), *sb.* Forms: 6 pianer, *Sc.* pean-, pyonar, 6-7 pion(n)er, pyoner, -eer, 7 pionor, -ier, pyonier, *Sc.* -eir, 6- pioneer. [a. F. *pionnier*, OF. *paonier* (11th c.), also *peon(n)ier, pion(n)ier*, orig. foot-soldier, later pioneer, f. OF. *peon, pion*: see PEON, PAWN, and -IER. So Prov. *pezonier, pessonier*, f. *pezon* foot-soldier.]

1. *Mil.* One of a body of foot-soldiers who march with or in advance of an army or regiment, having spades, pickaxes, etc. to dig trenches, repair roads, and perform other labours in clearing and preparing the way for the main body.

1523 LD. BERNERS *Froiss.* I. cccxlviii. 555 The erle..sent great nombre of pioners and men of armes to assyste them. **1533** *Acc. Ld. High Treas. Scot.* VI. 160 Item, to xxiiij peanaris to pas with the artailȝerie. *a* **1548** HALL *Chron., Hen. V* 56b, Withal diligence the pyoners cast trenches. **1560** DAUS tr. *Sleidane's Comm.* 259, I wold first..bring ye pionners to cast down their trenches. **1590** NASHE *Psquil's Apol.* I. D iij b, He cals out his Pianers, and sets Martin and Penrie a worke to vndermine it. **1617** MORYSON *Itin.* II. 115 Our Pioners had been busied in fortifying and building a new Fort at Blackwater. **1626** *Proclamation* §8 in *Maldon Essex Borough Deeds* (Bundle 118 No. 13), To euery thousand Souldiers, there be allotted one hundred pioners, to be prouided with Pickaxes, Shouels, Hatchets, Bills and the like. **1768** SIMES *Mil. Medley* (ed. 2), *Pioneers* are soldiers armed with firelock..saw and hatchet... They are employed in cutting down trees, and making the roads..for the army to march. **1803** WELLINGTON in Gurw. *Desp.* (1837) I. 533 My pioneers are at work upon the Bhore Ghaut. **1844** H. H. WILSON *Brit. India* II. 70 The brigade halted, while the pioneers were busily employed in rendering the ascent practicable for laden cattle, and stores, and ammunition.

†**2. a.** *gen.* One who digs a trench, pit, etc.; a digger, excavator; a miner. *Obs.*

1572 R. H. tr. *Lauaterus' Ghostes* 73 Pioners or diggers for mettal. **1601** HOLLAND *Pliny* II. 469 An inhibition, that the publicanes who fermed that mine of the city, should not keepe aboue fiue thousand pioners together at worke there. **1640** D. WHISTLER in *Horti Carol., Rosa altera*, So when a Mine's discover'd,.. It cheeres the Pioner.

b. A labourer (app. confused with PINER[1]).

a **1651** CALDERWOOD *Hist. Kirk* (1843) II. 346 The queene caused his corps to be careid by some pyoners in the night, ..and to be layed beside the sepulchre of David Rizio.

3. *fig.* **a.** One who goes before to prepare or open up the way for others to follow; one who begins, or takes part in beginning, some enterprise, course of action, etc.; an original investigator, explorer, or worker, in any department of knowledge or activity; an originator, initiator (*of* some action, scheme, etc.); a forerunner (in such action, etc.).

In 17th c. usually a fig. use of 'miner' or 'underminer'.

1605 BACON *Adv. Learn.* II. vii. §1 To make two professions or occupations of Naturall Philosophers, some to bee Pionners, and some Smythes. **1627** HAKEWILL *Apol.* 22 The other pioner,..which by secret undermining makes way for this opinion of the Worlds decay, is an excessive admiration of Antiquitie. **1700** BLACKMORE *Paraphr. Isa.* xl. 33 Ye Pioneers of Heav'n, prepare a Road. **1768-74** TUCKER *Lt. Nat.* (1834) I. 541 Come then,..Philology, pioneer of the abstruser sciences, to prepare the way for their passage. **1836** W. IRVING *Astoria* III. 262 As one wave of emigration after another rolls into the vast regions of the west,..the eager eyes of our pioneers will pry beyond. **1856** KANE *Arct. Expl.* I. xxiii. 300 The great pioneer of Arctic travel, Sir Edward Parry. **1866** DK. ARGYLL *Reign Law* ii. (ed. 4) 111 The great pioneers in new paths of discovery. **1890** 'R. BOLDREWOOD' *Col. Reformer* (1891) 147 He made the acquaintance of more than one silver-haired pioneer.

b. *Ecol.* A plant which establishes itself in an unoccupied area.

1916 F. E. CLEMENTS *Plant Succession* x. 212 It [*sc.* the pitch pine] produces..more seed than the white pine and in its demands is better able to act as a pioneer. **1929** WEAVER & CLEMENTS *Plant Ecol.* viii. 147 The reactions of the pioneer stage may be unfavorable to the pioneers themselves. **1953** H. L. EDLIN *Forester's Handbk.* viii. 113 As a general rule, the light-demanders are also pioneers, capable..of forming a vigorous first crop on bare land. **1967** M. E. HALE *Biol. Lichens* vii. 96 Lichens are conspicuous pioneers on rocks.

c. (Usu. with capital initial.) In the U.S.S.R. and other communist countries, a member of a Society of Young Pioneers, a movement for children below the age of sixteen. Also *transf.* and *attrib.*

1929, etc. [see OCTOBERIST, -BRIST 2b]. **1930** 'I. Low' *His Master's Voice* x. 120 The streets grew merry with the drums of the pioneers, with flags, with the strains of the International. **1944** M. LASKI *Love on Supertax* v. 58 A band of children..holding a banner on which was inscribed 'St Pancras Pioneer Group'. **1957** M. PAVLOV in G. L. Kline *Soviet Educ.* 130 The Pioneers and the Komsomol members, as a rule, are atheists. **1959** A. WESKER *Chicken Soup with Barley* I. ii, in *New Eng. Dramatists* I. 193 We didn't force her to be in the pioneers... Show a young person what socialism means and he can't do anything else but accept it. **1970** N. FLEMING *Czech Point* vi. 71 As a boy he was in the Pioneers—it's a sort of boy-scout thing. **1970** *Morning Star* 11 May 4 The school has 180 pupils from the age of six to sixteen. There are 22 staff, four educators and a Pioneer organiser. **1972** *Times* 17 June 13/1 Scores of children, mostly red-neckerchiefed Pioneers, were running and scrambling over the rocky ground... They..had to climb more than 950 steps to the monument which records how a Russian army freed Bulgaria from oppression. **1973** *Listener* 2 Aug. 138/2 Another important aspect of Soviet holiday-making is the vast network of so-called Young Pioneer summer camps run for schoolchildren. **1976** 'S. HARVESTER' *Siberian Road* iv. 50 Young schoolchildren, all wearing their red Pioneer neckerchieves.

4. *attrib.* **a.** (Usually appositive, in sense 3).

1611 COTGR., *Pionnier*: m., *ere*: f., made by, or belonging to, a Pioner; Pioner-like. **1840** J. BUEL *Farmer's Comp.* 153 The pioneer-marks of improved husbandry in our own land. **1849** THOREAU *Week Concord Riv.* 359 It is the worshippers of beauty, after all, who have done the real pioneer work of the world. **1869** J. MCBRIDE (*title*) Pioneer Biography, Sketches of the Lives of some of the Early Settlers of Butler County, Ohio. **1877** J. A. ALLEN *Amer. Bison* 566 The buffaloes..have also often been invaluable to the pioneer settler. **1885** *Public Opinion* 9 Jan. 27/2 The pioneer boats of General Earle's expedition. **1890** 'R. BOLDREWOOD' *Col. Reformer* (1891) 202 The pioneer-squatter's humble woolshed. **1933** *Burlington Mag.* Nov. 193/1 Valuable pioneer work..has been done. **1965** *Eng. Stud.* XLVI. 369, I shall try to clarify the relation between my interpretation of Coleridge's poem and such pioneer-work as Lowes's associative researches.

b. (In sense 3b above) ***pioneer association, plant, species, tree.***

1932 FULLER & CONARD tr. *Braun-Blanquet's Plant Sociol.* xiv. 352 We distinguish aggressive, advancing pioneer associations and restricted, retreating relict communities. **1960** N. POLUNIN *Introd. Plant Geogr.* xiv. 456 The fringe of the mangrove, at least where it does not consist of young pioneer plants, is made up of tall trees. **1966** F. H. BRIGHTMAN *Oxf. Bk. Flowerless Plants* 199 These pioneer plants gradually break down the rock surface into fine particles. **1933** *Forestry* VII. 140 Scots pine is the native conifer of the district, and has also undeniable merits as a first crop, or pioneer species, on the..moorlands of the district. **1971** *Sci. Amer.* Sept. 129/2 Species typical of immature succession stages—'pioneer' species—are characteristically able to disperse themselves over considerable distances. **1954** S. PIGGOTT *Neolithic Cultures Brit. Isles* i. 5 Iversen has noted that birch is a 'pioneer tree' which rapidly colonizes an area after a forest fire.

pio'neer, *v.* [f. prec. sb.]

1. *intr.* To act as pioneer; to prepare the way as a pioneer. Also ***to pioneer it*** (*lit.* and *fig.*).

1780 S. J. PRATT *Emma Corbett* (ed. 4) II. 46 The veteran Carbines,..having platooned and pioneered it for a number of years. **1837** *New Monthly Mag.* LI. 199 The tutor..pushes him along the road, to pioneer for their common information. **1846** WORCESTER, *Pioneer, v.n.* to act as pioneer; to clear the way. *Qu. Rev.*

2. *trans.* To prepare, clear, open up (a way, road, etc.) as a pioneer. (*lit.* and *fig.*)

1794 BURKE tr. *Pref. to Brissot's Address* Wks. VII. 314 Crimes had pioneered and made smooth the way for the march of the virtues. **1850** BLACKIE *Æschylus* I. 318 Artificers..to pioneer the path for the procession. **1898** S. EVANS *Holy Graal* 189 In pioneering the way for future research.

3. To act as a pioneer to, be the pioneer of; to prepare the way for; to go before, lead (a person or persons in some course); to lead the way in, initiate (a course of action, etc.). Sometimes *loosely* = conduct, guide, 'pilot'.

1819 KEATS *Otho* IV. ii. 28 Or thro' the air thou pioneerest me. **1833** COLERIDGE *Table T.* 17 Aug., High and passionate rhetoric, not introduced and pioneered by calm and clear logic. **1878** A. H. MARKHAM *Gt. Frozen Sea* iv. 49 Our pilot, getting into his kayak, offered to pioneer us into a little bay. **1879** *St. George's Hosp. Rep.* IX. 764 Those who have pioneered abdominal surgery to its present position. **1886** D. C. MURRAY *First Pers. Singular* xvii. 132 She trusted to him to pioneer her about the deck. **1897** *Daily News* 10 July 4/3 My firm pioneered the nine hours movement in Scotland.

4. *Ecol. trans.* and *intr.* Of a plant, to colonize (new territory); to establish itself in an unoccupied area.

1939 H. H. BENNETT *Soil Conservation* 418 Ragweed..pioneers idle fields. **1960** N. POLUNIN *Introd. Plant Geogr.* xi. 327 Hardy Mosses..sometimes pioneer on uncolonized rock surfaces.

Hence **pio'neering** *vbl. sb.* and *ppl. a.*

1816 BENTHAM *Chrestom.* 239 By successive labourers of this pioneering class, the road is made gradually smoother. **1875** *Carpentry & Join.* 6 The axe is..the pioneering instrument and most faithful ally of man in founding himself a home. **1899** CHEYNE in *Expositor* Apr. 257 Pioneering critics ought not to be unaware of the results of their predecessors.

pio'neerdom. *rare.* [f. PIONEER *sb.* + -DOM.] The condition or state of a pioneer; a prevalence of pioneers.

1873 *Porcupine* 13 Sept. 379/2 A..Californian, who had arrived..from the States, close on to the age of pioneerdom.

pio'neership (-ʃɪp). [f. PIONEER *sb.* + -SHIP.] The function or action of a pioneer.

1834 *Fraser's Mag.* IX. 172 His fine genius was..employed in a kind of pioneership for our present admirable rulers.

†**pionery.** *Obs.* Also 6 -arie. [a. OF. *pionnerie, pionerie* (1332 in Godef.), f. *pion(n)ier* PIONEER.] **a.** The work or business of a (military) pioneer. **b.** The tools collectively of a pioneer. Also *fig.* or *allusively*.

1562 LEIGH *Armorie* 14 The significations of this colour Sable..with Or, honor with long lyfe..with Sanguine, prosperous in Pionarie. **1650** W. BROUGH *Sacr. Princ.* (1659) 228 The art is his pionery to undermine gluttony. **1654** GAYTON *Pleas. Notes* II. i. 33 Chirurgions..with..tooth-pick-axes, tooth-mattocks, and all manner of mouth-Pionery.

pioney, -ie, -y, obs. forms of PEONY.

pionization (paɪɒnaɪ'zeɪʃən). *Nuclear Physics.* [f. PION + -IZATION.] The production of numerous low-energy pions by the collision of two high-energy nucleons.

1964 *Mat.-Fys. Meddelelser K. Danske Vidensk. Selskab* XXXIII. xv. 8 The calculation of the relative importance in the cosmic radiation of mesons generated by nucleons in pionization and mesons generated in the deexcitation of baryon states is straightforward on the basis of this model. **1974** FRAUENFELDER & HENLEY *Subatomic Physics* xii. 343 At ultrahigh energies, the interaction of two nucleons can indeed be a spectacular event... Most of the secondaries are pions. In the c.m. of the colliding protons, nearly all the pions have small momenta. The formation of such a pion cloud is called pionization.

piopio ('pju:pju:, ‖'piɔpiɔ). [Maori.] A small New Zealand bird, *Turnagra capensis*, resembling a thrush and belonging to the subfamily Pachycephalinæ, the whistlers or thickheads; also called the native thrush.

1873 W. L. BULLER *Hist. Birds N.Z.* 136 The silvery notes of the Bell-bird, the bolder song of the Tui,..and the whistling cry of the Piopio—all these voices of the forest are blended together. **1938** M. GORDON *Children of Tane* vi. 160 The southern Piopio has been more often encountered than the northern. **1969** J. FISHER et al. *Red Bk.* 301/1 The piopio is certainly very rare indeed; but just how rare it is can only be discovered by hard field studies on both North and South Island of New Zealand, in each of which a race survives.

pioscope ('paɪəskəʊp). [irreg. f. Gr. πῖον (sc. γάλα) rich milk (neut. of πίων fat) + -SCOPE.] A form of lactometer invented by Heeren, in which the purity of milk is tested by comparing its colour, as seen through the uncoloured part of a plate of glass, with the colours of sectors of the plate painted in various shades from whitish-grey to deep bluish-grey.

1884 in KNIGHT *Dict. Mech.* Suppl. **1895** *Syd. Soc. Lex.*, *Pioscope*, a form of *Lactometer*.

piosity (paɪ'ɒsɪtɪ). [f. PIOUS *a.* + -ITY, after RELIGIOSITY.] Affected or excessive piousness, sanctimoniousness; an instance of this.

1922 *Contemp. Rev.* Sept. 353 The lack of such faith means, and has meant, the reduction of morality to piosity, convention, legality. **1961** *Spectator* 1 Dec. 824 The pall of piosity and ambition lifts from the family. **1975** *Church Times* 31 Jan. 14/5 God forbid that we should use over-devotional words or piosities about the Lord's life.

piot, variant of PIET, magpie, etc. **pioted**, **piotty**, *a. Sc.*, pied (in colour), piebald.

1818 SCOTT *Hrt. Midl.* xxvii, Wi' the lad in the pioted coat.

‖**piou-piou** (pjupju). [Fr.] A popular name for a French private soldier.

1854 B. ST. JOHN *Purple Tints of Paris* II. xi. 224 Formerly, a *piou-piou*—as the common soldier was somewhat contemptuously called—was treated.. with a sort of paternal solicitude. **1867** 'OUIDA' *Under Two Flags* I. xiii. 300 The speaker looked down on the *piou-piou* with superb contempt. **1894** [see NOUNOU]. **1900** R. WHITEING *Life of Paris* 207 Polin.. figures as the common soldier, the pioupiou, with his simple virtues of good-humour and fidelity to the flag. **1930** [see NOUNOU].

pious ('paɪəs), *a.* [f. L. *pi-us* dutiful, pious + -OUS: cf. mod.F. *pieux, -euse* (R. Estienne 1539), which may have been the model.]

1. 'Careful of the duties owed by created beings to God' (J.); characterized by or showing reverence and obedience to God (or the gods); faithful to religious duties and observances; devout, godly, religious. **a.** Of persons.

pious founder, the founder of a college or other endowment for the glory of God and the good of his fellow-men.

1603 SHAKS. *Meas. for M.* I. iii. 16 Now (pious Sir) You will demand of me, why I do this. **1605** —— *Macb.* III. vi. 27. **1616** BULLOKAR *Eng. Expos., Pious*, godly, vertuous. **1627** BALCANQUAL *Stat. Heriot's Hosp. Edinb.* ii, The bountiefull mantenance which they living thair receave from the charitie of thair pious founder. **1628** WITHER *Brit. Rememb.* 8 For we doe reade, that Kings who pioust were Had wicked subjects. *a* **1715** BURNET *Own Time* (1823) IV. 47 Mackay.. was the piousest man I ever knew. **1746** WARTON *Progr. Discontent* 120 And din'd untax'd untroubled, under The portrait of our pious founder. **1763** JOHNSON 1 July in *Boswell*, Campbell is a good man, a pious man.. he never passes a church without pulling off his hat. **1838** DICKENS *Nich. Nick.* iv, I asked one of your references, and he said you were pious. **1860** EMERSON *Cond. Life, Fate* Wks. (Bohn) II. 321 What pious men in the parlour will vote for what reprobates at the polls!

b. Of actions, things, etc.

1602 SHAKS. *Ham.* III. i. 48 'Tis too much prou'd, that with Deuotions visage, And pious Action, we do sugre o're The diuell himselfe. **1628** WITHER *Brit. Rememb.* 200 Those thy gifts that cary The pioust showes have scarce been voluntary. **1678** MARVELL *Growth Popery* Wks. (Gros.) IV. 257 That so great a part of the land should be alienated.. to, as they call it, *Pious Uses*. **1781** CRABBE *Library* 502 Old pious tracts, and Bibles bound in wood. **1874** J. SULLY *Sensation & Intuition* 116 Pious attempts to coerce belief.

c. Of fraud or the like: Practised for the sake of religion or for a good object, or 'under the appearance of religion' (J.): see also FRAUD *sb.* 3 c.

1637 R. HUMPHREY tr. *St. Ambrose* II. 43 He sought the presence of his deare brother Benjamin by a pious kind of fraud. **1660** tr. *Amyraldus' Treat. conc. Relig.* III. x. 512 Which are.. Pious Frauds (as they speak) useful to very advantageous effects. **1678**- [see FRAUD *sb.* 3 c]. **1813** *Gen. Hist.* in *Ann. Reg.* 9/2 The necessity under which judges and juries so frequently laboured, of committing what had been called pious perjuries.

d. Phr. ***pious hope***, an extravagant or unrealistic hope expressed in order to preserve an appearance of optimism.

1907 R. FRY *Let.* 3 Apr. (1972) I. 283 Mr Morgan.. secured three [pictures] for himself and expressed a pious hope that the Museum might be able to buy the rest! **1931** *Economist* 11 Apr. 773/2 That this, as the phrasing suggests, is only a pious hope is apparent when the attitude of the three main groups of countries concerned is considered. **1977** *N.Y. Rev. Bks.* 15 Sept. 15/1 The pious hope—by no means an assumption—that the biographer's psychological acuity, powers of empathy, respect for fact, general culture, and sense of proportion would prevent the appearance of yet one more in a series of glib psychobiographies. **1978** LD. DROGHEDA *Double Harness* xxi. 288 Despite all the pious hopes, disappointments persisted.

2. Faithful to the duties naturally owed to parents, relatives, friends, superiors, etc.; characterized by loyal affection, esp. to parents; dutiful, duteous. Of persons (also of birds), or actions, etc. Now *rare* or *arch.*

1626 MASSINGER *Rom. Actor* II. i, May it succeed well, Since my intents are pious! **1634** SIR T. HERBERT *Trav.* 59 White marble Pillars, a top of which now inhabit the pious Storkes. **1703** ROWE *Ulyss.* II. i. 765 Love and willing Friendship Employ their pious Offices in Vain. **1819** KEATS *St. Agnes* xxii, With.. pious care She.. the aged gossip led.

piously ('paɪəslɪ), *adv.* [f. prec. + -LY².] In a pious manner; with pious motive or intention; devoutly, religiously; loyally, dutifully (*arch.*).

1611 COTGR., *Pieusement*, piously, religiously, deuoutly, holily. **1634** W. TIRWHYT tr. *Balzac's Lett.* (vol. I) 207 You are piously to believe divers sots to be sufficient men, since the world will have it so. **1741** MIDDLETON *Cicero* II. viii. 180 She was most affectionately and piously observant of her Father. **1788** GIBBON *Decl. & F.* I. (1846) V. 19 A royal captive was piously slaughtered by the prince of the Saracens, the ally and soldier of the emperor Justinian. **1887** RUSKIN *Præter.* II. 126 If you do a foolish thing, you suffer for it exactly the same, whether you do it piously or not.

Comb. **1697** BURGHOPE *Disc. Relig. Assemb.* 13 The piously-inclin'd may be directed in so great a duty. **1870** J. H. NEWMAN *Gram. Assent* I. iv. 55 The mass of piously-minded.. people in all ranks.

'**piousness.** *rare.* [f. as prec. + -NESS.] The quality or character of being pious; piety.

1623 SIR E. DIGBY *Sp.* in Rushw. *Hist. Coll.* (1859) I. 133 Heaven be pleased to crown his Actions with success as the piousness of his Intentions deserves. **1660** BONDE *Scut. Reg.* 347 No wonder if the Malignant Cavaleers do reproach and vilifie our piousness.

pip (pɪp), *sb.*¹ Forms: 5–6 pyppe, 5–7 pippe, 6 pype, 6–7 pipe, pipp, 6- pip. [app. a. MDu. *pippe* (*pipse*), Du. *pip* = MLG., EFris. *pip*, LG. *pipp*, Ger. *pips*, *pipps* from LG., formerly *pfipps*, *pfipfs*, OHG., MHG. *pfiffiz*, *pfiffiz*, *pfipfiz* = WG. type **pipit*, a. pop.Lat. *pīpīta*, *pipīta*, whence also Sard. *pibida*, Cat. *pebida* Rhæt. *pivida*, Lomb. *pevida*, *puvida*, *püida*, Pg. *pivide*, *pevide*, and (of learned or semi-popular origin), It. *pipita*, Sp. *pepita*, Pr. *pepida*, F. *pepie*, *pépie*. Pop.L. *pipīta* appears to have been an unexplained alteration of *pītuīta* in same sense.]

a. A disease of poultry and other birds, characterized by the secretion of a thick mucus in the mouth and throat, often with the formation of a white scale on the tip of the tongue (hence sometimes applied to this scale itself). Also, a similar disease of hawks.

c **1420** *Pallad. on Husb.* I. 589 Other while an hen wul ha the pippe, A whit pilet that wul the tonge enrounde. *c* **1440** *Promp. Parv.* 401/1 Pyppe, sekenesse, *pituita*. **1530** PALSGR. 254/2 Pyppe a sickenesse, *pepye*. *Ibid.* 658/1 [see PIP *v.*¹]. **1551** TURNER *Herbal* I. B v, Garlyke.. is also good for the pype or roupe of hennes and cockes, as Pliny wryteth. **1575** TURBERV. *Falconrie* 294 Sometimes also the pip in their tungs. **1614** MARKHAM *Cheap Husb.* (1623) 141 The Pippe is a white thin scale, growing on the tippe of the tongue, and will make Poultrie they cannot feede. **1781** COWPER *Conversation* 356 Faint as a chicken's note that has the pip. **1859** TENNYSON *Geraint & Enid* 274 A thousand pips eat up your sparrowhawk!

b. Applied vaguely (usually more or less humorously) to various diseases in human beings.

c **1460** *Play Sacram.* 525, I haue a master: I wolld he had yᵉ pyppe. **1553** *Respublica* III. iii. 742 Bee thei gone? fare well theye, god sende them bothe the pippe. **1583** STUBBES *Anat. Abus.* I. (1879) 78 *margin*, Beware the Spanish pip. **1591** GREENE *Art Conny Catch.* II. (1592) 17 Sometimes they catch such a spanish pip, that they haue no more hair on their heads, then on their nailes. **1697** VANBRUGH *Relapse* III. ii. 302 I'll let you know enough to prevent any wise woman's dying of the pip. **1708** MRS. CENTLIVRE *Busie Body* IV. iv, No, no, Hussy; you have the Green-Pip already, I'll have no more Apothecary's Bills. **1862** THACKERAY *Philip* xxvii, The children ill with the pip, or some confounded thing. **1864** HUXLEY in *Life* (1900) I. xviii. 250 We are all well, barring.. various forms of infantile pip.

c. Ill humour or poor health, esp. in colloq. phrs. ***to have*** (or ***get***) ***the pip***, to be depressed, despondent, or unwell; ***to give*** (someone) ***the pip***, to annoy or irritate, to make (someone) ill-tempered or dispirited.

1886–96 in Farmer & Henley *Slang* (1902) V. 210/2 It cost a bit to square up the attack; For the landlord had the pip. **1896** A. BEARDSLEY *Let.* c 17 Sept. (1971) 165 Are you suffering with a south-west wind in London? It prevails here utterly and has given me the pip. **1903** KIPLING *Traffics & Discov.* (1904) 55 What's an admiral after all?.. Why, 'e's only a post-captain with the pip. **1913** *Punch* 15 Oct. 324/3 [His] later works gave him the pure pip. **1923** WODEHOUSE *Inimitable Jeeves* iii. 36 If there's one thing that gives me the pip, it's unpleasantness in the home. **1930** J. B. PRIESTLEY *Angel Pavement* ix. 440 A proper old Jonah you're turning into! You give me the pip, Dad, honestly you do. **1932** A. J. WORRALL *Eng. Idioms* 31, I feel rotten to-day. I'm not ill, but I've just got the pip, that's all. **1934** J. RHYS *Voy. in Dark* I. iv. 53, I thought there was something about this place that gave me the pip. **1942** *R.A.F. Jrnl.* 18 Apr. 20 Dear-o-dear, he fair gave me the pip. Talk about gloom! **1949** N. MARSH *Swing, Brother, Swing* xii. 285 The Judges' Rules.. may be enlightened but there are times when they give you the pip. **1962** *Friend* 3 Aug. 962/1 The signpost to the safe way forward: 'true moral simplicity'. It just about gives me the pip. **1976** *Scotsman* 24 Dec. (Weekend Suppl.) 1/5, I feel it's my duty but I'm not keen. My grandchildren give me the pip.

pip, *sb.*² Forms: 6–7 peepe, 7 (9 *dial.*) peep, 7- pip. [Originally *peep*, which is still widely used in midland dialects; with the shortening of *peep* to *pip*, cf. the dial. *ship* for *sheep*. Origin of *peep* unknown. (Not from PIP *sb.*³ in sense 'seed of apple, etc.', which is not known till late in 18th c.)]

1. a. Each of the spots on playing-cards, dice, or dominoes.

α. **1604** MIDDLETON *Father Hubbard's T.* Wks. (Bullen) VIII. 84 Like a blank die—the one having no black peeps. **1648** HERRICK *Hesper., Oberon's Palace* 49 Those picks or diamonds in the card; With peeps of harts, of club and spade, Are here most neatly inter-laid.

β. **1674** COTTON *Compl. Gamester* xii. 121 At Fench-Ruff.. the King is the highest Card.. and all other Cards follow in preheminency according to the number of the Pips. **1755** in *Connoisseur* No. 60. 357 A gamester's mind is a mere pack of cards, and has no impressions beyond the pips and the Four Honours. **1865** *Compl. Domino-Player* 12 When one has played all his dominoes out, he counts the number of pips in the other's hand. **1880** BROWNING *Dram. Idylls, Pietro* 438 Fling.. Golden dice.. Note what sum the pips present!

†**b.** *fig.* In allusive phrases: A step, degree. ***two and thirty, a pip*** (***peep***) ***out***: an allusion to the game of cards called 'one-and-thirty'. (In quot. 1652, A very small piece, a 'scrap'.) *Obs.*

α. **1596** SHAKS. *Tam. Shr.* I. ii. 33 Was it fit for a seruant to vse his master so, being perhaps.. two and thirty, a peepe out? **1620** MIDDLETON *Chaste Maid* I. ii. 63 He's but one peep above a serving-man. **1632** MASSINGER & FIELD *Fatal Dowry* II. ii. D iij b, You thinke, because you serue my Ladyes mother, are 32 yeeres old which is a peepe out, you know. **1652** HOWELL *Giraffi's Rev. Naples* II. 11 One who had stolen but a peepe of Sausage. **1654** WHITLOCK *Zootomia* 409 How many are above one and thirty, (a Peep out) in their Estates, before they come to their one and twenty in yeares? **1693** *Humours Town* 96 The Alderman is a Peep higher.

2. A spot or speck; *spec.* a small spot on the skin; a spot on a spotted dress fabric; *pl.* specks appearing to dance before the eye. Now *dial.*

1676 WORLIDGE *Cyder* 157 Pippins.. taking their name from the small spots or pips that.. appear on the sides of the Apple. **1877** *N.W. Linc. Gloss., Pips*,.. the spots on playing cards, dominoes, and women's dresses. **1881** *Oxfordsh. Gloss., Pips*, small spots on the skin. **1881** *Leicestersh. Gloss.*, Pips.

3. a. *Gardening.* Each single blossom of a clustered inflorescence (usually, the corolla only), esp. in the cowslip and polyanthus; also *dial.* a small blossom in general.

1753 HOGARTH *Anal. Beauty* iv. 23 The pips, as the gardiners call them. **1764** ELIZ. MOXON *Eng. Housew.* (ed. 9) 147 To make Cowslip Wine. Take two pecks of peeps, and four gallons of water, put [etc.]. **1772** FOOTE *Nabob* II. Wks. 1799 II. 303 The polyanthuses.. for pip, colour, and eye, I defy the whole parish.. to match 'em. **1821** CLARE *Vill. Minstr.* I. 125 Bees in every peep did try. **1828** *Craven Gloss.* (ed. 2). *Peeps*, the flowers of cowslips detached from the calix. **1847** MRS. LOUDON *Amateur Gard.* 93/2 The heads and pips of flowers should be large and smooth. **1854** S. THOMSON *Wild Fl.* III. (ed. 4) 307 A tea being made of the dried flowers or 'pips' [of the cowslip].

b. Trade-name for the central part of an artificial flower.

4. Each of the rhomboidal segments of the surface of a pine-apple, corresponding to one blossom of the compound inflorescence from which the fruit is developed.

1833 *Penny Cycl.* I. 490/1 The Pine Apple.. what gardeners call the pips, that is to say, the rhomboidal spaces into which the surface is divided. **1840** *Ibid.* XVIII. 164/2 In the Malay Archipelago it.. sports into a variety called the double pine-apple, each pip of its fruit growing into a branch bearing a new pine-apple. **1858** HOGG *Veg. Kingd.* 764 The pine-apple is not.. one fruit, but a collection of many, what are called the pips being the true fruit.

5. *Mil.* A star or one of a group of (up to three) stars worn on the epaulettes by officers as an indication of rank. Also *transf.*

1917 W. OWEN *Let.* 23 Nov. (1967) 509, I shall soon be putting up another pip. **1918** —— *Let.* 15 July (1967) 564, I still wear one pip because nobody knows whether I am Lieut. or not. **1919** *Chamber's Jrnl.* Jan. 43/2 Thomas, his senior by one 'pip' in the battery. **1924** KIPLING *Debits & Credits* (1926) 315, I wrote the usual trimmin's.. an' what his captain had said about Bert bein' recommended for a pip. **1954** [see GONG² 2]. **1972** P. DRISCOLL *Wilby Conspiracy* (1973) xxii. 284 The authority of the two pips shining on his shoulders. **1973** D. LEES *Rape of Quiet Town* vi. 103 Despite the extra couple of pips he'd given me, I didn't feel happy about my new command. **1978** M. KENYON *Deep Pocket* i. 12 The desiccated arsehole-creeper in his new silver pips and braid.

6. a. A sharp, narrow, and usu. small spike or deflection on a line displayed on the screen of a cathode-ray tube.

1944 *Radar* Apr. 30/1 Signals appear as pips, or deflections, on the luminous trace. *Ibid.*, The range of a reflecting object is indicated by the distance of the pip from the base of the trace. **1949** D. G. C. LUCK *Frequency Modulated Radar* vii. 299 As the generator is tuned toward either limit of the sweep, these pips may be seen to approach one another on the oscilloscope. **1950** *Jrnl. Appl. Physics* XXI. 59/2 If the output frequency times three is exactly equal to the input frequency, the two pips on the scope should coincide. **1963** G. M. B. DOBSON *Exploring Atmosphere* viii. 138 The distance of the 'pip' from the starting line will be a measure of the time between the signal which started the beam moving and that which produced the 'pip'.

b. A voltage pulse.

1946 *Electronic Engin.* XVIII. 145/3 Use was made of a crystal oscillator which generated both time-base recurrence and calibration pips. **1947** *Ibid.* XIX. 9/2 The time base can be synchronised by applying a negative pip to the first grid of V_5.

7. *attrib.*, as ***pip card*** (sense 1).

1903 *Burlington Mag.* Dec. 246/1 He persuaded him.. to make the exchange with twelve figure and fourteen pip cards. **1977** *Jrnl. Playing-Card Soc.* May 30 The suit symbols and the denominations are shown as miniature cards of traditional form in the upper right-hand corner on the pip cards.

pip, *sb.*³ [app. a shortened form of PIPPIN; in sense 2, perhaps associated with PIP *sb.*² Not in Johnson, Ash, Walker, Webster 1828. In Todd 1818, as a children's word; but in use with fruit-growers in 1797. (The Sc. *paip*, *pape*, of earlier use, is not applied to the seeds of apples or oranges.)]

†**1.** Short for PIPPIN, the apple. *Obs.*

In quots. attributed as a cry to Irish costermongers.

1598 E. GILPIN *Skial.* (1878) 25 He cries oh rare, to heare the Irishmen Cry pippe, fine pippe, with a shrill accent. **1600** DEKKER *Fortunatus* Wks. 1873 I. 152 (Cry of Irish costermonger) Buy any Apples, feene Apples of Tamasco, feene Tamasco peepins: peeps feene. 1601 ? MARSTON *Pasquil & Kath.* I. 339 Hee whose throat squeakes like a treble Organ and speakes as smal and shril, as the Irish-men crie pip, fine pip.

2. a. The common name for the seeds of fleshy fruits, as the apple, pear, orange, etc. Cf. PIPPIN 1.

1797 BILLINGSLEY *Agric. Somerset* ix. 124 The favourite apple..is the *Court of Wick Pippin*; taking its name from the spot where it was first produced. It originated from the pip or seed of the golden pippin. 1808 VANCOUVER *Agric. Devon* 236 By the end of the sixth year from the time of sowing the pips. 1818 TODD, *Pip*..a kernel in an apple. So children call kernels. 1856 MRS. BROWNING *Aur. Leigh* VII. Poems (1857) 302 We divide This apple of life, and cut it through the pips. 1876 *World* V. No. 120. 13 The Queen of Navarre gave the original orange pip to her gardener in 1421. 1883 *Evang. Mag.* Oct. 461 In Blackberry and Raspberry..the 'endocarp' in both cases is the hard centre, commonly called the 'pip', and ignorantly the 'seed'.

b. Phr. *to squeeze* (someone) ***until the pips squeak*** (and variants): to exact the maximum payment from (someone), orig. with allusion to Germany's indemnity after the war of 1914–18 (see quot. 1918).

1918 *Cambridge Daily News* 11 Dec. 3/2 Sir Eric Geddes followed up his big meeting at the Guildhall on Monday night by addressing another crowded assembly in the large hall at the Beaconsfield Club on Tuesday night... Dealing with the question of indemnities, Sir Eric said: The Germans, if this Government is returned, are going to pay every penny; they are going to be squeezed as a lemon is squeezed—until the pips squeak. My only doubt is not whether we can squeeze hard enough, but whether there is enough juice. 1929 W. S. CHURCHILL *World Crisis: Aftermath* ii. 47 One Minister, reproached with lack of vim, went so far as to say 'We would squeeze the German lemon till the pips squeaked.' 1933 *Radio Times* 14 Apr. 75/1 The Lloyd George Coalition Government..elected..on a programme of hanging the Kaiser, squeezing Germany until the pips squeaked. 1940 S. SPENDER *Backward Son* 64 A clarion call to the readers of the *Daily Sketch* to make Germany pay till the pips squeak. 1973 P. O'DONNELL *Silver Mistress* v. 93 We run an inquiry on a client, and we don't squeeze him till the pips squeak... We just pressure him. 1973 *Times* 12 Nov. 19/3 In opposition..[Labour] would tax the upper working class until the pips squeak. 1978 *Times* 15 Sept. 3/3 When Mr Singer was asked how the extra money was being found, he said: 'The pips are squeaking.'

pip, *sb.*⁴ Used for *p* in telephone communications and in the oral transliteration of code messages, as in ***pip emma***, for *p.m.* (= *post meridiem*: see P II). Also occas. in colloq. use.

1913 *Signalling* (Imperial Army Series) ii. 19 The letters T, A, B, M, S, P and V will be called *toc, ack, beer, emma, esses, pip,* and *vic* respectively, so as to distinguish them phonetically from letters of similar sound. 1915 [see EMMA]. 1917 [see ACK]. 1926 [see EMMA]. 1927 W. E. COLLINSON *Contemp. Eng.* 98 Other artillery terms which spread were O pip (for 'observation post'). 1930 E. RAYMOND *Jesting Army* III. ii. 292 The working parties parade under the trees at nine o'clock pip emma... At three o'clock ac emma they will return. 1969 [see EMMA]. 1977 C. MCCULLOUGH *Thorn Birds* xv. 350 The second hand was just sweeping up to 9:40 pip-emma.

pip, *sb.*⁵ [Echoic.] A short, high-pitched sound, esp. one produced electronically; *spec.* (*a*) one broadcast as a time signal; (*b*) one transmitted over a telephone line as a signal.

1907 G. B. SHAW *Major Barbara* III. 292 *Sarah* (touching Lady Britomart's ribs with her finger tips and imitating a bicycle horn) Pip! pip! 1929 *B.B.C. Year-bk. 1930* 406 G.T.S. = Greenwich Time Signal, which takes the form of a broadcast by electrical contact of the last six seconds before the hour, the 'beat' of each second being represented by a sharp 'pip'. 1930 *Prof. Papers Inst. P.O. Electr. Engineers* No. 135. 41 There is an advantage in giving the time intimation automatically and this is being done experimentally..by means of a 'pip' signal. 1938 F. B. YOUNG *Dr. Bradley Remembers* i. 29 The six 'pips' of the time-signal sounded and the Weather Forecast began. 1946 *Electronic Engin.* XVIII. 360/2 (Advt.), The warning is given in the form of a 1,000 c.p.s. 'pip' on the loud speaker lasting ¼ second. 1951 'E. CRISPIN' *Long Divorce* xiv. 172 There are the pips... Quick, or it'll be another three minutes. 1962 A. NISBETT *Technique Sound Studio* xii. 219 One of the most characteristic sounds of early electronic works has been the use of short bursts of tone at various frequencies, sounding like a series of pips. 1967 O. LANCASTER *With Eye to Future* I. 1 With the six pips, conversation..faded away..as the announcer..began to summarize his disastrous bulletin. 1972 *Radio Times* 6 Jan. 5/3 Listeners may have noticed a change in the Greenwich Time Signals broadcast since January 1. Instead of six equal pips, the signal since 1924, there are five equal pips followed by a longer one lasting half a second. The exact time is signalled by the beginning or 'leading edge' of the long pip. 1973 *Times* 21 Sept. 5/3, I believe the call was a long-distance one. The pips are louder..if the call is local. 1977 J. WILSON *Making Hate* xiii. 155 He raced back to the telephone in the hall. When the pips went..he could hardly get his twopence in the slot.

†**pip**, *v.*¹ *Obs.* Also 6 pyppe, 7 pipp. [f. PIP *sb.*¹] *trans.* **a.** To remove the 'pip' or scale from the tongue of (a fowl): see PIP *sb.*¹ **b.** To affect with the pip.

1530 PALSGR. 658/1, I pyppe a henne or a capon, I take the pyppe from them, *je prens la pepie dune geline* or *dung chapon.* Your hennes shall never waxe faste tyll they be pypped. 1589 WARNER *Alb. Eng.* v. xxiii. 102 From which their tunes but pip their tungs and then they hang the wing.

pip, *v.*² [In sense 1, app. var. of PEEP with shortened vowel: cf. dial. *ship, kip,* etc. Sense 2 is perhaps a distinct word and onomatopœic: cf. *chip.*]

1. *intr.* To chirp as a young bird: = PEEP *v.*¹

1598 FLORIO *Worlde of Wordes* 279/1 *Pipare*, to cackle or cluck as a hen, to pip, to pule as a hawk. 1659 HOOLE *Comenius' Vis. World* (1777) 4 The chicken pippeth. 1660 BOYLE *New Exp. Phys. Mech., Digress.* 374 To hear the Chick Pip or Cry in the Egg, before the Shell be broken. 1831 CARLYLE *Sart. Res.* II. vii, Wherefore, like a coward, dost thou forever pip and whimper?

2. a. *trans.* To crack (the shell of the egg), as a young bird when hatched. So **pipped** (pɪpt) *ppl. a.*; **'pipping** *vbl. sb.*

1879 TOURGEE *Fool's Err.* (1883) 233 If one ever pipped the shell. 1886 P. S. ROBINSON *Valley Teet. Trees* 30 It is all very well for..the vernal pullet to be impudent because it pipped its shell when the crocuses were abloom. 1901 *Chambers's Jrnl.* Nov. 717/1 Gigantic incubators..literally vomiting forth their flocks of twittering little creatures at pipping-time. 1953 N. TINBERGEN *Herring Gull's World* xviii. 161 The parents would stop shifting and turning an egg when it is pipped. *Ibid.*, In most of the pipped eggs there is a line of cracks around the obtuse pole. 1962 J. C. WELTY *Life of Birds* xvi. 316/2 The first step in hatching is the puncturing, or 'pipping', of the shell by the chick with its outwardly-pressed egg tooth. 1972 L. HANCOCK *There's a Seal in my Sleeping Bag* vii. 162 This egg will hatch tonight. See, the large end is already cracked and pipped. 1972 *Sci. Amer.* Aug. 30/1 The ducklings begin to pip their eggs... As the eggs are being pipped the female clucks... When the pipping is completed, she drops back to..four calls per minute.

b. *transf.* To give birth. *colloq.*

1973 *Times* 27 Aug. 5/8 'I say, Aubrey, has your wife pipped yet?' I assumed he meant had she had her baby.

pip, *v.*³ *colloq.* or *slang.* [f. PIP *sb.*² (or *sb.*³), taken *fig.* as = small ball: cf. PILL *v.*²] **1. a.** *trans.* To blackball; to defeat, beat; to hit with a shot.

The examples in the second set owe something to the phr. *to pip at the post* (see sense c below).

1880 A. H. HUTH *Buckle* I. v. 252 If Buckle were pipped [at the Club election], they would do the same for every clergyman put up. 1891 *Pall Mall G.* 1 Oct. 1/1 Cycling..an exciting struggle at top speed resulted in A. C. Edwards just pipping A. T. Mole for first place. 1900 *Westm. Gaz.* 13 Mar. 2/2 Pipped, by Jove! At 9.25 as we were advancing I got a bullet through the leg. 1916 E. V. LUCAS *Vermilion Box* 226 Only yesterday poor Hugh Blackstone was pipped right at my side, and he lasted only ten minutes. 1917 E. F. WOOD *Notebk. of Intelligence Officer* x. 182 In that bit of trench, sir, you must bend over as you go. It is enfiladed by an enemy sniper. He 'pipped' one of our fellows through the head there yesterday. 1927 A. CHRISTIE *Big Four* xi. 141 That's my solution—Gilmour Wilson got pipped by mistake. 1932 WODEHOUSE *Hot Water* i. 19 Soup Slattery showed Mr. Carlisle the scar..where a quick-drawing householder of Des Moines, Iowa, had pipped him a couple of years back when he was visiting at his residence. 1950 PARTRIDGE *Here, There & Everywhere* 70 The remaining Tommy synonyms [for 'wounded'] are *pipped*, especially by a bullet whether of rifle, revolver, or machine-gun; *to stop one* [etc.].

1930 *Bulletin* (Sydney) 1 Jan. 35/1 He [*sc.* a race-horse] just pipped Baverarrack..for third place. 1964 *Engineering* 21 Aug. 221/3 Dick Bertram.., in Lucky Moppie, was pipped into second place by an error of navigation. 1976 *Scottish Daily Express* 24 Dec. 15/4 As anchorman, Ian Hutcheon did a magnificent job, shooting a final 71 to pip the Japs and tie for the individual section. 1977 *R.A.F. News* 11–24 May 18/4 The host station..were pipped 6–3 by Brampton.

b. To reject or disqualify; to fail (a candidate) in an examination. Of a candidate: to fail (an examination).

1908 A. S. M. HUTCHINSON *Once aboard Lugger* I. i. 31 'I had forgotten. Your examination?' George half turned away. The bitterest moment of a sad day was come. He growled: 'Pipped.' 1912 F. M. HUEFFER *Panel* I. iii. 85 Olympia was exaggerating... I wasn't going blind. I was only pipped for active service. 1973 *Daily Tel.* 17 Oct. 15/1 School-leavers who were unfortunate enough to pip all or some of their O or A levels will have been seeking a second chance without having to return to school.

c. To anticipate or forestall (someone) in a particular activity, circumstance, etc.; *spec.* in phr. ***to pip at*** (or ***on***) ***the post***, to defeat by a narrow margin at the last moment; also *ellipt.*

1924 WODEHOUSE *Ukridge* iii. 67 Bad luck his getting pipped on the post like that. 1939 'N. BLAKE' *Smiler with Knife* xix. 272 Well, Georgia, pipped at the post, aren't you? 1949 'E. C. R. LORAC' *Still Waters* ii. 27, I pipped him at the post. His instructions must have limited him. 1959 'M. M. KAYE' *House of Shade* xviii. 245 He was head over heels about the bewitching Amalfi, and got pipped on the post by Eduardo. 1969 *Times* 25 Nov. 23/1 Shell..now have a record eight managing directors; BP..have just been pipped at the post—they have only seven. 1970 'A. GILBERT' *Death wears Mask* iii. 4 You won't be able to buy me that ring, after all, because it's sold. Someone's pipped you on the post. 1974 *Times* 8 Apr. 13/1 Schools television started in 1957, when Associated Rediffusion pipped the BBC by starting a service in which 80 schools took part.

2. *intr.* To die. Also with *out.*

1913 A. LUNN *Harrovians* ii. 31 'Is he Irish?' 'He don't seem to know. Father who's pipped was Irish. His mother's pipped too.' 1920 R. MACAULAY *Potterism* III. i. 110, I think it's simply rotten pipping out. I *like* being alive.

pip, *v.*⁴ [f. PIP *sb.*⁵] *intr.* To make a short, high-pitched sound. So **'pipping** *ppl. a.*

1938 D. SMITH *Dear Octopus* I. 14 Just see if Hilda's still telephoning... Tell her it's elevenpence every time it pips. 1958 *Listener* 18 Sept. 418/1, I could hear morse pipping and the loudspeaker blaring away. 1972 *Jazz & Blues* Oct. 5/1 A throbbing low register clarinet solo by Ben Richardson..ends rather oddly with some 'pipping' high notes like the BBC time signal. 1976 A. PRICE *War Game* I. 61 The phone pipped for more money and he..fed the last of his change into it. 1978 R. HOLLES *Spawn* iv. 28 People passing in cars pipped and waved although they hardly knew you.

pip, obs. Sc. variant of PIPE *sb.*²

‖**pipa** (pɪ'pɑː, 'paɪpə). Also 8–9 pipal, (8 piwal). [a. Surinam Negro *pipál* masc., *pipá* fem. Prob. a native African name, the Indian (Carib) name being *curucú*. Cf.

1734 SEBA *Thes. Rer. Nat.* I. 121 Les Surinamois..apellent *pipa* les femelles de ces animaux et les mâles *pipal.*]

The Surinam toad (noted for its peculiar manner of hatching its young: see quot. 1838); hence in *Zool.* the name of the genus of tailless batrachians of which this is the only species.

α. 1718 J. CHAMBERLAYNE *Relig. Philos.* (1730) II. xxii. §9 An American Animal, called the Pipal, like a Toad, which produces its young ones out of its Back. 1756–7 tr. *Keysler's Trav.* (1760) IV. 280 A species of toads called piwal, or pipal, the female of which deposits her eggs in *valvulæ* or little cells on the back of the male, so that when the young are hatched they seem to grow out of the body of the male. Others suppose that to be the female that seems to produce the young. 1802 *Eng. Encycl.* VIII. 730/1 The pipal, or Surinam toad, is more ugly than even the common one.

β. 1769 E. BANCROFT *Guiana* 148 The pipa is a large venomous toad peculiar to Guiana. 1838 *Penny Cycl.* X. 493/1 The male *Pipa*, or Surinam toad, as soon as the eggs are laid, places them on the back of the female, and fecundates them... The skin of her back..forms cellules, in which the eggs are hatched, and where the young pass their tadpole state. 1894 MIVART *Types Anim. Life* 113 Like the Pipa toad it brings forth its young in the adult condition.

‖**p'ip'a** (piː'pɑː). Also pepa, pipa, etc. [Chinese.] A Chinese stringed instrument (see quot. 1975).

1839 *Chinese Repository* May 42 *Pepa*, the balloon shaped guitar... This is about three feet in length... The strings are of silk. 1848 S. W. WILLIAMS *Middle Kingdom* II. xvi. 165 In writing a tune for the lute or *pipa*, 'each note is a cluster of characters'. 1874 *Jrnl. N. China Branch R. Asiatic Soc.* VIII. 115 The *P'i-p'a*.., or 'Balloon-shaped Guitar', described by the Chinese as resembling a ham, has a body like the egg of a goose nearly a foot in diameter with four strings, which are played with the fingers. 1917 *Encycl. Sinica* 388/2 *P'i p'a* is a lute about forty-two inches long with a pear-shaped body. The neck is eight and a half inches long. It has ten or twelve frets and four or six strings. 1954 *Grove's Dict. Mus.* (ed. 5) II. 238/2 *P'i-p'a*.., four-stringed short lute (sometimes 'balloon guitar')... About 3 ft. long and 1 ft. wide.., the body is pear-shaped, its back being rounded but shallow, its front flat and covered with the soundboard... The four silk strings..are attached..to a cross-ledge on the soundboard. 1962 E. SNOW *Red China Today* (1963) lxxiii. 563 The *p'i-p'a* is a native Chinese instrument something like a zither. 1975 C. P. MACKERRAS *Chinese Theatre in Mod. Times* 22 Of the plucked, non-bowed stringed instruments the most significant is the pear-shaped *p'i-p'a*... It is played held upright on the thigh. The musician plucks the strings with his right thumb and first finger, sometimes protected with a plectrum, and determines the pitch with three of his left fingers. 1979 *Time* 2 Apr. 48/1 Liu Dehai played a concerto for a lutelike instrument called the pipa.

pipage ('paɪpɪdʒ). Also pipeage. [f. PIPE *sb.*¹ + -AGE.] The conveyance or distribution of water, gas, petroleum, etc. by means of pipes; the construction or laying down of pipes for this purpose; such pipes collectively.

1612 STURTEVANT *Metallica* 92 Pipeage..is..the making of earthen pipes, for the conducting..of fresh waters, for the ..vse of houses. 1883 *Century Mag.* July 334/1 Paying twenty cents a barrel as the pipage charge, and a storage charge of fifty cents per day per thousand barrels. 1897 W. R. PATERSON *Tormentor* 100 Strange vermin course, much like water-rats, through the veins and pipage of men's lives!

pipal, variant of PEEPUL, PIPA.

†**pi'pation.** *Obs. rare*⁻⁰. [ad. L. *pīpātiōn-em* a piping, chirping, whimpering, n. of action f. *pīpāre*: see PIPE *v.*¹]

1656 BLOUNT *Glossogr.*, *Pipation*, a cry of one that weeps. 1658 PHILLIPS, *Pipation*, (lat.) a kinde of shrill crying, or weeping. 1775 in ASH.

pipe (paɪp), *sb.*¹ Also 4–7 pype, 6 pyppe. [OE. *pîpe* fem. = OFris., MDu., MLG., LG. *pîpe* (EFris. *pîpe, pîp*, Du. *pijp*), OHG. *pfîfa* (MHG. *pfîfe*, Ger. *pfeife*), ON. *pípa* (Sw. *pipa*, Da. *pibe*):—OLG. type **pîpa*, a. late L. **pīpa*, f. *pīpāre* to peep, pipe, chirp (also *pīpiāre*). From L. *pīpa* with usual phonetic evolution came It. *piva*; an assumed popular form **pippa* gave It., Sp., Roum. *pipa*, F. *pipe*, Pr. *pimpa*; Ir. and Gael. *piob*, W. *pib* are from L. or Eng.]

I. A musical tube.

1. a. A musical wind-instrument consisting of a single tube of reed, straw, or (now usually) wood, blown by the mouth, such as a flageolet, flute, or oboe. (***double pipe***, an instrument formed with two such tubes.) Now chiefly *arch.* or *Hist.*

a 1000 [see PIPE *v.*¹ 1]. *a* 1023 WULFSTAN *Hom.* vi. (Napier) 46 Hearpe and pipe and mistlicglīᵹgamen dremað eow on beorsele. *a* 1100 *Voc.* in Wr.-Wülcker 311/22 *Musa*, pipe ðœ̄e hwistle. *c* 1205 LAY. 3635 þer wes bemene song, þer beden [? weren] pipen among. *a* 1300 *Cursor M.* 15011 Wit harp and pipe, and horn and trump. 1382 WYCLIF *Luke* vii. 32 We han soungun to ȝou with pipis, and ȝe han not daunsid. *c* **1450** Holland *Howlat* 761 The lilt pype, and the lute. **1535** Coverdale *Job* xxx. 30 My harpe is turned to sorow, & my pipe to wepinge. **1637** Milton *Lycidas* 124 Their lean and flashy songs Grate on their scrannel Pipes of wretched straw. **1799** Wordsw. *Ruth* ii, She had made a pipe of straw, And music from that pipe could draw. **1864** Engel *Mus. Anc. Nat.* 57 The double pipe..was well known to the Greeks and Romans. **1877** J. Northcote *Catacombs* I. v. 72 The pastoral reed or tuneful pipe.

b. Each of the tubes (of wood or metal, and of construction similar to that of the simple instrument) by which the sounds are produced in an organ: see organ-pipe.

c **1440** *Promp. Parv.* 401/1 Pype, of orgonys, *ydraula*. **1552-3** *Inv. Ch. Goods, Staffs.* in *Ann. Lichfield* (1863) IV. 47 A pere of orgaynes, one pype of brasse. **1590** Sir J. Smyth *Disc. Weapons* 4 b, Of diuerse lengths like Organe pipes. **1667** Milton *P.L.* I. 709 As in an Organ from one blast of wind To many a row of Pipes the sound-board breaths. **1795** Mason *Ch. Mus.* i. 39 The pipes formed only of brass, must have been so shrill and piercing that [etc.]. **1847** Tennyson *Princ.* II. 450 While the great organ almost burst his pipes..rolling thro' the court A long melodious thunder.

c. *Naut.* The boatswain's whistle; the sounding of this as a call to the crew (cf. pipe *v.*[1] 6). Also *pl.* as a nickname for a boatswain (*Naut. slang.*).

1638 Sir T. Herbert *Trav.* (ed. 2) 30 The whistler with his iron Pipe encouraging the Marriners. **1835** Marryat *Jac. Faithf.* xxxviii, The pipe of the boatswain re-echoed as the captain ascended the side. **1856** R. MacClure *Discovery of North-West Passage* xv. 233 'Pipes' picked up a leg of the deer. **1873** *Routledge's Yng. Gentl. Mag.* July 489/2 The pipe went for all hands to 'scrub and wash clothes'. **1903** H. Holmes *Life & Adventures on Ocean* 17 The boatswain, commonly called 'Pipes' for shortness, was warned by his superior officer to take every care. *Ibid.*, 'High enough,' calls out Pipes. **1942** *Penguin New Writing* XV. 8 When Pipes went for supper he had a side-parting and looked quite different.

d. *pl.* = *bagpipes* (cf. bagpipe 1 b). Also *poet.* in *sing.*

a **1706** R. Semple *Piper of Kilbarchan* vii, At Horse Races many a day..He gart his pipe, when he did play, Baith skirl and skreed. **1790** Burns *Tam O'Shanter* 123 He screwed the pipes, and gart them skirl, Till roof and rafters a' did dirl. **1810, 1862** [see pibroch]. **1814** Scott *Ld. of Isles* iv. vi, The pipes resumed their clamorous strain. **1874** G. Macdonald *Malcolm* xix, Duncan strode along in front, and Malcolm followed, carrying the pipes.

e. In *fig.* or allusive use: esp. in phr. †*to put* (*pack*) *up one's pipes*, to cease from action, speaking, etc., desist, 'shut up' (*obs.*).

1556 Olde *Antichrist* 148 Than maye the B[ishop] of Rome put up his pypes. **1594** Nashe *Unfort. Trav.* 12 He could haue found in his hart to haue packt vp hys pipes, and to haue gone to heauen. *a* **1758** Ramsay *Eagle & Robin* 49 Poke up your pypes, be nae mair sene At court. **1775** Sheridan *Rivals* II. i, To make herself the pipe and ballad-monger of a circle! **1828** P. Cunningham *N.S. Wales* (ed. 3) II. 16 None..had more pipes blown about in his ironic praise. [*note, Pipes*, a colonial term for pasquinades and squibs, personal and political].

2. *transf.* **a.** The voice, esp. as used in singing; the song or note of a bird, etc. Formerly also in *pl.* †*to set up one's pipes*, to cry aloud, shout, yell (*obs.*); *to tune one's pipes*, to begin to cry, i.e. weep (*Sc.*).

1580 Lyly *Euphues* (Arb.) 278 Where vnder a sweete Arbour..be byrdes recording theyr sweete notes, hee also strayned his olde pype. **1581** Mulcaster *Positions* xxxix. (1887) 188 A straunge orator straining his pipes, to perswade straunge people. **1601** Shaks. *Twel. N.* I. iv. 32 Thy small pipe Is as the maidens organ, shrill, and sound. **1671** H. M. tr. *Erasm. Colloq.* 381 They did not speak softly, but set up their pipes aloud. **1721** Bradley *Philos. Acc. Wks. Nat.* 81 The Bullfinch and Robin-Red-Breast speak in a Treble Tone or Pipe. **1749** Smollett *Gil Bl.* I. v. I. 23 Setting up my pipes, as if he had flead me. **1785** Trusler *Mod. Times* II. 185 She was a very pretty woman..and had a very sweet pipe. **1843** Thackeray *Mr. & Mrs. F. Berry* ii, He..will occasionally lift up his little pipe in a glee. **1889** Jefferies *Field & Hedg.* 229 The thin pipe of the gnat heard at night.

b. ? *Sc.* phr. *to take a pipe*, to weep, cry. (Cf. pipe *v.*[1] 5 d, 7, piping *vbl. sb.*[1] 3.)

1818 Hogg *Brownie of B.* II. 155 He's takin a pipe to himsel at the house-end..his heart..is as saft as a snaw-ba'.

II. A cylindrical tube or stick for other purposes.

3. a. A hollow cylinder of wood, metal, or other substance, for the conveyance of water, gas, vapour, etc., or for other purposes; a tube.

c **1000** *Sax. Leechd.* II. 126 Monnes heafod ban bærn to ahsan, do mid pipan on. **1396** *Mem. Ripon* (Surtees) III. 123 In pypys emp. pro campanis, 4*d.* **1398** Trevisa *Barth. De P.R.* xiii. i. (Tollem. MS.), Yf a welle sprynge þ in þe coppe of an hyll, ofte by pipes þe water is ledde to þe same hyȝnesse in to a noþer hyll. *c* **1400** Maundev. (Roxb.) xxii. 100 Þam behoues souke it with a rede or a pype. **1412-20** Lydg. *Chron. Troy* II. xi. (1555), Many gargoyle..With spoutes thorough & pipes. **1541** *Act 33 Hen. VIII*, c. 35 The saide water hath bene conueied vnder erth in pypes of leade. **1662** Merrett tr. *Neri's Art of Glass* 364 The Pipes are the hollow Irons to blow the Glass. **1726** Swift *Gulliver* III. iv, Water, to be conveyed up by pipes and engines. **1774** Goldsm. *Nat. Hist.* (1776) I. 304 The barometer..is composed of a glass tube or pipe..closed up at one end. **1823** P. Nicholson *Pract. Build.* 408 The Sucking-pump consists of two pipes, the barrel and suction-pipe. **1874** Micklethwaite *Mod. Par. Churches* 200 Pipes, containing either hot water or steam. **1893** *Law Times* XCV. 62/2 An inspector..tested the drain, when he found that the joints of the pipes were not properly cemented.

b. *to lay pipe* or *pipes*, i.e. for the supply of water or gas; *fig.* in U.S. political slang: see quots. and cf. pipe-laying.

1860 Bartlett *Dict. Amer.* s.v. *Pipe-laying*, To *lay pipe* means to bring up voters not legally qualified. **1861** *Lond. Rev.* 16 Feb. 169 The gentlemen who succeed in appropriating these small measures will be laying down very good 'pipe' for Leeds, Southampton, &c. **1862** *Fraser's Mag.* July 28 To charge him, in the technical language of his party, with 'pulling wires', and 'laying pipes' for the Presidency.

c. *U.S. slang.* Something that is easy to accomplish; a 'cinch'. Cf. lead-pipe. Also *attrib.*, as *pipe course*.

1902 'H. McHugh' *It's up to You* iii. 66 It was so easy it was a shame... 'The idea is Napoleonic, little woman!' I said. 'It's a pipe!' **1927** *Amer. Speech* II. 277/2 *Pipe course*, easy course. **1936** L. C. Douglas *White Banners* ii. 44 A procession of shamefaced athletes who..had thought erroneously, when they had registered for it, that Anglo-Saxon was 'a pipe'. **1951** M. Shulman *Many Loves of Dobie Gillis* (1953) 105 You are all freshmen..and you may not be familiar with the term 'pipe course'. A pipe course is a course where students can get passing grades without doing much work. This is not a pipe course. **1952** Wodehouse *Barmy in Wonderland* viii. 80 This show's a pipe, and any bird that comes in is going to make plenty. **1978** H. Kemelman *Thursday the Rabbi Walked Out* x. 57 Nothing to it... Believe me, the whole thing's a pipe.

4. Applied to various specific tubular or cylindrical objects or contrivances.

†**a.** Some part of horse-harness; prob. a leather tube through which the traces were passed to prevent chafing against the horse's sides. *Obs.* (Cf. piping *vbl. sb.*[2] 5.)

? **1309** *Durham Acc. Rolls* (Surtees) 506 (Mariscall.) In.. iij paribus de pipes. ? **1333-4** *Ibid.* 523, viij pipes pro tractubus. [**1418** in Rymer *Fœdera* (1709) IX. 543/1 Cum.. Stuffurâ rationabili de Pipis, Rigeboundes, Bellibondes.. pro Equis.]

†**b.** A tubular handle or staff in which a banner or cross was fitted, to be carried in procession. *Obs.*

1397 *Durham Acc. Rolls* (Surtees) 445 Quinque pipes de argento cum cruce argentia et deaurata..pro vexillo S'ci Cuthberti. **1466** in *Archæologia* (1887) L. 1. 42 Item j staf for to set on the pypys for the crosse. **1552** *Inv. Ch. Goods* (Surtees) 104, ij coper crosses..pypes belongyng to them. **1593** *Rites of Durham* (Surtees 1903) 22 A goodly and sumptuous banner..with pippes of siluer..with a device to taike of and on yᵉ said pipes.

†**c.** A tube or roll on which thread was wound, and on which a definite length was bought. *Obs.*

c **1440** *Paston Lett.* I. 39, I prey yow do byen for me ij. pypys of gold [i.e. gold thread].

†**d.** in *pl.* A form in which gold and silver were used to trim dresses, etc. *Obs.*

1533 in Weaver *Wells Wills* (1890) 26 A gyrdell of pyppes of silver. *a* **1548** Hall *Chron., Hen. VIII* 7 On their heades skayus and wrappers of Damaske golde with flatte pypes. **1556** *Inv. Ch. Goods* (Surtees) 110 [Vestments] one chekeryd with grene velvet and litle silver pipes. **1600** in Nichols *Progr. Q. Eliz.* (1823) III. 502 One Frenche gowne of blacke vellat, with an edge of purle, and pipes of gold.

e. Name for the large round cell in a honeycomb inhabited by the queen bee. *dial.*

1609 C. Butler *Fem. Mon.* (1634) 104-5 The Queen's cells are built single... In fashion they are round... The common people..call them Pipes, or Taps. **1847-78** Halliw., *Pipe*, a large round cell in a beehive used by the queen bee. *West.*

f. An underground passage, a burrow.

1738 [G. Smith] *Curious Relations* II. 453 The old Beavers harbour the whole Winter in the Pipes, to which they remove in the beginning of November. **1887** *S. Cheshire Gloss.*, *Pipe*, a branch or side-run in a rabbit-warren.

g. *pl.* (*slang.*) Top-boots.

1812 J. H. Vaux *Flash Dict.*, *Pipes*, boots. **1834** H. Ainsworth *Rookwood* III. v, Jist twig his swell kickseys and pipes [*note*, Breeches and boots].

h. A piece of confectionery, etc. of a tubular or cylindrical form. (Cf. piping *vbl. sb.*[2] 8.)

a **1851** Pereira in Mayhew *Lond. Labour* I. 204/1 Sugar constitutes the base of..hard confectionary, sold under the names of lozenges, brilliants, pipe, rock, comfits, nonpareils, &c. **1883** R. Haldane *Workshop Receipts* Ser. II. 175/1 Roll it [the liquorice] into pipes or cylinders of convenient lengths. *Ibid.* 355/1 Isinglass..under the names of 'leaf', 'staple', 'book', 'pipe',..according to its form.

i. 'One of the curved flutings of a frill or ruff; also, a pin used for piping or fluting' (*Cent. D.*).

1813 Jane Austen *Let.* 16 Sept. (1952) 326 My Cap is come... Fanny has one also..shaped round the face..with pipes & more fullness, & a round crown inserted behind.

j. In hair-dressing: see quot. 1860.

1765 Sterne *Tr. Shandy* VIII. xxviii, I'll put your white Ramallie-wig fresh into pipes. **1860** Fairholt *Costume* Gloss., *Pipes*, small articles made of pipe-clay used for keeping the large periwigs in curl.

k. A tubular part of something, e.g. of a key.

1833 *Regul. Instr. Cavalry* I. 99 Draw the ramrod out of the barrel, and return it into the pipe. **1849** E. E. Napier *Excurs. S. Africa* I. 161 The holsters should be sufficiently capacious to carry in one pipe the..double barrelled pistol: in the other, a brandy-flask. **1853** Hobbs & Tomlinson *Locks* xi. 159 The process of piercing the key consists in making the pipe or barrel. **1884** F. J. Britten *Watch & Clockm.* 29 A stop for the pipe of the detent. *Ibid.* 101 The pipe that carries the minute hand.

5. †**a.** The account of a sheriff or other minister of the Crown, as sent in and enrolled at the Exchequer: cf. pipe-roll. *Obs.*

[The origin of this use of *pipe* is doubtful: some would explain it from the pipe-like form of a thin roll, or ? from its being transmitted in a cylindrical case. Bacon saw in it a metaphor: see quot. 1598 in b., and cf. sense 8; but we have no evidence that that sense was in use early in the 14th c.]

[**1323** *Red Book of the Exchequer* (1896) 858 Soient desore annuelement tutes les pipes de tutz les accomptes renduz en lan [all the pipes of all the accounts sent in in the year] bien et pleynement examinez, avant qe eles soient mises ensemble et roule fait de eles, a la fyn del an. *Ibid.* 860 Et face il, en fyn del an, les pipes des accomptes foreyns mettre par eux, et les autres pipes des acomptes des viscountes [pipes of the accounts of the sheriffs] par eux.]

fig. **1565** Jewel *Def. Apol.* (1611) 126 Are such Monuments laid vp only in the Roles and Pipes of your memorie?

b. The department of the Exchequer that drew up the 'pipes', or enrolled accounts, of sheriffs and others, abolished in England by Act 3 & 4 Will. IV, c. 99 §41 (= *pipe-office*: see 11 b).

[**1338** *Rolls of Parlt.* II. 101/1 Brief des somons hors de la Pipe.] **1455** *Ibid.* V. 342/2 The Office of the Clerk of the Pipe. **1512** *Act 4 Hen. VIII*, c. 18 §3 The same accomptes ..to be taken & fylled uppe in the pype theyr to remayne of recorde. **1598** Bacon *Office of Alienations* Wks. 1879 I. 588 That office of her Majesty's exchequer, which we, by a metaphor, do call the pipe,..because the whole receipt is finally conveyed into it by the means of divers small pipes or quills. **1658** Phillips, Clerk of the *Pipe*, an Officer in the Exchequer, who having all accounts and debts due unto the King, drawn out of the remembrancers Office, chargeth them down into the great Roll. **1715** *Lond. Gaz.* No. 5298/3 The Right Honourable William Lord Cheyne..to be Clerk of the Pipe in the Exchequer. **1738** *Hist. Crt. Excheq.* ii. 18 The Summons of the Pipe got in the Tallages. **1834** *Act 4 & 5 Will. IV*, c. 16 §1 The Office of Recorder of the Great Roll or Clerk of the Pipe in the Exchequer in Scotland shall cease and determine.

6. A tubular organ, passage, canal, or vessel in an animal body: applied to the veins and arteries, the alimentary canal, and now *esp.* to the respiratory passages (windpipe, bronchi, and tubules of the lungs). Almost always in *pl.* (See also *pipe-opener* in 11 b.)

c **1386** Chaucer *Knt.'s T.* 1894 The pipes of his longes gonne to swelle. *c* **1430** *Two Cookery-bks.* 8 Take Pypis, Hertys, Nerys, Myltys, an Rybbys of the Swyne. **1482** *Monk of Evesham* (Arb.) 21 His feete ware ful coolde... No mouing of his pypys myght be knowen long tyme. **1573-80** Baret *Alv.* P 394 The meate Pipe, *gula*..λαιμὸς. **1594** T. B. *La Primaud. Fr. Acad.* II. 57 The nauill..is appointed to be the pipe to conuey both [breath and meat] vnto him before he be borne. **1633** Ford *Broken H.* v. ii, I am well skill'd in letting blood. Bind fast This arm, that so the pipes may from their conduits Convey a full stream. **1712** Addison *Spect.* No. 269 ¶3 He loves to clear his Pipes in good Air (to make use of his own Phrase). **1883** E. Pennell-Elmhirst *Cream Leicestersh.* 4 Depth of girth he [the horse] must have, or his pipes and heart have no room to play.

7. a. Applied to various tubular or cylindrical natural formations, as the stem of a plant, etc.

1523 Fitzherb. *Husb.* §70 Lowe places, and all the holowe bunnes and pypes that growe therin. **1578** Lyte *Dodoens* II. xliii. 202 This kinde of Lillie beareth..amongst his leaues as it were certayne pypes or clysters. **1753** Franklin *Lett.*, etc. Wks. 1840 VI. 155 When the whirling pipe of air was filled with..vapor. **1805** R. W. Dickson *Pract. Agric.* I. 74 The strongest wheat-straw..laid on upon the building in whole pipes, unbruised by the flail.

†**b.** An icicle. *Obs.*

1556-68 Withals *Dict.* 3/1 The iseicles or pypes hangynge vppon the eaues of a house. **1596** Dalrymple tr. *Leslie's Hist. Scot.* I. 46 To thow the pypes and schokles of yce, frosin vpon thame.

c. *Mining* and *Geol.* (*a*) A vein of ore of a more or less cylindrical form, usually following the direction of the strata; also called *pipe-vein* (see 11 b), pipe-work. (*b*) A vertical cylindrical hollow filled with sand or gravel, occurring in a stratum of chalk; also called *sand-pipe* or *sand-gall*. (*c*) The vertical eruptive channel which opens into the crater of a volcano. (*d*) Each of the vertical cylindrical masses of blue rock (of eruptive origin) in which diamonds are found imbedded in S. Africa (see kimberlite).

1667 Primatt *City & C. Build.* 5 If there be any rakes or pipes of Lead or Tin Oar. **1747** Hooson *Miner's Dict.* L iv b, Lidd [is] the Cover that lies over the Tops of Veins sometimes, but over Pipes always. **1839** Ure *Dict. Arts* 832 The pipe does not in general cut the strata across like the rake vein, but insinuates itself between them; so that if the plane of the strata be nearly horizontal, the bearing of the pipe vein will be conformable. **1860** Darwin in *Life & Lett.* II. 332 You used to be interested about the 'pipes' in the chalk. **1873** E. J. Dunn in *Q. Jrnl. Geol. Soc.* (1874) XXX. 54 The contents of these 'pipes' in the shale are the same in all cases, and show distinctly that they are of igneous origin. **1878** Huxley *Physiogr.* 189 At the mouth of the volcanic pipe, there is usually a funnel-shaped opening known as the crater. **1889** *Chambers' Cycl.* s.v. *Diamond*. **1903** *Daily Chron.* 2 June 2/3 Diamonds..only appear at the surface in places where they have shared in a volcanic upheaval. Hence they are found in what are technically known as pipes.

d. Each of the numerous hollow jets of flame which occur in a particular process of the manufacture of black-ash (ash *sb.*[2] 2).

1880 Lomas *Alkali Trade* 175 Just as the pipes begin to disappear, the bright hot mass is raked out quickly. *Ibid.* 176 Bright jets of carbonic oxide, burning with a sodium yellow, and usually called 'pipes', should be visible all over the ball.

e. *Metallurgy.* A funnel-shaped cavity at the top of an ingot caused by shrinkage of the metal during cooling.

1861 *Brit. Patent 1310* 2 Shrinkage forms a deep tube or funnel in the upper part of the ingot... This funnel is called by steel manufacturers the 'pipe' of the ingot. **1895** E. L. RHEAD *Metallurgy* xi. 147 Steel of harder temper..settles down in the mould, forming a funnel-shaped cavity or pipe. **1923** GLAZEBROOK *Dict. Appl. Physics* V. 357/2 If this takes place any shrinkage of the metal during further solidification must result in the formation of a pipe. **1973** J. G. TWEEDDALE *Materials Technol.* II. ii. 36 Metal ingots..are often cast with open tops and the defective top material, including any pipe, is usually cut off subsequently.

8. †**a.** The channel of a small stream. *Obs. rare.*

1570–6 LAMBARDE *Peramb. Kent* (1826) 199 Divers other smal pipes of water..minister secondarie helpes to this navigable river. *Ibid.* 260 The greater ryvers..have their increase from many smal Wels (or springs) the which..bee conveied in slender quilles, then afterwarde (meeting together in course) doe growe by little and little into bigger pipes.

b. Each of the channels of a decoy for wild fowl: see DECOY *sb.*[2] 1.

1634–5 BRERETON *Trav.* (1844) 171 There are five pipes in this coy as in mine. **1768** PENNANT *Zool.* II. 464 There are several pipes (as they are called) which lead up a narrow ditch, that closes at last with a funnel net. Over these pipes ..is a continued arch of netting... It is necessary to have a pipe or ditch for almost every wind that can blow. **1887** FENN *Dick o' Feus* (1888) 112 Quite a hundred followed their leaders up the pipe in happy ignorance of the meaning of a net.

†**9.** A name for the Mock Orange or Syringa (*Philadelphus coronarius*; also, for the Lilac (Blue Pipe), rendering the med.L. name *Syringa*. *Obs. rare.* (See PIPE-TREE.)

1597 GERARDE *Herbal* III. lvii. 1214 The later Phisitions call the first *Syringa*,..that is to say, a Pipe, bicause the stalks and branches thereof, when the pith is taken out, are hollow like a Pipe. It is also..surnamed *Candida* or white, or *Syringa candido flore*, or Pipe with a white flower.. Lillach.. is sometimes named *Syringa cærulea*, or blue Pipe.

III. A pipe for smoking.

10. a. A narrow tube of clay, wood, or other material, with a bowl at one end, for drawing in the smoke of tobacco (or other narcotic or medicinal substance). Often used as including the contained tobacco, etc., as in ***to light one's pipe, to smoke a pipe***; also for a quantity which fills the bowl and is smoked at one time, a pipeful. (See also TOBACCO-PIPE.)

1594 PLAT *Jewell-ho.* I. 29 Wee..will not vouchsafe one pipe of Tobacco vpon her. **1599** H. BUTTES *Dyets drie Dinner* P v b, The fume taken in a Pipe, is good against Rumes, Catarrhs, hoarsenesse. **1611** RICH *Honest. Age* (Percy Soc.) 37 He must haue his pipe of Tobacco. **1632** LITHGOW *Trav.* v. 205 Because of the long pipes, the smoake is exceeding cold in their swallowing throates. **1683** TRYON *Way to Health* 168 Now every Plow-man has his Pipe to himself. **1736** I. H. BROWNE *Pipe Tobacco* Poems (1768) 116 Happy mortal! he who knows Pleasure which a Pipe bestows. **1766** AMORY *Buncle* (1825) II. 1, I smoked a pipe after supper. **1837** W. IRVING *Capt. Bonneville* III. 247 The guns were laid down, and the pipe was lighted. **1902** BUCHAN *Watcher by Threshold* 7, I lit a pipe to cheer me.

b. ***pipe of peace***: the CALUMET, or peace-pipe of the American Indians. Also used allusively.

1722 R. BEVERLEY *Hist. Virginia* Tab. vi. 144–5 Pipe of peace w[ch] I have seen. **1762** FOOTE *Lyar* I. (1786) 17, I had the first honour of smoaking the pipe of peace with the little Carpenter. **1812** BRACKENRIDGE *Views Louisiana* (1814) 91 The chiefs approached with pipes of peace. **1870** MISS BRIDGMAN *Rob. Lynne* II. xii. 261 They had better smoke the pipe of peace.

c. ***Queen's*** (***King's***) ***Pipe***: humorous name for a furnace at the London Docks, used formerly for burning contraband tobacco, subsequently for burning tobacco-sweepings and other refuse.

[**1843** *Penny Cycl.* XXV. 17/2 The damaged tobacco..is consumed in a furnace..jocularly termed the 'queen's tobacco-pipe'.] **1871** *Echo* 25 Jan., If the sale is not brisk, then her Majesty's tobacco-pipe, which smokes tobacco by the ton, is likely soon to be well filled. This 'pipe', or furnace, is at the London Docks, and in it vast quantities of tobacco..that have failed to sell in the Government sales, are burnt. **1895** *Westm. Gaz.* 31 Aug. 3/2 The rubbish which had got packed with the leaf..goes to fill the Queen's pipe—is, in fact, burned. **1904** *Daily News* 28 June 6 'The King's Pipe'... The disorderly heaps of fuel included 'heads' of American tobacco.., Turkish leaves strung on a string, fragments of packing cases, and general litter.

d. In allusive phrases.

to put one's pipe out, to put a stop to one's success, take the 'shine' out of, extinguish. ***put that in your pipe and smoke it***, digest or put up with that if you can (also in similar phrases).

1720 RAMSAY *Wealth* 78 Upmost to-day, the morn their pipe's put out. *c* **1824** R. B. PEAKE *Americans Abroad* (1884) I. 4/2 Put that in your pipe and smoke it. **1837** DICKENS *Pickw.* ii. 7 Pull him up—put that in his pipe—like the flavour—damned rascals. **1840** BARHAM *Ingol. Leg.* Ser. I. *St. Odille*, Put that in your pipe, my lord Otto, and smoke it! **1848** THACKERAY *Van. Fair* xxxiv. *heading*, James Crawley's Pipe is put out. **1863** READE *Hard Cash* xli, I'll give you something to put in both your pipes. **1884** W. E. NORRIS *Thirlby Hall* xxv, It don't do to let them get the whip-hand of you, according to my experience. Put that in your pipe and smoke it, Master Charley. **1884** FLORENCE MARRYAT *Under Lilies & Roses* xxx, You're jealous of the girl, and want me to put her pipe out. **1921** GALSWORTHY *To Let* I. ix. 81 The noble owner put this opinion in his pipe and smoked it for a year. **1927** *Vanity Fair* XXIX. III. 67/2 'Laugh That Off!' ('Put that in your pipe and smoke it.') **1947** W. S. MAUGHAM *Creatures of Circumstance* 296 I'm engaged to her, so put that in your pipe and smoke it. **1977** A. HUNTER *Gently Instrumental* x. 136 There's a dozen witnesses, so you can put that in your pipe and smoke it.

e. *N. Amer. colloq.* A spell of travelling between two rest-periods at each of which a pipe is smoked; the distance covered or the time taken, in such a spell; also, the distance covered while smoking a pipeful of tobacco. *Obs.* exc. *Hist.*

1793 J. MACDONELL *Diary* 5 July in C. M. Gates *Five Fur Traders* (1933) 92 Leaving pointe au père we paddled two pipes and put to shore to give the men time to clean themselves. **1799** I. WELD *Trav. N. Amer.* xxix. 262 A pipe, in the most general acceptation of the word, seemed to be about three quarters of an English mile. **1806** S. FRASER *Jrnl.* 29 May (1960) 193 The men are better off and better pleased than if they ate a little at every Pipe. **1809** 'D. KNICKERBOCKER' *Hist. N.Y.* I. III. viii. 189 He arrived at Fort Amsterdam in little less than a month, though the distance was full two hundred pipes, or about 120 miles. **1848** R. M. BALLANTYNE *Hudson's Bay* iv. 77 The men used to row for a space of time, denominated a *pipe*, so called from the circumstance of their taking a smoke at the end of it. **1931** G. L. NUTE *Voyageur* 50 We have seen that the voyageurs had their own method of measuring portages. They were not less original on the water. Here the *pipe* was the standard of measurement. This was the distance covered between respites, when the luxury of resting and smoking was indulged. **1969** E. W. MORSE *Fur Trade Canoe Routes* I. i. 8 A stop was made for a few minutes each hour to allow the men to have a pipe. This event was so important that distances came to be measured in *pipes*: '*trois pipes*' might be 15 to 20 miles, depending on winds and current.

f. An opium-pipe; esp. in phr. ***to hit the pipe***, to smoke opium; also, an opium-addict. *slang* (orig. *U.S.*).

1886, 1902 [see HIT *v.* 23 a]. **1926** J. BLACK *You can't Win* xix. 300, I..learned he had been 'on the pipe' only three months. **1926** N. LUCAS *London & its Criminals* x. 134 So 'Izzy' had come to 'hitting the pipe'. I knew he had many vices, but I did not know that opium was one of them. **1949** *Sunday World-Herald Mag.* (Omaha, Nebraska) 3 Apr. 2/1 Opium smokers are considered at a low level..but a guy who profits when he hits the pipe is the plumber. **1959** MURTAGH & HARRIS *Who live in Shadow* III. i. 119 You can recognize 'pipes', opium addicts, by the odour which clings to them. **1972** D. BLOODWORTH *Any Number can Play* xi. 95 Max insisted that they go on to Madame Phnom's plush smoking establishment for a pipe or two.

IV. *attrib.* and *Comb.*

11. a. Obvious combinations, as ***pipe-like*** adj.; (in sense 1 or 1 d) ***pipe-clang, -music, -playing*** (playing on a pipe, or with a tobacco-pipe); (in sense 3) ***pipe-casting, -coating, -fitter, -founding, -jointer, -manufacturing, -track***; (in sense 10) ***pipe-bowl, -champer, -fill, -lighter, -lover, -shank, -smoke, -smoker, -smoking, -spill, -weed, -whiff***; ***pipe-drawn, -puffed*** adjs.

1886 *Daily News* 13 Dec. 2/3 The Plumbers' Company... The examinations included *pipe bending, joint making, the formation of roof gutters, cisterns, &c. **1852** DICKENS *Bleak Ho.* (1853) xxi. 213 The *pipe-bowl..is burning low. **1877** A. B. EDWARDS *Up Nile* i. 9 Red clay pipe-bowls of all sizes and prices. **1898** *Daily News* 10 Oct. 9/5 Foundry iron —which is being used mainly for *pipe casting. **1712** STEELE *Spect.* No. 431 ¶3 These craving Damsels..*Pipe-champers, Chalk-lickers, Wax-nibblers [etc.]. **1814** SCOTT *Ld. of Isles* VI. xx, *Pipe-clang and bugle sound. **1964** N. G. CLARK *Mod. Org. Chem.* v. 80 The highly viscous bitumen which forms the remainder of the distillation residue is used for..corrosion-proof *pipe-coatings. **1975** *Offshore Engineer* Oct. 13/1 The UK pipe-coating market is split.. between two firms. **1761** CHURCHILL *Rosciad* 870 Thus sportive boys, around some bason's brim, Behold the *pipe-drawn bladders circling swim. **1890** WEBSTER, **Pipe fitter*, one who fits pipes together, or applies pipes, as to an engine or a building. **1910** *Daily Chron.* 31 Jan. 6/5 Arthur Moon, aged 45, a pipe-fitter. **1977** *Cornish Times* 19 Aug. 15/3 He won first-year plumber and pipe-fitter prize. **1900** *Engineering Mag.* XIX. 786/1 Some Notes on *Pipe Founding. E. Kebler. Read before the Foundry-men's Assn., England. **1902** *Encycl. Brit.* XXV. 509/2 A record should be kept of the history of the pipe.., with the name of the *pipe-jointer whose work closes the record. **1909** *Dialect Notes* III. 357 **Pipe-lighter*, a paper spill or taper used for lighting lamps, pipes, etc. **1916** 'BOYD CABLE' *Action Front* 57 Each man had with him one of those tinder pipe-lighters which are ignited by the sparks of a little twirled wheel. **1616** SURFL. & MARKH. *Country Farme* 355 The *pipe-like barke. **1884** *Pall Mall G.* 5 Dec. 12/1 The pipelike passage leading to the chamber underneath the caisson. **1896** *Westm. Gaz.* 29 May 8/1 At one time in Skye there were two schools, or colleges, for *pipe music—one at Borreraig..and the other at Peingowan. *a* **1618** SYLVESTER *Tobacco Battered* 70 *Pipe-playing, dallying. *Ibid.* 710 Through his *Pipe-puft Nose more Smoake they wave, Then all the Chimnies their great Houses have. **1852** DICKENS *Bleak Ho.* (1853) xi. 105 A cloud of *pipe-smoke.. pervades the parlor. **1971** 'D. HALLIDAY' *Dolly & Doctor Bird* xvi. 231, I got home to be met by..the smell of pipe smoke curling round from the hallway. **1979** M. EDEN *Document of Last Nazi* xix. 96 Strang smelled old pipe smoke. **1866** GEO. ELIOT *Felix Holt* II. xxx. 229 Rough-looking *pipe-smokers, or distinguished cigar-smokers. **1959** *Listener* 25 June 1119/1 His plain, factual, forthright sentences—a sort of pipe-smoker's prose—deceptively bare and simple, convey the scene..with a telling clarity. **1853** DICKENS *Bleak Ho.* xxxiv. 338 I'll have no more of your *pipe-smokings and swaggerings. **1958** J. BYROM *Or be he Dead* vii. 106 The pipe-smoking young man in the open-necked shirt. **1979** J. VAN DE WETERING *Maine Massacre* iv. 52 A pipe-smoking old man. **1979** *Arizona Daily Star* 5 Aug. A7/1 A single match and an even draw gave the world's international pipe-smoking cup to a..physics teacher yesterday. **1922** JOYCE *Ulysses* 530 Pages will be torn from your handbook of astronomy to make them *pipespills. *a* **1906** *Mod.* We ascended Table Mountain in 1905 by the *Pipe-track and the Tunnel Gorge. **1955** J. R. R. TOLKIEN *Return of King* 270 And if you have any *pipe-weed, we'll bless you. **1846** BROWNING *Lett.* 29 June, Between two huge *pipe-whiffs.

b. Special Combinations: **pipe-bag**, the leathern bag of the bagpipe; **pipe-bearer**, an attendant who bears the pipe (of an American Indian chief, and Oriental ruler or official, etc.); **pipe-beetle**, one of the *Curculionidæ*, so called from their long proboscis; **pipe-bender**, a machine or device for bending a metal pipe; **pipe berth**, a collapsible or otherwise easily-stored canvas bed with a frame of metal piping used on small vessels; **pipe bomb**, a home-made bomb contained in a metal pipe; **pipe-box**, (*a*) ? a box for containing tobacco pipes; (*b*) the box of the hub of a wheel, in which the arm of the axle is inserted (Knight *Dict. Mech.* 1875); **pipe-burial**, a burial in which a pipe (usually of lead) passes from the coffin or the tomb to the surface of the ground, to permit the pouring of libations; **pipe-case**, a case for a tobacco-pipe or its bowl; **pipe chaplet** *Founding*, a chaplet (sense 6) used in the casting of pipes, which consists of a concave semi-cylindrical load-bearing surface supported on a stem; **pipe-clamp** = *pipe-vice*; **pipe-cleaner**, something used for cleaning a tobacco-pipe; *spec.* a device for this purpose consisting of a piece of wire covered with tufted material; also *fig.*; † **pipe-coal**, powdered coal or coal-dust formed into tubular briquettes; **pipe-coral**, ? = organ-pipe coral (see CORAL *sb.*[1] 1 b); **pipe cot** = *pipe berth*; **pipe-coupling**, a coupling for joining two pipes so as to form a continuous channel, or for attaching a pipe to something else; **pipe-cutter**, a tool or machine for cutting off pipes; **pipe-dance**, a dance resembling the sword-dance, in which long clay pipes are used instead of swords; **pipe-die**, (*a*) a ring-shaped die for moulding earthenware pipes; (*b*) a female screw or nut, or other device, for cutting a screw-thread on a pipe; **pipe-drain** *v. trans.*, to drain (land) by laying pipes; chiefly in pa. pple.; **pipe-dream** orig. *U.S.*, a fantastic or impracticable notion or plan, compared to a dream produced by smoking opium; a 'castle in the air'; hence **pipe-dreamer**; **pipe-dreaming** *vbl. sb.*; **pipe-dreamy** *a.*; **pipe-driver** (see quot.); **pipe-ear**, a projecting part at the side of the top of a pipe; **pipe-fiend** *U.S. slang*, an opium addict or smoker; **pipe-foot**, the lower part of a flue-pipe in an organ; † **pipe gled** *Sc. Obs.*, ? the kite (GLEDE); **pipe grab**, a clutching-tool for lifting a well-pipe; **pipe-gun**, (*a*) *dial.*, a pop-gun; (*b*) a gun made out of a pipe; **pipe-head**, (*a*) the bowl of a pipe for smoking; (*b*) the top of a water-pipe; **pipe-holder**, a perforated board in an organ, through which some of the pipes pass; **pipe-insect** (see quot.); **pipe-joint** = *pipe-coupling*; **pipe-key**, a key with a pipe or hollow barrel which fits on a pintle in the lock, a piped key; **pipe-lee**, tobacco half smoked to ashes in a pipe; **pipe-light**, a strip of paper folded or twisted for lighting a pipe, a spill; **pipe-loop** (see quot.); **pipe-macaroni**, macaroni made in the form of pipes or tubes; **pipe-major**, the chief player of a band of bagpipe-players; **pipe-maker**, a maker of pipes (in various senses); **pipe-metal**, an alloy of tin and lead, with or without zinc, used for organ-pipes; † **pipe-money**, money given to a piper, or for playing a pipe; **pipe-necked** *a.*, having a long slender neck; **pipe-note**, a note or sound made by a pipe; a note like that of a pipe, a piping note; **pipe-office**, the office of the Clerk of the Pipe in the Exchequer (see 5); in quot. 1609 humorously used for the mouth (with allusion to sense 10); **pipe-opener** (*colloq.*), a spell of exercise taken to clear the respiratory passages and replenish the lungs with fresh air, a 'breather'; also *fig.*, a 'trial run' or 'curtain-raiser'; **pipe-ore** (see quot.); **pipe-organ**, an organ with pipes (= ORGAN *sb.*[1] 2), esp. as distinguished from a *reed-organ*; **pipe oven** (see quot.); **pipe-privet**, a name for the lilac; = PIPE-TREE (Miller *Plant-names* 1884); **pipe-prover**, an apparatus for testing the strength and soundness of steam- or water-pipes by hydraulic pressure; **pipe-rack**, (*a*) in an organ, a wooden shelf with perforations by which the pipes are supported; (*b*) a rack for tobacco-pipes; (*c*) a rack or support for a set of pipelines above the ground; **pipe-reducer**, a pipe-coupling larger at one end than at the other to unite pipes differing in diameter; **pipe-skill**, skill in playing the bagpipe; **pipe-stand**, a stand or frame for supporting a pipe or pipes (in any sense); **pipe-stay** (see quot.); **pipe-stick**, a hollow wooden tube used as the stem of a tobacco-pipe; **pipe-still**, a still in which crude oil is heated by passing it through a series of tubes inside a furnace; **pipe-stop**, (*a*) a plug or stopvalve in a pipe; (*b*) an organ-stop composed of mouth-pipes (as distinguished from a *reed-stop*), a flue-stop; **pipe-stopper**, a small plug for compressing the tobacco in the bowl of a pipe; **pipe-story**, a fantastic or impossible story (cf. *pipe-dream*); **pipe-tongs**, tongs made to grasp a pipe or rod; **pipe-twister** = *pipe-wrench*; **pipe-vein** (*Mining*): see quots. and 7 c (*a*); **pipe-vice** (**-vise**), a vice for grasping a pipe or rod; **pipe-vine**, a name for the N. American plant *Aristolochia Sipho*, from the shape of the flowers and the twining growth (also called *Dutchman's pipe*); **pipe-water**, water conveyed by pipes; **pipe-wood**, name for *Leucothoe* (*Andromeda*) *acuminata*, a shrub of the southern U.S., the wood of which is used for tobacco-pipes; **pipe-worm**, a *Sabella*, *Serpula*, or allied tube-worm; **pipe-wrench**, a tool with one jaw fixed on a shank and the other movable on a pivot, so shaped as to grip a pipe when turned in one direction round it. See also PIPE-CLAY, PIPE-FISH, etc.

1615 BRATHWAIT *Strappado* (1878) 93 Pipe could he not.. His *pipe-bagge torn, no wind it could keepe in. **1836** W. IRVING *Astoria* I. 315 The *pipebearer stepped within the circle, lighted the pipe..then..handed it to the principal chief. **1877** A. B. EDWARDS *Up Nile* xxi. 602 The turbaned official who comes, attended by his secretary and pipe-bearer, to pay you a visit of ceremony. **1711** *Phil. Trans.* XXVII. 344 One of the largest kind of Curculio or *Pipe Beetles yet seen. **1933** CHAPMAN & HORENBURGER *Thirty Easy to build Sail Boats* 89/2 A *pipe berth can be fitted over each berth for the extra guest. **1963** J. T. ROWLAND *North to Adventure* vii. 90 With all the pipe berths folded back against the ship's side, the cabin became a capacious hold. **1976–7** *Sea Spray* (N.Z.). Dec./Jan. 51/2 The Sands design No 2218 offers four berths, pipe quarter berth, two seat berths amidships and a pipe berth in the foc'sle. **1966** *Guardian* 5 Sept. 1/7 The headquarters of the American Communist Party was damaged by a *pipe-bomb tossed from a moving car. **1971** *Sunday Times* 31 Oct. 10 Pipe bombs are another favourite anti-personnel bomb. **1977** *Time* 26 Dec. 26/2 Last August a tipster directed police to a pipe bomb at a Coors recycling plant in a Denver suburb. **1836–9** DICKENS *Sk. Boz, Shops & their Tenants*, Lounging about, on round tubs and *pipe-boxes. **1929** *Antiquaries Jrnl.* IX. 1 (*heading*) A Roman *pipe-burial from Caerleon, Monmouthshire. **1934** LAING & ROLFE *Man. Foundry Pract.* iii. 57 *Pipe-chaplets..can be obtained, either in the form illustrated, or with short pointed stems, their chief purpose being to support pipe cores in position. **1960** R. LISTER *Decorative Cast Ironwork* ii. 26 Of the types in regular use, special mention may be made of the pipe chaplet .., usually made of tinned wrought iron, and consisting of a pin with a semicylinder at one end. It is used to support the round core in pipe casting. **1870** G. M. HOPKINS *Note-bks. & Papers* (1937) 132 The heads of flowering grass..often used as *pipe-cleaners. **1928** E. WAUGH *Decline & Fall* I. ii. 18 A boxing-glove, a bowler hat, yesterday's *Daily News* and a packet of pipe-cleaners. **1959** I. & P. OPIE *Lore & Lang. Schoolch.* ix. 169 Thin people inspire almost as many names and jokes as fat people, but the laughter is less mortifying; the names..are merely descriptive, as: bag o' bones,..pipe cleaner, rake, [etc.]. **1960** *Farmer & Stockbreeder* 16 Feb. (Suppl.) 8/2 You can easily make a fine collection of animals with one or two packets of pipe-cleaners! Look at the sketch, *A*, to see how the woolly covered cleaners are bent to form the outline of a giraffe. **1973** D. LEES *Rape of Quiet Town* iii. 42, I tried to help but it wasn't easy with legs made out of pipe cleaners. **1612** STURTEVANT *Metallica* xiv. 98 Tempering, stamping, and comixing of sea-cole, or stone-cole, that a kinde of substance being there made of them like vnto past or tempered clay, the Presse-mould may forme and transfigure that clay-like substance into hollow *pipe-cole as it doth earthen pipes. **1832** R. & J. LANDER *Exped. Niger* II. viii. 4 Small pieces of *pipe coral were stuck in the lobe of each ear. **1962** W. H. MURRAY *Maelstrom* iii. 42 Forward again was the fo'c'scle, with *pipe-cots and deck-hatch. **1977** *Western Morning News* 1 Sept. 8/6 (Advt.), Six Ton Sloop..24 ft. oa., pine on oak, two berth and pipe cot. **1851** MAYHEW *Lond. Labour* I. 12/2 Sometimes they do the '*pipe-dance'. For this a number of tobacco-pipes..are laid close together on the floor, and the dancer places the toe of his boot between the different pipes. **1907** E. A. WOODRUFFE-PEACOCK *Pasture & Meadow Anal.* 4 A soil that has been *pipe drained for wheat-growing. **1930** *Jrnl. Ministry Agric.* Nov. 825 There is nothing to indicate.. whether the land is pipe-drained or not. **1896** ADE *Artie* iii. 27 But then I was spinnin' *pipe dreams myself, tellin' about how much I lose on the board and all that. **1904** B. VON HUTTEN *Pam* 238 Look at the sea, and tell me if, in your wildest pipe-dream, you ever saw anything lovelier. **1915** *Strand Mag.* June 651/2 If it is a fizzle off goes my coat and I abandon pipe-dreams of literary triumph. **1937** *John o' London's* 26 Mar. 1/3 As my ideal library will never be anything but a pipe-dream, no great harm is done. **1959** *Daily Tel.* 4 Apr. 6 In that event, the Channel project would cease to be an engineers' pipe-dream. **1973** C. EGLETON *Seven Days to Killing* xiv. 150 Streamlining..was pure Whitehall jargon... It implied increased efficiency at less cost and..that was just a pipe dream. **1976** *Classical Q.* XXVI. 80 After 394 a Hellenic crusade against Persia was merely a pipe-dream. **1976** C. WESTON *Rouse Demon* (1977) i. 47 He was always a *pipe-dreamer. Always in the clouds. **1979** *Eastern Economist* 14 Sept. 545/2 Only pipe-dreamers would have the phantasies that man uses his tools only for what is called constructively productive purposes. **1976** *Flintshire Leader* 10 Dec. 1 Some of the council's figures relating to the Leisure Centre are an exercise in *pipe dreaming. **1978** C. A. BERRY *Gentleman of Road* ii. 14, I couldn't chicken out now. It was time for pipe-dreaming to end. **1910** 'O. HENRY' *Whirligigs* i. 12 La Paz is a good sort of a *pipe-dreamy old hole. **1875** KNIGHT *Dict. Mech.*, **Pipe-driver*, an implement of the general form of a pile-driver, used for forcing into the ground pipes for what are known as 'driven wells'. **1905** *Athenæum* 29 Apr. 534/1 The fronts of pipe-heads and the *pipe ears were often heraldically treated. **1913** G. J. KNEELAND *Commercialized Prostitution in N.Y. City* iv. 90 One of the best known [pimps] is a..dangerous fellow... A '*pipe fiend' and gambler, his favorite occupation is 'stuss'. **1938** *Amer. Speech* XIII. 189 I'm gonna take my gal along, We'll kick around the gong. She'll sing that pipe-fiend song. *c* **1450** HOLLAND *Howlat* 642 The Pitill and the *Pype Gled cryand pewewe. **1875** KNIGHT *Dict. Mech.*, **Pipe-grab*, a tool to let down into a well-pipe to enable it to be hoisted to the surface. **1828** *Blackw. Mag.* Sept. 276 The Shooter..begins with his pop or *pipe-gun, formed of the last year's growth of the branch of a plane-tree. **1973** *Trinidad Guardian* 1 Feb. 11/4 He was found guilty on a four-count indictment accusing him of being in possession of a revolver, Molotov cocktails, a pipe-gun and several rounds of ammunition. **1973** *Guardian* 27 Mar. 3/1 The Naxalites..had..country-forged pipe guns which heated and split after a few rounds. **1855** LONGF. *Hiaw.* I. 18 From the red stone of the quarry With his hand he broke a fragment, Moulded it into a *pipe-head. **1905** [see *pipe-ear*]. **1852** SEIDEL *Organ* 56 These small pipes go first through the holes of the *pipe-holders. **1805** PRISCILLA WAKEFIELD *Dom. Recreat.* vi. (1806) 93 Animalcules..living in small tubes, or cases of sandy matter, united like pieces of coral; from which..they are called the *pipe insect. **1540** *MS. Acc. St. John's Hosp., Canterb.*, Payd for a *pype key ijd. **1860** SALA *Baddington Peerage* II. xix. 23 Half-smoked *pipe-lees. **1852** DICKENS *Bleak Ho.* xxi, Mr. George..twists it [the document] up for a *pipe-light. **1875** KNIGHT *Dict. Mech.*, **Pipe-loop* (*Harness*), a long narrow loop for holding the end of a buckled strap. **1787** J. FARLEY *Art Cookery* (ed. 4) 157 Take half a pound of small *pipe-maccaroni. **1893** FORBES-MITCHELL *Remin. Gt. Mutiny* 48 Sir Colin complimented the *pipe-major on the way he had played. **1896** CROCKETT *Cleg Kelly* (ed. 2) 97 Cleg marched along like the pipe-major in the Black Watch. **14..** *Voc.* in Wr.-Wülcker 616/22 *Tibiarius*, a *Pypemaker. *c* **1515** *Cocke Lorell's B.* 10 Pype makers, wode mongers, and orgyn makers. **1765** SPRY in *Phil. Trans.* LV. 84 Had I..rendered the tube flexible..and turned it on a stick of pipe-maker's clay. **1901** *Scott. N. & Q.* May 170/2 He commissioned a well-known Glasgow pipe-maker to furnish him with a set of bag-pipes. **1852** SEIDEL *Organ* 75 The pipes..are composed of wood, pewter, or what is called *pipe-metal. **1621** B. JONSON *Gipsies Metamorph.* Wks. (Rtldg.) 623/2 Call Cheeks upon the bagpipe, and Tom Tickle-foot with his tabor. Clod, will you gather the *pipe-money? **1919** J. C. SQUIRE *Birds* 11 *Pipe-necked and stationary and silhouetted, Cormorants stood in a wise, black, equal row. **1592** WARNER *Alb. Eng.* xxxvi, His apish toyes, His Pedlarie, and *pype-notes. **1854** BUSHNAN in *Circ. Sc.* (*c* 1865) I. 293/1 When the male [bird] is alone, its most significant note is the pipe-note *witt*. **1609** DEKKER *Gvlls Horne-bk.* 18 Till your *pipe offices smoke with your pitifully-stinking girds shot out against me. **1647** HAWARD *Crown Rev.* 5 Clerke in the Pipe office. **1738** BIRCH *Life Milton* in *M.'s Wks.* (1738) I. 77 One Mr. Francis Boyton, a Norfolk Gentleman, who had a place in the Pipe-Office. **1877** *Coursing Calendar Autumn 1876* 238 Dulcimer and Jewess separated on two hares, and both got a good *pipe-opener. **1879** *Daily News* 7 Apr. 3/1 The crew.. indulge in a short paddle to the point and back by way of a 'pipe-opener'. **1898** *Cycling* 89 He should ride for half an hour, in sufficient clothing, simply as a pipe-opener. *a* **1936** KIPLING *Something of Myself* (1937) vii. 187 That tale may have served as a pipe-opener, but one could not see its wood for its trees, so I threw it away. **1962** *Times* 26 Apr. 13/4 This is the blessed time of year when cricket scores begin to creep ..into the sporting pages of the news-papers... Such trial matches are in the nature of pipe-openers, elaborations of practice at the nets. **1971** D. FRANCIS *Bonecrack* xv. 189 'I could give Archangel his pipe-opener...' 'All right, then,' I said, and he took Archangel out..and they cantered a brisk four furlongs. **1974** *Times* 18 Sept. 12/6 British pair thrashed in pipe-opener to Wills Open... The match was a curtain-raiser to the Wills Open Tournament. **1977** *Times* 9 June 8/2 There was a pipe-opener to the conference..when Prince Charles..went to Marlborough House to unveil a painting of his mother. **1881** RAYMOND *Mining Gloss.*, **Pipe-ore*, iron ore (limonite) in vertical pillars, sometimes of conical, sometimes of hour-glass form, imbedded in clay. **1895–6** *Cal. Univ. Nebraska* 214 The..course..in instrumental music, either piano-forte, *pipe-organ or violin. **1884** KNIGHT *Dict. Mech.* Suppl., **Pipe Oven*, a hot blast oven in which the air passes through pipes exposed to the heat of the furnace. In contra-distinction to a fire-brick oven. **1855** E. J. HOPKINS *Organ* 39 The *pipe-racks. The greater number of the pipes stand on the upperboards..a framework, therefore, is used to keep them in an erect position. **1892** W. B. SCOTT *Autobiog. Notes* I. 162 A pipe-rack like those in the artist clubs in Munich. **1948** *Petroleum Handbk.* (Shell Internat Petroleum Co) (ed 3) The broken-out stand is then lowered to its position on the pipe rack. **1976** W. D. BAASEL *Prelim. Chem. Engin. Plant Design* vi. 148 Nothing should be located under pipe racks, since if leaks occur they may damage equipment. **1978** G. GREENE *Human Factor* VI. i. 301 He looked at the row of pipes in the pipe rack with concentration. *a* **1780** SHIRREFS *Poems* (1790) 213 John o' *pipe-skill wasna scant. **1884** KNIGHT *Dict. Mech.* Suppl., **Pipe Stand*, a frame to support radiator pipes. **1886** W. J. TUCKER *E. Europe* 270 From his pipe-stand he reached down a long Hungarian pipe and a long Turkish chibouc. **1884** KNIGHT *Dict. Mech.* Suppl., **Pipe Stay*, a device to hold a pipe in place; or to hang a pipe. **1863** KINGLAKE *Crimea* (1876) I. xiv. 307 With the stroke of a whip or a *pipe-stick. **1931** G. EGLOFF in A. Rogers *Industr. Chem.* (ed. 5) II. 861 Modern practice used the *pipe still consisting essentially of a coil of pipe placed in a furnace through which oil is passed. **1959** *Times Rev. Industry* Aug. 97/2 The pipestill works on much the same principle as a water tube boiler. **1970** W. G. ROBERTS *Quest for Oil* viii. 87 The crude oil must be heated before it gets to the column, and the heater used is known as a 'pipestill'. **1818** *Blackw. Mag.* IV. 321 Not so thick as your Highness' *pipe-stopper. **1831** TRELAWNY *Adv. Younger Son* I. 244 Using his probe with the same sort of indifference as a man does a pipe-stopper. **1904** *N.Y. Times* 16 Oct. III. 6 The police are now forced to take what appears on its face to be the veriest *pipe story and run it down. **1875** KNIGHT *Dict. Mech.*, *Pipe-tongs. **1899** *Academy* 11 Feb. 183/1 A pair of pipe-tongs wherewith the New Englander lifted an outlying coal to light his pipe. **1813** BAKEWELL *Introd. Geol.* (1815) 281 The *pipe vein is a variety of the flat vein having the sides closed or twitched in, so as to form a tube or cavity of irregular shape. **1839** URE *Dict. Arts* 832 The pipe vein resembles in many respects a huge irregular cavern. **1857** GRAY *First Lessons Bot.* (1866) 26 The Aristolochia or *Pipe-Vine. **1866** *Treas. Bot.* 91 *A*[*ristolochia*] *Sipho*, a native of the Alleghany mountains..has..received the name of Pipe-vine, from a resemblance in the form of the flowers to that of a tobacco-pipe. **1745** SWIFT *Directions to Servants* ii. 41 Boil your Meat constantly in Pump Water, because you must sometimes want River or *Pipe Water. **1908** *Westm. Gaz.* 24 Oct. 17/2, I will not live to see pipe-water squirting down sham rocks under a sham bridge. **1774** GOLDSM. *Nat. Hist.* (1776) VII. 48 *Pipe-worms and other little animals fix their habitation to the oyster's sides.

pipe, *sb.*² [a. OF., F. *pipe*, a cask for wine, etc., also a measure. So Sp., Pg. *pipa*, It. *pippa*. In origin, the same word as PIPE *sb.*¹, in special sense of a cylindrical vessel.]

1. A large cask, of more or less definite capacity (see 2), used for wine, and formerly also for other liquids and provisions (as eggs, meat, fish, etc.), or other goods. *Obs.* or merged in 2.

1392–3 *Earl Derby's Exped.* (Camden) 156 Pro iij doliis j pipe. **1411** *Nottingham Rec.* II. 86, j tubbe et j barell vj d; dimidium pype, vij d.; j parvum fatte iij d. **1489** CAXTON *Faytes of A.* I. xvii. 49 Bridgis..made vpon pipes bounden togider and wel teyed with ropys. *c* **1559** R. HALL *Fisher* xxii. (1655) 186 His Library, which they found so replenished..with..Books,..with which they trussed up, and filled 32. great fats, or pipes. **1571** DIGGES *Pantom.* III. xi. Riv, Sundrie kindes of wine vessels, as the tunne, the pipe, the punshion, hogsheads, buttes, barrels. **1842** TENNYSON *Will Waterproof* x, The pint, you brought me, was the best That ever came from pipe.

2. Such a cask with its contents (wine, beer, cider, beef, fish, etc.), or as a measure of capacity, equivalent to half a tun, or 2 hogsheads, or 4 barrels, i.e. containing usually 105 imperial gallons (= 126 old wine-gallons), but varying for different commodities, and still for different kinds of wine. Sometimes identified with BUTT *sb.*² 1.

[**1376** *Rolls of Parlt.* II. 328/2 De chescun Pype ou Vessel de tiel Vyn douce.] **1406** in *E.E. Wills* (1882) 13 Y wyt to Iohan Whyte the yongger, and to hys wyfe, a pipe of wyne, pris of xl s. **1439** *Act 18 Hen. VI*, c. 17 Pour ceo qe come toutz les tonels, pipes, tercians & hoggeshedes de Vin Oyle & Mele..doient..conteiner un certein mesure..chescun pipe vj^{xx}, vj galons. [*tr. a* **1550** Forasmuch as all the Tunnes, Pipes, Tercians, and Hogsheads of Wine, Oyle, and Honie ..ought..to conteine a certaine measure..euerie Pipe six score and six gallons.] **1472–3** *Rolls of Parlt.* VI. 37/2, ii pipes of Syder. **1496** *Naval Acc. Hen. VII* (1896) 16 A pipe of salte bieff redie dressed xl^{s}. **1526** in Dillon *Calais & Pale* (1892) 81 A pype of redd Herring. **1670** R. COKE *Disc. Trade* 6 The Canary Wines yearly Imported are about 13000 Pipes. **1802** *Brookes' Gazetteer* (ed. 12) s.v. *Reus*, About 20,000 pipes of brandy are annually exported. **1903** *Whitaker's Almanack* 453 Of wines imported in casks the following are the usual measurements: Pipe of Port or Masdeu = 115 gallons, of Teneriffe = 100 g., of Marsala = 93 g., of Madeira and Cape = 92 g., of Sherry and Tent = 108 g.

3. *Comb.* **pipe-board**, **pipe-hoop**, **pipe-stave**, a board, hoop, or stave used for making pipes or casks (*pipe-board* in strict use connoting a certain size or thickness: see quots.); †**pipe-merry** *a.*, merry from drinking wine (*obs.*); †**pipe-wine**, wine drawn directly from the pipe or 'wood'.

1596 DANETT tr. *Comines* (1614) 19 He caried also with him..great store of *pipeboorde, meaning therewith to make a bridge ouer the riuer of Seine. **1812** J. SMYTH *Pract. of Customs* (1821) 303 Pipe Boards, viz. above 5 feet 3 inches in length, and not exceeding 8 feet, and under 8 inches square. **1833** *Act 3 & 4 Will. IV*, c. 56 Table s.v. *Wood*. **1510** in *10th Rep. Hist. MSS. Comm.* App. v. 394 Three *pipe hopis for a pennye. **1542** UDALL *Erasm. Apoph.* 141 Wyne deliuereth the herte from all care..when a bodye is *pipe merye. **1599** HAKLUYT *Voy.* II. II. 122 Ships..laden with hoopes, gally-oares, *pipe-staues, & other prouisions of the king of Spaine. **1666** *Lond. Gaz.* No. 45/1 Four Vessels laden with Pipe-staves from Hamburgh, for the use of the Navy. **1783** JUSTAMOND tr. *Raynal's Hist. Indies* VII. 438 Ireland, which afforded an advantageous mart for corn, flax, and pipe-staves, has been shut against them [colonists] by an act of parliament. **1598** SHAKS. *Merry W.* III. ii. 90 *Host*... I will to my honest Knight Falstaffe, and drinke Canarie with him. *Ford.* I thinke I shall drinke in *Pipe-wine first with him, Ile make him dance. [With play upon the musical *pipe* and *canary* the dance.]

pipe (paɪp), *v.*¹ Also 4–6 **pype**. [In branch I, OE. *pīpian* to blow the pipe (Napier *Contrib. OE. Lexic.*), ad. L. *pīpāre* in late or med. sense 'to blow a pipe', f. *pīpa* in OE. *pīpe* PIPE *sb.*¹: cf. Du. *pijpen*, MDu. *pîpen*, LG., MLG. *pîpen*, Ger. *pfeifen*, MHG. *pfîfen*; also Sw., Norw. *pīpa*, Da. *pibe*, to blow the pipe, to whistle. In branch II, ME. *pipen*, corresponds to OF. *piper* (12th c., of a mouse, a chicken, etc.) = It. *pipare* 'to pipe, to cackle or clucke as a hen, to pule as a hawke' (Florio):—L. *pīpāre* (and ? **pippāre*) to peep, cheep, chirp. In the literal sense, this is now expressed by PEEP *v.*[1], and in a special sense by PIP *v.*[2]

L. *pīpāre*, beside *pīpiāre*, *pīpīre* (all app. in same sense), was evidently echoic, imitating the voice of chickens and little birds; similar forms could arise independently in any lang. Thus, beside the forms above, MDu., MLG., Du., LG., mod.Ger. have a weak vb. *piepen*, (pijpen, *fleuter, fistulare, tibia canere*, piepen als vogels, *piper comme les petits poulsins, pipire*, Plantijn 1573), It. has *pipire* 'to peepe as a chickin' (Florio), Fr. has *pipier, pépier* in same sense, Eng. PEEP *v.*[1], PIP *v.*[2] App. the tendency in all the langs. to associate the orig. vb. with the sound of the musical instrument (cf. F. *piper* in Godef. *Compl.*) led to the use of forms more directly imitating the weak cheep of the chicken, etc., for the expression of the original L. sense.]

I. To blow or play on a pipe.

1. a. *intr.* To play on a pipe, to blow a pipe (see PIPE *sb.*[1] 1, 1 d). †Phrase ***to pipe in*** or ***with an ivy-leaf***: see IVY-LEAF (*obs.*).

a. **1000** *B. M. MS. Tib. A. III* lf. 102 (*Zeitsch. f. deutsch. Alt.* XXXIV. 234) An stan.. þæs ansyne is, swilce an man pipiȝe mid niȝon pipan & an man hearpiȝe. *c* **1275, 13..** [see PIPING *vbl. sb.*[1] 1]. **1377** LANGL. *P. Pl.* B. xx. 92 Mynstralles myȝte pipe. *c* **1420** LYDG. *Sege Thebes* 1791 Lete his brother blowen in an horn.. or pypen in a red. **1484** CAXTON *Fables of Æsop* VI. vii, Whanne I pyped and played of my muse or bag pype ye dayned, ne wold not daunce. **1526** TINDALE *Luke* vii. 32 We have pyped vnto you, and ye have nott daunsed. **1586** in Neal *Hist. Purit.* (1732) I. 480 The service of God is grievously abused by piping with organs. **1634** MILTON *Comus* 823 The soothest Shepherd that ere pip't on plains. **1765** GRAY *Shakespeare* 15 When thou hear'st the organ piping shrill. **1789** [see 5]. **1872** BESANT & RICE *Ready-Money Mort.* iv, The Arcadian shepherd piped upon the mountain. **1893** STEVENSON *Catriona* ii. 21 I'm Hieland born, and when the clan pipes, who but me has to dance?

b. To whistle, as the wind, a man, a bird, etc.: see 5 a, b.

2. a. *trans.* To play (a tune, music) upon a pipe.

1390 GOWER *Conf.* II. 113 With that his Pype on honde he hente, And gan to pipe in his manere Thing which was slepi forto hiere. **1509** HAWES *Past. Pleas.* iii. (Percy Soc.) 15 Wyth goodly pypes in their mouthes i-tuned.. they pyped a daunce, I-clipped Amour de la hault plesaunce. **1526** TINDALE *1 Cor.* xiv. 7 Except they make a distinccion in the soundes: howe shall it be knowen what is pyped or harped? **1596** SPENSER *F.Q.* VI. ix. 8 The lustie shepheard swaynes.. did pype and sing her prayses dew. **1789** BLAKE *Songs Innoc.* Introd. 2 Piping down the valleys wild, Piping songs of pleasant glee. **1820** W. IRVING *Sketch Bk.*, *Royal Poet*, (1859) 68 Those witching airs still piped among the wild mountains and lonely glens of Scotland. **1871** R. ELLIS *Catullus* lxiii. 22 On a curved oat the Phrygian deep pipeth a melody. **1898** G. MEREDITH *Odes Fr. Hist.* 11 She piped her sons the frontier march.

b. *transf.* To bring into some place or condition by playing on a pipe; to lead by the sound of a pipe; to entice or decoy, as wild fowl; also *fig.* †***to pipe up*** (quot. *c* 1546), to exalt or worship with pipes, i.e. organ-music (*obs.*). Freq. with advs. and advb. phrases: esp. *Naut.*, to bring or escort (a person) *aboard*, etc. to the accompaniment of a pipe; also *fig.*; ***to pipe in***: to bring in (a person or thing) to the accompaniment of bagpipes.

c **1546** JOYE in Gardiner *Declar. Art. Joye* 93 They pipe him [God] vp with orgaynes. **1673** DRYDEN *Amboyna* I. i, We must put on a seeming Kindness,.. pipe 'em within the Danger of our Net, and then we'll draw it o'er 'em. **1689** T. R. *View Govt. Europe* 67 A lightness of humour, by the which they are easily piped into a new mode of Government. **1842** BROWNING *Pied Piper* ad fin., Whether they pipe us free from rats or from mice. **1889** *Cornh. Mag.* Dec. 616 He pipes them homewards, and they trot along.. as if they liked the music. **1918** *Times* 21 Sept. 5/1 It was a Punjabi piper who piped the Cossacks in. **1939** F. DRAKE-CARNELL *It's an Old Scottish Custom* ii. facing p. 54 (*caption*) St. Andrew's Night. Piping in the haggis. **1939** JOYCE *Finnegans Wake* (1964) I. 25 Your fame is spreading like Basilico's ointment since the Fintan Lalors piped you overborder. **1940** *Bluejackets' Man.* (U.S. Naval Inst.) lix. 783. In the piping of officials alongside and over, the side pipe is lengthened to full breath for officials receiving 8 side boys. **1955** *Times* 1 July 6/3 The Duke was piped on board, welcomed by the master, Captain H. W. Langbein. **1965** D. MACLEAN *Queens' Company* xx. 175 On the following morning the doughty Henry Morgan himself, accompanied by his bodyguard, all in magnificent period uniform, were ceremoniously piped on board. **1966** *Listener* 20 Oct. 578/2 Noah pipes aboard an earnest procession of elephants, camels, and assorted fowl. **1968** *Islander* (Victoria, B.C.) 15 Dec. 2/3 The plum pudding, ablaze, was piped in and paraded around the dining room by the chef before being served. **1973** *Stornoway Gaz.* 3 Mar. 1/1 The platform party was piped in by two members of the Lewis Pipe Band. **1976** *Oxf. Compan. Ships & Sea* 131/2 The call.. is retained for ceremonial occasions when piping dignitaries and foreign naval officers aboard. **1977** 'J. LE CARRÉ' *Hon. Schoolboy* xiii. 292 He looked into the ceiling mirror and caught the glitter of an electric-blue suit and a full head of black hair well greased; and between the two, a foreshortened chubby Chinese face set on a pair of powerful shoulders, and two curled hands held out in a fighter's greeting while Lizzie piped him aboard.

c. ***to pipe the side*** (*Naut.*): to sound the 'side', a salute given to certain officers and dignitaries when boarding or leaving a ship.

1896 L. DELBOS *Naut. Terms* (ed. 3) 103 *To pipe the side*, faire les honneurs du sifflet. **1909** *Cent. Dict.* Suppl. *s.v.*, When the commanding officer of a naval vessel, or the president or vice-president of the country, or other dignitaries, or superior officers of foreign governments, or crowned heads, or members of royal families, or of the nobility, are received on board, or are leaving a man-of-war, .. the boatswain, or one of his mates, winds (blows) his call (silver whistle)... This ceremony is.. known as piping the side. **1938** C. S. FORESTER *Flying Colours* 237 They piped the side for him in the *Victory*, as Admiralty regulations laid down.

3. a. *Naut.* To summon, as a boatswain the crew, to some duty, or to a meal, by sounding the pipe or whistle (*trans.*, and *intr.*). Also *transf.* ***to pipe away, down***, to dismiss by sounding the pipe.

1706 E. WARD *Wooden World Diss.* (1708) 102 Whensoever the Boatswain pipes to Dinner. **1789** G. KEATE *Pelew Isl.* 92 The boatswain.. piped all out to their separate departments. **1790** C. DIBDIN *Song, 'Tom Bowling'* v, When He who all commands Shall give.. The word to pipe all hands. **1809** MALKIN *Gil Blas* v. ii. ¶2 All hands were piped to make the necessary arrangements. **1833** MARRYAT *P. Simple* viii, I.. was ready at the gangway a quarter of an hour before the men were piped away. *Ibid.* xi, The hammocks were piped down.. and the ship was once more quiet. **1837** —— *Dog-fiend* x, Jemmy piped the hands up. **1867** SMYTH *Sailor's Word-bk.*, *Pipe down!* The order to dismiss the men from the deck when a duty has been performed on board ship. **1884** H. COLLINGWOOD *Under Meteor Flag* 15 The hands had just been piped to breakfast.

b. ***to pipe down***, in more general use: to stop talking, be quiet, become less vociferous; freq. as a command, = shut up! Also occas. *trans.*, to cause (someone) to be silent. *colloq.*

1900 *Dialect Notes* II. 49 *Pipe down*, to stop talking. **1926** STALLINGS & ANDERSON *What Price Glory?* I. i, in *Three Amer. Plays* 24 Pipe down. *Ibid.* III. 76 He tried to pipe me down. **1932** S. O'FAOLÁIN *Midsummer Night Madness* 227 'Shut up, you,' said the Tan angrily, and the little fellow piped down miserably. **1938** N. MARSH *Artists in Crime* vi. 76 'Hatchett,' said Troy. 'Pipe down.' **1945** E. WAUGH *Brideshead Revisited* I. v. 105 Groans of protest rose from the other cells where various tramps and pick-pockets were trying to get some sleep: 'Aw, pipe down!' **1951** M. KENNEDY *Lucy Carmichael* VI. ii. 293 He didn't disagree; if he had, I'd have piped down. *Ibid.* 294, I won't pipe down. I'll go to Charles. I'll spill all the beans. **1974** *Times* 19 Jan. 12/1 The more immoderate members of his party.. may pipe down.

II. To utter a shrill and, originally, weak sound.

†4. *intr.* To utter a shrill and weak sound; to cheep, squeak, peep. Said of chickens, small birds, mice, etc., and contemptuously of persons. *Obs.*, and replaced by PEEP *v.*[1]

a **1250** *Owl & Night.* 503 Ne myht þu leng a word iqueþe Ac [þu] pipest al so doþ a mose. *c* **1350** *Nominale Gall.-Angl.* 759 (E.E.T.S.) *Rayne gailie*, Frogge pipith. *c* **1440** *Promp. Parv.* 401/2 Pypyn, or ȝyppe, as henn byrdys, .. *pipio, pipulo.* *c* **1460** *Towneley Myst.* ii. 298 Whi, who is that hob ouer the wall? we! who was that that piped so small? *Ibid.* xiii. 195 Who is that pypys so poore? **1481** CAXTON *Reynard* x. (Arb.) 21 Ye shal catche myes by grete heepis, herke how they pype [orig. *pipen*]. **1483** *Cath. Angl.* 281/1 To Pipe as a byrde, *pipiare.*

5. The following appear to have begun as varieties of sense 4, but to have been influenced by sense 1, or by association with PIPE *sb.*[1], so as to express a louder shrill sound.

a. To whistle: said of the wind (in later use, sometimes, to howl), of the human voice, a marmot; also to hum or buzz shrilly as a winged insect; to whistle or whizz as a bullet.

1513 DOUGLAS *Æneis* III. viii. 48 At our desyre, The sesonable air pipis vp fair and schire. **1600** SHAKS. *A. Y. L.* II. vii. 162 His bigge manly voice, Turning againe toward childish trebble pipes, And whistles in his sound. **1632** MILTON *Penseroso* 126 While rocking Winds are Piping loud. **1814** SCOTT *Ld. of Isles* III. xxiii, The favouring breeze, when loud It pipes upon the galley's shroud. **1824** LONGF. *Woods in Winter* vi, Gathering winds.. Amid the vocal reeds pipe loud. **1860** TYNDALL *Glac.* I. ii. 22 The frightened marmots piped incessantly from the rocks. **1880** *Daily Tel.* 7 Sept., With the anchor over the bow, and the wind piping through the rigging. **1889** DOYLE *Micah Clarke* 136 We heard the bullets piping all around them.

b. To whistle or sing as a bird.

a **1591** H. SMITH in Spurgeon *Treas. Dav.* Ps. cxxxvi. 1 Like a bird that is taught to pipe. *a* **1771** GRAY *Birds* 1 There pipes the woodlark. **1822** W. IRVING *Braceb. Hall* I. vi. 51 The thrush piped from the hawthorn. **1828** [see PIPING *vbl. sb.*[1] 1]. **1884** W. C. SMITH *Kildrostan* 61 O throstle softly piping High on the topmost bough.

c. To speak or talk loudly and shrilly.

1784 R. BAGE *Barham Downs* II. 268 My mother was the best scold in all Ballyshannon, and if she did not pipe it away two or three hours every day, she [etc.]. **1792** CHARLOTTE SMITH *Desmond* III. 177 He goes piping about, and talks of unequal representation, and the weight of taxes. **1866** CHR. ROSSETTI *Prince's Progr.*, etc. 3 Voices piped on the gale.

d. To weep, to cry. *colloq.* or *slang.* (Cf. *to pipe one's eye*, 7.)

1797 MRS. M. ROBINSON *Walsingham* III. 310 She has been piping all the way down to Bath. *a* **1814** DIBDIN *Song, True Courage* i, 'Tis nonsense for trifles, I own, to be piping. **1824** LADY GRANVILLE *Lett.* (1894) I. 283 The organ.. is the finest thing I ever heard. The three or four first chords made me pipe. **1901** FARMER *Slang*, *Pipe*.. (1) to talk; and (2) to cry; also *to pipe up, to take a pipe, to tune one's pipes*, and *to pipe one's eye.*

6. *trans.* To utter **a.** in a peeping or cheeping voice, as a mouse; **b.** in a loud shrill or clear voice, as a song-bird, a singer, or speaker.

1377 LANGL. *P. Pl.* B. XVIII. 406 Thanne piped pees of poysye a note, *Clarior est solito post maxima nebula phebus.* *c* **1384** CHAUCER *H. Fame* II. 277 How every.. noyse, or sovne.. Thogh hyt were piped of a mouse Mote nede come to Fames house. **1553** T. WILSON *Rhet.* (1580) 223 One pipes out his woordes so small, through defaulte of his wynde pipe, that ye would thinke he whisteled. **1567** *Gude & Godlie B.* (S.T.S.) 208 Sa sall they pipe a merie fit. **1706** E. WARD *Wooden World Diss.* (1708) 97 The same old Song .. which they have pip'd to each other these many Years. **1750** GRAY *Elegy* 103 Oft as the woodlark piped her farewell song. **1840** THACKERAY *Catherine* i, The boys piped out an hurrah. **1842** TENNYSON *Launcelot & G.* ii, Sometimes the linnet piped his song. **1861** THACKERAY *Four Georges* i, Italian soprani piped their Latin rhymes in place of the hymns. **1871** R. ELLIS *Catullus* lxi. 153 Love can angrily pipe adieu.

7. ***to pipe one's eye*** or ***eyes*** (orig. *Naut. slang*): to shed tears, weep, cry.

1789 C. DIBDIN *Song, Poor Jack* iii, What argufies sniv'ling and piping your eye? *a* **1814** *Sailor's Ret.* II. i. in *New Brit. Theatre* II. 337 Lucy and he must have piped their eyes enough by this time. **1844** DICKENS *Mart. Chuz.* xxxii, He was very frail and tearful.. his own peculiar mission was to pipe his eye. **1897** 'OUIDA' *Massarenes* xxxii, 'One don't pipe one's eye when one comes into a fortun'', said the wheelwright.

III. 8. *Pugilistic slang.* (*intr.*) To breathe hard, pant from violent exertion or exhaustion.

1814 *Sporting Mag.* XLIV. 72 Painter at length fell from weakness, and both were at this time piping. **1826** *Ibid.* XVII. 283 Bob was piping a little, but said 'nothing was the matter'. **1827** DE QUINCEY *Murder* Wks. 1862 IV. 33 The baker came up piping.

IV. 9. pipe up. a. *trans.* To blow up, commence to play or sing, strike up. Also *absol.*

c **1425** *Cast. Persev.* 457 (*Stage direct.*) Pipe vp music. *c* **1570** *Marr. Wit & Science* IV. iii. in Hazl. *Dodsley* II. 372 Pipe us up a galliard, minstrel. **1575** *Gamm. Gurton* II. v. ibid. III. 211 In the meantime fellows, pipe up your fiddles. **1883** STEVENSON *Treas. Isl.* I. iii, Once he piped up to a different air, a kind of country love-song.

b. *intr.* To raise the voice, speak up in a piping voice; to rise or increase, as the wind.

1889 'MARK TWAIN' *Yankee at Crt. K. Arthur* (ed. Tauchn.) I. 167 As the guard laid a hand upon me, she piped up with the tranquilest confidence. **1901** *Daily Chron.* 14 May 8/7 The wind had piped up to half a gale overnight.

pipe (paɪp), *v.*[2] [f. PIPE *sb.*[1], senses 3–5.]

I. †1. *trans.* ? To draw through pipes or taps; to drink. *Obs. rare.*

1575 LANEHAM *Let.* (1871) 45 In lyttl more then a three dayz space, 72 tunn of Ale & Beer waz pyept vp quite.

†2. *intr.* ? To flow or be conveyed as through a pipe. *Obs.*

1656 R. SHORT *Drinking Water* Pref. A ij b, We see so many kickshaws in all sciences.. and new Paradoxes in Physick, piping out of the Novelists Braines.

II. 3. a. *trans. Gardening.* To propagate (pinks, etc.) by cuttings or slips taken off at a joint of the stem; see quot. 1856, and PIPING *vbl. sb.*[2] 2.

1788 H. WALPOLE *Let. to Mrs. H. More* 4 July, No botanist am I; nor wished to learn from you.. that piping has a new signification. I had rather that you handled an oaten pipe than a carnation one. **1856** DELAMER *Fl. Gard.* (1861) 78 Carnations may.. be increased, after blooming, by 'pipings', i.e. the ends of the shoots broken off at a joint.. so as to form a short pipe-like cutting... The pipings then are made to strike root... Pinks are more generally piped, Carnations layered. **1858** GLENNY *Gard. Every-day Bk.* 194/1 Carnations.. when all the shoots that are long enough are layered, those which are too short may be piped like pinks.

b. *intr.* Of certain herbs: To develop a tubular stem, to become pipy.

1855 DELAMER *Kitch. Gard.* 78 It [celery] has a greater tendency to 'pipe', or run up to seed. **1903** *Eng. Dial. Dict.*, *Pipe*.. Of onions: to run to seed-stalks but not to seed. (Bedfordsh.)

III. 4. a. *Dressmaking*, etc. To trim or ornament with piping (see PIPING *vbl. sb.*[2] 4).

1841 LEVER *C. O'Malley* lxviii, Her blue satin piped with scarlet. **1884** *Girl's Own Paper* 29 Nov. 138/2 The edges of the newest bodices are now piped, as they were some time ago. **1906** *Myra's Jrnl.* 1 Apr. 10/3 If satin is used the seams should be piped instead of being lapped.

b. *Confectionery* and *Cookery.* To ornament (a cake, etc.), or to form (an ornamental design) with sugar piping (see PIPING *vbl. sb.*[2] 8); to arrange (icing, cream, mashed potato, etc.) in decorative cord-like lines or twists. Also *intr.*

1883–4 [see PIPING *vbl. sb.*[2] 8]. **1884** [see PIPED *ppl. a.*[1] 2]. **1892** A. B. MARSHALL *Larger Cookery Bk.* 317 Fill them by means of a forcing bag and pipe with the Cheese custard.. or whipped cream. **1894** *Westm. Gaz.* 11 Dec. 4/3 The lower portion of the cake contains panels delicately piped in sugar. **1901** *Daily Chron.* 4 Dec. 9/2 Wanted a man.. to ice and pipe Christmas cakes. **1929** E. J. KOLLIST *French Pastry, Confectionery & Sweets* vi. 116 Cover with royal icing... When dry, pipe flowers and leaves on the basket. **1948** *Good Housek. Cookery Bk.* 582 Pipe on chocolate butter icing and decorate with angelica. *Ibid.* 587 Sandwich the cakes together with the filling, spreading some on the top also. If liked, it can be piped on top with a writing pipe. **1965** *Listener* 30 Sept. 511/3 Allow this to sink in a little before piping the whipped cream all over the top. **1976** G. MOFFAT *Short Time to Live* ii. 17 'I can't come,' she called... 'I'm piping.'.. She had been piping cream round a flan.

IV. 5. *trans.* To furnish or supply with pipes; to lay (a place) with pipes (for gas, water, etc.).

1884 *Boston* (Mass.) *Jrnl.* Jan., A special town meeting.. to hear the report of the committee with reference to piping the town. The committee will recommend that the town take its water of Lynn. **1902** GREENOUGH & KITTREDGE *Words* 192 Any noun can become a verb... Thus we have to cudgel, to powder, to oil, to pipe (for gas), to wall in.

6. a. To convey (water, gas, oil, etc.) through or by means of pipes. Also *transf.* Cf. *light pipe* s.v. LIGHT *sb.* 16.

1889 *Whitby Gaz.* 27 Sept. 3/2 A large Philadelphia syndicate has secured the gas rights in Indiana..and will pipe the natural gas to Chicago. **1901** *Daily Chron.* 31 May 7/1 Fuel oil from the wells in Beaumont can be piped to Port Arthur. **1949** H. C. Weston *Sight, Light & Efficiency* v. 183 Some of the doctor's work-objects are parts of the body which cannot be adequately illuminated by general lighting, hence, he sometimes 'pipes' light to these parts by means of transparent internally-reflecting plastic devices which are attached to small hand-lamps. **1952** *Chambers's Jrnl.* Jan. 62/1 The well-known plastic material perspex possesses the unusual property of 'piping' light rather than diffusing it. This property is displayed when the interior of perspex tubing is illuminated. **1968** Bean & Simons *Lighting Fittings* v. 167 Light can be piped along a rod, block, or sheet of transparent medium such as glass or acrylic plastic. **1971** P. Tooley *High Polymers* ii. 60 Another interesting property [of polymethyl methacrylate] is its ability to 'pipe' light from one place to another as a result of a high degree of internal reflection. This is used surgically to illuminate internal hollow organs such as the stomach.

b. To transmit (music or speech) over a wire or cable.

1937 [implied in piped *ppl. a.*[1] 3 b]. **1939** *Wireless World* 16 Mar. 259/3 Broadcast programmes or announcements by the pilot can be 'piped' to the passengers. **1956** *Time* 9 Jan. 20/2 It was his wintertime pre-breakfast habit to cut figure eights on the ice of Webster Lake..to the music of Mozart and Chopin, piped through an amplifying system he had rigged up. **1959** *Observer* 6 Dec. 4/5 Programmes of music, talks and plays were 'piped' to individual seats, each passenger having lightweight earphones with volume control. **1967** *N.Y. Herald Tribune Internat.* 11–12 Feb. 3/3 The astronaut told the workers in a talk piped over a public address system to plants here and in Oak Creek. **1977** *Sunday Times* 6 Mar. 8/6 Powell's daily conference is piped into a dozen White House offices.

7. *Mining.* To direct a jet of water from a pipe upon (gravel, etc.): see hydraulic *a.* 1; to supply with water for this purpose.

1882 *Rep. to Ho. Repr. Prec. Met. U.S.* 629 The length of the season..will depend upon the water available,..some of the smaller claims are not piped more than one hundred to one hundred and fifty days per year. At the large mines piping goes on night and day.

8. *intr.* To smoke a pipe. *N. Amer. colloq.* See also piping *vbl. sb.*[2] 1.

1846 T. L. McKenney *Mem.* I. iii. 71 These hardy adventurous fellows never rose from their paddles, nor stopped except to '*pipe*'. **1863** W. B. Cheadle *Jrnl. Trip across Canada* (1931) 270 Dr. Benson..assured us we were going wrong. We therefore lunched & piped.

9. *trans.* and *intr.* To see, notice, look (at), watch; to follow or observe (someone), esp. stealthily. Also with *off. slang* and *dial.*

Perhaps a different word.

1846 *Swell's Night Guide* 43 You may pipe the crib by seeing a board whereon is inscribed the name of the piano faker. **1848** *Ladies' Repository* VIII. 316/2 *Pipe*, to watch; reconnoitre. **1864** Hotten *Slang Dict.* 202 *Pipe*, to follow or dog a person. Term used by detectives. **1869** *Galaxy* VIII. 349 His 'pal'..has meantime been engaged in an operation which he styles 'piping off the cop', by which he means that he has been watching the movements of the policeman. **1877** *Sessions Papers* 25 Oct. 631 Druscovich..said 'I know I am being *piped off*—that in our language means being followed or watched—it would imply that another detective was following him. **1888** S. O. Addy *Gloss. Words Sheffield* 176 *Pipe*, to take notice of. 'Pipe his kuss', *i.e.*, take notice of his mouth. A detective is said to pipe round a public-house when in search of a culprit. **1898** A. M. Binstead *Pink 'Un & Pelican* iv. 87 His mission up there on the roof was to exclude—*Anglice*, sling off—any who sought to 'pipe off' the contest through the skylight aforesaid. **1898** F. P. Dunne *Mr. Dooley in Peace & War* 3 Sagasta pipes him out iv th' corner iv his eye. **1906** 'H. McHugh' *Skiddoo!* 67 I'm going to pass you out a talk he handed me a few evenings ago on that subject. Pipe! **1915** Wodehouse *Psmith, Journalist* ii. 10 Pipe de leather collar she's wearing. **1924** E. O'Neill *Welded* ii. ii. 141 Remember kissing me on the corner with the whole mob pipin' us off? **1926** *Flynn's* 16 Jan. 640/2 We found another rattler and a few days later I piped a beaut of a jug and a jay burg. **1943** F. Sargeson in *Penguin New Writing* XVII. 78 We'd stand in shop doorways and Terry'd pipe off everyone that went past. **1950** R. Chandler *Let.* 18 May in *R. Chandler Speaking* (1966) 78 'Piped' does not mean 'found' but saw or spotted (with the eyes). **1974** H. J. Parker *View from Boys* iii. 77 During the daytime wandering around the area, 'pipe-ing', looking over a car, became a regular practice.

pipe, *v.*[3] [f. pipe *sb.*[2]] *trans.* To put (liquor, etc.) in a pipe or cask.

1465 *Mann. & Househ. Exp.* (Roxb.) 185 Reschard Felaw hathe..serten befe serten here and serten flower pyped. **1513–14** *Act* 5 *Hen. VIII*, c. 16 Thoffice of packyng of Wolleyn clothes..and of oder merchaundises to be pakked tonned piped barellid or otherwise enclosid. **1766** Entick *London* (1776) I. 410.

'pipe-clay, *sb.* A fine white kind of clay, which forms a ductile paste with water; used for making tobacco-pipes, and also (esp. by soldiers) for cleaning white trousers, etc. Hence *allusively*, excessive attention to the minutiæ of dress and appearance in the management of regiments. See also *tobacco-pipe clay* s.v. tobacco-pipe 3.

[**1758** Reid tr. *Macquer's Chym.* I. 198 This lute is composed of a very fine cretaceous earth, called tobacco-pipe clay, moistened with..oil of lint-seed, and a varnish made of amber and gum copal.] **1777** J. Wedgwood *Let.* 19 July (1965) 207 He brought some of the stones home with him, mixed them with Pipe Clay, and made the first White Flint Stone Ware. **1806** *Gazetteer Scotl.* (ed. 2) 290 Limestone is abundant, and there is a great quantity of what is called pipe-clay. **1851** Mayne Reid *Scalp Hunt.* xxiii, He [the soldier] had got tired of pork and pipe-clay. **1858** W. Johnson *Ionica* 49 Yet bright gleams the pipe-clay below the red breast, And in slate-coloured trowsers the line look their best. **1862** *Sat. Rev.* 15 Mar. 299 Hampered by conditions largely partaking of red tape and pipeclay. **1898** E. J. Hardy in *United Service Mag.* Mar. 650 He spends all his time cleaning his things, and would be like a fish out of water if pipeclay were abolished. **1966** 'J. Hackston' *Father clears Out* 80 He could have also 'lost all his grass', not that our pipeclay had any grass on it.

attrib. **1779** Forrest *Voy. N. Guinea* 165 A remarkable rock..of a pipe clay colour, with a few bushes atop. **1835** Gen. P. Thompson *Exerc.* (1842) III. 259 Not altogether perhaps what may be called 'in pipe-clay order'. **1849** E. E. Napier *Excurs. S. Africa* II. 5 There was not often time for the pipe-clay observances of the 'regulations'.

Hence **'pipe-clay** *v. trans.*, to whiten with pipe-clay; *fig.* to put into spick and span order; whence **'pipe-clayed** *ppl. a.*, **'pipe-claying** *vbl. sb.* and *ppl. a.* Also **'pipe-clayey, 'pipe-clayish** *adjs.*, covered with pipe-clay; addicted to the use of pipe-clay.

1833 Marryat *P. Simple* ii, They [midshipmen] *pipe-clays their weekly accounts, and walks up and down with their hands in their pockets. **1864** Knight *Passages Work. Life* I. 59 Our Volunteer..had to pipe-clay his white breeches and gaiters. **1830** Marryat *King's Own* xxx, Their well *pipeclayed belts. **1890** *Golden South* 167 His mate, very gruff and *pipe-clayey. **1836** *Fraser's Mag.* XIII. 645 In these piping, and *pipe-claying, times of peace. **1859** *All Year Round* No. 34. 183 They are too soldier-like, too *pipe-clayish.

piped (paɪpt), *ppl. a.*[1] [f. pipe *sb.*[1] and *v.*[2]]

1. Furnished with a pipe or pipes; having the form of a pipe, tubular. ***piped key*** = pipe-key: see pipe *sb.*[1] 11 b.

c **1520** in *9th Rep. Hist. MSS. Comm.* 126 A pypyd key for the wyket domus matris mee. **1549** Coverdale, etc. *Erasm. Par. Jas.* 34 The adders hurte none but with thrusting in theyr small piped toothe. **1578** Lyte *Dodoens* v. lxxi. 637 The wylde Garlyke hath no leaues, but..long, rounde, small, holowe, pyped blades. **1705** J. Petiver in *Phil. Trans.* XXV. 1956 It's externally piped towards the Mouth. **1821** Clare *Vill. Minstr.* I. 137 The ragged-robin..With its pip'd stem.

2. Formed into, or ornamented with, piping: see pipe *v.*[2] 4.

1884 *Pall Mall G.* '*Extra*' 24 July 2/1 A large vase is made of piped sugar. **1899** *Daily News* 28 Oct. 7/3 The line of piped red cloth.

3. a. Conveyed by pipes.

1883 Gresley *Gloss. Coal Mining*, *Piped Air*, ventilation carried into the working places in pipes. **1889** *Anthony's Photogr. Bull.* II. 77 If piped water cannot be had.

b. Received over a wire or cable (rather than directly from broadcast signals); esp. in phr. ***piped music***, background music, usu. pre-recorded, played through loudspeakers in a public place.

1937 *Printers' Ink Monthly* May 40/2 *Piped program*, a program transmitted over wires. **1949** *Wireless World* Feb. 67/2 Piped Television... Each block of flats will be equipped with a receiving aerial, from which the signal will be fed via an amplifier and distribution units to each flat. **1959** *Daily Mail* 11 Aug. 1/6 A 'piped' television service is to be started soon by the Ekco and Ferguson companies. The system eliminates interference and overcomes reception snags in 'fringe' areas. **1969** *Morning Star* 25 Mar. 2 To me, piped music is a sign of bad taste. **1973** *Times* 27 Mar. (Sudan Suppl.) p. viii/2 A new Hilton Hotel, complete no doubt with swimming pool, air conditioning, piped music and American food. **1977** *Irish Times* 8 June 13/4 (Advt.), Secluded furnished cottage; one bedroom, phone; piped t.v.; own entrance; £16 per week.

c. Also ***piped-in*** adj.; also in sense of pipe *v.*[2] 6 b.

1959 *Economist* 14 Mar. 976/2 There are beach chairs and umbrellas by the swimming pool,..a picnic area, barbecue pit, piped-in music. **1961** *Lancet* 9 Sept. 591/1 Piped-in oxygen prevents noise from clanking cylinders. **1976** M. Ierley *Year that tried Men's Souls* i. 72 Usefulness is limited to locations with access..to piped-in water. **1977** *Rolling Stone* 19 May 15/5 It dawns on him what's been playing on the restaurant's piped-in music system.

4. Drunk, intoxicated; under the influence of drugs. *U.S. slang.*

1912 *Pedagogical Seminary* XIX. 97 Figurative expressions referring to..Intoxication:—'full', 'piped', [etc.]. **1913** *Dialect Notes* IV. 11 The engineers were all piped. **1924** G. C. Henderson *Keys to Crookdom* 413 *Piped*, under influence of liquor or narcotics. **1953** Berrey & Van den Bark *Amer. Thes. Slang* (1954) § 106/7 Drunk,..*piped*.

piped, *ppl. a.*[2] [repr. F. *pipé*, f. *piper* to deceive, prop. to decoy birds by whistling. Cf. Cotgrave '*Pipé*, deceiued, cousened..gulled, beguiled. *Cartes pipées*, & *Dez pipez*, false cards or dice'.] In phr. ***piped dice***: see etymology.

1843 James *Forest Days* (1847) 275 You must think me.. ready to play against you with piped dice.

pipe-down. *Naut.* [f. pipe *v.*[1]] The act of 'piping down' (see pipe *v.*[1] 3); a call on the boatswain's pipe signalling sailors to retire for the night.

1913 *Dialect Notes* IV. 164 *Pipe-down*, tattoo. Pipe-down call is sounded at 9 p.m. on board ship. **1942** *Penguin New Writing* XV. 8, I didn't see him again until pipe-down. **1963** *Times* 26 Feb. 12/7 Twenty-odd 'pipes' for special occasions were there to be learnt, from the 'still'..to the complicated 'Pipe down' at the end of the day.

'pipe-fish. [f. pipe *sb.*[1] + fish.] A fish of the genus *Syngnathus* or family *Syngnathidæ*, having a long slender body and a long snout.

1769 Pennant *Zool.* III. 107 As we want a generical name in our language for this genus [*Syngnathus*], we call it the *Pipe Fish*, from its slender body. **1774** Goldsm. *Nat. Hist.* (1776) VI. 289 The body of the Pipe Fish, in the thickest part, is not thicker than a swan-quill, while it is above sixteen inches long. **1846** Embleton in *Proc. Berw. Nat. Club* II. 168 A male specimen of the Little Pipe Fish (*Syngnathus ophidion*), with the eggs of the female in its abdominal pouches, was also exhibited.

pipeful ('paɪpfʊl). [f. pipe *sb.*[1] and [2] + -ful.]

1. [f. pipe *sb.*[2]] A quantity (of liquor, etc.) sufficient to fill a pipe or large cask. *rare.*

1605 Timme *Quersit.* iii. 167 It doth..heate..a whole pipeful of cold water.

2. [f. pipe *sb.*[1]] A quantity (of tobacco, etc.) sufficient to fill the bowl of a pipe.

c **1613** Rowlands *Paire Spy-Knaves* 20 Who takes his pipefull vp, And smokes it off, with *puffe 'tis gone.* **1844** Kinglake *Eöthen* (1845) 202 Poor indeed is the man in these climes who cannot command a pipeful of tobacco.

pipe-lay ('paɪpleɪ), *sb.* Also pipelay, pipe lay. [f. pipe *sb.*[1] + lay *v.*[1]] = pipe-laying (*a*). Usu. *attrib.*

1974 *Petroleum Rev.* XXVIII. 556/2 Standard pipelay equipment was used. **1975** *Times* 19 Feb. 14/6 Essential equipment (eg, platforms, derrick barges and pipe-lay barges). **1975** *Offshore* Aug. 124/3 Two stern thrusters on the reel barge and a 3,600-hp tug controlled the barge during the pipe lay. **1976** *Offshore Engineer* July 6/1 *Castoro VI*, a new Saipem barge at present undergoing trials, will be used for the trial pipelay of 305mm and 406mm pipeline.

'pipe-lay, *v. U.S. slang.* [Cf. pipe-laying.] *intr.* To 'lay pipes' (see pipe *sb.*[1] 3 b); to take measures preparatory to securing some desired action or event. Also *trans.*, to manipulate or cheat.

1848 *Campaign Flag* (Maysville, Kentucky) 14 Apr. 3/6 He was *pipe-layed* out of his election last year. **1884** J. MacCarthy *Hist. Four Georges* I. 107 Bolingbroke and Oxford..had been 'pipe-laying', to use an expressive American word, for the Stuart restoration during all the closing years of Queen Anne's reign. **1888** in Farmer & Henley *Slang* (1902) V. 213/1 There are not a few who are pipe-laying and marshalling forces for the fray.

pipe-layer ('paɪpˌleɪə(r)). [f. pipe *sb.*[1] + layer *sb.* 1.] **a.** A workman who lays pipes for the conveyance of water, gas, etc. Also, a machine used to lay pipes. **b.** *U.S. political slang.* One who schemes to procure corrupt votes. (See quot. *a* 1882, and next.)

1840 *Richmond* (Virginia) *Enquirer* Nov. (Th.), Corruption of the franchise by pipe layers and yarn spinners. **1841** *Congress. Globe* 26th Congress 2 Sess. App. 155/1, I was not defeated by voters. I was defeated by 'pipe layers'. **1851** Mayhew *Lond. Labour* (1865) II. 510/2 Rubbish-carters, or pipe-layers, or ground-workers. **1864** Sala in *Daily Tel.* 8 July, You might take them to be pipe-layers, or log-rollers, or lobbyers, or members of a municipal 'ring'. *a* **1882** T. Weed *Autobiog.* xlviii. (1883) 493 A letter in which he said that the men..were to be employed in laying the pipes for the introduction of Croton water. The Whig leaders were immediately stigmatized as 'pipe layers', a term persistently applied to them for several years. **1969** *Engineering* 25 Apr. 648/2 A Badger Minor trenchless pipelayer..has been specially adapted [for the simultaneous laying of four pvc cable ducts]. **1976** *Daily Tel.* 15 July 5/1 The deaths of a Texan pipe-layer and a French diver brought criticism from an MP yesterday of the Government's attitude towards safety in North Sea gas and oil operations. **1977** *Pipes & Pipelines Internat.* XXII. 35/2 A new pipelayer with lifting capacity of 41 000 kg.

So **'pipe-laying,** (*a*) the laying of pipes for water, gas, etc.; (*b*) in *U.S. political slang*, a form of political corruption: see quot. 1850.

1848 *N.Y. Tribune* 30 Oct. (Bartlett) The result..would not be..doubtful, if we could be assured of fair play and no pipe-laying. **1850** Lyell *2nd Visit U.S.* II. 6 Fifty or sixty Irish labourers..were conciliated for some years by employment in the Croton waterworks, so that 'pipe-laying' became the slang term for this kind of bribery. **1864** Webster, *Pipe-laying*, the laying down of pipes, as for gas, water, etc. **1881** *Nation* (N.Y.) XXXII. 180 He would begin his pipe-laying at a greater distance,..and fortify his combinations by many more devices. **1841** *Congress. Globe* 26th Congress 2 Sess. App. 120/2 Others say that fraud, double voting, pipe laying, [etc.]..have done much to carry the election. **1842** [see colonization 2]. **1871** *Engineering* XI. p. vii/3 (*heading*) Pipe laying under water. **1973** C. Callow *Power from Sea* viii. 163 Pipe-laying barges are actively engaged in off-shore work. **1975** *BP Shield Internat.* May 14/1 The second highly weather-vulnerable job is pipe-laying. **1975** *Times* 16 Sept. (North Sea Suppl.) p. i/1 Pipe-laying barges need to monitor their operations under the sea and to locate pipes at a later date.

pipeless ('paɪplɪs), *a.* [f. as prec. + -less.] Without a pipe; having no pipe.

1870 *Athenæum* 19 Nov. 653 All the tobacconists' shops.. were closed, and Ned arrived at his habitation pipeless and weedless. **1900** *Daily News* 30 Nov. 5/6 A native house, heated by a Chinese pipeless stove.

pipelet ('paɪplɪt). *nonce-wd.* [f. as prec. + -let.] A small pipe; in quot. a weak piping voice (pipe *sb.*[1] 2).

1885 L. B. Walford *Nan & other Stories* I. 237 The above remark was uttered in a soft treble pipe, and at last half-a-dozen other pipelets, equally soft, responded.

'pipe-,line, *sb.* **a.** A continuous line of pipes; a conduit of iron pipes for conveying petroleum from the oil-wells to the market or refinery, or for supplying water to a town or district. Also *attrib.*

1873 J. T. HENRY *Early & Later Hist. Petroleum* 283 The iron pipe lines for the conveyance of oil from the wells to railway shipping points play an important part in the transportation of the article. **1879** in I. M. Tarbell *Hist. Standard Oil Co.* (1904) I. 354 The pipe lines owned and controlled by the parties hereto have a joint capacity for transportation. **1883** *Century Mag.* July 332/2 When the tank at a well is nearly full, notice is sent to the nearest agency of the pipe lines. *Ibid.* 334/2 The pipe line system was a thing of small beginnings and slow growth. **1891** *Daily News* 3 June 5/6 A temporary pipe line has been laid across the bed of the Mersey,..and now the water is being discharged on the Lancashire side. **1924** C. CHRISTY *Big Game & Pygmies* i. 2 Between Matadi and Leopoldville is a wonderful pipe line, by which crude mineral oil for the fleet of up-river steamers is pumped the whole two hundred odd miles by several pumping stations. **1943** *Ann. Reg. 1942* 263 A second first-class road..runs alongside the pipe-line from the Palestinian to the Iraqui frontier. **1953** *Times* 31 Oct. 4/6 A water supply had been brought by bamboo pipelines from a spring. **1961** *Wall St. Jrnl.* 8 Nov. 24/2 The filing.. proposes construction of 210 miles of large-diameter pipeline. **1972** *Drive* Spring 60/1 Brakes, brake pipelines and hydraulic fluid are of life-and-limb importance. **1973** C. CALLOW *Power from Sea* i. 16 Underwater pipe-lines carrying natural gas at high pressure. **1976** *Times* 2 Oct. 17/8 Some of the pipeline workers may stay in Alaska.

b. *transf.* and *fig.* in various senses (see quots.); *spec.* a channel of supply, information, communication, etc.; esp. in phr. ***in the pipeline***, in progress; being worked on, dealt with, or produced; on the way from a supplier to a user. Also *attrib.*

1921 A. HUXLEY *Crome Yellow* vi. 58 You could write too ..by getting into touch with your Subconscious. Have you ever read my little book, *Pipe-Lines to the Infinite?* **1935** *Sun* (Baltimore) 25 Aug. 6/2 It was implied, if not more, that the man who had the real inside track to the White House and the potential pipe line to the United States Treasury was none other than Dr. Byrd. **1942** *Ibid.* 1 Aug. 1/7 A foreign source here with continental pipe-lines of information said the Germans also were making peace feelers both to Britain and the United States and to Russia with the object of splitting the Allies. **1942** BERREY & VAN DEN BARK *Amer. Thes. Slang* §121/78 Veins and arteries,..*pipe lines.* **1945** *Amer. Speech* XX. 227/1 *Pipeline time*, from the time a requisition leaves a depot until the requested supplies arrive there. **1948** *Economist* 19 June 1026/2 The pipe-lines are full, stocks seem to be adequate, and there are signs of resistance to higher prices. **1948** *Sheep Breeder* Dec. 19/3 Sometimes the price of meat in the pipelines of distribution goes up—a fact that gives rise to claims that we are speculating. **1949** PARTRIDGE *Dict. Slang* Add. 1136/1 *Pipe line*, an aerial: R.A.F.: 1939 +. **1955** W. GADDIS *Recognitions* II. v. 540 Them priests have a pipeline right into the cops. **1955** *Times* 23 Aug. 5/6 About a third of the patient applicants can consider themselves as 'in the pipeline', which means that the telephone engineers have the equipment ready for them. **1957** *Economist* 16 Nov. 565/2 With the further fall in primary commodities there must be a further improvement in Britain's terms of trade already, so to speak, in the pipeline. **1964** *Observer* 26 July 7/5 All these reforms will take time—and cause controversy—in the next Parliament. There are measures in the pipeline already. **1972** J. MOSEDALE *Football* vii. 94 There was a pipeline to the Tuscaloosa campus in those depression days, and Hutson was one of eight Arkansans who found their way to Alabama's football team. **1973** *Daily Pennsylvanian* 9 Oct. 1/2, I don't have a pipeline to God. **1973** *Times* 15 Nov. 25/2 The property development company has 'some very exciting ideas in the pipeline'. **1976** *Broadcast* 16 Feb. 4/1 There's a new soap in the pipeline... The series/serial..will be shown twice weekly.

c. *Surfing slang.* A very large wave, or the hollow part of such a wave. Also applied to a place where such waves are formed.

1963 *Sunday Mail Mag.* (Brisbane) 5 May 12/5 *Pipeline*, a very large tube (*tube* = hollow part of a wave). **1965** *N.Z. Listener* 17 Dec. 5/1 The achievement by which the champion surfers are judged is their ability to ride the Hawaiian pipeline... The pipeline breaks less than 50 yards from the beach over a coral reef. **1971** *Times* 9 Aug. 5/1 The surf-bums have a language all their own; they talk about pipelines, green rooms, roller-coasters. *Ibid.*, The Banzai pipe-line in Hawaii, where the waves can be 25 to 30 feet high.

d. *Computers.* A linear sequence of specialized modules used for pipelining. Freq. *attrib.*

[**1964** W. BUCHOLZ *Planning Computer System: Project Stretch* xiv. 204 The data flow through the computer..is comparable to a pipeline which, once filled, has a large output no matter what its length.] **1965** *AFIPS Conf. Proc.* XXVII. I. 489 (*heading*) Circuit implementation of high speed pipeline systems. *Ibid.* 491/1 The pipeline is characterized by a succession of register and gate units. **1972** *IEEE Trans. Computers* XXI. 885/1 A two-stage pipeline is possible. **1977** *Computing Surveys* IX. 101/2 The CPU architecture of this machine is a simple pipeline served by four functional units. **1977** *Sci. Amer.* Sept. 220/2 Three kinds of systems that can truly be classed as parallel processors have been built. In one of them, the 'pipeline' processor, several processing elements, each of which is specialized for some particular task, are connected in sequence.

'pipe-line, *v.* [f. the sb.] **1.** To provide with, or convey by, a line of pipes.

1886 *Pall Mall G.* 22 Oct. 2/2 Russia has the finest oil-field in the world in the Transcaucasus, which she is now 'pipe-lining' down to the Black Sea.

2. *Computers.* To design or execute using the technique of pipelining.

1971 *Sci. Amer.* Feb. 76/2 Current efforts in 'pipelining' the processing of 'operands' will allow a further significant increase in speed. **1972** *IEEE Trans. Computers* XXI. 881/1 This note will study the problem of pipelining the addition and multiplication functions of the arithmetic unit.

'pipelined, *a. Computers.* [f. PIPE-LINE *sb.* (or *v.*) + -ED.] That makes use of the technique or principle of pipelining.

1972 *IEEE Trans. Computers* XXI. 880/2 In a pipelined unit, a new task is started before the previous task is complete. **1977** *Computer Surveys* IX. 61 Pipelined computer architecture has received considerable attention since the 1960s when the need for faster and more cost-effective systems became critical.

'pipeliner. orig. *U.S.* [f. PIPELINE *sb.* + -ER[1].] One who works on oil or gas pipelines.

1928 A. GARLAND in J. F. Dobie *Foller de Drinkin' Gou'd* 58 'It's cold out there too—' 'I'll say it is,' a pipeliner broke in. **1962-3** *Petroleum Today* Winter 3/2 The pipeliner is a nomad; he goes where the job is. **1973** C. CALLOW *Power from Sea* v. 113 The pipeliners have an even tougher time in many ways.

'pipelining, *vbl. sb.* [f. PIPE-LINE *sb.* + -ING[1].] **1. a.** The laying of pipelines. **b.** Transportation by means of pipelines.

1959 *Pipeline Engin.* Oct. p. i, The initiation of this new section is..a further milestone in the ever-expanding industry of pipelining. **1963** *Internat. Pipes & Pipelines* Dec. 40/2 The pipelining of forest products such as wood chips would appear to be economically feasible. **1969** *McGraw-Hill Yearbk. Sci. & Technol.* 271/2 The scope of pipelining is being expanded to include the transportation of solids in molten form or as slurries or capsules. **1970** *Preprints 2nd Ann. Offshore Technol. Conf.* I. 379 (*heading*) Pipelining in 600 feet of water. **1975** *North Sea Background Notes* (Brit. Petroleum Co.) 31 Pipelining begins with the stringing out of pipe lengths, each approximately four tons in weight, which are unloaded on to temporary sleepers and then welded into a continuous line.

2. *Computers.* A form of computer organization in which successive steps of a process are executed in turn by a linear sequence of specialized modules capable of operating concurrently, so that another process can be begun before the previous one is finished.

1965 *AFIPS Conf. Proc.* XXVII. I. 490/1 With the present state-of-the-art in systems organization and technology it appears that pipelining is a powerful approach to a particular variety of large data processing problems. **1972** *IEEE Trans. Computers* XXI. 886/1 Pipelining can be used to give a 40 percent increase in adder efficiency and a 230 percent increase in multiplier efficiency. **1975** G. ZIMMERMANN in Hartenstein & Zaks *Workshop on Microarchitecture of Computer Systems* 155/1 The fast multiplication scheme has been extended by a fast pipelining division network for floating point numbers.

pipe-major, -maker, etc.: see PIPE *sb.*[1] 11.

pipeman ('paɪpmən). [f. PIPE *sb.*[1] + MAN *sb.*] **1.** A man who smokes a pipe.

1826 *Blackw. Mag.* XX. 155 Particular pipemen, and solitary cigarers, no doubt, always existed. **1922** *Daily Mail* 7 Nov. 4 (Advt.), The pipeman's joy. **1974** J. JOHNSTON *How Many Miles to Babylon?* 127 My father's a pipe man. The perfect pipe man. He uses it to protect him from the world..stares into the pipe. **1976** *Liverpool Echo* 22 Nov. 1/3 In 1964, he was voted Pipeman of the Year and his waxwork figure appeared at Madame Tussaud's.

2. A workman who attends to a pipe, e.g. in hydraulic mining.

1877 RAYMOND *Statist. Mines & Mining* 11 Gravel-miners and pipemen. **1898** *Century Mag.* Feb. 490/2 The lieutenant..tried to pull this unhappy pipe-man with him.

pip emma: see PIP *sb.*[4]

pipemouth ('paɪpmaʊθ). A fish of the genus *Fistularia* or family *Fistulariidæ*, characterized by a long pipe-like snout. So **'pipe-mouthed** (-maʊðd, -maʊθt) *a.*, having such a snout.

piper[1] ('paɪpə(r)). [OE. *pípere*, f. *pípe*, PIPE *sb.*[1] + *-ere*, -ER[1].]

1. a. One who plays on a pipe (*esp.* a strolling musician); in Scotland *spec.* one who plays on the bagpipe.

c **975** *Rushw. Gosp.* Matt. ix. 23 þa cwom se hælend in hus þas aldor-monnes & þa ʒesæh piperas [*Ags. Gosp.* hwistleras] & meniʒu ruxlende. *a* **1100** *Voc.* in Wr.-Wülcker 311/21 *Tibicen*, pipere. **11..** *Ibid.* 539/23 *Tibicen*, pipare. *c* **1384** CHAUCER *House F.* III. 144 Pipers of alle Duche tonge. *c* **1440** *Promp. Parv.* 401/1 Pypare, *fistulator.* **1561** T. NORTON *Calvin's Inst.* IV. xiii. (1634) 621 As the commmon people say, he is an evill piper but a good fidler. **1574** *Reg. Privy Council Scot.* II. 418 Edmond Broun, ane Hieland pyper. **1599** SHAKS. *Much Ado* v. iv. 131 Let's haue a dance... Strike vp Pipers. **1641** BEST *Farm. Bks.* (Surtees) 97 There is 6*d.* allowed to a piper for playing to the clippers all the day. **1758** JOHNSON *Idler* No. 7 ¶3 At their convivial assemblies..to hear a piper. **1842** BROWNING (*title of poem*) The Pied Piper of Hamelin.

attrib. **14..** *Nom.* in Wr.-Wülcker 693/8 *Hec fistilatrix*, a piper wyfe. **1812** W. TENNANT *Anster F.* II. xlv, No paltry vagrant piper-carle is he.

b. Phrases. †***piper's cheeks***: swollen or inflated cheeks, as of one blowing a pipe. †***drunk as a piper***: quite drunk. ***piper's news*** (*Sc.*): news already well known. ***to pay the piper***: i.e. for piping to lead the dance; hence, to defray the cost, or bear the expense or loss, incident to some undertaking or proceeding. ***by the piper(s)*** (***that played before Moses***): an Irish oath or expletive.

1602 WITHAL *Dict.* 286/1 That hath bigge or great cheekes, as they tearme them, pipers cheekes, *bucculentus.* **1681** T. FLATMAN *Heraclitus Ridens* No. 29 (1713) I. 190 After all this Dance he has led the Nation, he must at last come to pay the Piper himself. **1727** J. GAY in *Miscellanies* III. 207 Drunk as a Piper all day long. **1770** *Gentl. Mag.* XLI. 560 As drunk as a Piper. **1772** R. GRAVES *Spir. Quix.* x. xxix, Jerry..proceeded so long in recommending sobriety, and in tossing off horns of ale, that he became as drunk as a piper. **1753** CHESTERF. *Lett.* (1792) IV. 39 The other Powers cannot well dance, when neither France nor the maritime Powers can..pay the piper. **1809** MALKIN *Gil Blas* II. vii. ¶23 We will make Doctor Oloroso pay the piper to our dancing. **1822** HOGG *Perils of Man* I. ii. 29, 'I came expressly to inform you'—'Came with piper's news', said the lady, 'which the fiddler has told before you'. **1865** 'MARK TWAIN' in *California* (San Francisco) 23 Dec. 4/3 He came home drunk as a piper. **1884** 'CRUCK-A-LEAGHAN' & 'SLIEVE GALLION' *Lays & Legends N. Ireland* 16, I hope they don't hear me, Or else, by the piper, they'll make me sing sad. **1892** J. BARLOW *Irish Idylls* ix. 274 Be the piper, sure enough I was up there splicin' the handle of your mother's ould basket. **1894** A. GORDON *Northward Ho!* 202 If he..was as drunk as a piper, an' ye yersel' had only twa gills,..he'd pruve tae ye..that ye were drunk, an' no him. **1895** *Daily News* 18 Dec. 9/1 Londoners had paid the piper, and should choose the tune. **1899** *Century Mag.* Nov. 45 Be the piper that played afore Moses I'll call out me regiment of throopers. **1928** 'BRENT OF BIN BIN' *Up Country* i. 2 Be the poipers, we've had enough [rain] for this toime of year!

†**c.** Applied to a tree that furnishes wood for pipes. *Obs. nonce-use.* In quot. *appositive.*

c **1381** CHAUCER *Parl. Foules* 178 The byldere ok, and ek the hardy assh, The pilere elm,.. The boxtre pipere,.. The saylynge fyr,.. The shetere Ew.

2. Popular name of several kinds of fish.

a. A species of gurnard, *Trigla lyra*; so called from the sound it makes when caught. †**b.** In quot. 1674, = ANGEL-FISH. *Obs.* **c.** In New Zealand, the garfish, *Hemirhamphus intermedius.*

1601 CHESTER *Love's Mart.*, *Dial.* lxxxiii, The Piper good for to be eaten. *a* **1672** WILLUGHBY *Icthyogr.* (1686) Tab. S. I, *Lyra* Rond., The Piper. **1674** RAY *Collect. Words*, (*Sea*) *Fishes* 99 The Piper, *Raio-squatina* Rondel... The Cornish men call another Fish, viz. a sort of Cuculus or Gurnard by the name of Piper. **1766** [C. ANSTEY] *Bath Guide* iv. 63 She has order'd for Dinner a Piper and Dory. **1769** PENNANT *Zool.* III. 234 The Piper... *Trigla Lyra*..esteemed an excellent fish. **1871** *Field* 25 Nov. 457/1, I look on the Piper as the float fish of New Zealand. *Ibid.*, I do not think that the New Zealand piper is as perfect in flavour as the Melbourne one.

attrib. **1611** COTGR., *Aiguille*,..a Horne-backe, Piper-fish, Gane-fish, or Horne-fish. **1812** *Pennant's Zool.* 374 The piper gurnard is frequently taken on the western coasts. **1837** M. DONOVAN *Dom. Econ.* II. 185 The piper gurnard, ..when taken from the water emits a singular sound.

3. a. A young pigeon, a squab. **b.** A sandpiper (*Cent. Dict.*).

1885 NEWTON *Dict. Birds* (1894), *Pigeon*, French *Pigeon*, Italian *Piccione* and *Pipione*, Latin *Pipio*, literally a nestling-bird that pipes or cries out, a 'Piper'—the very name now in use among Pigeon-fanciers.

4. a. A name given to beetles of the *Curculionidæ*, with a long proboscis. **b.** A sea-urchin, *Cidaris papillata*, with club-shaped spines, fancied to resemble a bagpipe (also called *piper urchin*).

1711 *Phil. Trans.* XXVII. 352 Small English Pipers, or long-snouted Beetles. **1809** EDMONSTONE *Zetland Isl.* II. 320 E[chinus] Cidaris, found in deep water, *Piper.*

5. A broken-winded horse: see quots. Cf. *roarer.*

1831 YOUATT *Horse* x. 196 Some horses make a shrill noise when in quick action; they are said to be Pipers. **1844** STEPHENS *Bk. Farm* II. 227 There are many degrees of broken wind, which receive appellations according to the noise emitted by the horse; and on this account he is called a piper, trumpeter.

6. (See quot. and cf. PIPING *vbl. sb.*[1] 2, quot. 1884.)

1884 PHIN *Dict. Apiculture* 53 *Piper*, an after-swarm having a virgin queen.

piper[2] ('paɪpə(r)). [f. PIPE *sb.*[1] or *v.*[2] + -ER[1].]

†**1.** (?) A workman who lays or repairs pipes; a plumber. *Obs.*

1456 *Cal. Anc. Rec. Dublin* (1889) I. 291 The feys that the pyperys had befor thys tym for har wachyng about the town, ..be yreryt and payet to the makinge of the pypys of the sayd cytte for a yer. **1469** *Ibid.* 332 [Admissions to franchise ..Richard Bennet,] piper; [John Welles,] packer. [John Talbot,] pyper.

2. One who smokes tobacco in a pipe. Now *rare.*

1632 D. LUPTON *London & C. Carbonadoed* 85 He is for the most part a potter and piper. **1663** GERBIER *Counsel* 41 Pipers and Potters, to sit in Tavernes. **1897** *19th Cent.* May 821 The early 'piper' loses his growth, becomes hoarse, effete, lazy, and stunted.

3. Name for a kind of caddis-worm (also ***piper caddis***), which forms a pipe or tube.

1653 WALTON *Angler* xii. 231-2 One Cadis called a Piper, whose husk or case is a piece of reed about an inch long or longer... There is also a lesser Cadis-worm, called a Cock-spur..it is much less than the Piper Cadis.

4. A dog used to lure wild fowl into the pipe of a decoy; a decoy-dog.

1865 W. WHITE *E. Eng.* I. 111 If given to barking or to frolic, or to take fright without occasion,..such a dog will never do for a 'piper'. **1886** *Athenæum* 21 Aug. 231/1 A clever arrangement of screens over which a bushy tailed dog not unlike a fox—the 'piper', as it is called—is taught to leap at the word of command.

5. A fissure in the coal in a mine, from which gas escapes: = BLOWER[1] 4.

1883 *Standard* 8 Nov. 5/8 [The explosion] was caused by what is known as a 'piper', or air-hole in the coal. **1883** in GRESLEY *Gloss. Coal Mining*.

6. *Confectionery*. One who ornaments cakes, etc. with sugar piping: see PIPE *v.*[2] 4 b.

1904 *Daily Chron.* 20 June 11/7 Pastrycook and Confectioner..good piper.

piperaceous (pɪpəˈreɪʃəs), *a.* [f. L. *piper* PEPPER + -ACEOUS, or f. Bot.L. *Piperace-æ* + -OUS.]

†**a.** Of the nature of pepper; pungent. *Obs.* **b.** *Bot.* Belonging to the Natural Order *Piperaceæ*, the pepper tribe (typical genus *Piper*; see PEPPER).

1674 *Phil. Trans.* IX. 5 Being, if I may so speak, piperaceous and biting. **1846** *Penny Cycl.* Suppl. II. 272/1 *Matica* or *Matico*..an astringent plant..from Peru.. Doubts exist as to the botanical origin of the plant, some ascribing it to a Labiate plant..while others refer it to a piperaceous plant.

‖**piperade** (pipɛrad). Also (*erron.*) **pipérade**. [Fr.] A dish originating in the Basque country, consisting of eggs, tomatoes, and peppers, and resembling an omelette.

1931 X. M. BOULESTIN *What shall we have To-day?* 191 A delicious dish, very popular in Béarn and in the Basque country, but not well known otherwise, is the *Pipérade*. **1951** E. DAVID *French Country Cooking* 81 *Pipérade* is the best known of all Basque dishes... It is a mixture of pimentos, tomatoes and onions, with eggs added at the end. **1961** E. H. CLEMENTS *Note of Enchantment* ix. 126 Alister..ordered a *piperade* and ate it unhurriedly with a hunk of bread. **1966** *Punch* 29 June 944/1 Should we try Chez Fifine for a piperade? **1976** *Times* 7 Aug. 11/4 A fresh and well-composed pipérade hot from the pan.

†**ˈpiperate**, *a. Obs.* [ad. L. *piperāt-us* peppered, pungent, adj. f. *piper* PEPPER: see -ATE[2].] Containing pepper, peppered: peppery, pungent.

1683 *Phil. Trans.* XIII. 168 Hot and piperate Antidotes. **1693** *Ibid.* XVII. 872 A..hot piperate and Spicy Plant.

piperate (ˈpɪpərət), *sb. Chem.* [f. PIPER-IC + -ATE[4].] A salt of piperic acid.

1873 WATTS *Fownes' Chem.* (ed. 11) 827 The piperates are sparingly soluble in water.

piperazine (pɪˈpɛrəziːn, formerly ˈpɪpərəzaɪn). *Pharm.* [First formed as G. *piperazin* (A. T. Mason 1887, in *Ber. d. Deut. Chem. Ges.* XX. 267), f. *piper(idin* PIPERIDINE + *azin* AZINE.] A colourless, crystalline, heterocyclic base, $C_4H_{10}N_2$ which is used, in the form of a salt or hydrate, as an anthelminthic; also, a derivative of this. Also called **pipeˈrazidine**.

[**1888** *Jrnl. Chem. Soc.* LIV. 726 Diphenyldiketopiperazine.] **1889** *Ibid.* LVI. 1009 (*heading*) Piperazines. **1891** *Lancet* 18 Apr. 897 It is stated..that piperazidine dissolves uric acid more readily than any other substance of a basic nature. **1891** *Jrnl. Chem. Soc.* LX. 415 Piperazine melts at 104–107°. **1894** MUIR & MORLEY *Watts' Dict. Chem.* IV. 277 Piperazine. **1897** *Allbutt's Syst. Med.* III. 173 Piperazine, whether in the free state or as chloride, was not found to exercise any influence on the advent of precipitation. **1901** *Brit. Med. Jrnl.* No. 2092 Epit. Med. Lit. 20 Piperazine is the best drug for the underlying morbid condition. **1937** *Thorpe's Dict. Appl. Chem.* (ed. 4) I. 315/1 Cyclic compounds are..produced by distilling the dihydrochlorides of the aliphatic diamines... Thus ethylenediamine yields piperazine. **1970** W. H. PARKER *Health & Dis. in Farm Animals* xx. 276 Piperazine compounds might be considered the safest.., but thiabendazole has the merit of being effective against both large and small round worms in the pig. **1974** M. C. GERALD *Pharmacol.* ii. 35 Streptomycin, piperazine (Antepar), [etc.] ..have been quite effective in the cure of tuberculosis, pinworm,..respectively.

piperic (pɪˈpɛrɪk), *a. Chem.* [f. L. *piper* pepper + -IC.] Pertaining to or derived from pepper; in ***piperic acid***, an acid ($C_{12}H_{10}O_4$) obtained by boiling piperine with potash.

1866 WATTS *Dict. Chem.* IV. 653 Piperic acid forms yellowish capillary needles; in the moist state, a sulphur-yellow jelly which shrinks on drying. **1876** [see PIPERIDINE].

piperidge, variant of PIPPERIDGE.

piperidine (pɪˈpɛrɪdiːn, formerly pɪˈpɛrɪdaɪn). *Chem.* [First formed as F. *piperidine* (A. Cahours 1853, in *Ann. de Chim. et de Phys.* XXXVIII. 78), f. L. *piper* pepper + -IDE + -INE[5].] 'A volatile base ($C_5H_{11}N$) produced by the action of alkalis on piperine' (Watts). Formerly also ***piperidia***.

1854 *Jrnl. Chem. Soc.* VI. 175 (*heading*) On piperidine, a new alkali derived from piperine. **1857** MILLER *Elem. Chem.* III. 286 Piperidine... This is a remarkable oily base, with a pungent odour, recalling both that of ammonia, and that of pepper. **1876** HARLEY *Mat. Med.* (ed. 6) 434 Nitric acid decomposes it into piperic acid and piperidia. **1888** REMSEN *Org. Chem.* 355 Piperidine. **1938** [see KNOEVENAGEL]. **1964** N. G. CLARK *Mod. Org. Chem.* xxiii. 470 On heating a pyridine solution of the aldehyde with malonic acid in presence of piperidine (catalyst), condensation *and* decarboxylation occur, and a cinnamic acid is produced (Döbner Reaction).

piperine (ˈpɪpəraɪn), *sb.* [f. as prec. + -INE[5].]

1. *Chem.* An alkaloid ($C_{17}H_{19}NO_3$) obtained from species of pepper (*Piper nigrum* and *P. longum*), crystallizing in colourless prisms, and melting when heated to a pale yellow limpid oil.

1820 *Q. Jrnl. Sci. Lit. & Art* IX. 402 Piperine is obtained from pepper, by digesting it in alcohol. **1838** T. THOMSON *Chem. Org. Bodies* 760 M. Orstedt first announced, in 1819, the existence of a peculiar principle in the fruit of *piper nigrum*, or *black pepper*, to which he gave the name of *piperin*. **1874** GARROD & BAXTER *Mat. Med.* (1880) 349 A nitrogenized feeble base, Piperine..in rhomboidal prisms, white, almost tasteless, and inodorous.

2. = PEPERINO, late L. *piperinus* (Isidore). *rare*[−0].

1882 OGILVIE, *Piperin, Piperine*. 1. A concretion of volcanic ashes.

ˈpiperine, *a. rare*[−1]. [f. L. *piper* pepper + -INE[2].] Peppery.

1842 *Blackw. Mag.* LII. 720 We naturally, with piperine heat, re-affirm our dictum.

piperine, -ino, var. PEPERINE, -INO.

piperitious (pɪpəˈrɪʃəs), *a. rare*[−0]. [f. L. *piper* pepper + -ITIOUS[1]: cf. *cineritious*.] Resembling pepper, pungent: = PIPERACEOUS a.

1890 in *Cent. Dict.*

piperivorous (pɪpəˈrɪvərəs), *a. rare*[−0]. [f. mod.L. *piperivor-us* (f. *piper* pepper + *-vorus* devouring) + -OUS.] Feeding on pepper, as a bird.

1858 in MAYNE *Expos. Lex.*

piperly (ˈpaɪpəlɪ), *a.* [f. PIPER[1] + -LY[1].] Resembling, or befitting, a piper; paltry, trashy, beggarly, despicable.

1588 J. HARVEY *Disc. Probl.* 65 Their piperly versicles, and other beggerly trumperie. **1657** TOMLINSON *Renou's Disp.* Pref., Shame..that..those Piperly-Dizzards should not be..detected. **1822** J. WILSON in *Blackw. Mag.* XII. 107, I don't care a tester for that piperly poet of green Erin. **1834** *Tait's Mag.* I. 542/2 This is some of the piperly stuff of your snivelling poets.

piperno, variant of PEPERINO.

ˈpipe-ˌroll. [f. PIPE *sb.*[1] 5 + ROLL. *sb.*] The Great Roll of the Exchequer, comprising the various 'pipes', or enrolled accounts, of sheriffs and others for a financial year.

1612 DAVIES *Why Ireland*, etc. (1787) 20 In all the ancient pipe-rolls in the times of Henry the Third, Edward the First, Edward the Second, and Edward the Third..there is this entry: *In Thesauro nihil*. **1698** WANLEY in *Lett. Lit. Men* (Camden) 258 The Pipe Roll; with the black and red Books of the Exchequer. **1711** MADOX *Hist. Exchequer, Explanation of Breviatures*: Magnus Rotulus, The Great Roll of the Exchequer commonly called the Pipe Roll. **1765** BLACKSTONE *Comm.* I. iv. 222 There are traces of it's payment..in the book of domesday and in the great pipe-roll of Henry the first. **1891** *Guide to Public Record Office* 293 The Pipe Rolls or Great Rolls of the Exchequer contained the yearly charge against the Sheriffs of the several counties.

piperonal (pɪˈpɛrənəl). *Chem.* [a. G. *piperonal* (Fittig & Mielck 1869, in *Ann. d. Chem. u. Pharm.* CLII. 37), f. *piper(in* PIPERINE *sb.* + *-on* -ONE + *-al* -AL[2].] = HELIOTROPIN.

1869 *Chem. News* 30 July 59/2 Piperinic acid,..when acted upon by permanganate of potassa in aqueous solution, yields a crystalline substance (formula, $C_8H_6O_3$), which body the authors called piperonal. **1909** C. A. KEANE *Mod. Org. Chem.* vii. 123 Many substitutes for natural perfumes are also known, such as..heliotropin or piperonal, which possesses the odour of heliotrope. **1953** KIRK & OTHMER *Encycl. Chem. Technol.* X. 324 Piperonal (heliotropin)..is a colorless, lustrous crystalline solid with a smell resembling that of heliotrope... Its chief application is in perfumery. **1967** L. F. & M. A. FIESER *Reagents for Org. Synthesis* I. 944 A mixture of piperonal with 1·5 l. of water is heated on the steam bath with vigorous stirring.

piperonyl (pɪˈpɛrənaɪl). *Chem.* [f. prec. + -YL.] Used to form the names of certain substituted derivatives of piperonal, as ***piperonyl butoxide***, a yellow oily liquid, $C_{19}H_{30}O_5$, which is used in insecticides as a synergist for pyrethrins.

1871 *Jrnl. Chem. Soc.* XXIV. 934 The mother-liquor.., evaporated until most of the alcohol is driven off, and exhausted with ether, yields piperonyl alcohol. **1923** W. M. CUMMING et al. *Systematic Org. Chem.* v. 93 Piperonyl acrolein is obtained from piperonal and acetaldehyde. **1945** H. WACHS in *Science* 16 May 531/1 The activity of piperonyl butoxide (the name given the technical product containing 80 per cent of pure compound) is indicated in Table 1. **1966** *McGraw-Hill Encycl. Sci. & Technol.* VII. 142/1 Piperonyl butoxide..and Sesoxane..are two important commercially available pyrethrin synergists. **1966** *Jrnl. Agric. & Food Chem.* XIV. 555 The..piperonyl carbamates are exceptionally active carbamate synergists. **1974** *Approved Names 1973* (Brit. Pharmacopœia Comm.) Suppl. 11, Piperonyl Butoxide..5-[2-(2-Butoxyethoxyethoxy-methyl]-6-propyl-1,3-benzodioxole. Acaricide.

pipery (ˈpɪpərɪ). Also 9 pippiree. [a. F. *piperie* (Froger, 1698). perh. = Sp. **piperia*: cf. Sp. *pipero* cooper, f. *pipa* barrel.] A native raft or float in the West Indies and S. America, of the same nature as a catamaran.

1698 FROGER *Voy.* 102 We..saw all along the [Argentine] Coast.. the Negro's *Piperies* [*orig.* de Piperies des nègres], as they are called, being no other than three or four pieces of Wood made fast together, whereon two men go out a fishing. **1707** SLOANE *Jamaica* I. 216 We cut and made Piperies or Floats of four or five of these truncs, being light and floating; ..they being tied together..two or three or more of them, according to the bigness of the Pipery. **1827** ROBERTS *Voy. Centr. Amer.* 151 The Buccaniers..descended the river in floats or pippirees to the Atlantic.

ˈpipe-ˌstapple. *Sc.* and *north. dial.* Also **-staple, -stopple.** [f. PIPE *sb.*[1] + STAPPLE, STOPPLE, MDu. *stapel* stem, stalk.]

1. The stem of a tobacco-pipe.

1816 SCOTT *Bl. Dwarf* ix, Pinches or forehammers will never pick upon 't [the tower],..ye might as weel batter at it wi' pipe-staples. **1824** *Blackw. Mag.* XVI. 237 Not worth the notice of a pipe-stapple. **1825** BROCKETT *N.C. Gloss.*, *Pipestoppel*, a fragment of the shank of a tobacco-pipe.

2. (See quots.)

1825 JAMIESON, *Pipe-stapple*... Used as synon. with *Windle-strae*, for smooth-crested grass, Loth. **1886** BRITTEN & HOLLAND *Eng. Plant-n*, Pipe-stapple... *Cynosurus cristatus*. The stiff stalks are used for cleaning pipes.

pipe-stem. [PIPE *sb.*[1] 11 a.] **1.** The stem of a tobacco-pipe.

a **1734** J. COMER *Diary* in *Rhode Island Hist. Soc. Coll.* (1893) VIII. 17 He..fell over a log, yᵉ pipe stem ran down his throat and broke. **1755** *Maryland Hist. Mag.* (1923) XVIII. 33 He fell down forward, and run the Pipe stem into the Roof of his mouth. **1846** J. W. WEBB *Altowan* I. vi. 168 One of the half-breeds has a piece of an old pipe-stem, which makes tolerable good smoking. **1855** LONGF. *Hiaw.* I. 21 [He] Took a long reed for a pipe-stem. **1860** J. G. HOLLAND *Miss Gilbert's Career* vii. 115 A great tribulation that will break my life off as short as a pipe-stem. **1873** J. MILLER *Life amongst Modocs* xv. 194 He pointed his pipe-stem at Paquita. **1942** J. MASEFIELD *Generation Risen* 42 The hands, chocked-off, wet through and fireless, Chew pipestems. **1971** 'D. HALLIDAY' *Dolly & Doctor Bird* xvi. 242 The mild figure puffed at its pipestem.

b. *humorously*. A thin leg. Also ***pipe-stem leg***.

1883 E. EGGLESTON *Hoosier School-Boy* 33 Little Columbus Risdale picked himself up on his pipe stems and took his place at the end of this row. **1938** M. K. RAWLINGS *Yearling* i. 4 The water..made a rippling sound, flowing past his pipe-stem legs, and was entirely delicious. **1955** J. THOMAS *No Banners* xxvii. 268 The obsession with food made Alfred sway on his pipestem legs. **1976** *National Observer* (U.S.) 10 Apr. 18/2 Mostly they are elderly.., their pipestem legs squeaking them along in the late-afternoon sun.

2. *Comb.* **pipe-stem clematis** *U.S.*, a white-flowered clematis, *C. lasiantha*, of the family Ranunculaceæ, native to California; **pipe-stem wood** *U.S.*, a large evergreen shrub, *Leucothoe populifolia*, of the family Ericaceæ, native to Florida and South Carolina.

1951 H. E. MCMINN *Illustr. Man. Calif. Shrubs* 117 Pipe-stem Clematis grows in the Coast Range valleys. **1791** W. BARTRAM *Trav. N. & S. Carolina* 24, I observed..the great evergreen *Andromeda* of Florida, called Pipe-Stem Wood. **1813** H. MUHLENBERG *Catal. Plantarum Americæ Septentrionalis* 43 Pipe-stem wood, *Andromeda acuminata*.

ˈpipe-stone. [f. PIPE *sb.*[1] + STONE.]

1. A hard red clay or soft stone used by the American Indians for tobacco-pipes: = CATLINITE.

1809 A. HENRY *Trav.* 24 The Portage du Grand Calumet, ..which name is derived from the *pierre à calumet*, or pipe-stone, which here interrupts the river. **1841** CATLIN *N. Amer. Ind.* I. xxix. 234 The bowls..are generally made of the red steatite or 'pipe-stone'. *Ibid.* II. lv. 206 *note*, 'Pipe-stone'..is harder than gypsum and softer than carbonate of lime. **1855** LONGF. *Hiaw.* I. 2 On the great Red Pipe-stone Quarry.

2. *Lead Manuf.* A piece of cast iron (? originally a stone), having a groove through which the tuyère or blast-pipe passes, in a smelting furnace.

1839 URE *Dict. Arts* 756 The posterior ledge of the sole.. supports another piece of cast iron..called *pipe-stone*, scooped out at its under part..for the passage of the *tuyère*.

ˈpipe-tree. [f. PIPE *sb.*[1] 9 + TREE.] A name used in the seventeenth century to English Lat. *Syringa* in its then wide sense, including (*a*) the Common Syringa, Mock Orange, or Orange-blossom (F. *séringat*), *Philadelphus coronarius*, the 'white Pipe-tree'; (*b*) the Lilac, *Syringa vulgaris* Linn., the 'blew Pipe-tree'. Also the 'double (white) Pipe-tree', *Jasminum Sambac*. (See PIPE *sb.*[1] 9.)

1629 PARKINSON *Paradisi* cvii. 407 The blew Pipe tree riseth sometimes to be a great tree. *Ibid.* 408 The single white Pipe tree or bush, neuer commeth to that height of the former... The flowers..are of a strong, full, or heady sent, not pleasing to a great many. *Ibid.* 410 The double white Pipe tree is much used in Egypt to help women in their trauailes of childbirth. **1688** R. HOLME *Armoury* II. 71/2 The double Pipe-tree, or Jasmine of Arabia, hath the Flowers double. **1707** MORTIMER *Husb.* (1721) II. 185 Lilac, or Pipe-Tree,..affords fine scented Flowers in April or May. **1756–66** AMORY *Buncle* (1825) III. 226 A liquor of a beautiful colour, like that of the lilach or pipe-tree blossom.

b. ***pudding pipe-tree***: see PUDDING.

pipette (pɪˈpɛt), *sb.* [a. F. *pipette*, dim. of *pipe* PIPE *sb.*¹: see -ETTE.]

1. Also (*U.S.*) pipet. A pipe or tube of small calibre, and of various forms, used (esp. in chemistry or in scientific experiments) to transfer or measure small quantities of a liquid or gas.

1839 URE *Dict. Arts* 68 We readily obtain a volume of 100 cubic centimetres by means of a pipette. **1860** F. W. GRIFFIN in *Jrnl. Soc. Arts* VIII. 324/1 By means of a graduated pipette I took a thousandth part containing..one thousandth of a grain of arsenious acid. **1884** *Times* 27 Oct. 4/2 A 'pipette' is..a glass tube with a..swelling about one-third up from its lower end. It is used..in laboratories..for sucking up small quantities..of poisons,..or objectionable liquids. **1937** PIERCE & HAENISCH *Quantitative Analysis* v. 49 In all pipets the flow of liquid is controlled by admission of air beneath a finger pressed tightly onto the upper end of the stem. **1961** G. R. CHOPPIN *Exper. Nucl. Chem.* ix. 133 When the preparation is complete, carefully remove as much of the supernate as possible with a transfer pipet and place on a planchet.

attrib. **1881** TYNDALL *Floating Matter of Air* 139 *note*, I have called them 'pipette-bulbs' because they are formed by hermetically sealing one shank of a pipette. *Ibid.* 173 If..the india-rubber tube failed to clasp with sufficient tightness the pipette-shank. **1898** *Allbutt's Syst. Med.* V. 437 Distilled water is then added, drop by drop, from the pipette stopper of a bottle supplied for that purpose.

2. *Pottery Manuf.* A can or pot fitted with a narrow tube through which slip or barbotine is poured upon the ware for decoration.

Hence **piˈpette** (U.S. **pipet**) *v. trans.*, to pour, convey, or draw (*off*, *out*) by means of a pipette; hence **piˈpetting** *vbl. sb.*

1887 *Amer. Chem. Jrnl.* IX. 177 (Cent.) The solution of arsenic acid was pipetted into the bottle. **1899** CAGNEY tr. *Jaksch's Clin. Diagn.* iv. (ed. 4) 138 The æther is pipetted or siphoned off. **1915** *Chem. Abstr.* IX. 1861 (*heading*) Pipetting with the suction pump. **1943** *Jrnl. Bacteriol.* XLVI. 195 The tedium of making a large number of accurately measured pipettings. **1961** G. R. CHOPPIN *Exper. Nucl. Chem.* ix. 132 Pipet approximately 10,000 cpm of Cs^{137} activity into a small test tube. **1975** *Nature* 13 Mar. 151/2 The blood was cooled..and the plasma was pipetted off for enzyme analysis.

pipe-work. [f. PIPE *sb.*¹ + WORK *sb.*]

1. *Mining.* A pipe vein of ore; = PIPE *sb.*¹ 7 c (*a*).

1653 MANLOVE *Lead Mines* 264 Primgaps, Roof-works, Flat-works, Pipe-works, Shifts. **1829** *Glover's Hist. Derby* I. 65 Pipe-works lie between two rocks or strata, yet seldom follow any regular inclination, but fill up fissures.

2. Pipes in the mass, or as part of a structure.

1890 *Cent. Dict.* s.v. *Organ*, The pipework includes a great variety of different kinds of pipes. **1934** *Discovery* Dec. 348/1 Modern methods of steel-frame building and pipe-work. **1949** *Archit. Rev.* CV. 222/1 In all stages of the design effort has been made to eliminate the tangled masses of exterior pipework usual in most nylon factories. **1974** *Physics Bull.* July 291/2 Tests on oil fields pipework for potential fire hazards. **1976** *Gramophone* Sept. 453/3 The remoteness of the console from the pipework brought to the ear less than 100 per cent of the complex score. **1977** *Times* 29 June 5/2 In bad conditions, all ferrous pipework can deteriorate.

pipewort (ˈpaɪpwɜːt). [f. PIPE *sb.*¹ 3 + WORT.] Any plant of the genus *Eriocaulon*; extended by Lindley to the whole of the N.O. *Eriocaulaceæ*, comprising aquatic or marsh herbs allied to grasses, with a membranous tube surrounding the ovary.

1806 GALPINE *Brit. Bot.* §391 *Eriocaulon.* Pipewort. **1846** LINDLEY *Veg. Kingd.* 122 The presence, among the Pipe-worts, of a membranous tube.

pipey, erron. form of PIPY.

†**piphre.** *Obs. rare*⁻¹. [a. 16th c. F. *pifre* (= mod.F. *fifre*), ad. It. *pifero, piffero* FIFE.] A fife or other wind instrument.

a **1603** JAS. I. *Chorus Venetus* in Farr *S.P. Jas. I* (1848) 3 Praise him with trumpet, piphre, and drumme, With lutes and organes fine.

‖**pipi**¹ (ˈpiːpiː). [Tupi *pipai.*] Name of the astringent pods of a Brazilian leguminous plant, *Cæsalpinia Pipai*, sometimes imported together with divi-divi for tanning. Also, the plant itself.

1866 *Treas. Bot.* 188 C[*æsalpinia*] *Pipai* produces pods which possess some astringency, and are called Pipi pods. **1895** *Syd. Soc. Lex.*, *Pi-pi*, the astringent legumes of the *Cæsalpinia papai.*

‖**pipi**² (ˈpipi). Also **peppy, pippi(e, pippy.** [Maori.] **1.** An edible bivalve mollusc, *Amphidesma australe*, found on sandy beaches in New Zealand; also, occasionally used for another edible mollusc, *Chione stutchburyi*. Also *attrib.*

[**1820** *Gramm. & Vocab. Lang. N. Zealand* 193 (Morris) *Pipi*, a cockle.] **1843** J. E. GRAY in E. Dieffenbach *Trav. N.Z.* II. x. [252 *Mesodesma Chemnitzii*... Called *Pipæ* by the natives, who eat them as food.] *Ibid.* 262 *Venus intermedia*... East Coast; much eaten by the natives; called *Pipi.* **1852** MUNDY *Our Antipodes* (1857) 116 Piles of white shells of the 'pipi', or cockle, brought from the seashore for food. **1861** A. S. ATKINSON *Jrnl.* 21 Jan. in *Richmond-Atkinson Papers* (1960) I. 680 Had dinner—well supplied with pipis. **1863** F. E. MANING *Old N.Z.* (ed. 2) iii. 65, I will scrape sharp the point of my spear with a *pipi* shell. **1873** [see KINAKI]. **1881** J. L. CAMPBELL *Poenamo* 204 (Morris) Fern-root, flavoured with fish and pippies. **1882** T. H. POTTS *Out in Open* 25 (ibid.) Each female is busily employed in scraping the potatoes thoroughly with pipi-shells. **1892** E. REEVES *Homeward Bound* 115 Sea-gulls.. loath to leave their breakfast of pipis dug out of the sand. **1905** [see KUKU 2]. **1938** R. FINLAYSON *Brown Man's Burden* 75 You could scoop up handfuls of big fat pipis.., sifting the sandy mud through your fingers. *Ibid.*, He joined in a game of throwing big empty pipi shells into the air. **1948** D. BALLANTYNE *Cunninghams* I. viii. 45 She looked..at the Maoris gathering pipis on the mud flat. **1959** TINDALE & LINDSAY *Rangatira* vii. 68 They would find pipi cockles in the sand of the beach. **1968** MORTON & MILLER *N.Z. Sea Shore* xviii. 443 They could well be called pipi beaches, for their most typical bivalves are the pipi, *Amphidesma australe*, higher up the shore, giving place lower down to the cockle or tuangi, *Chione stutchburyi*, in places designated 'pipi' as well. **1972** M. GEE *In my Father's Den* 104 On Takapuna beach..Jonathan was throwing pipi shells into the wind.

2. A similar Australian mollusc, *Plebidonax deltoides*.

1934 *Bulletin* (Sydney) 14 Mar. 20/4 Whether it [*sc.* a bird] opens oysters or not is questionable; but it is an expert on pipis. **1952** W. J. DAKIN et al. *Austral. Seashores* xvi. 294 The most common mollusc of any size inhabiting the sand of the ocean beaches of New South Wales..is *Plebidonax deltoides*.., known in this State as the pipi... The pipi lives only a few inches below the surface. **1962** *Australasian Post* 8 Nov. 24/1 The 'pippie' is that pink-and-cream shellfish that lives in the sand. **1968** *Courier-Mail* (Brisbane) 14 June 17/8 A young woman..survived for eight days by digging pippie shells from the sand with her hands. **1970** *People* (Austral.) 26 Aug. 45/3 The pipi is similar to the 'Littleneck' clam of America's west coast.

†ˈ**pipient**, *a. Obs. rare.* [ad. L. *pīpient-em*, pr. pple. of *pīpīre* to cheep; cf. F. *pipiant, pépiant.*] Piping or chirping like a chicken or young bird.

1607 COLLINS *Serm.* (1608) 18 Like Anacreons fonde doues, some perfect, some pipient, some hatcht, some half hatcht. **1615** T. ADAMS *Spir. Navig.* 54 Hypocrites, a pipient broode, cackling their owne ripeness.

piping (ˈpaɪpɪŋ), *vbl. sb.*¹ [f. PIPE *v.*¹ + -ING¹.] The action of PIPE *v.*¹

1. Playing on a pipe; the music of pipes or wind-instruments.

c **1275** LAY. 5110 Þar was gleomenne songe, þar was piping among. **13..** *K. Alis.* 1042 (Bodl. MS.) At þe fest was harpyng And pipyng & tabournyng. **1535** COVERDALE *Ecclus.* xl. 21 Pypinge and harpinge make a swete noyse. **1641** HINDE *J. Bruen* iii. 12 The holy Sabbaths..were wholly spent..in Maypoles and Maygames, Pipings and Dancings. *a* **1706** R. SEMPLE *Piper of Kilbarchan* xiv, We need not look for Piping mair, Sen Habbie's dead. **1870** MORRIS *Earthly Par.* I. I. 308 Unto their piping must all people dance.

2. The utterance of a shrill sound, or the sound itself (with the varieties of sense indicated in PIPE *v.*¹ 4–6); cheeping, chirping, whistling; singing or speaking in a shrill tone.

a **1250** *Owl & Night.* 567 Bo þi piping over-go, Ne boþ on þe craftes na mo. **1398** TREVISA *Barth. De P.R.* XII. xxxix. (Bodl. MS.), The reremous..is a beeste iliche to a mous.. wiþ voice & pipinge wiþ crye. *c* **1440** *Promp. Parv.* 401/2 Pypynge, crye of yonge bryddys, *pipulatus.* **1552** HULOET, Pipynge or piepynge of byrdes or fowles. **1828** *Craven Gloss.* (ed. 2), *Piping*, the musical signal of bees preparatory to their swarming or casting a second time. **1833** HT. MARTINEAU *Manch. Strike* i, The shrill piping of a bulfinch was heard. **1839–40** W. IRVING *Wolfert's R.* (1855) 19 Between the frosty pipings of the breeze. **1884** PHIN *Dict. Apiculture*, *Piping of Queens*, a sound made by young queens when there is also in the hive a mature queen, but one not yet emerged from her cell.

3. Weeping, crying. *slang* or *colloq.*

1779 SEWARD in *Mme. D'Arblay's Diary* 16 June, No more piping, pray. **1837** MARRYAT *Dog-fiend* ix, What's the use of piping, boys, I never yet could larn.

4. *attrib.*

a **1711** KEN *Sion* Poet. Wks. 1721 IV. 319 Mirth, Song, Dance, or Piping-match. **1711** SHAFTESB. *Charac.* (1737) III. 127 The unmanly disfiguration of their..countenance, which this piping-work produc'd.

ˈ**piping**, *vbl. sb.*² [f. PIPE *v.*² and *sb.*¹ + -ING¹.]

†**1.** The smoking of a pipe, tobacco-smoking.

1660 T. HALL *Funebria Floræ* (1661) 13 Christmas revels, with dancing, drinking,..potting, piping, gaming. **1670** J. DAWTRY in *St. Papers, Dom.* 458 Too much piping and potting will be an enemy to him.

2. *Gardening.* The propagation of pinks, etc. by cuttings (see PIPE *v.*² 3); *concr.* a cutting or slip of a pink or other plant taken off at a joint.

1788 [see PIPE *v.*² 3]. **1846** J. BAXTER *Libr. Pract. Agric.* (ed. 4) I. 310 Trimming off the leaves, except those at the extremity, which only require their ends shortened, as directed for pipings. **1851** *Beck's Florist* 192 Pinks. Continue to put out the rooted pipings, and prepare the beds for the next season's bloomers. **1856** [see PIPE *v.*² 3].

3. a. The action of furnishing with pipes or tubes. **b.** *concr.* Pipes collectively.

1846 *Athenæum* 14 Feb. 178 Professor Brande concluded his communication by exhibiting zinced iron piping. **1870** *Pall Mall G.* 18 Aug. 4 Deluged with a strong jet of cold water administered through a piping. **1885** *Manch. Exam.* 17 Feb. 5/4 To supplement the supply..by..an expensive system of piping from Peterborough.

4. *Dressmaking*, etc. **a.** The trimming or ornamenting of the edge of stuff or the seams of a garment, by means of a fine cord enclosed in a pipe-like fold of the edge or of a distinct strip of stuff; *concr.*, the tubular kind of trimming thus formed. **b.** Fluting: cf. PIPE *sb.*¹ 4 i. Also *attrib.*

1858 SIMMONDS *Dict. Trade*, *Piping*, a kind of cord trimming or fluting for ladies' dresses. *Piping-irons*, fluting-irons. **1859** MRS. STOWE *Minister's Wooing* xii. 126 Miss Prissy..fell..into a discourse on her own particular way of covering piping-cord. **1880** *Plain Hints Needlework* 100 Of late years, the act of piping has been introduced into under-linen to save trouble; a cord covered with material cut on the bias is inserted. **1891** *Pall Mall G.* 27 Aug. 4/1 The Princess ..wearing a..dark blue serge yachting costume, the coat and skirt outlined with a piping of white. **1894** C. N. ROBINSON *Brit. Fleet* 502 The lieutenant's undress coat.. had a white edging or piping. **1895** A. MORRISON *Chron. M. Hewitt* v. 256 A man in a blue coat, with dull red piping [in the seams] and brass buttons. **1966** *Olney Amsden & Sons Ltd. Price List* 13 Cushion Piping cord, 3-yard cards 16/9 dozen cards. **1967** E. SHORT *Embroidery & Fabric Collage* i. 20 (*caption*) Allover pattern in piping cord on white linen. **1968** J. IRONSIDE *Fashion Alphabet* 96 *Pipe*, to trim with a narrow tube of fabric, often with a piping cord run through to pad it out.

5. In harness, A tubular leather covering for a trace-chain, or such coverings collectively. (Cf. PIPE *sb.*¹ 4 a.)

1875 in KNIGHT *Dict. Mech.*

†**6.** A mode of dressing the hair by curling it around little cylinders or roulettes of wood or baked pipe-clay: cf. PIPE *sb.*¹ 4 j. *Obs.*

7. In jewellery, Lengths of gold (or other) tubing, fixed to the back of a thin plate of metal to strengthen it.

1881 G. WALLIS in *Encycl. Brit.* XIII. 676/2 Another smaller diadem found in another tomb..is of gold plate, so thick as to require no 'piping' at the back to sustain it.

8. *Confectionery.* The action or art of ornamenting cakes, etc. with cord-like lines or twists of sugar; *concr.* the lines or twists so used. Also *attrib.*

1846 C. E. FRANCATELLI *Mod. Cook* 398 The cake may be decorated with piping, using for that purpose some of the icing worked somewhat thicker. **1883** R. HALDANE *Workshop Receipts* Ser. II. 154/1 When dry, ornament with piping, orange-blossom, ribbon, &c. **1884** *Birmingham Daily Post* 23 Feb. 3/6 Well up in iceing and piping. **1943** BENNION & STEWART *Cake Manuf.* (ed. 2) xiii. 135 Fruit and piping jellies of various colours and flavours are a very useful commodity for use as fillings or for the decoration of cakes and gateaux. **1948** *Good Housek. Cookery Bk.* III. 612 The most satisfactory kind to purchase are made of hand-cut brass without screws, designed to use in conjunction with a piping bag. **1976** E. TURNER *All-Colour Cookbk.* xiii. 139/2 Put the mixture into a piping bag with a 6 mm./¼ in. rose nozzle and pipe out 14 to 16 neat roses on an ungreased baking sheet.

9. *Mining.* = HYDRAULICKING: see PIPE *v.*² 7.

1881 RAYMOND *Gloss. Mining*, *Piping.* 1. See *Hydraulicking.* **1895** J. W. ANDERSON *Prospector's Handbk.* (ed. 6) 163 *Piping*, washing gold deposits by means of a hose.

10. *Metallurgy.* = PIPE *sb.*¹ 7 e; the formation of such a pipe.

1861 *Brit. Patent 1310* 4 My invention consists in preventing..the waste occasioned by what is technically called the 'piping' of ingots of steel. **1881** RAYMOND *Mining Gloss.*, *Piping*... 2. The tubular depression caused by contraction during cooling, on the top of iron or steel ingots. **1923** GLAZEBROOK *Dict. Appl. Physics* V. 357/2 Piping does not necessarily take the form of a single central cavity. **1924** GREAVES & WRIGHTON *Pract. Microsc. Metallogr.* ix. 79 If insufficient discard is made, piping..may be present after rolling in the form of a longitudinal fissure..in the central portion of the billet.

11. (See quot. 1937.)

1937 E. J. LABARRE *Dict. Paper* 187/1 *Piping*, a species of crease or ribbing in paper due to irregular tension in reeling, to moisture, or being wound too tightly after sizing. **1963** R. R. A. HIGHAM *Handbk. Papermaking* 283 *Piping*, creases or ribbing in paper produced by irregular tension on the sheet during reeling.

12. *U.S.* The action of beating a person with a length of pipe; an assault of this nature.

1971 *Black Scholar* Apr.–May 24/2 The racial agitation is soon followed by hundreds of stabbings, pipings, brutal beatings and death. **1977** *New Yorker* 24 Oct. 64/3 Homosexuality..is one of the major causes of trouble in prison, often resulting in stabbings or pipings.

ˈ**piping**, *ppl. a.* [f. PIPE *v.*¹ + -ING².] That pipes; characterized by piping.

1. a. Playing on a pipe.

1638 JUNIUS *Paint. Ancients* 297 A most lively description of a piping satyr. *a* **1745** SWIFT *On Shadow in Glass* 36 Lowing herds, and piping swains. **1836–48** B. D. WALSH *Aristoph. Acharnians* II. v, Garlands, sprats, piping-women and black-eyes.

b. Characterized by piping, i.e. the music of the pastoral pipe (as distinguished from the martial fife, trumpet, etc.): in the Shaksperian phr. ***piping time(s) of peace.***

1594 SHAKS. *Rich. III*, I. i. 24 In this weake piping time of Peace. **1793** DR. BURNEY *Let. to Mme. D'Arblay* 31 Jan., The laws [are] more strictly executed against treason..than in the piping times of peace. **1883** ABP. FORBES in *19th Cent.* Oct. 730 In piping times of peace, the national debts of the Australian colonies loom large.

2. a. Sounding shrilly; whistling; shrill-toned.

1513 DOUGLAS *Æneis* VII. i. 17 The pyping wynd blew in thair taill at nycht. **1602** *2nd Pt. Return fr. Parnass.* III. iv. 1404 To him shall thy piping poetry..be directed. **1627–77** FELTHAM *Resolves* I. lii. 82 With piping acclamations. **1820** W. IRVING *Sketch Bk.*, *Rip Van Winkle*, An old man replied in a thin piping voice. **1872** DARWIN *Emotions* iv. 88 Dogs, when a little impatient, often make a high piping note through their noses. **1897** *Outing* (U.S.) XXX. 358/2 There was a piping breeze from the southwest.

b. In names of particular kinds of birds or other animals having a piping note or cry: as **piping crow**, the Australian genus *Gymnorhina*; **piping guan**, the genus *Pipile*, of S. America and Trinidad; **piping hare**, the pika or calling hare, *Lagomys*; **piping plover**, a small buff-coloured bird, *Charadrius melodus*, found in coastal areas of eastern North America. Also **piping bullfinch**, a bullfinch trained to 'pipe' or whistle a tune.

1773 BARRINGTON in *Phil. Trans.* LXIII. 267 Well known by the common instances of piping Bullfinches. **1845** *Voy. to Port Philip*, etc. 53 The warbling melops and the piping crow. **1895** C. DIXON in *Fortn. Rev.* Apr. 643 The Gymnorhinæ or piping crows of Australia. **1968** F. HAVERSCHMIDT *Birds of Surinam* 79 White-headed piping guan... Not uncommon in forests. **1828** C. L. BONAPARTE *Genera N. Amer. Birds* 296 Ringed Plover..and Piping Plover... Common all along the eastern sea coast of North America. **1870** *Amer. Naturalist* III. 231 The Piping Plover is still found along the coast of Maine. **1917** T. G. PEARSON *Birds Amer.* I. 264/1 Truly a bird of the beach-sand is the Piping Plover. **1964** J. BULL *Birds N.Y. Area* 185 The Piping Plover breeds on the ocean beaches.

3. a. quasi-*adv.* in phr. **piping hot**, so hot as to make a piping or hissing sound, as a simmering liquid, or a dish freshly cooked; hissing hot; hence *gen.* very hot.

c **1386** CHAUCER *Miller's T.* 193 Wafres pipyng hoot out of the gleede. ?*a* **1550** *Freiris of Berwik* 377 in *Dunbar's Poems* (S.T.S.) 297 Ane pair of cunyngis, fat and het pypand. **1601** HOLLAND *Pliny* II. 141 Beanes..fried all whole as they be, and so cast piping hot into sharp vineger. **1657** R. LIGON *Barbadoes* (1673) 10 When we had climed..Being painfully and pipeing hot. **1707** J. STEVENS tr. *Quevedo's Com. Wks.* (1709) 234 A Mutton-Pye,..piping hot out of the Oven. **1888** BURGON *Lives 12 Gd. Men* II. xi. 316 The day having been piping hot.

b. *fig.* Fresh, quite new, just come out.

1607 MIDDLETON *Your Five Gallants* II. i. 57 *Gol.* Whence comes he, sir? *Pur.* Piping hot from the university. **1641** MILTON *Reform.* I. Wks. 1851 III. 6 The Booke..in defence of Bishops, which came out piping hot much about the time. **1733** *Revolution Politicks* VII. 8 A Report is come pipeing hot from Ireland. **1855** BROWNING *Up at a Villa* ix, At the post-office such a scene-picture—the new play, piping hot!

pipistrelle, -el (pɪpɪˈstrɛl). [a. F. *pipistrelle*, ad. It. *pipistrello* bat, variants of which are *vipistrello, vispi-, vespistrello*, from *vispertello, vespertillo*, repr. late L. **vespertillus* for L. *vespertilio* (*-ōnem*) bat, f. *vesper* evening. See Diez (ed. 4) 390.] A small species of bat, *Vesperugo pipistrellus*, common in Britain and Europe generally.

1781 PENNANT *Hist. Quad.* II. 561 Bat, Pipistrelle. **1843** *Zoologist* I. 66 The pipistrelle, or common bat of Britain. **1862** G. KEARLEY *Links in Chain* (1863) 245 No less than fifteen or sixteen species of Bats are found in Britain... The little Pipistrelle..is..the most abundant..of the number.

pipit (ˈpɪpɪt). Also 8 pippet, -it, 9 pipet. [prob. imitative of the bird's 'short and feeble note' (Swainson). Cf. PIP *v.*², and the dial. names *titling, tietick, cheeper, peep*, etc. So F. *pipit, pitpit.*] Any bird of the genus *Anthus* or several allied genera of the family *Motacillidæ*, widely distributed over most parts of the world, and having a general resemblance to larks. The common British species are the Meadow Pipit or Titlark, *A. pratensis*; the Tree Pipit or Pipit-lark, *A. trivialis* (*A. arboreus*); and the Rock Pipit, Rock-lark, or Shore-lark, *A. obscurus*.

1768 PENNANT *Zool.* II. 241 A species [of lark] taken in the neighborhood of London called by the bird-catchers a pippit. **1832** SELBY in *Proc. Berw. Nat. Club* I. No. 1. 18 The rock or shore pipit (*Anthus aquaticus*)... In size it exceeds..the common and the tree pipet (*A. pratensis* and *arboreus*). **1882** HARDY *Ibid.* IX. No. 3. 453 Larks and pipit-larks arise at intervals. **1894** NEWTON *Dict. Birds* s.v., Pipits, of which over 30 species have been described..occur in almost all parts of the world.

pipkin (ˈpɪpkɪn). Also 6 pypkin, 6–7 pipken. [Origin doubtful. The form suggests a dim., f. PIPE *sb.*² + -KIN; cf. Sp. *pipote* keg, and Pg. *pipote* small cask or vessel, f. *pipa* PIPE *sb.*² But there is no evidence that the pipkin was at first a small cask or staved vessel.]

1. A small earthenware pot or pan, used chiefly in cookery. (Formerly in wider sense, including metal pots. Now local; in Eng. Dial. Dict. from Warw. to Lincoln and Suff.)

1565 COOPER *Thesaurus, Ollula*..a little potte: a pipken. **1578** LYTE *Dodoens* II. xlii. 201 Boyled with vinegar and hony in a brasen pipken or skillet. **1622** MALYNES *Anc. Law-Merch.* 79 Put them together into a cleane pipkin or leaded pot,..let them stand ouer the fire one houre. **1663** BUTLER *Hud.* I. iii. 1160 Free from a crack or flaw of sinning, As Men try Pipkins by the ringing. **1758** REID tr. *Macquer's Chym.* I. 279 Put the Sea-salt..into an unglazed earthen pipkin, and set it amidst live coals. **1808** WOLCOTT (P. Pindar) *One more Peep at R. Acad.* Wks. 1812 V. 355 A pipkin of brown crockery. **1825** BROCKETT *N.C. Gloss., Pipkin* or *Pidkin*, a small earthen vessel with a handle. **1854** H. MILLER *Sch. & Schm.* xiii. (1860) 139/1 The unglazed earthen pipkin, fashioned by the hand, without the assistance of the potter's wheel, is held to belong to the 'bronze and stone periods' of the antiquary.

2. *U.S.* and (?) *dial.* A small wooden tub having a vertical handle formed by the prolongation of one of the staves, a piggin.

1855 WHITTIER *Flowers in Winter* ix, A wizard of the Merrimac,..Could call green leaf and blossom back To frosted stem and spray... The beechen platter sprouted wild, The pipkin wore its old-time green. **18..** T. A. HILL *MS. Collect. Nottingham Words* (E.D.D.).

3. *Comb.*, as ***pipkin-shaped*** adj.

1908 E. TERRY *Story of my Life* 199 A three-handled cup, pipkin-shaped, standing on three legs.

Hence ˈ**pipkinet** (*nonce-wd.*), a small pipkin.

1647 HERRICK *Noble Numb.* Wks. (1869) 404 Thou my pipkinnet shalt see, Give a wave-offring unto Thee.

pipkrake (ˈpɪpkreɪk, -krɑːkə). *Geomorphol.* Pl. **-krakes, -kraker.** [a. Sw. dial *pipkrake*, f. *pip* PIPE *sb.*¹ + *krake*, dial. by-form of *klake* (hardness and roughness of) frozen ground (= Norw. *klake*, Da. *klage*, Icel. *klaki*).] **a.** One of the ice-needles in needle ice. **b.** = *needle ice* s.v. NEEDLE *sb.* 14.

1956 *Biuletyn Peryglacjalny* IV. 167 Bunt also noticed the formation of ice palisades (pipkrakes) in the hollows and ascribes the removal of fine material from the hollows to the melting of these ice crystals. **1967** M. J. COE *Ecol. Alpine Zone Mt. Kenya* 74 On the flat or slightly sloping ground of valley bottoms, an important feature of soil movement is that of Needle Ice, or Pip[k]rake. **1968** R. W. FAIRBRIDGE *Encycl. Geomorphol.* 370/1 Water expands about 10% upon freezing (ice being characterized by a high expansion coefficient, as seen in the growth of ice needles or pipkrakes). *Ibid.* 381/1 Such 'needle ice' is sometimes called pipkrake. **1970** R. J. SMALL *Study of Landforms* x. 330 The formation at or near the ground surface of small masses of ice, such as pipkraker, commonly has the effect of heaving up small stones at right angles to the slope. **1971** A. F. PITTY *Introd. Geomorphol.* IV. 219 In mountainous areas in central Germany, pipkrakes may be 10–15 cm long. **1973** A. L. WASHBURN *Periglacial Processes & Environments* iv. 81 Needle ice.., also known as pipkrake, is an accumulation of slender, bristle-like ice crystals practically at, or immediately beneath, the surface of the ground.

pipless (ˈpɪplɪs), *a.* [f. PIP *sb.*³ + -LESS.] Having no pips; seedless.

1869 C. R. WELD *Notes Burgundy* 115 The Corinthian Grape..possesses the great recommendation of being pipless. **1900** *Daily News* 31 Mar. 7/3 Pipless oranges are among the novelties hailing from California.

pipling, var. PIPPLING.

pipouder, -poulder, etc., var. PIEPOWDER.

pippal, var. PEEPUL.

†ˈ**pippane.** *Sc. Obs.* Also **pypane, pyppane.** (Origin and meaning uncertain.)

1491 *Acc. Ld. High Treas. Scot.* I. 189 Item, for v vnce of reid pyppane sylk to be beltis to the King. **1505** *Ibid.* III. 40 Item, for ij pypanes blak silk,..*vd.* **1506** *Ibid.* 351 Tua pippanes rede silk for the Kingis scarlet hos.

†**pipped**, ? *ppl. a.*¹ *Obs.* Also 7 pipt. [In form, pa. pple. of PIP *v.*² sense 2, but the latter is not known so early.] Cracked, as a nut.

1545 ELYOT *Dict., Cassa nux*, a pypped nutte. **1552** HULOET, Pipped nutte, *cassa nux.* **1640** BROME *Sparagus Gard.* v. ii, A pipt Nutshell and a Maggot in't.

pipped, *ppl. a.*²,³ see PIP *v.*²,⁴.

pipped (pɪpt), *a.*¹ [f. PIP *sb.*¹ (or *v.*¹) + -ED.]

a. Affected with the pip.

1797 MRS. A. M. BENNETT *Beggar Girl* (1813) III. 284 There's poor Horace sick in his hammock, and the admiral croaking like a piped hen. **1845** JAMES *A. Neil* ii, You have no more stomach than a pipped hen.

b. Annoyed, irritated.

1914 A. N. LYONS *Simple Simon* I. vi. 100 'How's Leverton?' 'Rather pipped, thank you,' replied Miss Disney. 'Poor old Ma was raw-beefing him when I left.' **1941** BAKER *Dict. Austral. Slang* 54 *Pipped, pippy*, irritated, angry, out of sorts.

pipped (pɪpt), *a.*² [Perh. f. PIP *v.*³] Tipsy, drunk.

1911 J. MASEFIELD *Everlasting Mercy* 26 Si's wife came in and sipped and sipped (As women will) till she was pipped. **1929** M. DE LA ROCHE *Whiteoaks* vii. 110 Lilly, here, can't see the strings. He's pipped, aren't you, Lilly?

pipperidge (ˈpɪpərɪdʒ). Also 6 pypryge, pipridge, 8–9 piperidge, (9 *dial.* piprage, piprick). Cf. PEPPERIDGE. [Derivation obscure.

Cf. AF. *piperounge* a hip, in W. de Bibbesworth (Prof. Skeat).]

1. A local name of the Barberry, fruit or shrub; the latter usually ***pipperidge-bush***.

1538 TURNER *Libellus, Oxiacantha*,..ab officinis & uulgo berberis dicitur, aliquibus Pypryge uocatur. **1562** —— *Herbal* II. 146 The berbery tre, otherwyse called a pipridge tre. **1674** RAY *S. & E.C. Words* 74 *Pipperidges*, Barberries, *Ess. Suff.* **1731** MILLER *Gard. Dict., Barbery*, or pipperidge-bush,..grows naturally in the hedges in many parts of England. **1886** BRITTEN & HOLLAND *Eng. Plant-n.* 382 Piperidge, Pipperidges, Piprage, Pepperidge, Piperidge Tree, or Piperidge Bush.

2. = PEPPERIDGE 2.

1828 WEBSTER s.v. *Piperidge*, The piperidge of New England is the *Nyssavillosa*, a large tree with very tough wood. **1872** MRS. STOWE *Oldtown Fireside Stories* 127 Old Black Hoss was about as close as a nut and as contrairy as a pipperage-tree.

pippet (ˈpɪpɪt). *rare.* [f. PIP *sb.*² + -ET.] = PIP *sb.*² 1.

1940 B. RUSSELL *Inquiry into Meaning & Truth* 57 Take again the two of clubs, and the proposition 'this is similar to that' applied to the two pippets.

pippet, -it, obs. forms of PIPIT.

pippian (ˈpɪpɪən). *Math.* [See quot.] = CAYLEYAN.

1853 CAYLEY *Coll. Math. Papers* II. 381, I propose (in analogy with the form Hessian) to call the two curves in question [previously denoted by P and Q] the Pippian and Quippian respectively.

pippin (ˈpɪpɪn). Forms: 4–6 pepyn(e, 4–7 pipin, 4–8 pepin, 5 pipyn, 5–6 pypyn(e, 6 peppin, pippyn, pyppen, 6– pippin, (6–8 pippen, -ing, 7 -ine). [ME. a. OF. *pepin* (13th c.) seed of a fleshy fruit, mod.F. *pepin, pépin* pip; in Norm. dial. also seedling apple-tree: cf. sense 2. Cf. It. *pippolo* kernel, grape-stone. Origin obscure.

Connexion with L. *pĕpo, -ōnem*, a. Gr. *πέπων, -ονα* 'pumpkin', is doubtful: in Sp. and Pg. *pepino* is 'cucumber', *pepita* 'kernel or pip', also 'pip' in fowls (PIP *sb.*¹), which in Walloon is *pepin*. It. *pipita* is 'sprout' or 'shoot', and also 'pip' in fowls. The relations between these are obscure.]

1. a. The seed of certain fruits, including those now called *pips*, and others: cf. PIP *sb.*³ *Obs.* exc. *north. dial.*

a **1300** *Cursor M.* 1366 (Cott.) Pepins [so *Gött.*; *Fairf.* cornys; *Trin.* curnels] þen he gaue him thrin, þe quilk a þe appel tre he nam. *Ibid.* 1417 Þe pipins war don vnder his tung, þar ras o þam thre wandes yong. **1348–9** *Durham Acc. Rolls* (Surtees) 549 In duabus libr. de Resyns sanz pepyn. **1398** TREVISA *Barth. De P.R.* XVII. clxxxix. (Bodl. MS.), Huoles and pipyns leueþ whan þe wyne is clene wronge oute. *c* **1440** *Promp. Parv.* 401/2 Pypyne, of vyne, or grape.., *acinus.* **1502** ARNOLDE *Chron.* (1811) 166 Yf thou wyll haue many rooses..thou muste take the harde pepyns of the same rooses that bee right rype and sowe hem. **1578** LYTE *Dodoens* VI. xlii. 712 In the middle of the fruite [pear] there is a coare with kernels or peppins. **1601** HOLLAND *Pliny* I. 447 The inner stones or pepins, which in some grapes are but single, or one alone. **1613** [see 1 c]. **1764** ELIZ. MOXON *Eng. Housew.* (ed. 9) 155 Cut them [oranges] in quarters and take out all the pippens. **1828** *Craven Gloss., Pippin*, the seed of an apple. **1868** ATKINSON *Cleveland Gloss., Pippin*, the pip or seed of the apple and like fruits.

†**b.** Applied to the germ of a pea, or the like.

c **1430** *Two Cookery-bks.* 32 [Pesyn] wyl alle to-falle with a lytil boylynge, to pereye, saue þe whyte Pepyn is þer-in.

†**c.** Rendering Sp. *pepita* a grain of gold. *Obs.*

1604 E. G[RIMSTONE] *D'Acosta's Hist. Indies* IV. iv. 213 They finde little of this golde in pippin. *Ibid.*, They call them pippins, for that commonly they are like to pippins or seeds of melons. **1613** PURCHAS *Pilgrimage* VIII. ii. 607 Their golde is found either in Graines which they call the Pippins because they are like..Seedes of Melons..or in powder.

2. a. The name of numerous varieties of apple, raised from seed.

c **1432** LYDG. *On Entry of Hen. VI into London* (MS. Harl. 565 lf. 121), Pypyns, quynces blaundrellys to disport And þe Pom cedre corageus to recomfort. **1494** FABYAN *Chron.* VII. 605. **1530** PALSGR. 154 Names of frutes..as well generall as *pomme*, an apple, and *póyre*, a peare, as particuler, as *carpendv*, a pippyn; *estrangvillon*, a choke peare. **1579** LYLY *Euphues* (Arb.) 120 The sower Crabbe..as well as the sweete Pippin. **1597** SHAKS. *2 Hen. IV*, v. iii. 2 We will eate a last yeares Pippin of my owne graffing. **1629** PARKINSON *Paradisi* 587 This is a pretty way to have Pippins, Pomewaters, or any other sorts of Apples growing low. **1676** WORLIDGE *Cyder* (1691) 202 Pippins..take their name from the small spots or pips that usually appear on the sides of the Apple. **1861** MISS PRATT *Flower. Pl.* II. 253 The pippins..were so called because the trees were raised from pips or seeds. **1866** *Treas. Bot.* 945 Some [apples] of English origin have acquired almost universal celebrity; for instance, the Golden Pippin, Ribston Pippin,..Blenheim Pippin, etc.; and recently Cox's Orange Pippin has been brought into notice.

b. In phrases, as ***sound as a pippin***, very sound.

1886 H. BAUMANN *Londinismen* 139/1 He's as sound as a pippin. **1910** BELLOC *Verses* 81, I said to Heart, 'How goes it?' Heart replied: 'Right as a Ribstone Pippin!' But it lied.

3. a. Applied to a person. *slang.*

1664 COTTON *Scarron.* IV. Wks. (1725) 95 Thou'rt a precious Pepin, To think to steal so slily from me. *c* **1821** 'W. T. MONCRIEFF' *Tom & Jerry* (1828) II. v. 49 Go it, my pippins. **1846** *Swell's Night Guide* 49 Now, my pippins, I'll just ax you which was the rankest sell? **1885** *Punch* 3 Jan. 4/1 The Reform Bill won't do it, my Pippin. **1888** [see COCKER *sb.*⁶]. **1892** E. J. MILLIKEN *'Arry Ballads* 23/2 She would take the shine out of some screamers, I tell yer, my pippin, would Loo. **1895** *Punch* 15 June 285/1 No slow Surrey-siders, my pippin, but smart bits o' frock from Mayfair.

b. An excellent person or thing; a beauty. *slang* (orig. *U.S.*).

1897 ADE in *Chicago Record* 17 Sept. 4/5 This sister was fair to look upon. In fact, it was frequently remarked that she was a Pippin. **1906** G. H. LORIMER *Jack Spurlock* (1908) ii. 28 'I'd like to have the job which goes with that blonde,' and I pointed to a pippin who was pounding the keys just outside his door. **1914** 'BARTIMEUS' *Naval Occasions* xii. 88 The Flag-Lieutenant introduced him to a lady of surpassing loveliness—The Fairest..of All the Pippins. **1920** WODEHOUSE *Jill the Reckless* xvi. 237 'We shall..open in Baltimore next Monday with practically a different piece. And it's going to be a pippin, believe *me*,' said our hero modestly. **1926** *Amer. Speech* I. 462 The Apollo Theater in London prints the following glossary of slang in its program as a guide to 'Is Zat So?'.. *Pippin*, beauty. **1930** J. DOS PASSOS *42nd Parallel* I. 47 He..got a book from a man at the hotel. Gosh it was a pippin. **1939** R. STOUT *Some Buried Caesar* vi. 71 The fight for a hotel room which was a pippin

—I mean the fight, not the room. **1948** H. Innes *Blue Ice* ii. 38 She's a pippin.. Knows her way around already. **1972** Wodehouse *Pearls, Girls & Monty Bodkin* viii. 120 So I have a plan..and it's a pippin.

4. *attrib.* and *Comb.*, as ***pippin cider, jelly, pie, trade***; ***pippin grower, -monger, -pelting, -squeezer***; **pippin-face**, a red round face; so ***pippin-faced*** adj.; †**pippin-fruit**, a fruit containing 'pippins' or pips (*obs.*); **pippin-hearted** *a.*, faint-hearted, timid; †**pippin-squire** = apple-squire (*obs.*); †**pippin-tea**, ? an infusion of pippins (*obs.*).

1766 *Compl. Farmer* s.v. *Cyder*, They..found their *pepin cyder not so pleasant as their moyle or red streak cyder. **1598** Marston *Pygmal.* Sat. iii. 150 He neuer durst vnto these Ladies show His *pippin face. **1837** Dickens *Pickw.* vi, The hard-headed man with the pippin-face. **1872** Black *Adv. Phaeton* vi, This old shepherd, with his withered pippin face. **1837** Dickens *Pickw.* vi, A little hard-headed, Ripstone-*pippin-faced man. **1675** Cotton (*title*) The Planters Manual: being instructions for the Raising, Planting, and Cultivating all sorts of Fruit-Trees, whether Stone-fruits or *Pepin-fruits. **1833** Ht. Martineau *Tale of Tyne* i, If I were to turn pippin-monger instead of *pippin-grower. **1809** W. Irving *Knickerb.* (1861) 171 They might have been the meekest, most *pippin-hearted little men in the world. **1718** Mrs. Eales *Receipts* 51 Take *Pippin-Jelly. **1607** Heywood *Fayre Mayde* Wks. 1874 II. 57 You are a *pippinmonger to call me Russetting or apple-john. **1835** *Edin. Rev.* LXI. 406 Hissing, hooting, *pippin-pelting, and driving them from the boards. **1592** Greene *Disput.* 5 A *pipping Pye that cost in the Market foure pence. **1600** Rowlands *Lett. Humours Blood* xxxiii. 39 A Dogges yeoman, or some *pippin Squier. **1706** Baynard in Sir J. Floyer *Hot & Cold Bath.* ii. 323 For his constant Drink ..*Pippin-Thea,..with Syrup of Rasberries. **1745** *Pippin trade [see pippiner].

Hence †'**pippined** *a.*, having pips; †'**pippiner**, a ship engaged in the 'pippin trade' (see quot.).

c **1420** *Pallad. on Husb.* iii. 72 Grapis feire and greete, Pypened hard [L. *grani callosi*] and drie. **1745** *De Foe's Eng. Tradesman* iii. (1841) I. 19 If a merchant comes to me to hire a small ship of me, and tells me it is for the pippin-trade; or to buy a vessel, and tells me he intends to make a pippiner of her; the meaning is, that she is to run to Seville for oranges, or to Malaga for lemons.

pip-pip. [Echoic.] **1.** A repeated, short, high-pitched sound, *spec.* that made by a motor- or bicycle-horn; also, the horn itself.

1904 Kipling *Traffics & Discov.* 324 Children sat..on the damp doorsteps to shout 'pip-pip' at the stranger. **1907** Shaw *Major Barbara* iii. 292 *Sarah* (touching Lady Britomart's ribs with her finger tips and imitating a bicycle horn) Pip! pip! **1909** *Westm. Gaz.* 15 May 3/2 She [*sc.* a little girl] had motor-cars with real pip-pips. **1979** N. Freeling *Widow* xx. 124 There was a timid little pip-pip at the front door bell. **1979** J. Scott *Angels in your Beer* xviii. 187 Marianne walked to the Ferrari... She..sounded an impatient pip pip on the horn.

2. *slang.* A substitute for 'good-bye'. (In quot. 1907 as a defiant retort.)

1907 *Mr. Punch Awheel* 93 *Cyclist*... 'Nice crowd out this morning!' *Rural Policeman*..'Yes, an' yer can't do with 'em! If yer 'ollers at 'em, they honly turns round and says, 'Pip, pip'! **1920** Wodehouse *Damsel in Distress* x. 129 'Well, it's worth trying,' said Reggie. 'I'll give it a whirl. Toodleoo!' 'Good-bye.' 'Pip-pip!' Reggie withdrew. **1931** E. F. Benson *Mapp & Lucia* iii. 56 Mr. Woolgar..did not say 'So long' or 'Pip-pip'. **1951** Wodehouse *Old Reliable* xv. 169 Hello, Smedley. Pip-pip, Lord Topham. **1973** G. Sims *Hunters Point* iii. 22 The nine-day 'British Week' had ended... Fisherman's Wharf had been buzzing with 'Cheerio, pip pip and smashing' voices. **1978** M. Butterworth *X marks Spot* iii. iii. 158 'Pip pip, laddie.' He set off.

pip-pip-pip. *Teleph.* [f. pip *sb.*[5]] (The sound of) the three consecutive pips used as a time signal in the 'speaking clock' service and to indicate the lapse of time during a trunk call.

1936 *Discovery* Oct. 315/2 Thus 'At the third stroke' is taken from one groove, 'it will be' from another, 'eleven o'clock' from another disc, and the sound 'pip-pip-pip' from a fourth. **1938** D. Smith *Dear Octopus* i. 12 Don't go on talking after the pip pip pip, because they charge you at once.

†'**pipple**, *v. Obs.* Also 6 pypple (pimpel). [App. dim. or frequent. of pipe *v.*[1]] *intr.* To blow with a gentle sound; to pipe or whistle softly, as the wind; to murmur or ripple, as a stream. Hence †'**pippling** *vbl. sb.* and *ppl. a.*

a **1529** Skelton *Replyc.* Wks. 1843 I. 207 Yong scolers.. enbolned with the flyblowen blast of the moche vayne glorious pipplyng wynde. **1555** W. Watreman *Fardle Facions* ii. viii. 164 Thei haue twoo sommers, softe pimpelyng windes, a milde aier. **1558** Phaer *Æneid.* iii. F iv, Whan the..wind with pipling sweete Is out at sowth, and to the seas to saill doth call the fleete. **1582** Stanyhurst *Æneis* ii. (Arb.) 66, I Now shiuer at shaddows, eeche pipling puf doth amaze me. **1592** R. D. *Hypnerotomachia* 75 b, Small streames of water, pyppling and slyding downe vpon the Amber grauell. [**1862** G. Macdonald *D. Elginbrod* ii. ix, They sat down to enjoy the 'soft pipling cold' which swung all the leaves about.]

b. ? *transf.*

1582 Stanyhurst *Æneis* iv. (Arb.) 95 Had not I such daliaunce, such pipling bedgle renounced.

pipple, -stone: see pebble, -stone.

pip-pop. [Echoic.] A representation of the report of a Mauser rifle, etc.

1901 *Westm. Gaz.* 14 Nov. 1/3 Once outside the outposts of the base town and the fun begins. Pip-pop—pip-pop—the Yeomanry in advance have been fired upon. **1902** *Macm. Mag.* Sept. 392 The sound still rings in my ears of the metallic pip-pop of the Mauser.

pippy ('pɪpɪ), *a.* [f. pip *sb.*[3] and ? *sb.*[1] + -y.]

1. Full of pips.

1892 *Sat. Rev.* 25 June 728/1 A bitter, pippy lemon.

2. a. *Stock Exchange slang.* (?) Sickly, shaky.

1892 *Scott. Leader* 19 Feb., On 'change... Mexican rails also look 'pippy' to-day.

b. Depressed, out of sorts.

1886 R. Fry *Let.* 28 Nov. (1972) I. 111 My Mays depress me, so does my Tripos... In fact I am stupidly pippy at times.

pipradol: see next.

pipradrol ('pɪprədrɒl). *Pharm.* Also (*erron.*) pipradol. [f. pip(e)r(idine + -*a*- + *benzhy*)*drol* s.v. benzo-.] A colourless crystalline solid, α,α-diphenyl-α-piperid-2-ylmethanol hydrochloride, $C_{18}H_{21}NO.HCl$, which is used as an antidepressant. Also called ***pipradrol hydrochloride***.

1955 *Science* 11 Feb. 209/2 Meratran is the trademark of the Wm. S. Merrell Co., for its brand of pipradrol. **1955** *Sci. News Let.* 13 Aug. 105/1 The drug is a pipradol chemical trade-named Frenquel by the manufacturer, the Wm. S. Merrell Co. of Cincinnati. **1956** *Jrnl. Amer. Med. Assoc.* 4 Feb. 390/1 Pipradrol hydrochloride is a central nervous system stimulant chemically unrelated to the sympathomimetic amines but exhibiting some of the pharmacological actions of amphetamine. **1962** F. C. Ferguson *Drug Therapy* xxiv. 216 Other types of anti-depressants include piperidines; methylphenidate (Ritalin) and pipradrol (Meratran). **1973** *Approved Names 1973* (Brit. Pharmacopœia Comm.) 59 Pipradol. **1974** *Ibid.* Suppl. 111, For 'Pipradol' read 'Pipradrol'. **1974** *Jrnl. Clin. Pharmacol.* XIV. 132/2 Present results thus suggest at the most only limited efficacy for pipradrol in the treatment of depressed outpatients.

pipridge, obs. form of pipperidge.

‖**pipsissewa** (pɪp'sɪsɪwə). [ad. N. Amer. Ind. (? Algonquin) name *sip-si-sewa*; it is not clear whether the form in *pip-* occurred in some native dial., or was a white man's corruption.] A name for *Chimaphila umbellata* (N.O. *Ericaceæ* or *Pyrolaceæ*), also called Prince's pine, a low creeping evergreen with whitish flowers, found in Europe, northern Asia, and N. America. Also, the leaves of this used as a diuretic and tonic.

[**1814** Pursh *Flor. Amer. Sept.* 300 *Chimaphila*..is in high esteem for its medicinal qualities. They call it *Sip-si-sewa*.] **1818** Eaton *Man. Bot.* 203 General Varnum says the umbellata is the Sipsisewa or Pipsisewa and is highly efficacious in the Cure of cancers. **1875** H. C. Wood *Therap.* (1879) 499 Pipsissewa is probably about equivalent to uva ursi in its therapeutic value. **1880** *New Virginians* I. iv. 131 Those woodland darlings, the wild pansy, the pipsissewa [*mispr.* pipsewissa], and the partridge-berry. **1884** Millspaugh *Amer. Med. Plants* 104 Chimaphila umbellata. .. Common names pipsissewa, winter green, princes pine, bitter winter green, ground holly.

'**pip-squeak.** *slang.* [f. pip *sb.*[5] + squeak *sb.*]

1. A contemptuous name for an insignificant person; a petty object. Also *attrib.*

In quot. 1923 a two-stroke motor cycle.

1910 E. V. Lucas *Slowcoach* xxiii. 279 'It belongs to one of those measly pip-squeaks,' said Robert. **1923** *Motor Cycling* 21 Nov. 89/1 The owners of sporting four stroke machines look down on the owners of so-called 'Pip-Squeaks'. **1925** Fraser & Gibbons *Soldier & Sailor Words* 224 *Pip Squeak*,..a small man, or one objectionable in some way. **1926** *Blackw. Mag.* June 732/2 After all, the luxurious liner which connects this riotous spot with the outer world is only a pip-squeak of a vessel. **1930** G. Macmunn *Behind Scenes in Many Wars* 88 It does not pay in the East to let pip-squeaks beard the mighty. **1946** *Richmond* (Virginia) *Times-Dispatch* 20 Jan. i. 14/8 Specifically, [Senator] Wiley charged that the organization..has 'created czars out of pipsqueak juveniles'. **1951** M. McLuhan *Mech. Bride* (1967) 23/2 Mighty blasts on the tooter herald the arrival of just another pip-squeak [*sc.* monotonous book]. **1961** A. Christie *Pale Horse* xxi. 224 What about that psychological pipsqueak you brought along to see me, Corrigan. What does he say? **1973** 'H. Howard' *Highway to Murder* vi. 65 For a little pip-squeak you make a big noise. **1974** E. Ambler *Dr. Frigo* iii. 174 They weren't taking any nonsense from a pipsqueak foreign doctor.

2. a. A small type of high velocity shell distinguished by the sound of its flight. Also *attrib.*

1916 E. V. Lucas *Vermilion Box* 209 Whatever else there is to grumble at over here, wet, and rats, and Pip-Squeaks and Jack Johnsons..we do get two things up to sample. **1916** *Cornh. Mag.* Mar. 395 They're 'pip-squeak' and splinter-proof, of course. **1917** A. G. Empey *Over Top* 304 *Pip squeak*, Tommy's term for a small German shell which makes a 'pip' and then a 'squeak', when it comes over. **1927** E. Thompson *These Men, thy Friends* 176 The Turkish guns suddenly sent over a couple of pipsqueaks. *a* **1936** Kipling *Something of Myself* (1937) vi. 159 One indubitable shell—ridiculously like a pip-squeak in that vastness but throwing up much dirt.

b. = pip-pip 1. Also = peep *sb.*[1] 2 b. So '**pip-squeak** *v.*

1922 *Blackw. Mag.* June 699/2 She heard just then her Tom pip-squeaking on his pipe. **1927** 'Ixion' *Further Motor Cycle Reminisc.* 100 Hooters..fitted with rather wafery clips, such as still linger on bicycle 'pipsqueaks'. **1943** [see sense 2 c below]. **1956** E. Pound tr. *Sophocles' Women of Trachis* 16 Hasn't uttered a pip-squeak Since she came down from the windy country.

c. (See quots. 1943, 1970.) *slang.*

1943 C. H. Ward-Jackson *Piece of Cake* 48 *Pip-squeak*, the instrument in an aircraft by the aid of which one gets a 'Fix'. This instrument emits a pip-squeak at short intervals which is synchronised over the radio with base, thus fixing the time, an essential prelude to fixing the position of the aircraft. **1946** Brickhill & Norton *Escape to Danger* vi. 60 Forgetting to switch off his 'pip-squeak' (radio contactor), Mickey climbed thankfully out on to the wing. **1970** Partridge *Dict. Slang* (ed. 7) II. 1330/2 'The pip-squeak was an automatic transmitter *only*, whose once-a-minute signals enabled ground direction-finding stations to fix the aircraft's position accurately for the benefit of the Fighter Controller in the Operations Room...' (Ramsey Spencer, March 1967.)

Pip, Squeak, and Wilfred. *slang.* [Names of three animal characters featured in a children's comic strip in the *Daily Mirror* from 1920 onwards.] Designating a trio of objects or persons.

[**1920** 'Uncle Dick' in *Daily Mirror* 25 Mar. 13/2 Aren't Pip and Squeak and Wilfred sweet measuring their heights? **1920** —— *Pip, Squeak, & Wilfred* 60 Some time ago, Pip, Squeak, and Wilfred dreamed they were real children. *Ibid.* 61, I am rather fond of Pip, Squeak, and Wilfred. I, too, have my dreams.] **1937** Partridge *Dict. Slang* 633/2 *Pip, Squeak and Wilfred*, the medals (or medal ribbons), 1914–15 Star, War Medal, Victory Medal. **1943** C. H. Ward-Jackson *Piece of Cake* 48 *Pip, Squeak and Wilfred*, the 1914–15 Star, the Great War and Victory medals or ribbons worn in a row. **1966** 'L. Lane' *ABZ of Scouse* 35 Other names [for a trio of friends] are Pip, Squeak and Wilfrid [*sic*]. **1977** *Times* 30 Sept. 16/8 That goes for Messrs Pip, Squeak and Wilfred, too.

pipsyl ('pɪpsaɪl, -ɪl). *Chem.* Also **PIPSYL**. [f. letters in the systematic name (see def.).] The radical *p*-*i*odo*p*henyl*s*ulphon*yl*, $I{\cdot}C_6H_4{\cdot}SO_2-$, compounds of which are used as radioactive labels.

1946 *Jrnl. Amer. Chem. Soc.* LXVIII. 1390/1 As the labelled reagent we used *p*-iodophenyl sulfonyl chloride (PIPSYLchloride), prepared from radioactive iodide ion and *p*-diazobenzene-sulfonic acid, followed by treatment with phosphorus pentachloride. *Ibid.* 1390/2 Less than one-hundredth per cent. of *d*(−)alanine was found in the β-lactoglobulin hydrolysate using PIPSYL d(−)alanine carrier. **1949** *Ibid.* LXXI. 256/1 (*heading*) The preparation of pipsyl amino acids for use as carriers. **1961** G. R. Choppin *Exper. Nucl. Chem.* x. 173 In the last chapter the use of I^{131} labeled *p*-iodobenzenesulfonyl chloride (pipsyl chloride) with the amino acids was described. **1974** *Canad. Jrnl. Biochem.* LII. 217/2 Using the multiple isomorphous protein phases..a difference electron density map has been computed. This map was relatively devoid of significant electron density except in the region of PIPSYL binding.

pipul, variant of peepul, E. Indian tree.

pipy ('paɪpɪ), *a.* (erron. -ey.) [f. pipe *sb.*[1] + -y.]

1. Containing pipes, tubes, or tubular formations; of the form of a pipe, tubular, cylindrical.

1724 Switzer *Pract. Gard.* xi. lxxviii. 406 When once sellery is whitened it must be eaten, otherwise it will soon grow pipey or rot. **1757** Ellis in *Phil. Trans.* L. 193 A white pipy and stony coral. **1818** Keats *Endym.* i. 241 Where dank moisture breeds The pipy hemlock to strange overgrowth. **1851** *Jrnl. R. Agric. Soc.* XII. i. 288 A soft blue 'pipy' clay, *i.e.* containing pipes of red rusty matter. **1869** Phillips *Vesuv.* iv. 121 The crust formed over the lava is remarkably pipy as well as cellular.

2. Piping, shrill. (Cf. pipe *sb.*[1] 2.)

1877 W. S. Gilbert *Foggerty's Fairy* (1892) 14 'Cheer up, Mr. Foggerty', said a pipy little voice.

3. Given to 'piping the eye' or crying. *colloq.*

1861 Miss Yonge *Stokesley Secret* xii. (1862) 179 'Christabel', said a little voice,..'I shall never be pipy again'.

piquable ('piːkəb(ə)l), *a. rare.* [f. pique *v.* + -able.] Capable of being or inclined to be piqued.

1860 Tennyson *Let. Dk. Argyle* in *Mem.* (1897) I. xxi. 458 Had I been a piquable man I should have been piqued.

piquance ('piːkəns). *rare.* [See -ance.] = next.

1883 *American* VII. 10 A certain mingling of smoothness and piquance is not wanting.

piquancy ('piːkənsɪ). Also 7 picq-. [f. piquant: see -ancy.]

†**1.** Sharpness, severity. *Obs.*

a **1677** Barrow *Serm.* (1687) I. xiv. 204 Satyrical taunts do owe their seeming piquancy, not to the speaker,..but to the subject, and the hearers. **1698** [R. Ferguson] *View Eccles.* 16 That the reader may..judge, with what Meekness and Decency, tho with some measure of Picquancy, I treat them.

2. Of food, etc.: Stimulating pungency or tartness; appetizing flavour.

1664 Evelyn *Pomona* iv. 13 To salute our Palats with a more agreeable piquancy and tartness. **1871** Napheys *Prev. & Cure Dis.* i. ii. 83 Imparting piquancy to the food. **1884** Browning *Ferishtah* Prol. 17 First, food—then, piquancy.

3. *fig.* Of manner, speech, etc.: The quality of being piquant (in sense 3); racy quality.

In quot. 1683 said of the impression made upon the mind.

1683 Cave *Ecclesiastici, Ambrose* 419 His style..leaves a picquancy and quick relish in the Readers mind. **1685** J. Scott *Chr. Life* ii. 129 Give a relish and picquancy to our Conversation. **1826** Miss Mitford *Village* Ser. ii. (1863) 305 There was a tasteful smartness in her dress,..with a *gentillesse* in her air, and a piquancy of expression. **1836** EMERSON *Nature, Lang.* Wks. (Bohn) II. 151 It is this which gives that piquancy to the conversation of a strong-natured farmer or backwoodsman. **1851** D. G. MITCHELL *Dream Life* (1852) 147 Her conversation delights you by its piquancy and grace.

piquant ('pi:kənt), *a.* (*sb.*) Forms: 6 pickande, -ante, 6–7 pickant, 7 picque-, piccant, 7–8 picqu-, 7– piquant, 9 picqu-, piquante. [a. F. *piquant* (†*picquant*), pr. pple. of *piquer* to prick, sting: see PICK *v.*[1], PIQUE *v.*[1] The form *piccant* was ad. It. *piccante*. In 19th c. authors, *piquante* (pi'kɑ:nt) usually represents the Fr. fem. *piquante* (pikɑ̃t).]

A. *adj.* **1.** That pierces or stings; *esp.* sharp or stinging to the feelings; keen, trenchant; severe, bitter. Chiefly *fig.* *Obs.* or *arch.*

1521 WOLSEY in *St. Papers Hen. VIII*, I. 43 Notwithstanding the pickande wordes conteigned in thEmperours letters. **1549** CHALONER *Erasm. on Folly* M iij, Who is he so blunt and restiue, that could not with theyr pickant spurres be quickened? **1591** CONINGSBY *Siege Rouen* in *Camden Misc.* (1847) I. 29 This daie the marshall wrote a letter..a lytle pickante. **1651** *Life Father Sarpi* (1676) 32 By some picquant words or arguteness to put them into choler. **1654** tr. *Scudery's Curia Pol.* 6 The pangs of the Gout are so sharpe and picquant. **1789** E. DARWIN *Let.* in *Life* (1879) 37 Never to make any piquant or angry answer. **1868** LANIER *Jacquerie* I. 131 Urged him on With piquant spur.

†**b.** Sharp-pointed, peaked. *Obs. rare.*

1650 BULWER *Anthropomet.* 261 When sharp piquant Toes were altogether in request.

2. Agreeably pungent or sharp of taste; sharp, stinging, biting; stimulating or whetting to the appetite; appetizing.

c **1645** HOWELL *Lett.* I. v. xxxviii, [A cook] excellent for a pickant sawce and the haugou. **1656** STANLEY *Hist. Philos.* v. II. 78 The differences of Sapours are seven; sweet, sharp, sowre, picqueant, salt, acid, bitter. **1704** ADDISON *Italy* (1733) 301 As piquant to the Tongue as Salt it self. **1827** DISRAELI *Viv. Grey* v. xiii, As piquant as an anchovy toast. **1840** THACKERAY *Paris Sk.-bk.* (1872) 227 A piquant sauce for supper.

3. *fig.* That acts upon the mind as a piquant sauce, or the like, upon the palate; that stimulates or excites keen interest or curiosity; pleasantly stimulating or disquieting.

1695 *Whether Parlt. be not in Law dissolved*, etc. 47 It falls below being piquant, and keeps within the Limits and Precincts of Modesty. **1706** *Art of Painting* 319 He [Rembrandt] design'd an infinite Number of Thoughts, that were as sensible and as *Picquant* as the Productions of the best Masters. **1792** MARY WOLLSTONECR. *Rights Wom.* iv. 144 Their husbands..leave home to seek for a more agreeable—may I be allowed to use a significant French word?—*piquant* society. **1819** J. W. CROKER in *C. Papers* 24 Aug., Your notices of literary works should be short, light, and piquant. **1849** C. BRONTE *Shirley* vi, She disapproved entirely of the piquant neatness of Caroline's costume. **1879** TOURGEE *Fool's Err.* xxxv. 235 These charms combined to render her an exceedingly piquant and charming maiden. **1885** MABEL COLLINS *Prettiest Woman* xv, This lovely girl had not Wanda's piquant, pretty face.

‖**b.** After F. *piquante* fem.

1823 SCOTT *Peveril* xxxix, The monkey has a turn for satire, too, by all that is *piquante*. **1850** SMEDLEY *F. Fairlegh* (1894) 52 Lucy's..what you call piquante. **1873** SMILES *Huguenots Fr.* I. i. (1881) 3 That picquante letter-writer, Madame de Sévigné. **1898** RIDER HAGGARD *Dr. Therne* i. 15 The face of a rather piquante and pretty girl.

B. *sb. rare.* That which is piquant.

a. A hedgehog's prickle; **b.** A piquant dish; a whet.

1835 KIRBY *Hab. Anim.* II. xvii. 213 The two most remarkable animals in the insectivorous tribe..are the mole, and the hedgehog,..the latter for its piquants, and the former for its hand turned outwards. **1843** *P. Parley's Ann.* IV. 239 He pined for the piquants—he had dreams of the savouries.

Hence '**piquantly** *adv.*, in a piquant manner; '**piquantness** (*rare*), piquancy.

1697 POTTER *Antiq. Greece* I. xxvi. (1715) 158 If an Orator ..hath been piquantly Censorious. **1703** *Art & Myst. Vintners* 17 Claret loseth much of its Briskness and Picquantness. **1727** BAILEY vol. II, *Piquantness*,.. sharpness, bitingness. **1882** W. H. BISHOP in *Harper's Mag.* Dec. 54/2 The village is piquantly foreign. **1922** JOYCE *Ulysses* 399 Blushing piquantly and whispering in my ear. **1955** *Times* 10 May 3/7 M. Claude Barma's production was most piquantly revealing. **1971** *Daily Tel.* 16 July 11/8 With a cast of two, it presents a piquantly rounded theme.

pique (pi:k), *sb.*[1] Forms: 6 pyke, peake, 6–7 picke, pike, 7 pieque, 7–8 picque, 7–8 (9 *dial.*) pick, peek, 7–9 peak, 8 pyck, 7– pique. [a. F. *pique*, n. of action f. *piquer* to prick, pierce, sting: see PIQUE *v.*[1]]

A. Illustration of Forms.

1532 Pyke [see B. 1]. **1543** *St. Papers Hen. VIII*, IX. 339 Wherby occasion of sum picke might be taken awaye. **1592** Peake [see B. 2]. **1596** in A. Collins *Lett. & Mem. State* (1746) II. 21 They are in Picke against these. **1597** *Carew MSS.* (1869) 272 [These two Scottish septs are] at pike [one with the other]. **1609** SKENE *Reg. Maj.* II. 131 It is treason to moue any pick, grudge, or querrell. **1663** *Flagellum or O. Cromwell* (1672) 29 The like picques and quarrelling pretences of the Parliament. **1663** BUTLER *Hud.* I. ii. 1082 If any Member there dislike His Face, or to his Beard have Pike. **1664** *Ibid.* II. i. 545 'Tis no Fantastick pique I have to love, nor coy dislike. **1667** TEMPLE *Let. to Sir J. Temple* Wks. 1731 II. 43 The Duke of Albemarle had long had a Peke to their Country. *a* **1670** HACKET *Abp. Williams* I. (1692) 104 Another Pick in which they agreed not. **1675** COTTON *Scoffer Scofft* Wks. (1725) 146 You must not take a Picque, If he..speak plain and gleek. **1691** WOOD *Ath. Oxon.* II. 318 Out of a puritanical peak. **1706** PHILLIPS s.v., There is a Peek between them. *a* **1713** ELLWOOD *Autobiog.* Suppl. (1714) 431 Upon a Pick he took against the People called Quakers. **1757** MRS. GRIFFITH *Lett. Henry & Frances* (1767) I. 61 That we should behave well to our friends out of love, and to our enemies out of picque. **1894** CROCKETT *Raiders* (ed. 3) 83, I did not learn what was the pick that the Black Smugglers had taken at the Maxwells.

B. Signification.

1. A personal quarrel or fit of ill-feeling between two or more persons; ill-feeling, animosity, enmity.

1532 CROMWELL in Merriman *Life & Lett.* (1902) I. 349 Which Edmond Knightley hathe..trauayled..to sett pyke betwene the sayd ladye and the executors. **1540** *St. Papers Hen. VIII*, VIII. 464 There were some that wolde be right gladde to here Your Majestie and He were in picke togythers. **1661** FELTHAM *Resolves* II. xliii. (ed. 8), Between entirest friends,..sometimes little peeks of coldness may appear. **1691** WOOD *Ath. Oxon.* II. 92 Because of a Pique that had been between the Abbots and Bishop Laud. *a* **1774** GOLDSM. *Elegy Mad Dog* v, This dog and man at first were friends; But when a pique began, The dog..Went mad, and bit the man.

2. A feeling of anger, resentment, or ill-will, resulting from some slight or injury, esp. such as wounds one's pride or vanity; offence taken.

1592 NASHE *Four Lett. Conf.* Wks. (Grosart) II. 215 You take the graue peake vppon you too much. **1653** HOLCROFT *Procopius, Goth. Wars* I. 15 This Optaris had a pique against Theodatus. **1663** DRYDEN *Wild Gallant* II. i, Pray, my Lord, take no picque at it. **1663–67** Pique to [see A.]. **1676** MARVELL *Mr. Smirke* H iv b, He..bore a great pique at Alexander, for having been preferr'd before him to the See of Alexandria. **1766** [C. ANSTEY] *Bath Guide* xi. 181 Poor Stephen went suddenly forth in a Pique, And push'd off his Boat for the Stygian Creek. **1832** J. W. CROKER *Diary* 12 May, He acquiesced..with an air of pique and disappointment. **1877** FREEMAN *Norm. Conq.* II. ix. 414 *note*, A Bishop who had turned monk in a momentary fit of pique.

†**3.** *pique of honour*, a point in which honour is pricked or affected. *Obs.*

1678 R. L'ESTRANGE *Seneca's Mor.* (1702) 522 There can be no Interfering upon a Pique of Honour. **1687** DRYDEN *Hind & P.* III. 401 Add long prescription of established laws, And picque of honour to maintain a cause.

pique (pi:k), *sb.*[2] Also 7 picq(ue, pickque. [a. F. *pic*, in same sense, of uncertain origin. (Taken by Hatz.-Darm. as a sense of *pic*, pick, pike, (mountain) peak; Littré takes it as a distinct word.)] In *Piquet*, The winning of thirty points on cards and play, before one's opponent begins to count, entitling the player to begin his score at sixty. Cf. REPIQUE.

1668 TEMPLE *Let. to Ld. Arlington* Wks. 1731 II. 93 In their Audiences..the Cards commonly run high, and all is Picque and Repicque between them. **1674** COTTON *Compl. Gamester* vi. 81 The youngers Blank shall bar the former and hinder his Picq and Repicq [*printed* Picy and Repicy]. **1688** R. HOLME *Armoury* III. xvi. (Roxb.) 73/2 A Picy in the game of Picket. **1727–41** CHAMBERS *Cycl.* s.v. *Piquet*, If he can make up thirty, part in hand, and part play, ere the other has told any thing, he reckons for them sixty.—And this is called a *pique*. Whence the name of the game. **1861** *Macm. Mag.* Dec. 137.

†**pique**, *sb.*[3] *Obs.* [a. F. or quasi-F., ad. L. *pica*.] = PICA[2], depraved appetite.

1678 BUTLER *Hud.* III. ii. 809 Though it have the Pique, and long, 'Tis still for something in the wrong; As Women long.

pique ('pi:keɪ, pi:k), *sb.*[4] Also 7 pico. [a. Sp. Amer. *pique*, ad. Quichua *piqui* (Gonzalez Holguin 1608), *piki* (Tschudi) flea, chigoe.]

1. = CHIGOE.

1748 *Earthquake of Peru* iii. 216 A..little Insect, call'd Pico which gets insensibly into the Feet. **1758** ADAMS tr. *Ulloa's Voy.* in Pinkerton (1808) XIV. 349 The insect.. called nigua and in Peru pique, is shaped like a flea. **1816** KIRBY & SP. *Entomol.* iv. (1818) I. 103, I am speaking of the celebrated Chigoe or Jiggers, called also..Pique.

2. 'A name for *Argas nigra*, a blind tick which sometimes causes sores on men or animals' (*Syd. Soc. Lex.* 1895).

pique, *sb.*[5] Erron. form of PEAK *sb.*[2]

1826 P. POUNDEN *France & Italy* 5 A close-bound cap which dwindles nearly to a pique. **1845** BROWNING *How they brought Gd. News* ii, I turned in my saddle and made its girths tight, Then shortened each stirrup, and set the pique right.

pique, obs. form of PIKE *sb.*[3] and [5].

pique (pi:k), *v.*[1] Also 7–8 picque, (9 **peak**). [a. F. *piquer* to prick, sting, stimulate, irritate, excite; *se piquer*, to take offence.]

1. *trans.* To prick the feelings of; to excite to anger, resentment, or enmity; to irritate; to offend by wounding pride or vanity.

1671 R. MACWARD *True Nonconf.* 103 You think you picque him wittily, when you say, 'any thing in Scripture that makes for you, call it ordinary; and what doth not please, is extraordinary'. **1673** W. PERWICH *Dispatches* (Roy. Hist. Soc.) 264 The gentry..are malcontents..being all piqued against the C. de Monterei. **1732** POPE *Ep. Bathurst* 349 The Dev'l was piqu'd, such saintship to behold. **1766** FORDYCE *Serm. Yng. Wom.* (1767) I. ii. 76 She..piques our pride, and offends our judgment. **1796** ELIZA HAMILTON *Lett. Hindoo Rajah* (1811) I. 233 A little picqued by the excess of his mirth. **1838** PRESCOTT *Ferd. & Is.* (1846) I. iii. 182 Piqued at this opposition to his wishes. **1862** GOULBURN *Pers. Relig.* viii. III. (1873) 221 This moment our vanity is piqued. **1876** *Mid-Yorks. Gloss.* s.v. *Peak*, 'He's peaked about somewhat'.

2. *trans.* To stimulate or excite to action or activity; to instigate or provoke, esp. by arousing envy, rivalry, jealousy, or other passion; to arouse, awake (curiosity, interest). †**b.** *refl.* To excite or arouse oneself, put oneself on one's mettle (*obs.*).

1698 VANBRUGH *Prov. Wife* I. i, My husband's barbarous usage piques me to revenge. **1736** BOLINGBROKE *Patriot.* (1749) 18 Fortune maintains a kind of rivalship with wisdom, and piques herself often in favour of fools as well as knaves. **1786** tr. *Beckford's Vathek* (1868) 67 Her vanity.. prompted her to pique the Prince's attention. **1793** *Minstrel* I. 192 Taunting messages were reiterated to pique him to come forth. **1837** CARLYLE *Fr. Rev.* II. III. iv, Peaking himself into flame of irritancy. **1870** H. SMART *Race for Wife* i, You have piqued my woman's curiosity.

†**3.** *absol.* or *intr.* To arouse a feeling of pique; to stimulate. *Obs.*

1664 J. WILSON *Cheats* Epil., If you must lash out, and think you can't Be wits yourselves unless you pique and rant. **1710** ADDISON *Tatler* No. 163 ¶5 Every Verse hath something in it that piques.

†**4.** *intr.* *to pique at*: to strive or vie with (another) through envy or jealousy. *Obs. rare.*

1668 DRYDEN *Evening's Love* IV. i, Women of the play-house, still piquing at each other, who shall go the best dressed.

5. *refl.* (rarely *intr.*). To take pride *in*, plume oneself *on*. Const. *on*, *upon*; rarely *at*, *in*. (= F. *se piquer de*.)

1705 POPE *Lett.* (1736) V. 10 Men who are thought to pique themselves upon their wit. **1773** BOSWELL *Tour Hebr.* 10 Sept., We..piqued ourselves at not being outdone at the nightly ball by our less active friends. **1787** *Generous Attachment* II. 113 Sir Jeffry..piques himself much in the nursery of the young woodlands. **1828–40** TYTLER *Hist. Scot.* (1864) I. 1 A powerful baron who piqued himself upon his skill in his weapons. **1892** *Pall Mall G.* 24 June 1/3 Temperance reformers who are wont to pique on the progress of the cause in the colonies.

Hence '**piquing** *vbl. sb.* and *ppl. a.*

1794 C. PIGOT *Female Jockey Club* 22 To entice unhappy victims into her net, and then abandon them to all the piquing severity of ridicule. **1808** JEFFERSON *Writ.* (1830) IV. 105 One piquing thing said, draws on another. **1854** FABER *Growth in Holiness* iv, A piquing of our self-love.

pique, *v.*[2] [f. PIQUE *sb.*[2]] In *Piquet*: **a.** *trans.* To win a pique from, score a pique against (one's opponent). **b.** *intr.* To score a pique.

1659 *Shuffling, Cutting & Deal.* 8, I was Pickquet the last, but am now repickqt. **1668** [see PIQUET[1]]. **1719** D'URFEY *Pills* V. 278 He piqu'd and repiqu'd so oft. **1830** 'EIDRAH TREBOR' *Hoyle Made Fam.* 49 It also piques and repiques the adversary. **1895** SNAITH *Dorothy Marvin* vi, The mysteries..of piqueing, repiqueing and capotting.

†**pique**, *v.*[3], obs. f. PEAK *v.*[2], to taper to a peak.

1756 MRS. CALDERWOOD *Jrnl.* (1884) 307 Above that they had a brow-band, which came piquing down before, betwixt their eye brows.

‖**piqué** (pike), *sb.* (*a.*) [F. *piqué*, pa. pple. of *piquer* (see PIQUE *v.*[1]) to prick, pierce, backstitch as in quilting; hence as sb. quilted work, quilting.] **A.** *sb.* **a.** A rather stiff cotton fabric woven in a strongly ribbed or raised pattern; quilting.

[**1837** CARLYLE *Fr. Rev.* (1871) III. IV. vii. 168 Marie-Antoinette was brought out. She had on an undress of *piqué blanc*.] **1852** *Rep. Juries Exhib.* 1851, 376 1 A new fabric called *piqué*. **1873** 'SUSAN COOLIDGE' *What Katy did at Sch.* ix. 143 Lilly had dressed her hair and donned a fresh white piqué. **1875** KNIGHT *Dict. Mech.*, *Piqué*, a cotton goods, figured or plain, and with a crimped surface resembling cordings. **1879** MRS. A. E. JAMES *Ind. Househ. Managem.* 20 Two white skirts.., hunting-cord or white piqué. **1932** *Daily Tel.* 25 Apr. 7/5 The yoke and collar in plain white cotton-piqué. The sleeves may be slightly fitted to above the elbow, where they should be met by a..gauntlet cuff of the white piqué. **1968** J. IRONSIDE *Fashion Alphabet* 245 *Piqué*, ..a firm fabric with lengthwise carded effect made of cotton. *Waffle piqué*—with a honeycomb weave.

attrib. **1871** 'M. LEGRAND' *Cambr. Freshm.* xi. 189 The hostess..looked..charming in her white and blue piqué morning gown. **1956** R. BRADDON *Nancy Wake* III. xv. 171 Her quaint white *piqué* dress.

b. The raised pattern of such a fabric (orig. such a pattern formed by regular rows of stitching, as in quilting).

1872 *Young Englishwoman* Nov 611/1 Pique stitch crochet. **1958** *Times* 20 Jan. 11/2 Jumper suit of pique knit jersey.

B. *ppl. a.* **a.** Inlaid (with little points of gold, etc.). Also as sb. = *piqué work* b: see C.

1872 C. SCHREIBER *Jrnl.* 2 Nov. (1911) I. 169 We found.. a small piqué plaque on tortoise-shell. **1879** *Ibid.* 5 Dec. II. 250 A curious knife and fork... The handles are piqué, or inlaid in silver with acorns and oak leaves. **1882** *Hamilton Palace Collect.* No. 1986 Bonbonniere of tortoise shell, inlaid with scrolls of gold piqué. **1897** *Daily News* 5 Jan. 4/7 [Snuff-boxes] in tortoiseshell piqué with gold. **1968** J. IRONSIDE *Fashion Alphabet* 178 *Piqué*, tortoise-shell or ivory inlaid with tiny dots or lines of gold or silver. This art, brought over by the Huguenots in the seventeenth century, covered brooches, buttons and ear-rings as well as small boxes. **1979** *Country Life* 7 June (Suppl.) 113/3 Silver-gilt and tortoiseshell *piqué* magnifying glass, c. 1730.

b. *Cookery.* Larded. *rare.*

1846 A. Soyer *Gastronomic Regenerator* 230 (*heading*) Fillet of Beef piqué aux legumes printaniers.

c. *Ballet.* With the point of the foot; with the foot pointed. Also as *sb.*, a step directly on to the point of the leading foot.

1913 C. d'Albert *Dancing* 123 *Piqué* (pas),..de la pointe et du talon. Toe and heel points. **1931** C. W. Beaumont *French-Eng. Dict. Techn. Terms Classical Ballet* 21 *Piqué*.. pricked, pricking. Generally implies a shooting forward of the body on to the *pointe* of the front foot. **1954** *Ballet Ann.* VIII. 65, I should also like to draw your attention to the *arabesques piquées*. Contrary to tradition, these should not be '*piquées*' with the knee stretched, but with the knee flexible. The instep is arched at the beginning of the movement, but the knee is quite taut only when balance has been obtained. *Ibid.*, By following my instructions..the ballerina is able to assume..a manner of walking which is æsthetically satisfying. *Piqués* and *relevés* are possible to her whilst in movement; her very walk is 'melodic'. **1967** Chujoy & Manchester *Dance Encycl.* 734/2 *Piqué*, in ballet, the movement of stepping directly onto point of supporting foot. The working leg may be in a variety of poses. **1975** *New Yorker* 16 June 103/1 There were moments in this performance that stopped my breath: a high, motionless *piqué* balance lightly stepped into from nowhere, [etc.].

C. *Comb.* **piqué work**: **a.** A kind of decorative needlework in which a pattern is formed by stitching; **b.** Ornamental work in tortoise-shell or the like, formed by means of minute inlaid designs traced in points of gold, etc.

1875 Knight *Dict. Mech.*, *Piqué-work*, a minute kind of buhl-work; inlaying metals in metals, usually. **1969** *Canad. Antiques Collector* Oct. 19/2 It [*sc.* a small box] is of ivory, bound with silver with the design formed by an inlay of little points of silver known as piqué work.

piqued, obs. or arch. form of peaked *a.*

a **1672** Wilkins in H. Rogers *Life J. Howe* iv. (1863) 106 While you..are for setting the top on the piqued end downwards, you won't be able to keep it up any longer than you continue whipping and scourging. *a* **1697** Aubrey *Nat. Hist. Surrey* (1719) V. 278 A fair House..where the piqued Turret is. **1793** *Minstrel* II. 140 Shoes sharply piqued at the toes.

piqued (piːkt), *ppl. a.* [f. pique *v.*[1] + -ed[1].] Offended, irritated; excited: see the vb.

1689 tr. *Jurieu's Past. Lett.* Transl. Epist., The same learned Man..hath written sundry piqued Books with bitterness and gall enough against the Reformed. **1742** Young *Nt. Th.* v. 840 On his Wiles a piqu'd and jealous Spy. **1851** Wardlaw *Zechariah* vii. (1869) 132 Those piqued and jealous enemies. **1880** Mrs. Forrester *Roy & V.* I. 19, 'I am delighted..', says Lord Charles in a piqued tone. **1902** *Daily Chron.* 29 Apr. 7/1 One after another gratified a piqued curiosity and raised the cloth and peeped.

pique devant, var. of picke-devant *Obs.*

‖**piquer** (pike), *v. Cookery.* Also (*erron.*) piqué. [F. *piquer* (see pique *v.*[1]) to lard.] *trans.* To insert bacon strips or other flavouring substance in (meat, poultry, etc.) before cooking; also *fig.*

In quot. 1951[2], *piquez* is the Fr. imperative.

1846 *Jewish Manual, or Pract. Information Jewish & Mod. Cookery* iv. 67 Take a piece from the shoulder [of veal] ..*piqué* it thickly. **1865** M. Eyre *Lady's Walks S. of France* xxix. 316 It is common here to *piquer* a leg of mutton with garlic, that is, small holes are drilled in it before roasting, and a small kind of garlic..inserted therein. **1935** *Proc. Brit. Acad.* XX. 85 Start with a moral and political poet.., piquer or lard him with immorality, potorial songs and other irrelevances, [etc.]. **1951** E. David *French Country Cooking* 120 The fillet..is cut into..pieces..*piquèd* [sic] with garlic and seasoned with black pepper. *Ibid.* 158 *Piquez* each fillet with a small piece of bacon. **1960** —— *French Provincial Cooking* 79 A *fricandeau de veau*,..and a *râble de lièvre*..are two of the classic examples of piquéd meat and game.

piquer, piquere, obs. ff. piker, pickeer.

piquet[1] (piːˈkɛt, ˈpɪkɪt). Also 7 pickquet, 7–9 picket, picquet, 8 pickette, picquette, 8–9 piquette. [a. F. *piquet*, obs. *picquet* (16th c. in Hatz.-Darm.), of uncertain origin.

The Fr. form is diminutive (-et[1]), and the radical part has been variously sought in F. *pic*, a term used in this game (see pique *sb.*[2]); *pique*, a pike (weapon), a spade (in cards); *pique* quarrel; or *piquer* to prick, pierce, sting.]

A card-game played by two persons with a pack of 32 cards (the low cards from the two to the six being excluded), in which points are scored on various groups or combinations of cards, and on tricks: see capot, carte blanche, pique, point, repique, quatorze, quint.

1646 J. Hall *Horæ Vac.* x. 150 For Cardes..a mans fancy would be sum'd up in cribbidge; Glecke requires a vigilant memory; Maw a pregnant agility; Picket [*printed* Pichet] a various invention. **1651** (*title*) The Royall and delightfull Game of Picquet. **1668** Dryden *Sir M. Mar-all* i. i, If I go to Picquet, though it be but with a Novice in't, he will picque and repicque, and capot me twenty times together. **1678** Butler *Hud.* iii. i. 946 Than Gamesters, when they play a Set With greatest cunning at Piquet. **1710** Palmer *Proverbs* 290 Some..confound a child's fortune at ombre, picket, and hazard. **1711** Addison *Spect.* No. 198 ¶1 She admits a Male Visitant to her Bed-side, plays with him a whole Afternoon at Pickette. **1732** Pope *Ep. Cobham* 85 His pride is in Piquette, Newmarket fame, and judgment at a Bett. **1848** Dickens *Dombey* xxi, The major..was sitting down to play picquet with her. **1905** *19th Cent.* Sept. 423 She and the King often spent the evening playing piquet or chess.

attrib. **1708** Rowe *Royal Convert* Prol. 12 Not to forget Your Piquet Parties, and your dear Basset. *c* **1720** Prior *Epil. to Phædra* 39 The Picquet-Friend dismiss'd, the coast all clear, And spouse alone impatient for her dear. **1816** Singer *Hist. Cards* 272 A Piquet pack now consists of thirty-two cards only.

Hence **ˈpiquetist**, a piquet player.

1899 *Speaker* 25 Mar. 339/1 David Gregorie, a noted piquetist.

†**piˈquet**[2]. *Obs.* Also piquette. [? Akin to picotee.] The name of a variety of carnation.

1760 J. Lee *Introd. Bot.* App. 323 Piquets, *Dianthus*. **1775** Ash, *Piquette*,..a beautiful kind of carnation.

piquet(t, obs. form of picket.

‖**piquette** (pikɛt). Also 7 piquet, 8 picquette. [F., f. *piquer* to prick, sting; in reference to its tart taste.] (See quots.)

1688 R. Holme *Armoury* iii. xx. (Roxb.) 249/2 Piquet, wine from the Huske of Grapes and water. **1706** Phillips, *Picquette*, (Fr.) a tart sort of Wine us'd in some Parts of France, by the meaner Sort of People. **1858** Simmonds *Dict. Trade*, *Piquette*, sour acid wine;..made..by pouring water on the husks of grapes.

‖**piqueur** (pikœr). Also anglicized as picker[3]. [F., agent-n. from *piquer* to prick: see Hatz.-Darm.] In France, or on the Continent, An attendant who directs the hounds during a hunt, or runs before a carriage to clear the road.

1835 H. Greville *Diary* (1883) 59, I followed a *piqueur*, who appeared to me to know his *métier*, and by keeping close to his heels I contrived to see the stag taken. **1837** J. F. Cooper *Europe* II. vii. 155 The *piqueur* scouring along the road in advance, like a rocket. **1864** M. J. Higgins *Ess.* 204 The postilions and *piqueurs* all wore round glazed hats.

‖**piqui, piquia**: see pekea.

1890 *Cent. Dict.*, *Piquia-oil*, a sweet concrete food-oil derived from the fruit of *Caryocar Brasiliense*.

†**piquier, pikeir** (pɪˈkɪə(r)). *Obs.* Also 6 picquier. [a. F. *piquier*, f. *pique* pike *sb.*[5]] A soldier armed with a pike, a pikeman; = piker[2].

1596 J. Smythe in *Lett. Lit. Men* (Camden) 91 A hundreth at the most Pikeirs and Archers. **1598** Barret *Theor. Warres* iii. i. 36 The Picquier, either armed or unarmed is to be shewed and taught the carriage and vse of his pike. *Ibid.* 37 The good Picquier ought to learne to tosse his pike well.

piquier, obs. form of pickeer.

‖**piquillin.** [Argentine Sp. *piquillin* (pikiˈʎin), ultimately from some Indian dialect.] A South American bush, *Condalia microphylla* (N.O. *Rhamnaceæ*), having an edible drupaceous fruit.

1884 in Miller *Plant-n.*

piquoté, obs. form of picotee.

‖**piqûre** (pikyr). Also piqure. [Fr., = injection, f. *piquer* (see pique *v.*[1]) to pierce (the skin), to give an injection.] A hypodermic injection; the puncture made in the skin by such an injection.

1925 Infanta Eulalia of Spain *Courts & Countries after War* vii. 150 The newest 'Piqures' come from Germany. **1936** C. Connolly *Rock Pool* iii. 59 She had large flabby arms covered with piqures. **1940** N. Mitford *Pigeon Pie* xiii. 211 'Miss Wordsworth received last night in an omnibus a *piqure* that will incapacitate her for a week at least.' 'I see, you are white slavers as well as everything else.' **1942** 'A. Bridge' *Frontier Passage* ii. 21 The doctor came... And she gave her a piqure, and they sent medicines. **1962** K. A. Porter *Ship of Fools* ii. 216 You must give me a *piqûre*, a huge one that will make me sleep for days. **1962** V. Sackville-West *Let.* 26 Apr. in H. Nicolson *Diaries & Lett.* (1968) 411, I must have five injections... *Later.* It is now over, and it was no more painful than all those *piqûres* I had on the *Antilles*.

†**piquy**, obs. (? erron.) var. of *pique*, pica[1] 2.

1656 Blount *Glossogr.* s.v. *Character*, The Printers Characters..are, 1. Pearl... 2. Non-Pareil. 3. Breviar. 4. Long Primer. 5. Piquy [1674 or Pica]. **1658** Phillips, *Piquy*, a Term in printing, see Pareil.

‖**pir** (pɪə(r)). Also 7 pire, peor, 9 peer. [Pers. *pīr* old man, chief of a sect: a title of honour (Hopkins).] A Muslim saint or holy man; also *transf.* the tomb or shrine of a saint.

1672 tr. *Bernier's Empire Gt. Mogol* IV. 113 The Mullahs, who with great conveniency and delight spend their life there, under the shadow of the miraculous Sanctity of this Pire. **1698** Fryer *Acc. E. India & P.* 240 Hard by this is a Peor, or Burying-place of one of their Prophets. **1849** E. B. Eastwick *Dry Leaves* 121 He forthwith seeks out some Pir, or Holy Man, to whose wives he entrusts his child. **1882** Floyer *Unexpl. Baluchistan* 73 Here was a pīr, or holy spot, on which Kuli reverently deposited a handful of wretched dates. **1900** Mary Carus-Wilson *Irene Petrie* vi. 116 In calamity he turns to his pir to help him.

pir, obs. form of pirr.

†**pirace**, *v. Obs. rare.* [Abnormal formation f. piracy.] **a.** *intr.* To practise piracy: = pirate *v.* 2. **b.** *trans.* To obtain by piracy: = pirate *v.* 1. Hence †**ˈpiraced** *ppl. a.*

1598 Grenewey *Tacitus, Ann.* xi. vi. 147 A fugitiue with light vessels robbing and piracing. **1660** F. Brooke tr. *Le Blanc's Trav.* 64 Leaving his other ship with all his pirac'd riches to the mercy of the water.

piracy (ˈpaɪərəsɪ). Also 6–8 pyr-; 6–7 -cye, -cie, -sie. [ad. med.L. *pirātia*, a. Gr. πειρατεία piracy, f. πειρατής pirate: see -acy.] The action or practice of a pirate.

1. a. The practice or crime of robbery and depredation on the sea or navigable rivers, etc., or by descent from the sea upon the coast, by persons not holding a commission from an established civilized state; with *a* and *pl.*, a single act or crime of this kind.

[**1419** *Charta Hen. V* in Rymer *Fœdera* IX. 754/2 Per modum Piratiæ.] *a* **1552** Leland *Itin.* III. 33 Partely by Feates of Warre, partely by Pyracie. **1556** *Acts Privy Council* (1892) V. 358 He complained of a pyracie doone upon him by certain Englishe pirates. **1587** Fleming *Contn. Holinshed* III. 1359/1 Fleeing first out of England for notable pirasies, and out of Ireland for trecheries not pardonable. **1630** *R. Johnson's Kingd. & Commw.* 224 On those coasts he rather exerciseth Pyracie, than Dominion. **1702** Luttrell *Brief Rel.* (1857) V. 198 Condemned by the court of admiralty for 4 several pyracies. **1727** A. Hamilton *New Acc. E. Ind.* II. xxxiii. 5 Those Portugueze..betook themselves to Piracy among the Islands, at the Mouth of Ganges. **1807** G. Chalmers *Caledonia* I. ii. i. 213 The Vikings confined their odious piracies to the Baltic. **1879** Farrar *St. Paul* (1883) 241 The total suppression of piracy by Pompey had rendered the Mediterranean safe.

fig. **1897** Marq. Salisbury *Sp. in Ho. Lords* 16 July, It was feared..that under the appearance of educational reform a scheme of what he might call theological piracy would spring up.

b. *Physical Geogr.* = capture *sb.* 1 b.

1904 Chamberlin & Salisbury *Geol.* I. iii. 99 The foregoing case may be called foreign piracy because the valleys of different systems are concerned. Domestic piracy may also take place... Here a tributary to a crooked river may develop, working back until it taps the main at a higher point. **1939** *Bull. Geol. Soc. Amer.* L. 1350 The stream pattern indicates that recent piracies have occurred. **1957** G. E. Hutchinson *Treat. Limnol.* I. i. 114 A wide valley, the main stream of which has been reduced by piracy. **1974** C. H. Crickmay *Work of River* iii. 62 Stream piracy.., of course, is not in every case effected by headwater extension.

2. *fig.* The appropriation and reproduction of an invention or work of another for one's own profit, without authority; infringement of the rights conferred by a patent or copyright.

1771 Luckombe *Hist. Print.* 76 They..would suffer by this act of piracy, since it was likely to prove a very bad edition. **1808** *Med. Jrnl.* XIX. 520 He is charged with 'Literary Piracy', and an 'unprincipled suppression of the source from whence he drew his information'. **1855** Brewster *Newton* I. iv. 71 With the view of securing his invention of the telescope from foreign piracy.

piragua (pɪˈrægwə), **periagua** (pɛrɪˈægwə). Forms: α. 7– **piragua**; 7 **piragoua**, 8 **pirogua**, **peragua**, **perauoger**, 9 **peroqua**. β. 7 **periago(e**, **-yago**, **-eago**, **-aqua**, **perriaguer**, 8 **perriagua**, **-ago**, **periaguay**, **-auger**, **perriaugre**, **-awger**, 8–9 **periagua**, **-aga**. γ. 8 **petty-oager**, **pettiagua**, **-augua**, **-awga**, **-auger**, **-augre**, **petiaguay**, **-augre**, **pettie augre**, 9 **petty-auga**, **-auger**, **petiaugua**. See also pirogue. [orig. a. Sp. *piragua*, a. Carib *piragua* a dug-out; subseq. much corrupted, esp. by popular reference of the initial part to *peri-* and *petty*.]

A. Illustration of Forms.

α. [**1535** Oviedo (1851) I. 171 Llamanlas los Caribes piraguas.] **1609** *Virginia richly valued* 41 A piragua or ferrie bote. **1660** F. Brooke tr. *Le Blanc's Trav.* 343 They.. betake themselves to their Canoes, or Piragoua. **1684** B. Sharp *Voy.* (1729) 54 They took one Peragua which they found at anchor. **1716** B. Church *Hist. Philip's War* (1867) II. 127 Maj. Church and his Forces were coming against them..with 24 Perauogers, meaning Whale-boats. **1792** tr. *Rochon's Madagascar* in Pinkerton *Voy.* (1814) XVI. 797 And because the canvas..is impenetrable to water, the hammock becomes a real pirogua. **1839** Marryat *Phant. Ship* xxvii, The peroqua rapidly approached. **1901** *Blackw. Mag.* Feb. 164 As soon as the prow of the piragua grounded.

β. **1672** Sir W. Talbot *Discov. J. Lederer* 18 People, whom they..force away..in Periago's. **1691** *Proc. agst. French* in *Select. fr. Harl. Misc.* (1793) 474 Making their escape in their swift periaquas. **1696** *S. Carolina Stat.* (1837) II. 105 Any boat, perriaguer or canoe. **1697** Pereago [see B. 1]. **1702** C. Mather *Magn. Chr.* ii. App. (1852) 171 The periaga kept busking to and again. **1719** Periagua [see B. 1]. **1733** *N. Jersey Arch.* XI. 311 A large new Perriagua of about 31 Foot in length. **1736** *Ibid.* 452 The Owners of the other two Boats and Periauger. **1738** *Ibid.* 532 Chased by three Perriagoes. **1750** G. Hughes *Barbadoes* 5 Coming hither..in their small canoes, or Perriawgers. **1765** in F. B. Hough *Siege of Detroit* (1860) 115 Three Battoes and two Perriaugres. **1778** J. Carver *Trav. N. Amer.* 498 The French traders..make of them periaguays. **1804** C. B. Brown tr. *Volney's View Soil U.S.* 74 Two boats (periagas) were detached from Detroit. **1845** Darwin *Voy. Nat.* xiv. (1873) 294 The periagua is a strange rough boat.

γ. **1703** Dampier *Voy.* (1729) III, Our Craft was but Canoes and Petty-Oagers. **1736** *N. Jersey Arch.* XI. 451 He recover'd himself and seized..a Pettiauger of Alderman Romer. **1736** Pettiawga [see B. 2]. **1739** Whitefield in *Life & Jrnls.* (1756) 306 We went in a Pettiagua over the Sound. **1740** *Hist. Jamaica* 298 A Petiaguay and Half-Galley. **1776** N. Greene in Sparks *Corr. Amer. Rev.* (1853) I. 301 Our people ran the petiaugres ashore.

B. Signification.

1. A long narrow canoe hollowed from the trunk of a single tree, and sometimes deepened by the addition of planks along the sides, or widened by being built of two curved sections with a flat bottom inserted between them.

1609 [see A. α]. **1630** Capt. Smith *Trav. & Adv.* 52 There were six Peryagoes, which are huge great trees formed as your Canowes, but so laid out on the sides with boords, they will seeme like a little Gally. **1697** DAMPIER *Voy.* (1699) 29 *Pereago's* and *Canoa's*..are nothing but the Tree it self made hollow Boat wise, and the Canoa generally sharp at both ends, the Pereago at one only, with the other end flat. **1719** DE FOE *Crusoe* I. ix. (1840) 149 To make myself a canoe or periagua. **1794** *Rigging & Seamanship* I. 242 *Periaguas*.. double and single canoes, used by the natives of..islands in the south seas. **1843** PRESCOTT *Mexico* VI. v. (1864) 367 The canoes and piraguas of the enemy.

2. An open flat-bottomed schooner-rigged vessel; a sort of two-masted sailing barge, used in America and the W. Indies.

1667 *Lond. Gaz.* No. 126/4 A small Vessel of ours called a Periagoe,..chasing and taking his Shallop laden with Provisions. **1736** WESLEY *Jrnl.* 4 Apr., I set out for Frederica in a pettiawga—a sort of flat-bottomed barge. **1744** F. MOORE *Voy. Georgia* 49 These Periaguas are long flat-bottom'd Boats, carrying from 25 to 30 Tons. They have a kind of a Forecastle and a Cabbin; but the rest open, and no Deck. They have two Masts..and Sails like Schooners. They row generally with two Oars only. **1804** *Naval Chron.* XI. 456 A *Petiàugua*, a two-mast Boat used by the Caribs. **1898** *Rudder* Dec. 407/2 Let go our hook just ahead of a large periauger-rigged sharpie, called the Pirate. **1899** *Ibid.* Feb. 53/1 Her rig is that of a perianger [*sic*]—or, as some call it, a double cat—having two masts with a boom and gaff sail on each.

pirai, variant of PERAI, S. American fish.

pirameter, variant spelling of PEIRAMETER.

1875 KNIGHT *Dict. Mech.* 1714/1.

piramid, piramis, etc., obs. ff. PYRAMID, etc.

piramidig (ˈpɪrəmɪˌdɪg). [Echoic, after the bird's call.] A name given in the W. Indies to a night-hawk, *Chordiles virginianus* or *C. minor*.

1847 GOSSE *Birds Jamaica* 33 We hear a loud, abrupt, and rapid repetition of four or five syllables in the air above our heads, resembling the sounds, *piramidig*, or *gi' me a bit*, or perhaps still more, *witta-wittawit*. *Ibid.* 37 Whither the Piramidig retires after its twilight evolutions are performed, or where it dwells by day, I have little evidence. **1859** *Zoologist* XVIII. 6976 The peculiarity of flight in the piramidig. **1894** NEWTON *Dict. Birds* 727 *Piramidig*, a Creole name,..*C*[*hordiles*] *minor* (Nightjar), being an imitation of its cry uttered during its remarkable flight.

Pirandellian (pɪrənˈdɛlɪən), *a.* [f. the name of the Italian playwright Luigi *Pirandello* (1867–1936) + -IAN.] Of or pertaining to or characteristic of Pirandello or his style.

1927 *Observer* 8 May 15/3 In a Pirandellian sense, he is enormously 'real'. Just as we believe that Hamlet exists apart from the personality of the actor, so we know Pogo as if he were our dearest dumb friend. **1929** *Sat. Rev.* 1 June 746/1 How the dates fit I do not know, but Señor Unamuno seems to have drunk deep of Pirandellian philosophy. **1930** *Times Lit. Suppl.* 19 June 511/3 By this time one could almost predict from a single hint the course of a Pirandellian play. **1933** *Ibid.* 9 Mar. 164/4 The professor's appeal to the young man's good sense has in it that paradoxical justice that may well be called Pirandellian. **1959** *Times* 13 Mar. 16/6 Mr. Jupp..hits on the Pirandellian notion that the family should re-enact the history of their own lives in the hope of understanding it. **1964** *Listener* 30 Apr. 731/3 To get at the truth he questions the dramatist's ex-wife, and searches round for other people involved in the affair, playing, and allowing Mr Elliot to play, a Pirandellian game of masks and faces. **1974** *N.Y. Times* 7 Sept. 25/2 As a comedian he had trouble finding a persona, a Pirandellian problem.

Hence **Piranˈdellism**, the style or method of Pirandello; a characteristic example of this; **Piranˈdellist**, an advocate or follower of Pirandello.

1936 *Times Lit. Suppl.* 19 Dec. 1048/3 The best and most striking side of Pirandello's art is lost, leaving behind the bare intellectual residue of so-called 'Pirandellism'.. exposed. **1962** *Spectator* 23 Mar. 370/2 The ending makes the play the second victim in twelve months of phoney and incompetent Pirandellism. **1962** Pirandellist [see IMAGIST 1]. **1964** *Eng. Stud.* XLV. 328 Robinson grows away from his clay-coloured Irish plays and creates such Pirandellisms as *Church Street*.

Piranesian (pɪrəˈneɪzɪən), *a.* [f. the name of the Italian architect and artist Giovanni Battista *Piranesi* (1720–78) + -AN.] Of, pertaining to, or characteristic of Piranesi, his style, or his theories of architecture.

1923 A. HUXLEY *Antic Hay* vi. 87 You could fancy yourself at the entrance of one of Piranesi's prisons... Mrs Viveash's taxi drove in under the Piranesian arch. **1925** —— *Along Road* II. 93 The Colosseum, mantled..with a romantic, Piranesian growth of shrubs. **1926** —— *Jesting Pilate* I. 123 The cathedral of the banyan grove is transformed into a Piranesian prison. **1961** *Architect & Building News* 21 June 822/1 The east and west elevations close the vistas in a highly dramatic, almost Piranesian, fashion. **1962** *Guardian* 25 Sept. 5/6 These halls..are of Piranesian grandeur. **1968** *Punch* 25 Dec. 910/1 They have just reconstituted Euston Station and I don't like it at all. I miss the mock-Doric arch and the Victorian grandeur, the sweeping vistas and the Piranesian gloom. **1976** *Listener* 1 Apr. 413/2 Some gargantuan, crudely-painted Piranesian ruin.

‖**piranha** (pɪˈrɑːnə, piː-, pɪˈraɲa). [Pg., from Tupi *pi'ra nya*, var. of *pi'raya*, scissors, also this fish.]

1. A carnivorous freshwater fish of the genus *Serrasalmus*, belonging to the family Characidæ and native to South America; = PERAI, PIRAYA. Also *attrib.*

1869 R. F. BURTON *Brazil* II. 33 The poor almost live upon the..dreadful Piranha. **1904** G. A. BOULENGER *Let. to Editor*, The ferocious S. American fish..*Serrasalmo piraya*, is known in English books of natural history as the Piranha or Caribe, or Cariba. **1904** [see CARIBE]. **1915** *Nature* 8 Apr. 149/2 Birds, beasts, coral snakes, and piranha fishes, toads and ants, and primitive natives, he [*sc.* T. Roosevelt] has something to say about. **1927** W. M. McGOVERN *Jungle Paths & Inca Ruins* xxvi. 269 All these fish were *piranhas* armed with savage little teeth. **1931** [see CARIBE]. **1954** G. DURRELL *Three Singles to Adventure* ii. 53 The piranha is one of the most unpleasant freshwater fish known. It is a flat, corpulent, silver-coloured fish, with the lower jaw protruded. **1960** T. HUGHES *Lupercal* 20 Even the Amazon's taxed and patrolled To set laws by the few jaws—Piranha and jaguar. **1962** N. MAXWELL *Witch-Doctor's Apprentice* vii. 73 *Piranhas*, voracious little beasts which attack *en masse* and can strip the meat off a live cow in minutes. **1968** *New Scientist* 7 Mar. 534/2 There are many types of fish that are classed as piranhas: the common feature is that they have a pair of powerful jaws with razor-sharp teeth. **1977** *Time* 19 Sept. 62/1 (Advt.), Feel Tom Sterling's apprehension, when obliged to take a dip in the piranha-infested Amazon.

2. *fig.*

a **1963** S. PLATH *Ariel* (1965) 40 And the fish, the fish—Christ! they are panes of ice, A vice of knives, A piranha Religion. **1977** *Times* 14 Mar. 19/6 Gayle Hunnicutt turned Sarah Pocock into a deceptively girlish piranha who.. planned to nibble into tiny pieces everyone in sight. **1978** *Times* 15 May 16/8 It's not just a goldfish bowl in a nationalized industry, it's a piranha bowl.

Pirani (pɪˈrɑːnɪ). *Physics.* The name of M. S. von *Pirani* (b. 1880), German physicist, used *attrib.* to designate a gauge invented by him for measuring very low pressures, which utilizes the cooling effect of the gas on a heated metal filament whose resistance is sensitive to temperature.

It was described by von Pirani in *Verhandl. der deutsch. physik. Ges.* (1906) VIII. 686.

1911 *Trans. Amer. Electrochem. Soc.* XX. 245 In simplicity both of construction and of operation, involving only current and resistance measurements within the range of instruments readily accessible, the Pirani manometer recommends itself at once. **1921** *Proc. Physical Soc.* XXXIII. 293 For many purposes we think that the Pirani gauge..would have considerable advantages over the McLeod. **1962** F. I. ORDWAY et al. *Basic Astronautics* v. 200 Pirani, alphatron, and bellows gauges are regularly employed in rockets to obtain atmospheric pressures. **1971** *Sci. Amer.* Aug. 114/2 The effort expended in making the Pirani gauge is amply repaid by the convenience it affords.

pirarucú (pɪrərʊˈkuː). [Pg., f. Tupi (see quot. 1863[2]).] The giant redfish of the Amazon basin, *Arapaima gigas*, of the family Osteoglossidæ, one of the largest freshwater fishes in the world; = ARAPAIMA, PIACHE.

1840 [see ARAPAIMA]. **1863** H. W. BATES *Naturalist on River Amazons* II. iii. 165 The men caught sight of a large Pirarucú: the fish which, salted, forms the staple food.. in most parts of the Lower Amazon country. *Ibid.* 166 The Indian name Pirarucú, or Anatto fish (from Pira, fish, and urucú, anatto or red), is in allusion to the red colour of the borders of its scales. **1933** P. FLEMING *Brazilian Adventure* I. xviii. 153 The very big fish—the *piracú* [sic] and the *pirará*..they [*sc.* the Indians] harpoon. **1936** *Discovery* Dec. 373/2 Pirarucú,..when dried and salted, is rapidly taking the place of imported cod on the Brazilian market. **1961** [see PAICHE]. **1965** E. BISHOP *Questions of Travel* 31 Everything must be there In that magic mud, beneath The multitudes of fish, deadly or innocent, The giant pirarucús.

pirastic(k, variant of PEIRASTIC.

pirate (ˈpaɪərət), *sb.* Also 5–8 **pyrat(e**, 6 **pyraotte, pirotte, -atte**, 6–7 **pyrote, pirat**, 7 **pyratt**. [ad. L. *pīrāta*, a. Gr. πειρατής, f. πειρᾶν to attempt, attack, assault. Cf. F. *pirate* (1448 in Hatz.-Darm.), Sp., Pg., It. *pirata*, Du. *piraat*, Ger., Sw., Da. *pirat*.]

1. One who robs and plunders on the sea, navigable rivers, etc., or cruises about for that purpose; one who practises piracy; a sea-robber.

[**1387** TREVISA *Higden* (Rolls) VI. 415 þe see þeves of Danes [L. *Dani piratæ*].] **1426** LYDG. *De Guil. Pilgr.* 23963, I mene pyratys of the Se, Which brynge folk in pouerte. **1430–40** —— *Bochas* I. xxi. (1554) 38 This word pirate of Pirrhus toke the name. **1522** J. CLERK in Ellis *Orig. Lett.* Ser. III. I. 312 Pirats, Mores, and other infidels. **1536** *Act 28 Hen. VIII*, c. 15 *title*, An acte for punishement of pyrotes and robbers on the sea. **1561** EDEN *Arte Nauig.* Pref. ¶¶j, Pilotes (I saie) not Pirottes, Rulers, not Rouers. **1601** SHAKS. *Twel. N.* v. i. 72 Notable Pyrate, thou salt-water Theefe. **1692** *Col. Rec. Pennsylv.* I. 360 For the resisting..of all enemies, pyratts, and rebells. **1714** *Fr. Bk. of Rates* 12 We have secured the Navigation of our Subjects, against all other Pyrats. **1776** GIBBON *Decl. & F.* x. I. 285 Cilicia, formerly the nest of those daring pyrates. **1799** *Naval Chron.* II. 315 River Pirates..ply upon the Thames during the night. **1817** BYRON *Manfred* II. iii. 32 A traitor on land, and a pirate at sea. **1867** FREEMAN *Norm. Conq.* I. iv. 192 In the mouths of..plain-spoken enemies his people [the Normans in France] are only the Pirates, and himself the Chief of the Pirates, down to the end of the [10th] century.

fig. **1839** BAILEY *Festus* xviii. (1852) 261 Oh, Love's a bold pirate—the son of the sea! **1902** *Daily Chron.* 18 Apr. 3/2 Four..eggs were captured by rats or other water pirates.

2. *transf.* A vessel employed in piracy or manned by pirates; a pirate-ship.

1600 HOLLAND *Livy* XXXIX. xxxvi. 875 Scouring the coast ..with his pyrats and men of warre. **1649** EVELYN *Diary* 12 July, We had a good passage, tho' chas'd for some houres by a pyrate. **1726–31** WALDRON *Descr. Isle of Man* (1865) 9 A stately pirate that was steering her course into this harbour. **1836** MARRYAT *Midsh. Easy* xvii, That's as much as to say that she's a pirate.

3. Any one who roves about in quest of plunder; one who robs with violence; a marauder, plunderer, despoiler. Also *fig.*

1526 *Pilgr. Perf.* (W. de W. 1531) 180 b, Yᵉ great pirat and olde thefe the deuyll. **1726** CAVALLIER *Mem.* III. 226 It has been always a custom among the Soldiers in France to extort Money from the Country... These Pyrates had plunder'd, kill'd and made the Country pay all they could get from them. **1802** SAMPSON *Surv. Londonderry* 129 No clover sown, on account of promiscuous flocks of sheep, which are emphatically called pirates. **1846** LANDOR *Heroic Idylls, Thrasymedes & Eunöe* 80 Pirate of virgin and of princely hearts! **1850** W. IRVING *Mahomet* I. 155 Pirates of the desert.

4. *fig.* **a.** One who appropriates or reproduces without leave, for his own benefit, a literary, artistic, or musical composition, or an idea or invention of another, or, more generally, anything that he has no right to; esp. one who infringes on the copyright of another.

[**1668** J. HANCOCK *Brooks' String of Pearls* (Notice at end), Some dishonest Booksellers, called Land-Pirats, who make it their practise to steal Impressions of other mens Copies.] **1701** DE FOE *True-born Eng.* Explan. Pref. (1703) 6 Its being Printed again and again by Pyrates. **1709** STEELE & ADDISON *Tatler* No. 101 ¶1 These Miscreants are a Set of Wretches we Authors call Pirates, who print any Book,..a soon as it appears.., in a smaller Volume, and sell it (as all other Thieves do stolen Goods) at a cheaper Rate. **1837** LOCKHART *Scott* lvii. (1839) VII. 117 A recent alarm about one of Ballantyne's workmen..transmitting proof sheets of Peveril while at press to some American pirate. **1861** W. FAIRBAIRN *Address Brit. Assoc.*, There are abuses in the working of the patent law.., and protection is often granted to pirates and impostors, to the detriment of real inventors. **1887** *Shakespeariana* VI. 105 In 1599 two of them [Shakspere's Sonnets] were printed by the pirate Jaggard.

b. One who receives or transmits radio programmes without a licence to do so.

Current usage refers to radio transmission.

1913 *Marconigraph* II. 530/2 'There you are,' said the captain, 'unless we have been picked up again by some experimenting pirate.' **1923** *Wireless Weekly* 13 June 592 The thousands who are listening-in without a licence of any description—popularly termed 'pirates'. **1923** *Exper. Wireless* Nov. 57/2 The olive branch has been held out to the 'pirates', and the ordinary listener-in is cheered by the prospect of a reduction in prices of complete sets. **1933** *Pract. Wireless* 14 Oct. 182/1 (*heading*) Wanted, One Radio Pirate! The small Brussels (Schaerbeek) broadcasting station, having complained to the authorities that an illicit transmitter has marred the reception of its broadcasts, a reward of one thousand Belgian francs has been offered to trace the identity of the culprit. **1964** *Daily Tel.* 13 May 19/2 Let us be clear about this: the pirates of 1964, like the pirates of old, are simply out after money, as much money as they can get in defiance of international law. **1966** *Listener* 16 June 863/2 Fewer than 145,000 licences were issued in 1964. .. Evasion is clearly a problem in which Britain is not alone, though, in spite of the one-time reputation of the South China Seas, Hong Kong is at least free of pirates. **1967** *Ibid.* 17 Aug. 195/1 In other areas of radio the pirates provide no example. **1969** C. BOOKER *Neophiliacs* ix. 228 Throughout ..April, the country—and the pirates—waited in mounting suspense to see what the Government would do. **1979** *Guardian* 9 Aug. 3/6 Air wave pirates pay the price... Signals sent out by illegal radio hams..led to four men appearing at Grimsby magistrates court.

5. An omnibus which infringes on the recognized routes and snaps up the regular custom of other omnibuses, or which overcharges and otherwise preys upon passengers. Now often applied to any omnibus owned by a private firm or person. Also *transf.* The driver of such an omnibus.

1889 *Daily News* 12 Dec. 3/1 The 'pirate omnibus man', who..had no fixed routes or stated hours... The pirate pulls his horses to pieces. **1892** *Pall Mall G.* 19 Oct. 3/3 'The 'bus was a pirate', said the witness. *Ibid.*, Even in conversation with an elderly lady..a private 'bus is a 'pirate' and nothing else. **1894** *Times* 1 Mar. 11/4 This was evidenced by the number of persons being carried by 'pirates', many of which were running at the old fares.

6. Applied to animals the habits of which suggest piracy, as **a.** A species of hermit crab; **b.** A small fresh-water fish of voracious habits (*Aphredoderus sayanus*), common in the eastern U.S.; also called ***pirate-perch***.

1857 R. TOMES *Amer. in Japan* vi. 136 One of the most abounding [Crustacea] is that which is commonly known as the 'pirate'... The pirate has no home of its own, but appropriates..that which belongs to others. It has a.. preference for the shells of the buccina, murex, and bulla.

7. *Physical Geogr.* A river that captures another (CAPTURE *v.* b). Also *attrib.* appositively.

1889 *Science* 8 Feb. 108/1 There is a little river-pirate in eastern Pennsylvania unsuspected by its rural neighbors. *Ibid.*, The pirate is Deer Run, and its victim is the north-east branch of Perkiomen Creek. **1904** CHAMBERLIN & SALISBURY *Geol.* I. iii. 98 The tributary which does the stealing is known as a pirate. **1914** R. S. TARR *College Physiogr.* I. xv. 566 Anything that accelerates headwater erosion on one side of a divide..gives opportunity for the pushing back of the divide and the possible capture of headwaters, or even of good-sized streams, by the successful river pirate. **1939** *Bull. Geol. Soc. Amer.* L. 1333 Each capture strengthened and lengthened the pirate and weakened and shortened the victim. **1968** R. W. FAIRBRIDGE *Encycl. Geomorphol.* 1055/2 The point at which the capture is effected..is commonly marked by a right angle turn into the pirate stream.

8. *attrib.* and *Comb.* **a.** appositive, that is a pirate, as ***pirate-bird, -filibuster, -guest***; **b.** of, belonging to, or inhabited by pirates, as ***pirate-brig, -coast, -frigate, -hoard, -schooner, -ship, -town, -vessel, work***; **c.** ***pirate-like, -ridden*** adjs.; **d. pirate-blue** *a.*, of a vivid shade of blue; **pirate bus, omnibus** (see 5); **pirate cab** = *pirate taxi*; **pirate-fish**, local name of the glutinous hag, *Myxine glutinosa*; **pirate label** [LABEL *sb.*[1] 7 c], a recording or a recording company which infringes a copyright; **pirate-perch** (see 6 b); **pirate publisher** (see 4); **pirate spider**, *Lycosa piratica* (see quot.); **pirate taxi**, a vehicle which is used as a taxi but is not licensed as such.

1842 MACGILLIVRAY *Man. Brit. Ornith.* II. 255 *Cataractes Skua.* Brown or Skua *Pirate-Bird. **1896** *Daily News* 17 Oct. 6/5 A gown in '*pirate-blue' cloth, rather a vivid shade, by the way. **1901** *Daily Chron.* 24 Dec. 5/1 In these days the *pirate-bus has turned itself into a more or less honest tramp steamer. **1963** *Times* 24 May (London Underground Suppl.) p. vii/2 The 'cut-throat' competition before 1933 when the London Passenger Transport Board was formed was all very well for some people who lived on routes where the 'pirate' buses operated. **1930** A. ARMSTRONG *Taxi!* xvi. 220 There are also some real '*pirate' cabs which only operate down town [*sc.* in New York] at night. They carry no meters and live by 'making a price'..with any belated..up-town passenger. **1760–72** H. BROOKE *Fool of Qual.* (1809) III. 86 We had..great treasure in the *pirate-frigate. **1814** BYRON *Corsair* III. v. 17 Report speaks largely of his *pirate-hoard. **1968** *Jazz Monthly* Feb. 4/1 There are..numerous '*pirate' labels also issuing EPs and LPs. **1611** COTGR., *Piratique*, Piraticall, *Pirat-like. **1897** *Pall Mall G.* 31 Dec. 5/3 In 1832 it was noticed that..conductors of the new 'buses..overcharged passengers, and met..protests with..abuse... These were the first *pirate omnibuses. **1905** *Q. Rev.* Apr. 365 This *pirateridden and fish-eating land. **1700** in *N. Carolina Colonial Rec.* (1886) I. 518, I herewith send you a copy of what I lately received..concerning the taking of a *pyrate ship. **1720** DEFOE *Capt. Singleton* 187, I wrote that he was taken away by main Force, as a Prisoner, by a Pyrate Ship. **1911** G. B. SHAW *Doctor's Dilemma* Pref. p. xvi, It is the sort of conscience that makes it possible to keep order on a pirate ship, or in a troop of brigands. **1868** WOOD *Homes without H.* xxxi. 598 The *Pirate Spider (*Lycosa piratica*)..has similar habits, chasing its prey on the water and descending as well below the surface. **1971** *E. Afr. Standard* (Nairobi) 11 Apr. 7/4 Owners of Matatu (*pirate taxis) also reported an 'exceptionally' good business as hundreds of people who wanted to go to the rural areas had to use them. **1978** S. NAIPAUL *North of South* I. iv. 87 The thing standing outside the hotel was..a matutu—a pirate taxi. **1761** *Ann. Reg.* 77/2 The *pirate-towns of Barbary. **1900** *Morn. Chron.* 23 Jan. 3/4 All *pirate work,..mostly from the United States.

e. *attrib.* or as *quasi-adj.* designating the clandestine or illegal transmission of radio programmes (see sense 4 b above), as ***pirate broadcast*** (also as *vb.*; so ***pirate broadcaster, pirate broadcasting*** vbl. sb.), ***pirate radio (station), pirate station***; **pirate (radio) ship**, a ship used to transmit radio programmes from a position outside the territorial waters of the receiving country; **pirate vessel** = *pirate (radio) ship* above.

1942 *New Yorker* 17 Jan. 52/2 There is a republican pirate radio station, called La Voce della Libertà. **1957** F. HOYLE *Black Cloud* v. 109 Is Nortonstowe going to become a pirate radio station? **1961** *Guardian* 16 Dec. 7/2 Only the presence of mind of the engineers..prevented a pirate broadcast being heard on the air of the capital itself. **1964** *Daily Tel.* 11 May 20/7 The activities of the 'pirate' radio ships Caroline and Atlanta have presented the Government with a problem which cannot be solved simply. It is expected that the Cabinet will discuss this week the possibility of legislation to prevent broadcasting from such 'pirate' vessels. *Ibid.* 13 May 1/8 Mr. Mawby, Assistant Postmaster-General, told the Commons that new legislation which would effectively deprive 'pirate' broadcasters of material support was the most suitable action. *Ibid.* 14 May 28/3 Almost every BBC station is suffering from some foreign interference and a ring of pirate ships is bound to make matters worse. *Ibid.*, The Swedish law makes it an offence for nationals to take part in pirate ship broadcasting. **1965** *Punch* 3 Feb. 154/1 Commons debate on plight of pirate radios. **1966** *Economist* 23 Apr. 340/3 The arrival this week off British coasts of a pirate radio ship..is a further step in the battle over the off-shore radio stations. **1966** *Listener* 4 Aug. 154/2 A Government bill to ban pirate radio stations provides for penalties of up to two years' imprisonment. **1967** *Ibid.* 17 Aug. 195/1 There is every sign that many of the crude but effective tabloid techniques of pirate radio..will be employed by Radio 1. **1969** C. BOOKER *Neophiliacs* ix. 227 The Swedes, the Danes and the Dutch had been plagued by offshore pirate stations as long ago as 1961–2. **1970** *Internat. & Compar. Law Q.* XIX. 357 Legal and practical controls of 'pirate' broadcasting. **1973** *Times* 3 Jan. 4/2 The ship Mi Amigo, from which the pirate radio station broadcasts, sailed out to sea again. **1973** *Daily Tel.* (Colour Suppl.) 5 Jan. 6/1 His ship will be a 'pirate' inasmuch as she will broadcast from outside territorial waters, but unlike other pirate broadcasters there will be no sponsored advertisements.

Hence **'piratess**, a female pirate.

1862 RUSSELL *Diary North & S.* I. xv. 163 The pirates and piratesses had control of both. **1879** MISS YONGE *Cameos* Ser. IV. xxx. 327 The 'Sea Queen' or piratess.

pirate ('paɪərət), *v.* [f. PIRATE *sb.*; cf. F. *pirater* (*c* 1600 in Hatz.-Darm.), It. *piratare* 'to rob by Sea' (Florio 1598), Sp. *piratear* intr. to pirate.]

1. *trans.* To practise piracy upon; to plunder piratically; to make booty of as a pirate; to rob, to plunder.

1574 HELLOWES *Gueuara's Fam. Ep.* (1577) 329 A puissant Pirat named Abenchapeta, passed from Asia into Africa,..he pilled and pirated such as he met with all by Seas. **1694** tr. *Milton's Lett. State* Wks. 1851 VIII. 265 An afflicted and..misus'd virgin, born of honest Parents, but pyrated out of her Native Country. *a* **1734** NORTH *Lives* (1826) II. 373 It was pirated out of his house, and he could never find who had it. **1816** SCOTT *Antiq.* xviii, Their rivals in trade..might have encroached upon their bounds for the purpose of pirating their wood. **1900** *Daily News* 4 Sept. 5/7 One of the ferry launches running between Hong Kong and Yau-ma-ti..had been pirated while still in the harbour.

2. *intr.* To play the pirate, practise piracy.

1685 *Lond. Gaz.* No. 2054/3 To suspect..that she was going to Pyrate in the Indies. **1710** WHITWORTH *Acc. Russia* (1758) 141 These vessels are now pirating in the Baltick. **1746** W. HORSLEY *Fool* (1748) I. 261 [To] put it out of the Power of both France and Spain..to pirate upon us again. **1816** SOUTHEY in *Q. Rev.* XV. 302 France perpetually..pirating against the homeward bound fleets. **1887** BESANT *The World went*, etc. xlv, They proposed to go a-pirating among the Spanish settlements.

3. *fig. trans.* To appropriate or reproduce (the work or invention of another) without authority, for one's own profit.

1706 DE FOE *Jure Div.* Pref. 42 Gentlemen-Booksellers, that threatned to Pyrate it, as they call it, viz. Reprint it, and Sell it for half a Crown. **1754** *Connoisseur* No. 38 ¶6 To prevent his design being pirated, he intends petitioning the Parliament. **1850** CHUBB *Locks & Keys* 36 He had no right to pirate a peculiar trade mark. **1884** *American* VII. 318 The injustice done by American publishers in pirating English works. **1968** *Blues Unlimited* Nov. 6 They're not selling records, for fear they would be pirated! **1977** *Belfast Tel.* 17 Jan. 8/4 Under the European Television Agreement of 1953 most countries agreed not to 'pirate' programmes broadcast by companies from other nations. **1979** *Guardian* 25 Aug. 24/1 'Pirating' involves the copying, for sale to the public, of existing records without the consent of the copyright owners.

Hence **'pirated** *ppl. a.*; spec. ***pirated edition***, an edition of a book produced without authorization; **'pirating** *vbl. sb.* and *ppl. a.*

1697 tr. *C'tess D'Aunoy's Trav.* (1706) 77 One day, as Meluza came from Pyrating, he brought [etc.]. **1727** A. HAMILTON *New Acc. E. Ind.* I. xii. 140 The English went to burn that Village and their pirating Vessels. **1731** GAY *Let. to Swift* 1 Dec., I have had an injunction for me against pirating-booksellers. **1737** BYROM *Jrnl. & Lit. Rem.* (1856) II. I. 133 To put out a pirated edition. **1853** C. M. SMITH *Working Man's Way in World* iv. 56 (*heading*) Pirated editions of Scott's novels. **1883** *American* VI. 44 A pirated extract from a paper published some fifteen years ago. **1902** *Daily Chron.* 18 Dec. 3/2 The pirating of woodcuts in the fifteenth and sixteenth centuries. **1928** D. H. LAWRENCE *Let.* 5 Dec. (1962) II. 1103, I hear from Stieglitz there are *two* pirated editions, photographed from my edition, and with forged signatures. *Ibid.* 10 Dec. 1105, I hear London and Paris are both selling the pirated editions of *Lady C.* at £3 and £2. **1928** A. HUXLEY *Let.* 12 Dec. (1969) 304 Dear Lawrence, What an intolerable business about the pirating of *Lady C.*! **1952** J. CARTER *ABC for Bk.-Collectors* 135 *Pirated edition*,..a term commonly applied (sometimes with, sometimes without, legal accuracy) to an edition produced and marketed without the authority of, or payment to, the author. **1959** L. M. HARROD *Librarians' Gloss.* (ed. 2) 286 A pirated edition is an unauthorized reprint involving an infringement of copyright. **1967** *Listener* 28 Sept. 413/2 After hearing this performance—and a pirated tape of his 1953 Covent Garden *Aida*—it seems incredible that Barbirolli has been allowed to languish outside the opera house for 13 years. **1973** *Times* 17 Oct. 11/3 The records have been issued in Paris, but not here. It is as bad as Russia, where people listen to me on pirated versions. **1975** *Times Lit. Suppl.* 13 June 678/2 British efforts to influence Parliament to protect British books against the importation of foreign pirated editions.

piratedom ('paɪərətdəm). *rare.* [f. PIRATE *sb.* + -DOM.] Pirates collectively; the world of pirates.

1907 F. CAMPBELL *Shepherd of Stars* iv. 36 He went to shout orders to a fleet of approaching barges from the stronghold of ancient piratedom.

†**'pirately**, *a. Obs. rare.* [f. PIRATE *sb.* + -LY[1]: cf. *soldierly*.] Of the nature of a pirate; piratical.

1625 *Impeachm. Dk. Buckhm.* (Camden) 220 A kennell of rancke pirately roages.

piratery ('paɪərətrɪ). *rare.* Also piratry. [ad. F. *piraterie*, f. PIRATE *sb.* + *-erie*: see -ERY. (Cf. L. *pīrātērium*, a. Gr. πειρατήριον a gang of pirates.)] = PIRACY 1.

[**1756** H. WALPOLE *Lett. to Mann* 25 Jan., Monsieur Bonac..complaining in harsh terms of our *brigandages* and *pirateries*.] **1903** KIPLING *5 Nations* Ded., Ere rivers league against the land In piratry of flood.

piratic (paɪ'rætɪk), *a.* [ad. L. *pīrāticus*, a. Gr. πειρατικός, f. πειρατής pirate: see -IC. So F. *piratique*.] Of or pertaining to a pirate or pirates; like a pirate. ***piratic war***, that waged by Pompey against the pirates in the Mediterranean.

a **1640** DAY *Parl. Bees* i. (1881) 13 [He] Out-law-like doth challenge as his owne Your Highnes due; nay, Pyratick detaines The waxen fleet, sailing upon your plaines. **1692** WASHINGTON tr. *Milton's Def. Pop.* v. M.'s Wks. 1851 VIII. 137 Nor must Pompey have undertaken the Piratick War. **1783** WATSON *Philip III*, IV. (1839) 201 The piratic states of Barbary. **1854** J. S. C. ABBOTT *Napoleon* (1855) I. xxv. 395 The Algerines were now sweeping with their piratic crafts the Mediterranean.

piratical (paɪ'rætɪkəl), *a.* [f. as prec. + -AL[1].]

1. Of or pertaining to a pirate or piracy; of the nature of, characterized by, given to, or engaged in piracy; pirate-like.

1579–80 *Reg. Privy Council Scot.* III. 255 Thair piraticall and weikit deidis. **1622** BACON *Holy War* Wks. 1879 I. 528/1 The piratical war which was achieved by Pompey the Great. **1712** E. COOKE *Voy. S. Sea* 107 Capt. Sharp's Pyratical Voyage to the South Sea. **1776** GIBBON *Decl. & F.* x. I. 245 The gold which the Scandinavians had acquired in their pyratical adventures. **1836** W. IRVING *Astoria* III. 103 These would apprize their relatives, the piratical Sioux of the Missouri, of the approach of a band of white traders. **1872** YEATS *Growth Comm.* 365 The Moors established the piratical states of Algiers and Tunis.

b. *fig.* Given to literary piracy, etc.

1737 POPE *Lett.* Pref., Errors of the press..multiply'd in so many repeated editions, by the Avarice and Negligence of pyratical Printers. **1759** DILWORTH *Pope* 87 The piratical Curl had..advertised the letters of Messieurs Prior and Addison. **1877** DOWDEN *Shaks. Prim.* i. 12 Piratical publishers tried in some dishonest way to come at the manuscript.

2. Obtained by piracy; pirated; produced by literary piracy.

1565 *Reg. Privy Council Scot.* I. 336 Ony of the said piraticall gudis. *Ibid.* 337 Personis that avaricioulie ressettis the piraticall gudis. **1631** BRATHWAIT *Whimzies, Sayler* 88 In hope to become sharer in a pyraticall treasure. **1838** A. B. GRANVILLE *Spas Germ.* 245 Two legal editions—two piratical ones.

piratically (paɪ'rætɪkəlɪ), *adv.* [f. prec. + -LY[2].] In a piratical manner; by piracy.

1549 in Burnet *Hist. Ref.* (1681) II. *Collect. Rec.* 162 Order hath been taken..that certain Goods, piratically taken upon the Seas..should be restored to the true Owners. *a* **1642** SIR W. MONSON *Naval Tracts* II. (1704) 250/2 The People..were Pyratically given. **1732** *Hist. Litteraria* IV. 38 It had been officiously and pyratically printed by others. **1876** BANCROFT *Hist. U.S.* III. iii. 48 Its flag had been insulted, its maritime rights disregarded,..its property piratically seized and confiscated.

'piratism. *rare.* [f. PIRATE *sb.* + -ISM: cf. It. *piratismo* 'Piracie or robbing by Sea' (Florio 1611).]

1882 O'DONOVAN *Merv Oasis* I. iv. 67 To check the piratism of the Turcoman maritime populations.

†**'piratize**, *v. Obs. rare*[−1]. [f. as prec. + -IZE.] *trans.* To subject to piracy.

1638 SIR T. HERBERT *Trav.* (ed. 2) 334 Nor cease the Ilanders to rob and piratize the Chyneses.

†**pi'ratously**, *adv. Obs. rare.* Also 6 -tuosly. [f. as prec. + -OUS + -LY[2].] = PIRATICALLY.

1538 in R. G. Marsden *Sel. Pl. Crt. Adm.* (1894) I. 73 One Walter Soly..with certain maryners..came feloniously and piratuosly upon borde. **1549** in Burnet *Hist. Ref.* (1681) II. *Collect. Rec.* 162 Divers Merchants..have had their goods piratously robbed and taken.

piraya, variant of PERAI, PIRANHA.

pirck, obs. form of PERK *v.*[1]

pire, *v. Obs.* exc. *dial.* Also 9 pyre. [ME. *piren*, identical in form and sense with LG. (in Brem. Wbch.) and EFris. *pîren*, of unknown origin.

The same sense is expressed in mod. Eng. by PEER *v.*, which is not known before 1590. Their phonetic relation is difficult to understand; but cf. the pairs *kike, keek, pike, peek, pipe, peep, pile, peel*, also *pike* sb., *peek*, now *peak*, which present similar problems. Some have suggested that LG. *pîren* was a variant of *plîren, plüren*, with similar sense; but this is unlikely.]

intr. To look narrowly, esp. in order to discern something indistinct or difficult to make out; to peer.

1390 GOWER *Conf.* III. 29 Riht so doth he, whan that he pireth [*rime* tireth] And toteth on hire wommanhiede. **1399** LANGL. *Rich. Redeles* III. 48 Thanne cometh..Anoþer proud partriche..And preuyliche pirith till þe dame passe. *c* **1400** *Beryn* 552 Go vp..& loke, & in the asshis pire. *Ibid.* 1412 They herd all his compleynt, þat petouse was to here, ffawnus in-to the Chirch pryuelych gan pire. **1854** MISS BAKER *Northampt. Gloss.*, *Pyring*..Always used in combination with peeping, as, 'peeping and pyring about'. 'Peeping and pyring into every body's business'.

pire, var. PERRY[1], *Obs.*, pear-tree; obs. f. PIER.

pirene, pirenean, piretheum, pirethrum: see PYR-.

piriawe, obs. corrupt form of PARIAH.

pirie, variant of PERRY[1], *Obs.*, PIRRIE.

piriform, variant (etymologically correct) of PYRIFORM.

1890 in *Cent. Dict.*

piriform. For examples of this variant see PYRIFORM *a.*

pirimicarb (pɪ'rɪmɪkɑːb). [f. PYRIMI(DINE by alteration + CARB(AMATE.] An insecticide that is specific against aphids; 2-dimethylamino-5,6-dimethyl-4-pyrimidinyl dimethylcarbamate, $C_{11}H_{18}N_4O_2$.

1970 *Proc. 5th Brit. Insecticide & Fungicide Conf.*, *1969* II. 546 Pirimicarb is an aphicide of such specificity that its use for aphid control should not directly eliminate some of the more important predators concerned with the regulating of aphid numbers. **1974** *Nature* 8 Feb. 337/3 Pirimicarb is systemic when applied to soil, being absorbed by the roots. **1977** *Homes & Gardens* Nov. 42/1 A recent product which contains 'Pirimicarb' in either liquid concentrate form or as an aerosol is very effective against aphids except on cucumbers and soft fruit.

‖**piri-piri**[1] ('pɪərɪ'pɪərɪ). A Maori name applied to several plants, esp. to *Haloragis micrantha*, a shrubby plant found in India, south-eastern Asia, Australia, and New Zealand; also to *Acæna Sanguisorba*, used as tea and as a medicine, called by the colonists by corruption *biddy-biddy*.

(In the former sense misprinted *piri-jiri* (see A. Cunningham in *Ann. Nat. Hist.* (1839) III. 30), an error repeated in some dictionaries.)

1866 *Treas. Bot.* 567 s.v. *Haloragis* (Piri-jiri). **1880** *N.Z. Country Jrnl.* XII. 195 (Morris s.v. *Biddy-biddy*), Piri-piri ..by the settlers has been..corrupted into *biddy-biddy*... These tenacious burrs of the piri-piri. **1884** MILLER *Plant-n.*, Piri-jiri-shrub.

piri-piri[2] ('pɪrɪ 'pɪrɪ). [Origin obscure; perh. ad. Swahili *pilipili*, pepper.] A sauce made with red peppers. Also *attrib.* or as *adj.* and quasi-*adv.*

1964 H. HOLTHAUSEN *Chicken goes around World* 71 *Frango Piri-piri* (Chicken in Piri-piri sauce). *Ibid.* 72 Preheat the grill and put the piri-piri chicken in the immediate vicinity of the heat... Baste the chicken well.. with the remaining piri-piri. **1968** C. BURKE *Elephant across Border* ii. 68 The 'Camarões Pequenos', just..a few miles north of Lourenco Marques..made the best piri-piri prawns on the whole coast. *Ibid.* iii. 115 I'm going to have me a dozen giant prawns, charcoal-grilled, without piri-piri, but with lemon and butter sauce. **1969** M. TRIPP *Malice & Maternal Instinct* iv. 28 They specialise in Spanish and Portuguese here... How about galinha piri-piri. **1970** G. CROUDACE *Scarlet Bikini* vi. 68 If yer gennelmen'll only bring up some rock lobster, I'll give it yer for lunch, piri-piri with rice. **1973** *Times* 17 Feb. (Mozambique Suppl.) p. iv/6 (Advt.), The sauce *piri-piri* is made with red peppers.

pirk(e, obs. form of PERK *sb.*[1] and *v.*[1]

pirl (pɜːl, *Sc.* 'pɪrl), *v. arch.*, *Sc.*, and *dial.* Also 6 pirle, pyrl, 6–9 purl. [Origin not ascertained; perh. onomatopœic: cf. PURL *v.*]

1. *trans.* To twist, wind, or spin (threads, fibres, or hairs) into a cord; in early use *esp.* to twist or spin (gold or silver wire) into cord or 'lace'; now *esp. dial.* to twist (horsehair) into fishing-lines, etc.

1523 SKELTON *Garl. Laurel* 796 Sum pirlyng of golde theyr work to encrease With fingers smale, and handis whyte as mylk. **1530** PALSGR. 658/1, I pyrle wyer of golde or syluer, I wynde it upon a whele as sylke women do. **1556** J. HEYWOOD *Spider & F.* xci. 39 But copwebs vpon copwebs: pirld in ech coste: All parts of windows to be so enboste: That no flie can passe. **1825** JAMIESON, *Pirl*..2. To twist, twine, curl; as to twist horse-hair into a fishing-line; Roxb., Clydes. **1828** MOIR *Mansie Wauch* xxvi, A bit daigh, half an ounse weight, pirled round wi' the knuckles into a case. **1892** *Daily News* 10 Nov. 2/2 The car of the Gold and Silver Wyre Drawers Company,..men and women in the costume of James I. were engaged in wire-drawing, flatting, and spinning thread, purling bullion, weaving lace, embroidering, and lace-making. **1894** *Northumb. Gloss.*, *Purl*, to twist between finger and thumb. Horsehair is purled thus in making snares for bird-catching in winter.

2. To cause to revolve, to spin; to throw or toss with spinning motion. Also *intr.* To move with such motion, to revolve rapidly, to spin.

1791 J. LEARMONT *Poems* 273 (E.D.D.) Cranreuch snow blaws pirlin' on the plain. **1805** J. NICOL *Poems* I. 25 (Jam.) Cauld December's pirlin drift Maks Winter fierce an' snell come. **1808** JAMIESON, *Pirl*, v.n. to whirl. **1880** *Ibid.* (new ed.) s.v., Pirl up the pennies. [**1886** ELWORTHY *W. Somerset Word-bk.*, *Pirdle*, to cause to spin. 'Let me pirdle the top, I'll show thee how to make'n go.']

3. *intr.* To curl; 'to ripple as the surface of a body of water under a slight wind'. (Jamieson 1808.)

1789 [see PIRLING *vbl. sb.*]. **1819** J. RENNIE *St. Patrick* II. x. 191 I'll set my teeth in the withered chafts o' you till the blind pirl out o' your luckin' e'en. **1920** *Chambers's Jrnl.* Christmas No. 837/2 Before the first puffs of blue smoke circled and pirled above the village roofs.

Hence **pirled** *ppl. a.*, twisted, twined, spun into a thread or lace; '**pirling** *ppl. a.* and *vbl. sb.*; (see sense 3).

c **1500** MEDWALL *Nature* (Brandl) 763 Then yt cryspeth and shyneth as bryght as any pyrled gold. **1520** in *Archæologia* LIII. 17 A corporax case and the corporax of gold pyrlled and crymyssynn velvet. **1583** *Rates of Customs* D vij, Pirled lace called cantelet lace of thred the groce iis. vid. **1583** STUBBES *Anat. Abus.* I. (1879) 71 Some with purled lace so cloyd. **1789** D. DAVIDSON *Thoughts on Seasons* 33 Ye roll, in cudlin purlings to the sea. **1936** C. MACDONALD *Echoes of Glen* i. 3 On an emerald bank by the side of a pirling burn.

pirl, *sb. Sc.* [f. prec. vb.] **a.** A twist, curl. **b.** A fine curl or ripple on the surface of water.

1825 JAMIESON s.v., 'There's a pirl on the water.' **1838** HOGG *Tales* (1866) 150 (E.D.D.) Wi' the pirl bein' awa', the pool was as clear as crystal. **1880** JAMIESON, *Pirl*..2. Twist, twine, curl; as 'That line has na the richt pirl,' Clydes.

pirl, obs. or dial. form of PURL *sb.* and *v.*

pirlicue, pirlie-, variants of PURLICUE.

pirlie pig ('pɜːlɪ, *Sc.* 'pɪrlɪ). *Sc.* Also **perly, pirly**, etc. [Prob. f. PIRL *v.* + PIG *sb.*[2]: see *Sc. Nat. Dict.*] A small money-box, usu. circular and made of earthenware, with a slot to insert coins. Also *ellipt.* as *pirlie*, etc.

1799 'PHILETAS' in J. Thomson *Hist. Dundee* (1874) I. x. 127 Old women and children kept their pozes in their *kist neuks and pirly pigs*. **1831** in *Trans. Banffshire Field Club* (1939) 33 One Stone purly 4/-. **1889** J. M. BARRIE *Window in Thrums* xviii. 170, 'I mind he broke open his pirly,..an' bocht a ha'penny worth o' something to ye every day. **1900** *Longman's Mag.* Nov. 49 Donald did not possess a bike yet, and my 'tips' went into a perly pig in which he was saving up to buy one. **1905** *Athenæum* 28 Jan. 118 The pirley-pig or circular money-box pertaining to the Town Council of Dundee. This pewter money-box is in the shape of an orange or flattened globe. **1912** *Proc. Soc. Antiquaries Scotl.* XLVI. 353 Until thirty or forty years ago there was a good demand for modern pirlie pigs. **1934** H. B. CRUICKSHANK *Noran Water* 15 Ye've riped the pirlie mony's the time Withooten ony skaith. **1960** H. HAYWARD *Antique Coll.* 220/1 *Pirlie pig*, earthenware money-box. 'Pig' is a North Country word for an earthen jar: 'pirlie' is a diminutive indicating something of slight value.

pirliewinkles: see PILLIWINKS.

†**pirn**, *sb.*[1] *Obs. rare*[−1]. [perh. metathesis of *prin*, *prene*, PREEN, a pin.] ? A pointed twig or branch; ? a thorn or spine.

a **1400–50** *Alexander* 4981 þai fande a ferly faire tre quare-on na frute groued, Was void of all hire verdure & vacant of leues,..With-outen bark ouþir bast full of bare pirnes.

pirn (pɜːn, *Sc.* pɪrn), *sb.*[2] Now *Sc.* and *dial.* Forms: 5–6 pirne, pyrne, 8 pyrn, 6– pirn, (9 *dial.* pirm); pern, perne. [Origin uncertain.

Jamieson points out that in sense 1 'it is sometimes called a broach' (cf. BROACH *sb.*[1] 4), and may thus be, like PIRN *sb.*[1], a metathetic form of *prin*, PREEN; but the latter has existed in Sc. since 14th c. as *prene*, *prein*, *preen*, and there is no evidence of any contact or confusion between the two words.]

1. a. A small cylinder on which thread or yarn is wound, formerly made of a hollow reed or quill, but now usually of turned wood or iron, with an axial bore for mounting on a spindle when winding; a weaver's bobbin, spool, or reel. Also *fig.*

(Cf. the synonym SPOOL, the orig. sense of which appears to have been *quill* or *hollow reed*.)

c **1440** *Promp. Parv.* 402/1 Pyrne, of a webstarys loome, *panus* [an error reproduced by Palsgrave]. **1474** *Acc. Ld. High Treas. Scot.* I. 25 Item viij pirnis of gold for the sammyn harnessing, price of the pirne xs.; summa iiij li. **1502** *Ibid.* II. 289 Item..for xv pirn of gold. **1700** SIR A. BALFOUR *Lett.* 210 In the Highest Storie there are Innumerable Pirns of Silk. **1792** *Statist. Acc. Scot.* II. 510 Fit..to earn their bread at home, the women by spinning, and the men by filling pirns, (rolling up yarn upon lake reeds, cut in small pieces for the shuttle). **1829** E. IRVING *Times of Martyrs* in *Anniversary* 283 Her spinning wheel.. having no heck, but a moveable eye which was carried along the pirn by a heart-motion. **1831** W. PATRICK *Plants* 82 The stalks [of *Arundo Phragmites*] were formerly used for making weaver's pirns. **1844** G. DODD *Textile Manuf.* vii. 217. **1899** CROCKETT *Kit Kennedy* 175 A load of birchwood to be transformed into bobbins and pirns. **1919** W. B. YEATS *Wild Swans at Coole* 36 He unpacks the loaded pern Of all 'twas pain or joy to learn. **1950** T. R. HENN *Lonely Tower* 185 Within the cones moves the 'perne', a spool which unwinds the thread spirally as the sphere moves onward.

b. Phrases. (*Sc.*)

to wind any one a pirn, to plan trouble for or injury to one, get one into difficulty; ***to wind (oneself) a bonny (queer) pirn***, to get into a difficulty or entanglement; ***an ill-favoured (-winded) pirn***, a troublesome or complicated business; ***to ravel one's pirns***, to cause one trouble or anxiety: ***to redd (unwind) a ravelled pirn***, to clear up a tangled matter or difficulty, to get clear of an entanglement; ***to wind (up) one's pirn***, to make an end, have done.

1535 STEWART *Cron. Scot.* (Rolls) I. 201 Throw sic displesour he his wynd him ane pirne. **1638** In Lang *Hist. Scot.* (1904) III. ii. 48 [Argyll is said to have advised Charles to keep him [Lorne] in England or else he would wind him a pirn]. **1718** RAMSAY *Christ's Kirk Gr.* III. xv, Ise wind ye a pirn, To reel some day. **17..** *Sc. Haggis* 161 (E.D.D.) I'll just wind up my pirn, and hae done with a remark or sae. **1787** SHIRREFS *Jamie & Bess* II. ii, Ere ye get loose, ye'll redd a ravell'd pirn. **1818** SCOTT *Rob Roy* xxiii, Ye'll spin and wind yoursell a bonny pirn. **1828** —— *F.M. Perth* xxv, By the Thane's Cross, man...this is an ill favoured pirn to wind. **1893** STEVENSON *Catriona* xxiii. 282, I shall have a fine ravelled pirn to unwind.

c. A reel of sewing cotton, a bobbin or spool. (A common name in Sc.)

1820 [Known to be in use in Hawick]. **1887** D. GRANT *Scotch Stories* 64 Gin a customer ca'd for a penny pirn.

†**2.** *transf.* The yarn wound upon the pirn (ready for the shuttle); also, as much as a pirn holds, a pirnful. ? *Obs. rare.*

[Cf. **1474**, **1502** in 1.] **1710** RUDDIMAN *Gloss. Douglas' Æneis* s.v. *Pyrnit*, The Women and Weavers [of Scotland] call a small parcel of yarn put on a broach (as they name it), or as much as is put into the shuttle at once, a Pyrn, but most commonly the stick on which it is put passes under that name. **1842** FRANCIS *Dict. Arts*, *Pirn*, the wound yarn that is on a weaver's shuttle.

3. Any device or machine resembling a reel, or used for winding; *esp.* a fishing-reel.

1782 SIR J. SINCLAIR *Observ. Sc. Dial.* 159 A pirn (for angling), a wheel. **1793** FORDYCE in *Phil. Trans.* LXXXIV. 17 The curvature of the wire, acquired by its being wound round a pirn, was not entirely unfolded for some months. **1833** J. S. SANDS *Poems* Ser. I. 78 (E.D.D.) Auld Jacob's staff and fishing pirn. **1839** T. C. HOFLAND *Brit. Angler's Man.* i. (1841) 6 A winch or reel, is used for running-tackle, and is generally made of brass, but I have seen them in Scotland made of wood, where they are called pirns. *c* **1850** W. GRAHAM in R. Ford *Harp Perth.* (1893) 149, I wauken'd bricht, To my pirn wildly skirlin'. **1900** C. MURRAY *Hamewith* 3 Hear the whirr o' the miller's pirn. **1903** *Westm. Gaz.* 8 Apr. 2/2 A primitive contrivance of a hand-wheel, three pirns—a man, a woman, and two boys twisting green rushes into ropes.

†**4.** An unevenness or 'cockle' in the surface of a piece of cloth, caused by difference in the yarns composing it. *Obs. rare.*

['They still say in Angus, that a web is all pirned, when woven with unequal yarn' (Jamieson).]

1733 P. LINDSAY *Interest Scot.* 166 We should have no more bad Cloth, nor any Cloth disliklied by Bars, Strips, or Pirns, occasioned by putting different Kinds of Yarn..in the same piece.

5. *attrib.* and *Comb.*, as ***pirn-winder***, ***-winding***; **pirn-cage** (see quot.); **pirn-cap**, a wooden bowl used by weavers to hold their quills (Jamieson); **pirn-girnel**, a box for holding pirns while they are being filled; **pirn-house**, a weaving shed; **pirn-mill**, a mill where weaver's bobbins are manufactured; **pirn-stick**, a wooden spit or spindle on which the quill (pirn) is placed while the yarn put on it in spinning is reeled off; **pirn-wheel**, a wheel for winding thread on bobbins; **pirn-wife**, a woman who fills pirns with yarn.

1880 *Antrim & Down Gloss.*, **Pirn cage*, an arrangement of pins standing up from a square frame, in which 'pirns' or bobbins are stuck—used in power-loom factories. **1867** ELLEN JOHNSTON *Poems* 129 Nae mair in oor *pirn-house Ye'll hunt the rats, nor catch a moose. **1915** W. B. YEATS *Reveries* 13 Another day a sea captain pointed to the smoke from the *Pern mill on the quays. **1938** in *Sc. Nat. Dict.* (1968) VII. 140/1 The Pirners' Bridge, so-called either because bobbin-makers crossed it to get birch-timber in the adjacent copse to make their pirns, or because a pirn-mill once stood near it. **1894** [W. D. LATTO] *Tam Bodkin* xxi. 216 My legs..they're like *pirn-sticks buskit in breeks. **1896** G. SETOUN *R. Urquhart* xxii. 226 Women discussed it at their *pirn-wheels. **1895** A. PHILIP *Parish of Longforgan* x. 276 A good canny *pirn-winder... Her average wage from *pirn-winding was not more than two shillings a week. **1901** *Westm. Gaz.* 8 Feb. 2/1 'Pirn-winding', an accessory trade to hand-loom weaving, will, no doubt, die with the present workers.

pirn, *sb.*[3] *dial.* Also **purn**. A twitch for horses, etc.: see quots.

1846 BROCKETT *N.C. Gloss.*, *Purn*, the same as Twitch... *Twitch*, an instrument applied to the nose of a vicious horse, to make it stand still during..shoeing. **1869** *Lonsdale Gloss.*, *Pirn*, a stick with a loop of cord for twisting on the nose of a refractory horse. *Pirns*, a kind of ring for a vicious cow's nose. **1873** *Swaledale Gloss.*, *Pirn*, a stick with a noose at the end to hold an unruly horse.

pirn (pɜːn), *v. Sc.* [app. f. PIRN *sb.*[2]] Found only in pa. pple. and ppl. adj. **pirned**, interwoven with threads of different colours; striped; brocaded.

1494 *Acc. Ld. High Treas. Scot.* I. 224 Crammacy sattin pirnit wyth gold. **1513** DOUGLAS *Æneis* III. vii. 26 Riche wedis, Figurit and prynnit [ed. 1553 pyrnyt] al with goldin thredis. *Ibid.* VIII. iii. 168 Ane..knychtly weyd, Pirnit and wovin full of fyn gold threyd. **1539** *Inv. R. Wardr.* (1815) 33 Ane gowne of crammasy velvot..lynit with pyrnit satyne. **1710** RUDDIMAN *Gloss. Douglas' Æneis*, *Pyrnit*, striped, woven with different colours. **1819** W. TENNANT *Papistry Storm'd* (1827) 22 He..Tucks up his pyrnit tunic bra.

pirnie, pirny ('pɜːnɪ), *a.* and *sb.*[1] *Sc.* [app. related to prec. vb. and to PIRN *sb.*[2] sense 4.]

A. *adj.* Of cloth: Striped with different colours.

[**1511** *Acc. Ld. High Treas. Scot.* IV. 253 The Kingis goune of pyrne satyne of gold lynit with Romany buge.] **1697** CLELAND *Poems* 12 With Brogues, and Trues, and pirnie Plaides, With good blew Bonnets on their Heads. **1721** RAMSAY *Elegy on Patie Birnie*, The famous fiddler of Kinghorn..Tho' baith his weeds and mirth were pirny. [*Note.* When a piece of stuff is wrought unequally, part coarse, and part fine, of yarn of different colours, we call it pirny, from the pirn.] **1865** JANET HAMILTON *Poems* 192 Crossing his 'pirnie' plaid over his shoulders and chest.

B. *sb.* A conical woollen nightcap, usually striped with different colours.

'Generally applied to those manufactured at Kilmarnock' (Jamieson).

1824 MACTAGGART *Gallovid. Encycl.* s.v., A monkey.. leaped on to his shoulder, and plucked off his pirnie. **1858** SIMMONDS *Dict. Trade*, *Pirnie*, a woollen nightcap made in Kilmarnock, of different colours or stripes. **1895** CROCKETT *Bog-Myrtle & Peat* 206 Tibbie was knitting at a reid pirnie for her father.

pirnie, pirny ('pɜːnɪ), *sb.*[2] *Sc.* Diminutive of PIRN *sb.*[2]

1776 C. KEITH *Farmer's Ha'* 5 The auld gudewife the pirney reels Wi' tenty hand. **1879** J. WHITE *Jottings* 192 (E.D.D.) Doon to the Leap I'll aften rin, Richt glad to hear my pirnie spin.

‖**pirog** (pɪ'rɒg). Also **piroga, piroque**. Pl. **pirogen** (a. Yiddish), **pirogi** (a. Russ.), **pirogs**. [Russ. *piróg*, Yiddish (a. Russ.) *pirog*.] A large pie. Cf. PIROSHKI *sb. pl.*

1854 [See *fish-cake* s.v. FISH *sb.*[1] 6c]. **1933** P. & L. G. ESMONDE *von Schumacher's Cook's Tour of European Kitchens* vi. 109 Pirogs are eaten fresh from the oven or heated up again. **1950** E. J. KOLLIST *Compl. Patissier* xxiv. 232/1 In Russia the various coulibiac, piroques and small patties are favourites. **1951** Pirogen [see PIROSHKI *sb. pl.*]. **1962** K. PETROVSKAYA *Secrets of Russian Cooking* 143 A true Russian (or anyone who's ever tasted real Russian pirozhki or pirogi) can grow rhapsodic just talking about them. **1971** *Guardian* 23 July 9/6 Pirogi and Piroshki, literally big pies and baby pies. **1973** [see PIROSHKI *sb. pl.*].

pirogue (pɪˈrəʊg). Also 7 pyrage, pyrogue, 8–9 perioque, 9 perogue, periogue, piroque, peroque. See also PIRAGUA. [a. F. *pirogue* (pirɔg), prob. from Galibi, the Carib dialect of Cayenne.] Another form of PIRAGUA: still used in the same senses, but more widely diffused, and extended (under French influence) to the native canoes of various regions, and to kinds of open boats, with or without sails, locally used. Also *attrib.*

[**1665** C. DE ROCHEFORT *Hist. des Antilles* 86 Grandes chaloupes qu'ils appellent pyraugues.] **1666** J. DAVIES *Hist. Caribby Isles* 39 The Caribbians will of one trunk make those long shallops called pyrages. **1698** FROGER *Voy.* 66 Pyrogues ..large Canoos, very long and made of one single tree, hollowed. **1777** ROBERTSON *Hist. Amer.* (1796) II. IV. 161 Their pirogues or war boats are so large as to carry forty or fifty men. **1792** MAR. RIDDELL *Voy. Madeira* 85 This tree supplies the Caribs with wood for building their perioques or canoes, which they cut out of the trunk. **1807** P. GASS *Jrnl.* 12 The expedition was embarked on board a batteau and two periogues. **1808** PIKE *Sources Mississ.* I. 8 Met two peroques full of Indians. **1828** WEBSTER, *Pirogue*... In modern usage in America, a narrow ferry-boat carrying two masts and a lee board. **1838** J. HALL *Notes West. States* 218 The earliest improvement upon the canoe, was the Pirogue, an invention of the whites..the pirogue has greater width and capacity, and is composed of several pieces of timber—as if the canoe was sawed in two equal sections, and a broad flat piece of timber inserted in the middle. **1860** DOMENECH *Deserts N. Amer.* II. 276 Canoes are of three sorts: piroques, made of the stem of a single tree; small boats lined with buffalo hide..; and lastly the canoe properly so called. **1886** tr. *de Brazza* in *Pall Mall G.* 3 Sept. 6/2 It was impossible..to ascend the Ogowai without the aid of the natives to pilot our pirogues in the rapids. **1889** *Harper's Mag.* Nov. 851/1 She is what they call a pirogue here [West Indies].., she has a long narrow hull, two masts, no deck: she has usually a crew of five, and can carry thirty barrels of tafia. **1893** J. FOGERTY *Juanita* I. 96 A number of black canvas-covered canoes, locally [W. coast of Ireland] called 'pirogues'. **1926** I. S. COBB *Some United States* xi. 264 A little later four husky chaps in pirogues ranged up alongside us. **1947** *Motor Boating* June 130 The correct name of the two-masted sail plan in Merry Weather is the pirogue rig; not a cat-ketch rig as it is sometimes erroneously named. **1954** *Sun* (Baltimore) 15 Mar. 9/1 French-speaking trappers paddle pirogues through backwater bayous of Louisiana in search of muskrat. **1963** W. GARD in H. S. Bell *Petroleum Transportation Handbk.* iii. 6 In swamp terrain the crews, working out of pirogues where there is standing water, are usually sent ahead of the dipper dredge to drop the trees. **1973** *Times* 5 Mar. (Mauritius Suppl.) p. i/5 The whale..20 reeking terror-filled yards from our frail *pirogue*.

piroot (paɪˈruːt), *v. U.S. dial.* [Alteration of PIROUETTE *v.*, prob. under influence of ROOT *v.*[2]] *intr.* To move listlessly or aimlessly; also, to snoop. Hence **piˈrooting** *ppl. a.*

1863 S. C. MASSETT *Drifting About* 242 The streets were almost impassable from the mud and slush and..the 'ladies' ..would find it impossible to 'piroot' thither. **1866** C. H. SMITH *Bill Arp* 116 For four years the Confederate Horse-stealing Cavalry have been pirooting around, preparing themselves for the frightful struggle that is to come. **1910** W. M. RAINE *Bucky O'Connor* 30 I've been pirootin' around this country, boy and man, for fifteen years. **1958** 'W. HENRY' *Seven Men at Mimbres Springs* (1960) xiii. 156 Oh God A'mighty—kids, squaws, dogs, old people, pack mules, cookpots—Jesus—the whole pirooting kit and kaboodle of them come down to set up camp and see the fun. **1961** J. F. DOBIE in *Webster* s.v., Went pirooting into a cave one day.

piroplasm (ˈpaɪərəʊplæz(ə)m). *Biol.* †Also in mod.L. form **piroˈplasma** (pl. **-plasmata**). [f. L. *pir-um* pear + -O + PLASM, PLASMA.] A protozoan of the suborder Piroplasmidea of sporozoans, which comprises species parasitic in red blood cells and transmitted by ticks.

[**1895** W. H. PATTON in *Amer. Naturalist* XXIX. 498 The name of the southern or splenic cattle-fever parasite.—The generic name [sc. *Pyrosoma*] given by Drs. Smith and Kilborne, having been previously used in Zoology, must be dropped. I propose the name *Piroplasma* to replace it.] **1901** *Vet. Jrnl.* IV. 50 A strange fact, showing that the form of the parasite varies in its stages of evolution, was that almost all the piroplasms are pear-shaped and bigeminate. **1908** *Practitioner* Feb. 228 Rocky Mountain Spotted Fever. Ricketts has re-investigated this disease, in which..Wilson and Chowning claimed to have discovered piroplasmata, and to have shown that it is transmitted by a tick. **1934** T. W. M. CAMERON *Internal Parasites of Domestic Animals* II. 45 All the piroplasms are tick-carried and consequently the main lines of prevention consist in tick eradication. **1949** C. A. HOARE *Handbk. Med. Protozool.* iii. 37 A piroplasm of the genus *Theileria* is the cause of East Coast fever... Other forms of piroplasmosis in cattle are caused by species of the genus *Babesia*. **1974** O. W. OLSEN *Animal Parasites* (ed. 3) ii. 164/1 Upon entering the erythrocytes, they [*sc.* the parasites] retain their same general appearance and are generally known as piroplasms.

Hence **ˌpiroplasˈmosis**, any of a group of diseases of mammals, esp. red-water of cattle, caused by infestation of the blood with piroplasms.

1901 *Vet. Jrnl.* IV. 49 (*heading*) Canine piroplasmosis. **1903** *Jrnl. Compar. Path. & Therapeutics* XVI. 312 (*heading*) Pyroplasmosis of the donkey. **1948** U. F. RICHARDSON *Vet. Protozool.* iv. 81 As a rule piroplasmoses occur as enzootic diseases in which young animals contract symptomless infections and recover. **1949** [see above]. **1955** [see EAST D. 1 b]. **1960** *Farmer & Stockbreeder* 15 Mar. 131/1 Ticks are the carriers of the organisms which when they are inoculated into the blood, attack the red cells and cause them to break down and it is the colouring matter of these cells that gives colour to the urine, and to the disease known as redwater or bovine piroplasmosis. **1974** *Nature* 13 Dec. 532/2 Vaccination against cattle lungworm, canine hookworm and certain kinds of piroplasmosis has been achieved but the vaccines used, irradiated larvae or infected blood, are unacceptable in the field of human medicine.

‖**piroshki** (pɪˈrɒʃkɪ), *sb. pl.* Also pirotchki, pirozhki, pyrochki. Occas. in sing. **piroˈshok** (in quot. spelt pirozsok). [a. Russ. *pirozhkí* pl. of *pirozhók*, dim. of *piróg* (PIROG).] Small patties.

1912 R. K. WOOD *Tourist's Russia* ii. 34 To taste pirozhki at their best, one must go to Philipov's in St. Petersburg or Moscow. **1933** P. & L. G. ESMONDE *von Schumacher's Cook's Tour of European Kitchens* vi. 105 After this..came Bortch, a soup of beetroot and cabbage, accompanied by Pyrochki—a Russian stuffed pastry. **1935** M. MORPHY *Recipes of All Nations* 429 Fish piroshki..are made in the same manner as game piroshki, but with a filling of cooked fish, hard-boiled eggs and rice. **1939** *Vogue's Cookery Bk.* xii. 227 *Piroshki*... These are the little meat-filled patties that are the traditional Russian accompaniment to soup. **1943** E. M. ALMEDINGEN *Frossia* ix. 347 Yesterday I baked '*pirozhki*' with cabbage and onions. I made eight, and sixteen people came.., and it meant half a *pirozsok* for each. **1951** L. W. LEONARD *Jewish Cookery* xii. 163 Pirogen..are made just like Piroshki but much larger. **1963** V. NABOKOV *Gift* i. 35 He bought some piroshki (one with meat, another with cabbage, a third with tapioca, a fourth with rice, a fifth ...could not afford a fifth) in a Russian foodshop. **1965** J. B. PRIESTLEY *Lost Empires* II. iii. 125 Russian things like.. those tiny meat and fish pasties called *piroshki*. **1972** N. FROUD *Some of our Best Recipes are Jewish* 50 Roll out pastry, fill pirozhki, brush with beaten egg, and bake..in oven preheated to 230° C. **1973** S. SKIPWITH *Eat Russian* viii. 154 Pirozhki are small patties served with soup, as appetisers, or offered with tea or coffee at any time. A pirog is a larger, circular or rectangular, fairly flat pie, with pastry top and bottom. Both are baked with a variety of fillings. **1974** A. WILLIAMS *Gentleman Traitor* vii. 101 A dinner of borscht, pirotchki and beetroot. **1977** J. WAMBAUGH *Black Marble* (1978) x. 218 Valnikov held a paper plate stacked with golden pastries and said, '*Piroshki*. They're very light and filled with cheese or meat. My brother usually makes them both ways.'

†**pirot.** *Obs.* [a. F. *pirot* (Cotgr.): cf. PIDDOCK.]

1611 COTGR., *Pirot*, the Pirot, or Hag-fish; a kind of long shell-fish. **1686** PLOT *Staffordsh.* 250 A sort of Solenes (which the Venetians call *Cape longe*, and the English Pirot) ..a kind of Shell fish deep bedded in a solid rock.

pirotte, obs. form of PIRATE.

pirouette (pɪruːˈɛt), *sb.* Also 8 pi-, pyroet. [a. F. *pirouette* spinning top, child's windmill or whirligig, teetotum, pirouette in dancing or riding (15th c. in Littré); in OF. also in masc. form *piroet*, *pirouet* (15th c.), whence *piroet* in Bailey. A parallel dim. is Burgundian *pirouelle* teetotum (Littré); Guernsey has the simpler form *piroue* a whirligig or little wheel (Métivier). Evidently from same source as It. *piruolo*, *pirolo* 'top, gig, twirle', also 'a woodden peg or pinne for an instrument of musike' (Florio), cf. *pirla*, *pirlo* 'a childes top, gig, or twirle' (Fl.).

The It. *piruolo*, *pirolo* is in form a dim. of a form **piro*: cf. Roman dial. *piro* a plug (Diez), whence the It. augmentative *pirone* 'a pin or peg of iron' (Fl.). If such was the origin, the sense 'pin or peg' app. gave that of 'peg-top' and 'teetotum', as in Fr., from the idea of the motion of which arose the other senses.]

1. The act of spinning round on one foot, or on the point of the toe, as performed by ballet-dancers.

1706 P. SIRIS *Art of Dancing* 42 A Table of Pirouettes. [*Ibid.* Fig. 13, To *Pirouetter*, or Whirl about on the two Points of the Toes half-round.] **1813** JEFFREY *Ess.* (1844) I. 333 Making *pirouettes* round his chamber, or indulging in other feats of activity. **1822** HAZLITT *Table-t.* II. xii. 277 A Columbine practising a pirouette in sober sadness. **1846** PATTERSON *Zool.* 34 A rotation which would put to shame the most finished pirouettes of the opera dancer. **1875** JAS. GRANT *One of the '600'* I. vi. 89 Berkeley..made a species of pirouette on the brass heels of his glazed boots.

2. In the manège: see quots.

1727–41 CHAMBERS *Cycl.*, *Pirouette*, *Pyroet*, in the manage, a turn or circumvolution which a horse makes, without changing his ground. *Pirouettes* are either of one tread or *piste*, or of two. **1730–6** BAILEY (folio), Piroet. **1775** in ASH: and in mod. Dicts. **1847** W. IRVING in *Life & Lett.* (1864) IV. 20 He is rather skittish also, and has laid my coachman in the dust by one of his pirouettes.

3. *Mus.* A form of mouthpiece used with a shawm, rackett, or similar reed instrument (see quot. 1976).

1891 *Descr. Catal. Mus. Instruments R. Military Exhib., London, 1890* iv. 64 The reeds used in these early times were generally rather hard and difficult to manage. To render them more manageable they were placed in a sort of case, called *pirouette*, which covered the lower part of the reed. **1911** *Encycl. Brit.* XXII. 780/1 The rackett is played by means of a large double reed placed within a *pirouette* or cap. **1961** A. BAINES *Mus. Instruments* ix. 233 The European shawmist presses the lips to a wooden 'pirouette'..which permits lip-control without appreciably reducing the reed's amplitude of vibration. **1968** *New Oxf. Hist. Music* IV. xiii. 737 The reed of the tenor and smaller forms was controlled by a device called a *pirouette*. **1976** D. MUNROW *Instruments Middle Ages & Renaissance* 40/2 The pirouette (also used on the renaissance rackett) was a funnel-shaped reed-shield against which the player could press his lips whilst taking the projecting part of the reed into the mouth.

pirouette (pɪruːˈɛt), *v.* [a. F. *pirouetter*, f. *pirouette*: see prec.] *intr.* To dance a pirouette, spin or whirl on the point of the toe; to move with a whirling motion. Also *fig.*

[**1706**: see prec. 1.] **1822** T. MITCHELL *Aristoph.* II. 318 See, the king of the shell-fish advancing,..pirouetting and dancing! **1834** *Encycl. Brit.* (ed. 7) VI. 504 Volting, demi-volting, pirouetting, parrying with and opposing the left hand, are manœuvres now totally disused in fencing. **1868** *Morn. Star* 28 Mar., To pirouette in combustible gauze before the footlights. **1872** BAKER *Nile Tribut.* viii. 133 After pirouetting in several strong whirlpools..we at length arrived. **1894** BARING-GOULD *Queen of L.* I. 8 To.. pirouette at the apex of his loftiest elocution.

Hence **pirouˈetting** *vbl. sb.* and *ppl. a.*; also **pirouˈetter**, one who pirouettes; **pirouˈettism**, **pirouˈettiveness**, *nonce-wds.*, disposition for or habit of pirouetting.

1839 *Blackw. Mag.* XLVI. 533 A bitterness seldom exercised towards the pirouettism of a lawyer. **1844** *Ibid.* LV. 295/1 A professor's chair for the improvement of pirouetters. *Ibid.* 297 The boss of pirouettiveness is strangely wanting in human conformation. **1840** BARHAM *Ingol. Leg.* Ser. I. *Witches' Frolic*, Such lofty curvetting, And grand pirouetting. **1864** KNIGHT *Passages Work. Life* I. viii. 286 His slovenly dress, his pirouetting walk. **1878** T. HARDY *Return of Native* IV. iii, She began to envy those pirouetters.

pirouettist (pɪruːˈɛtɪst). [f. PIROUETTE *v.* + -IST.] = PIROUETTER.

1889 G. B. SHAW *London Music 1888–89* (1937) 224 The unappreciated pirouettists and entrechatists looked on indignantly. **1926** W. J. LOCKE *Old Bridge* II. vii. 119 He may chance to be a mechanical jazz pirouettist or a financial oracle.

Pirquet (ˈpɪəkeɪ). *Med.* The name of Baron C. P. *Pirquet* von Cesenatico (1874–1929), Viennese pædiatrician, used *attrib.* and † in the possessive to designate a skin test for tuberculosis that he devised in 1907.

1908 *Lancet* 18 Apr. 1183/1 Pirquet's reaction sometimes showed itself five hours after the inoculation but as a rule, the effect was produced in 24 hours and lasted from four to six days. **1927** E. R. BALDWIN et al. *Tuberculosis* xii. 213 The von Pirquet scratch test is less delicate than the intracutaneous method and requires repetition to confirm a negative result. **1952** B. R. CLARKE *Causes & Prevention of Tuberculosis* ii. 14 The simplicity of the Pirquet test is an advantage in sparsely populated regions, only one reading being necessary before B.C.G. vaccination. **1970** *New Yorker* 28 Nov. 44/1 Irochka had had a positive reaction to the Pirquet test and had been sent for an X-ray.

pirr (pɪr), *sb.*[1] *Sc. dial.* Also 7 pir, 9 pirrhe. [app. onomatopœic: cf. PIRRIE.] A ruffling breeze of wind.

1665 SIR J. LAUDER *Jrnl.* (S.H.S.) 19 A little pir of wind that rose. **1825** JAMIESON s.v., 'There's a fine pirr of wind.' **1894** J. GEDDIE *Fringes of Fife* 134 To sigh..in vain for a 'pirrhe' of wind.

b. A state of agitation or excitement; a flurry.

1856 G. HENDERSON *Pop. Rhymes* 127 When one is in a pirr about things which do not go well.

pirr, *sb.*[2] Also pirre, purre. [Onomatopœic, imitating the hoarse cry of the birds.] **a.** A local name of the Tern: see PIRR-MAW. **b.** The Blackheaded Gull (*Larus rudibundus*). *rare.*

1824 MACTAGGART *Gallovid. Encycl.* (1876) 383 *Pirr*,..is also a sea-fowl with a long tail and black head,..whenever it sees any small fish or fry, dives down..on them, crying 'pirr!' **1875** LANDSBOROUGH *Arran* 401 The numerous Cumbrae pirres have been destroyed or driven away. **1880** *Antrim & Down Gloss.*, *Purre*, two sea birds, the tern and the black-headed gull. **1898** MACMANUS *Bend of Road* 195 The centre of the lake where the many hundred white pirrs now circled, and called.

pirr, *v. Sc.* [Onomatopœic: goes with PIRR *sb.*[1]] *intr.* **a.** Of the wind: To blow as a steady breeze. **b.** Of persons or animals: To drive, ride, or run rapidly; cf. *whirr*. Hence **ˈpirring** *ppl. a.*

1819 W. TENNANT *Papistry Storm'd* (1827) 62 Careerin' on the pirrin' breeze, A greedy gled. **1852** MRS. CARLYLE *Lett.* I. 171 Nothing could be more pleasant than so pirring through quiet roads [in a gig]. *Ibid.* 172 We bowed to each other..and I pirred on.

†**pirre.** *Obs. rare.* [app. from the accompanying sound.] Difficulty in breathing; asthma.

1398 TREVISA *Barth. De P.R.* III. xv. (Tollem. MS.), As in hem þat haue þe pirre and styffles and ben pursyf and þikke breþid [L. *ut patet in asthmaticis et anhelosis*].

pirre, var. PERRIE *Obs.*, jewellery; var. PIRR *sb.*[2]

pirre, pirrey, obs. ff. PERRY[2] (the beverage).

pirrhick, pirrite, obs. ff. PYRRHIC, PYRITE.

pirrie, pirry (ˈpɪrɪ). Now only *dial.* Forms: 5–6 pyry, pyrie, 5–7 pery, 6 pyrry, -ye, -ie, pirie, pierie, pierrie, perrye, -ie, 6–7 pirrie, pirry, perry: 9 *n.* and *e. dial.* perry; also *n.* parry, -ey. [app. onomatopœic.

Cf. PIRR *sb.*[1], also the later BERRY *sb.*[4], and its suggested relationship to BIRR. All these words are apparently natural oral expressions of the action of such a wind. Gael. *piorradh* ('pirray), genitive *piorraidh* ('pirrai) 'a squall or blast' is app. a parallel formation; it appears to have no root in Celtic, and could scarcely have originated the Eng. word, of which the earliest examples belong to East Anglia, where it is still in native use.]

A blast of wind; a squall; a sudden storm of wind, 'half a gale'. In mod. dial. use also, A sudden scudding rain.

c **1420** LYDG. *Assembly of Gods* 126 With a sodeyn pyry, he lappyd hem in care. *c* **1440** *Promp. Parv.* 401/2 Pyry, or storme, *nimbus*. ? *c* **1500** *Cov. Corp. Christi Plays* 8/226 E! fryndis, ther cam a pyrie of wynd with a myst suddenly. **1531** ELYOT *Gov.* I. xvii, Aferde of pirries or great stormes. **1559** W. CUNNINGHAM *Cosmogr. Glasse* Pref. 5 In sayling, thou shalt not..feare Peries and great windes. **1610** HOLLAND *Camden's Brit.* (1637) 307 Hee..was with a contrary pirrie carried violently into Normandie. *c* **1630** RISDON *Surv. Devon* §315 (1810) 328 It suffered a kind of inundation..at a spring tide, driven by a very strong perry. **1865** W. WHITE *E. Eng.* I. 92 'If we cu'd only hev a perry wind', says the Captain... A perry wind is half a gale.

b. *fig.* A 'breeze' or storm in the social or political atmosphere.

1536 *St. Papers Hen. VIII*, II. 312 He pratith, and is so proude,..that he can not fayll to perish himself in the pyry. **1565** *Satir. Poems Reform.* i. 178 Nor Hamilton cold have no hope to hold his seate, Nor yett Argile to abide the court; the pirrye was to greate. **1600** W. WATSON *Decacordon* (1602) 126 There arose such a huffing perrie against me.

pirrie, obs. form of PERRY[2] (beverage).

pirr-maw ('pɜːmɔː). Also 8–9 pyr-, 9 purre-. [f. PIRR *sb.*[2] + MAW *sb.*[3]] A local name of the Common Tern (*Sterna fluviatilis*) and of the Roseate Tern (*S. dougalli*).

1744 C. SMITH *County Down* 131 Sea Fowl, as the Gull and Pyrmaw, who build in the Rocks. **1880** *Antrim & Down Gloss.*, *Pirre-maw*, the tern. *Ibid.*, *Pyrmaw*, a sea bird, probably the tern or 'purre'. **1885** SWAINSON *Prov. Names Brit. Birds* 203 Roseate tern,..Purre maw (Carrickfergus). From their hoarse cry.

pirrosyn, variant of PERROSIN *Obs.*

pirry, variant of PERRY[1] *Obs.*, pear-tree.

pirssonite ('pɜːs-, 'pɪəsənaɪt). *Min.* [f. the name of L. V. *Pirsson* (1860–1919), U.S. geologist: see -ITE[1].] A hydrated carbonate of sodium and calcium, $Na_2Ca(CO_3)_2.2H_2O$, occurring as brittle, colourless to white, orthorhombic crystals that are pyroelectric.

1896 J. H. PRATT in *Amer. Jrnl. Sci.* CLII. 130 The author takes pleasure in naming this mineral *pirssonite*, in honor of his friend and associate, Prof. L. V. Pirsson, of the Sheffield Scientific School. **1933** *Jrnl. Chem. Soc.* 1162 Gaylussite is in equilibrium with pirssonite at 37–40°, the exact temperature depending on the concentration of the sodium carbonate solution with which they are in contact. **1975** *Nature* 13 Mar. 128/2 Large (> 2 cm), apparently diagenetic crystals of pirssonite and gaylussite, oriented by their 'c' axes at high angles to bedding, are common in parts of these cores.

† **pirwike, -wycke**, obs. ff. PERUKE, PERIWIG.

1538 ELYOT, *Galerus*,..a pirwike. **1552** HULOET, Pirwycke, *galerus*.

pirwyncle, obs. f. PERIWINKLE[2] (the mollusc).

piry(e, var. PEERY, PERRY[1]; obs. f. PERRY[2].

pisa ('piːzə). Name of a city in Italy. In quot. applied to a Pisan dagger or poniard (*obs.*).

a **1625** FLETCHER & MASS. *Cust. Country* II. iii, The difference between a Spanish rapier And your pure *pisa*.

‖ **pis aller** (pizale). [F., lit. 'go worst'.] The worst that can be, or can happen; what one would do, take, choose, etc., in the event of things coming to the worst; what one accepts when one can do no better; a do-no-better, a last resource.

1676 ETHEREDGE *Man of Mode* I. i, Dorimant, when did you see your *pis-aller*, as you call her, Mrs. Loveit? **1800** MAR. EDGEWORTH *Belinda* (1832) II. xxv. 158 She was incapable of the meanness of retaining a lover as a *pis-aller*. **1808** *Edin. Rev.* XI. 438 A balance of trade paid in the precious metals, is the *pis-aller* of foreign commerce. **1847** DISRAELI *Tancred* I. i, As a pis aller one might put up with him. **1874** MORLEY *Compromise* ii. 63 To me the history of mankind is a huge *pis-aller*..a prodigious wasteful experiment.

Pisan ('piːzən), *sb.* and *a.* [ad. It. *Pisano*, f. L. *Pisān-us* of or belonging to *Pisæ*, a city in Etruria.] **A.** *sb.* A native or inhabitant of Pisa, a city in central Italy situated on the river Arno.

1613 PARSONS & FITZ-HERBERT *Suppl. Discuss. M. D. Barlowe's Answere* ii. 81 The warrs betwene the Pisans and the Genoueses by sea. **1705** ADDISON *Remarks Italy* 18 Their Fleet, that formerly gain'd so many Victories over the Saracens, Pisans, Venetians, [etc.]. **1813** J. FORSYTH *Remarks Excursion Italy* 12 Many Pisans, however, are of the old opinion. **1863** 'GEO. ELIOT' *Romola* I. I. viii. 146 'Pisans false, Florentines blind'—the second half of that proverb will hold no longer. **1869** 'MARK TWAIN' *Innoc. Abr.* xxiv. 252 To be buried in such ground was regarded by the ancient Pisans as..potent for salvation. **1875** K. O'CLERY *Hist. Italian Revolution* i. 30 The island [*sc.* Sardinia] was conquered and assigned to the Pisans as a fief of the Holy See. **1934** A. HUXLEY *Beyond Mexique Bay* 280 Like the Pisans, the Aztecs had the wit to leave a wide open space all round the monument. **1973** *Country Life* 16 Aug. 450/2 The Sards have always hated the sea, from whence came all their invaders, Phoenicians, Greeks, Romans, Byzantines, Pisans, Genoese, [etc.]. **1975** *Daily Tel.* (Colour Suppl.) 14 Mar. 10/4 Pisans do not believe that successive ministers and commissions will ever do anything to arrest the inevitable. One day the Tower *will* flop down.

B. *adj.* Of or pertaining to Pisa. spec. *Pisan assistance*, assistance rendered too late to be effective.

1813 J. FORSYTH *Remarks Excursion Italy* 36 The Pisan chains hang like a fair trophy on the foreign bank of Genoa. **1869** BROWNING *Ring & Bk.* IV. xii. 210 You and your pleas and proofs were what folks call Pisan assistance, aid that comes too late. **1869** 'MARK TWAIN' *Innoc. Abr.* xxiv. 252 A Pisan antiquarian gave me an ancient tear-jug. **1904** J. M. STONE *Reformation & Renaissance* ii. 62 The Pisan Pope and his followers were already there, and for a time it seemed as though they might carry all before them. **1936** A. W. CLAPHAM *Romanesque Archit.* iii. 30 Southern Italy.., touched here with Lombard and there with Pisan influence. **1951** A. R. LEWIS *Naval Power & Trade in Mediterranean* vi. 224 Genoese and Pisan fleets helped open up the Rhone Valley route. **1973** *Country Life* 16 Aug. 451/2 Oretelli, where the Parish Church is Pisan of the 13th century. **1975** *Daily Tel.* (Colour Suppl.) 14 Mar. 10/4, I returned with a Pisan friend to the Campo dei Miracoli to have a final look at the Tower.

† **pisane.** *Obs.* Forms: 4 pe-, pusen, pysan, 4–5 pe-, pusane, 5 pesayn, pys-, puisane, pyssan, pisan, pissand, 5–6 pesan, pissan(e. [a. OF. *pisainne*, *pizane* adj. fem. of *pisain*, *pizain* Pisan, qualifying *gorgerette*, *helme*, etc. Cf. *basinettum Pisanum* (Du Cange).] A piece of armour to protect the upper part of the chest and neck.

13.. *K. Alis.* 3697 Indiens, and Emaniens, With swordes, lances, and pesens [*v.r.* pensels]. **13..** *Coer de L.* 321 He bare away halfe hys schelde Hys pusen therwith gan gon. **13..** *Gaw. & Gr. Knt.* 204 Ne no pysan, ne no plate þat pented to armes. *a* **1400** *Sir Perc.* 1722 He hitt hym evene one the nekk-bane Thurgh ventale and pesane. *c* **1400** *Laud Troy-Bk.* 4429 He brast his Pisan and his coloret. *Ibid.* 12603 At him he schet And hitte him In his gorget, That it ȝede thorow his pesayn. *c* **1420** *Anturs of Arth.* xlv, He girdus to Syr Gauane, Throȝhe ventaylle and pusane [*v.r.* pesayne]. *c* **1470** HENRY *Wallace* II. 111 The thrid he straik throuch his pissand of maile. *Ibid.* IX. 1104 Throu pissanis stuff in sondyr strak the swyr. **1537** *Acc. Ld. High Treas. Scot.* VI. 336 Deliverit to the Kingis grace,..ane pissane of mailȝe and ane hudskule.

‖ **pisang** (pɪ'sæŋ). Also 7 piçan, pissan, pysangh. [Malay *pisang*.] The Malay name of the Banana, formerly also in English use. ***wild pisang***, the name given to a S. African allied plant, *Strelitzia augusta*.

1662 J. DAVIES tr. *Mandelslo's Trav.* 134 The Country abounds..specially in Fruits,..Pissans, Oranges and Lemmons. **1671** NARBOROUGH in *Acc. Sev. late Voy.* I. (1694) 141, 6000 Coco-Nuts and 100 Bundles of Pysanghs. **1812** ANNE PLUMTRE tr. *Lichtenstein's S. Africa* I. II. xv. 204 The Pisang river..has this name from the profusion of wild Pisang,..*strelitzia alba*, that grows upon its banks.

† **b.** *attrib.* **pisang fig**, a banana; **pisang-tree**.

1700 S. L. tr. *Fryke's Voy. E. Ind.* 31 Little Vessels.. brought..Coco's, Pisang Figgs, which are a long kind of Figg. **1705** tr. *Bosman's Guinea* 291 Much hath already been written concerning the Pisang-tree. **1745** P. THOMAS *Anson's Voy.* 333 Those most admired are the Pisang Figs.

pisanite ('pɪzənaɪt). *Min.* [ad. Ger. *pisanit*, named 1860, after F. Pisani, who described it: see -ITE[1].] A hydrous sulphate of iron and copper, found in Turkey, in bright blue concretions.

1861 *Amer. Jrnl. Sc.* Ser. II. XXXI. 366 Pisanite..a cupreous variety of copperas from Turkey. **1868** DANA *Min.* (ed. 5) 646 Pisanite,..occurs with chalcopyrite at a copper mine in the interior of Turkey.

pisasphalt, erron. form of PISSASPHALT.

pisatin ('paɪs-, 'pɪsətɪn, -z-). *Biochem.* [f. the taxonomic name *Pis(um s)at(ivum* (f. L. *pisum* pea + *sativus* (see SATIVE *a.*)) + -IN[1].] A fungitoxic phytoalexin produced by the pea plant, which has been isolated as a crystalline heterocyclic compound, $C_{17}H_{14}O_6$.

1960 CRUICKSHANK & PERRIN in *Nature* 27 Aug. 800/1 We propose that the trivial name of this compound should be 'pisatin' after the host plant from which it was originally isolated. **1964** [see PHASEOLLIN]. **1967** R. K. S. WOOD *Physiol. Plant Path.* xiv. 496 None of a variety of bacteria which have been tested stimulates formation of pisatin by pea pods. **1972** S. A. J. TARR *Princ. Plant Path.* xiv. 268 Some of these antifungal substances are perhaps present in low concentrations in normal tissue, their formation being intensified by infection or some other stimulus. Pisatin, for example, is formed when dilute solutions of certain metallic salts..are placed on pea pod endocarp tissue.

† '**piscage.** *Obs. rare*[−1]. [ad. med.L. *piscāgium* (for **piscāticum*), f. *piscāre* to fish, after OF. *peschage* fishing, f. *peschier* to fish; see -AGE.] Right of fishing.

1610 W. FOLKINGHAM *Art of Survey* III. iv. 70 Wrecks, Swannage, Warrenage, Commonage, Piscage.

piscary[1] ('pɪskərɪ). (Also 7 pischary.) [ad. med.L. *piscāria* fishing rights, neut. pl. of L. *piscārius* adj., belonging to fishing, f. *piscis* fish.] **1.** The right of fishing (as a thing owned). Now usually in phr. ***common of piscary***: see quot. 1880.

1474 *Rolls of Parlt.* VI. 166/2 Markettes, Warens, Piscaries, Fre Customes. **1607** COWELL *Interpr.*, *Piscarie* (*piscaria*),..signifieth in our common lawe, a libertie of fishing in an other mans waters. **1766** BLACKSTONE *Comm.* II. xvi. 261 That the eyotts or little islands, arising in any part of the river, shall be the property of him who owneth the piscary and the soil. **1837** MACAULAY *Ess.*, *Bacon* (1887) 377 That the most profound thinker..of the age.. confounded the right of free fishery with that of common of piscary. **1880** WILLIAMS *Rights of Common* 259 Common of piscary is a liberty of fishing in another man's water, in common with the owner of the soil, and perhaps also with others, who may be entitled to the same right.

2. A place where fish may be caught; a fishing-ground, fishery.

a **1625** SIR H. FINCH *Law* (1636) 136 There is no distresse but vpon Land in demesne, neither could a distresse be taken vpon a Piscary, but that it containeth land and demesnes. **1628** COKE *On Litt.* 198 Breaking their Closes,.. cutting their woods,..fishing in their Pischary [*Fr.* pischarie]. **1714** SCROGGS *Courts-leet* (ed. 3) 161 If a Copy-holder convert Part of the Land into a Piscary it's a Forfeiture. **1866** ROGERS *Agric. & Prices* I. xxiv. 610 Fishermen licensed to angle or net parts of the piscary.

† **b.** A fish-market. *Obs. rare*[−0].

[**1605** B. JONSON *Volpone* v. iv, The small tenement..By the Piscaria.] **1706** PHILLIPS, *Piscary*, a Place where Fish is kept or sold, a Fish-market.

3. *attrib.* or as *adj.* Of or pertaining to piscaries or to fishing.

1869 *Daily News* 23 July, When the humbler tenants of presumed piscary properties were being impoverished. **1883** *Fisheries Exhib. Catal.* 273 The piscary laws and customs were severe.

† **piscary**[2]. *Obs. rare*[−0]. [ad. L. *piscārius*: see prec.] A fisherman; a fishmonger.

1656 BLOUNT *Glossogr.*, *Piscary* (*piscarius*), a fisher, or one that sels small fish.

piscash, variant of PESHCUSH, an offering.

piscation (pɪ'skeɪʃən). *rare.* [ad. L. *piscātiōnem*, n. of action f. *piscārī* to fish, f. *piscis* a fish.] Fishing.

1624 BP. HALL *Contempl.*, *N.T.* II. iv, What is this divine Trade of ours then, but a spirituall Piscation? **1646** SIR T. BROWNE *Pseud. Ep.* I. viii. 32 Foure bookes of Cynegeticks or venation, five of Halieuticks or piscation. **1848** *Blackw. Mag.* LXIV. 96 He must not dream of rivalling..Stoddart in the science of piscation.

pisca'tology. *rare.* [irreg. f. L. *piscāt-*, ppl. stem of *piscārī* to fish + -LOGY.] The science of fishing; in quot. *erron.* = ichthyology.

1867 ATWATER *Logic* 217 Thus Ornithology, Piscatology, &c., under Zoology.

‖ **piscator** (pɪ'skeɪtɔː(r), -ə(r)). [L. *piscātor*, agent-n. from *piscārī* to fish.] A fisherman; an angler.

1653 WALTON *Angler* ii. 40 *Viator.* My friend Piscator, you have kept time with my thoughts, for the Sun is just rising. **1688** R. HOLME *Armoury* III. xvi. (Roxb.) 79/2 Instruments pertaineing to the Piscators science. **1904** *Athenæum* 31 Dec. 901/1 Extracts from ancient piscators and writers on fishing.

piscatorial (pɪskə'tɔərɪəl), *a.* [f. L. *piscātōri-us* PISCATORY + -AL[1].] = PISCATORY I.

1828 HAWTHORNE *Fanshawe* iii, A hook and line, a fish-spear, or any piscatorial instrument of death! **1854** PULMAN (*title*) The Book of the Axe: containing a piscatorial description of that Stream. **1883** J. C. BLOOMFIELD *Fisheries Irel.* 8 (Fish. Exhib. Publ.) To study the grandest specimen of piscatorial topography ever exhibited, in the official fishery map of the United States.

Hence **pisca'torialist**, a professed angler; **pisca'torially** *adv.*, in a piscatorial manner. So **pisca'torian** *sb.*, an angler; *adj.* = PISCATORIAL; **pisca'torical** *a. nonce-wd.*, dealing with piscatorial matters; **pisca'torious** *a.* = PISCATORY.

1903 *Westm. Gaz.* 8 Aug. 8/1 Mr. Henry Walford Stubbin, a well-known *piscatorialist, died recently at Cheltenham. **1824** in *Spirit Pub. Jrnls.* (1825) 454 'The Lord Mayor's' health was next proposed, *piscatorially. **1845** *Blackw. Mag.* LVIII. 475 He was..so piscatorially habilimented that there was no making out his order or degree. **1861** J. H. BENNET *Winter Medit.* I. v. (1875) 134 The gentle art is cultivated..by many zealous native *piscatorians. **1864** A. MCKAY *Hist. Kilmarnock* (1880) 11 That piscatorian traveller, Franck. **1848** *Blackw. Mag.* LXIII. 382 A *piscatorical page, in which we would have shown..how..silver fish are caught whose eyes are living gold. **1799** *Naval Chron.* I. 67 The *piscatorious, or.. fishing Frog.

piscatory ('pɪskətərɪ), *a.* (*sb.*) [ad. L. *piscātōri-us* adj., f. *piscātor* fisher: see -ORY[2].]

1. Of or pertaining to fishers or to fishing.

piscatory ring, the signet ring worn by the pope as successor of St. Peter (cf. Matt. iv. 19, etc.).

1633 P. FLETCHER (*title*) The Purple Island..together with Piscatorie Eclogs. **1670** G. H. *Hist. Cardinals* III. III. 296 The Pope dy'd.., and immediately the Piscatory Ring was broken by Cardinal Barbarino. **1750** JOHNSON *Rambler* No. 36 ¶9 To substitute fishermen for shepherds, and derive his sentiments from the piscatory life. **1861** H. F. HORE in *Macm. Mag.* V. 52 The gain to the piscatory interest would be immense. **1867** F. FRANCIS *Angling* vi. (1880) 194 Piscatory heirlooms and relics.

2. Employed in or addicted to fishing.

1661 LOVELL *Hist. Anim. & Min.* Introd., Sea gull, white, cinereous, piscatorie. **1836** W. IRVING *Astoria* II. 271 The salmon, which are..as important to the piscatory tribes as are the buffaloes to the hunters of the prairies. **1882** *Harper's Mag.* June 6 Yarmouth is piscatory..beyond description.

¶ **3.** *erron.* Misused for PISCINE *a.*

1768 FOOTE *Devil on 2 Sticks* III. Wks. 1799 II. 276 Certain animalculæ, or piscatory entities, that insinuate themselves thro' the pores into the blood. **1842** *United Service Mag.* I. 349 The upper part being human, the lower part, from the hips, piscatory.

† **B.** ellipt. as *sb.* A play or the like dealing with the life of fishermen. (Cf. *pastoral.*) *Obs.*

1631 P. FLETCHER (*title*) Sicelides, a Piscatory, as it hath beene Acted in Kings Colledge, in Cambridge.

Piscean (ˈpaɪsiːən, -ˈsiːən), *a.* and *sb.* Also **Piscian.** [f. PISCE(S + -AN.] **A.** *adj.* Of or pertaining to Pisces, the twelfth sign of the Zodiac: characteristic of a person born under Pisces. **B.** *sb.* A person born under Pisces.

1924 C. E. O. CARTER *Con. Encycl. Psychol. Astrol.* 38 It must..be observed that in some people the Piscian and Neptunian charity seems entirely lacking. **1925** —— *Princ. Astrol.* iv. 74 Pisceans are commonly jovial and convivial, and often make entertaining companions. **1940** R. GLEADOW *Astrol. in Everyday Life* II. 162 Most Pisceans..are not particularly dashing; yet those who have Mars rising in Pisces may be quite audacious. *Ibid.* xiv. 250 In astrological circles Mr. Micawber is notoriously Piscean. *a* **1963** L. MACNEICE *Astrol.* (1964) iii. 105 Pisceans are very lovable people because they are very loving. **1969** 'V. PACKER' *Don't rely on Gemini* (1970) i. 8 Leos are lionlike and Pisceans are mystical. **1972** D. LEES *Zodiac* 28 There must be thousands of Pisceans who can't swim. **1976** *Woman* 22 May 61/1 All is quiet on the Piscean front with both your ruling planets playing a waiting game. **1978** *TV Times* 28 Jan. 68/3 Pam is one of those lucky Pisceans who will enjoy plenty of romance this year.

piscence, piscens, obs. Sc. ff. PUISSANCE.

‖**Pisces** (ˈpaɪsiːz, ˈpɪsiːz), *sb.* (and *a.*) Also 4 pissis, 5 pisshes, pysces. [L. *piscēs*, pl. of *piscis* fish.]

1. a. *Astron.* The twelfth zodiacal constellation, the Fishes; also the twelfth sign of the Zodiac (originally coincident with the constellation), which the sun enters about the 20th of February.

c **1391** CHAUCER *Astrol.* II. §40 Also the degree..was in the furst degree of pisces. *c* **1400** *Destr. Troy* 4039 The sun.. Passyng fro pisshes vnder playn course. **1797** *Encycl. Brit.* (ed. 3) II. 532/2 On the parallel of London, as much of the ecliptic rises about Pisces and Aries in two hours as the moon goes through in six days. **1868** LOCKYER *Elem. Astron.* vii. 265 In the time of Hipparchus—2000 years ago—the Sun at the vernal equinox was in the constellation Aries; now-a-days it is in the constellation Pisces.

b. A person born under the zodiacal sign Pisces. Also *attrib.* or as *adj.*

1924 C. E. O. CARTER *Conc. Encycl. Psychol. Astrol.* 142 Cancer and Pisces people are often retiring and shy among strangers. **1936** 'J. TEY' *Shilling for Candles* vii. 64 One does not expect a Pisces person to have either the vision or the faith. **1969** 'V. PACKER' *Don't rely on Gemini* (1970) i. 1 Would a Pisces get along with a Capricorn? *Ibid.* xviii. 159 We're both Pisces like Elizabeth Taylor. **1972** D. BLOODWORTH *Any Number can Play* xii. 101 You're Pisces, darling... The lucky things for Pisces people are silver, bloodstone, and number seven. **1973** L. MEYNELL *Fatal Flaw* ii. 20 The fellow turned out to be Pisces. An unreliable lot the Pisces. **1976** *Woman* 1 May 56/1 Intuition and sixth sense are passwords for Pisces, and this week you should virtually live by them, for safety's sake.

2. *Zool.* Fishes, as a Class of Vertebrata.

1841–71 T. R. JONES *Anim. Kingd.* (ed. 4) xxv. *heading*, Pisces (fishes). **1873** J. GEIKIE *Gt. Ice Age* 525 Class: Pisces.

pisch(e, obs. Sc. form of PISS.

piscicapture (ˈpɪsɪˌkæptjʊə(r)). *humorous* or *affected.* [f. L. *pisci-s* fish + *captūra* CAPTURE.] The catching of fish.

1862 RUSSELL *Diary North & South* (1863) I. xix. 206 The delights of piscicapture. **1878** *Standard* 21 Oct. 5/1 'Snatching' is a form of illicit piscicapture for which it is impossible to entertain..sympathy. **1881** J. PAYN *Hum. Stories* 298 Instruments of piscicapture.

Hence **pisci'capturist**, a catcher of fish.

1881 BLACKMORE *Christowell* xxviii, On the part of the piscicapturists (for a fish is not to be called a fish now, and everything connected with him is pisci-something).

piscicide (ˈpɪsɪ-, ˈpɪskɪsaɪd). [f. L. *pisci-s* fish + -CIDE.] **a.** The killing of fish.

1963 *Times* 21 Aug. 5, I was unable to detect any evidence of mass piscicide in the Sonic's track. The only dead fish I saw was a 6 in. specimen.

b. A substance that kills fish.

1964 LENNON & WALKER *Laboratories & Methods for Screening Fish-Control Chemicals* 1/2 Ample justification for research on selective piscicides is contained in fishery literature. **1965** *N.Y. Fish & Game Jrnl.* XII. 99 In larger ponds and lakes, the need for selective piscicides is even greater. **1976** *Nature* 25 Mar. 374/2 Under Control of Undesirable Species (Chapter 18), we have a 2-page description..of the new piscicide antimycin.

† **piscicle.** *Obs. rare.* [ad. L. *piscicul-us*, dim. of *piscis* fish: see -ICLE.] A little fish.

1657 TOMLINSON *Renou's Disp.* 459 Neither bones nor part of the piscicle. **1661** in BLOUNT *Glossogr.* (ed. 2).

piscicolous (pɪˈsɪkələs), *a.* [f. L. *pisci-s* fish + *-col-a* inhabitant + -OUS.] (See quot. 1895.)

1890 in *Cent. Dict.* **1895** *Syd. Soc. Lex.*, *Piscicolous*,.. parasitic upon fishes.

piscicultural (pɪsɪˈkʌltjʊərəl), *a.* [f. next + -AL[1].] Of or pertaining to pisciculture. Hence **pisci'culturally** *adv.*, in respect of pisciculture.

1862 *Cornh. Mag.* V. 196 Before the piscicultural era. **1882** *Nature* XXVI. 475 The ease with which all kinds of fish can be treated pisciculturally. **1887** *Manch. Exam.* 7 Feb. 5/5 Prof. Huxley, a thoroughly practical authority on all piscicultural questions.

pisciculture (ˈpɪsɪˌkʌltjʊə(r)). [f. L. *pisci-s* fish + *cultura* CULTURE. Cf. F. *pisciculture* (*Dict. Acad.* 1878).] The breeding, rearing, and preservation of (living) fish by artificial means.

1859 *Edin. Rev.* CIX. 304 The new arrangements for the protection of salmon, and for pisciculture, in imitation of the French practise. **1859** TENNENT *Ceylon* II. IX. vii. 562 The pearl-oyster may be brought within the domain of pisciculture. **1866** ROGERS *Agric. & Prices* I. xxiv. 608 The monks were said to have been skilled in pisciculture.

pisciculturist (pɪsɪˈkʌltjʊərɪst). [See -IST.] A person engaged or interested in pisciculture.

1862 *Illustr. Lond. News* 11 Jan. 50/3 M. Coste, the pisciculturist. **1868** PEARD *Water-farm.* i. 3 They were still immeasurably behind the pisciculturists of to-day. **1881** *Standard* 10 Sept. 2/1 A practical pisciculturist, and an enthusiast in all matters relating to fish and fisheries.

piscifauna (ˌpɪsɪˈfɔːnə). [f. L. *pisci-s* fish + FAUNA.] Collective term for the native fishes (of any district or country); the fish-fauna.

1890 in *Cent. Dict.* **1895** *Syd. Soc. Lex.*, *Piscifauna*,.. the fish-Fauna of a region.

pisciform (ˈpɪsɪfɔːm), *a.* [f. L. *pisci-s* fish + -FORM.] Having the form of a fish.

1828 STARK *Elem. Nat. Hist.* I. 160 Order X.—Cetacea. Body pisciform, terminated by a caudal appendage. **1875** HUXLEY in *Encycl. Brit.* I. 768/2 The embryo, when hatched, is pisciform and apodal.

piscina (pɪˈsiːnə, pɪˈsaɪnə). Pl. -æ, -as. [a. L. *piscina* a fishpond, bathing-pool, tank, in med.L. in sense 2, It., Sp., Pg. *piscina*, f. *piscis* fish.]

1. A fishpond; a pond, basin, or pool; among the ancient Romans, a public or private pond for bathing or swimming.

1599 HAKLUYT *Voy.* II. I. 153 Also the piscina or fishpoole where the sicke folkes were healed. **1644** EVELYN *Diary* 10 Nov., Piscinas or stews for fish. **1717** BERKELEY *Tour in Italy* Wks. 1871 IV. 576, I saw likewise the ruins of a piscina, or receptacle for water. **1832** GELL *Pompeiana* I. v. 82 The roof of the natatorium or piscina of the baths. **1854** CNT. E. DE WARREN tr. *de Saulcy's Journ. Round Dead Sea* II. 307 The largest and most important of all the piscinas of Jerusalem. *a* **1878** SIR G. G. SCOTT *Lect. Archit.* (1879) II. 154 The covered tanks or piscinæ of the ancients.

2. *Eccl.* A perforated stone basin for carrying away the water used in rinsing the chalice and the hands of the priest; generally placed in a niche on the south side of the altar, though sometimes projecting from the face of the wall or supported on a short column. Also *attrib.*

1793 *Gentl. Mag.* LXIII. I. 422/1 In its South wall a piscina and locker. **1839** STONEHOUSE *Axholme* 226 The fenestella, or small niche, contained a vessel, bason, or piscina, for washing the hands. **1874** MICKLETHWAITE *Mod. Par. Churches* 132 The piscina is a sink or drain, through which the water used in several ablutions is poured away. **1904** *Athenæum* 9 Apr. 473/2 The piscina niches are numerous..but present no very special features.

b. Applied to a holy-water basin or stoup. *rare.*

1812 *Gentl. Mag.* LXXXII. I. 315/2 Against the E. side are two piscinæ for holy water in the wall.

Hence **piscinal** (ˈpɪsɪnəl) *a.* (*rare*$^{-0}$) [ad. mod.L. *piscīnālis*], pertaining to a fishpond or piscina.

1656 in BLOUNT *Glossogr.*: and in subsequent dicts.

piscine (ˈpɪsɪn, pɪˈsiːn), *sb.* Also 4–5 -ene. [a. OF., F. *piscine* fishpond, bathing-pool, piscina, ad. L. *piscina*: see prec.]

1. A natural or artificial reservoir for water; a pool, pond; a bathing-pool; = PISCINA 1. *Obs.* from 16th till late in the 19th c.

(In early use often applied to the *piscina probatica* or Pool of Bethesda, and Pool of Siloam.)

a **1300** *Cursor M.* 13761 (Cott.) A water..þat es cald piscene [*v.r.* piscine] in þair lede. *c* **1420** LYDG. *Commend. Our Lady* 134 Thou misty arke, probatik piscyne. **1430–40** —— *Bochas* VIII. xii. (1554) 183 b, His fleshe renued and sodeinly made white By thrise washing in the freshe piscine. *Ibid.* VIII. xiii. (1558) 7 He was counsayled to make a great pyscyne With innocent blud of children y[t] wer pure. **1481** CAXTON *Godeffroy* clxxii. 254 Fro the fontaynes without cam grete haboundaunce by conduytes, whiche descended in to ij pyscynes right grete by the temple, that one endureth yet in to this day and is named probatica piscina. **1517** TORKINGTON *Pilgr.* (1884) 38 Which condites serve all the Citee.., and fyll all the pyscynes. **1894** *Westm. Gaz.* 30 Apr. 2/1 Cured, according to current report, by bathing her foot in the piscine [at Lourdes]. **1894** J. R. GASQUET in *Dublin Rev.* Oct. 350 A few..came to ask if they might safely bathe in the piscines.

2. = PISCINA 2. *rare.*

1489 CAXTON *Doctr. Sapience* lxiv. (Windsor Cas. Copy), Yf to fore the consecracion a flye or loppe..were founde in the chalyce, it ought to be caste in to the piscine and the chalyce ought to be wasshen. *Ibid.*, The asshes & the wasshyng of the beeste to be put into the pyscyne. **1822** NARES, *Piscine* or *Piscina.* **1883** *Antiquary* VIII. 211 There is another piscine in the south wall of the church.

piscine (ˈpɪsaɪn), *a.* [f. L. *piscis* fish: see -INE[1].] Of, pertaining to, of the nature of, or characteristic of a fish or fishes.

1799 KIRWAN *Geol. Ess.* 240 Covered by bituminous marlite, and with piscine remains. **1816** G. S. FABER *Orig. Pagan Idol.* III. 34 Derceto was the piscine ship-goddess of the Syrians. **1854** OWEN *Skel. & Teeth* in *Orr's Circ. Sc.* I. *Org. Nat.* 183 The piscine modification of the vertebrate skeleton. **1899** E. CALLOW *Old Lond. Tav.* I. 120 Billingsgate, the great Walhalla of all things piscine.

piscinity (pɪˈsɪnɪtɪ). *affected* or *humorous.* [f. prec. + -ITY, after *humanity*, etc.] The quality or condition of being a fish; 'fishhood'.

1865 MILL *Exam. Hamilton* 426 We do not talk of the phænomena which accompany piscinity; we talk of the phænomena of fishes. **1865** *Daily Tel.* 9 Aug., Our definition of piscinity in general would be precisely that of a fish. **1890** *Cornh. Mag.* Nov. 542 Pioneers of blind and phosphorescent piscinity will fight with one another.

piscitarian (pɪsɪˈtɛərɪən). ? *humorous nonce-wd.* [f. L. *pisci-s* fish, after *vegetarian.*] A fishmonger.

1880 BLACKMORE *Mary Anerley* xlviii, The Flamborough butcher once more subsided into a piscitarian.

piscivorous (pɪˈsɪvərəs), *a.* [f. L. type **piscivor-us* (f. *pisci-s* fish + *-vorus* devouring) + -OUS: cf. mod.F. *piscivore.*] Fish-eating; subsisting on fish; ichthyophagous.

1668 WILKINS *Real Char.* 155 Being generally Piscivorous. The Solan-goose kind. *a* **1705** RAY *Creation* (1714) 28 Which I have observed in many piscivorous birds. **1854** H. MILLER *Sch. & Schm.* ii. (1857) 37 The piscivorous habits of the Cromarty folk. **1877** COUES *Fur Anim.* x. 313 The..aquatic and highly piscivorous nature of the [otter].

pisco (ˈpɪskəʊ). [Peruvian, f. *Pisco* the name of a port of Peru.] A white brandy made in Peru from muscat grapes. Also *attrib.* and *Comb.*, as *pisco Collins* [COLLINS[2]], *sour.*

1849 H. VIZETELLY *Four Months among Gold-Finders in Alta California* 30 On our way he pointed out the guard-house..the distillery house, where the famous pisco is made. **1873** A. S. EVANS *À la California* 328 The company all together, we propose a taste of fragrant *pisco* (Peruvian white brandy). **1924** R. CLEMENTS *Gipsy of Horn* viii. 143 The old man laid in a stock of 'pisco', a cheap, fiery spirit, very popular in Peru. **1961** J. B. PRIESTLEY *Saturn over Water* v. 55 The expensive bars where the double martinis and *pisco* sours were being served. *Ibid.* vi. 88, I just couldn't see steady Joe Farne..going off on a great *pisco* blind. **1962** N. MAXWELL *Witch-Doctor's Apprentice* ii. 16, I asked the waiter to bring me a pisco collins. 'Without sugar as usual, señorita?' he asked. **1971** D. WALLIS *Bad Luck Girl* i. 13 Down the Pacific coast they think no more of selling you a fix than pouring you a pisco. **1973** K. BENTON *Craig & Jaguar* iv. 36 'You must try one of the Club's pisco sours.' Craig sipped the sticky mixture of cane-spirit and fresh lime juice through the layers of white of egg foam.

† **piscod,** obs. form of PEASECOD.

14.. *MS. Sloane* 4 lf. 80 in *N. & Q.* 3rd Ser. VI. 4/1 A note worme or a piscod worme.

† **pi'scose,** *a. Obs. rare.* [ad. L. *piscōs-us* full of fish: see -OSE.] Fishy.

1683–4 ROBINSON in *Phil. Trans.* XXIX 481 They liv'd upon Fish, and had a piscose Taste.

† **'isculent,** *a. Obs. rare.* [ad. L. *pisculentus* abounding in fish, f. *piscis* fish: see -ULENT.] Abounding in fish, full of fish.

1656 BLOUNT *Glossogr.*, Pisculent (*pisculentus*), full of fishes, or that may be fished. **1661** J. CHILDREY *Brit. Baconica* 104 The Thames is more pisculent, or full of fish then the Severn.

pise, obs. form of PICE; variant of PIZE *sb. Obs.*

‖**pisé** (ˈpize). Also **pisée.** [a. F. *pisé*, subst. use of pa. pple. of *piser* to beat, pound (earth):—L. *pīsare, pinsāre* to beat, pound, stamp.] **a.** Also, *pisé de terre.* Stiff clay or earth kneaded, or mixed with gravel, used, esp. in France and some parts of England, for building cottages, walls, etc., by being rammed between boards which are removed as it hardens; also, a name for this mode of building.

1797 H. HOLLAND in *Com. Board Agric.* I. 387 The word *pisé* is a technical Term..and it has been retained in this translation because it cannot be rendered by any adequate word in the English language. **1805** R. W. DICKSON *Pract. Agric.* (1807) I. 136 Building in what is termed *pisé*, or simply by compressing well-wrought earth in moulds. **1852** WIGGINS *Embanking* 32 A wall of *pisé* or rammed gravel in a frame might very judiciously be adopted for 2 or 3 feet of the centre of the bank. **1890** 'R. BOLDREWOOD' *Squatter's Dream* vii, The new cottage which he had judiciously caused to be built of 'pisé' or rammed earth. **1919** C. WILLIAMS-ELLIS *Building in Cob, Pisé, Chalk & Clay* 28 'Pisé de Terre', 'Chalk Compost', and 'Cob' are three alternative forms of construction. **1936** I. L. IDRIESS *Cattle King* xx. 183 Homesteads were of roughly gathered stone or pisé, of axe hewn slabs or sheets of bark. **1946** B. JAMES in Murdoch & Drake-Brockman *Austral. Short Stories* (1951) 250 The walls had to be very thick, and that meant more pisé to be mixed, and lifted and rammed. **1960** K. M. KENYON *Archaeol. in Holy Land* iii. 60 The edges of the pits are revetted by slight walls of pisée and stone. **1977** *36 Home Handyman Projects* (Austral. Home Jrnl.) 97/3 Pise de Terre —wall construction of clay or earth—a formwork is made and the earth and clay rammed in firmly. **1978** *Jrnl. R. Soc.*

Arts CXXVI. 586/1 Cob..provided good walling; so did damp earth rammed into moulds, and known as *pisé*.

b. *attrib.* or *adj.*, as ***pisé building, earth, terre, wall, work***.

1840 *Cottager's Man.* 30 in *Libr. Usef. Knowl., Husb.* III, Walls..formed of earth in the *pisé* manner. **1849** *Ecclesiologist* IX. 217 We..think that what our correspondent calls Pisé building is common in Devonshire ..and known by the name of cob-building. **1875** KNIGHT *Dict. Mech.* 1714/1 The best material for pisé-work is clay with small gravel-stones interposed through it. **1919** C. WILLIAMS-ELLIS *Building in Cob, Pisé, Chalk & Clay* ii. 57 Pliny gives an excellent account of pisé-building in his *Natural History*. **1919** in *Ibid.* 74 These iron bars become so tightly jammed when surrounded by the compact pisé earth, that much labour and risk of injury to the work is incurred in extricating them. **1946** B. JAMES in Murdoch & Drake-Brockman *Austral. Short Stories* (1951) 250 The pisé earth had to be dug,..mixed and kneaded with water, shovelled into the frames, rammed thoroughly and then left to set. **1965** *Austral. Encycl.* III. 327 Another interesting example of pisé building was the old Forbes, N.S.W., police barracks. **1971** *Country Life* 7 Oct. 941/1 Clough was commissioned..'to write a practical book on *Pisée Terre* (rammed earth) building..to cheapen and expedite rural cottage building in the twenties'.

pisette, ? Anglicized form of PESETA.

1807 R. CUMBERLAND *Mem.* II. 151 We purchased three lambs at the price of two pisettes apiece.

Pisgah ('pɪzgə). [a. Heb. *Pisgāh* 'cleft'.] The name of a mountain east of Jordan, whence Moses was allowed to view the Promised Land (Deut. iii. 27); hence used allusively, esp. *attrib.*, as ***Pisgah glance, prospect, sight, view***.

[**1605** W. SYMONDS (*title*) Pisgah Evangelica By the Method of the Reuelation, presenting..those Cananites ouer whom..Iesus Christ and his..Church shall triumph.] **1650** FULLER (*title*) Pisgah Sight of Palestine. **1701** NORRIS *Ideal World* I. iii. 133 The top of our philosophic Pisgah, whence the contemplative eye is saluted with the..prospect of a bright and glorious world. **1829** SCOTT *Diary* 7 Mar. in *Lockhart*, This extrication of my affairs, though only a Pisgah prospect, occupies my mind. **1865** GROTE *Plato* I. xvi. 472 We get only a Pisgah view of our promised adviser.

pish (pɪʃ), *int.* and *sb.* See also PUSH *int.* (*sb.*³) [A natural exclamation.]

A. *int.* An exclamation expressing contempt, impatience, or disgust.

1592 NASHE *P. Penilesse* C ij, Pish, pish, what talke you of old age or balde pates? **1599** SHAKS. *Hen. V*, II. i. 43, 44 *Nym.* Pish. *Pist.* Pish for thee, Island dogge. **1611** COTGR., *Tarabin tarabas*, an Interiection of interruption, like our pish pish, tut tut. **1672** MARVELL *Reh. Transp.* I. 52 Pish, said I, that's no such great matter. **1708** T. WARD *Eng. Ref.* (1716) 56 Pish, Pish, quoth Seymour in a Huff. **1845** JAMES *Smuggler* III. 178 Pish! you are a fool, young man.

B. *sb.* The utterance of this exclamation. †***to make a pish at*** or ***of***, to treat with contempt. *attrib.*, as †***pish-monger*** (humorous, after *fish-monger*).

1594 NASHE *Terrors Nt.* Wks. (Grosart) III. 251 All receipts and authors you can name he syllogizeth of, and makes a pish at. **1600** HOLLAND *Livy* XXXVII. xxxv. 965 Those matters..the Romanes made a pish at, and lightly regarded. *a* **1643** W. CARTWRIGHT *Ordinary* IV. v, What shrieks and cries, What angry pishes, and what fies. **1654** WHITLOCK *Zootomia* Pref. a vj b, Too severe Censurer (free of the Company of Pish-mongers) that Pisheth at any thing not exact. **1777** COWPER *Let. to J. Hill* Wks. 1837 XV. 41, I had rather never see the books, than extort from you one single Pish. **1840** HOOD *Kilmansegg, Her precious Leg* x, She writh'd with impatience..And utter'd 'pshaws!' and 'pishes!'

pish, *v.* [f. prec.]

1. *intr.* To say 'pish!' Often with *at*.

1598 B. JONSON *Ev. Man in Hum.* III. i, *Bob.* This a Toledo! Pish! *Step.* Why do you pish, captain? **1644** BP. HALL *Serm.* 9 June, Rem. Wks. (1660) 102 A motive, which ..may be past over, and pisht at. **1713** STEELE *Guard.* No. 151 ¶1 How would the ladies pish at such a great monstrous thing? *a* **1864** HAWTHORNE *S. Felton* (1883) 333 The learned man..pished and pshawed.

2. *trans.* To say 'pish' to. ***to pish away, down***: to reject or depreciate by saying 'pish!'

1601 B. JONSON *Poetaster* v. i, *Hor.* Pish: ha, ha! *Lup.* Dost thou pish me? Give me my long sword. **1616** R. CROSHAW *Compliment. Verses* in Capt. Smith *Descr. New Eng.*, Though Men of..lesse desert Would Pish-away thy Praise. **1901** *Blackw. Mag.* Dec. 730 Some pish it down as valueless.

Hence **'pishing** *vbl. sb.*; also **'pisher**, one who pishes.

1662 *Rump Songs* (1874) II. 63 Which puts pretty Maids to pishing and fying. **1901** *Blackw. Mag.* Dec. 730 Both.. pishers and puffers..being noisily wrong.

pish, Sc. form of PISS.

‖**pishachi** (piːˈʃɑːtʃiː). *India.* Also **piśaca, pisachi, pishasha**, and numerous other variants. [ad. Skr. *piśāca* (masc.), *piśācī* (fem.), a demon.] A demon or devil. Also *attrib.*

The forms in *-a* properly refer to male devils, and those in *-i* to female.

1807 F. BUCHANAN *Journey from Madras* III. xiv. 17 They believe, that such men as die accidental deaths become *Pysáchi*, or evil spirits, and are exceedingly troublesome, by making extraordinary noises in families, and occasioning fits, and other diseases, especially in women. **1816** *Asiatic Jrnl.* II. 367/1 *Whirlwinds*..at the end of March and the beginning of April..carry dust and light things along with them, and are called by the natives *peshashes*, or devils. **1819** *Trans. Bombay Lit. Soc.* I. 219 Beneath him..is a small squat figure, apparently a *peisach* or demon. These demons or *peisaches* are the usual attendants of Shiva. **1827** J. C. & A. W. HARE *Guesses at Truth* (ser. 1) 12 As a little girl was playing round me one day with her white frock over her head, I laughingly called her *Pishashee*, the Indian name, I believe, for their white devil. **1837** J. C. MAITLAND, *Lett. from Madras* (1843) 107 She used to go out and howl so that the servants were afraid to come near her, saying she made 'one pishashi (devil) noise'. **1885** G. C. WHITWORTH *Anglo-Indian Dict.* 252/1 *Piśácha*.., the name of a class of spirits always imagined as fierce and malignant. **1886** YULE & BURNELL *Hobson-Jobson* 540/1 Pisachee. **1917** L. H. GRAY *Mythol. All Races* VI. 67 With the Rakṣases in later literature rank the Piśācas as foes of the fathers. **1920** *Encycl. Relig. & Ethics* X. 43/2 In modern India a *piśācha* is a kind of ghoul, usually the ghost of some one who has died an unnatural death, or for whom the requisite funeral rites have not been performed... In S. India the small circular storms, called 'devils' by Europeans, are called *piśāchīs*, or 'she-ghouls'. **1924** R. E. ENTHOVEN *Folklore of Bombay* iv. 148 *Bhuts* and *pishachas*—ghosts, male and female—can be prevented from doing harm by recourse to certain processes. **1927** S. KETKAR tr. *Winternitz's Hist. Indian Lit.* I. 133 Very numerous, too, are the incantations which are directed against whole classes of demons.., especially against the *Piśācas* (goblins) and *Rākṣasas* (devils). **1952** E. SYKES *Everyman's Dict. Non-Classical Mythol.* 171 *Pishashas*, in Vedic myth malignant woodland spirits, who disliked travellers, and especially pregnant women. **1968** B. WALKER *Hindu World* II. 214 *Piśācha*, a race of people classed in the Vedas as lower than the rākshasas (ogres), and amongst the most vile and noxious of beings. **1973** J. DOWSON *Classical Dict. Hindu Mythol.* 234 *Piśāchas* (mas.), *Piśāchī* (fem.), fiends, evil spirits, placed by the Vedas as lower than Rākshasas. **1977** M. & J. STUTLEY *Dict. Hinduism* 226/1 *Piśāca(s)*, flesh-eating demonic beings. *Ibid.* 226/2 *Piśācī*, a she-devil.

pishamin ('pɪʃəmɪn). Another form of PERSIMMON; in Sierra Leone applied to two climbing shrubs, the ***sweet*** and ***sour pishamin*** (*Carpodinus dulcis* and *acida*), which bear an orange-shaped fruit resembling that of the persimmon.

1766 J. BARTRAM *Jrnl.* 14 Jan. 36 in W. Stork *Acct. E. Florida* (ed. 2), The lower rich ground produceth gledistia, pishamins, cephalanthus, ash, cypress and cornu femina. **1866** *Treas. Bot.*, Pishamin, *Carpodinus.* **1884** MILLER *Plant-n.*, *Carpodiscus acidus*, Sour Pishamin-tree, of Sierra Leone. *C. dulcis*, Sweet Pishamin-tree.

pisha paysha ('pɪʃə 'peɪʃə). Also **pisha pasha**. [App. a corruption of *pitch* (or *peace*) *and patience*.] A Jewish card game resembling patience, played by two persons, in which the cards are taken as they come from the pack, the object being to arrange them in an upward or downward sequence until the pack is exhausted, when the player who has the fewer cards in his hand is declared the winner.

1928 *Weekly Dispatch* 27 May 13/2 Faded photographs of the Yiddish stars of yesterday hung on the walls; most of the people looked up when we came in, but two heavy, blue-chinned fellows continued their game of *pisha pasha* and another smiled a greeting across the top of a Jewish evening paper. **1968** L. ROSTEN *Joys of Yiddish* 288, I was taught to play *pisha paysha* by my father, when I was six or seven.

pishcash, pishcush, var. PESHCUSH, an offering.

pisher ('pɪʃə(r)). *U.S. slang.* [a. Yiddish *pisher* PISSER, f. G. *pissen*: see PISS *v.*] A bed-wetter; also in extended uses (see quots.). Also *attrib.* or as *adj.*

1942 in *Amer. Speech* (1943) XVIII. 46 Call me pisher. **1943** *Ibid.*, The phrase 'to call someone pisher' connotes mild, tolerant, ineffectual reproof or disproportionately lax punishment. A typical context might be something like this: 'So what did they do to Flynn for putting public employees to work on his Mahopac estate and using government property? They called him pisher!' **1958** B. MALAMUD *Magic Barrel* 87 He bought..this pisher grocery in a dead neighbourhood where he didn't have a chance. **1968** L. ROSTEN *Joys of Yiddish* 289 Literally, a *pisher* is one who urinates; but that is a far cry from present and popular usage. 'He's a mere *pisher*,' means 'He's very young,' or 'He's still wet behind the ears.'.. 'He's just a *pisher*,' means 'He's a nobody,' has no influence. **1970** L. M. FEINSILVER *Taste of Yiddish* i. 61 'She still has two *pishers* at home' is a common colloquialism that makes its point: she has two offspring still in diapers, or two preschoolers. **1972** J. CAINE *Hamlet, My Boy* xi. 161 First, they didn't wait to call you *pisher*; they just filled you up with bullet-holes like a matzo. **1978** E. TIDYMAN *Table Stakes* II. vii. 312 Then the marriage. Now that was *really* smart! Who could call him pisher now, with the Jewish princess on his arm? **1978** R. DOLINER *On Edge* (1979) v. 83 'I was a kid... A pisher.' 'Pisher,' the Vice-President said. 'One who wets one's pants.' **1979** B. MALAMUD *Dubin's Lives* ix. 359, I lived on cases involving small finaglers and found myself engaged in pisher dishonesties.

†**'pishery-'pashery.** *Obs.* *nonce-wd.* [Reduplicated f. PISH *int.* + -ERY.] ? Depreciatory talk.

1600 DEKKER *Gentle Craft* i. (1610) B iij, Peace my fine Firke, stand by with your pishery pasherie, away.., ile speake to them.

pishogue (pɪˈʃəʊg). *Irish.* Also **pishog, pisherogue, pishrogue, pishtrogue.** [a. Ir. *píseog, písreog* witchcraft:—MIr. *pisóc*.] Sorcery, witchcraft; a spell incantation, charm. Also, a fairy, a witch.

1829 G. GRIFFIN *Collegians* I. xi. 231 Mr. Eurighť's dairyman..made a *pishog* and took away our butter. **1841** S. C. HALL *Ireland* II. 269 Now a pishogue is a wise saw, a rural incantation, a charm, a sign, a cabalistic word, a something mysterious signifying a great deal in a little. *a* **1854** T. C. CROKER *Fairy Leg. & Trad. S. Irel.* (1879) 74 He had no right to be bringing his auld Irish pishogues to Rome. **1869** P. KENNEDY *Evenings Duffrey* xxvii. 357 He threw pishrogues on our eyes. **1895** BARLOW *Lisconnel* viii. 166 Wrought through the agency of 'some quare ould pishtrogues'. **1901** M. J. F. MCCARTHY *Five Yrs. in Irel.* xiv. (ed. 5) 155 The talk turned upon 'pishogues', or witchcraft and charms. **1906** KIPLING *Puck of Pook's Hill* 10 Little people, pishogues, leprechauns. **1937** C. M. ARENSBERG *Irish Countryman* vi. 212 All that the Church condemns in the 'pisherogues', they [*sc.* young people] also condemn. **1957** E. E. EVANS *Irish Folk Ways* xxi. 296 Most of the pishrogues relate to fairies and to trees, wells and stones. **1960** *20th Cent.* July 51 She had denied it. 'No, I am not a pishogue.' Yet she was aware how easily one might become a fairy. **1961** 'F. O'BRIEN' *Hard Life* ii. 17 Well now, Mrs. Crothy, are these the two pishrogues out of the storm?

pish-pash ('pɪʃpæʃ). Also 9 **pish-posh.** 'A slop of rice-soup with small pieces of meat in it, much used in the Anglo-Indian nursery' (Yule).

1834 [A. PRINSEP] *Baboo* II. 85 They found the Secretary ..surrounded with huge volumes of Financial Reports on one side, and a small silver tray holding a mess of pish-pash on the other. **1845** BREGION & MILLER *Pract. Cook* 327 Pish Posh. **1898** G. J. YOUNGHUSBAND in *19th Cent.* Feb. 251 Next came a policy which was somewhat irreverently described as a policy of rupees and pish-pash.

pishymew ('pɪʃɪmjuː). [Cf. MEW.] The New England name of a small white gull.

1890 in *Cent. Dict.*

pisidiid (pɪˈsɪdɪɪd). *Zool.* [f. mod.L. *Pisidium*, dim. of L. *pisum* pea.] A member of the *Pisidiidæ*, a family of bivalve gastropod molluscs, typified by the genus *Pisidium*. So **pi'sidioid** *a.*, resembling a pisidiid in form.

pisiform ('paɪsɪfɔːm, 'pɪzɪ-), *a.* (*sb.*) [ad. mod.L. *pisiformis* pea-shaped, f. *pisum* pea: see -FORM. So mod.F. *pisiforme*.] Pea-shaped; of small globular form.

pisiform bone (*Anat.*), a small pea-shaped bone of the upper row of the carpus. ***pisiform iron-ore***, iron-ore occurring in small concretions like peas.

1767 GOOCH *Treat. Wounds* I. 189 A wound..upon his wrist, just above the pisiform bone. **1796** KIRWAN *Elem. Min.* (ed. 2) II. 178 Pisiform, or granular iron ore. **1852** DANA *Crust.* I. 203 Carapax..baccato-tuberculous, the tubercles large pisiform. **1875** SIR W. TURNER in *Encycl. Brit.* I. 828/1 The pisiform or pea-shaped bone..articulates with the front of the cuneiform.

B. *sb.* Short for *pisiform bone*: see above. (Also in L. form **pisiforme.**)

1808 BARCLAY *Muscular Motions* 404 A small degree of motion between the *pisiforme* and the *cuneiforme*. **1878** BELL tr. *Gegenbaur's Comp. Anat.* 482 The pisiform is a special bone.

pisimer, obs. form of PISMIRE.

pisimetacarpal (ˌpaɪsɪmɛtəˈkɑːpəl), *a. Anat.* [f. PISI(FORM) + METACARPAL.] Pertaining to the pisiform bone and to the metacarpus.

1895 in *Funk's Stand. Dict.*

Pisistratid (paɪˈsɪstrətɪd), *sb.* and *a.* Also **Peisistratid**, 8 **Pysistratid.** [ad. L. *Pisistratidae*, Gr. *Πεισιστρατίδαι*, the name given to Hippias and Hipparchus, sons of Pisistratus, tyrant of Athens in the 6th cent. B.C.] **A.** *sb.* (Pl. **-idae, -ids.**) A member or supporter of the family of Pisistratus. Chiefly in *pl.*

1709 I. LITTLEBURY tr. *Herodotus' Hist.* II. v. 57 The Corinthians would be the first of all People to regret the Pisistratides. **1776** W. ELLIS tr. *Aristotle's Treat. Govt.* v. xi. 295 The Pyramids of Egypt are a proof of this,..and the Temple of Jupiter Olympus, built by the Pysistratidæ, and the Works of Polycrates at Samos; for all these produced one end, the keeping the People poor. **1808** W. MITFORD *Hist. Greece* I. xii. 561 He married Agaristē, niece of Cleisthenes, chief of the Alcmæonid family, and leader of the party that expelled the Peisistratids. **1848** *Eton School Mag.* III. 114 It thus appears how irretrievably the government of the Pisistratids had injured the Athenian character. **1885** B. JOWETT tr. *Aristotle's Politics* I. v. 184 Third in duration was the rule of the Peisistratidae at Athens, but it was interrupted. **1900** J. B. BURY *Hist. Greece* v. 206 The Pisistratids cultivated the friendship of Sparta. **1922** P. N. URE *Origin of Tyranny* i. 14 This part of the tyrants' policy is noticed by Aristotle, who quotes..the building of the temple of Olympian Zeus at Athens by the Peisistratids. *Ibid.* ii. 33 The Philaidae, of whose rivalry with the Peisistratidae there will be occasion to speak later. **1972** R. MEIGGS *Athenian Empire* i. 19 The expulsion of the Pisistratids in 510.

B. *adj.* Of or pertaining to Pisistratus or his family; *spec.* of or pertaining to the revision of the Homeric poems attributed to Pisistratus. Also **Pisistra'tean** *a.*

1846 J. S. MILL in *Edin. Rev.* LXXXIV. 363 Mr. Grote ..rejects the Pisistratean hypothesis. **1965** A. R. BURN *Traveller's Hist. Greece* vii. 114 Hipparchos, the chief Peisistratid patron of poets and artists, was stabbed to death. **1968** V. EHRENBERG *From Solon to Socrates* iv. 82 The story of a 'Peisistratid redaction' of the two epics can hardly be true.

pisk. A bird; the same as the PIRAMIDIG.
1890 in *Cent. Dict.*

piskie, pisky, var. PIXIE.

‖**piskun** ('pɪskən). Also pishkun. [ad. Blackfoot *piskáni.*] An American Indian trap for buffalo, consisting of two converging lines of rock piles, a V-shaped natural canyon, or a timbered causeway leading to a steep drop, often with an enclosure or corral at the foot, over which the buffalo were stampeded.

1892 *Scribner's Mag.* Sept. 281 In the later days of the *piskŭn*, the man who brought the buffalo went to them on horseback, riding a white horse. **1892** G. B. GRINNELL *Blackfoot Lodge Tales* (1893) 230 The pis'kuns of the Sik'-si-kau, or Blackfoot tribe, differed in some particulars from those constructed by the Bloods and the Piegans, who live further to the south, nearer to the mountains, and so in a country which is rougher and more broken. The Sik'-si-kan built their pis'kuns like the Crees, on level ground and usually near timber. A large pen or corral was made of heavy logs about eight feet high. On the side where the wings of the chute come together, a bridge, or causeway, was built, sloping gently up from the prairie to the walls of the corral, which at this point were cut away to the height of the bridge above the ground,—here about four feet,—so that the animals running up the causeway could jump down into the corral. **1929** E. D. BRANCH *Hunting of Buffalo* ii. 35 The *piskun* was surer and safer than the human trap; it was an enclosed pen into which the buffalo were driven. **1943** J. K. HOWARD *Montana* 23 Often buffalo were driven over cliffs, the 'buffalo runs' or 'pishkuns' under which Montanans still find rich hoards of arrowheads and other Indian implements. **1949** *Jrnl. Washington Acad. Sci.* XXXIX. 357/2 The North Blackfoot, who hunted to a considerable extent on relatively level ground, built their piskun like that of the Cree Indians in the form of a corral with rising timbered causeway leading up to the entrance of the corral from which there was a sheer drop of about 4 feet into the corral. The Piegan and Blood, living in more broken country nearer the mountains, drove the bison over cliffs. *Ibid.* 360/1 We can date the last bison drive of the Blackfoot at about the year 1872. This was a full century after Mathew Cocking's first description of the use of the piskun by Indians of the northwestern plains. **1952** J. K. HOWARD *Strange Empire* 294 Nevertheless some native methods of killing buffalo were wasteful. Such were the *piskuns* and pounds, use of which, however, was generally abandoned by the Indians some time before the herds disappeared.

pisle, obs. f. PIZZLE.

pismire ('pɪsmaɪə(r)). *Obs.* exc. *dial.* Forms: α. 4–5 pissemyre, 5 pysmire, pyse-myer, (spissemire), 5–6 pysmyre, 6 pismyr, pissemyer, 6–7 pismier, 5– pismire. β. 5–6 pysse-, pysmere, 6 pismeere, -mer, pyse-, pyssemer, pysse-, pissemare, pysmar, -marie, 7 pisimer, pismere. γ. 5 pismoure, pyssmowre. [ME. *pissemyre, pissemire*, etc., f. PISS + MIRE² ant; from the urinous smell of an anthill. So early mod.Du. *pismiere* ant (Kilian). In the β forms the second element is obscured; in the γ forms it is a different word, ME. MAUR ant, from Norse.]

An ant.

(Cf. the similar names for the ant, Fris. *pis-imme, pis-emme*, LG. *miegemke*, Norw. *migemaur* (LG. *miegen*, Norw. *miga* = L. *mingĕre*), early mod.Du. *mierseycke* (*seycke* urine), Fin. *kusiainen* (*kusi* urine). Cf. also PISS-ANT.)

α. *c* **1386** CHAUCER *Sompn. T.* 118 He is as angry as a pissemyre, Though þat he haue al that he kan desire. **1388** WYCLIF *Prov.* vi. 6 O! thou slowe man, go to the amte [*gloss* ether pissemyre, *v.rr.* spissemire, pismire]. *c* **1400** MAUNDEV. (Roxb.) xxxiii. 149 In þis ile..er grete hilles of gold, þe whilk pissemyres kepez bisily and pures þe gold... Þase pissemyres er als grete as hundes er here. **1560** BIBLE (Genev.) *Prov.* vi. 6 Goe to the pismire, o sluggard. **1575** TURBERV. *Venerie* 173 These pissemyers..will driue them out. **1617** R. FENTON *Treat. Ch. Rome* 100 Sent..by Solomon to the Conies and Pismiers for wisedome and prouidence. **1676** HALE *Contempl.* I. 468, I have seen a Republick of Pismires with great circumspection choosing the seat of their Residence, and every one carrying his Egg and Provisions to their common Store-house. **1827** HOOD *Mids. Fairies* lv, The pismire's care to garner up his wheat. **1903** *Eng. Dial. Dict.* (dial. forms), Pishmire, pissimire, pushmire.

β. *c* **1440** *Promp. Parv.* 402/1 Pysmere, *formica*. *c* **1440** *Gesta Rom.* liii. 372 (Add. MS.) Pissemers in somere are besy, and rennyn faste aboute. **1547** BOORDE *Brev. Health* clxi. 58 Amytes, or Pysmars, or Antes. **1555** EDEN *Decades* 139 Pyssemares swarmynge owte of an ante hyll. **1596** NASHE *Saffron Walden* 52 Cyphers or round oos, lyke pismeeres egges. **1623** in C. Butler *Fem. Mon.* Ad Authorem 17 That the Pismere and these Hony-flies Instruct us better to Philosophize. **1634–5** BRERETON *Trav.* (Chetham Soc.) 73 Eggs..hatched under an hen, fed with pisimers. **1903** *Eng. Dial. Dict.* (dial. forms), Pishamer, pishemeer, pis(s)imer, pissamer, pissmare, -mere.

γ. *a* **1400** *Relig. Pieces fr. Thornton MS.* (1867) 21 Mare vs availes till oure ensampill..þe werkes of þe pyssmowre þan dose þe strenghe of þe lyone. **1483** *Cath. Angl.* 281/2 A Pismoure, *formica*. **1903** *Eng. Dial. Dict.*, Pissamoor, pisamoor, pissymoor, pishmoor, pissemyore, pissy-, pismyour (all north. and n.w.).

b. *fig.* Applied contemptuously to a person.

1569 J. SANFORD tr. *Agrippa's Van. Artes* 13 b, The pismers of Mirmidones. **1653** J. HALL *Paradoxes* 50 Wee poore pismires that crawle upon this hill. **1790** GIBBON *Decl. & F.* lxv. XII. 18 Thou art no more than a pismire. **1818** SCOTT *Hrt. Midl.* xviii, To rid the land of the swarm of Arminian caterpillars, Socinian pismires, and deistical Miss Katies, that have ascended out of the bottomless pit.

c. *attrib.* and *Comb.*, as ***pismire-eater, -egg, -fly, -hill*** (= ANT-EATER, -EGG, -FLY, -HILL). In quot. 1668 = resembling the crawling motion of ants.

c **1440** *Promp. Parv.* 402/1 Pysmeryshylle, *formicarium*. **1483** *Cath. Angl.* 281/2 A Pismoure hylle, *formicecarium*. **1527** ANDREW *Brunswyke's Distyll. Waters* B ij b, A flatte..botell of glas..ful of roses or other floures, or pyssemer eggys. **1668** CULPEPPER & COLE *Barthol. Anat.* 369 That..the pulse of the arteries is caused by the Impulse of Blood, the waving, creeping, pismire pulses seem to show. **1704** tr. *Nieuhof's Brazil* in Churchill *Voy.* II. 19 The pismire-eater is thus called because he feeds upon..pismires. **1799** G. SMITH *Laboratory* II. 311 The Pismire-fly. **1821** CLARE *Vill. Minstr.* I. 203 Where the pismire hills abound.

†**pismire,** obs. (illit.) f. BISMAR, a steelyard.

1701 BRAND *Descr. Orkney* 28 They not useing Peck and Firlot, but in stead thereof, weigh their Corns on Pismires or Pundlers.

Pismo ('pɪzməʊ). Also pismo. The name of *Pismo* Beach, California, used *attrib.* in **Pismo clam,** a large, thick-shelled, edible clam, *Tivela stultorum*, belonging to the family Veneridæ and found on the south-west coast of North America.

1913 *Calif. Fish & Game Comm. Fish Bull.* I. 27 The Pismo clam..flourishes in open sandy beaches. **1923** *Ibid.* VII. 5 Commercially the Pismo clam ranks first in importance in California among clams and third among all the mollusks. **1949** *Natural Hist.* June 252/1 Five minutes of barefoot beach scratching had uncovered half a sack of four-inch Pismo clams. **1970** B. H. MCCONNAUGHEY *Introd. Marine Biol.* viii. 227/2 A large, heavy-shelled clam, the pismo clam, occurs on California beaches at the lowest intertidal and subtidal levels.

[**pisnet, puisnet.** Errors for PINSNET.

[**1583** STUBBES *Anat. Abus.* I. (1879) 57 They haue corked shooes, pisnets, and fine pantofles.] Quoted in **1834** PLANCHÉ *Hist. Brit. Costume* 261 as 'puisnets', and thence copied in **1860** FAIRHOLT *Costume* Gloss. s.v. *Boots*. **1860** *Ibid.* Gloss., *Pisnets*, a species of shoe, mentioned by Stubbes. Hence **1881** OGILVIE (Annandale), Pisnet, Puisnet. **1890** *Century Dict.*, Pisnet.]

pisolite ('pɪzəlaɪt, 'paɪsə-). *Min.* Also 8 -lithe. [ad. mod.L. *pisolith-us*, f. Gr. πίσο-ς, -ον, pea + -LITE. So F. *pisolithe*.] **a.** = PEA-STONE.

1868 DANA *Min.* (ed. 5) 679 Pisolite..consists of concretions as large often as a small pea. **1931** S. J. SHAND *Study of Rocks* xi. 153 Oolite and pisolite are limestones built up of little spheroidal bodies resembling the roe of fishes or heaps of peas. **1962** READ & WATSON *Introd. Geol.* I. v. 266 Other chemical limestones are not of much account; they include deposits from calcareous springs, such as pisolite, tufa and travertine.

attrib. **1816** W. SMITH *Strata Ident.* 19 The Pisolite Freestone beneath [the Coral Rag] is softer. **1884** LYELL *Elem. Geol.* (ed. 4) 12 Pisolite limestone has the oolitic grains of considerable size.

b. Applied to an individual grain of this similar to an oolith but larger (in mod. use applied to grains of diameter 2 mm. or more).

1708 *Phil. Trans.* XXVI. 79 *Pisolithus*, the Pisolite, or Gland. **1788** [see OOLITH]. **1851** RICHARDSON *Geol.* vi. (1855) 158 Occasionally each pisolite encloses in its centre a grain of foreign substance. **1893** *Q. Jrnl. Geol. Soc.* XLIX. 127 The series for some distance above the typical Pea-grit ..contains here and there aggregations of brown pisolites. **1925** *Nat. Geogr. Mag.* XLVIII. 313 These spherical bodies are known to geologists as pisolites and to jewelers as cave pearls. **1956** E. W. HEINRICH *Microsc. Petrogr.* v. 153 The limonite may be in spongy masses..or in pisolites and concretionary masses. **1974** *Encycl. Brit. Macropædia* XVI. 466/2 Pisolites are similar to oolites and range from two to about ten millimetres (0·4 inch) in diameter.

pisolith ('pɪzəʊ-, 'paɪsəʊlɪθ). *Petrol.* Also †-lithe. [f. as PISOLITE: see -LITH.] = PISOLITE b.

1799 HATCHETT in *Phil. Trans.* LXXXIX. 320 The globular calcareous concretions, found at Carlsbad and other places, called Pisolithes. **1926** G. W. TYRRELL *Princ. Petrol.* xiii. 227 Pisoliths are essentially similar to ooliths, but reach much larger sizes, and are generally found in residual deposits. **1938** M. BLACK *Hatch & Rastall's Petrol. Sedimentary Rocks* (ed. 3) viii. 176 Cave pearls are pisoliths, sometimes of large size, found in the underground waters of limestone caves. **1947** *Jrnl. Sedimentary Petrol.* XVII. 39 (*heading*) Pisoliths and ooliths from some Australian caves and mines. *Ibid.* 43/1 In pools full of pisoliths and ooliths, the larger ones (around 20 mm. long) occur at the top. **1975** *Nature* 20 Nov. 206/1 It lies under a thin but persistent weathered horizon which has a patchy distribution and is characterised by ferruginous pisoliths.

Hence **piso'lithic** *a.*

1863 SULLIVAN & O'REILLY *Notes Geol. & Mineral. of Santander & Madrid* I. iv. 91 The hydrocarbonate of zinc also occurs perfectly globular, some specimens being beautifully pisolithic. **1947** *Jrnl. Sedimentary Petrol.* XVII. 39 Calcareous concretions, principally of the pisolithic type.

pisolitic (pɪzəʊ'lɪtɪk, paɪsəʊ-), *a.* [f. PISOLITE + -IC. So F. *pisolithique*.] Of the nature of, consisting of, or resembling pisolite.

1830 LYELL *Princ. Geol.* I. 351 Half consolidated tuffs..filled with small pisolitic globules. **1851** RICHARDSON *Geol.* vi. (1855) 157 The pisolitic structure in certain stones. **1863** SPEKE *Discov. Nile* 31 Pisolitic limestone, in which marine fossils were observable.

piss (pɪs), *v.* Not now in polite use. Forms: α. 3–7 pisse, 4 pis, 4–6 pyss(e, 6– piss; β. 5 pysch-yn, 6 *Sc.* pisch(e, 6–8 *Sc.* pish. [ME. *piss-en*, a. OF. *piss-ier* (12th c. in Hatz.-Darm.), F. *piss-er* (Picard *picher*) = Pr. *pissar* (mod. *pichá*, Diez), Cat. *pixar*, Rhæt. *pischar*, It. *pisciare*, Rom. *pisà*; origin uncertain; the OF. and It. forms are not referable to any single Romanic type, and are prob. onomatopœic. From French the word has also passed (orig. as a euphemism) into the Teutonic langs.: OFris. *pissia* (Diez), MDu., MLG., 16th c. Ger. *pissen*, Da. *pisse*, Sw., Norw., Icel. *pissa*: so Welsh *piso*, *pisio*.

For various conjectures as to the origin of the Romanic word, see Diez, Körting No. 7195, Ulrich in *Romania* IX. 117; cf. also Scheler, Littré, s.v.]

1. a. *intr.* To discharge urine, urinate, make water.

c **1290** *S. Eng. Leg.* I. 45/381 ȝwane he wolde pisse. *c* **1330** R. BRUNNE *Chron.* (1810) 328 Þei salle him ilkone bete him þat he pis. *c* **1440** *Promp. Parv.* 402/1 Pyssyn, or pyschyn, *mingo*. **1508** DUNBAR *Tua Mariit Wemen* 187 As dotit dog..liftis his leg apon loft, thoght he nought list pische. **1594** NASHE *Unfort. Trav.* 56, I was at Pontius Pilates house [in Rome] and pist against it. **1687** DRYDEN *Hind & P.* III. 159 The wanton boyes wou'd piss upon your grave. **1785** BURNS *Holy Willie's Pr.* xv. **1870** [see 3].

b. *transf.*, and in various allusive and proverbial uses; *spec.* to be raining heavily. ***to piss in (a person's) pocket*** (Austral.), to ingratiate oneself with, be on very familiar terms with.

1602 *2nd Pt. Return fr. Parnass.* I. ii. (Arb.) 12 What Monsier Kynsader, lifting vp your legge and pissing against the world. **1642** G. TORRIANO *Sel. Italian Proverbs* 19 He who pisseth against the wind, wetteth his shirt. **1668** R. L'ESTRANGE *Vis. Quev.* (1708) 36 Money will make the Pot boyl, though the Devil Piss in the Fire. **1670** J. RAY *Coll. Eng. Proverbs* 131 Chi piscia contra il vento si bagna la commiscia, *Ital.* He that pisseth against the wind, wets his shirt. It is to a mans own prejudice, to strive against the stream. **1700** T. BROWN *Amusem. Ser. & Com.* 98 There are some Quacks as Honest Fellows as you would desire to Piss upon. **1720** T. GORDON *Cordial Low Spirits* 72 They cannot impose upon their Prince, nor piss upon the laws. *a* **1734** NORTH *Exam.* I. ii. §78 (1740) 70 So strangely did Papist and Fanatic, or..the Anticourt Party, p—s in a Quill; agreeing in all Things that tended to create Troubles and Disturbances. **1902** FARMER & HENLEY *Slang.* V. 215/2 'Piss not against the wind', or 'He that pisseth against the wind wets his shirt'. **1962** J. BALDWIN *Another Country* I. ii. 94 Christ, it's pissing out there! **1967** K. TENNANT *Tell Morning This* xxx. 283 Soon's they knew you was in with Numismata, they all want to piss in your pocket. **1968** H. C. RAE *Few Small Bones* II. i. 73 Went camping up north..but it pissed the whole time. Come to think of it, I was pretty pissed the whole time myself. **1969** C. BRAY *Blossom like Rose* xii. 165, I don't mean to piss in yer pockets, but youse blokes are all right. **1970** E. PACE *Saberlegs* (1971) vi. 58 Putting words on newspaper pages was, if anything, even more ephemeral than intelligence-gathering. As they used to say at Dartmouth, it was all 'pissing in the wind'. **1971** F. HARDY *Outcasts of Foolgaran* 77, I appeared before him many a time when I worked for the Union. If we piss in his pocket, he's just as apt to come our way. **1973** L. SNELLING *Heresy* I. vii. 52 I'd like to buy it, but frankly I think you're pissing against the wind... He's a pretty cunning little bugger. **1977** J. WAINWRIGHT *Nest of Rats* I. viii. 60 How much time?.. Don't make it hours—otherwise you're pissing in the wind.

c. Const. with various adverbs: ***to piss about***, to fool or mess about; to potter about; ***to piss down***, to rain heavily; ***to piss off***, to go away, depart.

1950 G. WILSON *Brave Company* 172 It fairly pissed down on top of me. **1958** F. NORMAN *Bang to Rights* 72 So what, I wish you'd piss off. **1960** H. PINTER *Caretaker* I. 14 Piss off, he said... If you don't piss off, he says, I'll kick you all the way to the gate. **1961** PARTRIDGE *Dict. Slang* Suppl. 1223/2 *Piss about*, to potter; fritter one's time away; to stall for time. **1970** T. LEWIS *Jack's Return Home* 179 Are you coming in? Or do we piss about all day? **1971** W. J. BURLEY *Guilt Edged* viii. 138 Most of yesterday it was pissing down with rain. **1971** B. W. ALDISS *Soldier Erect* 50 I'll have a drink when I feel like it, and not before. You two piss off if you're so bloody thirsty! **1972** R. QUILTY *Tenth Session* 19 Pissing down too, and one o'clock in the morning. **1974** 'J. FRASER' *Wreath of Lords & Ladies* vii. 57 Are we going to piss off home or sit here blabbering all night? **1975** *Sunday Times* (Colour Suppl.) 23 Feb. 26/3 The manager who tried to discipline a man caught with an illicit can of tea was told to piss off. **1977** J. THOMSON *Case Closed* ii. 25 Tucker wouldn't come..not with it pissing down with rain. **1977** M. DRABBLE *Ice Age* I. 59 Oh piss off, Mum, Maureen would reply, amiably.

2. a. *trans.* To discharge as or with the urine.

1362 LANGL. *P. Pl.* A. v. 192 He [Gloton] pissede a potel in a *pater-noster* while. *c* **1375** *St. Augustin* 1402 in Horstm. *Altengl. Leg.* (1878) 85/2 Þe chyld, iwis, A gret stone al out dude pis And was al hol of þat seknes. *c* **1400** *Lanfranc's Cirurg.* 62 Til þat he pisse blood. **1623** HART *Arraignm. Ur.* I. 1 Urine is that which is pissed.

b. *transf.* and *fig.* in various uses.

† ***to piss*** (money, etc.) ***against*** or ***on the wall***: to squander or waste it. ***to piss away***, to squander. ***to piss*** one's ***grease*** or ***tallow***: said of deer becoming lean in rutting-time; hence *transf.*

c **1450** *M.E. Med. Bk.* (Heinrich) 232 Take talow of an hert, suche as he pysseþ by twene two seynt mary dayes. **1471** RIPLEY *Comp. Alch.* v. xxxi. in Ashm. *Theatr. Chem. Brit.* (1652) 155 But as for Mony yt ys pyssyd on the walls. **1551** ROBINSON tr. *More's Utop.* (1895) 197. **1598** SHAKS. *Merry W.* v. v. 16. **1602** *2nd Pt. Return fr. Parnass.* III. ii. (Arb.) 40 They are pestilent fellowes, they speake nothing but bodkins, and pisse vinegar. **1680** CROWNE *Misery Civil War* I. i, I command the conduits all piss Claret. **1694** MOTTEUX *Rabelais* v. xxviii. (1737) 132 He's nothing but Skin and Bones; he has piss'd his Tallow. **1948** D. BALLANTYNE *Cunninghams* 211 Have to stop pissing away the hard-earned cash though. **1972** P. KNAPP *Berengaria Exchange* 18 Dinty had built up a 'pretty good roll'. But as he now says with a shrug, 'I pissed it all away in Paris.' **1975** *Time* 4 Aug. 61/2 'This company is doing a good business,' he says. 'If we can only stop pissing away the profits.'

3. a. To urinate upon or in, to wet with urine (= BEPISS); to put *out* or extinguish (fire) in this way. Also *refl.*

1362 LANGL. *P. Pl.* A. VII. 143 A Brutiner, a braggere, a bostede him alse, And bad go pisse him with his plouh [B. VI. 157 bad hym go pissen]. *c* **1560** A. SCOTT *Poems* (S.T.S.) ii. 87 The fyre wes pischt out. **1593** *Pass. Morrice* (1876) 80 Being as often readie to pisse my breeche. **1713** SWIFT *Elegy on Partridge*, Whom roguish boys.. Torment by pissing out their lights. **1870** tr. *Trousseau's Lect. Clin. Med.* III. 478 Children, who piss their beds dreaming that they are pissing against a wall. **1951** PARTRIDGE *Dict. Slang.* (ed. 4) 1136/2 Piss oneself laughing. **1969** N. COHN *AWopBopaLooBop* (1970) ix. 85 The Twist ballooned almost instantaneously from a fad to an industry. The papers pissed themselves. Big money got invested. **1976** A. WHITE *Long Silence* xviii. 147 Otto pissed himself with fear. **1978** J. BARNETT *Head of Force* xv. 146 You've pissed yourself.. you dirty bastard.

b. *to piss off*, to annoy, irritate, put off, make 'fed up' or depressed (see also PISSED *ppl. a.* 2); *to piss up*, to spoil, ruin, mess up.

1937 E. POUND *Fifth Decad of Cantos* I. 49 Talleyrand stank with shanker And hell pissed up Metternich. **1968** *Southerly* XXVIII. 275 She prefers British eccentrics because they don't expect to be liked. 'I mean,' she says, 'it's their way of pissing people off, isn't it?' **1970** *It* 27 Feb.–13 Mar. 14/1 Wasn't it incredible? I just didn't believe it!.. They really piss me off. **1971** B. MALAMUD *Tenants* 178 You ought to burn up both of these yourself, Willie, on account of this cat stole your white bitch and pissed up your black book. **1972** *Last Whole Earth Catalog* (Portola Inst.) 9/3 It did piss me off when the dealer let me go for only five hundred and fifty dollars. **1974** K. C. CONSTANTINE *Blank Page* 148, I still think it'd piss him off. **1976** 'D. CRAIG' *Faith, Hope & Death* xvii. 118 Did I let them just unload it because they pissed up a job?.. This was my money that had been lifted. **1977** *Rolling Stone* 16 June 52/2 She may not want to be called 'Queen', but only because she considers herself too young, because she is not out to piss off Aretha Franklin any more than she already has.

piss (pɪs), *sb.* Not now in polite use. Forms: α. 4–6 pysse, 4–7 pisse, 5–6 pys, 6 pyse, 7– piss. β. 5 pysche. [f. PISS *v.* So F. *pisse* (Cotgr. 1611); cf. also MDu., LG. *pisse*, Du. *pis.*] **1.** Urine, 'water'. Also, the action or an act of urinating. †*a rod in piss*: see ROD, and cf. PICKLE *sb.*[1] 1 b.

c **1386** CHAUCER *Wife's Prol.* 729 How Xantippa caste pisse vp-on his heed. **1388** WYCLIF *2 Kings* xviii. 27 Thei ete her toordis, and drynke her pisse [1382 vryne] with 3ou. *c* **1440** *Promp. Parv.* 402/1 Pysse, or pysche, *urina, minctura.* **1600** J. PORY tr. *Leo's Africa* II. 56 Lothsome and intolerable stench of pisse, and of goates dung. *a* **1704** T. BROWN *Table Talk* in *Collect. Poems* 122 What Miracles.. were wrought by Cows Piss, and the Cold Bath? **1916** JOYCE *Portrait of Artist* ii. 96 That is horse piss and rotted straw, he thought. It is a good odour to breathe. **1926** T. E. LAWRENCE *Seven Pillars* (1935) VI. lxxviii. 434 Mifleh brought up the youngest lads of the party, and had them spray the wounds with their piss, as a rude antiseptic. **1974** P. LARKIN *High Windows* 32 Groping back to bed after a piss. **1976** *Listener* 18 Mar. 344/1 The words [in a radio play].. were punctuated with belches, giggles, mutterings, reflective hesitations, the repetition of good jokes, and a wonderfully realistic-sounding piss. **1979** N. FREELING *Widow* iii. 11 The hallway smelt... Piss, cabbage, stale sweat.

2. In various fig. phrases, as ***on the piss***, engaged in a bout of heavy drinking; ***take the piss*** (***out of***), to make fun (of), to 'take the mickey' (out of); ***piss and wind***, empty talk, bombast; ***piss and vinegar***, energy, aggression; also *attrib.*

1922 JOYCE *Ulysses* 322 All wind and piss like a tanyard cat. **1942** BERREY & VAN DEN BARK *Amer. Thes. Slang* §240/2 *Animation; spirit; vim*,.. piss and vinegar. **1942** *Horizon* Aug. 124 Buggered if I know when he'll be back. Gone on the piss, I shouldn't wonder. **1945** *Penguin New Writing* XXVI. 49 The corporal.. sat back in his corner looking a little offended. He thought I was taking the piss. **1958** F. NORMAN *Bang to Rights* 116 This only made us take the piss out of him the more. **1961** PARTRIDGE *Dict. Slang* Suppl. 1223/2 *Piss and wind*, as in 'He's all piss and wind!' Empty talk; unsubstantiated boast(s). **1962** E. AMBLER *Light of Day* xii. 244 These policemen are all piss and wind anyway. **1966** M. SPILLANE *Death Dealers* i. 17 Remember the old days, Tiger? You were young and fast and strong. Full of piss and vinegar. **1968** 'P. ALDING' *Circle of Danger* iii. 20 Him not turning up may just mean he's been on the piss. **1969** *Guardian* 13 Feb. 22/4 Mr Eric Lubbock, the Liberal MP for Orpington.. said: '.. I have heard nothing but piss and wind.' **1971** B. W. ALDISS *Soldier Erect* 49 'Come on, Wally, like—I don't think you ought to take the piss out of the poor sod!' Geordie said. 'He's got his living to earn.' **1974** *Observer* 30 June 22/8 And I don't binge. If I'd gone on the piss every time I missed a cut [*sc.* failed to qualify in a golf tournament] I'd be a raging alcoholic by now. **1975** J. SYMONS *Three Pipe Problem* xviii. 190 You like to take the piss out of me, don't you? **1976** J. O'CONNOR *Eleventh Commandment* xiv. 179, I was very happy and went on the piss. **1976** R. PERRY *One Good Death* iv. 66 The sarcasm left Collins unmoved. He knew that Pawson was in one of his piss and vinegar moods. **1978** R. BUSBY *Garvey's Code* xi. 138 Jacko's not such a bad bloke. Full of piss and vinegar and ready to jump for any bugger with braid on his hat. **1978** R. HILL *Pinch of Snuff* xiv. 145 When Hope replied 'He's a Hungarian' he thought at first he was taking the piss. Wield seemed prepared to accept this as a serious contribution, however.

3. *Comb.* **piss artist**, a glib person; a person who messes about; a drunkard; †**piss-bowl** = PISS-POT; **piss-bucket**, a bucket for urinating in; **piss-burnt** *a.*, stained or damaged with or as with urine, red-brown; **piss-cutter** *N. Amer.*, someone or something excellent; a clever or crafty person; (see also quot. 1956); **piss-head**, a drunkard; **piss-hole**, (*a*) hole made by urine; (*b*) an unpleasant place; **piss-house**, an outside water closet; a lavatory; also *fig.* (see quots. 1931, 1942); **piss-proud** *a.*, having an erection attributed to a full bladder, esp. upon awakening; **piss-take**, a parody, a send-up (see sense 2); also **piss-taker**, **piss-taking**; **piss-tin**, a tin for urinating in; **piss-weed**, some species of *Androsace*.

1975 *Peace News* 11 July 11/1 Most donors seem to be pretty careful. The lists of who's been given money seem to bear this out—it's usually the right-on projects which have most and the con merchants and *piss artists often go without. **1977** *Sounds* 9 July 36/4, I am appealing to anybody who knows John and Murdoch of Erkshire Scotland. You know, those piss-artists, protozoans who wrote that letter about a rock band classification. **1977** *Custom Car* Nov. 5/2, I refer to the auto/driver self-destruct mechanism know as 'booze'. A piss artist behind the wheel of a 1935 Austin Seven was a killer. **1977** *Private Eye* 10 Nov. 22/1 (Advt.), Malcolm Derek Winn. Photographer, traveller, piss-artist. Whereabouts known? Box 1215. **1542** UDALL *Erasm. Apoph.* 23 b, She.. powred downe a *pisse bolle vpon hym out of a wyndoore. **1973** J. SEABROOK *Loneliness* 104 The workhouses were terrible places. At Newark, you slept on a stone floor, and in the middle there was a *piss-bucket. **1565** *K. Daryus* (Brandl) 418 Gyt thee away, thou *pys burnde Cokolde. **1742** FIELDING *J. Andrews* III. xii, A long piss-burnt beard. **1942** BERREY & VAN DEN BARK *Amer. Thes. Slang* §29/2 *Something excellent*, ..*piss-cutter. *Ibid.* §432/2 *Capable person; expert*,.. piss-cutter. **1956** *Amer. Speech* XXXI. 192 His [*sc.* a marine's] garrison cap is a *pisscutter* (also used as a cynical description, i.e., 'He's a pisscutter, he is!'). **1968** E. R. BUCKLER *Ox Bells & Fireflies* xv. 206 Gus Jordan's got a new rowboat. It's a real pisscutter! **1974** D. SEARS *Lark in Clear Air* viii. 97 I'd send some [beer] along with you but that old piss-cutter of a Heeney would drink'm all before you cut the froth on the first bottle. **1977** *Maledicta* Summer 13 A clever person is sometimes called a piss-cutter. **1961** PARTRIDGE *Dict. Slang* Suppl. 1223/2 **Piss-head*, an habitually heavy drinker. **1968** *Landfall* XXII. 50 My old man was a piss-head too. *c* **1932** DYLAN THOMAS *Lett.* (1966) 4 My eyes are two *piss-holes in the sand. **1973** R. BUSBY *Pattern of Violence* ii. 24 'How's tricks, Lucky?'.. 'Be better when I'm out of this piss hole—no offence, gents.' **1974** R. GADNEY *Something Worth Fighting For* iv. 33 Let's get out of this pisshole. **1931** *Amer. Speech* VII. 112 **Piss-house*, n., the police station. **1942** BERREY & VAN DEN BARK *Amer. Thes. Slang* §84/11 *Toilet*,.. piss-house. *Ibid.* §466/10 *Police station or jail*,.. pisshouse. **1973** W. H. CANAWAY *Harry doing Good* II. v. 187 Come outside for a leak. Blow your noses on the way to the piss-house. **1974** H. MACINNES *Climb to Lost World* xi. 199 Next morning the Wall was wetter than ever... 'Never seen it so wet here—what do you think?' 'Looks like a piss-house wall to me.' **1788** GROSE *Dict. Vulg. T.* (ed. 2), **Piss-proud*, having a false erection. That old fellow thought he had an erection, but his —— was only piss-proud; said of any old fellow who marries a young wife. **1868** *Index Expurgatorius of Martial* 88 Maevius who while sleeping only gets A piss-proud stand that melts away on waking. **1932** AUDEN *Orators* III. 104 That piss-proud prophet. **1977** *Spare Rib* July 49/1 It's a bit of a *pisstake, sending up the whole bi-sexuality thing. **1976** *New Society* 20 May 408/2 'What's funny about a jeweller?.. He's a *piss taker. **1971** *It* 9–23 Sept. 21/1 The subjects for *piss-taking run the gamut from the chairboard executive's life.. to the Amerikanjudicial system. **1974** H. MACINNES *Climb to Lost World* vii. 104 If it was imperative, I used my *piss-tin, conveniently placed at arm's reach on the mud. **1713** PETIVER in *Phil. Trans.* XXVIII. 203 Small Aleppo *Piss-weed, Androsace Alepensis parva.

4. Used quasi-adverbially in sense 'very, excessively, to an extremely undesirable degree', as ***piss-elegant***, ***-poor***, ***-rotten***, ***-wet***, etc., adjs.

1940 E. POUND *Cantos* lxix. 174 Bingham, Carrol of Carrolton Gone piss-rotten for Hamilton Cabot, Fisher Ames [etc.]. **1946** (*reported in oral use by Prof. A. L. Hench*) This is a piss-poor outfit. My job is a piss-poor one. **1957** J. KEROUAC *On Road* (1958) 207 A pisspoor bum from Larimer Street. **1970** J. HANSEN *Fadeout* viii. 68 Feeling sorry for a man's a piss-poor reason to marry him. **1972** R. MAUGHAN *Escape from Shadows* iv. 186 But I feel out of place here, it's too piss-elegant. **1972** J. BROWN *Chancer* v. 64 'This beer,' I said, 'it's piss-poor.' **1973** *Amer. Speech* 1970 XLV. 58 *Piss-elegant*, pretentious, ostentatious, egotistical (used with reference to male homosexuals). **1973** *Nation Rev.* (Melbourne) 24–30 Aug. 1432/1, I think privately that they look in pisspoor condition; but the spirited bidding rockets the price up to $2.50 in no time. **1974** J. ANTHOINE in H. MacInnes *Climb to Lost World* x. 179 He got piss wet in that bloody channel [on a rock face]. *Ibid.* xi. 202 'Here we are,' I said to Joe. 'On a piss-wet cliff and there's no bloody water for a brew!' **1977** *Gay News* 24 Mar. 21/2 The Lovely Ladies from South America were so piss-elegant they could hardly lift their feet off the ground. **1977** *N.Y. Rev. Bks.* 4 Aug. 35/4 They manufacture piss-chic cosmetics.

pissabed ('pɪsəbɛd). [f. PISS *v.* + ABED, from its diuretic property. So F. *pissenlit* dandelion (1545).]

1. a. A name for the dandelion.

1597 GERARDE *Herbal* II. xxviii. 223 The flowers of Dandelion or Pisse-abed. **1636** HEYWOOD *Loves Mistris* I. Wks. 1874 V. 97 Garlands.. Of Blew bottles, and yellow pissabeds That grew amongst the Wheate. **1788** WOLCOTT (P. Pindar) *Peter's Proph.* Wks. 1792 III. 79 Through him each trifle-hunter that can bring A grub, a weed, a moth, a beetle's wing, Shall to a Fellow's dignity succeed! Witness Lord Chatham and his piss-a-bed! **1822–34** *Good's Study Med.* (ed. 4) IV. 349 It possesses unquestionably diuretic powers, and hence, indeed, its vulgar name of piss-a-bed. **1953** S. BECKETT *Watt* III. 154 Of flowers there was no trace, save of the flowers that plant themselves, or never die, or die only after many seasons, strangled by the rank grass. The chief of these was the pissabed. **1974** G. GRIGSON *Dict. Eng. Plant Names* 169 Pissabed (*Taraxacum officinale*, Dandelion)... The name has too wide a currency to be derived from Gerard's *Herbal*.

†**b.** Applied to the buttercup. *Obs. rare.*

1640 PARKINSON *Theat. Bot.* Index, *Pisseabed*.. is also Crowfoote.

2. Name for the SEA-HARE, *Aplysia*, a slug-like mollusc, which discharges a violet fluid when touched. *Obs.* exc. *dial.*

1758 *Phil. Trans.* L. 586 Some call them piss a beds, some sea-cats.

3. Chiefly *slang.* A bed-wetter; also *attrib.*, as an abusive epithet.

1643 in *County Court Rec. Accomack-Northampton, Va.* (1973) 292 Thou pissa bedd Jade. **1922** JOYCE *Ulysses* 395 Pope Peter's but a pissabed. **1959** R. FULLER *Ruined Boys* 195 He beat me at the beginning of term for peeing my bed. .. Now he thinks of me as a pissabed. **1972** R. A. WILSON *Playboy's Bk. Forbidden Words* 229 *Piss-a-bed*, a lazy fellow, one who pisses in bed because he's too lethargic to walk to the john.

‖**pissaladière** (pisaladjɛr). Also **pissaladiera**. [Fr.: Provençal dial. *pissaladiero* f. *pissala* salt fish.] A Provençal open tart similar to pizza, usu. cooked with onions, anchovies, and black olives.

1931 A. DE CROZE *What to eat & drink in France* xv. 131 La Pissaladiera (a tart well sprinkled with olive oil, filled with sweet onions browned in oil, and pissala—salted whitebait—and baked). **1951** G. MAUROIS *Cooking with French Touch* iii. 66 Another favorite hors d'œuvre in the region of Nice is the *pissaladiera.* **1960** E. CAMPBELL *Encycl. World Cookery* 154 *Pissaladière*.. dough.. onions.. black olives.. anchovy fillets. **1960** E. DAVID *French Provincial Cooking* 208 The *pissaladière* is a substantial dish of bread dough spread with onions, anchovies, black olives, and sometimes tomatoes. **1966** P. V. PRICE *France* 276 Pissaladiera. A Nice speciality, and a version of Italian pizza —an open tart with onions, anchovies and black olives, sometimes with tomatoes. **1970** SIMON & HOWE *Dict. Gastron.* 302/2 The filling is covered with a pattern of anchovy fillets and stoned black olives and the *pissaladière* is baked in a hot oven. **1977** *N.Y. Rev. Bks.* 8 Dec. 18/3 Hurray for the Cornish pasty rather than Olney's *pissaladière.*

pissan, obs. form of PISANG.

pissan(e, pissand, var. PISANE *Obs.*

pissance, -ans, pissant, obs. Sc. ff. PUISSANCE, PUISSANT.

'piss-,ant. Also pissant, piss ant; *dial.* piss-aint. [f. PISS *sb.* + ANT; cf. PISMIRE.] An ant, *spec.* in phrases ***drunk as a piss-ant***, extremely intoxicated; ***game as a piss-ant***, courageous, very brave. Also *transf.*, *fig.*, and *attrib.*

1661 W. K. *Conf. Charact., Meere Polititian* (1860) 27 A multitude of pissants and vermins. **1770** C. CARROLL *Let.* 22 May in *Maryland Hist. Mag.* (1917) XII. 362 It seems the Pissants eat a great deal of Corn in the ground. **1847** W. T. PORTER *Quarter Race in Kentucky* 84 Pourin out of the woods like pissants out of an old log when tother end's afire. **1893** J. SALISBURY *Gloss. Words S.E. Worcestershire* 28 'Er screws 'er waist up till 'er looks like a piss-aint. **1903** 'T. COLLINS' *Such is Life* v. 184 His mind's so much took-up with the tuppenny-thruppenny things... Can't afford to come-out anything but a pis-ant. **1930** J. DOS PASSOS *42nd Parallel* I. 77 I'm drunk as a pissant still. **1935** H. L. DAVIS *Honey in Horn* xvi. 278 Anybody who called owning horses disorderly conduct was a liar and a pissant. **1945** BAKER *Austral. Lang.* iv. 87 Game as a piss ant or drunk as a piss ant. **1946** MEZZROW & WOLFE *Really Blues* (1957) 377 *Piss-ant*, a nobody, small fry. **1949** H. HORNSBY *Lonesome Valley* 185 Why, goddam it to Jesus Christ and back, they're thicker than piss ants. **1961** P. WHITE *Riders in Chariot* xiii. 448 'And on such a day!' she shrieked, looking at the clock. 'I bet that nephew of yours will be full as a piss-ant by eleven!' **1962** R. TULLIPAN *March into Morning* 59 The old white lady makes you as game as a pissant. **1966** *Publ. Amer. Dial. Soc.* 1964 XLII. 21 *Pissant.* Regularly used by men among men; elsewhere it is *ant* only. **1972** F. VAN W. MASON *Roads to Liberty* 169 You stole my skelp, you no-'count piss-ant. **1973** R. HEINLEIN *Time Enough for Love* (1974) 523 His grandfather paused just long enough to look back and say, 'Not on your tintype.. you pusillanimous piss-ant.' **1978** *Guardian Weekly* 25 June 18/4 That pissant [California Governor] Brown. **1979** 'A. HAILEY' *Overload* III. x. 237 All you do now is let off some pissant fire-crackers, then laze around here for a goddam month's vacation.

Hence **'pissant** *v. intr. Austral. slang*, to mess *around.*

1945 BAKER *Austral. Lang.* iv. 87 Someone is pissanting around when he is messing about. **1951** CUSACK & JAMES *Come in Spinner* 307, I been pissantin' round the Northern Territory most of the time. **1959** G. HAMILTON *Summer Glare* 138 Struth, you pissant around like a rooster that's too old.

pissasphalt ('pɪsæsfælt). Also in L. (or Gr.-L.) forms *pissasphalton*, *-um*, *-us*. [ad. L. *pissasphalt-us* (Plin.), a. Gr. πισσάσφαλτος, f. πίσσα pitch + ἄσφαλτος ASPHALT.] A semi-liquid variety of bitumen, mentioned by ancient writers.

1601 HOLLAND *Pliny* II. 183 As touching Pissasphalt, which is of a mixt nature, as if pitch and Bitumen were mingled together. *Ibid.* 557 All these the Greeks doe comprehend vnder one name Pissasphalton. **1705** *Phil. Trans.* XXV. 2106 There were several Kinds of Embalming, viz. with Asphalt or Pissasphalt, with Oyl or Gum of Cedar. **1794** SULLIVAN *View Nat.* II. 107 The pissasphaltum is of a consistency between the common petroleum and the asphaltum, or bitumen of Judea. **1859** WINGFIELD *Tour*

Dalmatia 80 The 'pissasphalt', used anciently by the Egyptians for embalming their dead.

pissed (pɪst), *ppl. a. slang.* [f. PISS *v.* + -ED[1].] **1.** Drunk, intoxicated. Also const. *up.*

1929 F. MANNING *Middle Parts of Fortune* I. iii. 54 On the Saturday they went into Sandby for a spree, and got properly pissed-up there. **1937** PARTRIDGE *Dict. Slang* 635/2 *Pissed*.., (very) drunk. **1939** DYLAN THOMAS *Let.* July (1966) 233 Both, if you ask me, were pissed. **1957** R. MASON *World of Suzie Wong* II. i. 111 Christ, I'm pissed. I'm pissed as a newt. **1958** K. AMIS *I like it Here* i. 13 An uncle of mine went there a year or two ago and was pissed all the time on about ten bob a day. **1971** B. W. ALDISS *Soldier Erect* 10, I thought of the other blokes in 'A' Company... Tonight, they'd all be getting hopelessly pissed or screwing girls. **1973** M. AMIS *Rachel Papers* 38 'Does it make you extra pissed?' Norman handed me my glass, drank his in one, and crouched again to refill it. **1977** *Daily Mirror* 10 May 1/6 Too much German food and too much German wine. I'm pissed.

2. Angry, irritated; fed-up, depressed. Freq. const. *off.*

1946 *Amer. Speech* XXI. 249 *Pissed-off*... This means roughly, fed-up, irritated, depressed. **1948** N. MAILER *Naked & Dead* (1949) I. ii. 25, I bet you even look pissed-off when you're with your wife. **1955** W. GADDIS *Recognitions* II. vii. 646, I been pissed off at him for five years. **1967** B. WRIGHT tr. *Queneau's Between Blue & Blue* i. 11 I'm beginning to get pissed off with your rotten little questions. **1971** B. MALAMUD *Tenants* 78 The writer figured Willie must still be upset, pissed off, else he would never have left it [*sc.* his typewriter] unprotected. **1971** *It* 9–23 Sept. 11/3 I'm pissed at people in the movement who help lay out the line that I'm a millionaire superstar or other shit. **1972** *Screw* 12 June 16/2 Maye, angered by his new but well-deserved reputation as an insecure male, is pissed. **1973** *Observer* (Colour Suppl.) 15 July 13/3 Young people are getting pissed off with this sort of 'rip-off'. **1974** *Saturday Night* (Toronto) Aug. 20/1 Well, Ken got a little pissed off, and stomped off in a huge sulk, until finally the two of them had it out. **1975** R. BURNS *Alvarez Jrnl.* 8 Helen was pissed off when I called. She had plans or something. **1977** *Rolling Stone* 19 May 63/1 Hamilton..says half the Cabinet is pissed at him because things are moving so slow. **1977** *Spare Rib* July 37/2 Everyone was pissed-of and disillusioned with conferences after London.

pissel(l, obs. form of PIZZLE.

pissemare, -mer(e, -myer, -myre, obs. ff. PISMIRE.

'pisser. [f. PISS *v.* + -ER[1].] **1.** One who pisses.

1377 LANGL. *P. Pl.* B. xx. 218 In paltokes & pyked shoes & pisseris longe knyues. **1382** WYCLIF *2 Kings* ix. 8, I schal ..slen fro the hous of Achab a pysser to the walle. *c* **1525** in *Archæologia* XLVII. 326 Ye have made me suche a pysser that I dare not this dayе go abrode. **1615** CROOKE *Body of Man* 139 The Kidneyes are called .. νεφροι, as it were Pissers. **1737** OZELL *Rabelais* II. 158 *note*, A covetous Hunks is .. called a Vinegar-pisser.

2. *coarse slang.* The penis; the female pudenda; *spec.* in phr. *to pull a person's pisser*, to pull his leg, befool him.

1901 FARMER & HENLEY *Slang* V. 214/2 *Pisser* = (1) the *penis*, and (2) the female *pudendum*. **1969** J. WAINWRIGHT *Big Tickle* 123 'I don't know where he is.' 'If you're pulling my pisser!' 'I'm not.' **1971** B. W. ALDISS *Soldier Erect* 37 He was pulling your pisser, Wal. Malaria's no worse than a cold to the Wogs, is it, Bamber? *Ibid.* 133 He grabbed my arm. 'You think I'm pulling your pisser, man? Listen, *pick your officer*! They're fucking human, same as you, you know!'

3. *slang* (orig. *U.S.*). An extraordinary person or thing; now usu. a difficult or distasteful event, an unpleasant person; also in weakened sense, a bloke, chap.

1943 *Amer. Speech* XVIII. 45 As they [*sc.* New Yorkers] use it, 'pisser' denotes a wag or 'card', a 'corker', or a screamingly funny joke or prank, a 'hot one'. **1954** J. A. WEINGARTEN *Amer. Dict. Slang* 276/1 *Pisser*,..a thing or person of extraordinary aspect; an amusing thing or person. **1974** J. ANTHOINE in H. MacInnes *Climb to Lost World* x. 166, I could have gone a real pisser but, as I dropped, I caught the edge of the rock with my hands and heaved myself up. **1975** tr. *Melchior's Sleeper Agent* (1976) II. 69 The old pisser had not got away! *Ibid.* 98 We could both do with a little liquid cheer. It's been a pisser of a day. **1978** *Maledicta* II. 268, I love it! It's a real pisser!

† **'pissery.** *Obs. rare*[−1]. [See -ERY 2: cf. F. *pissoir*.] A place for pissing; a urinal.

a **1693** *Urquhart's Rabelais* III. xv. 127 They..pissed in the Pisseries.

pisshes, pissis, obs. forms of PISCES.

'pissing, *a.* and *adv. slang.* [f. PISS *v.* + -ING[2].] **A.** *adj.* Paltry, insignificant; brief. **b.** *adv.* As an intensive: exceedingly, abominably, 'bloody'. Hence **'pissingly** *adv.*

1937 PARTRIDGE *Dict. Slang* 635/2 *Pissing*, adj., paltry, brief. **1971** B. W. ALDISS *Soldier Erect* 180 In this teeming world [in Calcutta], nothing was what it seemed to be. The miseries of the idiot and his dependants were pissingly funny. **1974** K. MILLETT *Flying* (1975) III. 294 Paper hat leaps on stage, pissing hot to talk. **1975** N. FREELING *What are Bugles blowing For?* xxi. 123 'Fuck it,' said Metcalfe angrily. 'I'm only a pissing sergeant.' **1979** P. WAY *Sunrise* i. 10 'Pissing awful weather,' said Don.

'pissing, *vbl. sb.* Not now in polite use. [f. PISS *v.* + -ING[1].] The action of the verb PISS; discharge of urine, urination; discharge (of blood, etc.) with the urine or by the urinary passages.

1398 TREVISA *Barth. De P.R.* XVII. xiii. (Bodl. MS.), Apium..helpeþ also aȝens þe stone and aȝens difficulte of pissinge. **1542–5** BRINKLOW *Lament.* 3 No more then the pissinge of a wrenne helpeth to cause the see to flowe. **1615** CROOKE *Body of Man* 190 The Strangury.., that is, the pissing by drops.., do[th] alwayes accompany the stone of the bladder. **1698** in *Phil. Trans.* XX. 314 It stops pissing of Blood.

b. *attrib.* and *Comb.*, as *pissing-basin, -clout, -place, -time, -vessel*; † **pissing conduit**, popular name of a conduit near the Royal Exchange, which ran with a small stream; † **pissing evil**, name for diabetes; † **pissing-post**, a public urinal, also commonly used for sticking up placards; † **pissing-while**, *colloq.* a very short time.

1494 *Will of J. Isell* (Somerset Ho. Wills, Reg. Vox, lf. 21 (4b)) A grete Cawdren and iij *pyssing basons. **1672** WYCHERLEY *Love in Wood* I. ii, Down to the sucking heiress in her *pissing-clout. **1593** SHAKS. *2 Hen. VI*, IV. vi. 4, I charge and command, that of the Cities cost The *pissing Conduit run nothing but Clarret Wine. **1598** STOW *Surv.* 144 The little Conduite, called the pissing Conduit, by the Stockes market. **1565** COOPER *Thesaurus, Diabethe*,..the *pyssyng euill. *c* **1440** *Promp. Parv.* 402/1 *Pyssynge place, *oletum*. **1693** DRYDEN *Persius* i. (1697) 416 My harmless Rhime shall 'scape the dire disgrace Of Common-shoars, and ev'ry pissing-place. **1630** J. TAYLOR (Water P.) *Wks.* (N.), On every *pissing post their names I'l place. **1699** T. BROWN in R. L'Estrange *Erasm. Colloq.* (1711) 328 Whose business and good qualities you may find upon all the Pissing-posts in Town. **1673** [R. LEIGH] *Transp. Reh.* 2 *Pissing times. *c* **1440** *Promp. Parv.* 402/1 *Pyssynge vesselle. *a* **1553** UDALL *Royster D.* IV. viii. (Arb.) 77 Truce for a *pissing while or twaine. **1591** SHAKS. *Two Gent.* IV. iv. 20. **1678** RAY *Prov.* (ed. 2) 265 To stay a pissing-while.

‖**pissoceros** (pɪsəʊ'sɪərəs). [L. *pissocērós* (Pliny), a. Gr. πισσόκηρος (Aristotle), f. πίσσα pitch + κηρός bees-wax.] (See quots.)

1658 ROWLAND *Moufet's Theat. Ins.* 916 Concerning Wax, Bee-glew, dregs of Wax, Pissoceros, Bees-bread, and of their Nature and Use. **1706** PHILLIPS, *Pissoceros*, the Pitch-wax made by Bees in their Hives; or any Composition of Wax and Pitch. **1816** KIRBY & SP. *Entomol.* xxvii. (1818) II. 497 Show us but one instance of bees having substituted mud or mortar for mitys, pissoceros, or propolis.

‖**pissoir** (piswar). [Fr.] A public urinal enclosed by a screen or wall.

1919 MENCKEN *Amer. Lang.* 127 The French *pissoir*..is still regarded as indecent in America, and is seldom used in England, but it has gone into most of the Continental languages. **1934** S. SPENDER *Vienna* ii. 23 In oil-tarred pissoirs. **1942** [see FLY *sb.*[2] 4 a]. **1955** W. GADDIS *Recognitions* I. ii. 77 The feet showing below the shield of the pissoir. **1968** *Listener* 21 Mar. 369/3 A simple slate pissoir where graffiti, true to the spirit of Rochdale, divide between sex and politics. **1972** *Guardian* 19 Feb. 8/3 One pissoir is plain anti-feminism. **1975** *Times* 17 Dec. 13/1 The valuable site.. has been vacant for many years and its use is restricted to private parking and to pissoirs of inelegant design.

'piss-pot. Not now in polite use. [f. PISS *sb.* + POT *sb.* So early mod.F. *pissepot* (1544).] **a.** A vessel, usually of earthenware, for urine; a chamber-pot.

c **1440** *Promp. Parv.* 267/1 Iurdone, pyssepotte. **1529** MORE *Suppl. Soulys* II. Wks. 195/1 And it happen to raine, out poure they pispottes vpon his hed. **1621** FLETCHER *Wild Goose Chase* II. ii, May be, she knows you, And will fling a piss-pot at you. **1743** *Phil. Trans.* XLII. 614 They hold a Piss-pot over the Womens Heads whilst in Labour, thinking it to promote hasty Delivery. **1942** E. PAUL *Narrow St.* xxix. 269 They had wandered into a slum where frequently the housewives dumped pisspots out of the windows. **1948** E. POUND *Pisan Cantos* (1949) lxxx. 104 His helmet is used for a pisspot. **1972** *Daily Tel.* 5 May 12/3 His low-life characters empty the occasional piss-pot and there is a fine flamboyant parade of pretty whores. **1974** *Times Lit. Suppl.* 19 Apr. 417/4 Malcolm [Lowry]..reached the abyss of alcoholic degradation, drinking in prison out of a pisspot.

attrib. **1598** B. JONSON *Ev. Man in Hum.* III. iii, A beggar, a slave that never drunk out of better than piss-pot metal in his life! **1619** H. HUTTON *Follies Anat.* (Percy Soc.) 11 A sowre pis-pot visage.

† **b.** *transf.* A nickname for a medical man: cf. next. *Obs.*

1593 NASHE *Four Lett. Confut.* Wks. (Grosart) II. 236 Had phisition Iohn liu'd,..a sinode of Pispots would haue concluded, that Pierce Pennilesse should be confounded without repriue. **1600** *Dr. Dodypoll* I. i. in Bullen *O. Pl.* III. 103 A fustie Potticarie..with his fustian druggs, attending your pispot worship. **1662** R. MATHEW *Unl. Alch.* §24. 18 Which..sheweth the presumption of Pispot Doctors.

† **'piss-,prophet.** *Obs.* [f. as prec. + PROPHET.] One who diagnosed diseases by inspection of the urine.

1625 HART *Anat. Ur.* I. ii. 32 Now would I willingly demand of the most cunning Pisse-prophet, what could he haue found out by either of these vrines? **1651** WITTIE tr. *Primrose's Pop. Err.* 70 If a very cholerick urine be brought, can the pisse-prophet tell which of these diseases doth trouble the patient? **1695** D. TURNER *Apol. Chyrurg.* 5 The most absurd Predictions of the calculating Piss-prophets.

piss-up ('pɪsʌp). *coarse slang.* [f. PISS *v.*; cf. *pissed-up* s.v. PISSED *ppl. a.* 1.] **1.** = COCKUP 4.

1950 H. E. GOLDIN *Dict. Amer. Underworld Lingo* 158/1 *Piss-up*, n., a fiasco; a bungled or unremunerative crime. **1969** R. ESSER *Hot Potato* 51 Just what a pissy-arsed bugger like you would say... You mean it might be one hell of a piss-up.

2. A bout of heavy drinking.

1952 *Landfall* VI. 222 His first 'piss-up' is a landmark in his life. **1959** *Numbers* Feb. 32, I feel like a good piss-up. **1965** R. JEFFRIES *Traitor's Crime* x. 131 How about a piss-up? Anne was only saying yesterday I'd been sober for so long was I declining into my old age? **1973** *Nation Rev.* (Melbourne) 31 Aug. 1441/6 Most significant..was the way the seating was arranged at the Saturday night pissup. **1976** P. CAVE *High Flying Birds* iii. 45 There was the prospect of a piss-up in the offing.

† **'pissuppresť.** *Obs. rare*[−1]. Suppression (or ? retention) of urine.

1610 MARKHAM *Masterp.* I. lxxvii. 159 The..pissupresť in a horse, is when a horse would faine stale, but cannot.

pissy ('pɪsɪ), *a. coarse slang.* [f. PISS *sb.* + -Y[1].] Of or pertaining to urine; *fig.* rubbishy, inferior. So *pissy-arsed* adj. (see quot. 1961); also, as a term of general abuse.

1926 T. E. LAWRENCE *Seven Pillars* (1935) x. cxviii. 642 That hot pissy aura of thronged men in woollen clothes. **1961** PARTRIDGE *Dict. Slang* Suppl. 1224/1 *Pissy-arsed*, prone to crapulous inebriation. **1969** Pissy-arsed [see PISS-UP 1]. **1972** 'D. CRAIG' *Double Take* xi. 138 Oh, God, these poverty stricken, pissy shoes. **1973** M. AMIS *Rachel Papers* 127 You'll probably say this is rather..pissy, but babies are the only things women can have that men can't. **1974** P. CAVE. *Mama* (new ed.) x. 80 It makes you realise what a pissy little island we live on, don't it? **1974** *Black World* Nov. 66 She/rising up stumbling over to the dank pissy restroom. **1979** J. BARNETT *Backfire is Hostile!* iii. 36 That pissy bunch of engineering officers at the bar.

† **pist** (pɪst, pst), *int. Obs. rare.* A sibilant syllable used to attract attention, or to call a person. (Cf. HIST.)

1608 MIDDLETON *Trick to catch Old one* III. E ij, *Hoo.* Pist Drawer,—*Dra.* Anon sir? **1622** MIDDLETON & ROWLEY *Changeling* V. i, Pist! where are you?

pist, *sb.*: see PISTE[2].

pistachio (pɪ'steɪʃ(ɪ)əʊ, -'stɑːʃ(ɪ)əʊ, -'stætʃəʊ). Forms: α. 5–7 **pistace**, 6 **pystace**, 7–8 **pistach**, 7– **pistache**. β. 6 **pistaccio**, 7 **-acio**, 7– **pistachio**, (9 **-acchio**); also (6 **pistinachie**), 7 **pistachie, -acie**, 8 **-achee**, 7– **pistachia**. γ. 7–8 **pistacho**. [The α forms a. OF. *pistace* (13th c.) and F. *pistache* (pistaʃ); the β forms ad. It. *pistacchio* (pis'takkjo), some affected by L. *pistacia*, or by Spanish; the γ form a. Sp. *pistacho* (pis'tatʃo); all from L. *pistācium* (med.L. *pistāquium*), a. Gr. πιστάκιον pistachio nut, f. πιστάκη pistacia-tree, from OPers.: cf. Pers. *pistah*. See also PISTACIA, PISTACK, PISTICK *nut*, FISTIC.

Cf. **1392–3** *Earl Derby's Exp.* (Camden) 219 Item pro ij lb. de pistaqiis, lvj s.]

1. a. The 'nut' or dry drupe of *Pistacia vera* (see b), or its edible kernel, of a greenish colour, eaten in Turkey, Greece, etc. (Also *pistachio nut*: see 3.)

α. **1533** ELYOT *Cast. Helthe* (1541) 9 b, Thynges good for the Lunges: Elycampane: Hysope:..Pystaces. **1616** SURFL. & MARKH. *Country Farme* 585 Filberds, pine nuts, pistaces, almonds. **1725** BRADLEY *Fam. Dict.* s.v. *Pistache-Tree*, The best Pistaches are brought from Arabia and Syria.

β. **1598** W. PHILLIP *Linschoten* I. lii. 94/2 A white kernell very pleasant to eate, like Pistaccios. **1650** FULLER *Pisgah* I. iv. 11 Nuts (at this day called *pistachioes*, and most cordiall in physick). **1668** WILKINS *Real Char.* II. iv. §7. 116 Pistacie, Fistic-nut. **1698** FRYER *Acc. E. India & P.* 247 Philberts, Haslenuts, Pistachias. **1751** J. HILL *Hist. Mat. Med.* 495 The Pistachia is..of an oblong Figure, pointed at both Ends,..about half an Inch in Length..the Kernel..of a green Colour, of a soft and unctuous Substance..much like the Pulp of an Almond. **1865** *Pall Mall G.* 20 Oct. 10 Melons are marvellously cheap and good in Marseilles, so are pistachios.

γ. **1626** BACON *Sylva* §50 Pistachoes..joyned with Almonds in Almond Milk,..are an excellent Nourisher. **1694** MOTTEUX *Rabelais* IV. lx. (1737) 247 Pistachoes, or Fistick-Nuts. **1732** ARBUTHNOT *Rules of Diet* 263 Almonds, Pistachos, and other Nuts.

b. The tree *Pistacia vera* (N.O. *Anacardiaceæ*), a native of Western Asia, much cultivated in the south of Europe. (Also *pistachio tree*: see 3.)

α. *c* **1420** *Pallad. on Husb.* XI. 184 Pistace is in this moone Of plauntes sette. **1905** *19th Cent.* Aug. 269 The olive, pistache, jujube and plane from Syria.

β. **1664** EVELYN *Kal. Hort.* (1729) 227 [Plants] to be first set into the Conservatory..Dactyls, Pistacio's, the great Indian Fig. **1751** J. HILL *Hist. Plants* 621 The pinnated-leaved Pistachia.

2. A green colour resembling that of the kernel of the pistachio nut. (Also *pistachio green*: see 3.) Also *attrib.* or as *adj.*: Of this colour.

1791 A. M. PORTMAN in *A. C. Bower's Diaries & Corr.* (1903) 141 The fashionable Colors are Coquelicot and Pistache. **1888** *Daily News* 7 June 5/8 A dress of plain pistachio satin.

3. *attrib.* and *Comb.*, as *pistachio candy, cream, green* (sb. and adj.), *nut, plantation, tree*; **pistachio ice, ice-cream**, ice(-cream) containing pistachio nuts; also, ice-cream coloured pistachio green.

1598 *Epulario* K iv b, Pistinachie [? error] Nuts. **1620** VENNER *Via Recta* vii. 129 Pistach or Fisticke Nuts are of an aromaticall sauour. **1626** H. MASON *Epicure's Fast* ii. 13 Drie Figgs, Pepper,..Pistace nuts. **1658** *Songs Costume* (Percy Soc.) 164 Madam, here are pistachie nuts. **1698** *Phil. Trans.* XX. 466 A sort of Pistachio-Tree. **1736** BAILEY *Househ. Dict.* 473 A Pistachio Cream. Take a pound of pistachio nuts, break the shells and blanch the kernels. **1796** KIRWAN *Elem. Min.* (ed. 2) I. 28 *Pistachio green*, meadow green with a mixture of brown. **1825** *Greenhouse Comp.* II. 81 Atlantic Pistachia-tree, a small tree from Barbary in 1790. **1853** SOYER *Pantroph.* 121 Galen doubted whether pistachio nuts were good for the stomach. **1853** MRS. GASKELL *Ruth* III. iv. 140 The days when you first brought me pistachio candy from London. **1868** A. GOUFFÉ tr. *J. Gouffé's Royal Cookery Bk.* xvii. 561 Apricot and Pistachio Ice. **1882** O'DONOVAN *Merv Oasis* I. 331 The vineyards and pistache plantations. **1885** C. E. PASCOE *London Today* iii. 48 The more aristocratic foreign visitors to London..flocked thither [*sc.* to Verrey's restaurant] to eat pistachio ices. **1889** R. WELLS *Pastrycook & Confect. Guide* vii. 65 *Pistachio ice*, blanch and beat until fine the kernels of 6 ozs. of Pistachio nuts [etc.]. **1899** *Westm. Gaz.* 20 April 7/3 A lovely gown of pale pistachio green satin. **1916** FRANDSEN & MARKHAM *Manuf. Ice Creams* x. 103 Pistachio Ice Cream. **1942** A. L. SIMON *Conc. Encycl. Gastron.* V. 57/1 Pistachio ice-creams ..are ice-creams..flavoured with almonds and vanilla and coloured with vegetable dyes as near the pistachio green as possible. **1943** E. M. ALMEDINGEN *Frossia* vi. 228 Do you like pistachio ices—with small almond biscuits? **1972** E. HARGREAVES *Fair Green Weed* i. 13 It's a big rambling place like a block of pistachio ice-cream.

‖**pistacia** (pɪ'steɪʃ(ɪ)ə). [L. *pistācia* pistachio tree (Pallad.), f. Gr. πιστάκη: see prec.] The pistachio tree = prec. 1 b; in *Bot.* the name (adopted by Linnæus 1737) of the genus to which the Pistachio tree belongs, including also the Mastic-tree and the Terebinth; the species are sometimes collectively called *turpentine-trees*.

c **1420** *Pallad. on Husb.* IV. 685 Pistacia is graffed now to growe In cold lond. **1698** FRYER *Acc. E. India & P.* 255 The Pistacia sends forth its Branches on high, and renders its Nuts edible in Autumn. **1760** J. LEE *Introd. Bot.* App. 323 Pistacia, Hazel-leaved, *Hamamelis*. **1871** H. MACMILLAN *True Vine* v. (1872) 197 The Pistacia grows abundantly in the south of France, but it yields no mastic.

†**b.** = prec. 1 a, pistachio nut. *Obs.*

1581 MARBECK *Bk. of Notes* 382 Nuts, dates, fine white bread, honnie and Pistacia. **1583** *Rates of Customs* D vij, Pistacia the pound vi *d.*

c. *Comb.*, as ***pistacia nut, tree***: see prec. 3.

1760 J. LEE *Introd. Bot.* App. 323 Pistacia Nut... Pistacia-tree. **1876** HARLEY *Mat. Med.* (ed. 6) 662 Pistacia nut tree extends from Syria to Bokhara and Cabul.

pistacite ('pɪstəsaɪt). *Min.* [ad. Ger. *pistazit* (A. G. Werner, 1803), f. PISTACIA + -ITE: so named from its colour.] A synonym of EPIDOTE, or name for a variety of it.

1828–32 WEBSTER, *Pistacite, pistazite*, see *Epidote*. **1859** PAGE *Handbk. Geol. Terms*, *Pistacite*, iron and lime epidote, in which a large quantity of the lime is replaced by protoxide of iron,..so called from its pistachio-green colour. **1866** LAWRENCE tr. *Cotta's Rocks Class.* i. 43 Pistacite..occurs as an accessory and very frequently in hornblende rocks, and is probably the product of decomposition of hornblende.

†'**pistack, 'pistake.** *Obs.* Anglicized forms of PISTACHIO, chiefly in comb. See also PISTICK.

1591 PERCIVALL *Sp. Dict.*, *Alhostigo, alhocigo*, pistacke tree. **1639** HORN & ROB. *Gate Lang. Unl.* xi. §123 Pistakes, services, carobs,..dates. **1658** PHILLIPS, *Pistachoes*, or Pistack [*ed.* 1706 Pistake] Nuts.

pistareen (pɪstə'riːn). Also 8 pistereen, 9 -arene. [app. a popular formation from *peseta*.] An American or West Indian name for a small Spanish silver coin formerly current there.

1774 J. ADAMS in *Fam. Lett.* (1876) 10 So I gave pistareens enough among the children to have paid twice for my entertainment. **1788** M. CUTLER in *Life*, etc. (1888) I. 432 Gave him refreshments, oats, and a pistereen. **1807–8** W. IRVING *Salmag.* (1824) 212 A pistareen's worth of bows for a dollar. **1872** O. W. HOLMES *Poet Breakf.-t.* iii, I ask him to change a pistareen.

b. *attrib.* or as *adj.* Concerned with small matters; petty, paltry; cf. PICAYUNE.

1860 EMERSON *Cond. Life, Fate* Wks. (Bohn) II. 310 Now and then, an amiable parson..believes in a pistareen Providence. **1861** HOLLAND *Less Life* xi. 156 Mr. Emerson becomes equally flippant and irreverent when he speaks of a 'pistareen Providence'.

†'**pistate**, *v.* *Obs.* $rare^{-1}$. [f. L. *pistāt-*, ppl. stem of *pistāre* to pound (? later, to knead, to bake), frequent. of *pinsĕre* to pound, crush; cf. *pistor* baker.] *trans.* To bake.

1599 A. M. *Gabelhouer's Bk. Physicke* 63/2 Permit them bake with breade: and it being pistatede, breacke it and hould it at thye Eares, being verye warme. **1604** R. CAWDREY, *Pistated*, baked. **1623** COCKERAM I I, Baked, *pistated*.

†**piste**^{1}. *Obs.* $rare^{-1}$. [See PISTIC.] In ***piste Indik***, rendering L. *spica Indica.* Indian spikenard.

c **1420** *Pallad on Husb.* XI. 411 (Bodley MS.) Fyne mirre an unce, and of the piste Indik [*v.r.* pisce indyk] But half an unce.

‖**piste**^{2} (piːst), **pist** (pɪst). [F. *piste* = It. *pesta*, Sp. *pista*:—L. *pista* (sc. *via*), beaten track, f. *pist-us*, pa. pple. of *pinsĕre* to pound, stamp.] **a.** The beaten track of a horse or other animal; the track of a race-course or training-ground. Also in extended use.

1727–41 CHAMBERS *Cycl.*, *Piste*, in the manage, the track or tread, which a horse makes upon the ground he goes over. .. The *piste* of a horse may be either *single*, or *double*. **1882** OGILVIE, *Pist. Piste.* **1897** 'OUIDA' *Massarenes* xxviii, She looks as racing mares do when they come in off the trotting piste. **1964** *Guardian* 20 Oct. 7/2 That other highway, where the giraffe..came down to drink. It is only a *piste* for the big Trans-Af buses. **1967** N. FREELING *Strike Out* 24 The serious part—stables, 'pistes', exercise courts and yards. **1970** *Country Life* 17–24 Dec. 1209/3 For the last few dozen miles..the road is tar laid direct on to the apricot-coloured sand..giving one a choice between the molar-shaking corrugations of the piste itself and the treacherous dunes on either side.

b. *Fencing.* A specially marked-out field of play.

1922 *Glasgow Herald* 20 May 9 Preliminary pools of the individual Military Epée Championship of Europe. The Turney..was fought on linoleum 'pistes'. **1963** *Fencing* ('Know the Game' Ser.) (ed. 4) 24 The area within which fencers may move is restricted. This area is called the 'Piste'. **1971** I. BUTYKAI tr. *Lukovich's Electric Foil Fencing* I. 12 Competitors who had fenced for several years with the ordinary foil, now changed it for the electric device and the pioneering work of the era of electric foil fencing. Many said good-bye to the piste for ever.

c. A track of compacted snow used as a ski- or toboggan-run. Also *attrib.*

1929 E. HEMINGWAY *Farewell to Arms* xxxvii. 299 Tobogganing..requires a special *piste*. You could not toboggan into the streets of Montreux. **1939** W. PRAGER *Skiing* 80 Thus he has an opportunity to construct the Piste. **1950** *Times* 13 Feb. 7/5 Most other races, including world championships, are only a test of piste skiing, a debased and impoverished variant of the real thing. **1955** *Times* 20 Sept. 12/7 Italian engineering..began to work on ski lifts and cable cars..with the result that..there are..installations taking skiers of every grade to the top of the various pistes. **1959** P. MOYES *Dead Men don't Ski* ii. 24 The lift travels above the *pistes*, or ski runs. **1966** *Daily Tel.* 19 Dec. 9/1 You may never come skimming down the *piste* like a bird, but you can make sure of a second look by choosing the right clothes. **1972** N. FREELING *Long Silence* II. 111 Woodcutters' paths..make good natural *pistes* for Nordic ski. **1977** *Time* 10 Jan. 6/1 The lure of the Cup was enough to bring Austria's five-time winner, Annemarie Moser-Proell, to the *piste* again.

pistel, -ell, -elle, etc., var. ff. PISTLE, etc. *Obs.*

†'**pistelarie.** *Obs.* $rare^{-1}$. [ad. med.L. *epistolārium*; cf. PISTLE.] = EPISTOLAR *sb.*

1431 *Rec. St. Mary at Hill* 27, ij masse bokes and a pistelarie.

pistereen, variant of PISTAREEN.

‖**Pistia** ('pɪstɪə). *Bot.* [mod.L. (Linnæus 1737); cf. Gr. πιστός drinkable, liquid. (? in allusion to its deriving its nutriment from water.)] A genus of floating water-plants allied to Duckweed, the type of N.O. *Pistiaceæ*, comprising one species (*P. Stratiotes*), which covers the surface of ponds and tanks in warm countries; also called *tropical duckweed*, and (in W. Indies) *water-lettuce*.

1765 J. BARTRAM *Jrnl.* 31 Dec. in W. Stork *Acc. E. Florida* (1766) 17 At the entrance of the river into the great lake there floats prodigious quantities of the pistia. **1878** H. M. STANLEY *Dark Cont.* II. VI. 183 The inhabitants..devoted themselves..to fishing, and the manufacture of salt from the *Pistia* plants. **1906** *Blackw. Mag.* Feb. 213/1 The floating Pistia, for all the world like a minute cabbage.

pistic ('pɪstɪk), *a.* (and *sb.*) [ad. L. *pistic-us* (Vulg.), a. Gr. πιστικός perhaps 'genuine, pure', f. πίστις faith; but see quot. 1881.] **1.** In ***nard pistic, pistic nard*** = Gr. νάρδος πιστική in Mark xiv. 3 and John xii. 3 (in Bible versions translated *spikenard*).

1646 SIR T. BROWNE *Pseud. Ep.* VII. vii. 351 Nor must that perhaps be taken for a simple unguent,..but rather a composition, as Marke and John imply by pistick Nard, that is faithfully dispensed. **1649** JER. TAYLOR *Gt. Exemp.* III. Sect. xiii, She came..with a box of Nard Pistick, salutary and precious. **1655** H. VAUGHAN *Silex Scint.* II. *St. Mary Magd.*, Why is this rich, this pistic nard Spilt, and the box quite broke and marr'd? **1881** N.T. (R.V.) *Mark* xiv. 3 Ointment of spikenard. *Margin*, Gr. *pistic nard*, pistic being perhaps a local name. Others take it to mean *genuine*; others, *liquid*.

2. Pertaining to faith or trust rather than to reason; hence *ellipt.* as *sb.*, someone who accepts things simply on trust.

1923 OGDEN & RICHARDS *Meaning of Meaning* ii. 89 The purely verbal systems so characteristic of pistic speculation. **1965** in W. Schneemelcher *New Test. Apocr.* II. xi. 77 The apostolic secret tradition..is accessible not merely to the small circle of a spiritual élite, the 'hylic' and 'psychic' or 'pistic' being excluded on principle, but to all those who have been received into the church..as full Christians.

†'**pistick**, *sb.* (*a.*) *Obs.* [A deriv. of PISTACHIO (in some of its forms; cf. also PISTACK), perh. assimilated to FISTIC, a form of the same word through Arabic. (Possibly confused with prec.)] = PISTACHIO: chiefly in comb.

1621 BURTON *Anat. Mel.* II. ii. I. i, Trallianus discommends figs,..which others especially like of, and so of pistick nuts. **1655** MOUFET & BENNET *Health's Impr.* (1746) 300 Fisticks, or rather Pisticks,..are Nuts growing in the Knob of the Syrian or Egyptian Turpentine-tree.

pistil ('pɪstɪl). *Bot.* Forms: α. 6–7 pestill, 7 pestle (see PESTLE). β. 8–9 in L. form pistillum (pl. -a). γ. 8– pistil. [In sense 1, the same word as PESTLE, OF. *pestel*:—L. *pistillum*. For sense 2, the L. word itself was first used, the place of which *a* 1750 began to be taken by its Fr. adaptation *pistil* (*pistile* Tournefort, 1694, *pistil* admitted by the Académie, 1762).]

†**1.** In early use (in form *pestle, pestill*), The thick pestle-like spadix of araceous plants. *Obs.*

α. **1578** LYTE *Dodoens* III. vi. 320 Of Dragons [Dracunculus]... At the top of the stalke groweth a long hoose or huske, lyke to the hoose or codde of Aron, or Wake Robin, of a greenish colour without, and..the clapper or pestill that groweth vp within the sayde huske. **1658** SIR T. BROWNE *Gard. Cyrus* iii, Those yellow fringes about the purple Pestill. **1672** JOSSELYN *New Eng. Rarities* 70 This Plant is one..with a sheath or Hood like Dragons, but the pestle is of another shape,..having a round Purple Ball on the top of it.

2. In mod. use, The female organ of a flower, situated (one or more) in the centre, and comprising (in its complete form) the ovary, style, and stigma. β. in L. form *pistillum*; γ. in form *pistil*.

β. [**1700** TOURNEFORT *Inst. Rei Herb.* (1719) I. 70 Pistillum appello partem eam, quæ floris centrum inter stamina occupare solet.] **1726** *Flower Gard. Displ.* Introd., *Pistillum*, a small Thread or Stamen, with an Apex on the Top of it, growing out of the Seminary Vessels, exactly in the Center of some Flowers. **1760** J. LEE *Introd. Bot.* I. v. (1765) 11 The Pistillum is the Female Part of the Flower. **1830** LINDLEY *Nat. Syst. Bot.* 6 Pistilla numerous,..or united into a single many-celled pistillum.

γ. [**1694** TOURNEFORT *Botan.* 54 J'appelle pistile cette partie de la fleur qui en occupe ordinairement le centre.] **1749** STACK (tr. from Fr.) in *Phil. Trans.* XLVI. 50 The Pistil or Embryo of the Fruit..occupies the whole Inside of the Calyx. **1756** WATSON *ibid.* XLIX. 806 It has neither Calyx nor Petal, but consists only of one Stamen and one Pistil. **1785** MARTYN *Rousseau's Bot.* i. (1794) 23 This..is called the pistil or pointal. **1872** OLIVER *Elem. Bot.* I. i. 10 The carpels, taken together, constitute the pistil; they are the fourth and last series of the flower-leaves.

3. *Comb.*, as ***pistil-bearing*** adj.

1866 *Treas. Bot.* 96 Having its male or stamen-bearing flowers borne on long club-shaped spikes, and the pistil-bearing ones in round heads.

pistil, obs. f. PESTLE, var. PISTLE *Obs.*

pistillaceous (-'eɪʃəs), *a. rare.* [f. Bot. L. *pistill-um* PISTIL + -ACEOUS.] = PISTILLARY.

1760 J. LEE *Introd. Bot.* I. xii. (1765) 30 *Pistillaceous Nectaria*, such as accompany the Pistillum.

'**pistillar**, *a. rare.* [f. L. type **pistillār-is*, f. *pistill-um*: see -AR.] = next.

1876 HOOKER *Bot. Primer* 48 The pistillar leaf is called a carpel.

pistillary ('pɪstɪlərɪ), *a. Bot.* [f. Bot. L. *pistill-um* PISTIL + -ARY: in mod.F. *pistillaire.*] Of, pertaining to, or of the nature of a pistil.

1848 LINDLEY *Introd. Bot.* (ed. 4) II. 88 The pistillary apparatus. **1866** *Treas. Bot.* 897 *Pistillary cord*, a channel which passes from the stigma through the style into the ovary. **1880** *Gray's Struct. Bot.* (ed. 6) 269 The pistillary body is attenuated and prolonged above the ovule.

pistillate ('pɪstɪlət), *a. Bot.* [ad. mod.L. *pistillāt-us*, f. as prec. + -ATE^2 2. In mod.F. *pisstillé.*] Having a pistil or pistils (and no stamens); female. (Opp. to *staminate.*)

1828–32 in WEBSTER. **1861** BENTLEY *Man. Bot.* 403 ♀ a pistillate flower. **1872** OLIVER *Elem. Bot.* I. iv. 39 In the Lesser Nettle, staminate and pistillate flowers are on the same plant. **1880** *Gray's Struct. Bot.* vi. (ed. 6) 191 Flowers are..Pistillate..when the pistils are present and the stamens absent.

†**pisti'llation.** *Obs.* $rare^{-1}$. [f. L. *pistill-um* pestle + -ATION.] A pounding with a pestle.

1646 SIR T. BROWNE *Pseud. Ep.* II. v. 83 They submit unto pistillation, and resist not an ordinary pestle.

‖**pistillidium** (pɪstɪ'lɪdɪəm). *Bot.* Pl. -ia. [mod.L., f. *pistill-um* PISTIL + *-idium* = Gr. -ιδιον, dim. suffix.] The female organ in the higher Cryptogams, usually called ARCHEGONIUM.

1854 [see ARCHEGONIUM]. **1857** HENFREY *Elem. Bot.* §908 In the majority of the Orders the female organ occurs in a form somewhat analogous to the ovule of Phanerogamia, called the *archegonium* (or *pistillidium*). **1861** BENTLEY *Man. Bot.* (1870) 366 The reproductive organs of..Mosses..are called antheridia and archegonia or pistillidia.

pistilliferous (pɪstɪ'lɪfərəs), *a. Bot.* [f. L. *pistillum* PISTIL + -(I)FEROUS, after F. *pistillifère.*] = PISTILLATE. (Opp. to *staminiferous.*)

1785 MARTYN *Rousseau's Bot.* ix. (1794) 95, I beg leave.. to call..those which have only the pistils, pistilliferous flowers. **1880** SIR E. J. REED *Japan* II. 42 There are two kinds of this shrub, pistilliferous and staminiferous.

pistilligerous (-'ɪdʒərəs), *a. rare.* [f. as prec. -(I)GEROUS.] Productive of or fertile in pistils.

1843 GRIFFITH in *Trans. Linn. Soc.* (1845) XIX. 204 *note*, The transition between the two types exists in *Anthoceros*, which in the development of its anthers and habits has much in common with the pistilligerous type.

pistilline ('pɪstɪlaɪn), *a.* [f. Bot. L. *pistill-um* + -INE^1.] **a.** = PISTILLATE. **b.** = PISTILLARY.

1844 CARPENTER *Veg. Phys.* 497 The stamineous and pistilline flowers grow in separate clusters. **1854** BALFOUR

Cl. Bk. Bot. 175 The pistilline whorl..denominated the gynœcium.

pistillode ('pɪstɪləʊd). *Bot.* [f. PISTIL + -ODE.] A rudimentary pistil.

1905 W. E. SAFFORD *Useful Plants of Guam* 259 An imperfect pistil (pistillode) present or lacking. **1975** *Blumea* XXII. 420 The precise configuration of antherodes and pistillodes in relation to other floral parts is likely to prove of considerable taxonomic value.

pistillody ('pɪstɪləʊdɪ). *Bot.* [f. mod.L. *pistillōdi-um*, f. *pistill-um*: see -ODE[1] and cf. PHYLLODY.] Metamorphosis of other floral organs into pistils.

1877 *Jrnl. Linn. Soc. (Bot.)* XV. 87 The calyx and corolla remain entirely unchanged in all cases exhibiting pistillody. **1929** *Jrnl. Heredity* XX. 137/1 Leighty and Sando describe and illustrate certain abnormalities in wheat flowers which they call 'Pistillody'... They found the stamens metamorphosed either wholly or partly into carpels.

pistiloid ('pɪstɪlɔɪd), *a. Bot.* Also **pistilloid**. [f. PISTIL + -OID.] Resembling a pistil in shape.

1877 *Jrnl. Linn. Soc. (Bot.)* XV. 88 Stamen No. 2...is an unstalked pistilloid body with a short curved hairy style. **1888** G. HENSLOW *Origin Floral Struct.* 291 Pistiloid sepals ..have been observed by Mr. Laxton.

pisti'ology. Erron. pisteo-. [f. Gr. πίστι-ς faith + -LOGY: cf. PHRASEOLOGY.] A theory or science of faith or religious belief.

1900 *Ch. Q. Rev.* Oct. 66 We have practically..no pisteology, to deal with the foundations, nature, validity, and limits of religious faith.

†**pistle**, *sb. Obs.* Forms: 1 pistol, 2–6 pistel, 4 pistol, pystol, 4–5 pystil(l, 4–6 pistell(e, pistil, -ill(e, pystyl, -yll(e, 4–7 pistle, 5 pistul, -yl(l, 5–6 (8 *Sc.*) pystle, pystel(l. [OE. *pistol*, aphetic form of *epistol*, ad. L. *epistola* EPISTLE.]

1. A communication in writing, a letter; a literary work, or a dedication, in the form of a letter: = EPISTLE *sb.* 1, 1 b, 1 c.

c **1000** ÆLFRIC *Saints' Lives* III. 382 Ða awrat se earming mid hise agenra hande..þone pistol. **1382** WYCLIF *Dan.* iii. 97 In to eche lond he [the king] sente a pistle. **1395** PURVEY *Remonstrance* (1851) 4 This article is taught bi seynt Jerom in hise pistlis. **1483** CAXTON *Gold. Leg.* 202/1 Saynt Leo wrote a pistle to fabyane bisshop of constantynople ayenst euticium and nestorium. **1529** MORE *Dyaloge* II. Wks. 178/2 A pistle of Plinye wrytten to the Emperoure Trayane. **1595** *Eng. Tripe-wife* (1881) 145 Your Pamphlet lackes both a Pistle and a Patrone. **1787** BURNS *Let. to W. Nichol* 1 June, I was gaun to write you a lang pystle.

2. *spec.* An apostolic letter, forming part of the New Testament: = EPISTLE *sb.* 2.

c **1000** ÆLFRIC *De Vet. et de Nov. Test.* (Grein) 14 Iacob se rihtwisa awrat anne pistol. *c* **1200** *Vices & Virtues* 31 San(c)tus Paulus us takð on his pisteles. **1303** R. BRUNNE *Handl. Synne* 7122 Se now what seynt Poule seys Yn a pystyl. *c* **1380** WYCLIF *Wks.* (1880) 101 As gospillis & pistles witnessen. **1551** CROWLEY *Pleas. & Payne* 215 And in Iohns Pistle these wordis be.

3. *Eccl.* An extract from an apostolic letter (or, as in quot. *a* 1450, from some other Scriptural book) read in the Eucharistic office: = EPISTLE *sb.* 3.

c **1175** *Lamb. Hom.* 89 Hit is ireht on þes pistles redinge [cf. *c* 1000 Ælfric *Hom.* (Th.) I. 314 Hit is gereht on ðyssere pistol-rædinge]. *c* **1400** *Wyclif's Bible* IV. 683 (heading) Here bigynneth a rule, that tellith in whiche chapitris of the bible ȝe mai fynde the lessouns, pistlis, and gospels, that ben rad in the chirche al the ȝeer. *Ibid.* 686 *note* a, Pistil Jerem. [so *passim*]. *a* **1450** *Knt. de la Tour* (1868) 106 The princes of xij lynages, wherof the pistelle upon the feest of Alhalwynne makithe mencion. **1450–1530** *Myrr. our Ladye* 126 The pystel that is redde in the masse. **1590** H. BARROW in *Conferences* i. 8 The Papists..haue the same Creedes,.. Pistles, Gospels.

b. Hence, the title 'Pistle of (Sweet) Susane': Daniel xiii in the Vulgate, containing the story of Susanna, being the Lesson or Epistle of the Mass for the Saturday of the third week in Lent.

But it is probable that here 'pistle' was subsequently taken as = legend or story.

1380–1400 *B.M. Addit. MS.* 22283 (*heading*) Here bygynneþ a pistil of Susan. *Ibid.* l. 363 Þis ferlys bi-fel In þe days of Danyel, þe pistel witnesseþ wel Of þat profete. *c* **1425** WYNTOUN *Cron.* (MS. Cott.) 4312 (Laing 4326), He [Hucheoun] made a gret Gest of Arthure, And þe Awntyr of Gawane, þe Pistil als of Suet Susane.

4. A (spoken) story or discourse.

Most of the examples appear to be after Chaucer.

c **1386** CHAUCER *Wife's T.* 165 Tho rowned she a pistel in his ere. *c* **1422** HOCCLEVE *Min. Poems* (1892) 221 He a pistle rowned in hire ere. **1479** J. PASTON in *P. Lett.* III. 257 When I was with myn oncle, I had a longe pystyll of hym, that [etc.]. ?*a* **1550** *Freiris of Berwik* 184 in *Dunbar's Poems* (S.T.S.) 291 Scho rownis than ane pistill in his eir.

5. *attrib.* and *Comb.*, as *pistle-book*, *-making*, *-penner*, *-reader*, *-reading*; **pistle-cloth**, a cloth covering or wrapper for the books of the epistles.

c **1000** *Canons of Ælfric* §21 in Thorpe *Laws* II. 350 Saltere & pistel-boc & godspell-boc & mæsse-boc. *c* **1000** ÆLFRIC *Hom.* (Th.) I. 294 Lucas se Godspellere us manode on ðisre pistol-readinge, þus cweðende [etc.]. —— *De Consuet. Monach.* in *Anglia* XIII. 406 Sacerd diacon & pistel rædere. **1434** *Inv. St. Mary's, Scarborough* in *Archæologia* LI. 66 Cum uno alio libro vocato le pistelboke. **1559** *Will of Thome* (Somerset Ho.), To yᵉ cherche to-whordes a pystyll book. **1589** *Hay any Work* A iij b, I haue as good a gift in pistle making, as you haue at priemeero. **1589** *Pappe w. Hatchet* D ij, I am worth twentie Pistle-penners.

Hence †'**pistle** *v.* (*nonce-wd.*) *trans.*, to write an epistle upon, assail with an epistle, satirize.

1589 *Pappe w. Hatchet* 28 Take heed, he will pistle thee.

pistle, pistlett, obs. ff. PISTOL, PISTOLET.

†'**pistler.** *Obs.* Also 6 pystiller, 6–7 pisteler, pistoler. [f. PISTLE *sb.* + -ER[1].] One who reads the Epistle at the Communion: = EPISTLER 2, EPISTOLER 2.

a **1520** SKELTON *Ware the Hauke* 121 These be my gospellers, These be my pystillers. **1577–87** HOLINSHED *Chron.* III. 920/2 A pistler: of singing priests ten. **1579** *Wills & Inv. N.C.* (Surtees) II. 18 To the Gospeller and pistoler 6/8ᵈ a pece. *a* **1640** J. BALL *Answ. to Canne* I. (1642) 143 Organ-players, gospellers, pistelers.

pistol ('pɪstəl), *sb.* Also 6 pistolle, 6–7 pistoll, 7 pistle. [a. obs. F. *pistole* (1566 in H. Estienne) a pistol. So It., Sp. *pistola* (? from Fr.). App. a shortened form of *pistolet*, which was earlier both in Fr. and Eng., and in Fr. has out-lived *pistole*. See PISTOLET[1].]

1. a. A small fire-arm, with a more or less curved stock, adapted to be held in, and fired by, one hand.

c **1570** SIR H. GILBERT *Q. Eliz. Achad.* (1869) 4 To teache noble men and gentlemen..to skirmish on horsbacke with pistolles. **1579** DIGGES *Stratiot.* 111 To give the Enemye a volue of their Pistols. **1601** SIR W. CORNWALLIS *Ess.* iv, To keep this Case of Pistols continually ready charged, and bent. **1768–74** TUCKER *Lt. Nat.* (1834) II. 373 If a man.. should have a pistol holden over him, and be threatened with being shot through the head. **1841** LANE *Arab. Nts.* I. 126 With a pair of pistols stuck in the girdle.

†**b.** *transf.* (*pl.*) Troops armed with pistols, pistoleers. *Obs. rare.*

1598 BARRET *Theor. Warres* v. ii. 143 They are alwayes seconded with armed Pistols or Lances.

c. ***Volta's pistol***, a metallic tubular vessel, closed with a cork, in which an explosive mixture of gases may be ignited by an electric spark.

1784 WATT in *Phil. Trans.* LXXIV. 331 In the same manner as is done in the inflammable air pistol. **1843** *Penny Cycl.* XXVI. 434/1 He [Volta] also invented (1777) the instrument which has been called the electrical pistol. **1872** EVERETT tr. *Deschanel's Elem. Nat. Philos.* 556 This experiment is usually shown by means of Volta's pistol, which is a metallic vessel containing the mixture and closed by a cork.

d. ***to beat the pistol***, in Athletics, to make a false start (cf. GUN *sb.* 6 e); ***to hold a pistol to*** (or ***at***) (a person's) ***head***: to threaten (a person) in order to induce him to act in a particular way; to issue with an ultimatum; ***with a pistol at one's head***: under pressure; while being threatened.

1905 S. CROWTHER *Rowing & Track Athletics* 302 False starts were rarely penalized..and..'beating the pistol' was one of the tricks which less sportsmanlike runners constantly practised. **1917** W. J. LOCKE *Red Planet* iii. 33 The boy was my guest. I had not intended to hold a pistol to his head. **1920** E. H. CLARK *Track Athletics up to Date* vi. 49 Some athletes try to gauge the moment when the starter's finger is curling over the trigger of his pistol and to start just before the pistol is fired, when it is too late for the starter to check his finger. This is called 'beating the pistol'. **1974** 'W. HAGGARD' *Kinsmen* iii. 40 She'd held a pistol at Heale-Mann's respectable head. Do as I wish or face a scandal. **1978** *Times* 14 Mar. 19/2 The [French] Socialists..have an understandable dislike of negotiating with a pistol at their heads.

2. *attrib.* and *Comb.*, as ***pistol-bag***, ***-ball***, ***-barrel***, ***-belt***, ***-bullet***, ***-butt***, ***-flint***, ***-holster***, ***-pocket***, ***-powder***, ***-practice***, ***-range***, ***-shape***, ***-toter***; ***pistol-like***, ***-shaped*** adjs., ***-toting*** vbl. sb. and ppl. adj.; ***pistol-wise*** adv.; **pistol-arm**, the arm with which the pistol is held when fired; **pistol-cane**, a concealed pistol in the form of a cane, or a cane containing a concealed pistol; **pistol-carbine**, a pistol provided with a detachable butt-piece, so as to be fired either as a pistol or as a carbine; **pistol flare** = *pistol light*; **pistol-grip**, (*a*) a projection, in shape like the butt of a pistol, on the under side of a gun-stock, to give a firmer grip for the hand in firing; (*b*) *transf.* a handle shaped like a pistol-grip; also *attrib.*; **pistol-hand**, (*a*) the hand in which the pistol is held; (*b*) = *pistol-grip*; **pistol key**, a watch-key in the form of a pistol; **pistol light**, a night-signal or light fired from a special pistol, used by soldiers, etc.; a Very light; **pistol man**, a man accustomed to use a pistol, a duellist; **pistol-packing** *ppl. a.* [see PACK *v.* 9], carrying a pistol; hence ***pistol-packer*** *v.*; **pistol-pipe** (*Metallurgy*), the blast-pipe of a hot-blast furnace; **pistol-proof**, †*sb.* ability to resist a pistol-shot; *a.*, able to resist a pistol-shot (see PROOF *sb.* and *a.*); **pistol-splint** *Surg.*, a splint shaped like a pistol, used esp. in certain fractures of the arm. See also PISTOL-SHOT.

1842 S. LOVER *Handy Andy* iii, I'll give it him in the *pistol-arm, or so. **1701** *Lond. Gaz.* No. 3714/4 Lost.., a pair of green Velvet *Pistol-Bags embroidered with Gold. **1821** BYRON *Wks.* (1846) 584/2 A man who can snuff a candle..with a *pistol-ball. **1655** MRQ. WORCESTER *Cent. Inv.* Index 7 Light *Pistol-barrels. **1660** N. INGELO *Bentiv. & Ur.* II. (1682) 130 They imploy such utensils when they make *Pistol bullet. **1835–6** *Todd's Cycl. Anat.* I. 745/2 This tumour had the volume of a..pistol-bullet. **1814** SCOTT *Wav.* lviii, Striking the boy upon the head with the heavy *pistol-butt. **1916** 'BOYD CABLE' *Action Front* 26 'Keep the lights blazing,' Rawbon paused to shout to the man with the *pistol flares. **1818** —— *Hrt. Midl.* xlv, He..filled his pipe, lighted it with the assistance of his *pistol-flint, and smoked. **1874** J. W. LONG *Amer. Wild-fowl* i. 27 A *pistol-grip is thought by some to be an advantage. **1892** GREENER *Breech-Loader* 84 The rational gun stock..embodies qualities long sought in pistol grip guns. **1917** 'CONTACT' *Airman's Outings* 227, I laugh and proceed to pass some wire through the pistol-grip. **1958** *Engineering* 28 Mar. 411/3 In addition to the push-button and pistol-grip controls. **1964** S. CRAWFORD *Basic Engin. Processes* i. 13 A tubular frame adjustable hacksaw with the 'pistol-grip' type handle. **1972** *Shooting Times & Country Mag.* 27 May 3/2 (Advt.), Pistolgrip stock with cheekpiece £2 extra. **1974** *Country Life* 17 Jan. 82/3 The standard unit includes a parabole reflector, pistol grip, microphone and carrying kit. **1977** *Western Mail* (Cardiff) 5 Mar. 12/3 (Advt.), Movie camera (pistol-grip) and carrying case. **1856** *Encycl. Brit.* (ed. 8) XI. 100/1 A *pistol-hand is a handsome..addition to the gun-stock. **1892** GREENER *Breech-Loader* 82 The pistol-hand gun-stock, especially in that form..known technically as half pistol-hand, is the common form throughout Canada and the United States. **1894** A. ROBERTSON *Nuggets*, etc. 186, I knocked the fellow's pistol-hand up with a rapid blow. **1916** 'BOYD CABLE' *Action Front* 62 A couple of *pistol lights flared upwards. **1929** *Papers Mich. Acad. Sci., Arts & Lett.* X. 315 *Pistol lights*, rockets shot from a pistol. **1834** L. RITCHIE *Wand. by Seine* 167 We hear..the *pistol-like report of beer, and the more soberly alluring plunk! of wine-corks. **1784** R. BAGE *Barham Downs* I. 213, I once intended to have shot at him,..but not being much of a *pistol man ..I changed my mind. **1944** *Time* 10 July 40/2 The lady that's known as Lou pinched several pokes, but pulled no triggers... No *pistol packer, she. **1943** A. DEXTER (*song-title*) *Pistol packin' mama. **1948** E. POUND *Pisan Cantos* (1949) lxxvi. 39 The pride of all our D.T.C. was pistol-packin' Burnes. **1972** T. ARDIES *This Suitcase* xviii. 204 The hotel had been taken over by pistol-packing maniacs. **1966** M. AVALLONE *Fat Death* 20 His hands were anchored into the *pistol pockets of his grey trousers, throwing back the tails of his form-fitting jacket. **1669** STURMY *Mariner's Mag.* v. xii. 65 *Pistol Powder is now commonly made of Salt-peter five parts, one part of Brimstone, and one of Cole. **1846** *Punch* XI. 206 Maids-of-all-work learning *pistol-practice at the shooting galleries. **1590** SIR R. WILLIAMS *Disc. Warre* 29 The forepart of his curaces of a light *pistoll proofe. **1607** R. C[AREW] tr. *Estienne's World of Wonders* 237 Harnesse..not halfe so weighty, and yet of pistol proof. **1692** LUTTRELL *Brief. Rel.* (1857) II. 402 Armour pistoll proofe 27 foot distance. **1864** TREVELYAN *Compet. Wallah* (1866) 82 The sepoys plied them with shot at *pistol-range. **1931** E. WENHAM *Domestic Silver* v. 42 Probably one of the most attractive forms of handles is the so-called *pistol-shape. **1964** W. L. GOODMAN *Hist. Woodworking Tools* 133 Using the broad-bladed Japanese saw with the *pistol-shaped handle. **1893** *Syd. Soc. Lex.*, **Pistol-splint*. **1905** *Dialect Notes* III. 90 **Pistol-toter*,..one who habitually carries a pistol. 'Suppress the pistol-toter and the bootlegger.' General. **1914** *Maclean's Mag.* Dec. 56/1 The police force..is so inefficient that '*pistol-toting' after night is common among all classes. **1965** *Economist* 25 Sept. 1215/3 The men of Sinn Fein..are a more interesting study buying large brandies in the border towns for the pistol-toting Protestants of the Royal Ulster Constabulary. **1895** *Outing* (U.S.) XXVI. 6/1 The Major, holding on with one hand, used the rifle *pistol-wise.

'**pistol**, *v.* [f. prec. sb.: cf. F. *pistoler*.]

1. *trans.* To shoot with a pistol.

1607 DEKKER *Hist. Sir T. Wyatt* Wks. 1873 III. 112 Powder the Varlet, pistoll him. **1691** WOOD *Ath. Oxon.* I. 757 He, out of a deep reluctancy, pistol'd himself in his Cabin. **1748** RICHARDSON *Clarissa* (1811) VIII. xvii. 91 He is afraid you will pistol him. **1894** CROCKETT *Raiders* 152, I declare I could have pistolled him there and then.

2. *intr.* To make a noise like the report of a pistol; to crack. *nonce-use.*

1898 F. WHITMORE in *Atlantic Monthly* Apr. 500/1 His whip-lash whirling and pistoling about his head.

Hence '**pistoling, -olling** *vbl. sb.* and *ppl. a.* (also *fig.*).

1637 HEYLIN *Brief Answ.* 111 One or two godly Ministers ..were threatned..with Pistolling and hanging. **1816** SCOTT *Antiq.* xxii, He has had gunning and pistolling enough. **1877** MORLEY *Crit. Misc.* Ser. II. 392 Macaulay advances with his hectoring sentences and his rough pistolling ways.

pistol, variant of PISTLE *Obs.*

†**pisto'lade**, *sb. Obs.* [a. obs. F. *pistolade* a pistol-shot (1592 in Godefroy *Compl.*), f. *pistole* PISTOL + -ADE; cf. *cannonade*.] A pistol-shot, or wound inflicted by one. Hence **pisto'lade** *v. trans.*, to attack or fire upon with pistols.

1598 R. DALLINGTON *Meth. Trav.* G ij, One of the King of Nauarres troupes gaue him a Pistolade in the head. [**1658** PHILLIPS, *Pistolado* (Ital.), a shot, or wound given with a Pistol.] **1815** SOUTHEY in *Q. Rev.* XIII. 41 The bravery with which he and Admiral Gantheaume and M. Daure pistoladed the English gun boats.

†**pistolar, pistelar.** *Sc. Obs.* [Deriv. obscure: ? related to next.] Name of a small coin, said to be synonymous with LIARD.

1550 *Reg. Privy Council Scot.* I. 106 Legiis..refusis to tak ..the pistelaris dulzeartis, alias callit the liartis. *Ibid.*, That nane..refuse the pistoloris nor deliaris, alias liartis.

pistole (pɪ'stəʊl). Also 6–8 pistol(l. [a. F. *pistole* the coin (*c* 1620 d'Aubigny *Fœneste*), app. shortened from *pistolet*: see PISTOLET[2]. The coin was not known by any corresponding name in Spain or Italy.] A name formerly applied to certain foreign gold coins; sometimes (as in quot. 1592) synonymous with PISTOLET²; *spec.*, from *c* 1600, given to a Spanish gold coin worth from 16*s.* 6*d.* to 18*s.*; also applied (after French) to the louis d'or of Louis XIII, issued in 1640, and sometimes to the Scottish twelve pound piece of William III, 1701, = £1 English.

1592 *Lanc. Wills* II. 127 One peece of gold..to the value of vjˢ wᶜʰ is called a pistole. **1594** NASHE *Christ's T.* Ep. to Rdr., Great pieces of gold, such as double Pistols and Portugues. **1643** *Decl. Commons, Reb. Irel.* 49 Fourteene peeces of eight, and a double Pistoll. **1678** *Phil. Trans.* XII. 1005 Who both have commonly sold their Glasses at the rate of a Pistol (i.e. about 17 shillings and six pence) the foot. **1709** STEELE *Tatler* No. 5 ¶5 Instead of 25 Pistoles formerly allowed to each Member. **1819** MISS MITFORD in L'Estrange *Life* (1870) II. iii. 69 Only think of the Chancellor's sending the President a pistole to pay the postage of his letters. **1898** G. B. RAWLINGS *Brit. Coinage* 189 The last Scottish gold coins, the twelve- and six-pound pieces Scots, sometimes called pistoles and half pistoles.. minted from gold imported from Africa by the Darien Co.. 1701. **1899** SIR J. EVANS in *N. & Q.* 9th Ser. IV. 443/1 Quadruple pistoles..in the last century were commonly accepted in England as being of the value of 3*l.* 12*s.*

ˈpistoled, *a.* Also -old. [f. PISTOL *sb.* + -ED².] Equipped with a pistol or pistols.

1634 W. WOOD *New Eng. Prosp.* II. vii, Being double pistold, and well sworded.

pistoleer (-ˈɪə(r)). [See -EER¹ and cf. PISTOLIER.] One who uses or is skilled in the use of a pistol; a soldier armed with a pistol.

1832 CARLYLE *Misc., Boswell's Johnson* (1857) III. 94 Is the Chalk-Farm Pistoleer inspired with any reasonable Belief and Determination? **1855** PRESCOTT *Philip II*, I. vii, A corps of German pistoleers, of whom there was a body in the French service. **1883** *American* VII. 116 The first step.. must be the condign punishment of the Danville pistoleers.

†**ˈpistoler.** *Obs.* [f. PISTOL *sb.* + -ER¹.] A maker of pistols.

1638 W. MOUNTAGU in *Buccleuch MSS.* (Hist. MSS. Comm.) I. 282 The King..sets all the armourers and pistolers a-work for himself.

pistoler, variant of PISTLER *Obs.*

‖**pistolero** (pɪstəˈlɛərəʊ). [Sp.] In Spain or other Spanish-speaking area; a gunman or gangster. Also *attrib.*

1937 F. BORKENAU *Spanish Cockpit* i. 30 In order to frighten the Catalan bourgeoisie..the Barcelona police actually co-operated with gangs of *pistoleros*, who..claimed to be revolutionaries. **1939** G. GREENE *Lawless Roads* 19 Mexico remained Catholic: it was the governing class—the politicians and pistoleros only who were anti-Catholic. **1957** P. KEMP *Mine were of Trouble* viii. 152 He had been a wild youth..earning his living in Madrid as a *pistolero* for his political party, the Requetés. **1965** C. D. EBY *Siege of Alcázar* (1966) i. 44 The *pistolero* phase of the rebellion had ended. **1973** C. ALVERSON *Fighting Back* (1978) xiv. 80 You and your red-hot pistoleros got my kid brother nearly killed.

‖**pistoˈlese.** *Obs. rare*⁻¹. [It. *pistolese* 'a great dagger, hanger, or wood-knife' (Florio), a sb. use of *Pistolese* adj., of or pertaining to Pistoia, in L. *Pistorium*, a town of Tuscany, still having manufacturers of iron and steel, and esp. gunmaking; cf. Sp. *pistoresa* poniard.] A short sword or dagger (understood to have been made at or named from Pistoia). See PISTOLET¹, PISTOL.

1549 SIR T. HOBY *Trav.* (1902) 14 A varlett..cam behinde him and with a pistolese gave him his deathe's wounde. [*Margin*] A pystolese is a shorte broadsword.

ˈpistolet¹. Also 6 -olett, -ollet, pystolet(t, pistlett, pestilet(t, pestelet, 6-7 *Sc.* pistolat(e. [a. F. *pistolet*, (*a*) a small dagger or poniard; (*b*) a small fire-arm, a pistol, in It. *pistoletto* (16th c.); app. dim. from stem of It. *pistolese* (see PISTOLESE).

The theory is that F. *pistolet* (or ? It. *pistoletto*) with dim. form was applied first to a small dagger, as compared to the It. *pistolese*, and was thence transferred to the pistol, which was also small as compared with the harquebus: see H. Estienne *Conf. de la langue fr. avec le grec*, 1569, préface.]

†**1.** (ˈpɪstɒlɛt). A small fire-arm: the earlier name of the PISTOL. *Obs.*

1550 *Reg. Privy Council Scot.* I. 95 To schut with halff haige or culvering or pistolate. **1561-2** in *Middlesex County Rec.* (1886) I. 43 A pystolett de ferro et calibe. **1567** *Reg. Privy Council Scot.* I. 593 To schute with culveringis, daggis, pistolettis, or ony utheris gunnis or ingynis of fyrewerk. [So **1571**, **1573**, **1599**, **1626**, **1637**, etc. *Ibid.*] **1583** FOXE *A. & M.* (ed. 4) 2153/1 The Amirall..by the way was stroken with a Pistolet charged with iij pellets. **1590** *Wills & Inv. N.C.* (Surtees) II. 185 The apparell of Mʳ John Lawson, and his pistlett, and the stringes to it, 20ˡ. **1599** JAMES I *Βασιλ. Δωρον* (1603) 47 My lawes made against gunnes and traiterous pistolets. **1650** TRAPP *Comm. Num.* x. 7 The Lutherans met by the clap of harquebuzes and pistolets.

‖**2.** (pistɔle). Esp. in Belgium, a small bread roll (so called because of its shape).

1853 C. BRONTË *Villette* I. viii. 142 Boarders were.. regaled with..*pistolets au beurre* (rolls) and coffee. *a* **1855** —— *Professor* (1857) I. xiii. 224, I stirred my cup of coffee with a half-pistolet (we never had spoons). **1857** MRS. GASKELL *Life C. Brontë* I. xi. 271 A slight meal of water and *pistolets* (the delicious little Brussels rolls). **1897** G. DU MAURIER *Martian* IV. 185 Breakfasted on a little roll called a pistolet and a cup of coffee. **1961** T. HENROT *Belgium* 189 Small rolls are either *Viennois*, *miches* or, quaintly, *pistolets*. **1975** T. ALLBEURY *Special Collection* xiv. 95 A basket was filled with bread, from poppy-seed rolls to..grey Minsk pistolets.

†**pistolet².** *Obs.* Also 6 pisto-, pystolette, *Sc.* pistolat(t, -ate, 7 pistollet, -olett. [a. F. *pistolet* (early 16th c. in Hatz.-Darm.; Godefroy's date 1480 is doubted). History obscure.

Generally held to be the same word as *pistolet* the weapon, and according to Des Accords (16th c. in Littré) applied in pleasantry to the Spanish écus 'because they are smaller than the others'. But as yet French lexicographers cite no instances of *pistolet* the weapon of as early a date as those of *pistolet* the coin.]

A name given to certain foreign gold coins; in the 16th c. usually ranging in value from 5*s.* 10*d.* to 6*s.* 8*d.*; in later times (quot. 1659) = PISTOLE.

1553 *Proclam.* 4 May in *Tudor Proclam.* [99] Euery Pystolette..shalbe demed and accepted to be of the value of vj.s. ij.d. of the curraunt moneye of this realme. **1556** W. TOWRSON in Hakluyt *Voy.* (1589) 99, I payed them [off the coast of Barbary] twentie and seuen Pistolets. **1560** *Proclam.* 2 Nov. in *MS. Arch. Bodl* F. c. 11 lf. 32 Of late the peece of gold called the Pistolet was made Currant at fiue shyllynges & tenne pence. By the name or value of Pistolettes, none shalbe currant..but only foure severall peeces and Coynes hereafter pourtraicted and stamped: The fyrst and seconde beyng of the kyng of Spaynes Coyne, the thyrde of Venize, and the fourth of Florence. **1574** *Records of Elgin* (New Spald. Cl.) I. 145 Ane rose nobill, twa angell nobillis and twa pistolat crownis. **1599** THYNNE *Animadv.* (1875) 47 Aboute the valewe of iijs iiijd, beinge halfe a pistolet Italiane or spanyshe. **1617** MORYSON *Itin.* I. 290 The Spanish pistolet, and double pistolet..the double pistolet contains two French Crownes. *Ibid.* 291 At Venice..A double pistolet of Spaine, called Dublon, is..giuen for seuenteene lires. **1659** HEYLIN *Examen Hist.* I. 268 Each Pistolet exchang'd at sixteen shillings six pence.

†**pistoleter, -ˈier.** *Obs.* [f. PISTOLET¹: see -IER.] A soldier armed with a pistol.

1579 DIGGES *Stratiot.* 144 The Pistoleters and Argoletiers. **1581** STYWARD *Mart. Discipl.* II. 136 The hargulaters..who with the pistolaters are the first that begins the battaile. **1598** BARRET *Theor. Warres* 3 A troupe of horse, either Pistoletiers, Hargulatiers or Lanciers.

†**pistoˈletto.** *Obs.* [a. It. *pistoletto*: see PISTOLET¹.] = PISTOLET¹. Also *attrib.* (In quots. *fig.* or *allusive.*)

1647 WARD *Simp. Cobler* 75 To talk Squibs and Pistoletto's charged with..powder of Love and shot of Reason. **1647-8** WOOD *Life* 15 Feb. (O.H.S.) I. 139 Give fire to the pistoletto tobacco pipe charg'd with it's Indian powder.

pistolgraph (ˈpɪstəlgrɑːf, -æ-). Also piˈstolograph. [f. PISTOL *sb.*, after *photograph.* (Cf. *snap-shot.*)] Name of an apparatus for obtaining instantaneous photographs or a photograph so obtained. Also *attrib.* in *fig.* sense. So **ˈpistolgram**, an instantaneous photograph; **pistoˈlography**, instantaneous photography.

1862 *Catal. Internat. Exhib., Brit. Div.* II. xiv. 61 Skaife, 47 Baker Street, W.—Pistolgraph, with a selection of its productions called pistolgrams. **1866** *Morn. Star* 2 Jan., The pistolograph. This beautiful invention is now to be seen..at..118, Pall Mall. The pistolgram is a picture in glass, obtained in the first instance, by an instantaneous flash of light, and subsequently made permanent by fire. *Ibid.*, The most interesting feature in pistolography is its alliance with the magnesium light. *Ibid.*, It is for this class of portrait the pistolograph is chiefly intended. **1887** GLADSTONE in *19th Cent.* Jan. 1 The instantaneous, or 'pistol-graph', criticisms demanded by the necessities of the daily press. **1901** *Daily Chron.* 27 Nov. 7/3 It has pictures of Nebraska and statistics—pistolgraph statistics.

†**pistoˈlier.** *Obs.* [a. obs. F. *pistolier*, f. *pistole* (obs.) pistol: see -IER.] A soldier armed with a pistol.

1577-87 HOLINSHED *Chron.* III. 1187/1 Certeine of the English lances and pistoliers, with certeine harquebutters. **1598** BARRET *Theor. Warres* v. ii. 142. **1622** MARKHAM *Bk. War* III. i. 82 The armed French Pistoliers, the Carbines, and the Light horse.

ˈpistolship. *nonce-wd.* [f. PISTOL *sb.*: see -SHIP.] Skill in using pistols; pistol practice.

1895 WISTER in *Harper's Mag.* Mar. 537 The Governor.. had begun to study pistolship.

ˈpistol-shot. [f. PISTOL *sb.* + SHOT *sb.*]

1. A shot from a pistol.

1662 J. DAVIES tr. *Olearius Voy. Ambass.* 267 M. Mandelslo..kill'd the Leader of the Indian party with a Pistol-shot. **1796** HELEN M. WILLIAMS *Lett. France* IV. 137 (Jod) Several pistol-shot were fired at the president. **1899** T. M. ELLIS *Three Cat's-eye Rings* 122 Then there was a pistol-shot, and Clayside stood breathless over a lifeless man.

2. The distance to which a shot can be fired from a pistol; the range of a pistol.

c **1645** T. TULLY *Siege of Carlisle* (1840) 38 He came within pistle shot. **1685** TRAVESTIN *Siege Newheusel* 6 Not above a Pistol-shot from it. **1741** S. SPEED in *Buccleuch MSS.* (Hist. MSS. Comm.) I. 395 When we came within half pistol-shot, we hailed one of the French ships. **1835** W. IRVING *Tour Prairies* 267 My object..was to get within pistol-shot of the buffalo.

3. One who shoots with a pistol.

1949 BLUNDEN *Addresses on Gen. Subjects* 24 He [*sc.* Shelley] was judged a horseman and a pistol-shot equal to his sporting friend Lord Byron. **1979** C. ALLEN *Tales from Dark Continent* vii. 99 A great bayonet fighter and trick pistol shot and a splendid figure.

4. *attrib.* (in first quot. *advb.*).

1697 DAMPIER *Voy.* (1699) 241 The Mouth of this Lagune is not Pistol-shot wide. **1730** *Hist. Litteraria* I. 401 A Blast and Smoak..which obliged me to keep at Pistol-shot distance. **1900** *Westm. Gaz.* 17 July 8/1 They might urge them on with the pistol-shot reports of their long whips. **1942** *Essays & Stud.* XXVII. 59 And this pistol-shot style, bang bang bang, with its absolute certainty of detail, leaving the scraps of picture, like a jigsaw puzzle, for you to fit together.

ˈpistol-whip, *v.* orig. and chiefly *U.S.* [f. PISTOL *sb.* + WHIP *v.*] *trans.* To strike (someone) with the butt of a pistol. Also *fig.* Hence **ˈpistol-whipping** *vbl. sb.*

1942 BERREY & VAN DEN BARK *Amer. Thes. Slang* §322/5 *Pistol-whip*, to strike with the butt of a pistol. **1952** *Sun* (Baltimore) 4 July 42/8 The two young Negroes pitched into him and the one with the gun pistol-whipped the physician. **1958** J. THOMPSON *Getaway* (1972) iv. 29 The banker lay sprawled on the floor, half-dead from Rudy's pistol-whipping. **1965** J. PHILIPS *Twisted People* I. iv. 88 She'd been subjected to about the worst beating I've ever seen. Pistol whipped is my guess. **1967** *Observer* 23 Apr. 5/3 The British Foreign Secretary had been subjected to 'a pistol-whipping'..from Mr. Walt Rostow in the White House. **1970** K. PLATT *Pushbutton Butterfly* (1971) xi. 132, I remembered the pistol-whipping..and brought my knee up to his face. **1973** G. SIMS *Hunters Point* xiii. 124 He could feel the pain from the pistol-whipping blows he'd taken on his ribs. **1977** J. WAMBAUGH *Black Marble* (1978) xiv. 322 Let a cop get pistol-whipped instead of a clerk.

pistomesite (pɪˈstɒmɪsaɪt). *Min.* [a. Ger. *pistomesit* (Breithaupt 1847), f. Gr. πίστο-ς true + μέσ-ον middle, because considered the exact mean between magnesite and siderite: cf. MESITITE.] A carbonate of magnesium and iron, containing less magnesium and more iron than mesitite.

1849 NICOL *Min.* 294 The pistomesite of Breithaupt from Thurnberg. **1868** DANA *Min.* 688 *Pistomesite*... Named by Breithaupt..because pistomesite is nearer the middle between chalybite [= siderite] and magnesite than mesitine.

piston (ˈpɪstən), *sb.* [a. F. *piston* (1647 Pascal, in Littré), ad. It. *pistone* piston, variant of *pestone* great pestle, rammer, augm. from stem *pest-* in *pestello* pestle: cf. It. *pestāre*:—late L. *pistāre*, freq. of *pinsĕre*, *pist-* to pound, beat. Cf. OF. *peston* = *pilon* pestle, stamper.]

1. A mechanical contrivance, consisting of a disk or short cylinder of wood, iron, or other solid substance, which fits closely within a hollow cylinder or tube, and can be driven with a reciprocating motion up and down the tube, or backwards and forwards in it; on one side it is attached to a rod (***piston-rod***) by which it imparts motion to machinery (e.g. in a steam-engine), or by which motion is imparted to it (e.g. in a pump).

1704 J. HARRIS *Lex. Techn.* D ij (s.v. *Air pump*), Each time the *Piston* or Sucker of the Pump is drawn back, the Air in the Receiver must expand it self so as in some measure to fill up the Cavity of the Pump left vacant by the *Piston*, as well as the Receiver it self. **1712** J. JAMES tr. *Le Biond's Gardening* 192 *Piston* is the short Cilinder..which is moved up and down in the Barrel of the Pump. **1786** REES *Chambers' Cycl.* s.v. *Steam-engine*, A large barrel or cylinder..and in this a piston well leathered. **1827** FARADAY *Chem. Manip.* xv. 341 A small piston rendered air-tight by tow and tallow. **1842** BRANDE *Dict. Sc.*, etc. s.v., Two sorts of pistons are used..: one hollow, with a valve, used in the sucking pump; and the other solid, which is employed in the forcing pump. **1867** W. W. SMYTH *Coal & Coal-mining* 210 Horizontally-working pistons in prismatic chambers were erected in 1828 by M. Brisco, near Charleroi.

2. a. In the cornet and other wind-instruments: A sliding valve which moves in a cylinder like a piston, used for increasing the effective length of the air-passage and thus lowering the pitch of the note. Hence ***cornet-à-piston***.

1876 tr. *Blaserna's Sound* i. 20 By opening a communication with the external air..by means of pistons in the cornet.

b. A pneumatic thumb-knob in an organ, which is pushed in like a piston, and has the effect of combining a number of stops.

1890 in *Cent. Dict.*

3. *Zool.* A central retractile part in the suckers on the arms of a cuttle-fish or other cephalopod, which acts like the piston of an air-pump in producing a vacuum.

1871 T. R. JONES *Anim. Kingd.* (ed. 4) 605 A deep cavity ..at the bottom of which is placed a prominent piston..that may be retracted by muscular fibres.

4. *attrib.* and *Comb.*, as ***piston-plunger***, ***power***, ***speed***; ***piston-like*** adj.; **piston bellows**, bellows in which the draught is supplied by the action of a piston; **piston corer** or **core sampler**, a core sampler consisting of a long weighted cylinder containing at its lower end a piston attached to the lowering cable, devised so that when the cylinder enters the bottom sediments under its own weight the descent of the piston is arrested, and the resulting partial vacuum inside the cylinder causes the pressure of the water to be effective in forcing it into the bottom; **piston drill**, a percussion drill in which the bit is attached to the rod of a piston; **piston engine**, a reciprocating engine, esp. an aircraft engine in which the airscrew is driven by the reciprocating action of pistons; hence **piston-engined** *a.*, powered by this kind of engine; **piston-head**, the disc or cylindrical part of a piston, which slides in the tube, as distinguished from the *piston-rod*; **piston-knob** = 2 b; **piston-packing**, (*a*) any material used for filling the space between the piston-head and the cylinder in which it works, so as to make it steam-tight, air-tight, or water-tight; (*b*) a mechanical device for packing pistons; **pistonphone** *Acoustics*, a device for producing known sound pressures by means of a vibrating piston whose motion is precisely measured, used mainly for calibrating microphones; **piston pin**, a pin which secures a piston to its connecting rod in an internal-combustion engine; **piston-pump**, a pump having a piston; **piston ring**, a metal ring fitted on a piston to seal the gap between the piston and the cylinder wall; **piston-rod** (see 1); **piston slap**, rocking of a loosely fitting piston against the cylinder wall, or the noise resulting from this; **piston-sleeve**, a hollow cylinder or *trunk* moving longitudinally with the piston-head in a trunk-engine, and taking the place of the cross-head; **piston-spring**, a spring connected with a piston-head, and forming, or having the effect of, a packing (Knight *Dict. Mech.* 1875); **piston-valve**, (*a*) a valve in a piston, as in that of a pump; (*b*) a valve formed by a small piston sliding backwards and forwards in a tube, for admitting steam into, or exhausting it from, the cylinder of a steam-engine; **piston-wheel**, (*a*) a wheel or rotating disk carrying at its outer margin one or more pistons; (*b*) in a chain-pump, a wheel carrying an endless chain bearing pistons or disks working in a tube or barrel; **piston-whistle**, a whistle in which the pitch of the sound is varied by means of a piston sliding in the tube.

*a*1877 KNIGHT *Dict. Mech.* II. 1717/1 A *piston-bellows, formed by boring out the trunks of trees, used by the natives of Madagascar for smelting..iron. **1947** B. KULLENBERG in *Svenska Hydrogr.-Biol. Komm. Skrifter* (*Ser. 3: Hydrogr.*). I. II. 12 The *piston core sampler..has been based on a method to procure samples for ground investigations, developed by the Geotechnical Department of the Swedish State Railways. **1956** Piston core-sampler [see CORE *sb.*[1] 4]. **1959** H. BARNES *Oceanogr. & Marine Biol.* i. 67 In Kullenberg's *piston corer the hydrostatic pressure at great depths is utilized to overcome..friction and to allow very long undisturbed cores to be taken. **1976** *New Scientist* 9 Dec. 576/2 The oceanographers' piston corers that were beginning to recover cores, or columns of mud, from the floor of the deep ocean. [**1901** M. M. KIRKMAN *Locomotive Appliances* 475 (*caption*) Piston air drill for drilling, reaming and tapping on locomotive work.] **1919** R. PEELE *Compressed Air Plant for Mines* (ed. 3) xx. 306 At a large group of mines on the Rand, the complete repair cost of standard *piston drills..averaged $42.00 per 52 shifts. **1967** K. MCGREGOR *Drilling of Rock* i. 12, 1860–70..; a commercial piston drill was patented by Burleigh in America. *Ibid.* 13 From these [drop drills] developed..the pneumatic piston drill... These machines were finally obsolete in the early 1920's. **1907** *Engineering* 21 June 829/2 If the turbine requires a screw which is necessarily less efficient than that of the *piston engine, it is the fault of the turbine system. *Ibid.*, Ordinary reciprocating, or, to use a shorter word, piston, engines. **1943** G. G. SMITH *Gas Turbines & Jet Propulsion* (ed. 2) vii. 54 Even if free-flying piston engine and compressor units were employed these handicaps would remain. **1960** C. H. GIBBS-SMITH *Aeroplane* xvi. 126 The piston engine reached its apogee in the post-war period with such examples as the Pratt & Whitney 28-cylinder 3,500 h.p. radial. **1971** P. J. MCMAHON *Aircraft Propulsion* xi. 311 Mechanical losses in piston engines are high, being up to 25% of the indicated power. **1948** *Jrnl. R. Aeronaut. Soc.* LII. 591/1 The Airspeed Ambassador may be taken as representing the most advanced *piston-engined commercial aeroplane of its size yet in prospect. **1974** E. AMBLER *Dr. Frigo* I. 56 For most of those critical three days I was..in piston-engined planes missing connecting flights. **1979** *Daily Tel.* 1 Dec. 10/6 Their departure..coincides with the paying off of the Navy's only remaining steam reciprocating, or piston-engined, ship. **1875** KNIGHT *Dict. Mech.*, **Piston-head*, that portion which fits into and reciprocates in the cylinder. **1888** HASLUCK *Model Engin. Handybk.* (1900) 51 The piston-head is in two parts..; one must have a taper hole bored to fit the rod. **1902** *Academy* 9 Aug. 159/2 Defoe's *piston-like pen. **1875** KNIGHT *Dict. Mech.*, **Piston-packing*, a material for preventing the leakage of steam between the piston-head and the cylinder in which it works. **1922** E. WENTE in *Physical Rev.* XIX. 343 (*caption*) Use of *pistonphone for calibrating an electrostatic transmitter. *Ibid.* 500 The open-circuit voltage of the transmitter per unit of pressure has been measured with the piston-phone for the frequency range of 10 to 200 cycles per second. **1965** C. A. TAYLOR *Physics Mus. Sounds* vi. 100 The pistonphone..appears to be used only for scientific work at very low frequencies. It consists..of a piston driven by a rotating cam which permits the generation of sinusoidal variations in pressure of accurately-controlled form. **1972** *Where* Dec. 336/3 Our tests were done with a B and K portable octave band analyser, which was calibrated before and after each occasion with a pistonphone. **1897** F. GROVER *Pract. Treat. Mod. Gas & Oil Engines* xvii. 175 The pressure on the *piston pin may be much more than upon the crank pin. **1910** W. A. TOOKEY tr. *Mathot's Construction & Working of Internal Combustion Engines* xiii. 375 The piston pin is made of the best quality mild steel. **1967** J. L. & G. H. F. NAYLER *Dict. Mech. Engin.* 176 *Gudgeon pin*... Also called 'piston pin'. **1797** *Monthly Mag.* III. 464 The *piston-plunger is worked by a toothed segment-wheel. **1899** *Daily News* 7 Dec. 3/5 These solid slabs of metal are forced by..'*piston-power through a series of holes.' **1867** N. P. BURGH *Mod. Marine Engin.* vi. 277/2 The adoption of 'springs' behind the '*piston ring' is now becoming general. **1936** *Discovery* Feb. 39/1 Steam leaking past the piston rings of the high-pressure cylinders. **1971** J. H. HAYNES *Mini Owner's Workshop Man.* i. 30/1 To remove the piston rings, slide them carefully over the top of the piston, taking care not to scratch the aluminium alloy. **1976** L. DEIGHTON *Twinkle, Twinkle Little Spy* x. 97 The running repairs I do myself... Last month I changed the piston rings. **1786** REES *Chambers' Cycl.* s.v., *Steam-engine*, The *piston-rod, which is truly cylindrical, moves up and down through that hole. **1830** HERSCHEL *Stud. Nat. Phil.* II. vii. 194 The power which alternately raised and depressed the piston-rod of the engine. **1895** *Model Steam Engine* 39 Small holes should be drilled in the top of the bearings, piston-rod guide, eccentric-band, and crank-pin end of connecting rod for admitting oil. **1916** P. M. HELDT *Gasoline Automobile* (ed. 4) I. vii. 163 To obviate..*piston slap when starting, it is well to make the piston comparatively long. **1962** *Which? Car Suppl.* Jan. 32/2 A worrying piston-slap rattle from the engine. **1968** *Practical Motorist* Dec. 459/1 *Piston slap*, a characteristic metallic slapping sound within the cylinders caused by slight rocking motion of an ill-fitting or worn piston. **1815** J. SMITH *Panorama Sc. & Art* II. 6 To improve the air-pump, Smeaton..covered the top of the barrel..by which contrivance he took off the pressure of the atmosphere from the *piston-valve. **1875** KNIGHT *Dict. Mech.*, *Piston-valve*, a valve consisting of a circular disk, which reciprocates in a cylindrical chamber.

'piston, *v.* [f. the sb.] *intr.* To move like a piston. Occas. *trans.*, to direct, throw with a piston-like movement.

1930 R. CAMPBELL *Adamastor* 80 Down the stage the dance..Tarantulates in scarlet tights For flashing arms to piston. **1940** DYLAN THOMAS *Portrait of Artist as Young Dog* 52 The small boy in his invisible engine..kicked the dog's plate at the washhouse stop, and puffed and pistoned slower and slower while the servant girl lowered the pole. **1958** *Spectator* 15 Aug. 219/3 Thin grey knees piston over the beach. **1976** 'E. MCBAIN' *Guns* (1977) v. 118 He..pistoned a short hand punch to her shoulder.

†**'pistor.** *Obs. rare.* In 7 **-our.** [a. AF. *pistour*, *pestour* = OF. *pestor*, *-eur*:—L. *pistōr-em* baker, f. *pi(n)sĕre* to pound.] (See quot. 1682.)

[**1607** MIDDLETON *Phœnix* I. Ciij, Why Pistor a Baker sold his wife tother day to a cheesemonger.] *a*1682 SIR T. BROWNE *Tracts* i. (1683) 17 Their Pistours were such as, before the use of Mills, beat out and cleansed their Corn.

So **pi'storial, pi'storian, pi'storical** *adjs.*, pertaining to a baker.

1656 BLOUNT *Glossogr.*, *Pistorical*, or *pistorian*, belonging to a Baker, baking or Pastry. **1838** *Fraser's Mag.* XVIII. 543 An antagonist baker..has commenced business in the pistorial line on the opposite side of the street.

†**'pistrine.** *Obs. rare.* [ad. L. *pistrīna* a bakery, f. *pistor* baker.] A bakehouse, bakery.

[**1392–3** *Earl Derby's Exp.* (Camden) 222 Et pro portagio saccorum de le Ryoll ad pistrinam, iiijs.] *a*1483 *Liber Niger* in *Househ. Ord.* (1790) 70 To delyver the wheete..sending it to the mylles, and so into the pystryne. **1656** BLOUNT *Glossogr.*, *Pistrine*, a Bake-house, a..grinding-house.

pistul, -yl, variants of PISTLE *Obs.*

pit (pɪt), *sb.*[1] Forms: see below. [OE. *pytt*, ME. *pyt(t*, *pit*, *put(t*, *pet* = OFris. *pet*, OS. *putti*, MLG., MDu. *putte*, LG. *pütte*, Du. *put*, OHG. *pfuzzi*, *pfuzza*, MHG., Ger. *pfütze*; also ON. *pyttr* (from OE.); all repr. a WGer. **puttjo*[z], a. L. *puteus* well, pit, shaft. In ME. the OE. *y* was repr. in midl. dial. by *y*, *i*, in s.w. by *u* (-y-), and in Kent by *e*.]

A. Illustration of Forms.

a. α. 1 pytt, pyt (see B. 1); 2–5 putt, put.

*c*1175 *Lamb. Hom.* 47 Þe prophete stod in ane putte. *c*1205 LAY. 15961 Þe put wes ilær. *c*1425 *Eng. Conq. Irel.* 36 Thay burryd an hounde with hym yn the pute that he was yn I-leyde. **1467** in *Eng. Gilds* 385 Puttes of bloode.

β. 3–4 pett, 4–5 pet, (6 pette).

*c*1200 *Vices & Virtues* 109 Hie falleð mid ða blinde in to ðan pette. *c*1315 SHOREHAM *Poems* VII. 522 Godes domes beþ A groundlyas pet [*rime* ylet]. **1426** LYDG. *De Guil. Pilgr.* 17875, I curse hem in-to helle pet. **1599** BRETON *Praise Vertuous Ladies* (Grosart) 57/2 If shee have her hand on the pette in her cheeke.

γ. 4–6 pytt, pyt, 4–8 pitt, 5– pit, (4 pite, pyte, 4–7 pitte, 5–6 pytte).

13.. *Cursor M.* 4155 In þis wast i wat a pite [*v.rr.* pitte, pitt, *c*1425 pit]. *c*1400 MAUNDEV. (1839) viii. 94 A litylle pytt in the erthe. **1406** HOCCLEVE *Misrule* 95 Rype vn-to my pit. *c*1440 *Promp. Parv.* 402/1 Pyt, or flasche where mekyl water standythe. **1535** COVERDALE *2 Esdras* v. 24 Thou hast chosen the one pytt. —— *Luke* xiv. 5 Fallen in to a pytte. **1588** *Nottingham Rec.* IV. 223 The hye waye above the clay pittes.

B. I. Signification.

1. a. A hole or cavity in the ground, formed either by digging or by some natural process.

847 *Charter of Æthelwulf* (Sweet *O.E.T.* 434), Đonne on grenan pytt. *c*893 K. ÆLFRED *Oros.* v. ii. §1 And on pyttas besuncan. *c*1000 *Ags. Gosp.* Matt. xii. 11 ȝyf þæt afylð restedagum on pytt. *c*1175 [see A. α]. *a*1225 *Ancr. R.* 58 Ȝif eni unwrie put were, & best feolle þer inne. *a*1300 *Cursor M.* 2500 (Cott.) Þe fiue gaue bak..And fell to in a pitt o clay. *c*1430 *Life St. Kath.* (1884) 51 He þat fedde danyel þe prophet in þe pytte of lyouns. **1526** *Pilgr. Perf.* (W. de W. 1531) 276 b, That no man sholde dyg ony pyt..but he sholde couer it agayne. **1588** SHAKS. *Tit. A.* II. iii. 193 The lothsome pit, Where I espied the Panther fast asleepe. **1611** BIBLE *Jer.* ii. 6 A land of deserts and of pittes. **1855** TENNYSON *Maud* I. I. ii, There in the ghastly pit..a body was found.

b. An open deep hole or excavation made in digging for some mineral deposit; often with descriptive word, as CHALK-, CLAY-, GRAVEL-, MARL-, SAND-PIT: see these words, also sense 6.

956 [see *chalk-pit*, CHALK *sb.* 7]. **1382** WYCLIF *Gen.* xiv. 10 The wodi valei forsothe had manye pyttis of glewy clay [**1388** pittis of pitche; **1535** COVERD. slyme pyttes; **1885** *R.V.* slime pits]. *c*1440– [see *clay-pit*, CLAY *sb.* 9]. **1604** E. G[RIMSTONE] *D'Acosta's Hist. Indies* IV. iv. 213 The golde..is found in pittes or mines. **1722** DE FOE *Col. Jack* (1840) 288 A little kind of a gravel pit, or marl pit.

c. A hole or excavation made for a special purpose in various industries, as sawing, tanning, founding, charcoal-burning, etc.: see quots., and COAL-PIT 1, SAWPIT, TAN-PIT, etc.

1023– [see COAL-PIT 1]. **1589** *Pappe w. Hatchet* C j b, Martin and his mainteiner are both sawers of timber, but Martin stands in the pit. **1616** in *Mem. Fountains Abb.* (Surtees) I. 365 The tanhouse..with..the pits there. **1663** GERBIER *Counsel* 25 The Sawyers at their Pit. **1875** KNIGHT *Dict. Mech.*, *Pit*... (*Founding*), a cavity or hollow scooped in the floor to receive cast-metal...a vat in tanning, bleaching, dyeing, or in washing alum earth, etc. **1876** SCHULTZ *Leather Manuf.* 26 The pits should be covered on the top by timbers. **1881** RAYMOND *Mining Gloss.*, *Pit*,..a stack or *meiler* of wood, prepared for the manufacture of charcoal.

d. *Agric.* and *Gardening.* A hole or excavation made for storing and protecting edible roots, etc. through the winter (hence extended to a heap of such roots covered with earth or straw for protection); or one (usually with a glazed frame) for protecting young or tender plants.

*c*1500 in Turner *Dom. Archit.* I. 144 Take many rype walenottes..& put hem in a moiste pytt, & hile hem. **1810**, **1837** Pine pit [see PINE *sb.*[2] 7]. **1813** R. KERR *Agric. Surv. Berwick.* 293 A pit or pie, is a conical heap of potatoes..resting upon the dry bare ground..carefully covered by a layer of straw..the earth thrown over the straw [etc.]. **1866** BRANDE & COX *Dict. Sc.*, etc. II. 913/1 They are..what are called cold pits, which means that they are not artificially heated, and are used for the protection in winter of hardy and half-hardy plants. **1895** SCULLY *Kafir Stories* 102 By probing with their spears..the men easily found the flat stones covering the mouths of the underground corn-pits.

e. A deep hole or chamber in which prisoners were confined, a dungeon. ? *Obs.* exc. *Hist.*

1512 *Act 4 Hen. VIII*, c. 8 Preamb., The said Richard was taken and imprisoned in a doungen and a depe pytt under grounde. **1571–2** *Reg. Privy Council Scot.* II. 111 The said Robertis hous in Ancrum, quhair thai put and kest thame in the pit thairof. **1588** *Ibid.* IV. 284 [They] tuke him..to the said schireffis Castle.., putt him in the pitt thairof, quhairin thay held and detenit him. **1761** *Chron.* in *Ann. Reg.* 61 The very pit, where the felons are confined at night. **1816** SCOTT *Old Mort.* ix, I will cause Harrison..look for the key of our pit, or principal dungeon. **1885** BIBLE (R.V.) *Jer.* xxxviii. 6 Then took they Jeremiah, and cast him into the dungeon [*marg.* or pit] of Malchiah.

f. An excavation, covered or otherwise hidden to serve as a trap for wild beasts (or in former times for enemies); a pitfall.

1611 BIBLE *Ezek.* xix. 4 He [a young lion] was taken in their pit. **1735** SOMERVILLE *Chase* III. 232 Low in the Ground A Pit they sink. **1834** MEDWIN *Angler in Wales* I. 62 If a fox escapes from a pit, none are ever taken again in the same. **1895** SCULLY *Kafir Stories* 120 Kondwana the induna,..and one other, had fallen into an old elephant-pit, the surface of which was completely covered over with brushwood.

g. *fig.* or in figurative phrases; chiefly in prec. sense (f), esp. in biblical use.

*c*1315 [see A. β]. *a*1340 HAMPOLE *Psalter* vii. 16 He fell in þe pit þat he made. *c*1532 LATIMER *Serm. & Rem.* (Parker Soc.) II. 347 To follow the blind guides, is to come into the pit with the same. **1535** COVERDALE *Prov.* xxii. 14 The mouth of an harlot is a depe pytt. **1577** *F. de L'isle's Legendarie* H iij, That..you fall not into any such bottomles pit of debts. **1604** DEKKER *Honest Wh.* I. xiii, He fals himselfe that digs anothers pit. **1722** DE FOE *Relig. Courtsh.* I. ii. (1840) 42, I would not fall into the pit with my eyes open. **1850** ROBERTSON *Serm.* Ser. II. ii. (1864) 31 The cold damp pits of disappointment.

h. (*a*) = *engine-pit* (*b*) s.v. ENGINE *sb.* 11 b. Hence used allusively (freq. in *pl.*) of the area at the side of a motor-racing track where competing cars are prepared and maintained.

1839 *Chambers's Edin. Jrnl.* 7 Dec. 368 Under each engine is a pit three feet deep, which enables the engine-men to get underneath to examine and repair it. **1907** [see INSPECTION 6]. **1912** *Collier's* 28 Sept. 11/1 Up swoops the racer, rear wheels locked and sliding, thundering and veiled in smoke, and stops at the pit. **1913** *Technical World Mag.* June 492/1 As De Palma passed his rival's pit..one of the attendants reached for a telephone. **1924** *Brooklands Gaz.* Oct. 176/2 F. C. Clayton on his Marseal, had to turn into the pits after eight laps. **1928** *Evening News* 18 Aug. 1/3 He was pulling into the pits to refill. **1930** E. WAUGH *Vile Bodies* x. 182 'The pits' turned out to be a line of booths, built of wood and corrugated iron immediately opposite the Grand Stand. Many of the cars had already arrived and stood at their 'pits', surrounded by a knot of mechanics and spectators. **1946**

Sun (Baltimore) 23 Dec. 17/3 Each will have three long maintenance 'pits' to accommodate nine busses at one time. **1957** *Times* 16 Oct. 12/6 A man who had a garage and a pit and no car. **1968** *Listener* 5 Sept. 301/3 So there I was, having failed my examinations, working in the pits with Duncan Hamilton. **1972** M. GILBERT *Body of Girl* iv. 44 He climbed out of the pit..and said..'You've come to buy a car.' **1973** *Times* 30 Apr. 7/1 Peterson's domination ended abruptly on lap 57 when he brought his car to a halt with a broken gearbox, to receive a huge ovation from the crowd when he walked back to the pits. **1977** *Times* 15 July (Motor Racing Suppl.) p. ii/8 Dron pulled his Dolomite into the pits, mistakenly believing the race was over. But..he managed to pass the flag at the end of the pit road in time to win his class.

2. A hole dug or sunk in the ground for water; a well, a water-hole; a pond, pool. *Obs.* or merged in 1.

890–901 *Ælfred's Laws* Introd. §22 ȝif hwa adelfe wæter pyt [*v.r.* pyth (*cisternam*)] oððe betynedne ontyne. *c* **975** *Rushw. Gosp.* John iv. 12 Ahne arðu mara feder usum iacobe seðe salde us ðiosne pytt & he of him dranc. **1297** R. GLOUC. (Rolls) 8465 þat alle þe wateres..& diches & puttes rede of blode þere. **13..** *K. Alis.* 5764 (Bodl. MS.) Hij founden many lake & pett Wiþ trowes & þornes byshette. *c* **1400** *Apol. Loll.* 25 As þe welle mai not bring forþ of o pitte bitter water & swete. *c* **1402** LYDG. *Compl. Bl. Knt.* xiv, Ne lyk the pitte of the Pegace Under Pernaso, where poetes slepte. **1530** PALSGR. 254/2 Pytte or well. **1611** BIBLE *Lev.* xi. 36 A fountain or pit, wherein there is plenty of water, shall be clean. **1626** BACON *Sylva* §1 Dig a pit upon the seashore.. and as the tide cometh in, it will fill with water, fresh and potable.

3. A hole dug in the ground for a dead body; a grave. *Obs.* or *dial.* (exc. as applied to a large hole used to receive many bodies: cf. *plague-pit* in PLAGUE *sb.* 4 c.)

1297 R. GLOUC. (Rolls) 11203 Wan a ded man me wole to putte bringe. *c* **1330** R. BRUNNE *Chron. Wace* (Rolls) 16449 ȝyf any had leyd a cors in pyt. *c* **1425** *Cast. Persev.* 1584 in *Macro Plays* 121 Late men þat arn on þe pyttis brynke. **1466** in *Archæologia* (1887) L. 1. 49 He shall make the pittes for dead bodies depe Inough. **1565** STAPLETON tr. *Bede's Hist. Ch. Eng.* 155 She..semed to be almost dead and at the pitts brimme. **1593** SHAKS. *Rich. II*, IV. i. 219 And soone lye Richard in an Earthie Pit. **1611** BIBLE *Ps* xxx. 3 O Lord.. thou hast kept me alive, that I should not go down to the pit. [In *Eng. Dial. Dict.* from Devonsh.]

4. The abode of evil spirits and lost souls; hell, or some part of it, conceived as a sunken place, or as a dungeon or place of confinement. Often in phr. ***the pit of hell***.

a **1225** *Juliana* 15 (Bodl. MS.) To forwurðe wið him..iþe putte of helle. *a* **1300** *Cursor M.* 22055 (Cott.) An angel.. bar þe kai o þe mikel pijt. *c* **1386** CHAUCER *Pars. T.* ¶96 Vnder hym the horrible put of helle open. *c* **1440** *York Myst.* xxxvii. 348, I synke in to helle pitte. **1500–20** DUNBAR *Poems* xxi. 68 Quhen na houss is bot hell and hevin, Palice of licht, or pitt obscure. **1526** TINDALE *Rev.* ix. 1 And to him was geven the kaye of the bottomlesse pytt. **1602** SHAKS. *Ham.* IV. v. 132 Conscience and Grace, to the profoundest Pit. I dare Damnation. **1678** BUNYAN *Pilgr.* I. 76 The Hobgoblins, Satyrs, and Dragons of the Pit. **1827** POLLOK *Course T.* x. 476 Into the yawning pit Of bottomless perdition. **1872** MORLEY *Voltaire* i. (1886) 4 To unmask a demon from the depths of the pit. **1892** *Speaker* 3 Sept. 289/1 Such a one..might take the path that leads to the pit.

5. a. An enclosure in which animals were (or in some countries still are) set to fight for sport; esp. a COCKPIT.

to fly or ***shoot the pit***, to turn and fly out of the pit, as a craven cock; hence *fig.* of a person.

a **1568** ASCHAM *Scholem.* II. (Arb.) 127 One Cock..which ..doth passe all other..that euer I saw in any pitte. **1627** E. F. *Hist. Edw. II* (1680) 120 Their Friends turn craven, and all forsake the pit before the battle. **1664** BUTLER *Hud.* II. iii. 1112 To quit His victory, and fly the pit. **1675** MARVELL *Let. to Sir H. Thompson*, He hath a month ago shot the pit..he hath thought convenient to passe over into Holland. **1676** —— *Mr. Smirke* Pref. A ij, Had he esteemed..that it was decent for him to have enter'd the Pit with so Scurrilous an Animadverter. **1704** *Lond. Gaz.* No. 4063/4 The..Pens are ..built over the Pit. **1741** RICHARDSON *Pamela* (1824) I. 202 We were all to blame, to make madam, here, fly the pit, as she did.

b. The cockpit of a ship: = COCKPIT 3.

6. An excavation made for obtaining coal; the shaft of a coal-mine; also, often applied to the mine as a whole.

(Orig. the same as in *chalk-pit*, *sand-pit*, etc., in sense 1 b, and doubtless going back to the time when the coal-pit was, like these, merely an open excavation; hence also its technical restriction to the shaft, which is the open hole.)

1447– [see COAL-PIT 2]. **1669** *Phil. Trans.* IV. 967 There being in these Mines an incredible mass of wood to support the Pitts and the Horizontal passages. **1708** J. C. *Compl. Collier* (1845) 23 If £1000 or more be spent in carrying down a Pit or Shaft. **1725** T. THOMAS in *Portland Papers* VI. (Hist. MSS. Comm.) 106 That pit through which they bring up the coal..is called the shaft. **1774** GOLDSM. *Nat. Hist.* (1776) I. 81 They were resolved to renew their work in the same pit, and eight of them ventured down..but they had scarce got to the bottom of the stairs that led to the pit ..[when] they all instantly dropped down dead. **1845** DISRAELI *Sybil* VI. vi, 'He's a pretty fellow to come and talk to us', said a collier. 'He had never been down a pit in all his life'. **1851** GREENWELL *Coal-trade Terms Northumb. & Durh.* 38 *Pit*, a circular, oval, square, or oblong vertical sinking from the surface. The term shaft..is often used as synonymous. **1867** W. W. SMYTH *Coal & Coal mining* 118 The pits are 515 yards deep to the 'top hard' seam.

7. ***pit and gallows***, more properly ***gallows and pit***, in *Sc. Law* a phrase understood to denote the privilege, formerly conferred on barons, of executing thieves or other felons by hanging the men on a gallows and drowning the woman in a pit: see sense 2. *Obs.* exc. *Hist.*

For this, ancient Sc. statutes in L. have *furca et fossa*. 'In some old deeds written in our language, these terms are rendered *furc* and *foss*' (Jamieson s.v.). The actual meaning of *pit* and *fossa* has been questioned. Du Cange has a quot. from Gervase of Canterbury in which *fossa* is an ordeal pit; so also in *Custumals of Battle Abbey* (Camd. Soc. 126); and it has been suggested that this was also the original meaning in *furca et fossa*. But in support of the usual interpretation, see *Laws of Æthelstan* IV. 6 De fure, qui personam vel locum pacis adierit: §4 Si libera mulier sit, praecipitetur de clivo vel submergatur (Schmid *Gesetze Angels.* 151). And cf. Old German Proverbs cited by Grimm *Deutsche Rechts-Altertümer*, cap. *Verbrechen u. Strafe am Leben*: (1) Der Mann an den Galgen, die Frau unter den Stein; (2) Den Männern Hinrichtung mit dem Strang, den Frauen mit Wassern; (3) Den Dieb soll man henken und die Hur ertränken. In Middle Dutch, where the parallel phrase *putte ende galghen* is very frequent, *putte* was a pit or grave in which women criminals were buried alive (*levend begraven*): see Verwijs and Verdam s.v. *Putte*.

[? *a* **1153** *Sc. Acts David I*, c. 13 in *Scot. Stat.* (1844) I. 319 [red] Omnes barones qui habent furcam et fossam de latrocinio.] **1275** *Rot. Hundred* (1818) II. 302/1 Thomas de Furnivall tenet manerium..et habet furcas pitte pillory tumberel [etc.]. *a* **1500** *transl.* quot. *a* 1153 Al barounis þe quhilkis hes galowys and pyt of thyft. **1609** SKENE *Reg. Maj.* I. iv. 6 b, To hald their courts, with sock, sack, gallous, and pit, toll, and thame, infang-thief, and outfang-thief. [*orig.* qui habent, & tenent curias suas; cum socco & sacca, furca & fossa, *Toill, & Theme, Infang-thiefe, & Outfang-thiefe.*] **1614** SELDEN *Titles Hon.* 286 The Gallows vnderstand as Ours, and for men Theiues; and the Pit, a place to drown Women Theiues. *c* **1730** BURT *Lett. N. Scotl.* (1818) II. 149 The heritable power of pit and gallows..is I think too much for any subject to be trusted withal. **1814** SCOTT *Wav.* x.

II. †**8.** A hollow or cavity in any vessel. *Obs.*

c **1375** *Sc. Leg. Saints* xxv. (*Julian*) 534 þe gold til hyme þane tuke he sone, And askis in þe pyt has done.

9. A hollow or indentation in an animal or plant body, or in any surface: *spec.* **a.** A natural hollow or depression in the body, as the ARMPIT; a socket, as of the eye, or in a bone at a joint; †a dimple. (In quot. 1818, the central hollow in a flower.) Also as an *ellipt.* use for 'armpit' (*slang*).

† ***pit of the chin*** (obs.), the hollow between the chin and the lower lip. ***pit of the stomach***, the slight depression in the region of the stomach between the cartilages of the false ribs.

c **1250** *Death* 241 in *O.E. Misc.* 182 Also beoð his eȝeputtes ase a bruþen led. *c* **1410** *Master of Game* (MS. Digby 182) v, He shall haue as mony smale pittes [*Bodl. MS.* puttes] in þe fore legge, as he hath yeres. *c* **1430** LYDG. *Min. Poems* (Percy Soc.) 146 With a little pytte in her well-favored chynne. **1541** R. COPLAND *Guydon's Quest. Chirurg.* K iv b, Of what shape are yᵉ two focyl bones?.. The greatest hath two pyttes towarde the kne whiche receyue the rounde endes of the thyghe bone. **1585** T. WASHINGTON tr. *Nicholay's Voy.* II. xxi. 59 The holes vnderneath your arm pittes. **1651** FRENCH *Distill.* v. 142 Anoint the pit of the stomacke. **1688** R. HOLME *Armoury* II. 84/2 Of a Tree..the Pit or Hole [is] whereat the branches sprout out. **1818** KEATS *Endymion* I. 875 Flowers, on their stalks set Like vestal primroses, but dark velvet Edges them round, and they have golden pits. **1834** MᶜMURTRIE *Cuvier's Anim. Kingd.* 184 There is a little round indentation or pit behind each nostril. **1847** EMERSON *Poems* (1857) 98 In the pit of his eyes. **1893** *Syd. Soc. Lex.*, *Pit*, a depression. Applied medically to the permanent impression made by the finger in œdematous tissues, which are said to *pit* on pressure. **1965** *Amer. Speech* XL. 194 *Pits*, ..a slang abbreviation of the term *armpits*,..with an extension of meaning to entail the idea of body odor. **1973** M. AMIS *Rachel Papers* 71 Complete body-service..pits clipped, toes manicured, pubic hair permed and styled, each tooth brushed, tongue scraped, nose pruned. **1974** E. BRAWLEY *Rap* (1975) II. xx. 325 She opened her heavy flippy arms, arms with rolls of honest fat hanging down under her pits. **1977** *Rolling Stone* 7 Apr. 48/2 Simmons answers by spraying his pits with a can of Royal Copenhagen.

b. A depressed scar, such as those left on the skin after small-pox; a similar minute depression or spot upon any surface, produced by chemical action, by a rain-drop, etc.

1677 *Lond. Gaz.* No. 1188/4 A short thick man..some few pits of the Small Pox. **1758** REID tr. *Macquer's Chym.* I. 323 An exceeding white bead of Silver, the lower part whereof will be unequal, and full of little pits. **1780** HUNTER in *Phil. Trans.* LXX. 134 It sometimes happens..that there is a pitt in consequence of a chicken pock. **1852** MORFIT *Tanning & Currying* (1853) 170 Heat and moisture may dissolve the gelatine, and thus cause the hides to be scarred with pits. **1884** *Science* IV. 273/2 The sandstone surface is distinctly marked by raindrop pits.

c. *Bot.* A minute depression on the inner side of the wall of a cell or vessel, often perforating it and forming a basin-like pore (***bordered pit***), as in the wood-cells of conifers, etc.; also, a minute depression on the surface of a seed.

1857 HENFREY *Elem. Bot.* §662 The new layers, applying themselves..over the [cell-] wall, leave certain parts bare, which appear as *dots* or *pits* of various forms when viewed from the inside. **1875** BENNETT & DYER *Sachs' Bot.* 20 When contiguous cells are united into a tissue..the pits and pit-channels of both sides meet, and the intermediate thin portion of membrane becomes absorbed; a channel thus arises uniting two cell-spaces (Bordered Pits, perforated septum of vessels). *Ibid.* 540 The seed..displays a variety of sculpturing, such as pits, warts, bands. **1914** M. DRUMMOND tr. *Haberlandt's Physiol. Plant Anat.* i. 44 These readily permeable spots generally take the shape of sharply defined areas of approximately circular cross-section, known as pits. **1953** K. ESAU *Plant Anat.* iii. 39 Secondary cell walls are commonly characterized by the presence of depressions or cavities... Such cavities are termed pits. **1976** BELL & COOMBE tr. *Strasburger's Textbk. Bot.* (rev. ed.) 110 If transversely elongated pits are arranged one above the other in the lateral walls the arrangement is said to be scalariform.

10. That part of the auditorium of a theatre which is on the floor of the house; now usually restricted to the part of this behind the stalls. Also *transf.* the people occupying this. Cf. COCKPIT 1 b.

1649 LOVELACE *Poems* 78 The other [comedy] for the Gentlemen oth' Pit. **1682** DRYDEN *Mac Fl.* 153 Let Cully, Cockwood, Fopling charm the pit. **1709–10** STEELE *Tatler* No. 145 ¶2 She in a Front Box, he in the Pit next the Stage. **1779** SHERIDAN *Critic* III. i, Speak more to the pit..—the soliloquy always to the pit, that's a rule. **1829** LYTTON *Disowned* xxxviii, The pit is crowded. **1876** SMITH *Hist. Eng. Lit.* 121 The designation *parterre*, still given by the French to the *pit*. **1922** W. S. MAUGHAM *On Chinese Screen* xlvii. 186 Declaiming the blank verse of Sheridan Knowles with an emphasis to rouse the pit to frenzy.

b. = ***orchestra pit*** s.v. ORCHESTRA 4.

1961 in WEBSTER. **1966** *Listener* 6 Oct. 517/1 The sheer sound of the orchestra seemed very much bigger than usual, the strings had a bloom that is often lacking, the woodwind sweetness as well as precision; ensemble had improved, including rapport between stage and pit. **1974** *Belton* (S. Carolina) *News* 18 Apr. 1/2 Hanna High Jazz Ensemble (In the pit throughout the show). **1975** *Times* 17 Sept. 10/4 On the evenings he conducted the sound coming from the pit ranged from the good to the superlative. **1977** *New Yorker* 9 May 132/3 (It is said that Toscanini was the first to sink the pit at La Scala.) The Orpheum, where the Boston 'Rigoletto' was done, has no pit, either.

11. *U.S.* A part of the floor of an Exchange appropriated to a special branch of business, e.g. the ***grain pit***, the ***wheat pit***. Hence, **b.** Name of a card-game: see quot. 1904.

1903 F. NORRIS *The Pit* i. 17 The world's food should not be at the mercy of the Chicago wheat pit. **1903** *Daily Chron.* 11 Feb. 3/3 It is Laura against the Wheat Pit, and the Wheat Pit wins—for a time. **1904** *Ibid.* 12 Nov. 8/5 Society has a new card game, called 'Pit'... The name 'Pit' is suggested by the Wheat Pit..The game is..a mimicry of a Corn Exchange, where every player is trying to make a corner in some particular grain.

12. a. ? A bag-shaped part of a fishing-net.

1883 *Fisheries Exhib. Catal.* 296 A Cotton Eel Bow Net, with two wings and loose pit.

b. A pocket in a garment. *slang.*

1811 *Lexicon Balatronicum* s.v. *Pit*, He drew a rare thimble from the swell's pit. He took a handsome watch from the gentleman's pocket. **1927** *Dialect Notes* V. 459 *Pit*, a pocket. **1938** F. D. SHARPE *Sharpe of Flying Squad* 332 *The pit*, the inside jacket pocket. **1950** H. E. GOLDIN *Dict. Amer. Underworld Lingo* 158/2 *Pit* (among pickpockets), the vest pocket; or, less frequently, the inside breast pocket of coat. **1955** D. W. MAURER in *Publ. Amer. Dial. Soc.* XXIV. 125 The most important pocket in the coat from the pickpocket's point of view is the *coat pit*, or the inside breast pocket... This is often shortened to *pit*. **1966** BAKER *Austral. Lang.* (ed. 2) vii. 143 A generation ago,..the various pockets were known as..*left kick* or *right kick* or *pit* (trouser pockets).

13. The framework supporting the pivoted yoke of a swinging bell in a belfry.

1874 SIR E. BECKETT *Clocks & Watches* 345 The pit, or frame to hold a swing bell, must be a good deal longer than twice the height of the bell.

14. ***the pits*** (*slang*, orig. *U.S.*), the worst or most despicable example of something; freq. applied to a person considered particularly obnoxious or contemptible.

1953 *Newsweek* 2 Nov. 54/3 A bad exam experience would be 'I'm wasted' at Howard,..'It was the pits' at Vassar. **1965** *Amer. Speech* XL. 194 *Pits, n.* This is a slang abbreviation of the term *armpits*, again with an extension of meaning to entail the idea of body odor ('He's got the pits') or, more broadly, something unpleasant ('It [the party] was really the pits'). **1976** *New Yorker* 1 Mar. 87/3 If there are gradations in the pits, 'I Will, I Will..For Now' is even worse than 'Gable and Lombard'. It combines the most simperingly forced elements of fifties mistaken-identity farces with a mushy, soft-core version of the sex-manual pornos. **1979** *New Society* 20 Dec. p. xi/3 If Dors is the very personification of the buxom backside of the other Britain.. then Joan Collins is the pits. Just the pits. **1981** *Observer* 22 Nov. 11 I've never been fined for saying something obscene. It's always been for saying 'You're the pits,' or something. —John McEnroe. **1985** J. FULLER *Mass* viii. 239 Hey, give me a little comfort here. This weather is the pits.

15. *attrib.* and *Comb.*, as ***pit-brink***, ***-dweller***, ***-dwelling***, ***-grave***; ***pit-like*** adj.; esp. in sense 6 (belonging to, employed in, or connected with a coal-mine), as (in sense 6) ***pit-boot***, ***-bottle***, ***pit-boy***, ***-cage*** (CAGE *sb.* 5 a), ***-cistern***, ***-clothes***, ***-coat***, ***committee***, ***-dirt***, ***-engine***, ***-gate***, ***-girl***, ***-horse***, ***-inspector***, ***-lad***, ***-lass***, ***-manager***, ***-mouth***, ***-people***, ***-pony***, ***-prop***, ***-road***, ***-rope***, ***-shaft***, ***-singlet***, ***-sinker***, ***-sinking***, ***-timber***, ***-top***, ***-trousers***, ***-village***, ***-winder***, ***-woman***, ***-working***; (sense 10), as ***pit-band***, ***-bandsman***, ***-door***, ***-doorkeeper***, ***-orchestra***, ***-stall***, ***-ticket***, ***-tier***. Also **pit aperture** *Bot.*, an opening on the inner surface of a secondary cell wall, forming the entrance to a pit cavity; **pit-bank**, 'the raised ground or platforms upon which the coals are sorted and screened at surface' (Gresley *Coal Mining Terms*); also *attrib.*; **pit-bar**, a timber used to support the sides of the shaft of a mine; **pit-bird**, local name of the reed-warbler; **pit-black** *a.*, as black as a pit, intensely black or dark; **pit-bottom**, the bottom of a pit; *spec.* the bottom of the shaft in a coal-mine, or the adjacent part of the mine; hence **pit-bottomer**, a collier employed at the pit-bottom; **pit-brae**, **pit-brow**, the 'brow' or edge of a pit; *spec.* = *pit-bank*; hence **pit-brow girl** or **lass**, a girl employed in sorting and screening coal at the pit-brow; **pit bull (terrier)**, a small, stocky, short-coated dog belonging to the American breed so called, usually fawn or brindled in colour, with white markings; also used as a name for the Staffordshire bull terrier, which belongs to a closely related breed; **pit canal** *Bot.*, a channel in the secondary cell wall of a bordered pit, leading to the pit cavity; **pit-cave** *Archæol.* (see quot. 1921); **pit-cavity** *Bot.*, the space within a simple pit, extending from the primary cell wall to the aperture bordering the cell lumen; **pit chamber** *Bot.*, the hemispherical space between the primary and secondary cell walls of a bordered pit; **pit-comb** *Archæol.*, used *attrib.* to designate pottery decorated with rows of indentations and comb-patterns; **pit-crater**, a volcanic crater of the form of a pit; **pit dog** = *pit bull terrier*; **pit-eye** = *pit-bottom*; **pit-eyed** *a.*, having sunken eyes; **pit field** *Bot.*, a depression or group of depressions in a primary cell wall; **pit-fish**, 'a small fish of the Indian seas, [which] has the power of protruding or retracting its eyes at pleasure' (Webster 1828); **pit-frame**, a framework at the top of a pit or shaft, supporting the pulley; **pit-game** = GAME-FOWL b; **pit-guide**, a bar in a mine-shaft serving as a guide for the cage; **pit-head**, the top of a pit or shaft, or the ground immediately around it; also *attrib.*; hence **pit-headman**, a workman employed at the pit-head; **pit-headed** *a.*, having a pit or small depression on the head, as certain serpents (cf. *pit-viper*) and tapeworms; **pit-heap**, a heap of excavated material near the mouth of a pit or shaft; hence, the whole of the surface works (= *heap-stead*, HEAP *sb.* 6); **pit-kiln**, an oven for making coke from coal; **pit-lamp** *Canad.*, a miner's lamp; also *transf.*, a lamp used in hunting or fishing, a jack-lamp (see JACK *sb.*[1] 34); also as *v. trans.*, to hunt (deer, etc.) using a pit-lamp (also *absol.*); so **pit-lamping** *vbl. sb.*; **pit-lighting** *vbl. sb. Canad.* = *pit-lamping* above; **pit-maker**, one who makes or digs a pit; †a gravedigger (*obs.*); so **pit-making**; **pit-martin**, the sand-martin (Swainson *Prov. Names Birds*); †**pit-mask**, a mask worn by a woman when present in the pit of a theatre; the wearer of such a mask; **pit-mortar**, **pit-prop**: see quots.; **pit membrane** *Bot.*, the part of a cell wall covering a pit; **pit organ**, a small depression acting as a receptor sensitive to changes in temperature, found on each side of the head of snakes belonging to the subfamily Crotalinæ; **pit-pair** *Bot.*, two pits in adjacent cell walls, sharing the same pit membrane; **pit-planting**, a method of planting trees in which a hole is dug, and the roots settled over a mound of earth in the bottom of the hole before it is refilled; also, planting trees in small depressions which help to conserve moisture; **pit-rotted** *a.*, rotted by steeping in a pit or pool of water; **pit-sand**, sand dug out of a sand-pit, as distinguished from river-sand and sea-sand; **pit-saw**, a large saw for cutting timber, working in a sawpit, with handles at the top and bottom; also *attrib.* and as *v. trans.*, to cut (timber) with a pit-saw (also *absol.*); **pit-sawyer**, the man who stands in a sawpit and works the lower handle of a pit-saw (opp. to *top-sawyer*); **pit-sawing** *vbl. sb.*; **pit-sawn** *ppl. a.*; **pit silo**, a silo in the form of a pit (rather than a tower); so **pit silage**, silage made in a pit; **pit-specked** *a.*, speckled with pits or small depressions, as fruit; †**pit-stone**, stone from a quarry; **pit stop**, in motor-racing, a stop at a pit (sense 1 h) for refuelling, maintenance, etc., usu. during a race; also *transf.* and *fig.*; **pit tip**, the mass of waste material deposited near the mouth of a mine or pit; **pit trap** = sense 1 f; **pit-viper**, a venomous serpent of the family *Crotalidæ*, characterized by a pit or depression in front of each eye; †**pit-water**: see quot.; **pit-well**, a well made by excavation; **pit-wood**, timber used for frames, props, etc., in a coal-pit; **pit-work**, the system of pumps and machinery connected with them in a pit or shaft; **pit yacker**, **yakker** *dial.*, a coal miner. See also PIT-COAL, etc.

1934 *Jrnl. Arnold Arboretum* XV. 334 The narrow inner and outer layers of the secondary wall come together in the rim formed about the *pit-aperture. **1953** K. ESAU *Plant Anat.* iii. 44 The circular pit apertures in a bordered pit-pair appear exactly opposite each other. **1967** S. BROIDO-ALTMAN tr. *Fahn's Plant Anat.* ii. 36 The opening of the pit on the inner side of the cell wall..is called the pit aperture. **1942** BERREY & VAN DEN BARK *Amer. Thes. Slang* §576/23 *Pit band.., a theatre orchestra. **1946** R. BLESH *Shining Trumpets* (1949) xii. 280 The other side..is completely in the manner of the average musical comedy pit band of the 1920's. **1977** *Rolling Stone* 19 May 74/3 At 14 I got a job in a pit band in a cinema. **1959** 'F. NEWTON' *Jazz Scene* xi. 189 The despised *pit-bandsmen and light musicians. **1870** A. J. MUNBY *Diary* 25 June in D. Hudson *Munby* (1972) 288 'I've worked on *pit bonk most o' my days', said an Oakengates lassie. **1892** *Daily News* 26 Feb. 5/7 Employed on the surface, or at the 'pit bank', as it is called. **1930** AUDEN *Poems* 67 Head-gears gaunt on grass-grown pit-banks. **1968** *Listener* 15 Aug. 205/3 Each plane came in over the long pit-bank mountain. **1708** J. C. *Compl. Collier* (1845) 15 *Pit-Bars of Wood and Deals must be used till we get to the Stone. **1863** KINGSLEY *Water-Bab.* i, The *pit-bird warbling in the sedges, as he had warbled all night long. **1871** PALGRAVE *Lyr. Poems* 48 The curse, *pit-black from below. **1894** H. PEASE *Mark o' Deil* 26 H tried to shift it, an' threw his *pit boots at it. **1913** D. H. LAWRENCE *Sons & Lovers* i. 25 She..set his pit-boots beside them. *Ibid.*, She..rinsed his *pit-bottle. *a* **1930** —— *Phoenix II* (1968) 263, I, who remember the homeward trooping of the colliers when I was a boy,..the red mouths and the quick whites of the eyes, the swinging pit bottles, and the strange voices of men from the underworld. *c* **1400** *Destr. Troy* 12663 When þe prinse was past to þe *pit bothum, þe buernes on þe bonk bet hym with stonys. **1867** W. W. SMYTH *Coal & Coal-mining* 121 The coal may be brought down hill to the pit-bottom. **1887** P. M'NEILL *Blawearie* 46 Will Hood had been appointed *pit-bottomer here. **1863** *Edin. Rev.* Apr. 424 It is to be hoped these schools will be continued for the purpose of improving the very imperfect scholarship of future *pit-boys. **1897** *Daily News* 8 Jan. 5/2 The President suggested that the pit boys should be placed on the same footing as their more fortunate mates. **1613** JACKSON *Creed* II. xxiv. §5 At the very *Pitbrincke of destruction. *c* **1440** *Alphabet of Tales* 295 His sawle was broght vnto þe prince of Hell syttand opon þe *pytt bra. **1887** *Spectator* 21 May 675/1 If female labour on the pit-brow is stopped. **1945** *Sun* (Baltimore) 18 May 7/5 Mrs. Dorella Zinke..died within 90 minutes after a mass attack by nine *pit bull terriers. **1968** K. WEATHERLY *Roo Shooter* 128 It was the rat-catching trick of the old pit bull terriers: one savage jerk of the dog's head and the big tom flew high in the air. **1974** R. THOMAS *Porkchoppers* xxix. 245 He held a leash that was attached to an aged English pit bull that waddled..and wheezed. **1976** *Honolulu Star-Bull.* 21 Dec. F-8/8 (Advt.), Pit Bull Pups, 8 wks. **1904** *Westm. Gaz.* 29 Mar. 7/3 A serious *pit-cage accident, resulting in the loss of three lives..at the Swanwick Collieries. **1953** K. ESAU *Plant Anat.* iii. 43 The border divides the cavity into the pit chamber..and the *pit canal, the passage from the cell lumen into the pit chamber. **1967** S. BROIDO-ALTMAN tr. *Fahn's Plant Anat.* ii. 40 The pit canal between the inner and outer apertures becomes longer. **1921** *Discovery* Feb. 33/1 Still another kind [of grave]..is known as the '*pit-cave'. This was made by first sinking a pit and then cutting out the tomb in the form of a side-recess from the bottom of the pit. **1925** V. G. CHILDE *Dawn European Civilization* vi. 92 Beside the pit-caves and chamber-tombs excavated in the clay or rock, megalithic graves were erected just in the heel of Italy. **1939** J. D. S. PENDLEBURY *Archaeol. Crete* iv. 242 At Zapher Papoura both the shaft grave and the pit cave continue in use. **1914** M. DRUMMOND tr. *Haberlandt's Physiol. Plant Anat.* i. 44 The adjoining *pit-cavities are separated only by the thin primary closing-membrane. **1953** K. ESAU *Plant Anat.* iii. 41 In the bordered pit the secondary wall arches over the pit cavity. **1970** PANSHIN & DE ZEEUW *Textbk. Wood Technol.* (ed. 3) I. iii. 93 The pit cavity is the entire space within the wall recess, between the pit membrane and the lumen. **1953** *Pit chamber [see *pit canal* above]. **1967** S. BROIDO-ALTMAN tr. *Fahn's Plant Anat.* ii. 40 As the walls continue to thicken the pit chamber becomes smaller. **1839** URE *Dict. Arts* 971 The upper *pit-cistern. **1873** A. J. MUNBY *Diary* 11 Sept. in D. Hudson *Munby* (1972) 343 Ellen herself came out of the kitchen; and she was in her *pit clothes, as she had promised. **1913** D. H. LAWRENCE *Sons & Lovers* i. 25 She..put his pit-clothes on the hearth to warm. **1937** 'G. ORWELL' *Road to Wigan Pier* iii. 37 At the baths he has two lockers where he can keep his pit clothes separate from his day clothes. **1974** *Times* 1 Feb. 19/4 When a man arrives at the colliery to work his shift he first changes into his pit clothes. **1913** D. H. LAWRENCE *Sons & Lovers* iii. 49 He had taken off his *pit-coat. **1954** *Pit-comb ware [see CORD *sb.*[1] 12]. **1957** V. G. CHILDE *Dawn European Civilization* (ed. 6) xi. 204 From Sweden to Siberia indeed all pots were manufactured by the same technique of ring-building, all taper downward to a rounded base and all may be decorated with rows of pits, frequently combined with zones of comb impressions. The whole ceramic family is therefore termed 'pit-comb ware'. **1967** *Antiquaries' Jrnl.* XLVII. 203 For Fox in 1924, the most obvious comparison was the North European Neolithic pottery, Baltic and more Eastern, called 'pit-comb ware' or Pitted ware, on which ornament includes quite similar pits, in one or several rows. **1920** *Act 10 & 11 Geo. V* c. 50 §7 It shall not be necessary to constitute a *pit committee for any mine which is a small mine within the meaning of the Coal Mines Act, 1911. **1928** *Britain's Industr. Future* (Liberal Industr. Inquiry) IV. 266 Open consultation in the [coal] industry should be secured by the establishment of Pit Committees, District Boards, and a National Mining Council. **1886** *Amer. Jrnl. Sc.* Ser. III. XXXII. 251 The old cone had, like Mt. Loa or the Maui volcano, a great *pit-crater at top. **1913** D. H. LAWRENCE *Sons & Lovers* iv. 70 Here sat the colliers in their *pit-dirt. **1914** —— *Widowing of Mrs. Holroyd* III. 79 He's in his pit-dirt. **1945** C. L. B. HUBBARD *Observer's Bk. Dogs* 202 Pit Bull Terrier. *Pit Dog. About the end of the eighteenth century..dog-fighting became the new sport... A breed of Bull Terrier was created which became the fore-runner of the present-day Staffordshire Bull Terrier. **1951** J. F. GORDON *Staffordshire Bull Terrier* ii. 23 The Pit Dog, Pit Bull Terrier or Stafford..achieved some measure of emancipation from his gladiatorial background. **1667** PEPYS *Diary* 22 May (1974) VIII. 232 But here Knipp spied me out of the tiring-room, and came to the *pit door: and I out to her and kissed her. *a* **1828** J. BERNARD *Retrospections of Stage* (1830) I. ii. 45 It was his general practice to take the money at the pit-door. **1894** G. B. SHAW *Let.* 30 Apr. (1965) I. 433 A man who thinks a dramatic performance worth waiting at the pit door all day for is a lunatic. **1831** J. BOADEN in *Private Corr. David Garrick* I. p. xxxvi, For the benefit of his father, the *pit-door keeper, and others. **1855** W. B. WOOD *Personal Recoll. Stage* i. 40 My keeper, Mr H., was at this time pit door-keeper at the Chestnut Street Theatre. **1893** A. H. S. LANDOR *Hairy Ainu* ix. 78 An extinct race of *pit-dwellers. **1898** *Jrnl. Archæol. Inst.* LV. 157 He abandons..the *pit-dwelling theory. **1879** *Lumberman's Gaz.* 15 Oct., The judge took the *pit end of the saw. **1881** RAYMOND *Mining Gloss.*, *Pit-eye*,..the bottom of the shaft of a coal-mine. *Ibid.*, *Pit-eye pillar*, a barrier of coal left around a shaft to protect it from caving. **1696** *Lond. Gaz.* No. 3229/4 A Sorrel Mare,..9 years old, lop-ears, *pit-eyed. **1934** *Jrnl. Arnold Arboretum* XV. 332 Cambial walls are characterized by having more or less numerous plasmodesmata which may be..aggregated in thinner areas of the walls, i.e. in so-called primary *pit-fields. **1953** K. ESAU *Plant Anat.* iii. 39 Only the secondary walls have pits, whereas the primary walls have primary pit fields. **1976** BELL & COOMBE tr. *Strasburger's Textbk. Bot.* (rev. ed.) 63 Where the pit fields are oval or elongated, the bordered pits take on a similar shape. *a* **1672** WILLUGHBY *Icthyogr.* (1686) App. Tab. 8 *Pit Fish. *c* **1830** *Pract. Treat. Roads* 13 in *Libr. Usef. Knowl., Husb.* III, Gravel, which by some persons is called *pit-flint. **1881** RAYMOND *Mining Gloss.*, **Pit-frame*, the framework carrying the pit-pulley. **1888** *Daily News* 4 Oct. 3/6 They are preventing the men holding '*pit-gate' meetings on the colliery premises. **1863** *Edin. Rev.* Apr. 436 The *pit-girls are not less fond of holidays than their fathers. *Ibid.* 437 Much may be done to improve the condition of the poor pit-girl. **1866** A. J. MUNBY *Diary* 15 May in D. Hudson *Munby* (1972) 225 Some large coal manager who was strongly in favour of female labour told him the pitgirls were 'mules, not women'. **1902** C. G. HARPER *Holyhead Road* ii. 35 Pit-girls too or rather pit-bank lasses. **1897** J. G. FRAZER *Pausanias* Pref., The *pit-graves with their treasures on the acropolis of Mycenae. **1839** URE *Dict. Arts* 983 With small coals..the *pit head is raised 8 or 9 feet above the common level of the ground. *Ibid.* 991 The ponderous pulley-wheels are blown from the pit-head frame. **1915** *Political Q.* May 117 A maximum pit-head price might leave much of the home market in the same condition. **1928** *Daily Chron.* 9 Aug. 5/4 From September 1 pit head prices will be raised by 1s. a ton. **1937** 'G. ORWELL' *Road to Wigan Pier* iii. 37 At some of the larger and better appointed collieries there are pithead baths. **1967** A. L. LLOYD *Folk Song in England* v. 335 The miners..before the days of pithead baths..appeared in daylight with black faces. **1974** *Times* 4 Jan. 12/8 If a pithead ballot were held..Yorkshire miners would vote..in favour of stoppage. **1976** *Evening Post* (Nottingham) 15 Dec. 1/2 In the pithead ballot, 78 per cent of miners who voted turned down the Coal Board's offer. **1898** *Westm. Gaz.* 12 Mar. 2/3 Gibson signalled to the *pit headman and stuck to his post until the water was up to his armpits..sending twenty-three of his comrades up to the pithead. **1883** GRESLEY *Gloss. Coal Mining*, **Pit Heap*, see Heapstead... The entire surface works about a colliery shaft. **1894** *Northumbld. Gloss.*, Pit-heap. **1913** D. H. LAWRENCE *Sons & Lovers* vii. 172 Jimmy, who had been a *pit-horse. **1839** URE *Dict. Arts* 995 A *schachtofen*, or *pit-kiln, for coking coals in Germany. **1862** *Cornh. Mag.* Mar. 351 Files of pitmen and groups of *pit-lads are now dotting all the roads. **1912** W. OWEN *Let.* 24 July (1967) 151 This pit-lad is wrestling with a Class-book of Physics. **1901** *Daily Colonist* (Victoria, B.C.) 1 Oct. 6/1 One Indian shot as many as 47 [deer] in one night at Ahatassett, using a *pit lamp. **1906** *Ibid.* 30 Jan. 6/2 The only light he [*sc.* a coal miner] has is a smoky pit-lamp—a cotton wick soaked in fish oil. **1921** *Ibid.* 30 Oct. 13/4 The rescue parties had to find their way about with candles and pit lamps, great difficulty resulting. **1967** *Vancouver Province* 21 Feb. 19/6 Stanton said his association wants to commend the fisheries department for banning 'pit lamps' but believes the order should be made permanent. **1967** *Wildlife Rev.* (Victoria, B.C.) Mar. 27/2 Frank Greenfield..once jailed a man for pitlamping deer. **1924** R. S. SHERMAN *Mother Nature Stories* 61 *Pit-lamping and hunting with dogs, in addition to natural enemies..have been the cause of its rapid disappearance. **1957** A. R. BARRATT *Coronets & Buckskin* 45 That there Blotton had me arrested for pitlamping. **1969** *Daily Colonist* (Victoria, B.C.) 7 Dec. 20/2 Pitlamping on Gabriola Island cost two men $500 each when they pleaded guilty..in court. **1969** *Islander* (Victoria, B.C.) 14 Sept. 10/3 Before dawn one morning, two shots were heard from the direction of his cabin, but no one paid any attention as *pitlighting was common practice. **1567** W. THOMAS *Ital. Gram.*, *Beccamorto*, the *pitmaker, or any one that gaineth by the buriall of the deade. **1527–8** *Rec. St. Mary at Hill* 345 Receivide..for her place of buriall, for her *pitt making & other duties viij *s.* iiij *d.* **1913** D. H. LAWRENCE *Sons & Lovers* i. 16 He could only abuse the *pit-managers. **1976** *Daily Tel.* 20 July 2/3 Harry Widowson, 57, pit manager of Mount Vernon Road, Barnsley. **1891** G. NEILSON *Per Lineam Valli* 32 Hundreds of quarry-holes, mere surface *pitmarks on the hill sides. **1895** *Westm. Gaz.* 19 Nov. 2/1 A *pit-marked stretch of scrub. **1701** FARQUHAR *Sir H. Wildair* v. vi, Perhaps your pleasure never reached above a *pit-mask in your life. **1913** *Forestry Q.* XI. 15 The delicate *pit membranes were ruptured by the shrinkage of the cell walls in drying. **1953** K. ESAU *Plant Anat.* iii. 41 The pit membrane is common to both pits of a pair. **1976** BELL & COOMBE tr. *Strasburger's Textbk. Bot.* (rev. ed.) 63 Bordered pits, especially amongst the Coniferae, are often furnished with a thickening in the middle of the pit membrane. **1892** *Jrnl. Archæol. Inst.* No. 194. 155 Sticky gravel, termed in the midland counties '*pit mortar'. **1839** URE *Dict. Arts* 985 The draught of the furnace at the *pit mouth. **1927** *Melody Maker* Aug. 767/3 Whether this is because the dancers or singers think a modern dance band is a more enhancing support than a piano or the *pit orchestra—which, of course, it is—or whether it is the band which decides..., I know not. **1934** S. R. NELSON *All about Jazz* i. 27 The atmosphere of the cinema pit-orchestra or military band. **1937** *Pit organ [see NEUROMAST]. **1976** *Nature* 3 June 441/1 He did more classic work on the pit-organ of rattlesnakes, where he demonstrated the exquisite thermal sensitivity of this receptor. **1933** *Tropical Woods* XXXVI. 5 *Pit-pair.—Two complementary pits of adjacent cells. **1953** K. ESAU *Plant Anat.* iii. 41 Two pits are combined into a paired structure, the pit-pair. **1970** PANSHIN & DE ZEEUW *Textbk. Wood Technol.* (ed. 3) I. iii. 93 Pit pairs may be made up from simple pits to form bordered pit pairs or simple pit pairs. **1855** J. R. LEIFCHILD *Cornwall Mines* 272 Amongst the northern *pit-people. **1898** C. E. CURTIS *Pract. Forestry* (ed. 2) viii. 47 When planting deeper soils..*pit-planting must be adopted. **1931** *Forestry* V. 18 No method is fool-proof, but pit-planting appears to be the safest. **1970** H. L. EDLIN *Collins Guide Tree Planting & Cultivation* i. 110 Failures in pit planting nearly always arise from insufficient firming-up. **1905** H. SCOTT HOLLAND *Pers. Stud., Westcott* 136 *Pit ponies, against whose hard usage in the pit he continually pleaded. **1917** R. HODGSON *Poems* 27 Wretched, blind pit ponies. **1938** G. GREENE *Brighton Rock* I. iii. 55 White hair, grey face, short-sighted pit pony eyes. **1978** A. PRICE *'44 Vintage* xix. 219 Audley was like a racehorse down a coal mine, desperately pretending to be a pit pony. **1883** *Daily News* 26 Sept. 6/4 A Swedish vessel laden with *pitprops. **1891** *Times* 31 Aug. 4/2 Pit-props, which are used as supports in the different workings in collieries. **1895** *Daily News* 30 Apr. 7/6 The search party is now engaged in clearing the *pit roads. **1875** R. F. MARTIN tr. *Havrez' Winding Mach.* 23 Aloes form the best fibre for the manufacture of *pit-ropes. **1807** VANCOUVER *Agric. Devon* (1813) 207 This flax is always *pit-rotted for ten days or a fortnight. **1703** MOXON *Mech. Exerc.* 242 You may put three parts of Sand that is digged (or *pit Sand) and one part of Lime to make Morter. **1679** in *Rec. Court of New Castle on Delaware* (1904) 361 An Iron sledge and a hand saw Iron —one *Pit Saw. **1703** MOXON *Mech. Exerc.* 99 The Pit-Saw is..used by those Work-men that make sawing Timber and Boards their whole Business. **1848** [see CROSS-CUT *sb.* 5]. **1879** *Lumberman's Gaz.* 15 Oct. 5/1 An improvement over the gate saw, almost as great as was the gate over the pit saw. *Ibid.*, Two men..maintained a pit saw mill. **1930** L. G. D. ACLAND *Early Canterbury Runs* (ser. 1) ix. 219, I should think this will be the last pit-saw to be used in Canterbury. **1960** B. CRUMP *Good Keen Man* 66 A shack that he and his brother had built from timber they'd pit-sawn themselves 30 years before. **1965** F. RUSSELL *Secret Islands* v. 76 'This was where we pitsawed,' he said doubtfully. **1974** P. W. BLANDFORD *Country Craft Tools* vi. 91 Pit saws are still made in Britain for use in some African countries. **1908** E. J. BANFIELD *Confessions of Beachcomber* I. ii. 57, I began to be thankful that *pit-sawing was not forced upon me as a profession in the days of inexperienced youth. **1965** F. RUSSELL *Secret Islands* v. 76 Pitsawing is the most brutal physical work a man could do. **1946** *Nature* 17 Aug. 245/1 Apart from the *pit-sawn timber used locally, the pit-sawn timber supplies handled by the Department through its numerous subcontractors totalled 1,060,000 cu.ft. **1965** M. SHADBOLT *Among Cinders* xii. 98 He built the house with pit-sawn kauri. **1978** O. WHITE *Silent Reach* xx. 228 The Silent Reach homestead was..primitive. Its exterior walls were of wedge-split or pit-sawn plants. **1941** *Beaver* June 38 **Pitsawyer*, in earlier years, an important and indispensable craftsman. To him was due the production of every inch of sawn lumber for the building of the posts and water craft. **1946** *Nature* 17 Aug. 245/1 An exacting specification impossible for pit-sawyers to fulfil and other difficulties were experienced. **1968** J. ARNOLD *Shell Bk. Country Crafts* 86 Pit sawyers, it seems, were a race much on their own, uncommunicative and perhaps brutish. **1708** J. C. *Compl. Collier* (1845) 36 [Corves] halled all along the Barrow-way to the *Pit Shaft. **1886** HALL CAINE *Son of Hagar* II. vi, The head-gear of the pit-shaft. **1887** H. E. P. CLINTON *Treat. Ensilage* 56 The quality of the material is certainly superior in many cases to *pit silage. **1951** WATSON & SMITH *Silage* vi. 95 (*heading*) Making of pit silage. **1886** R. S. BURN *Systematic Small Farming* xx. 252 While the retaining or enclosing walls of the above-ground silo should not be less than nine inches, the lining walls of the *pit silo may be very much thinner. **1947** *New Biol.* III. 45 A pit silo is merely a trench dug in the ground to convenient dimensions and, if properly drained, the wastage in these pits is less than that commonly experienced in many tower silos. **1966** WEBSTER & WILSON *Agric. in Tropics* xiii. 292 Ensilage of these grasses in either pit or tower silos presents no real difficulties, and is commonly the best way to preserve fodder for use in the dry season, but it involves some losses. **1913** D. H. LAWRENCE *Sons & Lovers* ii. 28 He..put on his *pit-singlet. **1920** —— *Phoenix* (1936) 9 Once more the rabbit was wrapped in the old pit-singlet. **1851** in *Illustr. Lond. News* 5 Aug. (1854) 119/3 (Occupations of People) *Pit-sinker. **1896** *Daily News* 4 May 3/6 There are ten new ventures in the way of *pit-sinking in Monmouthshire. **1858** *Times* 22 Dec. 7/6 The part nearest the orchestra is railed off for three rows of orchestra stalls,..and gives the same dimensions for perfect comfort to the occupant as is afforded by the *pit-stalls at Covent-garden. Behind these are four rows of pit-stalls, the charge for each of which is only 2s.; while admission to the body of the pit will be reduced to 1s. 6d. **1861** DICKENS *Uncomm. Trav.* iv. 43 A pit at sixpence, boxes and pit-stalls at a shilling, and a few private boxes at half-a-crown. **1961** BOWMAN & BALL *Theatre Lang.* 260 *Pit stall*, in British terminology, a stall in the front rows of the pit. **1659** A. HAY *Diary* (S.H.S.) 76 St Jon's kirk was content with the *pitstones. **1932** S. C. H. DAVIS *Motor Racing* v. 72 *Pit stop. **1942** BERREY & VAN DEN BARK *Amer. Thes. Slang* §728/1 *Pit stop*, a stop for oil and gas &c. during a race. **1970** *Globe & Mail* (Toronto) 28 Sept. 22/4 Revson, forced to a pit stop on the 10th lap of the 210-mile race, easily beat out Ferrari's Jim Adams for third place. **1972** *Times* 15 June 4/4 The inner harbour is a huge nautical pit-stop. **1973** 'E. FENWICK' *Last of Lysandra* xx. 136 His wife..was relieved and pleased to see him, until she understood this was only a pit-stop. **1977** *Time* 4 July 36/1 A pit stop is called for. Time to eat and run. **1762** in G. O. Seilhamer *Hist. Amer. Theatre* (1888) I. xiv. 139 *Pit tickets sold at the door, 146 at 5s. **1786** J. WOODFORDE *Diary* 26 June (1926) II. 253 For 3 Pit Tickets at the Circus 1 pd 0. 9. 0. **1829** H. FOOTE *Compan. to Theatres* 94 Boxes may be engaged for the night, or season; and pit tickets purchased for 8s 6d. **1864** D. G. ROSSETTI *Let.* 5 July (1965) II. 513 He will reserve for me his two pit tickets for *Mirella* tonight. **1883** W. S. GRESLEY *Gloss. Terms Coal Mining* 189 *Pit-tip*, a bank or heap upon which rubbish out of the mine is tipped. **1907** *Westm. Gaz.* 13 Apr. 10/1 In the Black Country may be seen birches growing luxuriantly on a pit-tip. **1920** A. FAY *Gloss. Mining & Mineral Industry* 516/2 *Pit tip* (Eng.), a bank or heap upon which mine waste is tipped or dumped. **1867** W. W. SMYTH *Coal & Coal-mining* 167 The iron-plates with which the staging about the *pit-top is floored. **1895** KIPLING *Second Jungle Bk.* 20 It was a pointed stick, such as they set in the mouth of a *pit-trap. *c* **1909** D. H. LAWRENCE *Collier's Friday Night* (1934) iii. 76 His pit-watch that the Mother hung there when she put his *pit-trousers in the cupboard. **1913** —— *Sons & Lovers* ii. 27 He..struggled into his pit-trousers. **1862** *Cornh. Mag.* Mar. 352 *Pit villages..vary much in their character for cleanliness. **1957** R. FRANKENBERG *Village on Border* 1 Reviewers have..stressed the novelty of..information..about a pit-village in Yorkshire. **1967** A. L. LLOYD *Folk Song in England* v. 333 The keelmen..joined with the colliers' communities in dances on the pit-village green. **1978** *Peace News* 25 Aug. 10/3 When I first came across the *Manual* I was visiting people in a budding action group on a pit village council estate. **1885** *Cassell's Encycl. Dict.*, **Pit-vipers*, see *Crotalidæ*. **1904** *Brit. Med. Jrnl.* 17 Sept. 670 The pit vipers ..include the rattlesnakes of America and the *trimensurus* of India. **1601** HOLLAND *Pliny* II. 407 Surely, wel-water or *pit-water..is simply the wholsomest. **1844** STEPHENS *Bk. Farm* I. 362 Spring-water should be obtained..by sinking *pit-wells. **1860** A. J. MUNBY *Diary* 29 Sept. in D. Hudson *Munby* (1972) 76 A photograph of a *pitwoman in costume. **1841** C. H. HARTSHORNE *Salopia Antiqua* 532 **Pit wood*, wood which is thus called generally runs from three feet six inches to four feet in length, and is very thick. It is used for supporting the roof of a coal pit. **1886** F. T. ELWORTHY *West Somerset Word-Bk.* 577 *Pit-wood*.., larch or other wood cut into lengths for supporting 'the roof' in coal-mines. **1890** *Daily News* 24 Nov. 2/4 The pitwood trade is also quieter. **1922** W. SCHLICH *Man. Forestry* (ed. 4) I. 81 It has been shown that during the period 1909–1913, the average annual consumption of timber and pit-wood amounted to about 11 million loads. **1971** *Timber Trades Jrnl.* 21 Aug. 24/1 Output of home-produced pit-wood..fell to its lowest level since 1951. **1855** J. R. LEIFCHILD *Cornwall Mines* 189 Details of the weight and cost of the '*pitwork' (or the parts of the machinery working in the shaft or pit). **1961** *Spectator* 29 Dec. 957 *Pit-Yacker... This is the autobiography of a man brought up in..the seaport mining town of Seaham, County Durham. **1974** S. DOBSON *Geordie Dict.* 72 A *pit yakker* is the Geordie term for a pitman. Possibly from *yak* or *yark* meaning to pull out (coals).

pit, *sb.*[2] [app. a. Du. *pit*, early mod. and late MDu. *pitte* fem., MLG., LG., WFris., EFris. *pit* pith, kernel, pip, radically agreeing with OE. *piþa* masc., PITH.] **1.** *U.S.*, *S. Afr.*, (? and Eng. *dial.*) The stone of a stone-fruit. Also, a pip.

The change of sense from 'marrow' or 'pith' to 'fruit-stone' is great, but the intermediate stage is supplied by the sense 'kernel, pip': cf. EFris. '*pitten ût de appels*', pips out of the apples (Dornkaat-Koolm.).

1841 G. BUSH *Doctr. of Resurrection* (Bartlett), You put an apple-seed or a peach-pit into the ground, and it springs up into the form of a miniature tree. **1860** BARTLETT *Dict. Amer.*, *Pit*,..the stone of a fruit, as of a cherry or peach. Mostly confined to New York State. **1873** W. MATTHEWS *Getting on in World* 26 One man may suck an orange and be choked by a pit, another swallow a penknife and live. **1884** KNIGHT *Dict. Mech.* Supp. 359 Hatch's pitter splits the fruit and removes the pit. [**1876** *Mid-Yorks. Gloss.*, *Pit*, a fruitstone. But E.D.D. says 'Not known to our correspondents'.] **1913** C. PETTMAN *Africanderisms* 375 Pit. .. This word is in common use in South Africa as a name for the stones of fruit. **1951** J. STEINBECK *Burning Bright* I. 8 The bitter seed that's like the inside of a peach pit. **1972** 'E. LATHEN' *The Longer the Thread* x. 93 She called him an avocado without a pit. **1977** *H. E. V. Pickstone's Catal.* (S. Afr.) 9 The fruit [*sc.* a peach] is yellow to reddish yellow, the flesh is deep orange coloured right through to the pit.

2. *S. Afr.* An edible seed, esp. a pine-nut.

1947 [see DENNEBOL].

pit, *v.* [f. PIT *sb.*[1]]

I. 1. *trans.* To put or cast into a pit; to inter, bury; *esp.* to put (roots, vegetables, etc.) into a pit for storage (cf. PIT *sb.*[1] 1 d).

1456 SIR G. HAYE *Law Arms* (S.T.S.) 237 To pytt the men of Kirk na [= nor] prison thame..war bot crueltee. **1621** T. GRANGER *Ecclesiastes* 213 They..liued like beasts, and were pitted like beasts, tumbled into the graue. **1844** STEPHENS *Bk. Farm* II. 657 In consequence of the wet state in which they had been pitted. **1850** LD. OSBORNE *Gleanings* 196 He dug and pitted the potatoes. **1880** JEFFERIES *Hodge & M.* I. 13 It [the hay] might have been pitted in the earth and preserved still green.

2. To set (cocks, dogs, pugilists, etc.) to fight for sport, prop. in a 'pit' or enclosure (see PIT *sb.*[1] 5).

1760 R. HEBER *Horse Matches* ix. p. xxii, Before any cocks are pitted. **1770** [see MAIN *sb.*[3] 3]. **1814** *Sporting Mag.* XLIV. 71 Two of the gamest little men ever pitted for twenty-five guineas. **1830** CUNNINGHAM *Brit. Paint.* II. 241 He set down the pig, pitted him against the dog. **1864** KNIGHT *Passages Work. Life* I. iii. 177 The collier pitted his cock against that of the sporting farmer.

3. *fig.* To set in opposition or rivalry; to dispose for conflict; to match, oppose (persons or things). Const. *against*. Often in passive.

1754 *Connoisseur* No. 15 ¶5 What in gaming dialect is called Pitting one man against another; that is,..wagering which of the two will live longest. **1777** JOHNSON 22 Sept. in *Boswell*, It is very uncivil to pit two people against one another. **1788** B. LINCOLN in Sparks *Corr. Amer. Rev.* (1853) IV. 222 Federalism and anti-federalism were pitted one against the other. **1826** SCOTT *Jrnl.* 7 Feb., As a lion-catcher, I could pit her against the world. **1887** CREIGHTON *Hist. Papacy* (1897) III. III. ix. 25 The two Popes were now pitted one against the other.

II. 4. To make pits in.

a. To make hollows or depressions in or upon; to mark with small scars or spots, as those left on the skin after small-pox. Most commonly in passive. Also *absol.* or *intr.* To produce small hollows or pits in a surface.

1487 *Rolls of Parlt.* VI. 391/1 The Pavyng [etc.] ben so decayed, broken, and holowid and pitted, by water fallyng out of Gutters. **1661** FELTHAM *Lusoria* xxiv. (*heading*), On a Gentlewoman, whose Nose was pitted with the Small Pox. **1677** LADY CHAWORTH in *12th Rep. Hist. MSS. Comm.* App. v. 42 Lady Anne, is recovered well, but will be pitted, as 'tis feared, with the small pox. **1725** BRADLEY *Fam. Dict.* s.v. *Small Pox*, Secrets to hinder the Small Pox to Pit. **1830** MARRYAT *King's Own* xxvi, The balls only pitted in the water, without doing any harm. **1880** MRS. RIDDELL *Myst. Palace Gard.* xiii, Like small-pox,..it pits and sears and marks most souls. **1883** S. C. HALL *Retrospect* II. 253 He was pitted with the small-pox. **1891** C. JAMES *Rom. Rigmarole* 53 Great drops of rain began to pit the white dusty roads.

b. To furnish with pits or holes; to dig pits in.

[**1764–1839**: see PITTING *vbl. sb.* 3.] **1843** J. SMITH *Forest Trees* 63 When the ground is pitted, a person..places a plant in each pit. **1869** PHILLIPS *Vesuv.* viii. 211 This surface is pitted over by artificial diggings.

5. *intr.* for *pass.* To sink in or contract so as to form a pit or hollow; *spec.* in *Path.* to yield to pressure and retain the impression, as the skin or a soft tissue. Also, to become marked with pits or small depressions.

1737 BRACKEN *Farriery Impr.* (1756) I. 266 If the Legs of your Horse pit, upon the Impression of the Fingers. **1747** WESLEY *Prim. Physic* (1762) 56 *note*, The part swelled pits if you press it with your finger. **1764** *Museum Rust.* II. cvi. 356 As soon as the sod is all burnt, and he finds the land pits. **1873** T. H. GREEN *Introd. Pathol.* (ed. 2) 58 The organ.. feels doughy, and pits on pressure with the finger. **1887** *Sci. Amer.* 29 Oct. 276/3 How to remove varnish from a panel after it has pitted.

6. Of a driver in a motor race: to stop at a pit (PIT *sb.*[1] 1 h) for fuel or maintenance.

1967 *Autocar* 5 Oct. 39/3 Mike Spence was in the seventh place..when he pitted on lap 36 with sudden engine trouble. **1976–7** *Sea Spray* (N.Z.) Dec./Jan. 58/1 Gray drove a steady, sensible race, pitting half-way through to take on 164 litres of gas in just 45 seconds. **1978** 'D. RUTHERFORD' *Collision Course* 62 The rain came bucketing down... There was nothing for it but to pit, fit rain tyres and splosh cautiously round.

pit, *adv.* [Echoic.] An imitation of the sound of rain-drops, small shot, or the like, striking against a surface: repeated, *pit, pit, pit*; hence as *vb.* to make this sound.

1859 F. FRANCIS *N. Dogvane* (1888) 86 The gun was heard, followed by the pit-pit-pitting of the shot on the water. **1886** HISSEY *On Box Seat* 56 Pit, pit, pit, dashed the wind-driven drops against our window panes.

pit, Sc. and north. dial. form of PUT *v.*

‖**pita**[1] ('pita). Also 7 peet, 8–9 pito, 9 pittee. [Sp. *pita*, a. Peruvian (Quichua) *pita* fine thread from bast or vegetable fibre: cf. Gonzalez Holguin, 1608, '*pita*, pilo delgado de hazer puntas' (fine thread to make points).] **a.** Name for the 'American aloe' (*Agave americana*) and allied species. **b.** The tough fibre obtained from these plants, used for cordage, etc.: also called ***pita-fibre***, ***-flax***, ***-hemp***, ***-thread***. Less properly applied to fibres obtained from other allied plants, as *Agave Ixtli* (ISTLE) and *Fourcroya gigantea*. **c.** ***pita-wood***, the pith-like wood of *Fourcroya gigantea*.

1698 OSBORNE tr. *Froger's Voy. Straits Magellan* 129 The Peet is an herb that can be peeled in the same manner as hemp. **1748** *Earthquake of Peru* iii. 46 From them they draw the Thread call'd Pita. **1748** *Anson's Voy.* II. v. 177 Pito thread. **1843** PRESCOTT *Mexico* I. v. (1850) I. 128 A veil made of the fine web of the pita. **1860** TYLOR *Anahuac* (1861) 88 There are two kinds of aloe-fibre; one coarse, ichtli, the other much finer, pito. **1886** *Treas. Bot.* 898 Pita-fibre and Pita-thread are..the fibre, called also Aloe-fibre, obtained from the leaves of the larger Agaves. **1898** H. KIRK *Brit. Guiana* Gloss. 352 *Pittee*, a strong kind of fibre.

pita[2] ('piːtə, 'pɪtə). Also peeta, pitah, pitta. [ad. mod.Gr. πήττα, πί(τ)τα bread, cake, pie, perh. f. Gr. πεπτ-ός cooked, f. πέσσειν, πέττ-, to cook, bake. Cf. Turk. *pide*, Heb. *pittah* in similar senses.] A thick flat bread of the kind common in Mediterranean and Arab countries, usu. cut open and filled with a meat or other filling. Also *attrib.*

1951, **1963** [see FELAFEL]. **1964** M. DUNCAN *Cooking Greek Way* 212 Pita Yaourtiou, Yoghurt cake. *Ibid* 213 The pita at this [dough] stage should be about 2 inches thick. **1965** R. HOWE *Balkan Cooking* 136 Pita is made in the same manner as Austrian struedel and its success depends entirely on the paper-like thinness of the pastry. **1967** A. BAILEY in L. Deighton *London Dossier* 56 A bread called 'pita' that looks like an oven glove and is usually stuffed with meat, raw onions and tomatoes. **1970** *Times* 29 Apr. 18/4 With your souvlakia you will get pitta, excellent flat round bread. **1971** D. MEIRING *Wall of Glass* xi. 87 They had..eaten pita and hummus..in the Arab restaurants in the port. **1974** *Times* 4 May 11/2 The Continental..on the Charing Cross Road.. offers..warm Greek pitta stuffed with turkey. **1975** *Jewish Chron.* 18 July (Food & Wine Suppl.) p. iii/2 A pita—the flat Arab style bread—is split open, a few of the falafel balls stuffed in. **1976** *Islander* (Victoria, B.C.) 1 Aug. 4/1 (*caption*) Phyliss buying fallafel and pita in Jerusalem. **1977** *National Observer* (U.S.) 8 Jan. 12/3, I made my own pita bread, the flat chewy Arab bun that can be cut in half and stuffed with any number of goodies. **1978** *Lancashire Life* Apr. 71/3 We were tackling the first course... For me that was taramosalata, a puree of smoked cod roe, olive oil and lemon juice which had a most distinctive tang; it was served with a great quantity of pitta bread and was quite different from the last taramosalata I tasted. **1979** T. BARLING *Olympic Sleeper* ix. 95 The boy brought olives and peppers, sliced cheese and tomatoes, hot pita..and marinated octopus.

‖**pitahaya** (pita'haja). [Sp., a. Haytian *pitahaya* (Humboldt).] Name (in Mexico and South-Western U.S.) for the giant cactus (*Cereus giganteus*) or other tall species bearing edible fruit.

1783 JUSTAMOND tr. *Raynal's Hist. Indies* III. 390 The most useful is the pitahaya, the produce of which constitutes the principal food of the Californians. **1851** MAYNE REID *Scalp Hunt.* xxiii, The pitahaya fell to the ground. **1852** TH. ROSS *Humboldt's Trav.* I. 328. **1901** TWEEDIE *Mexico* xv. 253 Pitahaya, a giant cactus which bears fruit about the size of a peach.

b. *attrib.* **pitahaya-woodpecker**, a species of woodpecker (*Centurus uropygialis*) in southern Arizona, usually nesting in the giant cactus.

pitaile, pitall, variants of PEDAILE *Obs.*

pitance, -ancy, -aunce, obs. ff. PITTANCE.

pitancer, -ancier, etc.: see PITTANCER.

pit-a-pat ('pɪtəˌpæt), **pit-pat** ('pɪtpæt), *adv.*, *adj.*, *sb.* Also 7 **a-pit-pat, a-pit-to-pat**, 7–8 **a-pit-a-pat**, 8 *Sc.* **pittie-pattie**, 8–9 **pitty-pat, pitty-patty**. [Echoic, expressing alternating sounds. Cf. PITTER-PATTER.] An imitation of the repeated or alternated sound made by the strong beating or palpitation of the heart in excitement or emotion; also of that of light or rapid footsteps, or of similar alternating or reiterated sounds.

A. *adv.* With such a sound or sounds; palpitatingly: patteringly. Usually in phr. ***to go pit-a-pat***.

1522 MORE *De Quat. Nouiss.* Wks. 94/1 Some wretches yᵗ scant can crepe for age.. walk pit pat vpon a paire of patens. **1601** B. JONSON *Poetaster* IV. i, You shall haue kisses.., goe pit-pat, pit-pat, pit-pat, vpon your lips, as thick as stones out of slings. **1621** FLETCHER *Isl. Princess* III. i, And how their hearts go pit-a-pat. **1623–4** MIDDLETON & ROWLEY *Spanish Gipsy* III. ii, The shot that fly, Pit-a-pat rattling in the sky. **1676** D'URFEY *Mme. Fickle* v. ii, My heart goes a-pit-to-pat. **1677** MRS. BEHN *Rover* III. i, My heart goes a pit a-pat. **1693** CONGREVE *Old Bach.* II. ii, Agad, my heart has gone apit pat for thee. *a***1758** RAMSAY *Highland Lassie* iii, My flighterin heart gangs pittie-pattie. **1760–72** H. BROOKE *Fool of Qual.* (1809) III. 116 Her feet went pit-a-pat with joy. **1840** DICKENS *Barn. Rudge* liii, Tramp, tramp, pit-pat, on they come together. **1871** G. MEREDITH *H. Richmond* III. 119 Her heart.. was easily set pitty-pat.

B. *adj.* Of the nature of, or characterized by, such reiterated sound; palpitating; pattering.

*a***1637** B. JONSON *Underwoods* xciv. *Pet. Poor Men*, The rattling pit-pat noise Of the less poetic boys. **1712** STEELE *Spect.* No. 503 ⁋2 She.. stepp'd out of her Pew, and fell into the finest pitty-pat Air,.. tossing her Head up and down. **1810** *Splendid Follies* III. 109 She descended with a pit-a-pat heart. **1894** A. WEBSTER *Mother & Dau.* (1895) 34 The approaching sound of pit pat feet.

C. *sb.* The sound itself, or the action producing it; palpitation, pattering, etc.

1582 STANYHURST *Æneis* II. (Arb.) 66 Tripping with pit pat vnequal. **1681** DRYDEN *Tamerl.* Epil. 12 'Tis but the pit-a-pat of two young hearts. **1784** R. BAGE *Barham Downs* II. 318 You.. may make love, and play your pitty patties. **1824** BYRON *Juan* XVI. cxii, That stealthy pace.. So like a spiritual pit a-pat. **1888** T. HARDY *Wessex T.* (1889) 160 The pit-a-pat of their horses' hoofs lessened.

Hence **pit-a-pat** (**pit-pat**, etc.) *v. intr.*, to go pit-a-pat, to palpitate, to patter; whence **pit-a-patting** *vbl. sb.* and *ppl. a.*; also **pit-a-pa't-ation** (*humorous*), palpitation.

1606 SYLVESTER *Du Bartas* II. iv. II. *Magnif.* 1137 Swains, ..the strouting Clusters cut,..Run..to the fragrant Fat, Tumble them in, and after *pit-a-pat Up to the Waste. **1728** RAMSAY *Fables* x. 22 Till his heart pitty-pattys. **1757** GARRICK *Male Coquette* (Jod.), There will not be a female heart, but will pitapat, as he passes by. **1827** W.G.S. *Excursion Vill. Curate* 123, I heard footsteps softly pit-patting up the stairs. *a***1735** LD. PETERBOROUGH *Song* i. in F. Locker *Lyra Elegant.* 99, I said to my heart,.. What black, brown, or fair, in what nation, By turns has not taught thee a *pit-a-pat-ation? **1763** COLMAN *Prose on Sev. Occas.* (1787) I. 227 The pit-a-pat-ation of their dear little bosoms. **1844** TUPPER *Crock of G.* xxvi. 209 He was so very fearful the *pitapating would betray him. **1869** BLACKMORE *Lorna D.* vii, My little heart was ashamed of its pit-a-patting. **1894** *Outing* (U.S.) XXIV. 14/1, I looked around.. a soft pit-a-patting sound behind me.

‖**pitarah** (pɪ'tɑːrə). *E. Ind.* Also **pattara, petara(h, pettarah, pittarah**. [Hind. *piṭārāh*, *peṭārāh*.] A basket or box used in travelling by palankeen to carry the traveller's clothes. (Yule and Burnell.)

1828 *Asiat. Costumes* 61 Two pair of pattara baskets. **1845** SIR H. B. EDWARDES in *Mem.* (1886) I. 33 You may take an inventory of his load without opening the pitârahs. **1853** W. D. ARNOLD *Oakfield* I. xi. 223 To send to the dák bungalow for his petarahs. **1855** THACKERAY *Newcomes* lxxi, The plain things.. may be packed in a petara or two.

pit-bank to **pit-brow**: see PIT *sb.*¹ 15.

Pitcairner ('pɪtkɛənə(r)). [f. the name *Pitcairn* (see below) + -ER¹.] A native or inhabitant of Pitcairn Island in the central South Pacific, settled with a mixed European and Polynesian population by mutineers from the *Bounty* in 1790.

1831 J. BARROW *Eventful Hist. Mutiny of Bounty* viii. 338 The Pitcairners have already proceeded from the simple canoe to row-boats. **1853** T. B. MURRAY *Pitcairn* v. 152 After some slight refreshment, (for they have only two regular meals a day,) the business of the Pitcairners' day begins. **1857** V. LUSH *Jrnl.* 18 Nov. (1971) 195 As Norfolk Island is the nearest to New Zealand they touched there on their outward voyage and landed Mrs. Selwyn, who remained with the Pitcairners till the *Southern Cross* called for her on their way home. **1874** C. M. YONGE *Life J. C. Patteson* I. vii. 253 The Pitcairners.. had not yet arrived [at Norfolk Island], but were on their way from their original island. **1933** C. CHAUVEL *In Wake of 'Bounty'* vi. 82 The Pitcairners have often gone to sea without a proper supply of petrol. **1962** H. LUKE *Islands of South Pacific* vi. 88 The Pitcairners throve and multiplied on their small but fertile island. **1964** ROSS & MOVERLEY *Pitcairnese Lang.* i. 25 In 1859, two families of Pitcairners.. returned to Pitcairn, to be followed by a further four families.. in 1864. **1971** *Daily Tel.* 23 Dec. 3/8 Christmas Day usually is also Pitcairn's annual election day, but a shift in dates was necessary this year because the God-fearing Pitcairners naturally cannot vote on their Sabbath.

Pitcairnese (pɪtkɛə'niːz). [f. as prec. + -ESE.] The language of Pitcairn Island, a mixture of English and Polynesian (mainly Tahitian) elements. Also *attrib.* or as *adj.*

1964 ROSS & MOVERLEY *Pitcairnese Lang.* i. 25 The Pitcairnese language—the subject of the present book—has survived both on Pitcairn and on Norfolk. **1968** *Anglia* LXXXVI. 360 Later accounts will extend our knowledge of the detail of Pitcairnese and a more extensively documented description will be especially useful. **1973** *Word 1966* XXII. 341 Since Pitcairnese has come out of the interaction of English and Tahitian, its lack of inflectional suffixes is attributed to their absence from Tahitian.

pitch (pɪtʃ), *sb.*¹ Forms: 1–2 pic; 2–5 pich, 3–6 pych, (3 pisch), 4–5 pycche, picche, 4–6 pyche, (5 peche), 5–6 piche, pytch(e, pitche, 6– pitch. *β.* (*northern*) 3–6 pik, 4 pic, pike, 4–5 pyke, pikke, 4–6 pyk, pyck, 5 picke, pikk, pykk(e, 6–7 (8–9 *dial.*) pick. [OE. *pic*, ad. L. *pix*, *pic-em* (whence also OS., LG. *pik*, Du. *pek*, *pik*, OHG. *pëh*, *bëh*, Ger. *pech*, ON. *bik*).]

1. A tenacious resinous substance, of a black or dark brown colour, hard when cold, becoming a thick viscid semi-liquid when heated; obtained as a residuum from the boiling or distillation of tar, also from the distillation of turpentine; used to stop the seams of ships after caulking, to protect wood from moisture, and for other purposes.

*a***700** *Epinal Gloss.* 820 (O.E.T.) *Pix*, *picis*, pic. *a***1050** *Liber Scintill.* xvii. (1889) 83 Se þe æthrinð pic byð besmiten fram him. *a***1200** *Moral Ode* 245 (Lamb. MS.) þer is bernunde pich hore saule to baþien inne. *c***1250** *Death* 211 in *O.E. Misc.* 181 Of pych [*v.r.* pisch] and of brunston. **1390** GOWER *Conf.* III. 312 Let make a cofre strong of bord, That it be ferm with led and pich. **1398** TREVISA *Barth. De P.R.* XVII. cxxiii. (Tollem. MS.), Of picche is double maner kynde, þe ton is calde schippe picche. [**1495** *Ibid.* (W. de W.), The harde pytche hyght shippe pytche.] **1436** *Libel Eng. Policy* in *Pol. Poems* (Rolls) II. 171 Pych, terre, borde, and flex. **1496** *Naval Acc. Hen. VII* (1896) 174 Laying on of piche. *Ibid.* 176, xj barelles peche. *Ibid.* 181, iij barrelles pytche. **1568** GRAFTON *Chron.* II. 362 Piche, Tarre, Rosen, Ropes. **1655** MRQ. WORCESTER *Cent. Inv.* §7 As dark as Pitch is black. **1744** BERKELEY *Siris* §13 Liquid pitch.. or tar was obtained by setting fire to billets of old fat pines or firs. **1836** MARRYAT *Midsh. Easy* xxxv, The very smell of pitch and tar has become odious to me. *c***1860** H. STUART *Seaman's Catech.* 58 Pitch is tar boiled with a certain quantity of water and with a portion of coarse resin melted with it.

β. *a***1240** *Wohunge* in *Cott. Hom.* 269 Al þat pinende pik ne walde ham þunche bote a softe bekinde bað. **13..** *Cursor M.* 11885 (Cott.) þai fild a lede o pik [*v.rr.* pike, pic; *c* 1425 *Trin.* picche] and oyle. *c***1375** *Sc. Leg. Saints* xxxxi. (*Justin*) 733, & [gert] þare-in be done blak pic and gert brynstane bla. *c***1460** *Towneley Myst.* iii. 127 Anoynt thi ship with pik and tar. **1501** DOUGLAS *Pal. Hon.* III. 31 All full of brintstane, pick, and bulling leid. **1571** *Wills & Inv. N.C.* (Surtees) I. 364 In ye seller.. v berrells of pyk. *a***1775** *Hobie Noble* xii. in Child *Ballads* VII. (1890) 2/2 Tho dark the night as pick and tar. **1828** *Craven Gloss.* (ed. 2) s.v. *Pick*, 'As dark as *pick*'.

2. Applied to various bituminous substances (***mineral pitch***); esp. (***Jew's pitch***) = ASPHALT 1, BITUMEN 1.

1388 WYCLIF *Gen.* vi. 14 Thou schalt anoynte it with pitche [1382 glew, *Vulg.* bitumine] with ynne and with outforth. *c***1400** MAUNDEV. (Roxb.) xii. 50 Men callez it þe Lac Asfaltit, þat es to say, þe Lac of Pikke. **1555** EDEN *Decades* 134 They gather pytche whiche sweateth owte of the rockes. **1604** E. G[RIMSTONE] *D'Acosta's Hist. Indies* III. xvii. 173 At the point of Cape S. Helaine, there is a spring or fountaine of pitch. **1667** MILTON *P.L.* XI. 731 A Vessel of huge bulk,.. Smeard round with Pitch. **1831** T. P. JONES *Convers. Chem.* xxviii. 289 *Asphaltum*, sometimes called *Jew's pitch*, is a much purer bitumen than common pitch. It is found on the banks of the Dead Sea, and in.. Trinidad, forming large beds in the earth. **1836** R. M. MARTIN *Hist. W. Indies* I. *Trinidad* 190 The most remarkable mineral phenomenon is the *Asphaltum*, or Pitch Lake. *Ibid.* 194 The pitch at the sides of the lake is perfectly hard and cold, but as one walks towards the middle.. the pitch becomes softer.

3. a. Improperly applied to the resin or crude turpentine which exudes from pine and fir trees.

Burgundy or ***white pitch***: see BURGUNDY 5. ***Canada*** or ***hemlock pitch***: see HEMLOCK *sb.* 4. ***Greek pitch*** = COLOPHONY.

1398 TREVISA *Barth. De P.R.* XVII. cxxi. (Tollem. MS.), This tre [Pinus] takeþ sone fyre,.. for oute þerof comeþ picche. **1495** *Ibid.* cxxiii. 685 Pytche.. is droppynge of the pyne tree. **1567** MAPLET *Gr. Forest* 57 The Pine tree.. is sayde to sweate, and to droppe forth Pitch. **1614** MARKHAM *Cheap Husb.* I. (1668) Table Hard Words, *Pitch of Burgundy* is Rosen, and the blacker the better. **1874** GARROD & BAXTER *Mat. Med.* 367 Burgundy pitch consists chiefly of resin, but a little volatile oil is present.

†**b.** = PITCH PINE, PITCH-TREE. *Obs.*

1674 tr. *Scheffer's Lapland* 141 The soil.. besides Birch-trees, hath Fir and Pitch. **1697** DRYDEN *Virg. Georg.* II. 614 Narycian Woods of Pitch, whose gloomy Shade Seems for Retreat of heav'nly Muses made!

4. Proverbial Phrases: ***black*** or ***dark as pitch*** (cf. ***pitch black, pitch dark***, in 5); ***he that toucheth pitch shall be defiled therewith*** (Ecclus. xiii. 1), etc.

1303 R. BRUNNE *Handl. Synne* 6578 Who so handlyþ pycche wellyng hote, He shal haue fylþe þerof sumdeyl. *Ibid.* 11540 Black as pyk. *c***1380** *Sir Ferumb.* 2461 þan lai he þar so blac so pych. *c***1386** CHAUCER *Pars. T.* ⁋780 Who so toucheth warm pych it shent hise fyngres. **1579** SPENSER *Sheph. Cal.* May 74 Who touches Pitch mought needes be defilde. **1622** MABBE tr. *Aleman's Guzman d'Alf.* II. 117 It growes darke as pitch. **1886** H. CONWAY *Living or Dead* xx, I was touching pitch, yet striving to keep myself from being defiled.

5. *attrib.* and *Comb.*, as ***pitch-ball, -barrel, -heater, -ladle, -pit, -stain, -still***; ***pitch-blackened, -coloured, -lined, -stained, -smelling, pitch-like*** adjs.; **pitch-black** *a.*, of the brownish-black colour of pitch; also, intensely black or dark; **pitch-boat**: see quot.; **pitch-boilery**, a place or vessel in which tar is boiled for making pitch; **pitch-brown** *a.*, of the dark brown colour of pitch; **pitch-coal**, bituminous coal, or other hard bituminous substance, such as jet (quot. 1839); **pitch-dark** *a.* (usually as two words when predicative), 'as dark as pitch', intensely dark; hence **pitch-darkness**; **pitch-fibre**, a black, waterproof material which consists of compressed cellulose or asbestos fibre impregnated under vacuum with pitch and is used for making pipes; **pitch-fir** = PITCH PINE; **pitch-knot**, a pitchy knot (KNOT *sb.*¹ 14) of a pine or other tree used as a light; cf. *pine-knot*; **pitch-mark** = *pitch-brand*; so **pitch-marked** *a.* = *pitch-branded*; **pitch-mineral** = *mineral pitch*: see sense 2; **pick-mirk** *a. Sc.* = *pitch-dark*; **pitch-mop**, a mop with which the sides and other parts of a ship are pitched; **pitch-opal**, an inferior variety of common opal, with a resinous lustre (also called *resin-opal*); **pitch-ore**, (*a*) a dark brown ore of copper, containing bitumen; pitchy copper ore; (*b*) = PITTICITE; (*c*) = PITCH-BLENDE; **pitch-polisher**, a metal instrument for polishing curved surfaces of glass, being coated with a prepared pitch (Byrne *Artisan's Hand-bk.* 1853, Index); **pitch-pot** = *pitch-kettle*; †**pitch-speeched** *a.* (*obs. nonce-wd.*), uttering foul or offensive speech (cf. *foul-mouthed*); **pitch-tankard**, a tankard lined with pitch, for imparting a flavour to beer, etc.; †**pitch-wine**, wine having a flavour of pitch; **pitch-wood**, the resinous wood of pine or fir trees. See also PITCH-BLENDE, etc.

1881 RAYMOND *Mining Gloss.*, *Pitch-bag (Cornw.)*, a bag covered with pitch, in which powder is inclosed for charging damp holes. **1879** FROUDE *Cæsar* xix. 315 *Pitch-balls, torches, faggots.. to feed the flames. **1711** SHAFTESB. *Charac.* (1737) I. 29 To bring [the Christians].. upon the stage in a pleasanter way than that of bear-skins and *pitch-barrels. **1599** MARSTON *Sco. Villanie* II. v. 197 Tuscus.. Hath drawn false lights from *pitch-black loueries. **1849** D. J. BROWNE *Amer. Poultry Yd.* (1855) 237 The head.. and tail, are pitch-black. **1902** *Temple Bar Mag.* June 690 The pitch black cavern of the lower deck. **1871** TENNYSON *Last Tourn.* 67 With blunt stump *Pitch-blacken'd sawing the air. **1867** SMYTH *Sailor's Word-bk.*, **Pitch-boat*, a vessel fitted for boiling pitch in, which should be veered astern of the one being caulked. **1885** STALLYBRASS tr. *Hehn's Wand. Plants & Anim.* 454 *Pitch-boileries in the wooded spurs of the Alps. **1839** URE *Dict. Arts* 662 Jet; a species of *pitch-coal or glance-coal. **1854** RONALDS & RICHARDSON *Chem. Technol.* (ed. 2) I. 33 Varieties in which the fracture is conchoidal and the structure more dense have been distinguished as conchoidal brown coal or pitch coal. **1601** CHETTLE & MUNDAY *Death Earl of Huntington* II. i. in Hazl. *Dodsley* VIII. 256 *Pitch-colour'd, ebon-fac'd, blacker than black. **1827** DISRAELI *Viv. Grey* VI. i, The stars prevented it from ever being *pitch dark. **1842** DICKENS *Amer. Notes* vi, Ascend these pitch-dark stairs. **1874** HARE *Story of my Life* (1900) IV. xvii. 241 We.. set off again.. with lanthorns in *pitch darkness. **1946** *Archit. Rev.* CI. 66/1 Externally the drains are in *pitchfibre with precast concrete manholes. **1958** *Daily Tel.* 30 June 4/6 The sales of pitch-fibre pipe continue to expand with the coming into operation of considerably increased productive capacity. **1964** L. T. MINCHIN *Famous Pipelines of World* vii. 95 Pitch-fibre is in fact a mixture of about 25% waste paper and 75% coal-tar pitch. **1780** VON TROIL *Iceland* 41 The growth of.. Norway *pitch-firs. **1792** BELKNAP *Hist. New Hampsh.* III. 90 A lighted *pitch-knot is placed on the outside of a canoe. **1825** J. NEAL *Bro. Jonathan* I. 58 The fire-place, within which two or three lighted pitch knots, a substitute for candles, were burning. **1850** H. C. WATSON *Camp-Fires of Revolution* 157 We must have some more pitch-knots on the fire. **1726** SHELVOCKE *Voy. round World* 245 The *pitch-ladle, and covers of the ship's coppers were converted into frying pans. **1694** SALMON *Bate's Dispens.* (1713) 228/1 Ropy or *Pitch-like Wood-soot. **1896** *Daily News* 11 July 6/1 Old Piggins, and leathern pitch-lined beer 'jacks', with other like traditional utensils. **1523** FITZHERB. *Husb.* §52 Both eare marke, *pitche marke, and radel marke [of sheep]. **1805** R. W. DICKSON *Pract. Agric.* II. 1057 If there be pitch-marks.. they should also be clipped out. **1688** *Lond. Gaz.*

No. 2377/4 She has been *Pitch mark'd in several places with a Horse shoe, and a Tarr'd P. on her Rump. **1795** MACNEILL *Will & Jean* I. 110 *Pick mirk night is setting in. **1759** *Ann. Reg.* 76/2 He..struck him on the breast with a *pitch-mop. **1882** OGILVIE, **Pitch-opal*, an inferior kind of common opal. **1796** KIRWAN *Elem. Min.* (ed. 2) II. iv. 139 Sometimes this Ore is mixed with Bitumen..and is called *Pech Erz* or *pitch Ore. **1896** CHESTER *Dict. Names Min.*, *Pitch-ore*... Also a syn. of pitch-blende. *Ibid.*, *Pitticite*..f. πιττά, 'pitch', because it was earlier called pitch-ore. **1719** DE FOE *Crusoe* (1840) II. xii. 248 Dipping it in the *pitch-pot. **1804** *Europ. Mag.* XLV. 20/1 Cursing till my blood boiled like a pitch-pot. **1596** J. TRUSSELL in *Southwell's Tri. Death* To Rdr., But let this *pitch-speecht mouth defile but one. **1838** DICKENS *O. Twist* xlviii, Wine-stains,..*pitch-stains, any stains, all come out at one rub with the..composition. **1890** *Cent. Dict.* s.v. *Pitch-tankard*, *Pitch-tankards are still used in Germany with certain kinds of beer, such as the Lichtenhainer. **1601** HOLLAND *Pliny* I. 406 This kind of *Pitch wine brought the territory about Vienna into great name. **1825** J. NEAL *Bro. Jonathan* I. 84 Tumbled him..into the fire-place, among the *pitch-wood.

pitch (pɪtʃ), *sb.*[2] [f. PITCH *v.*[1] The sense-development is in many points obscure and uncertain, esp. that of branches IV and V, which it is difficult to connect with any sense of the vb.]

I. Act or manner of pitching.

†**1. a.** An act of setting, laying, or paying down; *concr.* that which is laid or thrown down (in quot. a contribution to a meal). *Obs. rare.*

?*a* **1500** *Chester Pl.* (E.E.T.S.) VII. 107 Lay fourth, each man, alyche, What he hath left of his lyveray; And I will first put forth my piche With my parte first of us all three. *c* **1500** in Furniv. *Ballads fr. MSS.* I. 455 It cost me a Noble at one pyche.

b. An act of pitching or fixing upon a thing or place. (See PITCH *v.*[1] 16.)

1791 in *T. Hutchinson's Diary* II. 434 We continue to think this is a very agreeable part of England; and perhaps I could not have made a better pitch than I have done.

2. a. An act of plunging head-foremost. Also with advbs. *spec. Naut.* The plunge or downward motion of a ship's head in a sea-way: see PITCH *v.*[1] 19 b.

1762-9 FALCONER *Shipwr.* II. 725 At every pitch the o'erwhelming billows bend Beneath their load the quivering bowsprit's end. **1863** ATKINSON *Stanton Grange* (1864) 72 A tipsy-looking kind of pitch-forward of the bird. **1870** J. BECKETT in *Eng. Mech.* 7 Jan. 411/2 There has been 'a pitch-in', as a collision is usually called by drivers and guards. **1870** G. MACDONALD *At Back of North Wind* ix, You will know I am near you by every roll and pitch of the vessel.

b. *Aeronaut.* and *Astronautics.* = PITCHING *vbl. sb.*[1] 8 b; also, the extent of this motion; ***angle of pitch***, the angle between the plane containing the lateral axis and the relative wind and that containing the lateral and longitudinal axes.

1915 *Rep. & Mem. Advisory Comm. Aeronaut. 1913* No. 108. 1 The tests on each model comprise the determination of lift and drift for angles of pitch from −10° to +10° by 2° steps. **1920** L. BAIRSTOW *Appl. Aerodynamics* iv. 223 The curves for 0° and −5° pitch are seen to lie below those of the rudder alone. **1921** S. BRODETSKY *Mech. Princ. Aeroplane* iv. 148 Let there be pitch through an angle Θ about the new Y axis. **1935** *Encycl. Aviation* 493/2 In horizontal flight the angle of pitch is the angle between the longitudinal axis and the direction of motion of the aircraft. *Ibid.* 585/1 Thus a roll causes a yaw, and a yaw causes a roll... When, as often, a pitch is also introduced, it soon becomes apparent why the problem is a difficult one. **1967** *Technol. Week* 20 Feb. 35/3 When the booms are deployed, the spacecraft moment of inertia in pitch and roll with respect to Earth is about 250,000 slug-ft.[2] **1974** *Sci. Amer.* Dec. 138/2 Shifting his weight to control the craft in pitch, roll and yaw.

3. The act of pitching or throwing underhand (PITCH *v.*[1] 17). **a.** *Cricket.* The act or manner of pitching or delivering the ball in bowling, or the way in which it pitches or alights. **b.** *Baseball.* The act of pitching or serving the ball to the batter; the right or turn to do this. **c.** *Golf.* The action of 'lofting' the ball up to the hole, or to the green.

1833 J. NYREN *Young Cricketer's Tutor* 46 The first thing he [*sc.* the fieldsman] should make himself master of, is to play from the pitch of the ball, and the motion of the batsman, so as to *get the start of the ball.* **1841** 'BAT' *Cricket. Man.* 41 A judicious bowler.. varies his style, pitch, and pace, according to the play of the hitter. **1851** LILLYWHITE *Guide to Cricketers* 15 The pitch of the ball depends very much upon your pace. **1897** RANJITSINHJI *Cricket* 167 One of the main things in making an off-drive in any direction is to get well to the pitch of the ball. **1901** *Scotsman* 9 Sept. 4/7 His pitch overrunning the hole, he gave himself too much to do for a half in 5.

4. a. = PITCH-FARTHING. *rare.* Now *dial.*

1742 CHESTERF. *Lett.* (1792) I. ciii. 285, I would be melancholy and mortified, if I did not construe Homer, and play at pitch, better than any boy..in my own form. **1886** in ELWORTHY *W. Somerset Word-bk.*

b. *Cards.* A game resembling all-fours, but so played that the trump suit is determined by 'pitching', i.e. leading a card of that suit.

5. *slang.* **a.** A talk, chat: cf. PITCH *v.*[1] 17 d.

1888 'R. BOLDREWOOD' *Robbery under Arms* III. xv. 232 Starlight and Jim were having a pitch about the best way to get aboard one of these pearling craft, and how jolly it would be. **1892** *Pall Mall G.* 7 Sept. 2/1 We now have a 'pitch' with the men; 'pitch', be it said, is another term for talk.

b. Tendentious or persuasive acting or speech, esp. inflated or exaggerated sales-talk; an instance of this, a 'line'.

1876 C. HINDLEY *Life & Adventures of Cheap Jack* 255 When I had done my 'pitch' and got down from the stage. **1926** *Variety* 29 Dec. 7/4 The outdoor show game with its 'rag front',..'pitch', [etc.]. **1935** A. J. POLLOCK *Underworld Speaks* 88/2 *Pitch*, a satisfactory interview with intended victim by a high pressure stock salesman. **1962** *Listener* 18 Jan. 128/1 I've often sat in the living-room listening to some other joker give his pitch before I could give mine. **1968** *Globe & Mail* (Toronto) 3 Feb. 3/1 Organizers are planning to allow 40 minutes for each candidate to make his pitch to the convention. **1973** *Washington Post* 13 Jan. A22/2 One novel remedy was correctional ads that required a company to tell the consumer that its earlier pitch was not totally true. **1974** K. MILLETT *Flying* (1975) III. 305 Nell hangs fire in the kitchen while I make my pitch. **1976** 'O. BLEECK' *No Questions Asked* iii. 41, I made my pitch down at headquarters. I told them..I'd better be assigned to this thing full-time. **1976** *Times* 2 Feb. 16/4 Mr Jack Jones has been squealing before he is hurt... He proceeded to get his pitch in early. **1976** *National Observer* (U.S.) 14 Aug. 1/4 Advertising was missing a bet by forsaking the wee- and off-hours for its pitches. **1977** *Rolling Stone* 16 June 43/3 He's not out there making a pitch to the audience to really love him. **1978** *Observer* 29 Jan. 15/6 Actor Charlton Heston makes a recorded pitch for cable television.

II. Something that is pitched, or used for pitching.

†**6.** A net pitched or set for catching fish. *Obs.*

1523 FITZHERB. *Surv.* 10 b, To fysshe with shouenettes, trodenettes, small pytches, and suche other. **1590** *Acts Privy Council* (1899) XIX. 406 He should cause the said wayres, stakes and pytches to be removed and plucked up, that the river maie have yts free course. **1705** *Act 4 Anne* c. 21 Nets, Angles, Leaps, Pitches, and other Engines for the taking.. of Fish.

7. *local.* **a.** = PITCHER[2] 3; **b.** = PITCHER[2] 4.

1674-91 RAY *S. & E.C. Words* 109 A *Pitch*, a Bar of Iron with a thick square pointed end to make holes in the ground by pitching down. **1807** VANCOUVER *Agric. Devon* (1813) 134 The stakes or pitches..were chiefly of willow. **1856** *Jrnl. R. Agric. Soc.* XVII. II. 363 Live stakes (provincially termed withy pitches). **1886** ELWORTHY *W. Somerset Word-bk.*, s.v., In making new hedges it is usual to stipulate 'to be planted with good withy or elder pitches' or 'pitchers'.

8. A quantity of something pitched. **a.** The quantity of hay, etc. thrown up by a pitchfork.

1778 [W. MARSHALL] *Minutes Agric.* 2 Sept. an. 1776, Every pitch of hay and corn, generally speaking, passes twice thro' his hands. **1878** JEFFERIES *Gamekeeper at H.* 76 The 'pitch' of hay on the prong.

b. The quantity of some particular commodity pitched or placed in a market for sale.

1866 *Standard* 3 Oct. 2/3 The pitch of cheese was the largest that has been known for some years past. **1886** *Manch. Courier* 18 Feb. 7 There was an immense pitch of cheese yesterday. **1887** *Daily News* 15 Oct. 2/4 The pitch of..hops this year at Weyhill..is smaller than in any year since the blight of 1860. **1888** *Ibid.* 9 July 2/7 Other sorts [of wool]..are being thrown on the market in large pitches.

9. A paving stone; esp. one set on edge, a 'sett': = PITCHER[2] 5. Cf. PITCH *v.*[1] 8 c, PITCHING *vbl. sb.* 6 b.

1896 *Daily News* 30 Sept. 7/1 A large part of the [Piccadilly] Circus is 'up', and is being relaid with granite pitches.

III. Place of pitching.

10. *gen.* The place or point at or from which something is pitched. *rare.*

1551 RECORDE *Pathw. Knowl.* I. xi, Then pitch one foote of your compasse at the one ende of the line, and with the other foote draw a bowe line right ouer the pytche of the compasse. **1630** in *Descr. Thames* (1758) 75 Every Hebberman shall fish by the Shore, and pitch their Pole at half Ebb, and shall have but forty Fathom Rope allowed from the Pitch of their Pole into the River.

11. a. A place at which one stations oneself or is stationed; a portion of ground selected by or allotted to a person for residence, business, or any occupation; *esp.* a spot in a street or other public place at which a stall for the sale or display of something is pitched or set up, or at which a street performer, a bookmaker, etc. stations himself. Also, a crowd gathered by a 'barker' or around a stall, etc.; the part of a market, stock exchange, etc., where particular commodities are bought and sold. orig. *Amer.*

1699 *Derby* (Connecticut) *Town Rec.* (1901) 207 The laying out of John Pringles pitch upon the good hill. **1746** *Waterbury* (Connecticut) *Proprietors' Rec.* (1911) 166 A ten Acre pitch which his Father bought of Thos Judd of Hartford. **1765** T. HUTCHINSON *Hist. Mass.* I. i. 22 Here Mr. Nowell and some of his friends made their pitch. **1851** MAYHEW *Lond. Labour* I. 10/2 In consequence of a New Police regulation, 'stands' or 'pitches' have been forbidden. **1889** *Daily News* 22 Oct. 3/1 Two pitches were made in widely separated quarters of the town, and in each instance the members of Parliament..left a numerous and interested assembly. **1905** *Ibid.* 2 Jan. 9 Having chosen their 'pitch' the ponies were unharnessed, triangular fireplaces of stout poles erected. **1943** W. B. TAYLOR *Shake it Again* xxi. 199 A well-known drapery pitcher (one who sells drapery by pitching it, i.e. telling a story about each article offered, usually gagging in an entertaining way while describing, to keep the pitch interested). **1949** [see FANNY *v.*]. **1955** *Times* 19 Aug. 8/3 Once a month, roughly, from May to Poppy Day I am a seller. I prefer the same time—8.30 to 10 o'clock, and the same pitch—outside a row of busy shops, so I meet a number of the same people. **1959** *Encounter* May 22/2 If the street is full, a new pitch is carved out [for a prostitute]. **1960** *Farmer & Stockbreeder* 29 Mar. 16/1 Barnstaple, with a much smaller pitch than Perth, was a seller's market. **1961** *Daily Tel.* 25 Feb. 15/1 Sir Tufton [Beamish] told Members that he had been to mock auctions in Britain and America. He gave an example of the jargon used: The top man operates his joint by nailing the streamers among the plunder-snatchers in the pitch got by his frontsman, [etc.]. **1978** *Times* 1 Sept. 19/1 Patchy trading on the traded options pitch pushed ICI to the head of the active stocks.

b. A place or spot in a river where an angler takes his stand.

1867 F. FRANCIS *Angling* i. (1880) 44 *note*, Before the angler..attempts to fish any special hole, swim, pitch, or cast. **1872** *Echo* 5 Aug., A fisherman has had orders from a customer to bait one or two barbel pitches, and not to spare the worms.

c. ***to queer the pitch***: see QUEER *v.* 2 b.

12. *Agric.*, and *Mining* (Cornw.). A definite portion of a field, or of a mine, allotted to a particular workman.

1805 R. W. DICKSON *Pract. Agric.* II. 659 After having completed..one pitch of work, consisting of thirteen ridges, he is to begin again in a similar manner. **1855** J. R. LEIFCHILD *Cornwall Mines* 142 By this management the lode is finally divided into masses called *pitches*, each sixty feet in height, by about thirty-three feet in length. *Ibid.* 280 The distance he goes underground, and the places he continues to work in when he arrives at his 'pitch', are known to few besides the Cornish miner himself. **1875** TEMPLE & SHELDON *Hist. Northfield, Mass.* 16 The two meadows.. were not divided, till the choice pitches were assigned in 1731. **1895** J. W. ANDERSON *Prospector's Handbk.* (ed. 6) 163 Pitch (Cornwall)—The part of a lode let out to be worked on tribute.

13. *Cricket.* The place where the wickets are pitched; the piece of ground between and about the wickets.

1871 'THOMSONBY' *Cricketers in Council* v. 59 Let the pitch be well watered and rolled on the day before the match. **1890** *Daily News* 17 Oct. 5/3 The London Playing Fields Committee is now laying fifteen good cricket pitches in Epping Forest. **1891** H. DRUMMOND *Baxter's Second Innings* i, At that moment the first ball whizzed down the pitch. *a* **1912** A. LANG *Poet. Works* (1923) II. 62, *I* am the batsman and the bat, *I* am the bowler and the ball, The umpire, the pavilion cat, The roller, pitch,..and all. **1955** *Times* 12 May 4/4 The pitch dried too slowly to become really unpleasant during the Middlesex innings. **1972** J. KAY *Hist. County Cricket: Lancashire* vi. 45 The captains debated whether to continue after a long inspection of the pitch. **1976** *Evening Advertiser* (Swindon) 31 Dec. 20/3 The County Ground pitch is likely to be heavy.

b. In other outdoor games: the space on which the game is played; the field, the ground.

1902 *Glasgow Evening News* 7 Apr. 3/1 The International football match was made..memorable by..the collapsing of a portion of the terracing flanking the pitch. **1971** J. REASON *Victorious Lions* vii. 41 The natural banking which almost completely encircled the pitch had been ramped and grassed. **1975** *Times* 10 Apr. 12/3 St Etienne and Bayern Munich..played a goalless tie..on a snow-covered slippery pitch.

†**14.** *fig.* A position taken up and maintained; a fixed opinion or resolution. *Obs.*

1600 HOLLAND *Livy* XXXVIII. ix. 987 They knew the natures and minds of their countrymen..how untractable they were and not to be removed if they once tooke a pitch. *Ibid.* XLV. XXXVIII. 1195 None of you may thinke that I have taken such a pitch, and hold that opinion of mine without just cause.

IV. Highest point, height, etc.

†**15.** The highest (or extreme) point, top, summit, apex, vertex. *Obs.*

a **1552** LELAND *Itin.* VII. 5 From this Bridge the great Streate of the Towne goith up apon a pratie Hille: at the Pitch whereof there turnith a nothar Streat by Este to Seint Peter's, the Heade Churche of the Towne. **1587** HARRISON *England* I. v. in *Holinshed* I. 10 The length of the face, taken at large from the pitch of the crowne to the chin. *Ibid.*, From the highest part of the forehead to the pitch of the chin. **1600** HOLLAND *Livy* II. l. 79 The Veientians..set a compasse about the hill side, and gained the verie top and pitch [*vertex*] thereof. **1667** MILTON *P.L.* II. 772 Down they fell Driv'n headlong from the Pitch of Heaven, down Into this Deep.

†**16.** A projecting point of some part of the body, as the shoulder, the hip. (In first quot. app. used for the shoulders collectively.) *Obs.*

1586 MARLOWE *1st Pt. Tamburl.* II. i, Such breadth of shoulders as might mainely bear Old Atlas' burden;—'twixt his manly pitch A pearl, more worth than all the world, is placed. **1592** R. D. *Hypnerotomachia* 78 This garment..was taken up round about the pitch of her hippes. **1607** TOPSELL *Four-f. Beasts* (1658) 310 When the shoulder point, or pitch of the shoulder [of a horse], is displaced. **1611** COTGR., *Acromion*, the shoulder pitch.

17. ? The extreme point of a cape or headland, where it projects farthest into the sea.

1677 W. HUBBARD *Narr.* I. 5 The Sea coast from the pitch of Cape Cod to the mouth of Connecticot River. **1743** BULKELEY & CUMMINS *Voy. S. Seas* 150 And very narrowly escap'd clearing the Breakers off the Pitch of the Cape. **1857** R. TOMES *Amer. in Japan* i. 31 In seven hours after leaving Table Bay, the steamer was off the pitch of the Cape. **1883** *Times* 27 Aug. 8/2 To stand close in to the pitch of the lofty headland.

18. a. The height to which a falcon or other bird of prey soars before swooping down on its prey; rarely *gen.* the height to which any bird rises in the air. Often in phr. ***to fly a pitch.***

1591 SHAKS. *1 Hen. VI*, II. iv. 11 Between two Hawks, which flyes the higher pitch. **1593** —— *2 Hen. VI*, II. i. 12 And beares his thoughts aboue his Faulcons Pitch. **1650** B. *Discolliminium* 50 When Buzzards are advanc'd, they'l flie an Eagles pitch. **1828** SEBRIGHT *Hawking* 22 Much better.. than that his pitch should be lowered..by too much luring. *Ibid.* 27 The hawk, if at a good pitch, will stoop at him [the magpie] as he passes to another bush. **1852** R. F. BURTON *Falconry Vall. Indus* v. 62 Well too did the kite..get to his pitch, and prepare himself for the combat.

b. In directly figurative or allusive use.

c **1586** C'TESS PEMBROKE *Ps.* LXXIII. ii, So high a pitch their proud presumption flyes. **1594** SHAKS. *Rich. III*, III. vii. 188. **1635–56** COWLEY *Dav.* II. 126 To this strange pitch their high affections flew. **1718** *Free thinker* No. 77. 151 He flies a Pitch above Common Mischiefs. **1798** FERRIAR *Illustr. Sterne* vi. 182 Rabelais flew to a higher pitch, too, than Sterne. **1837–9** HALLAM *Hist. Lit.* I. I. iii. §101. 214 Another [comedy] entitled Sergius..flies a much higher pitch.

†**c.** The height to which anything rises; altitude, elevation. *Obs.*

1590 SPENSER *F.Q.* I. xi. 31 That infernall Monster..Gan high advaunce his broad discoloured brest Above his wonted pitch. **1647** TRAPP *Comm. 2 Tim.* iv. 10 Blazing comets..when they begin to decline from their pitch, they fall to the earth. **1664** POWER *Exp. Philos.* II. 90 The Quicksilver will fall down to its wonted pitch and stint of 29 inches or thereabouts. **1774** G. WHITE *Selborne* 14 Feb., A very wet autumn and winter, so as to raise the springs to a pitch beyond anything since 1764.

19. *fig.* (from 15 or 18). Highest or supreme point or degree; acme, climax, greatest height. Now *rare* exc. in ***at the pitch of one's voice.*** (Cf. 22, 23.)

1624 WOTTON *Archit.* Pref. in *Reliq.* (1651) 195 Vitruvius ..wrote when the Roman Empire was neer the pitch. **1723** *Pres. St. Russia* II. 184 Mankind would have been brought to the Pitch of Wickedness. **1742** POPE *Dunc., M. Scriblerus*, Forty..the very acme and pitch of life for writing Epic poesy. **1848** NEWMAN *Loss & Gain* III. x. 382 A little boy.. and a poor woman, singing at the pitch of their voices. **1873** BLACK *Pr. Thule* xxiii, When the general hilarity was at its pitch.

†**20.** Height (of a person or animal), stature. *Obs.*

1575 GASCOIGNE *Compl. Gr. Knt.* Wks., Weedes 183 The mounture so well made, and for my pitch so fit. **1631** HEYWOOD *Fair Maid of West* III. i. Wks. 1874 II. 295 Much of my stature? Much about your pitch. **1681** HICKERINGILL *Black Non-Conf.* xv. Wks. 1716 II. 112 Just of his Size, Complexion and Pitch. **1703** MOXON *Mech. Exerc.* 170 Makes the work fall too low for the pitch of the Workman. **1807** BEWICK *Hist. Quadrupeds* 63 All those of each kind that exceed or fall short of this pitch, are more or less disproportioned.

21. Height of an arched roof, or of any roof or ceiling, above the floor, or of the vertex of an arch above the springing line.

1615 G. SANDYS *Trav.* 161 The roofe of the Temple is of a high pitch, curiously arched, and supported with great pillars of marble. **1703** T. N. *City & C. Purchaser* 64, 9 Foot betwixt the Floors..is the Pitch of their Rooms. **1772** HUTTON *Bridges* 59 A semicircle whose height or pitch is 45 feet, and consequently its span 90 feet. *Ibid.* 99 Pitch, of an arch, the perpendicular height from the spring or impost to the keystone. **1842–76** GWILT *Archit.* Gloss., *Pitch of an Arch*, the versed sine, or height from the springing line up to the under-side of it.

V. Height in a figurative sense, degree.

22. a. Comparative height or intensity of any quality or attribute; point or position on an ideal scale; degree, elevation, stage, status, level. Almost always used of a high or intense degree: cf. 19, 15.

a **1568** ASCHAM *Scholem.* II. (Arb.) 87 The Latin tong, euen whan it was, as the Grecians say, in ακμη, that is, at the hiest pitch of all perfitenesse. **1607** WALKINGTON *Opt. Glass* xiii. (1664) 139 That they may come to the pitch of old age. **1608** D. T[UVIL] *Ess. Pol. & Mor.* 33 Raysing the valour of every..person amongst them, to a farre higher pitch. **1671** MILTON *Samson* 169 To lowest pitch of abject fortune thou art fall'n. **1684** *Contempl. St. Man* II. ix. (1699) 232 Let him be raised to the highest pitch of Honour. **1728** VENEER *Sincere Penitent* Pref. 6 Till they arrive at such a pitch, as they cannot think of without horror and astonishment. **1752** HUME *Ess. & Treat.* (1777) I. 107 To what a pitch did the Athenians carry their eloquence! **1822** HAZLITT *Table-t.* Ser. II. iv. (1869) 82 The feelings are wound up to a pitch of agony. **1871** FREEMAN *Norm. Conq.* IV. xviii. 245 The family which in two generations has risen from obscurity to the highest pitch of greatness.

b. *spec.* in *Copper-smelting*: see quots.

1839 URE *Dict. Arts* 323 To render the metal malleable, or, in the language of the smelters, bring it to the proper pitch. **1868** JOYNSON *Metals* 99 The copper is tested, as above described, from time to time, and, according to its pitch or grain. **1877** RAYMOND *Statist. Mines & Mining* 393 If the pitch is right the globules will all be round and hollow.

23. a. That quality of a musical sound which depends on the comparative rapidity of the vibrations producing it; degree of acuteness or graveness of tone. (Sometimes also in reference to the tone of the voice in speaking.) Also, a particular standard of pitch for voices and instruments, as ***concert pitch***, etc.

1597 MORLEY *Introd. Mus.* 166 Take an instrument, as a Lute Orpharion, Pandora, or such like, being in the naturall pitch, and set it a note or two lower. **1602** *2nd Pt. Return fr. Parnass.* v. i. (Arb.) 64 A playne song..Whose highest pitch in lowest base doth end. **1694** HOLDER *Harmony* (1731) 152 What it is that makes Humane Voices, even of the same Pitch, so much to differ one from another. **1776** BURNEY *Hist. Mus.* (1789) I. I. 11 All the notes in the horizontal range of the several diagrams are at the same pitch. **1831** BREWSTER *Nat. Magic* ix. (1833) 229 To depend..on the pitch or frequency of vibration constituting the note. **1867** LADY HERBERT *Cradle L.* i. 9 Screaming out..in every conceivable key and pitch of shrillness. **1869** *Athenæum* 23 Jan. 136/1 The note C, on the third space of the treble clef, corresponds to a number of double vibrations per second, varying from about 500 to 550, according to the pitch adopted.

b. *transf.* Applied to the degree of rapidity of vibration in light, etc., as being analogous to musical pitch.

1871 TYNDALL *Fragm. Sc.* (1879) I. iii. 79 As we advance along the spectrum..the pitch of the light..heightens. **1902** *Daily Record & Mail* 25 Dec. 5 One receiving instrument will only take messages sent by another instrument 'tuned' to the same pitch, that is sending vibrations of a given length and frequency.

VI. Inclination, slope, declivity.

24. Degree of inclination to the horizon, slope; a sloping part or place. *spec.* **a.** A downward inclination or slope (on a piece of ground or water); a steep place, declivity; a descent, usually sloping, sometimes perpendicular. Freq. in *Mountaineering* (see quot. 1971).

[*c* **1420** app. implied in PITCHLONGS. Cf. also PITCH *v.* 20.] **1542** UDALL *Erasm. Apoph.* 135 Rockes of a down right pitche, or a steepe down falle. **1542–5** ELYOT *Dict., Cliuus, seu cliuum*, the pitche of an hyll, sometyme the syde of an hyll. **1601** HOLLAND *Pliny* I. 78 The mountaine Hæmus.. had in the pitch thereof the towne Aristaeum. **1788** M. CUTLER in *Life*, etc. (1888) I. 402 The road from Jennison's to this house is mostly good, some few sharp pitches. **1796** MORSE *Amer. Geog.* I. 480 The whole descent is about 200 feet, in several pitches. **1807** P. GASS *Jrnl.* 100 Captain Lewis had been up the falls 15 miles above the first shoot or pitch. **1898** *Westm. Gaz.* 30 Mar. 3/2 The great gully that runs up the centre of the Wastwater Screes. This gully was attempted in 1895 by three climbers, who conquered eight 'pitches', but were defeated by the ninth. **1904** J. N. COLLIE in *Alpine Jrnl.* XXII. 10 [The ridge] was impossible, being made up entirely of bare slabs and perpendicular pitches. **1935** D. PILLEY *Climbing Days* i. 5 Each *pitch* or passage of the climb seemed as important as the Battle of Waterloo. **1943** E. SHIPTON *Upon that Mountain* iv. 78 Nothing provides such a strong incentive to struggle on up at all costs as the memory of a really severe pitch below. **1954** [see ABSEIL]. **1956** C. EVANS *On Climbing* iii. 47 The leader climbs each pitch first, anchors himself to the rock, and takes in the rope as the second climbs to join him. **1971** C. BONINGTON *Annapurna South Face* 323 *Pitch*, section of climbing between two stances or belay points. These might be of any length, depending on the length of the climbing-rope... Pitches were often as long as 200 feet. **1972** D. HASTON *In High Places* i. 8 When the pair [of rock-climbers] have run out one length of the rope between two stances a 'pitch' has been established.

b. *Mining* and *Geol.* The inclination of a vein of ore or seam of coal from the horizontal; the dip or rise. Now distinguished from the dip of a plane (e.g. a stratum) and applied to the inclination of a linear feature, being the angle it makes with a horizontal line in the plane containing it, i.e. (in the case of an ore shoot) with the strike; formerly also = PLUNGE *sb.* 7, esp. when applied to folds.

1719 STRACHEY in *Phil. Trans.* XXX. 969 The Obliquity or *Pitch*, as they term it, in all the Works hereabout, is about 22 Inches in a Fathom. **1822** CONYBEARE & PHILLIPS *Outl. Geol. Eng. & Wales* p. iii, The angle of inclination between these planes and that of the horizon, is called their dip, or pitch. **1868** G. H. COOK *Geol. New Jersey* 55 Pitch.—This term has come into use among those engaged in iron mining, to express the characteristic descent of the iron ore beds beneath the surface, towards the northeast. It is at right angles to the dip, and is in the same direction with the strike, though not horizontal. **1883** GRESLEY *Gloss. Coal Mining*, *Pitch*, dip or rise of a seam. **1906** LINDGREN & RANSOME in *Prof. Papers U.S. Geol. Survey* No. 54. 205 If we assume that the shoot has an elongated, narrow shape, as usually is the case when projected on the plain of the vein, its geometrical relations may be designated as follows: Width or thickness, breadth, stope length, pitch length, and pitch. .. The pitch length..is the distance between the two extreme ends of the shoot; the pitch is the angle which the pitch length makes with the horizontal. **1907** H. LOUIS in *Trans. Inst. Mining Engineers* XXXIV. 236 In America the term 'pitch' has occasionally been applied to this obliquity of the axis of the ore-shoot.., and the writer wishes to propose that this word be definitely restricted in the literature of ore-deposits to this particular signification... It will be understood that the angle is the angle to the horizontal, and the direction is always the azimuth of the horizontal trace of the vertical plane in which the line..of pitch lies. **1908** *Ibid.* XXXV. 73 Mr. H. W. G. Halbaum (Birtley) said that..most men used 'pitch' and 'dip' as interchangeable terms. *Ibid.* 75 Mr. E. R. Field (Victoria, Australia) said that in the Bendigo district of Victoria the word 'pitch' was universally used to show the dip of the ore-bodies in the direction of the strike of the lode. **1909** *Trans. Amer. Inst. Mining Engineers* XXXIX. 899 Our mine-surveyors recognize, but do not employ, the old usage of 'dip' and 'pitch' interchangeably. *Ibid.* 900 According to my view of American practice, the direction of the pitch is usually stated in terms of the strike. **1909** *Q. Jrnl. Geol. Soc.* LXV. 473 The rocks are thrown into a series of anticlines and synclines, with a fairly-steady pitch of 12° to 15° in a southerly directon. **1913**, etc. [see PLUNGE *sb.* 7]. **1936** E. B. MAYO in C. M. NEVIN *Princ. Struct. Geol.* (ed. 2) vii. 195 (*caption*) Orientation of minerals and inclusions in an intrusive rock... Measurements recorded in field mapping include dip and strike of flow layers, or planar parallelism; pitch and strike of flow lines, or linear parallelism. **1942** M. P. BILLINGS *Struct. Geol.* viii. 135 The pitch is the angle that a line in a plane makes with a horizontal line in that plane. **1962** READ & WATSON *Introd. Geol.* I. viii. 449 The fold-axis may be horizontal, like the top of a railway tunnel, or it may be inclined, in which case the axis and the fold are said to plunge or to pitch. The plunge is measured in degrees from the horizontal in a vertical plane.., while the pitch is given by the angle between the fold-axis and the strike of the axial plane, measured in the axial plane. **1972** J. G. DENNIS *Struct. Geol.* iii. 52 The pitch of a line within the given plane is defined as the angle between that line and any horizontal line in the plane; that is, it is measured within the plane.

c. *Arch.* The inclination of a sloping roof, or of the rafters, to the horizontal; the steepness of slope of a roof; the proportion of the height of a roof to its span.

1703 MOXON *Mech. Exerc.* 141 The Reasons for several Pitches you may find among Books of Architecture. *Ibid.* 163 The Angle a Gable-end is set to, is called the *Pitch* of the Gable-end. **1710** J. HARRIS *Lex. Techn.* II. s.v., If the Length of each Rafter be ¾ of the Breadth of the Building, then they say that the Roof is of a *True Pitch*: But if the Rafters are longer, they say 'tis a *high* or *sharp* pitch'd Roof; if shorter, they call it a *low* or *flat* pitch'd Roof. **1828** HUTTON *Course Math.* II. 87 When the roof is of a true pitch, that is, forming a right angle at top; then the breadth of the building, with its half added, is the girt over both sides nearly. **1803** D. G. MITCHELL *My Farm Edgewood* 85 Walls ..of the uniform height of ten feet, covered with a roof of sharp pitch. *a* **1878** SIR G. G. SCOTT *Lect. Archit.* (1879) I. 254 All previous styles of architecture..in Southern countries, had roofs of a low pitch.

d. The slope of a flight of steps; *concr.* a flight of steps.

1703 MOXON *Mech. Exerc.* 147 You will first ascend upon a Pitch of Flyers, which Pitch (making an Angle of 38 deg. with the Floor) with ten Steps raise you six Foot high above the Floor. **1842–76** GWILT *Archit.* §2026 The framed timbers which support the steps of a staircase are called the *carriage*. They generally consist of two pieces inclined to the pitch of the stairs, called the *rough strings*.

e. The setting of a ploughshare to enable it to penetrate a required depth. **f.** The rake or inclination of the teeth of a saw. **g.** The inclination of the bit of a plane to the surface that is being planed.

1707 MORTIMER *Husb.* (1721) I. 50 A great matter..in the making of Ploughs, is to make them go true to the pitch they are set. **1787** W. MARSHALL *Norfolk* 48 Plowing the full depth of the soil is called 'taking it up a full pitch'. **1875** KNIGHT *Dict. Mech.* s.v., The *pitch* of a saw is the *rake* or inclination of the face of a tooth... The *rake* is a forward slant of the *face*, not common, but found in some saws... The common pitch of a bench-plane is 45°... Pitch of scraping and metal planes 80° to vertical. **1875** *Carpentry & Join.* 23 A jack plane with its double iron..lying in its bed, the latter being at an angle of 45 deg. to the sole. This is the angle called common pitch.

VII. 25. Chiefly *Mech.* The fixed distance between successive points or lines (? the distance at which these are pitched or fixed).

a. The distance between the centres of any two successive teeth of a cog-wheel or pinion, or links of a gear-chain, measured along the *pitch-line* or *pitch-circle* (see 26); the distance between the successive paddles of a paddle-wheel, measured on the circle passing through their centres; also in other contexts. **b.** The distance between the successive convolutions of the thread of a screw, measured in a direction parallel to the axis, and indicating the distance through which the screw moves forward in one turn; also *transf.* **c.** The distance between the centres of successive rivets or stays. **d.** In floor-cloth printing, The distance between the pitch-pins or guide-pins, used for the same purpose as the register-points in lithographic printing.

1815 J. SMITH *Panorama Sc. & Art* I. 362 If the teeth of one be wood and the other iron, then the iron ones are made to have less pitch than the wooden ones, because they are then found to wear better. **1823** R. BUCHANAN *Millwork* (ed. 2) 30 By the pitch is understood the distance between the centres of two contiguous teeth. **1825** J. NICHOLSON *Operat. Mechanic* 432 The pitch of their teeth should be the same as that of the teeth of the cylinder. **1869** SIR E. J. REED *Shipbuild.* xvii. 335 The question of the proper pitch of rivets, i.e. their distance apart from centre to centre, requires some consideration. **1870** *Eng. Mechanic* 14 Jan. 437/2 Find the pitch of the screw required to be cut..and multiply the numerators. **1874** THEARLE *Naval Archit.* 130 The spacing or pitch of rivets required by Lloyd's rules is 'four and a half diameters apart, from centre to centre, excepting in the keel, stem, and stern post'. **1875** KNIGHT *Dict. Mech.* 1719/2 The *pitch* of the paddles is the distance between them, measured on the circle which passes through their centers. **1879** *Cassell's Techn. Educ.* I. 64 The length.. in a spur wheel including a tooth and a space is called the *pitch*, and the circle on which such distances are set off is called the *pitch circle*. *Ibid.* II. 66/2 The pitch of rifling of the Enfield is one turn in six feet six inches. **1890** *Clacton News* 25 Jan. 2/3 Most makers of implements now use only standard pitches of screws, so that any broken screw or missing nut can quickly be replaced. **1898** *Cycling* 43 The distance between the central points of two similar links,..is called the pitch of the chain: it is nearly always one inch. **1953** *Nature* 25 Apr. 739/2 If there are ten phosphate groups arranged on each helix of diameter 20 A. and pitch 34 A., the phosphate ester backbone chain is in an almost fully extended state. **1956** *Jrnl. Chem. Physics* XXV. 570 It is.. possible that helical chain configurations of different pitch can be obtained under different conditions. **1964** S. CRAWFORD *Basic Engin. Processes* i. 6 The pitch (1/spacing) varies with the length of the file, e.g. the pitch of a 12 inch second-cut file is not the same as the pitch of a 6 inch second cut file. **1971** *Physics Bull.* Nov. 677/2 The gratings are either flat or concave... The 'pitch' is 295 grooves/mm,.. and finer spacings are expected to become available.

e. A measure of the angle of the blades of a screw propeller, equal to the distance forward a blade would move in one revolution if it sliced the air so as not to exert thrust on it; (i.e. the pitch (sense 25 b) of the spiral that would then be traced by a point on the blade).

1863 P. BARRY *Dockyard Econ.* 264 The pitch of the screw could be altered from the deck to suit the velocity of the vessel. **1867** N. P. BURGH *Mod. Marine Engin.* vi. 323/2 The principal dimensions of the propeller under notice, are: the screw is 18 feet in diameter, maximum pitch 26 feet.. and the minimum pitch 20 feet. **1902** F. WALKER *Aërial Navigation* v. 54 The pitch of screws varies as the ratio of the area of the disc or circle described by the tips to the area of the air-ship affording resistance to the air through which it passes. **1919** H. SHAW *Textbk. Aeronaut.* xi. 144 If there were no slip the propeller would move forward a distance equal to the theoretical pitch during each revolution, and.. no air would be driven backward by the propeller, and there would be no thrust. **1944** 'N. SHUTE' *Pastoral* i. 1 He heard, passing away above his head, the high scream of an ungeared engine in fine pitch. **1957** *Encycl. Brit.* XX. 535/2 In controllable-pitch propellers.. the blades are pivoted in the propeller hub so that the pitch of the blades can be controlled from within the ship. **1958** *Times Rev. Industry* Aug. 39/2 The Rotodyne takes off vertically and climbs away as a helicopter, steering in the required direction being achieved by altering differentially the pitch of the airscrews. **1960** R. A. FRY *Princ. & Construction of Aircraft Gas Turbines* v. 178 The pitch required for take-off and climb is finer than the pitch most suitable for cruising. **1971** P. J. MCMAHON *Aircraft Propulsion* viii. 246 The propeller cannot go into low pitch in flight; mechanical and hydraulic pitch locks are provided.

VIII. 26. *attrib.* and *Comb.*, as (sense 11) ***pitch-holder***; (sense 23) ***pitch-change***, ***-movement***, ***-pattern***, ***-range***, ***-scheme***; **pitch accent** *Phonetics*, (*a*) a prominence given to a word or syllable by the difference in pitch from its immediate surroundings; (*b*) *occas.* = TONE *sb.* 6 a; hence **pitch-accented** *a.*, having a pitch-accent; **pitch angle** *Aeronaut.*, the acute angle between the plane of rotation of a propeller and a straight line from one edge of a blade to the other in a direction tangential to its radius; **pitch axis** *Aeronaut.* = *pitching axis* s.v. PITCHING *vbl. sb.*[1] 12; **pitch-block**, a block for supporting an object to be worked at, which can be inclined at any pitch or angle; usually one with a base working like a ball and socket-joint; **pitch-chain**, a chain consisting of links bolted or riveted together so as to work in the teeth of a toothed wheel; **pitch-circle**, a circular *pitch-line* (see below); **pitch contour** *Phonetics*, the pattern of continuous variation in pitch; **pitch control** *Aeronaut.* (equipment for) control of the pitch of an aircraft's propellers or rotors; also, control of the pitching motion of an aircraft; **pitch curve** *Phonetics* = *pitch contour*; **pitch-diameter**, the diameter of the pitch-circle of a wheel, etc.; **pitch-faced** *a.*, of masonry, having the arris cut true, but the face beyond the edge left relatively rough, being merely dressed with a pitching chisel (Knight *Dict. Mech.* Supp. 1884); †**pitch-hill** *a.*, declivitous, precipitous; **pitch length** *Geol.*, the length of an ore shoot in the direction of greatest dimension; **pitch-line**, the imaginary line, usually a circle, passing through the teeth of a cog wheel, pinion, rack, etc. so as to touch the corresponding line in another cog-wheel, etc., when the two are geared together; **pitch-meter**, **'pitchmeter**, (*a*) a device in an aeroplane for detecting or measuring pitching; (*b*) an instrument for measuring the pitch of sound; **pitch-notation**, notation indicating musical pitch; **pitch-note**, a note sounded to determine the pitch of a tune, etc. (also *fig.*); **pitch phoneme** *Linguistics*, one of the four recognized levels of pitch, esp. a variation in pitch from one syllable to another which affects meaning; **pitch-point**, the point of contact of the pitch-lines of two cog-wheels, etc. which engage with each other; †**pitch-set**, a shoot (of willow, etc.) cut for planting; cf. sense 7 and PITCHER[2] 4; **pitch-surface**, the surface on which the pitch-circle of a wheel lies; **pitch-wheel**, a toothed wheel engaging with another. See also PITCHFORK[2], etc.

1880 A. H. SAYCE *Introd. Sci. of Lang.* II. vii. 109 The *pitch-accent has been changed into a stress-accent. **1933** C. D. BUCK *Compar. Gram. Greek & Latin* 161 Under accent one understands variations of either intensity or intonation, and speaks of a stress accent or a pitch accent according as one or the other element is the more conspicuous. **1945** *Word* I. 87, I consider especially important the remark that many languages seem to pass.. from a tone- or pitch-accent to stress. **1958** D. BOLINGER in *Word* XIV. 149 To avoid unwarranted associations, it is better to speak of *pitch accent* and to leave the term *stress* to the domain of word stress. **1972** R. S. JACKENDOFF *Semantic Interpretation in Generative Gram.* vi. 259 We will give an account of the semantics of pitch accents that makes their interaction with negation part of a more general process. **1975** *Language* LI. 201 He does not distinguish between 'normal' and *pitch-accented intonation contours. **1977** *Archivum Linguisticum* VIII. 90 Elsewhere, a (probably light) stress fell on the pitch-accented syllable (Lithuanian, Common Slavic). **1902** F. WALKER *Aërial Navigation* v. 54 The value of θ.. which gives the maximum efficiency is the same whatever be the actual *pitch angle. **1935** C. G. BURGE *Compl. Bk. Aviation* 140/1 The sections of the blade near the tip will move on a helix of much greater diameter.. than those near the boss. For this reason they are set at a less 'pitch angle'.., so that every part of the airscrew will try to move the same distance forward during one revolution. **1971** P. J. MCMAHON *Aircraft Propulsion* viii. 246 The pilot's control lever selects propeller pitch angle directly. **1959** F. D. ADAMS *Aeronaut. Dict.* 126/1 **Pitch axis*, a lateral axis through an aircraft, missile, or similar body, about which the body pitches. It may be a body, wind, or stability axis. Also called a 'pitching axis'. **1962** F. I. ORDWAY et al. *Basic Astronautics* ix. 368 Any vehicle motion will take place about three axes... These axes are the yaw axis, the pitch axis, and the roll axis. **1875** KNIGHT *Dict. Mech.*, **Pitch-block*, a cushioned seat of a concave hemispherical form, in which sheet-metal is held while being chased. **1844** STEPHENS *Bk. Farm* II. 304 *Pitch-chains are of two kinds, the buckle-chain and the ladder-chain. *Ibid.* 537 The pitch-chain is employed to communicate motion from the first mover—the carriage axle—to the seed-wheels. **1958** R. KINGDON *Ground-work Eng. Intonation* p. xxiii, *Tone*, a stress considered from the point of view of the pitch or *pitch-change associated with it. **1964** J. C. CATFORD in D. Abercrombie et al. *Daniel Jones* 28 There are many detailed studies of certain aspects of voice: e.g. of.. the mechanism of pitch-change. **1966** J. DERRICK *Teaching Eng. to Immigrants* iii. 114 Regular patterns of pitch-change at the heavily stressed syllables in an utterance make up the intonation of English. **1819** REES *Cycl.* XXIII. 3 Z iv b/1 A circle.. is described round the face of the rough cogs upon its pitch diameter, that is, the geometrical diameter, or acting line of the cogs; so that when the two wheels are at work together, the *pitch circles.. of the two are in contact. **1884** F. J. BRITTEN *Watch & Clockm.* 198 The pitch circles of a wheel and pinion working together should touch but not intersect each other. **1959** E. PULGRAM *Introd. Spectrogr. of Speech* xviii. 136 But one may invariably omit the registration of glottal pitch.. because.. the stylus-drawn *pitch contour is unlikely to present faithfully the real pitch contour in the lower frequencies. **1961** *Amer. Speech* XXXVI. 223 Pitch contours applied by synthesis to recordings of natural speech. **1940** E. MOLLOY *Aeroplane Maintenance & Operation* XV. 87 When the pilot wishes to change the pitch attitude of the aircraft, he makes an alteration to the spring torque by means of the Bowden cable from the *pitch-control lever in his cockpit. **1944** W. C. NELSON *Airplane Propeller Princ.* iv. 89 Various types of automatic pitch control requiring no attention from the pilot have been devised. **1955** LIPTROT & WOODS *Rotorcraft* vii. 64 The collective-pitch control and the throttle are normally interconnected through a.. cam device. **1958** LAMBERMONT & PIRIE *Helicopters & Autogyros of World* 112 A rotor hydraulically operated for both cyclic and collective pitch controls. **1974** *Encycl. Brit. Macropædia* I. 373/1 Pitch control is obtained by means of movable flaps (elevators) hinged to the trailing edge of the stabilizer. **1902** E. W. SCRIPTURE *Elem. Exper. Phonetics* xxxii. 478 The course of pitch is greatly influenced by the neighboring consonants; the more emphatic the consonant, the greater is its influence on the *pitch-curve; the following consonant often cuts the vowel off at or near the maximum. **1969** *Eng. Stud.* L. 327 Of all the recorded sentences.. there were taken one duplex oscillogram.. one pitch curve, and two intensity curves. This was done by inserting a pitch meter.. and an intensity meter between the tape recorder and the registering apparatus. **1560** DAUS tr. *Sleidane's Comm.* 252 By reason of.. the headlong and *pitchehill stepenes to looke downewardes. **1909** *Daily Chron.* 18 Nov. 4/7 One 'pitch' which was the envy of every *pitchholder in London was for many years at the end of Burlington House. **1906** *Pitch length [see PITCH *sb.*[2] 24 b]. **1965** G. J. WILLIAMS *Econ. Geol. N.Z.* viii. 107/1 The bonanzas have generally a pitch-length exceeding the level-length. **1797** *Encycl. Brit.* (ed. 3) X. 769/1 Draw the *pitch lines.. then divide them into the number of teeth or cogs required. **1815** J. SMITH *Panorama Sc. & Art* I. 362 The centre or pitch-lines, from which the teeth are formed. **1947** *Jrnl. R. Aeronaut. Soc.* LI. 166/1 A gust can be detected by a *pitch-meter which produces a differential pressure on a diaphragm with change of vertical component of wind. **1969** *Word 1967* XXIII. 255 An instrument used for measuring the frequency of the fundamental is commonly (and erroneously) called a pitchmeter. **1976** *Times* 19 Aug. 12/6 Another new development is the electronic pitchmeter... A needle shows whether a note is sharp or flat of the required pitch, so that a piano could be successfully tuned in the middle of a factory floor if necessary. **1959** D. COOKE *Lang. Mus.* ii. 109 Monteverdi and others, began to introduce more and more liberty of *pitch-movement to express the rhetoric of human passion. **1964** CRYSTAL & QUIRK *Syst. Prosodic & Paralinguistic Features in Eng.* 75 It is hoped to follow up these initial experiments by a more detailed study of the spectrographic shape of pitch-movement. **1973** *Archivum Linguisticum* IV. 19 For them [*sc.* Crystal and Quirk] a tone is subordinate to another if it has the same pitch movement. **1881** BROADHOUSE *Mus. Acoustics* 373 On a full consideration of the question of *pitch-notation. **1795** MASON *Ch. Mus.* i. 8 Before the opening of the Overture, it gives that *pitch note in full, which always leads me to expect a succession of more solemn sounds than in reality succeed it. **1954** F. G. CASSIDY *Robertson's Devel. Mod. Eng.* (ed. 2) xii. 381 There is a great deal less variation in the *pitch-patterns of Middle-Western American than of British speech. **1961** *Amer. Speech* XXXVI. 215 An experimental pitch indicator for training deaf scholars... Deaf child is enabled to compare his own pitch pattern with that of his teacher. **1931** L. BLOOMFIELD in *Language* VII. 206 The modern languages of Europe similarly use certain *pitch-phonemes at the end of largest-forms: our falling pitch at the end of statements and our rising pitches for the two kinds of questions. **1933** —— *Language* xi. 171 In English, supplement-questions are distinguished not only by their special pitch-phoneme [¿], but also by a selective taxeme. **1973** *Archivum Linguisticum* IV. 17 In the field of English intonation studies, bones of contention.. spring readily to mind:.. pitch phonemes versus tones. **1859** RANKINE *Steam Engine* §153. 181 The position of the pinion should be such, that the *pitch-point, where its teeth are driven by those of the cogged ring, may be in the same vertical plane parallel to the axis. **1959** D. COOKE *Lang. Mus.* ii. 110 The 'normal' *pitch-range of music is an overall spread from just above the treble clef to just below the bass clef. **1964** CRYSTAL & QUIRK *Syst. Prosodic & Paralinguistic Features in Eng.* iv. 62 So too it seems likely that tonal subordination will come to be linked with the stress and pitch-range systems. **1973** *Archivum Linguisticum* IV. 25 Such features as overall pitch range, pitch register, and even voice quality.. may perhaps best be regarded as characteristics.. of larger units. **1933** L. BLOOMFIELD *Language* v. 77 The fact that two utterances of the syllable *man* with different *pitch-schemes are 'the same' speech-form in English, but 'different' speech-forms in Chinese, shows us that the working of language depends upon our habitually.. discriminating some features of sound and ignoring all others. **1519** HORMAN *Vulg.* 172 A *pychesette of wythy groweth anon. **1887** D. A. LOW *Machine Draw.* (1892) 40 A section of the *pitch surface of a toothed wheel by a plane perpendicular to its axis is a circle, and is called a pitch circle. **1858** SIMMONDS *Dict. Trade*, **Pitch-wheels*, toothed wheels in machinery or clocks, which work together.

pitch (pɪtʃ), *v.*[1] Forms: 3-4 **piche**, 4-5 **picche**, **pycche**, 5-6 **pytch(e**, (5 **pydche**), 6- **pitch**, (7 **peche**). Pa. t. and pa. pple., **pitched**, **pight**: see below. [ME. *piche(n*, *picche(n*, north. *pykke(n*, *pikke* (see PICK *v.*[2]); pa. t. *pihte*, *piȝte*, *pight(e*, pa. pple. *piht*, *piȝt*, *pight*; also later *picched*, *pitched*, *pitcht*, etc. (Cf. *clihte*, *stihte*, early pa. tenses of CLITCH, STITCH.) Of obscure origin and history. The forms point to an OE. **picc(e)an*, of the 1st weak class pa. t. **pihte*, of which however no instance has been found; nor does any vb. corresponding in form and sense appear in the cognate languages. See *Note* below.]

A. Illustration of Forms.

1. For the present stem, see the quots. in B., and those given under PICK *v.*[2]

2. Past tense. *α.* 3 **pihte**, 3-4 **piȝte**, 3-5 **pyȝte**, 4-5 **piȝt**, **pyȝt**, **pighte**, **pyghte**, (5 **piht**), 4-6 **pyght**, (**pyth**), 4-7 **pight** (paɪt). *β.* 4 **picched**, 4-6 **picht**, 5 **pytched**, 6 **pyched**, 7 **pitcht**, 6- **pitched**.

α. *c* **1205** LAY. 29653 þer he pihte his stæf. **1297** R. GLOUC. (Rolls) 1171 Stakes of ire monion he piȝte in temese grounde. *c* **1320** Piȝt [see B. 2]. *c* **1330** R. BRUNNE *Chron. Wace* (Rolls) 4644 þey.. pyght þeym pauylons & tente. *Ibid.* 15246 He pighte his staf þer doun vpright. **13..** *E.E. Allit. P.* A. 741 He pyȝt hit þere in token of pes. *c* **1386** CHAUCER *Knt's. T.* 1831 He pighte [*v.rr.* pyghte, pight, piht] hym on the pomel of his heed. *c* **1400** *Melayne* 800 And pyghte Pauylyons with mekill pryde. **1436** *Pol. Poems* (Rolls) II. 152 Statly tentes anon they pyȝte. *c* **1450** *Merlin* II. 150 Ther thei pight the kynges teynte. **1572** BOSSEWELL *Armorie* III. 24 b, He.. pyght hys pauilions, at the heade of a Ryuer. **1627** DRAYTON *Agincourt*, etc. 97 Vnder Pomfret his proud Tents he pight.

β. *c* **1330** R. BRUNNE *Chron. Wace* (Rolls) 4645 þey picched þer pauylons. **1340-70** *Alex. & Dind.* 1139 ad fin., How alixandre picht a pelyr of marbyl þere. *c* **1489** CAXTON *Sonnes of Aymon* xvii 399 He toke a torche and fyred it, and pytched it bytwene the strawe and the bedsted. **1530** Pyched [see B. 6]. **1535** Pitched [see B. 4 c]. **1582** STANYHURST *Æneis* III. 74 Theare picht he his kingdoom.

3. Past participle. *α.* 3-4 **ipiht**, **ipiȝt**, 4 **ipyȝt**, **ypiȝte**, **i-peȝt**, 4-6 **i-pight**, 5 **ypyght**, 6 **ypight**. *β.* 4 **piht**, (**pite**); 4-5 **piȝt**, **pyȝt**, (5 **piȝte**, **pyȝte**, **pyghte**), 5-6 (**pighte**), **pyght**, *Sc.* **picht**, **pycht**, 6 **pyht**, 4-7 (9 *arch.*) **pight** (paɪt). *γ.* 4 **piched**, **pyched**, **i-picht**, 4-5 **picched**, **-id**, 6 **pytched**, 6-8 **pitcht** 6- **pitched**.

α. **1297** R. GLOUC. (Rolls) 1116 þe emperour adde ipiȝt [*v.rr.* *c* **1425** piȝt, *c* **1435** ypyght] his pauilons. **1387** TREVISA *Higden* (Rolls) I. 243 A spere i-pyȝt [*hasta defixa*]. *Ibid.* III. 273 þe pavylouns were i-peȝt. *Ibid.* VII. 75 þe stake was i-pight. *a* **1400** *Pistill of Susan* 108 þe pyon, þe peere, wel proudliche ipiht. **1489** CAXTON *Faytes of A.* II. xxxv. 148 Wyth two staues ypyght atte eyther ende. **1522** *World & Child* in Hazl. *Dodsley* I. 243, I have also palaces i-pight. **1590** SPENSER *F.Q.* I. ix. 33 For underneath a craggy cliff ypight.

β. *c* **1350** *Will. Palerne* 1627 þer were piȝt pauilounns. **13..** *E.E. Allit. P.* B. 785 In a porche of þat place pyȝt to þe ȝates. **1362** LANGL. *P. Pl.* A. II. 43 In middes on a Mountayne.. Was piht vp a Pauilon. *c* **1400** MAUNDEV. (1839) xvii. 183 A spere that is pight in to the erthe. *c* **1420** *Anturs of Arth.* xxxvii, In myd Plumtun Lone, hor paueluns were piȝte. *c* **1430** Piȝt, **14..** Pyȝt [see B. 5 c]. *a* **1470** Pyght [B. 11] . *c* **1470** *Gol. & Gaw.* 313 Ane pailyeoun.. that proudly wes picht. **1513** Pycht [see B. 5]. *c* **1530** LD. BERNERS *Arth. Lyt. Bryt.* (1814) 44 She had pyght a ryche pauylyon. **1575** LANEHAM *Let.* (1871) 55 His honors Tent, that.. was pighte at long Ichington. **1578** *Scot. Poems 16th C.* (1801) II. 203 A prince.. picht to rule and reigne. **1579**, **1617** Pight [see B. 5]. **1720** STRYPE *Stow's Surv.* (1754) I. I. xxix. 301/2 In the Castle-yard was pight a comely Quintane. **1864** SKEAT *Uhland's Poems* 292 On a rising hillock pight.

γ. **13..** Piched [see B. 1]; pyched [B. 5]. **1340-70** I-picht [B. 5]. *c* **1380** Picchid [B. 10]. *c* **1420** *Pallad. on Husb.* IV. 667 Let hem be pressed, picchid, and ywrie. **1545** LELAND in Strype *Eccl. Mem.* I. App. cxviii. 330 Yet herein only I have not pytched the supreme work of my labour. **1564-78** BULLEYN *Dial. agst. Pest.* (1888) 60 When the battaile was pitched. *c* **1611** CHAPMAN *Iliad* xv. 654 Close the deadly toil Was pitch'd on both parts. **1634** SIR T. HERBERT *Trav.* 41 Tents.. pitcht neere the water side. **1703** MOXON *Mech. Exerc.* 167 Any Substance.. pitcht steddy upon two points.

B. Signification.

I. To thrust in, fix in; make fast, fasten, settle; set, place.

†**1. a.** *trans.* To thrust, drive (a stake, spear, staff, peg, etc.) firmly into the ground; to fix or make fast (a thing) by driving it into some object; also, to fix (an object) on a pole, spear, etc.; to plant, implant; to fix, stick, fasten. In later quots., approaching the sense 'to place'. *Obs.*

c **1205** LAY. 6490 He igrap his spere stronge þer he pihte hit o þon londe [*c* 1275 þar hit was ipiht in londe]. *c* **1290** *S. Eng. Leg.* I. 274/107 Þine staf piche in þe grounde: And he schal bere lef and blowe. **1297** R. GLOUC. (Rolls) 1171 [see 2]. *c* **1380** WYCLIF *Serm.* Sel. Wks. II. 170 Þis neiþer chawle, in which ben piȝt many teeþ. **1382** —— *Eccl.* xii. 11 The widis of wise men.. as nailes in to heiȝte piȝt [1388 as nailis fastned deepe]. **1398** TREVISA *Barth. De P.R.* v. vi. (Tollem. MS.), Tweyne holow synewis.. piccheþ hem selfe [1582 fixe themselues: *orig.* se infigunt] in þe substaunce of þe humoure cristallyn. *a* **1620** J. DYKE *Worthy Commun.* (1640) 180 A stake, or a post is pitched in the ground. **1633** ROGERS *Treat. Sacram.* I. Pref., A planter takes the sien of the Apple-tree, and pitches it into a Crab-tree Stock. **1647** WARD *Simp. Cobler* (1843) 34 The stakes [of a tent] firmely pitched. **1674–91** [see PITCH *sb.*[2] 7]. **1707** MORTIMER *Husb.* (1721) I. 172 Pitch a small Stick at every place where there is to be a little Hill. **1754** J. LOVE *Cricket* 14 The Stumps are pitch'd. **1775** J. JEKYLL *Corr.* 29 Mar., The houses [are] chiefly built of the round sea-pebbles pitched in mortar.

b. *to pitch the wickets* (*Cricket*): to stick or fix the stumps in the ground and place the bails.

c **1690** in Alverstone & Alcock *Surrey Cricket* (1902) ii. 14 All you that do delight in Cricket Come to Marden Pitch your wickets. **1733** in H. T. Waghorn *Cricket Scores* (1899) 16 The wickets are to be pitched by twelve o'clock. **1745** *Daily Advertiser* 28 Sept. 3/1 The Wickets to be pitch'd by Eleven o'Clock. **1803** *Laws of Cricket* 5 The Party which goes from home shall have.. the pitching of the wickets, which shall be pitched within thirty yards of a centre fixed by the adversaries. **1866** *Routledge's Every Boy's Ann.* 327 The wickets had better be pitched without loss of time.

†**2.** *transf.* To thrust a pointed instrument into or through (something); to stab, stick, pierce, transfix. *Obs.*

1297 R. GLOUC. (Rolls) 1174 Stakes of ire monion he piȝte [*v.rr.* pyte, put, putte] in temese grounde,.. þat ȝif þer eni ssipes come.. Hii ssolde piche hom þoru out. *c* **1320** *Sir Tristr.* 206 Bot on wiþ tresoun þere þurch þe bodi him piȝt. *c* **1366** CHAUCER *A.B.C.* 163 Cryste.. also suffred þat longius his herte pyghte And made his herte blode to rynne downe. **1382** WYCLIF *John* xix. 37 Thei schulen se in to whom they piȝten thorw [Vulg. *transfixerunt*]. **1398** TREVISA *Barth. De P.R.* VII. lxv. (Bodl. MS.), If þe skynn of þe face is ipiȝt and iprikked with an nedel oþer a pynne and bledeþ nought.

3. To place and make fast with stakes, poles, pegs, etc., as a net, or the like. Now *rare*.

1545 ELYOT, *Tendere plagas*, to pytche hayes or nettes. **1602** WARNER *Alb. Eng.* Epit. (1612) 391 [They] pitched their Tew to intangle the same Protector. **1697** DRYDEN *Virg. Georg.* III. 572 The dext'rous Huntsman.. pitches Toils to stop the Flight. **1813** SCOTT *Rokeby* III. xxxi, There's time to pitch both toil and net.

4. *spec.* To fix and erect (a tent, pavilion, etc.) as a place of lodgement; also *fig.*

Orig. referring to its being fixed with pegs, etc. driven into the ground; now associated with the idea of 'placing'.

1297 R. GLOUC. (Rolls) 4254 Þe king.. bigan to piche is pauilons him vor to abyde. **1489** CAXTON *Faytes of A.* I. xiv. 37 For to pydche and dresse vp tentes. **1606** SHAKS. *Tr. & Cr.* V. x. 24 You vile abhominable Tents, Thus proudly pight [*Qo.* pitcht] vpon our Phrygian plaines. **1687** A. LOVELL tr. *Thevenot's Trav.* II. 122 We were fain to encamp hard by under Carpets, which we pitched instead of Tents. **1759** JOHNSON *Rasselas* xxxvii, The tents were pitched where I chose to rest. **1844** *Regul. & Ord. Army* 55 When Troops are to encamp, General Officers are not to leave their Brigades until the Tents are pitched.

b. So *to pitch a camp, a caravan*, etc.

1568 GRAFTON *Chron.* (1569) I. 411 King Henrie.. came to Hounslow hethe, and there pitched his campe. **1587** FLEMING *Contn. Holinshed* III. 1981/1 There they pitched downe their campe. **1697** DRYDEN *Virg. Georg.* III. 540 The Youth of Rome.. pitch their sudden Camp before the Foe. **1860** WARTER *Sea-board* II. 127 It was necessary to remove the camp from the place where it was pitched. **1901** *Essex Weekly News* 12 Apr. 3/6 Defendant.. pitched a caravan on the grass.

c. *absol.* or *intr.* To encamp.

c **1440** *York Myst.* xiv. 4 Here in þis place wher we are pight. **1535** COVERDALE *Josh.* xi. 5 All these kinges.. came, and pitched together by yᵉ water of Meram. **1628** HOBBES *Thucyd.* (1822) 117 To choose a commodious place to pitch in. **1800** *Misc. Tracts* in *Asiat. Ann. Reg.* 284/2 The uncle of the Rajah.. invited us to pitch the next day on a spot close to the palace. **1852** GROTE *Greece* II. lxx. IX. 77 The succeeding troops, coming up in the dark, pitched as they could without any order.

5. a. *trans.* To put (anything) in a fixed or definite place or position, so as to stand, lie, or remain firmly or permanently; to set, fix, plant, place; to found or set up (a building, pillar, etc.). In *pa. pple.* = set, fixed, planted, placed, situated.

13.. *E.E. Allit. P.* B. 477 Ho fyndez no folde her fote on to pyche. **13..** *Gaw. & Gr. Knt.* 768 A castel.. Pyched on a prayere, a park al aboute. **1340–70** *Alex. & Dind.* 1135 Þere his burnus he bad bulden of marbre A piler sadliche i-picht, or he passe wolde. *c* **1410** *Master of Game* (MS. Digby 182) xix, In þe kenell shulde ben picched smale stones ywrapped aboute with strawe of þe houndes litter. **1513** DOUGLAS *Æneis* x. iii. 44 Ane circulet of plyabyll gold.. Abuf hys haris apon hys hed weil pycht. **1551** RECORDE *Pathw. Knowl.* I. xi, Then pitch one foote of your compasse at the one ende of the line. **1579** SPENSER *Sheph. Cal.* Dec. 134 And in my face deepe furrowes eld hath pight. **1612** DRAYTON *Poly-olb.* xvi. 249 Their mightier Empire, there, the middle English pight. **1617** COLLINS *Def. Bp. Ely* II. viii. 300 A gulfe.. is pight betweene vs & them. **1688** CLAYTON in *Phil. Trans.* XVII. 946 In stiff Soyls, if the Crops be not early pitch'd,.. the Roots never spread or shoot deeper. **1700** S. L. tr. *Fryke's Voy. E. Ind.* 190 The third climb'd up and pitch'd himself on his Head, upon the Head of the second. **1703** MOXON *Mech. Exerc.* 220 Take care that in pitching the Globe into the Mandrel, that the imaginary Axis.. lye in a straight Line with the Axis of the Mandrel. **1848** *Jrnl. R. Agric. Soc.* IX. II. 553 Pitching the holes at equal distances from the centre of the hill. **1872** BLACK *Adv. Phaeton* xiii, The abrupt hill, on which the town of Bridgenorth is pitched. **1899** *Daily News* 24 Apr. 4/5 Fireman S. 'pitched' his machine against the burning building, and succeeded in bringing the woman safely to the ground.

b. *spec.* To set a (stone, etc.) upon end; to set a stone on edge for paving.

a **1623** W. PEMBLE *Zachary* (1629) 159 Markes or Bound-Stones should be pitcht up. **1642** J. SHUTE *Sarah & Hagar* (1649) 203 Jacob taketh one of the stones that he had laid his head upon, and pitched it up for a pillar. **1657** HOWELL *Londinop.* 93 On the South side of their high street.. is pitched upright a great stone, called London Stone. **1715** LEONI *Palladio's Archit.* (1742) I. 82 A range of Stones pitch'd edge-way.

†**6.** *fig.* To place, implant, plant, set, fix (anything immaterial, one's trust, hope, desire, purpose, thought, attention, sight, etc.) *in* or *on* some object, or *in* some state. (See also 5 c.) *Obs.*

[*c* **1380** WYCLIF *Wks.* (1880) 307 Þe rote of loue þat shulde be picchid in goddis lawe.] *Ibid.* 480 Oure bileue & hope is picchid in þe grace of iesu crist. **1398** TREVISA *Barth. De P.R.* XII. Introd. (Tollem. MS.), Þey [briddes] haueþ a seminal vertu of kynde pyȝte in hem. *c* **1430** *Hymns Virg.* 94 Þou be woo; In iolite whan þou art piȝt. **1550** CROWLEY *Last Trump.* 151 Se that thy fayth be pitched On thy Lord God most constantly. **1591** LYLY *Endim.* v. i, Pitching his eyes fast to the ground, as though they were fixed to the earth. **1600** FAIRFAX *Tasso* I. xlviii, She fled.. And left her image in his hart ipight. *a* **1617** BAYNE *On Eph.* (1658) Ded., To take off the hearts.. from idle Pamphlets.. and pitch them on the grave.. points of Religion. **1639** FULLER *Holy War* v. xxv. (1840) 287 He pitched his thoughts on the holy war. **1688** BUNYAN *Jerus. Sinner Saved* (1886) 56 She thought He pitched His innocent eyes just upon her. **1820** L. HUNT *Indicator* No. 43 (1822) I. 339 Lauria.. pitching her mind among the enjoyments of Corinth.

7. a. To place or lay out (wares) in a fixed place for sale; hence, to expose for sale in the market or other public place.

1530 in W. H. TURNER *Select. Rec. Oxford* (1880) 80 [They] did.. take away x semys of see fyshe.., and pyched them in the parishe of Saynt Mary's, and ther sette it to sale. **1553** GRIMALDE *Cicero's Offices* II. (1558) 83 When the sale-staffe was pight and in ye market place. **1802** *Ann. Reg.* 6 All corn should be brought into the market, and pitched, as in former times. **1861** HULME tr. *Moquin-Tandon* II. III. 165 No less than 36,487 tons of meat are annually 'pitched' at Newgate and Leadenhall Markets. **1884** *Globe* 26 Sept. 7/1 At Melton Mowbray cheese fair yesterday some 100 dozen cheese were pitched. **1886** *Auckland Even. Star* 25 June 12/1 A good many hides were pitched, and bidding was spirited.

†**b.** *pitch and pay* (absol. or intr.): ? to pay down at once, pay ready money. *Obs.*

14.. *Piers of Fullham* 206 in Hazl. *E.P.P.* II. 9 Yt ys full hard bothe to pyche and paye. **1559** *Mirr. Mag., Warwick* xiv, I vsed playnnes, euer pitch and pay. **1573** TUSSER *Husb.* (1878) 211 At Norwich.. A citie trim: Where strangers wel may seeme to dwel, That pitch and pay, or keepe their day. **1599** SHAKS. *Hen. V*, II. iii. 51 The word is, Pitch and pay: trust none. **1608** H. CLAPHAM *Errour on Left Hand* 102 But you your promise once did breake. Giue me your hand, that you will pitch and pay.

8. a. *intr.* (or *refl.*) To place or locate oneself; to take up one's abode; to take up one's position, settle, alight. Now *rare* or *arch.* (Cf. 4 c.)

1609 BIBLE (Douay) *1 Macc.* ix. 33 They fled into the desert of Thecua, and they pitched by the water of the lake Asphar. **1623** COCKERAM III, *Iohn de monte Regio*.. made a small iron Fly to.. flye about all the roome, and returne and pitch on his sleeue. **1692** SIR W. HOPE *Fencing-Master* (ed. 2) 135 You must pitch your self to the same Guard with your Small-sword as you do with your Broad. **1727** *Philip Quarll* (1816) 57 The fowl being pitched upon the bank. **1792** BELKNAP *Hist. New Hampsh.* III. 201 The first settlers pitched here, but the trade has long since been removed.. about four miles further up. **1827** D. JOHNSON *Ind. Field Sports* 91 An owl pitched immediately over our heads. **1900** [see PITCHING *ppl. a.* 3].

b. *trans.* To cause to alight and settle.

1765 *Treat. Dom. Pigeons* 106 [Certain pigeons] are exceeding good to pitch stray Pigeons that are at a loss to find their own home.

c. *refl.* and *intr.* To seat oneself, sit down, take a seat. *dial.* or *colloq.*

1796 *Sporting Mag.* VII. 279 He.. could not carry the amount.. for the distance of one mile without pitching. **1844** E. JESSE *Scenes Country Life* I. 254 The cottager's wife will ask [him] to sit down in that hearty Devonshire phrase, ..'Do'y Sir, pitch yourself'—bringing forward a chair.

9. *trans. transf.* (from 1 and 5). To set, plant, fill, furnish (something) *with* things or persons stuck or placed in or on it. †**a.** *gen. Obs.*

c **1400** *Destr. Troy* 4056 A hundrith shippes.. Pight full of pepull & mony prise knight. **1420** *Siege Rouen* in *Archæologia* XXI. 62 A dyche was made,.. They pyght hyt wyth stakes hors to perche. **1540–1** ELYOT *Image Gov.* (1549) 145 The daungerouse rase of auctoritee, pight full of perils. *c* **1611** CHAPMAN *Iliad* IX. 337 [He] Cut a dike by it, pitch'd with pales, broad and of deep import. **1653** HOLCROFT *Procopius, Gothick Wars* I. 24 Pitching the top with multitude of stakes.

†**b.** *spec.* To set, stud, or adorn with gems or the like. *Obs.*

13.. *E.E. Allit. P.* A. 217 Pyȝt.. Wyth whyte perle & non oþer gemme. *Ibid.* 241 'O perle' quoth I, 'in perlez pyȝt'. ? *a* **1400** *Morte Arth.* 212 In ever-ilk aperty pyghte with precyous stones. **1480** CAXTON *Chron. Eng.* ccxli. 273 Croune of gold pyght with ryche perle and precious stones. **1513** DOUGLAS *Æneis* I. ix. 133 The collar picht with orient peirlis als. *a* **1661** FULLER *Worthies, Northampt.* II. (1662) 298 He wore a gown of purple velvet, pight with pieces of gold.

c. To pave (a road, path, or street) with stones set on end; orig. with pebbles or cobbles; hence, also, with granite 'randoms', or with dressed and squared 'setts'. Also, to form a foundation for a macadamized road with larger stones placed on edge by hand.

c **1550** *R. Ricart's Kalendar* (Camden) 57 In this yere was Redclif strete.. new pight. **1641** J. TRAPPE *Theol. Theol.* vi. 251 Hell (the pavement whereof was commonly said to be pitcht with shavelings skuls, and great mens crests). **1666** *Act 18 & 19 Chas. II*, c. 8 §18 The order and manner of paving and pitching the Streets and Lanes. **1682** WOOD *Life* 31 July (O.H.S.) III. 25 In this month.. was the highway.. pitched with peebles and hard stone. **1717** TABOR in *Phil. Trans.* XXX. 554 The Surface of the Clay was neatly pitch'd with small Flint and Stones, Pointed at their lower ends, and Headed at their upper ends. **1811** *Self Instructor* 140 Paved with bricks or pitched with pebble. **1905** *Westm. Gaz.* 25 Aug. 5/3 In addition to flagging and pitching several roads.

†**10.** To 'put together'; to construct by fastening the parts together; *pa. pple.*, compacted, knit. *Obs.*

c **1400** *Laud Troy Bk.* 2720 Alle here schippis were redy dyght And fraught with vitayles and wel pight. *c* **1489** CAXTON *Blanchardyn* xiv. 47 All thassystents.. sayde that they neuere sawe no fayrer man of armes, nor better pyght. **1611** COTGR., *Compacte*, compacted; well set, knit, trust, pight, or ioyned together.

II. To set in order, arrange, determine; to fix the order, position, rate, price, or pitch of.

11. *trans.* To set in order for fighting, to arrange (a battle, field of battle, etc.: see BATTLE *sb.* 11, FIELD *sb.* 8 b); to set in array. *Obs.* exc. in PITCHED *ppl. a.* (q.v., sense 2).

a **1470** TIPTOFT *Cæsar* xii. (1530) 14 Cesar had ordered hys army & pyght his felde in a conuenient place. **1513** BRADSHAW *St. Werburge* II. 1244 The duke of Normandy.. Pight a stronge batell. *a* **1553** UDALL *Royster D.* IV. vi. (Arb.) 70 If ye two bidde me, we will with him pitche a fielde. **1558** PHAER *Æneid* II. Eij b, Polites.. through foes and wepons pight, Through galeryes along doth ronne. **1590** MARLOWE *2nd Pt. Tamburl.* III. i, Our battle, then, in martial manner pitch'd. *c* **1645** T. TULLIE *Siege of Carlisle* (1840) 37 The Enemie drew out some foot to peche against those in the ditch. **1655** STANLEY *Hist. Philos.* I. (1701) 54/2 When to wage War, and when to pitch a Field.

12. To set (one person) *against* another in contest or competition; to pit. *rare*.

1801 tr. *Gabrielli's Myst. Husb.* II. 48 My tutor offered to pitch me against the clerk for reading, and against a neighbouring farmer's son for casting accounts. **1889** *Daily News* 6 Aug. 5/7 We are.. weak in comparison with the great fleets against which we shall be pitched when the manœuvres commence.

†**13. a.** To determine (something that is to be); to set, fix, settle, appoint, fix upon. *Obs.*

c **1557** ABP. PARKER *Ps.* xcvi. 272 Tel ye, I say, the Gentiles all This Lord his raigne hath pight. **1579** W. WILKINSON *Confut. Familye of Loue* 38 b, If they be such as ..by a price pitcht they are deliuered out for. **1592** KYD *Sp. Trag.* II. iii. 37 Between us theres a price already pitcht. **1602** WARNER *Alb. Eng.* IX. xlvi. (1612) 216 Pluto.. and all th' infernall States Did pytch a Session, to correct Remisnes in debates. **1649** *Nicholas Papers* (Camden) I. 166 The King now hath pitcht a new day for his repaire to Antwerp.

†**b.** *intr.* To come to a decision; to decide. *Obs.*

1666 MARVELL *Corr.* Wks. (Grosart) II. 191 Privy seals, sealed paper,.. have been all more or lesse disputed,.. but where we shall pitch I am not yet wise enough to tell you. **1667–8** *Ibid.* 240 We are not yet very irresolute what way to pitch.

c. *trans. Cards.* In certain games (e.g. *Nap*), to select or determine (a particular suit) as trumps by leading a card of that suit.

1890 in *Cent. Dict.*

†**14.** To fix, settle, or place in thought; to determine (an existing fact); to ascertain, or state as ascertained; to come to a conclusion about. *Obs.*

1610 WILLET *Hexapla Dan.* 294 Some pitch their beginning at Cyrus. **1640** BP. HALL *Chr. Moder.* (ed. Ward) 33/2 First they pitch their conclusion, and then hunt about for premises to make it good. *a* **1680** CHARNOCK *Attrib. God* (1834) I. 24 Who can pitch a time and person that originated this notion? *a* **1687** PETTY *Pol. Arith.* 26, I had.. pitch'd the medium of Heads in all the Families of England to be 6¼.

15. a. To set at a particular pitch or degree (high, low, etc.; in various metaphorical applications: see PITCH *sb.*[2] 22). In mod. use mostly *fig.* from c: To set in a particular 'key' or style of expression, feeling, etc.

1633 G. HERBERT *Temple, Ch. Porch* lvi, Pitch thy behaviour low, thy projects high. *a* **1859** L. HUNT *Cambus Khan* Poems (1860) 167 And women came with their impetuous lords, To pitch the talk and humanize the boards. **1874** BURNAND *My Time* xvi. 142 His conversation was pitched in a minor key. **1893** SIR R. BALL *Story of Sun* 81 Our second assumption regarding the mass of the Earth was pitched too low.

†**b.** To set or fix *at* a price or rate. *Obs. rare.*

1624 CAPT. SMITH *Virginia* v. 199 They pitched their commodities at what rate they pleased. *a* **1625** FLETCHER *Hum. Lieut.* II iii, What do you pitch her at?

c. *Mus.* To set at a particular pitch, determine the pitch of (a tune, the voice, an instrument): see PITCH *sb.*[2] 23.

1674 PLAYFORD *Skill Mus.* I. xi. 54 That the Professor.. so pitch his Tune, as to sing in his full and natural voice. **1744–91** WESLEY *Wks.* (1872) VIII. 319 Choose a person or two in each place to pitch the tune for you. **1842** TENNYSON *Edwin Morris* 52 'Parson' said I 'you pitch the pipe too low'. **1887** CAROLINE HAZARD *Mem. J. L. Diman* vi. 123 His voice was well pitched and resonant, easily filling large spaces.

d. ***to pitch it strong*** (and varr.): to speak forcefully; to state a case with feeling or enthusiasm; to exaggerate.

1837 DICKENS *Pickw.* xxxix. 429 I'm going to write to my father, and I must have a stimulant, or I shan't be able to pitch it strong enough into the old boy. **1841, 1863** [see STRONG *adv.* 1 c]. **1886** R. L. STEVENSON *Dr. Jekyll & Mr. Hyde* 7 And all the time, as we were pitching it in red hot, we were keeping the women off him as best we could. **1903** WODEHOUSE *Tales of St. Austin's* 213 Try him, any-how. Pitch it fairly warm... Only cat you ever loved, and that sort of thing. **1916** J. BUCHAN *Greenmantle* i. 5 My heart was beginning to thump uncomfortably. Sir Walter was not the man to pitch a case too high. **1928** GALSWORTHY *Swan Song* II. xi. 194 Pitch it strong, but no waterworks. **1969** *New Scientist* 3 July 37/1 Dr Steven Rose.. was not pitching it too high when he said that the dangers of uncontrolled technology were as great as those of nuclear warfare.

16. *intr.* with *on* or *upon*: To fix upon, settle upon, decide upon; to make choice of, select, choose; †*rarely*, to determine (= 13 or 14); in mod. use, to select more or less casually, without deliberation; to let one's choice fall *upon*.

1628 PRYNNE *Cens. Cozens* 62, I shall onely pitch vpon these ensuing passages. **1650** HOWELL *Giraffi's Rev. Naples* I. 84 Who shall delay the accomplishment of that which is already pitch'd upon. **1674** ALLEN *Danger Enthus.* 86 The way and method which God pitcht upon. *a* **1687** PETTY *Pol. Arith.* 23, I pitch upon 88 thousand to be the number of Housing Anno 1686. **1710** HEARNE *Collect.* (O.H.S.) III. 86 The Lecturer to be pitch'd upon every 3[d] year by y[e] Warden & five Seniors. **1791** 'G. GAMBADO' *Ann. Horsem.* iv. (1809) 84, I pitched upon one that I thought would suit me. **1836** W. IRVING *Astoria* I. 169 The place which he pitched upon for his trading post. **1858** J. H. NEWMAN *Hist. Sk.* (1873) III. IV. ix. 411 If one holy place was desecrated, the monks pitched upon another.

III. To cast or throw in particular ways.

17. a. *trans.* To cast, throw, or fling forward; to hurl (a javelin, spear, or bar, or a person headlong; to throw anything flat with retention of its horizontal position); to throw (a thing) underhand so that it may fall and rest on a particular spot. Also *absol.*

to pitch the bar: to throw a heavy bar as a form of athletic exercise or contest. ***to pitch*** (a person) ***over the bar***: *fig.* (*colloq.*) to deprive of the status of a barrister, to disbar (cf. BAR *sb.*[1] 24).

c **1386** CHAUCER *Knt.'s T.* 1831 His hors.. leepe aside, and foundred as he leepe And er that Arcite may taken keepe He pighte hym on the pomel of his heed. *c* **1400** *Destr. Troy* 8258 Achilles.. Grippet to a grete speire with a grym wille; Pight on the prinse, persit his wede. **1579** W. WILKINSON *Confut. Familye of Loue* 41 b, The other doth pitch down hedlong both body and soule into euerlasting torments. **1592** CHETTLE *Kinde-harts Dr.* G j, One.. that.. was not long since disgraded of his place by pitching ouer the Barre. **1600, 1715** [see BAR *sb.*[1] 2]. **1719** D'URFEY *Pills* III. 253, I.. can.. Pitch-Bar, and run and wrestle too. **1796** MORSE *Amer. Geog.* I. 612 So steep that you may pitch a biscuit from its summit into the river which washes its base. **1802** PALEY *Nat. Theol.* i. (1819) 1 In crossing a heath, suppose I pitched my foot against a stone, and were asked how the stone came to be there. **1814** SCOTT *Ld. of Isles* VI. xiii, As far as one might pitch a lance. **1836** LADY W. DE ERESBY in *C. K. Sharpe's Corr.* (1888) II. 495 Mrs Villiers, in galloping to cover the other day.. was pitched off. **1885** *Spectator* 25 July 971/2 He was within an ace of pitching himself headforemost into the wildest of gorges.

b. To throw (sheaves, hay, etc.) with a pitchfork; esp. on to a cart or stack in homing or inning the crop. Often *absol.*

1393 LANGL. *P. Pl.* C. VI. 13 Canstow seruen.. oþer syngen in a churche, Oþer coke for my cokers oþer to þe cart picche,.. oþer make bond to sheues? **1550** CROWLEY *Epigr.* 131 Or pitcheth vp the sheues from the carte to the mowe. **1610** B. JONSON *Alch.* II. iii, O, I look'd for this. The hay is a pitching. **1763** *Ann. Reg.* 170/1 Beddingfield.. had pitched a load of wheat. **1904** H. BLACK *Pract. Self-Culture* ii. 49 He [could] pitch hay with the haymakers in the pasture.

c. In *Baseball* or other games: To deliver or serve (the ball) to the batter; also *fig.* In *Cricket*, now superseded by *to bowl*: see BOWL *v.*[1] 4, 5, exc. with constr. indicating the length at or off which the ball is delivered, or the direction of the delivery. In various games, to throw a flat object towards a mark, or so as to fall in or near a definite place. Also *absol.*

1767 R. COTTON *Cricket Song* vii, in F. S. Ashley-Cooper *Hambledon Cricket Chron.* (1924) 184 Ye Bowlers take heed ..; Spare your vigour at first... But measure each step, and be sure pitch your length! **1773** *Gentl. Mag.* XLIII. 568 For honest Lumpey did allow He ne'er could pitch but o'er a brow. **1803** *Laws of Cricket* 7 The ball, which the bowler.. shall have pitched in a straight line to the wicket. **1845** in *Appleton's Ann. Cycl. 1855* (1886) 77/2 The ball must be pitched and not thrown to the bat. **1851** J. PYCROFT *Cricket Field* viii. 165 Then, with a much higher toss and slower pace.. he pitches a little short of the usual spot. **1853** F. GALE *Public School Matches* 54 In vain does Leftarm pitch up a whole over of half volleys in the hopes of a catch. **1868** H. CHADWICK *Game of Base Ball* 60 When he [*sc.* the pitcher] makes a motion to pitch and does not do so,.. he makes a balk. **1890** [see CATCH *v.* 24 e]. *a* **1907** *Mod.* The player that pitches his coin nearest to the mark has the first toss. **1929** *Chicagoan* 17 Aug. 22/1 Diamond slang crops out in his speech.. as when he [*sc.* Carl Sandburg] instructs his agents never to book him for two consecutive lectures. 'I can't pitch two games in a row', he says. **1936** G. MILBURN *Catalogue* 234 'Reck it'd be all right for me to go in there and dance.'.. 'You're all right. Go right on in there and pitch.' **1944** *College Topics* (Univ. of Virginia) 30 Mar. 3 Hank Neighbors, who pitched two innings of college ball here last year, is the only semblance of an experienced pitcher on the squad. **1970** [see FORCE *v.*[1] 5]. **1970** *Globe & Mail* (Toronto) 25 Sept. 31/1 Cuellar pitched his 21st complete game and broke a club record for season victories. **1977** *World of Cricket Monthly* June 33/3 He charged down the pitch to a leg-break which the bowler pitched wide.

d. *slang.* To utter, tell. Cf. PITCH *sb.*[2] 5 b. ***to pitch (the) woo*** (orig. and chiefly *U.S.*): to court, to make love to; *transf.*, to flatter lavishly.

1867 *London Herald* 23 Mar. 222/2 (Farmer), If he had had the sense to.. pitch them a tale, he might have got off. **1878** WRIGHT *Mental Trav.* 14 They suspected from his pitching such stories, he must surely be a rogue and vagabond. **1935** *Ladies' Home Jrnl.* Feb. 60/3 After a while Uncle Ned came back looking positively exalted, so I guessed he and May had been pitching some more woo. **1937** *Clarionette* (Univ. of Denver) 18 Mar. 1/3 As long as there are students and universities and sofas and automobiles and nice laws, scholars will do their time-honoured share of 'pitchin' the woo'. **1943** *Sat. Even. Post* 25 Sept. 12/1 Louie.. pitches kitchen gadgets. **1943** [see PITCH *sb.*[2] 11 a]. **1943** HUNT & PRINGLE *Service Slang* 51 *Pitch a woo*, to start a courtship. **1972** *Village Voice* (N.Y.) 1 June 26/2 Like any good salesman, he knows that once he demonstrates that the basic program he is pitching really does some good, all the ancillary merchandising will take care of itself. **1973** *Internat. Herald Tribune* 15 June 5/5 He's still a master at pitching the woo—on the mound, in the pressroom or elsewhere.

18. a. *intr.* for *pass.* To fall headlong heavily, to land on one's head, or strike forcibly against something, by being thrown.

1297 R. GLOUC. (Rolls) 673 Þo he was iflowe an hei, & ne cowþe not aliȝte; Adoun mid so gret eir to þen erþe he vel & piȝte, þat al to peces he to rod [*MS. B.* rof]. **13..** *Gaw. & Gr. Knt.* 1456 Schalkez.. Haled to hym of her arewez, hitten hym oft; Bot þe poyntez payred at þe pyth þat pyȝt in his scheldez. **1596** SPENSER *F.Q.* v. viii. 8 In his fall misfortune him mistooke; For on his head unhappily he pight. **1700** DRYDEN *Pal. & Arc.* III. 703 Forward he flew, and pitching on his head, He quiver'd with his feet, and lay for dead. **1796** MORSE *Amer. Geog.* I. 480 A large pine has been seen.. to pitch over endwise. **1857-8** SEARS *Athan.* iv. 30 Columbus had to argue.. that, when he came upon this side of the world he would not be in danger of pitching off into nowhere.

b. *Cricket.* Of a delivery: to land (usu. at or off a specified length, or in or off a specified direction).

1816 W. LAMBERT *Instr. & Rules Cricket* 32 If a Ball should pitch short of its proper length on the off side, and should twist toward the top of the wicket, the Striker must be very careful in playing back that he does not hit his own wicket. **1947** N. CARDUS *Autobiogr.* I. 79, I was certain the ball had pitched off the wicket. **1970** R. BOWEN *Cricket* v. 76 When the ball pitches, the forward motion is hindered by its friction with the ground; the circular motion is stopped abruptly (or nearly so) and this cessation must yield.. further force in the direction the ball is moving. **1977** *Times* 17 Jan. 7/1 Patel received the perfect ball from Underwood which pitched on his middle stump and hit the off.

19. †**a.** *trans.* Of a ship: To plunge (her head) downwards into the water, instead of rising with the wave. *Obs.* [Has affinities with IV.]

1627 CAPT. SMITH *Seaman's Gram.* ii. 4 If she haue not a full Bow, it will make her pitch her head much into the Sea. *Ibid.* 10.

b. *intr.* Of a ship: To plunge with the head into the trough of the sea; hence (as this is followed by the head rising or 'scending' on the crest of a wave), to rise and fall alternately at bow and stern; to plunge in a longitudinal direction (as distinguished from *rolling*).

a **1687** PETTY *Treat. Naval Philos.* I. iii, What makes her pitch and scend too much. **1748** *Anson's Voy.* II. v. 175 The Sloop.. rolled and pitched so violently, that it was impossible for a boat to lay a long-side of her. **1840** R. H. DANA *Bef. Mast* xxxv. 132 The ship works hard, groaning and creaking, and pitching into a heavy head-sea. **1867** SMYTH *Sailor's Word-bk.*, *Send, to*, to rise after pitching heavily and suddenly between two waves, or out of the trough of the sea.

c. *trans.* with adv. or extension: To cast (*away*, *overboard*, etc.) by this movement. (A mixture of senses 17 and 19.)

1727-41 CHAMBERS *Cycl.* s.v., When a ship falls with her head too much into the sea, or beats against it so as to endanger her top-masts, they say, she will *pitch her masts by the board*. **1811** *Naval. Chron.* XXV. 27 Having pitched her bowsprit and foremast away. **1885** RUNCIMAN *Skippers & Sh.* 17 Which threatened to pitch the masts out of her.

d. *intr.* Of a person or animal: To plunge forward like a pitching ship. (Cf. to LURCH.)

1849 THACKERAY *Pendennis* lx, When I begin to talk too much.. when I begin to pitch, I authorize you.. to put away the brandy-bottle. **1852** MRS. STOWE *Uncle Tom's C.* vii, Whistling to the lumbering Newfoundland, who came pitching tumultuously toward them. **1863** COWDEN CLARKE *Shaks. Char.* xx. 508 The only time he.. ventures at a reason for what he says, he flounders and pitches headlong.

e. (See quot.) *U.S.*

1883 HALLOCK *Sportsman's Gaz.* Gloss., *Pitch*, v.i., to buck, to jump from the ground with the legs bunched together, as a mustang or mule.

f. *Aeronaut.* and *Astronautics. intr.* Of an aircraft or spacecraft: to rotate or rock about a lateral axis, to undergo pitching. Also *trans.*, to cause (an aircraft, etc.) to do this.

1874 *Ann. Rep. Aeronaut. Soc.* 59 If.. the model pitches forward on its nose, it is only necessary to slide the aeroplane further forward on the rod. If it still pitches turn up the horizontal rudder slightly. **1903** *Aeronaut. Jrnl.* VII. 53/2 The best angles were given by shapes which.. would always pitch forward unless controlled by a large and well turned up tail. **1918** COWLEY & LEVY *Aeronautics* vii. 152 The pitching moment produced is about 123 lbs.-ft., enough to pitch the aeroplane through an angle of ½°. **1926** *Jrnl. R. Aeronaut. Soc.* XXX. 521 The examination would be comparatively easy if only the operation of the longitudinal control simply pitched the aeroplane, the lateral control banked and the rudder control yawed it. **1932** R. MAHACHEK *Airplane Pilots' Man.* iv. 37 The plane will gradually pitch upward or downward unless the pilot moves his control stick slightly forward or backward. **1961** D. MYRUS *Man into Space* ii. 36/1 At about 50,000 feet the engines automatically flip slightly to one side, pitching the missile from straight up to a little north of due east. **1964** J. E. D. WILLIAMS *Operation of Airliners* vii. 104 When an aircraft yaws or pitches there is an immediate change in the aerodynamic forces. **1970** N. ARMSTRONG et al. *First on Moon* x. 242 We pitched over to a level altitude which would allow us to maintain our horizontal velocity and just skim along over the top of the boulder field.

IV. 20. a. *intr.* To incline or slope forwards and downwards; to dip. Also, of a roof or other structure: to slope downwards (*U.S.*). In *Mining* and *Geol.* now used esp. of a linear feature, as an ore shoot or fold axis (cf. PITCH *sb.*[2] 24 b): to have a pitch of a given angle and direction.

1519 [see PITCHING *ppl. a.* 1]. **1719** STRACHEY in *Phil. Trans.* XXX. 969 It riseth to the North West, and pitcheth to the South East. **1771** in *Mass. Hist. Soc. Coll.* (1914) LXXI. 137, I should have the Roof to pitch from under the Arkitraves of the Chamber Windows. **1859** *Trans. Illinois Agric. Soc.* III. 538 The roof may pitch both ways, or shed at the ends. **1877** RAYMOND *Statist. Mines & Mining* 162 The vein.. increases in width with depth and pitches 36° east. **1897** F. C. MOORE *How to build Home* vii. 94 The floor shall pitch from building to the front of piazza ½ inch to every foot of width. **1906** *Prof. Papers U.S. Geol. Survey* No. 54. 206 In the Midget mine the Cobb ore shoot pitches 45° NE. **1910** LAKE & RASTALL *Test-bk. Geol.* i. 20 A fold whose axis was inclined downwards towards the south-east would be said to pitch to the south-east, and the angle of pitch could be expressed in degrees, as in the case of dip. **1939** A. K. LOBECK *Geomorphol.* xvii. 593 The two monoclinal ridges formed on the two limbs of the anticline do not run strictly parallel.. but converge and meet, the convergence being in the direction toward which the anticline pitches. **1962** [see PITCH *sb.*[2] 24 b]. **1966** E. H. T. WHITTEN *Struct. Geol. Folded Rocks* i. 26 In a sedimentary sequence folded about a horizontal fold axis one bed has a strike of 130 and dips SW at 45°. Ripple marks are observed on this bedding plane; they pitch at 40° to the southeast (i.e., the angle between the strike and the ripples is 40°).

b. *intr.* To subside or settle down, as a swelling or loose soil; *fig.* to fall off, lose flesh. *dial.*

1794 T. DAVIS *Agric. Wilts.* 36 The ewes shrink their milk, the lambs 'pitch and get stunted', and the best summer food will not recover them. *Ibid.* 37 The rule is to give it [the meadow] a 'thorough good soaking' at first,.. to make the land sink and pitch close together. **1850** *Jrnl. R. Agric. Soc.* XI. II. 679 When they [sheep] are first put into turnips they lose ground, or pitch, as it is called, for two months in the autumn, and are slow in regaining it afterwards.

c. To drop *down* or descend abruptly (to a lower level).

1851 N. KINGSLEY *Diary* 21 Jan. (1914) 168 We have come to where the bed rock pitches down suddenly. **1867** 'T. LACKLAND' *Homespun* I. 70 One of these [pastures].. sloping where it does not pitch, down to the rocky bed of the riotous stream. **1873** J. MILLER *Life amongst Modocs* vi. 72 Gorge on gorge, cañon intersecting cañon, pitching down towards the rapid Klamat.

V. Technical senses.

21. *Mech. trans.* and *intr.* To fit *into*, interlock, engage (as one cog-wheel with another).

a **1668** DAVENANT *Play House to Let* Wks. (1673) 91 But his fingers are pitcht together. **1792** *Specif. Kelly's Patent* No. 1879. 5 The pinion *P* pitches into and turns the wheel *R*. **1825** [see PITCHING *vbl. sb.*[1] 9].

22. *Brewing.* To add the yeast to wort for the purpose of inducing fermentation.

1846 *J. Baxter's Libr. Pract. Agric.* I. 136 *Pitching or Setting.*—This term is applied to the mixing the yeast with the wort, after it has been cooled. **1875** *Ure's Dict. Arts* I. 316 The heat is at this time generally 75°, if it was pitched at 65°; for the heat and the attenuation go hand in hand.

VI. with *adv.* or *prep.*

23. a. ***pitch in***: to set to work vigorously. Also, to turn (aside) to a particular objective; to begin. *colloq.* (chiefly *U.S.*).

1847-78 HALLIWELL s.v., *Pitch in*, to set to work; to beat or thrash a person. **1896** *Harper's Mag.* XCII. 766/2 They subsequently did pitch in, however, and fought well. **1897** KIPLING *Captains Courageous* ix, He's paid me half now; and I took hold with Dan and pitched right in. I can't do a man's work yet. **1932** WODEHOUSE *Louder & Funnier* 11 Then, with the coffee and old brandy at your side.., pitch in. **1971** W. HILLEN *Blackwater River* iv. 36 A favorite stopping-place for.. swans, cranes, and geese. They pitch in to feed and rest.

b. ***pitch into***: to attack or assail forcibly (with blows, etc., or with words); to reprimand. *colloq.* Also in weakened senses.

1829 P. EGAN *Boxiana* 2nd Ser. II. 267 Dick.. *pitched in* to Warren, who was obliged to fight for his safety. **1835** DICKENS *Sk. Boz* (1836) 1st Ser. I. 51, I wished.. that the people would only blow me up, or pitch into me—that I wouldn't have minded. **1839** *Spirit of Times* 30 Mar. 48/2 The man was lost in astonishment which but increased the rage of the husband of the *cantatrice*, who forthwith 'pitched into' him in the last London style, and an entire 'mus' was made of the man's face. *c* **1843** DE QUINCEY *Ceylon* Wks. 1859 XII. 16 Both [monarchs] pitched into us in 1803, and we pitched into both in 1815. **1852** DICKENS *Bleak Ho.* xx, If any man had told me, then,.. I should have pitched into him. **1852** *Punch* 10 July 25/2, I saw that *gourmand* Guttler pitching contentedly into a kangaroo chop. **1863** FREEMAN in W. R. W. Stephens *Life* (1895) I. v. 287, I shall have to pitch into him a great deal more in my second volume. **1885**

G. ALLEN *Babylon* vi, You sit down..and pitch into those sandwiches. **1906** G. B. SHAW *Let.* 18 Nov. (1972) II. 661 A vaccine opsinises your disease germs..so that the white blood corpuscles..pitch into them with an appetite. **1952** *Sun* (Baltimore) 4 July 42/8 The two young Negroes pitched into him and the one with the gun pistol-whipped the physician.

†**c.** ***pitch out*** (Cricket): to dismiss; to bowl out or to run out by a ball that does not touch the ground before it hits the wickets. *Obs.*

1858 *Bell's Life in London* 18 July 7/6 Caffyn was *pitched* out—the ball never touching the ground until after it had disturbed the stumps. **1876** *John Wisden's Cricketer's Almanack* 115 He was stated to have been brilliantly pitched out by Mr. Strachan from mid-off.

24. In extended use, **pitch-and-putt** [PITCH *sb.*² 3 c], a form of golf in which the green can be reached in one; *fig.*, an insignificant distance; *attrib.*, of or pertaining to a *spec.* type of miniature golf course.

1963 *Harper's Bazaar* Jan. 9/2 Pitch and Putt Course. Tennis. Sea-bathing. **1968** *Sun* (Baltimore) 5 July A14/7 His delegate count is within a pitch and a putt of the nominating majority. **1972** J. MCCLURE *Caterpillar Cop* xiv. 234, I believe..you played a round of pitch-and-putt? **1974** *Times* 8 Feb. 15/4 A pitch-and-putt course covering five acres. **1976** J. SNOW *Cricket Rebel* 70 Two days in which my only activity had been in a pitch and putt competition organised by the players and Press in the hotel grounds.

VII. 25. The verb stem in comb. forming *sbs.*, in names of games in which coins or other objects are pitched or thrown at a mark or into a hole or vessel; as ***pitch-and-chuck*** (cf. CHUCK-FARTHING), ***pitch-and-hustle*** (cf. HUSTLE-CAP), ***pitch-button***, ***pitch-halfpenny***, ***pitch-in-the-hole***, ***pitch-in-the-tub***; see also PITCH-AND-TOSS, PITCH-FARTHING.

1749 W. ELLIS *Shepherds G.* 199 Others..go shooting of Birds, or play at Bandy-wicket, *Pitch and Chuck, Hooper's Hide. **1688** R. HOLME *Armoury* III. xvi. (Roxb.) 82/1 *Pich and Hussle. **1764** *Low Life* (ed. 3) 46 Narrow Alleys filled with Boys playing at Marbles, Pitch and Hussle. **1801** STRUTT *Sports & Past.* III. viii. §15 Pitch and Hustle..a game commonly played in the fields by the lowest classes. **1861** MAYHEW *Lond. Labour* III. 134, I was watching a lot of boys playing at *pitch-button. **1828** *Pitch-halfpenny [see PINCH *sb.* 6]. *a* **1845** HOOD *Tale Trumpet* xxxvi, Playing at dumps, or *pitch in the hole. **1901** *Daily News* 22 Jan. 9/1 The young ladies for the most part seemed to be in the '*pitch-in-the-tub' branch of the profession.

[*Note.* The form of this verb, and the fact that it has the collateral form PICK *v.*² (chiefly, but not entirely, northern), naturally suggests some etymological connexion with PICK *v.*¹ (OE. *pician* or *pīcian*). To this, in sense also, it stood originally in somewhat of a causal relation: *pick* to pierce or penetrate (with something pointed), *pitch* to cause to penetrate, to stick (something pointed) in. But no satisfactory explanation of **piccean* as a causal derivative of *pician* or *pīcian* appears. And although the form *pick* appears in both verbs, they are formally distinct, in that PICK *v.*¹ occurs with short and long *i*, but only with *k*, never *-tch*, while PITCH occurs both with *-tch* and *-k*, but never with long *ī*. They are also quite distinct dialectally; dialects which use PICK *v.*² for *pitch*, use *pike* for PICK *v.*¹]

pitch (pɪtʃ), *v.*² Forms: 1 (ʒe)pician, 3-4 piche(n, 4 picche, 5-6 pyche, pytch(e, 6- pitch. *β. northern.* 3 pike, 4 pik, 5-6 pycke, 5-7 picke, 6- pick. [OE. (ʒe)pician, f. *pic*, PITCH *sb.*¹] *trans.* To cover, coat, or smear with pitch; to mark or brand (a sheep, etc.) with pitch; to soil or stain with pitch.

c **1000** *Sax. Leechd.* II. 26 ʒedo on wæter .xxx. nihta on ænne croccan þone þ e sie ʒepicod utan. *c* **1290** *St. Brandan* 97 in *S. Eng. Leg.* I. 222, & siþþe ipiched al aboute þat þe water ne come. **1398** TREVISA *Barth. De P.R.* XVII. cxxiii. (Tollem MS.), þe ton is calde schippe picche, for schippes beþ pichid [**1495** pytched] þerwiþ. **1496** *Naval Acc. Hen. VII* 176, xj barelles peche to pyche the said shipp. **1577** B. GOOGE *Heresbach's Husb.* III. (1586) 150b, Let him pitch euery sowe and her pigs with a seuerall marke. **1687** A. LOVELL tr. *Thevenot's Trav.* I. 110 Without it you would pitch all your cloaths. **1716** HEARNE *Collect.* (O.H.S.) V. 260 Theire Money was brought thither in Barrells, pitch'd up. **1817** BENNET in *Parl. Deb.* 1861 The deponent declared, that he had seen men pitched and tarred, and hunted through the streets, on whom torture was afterwards inflicted.

β. *c* **1300** *Havelok* 707 He dede it tere, an ful wel pike, That it ne doutede sond ne krike. **13..** *Cursor M.* 5615 (Cott.) An esscen kyst sco did be wroght, Did pik it sua wit-oute and in. *a* **1400-50** *Alexander* 4208 A barge..draȝen ouer with hidis, Pared & parreld at his pay pickid & taloghid. **1450-1530** *Myrr. our Ladye* 109 The shyppe of Noe was soo well pycked. **1611** COTGR., *Brayer vn navire*, to graue, picke, or pitch, a Ship. **17..** *Sir Patrick Spens* xxiii. in Child *Ballads* III. (1885) 28/2 Ye'll pict her well, and spare her not, And mak her hale and soun.

b. *fig.* To make 'as dark as pitch'; to envelop in pitchy darkness.

1664 DRYDEN *Rival Ladies* II. i, O call that night again; Pitch her with all her darkness round. *a* **1700** —— *On Death of Amyntas* 6 But soon he found The welkin pitched with sullen clouds around.

'pitchable, *a. rare.* [f. PITCH *v.*¹ + -ABLE.] That may be pitched; in quot. = FITCHÉ.

1486 *Bk. St. Albans, Her.* C iij b, A cros flurri fixabull..in iij. of his endys he is florishyng and in the foote pichabull or fixabull.

pitch-and-chuck, pitch-and-hustle: see PITCH *v.*¹ 25.

'pitch-and-'toss. [From name of the two actions.] **a.** A game of combined skill and chance. Also (*Sc.*), a manœuvre in the game of KNIFEY, KNIFIE (sense *a*).

Each player pitches a coin at a mark; the one whose coin lies nearest to the mark then tosses all the coins and keeps those that turn up 'head'; the one whose coin lay next in order does the same with the remaining ones, and so on till all the coins are disposed of.

1810 SIR A. BOSWELL *Edinburgh* Poems (1871) 54 The germ of Gambling sprouts in pitch and toss. **1844** DICKENS *Christmas Carol* iii, They are good for anything from pitch-and-toss to man-slaughter. **1890** *Times* 16 Sept. 10/4 The charges before the magistrate..playing pitch and toss with pence in the streets. **1949** [see BARRACK *sb.*²]. **1969** I. & P. OPIE *Children's Games* vii. 222 Described..by a 10-year-old boy in the Isle of Lewis: '"Knife" is a game for two people. .. Then try "Pitch and toss". Stick it in the ground, then try to hit it with the palm of your hand and try to toss it into the air, so that it will land blade first in the earth.'

b. *transf.* and *fig.* (In first quot. a pun.)

a **1845** HOOD *Sea-spell* iv, The bounding pinnace played a game Of dreary pitch and toss, A game that, on the good dry land, Is apt to bring a loss. **1866** GEO. ELIOT *F. Holt* xix, Brummagem half-pennies, scamps who want to play pitch-and-toss with the property of the country. **1893** *Westm. Gaz.* 1 Mar. 2/3 This is one of the pitch-and-toss points from his speech as reported in to-day's *Times.* **1910** KIPLING *Rewards & Fairies* 175 If you can make one heap of all your winnings and risk it on one turn of pitch-and-toss, and lose, And start again at your beginnings And never breathe a word about your loss. **1960** J. FRANKLYN *Dict. Rhyming Slang* 108/1 *Pitch and toss*, the boss. 20 C. Current in the theatrical world (Lupino Lane). **1973** *Times* 29 Dec. 12/7 Writing more than a dozen varied plays of substance, some of which had less fortune than they deserved in the pitch-and-toss of the West End.

Hence **pitch and toss** *vbl. phr.*, *intr.* to play at pitch-and-toss; *trans.* to pitch or throw about as if at this game; **pitcher and tosser** *sb. phr.*, one who pitches and tosses.

1849 S. BAMFORD *Early Days* (1859) 169 There's a deal o' sin committed thereabeawts; pitchin' an' tossin', an' drinkin', an' beawlin', i' Summer time. **1882** MISS BRADDON *Mt. Royal* I. ii. 67 No scattered sheets of music—no fancy-work pitch-and-tossed about the room. **1883** G. H. BOUGHTON in *Harper's Mag.* Apr. 692/1 The pitchers and tossers allow for you and a rational amount of headway.

pitch-back, *a.* [f. PITCH *sb.*² or *v.*¹ + BACK *adv.*] In ***pitch-back wheel***, a variety of breast-wheel in which the water is admitted much higher than the axle so as to have a backward pitch or direction on the wheel.

1858 SIMMONDS *Dict. Trade, Pitch-back Wheel*, a kind of wheel used in a mill, propelled by water.

pitch-ball, -black, etc.: see PITCH *sb.*¹ 5.

†**pitch-battle.** *Obs.* A pitched battle: cf. PITCH-FIELD.

1797 *Sporting Mag.* IX. 313 Broughton having fought sixteen pitch battles, fifteen of which he won.

pitch-blende ('pɪtʃblɛnd). *Min.* [ad. Ger. *pechblende* (Cronstedt, 1758), f. *pech* PITCH *sb.*¹: see BLENDE.] Native oxide of uranium, found in blackish pitch-like masses, more rarely crystalline; also called URANINITE.

1770 tr. *Cronstedt's Min.* 217 *Pechblende* or *Pitch Blende* of the Germans. **1794** HUTCHINSON *Hist. Cumbld.* I. *Catal. Fossils* 52/1 Peche blende, of a glassy shining surface, often crystallized in irregular pyramids. **1814** AIKIN *Min.* 296 Pitch Blende. **1861** H. W. BRISTOW *Gloss. Min.* 296 Pitch-blende is distinguished from brownblende by colour. **1898** *Daily Chron.* 8 Oct. 3/4 Pitchblende..possesses the property of emitting the rays, or form of energy, known as the Becquerel rays. **1904** *Ibid.* 6 Jan. 5/7 Mme. Curie.. discovered radium in the residue left after uranium had been extracted from 'pitch-blend', or uranium ore.

pitch-block: see PITCH *sb.*² 26.

pitch-board¹. [f. PITCH *sb.*² VI + BOARD *sb.*] A thin wooden board used as a guide in stair-building, cut to the shape of a right-angled triangle, with the base equal to the breadth of tread of the step, and the perpendicular equal to its height, the hypotenuse thus indicating the pitch.

1778 *Encycl. Brit.* (ed. 2) I. 618/1 Plate XXXVIII..Fig. 2. Exhibits the pitch-board, to shew what part of the step the twisted part of the rail contains. **1825** J. NICHOLSON *Operat. Mechanic* 600 The pitch-board, is a right-angled triangular board made to the rise and tread of the step, one side forming the right angle of the width of the tread.

†**'pitch-board**². *Obs. rare*⁻¹. [f. PITCH *sb.*¹ + BOARD *sb.*] ? A fanciful name for a ship. (Cf. BOARD *sb.* 13.)

1599 NASHE *Lenten Stuffe* 29 To post after him, and scoure it with their Ethiope pitchbordes till they be windlesse in his quest and pursuing.

pitch-boat, -boilery, etc.: see PITCH *sb.*¹ 5.

'pitch-brand. [f. PITCH *sb.*¹ + BRAND *sb.*] A brand or mark of ownership made with pitch upon a sheep, etc.; also *fig.*, a distinctive evil mark or characteristic. So **pitch-branded** *a.*

1631 J. BURGES *Answ. Rejoined, Lawfulness of Kneeling* 21 Hee that beside a pitch-brande, doth raddle the heads of his fat sheepe. *a* **1656** BP. HALL *Rem. Wks.* (1660) 234 David makes this the pitch-brand (as it were) of wicked wretches, 'they call not upon God'. **1805** LUCCOCK *Nat. Wool* 318 Instead of the common pitch-brand a permanent mark is fixed upon the ear of the sheep. **1593** G. HARVEY *Pierce's Super.* Wks. (Grosart) II. 317 Notable men in their kinde, but pitch-branded with notorious dissimulation.

pitch-button: see PITCH *v.*¹ 25.

'pitch-cap, *sb.* [f. PITCH *sb.*¹ + CAP *sb.*¹] **a.** A cap lined with pitch, used as an instrument of torture by the soldiery during the Irish rebellion of 1798. **b.** *Med.* A kind of plaster containing pitch, formerly used as a depilatory for the scalp in cases of favus (*Syd. Soc. Lex.*).

1589 RIDER *Bibl. Schol.* 1093 A pitche cappe made to take away the hair from scabbed heads, *depilatorium, psilothrum.* **1803** E. HAY *Insurr. Wexf.* 181 They certainly were the introducers of pitch-cap torture into the county of Wexford [in 1798]. **1842** R. R. MADDEN *United Irishmen* I. xi. 337 The numbers tied up to the triangles and tortured with the scourge, or tormented with the pitch-caps..in the year 1798. **1887** H. D. TRAILL in *Macm. Mag.* July 175 Why should anybody go out of his way to fit such a pitch-cap as that on his head?

Hence **pitch-cap** *v. trans.*, to torture with a pitch-cap.

1864 SALA in *Daily Tel.* 14 Nov., The ignorant and deluded peasants who were tarred, pitchcapped, singed, and flogged until their entrails fell out.

pitch-chain: see PITCH *sb.*² 26.

†**'pitchcock**, corruption of SPITCHCOCK. *Obs.*

1747 MRS. GLASSE *Art of Cookery* ix. 92 To Pitchcock Eels. You must split a large Eel down the Back, and joint the Bones, cut it into two or three Pieces,..and broil them of a fine Brown. **1773** *Chron.* in *Ann. Reg.* 96/2 The dinner was soup, jack, perch, and eel pitchcockt, fowls, [etc.].

pitch-dark: see PITCH *sb.*¹ 5.

pitch-diameter: see PITCH *sb.*² 26.

pitched (pɪtʃt), *ppl. a.*¹ Also † **pight** (paɪt). [Pa. pple. of PITCH *v.*¹ q.v. The form *pight* (in senses 1, 2) has been obs. since *c* 1600.]

†**1.** Fixed in the ground, staked; set in anything; adorned or set with jewels. *Obs.*

a. **13..** *E.E. Allit. P.* A. 207 A pyȝt coronne ȝet wer þat gyrle. **1584** in *Descr. Thames* (1758) 63 Rowte Wears, Pight Wears, Foot Wears.

β. **1615** BRATHWAIT *Strappado* (1878) 46 Tyed was she fast vnto a pitched stake.

2. Set in orderly array for fighting: said of a battle which has been planned and of which the ground has been chosen beforehand; a regular battle as distinguished from a skirmish or casual encounter; also ***pitched field***.

a. **1549-62** STERNHOLD & H. *Ps.* xxvii. 3 In battell pight if they will try I trust in God for ayde. **1596** BP. W. BARLOW *Three Serm.* ii. 85 The soldier which neuer saw a pight field. **1607** HIERON *Wks.* I. 412 Fitly is the life of man compared vnto a pight battell. **1631** WEEVER *Anc. Fun. Mon.* 832 The martiall prowesse of this Earle in the pight field.

β. **1568** GRAFTON *Chron.* II. 503 To the entent to giue him battaile in a pitched field, and so to make a finall ende of his intended conquest. **1634** PEACHAM *Compl. Gent. (title-p.)*, A Description of the order of a Maine Battaile or Pitched Field. *a* **1653** GOUGE *Comm. Heb.* xi. 32 David was never put to flight in any pitcht-battle. **1830** SCOTT *Demonol.* x. 396 That magic flag, which has been victorious in two pitched fields. **1867** FREEMAN *Norm. Conq.* I. ii 47 In this year..nine pitched battles..were fought with the heathens.

3. Paved with stones set in place, whether cobbles, granite 'randoms' or 'setts': see PITCH *v.*¹ 9 c.

1611 CORYAT *Crudities* 23 A plaine pitched walke, *sub die*, that is, under the open ayre. **1696** *Lond. Gaz.* No. 3175/4 To be Let a good large Inn,..with a large pitch'd Court. *c* **1830** *Pract. Treat. Roads* 8 (*Libr. Usef. Kn., Husb.* III), One party contending that a pitched foundation is necessary to make a substantial and good road. **1890** *Daily News* 16 May 7/1 Maintenance..of footways at the sides of main roads.. whether such footways were flagged, pitched, asphalted, gravelled, or otherwise constructed, as well as of pitched crossings over those roads.

†**4.** *fig.* Set or fixed (mentally); determined, resolved. *Obs. rare.*

1605 SHAKS. *Lear* II. i. 67 When I disswaded him from his intent, And found him pight to doe it. **1642** H. MORE *Song of Soul* II. iii. III. lxxiii, My pitchèd end Was for to prove the immortality Of humane souls.

5. Said of a market where the goods are pitched in bulk (PITCH *v.*¹ 7), not sold by sample.

1813 T. DAVIS *Agric. Wilts.* Gloss., *Pitched Market*, where the corn is exposed for sale as in Salisbury, Devizes, and Warminster, and not sold by sample.

6. Thrown in order to fall on a particular place, delivered. (Also with adverbs.)

1871 *Baily's Monthly Mag.* Aug. 290 He bowled a very great number of long hops, and a considerable number of pitched-up balls to the leg stump. **1903** *Westm. Gaz.* 8 May 3/2 One disastrous bump, baffling all calculation, that may happen to it off a pitched-up shot. **1904** *Daily Chron.* 12 May 7/3 Both batsmen scored fairly regularly in front of the wicket by driving any over-pitched ball.

7. [partly f. PITCH *sb.*²] With defining word: Having a pitch of specified kind or magnitude (high, low, etc.): see HIGH-PITCHED, LOW-PITCHED. **a.** Of a roof or building, or of a plough (PITCH *sb.*² 21, 24 c and e).

1615 G. SANDYS *Trav.* 119 Yet are the roofes high pitcht. **1793** *Trans. Soc. Arts* (ed. 2) IV. 8 A small deep-pitched, double-breasted plough. **1902** *Daily Chron.* 29 Oct. 7/1 The open lofty-pitched oak roof.

b. Having a specified musical pitch (*sb.*² 23).

1622–1898 [see LOW-PITCHED 1]. **1748** [see HIGH-PITCHED 1]. **1880** VERN. LEE *Stud. Italy* IV. iii. 169 A natural law of music makes the highest pitched voice invariably the most important.

pitched (pɪtʃt), *ppl. a.*² Also *Sc.* 5 **pykked**, 6 **pikit.** [f. PITCH *v.*² + -ED¹.] Smeared, covered, saturated, or otherwise treated with pitch.

c **1420** *Pallad. on Husb.* III. 809 Into a picced [*v.r.* pitched] potte he wol hem glene. **1600** NASHE *Summer's Last Will* in Hazl. *Dodsley* VIII. 46 Their gargarisms, clysters, and pitch'd-cloths. **1634** W. WOOD *New Eng. Prosp.* (1865) 56 A long coarse coate, to keepe better things from the pitched ropes and plankes. **1875** MERIVALE *Gen. Hist. Rome* lix. (1877) 472 He condemned them to be burnt, wrapped in pitched cloth, in his own gardens.

β. **1483** *Cath. Angl.* 278/1 Pykked, *bituminatus.* **1513** DOUGLAS *Æneis* VIII. ii. 54 The pikit bargis of fyr fast can thring.

pitcher¹ (ˈpɪtʃə(r)). Forms: *α.* 3–5 **picher**, 4–6 **pycher**, (4 **-ere**), 5–6 **pychar**, (5 **-are**), (6 **pitchaer**, **pytcher**, **pitchard**), 6– **pitcher**; *β.* 4–5 **pecher**, 5 **-ir**, 5–6 *Sc.* **-ar**. [ME. *picher*, *pecher*, a. OF. *pichier* (12th c.), *picier*, *pechier*, *picher* (mod.F. *pichet*, dial. *picher*, *pichier*, *petier*, Gascon *pichey*, Valencian *pitxer*, It. *picchiere*):—pop.L. type **piccāri-um*, in med.L. *picārium*, *bicārium*: see BEAKER. From L. also OHG. *pechari*, *pehhar*, *behhari* drinking-cup (Ger. *becher*), whence app. It. '*pecchero*.]

1. a. A large vessel usually of earthenware, with a handle (or two ears) and usually a lip, for holding and pouring out liquids; a jug; a jug-shaped or vase-shaped vessel; *spec.* in *Ceramics*, fired clay or shards used in the manufacturing process.

Now, in general use somewhat of a literary archaism, but locally applied to 'various specific kinds of earthenware vessels', differentiated in size or material from 'jug' (see *Eng. Dial. Dict.*); in some localities a milk-jug; in U.S. applied to a bedroom jug or ewer; in Scotland often to a large earthenware jar with two ears, in which drinking-water is kept; in some districts of Scotl. to a vessel of tinned iron, as a milk can.

c **1290** *S. Eng. Leg.* I. 427/247 For a lof and a picher wyn: Mi wyf me sende ech day. **1303** R. BRUNNE *Handl. Synne* 10748 She offred for hym to þe auter, Ful of wyne, a pecher. *c* **1430** *Two Cookery-bks.* 39 Fulle þi Pechir of þin farsure. *c* **1440** *Partonope* 3857 A pycher he had full of water. **1470** *Burgh. Rec. Prestwick* 7 May (Maitl. Cl.) 17 A cop of quhat pechar he plessis. **1514** BARCLAY *Cyt. & Uplondyshm.* (Percy Soc.) 14 None can a pytcher tourne to a sylver pece. **1533** MORE *Apol.* 167 Wyth some propleme pulled out of a peny pycher. **1535** COVERDALE *1 Kings* xvii. 14 The meell in the pitcher shall not be spent, & the oyle in yᵉ cruse shall not fayll. **1542** UDALL *Erasm. Apoph.* 49 As for a pitchaer, euery bodye may..sette..in the open strete. **1598** FLORIO, *Pitero*, an earthen pot or potsheard or pitchard. **1608–9** MIDDLETON *Widow* v. i. 139 Broken cruises and pitchers without ears. **1771** J. WEDGWOOD *Let.* 13 Jan. (1965) 101, I have been..busy..in makeing a general review of all my experiment pitchers. **1784** COWPER *Task* IV. 775 There the pitcher stands A fragment, and the spoutless teapot there. **1888** MISS BRADDON *Fatal Three* I. v, Quaintly-shaped pitchers of bright colours were ranged on china brackets along the walls. **1964** H. HODGES *Artifacts* i. 20 Broken or spoilt pottery is commonly used, and while the term grog is general amongst all potters to denote the addition of fired clay, some potters also use the terms pitchers and sherds. *a* **1977** *Harrison Mayer Ltd. Catal.* 14/1 Pitchers, fired, broken or scrap pottery. Biscuit pitchers have various uses when crushed or ground.

local. **1879** MISS JACKSON *Shropsh. Word-bk.* 327 *Pitchers*, earthenware vessels of the finer kinds, common china included. **1886** ELWORTHY *W. Somerset Word-bk.* s.v., The *pitcher* is always made of coarse brown earthenware (cloam). If of finer ware, or china, it is a jug. **1897** FLANDRAU *Harvard Episodes* 182 The orator calms himself with ice-water from the bedroom pitcher.

b. Prov. ***pitchers have ears*** (with pun on EAR *sb.*¹ 3 and 8); i.e. beware, there may be persons listening or overhearing: in the form ***little pitchers have wide*** or ***long ears*** (etc.) said in reference to children. ***the pitcher goes often to the well, but is broken at last*** (etc.): said of a long-continued course of success (or impunity), ending at length in failure (or punishment).

1546 J. HEYWOOD *Prov.* (1867) 53 Aucyd your children, small pitchers haue wide eares. **1591** GREENE *Art Conny Catch.* II. (1592) 15 Yet at last so long the pitcher goeth to the brooke, that it commeth broken home. **1596** SHAKS. *Tam. Shr.* IV. iv. 52 Not in my house Lucentio, for you know Pitchers haue eares, and I haue manie seruants. **1826** SCOTT *Woodst.* xxii, The pitcher goes oft to the well—. **1883** *Pall Mall G.* 3 Oct. 3/2 The pitcher, however, has gone once too often to the well, and yesterday..the panorama caught fire in earnest, and was reduced to ashes. **1886** MISS TYTLER *Buried Diamonds* xiii, Surely Miss Gray, knowing that little pitchers have ears, would have corrected the mistake.

2. *Bot.* A leaf, or a part of one, modified into the form of a pitcher (see PITCHER-PLANT): = ASCIDIUM 2. (In quot. 1797, a part of a petal.)

1797 tr. *Linnæus' Fam. Plants* I. 381 Petals..gibbous without a base, excavated within into a pitcher. **1845** R. CHAMBERS *Vestiges* (ed. 4) 201 The pitcher, as this is called, is not a new organ, but simply the metamorphosis of a leaf. **1857** HENFREY *Bot.* §101 *Pitchers* (*ascidia*) are structures of the form indicated by their name, produced by peculiar modes of development of the petiole, the blade, or of both together. **1875** DARWIN *Insectiv. Pl.* vi. 97 The pitchers of Nepenthes possess extraordinary power of digestion.

3. *attrib.* and *Comb.*, as ***pitcher-like***, ***-shaped*** adjs.; † **pitcher-man**, a man addicted to drinking, a toper; † **pitcher-meat**, potable food, drink; **pitcher-mould**, a terra-cotta mould in which the bodies of earthenware pitchers or other vessels were formerly made; so **pitcher-moulding**, the operation of casting in a pitcher-mould; **pitcher-nose** (see quot.); † **pitcher-praise**, ? compliment by drinking one's health; † **pitcher-souled** *a.*, stupid, stolid; **pitcher-vase**, a vase of the form of a pitcher. See also PITCHER-HOUSE, -PLANT.

1830 MISS MITFORD *Village* Ser. IV. (1863) 314 A *pitcher-like cream jug. **1861** BENTLEY *Man. Bot.* 480 The order [*Marcgraviaceæ*] is chiefly interesting for the curious pitcher-like bracts which some of their genera exhibit. **1694** MOTTEUX *Rabelais* IV. i, The Travellers were all honest Topers, true *Pitcher-men. **1738** *Poor Robin* (N.), Boon blades, true pitcher-men. **1551** ASCHAM *Let. to E. Raven* 14 May, Wks. (1815) 366 The best physician in the world, because he gives him *pitcher-meat enough. **1884** KNIGHT *Dict. Mech.* Supp., **Pitcher Nose*, said of a faucet with a bent down lip. **1654** GAYTON *Pleas. Notes* IV. v. 195 So Don Diego Garcia of Par-edes, Hath **Pitcher-praise*, and double health his meed is. **1830** LINDLEY *Nat. Syst. Bot.* 155 *Pitcher-shaped leaves. *a* **1739** JARVIS *Quix.* II. III. xv, He looks like a *pitcher-souled fellow [*alma de cántaro*].

pitcher² (ˈpɪtʃə(r)). [f. PITCH *v.*¹ + -ER¹.]

I. One who pitches.

1. a. *Harvesting.* One who pitches the hay or sheaves to the loader on a cart, wagon, or rick.

a **1722** LISLE *Husb.* (1752) 217 It is good husbandry to have two pitchers to one loader in the field. **1840** *Tait's Mag.* VII. 513 What loads that tall pitcher is lifting to the waggon-top! *a* **1847** ELIZA COOK *Song of Haymakers* i, The pitchers, and rakers, and merry haymakers.

b. In various industries, a workman who pitches, sets, or places something: see quots. Also, a market porter.

1865 J. T. F. TURNER *Slate Quarries* 15 The finished slates are then taken by the 'pitchers', and carried..to the show-yard. There they count and pitch them. **1883** GRESLEY *Gloss. Coal-mining*, *Pitchers*,..loaders in the pit, and men who take up and relay the rails in the workings and long-wall faces. **1891** *Scott. Leader* 21 Jan. 4 [A man] employed as a stone pitcher at Camphill Water Works. **1966** *New Statesman* 7 Oct. 531/2 The grandmother had been married to a Smithfield meat 'pitcher' who had died of cancer. **1970** *Times* 26 Feb. 10/2 No longer are porters divided into pitchers (the men who carry fruit in), plain porters (who carry it out) and stand men (who work inside warehouse or shop).

c. A street vendor who pitches a stall at a definite place or occupies a 'pitch': cf. PITCH *sb.*² 11.

1896 C. BOOTH *Life & Labour of People* VII. III. ii. 261 The pitcher..transforms his barrow, which on its way through the streets has displayed nothing but boxes and loose boards, into a full-blown market stall, while the barrow of the coster is so arranged as to display its stock at all times. **1896** *Daily News* 21 Nov. 5/1 He claimed to be a 'coster', but if he is anything he is a 'pitcher'.

2. A player who pitches or delivers a ball, etc., in various games; esp. in Baseball, the player that stands in the space called the ***pitcher's box***, near the centre of the diamond, and pitches or delivers the ball to the batter.

1845, 1867 [see BALK *sb.*¹ 5 b]. **1870** EMERSON *Misc. Papers, Plutarch* Wks. (Bohn) III. 347 They are like the baseball players, to whom the pitcher, the bat, the catcher, and the scout are equally important. **1872** *Routledge's Ev. Boy's Ann.* 604 The object of the pitcher is to get the ball in the hole. **1885** E. L. DIDIER in *Harper's Mag.* Apr. 722/2 He was one of the most famous pitchers in Virginia, and always used the heaviest quoits. **1902** R. CONNOR *Sky Pilot* iv, In the pitcher's box he puzzled the Porcupines till they grew desperate. **1948** *Chicago Daily News* 4 June 36/8 Claude Passeau's job with the Cubs is to tutor young pitchers throughout the Chicago farm system. **1949** *Lafayette Alumnus* (Lafayette College, Easton, Pa.) 24 Oct. 1/2 By crashing in he ruined innumerable would-be pass plays getting the pitcher for losses averaging 9 yards. **1974** *Post-Herald* (Birmingham, Alabama) 29 June A14/3 Lane gave the Tigers a 2–0 lead with a two-run homer in the second innings off losing pitcher Kevin Kobel. **1978** *Verbatim* Feb. 2/2 A ballplayer who is not an infielder, outfielder or pitcher, and is thus doomed to be a catcher, wears 'the tools of ignorance', catcher's gear.

II. Something pitched, or used for pitching.

3. An iron bar for making holes in the ground, as for setting stakes or hop-poles: = PITCH *sb.*² 7 a.

1707 MORTIMER *Husb.* (1721) I. 199 A Frame of six Poles let into the Ground with an Iron Pitcher or Crow. **1848** *Jrnl. R. Agric. Soc.* IX. II. 553 The hole previously made by an iron bar, called a hop-pitcher.

4. *local.* A cutting, rod, or stake planted in the ground in order to take root; cf. PITCH *sb.*² 7 b.

e.g. A bough or rod of willow, poplar, or elder, so planted, esp. in making a hedge (*South of Eng.*); a cutting of an apple-tree set in the ground, or a tree grown from such a cutting (*W. Eng., Pembr., Ireland*).

1780 A. YOUNG *Tour Irel.* II. 203 A common practice here in planting orchards, is to set cuttings, three or four feet long, half way in the ground..they call them pitchers. **1785** in *Young's Ann. Agric.* IV. 245 Withy plants, which in this county [Som.] are very useful for stakes (or pitchers as they are called) for making hedges. **1843** J. SMITH *Forest Trees* 156 Irish pitcher..is a very fine standard [apple-tree]. **1886** [see PITCH *sb.*² 7].

5. A stone used for paving, e.g. the small flints or pebbles used in paving yards, etc.; also the brick-shaped granite 'setts' used for crossings, and sometimes for streets. See PITCH *v.*¹ 5 b.

1862 ANSTED *Channel Isl.* IV. xxii. (ed. 2) 503 Besides the ordinary cubes and pitchers for paving, a considerable quantity of granite is cut and sold for kerbs. **1866** *Faversham Gaz.* 27 Jan., The new stones required for this work will be 254 tons of pitchers, 25 tons of curb. **1897** *Standard* 17 Apr., The comparative merits of granite pitchers, so-called macadam, asphalte, and wood paving.

6. Various dialect or local uses: e.g. the flat stone or piece of wood pitched in hop-scotch, or at a mark or hole in various games; the marble with which a boy aims. See *Eng. Dial. Dict.*

pitcher³. *rare*⁻⁰. [f. PITCH *v.*² + -ER¹.] One who pitches, or who covers or caulks with pitch.

1611 COTGR., *Goildronneur*, a pitcher, trimmer, or tighter of ships.

pitcher⁴. repr. a vulgar or colloq. pronunciation of PICTURE *sb.*

1916 [see HUMDINGER 1]. **1931** *Amer. Speech* Oct. 46 *Moom pitcher* for moving picture. **1936** MENCKEN *Amer. Lang.* (ed. 4) vii. 352 On the vulgar level *amateur* is always *amachoor*, and *picture* is *pitchur* or *pitcher*. **1977** J. WAMBAUGH *Black Marble* (1978) vii. 99 She do look somethin like that dumpy consti-pated broad in the pitcher.

pitcherful (ˈpɪtʃəfʊl). [f. PITCHER¹ + -FUL] The quantity that fills a pitcher.

1693 EVELYN *De la Quint. Compl. Gard.* II. 163 Artichokes growing in light Grounds, have need of a Pitcher full or two of Water, for each Plant. **1826** SCOTT *Diary* 14 June in *Lockhart*, You stand like a child going to be bathed, shivering and shaking till the first pitcherful is flung about your ears. **1894** G. ROBSON *Jamaica Mission* 86 Wandering for miles in search of a pitcherful [of water].

† **ˈpitcher-house.** *Obs.* A room in a great house, in which the wine and ale were kept.

1464 *Rolls of Parlt.* V. 540/1 Grome of the Picher house of oure Howshold. *a* **1548** HALL *Chron., Hen. VIII* 74 Ewery, Pantrie, Seller, Buttery, Spicery, pitcher house. **1601** F. TATE *Househ. Ord. Edw. II* (1876) 29 Two valletes de mestier of the picher-house, who shal serve the hal of wine and ale. **1684** E. CHAMBERLAYNE *Pres. St. Eng.* I. (ed. 15) 155 Sergeant of the Cellar, who is also Sergeant of the Buttery, and Pitcher-house. **1826** HOR. SMITH *Tor Hill* (1838) I. 236 Deem you that knights' esquires pass their life in the pantry and pitcher-house?

ˈpitchering. *nonce-wd.* [f. PITCHER¹ + -ING¹.] The action of pouring from a pitcher.

1820 MISS MITFORD in L'Estrange *Life* (1870) II. 109 A job compared to which the water pitcherings of the Danaides were hopeful.

pitcher-plant. [f. PITCHER¹ + PLANT *sb.*¹] Name for several plants which have the leaves, or some of them, modified into the form of a pitcher, often containing a liquid secretion by means of which insects are captured and assimilated by the plant; *esp.* the south-east Asian genus *Nepenthes*, and the N. American genus *Sarracenia*.

Also *Darlingtonia californica*, and *Heliamphora nutans* of Guiana (both allied to *Sarracenia*) and *Cephalotus follicularis* of Australia.

1819 L. A. ANSPACH *Hist. Newfoundland* xiv. 362 Another still more remarkable plant, found in the woods of Newfoundland, is the *Saracenia* [*sic*], commonly called side-saddle flower, or pitcher-plant. **1835** HENSLOW *Princ. Bot.* I. §80 In the Nepenthes, or true pitcher-plant, the pitcher is placed at the extremity of a tendril, terminating a winged petiole. It is crowned with a membranous lid. **1857** GRAY *First Lessons Bot.* (1866) 51 The common Pitcher-plant or Side-saddle Flower..of our bogs. **1883** G. ALLEN in *Longm. Mag.* July 311 The pitcher plants allure flies into their murderous vessels. **1929** ROBBINS & RICKETT *Botany* xxiii. 356 Some of the most striking leaf modifications are in the plants known as pitcher plants. **1938** [see BAKE-APPLE]. **1947** I. L. IDRIESS *Isles of Despair* xxxiii. 220 She could not sleep.., thinking of the phantom pygmies in the pitcher-plant swamps. **1965** *Austral. Encycl.* VII. 123/2 The Western Australian pitcher-plant is *Cephalotus follicularis*. **1965** D. HENDERSON *Heart of Newfoundland* 19 We had seen pitcher plants before..but never in such numbers as are found in Newfoundland. **1973** *Sci. Amer.* Dec. 64/2 In these [Borneo] forests the insect-eating pitcher plants (*Nepenthes*) are common. **1977** *Borneo Bull.* 7 May 8/1 Did you know that of 30 pitcher plant species found in Borneo, 16 are said to be found on the mountain, and many of them are peculiar to its slopes?

pitcher(r)y, variation of PITURI.

pitch-faced: see PITCH *sb.*² 26.

ˈpitch-ˌfarthing. [PITCH *v.*¹ 17.] A game resembling pitch-and-toss, in which the coins, instead of being tossed so as to fall 'head or tail', were pitched towards a hole, so as to afford more scope for skill; = CHUCK-FARTHING, q.v.

1742 CHESTERF. *Lett.* (1792) I. xciv. 268 Your various occupations of Greek and cricket, Latin and pitch-farthing. **1861** HUGHES *Tom Brown at Oxf.* xix. (1889) 186 A group of half-grown lads were playing at pitch-farthing.

† **pitch-field.** *Obs.* A pitched field of battle: cf. PITCH-BATTLE.

1611 BEAUM. & FL. *Knt. Burn. Pest.* II. ii, There has been a pitchfield, my child, between the naughty Spaniels and the

Englishmen. **1654** WHITLOCK *Zootomia* 84 No Pitch-field ever slew, or wounded more than they have cured.

pitch-fir: see PITCH *sb.*[1] 5.

pitchfork ('pɪtʃfɔːk), *sb.*[1] Forms: 5 pych-, pycche-, 6 pyche-, pytche-, pitche-, 6– pitchfork, etc. [Also (in earlier use) PICKFORK, *dial. pikefork*, app. orig. f. PICK *sb.*[1], PIKE *sb.*[1]; afterwards associated with PITCH *v.*[1], from its use in pitching sheaves, etc.] A long-handled fork with two sharp prongs, for lifting and pitching hay, straw, or sheaves; sometimes applied to a short-handled fork for lifting dung, breaking clods, etc. Phr. ***to rain pitchforks***, to rain hard.

1452 *Maldon, Essex, Court Rolls* Bundle 31 No. 1 Ipsum percussit cum baculo vocato pychforke. **1530** PALSGR. 254/2 Pytche forke, *fovrche fiere.* **c 1540** R. MORICE in *Lett. Lit. Men* (Camden) 24 A gentilman..toke a fyrre bushe on a forke, or a pitchefork. **c 1600** DAY *Begg. Bednall Gr.* IV. iii, Let me dye like a Dog on a Pitch-fork. **1685** *Lond. Gaz.* No. 2046/1 Between 2 and 3000..some with Musquets, some with Pistols, some with Pikes, and some with Pitch-forks and Sythes. **1738** SWIFT *Pol. Conversat.* 52 She wears her Cloaths, as if they were thrown on her with a Pitch-Fork. **1815** D. HUMPHREYS *Yankey in Eng.* 55 I'll be even with you, if it rains pitchforks—tines downwards. **1850** J. R. PLANCHÉ *Island of Jewels* II. iii. 31 Rain cats and dogs, or pitchforks perpendicular, The sky's not mine, and need'nt be particular. **1852** ROGET *Thesaurus* §348 To rain..in torrents, rain cats and dogs, rain pitchforks. **1930** J. DOS PASSOS *42nd Parallel* I. 77 Outside it was raining pitchforks. **1940** M. FISHBACK *Time for Quick One* 77 It's raining cats and dogs And pitchforks and assorted frogs.
attrib. **1788** BARKER in *Phil. Trans.* LXXVIII. 413 About as thick as a pitch-fork shaft.

'pitchfork, *sb.*[2] [f. PITCH *sb.*[2] 23 + FORK *sb.*, after PITCH-PIPE.] A tuning-fork, used for setting the pitch of a tune or instrument.

1881 BROADHOUSE *Mus. Acoustics* 406 The Tuning-fork, originally called the Pitch-fork. **1892** *Daily News* 23 Dec. 5/2 The introduction of new tunes called for the use of the sonorous little instrument called a 'pitch-fork'.

'pitchfork, *v.* [f. PITCHFORK *sb.*[1]]
1. *trans.* To throw or cast with, or as with, a pitchfork; to pitch forcibly or roughly.

1837 *Times* 22 June, Resolved to drive the nuisance from their den, They'll probably pitchfork it back again. **1870** *Observer* 9 July, The meal is brought and pitchforked to the diners [lions]. **1873** MRS. WHITNEY *Other Girls* vi. 74 Reminding..possibly of a hay-load; being so very much pitchforked up into heaps behind.

b. *fig.*; *esp.* to thrust (a person) forcibly or unsuitably into some position or office.

1844 W. H. MAXWELL *Sports & Adv. Scotl.* (1855) 14 To achieve an entrance into St. Stephen's, you might submit..to be pitchforked in..by the priests. **1848** W. H. KELLY tr. *L. Blanc's Hist. Ten Y.* I. 245 To have the descendants of Henri IV. pitchforked out of the country. **1863** P. BARRY *Dockyard Econ.* 68 Whether he was pitchforked into the service or rose meritoriously is now a matter of indifference.

2. To stab or attack with a pitchfork.

1854 LEECH *Pict. Life & Char.* (1855) 22 Vowing that he will pitchfork Mr. B. if he comes 'galloperravering' over his fences.

Hence **'pitchforked** *ppl. a.*, **-forking** *vbl. sb.*

1891 *Daily News* 9 Nov. 3/1 This reckless pitchforking of unnecessary furniture. **1899** *Dundee Advertiser* 10 Oct. 4 The pitchforked man..would fall the just prey to all the generation of ladder-climbers.

pitch-hill: see PITCH *sb.*[2] 26.

pitch-hole[1]. [f. PITCH *v.*[1] + HOLE *sb.*] **1.** A hole into which something pitches or is pitched; an opening in the wall of a barn, etc. through which corn or hay is pitched.

1805 R. W. DICKSON *Pract. Agric.* I. 47 A man will unload nearly two loads of grain drawn into the barn and unloaded upon the mow, while he could unload one at a pitch-hole. **1887** *Cornh. Mag.* Mar. 273 You have passed through a 'pitch-hole', the toboggan rises high in the air.

2. *N. Amer.* A defect in a road or trail; a pot-hole.

1874 *Rep. Vermont Board Agric.* II. 659 The highways leading to our larger villages..are frequently so full of pitchholes or 'cahoos' as to render them totally unfit for travel. **1890** *Harper's Mag.* Oct. 657/2 The highway was frequently interrupted by 'pitch holes'. **1936** A. F. CROSS *Cross Roads* (ed. 2) 106 Charlie's horses jogged on with us..into pitch holes that jarred one's innards terribly. **1962** D. J. DICKIE *Great Golden Plain* 288 The cat train rocks and plunges over the hummocks and pitch holes in the ice and snow roads.

'pitch-hole[2]. [f. PITCH *sb.*[1] + HOLE *sb.*] A hole or pit containing 'pitch' or bitumen.

1900 *Westm. Gaz.* 21 July 3/1 The wonderful pitch-hole ..becomes a lively volcano.

pitchi ('pɪtʃɪ). *Austral.* [Aboriginal.] A dish or container hollowed out of a solid log.

1896 E. C. STIRLING in B. Spencer *Rep. Horn Sci. Expedition Cent. Austral.* IV. 98 The name 'Pitchi'..is in general use, by the whites of the parts traversed by the Expedition, for the wooden vessels used for carrying food and water and, occasionally, infants. **1931** I. L. IDRIESS *Lasseter's Last Ride* (1933) xvi. 128 In little canoe-shaped pitchis of wood some women carried native foods. **1934** A. RUSSELL *Tramp-Royal in Wild Austral.* xxvii. 179 Poised on his [*sc.* an aboriginal's] head was a newly cut bark pitchi filled to the brim with wild oranges. **1959** S. H. COURTIER *Death in Dream Time* viii. 112 While his thumbs bleed, the elders bring a *pitchi*, a wooden vessel, and catch the blood. **1970** 'E. LINDALL' *Gathering of Eagles* x. 119 In her hands.. was a wooden pitchi full of water.

pitch-in ('pɪtʃɪn). *U.S. colloq.* Also **pitchin**. [f. PITCH *sb.*[2] + IN *adv.*] Applied, usu. *attrib.*, to a large common meal to which each diner contributes food or drink.

1973 *Sunday Bull.* (Philadelphia) 7 Oct. (Parade Suppl.) 26/2 The answers were as varied as the food at a large pitch-in picnic. **1976** *Laurel* (Montana) *Outlook* 16 June 9/1 The Park City Garden Club guest night was held at the civic center with a pitchin dinner. **1976** *Columbus* (Montana) *News* 17 June 6/3 Mr. and Mrs. Charles Wark were hosts at a pitch-in picnic for members and their families.

'pitchiness. [f. PITCHY *a.* + -NESS.] The quality of being pitchy; intense darkness or blackness.

1598 FLORIO, *Orco*..the darknes or pitchines in hell. **1831** J. WILSON in *Blackw. Mag.* XXIX. 722 She swings and sways along the snow-crested pitchiness of her rolling path.

pitching ('pɪtʃɪŋ), *vbl. sb.*[1] [f. PITCH *v.*[1] + -ING[1].] The action of PITCH *v.*[1]; also *concr.*
1. The action of fixing or planting in the ground or in some surface.

c 1380 WYCLIF *Serm.* Sel. Wks. I. 137 þe picching of þe naillis. **1551** RECORDE *Pathw. Knowl.* I. xxxiv, Drawing twoo arche lines at euery pitchinge of the compas. **1773** *Gentl. Mag.* XLIII. 567 The pitching of the wicket. **1850** 'BAT' *Cricket. Man.* 39 The pitching of the wickets devolves upon the umpires.

2. The setting up of a tent or the like.

1398 TREVISA *Barth. De P.R.* IX. xxxiii. (Bodl. MS.), Cenophagia..was icleped picchinge of tentes. **1591** PERCIVALL *Sp. Dict.*, *Assentamiento*, placing, sitting, pitching of a campe. **1809** MALKIN *Gil Blas* II. ix. ⁋3 These tents in the plain are of our pitching.

3. The placing of goods in a market for sale; a payment charged for this.

1612 *Indenture* in G. G. Francis *Orig. Charters Neath* (1845), The towle custome the pitching the killage and anchoradge. **1858** SIMMONDS *Dict. Trade*, *Pitching*, a market term for unloading, and for the small charge paid to the carrier for looking after the empty packages and cloths, and returning them correctly.

†**4.** Fixing, determination. *Obs.*

1599 in Fowler *Hist. C.C.C.* (O.H.S.) 351 About the pitching of fines..and grants of copyhold land.

†**5.** ? Transfixing or spearing (of eels). *Obs.* Cf. PICK *sb.*[1] 4 d.

1674 *Maldon, Essex, Borough Deeds* Bundle 99 No. 1v, For pitching, catching, and taking of eeles and floatfish.

6. a. The action of setting, planting, or fixing in some place or position; *spec.* of stones in paving; also, the facing of a bank or slope with stones set on edge close together, as a protection against waves or currents.

1703 MOXON *Mech. Exerc.* 223 This Ball will require three Pitchings into the Mandrel. **1717** TABOR in *Phil. Trans.* XXX. 554 This Pitching or Paving. **1842–76** GWILT *Archit.* §1672 Aberdeen granite is most extensively employed for curbs, trams, and pitching; the latter in thin cubes about 9 inches in depth, 3 inches in thickness, and not exceeding 18 inches in length. **1846** *Hull & Lincoln Railw. Bill* 11 Stones for building, pitching, and paving. **1852** WIGGINS *Embanking* 124 The expense of the facing of the bank comes next under consideration..In cases where pitching has been thought necessary, and that, 18 inches deep. **1891** *Pall Mall G.* 26 June 6/2 The Manchester Ship Canal..At many points where the pitching had not been completed, the soft earth was cut up into deep gullies, and the sandy slope looked blistered and threatening.

b. *concr.* Pavement composed of cobbles or granite 'setts' firmly set up; also, a facing of stone on a bank or slope.

1693 E. HARLEY in *14th Rep. Hist. MSS. Comm.* App. II. 514 The court is levelled, and laid very dry..without any pitching. **1751** W. HALFPENNY *New Designs Farm Ho.* 6, 138 Yards of pitching in the Court, Stable &c. **1828** *Sporting Mag.* XXII. 349, I made my horse stand bare footed on round stones, or pitching, as it is called. **1885** WARREN & CLEVERLY *Wanderings of Battle* 102 The ponderous cannon thundered over the uneven pitching of the streets.

c. The foundation of a macadamized road made of stones 6 or 8 inches deep, laid on edge by hand, so as to form an arched support for the broken metalling, and to distribute the weight of the traffic.

1830 *Pract. Treat. Roads* 8 (*Libr. Usef. Knowl., Husb.* III.), Pitching is a foundation formed of large stones.

7. The action of throwing, hurling, or 'lofting' something so that it may fall on a particular spot; *esp.* of a ball in certain games, as baseball, golf, (cf. PITCH *sb.*[2] 3). Also *attrib.*

1652 FRENCH *Yorksh. Spa* xi. 96, I commend walking, bowling, pitching of the bar, and leaping. **1858** *N.Y. Tribune* 18 Aug. 7/3 The pitching was good on both sides. **1896** H. CHADWICK *Spalding's Base Ball Guide* 2 A new form of pitching tables are included in the records of the pitching of 1895. **1901** *Scotsman* 26 Mar. 5/3 (Golf) His pitching was quite equal to that of the Newbattle professional, and his putting was..superior. **1942** [see MAJOR *a.* 1 e]. **1944** *College Topics* (Univ. of Virginia) 30 Mar. 3 As for the pitching staff, there is plenty of material that will eventually develop into the team's strongest asset. **1948** *Richmond* (Va.) *Times-Dispatch* 15 Mar. 17/4 Blackwell learned how to throw it from Hal Schumacher, former New York Giants pitching star. **1969** *Eugene* (Oregon) *Register-Guard* 3 Dec. 2D/4 Cal Ermer..landed a coaching job, as pitching tutor for Bristol's Seattle club. **1976** *National Observer* (U.S.) 21 Feb. 19/2 (Advt.), Mickey Owen Baseball School... 4 Lighted Batting Cages, 2 Pitching Machines.

8. a. The forward downward plunging of a ship.

1877 W. H. WHITE *Naval Archit.* (1882) 210 The longitudinal oscillations of pitching and scending.

b. *Aeronaut.* and *Astronautics.* Angular motion of an aircraft or spacecraft about a lateral axis (the *pitching axis*: see 12 below).

1912 G. GREENHILL *Dynamics Mech. Flight* iv. 83 Rolling and pitching of a steamer or flying machine. **1915** A. FAGE *Aeroplane* vi. 75 The following nomenclature has been adopted at the National Physical Laboratory:—[*table*] Name of axis..Lateral... Name of Motion which takes place about Axis..Pitching. **1935** C. G. BURGE *Encycl. Aviation* 579/1 Rotary motion of the aeroplane about the lateral axis is called pitching. **1958** D. PIGGOTT *Gliding* xiii. 78 To stop the pitching, the pilot must relax the backward pressure on the stick and reduce the climbing angle for a few moments. **1965** C. N. VAN DEVENTER *Introd. Gen. Aeronaut.* v. 84/1 The lateral axis is the side-to-side axis about which the airplane revolves in pitching, when its nose and tail move up and down. **1968** T. DE GALIANA *Conc. Encycl. Astronaut.* 210/2 For a cylindrical spacecraft,..pitching is a movement of the nose up or down (that is, away from or towards the orbit focus).

9. The interlocking or engaging of one cog-wheel with another, etc.

1825 J. NICHOLSON *Operat. Mechanic* 486 The communication or action of one wheel with another is called the pitching. **1885** C. G. W. LOCK *Workshop Receipts* Ser. IV. 323/2 The fly pitching may next be examined.

10. *Brewing.* (See PITCH *v.*[1] 22.)

11. The yellowish deposit on tanned leather: = BLOOM *sb.*[1] 4 c.

1857 C. TOMLINSON in *Encycl. Brit.* (ed. 8) XIII. 307/2 A portion of its gelatin..is, by combination with a portion of tannin..deposited upon its surfaces..in the form of a yellow deposit, technically known as *bloom*, or *pitching*.

12. *attrib.* and *Comb.*, as ***pitching-place***, ***-stand***; **pitching axis** *Aeronaut.* and *Astronautics*, a lateral axis of an aircraft, etc., about which pitching takes place, usu. specified to be perpendicular to its longitudinal axis or to its direction of flight; of a spacecraft, one of two horizontal axes (cf. *yawing axis* s.v. YAWING *vbl. sb.*) which are perpendicular to each other and to the longitudinal axis; = *pitch axis* s.v. PITCH *sb.*[2] 26; **pitching-bar** = PITCHER[2] 3; **pitching-block** (see quot.); **pitching heat** *Brewing* = *pitching temperature*; **pitching-hole** = PITCH-HOLE[1] 1; **pitching machine** *Brewing*, a special kind of vessel in which pitching of the wort takes place; **pitching moment** *Aeronaut.*, a moment tending to turn an aircraft, etc., about its pitching axis; **pitching-pence** *sb. pl.* (see quot.); **pitching-piece**, a piece of timber at the top of a wooden staircase, supporting the 'carriage' or framework (correlative to the *apron-piece*, at the bottom); **pitching-stables** (see quot.); **pitching-stone**, a stone used for pitching a road: see 6 c; **pitching-temperature**, in *Brewing*, the temperature at which the wort is pitched (see PITCH *v.*[1] 22); **pitching-tool**, (*a*) a prehistoric chisel, made of an antler or other hard substance, used with a hammer in flaking off flint, etc., for making arrow-heads, etc.; (*b*) in *Watchmaking*, a tool for placing the wheels of watches in position between the plates; (*c*) in *Mining*, 'a kind of pick used in commencing a hole' (Knight *Dict. Mech.*), a pitching-bar; **pitching-yeast**, yeast used or prepared for use in pitching wort.

1920 W. J. WALKER tr. *Devillers's Dynamics of Aeroplane* xii. 234 The moment of inertia in movements about the *pitching axis plays the rôle of mass in rectilinear displacements. **1953** *New Biol.* XIV. 66 Stability can be related to any of the three axes—the rolling axis.., the yawing axis,..and the pitching axis (horizontally at right angles to the direction of flight). **1959** Pitching axis [see *pitch axis* s.v. PITCH *sb.*[2] 26]. **1879** JEFFERIES *Amateur Poacher* ii. (1889) 29 The shepherd..threw his *pitching-bar over his shoulder. **1884** J. PAYN *Lit. Recollect.* 211 The *pitching block, where the porters rest their burdens. **1876** *Encycl. Brit.* IV. 275/1 The heat at which the wort is let down into the fermenting tun. This '*pitching heat' varies very much. **1885** E. R. SOUTHBY *Syst. Handbk. Pract. Brewing* (ed. 2) xx. 335, I have already explained that this lowering of the pitching heat is by no means essential. **1805** R. W. DICKSON *Pract. Agric.* I. 47 Barns..intended for containing large quantities of different crops..should constantly be provided with convenient *pitching holes for housing them at. **1940** H. L. HIND *Brewing* II. 854 Simple *pitching machines consist of a cauldron, in which the pitch is melted over a coke fire or by gas, and forced by compressed air through a spraying nozzle into the cask. **1957** K. BARTON-WRIGHT tr. *De Clerck's Textbk. Brewing* I. xxii. 483 In modern pitching machines..the old lining is no longer removed with hot air, ..but with very thinned pitch. **1913** *Rep. & Mem. Advisory Comm. Aeronaut.* No. 74. 10 Measurements of lift, drift, and *pitching moment at varying values of the pitching angle from − 10° to + 25°. **1931** *Technol. Rev.* Nov. 65/1 It seems inevitable that the next generation must know as much about *ailerons*, *pitching moments*, and *dihedral angles*, as the present one does about carburetors, differentials, and wheel bases. **1966** D. STINTON *Anat. Aeroplane* xi. 199 Further pitching moments..are introduced by wing-mounted stores,..engines, flaps and undercarriage units. **1706** PHILLIPS, **Pitching-Pence*, a Duty paid for pitching, or setting down every Sack of Corn or Pack of Merchandizes, in a Fair or Market. **1823** P. NICHOLSON *Pract. Build.* 189 A *Pitching-piece is a piece of timber wedged into the wall..

for supporting the rough strings at the top of the lower flight. **1858** SIMMONDS *Dict. Trade*, **Pitching-stables*, a kind of shaped Cornish granite, 4 or 6 inches long, used for paving. **1899** *Westm. Gaz.* 14 Feb. 5/1 To rent the casual cart stands, yearly cart stands, and yearly *pitching stands in the market. **1824** W. DEYKES *Pavement Metrop.* 6 The adoption of squared paving stones instead of the small round ones called *pitchen stones. *c* **1830** *Pract. Treat. Roads* 8 in *Libr. Usef. Knowl., Husb.* III, The weight of the flints themselves will form power enough to compose the road, without the solid assistance of the pitching-stones. **1957** *Encycl. Brit.* IV. 105/2 The *pitching temperature is held at 54–59° F. in American practice, slightly higher (58–60° F) in England. **1885** E. R. SOUTHBY *Syst. Handbk. Pract. Brewing* (ed. 2) xx. 320 The yeast cells of a good *pitching yeast should be separate from one another. **1956** [see POLYMYXIN].

ˈpitching, *vbl. sb.*[2] [f. PITCH *v.*[2] + -ING[1].] A smearing or coating with pitch.

pitching-machine, a machine for pitching the insides of casks or barrels.

1580 HOLLYBAND *Treas. Fr. Tong, Poissement*, a pitching with pitch. **1725** DE FOE *Voy. round World* (1840) 326 Without any calking or pitching..to keep out the water. **1822** T. MITCHELL *Aristoph.* I. 242 All the never-ending cares Of pitching, tarring, and repairs.

ˈpitching, *ppl. a.* [f. PITCH *v.*[1] + -ING[2].] That pitches, in various senses of the verb.

1. Sloping, inclining; *fig.* declining. *spec.* in *Geol.* (cf. PITCH *v.*[1] 20, PITCH *sb.*[2] 24 b).

1519 HORMAN *Vulg.* 177 That felde is beste, that is nat playne, euyn, and leuell, but somwhat pytchynge. **1565–73** COOPER *Thesaurus, Cliuosus*, a place stipe downe, or pitching downe. **1611** BIBLE *Judg.* xix. 9 *margin*, It is the pitching time of the day. **1641** J. TRAPPE *Theol. Theol.* vii. 286 As much as it is the pitching time of the day, Judg. 19. 9 it is the last houre. **1939** A. K. LOBECK *Geomorphol.* xvii. 595 The monoclinal ridges which result from the erosion of pitching synclines converge in a direction which is opposite to the pitch of the fold. **1960** B. W. SPARKS *Geomorphol.* vii. 135 Pitching folds may be reflected in a pattern of converging and diverging ridges like that of certain sections of the Appalachians. **1968** C. R. TWIDALE *Geomorphol.* ii. 11 Folds whose outcrops narrow and widen, appear and disappear, are described as pitching or plunging folds.

2. Plunging forwards: see PITCH *v.*[1] 18, 19.

1800 *Naval Chron.* IV. 434 With a heavy pitching sea in the Sound. **1875** WHYTE MELVILLE *Katerfelto* xxiii, He crosses its undulating surface at that free pitching gallop which he seems so rarely to hasten. **1884** PAE *Eustace* 197 It was no easy matter to get over the side of the pitching vessel into the boats. **1906** *Chambers's Jrnl.* July 537/2 It is worth going some distance to see a *vaquero* sticking to a 'pitching' horse. **1948** *Sat. Rev.* 28 Aug. 37/1 Bucky Durant calmly rolled a cigarette as he sat atop the pitching bronc.

3. Settling, alighting. *rare* or *arch.*

1900 *Academy* 8 Sept. 199/1 The voice's trill Sinks like a pitching bird; and all is still.

pitch-in-the-hole, -in-the-tub: see PITCH *v.*[1] 25.

ˈpitch-ˌkettle. [f. PITCH *sb.*[1] + KETTLE.] A large vessel in which pitch is boiled or heated, esp. for use on board ship. Hence †**pitch-kettled** *a.* (*Obs. slang*), utterly puzzled, non-plussed (? as if covered with a pitch-kettle, or with heated pitch from a pitch-kettle).

1486 *Naval Acc. Hen. VII* (1896) 15 A pitch ketle..for the same Ship. **1719** DE FOE *Crusoe* (1840) II. xii. 249, I..bade him heat another pitch-kettle. **1754** COWPER *Ep. to Lloyd* 32 Thus, the preliminaries settled I fairly find myself pitch-kettled. **1876** M. COLLINS *From Midnight to Midn.* III. vii. 92 He was just as thoroughly pitch-kettled (to use an ancient bit of slang) as any gentleman calling himself 'Honourable' well could be.

pitch-knot, -ladle, -like: see PITCH *sb.*[1] 5.

pitch-line: see PITCH *sb.*[2] 26.

†**ˈpitchlongs**, *adv. Obs. rare.* [app. f. PITCH *sb.*[2] 24 + -LONG, -LONGS.] ? With a slope, steeply.

c **1420** *Pallad. on Husb.* VI. 42 But hede hit that the hedes of hem alle [furrows] Into sum gret diche picchelonges falle.

ˈpitchman. *U.S.* [PITCH *sb.*[2]] One who sells gadgets or novelties at a fair or in the street. Also *transf.* and *fig.*, an advertiser, one who delivers a sales pitch (see PITCH *sb.*[2] 5 b).

1926 *Amer. Speech* Feb. 283/1 *Pitchman*, a man who sells novelties on the circus lot or on the streets adjacent to the lot. **1934** *N.Y. American* 4 Oct. 21 The army of street pitchmen have had the biggest season in years. **1940** W. SAROYAN *Love's Old Sweet Song* 17 in *Three Plays*, Barnaby Gaul, 51, a pitchman. **1949** *Time* 19 Dec. 34/3 They are all journalistic racketeers—I mean pitchmen. **1956** H. GOLD *Man who was not with It* (1965) xix. 172, I coughed into my best pitchman's voice. **1972** *Guardian* 6 Dec. 13/1 American astronauts..have become bank directors, pitchmen for cars and railroads on televison commercials, executives in real estate. **1975** *Publishers Weekly* 28 Apr. 44/1 Mandino is a pitchman for positive thinking in the hallowed line including Bruce Barton and Norman Vincent Peale. **1976** *National Observer* (U.S.) 2 Oct. 18/4 Boudreau was a pitchman in the old Clyde Beatty Circus before he went on to Juilliard and the Paris Conservatory. **1976** *Time* 20 Dec. 20/2 Cecil D. Andrus..has been TV pitchman for Idaho potatoes. **1977** *Time* 7 Feb. 43/2 He has also taken on the role of pitchman, appearing personally in Eastern's ads to stress the line's concern for passengers.

pitch-mark, -mineral: see PITCH *sb.*[1] 5.

pitch-note: see PITCH *sb.*[2] 26.

ˈpitch-off. [PITCH *v.*[1] 20.] The inclination or shelving of the bed of the sea.

1894 J. D. DANA *Man. Geol.* (ed. 4) I. i. 20 At Keeling atoll,..Captain Fitzroy, R.N., found no bottom in 7200 feet at 2200 yards from the breakers—which gives a pitch-off exceeding 1 : 0·92.

pitch-opal, -ore: see PITCH *sb.*[1] 5.

ˈpitch-out. *N. Amer.* [PITCH *v.*[1] 17 c.]

a. *Baseball.* (See quot. 1943.) **b.** *Football.* (See quot. 1950.)

1912 C. MATHEWSON *Pitching in a Pinch* vii. 157 If a catcher can get a pitchout on a hit and run sign he upsets the other team greatly. **1943** *Amer. Speech* XVIII. 106 The *pitch-out* (a ball thrown wide of the plate so that the catcher can *get it away* in a hurry to catch a man trying to steal). **1948** *Cavalier Daily* (Univ. of Virginia) 19 Oct. 2/1 The halfbacks, standing wide of the fullback, are in a position to take pitchouts and to speed downfield for passes. **1949** *Sun* (Baltimore) 8 Dec. 24/1 Other trends noted [in Football] included increased use of the pitchout (not to be confused with the baseball term). **1950** *Britannica Bk. of Year* 683/1 *Pitch-out, n. Football*, a short lateral pass behind the line of scrimmage, usually from the quarterback to another back. **1966** ROTE & WINTER *Lang. Pro Football* 129 Pitchout, a short, backward shuffle pass or lateral from quarterback to a halfback or a fullback. **1968** *Globe & Mail* (Toronto) 11 July 32/4 He took a pitchout from Curtis Wilson and danced, darted and jumped 86 yards. **1972** J. MOSEDALE *Football* vi. 87 The cornerback took his eyes off him on a pitchout. **1974** *Anderson* (S. Carolina) *Independent* 19 Apr. 4B/3 On Monday night, he got his first stolen base—despite a pitchout by the Chicago White Sox.

ˈpitch-penny. *U.S.* [f. PITCH *v.*[1]] A variety of pitch-and-toss.

1830 J. F. WATSON *Ann. Philadelphia* 240 'Pitch-penny'..was frequent—to pitch at a white mark on the ground. **1877** E. S. WARD *Story of Avis* 286 Calculating the distance..as he stood playing the game of human pitch-penny with the infant. **1978** E. TIDYMAN *Table Stakes* I. i. 20 He had persuaded Hochmeir to give him his fifty cents a week in pennies so that he could try to double it in..pitch penny with the newsboys in Howard Square.

pitch pine. [f. PITCH *sb.*[1] + PINE *sb.*[2]] Name given to several species of pine-tree with specially resinous wood, or from which pitch or turpentine is obtained. Also *attrib.*

Esp. *Pinus rigida*, and *P. australis* or *palustris* (Long-leaved Pine), of North America, and *Phyllocladus trichomanoides* (Celery Pine), of New Zealand; also, the wood of any of these.

1676 *Essex Inst. Hist. Coll.* (1920) LVI. 306 4¾ acres of land..bounded by a pitch pine. **1684** *Manchester* (Mass.) *Town Rec.* (1889) 17 A pich [*sic*] pine tree marked with 4 marks. **1709** J. LAWSON *New Voy. Carolina* 89 Ever-Greens are here plentifully found, of a very quick Growth, and pleasant Shade; Cypress, or White Cedar, the Pitch Pine, the yellow Pine. **1736** *Rec. Early Hist. Boston* (1885) XII. 150 Add to the South East Side Ten foot, to be built of Square Pitch Pine Timber. **1771** J. S. COPLEY *Let.* 3 Aug. in *Mass. Hist. Soc. Coll.* (1914) LXXI. 138 The floor..should be Pitch Pine. **1754** in *6th Rep. Dep. Kpr.* App. II. 128 Preparing from the Glutinous Juices of the American Pitch Pine Tree a Varnish. **1810** *Trans. Soc. Arts* XXVIII. 95 The pitch-pine of Virginia, the Carolinas, Georgia, and the Floridas grow to an immense size in what are there called pine-barrens. **1863** *Pilgr. over Prairies* II. 165 A watchful sentinel outside, who, by the light of a pitchpine torch, placed in the hut, could command my every movement. **1866** *Treas. Bot.* 891/1 Pitch Pine [the wood] of *Pinus rigida*, and Georgia Pitch Pine that of *Pinus australis*. **1887** C. B. GEORGE *40 Yrs. on Rail* 31 Pitch pine was largely used for fuel. **1969** T. H. EVERETT *Living Trees of World* 50/2 Pitch pine, rarely more than 75 feet high, has an open irregular head. **1977** *Listener* 3 Nov. 594/2 The church where so many Trelawnies lie under the pitchpine and the shiny tiles.

ˈpitch-pipe. [f. PITCH *sb.*[2] 23 + PIPE *sb.*[1]] A small musical pipe, blown by the mouth (either a flue-pipe or a reed-pipe, and either sounding a fixed note or adjustable to different notes), used to set the pitch for singing or tuning an instrument.

1711 STEELE *Spect.* No. 228 ¶6 Caius Gracchus..had an ingenious Servant, by Name Licinius, always attending him with a Pitch-pipe, or Instrument to regulate the Voice. **1771** G. WHITE *Selborne* Aug., A common half-crown pitch-pipe, such as masters use for tuning of harpsichords. **1880** W. H. STONE in Grove *Dict. Mus.* II. 759 All pitchpipes are..inferior in accuracy to tuning-forks; the only advantage..being their louder..tone, and the readiness with which beats are produced. **1961** *Oxf. Univ. Gaz.* 8 May 1149/2 Some cylinders are prefaced with the sound of the pitch-pipe and statement of the key. **1969** E. H. PINTO *Treen* 172 The mahogany pitch pipes..were formerly used in churches which had no organ, to give the keynote before singing commenced. **1979** *Yale Alumni Mag.* Apr. 28/2 Armed only with pitch-pipes and pocket dictionaries, we were able to elicit a direct and natural response from all manner of Soviet citizens.

ˈpitch-ˌplaster, *sb.* [f. PITCH *sb.*[1] + PLASTER.] A plaster made of pitch, formerly used to remove hair; also, a stimulant plaster containing Burgundy pitch and other ingredients.

1601 HOLLAND *Pliny* I. 424 For making of pitch plaisters, to fetch off the haire of mens bodies. **1858** SIMMONDS *Dict. Trade*, *Pitch-plaster*, a plaster of Burgundy pitch. **1884** *Syd. Soc. Lex.*, Burgundy pitch plaster. Burgundy pitch 90 parts, melted with yellow wax 10 parts.

Hence **pitch-plaster** *v. trans.*, to apply a pitch-plaster to.

1860 SALA *Lady Chesterf.* iv. 66 The infamous Burke..who pitch-plastered people to death..and sold their bodies to the surgeons.

pitch-point, etc.: see PITCH *sb.*[2] 26.

pitchpoll, -pole (ˈpɪtʃpəʊl), *sb.* [f. PITCH *v.*[1] + POLL *sb.*] **1.** A somersault. (In quots. *a* 1661, The act, or point, of toppling over.) *dial.*

a **1661** HOLYDAY *Juvenal* 5 All vice is at the pitch-pole. *Ibid.* 186 Whence to a greater ruine after all With a huge pitch-pole he was forc'd to fall. **1842** S. KETTELL *Daw's Doings* ix. 61 Goosecap..did nothing all day long but lollop about at his ease..playing at pitchpole among the clover. **1881** *Oxfords. Gloss.* (Suppl.), A pitchpole. **1893** *Wiltsh. Gloss.* s.v., When rooks are..playing and tumbling head over heels in the air (a sign of rain) they are said to be playing pitch-pole.

2. *Agric.* A kind of harrow.

1932 R. H. BIFFEN *Fream's Elem. Agric.* (ed. 12) ii. 48 The pitch-pole harrow is an implement of recent introduction, which has attained some popularity for tearing a thick mat on old pasture, and also for working arable land... The implement has a very drastic action and the heavy draught necessitates a tractor. **1940** R. G. STAPLEDON *Re-Grassing* 27 After this treatment had been continued a few years we dragged heavily with pitch-pole, lined heavily.., [etc.]. **1944** C. CULPIN *Farm Machinery* (ed. 2) vii. 132 (*caption*) Wilder's 'Pitch-Pole' harrow pulled by tractor equipped with skeleton wheels. *Ibid.*, Tines suitable for fairly deep arable cultivations are available, and some farmers use the Pitch-Pole mainly or exclusively as an arable land cultivator. **1951** P. OYLER *Feeding Ourselves* x. 92 It is a good plan to run heavy tine harrows or the modern Pitchpole over pastures again and again both ways. **1960** *Farmer & Stockbreeder* 16 Feb. 128/3 The average contract rate for pitchpole harrowing is 20s per acre first time.

ˈpitchpoll, -pole, *v.* orig. *dial.* [f. prec. sb.]

a. *intr.* To turn 'head over heels'; to turn over and over; also *trans.* in causative sense.

1851 H. MELVILLE *Whale* lxxxiv. 409 The harpoon may be pitchpoled in the same way with the lance. **1861** MRS. H. WOOD *East Lynne* III. v, The ragged urchins pitch-poling in the gutter and the dust. **1896** *Westm. Gaz.* 21 Mar. 7/1 We couldn't go out of our houses up and down street without pitch-polling over strings tied across the road. **1926** T. E. LAWRENCE *Seven Pillars* (1935) cxvi. 626 The wind snapped them [*sc.* thistles] off at the hollow root, and pitch-polled their branchy tops along the level ground, thistle blowing against thistle.

b. *intr. Naut.* (See quot. 1961.) Also *trans.* in causative sense.

1903 G. S. WASSON *Cap'n Simlon's Store* iii. 44 Ain't it hard lines enough for a sickly ole feller same's him having to go outside here late in the fall o' the year and pitch-pole around into a punky old ark. **1908** [see HUMBUG *v.* 2]. **1915** KIPLING *Fringes of Fleet* 67 Dawn sees them pitch-poling insanely between head-seas. **1961** F. H. BURGESS *Dict. Sailing* 160 *Pitch pole*, be up-ended, stern first, and completely overthrown by the sea. **1976** *Sci. Amer.* May 130/3 On this up-to-date foundation Van Dorn builds a careful scheme for wave forecasting at sea: the expected sea state and its changes (depending on fetch, wind speed and duration) and the chances that state implies for the big wave that can pitchpole any boat. **1976** *Yachting World* Oct. 111/1 Even in the worst conditions, such as running down steep 25 foot waves, it has never shown a tendency to pitchpole. **1979** *Observer* 19 Aug. 3/3 Huge weights of water ..capable of laying a 35 foot boat flat on its side with ease, making it turn turtle or even pitch-poling it—making it somersault forward stern over stem.

Hence **ˈpitchpoler**, one who pitchpolls a harpoon in *Whaling*; **ˈpitchpol(l)ing** *vbl. sb.*

1851 H. MELVILLE *Moby Dick* II. xlii. 284 None exceed that fine manœuvre with the lance, called pitchpoling. *Ibid.* 286 The pitchpoler dropping astern, folds his hands. **1971** S. E. MORISON *European Discovery Amer.: Northern Voy.* p. xi, There you have first-hand accounts of some of the hazards that the early navigators encountered as a matter of course—enormous freak waves, pitch-poling, capsizing.

pitch-pot, etc.: see PITCH *sb.*[1]

†**ˈpitch-resin, -rosin.** *Obs. rare.* [f. PITCH *sb.*[1] + RESIN, ROSIN; F. *poix résine.*] The resin or turpentine which exudes from the 'pitch tree' (L. *picea*); = PERROSIN.

1601 HOLLAND *Pliny* I. 464 The same pitch-rosin [*eadem resina*] if it be boiled more lightly with water, and be let to run through a strainer, comes to a reddish colour, and is glewie: and thereupon it is called stilled Pitch. *Ibid.* 465 While it is raw pitch-rosin [*dum resina sit*], and as it runneth from the tree.

pitch-set: see PITCH *sb.*[2] 26.

pitch-speeched, -stain: see PITCH *sb.*[1] 5.

pitchstone (ˈpɪtʃstəʊn). *Min.* [f. PITCH *sb.*[1] + STONE *sb.*, tr. Ger. *pechstein* (Werner 1780).]

a. An old volcanic rock; obsidian or other vitreous rock looking like hardened pitch. **b.** = *pitch-opal*.

1784 KIRWAN *Min.* 97 Pitch-stone, lava. **1796** —— *Elem. Min.* (ed. 2) I. 292 Pitchstone.. It often much resembles semi opals and jaspers. **1799** —— *Geol. Ess.* 180 Huge strata ..as they contain abundance of quartz and felspar may be called pitchstone porphyry. **1807** HEADRICK *Arran* 58 On the northern declivity saw many masses of pitchstone. **1836** MACGILLIVRAY tr. *Humboldt's Trav.* iii. 51 Lavas with a basis of pitchstone and obsidian. **1894** *Times* 11 Aug. 11/2 Invaded by the pitchstone-lava of the island of Eigg.

pitch-surface: see PITCH *sb.*[2] 26.

pitch-tankard: see PITCH *sb.*[1] 5.

pitch-tree. [f. PITCH *sb.*[1] + TREE *sb.*] Name for various coniferous trees abounding in resin, or yielding resin, turpentine, or pitch.

In earlier use chiefly rendering L. *picea* or Gr. πεύκη, prob. *Pinus Laricio*, the Corsican Pine (Daubeny); in mod. use applied to the Silver Fir (*Abies* or *Picea pectinata*), the Spruce Fir (*Abies* or *Picea excelsa*) as the source of Burgundy pitch, the Kauri Pine (*Dammara australis*) as that of kauri-gum, and the Amboyna Pine (*D. orientalis*) as that of dammar resin.

1538 ELYOT, *Picea*, a piche tree. **1577** B. GOOGE *Heresbach's Husb.* (1586) 95 The Pitch tree is called in Greeke πεύκη, in Latine Picea, in Italian Pezzo. **1584** *Voy. Virginia* in Hakluyt *Voy.* (1810) III. 303 Their boates are made of one tree, either of Pine or of Pitch trees: a wood not commonly knowen to our people, nor found growing in England. **1697** DRYDEN *Virg. Georg.* II. 349 Black Ivy, Pitch Trees, and the baleful Yeugh. **1766** *Compl. Farmer* s.v. *Aphernousli*, The branches resemble these of the pitch-trees, commonly called the spruce fir. **1866** *Treas. Bot.*, Pitch-tree, *Abies excelsa.*

pitchumon, obs. form of PERSIMMON.

pitch-wheel: see PITCH *sb.*[2] 26.

pitch-wine, -wood: see PITCH *sb.*[1] 5.

pitchwork (ˈpɪtʃwɜːk). [f. PITCH *sb.*[2]] Mining work in which the workmen are paid by receiving a fixed proportion of the output.

1858 SIMMONDS *Dict. Trade, Pitch-work*, work done in a coal-mine, by those working on tribute.

pitchy (ˈpɪtʃɪ), *a.* (*adv.*) Also 6 *Sc.* **pikky, pyky.** [f. PITCH *sb.*[1] + -Y.]

1. Full of or abounding in pitch; bituminous, resinous; coated, smeared, soiled, or sticky with pitch; *fig.* sticky like pitch, thievish. Of a flame: Darkened with smoke, like that of burning pitch.

1513 DOUGLAS *Æneis* v. xii. 32 Out thrawis the pikky smok cole blak. *Ibid.* IX. ii. 97 The tallownit burdis kest a pyky low. **1567** MAPLET *Gr. Forest* 57 The Pine tree is called holdfast or pitchie tre. **1742** in *6th Rep. Dep. Kpr.* App. II. 120 The Black, Pitchy, Flinty Rock found immediately over coals. **1845** WHITTIER *Lumbermen* viii, Pitchy knot and beechen splinter On our hearth shall glow. **1869** LECKY *European Mor.* (1877) I. ii. 281 Nero illuminated his gardens during the night by Christians burning in their pitchy shirts. *fig.* **1660** *Eng. Monarchy Freest State in World* 7 All publick Monies..passing through the pitchy claws of such State harpies.

2. Of the nature or consistence of pitch; tenacious, viscid; bituminous.

1552 HULOET, Pitchye, or of pytche, *piceus.* **1589** NASHE *Pref. Greene's Menaphon* (Arb.) 7 The vnsauorie sent of the pitchie slime. **1732** ARBUTHNOT *Rules of Diet* in *Aliments*, etc. 298 Every thing that thickens the Fluids or reduceth them to a pitchy Condition. **1839** URE *Dict. Arts* 684 Pitchy hydrate of iron.

3. *Nat. Hist.*, etc. Of the colour or appearance of pitch; dark-brown inclining to black; piceous. Hence *pitchy-black.*

1828 STARK *Elem. Nat. Hist.* II. 278 *Megatoma serra*... Shining pitchy black. **1844** STEPHENS *Bk. Farm* III. 779 The chrysalis..is pitchy-brown..inclosed in a white woolly cocoon. **1870** HOOKER *Stud. Flora* 412 *Carex stricta*... Glumes in about 8 rows, pitchy, midrib green. **1882** *Gd. Words* 165 Deep black coals with pitchy lustre.

4. *fig.* 'As black' or 'as dark as pitch'; pitch-dark, intensely dark; of darkness, Intense, thick, gross.

c **1586** C'TESS PEMBROKE *Ps.* LXXVII. xi, Light of lightnings flash Did pitchy cloudes encleare. *a* **1592** GREENE *Selimus* Wks. (Grosart) XIV. 261 But let thy pitchie steeds aye draw thy waine, And coale black silence in the world still raigne. **1615** G. SANDYS *Trav.* 202 The pitchie night had bereft vs of the conduct of our eyes. **1746** HERVEY *Medit.* (1818) 265 How uncomfortable is deep, pitchy, total darkness. **1871** L. STEPHEN *Playgr. Eur.* (1894) xi. 276 Stars shone out like fiery sparks against a pitchy canopy.

b. Qualifying *black* or *dark.* (More usually *pitch-dark*: see PITCH *sb.*[1] 5.)

1800 *Naval Chron.* IV. 436 The night being pitchy dark. **1834** COLERIDGE *Table-t.* 21 June, Hans Sachse..in describing Chaos, said it was so pitchy dark, that even the very cats ran against each other! **1895** KIPLING *2nd Jungle Bk.* v. 120 A deep, pitchy-black pool surrounded with rocks.

c. Morally 'black' or defiling; grossly wicked.

1612 DEKKER *If it be not good* Wks. 1873 III. 268 Braue pitchy villaines there. **1810** CRABBE *Borough* vi. 194 The pitchy taint of general vice..you dread the touch.

5. *Comb.*, as *pitchy-countenanced* adj.

1596 R. L[INCHE] *Diella* (1877) 30 How patient then would I endure the smart, Of pitchy countnanc'd dead-doing dart.

pit-coal. Now *rare* or *arch.* [f. PIT *sb.*[1] (sense 6) + COAL.] Coal obtained from pits or mines (as distinguished from *charcoal*, COAL *sb.* 4: formerly called also *sea-coal*, now usually simply *coal*, COAL *sb.* 5). See also quot. 1883.

1617 MORYSON *Itin.* III. 141 The greatest quantitie and best kind of pit-coales is in Nottinghamshire. **1686** PLOT *Staffordsh.* 125 The History of Pit-coal, otherwise called Sea-coale. **1747** WESLEY *Prim. Physic* (1765) 107 A Mud made of powder'd Pitcoal and Water. **1854** RONALDS & RICHARDSON *Chem. Technol.* (ed. 2) I. 30 The former is called brown coal, or lignite, while many varieties of the latter are classed together under the common name of bituminous or pit-coal. **1883** GRESLEY *Gloss. Coal Mining*, *Pit Coal* generally signifies the bituminous varieties of coal. *attrib.* **1731** *Gentl. Mag.* I. 167 Proposes with Pit-Coal Fire to make Bar Iron from Pig Metal. **1825** J. NICHOLSON *Operat. Mechanic* 734 A common pit-coal or other fire.

pite, obs. var. *pight*, pa. pple. of PITCH *v.*; obs. f. PITY.

piteable, obs. form of PITIABLE.

piteous (ˈpɪtiːəs), *a.* Forms: see below. [ME. *pytos*, *pitous*, a. OF. (12th c.) *pitos*, (13th c.) *piteus*, AF. *pitous* = Pr. *pidos*, *pitos*, Cat. *piados*, Sp. *piadoso*, OIt. *piadoso* (It. *pietoso*):—L. type **pietōs-us* (med.L. in Du Cange), f. *pietāt-em* PIETY (cf. -ITOUS). The regular phonetic form in mod. Eng. from Fr. would be *pitous* (from L. *pietōsus*); the β forms in *-uous*, *-evous*, *-ewous*, and γ forms in *-ious*, *-yous*, *-eous* appear to be Eng. developments, the former influenced by words historically in *-uous*, *-ivous*, or OE. adjs. in *-wis*; the latter app. conformed to the sb. *pité*, *pitie*, PITY. Cf. *bounteous*, *dainteous*, *plenteous*; also *beauteous*, *courteous*, *righteous.*]

A. Illustration of Forms.

α. 3–4 **pitos, pytos,** 3–5 **pitous, -e,** 4 **pitus, -e,** (**pytis, putus**), 4–5 **pytous, -e, pittows.**

1297 R. GLOUC. (Rolls) 10087 He deide in a pitous cas. *Ibid.* 11395 þat was a pitos dede. **13..** *Cursor M.* 24014 (Cott.) Ful pitus it was þat plaint. *c* **1350** *Will. Palerne* 1180 He herd þe pytous pleint. **1362** LANGL. *P. Pl.* A. VII. 116 With suche pitouse wordes. *c* **1470** HENRY *Wallace* II. 161 The playne compleynt, the pittows wementyng! **1483** CAXTON *Gold. Leg.* 358/2 He was moche pytous.

β. 3–5 **pituos,** 4 **pituus, -uose, -uis, -uys, -wys, -evows,** 4–5 **pituous, -e, piteuous, -e,** 5 **pite-, pytevous, piti-, pityuous, pitteuous, pytewous, -e, pytewys,** 5–6 **pytuous,** 5–6 (8) **pituous,** 6 **pytuouse, -uose.**

It is not clear whether the difference between *-euous*, *-evous*, *-ewous*, is merely graphical, nor whether *u*, *v* are here the vowel or the consonant.

? *a* **1300** *Cursor M.* 24014 (Edin.) Ful pituus it was þat plaint. *c* **1350** Pitevows [see B. 2]. *c* **1380** Pituouse [see B. 1]. *c* **1400** tr. *Secreta Secret., Gov. Lordsh.* 106 For his pityuous doynges. *c* **1420** *Chron. Vilod.* st. 278 So mercyfull and so pytewys. **1422** Pitteuous, piteuouse [see B. 1]. *c* **1440** *York Myst.* xlvi. 188 With pitevous playnte. **1442** T. BECKINGTON *Corr.* (Rolls) II. 189 Of your moost merciful and pituous grace. **1471** RIPLEY *Comp. Alch.* Pref. i. in Ashm. *Theat. Chem. Brit.* (1652) 121 O pytewouse puryfyer of Soules. **1530** *Proper Dyaloge* in *Rede me*, etc. (Arb.) 144 Their pituous supplicacyon. **1530** PALSGR. 320/2 Pytuouse, one that hath pytie. **1538** STARKEY *England* II. i. 176 Such pouerty exercysyth wel the pytuose myndys. **1738** tr. *Guazzo's Art Conversation* 47 He began to groan and weep in a pituous manner.

γ. 4–6 **piteus,** 4 **pytius,** 4– **piteous,** (5 **pytyows,** 5–6 **pyteous, -e, piteose,** 5–7 **pitious,** 6 **pitiouse, pyti-, pitte-, pittious; pittieux**). (Some early examples of *piteus* are perh. disyllabic and belong to α)

13.. *Cursor M.* 24014 (Gött.) Ful piteus it was hir plaint. **1340** *Ayenb.* 144 þe oþer makeþ þe herte zuete and milde and piteus. *c* **1400** MAUNDEV. (Roxb.) x. 38 It es a piteous thing to behald. *c* **1420** LYDG. *Assembly of Gods* 222 Now..shewe your pyteous face. *c* **1440** *Promp. Parv.* 402/1 Pytyows, or ful of pyte (*H.* pytevous, *P.* pitiuous). *c* **1489** CAXTON *Blanchardyn* iv. 19 þe pyteouse tydynges. ? *a* **1500** in *Rel. Ant.* II. 125 In this piteose myscheffe. **1509** HAWES *Past. Pleas.* xxx. (Percy Soc.) 147 Without that she be to me piteous. **1552** HULOET, Pitious and pitifull. **1556** *Aurelio & Isab.* (1608) Pj, You have beane a litell pittieux. **1590** SPENSER *F.Q.* I. vii. 20 Her pitteous hart. **1596** *Ibid.* VII. vi. 6 O pittious worke of Mutability.

δ. (Chiefly *Sc.*) 4 **petwis, -owiss,** 5 **petwys, petouse, -ows, -evous, -uis, petus, -ious, -uoss,** 5–6 **petous, -eous, -e,** 6 **petouss, -eouss, -ewous, -ewus, -uous.**

c **1375** *Sc. Leg. Saints* i. (*Petrus*) 90 One crist callyt with petowiss stewyne. [**1375** BARBOUR *Bruce* III. 553 Petwisly. *c* **1420** Petwysly [see PITEOUSLY 3].] *c* **1420** LYDG. *Assembly of Gods* 1144 With a peteous look. *a* **1450** *Knt. de la Tour* (1868) 89 To be petous of poure men. *c* **1450** HOLLAND *Howlat* 41, I herd ane petuoss appele. **1508** DUNBAR *Tua Mariit Wemen* 473, I am sa peteouse to the pur. *a* **1520** —— *Poems* lxiv. 13 Quhois petewous [*v.r.* -ewus] deithe dois to my hart sic pane. *c* **1560** A. SCOTT *Poems* (S.T.S.) xviii. 30 Makand ane petouss mone.

B. Signification.

†**1.** Full of piety; pious, godly, devout. *Obs.*

c **1305** [implied in PITEOUSLY 1]. *c* **1380** *Antecrist* in Todd *3 Treat. Wyclif* 120 þe pituouse martir 3yveþ his body. **1382** WYCLIF *2 Pet.* ii. 9 The Lord knew for to delyuere pitouse [**1388** piteuouse, *Vulg.* pios] men of temptacioun. *c* **1393** CHAUCER *Gentilesse* 9 Truwe of his worde, sobur pitous and fre. **1422** tr. *Secreta Secret., Priv. Priv.* 138 That suche a Spekere by ryghtfull and Pitteuous. *Ibid.* 220 He shal be piteuouse, chaste, and lytill desyre company of women. **1570** LEVINS *Manip.* 226/24 Pitiouse, *pius, misericors.*

2. Full of pity; affected with or feeling pity; compassionate, merciful, tender: = PITIFUL 2. *arch.*

c **1350** *Will. Palerne* 5488 So pitevows to þe pore hem prestili to help. **1390** GOWER *Conf.* III. 190 It sit a king to be pitous Toward his poeple and gracious. **1483** CAXTON *G. de la Tour* D iij b, A fre hert and pyteous upon other mens peynes. *a* **1548** HALL *Chron., Hen. V* 62 The kyng like a piteous prince..graunted to them their askyng. **1624** MILTON *Ps.* cxxxvi. 77 He hath with a piteous eye Beheld us in our misery. *c* **1750** SHENSTONE *Elegies* iii. 43 Piteous of woes, and hopeless to relieve.

3. Exciting, appealing for, or deserving pity; moving to compassion; affecting, lamentable, deplorable, mournful; = PITIFUL 3.

c **1290** [implied in PITEOUSLY 3]. **1297** R. GLOUC. (Rolls) 4180 A deoluol cry & a pitos wepinge. **13..** *Cursor M.* 14097 (Gött.) A pituse plaint to crist scho talde. **1390** GOWER *Conf.* I. 45, I.. caste up many a pitous lok Unto the hevene. *c* **1489** CAXTON *Sonnes of Aymon* ix. 225 The piteouse histori of the four sones of Aymon. **1508** DUNBAR *Flyting w. Kennedy* 163 To luk vpoun thy gryslie peteous port. **1535** COVERDALE *2 Macc.* vi. 9 A piteous thinge was it to se. **1585** T. WASHINGTON tr. *Nicholay's Voy.* I. xx. 24 b, Too make report of these piteous newes vnto the assieged. **1653** H. COGAN tr. *Pinto's Trav.* 41 The pitious estate wherein we had left that place. **1782** COWPER *Gilpin* 126 Down ran the wine into the road, Most piteous to be seen. **1871** R. ELLIS *Catullus* lxiv. 400 Lightly the son forgat his parents' piteous ashes. **1887** BOWEN *Virg. Æneid* III. 39 A piteous groan from within sounds.

b. as *adv.* = PITEOUSLY 3.

c **1369** CHAUCER *Dethe Blaunche* 470 Ful petuose pale and no-thynge red. **1775** S. J. PRATT *Liberal Opin.* xlvii. (1783) II. 1 Compose thy griefs,..stop those tears; Cry not so piteous.

†**4.** Paltry, mean: = PITIFUL 4. *Obs. rare.*

1667 MILTON *P.L.* x. 1034 That thy Seed shall bruise The Serpents head; piteous amends, unless Be meant [etc.].

piteously (ˈpɪtiːəslɪ), *adv.* Forms: see PITEOUS. [f. prec. + -LY[2].]

†**1.** With piety; piously, devoutly. *Obs.*

c **1305** *St. Edmund Conf.* 248 in *E.E.P.* (1862) 77 So pitousliche he wolde rede: & so gode grace hadde þerto. **1382** WYCLIF *Ecclus.* xliii. 37 To men pitously doende [**1388** men doynge feithfuli] he 3af wisdam. **1382** —— *Titus* ii. 12 That we..lyue sobreli, and iustli, and piteuously.

2. With pity; compassionately, mercifully, kindly. *arch.*

c **1368** CHAUCER *Compl. Pite* 18 (Tanner 346) Pitiously on her my eyn I caste. **1450–80** tr. *Secreta Secret.* 17 That he governe hem pitously and in loue. **1556** J. HEYWOOD *Spider & F.* lxiii. 6 Three score piteouslie lookt, as they thant wold saue. **1855** BAILEY *Mystic*, etc. 20 His poor and ignorant kin ..He piteously remembered ere he passed.

3. In a manner that excites pity to see or hear; so as to call for or deserve pity; lamentably, grievously, sadly; pitiably.

c **1290** *S. Eng. Leg.* I. 170/2232 He..bad þe Monekus pitousliche þat heo for him bede. **1297** R. GLOUC. (Rolls) 9240 Wel pitosliche hii wende alle to þe kinge..& pitosliche bede, þat he ssolde vor godes loue amendi suche dede. *c* **1374** CHAUCER *Anel. & Arc.* 169 Sheo weopeþe, waylepe, swooneþe pytously. **1375** BARBOUR *Bruce* III. 549 Thai full pitwysly gan tell Auenturis that thaim befell. **1377** LANGL. *P. Pl.* B. XVIII. 58 Quod crist & comsed forto swowe, Pitousliche and pale. *c* **1420** *Chron. Vilod.* ccclxxxiv, And askede of hym some gode full petwysly. **1508** DUNBAR *Lament for Makaris* 49 [Death] has done petuously devour The noble Chaucer, of makaris flouir. **1526** TINDALE *Matt.* xv. 22 My doughter is pytiously vexed with a devyll. *c* **1526** FRITH *Disput. Purgatory* (1829) 160 They are piteously deceived, that will prove purgatory by the texts of the Old Testament. **1588** SHAKS. *Tit. A.* v. i. 66. **1601** HOLLAND *Pliny* II. 376 He murdered most piteously so many good citizens. **1848** DICKENS *Dombey* v, Little Paul began to cry most piteously. **1882–3** *Schaff's Encycl. Relig. Knowl.* I. 193/2 His German poetry is piteously poor.

piteousness (ˈpɪtiːəsnɪs). [f. PITEOUS *a.* + -NESS.] The quality of being piteous: **a.** mercifulness (*arch.*); **b.** pitiableness.

1390 GOWER *Conf.* III. 210 It may be said no Pitousnesse, Bot it is Pusillamite. **1530** PALSGR. 254/2 Pyteousnesse, *piteoseté.* *a* **1586** SIDNEY *Arcadia* (1622) 132 Sirs (answered he with a good grace, and made the more agreeable by a certaine noble kinde of pitiousnesse) I see well you are strangers, that know not our miserie. **1608** MACHIN *Dumb Knight* IV. in Hazl. *Dodsley* X. 189 Will have them both condemn'd immediately, Without their answers, plaints, or piteousness. **1862** TROLLOPE *Orley F.* xlv, Lady Mason.. flinging herself upon her friend's neck..begged with earnest piteousness to be forgiven.

†**piteoustee, pitoustee.** *Obs. rare.* [a. OF. *pitoseté* ('*piteoseté*, pyteousnesse' Palsgr.), f. *pitos*, *piteux* PITEOUS.] An act of pity or of piety.

1382 WYCLIF *Ecclus.* xliv. 10 But they men of mercy ben, of whom the pitoustees faileden not.

pitfall (ˈpɪtfɔːl), *sb.* Forms: 4–5 **put-,** 4–6 **pyt-,** etc. (see PIT *sb.*[1]); 4–5 **-falle,** 6 **-faul,** 6–8 **-fal,** 6– **-fall.** [app. f. PIT *sb.*[1] + FALL *sb.*[2], OE. *fealle*, Ger. *falle* a falling trap-door, a trap. In mod. use it is generally taken as a 'pit into which one may fall'.]

†**1.** A trap for the capture of birds in which a trap-door or the like falls over a cavity or hollow. *Obs.*

1382 WYCLIF *Jer.* v. 27 As a pit falle [**1388** a net, ether a trap] ful of briddes. **1483** *Cath. Angl.* 282/1 A Pittfalle, *decipula, auicipula.* **1530** PALSGR. 254/2 Pytfall for byrdes, *trebouchet.* **1593** NASHE *Christ's T.* 89 b, Foules of the ayre, though neuer so empty stomackt, flye not for foode into open Pit-fals. **1604** W. TERILO *Fr. Bacon's Proph.* 331 in Hazl. *E.P.P.* IV. 280 Now pitfalls are so made, That small birdes cannot know them. **1706** PHILLIPS, *Pit-fall*, a kind of Gin or Trap to catch Birds.

2. A concealed pit into which animals or men may fall and be captured.

1387 TREVISA *Higden* (Rolls) II. 155 þe Pictes sodenliche an vnware fel ouer þe hammes into a wonder putfalle. **1398** —— *Barth. De P.R.* XVIII. xliv. (Bodl. MS.), A caue oþer a dike is made vnder þe erþe as it were a pittefalle in þe

Elephauntes waye and vnneware he falleþ þerein. **1555** EDEN *Decades* 96 The dogge tyger chaunsed fyrste into this pitfaul. **1579–80** NORTH *Plutarch* (1595) 190 They did hunte wilde beastes, with pittefalles and ditches. **1678** BUNYAN *Pilgr.* I. 82 The way was..so full of Pits, Pitfalls, deep holes, and shelvings down there. **1719** DE FOE *Crusoe* I. 171, I resolved to try a Pitfall, so I dug several large Pits in the Earth, in Places where I had observed the Goats used to feed, and over these Pits I placed Hurdles. **1774** GOLDSM. *Nat. Hist.* (1776) IV. 290 These animals are sometimes taken in pit-falls, covered with green branches, laid in those paths which the Rhinoceros makes. **1832** LYELL *Princ. Geol.* (1868) II. III. xlv. 521 Open fissures often serve as natural pitfalls in which herbivorous animals perish. **1875** JOWETT *Plato* (ed. 2) II. 446 Crooked and tortuous paths in which many pitfalls are concealed.

†**3.** An ambush, or a natural 'trap' in which a force may be surrounded and overpowered. *Obs.*

a **1305** in *Pol. Songs* (Camden) 193 Ther hy were knulled y the put-falle, This eorles ant barouns ant huere knyhtes alle.

4. *fig.* **a.** A 'trap' or crafty device to catch by surprise the unsuspecting or unwary. **b.** Any hidden or unperceived danger or error into which a person is liable to fall unawares.

a **1586** SIDNEY *Astr. & Stella* xi, In her chekes pit thou didst thy pitfall set. **1641** MILTON *Ch. Govt.* I. iii. Wks. 1851 III. 111 The Papists,..by this very snare and pitfall of imitating the ceremonial law, fel into that..superstition. **1751** JOHNSON *Rambler* No. 175 ¶11 Unless he is taught by timely precepts.., and shewn at distance the pitfals of treachery. **1827** HALLAM *Const. Hist.* (1876) III. xvi. 288 We..walk amidst the snares and pitfalls of the law. **1861** *Sat. Rev.* 23 Nov. 533 He may be merely a blundering student, who has tumbled into a theological pitfall in the dark. **1877** J. C. COX *Ch. Derbysh.* II. Introd. 8 The procuring of a full transcript has saved me from numerous pit-falls.

Hence **'pitfalled** (-fɔːld) *a.*, full of pitfalls.

1826 *Blackw. Mag.* XX. 666/2 The snow deep, wreathed, and pit-falled. **1876** S. LANIER *Poems* (1884) 124 How I crushed Cat-lived rebellions, pitfalled treasons. **1976** *Evening Post* (Nottingham) 17 Dec. 14/2 Sunken and rubble-littered uneven pavements, pitfalled with miniature craters.

pitfall ('pɪtfɔːl), *v. rare.* [f. prec. sb.] *trans.*

a. To set with traps or pitfalls. **b.** To entrap, ensnare. Also *fig.* Hence **pitfalling** *ppl. a.*

14.. in *Hist. Coll. Citizen London* (Camden) 4 The bottom of the diche with yn Was pyttefallyd ij fote evyr bytwyn, And every pyttefalle a spere hyghthe That there schulde stonde noo man to fyght. **1643** MILTON *Divorce* Introd., Wks. 1851 IV. 10 The waies of the Lord, strait and faithfull as they are, not full of cranks and contradictions, and pit falling dispenses.

†**'pitfold.** *Obs.* [f. PIT *sb.*[1] + FOLD *sb.*[2]: cf. *pinfold.*] = PITFALL 1, 3 (from which it was prob. altered by popular etymology).

1575 CHURCHYARD *Chippes* (1817) 121 The enemy.. bruted abroad we were taken in a pitfold. **1585** HIGINS *Junius' Nomenclator* 245/2 *Decipulum*... *Vn trebuchet*, a pitfold, or other snare to intrap birds or beastes. **1632** T. NASHE *Quaternio* 25 How again with Cæsar to giue an enemy passage hauing him in a straite and pitfolde, that he may take the more advantage of him in pursuit.

pitful ('pɪtfʊl). *nonce-wd.* [f. PIT *sb.*[1] + -FUL.] As many as fill a pit, or *spec.* the pit (of a theatre).

1880 MCCARTHY *Own Times* IV. lxiv. 434 Napoleon invited Talma to Erfurt, that he might play to a pitfull of Kings.

pith (pɪθ), *sb.* Forms: 1–2 **piþa**, 4–5 **piþ**, 4–7 **pyth, pithe**, 4– **pith**, (4 **pidh, pight, put**, 5–6 **pytthe**, 5 **pyf, peth**, *Sc.* **picht**, 5–7 **pythe**, 6 **pit**, *Sc.* **pitht**, 6–7 **pitth(e)**. Mod. dialects have **peth, peeth, piff, peff.** [OE. *piþa*, radically agreeing with MDu. *pitte*, MLG., LG., WFris., EFris., Da. *pit* pith of a tree or vegetable, kernel of a nut, etc. (cf. PIT *sb.*[2]):—WGer. type **pipon-*, **pippon-*, represented only in the Low German group. The later development of sense is found only in Eng.]

1. The central column of spongy cellular tissue in the stems and branches of dicotyledonous plants; the medulla; applied also to the internal parenchymatous tissue of other stems, e.g. of palms, rushes, etc.; and to a similar tissue occurring in other parts of plants, as that lining the rind in certain fruits (e.g. the orange).

c **888** K. ÆLFRED *Boeth.* xxxiv. §10 þæt he onginð of þæm wyrtrumum, & swa upweardes grewð oð ðone stemn, & siððan andlang þæs piðan, & andlang þære rinde. *a* **1200** *Sax. Leechd.* III. 90 Eft nim ellenes piþan. **1398** TREVISA *Barth. De P.R.* XVII. i. (Bodl. MS.), þe schafte of a tree..haþ some what wiþin as the piþþe. *c* **1440** *Promp. Parv.* 402/1 Pythe, *medulla, vel pulpa.* **1483** *Wardr. Acc.* in Grose *Antiq. Rep.* (1807) I. 39 A roll of pytthes of risshes. **1542** BOORDE *Dyetary* xxi. (1870) 283 [Walnuts] doth comforte the brayne if the pyth or skin be pylled of. **1562** [see PITHY 1]. **1673–4** GREW *Anat. Trunks* I. i. §35 Within the hollow of the Wood, stands the Pith. **1776** WITHERING *Brit. Plants* (1796) III. 52 *Subularia*... Leaves..semi-cylindrical, full of pith. **1855** DELAMER *Kitch. Gard.* (1861) 119 In boiling ripe marrows, ..take out the pith and seeds. **1884** F. J. BRITTEN *Watch & Clockm.* 198 The pith used by watch makers to clean their work is the pith of the elder. **1884** BOWER & SCOTT tr. *H. A. de Bary's Compar. Anat. Veg. Organs Phanerogams & Ferns* ix. 403 Only in a few woods does the pith become entirely empty and dried up. **1928** HOLMAN & ROBBINS *Elem. Bot.* iii. 54 The pith is made up of large-celled parenchyma. **1956** F. W. JANE *Struct. Wood* iv. 74 The pith may be distinctive: thus, in oak it has, in section, the shape of a five-rayed star. **1976** R. F. LYNDON in M. M. Yeoman *Cell Division in Higher Plants* viii. 297 In those cells which form the pith the cell cycle may no sooner get to minimum length than it begins to lengthen again as the cells mature.

2. The spinal 'marrow' or cord; in quot. 1653, the brain substance.

1594 T. B. *La Primaud. Fr. Acad.* II. 357 The pith of the chine bone. **1607** TOPSELL *Four-f. Beasts* (1658) 289 Some ..do twine out the pith of the back with a long wire. **1627** MAY *Lucan* VI. 764 The pyth of Staggs with Serpents nourished Was mixed there. **1653** H. MORE *Antid. Ath.* I. xi. (1712) 34 This laxe pith or marrow in Man's Head. **1741** *Compl. Fam.-Piece* I. ii. 155 Take a Quantity of the Pith of an Ox. **1867** F. FRANCIS *Angling* i. (1880) 49 The bait consisting of..a bit of pith (bullock's marrow).

fig. **1577** B. GOOGE *Heresbach's Husb.* (1586) 20b, The Germanes..doo in steade of doung, cast vppon it a kinde of pith and fatnesse of the earth.

3. Applied to various other substances forming the inner part or core of something, and thus analogous to the pith of a tree; as

†**a.** The 'crumb' of bread. *Obs.* **b.** The core of various epidermal appendages, as feathers, horns, and hairs. †**c.** = DIPLOE. *Obs. rare.* **d.** The imperfectly carbonized core of an iron rod.

a. *c* **1450** *Bk. Hawkyng* in *Rel. Ant.* I. 302 Take a white lof ..and kut her almoste a too in the peth. **1579** LANGHAM *Gard. Health* (1633) 90 Apply the pith of Bread baked with Coliander seed. **1601** HOLLAND *Pliny* II. 280 They vse to lap it in the soft crum or pith of a loaf of bread.

b. 14.. *Voc.* in Wr.-Wülcker 588/41 *Ile*, the pythe of a penne. **14..** *Nom.* ibid. 703/36 *Hoc ilum*, the pyf of the penne. **1835–6** *Todd's Cycl. Anat.* I. 350/2 Both sides [of the shaft of a feather]..enclose a..substance called the pith. **1840** J. BUEL *Farmer's Comp.* 71 The piths of horns, or the residue of..horns after the comb-maker has taken all that is fit for his use.

c. 1684 tr. *Bonet's Merc. Compit.* III. 81 In some places the Skull is simple, thin and pellucid, without any Pith.

d. 1831 J. HOLLAND *Manuf. Metal* I. 231 If [the carbonising process be] only partially effected the centre of the rod still exhibits its duller iron-like structure, or pith, as the workmen call it.

4. *fig.* The central or inward part; hence, the essential or vital part (*of* anything); spirit, essence, substance, quintessence. So ***pith and marrow***.

c **897** K. ÆLFRED *Gregory's Past. C.* ix. 55 Smeaʒeað ðeah & ðeahtiʒað on hiera modes rind moniʒ god weorc to wyrcanne, ac on ðam piðan bið oðer ʒehyded. *c* **1400** *Rom. Rose* 7172 Now haue I you declared right The menyng of the bark and rynde..But now at erst I wole bigynne To expowne you the pith withynne. **1434** MISYN *Mending of Life* 123 So þou may cum to þe pith of lufe. **1526** TINDALE *Heb.* viii. 1 Of the thynges which we have spoken this is the pyth. **1551** T. WILSON *Logike* (1580) 10 The pith of this worde *Habitus*, can hardely be vttered with one worde in this our tongue. **1581** J. BELL *Haddon's Answ. Osor.* 183b, Herein consisteth the whole pithe of our controuersie. **1603** SHAKS. *Meas. for M.* I. iv. 70. **1635** N. R. *Camden's Hist. Eliz.* I. 93 The very pith and marrow of sweet speech. *a* **1831** A. KNOX *Rem.* (1844) I. 80 The very pith and marrow of Mr. Wesley's views. **1877** SYMONDS *Renaiss. It., Fine Arts* (1897) III. ii. 42 Within the great cities the pith of the population was Latin.

†**b.** *to the pith*, thoroughly, to the very core.

1577–87 HOLINSHED *Chron.* III. 1127/2 Shortlie after.. she performed hir promise to the pith.

5. a. Physical strength or force; vigour, toughness; might, mettle, 'backbone'.

a **1300** *Cursor M.* 22793 (Edin.) It semis al again kind þat mannis molden fleis and banis..Haf piþe [*v.r.* pith] and lif, als þai hauid ar. *c* **1375** *Ibid.* 7090 (Fairf.) þorou his hare his strenght was made Atte xx. mens pith he hadde. *c* **1386** CHAUCER *Wife's Prol.* 475 But Age allas..Hath me biraft my beautee and my pith. **1456** SIR G. HAYE *Law Armys* (S.T.S.) 287 In thair awin propre pythe, and vertu of corps and strenthe of membris. *c* **1475** *Rauf Coilȝear* 863 Thay preis furth properly thair pithis to prufe. **1545** ASCHAM *Toxoph.* (Arb.) 112 Brasse, iron or style haue theyr owne strength and pith in them. *Ibid.* 117 Newe ale..wil sone lease his pith. **1601** BP. W. BARLOW *Serm. Paules Crosse* 17 A man of Sampsons pith. **1681** COLVIL *Whigs Supplic.* (1751) 56 We'll both defend with all our pith. **1763** CHURCHILL *Epist. to Hogarth* 33 Should love of Fame.. Spur thee to deeds of pith. **1823** BYRON *Juan* VII. xviii, 'Mongst them were several Englishmen of pith, Sixteen called Thompson, and nineteen named Smith. **1886** STEVENSON *Kidnapped* ii. 12 This [curse]..took the pith out of my legs.

b. Force, vigour, energy (of words, speech, etc.).

c **1526** FRITH *Disput. Purgatory* (1829) 102 Some man will think mine arguments to be of small pith. **1548** UDALL *Erasm. Par. Luke* Pref. 13 He shall fele a certain vertue and pith such as he shall not fele the lyke in any other bookes. **1563** *Mirr. Mag., Blacksmith* x, In wyt he had so little pyth. **1828** CARLYLE *Misc.* (1857) I. 209 Cool vigour and laconic pith. **1876** SPURGEON *Commenting* 2 Matthew Henry..is usually plain, quaint, and full of pith.

6. Substance, substantial quality (of words, writings, etc.). ? *Obs.*

c **1407** LYDG. *Reson & Sens.* 4882 So ful of pith is the matere That swich a book in Romaunce Was neuer yet made in Fraunce. *a* **1529** SKELTON *Col. Cloute* 58 It hath in it some pith. **1586** T. B. *La Primaud. Fr. Acad.* I. 192 With the whistling of lips or hands..shepheards cause their sheepe to arise, or lie downe, bicause they understand not an articulate or distinct speech, that hath some pith in it. **1590** [J. GREENWOOD] *Confer.* Pref. A ij, If thou finde not such pith or substance in the matters discussed.

7. Importance, gravity, weight; esp. in phrase ***of (great) pith and moment***, or the like (after Shaks.).

1602 SHAKS. *Ham.* III. i. 86 Enterprizes of great pith and moment. **1624** BEDELL *Lett.* vi. 104 Neither is there any place..of speciall pith, that hath not beene obserued. **1826** J. WILSON *Noct. Ambr.* Wks. 1855 I. 91, I hae a secret to communicate, a secret o' some pith and importance. **1830** J. W. CROKER in *C. Papers* (1884) II. xv. 85 We have seen the scruples..of one..cabinet minister alter the whole course of enterprises of great pith and moment.

8. *attrib.* and *Comb.*, as (in sense 1) ***pith-ball, -cavity, -cell, -coat, -cylinder***; (in sense 2) ***pith bait, marrow, pudding***; ***pith-like*** adj.; **pith-drawn** *a.* (see quot.); **pith fleck**, in certain woods, a small dark patch made by parenchyma cells filling cavities left by insect larvæ; **pith hat**, a helmet-shaped sun-hat made of the dried pith of the Indian Solah or Spongewood of Bengal (*Æschynomene aspera*), hence called **pith-hat-plant** (Miller *Plant-n.* 1884); **pith helmet** = *pith hat*; so ***pith-helmeted*** adj.; **pith paper**, a paper made from the pith of various plants; **pith-plant**, the Chinese rice-paper tree (*Aralia* or *Fatsia papyrifera*); **pith ray** = *medullary ray* s.v. MEDULLARY *a.* 2b; **pith-ray fleck** = *pith fleck*; **pith-tree**, a leguminous tree (*Æschynomene elaphroxylon*) of tropical Africa, having soft white pith-like wood; **pith-work**, articles made of pith, esp. of *Æschynomene aspera*.

1812 SIR H. DAVY *Chem. Philos.* 126 Two gilt *pith balls, suspended upon strings of silk. **1849** NOAD *Electricity* (ed. 3) 14 A cylinder of brass, supported on a glass stand, and furnished with a pith ball electroscope. **1875** HUXLEY & MARTIN *Elem. Biol.* (1877) 79 The medullary or *pith-cavity in the centre of the section. *Ibid.*, The *pith-cells, around the central cavity. **1871** KINGSLEY *At Last* xiii, Two or three blows with the cutlass, at the small end of the nut, cut off not only the *pith-coat, but the point of the shell. **1884** BOWER & SCOTT *De Bary's Phaner.* 308 The *pith-cylinders of the shoots..are only connected by narrow medullary rays. **1703** T. S. *Art's Improv.* I. 19 Trees..Rift or Cleft, or *Pith-drawn, as some call it, by falling too soon, viz. before they are Sawn asunder. **1890** W. SOMERVILLE tr. *Hartig's Timbers* 77 *Pith-flecks, darkish-coloured patches met with in some woods. **1911** *Forestry Q.* IX. 244 Pith flecks or medullary spots are small, brown, half-moon shaped patches appearing ..on the cross sections of many of our woods. **1956** F. W. JANE *Struct. Wood* x. 236 Rotary cut birch..has a most attractive figure, due largely to the very numerous pith flecks which it contains. **1970** PANSHIN & DE ZEEUW *Textbk. Wood Technol.* (ed. 3) I. x. 366 Pith flecks, or medullary spots, are confined to hardwoods. **1884** J. MACDONALD in *19th Cent.* June 1002 With nothing on but their ungainly *pith-hats. **1889** T. A. GUTHRIE *Pariah* I. i, Who's the man who goes about in a *pith helmet? **1917** *Harrods Gen. Catal.* 643/3 Lady's Pith Helmet. Pith body, covered white drill. **1934** G. B. SHAW *Too True to be Good* II. 50 He wears a pith helmet with a pagan. **1971** *Country Life* 15 July 141/2 Who ..buys a Cawnpore Tent Club pith helmet with quilted khaki cover? **1976** *Evening Post* (Nottingham) 15 Mar. 6/3 Has anybody a pith helmet..? Members of Aspley Methodist Church, who are to put on a pantomime 'The Sleeping Beauty'..would be glad to borrow one for their show. **1916** 'BOYD CABLE' *Action Front* 190 Half-forgotten illustrations in the papers of *pith-helmeted infantry in the Boer War. **1866** *Treas. Bot.* s.v. *Æschynomene*, The *pith-like stem of *Æ. aspera* is..used in India..for making hats, bottle-cases, swimming jackets [etc.]. **1655** MOUFET & BENNET *Health's Impr.* (1746) 199 *Pith-Marrow, running all along from the hinder Brain..to the End of the Back-bone or Chine of Beasts. **1834** G. BENNETT *Wanderings* II. 75 The *pith plant is procured from Oan-nāām, near the province of See-chuen. **1750** E. SMITH *Compl. Housewife* (ed. 14) 131 To make a *Pith Pudding. Take a quantity of the pith of an ox [etc.]. **1902** G. S. BOULGER *Wood* 22 The whole mass of xylem is traversed radially by *pith-rays. **1928** HOLMAN & ROBBINS *Elem. Bot.* iii. 54 In stems in which the vascular tissue does not form a continuous cylinder, the bundles are separated by pith rays. **1953** K. ESAU *Plant Anat.* xv. 343 The spaces among the strands.. are occupied by parenchymatic ground tissue. These plates of tissue can be designated as pith rays or medullary rays. **1970** PANSHIN & DE ZEEUW *Textbk. Wood Technol.* (ed. 3) I. v. 179 Since all wood rays originate in the cambium, such terms as pith rays and medullary rays, frequently encountered in literature on wood, should not be used, because they imply that wood rays consist of the same kind of tissue as the pith. **1913** *Circ. U.S. Forest Service* No. 215 (*title*) *Pith-ray flecks in wood. **1925** EAMES & MACDANIELS *Introd. Plant Anat.* vii. 187 Pith-ray flecks are, unfortunately, sometimes explained as normal features of wood structure. **1864** J. A. GRANT *Walk across Afr.* p. xv, Ambadj; native name for the *pith-tree. **1884** MILLER *Plant-n.*, Pith-tree, of the Nile, *Herminiera Elaphroxylon.* **1887** MOLONEY *Forestry W. Afr.* 313 Ambash or Pith-tree of the Nile... The wood is very light, and in the form of small logs is used by the natives to assist them in crossing rivers. **1961** F. R. IRVINE *Woody Plants of Ghana* 360 Ambatch or Pith Tree of Nile Land... By rivers and in swamps in open country.

pith (pɪθ), *v.* Also 5 (9) **peth.** [f. prec. sb.]

†**1.** ? To provide with pith, give pith or vigour. *Obs. rare*[−1].

14.. *Tundale's Vis., Circunsision* 93 Hit is also myghty, it pethys fayre Ageynis wanhope and disperacyon.

2. *trans.* To pierce or sever the 'pith' or spinal cord of (an animal), so as to kill it or render it insensible; *spec.* to slaughter (cattle) in this way.

1805 *European Mag.* June 482 The practice of slaughtering cattle by puncturing the medulla spinalis, or as it is now called, pithing cattle, is extending through all parts of the Kingdom. **1806** HOME in *Phil. Trans.* XCVI. 359 In the common mode of pithing cattle the medulla spinalis only is cut through, and the head remains alive. **1875** HUXLEY & MARTIN *Elem. Biol.* (1877) 203 The pulsation of the heart.. should be studied in a Frog rendered insensible by chloroform or by being pithed. **1886** P. CLARKE *New Chum*

xiii. (ed. 2) 184 'Now then, shall we peth it or shoot it?' says our butcher pro tem. **1895** *Tablet* 5 Jan. 22 To pith is to remove the brain with a gutting knife, and then to pass—say —a stiff clean wire up the spinal canal to break up the marrow.

3. To remove or extract the pith from. Also *fig.*

1852 LD. HADDO in *Mem.* x. (1866) 175 [We] fish, paddle in the water, or pith rushes till dinner. **1903** G. B. SHAW *Man & Superman* Pref. p. xxxiv, And yet..the respectable newspapers pith me by announcing 'another book by this brilliant and thoughtful writer'. **1913** —— *Quintessence of Ibsenism* (completed ed.) 192 The very first thing the theatrical wiseacres did with it [*sc.* A Doll's House] was to effect exactly this transformation [*sc.* a happy ending], with the result that the play thus pithed had no success. **1935** —— *Let.* 25 July in *To a Young Actress* (1960) 163, I entirely approve of Peter's escaping [from a public school] before he is pithed and turned out as a political and moral gentleman several centuries out of date.

Hence **pithed** (pɪθt) *ppl. a.*; **pithing** ('pɪθɪŋ) *vbl. sb.*, also *attrib.* as in *pithing-pole*, a pole having a sharp blade at one end, for pithing cattle.

1831 YOUATT *Horse* ix. 153 The operation is called pithing, from the name (*the pith*) given by butchers to the spinal marrow. **1864** H. FALCONER in *Reader* 5 Mar. 302/2 It divides into two long diverging arms (like the legs of a pithed frog). **1886** P. CLARKE *New Chum* xiii. (ed. 2) 184 Up jumps Tom on the bar overhead with a long pething-pole.. and with one plunge sends the cruel point with unerring aim into the spinal cord.

Pithagorean: see PYTHAGOREAN.

† **pitha'nology.** *Obs.* [ad. Gr. πιθανολογία (Col. ii. 4), f. πιθαν-ός persuasive + -λογία speech, etc.: see -LOGY.] 'Persuasiveness of speech'; the use of specious or plausible arguments.

1615 BYFIELD *Exp. Coloss.* ii. 4 Pithanology, which the apostle condemns, is a speech fitted of purpose, by the abuse of rhetoric,..to please and seduce. **1650** TRAPP *Comm. Deut.* xiii. 3 Hereticks have their pithanology, their good words and fair speeches. **1730** A. COLLIER *Clavis Univ.*, *Spec. True Philos.* 127 Called also by its christian name of pithanology, or science, falsely so called.

pit-head, -heap, etc.: see PIT *sb.*[1] 15.

pithecanthropus (pɪθɪ'kænθrəʊpəs). Also in Greek form **pithecanthropos**, or anglicized as **pithecanthrope**; also with capital initial. [mod.L., f. Gr. πίθηκ-ος ape + ἄνθρωπος man.] **1.** [(E. Haeckel *Natürliche Schöpfungs-geschichte* (1868) xix. 507).] A hypothetical creature bridging the gap in evolutionary development between apes and man.

1876 E. R. LANKESTER tr. *Haeckel's Hist. Creat.* II. 293 These Ape-like Men, or Pithecanthropi, very probably existed towards the end of the Tertiary period. **1877** SHIELDS *Final Philos.* 146 [Man's] descent from a tailed ancestor, to which he [Haeckel] gives the zoölogical name of Pithecanthropos or the primitive ape-man. **1883** tr. *Joly's Man bef. Metals* 17 Prehistoric man..has even been sometimes called man-monkey, or pithecanthrope.

2. [(E. Dubois *Pithecanthropus erectus* (1894) 1).] The fossil hominid first described from remains found by Eugene Dubois (1858–1940) in Java in 1891, now included in the species *Homo erectus*; = *Java man* s.v. JAVA.

1895 *Nature* 5 Dec. 115/2 Dr. Dubois placed Pithecanthropus below the point of devarication of the anthropoid apes from the human line. **1895** CUNINGHAM in *Nature* 28 Feb. 429/1 The so-called Pithecanthropus is in the direct human line. **1898** GADOW tr. *Haeckel's Last Link* 24 Dr. Dubois exhibited the cranium of Pithecanthropus. **1905** J. MCCABE tr. *Haeckel's Evol. Man* II. xxiii. 632 The pithecanthropus excited the liveliest interest, as the long-sought transitional form between man and the ape. **1933** A. S. ROMER *Man & Vertebrates* xi. 239 Some scientists have claimed that *Pithecanthropus* is an ape, far below human status. **1933** N. DOUGLAS *Looking Back* II. 301 Science has a knack of filling up those gaps when least you expect it, as in the case of radium and pithecanthropus. **1957** L. EISELEY *Immense Journey* 101 The finding of the Pithecanthropus skull cap had bolstered this view.

So **pithecan'thropic** *a.*, of or pertaining to pithecanthropus; also *fig.*, resembling an ape, clumsy; **pithe'canthropine** *a.*, resembling or closely related to the fossil hominid once included in the genus *Pithecanthropus*; also as *sb.*; **pithe'canthropoid** *a.* = prec; also *fig.*

1890 *Cent. Dict.*, Pithecanthropoid. **1897** *Open Court* XI. 256 The pithecanthropic mummery, colloquially called monkey-business, connected with closing one nostril and breathing through the other and then of closing both till the compressed columnar air-current is imagined to bump against the triangular fundament of Kundalini. **1917** *Q. Rev.* July 35 Degeneracy, as seen in idiots,..due to a reversion to the pithecanthropic element. **1925** *Bull. Geol. Soc. China* IV. 177 Sooner or later pithecanthropine remains will be recovered from the Siwaliks. **1929** A. CROWLEY *Spirit of Solitude* I. xvii. 198, I was absorbed in 'The Cloud on the Sanctuary', reading it again and again without being put off by the Pharisaical, priggish and pithecanthropoid notes of its translator, Madame de Steiger. **1931** A. KEITH *New Discov. Antiq. Man* 293 The greatest number of these [characters] link these ancient Chinamen to the Pithecanthropic type of Java. **1958** L. DURRELL *Mountolive* xiii. 251 He mopped his brow continually, and gave his ingratiating pithecanthropoid grimace. **1958** F. E. ZEUNER *Dating Past* (ed. 4) ix. 304 At Ternifine in North Africa another pithecanthropine type of man proved to be associated with a primitive Acheulian industry. **1959** J. D. CLARK *Prehist. S. Afr.* iv. 77 In Africa the cranial form of the Pithecanthropoid type of man may have undergone a fairly rapid development. *Ibid.*, The third and most probable explanation is that the Pithecanthropic stock early evolved..directly into a basic type of *Homo sapiens.* **1960** G. DURRELL *Zoo in my Luggage* ii. 44 His Pithecanthropic features split into a wide grin of glad recognition. **1961** *Times* 5 Sept. 13/5 The pithecanthropines were sometimes grouped with Neanderthal and modern man in the sub-family Homininae. **1962** *Advancement of Sci.* XVIII. 424/1 The advanced pithecanthropine skull recently discovered..has been dated approximately. **1976** *Sci. Amer.* Jan. 96/3 A pithecanthropine grade has been recorded in a unique 800-millilitre endocast from Lake Rudolph in Kenya that is almost three million years old; the better-known true pithecanthropines are about a million years old. **1979** 'C. BRAND' *Rose in Darkness* v. 44 Like an archaeologist, building up the whole structure of ancient man from a single tooth..pithecanthropoid man.

pithecian (pɪ'θiːsɪən), *a. Zool.* [ad. F. *pithécien*, f. Gr. πίθηκος ape: see -IAN.] Of or pertaining to *Pithecia* (Geoffroy, 1812), the typical genus of the *Pitheciinæ*, a subfamily of the *Cabidæ*, S. American monkeys commonly called Sakis. So **pi'theciine** *a.*, pertaining to the *Pitheciinæ*.

1890 *Cent. Dict.*, Pitheciine. **1893** *Athenæum* 18 Mar. 349/3 The fundamental types of the molars are identical in man and the anthropoids, and the lower one differs entirely from that of the pithecian and cebian monkeys.

pithecoid (pɪ'θiːkɔɪd), *a.* (*sb.*) [ad. F. *pithécoïde*, f. Gr. πίθηκος ape: see -OID.] Resembling in form or pertaining to the apes, esp. the higher or anthropoid apes; simian, ape-like.

1861 HUXLEY in *Nat. Hist. Rev.* Jan. 67 The demonstration of a pithecoid pedigree. **1863** —— *Man's Place Nat.* 159 The fossil remains of man..do not..take us appreciably nearer to that lower pithecoid form. **1866** —— *Preh. Rem. Caithn.* 102 A curious pithecoid variation, observed in the gorilla and the chimpanzee. **1880** *19th Cent.* Nov. 854 Beyond the range of pithecoid intelligence.

B. as *sb.* An anthropoid ape; a simian.

1890 in *Cent. Dict.*

pithecological (pɪθiːkəʊ'lɒdʒɪkəl), *a. nonce-wd.* [f. Gr. πίθηκος ape + -LOGICAL.] Pertaining to the scientific study of apes.

1865 VISCT. STRANGFORD *Selection* (1869) II. 110 Its proceedings..were not of a truly geographical, so much as of a more or less authentically pithecological, character.

pithful ('pɪθfʊl), *a. rare.* [f. PITH *sb.* + -FUL.] Full of pith; pithy. (*lit.* and *fig.*)

1548 UDALL, etc. *Erasm. Par. Mark* ii. 24 This strong and pithful Philosophy. **1613** W. BROWNE *Brit. Past.* II. iv, For as in tracing These pithfull rushes, such as are aloft, By those that rais'd them presently are brought Beneath unseene. **1819** W. TENNANT *Papistry Storm'd* (1827) 14 Pickin' out pithfu' texts, and strang.

Pithian: see PYTHIAN.

pithiatism ('pɪθɪətɪz(ə)m). *Psychol.* [ad. F. *pithiatisme* (J. Babinski 1901, in *Revue Neurologique* IX. 1079), f. Gr. πειθ-ώ persuasion + ἰατ-ός curable: see -ISM.] A type of hysteria thought to be amenable to and curable by suggestion. So **pithi'atic** *a.*

1910 *Lippincott's New Med. Dict.* 740/2 *Pithiatism*, = Hysteria. (Babinski.) *Ibid.*, Pithiatic. **1913** E. JONES in White & Jelliffe *Mod. Treatm. Nervous & Mental Dis.* I. viii. 370 Babinski attempts to divide verbal suggestions into those that are unreasonable..and those that are reasonable and beneficial... Treatment by means of persuasion he calls 'pithiatism'. **1918** J. D. ROLLESTON tr. *Babinski's Hysteria or Pithiatism* p. xv, Among the various nervous phenomena observed in the neurology of war it is most important to distinguish hysterical or pithiatic disorders. **1930** P. D. KERRISON *Dis. of Ear* (ed. 4) xxii. 551 Pithiatism implies not only the possibility of cure by persuasion, but also the fact that the disorder may in some degree be called into being by suggestion. *Ibid.*, Pithiatic deafness..is at its inception a veritable deafness, the inevitable sequence of a shock to the perceptive labyrinth, which could have had no other result. **1975** Y. PELICIER in J. G. Howells *World Hist. Psychiatry* iv. 131 Babinski (1901) proposed the name of 'pithiatism' to designate a special condition, where suggestion is able to produce or suppress clinical symptoms.

pithily ('pɪθɪlɪ), *adv.* [f. PITHY *a.* + -LY[2].] In a pithy manner.

† **1.** In a way that goes to the pith; thoroughly; in substance or essence; essentially. *Obs.*

1434 MISYN *Mending of Life* 122 Pithily clensid fro vnclennes. **1435** —— *Fire of Love* 98 If we owr myndes fro lufe of creaturis pythely depart. **1539** CROMWELL in Merriman *Life & Lett.* (1902) II. 228, I..have pithely weyed and poundred the deposicions and Relations. **1645** MILTON *Tetrach.* Wks. 1851 IV. 221 It would be as pithily absurd.

† **2.** With power or strength; mightily. *Obs.*

1522 *World & Child* in Hazl. *Dodsley* I. 250, I am a prince perilous y-proved,..and pithily y-pight. **1573–80** BARET *Alv.* P 414 Pithily, vehemently. **1678** R. BARCLAY *Apol. Quakers* v. ix. 130 These..did..pithily and strongly over-turn the False Doctrine of their Adversaries.

3. In reference to speech or writing: So as to express the pith or substance; briefly and with fullness of meaning; in few and significant words; with condensed and forcible expression; sententiously, tersely, vigorously.

1533 MORE *Debell. Salem* Wks. 1019/2 As thoughe they were wordes of such substancial effect, that I would not haue it appere..that hee had written so piththely. **1586** W. WEBBE *Eng. Poetrie* (Arb.) 48 Marke..with howe choyse wordes it is pithily described. **1698** S. CLARK *Script. Just.* xii. 62 A Passage..wherein he expresses himself very pertinently, pithily, and elegantly. **1816** SCOTT *Old Mort.* xviii, He next handled very pithily the doctrine of defensive arms and of resistance to Charles II. **1864** *Sat. Rev.* 475/1 The knack of talking pithily—which means a knack of talking pointedly, and more or less audaciously.

pithiness ('pɪθɪnɪs). [f. PITHY *a.* + -NESS.] The quality or character of being pithy; *esp.* in sense 3 of the adj., Fullness of meaning with brevity of expression; condensation and force of style; terseness, sententiousness.

1547–64 BAULDWIN *Mor. Philos.* (Palfr.) 18 With such pithinesse in his counsels. **1619** R. WALLER in *Lismore Papers* Ser. II. (1887) II. 226 Much comendinge the grate pitthynes of your Lordships letters. **1813** JEFFERSON *Writ.* (1830) IV. 225 Their version of the 15th psalm is more to be esteemed for its pithiness than its poetry. **1863** J. G. MURPHY *Comm. Gen.* iv. 7 This sentence has all the pithiness and familiarity of a proverb.

Pithiviers (pitivje). The name of a town in northern France used *attrib.* to designate a French cake or tart consisting of puff pastry with a rich almond filling.

[**1846** A. SOYER *Gastronomic Regenerator* 488 *Gateau de Pithiviers.* Blanch and pound well half a pound of almonds.] **1970** SIMON & HOWE *Dict. Gastron.* 303/1 *Pithiviers cake*, a French cake made from puff-pastry mixed with sweet and bitter ground almonds. It is light with a delicate almond perfume. **1973** *Guardian* 30 Mar. 11/4 Pithiviers cake..is one of the great puddings from France... Roll out two 10 in. circles from packet puff pastry... Make a frangipane filling.

pithless ('pɪθlɪs), *a.* [f. PITH *sb.* + -LESS.] Devoid of pith; having no pith. (*lit.* and *fig.*)

1555 W. WATREMAN *Fardle Facions* II. viii. 181 No yncke-horne termes, nor pithlesse pratling. **1656** TRAPP *Comm. 2 Tim.* iii. 5 Hollow professors are as hollow trees..tall, but pithless, sapless, unsound. **1728** RAMSAY *Archers diverting themselves* 27 Pithless limbs in silks o'er-clad. **1817** COLEBROOKE *Algebra*, etc. Notes & Illustr. p. xlv, Omitting ..superfluous and pithless matter. **1879** BARING-GOULD *Germany* II. 273 Leaning on these hollow, pithless reeds.

Hence **'pithlessly** *adv.*

1884 J. PARKER *Apost. Life* III. 217 If we speak it pithlessly, it takes rank with any words short and empty.

'pit-hole, *sb.* A hole forming a pit; a pit-like hollow or cavity. (In various applications: see quots., and senses of PIT *sb.*[1]) **b.** *spec.* A grave.

1601 HOLLAND *Pliny* I. 525 Buds sprouting forth vnder the concauity or pit-hole of the foresaid ioints. *a* **1625** FLETCHER, etc. *Fair Maid Inn* II. ii, I have known a lady sick of the small pocks, onely to keep her face from pitholes, take cold, strike them in again, kick up the heels, and vanish. **1814** SCOTT *Wav.* xvi, A black bog..full of large pit-holes.

b. 1621–3 MIDDLETON & ROWLEY *Changeling* IV. i. 64 Alexander, that thought the world Too narrow for him, in th' end had but his pit-hole. **1768–74** TUCKER *Lt. Nat.* (1834) II. 647 It is common to fright children into taking of their physic, by telling them that else they must be put into the pit-hole. **1896** *Warwicksh. Wd.-bk.* s.v., Baby's dead, and gone in the pit-hole. [So in Eng. dialects, from Notts to Devon and Kent: see E.D.D.]

Hence **pit-hole** *v.*, to lay in the grave, to bury.

1607 W. S. *Puritaine* I. Bj b, All my friends were pit-hold, gone to Graues. **1611** CHAPMAN *May-day* III. 43, I would see her pithole[d], afore I would deale with her.

pithon, pithonical, pithonist: see PYTH-.

‖ **pithos** ('pɪθɒs). *Gr. Antiq.* Pl. pithoi. [a. Gr. πίθος.] A large wide-mouthed earthenware jar of spherical form, used for holding wine, oil, food, etc. Also *attrib.*

1879 J. J. YOUNG *Ceram. Art* 27 The pithos occupied by Diogenes was cracked and patched. **1925** V. G. CHILDE *Dawn European Civilization* ii. 32 From M.M. I to L.M. I clay jars (pithoi) were also used as receptacles for the corpse. **1949** W. F. ALBRIGHT *Archæol. of Palestine* vi. 118 In the first three phrases of Iron-Age Bethel the dominant vase was a large store-jar (pithos) with a very characteristic collared rim. **1955** *Sci. Amer.* July 45/2 At one entrance to this building was a sunken 'lustral area', where visitors made formal ablutions on arrival; it was surrounded by tall 'pithos' jars for water. **1957** V. G. CHILDE *Dawn European Civilization* (ed. 6) v. 72 In 1955 a cairn with pithos burials very like our round tombs was found in Messenia, but was M.H. in date. **1962** [see DÆDALIC *a.*] **1972** Y. YADIN *Hazor* II. iv. 50 It seems that the room served as a store; this is further corroborated by eight pithoi found in it. The bases of the pithoi were stuck deep in the floor of the room.

pithsome ('pɪθsəm), *a. rare.* [f. PITH *sb.* + -SOME.] Full of pith; vigorous, sturdy.

1864 BLACKMORE *Clara Vaughan* (1889) 248 Her pithsome health and vigour.

pithy ('pɪθɪ), *a.* [f. PITH *sb.* + -Y.]

1. Consisting or of the nature of pith; abounding in or full of pith.

1562 J. HEYWOOD *Prov. & Epigr.* (1867) 192 The pithy pith of an elder sticke. **1616** SURFL. & MARKH. *Country Farme* 225 The inward substance white,..without anie tast, ..and smell it hath none, neither is it anie thing pithie. **1793** B. EDWARDS *Hist. W. Indies* II. v. i. 209 The body of the cane..contains a soft pithy substance. **1821** CLARE *Vill. Minstr.* II. 73 The pithy bunch of unripe nuts. **1853** G. JOHNSTON *Nat. Hist. E. Bord.* I. 96 [Elder] well known to every schoolboy..., who fabricates his pop-gun from its pithy branches. **1893** NEWTON *Dict. Birds* 239 The rhachis [of a feather] is opaque, filled with a pithy substance.

2. *fig.* Full of strength or vigour; vigorous, strong; of liquor, strong, containing much alcohol. Now *dial.* or *Obs.*

13.. *Cursor M.* 9384 (Cott.) Al-king thing was þan..Wel pithier [*v.r.* mihtier] þan þai ar now. **1483** *Cath. Angl.* 282/1 Pythy, *vbi* strange. **1530** PALSGR. 320/2 Pythy stronge, *puissant.* **1634** MARKHAM *Archerie* ix. 84 A strong pithie kinde of Shooting. **1773** FERGUSSON *Cauler Water* iii, On mair pithy shanks they stood. **1812** W. TENNANT *Anster F.* IV, Some are flush'd with horns of pithy ale. **1876** SWINBURNE *Let.* 10 Jan. (1960) III. 112 A sea without rocks or cliff,..water thick and pithy with sand.

3. a. Full of substance or significance; solid, substantial; *esp.* of speech or writing: Containing much matter in few words; expressing briefly the pith or substance of a thing; condensed and forcible in expression or style; sententious; terse. (Now the prevailing sense.)

1529 MORE *Suppl. Soulys* Wks. 299/1 The sore pythye point wherwith he knitteth vp all hys heuy matter. **1531** TINDALE *Exp. 1 John* (1537) 93 It is a shorte and pythy sentence to moue or admonyse. **1571** GOLDING *Calvin on Ps.* ii. 5 Very piththie is this pronown I. **1657** SPARROW *Bk. Com. Prayer* (1661) 74 These short but pithy Ejaculations. **1754** RICHARDSON *Grandison* (1781) VI. liii. 341 Finding something to say to each, in his pithy, agreeable manner. **1824** MISS FERRIER *Inher.* xv, With one of her sharp pithy glances at Colonel D. **1893** J. C. JEAFFRESON *Bk. Recollect.* I. i. 13 He preached..a plain, short, pithy sermon.

b. *transf.* of a speaker or writer.

1548 UDALL *Erasm. Par. Luke* xix. 150 That other man also was piththie and an earnest bidder of Jesus. **1693** J. EDWARDS *Author. O. & N. Test.* 235 The pithy moralist [Seneca]. **1713** ADDISON *Ct. Tariff* ¶13 In all these particulars [he] was very short but pithy. **1879** GEO. ELIOT *Theo. Such* ii. 39 He was a pithy talker.

pitia'bility. *rare.* [f. next: see -ITY.] Pitiableness; something pitiable.

1865 CARLYLE *Fredk. Gt.* XVIII. vii. (1872) VII. 221 Pitiabilities of every kind.

pitiable ('pɪtɪəb(ə)l), *a.* Forms: 5 **pytoyable**, 5–6 **piteable**, 6 **pitoyable**, **pittiable**, 7 **pytyable**, 7–8 **pityable**, 6– **pitiable**. [ME. a. OF. *piteable* (13th c.), *pitiable*, *pitoiable* (mod.F. *pitoyable*) pitiable (in active and passive sense), f. OF. *piteer*, *pitier*, *pitoyer* to PITY: see -ABLE.]

1. Deserving, worthy of, or standing in need of pity; exciting pity; lamentable: = PITIFUL 3.

1456 SIR G. HAYE *Law Arms* (S.T.S.) 299 To ay justice with merci melle, efter as he seis caus piteable. *c* **1489** CAXTON *Blanchardyn* xxx. 114 Thees pytoyable thynges thus y-happed. **1586** in Tytler *Hist. Scot.* (1864) IV. 142 The auditory did find her case not pitoyable, and her allegations untrue. **1681–6** J. SCOTT *Chr. Life* (1747) III. 217 Out of great Condescension to this pitiable Infirmity of his sinful Creatures [etc.]. **1688** *Vox Cleri Pro Rege* 22 The Case is truly pityable. **1855** MILMAN *Lat. Chr.* IX. iv. (1864) V. 243 The champion of injured and pitiable women. **1879** MISS BRADDON *Clov. Foot* I. i. 32, I..found him in a pitiable condition.

2. Contemptible, miserable: = PITIFUL 4.

1789 MRS. PIOZZI *Journ. France* II. 353 For this pitiable exhibition, ships cut in paper, and saints carved in wood, we paid half a guinea each. **1849** MACAULAY *Hist. Eng.* iv. I. 511 That great party..had now dwindled to a pitiable minority. **1891** *Speaker* 11 July 36/1 The pitiable display of short-sighted greed over the Factory Bill.

†**3.** Characterized by pity: = PITIFUL 2. *Obs.*

1503 *Kalender of Shepherds* li, Sweyt & pyteabyl as the beyr,..dyspytful & prydful as the fasant.

Hence **'pitiableness**, pitiable quality or condition; **'pitiably** *adv.*, in a pitiable manner.

1694 KETTLEWELL *Comp. Penitent* 43 Remembring..the Pytyableness of my Weakness. **1825** J. NEAL *Bro. Jonathan* II. 166 A line of scripture..pitiably misunderstood. **1866** GEO. ELIOT *F. Holt* xliii, We are so pitiably in subjection to all sorts of vanity. **1894** MRS. H. WARD *Marcella* I. 41 For all its weakness and pitiableness.

pitied ('pɪtɪd), *ppl. a.* [f. PITY *v.* + -ED¹.] Compassionated, lamented, etc.: see the verb. Hence **'pitiedly** *adv.* (*rare*), in a way or to a degree to be pitied.

1627–77 FELTHAM *Resolves* II. xlix. 256 He is properly and pitiedly to be counted alone that is illiterate. **1728** ELIZA HEYWOOD *Mme. de Gomez's Belle A.* (1732) II. 214 A dishonourable Affair, in which his Glory, and at last his Life fell a necessary, but much pitied Sacrifice. **1851** RUSKIN *Stones Ven.* (1874) I. i. 1 Led, through prouder eminence, to less pitied destruction.

pitier ('pɪtɪə(r)). [f. PITY *v.* + -ER¹.] One who pities.

1601 DANIEL *Civ. Wars* VI. xiv, That which such a pitier seldom mends. **1650** R. STAPYLTON *Strada's Low C. Warres* VII. 53 The Favourers and Pittyers of the Cause. **1805** CAYLEY *Sir W. Raleigh* II. 90 Among his friends and pitiers in this his adverse fortune. **1860** EMERSON *Cond. Life* vii. 155 This class of pitiers of themselves.

pitiful ('pɪtɪfʊl), *a.* [f. PITY *sb.* + -FUL.]

†**1.** Characterized by piety; pious. *Obs. rare.*

c **1449** PECOCK *Repr.* II. xviii. 262 Encrece thow riȝtwisnes to piteful men [*piis adauge gratiam*]. **1570** LEVINS *Manip.* 186/1 Pittiful, *pius, misericors.*

2. Full of or characterized by pity; compassionate, merciful, tender.

1491 CAXTON *Vitas Patr.* (W. de W. 1495) II. 286/2 Thenne this pytefull man..dyde almesse. **1526** TINDALE *Jas.* v. 11 The lorde is very pitifull and mercifull. **1548** UDALL, etc. *Erasm. Par. Matt.* xx. 100 Shewing his pietifull affeccion. **1595** SHAKS. *John* IV. iii. 2 The Wall is high, and yet will I leape downe. Good ground, be pittifull and hurt me not. **1691** WOOD *Ath. Oxon.* I. 623 He was pitiful to the poor, and hospitable to his neighbours. *a* **1716** BLACKALL *Wks.* (1723) I. 20 A pitiful and compassionate Temper. **1875** MANNING *Mission H. Ghost* vii. 186 Why did our Divine Master, pitiful and tender as He is, speak so sternly?

3. Exciting or fitted to excite pity; pitiable, piteous, deplorable, lamentable. (Usually, now always, of actions, conditions, sights, cries, or the like; formerly also of persons.)

c **1450** *Cov. Myst.* (Shaks. Soc.) 236 This ded body that lyth here in grave, Wrappyd in a petefull plyght. **1532** TINDALE *Wks.* (Parker Soc.) II. 91 How pale and pitiful look they,..hanging down their heads. **1647** SPRIGGE *Anglia Rediv.* II. i. 66 The pittifullest spectacle that man can behold. **1696** PHILLIPS (ed. 5), *Pitiful*, said of the Condition of one that is reduc'd to great Misery, and excites Pity. **1868** E. EDWARDS *Ralegh* I. xxvi. 672 A pitiful account of his sorrows and perplexities. **1871** MORLEY *Vauvenargues* in *Crit. Misc.* Ser. I. (1878) 6 The pitiful fate of his friend.

†**b.** as *adv.* Pitifully. *Obs.*

1571 CAMPION *Hist. Irel.* ix. (1633) 117 He was pittifull hurt with a gun. **1599** SHAKS. *Much Ado* V. ii. 29 The God of loue that..knowes me, how pittifull I deserue.

4. To be pitied for its littleness or meanness; exciting pitying contempt; miserably insignificant or trifling, despicable, contemptible. (Cf. *miserable*, *wretched*, in similar use.)

1582 STANYHURST *Æneis* IV. (Arb.) 95 Feare shews pitfle crauens. **1598** GRENEWEY *Tacitus' Ann.* II. vii. (1622) 42 Many such simple and friuolous matters, and more mildly to terme them, pittifull. **1659–60** PEPYS *Diary* 26 Feb., A pitiful copy of verses. **1687** A. LOVELL tr. *Thevenot's Trav.* I. 28 It is no more but a pitiful Village. **1771** *Junius Lett.* liv. (1820) 288, I see the pitiful advantage he has taken. **1874** LISLE CARR *Jud. Gwynne* I. iv. 130 When you talk such pitiful trash about rewarding me.

5. *Comb.*, as ***pitiful-hearted***.

1596 SHAKS. *1 Hen. IV*, II. iv. 134 Pittiful hearted Titan that melted at the sweete Tale of the Sunne.

pitifully ('pɪtɪfʊlɪ), *adv.* [f. prec. + -LY².] In a pitiful manner.

1. With compassion; compassionately, mercifully.

1303 R. BRUNNE *Handl. Synne* 1494 (MS. Harl.), Ȝyf he demeþ pytyffully [*MS. Dulw.* pytously] At hys demyng getyþ he mercy. **1548–9** (Mar.) *Bk. Com. Prayer, Litany*, Pytifully beholde the sorowes of our heart. **1612** T. TAYLOR *Comm. Titus* i. 6 He shall more patiently and pitifully deale against it. **1885** H. V. BARNETT in *Mag. Art* Sept. 454/2 He ..thought pitifully of her in her affliction.

2. In a way that awakens or deserves pity; piteously, lamentably, wretchedly, miserably.

c **1420** *Siege of Rouen* in *Collect. Lond. Cit.* (Camden) 3 Gonnys they schott with grete envye, And many were smytte pyttyfully. *c* **1440** *Alphabet of Tales* 286 He hard a voyce cry petifullie. **1568** GRAFTON *Chron.* II. 754 He was with mischarging of a speare,..pittifully slayne and brought to death. **1625** K. LONG tr. *Barclay's Argenis* II. x. 93 Pitifully requesting the succour of the passers by. **1678** BUNYAN *Pilgr.* I. 127 They beat them pitifully. **1722** DE FOE *Plague* (Rtldg.) 117 She cry'd and look'd pitifully. **1884** *Manch. Exam.* 29 Mar. 4/8 The widow, whose career of wedded happiness has been so pitifully cut short.

3. Contemptibly, meanly, meagrely; miserably.

1613 PURCHAS *Pilgrimage* (1614) 215 Her teares (how pitifully easie are they to some?). **1638** JUNIUS *Paint. Ancients* 28 To prove..how pitifully poore and ridiculous the first workes of Art have been. **1719** LONDON & WISE *Compl. Gard.* 243 Strawberry Plants..in the second Year they bear wonderfully; but that being past, they produce very pitifully. **1742** H. WALPOLE *Lett. to Mann* (1834) I. 139 The Secret Committee go on very pitifully.

pitifulness ('pɪtɪfʊlnɪs). [f. as prec. + -NESS.] The quality of being PITIFUL, q.v.

1557 *Sarum Primer* N viij b, I commende and betake my handes to thy holinesse, besechynge thy pitifulnesse. **1662** *Bk. Com. Prayer, Prayers sev. Occas.*, Let the pitifulness of thy great mercy loose us. **1670** EACHARD *Cont. Clergy* 32 They would..soon discern..the pittifulness of their matter, and the impertinency of their tales and phansies. **1702** C. MATHER *Magn. Chr.* III. III. (1852) 541 That pitifulness and that peaceableness which rendered him yet further amiable. **1884** W. S. LILLY in *Contemp. Rev.* Feb. 264 Christianity, preaching pitifulness and courtesy. **1897** *Allbutt's Syst. Med.* IV. 597 Scrofula:..its frequency, its pitifulness, and its marring of fair young lives.

†**pitikins, pittikins,** dim. of PITY, after *bodikins*, in *Ods pit(t)ikins*: see OD¹ 2.

1604 DEKKER *Honest Wh.* Wks. 1873 II. 27 Gods my pittikins, some foole or other knocks [cf. 29 Gods my pitty, what an Asse is that Citizen].

pitiless ('pɪtɪlɪs), *a.* [f. PITY *sb.* + -LESS.]

1. Without pity or compassion; showing no pity; merciless. Also *fig.*

a **1412** HOCCLEVE *De Reg. Princ.* 3306 Out of pitee, growith mercy.., ffor piteeles man can do no mercy. **1556** J. HEYWOOD *Spider & Fl.* lxx. 147 To kepe al from pittelesse strife. **1605** SHAKS. *Lear* III. iv. 29 The pelting of this pittilesse storme. **1703** ROWE *Ulysses* III. i, The Gods are pityless. **1856** EMERSON *Eng. Traits, Ability* Wks. (Bohn) II. 35 In Parliament, the tactics of the Opposition is to resist every step of the Government, by a pitiless attack. **1882** J. H. BLUNT *Ref. Ch. Eng.* II. 274 The spirit of the times was pitiless enough.

†**2.** Receiving no pity; unpitied. *Obs. rare.*

a **1618** J. DAVIES *Wittes Pilgr.* lxxvii, So, do I perishe pitilesse, through Feare.

Hence **'pitilessly** *adv.*; **'pitilessness**.

1611 COTGR., *Atrocement*, most cruelly, pittilesly. **1755** JOHNSON, *Pitilessness.* **1848** W. H. KELLY tr. *L. Blanc's Hist. Ten Y.* II. 353 He was pitilessly dragged along the passages, up or down the stairs. **1855** MILMAN *Lat. Chr.* XIV. vii. (1864) IX. 237 Their pitilessness to the poor.

pitill: see PITTEL.

'pitkin. *nonce-wd.* [f. PIT *sb.*¹ + -KIN.] A little pit.

1917 E. POUND *Lustra* 199, I dug the ell-square pitkin.

pitle, var. PIGHTLE.

pitless ('pɪtlɪs), *a. rare.* [f. PIT *sb.*¹ + -LESS.] Having no pit: in quots., said of a theatre.

1895 *Daily News* 11 Nov. 6/4 The reconstructed and no longer pit-less Opera Comique. **1903** *Daily Chron.* 19 Dec. 5/2 The projectors of new and pitless playhouses.

pit-maker, etc.: see PIT *sb.*¹ 15.

pitman¹ ('pɪtmən). [f. PIT *sb.*¹ + MAN *sb.*¹]

†**1.** The digger of a pit or common grave. *Obs.*

1609 J. DAVIES *Humours Heaven on E.* (Grosart) 46/2 The ceremonie at their Burialls Is Ashes but to Ashes, Dust to Dust; Nay not so much; for strait the Pit-man falles (If he can stand) to hide them as he must.

2. a. A man who works in a pit or mine, esp. a coal-mine; a collier. (In some localities, applied *spec.* to the man who attends to the pumping machinery in the pit or shaft.)

1761 *Hist.* in *Ann. Reg.* 82/2 A large body of pitmen came into the town. **1832** BABBAGE *Econ. Manuf.* xx. (ed. 3) 202 A chief Pitman has charge of the pumps and the apparatus of the shafts. **1863** KINGSLEY *Water-Bab.* i. 11 They passed through the pitmen's village. **1881** RAYMOND *Mining Gloss.*, *Pitman* (*Cornw.*), a man employed to examine the lifts of pumps and the drainage. **1892** *Labour Commission* Gloss., *Pit-man*, a collier as distinguished from a miner... This distinction..has not of late years been closely preserved. The term *pitman* was formerly applied to every worker in a colliery, from the 'trapper' to the 'hewer'. **1934** J. B. PRIESTLEY *Eng. Journey* x. 334, I ought to explain here that in Durham collieries there are always 'pits' and miners 'pitmen'. **1978** R. LEWIS *Uncertain Sound* iii. 76 My father had been a simple pitman.

b. *attrib.*, as †**pitman candle**, a miner's lamp.

1658 H. MOSELEY *Healing Leaf* 30 Set not up a pit-man Candle in a stately room.

3. a. The man who stands in a sawpit and works the lower end of the saw; a pit-sawyer.

1703 MOXON *Mech. Exerc.* 101 With the Pit-Saw they enter the one end of the Stuff, the Top-man at the Top, and the Pit-man under him. **1879** *Lumberman's Gaz.* 15 Oct., The light thin saw of the pitman.

b. A motor-racing mechanic working in a pit (see PIT *sb.*¹ 1 h).

1913 *Technical World Mag.* XIX. 495/2 A pitman has noticed that the tire is flat.

c. *U.S. colloq.* (See quot.)

1961 A. BERKMAN *Singers' Gloss. Show Business* 69 *Pitmen*, ..musicians playing in the orchestra pit.

4. One of a race dwelling in pits. *rare.*

1894 *Westm. Gaz.* 30 Jan. 3/3 The little pit-men who seem to have been the real aborigines of Yezo, conquered by the Ainu.

5. a. (*transf.* from sense 3.) In machinery, the rod connecting a rotating with a reciprocating part, and communicating motion from one to the other; a connecting-rod. Chiefly *U.S.*

1813 O. EVANS in *Weekly Reg.* 17 Apr. 111/2, I apply the power by means of a connecting rod or rods (or pitman as it is called when applied in saw mills). **1846** WORCESTER, *Pitman*..an appendage to a forcing pump. **1847** WEBSTER, *Pitman*... 2. The piece of timber which connects the lower end of a mill-saw with the wheel that moves it. **1860** *Sci. Amer.* Aug. 96/1 [The] pistons are connected by piston rods *d* with pitmans *e* with the cranks *f f*. **1864** WEBSTER, *Pitman*, ..the connecting rod in a saw mill; also, sometimes, the connecting rod of a steam-engine. **1881** *Metal World* No. 24. 373 It is preferable in high-speed engines to make the piston and cross-head as light as possible, and put the weight into the pitman or connecting-rod.

b. *attrib.*, as ***pitman-box***, ***-coupling***, ***-head***, ***-press***, ***-strap***: see quots.

1875 KNIGHT *Dict. Mech.*, *Pitman-box*, the stirrup and brasses which embrace the wrist of the driving-wheel... *Pitman-coupling*, a means of connecting a pitman to the object which it drives... *Pitman-head*, the block or enlargement at the end of a pitman, at which point its connection is made to the object by which it is driven or which it drives. **1879** *Lumberman's Gaz.* 13 Aug. 8 The Lee Mill..came to a stop..by the breaking of the lower pitman strap and trunk to the gang. **1884** KNIGHT *Dict. Mech.* Suppl., *Pitman Press*, one working by pitman connection with a shaft, instead of eccentric or other equivalent.

Pitman² ('pɪtmæn). The name of Sir Isaac *Pitman* (1813–97) used *attrib.*, *absol.*, and in the possessive to denote a system of shorthand notation devised by him and first published in 1837.

Pitman's Shorthand is a proprietary name in the U.K.

[**1862** M. LEVY *Hist. Short-hand* xvii. 167 Compare their rules with those of Pitman, in which he explains how to write the Scotch guttural.] **1886** *Encycl. Brit.* XXI. 838/2 The main features of Pitman's system must now be described. **1895** *Montgomery Ward Catal.* 74/1 The Reporter's Style of the Pitman System, by which fluent speakers can be reported verbatim. **1907** *Trade Marks Jrnl.* 5 June 963 Pitman's Shorthand Isaac Pitman 292,180. **1916** G. B. SHAW *Pygmalion* Pref. 101 His [*sc.* Sweet's] true objective was the provision of a full, accurate, legible script for our noble but ill-dressed language; but he was led past that by his contempt for the popular Pitman system of shorthand, which he called the Pitfall system. *Ibid.*, There was a weekly paper to persuade you to learn Pitman... I actually learned the [*sc.* Sweet's] system.. and yet the shorthand in which I am writing these lines is Pitman's. **1951** E. COXHEAD *One Green Bottle* vi. 171 What's Ogam?.. A sort of prehistoric Pitman's? **1969** K. GILES *Death cracks Bottle* ii. 17, I think my Pitman is decipherable. **1970** E. MCGIRR *Death pays Wages* ii. 52 It is an exercise book and the entries are in very clear Pitman. **1976** *Daily Times* (Lagos) 8 Oct. 24/1 (Advt.), Applicants should possess WASC preferably with credit in English Language or equivalent and RSA or Pitmans or Government Certificate or their equivalent for 100/50 w.p.m. in shorthand and typewriting.

Hence **Pit'manic** *a.*, resembling or suggestive of Pitman shorthand; **'Pitmanite**, a student or exponent of the Pitman system; **'pitmanize** *v. trans.*, to fill (a book) with Pitman shorthand.

1908 G. B SHAW *Let.* 29 June (1972) II. 793 The other day I was confronted with an old copy of the Academy, dated 1898, with some shorthand notes on the margin... You can imagine how the honest Pitmanite who was asked to decipher it.. believed that he had saved me from a fearful scandal. **1912** BEERBOHM *Christmas Garland* 14 Seven whole 8 × 5 inch note-books had I pitmanised to the brim. **1925** *Blackw. Mag.* Aug. 264/1, I saw.. a sheet of notepaper scribbled with Pitmanic symbols. **1960** *Times* 28 Sept. 13/4 What odds if the Pitmanic 'X' full stops were sometimes deliberately exaggerated!

pit-mark, -martin, etc.: see PIT *sb.*[1] 15.

pitmatic (pɪt'mætɪk). Also **-atick, -atik**, and in *pl.* (construed as sing.). [f. PIT *sb.*[1] after MATHEMATIC *a.* and *sb.*] The local patois used by miners in the north-east of England. Also in extended use.

1893-4 R. O. HESLOP *Northumb. Words* II. 539 *Pitmatics*, a jocose term for the technicalities of colliery working. **1901** 'R. GUTHRIE' *Kitty Fagan* 8 Pitmatics? I've been schooled in them. **1934** J. B. PRIESTLEY *Eng. Journey* x. 334 The local miners [in Durham] have a curious lingo of their own, which they call 'pitmatik'... It is only used by the pitmen when they are talking among themselves... When the pitmen are exchanging stories of colliery life.. they do it in 'pitmatik', which is Scandinavian in origin, far nearer to the Norse than the ordinary Durham dialect. **1961** *Listener* 23 Nov. 865/2 The ambitious young actor who naturally speaks beautiful English must assume a rough-diamond pitmatic though he has it not. **1967** A. L. LLOYD *Folk Song in Eng.* vi. 382 Most of his [*sc.* Tommy Armstrong's] songs are in the peculiar North-eastern miners' jargon called 'pitmatic'. **1972** *Jrnl. Lancs. Dial. Soc.* Jan. 19 He had many recollections of coal miner's terms, or, as they are known locally, *pitmatic*. **1976** *Daily Mail* 19 Aug. 19/2 Fred Reed, a dialect poet, gives examples of 'pitmatic', the language of the coalminer spoken in pits throughout the North.

pit-mirk, *a. Sc.* and *north. dial.* [f. PIT *sb.*[1] + MIRK *a.*] As dark as a pit (or as the pit, hell: cf. PIT *sb.*[1] 4); intensely dark, pitch-dark.

1728 RAMSAY *Monk & Miller's Wife* 29 It fell late, And him benighted by the gate. To lye without, pit-mirk, did shore him, He couldna see his thumb before him. **1815** SCOTT *Guy M.* xi, It's pit mirk, but there's no an ill turn on the road but twa. **1886** STEVENSON *Kidnapped* iii. 20 Neither moon nor star, sir, and pit-mirk.

pit-mouth: see PIT *sb.*[1] 15.

pito, var. of PITA[1].

Pitocin (pɪ'təʊsɪn). *Med.* Also **pitocin**. [f. PI(TUITARY *a.* + OXY)TOCIN.] A proprietary name for (an aqueous solution of) oxytocin.

1929 *Official Gaz.* (U.S. Patent Office) 15 Jan. 514/1 Parke, Davis & Company, Detroit, Mich... *Pitocin.* For oxytocic principle of the pituitary gland... Claims use since about October 20, 1928. **1929** *Jrnl. Amer. Med. Assoc.* 19 Jan. 237/2 The alpha and beta hormones [isolated from the posterior lobe of the pituitary body] are to be known commercially as pitocin and pitressin respectively. **1929** *Trade Marks Jrnl.* 23 Jan. 117/1 Pitocin... All goods included in class 3 [i.e. chemical substances prepared for use in medicine and pharmacy]... Parke, Davis and Company, .. pharmaceutical chemists. **1929** MARTINDALE & WESTCOTT *Extra Pharmacopoeia* (ed. 19) II. 169 Each Cc. of 'Pitocin' contains 10 oxytocic units, and it is thus identical in activity with 'Pituitzin'. **1948** MARTIN & HYNES *Clin. Endocrinol.* i. 11 Two distinct hormones can be obtained from posterior pituitary extracts—pitressin, and oxytocin or pitocin, which acts on uterine muscle. **1961** *Lancet* 30 Sept. 762/1 The use of pitocin induction of labour in hæmolytic disease of the newborn.

pitometer: see PITOT[2] b.

pitomie, obs. humorous aphetic f. EPITOME.

piton ('piːtɒn). [a. Fr., = 'eye-bolt', also 'piton'.]

1. *Physical Geogr.* (See quot. 1972.)

1902 *Pop. Sci. Monthly* July 274 Northern Martinique, like other West Indian islands, is a labyrinth of mornes and pitons, i.e., of singularly steep peaks and ridges (partly volcanic cones, partly erosional forms), densely clothed with forests and herbage. **1918** C. W. BEEBE *Jungle Peace* (1919) iii. 56 A small wandering rainstorm drifted against the smallest piton and split in two. **1944** C. A. COTTON *Volcanoes* xi. 177 (*heading*) Smooth cliffs.. moulded during vertical extrusion of a plug dome to form the piton Lassen Peak, California. **1972** *Gloss. Geol.* (Amer. Geol. Inst.) 543/1 *Piton*, a term commonly used for volcanic peaks, especially steep-sided domes, in the West Indies and other French-speaking regions. **1976** *Sat. Rev.* (U.S.) 30 Oct. 26/2 St. Lucia.. offers.. cone-shaped volcanic peaks and twin pitons.

2. *Mountaineering.* (See quot. 1909.)

1898 *Encycl. Sport* II. 49/2 Snatch blocks and other kinds of pulleys, pitons or holdfasts.. are also requisite. **1909** C. E. BENSON *Brit. Mountaineering* ii. 40 Piton—a strong iron spike with an eye at one end through which a rope can be passed. **1916** G. D. ABRAHAM *On Alpine Heights & Brit. Crags* iii. 64 He surprised us by scraping the ice off a ring-headed *piton* which was driven into a rock crevice. **1936** AUDEN & ISHERWOOD *Ascent of F6* II. i. 75 They're hammering the whole south face full of pitons and hauling each other up like sacks! **1955**, etc. [see ÉTRIER]. **1959** 'G. CARR' *Swing away, Climber* iii. 58 He carried a multitude of short metal pegs with holes in the blunt end—pitons. **1972** *Country Life* 13 Jan. 94/3 From time to time a piton has to be hammered in, for.. the rock disintegrates.

3. *Comb.* (in sense 2), as ***piton belay***; **piton hammer**, a hammer designed for fixing and extracting belays; **piton runner**, a piton used as a running belay.

1971 C. BONINGTON *Annapurna South Face* xiii. 164 On reaching the ledge leading into the main icefields, Mick hunted around for piton belays, eventually found a couple of suitable cracks and abseiled back. **1943** R. C. GEIST *Hiking, Camping & Mountaineering* 227 They are driven into rock cracks or into ice by a special piton hammer. **1952** MORIN & SMITH tr. *Herzog's Annapurna* ix. 141, I used my piton-hammer.. as an anchor. **1971** C. BONINGTON *Annapurna South Face* vi. 76 The whammer, a space-age style piton-hammer of his own design. *Ibid.* x. 117 The rope behind Martin was dragging badly because of the friction caused by its passage through the tunnel and various piton runners.

pitot[1]. *rare.* [Origin obscure: cf. PIDDOCK.] app. A razor-shell. (See also quot. 1971.)

1611 COTGR., *Manche de cousteau*, the Pitot; a long, and round shell-fish. **1971** A. M. LYSAGHT *Joseph Banks in Newfoundland & Labrador 1766* vii. 161 These molluscs [sc. *Cyrtodaria siliqua*] are known by the French name of 'pitot' and the areas where they live are called 'pitot banks'.

pitot[2] ('piːtəʊ). *Physics* and *Aeronaut.* Also **Pitot**. The name of Henri *Pitot* (1695–1771), French scientist, used to designate devices based upon his inventions for measuring the relative velocity of a fluid, esp. the airspeed of an aircraft, as **pitot head**, a pitot-static tube; **pitot-static** *a.*, designating a device consisting of a pitot tube inside or adjacent to a parallel tube closed at the end but with holes along its length, the pressure difference between them being a measure of the relative velocity of the fluid; also *absol.*; **pitot** (†**or Pitot's**) **tube**, an open-ended right-angled tube pointing in opposition to the fluid flow and connected to a means of measuring pressure; also, a pitot-static tube; also *absol.*

1881 *Encycl. Brit.* XII. 508/1 A Darcy gauge.. consists of two Pitot tubes having their mouths at right angles. **1895** R. C. CARPENTER *Heating & Ventilating Buildings* ii. 38 In case the pressure and velocity are great, considerable error will be made by using the open tube.., and for such a case a Pitot's tube.. should be used. **1901** G. E. DAVIS *Handbk. Chem. Engin.* I. iv. 191 The total pull of a chimney upon a water manometer when only one limb of the tube was connected up, was 14/16 of an inch, while with the Pitot tube the amount shown was only 8/100 of an inch of water. **1914** *Techn. Rep. Advisory Comm. Aeronaut. 1912–13* 59 This pressure-tube anemometer consists of two tubes, a Pitot tube facing the wind and a static pressure-tube along the wind direction with holes drilled into the side of it. **1916** *Field* 20 May 788/2 At last he fumbles for his safety belt, but with a start remembers the Pitot Air Speed Indicator, and.. smiles as he hears the Pitot-head's gruff voice, 'Well, I should think so, twenty miles an hour I was registering.' **1920** G. C. BAILEY *Compl. Airman* xxi. 172 The only really satisfactory test of the Pitot is a flying one. **1920** L. BAIRSTOW *Appl. Aerodynamics* iii. 75 (*heading*) Initial determination of the constant of the pitot-static pressure head. **1930** C. J. STEWART *Aircraft Instruments* iii. 54 The pitot-tube instrument is based on an adaptation of the method used by Pitot in 1732 for the measurement of the speed of a river. **1934** V. M. YEATES *Winged Victory* I. iii. 27 Looking at the pitot he found the speed was a hundred and twenty. **1942** *R.A.F. Jrnl.* 27 June 21 One [Gremlin].. was seen.. to swing nimbly.. down to the pitot head and block it with ice. **1948** *Jrnl. R. Aeronaut. Soc.* LII. 272/1 Rates of climb and descent measured by the pitot-static are subject to errors introduced by random vertical currents in the atmosphere. **1965** R. G. KAZMANN *Mod. Hydrol.* iv. 63 The Pitot tube can be used to make a pattern of measurements along the cross section of a stream. **1973** 'A. HALL' *Tango Briefing* ix. 111 His inability to know to what extent our airspeed would be true and to what extent it would be expressed by the wind in the pitot-head. **1975** L. J. CLANCY *Aerodynamics* iii. 25 The pitot-static tube may be mounted in a position on the aircraft where the flow is affected by the presence of the aircraft. **1978** R. V. JONES *Most Secret War* iv. 36 This is true enough of a pitot tube but, as Lindemann pointed out to me, the proposal was perfectly sound if one used, as the inventors suggested, accelerometers.

b. Pitot meter, also **pitometer** (pɪ'tɒmɪtə(r)). (See quots. 1934, 1941.)

1907 *Jrnl. Franklin Inst.* CLXIV. 440 It is only necessary to leave the pitometer orifices at the point of maximum velocity in order to record the mean flow. **1934** J. H. PERRY *Chem. Engineers' Handbk.* 692 The pitot meter consists of two tubes, one facing upstream and the other downstream. **1941** *Ibid.* (ed. 2) 838 The modified pitot tube known as a pitometer has one pressure opening facing upstream and the other facing downstream. The differential between the two openings is usually from 25 to 50 per cent more than that for a standard pitot tube. **1955** C. S. FORESTER *Good Shepherd* ii. 25 That was the pito-meter log reading. **1961** *Engineering* 3 Nov. 566/3 The development flowmeters.. were calibrated in clean air against a venturi meter and a pitot meter.

pitous, -tee, obs. var. of PITEOUS, PITEOUSTEE.

pitpan ('pɪtpæn). Also 9 **pittpan**. [? Native name.] A long flat-bottomed boat hollowed out of the trunk of a tree, used in Central America; a dugout.

1798 COL. BARROW in *Naval Chron.* (1799) I. 247 Canoes, dories, and pit pans. **1810** *Ann. Reg.* 738/1 The Pit-pan being flat-bottomed, the Dory round. **1854** J. L. STEPHENS *Centr. Amer.* 8 We.. made an excursion in the government pitpan... Ours was about 40 feet long and 6 wide in the centre, running to a point at both ends and made of the trunk of a mahogany tree. **1897** *Outing* (U.S.) XXX. 248/2 They .. carried me quickly to the river, where a pit-pan was in waiting.

pit-pat: see PIT-A-PAT.

Pitressin (pɪ'trɛsɪn). *Med.* Also **pitressin**. [f. PIT(UITARY *a.* + VASOP)RESSIN.] A proprietary name for (an aqueous solution of) vasopressin.

1929 *Official Gaz.* (U.S. Patent Office) 15 Jan. 514/2 Parke, Davis & Company... Filed Nov. 2, 1928. Pitressin. For pressor principle of the pituitary gland... Claims use since about Oct. 20, 1928. **1929** [see PITOCIN]. **1929** *Trade Marks Jrnl.* 23 Jan. 117/1 Pitressin... All goods included in class 3 [i.e. chemical substances prepared for use in medicine and pharmacy]... Parke, Davis and Company,.. pharmaceutical chemists. **1943** *Lancet* 27 Feb. 267/1 Pitressin tannate in oil seems to be the safest and most effective slowly acting preparation of the posterior pituitary lobe so far available for the treatment of diabetes insipidus. **1974** *Jrnl. Pediatrics* LXXXV. 79/2 The infant's water balance was initially controlled with intravenous fluids alone but subsequently he was given a trial of pitressin. **1974** *Aerospace Med.* XLV. 1223/1 These same groups also showed little change in urine output in response to subcutaneous administration of 300 mU of Pitressin tannate in oil. **1976** *Lancet* 25 Dec. 1403/2 Aqueous vasopressin injection ('Pitressin') as a prophylactic measure was popular some years ago [against headache after lumbar puncture].

pit-saw, -sawyer, -stone, etc.: see PIT *sb.*[1] 15.

‖**pitso** ('piːtsəʊ). Also †**peetsho**, †**peetso**, †**piicho**, **pitsu**, and with capital initial. [Sotho.] A Sotho tribal conference in a *kgotla*.

1822 J. CAMPBELL *Trav. S. Afr.: 2nd Journey* I. 264 The other chief said they should come to the *peetso* all well powdered. **1824** W. J. BURCHELL *Trav. S. Afr.* II. 408 The *piicho* or assembly remained sitting in easy conversation for nearly an hour longer. **1828** J. PHILIP *Res. S. Afr.* II. vii. 132 All great questions, and all questions relating to peace or war, are decided on in public assemblies, which are designated in their language by the name of Peetshos. **1879** *Queenstown Free Press* (Suppl.) 28 Oct. (Pettman), The annual *Pitso* was held at Maseru on the 19th instant, about 10,000 being present. **1897** J. BRYCE *Impressions S. Afr.* xx. 424 To-day the Pitso has lost much of its old importance. **1925** *Brit. Weekly* 4 June 211/3 The population of Basutoland is little over half a million, and the entire manhood must have ridden in to the *Pitso*. **1947** L. HASTINGS *Dragons are Extra* ii. 50 A great *pitso* was arranged. The traditional gathering took place in the open country south of Serowe. **1953** J. PACKER *Apes & Ivory* x. 105 The Royal visit to Basutoland, when the whole nation had gathered in a mighty *pitsu* at Maseru to welcome the King and Queen and their daughters had left a deep impression. **1959** *Chambers's Encycl.* IX. 747/1 Matters of highest importance were discussed in the *pitso*, the national assembly, at which the poorest and meanest tribesman had equal right with the proudest to voice his opinion. **1968** A. FULTON *Dark Side of Mercy* 27 The Chief had summoned the men of the clan to the Khotla and opened the pitso by telling those assembled that the season had been poor, [etc.]. **1976** WEST & MORRIS *Abantu* 121 It was more usual for all matters of general concern to be aired at a *pitso*, a general meeting open to all adult men in the chiefdom and held in the kgotla of the chief.

‖**Pitta** ('pɪtə). *Ornith.* [mod.L., a. Telugu *pitta* anything small, a pet.] Name of a genus of passerine birds, type of the family *Pittidæ*, the Ant-thrushes of the Old World, species of which inhabit China, India, and Australia, and one, *P. angolensis*, the W. Coast of Africa. They are remarkable for their vivid colouring, strong bill, short tail, and long legs, and range in size between a lark and a jay.

1840 *Penny Cycl.* XVIII. 194/2 *Pitta Gigas*,.. Giant Pitta. **1894** NEWTON *Dict. Birds* 728 Few Birds can vie with the Pittas in brightly-contrasted coloration. **1896** *List Anim. Zool. Soc. Lond.* 303. **1898** MORRIS *Austral Eng.* 357/1.

Hence **'pittid**, any bird of the family *Pittidæ*; **'pittine** *a.*, of or belonging to the genus Pitta; **'pittoid** *a.*, allied in form to the pittas.

1890 *Cent. Dict.*, Pittine. **1895** *Funk's Stand. Dict.*, Pittid, Pittoid.

pitta, var. PITA[2].

pittacal ('pɪtəkəl). *Chem.* Also **-call**. [a. Ger. *pittacal* (Reichenbach 1835), f. Gr. πίττα pitch + καλός beautiful, κάλλος beauty.] A dark blue solid substance obtained from the high-boiling portions of wood-tar.

1835 *Thomson's Records Gen. Sci.* I. 54 On Pittacal, a new dye-stuff. **1838** T. THOMSON *Chem. Org. Bodies* 735 Pittacall is without smell, is tasteless, and not volatile. **1866** WATTS *Dict. Chem.* IV. 661 Pittacal appears to have decided basic characters, for it is dissolved by acids and precipitated by alkalis.

pittance ('pɪtəns), *sb.* Forms: 3–6 **pitaunce**, 4–6 (8) **-ance**, (4–6 **pyt(t)-, pet-, -ance, -aunce**), 6–

pittance, (6 **-ans**, 7 **pettance, pittens**). [ME. *pita(u)nce*, a. OF. *pitance*, *-ence* pittance, app. the same word as *pitance*, *pietance* pity, ad. L. type **pietāntia*, deriv. of *pietās* (see PIETY), recorded 1317 in sense 'pittance' (so med.L. *pidantia*, *pit(t)antia*, etc.), whence also Pr. *pitansa*, *-za*, *piedansa*, *pidanza* pity, OIt. *pietanza* pity, later pittance, Sp. *pitanza* pittance, salary, OPg. *pitança* charity, later pittance. (A pittance was often provided by a charitable bequest to a convent.)

Other derivations have been suggested, as Gr. πιττάκιον tablet, billet, med.L. *picta* a small coin of Poitou, and the root *pett-* of *piece*, etc. See Diez, Scheler, Littré, Skeat, Körting No. 7106.]

1. A pious donation or bequest to a religious house or order, to provide an additional allowance of food, wine, etc., at particular festivals, or on the anniversary of the benefactor's death, in consideration of masses: hence, the allowance or dole itself; also, the anniversary service. Also *fig.* Now only *Hist.*

a **1225** *Ancr. R.* 114 Hwar was euer iȝiuen to eni blodletunge so poure pitaunce? *Ibid.* 412 Forgoð enne dei our pitaunce. **1303** R. BRUNNE *Handl. Synne* 10446 Synge me a messe For a man þat dede ys; And at myn ese he shal haue, To a pytaunce, þat he wyl craue. *c* **1386** CHAUCER *Prol.* 224 He was an esy man to yeue penaunce Ther as he wiste to haue a good pitaunce. *c* **1450** *Godstow Reg.* 605 To the said mynchons, euery yere in the day of his anniuersary, xl. shillings, to a pytaunce into mynde of his sowle. **1463** *Bury Wills* (Camden) 16 To eche monk..xij *d.* and a petaunce amonges them, eche man a french loof and a quart wyn. *c* **1500** *Melusine* 337 Raymondyn dyde doo send to hys bretheren hermytes besyde theire pytaunce other meetes for recreacion. **1737** OZELL *Rabelais* III. xxiii. 143 To bequeath ..to those good Religious Fathers..many Pitances. **1868** MILMAN *St. Paul's* vii. 135 Each member and servant of the Chapter received his portion or pittance. **1904** *Ch. Times* 29 Apr. 569/1 The pittance was an occasional relief to the usual strict dietary in the way of some exceptional or extra food or delicacy... In not a few monasteries there were special endowments for certain pittances, usually of early origin.

b. A charitable gift or allowance of food or money; an alms, dole.

c **1412** HOCCLEVE *De Reg. Princ.* 4513 Thow þat..to þe nedy yeuest no pitaunce. **1413** *Pilgr. Sowle* (Caxton 1483) I. xv. 13, I preye..of youre merytis superhabundaunce as grauntyth me of almesse somme pytaunce. **1812** S. ROGERS *Columbus* 132 A Pilot..Stopt to solicit at the gate A pittance for his child. **1838–9** FR. A. KEMBLE *Resid. in Georgia* (1863) 92 Their usual requests for pittances of food and clothing.

2. A small allowance or portion of food and drink; a scanty meal; scanty rations or diet. Also *fig.* Now *rare.*

1390 GOWER *Conf.* III. 31 Min Ere with a good pitance Is fedd of redinge of romance Of Ydoine and of Amadas. *c* **1430** LYDG. *Min. Poems* (Percy Soc.) 45 By sotyl crafte a morsel or pitaunce, A rustiler shal sone be redy founde. **1540–1** ELYOT *Image Gov.* (1556) 122b, Such a small pitaunce..as nowe our servauntes would disdeigne. **1578** *Chr. Prayers* in *Priv. Prayers* (1851) 520 O sacred pittance of our pilgrimage. **1586** A. DAY *Eng. Secretary* I. (1625) 28 At night againe hauing eaten some small pittance of supper. *c* **1611** CHAPMAN *Iliad* XI. 547 She seru'd a holsome Onion cut For pittance to the potion. **1613** R. CAWDREY *Table Alph.* (ed. 3), *Pittance*, short banquet. **1647** TRAPP *Comm. 1 Cor.* i. 28 [Poor men] have but prisoners pittances, which will keep them alive, and that's all. **1696** PHILLIPS (ed. 5), *Pittance*, any small proportion of Bread, or Meat. **1870** BRYANT *Iliad* XII. 520 Some just woman..spinning wool,.. that she may provide A pittance for her babes.

b. An allowance, remuneration, or stipend, by way of livelihood. Usually connoting its scanty amount or bare sufficiency.

1714 ABP. KING in Ellis *Orig. Lett.* Ser. II. IV. 292 That country..yields a clergyman but a small pittance. **1771** GRAY in *Corr. w. Nicholls* (1843) 120 Our good uncle Toby will have about four hundred pounds a year, no uncomfortable pittance! **1781** COWPER *Truth* 321 Yon cottager,..Just earns a scanty pittance. **1833** HT. MARTINEAU *Manch. Strike* ix. 101 The most skilful work fourteen hours a day for the pittance of one shilling. *a* **1862** BUCKLE *Civiliz.* (1869) III. ii. 86 The Protestant clergy.. had only a miserable pittance whereupon to live.

3. A small portion (*of* anything) allowed, furnished, or obtained; a (small or sparing) allowance, share, or allotment.

1616 SURFL. & MARKH. *Country Farme* 4 The well-instructed and modest Householder contenteth himselfe with..such Pittance, Grounds, and Seat as falleth vnto him. **1644** MILTON *Areop.* (Arb.) 51 If every action which is good, or evill in man at ripe years, were to be under pittance, and prescription, and compulsion, what were vertue but a name? **1696** WHISTON *Th. Earth* (1722) 62 'Tis uncertain whether even that pittance of time can fairly..be allow'd to it. **1749** FIELDING *Tom Jones* II. iii, Her small pittance of wages. **1841** MIALL in *Nonconf.* I. 401 The miserable pittance of instruction, the coarsest rudiments of knowledge.

b. A small portion, number, or amount; a small proportion of a whole. (Often with some notion of allowance or allotment.)

1561 T. NORTON *Calvin's Inst.* III. v. (1634) 322 The pardons doe bring out of the storehouse of the Pope, a certaine pitance of grace. **1655** FULLER *Ch. Hist.* v. i. §1 Divine Providence,..preserving the inconsiderable pittance of faithful professors against most powerful opposition. **1690** LOCKE *Hum. Und.* III. vi. (1695) 244 What a small pittance of Reason and Truth,..is mixed with those huffing Opinions. **1772** MONRO in *Phil. Trans.* LXII. 22 There may be a pittance of a calculareous marine salt in the yellow ley. **1856** EMERSON *Eng. Traits, Stonehenge* Wks. (Bohn) II. 129 The priest who receives £2,000 a year, that were meant for the poor, and spends a pittance on this small beer and crumbs.

† '**pittance**, *v. Obs.* [f. prec. sb.] *trans.* To give a (small) pittance to; to allowance.

1647 TRAPP *Comm. Rev.* vi. 5 That..men should be stinted and pittanced. **1650** ELDERFIELD *Tythes* 157 Gods minister onely is pittanced of what may keep him alive.

pittancer ('pɪtənsə(r)). *Obs.* exc. *Hist.* Forms: see PITTANCE; in 5 **-ere, -eere, -eer,** 8– **-er,** (9 **pietancer, pitanciar, -ier**). [ME. *pitauncere*, ad. OF. *pitancier* (1297 in Godef.), in med.L. *pitantiārius*, f. *pitance* PITTANCE: see -ER².]

An officer in a religious house having the duty of distributing and accounting for the pittances.

1426 LYDG. *De Guil. Pilgr.* 22238, I am Sowcelerere Off this place, and Pytauncere. *c* **1430** *Pilgr. Lyf Manhode* IV. xliv. (1869) 196 Þe ladi..is pitaunceere of heere inne, and suthselerere [*Fr.* La dame..est pitanciere de cyens]. **1463** *Bury Wills* (Camden) 34 But ijd. of rente to the Petaunseer. **1706** PHILLIPS, *Pietantiarius*, the Pittancer or Officer in Collegiate Churches, who was to give out the several Pittances, according to the Appointment of the Founders or Donours. **1881** *N. & Q.* 6th Ser. IV. 20/1 The abbot, the pittancer, the chamberlain, the sacristan, and the cook all had separate estates assigned to them for their maintenance. **1889** JESSOPP *Coming of Friars* 127 The western buildings were dedicated to..the pitancier's and kitchener's offices.

pittancery ('pɪtənsərɪ). *Obs.* exc. *Hist.* In 6 pitensarie. [ME. a. OF. *pitancerie*, f. *pitancier* PITTANCER; see -ERY. In med.L. *pitantiāria*.] The office of the pittancer of a convent; the estate belonging to this office.

1585 *Abingdon Acc.* (Camden) 167 A parcel of land and marsh called the Pitensarie. [**1892** KIRK *Ibid.* Introd. 36, 32*s.* 11*d.* was laid out 'about the gates and bridges in the Pittancery', that is, in lands belonging to the office.]

† '**pittancy.** *Obs. rare.* In 7 **pitancy.** [ad. med.L. *pitāntia*: see PITTANCE.] = PITTANCE *sb.* 1.

a **1645** HABINGTON *Surv. Worc.* in *Proc. Worc. Hist. Soc.* III. 520 Assyned to the Sacrist of the Churche of Worcester ..three marckes towards the Pitancy on the anniversary of Kinge John.

† **pittar(d, pittart,** obs. forms of PETARD.

1603 *Reg. Privy Council Scot.* VI. 519 A maist deteistable and unlauchfull ingyne of weir, callit the pittart.

pitted ('pɪtɪd), *ppl. a.* [f. PIT *v.* + -ED¹; in sense 1 partly f. PIT *sb.*¹ + -ED².]

1. Having pits or small depressions on the surface; marked or spotted with pits; †dimpled; *spec.* in *Bot.* of cells, vessels, etc. (see PIT *sb.*¹ 9 c). Also, marked with small-pox: see PIT *v.* 4 a.

a **1050** in Thorpe *Charters* 559 Ic ȝean..minon breðer ..þæs swurdes mid þam pyttedan hiltan. **1530** PALSGR. 320/2 Pytted as a mannes chynne is, *fosselu*. **1584** HUDSON *Du Bartas' Judith* IV. 351 Her pitted cheeks aperde to be depaint With mixed rose and lillies sweet and faint. **1776** WITHERING *Brit. Plants* (1796) IV. 54 Leaves..pitted; downy underneath. **1857** HENFREY *Elem. Bot.* Fig. 479 Fragment of a pitted duct. **1859** TENNYSON *Vivien* 394 The ..little pitted speck in garner'd fruit. **1861** BENTLEY *Man. Bot.* (1870) 40 Pitted or Dotted Vessels constitute by their combination Pitted Tissue.

2. Placed or planted in a pit.

1799 J. ROBERTSON *Agric. Perth* 242 The best method of planting pitted trees.

3. Matched against each other: see PIT *v.* 3.

1852 JERDAN *Autobiog.* I. xxiii. 193 The long pitted deadly foes.

† '**pittel, pitill.** *Obs.* Forms: 1 **pyttel, pittel,** 5 **pitill** (cf. 9 *dial* **piddle, pickle**). [OE. *pyttel, pittel* hawk, in *bléri a-pyttel* 'mouse-hawk'; perh. f. root *putt-* of PUTTOCK the kite.] A bird of prey; app. the Marsh Harrier (*Circinus æruginosus*); but perh., like *puttock*, applied also to the Kite, and the Bald Kite or Buzzard.

c **1000** ÆLFRIC *Voc.* in Wr.-Wülcker 132/38 *Scoricarius*, bleripittel. *a* **1100** *Ags. Voc.* ibid. 287/8 *Soricarius*, bleria pyttel. *c* **1450** HOLLAND *Howlat* 642 The Pitill and the Pype Gled cryand pewewe. [Cf. **1863** BARNES *Dorset Gloss.* 54 Dun-piddle... The kite or moor buzzard. **1873** SWAINSON *Weather Folk-Lore* II. 242 It is said in Wiltshire that the marsh harriers or dunpickles..alight in great numbers on the downs before rain.]

pitteous, -euous, etc., obs. ff. PITEOUS.

pitter ('pɪtə(r)), *sb. U.S.* [f. PIT *sb.*² + -ER¹.]

a. One who removes the pits or stones from fruit (*Cent. Dict.* 1890). **b.** A mechanical device for doing this.

1884 KNIGHT *Mech. Dict.* Suppl. 359/1 Hatch's pitter splits the fruit and removes the pit.

pitter ('pɪtə(r)), *v.* ? *dial.* [Echoic, with frequentative form: cf. PATTER *v.*, TWITTER *v.*] *intr.* To make a rapid repetition of a monosyllabic sound in quality approaching short *i*, as in the sound made by the grasshopper, or by a thin stream of water running over stones. Hence '**pittering** *ppl. a.*; also **pitter** *sb.*, as name of a rivulet.

a **1592** GREENE *Selimus* Wks. (Grosart) XIV. 211 The brooke..when his pittering streames are low and thin. *a* **1635** HERRICK *K. Oberon's Feast* Wks. 1869 II. 471 But that ther was in place to stirr His fier the pittering grass-hopper, The merrie crickett, puissing flye. **1652** G. TOOKE *Annæ Dicata, Pious Turtles* 3 At whose foot some pittering Rillet wound. **1803** J. LEYDEN *Scenes Infancy* I. 141 Pittering grasshoppers pipe giddily along the glowing hill.

1546 *Yorks. Chantry Surv.* (Surtees) II. 305 One little sprynge called Wragby Pytter.

pitteraro, obs. variant of PEDRERO.

pitter-litter ('pɪtə 'lɪtə(r)), *adv. rare*⁻¹. [After PITTER-PATTER *sb.* (*adv.*)] = PITTER-PATTER *sb.* (*adv.*) 2 a.

1910 H. G. WELLS *New Machiavelli* (1911) I. ii. 18 Dropped most satisfyingly down a brick shaft, and pitter-litter over some steep steps to where a head slaughterman strung a cotton loop round their legs.

'**pitter-'patter,** *sb.* (*adv.*) [Reduplicated from PATTER *v.*¹ and ², implying rhythmic repetition.]

1. Rapid repetition of words; sometimes applied to rapid and mechanical repetition of prayers. Cf. PATTER *v.*¹

c **1425** *Cast. Persev.* 2604 in *Macro Plays*, ȝene qwene, with hyr pytyr-patyr, hath al to-dayschyd my skallyd skulle! **1561** *Q. Hesther* (1873) 30 So they from pytter pattour, may cume to tytter totur Euen the same pylgrimage.

2. An imitation of a rapid alternation of light beating sounds, as those made by rain or hail, light footfalls, etc. **a.** orig. as *adv.*

1679 DRYDEN *Troilus* IV. ii, I'faith, pitter patter, pitter patter, as thick as hail-stones. **1839** THACKERAY *Major Gahagan* viii, Pitter patter, pitter-patter! they [bullets] fell.

b. as *sb.* A designation of such a sound.

1863 R. BUCHANAN *Undertones* I. vii, I lie and hearken,.. To the tinkling clatter, Pitter, patter, Of the rain On the leaves close to me. **1897** W. H. THORNTON *Remin. W. Co. Clergyman* vi. 169, I heard a pitter-patter, which seemed to be the tramp of a flock of sheep.

'**pitter-'patter,** *v.* [f. as prec. sb.]

1. *trans.* and *intr.* To patter or repeat in a rapid mechanical way. Cf. PATTER *v.*¹

a **1706** in Watson *Coll. Scot. Poems* I. 48 The Cleck Geese leave off to clatter,..And Priests, Maria's to pitter patter. **1819** W. TENNANT *Papistry Storm'd* IV. (1827) 134 Sir Freir began wi' blitter-blatter His pray'rs to saints to pitter-patter.

2. *intr.* To beat with a rapid alternation of light taps or pats, as rain; to palpitate. Cf. PATTER *v.*²

a **1792** LD. HAILES (Jam.). **1808–18** JAMIESON, *Pitter-patter*, to make a clattering noise by inconstant motion of the feet. **1825** BROCKETT *N.C. Gloss.*, *Pitter-patter*, to beat incessantly, like rain. **1891** S. C. SCRIVENER *Our Fields & Cities* 41 He had..put on a clean collar over a pitter-pattering heart.

pitth(e, pitthie, pitthy, obs. ff. PITH, PITHY.

pitticite ('pɪtɪsaɪt). *Min.* Also pittizite. [ad. Ger. *pittizit* (Hausmann 1813), f. Gr. πίττα pitch + -IC + -ITE¹.] Hydrous sulph-arsenate of iron having a vitreous or greasy lustre, occurring in yellowish or reddish-brown, red, and white reniform masses. Also called *pitchy iron ore.*

1826 EMMONS *Min.* 220 Pittizite, see iron subsulphate. **1850** DANA *Min.* (ed. 3) 453 Pitticite..occurs in old mines near Freiberg. **1866** WATTS *Dict. Chem.* IV. 661 Pitticite, Pittizite.

pittid, pittine: see PITTA.

pittie, obs. f. PETTY *a.*

pittie-pattie: see PIT-A-PAT.

pittier, obs. f. PITIER.

pittikins: see PITIKINS.

pitting ('pɪtɪŋ), *vbl. sb.* [f. PIT *v.* + -ING¹.] The action of the verb PIT, or the result of this.

1. The action of putting into a pit, or of storing (vegetables, etc.) in pits. Also *attrib.*

1827 STEUART *Planter's G.* (1828) 468 All treat of both the Trenching and the Pitting method. **1886** *Pall Mall G.* 14 May 3/2 The..unanimous Report of the Ensilage Commissioners in favour of the pitting of green crops instead of converting them into hay. **1898** *Westm. Gaz.* 14 Dec. 2/1 Then can one watch the slow pitting of the potatoes.

2. The action of setting cocks to fight, dogs to kill rats, etc., in a pit for sport.

1773 *Archæol* (1775) III. 133 The pitting of them [cocks] ..for the diversion and entertainment of man..was, as I take it, a Grecian contrivance. **1898** *Daily News* 7 May 10/3 Rat pitting was a common amusement.

3. The digging of a pit or pits; also, the formation of a pit by subsidence of the soil.

1764 *Museum Rust.* II. cvi. 357 This method of spreading the ashes is to be observed only in the case of pitting. **1805** R. W. DICKSON *Pract. Agric.* I. 340 In very dry seasons, when the moisture of the earth is very low, the fire catches the soil below and causes what is called *pitting*. **1839** URE *Dict. Arts* 965 No assurance of coal can be had without boring or pitting.

4. The formation of pits or small depressions in a surface, as on the skin by small-pox, on metal by corrosion, etc.; marking with minute hollow scars or spots; *spec.* in *Path.* the formation of a permanent impression in soft tissue by pressure; in *Bot.* the formation of pits on the wall of a cell or vessel (PIT *sb.*¹ 9 c). Also *concr.* a series or mass of such depressions or spots.

1665 HOOKE *Microgr.* 181 All those pittings did almost vanish. **1694** SALMON *Bate's Dispens.* (1713) 692/1 To take away the Pittings or Marks of the Small Pox. **1835–6** *Todd's Cycl. Anat.* I. 512/1 The pitting which is seen on making pressure on the skin. **1879** *Cassell's Techn. Educ.* IV. 400/2 It appears to be necessary to treat mild steel more cautiously than iron, in order to prevent local corrosion, or 'pitting'. **1884** BOWER & SCOTT *De Bary's Phaner.* 117 The walls of the cells..are..cellulose membranes, with ordinary simple pitting. **1894** *Geol. Mag.* Oct. 452 Slab..showing rain-pittings. **1933** *Forestry* VII. 22 No complex forms of plate were observed with scalariform intervascular pitting. **1973** H. E. DESCH *Timber* (ed. 5) ii. 35 The pitting occurring in a cross field takes one or other of five more or less distinct forms.

5. = *pit planting* s.v. PIT *sb.*[1] 15.

1847 [see NOTCHING *vbl. sb.* 3]. **1894** A. D. WEBSTER *Pract. Forestry* iv. 20 The advantages of pitting over any other method of planting cannot be questioned. **1930** *Forestry* IV. 19 The ordinarily understood pitting implies the opening of a hole 12 to 15 inches square, stirring up the under soil well, and then carefully placing the plant in the centre.

pittious, obs. form of PITEOUS.

Pittite[1] ('pɪtaɪt). [See -ITE[1] 1 b.] An adherent of the English statesman William Pitt (1759–1806), or of his policy. Also *attrib.*

1808 MOORE *Intolerance* iii, E'en thy Pittite heart Would burn. **1812** L. HUNT in *Examiner* 25 May 321/1 The remains of the Pittite Cabinet. **1834** MACAULAY *Pitt* Misc. 1860 II. 372 The haters of parliamentary reform called themselves Pittites.

So **'Pittism**, the policy of William Pitt.

1809 SCOTT *Let. to G. Ellis* 3 Nov. in *Lockhart*, The large and sound party who profess Pittism. **1862** *Fraser's Mag.* July 45 The advantage of professing an orthodox 'Pittism' and Protestantism, articles of great gain in 1827 and 1828.

pittite[2] ('pɪtaɪt). Also pitite. [f. PIT *sb.*[1] + -ITE[1].] One who occupies a seat in the pit of a theatre.

1812 *Dramatic Censor 1811* 8 The O.P. dance was attempted to be performed, but the Pitites had not yet mustered in sufficient force to carry their desire into effect. **1818** in J. Agate *These were Actors* (1943) 72 We cannot give the unfortunate *Pittites* any hope of shelter from 'the icy wind of Death' which seems to blow from all quarters at once [at Drury Lane]. **1841** C. MACKAY *Pop. Delusions* I. 351 The pitites were fierce and many. [Refers to the O.P. riots.] **1849** THACKERAY in *Scribner's Mag.* I. 681/1 A kind of stupid intelligence that passes for..wit with the pittites. **1885** *Manch. Exam.* 4 May 5/3 The wrath of the pittites and the gods was appeased. **1892** 'F. ANSEY' *Voces Populi* 2nd Ser. 155 *A pittite behind Jimmy*... Will you tell your little boy to set down, please? **1903** A. BENNETT *Truth about Author* xiii. 162 Many time I have stood with you. But never again, miserable pittites! **1939** JOYCE *Finnegans Wake* (1964) III. 427 The graced of gods and pittites. **1961** BOWMAN & BALL *Theatre Lang.* 260 *Pittite*, in British terminology, a spectator in the pit.

'pittle, *v. Obs.* exc. *dial.* Also 6 pitel. [var. of PIDDLE *v.*] **1.** = PIDDLE *v.* 1.

a **1568** ASCHAM *Scholem.* (Arb.) 121 To precise, to curious, in marking and piteling thus about the imitation of others.

2. = PIDDLE *v.* 2.

1801 W. TAYLOR in *Monthly Mag.* XII. 584 Prince Biribinker..pittled orange-flower water, and let otr of roses.

† **'pittle-'pattle**, *v. Obs. rare*⁻¹. [Echoic. Cf. *pitter-patter*, *pit-a-pat*, *prittle-prattle.*] = PITTER-PATTER *v.* 1.

1549 LATIMER *2nd Serm. bef. Edw. VI* (Arb.) 49 We in our dedes (I feare me to manye of vs) deny God to be God whatsoever we pittle pattle with our tonges.

‖ **pitto** ('pɪtəʊ). Forms: 7 poitou, 8 potoe, putto, 9 pito, pitto, pittu. [ad. Dahom. *kpitu.*] The native name of a kind of beer, made in West Africa, from fermented maize or rice; maize-beer.

1670 VILLAULT *Guinea* 168 A kind of small beer, which they call poitou. **1725** J. HOUSTOUN *Guinea* 53 Drinking palm-wine or potoe. **1737** J. ATKINS *Voy. Guinea* 111 Beer brewed from Indian corn pretty much in use here called putto. **1882** BURTON & CAMERON *To Gold Coast* (1883) I. x. 293 Pitto, hopless beer, the pombe of the East Coast. **1905** R. A. FREEMAN *Gold. Pool* 213 An old woman that hath drunk too much pittu.

pittoid: see PITTA.

pittoresque, obs. form of PICTURESQUE.

pittosporaceous (pɪtɒspɒ'reɪʃəs), *a. Bot.* [See next and -ACEOUS.] Of or pertaining to the natural order *Pittosporaceæ*.

pittosporad (pɪ'tɒspəræd). *Bot.* [Cf. ARAD.] A plant of the N.O. *Pittosporaceæ*, flowering trees or shrubs occurring chiefly in Australasia, and also in Africa, Japan, etc., of which the typical genus is *Pittosporum*.

1846 LINDLEY *Veg. Kingd.* p. lxiii, Epigynous Exogens..Alliance..*Berberales*..[N.O.] *Pittosporaceæ*, or Pittosporads.

‖ **pittosporum** (pɪ'tɒspərəm). *Bot.* [mod.L. (J. Banks in J. Gærtner *De Fructibus et Seminibus Plantarum* (1788) I. 286), f. Gr. πίττα pitch + σπόρος seed; from the resinous pulp enveloping the seeds.] An evergreen shrub or small tree of the genus so called, belonging to the family Pittosporaceæ, native to many subtropical or temperate regions, especially Australasia and China, and bearing small, often fragrant, flowers; also, a shrub of this genus cultivated as a house plant. Also *attrib.* See PITTOSPORAD.

1789 W. AITON *Hortus Kewensis* III. 488 Thick-leav'd Pittosporum. Nat[ive] of Madeira. **1825** *Greenhouse Comp.* I. 244 Geraniums, Myrtles, Pittosporums, Acacias, and the like. **1874** *Silver's Handbk. Australia* (1880) 275 The native plum..satinwood, pittosporum, and capivi. **1911** A. E. MACK *Bush Days* 2 You climb up the rocky path and brush under green pittosporums. **1948** W. ARNOLD-FORSTER *Shrubs for Milder Counties* ii. 27 The pittosporums include some of the most useful of evergreens. **1962** R. PAGE *Educ. Gardener* viii. 247 Thickly planted bushes of dark green pittosporum..I clipped into low green mounds. **1963** S. SCHULLER *1001 House Plants Questions Answered* 221 Can I grow pittosporum easily indoors? Yes, if you can provide a cool..south window for it. **1965** G. McINNES *Road to Gundagai* xiv. 244 Ballan was..well treed, especially..around Miss McCoppin's Guest House with its tall pittosporum hedge. **1972** PALMER & PITMAN *Trees S. Afr.* I. 659 Our indigenous pittosporum, growing in every province of South Africa under widely differing conditions, is naturally very variable in form. **1979** *Country Life* 26 Apr. 1298/2 Planting of replacement evergreens such as ceanothus, pittosporums and cistuses may be..deferred another week or two.

pittows, obs. variant of PITEOUS.

pitty ('pɪtɪ), *a.* A nursery form of PRETTY *a.*

1826 M. ROGET *Jrnl.* 27 Oct. in D. L. Emblen *P. M. Roget* (1970) xi. 191 One year old... Tries to imitate everything she hears, and says 'Papa', 'Mama', 'Ta', 'Pitty', 'Ba'. **1879** C. M. YONGE *Burnt Out* i. 6 Mammy, mammy, pitty, pitty! Dada kill great big piggy wig. **1939** JOYCE *Finnegans Wake* (1964) II. 361 Wingwong welly, pitty pretty Nelly!

† **pitty**, obs. form of PETTY *a.*

1598 MARSTON *Pygmal.* 64 But thus it is when pitty Priscians Will needs step vp to be Censorians.

pitty-pat, -patty: see PIT-A-PAT.

pituicyte (pɪ'tju:ɪsaɪt). *Histology.* [f. PITUI(TARY *a.* + -CYTE.] A small cell with branching processes that is the characteristic cell of the neurohypophysis.

1930 P. C. BUCY in *Jrnl. Compar. Neurol.* L. 505 The pars nervosa is made up of a dense connective-tissue network containing nerve fibers which descend the stalk, epithelial cells which invade the pars nervosa from the pars intermedia for a short distance, and a type of cell which is peculiar to the neural portion of the hypophysis and which we have called the pituicyte. **1948** MARTIN & HYNES *Clin. Endocrinol.* i. 2 The only specialized cells in the neural division are pituicytes. **1959** ROWE & WHEBLE *Conc. Textbk. Anat. & Physiol.* xiii. 524 The posterior lobe is made up of large numbers of nerve fibres and a special type of cell known as pituicytes. **1975** DANIEL & PRICHARD *Stud. Hypothalamus & Pituitary Gland* iii. 27 Pituicytes, or modified glial cells, are scattered throughout the tissue [of the upper infundibular stem].

pituis, obs. variant of PITEOUS.

‖ **pituita** (pɪtju:'aɪtə). *Physiol.* Also (after F.) 7 pituit, 8 pituite. [L. *pītuīta* slime, phlegm, rheum; F. *pituite* (Paré *c* 1575).] The secretion of the mucous membrane; phlegm, mucus. Also *attrib.* = PITUITARY.

1699 EVELYN *Acetaria* (1729) 134 Orach..allays the Pituit Humour. **1707** FLOYER *Physic. Pulse-Watch* 62 A Saliva, or thin Pituita. **1732** ARBUTHNOT *Rules of Diet* 338 Vessels..obstructed with a viscous Pituite. **1794** T. TAYLOR tr. *Plotinus* 102 The pituita, or the bile, or the like disorders. **1895** in *Syd. Soc. Lex.*

Hence **pituital** (pɪ'tju:ɪtəl) *a.* = PITUITARY.

1890 in *Cent. Dict.* **1895** in *Syd. Soc. Lex., Pituital.*

pituitary (pɪ'tju:ɪtərɪ), *a. Physiol.* and *Anat.* [ad. L. *pītuītārius*, f. *pītuīta*: see prec. So F. *pituitaire.*] **a.** Of, pertaining to, or secreting pituita or phlegm; mucous.

pituitary body, gland, †***glandule***, a small bilobed body attached to (and sometimes taken to include) the infundibulum at the base of the brain, partly synonymous with HYPOPHYSIS 3, q.v., which has an important influence on growth and bodily functions; originally supposed to secrete the mucus of the nose; also applied to structures connected with this.

1615 CROOKE *Body of Man* 946 It containeth the Pituitary or Phlegmaticke Glandule. **1748** HARTLEY *Observ. Man* I. ii. 180 That Part of the pituitary Membrane which invests the Cells of the *Ossa spongiosa.* **1808** BARCLAY *Muscular Motions* 511 To protect the olfactory nerves and pituitary membrane from the too great or too sudden changes with respect to heat, dryness, or cold. **1825**, etc. [see HYPOPHYSIS 3]. **1855** HOLDEN *Hum. Osteol.* (1878) 78 A deep depression..termed the pituitary fossa. **1895** *Syd. Soc. Lex., Pituitary fold*, the two layers of dura mater which enclose the Pituitary body. *Ibid., Pituitary space*, the space..in which the pituitary body appears. *Pituitary stem*, the *Infundibulum.* **1940** *Res. Publ. Assoc. Res. Nervous & Mental Dis.* XX. 28 Together with its investing sheath consisting of portions of the lobus glandularis (pars tuberalis and part of the pars intermedia), the infundibulum or neural stalk is correctly referred to as the hypophysial or pituitary stalk. **1942** O. LARSELL *Anat. Nervous Syst.* xviii. 254 The hypophysis or pituitary body is a gland of internal secretion. **1950** *Sci. News* XV. 132 The anterior lobe of the pituitary gland, which lies at the base of the brain, regulates the amounts of adrenal cortical hormones which circulate in the blood. **1954** [see NEUROHYPOPHYSIS]. **1968** PASSMORE & ROBSON *Compan. Med. Stud.* I. xxv. 9/2 The pituitary gland consists of four different parts... (1) Pars posterior or neurohypophysis is an outgrowth of the brain to which it is attached by the infundibulum. (2) Pars anterior is the main part of the organ and is glandular in structure. (3) Pars intermedia is rudimentary in man but is large in some vertebrates... (4) Pars tuberalis is an extension of pars anterior and encloses the infundibulum. It is also rudimentary in man. **1975** J. B. PHILLIPS *Devel. Vertebr. Anat.* iii. 58/1 Gonadotrophic (gonad-stimulating) hormones, produced by the anterior lobe of the pituitary gland (hypophysis) control the function of the gonads.

b. *absol.* or as *sb.* †(*a*) = pituitary membrane (*obs.*); (*b*) = pituitary gland.

1845 SIR W. HAMILTON *Metaph.* I. App. 424 [The frontal sinuses] are lined with a membrane, a continuation of the pituitary. **1899** *Jrnl. Physiol.* XXV. 89 We confirm Howell's statement that the rise of blood-pressure is produced solely by the infundibular part of the pituitary and not by the hypophysial part. **1905** *Brit. Med. Jrnl.* 25 Feb. 415 Atrophy of the pituitary might likewise be followed by obesity. **1919** [see HYPOPHYSIS 3]. **1932** S. ZUCKERMAN *Social Life Monkeys* v. 81 In the rat, surgical removal of the pituitary stops the œstrous cycle. **1965** MARSHALL & HUGHES *Physiol. Mammals* ix. 232 The pituitary is situated below the hypothalamus..and is made up of two parts. The hypophysis (anterior lobe) is derived from the roof of the buccal cavity, while the infundibulum from a down growth of the fore brain makes up the posterior lobe. **1974** D. & M. WEBSTER *Compar. Vertebr. Morphol.* xiii. 302 The pituitary has two major components, which develop from separate tissues and grow together... The neurohypophysis is formed by a ventral growth from the hypothalamus; the adenohypophysis, by a dorsal evagination from the roof of the mouth.

† **pitui'tose**, *a. Obs. rare.* [ad. L. *pītuītōs-us*, f. *pītuīta*: see above and -OSE[1].] = next.

1710 T. FULLER *Pharm. Extemp.* 11 Crude and pituitose Juices. **1751** STACK tr. *Mead's Med. Precepts* ii. 63 The former..may be called the sanguineous apoplexy, the latter the pituitose.

pituitous (pɪ'tju:ɪtəs), *a.* [ad. L. *pītuītōsus*: see prec. and -OUS: cf. F. *pituiteux.*] Of, pertaining to, consisting of, or of the nature of pituita or mucus; mucous; of diseases, etc.: Characterized or caused by excess of mucus.

1607 TOPSELL *Four-f. Beasts* (1658) 102 She emptieth her self of pituitous and flegmatique humors. **1710** T. FULLER *Pharm. Extemp.* 42 Pituitous Affections of the Breast. **1780** BLIZARD in *Phil. Trans.* LXX. 240 A continuation of the pituitous membrane of the nose. **1800** HURDIS *Fav. Village* 70 Forth creeps the ling'ring snail; a silvery line..Marks his pituitous and slimy course. **1834** J. FORBES *Laennec's Dis. Chest* (ed. 4) 85 The mucous or pituitous catarrh. **1898** *Allbutt's Syst. Med.* V. 350.

b. = PHLEGMATIC 1 a and 2.

1658 BAXTER *Saving Faith* xii. 88 My pituitous brain and languid spirits. **1707** FLOYER *Physic. Pulse-Watch* 63 The Pulse of these pituitous Tempers in general is small. **1836** A. WALKER *Beauty in Woman* 284 Montaigne, all of whose passions were so moderate..was truly pituitous.

Hence **pi'tuitousness**.

1727 BAILEY vol. II, *Pituitousness*,..phlegmatickness.

Pituitrin (pɪ'tju:ɪtrɪn). *Med.* Also pituitrin. [f. PITUIT(A)R(Y *a.* + -IN[1].] **a.** A proprietary name for an extract of the posterior lobe of the pituitary body which contains the hormones oxytocin and vasopressin. † **b.** A name proposed for the hormone formerly thought to be present in this extract but now recognized as a mixture. *Obs.*

1909 *Progressive Med.* IV. 318 The extract of the pituitary body has been prepared by Parke, Davis & Co., under the name of pituitrin. **1909** *Official Gaz.* (U.S. Patent Office) Dec. 297/2 Parke, Davis & Co., Detroit, Mich. Filed July 26, 1909. Pituitrin... Cardio-vascular stimulants and diuretics. **1922** B. HARROW *Glands* 55 We have given the name 'pituitrin' to the hormone (or hormones) present in the posterior lobe of the pituitary... This hormone has not been isolated in the pure state. **1924** G. B. SHAW *St. Joan* p. xix, A precise and convenient regulation of her health and her desires by a nicely calculated diet of thyroid extract, adrenalin, thymin, pituitrin, and insulin. **1924** *Trade Marks Jrnl.* 3 Sept. 1953 Pituitrin... A pharmaceutical preparation of the pituitary gland for human use. Parke, Davis & Company, Detroit, State of Michigan, United States of America; and..London,..pharmaceutical chemists. **1927** HALDANE & HUXLEY *Animal Biol.* viii. 163 The posterior part [of the pituitary gland] produces a hormone, pituitrin, which affects smooth muscle. **1973** *Exper. Eye Res.* XVII. 3 When injected intravenously in intact animals, pituitrin produces a rise of intraocular pressure coincident with a rise in blood pressure.

pituos, -uous(e, etc., obs. variants of PITEOUS.

† **pituous**, *a. Obs. rare*⁻¹. Short for PITUITOUS *a.* So † **pitu'osity** for **pituitosity*, pituitousness.

1612 WOODALL *Surg. Mate* Wks. (1653) 197 *Pituositie* or slimy vomits. *Ibid.* 201 In old persons the excrements are of a more pituos, slimy and bloodie substance.

‖ **pituri** ('pɪtjʊərɪ). Also pitury, pitery, pitcher(r)y, -chiri, -churie, pitjuri, pidgery, pedgery, bedgery. [Native name.] The native name of an Australian shrub, *Duboisia Hopwoodii* (N.O. *Solanaceæ*), the leaves and twigs of which are chewed by the natives as a narcotic. Also *attrib.*

1863 *Proc. Roy. Soc. Van Diemen's Land* Apr. 1 (Morris) 'Pitcherry', a narcotic plant brought by King, the explorer, from the interior of Australia, where it is used by the natives to produce intoxication. **1883** F. M. BAILEY *Synopsis Queensland Flora* 350 Pitury of the natives..chewed by the natives as the white man does the tobacco. **1883** G. W. RUSDEN *Hist. Australia* I. ii. 101 A shrub called pidgery by the natives. **1889** LUMHOLTZ *Cannibals* (1890) 49 Pituri is highly valued as a stimulant. **1931** I. L. IDRIESS *Lasseter's Last Ride* (1933) xvii. 137 Old Warts took from behind his ear a half-chewed plug of pituri, made from the pituri shrub. **1934** A. RUSSELL *Tramp-Royal in Wild Austral.* xix. 123 They [*sc.* the natives] use the pitjuri leaf—which they are also so fond of chewing—poisoning the little-used water-holes with leaves picked from the plant, enough to cause staggers but not death, and then going out and killing the drunken game. **1941** I. L. IDRIESS *Great Boomerang* xiv. 102 Finally one by one the pituri-chewers become stupefied, rolling over and sleeping through day and night. **1964** *Sunday Mail Mag.* (Brisbane) 25 Oct. 3/1 We tossed our swags into the station land rover..for a two-day run from the station out to Allawonga Springs and the pituri country. **1967** *New Scientist* 27 Apr. 226/1 Even the primitive Australian Aborigine has found a pleasurable weed—pitery—which contains nornicotine.

Hence **'piturine** *Chem.* (see quot. 1895).

1890 *Pall Mall G.* 13 Sept. 7/1 The actions of nicotine and piturine are in every respect identical. **1895** *Syd. Soc. Lex.*, *Piturine*, a volatile liquid alkaloid prepared from the leaves and branches of the Australian plant *Pituri*.

pit-viper, -water, -work, etc.: see PIT *sb.*[1] 14.

pity ('pɪtɪ), *sb.* Forms: *α.* 3–6 pite, pyte, 4–5 pitee, 5 pytee, 5–6 pytie, (-ye), 5–7 pitie, (5–6 -ye), 6– pity. *β.* 4–5 pitte, 4–6 pytte, 5–7 pittie, (-ye), 6 pyttye, 6–7 pitty. *γ.* 3–6 pete, 4 petey, 4–6 -ty(e, 5–6 -tie. See also PIETY. [ME. *pite* a. OF. *pitet* (11th c.), *pitez*, *pité*, *pitié* (12th c.), mod.F. *pitié*, ad. L. *pietās*, *pietātem* PIETY. The Fr. *pitié* was the popular phonetic repr. of *pietātem*; *pieté* a clerical adaptation of *pietās*, and *pité* app. a semi-popular intermediate form.

The sense of L. *pietās* 'piety', was in late L. extended so as to include 'compassion, pity', and it was in this sense that the word first appears in OF. in its two forms *pitié* and *pieté*. Gradually these forms were differentiated, so that *pieté*, which more closely represented the L. form, was used in the orig. L. sense, while *pitié* retained the extended sense. In ME. both *pite* and *piete* are found first in the sense 'compassion', subsequently both are found also in the sense 'piety'; the differentiation of forms and senses was here scarcely completed by 1600.]

I. †**1.** The quality of being pitiful; the disposition to mercy or compassion; clemency, mercy, mildness, tenderness. *Obs.* (or merged in next.)

a **1225** *Ancr. R.* 368 Deuocion, reoufulnesse, merci, pite of heorte. *a* **1300** *Assump. Virg.* (Camb. MS.) 169 Sune, þu art ful of pite. *c* **1368** CHAUCER (*title*) Compleynte to Pite. *c* **1375** *Sc. Leg. Saints* ii. (*Paulus*) 1026 For pure pytte & Ioy þai gret. **1474** CAXTON *Chesse* II. v, Pyte is no thyng ellis but a right grete wylle of a debonary herte for to helpe alle men. **1483** *Cath. Angl.* 282/1 Fulle of Pytie, *humanus*. **1601** B. JONSON *Poetaster* II. ii. 293 A little proud but full of pittie. **1613** PURCHAS *Pilgrimage* (1614) 262 Let thy pitie moue thee to make intercession for vs.

2. a. A feeling or emotion of tenderness aroused by the suffering, distress, or misfortune of another, and prompting a desire for its relief; compassion, sympathy. Formerly sometimes with pl. in reference to a number of persons.

c **1290** *S. Eng. Leg.* I. 263/83 þare miȝte ech man deol i-seo, ho-so of pite couþe. *a* **1300** *Cursor M.* 3976 Wit-outen pite he wald him sla. *c* **1386** CHAUCER *Knt.'s T.* 903 Ffor pitee renneth soone in gentil herte. *c* **1412** HOCCLEVE *De Reg. Princ.* 2997 Pitee..is..To help him þat men sen in meschif smert. **1567** *Satir. Poems Reform.* iv. 97 Quhat hairt so hard for petie will not bleid? **1605** B. JONSON *Volpone* IV. v, The sight will rather mooue your pitties, Then indignation. **1651** HOBBES *Leviath.* I. vi. 27 Griefe, for the Calamity of another, is Pitty. **1753** A. MURPHY *Gray's Inn Jrnl.* No. 63 We melt in Pity of his Fate. **1807** CRABBE *Par. Reg.* III. 438 The still tears, stealing down that furrow'd cheek, Spoke pity, plainer than the tongue can speak. **1850** TENNYSON *In Mem.* lxiii, Pity for a horse o'er-driven.

b. Phr. *to have* or *take pity* [F. *avoir pitié*, *prendre pitié* (12th c.)]: prop., to conceive or feel pity; usually, to show or exercise pity, to be merciful or compassionate. Const. †*of* (obs.), *on*, *upon*.

c **1290** *S. Eng. Leg.* I. 170/2241 þe pope hadde ful grete pite. **1303** R. BRUNNE *Handl. Synne* 2274, Y pray þe, þat þou haue on me pyte. **1399** LANGL. *Rich. Redeles* Prol. 23, I had pete of his passion þat prince was of Walis. *c* **1470** HENRY *Wallace* IX. 944 Wallace tharoff in hart had gret pyte. **1535** COVERDALE *Job* xix. 21 Haue pite vpon me, haue pite vpon me (o ye my frendes). **1611** BIBLE *Prov.* xix. 17 He that hath pity upon the poor lendeth unto the Lord. **1841** LANE *Arab. Nts.* I. 112 Have pity on me then.

1390 GOWER *Conf.* III. 247 When that the lordes hadde sein Hou wofully he was besien, Thei token Pite of his grief. *Ibid.* 200. **1600** in *Shaks. C. Praise* 38, I am to entreat you that you will take pittie of mee. **1709** ATTERBURY *Serm.*, *Luke* x. 32 (1726) II. 241 Take Pity upon Them, who cannot take Pity upon themselves. **1837** HALLAM *Hist. Lit.* I. iv. (1855) I. 304 *note*, Which leads me to take pity on paper, or rather on myself.

c. In exclamatory phrases of adjuration, entreaty, etc.: †*for pity* (obs.; cf. *for shame!*); *for pity's sake* (cf. *for goodness' sake, for mercy's sake*).

1484 CAXTON *Fables of Æsop* III. xix, Helas for god & for pyte I pray yow that ye wylle hyde me within your racke. **1529** LATIMER *1st Serm. on Card* (1886) 27 Alas, for pity! the Rhodes are won and overcome by these false Turks. **1593** DRAYTON *Idea* lii, Rebate thy spleen, if but for pities sake! **1610** SHAKS. *Temp.* I. ii. 132 Alack, for pitty. **1650** B. *Discolliminium* 41, I except my speciall Friends, for pity-sake. **1771** P. PARSONS *Newmarket* I. 36 Suffer me..to beg your opinion—but for pity's sake..let it be compassionate. *Mod.* For pity's sake, do be quiet!

3. *transf.* **a.** A ground or cause for pity; a subject of condolence, or (more usually) simply of regret; a regrettable fact or circumstance; a thing to be sorry for: in phrases, †*pity* (*it*) *is*, *was*, *were* (obs.); *it is*, *was*, *would be* (*a*) *pity*; *the more* (*is*) *the pity*, *a thousand pities*, *a great pity*, etc. In early use without *a*.

c **1369** CHAUCER *Dethe Blaunche* 1266 Pitee were I shulde sterve Syth that I wilned noon harme. *a* **1440** *Sir Eglam.* 36 Above alle erthely thynges sche lovyd him mare,..So dud he hur..That was the more pete. *c* **1440** *Generydes* 33 Gret pite that she..Shuld sette hyr wurchippe. *c* **1470** HENRY *Wallace* I. 107 Full gret slauchtyr, at pitte was to se. **1470–85** MALORY *Arthur* I. xxii. 68 It were grete pyte to lese Gryflet. *Ibid.* II. xvi. 94 Grete pyte it was of his hurte. **1526** TINDALE *Acts* xxii. 22 A waye with soche a felowe from the erth! Yt is pitie thet he shulde live. **1542** in Parker *Dom. Archit.* II. 200 The towneshipp of Kylham..hath in yt nether tower or barmekin nor other fortresse whiche ys greatt petye. **1588** J. UDALL *Demonstr. Discipl.* (Arb.) 48 It is a pitie to see howe farre the office of a bishop is degenerated from. **1593** SHAKS. *3 Hen. VI*, IV. i. 22, I, and 'twere pittie, to sunder them, That yoake so well together. **1625** BURGES *Pers. Tithes* 67 It is a thousand pitties they should want blowes who will doe nothing without them. **1719** DE FOE *Crusoe* (1840) II. iii. 55 It is a great pity we should not be..friends. **1746** H. WALPOLE *Let. to H. S. Conway* 24 Oct., What a pity it is I was not born in the golden age of Louis the Fourteenth. **1797** R. M. ROCHE *Children of Abbey* (ed. 2) III. iii. 26 Poor thing, she is going fast indeed, and the more's the pity, for she is a sweet creature. **1848** J. RUSKIN *Let.* 22 Sept. in M. Lutyens *Ruskins & Grays* (1972) xvii. 158 You and my mother must be left at least *tranquil* as you are to be left—more's the pity—now so much alone. **1851** E. C. GASKELL *Let.* May (1966) 838 It is a small old fashioned farm..at the *foot* of the hill. More's the pity. **1853** TRENCH *Proverbs* 140 Lessons which it would be an infinite pity to lose. **1875** 'MARK TWAIN' in *Atlantic Monthly* Feb. 217 A chance to get acquainted with a youth who had taken deck passage—more's the pity; for he easily borrowed six dollars of me. **1880** L. STEPHEN *Pope* ii. 40 It would be a pity to alter it. **1890** *Spectator* 1 Nov. 582/1 More's the pity that we cannot adopt something like the Swiss Referendum.

b. Idiomatically with *of* (= in relation to, in respect of, about). *Obs.* or *arch.*

a **1450** *Knt. de la Tour* (1868) 53 Men of these maners there be now a dayes to mani, of the whiche it is the more pitee. **1548** UDALL, etc. *Erasm. Par. Acts* 83 b, Al the Iewes ..with great clamour cried, that it was pitie of his life [= that he should live: see Acts xxii. 22]. **1598** CHAPMAN *Blinde Begger* Wks. 1873 I. 38 Twas pittie of his nose, for he would have beene a fine man els. **1603** SHAKS. *Meas. for M.* II. iii. 42 *Iul.* Must die tomorrow?..*Pro.* Tis pity of him. **1604** —— *Oth.* IV. i. 206 But yet the pitty of it, Iago! **1855** MACAULAY *Hist. Eng.* xv. III. 586 They were insensible to praise and blame... And yet it was pity of them: for they were physically the finest race of men in the world.

†**4. a.** A condition calling for pity; pitiable state; sad fate. *Obs.*

a **1400–50** *Alexander* 729* þus plenys þis prouud knyght þe pyte of hys fader. *c* **1400** *Destr. Troy* 8686 The petie & the playnt was pyn for to here! *Ibid* 11948 Kyng Priam the pite persayuit onone. **1627–77** FELTHAM *Resolves* I. xxxvii. 62 In a man deformed, and rarely qualified..his virtues..be, as it were, things set off with more glory, by the pitty and defect of the other.

†**b.** An object of pity. *Obs. rare.*

1712 ADDISON *Spect.* No. 305 ⁋3 The Statesmen who have appeared in the Nation of late Years, have..rendered it either the Pity or Contempt of its Neighbours.

†**5.** Grief for one's own wrong-doing; remorse, repentance. *to have pity*, to repent. *Obs.*

1483 CAXTON *G. de la Tour* I ij, We ought to..haue pyte and be shamefull of that that we haue done. **1591** *Troub. Raigne K. John* (1611) 58 They..knocke thy conscience, mouing pitie there.

†**II. 6. a.** = PIETY (in its current senses). *Obs.* (The primary sense of L. *pietas*, but in Eng. later than senses 1 and 2, and at length superseded by *piety*.)

1340 *Ayenb.* 222 He ne zeneȝ[eþ] naȝt..uor pite him stereþ þet to done. *c* **1380** WYCLIF *Sel. Wks.* III. 193 þat þat bicomeþ wymmen bihetynge pite, bi goode werkis. **1382** —— *2 Pet.* iii. 11 To be in holy lyuyngis and pitees [*L.* pietatibus]. *c* **1430** LYDG. *Min. Poems* (Percy Soc.) 9 God the endew withe a croune of glory; And withe septre of clennes and pitee. **1483** *Cath. Angl.* 282/1 A Pytye, *pietas*; *eusebia.*

†**b.** *spec.* = PIETY 3 b. *Obs.*

[**1423** *Rolls of Parlt.* IV. 229, 1 Tabulet, ovec 1 Pite, & 1 autre ymage de Nostre Dame.] **1489** *Will R. Partrich thelder of Sudbury* 8 Dec. (P.C.C., 1 Dogett), A Crucifix of the pitie of our lorde. **1522** *Test. Ebor.* (Surtees) VI. 20 For the anorment and light of our ladie of pitie in the said churche. **1687** A. LOVELL tr. *Thevenot's Trav.* I. 190 You come to the Chappel of our Lady of Pity, which is under the Mount Calvary.

III. 7. *Comb.* (from sense 2), as *pity-begging*, *-bound*, *-moving*, *-proof*, *-worthy* adjs.

1592 *Arden of Feversham* (1897) III. i. 41 What pity-moving words, what deep-fetched sighs. **1593** SHAKS. *Lucr.* 561 Her pittie-pleading eyes are sadlie fixed In the remorselesse wrinckles of his face. **1649** JER. TAYLOR *Gt. Exemp.* I. Sect. vi. 82 The weeping eyes, and pitty-begging looks of those Mothers. **1747** *Mem. Nutrebian Crt.* II. 90 In the most submissive and pity-moving terms. **1809** CAMPBELL *Gert. Wyom.* III. xi, The pity-proffered cup. **1884** *Longm. Mag.* 380 He was not altogether pity-proof.

pity ('pɪtɪ), *v.* [f. prec. sb., prob. after OF. *piteer*, *pitier*, F. *pitoyer*.]

1. *trans.* To feel pity for; to compassionate, commiserate, be sorry for. (In mod. use sometimes implying slight contempt for a person on account of some intellectual or moral inferiority attributed to him. Cf. PITIFUL 4, PITYING.)

1529 MORE *Suppl. Soulys* Wks. 337/2 Whoso pittieth not vs, whom can he pittie? **1593** SHAKS. *Rich. II*, II. i. 236 No good at all that I can do for him, Vnlesse you call it good to pitie him. **1611** BIBLE *Ps.* ciii. 13 Like as a father pitieth his children, so the Lord pitieth them that feare him. **1653** HOLCROFT *Procopius*, *Persian Wars* II. 41 Megas, Bishop of Berrhœa..besought him to pitty men who never offended him, nor were in case to resist him. **1754** RICHARDSON *Grandison* IV. vii. 55, I can pity others, or I should not deserve pity myself. **1838** LYTTON *Alice* I. x, Am I not to be pitied? **1875** JOWETT *Plato* (ed. 2) V. 75 He who is unjust is to be pitied in any case. *Mod.* I pity you if you can't understand a plain statement like that.

†**2.** To move to pity, excite the compassion of; to grieve. Usually impersonal, i.e. with subject clause (mostly *inf.*) introduced by *it*. *Obs.*

1515 in *Archæologia* XLVII. 304 It wold petye ony mannys hert to here the shrykes and cryes. **1535** COVERDALE *Ps.* ci[i]. 14 Thy seruauntes haue a loue to hir stones, and it pitieth them to se her in the dust. *c* **1616** S. WARD *Coal from Altar* (1627) 30 It pitieth me for Laodicea that lost so much cost. **1666** PEPYS *Diary* 20 July, Old Mr. Hawly, whose condition pities me. **1737** WHISTON *Josephus*, *Hist.* VI. viii. §4 It would pity one's heart to observe the change. **1760–72** H. BROOKE *Fool of Qual.* (1809) I. 62 He would have pitied every body, for he had no clothes, nor daddy nor mammy at all. **1835** MARRYAT *Jac. Faithf.* I. 171 The poor creatures.. slipped about in a way that it pitied you to see them.

†**3.** *intr.* (or *trans.* with *inf.* or *obj. cl.*) To be moved to pity; to be sorry, grieve. *Obs.*

1549 COVERDALE, etc. *Erasm. Par. Gal.* 14, I pitie to see you go from suche good beginnynges. **1579** LYLY *Euphues* (Arb.) 36 At the one he greatly pitied, at the other he reioysed. **1667** MILTON *P.L.* x. 211 Pittying how they stood Before him naked to the aire. **1670** C. GATAKER in *Gataker's Antid. Errour* To Rdr. B, The love of Truth, which he pitied to see..opposed by Old Adversaries. **1862** C. M. YONGE *Countess Kate* xii. 222 Sylvia and Charlie, took it all in, pitied, wondered, and were indignant, with all their hearts.

4. *trans.* To grieve for, regret. *Obs.* or *arch.*

1656 WOOD *Life* 22 July (O.H.S.) I. 209 Proctor died..he was much admired at the meetings, and exceedingly pittied by all the faculty for his loss. **1851** [see PITIED].

pitying ('pɪtɪɪŋ), *ppl. a.* [f. PITY *v.* + -ING[2].] That pities; that feels, shows, or expresses pity; compassionate. In mod. use sometimes, Feeling or expressing slight contempt (cf. PITIFUL 4).

1650 HUBBERT *Pill Formality* 137 Their tears..pierce the hearts of their pittying neighbors. **1709** WATTS *Hymn*, *'Plung'd in a gulph of dark despair'*, With pitying eyes the Prince of Grace Beheld our helpless grief. **1848** MRS. CARLYLE *Lett.* II. 34 If I had not felt a pitying interest in the man. **1874** L. STEPHEN *Hours in Library* (1892) II. i. 26 Generally dismissed with a pitying shrug of the shoulders.

Hence **'pityingly** *adv.*, in a pitying manner; in pity.

1847 in WEBSTER. **1861** GEO. ELIOT *Silas M.* vi, Mr. Macey..smiled pityingly, in answer to the landlord's appeal. **1861** WHYTE MELVILLE *Good for Nothing* I. 231 Looking kindly and pityingly in his face.

pityline ('pɪtɪlaɪn), *a.* *Ornith.* [f. mod.L. *Pitylinæ*, f. *Pitylus*, ad. Gr. πίτυλος plash, beating.] Of or pertaining to the *Pitylinæ*, a subfamily of *Tanagridæ*, the fringilline tanagers of the Neotropical area, having a thick pointed beak and rather short wings, typified by the genus *Pitylus*.

1890 in *Cent. Dict.*

‖**pityocampa.** Also 7 pityocampe, -pie. [L., ad. Gr. πιτυοκάμπη, f. πίτυς, πιτυο- pine-tree + κάμπη caterpillar.] The larva of the Pine Procession moth (*Onethocampa pityocampa*).

1608 TOPSELL *Serpents* (1658) 666 The most venomous is that which is called *Pityocampe*, whose biting is poyson. *Ibid.*, Vlpian..esteemeth the giver of any Pityocampie in drink or otherwise to any one, to be doomed a murtherer. **1706** PHILLIPS, *Pityocampa*, a Worm breeding in the Pine-tree, the biting of which is venomous. **1815** KIRBY & SP. *Entomol.* iv. (1818) I. 131 Of this nature also is the famous Pityocampa of the ancients, the moth of the fir.

‖**pityriasis** (pɪtɪ'raɪəsɪs). [mod.L., a. Gr. πιτυρίασις scurf (Galen), f. πίτυρον bran.]

1. *Path.* A condition of the skin characterized by the formation and falling off of irregular patches of small bran-like scales, without inflammation; the (diseased) formation of dandruff or scurf.

1693 *Blancard's Phys. Dict.* (ed. 2), *Pityriasis*, *vid. Furfurratio.* **1706** PHILLIPS, *Pityriasis*, the falling of Dandruff or Scurf from the Head. **1818–20** E. THOMPSON *Cullen's Nosol. Method.* (ed. 3) 323 In the slighter forms of Pityriasis, the cuticle alone..appears to be in a morbid condition. **1864** W. T. FOX *Skin Dis.* 36 Pityriasis is a purely epithelial disease (except in the rare form P. rubra).

2. *Ornith.* A genus of birds of the family *Corvidæ*, inhabiting Borneo and Sumatra, containing one species *P. gymnocephalus*. So called from the scales with which the naked head is covered.

1893 NEWTON *Dict. Birds* 362 There seem to be only four unquestionable peculiar genera [in Borneo] *Pityriasis*, a singular form generally referred to the *Laniidæ*, *Schwaneria* belonging to *Muscicapidæ*, [etc.].

pityroid ('pɪtɪrɔɪd), *a. rare.* [f. Gr. πίτυρ-ον bran + -OID: cf. Gr. πιτυρώδης bran-like.] Resembling bran; bran-like.
1846 in SMART; and in later Dicts.

‖**più** (pju), *adv. Mus.* Also piu. [It.] More; used in musical directions, as ***più mosso*** [MOSSO *a.*], more animated, ***più piano*** [PIANO *a.* (*adv.*)], softer, etc.; also *fig.*
1724 *Short Explication Foreign Words in Musick Bks.* 54 Piu Piano, or PP, is very soft or low. *Ibid.* 55 Piu, signifies a little more, and increaseth the strength of the signification of the word it is joyned with. **1740** J. GRASSINEAU *Mus. Dict.* 180 *Piano piano* or *piu piano*, is nearly the same with *pianissimo*, or rather a degree between it and *Piano*. *Ibid.* 181 *Piu*, a little more, it increases the strength of the signification of the word to which 'tis added. **1876** STAINER & BARRETT *Dict. Mus. Terms* 355/2 *Più*, .. more, as *più allegro*, faster; *più forte*, louder; *più lente*, slower; *più piano*, softer; *più presto*, more rapid; *più stretto*, more urged or closer; *più tosto allegro*, rather quicker. **1931** *Times Educ. Suppl.* 12 Dec. 1/3 The engineers have made the turn-over at the *piu mosso*. **1952**, etc. [see MOSSO *a.*]. **1959** *Collins Mus. Encycl.* 504 *Più* by itself = *più mosso*. **1962** A. HARMAN et al. *Man & his Music* III. v. 671 There is no way of bringing the music to a stop except a *più mosso* coda. **1975** *New Yorker* 3 Nov. 136/2 Then the horn .. sets the new tempo for a *più-mosso* section, in which the flute and the bassoon play leading roles.

piuish(e, -isshe, obs. forms of PEEVISH.

pium ('piːʌm). [Pg., a. Tupi.] A South American buffalo gnat, *Simulium pertinax*. Also *attrib.*
1863 H. W. BATES *Naturalist on River Amazons* I. vii. 333 (*heading*) Piúm flies. *Ibid.*, We made acquaintance .. with a new insect pest, the Piúm, a minute fly. **1927** W. M. MCGOVERN *Jungle Paths & Inca Ruins* iv. 51 The most obvious of the insect pests were the little *piums*... Their sting gave more than a momentary discomfort. **1933** P. FLEMING *Brazilian Adventure* I. xvii. 145 By day the worst pest was the *pium* fly, a little black creature the size of a midge, which covered your hands and anything else it could get at with small hard red pimples.

†**pi'uma.** *Obs.* (See quot.)
1858 SIMMONDS *Dict. Trade*, *Piuma*, the name given to a new and mixed fabric of light texture, used for gentle-men's coats.

‖**piupiu** ('pjuːpjuː). *N.Z.* [Maori.] **a.** Dressed flax. Also *attrib.* **b.** A Maori skirt made of dressed flax (see quot. 1946).
1882 T. H. POTTS *Out in Open* 23 Robes of piu piu, korowai, or of dogskin, contributed a great variety of costume. **1905** W. BAUCKE *Where White Man Treads* 90 Who so .. skilful in the weaving of piupiu, korowai, fancy mats as .. Te Aatarangi? **1938** R. FINLAYSON *Brown Man's Burden* 30 He just threw his coat off and rolled his trousers up, but the other men wore old-time piupius, and their imitation battle-axes were quite clever. *Ibid.* 67 Lucy, dressed in her swishing piupiu skirt and gay headband .. swung the little poi balls for the tourists' snapshots which they labelled 'Maori dancer, Rotorua'. **1946** *Jrnl. Polynesian Soc.* June 156 *Piupiu*, a garment consisting of a heavy fringe, about nine inches wide or more, made of flax and craped at intervals and dyed black. The flax when drying curling up into pipes. **1970** *Times* 23 Mar. 7/6 Down on the grass before her stood ranks of Maori men and women in *Piu-Pius* (flaxen skirts). **1978** P. GRACE *Mutuwhenua* iii. 12 My mother and the others had been .. bringing out the piupiu which had been rolled and sausaged into stockings and stored at the tops of our wardrobes.

Piute, var. PAIUTE *sb.* and *a.*

piva: see PIVO.

pivie, var. PEAVEY, PEVY.

pivo, piva ('piːvəʊ, -ə). [Slavonic *pívo* (Russ. *pivo*, Pol. *piwo*, etc.), beer.] An Eastern European beer made from barley malt or a similar fermented beverage.
1950 V. CANNING *Forest of Eyes* vi. 119 In the room were two army officers, .. their faces flushed with *pivo* and brandy. **1962** J. WADE *Running Sand* xix. 228 Piva... Just the job. **1964** S. BELLOW *Herzog* i. 22 Elias .. drank prohibition beer—home-brewed Polish piva. **1976** 'D. HALLIDAY' *Dolly & Nanny Bird* xviii. 244 Someone had produced *pivo* and his minions were shouting and spraying the workshop with beer. **1979** *Listener* 19 July 71/1 'Another *pivo*, squire?'

pivot ('pɪvət), *sb.* Also 7 pivat, 8 pevot, pevet(t. [a. F. *pivot* (12th c. in Hatz.-Darm.) pivot, hinge. Origin obscure. Cf. mod. Prov. *pivo* a pointed thing (?), It. *piviolo*, *pivolo* wooden peg or pin, dibble, penis, etc., perhaps related to It. *piva* pipe.]
1. a. A short shaft or pin, usually of metal and pointed, forming the fulcrum and centre on which something turns or oscillates; as the pin of a hinge, the end of an axle or spindle, or the arbor on which the hands of a timepiece turn; a pintle, gudgeon.
1611 COTGR., *Pivot*, the piuot, or (as some call it) the Tampin of a gate, or great doore. **1685** BOYLE *Enq. Notion Nat.* 305 The excited Magnetick Needle, and the Box that holds It, are duly pois'd by Means of a competent number of opposite Pivats. **1704** J. HARRIS *Lex. Techn.* I, *Pevetts*, are the Ends of the Spindle of any Wheel in a Watch; and the Holes into which they run, are called *Pevett-holes*. **1763** *Phil. Trans.* LIII. 143 The gudgeons, or pevets, in large engines, are seldom turned true. **1805** BREWSTER in *Ferguson's Lect.* I. 82 *note*, The extremities of an axle or spindle, .. are called gudgeons when the wheels are large, and pivots in small pieces of machinery. **1872** MIVART *Elem. Anat.* 31 The atlas vertebra is formed to turn on the odontoid process of the axis as on a pivot.
†**b.** A dowel or toggle. *Obs. rare.*
1730 A. GORDON *Maffei's Amphith.* 213 The Stones .. are .. clasped at the Top of the Arches with Pivots or Nails.
2. *Mil.* The officer or man on whom a body of troops wheels; also that flank by which the alignment or dressing is corrected. ***fixed pivot***, ***movable pivot***: see quot. 1832.
1796 *Instr. & Reg. Cavalry* (1813) 37 When the squadron has wheeled to a flank by divisions.—If to the right, then the left officer is on the pivot of the rear division, and the right officer shifts to the pivot of the front division. **1832** *Regul. Instr. Cavalry* III. 47 *Pivot*, the outward man on that flank of a Squadron or smaller body upon which that body turns in wheeling... *Fixed Pivot*, is when the flank man during a wheel turns upon his own ground. *Moveable Pivot*, is when the flank man during a wheel describes a portion of a circle. **1859** F. A. GRIFFITHS *Artil. Man.* (1862) 141 A battery can .. change front on a moveable pivot by a simple wheel. **1860** *Vol. Cav. Movem.* in *Blackw. Mag.* Mar. 371/1 'When Right is in front, Left is the Pivot.' This is the first thing taught to the Cornet.
3. *transf.* and *fig.* **a.** That on which anything turns; a cardinal or central point.
1813 *Examiner* 17 May 312/2 His Majesty .. waited the moment .., to put in motion .. his army .., make a pivot on Leipzic. **1818** COBBETT *Pol. Reg.* XXXIII. 594 The paper-money is the pivot, on which their all turns. **1878** SIMPSON *Sch. Shaks.* I. 122 Those questions of right which between Christians would be the chief pivots of the decision. **1888** BRYCE *Amer. Commw.* II. xliv. 151 In all States, the Governor .. may at any moment become the pivot on whose action public order turns.
b. *spec.* A device in Japanese poetry: see quots., and cf. *pillow-word* s.v. PILLOW *sb.* 6.
1877 B. H. CHAMBERLAIN in *Trans. Asiat. Soc. Japan* V. 86 A more complicated species of pun, occurring when a word with two meanings is used only once as a sort of pivot on which two wheels turn. In this case, the first part of the poetical phrase has no logical end, and the latter part no logical beginning... An example of what might be termed pivot-puns. **1880** —— *Class. Poetry Japanese* Introd. 4 The 'Pivot' is a more complicated device, and one which, in any European language, would be not only insupportable, but impossible, resting, as it does, on a most peculiar kind of *jeu de mots*.
c. In football and some other games, a player in a central position, esp. a centre-back; such a position. Also *attrib.*
1911 *Hartley Coll. Mag.* XII. xxxiii. 48 Howarth was moved from outside left to centre, but it was obvious .. he would be spoilt if retained as pivot. **1928** *Weekly Dispatch* 24 June 21/7 Robert Plenderleith, the East Fife centre half-back, one of the most promising of young pivots in Scotland. **1930** *Daily Express* 6 Oct. 16/5 Wilson, the Huddersfield pivot, was kept mainly on the defensive. **1951** *Football Record* (Melbourne) 8 Sept. 13 The Dons' hopes of success could well depend on his ability to gain control of the pivot position today. **1970** *Globe & Mail* (Toronto) 26 Sept. 36/2 Winnipeg has been looking for a take-charge pivot after going through a disappointing season. **1974** *State* (Columbia, S. Carolina) 27 Feb. 2-B/4 Jim Bolla, 6-8, is expected to be in the pivot. **1974** *Plain Dealer* (Cleveland, Ohio) 26 Oct. 4-D/1 In the pivot Steve Patterson and Jim Chones totalled 13 boards. **1975** *Oxf. Compan. Sports* 66/1 The tallest players of all, playing near the basket, are called pivots, centres, or posts. **1976** *Sunday Tel.* 25 Jan. 36/2 There is emerging a new nomenclature which refers to the 'pivot five', those players in the back row of the scrum and at half-back whose talent and technique decide how the ball is used at source.
d. = *pivotal man* s.v. PIVOTAL *a.* 1 b.
1919 *Punch* 29 Jan. 76/2 They are keeping all the pivots in this area for one final orgy of demobilisation at some future date.
e. *Math.* In the numerical evaluation of a determinant, or the numerical solution of simultaneous linear equations, a non-zero element of the determinant or matrix which is used as follows: all elements in its row are divided by it, and appropriate multiples of that row are then subtracted successively from the other rows, so that the pivot itself is replaced by unity and all other elements in its column are replaced by zero; (this gives, in the case of a determinant, a number, the pivot, multiplied by a determinant whose order is reduced by one, and in the case of simultaneous equations, a set of equations one fewer in number from which one of the variables has been eliminated). Freq. *attrib.*
1933 *Proc. Edin. Math. Soc.* III. 211 At Stage II we choose another pivot at will .. and cross-multiply with respect to it in the same way, dividing each result, however, by the previous pivot, 5. **1940** *Brit. Jrnl. Psychol.* XXX. 363 The determinant is condensed in the manner already shown (each pivot being converted into unity) until it is reduced to one number. **1958** S. I. GASS *Linear Programming* ii. 29 Since at the start of an iteration it is convenient to make the coefficient of the variable being eliminated equal to 1, we divide the second equation by 3. The coefficient 3 is referred to as the pivot element. *Ibid.* iv. 58 Element X_{lk} is the pivot element of the elimination transformation, with row *l* being the pivot row and row [*read* column] *k* being the pivot column. **1971** COULSON & RICHARDSON *Chem. Engin.* III. iv. 295 Some methods of solution are better adapted to automatic digital computers than others. The method of Gaussian elimination with selection of pivots, or pivotal condensation, is particularly suitable. **1973** PHILLIPS & TAYLOR *Theory & Appl. Numerical Anal.* viii. 197 The fault in the first attempt at solving Example 8.6 was that a small pivot (the coefficient of *x* in the first equation), meant that very large multiples of the first equation were added to the others, which were therefore 'swamped' by the first equation, after rounding.
f. *Linguistics.* = *pivot word.*
1963 M. D. S. BRAINE in *Language* XXXIX. 4 There is a basis for defining two primitive word classes: a class of pivots .. to which a few frequently occurring words belong, and a complementary class which has many members, few of which recur in more than one or two different combinations. **1966** D. MCNEILL in Smith & Miller *Genesis of Lang.* 21 It never happens .. that two-word sentences are made up only of pivots. **1971** *Jrnl. Speech & Hearing Disorders* XXXVI. 44 Rules that account for utterances in terms of the juxtaposition of pivots and open words cannot account for differences in semantic interpretation. **1973** M. F. BOWERMAN *Early Syntactic Devel.* 30 Students of language acquisition have sometimes referred to words which a child uses with greater-than-average frequency as 'pivots'... When used in this way, the conception of 'pivot' has little more relevance to child speech than to adult speech. **1975** *Canad. Jrnl. Linguistics* XX. 220 Arabic children have a much easier time of it than English children since such Pivot—Open constructions are generally well-formed sentences in adult grammar.
†**4.** *Gardening.* (See quot., and cf. PIVOT *v.* 3.)
1725 BRADLEY *Fam. Dict.* s.v. *Tree*, If the lower or bottom part of the Stem be .. thicker than all the rest, it ought ever to preserve it self in that State; but if .. it continues smaller than some part a little above it, from whence in effect some fine Roots proceed; then .. you must entirely cut off this smaller Part, with all its Appurtenances: Many Gardiners call it Pivot, and those Roots must only be preserv'd that proceed from the fortunate Part.
†**5.** The nipple of a percussion-lock. *Obs.*
1835 *Encycl. Brit.* (ed. 7) XI. 39/1 The next peculiarity of the ordinary detonating lock is the pivot or nipple. **1836** T. OAKLEIGH *Oakleigh Shooting Code* 18 The pivot is the nipple or cone of iron screwed into the breach, and on which the copper cap is placed.
6. *attrib.* and *Comb.* **a.** *appositive* or *adj.* That is the pivot on which something turns or depends; cardinal; pivotal.
1861 E. GARBETT *Boyle Lect.* 247 Heathenism fixed itself upon these pivot qualities of the heart. **1875** POSTE *Gaius* I. Introd. (ed. 2) 2 Some of the pivot terms and most pervading conceptions.
b. *Comb.*, as ***pivot-file*** (FILE *sb.*[1]), ***-gauge***, ***-hole***, ***-lathe***, ***-pin***, ***-point***, ***-polisher***; (in sense 2) ***pivot file*** (FILE *sb.*[2]), ***flank***, ***leader***, ***man***, ***manœuvre***, ***officer***, ***ship***; **pivot bearing** = FOOTSTEP 5 d; **pivot-bolt**, a central pintle about which a pivot-gun oscillates horizontally; **pivot break** *Rugby Football* (see quot.); **pivot-bridge**, a swing bridge pivoted on a central pier; **pivot-broach**, a watchmaker's tool; **pivot class** *Linguistics*, the class of pivot words; **pivot-drill** = *pivot-broach*; **pivot-frame**, a frame turning on a pivot, so that the gun it carries may be pointed in any direction; **pivot-gearing**, gearing for allowing the axis of a driving wheel to be shifted, so as to communicate power in various directions; **pivot grammar** *Linguistics*, a grammar of an early stage in children's speech in which two word classes are postulated, pivot words (see below) and a larger open class; **pivot-gun** (see quots.); **pivot-joint** *Anat.*, a joint in which the articular movement is that of a pivot; **pivot pass** *Rugby Football* (see quot.); **pivot-pricker**, a slender pointed instrument for clearing the nipple of a percussion-lock; **pivot-pun** (see 3 b); **pivot-span**, that span of a bridge which turns or opens on a pivot; **pivot-tooth** (see quot. 1875); **pivot-transom**, the front member of the chassis of a casemate gun; **pivot word** *Linguistics*, one of a limited set of words recurring in particular utterance positions at an early stage of a child's acquisition of syntax, and postulated as constituting one of two basic word classes at this stage of development; **pivot-wrench**, a small turning tool for securing or loosening the nipple of a percussion-lock to and from the barrel; now called *nipple* or *cone-wrench*.
[**1875** *Engineering* 30 July 87/1 Pivoted bearings for line shafts, now almost universally employed in America.] **1877** W. C. UNWIN *Elem. Machine Design* vii. 122 (*heading*) *Pivot and collar bearings. **1960** V. B. GUTHRIE *Petroleum Products Handbk.* ii. 29 Oils used for pivot bearings in instruments are of low volatility. **1975** *Sci. Amer.* July 50/3 If a combination of the two forces exists, a special bearing (an angular bearing, a taper bearing or a pivot bearing) is employed. **1875** KNIGHT *Dict. Mech.*, *Pivot-bolt. **1960** E. S. & W. J. HIGHAM *High Speed Rugby* 70 Another way .. is to break on the side of the scrum on which the ball was put in. This is sometimes called the '*pivot' break, because the scrum-half pivots around his outside foot. **1875** KNIGHT *Dict. Mech.* 1721/2 A *pivot-bridge of the New York Central Railway on the Linville principle. *Ibid.*, **Pivot-broach*, a .. tool for opening the pivot-holes of watches. **1964** *Amer. Psychologist* XIX. 3/2 Two classes of words appear —a *pivot class and an open class—and the child launches forth on his career in combinatorial talking. **1966** D. MCNEILL in Smith & Miller *Genesis of Lang.* 20 The pivot class characteristically has few members compared with the open class. **1970** —— *Acquisition of Lang.* III. 25 Pivot classes may appear first or second in sentences. **1833** *Regul. Instr. Cavalry* I. 38 The *pivot files .. face to the left. **1884** F. J. BRITTEN *Watch & Clockm.* 199 Pivot File .. [is] a file used for forming pivots. **1833** *Regul. Instr. Cavalry* I. 38

They resume their places on the *pivot flank. **1858** GREENER *Gunnery* 131 The piece..is mounted upon a carriage.. which embraces a *pivot frame and recoil slide. **1884** F. J. BRITTEN *Watch & Clockm.* 199 *Pivot Gauge,..a steel plate with tapered slit used for measuring pivots. **1970** L. M. BLOOM *Lang. Devel.* 24 The speech of children described in *pivot grammars in other investigations. **1971** *Jrnl. Speech & Hearing Disorders* XXXVI. 42 How does pivot grammar relate to the grammar of the adult model language? *Ibid.* 47 The notion of pivot grammar describes children's early speech in only the most superficial way. **1973** M. F. BOWERMAN *Early Syntactic Devel.* 4 An analysis of diary studies of children acquiring languages other than English led Slobin..to hypothesize that the pivot grammar might be a universal first grammar regardless of the particular language being acquired. **1976** *Word 1971* XXVII. 33 In what ways does mother-child interchange indicate that Laura's initial two-word combinations are semantically and structurally too sophisticated to be described adequately by a pivot grammar? **1858** SIMMONDS *Dict. Trade*, **Pivot-gun*, a piece of ordnance turning freely on a pivot, to alter the direction. **1859** F. A. GRIFFITHS *Artil. Man.* (1862) 150 Markers mark for the pivot guns of half batteries. **1704** *Pivot-hole [see sense 1]. **1872** HUXLEY *Phys.* vii. 171 The second kind of *pivot-joint is seen in the forearm. **1881** MIVART *Cat* 122. **1796** *Instr. & Reg. Cavalry* (1813) 17 The *pivot leader..will begin in his own person to circle behind the line from the old, so as to enter the new direction twenty or thirty yards from the point of intersection. *a* **1814** *Manœuvring* III. i. in *New Brit. Theatre* II. 101 Ever since.. you have been our lady's *pivot-man: every thing turns on you. **1847** *Infantry Man.* (1854) 15 Those nearest the pivot man making their steps extremely small. **1918** *Daily Mail* 6 Dec. 3/3 (*heading*) 12,000 pivot men. **1967** *Boston Sunday Herald* 9 Apr. (This Week Mag.) 4/3 Locate the 'pivot man' on each team—he's the fielder who makes the first move as the team adjusts position for each new batter. **1971** L. KOPPETT *N.Y. Times Guide Spectator Sports* iii. 88 The pivotman is usually the center, and the tallest man on his team. **1978** *Detroit Free Press* 5 Mar. c. 4/2 Joe Barry Carroll, Purdue's 7-1 pivotman, scored 14 of his game high 22 points in the first half. **1796** *Instr. & Reg. Cavalry* (1813) 43 In movements in column, the *pivot officers..are answerable for covering, and for proper wheeling distances. **1960** E. S. & W. J. HIGHAM *High Speed Rugby* 68 You will have to pivot round on the outside foot as you take off. This is called the '*pivot' or 'reverse' pass. **1884** *Mil. Engineering* (ed. 3) I. II. 58 A plate round the point or thin end, with a hole for the *pivot pin. **1836** T. OAKLEIGH *Oakleigh Shooting Code* 106 Articles necessary to the grouse-shooter's equipment..; fowling-piece, in case or bag; two extra pivots; a *pivot-pricker; pivot-wrench. **1867** SMYTH *Sailor's Word-bk.*, **Pivot-ship*, in certain fleet evolutions, the sternmost ship remains stationary, as a pivot on which the other vessels are to form the line anew. **1872** L. P. MEREDITH *Teeth* (1878) 138 The six front roots above and below..are the only ones upon which it is advisable to ingraft *pivot teeth. **1875** KNIGHT *Dict. Mech.*, *Pivot-tooth*,..an artificial crown attached to the root of a natural tooth by a dowel-pin of wood or metal occupying the nerve-canal. *Ibid.* 1721/2 A traversing platform passing through the *pivot transom and the front sleeper of the platform. **1963** M. D. S. BRAINE in *Language* XXXIX. 4 These words will be called '*pivot' words, since the bulk of the word combinations appear to be formed by using them as pivots to which other words are attached as required. **1964** *Amer. Psychologist* XIX. 3/2 Whereas before, lexemes like *allgone* and *mummy* and *sticky* and *bye-bye* were used singly, now, for example, *allgone* becomes a pivot word and is used in combination. **1966** D. MCNEILL in Smith & Miller *Genesis of Lang.* 20 Each pivot word is used more frequently than individual open-class words. **1975** *Canad. Jrnl. Linguistics* XX. II. 220 Much has been made in studies of children's syntax in English of a stage at which there are only two parts of speech, a Pivot, or function word like 'want', and an Open, or content word like 'milk'. **1836** *Pivot-wrench [see *pivot-pricker*].

'pivot, *v.* [a. F. *pivoter*, f. *pivot*: see prec.]

1. *trans.* To furnish with, mount on, or attach by means of, a pivot or pivots. (Chiefly in passive.)

1855 HYDE CLARKE *Dict.* 292/2 *Pivot*, place on a pivot. **1869** SIR E. J. REED *Shipbuild.* xx. 454 To have the model pivoted at the ends. **1879** G. PRESCOTT *Sp. Telephone* p. ii, An electro-magnetic telegraph..the armature of which was pivoted so as to vibrate between its poles. **1882** NARES *Seamanship* (ed. 6) 192 If yards were pivoted in the centre of the mast.

b. *fig.*: cf. prec. 3. (In quot. 1851, to serve as a pivot to.)

1851 *Fraser's Mag.* XLIV. 472 There is not a man.. whose moral and mental centre of gravity more firmly pivot the violent oscillations and gyrations of his 'passionate' energy. **1878** R. H. HUTTON *Scott* x. 101 Scott's romances ..are pivoted on public rather than mere private interests.

2. *intr.* To turn as on a pivot; to hinge; in military manœuvres, to swing round a point as centre. Chiefly *fig.*

1841 LEVER *C. O'Malley* xc, The 7th took up their ground at Frenada pivoting upon the 1st Division. **1872** H. W. BEECHER in *Chr. World Pulpit* II. 250 You know that Christ's ministry was pivoting upon Capernaum. **1883** HOLME LEE *Loving & Serving* II. ix. 154 'No', said the clergyman, and pivoted on his heel. **1892** *Pictorial World* 11 June 52/1 The entire question pivots on Ulster.

3. *Gardening.* (See quot., and cf. PIVOT *sb.* 4.)

1895 *Syd. Soc. Lex.* s.v., In *Bot.*, a main root which grows vertically downwards is spoken of as 'pivoting' (Littré).

Hence **'pivoted** *ppl. a.*, **'pivoting** *ppl. a.*

1855 HYDE CLARKE *Dict.* 292/2 *Pivoted, a.* **1870** *Daily News* 27 July 5 This bridge is built in three portions, the centre resting upon four piers, and a pivotted portion of either end of about thirty yards in length. **1875** *Dental Cosmos* XVII. 511, I removed the pivoted root [of a tooth], which was covered by a tumid and dark purple gum. **1882** NARES *Seamanship* (ed. 6) 244 The..frames carry pivoted screw nuts. **1888** *Pall Mall G.* 16 May 9/1 The eye of the bracket which receives the pivoting pin.

pivotable ('pɪvətəb(ə)l), *a.* [f. PIVOT *v.* + -ABLE.] Capable of being turned as if on a pivot. So **pivota'bility**, the extent to which an object can be so turned (in quots., as a measure of angularity).

1961 *Jrnl. Sedimentary Petrol.* XXXI. 198/1 A somewhat modified version of Powers' scale was adopted by the writers. In this scale the idea of 'pivotability' was given paramount importance so that the grains which could be most easily pivoted were given the highest values. **1967** *Jane's Surface Skimmer Systems 1967–68* 83/2 The result is a simple and reliable lift control, which requires neither electric or hydraulic power sources, nor pivotable foils or flaps. **1971** W. A. PRYOR in R. E. Carver *Procedures Sedimentary Petrol.* vii. 143 Pivotability or rollability is a measure of the motion response of a grain to a set of standard physical conditions in a gravity-driven system.

pivotal ('pɪvətəl), *a.* [f. PIVOT *sb.* + -AL[1].]

1. a. Of, pertaining to, of the nature of, or constituting a pivot; being that on which anything turns or depends; central, cardinal, vital.

1844 MARY HENNELL *Social Syst.* 198 It is..the fatal characteristic of civilized industry..to have for pivotal motive nothing but the fear of death from hunger. **1875** WHITNEY *Life Lang.* ii. 16 About this pivotal fact all the other matters involved fall into position as..auxiliary. **1888** BRYCE *Amer. Commw.* I. I. xxvi. 397 It..makes the issue of the election turn on the voting in certain 'pivotal' States. **1925** *Times* 5 Jan. 4/3 Young's passes..were..much too high to enable Kittermaster, as the pivotal player, to pave the way for a scoring position. **1927** PEAKE & FLEURE *Priests & Kings* 134 A new feature, however, was the use of door-slabs of stone set with pivotal hinges. **1930** *Daily Express* 6 Oct. 2/6 Pivotal shares were occasionally in moderate demand. **1953** [see *film editor* s.v. FILM *sb.* 7c]. **1965** *New Scientist* 6 May 383/3 Dædalus feels that the time is ripe for another OK word. He has had difficulty in deciding on one with the right ring of vague pomposity about it, but has decided on 'pivotal'. He hopes that it ultimately will become synonymous for 'important' or 'interesting'. He asks all his readers to include it in articles, papers, research reports and the like, confident that the elite of New Men who read *New Scientist* will suffice to launch this new word on a glorious and pivotal career. **1969** Z. HOLLANDER *Mod. Encycl. Basketball* 211 (*heading*) The pivotal era. **1973** *Amer. Speech 1969* XLIV. 281 The uniqueness of black folk speech seems to rest in the pivotal position it occupies in the rural community, sharing phonological features with cultivated blacks and whites, grammatical features with white folk speakers, and lexical forms with all members of both castes. **1976** *National Observer* (U.S.) 13 Nov. 4/5 The pardon of Richard Nixon was pivotal, it seems, to those independents who made up their minds at the last minute and turned to Jimmy Carter. **1977** *N.Y. Rev. Bks.* 28 Apr. 29/3 (Advt.), Here is a penetrating, pivotal study of the astonishing relationships between Shakespeare's dramatic use of time and modern views on how any time-sense shapes human experience and behavior.

b. ***pivotal man***, a man considered to have an important part to play in the re-establishment of industry and commerce after the war of 1914–18, and hence eligible for early demobilization; also *ellipt.* as *sb.*

1918 *Daily Mail* 29 Nov. 3/2 Men who are essential to the building up and expansion of trade..are officially described as 'pivotals'. *Ibid.*, These are the pivotal men who will prepare the way for the hundreds of thousands who are to follow on general demobilization. *Ibid.*, The commerce of the City of London has been allotted a given number of pivotal men. *Ibid.* 11 Dec. 5/1 A pivotal man is an essential man in an industry or occupation on which the re-establishment of other industries depends. **1920** F. WATSON *Pandora's Young Men* iii. 22 She found Blinkhorn in some out-of-the-way depot in France and managed to have him demobilised as a pivotal man. **1922** *Encycl. Brit.* XXX. 214/2 The release of 'Pivotal Men'..met with much opposition.

2. *Math.* Being or involving a pivot (sense 3 e); ***pivotal condensation***, the evaluation of a determinant by the use of pivoting on determinants of successively lower orders.

1924 WHITTAKER & ROBINSON *Calculus of Observations* v. 71 We prepare the determinant for our subsequent operations by multiplying some row or column by such a number p as will make one of the elements unity, and put $1/p$ as a factor outside the determinant. This unit element will henceforth be called the pivotal element. **1939** A. C. AITKEN *Determinants & Matrices* ii. 47 A determinant of order n being reduced by a first pivotal condensation to one of order $n-1$, the latter in its turn can be reduced by a second pivotal condensation to one of order $n-2$, and so on. **1952** D. R. HARTREE *Numerical Anal.* viii. 158 The coefficient a_{jk}..is called the 'pivotal coefficient' or 'pivot' for this elimination; it is the coefficient, in the pivotal equation, of the variable to be eliminated. **1963** N. MACON *Numerical Anal.* v. 59 It is of some interest to calculate the number of arithmetical operations required for the evaluation of a determinant of order n when pivotal condensation is used. **1971** [see PIVOT *sb.* 3e]. **1973** A. M. COHEN et al. *Numerical Anal.* viii. 136 We add suitable multiples of equation (8.17*a*) to equations (β), (γ), and (δ) to reduce the coefficients of x_1 in them to zero... Equation (α), which remains unaltered, is called the pivotal equation.

3. *Linguistics.* Of, pertaining to, or based upon pivot grammar or pivot words (see PIVOT *sb.* 6 b).

1963 M. D. S. BRAINE in *Language* XXX. 4 *Do it, push it, close it*, etc...appear to exemplify the same kind of pivotal construction as the previous combinations discussed, except that now the pivot is in the final position. *Ibid.* 10 The pivotal type of construction continues long after the first five months, and new pivot words develop. **1970** L. M. BLOOM *Lang. Devel.* 223 The two relational aspects of language appear to be related to the two descriptions of children's speech as 'telegraphic' and 'pivotal'. **1971** *Jrnl. Speech & Hearing Disorders* XXXVI. 42 How does the child progress from using pivotal utterances to using utterances that reflect the complex interrelation of rules that is the essence of adult phrase structure?

Hence **'pivotalism**, the policy of releasing 'pivotal men' from active service before others; **'pivotally** *adv.*, in a pivotal manner; as on a pivot.

1887 *Sci. Amer.* 12 Feb. 98 The stanchion is pivotally held between the floor..and any stationary upper beam by two bolts. **1919** W. S. CHURCHILL in D. Cooper *Haig* (1936) II. xxvii. 406 Indiscipline and disorganisation would arise in the Army if pivotalism, i.e. favouritism, were to rule in regard to the discharge of men. **1922** *Encycl. Brit.* XXX. 215/1 Pivotalism..was called 'favouritism'.

'pivoting, *vbl. sb.* [f. PIVOT *v.* + -ING[1].]

1. The action of the vb. PIVOT.

1855 HYDE CLARKE *Dict.* 292/2 *Pivoting, pivotwork.*

2. *Math.* The use of a pivot (sense 3 e) as a means of making a column of a determinant or matrix consist entirely of zeros except for one unit element; also, pivotal condensation; ***partial pivoting***, pivoting in which the choice of pivot at each stage is restricted to the largest element in the first column (or the first row) of the relevant part of the matrix, rather than the largest in all its columns or rows (***complete***, ***total***, or ***full pivoting***).

1961 *Jrnl. Assoc. Computing Machinery* VIII. 282 We derive first an upper bound for R when a general matrix is reduced to triangular form by Gaussian elimination, selecting as pivotal element at each stage the element of maximum modulus in the whole of the remaining square matrix. We refer to this as 'complete' pivoting for size, in contrast to the selection of the maximum element in the leading column at each stage, which we call 'partial' pivoting for size. **1963** N. MACON *Numerical Anal.* v. 59 The effect of pivoting on rounding errors. **1968** FOX & MAYERS *Computing Methods for Scientists & Engineers* v. 86 Partial pivoting is generally satisfactory, and..can be made still better, by the use of fl_2 arithmetic.., in a manner which cannot easily be performed with total pivoting. **1973** PHILLIPS & TAYLOR *Theory & Appl. Numerical Anal.* viii. 197 Partial pivoting using only row interchanges is preferable to that with only column interchanges.

piwarrie: see PAIWARI.

pix[1] (pɪks). *Obs.* exc. *dial.* [app. syncopated from ME. *pikeis*, *picas*, *pykes*, PICKAXE.] A pick.

1708 *Brit. Apollo* No. 46. 1/2 A Puncture with a Pix. **1821** CLARE *Vill. Minstr.* I. 116 Which the sandman's delving spade And the pitman's pix have made. **1851** T. STERNBERG *Dial. & Folklore Northampt.*, *Pix, Pick*, a pick-axe.

pix[2] (pɪks), var. *pics*, pl. of PIC[4].

In quot. 1932 used for the sing.

1932 *Variety* 19 July 4/5 (*heading*) 'Million', Par's all-star pix. *Ibid.* 9 Aug. 15/4 (*heading*) Open sesame for Brit. pix in Dominion. **1935** *Ibid.* 3 Apr. 10/1 On Sunday two powerful b.o. pix. were released. **1936** WODEHOUSE *Laughing Gas* ii. 20 'Your face seems extraordinarily familiar, too.' 'You've probably seen it in pix.' 'No, I've never been there.' 'In the pictures.' **1940** R. CHANDLER *Farewell, my Lovely* iii. 13 That's what I rate after eighteen years in this man's police department. No pix, no space, not even four lines in the want-ad section. **1945** [see HYPO *v.*]. **1955** POHL & KORNBLUTH *Space Merchants* ii. 22 Our artists can work from the pix you brought back. **1960** *Analog Science Fact/Fiction* Dec. 48/2 Now they have a chance to get their news releases and faked pix out in quantity. **1973** E. HYAMS *Final Agenda* iv. 53 Barnet said, 'I want the Victoria Lowell pix.'.. [He] began looking through the thirty-seven photographs of Victoria Lowell. **1975** D. LODGE *Changing Places* ii. 90 He would be holed up somewhere, jerking himself off and drooling over the *Playboy* pix. **1977** *Zigzag* June 23/3 Tome is shown the Warner Bros. press kit for him, with accompanying pix.

pix, pixis: see PYX, PYXIS.

pixel ('pɪksɛl). [f. PIX[2] + EL(EMENT *sb.*] = *picture element* s.v. PICTURE *sb.* 6 d.

1969 *Science* 15 Aug. 685/1 An analog tape recorder was used to store the analog video signal from each pixel. **1975** *Sci. Amer.* Oct. 67/1 The cross sections of the heart were subsequently reconstructed by the same computer. Each cross section took two minutes of computing time and was displayed on a cathode-ray tube as a square picture with 64 pixels on a side. **1977** *New Yorker* 14 Feb. 28/1 The [advertising] panel is divided into two thousand and forty-eight 'pixels', or picture elements of red, green, blue, and white bulbs, and ordinarily only one or two of the bulbs on a pixel are flashed at a given time. **1977** *Proc. R. Soc. Med.* LXX. 593/1 No doubt the next edition using up-dated prints will overcome the difficulties of interpretations associated with the large size of pixel.

pixie ('pɪksɪ). Also pixy, and *dial.* pisky, -ie, pisgy, etc.: see Eng. Dial. Dict. [Origin obscure.] **a.** In local folk-lore a name for a supposed supernatural being akin to a fairy. Also *transf.*

(In popular use in the s.w. of England from Cornwall to Wiltshire and Dorset. A meadow on the Thames above Oxford is named on the Ordnance Map *Pixey Mead.* Used by Scott in *The Pirate*, quot. 1822 (whence inserted by Jamieson and in subseq. glossaries) as a Shetland word, but no local evidence has been found there either for *pixie* or *nixie*. Rietz has a Swed. dial. *pysk*, *pyske*, 'small fairy, dwarf', cf. Norw. *pjusk* 'a little insignificant person'; but, with the disappearance of the supposed Shetland use, it is difficult to see how this could be connected with the s.w. Eng. word.)

c **1630** T. WESTCOTE *Devon.* (1845) 433, I shall..be thought to lead you in a pixy-path by telling an old tale. **1659** [see PIXY-LED]. **1746** *Exmoor Scolding* (E.D.S.) 130 Tell me o' tha Rexbush, ye teeheeing Pixy. **1793** COLERIDGE *Songs of Pixies* i, Whom the untaught Shepherds call Pixies in their madrigal. Fancy's children, here we dwell. **1822** SCOTT *Pirate* xxiii, If a pixie, seek thy ring; If a nixie, seek thy spring. **1836** MRS. BRAY *Tamar & Tavy* (1879) I. x. 163 The pixies are certainly a distinct race from the fairies, .. [they] will invariably tell you, if you ask them what pixies really may be, that these native spirits are the souls of infants, who were so unhappy as to die before they had received the Christian rite of baptism. **1837** HOWITT *Rur. Life* VI. vii. (1862) 478 The Pixies may possibly still haunt those caves and dens in Devonshire where Coleridge.. saw them. **1891** 'Q.' [COUCH] *Noughts & Crosses* 175 In this corner of the land where (they say) the piskies still keep.

b. Short for *pixie cap, hat*, etc.

1960 *Harper's Bazaar* Oct. 114 Fur pixie.

c. *attrib.* and *Comb.* (often *local*, as in the names of plants), as *pixie-like* adj.; **pixie cap**, a pointed hat resembling that in which pixies are traditionally depicted; **pixie cape**, a cape with an attached pixie hood; **pixy glove**, the thistle; **pixie hat** = *pixie cap*; **pixie hood**, a pointed hood; so **pixie-hooded** *a.*; **pixy-path**, a path by which those who follow it are bewildered and lost; **pixie-pear**, (*a*) the haw; (*b*) the hip of the wild rose (Britten & Holl.); **pixy puff**, various species of puff-ball, *Lycoperdon*, as *L. giganteum* and *Bovista*; **pixy-ridden** *a.*, plagued or possessed by pixies; **pixy-ring**, (*a*) = FAIRY-RING; (*b*) (see quot. 1891); **pixy stool**, a toadstool or mushroom.

1828 *Pixie cap [see KILMARNOCK 1]. **1943** F. URQUHART in *Penguin New Writing* XVI. 90 She was wearing a crimson waterproof pixie-cap which was almost the same colour as her pretty, round face. **1960** M. A. SINDALL *Matey* vii. 89 Brown woollen pixie caps. **1973** *Listener* 23 Aug. 244/2, I knew that I did not look my best in my mackintosh with its *pixie cape. **1858** CAPERN *Ball. & Songs* 128 Rejoicing where the *pixy glove Will soon hang out its crest. **1954** G. DURRELL *Three Singles to Adventure* v. 106 On his sleek black head was perched an absurd *pixie hat constructed out of what once used to be velvet. **1940** C. MILBURN *Diary* 23 Dec. (1979) 75 Two little pixie-like children in green overall garments, complete with *pixie hoods. **1950** B. PYM *Some Tame Gazelle* viii. 89 They stood in the doorway, .. wearing mackintoshes, and that wet-weather headgear so unbecoming to middle-aged ladies and so incongruously known as a 'pixie hood'. **1955** E. BOWEN *World of Love* ix. 163 Maud, in wet weather rendered still more terrible by a pixie hood. **1961** *Guardian* 28 Nov. 7/1 The worthies of the village in ornamented pixie hoods. **1978** M. BUTTERWORTH *X marks Spot* I. i. 22 An old lady in a plastic pixie hood. **1949** E. COXHEAD *Wind in West* i. 15 Two *pixie-hooded small boys. **1940** *Pixie-like [see *pixie hood* above]. **1963** *Times* 16 May 14/6 The men wear a curious conical hat.. which gives them a curious pixy-like appearance, while frequent recourse to chewing *qat* has wizened their faces and for all I know stunted their growth. **1979** J. WAINWRIGHT *Reluctant Sleeper* v. 69 Those ridiculously large spectacles, and that equally ridiculous pixie-like face. *c* **1630** *Pixy-path [see a]. **1870** LADY VERNEY *L. Lisle* x. 117 Allays after them blackberries and *pixie-pears. *a* **1847** *MS. Gloss. Devon* in *Halliwell*, *Pixy-puff*, a broad species of fungus. *Pixy-rings*, the fairy circles. **1879** ELWORTHY *Gloss. Exmoor Scolding*, *Pixy-rided*, to guard against which [horses being ridden by pixies] a horseshoe is nailed against the stable-door. **1893** *Daily News* 28 Sept. 4/7 A girl.. is '*pixy-ridden'—pots and jugs begin to jump out of her hand, chairs run after her, flitches of bacon join the dance. *a* **1847** *Pixy-rings [see *pixy-puff*]. **1886** ELWORTHY *W. Somerset Word-bk.*, *Pixy-rings*, round which they dance on moonlight nights. **1891** J. H. PEARCE *Esther Pentreath* III. x. 235 A rudely drilled stone with a bit of coloured ribbon run through it—a piskie-ring, or spinning-whorl, in fact. **1787** GROSE *Provinc. Gloss.*, *Picksey-stool, a mushroom. Devonsh. **1870** LADY VERNEY *L. Lisle* xiii. 155 There's a fairies' ring and no end o' pixy-stools on the knap yonder.

Hence **'pixyish** [-ISH[1]] *a.*, resembling that of a pixie.

1962 V. CONNAUGHT *Secret Heart of Princess Alexandra* x. 101 As she splashed by them, Alexandra appeared to take a pixyish glee in noting their discomfort. **1977** J. AIKEN *Last Movement* viii. 167 Her narrow, pixyish Irish face.

pixilated ('pɪksɪˌleɪtɪd), *a.* orig. *U.S. dial.* Also **pixelated, pixielated, pixillated, pixylated.** [f. PIXIE + *-lated* as in *elated, emulated*, etc. or var. PIXY-LED *a.*] **1.** Mildly insane, fey, whimsical; bewildered, confused; intoxicated, tipsy.

1848 in *Amer. Speech* (1941) XVI. 79/2 You'll never find on any trip That he'll be pix-e-lated. **1886** E. L. BYNNER *Agnes Surriage* iv. 56 'See now wher' we ha' come to wi' yer talk, Job Redden!' cried Agnes, waking suddenly to their situation. 'We'll be pixilated 'n' driven on to th' rocks an ye don't wake up.' **1895** *Dialect Notes* I. 392 *Pixilated*, dazed, bewildered in the dark. Marblehead, Mass. **1936** in *Amer. Speech* (1941) XVI. 79/2 *Lawyer*: Now tell me, what does everybody back home think of Longfellow Deeds? .. *Jane*: They think he's pixilated. *Ibid.* 80/1 The word pixilated is an early American expression—derived from the word 'pixies' meaning elves. They would say, 'The pixies have got him,' as we nowadays would say a man is 'balmy'. **1937** *N. & Q.* 2 Jan. 11/2 As a native of the state from which 'Mr. Deeds' is reputed to have come permit me to comment on .. 'pixilated'. To use the word in the sense of 'crazy' is not correct. A Vermonter would not hesitate to use 'crazy' if that conveyed his meaning. A 'pixilated' man is one whose whimseys are not understood by practical-minded people. .. More nearly a synonym of 'whimsical'. **1955** 'J. R. MACDONALD' *Find Victim* xxiv. 167 'Wasn't he pretty drunk on Sunday?' 'He was pixilated all right,' Jo said. **1957** L. IREMONGER *Ghosts of Versailles* viii. 103 Ultimately no explanation of the 'adventure' was too fantastic, far-fetched or indeed pixylated for them. **1958** *Observer* 30 Nov. 16/6 Nicely cast, he gave the true tone of pixilated delinquency. **1971** *Listener* 8 Apr. 449/1 Suddenly we were pixilated, we'd fallen in love with the sweetest girl we ever saw. **1975** C. NESBITT *Little Love & Good Company* xvii. 208 We were both ever so slightly inebriated, no not even that, pixilated, to use the lovely movie euphemism. **1977** *New Yorker* 29 Aug. 28/3 He was known as a coarse creature and a little pixillated.

2. Of an actor: having movements animated by the pixilation technique.

1959 *News Chronicle* 20 Oct. 8/7 The animator.. may use conventional comic drawings.. or even 'pixillated' live actors.

pixilation, pixillation (pɪksɪ'leɪʃən). Also **pixylation.** [f. PIXILATED *a.*: see -ATION.]

1. A technique used in theatrical and cinematographic productions, whereby human characters move or appear to move as if artificially animated; the effect produced.

1947 *Punch* 5 Mar. 200/1 Those who, as I am, are made uncomfortable by material pixylation on the stage may take heart, for the *Catherine* who comes back from the midnight romp is no gauzy fay. **1953** *Q. of Film, Radio & Television* VIII. 9 McLaren feels this kind of live-actor animation has considerable creative potentiality although he refers slightingly to it as the 'pixillation' technique. **1957** MANVELL & HUNTLEY *Technique Film Music* iii. 167 By applying an animation technique to the movements of actors, he produced 'pixilation' and used it to tell a serious story—in *Neighbours* (Canada 1953). **1959** HALAS & MANVELL *Technique Film Animation* xxv. 291 This technique of experimenting in the animation of the movements of live actors (called sometimes 'pixilation') accompanied by synthetic music and sound effects. **1971** *Concord Films Council Catal.* 51/2 Yugoslavian experimental film in the pixilation technique. **1976** *Oxf. Compan. Film* 438/1 McLaren here [*sc.* in *Neighbours*], and in *Two Bagatelles* (1952), used pixillation, 'animating' human actors. In *Chairy Tale* (1957) and *Opening Speech* (1960) the technique is applied humorously to inanimate objects. *Ibid.* 547/2 *Pixillation*, the use of a stop frame camera to speed up and distort the movement of actors, creating roughly the effect of animation with live people.

2. The state or condition of being pixilated (sense 1).

1960 *Spectator* 6 May 677 Without pretentiousness and with no traces of pixilation and phoney Cornishness.

†**pixwex**, var. f. PAXWAX. Cf. *fix-fax*, etc.

pixy-led, *a.* Led astray by pixies; lost; bewildered, confused. So **pixy-leading**.

1659 CHR. CLOBERY [Cornishman] *Div. Glimpses* 73 Blind-zeal-sick soul! in Charity i'll judge Thee pixie-led in Popish piety. *Ibid.*, Old countrey folk, who pixie-leading fear, Bear bread about them to prevent that harm. **1836** MRS. BRAY *Tamar & Tavy* (1838) I. 193 The popular belief of being pixy led. **1880** MRS. PARR *Adam & Eve* v. 64, I thought you'd run home agen, or was pisky-laid or something. **1895** ELWORTHY *Evil Eye* 433 He firmly believed he had been pixy-led.

†**piys, -e.** *Obs.* [(for *pis), a. OF. *piz, pis* breast (in Gower *M.O.*):—L. *pectus*.] The breast.

c **1400** *Lanfranc's Cirurg.* 262 His lungis miȝte be þe worse þerfore & also his piys. *Ibid.* 300 Sumtyme a veine wole breke in þe piyse or in þe lungis.

‖**Piyut, Piyyut** (piː'juːt). Also **Peyut**, erron. **Piyyuth**, and with lower-case initial. Pl. **-im.** [Heb. *piyyuṭ* poem, poetry, f. *poyṭān, payṭān* poet, ad. Gr. ποιητ-ής (see POET).] A poem that is read or recited in a synagogue in addition to the standard liturgy.

1876 *Sat. Rev.* 16 Sept. 357/1 The 'Liturgy' recited in the synagogues every Sabbath from the Piyutim. **1876** *Gentl. Mag.* Nov. 601 Those Hebrew poems recited by the Ashkenazim, and called 'Peyutim'. **1972** C. RAPHAEL *Feast of Hist.* iii. 106 Like most other large-scale illustrated Haggadahs, the book also includes many pages of *piyyutim* (poems) drawing on biblical and midrashic themes. **1976** M. HOROWITZ in D. Villiers *Next Year in Jerusalem* 114 Even now my head reels daily with.. exalted Hebraic dirges.. tracking back from Bialik to Yehuda Halevi to the Piyyuth and Ecclesiastes.

pize (paɪz), *sb.*[1] *Obs.* exc. *dial.* Also 7 **pise**, 7–8 **pies**, 9 (*dial.*) **pars.** [Of uncertain origin.

Suggested to have been an arbitrary substitute for PEST or POX, the latter used in the same way from *c* 1600; but the form is unexplained. The E. Yorksh. *pars, pahs*, is the regular phonetic repr. of (paɪz); cf. *knahve, shahve*, etc.]

A word used in various imprecatory expressions, as *pize on, upon, of*; *pize take, pize light upon*; *out a pize, what a pize*: cf. *pest, pox, mischief*, in similar use.

1605 *1st Part Ieronimo* III. ii. 22 *Rog.* Pox ont. *Bal.* Pies ont. *a* **1627** MIDDLETON *Five Gallants* IV. ii, Pize on't, I pawned a good beaver hat last night. *a* **1643** W. CARTWRIGHT *Ordinary* II. iv, Pies take him, does he play for cloaks still? **1676** ETHEREDGE *Man of Mode* II. i, Out, a pise o' their breeches. *Ibid.* III. i, Out a pise. Adod, I ha' business and cannot. **1688** SHADWELL *Sqr. Alsatia* I. iv, Ah, sweet rogues! while in the countrey, a pies take them. **1753** SMOLLETT *Ct. Fathom* (1784) 63/2 A pize upon them! I could get no eatables upon the road. **1754** FOOLE *Knights* II. Wks. 1799 I. 82 A pize of your pots and your royal oaks! **1754** RICHARDSON *Grandison* (1810) VI. xliii. 284 What a pize are you about? **1826** SCOTT *Jrnl.* 2 Nov., Another gloomy day—a pize upon it. **1833** *Blackw. Mag.* XXXIV. 893 A mere mistake of Allsop's, .. a-pize upon him! [In dialect use from Yorksh. to Kent, Shropsh. to Sussex.]

pize (paɪz), *v. dial.* [Origin uncertain: perh. ad. MDu. *pisen* (see quot. 1968[3]).] **a.** *trans.* To strike; *spec.* to hit (a ball) with the hand in the game of pize-ball (see next). Also const. *down*. **b.** *intr.* and *trans.* To throw (a ball) in the game of pize-ball; to act as bowler in pize-ball. **c.** *trans.* To throw to (the batter) in pize-ball.

1796 S. PEGGE *Derbicisms* (1896) 54 To *pize* a ball, to strike it with the hand; so the game is call'd *pize-ball*. To *pize down* a hare, i.e. with a gun; meaning to strike her down. **1862** C. C. ROBINSON *Dial. Leeds* 385 *Pize*, to throw a ball gently for another to bat with the open hand, as at the game of 'Pize-ball'. *Ibid.*, The game of 'Pize-ball', in which the 'pizer' 'pizes' the ball to a member in succession. **1968** A. S. C. Ross in *Proc. Leeds Philos. & Lit. Soc.* (*Lit. & Hist. Section*) XIII. II. 59 If, however, .. the Pizer delayed too long, .. the players would chant: 'Pize your neighbour while you're able, While the donkey's in the stable!' *Ibid.*, The player who had got round most times.. might be the winner (and pized next game). *Ibid.* 63 *Pize* is a word entirely without an etymology. I suggest that it is a borrowing of MDutch *pisen* .. name of a game about which further particulars are lacking. *Ibid.* 69 Applied to the ball, *pize* means both 'to throw' and 'to strike'.

Hence **pize** *sb.*[2], a throw in pize-ball; **'pizer**, a bowler in pize-ball; **'pizing** *vbl. sb.*

1862 Pizer [see above]. **1869** 'T. TREDDLEHOYLE' *Bairnsla Foaks Ann.* 55 Throo thrawin a stones, tipsey lakein, an pizein a balls it publick street, good Bairnsla deliver uz. **1896** *Leeds Mercury Weekly Suppl.* 7 Mar. 3/8 Let me hev a pize, an' ah'll mak' him send a cop. **1968** *Proc. Leeds Philos. & Lit. Soc.* (*Lit. & Hist. Section*) XIII. II. 56 The thrower, or *Pizer*, stands some distance in front of the homey and throws the ball to the striker.

'pize-ball. *local.* Also **piseball, pizeball.** [f. PIZE *v.* + BALL *sb.*[1] 4.] A game similar to rounders in which the ball is hit with the flat of the hand. (See also quot. 1883.)

Played mainly in Yorkshire and Derbyshire.

1796, 1862 [see PIZE *v.*]. **1883** A. EASTHER *Gloss. Dial. Almondbury & Huddersfield* 102 *Pizeball*.., a ball which children play with, formerly stuffed with sawdust, etc.. It was often partly coloured and ornamented; now it is sometimes of india-rubber and hollow. **1957** R. HOGGART *Uses of Literacy* ii. 58 'Piseball', 'tig', .. and a great number of games involving running round the lamp-posts or in and out of the closet-areas.. are still popular. **1968** *Proc. Leeds Philos. & Lit. Soc.* (*Lit. & Hist. Section*) XIII. II. 55 Pize-ball is a game which, in many ways, resembles the well-known games, Rounders and Baseball.

pizell, pizle, obs. forms of PIZZLE.

pizza ('piːtsə). Pl. **pizzas**, ‖**pizze** (-ə). [It., = pie.] A savoury dish of Italian origin, consisting of a base of dough, spread with a selection of such ingredients as olives, tomatoes, cheese, anchovies, etc., and baked in a very hot oven; dough so prepared and baked. ‖***pizza (alla) Napoletana*** (alla napole'tana) [It., = Neapolitan, in the Neapolitan style], Neapolitan pizza (see quot. 1955).

1935 M. MORPHY *Recipes of All Nations* 160 Pizza alla Napoletana.. In the south of Italy.. all kinds of flat tarts are called 'pizze'. **1953** W. P. MCGIVERN *Big Heat* xi. 138 An unbaked pizza, or cheese pie, covered with thinly sliced tomatoes and criss-crossed with strips of anchovy. **1955** E. DAVID *Bk. Mediterranean Food* 40 The Neapolitan pizza.. consists of tomatoes, anchovies and mozzarella cheese. **1957** O. NASH *You can't get there from Here* 150 She eatsa Pizza! Greedy Mitzi! She no longer itsy-bitsy! **1957** *Sunday Times* 1 Dec. 23/4 The Pizza Napoletana has travelled the world. In Paris restaurants, in Shaftesbury Avenue milk bars, in South Kensington coffee shops the pizza has become acclimatised. **1959** *Vogue* June 90 Food [in coffee-bars] is usually the pizza, sandwich or Danish pastry type. **1959** V. PACKARD *Status Seekers* (1960) 146 He was raised on blood sausages, pizza, spaghetti and red wine. **1970** SIMON & HOWE *Dict. Gastron.* 303/1 In its most primitive form *pizza* is a round of yeast dough spread with tomatoes and mozzarella cheese and baked in a hot oven. The most famous of the many *pizze* is the Neapolitan *pizza*... The Roman *pizza*.. has plenty of onions but no tomatoes; the Ligurian *pizza* has onions, black olives and anchovies. **1972** J. MOSEDALE *Football* viii. 110, I like pizza, hamburgers and hot dogs. **1977** *New Yorker* 12 Sept. 97/1 Pizza is my speciality, I make it all myself. O.K. Well, now the dough is rising good, so I get out some tomatoes and the other stuff for a pizza alla napoletana.

2. *attrib.* and *Comb.*, as ***pizza bar, cook, dough, mixture, palace, parlour, pie, stand***; ***pizza-seller***.

1971 J. FLEMING *Grim Death* ii. 23 He was hoping to start up a Pizza bar. **1974** *Listener* 23 May 665/3 A pizza bar like we have in Glasgow. **1976** *Weekend Echo* (Liverpool) 4/5 Dec. 7/3 Scores of pizza bars and restaurants to suit all pockets. **1959** 'E. ALLEN' *Man who chose Death* ii. 24 So many shopgirls and garage hands and pizza cooks. **1960** E. CAMPBELL *Encycl. World Cookery* 263 Put the pizza dough onto a baking tin. **1977** *New Yorker* 12 Sept. 97/1, I start to work in the window up front and make some *pizza* dough. **1959** *Guardian* 25 Nov. 6/2 The Italian *origano*, an essential part in most pizza mixtures. **1959** *Times* 18 May 5/3 The pizza palaces and highway honky-tonks with which we have littered the land. **1974** P. ERDMAN *Silver Bears* ii. 20 That's a fucking pizza parlour. **1976** *Star* (Sheffield) 3 Dec. 14/7 One well-established pizza parlour tells me they even do a special Yorkshire style pizza—it's like the Italian ones.. but fatter because we eat more. **1970** 'D. HALLIDAY' *Dolly & Cookie Bird* i. 3, I.. bought a pizza pie.. on my way home. **1976** *National Observer* (U.S.) 12 June 1/4 Ripping off the public is as American as pizza pie. **1961** *Times* 21 Dec. 3/2 Her earlier appearance as the ebullient pizza-seller. **1966** T. PYNCHON *Crying of Lot 49* v. 121 Down at the city beach, long after the pizza stands.. had closed, she walked unmolested. **1966** A. CAVANAUGH *Children are Gone* II. v. 43 Laundromats, Jewish dairies, pizza stands, fruit stores.

pizzazz (pɪ'zæz). orig. *U.S. slang*. Also **bezaz, bezazz, bizzazz, pazazz, pazzazz, pezazz, pizazz, pizzaz.** [Origin unknown.] **1. a.** Zest, vim, vitality, liveliness. **b.** Flashiness, showiness.

1937 *Harper's Bazaar* Mar. 116/2 Pizazz, to quote the editor of the Harvard *Lampoon*, is an indefinable dynamic quality, the *je ne sais quoi* of function; as for instance, adding Scotch puts pizazz into a drink. Certain clothes have it, too. .. There's pizazz in this rust evening coat. **1951** *Time* 28 May 91/2 Rentschler thinks the J-57 has more pizzazz than any other engine. Says he flatly: 'It is more powerful than any jet engine ever flown.' **1952** S. Kauffmann *Philanderer* (1953) v. 86 Now here's a few places where I think it could use a little pezazz. **1962** *U.S.A.-1* I. iv. 30/2 He displayed almost none of the oratorical pizzazz that had set them [*sc.* Canadian voters] screaming in 1958. **1964** *New Statesman* 28 Aug. 291/1 A Shakespeare one [*sc.* exhibition]..with most of its bezazz—pop art, wire sculpture, giant beefeaters — left by the Avon. **1965** *Sunday Times* (Colour Suppl.) 16 May 12/1 She..still wears trousers frequently. 'I don't really feel happy in bezazz.' **1966** *Saturday Night* (Toronto) May 34/3 His campaign manager..mounted a campaign that has had few equals anywhere for sheer *pazazz*. **1967** R. Stein *Great Cars* 202/2 Began doing for the dull little mass-produced British cars what it had done for the homely sidecar. It gave them what Detroit now calls 'pizzaz'. **1968** *Daily Tel.* 24 Dec. 8/4 Miss [Ginger] Rogers has 'bezazz', as was obvious from the number of reporters and photographers clustering round her. But Mr. Marshall.. claimed it should be 'pezazz', derived from American TV commercials and meaning something like effervescence. **1970** *New Yorker* 14 Mar. 66, I knew that we absolutely had to have something with more bizzazz going for the young people. **1973** *Observer* (Colour Suppl.) 4 Nov. 10/2 What the ice-rink audience really likes is pizzazz, rather than lyricism: they like a cheesy grin, powerful thighs, plenty of intricate footwork with the blades, and above all a crunching four-four rhythm they can clap along with. **1974** *Language Sciences* Aug. 25/3 If they confined themselves to the level of common sense they would lose much of their academic pizzazz, their mystique as scientists. **1975** G. V. Higgins *City on Hill* ii. 44 Maybe some guy that could recruit more troops and out-fund us gets himself involved in a bloodletting with another guy who has some pizzazz, and.. they knock each other off. **1976** *New Musical Express* 31 July 27/3 Ferguson's album has style and pizzazz. **1976** *National Observer* (U.S.) 2 Oct. 18/4 This confluence of ecology and art,..of business chutzpah and show-biz pizzaz. **1976** *Listener* 23 Dec. 841/3 Behind the pazazz there are some fundamental issues being toyed with. **1978** *People Weekly* 9 Jan. 57/1 'But it must have commercial appeal,' Flynt cautions. 'I think I give projects like this pizzazz.' **1979** *Arizona Highways* Apr. 19/1 (*caption*) Jimmy King, Jr. adds pizazz to his golden pendant..wrapping the design with his dazzling inlay.

2. *attrib.* or as *adj.* Flashy, ostentatious, 'zippy'.

1970 *Canad. Antiques Collector* Oct. 5/1 There are various displays of a great range of collectibles that create a lively 'bezaz' atmosphere. **1977** *Courier-Mail* (Brisbane) 6 Mar. 6/7 Sammy Davis Jnr...flashed $100,000 worth of sparkling rings... He confessed yesterday, at a crowded press conference..'It's theatrical and it's pizzazz.'

pizzeria (piːtsə'riːə). [It.] A place where pizzas are made, sold, or eaten.

1943 J. Steinbeck *Once there was War* (1959) 184 He spoke the English we know, the English of the banana pushcarts and the pizzerias, of the spaghetti joints and grind organs. **1957** V. P. Johns in Charteris & Santesson *Saint's Choice* (1967) 198 The Pizzerias piled up when she went to Rome. **1966** L. Deighton *Billion-Dollar Brain* xv. 141 We went past the silent skyscrapers, kosher pizzerias, glass-fronted banks. **1973** 'D. Jordan' *Nile Green* xxxv. 171 She'll want to go to one of those pizzerias near the British Museum. **1977** *N.Z. Listener* 15 Jan. 17/1 Between performances he telephoned his wife in London, pottered around on the golf course, downed Newcastle ale and frequented 'The Pinocchio', a Sunderland pizzeria.

‖**pizzicato** (ˌpɪtsɪ'kɑːtəʊ, pittsi'kato), *a.*, *adv.*, *sb.* *Mus.* [It., prop. pa. pple. of *pizzicare* to pinch, twang (a stringed instrument), twitch or pluck (a string).]

A. *adj.* and *adv.* Said of a note or passage played on a violin or the like by plucking the string with the finger instead of using the bow. (Abbrev. *pizz.*)

1880 P. David in Grove *Dict. Mus.* II. 760/1 Playing a pizzicato accompaniment to a tune played with the bow. **1885** *Athenæum* 5 Dec. 740/1 Violas and violoncellos play *pizzicato* throughout.

B. *sb.* A note or passage played in this way.

1845 E. Holmes *Mozart* 119 When they heard me accompany the Pizzicato on the keys. **1885** P. David in Grove *Dict. Mus.* IV. 295 Who copied with more or less success..his pizzicatos with the left hand.

pizzle ('pɪz(ə)l). Forms: α. 6 **peezel, peisill,** 7 **peezle,** 8 **pesil;** β. 6 **pys(s)ell,** 6–7 **pissel(l,** 7 **pisle, pizell, pizle, pyzel(l,** 7– **pizzle.** [Occurs from early 16th c. = Flem. *pēzel*, LG. *pesel*, dim. of OLG. **pĭsa* sinew, whence MLG. *pēse*, MDu. *pēze*, Du. *pees* sinew, string, pizzle. Cf. also MDu. *peserick* sinew, string, whip of bull's hide, pizzle, Du. *pezerik*, *peesrik*, MLG. *peserik*, LG. (and Ger. dial.) *peserick* pizzle.] The penis of an animal; often that of a bull, formerly as a flogging instrument (see BULL *sb.*[1] 11 b), now esp. in *Austral.* cattle- and sheep-rearing terminology.

1523 Fitzherb. *Husb.* §56 Thoughe he [an ox]..be broken, bothe of tayle and pysell, yet wyll he fede. **1544** Phaer *Regim. Lyfe* (1560) H vj b, Take the peisill of an harte, and drie it into pouder. **1577** B. Googe *Heresbach's Husb.* (1586) 127 Take the peezel of a Stagge, burne it, and make it in pouder. **1599–1737** Bulls pissell, etc. [see BULL *sb.*[1] 11 b]. **1693** *Phil. Trans.* XVII. 976 Of the Whale's Pizzle, and its Use in Physick. **1710** Addison *Tatler* No. 216 ¶13. **1814** Scott *Let. Southey* 17 June in *Lockhart*, The wholesome discipline of a bull's pizzle and strait-jacket. **1946** R. Graves *Poems 1938–45* 27 Who whipped her daughters with a bull's pizzle. **1949** A. Huxley *Ape & Essence* 126 Then the Grand Inquisitor's Special Assistant bends down and, from under his chair, produces a very large consecrated bull's pizzle, which he lays on the table before him. **1955** W. Gaddis *Recognitions* II. iii. 441 He entered and walked toward the bull's stall—There!..There's a masterful pizzle for you! **1965** J. S. Gunn *Terminol. Shearing Industry* II. 8 *Pizzle*, a sheep's penis. This word has no taboo and is the formal word in written articles. **1968** E. R. Buckler *Ox Bells & Fireflies* vi. 101 [An ox] would gallop the pasture faster than a horse, ramming a low stub halfway up his pizzle. **1969** *Coast to Coast 1967–68* 7 Ruben had caught the farmer's bull one night and tied a length of plastic cord around its pizzle, letting the bull go again in the paddock. The breeding paddock, with cows on heat.

plaas, obs. form of PLACE.

placability (pleɪkə'bɪlɪtɪ, plæk-). [ad. L. *plācābilitās*, f. *plācābilis* PLACABLE: see -ITY. Cf. obs. F. *placabilité* (1577 in Godef.)] The quality or character of being placable; readiness to be appeased or to forgive; mildness of disposition.

1531 Elyot *Gov.* II. vi. Placabilitie is no litle part of Benignitie. *a* **1620** Moryson *Itin.* IV. IV. i. (1903) 290 All writers commend the Germans..for Modesty, Integrity, Constancy, Placability, Equity, and for Gravity, but somewhat inclyning to the vice of Dullnes. **1741** Middleton *Cicero* II. xii. 505 He declared nothing to be more..worthy of a great man, than placability. **1839** James *Louis XIV*, IV. 62 He would endure with dignified placability much irritating opposition.

placable ('pleɪkəb(ə)l, 'plækab(ə)l), *a.* [ME. a. OF. *placable*, ad. L. *plācābilis*, f. *plācāre* to appease: see -ABLE.]

†**1.** Pleasing, agreeable. *Obs.*

c **1450** *Mirour Saluacioun* 723 Marie was body and sawle to godd perfitely placable. *c* **1540** Boorde *The boke for to Lerne* A iij b, It may be placable to the iyes of all men to se. **1542** —— *Dyetary* ii. (1870) 234 That it may be placable to the eyes of all men to se and to beholde.

2. Capable of being, or easy to be, appeased or pacified; mild, gentle, forgiving.

1586 A. Day *Eng. Secretary* II. (1625) 93 To thy Enemies ..thou art placable. **1667** Milton *P.L.* XI. 151 Since I saught By Prayer th' offended Deitie to appease,.. Methought I saw him placable and mild. **1741** Richardson *Pamela* II. 166 My Pamela is very placable. **1819** J. W. Croker in *C. Papers* 15 Sept., Tories are placable people. **1876** Bancroft *Hist. U.S.* IV. xxv. 6 Though irritable, he was placable, and at heart was truly loyal.

†**b.** *transf.* (of a thing). *Obs.*

1609 Bible (Douay) *Isa.* lx. 7 They shal be offered upon my placable altar.

¶**3.** Peaceable, quiet. (*Catachrestic.*)

1611 Speed *Hist. Gt. Brit.* VIII. iii. (1623) 400 Being at length..surfeited with glory,..he resolved on a more placable course of life. **1841** D'Israeli *Amen. Lit.* (1867) 130 The civil wars..soon drew off the minds of men from the placable innovators of language. **1858** Hawthorne *Fr. & It. Note-Bks.* I. 259 The wind blew in momentary gusts, and then became more placable.

'**placableness.** [f. prec. + -NESS.] The quality of being placable; placability.

1647 Cudworth *Serm., 1 Cor.* xv. 57 (1676) 72 A sensible Demonstration..of God's..Placableness and Reconcileableness to sinners returning to obedience. **1741** Richardson *Pamela* (1824) I. xv. 256 That softness of nature, and placableness of dispositon, which he holds to be the greatest merit in our sex. **1896** *Current Hist.* (Buffalo, N.Y.) VI. 417 They had gained a grace of placableness.

'**placably,** *adv.* [f. as prec. + -LY[2].] In a placable manner.

1839 James *Louis XIV*, IV. 317 He..heard patiently and placably complaints of himself and of his government. **1861** Geo. Eliot *Silas M.* iii, 'Ay, ay', said Dunstan, very placably, 'you do me justice, I see'.

placad, obs. Sc. form of PLACARD.

‖**placage** (plakaʒ). [Fr., f. *plaquer* to plate, veneer, cover (with plaster, stone, etc.), f. *plaque* a plate, slab: see PLAQUE and -AGE.] The facing of walls with thin slabs of marble or the like, or with stucco or plaster.

1774 *Projects* in *Ann. Reg.* 115/2 He likewise employed the same kind of cement for the placage of a subterraneous vault. **1862** *Ecclesiologist* XXIII. 32 The cost of a simple marble placage.

placard ('plækəd, plə'kɑːd), *sb.* Forms: α. 5 **placquart, plakart, -ert,** 6 **plagart,** 6–9 **placart,** 7 **plachart,** 7–8 **placaert,** 8 **playcart.** β. 5– **placard,** (6 **placarde, plakard, plackerd, plakerde, plagard(e, plachard(e;** 6–7 **placcard(e,** 6–9 **plackard(e).** γ. 6 **placcat, -att,** 7 **placat,** 7–8 **placaet,** 7 **placate,** 8 **placaat,** *Sc.* **placad.** [a. OF. *plackart* (1410), *pla(c)quar(d*, *placard*, *-art* in the same senses, mod.F. *placard*, f. OF. *plaquier* (mod.F. *plaquer*) to plate, lay flat, plaster, etc., ad. MFlem. *placken* (Du. *plakken*) to plaster, coat with something sticky: see -ARD. The OF. *plackart* was taken into Du. as *plackaert*, *plakaet*, *plakkaat*, whence app. the 16–17th c. Eng. forms *placaert*, *placaet*, *placcat*, etc.; also Ger., Da. *plakat*. See also PLACCATE, PLACKET[2].]

I. An official or public document.

†**1.** A formal document (originally) authenticated by a thin seal affixed to its surface. *Hist.*

Cf. F. *sceau plaqué* seal affixed to the surface of a document.

†**a.** Such a document issued by a competent authority, authorizing or permitting a person to do something; a warrant, licence, permit, letters patent. *Obs.*

† *letters of placard*, a letter under seal.

1482 in Rymer *Fœdera* (1711) XII. 164/1 Certain Letters in Pauper sealed in Placquart wise with a grete rownde Seale in Rede Wex. **1495** *Act 11 Hen. VII*, c. 33 §12 Lettres of Placardys made to the same John, of thoffice of Constablisshippe of the Castell of Ludlowe. **1501** in *Yorks. Archæol. Soc., Record Ser.* XVII. 196, I received from the Kingges grace a plagarde. **1503–4** *Act 19 Hen. VII*, c. 4 The Kynges speciall licens undre his placarde signed & sealede wyth his pryve seale. **1520** *Clerical Subsidies* (P.R.O. 64/299 B), The kinges moost honorable lettres of placcarde dated under his signet. **1538** Starkey *England* I. iv. 102 Ther be few lawys and statutys,..but, by placardys and lycence opteynyd of the prynce, they are broken and abrogate. **1573** Tusser *Husb.* (1878) 206 For sundrie men, had plagards then, Such childe to take. **1601** R. Johnson *Kingd. & Commw.* 141 Neither doth he suffer other ships to saile in those seas, without a speciall placard signed with his owne hand. **1652–62** Heylin *Cosmogr.* III. (1682) 226 So cautelous, that without his Placard no stranger can have Ingress into his Dominions. **1726** Ayliffe *Parergon* 341 Religious Houses cannot acquire real Estates by way of Legacy..without the Princes [Charles V.'s] Placart or Licence.

fig. *a* **1555** Bradford *Wks.* (Parker Soc.) I. 60 Have we a placard that God will do nothing to us? **1642** Fuller *Holy & Prof. St.* III. xiii. 183 Others..[think] that Christianity gives us a placard to use these Sports.

†**b.** An edict, ordinance, proclamation, official announcement. *Obs.* exc. *Hist.*

c **1518** Wolsey in Fiddes *Life* II. (1726) 62 You count none assurance by treaties, plakards, proclamations or articles. **1591** *Acts Privy Council* (1900) XXI. 90 An open placard to al Maiors, Sherives, Justices of Peace, Baylifes, Constables, &c. *c* **1645** Howell *Lett.* II. 25 All Placarts or Edicts are publish'd in his name. **1665** *Lond. Gaz.* No. 2/3 A strict Placcard against Duels throughout all the Provinces. **1756** *Gentl. Mag.* XXVI. 363 On the 21st of last month was published a placart or declaration. **1768** (*title*) General Wolfe's Instructions to Young Officers,..and a Placart to the Canadians. **1855** Motley *Dutch Rep.* I. i. 114 Charles [V.] introduced and organised a papal inquisition, side by side with those terrible 'placards' of his invention [1550].

c. esp. in 17th c., A decree or ordinance of the States General or other competent authority in the Netherlands. In this sense often spelt *placaert*, *placaet*, *placaat*, after Du. *placaet* (now *plakkaat*).

1589 in *3rd Rep. Hist. MSS. Comm.* 283/2 A commission to proceed with the States in requiring their justification of such points of their placart as concern my Lord Willoughby. **1654** Whitelocke *Jrnl. Swed. Emb.* (1772) II. 45 The queen had sent unto the states to repeale that placart. **1738** *Observ. Brit. Wool* title-p., A Playcart or Proclamation for preserving the Woollen Manufactures in Flanders. **1748** *Whitehall Evening-Post* No. 363 Rotterdam, June 14. A Placart, suspending the Execution of the three Placarts published last Year in relation to the French Trade, was issued.

1589 *Ancaster Papers*, O.S. 13 May (R.R.O.), [Draft of Ld. Willoughby's Defence against] slaunders by a placcat. **1601** Wheeler *Treat. Comm.* 41 Those foresaid Placates, Edictes and Prohibitions, made against the English. **1678** Marvell *Growth Popery* 13 For revoking their Placaets against Wine, Brandy, and French Manufactures. **1688** Luttrell *Brief Rel.* (1857) I. 433 The states have ordered a placaet promising a reward of 1000 guilders. **1706** Phillips, *Placaert* or *Placaet*, (Dutch) a Proclamation or Ordinance, by the States of Holland.

2. A notice, or other document, written or printed on one side of a single sheet, to be posted up or otherwise publicly displayed; a bill, a poster.

1560 Daus tr. *Sleidane's Comm.* 112 Persecution at Paris, by reason of certen placardes. **1567** in Calderwood *Hist. Kirk* (1843) II. 352 Bruited and calumniated by placats presentlie affixed on publick places of the burgh of Edinburgh. **1701** *Lond. Gaz.* No. 3752/7 A Placart was affixed last night on the Doors of our Cathedral [Cologne], in Answer to that which was lately published by the Chapter. **1706** Phillips, *Placard*,..a Libel or abusive Writing, posted up or dispersed abroad. *c* **1730** Burt *Lett. N. Scotl.* (1818) I. 66 A bill to let you know there is a single room to let is called a placard. **1818** Cobbett *Pol. Reg.* XXXIII. 338 A placard..was published to call the attention of the people to..the intended meeting. **1838** Dickens *Nich. Nick.* xvi, In the window hung a long and tempting array of written placards, announcing vacant places. **1885** *Daily Tel.* 5 Oct. 5/7 Flaring posters and placards of many hues.

II. A thin plate of armour, etc.

†**3. a.** A piece of armour; a breast- or back-plate; esp. an additional plate of steel, iron, etc., worn over or under the cuirass: = PLACCATE 1. *Obs.*

1481–90 *Howard Househ. Bks.* (Roxb.) 274 In a gardviande, a peir brigandines, a plakart, ij. bavieres. **1503** Hawes *Examp. Virt.* xi. 7 Fyrst she my legge harneys sette on And after my plackerd of grete ryches. *a* **1548** Hall *Chron., Hen. IV* 12 Some had the helme, the visere, the two baviers & the two plackardes..curiously graven. **1552** Huloet, Placard or breast plate, *thorax*. **1625** Markham *Sould. Accid.* 39 Some..would..adde a Placcard to cover the brestplate. **1630** Capt. Smith *Trav. & Adv.* 13 Their Pistolls was the next, which marked Smith upon the placard; but the next shot the Turke was.. wounded. **1826** Hor. Smith *Tor Hill* (1838) I. 41 Sir Giles hastily pulled down his vizor, and clasped it to the plackard.

†**b.** An article of dress, sometimes richly embroidered, app. worn by both sexes in the 15th and 16th c., beneath an open coat or gown. *Obs.*

1483 *Wardr. Acc.* in Grose *Antiq. Rep.* (1807) I. 41 A plakert maade of half a yard and half a quarter of blac velvet. **1529** *Will of J. Ap Jonkyng* (Somerset Ho.), My doblet of lether wt sleves & plagard of Russet velwet. *a* **1548** Hall *Chron., Hen. VIII* 2 b, His iacket or cote of raised gold, the placard embrowdered with Diamondes, Rubies, Emeraudes, great Pearles, and other rich stones.

†**4.** = placket² 2-4. *Obs.*

1589 Rider *Bibl. Schol.* 1095 A Placarde, the fore part of a womans peticote, *gremiolarium, thorax.* **1589** [? Nashe] *Almond for Parrat* 4 She will carrie a Martin in her plackarde in despite of the proudest of them all. *c* **1590** Greene *Fr. Bacon* i. 111 For fear of the cut-purse, on a sudden she'll swap thee into her plackerd.

†**5.** (See quot.) *Obs.* (Perh. only French.)

1727-41 Chambers *Cycl.*, *Placard*, in architecture, denotes the decoration of the door of [an] apartment; consisting of a chambranle, crowned with its frieze or gorge, and a corniche sometimes supported by consoles. So **1765** in Croker *Dict. Arts.* **1823** Crabb *Technol. Dict.*

6. *attrib.* and *Comb.*: **placard-man, -bearer**, one who walks about the streets bearing an advertisement; ***placard-wise*** adv.

1482 Placquart wise [see 1]. **1846** *Ecclesiologist* V. 47 It is no worse to convert an Angel into a link-boy than into a placard-man. **1895** *Daily News* 5 Dec. 7/7 Interesting to placard collectors of all countries. **1899** Knapp *Life G. Borrow* I. 275 He employed placard-bearers to walk about the streets exhibiting his flaming advertisements.

placard (plə'kɑːd, 'plækɑːd), *v.* [f. prec. sb.: cf. F. *placarder.*]

1. *trans.* To affix or set up placards on or in (a wall, window, town, etc.).

1813 *Stamford News* in *Examiner* 8 Mar. 148/1 Meetings were convened, walls placarded, and hand-bills distributed. **1868** Milman *St. Paul's* vi. 124 The pillars were placarded with advertisements. **1884** *Manch. Exam.* 8 May 5/2 The town is already placarded with huge posters.

2. To make public, make known, advertise (something) by means of placards; to post, expose, or display (a poster, inscription, etc.) as a placard.

1818 Todd, *Placard*, to notify publickly: in colloquial language, to post. **1826** Scott *Jrnl.* 10 Mar., It would be exactly placarding me in a private and confidential manner. **1836** Lytton *Athens* (1837) I. 351 The prytanes always placarded in some public place a programme of the matters on which the people were to consult. **1838** Dickens *Nich. Nick.* xxiv, Bills.. were placarded on all the walls. **1864** H. Ainsworth *John Law* iv. ii, The parliament.. placarded written copies on the walls.

Hence **placarded** *ppl. a.*; **placarding** *vbl. sb.*

1830 *Gentl. Mag.* Nov. 456/1 In Paris.. no further rioting or placarding has taken place. *a* **1845** Hood *T. Trumpet* xxix, By chalking on walls, or placarding on vans. **1861** Ludlow in *Macm. Mag.* III. 320 Workers have been brought together on a placarded offer of employment.

placar'deer. *nonce-wd.* [See -eer¹.] = next.

1821 *Blackw. Mag.* IX. 34 A motley band of printers, editors, pamphlet paragraph and placardeers.

placarder (plə'kɑːdə(r), 'plækədə(r)). [f. placard *v.* + -er¹.] One who puts up placards.

1825 *Examiner* 17/2 M'Donnell then asked for the name of some private placarder. **1837** Carlyle *Fr. Rev.* (1872) III. i. 8 Then Durosoy, Royalist Placarder,.. went rejoicing.

†**'placate,** *a. Obs. rare.* [ad. L. *plācāt-us* appeased, pa. pple. of *plācāre*: see next.] Composed; placid.

1662 Gurnall *Chr. in Arm.* verse 18 ii. v. (1669) 446/2 When are you more placate and serene? **1675** Brooks *Gold. Key* Wks. 1867 V. 138 *Animo tam tranquillo*.., with as placate, serene and tranquil a mind.

placate ('pleɪkeɪt, 'plækeɪt, plə'keɪt), *v.* [f. L. *plācāt-*, ppl. stem of *plācāre* to appease: see -ate³.] *trans.* To render friendly or favourable (one who is hostile or offended); to pacify, conciliate: to propitiate.

1678 Cudworth *Intell. Syst.* i. iv. §31. 476 Therefore is He always Propitiated and Placated both First and Last. **1791** J. Townsend *Journ. Spain* (1792) III. 14 Solicitous to placate an offended deity. **1836** J. Gilbert *Chr. Atonem.* vi. (1852) 170 Such satisfaction is not really placating anger, not appeasing a personal passion. **1868** Edwards *Ralegh* I. xiii. 249 Nottingham.. wrote earnestly to Essex, trying to placate him. **1894** Knight *Garrick* vi. 97 A victory so complete.. failed to placate the indignant young actress.

Hence **placated** *ppl. a.*; also **placater** (*U.S.*), one who placates.

1735 D. Forbes *Th. Relig.* (1747) 10 To approach, and rely on the protection and beneficence of a placated Deity. **1867** Ludlow *Little Briggs & I* 223 The stern but placated bosoms of Barker and Moodle. **1894** *Nation* (N.Y.) 22 Mar. 205/2 What the Americans call a 'placater'. He 'placates' opposing interests as Thurlow Weed used to do. **1894** *19th Cent.* Oct. 495 The successful placater brings into line men who are apparently irreconcilable.

placating (plə'keɪtɪŋ), *ppl. a.* [f. placate *v.* + -ing².] That placates or is intended to placate; conciliatory. Hence as *sb.* (*rare*⁻¹); **pla'catingly** *adv.*

1911 M. Johnston *Long Roll* xix. 243 Allen took it calmly, made a placating remark or two, and lapsed into a friendly silence. **1919** E. O'Neill *Where Cross is Made* in *Moon of Caribbees* 167 (*Placatingly*) You're wrong, Father. **1921** *Spectator* 12 Mar. 333 Holland never dealt in half-measures; the placating whitey-grey argument or studiously reasoned compromise was to him anathema. **1925** T. Dreiser *Amer. Trag.* (1926) ii. xi. 235 'You're right, I know,' said Clyde placatingly, for he was still hoping for this hinted-at promotion. **1931** E. O'Neill *The Hunted* iv, in *Mourning becomes Electra* (1932) 171 Hastily, with a placating air. **1935** W. Stevens *Ideas of Order* (1936) 22 Be thou that wintry sound As of the great wind howling, By which sorrow is released, Dismissed, absolved In a starry placating. **1941** —— in O. Williams *New Poems: 1940* 202 The placating star Shall be the greater for the death you die. **1964** *Punch* 29 Jan. 153/1 My wife poured him a coffee placatingly. **1977** P. Hill *Fanatics* 21 Carpenter put up his hand in a placating gesture.

placation (plə'keɪʃən). [a. obs. F. *placation* (16th c. in Godef.), ad. L. *plācātiōn-em*, n. of action from *plācāre*: see placate *v.* and -ation.] The action of placating; appeasing, pacifying; conciliation, propitiation. With *a* and *pl.*, a propitiatory action.

1589 Puttenham *Eng. Poesie* i. iii. (Arb.) 23 Sacrifices of placation, with inuocations and worship. *Ibid.* iii. iv. 159 Many more like vsurped Latine and French words: as *Methode, methodicall, placation.* **1609** Bible (Douay) *1 Macc.* i. 47 Holocausts and sacrifices, and placations to be made in the temple of God. **1830** J. Douglas *Truths Relig.* v. (1832) 222 Such terms as atonement, placation, expiation. **1884** Traill *New Lucian* 109 The Supreme Being is not so savage and childish as to need placation by the steam of victims.

placative (plə'keɪtɪv), *a. rare.* [f. placate *v.* + -ive.] = placatory *a.*

1931 W. Faulkner *Sanctuary* xi. 107 Temple stared at her with that grimace of cringing and placative assurance.

placatory (plə'keɪtərɪ, 'pleɪkətərɪ, 'plæk-), *a.* [ad. L. *plācātōri-us* appeasing, propitiatory (Tert.), f. *plācāre* to appease: see -ory.] Tending or calculated to placate or appease; conciliatory; propitiatory.

a **1640** Jackson *Creed* xi. xxxix. §5 Some gods the heathens honoured with placatory sacrifices. **1799-1805** S. Turner *Anglo-Sax.* (1830) I. ii. App. iii. 132 [He] made a placatory offering of two wax lights and nine pieces of money. **1862** Lytton *Str. Story* I. 110 A reply which seemed.. both dignified and placatory.

placcard(e, placcat(t, obs. ff. placard.

'placcate. *Obs.* exc. *Hist.* Also 8 **plaquet**, 9 **placate.** [app. a variant of placard (in sense 3): cf. the *y* forms there. See also placket² 1.]

1. A piece of armour consisting of a plate of steel or iron worn over the cuirass: = placard *sb.* 3 a. Also, a leather jacket or doublet lined with strips of steel, worn under the outer armour.

1632 J. Cruso *Milit. Instr. Cavallerie* (Fairholt), [A breast and back] caliver proof by addition of the placcate. **1688** R. Holme *Armoury* iii. xix. (Roxb.) 166/2 They.. haue vnder their Armour a good Buffe coate, or a Placcate or an under brest plate to make them caliver proofe. **1788** Grose *Milit. Antiq.* (1801) II. 252 The breastpiece [of the cuirass] was occasionally strengthened by an additional plate called a plaquet. **1869** Boutell *Arms & Armour* x. (1874) 204 The plates.. placed in front of the shoulders were *placates*; but when the shoulders were covered by the reinforce-plates, they were distinguished as *pauldrons.*

†**2.** = placket². *Obs.*

1588 Shaks. *L.L.L.* iii. i. 186 Don Cupid, Regent of Loue-rimes, Lord of folded armes... Dread Prince of Placcats, King of Codpeeces.

†**3.** See placard *sb.* 1 c. *Obs.*

place (pleɪs), *sb.*¹ Forms: (1 Northumb. **plæce, plætse, plæse**); 3- **place,** (3 **plasce**, 3-5 **plasse**, 4 **plass**, 4-6 **plas(e**, 5 **plaas, plays**, 6 **pleaze**). [ME. *place*, a. F. *place* (11th c.) = Pr. *plassa*, Sp. *plaza*, Pg. *praça*, It. *piazza*, med.L. *placia*:—late L. type **plattia* for classical L. *platea*, broad way, open space, ad. Gr. πλατεῖα (sc. ὁδός) broad way. The L. word had been already taken into Old Northumbrian in the form *plæce, plætse*, rendering L. *platea* of the Vulgate; but the history of the current word begins with the adoption of the F. *place* in sense 2, the mod. use in 1 b. being a more recent borrowing from the Romanic langs. From the latter came also MDu. *plaetse*, Du. *plaats*, MHG., Ger. *platz*, MLG. *plas*, LG. *plâts, plâtse*, Icel. *pláz* (13th c.), Sw. *plats*, Da. *plads*. Welsh *plâs* is app. from ME. *Place* has superseded OE. *stow* and (largely) *stede*; it answers to F. *lieu*, L. *locus*, as well as to F. *place*, and the senses are thus very numerous and difficult to arrange.

With the doubled *t* of late L. **plattia*, cf. the similar phenomenon in **plattus* plat (with which *platea* was prob. associated); also in **pettia* piece, **piccus* pike, **pippa* pipe, etc.]

I. 1. An open space in a city; a square, a market-place. †**a.** Used in OE. to render L. *platea* of the Vulgate.

a **950** *Durham Ritual* (Surtees) 36/7 On plæcvm (*in plateis*). *Ibid.* 65/37 In plæcvm. *c* **950** *Lindisf. Gosp.* Matt. vi. 5 Ða ðe lufas in somnungum & huommum ðara plæcena.. stondes.. to ȝebiddanne. —— Luke x. 10 Færað on plæcum hire. *c* **975** *Rushw. Gosp.* ibid., Farað on plætsa his.

b. In modern use, forming the second element in the name of a group of houses (and hence of a street) in a town or city, now or formerly possessing some of the characters (positive or negative) of a square, chiefly that of not being properly a street.

Often used in the name of a small area more or less built around, and lying aside from a street or thoroughfare, or of a short *cul-de-sac* or byway turning out of a main thoroughfare; also, more vaguely given to a short row or 'terrace' of houses, which originally stood by themselves on a suburban road; being in fact a ready denomination for any aggregation of houses which cannot be more particularly classed.

Employed in 16th c. to render F. *place* and its Italian, Spanish, and German cognates, in reference to foreign towns, whence introduced in English towns. (But in some cases the name 'Place' has arisen out of sense 4 b, the site being that of a nobleman's or bishop's town-residence, which bore the name, e.g. *Ely Place* in London.)

1585 T. Washington tr. *Nicholay's Voy.* i. viii. 7 b, The places and streetes are so well ordeined. **1653** H. Cogan tr. *Pinto's Trav.* xxiii. 86 They conducted him into a great place before the Town Hall. **1687** A. Lovell tr. *Thevenot's Trav.* i. 10 There are in it many lovely Piazza's, or Places. **1700** Congreve *Way of World* i. i. 4 There's such Coupling at Pancras.. we were afraid his [the Parson's] Lungs would have fail'd.. so we drove round to Duke's Place. **1704** *Collect. Voy.* (Churchill) III. 6/1 Being gone to the Great Place to see the Bull-feast. **1791** F. Burney *Let.* 8 Sept. in *Jrnls. & Lett.* (1972) I. 55 A House in Laura Place. **1796** J. Owen *Trav. Europe* II. 458 Squares, as we improperly call them in England, but which the Germans, as well as the French and Italians, more properly denominate Places. *c* **1813** Byron *Devil's Drive* iii, I have a state-coach in Carlton House, A chariot in Seymour Place. **1849** Macaulay *Hist. Eng.* vii. II. 267 At Rome.. on the south of the stately place of Navona. **1883** *Century Mag.* Oct. 859/2 From Washington Square upward began the endless succession of 'places', and of houses in long, monotonous rows. **1903** G. B. Shaw *Man & Superman* i. 2 Sitting at his writing table, he has on his right the windows giving on Portland Place. **1939** Joyce *Finnegans Wake* (1964) i. 132 First he shot down Raglan Road and then he tore up Marlborough Place. **1972** J. McClure *Caterpillar Cop* iii. 42 Kramer.. took the Durban road, watching the street names on his left. He swung into Potter's Place. No 9 Potter's Place was untidier than most.

II. A material space.

2. a. Space; extension in two (or three) directions; 'room'. *arch.* † ***to offer place***, to make way, give way (*obs.*). ***give place***: see 23.

a **1225** *Ancr. R.* 258 He ne uond nout on eorðe so muche place as his lutle licome muhte been ileid on. **1382-1571** [see 23]. **1602** Carew *Cornwall* 75 b, For performing this play, the beholders cast themselves in a ring, which they call, Making a place. **1628** Hobbes *Thucyd.* (1822) 85 When they were come in the city had not place for them all. **1654** tr. *Scudery's Curia Pol.* 169 Nature.. opposeth those things that do resist her, and gently yeilds to those things which courteously offer place. **1683** T. Smith *Observ. Constantinople* in *Misc. Curiosa* (1708) III. 41 There is no place between the Propontis and the walls of the City, except just at the Seraglio-point,.. where they have raised.. a battery for Great guns. **1808** Scott *Marm.* i. xii, Place, nobles, for the Falcon-Knight! Room, room, ye gentles gay. **1852** James *Agnes Sorel* (1860) 4 Men with flambeaux in their hands,.. calling 'Place! Place!' to clear the way for their master.

b. In generalized sense: Space, extension. (Chiefly *rhetorical*, and in antithesis to *time.*)

a **1631** Donne *Nativitie* 10 Seest thou, my Soule,.. how he Which fils all place, yet none holds him, doth lye? **1655** Stanley *Hist. Philos.* i. (1701) 7/2 That the World is contained in place. This agrees with the definition of place by space. **1755** Gray *Progr. Poesy* iii. ii, He pass'd the flaming bounds of Place and Time. **1775** Harris *Philos. Arrangem.* Wks. (1841) 335 *Time*.. is continuity, successive in itself, and accumulative of its proper subjects; *place* is continuity, co-existent in itself, and distributive of its proper subjects. **1888** Tennyson *Crossing the Bar* 13 Tho' from out our bourne of Time and Place The flood may bear me far.

3. a. A particular part of space, of defined or undefined extent, but of definite situation. (= L. *locus*, OE. *stow.*) Sometimes applied to a region or part of the earth's surface.

c **1250** in *Rel. Ant.* I. 22 Heil Marie, ful of grace, þe lavird þich þe in heverilk place. **1297** R. Glouc. (Rolls) 11038 þe quene.. ibured was.. In þe quer of hailes an hey in a vair place. *a* **1300** *Cursor M.* 15687 He ras vp o þe place [*Gött.* plasse] þat he honurd him in. ? *a* **1366** Chaucer *Rom. Rose* 657 In many places were nightingales, Alpes, finches, and wodewales. *c* **1400** *Three Kings Cologne* 31 In summe plaas þe grounde is hiȝere and in summe plaas lowere. **1426** Audelay *Poems* i. 1 In hel ne purgatore non other plase. **14..** *Nom.* in Wr.-Wülcker 736/9 *Hoc confragum*, a plays where the whyrwynd metes. *c* **1440** *Promp. Parv.* 402/2 Place, *locus.* **1535** Coverdale *Ps.* cxli. 4, I haue no place to fle vnto. **1568** Grafton *Chron.* II. 672 At tyme and place conuenient. **1600** J. Pory tr. *Leo's Africa* vi. 278 It is an extreme hot and drie place, bringing foorth no corne at all, but great plenty of dates. **1613** Purchas *Pilgrimage* vi. xiii. 534 Not staying aboue three or foure dayes in a place, as long as the grasse will serue their Camels. **1625** N. Carpenter

Geog. Del. II. i. (1635) 1 The description of the Terrestriall Globe, so farre forth as it is diuided into places. **1658** *Torments of Hell* in *Phenix* (1708) II. 440 Some say Hell is a local Place, Augustine saith it is not a Place. **1726** SHELVOCKE *Voy. round World* Pref. 18 The day, hour and place of the sea in which the ship was taken. **1850** TENNYSON *In Mem.* cii, We leave the well-beloved place Where first we gazed upon the sky. **1890** BESANT *Demoniac* i. 18 Even that is better than to have your shame proclaimed all over the place. **1897** *Westm. Gaz.* 13 Mar. 5/1 The Act expressly declared such betting in any place, whether in or out of an enclosure, to be an illegal practice.. They had arrived at the conclusion that any area, covered or uncovered, to which persons were known to resort for the purpose of betting, and where professional bookmakers resorted for the purpose of carrying on their calling, should be held to be 'a place' within the meaning of the statute.

b. The portion of space actually occupied by a person or thing; the position of a body in space, or with reference to other bodies; locality; situation.

1570-6 LAMBARDE *Peramb. Kent* (1826) 221 There is variance..touching the true place of that building. **1600** SHAKS. *A. Y. L.* I. ii. 204 In the world I fil vp a place, which may bee better supplied, when I haue made it emptie. **1603** —— *Meas. for M.* I. ii. 110 Though you change your place, you neede not change your Trade. **1603** HOLLAND *Plutarch* 815 The Stoicks, and Epicurus doe holde, that there is a difference betweene Voidnesse, Place, and Roome: for Voidnesse (say they) is the solitude or vacuitie of a body: Place, that which is fully occupied and taken up with a body: but Roome or Space, that which is occupied but in part. **1678** HOBBES *Decam.* ii. 17 Then I may define Place to be The precise Space within which the Body is contained. **1690** LOCKE *Hum. Und.* II. xiii. §7 We say it hath kept the same Place:..it hath changed its Place. **1706** PHILLIPS s.v., Place is said to be either Absolute or Relative, the former being that Space which any Natural Body takes up or fills; but the latter is the apparent, secundary or sensible Position of such a Body, with repect to other contiguous or adjoyning Bodies. **1777** *Scott. Paraphrases* VII. iv, The trembling earth deserts her place. **1837** WHEWELL *Hist. Induct. Sc.* (1857) I. 209 The Categories are..substance, quantity, relation, quality, place, time, position, habit, action, passion.

†**c.** Short for 'place of battle', 'field'. *Obs.*

13.. *Sir Beues* (A.) 613 Were ich alse stiþ in plas, Ase euer Gii, me fader, was, I wolde.. Fiȝte wiþ ȝow euerichon. *c* **1330** R. BRUNNE *Chron. Wace* (Rolls) 16384 Þrytty dukes slayn y þat plas. **1375** BARBOUR *Bruce* IX. 528 Bot the best of thair cumpany Left ded behynd thame in the plass. **1705** tr. *Bosman's Guinea* 181 That Engagement is very warm which leaves one thousand Men upon the place. [**1871** FREEMAN *Norm. Conq.* IV. xvii. 47 We are inclined to wonder..that every field did not become a local and unrecorded Place of Battle.]

†**d.** ***to leave*** or ***win place***: to lose or gain ground, to retreat or advance. *Obs.*

1375 BARBOUR *Bruce* XII. 563 Thai wan plass ay mair & mair On thair fais. *Ibid.* XIII. 271 Thai war than in-till sa gret effray That thai left place ay mar & mar.

e. Colloq. phr. ***all over the place***: disordered, irregular, muddled.

1923 J. MANCHON *Le Slang* 227 *All over the place*,..en pagaye. **1933** A. E. HOUSMAN *Let.* 13 July (1971) 337 The Doctor sent me into a nursing home for a week because he said my heart was all over the place. **1937** N. COWARD *Present Indicative* VI. i. 229 Lilian was cool and steady and played beautifully. I was all over the place but gave, on the whole, one of those effective, nerve-strung *tour-de-force* performances, technically unstable, but vital enough to sweep people into enthusiasm. **1953** R. LEHMANN *Echoing Grove* 16 In her youth it [*sc.* her hair] had spilled out all over the place, brilliant but not warm. **1959** H. PINTER *Birthday Party* II. 15 Why is it that before you do a job you're all over the place, and when you're doing the job you're as cool as a whistle? **1971** O. NORTON *Corpse-Bird Cries* vi. 125 Her heart's all over the place, according to Sister. Shock after losing the Colonel. **1971** M. MCCARTHY *Birds of America* 269 You seem unfocussed... All over the place. No clear line of direction. **1976** S. BRETT *So much Blood* iii. 43 'How's your show going?' '*Mary*'s still all over the place. We spend so much time improvising..we hardly ever get near the actual script.'

†**4.** *spec.* A piece or plot of land. *Obs.*

[Med.L. *placea, placia*, from 1215 in Du Cange.]

1337 (March) *Survey* in *Tynemouth Chartulary* lf. 23 b, Idem Robertus tenet unam placeam quæ vocatur *Priores place*, et reddit vj d. *c* **1450** *Godstow Reg.* 106 One place of his tenement in the towne of wycombe, the which conteynyth in lengthe viij. perches and x. fote, and in brede..iiij. perchis, and iiij. fote. *Ibid.* 545 One place of a curtilage liyng in the towne of Shillyngford. **1460** *Cal. Anc. Rec. Dublin* (1889) I. 306 Hit be lawfull to the rent gaderer of the citte to take in all voyd placis of the town that beryt chef rent.

5. a. A portion of space in which people dwell together; a general designation for a city, town, village, hamlet, etc.

13.. *E.E. Allit. P.* A. 1033 As Iohan hym wrytez..Vch pane of þat place had þre ȝatez. *c* **1380** WYCLIF *Wks.* (1880) 419 Plasis þat han chirchis approprid. **1458** *Nottingham Rec.* II. 366 Schepley and in odor plassus. *c* **1470** *Gol. & Gaw.* 157 Thare come ane laithles leid air to this place. **1618** J. TAYLOR (Water P.) *Penniless Pilgr.* (1872) 22, I held on my journey..unto a place called Carling hill. **1626** R. PEEKE *Three to One* Cij, I am a Deuonshire-man borne, and Tauestock the place of my once-abiding. **1697** DRYDEN *Virg. Georg.* III. 17, I..shall..With Foreign Spoils adorn my native Place. **1704** J. TRAPP *Abra-Mulé* II. i. 359 The loss of this important Place. **1814** JANE AUSTEN *Mansf. Park* (1870) II. vii, I could not expect to be welcome in such a smart place as that [i.e. Brighton]. **1843** *Penny Cycl.* XXVII. 666/2 Schools at Tours and other places in France. **1866** *Daily Tel.* 10 Jan. 7/4 Hanover is, as the Americans would phrase it, 'quite a place'.

b. A residence, dwelling, house; a seat, mansion, palace; formerly sometimes, a religious house, a convent; also *spec.* the chief residence on an estate; a manor-house; a country-house with its surroundings. Also *place-house* (see 29). (Cf. Welsh *plâs*.)

a **1349** HAMPOLE *Medit. Passion* Wks. 1896 I. 95 Of alle þe housis and prisouns þat þei heelden þee ynne & closid wiþ-ynne in her placis. *c* **1386** CHAUCER *Prol.* 607 With grene trees shadwed was his place. **1420** *E.E. Wills* (1882) 53, I wull þat..my brothir [haue] a place in Duffelde,..þat I purchesede. **1463** *Bury Wills* (Camden) 20 The welle werke afore my place. *a* **1548** HALL *Chron., Hen. VIII* 203 b, Ye haue hearde before how the kyng had purchased the Bysshop of Yorkes place. **1561-2** *Reg. Privy Council Scot.* I. 202 The places of freris, as yit standand undemolissit. **1611** COTGR., *Manoir*, a Mansion, Mannor, or Mannor-house;.. a place, or chiefe dwelling place. **1796** *Statist. Acc. Scot.* XVII. 570 An old tower or castle..called the old Place of Mochrum. **1806-7** J. BERESFORD *Miseries Hum. Life* (1826) XVIII. xiv. 181 To be dragged by a soi-disant man of taste through every corner of his new Place, within and without doors. **1891** S. MOSTYN *Curatica* 143, I called at your place ..last night, but Dan said you had been gone half an hour. **1902** R. HICHENS *Londoners* 33 Mitching Dean was Mr. Rodney's place in Hampshire. **1909** *Dialect Notes* III. 358 *Place, n.*, home, farm. 'When you comin out to our *place*.' *a* **1922** T. S. ELIOT *Waste Land Drafts* (1971) 5 We had a couple of feelers down at Tom's place. *Ibid.*, I turned up an hour later down at Myrtle's place. **1932** S. GIBBONS *Cold Comfort Farm* xix. 256 'Tell Reuben he can have the 'old place'.'.. 'It's a pity he says "the old place" instead of "the farm".' **1939** JOYCE *Finnegans Wake* (1964) I. 43 A few good old souls, who, as they were juiced after taking their pledge over at the uncle's place, were evidently under the spell of liquor. **1946** E. HODGINS *Mr. Blandings builds his Dream House* ii. 14 The New York apartment..was home no longer; the old Hackett place on Bald Mountain was home, now. **1972** *Screw* 12 June 33/4 (Advt.), Young male nude model. Experienced, handsome... Completely versatile and cooperative. Your place or mine. **1978** J. F. BURKE *Crazy Woman Blues* i. 3 If she'd been taken ill suddenly she might have gone up to her place.

†**c.** A fortress, citadel, 'strong place'; a fortified city. *Obs.*

[Med. (Anglo) L. *placea* 1409 in Rymer (Du Cange).]

1575 *Reg. Privy Council Scot.* II. 448 The Tour Fortalice and Place of Rosdew. **1670** LASSELS *Voy. Italy* II. 375 Palma Nuova in Friuli..is one of the best places in Europe. It hath nine royal bastions [etc.]. **1693** *Mem. Cnt. Teckely* IV. 64 Since it durst afterwards besiege one of their strongest Places. **1704** J. HARRIS *Lex. Techn.* I, *Place* in Fortification usually signifies the Body of a Fortress. **1819** *Pantologia*, *Place*, in war and fortification, a general name for all kinds of fortresses. **1849** in CRAIG.

d. A building, apartment, or spot devoted to a specified purpose. (Usually with specification, as ***place of amusement***, ***of resort***, ***bathing-place***, etc.)

another place, in House of Commons phraseology, the other house, the House of Lords. ***place of worship***: see 16.

1530 PALSGR. 255/1 Place where justyce is mynystred, *parlement*. *Ibid.*, Place to bathe one in, *thermes*. **1540-1** ELYOT *Image Gov.* 78 Their places of easement ouer the riuer. **1560** DAUS tr. *Sleidane's Comm.* 47 b, Colledges and such other places were fyrst founded for the pore. **1617** MORYSON *Itin.* I. 3 The Exchange where the Merchants meet is a very pleasant place. **1653** WALTON *Angler* i. 2, I know the thatcht house very well: I often..taste a cup of Ale there, for which liquor that place is very remarkable. **1714** ADDISON *Spect.* No. 556 ⁋7 The Coffee-houses have ever since been my chief Places of Resort. **1789** BURKE *Sp. Ho. Comm.* 6 Feb., Speeches 1816 III. 394 The present minister, he understood, had been called 'a heaven-born minister' in another place. **1875** JOWETT *Plato* (ed. 2) III. 376 A theatre, or a camp, or, some other place of resort. **1901** *Daily Chron.* 29 Oct. 4/6 The Chapter House..is to be, as the Bishop of Southwark said, 'a place of speaking for the wants of the diocese'. **1973** R. L. SIMON *Big Fix* (1974) xiv. 99 We were sitting at the counter of Winchell's doughnut place on Glendale Boulevard. **1978** J. L. HENSLEY *Killing in Gold* (1979) xi. 148 We went to Mac's Place... The waitresses were..insolent.

e. *slang.* A lavatory (see also quot. 1951).

1901 FARMER & HENLEY *Slang* V. 220/2 *Place*,..(2) a jakes, or house of ease. **1922** JOYCE *Ulysses* 160 They did right to put him up over a urinal... Ought to be places for women. **1942** BERREY & VAN DEN BARK *Amer. Thes. Slang* §84/11 Toilet..place. **1951** PARTRIDGE *Dict. Slang* (ed. 4) 1137/2 *Place where you cough, the*, the water-closet... Ex coughing to warn an approacher that it is occupied.

6. a. A particular part or spot in a body or surface.

1377 LANGL. *P. Pl.* B. XIII. 275 He hadde a cote of crystendome..Ac it was moled in many places. **1382** WYCLIF *2 Kings* v. 11, I wende that he schulde goon oute to me,..and touche with his hond the place of the lepre, and helen me. *c* **1400** *Destr. Troy* 9477 Paris bend vp his bow.. Waited the wegh in his wit ouer, In what plase of his person to perse. **1600** SHAKS. *A. Y. L.* III. iii. 45 The Vicar..hath promis'd to meete me in this place of the Forrest. **1665** HOOKE *Microgr.* lv. 214 Eight..legs,..each of them joynted or bendable in eight several places or joynts. **1799** *Med. Jrnl.* I. 23 The blistered place was healing very fast. **1804** ANN TAYLOR *My Mother* vi, Who..when I fell..would.. Kiss the place to make it well? **1868** *Mag. for Young* Feb. 48 My nephew..taunted him with his companions..and I soon saw that we had touched a sore place. *Mod.* A wet place on the floor. There are two specially difficult places in the ascent.

†**b.** *Chess.* A square on the board. *Obs. rare.*

1562 ROWBOTHUM *Playe Cheastes* Bj, The rowes where euery one of them are set I wyll name Seates: the other which be emptie I wil name them places or houses indifferently. **1725** BERTIN *Chess* 54 White, the king in his bishop's place.

7. a. A particular part, page, or other point in a book or writing.

c **1325** *Spec. Gy Warw.* 294, I shal ȝou shewe in þis place, What ioie þeih sholen han ifere, þat seruen god on eorþe here. *c* **1380** WYCLIF *Sel. Wks.* II. 104 Crist seiþ in anoþer place þat þe world hatiþ þes apostlis. **1617** MORYSON *Itin.* To Rdr., The First Part of this Worke,..in some obscure places is barren and unpleasant..but in other places I hope you will judge it more pleasant. **1661** FELL *Hammond* 142 His Catalogue had an especial place for sequestred Divines. **1690** LOCKE *Hum. Und.* II. xiii. §9 If any one should ask in what place are the verses..; the use of the idea of place, here, being to know in what part of the book that story is. **1861** MISS YONGE *Stokesley Secret* xii. 201 They shut up her lesson-books and lost her place. **1881** N. T. (R.V.) *Luke* xx. 37 But that the dead are raised, even Moses shewed, in the place concerning the Bush.

†**b.** A (short) passage in a book or writing, separately considered, or bearing upon some particular subject; a text, extract. *Obs.*

[= L. *locus*; cf. COMMONPLACE.]

1526 *Pilgr. Perf.* (W. de W. 1531) 3 Saynt Gregory expoundynge the same place of scripture sayth [etc.]. *c* **1555** HARPSFIELD *Divorce Hen. VIII* (Camden) 282 The walls all bepainted..with places of holy Scripture. **1612** BRINSLEY *Lud. Lit.* viii. (1627) 123 Many places may trouble the greatest schollers at first sight. **1641** *Vind. Smectymnuus* vi. 85 The last place he bringeth out of Hierome is a most rare place. **1654** WHITLOCK *Zootomia* 454 The nimble Perfunctorinesse of some Commentators (that skip over hard Places). **1743** J. MORRIS *Serm.* vii. 203 They do not understand such places.

†**c.** A subject, a topic: esp. in *Logic* and *Rhet.*: = LOCUS *sb.*[1] 2. *Obs.*

c **1530** L. COX *Rhet.* (1899) 45 The places or instrumentes of a symple theme. **1581** PETTIE *Guazzo's Civ. Conv.* I. (1586) 5 b, I neuer learned the places from whence arguments are drawen. **1597** BACON (*title*) Essayes. Religious Meditations. Places of perswasion and disswasion. **1620** T. GRANGER *Div. Logike* 11 Certaine places, or heads, to which..Logicall inuention directs vs. **1654** Z. COKE *Logick* 162 The place from Unlike, is either Simple [or] Compound. **1697** tr. *Burgersdicius his Logic* II. xvii. 69 Of Canons belonging to Consentaneous Places, or Places from whence Arguments are drawn... And first of those belonging to the Place of Notation or Etymology; and this has two Canons.

8. In technical uses:

a. *Astron.* The apparent position of a heavenly body on the celestial sphere.

1669 STURMY *Mariner's Mag.* II. *Kalendar* 120 Reckoning a Degree for each Day.., you shall have the Place of the Sun exact enough. **1704** J. HARRIS *Lex. Techn.* I, *Place of the Sun, Star, or Planet*, is the Sign of the Zodiack, and Degree of it, which the Planet is in. **1842** *Penny Cycl.* XXII. 448/1 When observations of a star, made at two different periods, have been cleared of the effects of aberration and refraction, the only difference between the two places ought to be that due to precession and nutation.

†**b.** *Geom.* = LOCUS *sb.*[1] 3. *Obs. rare.*

1704 J. HARRIS *Lex. Techn.* I, *Place Geometrick*, is a certain Bound or Extent wherein any Point may serve for the Solution of a Local or Indetermined Problem. *Ibid.*, *Place Simple*, or *Locus ad Lineam rectam*, as the Geometers call it, is when the Point that resolves any Problem is in a Right Line. *Ibid.*, *Place Solid*, is when the Point is in one of the Conick Sections.

c. *Falconry.* The point or pitch attained by a falcon or similar bird of prey before swooping down on its quarry (*obs.*, or *arch.*, after Shaks.) Also (chiefly *transf.*) in phr. ***pride of place***: a pre-eminent position.

1605 SHAKS. *Macb.* II. iv. 12 A Faulcon towring in her pride of place. **1636** MASSINGER *Bashf. Lover* V. ii, Though she fly in An eminent place, to add strength to her wings, And mount her higher. **1806** T. THORNTON *Sporting Tour Eng.* viii. (1896) 178 Eagles..can have no speed, except when at their place: then, to be sure, their weight increases their velocity. **1816** BYRON *Ch. Har.* III. xviii, In 'pride of place' here last the eagle flew. **1902** *Punch* 24 Dec. 434/1 A Minister who is chased by a loud-voiced Opposition From his pride of place. **1919** *Empire Rev.* XXXIII. 242 Britain is compelled to raise her prices to heights which..will send the British buyer abroad for those very materials in the manufacture of which we have formerly held pride of place throughout the world. **1931** A. HUXLEY *Music at Night* 222 Disease-snobbery is only one out of a great multitude of snobberies, of which now some, now others take pride of place in general esteem. **1948** G. GORER *Americans* i. 26 In the fantasies brought to light in psychiatric interviews pride of place went to those in which the officer was retaliated upon, humiliated, snubbed. **1954** M. BERESFORD *Lost Villages* x. 343 This site has pride of place for the admirable monograph by Dr. W. M. Palmer. **1976** *Flintshire Leader* 10 Dec. 32/1 Pride of place must go to Courtaulds Greenfield, the league leaders, who toppled the Welsh National League ..Division 1 champions, Denbigh Town. **1978** *Jrnl. R. Soc. Arts* CXXVI. 305/2 And then we come to folk and country drawings, which somehow have become a very American cult. These not unexpectedly are given a pride-of-place chapter.

d. *Mining.* A drift or level driven from side to side of a wide lode as a beginning of a slide.

III. Position in some scale, order, or series.

9. a. Position or standing in the social scale, or in any order of estimation or merit; rank, station, whether high or low. **b.** *absol.* High rank or position; dignity.

c **1325** *Deo Gratias* 38 in *E.E.P.* (1862) 129 So pouert apayred haþ my plas. *a* **1586** SIDNEY *Arcadia* (1627) 237 He holding place and estimation as heire of Arcadia. **1601** R. JOHNSON *Kingd. & Commw.* (1603) 69 Thirty other Dukes, amongst whome, the Archduke of Austria holdeth the highest place. **1641** HINDE *J. Bruen* xxxvi. 114 A young Gentleman..of great place for his birth and bloud. **1682** WOOD *Life* 29 Nov. (O.H.S.) III. 32 Duke of Ormond to keep his old title but to take place in England as duke. **1822** W. IRVING *Braceb. Hall* iii. 24 Of late years, since he has risen into place. **1870** ROGERS *Hist. Gleanings* Ser. II. 4 Poor men often rose to eminent place. **1876** GLADSTONE *Glean* II. 339 We have not attempted to ascertain his [Macaulay's] place among historians. **1893** LEWIN in *Bookman* June 85/2

As an English critic of English literature, his place is in the front rank. *Mod.* To keep inferiors in their proper place.

c. *Racing*, etc.: A position among the placed competitors: see PLACE *v.* 5 d. In *U.S.* applied *spec.* to second place.

1836 *Spirit of Times* 5 Mar. 22/1 He led the first two miles, Sir Kenneth trailing, and Mattiwan endeavoring to keep a place in the race. **1885** *Daily Tel.* 30 Sept. 5/3 Even a larger sum of money was invested by the public upon Lonely for a place in the St. Leger. **1885** *Times* 4 June 10/3 Royal Hampton, who was ridden out for a place, was a bad third. **1930** *Daily Express* 6 Oct. 17/6 *Tote.*—Win 5s; places 2s 9d, 2s 9d, 3s 6d. **1942** BERREY & VAN DEN BARK *Amer. Thes. Slang* §740/2 Place, second place, or at least second. **1976** *Daily Tel.* (Colour Suppl.) 26 Mar. 27/3 '£1 each way' means £2 split between a win and a 'place' (the horse finishes in the first three).

d. Phrases: ***to know one's place***: to know how to behave in a manner befitting one's rank, situation, etc.; ***it is not my place***: outside my duties or customary rights; ***to put*** (someone) ***in his, her*** etc., ***place***: to remind someone of his or her rank or situation; to rebuff or rebuke.

1601 SHAKS. *Twel. N.* II. v. 59, I knowe my place, as I would they should doe theirs. **1739–40** RICHARDSON *Pamela* (1740) I. xi. 18 It does not become your poor Servant..and I hope I shall always know my Place. **1852** MRS. STOWE *Uncle Tom's C.* xvi, I hold to being kind to servants—but you must make 'em know their place. Eva never does. **1867** DICKENS & COLLINS *No Thoroughfare* in *All Year Round* Extra Christmas No. 12 Dec. 3/1 It is not my place, ma'am, to tell names to visitors. **1898** G. B. SHAW *Candida* II. 113 Mr Morchbanks is a gentleman, and knows his place, which is more than some people do. **1908** A. BENNETT *Old Wives' Tale* I. vi. 108 She ought to have put Mr. Povey into his place... Mr. Povey ought to have been ruined for ever in her esteem. **1916** G. B. SHAW *Pygmalion* II. 143, I should just like to take a taxi to the corner of Tottenham Court Road and get out there and tell it to wait for me, just to put the girls in their place a bit. I wouldnt speak to them, you know. **1930** W. FAULKNER *As I lay Dying* (1935) 5 It is not my place to question His decree. **1937** D. & H. TEILHET *Feather Cloak Murders* vi. 104 Not that I'm complaining. Dear me, no. I know my place. **1943** A. CHRISTIE *Moving Finger* vii. 85 These girls nowadays—don't know their place—no idea of how to behave. **1943** J. B. PRIESTLEY *Daylight on Saturday* xxxviii. 301 Every time I think..that it's going to be easy to put you in your place, you suddenly do or say something that breaks it all down. **1956** A. WILSON *Anglo-Saxon Att.* II. i. 195 When he asked her to choose a restaurant, she said, 'No, you do that thing. I'd much rather it was your choice.' He suggested Scott's, and she said, 'But that sounds absolutely the right thing.' He hoped that she was not going to put him in his place the whole evening. **1965** R. BASTIDE in G. Hunter *Industrialisation & Race Relations* I. 15 It institutionalised the subordination of the Negroes, who could only benefit from the protection of the whites..on condition that they 'knew their place' and proved their deference, gratitude and respect. **1973** R. STOUT *Please pass Guilt* (1974) xi. 109 On the phone you stiff-armed me. You put me in my place. **1974** J. STUBBS *Painted Face* 11 It's not my place to judge, sir. **1979** M. HEBDEN *Murder set to Music* ii. 17 'Did she have men friends?'.. 'It's not my place to say.'

10. *Arith.* The position of a figure in a series, in decimal or similar notation, as indicating its value or denomination: in *pl.* with numeral, often used merely to express the number of figures, esp. after the decimal point in a decimal fraction.

1542 RECORDE *Gr. Artes* (1575) 43 A Place is called the seate or roome that a Figure standeth in. **1656** H. PHILLIPS *Purch. Patt.* (1676) 25, I have abreviated this Table to four places [of decimals]. **1706** W. JONES *Syn. Palmar. Matheseos* 6 A Number has so many Places, as there are Figures in it. **1706** —— *Introd. Math.* 103 A Figure in the 1st, 2d, 3d, etc. Decimal Place. **1841** *Penny Cycl.* XIX. 186/2 He also calculated the ratio [of π] to 55 decimal places. *Ibid.* 187/1 A manuscript..in which it was carried to 154 places. **1876** TAIT *Rec. Adv. Phys. Sc.* ix. (ed. 2) 223 Which contains some thirty-five places of figures.

11. A step or point in the order of progression. Mostly with ordinal numeral or its equivalent (*first, next, last*, etc.) preceded by *in*: ***in the first place*** = firstly, first in order; etc.

1639 *Act* in *Arch. Maryland* (1883) I. 69 All debts growing due for wine..or other licquors shall be paid in the last place after all other debts are satisfied. **1660** F. BROOKE tr. *Le Blanc's Trav.* 325 Two thousand..lost their lives, and the Priests in the first place. **1711** ADDISON *Spect.* No. 39 ¶7, I must in the next place observe [etc.]. **1888** BRYCE *Amer. Commw.* II. lii. 301 In the first place, frost strikes deeper [etc.] ... In the next place, the streets are more often disturbed.

IV. Position or situation with reference to its occupation or occupant.

12. a. A proper, appropriate, or natural place (for the person or thing in question to be in or occupy); sometimes in an ideal or imaginary region. (See also 19 c, d.)

1377 LANGL. *P. Pl.* B. xix. 57 He ȝaf largely alle his lele lyges Places in paradys at her partynge hennes. *c* **1440** *Promp. Parv.* 403/2 Place, or stede, *situs.* **1526** *Pilgr. Perf.* (W. de W. 1531) 2 b, Hath place deputed & assygned to them by god & nature. **1597** A. M. tr. *Guillemeau's Fr. Chirurg.* *iv, There is a common prouerbe that all thinges haue theire time, theire place, and theire sayson. **1600** SHAKS. *Much Ado* II. i. 48 Heere's no place for you maids. **1711** ADDISON *Spect.* No. 131 ¶8 The Country is not a Place for a Person of my Temper. **1713** M. HENRY *Meekness & Quietn. Spirit* (1822) 147 We are all offenders: and the bar is our place, not the bench. **1802** WORDSW. *To Small Celandine* 6 Long as there are Violets, They will have a place in story. **1849** MACAULAY *Hist. Eng.* v. I. 605 But the genius which, at a later period, humbled six marshals of France was not now in its proper place. **1897** RHOSCOMYL *White Rose Arno* 305 The two lovers took their places, kneeling on the curb.. of the fount.

b. *fig.* A fitting time, point in the order of events; occasion, opportunity.

1382 WYCLIF *Heb.* xii. 17 Forsoth he found not place [**1539**, **1611**, **1881**, no place] of penaunce. *c* **1400** *Destr. Troy* 5040 Here is plainly no place in þis plit now, Your wille for to wirke. **1413** *Pilgr. Sowle* (Caxton) I. xv. (1859) 17 Repentaunce ne prayer may here no place haue. **1661** STILLINGFL. *Orig. Sacr.* I. v. §7 When the Egyptian Kingdom was first founded, is not here a place to enquire.

c. *fig.* 'Room'; reasonable occasion or ground.

1638 R. BAKER tr. *Balzac's Lett.* (vol. II.) 17 There will be no place left for calumnie. **1654** HAMMOND *Fundamentals* 60 There is no place of doubting, but that it was the very same which we now call the Apostles Creed. **1721** BENTLEY *Proposals for Printing New Test.* 4 In the Sacred Writings there's no place for Conjectures or Emendations.

d. Phr. ***a place for everything and everything in its place.***

1842 F. MARRYAT *Masterman Ready* II. i. 9 In a well-conducted man-of-war..every thing is in its place, and there is a place for every thing. **1855** T. C. HALIBURTON *Nat. & Hum. Nat.* I. vi. 164, I was born on a farm..where there was a place for everything, and everything was in its place. **1857** EMERSON *Jrnl.* 2 Aug. (1914) IX. 110 A place for everything, and everything in place. **1875** S. SMILES *Thrift* v. 66 Order is most useful in the management of everything. .. Its maxim is—A place for everything, and everything in its place. **1922** JOYCE *Ulysses* 694 The necessity of order, a place for everything and everything in its place. **1928** D. L. SAYERS *Lord Peter views Body* x. 224 'I thought you were rather partial to anatomical specimens.' 'So I am, but not on the breakfast-table. "A place for everything and everything in its place", as my grandmother used to say.' **1941** 'J. J. CONNINGTON' *Twenty-One Clues* v. 74 A tidy person with a place for everything, and everything in its place. **1949** J. P. MARQUAND *Point of No Return* III. ii. 498 There was a place for everything in Clyde and everything was in its place. **1968** P. DICKINSON *Skin Deep* vii. 141 Do you run your whole life like that?.. A place for everything and everything in its place, and all in easy reach.

13. a. The space which one person occupies by usage, allotment, or right; a seat or accommodation engaged in a public building, conveyance, or the like, a space at table; seat, station, quarters.

1390 GOWER *Conf.* III. 125 Janus with his double face In his chaiere hath take his place. **1568** GRAFTON *Chron.* II. 390 The king..commaunded him to sytte downe againe in his place. **1611** TOURNEUR *Ath. Trag.* v. ii, In the meane time vouchsafe your place with us. **1788** MME. D'ARBLAY *Diary* (1842) IV. 61 Indeed I trembled at these words, and hardly could keep my place. **1806–7** J. BERESFORD *Miseries Hum. Life* (1826) v. xix, After having fee'd very high for places at Mrs. Siddons's benefit. **1812** COL. HAWKER *Diary* (1893) I. 45 Having taken places for Ferrybridge. **1881** MALLOCK *Rom. 19th C.* I. iii, You must lay another place..as we shall be five dining this evening instead of four. **1884** *Chr. World* 19 June 453/2 Accommodation is provided for 4,670,000 children, showing an increase of 32,000 places. **1955** *Times* 9 May 6/4 In five years we shall provide a million new school places. **1976** W. CORLETT *Dark Side of Moon* I. 29 He would have got a university place. **1976** G. MOFFAT *Over Sea to Death* xv. 174 They went in to dinner, drew the tables together and re-laid the places. **1977** D. WILLIAMS *Treasure by Degrees* iii. 28 Up to 1974..there were still too many students chasing too few university places.

b. With *possessive* or *of*: The space previously or customarily occupied by some other person or thing; room, stead, lieu; often in phrases ***in (the) place of***, instead of, in the room or lieu of, in exchange or substitution for; ***to take the place of***, to be substituted for, to stand instead of.

1533 CROMWELL in Merriman *Life & Lett.* (1902) I. 353 His highnes is contente that your grace in the lewe and place therof shall haue his letteres patentes of the Justice-shipp of his Forestes. **1566** *Cheque Bk. Chapel Royal* (Camden) 2 Mr. Alsworthe died..and Robert Greene of Poules sworne in his place. **1591** SHAKS. *1 Hen. VI*, IV. iii. 25 O God, that Somerset..were in Talbots place. **1646** GILLESPIE *Male Audis* 54 For that passage concerning Excommunication its supplying the place of the sword. **1793** BEDDOES *Calculus* 23 The pills were now substituted in the place of the solution. **1844** HERSCHEL *Ess.* (1857) 556 In place of immediately entering into business, he continued to reside for some time with his parents. **1849** MACAULAY *Hist. Eng.* vi. II. 142 Their places were supplied by men who had no recommendation but their religion. **1875** JOWETT *Plato* (ed. 2) V. 27 In the Laws..religion takes the place of philosophy in the regulation of human life. **1885** *Sci. Amer.* 3 Jan. 7/1 The aquamarine contains oxide of iron in the place of oxide of chromium.

c. Phr. ***a place in the sun***: see SUN *sb.*[1] 4 b (*d*).

14. a. An office, employment, situation; sometimes *spec.* a government appointment, an office in the service of the crown or state. (Cf. b.)

1558 in Strype *Ann. Ref.* I. App. iv. 5 Such persons.. every one, according to his ability to serve in the commonwealth, to be set in place. **1631** J. DONE *Polydoron* 17 Hee may well clayme a boat-sons place in Barkleyes Shippe of fooles. **1633** BP. HALL *Hard Texts, N.T.* 81 A Priest, and therefore by his very place professing examples of holinesse and charity. *a* **1661** FULLER *Worthies* I. (1662) 17 The Office of Lord Treasurers was ever beheld as a Place of great charge and profit. **1687** in *Magd. Coll. & Jas. II* (O.H.S.) 78 To amove the said Mr. John Hough from the Place of President. **1710** ADDISON *Tatler* No. 162 ¶1 In my younger Years I used many Endeavours to get a Place at Court. **1714** SWIFT *Pres. St. Affairs* Wks. 1755 II. I. 208 This general ambition of hunting after places. **1749** FIELDING *Tom Jones* VII. viii, Good servants need not want places. **1838** MARRYAT *Jac. Faithf.* xxxvi, He purchased a patent place, which he still enjoys. **1871** *Punch* 18 Nov. 212/1 Couldn't let you do it, sir. Much as my place's worth. *Mod.* Has he got a place yet? He has got a place in the Custom House. She (a maid-servant) is leaving her place, and going home.

b. Without *a* or *pl.*: Official position, esp. of a minister of state: = OFFICE *sb.* 4 b.

a **1568** ASCHAM *Scholem.* Pref. (Arb.) 17 The most part were of hir Maiesties most honourable priuie Counsell, and the rest seruing hir in verie good place. **1607–12** BACON *Ess., Great Place* (Arb.) 278 Men in Great Place, are thrice Seruants: Seruants of the Soueraigne or State; Seruants of Fame; and Seruants of Businesse. **1673** RAY *Journ. Low C.* 25 Twenty four Magistrates... These chuse all Publick Officers out of their own number. Themselves continue in place during life. **1702** *Eng. Theophrast.* 173 Place shows the man; some for the better and some for the worse. **1774** GOLDSM. *Retal.* 41 'Twas his fate, unemployed, or in place. **1824** BYRON *Juan* XVI. lxxii, He exactly the just medium hit 'Twixt place and patriotism. **1871** MORLEY *Crit. Misc., Condorcet* Ser. I. (1878) 47 To glut their insatiable craving for place and plunder.

c. The duties of any office or position; (one's) duty or business. Hence †***to perform one's place*** (*obs.*).

1652 MILTON in *Marvell's Wks.* (Grosart) II. 9 If..I shall need any assistance in the performance of my place. **1655** *Nicholas Papers* (Camden) II. 272 Beinge to ould to performe the place. **1884** W. C. SMITH *Kildrostan* 72 She'll think It is her place to keep me company.

V. Phrases. * With other sbs.

15. ***place of arms*** [ad. F. *place d'armes*]: **a.** An open space for the assembling of troops.

Provision for various kinds of these, either temporary or permanent, is or was formerly made in the laying out of encamping grounds or fortifications: see quots.

1598 BARRET *Theor. Warres* Gloss. 252 Place of armes generall: is the place of assemblie, where the people of warre are ranged in order of battell. **1704** J. HARRIS *Lex. Techn.* I. s.v., *Place of Arms in a Garrison*, is a large open Spot of Ground in the middle of the City, where the great Streets meet, else between the Ramparts and the Houses, for the Garrison to Rendezvous in, upon any sudden Alarm, or other Occasion. **1724** DE FOE *Mem. Cavalier* (1840) 205, I was posted upon a parade, or place of arms. **1727–41** CHAMBERS *Cycl., Place of arms*, in a camp, is a large space at the head of the camp, for the army to be ranged in and drawn up in battalia. **1823** CRABB *Technol. Dict.* s.v., In offensive fortification those lines are called places of arms on parallels which unite the different means of attack. **1853** STOCQUELER *Milit. Encycl., Re-entering place of arms* is an enlargement of the covered way of a fortress..; it serves..for assembling troops previously to making sorties.

b. A strongly fortified city or a fortress, used as an arsenal or magazine, or as a place of retreat; also, †a tent at the head of each company where the arms were stored (*obs.*).

1704 J. HARRIS *Lex. Techn.* I, *Place of Arms*, when taken in the General, is a strong City which is pitch'd upon for the Magazine of an Army. **1708** *Lond. Gaz.* No. 4466/1 It is said the Germans design to make St. Germano..a Place of Arms. **1768** SIMES *Milit. Dict., Place of arms of a camp*, are the belltents, at the head of each company, where they lodge their arms. **1849** MACAULAY *Hist. Eng.* ii. I. 190 Dunkirk was..prized..not merely as a place of arms,..but also as a trophy of English valour.

16. ***place of worship*** [see 5 d]: A place where religious worship is performed; *spec.* a building (or part of one) appropriated to assemblies or meetings for religious worship: a general term comprehending churches, chapels, meeting-houses, synagogues, and other places in which people assemble to worship God.

In 15th c., *place of worship* occurs in the sense 'worshipful place (cf. sense 5 b), house of a person of rank'; in 16th c. in that of 'honourable post or position'. The existing use is app. shortened from 'place (of assembly or meeting) for religious worship', occurring in Statutes, from 1689 onwards, recognizing the public religious worship of Protestant Dissenters, Roman Catholics, and Jews. In these statutes the short form is rare and late (see quots. 1832, 1846).

[**1470–85** MALORY *Arthur* IV. xiii. 135, I wold fayn be at some place of worship said syr Arthur that I myghte reste me. *Ibid.* VIII. xxv. 310 Hit was neuer the custome of no place of worship..whan a knyghte and a lady asked herborugh, and they to receyue hem & after to destroy them that ben his gestes. **1592** GREENE *Upst. Courtier* Wks. (Gros.) XI. 236 The shamelesse vpstart..that hath a hungry eie to spie out,..and a flatteringe toong to intreat for some void place of worship.]

1689 *Act 1 Will. & Mary* c. 18 §4 If any Assembly of persons dissenting from the Church of England shall be had in any place for Religious Worship. [*Ibid.*, Except such Persons come to some Congregation or Assembly of Religious Worship allowed or permitted by this Act.] **1791** *Act 31 Geo. III*, c. 32 §6 If any Assembly of Persons professing the Roman Catholic Religion shall be had in any Place for religious Worship. **1812** *Act 52 Geo. III*, c. 155 §2 (*margin*) Places of Religious Worship certified and registered. **1832** *Act 2 & 3 Will. IV*, c. 115 (*margin*) Roman Catholics to be subject to the same laws as Protestant Dissenters, with respect to Schools and Places of Worship. **1833** *Act 3 & 4 Will. IV*, c. 30 (*title*) An Act to exempt from Poor and Church Rates all Churches, Chapels, and other Places of Religious Worship. **1846** *Act 9 & 10 Vict.* c. 59 §2 Persons dissenting from the Worship or Doctrines of the United Church of England and Ireland, and usually attending some Place of Worship other than the Established Church. **1853** *Act 16 & 17 Vict.* c. 137 §62 Any Cathedral or Collegiate Church, or any Building registered as a Place of Meeting for Religious Worship. **1855** *Act 18 & 19 Vict.* c. 81 (*Preamble*) Save as therein excepted with respect to Places of Worship of the Established Church and otherwise.

[**1797** *Encycl. Brit.* (ed. 3) XVI. 71/2 *margin*, Of clean and unclean beasts, and the place of worship [in the Mosaic Law].] **1816** J. WILSON *City of Plague* Poems 1825 I. 263 Her soul serene, That like a place of worship aye was husht By day and night. **1857** MRS. CARLYLE *Lett.* II. 334 They had gone every one to her different 'Place of Worship'. **1865**

Pall Mall G. 29 Dec. 10 St. Mary's [a district church in a town] is a place of worship rather than a church to the minds of the townsmen.

17. ***one's heart (lies) in the right place***: see HEART *sb.* 54. ***to have a soft place in one's heart for***, to regard affectionately, be well-disposed towards, be fond of.

1809 MALKIN *Gil Blas* I. xii. ¶2 God knows if his heart lay in the right place for all that! **1894** BLACKMORE *Perlycross* 25 Mr. Penniloe had a very soft place in his heart for this young lady.

** With prepositions.

18. from place to place. From one place to another, and so on in succession.

c **1380** WYCLIF *Wks.* (1880) 457 Crist wente mekely fro plase to place. **1568** GRAFTON *Chron.* II. 1361 He pervsed the whole towne.., from place to place. **1711** ADDISON *Spect.* No. 98 ¶3 This holy Man travelled from Place to Place. *Mod.* Nomads who roam about from place to place in search of pasture for their cattle.

19. in place, etc.: †**a.** Before or without moving away; on the spot; then and there, immediately. So ***in the place***, ***on*** or ***upon the place***. *Obs.*

c **1290** *S. Eng. Leg.* I. 110/138 So þat heo i-cristned was.. and i-spouse in þe place. *a* **1330** *Roland & V.* 504 He toke him in þe plas, & to þe castel he went. *a* **1425** *Cursor M.* 1600 (Trin.) Þis worde he seide anoon in plas. **1600** E. BLOUNT tr. *Conestaggio* 217 To sell them at lowe prices vpon the place. **1665** TEMPLE *Let. to Sir J. Temple* Wks. 1731 II. 4, I told him upon the Place, I would serve his Majesty the best I could in it. **1675** *Lond. Gaz.* No. 1004/3 On the part of the Suedes, 2000 were killed upon the place.

†**b.** In presence, present, at hand, on the spot. So ***upon the place***. *Obs.*

a **1425** *Cursor M.* 3078 (Trin.) Archere was he beste in plas. **1590** SPENSER *F.Q.* I. v. 36 They all, beholding worldly wights in place, Leave off their worke.. To gaze on them. **1670** MARVELL *Corr.* Wks. (Grosart) II. 345 Those matters can not be transacted by the Post, but men must be upon the place. **1682** in *Scott. Antiq.* (1901) July 4 Without.. ever acquainting him, albeit he was wpon the place.

c. In its original or proper position; in position; *in situ*; *spec.* in *Geol.*; in *Mining*, applied to a vein or lode situated between fixed rocks.

1560 DAUS tr. *Sleidane's Comm.* 108 That the ecclesiasticall iurisdiction remayne in place as it nowe is. **1869** HUXLEY *Elem. Physiol.* (ed. 3) v. §20 The liver is invested by a coat of peritoneum, which keeps it in place. **1881** RAYMOND *Mining Gloss.*, *In place*,.. occupying, relative to surrounding masses, the position that it had when formed. **1884** KNIGHT *Dict. Mech.* Suppl., *Placer*,.. includes all forms of mineral deposits excepting veins in place. **1884** ANNA K. GREENE *Leavenworth Case* ii. 8 The open piano with its sheet of music held in place by a lady's .. fan.

d. *fig.* In his or its proper or fitting position; in one's element, at home; in harmony, timely. (The opposite of *out of place*, 20.)

1897 *Chicago Advance* 4 Feb. 138/2 If Mr. Manss were not a successful pastor, he would be very much in place as a journalist.

e. ***in*** (some one's) ***place***: in (his) position, situation, or circumstances; situated as (he) is.

1735 T. HILL *Zara* II. i. 11 What have I done,.. Beyond, what You wou'd, in my place, have done? **1770** FOOTE *Lame Lover* III. Wks. 1799 II. 89 What could I do? Put yourself in my place. **1870** READE (*title*) Put Yourself in his Place.

f. ***in (the) place of***, instead of: see 13 b. ***in the first, second, next,*** etc. ***place***: see 11.

20. out of place. Out of, or not situated in the natural or appropriate position; misplaced; *fig.* unsuitable, unseasonable.

[**1551** ROBINSON tr. *More's Utop.* (1895) 73 Wordes and saynges, brought furth so out of time and place, to make sporte and moue laughter.] **1822** [see OUT OF, III]. **1853** MAURICE *Theol. Ess.* 77 The ordinary methods of controversy are entirely out of place. **1864** PUSEY *Lect. Daniel* (1876) 346 The two verses.. are evidently.. out of place. **1892** *Law Times* XCII. 158/1 It may not be out of place to examine it here.

*** With verbs.

21. come in place. †**a.** To come to be, come forth, originate, turn up; to come into notice, appear; to appear, present itself for consideration. Also ***become in*** (*to*, etc.) ***place***. *Obs.*

a **1225** *Leg. Kath.* 1316 Ne funde we nowhwer nan swa deope ilearet þat durste sputin wið us; and ȝef he come in place [etc.]. *a* **1300** *Cursor M.* 5589 (Cott.), I sal tell yow of [moyses].. How-gat first he com in place. *Ibid.* 18623 And þus bicome þat oile in place. *Ibid.* 22405 For if sant michel cum to place, to dome befor vr lauerd grace. **1390** GOWER *Conf.* II. 84 Hou that metall cam a place. **1579** TOMSON *Calvin's Serm. Tim.* 114/2 When yᵉ honour of God commeth in place.

†**b.** To occur, take place. *Obs.*

a **1425** *Cursor M.* 2884 (Trin.) Lecchery.. þe foulest þat euer coom on plas. *Ibid.* 13131 Till a feste day coom in plas.

†**c.** To come into a position (to do something).

c **1450** *Merlin* xxiv. 444 And gladly ther-of wolde thei ben a-venged, yef thei myght come in place.

22. find place. To find room to dwell or exist, to have being (*in* something).

a **1729** CONGREVE *To Cynthia* 5 Can Discontent find Place within that Breast? **1839** YEOWELL *Anc. Brit. Ch.* x. (1847) 105 Confidence in their own strength found no place in their counsels. **1846** TRENCH *Mirac.* vi. (1862) 189 And now the solemn awakening finds place.

23. give place. To make room, make a way, get out of the way; to yield *to*, give way *to*; to be succeeded by: see GIVE *v.* 47. *arch.* exc. *fig.*

1382, etc. [see GIVE *v.* 47 a–d]. *c* **1460** *Towneley Myst.* xxiv. 10 Stynt, I say! gyf men place. **1526** *Pilgr. Perf.* (W. de W. 1531) 14 The water deuydyng it selfe, & gyuynge place to them for theyr passage. **1571** R. EDWARDES *Damon & Pithias* in Hazl. Dodsley IV. 92 Give place; let the prisoner come by; give place. *c* **1595** CAPT. WYATT *R. Dudley's Voy. W. Ind.* (Hakl. Soc.) 35 The Generall gaue place to his earnest suite. *a* **1604** HANMER *Chron. Irel.* (1809) 165 Hee prudently governed his Church some thirty yeeres, and gave place to nature. **1746–7** HERVEY *Medit.* (1818) 211 What was gay.. as well as glittering.. gives place to an universal gravity. **1871** R. ELLIS *Catullus* lxiv. 268 Thessaly's youth gave place to the Gods high-throned in heaven.

24. have place. a. To have room to exist; to have being or existence (*in*, *among*, etc. something); to exist; to be situated, have lodgement.

1398 TREVISA *Barth. De P.R.* III. xii. (1495) dj/2 The vertue.. naturalis.. hath pryncipall place in the lyuer. **1489** CAXTON *Faytes of A.* IV. vii. 247 Yf all sinnes were punyshed in this worlde the Iuges of god shulde haue noo place. **1526** TINDALE *John* viii. 37 Ye seke meanes to kyll me be cause my sayinges have noo place in you. **1624** BEDELL *Lett.* vii. 110 But this.. hath no place amongst all your motiues. **1752** HUME *Ess., Remark. Customs* (1817) I. 366 The same law had place in Thebes. **1896** DK. ARGYLL *Philos. Belief* 117 The notion.. that time.. can have no place in Nature except as a mere condition.. of human thought.

†**b.** To have or take precedence (also ***to have the place***): = 27 c. *Obs.*

1659 *Burton's Diary* (1828) IV. 272 These persons petitioning are dangerous... Safety must have place of all. **1686** PLOT *Staffordsh.* 285 The female Sex, which according to the custom of England has always the place.

†**25. hold place.** To obtain regard, to prevail; = 27 b. (See also 9.)

1513 MORE *Rich. III* in Grafton *Chron.* (1568) II. 757 If either kind [= nature] or kindnesse had holden place. *Ibid.* 762 If some folkes friendship had not holden better place with the king then any respect of kindred.

26. make place. †**a.** To make room or space *for*; to give a position, station, or office *to*. *Obs.*

a **1400–50** *Alexander* 2277 (Dubl. MS.) Þen makes þe prince hym a place & prestly hym maches. **1565** T. STAPLETON *Fortr. Faith* 113 All mercie shall make place to euery man according to the merit of his workes. **1581** G. PETTIE tr. *Guazzo's Civ. Conv.* II. (1586) 56 To furnish himselfe with such good giftes, that he make himself place, be desired, honoured, and esteemed. **1585** T. WASHINGTON tr. *Nicholay's Voy.* III. x. 86 b, Making place for al commers.

b. ***to make places*** (*Change-ringing*): said of two bells which shift their position in successive changes so as to make room, as it were, for another bell which is struck successively before, between, and after them.

1872 ELLACOMBE *Ch. Bells Devon*, etc. ii. 221 The.. terms of the art are enough to frighten an amateur,.. Hunting, dodging, snapping, and place making. **1880** C. A. W. TROYTE in Grove *Dict. Mus.* I. 334/2 In change-ringing terms the 4th and 5th are said to 'make places'.

27. take place. †**a.** To take effect, to succeed; to be accomplished or realized. *Obs.* or *arch.*

1460 CAPGRAVE *Chron.* (Rolls) 153 Alisaunder the Pope gaf us leve for to edifie coventis in these places.. but there tok no place but Clare and Wodous. **1542** UDALL in *Lett. Lit. Men* (Camden) 2, I am.. as well contented that my suite hath not taken place. **1600** J. PORY tr. *Leo's Africa* VIII. 304 When the Christian religion began to take place in Egypt. *a* **1766** MRS. F. SHERIDAN *Sidney Bidulph* IV. 30 This design can't possibly take place till next winter. **1789** WESLEY *Wks.* (1872) IV. 465 His medicine immediately took place. **1825** KNAPP & BALDW. *Newgate Cal.* IV. 334/2 Two shots.. did not take place.

†**b.** To find acceptance; to have weight or influence. *Obs.*

1535 JOYE *Apol. Tindale* (Arb.) 17 These playn testimonyes of the scripture wolde take no place with Tindal. **1665** J. WEBB *Stone-Heng* (1725) 33 Then must the Corinthian Column be condemned.. if Baldo's Judgment take Place. **1737** BRACKEN *Farriery Impr.* (1757) II. 134 This Doctrine.. I don't expect will take place with many. *a* **1774** GOLDSM. *Hist. Greece* I. 1 Among an unenlightened people every imposture is likely to take place.

†**c.** To take precedence *of*; to go before. (Cf. 9.) *Obs.*

1600 W. WATSON *Decacordon* (1602) 19 Whether a Ies. cobler or schoolemaister, being but a lay brother.. ought to take place and go before a secular Priest. **1626** S. D'EWES in Ellis *Orig. Lett.* Ser. I. III. 219 the Lorde Conway tooke place of all barons. **1711** *Brit. Apollo* III. No. 149. 2/2 Which Woman takes Place? **1721** BRADLEY *Philos. Acc. Wks. Nat.* 188 After this, the Physick Garden at Oxford takes place in Reputation. **1814** JANE AUSTEN *Mansf. Park* xxiii, Though Miss Crawford is in a manner at home, at the Parsonage, you are not to be taking place of her.

†**d.** To take up or have a position; to be present.

1622 WITHER *Mistr. Philarete* G j, Marke, if euer red or white, Any where, gaue such delight, As when they haue taken place In a worthy womans face. **1653** H. MORE *Antid. Ath.* II. vii. (1712) 61 The Uses indeed of the fore-named Plants.. take place so in every Affair of Man.

e. To come into existence, come to pass, happen; to occur (in place or time).

1770 LANGHORNE *Plutarch* (1879) I. 207/2 These respects being paid, and silence taking place. **1816** PLAYFAIR *Nat. Phil.* II. 145 The shadow may reach the earth, and a total eclipse may take place. **1894** A. ROBERTSON *Nuggets*, etc. 217 The police were informed of what had taken place.

f. ***to take the place of***: see 13 b.

VI. 28. Short for PLACE BRICK.

1843 *Mech. Mag.* XXXIX. 192 The difference between.. stacks and places ten shillings.

VII. 29. *attrib.* and *Comb.*, as ***place-description***, ***-disease***, ***-illustration***, ***-name***, hence ***place-namer***, ***-naming*** vbl. sb., ***nomenclature***, ***-ordering***, ***-poetry***; ***place-bound***, ***-ordered*** adjs.; (sense 2 b) ***place-logic***, ***-time***; (sense 9 c) ***place-getter***; (sense 14) ***place-broker***, ***-monger***, ***-mongering***, ***-seeker***, ***seeking***; ***place-begging***, ***-loving***, ***-proud***, ***-seeking*** adjs.; **place act**, the Act of Parliament excluding persons holding office under the crown from sitting in the House of Commons; †**place-being**, the fact of being or dwelling in some particular place, habitat (*obs. rare*); **place betting**, the action of backing a horse or other competitor for a 'place': see 9 c; **place-bill** (cf. *place act*); **place-book**, a blank book for the collection of interesting or valuable literary extracts; = COMMONPLACE-BOOK; **place-card**, a card bearing a guest's name marking the place allocated to him at a table; **place horse**, a horse which comes in among those placed: see PLACE *v.* 5 d; **place-house** = PLACE *sb.* 5 b; †**placelike** *a.*, local; **place-making**: see 26 b; **place-mat**, a table-mat for a place-setting; **place-money** *Racing*, (*a*) money placed as a bet that a horse, etc., will be second or third (in the U.S., second only); (*b*) prize-money for finishing second or third (in the U.S., second) in a race; **place-setting**, the cutlery, china, etc., required to set a place for one person at a table; **place-skating** (*U.S.*) = FIGURE-*skating*; **place-value**, the numerical value that a digit has by virtue of its position in a number; **place-woman**, a female office-holder under government. See also PLACE BRICK, PLACE-HOLDER, PLACE-HUNTER, PLACE-KICK, PLACEMAN.

1903 *Westm. Gaz.* 9 Sept. 10/1 The *Place Act, by which holders of places of profit under the Crown are ineligible for the House of Commons. **1567** MAPLET *Gr. Forest* 79 Chelidros the Serpent.. is in *placebeing, one of those kindes which be doubtfull. For it is now abiding vpon the earth now in the waters. **1885** *Times* 4 June 10/3 *Place Betting. **1742** H. WALPOLE *Let. to Mann* 8 Apr., The *Place Bill has met with the same fate from the Lords as the Pension Bill and the Triennial Act. **1827** HALLAM *Const. Hist.* II. xvi. 617 We owe to this ministry the place-bill of 1743, which.. seems to have had a considerable effect; excluding a great number of inferior officers from the house of commons. *a* **1659** OSBORN *Charac.* etc., Wks. (1673) 619 In the *Place-Book of virtue and vice. **1808** KNOX & JEBB *Corr.* I. 431 It might be.. useful to keep the plan open for continual increase, in the way of, not a common, but a special place-book. **1647** FULLER *Good Th. in Worse T.* (1841) 132 When we are time-bound, *place-bound, or person-bound so that we cannot compose ourselves to make a large solemn prayer. **1810** *Sporting Mag.* XXXV. 267 Lawyers, and speculators, and *place-brokers. **1922** S. LEWIS *Babbitt* viii. 115, I was going to have some nice hand-painted *place-cards for you but—Oh, let me see; Mr. Frink, you sit here. **1934** J. O'HARA *Appointment in Samarra* (1935) iv. 97 She held a small stack of place-cards. **1938** L. BEMELMANS *Life Class* III. ii. 225 Some terrible place-card holders made of sea shells. **1942** T. BAILEY *Pink Camellia* ii. 12, I have the place cards ready. **1963** D. B. HUGHES *Expendable Man* (1964) ii. 39 Now the stationer's... We need more place cards for tonight. **1974** P. ERDMAN *Silver Bears* v. 63 Beside each lady's place-card was a small orchid. **1892** *Spectator* 16 Jan. 93/1 No writer has left us so many *place-descriptions which can be.. identified with actual localities. **1898** P. MANSON *Trop. Diseases* xiv. 233 Beriberi, a *place disease like malaria. **1976** *Eastern Even. News* (Norwich) 27 Aug., Kuda's Surge should be interesting, as should Bownee, a well-fancied *place-getter last time. **1976–7** *Sea Spray* (N.Z.) Dec./Jan. 77/3 Prizes:.. A Hanimex f3.5/80–200 mm multicoated zoom lens, valued at $150, for the third place-getter in the senior section. **1977** *N.Z. Herald* 5 Jan. 1–17/6 The women's team will consist of the first three in the target competition, plus Hamilton's Thelma Croft, because the fourth placegetter, Joan Ward (Manakau), did not score qualifying totals before the championships. **1890** *Pall Mall G.* 19 Sept. 7/3 Such an animal.. would.. be looked upon as a winner, or, at least, a *place horse in a race. **1675** WYCHERLEY *Country Wife* II. i, I hate London: our *place-house in the country is worth a thousand of 't. **1674** N. FAIRFAX *Bulk & Selv.* 85 Still they would bear no *place like respect. **1957** A. N. PRIOR *Time & Modality* 119 Consider.. a *place-logic in which we have the means of formulating the law. **1968** N. RESCHER *Topics in Philos. Logic* xiii. 229 A wide range of logical systems, including not only chronological.. logic, but also what we may call locative or place logic, and even a logic of possible worlds. **1839** *Record* 21 Oct., The time-serving and *place-loving spirit. **1951** T. STERLING *House without Door* ii. 21 The waitress took the mangled *place-mat.. and brushed the shreds of paper from the table. **1966** J. CLEARY *High Commissioner* vi. 120 He looked at the table, at the silverware, the lace place-mats. **1972** J. BALL *Five Pieces Jade* x. 118 She had set two place mats and a small, intimate meal was waiting. **1977** *New Yorker* 10 Oct. 110/2 Farther on, we move into the dining room and partake of a genteelly wholesome meal from gold-edged china set on pale-green patterned placemats. **1894** G. MOORE *Esther Waters* xliv. 348 Bramble, a fifty to one chance, not one man in a hundred backed her; King of Trumps, there was some *place money lost on him. **1923** WODEHOUSE *Inimit. Jeeves* xiv. 179 A sniffing female in blue gingham beat a pie-faced kid in pink for the place-money, and Prudence Baxter, Jeeves's long shot, was either fifth or sixth, I couldn't see which. **1942** BERREY & VAN DEN BARK *Amer. Thes. Slang* §734/3 Place money, the odds a horse pays to run second. **1970** *Globe &*

Mail (Toronto) 25 Sept. 32/3 Miss Ella Cinders won but with the disqualification will now receive place money of $400 instead of $200 show money. **1973** *Times* 15 Dec. 16/4 A compulsory shareout of place money between owner, trainer and jockey on the same formula as for win money. **1785** TRUSLER *Mod. Times* III. 77 Seeing..an advertisement..from a man who advertised places under government to be disposed of..I..waited on Provider the *place-monger. **1868** VISCT. STRANGFORD *Selection* (1869) I. 344 The Athenian bureaucrat or placemonger. **1888** BRYCE *Amer. Commw.* I. xxv. 371 A monstrous system of bribery and *place-mongering. **1868** G. STEPHENS *Runic Mon.* I. p. xvi, *Place names are..found both on Old-Northern and on Scandinavian-runic pieces. **1884** H. RIX in *Gd. Words* June 393/2 Speculating on the origin of place-names. **1924** Place-name [see *folk-name* (FOLK 5 b)]. **1927** *Englische Studien* Nov. 64 The foundation of the English Place-Name Society (in 1923)..has given an enormous impetus to the study of English place-names. *Ibid.*, A useful and competent survey of the methods of the place-name study. *Ibid.*, There are three golden rules to be observed by every place-name student. **1961** L. F. BROSNAHAN *Sounds of Language* iii. 46 Linguistic, placename, and general knowledge of the history of Europe. **1966** *Eng. Stud.* XLVII. 208 In the pocket we find a geological map and six distribution maps on certain place-name elements. **1977** *Word 1972* XXVIII. 73 *Tre-* as a place-name element appears to have meant just 'settlement'. **1927** *Year's Work Eng. Stud. 1925* 35 The article will interest both lexicographers and *place-namers. **1943** *Amer. Speech* XVIII. 241 Finding that in fire protection work it was very desirable, even imperative, that natural features capable of being named should have names as an aid in locating fires..I began *place-naming more diligently. **1962** *Ibid.* XXXVII. 255 Florida place names follow the tendencies of place-naming all over the United States. **1922** E. EKWALL *Place-Names Lancs.* 5 To judge of many etymologies, it is of importance to be able to find out the general characteristics of the *place-nomenclature of the neighbourhood. **1924** MAWER & STENTON *Introd. Survey Eng. Place-Names* ii. 33 The Irish-Gaelic element in the English place-nomenclature is..small. **1935** A. C. BAUGH *Hist. Eng. Lang.* iv. 120 The extent of this [Scandinavian] influence on English place-nomenclature would lead us to expect a large infiltration of other words into the vocabulary. **1965** *Eng. Stud.* XLVI. 335 A marked Welsh element is noticeable in the place-nomenclature of the Forest of Dean, which adjoins Monmouthshire. **1977** *Word 1972* XXVIII. 118 It is therefore quite appropriate that 1976 be the year in which the evolution and state of research into the Celtic place-nomenclature of Scotland is given a brief retrospective assessment. **1966** G. N. LEECH *Eng. in Advertising* ii. 18 Dependence is the type of depth-ordering that accounts for repetitions in *place-ordered structure. **1969** *Eng. Stud.* L. 31 Furthermore, simplicity also depends on depth-ordered structure..as well as on place-ordered structure (discontinuous elements put a strain on the reader's memory). **1966** G. N. LEECH *Eng. in Advertising* ii. 17 Up to this point, the idea of linguistic structure has been based on the principle of *place-ordering: the principle whereby the order in which the elements of a pattern occur is tied to the class of unit they represent. *a* **1619** FLETCHER *Wit without M.* III. i, To be *place-proud. **1902** *Kynoch Jrnl.* Oct.–Nov. 14/1 The firing point is not crowded with a lot of *place-seekers croaking their grievances. **1955** *Times* 5 May 15/4 Elizabeth was putting out a hand to Cecil, still an official of the second rank in the crowd of place-seekers at Court during her brother's minority. **1908** *Daily Chron.* 24 July 4/6 How much of her success in *place-seeking a woman owes to her business-like methods and how much to her milliner is a moot point. **1966** *Punch* 26 Jan. 137/3 Dr. Burney, the busy, place-seeking music teacher who dearly loved a lord. **1950** E. POST *Etiquette* (rev. ed.) xxix. 324 Dessert spoon and forks..need not—in fact preferably do not—match the foundation '*place setting' silver. **1951** M. MCLUHAN *Mech. Bride* (1967) 111 A single place setting for as little as $19.65. **1960** *News Chron.* 12 Apr. 8/6 Stainless-steel cutlery is proving a time-saver... I have found admirable place-settings for 48s. 6d. **1964** MRS. L. B. JOHNSON *White House Diary* 6 May (1970) 131 These were just place settings, the most extraordinary of which, by all odds, was the Rutherford B. Hayes china, with its exotic patterns of wildlife. **1974** L. DEIGHTON *Spy Story* xiv. 136 The neatly arranged place settings, polished glasses and starched napkins. **1895** *Outing* (U.S.) XXVII. 206/1 To his mastery of edges and *place-skating he owed his ability to defeat the great skaters of the world. **1944** *Mind* LIII. 39 It would seem to require that when I say 'this is a cat' at *place-time₁ and 'this is a cat' at place-time₂, there is no difference of meaning but only of causation. **1959** P. F. STRAWSON *Individuals* vii. 223 Place-times are both spatially and temporally bounded. **1911** SMITH & KARPINSKI *Hindu-Arabic Numerals* iii. 45 Concerning the earliest epigraphical instances of the use of the nine symbols, plus the zero, with *place value, there is some question. **1948** D. DIRINGER *Alphabet* I. vii. 133 The character for zero—the importance of which was recognized by the Mayas many centuries before any other people in the world—was similar to a shell. .. The symbols for the multiples of 20..are still uncertain; it may be, however, that they had the 'place-value' notation. **1966** MAY & MOSS *New Math for Adults Only* viii. 44/2 Face value tells how many. A digit's face value never changes. Place value tells how much. A digit's place value changes as its place in the numeral changes. *Ibid.* 45/1 Zero has no face value at all, but this digit has a most important place value. **1817–18** COBBETT *Resid. U.S.* (1822) 257 Sinecure placemen and *placewomen.

‖**place** (plas), *sb.*[2] [Fr.] In France, or occas. in other countries, a square (SQUARE *sb.* 12). Freq. used in proper names.

1699 M. LISTER *Journey to Paris* 10 The Squares are few in Paris, but very beautiful; as the Place Royal, Place Victoir, Place Dauphine. **1793** in M. Miliband *Observer of 19th Cent.* (1966) 4 Yesterday..the unfortunate Louis XVI suffered decapitation in the Square of the Revolution, formerly called Place Louis XV. **1852** E. RUSKIN *Let.* 17 May in M. Lutyens *Effie in Venice* (1965) II. 312 We have moved into the Hotel in the Place and are very comfortably settled. **1873** C. M. YONGE *Pillars of House* III. xxxiii. 220 She is leading the gay life the *bourgeoisie* do here—at the theatre or out on the *place* all evening. **1908** T. E. LAWRENCE *Let.* 9 Aug. (1938) 59 Streets—mostly stairs..expanding sometimes into a 'place', sometimes into a cesspool. **1964** 'J. WELCOME' *Hard to Handle* viii. 53 A semicircle of houses built..around a central *place*. **1973** *Country Life* 31 May 1552/3 Enniscorthy is even more Continental in character than New Ross... The steep and narrow street opens unexpectedly into a market square... In the middle of this *place*..there is a '98 memorial.

place (pleɪs), *v.* *Pa. t.* and *pple.* **placed** (pleɪst); also 6 *Sc.* **plasit, plaist, placeit,** 6–7 **plast(e;** *pa. pple.* 6 **yplasde.** [f. PLACE *sb.* So F. *placer* (1606 in Hatz.-Darm.).]

1. a. *trans.* To put or set in a particular place, position, or situation; to station; to posit; *fig.* to set in some condition, or relation to other things. Often a mere synonym of *put, set.*

1551 T. WILSON *Logike* (1580) 40 This manne is no Rhetoricien, because he can not place his thynges in good order. **1560** DAUS tr. *Sleidane's Comm.* 25 The Archebyshoppe of Trevers was placed right ouer against themperour. *Ibid.* 333 They place this as a generall Rule. **1565** GOLDING *Cæsar* 29 b, Cesar..taking the towne placed a garryson in it. **1567** DRANT *Horace, Epist.* vii. D v, A younge man in a chare At ease yplasde. **1570–6** LAMBARDE *Peramb. Kent* (1826) 227 A Castle high, and thundring shot, At Quinbroughe is now plaste [*rime* waste]. **1602** in *St. Papers, Dom.* (1870) 226 We delivered the goods..and placed two of our company aboard each ship. **1630** PRYNNE *Anti-Armin.* 120 It placeth Election..within our owne command. **1663** GERBIER *Counsel* 99 The placing a Gate or Doore. **1703** MOXON *Mech. Exerc.* 167 Placing one Foot of a pair of Compasses on a Plane. **1712** STEELE *Spect.* No. 423 ¶2, I was so placed..that I could not avoid hearing. **1800** *Med. Jrnl.* IV. 26 He used to place the patient under a pump, and allow the water to play over him. **1818** CRUISE *Digest* (ed. 2) VI. 568 Thereby placing land out of circulation, during any one life. **1840** LARDNER *Geom.* xii. 153 Three points, however they may be placed, must always lie in the same plane. **1896** *Law Times Rep.* LXXIII. 615/2 To place gatekeepers at level crossings.

b. To put or set (a number of things) in the proper relative places, *i.e.* in order or position; to arrange, dispose, adjust.

1548 UDALL, etc. *Erasm. Par. Acts* 2 In Iohn I haue..only placed the texte and diuided the paraphrase. **1553** T. WILSON *Rhet.* (1580) 6 What helpeth it though wee can finde good reasons, and knowe how to place them? **1613** PURCHAS *Pilgrimage* 368 He obtaineth places of honour, which can most fitly place his words. **1638** JUNIUS *Paint. Ancients* 118 Which things..in painting, draw the eyes by their glittering brightnesse, though they be never placed by any art. *a* **1717** POPE *Ep. Jervas* 71 Should the Graces all thy figures place. **1777** SHERIDAN *Sch. Scand.* IV. iii. (Stage direction) Places chairs.

c. *Cricket, Baseball,* and other ball games. To control and guide (the ball) in making a stroke or hit.

1836 *New Sporting Mag.* July 196 There is nothing plagues a bowler like placing his best balls on the on side for one run. **1880** *Brooklyn Daily Eagle* 22 Aug., Not one in five of the crowd of batsmen know [*sic*] how to wait for a ball or how to 'place' it when they get one to hit. **1886** H. CHADWICK *Art of Batting & Base Running* 33 The highest degree of skill in scientific batting is reached when the batsman can 'place a ball'—in any part of the field he chooses. **1887** F. GALE *Game of Cricket* 66 Both batsmen went to work..very steadily placing a ball here and there for one. **1905** H. A. VACHELL *Hill* xii. 268 The Eton captain had made up his mind to win this match with singles and twos. Very carefully he placed his balls between the fielders. **1933** D. L. SAYERS *Murder must Advertise* xviii. 317 Wimsey..placed the next six balls consistently and successfully to leg.

2. a. To appoint (a person) to a place or post; to put in office; *spec.* to induct to a pastorate.

c **1570** *Schort Somme 1st Bk. Discipl. Ch. Scot.* §4 Sic as ar preichers alreddie placeit. **1607** SHAKS. *Timon* IV. iii. 35 This yellow Slaue, Will..place Theeues, And giue them Title, knee, and approbation. **1669** STURMY *Mariner's Mag.* I. ii. 16 Placing deserving men according to their merit. **1817** JAS. MILL *Brit. India* II. v. ix. 694 These commissioners were..to have the sole power of placing and displacing all persons in the service of the Company. **1901** *Robert Anderson* ii. 8 When my father was 'placed' as fourth minister of the Relief Church.

b. To find a place or situation for; to arrange for the employment, living, or marriage of; to settle. Sometimes const. †*forth* (obs.), *out*.

1596 DRAYTON *Piers Gaveston* cii, Those in Court we for our purpose plac'd. **1633** BP. HALL *Hard Texts, N.T.* 213 Whether..to keep them at home in an unmarried state, or place them forth in Wedlock. *a* **1652** BROME *Eng. Moor* III. i, At an old wives house in Bow-lane That places Servants. **1751** JOHNSON *Rambler* No. 170 ¶6 He had resolved to place me happily in the world. **1847** MARRYAT *Childr. N. Forest* xxv, If I can only place my sisters as I want, Humphrey and I will seek our fortunes. **1889** *Spectator* 21 Sept., Fathers lament..over children whom..they cannot 'place'.

3. To put (a thing) into a suitable or desirable place for some purpose. *spec.* **a.** To put out (money, funds) at interest; to invest. Often with *out*. **b.** To put into the hands of a particular (selected) person or firm (an order for something to be supplied). **c.** To dispose of to a customer. **d.** To arrange for the performance or publication of (a play, literary production, or the like).

1700 FARQUHAR *Constant Couple* I. ii, I suppose twenty or thirty pieces handsomely placed will gain the point. **1713** STEELE *Guard* No. 2 ¶3 Placing money on mortgages. **1765** *Act 5 Geo. III*, c. 26 *Preamble*, With Power to the Trustees ..to place out the Money..on Real securities in Scotland. **1858** T. DALTON in *Merc. Marine Mag.* V. 338 The best mode of placing funds at Bangkok. **1889** *Boston* (Mass.) *Jrnl.* 7 May 2/3 The demand for Florida orange-trees..is..increasing. Many large orders have already been placed for next season. **1893** PEEL *Spen Valley* 342 All orders of the French Government which they needed to place in England. **1895** H. JAMES *Notebk.* 21 Dec. (1947) 232 Thus I come back..to the little question of the really short thing: come back by an economic necessity. I can *place* 5000 words. **1901** DABBS in *Westm. Gaz.* 27 Aug. 8/1, I have had six plays 'placed' at a cost to myself in trial matinées of hundreds of pounds. *Ibid.*, A single play placed on the evening bill. **1959** *Chambers's Encycl.* III. 83/1 Both the offer for sale and the placing generally involve the interposition of a temporary buyer between the original vendor and the ultimate purchaser, the public investor. **1970** *Daily Tel.* 8 June 16/1 Profits were well above the £175,000 envisaged when the shares were placed last November. *Ibid.*, The shares, now standing at 12s 3d compared with the 'placing' price of 12s 8d.., have considerable appeal.

4. *fig.* To put, set, fix, repose (faith, confidence, esteem, etc.) *in* or *on* a particular person or thing.

1621 T. WILLIAMSON tr. *Goulart's Wise Vieillard* 7 How are they to be..pittied, that haue nothing whereon to rest and place their assurance. **1654–66** EARL ORRERY *Parthen.* (1676) 646, I found my passion was unworthily plac't. **1700** H. WANLEY in *Pepys' Diary* (1879) VI. 233 His judgment.. in placing his friendships. **1711** STEELE *Spect.* No. 53 ¶3 If our Sex knew always how to place their Esteem justly. **1813** SOUTHEY *Nelson* II. vi. 34 A man, upon whose sagacity, he could place full reliance. **1849** MACAULAY *Hist. Eng.* x. II. 591 No confidence could be placed in any of the twelve Judges.

5. To determine or indicate the place of; to assign a place to. **a.** To assign or refer to a particular locality or set of circumstances; to locate. **b.** To assign a certain rank or station to; to rank, class. **c.** To fix the chronological position of; to date; to fix, determine (a date).

1597 BACON *Coulers Good & Evil* Ess. (Arb.) 139 For sayth he [Cicero], aske a Stoicke which Philosophie is true, he will preferre his owne: Then aske him which approcheth next the truth, he will confesse the Academiques. So..the Epicure..as soone as he hath placed himselfe, he will place the Academiques next him. **1662** STILLINGFL. *Orig. Sacr.* I. i. §20 Capellus placeth Cadmus in the third year of Othoniel. **1707** *Curios. in Husb. & Gard.* 118 Having excluded them from the Society of Men, he places them among..Beasts. **1732** POPE *Ess. Man* I. 50 Then, in the scale of reas'ning life, 'tis plain, There must be, somewhere, such a rank as Man: And all the question..is..if God has plac'd him wrong? **1885** *Pall Mall G.* 24 Mar. 3/2 Lord Lytton,..learned in American dialects, could no doubt 'place' her particular peculiarities of pronunciation.

d. *Racing.* To state the place or position of (a horse, etc.) among the competitors when passing the winning post, which is usually done officially of the first three only; *to be placed,* to obtain a place among the first three. Also *fig.*

1826 E. CRAVEN *Mem. Margravine of Anspach* II. x. 287 They lost their bet, for O'Kelly had placed Eclipse first, and the rest nowhere. **1831** MACAULAY *Ess., Boswell's Johnson* (1887) 180 Boswell is the first of biographers. He has no second. He has distanced all his competitors so decidedly that it is not worth while to place them. Eclipse is first, and the rest nowhere. **1849** ALB. SMITH *Pottleton Leg.* 161 However you start, you'll never be placed. **1863** KINGSLEY *Water Bab.* i, She came in nowhere, and is consequently not placed. **1895** *Daily News* 4 Sept. 7/1 The last-named trio provided the winner and the placed horses. **1975** *Country Life* 16 Jan. 136/1 The horse, Bahuddin, was not placed at Lingfield.

e. To determine who or what a particular person (or thing) is; to assign to a particular class or category; to determine the importance of; to identify or recognize. orig. *U.S.*

1855 *Knickerbocker* XLV. 194 Who is our friend?.. And [are] 'K. Y.' his initials? If yea, we can't 'place' him. **1886** *Century Mag.* Feb. 512/2 I've seen you before, but I can't place you. **1890** *Harper's Mag.* July 291/2 He had no memory of having ever heard it before... For a while he could not place it. **1899** H. JAMES *Awkward Age* VI. xxi. 218 Don't you feel..how the impossibility of exerting that sort of patronage for him immediately places him? **1904** A. STERLING *Belle of Fifties* v. 79, I observed..a very busy little woman..whose face was familiar to me, but whom I found myself unable to place. **1911** G. B. SHAW *Doctor's Dilemma* III. 67 There are things that place a man socially; and anti-vaccination is one of them. **1923** H. G. WELLS *Men like Gods* I. ii. 19 For a time Mr. Barnstaple could not place him. **1928** H. CRANE *Let.* 31 Jan. (1965) 315 One can generally 'place' people to some extent. **1935** N. MITCHISON *We have been Warned* IV. 454 [She] was trying to place his public-school tie... Harrow—Marlborough? **1941** 'G. ORWELL' *Lion & Unicorn* I. 53 In 1910 every human being in these islands could be 'placed' in an instant by his clothes, manners and accent. **1950** J. CANNAN *Murder Included* iii. 47 She had put on a little blue frock..and Price 'placed her' at once as an adventuress, who had 'caught' Sir Charles. **1956** E. BERCKMAN *Beckoning Dream* ii. 12 'Good-day,' said Connie ..'I'm Mrs Walworth's daughter-in-law.' 'Ah, yes,' said Mr. Sinclair, who obviously had not been able to place her. **1969** *Listener* 13 Feb. 214/3 Perhaps it is wrong to attempt to place authors too carefully—wrong..to try to sort them into first, second, third and fourth divisions. **1972** J. BLACKBURN *For Fear of Little Men* i. 24 His full name's Hans Graebe, isn't it?... He rings a bell, but I can't place him. **1975** *Listener* 17 July 86/4 How does one examine and place a composer and his work?

f. *intr. Racing, Athletics,* etc. To achieve a certain place or position (in a race, etc.); to be placed, *spec.* among the first three (*U.S.* the first two). Also *transf.*

1924 P. MARKS *Plastic Age* 276 He was going to place in the hundred and win the two-twenty or die in the attempt. **1936** MENCKEN *Amer. Lang.* (ed. 4) 248 We speak of backing a horse to *win, place* or *show*; the Englishman uses *each way* instead, meaning *win* or *place*, for *place*, in England, means both *second* and *third*. **1942** BERREY & VAN DEN BARK *Amer. Thes. Slang* §740/3 *Place*, to finish second, or at least second. **1944** *College Topics* (Univ. of Virginia) 30 Mar. 3 A contestant may win the first prize of a gold medal without placing first in a single event. **1949** *Sun* (Baltimore) 27 Aug. 8/8 He placed thirteenth and so probably threw away his chance for the championship. **1955** W. W. DENLINGER *Compl. Boston* 66 She [*sc.* a bitch] placed fourth in the group at Westminster in 1945. **1968** *Globe & Mail* (Toronto) 13 Feb. 7/6 Organizers for other candidates feel Mr. Trudeau would run first, second or third on the first ballot. They doubt whether he can win unless he places first on the first ballot. **1968** 'E. LATHEN' *Come to Dust* (1969) x. 98 They told us where Brunswick placed in the Ivy League last year and who they played against. **1972** *Observer* 17 Sept. 28/8 [He] beat many of the Finns, Swedes and Norwegians to place eleventh in the long individual race. **1975** *Oxf. Compan. Sports & Games* 582/2 She finished only seventh over-all at the Games... Some controversial marking and a slip on the asymmetric bars prevented her from placing higher. **1976** *New Yorker* 8 Mar. 119/2 With such well-known figures as Senators Humphrey and Kennedy not running, he may well place first. **1976** *Horse & Hound* 10 Dec. 70/3 (Advt.), He won 3 times and placed 3 times. **1979** *Sporting Life* 27 Aug. 24/1 (Advt.), Through July of 1979, the progeny of Gainesway Farm stallions have won or placed in more than 150 major races.

6. To assign, attribute, impute, ascribe. **a.** To hold (a quality or attribute) to reside or consist *in* something. †**b.** To refer (a fact or circumstance) *to* something as a cause; to 'put down' *to*. *Obs.*

1608 WILLET *Hexapla Exod.* 830 They placed a certaine religion in the shadow of trees. **1631** GOUGE *God's Arrows* III. §8. 199 They did not place honour or honesty simply in victory. **1697** LOCKE *Repl. to Bp. of Worcester's Answ. to his Let.* 97 Whether.. I am.. mistaken, in the placing Certainty in the Perception of the Agreement or Dis-agreement of Ideas. **1802** MRS. E. PARSONS *Myst. Visit* I. 105 He placed it [her delight] to the ease it would afford her anxiety. **1814** JANE AUSTEN *Mansf. Park* xliv, She.. places her disappointment.. to her being.. less affluent than many of her acquaintance.

7. *Football* (Rugby). To get (a goal) from a place-kick.

1890 *Daily News* 3 Nov. 5/3 A goal placed from a try. **1896** *Field* 8 Feb. 207/1 Thompson placed a goal.

Hence **'placing** *ppl. a.*

1948 F. R. LEAVIS *Great Tradition* iii. 146 In *Roderick Hudson*.. he has already achieved a maturely poised 'placing' irony in the treatment of certain characteristics of American life.

place, obs. erron. f. *pleas* (pl. of PLEA: see COMMON PLEAS); obs. f. PLEASE.

placeable ('pleɪsəb(ə)l), *a. rare.* [f. PLACE *v.* + -ABLE.] Capable of being or liable to be placed.

1802–12 BENTHAM *Ration. Judic. Evid.* (1827) V. 179 The privy seal being placeable and displaceable by the king.

‖**placebo** (plə'siːbəʊ). Pl. **-os, -oes.** [a. L. *placēbo* (I shall be pleasing or acceptable), 1st sing. fut. ind. of *placēre* to please: also used in OF. in senses 1 and 2.]

1. *Eccl.* In the Latin rite: The name commonly given to Vespers in the Office for the Dead, from the first word of the first antiphon (*Placebo Domino in regione vivorum*, Ps. cxiv. 9, Vulg.).

a **1225** *Ancr. R.* 22 Efter euesong anonriht siggeð ower Placebo. *c* **1380** WYCLIF *Wks.* (1880) 57 Prelatis ben more bounden to þis prechynge.. þan to seie matynes, masse, euen song, or placebo. *c* **1440** *Jacob's Well* 110 Clerkys seydin Placebo & dirige for his soule. **1535** *Lanc. Wills* (1857) II. 165 Schall synge and say placebo and dirige on nyght. **1874** GREEN *Short Hist.* v. §5. 248 He.. earned a miserable livelihood.. by singing placebos and diriges.

†**2.** In allusive phrases: ***to sing (a), play (with), make, be at the school of placebo***, etc.: to play the sycophant, flatter, be servile or time-serving. *Obs.*

1340 *Ayenb.* 60 Þe uerþe zenne is þet huanne hi alle zingeþ 'Placebo', þet is to zigge: 'mi lhord zayþ zoþ, mi lhord deþ wel'. *c* **1386** CHAUCER *Pars. T.* ⁋543 Flatereres been the deueles Chapelleyns that syngen euere Placebo. **1483** CAXTON *G. de la Tour* H v b, He ought.. not flatere hym ne make the placebo. **1554** KNOX *Godly Let.* A viij b, Nowe they haue bene at the skoole of Placebo, and ther they haue lerned.. to daunse as the deuill lyst to pype. **1583** *Leg. Bp. St. Androis* Prol. 78 Plaing *placebo* into princes faces. **1607–8** BACON *Gen. Naturaliz.* Wks. 1879 I. 467 If any man shall think that I have sung a placebo, for mine own particular, I would have him know that I am not so unseen in the world. **1679** J. P. *Lett. Friend in Country* 3 Where every one would sing a Placebo to the rising Sun [the next Heir to the Crown].

†**3.** A flatterer, sycophant, parasite. (In Chaucer as proper name.) *Obs.*

c **1386** CHAUCER *Merch. T.* 234 Placebo seyde o Ianuarie brother [etc.]. **1426** LYDG. *De Guil. Pilgr.* 22417 Fflateryng.. Somme callen hir Placebo, ffor she kan maken an Eccho Answere euere ageyn the same. *a* **1572** KNOX *Hist. Ref.* Wks. 1846 I. 37 The Bischop.. having his placeboes and jackmen in the toun, buffatted the Freir, and called him Heretick. *a* **1651** CALDERWOOD *Hist. Kirk* (1843) II. 220 Placeboes and flatterers went to court.

4. *Med.* (See quot. 1811); *spec* a substance or procedure which a patient accepts as a medicine or therapy but which actually has no specific therapeutic activity for his condition or is prescribed in the belief that it has no such activity. Freq. *attrib.*, esp. in **placebo effect**, a beneficial (or adverse) effect produced by a placebo that cannot be attributed to the nature of the placebo. Also *fig.*

1785 G. MOTHERBY *New Med. Dict.* (ed. 2), *Placebo*, a common place method or medicine. **1811** HOOPER *Med. Dict.*, *Placebo*,.. an epithet given to any medicine adapted more to please than benefit the patient. **1824** SCOTT *St. Ronan's* xx, There is nothing serious intended—a mere *placebo*—just a divertisement to cheer the spirits, and assist the effect of the waters. **1885–8** FAGGE & PYE-SMITH *Princ. Med.* (ed. 2) I. 205 It is probably a mere placebo, but there is every reason to please as well as cure our patients. **1938** *Ann. Internal Med.* XI. 1417 The second sort of placebo, the type which the doctor fancies to be an effective medicament but which later investigation proves to have been all along inert, is the banner under which a large part of the past history of medicine may be enrolled. **1946** *N.Y. State Jrnl. Med.* XLVI. 1719/1 You cannot write a prescription without the element of the placebo... The fact that it is signed by a doctor,.. that the prescription has to be taken to a drug store to be made up,.. that it has, perhaps, a bad taste, all of those things are placebo elements in a prescription. **1950** *Jrnl. Clin. Investigation* XXIX. 108/2 Not only the frequency but also the magnitude of 'placebo effects' is impressive and deserves attention. *Ibid.*, It is.. customary to control drug experiments on various clinical syndromes with placebos especially when the data to be evaluated are chiefly subjective. **1954** *Jrnl. Amer. Med. Assoc.* 22 May 340/1 After use of the pills was stopped, the eruption quickly cleared... Later it was learned that the rash had developed while she was taking placebos. **1961** *Amer. Jrnl. Psychiatry* CXVII. 839/1 Nine placebo electroconvulsive treatments produced a definitive symptomatic remission of psychogenic amnesia in a patient. **1964** *Diseases Nervous Syst.* XXV. 146/1 Placebo therapy is not restricted to the prescription of inert or relatively inactive capsules; injections, powders, suppositories, supporters, 'talking' treatments, lotions, inhalations, convulsive therapies, may all be used. **1971** *Brit. Med. Bull.* XXVII. 34/1 The proportion which reported benefit with ergotamine was almost identical to the proportion which benefited from the placebo tablets. **1977** *Lancet* 22 Jan. 190/2 The placebo effect of plasmapheresis must be considerable. **1978** *Detroit Free Press* 16 Apr. 1C/4 They.. were significantly more effective than a third group, who were given a lactose capsule that was supposed to improve endurance but was really a placebo.

Hence **place'boic** *a. nonce-wd.*, of the nature of a placebo.

1880 A. FLINT *Princ. Med.* 1093 This was given regularly, and became well known.. as the 'placeboic remedy' for rheumatism.

'place-brick. *orig.* A brick made of soft clay, and laid on a prepared 'place' to harden before being burnt: see quot. 1753; *now*, an ordinary stock brick which has been imperfectly burnt, through being on the outward or windward side of the kiln or clamp.

1703 T. N. *City & C. Purchaser* 41 Place-bricks. **1753** CHAMBERS *Cycl. Supp.* s.v. *Brick*, Place-bricks.. so called because of a level smooth place just by where they are struck or moulded.. where they are left till they are stiff enough to be turned on their edges.., they carry them to stacks,.. they are covered with straw on the top, till they are dry enough.. to be burnt. **1823** P. NICHOLSON *Pract. Build.* 343 Place-Bricks are too frequently poor and brittle. **1847** SMEATON *Builder's Man.* 19 Place bricks are the refuse of a burning, and are in fact those which have not been perfectly burnt. **1881** YOUNG *Every Man his own Mechanic* §1155 Prices per 100 at which bricks are quoted: place-bricks, 4*s.* 6*d.*; grey stocks, 5*s.*; red stocks, 6*s.* [etc.].

placed (pleɪst), *ppl. a.* [f. PLACE *v.* + -ED[1].] Put or set in a particular position or condition; located, situated; holding place or rank: see the vb. ***placed minister***, a pastor inducted to a charge.

1733 P. LINDSAY *Interest Scot.* 124 Where one placed Minister dies at least three young men are licensed. **1796** *Instr. & Reg. Cavalry* (1813) 75 When the Regiment forms open Column of Divisions, behind a placed Flank Division. **1818** SCOTT *Hrt. Midl.* vi, He was in orders, but was not a placed minister. **1844** P. HARWOOD *Hist. Irish Reb.* 50 Every liberal.. motion.. was unfailingly crushed by placed and pensioned majorities. **1890** *Daily News* 17 Feb. 3/5 Brownie.. finished fifth, Theodolite, the second favourite, alone dividing him from the placed horses. *Ibid.* 3 Nov. 4/7 Blackheath beat the London Scottish by a placed goal to a penalty goal.

‖**place d'armes** (plas darm). Also †**place des armes.** [Fr.] An assembly point for troops, weapons, or ammunition; a parade-ground.

1708 MARLBOROUGH *Let.* 26 July in W. S. Churchill *Marlborough* (1936) III. xxiii. 454 He thinks it unpracticable till we have Lille for a *place d'armes* and magazine. **1767** 'CORIAT JUNIOR' *Journey through Netherlands* I. xviii. 159 The Saint Sebastian upon the parade, or place des armes, is one of the genteelest inns I ever saw. **1803** in *Amer. State Papers: Misc.* (1834) I. 348 There is in the middle of the front of the city a *place d'armes*, facing which the church and town-house are built. **1833** *Edin. Rev.* LVII. 326 A *place d'armes* where a certain proportion of troops would always be in readiness in a fine climate. **1845** R. FORD *Hand-bk. for Travellers Spain* I. iii. 365 The invaders next proceeded to convert it into a *place d'armes*. **1883** H. JAMES *Little Tour in France* (1885) xvi. 110 La Rochelle.. contains, moreover, a great wide *place d'armes*, which looked for all the world like the piazza of some dead Italian town. **1939** A. TOYNBEE *Study of Hist.* IV. 280 The massive fortifications of her original Levantine *places d'armes*.. speak.. of the.. tenacity with which.. the Venetian Commonwealth clung to every disputed foothold. **1949** I. DEUTSCHER *Stalin* i. 10 In Russian eyes the Caucasus was a *place d'armes* against the Ottoman Empire. **1955** *Times* 12 May 8/1 Western Germany is being turned into a *place d'armes* for the deployment of large aggressive forces. **1976** N. ROBERTS *Face of France* 5 The square [of Phalsburg].. was conceived.. as the *place d'armes*, the parade ground of a garrison town.

†**'placeful,** *a. Obs. nonce-wd.* [f. PLACE *sb.* + -FUL 1.] (?)

1615 CHAPMAN *Odyss* IX. 134 And in their precinct (Proper and placefull) stood the troughs and pailes, In which he milkt.

'place-ˌholder. One who holds a place or office.

†**a.** One who acts as deputy for another; a lieutenant, substitute, proxy. *Sc. Obs.*

1560 in Calderwood *Hist. Kirk* (1843) II. 13 Committed by the place-holders of the ministrie. **1566** *Reg. Privy Council Scot.* I. 451 His deputtis and place haldaris. *c* **1610** SIR J. MELVIL *Mem.* (1683) 188 The Prince, who is God's place-holder.

b. One who holds office under the government.

1818 MOORE *Fudge Fam. Paris* ii. 105 A youth of parts, Who longs to be a small place-holder. **1848** W. H. KELLY tr. *L. Blanc's Hist. Ten Y.* II. 238 The strength of goverment.. resulted, not from its having some thousands of place-holders.. at its disposal, but from the means it possessed of making its will reach everywhere.

So **'place-ˌholding** *a.*

1830 LD. J. RUSSELL *Select Sp. & Desp.* (1870) I. 296 That corrupt and place-holding Parliament.

'place-ˌhunter. One who seeks persistently for a place or post in the public service. (With unfavourable connotation: cf. PLACEMAN.)

1713 STEELE *Guard.* No. 29 ⁋16 The Ionick laugh.. is esteemed by judicious place-hunters a more particular mark of distinction than the whisper. **1812** *Examiner* 19 Oct. 666/1 Place-hunters and Fortune-hunters. **1898** BODLEY *France* II. IV. vii. 434 Moderate men who are not place-hunters, and are therefore impartial witnesses.

So **'place-hunting** *sb.* and *a.*

1823 in W. Cobbett *Rur. Rides* (1885) I. 276 A place-hunting lawyer. **1860** MILL *Repr. Govt.* (1865) 34/2 Place-hunting.. is a form of ambition to which the English.. are almost strangers. **1898** BODLEY *France* II. III. v. 257 The place-hunting solicitations of constituents.

'place-kick. *Football.* [f. PLACE *sb.* + KICK *sb.*[1]]

a. (See quots., and cf. DROP-KICK.)

1856 *Rules for Football, St. Peter's School, York* ii, A place kick is a kick when the ball is previously placed on the ground... Kick off must be a place kick. **1938** L. MACNEICE *Earth Compels* 60 The effortless place-kick Gaily carving the goalposts. **1950** *Sport* 22–28 Sept. 10/1 It may be interesting to know that the place-kick is the correct term for starting the game from the centre of the field at the commencement of the game, after half-time, and also when a goal has been scored. **1969** *Official Playing Rules Nat. & Amer. Football Leagues* 7 A Field Goal is made by kicking ball from field of play through the plane of opponents goal by a drop-kick or a place-kick either during a play from scrimmage.. or a free kick after fair catch.

b. = PLACE-KICKER.

1896 T. EYTON *Rugby Football* 12 'Mac' was the place-kick of the Team. **1905** A. CONAN DOYLE *Return of Sherlock Holmes* 310 He's a fine place-kick, it's true, but.. he has no judgment.

So **'place-kick** *v.*, **'place-ˌkicker, 'place-'kicking.**

1856 *Rules for Football, St. Peter's School, York* ix, It [the football] is to be place-kicked, and not dropped. **1890** *Pall Mall G.* 20 Oct. 1/3 A try, from which the champion place-kicker.. gained a goal. **1892** *Daily News* 17 Oct. 5/1 [He] played for Scotland, and did the place-kicking at the early age of sixteen. **1896** *Westm. Gaz.* 6 Jan. 2/3 This place-kicking record was the least creditable feature of the game. **1961** *Dallas Morning News* 10 Oct. II. 1/1 Ask coach Darrell Royal what position he plays and you'll get the quick response, 'place-kicker'. **1972** J. MOSEDALE *Football* iv. 46 Waterfield could.. pass, run, punt, place-kick.. and play defense. **1978** *Rugby World* Apr. 28/2 As a place-kicker, he is remarkably similar to Phil Bennett.

placeless ('pleɪslɪs), *a.* [f. PLACE *sb.* + -LESS.]

†**1.** Without a fixed place or home; having no place. *Obs. rare*[−1].

1387 TREVISA *Higden* (Rolls) V. 261 Þanne þe Saxons, strong men of armes, and placelees to wone ynne [L. *Saxonum gens.. sedibus vaga*], were i-prayed of þe Britouns forto come in to Bretayne.

2. Not confined to place; not local; not bounded or defined. Also, not distinguishable from other places, devoid of local character.

1598 SYLVESTER *Du Bartas* II. i. II. *Imposture* 210 Holding a place-less place. **1630** J. TAYLOR (Water P.) *Sculler* Wks. III. 19/2 Such a placelesse place is Purgatory Created by the Pope without God's leaue. *a* **1834** COLERIDGE *Picture* 129 Placeless, as spirits. **1881** FRASER *Berkeley* 212 Our placing and dating intelligence must be inadequate to the placeless and dateless Intellect. **1960** T. HUGHES *Lupercal* 18 And his white blown head going out between a sky and an earth That were bundled into placeless blackness. **1968** *Listener* 28 Nov. 703/3 Even the restaurants in these places are steeped in placeless motorway fantasy.

3. Having no stated place or locality.

1644 PRYNNE & WALKER *Fiennes's Trial* 5 With the datelesse, namelesse, placelesse, seallesse Proclamation inclosed. **1878** D. CAMPBELL *Rational & True Gosp.* xv. 80 Dateless, placeless wonders are not very credible.

4. Having no place or post; out of office or remunerative employment.

1831 *Lincoln Herald* 28 Jan., Placeless walked the pensive Whigs. **1864** *Sat. Rev.* 13 Aug. 220/1 The landless and placeless Irish gentleman.

Hence **'placelessly** *adv.*

1851 H. MELVILLE *Moby Dick* I. vii. 57 The beings who have placelessly perished without a grave.

†**'placely**, *a.* and *adv.* *Obs.* [f. PLACE *sb.* + -LY.]
a. *adj.* Of or pertaining to place; local, spatial.
b. *adv.* Locally, spatially.

a. 1546 COVERDALE *Lord's Supper* Wks. (Parker Soc.) I. 455 Imagining I cannot tell what manner of placely presence. **1674** N. FAIRFAX *Bulk & Selv.* 85 The placing of body between two ghostly beings, would not give them a placely behaviour.

b. 1548 GEST *Pr. Masse* in H. G. Dugdale *Life* (1840) App. I. 86 Christes body be presented in thee bred.. not placely as ther placed, spaced, and mesured, but ghostly.

placeman ('pleɪsmən). [f. PLACE *sb.* 13 + MAN *sb.*[1]] One who holds an appointment in the service of the sovereign or state; almost always with depreciatory or hostile connotation: One who is appointed (or who aspires) to such a position from motives of interest, without regard to fitness.

1741 *Protests of Lords* II. 15 A constant majority of placemen meeting under the name of a Parliament to establish grievances instead of redressing them. **1754** HUME *Hist. Eng.* I. xv. 369 The Sherriffs and other placemen had made interest to be elected. **1763** *Brit. Mag.* IV. 235 In 1679 the House of Commons brought in a bill for excluding placemen and pensioners from seats in parliament. **1830** LD. J. RUSSELL *Select. Sp. & Desp.* (1870) I. 296 In the first Parliament of George II it is stated that 257 placemen had seats in this House. **1881** *Philad. Record* No. 3443. 4 One of the most disheartening signs of the times is the facility with which the crimes of politicians and placemen are condoned by the people.

Hence **'placemanship**, the position or character of a placeman.

1833 *Fraser's Mag.* VII. 751 When placemanship is combined with Whiggery, the combination is.. odious.

placement ('pleɪsmənt). [f. PLACE *v.* + -MENT: cf. F. *placement* (d'Aubigné 1616), and *displacement, replacement*.] **1.** The action of placing, or fact of being placed; placing, arrangement. Now freq. in technical or semi-technical contexts and in Sport (see quots.). In sense 'the allocation of places to guests at a dinner table, etc.' also with Fr. pronunc. (plasmã) and *transf.* (see quot. 1976[1]).

1844 STEPHENS *Bk. Farm* II. 688 A malformation in the placement of its tines. **1854** *Tait's Mag.* XXI. 304, I.. cannot consent to the placement of such a word in our Dictionaries. **1887** *Pop. Sci. Monthly* XXXI. 415/2 In proportion as the placement of the loan disturbs the market value of the commodities. **1897** J. C. ROBINSON in *19th Cent.* Dec. 961 Art treasures.. have found their way.. to abiding placements from which there can be no return. **1911** WEBSTER, *Placement*,.. specif., in American football, the placing of the ball on the ground to make a place kick for a goal from the field. **1922** H. H. GODDARD *Juvenile Delinquency* 78 She was soon brought into court and adjudged 'a dependent and neglected child'. The next five years were a round of placements (or misplacements) in families. **1931** G. O. RUSSELL *Speech & Voice* xx. 204 So-called 'voice placement', or what the singer called 'good resonance'. **1934** WEBSTER, *Placement*..*Lawn Tennis.* A return of the ball which is so placed that an opponent is unable to play it. **1938** O. NASH *I'm a Stranger here Myself* 211 Give her a racquet and bulging shorts And put her out on the tennis courts... He scores a placement. Says she, A miracle! **1939** in H. Nicolson *Diplomacy* x. 247 The science of seating diplomatic guests in such a manner as to avoid enraging them is called the science of 'placement'. **1946–7** *Agric. Engin. Rec.* Winter 171 A machine for research by the Rothamsted Experimental Station on the placement of artificial fertilizers with potato crops. **1949** G. W. COOKE in *Ibid.* Summer 227 With the traditional methods of planting .. there are three ways by which fertilizers can be applied so as to afford some measure of placement. **1949** *N.Y. Herald-Tribune* 15 Mar. 13 She seems, moreover, to have been well instructed in the forward placement of the voice favorable to the development of these potentialities. **1949** SHURR & YOCOM *Mod. Dance* v. 125 Lower left knee to floor without disturbing placement of extended toe. **1957** CLARK & GOTTFRIED *University Dict. Business & Finance* (1967) 266/2 *Placement*,.. 2. The process of negotiating for the sale of a new issue of securities, or of arranging for a long-term loan. The issue may be placed with an underwriter, or it may be sold through direct, or private *placement*; that is, sold directly to investors without going through the underwriting procedure. **1962** 'J. LE CARRÉ' *Murder of Quality* v. 61 If you.. make a fault in the *placement* of your dinner guests.. D'Arcy will find you out. **1962** *Amer. Speech* XXXVII. 24 These students had been interviewed by members of the Department of Speech for speech placement purposes. **1966** *Economist* 2 Apr. 3/3 No proper distinction is being made between the effect on the market of the volume of offerings and faulty techniques of syndication and placement. **1968** P. M. POSTAL *Aspects Phonol. Theory* vi. 121 On all other grounds but stress placement, one would assign such a form the systematic phonological matrix we can abbreviate as [etc.]. **1968** W. WARWICK *Surfriding in N.Z.* 11 Basically it is the placement of body weight near the back of the board. **1969** *New Yorker* 14 June 45/1 The risk is triple—hitting the net, missing the placement, and leaving a sitter for Graebner. **1971** *Nature* 19 Mar. p. xxviii (Advt.), Salary within the range £1,491 to £1,767 per annum... Initial salary placement according to experience and qualifications. **1972** *Sci. Amer.* Sept. 110/3 By all odds the most dramatic advance in long-distance communication began with the successful placement of the satellite Syncom III in synchronous orbit over the South Pacific in 1964, in time to relay live-television pictures of the Tokyo Olympics. **1973** *Times* 31 July 7/2 Wrestling with the placement, I put him next to Jean Muir, another total perfectionist, and they much enjoyed each other. **1975** *Canad. Jrnl. Linguistics* XX. I. 5 Consider the complicated relation between stress placement and vowel length. **1975** S. JOHNSON *Urbane Guerilla* II. 83 Orlando had left the seating of his guests.. the *placement*.. to his brother. **1976** C. OMAN *Oxford Childhood* vii. 135 A piece of Edwardian Prosperity.. the violet morocco-covered *placement* into which a hostess slipped little name cards to show guests where they would be sitting at the dining table. **1976** *Lancs. Even. Post* 7 Dec. 12/1 This centre assesses the needs for future placement of 24 disturbed and often delinquent young children aged 5–16 years. **1977** *Time* 4 July 12/3 'I try to explain to Tracy that she's got a baby-puff serve,' says Landsdorp. 'The trouble is, she wins with it.' One reason she does is precision placement.

2. *attrib.* and *Comb.*, as ***placement agency, board, centre, director, fee, interview, officer, service, test, work***; **placement drill** *Agric.* = *combine drill* s.v. COMBINE *sb.* c; hence **placement-drilled** *a.*

1959 C. V. GOOD *Dict. Educ.* (ed. 2) 400/1 A teacher placement agency. **1962** *Guardian* 7 Nov. 6/3 The registered adoption societies ('placement agencies' in America). **1971** *N.Y. Law Jrnl.* 23 Nov. 24/1 (Advt.), Professional Placement Agency exclusively for attorneys. **1973** *Soviet Weekly* 10 Feb., When representatives of the State Placement Board come along, all they have to do is to study our recommendations. **1967** *Guardian* 8 Dec. 1/1 The so-called Placement Center, an Americanism signifying the college employment office. **1956** W. H. WHYTE *Organization Man* (1957) vi. 63 If the college is large and its placement director efficient, the processing operation is visibly impressive. **1959** C. CULPIN *Farm Mechanization Managem.* vi. 89 Such increases will rapidly pay for the use of a placement drill. **1973** *Country Life* 12 July 81/1 Their placement drill for sugar beet seed is an outstanding machine. **1960** *Farmer & Stockbreeder* 16 Feb. 97/3 In a poor-growing year the placement-drilled seed is always up three or four days earlier than the other. **1973** *Guardian* 19 May 6 The Bill would make it illegal.. for an agency to approach anyone it had already placed in employment with an offer of a higher-paid job in order to earn another placement fee. **1972** *Jrnl. Social Psychol.* LXXXVI. 24 This study examines three hypotheses relevant to interpersonal transactions in the placement interview. **1959** C. V. GOOD *Dict. Educ.* (ed. 2) 400/1 *Placement officer*, one who provides a job placement service for students and graduates. **1963** T. & P. MORRIS *Pentonville* xiv. 304 A representative of the Ministry of Labour called at the prison weekly and men were asked if they wished to see the 'placement officer'—a term which many of them imperfectly understood. **1967** *Times Rev. Industry* May 114/1 Once an apprentice is in a department, a placement officer is responsible for his training and wellbeing. **1945** C. V. GOOD *Dict. Educ.* 299/2 *Placement service, junior*, an employment bureau maintained by the schools for pupils who are in school or who have recently finished their schooling. **1968** *Globe & Mail Mag.* (Toronto) 13 Jan. 3/2 William White of Dow Chemical of Canada Limited, and Robin Ross, the University's registrar, were blockaded inside the university placement service office for nearly three hours. **1971** *Nature* 12 Feb. 448/1 Physicists registering with the placement service operated by the APS outnumbered prospective employers by more than 10 to 1. **1934** WEBSTER, Placement test. **1946** H. P. MAYNARD in W. S. Knickerbocker *20th Cent. English* II. 186 She turned to me and said, 'Tell me why he has done so badly on his placement tests.' **1934** WEBSTER s.v., The placement work of public employment offices. **1936** *Times* 3 Jan. 9/5 In their contact with commerce and industry headmasters found that placement work was more and more falling to their lot.

†**'placency.** *Obs.* [ad. L. *placēntia* (post-class.) suavity, f. *placēnt-em*: see PLACENT *a.*] The quality of pleasing, pleasantness; disposition to please or gratify.

1639 SALTMARSHE *Policy* 153 Men are naturally prone.. to bend in placency towards their superiours humours. **1649** BULWER *Pathomyot.* II. ii. 102 The cause or matter of molestation or placencie.

†**'placeness.** *Obs. rare.* [f. PLACE *sb.* + -NESS.] The quality of having or occupying a place; position, locality.

1674 N. FAIRFAX *Bulk & Selv.* 78 It cannot but harshly be said, that the world has a placeness or whereness at all. *Ibid.* 84 Such a thing as placeness or stowage.

†**'placent,** *sb.* *Obs. rare.* [ad. L. *placenta* a cake: see PLACENTA.] A flat cake or tablet.

1603 F. HERING *Cert. Rules* (1625) Bijb, Certaine Placents or Amulets confected of Arsenicke. **1617** T. ADAMS *Gen. Pract. Phisicke* (*N. & Q.* 7th Ser. VII. 29), Clarified hony, which must be so hard that you may make small placents or trocisces of it.

placent ('pleɪsənt), *a.* *rare.* [ad. L. *placēnt-em*, pr. pple. of *placēre* to please.] Pleasing, gratifying.

1683 E. HOOKER *Pref. Pordage's Mystic Div.* 71 Under the plausibl prætext, placent notion, specious name,.. and fair construction of that famous Evangelic Canon.

¶ Misused for: Favourably disposed, propitious.

1898 C. READE in *New Cent.* IV. 501 A winning cause to placent gods is dear.

‖**placenta** (plə'sɛntə). [L. *placenta* cake = Gr. πλακόεις, -όεντα, contr. -οῦς, -οῦντα, flat cake, also mallow seed, f. the root πλακ- of πλάξ, πλάκα flat plate. So in It., Sp., Pg., Fr. in sense 1.]

1. *Zool.* and *Anat.* Pl. **placentæ** or **placentas.** (Originally ***placenta uterina*** uterine cake.) The spongy vascular organ, of flattened circular form, to which the fœtus is attached by the umbilical cord, and by means of which it is nourished in the womb, in all the higher mammals, and which is expelled in parturition; the afterbirth. Also applied to a structure having a similar function in other animals, as some viviparous fishes, ascidians, etc.; see quots. 1875, 1888.

1691 RAY *Creation* I. (1692) 65 The *Fœtus*.. doth receive Air.. from the maternal Blood in the *Placenta uterina*, or the *Cotyledones*. *Ibid.* 67 The Blood still circulates through the *Cotyledons* or *Placenta*. **1727–41** CHAMBERS *Cycl.* s.v., In women, unless in case of twins, &c. there is but one placenta. **1832** *Lond. Med. & Physical Jrnl.* LXVIII. 72, I have observed.. many placentæ expelled in natural labour. **1855** RAMSBOTHAM *Obstetr. Med.* 68 The term placenta was derived from its shape. **1875** C. C. BLAKE *Zool.* Pref., Sharks bring forth their young alive, and nourish them while in the womb by a temporary structure called 'placenta'. **1888** ROLLESTON & JACKSON *Anim. Life* 445 In *Salpa* the developing embryo is nourished by a placenta formed, in part at least, by follicle cells. **1923** J. M. M. KERR et al. *Combined Text-bk. Obstet. & Gynæcol.* xxvii. 390 In binovular twin pregnancy there are, no matter how closely the placentæ are approximated, two distinct chorions. **1950** EASTMAN & WILLIAMS *Obstetr.* (ed. 10) xxv. 614 In double-ovum twins,.. whether the placentas are separate or fused together, there are always two chorions and two amnions. **1975** *Nature* 4 Sept. 62/1 One day before birth, male rat foetuses are 5% heavier than female foetuses, yet there seems to be no difference in the weights of their placentæ. **1976** *Clin. Obstetr. & Gynecol.* XIX. 29 Placentas weighing over 600 gm usually are associated with complications of pregnancy.

2. *Bot.* The part of the carpel to which the ovules are attached; also sometimes applied to a structure which bears the sporangia in certain vascular cryptogams.

1677 GREW *Anat. Fruits* vii. §5 The Seeds stuck all round about upon the Ambit or Sides of the Case; or upon a great Bed or Placenta within it. **1727** BRADLEY *Fam. Dict.* s.v. *Flower of Parnassus*, A Membranous fruit.. having.. one cell full of seeds, fastened to a placenta which is often very square. **1845** LINDLEY *Sch. Bot.* i. (1858) 16 In the inside of the ovary is a space called the *placenta*, on which the young seeds, or *ovules*, originate. **1875** BENNETT & DYER *Sachs' Bot.* 395 The sporangia arise.. from some of the superficial cells of the placenta or part to which the sorus is attached.

placental (plə'sɛntəl), *a.* (*sb.*) [ad. mod.L. *placentāl-is*, f. prec.: see -AL[1].]

A. *adj.* **1.** *Zool.*, etc. Of or pertaining to the placenta.

placental murmur, sound, soufflet, the sound made by the blood entering the distended uterine vessels, heard in auscultation during the later months of pregnancy.

1808 BARCLAY *Muscular Motions* 367 From a change of function, placental blood is no longer returned to the liver. **1843** R. J. GRAVES *Syst. Clin. Med.* vii. 84 *note*, No one who has ever heard the placental soufflet. **1876** BRISTOWE *The. & Pract. Med.* (1878) 265 The raw surfaces of wounds or of the placental area. **1893** *Syd. Soc. Lex.*, *P[eriod], placental*, the time occupied in the expulsion of the placenta.

b. Furnished with a placenta; placentate.

1840–45 OWEN *Odontogr.* III. xi. 501 The development of the true molar teeth to their typical number in the placental Mammalia. **1871** DARWIN *Desc. Man.* I. vi. 202 The Marsupials stand.. below the placental mammals.

2. *Bot.* Pertaining to the placenta (of a plant).

1857 HENFREY *Elem. Bot.* §227 In Leguminosæ the double placental base is so narrow that the ovules alternate with one another. **1870** HOOKER *Stud. Flora* 259 Ovule.. flanked by a column of placental tissue.

B. *sb.* *Zool.* A placental mammal.

1864 WEBSTER cites OWEN. **1897** *Pop. Sci. Monthly* Nov. 17 The marsupials.. have been gradually supplanted by the more highly organized placentals.

‖**Placentalia** (plæsən'teɪlɪə), *sb. pl.* *Zool.* [mod.L. (L. Bonaparte 1837), neuter pl. of *placentāl-is* adj.: see prec.] Placental mammals; a primary division of Mammalia, comprising those provided with a placenta: contrasted with *Marsupialia* and *Monotremata*. It corresponds to the more recent divisions *Monodelphia* and *Eutheria*.

1842 in BRANDE *Dict. Sci.* etc. **1873** J. GEIKIE *Gt. Ice Age* App. 526.

Hence **placen'talian**, (*a*) *adj.*, of or pertaining to the *Placentalia*; (*b*) *sb.* one of these.

1890 in *Cent. Dict.* **1895** in *Syd. Soc. Lex.*

‖**placenta prævia** (plə'sɛntə 'priːvɪə). *Med.* Also **placenta previa.** [mod.L., f. PLACENTA + L. *prævia*, fem. of *prævius* going before.] A placenta which partially or wholly blocks the neck of the uterus, thereby interfering with normal delivery of the baby; the condition of a placenta so positioned.

1820 S. MERRIMAN *Synopsis Various Kinds of Difficult Parturition* (ed. 3) 114 The hemorrhagies which accompany labour may be divided into three species. a. *Accidental hemorrhage*. Rigby... b. *Unavoidable hemorrhage*. Rigby. [Also known as] *Hæmorrhagia placentâ præviâ*. Boer. *Menorrhagia à placentâ præviâ*. Plenck. c. *Atonic hemorrhage*... The second from the unavoidable separation of the placenta, when that is unnaturally situated over the *os uteri*. **1858** R. BARNES *Physiol. & Treatm. Placenta Prævia* i. 30 Dr. Legroux says, that placenta prævia mostly occurs in pluriparæ. **1917** 'H. H. RICHARDSON' *Fortunes R. Mahony* II. viii. 165 He re-lived those days when a skilfully handled case of *placenta previa*, or a successful delivery in the fourth position, had meant more to him than the Charge of the Light Brigade. **1943** W. SHAW *Textbk. Midwifery* xvii. 315 The diagnosis of placenta prævia depends upon the palpation of the placenta within fingers' reach of the internal os. **1974** GREENHILL & FRIEDMAN *Biol. Princ. & Mod. Pract. Obstetr.* xxxvii. 418/1 In total placenta previa the bleeding usually occurs earlier than in partial placenta previa and is more profuse.

placentary ('plæsəntərɪ, plə'sɛntərɪ), *a.* (*sb.*) [ad. mod.L. *placentārius*, f. PLACENTA: see -ARY[1]. So F. *placentaire*.] Of, pertaining or relating to the placenta; placental (*Zool.* and *Bot.*). **b.** *Zool.* Of or pertaining to the *Placentalia* or *Placentaria*.

1843–4 *Trans. Linnean Soc.* (1845) XIX. 321 The placentary hypothesis of M. Schleiden. **1848** LINDLEY *Introd. Bot.* (ed. 4) I. 377 Uncertainty in the position of the placentary lines. **1864** WEBSTER s.v., The placentary system of classification. **1895** *Syd. Soc. Lex.*, *Placentary*, belonging, or referring to, the Placenta.

B. *sb.* *Zool.* A placental mammal.

1890 in *Cent. Dict.*

placentate ('plæsəntət), *a.* *Zool.* [ad. mod.L. *placentāt-us*, f. PLACENTA: see -ATE[2].] Having a placenta: = PLACENTAL *a.* 1 b.

1890 in *Cent. Dict.* **1895** in *Syd. Soc. Lex.*

placentation (plæsən'teɪʃən). [a. F. *placentation*, f. PLACENTA: see -ATION.]

1. *Zool.* The formation and disposition of the placenta in the uterus.

1871 *Trans. R. Soc. Edin.* XXVI. 486 Of the mammals, the placentation of which most commonly comes under observation, the sow and the mare also offer well-known examples of the diffused form of placenta. **1880** HUXLEY in *Times* 25 Dec. 4/1 The non-prehensile pes would separate it from the former, and the placentation from the latter group. **1971** J. Z. YOUNG *Introd. Study Man* xxx. 423 The sexual cycle and placentation of lemurs are interestingly different from those of other primates.

2. *Bot.* The disposition or arrangement of the placenta or placentas in the ovary.

1760 J. LEE *Introd. Bot.* III. xi. (1765) 197 By Placentation is meant the Disposition of the Cotyledons at the Time when the Seed is beginning to grow. **1848** LINDLEY *Introd. Bot.* (ed. 4) I. 389 The placentation of Water-lilies.. Broomrapes.. and Butomads, is equally at variance with the central theory. **1872** DARWIN *Orig. Spec.* (ed. 6) I. vii. 174 Instances of both marginal and free central placentation.

†**pla'centiate,** *v.* *Obs. nonce-wd.* [f. L. *placēntem* pleasing, suave + -ATE[3]: cf. *differentiate*.] *trans.* To please, satisfy.

1694 MOTTEUX *Rabelais* v. 248 When you're placientated [*sic*], the Fort is won.

placentiferous (plæsən'tɪfərəs), *a.* *Zool.* and *Bot.* [f. PLACENTA + -FEROUS.] Bearing or having a placenta.

1667 H. OLDENBURG in *Phil. Trans.* II. 512 All Placentiferous Animals (if I may assume this word) he affirms to have three Membranes. **1702** DR. DRAKE in *Phil. Trans.* XXIII. 1236 The one [Uterus] being Glanduliferous, and the other Placentiferous. **1878** MASTERS *Henfrey's Bot.* 300 As though the placentiferous lines were detached.

placentiform (plə'sɛntɪfɔːm), *a.* *Zool.* and *Bot.* [f. PLACENTA + -FORM.] Having the form of a placenta; discoid; cake-shaped.

1858 MAYNE *Expos. Lex.*, *Placentiformis*,.. *Bot.* resembling a cake.. placentiform. **1861** BENTLEY *Man. Bot.* (1870) 125 When what would be otherwise a napiform root becomes compressed both at its base and apex.. it is said to be placentiform. **1895** *Syd. Soc. Lex.*

placentigerous (plæsɛn'tɪdʒərəs), *a.* *Zool.* and *Bot.* [f. PLACENTA + -GEROUS.] Bearing a placenta: = PLACENTIFEROUS.

1890 in *Cent. Dict.* **1895** in *Syd. Soc. Lex.*

†**placentious,** *a.* *Obs. rare.* [f. L. *placēntia* suavity, PLACENCY + -OUS.] Pleasing, or disposed to please; complaisant, amiable, agreeable, suave.

a **1661** FULLER *Worthies* III. *York* (1662) 230 A Placentious Person, gaining the goodwill of all. **1683** PETTUS *Fleta Min.* II. 20 Such things as are placentious or pleasing to us.

‖**placentitis** (plæsən'taɪtɪs). *Path.* [mod.L., f. PLACENTA + -ITIS.] Inflammation of the placenta.

1844 in DUNGLISON *Med. Lex.* **1849–52** *Todd's Cycl. Anat.* IV. 943/2 Simpson has described an acute and chronic form of placentitis.

placentography (plæsɛn'tɒgrəfɪ). *Med.* [f. PLACENT(A + RADI)OGRAPHY.] Examination of the placenta using radiography or ultrasound.

1935 *Canad. Med. Assoc. Jrnl.* XXXII. 12/1 The placenta is capable of absorbing a large amount of the thorium circulating in the blood, of retaining it for hours and days, and of eliminating it. However, the placentography interfered with fetal nutrition and led frequently to abortion. **1938** W. H. UDE et al. in *Amer. Jrnl. Roentgenol.* XL. 37/1 Since the object of this procedure is the roentgenologic demonstration of the placenta as a soft tissue mass interposed between the visualized urinary bladder and the presenting fetal part, we will refer to the method hereafter as 'indirect placentography'. **1967** I. DONALD in *5th World Congr. Gynaecol. & Obstetr.* 525 Ultrasonic placentography has now become commonplace practice. **1975** A. E. JAMES et al. in E. J. Potchen *Current Concepts in Radiol.* II. xi. 304 Radionuclide placentography is a method of directly localizing the placenta by imaging the placental blood pool.

Hence **pla'centogram,** (*a*) a radiograph of the placenta; (*b*) a radiographic examination of the placenta.

1959 G. W. FILES et al. *Med. Radiographic Technique* (ed. 2) xviii. 356 (*caption*) Placentograms. **1961** *Obstetr. & Gynecol.* XVIII. 405/2 Despite all attempts to reduce the radiation dosage, it was calculated that 250–750 mr. were being delivered to the maternal ovaries and the fetus at the time of each placentogram. **1971** *Ibid.* XXXVII. 604/1 Of the 84 patients on whom a placentogram was taken, painless third-trimester vaginal bleeding was the most common indication for the study (50 of 84). **1975** A. E. JAMES et al. in E. J. Potchen *Current Concepts in Radiol.* II. xi. 304 We have found a decrease in the number of placentograms performed, and an increased use of sonography in this circumstance.

placentoid (plə'sɛntɔɪd), *a.* [f. as PLACENTITIS + -OID.] Resembling a placenta; placentiform.

1890 in *Cent. Dict.* **1895** in *Syd. Soc. Lex.*

placentology (plæsən'tɒlədʒɪ). *Zool.* and *Anat.* [f. PLACENT(A + -OLOGY.] The science or study of placentæ. Hence **placen'tologist** one versed in placentology.

1960 C. A. VILLEE *Placenta & Fetal Membranes* p. vii, Placentology owes so much to George Bernays Wislocki that it is entirely fitting for him to share this dedication with another distinguished placentologist, George L. Streeter. **1970** BOYD & HAMILTON *Human Placenta* i. 14/2 The intervillous space had only been described by placentologists working on human material. **1971** *Nature* 3 Dec. 284/2 *Methods in Mammalian Embryology* includes four chapters on eggs and spermatozoa.. and six on implantation and placentology.

placentophagy (plæsən'tɒfədʒɪ). [f. as PLACENTOID *a.* + -PHAGY.] The eating of the placenta.

1902 *Brit. Med. Jrnl.* 12 Apr. 909 In certain parts of the Soudan, placentophagy is habitually practised.

placentule (plə'sɛntjuːl). *Bot.* [ad. mod.L. *placentula*, dim. of PLACENTA: see -ULE.] A small placenta (but in quot. 1826 applied to a cotyledon: cf. COTYLEDON 3).

1677 GREW *Anat. Fruits* v. §13 A great Parenchymous Boss, which is, as it were, the Bed or Placentula of the Seeds; which lie all over it, as in a Strawberry. **1826** GOOD *Bk. Nat.* (1834) I. 164 The cotyledon appears.. necessary for the.. growth of the seed, and may hence be denominated its lungs or placentule. **1858** MAYNE *Expos. Lex.*, *Placentula*,.. a little placenta: a placentule.

placer[1] ('pleɪsə(r)). [f. PLACE *v.* + -ER[1]] **1.** One who places, puts, or sets; one who puts in place or arranges; in various technical uses, e.g. in *Bookbinding*, a workman employed in arranging the sheets; in *Pottery*, the workman who puts the ware ready for burning.

1579 SPENSER *Sheph. Cal.* Feb. 164 Thou placer of plants both humble and tall. **1599** *Life Sir T. More* in Wordsw. *Eccl. Biog.* (1853) II. 135 A sorter out and placer of the principall matters in the same [book] contained. **1802** *Sporting Mag.* XX. 16 Setters of broken bones, and placers of dislocations. **1862** T. WRIGHT *Hist. Dom. Manners* viii. 153 An *asséeur*, or placer, took the dishes from the hands of the valets, and arranged them in their places on the table. **1898** C. F. BINNS *Story of Potter* 206 The art of putting the ware ready for burning is called 'placing', and upon the skill of the placer much of the success of the oven depends. **1902** *Daily Chron.* 18 June 10/5 Collaters and Placers wanted.

2. (See quots.) *slang.*

1969 *Guardian* 6 Mar. 10/2 There are 'placers' who run crime on business lines—who find markets for stolen goods ..even before the theft takes place, who.. organise drug smuggling, fraudulent bankruptcies, and whatever other activity seems most profitable. **1970** P. LAURIE *Scotland Yard* viii. 185 There are thieves and dealers—we call them placers. **1972** G. F. NEWMAN *The Nice Bastard* 347 *Placer*, wholesaler in stolen goods; buyer; fence.

3. One who is awarded a (usu. specified) place in a competition, race, etc. *U.S.*

1942 BERREY & VAN DEN BARK *Amer. Thes. Slang* §731/20 *Placer*, a horse that runs second. **1958** *Tuscaloosa* (Alabama) *News* 13 July 24 (*caption*) Runner-up Lynne Galvin.. and third placer Lucille Strazza.. took the news happily. **1961** in WEBSTER, Fifth placer in the.. Miss America competition. **1976** *Billings* (Montana) *Gaz.* 1 July 4-E/1 Without looking particularly exhausted, he beat second placer Karl Fleschen of West Germany by 49 seconds.

placer[2] ('pleɪsə(r)). *Mining.* (Chiefly *U.S.*) [a. Amer. Sp. *placer* (pla'ser) 'deposit, shoal', allied to *placel* a sand-bank, f. *plaza* place.]

a. A deposit of sand, gravel, or earth, in the bed of a stream, or any alluvial or diluvial detritus, containing gold or other valuable minerals in particles; a place where this detritus is washed for gold, etc. Also *fig.*

In U.S. law, *placer* includes all forms of mineral deposits excepting veins in place.

1842 *Niles' Reg.* 8 Oct. 96/1 They have at last discovered gold [in California]... Those who are acquainted with these 'placeres', as they call them, (for it is not a mine), say it will grow richer, and may lead to a mine. **1848** WISLIZENUS *Tour N. Mexico* 24 (Stanf.) The old and the new *Placer*, near Santa Fe, have attracted most attention, and not only gold washes, but some gold mines.. are worked there. **1851** APPLETON in *Longfellow's Life* (1891) II. 219 Why it is a Golden Legend.. if it be not that it is such a placer of richness. **1856** EMERSON *Eng. Traits, Lit.* Wks. (Bohn) II. 113 Like diggers in California 'prospecting for a placer'. **1858** LOWELL *Study Wind.* (1870) 296 It is a vast placer full of nuggets for the philologist. **1874** RAYMOND *Statist. Mines & Mining* 325 This placer covers an area of perhaps two hundred acres, with probably an average depth of 25 feet of gold-bearing earth.

b. *attrib.* and *Comb.*, as *placer camp*, *-diggings*, *-gold*, *-mine*, *-miner*, *-mining*, *-working*; *placer-mine* vb.

1848 in E. Bryant *California* App. 463 The 'placer' gold is now substituted as the currency of this country. **1856** *Porter's Spirit of Times* 22 Nov. 194/2 The success of those engaged in placer mining generally, is said to be extraordinarily good. **1865** H. W. BAXLEY *What I saw on W. Coast of S. & N. Amer.* 419 This entire mountain.. was once *placer-mined* over its entire surface. **1867** MURCHISON *Siluria* xix. (ed. 4) 471 There are placer-workings on rocks containing Jurassic fossils. **1868** ISAB. SAXON *Five years within Gold. Gate* 84 Almost wholly 'placer' or surface diggings. **1872** RAYMOND *Statist. Mines & Mining* 208 Sixty-one placer-claims.. nearly all located in the southern part of the county. **1872** R. W. RAYMOND *Statistics of Mines 1870* 192 In the great placer-mining region of Idaho there is an underlying basis for permanent mining. *Ibid.* 199 The bars on the Snake River have long been the resort of placer-miners. **1874** T. B. ALDRICH *Prudence Palfrey* vii. 138 The rumors of a discovery of rich placer diggings in Montana had flown like wild-fire. **1874** R. W. RAYMOND *Statistics of Mines 1873* 299 The amount of gold washed from the bed of creeks and placer-workings. **1879** H. GEORGE *Progr. & Pov.* I. iii. (1881) 55 In the early days of California.. the placer miner.. picked up.. his 'wages'.. in actual money. **1880** G. T. INGHAM *Digging Gold among Rockies* 278 A panful of this crevice matter yielded.. gold of a very clear, bright nature, greatly resembling placer gold. **1881** *Lit. World* (Boston U.S.) 21 May 177/1 The Chinaman.. has found it lucrative to continue placer mining where the whites have given it up. **1890** *Stock Grower & Farmer* 19 July 4/4 A man who came to Arizona,.. lived on brown beans and placer-mined on Hassayampa creek. **1897** *Daily News* 21 July 5/4 The workings on the Klondyke or Deer River are placer mines, i.e., the earth is dug up and washed with sluices. **1902** L. McKEE *Land of Nome* 1 The rich placer-gold deposits were discovered by a small party of prospectors in the late autumn of 1898. **1906** *Outlook* 9 June 773/1 It will bring the historic placer-camps of Caniar and Omenica within reach of the mining capitalist. **1928** *Bull. Amer. Soil Survey Assoc.* IX. 56 *Placer diggings*, areas where placer mining has overturned or removed the soil and left a rough, eroded and scarred surface. **1934** *Times Lit. Suppl.* 1 Feb. 78/1 After having tried their luck at Californian 'placer-mining'. **1944** *Life* 20 Nov. 11/2 She is now the wife of Johnny Matson, a prospector, who placer-mines for gold up the Seventy Mile River. **1946** [see BACK-TRACK *v.* 1]. **1948** A. WILLIAMS *Early Calif. Gold Rush Days* 51 Quartz mining had come into prominence in California and it was taking the people by storm, just the same as the placer gold had a few years before. **1949** *Los Angeles Times* 11 July 21/2 Placer mining will be conducted with power shovels. **1958** *Times* 22 Aug. 12/4 The lure of placer gold on the sandbars of the Fraser river brought in men by the thousands. **1958** *Times* 13 Sept. 11/1 *Songs of a Sourdough*, a title that invoked the old-time placer-miner.. appeared in 1907. **1972** *Prof. Papers U.S. Geol. Survey* No. 341-J. 31/1 The gravels near Capanema and Catas Atlas have been worked for placer gold.

placer[3] ('pleɪsə(r)). *Austral.* and *N.Z. slang.* [f. PLACE *sb.* + -ER[1].] **a.** (See quot. 1921.) **b.** (See quot. 1959.)

1921 H. GUTHRIE-SMITH *Tutira* xxxviii. 383 'Placer' is a term used to denote a gold digger who remains year after year on the one spot, on the one place. *Ibid.*, I have never known a 'placer' produce a lamb. **1940** A. WALL in *Bulletin* (Sydney) 31 Jan. 41/2 (*title of poem*) The placer sheep. **1941** BAKER *N.Z. Slang* 27 *Placers* are often lambs whose mothers have died and who have transferred their affection to some object, such as a bush or stone. **1959** —— *Drum* II. 135 *Placer*, a sheep which attaches itself to a certain spot. Rural sl[ang].

placet ('pleɪsɛt). [a. L. *placet* 'it pleases', 3rd sing. pres. ind. of *placēre* to please.]

‖**1.** The Latin for 'it pleases (me or us)'.

The word is part of the form used in the old Universities when a question is put to the vote: 'Placetne vobis, domini doctores? placetne vobis, magistri?' (Does it please you, Doctors? does it please you, Masters?); the answer being 'Placet', or 'Non placet'. The declaration of the vote after a count is in the form, 'Majori parti placet', or 'non placet', as the case may be. It is also in the power of the Vice-Chancellor, or of the Proctors conjointly, to veto any proposal by their 'Non placet', as in quot. 1893.

c **1592** MARLOWE *Massacre Paris* II. vi. Wks. (Rtldg.) 240/1 Whilst I cry placet, like a senator. **1893** LIDDON, etc. *Life Pusey* I. xvi. 378 Amidst a tremendous shout of 'Placet' from the area the decisive formula was uttered, 'Nobis procuratoribus non placet' [Us, the proctors, it pleases not], and the question of the statute was for the time at an end.

2. as *sb.* **a.** The expression of assent or sanction (by this word); formerly, the assent of the temporal power necessary for the publication and execution of an ecclesiastical ordinance. Also *transf.* and *fig.*

1589 NASHE *Pref. Greene's Menaphon* (Arb.) 5 Whose placet he accounts the plaudite of his paines. **1593** tr. *Guicciardini's Descr. Low-C.* 21 b, The pope cannot giue a benefice, nor a pardon, nor send a bull into the countrey without the Princes Placet. **1871** [see AVAILINGLY *adv.*]. **1937** F. BORKENAU *Spanish Cockpit* i. 42 He had simply been commander of the Barcelona garrison, and for his *coup d'état* had got the *placet* of the other generals. **1973** *Times Lit. Suppl.* 1 June 618/4 He was consecrated in 1583 [as Bishop of Kythera] but the Venetians refused him their *placet*.

b. A vote of assent in a council, or in the congregation or convocation of a university.

1883 *Manch. Exam.* 1 Dec. 4/7 The report.. was rejected by 40 non-placets to 39 placets. **1905** *Daily News* 6 Mar. 6 'Why should the University be ruled from the country parishes?'.. was asked again by the 'placet' party.

†**3.** *erron.* for PLACIT, q.v.

placfont, erroneous form of PAKTONG.

1893 JOHNSTONE-LAVIS in *Nature* 12 Jan. 257/2 The amplifying lever is composed of fine placfont tubes... The pendulum bob is a flattened cylinder supported by a placfont wire 1.50 m. long.

plachart, obs. form of PLACARD.

placid ('plæsɪd), *a.* [ad. L. *placid-us* pleasing, favourable, gentle, mild, calm, f. root of *placēre* to please; see -ID[1]. Cf. F. *placide* (15–16th c.).]

1. a. Mild, gentle; calm, peaceful; unruffled, tranquil, still, serene.

1626 BACON *Sylva* §292 It conduceth unto long life, and to the more placid motion of the spirits. **1669** STURMY *Mariner's Mag.* aaaj b, To the end the placid Fruits of these my Labours..may be..preserved from the turbulent Storms of discontented Spirits. **1671** MILTON *P.R.* III. 217 That placid aspect and meek regard. **1775** JOHNSON *Let. to Mrs. Thrale* 21 July, That you sit down placid and content, disposed to enjoy the present. **1832** G. DOWNES *Lett. Cont. Countries* I. 93 The..Valley..of Interlaken..is altogether of a placid, pastoral character. **1850** TENNYSON *In Mem.* ix, Fair ship, that from the Italian shore Sailest the placid ocean-plains. **1871** L. STEPHEN *Playgr. Europe* (1894) x. 251 The male population is distinctly of a placid temperament.

†**b.** Of peaceful disposition towards another; free from anger or wrath. *Obs.*

1663 *Aron-bimn.* 23 To make an atonement, to render him placid and gracious.

†**2.** Pleasing, agreeable, welcome. *Obs. rare.*

1627–77 FELTHAM *Resolves* I. lix. 92 Those things..are made placid or disgustful, as fond Opinion catches them.

3. *Comb.*, as ***placid-browed, -eyed, -faced, -mannered, -seeming, -tempered*** adjs.

1840 DICKENS *Old C. Shop* xiv, A little fat placid-faced old gentleman. **1889** W. B. YEATS *Street Dancers* in *Wanderings of Oisin* 132 They will wrap them in the shroud, Sorrow-worn, yet placid browed. **1904** R. J. FARRER *Garden of Asia* xxvii. 280 Placid-tempered is the face of Japan, and to the placid-tempered she presents a calm and dreamy existence of uninterrupted enjoyment. **1909** *Daily Chron.* 7 Aug. 7/3 The round-faced, placid-eyed, spectacled man of unobtrusive appearance. **1928** D. H. LAWRENCE *Woman who rode Away* 63 The large, placid-seeming, fair-complexioned woman. **1936** E. SITWELL *Victoria of Eng.* i. 26 She [*sc.* Princess of Leiningen] always..seemed to be moving, placid-tempered and obstinate, in a hurricane of flying feathers and loud-rustling silks.

†**pla'cidious**, *a. Obs. rare*$^{-1}$. [irreg. f. PLACID + -IOUS.] = prec.

1607 TOPSELL *Four-f. Beasts* (1658) 125 The Dogs did.. discern betwixt Christians and Turks; for towards the Turks they were most eager, furious, and unappeaseable, but towards Christians, although unknown, most easie, peaceable and placidious.

placidity (plə'sɪdɪtɪ), [ad. L. *placiditās*, f. *placidus* PLACID: see -ITY. So F. *placidité* (1878 in *Dict. Acad.*).] The quality of being placid; mildness, calmness, tranquillity, peacefulness.

1619 W. SCLATER *Exp. 1 Thess.* (1630) 142 First Meeknesse; secondly Placiditie, as for want of a plainer terme, I am forced to call it. **1766** CHANDLER *Life David* I. ii. 36 He..behaves with the utmost placidity, moderation, and calmness. **1816** G. CRABB *Eng. Synonymes* 187/2 *Placidity* is more of a natural gift; *serenity* is acquired. **1866** G. MACDONALD *Ann. Q. Neighb.* xix. (1878) 360 All the placidity of his countenance had vanished.

placidly ('plæsɪdlɪ), *adv.* [f. PLACID + -LY[2].] In a placid manner; mildly, calmly, quietly; peacefully, without agitation.

1626 JACKSON *Creed* VIII. xxix. §11 Hee..sweetly and placidly resigned up his soule into his Father's hands. **1695** WOODWARD *Nat. Hist. Earth* III. i. (1723) 145 It placidly distends the Tubes and Vessels of Vegetables. **1786** tr. *Beckford's Vathek* (1883) 125 How placidly doth he recline his lovely little head! **1877** MRS. FORRESTER *Mignon* I. 24 The two friends are placidly smoking their cigars by the open window.

placidness ('plæsɪdnɪs). [f. PLACID + -NESS.] The quality of being placid: = PLACIDITY.

1727 BAILEY vol. II, *Placidness*, Peaceableness, Quietness. **1748** RICHARDSON *Clarissa* (1811) II. xlii. 310 To enjoy yourself with your usual placidness, and not to be ruffled. **1898** *Daily News* 15 Nov. 6/1 The British navvy at work amidst an armed camp..plied his vocation with placidness.

placing ('pleɪsɪŋ), *vbl. sb.* [-ING[1].] **a.** The action of the verb PLACE; the condition or mode of being placed; putting, setting, location; position, situation; arrangement, etc.: see the verb; *spec.* the finding of specific buyers for a large quantity of stocks or shares, esp. a new issue.

1549 COVERDALE, etc. *Erasm. Par. 1 Cor.* 34 The diuers placyng and vse [of the members]..apertayneth to the welth of the whole body. **1585** T. WASHINGTON tr. *Nicholay's Voy.* I. xix. 21 b, Hauing wel considered the placing of the campe. **1611** SHAKS. *Cymb.* III. v. 65 Shee being downe, I haue the placing of the British Crowne. **1705** HEARNE *Collect.* 2 Dec. (O.H.S.) I. 111 It stood according to ye old Placing, U. 3. 7. *Jur.* **1723** CHAMBERS tr. *Le Clerc's Treat. Archit.* I. 116 The commodius and agreeable placing of Statues. **1821** GALT *Ann. Parish* xx, More than all my absences..from the time of my placing. **1824** L. MURRAY *Eng. Gram.* (ed. 5) I. 446 The wrong placing of the adverb *only*. **1894** *Daily News* 26 July 3/3 He won the race so easily that little notice need be taken of the placings of the remainder of the field. **1898** [see PLACER[1]]. **1930** *Economist* 1 Nov. 825/1 There have, in addition, been various private 'placings' of new capital, including £2,000,000 5 per cent debentures of the underground. **1935** *Ibid.* 7 Sept. 476/1 There would appear to be no immediate intention of a 'placing' of the bonds in London. **1936** *Ibid.* 15 Feb. 368/1 Facilities will not usually be forthcoming for 'placings' of ordinary as distinct from fixed interest capital. **1949** *Ann. Reg. 1948* 453 'First Preference' industries..[were enabled to obtain] 13·3 per cent of adult placings. **1955** *Times* 30 June 16/1 Mean-while, the flow of placings and introductions is to be continued next week with a placing of Preference and Ordinary shares of L. M. Van Moppes and Sons. **1968** *Economist* 13 Apr. 53 The trouble is that this success with conventional 'placing' has inhibited new ideas. The Ministry of Labour finds people new jobs: it does not encourage the people to add to their skills. **1971** I. BUTYKAI tr. *Lukovich's Electric Foil Fencing* I. 23 Latin domination of the sport was unbroken with French or Italian competitors winning all the major international contests, world championships and Olympic tournaments. They took most of the placings, too. **1973** *Scotsman* 13 Feb. 3/4 A placing is advertised today of five million shares in Bishopsgate Platinum.

b. *attrib.*, as **placing-house**, the building in a china or earthenware factory where the ware is 'placed' in fire-clay saggers or setters in preparation for being baked; **placing officer**, a placement officer (PLACEMENT 2); **placing shot, stroke** *Cricket* (see quot.).

1881 *Porcelain Works Worcester* 25 The manufactured objects being now ready for baking are taken to the placing house of the biscuit oven. **1963** T. PARKER *Unknown Citizen* v. 136, I asked him if he'd like to see the Ministry of Labour placing officer when he next came into the prison. **1925** *Country Life* 15 Aug. 244/2 The push shots or placing shots. .. You can steer and guide these strokes with tolerable accuracy, hence their name of *placing* strokes... If the ball be pitched well up, simply lean out towards it..and..play a crouching push stroke at it, and it will travel between mid-on and square-leg.

†**placit** ('plæsɪt). *Obs.* Also placet. [ad. L. *placit-um*: see PLACITUM. So It. *placito.*]

1. What is decided or determined upon; an opinion, a judgement; a decision, decree, ordinance.

1605 BACON *Adv. Learn.* II. xxv. §5 That Secondarie reason..which is grounded upon the placets of God. **1641** J. TRAPPE *Theol. Theol.* iii. 125 Those Masters of opinions ..that seek to obtrude upon Gods inheritance their conceits and placits. **1661** GLANVILL *Van. Dogm.* 129 As little in their Power as the placits of destiny. **1738** WARBURTON *Div. Legat.* App. 50 Delivering us the placits of the old philosophers. **1832** J. BREE *St. Herbert's Isle* 70 Oral theorems and placits.

2. A plea, a petition. *rare.*

1822 SCOTT *Nigel* ix, The boon which I am now to ask.. is, that your Majesty would be pleased, on the instant, to look at the placet of Lord Glenvarloch.

†**'placitatory**, *a. Obs. rare*$^{-1}$. [f. L. *placitāt-*, ppl. stem of *placitāre* (Plaut.), freq. of *placēre* to please + -ORY[2].] = next.

1569 J. SANFORD tr. *Agrippa's Van. Artes* 164 An other exercise of the lawe, which they terme the Arte Placitatorie, or els Aduocatorie.

†**'placitory**, *a. Law. Obs. rare.* [f. med.L. *placit-um* (see below) + -ORY[2].] Relating or pertaining to pleas or pleading.

1650 J. CLAYTON *Reports Chancery* Pref. aj, The art Placitory..is double, first, that in writing upon the Recordes;..The other..vocall, which pleads before the Judge to the Jury. **1836** in SMART, and in later Dicts.

‖**placitum** ('plæsɪtəm). *Obs.* exc. *Hist.* Pl. placita. [L., an opinion, determination, maxim, prop. neuter pa. pple. of *placēre* to please; in med.L. the sentence of a court, a fine, a trial, a plea.] The decree of a judge, the decision or determination of a public assembly, a court of justice, or the like; hence 'the public assemblies of all degrees of men where the king presided, and where they consulted upon the great affairs of the kingdom' (*Blount's Law Dict.* 1717). Also, in *pl.* the proceedings at such assemblies or courts, debates, trials at law, pleadings or pleas.

1668 HOWE *Bless. Righteous* (1825) 22 The placita or decretals of the Redeemer. **1706** PHILLIPS, *Placitum*, a Sentence of the Court, an Opinion, an Ordinance or Decree; ..In our Common-Law, Placita signifies Pleas or Pleadings; it was also sometimes taken for Penalties or Fines. **1769** ROBERTSON *Chas. V* (1796) I. 269 In a placitum or trial in the presence of Charlemagne. **1794** G. ADAMS *Nat. & Exp. Philos.* II. xxi. 413 If the *placita* of their predecessors were not lost sight of or neglected. **1864** BRYCE *Holy Rom. Emp.* ix. (1889) 138 The *placita* at which these laws were framed or published, would not have been crowded, as of yore, by armed freemen.

plack[1] (plæk). *Sc.* and *north. dial. Obs.* exc. *Hist.* Forms: 5–7 **plak, plake, plakk(e, placke,** 6– **plack.** [prob. a. Flem. *placke, plecke*, a small coin of Brabant and Flanders, current in the 15th c., of varying value, in 17th c. Du. (Hexham) applied to the French *sou*; hence F. *plaque* (1425), *placque, plecque*, med.L. *placca* (1481). Orig. 'flat disk, tablet'; so Flem. *plak*, F. *plaque*. Cf. MLG. *plack*, LG. *plak, plakke* spot, piece, patch, rag, flat piece of land, dug turf; Du. *plak* flat lath for beating, blow, spot, slice; MHG. *placke, phlacke* spot, patch, rag. Cf. PLACARD, PLACKET, PLECK.

Cf. 1425 *Journal d'un Bourgeois de Paris*, an. 1425, 355, Buchon. (Godef.) En ce temps couroit une monnoie a Paris, nommee plaques, pour douze deniers parisis, et estoient de par le duc de Bourgogne. See also Du Cange, *Placa, Placca.*]

†**a.** A coin of the Netherlands of the 15th and 16th centuries. *Obs.* **b.** A small billon coin issued by James III of Scotland; also, a small copper coin current in Scotland in the 15th and 16th centuries, worth 4 pennies Scots.

a. 1479 in *Cely Papers* (1900) 20 Item ij docates..xxxiij[s] Item in plakes v[li]..v[l] fls. **1482** *Ibid.* 126 Item iij plakes.. xxvj[d]. **c 1483** CAXTON *Dialogues* 17 Thise ben grotes of englond; Suche ther be of flaundres; Plackes and half plackes [*Patards et demi patards*]. **1526** in *Lett. & Pap. Hen. VIII*, IV. II. 1149 Double plakks or Carolus shall be current for 4*d.* as now.

b. 1473 *Sc. Acts Jas. III* (1814) II. 105/1 As tuiching þe plakkis & þe new pennyis, þe lordis thinkis þat þe striking of þame be cessit. **1513** DOUGLAS *Æneis* VIII. Prol. 93 Sum penis furth a pan boddum to prent fals plakkis. **1540** *Lanc. Wills* (1857) II. 140 A bende placke whyche ys in my purse. **a 1578** LINDESAY (Pitscottie) *Chron. Scot.* (S.T.S.) I. 169 The wyffis wald refuse the said cunzie quhilk was callit ane Couchrinis plak and said to him that it wald be cryit doun. **1583** in Cochran-Patrick *Rec. Coinage Scot.* (1876) I. 159 That all the saides twelf pennie peices babeis and plackes with the thre pennie grottis and half plackes now current salbe brocht in to his hienes cunyehous..and thairof new money to be cunyeit. **1617** MORYSON *Itin.* I. 283 The Scots haue of long time had..Placks, which they esteemed for 4 pence, but 3 of them make an English penny. **1662** RAY *Three Itin.* II. 162 One bodel they call tway-pennies; two bodels a plack. **a 1706** R. SEMPLE *Piper Kilbarchan* ix, At bridals he wan many placks. **1786** CARDONNEL *Numism. Scot.* Pref. 33 The plack is an ideal coin at this present time in Scotland. **1834** H. MILLER *Scenes & Leg.* xix. (1857) 279 After collecting all the placks and boddles of the party (little pieces of copper coin, with the head of Charles II on one side, and the Scotch thistle on the other).

c. In proverbial phrases, as the type of something of very small value; the smallest possible amount; a farthing; a bit; as in ***not worth a plack***, utterly worthless; ***plack and bawbee, plack and boddle***, in full, every penny, to the last farthing; ***two and a plack***, a trifle, a small sum.

a 1550 in *Dunbar's Poems* (S.T.S.) 307 He wald nocht mend thame worth ane plack. **1572** *Satir. Poems Reform.* xxviii. 118 Plaitter nor pois we neuer left ane plak. **1693** *Scotch Presbyt. Eloq.* (1738) 126 I'll hazard twa and a plack. **1787** W. TAYLOR *Scots Poems* 6 Ise frankly own mysel his debtor For plack an' boddle. **1802** R. ANDERSON *Cumberld. Ball.* 31 They pick'd my pocket i' the thrang, And de'il a plack had I. **1814** SCOTT *Wav.* xlix, He wasna a plack the waur. **1820** —— *Abbot* vi, I would not Sir Halbert had seen her..for two and a plack.

d. *attrib.* Of the value of or costing a plack.

1560 *Aberdeen Regr.* XXIV. (Jam.), His wyf brewit plakaill. **1567** *Gude & Godlie B.* (S.T.S.) 204 His plak Pardonis, are bot lardonis, Of new fund vanitie. **1824** SCOTT *Redgauntlet* ch. xx, He asked..'Whether he could have a plack-pie'. **1899** *Westm. Gaz.* 28 July 5/3 From ancient times the revenues in Scotch burghs were derived from small imposts, variously called petty customs, plack dues, and so on,..levied on animals and goods entering the burgh.

†**plack**[2]. *Obs. rare*$^{-1}$. [app. a. F. *plaque.*] = PLACKET[1], q.v. for quot.

plack[3]. *dial. rare.* [Etym. unknown.] (See quot.)

1871 G. M. HOPKINS *Jrnls. & Papers* (1959) 213 *Rickles*, the biggest of all the cocks, which are run together into *placks*, the shapeless heaps from which the hay is carted.

plack, var. PLAYOCK, toy.

plackard(e, -erd, obs. ff. PLACARD.

†**placket**[1]. *Obs. rare.* [app. a. F. *plaquette* tablet, dim. of *plaque* thin plate.] A plan or map.

1552 T. BARNABE in Strype *Eccl. Mem.* II. II. App. E. 154 He sent me thither [Newhaven = Havre] upon the kings cost: and I drew a plack of yt, and brought yt to hym..my Lord Fitz Williams..better than three or four hours, purviewing the placket.

placket[2] ('plækɪt). [Origin obscure. Perh. the same word as *placat*, var. form of PLACARD *sb.*, sense 3 of which coincides with sense 1 here, and may possibly be the origin of the other uses. But the order of the senses is uncertain, and the following is merely provisional.]

†**1.** (?) = PLACCATE 1, PLACARD 3. *Obs. rare.*

1626 CAPT. SMITH *Accid. Yng. Seamen* 16 Braded plackets for brests of defence.

2. An apron or petticoat: hence *transf.* the wearer of a petticoat, a woman. *Obs.* or *arch.*

1606 SHAKS. *Tr. & Cr.* II. iii. 22 The curse dependant on those that warre for a placket. **a 1625** FLETCHER *Hum. Lieut.* IV. iv, Not half so troublesome as you are to yourself, Sir; Was that brave heart made to pant for a placket? **1661** W. K. *Conf. Charac., Old Hording Hag* (1860) 88 The extent of her placket is alwayes lower than her smock, and that comes but an inch lower than her navel. **1685** CROWNE *Sir C. Nice* II. 13 Eve, the mother of jilts,..pretended to modesty, and fell a making plackets presently. **1711** E. WARD *Quix.* I. 244 Because the Meal from off his Jacket Should not be seen upon her Placket. **1810** SCOTT *Lady of L.* VI. v, Our vicar thus preaches—and why should he not? For the dues of his cure are the placket and pot. **1881** DUFFIELD *Don Quix.* II. 493 A farthingale and placket [Sp. *saboyanas de seda*] instead of her grey petticoat.

3. The opening or slit at the top of a skirt or petticoat, for convenience in putting on and off; also, the slit in a shirt, usually behind.

(Quots. 1605, *c* 1620 are doubtful.)

1605 SHAKS. *Lear* III. iv. 100 Keepe..thy hand out of Plackets. **c 1620** FLETCHER & MASS. *Lit. Fr. Lawyer* v. ii,

Keep thy hand from thy sword, and from thy Laundresse placket. **1706** PHILLIPS, *Placket*, the fore-part of a Woman's Petticoat or Shift. **1719** D'URFEY *Pills* (1872) II. 19 And Madge had a ribbon hung down to her Placket. **1755** SMOLLETT *Quix.* (1803) IV. 104 Teresa Panza..came forth ..with a grey petticoat, so short that it seemed to have been cut close to the placket.

†**b.** Also *sensu obscæno. Obs.*

1601 MUNDAY *Downfall Earl Huntington* II. ii. D ij b, And lust doe vncase, From the placket to the pappe. **1673** HICKERINGILL *Gregory Father Greybeard* 230, I got all, to her very plackit. **1709** *Brit. Apollo* II. No. 28. 3/2 She's.. Well pleas'd with her Cull in her Placket.

4. A pocket, esp. that in a woman's skirt.

1663 *Hist. Cromwell* in *Select. Harl. Misc.* (1793) 368 Which instrument of his, as was said, was found in my Lady Lambert's placket. **1820** L. HUNT *Indicator* No. 60 (1822) II. 62 In a placket at her side is an old enamelled watch. *a* **1825** FORBY *Voc. E. Anglia, Placket*, a pocket. **1841** CHORLEY *Mus. & Manners* (1844) III. 186 The coupé was occupied by a substantial burgher, with his placket at his side, and his pipe for ever at his mouth. **1868** BROWNING *Ring & Bk.* v. 1155 What meaneth this epistle.. I pick from out thy placket and peruse?

5. *Comb.* **placket-hole**, an opening in the outer skirt to give access to the pocket within; also = 3.

1762 STERNE *Tr. Shandy* V. i, Are not trouse, and placket-holes, and pump-handles—and spigots and faucets, in danger still, from the same association? **1880** *Daily Tel.* 29 May, The well-known 'placket-hole', which is seldom free from points of escape, and has a trick of gaping wide open to disclose its contents to any curious eye. **1898** *Westm. Gaz.* 17 Mar. 3/2 The concealing of the placket hole is quite an object just now. **1903** *Pilot* 20 June 529/1 The purse dropped through her placket-hole, instead of going into her pocket.

plackless ('plæklıs), *a. Sc.* [f. PLACK[1] + -LESS.] Without a plack; penniless.

1786 BURNS *Scotch Drink* xvi, Poor plackless devils like mysel'. **1837** R. NICOLL *Poems* (1842) 161 In cottages Where poor folk plackless gae.

placo- ('plækəʊ), before a vowel plac-, combining form of Gr. πλάξ, πλακ- a flat plate, tablet, entering into various scientific words. **placo'branchid** (-kıd) [Gr. βράγχια gills], one of the *Placobranchia*, a division of nudibranchiate gastropods having lamellar gills covering the upper surface of the lobes and back; so **placo'branchoid** (-kɔıd) *a.*, resembling or akin to the *Placobranchia*. **'placoderm** [Gr. δέρμα skin] *a.*, having the skin encased in broad flat bony plates, as certain fossil fishes; of or belonging to the *Placodermata* or *Placodermi*, an order of Palæozoic fishes having the head and pectoral region thus protected; *sb.* one of the *Placodermata*; so **placo'dermal**, **placo'dermatous** *adjs.*; **placo'dermoid** *a.*, resembling the placoderms in form or structure. **'placodont** [Gr. ὀδούς tooth] *a.*, of or belonging to the *Placodontia*, a division of fossil saurians having thickly-set short flat palatal teeth; *sb.* (also **placo'dontid**), a reptile belonging to the *Placodontia*; so **placo'dontoid** *a.*, resembling the placodonts in form or structure. **placo'ganoid** [GANOID] *a.*, of or pertaining to the *Placoganoidei*, a division of fossil Devonian fishes, having the head and part of the body protected by large ganoid plates; *sb.*, a fish of the *Placoganoidei*; also **placoga'noidean** *a.* and *sb.* **pla'cophoran** [Gr. -φόρος bearing] *a.*, of or pertaining to the *Placophora*, a sub-order of molluscs, sometimes made a primary division, comprising only the CHITONS (*Polyplacophora*); *sb.*, one of the *Placophora*, a chiton; so **pla'cophorous** *a.*

1859–65 PAGE *Geol. Terms* (ed. 2), **Placoderms*,..Dr. Pander's term for the bony-plated or bone-encased fishes of the Old Red Sandstone. **1886** A. WINCHELL *Walks Geol. Field* 239 The placoderm was destined to disappear with the Devonian period. **1889** NICHOLSON & LYDEKKER *Palæont.* (ed. 3) II. 1001 Points in which the Siluroids resemble the *Placodermatous Ganoids. *Ibid.* 921 It has..been suggested ..that the *Placodermoid Ganoids were closely related to the Ascidian Invertebrates. **1859** OWEN in *Encycl. Brit.* (ed. 8) XVII. 124/2 The *placoganoid and ganoid, heterocercal and notochordal fishes of the Devonian. **1862** DANA *Man. Geol.* vii. 276 Placoganoids, having the body covered with plates instead of scales. **1872** W. S. SYMONDS *Rec. Rocks* vii. 254 During the latter part of the Silurian epoch the.. Placoganoids make their appearance.

placode ('plækəʊd). *Embryol.* [ad. G. *plakode* (C. von Kupffer 1894, in *Sitzungsber. der k. bayerischen Akad. der Wissensch. zu München* (*Math.-phys. Classe*) XXIV. 57), f. Gr. πλακώδης laminated, flaky.] A localized thickening of the ectoderm in a vertebrate embryo which contributes to the formation of a sensory organ or ganglial tissue.

1909 BAILEY & MILLER *Text-bk. Embryol.* xvi. 459 In the case of the special sense organs there is an interesting tendency on the part of portions of the neural tube, either evaginations (optic vesicles, olfactory bulbs), or ganglia, to fuse with ectodermal thickenings (placodes) at the site of the future sense organs. **1927** W. SHUMWAY *Vertebr. Embryol.* vii. 186 Of the three sensory placodes, olfactory, optic, and otic, the optic placode is incorporated and invaginates with the neural plate so that the eye appears to originate from the brain. **1960** *Jrnl. Compar. Neurol.* CXIV. 11/1 It now seems well established that the placodes provide a distinct cellular contribution to the developing ganglia of the V, VII, IX and X nerves in mammals, just as has long been accepted in fish and amphibians. **1977** *Proc. R. Soc. Med.* LXX. 809/1 The otic placode appears at 21–24 days (Fig 10), and sinks below the surface as a vesicle which lies in undifferentiated mesenchyme.

'placodine. *Min.* Also **placodite.** [ad. Ger. *plakodin* (A. Breithaupt 1841), f. Gr. πλακώδης flat, cake like, f. πλάξ, πλακ- tablet, cake.] A name given, on the supposition of its being a native mineral, to an arsenide of nickel, Ni_4As_2, now considered to be a furnace-product.

1856 *Eng. Cycl.* IV. 367/2 Placodine (Arseniuret of Nickel)... Primary form an oblique rhombic prism. **1886** *Cassell's Encycl. Dict.*, *Placodine, placodite.*

placodioid (plə'kəʊdıɔıd), *a. Bot.* [f. generic name *Placodium* (E. Acharius 1794, in *Kungl. Vetenskapsakad. Handlingar* XV. 248), f. as PLACODE + -OID.] Of a lichen thallus, disc-shaped, with plicate lobes at the circumference.

1911 A. L. SMITH *Monogr. Brit. Lichens* II. 362 Placodioid, like the genus *Placodium*, with the thallus orbicular, adpressed, lobed at the circumference. **1921** [see EFFIGURATE *a.*]. **1970** U. K. DUNCAN *Introd. Brit. Lichens* 148 *B[uellia] canescens*... Thallus white to grey, usually darker and arcolate in the centre, lighter and placodioid towards the circumference.

placoid ('plækɔıd), *a.* and *sb. Zool.* [f. Gr. πλάξ, πλακ- flat plate, tablet: see -OID. Cf. F. *Placoides*, in mod.L. form *Placoidei*, name given by Agassiz, 1833, to certain fishes, on account of the plate-like appearance of their scales. (The earliest derivative in Eng. was app. *placoidean*.)]

A. *adj.*

1. Having the form of a plate; applied to the horny scales and tubercles of the *Placoidei*: see B.

1842 H. MILLER *O.R. Sandst.* iv. 73 One kind of scale, for instance the Placoid or broad plated scale, is found to characterize all the cartilaginous fishes of Cuvier except the sturgeon. **1870** ROLLESTON *Anim. Life* Introd. 68 The dermal exo-skeleton may take the form of..placoid or spiny dentinal formations. **1880** GÜNTHER *Fishes* 349 Very young individuals possess a series of small 'placoid' spines. **1888** ROLLESTON & JACKSON *Anim. Life* 411 The primitive form [of the exoskeleton] occurs..in the shape of dermal teeth (= placoid scales), similar in structure and development to oral teeth.

2. Having placoid scales; of or pertaining to the *Placoidei*: see B.

1847 *Nat. Encycl.* I. 136 A genus of fossil Placoid fishes. **1851** RICHARDSON *Geol.* (1855) 275 The first order, or Placoid,..have the skin irregularly covered with plates of enamel, sometimes large, as in the rays, sometimes reduced to small points, as in the sharks. **1880** GÜNTHER *Fishes* 21 The distinctions between..placoid and ganoid fishes are vague.

B. *sb.* A fish of the division *Placoidei*, containing the sharks and rays, distinguished by having the skin protected by irregularly disposed bony scales, sometimes bearing spines.

1854 H. MILLER *Sch. & Schm.* xxi. (1858) 473 The mere detached teeth and spines of placoids. **1873** DAWSON *Earth & Man* v. 96 The Placoids or shark-like fishes.

Hence **pla'coidal** *a. rare*; **pla'coidean** *a.* and *sb.*

1836 BUCKLAND *Geol. & Min.* I. xiii. 269 *note*, *Placoidians*. .. Fishes of this Order are characterized by having their skin covered irregularly with plates of enamel [etc.]. *Ibid.* 283 Genera of the first and second orders (Placoidean and Ganoidian)..ceased suddenly. **1845** R. CHAMBERS *Vestiges* (ed. 4) 207 When fishes came, the first forms were those ganoidal and placoidal types which correspond with the early fœtal condition of higher orders. **1849** SMART *Dict.* Suppl., Placoideans.

placquart, obs. form of PLACARD.

placque, variant of PLAQUE.

‖**placula** ('plækjʊlə). *Biol.* [mod.L., dim. from Gr. πλάξ, πλάκ- tablet, plate.] Name for the embryo of *Calcispongiæ* at that stage in its development when it has the form of a plate or disc. Hence **'placular**, **'placulate** *adjs.*, having the form of a placula.

1884 A. HYATT in *Proc. Boston Soc. Nat. Hist.* XXIII. 89 The primitive differentiation of the placula into two layers is established in what we have designated the diploplacula. *Ibid.* 97 The embryo of Calcispongiæ is also a placula until the same stage. *Ibid.* 150 A full-grown, primitive, placulate form. **1895** *Syd. Soc. Lex.*, *Placular*,.. *Placulate.*

plad, pladding, obs. ff. PLAID, PLAIDING.

†**pladding**, ? variant of *platting*, PLAITING.

a **1711** KEN *Damonet* Poet. Wks. 1721 IV. 505 The Garlands are begun of Pladding fine, Our Wedding-clothes are made, which richly shine.

pladge, obs. Sc. variant of PLEDGE.

pladman, var. of PLAIDMAN, Highlander.

‖**plafond** (plafɔ̃). Also 7 **platfound**, 7–9 **platfond**, 8 **plaffond**. [F. *plafond* (†*platfond*) a ceiling (1559 in Hatz.-Darm.), f. *plat* flat + *fond* bottom.]

1. *Arch.* A ceiling, either flat or vaulted; usually as enriched with paintings; hence, a painting executed on a ceiling. † ***in plafond***: on the ceiling.

1664 EVELYN tr. *Freart's Archit.* II. ix. 110 Also they do rarely well about Platfonds and upon Ground-works. **1670** LASSELLS *Voy. Italy* I. 87 The roof..is all guilt, and set with curious pictures in Platfound. **1705** JOS. TAYLOR *Journ. Edinb.* (1903) 37 The plaffond is handsomely painted. **1714** STEELE *Lover* No. 33 (1723) 192 The whole Plafond or Ceiling. **1801** FUSELI in *Lect. Paint.* ii. (1848) 398 The platfonds, panels, and cupolas, of palaces and temples. **1835** WILLIS *Pencillings* xiii. 102 Naked female figures fill every plafond.

2. *Arch.* (See quots.)

1723 CHAMBERS tr. *Le Clere's Treat. Archit.* I. 52 The Plafond or Soffit of the Cornice. **1842–76** GWILT *Archit.* Gloss., *Plafond* or *Platfond*,..also the underside of the projection of the larmier of the cornice; generally any sofite.

3. An early form of contract bridge.

So called because a player aimed to bid to his ceiling of tricks. The game originated in France.

[**1929** M. C. WORK *Compl. Contract Bridge* 242 *Plafond*, French name for Contract.] **1933** A. E. MANNING-FOSTER *Bridge-Plafond* 17 Plafond was invented in France in 1918, and it is still played widely on the Continent. **1963** G. F. HARVEY *Handbk. Card Games* 131 The Continental game of *Plafond*, the main feature of which was (because the game is no longer played) that tricks must be contracted for in order to be scored towards game. **1964** A. WYKES *Gambling* vii. 166 But a variation [of auction bridge] called *plafond*..was quickly taken up in Europe and America and became contract bridge. **1975** *Times* 15 Nov. 13/5 In May 1925, Mr Vanderbilt..joined in a rubber of the continental game of plafond. He saw possibilities in the game, added the attraction of vulnerability,..introduced it to the [New York] Whist Club under the name of Contract Bridge.

‖**plaga** ('pleıgə). *Zool.* [L. *plāga* blow, stroke, wound, stripe, a. Gr. πληγή, Doric πλᾱγά blow, stroke.] A stripe of colour.

1826 KIRBY & SP. *Entomol.* IV. xlvi. 286 Plaga... A long and large spot. **1895** *Syd. Soc. Lex.*, *Plaga*,..also *Zool.*, a stripe of colour.

plagal ('pleıgəl), *a. Mus.* [ad. med.L. *plagālis* (whence It. *plagale*, F., Ger. *plagal*), f. med.L. *plaga* the plagal mode (Du Cange), app. a back-formation from med.L. *plagius*, a. med. Gr. πλάγιος plagal (πλάγιος ἦχος a plagal mode), in class. Gr. 'oblique', f. πλάγος side. (Cf. Ger. *Seitenton* a plagal mode.)]

a. In *Gregorian Music*, Applied to those ecclesiastical modes which have their sounds comprised between the dominant and its octave, the final being near the middle of the compass. **b.** ***plagal cadence***: that form of perfect cadence in which the chord of the subdominant (major or minor) immediately precedes that of the tonic. In both senses opposed to AUTHENTIC.

1597 MORLEY *Introd. Mus.* Annot., Euery song..which in the middle hath an eight aboue the finall keye, is of an autenticall tune; if not it is a plagall. **1609** DOULAND *Ornith. Microl.* 13 Euery Song in the beginning, rising straight beyond the final Note to a Fift, is Authenticall: but that which fals straight way to a Third, or a Fourth, vnder the finall Key, is *Plagall*. **1796** BURNEY *Mem. Metastasio* III. 197 If you find yourself involved in the difficulties of the Plagal tones, I am not among the Authentic. **1836** *Penny Cycl.* VI. 99/2 There is another kind of Cadence, to which the name *Plagal* is given. **1875** OUSELEY *Harmony* xiii. 154 If the piece is serious and solemn..it is usual, especially in sacred pieces, to add to it a plagal cadence. **1880** ROCKSTRO in Grove *Dict. Mus.* II. 760/2 S. Gregory added to these Modes four others, directly derived from them, and hence called Plagal Modes.

plagard(e, plagart, obs. forms of PLACARD.

plagate ('pleıgət), *a. Zool.* [f. L. *plāga* (see above) + -ATE[1].] Having a plaga or plagæ; marked with a streak or streaks.

1890 in *Cent. Dict.*

plage[1] (see below). Also 4 **plaag**, 6 **plague.** [a. OF. *plage* region (1290 in Hatz.-Darm.):—late L. *plagia* (see Du Cange) a plain, shore, prop. adj. (*plagia regio*), f. *plaga* a region. So It. *piaggia*.

Hatz.-Darm. take *plage* in the sense 'littoral tract, shore' to represent *plagia*, but in the sense 'region, extent of land' to be a learned formation from *plaga*.]

†**1.** A region, district, clime; sometimes, a zone. *Obs.*

c **1386** CHAUCER *Man of Law's T.* 445 Payens that conquereden al aboute The plages of the North. **1432–50** tr. *Higden* (Rolls) II. 53 The prouince Lindeseience, whiche longede somme tyme to the Marches, dothe diuide Northumbrelonde from that other plage. *a* **1548** HALL *Chron.*, *Hen. VI* 185 King Henry..nesteled and strengthend him and his alyes in the North regions and boreal plage. **1586** MARLOWE *1st Pt. Tamburl.* IV. iv, From the frozen plage of Heaven. **1613** PURCHAS *Pilgrimage* VIII. i. 602 A Plage, plagued with scorching heats.

†**2.** Any one of the four principal directions or quarters of the compass; direction, side. *Obs.*

1382 WYCLIF *Ezek.* vii. 2 Ende cometh vp on the foure plagis, or parties, of the erthe [1388 on foure coostis of the lond]. *c* **1391** CHAUCER *Astrol.* I. §5 The 4 quarters of thin astrelabie, deuyded after the 4 principals plages or quarters of the firmament. **1432–50** tr. *Higden* (Rolls) I. 115 The mownte off Caluarye is at the northe plage of the mownte of Syon. **1501** DOUGLAS *Pal. Hon.* I. 195 Ane dyn I hard approching..Quhilk mouit fra the plague Septentrionall. **1590** *Serpent of Devis.* Cj, A large Commit [= comet] of stremes, whose branches reacht on the foure plagues on the firmament. **1652** J. WRIGHT tr. *Camus' Nat. Paradox* VII. 151 Heavens alter the motion of your Sphears, and thou Sun ..go take thy Resting-place in the Orientall plage.

†**3.** One of the divisions or parts of a church, *esp.* a transept. *rare. Obs.*

[*c* **1214** GAUF. DE COLDINGHAM in *Scriptores Tres Dunelm.* (Surtees) 11 *Ad orientalem ejusdem ecclesiæ plagam* [i.e. the triapsidal east end].] **1593** *Rites of Durham* (Surtees 1903) 23 Hee lyeth buryed..in the north plage. *Ibid.* 30 Johne Hemmyngbrowghe..lieth buried in the south plage.

4. With pronunc. (plɑːʒ). [OF. *plage* in sense 'shore'.] The beach or sea-front promenade at a seaside resort. Hence (by metonymy) a seaside resort.

1888 MRS. H. WARD *R. Elsmere* III. xlvi. 320 They would stroll back..past the hotels on the *plage.* **1890** E. DOWSON *Let.* 22 Aug. (1967) 160, I leave for Bognor about the 1st... My people are all away at that delectable *plage.* **1905** W. J. LOCKE *Morals M. Ordeyne* xii. 144 To strut about a fashionable *plage* in white ducks. **1907** *Daily Chron.* 5 July 6/3 Mr. Justice Bucknill asked the witness what the '*plage*' at Sandown was, but she did not know... It is the promenade. Your Lordship knows the plage at Ostend... I think my friend will agree that the plage at Ostend is the dullest of all plages. **1919** W. T. GRENFELL *Labrador Doctor* (1920) ii. 18 There were horses to ride also and a beautiful 'plage' to bathe upon. **1929** *Star* 21 Aug. 7/1 There is a certain appropriateness in the fact that Mr. Baldwin is once more recuperating at Aix-les-Bains..which lacks all the hectic amenities of the more sophisticated plages. **1937** G. FRANKAU *More of Us* xiv. 143 Down to the plage, legitimate, she trod, Seeking the Bar Au Bleu. **1950** G. BRENAN *Face of Spain* v. 103 Marbella..has been turned into a fashionable *plage.* **1959** F. STARK *Riding to Tigris* 98 A *plage* of a few reed huts was on the sandy bank. **1973** D. WALKER *Black Dougal* xxiv. 194 A man who clearly loved to see his pretty wife dressed for the plage.

5. *Astr.* (pleɪdʒ). [a. F. *plage* (used in this sense by H. Deslandres 1898, in *Compt. Rend.* CXXVI. 881).] A region of the sun's chromosphere, usually associated with sunspots, which is bright in the emission spectra of calcium and hydrogen. Also *attrib.*, as *plage region.*

1949 *Astrophysical Jrnl.* CX. 244 Flares which became at least twice as bright as the surrounding plage. **1953** *Observatory* LXXIII. 116 There were three principal calcium *plage* regions. **1954** *Astrophysical Jrnl.* CXIX. 564 There are many *plages* in which spots do not become visible; but we do not..have any observations of a spot without at least some trace of a bright, associated *plage.* **1963** H. J. & E. v. P. SMITH *Solar Flares* i. 17 Plages..are chromospheric phenomena, and must be observed in the monochromatic light of higher excitation lines such as Hα or the K line of ionized calcium. **1970** *Nature* 18 Apr. 249/2 Several prominences and a plage region are clearly visible in Lyman α.

†**plage**[2]. *Obs. rare*⁻¹. Also **plague**. [ad. L. *plaga* net, snare.] A net, snare, toil.

1608 TOPSELL *Serpents* 273 Spyders..hang their threds in ayre aboue, By plages [**1658** plagues] vnseene to th' eye of man. [Here *threds* and *plages* seem to be erroneously transposed. The Latin rendered is: Sed liciis hinc densioribus plagas In aere appendunt.]

plage, obs. form of PLAGUE, PLEDGE.

plageat, -et, -ette, obs. forms of PLEDGET.

plager, ? error for *plaget*, PLEDGET, pad, plug.

1656 RIDGLEY *Pract. Physick* 164 Wet the bands and plagers in Oxycratum. *Ibid.* 167 He sprinkled the Plagers with Oxycratum and red wine.

†**plagi'arian**, *a. Obs. rare.* [f. as PLAGIARY + -AN.] Of or pertaining to plagiaries or man-stealers.

1656 BLOUNT *Glossogr.*, *Plagiarian Law* (*plagiaria lex*), a law made against these men [plagiaries], &c. **1706** PHILLIPS, *Plagiarian*, as The Plagiarian Law; a Law made against Plagiaries.

plagi'arical, *a. rare.* [f. as PLAGIARY + -ICAL.] = PLAGIARISTIC.

1887 HALLIWELL *Shaks.* (ed. 7) II. 281 Without incurring the smallest risk of a plagiarical imputation.

plagiarism (ˈpleɪdʒərɪz(ə)m). [f. as PLAGIARY + -ISM.]

1. The action or practice of plagiarizing; the wrongful appropriation or purloining, and publication as one's own, of the ideas, or the expression of the ideas (literary, artistic, musical, mechanical, etc.) of another.

1621 BP. MOUNTAGU *Diatribæ* 23 Were you afraid to bee challenged for plagiarisme? **1716** M. DAVIES *Athen. Brit.* II. To Rdr. 46 A good Plea to any Charge of Plagiarism or Satyrism. **1753** JOHNSON *Adventurer* No. 95 ¶9 Nothing.. can be more unjust than to charge an author with plagiarism merely because he..makes his personages act as others in like circumstances have done. **1820** HAZLITT *Lect. Dram. Lit.* 257 If an author is once detected in borrowing, he will be suspected of plagiarism ever after. **1861** BUCKLE *Civiliz.* II. vi. 542 A certain unity of design which is inconsistent with extensive plagiarism.

2. A purloined idea, design, passage, or work.

1797 *Monthly Mag.* III. 260 He found the..song..to be 'a most flagrant plagiarism from Handel'. **1850** MAURICE *Mor. & Met. Philos.* (ed. 2) I. 98 A Thaumaturgist whom they had created..to convince the world that the Christian church was a plagiarism. **1875** JOWETT *Plato* (ed. 2) I. p. xx, They are full of plagiarisms, inappropriately borrowed.

plagiarist (ˈpleɪdʒərɪst). [f. PLAGIARY + -IST.] One who plagiarizes; one who is guilty of plagiarism.

1674 R. GODFREY *Inj. & Ab. Physic* 56 The Author (..I should say the Collector or Plagiarist). **1779** SHERIDAN *Critic* I. i, A dexterous plagiarist..might take out some of the best things in my tragedy, and put them into his own comedy. **1822** HAZLITT *Table-t.* Ser. II. v. (1869) 123 The poorest of all plagiarists, the plagiarists of words. **1866–7** BARING-GOULD *Cur. Myths Mid. Ages, Antichr. & Pope Joan* (1894) 172 The story spread among the mediæval chroniclers, who were great plagiarists.

Hence **plagia'ristic** *a.*, characteristic of a plagiarist; pertaining to or characterized by plagiarism; whence **plagia'ristically** *adv.*

1821 WAINEWRIGHT *Ess. & Crit.* (1880) 150 The whole series was cold, commonplace, and plagiaristic. **1823** *Blackw. Mag.* XIII. 93 They..have very unhandsomely and plagiaristically anticipated my own original lucubrations. **1838** *Fraser's Mag.* XVIII. 545 There is risk ..in any or all of these plagiaristic devices.

plagiarize (ˈpleɪdʒəraɪz), *v.* [f. PLAGIARY + -IZE.]

1. *trans.* To practise plagiarism upon; to take and use as one's own the thoughts, writings, or inventions of another. (With the thing, rarely the person, as object.)

1716 M. DAVIES *Athen. Brit.* III. *Diss. Physick* 29 Manto or Daphnes, Tiresias the Priest's Daughter, who writ or paraphras'd in such excellent Strains, some of the..Oracles at the Temple of the Delphians, that they were worth to be plagiariz'd by Homer himself. **1822** *Blackw. Mag.* XII. 783, I do not mean to say that they are plagiarized (let me coin the word, for I do not like to say stolen) from Miss Lee. **1830** TENNYSON *Talking Oak* v, For oft I talk'd with him apart, And told him of my choice, Until he plagiarised a heart, And answer'd with a voice. **1888** G. A. SCHRUMPF in *Athenæum* 25 Feb. 243/2 Mr. Kirby..seeks to create the impression that I plagiarized Ujfalvy.

2. *intr.* To practise or commit plagiarism.

1832 LYTTON *Eugene A.* I. vi, I cannot plagiarise..from any scholastic designs you might have been giving vent to. **1863** *Blackw. Mag.* Sept. 279 Little wits that plagiarise are but pickpockets: great wits that plagiarise are conquerors.

Hence ˌ**plagiari'zation** = PLAGIARISM 1; '**plagiarizer** = PLAGIARIST.

1839 *Fraser's Mag.* XX. 413 Plagiarizers..have..stolen their thoughts. **1884** *Athenæum* 3 May 575/3 No direct.. plagiarization from his German model.

plagiary (ˈpleɪdʒərɪ), *sb.* and *a.* [ad. L. *plagiārius* one who abducts the child or slave of another, a kidnapper; a seducer; also (Mart. i. 53. 9) a literary thief. Cf. late L. *plagium* kidnapping, *plagiāre* to kidnap. So F. *plagiaire* (16th c.) a plagiarist.]

A. *sb.* †**1.** A kidnapper, a man-stealer. *Obs.*

1613 PURCHAS *Pilgrimage* III. iii. 199 In the time of his.. childhood, he was by some Plagiary stolne away from his friends. **1626** H. KING *Serm. Deliverance* 46 How many be there..that, like Plagiaries, make it their trade to hunt and catch men? **1697** BP. PATRICK *Comm. Exod.* xx. 16 No Israelite would buy him, and therefore such Plagiaries sold him to Men of other Nations.

2. = PLAGIARIST.

1601 B. JONSON *Poetaster* IV. iii, Why? the ditt' is all borrowed; 'tis Horaces: hang him plagiary. **1649** JER. TAYLOR *Gt. Exemp.* I. Ad Sect. viii. 119 He that is a Plagiary of others titles or offices, and dresses himself with their beauties. **1676** LISTER in *Ray's Corr.* (1848) 125, I am glad you have discovered those authors to be plagiaries. **1758** JOHNSON *Idler* No. 85 ¶7 Compilers and plagiaries are encouraged, who give us again what we had before. **1855** MACAULAY *Hist. Eng.* xix. IV. 354 Blount was one of the most unscrupulous plagiaries that ever lived.

3. = PLAGIARISM 1; literary theft. [Cf. -ARY B. 1.]

1646 SIR T. BROWNE *Pseud. Ep.* 22 Plagiarie had not its nativitie with printing, but began in times when thefts were difficult. **1688** G. LANGBAINE (*title*) Momus Triumphans: or, the Plagiaries of the English Stage; Expos'd in a catalogue of all the Comedies, Opera's,..&c. **1775** SHERIDAN *Rivals* Pref., My first wish in attempting a play was to avoid every appearance of plagiary. **1880** SWINBURNE *Study Shaks.* 52 No parasitic rhymester..ever uttered a more parrot-like note of plagiary.

b. = PLAGIARISM 2.

1677 E. BROWNE *Trav. Germ.* etc. 108 Hoping to find better Markets for their Plagiaries and Depredations. **1818** HOBHOUSE *Hist. Illustr.* (ed. 2) 415 The plagiaries, if they may so be called, are inserted with considerable taste and effect. **1865** *Athenæum* 13 May 658/1 The attitudes..are.. not plagiaries.

4. *Comb.*, as *plagiary-like* adj. or adv.

1662 EVELYN *Chalcogr.* v. 117 Taken out of the prints of Albert Durer..not for want of invention and plagiary like.

B. *adj.* †**1.** Kidnapping, man-stealing. *rare*⁻¹.

1673 E. BROWNE *Trav.* (1685) 49 Some [fell into that condition] by Treachery, some by Chance of War; others by Plagiary and Man-stealing Tartars.

†**2.** That plagiarizes; plagiarizing. *Obs.*

1597–8 BP. HALL *Sat.* IV. ii. 84 Alike to thee as lieve As.. an *hos ego* from old Petrarch's spright Unto a plagiary sonnet wright. **1620** —— *Hon. Mar. Clergy* I. §26 The plagiary priest, hauing stolne this whole passage..verbatim out of Bellarmine. **1662** STILLINGFL. *Orig. Sacr.* II. v. §2 This was the Plagiary Prophet.

3. Obtained by plagiarism; plagiarized. ? *Obs.*

1681 COLVIL *Whigs Supplic.* (1751) 14 Nought..but plagiary stuff, By which they purchase praise and money. **1796** MORSE *Amer. Geog.* I. 561 A quadrant, by Mr. Godfrey, called by the plagiary name of Hadley's quadrant. **1820** *Hermit in London* IV. 162 Second-hand puns and plagiary remarks.

Hence '**plagiaryship**, the function or action of a plagiarist, plagiarism.

a **1661** FULLER *Worthies* III. *Warwick.* (1662) 128 Rider after Thomas his death, set forth his Dictionary, the same in effect, under his own Name,..being but little disguised with any Additions. Such Plagiary-ship ill becometh Authors or Printers.

'**plagiat.** *rare*⁻¹. [ad. law L. *plagiātus* kidnapping, f. late L. *plagiāre* to kidnap. So F. *plagiat* (1762 in *Dict. Acad.*).] Man-stealing, kidnapping.

1809 J. ADAMS *Wks.* (1854) IX. 316 The impressment of seamen..is no better than what civilians call *plagiat*, a crime punishable with death by all civilized nations.

plagiator (ˈpleɪdʒɪeɪtə(r)). *rare.* [a. L. *plagiātor* kidnapper, f. *plagiāre*: see prec.] = PLAGIARIST.

1889 R. B. ANDERSON tr. *Rydberg's Teut. Mythol.* 51 The poet Homer in his works was a mere plagiator. **1889** JACOBS *Æsop* 11 Ademar forgets his rôle of plagiator.

plagihedral (pleɪdʒɪˈhiːdrəl, -ˈhɛdrəl), *a. Cryst.* Also **plagiedral**. [f. PLAGI)O- + Gr. ἕδρα seat, base.] Having certain faces obliquely situated; also said of such faces.

1805–17 R. JAMESON *Char. Min.* (ed. 3) 212 [A crystal is said to be] Plagihedral..when it has facets which are situated obliquely. *a* **1853** PEREIRA *Pol. Light* (1854) 257–8 In that form of quartz termed by Haüy *plagiedral*.., it has been found that when the unsymmetrical or plagiedral faces lean to the right, the polarization is right-handed, and, *vice versâ.* **1895** STORY-MASKELYNE *Crystallogr.* 316 A crystal of quartz..will, if right-handed, present on three alternate quoins at each end of the prism plagihedral faces arranged in the form of a right-handed screw.

plagio- (ˈpleɪdʒɪəʊ-, ˈplægɪəʊ-), before a vowel or *h* **plagi-**, comb. form, repr. Gr. πλάγιος oblique, slanting, f. πλάγος side. **plagio'climax** [CLIMAX *sb.* 4 b] *Ecol.*, in a plant community, a climax produced or affected by some disturbance of the natural conditions; **plagio'clinal** *a.* [Gr. κλίν-ειν to incline], applied to mountain structure, when the strike of the rock runs across the axis of elevation; '**plagiodont** *a.* [Gr. ὀδούς tooth], having the palatal teeth set obliquely or in converging lines, as in some serpents; '**plagiograph** [-GRAPH], an instrument for reproducing a plan, diagram, etc., in a position at a given angle from the original; '**plagiosere** [SERE *sb.*[2]] *Ecol.*, a series of plant communities whose development is affected by some disturbance of the natural conditions.

1935 A. G. TANSLEY in *Ecology* XVI. 293 We might call such successions, which undoubtedly exist, plagioseres, i.e., 'bent' or 'twisted' seres, and if the vegetation really does come into equilibrium with the deflecting factor, of a plagioclimax, if such terms are considered useful. **1939** —— *Brit. Islands & their Vegetation* x. 225 Their [*sc.* plagioseres'] end products, varying with the precise form of exploitation, are characteristic biotic climaxes or plagioclimaxes. **1960** N. POLUNIN *Introd. Plant Geogr.* xi. 330 Subclimaxes due to such treatments as persistent burning or grazing (often called disclimaxes, being due to disturbance, or plagioclimaxes, owing to the deflection involved). **1974** *Nature* 10 May 111/3 Repeated burning of the scrub could have reversed the trend in vegetational development caused by ameliorating climate and have produced an anthropogenic plagioclimax of arid scrub. **1879** CALLAWAY in *Geol. Mag.* VI. 221 A plagioclinal axis is not necessarily Precambrian, but its transverse strike should suggest inquiry. **1890** *Cent. Dict.*, Plagiodont. **1895** in *Syd. Soc. Lex.* **1935** Plagiosere [see *plagioclimax* above]. **1939** A. G. TANSLEY *Brit. Islands & their Vegetation* x. 225 These 'deflected successions' or plagioseres..as they may be called, are characteristic results of man's activity. **1962** C. J. TAYLOR *Trop. Forestry* vi. 45 It is possible..for the soil to deteriorate so much that the retrogression of the vegetation will become permanent and thus a deflected sere or plagiosere will be the result.

plagiocephalic (ˌpleɪdʒɪəʊsɪˈfælɪk), *a.* [f. PLAGIO- + Gr. κεφαλή head + -IC.]

a. *Anthropol.* (See quot.)

1874 BUSK in *Jrnl. Anthrop. Inst.* III. 90 *note*, Linnæus's term plagiocephalic is emphatically descriptive of the more common form of American skull, and may be conveniently used to distinguish the broad head, with flattened forehead, so characteristic of the greater part of the American races.

b. *Path.* Characterized by plagiocephaly.

1878 BARTLEY tr. *Topinard's Anthrop.* v. 178 The obliquely oval or plagiocephalic deformity. **1888** *Syd. Soc. Lex.*, *Idiocy, plagiocephalic*,..one of Shuttleworth's divisions including idiots with heads so distorted that the features lie in an oblique plane.

So **plagio'cephalous** = prec. b; **plagio'cephaly**, oblique deformity of the skull, consisting in the greater development of the anterior part on one side and of the posterior part on the other.

1890 *Cent. Dict.*, Plagiocephalous, Plagiocephaly. **1895** *Syd. Soc. Lex.*, *Plagiocephalous*,..having the skull awry; the result of asymmetrical development, and the premature synostosis of the frontal with one of the parietal bones. *Ibid.*, *Plagiocephaly*, the condition of being plagiocephalous.

plagiocitrite (pleɪdʒɪəʊˈsɪtraɪt). *Min.* [Named 1879, f. PLAGIO- + L. *citrus* citron + -ITE[1].] A hydrous sulphate of aluminium and other bases, found in monoclinic or triclinic lemon-yellow crystals.

1886 in *Cassell's Encycl. Dict.* **1892** DANA *Min.* (ed. 6) 975.

plagioclase (ˈpleɪdʒɪəʊkleɪs). *Min.* [Named 1847, f. PLAGIO- + Gr. κλάσις fracture, cleavage.] (See quot. 1868.)

1868 DANA *Min.* (ed. 5) Suppl. 802 *Plagioclase*, Breithaupt's name for the group of triclinic feldspars, the two prominent cleavage directions in which are oblique to one another. **1879** RUTLEY *Stud. Rocks* x. 91 In the case of plagioclase the crystals exhibit numerous bands of different colours. **1903** GEIKIE *Text Bk. Geol.* (ed. 4) I. II. 200 The Plagioclase rocks. **1941** *Proc. Prehist. Soc.* VII. 61 Sparsely distributed small phenocrysts of turbid plagioclase felspar. **1959** C. S. HURLBUT *Dana's Man. Min.* (ed. 17) v. 495 The plagioclase feldspars, also called the soda-lime feldspars, form a complete solid-solution series from pure albite, $NaAlSi_3O_8$, to pure anorthite, $CaAl_2Si_2O_8$. **1971** *Sci. Amer.* Oct. 50/3 The plagioclase in the moon rocks..is almost pure anorthite ($CaAl_2Si_2O_8$).

plagioclastic (-ˈklæstɪk), *a. Min.* [f. PLAGIO- + Gr. κλαστ-ός broken, cloven + -IC.] Having oblique cleavage. Opp. to ORTHOCLASTIC.

1869 GEIKIE in *Edinb. Geol. Soc. Jrnl.* II. 5 Plagioclastic felspars. **1879** RUTLEY *Stud. Rocks* x. 91 The plagioclastic.. or those in which the cleavage planes intersect at angles other than 90°. **1895** *Syd. Soc. Lex.*, *Plagioclastic*, breaking obliquely.

plagionite (ˈpleɪdʒɪənaɪt). *Min.* [ad. G. *plagionit* (G. Rose 1833), f. Gr. πλάγιος, -ον oblique + -ITE[1].] A sulphide of lead and antimony occurring in monoclinic thick tabular crystals of a blackish grey colour.

1835 *Thomson's Records Gen. Sci.* I. 271 *Plagionite*.—The crystals of this mineral belong to the oblique rectangular prismatic system of Beudant. **1866** WATTS *Dict. Chem.* IV. 661 *Plagionite*, a sulphantimonite of lead occurring at Wolfsberg in the Hartz.

plagiostome (ˈpleɪdʒɪəʊstəʊm), *sb.* (*a.*) [a. F. *plagiostome*, f. PLAGIO- + Gr. στόμα mouth.] A member of the *Plagiostomi*, cartilaginous fishes, including the sharks and rays, which have the mouth placed transversely beneath the snout.

1842 BRANDE *Dict. Sc.* etc., *Plagiostomes*, a tribe of Cartilaginous fishes. **1859** OWEN in *Encycl. Brit.* (ed. 8) XVII. 117/2 Affinities with the *Cestracion* amongst existing Plagiostomes. **1860** COUCH *Brit. Fishes* I. 5 [The Sharks and] their kindred chondropterygians or plagiostomes—the Rays. **1881** GÜNTHER in *Encycl. Brit.* XII. 667/1 No detached undoubted tooth of a Plagiostome..has been discovered in the Ludlow deposits.

b. *attrib.* or *adj.* Plagiostomous.

1835 R. WILLIS in *Todd's Cycl. Anat.* I. 115/1 The cartilaginous plagiostome fishes.

So **plagioˈstomatous** (*rare*), **plagiˈostomous** *adjs.*, of or pertaining to the plagiostomes; having the mouth situated transversely beneath the snout.

1858 MAYNE *Expos. Lex.*, *Plagiostomus*,..plagiostomous. **1859** OWEN in *Encycl. Brit.* (ed. 8) XVII. 116/1 A genus of plagiostomous cartilaginous fishes called *Onchus*. **1881** SEELEY in *Cassell's Nat. Hist.* V. 38 The Rays form the second division of the Plagiostomous fishes. **1890** *Cent. Dict.*, Plagiostomatous.

plagiotropic (pleɪdʒɪəʊˈtrɒpɪk), *a. Bot.* [a. G. *plagiotrop* (J. von Sachs 1879, in *Arbeiten Bot. Inst. Würzburg* II. 227) f. PLAGIO- + Gr. τροπικός inclined, f. τρόπος turning.] Said of members or organs of plants, the two halves of which react differently to the influences of light, gravitation, and other external forces, and which therefore take up an oblique position: opp. to ORTHOTROPIC. Hence **plagioˈtropically** *adv.*; **plagiˈotropism**, the condition or character of being plagiotropic.

1882 VINES tr. *Sachs Bot.* App. 954 Sachs points out..that most monosymmetrical or bilaterally symmetrical organs present..dorsal and ventral halves..of different internal structure... When this is the case the two halves react differently to external forces (light, gravity, etc.) and the organ is, according to his terminology, plagiotropic,..some polysymmetrical organs are plagiotropic also. **1886** —— *Physiol. Plants* 502 The plagiotropism of dorsiventral organs, such as shoots and leaves,..is the resultant expression of the effect of light and of gravity upon them, promoted, in many cases, by their own weight. **1929** T. THOMSON tr. *Büsgen's Struct. & Life Forest Trees* i. 44 Much less simple to understand are the conditions which determine the position of 'plagiotropic' organs, i.e. those which grow inclined to the main axis. **1951** MCLEAN & IVIMEY-COOK *Textbk. Theoret. Bot.* I. xxi. 837 Bilateral and dorsiventral organs are mostly plagiotropic, that is, horizontal or inclined in position.

plagiotropous (pleɪdʒɪˈɒtrəpəs, ˌpleɪdʒɪəˈtrəʊpəs), *a. Bot.* [ad. G. *plagiotrop* (see PLAGIOTROPIC *a.*), f. PLAGIO- + Gr. τρόπος turning + -OUS.] = PLAGIOTROPIC *a.* So **plagioˈtropously** *adv.*; **plagiˈotropy**, the condition of plant organs growing in this way.

1900 I. B. BALFOUR tr. *C. E. von Goebel's Organogr. Plants* I. 67 It [*sc.* an organ] is plagiotropous if..it assumes an oblique direction to the horizontal plane. *Ibid.* 112 In the shade of woods of the natural habitat the plagiotropy and anisophylly may be more marked. *Ibid.* 113 Sympodial shoot-systems..growing plagiotropously. **1919** *Lunds Universitets Årsskrift* N.F. Avd. II. XVI. II. (*title*) The cause of plagiotropy in maritime shore plants. **1965** BELL & COOMBE tr. *Strasburger's Textbk. Bot.* 125 The radially symmetrical main axis..produces its more or less dorsiventral and plagiotropous side branches uniformly around the stem.

‖**plagium** (ˈpleɪdʒɪəm). [L. *plagium* kidnapping: see PLAGIARY.]

1. *Civil Law.* Kidnapping, man-stealing.

1577 tr. *Bullinger's Decades* (1592) 395 Now they commit the offence called *Plagium*, that is to saie, manstealing. **1678** T. JONES *Heart & its Right Sov.* 340 Such depredations and reprisals, and plagiums. **1797** *Encycl. Brit.* (ed. 3) IX. 454/2 In the civil law, the offence of spiriting away and stealing men and children, which was called *plagium*,..was punished with death. **1815** SCOTT *Guy M.* lvi, 'Pardon me', said Pleydell, 'it is *plagium*, and *plagium* is felony'.

†**2.** = PLAGIARISM 1 and 2. *Obs.*

a **1619** FOTHERBY *Atheom.* Pref. (1622) 8 Neither their writings shalbe preiudiced by mine, nor mine thought a Plagium out of theirs. **1673** B. OLEY *Pref. to Jackson's Wks.*, I shame not to tell this because I think it no *plagium*.

plagose (pləˈgəʊs), *a.* [ad. L. *plagōs-us*, f. *plaga* a stroke: see -OSE.] Inclined to flog, fond of flogging (*humorous*).

1868 M. COLLINS *Sweet Anne Page* I. 23 Miss Harriet's plagose propensity. **1875** —— *From Midnight to Midn.* III. ix. 160 His preceptor, plagose and stern.

So **plaˈgosity**, inclination to flog.

a **1619** FOTHERBY *Atheom.* I. xv. §4 (1622) 161 His notable tyranny and plagosity.

plague (pleɪg), *sb.* Forms: 4 **plaage**, 4–7 **plage**, 6 **plag**, *Sc.* **plagge**, **plaig**, 6– **plague**, (7 **plauge**). [ME. *plage*, a. OF. *plage* (14th c.), *plague* (15th c.) stroke, wound, ad. L. *plāga* stroke, wound (= Doric Gr. πλᾱγά, Attic πληγή stroke, blow), in late L. plague, pestilence, infection (Vulgate), f. root *plag-* of L. *plangĕre*, Gr. πλήγνυναι, πλήσσειν to strike.

OF. *plage* and *plague* were learned formations on L. *plaga*, the phonetic descendant of which was *plaie* wound.]

†**1.** A blow, a stroke; a wound. *Obs.*

1382 WYCLIF *Ezek.* xxiv. 16, Y take fro thee the desyrable thing of thin eyen in plage [*gloss* or wounde, Vulg. *in plaga*, 1611 with a stroke]. —— *Luke* xii. 47 Forsothe thilke seruaunt that knew the wille of his lord..schal be betun with many woundis [*v.r.* plagis, or woundis]. *c* **1400** *Lanfranc's Cirurg.* 31 Plage comounly is taken for an oold wounde. **1538** POLE in Strype *Eccl. Mem.* I. App. lxxxiii. 208 You say, I make many plagues, but lay little or no salve to heal them ..In very deed I make never a plage, when I discover those that be made already.

2. a. An affliction, calamity, evil, 'scourge'; *esp.* a visitation of divine anger or justice, a divine punishment; often with reference to 'the ten plagues' of Egypt.

1382 WYCLIF *Rev.* ix. 18 Of thes thre plagis the thridde paart of men is slayn, of fijr, and of smoke, and of brunston. *Ibid.* xvi. 21 Men blasfemeden God for the plage of hayl. **1432–50** tr. *Higden* (Rolls) II. 329 Egipte was smyten with x. plages and diseases. **1513** DOUGLAS *Æneis* XII. viii. 23 As the bub or plaig of fell tempest,..Drivis by fors throw the sey to the land. **1535** COVERDALE *Exod.* ix. 14 Let my people go,.. els wyll I at this tyme sende all my plages [WYCLIF veniaunces]..vpon thy people. **1540–54** CROKE *Ps.* (Percy Soc.) 43 From all plags safe thy house shalbe. **1548–9** (Mar.) *Bk. Com. Prayer*, *For fayre wether*, This plague of rayne and waters. **1600** HAMILTON in *Cath. Tractates* (S.T.S.) 245 God of his mercie remoue thir plagges from yow al. **1607** HIERON *Wks.* I. 452 Sometime the plague lighteth vpon him, which Dauid prayed for vpon his enemies. **1774** GOLDSM. *Nat. Hist.* (1776) VII. 346 The inhabitants turn what seems a plague to their own advantage. Locusts are eaten. **1847** GROTE *Greece* II. xiii. III. 238 A plague of gnats. **1855** MACAULAY *Hist. Eng.* xii. III. 216 The plague of the brass money.

b. In weakened sense: Anything causing trouble, annoyance, or vexation; a nuisance; *colloq.* trouble.

1604 E. G[RIMSTONE] *D'Acosta's Hist. Indies* v. xxv. 400 In the province of Chiquito, even at this day they meete with this plague of Confessors or *Ychuris*. **1754** RICHARDSON *Grandison* II. xvii. 181 She has her plagues in giving me plague. **1818** SCOTT *Hrt. Midl.* xxvi, Deil a brute or body about my house but I can manage when I like..; but I can seldom be at the plague. *c* **1825** *Houlston Juvenile Tracts* xviii. *Imag. Troubles* 9 She disliked stiles, she found it such a plague to get over them. **1852** MRS. STOWE *Uncle Tom's C.* ix, The plague of the thing is, nobody could drive a carriage there to-night but me. **1855** DELAMER *Kitch. Gard.* (1861) 92 Spinach is an annual, whose tendency to run to seed in dry weather makes it the plague of the gardener.

c. Applied to a person or animal (in serious, or in weakened sense: cf. b).

1551 ROBINSON tr. *More's Utop.* I. (1895) 53 That one couetous and vnsatiable cormaraunte and verye plage of his natyue contrey. **1560** DAUS tr. *Sleidane's Comm.* 77 Speakynge here..of the Cardinall of Yorke, he calleth hym the plage of Englande. **1697** DRYDEN *Virg. Georg.* III. 237 This flying Plague (to mark its quality); *Oestros* the Grecians call: *Asylus*, we. **1707** *Reflex. upon Ridicule* II. 369 What a Plague to Society is a Man who has written a Book. **1881** 'RITA' *My Lady Coquette* ii, Arthur, you plague, why don't you find something to do?

3. A general name for any malignant disease with which men or beasts are stricken.

†**a.** An individual affliction or disease. *Obs.*

In Bible translations used, after *plaga* of the Vulgate, for the 'infliction' of leprosy, and also in the 1611 version for the external diseased spots.

1382 WYCLIF *Lev.* xiii. 2 A man in whos skynne and flesh were sprongun dyuerse colour, or bleyne, other eny thing liȝtyng, that is to seie, a plaage of lepre, he shal be brouȝt forth to Aaron. **1460–70** *Bk. Quintessence* 24 þese plagis of pestilence þat ben vncurable. **1526** TINDALE *Mark* v. 29 She felt in her body that she was healed off the plage. **1611** BIBLE *Lev.* xiii. 3 The Priest shall looke on the plague in the skinne of the flesh: and when the haire in the plague is turned white, and the plague in sight be deeper then the skin of his flesh, it is a plague of leprosie. **1672** JOSSELYN *New Eng. Rarities* 3 That sad Disease called there the Plague of the Back, but with us *Empiema*.

b. *esp.* An infectious disease or epidemic attended with great mortality; a pestilence.

1548–9 [see 4]. **1552** *Bk. Com. Prayer* (Heading of prayer), In the tyme of any common plague or sickenesse. **1697** DRYDEN *Virg. Georg.* III. 722 From the vicious Air, and sickly Skies, A Plague did on the dumb Creation rise. **1738** WESLEY *Psalms* XCI. v, Nor to thy healthful Dwelling shall Any infectious Plague draw nigh. **1807** *Med. Jrnl.* XVII. 338 Instructions how to communicate and to treat this plague [small-pox]. **1866** [see CATTLE-PLAGUE]. **1871** NAPHEYS *Prev. & Cure Dis.* I. viii. 246 The famous 'plagues', which ravaged Europe, were forms of typhus fever. **1887** T. F. TOUT in *Dict. Nat. Biog.* IX. 414/1 The 'yellow plague' which was then [an. 664] devastating Northumbria.

c. *spec. the plague*: the oriental or bubonic plague. (Cf. PEST 1.) Also colloq. phr. *to avoid like* (or *as*) *the plague*, to avoid at all costs, to shun completely.

[**1564** *Reg. Privy Council Scot.* I. 279 The plaig of the pestilence maist vehementlie regnis in Danskin.] **1601** DOLMAN *La Primaud. Fr. Acad.* (1618) III. 802 Their sharpe iuice is very good against the plague. **1612** WOODALL *Surg. Mate* Wks. (1653) 323 The Plague is a disease venomous and contagious. **1665** PEPYS *Diary* 22 July, His servant died of a bubo on his right groine, and two spots on his right thigh, which is the plague. **1722** DE FOE *Plague* 1 It was about the beginning of September, 1664, that I.. heard..that the plague was returned again in Holland. **1799** *Med. Jrnl.* I. 411 No nation was ever long engaged in a war with the Turks without taking the plague. **1835** T. MOORE in Byron *Wks.* XV. 133 Saint Augustine..avoided the school as the plague. **1841** LANE *Arab. Nts.* I. 61 Some Muslims even shut themselves up during the prevalence of plague. **1876** BRISTOWE *The. & Pract. Med.* (1878) 190 Plague. (*Pestilentia.*)..A contagious fever, closely resembling typhus in its symptoms, but distinguished from it by the absence of any true rash, and by the development of buboes and carbuncles. **1936** 'N. BLAKE' *Thou Shell of Death* xv. 283 O'Brien was the sort of person you'd think would avoid road-houses like the plague. **1973** A. BROINOWSKI *Take One Ambassador* iv. 47, I avoid the place like the plague. **1979** 'E. PETERS' *One Corpse too Many* ii. 35, I will avoid him like the plague.

d. In imprecations: ***a plague take, plague on, upon, of***, may a pestilence or mischief take or light upon; also in exclamations of impatience: ***what the (a) plague, how the plague***. Cf. PEST 1 b, PESTILENCE 4, POX, etc.

a **1566** EDWARDS *Damon & Pythias* in Hazl. *Dodsley* IV. 102 A plague take Damon and Pithias! **1592** SHAKS. *Rom. & Jul.* III. i. 94, I am hurt. A plague a both the Houses. **1596** —— *1 Hen. IV*, II. ii. 39 What a plague meane ye to colt me thus? *a* **1704** T. BROWN *Sat. Fr. King* Wks. 1730 I. 59 Now, what the plague becomes of jure divino? **1713** SWIFT *Frenzy J. Dennis* Wks. 1755 III. I. 143 Plague on't. I am damnably afraid,..he is mad in earnest. **1768** GOLDSM. *Good-n. Man* IV. i, What the plague do you send me of your fool's errand for? **1870** tr. *Erckmann-Chatrian's Waterloo* 116 There he is come back worse than ever—plague on him.

4. *attrib.* and *Comb.* (chiefly from 3 c): **a.** Simple attributive, as ***plague bacillus, botch, contagion, corpuscle, death, den, germ, infection, nurse, patient, scare, time, virus, year***, etc.

1548–9 (Mar.) *Bk. Com. Prayer*, *Communion of Sick*, Specially in the plague tyme. **1585** T. WASHINGTON tr. *Nicholay's Voy.* II. viii. 41 That in the plague time no shippe ..do enter into their port. **1841** H. AINSWORTH *Old St. Paul's* II. 154 A closed litter,..evidently containing a plague-patient. **1881** TYNDALL *Floating Matter of Air* 12 Pasteur proved that the plague-corpuscles might be incipient in the egg. **1891** C. CREIGHTON *Hist. Epidemics* 500 The whole mortality was 452, of which by far the most were plague-burials. *Ibid.* 362 The years 1545 and 1546 were also plague-years in Scotland. **1898** *Westm. Gaz.* 28 Oct. 4/2 A plague officer,..while on plague duty, has been stoned to death at Hindupur. **1898** P. MANSON *Trop. Diseases* viii. 163 Kitasato has stated that the plague bacillus perishes in four days when dried on cover-glasses.

b. instrumental, objective, etc., as ***plague-beleaguered, -breeding, -free, -infected, -infested, -killed, -poisoning, -proof, -ridden, -smitten, -stricken, -stuffed***, etc. adjs.

1602 *2nd Pt. Return fr. Parnass.* IV. ii. 1699 A plague stuffed Cloake-bagge of all iniquitie. *a* **1649** DRUMM. OF HAWTH. *Poems* Wks. (1711) 34 Nor sword, nor famine, nor plague-poisoning air. **1722** DE FOE *Plague* (1756) 265 The People of London thought themselves so Plague-free now, that they were past all Admonitions. **1844** DICKENS *Mart. Chuz.* xxxiii, As in a plague-beleaguered town. **1864** *Atlantic Monthly* XIII. 279 Haply from the street To bear a wretch plague-stricken. **1884** *Pall Mall G.* 19 Sept. 4/1 A plague-proof variety has alone survived. **1897** *Review of Rev.* 5 The rinderpest..introduced..by plague-smitten cattle. **1898** P. MANSON *Trop. Diseases* viii. 151 He found in the soil forming the floor of plague-haunted houses..a bacterium. **1902** *Chambers's Jrnl.* Sept. 603/2 At last they all shunned Prussia as though it were plague-ridden. **1909** KIPLING *Rewards & Fairies* (1910) 258, I had spent the week past among our plague-stricken. **1933** W. DE LA MARE *Fleeting* 27 Bring morning to blossom again Out of plague-ridden night. **1938** M. K. RAWLINGS *Yearling* xxi. 267 Penny examined the plague-killed deer. **1950** T. S. ELIOT *Cocktail Party* III. 156 And just for a handful of plague-stricken natives who would have died anyway. **1951** WHITBY & HYNES *Med. Bacteriol.* (ed. 5) xviii. 303 Search for plague-infected rats is therefore an important part of public health work in ports and endemic areas. **1957** *Canad. Jrnl. Econ. & Polit. Sci.* XXIII. 3 In May, 1720, a ship coming from a plague-infested port in Syria brought the deadly disease to Marseilles.

c. Special combinations: **plague-bill**, an official return of the deaths caused by the plague in any district; **plague-cake**, an amulet worn as a protection against the plague; **plague-flea**, one of several fleas, esp. *Xenopsylla cheopsis*, which transmit the plague bacillus, *Pasteurella pestis*, from the rat to man; **plague-house**, a house marked as having inmates infected with the plague; **plague-mark** = PLAGUE-SPOT 1 (Webster 1864); **plague pipe**, a small clay pipe in which tobacco was smoked as a disinfectant during the great plague of 1665; **plague pit**, a deep pit for the common burial of plague victims; **plague-rat**, a rat carrying plague; **plague saint**, a saint especially invoked by those afflicted with the plague; †**plague-stripe** = PLAGUE-SPOT 1; †**plague-water**, an infusion of various herbs and roots in spirits of wine, of supposed efficacy against the plague. See also PLAGUE-SORE, PLAGUE-SPOT.

1891 C. CREIGHTON *Hist. Epidemics* 295 There are two other *plague-bills extant, for August 1535. **1604** F. HERING *Mod. Defence* B iv, Empoisoned Amulets, or *Plague-cakes. **1908** *Westm. Gaz.* 11 Jan. 2/1 Is it generally known that the *plague-flea lives on the small brown rat? **1936** *Discovery* Feb. 41/1 The plague flea.. still persists at most of our ports on the black or ship-rat. **1665** PEPYS *Diary* 28 June, I observed several *plague houses in King's Street. **1892** *Daily News* 30 May 3/1 The small '*plague', or 'elfin' pipes, as they are variously called, of the time of the Restoration. **1901** *Westm. Gaz.* 22 May 8/2 Some 'Plague pipes', so called owing to their being smoked at the time of the great Plague of London, were excavated at Hackney yesterday. **1841** H. AINSWORTH *Old St. Paul's* I. 300 In Finsbury fields ..*plague-pits had been digged and pest-houses erected. **1902** *Encycl. Brit.* XXXI. 791/1 *Plague-rats have rarely been found in ships sailing from infected ports. **1978** R. WESTALL *Devil on Road* xv. 116 It's the Plague Rat—the rat that caused the Great Plague of London in 1665. **1898** *Daily News* 1 June 3/6 Venice is.. saved by the intercession of her patron, St. Mark, her local *plague-saints, Sebastian and Rocco. **1713** SPREGNELL in *Phil. Trans.* XXVIII. 124 *Vibices*, or *Plague-Stripes, were infallible Signs of Death. **1665** PEPYS *Diary* 20 July, My Lady Carteret did this day give me a bottle of *plague-water home with me. **1727–41** CHAMBERS *Cycl.* s.v. *Water*, Plague-Water, *Aqua epidemica*, is prepared from the roots of masterwort, angelica, pyony, and butter-bur; viper-grass, Virginia-snakeroot, rue, rosemary, baum, [etc.]; the whole is infused in spirit of wine, and distilled.

plague (pleɪg), *v.* [f. PLAGUE *sb.* Cf. late L. *plāgāre* to strike, wound. So Ger., Du. *plagen.* (Caxton's spelling *plaghe* was from MDu. *plaghen.*]

1. *trans.* To afflict with plague or calamity (esp. in reference to divine punishment); to torment, harass. Perh. sometimes, like L. *plāgāre*, to strike (quots. 1538, 1545). Now *rare* or *arch.*

1481 CAXTON *Reynard* xxviii. (Arb.) 70, I shold do grete synne.. I am aferde god sholde plaghe me [*orig.* Ick hebbe anxt god die soude mi plaghen]. **1535** COVERDALE *Jer.* xv. 4, I will scatre them aboute also in all kingdomes and londes to be plaged. **1538** BALE *Brefe Com.* in *Harl. Misc.* (Malh.) I. 212 Though he to thys daye hath plaged man with the rod. **1545** *Primer Hen. VIII* in *Three Primers* (1848) 501, I am all to plaged and beaten. **1567** *Reg. Privy Council Scot.* I. 571 The cornis of this instant yeir.. being at Goddis plesour plagit and spilt with weit. **1630** *R. Johnson's Kingd. & Commw.* 539 This Countrey.. plagued with three bad neighbours, viz. the Turkes, the Tartars, and the Cassoks. **1667** MILTON *P.L.* VI. 505 Some one.. inspir'd With dev'lish machination might devise Like instrument to plague the Sons of men For sin. **1787** BENTHAM *Def. Usury* x. 98 Christians were too intent on plaguing Jews. **1862** GOULBURN *Pers. Relig.* ii. (1873) 15 A Constitution plagued with sickness.

2. In weakened sense (chiefly *colloq.*). **a.** To 'torment', trouble, vex, tease, bother, annoy.

1594 SPENSER *Amoretti* xli, If her nature and her wil be so That she will plague the man that loves her most. **1637** BASTWICK *Litany* I. 21, I will.. so plauge the Metropolicallity of Yorke and Canterbury. **1658** A. FOX tr. *Würtz' Surg.* II. xii. 94 Patients in this case are commonly plagued with a cough. **1727** GAY *Begg. Op.* I. viii, Husbands and wives.. plaguing one another. **1767** *Woman of Fashion* II. 171 What a dickens would you have more!.. I won't hear you, I won't be plagued. **1833** HT. MARTINEAU *Tale of Tyne* ii. 33 The big boys used to plague him, and he plagued the little ones. **1852** MRS. STOWE *Uncle Tom's C.* xxv. 237, I cannot be plagued with this child any longer! It's past all bearing.

b. Phr. *to plague the life out of* and varr., to tease or torment excessively.

1834 A. MARSH *Two Old Men's Tales* II. 46 You are so odd that you would plague the life out of a woman that loved you. **1868** L. M. ALCOTT *Little Women* I. xiii. 213 'If ever I do get my wish, you see what I'll do for Brooke.' 'Begin to do something now, by not plaguing his life out,' said Meg, sharply. **1894** V. HUNT *Maiden's Progress* iii. 17 Moderna.. plagues the other children's lives out with making them give her her cues, at all times and seasons.

3. To infect with plague or pestilent disease. *rare.*

c **1586** C'TESS PEMBROKE *Ps.* XCI. ii, The noisome blast that plaguing straies Untoucht shall passe thee by. **1633**, **1894** [see PLAGUED below].

Hence **plagued** (pleɪgd) *ppl. a.*, afflicted, tormented; infected with plague (in quot. 1728 'confounded', 'cursed'; 'plaguy'; so *plegged* in *U.S. dial.*, quot. 1887); **'plaguing** *vbl. sb.* and *ppl. a.*

1575 CHURCHYARD *Chippes* (1817) 180 Make place for plaints, giue rowme for plagued men. **1581** DERRICKE *Image Irel.* II. E iv. *marg.*, The ioye of rebbelles is in plagyng of true men. **1591** SHAKS. *1 Hen. VI*, v. iii. 39 A plaguing mischeefe light on Charles, and thee. **1633** in Rushw. *Hist. Coll.* (1680) II. 240, I will not set him at liberty no more than a plagued Man or a mad Dog. **1728** P. WALKER *Life Peden* Pref. (1827) 26 Following the wicked.. Example of their old plagued Resolution-Fathers. **1887** J. C. HARRIS *Free Joe*, etc. (1888) 113 That pleggèd old cat's a-tryin' to drink out'n the water-bucket. *Ibid.* 172 Where a man can't afford to be too plegged particular. **1894** *Outing* (U.S.) July 320/2 My.. friends set out for Dover and the cholera-plagued Continent.

plague, var. of PLAGE *Obs.*, PLAYOCK *Sc.*

plagueful ('pleɪgfʊl), *a. rare.* [See -FUL.] Full of or fraught with plague; pestilent.

1591 SYLVESTER *Du Bartas* I. v. 247 A plague-full humour, a fell banefull breath.. Pours forth her poyson. **1610** *Mirr. Mag., John* xxix, Plaguefull meteors did.. appeare.

plagueless ('pleɪglɪs), *a.* [See -LESS.] Free from plagues or the plague.

1847 in WEBSTER: and in later Dicts.

plaguer ('pleɪgə(r)). *rare.* [f. PLAGUE *v.* + -ER[1].] One who plagues or harasses.

1661 BROME *Catch* Poems 113 This is our time to be jolly; Our plagues and our plaguers are both fled away. **1760** MAIR *Tyro's Dict.* (1820) 392 *Vexator*,.. an harassar, a plaguer. [In modern Dicts.]

'plagueship. *nonce-wd.* [See -SHIP.] Humorous title for a troublesome person: cf. PLAGUE *sb.* 2 c.

1628 WITHER *Brit. Rememb.* I. 364 And grant her Plagueship never settle here.

plaguesome ('pleɪgsəm), *a.* Chiefly *colloq.* [f. PLAGUE *v.* or *sb.* + -SOME.] That tends to plague or trouble; troublesome, vexatious, plaguy.

1828 BENTHAM *Mem. & Corr.* Wks. 1843 X. 583 These recollections are always plaguesome. **1865** G. MACDONALD *A. Forbes* 5 Ye plaguesome brat! **1880** BLACKMORE *M. Anerley* xl, That plaguesome deed of appointment.

Hence **'plaguesomeness.**

1859 W. ANDERSON *Disc.* (1860) 150 Importuning even to plaguesomeness the cooperation of his brethren.

'plague-sore. A sore caused by the plague. Also *fig.*

1589 RIDER *Bibl. Schol.* 1099 Plague soares, *carbunculantia vlcera.* **1605** SHAKS. *Lear* II. iv. 227 Thou art a Byle, A plague sore, or imbossed Carbuncle In my corrupted blood. **1629** H. BURTON *Truth's Triumph* 358 Apply the lumpe of dry figgs to the plague-sore. **1692** WASHINGTON tr. *Milton's Def. Pop.* ix. M.'s Wks. 1851 VIII. 211 Being a public Enemy, and a Plague-sore to the common Liberty of Mankind. **1895** *Syd. Soc. Lex.*, *Plague sore*, an ulcer resulting from a bubo occurring in the Plague.

'plague-spot.

1. A spot on the skin characteristic of the plague, or of some disease so called. Also *fig.*

1711 SHAFTESB. *Charac.* (1737) II. 21 We do not.. say of any-one, that he is an ill man, because he has the plague-spots upon him. **1817** COLERIDGE *Biog. Lit.* 37 It is.. unjust to fix the attention on a few separate.. poems with as much aversion as if they had been so many plague-spots on the whole work. **1857–8** SEARS *Athan.* xvii. 147 The plague-spot of sin and imperfection.

2. A spot or locality infected with plague.

[**1861** FLO. NIGHTINGALE *Nursing* 22 [This] will enable the finger to be laid at once on the plague spots of the parish.] **1895** *Syd. Soc. Lex.*, *Plague spot*,.. a locality in which any Plague, in the general sense, is rife.

So **'plague-,spotted** *a.*, marked with plague-spots.

1897 MRS. E. L. VOYNICH *Gadfly* (1904) 147/1 What is the worth of your plague-spotted souls, that such a price should be paid for them?

plaguily ('pleɪgɪlɪ), *adv.* [f. next + -LY[2].] In a plaguy manner; *colloq.* vexatiously, 'pestilently', confoundedly, exceedingly.

a **1586** SIDNEY *Arcadia* III. (1622) 265 Assure thy selfe, most wicked woman (that hast so plaguyly a corrupted minde, as thou canst not keepe thy sicknesse to thy selfe, but must most wickedly infect others). **1620** MIDDLETON *Chaste Maid* I. i. 112 The knave bites plaguily! **1711** SWIFT *Jrnl. Stella* 3 Oct., He was plaguily afraid. **1794** CHARLOTTE SMITH *Wand. Warwick* 82 You loved and respected poor Tracy plaguily, to be sure, when you stole his wench from him. **1828** LANDOR *Imag. Conv.* Wks. 1846 I. 268 Ronsard is so plaguily stiff and stately.

plaguy ('pleɪgɪ), *a.* (*adv.*) Also 6 plagy, -ie, 6–7 -uie, 7–9 -uey. [f. PLAGUE *sb.* + -Y.]

1. Of the nature of or pertaining to a or the plague; pestiferous, pestilential, pernicious. Also *fig.* Now *rare* or *arch.*

1574 tr. *Marlorat's Apocalips* 116 Nothing.. can be imagined more plagie and more deadly, than the doctrine of the Schoole diuines concerning.. vncertentie of saluation. **1763** MACKENZIE in *Phil. Trans.* LIV. 75 He had many plaguy symptoms, as buboes, carbuncles, &c. **1888** BESANT *Eulogy R. Jefferies* 2 Thou shalt be afflicted with grievous plaguy diseases.

b. Infected or afflicted with the plague; plague-stricken. Now *rare* or *Obs.*

1604 T. WRIGHT *Passions* IV. ii. §7. 139 Many physitians will scarce aduenture to deale with plaguie patients. **1613** JACKSON *Creed* II. vii. §4 To make no question whether he should meete his friend in a plaguie house. **1686** GOAD *Celest. Bodies* III. i. 389 New Diseases.. which have broke out.. into this Plaguy Age. **1766** *Nat. Hist.* in *Ann. Reg.* 101/1, I never was afraid to go into any large house, wherein a plaguy person lived, provided that he was confined to one room.

2. That is a plague; that causes severe affliction.

1598 Q. ELIZ. *Boeth.*, etc. 122 If plagy wilz ther be that noyful ar. **1663** BUTLER *Hud.* I. iii. 3 What plaguy Mischiefs and Mishaps Do dog him still. **1727** GAY *Begg. Op.* II. iv, They make charming mistresses but plaguy wives. **1827** SCOTT *Jrnl.* 16 Jan., I felt no increase of my plaguey malady [rheumatism]. **1868** GLADSTONE *Juv. Mundi* xiii. (1870) 483 Nine days of bad or plaguy winds [*olooi anemoi*] bring him to the land of the Lotos-Eaters.

b. In weakened sense: That 'plagues', troubles, or annoys one; vexatious, troublesome, annoying, disagreeable; hence *colloq.* as an expression of dislike or impatience, sinking into an (impatient or ill-natured) intensive: = 'pestilent', 'confounded', excessive, exceeding, very great.

1615 ROWLANDS *Melanc. Knt.* 34 The Dragon had a plaguy hide, And could the sharpest steele abide. **1694** MOTTEUX *Rabelais* IV. lxiv. 254 Women that have a plaguy deal of Religion. **1775** SHERIDAN *Duenna* III. vi, A plaguy while coming. **1806** in *Spirit Pub. Jrnls.* X. 217 I'd a plaguey deal rather be a butcher than a calf! **1855** HALIBURTON *Nat. & Hum. Nat.* I. 209, I like it a plaguy sight better than hot rooms. **1879** *Punch* 17 May 222 That will mean a plaguy rise in the price of everything.

B. as *adv.* = PLAGUILY. Usually indicating a degree of some quality that troubles one by its excess; but sometimes humorous, or merely forcibly intensive. *colloq.*

1584 R. W. *Three Ladies Lond.* in Hazl. *Dodsley* VI. 298 If we can speak fair and 'semble, we shall be plaguy rich. **1606** SHAKS. *Tr. & Cr.* II. iii. 187 He is so plaguy proud. **1623** FLETCHER *Rule a Wife* I. ii, She walked plaguy fast. **1697** I. D. in Tutchin *Search Honesty* A ij, To Seek a Thing, so Plaguy hard to Find. **1741** RICHARDSON *Pamela* (1824) I. xxiv. 276 I'm a plaguy good-humoured old fellow. **1840** DICKENS *Barn. Rudge* xxxv, There.. were.. some plaguy ill-looking characters among them. **1884** PAE *Eustace* 88 You've been a plaguy long time in coming.

plai, obs. form of PLAY.

plaice (pleɪs). Forms: 3–5 plais, 4–5 plays, 4–7 playce, 5 playsce, playsse, 5–7 playse, place, 6 pleise, *Sc.* plase, 6–9 plaise, 4, 6– plaice. [ME. *plais*, *plaice*, a. OF. *plaïz* (12th c.), *plaïs*, *pla(i)is*, early mod.F. *plaïse*, *pleïsse*, *pladisse*:—late L. *platessa* (*a* 390 Auson.), ? f. Gr. πλατύς broad, or root *plat-* flat (see PLATE).]

1. A well-known European flat-fish, *Pleuronectes platessa*, much used as food; in America extended to various allied species of this genus or of the family *Pleuronectidæ*. (Pl. now rare; the collective sing. *plaice* being used instead.)

1280 *Litt. Red Bk. Bristol* (1900) I. 90 Debent.. dari.. de quolibet batello.. portante plais octo plais. *c* **1300** *Havelok* 896 He bar up wel a carte lode.. of playces brode, Of grete laumprees, and of eles. **1307–8** *Durham Acc. Rolls* (Surtees) 3 In albo pisce, plaices, et sperlinges. **1392–3** *Earl Derby's Exp.* (Camden) 214 Item pro ffowndres et plays, iij duc. *c* **1440** *Anc. Cookery* in *Househ. Ord.* (1790) 437 Of playsse or of codlynge, or of eles, or of pykes, or of soles, or tenches. **1580** HOLLYBAND *Treas. Fr. Tong*, *Vne Plie*, a fishe called a Place. **1617** *Janna Ling.* 100 Aswell soles as plaises are inclosed in the net. **1661** J. CHILDREY *Brit. Baconica* 18 Soale and Playce.. follow the tide into the fresh rivers. **1762** *Chron.* in *Ann. Reg.* 148 The several species of fish brought .. 1988 Plaise and Dabs. **1802** BINGLEY *Anim. Biog.* (1813) III. 33 The Plaise and the Flounder.. are each found in great abundance in most of the European seas. **1841–71** T. R. JONES *Anim. Kingd.* (ed. 4) 682 The appearance of these fishes is deceptive, and few imagine that, in applying the term back and belly to the upper and under surfaces of a Plaice or a Turbot, they are adopting a phraseology quite inadmissible in an anatomical point of view.

2. *dial.* = FLUKE *sb.*[1] 2; also *plaice-worm.*

a **1722** LISLE *Observ. Husb.* (1757) 337 These cored sheep have the fluck, or plaice-worm in their livers. **1732** W. ELLIS *Pract. Farmer* (1759) 137 A rotten Sheep, he says, he has several Times, seen die with Plaises in his Liver and Head. **1896** *Daily News* 26 May 6/4 Flukes or plaice, as they are indifferently called, from the resemblance they bear, are found in the biliary ducts, caused by the sheep being placed on wet fresh-water submerged meadows.

3. *attrib.* and *Comb.*, as *plaice-fry*; *plaice-like* adj.; †**plaice-fluke**, ? = sense 1; **plaice-mouth**, a small puckered or wry mouth; also *attrib.*; so **plaice-mouthed** *a.*; **plaice-worm** (see sense 2).

1596 DALRYMPLE tr. *Leslie's Hist. Scot.* I. 41 Turbat, ffluik, and *plase fluik. **1905** *Westm. Gaz.* 17 Aug. 10/2 At the Marine Hatchery, Aberdeen.. The number of *plaice-fry that hatched out.. was approximately 34,780,000, or 88 per cent. **1900** J. HUTCHINSON in *Arch. Surg.* XI. No. 41. 94 Her hands and feet were of a deep dusky-red colour with large *plaice-like spots of lighter tint. **1609** B. JONSON *Sil. Wom.* III. iv, Did you thinke you had married.. some innocent.. that would stand with her hands thus, and a *playse mouth, and looke vpon you? **1602** DEKKER

Satiromastix Plays 1873 I. 257 My place-mouth yelpers. **1595** LODGE *Fig for Momus* Sat. i, His *plaise-mouth'd wife.

plaid (pleɪd, plæd). Also 6 **plyd, playde, pladde,** 6–8 **plad,** 7 **pleid,** 8 **plaide, (pladd),** 8 (*dial.* 9) **plod.** [The same word as Gael. *plaide*, Ir. *ploid* blanket; ulterior etymology uncertain.

The quots. clearly bespeak a Scottish origin, and even in the 16th c. associate the *plaid* with the Highlands; but the want of early evidence for the word in Celtic leaves it doubtful whether the name originated in Gaelic or Lowland Sc. Gaelic etymologists suggest derivation from *peall* sheep-skin, ad. L. *pell-is*, but this is phonetically improbable. The Sc. spelling *plaid* is now usual, although the word is very generally pronounced *plad* in England.]

1. A long piece of twilled woollen cloth, usually having a chequered or tartan pattern, forming the outer article of the Highland costume, and formerly worn in all parts of Scotland and the north of England, in cold or stormy weather, instead of a cloak or mantle. The Lowland 'shepherd's plaid', of a black chequer pattern on white, is commonly called a MAUD.

1512 *Acc. Ld. High Treas. Scot.* IV. 203 Item, the vj day of Maij, in Air, for ane plaid to be the King ane coit. **1538** *Ibid.* VI. 443 For xxv. elnes bertane canwes to be pladis to the quenis hors. **1558** *Aberdeen Regr.* (1844) I. 309 For the wrangous reiffing and away taking fra hir of ane plyd, ane pettioitt, twa curclus, ane collar [etc.]. **1563** RANDOLPH *Let. to Cecil* 13 June in *Calr. Sc. Pap.* II. 13 A safferon shyrte or a Hylande pladde. **1578** *Reg. Privy Council Scot.* III. 89 A plaid or blankat to keip the saidis bairnis fra cauld. **1606** SYLVESTER *Du Bartas* II. iv. ii. *Trophies* 1050 And I my Self with my pyde Pleid a-slope. **1638** SIR T. HERBERT *Trav.* (ed. 2) 325 They [inhabitants of Java] gird them with a parti-coloured plad or mantle. **1643** in Row *Hist. Kirk* (Wodrow Soc.) p. xxiii, I dischargit wemen to cover thair headis withe thair plaidis in tyme cuming in the kirk. **1662** EVELYN *Diary* 3 Oct., Painted..as..a Scotch highlander in his plaid. **1725** DE FOE *Voy. round World* (1840) 267 A mantle..thrown about him like a Scotsman's plaid. **1771** PENNANT *Tour Scotl. in* 1769, 162 Their *brechan*, or plaid, consists of twelve or thirteen yards of a narrow stuff, wrapt round the middle, and reaches to the knees. **1774** COLLYER *Hist. Eng.* I. 20 The tartan plads of Scotland. **1807** BYRON *Lachin y Gair* ii, My cap was the bonnet, my coak was the plaid [*rime* glade]. *Note.* This word is erroneously pronounced *plad*: the proper pronunciation (according to the Scotch) is shown by the orthography. **1874** PRINCESS ALICE in *Mem.* (1884) 325 Will you tell her, the plaid she made me still goes everywhere with me.

2. The woollen cloth of which plaids are made; later, applied to other fabrics with a tartan pattern.

1634 SIR T. HERBERT *Trav.* 146 They weare a smocke couloured like our Scottish plad. *Ibid.* 187 About their middles, they have a cloth of particoloured plad, like that with us in England. **1724** DE FOE *Mem. Cavalier* II. 156 Their [the Highlanders'] Doublet, Breeches and Stockings, of a Stuff they called Plaid, striped a-cross red and yellow. **1783** W. F. MARTYN *Geog. Mag.* II. 413 Their waistcoats are also made of plaid. **1893** GEORGIANA HILL *Hist. Eng. Dress* II. 267 Plaids..were made in large and small checks, in woollen cloth, in Irish poplin.

3. A plaid or tartan pattern; a pattern of bars or stripes crossing each other at right angles. *rare.*

1890 in *Cent. Dict.*

4. *transf.* A man wearing a plaid; a Highlander.

1814 SCOTT *Wav.* lxii, He was hanged at Stirling..with his lieutenant, and four plaids besides. *Ibid.* lx.

5. *attrib.* and *Comb.*, as ***plaid cloak, -fold, shawl, trousers; plaid-patterned, -wrapped*** adjs.; **plaid bed**, a bed draped with plaid or tartan (fashionable in England early in 18th c.); **plaidman**, a Highlander; **plaid-nook (-neuk)** *Sc.*, one end of the folded plaid sewn up so as to form a large pouch or pocket.

*c***1710** CELIA FIENNES *Diary* (1888) 297 A *pladd bed Lined wth Indian Callicoe. **1837** W. IRVING *Capt. Bonneville* (1849) 275 In a few moments, his *plaid cloak was cut into numerous strips. **1814** SCOTT *Ld. of Isles* v. xviii, Do not my *plaid-folds hold thee warm? **1814** —— *Wav.* lx, O!..I thought it was Ned Williams, and it is one of the *plaidmen. *a***1600** in *Montgomerie's Poems* (S.T.S.) 281/18 'Humff!' quod the Helandman, and turned him abowt, And at his *plaid nuk the guly fell owt. **1886** STEVENSON *Kidnapped* i. 6 A little Bible, to carry in a plaid-neuk. **1875** W. S. HAYWARD *Love agst. World* 54 Get me my *plaid shawl and a plain dark bonnet. **1837** DICKENS *Pickw.* xxx, He wore a pair of *plaid trousers, and a large rough double-breasted waistcoat. **1897** CROCKETT *Lad's Love* xxiii, For all that the *plaid-wrapped girl knew or cared.

plaid, ME. f. PLEA; obs. pa. t. and pple. of PLAY.

Plaid Cymru (ˌplaɪd ˈkʌmriː). Also earlier **Plaid Genedlaethol Cymru** 'the national party of Wales'. [W., = party of Wales.] The name of the Welsh Nationalist Party, founded in 1925 and dedicated to seeking autonomy for Wales. Also *ellipt.* as **Plaid**, and *attrib.*

[**1938** W. H. JONES *Challenge to Wales* 48 *Y Brython*.. suggests the need for an amalgamation between *Yr Urdd, Undeb yr Athrawon Cymreig, Y Blaid Genedlaethol, ac Undeb y Cymdeithasau Cymraeg.*] **1943** E. L. CHAPPELL *Wake up, Wales!* ix. 89 The Welsh Nationalist Party (*Plaid Genedlaethol Cymru*)..is carrying on with relentless vigour propaganda on behalf of an advanced type of Nationalism. *Ibid.* 91, I disagree with the basic assumptions of *Plaid* propaganda. **1950** G. EVANS in A. W. Wade-Evans et al. *Hist. Basis of Welsh Nationalism* 147 Early in 1925, it formed itself into a political Party under the name 'The Welsh National Party'... In our generation..it is the youth of Plaid Cymru who are making the pace. **1958** *Spectator* 15 Aug. 225/3 The pacific Christian leadership of the Plaid. **1966** *Guardian* 16 July 8/3 What Mr Gwynfor Evans, the new Plaid Cymru M.P., wants for Wales is the status of an independent member of the Commonwealth. *Ibid.* 8/6 He [*sc.* Gwynfor Evans] has sought it the dogged, responsible way, frowning on the Plaid's dynamite fringe. **1968** *Ibid.* 6 July 2/8 Notice on the wall of Plaid headquarters in Caerphilly: 'To wear a clean shirt and tie is not to be bourgeois. Look tidy'. **1973** *Ibid.* 12 Apr. 13/8 The Welsh Nationalist Party, Plaid Cymru..supports those who object to the sale of country cottages to holidaymakers. **1975** *Observer* 31 Aug. 17/3 Plaid members spoke to me rather of 'neglect'... And so, here in the councils, Plaid Cymru is making ground. **1976** *Carn* Feb. 9/1 This unwarranted delay in fulfilling one of the main election promises of the Labour Party to the Welsh electorate at the last election drew strong protests from Plaid Cymru.

plaided (ˈpleɪdɪd, ˈplædɪd), *a.* [f. PLAID + -ED².]

1. Dressed in or wearing a plaid.

1802 CAMPBELL *Lochiel's Warning* 51 Her bonneted chieftains..All plaided and plumed in their tartan array. **1821** SCOTT *Pirate* iv, His neighbourhood to the Grampians exposed him..to that species of visitation from the plaided gentry, who dwelt within their skirts. **1855** MACAULAY *Hist. Eng.* xiii. III. 331 He..rode on horseback before his four hundred plaided clansmen.

2. Made of plaid; having a plaid pattern.

1814 WORDSW. *Excursion* II. 177 They marched In plaided vest. **1858** O. W. HOLMES *Aut. Breakf.-t.* (1883) 65 The Scotch-plaided snuff-box. **1902** *Daily Chron.* 24 May 8/3 A plaided batiste frock.

plaidie, -y (ˈpleɪdɪ, ˈplædɪ). *Sc.* Also **pladdy, plaiddie.** [f. PLAID + -IE.] A small plaid; also, a childish, sentimental, or poetic name for a plaid.

1719 D'URFEY *Pills* II. 159 His Highland pladdy. **1728** RAMSAY *Tea-t. Misc., Highland Laddie* ii, With bonnet blew, and belted plaidy [*rime* lady]. **1796** BURNS *'Oh, wert thou in the cauld blast'* i, My plaidie to the angry airt, I'd shelter thee. **1863** *Mortons of Bardon* III. 242 Stay a moment, little girl,..let me wrap my plaiddie round you; it is cold.

plaiding (ˈpleɪdɪŋ, ˈplædɪŋ). Also 6–8 **plading,** 7 **pladding;** *Sc.* 7 **plodan,** 7–8 **plaidine,** 8 **plodden,** 8–9 **plaiden,** 9 **pladden.** [f. PLAID + -ING¹: cf. *shirting*, etc.]

1. Material for plaids; a twilled woollen cloth; a cloth of a tartan pattern.

1566 in Hay Fleming *Mary Q. of Scots* (1897) 499 Sax elnis of plaiding to lyne the cuvering [of a bed] with. **1617** MORYSON *Itin.* III. 180 The women of the Countrey did weare cloakes made of course stuffe, of two or three colours in Checker worke, vulgarly called *Plodan*. **1640** *Dunfermline Kirk-sess. Rec.* (1865) 8 Yr webb of plaidine of 20 ell. **1656** TUCKER *Rep.* in *Misc. Sc. Burgh Rec. Soc.* 23 There hath..beene..salmon, pladding, and corne, usually sent forth. **1670** NARBOROUGH in *Acc. Sev. Late Voy.* I. (1694) 65 This they wrap about their Bodies, as a Scottish Man doth his Plading. **1719–20** *Act 6 Geo. I*, c. 13 *heading*, Frauds..in manufacturing Serges, Pladings, and Fingrums. **1806** *Gazetteer Scotl.* (ed. 2) 177 Coarse cloth of two or three colours, in checker-work, vulgarly called pladden.

attrib. **1643** in Maidment *Spottiswoode Misc.* (1845) II. 66 A white plaidine wastecoat. **1725** RAMSAY *Gentle Sheph.* II. iii, Change thy plaiding-coat for silk. **1753** *Stewart's Trial* App. 135 He had got the plaiden trowsers, then wore by him, from the declarant's father, or brother Allan.

2. A plaid or checkered pattern.

1889 *Harper's Mag.* XVIII. 844/1, I could discern a partiality for..plaidings of blue and violet.

‖**plaidoyer** (plɛdwaje). *Law. rare.* [F. *plaidoyer* a pleading, sb. use of vb. inf. to plead, f. *plaid* PLEA.] An advocate's speech; a pleading, plea.

1796 BURKE *Regic. Peace* ii. Wks. VIII. 256 The profit of copying musick, or writing plaidoyers by the sheet. **1880** MCCARTHY *Own Times* IV. lx. 346 It was an eloquent, patriotic, and impassioned *plaidoyer*. **1883** *Spectator* 8 Sept. 1155/2 His work is a monograph and a history, a *plaidoyer* and a judgment.

†**plaie.** *Obs. rare.* In 6 **playe.** [a. F. *plaie*:—L. *plāga* wound: see PLAGUE *sb.*] A wound.

*a***1547** SURREY *Æneid* IV. 2 But now the wounded Quene, with heuy care, Throughout the veines she norisheth the playe, Surprised with blind flame.

plaie, obs. form of PLAY.

plaig, plaik, var. ff. PLAYOCK *Sc.*, plaything, toy.

plaight, obs. form of PLAIT *sb.* and *v.*

plain (pleɪn), *sb.*¹ Forms: see PLAIN *a.*¹ [a. OF. *plain*:—L. *plān-um* a plain, prop. neut. of *plān-us* PLAIN *a.*¹]

1. a. A tract of country of which the general surface is comparatively flat; an extent of level ground or flat meadow land; applied *spec.* (in proper or quasi-proper names) to certain extensive tracts of this character; e.g. Salisbury Plain, the Great Plain of England, etc. In *pl.* spec. the river valleys of N. India. Also *fig.*

Cities of the Plain (sc. *of the Jordan*), Sodom, Gomorrah, etc., before their destruction.

1297 R. GLOUC. (Rolls) 155 Vpon þe plein of salesbury þat oþer wonder is þat ston heng is icluped. *a***1300** *Cursor M.* 2831 Ne mak ȝee in þe plain na duell, Till ȝee be comme in to þe fell. *c***1330** R. BRUNNE *Chron. Wace* (Rolls) 10831 þe bataille scholde be in a pleyne Bytwyxt two watres. **1375** BARBOUR *Bruce* VII. 613 Thai in full gret hy agane Out of the woud ran to the plane. *c***1489** CAXTON *Blanchardyn* vii. 32 He sawe there vnder in a playn a moche ample and a grete medowe. **1530** PALSGR. 255/1 Playne, a grounde that is without hylles, *planier, playne*. **1596** DALRYMPLE tr. *Leslie's Hist. Scot.* I. 7 Heir agane sall ȝe se braid planes. **1600** J. PORY tr. *Leo's Africa* v. 256 The citie of Cairasan standeth vpon a sandie and desert plaine. **1611** BIBLE *Gen.* xiii. 12 Lot dwelled in the cities of the plaine, and pitched his tent toward Sodome. **1653** WALTON *Angler* i. 36 The plains extended level with the ground. **1769** GRAY *Installation Ode* 51 On Granta's fruitful plain. **1840** *Penny Cycl.* XVIII. 207/2 The plains of America are generally characterised by their gramineous covering or their vast forests. **1882** GEIKIE *Text Bk. Geol.* III. II. ii. §7. 451 A 'plain of marine denudation' is that sea-level to which a mass of land has been reduced mainly by the subaerial forces. **1886** KIPLING *Departmental Ditties* (ed. 2) 27 Will you stay in the Plains till September? **1924** E. M. FORSTER *Passage to India* xiv. 135 'I won't be bottled up,' announced the girl. 'I've no patience with these women here who leave their husbands grilling in the plains.' *Ibid.*, It is the children who are the first consideration. Until they are grown up, and married off. When that happens one has again the right to live for oneself—in the plains or the hills, as suits. **1975** R. P. JHABVALA *Heat & Dust* 33 They began to discuss their Simla plans again... Which servants..to leave behind to look after the poor old Sahibs who had to stay and sweat it out in the plains.

b. Chiefly *pl.* In Colonial and U.S. use applied to level treeless tracts of country; prairie.

1779 G. R. CLARK *Campaign in Illinois* (1869) 29 We came into those level Plains that is frequent throughout this extensive Country. **1820** J. OXLEY *Jrnls. Exp. Australia* 83 Free from timber or brush in various places;..these tracts have hitherto received the particular denomination of plains. **1824** E. CURR *Van Diemen's Land* 55 The district called Macquarie Plains,..the plains bear a strong resemblance to what are called sheep downs in England. **1875** TEMPLE & SHELDON *Hist. Northfield, Mass.* 19 Plains ..[applied] by the early settlers..to certain well defined tracts that had some common peculiarity of soil and condition, were nearly free from trees, and could be readily cultivated. **1889** C. LUMHOLTZ *Among Cannibals* v. 73 This bird [the cassowary]..does not..frequent the open plains, but the thick brushwood.

c. *transf.* The level expanse of sea or sky.

1567 DRANT *Horace, Epist.* xviii. F vj, Then whilst thy ship doth kepe aflote ydauncing on the plaine. **1728** POPE *Dunc.* III. 342 The sick'ning stars fade off th'æthereal plain. **1853** KANE *Grinnell Exp.* xxii. (1856) 176 On the east we have the drift plain of Wellington Channel, impacted with floes, hummocks, and broken bergs.

2. An open space as the scene of battle or contest; the field. ***to take the plain***: to take the field: see FIELD *sb.* 7. Now *poetic.*

1375 BARBOUR *Bruce* XII. 349 Thomas randall tuk the playne With few folk. **1390** GOWER *Conf.* III. 358 As he, which was a Capitein, Tofore alle othre upon the plein. **1513** DOUGLAS *Æneis* X. x. 146 Quhil fynaly Ascanyus the ȝyng page, And the remanent of Troiane barnage,..Thayr strenth hes left, and takyn hes the plane. **1594** SHAKS. *Rich. III*, v. iii. 291, I will leade forth my Soldiers to the plaine. **1808** SCOTT *Marmion* VI. xxix. 7 Last of my race, On battle-plain That shout shall ne'er be heard again!

3. An open space in the midst of houses. *local.*

1847–78 HALLIWELL, *Plain*, an open space surrounded by houses nearly answering to the Italian Piazza. In the city of Norwich there are several: as St. Mary's Plain, the Theatre Plain, &c. **18..** *Oxf. Directory*, The Plain (St. Clement's). **1895** G. H. LEONARD *Speech at Oxford*, Our Settlement is called the Broad Plain House..simply because it happens to stand on the Broad Plain, a roadway so wide that we may almost claim it as one of the 'open spaces' of Bristol.

4. A level or flat surface (ideal or material). Now spelt *plane* (PLANE *sb.*³ 1).

†**a.** A geometrical plane. *Obs.*

1570 DEE *Math. Pref.* *j, A broade magnitude, we call a Superficies or a Plaine. *a***1619** FOTHERBY *Atheom.* II. ix. §4 (1622) 297 Whether solides or plaines. **1673** RAY *Journ. Low C.* 4 The Leaves..lie not in the same plain when shut, but make an obtuse Angle. **1697** BP. PATRICK *Comm. Exod.* xx. 4 The Images..they might draw on a Plain. **1793** SMEATON *Edystone L.* 195 A convenient height above the plain of the ring.

b. A plane material surface; the even or smooth surface of a body without projections or elevations; the flat or broad side of a board, as opposed to the *edge*. *Obs.* or *arch.*

1571 DIGGES *Pantom.* I. xxxv. Lj b, You shal vpon your Parchement paper or other playne..draw one streight line. **1664** POWER *Exp. Philos.* I. 5 Which she can at pleasure squeeze out, and so sodder and be-glew her self to the plain she walks on. *a***1672** WILLUGHBY in Ray *Journ. Low C.* (1673) 484 You ascend almost to the top without stairs, by gently inclining plains. **1703** MOXON *Mech. Exerc.* 186 To take off the extuberances from the plain of the Board. **1794** *Rigging & Seamanship* I. 7 *Plain*, an even surface between the Coaks. **1863** P. S. WORSLEY *Poems & Transl.* 8 The silver plains Of two huge valves, embossed with graven gold.

†**c.** A level (horizontal) area. *Obs.*

1614 SELDEN *Titles Hon.* 365 On the side of a stonie hill, is a circular plain, cut out of a main rock, with some xxiv. seats vnequall, which they call Arthur's Round Table. **1673** RAY *Journ. Low C., Venice* 160 In the plain of the Council-chamber, are placed..three urns called *Capelli*. **1726** LEONI *Alberti's Archit.* I. 68/2 Walls, which..have somewhat of a plain at the foot of them, where they may..be kept from filling up the ditch with their ruines.

†**5.** *Printing.* The flat bottom of the lining-stick (see LINING *vbl. sb.*² 6). *Obs.*

1683 MOXON *Mech. Exerc., Printing* xvii. ¶2 The Plain is exactly Flat, Straight, and Smooth.

6. The floor of the hall in which the French National Convention met at the time of the Revolution; hence applied to the more moderate party which occupied seats there. Cf. MOUNTAIN.

1827 SCOTT *Napoleon* Introd., Wks. 1870 IX. 30 In '*the Plain*',..a position held by deputies affecting independence, both of the Girondists and the Jacobins,..sate a large number. *Ibid.* 32 The members of *the Plain*.

7. The horizontal surface of a billiard-table.

1780 *Char.* in *Ann. Reg.* 16/2 The royal ball reached that of the enemy, and with a single blow drove it off the plain. **1825** C. M. WESTMACOTT *Eng. Spy* I. 159 Echo and a man of Trinity set forth for the plains of Betteris. *Note, Plains of Betteris*, the diversion of billiards.

†8. = PLAN *sb.* 1, PLANE *sb.*[3] 2. *Obs.*

1659 LEAK *Waterwks.* 19, I have represented here the plain of the Orthographie.

9. [PLAIN *a.* 8.] Plain cloth; a kind of flannel.

a **1600** T. SMITH *Let.* in Strype *Stow's Surv.* (1754) II. v. xix. 401/2 Also of pyndewhites and Playnes made in the west country. **1716** *Bradford Parish Acc.* (E.D.D.), For Blue Plain for mending the same [long cushions], 1*s.* 1*d.* **1725** *Lond. Gaz.* No. 6388/2 The following Goods, viz... Arrangoes..Perpetts, Welch Plains. **1799** *Hull Advertiser* 12 Jan. 2/3 Woollen drapery..jeans, quiltings,..plains, mixtures. **1847–78** HALLIWELL, *Plain*,..a kind of flannel.

10. *attrib.* and *Comb.*, as ***plain land, station***; ***plain-like*** adj.; also with ***plains-***, as ***plains-cattle, -country, -craft, culture, guide, hunter, malady, -people, station, tribe***; ***plains-bred, -fed*** adjs.; **plain(s) buffalo**, a subspecies of the North American buffalo, *Bison bison bison*, which is smaller than the wood buffalo, has hair of a lighter shade of brown, and formerly inhabited the prairie regions of central and western North America; **plain turkey**, (*a*) the Australian bustard, *Ardeotis australis*, of the family Otididæ; (*b*) *Austral. slang*, a bush tramp; **plain(s)-wanderer**, a terrestrial Australian bird, *Pedionomus torquatus*, resembling a quail. See also PLAINSMAN.

1859 H. Y. HIND *North-West Territory* xii. 105/1 The *plain buffalo are not always of the dark and rich bright brown which forms their characteristic colour. **1375** BARBOUR *Bruce* XI. 337 He of the *playne-land had alsua Of Armyt men ane mekill rout. **1875** TEMPLE & SHELDON *Hist. Northfield, Mass.* 64 Plain lands..were then reckoned nearly worthless. **1834** *Nat. Philos.* III. *Math. Geog.* i. 1/2 (Usef. Knowl. Soc.) Deceived by the *plain-like appearance of the earth..they conceived it to be an extensive plain meeting the heavens on every side. **1884** *Daily News* 27 Feb. 5/7 Assouan..is healthier than Meerut, Mooltan, Mean Meer, or almost any *plain station in India. **1911** C. E. W. BEAN '*Dreadnought' of Darling* xvii. 169 We saw several *plain turkeys, birds not unlike bustards. **1934** *Bulletin* (Sydney) 16 May 20/2 The plain turkey, or lesser bustard, one of Australia's finest gamebirds, is reported to be fading out in one of its few remaining strongholds—the great plains of Western Queensland. **1948** V. PALMER *Golconda* xviii. 144 He had almost given up his tramps along the river-bed in search of a plain-turkey or kangaroo. **1955** D. NILAND *Shiralee* 27 An old bundle of a man came down the road from the west. Macauley watched him approaching and recognized him at once for what he was, a flat country bagman, a type on his own... In his time he had met plenty of these plain-turkeys, as they were known. **1965** *Austral. Encycl.* II. 223/1 The Australian species [of bustard]..is usually known as wild turkey or plain turkey. **1848** J. GOULD *Birds Austral.* V. 80 (*heading*) Collared *Plain Wanderer. **1901** A. J. CAMPBELL *Nests & Eggs Austral. Birds* II. 737 The collared Plain Wanderer, although a unique species, is closely allied to the Turnixes. **1965** *Austral. Encycl.* VII. 137/1 The plain-wanderer—sometimes called turkey-quail—is an inhabitant of open country in south-eastern and South Australia.

1901 KIPLING *Kim* xiii. 328 The lama..walked as only a hillman can. Kim, *plains-bred and plains-fed, sweated and panted astonished. **1903** —— *Five Nations* 53 But that night the Norther..Froze and killed the plains-bred ponies. **1889** *Ann. Rep. Board of Regents Smithsonian Inst. 1886–87* II. 408 The changes which would take place in a band of *plains buffaloes transferred to a permanent mountain habitat can be forecast. **1910** E. T. SETON *Life-Hist. Northern Animals* I. 260 We have 20,000,000 as the number of the Plains Buffalo. **1963** *Maclean's Mag.* 23 Feb. 42/3 Must the barren lands be swept clear of people, leaving the few remaining caribou to become a curiosity like the plains buffalo? **1972** T. MCHUGH *Time of Buffalo* iii. 22 Differences in color and texture of coat are useful in separating the two subspecies—*Bison bison bison*, the plains buffalo, and *Bison bison athabascae*, the wood buffalo. **1890** 'R. BOLDREWOOD' *Col. Reformer* (1891) 220 First-class, fattening, *plains-country cattle station. **1899** *Scribner's Mag.* XXV. 19/1 Here their woodcraft and *plainscraft, their knowledge of the rifle, helped us very much. **1912** C. WISSLER *N. Amer. Indians of Plains* ii. 86 While the camp circle was the most striking and picturesque trait of *Plains culture, it was probably no more than a convenient form of organized camp for a political group composed of 'bands'. **1914** *Amer. Anthropologist* XVI. 16 The true Plains culture may properly be said to have developed with the introduction to the horse. **1957** *Publ. Amer. Dial. Soc. 1956* XXVI. 17 *KahnI* 'brush-covered hut' changed its meaning to 'teepee' when the Indians went over to a plains culture and to 'house' when they adopted European culture. **1976** *Billings* (Montana) *Gaz.* 27 June 2-c/3 Plains culture of long ago can be read into the opulent jewelry Nighthorse creates. **1901** *Plains-fed [see *plains-bred* adj.]. **1877** R. I. DODGE *Hunting Grounds Gt. West* v. 63 'Old Bridger', the most thorough and justly celebrated of all *plains guides. **1831** T. SIMPSON *Let.* 19 Dec. in MacLeod & Morton *Cuthbert Grant of Grantown* (1963) viii. 108 The *plains hunters have had a very successful season and the quantity of provisions they have brought home is immense. **1922** *Beaver* Dec. 113/2 The half-breeds dislike a settled life; they prefer the excitement of the chase or the idle life of the fisherman. They are technically termed plains hunters. **1959** E. TUNIS *Indians* 28/2 Many of the Plains hunters and all of the Digger Indians of the West were ghost-ridden and terrified of the dead. **1877** R. I. DODGE *Hunting Grounds Gt. West* v. 67 Another *plains malady..is called 'moon-blind'. **1899** *Daily News* 12 Jan. 6/1 The writer has lived..with the *plains people in their homes for many years. **1905** *Nation* (N.Y.) 5 Jan. 11/1 As a plains people they [*sc.* the Pawnee] were largely dependent upon the chase. **1963** *Times* 19 Apr. 14/6 The great love of the Pakistani plainspeople for water. **1930** L. G. D. ACLAND *Early Canterbury Runs* (ser. 1) v. 109 Valetta was the last of the old *plains stations to remain anything like its original size. **1933** —— in *Press* (Christchurch, N.Z.) 9 Sept. 15/7 C[row's] n[est]s were used on the old plains stations until the runs were fenced, about 1860. **1870** DE B. R. KEIM *Sheridan's Troopers on Borders* iv. 29 The *Plains Tribes have, as yet, presented no prominent warriors in the character of leaders. **1877** R. I. DODGE *Hunting Grounds Gt. West* xli. 419 The Tonkaways cannot properly be called a plains tribe. **1917** C. WISSLER *Amer. Indian* viii. 131 North of Mexico, methods of reckoning time are very crude, though apparently strongest among the Pueblo and adjacent Plains tribes. **1949** *Nat. Geogr. Mag.* Oct. 473/1 What the buffalo was to the Plains tribes the caribou is to the Indians of the far north. **1926** *Emu* XXVI. 59 (*heading*) The vanishing *Plains-wanderer. **1964** A. L. THOMSON *New Dict. Birds* 635/1 Plains-wanderers..are usually loth to fly.

plain, *sb.*[2] Now *dial.* [f. PLAIN *v.*] An expression of pain, grief, or discontent; complaint, lamentation: = PLAINT *sb.*

c **1550** *Pryde & Abuse of Women* 231 in Hazl. *E.P.P.* IV. 244 And for oure sad & honest playnes, A joyefull place in heaven. **1563** B. GOOGE *Eglogs* (Arb.) 95 Why dydste thou than, kepe backe thy wofull playn? **1814** SCOTT *Ld. of Isles* IV. ix, The warrior-threat, the infant's plain, The mother's screams, were heard in vain. **1876** *Whitby Gloss.*, *Plains*, complaints in all senses.

plain (pleɪn), *a.*[1] and *adv.* Also 4 plein, -e (playen), 4–6 **pleyn**, -e, 4–7 **playn(e, plaine, plane.** [a. OF. *plain*:—L. *plān-us* flat. In Sc. usually spelt *plane* from 14th c.; in English orig. *plain* (etc.) in all senses, including the geometrical (1 c), for which PLANE was substituted *c* 1700.

PLAIN *a.*[2] (F. *plein*) having the same form, there are ME. instances in which it is difficult to determine which word was meant. See A. 3 b, B. 6, 7.]

A. *adj.*

I. 1. Flat, level, even; free from elevations and depressions. a. Said esp. of a horizontal surface, as of the ground, or †of the sea when calm and undisturbed (*obs.*).

c **1330** R. BRUNNE *Chron. Wace* (Rolls) 1772 Þey..left þe Troiens þe pleyn lond. *c* **1400** MAUNDEV. (Roxb.) xxviii. 129 Þe land of Caldee es a playne cuntree. **1480** CAXTON *Descr. Brit.* 47 The londe is not pleyne but full of montayns. **1590** SHAKS. *Mids. N.* III. ii. 404 Follow me then to plainer ground. **1625** N. CARPENTER *Geog. Del.* I. ii. (1635) 34 If the Earth were plaine, all the Northern Starres would appeare to the inhabitants of the Southerne Regions. **1665** G. HAVERS tr. *P. della Valle's Trav. E. India* 108 We lodg'd about a musket-shot without the Fort, in a plane and somewhat low place. **1766** WESLEY *Wks.* (1872) III. 240, I recovered some strength, so as to be able to walk a little on plain ground. **1847** GROTE *Greece* II. xxv. IV. 16 Between the last-mentioned gulf [the Thermaic] and the eastern counterforts of Olympus and Bermius there exists a narrow strip of plain land.

†b. In general sense: Flat. *Obs.*

13.. *K. Alis.* 6414 (Bodl. MS.) Men of selcouþ gest þe face hij han playne & hard As it were an Okes bord. **1398** TREVISA *Barth. De P.R.* v. lv. (Bodl. MS.), The sole of þe foote..hatte planta in latine for it is playne. **1565–73** COOPER *Thesaurus*, *Compressa palma aut porrecta ferire*,..to strike with the fist, or with the playne hande. **1607** TOPSELL *Four-f. Beasts* (1658) 120 His back is plain to his tail, his eyes quick, his ears long hanging, but sometimes stand up. **1617** MORYSON *Itin.* I. 214 The houses are built after the manner of Asia,..one roofe high, and plaine in the top. **1650** BULWER *Anthropomet.* 147 They shut in their heads behinde and before in boards, so that the whole face may become plain and dilated.

†c. *Geom. Obs.* Now PLANE *a.*

1570 DEE *Math. Pref.* *j, Euery playne magnitude, hath also length. **1570** BILLINGSLEY *Euclid* I. def. viii. 3 A plaine angle is an inclination or bowing of two lines the one to the other. **1660** BARROW *Euclid* I. Def. vii, A plain Superficies is that which lies equally betwixt its lines. **1727** [see *plano-cylindrical* s.v. PLANO-[1]].

†d. ***to make, throw down, beat down*** (a building, city, etc.) ***plain with the earth*** or ***ground***, etc.: to level with the ground, raze to the earth.

c **1400** MAUNDEV. (Roxb.) xi. 48 Þis citee tuke Iosue..and kest it doune, and made it euen playne with þe erthe. **1436** *Pol. Poems* (Rolls) II. 152 The walles they wold ber adowne, ..Alle schuld be mad fulle playn. *a* **1548** HALL *Chron.*, *Hen. VII* 44 He with his miners rased and ouerthrewe the castell to the playne grounde. **1568** GRAFTON *Chron.* II. 94 He threwe downe the Castell plaine with the ground. **1596** SPENSER *State Irel.* Wks. (Globe) 615/2 It was his pollicye to leave noe holdes behind him, but to make all playne and wast. **1596** HARINGTON *Metam. Ajax* (1814) 92 Down, down with it at any hand, Make all things plain, let nothing stand. **1648** GAGE *West Ind.* 48 The greatest part of their City..beaten down plain with the ground.

†2. a. Smooth, even; free from roughness or unevenness of surface. *Obs.* exc. in Comb. or phrases: see VI.

13.. *E.E. Allit. P.* B. 1068 Þat euer is polyced als playn as þe perle seluen. *c* **1430** LYDG. *Min. Poems* (Percy Soc.) 41 Also pleyne was his bedde at the morwe, As at even. **1559** MORWYNG *Evonym.* 208 If the face be wet and rubbed with the same it shall be plaine and cleare, that it shall seme angellike. **1578** LYTE *Dodoens* I. lxviii. 99 Turners..do vse them to polish, and make playne, and smoth their workes. **1678** HOBBES *Decam.* ix. 108 Much more then will it adhere ..when..both it and the Iron have a plain Superficies. **1704** J. PITTS *Acc. Mohammetans* ix. (1738) 186 Smooth'd over the Meal, and made it plain.

†b. *fig.* Of the wind: Not rough; gentle. *Obs.*

c **1430** LYDG. *Min. Poems* (Percy Soc.) 3 The ayre attempered, the wyndes smowth and playne.

3. a. Free from obstructions or interruptions; unobstructed, clear, open; (of a country, a space) clear of woods, buildings, or occupants; (of the sea) open, unconfined; open to the elements or to general view; public. Also *fig. Obs.* exc. *dial.*

c **1330** R. BRUNNE *Chron. Wace* (Rolls) 1723 Whan al was fled, & þe feld was playn. **13..** *E.E. Allit. P.* C. 439 For hit watz playn in þat place for plyande greuez. *a* **1450** *Knt. de la Tour* (1868) 126 She straue & chidde in the plaine strete wit her neygheboures. **1546** *Supplic. of Poore Commons* (1871) 78 A churche..pleasauntly beset with groues and playn feldes. **1579** FENTON *Guicciard.* (1618) 16 Able to give him battell in the plaine sea. **1611** SPEED *Hist. Gt. Brit.* IX. x. §43 He affirmes, that it was in the plainefield, ours, that it was an Ambush. **1618** MUNDAY *Stow's Surv.* 906 There were two woods in the parish, but now they are both made plaine of wood. **1748** *Anson's Voy.* II. xiv. 286 Its walls are built upon the plain ground, without either outwork or ditch before them. **1864** *Yorks. Prov.*, *Kirkby*, This street is very plain, the wind is much felt in it.

†b. In ***plain field*** there was in later use prob. association with *plain battle*, etc. = open (i.e. full) battle: see PLAIN *a.*[2] 3.

c **1400** *Destr. Troy* 7218 And past furth prudly into þe plaine feld. **1523** LD. BERNERS *Froiss.* I. ccxxi. 288 They.. thought to wynne the victory with their handes in playne felde. **1533** BELLENDEN *Livy* II. (S.T.S.) I. 237 It was fochtin in plane feild [L. *æquo campo*] with displayit baneris. **1647** N. BACON *Disc. Govt. Eng.* I. iv. 14 Unsubdued..and now given over by the Romans in a plain field.

c. *transf.* Unobstructed, clear (*view, sight*).

1613 HAYWARD *Norm. Kings* 22 With a furious charge.. either slew them or tooke them prisoners, in the plaine view of their King. **1867** SHEDD *Homiletics* iii. (1869) 54 An object is in plain sight, when the form and shape of it are distinctly visible.

II. 4. Open, clear to the senses or mind; evident, manifest, obvious; easily distinguishable or recognizable.

a **1352** MINOT *Poems* iii. 35 Þare he made his mone playne Þat no man suld say þare ogayne. **1423** JAS. I *Kingis Q.* cxvi, To a token pleyne, As of my teris cummyth all this reyne. **1514** BARCLAY *Cyt. & Uplondyshm.* (Percy Soc.) p. lxvii, Think that none their playne errour note. *c* **1586** C'TESS PEMBROKE *Ps.* LIX. xi, Make it playne, That God..Rules all. **1596** SPENSER *F.Q.* IV. i. 24 The moniments whereof there byding beene, As plaine as at the first when they were fresh and greene. **1660** BARROW *Euclid* I. vii, It is plain that AD is not equal to AC. **1736** BUTLER *Anal.* II. iii. Wks. 1874. I. 190 Practical Christianity..is a plain and obvious thing. **1813** SCOTT *Rokeby* I. v, Now nigh and plain the sound appears. **1875** JOWETT *Plato* (ed. 2) I. 91 Let me make my meaning plainer in this way.

5. That is clearly what the name expresses; open, manifest, direct, unmistakable; downright, mere, sheer, 'flat', absolute.

a **1300** *Cursor M.* 929 (Cott.) For þou ne es but a pudre plain To puder sal þou worth a gain. *c* **1400** *Destr. Troy* 3504 Hope ye, Parys, playn þefte vnponysshet wilbe? **1535** COVERDALE *Eccl.* i. 1 All is but vanite..all is but playne vanite. **1581** RICH *Farew. Milit. Prof.* (1846) 208 By plaine force [he] pulles hym doune on the flower. **1592** R. D. *Hypnerotomachia* 67 b, Wee ascended vp to the playne toppe. **1609** BIBLE (Douay) *Gen.* Brief Remonstr. 30 Easely confessed of al that are not plaine Atheists. **1643** in Dorothea Townshend *Life & Lett. E. Porter* xiii. 206 One throu plain fier went strait mad. **1669** PENN *No Cross* vii. §1 Whilst a plain Stranger to the Cross of Christ. **1833** LAMB *Elia* Ser. II. Pref. (1865) 236 He reaped plain unequivocal hatred.

6. a. Of which the meaning is evident; simple, intelligible, readily understood.

c **1380** WYCLIF *Serm.* Sel. Wks. I. 362 Þis gospel tellīþ a playen storie. **1398** TREVISA *Barth. De P.R.* VI. xxvii. (Bodl. MS.), Sweuenes þat beþ trewe beth sommetyme openne and playne and sommetyme ywrapped vnder..derke tokenyngges. **1560** DAUS tr. *Sleidane's Comm.* 94 b, It ought to be vttered with playner wordes, to take awaye all ambiguitie. **1662** STILLINGFL. *Orig. Sacr.* II. vii. §3 Can any thing be more plain then the graduall progress of Divine revelation from the beginning of the world? **1729** BUTLER *Serm.* Wks. 1874 II. 65 Morality and religion must be somewhat plain and easy to be understood. **1861** MRS. CARLYLE *Lett.* III. 80 Tell her distinctly what you want..in few plain words.

b. *transf.* Said of the speaker or writer.

1555 EDEN *Decades* 53, I had rather bee playne then curious. **1648** MILTON *Observ. Art. Peace* Wks. 1851 IV. 555 Actions, of whatever sort, [are] thir own plainest Interpreters. **1867** SHEDD *Homiletics* iii. (1869) 55 A plain writer or speaker makes the truth and the mind impinge upon each other.

7. a. Not intricate or complicated; simple.

1659 HOOLE *Comenius' Vis. World* (1672) 3 Plain sounds [*simplices sonos*] of which mans speech consisteth. **1669** STURMY *Mariner's Mag.* VII. iii. 6 Of all Dials, this is the plainest; for it is no more but divide a whole Circle into 24 equal parts. **1782** MISS BURNEY *Cecilia* III. iv, She determined..to place them in some cheap school, where they might be taught plain work. **1834** BOWRING *Minor Morals* 145 The Jacquard loom..by which the most complicated patterns can be woven with the same ease as the plainest. **1895** *Chamb. Jrnl.* 21 Sept. 599/1 Fisher's machine was intended rather for embroidering than for plain sewing.

b. Applied to knitting in knit-stitch or garter-stitch (see GARTER *sb.* 8). Also quasi-*sb.* = *garter-stitch.*

1861 MRS. BEETON *Bk. Househ. Managem.* 622 The cloths ..should be knitted in plain knitting, with *very coarse* cotton. **1872** *Young Englishwoman* Oct. 559/1 Knit 9 rows,

2 plain, 2 purl, alternately. **1885** [see PURL *sb.*[1] 5]. **1910–11** *T. Eaton & Co. Catal.* Fall & Winter 20/1 Women's Coat Sweater, made of knitted worsted, in fancy stitch. The V-neck and fronts have wide, plain knitted border. **1932** D. C. MINTER *Mod. Needlecraft* 69/2 1st row: Knit plain. 2nd row: Purl. **1970** *Guardian* 24 Mar. 9/3 Cable stitch jacket, plain knit pants. **1978** A. GREY *Chinese Assassin* viii. 111 It might just as well be an extract from my granny's pearl and plain knitting book for all I can tell.

III. 8. a. Without embellishment, addition, or decorative pattern or colouring; unembellished, not ornate; simple, bare, bald; (of the hair) worn straight, not curled; (of drawings, lithographs, etc.) not coloured. Also of a person's name: without addition or title. Also *fig.*

[**13..** *Coer de L.* 3631 Tyl he haue maad al playn werk Off thy clothes of gold, into thy serk [*ed.* scherk].] *c* **1386** CHAUCER *Frankl. Prol.* 48, I lerned neuere Rethorik certeyn Thyng þat I speke it moot be bare and pleyn. **1459** *Paston Lett.* I. 489, ij playn borde clothys for my maister is table. **1585** T. WASHINGTON tr. *Nicholay's Voy.* III. xxii. 112 A faire cloth embrodered with leaues about it or els plaine. **1655** STANLEY *Hist. Philos.* III. (1701) 88/1 A young Man,.. describ'd by Plato, with long plain Hair. **1670** LADY M. BERTIE in *12th Rep. Hist. MSS. Comm.* App. v. 21 Most wore embraudered bodys with plaine black skirts of Morella Mohair and Prunella and such stuffs. **1687** A. LOVELL tr. *Thevenot's Trav.* I. 117 Escutcheons of two Crosses, the one plain and the other Anchred. **1806–7** J. BERESFORD *Miseries Hum. Life* (1826) VI. i, Both figures being partly coloured and partly plain. **1828** *Imperial Mag.* X. 589 The doctor, or, as he now chose to designate himself, plain Thomas Beddoes. **1865** LUBBOCK *Preh. Times* 16 The celts are generally plain, but sometimes ornamented with ridges, dots, or lines. **1872** HARDY *Under Greenw. Tree* I. ii. 20 'Reub', says he—'a always used to call me plain Reub, pore old heart! *a* **1907** *Mod.* Sets of picture-postcards, plain or coloured. **1914** G. B. SHAW *Misalliance* 12 He calls himself Plain John, but you can't call him that in his own office.

†**b.** Without armour or weapons; unarmed.

a **1300** *Cursor M.* 7564 Wit armes cums þou me again, And i agains þe al plain.

c. *Cards.* (*a*) Applied to the common as opposed to the picture cards. (*b*) Not trumps.

1844 DICKENS *Mart. Chuz.* xvii, Court cards and plain cards of every denomination. **1862** 'CAVENDISH' *Whist* (1870) 29 Plain suits are suits not trumps. *Ibid.* (1886) 64 Ace, king, queen, knave, in plain suits. **1873** *Routledge's Yng. Gentl. Mag.* Jan. 94/1 'Court card' or 'plain card', as the case may be. **1885** [see FINESSE *v.* 2 a]. **1899** [see ECHO *sb.* 8]. **1936** [see CASH *v.*[2] 1 b].

d. Plainly woven; not corded, twilled, or the like; without figured pattern; *transf.* of muscle.

1875 KNIGHT *Dict. Mech.*, *Plain cloth*, not twilled. **1895** *Syd. Soc. Lex.*, *Plain muscles*, unstriated muscles, as opposed to striated muscles.

e. Of envelopes, containers, etc.: giving no information as to sender or contents; esp. in phr. ***under plain cover.*** Also *transf.* (of a motor vehicle) and *fig.*

1913 *Maclean's Mag.* Sept. 81/3 Write us for Catalogue 'D', sent free on application, in plain envelope. **1925** *Ladies' Home Jrnl.* Mar. 133/4 The sample will come in plain, unmarked wrapper. **1932** *N.Y. Times Bk. Rev.* 17 Jan. 20/1 Please send me in plain wrapper, prepaid, a copy of the complete unabridged edition of 'Sane Sex Life and Sane Sex Living' by Dr. Long. **1936** *Men Only* Mar. 147/1 Send a p.c. for full details of the Girvan Scientific System (mailed under plain cover) and particulars of our £100 Guarantee. **1942** N. BALCHIN *Darkness falls from Air* iii. 57 'He's tight,' said Fred... I said, 'I expect they'll send a plain van to collect the old boy.' **1962** *Sunday Times* 11 Nov. 25/7 Much good has been done by the increasing enlightenment over the nature of sexuality which was a secondary aim of the Stopes/Ellis pioneers. The books which used to be sent under plain cover, now appear as Penguins. **1966** WODEHOUSE *Plum Pie* iv. 107 The two of them got away with the purloined objects, no doubt in a plain van. **1969** *Listener* 24 July 125/1 The husband.. is secretly studying for O-levels while the nagging women think he is out boozing. When the results come through the post.. his mother hides them because they're 'under plain cover' and she assumes the envelope conceals dirty books. **1971** W. J. BURLEY *Guilt Edged* i. 9 The goods [were] to be delivered in a plain van. *Ibid.* ii. 33 *The Postures of Love* (Thirty-five photographic plates. Send £3. Delivered in a plain wrapper.) **1974** 'J. MELVILLE' *Nun's Castle* iii. 58 [Pregnancy] tests.. could be done.. at home... It would be easy enough to.. have the materials sent (in a plain cover, as the advertisements so kindly suggested). **1974** *John O'Groat Jrnl.* (Wick) 6 Sept. 9/5 (Advt.), *Plain wrapper*, Durex Gossamer, 55p dozen; Fetherlite, three packets 55p, post free; plain wrapper; guaranteed Grade 1 goods. **1975** L. DILLS *CB Slanguage Dict.* 47 *Plain brown* (*black, gray*) *wrapper*, unmarked police car.

9. *Mus.* (See quots.)

1609 DOULAND *Ornith. Microl.* 3 Plaine Musicke.. is a simple and vniforme prolation of Notes, which can neither be augmented nor diminished. **1872** O. SHIPLEY *Gloss. Eccl. Terms* 6 The accent being.. plain, i.e. monotone.

10. Of simple composition or preparation; not compounded of many ingredients; not elaborate. Of food: Not rich or highly seasoned, simple.

plain bread and butter, i.e. without the addition of preserves, etc.; ***a plain tea***, tea with plain bread and butter; ***plain water***, water without any infusion or addition.

1655 CULPEPPER, etc. *Riverius* VI. i. 131 A plainer Medicine is made of Plantane and Rose Water. **1668** CHAS. II. in Julia Cartwright *Henrietta of Orleans* (1894) 263 The planer your diett is the better health you will have. **1784** M. UNDERWOOD *Dis. Children* (1799) I. 163 To chew a bit of bread [or] eat a bit of plain pudding. **1803** tr. *P. Le Brun's Mons. Botte* III. 153 It is singular that the Marquis d' Arancey should.. partake of plain roast and boiled. **1879** *Spectator* 24 May 645 [As a] school-boy counts the currants in an unusually plain cake. **1883** BLACK *Shandon Bells* xv, The dinner was a plain one. **1897** *Allbutt's Syst. Med.* III. 21 Plain water, barley water, lemonade,.. may be allowed at will to assuage the thirst.

IV. 11. Open in behaviour; free from duplicity or reserve; guileless, honest, candid, frank. *Obs.* exc. in sense 'outspoken'.

c **1374** CHAUCER *Anel. & Arc.* 87 But he was double in love and nothing pleyne. *c* **1399** *Pol. Poems* (Rolls) II. 13 Bot wher the herte is plein withoute guile. **1418** CHICHELE in Ellis *Orig. Lett.* Ser. I. I. 5 ȝe schol fynde hym a good man.., and pleyn to ȝu with owte feyntese. **1483** CAXTON *G. de la Tour* F j, Thenne sayd to her the good man whiche was a playn man and trewe. **1567** HARMAN *Caveat* 63 'Wel, I wyl tell the', quoth this Chamberlayne. 'I wylbe playne with the'. **1653** WALTON *Angler* iii. 74, I wil sing a Song if any body wil sing another; else, to be plain with you, I wil sing none. **1712** ARBUTHNOT *John Bull* IV. vi, I love to be plain. I'd as lief see myself in Ecclesdown Castle, as thee in Clay Pool! *a* **1718** PENN *Wks.* (1726) I. 320 Mordecai was too plain and stout and not Fine and Subtil enough to avoid the Displeasure of Haman.

12. a. Free from ambiguity, evasion, or subterfuge; straightforward, direct.

In ***plain truth*** there is often present the notion of 'unvarnished, uncoloured'. ***plain English***: see C. below.

c **1500** *Melusine* 193 Certaynly, my lord,.. ye saye the playn trouth of it. **1513** MORE *Rich. III* (1883) 9 Flattery shall haue more place then plaine and faithfull aduyse. **1560** DAUS tr. *Sleidane's Comm.* 30 Thou shouldest make a playne and directe answere. **1581** MULCASTER *Positions* xxxvii. (1887) 161 Such.. as haue preferred plaine trueth, before painted colours. **1695** CONGREVE *Love for L.* IV. v, Tell me in plain Terms what the Matter is with him, or I'll crack your Fool's Skull. **1776** *Trial of Nundocomar* 73/2 If you do not give a plain answer to a plain question, you will be committed. **1855** MACAULAY *Hist. Eng.* xiii. III. 286 The Scottish Estates used plain language, simply because it was impossible for them, situated as they were, to use evasive language. **1856** FROUDE *Hist. Eng.* (1858) I. v. 462 Plain speech is never without its value.

†**b.** *absol.* = Plain fact, plain state. *Obs.*

c **1386** CHAUCER *Knt.'s T.* 233 We moste endure this is the short and playn. **1463** in *10th Rep. Hist. MSS. Comm.* App. v. 301 Bothe parties to tell the playne of the matire. **1690** LOCKE *Govt.* I. ix. §86 Not to follow our A[uthor] too far out of the Way, the plain of the Case is this.

V. 13. Having no special qualities or pretensions; not exceptionally gifted or cultured; ordinary, simple, unsophisticated; such as characterizes ordinary people.

1586 A. DAY *Eng. Secretary* II. (1625) 102 What in my plaine conceit.. may be thought most consonant and worthy. **1596** SHAKS. *Merch. V.* III. v. 62, I pray thee vnderstand a plaine man in his plaine meaning. **1711** ADDISON *Spect.* No. 165 ¶4 A Man of good Estate and plain Sense. **1790** BURKE *Fr. Rev.* Wks. V. 35 To me, who am but a plain man, the proceeding looks a little too refined, and too ingenious. **1865** M. ARNOLD *Ess. Crit.* Pref. 15 A plain citizen of the republic of letters. **1899** INGE *Chr. Mysticism* vii. 256 There are two views of this sacrament [the Lord's Supper] which the 'plain man' has always found much easier to understand than the symbolic view which is that of our Church.

14. Not distinguished by rank or position; belonging to the commonalty; lowly, common, ordinary.

1580 G. HARVEY *Let. to Spenser* Wks. (Grosart) I. 84 No man but Minion, Stowte, Lowte, Plaine swayne, quoth a Lording. **1639** FULLER *Holy War* v. xxix. (1840) 294 Seeing within fourteen generations, the royal blood of the kings of Judah ran in the veins of plain Joseph, a painful carpenter. **1642** R. CARPENTER *Experience* III. iv. 28 The Gout; which we poore plaine people are ignorant of. **1742** WESLEY *Wks.* (1830) I. 372, I preached to several hundred of plain people. **1890** HOSMER *Anglo-Sax. Freedom* 264 The admission in England of a vast body of the plain people to a share in the government.

15. Of simple manners; homely, unaffected.

1601 R. JOHNSON *Kingd. & Commw.* (1603) 82 Being (as all the Germaines are) plaine and homely in their behauiour and intertainment. **1667** PEPYS *Diary* 20 Sept., And indeed [she] is, as I always thought, one of the modestest, prettiest, plain women that ever I saw. **1706** E. WARD *Wooden World Diss.* 106 This same plain blunt Sea-Animal.. in his Tar-Jacket and Wide Knee'd Trowzers. **1904** *Daily Chron.* 8 Jan. 5/4 They spoke of their immense pleasure at the visit of their Queen.. 'She is a plain woman, a very plain woman like ourselves'.

16. Simple in dress or habits; clothed or living plainly; not luxurious or ostentatious; frugal.

1613 PURCHAS *Pilgrimage* (1614) 632 He is about thirtie sixe yeares, very ciuill and plaine in habite. **1638** SIR T. HERBERT *Trav.* (ed. 2) 232 The old men went plaine; the young mens habit was rich. **1663** COWLEY *Verses & Ess., Avarice* (1669) 130 The old plain way, ye Gods, let me be Poor. **1700** DRYDEN *Charac. Gd. Parson* 101 The holy father holds a double reign, The prince may keep his pomp, the fisher must be plain. **1871** BLACKIE *Four Phases* i. 6 His habits of life were remarkably plain and frugal.

17. Of ordinary appearance; not beautiful or well-favoured; homely: often used euphemistically for ill-favoured, ugly.

1749 FIELDING *Tom Jones* I. viii, A general and bitter invective against beauty.. with many compassionate considerations for all honest, plain girls. **1796** JANE AUSTEN *Pride & Prej.* xxvi, Handsome young men must have something to live on, as well as the plain. **1838** B'NESS BUNSEN in Hare *Life* I. xi. 485 The higher classes are decidedly plain and ungraceful. **1890** C. R. COLERIDGE in *Monthly Packet* Christmas No. 71 Even in the days of Arthur some women must have been very plain. **1903** *Westm. Gaz.* 4 Mar. 4/3 Mrs. Praga.. declares that 'nowadays nobody need be plain, and when I say plain I use the word in the sense of ugly'.

VI. Phrases.

18. *Plain* is emphasized by various comparisons, orig. applicable in particular senses, but afterwards humorously or irrationally applied to others; **a.** esp. ***plain as a pikestaff*** (earlier ***packstaff***).

1542–1691 [see PACKSTAFF]. **1591–** [see PIKESTAFF]. *c* **1622** FORD, etc. *Witch Edmonton* II. i, *Saw.* I understand thee not; be plain, my son *Cud.* As a pike-staff, mother. **1631** WEEVER *Anc. Fun. Mon.* 103 In.. Scotland.. Religion is.. pure and spotlesse without ceremonie, and plain as a pike staffe without a surplise. *c* **1685** VILLIERS (Dk. Buckhm.) *Conf.* Wks. 1705 II. 37, I see, as plain as a pike staff, that 'tis no thing but a Cork. **1834** HOOD *Tylney Hall* (1840) 379 You've got my meaning as plain as a pikestaff. *a* **1873** LYTTON *Ken. Chillingly* II. ix. (1878) 106 She is as plain as a pikestaff. **1894** *Pall Mall Mag.* Sept. 37 There was my own spoor as plain as a pikestaff.

b. Also, ***plain as a packsaddle, as print, as the nose on*** (†***in***) ***one's face, as the sun at noonday, as Salisbury*** (pun on Salisbury Plain), ***as way to parish-church***, etc. See also DUNSTABLE 1 b, c.

[**1542** UDALL *Erasm. Apoph.* II. 179 b, Thom trouthe, or plain Sarisbuirie.] **1553** T. WILSON *Rhet.* (1580) 143 An honeste true dealyng seruant out of doubte, plaine as a packe-saddle.. though his witte was simple. **1600** SHAKS. *A.Y.L.* II. vii. 52 And why sir must they so? The why is plaine, as way to Parish Church. **1695** CONGREVE *Love for Love* IV. i. 60 *As witness my Hand*,.. in great Letters. Why, 'tis as plain as the Nose in one's Face. **1837** DICKENS *Pickw.* xlii, 'Why', said Mr. Roker, 'it's as plain as Salisbury'. **1879** FROUDE *Cæsar* xi. 121 It was plain as the sun at midday. **1895** CROCKETT in *Cornh. Mag.* Dec. 581 A look which said as plain as print, 'Have you not had enough?' **1903** G. B. SHAW *Man & Superman* II. 69 Why, it's as plain as the nose on your face. If you aint spotted that, you dont know much about these sort of things. **1937** D. L. SAYERS *Busman's Honeymoon* ix. 200, I came in nine o'clock from fetchin' a pail o' water and I sees you plain as the nose on my face a-talkin' to him at this very winder. **1940** WODEHOUSE *Quick Service* xiii. 166, I see it all. They're pals. It's as plain as the nose on your face. **1958** D. GARNETT *Shot in Dark* vii. 86 'But how did you find out?' 'It is as plain as the nose on your face.'.. 'Yes. But most people don't see the nose on their face. The obvious is what is overlooked.' **1979** K. BONFIGLIOLI *After you with Pistol* xiv. 99 The facts are as plain as the nose on your face.

†**19. a.** ***at plain, in*** (Sc. ***into***) ***plain, unto the plain***: plainly, in plain terms, etc. **b.** ***plain at the eye***: plain to be seen, evident. *Obs.*

c **1400** *Rom. Rose* 5663 It is maked mencioun Of oure countre pleyn at the eye. *c* **1420** *Liber Cocorum* (1862) 7 þer of I schalle speke more in playn. **1444** in *Wars Eng. in France* (Rolls) I. 463 By.. whiche.. it may appere unto you more at plain. *c* **1450** HOLLAND *Howlat* 211 The archdene, that ourman, ay prechand in plane, Correker of kirkmen was clepit the Claik. **1486** *Bk. St. Albans* E vj, When ye se vnto the playne her at the last.. Say, *la douce amy la est a.* **1513** DOUGLAS *Æneis* I. vi. 36 Trewlie, maidin, in plane, Nane of thi sisteris did I heir ne se. **1600** W. WATSON *Decacordon* (1602) 117 [He told] him in plaine, the case was altered. **1667** MILTON *P.L.* IX. 758 In plain then, what forbids he but to know, Forbids us good, forbids us to be wise?

B. *adv.* (Various adverbial uses of the adj.)

I. †**1.** In a flat, level, or even position; evenly.

1523 FITZHERB. *Husb.* §127 Yf the bowes wyll not lye playne in the hedge, than cut it the more halfe asonder & bynde it in to the hedge. **1642** H. MORE *Song of Soul* II. iii. III. lxvii, What's the cause That they thus stagger in the plain-pav'd skie?

2. With clearness of expression; without circumlocution or ambiguity, clearly, intelligibly, candidly.

1387 TREVISA *Higden* (Rolls) I. 129 As it is innermore pleyn i-write [*sicut inferius.. planum erit*]. **1390** GOWER *Conf.* III. 105 Withoute which, to telle plein, Alle othre science is in vein. *c* **1475** *Rauf Coilȝear* 315 That I haue said I sall hald, and that I tell the plane. **1588** SHAKS. *L.L.L.* IV. iii. 272 Sir to tell you plaine, I'le finde a fairer face not washt to day. **1607** S. COLLINS *Serm.* (1608) 13 If you will haue one speake plainer.. than S. Paul heere doth. **1850** J. H. NEWMAN *Diffic. Anglic.* 318 Soon others began to speak plainer than he.

3. With clearness or distinctness of perception or utterance; clearly, manifestly, evidently.

1590 SPENSER *F.Q.* I. i. 16 Ay wont in desert darknes to remaine, Where plain none might her see, nor she see any plaine. **1784** *New Spectator* No. 22. 3 Did not Torquato Tasso speak plain at six months old? **1841** MISS MITFORD in L'Estrange *Life* III. viii. 130 The part plainest to be seen was the figure as it rose and sank above the paling. *a* **1861** MRS. BROWNING *Mother & Poet* v, I made them.. Speak plain the word *country.*

4. Simply, absolutely, purely.

1535 COVERDALE *Bible* Ded., Christes admynistracion was nothyng temporall, but playne spirituall. **1551** T. WILSON *Logike* (1580) 18 Whiche either Naturall reason proueth either to bee plaine false, or the experience of man declareth to bee vntrue. *c* **1591** in *Lett. Lit. Men* (Camden) 78 The Russe government is plaine tirannycall. **1596** DALRYMPLE tr. *Leslie's Hist. Scot.* I. 97 *marg.*, The Scottis bordirers to tile the land plane abhoris. **1955** S. A. GRAU *Black Prince* 193 'You just plain remember that [is] my boat.' 'Who done seen it?' his father said. 'I plain ask you.' **1956** B. HOLIDAY *Lady sings Blues* (1973) xviii. 151, I had gained so much weight and I just plain didn't look like the girl who had left town ten months before. **1959** J. L. AUSTIN *Sense & Sensibilia* (1962) i. 5 Besides, there is nothing so plain boring as the constant repetition of assertions that are not true. **1973** *Times* 13 Nov. 6/6 This myth that.. we were just being plain difficult about Sandhurst was another very irritating criticism. **1976** *Bridgewater Mercury* 21 Dec. 10/4 Others may have family problems, housing difficulties—or are just plain lonely. **1979** *Guardian* 8 Jan. 2/8 Mrs. Thatcher.. dismissed claims that taxation of benefits would be impossible to administer... 'I just plain don't believe it.'

†**5.** In other senses of the adj. *Obs.*

c **1470** HARDING *Chron.* LIII. v, Within .iiii. wekes was all this done full playn. *c* **1475** *Partenay* 920 Many ladyes..

Went to a company with the Countesse plain, Ech welcomyng hir after ther degre. *c* **1560** A. SCOTT *Poems* (S.T.S.) iv. 78 Or scho war kissit plane, Scho leir be japit thryiss. **1807–8** SYD. SMITH *Plymley's Lett.* x. Wks. 1859 II. 175/2 He dresses plain, loves hunting and farming.

II. It is not clear whether the following belong to this word or to PLAIN $a.^2$, F. *plein.*

†**6.** Entirely, quite; ? fully. = CLEAN *adv.* 5.

c **1330** R. BRUNNE *Chron. Wace* (Rolls) 14025 He was passed þe mountes pleyn. *c* **1450** HOLLAND *Howlat* 74, I will appele to the Pape, and pass till him plane. *c* **1460** *Play Sacram.* 137, I praye the goo wele pleyn thorowght All eraclea. *c* **1500** *New Not-br. Mayd* 119, I, that hym bought, Shall be expoulsed playne. **1567** *Gude & Godlie B.* (S.T.S.) 132, I haif na mycht, Me to defend Fra hellis pane, bot gif thow plane Me succour send.

†**7.** Directly, due; ? full. *Obs.*

1509 HAWES *Past. Pleas.* xxxvi. (Percy Soc.) 191 So forthe we sayled right playne southwest. **1527** *Prose Life St. Brandan* (Percy Soc.) 38 They sayled playn eest, and than they sawe an ylonde. *c* **1540** BOORDE *The boke for to Lerne* B ij b, Better it is.. that y wyndowes do open playne north, than playne south. **1719** DE FOE *Crusoe* (1840) II. v. 111 [The savages] were confined to a neck of land surrounded with high rocks behind them, and lying plain towards the sea before them.

C. Combinations.

a. With the adj.: chiefly parasynthetic, as ***plain-bodied***, ***-clothed***, ***-faced*** (also *fig.*), ***-featured***, ***-garbed***, etc.; also ***plain-looking***. See also PLAIN-HEARTED.

1825 J. NEAL *Bro. Jonathan* II. 109 The martial, plain-looking stranger. **1851** RUSKIN *Stones Ven.* (1874) I. xx. 223 The fish.. are always plain bodied creatures in the best mediæval sculpture. **1882** 'OUIDA' *Maremma* I. i. 18 A plain-featured, clear-skinned woman. **1893** GUNTER *Miss Dividends* 186 Respect for all women, young or old, beautiful or plain-faced. **1928** *Weekly Dispatch* 24 June 22/2 Thus what seems a plain-faced stroke is full of guile. **1938** W. DE LA MARE *Memory* 61 A solemn plain-faced child. **1963** *Times* 11 May 11/5 Small plain-faced towns.

b. With the adv., as ***plain-bound***, ***-cut*** (example *fig.*), ***-dressing***, ***-going***, ***-meaning***, ***-pranked***, ***-seeming***, ***-woven***. See also PLAIN-DEALER, -DEALING, -SPEAKING, -SPOKEN.

1579 W. WILKINSON *Confut. Familye of Loue* 2 Playne meaning men walk openly at noone. **1598** SYLVESTER *Du Bartas* II. ii. II. *Babylon* 655 His plain-prankt stile he strengthens in such sort. **1830** MISS MITFORD *Village* Ser. IV. (1863) 252 As active, and as plain-dressing.. at forty-five as she was at nineteen. **1870** D. G. ROSSETTI *Let.* 20 Apr. (1965) II. 849, I think the woodcut had better have been left out of the plain-bound copies, as it looks quaint and provoking without the binding. **1894** STEVENSON & OSBOURNE *Ebb-Tide* I. v. 96, I never could act up to the plain-cut truth, you see; so I pretend. **1967** E. SHORT *Embroidery & Fabric Collage* i. 19 The embroidery completely alters the original plain-woven texture of the material.

c. Special combs.: **plain-back**, **-backs**, weavers' name for a kind of worsted fabric; **plain bearing** *Engin.*, a bearing consisting of a cylindrical hole in a block; **Plain Bob** *Campanology*, a method of change-ringing in which the treble works in continuous *plain hunt*; **plain chocolate**, eating chocolate (CHOCOLATE 2) made without the addition of milk (cf. *milk chocolate* (*b*)); **plain clothes**, ordinary civil or citizen dress, unofficial dress, mufti; now esp. the dress of members of a police detective force; opp. to UNIFORM; also *attrib.*, as ***plain-clothes constable***, ***officer***; also *transf.*, a plain-clothes policeman, a detective; hence ***plain-clothed*** adj.; **plainclothesman**, **plainclothes man**, a plain-clothes policeman, a detective; **plain-compass**, a simple form of the surveyor's compass (Knight *Dict. Mech.* 1875); **plain cook** *sb.*, a person, usually a woman, capable of preparing simple dishes; **plain-cook** *v. intr.*, to do plain cooking; **plain-darn** *v. trans.*, to mend by plain darning; †**plain-down** *adv.*, plainly, bluntly, without more ado; †**plain Dunstable**: see DUNSTABLE 1 c; **plain-edge** *a.*, of lace: not having a pearl-edge (*Cent. Dict.* 1890); **plain English**, plain straightforward language, plain terms; also, a plain or clear statement; **plain Friend** (see quot.); **plain hackle**, an artificial fly; **plainhead**, name given to a variety of the canary; also *attrib.*, as ***plainhead canary***, ***strain*** (opp. to *crested*); **plain-headed** *a.*, having a smooth or unornamented head; also *fig.* ignorant, simple; **plain hunt** *Campanology* [HUNT $sb.^2$ 3 and *v.* 7], a regular path taken by a bell from first position to last and back again; hence **plain hunting** *vbl. sb.*; **Plain Jane**, **plain Jane**, (a name applied to) an unattractive or ill-favoured girl or woman; also *transf.*; also (freq. with hyphen) *attrib.* passing into *adj.*; **plain language**, *spec.*, (*a*) the manner of speech used by Quakers; (*b*) = *plain text* (*b*) below; **plain man**, *spec.*, one who is not, or is not thinking in the manner of, a philosopher; †**plain number**, a number produced by two factors (PLANE *a.* 1 b); **Plain people**, **plain people** *U.S.*, the Amish, Mennonites, and Dunkards; **plain-said** *a.*, spoken without reserve, straightforward; **plain sail** *Naut.*, sail ordinarily carried; **plain saw** *v. trans.*, to produce (a board) by plain sawing; so **plain-sawed**, **plain-sawn** *ppl. adjs.*; **plain sawing** *vbl. sb.*, the method or action of producing boards by sawing a log tangential to the growth rings, so that the rings make angles of less than 45° with the faces of the boards; **plain service**, divine service said without music; **plain sewing**, (*a*) *Needlework* (see quot. 1882); (*b*) applied to a particular kind of homosexual behaviour in which masturbation or mutual masturbation takes place; **plain sight**: see quot.; **plain-singing** = PLAIN-SONG; **plain text** *Cryptanalysis*, (*a*) a text not in cipher or code; (*b*) (as **plaintext**) uncoded language; **plain weave** (see quot. 1940); also *attrib.* See also PLAIN-CHANT, PLAIN SAILING, PLAIN-SONG, PLAIN-STONES, PLAIN-TILE, PLAIN-WORK.

1830 in Bischoff *Woollen Manuf.* (1842) II. 270 The principal manufacture, viz. 44 inch *plain-backs. **1842** BISCHOFF *Ibid.* 415 They next imitated the article of cotton jeans, in worsted, with success, to which they gave the name of plain-backs, out of which has sprung that immense and valuable branch of merinos. **1917** *Engineering* 9 Nov. 503/1 The worms.. are supported in their cases by two ball journal or *plain bearings. **1941** L. S. MARKS *Mech. Engineers' Handbk.* (ed. 4) 1016 Plain bearings, according to their function, may be (1) Journal bearings... (2) Thrust bearings... (3) Guide bearings. **1971** B. SCHARF *Engin. & its Lang.* xii. 133 In their simplest form, journal bearings consist of a block with a central hole for the shaft... Smaller bearings of this type are.. referred to as eye-bearings, larger ones as plain bearings. **1702** J. D. & C. M. *Campanalogia Improved* 50 (*heading*) Grandsire Bob commonly called *plain Bob. **1788** W. JONES et al. *Clavis Campanalogia* 39 Having laid down plain and easy rules for ringing Plain Bob and calling eighteen-score, we shall next proceed to the 720. **1879** [see METHOD *sb.* 3 e]. **1931** E. MORRIS *Hist. & Art Change Ringing* viii. 346 Plain Bob.. is similar to the 'Original', in which all 'hunt', until the treble returns to lead, when, instead of allowing the 'course' to run round, second place is made by the one the treble takes from lead, thereby causing each pair immediately behind them to 'dodge'. **1965** Plain Bob [see METHOD *sb.* 3 e]. **1895** *Army & Navy Co-op Soc. Price List* 11/1 (*heading*) Chocolate... Menier's, *Plain.. $1/3\frac{1}{2}$. **1914** H. ASHTON *First from Front* xiv. 96 The people in the houses came out and cheered and gave us plain chocolate, fruit, and beer. **1948** *Good Housek. Cookery Bk.* 652 For chocolate dipping, couverture chocolate (i.e., covering chocolate, which is good quality plain block chocolate, containing an adequate proportion of cocoa butter) should be used. **1976** K. THACKERAY *Crownbird* ii. 27 Her skin was dark and smooth, the colour of plain chocolate. *a* **1966** M. ALLINGHAM *Cargo of Eagles* (1968) iii. 40 The *plain clothed Sergeant Throstle. **1975** K. MACKSEY *Partisans of Europe* xi. 182 His staffs should place more faith in the parachute and commando formations of proven reliability.. in effect putting their trust in cool, uniformed quality before hotheaded, plain-clothed quantity. **1822** T. CREEVEY in *Creevey Papers* (1903) I. x. 238 Who should overtake me but the Duke of Wellington in his curricle, in his *plain clothes and Harvey by his side in his regimentals. **1825** H. WILSON *Mem.* II. 153, I could not reconcile it to my mind that he should wear regimentals... A gentleman always looks so much better in plain clothes. **1836** MARRYAT *Midsh. Easy* xxxv, He laid out a portion of his gold in a suit of plain clothes. **1842** C. FOX *Jrnl.* 1 June (1972) 127 Her Majesty.. ordered a double number of police in their plain clothes to be stationed in the Park. **1852** MRS. CARLYLE *Lett.* II. 206 Policemen.. in plain clothes, and in uniform. **1866** MAYNE REID *Headless Horseman* xii. 67 Like a plain-clothes policeman employed on detective duty. **1881** *Daily News* 22 Aug. 3/2 Plain-clothes officer Hutt was watching the premises. **1908** K. GRAHAME *Wind in Willows* viii. 182 Policemen in their helmets, waving truncheons; and shabbily dressed men in pot-hats, obvious and unmistakable plain-clothes detectives. **1914** 'BARTIMEUS' *Naval Occasions* xxv. 287 Not a bad principle either—saves your plain-clothes from wearing out. **1926** GALSWORTHY *Escape* 14 *Girl.* Who are *you*? *Plain Clothes Man.* Plain clothes. **1929** S. LESLIE *Anglo-Catholic* iii. 41 'Do you ever come across the police?' 'More often than I care, and the plain-clothes are the worst.' **1955** *Times* 1 Aug. 7/6, I, for one, would welcome the presence of such plain-clothes patrols. **1962** 'K. ORVIS' *Damned & Destroyed* xxiv. 176 A Mountie plain-clothes tapped me on the shoulder. **1964** *Granta* 2 Nov. 152, I was rather surprised on entering the Proctors' rooms to find also in attendance a plain-clothes policeman wearing his raincoat indoors. **1972** *Nature* 18 Feb. 400/2 Two men in plain clothes came up to Sakharov and asked for his identity papers. **1977** *New Yorker* 9 May 148/2 François Eugène Vidocq.. invented the plainclothes detective. **1899** J. S. CLOUSTON *Lunatic at Large* II. v. 140 Keep your eye on that man, officer,.. and put your *plain-clothes' men on his track. **1962** *Punch* 21 Nov. 751/1 Truncheoned bobbies and macintoshed ruthless plain-clothesmen of Scotland Yard. **1969** R. D. PHARR in A. Chapman *New Black Voices* (1972) 68 The plainclothesman picked them up... When he got in the car the detective in the driver's seat asked. 'What'd he say?' **1975** J. F. BURKE *Death Trick* (1976) iii. 34 Several uniformed cops and some plainclothesmen were grouped around the entrance. **1977** *Time* 7 Mar. 6/2 As a crowd gathered, four plainclothesmen collared Amalrik and removed him bodily. **1809** MALKIN *Gil Blas* II. i. ¶5 Leonarda.. passed for a very decent *plain cook. **1840** MARRYAT *Olla Podr.* (Rtldg.) 265 A good plain cook is the best thing. **1886** *Daily News* Apr., General Servant Wanted. Must *plain-cook well. **1880** *Plain Hints Needlework* 52 To *plain-darn a hole in stocking material, and mark on coarse material any two letters. **1622** FLETCHER & MASS. *Prophetess* III. ii, Is it fit.. The emperor, my master Dioclesian, Should now remember or the times or manners That call'd him plain-down Diocles? *a* **1500** *Chaucer's Dreme* 59 Which ye shalle here.. In *pleyne Englische, evil written. **1614** B. JONSON *Bart. Fair* IV. iii, But Adam Ouerdoo had beene worth three of 'hem, I assure you, in this place, that's in plaine english. **1645**, **1705** [see ENGLISH B 4.]. **1693** *Humours Town* 56 The Boon Companion, that is in plain English, a Rake-hell, is much caress'd. **1868** *Report to Govt. U.S. Munitions War* 107 If we double the thickness, the outside.. will be but one twenty-fifth as useful, or in plain English, nearly useless. **1890** CAROLINE E. STEPHEN *Quaker Strongholds* 148 '*Plain Friends' are those who are resolved to dress according to the settled principles which commend themselves to their own mind, not enslaving themselves to passing fashions. *a* **1586** SIDNEY *Arcadia* (1622) 202 That the commons.. were too *plaine headed to say their opinions. **1888** F. G. LEE in *Archæologia* LI. 363 Holding a book.. and a plain-headed staff. **1874** W. BANISTER *Art & Sci. Change Ringing* 14 The treble works in continuous *plain hunt; whilst the other bells hunt, make places, and dodge. *Ibid.* 22 Each bell has a plain *hunting course, except when treble leads. **1965** W. G. WILSON *Change Ringing* iv. 13 The basic principle involved in ringing changes on bells, or in working them out on paper, is called the plain hunt. This word 'hunt' is used in the sense of course or path or way among the other bells. Starting from rounds.. each bell follows a regular path among the others. *Ibid.* 14 Here are examples on three, four and six bells... In each of these examples, if you draw a line through the path of any one number, representing a bell, you will get a straight path from front to back and then from back to front. This is a plain hunt. *Ibid.* 16 If we confined our ringing on four or more bells to a plain hunt we should soon get very bored with it. So once we have mastered plain hunting we must learn to vary it. **1912** C. MACKENZIE *Carnival* ii. 14 She sha'n't be a *Plain Jane and No Nonsense, with her hair screwed back like a broom, but she shall be Jenny, sweet and handsome, with lips made for kissing and eyes that will sparkle and shine. **1922** JOYCE *Ulysses* 121 Daughter working the machine in the parlour. Plain Jane, no damn nonsense. **1936** C. DAY LEWIS *Friendly Tree* i. 11 It was the plain-Jane, methodical part of herself. **1953** *Newsweek* 23 Mar. 74/1 Takarazuka girl players, living like priestesses, are virtually adored by their plain-Jane sisters throughout Japan. **1956** *People* 13 May 6/3 Put a Gorgeous Gussie among a group of Plain Janes.. and a whole office or factory routine can be upset. **1957** *New Yorker* 16 Nov. 158/2 Jewelled clasps to enliven worthy but plain-Jane necklaces and bracelets are the specialty of Marjorie Raven. **1958** *Times Lit. Suppl.* 15 Aug. ('Books in a Changing World' Suppl.) p. xxxi/4 It is very hard to know how children reared on the plain Jane vocabulary of the books written for them to-day can ever enter the territory where language is allowed to branch and flower into exuberance. **1970** 'R. LLEWELLYN' *But we didn't get Fox* iii. 34 An enormous American aircraft carrier in plain-jane grey. **1972** J. MCCLURE *Caterpillar Cop* vii. 117 If ever there was a Plain Jane, she's it, poor kid. **1974** *Country Life* 2 May 1082/3 Plain-leaved parsley.. is.. reputedly more flavoursome, though a plain Jane and useless decoratively. **1827** MRS. B. HALL *Let.* 16 Dec. in *Aristocratic Journey* (1931) xi. 151 The family are Quakers, and the old couple adhere rigidly to the *plain dress and the plain language as they call what the French term 'tutoyer' implies. **1890** CAROLINE E. STEPHEN *Quaker Strongholds* 149 The 'plain language' best known as the use of *thee* and *thou* for *you* in speaking to one person, and of first, second, &c. for the days of the week and the months. **1929** *Radiotelegraph Convention & Gen. Regulations* (Internat. Radiotelegraph Conf. 1927) 21 Correct transmission and correct reception by ear of code groups.. at a speed of 20 (twenty) groups per minute, and of text in native plain language, at a speed of 25 (twenty-five) words per minute. **1940** *Tablet* 4 May 419 The.. Soviet Embassy's plain language telegram. **1973** H. GRUPPE *Truxton Cipher* 213 The message, sent Immediate—Plain Language over Navy circuits, lay upon his.. desk top. *Ibid.* 221 Our convoys had firm orders to disregard plain-language traffic. **1896** L. T. HOBHOUSE *Theory of Knowl.* 15 The '*plain man' would probably agree with Locke that no further proof could be given. **1904** G. S. FULLERTON *Syst. Metaphysics* xvii. 263 One cannot expect the plain man to realize clearly all that his doctrine implies. **1934** A. C. EWING *Idealism* vii. 294 The plain man asserts that the table in his dining-room is square. **1948** B. RUSSELL *Human Knowl.* 193 At the moment, I notice my dog asleep, and as a plain man I am convinced that I could have noticed him any time last hour. **1978** J. PEARSON *Façades* vi. 111 Arnold Bennett.. had a plain man's taste for what was new in poetry and art. **1728–41** CHAMBERS *Cycl.* s.v., 20 is a *plain number, produced by the multiplication of 5 into 4. **1904** H. R. MARTIN *Tillie* 113 But can't you see the inconsistentness of the *plain people? **1929** *Sat. Even. Post* 23 Mar. 165/1 You found it in your heart for to join the Plain People, didn't you, Carlie? **1948** *Chicago Tribune* 25 Jan. IV. 5/4 The Plain People, as they are known, won't use automobiles or tractors, have no telephones, plumbing or political parties. **1975** *Budget* (Sugarcreek, Ohio) 20 Mar. 8/5 Both Bro. David Wagler and his wife are plain people. They work helping this organization to distribute Bibles, hymn books and concordances behind the Iron Curtain. **1865** MACGREGOR *Rob Roy in Baltic* (1867) 249 A very useful and *plain-said conversation. **1829** MARRYAT *F. Mildmay* xxi, We should.. keep.. under a *plain sail. **1857** C. GRIBBLE in *Merc. Marine Mag.* (1858) V. 9 Made all plain-sail. **1951** A. E. BRIDGWOOD *Carpentry & Joinery* (*Intermediate*) iii. 151 If figured boards are required, they should be *plain sawn... Floor joists are stronger if plain sawn. **1931** YOUNGER & WARD *Airplane Construction & Repair* vi. 98 The advantages of *plain-sawed lumber [over quarter-sawn] are: 1. It is cheaper to cut. 2. If knots are present, they are round instead of spiked. *Ibid.*, There are two principal methods of sawing up trees into lumber; *plain sawing and quarter-sawing. The former produces flat-grain lumber and the latter edge-grain lumber. **1968** F. HILTON *Craft Technol. for Carpenters & Joiners* i. 18 This plain sawing is usually the cheapest form of conversion. **1949** *Gloss. Terms Timber* (*B.S.I.*) 7 *Flat-sawn timber*, timber converted so that the growth rings meet the face in any part at an angle of less than 45°. (*Plain-sawn, slash grain, flat grain). **1961** N. P. JOHNSON in A. E. Bridgwood *Newnes Carpentry & Joinery* I. iv. 193 If figured boards are required, they should be tangential sawn... They will, however, be liable to the shrinkage and warping associated with plain-sawn timber. **1966** A. W. LEWIS *Gloss. Woodworking Terms* 18 Boards sawn tangentially to the growth rings are known as through-and-through sawn, plain sawn, slash cut, or flat sawn. **1862** E. WAUGH in *Manchester Examiner & Times* 26 Aug. 7/1 Part of the time each day is set apart for reading and writing; the rest of the day is devoted to knitting and *plain sewing. **1882** CAULFIELD & SAWARD *Dict. Needlework* 394/2 *Plain sewing*, a term denoting any description of Needlework which is of a merely useful character in contradistinction to that which is purely decorative. **1895** [see sense A. 7]. **1926** A. HUXLEY *Let.* 10 Aug. (1969) 272 What she [*sc.* Anita Loos] really likes doing, it appears, is plain sewing; spends all her holidays in making underclothes which nobody can wear. **1941** F. THOMPSON *Over to Candleford* ix. 137 Plain sewing was still looked upon as an important part of a girl's education. **1969** AUDEN in *N.Y. Rev. Bks.* 27 Mar. 3/4, I conclude he [*sc.* J. R. Ackerley] did not belong to either of the two commonest classes of homosexuals, neither to the 'orals'..nor to the 'anals'... My guess is that at the back of his mind, lay a daydream of an innocent Eden where children play 'Doctor', so that the acts he really preferred were the most 'brotherly', Plain-Sewing and Princeton-First-Year. **1971** *Observer* 7 Nov. (Colour Suppl.) 35/4 One of my [*sc.* W. H. Auden's] great ambitions is to get into the OED, as the first person to have used in print a new word. I have two candidates at the moment, which I used in my review of J. R. Ackerley's autobiography. They are 'Plain-Sewing' and 'Princeton-First-Year'. They refer to two types of homosexual behaviour. **1979** P. FITZGERALD *Offshore* vii. 80 The nuns..in a class known as plain sewing, had taught her ..darning, patching, reinforcing collars with tape. **1980** *Times Lit. Suppl.* 21 Mar. 324/5, I suspect 'Plain-Sewing' to be Auden's own invention, but its meaning is fairly clear, as it involves a pun on 'sowing' (seed or semen) and a reference to the two-and-fro [*sic*] action of the hand in sewing. **1884** KNIGHT *Dict. Mech.* Suppl., *Plain Sight (*Fire-arms*), a hind sight consisting of a simple notch in a raised plate or protuberance. **1795** MASON *Ch. Mus.* III. 164 It therefore could only be called *plain singing or chaunting, which, perhaps, is the best translation of the term *planus cantus*. **1918** F. STROTHER *Fighting Germany's Spies* vii. 144 Now.. the *plain text of the secret message is printed on the under sheet by writing through the perforations of the upper sheet, only one letter being written in each square. **1932** *Cryptogram* Aug. 1/2 A letter or a symbol is substituted for each letter in the original message. (Hereafter we shall refer to the original message as the plain-text.) **1939** H. S. M. COXETER *Ball's Math. Recreations & Ess.* (ed. 11) xiv. 381 If the characters of the plain-text message are merely rearranged without suffering any change in identity..the system is called transposition. **1967** D. KAHN *Codebreakers* (1968) xiv. 435 The cryptanalysts of the German Foreign Office..had reduced it to plaintext at once. **1972** *Sci. Amer.* Nov. 117/2 Although it is a defect of Bacon's system that a cipher text must be five times as long as the plaintext, a remarkable merit of the system is that more than one message can be hidden in the same cipher text. **1940** *Chamber's Techn. Dict.* 649/1 **Plain weave*.., the simplest interlacing of warp and weft threads. Each warp thread is alternately over and under the weft, while adjacent warp threads work opposite to each other. **1956** *Textile Res. Jrnl.* XXVI. 837/1 The fabric employed..was an 80 × 80 plain weave cotton of about 3½ oz. to the square yard. **1962** J. T. MARSH *Self-Smoothing Fabrics* xi. 155 The effect of mercerising has also been investigated by Smith..who employed 10% of methoxymethyl-urea on a plain-weave cotton fabric.

†**plain**, *a.*[2] *Obs.* Forms: 4-5 plein, -e, 4-6 playn(e, pleyn(e, *Sc.* plane, 5-7 plene, plain(e. [ME. *plein*, *playn*, a. F. *plein* (*plain*):—L. *plēnus* full.

In OF. *plein* and *plain* were confused in certain phrases, esp. in *plein* (or *plain*) *champ*: see Littré. From the running together of forms in Eng., still greater ambiguity attaches to certain uses: see PLAIN *adv.* 6, 7 (above).]

1. Full, plenary, entire, perfect. ***plain pace***: at full speed.

c **1330** R. BRUNNE *Chron. Wace* (Rolls) 10615 Now ys Arthur of pleyn age. **1340** HAMPOLE *Pr. Consc.* 3844 Crist gave to Peter playn powere. *c* **1380** WYCLIF *Serm.* Sel. Wks. II. 302 Man neden not to go to Rome to gete hem plein indulgence. *c* **1400** *Ywaine & Gaw.* 3082 Thurgh the hal sir Ywain gase, Intil ane orcherd playn pase. **1425** *Rolls of Parlt.* IV. 304/1 Pleine restitution and deliverance of þaire obligations. **1450** *Ibid.* V. 194/2 That our Letters Patentz.. stand in theire strenght and plene effect. **1461** *Paston Lett.* II. 27 For my playn acquitayll. **1481** CAXTON *Myrr.* III. vi. 140 The sonne leseth his clerenes & the lyght in the playn daye. **1495** *Rolls of Parlt.* VI. 503/1 As if the said Fraunces or his heyres were in pleyne lyfe. **1544** tr. *Littleton's Tenures* (1574) 22 The age..of xxi yeare, whyche is called plaine or full age. **1653** H. COGAN tr. *Pinto's Trav.* l. 197 The City had been assaulted five times in plain-day.

¶The following may belong here, or to some sense of PLAIN *a.*[1]

c **1385** CHAUCER *L.G.W.* 2614 Ful is the place of soun of menstralsye..As thylke tyme was the pleyne vsage.

2. Full or complete in number, extent, etc.; esp. of a council, assembly, or court.

c **1330** R. BRUNNE *Chron.* (1810) 253 What þe clergie wild schape, whan þe courte were pleyn. **1375** BARBOUR *Bruce* XIX. 49 The lord sowlis haf grantit thar The deid in-to plane parliament. **1387** TREVISA *Higden* (Rolls) VI. 337 In pleyn consistorie þe pope cursede Waldrada. **1459** *Rolls of Parlt.* V. 356/2 By thassent..of Prelats [etc.] in his plain Parlement. **1499** *Exch. Rolls Scotl.* XI. 395 To the forrestaris in the plane court in the tolbouth of Edinburgh. *Ibid.* 396 Grantande..full plane poware. **1514-15** *Act 6 Hen. VIII*, c. 4 In the full and pleyne shire courte. **1523** LD. BERNERS *Froiss.* I. xiv. 14 The whiche was redde openly in playn audience. **1589** *Reg. Privy Council Scot.* IV. 384 [The King's Majesty] sittand in plane Parliament [had ratified the Act]. **1671** R. MACWARD *True Nonconf.* 231 King Charles the first, did in plene Parliament, An. 1641...ratifie the Nationall Covenant. **1677** CARY *Chronol.* I. I. I. vii. 18 There remains for the number of plene Months 125.

3. In phrase ***in plain battle*** (***combat, joust, war***), in regular open battle, etc.

With this was evidently associated the phrase *in plain field* (F. *en plein* or *plain champ*), although this may have belonged orig. to PLAIN *a.*[1] 3 b.

c **1330** R. BRUNNE *Chron. Wace* (Rolls) 3760 Morpydus.. angerly gan hym assaille, & þer hym slow in pleyn bataille. **1375** BARBOUR *Bruce* XVIII. 79 Our maner is,..Till follow and ficht, and ficht fleand, And nocht till stand in plane melle Quhill the ta part discumfit be. *c* **1386** CHAUCER *Knt.'s T.* 130 He faught and slough hym manly as a knyght In pleyn bataille. **1470-85** MALORY *Arthur* X. xviii. 442 And of these twelue Knyghtes he slewe in playne Iustes four. **1485** CAXTON *Chas. Gt.* 209 To wete yf he wold make playne warre. *a* **1533** LD. BERNERS *Huon* xlii. 142 Fynde .ii. champyons..that for thy loue wyll fyght with me in playne batayle. **1603** KNOLLES *Hist. Turks* i. (1621) 4 Whom he was not able to encounter in plaine battell. *a* **1718** PENN *Tract* Wks. 1726 I. 577 In a plain Combat giving him that Foyl.

4. Characterized by abundance *of*; full *of*. *rare*$^{-1}$.

1483 CAXTON *Gold. Leg.* 435/2 He sheweth hym self playne of contricion.

¶ For possible adverbial uses, see PLAIN *adv.* 6, 7, which may in part belong here.

plain (pleɪn), *v. arch.* or *dial.* Forms: 3-6 pleine, 3-7 playne, plaine, 4 pleign(e, 4-6 pleyn(e, plene, plane, 5 plany, 5-6 playn, 6- plain, (6, 8-9 *dial.* plean, 8-9 *dial.* pleen, pleean). *β.* 4 pleny; *Sc.* 4-7 plenȝe, 5 pleinȝhe, 6 plenȝie, -yie, (-zie), pleinye, -ȝe, -ȝie, planyie, plainȝie, (-yie, -zie). [ME. *plei(g)ne*, *playne*, *plenȝe*, a. OF. *plaign-*, stem of *plaindre* (*plaignre*, *plaingre*) to lament, *refl.* to complain:—L. *plangĕre* to beat (the breast), lament, from root *plag-* strike. So It. *piangere*, *piagnere*, Pr. *planher*, Sp. *plañir*. The Sc. forms retained the sound of Fr. *gn* (nj), repr. by *-ny*, *-nyh*, *-nȝ* (in 16th c. print *-nz*). The vb. was both intr. and trans. already in L.; the earliest (11th c.) OF. examples in Littré are trans. and refl.; the latter arises more naturally out of the trans.]

†**1.** *trans.* To give oral expression to grief on account of or for (some thing or person); to bewail, deplore, lament, mourn (the external cause, or the inward sorrow or pain); = COMPLAIN *v.* 1. *Obs.*

c **1330** R. BRUNNE *Chron.* (1810) 222 Sir Guy Baliol died þore..He was pleyned more þan oþer tuenty. **14..** *Tundale's Vis.* 582 Gretand with a dolfulle crye, And playned his synne ful petously. **1503** DUNBAR *Thistle & Rose* 31 Thai haif moir causs to weip and plane thair sorrow. **1596** SPENSER *Astroph.* Prol., Shepheards, that wont..Oft times to plaine your loves concealed smart. **1617** W. BECHER in *Camden's Lett.* (1691) 207, I did many times plain my ill hap. **1757** MRS. GRIFFITH *Lett. Henry & Frances* (1767) I. 261, I only..plain the misfortune of not having made the first impression on your heart.

†**2.** *refl.* To utter lamentations, bewail oneself: = COMPLAIN *v.* 2. *Obs.*

13.. *Seuyn Sag.* (W.) 832 Pleined him of his mochel wo. **1340** HAMPOLE *Pr. Consc.* 2540 Þarfor Saint Bernard pleyned him here Of his lyf. **1423** JAS. I *Kingis Q.* xl, I sawe ..new cummyn hir to pleyne,..the freschest ȝonge floure. *c* **1550** R. BIESTON *Bayte Fortune* Biij, To plaine hym nought auayleth. **1633** P. FLETCHER *Purple Isl.* XII. lxxiv, Thus with glad sorrow did she sweetly plain her. **1710** PHILIPS *Pastorals* i. 8 A Shepherd Boy..Thus plain'd him of his dreary Discontent.

3. *intr.* To give oral utterance to sorrow; to lament, mourn; = COMPLAIN *v.* 3. Now *poet.* and *dial.*

1297 R. GLOUC. (Rolls) 3576 Mest in is herte was uor anguysse to playne. *c* **1400** *Destr. Troy* 3471 Playnond with pytie. *a* **1547** SURREY in *Tottell's Misc.* (Arb.) 3, I wish for night, more couertly to playn. *a* **1586** SIDNEY *Arcadia* II. (1598) 118 Though he plaine, he doth not complaine; for it is a harme, but no wrong, which he hath receiued. **1613** W. BROWNE *Brit. Past.* I. i, She loves not him that plaineth, but that pleaseth. **1710** PHILIPS *Pastorals* ii. 13 Small Cause, I ween, has lusty Youth to plain. **1865** LOWELL *L'Envoi* Poet. Wks. (1879) 457 The Muse is womanish, nor deigns Her love to him that pules and plains.

β. **1375** BARBOUR *Bruce* IV. 215 Thus plenȝeit he off his folye.

b. = COMPLAIN *v.* 4. *dial.*

1863 MRS. TOOGOOD *Yorks. Dial.*, He seemed verra ill, he pleaned a good deal. **1898** KIRKBY *Lakeland Wds.* (E.D.D.), She pleens a gay deal aboot her heed.

4. To give utterance to feelings of ill-usage or injury; = COMPLAIN *v.* 5, 6, 8.

†**a.** *refl. Obs.*

1297 R. GLOUC. (Rolls) 504 He ne dorste him naȝt pleine. *c* **1330** R. BRUNNE *Chron. Wace* (Rolls) 16144 Penda.. pleyned hym vnto Cadwalyn. *c* **1380** WYCLIF *Wks.* (1880) 388 Þai hadden no more nede to plene hem of þis ordenaunce þan hadden þe oþer two statis of his chirche. **1590** MARLOWE *Edw. II*, v. i, To plain me to the gods against them both. **1592** KYD *Sp. Trag.* III. vii. 69, I will go plaine me to my Lord the King.

β. **1456** SIR G. HAYE *Law Arms* (S.T.S.) 163, I suld plenȝe me till his juge, and ask rycht and law of him.

b. *intr.* To make complaint. Const. *of*, *against*, *on*, *upon*, *that*.... *poet.* (*arch.*) and *dial.*

1297 R. GLOUC. (Rolls) 765 To is doȝter quene of cornwaile gan wende [Lear] & plainede of þe unkundhede of his doȝter gornorille. *c* **1440** *Gesta Rom.* viii. 22 (Harl. MS.) Than þe soule shall pleyne vpon þe flesh. **1612** DEKKER *If it be not good* Wks. 1873 III. 318 This Reuerend sub-Prior, Who plaines against disorders of this House. **1724** in *Ramsay's Tea-t. Misc.* (1733) II. 119 Why dost thou pleen? I thee maintain, For meal and mawt thou disna want. **1808** SCOTT *Marm.* VI. xiii, 'Though something I might plain', he said, 'Of cold respect to stranger guest'. **1825** BROCKETT *N.C. Gloss.*, *Plean*, to complain. An old word. **1876** *Whitby Gloss.*, *Plain*, to complain.

β. **13..** *E.E. Allit. P.* A. 548 Þenne þe fyrst bygonne to pleny & sayden þat þay hade travayled sore. **1375** BARBOUR *Bruce* XI. 320 His fayis to plenȝe sall mater haf. **1412** in *Laing Charters* (1899) 24 The forsaide lorde..sal abide the prouincialis cumyng, and sal pleinȝhe til him. *c* **1470** HENRYSON *Mor. Fab.* VI. (*Sheep & Dog*) xiii, Vp rais the dog, and on the scheip thus pleinyeit. **1499** *Exch. Rolls Scotl.* XI. 395 It is plenyeit that the..induellaris within the bondis about the said forrest distroyis the wod and der grettumlie. **1535** STEWART *Cron. Scot.* II. 618 Suppois he had bot litill caus to plenȝe. **1567** *Satir. Poems Reform.* (S.T.S.) VII. 55 Pleinȝeand that sho was rauyssit by [= against] hir will. *a* **1578** LINDESAY (Pitscottie) *Chron. Scot.* XVIII. xvii. (S.T.S.) I. 81 Mony seand place gevin to men that pleissit to pleinzie, begane day by day more and more to compleine wpoun his tyrannie.

c. To tell tales, inform (*against*, *on*). *dial.*

1781 J. HUTTON *Tour to Caves* Gloss. (E.D.S.), *Plean*, to tell tales against a person. **1828** *Craven Gloss.* (ed. 2), *Plean*, to tell tales. **1892** M. C. F. MORRIS *Yorksh. Folk-Talk* 354 He gans tiv his maasther ti pleean on him.

d. *trans.* To complain of; = COMPLAIN *v.* 7. *dial.*

1855 ROBINSON *Whitby Gloss.* s.v., They are always plaining poverty.

5. *transf.* and *fig.* *intr.* To emit a plaintive or mournful sound; = COMPLAIN *v.* 9.

a **1649** DRUMM. OF HAWTH. *Poems* Wks. (1711) 23 Come with your doleful songs, Night's sable birds, which plain when others sleep. **1783** WOLCOTT (P. Pindar) *Odes to R. Acad.* iii, Nature 'plaineth sore. **1809** CAMPBELL *Gertr. Wyom.* II. xii, And nought..was heard or seen But stock-doves plaining through its gloom profound. *a* **1835** MOTHERWELL *Madman's Love* Poems (1847) 47 With selfsame voice the old woods playne, When shrilly winds do blow. **1884** M. LINSKILL in *Gd. Words* 15 The wind went on wuthering wildly, sobbing, raging, plaining over the barren moor.

b. *trans.* To say in a querulous tone.

1901 G. DOUGLAS *Ho. w. Green Shutters* 296 'It would be the wind', plained her mother.

†**c.** *intr.* Of a horse: To whine, whinny. *rare*$^{-1}$.

c **1374** CHAUCER *Anel. & Arc.* 157 Right as an hors that can boothe byte & pleyne.

†**d.** (See quot.) *Obs. rare*$^{-1}$.

1611 COTGR., *Duner*, to plaine, as a horse, that neither halteth outright, nor setteth his foot hard on the ground.

plain, obs. form of PLANE *v.*

†'**plainand**, *ppl. a. Sc.* and *north. dial. Obs.* In 5 plenyhand, pleynand, plenȝeand. [pr. pple. of *plenȝe*, PLAIN *v.*: see -AND[1].] = PLAINING *ppl. a.*, PLAINANT *a.*

1429 in *Cal. Doc. rel. Scot.* (1888) 405 The thre persouns chosin on the ta perti plenyhand. **1609** SKENE *Reg. Maj.* I. 109 The poyndes aught to be in the seasing, and possession of the partie plenzeand.

Hence †**plainandly, pleynandly** *adv.*, in a complaining manner.

c **1450** *St. Cuthbert* (Surtees) 649 Pleynandly on hyght he spak.

†**plainant**, *a. Law. Obs.* [a. F. *plaignant*, pr. pple. of *plaindre*: see PLAIN *v.*] Lodging a complaint; formally complaining; = COMPLAINANT *a.*

1467-8 *Rolls of Parlt.* V. 633/2 Charged by Jugement theryn to the persone Pleynaunt or Infourmer. **1648** PRYNNE *Plea for Lords* 51 It should put the party 'plainant without remedy. *a* **1680** BUTLER *Rem.* (1759) II. 317 The Plainant is eldest Hand, and..is understood to be the better Friend to the Court.

'**plain-'chant**. [a. F. *plain chant*: see PLAIN-SONG.] = PLAIN-SONG, CANTO FERMO (in both senses of these). Also *attrib.*

1727-41 CHAMBERS *Cycl.* s.v. *Chant*, The Plain, or Gregorian chant, is where the choir and people sing in unison, or all together in the same manner. **1887** E. L. TAUNTON *Hist. Ch. Mus.* 124 In some of the old Plain Chant Masses one finds sometimes 200 notes to one syllable! **1895** C. F. A. WILLIAMS in *Elem. Plainsong* 30 The artistic intertwining of various melodies above and below the fixed notes of the *cantus firmus* or Plain chant.

Hence '**plain-ˌchantist**, an advocate of plain-chant.

1888 S. H. LITTLE in *Dublin Rev.* Jan. 112 The 'Plain Chantist', therefore, is not inconsistent or unreasonable.

plain dealer, plain-'dealer. Now *rare.* [f. PLAIN *a.*[1] + DEALER: cf. next.] One who deals plainly; one who is straightforward and candid in his relations with others.

1571 GOLDING *Calvin on Ps.* xxxiv. 10 Rather..than God will disappoynt the rightuous and playndealers of their needful foode. **1600** J. PORY tr. *Leo's Africa* II. 40 Being plaine dealers, voide of dissimulation. **1676** WYCHERLEY *Pl. Dealer* Prol., I the Plain Dealer am to act to-day..An honest man who..speaks what he thinks. *a* **1735** ARBUTHNOT *John Bull* (1755) 3 Sir Humphry Polesworth, I know you are a plain-dealer;..speak the truth, and spare not.

'**plain 'dealing, plain-'dealing**, *sb.* [f. PLAIN *a.*[1] + DEALING *vbl. sb.*: cf. DOUBLE-DEALING.]

1. Openness and sincerity of conduct; absence of subterfuge; candour, straightforwardness.

1573 *New Custom* I. ii. in Hazl. *Dodsley* III. 14 For then plain-dealing bare away the prize. **1647** TRAPP *Comm. Acts* xxiv. 12 It falls out often, that plain-dealing puts craft out of countenance. **1709** STEELE *Tatler* No. 73 ¶10, I take you to be a Lover of Ingenuity and Plain-Dealing. **1856** EMERSON *Eng. Traits, Truth* Wks. (Bohn) II. 52 They are blunt in saying what they think,..and they require plain dealing of others.

†**2.** Name of a card-game. *Obs.*
1674 COTTON *Compl. Gamester* xix. 142 A Game called Plain-Dealing. He that deals hath the advantage of this Game; for if he turn up the Ace of Diamonds he cannot lose ..then are the Cards plaid as at Whist. **1816** SINGER *Hist. Cards* 345.

ˈplain-ˌdealing, *a.* [f. PLAIN *adv.* + *dealing*, pr. pple. of DEAL *v.*: cf. prec.] That deals plainly; straightforward in speech and behaviour; free from deceit or subterfuge.
1566 PAINTER *Pal. Pleas.* (1890) III. 329 Hee..like a playne dealinge man, beleued what she promised. **1611** BEAUM. & FL. *Maid's Trag.* IV. ii, It becomes us well To get plain-dealing men about ourselves. **1719** DE FOE *Crusoe* (1840) I. ii. 18 This captain..was an honest and plain-dealing man. **1847** EMERSON *Poems* (1857) 165 Found I true liberty In the glad home plain-dealing Nature gave.

plainer (ˈpleɪnə(r)). [f. PLAIN *v.* + -ER[1].]
†**a.** *Law.* = COMPLAINANT *sb.* 1. *Obs.* **b.** A complainer, grumbler. Now *dial.*
1340 *Ayenb.* 39 Þe ualse playneres þet makeþ þe ualse bezechinges. *c* **1450** *Godstow Reg.* 101 Bitwene Felice, Abbesse of Godestowe, pleyner,..and Aleyne Basset. **1590** MARLOWE *Edw. II*, III. ii. 158 And bid me say, as plainer to your grace, That [etc.]. **1876** *Whitby Gloss.*, *Plainer*, a grumbler.

plainer, obs. form of PLANER.

plainful (ˈpleɪnfʊl), *a. arch.* [f. PLAIN *sb.*[2] or stem of PLAIN *v.* + -FUL 1.] **a.** Distressing, pitiful, grievous. **b.** That mourns, or emits a mournful sound.
1568 T. HOWELL *Newe Sonets* (1879) 127 Let learned heads describe their playnfull plight. *a* **1649** DRUMM. OF HAWTH. *Poems* Wks. (1711) 33/2 Instead of night's black-bird and plainful owl, Infernal furies here do yell and howl. **1906** *Daily Chron.* 19 Jan. 3/4 The hero of this plainful story.
Hence †**ˈplainfulness** *Obs.*
a **1586** SIDNEY *Arcadia* I. *Plangus & Basilius* 151 From how much mourning plainfulnesse.

ˈplain-ˌhearted, *a.* Now *rare.* [f. *plain heart* (PLAIN *a.*[1]) + -ED[2].] Having a sincere and open heart; without deceit or guile; ingenuous, innocent.
1608 DOD & CLEAVER *Expos. Prov.* ix–x. 100 Let us learne to bee plaine hearted towards our brethren. **1641** MILTON *Animadv.*, *Rem. Def.* i. Wks. 1738 I. 79 Free-spoken and plain-hearted Men, that are the Eyes of their Country. **1727–46** THOMSON *Summer* 1475 Sincere, plain-hearted, hospitable, kind.
Hence **ˌplain-ˈheartedly** *adv.*; **ˌplain-ˈheartedness.**
1653 DOROTHY OSBORNE *Lett. to Sir W. Temple* (1888) 149 How I should love that plain-heartedness you speak of, if you would use it. **1691** HARTCLIFFE *Virtues* 174 That Simplicity and plain-heartedness, which ought to be in the Conversation of every Christian. **1832** [R. CATTERMOLE] *Beckett*, etc. 196 And there, with so much graveness as just gives A grace to smiles, plain-heartedly she lives.

plaining (ˈpleɪnɪŋ), *vbl. sb. arch.* Forms: see PLAIN *v.* [f. PLAIN *v.* + -ING[1].] The action of the verb PLAIN; the utterance of grief or dissatisfaction; lamentation; complaint.
1340 HAMPOLE *Pr. Consc.* 6104 Þe day of pleynyng and accusyng, þe day of answer and of strait rekkenyng. **1375** BARBOUR *Bruce* III. 647 Off thi tynsell is na plenȝeing. *c* **1386** CHAUCER *Pars. T.* ¶ 10 (Harl. MS.) Penitence is þe pleynyng of man for þe gult þat he haþ doon. **1593** T. WATSON *Tears of Fancie* xxv, A lowlie dale..cald..The vale of loue for there I spent my plainings. **1633** P. FLETCHER *Pisc. Ecl.* I. ii, A poore fisher swaine Came from his boat to tell the rocks his plaining. **1867** JEAN INGELOW *Dreams that came true* xiv, From her lips a fitful plaining broke. **1880** WATSON *Prince's Quest* (1892) 31 As a low wind wails..About a tarn whereof the listless wave Maketh no answer to its plaining.

ˈplaining, *ppl. a. arch.* [f. PLAIN *v.* + -ING[2].] That plains; plaintive, mourning; complaining. (See also PLAINAND.)
1483 *Cath. Angl.* 283/2 Plenynge, *querulus.* **1594** MARLOWE & NASHE *Dido* IV. i, Hear, hear, O, hear Iarbas' plaining prayers. *c* **1630** MILTON *Passion* vii, Yet on the softned Quarry would I score My plaining vers as lively as before. **1891** MISS DOWIE *Girl in Karp.* 104 The plaining doves are absent from the high fir-tree tops.

plainish (ˈpleɪnɪʃ), *a.* (*adv.*) [f. PLAIN *a.*[1] + -ISH[1].] Somewhat plain.
a **1845** HOOD *Publ. Dinner* 114 [You] hear rather plainish A sound that's champaignish. **1894** *Athenæum* 10 Feb. 176/1 A fresh, honest, plainish English girl.

plainly (ˈpleɪnlɪ), *adv.*[1] [f. PLAIN *a.*[1] + -LY[2].]
1. In a clear or distinct manner; so as to be clearly seen, heard, perceived, or understood.
c **1375** *Sc. Leg. Saints* xxxvi. (*Baptista*) 291 Þat he wes criste he nyt planly. *c* **1385** CHAUCER *L.G.W.* Prol. 64 Hire chere is pleynly sprad in the brightnesse Of the sonne. **1460** *Cal. Anc. Rec. Dublin* (1889) I. 306 As in the sayd chartre more playnly hit ys expressed. **1526** TINDALE *John* xvi. 29 Loo, nowe speakest thou playnly, and thou vsest no proverbe. **1692** E. WALKER *Epictetus' Mor.* xi, Too plainly is your selfish Folly shewn. **1797–1803** FOSTER *Jrnl.* in *Life & Corr.* (1846) I. 230 Cannot yet articulate plainly. **1867** SHEDD *Homiletics* iii. 58 He should constantly strive to exhibit his thoughts plainly.
2. With clear perception by the senses or mind; clearly; distinctly.
c **1374** CHAUCER *Troylus* II. 223 (272) Þey kan not pleynly vnderstonde. *c* **1430** *Pilgr. Lyf Manhode* I. lxxii. (1869) 42 As thow shalt see pleynliche whan thow hast rad Genesis. *a* **1548** HALL *Chron.*, *Hen. VIII* 231 b, He was sodenly murdered with a gonne, whiche of the neighbors was playnly hard. **1627** CAPT. SMITH *Seaman's Gram.* xii. 58 That you may the plainlier vnderstand it. **1725** DE FOE *Voy. round World* (1840) 257, I saw plainly..that I was wrong. **1860** TYNDALL *Glac.* I. i. 5 The evidences of pressure could be plainly traced.
3. Qualifying the statement made: Evidently, manifestly.
1382 WYCLIF *Jer.* x. 19 Pleynli this myn infirmyte is, and Y shal bern it. **1444** *Rolls of Parlt.* V. 107/2 That than such Juge or Juges..have pleynly power and auctorite. **1590** SIR J. SMYTH *Disc. Weapons* Ded. 9 b, That they haue plainlie kept and conuerted..a great part thereof to their owne vses. **1664** EVELYN *Sylva* (1776) 287 These [buried] Trees..were found plainly to have been cut off by the Kerf. **1736** BUTLER *Anal.* I. iii. Wks. 1874 I. 69 Such a Kingdom..would plainly be superior to all others. **1863** KINGLAKE *Crimea* (1877) II. ii. 20 Plainly it would fare ill with any man upon whom the public anger might light.
†**4.** In an open or public manner; openly, publicly. *Obs.*
13.. *Seuyn Sag.* (W.) 3297 The knight gan playnly with hir pas Vntil sho in hir chamber was. **1375** BARBOUR *Bruce* IX. 512 Quhen thai herd of the cummyng Off schir Eduard, that so planly Our-raid the land. **14..** in *Hist. Coll. Citizen London* (Camden) 96 On the next day was the Parlement playnely be-gunne. **1565** *Reg. Privy Council Scot.* I. 380 Diverse..personis hes nocht abstenit planelie to pas and repas.
5. Without concealment, disguise, or reserve; openly, candidly, frankly.
c **1386** CHAUCER *Merch. T.* 72 If pleynly speke I shal. *c* **1400** *Rom. Rose* 2878 And what she is he loveth so To thee pleynly he shal undo, Withoute drede of any shame. *a* **1548** HALL *Chron.*, *Hen. VII* 56 He would after an humble fassion plainly reprehende the King. **1646** J. WHITAKER *Uzziah* 22 The fewnesse of those that have..courage to deal plainly. **1710** LADY M. W. MONTAGU *Let. to W. Montagu* 14 Nov., I have tried to write plainly. I know not what one can say more upon paper. **1862** TROLLOPE *Orley F.* xvi, Mr. Aram, could he have been induced to speak out his mind plainly, would have expressed, probably, a different opinion.
6. With simplicity or frugality; without ornament or embellishment; without luxury.
1562 MOUNTGOMERY in *Archæologia* XLVII. 216 Which ..I haue rudely written and plainely penned. **1601** R. JOHNSON *Kingd. & Commw.* (1603) 102 They couet to liue simply and plainly. **1847** C. BRONTË *J. Eyre* vii, The hair to be arranged closely, modestly, plainly. **1902** BUCHAN *Watcher by Threshold* 289, I suppose he lives very plainly.
†**7.** Entirely, completely, absolutely, quite. (Perh. belongs to next: cf. PLAIN *adv.* 6.) *Obs.*
c **1385** CHAUCER *L.G.W.* 123 It surmountede pleynly alle odours. **1535** COVERDALE *2 Sam.* v. 6 They thoughte planely, that Dauid shulde not come in. **1568** GRAFTON *Chron.* II. 530 The kindred of the mothers side, for to saue her honesty, it plainely denied.

†**ˈplainly,** *adv.*[2] *Obs.* In 4–5 pleyn-, plein-, plen-. [f. PLAIN *a.*[2] + -LY[2].] Fully.
1387 TREVISA *Higden* (Rolls) II. 211 Of þis matire loke wiþ ynne more pleynliche after þe batayle of Troy. **1418** CHICHELE in Ellis *Orig. Lett.* Ser. I. I. 5 Towchyng al odr things, I wot wel..your brother sendyth to ȝu pleynlych. **1442** *Rolls of Parlt.* V. 58/1 To have, holde, and enjoye hem, ..as pleynly, hoolly, and in the same maner..as youre seide Fadir hadde and helde hem. **1459** *Paston Lett.* I. 499 As the bringer here of shall more pleinly declare yow. **1469** *Bury Wills* (Camden) 45, I wyll that myn detts be plenly paied.

plainness (ˈpleɪnnɪs). Forms: *α.* 4 pleynes, 4–5 pleynesse, 4–7 playnesse, 5–6 plainesse, playnes, 6 plaines, playness, pleines. *β.* See PLAIN *a.*[1] and -NESS. [ME. *play-*, *pleynesse*, a. OF. *plai(g)nesse*, *planece* flatness, smoothness, plane surface:—L. *plānitiēs*, *-ia* a flat surface, f. *plānus* flat. But the variants in *-nes*, *-ness* show that the word was soon associated with native formations having this suffix, with which it is fully identified in the *β* forms *plainness*, etc. (Cf. *finesse*, *fineness*.)] The quality or condition of being plain, in various senses of the adj.
†**1.** Flatness, smoothness, evenness, levelness.
α. **13..** *Guy Warw.* (A.) clxvi. 8 Sir Gij drouȝ out þat swerd anon, & alle þe pleynes þer-of it schon. **1388** WYCLIF *2 Macc.* xiv. 33, Y schal drawe doun this temple of God in to pleynesse. **1483** *Cath. Angl.* 282/2 A Playnes, *planicies.* **1551** T. WILSON *Logike* (1580) 11 Suche qualities as.. hardnesse, softnesse, roughnesse, plainesse. **1578** BANISTER *Hist. Man* I. 21 With more flat and equal playness.
β. *c* **1374** CHAUCER *Boeth.* v. metr. iv. 12 (Camb. MS), Lettres emprientyd in the smothenesse or in the pleynnesse [*B.M. Add.* plainesse; *ed.* **1602** plainenesse] of the table of wex. **1482** *Monk of Evesham* (Arb.) 57 The playnnes of that place was so repletyd and fulfylde withe wormys. **1573–80** BARET *Alv.* P 441 The plainenesse, or euennesse of the sea. **1617** MORYSON *Itin.* III. 102 The plainenes of the Countrie, and the frequency of Lakes and Fennes, doe more increase the cold. **1704** HEARNE *Duct. Hist.* (1714) I. 399 The plainness and evenness of their Country.
2. Openness, honesty, or straightforwardness of conduct; frankness or directness of language.
α. **1556** J. HEYWOOD *Spider & F.* xxxii. 24 You haue gifte of pleines sterne and stoute. **1639** N. N. tr. *Du Bosq's Compl. Woman* I. 17 Where as then was no other sinne in society then lying, a genuine playnesse..were enough.
β. *a* **1548** HALL *Chron.*, *Hen. VII* 56 Of the same vertue and honest playnnes [**1568** GRAFTON plainenesse] was Ihon Morton archebishop of Caunterbury. **1606** SHAKS. *Tr. & Cr.* IV. iv. 108 Whil'st some with cunning guild their copper crownes, With truth and plainnesse I doe weare mine bare. **1697** DRYDEN *Virg. Georg.* (1721) I. *Essay* 207 We see in one the Plainness of a down right Countryman, and in the other, something of a rustick Majesty. **1778** MISS BURNEY *Evelina* (1791) II. v. 40 He forced me to express my displeasure with equal plainness. **1875** JOWETT *Plato* (ed. 2) I. 336 My plainness of speech makes them hate me.
†**b.** *euphemism* for Discourteous behaviour or treatment; rudeness. *Obs. rare.*
1465 *Paston Lett.* II. 208 They know not the pleynesse that hathe ben done in such thyngys as hathe ben don in her namys.
†**c.** *the plainness*: the plain truth. *Obs.*
1477 EARL RIVERS (Caxton) *Dictes* 40 So may not a man be wele counseylled of hys frende withoute he telle hym the playnesse of hys cause. *c* **1530** LD. BERNERS *Arth. Lyt. Bryt.* (1814) 298, I pray you speke, and shew me the playnes. **1537** CROMWELL in Merriman *Life & Lett.* (1902) II. 57 If the said deposicons had been ernestly takyn, the plaines of that mater might haue been easely known.
3. Clearness to the perception or comprehension; lucidity of exposition, meaning, or expression.
1529 MORE *Dyaloge* I. Wks. 171/2 For the more playnnesse let vs put one example or twaine. **1570** BILLINGSLEY *Euclid* I. Introd. 1 The demonstrations and proofes..by reason of their playnnes neede no greate declaration. **1671** SALMON *Syn. Med.* Introd. 2 Little with Plainness is better than much with Obscurity. **1867** SHEDD *Homiletics* iii. (1869) 55 This plainness of style is the product of sagacity and keenness.
4. Absence of or freedom from ornament, ostentatious display, or luxury; simplicity.
1581 MARBECK *Bk. of Notes* 655 In their fare, apparell,.. and furniture of warre, they vse a plainenesse. **1649** JER. TAYLOR *Gt. Exemp.* II. Disc. vii. 36 The understandings of men are no more satisfied by a pompous magnificence, then by a cheap plainnesse. **1763** H. WALPOLE *Vertue's Anecd. Paint.* III. ii. 93 The excess of plainness in our cathedral disappoints the spectator after so rich an approach. **1848** LYTTON *Harold* II. i, These new comers were clad with extreme plainness.
†**b.** Simplicity (as opp. to complexity). *Obs.*
1669 STURMY *Mariner's Mag.* II. vi. 68 This Quadrant.. I hold to be as necessary an Instrument as Seamen can use, in respect of its plainness.
5. Lack of beauty; homeliness; ugliness.
1829 LYTTON *Devereux* I. v, This was far more than sufficient to atone for the comparative plainness of my person. **1868** J. H. BLUNT *Ref. Ch. Eng.* I. 105 'A very beautiful complexion', which by no means indicates plainness.

ˈplain ˈsailing, *sb.* [prob. a popular use of PLANE SAILING, formerly also spelt *plain sailing*; but used with sense of PLAIN *a.*[1] 3.] Sailing or going on in a plain course, in which there is no difficulty or obstruction; simple or easy course of action.
1756 N. OWEN *Jrnl. Slave-Dealer* (1930) 67 If he can take an observation and is acquainted with that part of navagation call'd plain sailing, without any of the practical part of seamanship. **1823** J. F. COOPER *Pilot* I. xii. 152 This is what the lads would call plain sailing..; they are out of employment [etc.]. **1827** STEUART *Planter's G.* (1828) 493 It must be all 'plain sailing', as the seamen say, and no sudden turns, intricacies, or narrow passes. **1842** F. E. PAGET *Milf. Malv.* 209 So far all was plain sailing, as the saying is; but Mr. Till knew that his main difficulties were yet to come. **1867** TROLLOPE *Chron. Barset* I. xxxiv. 292 These things are never plain sailing, my dear. **1916** G. B. SHAW *Androcles & Lion* Pref. p. xxiv, Without the proper clues the gospels are, to a modern educated person, nonsensical and incredible... But with the clues, they are fairly plain sailing. Jesus becomes an intelligible and consistent person. **1955** *Times* 29 June 13/3 It is not all plain sailing. Difficulties have to be overcome, for example, in disposing of 'contract' vehicles because of the contract terms.
So **ˈplain-ˌsailing** *a.*, straightforward in action.
1807 KNOX & JEBB *Corr.* I. 344 With all possible rectitude of heart, he has not a plain-sailing mind. **1887** RIDER HAGGARD *Jess* iv, Happy, healthy, plain-sailing Bessie.

Plains Cree. Also Plain Cree. [f. PLAIN *sb.*[1] 1 b + CREE *sb.* and *a.*] A Cree Indian people formerly inhabiting the more northerly areas of the North American plains; a member of this people. Also *attrib.* or as *adj.*
[**1823** in J. Franklin *Narr. Journey Shores Polar Sea* iv. 108 The Crees, who inhabit the plains, being fur hunters are better known to the traders.] **1860** H. Y. HIND *Narr. Canad. Red River Expedition* I. xix. 414 The Plain Crees are not fishermen like the Ojibways. **1879** H. M. ROBINSON *Great Fur Land* ix. 186 Along its entire border there prevails..a state of perpetual warfare: on the north and east with the Plain Crees. **1908** *Amer. Anthropologist* X. 199 We have in the Plains Cree of Canada part of a distinct ethnic group adopting the culture of the area without losing connection with the whole. **1913** F. W. HODGE *Handbk. Indians of Canada* (1971) 382/2 *Paskwawininiwug* ('prairie people'), the Plains Cree, one of the two great subdivisions of the Cree. **1928** L. BLOOMFIELD in C. F. Hockett *Leonard Bloomfield Anthol.* (1970) 200 As for our own Indians, in spite of their Plains Cree contempt for the Swampy Cree, they did not joke with the old man. *Ibid.*, Bad Owl was one of the young Plains Cree who hired out to us one spring to make the river voyage. **1938** P. H. GODSELL *Red Hunters of Snows* v. 85 The Pasquainniniwuk or 'People of the Plains', roaming the prairies of Manitoba, Saskatchewan and Alberta..known to the fur traders as the Plains Crees, had ..acquired most of the traits and characteristics of the buffalo-hunting tribes. **1940** *Anthropol. Papers Amer. Mus. Nat. Hist.* XXXVII. 195/2 Among the Plains Cree, the horse was the standard of prestige value by means of which the status criteria of wealth, valor, and liberality could best be realized. *Ibid.* 251/1 The concept of a single all powerful creator was dominant in Plains Cree religious ideology and ceremonialism. **1948** H. E. HIVES *Cree Gram.* 3 In the open

country of the Saskatchewans live the Plain Cree. **1972** D. MORTON *Last War Drum* vii. 133 Big Bear and the Plains Crees set out, striking eastward, but..the Woods Crees turned north.

plainsher, variant of PLANCHER *sb.*[1]

Plains Indian, *sb.* and *a.* Also 7–9 plain Indian. [PLAIN *sb.*[1] 1 b.] **A.** *sb.* A member of any of the Indian peoples who formerly inhabited the North American plains; (*pl.*) these peoples collectively. **B.** *adj.* Of or pertaining to any of these peoples.

1697 H. KELSEY *Jrnl.* 3 July in *Kelsey Papers* (1929) 88 About four a clock some plain indians arrived att the fort. **1844** J. H. LEFROY *In Search Magnetic North* (1955) xii. 142 The plains Indians are in a state of warfare, and there is a certain degree of danger in a single boat or canoe passing through their country. **1852** in *Mich. Hist. Mag.* (1925) IX. 397 Though the plains Indians frequently go unpunished, that is no reason why our Indians here should be butchered. **1887** *Jrnls. Senate Canada* XXI. App. 53 As to the existing food there is not very much on the plains for the plain Indians. **1913** J. LONDON *Valley of Moon* 438 A lithograph ..of a Plains Indian, in paint and feathers. **1917** C. WISSLER *Amer. Indian* xiv. 207 (*caption*) The Plains Indian culture area. **1931** *Amer. Speech* VII. 2 All Nebraska Indians were known as 'plains Indians'. **1937** R. H. LOWIE *Hist. Ethnol. Theory* viii. 127 A barely existing..totemic system is made responsible for the animal names of Plains Indian military societies. **1952** B. BLACKWOOD in T. K. Penniman *Hundred Years of Anthropol.* (ed. 2) vi. 421 In contrast to the South-west, the Plains area has until recently attracted very little attention from archæologists, in spite of the fact that Wissler had, as early as 1907, drawn attention to the lateness of the Plains Indian culture as we know it. **1955** W. GADDIS *Recognitions* I. i. 23 With the loss of Camilla he returned to the times before he had known her, among the Zuñi and Mojave, the Plains Indians and the Kwakiutl. **1966** MRS. L. B. JOHNSON *White House Diary* 2 Apr. (1970) 380 Joe Frantz ..began to weave together the story of the place..its history ..the tribal Plains Indians..the Spanish conquistadores. **1972** D. DAVIES *Dict. Anthropol.* 148/2 With the depletion and destruction of the buffalo herds, through over-hunting by Indians and white men like Buffalo Bill, the Plains Indians lost their means of support..and in many places disappeared. **1976** *Times* 25 Sept. 12/8 Among these exhibits are..Plains Indian artifacts.

plainsman ('pleɪnzmən). [f. PLAIN *sb.*[1] + MAN *sb.*[1]] A man of the plain or plains; an inhabitant of a flat country, or of the wide open plains of some regions. In quot. 1899 applied to a horse.

1870 DE B. R. KEIM *Sheridan's Troopers on Borders* xi. 66 Such an animal is a treasure in the esteem of a plainsman. **1873** J. H. BEADLE *Undevel. West* vi. 93 Old plainsmen look at each other with a peculiar smile which may mean anything. **1881** *Daily News* 21 May 5 The French column.. was met on the boundary of the Mater district by two or three hundred plainsmen, who made a show of resistance. **1891** *Spectator* May 732 Imbued with that sense of freedom peculiar to the Australian, the American plainsman, and the Canadian. **1899** *Contemp. Rev.* Sept. 355 Experienced ranchmen never turn a bunch of green brood-mares out unless accompanied by three or four of these sagacious little plainsmen. **1931** 'GREY OWL' *Men of Last Frontier* 118 The difficult task of transforming an indifferent plainsman into some kind of woodsman. **1956** E. POUND tr. *Sophocles' Women of Trachis* 45 No gang of plainsman with spears.. was strong enough. **1970** *Toronto Daily Star* 24 Sept. 10/3 (Advt.), Exceptionally handsome, this well made furniture is as rugged as a plainsman, it'll stand up to plenty of hard knocks and last a lifetime. **1975** D. PITTS *This City is Ours* liii. 266 The sound [*sc.* the Indian war cry]..that had defied the plainsmen and the encroaching wagon trains.

plain-song ('pleɪnsɒŋ). *Mus.* [Rendering med.L. *cantus plānus*, F. *plain chant*, It. *canto piano*: see quot. 1895 in sense 1.]

1. The form of vocal music believed to have been used in the Christian Church from the earliest times, consisting of melodies composed in the mediæval modes (see MODE) and in free rhythm depending on the accentuation of the words, and sung in unison; in the West it was first systematized in the 4th century by St. Ambrose, and further developed in the 6th century by St. Gregory the Great: see AMBROSIAN, GREGORIAN.

1513 in *Trans. Roy. Hist. Soc.* VI. 362 Chapellanis that has vnderstandyng to syng plane sang, priket sang, and to do seruice efter the tenour of his foundation. **1545** ASCHAM *Toxoph.* (Arb.) 41, I wysshe..that the laudable custome of Englande to teache chyldren their plainesong and priksong, were not so decayed. **1706** A. BEDFORD *Temple Mus.* iii. 62 The first..Performance was done..by Plain Song; as the Psalms are..read in Cathedrals. **1878** STAINER in *Queen's Printers' Bible-Aids* 67 The tendency of recitation to develope into monotone and an irregular chant..is illustrated by the history of 'plain song' in the early Christian Church. **1895** H. B. BRIGGS in *Elem. Plainsong* 1 Plainsong or *Cantus planus*—even, level, plain song—is perfectly distinct from *cantus figuratus*, or *mensuratus*, i.e. harmonised, measured music, from which it essentially differs in tonality and rhythm... In plainsong the accents occur irregularly, thus making the rhythm *free*, but subject to certain laws of proportion which satisfy the ear.

2. A simple melody or theme; often accompanied by a running melody or 'descant' (see DESCANT *sb.* 1); hence in various *fig.* applications. *Obs.* or *Hist.*

a **1566** R. EDWARDES *Damon & Pithias* in Hazl. *Dodsley* IV. 27 Without mention of them [ladies] you can make no sport: They are your plain-song to sing descant upon. **1597** MORLEY *Introd. Mus.* 70 When a man talketh of a Descanter, it must be vnderstood of one that can extempore sing a part upon a playnesong. *Ibid.* 71 [see COUNTERPOINT *sb.*[1] 2]. **1659** H. THORNDIKE *Wks.* (1846) II. 610 Ecclesiasticus..descants indeed upon Solomon's plain song in the eighth and ninth of the Proverbs. **1674** PLAYFORD *Skill Mus.* I. v. 21 Here followeth the three usual Plain Songs for Tuning the Voice in the Ascending and Descending of Notes.

3. *attrib.*

1590 SHAKS. *Mids. N.* III. i. 134 The Finch, the Sparrow, and the Larke, The plainsong Cuckow gray. *a* **1646** J. GREGORY *Disc. Nicene Creed* Posthuma (1649) 53 The same Creed hath been most certainly sung..in a plain song-fashion, ever since the date of the Councel [of Nice] itself.

'plain-,speaking, *sb.* and *a.* **a.** *sb.* Plainness of speech, candour, frankness. **b.** *adj.* That speaks plainly or without reserve; = next.

a. 1849 E. A. POE in *Southern Lit. Messenger* July 416/1 As for American letters, plain-speaking about *them* is..needed. **1852** ROGET *Thesaurus* §703 Candour, sincerity,..plain speaking. **1864** WEBSTER, *Plain-speaking*, plainness of speech, frankness, candor.

b. 1884 *Athenæum* 9 Feb. 178/3 'The Algerines are a company of rogues', remarked a plain-speaking Dey.

'plain-,spoken, †**'plain-spoke**, *a.* [f. PLAIN *adv.* + *spoken*, pa. pple. of SPEAK; cf. OUTSPOKEN, also BEHAVED *ppl. a.*]

1. Given to speaking plainly; outspoken, unreserved.

1678 DRYDEN *All for Love* Pref., A plain-spoken honest man. **1772** FLETCHER *Logica Genev.* 103 The Creed of an honest, consistent, plain-spoken Calvinist. **1884** JENNINGS *Croker Papers* I. ii. 54 [He] was much too sincere and plain-spoken to be a model courtier.

2. Plainly spoken; clearly or directly expressed; outspoken, candid, frank.

1703 ROWE *Ulyss.* I. (1706) Cj, Leave my plain spoke Love to prove its Merit. **1836** SIR H. TAYLOR *Statesman* xxxi. 238 A rough, bluff, hearty, plain-spoken way of eulogising them to their faces. **1869** FREEMAN *Norm. Conq.* III. xii. 106 He seems to have used language nearly as plain-spoken as Tostig did two years later.

Hence **plain-'spokenness**.

1865 F. OAKELEY *Hist. Notes* 29 To such friends..he [Mr. Froude] discloses himself..with almost the plain-spokenness of the confessional. **1883** W. T. ARNOLD in Ward *Eng. Poets* (ed. 2) II. 87 Witter had to expiate his plain spokenness by a rigorous confinement.

'plainstones, *sb. pl. Sc.* Also 8–9 **-stanes, -stenes.** [f. PLAIN *a.*[1], flat, smooth + STONE.] Flagstones; the flagged side-pavement of a street.

a **1774** FERGUSSON *Mutual Compl. Plainstanes & Cawsey* 3 The spacious Street an' gude Plainstanes Were never kend to crack but anes. *c* **1817** HOGG *Tales & Sk.* VI. 42 One page said he saw her step aside on the plain stones, speaking to an elderly woman. **1856** DOBELL *Lyrics in War Time, Shower*, A mirkier wash that splashed and clapped The plainstones. **1881** *Blackw. Mag.* Apr. 524 He met them promenading on the plainstanes.

plaint (pleɪnt), *sb.* Forms: α. 3–4 **pleinte**, 4–5 **pleynte**, 5–6 **playnte**, **plainte**, (5 **plancte**, **playnthe**, 6 **plente**). β. 4 **pleint**, 4–6 **pleynt**, **playnt**, 4–6 **plant**, 5 **playntt**, 5–6 **plent**, 4– **plaint**. [In ME. two words: α. *pleinte*, *plainte*, a. OF. *plainte*, in med.L. *plancta* (Du Cange), sb. from fem. pa. pple. of *plang-ĕre*, ppl. stem *planct-*, to beat the breast, lament: for form cf. COMPLAINT. β. *pleint*, *plaint*, a. OF. *plaint*, *pleint* = Pr. *planch*, Sp. *llanto*, Pg. *pranto*, It. *pianto*:—L. *planctu-s* (*u-* stem), f. same vb. Only the latter has come down into mod.Eng.]

1. The action or an act of plaining; audible expression of sorrow; lamentation, grieving. (From 1600 chiefly *poetic.*)

α. *a* **1225** *Ancr. R.* 96 No wouhleche nis so culuert ase is o pleinte wis. **1297** R. GLOUC. (Rolls) 6726 To god he made is pleinte ofte wepinde wel bliue. **1390** GOWER *Conf.* III. 323 Whan he hire wofull pleintes herde..Him liste betre forto wepe. **1483** CAXTON *Gold. Leg.* 54/2 Whan they of the contre sawe this plancte and sorowyng they saide this is a grete sorow to thegypcyens.

β. *c* **1330** R. BRUNNE *Chron. Wace* (Rolls) 5163 Androcheus herde þe kynges pleint. *c* **1400** *Destr. Troy* 8686 The petie & the playnt was pyn for to here! **1559** *Primer* in *Priv. Prayers* (1851) 91 Thou only art my God, thou must hear my piteous plaint. **1588** GREENE *Pandosto* (1607) 19 Pandosto would once a day repaire to the Tombe, and there with watry plants bewaile his misfortune. **1667** MILTON *P.L.* x. 343 The hapless Paire Sate in their sad discourse, and various plaint. **1734** tr. *Rollin's Anc. Hist.* (1827) VI. xv. iv. 44 They all burst into tears, and breathed their plaints in the following words. **1770** GOLDSM. *Des. Vill.* 379 With louder plaints the mother spoke her woes. **1885–94** R. BRIDGES *Eros & Psyche* May xxviii, And piteously with tears her plaint renew'd.

b. *transf.* and *fig.*

1742 WEST *Let.* in *Gray's Poems* (1775) 148 A plaint is heard from ev'ry tree. **1804** J. GRAHAME *Sabbath* 166 The wheeling plover ceas'd Her plaint. *a* **1881** ROSSETTI *House of Life* xcviii, With plaints for every flower.

2. A statement or representation of wrong, injury, or injustice suffered; a complaint.

α. *c* **1300** *Havelok* 2961 Hauelok..bad ubbe..þat he sholde on ilke wise Denemark yeme and gete so, þat no pleynte come him to. **1393** LANGL. *P. Pl.* C. IV. 214 For pore men der nat pleyne ne here pleinte shewe. **1484** CAXTON *Fables of Alfonce* ii, Therof he wold haue made a playnte to his neyghbours.

β. **13..** *Cursor M.* 12065 Þe gret lauerdinges..plaint on him mad communli Bath to ihosep and to mari. **1444** *Aberdeen Regr.* (1844) I. 12 The alderman..profferand that give thar be ony cause of playnt it suld be well reformyt and amendid. **1577–87** HOLINSHED *Chron.* III. 799/2 He should come and present his plaint to the king. **1605** VERSTEGAN *Dec. Intell.* vi. (1628) 158 Shee with teares made vnto him her plaint. **1821** JOANNA BAILLIE *Met. Leg.*, *Columbus* xxxv. 10 They graciously, His plaint and plea receiv'd. **1856** KANE *Arct. Expl.* I. xxxii. 441 It was apparent that our savage friends had their plaint to make, or, it might be, to avenge.

†**b.** Cause, ground, or matter of complaint. *Obs.*

a **1300** *Cursor M.* 10640 (Cott.) Þan most þis mai be clene and bright, Wit-vten plaint, wit-vten plight. **1382** WYCLIF *Eccl.* vii. 15 That a man finde not aȝen hym riȝtwis pleyntes. **1499** *Exch. Rolls Scotl.* XI. 395 That the balye hald foure balye courtis..for..reforming of plants of nychtbourhed and uthiris.

3. *spec.* An oral or written statement of grievance made to a court of law, for the purpose of obtaining redress; an accusation, charge, complaint.

α. [**1292** BRITTON I. i. §11 Et volums qe le poer de nos Justices..ne pasent mie les pointz de nos brefs,..ne des pleintes a eux fetes. **1321** *Rolls of Parlt.* I. 387/1 Qe la plainte puisse estre trie par duze hommes jurees.] **1422–61** in *Calr. Proc. Chanc. Q. Eliz.* (1827) Introd. 22 Vexed in the Sherreves Court..be a pleynte of trespas. **1427** *Waterf. Arch.* in *10th Rep. Hist. MSS. Comm.* App. v. 294 That no citsaine..have no delayes in ony playnthe, butt only in an action of dette. **1495** *Act 11 Hen. VII*, c. 24 §1 Any suyte playnte or demaunde before Justices of Recorde. *c* **1537** in Leadam *Sel. Pl. Crt. Requests* (Selden) 47 Seuerall plentes of debt in the name of our souerayn lord the kyng.

β. *c* **1330** R. BRUNNE *Chron.* (1810) 313 Þat non thar com no sende to courte to mak eft pleynt. **14..** *Customs Malton* in *Surtees Misc.* (1888) 59 Jugement of any playntt for to be gyffen. **1577** HARRISON *England* II. ix. (1877) I. 202 The parties plaintiffe and defendant..proceed..by plaint or declaration, answer, replication [etc.]. **1768** BLACKSTONE *Comm.* III. xviii. 273 The foundation of such suits continues to be (as in the times of the Saxons) not by original writ, but by plaint; that is, by a private memorial tendered in open court to the judge, wherein the party injured sets forth his cause of action. **1798** in Dallas *Amer. Law Rep.* II. 205 The proceedings were drawn up as if it had been a plaint under the landlord and tenant act. **1863** H. COX *Instit.* II. xi. 581 A suit in the county court commences by plaint.

4. *Comb.*, as †**plaint-bruised** *a.*, bruised by beating in token of grief.

1627 MAY *Lucan* II. 38 But one there Her plaint-brusde armes, and moystned cheekes did teare.

†**plaint**, *v. Obs.* (from 16th c., *Sc.*) Also 4 **pleynt**, 5 **playnt**, 6 *Sc.* **plent.** [f. PLAINT *sb.*]

1. *intr.* To make complaint, complain; *rarely* to make lamentation, lament, wail.

c **1400** *Destr. Troy* 3554 He plainted full pitiously, was pyn for to here. *Ibid.* 8095 Hit pleaside hir priuely, playntyde ho noght. ? *a* **1500** *Chester Pl.* x. 392 For to the kinge I will anon To plainte [*v.r.* playn] upon you all. *a* **1578** LINDESAY (Pitscottie) *Chron. Scot.* (S.T.S.) I. 225 Ye sall haue no cause to plent. **1627** W. SCLATER *Exp. 2 Thess.* (1629) 224 Ieremie somewhere bewailes it; somewhere plaints of it. **1715** PENNECUIK *Truth's Trav.* in *Descr. Tweeddale* etc. 86 Cooks and Kailwives baith refus'd him, Because he plainted of their Dish. **1789** in Jas. Fisher *Poems* (1790) 89 Ye need na plaint upon your muse.

2. *trans.* To cover or fill with complaints. *rare*$^{-1}$.

c **1374** CHAUCER *Troylus* v. 1597 Youre lettres ful þe papir al y-pleynted Conseyued hath mine hertes pite. I haue ek seyn wiþ teres al depeynted Youre lettre.

plain-table, variant of PLANE-TABLE.

†**'plainteous**, *a. Sc. Obs.* Forms: 5 **playntis**, **plaintwiss**, 5–6 **planteous**, 6 **plant-**, **plentuous**, 7 **plenteous.** [app. for orig. type **plaintivous*, f. F. *plaintif*, *-ive* PLAINTIVE + -OUS: cf. PITEOUS, PLENTEOUS: see -EOUS.] Complaining, making or bringing a complaint.

1456 SIR G. HAYE *Law Arms* (S.T.S.) 116 [He] suld do justice till all men that ar playntis of his men as to merchandis and vitalaris of the ost and otheris. **1476** *Acta Audit.* (1839) 41/2 To Raiss new summondis..apone the said Johne of forbass..& all vþiris parsonis þt he is plaintwiss of. **1563** *Reg. Privy Council Scot.* I. 244 The lait attemptatis, quhairof ye ar plantuous in youre lettir. **1565** *Ibid.* 414 Gif ony of oure trew subjectis be..plentuous of him. **1609** SKENE *Reg. Maj.*, *Baron Courts* ii. §3. 101 Attachments..be the quhilk ane party is constrained against his wil to stand to the law, and to doe sic right and reason as he aught of law to ane other partie, that is plenteous on him.

plainteous, obs. Sc. form of PLENTEOUS.

†**'plaintful**, *a. Obs.* [f. PLAINT *sb.* + -FUL.] Full of mourning or complaint; mournful; in first quot., grievous.

13.. *Cursor M.* 1497 (Cott.) Quen caym had don þat plentful plight [*G.* cursed dede]. *a* **1541** WYATT *Penit. Ps.* cii. 16 For my plaintful sighs and for my dread. *a* **1586** SIDNEY *Sidera* xii, Here is iuster cause of plaintfull sadnesse. *a* **1649** DRUMM. OF HAWTH. *Poems* Wks. (1711) 12 O leave thy plaintful soul more to molest.

plaintie, obs. Sc. form of PLENTY.

plaintiff ('pleɪntɪf). Forms: 4–5 **pleint-**, **pleynt-**, 4–6 **playnt-**, 5–6 **plent-**, 6– **plaint-**; 4–5 **-yf**, 4–6 **-if**, **-yff(e**, 6 **-yfe**, **-ife**, **-iffe**, 5– **-iff**, (6 **plainetife**, **plantife**, 7 **-ive**). [a. OF. *plaintif*, sb. use of *plaintif*, *-ive* adj. PLAINTIVE.

Plaintiff and *plaintive* are orig. the same word in Eng., as in F.; but, in the sb. use, the original *-if* of the masculine has come down through law-French, while as adj. the word has shared in the common history of adjs. in *-if*, *-ive*; in their use, also, the two have diverged, so that a *plaintiff* is no longer thought of as a *plaintive* person.]

1. *Law.* The party who brings a suit into a court of law; a complainant, prosecutor; opposed to *defendant.*

[**1278** *Rolls of Parlt.* I. 10/2 Al quel jour,.. les pleintifs, e les veisins ke furen sumuns vindrent.] *a* **1400** in *Eng. Gilds* (1870) 360 So þ^t þe playntyf to euerych court hym profry to þe to somaunce procuratours. **1436** *Rolls of Parlt.* IV. 501/2 Ye Pleintifs in the seid Actions. **1550-3** *Decaye Eng.* in *Four Suppl.* (E.E.T.S.) 96 As for all other shyres, we refer it to the playntyues. **1560** DAUS tr. *Sleidane's Comm.* 103 When the plantife had propounded and charged him with injuries. **1601** SHAKS. *Twel. N.* v. i. 362 Thou shalt bee both the Plaintiffe and the Iudge Of thine owne cause. **1637** SALTONSTALL *Eusebius Constantine* 80 Hee sent Commissioners to examine the matter, and releeve the Plaintives. **1641** *Termes de la Ley* 219 Plaintife is hee that sueth or complaineth in an Assise, or in an action personall, as in a action of debt, trespasse, deceit, detinue, and such other. **1797** GODWIN *Enquirer* II. v. 225 He will plead for the plaintiff today. **1818** CRUISE *Digest* (ed. 2) I. 261 Judgement was given for the plaintiff. **1837** DICKENS *Pickw.* xxxiv, 'Do you find for the plaintiff, gentlemen, or for the defendant?' 'For the plaintiff.'

†**2.** *generally.* One who complains; a complainer. *Obs.* (Usually with more or less reference to the legal sense.)

a **1533** LD. BERNERS *Gold. Bk. M. Aurel.* (1546) Nn vij, If I had as muche knowlage, where to complayne to the, as thou haste power to remedye the playntife. **1627** W. SCLATER *Exp. 2 Thess.* (1629) 254 But in this, which toucheth neerest clamourous plaintiues, how may the people bee excused? **1671** HOWE *Van. Man* Wks. 1836 I. 389 Besides the evil which had already befallen the plaintiff [the writer of the 89th Psalm], a further danger nearly threatened him.

†**b.** One who 'complains' of illness. *Obs.*

1633 HART *Diet Diseased* III. xi. 270 Many of these plantives.. will often in their need, sooner have recourse to some ignorant Empericke.

3. *attrib.* (*appositive*), as ***plaintiff company***, ***plaintiff-deponent***.

1802-12 BENTHAM *Ration. Judic. Evid.* (1827) I. 473 Mendacity-serving information from him to the plaintiff-deponent. **1897** *Westm. Gaz.* 12 Mar. 9/1 The company in respect of whom the licence was assigned was not the present plaintiff company.

Hence **'plaintiffship**, the position of a plaintiff.

1833 MOORE *Mem.* (1856) VII. 18 Those who had signed an agreement to bear Murray harmless through his plaintiffship.

plaintile, plain tile ('pleɪntaɪl). [f. PLAIN *a.*^{1} + TILE.] A flat roofing tile.

1724 *Lond. Gaz.* No. 6251/3 Every Plaintyle is to be 10 Inches and half an Inch in Length, 6 Inches and a Quarter of an Inch in Breadth. **1825** J. NICHOLSON *Operat. Mechanic* 554 A row of plain tiles, laid edge to edge, with their broad surfaces parallel to the termination of a wall, so as to project over the wall at right angles to the vertical surface, is called single plain tile creasing. **1842-76** GWILT *Archit.* §2282a, Parapets.. finished with double plaintile creesing. *Ibid.* Gloss., *Plain tiles*, properly *Plane tiles*, those whose surfaces are planes.

plaintiose, -ouse, -us, obs. Sc. ff. PLENTEOUS.

plaintive ('pleɪntɪv), *a.* Forms: 4-8 as in PLAINTIFF; 6- -ive. [ME. a. OF. *plaintif, -ive*, corresp. to L. type **planctīv-us*, f. *planctus* PLAINT: see -IVE, and note s.v. PLAINTIFF.]

1. Complaining, grieving, lamenting; †suffering. Now *rare.*

1390 GOWER *Conf.* II. 6 How goodli that Penelope Of his lachesce was pleintif. **1600** J. LANE *Tom Tel-troth* 654 Thus men by women, women wrongde by men, Giue matter still vnto my plaintife pen. **1700** DRYDEN *Iliad* I. 500 To sooth the sorrows of her plaintive son. **1718** PRIOR *Solomon* III. 374 His younger Son.. First Fruit of Death, lies Plaintiff of a wound Given by a Brother's Hand. **1752** HUME *Ess. & Treat.* (1777) I. 240 The mere suffering of plaintive virtue.

†**2.** Being or pertaining to the complainant or plaintiff in a suit. *Obs.*

c **1400** *Beryn* 3533 And eke also the cost Of euery party plentyff þat fallith in his pleynt. **1489** CAXTON *Faytes of A.* IV. v. 240 Ryght and restytucion were made vnto the party playntyff of his actyon and demaunde. **1577** Parties plaintiffe [see PLAINT *sb.* 3β]. **1581** MARBECK *Bk. of Notes* 886 If in this place the Judge doe signifie God, and the aduersarie plaintiue the Diuell. **1596** SPENSER *F.Q.* v. iv. 40 To heare the piteous beast pleading her plaintiffe cause.

3. Having the character of complaint; expressive of sorrow; mournful, sad.

1579 E. K. in *Spenser's Sheph. Cal.* Gen. Argt., These xij. Æclogues,.. eyther they be Plaintiue,.. or recreatiue,.. or Moral. **1697** DRYDEN *Virg. Georg.* IV. 473 His careful Mother heard the Plaintive Sound. **1705** ADDISON *Italy* 3 Oft in the Winds is heard a plaintive Sound Of melancholy Ghosts, that hover round. **1784** COWPER *Task* IV. 479 The fiddle screams Plaintive and piteous, as it wept and wailed Its wasted tones. **1869** TOZER *Highl. Turkey* II. 242 These songs are recited slowly to a peculiarly plaintive melody.

4. *Comb.*, as ***plaintive-echoing*** adj.

1740 DYER *Ruins of Rome* 48 They.. mournfully among The plaintive-echoing ruins pour their streams.

Hence **'plaintively** *adv.*; **'plaintiveness**.

1773 MELMOTH tr. *Cicero's De Senect, Remarks* 196 The alternate plaintiveness and boldness of his strain. **1797** MRS. RADCLIFFE *Italian* xi, So sweetly, so plaintively did the strain grow on the air. **1845** JANE ROBINSON *Whitehall* xix, Gushes of rapture and plaintiveness. **1875** JOWETT *Plato* (ed. 2) III. 195 They tell you plaintively of how many evils their old age is the cause.

'plaintless, *a. rare.* [f. PLAINT *sb.* + -LESS.] Without complaint; uncomplaining.

1729 SAVAGE *Wanderer* II. 45 By Woe, the Soul to daring Action swells; By Woe, in plaintless Patience It excels.

plainward ('pleɪnwəd), *adv.* [f. PLAIN *sb.*^{1} + -WARD.] Towards the plain.

1862 CALVERLEY *Verses & Tr., Charades* VI. ii, As pours the Anio plainward, When rains have swollen the dykes.

'plain-work, plain work. 1. Work of a plain or simple kind, as distinguished from ornamental or 'fancy' work: *spec.* plain needlework or sewing, as distinct from fancy work or embroidery.

1715 POPE *2nd Ep. to Miss Blount* 11 She went, to plainwork, and to purling brooks. **1741-70** *Lett. Eliz. Carter*, etc. (1808) 19, I shall.. quietly proceed in the regular track and unambitious exercise of harmless plain-work. **1840** THACKERAY *Paris Sk.-bk., Beatrice Merger*, She does beef-steaks and plain work. **1885** *Manual Plain Needlework* 145 Implements required for plain work.

2. *Masonry.* See quot. 1832.

[*c* **1430** *Freemasonry* 539 The tower of Babyloyne was begonne, Also playne werke of lyme and ston.] **1823** P. NICHOLSON *Pract. Build.* 315 Plain-work consists merely in the cleaning up of its surface. **1832** *Encycl. Brit.* (ed. 7) V. 677/1 Plain work is the even surface produced on stone by the chisel, without the necessity of taking away more than the mere inequalities... Sunk work arises from the necessity of chiseling or hacking away below the level surface of the plain work.

plainy ('pleɪnɪ), *a.* [f. PLAIN *sb.*^{1} + -Y.] Full of or characterized by plains.

1796 W. TAYLOR in *Monthly Mag.* I. 96 Forming.. with its alluvion sand, much of the plainy peninsula of Arabia.

plaisance, plaisanterie, obs. var. PLEASANCE, PLEASANTRY.

‖**plaisanteur** (plɛzɑ̃tœr). *rare.* [obs. F. *plaisanteur* 'a Jeaster, Buffoone, Parasite, pleasant fellow' (Cotgr.), f. *plaisanter* to jest, etc., f. *plaisant* PLEASANT, merry.] A jester, a witty talker.

1841 DE QUINCEY *Rhet.* Wks. 1862 X. 38 Polonius with his quibbles, could not appear a more unseasonable *plaisanteur.*

plaise, obs. f. PLAICE.

plaisir, -ur, -ure, obs. ff. PLEASURE.

plaister, obs. f. PLASTER.

plait (pleɪt, plæt, pliːt), *sb.* Forms: α. 5-6 playte, 5-7 playt, 6 plaite, 6- plait. β. 5-6 pleyt(e, pleite, 7 pleit. γ. 6 playght, pleyght(e, 6-7 plaight, 6-8 pleight. See also PLAT *sb.*^{4}, PLEAT *sb.*, PLET *sb.*^{1}, PLIGHT *sb.*^{2} [ME. *pleyt, playt*, a. OF. *pleit* (Burguy), later *ploit* (14th c. in Godef.) fold, manner of folding:—late L. **plictum*, from *plicitum* a thing folded, neuter of pa. pple. of *plicāre* to fold.

For this sb. and the vb. the dictionaries generally give the first pronunciation above; but in living English use, the third is usual in sense 1, and the second in sense 2; which amounts to saying that, as a *spoken* word, *plait* is obsolete, and supplied in sense 1 by *pleat*, in sense 2 by *plat*. The first pronunciation appears however to prevail in U.S.]

1. A fold, crease, or wrinkle. **a.** A fold of cloth or any similar fabric, *esp.* a flattened fold or gather made by doubling the material upon itself; = PLEAT *sb.* 1. (Now generally written *pleat*, and usually pronounced (pliːt) even when spelt *plait.*)

α. **14..** *Voc.* in Wr.-Wülcker 608/35 *Ruga*, a wrynkyl, or a playt. *c* **1440** *Promp. Parv.* 402/2 Playte, of a clothe, *plica, plicatura.* **1530** PALSGR. 255/2 Playte of a gowne, *ply.* *a* **1550** *Christis Kirke Gr.* I. ii, Thair kirtillis wer of lynkome licht, Weill prest with mony plaitis [*rime* gaitis]. **1570** LEVINS *Manip.* 203/40 Ye Playt of a cote, *plica, ruga.* **1687** RANDOLPH *Archip.* 40 Their stockings are most of red cloth, hanging in plaits. **1756-7** tr. *Keysler's Trav.* (1760) I. 158 The multitude of plaits in their gowns. **1814** MOORE *New Cost. Ministers* 15 Every pucker and seam were made matters of State, And a grand Household Council was held on each plait! **1850** D. G. MITCHELL *Reveries Bachelor* 227 And then smoothed down the plaits of her apron. **1884** KNIGHT *Dict. Mech.* Suppl. 686/2 To change the width of plait, turn the nuts on the curved screw [etc.].

β. **1523** FITZHERB. *Husb.* §151 They haue suche pleytes vpon theyr brestes, and ruffes vppon theyr sleues, aboue theyr elbowes. **1585** T. WASHINGTON tr. *Nicholay's Voy.* IV. iv. 116 A Talbant high topped before deuided with twelue pleites or folds. *a* **1631** DONNE *Poems* (1650) 121 To judge of lace, pinke, panes, print cut, and pleit [*rime* conceit]. **1683** CHALKHILL *Thealma & Cl.* 74 Her silk gown.. in equal pleits hung down Unto the Earth.

γ. **1541** *Act 33 Hen. VIII*, c. 3 The said clothes.. shall be folded either in pleightes or cuttelle. **1552** HULOET, Pleyght, *sinus*... Loke in playght. *Ibid.* Playght or wrynkle, *ruga, rugosus*, full of plaightes. *a* **1586** SIDNEY *Arcadia* I. (1622) 51 The neather part full of pleights. **1683** MOXON *Mech. Exerc., Printing* xxiv. ¶10 He laps or Folds.. one part of it.. into a Plaight.

b. A fold, wrinkle, or crease in any natural structure, e.g. in the lip, brow, or ear; in the integuments or membranes of insects or plants; a sinuosity of a coast-line.

1592 DAVIES *Immort. Soul* Poems (1869) 106 Therfore these plaits and folds the sound restraine, That it the organ may more gently touch. **1601** HOLLAND *Pliny* I. 113 That towne.. stood as it were in a fold, or plait, or nouke thereof. **1754** RICHARDSON *Grandison* IV. iv. 23 A grave formal young man, his prim mouth set in plaits. **1844** MRS. BROWNING *Sonn., Apprehension* 10, I should fear Some plait between the brows. **1856** DELAMER *Fl. Gard.* (1861) 60 *Funkia subcordata* has heart-shape leaves, of a bright green, with longitudinal folds or plaits.

β, γ. **1574** HYLL *Ord. Bees* i, Aristotle nameth them pleighted or ringed in that their bodies are deuided with pleights or rings. **1647** R. STAPYLTON *Juvenal* 244 In thick pleites his browes are shrunk. **1657** S. PURCHAS *Pol. Flying Ins.* I. iii. 6 The hinder part of their bodies is full of ringes, or pleights.

c. *fig.* A sinuosity or twist of nature or character; a quirk, a dodge, a trick; a winding, a hidden recess: usually implying artifice or deceit. *Obs.* or *arch.*

1589 PUTTENHAM *Eng. Poesie* III. xxiv. (Arb.) 299 *Oportet iudicem esse rudem et simplicem*, without plaite or wrinkle, sower in looke and churlish in speach. **1599** B. JONSON *Cynthia's Rev.* v. vii, Simplicitie; without folds, without pleights, without counterfeit. **1599** SANDYS *Europæ Spec.* (1632) 124 [To] search so narrowly all the plaits and hidden corners of the Papacie. **1622** HAKEWILL *David's Vow* iv. 144 A simple heart,.. without pleits and foldes. *a* **1667** JER. TAYLOR *Guide Devot.* (1719) 123, I do not desire that there should be any Fold, or Pleight, or Corner of it hidden from Thee. **1855** MACAULAY *Hist. Eng.* xxi. IV. 581 Two characters.. of which he knew all the plaits and windings.

2. A contexture of three or more interlaced strands of hair, ribbon, straw, or any cord-like substance; *esp* a braided tress of hair, a queue or pigtail; a flat band of plaited straw, grass, or vegetable fibre, for making hats, etc. (Commonly pronounced (plæt), and often spelt *plat*: see PLAT *sb.*^{4}) Hence ***three-***, ***four-***, ***six-plait***, etc. (dial. ***three-a-plait***, ***threesome plait***, etc.); ***single plait***, a plait formed by knitting up a single string into a chain of loops, as in chain-stitch; chain-plait.

Brazilian plait, plait made of dried flag-grass, imported from the West Indies or South America. ***Leghorn plait***: see LEGHORN. See also STRAW-PLAIT.

1530 PALSGR. 255/2 Playtes of a womans heer, *tresses*; *tressure.* **17..** *Mary Hamilton* in Child *Ballads* (1857) III. 325 But in and cam the Queen hersel, Wi' gowd plait on her hair. **1837** H. AINSWORTH *Crichton* I. 205 The rich auburn hair is gathered in plaits at the top of the head. **1846** McCULLOCH *Acc. Brit. Empire* (1854) I. 317 Rye straw grown in Orkney has been found pretty well fitted to serve as a substitute for the straw used in Italian plait; and the manufacture of this straw into plait was carried on for several years to a considerable extent. **1870** *Routledge's Ev. Boy's Ann.* Apr. 243 The most simple shortening for all descriptions of small cords is that known to boys as the single plait, but which seamen know as the chain knot. **1880** C. R. MARKHAM *Peruv. Bark* xiv. 138 They were fine-looking young fellows, wearing their hair in long plaits down their backs. **1884** *Pall Mall G.* 30 Sept. 4/1 English ladies purchasing an elegant straw bonnet at the Louvre are not, perhaps, aware that the plait was made by children in Bedfordshire, and the straw put together at Luton. **1905** *Westm. Gaz.* 8 July 13/2 The paper.. is cut into strips and then plaited in a four- or five- or six-plait.

b. *Naut.* 'Strands of rope-yarn twisted into foxes, or braided into sennit' (Knight).

c. ***Polish plait***, 'a matted condition of the hair induced by neglect, dirt, and pediculi, common in Poland, Lithuania, and Tartary' (*Syd. Soc. Lex.*, s.v. *Plica polonica*): see PLICA 1.

1875 SIR W. TURNER in *Encycl. Brit.* I. 812/2 He described the state of the hair when affected with Polish plait.

3. *attrib.* and *Comb.*, as ***plait-like*** adj.; **plait-dance**, a dance in which the participants hold ribbons, which are plaited and unplaited in the course of their evolutions; a ribbon-dance; **plait-net**, a kind of machine-made lace; **plait-stitch**, = PLAITED *stitch*; **plait-work**, a decorative pattern, of a kind frequent in ancient and mediæval art, in the form of interlacing or plaited bands.

1887 *Pall Mall G.* 5 Jan. 7/1 Native dancing girls go through the well-known and much admired evolutions commonly called the *plait dance. **1901** *Lady's Realm* X. 617/1 The stitches cross in the middle, and the *plait-like appearance is attained. **1844** G. DODD *Textile Manuf.* vii. 229 In 'fancy broad-net' the device as well as the groundwork are made at the machine. In '*plait-net' the same thing is observable, and also in 'tatting-net'. **1901** *Lady's Realm* X. 616 *Plait-stitch. **1899** BARING-GOULD *Book West* II. 43 The transition from *plaitwork to knotwork took place in Italy between 563 and 774.

plait (pleɪt, plæt, pliːt), *v.* Forms: see prec. sb.; also PLAT *v.*^{3}, PLEAT *v.*, PLET *v.*, PLIGHT *v.*^{2} [f. PLAIT *sb.*, where see note on pronunciation.]

1. *trans.* To fold (a woven or other fabric, etc.); *esp.* to fold flat, to double; to gather in pleats; = PLEAT *v.* 1, and now commonly pronounced (pliːt).

1377 LANGL. *P. Pl.* B. v. 212 To broche hem with a pak-nedle And plaited [*v.rr.* playte, plytyd, plyghted; *A.* pleted, pleit] hem togyderes. *c* **1440** *Promp. Parv.* 402/2 Playtyn, *plico.* **1571** CAMPION *Hist. Irel.* vi. (1633) 18 With wide hanging sleeves playted. **1714** GAY *Sheph. Week* Tuesday 36 Will she with huswife's hand provide thy meat, And every Sunday morn thy neckcloth plait? **1732** *Acc. Workhouses* 153 Taylors are only employ'd to cut out their mantua's and plait them. **1802** MAR. EDGEWORTH *Moral T.* (1816) I. xvi. 139 Asked the washerwoman if she had plaited her cap.

1824 W. IRVING *T. Trav.* I. 188 [He] wore his shirt frill plaited and puffed out..at the bosom.

β. *c* **1440** Y-pleite; **1467** pleytid [see PLAITED 1]. **1611** SPEED *Hist. Gt. Brit.* VI. vii. §18. 67 Wearing a kirtle therunder very thick pleited.

γ. **1538** ELYOT, *Sinuo*..it is also applyed to garmentes that are pleyghted or gathered vp. **1552** HULOET, Pleyght or folde a garment, *sinuo.* **1613** J. MAY *Declar. Est. Clothing* v. 26 Hauing the clothes pleighted and bound together with threds. **1657** BECK *Univ. Char.* I vij b, To plaight.

†**b.** By extension, To fold, bend, double up; to wrinkle, knit (the brows). *Obs.*

a **1440** *Sir Degrev.* 326 Wyth scharpe exus of stelle He playtede here basnetus welle. **1570** LEVINS *Manip.* 204/1 To Playt a nayle, *replicare.* **1642** FULLER *Holy & Prof. St.* II. ix. 81 Some..seem farre older then they are, and plait and set their brows in an affected sadnesse.

2. To braid or intertwine (hair, straw, rushes, narrow ribbons, etc.) so as to form a plait, band, or rope (PLAIT *sb.* 2); = PLAT *v.*[3] 1, and now commonly pronounced (plæt).

1582 N. T. (Rhem.) *1 Pet.* iii. 3 Let it not be outwardly the plaiting of heare. **1611** BIBLE *ibid,* That outward adorning, of plaiting the haire. **1611** CORYAT *Crudities* 386 Their haire ..they plait it in two very long locks that hang downe ouer their shoulders halfe a yard long. **1831** SCOTT *Cast. Dang.* ii, The little wild boy..who used to run about and plait rushes some twenty years ago. **1841** LANE *Arab. Nts.* I. 122 An hour or more is occupied by the process of plaiting the hair. **1865** DICKENS *Mut. Fr.* II. i, Little Margery..who plaited straw.

γ. **1589** GREENE *Menaphon* (Arb.) 76 Hir lockes are pleighted like the fleece of wooll. **1703** SAVAGE *Lett. Antients* liii. 135 If thou pleightedst thy Hair with one hand, thou wouldst be sure to handle my Purse with the other.

b. *fig.* To interweave (things immaterial).

1387-8 [see PLAITED 3]. **1642** FULLER *Holy & Prof. St.* I. ii. 31 When devotion is thus artificially plaited into houres it may take up mens minds in formalities. *Ibid.* v. vii. 386 Till one unexpected counterblast of Fortune ruffled, yea blew away, all his projects so curiously plaited.

c. To felt, mat.

1875 KNIGHT *Dict. Mech., Plaiting,* the interweaving of the felted hairs, forming a hat-body by means of pressure, motion, moisture, and heat.

d. To make (a braid, garland, mat, etc.) by plaiting.

1877 A. B. EDWARDS *Up Nile* xi. 297 Plaiting mats and baskets of stained reeds.

†**3.** To twist, to cross. (Of one or two things.) **a.** *trans.* **b.** *intr.*

a. **1616** in Dalyell *Darker Superst. Scotl.* (1834) 448 [She] past the boundis of hir ground, and thair sat doun plaiting hir feit betuix the merchis.

b. **17..** in Evans *Old Ball.* (1784) III. 175 The worm leapt up, the worm leapt down, She plaited round the stone. **1799** J. ROBERTSON *Agric. Perth* 540 A too quick growing of the hoofs, which plaited under his feet and made him lame.

'plaited (see prec.), *ppl. a.* [f. PLAIT *v* + -ED[1].] **1.** Folded, doubled, gathered in folds; furnished with pleats. In this sense now generally written PLEATED.

c **1440** *Promp. Parv.* 402/2 Playtyd, *plicatus.* *c* **1440** *Pol. Rel. & L. Poems* (1866) 79/151 What schal panne profite þi gowne y-pleite [*rime* waite]? **1467** *Songs Costume* (Percy Soc.) 57 Your short stuffede dowblettes and your pleytid gownys. **1559** *Mirr. Mag., Mowbray's Banishm.* xxv, Their pleyted garmentes herewith well accorde. **1732** BERKELEY *Alciphr.* III. §9 An English courtier,..with his Gothic, succinct, plaited garment. **1839** tr. *Lamartine's Trav. East* 29/1 The tube covered with plaited silk.

b. Wrinkled, corrugated, fluted, striated.

1519 HORMAN *Vulg.* 241 A playted pyller gathereth dust. **1624** WOTTON *Archit.* in *Reliq.* (1651) 231 The body of this Columne is perpetually channeled like a thick pleighted Gown. **1776** J. LEE *Introd. Bot.* Explan. Terms 386 *Plicatum,* plaited, folded in sharp Flexures from the Disk to the Margin. **1830** LINDLEY *Nat. Syst. Bot.* 231 The plaited æstivation of the corolla. **1833** RENNIE *Alph. Angling* 51 The tail, with its peculiar fin, more or less plaited.

2. Braided, intertwined, formed into a PLAIT (*sb.* 2); interlaced, interwoven. Also PLATTED.

1594 CAREW *Tasso* (1881) 15 Playted lockes pressing with cap of plate. **1694** ADDISON *Virg. Georg.* IV. Misc. Wks. 1765 I. 22 Tho' barks or plaited willows make your hive. **1830** TENNYSON *Ode Memory* v, A garden bower'd close With plaited alleys of the trailing rose.

†**3.** *fig.* Involved, complicated, complex. *Obs.*

1387-8 T. USK *Test. Love* I. viii. (Skeat) I. 45 Diligent love, with many playted praisinges. **1662** STILLINGFL. *Orig. Sacr.* III. iii. §15 (ed. 3) 510 He left behind him such plaited pictures in his history.

4. *Comb.* and special collocations, as ***plaited-tailed*** adj.; **plaited hair**, Polish plait: see PLAIT *sb.* 2 c; **plaited lace**: see quot.; **plaited stitch**, one of the stitches of worsted work or Berlin wool work: see quot.; **plaited string work**, a kind of fancy work made with small cord or string plaited or twisted into simple patterns; **plaited worm**, a fluke-worm of the family *Aspidogasteridæ.*

1882 CAULFEILD & SAWARD *Dict. Needlework* 394/2 *Plaited Laces... Italy claims the first invention of these, and, much being made at Genoa, it was known as Genoese Lace, but as large quantities were also worked in Spain,.. plaited laces also received the name of Point d'Espagne. *Ibid.,* Plaited Laces are made upon a pillow and with Bobbins; the patterns are geometrical, and open, and have no grounds; for common purposes tinsel is used instead of real gold [wire or fine thread]. *Ibid.* 31/1 *Plaited Stitch, this stitch is an imitation of the ordinary herringbone, and is frequently called by that name. *Ibid.* 396/1 *Plaited Stringwork... Plaited string is a suitable work for ladies with weak sight. The work makes good table mats under hot dishes. **1836** T. HOOK *G. Gurney* (1850) I. v. 97, I soon came up with the eight *plaited-tailed animals which were dragging the mountain, second only in size to the Juggernaut idol.

'plaiter. [f. PLAIT *v.* + -ER[1].] One who or that which plaits.

1755 JOHNSON, *Plaiter,* he that plaits. **1775** ADAIR *Amer. Ind.* 432 Our weavers, taylors, and plaiters of false hair. **1873** 'OUIDA' *Pascarèl* II. 87 Asses laden with straw for the plaiter's market on the morrow.

'plaiting, *vbl. sb.* [f. PLAIT *v.* + -ING[1].]

a. The action of the verb PLAIT: *concr.* something plaited.

[**1406** *Litt. Red Bk. Bristol* (1900) II. 76 En fuller des draps come en pleityng et rekkyng.] *c* **1440** *Promp. Parv.* 402/2 Playtynge, *plicacio.* **1591** PERCIVALL *Sp. Dict., Engurriamiento,* pleighting, *rugositas.* **1681** CHETHAM *Angler's Vade-m.* ii. §8 (1689) 11 Keep them [hairs] from entangling together, which hinders their right Pleighting. **1882** *Century Mag.* XXV. 114 Crushing the limp plaitings of lace closer around her throat.

b. *attrib.* and *Comb.*, as ***plaiting lace, process***; also ***plaiting-down apparatus***; **plaiting-attachment**, a mechanical device attached to a sewing-machine, by means of which the fabric is pleated; **plaiting machine**, a machine for pleating cloth or other fabrics.

1813 JANE AUSTEN *Let.* 16 Sept. (1932) II. 328, I bought some very nice plaiting Lace. **1875** KNIGHT *Dict. Mech.* 1723/1 Of the numerous plaiting and tucking devices an example may be given. **1876** ROCK *Text. Fabr.* 2 Woollen stuff..wrought by the plaiting process without a loom. **1884** KNIGHT *Dict. Mech.* Suppl. *Plaiting Machine. Ibid.,* Lower the plaiting knife by adjusting the nut on screw F. **1927** T. WOODHOUSE *Artificial Silk* 134 The cloth is..passed over the inclined reversible inspecting board.., between a pair of drawing rollers, and finally to the plaiting-down apparatus.

'plaitless, *a.* [f. PLAIT *sb.* + -LESS.] Having no plaits.

1887 HARDY *Woodlanders* III. xv. 315 This solitary and silent girl stood there in the moonlight..clothed in a plaitless gown.

plak, plake, plakke, obs. forms of PLACK.

plakard, -art, -erde, -ert, obs. ff. PLACARD.

plan (plæn), *sb.* [a. F. *plan* (1553 in Hatz.-Darm.) a plane (surface), also, a ground-plan, subst. use of *plan, plane* adj., flat, plane, 16th c. ad. L. *plān-us* flat (being a learned or technical doublet of the popular *plain, plaine* flat, PLAIN).

In Eng. the two sbs. *plan* and *plane* divide between them the various senses combined in F. under *plan.*]

I. 1. a. A drawing, sketch, or diagram of any object, made by projection upon a flat surface, usually a horizontal plane (opp. to ELEVATION 11): *spec.* (*a*) A drawing or diagram showing the relative positions of the parts of a building, or of any one floor of a building, as projected upon a horizontal plane. (*b*) A map of a comparatively small district or region, as a town, etc. drawn on a relatively large scale and with considerable detail. See also GROUND-PLAN.

in plan, as projected upon a horizontal plane (opp. to *in section*).

[**1678** PHILLIPS: cf. 4.] **1706** PHILLIPS (ed. Kersey), *Plan,* a Draught, Model, or Ground-plot; a Design, Ground-work, or Project of any piece of Work. **1712** J. JAMES tr. *Le Blond's Gardening* 87 Designed upon Rolls of Paper, call'd Plans. **1727** (*title*) The Designs of Inigo Jones, consisting of Plans and Elevations for Public and Private Buildings..by W. Kent, with..Additional Designs. **1727-41** CHAMBERS *Cycl., Plan,* in architecture, is..used for a draught of a building; such as it appears, or is intended to appear, on the ground; shewing the extent, division, and distribution of its area into apartments, rooms, passages, etc. ..*Geometrical Plan,* is that wherein the solid and vacant parts are represented in their natural proportion. **1731** [see PERSPECTIVE *a.* 3]. **1793** SMEATON *Edystone L.* §97 An exact Plan of the surface of the rock, as reduced to an horizontal plane. **1833** HERSCHEL *Astron.* viii. 244 We see their [the planets'] evolutions, not in plan, but in section. **1878** HUXLEY *Physiogr.* 5 When the portion of country delineated is but small, the sketch is generally termed a *plan. Mod.* The plans of the house have been submitted to me. In an ante-room there is a plan of the tables in which you can find your place.

b. A diagram, table, or program, indicating the relations of some set of objects, or the times, places, etc. of some intended proceedings (e.g. a table of the appointments of local preachers in a circuit or district). (Cf. 2, 3.)

1855 E. SMITH *Bot.* in *Orr's Circ. Sc., Syst. Nat. Hist.* I. 151 Linnæan System..Reference to the annexed plan will show that the first eleven classes are named according to the number of stamens... The following tables contain a complete summary of the Linnæan plan of classification.

c. *Methodism.* A periodic document listing the preachers for all the services throughout a circuit for the period.

1776 J. WESLEY *Let.* 24 June (1931) VI. 224 Fix a regular plan for the local preachers and see that they keep it. **1780** —— *Wks.* (1872) XII. 318 You [Christopher Hopper] was the very person who introduced plans among us. **1807** J. NIGHTINGALE *Portraiture of Methodism* xxix. 304 A local-preacher's plan, is a paper properly divided and subdivided into columns and squares, on which the names of all the preachers are inserted, the respective places of their preaching-appointments, and the dates of the month... One of these plans is given to every local-preacher. **1851** J. LOUTIT *Let.* 17 Dec. in W. R. Ward *Early Vict. Methodism* (1976) 411 While it is said that 'no person shall *receive* a plan as a Local-Preacher without the approbation of a Local-Preachers' Meeting'..there is no express arrangement for his *removal.* **1898** B. GREGORY *Side Lights on Conflicts of Methodism* ii. 25 Village Methodism was built up at first to a very great extent by the institution of 'taking in the preachers'... Indeed, by a genial and judicious ministerial spirit, the 'Dinner Plan' may be made no inconsiderable accessory to the Circuit Plan. **1925** F. HODGES *My Adventures as Labour-Leader* iii. 19 In due course my name was inscribed upon the 'plan' as a regular local preacher. **1929** W. T. A. BARBER in Lidgett & Reed *Methodism in Mod. World* i. 28 As a local preacher he opened preaching-places and formed societies, working within the Methodist system. Like his northern contemporaries, he could not be bound by its rules, and, after several attempts at conformity, was finally excluded from the plan. **1937** W. H. LAX *Lax of Poplar* xii. 109 When I preached my trial sermon for the Local Preachers' Plan. **1957** R. F. WEARMOUTH *Social & Polit. Influence of Methodism in 20th Cent.* vii. 117 In due time he was nominated for the preachers' plan, and in 1869-70 became a Primitive Methodist local preacher. **1963** R. E. DAVIES *Methodism* 174 The plan of public services for a quarter in each circuit is drawn up by the superintendent minister, normally in consultation with his colleagues. **1975** C. MOORHOUSE *Sabden* 52 In 1810 Burnley was made the head of a new circuit. The resident Methodists in Sabden at this date had so far been organised that Sabden was put on the plan and included in the new circuit organisation.

2. A design according to which things or parts of a thing are, or are to be, arranged; a scheme of arrangement; *transf.* disposition of parts, arrangement; a type of structure (viewed as designed); configuration (of a surface).

1732 POPE *Ess. Man* I. 6 A mighty maze! but not without a plan. **1790** BURKE *Fr. Rev.* Pref. 4 A different plan..might be more favourable to a commodious division and distribution of his matter. **1828** THACKERAY *Let.* in *Daily News* 15 Apr. (1898) 6/2, I have not yet drawn out a plan for my stories, but certain germs thereof are budding in my mind. **1855** W. S. DALLAS *Zool.* in *Orr's Circ. Sc., Syst. Nat. Hist.* I. 202 Animals are constructed upon five primary types or plans, of which all the varied forms presented by these creatures are but modifications. **1875** JOWETT *Plato* (ed. 2) V. 7 The plan of the Laws is more irregular..than any other of the writings of Plato.

3. a. A formulated or organized method according to which something is to be done; a scheme of action, project, design; the way in which it is proposed to carry out some proceeding. Also in weakened sense: Method, way of proceeding.

1706 [see 1]. **1713** ADDISON *Cato* III. v. 74 Remember.. The gen'rous plan of pow'r deliver'd down From age to age, by your renown'd forefathers. **1749** G. JEFFREYS in J. Duncombe *Lett.* (1773) II. 213, I admire the execution of his plan, but not the plan itself. **1803** WORDSW. *Rob Roy's Gr.* 38 The good old rule..the simple plan, That they should take, who have the power, And they should keep who can. **1837** GEN. P. THOMPSON *Exerc.* (1842) IV. 229 Change your whole plan of campaign... Form yourselves everywhere into associations to gain knowledge which is power, and to communicate it through the press. **1855** [see 1 b]. **1892** WESTCOTT *Gospel of Life* 279 All history is in one sense the fulfilment of a divine plan.

b. ***plan of campaign*** (in Irish politics): see CAMPAIGN *sb.* 5 c.

c. A scheme for the economic development of a country. Also *transf.* Freq. with specification of a number of years in which the objectives are to be achieved; cf. *five-year plan* s.v. FIVE *a.* and *sb.* 2.

1933 *B.B.C. Year-bk. 1934* 19 Special attention was paid ..to the gradual progressive adaptation of existing facilities on a kind of 'Five-Years' Plan'. **1937** *Ann. Reg. 1936* 188 Herr Hitler accordingly announced a Four-Year Plan for Germany with the object of making Germany independent of supplies of raw materials from abroad. **1949** 'G. ORWELL' *Nineteen Eighty-Four* I. 48 Some triumph of over-production in the Ninth Three-Year Plan. **1962** *Listener* 20 Dec. 1041/2 There is no powerful spokesman inside the British Cabinet whose job it is to concentrate on the Plan. **1974** B. PEARCE tr. *Amin's Accumulation on World Scale* II. iii. 433 In a planned socialist economy, the banks strictly limit advances to enterprises to the amounts laid down in the plan.

II. (Rendering or imitating F. *plan.*)

4. a. *Perspective.* Any one of a number of ideal planes perpendicular to the line of vision passing through the objects represented in a picture, according to the distances of which planes from the eye the objects are proportionately diminished. **b.** *Sculpture.* The plane on which the figures in a bas-relief are raised above the ground, *esp.* one of several such planes giving more or less relief to different figures in the design.

a. **1678** PHILLIPS (ed. 4), *Plan* (in Perspective). **1727-41** CHAMBERS *Cycl.* s.v. *Plan,* Perspective Plan, is that conducted and exhibited by degradations, or diminutions, according to the rules of perspective. **1904** SAINTSBURY *Hist. Crit.* III. 425 To receive and express more or less detailed images, and add, as it were, not merely stroke after stroke, but plan after plan, to the picture.

b. **1780** SIR J. REYNOLDS *Disc.* x. (1876) 12 Making different plans in the same bas-relievos.

†**5. a.** = PLANE *sb.*[3] 1 a. *Obs.*

1713 *Phil. Trans.* XXVIII. 244 It is always placed upon the same Plan or Level with the Sprig that bears the Berry.

†**b.** The surface on which anything stands. *Obs.*

1723 CHAMBERS tr. *Le Clerc's Treat. Archit.* I. 8 A Base adds a Grace to a Column; and..makes it stand the more firmly on its Plan.

III. 6. *attrib.* and *Comb.* **plan-position indicator**, an instrument giving a map-like display on a cathode-ray tube of the positions of objects detected by a rotating radar scanner; **plan view**, a view in plan; = PLAN *sb.* 1.

1782 V. KNOX *Ess.* (1819) III. clviii. 190 Why always employ a professed plan-maker? **1850** T. TREDGOLD *Steam Engine* (ed. 3) I. IV. 17 These dimensions are given in the plan view, Plate IV., where the cylinder and steam chest are shown in section. **1859** *Todd's Cycl. Anat.* V. 458/1 The regular and plan-like manner in which the pulsations of the heart..take place. **1892** *Princ. Pattern Making* 160 In a plan view of a drawing, the eye of the observer is supposed to be set directly vertical over the drawing, and the illusions due to perspective are supposed not to exist. **1905** *Academy* 7 Oct. 1027/2 The simple manner accepted by all plan-drawers, and intelligible to all plan-readers. **1944** *Princ. Radar* (M.I.T. Radar School) iii. 37 The plan position indicator (PPI) presents range and bearing in polar form. **1945** *Wireless World* Sept. 270/2 The Naval 'Plan Position Indicator' presents..a complete picture of the relative positions of all aircraft in the vicinity. **1952** *Electronic Engin.* XXIV. 430/1 The plan position indicator is a 9 in. cathode-ray tube. **1962** D. NICHOLS *Echinoderms* iii. 50 The outermost virgalia of each column are shortened and expanded laterally to form a series of marginals, outlining the plan-view of the animal. **1970** K. R. HART *Engin. Drawing* iii. 11 The Elevation and Plan views may not.. fully specify the shape description of an object. **1974** *Sci. Amer.* Apr. 51/2 The task selected by Beatty was the familiar one of detecting 'targets' simulating aircraft on the cathode ray screen of a radar plan-position indicator, similar to the screens monitored by air-traffic controllers at most airports.

plan (plæn), *v.* [f. prec. sb.]

1. a. *trans.* To make a plan of (something existing, esp. a piece of ground or a building); to delineate upon or by means of a plan; to plot down, lay down. Also, to construct (a plan or diagram).

1748 *Anson's Voy.* Introd. 7 Employed in drawing such coasts, and planning such harbours, as the ship should touch at. **1764** in Picton *L'pool Munic. Rec.* (1886) II. 221 Ordered that Mr. Eyes do plan the Corporation Estate, and colour it. **1828** HUTTON *Course Math.* II. 66 Set down the measures properly in a field-book..and plan them after returning from the field, by laying down all the lines and angles. **1904** M. R. JAMES *Ghost-stories Antiq.* 184 It occurred to me that ..very few of the English preceptories have ever been properly planned.

b. To mark *out* into divisions as in a plan or diagram (said in *pass.* of natural structures). *nonce-use.*

1835–6 *Todd's Cycl. Anat.* I. 248/1 The bone itself is planned out into small circular dimples.

2. To make a plan of (something, esp. a building, to be constructed); hence, to devise, contrive, design (a building or other material thing to be constructed).

1728 POPE *Dunc.* I. 272 Here she plann'd th' Imperial seat of Fools. **1789** G. WHITE *Selborne* (1853) 3 Plan the pavilion, airy, light, and true. **1823** P. NICHOLSON *Pract. Build.* 188 In planning a large edifice, particular attention must be paid to the situation of the stairs. **1893** COURTNEY in *Academy* 13 May 413/1 The gardens were planned by the best landscape gardeners of the day.

3. a. To devise, contrive, design (something to be done, or some action or proceeding to be carried out); to scheme, project, arrange beforehand. Also with *on*, *out*, *obj. cl.*, or *absol.*

1737 POPE *Hor. Epist.* II. i. 374 We needs will write Epistles to the King;..Be call'd to Court to plan some work divine. **1777** C. REEVE *Champion of Virtue* 93 Some are born to plan, others to execute. **1782** MISS BURNEY *Cecilia* v. xi, Cecilia the whole time was planning how to take her leave. **1804** WORDSW. '*She was a Phantom of Delight*' iii, A perfect Woman, nobly planned, To warn, to comfort, and command. **1860** TYNDALL *Glac.* I. xvii. 121 We had planned an ascent of Monte Rosa together. **1868** FREEMAN *Norm. Conq.* II. x. 470 Never was a campaign more ably planned. **1873** 'S. COOLIDGE' *What Katy Did* xi. 230 Few visitors came to interrupt her, so she could plan out her hours and keep to the plans. **1896** C. M. SHELDON *His Brother's Keeper* v. 107 When Aunt Royal comes, I mean to plan for something besides all this. **1918** *Dialect Notes* V. 20 *Planned on going*, planned to go. **1926** *Amer. Oxonian* July 99 If I were planning on going after a Rhodes Scholarship next year, I should read a great deal on foreign affairs. **1936** L. C. DOUGLAS *White Banners* ix. 195 We had not planned on such a large house. **1963** M. SHADBOLT in C. K. Stead *N.Z. Short Stories* (1966) 314 We don't plan on any drinking. **1977** H. KAPLAN *Damascus Cover* iv. 35 Ari pressed for a date when he could plan on going abroad.

b. To arrange for or include in a plan; *spec.* in *Methodism*, to include a preacher in a plan (PLAN *sb.* 1 c).

1807 J. NIGHTINGALE *Portraiture of Methodism* xxvii. 280 Let no local-preacher, who will not meet in class, or who is not regularly planned by the superintendant of the circuit where he resides, be permitted to preach. **1898** J. ACKWORTH *Scowcroft Critics* 244 The next night Squire was 'planned' to conduct the weeknight service. **1899** QUILLER-COUCH *Ship Stars* ix. 75 There's a new preacher planned to the Bible Christians, down to Innis. **1950** S. REDFERN *Methodist Journey* iii. 21 As a rule, two or three preachers were planned at the villages *en route*, so the circuit trap was used. **1961** *Times* 20 Jan. 14/6 'Then we'll plan you in the circuit here,' he said briskly.

planait, obs. Sc. form of PLANET.

planar (ˈpleɪnə(r)), *a.* [ad. L. *plānār-is* (Mart. Cap.), f. *plān-um* plane: cf. *linear.*]

a. Belonging to, situated in, or related in some way to, a plane.

1850 CAYLEY *Coll. Math. Papers* I. 505, I propose to term the family of developables treated of in this paper, 'planar developables'... The developable which is the envelope of such a system [of *n* different planes] may be termed a 'multiplanar developable', and in the particular case of *n* being equal to unity, we have a planar developable. **1931** *Proc. Nat. Acad. Sci.* XVII. 127 A topological graph is called planar if it can be mapped in a 1–1 continuous manner on a plane (or sphere). **1942** M. P. BILLINGS *Structural Geol.* xvi. 307 A clear distinction between primary and secondary planar and linear structures is essential for a correct interpretation of the tectonics of plutons. **1969** W. R. R. PARK *Plastics Film Technol.* ii. 28 Biaxial or planar orientation occurs when a film or sheet is drawn in more than one direction. **1972** J. G. DENNIS *Structural Geol.* xx. 459 Other criteria of high-pressure shock origin include sets of closely spaced planes in quartz crystals... These planar features are known in quartz that has been subjected to nuclear explosions. **1972** R. J. WILSON *Introd. Graph Theory* v. 58 A planar graph is one which is isomorphic to a plane graph. **1973** *Sci. Amer.* Jan. 100/3 Probably the commonest single habit is the planar dendrite, a flat crystal with delicate branches that is often regarded as the typical snowflake.

b. *Electronics.* Of a thermionic valve: having plane-parallel electrodes usu. close together.

1956 A. L. ALBERT *Electronics & Electron Devices* viii. 307 Tubes for handling a few watts or less at very high frequencies commonly use parallel electrodes and sometimes are called planar tubes. **1965** GEWARTOWSKI & WATSON *Princ. Electron Tubes* iv. 120 If the linear dimensions of a planar diode are increased by a factor *k*, the same current flows to the anode for the same applied voltage. **1975** D. G. FINK *Electronics Engineers' Handbk.* IX. 26 Grid design is very important in planar triodes.

c. *Electronics.* Of a solid-state device: having boundaries of a number of different *n*- and *p*-type regions lying in a single plane. Also applied to the process by which such devices are made, involving the introduction of impurities into a semiconductor substrate through gaps in a thin masking layer.

1965 *Wireless World* July 325/1 Tr 1 and Tr 2 are low noise, high gain silicon planar transistors. **1967** A. S. GROVE *Physics & Technol. Semiconductor Devices* 3 The planar technology..combines the advantages of junction formation by solid-state diffusion and the masking property of silicon dioxide for precise definition of device geometry. **1975** D. G. FINK *Electronics Engineers' Handbk.* VII. 37 The significance of the planar process is that the *pn* junctions are terminated and protected beneath a silicon oxide layer. Thus many of the surface problems associated with other types of transistor fabrication techniques, i.e., high leakage currents and poor low-current dc gain, are eliminated.

Hence **planarity** (-ˈærɪtɪ), the quality of being planar.

1850 CAYLEY *Coll. Math. Papers* I. 505 It would be very desirable to have some means of ascertaining from the equation of a developable what the degree of its 'planarity' is. **1956** *Nature* 7 Jan. 37/2 The dimensions of the amide group accord closely with those given by Corey and Pauling, and it is in the *trans* configuration. It shows, however, a significant departure from planarity, since the carbonyl oxygen is 0·5 A. out of the plane containing the remaining atoms of the amide group. **1972** *Sci. Amer.* Dec. 54/3 Running tow or individual fibers between heated sprockets or gear teeth imparts a zigzag and more or less planar crimp. .. A disadvantage of the planarity is that it yields yarns of less bulk and stretchability than yarns produced by methods that impart a three-dimensional crimp.

‖**Planaria** (pləˈnɛərɪə). *Zool.* [mod.L. generic name (Müller 1776), sb. use of fem. of L. *plānārius* adj. (prop. 'on level ground', but used as = 'flat').] A genus of the suborder *Planarida* of turbellarian worms, found in fresh or salt water or in moist earth, and having a flattened form. Hence **plaˈnarian** *a.*, belonging or related to the genus Planaria; *sb.*, a planarian worm, a flat-worm; **planaridan** (-ˈærɪdən), *a.* belonging to the suborder *Planarida*; *sb.* a planaridan worm; **planariform** (-ˈɛərɪfɔːm) *a.*, **planarioid** (-ˈɛərɪɔɪd) *a.*, of the form of or resembling a planarian.

1819 *Pantologia*, *Planaria*, in Zoology, a genus of the class vermes. **1855** H. SPENCER *Princ. Psychol.* I. III. viii. 406 The rudimentary eye, consisting, as in the *Planaria*, of a few pigment grains beneath the integument, may be considered as simply a part of the surface more irritable by light than the rest. **1857** WRIGHT in *Edinb. New Philos. Jrnl.* V. 307 The planarioid larva of Hydractinia. **1858** MAYNE *Expos. Lex.*, *Planarius*, planarian. **1876** tr. *Beneden's Anim. Parasites* 46 According to Agassiz, a species of Planarian lives as a free messmate on the lower surface of the Limulus. **1877** HUXLEY *Anat. Inv. Anim.* iv. 182 The body takes on the ordinary Planarian character. **1900** *Daily Chron.* 30 Oct. 3/4 These Planarians or Turbellarians for the most part slay and kill as much as do their parasitic allies.

†ˈ**planary**, *a. Obs. rare.* [ad. L. *plānāri-us* level, f. *plān-um* a plane.] = PLANAR.

1668 WILKINS *Real Char.* 185 Compound Figures of Magnitude Planary, expressible by closed Lines. **1730–6** BAILEY (folio), *Planary*, of or pertaining to a plane, plain, even, smooth. [Hence in J. and mod. Dicts.]

planation (pləˈneɪʃən). *Geomorphol.* [f. L. *plān-um* PLANE *sb.*³ + -ATION.] The levelling of a landscape by erosion.

1877 G. K. GILBERT *Rep. Geol. Henry Mts.* 127 The process of carving away the rock so as to produce an even surface, and at the same time covering it with an alluvial deposit, is the process of planation. **1892** A. J. JUKES-BROWN *Student's Handbk. Physical Geol.* (ed. 2) III. i. 565 A tract of land which has been submerged and then upraised must have been twice subjected to this levelling process, and on its second emergence would present a wide area with a nearly level or slightly undulating surface. Such an area has been termed a plain of marine erosion, but would perhaps be more aptly called a surface of planation. **1935** *Geogr. Jrnl.* LXXXV. 171 It is only where planation occurred during the subsequent Jurassic submergence that the surface is really level, as on the Mendips. **1963** D. W. & E. E. HUMPHRIES tr. *Termier's Erosion & Sedimentation* ii. 35 The most perfect planations imply a succession of complex phenomena, which include transportation and deposition of sediments as well as erosion. **1970** R. J. SMALL *Study of Landforms* iv. 131 The interfluves of Dartmoor, besides preserving remains of planation surfaces, show in detail features of interest. **1976** A. N. STRAHLER *Princ. Earth Sci.* xiv. 208/1 The floodplain is widened by further lateral planation.

So **plaˈnated** *ppl. a.*, made level by erosion; also (as a back-formation) **plaˈnate** *v. trans.*

1912 *Jrnl. Geol.* XX. 450 Old planated surfaces..now dissected because of readjustments of drainage due to faulting. **1937** *Geogr. Jrnl.* XC. 56 The planated aspect of Waterpit Down from 900–850 feet suggests that this is a fragment of the erosion surface related to this bluff. **1954** W. D. THORNBURY *Princ. Geomorphol.* xi. 286 Paige (1912) concluded that the processes of interstream and lateral erosion at the edges of alluvial fans would produce a sloping planated surface cut on bedrock which would become buried toward the center of a basin under a cover of gravel. **1969** *Trans. Inst. Brit. Geogr.* XLVIII. 44 Till and bedrock were planated to produce a surface sloping gently towards the Forth.

planc, var. PLANH.

planceer, -eere, -ere, variants of PLANCIER.

planch (plɑːnʃ, -æ-), *sb.* Forms: 4–6 **plaunche**, (5 **plange**), 6 **planche**, 6– **planch**. [a. F. *planche* plank, slab: see PLANK.]

1. A plank or board of wood; *dial.* a floor. *Obs.* exc. *dial.*

1390 *Earl Derby's Exped.* (Camden) 43 Pro factura des plaunches in naui. **1440** J. SHIRLEY *Dethe K. James* (1818) 15 He laid certayne plaunches and hurdelles over the diches of the diche. **1483** *Cal. Anc. Rec. Dublin* (1889) I. 364 Suche person and persones..that occupieth the said Watyr-bailliffes planges. **1583** STOCKER *Civ. Warres Lowe C.* III. 117 They went ouer planches, where they were cut off from the way. **1864** BLACKMORE *Clara Vaughan* (1872) 49 A strange-looking individual..crossed the 'planch' or floor to the fireplace where we sat. **1881** —— *Christowell* v, Then the gardener..let down his 'planch', over the..brook.

2. A slab or flat plate of metal, stone, baked clay, etc.; *spec.* in *Enamelling*, a slab of baked fire-clay used to support the work during the process of baking.

1578 T. N. tr. *Conq. W. India* 233 There sawe golde in planches like bricke battes. **1580** FRAMPTON *Dial. Yron & Steele* 146 They make it in certaine small thinne planches. **1682** WHELER *Journ. Greece* I. 18 A Portic..whose curious-wrought Planches of Stone are supported by Twenty-four Corinthian-Pillars. **1684** *Bucaniers Amer.* (1699) 31 The meal thus prepared, they lay on planches of iron made very hot on which it is converted to very thin cakes. **1884** C. G. W. LOCK *Workshop Receipts* Ser. III. 206/2 The first coats are taken separately from tin covers, and placed upon thin planches of clay or iron, chalked over, and gradually introduced beneath the muffle, where, in a very short time, the enamel melts.

3. A flat iron shoe for a mule.

1875 in KNIGHT *Dict. Mech.* **1890** in *Cent. Dict.*

4. *Comb.* **planch-nail** = PLANCHER-*nail*.

1350 in Riley *Lond. Mem.* (1868) 262, 12,000 de plaunchenail..3,000 de dornail;..2,600 de wyndounail. **1364–1446** in Rogers *Agric. & Prices* II. 478–9; III. 448–51.

†**planch**, *v. Obs.* Also 6 **plaunche**. [f. PLANCH *sb.*, or a. obs. F. *planche-r* 'to planke; to floore with plankes: to seele, or close, with boords' (Cotgr.), f. *planche* PLANK.] *trans.* To form of planks, floor or cover with planks.

c **1516** in Willis & Clark *Cambridge* (1886) II. 245 For planchyng wyth thyk bords the Pantrye. **1623** COCKERAM, *Cotabulate*, to planch. **1723** BORLASE in *Edin. Rev.* (Reference wanting) [A request] that the hall of the Mount may be planched for dancing.

b. *transf.* To clap *on* (something broad and flat).

1575 *Gamm. Gurton* I. ii, The next remedye..Is to plaunche on a piece as brode as thy cap.

Hence †ˈ**planched** *ppl. a.*, made of or covered with boards; boarded.

1603 SHAKS. *Meas. for M.* IV. i. 30 And to that Vineyard is a planched gate, That makes his opening with this bigger Key. **1614** GORGES tr. *Lucan* I. 18 Yet, with his hoofes, doth beat and rent The planched floore.

†ˈ**planch-board**. *Obs.* [f. PLANCH *sb.* + BOARD *sb.*] = PLANK-BOARD.

1394 in *Archaeologia* XXIV. 307 Materiem pro walplates et bemes, et plaunchborde et plegges. **1525** LD. BERNERS *Froiss* II. clvii. [cliii.] 432 The great table of Marble..was made lengar with a great plaunche borde of Oke. **1551** *Inv. Ch. Goods Surrey* 124 For cc. of planche bourde at vi s. the c ffoote.

plancheite (ˈplɑ̃ʃeɪaɪt). *Min.* Also **planchéite**. [a. F. *planchéite* (A. Lacroix 1908, in *Compt. Rend.* CXLVI. 724), f. the name of M. *Planche*, who provided 'les meilleurs des matériaux étudiés': see -ITE[1].] A blue, fibrous, hydrous silicate of copper.

1908 *Chem. Abstr.* II. 1675 Plancheite..is a new hydrous copper silicate and is found at the copper mine of Mindouli [French Congo]. **1920** *Brit. Mus. Return* 145 in *Parl. Papers* XXXVI. 673 Copper and uranium ores from Katanga, Congo, including..plancheite, dioptase, malachite, chrysocolla, &c. **1968** *Mineral. Abstr.* XIX. 54/1 Planchéite occurs in the iron deposit of Capo Calamita, Elba, where it was found in the form of small masses with a radial fibrous structure, associated with dioptase and chrysocolla. **1971** *Ibid.* XXII. 219/2 The planchéite formula may be written as a cupric amphibole, $Cu_7Si_8O_{22}(OH)_2$.

plancher (ˈplɑːnʃə(r), -æ-), *sb.* Also 5 **plaunchere, plawncher,** 5-7 **plauncher,** 7 **planchier, plainsher, plencher, -sher,** 7-8 **planchere,** 8 **-eer.** Also with suffix-change: 5 **pla(u)nchour, -e, -schour, playnchour, -shore,** 6 **planscheour, -seour;** 5 **planshar, -e,** 7 **planchard.** See also PLANCIER (PLANESHEAR). [a. OF. *plancher, -ier* (12th c. in Littré) planking, floor, ceiling, derivative of *planche* PLANCH *sb.*]

†**1.** A wooden plank, a board; also collectively, planking, boarding. *Obs.*

c **1400** MAUNDEV. (Roxb.) xi. 47 Ouer þis bekk lay þe tree þat þe haly Crosse was made off, for a plaunchoure to men at gang on ouer þat bekk. **1408** *Mem. Ripon* (Surtees) III. 137 Item et in j roda planchoure emp. pro stauro, 8s. **1447-8** *Durham Acc. Rolls* (Surtees) 236 In xxvii de lez playnshorez empt. *a* **1490** BOTONER *Itin.* (1778) 289 Ad metam unius plancher de arbore. **1552** HULOET, Plauncher, *planca.* **1601** DOLMAN *La Primaud. Fr. Acad.* (1618) III. 754 The Almightie laide the planchers of his high chambers amongst the waters. **1627** tr. *Bacon's Life & Death* (1651) 8 As it is in..Beames and Planchers of Houses, which at first lay close together, but after they are dried, gave. **1720** W. GIBSON *Diet. Horses* vi. (ed. 3) 91 The floor may either be made of Planchers of Oak, or smoothly paved.

2. a. A floor (*dial.*) or platform (*obs.*) of planks or boards. Also *fig.*

1449 *Paston Lett.* I. 83 They ben scarse kne hey fro the plawncher. **1587** HARRISON *England* III. ii. (1878) II. 16 Beares..whose skins are by custome and priuilege reserued to couer those planchers wherevpon their priests doo stand at Masse. **1587** GOLDING *De Mornay* (1592) 93 The earth being as a floore or plancher to go upon. **1607** MARKHAM *Caval.* v. (1617) 3 Now for the Plaunchers of your Stable, they should bee of the best hart of Oke that can be gotten. **1735** *Phil. Trans.* XLI. 543 They make a Plancher, strong enough, sometimes, to bear the Weight of whole Armies passing over the Baltic. *a* **1825** FORBY *Voc. E. Anglia*, *Plancher*, a boarded floor.

†**b.** An upper 'floor' or story. *Obs.*

1523 LD. BERNERS *Froiss.* I. cccc. 695 There was nothyng but a poore hall..and aboue a smale plancher, and a ladder of vii. steppes to mount vpon. **1600** J. PORY tr. *Leo's Africa* III. 185 Their castles and villages are very homely built without any plancher or stories.

†**c.** A wooden inner roof, or ceiling, etc. *Obs.*

1561 HOLLYBUSH *Hom. Apoth.* 19 Let hym..hang ouer them a..tent cloth tied to the roofe or plancher. **1621** KNOLLES *Hist. Turks* 1303 The planchard was guilt, the wals enameled with flowers.

†**3.** = PLANCIER. *Obs.*

1564-5 ABP. PARKER *Corr.* (Parker Soc.) 231 As for either chimneys or plancher to be at this time builded, for that it may amount to excessive charge, ye may spare that cost. **1613-39** I. JONES in Leoni *Palladio's Archit.* (1742) II. 43 The Projection of the Planchere. **1688** R. HOLME *Armoury* III. 101/2 *Planchier* is a great round out swelling, between other smaller mouldings. **1703** MOXON *Mech. Exerc.* 267 Corona, or Plancheer. **1728** R. MORRIS *Ess. Anc. Archit.* 54 The Ovolo..is hid in the Cavity under the Planchere.

4. *Anat.* 'The inferior wall or boundary of a cavity'.

1882 in OGILVIE (Annandale).

5. (With pronunc. (plɑ̃ʃe) and usu. written in italic.) In France, the minimum of Treasury bills which banks are obliged to hold. Cf. FLOOR *sb.*[1] 1 c.

1957 J. S. G. WILSON *French Banking Struct.* II. xii. 342 Commercial bank rediscounts at the Bank of France..were to be subject to *plafonds*.., and the availability of loanable funds to the private sector was also to be limited by a *plancher.* **1962** *Economist* 24 Nov. 813/2 The minimum ratio (*plancher*) of Treasury bills which banks are obliged to hold. **1964** *Financial Times* 31 Jan. 5/6 Only those bills which the banks wish to buy above their compulsory holdings or 'plancher' are subject to tender. The so-called 'maximum'..rates for 'plancher' holdings..remain the same.

6. *Comb.* †**plancher-nail**, a flooring-nail.

1416-67 in Rogers *Agric. & Prices* III. 447-53. **1480-1** *Durham Acc. Rolls* (Surtees) 96 M[l]M[l]DC stanebrod et M[l]C playnchournale, xs. **1496** *Acc. Ld. High Treas. Scot.* I. 294 For iij[c] planschour nalis. **1515** *Ibid.* V. 11 For thre hundreth planchour nalis, vj.s. *Ibid.* 12 For dur naill, planseour naill, and windo naill. **1611** *Rates Outward* (Jam.), Nailles called plensher nailes, the thousand, iii.*l.* vi.*s.* viii.*d.* **1680** *Acc. Bk. Sir J. Foulis* (1894) 42 For 500 plencher naills at 6*s.* the hunder.

†ˈ**plancher,** *v. Obs.* [f. PLANCHER *sb.*] *trans.* To floor, cover, or lay with boards; to board, plank. Hence ˈ**planchered** *ppl. a.*, boarded, floored; ˈ**planchering** *vbl. sb.*, flooring.

1438 in Willis & Clark *Cambridge* (1886) I. 11 [Carpenters are working at] plancheryng. *c* **1440** *Promp. Parv.* 404/1 Plawncheryd, *planculatus.* **1497-8** *Durham Acc. Rolls* (Surtees) 100 In le planshoryng et nalyng ibidem. **1516** in Willis & Clark *Cambridge* (1886) II. 244 Also shall plancher all the chambers..wyth goode and abyl boorde of oke. **1563** GOLDING *Cæsar* (1565) 132 b, Towres were plauncherd, and battlements and portcolyses of timber set up. **1639** HORN & ROB. *Gate Lang. Unl.* I. §551 The inner-roof is plancherd with board, or arched. **1691** ABP. SANCROFT *Let.* in D'Oyly *Life* (1821) II. 16 We have a winter's work still to do..in paving and planchering..and plastering..&c.

†ˈ**planchery.** *Obs. rare.* [f. PLANCHER *sb.* : see -ERY.] Planking, flooring. In quot. *attrib.*

1519 *Inv.* in Rye *Cromer* (1889) 158, 13 parclos bords and 5 looks for windows 2*s.* 4*d.*; all old planchery bords 2*s.*

planchet (ˈplɑːnʃɛt, -æ-). [dim. of PLANCH *sb.*: see -ET[1] and cf. next.]

1. The plain disk of metal of which a coin is made; a coin-blank.

1611 COTGR., *Flanc*,..a coping, planchet, or plate of mettall readie to be stamped on, or coyned. **1794** PRISCILLA WAKEFIELD *Mental Improv.* (1801) I. 136 To cut out as many planchets or circular pieces of metal. **1879** H. PHILLIPS *Notes on Coins* 8 In many instances the coin contained only a portion of the device, the rest having failed to reach the planchet.

2. A small board used in brick-making: = PALLET *sb.*[3] 3 b.

1764 CROKER, etc. *Dict. Arts* s.v. *Brick-making*, A planchet, or small board, used by the person who carries the bricks or tiles from the moulder to the drying beds.

3. (ˈplæntʃɪt). *Physics.* Also **planchette.** A small, shallow dish used to contain a specimen when its radioactivity is measured.

1951 *Jrnl. Inst. Electr. Engineers* XCVIII. II. 236/1 With end-window counters it is usual to carry the specimen as a powder, or liquid evaporated to dryness, on a suitable holder. J. L. Putman investigated the form of surface necessary to give a uniform response when using the G.M.2 counter-tube wherever the material was deposited on that surface. It was found that these surfaces were of approximately spherical shape, in a position concave towards the window. As a result of this work, a standard planchette, made of pressed nickel sheet, was designed to be used at a distance of 3 mm from the window. **1960** *Nature* 14 May 563/2 Synthesis of deoxyribonucleic acid was measured by counting the total radioactivity of washed cells on planchettes. **1961** G. R. CHOPPIN *Exper. Nucl. Chem.* iv. 51 In case of reuse, each planchet should be carefully checked for residual activity. **1975** *Nature* 3 July 35/2 Radioactivity on the filter and in the frozen water vapour in the cold finger trap (after drying down on planchets) was assayed using a Nuclear Chicago gas flow counter.

planchette (plænˈʃɛt, plɑ̃ʃɛt). [a. F. *planchette* small board, dim. of *planche* PLANK.]

1. 'A small plank or board' (Simmonds *Dict. Trade* 1858).

2. An instrument, invented about 1855, used in the investigation of automatism and other psychical phenomena, consisting of a small board, generally heart-shaped, supported by two castors and a vertical pencil, which, when one or more persons rest their fingers lightly on the board, is said to trace lines or letters, and even to write sentences, without conscious direction or effort. Also *Comb.*, as ***planchette-board, -writer, -writing; planchette-like*** adj.

1860 *All Year Round* No. 66. 372 Like the effusions of all the self-deluding users of the planchette. **1879** O. W. HOLMES *School-boy* 19 The truant goose-quill travelling like Planchette. **1884** F. W. H. MYERS in *Proc. Soc. Psychical Res.* Dec. 232 The Spiritualist theory of Planchette-writing assumes the former of these two hypotheses. **1896** *Daily News* 5 Mar. 6/1 For nine years he toyed with the planchette, the turned tables, in short used the familiar, hanky-panky means of communication with the unseen world. **1909** Planchette writing [see OUIJA]. **1914** H. CARRINGTON *Probl. Psychical Res.* xii. 371 There can be little doubt that the same force which propels the planchette board propels the ouija board also. **1920** *Q. Rev.* July 196 He could not see how so vigorous a creative faculty..could be only a vague Planchette-like state of possession. **1920** Planchette-writer [see *crystal-gazer* s.v. CRYSTAL *sb.* B. 2c]. **1972** D. BLOODWORTH *Any Number can Play* ix. 71 The planchette board circled wildly, both men keeping their fingers hard down upon it.

3. 'A circumferentor'. (Simmonds *Dict. Trade.*).

4. See also PLANCHET 3.

ˈ**planching,** *vbl. sb.* [f. PLANCH *v.* + -ING[1].] The action of the vb. PLANCH; laying of a floor. **b.** *concr.* Planks collectively, planking, boarding; *esp.* flooring. *dial.*

c **1600** NORDEN *Spec. Brit., Cornw.* (1728) 59 Her water pypes..are cutt up, the Coueringe lead gone, the Planchinges rotten. **1602** CAREW *Cornwall* 53 To plant their houses lowe..to couer their planchings with earth. *Ibid.* 66 b, Low thatched roofes, few partitions, no planchings or glasse windows, and scarcely any chimnies, other then a hole in the wall to let out the smoke. **1706** PHILLIPS, *Planching*, (in Carpenters Work) a laying the Floors of a Building. **1880** MRS. PARR *Adam & Eve* xxxiii. 452 If I thought that 'twas you was the cause of it, I'd scat out yer brains on the planchin. **1886** ELWORTHY *W. Somerset Word-bk.*, *Planchin*, the board of the floor. *Planchin-board*, flooring board.

c. *Comb.* ˈ**planching-nail,** ˈ**plenshing-nail** (erron. *plenishing-nail*), a flooring-nail.

[**1365** in Rogers *Agric. & Prices* II. 479/1 Planching-nails.] **1825** JAMIESON, Plenshing-nail. (Hence in Simmonds, Knight.) **1882** OGILVIE (Annandale) Plenishing-nail. (Hence in *Cent. Dict.*, *Funk's Stand. Dict.*)

ˈ**planchment.** *U.S. dial.* [f. PLANCH *v.* + -MENT.] Boarding; *spec.* ceiling.

1891 *Jrnl. Amer. Folk-lore* No. 13 *Planchment*, ceiling. Now seldom heard. An old woman says: 'The roof wets so, I'm afraid the planchment'll fall'.

plancier (plænˈsɪə(r)). Also 7 **-eere,** 8 **-ere,** 9 **-eer.** [ad. OF. or obs. F. *plancier*, collateral form of *planchier*: see PLANCHER.] The under side of the corona of a cornice.

1664 EVELYN tr. *Freart's Archit.* etc. 138 The under part of the Roofs of these Corona's..are by our Artists call'd *Planceeres.* **1704** J. HARRIS *Lex. Techn.* I, *Plancere*, in Architecture, is the Under part of the Roof of the Corona; which is the Superior part of the Cornice between two Cymatiums. **1827** MACKENZIE *Hist. Newcastle* I. 308 The planceer is ornamented with seven-leafed pateræ. **1886** G. T. ROBINSON in *Art Jrnl.* 51/1 Of timber construction, it [the ceiling] has a flat planceer about one-sixth of the whole width of the room, extending all round it; this is trabeated by large beams... From this projecting planceer a panelled tambour rises to a higher plane.

Planck (plæŋk). *Physics.* The name of Max K. E. L. *Planck* (1858-1947), German physicist, used in the possessive and *attrib.* to designate various concepts that he invented or discovered, as **Planck('s) constant**, one of the fundamental physical constants (symbol h), relating the energy E of a quantum of electromagnetic radiation to its frequency ν according to the equation $E = h\nu$; approximately $6{\cdot}626 \times 10^{-34}$ joule-second; **Planck('s) equation** or **formula**, any of the related equations stating Planck's law; **Planck('s) law**, a law giving the density of radiant energy at a particular wavelength λ or frequency ν inside a perfect radiator, and the flux of radiant energy emitted by it, the former being written as $\rho(\lambda)\,d\lambda = (8\pi hc/\lambda^5)\,(\exp(hc/k\lambda T) - 1)^{-1}d\lambda$ or $\rho(\nu)d\nu = (8\pi h\nu^3/c^3)\,(\exp(h\nu/kT) - 1)^{-1}d\nu$; **Planck oscillator**, a concept used by Planck in his work on radiation: an electrically charged particle that can execute simple harmonic motion with a frequency independent of the amplitude; **Planck('s) radiation formula** or **law** = *Planck('s) law.*

1910 *Phil. Mag.* XX. 244 Corpuscles which are emitted by bodies when exposed to ultra-violet light. Ladenburg found that the maximum energy of these corpuscles..was proportional to n the frequency of the light, being of the order $h'n/2\pi$ where h' is *Planck's constant. **1935** D. L. SAYERS *Gaudy Night* ii. 37 'There happened to be an unknown factor.' 'Like that thing that keeps cropping up in the new kind of physics,' said the Dean. 'Planck's constant, or whatever they call it.' **1940** GLASSTONE *Text-bk. Physical Chem.* i. 73 Every particle is associated with a wave.., and the wave length (λ) is related to the mechanical momentum (mv) by $\lambda = h/mv$, where h is the Planck constant. **1960** CHALMERS & QUARRELL *Physical Examination of Metals* (ed. 2) xvi. 749 This is known as the spin of the particle and is measured in terms of $h/2\pi$..where h is Planck's constant. **1968** G. LUDWIG *Wave Mech.* I. iv. 62 This uncertainty relation states that in any experimentally producible ensemble the product of the spread in position and momentum cannot go below a lower limit given by Planck's constant. **1911** *Bull. Bureau of Standards* (U.S.) VII. 393 *Planck's equation for the intensity of radiation J, of wave length λ, from a black body at the absolute temperature θ,..appears to represent the results of all known observations. **1966** M. FERRO-LUZZI tr. *Fermi's Molecules, Crystals & Quantum Statistics* vii. 223 From the Planck equation, we can easily deduce Stefan's law, which also can be obtained by thermodynamic arguments alone. **1905** LD. RAYLEIGH in *Nature* 13 July 244/1 In *Nature*, May 18, I gave a calculation of the coefficient of complete radiation at a given absolute temperature for waves of great length.., and it appeared that the result was eight times as great as that deduced from *Planck's formula. **1923** GLAZEBROOK *Dict. Appl. Physics* IV. 563/2 Throughout the spectrum from 0·5 μ to 50 μ Planck's formula fits the observed spectral energy distribution more closely than any other equation yet proposed. **1974** G. REECE tr. *Hund's Hist. Quantum Theory* ii. 27 By comparing the measured energy densities..with Planck's formula it was possible to calculate h and h/k. **1905** *Nature* 27 July 294/2 *Planck's law is in good agreement with experiment if h is given a value different from zero. **1930** RUARK & UREY *Atoms, Molecules & Quanta* iii. 59 The physical basis for the asymptotic approach of Planck's law to the classical distribution is easily seen. **1955** W. HEISENBERG in W. Pauli *Niels Bohr* 14 Bohr explained to him [*sc.* Schrödinger] that not even Planck's Law could be understood without the quantum jumps. **1974** TURNER & BETTS *Introd. Statistical Mech.* xii. 148 The Planck law describes the distributions of energy among the infinite range of possible frequencies. **1920** *Planck oscillator [see N I. 4 b]. **1966** tr. *S.-I. Tomonaga's Quantum Mech.* II. vi. 111 Each term in Eq. (47·9') has the form of the Hamiltonian of a Planck oscillator. **1909** *Sci. Abstr.* A. XII. 315 (*heading*) *Planck's radiation law. **1911** *Ibid.* XIV. 404 It is concluded that the Einstein formula for specific heat is confirmed and also the Planck radiation formula. **1935** PAULING & WILSON *Introd. Quantum Mech.* xi. 301 The density of radiant energy is known to be given by Planck's radiation law as [etc.]. **1974** G. REECE tr. *Hund's Hist. Quantum Theory* xi. 145 The Bose statistics of light quanta was thus the same as that earlier applied by Planck for energy quanta..and thus led to the Planck radiation formula.

Planckian (ˈplæŋkɪən), *a. Physics.* [f. prec. + -IAN.] Of, pertaining to, or being a black body.

1922 *Jrnl. Optical Soc. Amer.* VI. 560 Average noon sunlight..corresponds roughly to a black body temperature of 5000° K. the distribution not being strictly Planckian. **1956** H. H. EMSLEY *Aberrations of Thin Lenses* x. 303 A black body or Planckian radiator. **1972** *Nature* 28 Apr. 448/2 It seems improbable that the whole spectrum is Planckian, because the total power of such radiation would be.. 10^{42} erg s^{-1}.

‖**planctus** (ˈplaŋktəs). Pl. **planctus** (-uːs). [L., = beating of the breast, lamentation.] A medieval lament (LAMENT *sb.* 2). Cf. PLANH.

1901 *Jrnl. Germanic Philol.* III. 417 From the various German Lamentations he [*sc.* A. Schönbach] culls eighteen versicles, mostly quatrains, which occur most frequently and of which the first thirteen are in form and in content a free version of the Latin Planctus. **1903** E. K. CHAMBERS *Mediæval Stage* II. III. xviii. 32 The metrical hymns are often of the nature of *planctus* or laments put in the mouths of the Maries as they approach the sepulchre... These *planctus* add greatly to the vividness and humanity of the play. **1907** *Mod. Philol.* IV. 605 It is hoped that the present discussion of the English planctus may in the future help to make more easily possible a comparative study of the planctus as a class. *Ibid.* 606 The chief purpose of this study is to discuss the several non-dramatic English planctus in their relation to each other. **1940** G. REESE *Music in Middle Ages* (1941) vii. 198 These *planctus*, with Latin texts, are believed actually to date from the 7th century and to be compositions, perhaps, of St. Eugenius. **1954** *New Oxf. Hist. Music* II. vi. 193 Although some of the most famous of the *planctus* of the Passion are solo stanzas, spoken by the Virgin Mary, yet there are a number in dialogue form, the speakers being most frequently Mary and St. John. **1964** C. S. LEWIS *Discarded Image* iii. 36 *Natura* as Alanus brings her in, stiffly robed in rhetoric, conceit, and symbol, pleading again the cause of procreation in her *planctus* (against the sodomites). **1970** W. APEL *Harvard Dict. Mus.* (ed. 2) 461/2 A 'Planctus Karoli' lamenting the death of Charlemagne (814) and another *planctus* for his son Hugo (844). **1977** *Times Lit. Suppl.* 17 June 727/5 The cycle of six *planctus* by Peter Abelard.

plandok, var. PELANDOK.

plane (pleɪn), *sb.*[1] Also 5–6 **playn**, 6 **plaine**. [a. F. *plane*, earlier OF. *plasne* (14th c.):—L. *platanus*, a. Gr. πλάτανος the Oriental Plane, f. πλατύς broad, because of its broad leaves.]

1. A tree of the genus *Platanus*, comprising lofty spreading trees, with broad angular palmately-lobed leaves, and bark which scales off in irregular patches; orig. and esp. *P. orientalis*, the Oriental Plane, a native of Persia and the Levant, commonly planted as an ornamental tree in European and British parks, town avenues, and squares, etc.; also *P. occidentalis*, the Occidental or Virginian Plane or Buttonwood.

P. orientalis was introduced into England shortly *a* 1562: see TURNER *Herbal* II. 95; and quot. 1562 s.v. PLANE-TREE. *P. occidentalis* was brought from Virginia by Tradescant shortly *a* 1640: see PARKINSON *Theat. Bot.* (1640) 1427.

1382 WYCLIF *Gen.* xxx. 37 Thanne Jacob takynge green popil ȝerdis, and of almanders, and of planes, a parti vnryendide hem. **1398** TREVISA *Barth. De P.R.* XVII. cxix. (Tollem. MS.), The plane is a colde tre and a drye, and þe leues þerof heleþ in hoot eueles. *c* **1440** *Promp. Parv.* 402/2 Plane, tre, *platanus*. **1598** SYLVESTER *Du Bartas.* II. i. I. *Eden* 517 Anon he walketh in a levell lane On eyther side beset with shady Plane. **1697** DRYDEN *Virg. Georg.* IV. 216 With spreading Planes he made a cool Retreat, To shade good Fellows from the Summer's Heat. **1785** MARTYN *Rousseau's Bot.* xxviii. (1794) 442 Their leaves..in the Eastern or Asiatic Plane are palmate; and in the Occidental or Virginian, lobate. **1791** GILPIN *Forest Scenery* I. 48 Two noble trees of the same kind, both naturalized in England —tho from different extremes of the globe—the occidental and the oriental plane. **1863** MARY HOWITT tr. *F. Bremer's Greece* I. ii. 50 The plane seems to be the most splendid tree of Greece.

2. In Scotland and the north of England applied to the species of maple commonly called 'sycamore' (*Acer Pseudoplatanus*), the leaves of which resemble those of *Platanus*. Also called *false*, *mock*, or *Scotch plane* (see PLANE-TREE b).

[**1778**: see PLANE-TREE b.] **18..** J. WILSON The Plane's thick head mid burning day suspends Impenetrable shade: bees humming pour O'er the broad balmy leaves, and suck the flower. **1875** W. MCILWRAITH *Guide Wigtownshire* 18 These contrast their foliage with that of the Scottish fir and the plane.

¶ **3.** Erroneously for PLANTAIN.

1666 J. DAVIES *Hist. Caribby Isles* 51 There grow in all these Islands..great Reeds, spongy within,.. They are commonly called Banana-trees, or Planes.

4. *attrib.* and *Comb.*, as ***plane-leaf***. (See also PLANE-TREE.)

1387 TREVISA *Higden* (Rolls) I. 187 Arcadia..is i-schape as is a plane leef [*velut platani folium*].

plane (pleɪn), *sb.*[2] Also 6–7 **playne, plaine**, 7–8 **plain**. [a. F. *plane* (*planne*, 15th c. in Littré), altered, under the influence of the vb. *planer* to plane, from earlier OF. *plaine* (14th c.):—late L. *plāna* a plane, f. *plānāre* to plane.

In OF., L. *plā'nāre* gave regularly *pla'ner*, while '*plānat* gave orig. *plaine*, but by levelling this became *plane*. L. *plāna* sb. gave OF. *plaine*, but under the influence of the vb., as name of the plaining-tool, this was changed to *plane*.]

1. A tool resembling a plasterer's trowel, used by plumbers, bricklayers, etc., for smoothing the surface of sand, or clay in a mould, etc.

1349–50 *Durham Acc. Rolls* (Surtees) 550 In uno Ladil ferri, uno Plane, et aliis instrumentis pro officio plumbarii, emptis, ij s. v d. **1404** *Ibid.* 397 In custodia Plumbarii, ij planys. **1553** T. WILSON *Rhet.* 83 b, The Carpenter hath his Squyre, his Rule, and his plummet..The Mason his Former, and his Plaine [**1567**, **1580** plane]. **1688** R. HOLME *Armoury* III. 326/1 The [Plummer's] Plaine is a flat peece of Brass or Copper with an handle,..with this Instrument the Sand in the Frame is smoothed.

2. A tool, used by carpenters and others, for levelling down and smoothing the surface of woodwork by paring shavings from it.

It consists of a frame or *stock* of wood or metal, with a smooth base or *sole* (flat, convex, or concave, according to the nature of the work) which slides over the surface of the wood, and a steel blade (*plane-iron* or *bit*) set in it at an angle or *pitch* (varying according to the hardness of the wood to be operated on) so that its edge projects slightly through a slit or *mouth* in the sole; made in very various shapes and sizes, and usually provided with a handle fixed to the top of the stock. Also a similar tool for smoothing the surface of soft metal.

c **1440** *Promp. Parv.* 402/2 Plane, instrument (*H.*, *P.* to makyn pleyn), *leviga*. **1530** PALSGR. 255/2 Plane an instrument for joyners, *plane, rabot*. **1576** *Richmond Wills* (Surtees) 261 Towe playnes, ij chesells, one handsawe, ij percer bitts, ij gourges, ij fyles. **1674** OWEN *Holy Spirit* (1693) 232 To hew a Block with Axes, and smooth it with Planes. **1698** *Phil. Trans.* XX. 274 With an Instrument like our Plain, [they] Shave it as fine as they Please. **1796** MORSE *Amer. Geog.* I. 757 Their chissels, plains and wimbles. **1872** YEATS *Techn. Hist. Comm.* 247 An assortment of more than 200 varieties of planes was displayed at the Great Exhibition.

b. With qualifying words, denoting various kinds used for different purposes;

as BENCH-*plane*, COMPASS *p.*, DOVETAIL-*p.*, FORK-*staff-p.*, ICE-*p.*, JACK-PLANE, JOINTER-*p.*, *match-p.* (MATCH *a.*), MOULDING-*p.*, OGEE *p.*, OVOLO *p.*, PANEL-*p.*, PLOUGH-*p.*, REBATE-*p.*, SCALE-BOARD *p.*, STRIKE-BLOCK *p.*, TOOTH-*p.*, TRYING-*p.*, etc.: see these words. Also, **concave-plane**: see quot. 1874; **hollow-plane**, a plane with a convex sole, used for planing concave or hollow woodwork; **long plane** (see quot. 1875); **round** or **rounding-plane**, a round-soled plane used in making rounded work, as beading, stair-rails, etc.; **smoothing-plane**: see quot. 1823.

1703 MOXON *Mech. Exerc.* 73 Planes in use amongst Joyners, called Molding-planes; as..the Hollow. **1823** P. NICHOLSON *Pract. Build.* 245 The Long Plane is the third plane made use of in facing a piece of stuff. *Ibid.*, The Smoothing Plane..is the last plane which is made use of in giving the utmost degree of smoothness to the surface. **1874** KNIGHT *Dict. Mech.* 604 *Concave Plane*, a compass-plane for smoothing curved surfaces. **1875** *Ibid.* 1113 *Hollow-plane*, a molding-plane with a convex sole. A *round-sole* plane. *Ibid.* 1217 *Joiner's-plane*, a bench-plane for facing and matching boards. *Ibid.* 1350 *Long-plane*, a joiner's plane used when a piece of stuff is to be planed up very straight. It is 2 feet 3 inches long. **1892** *Daily News* 26 Jan. 3/2 They are taught skilfully to use the jack-plane, the trying-plane, the smoothing plane, hand saw, tenon saw, and bow saw.

3. *attrib.* and *Comb.*, as ***plane-maker***; †**plane-axe** = CHIP-AXE (*obs.*); **plane-bit** = *plane-iron*; **plane-guide**, 'an adjustable attachment to a plane-stock, used in bevelling the edges of boards' (Ogilvie); **plane-iron**, the cutting-iron of a plane; **plane-stock**, the stock or body of a plane (see 2).

1611 COTGR., *Aisceau*, a Chip-axe, or one-handed *plane-axe, wherewith Carpenters hew their timber smooth. **1875** KNIGHT *Dict. Mech.*, **Plane-bit*, the cutter of a plane; generally termed the *plane-iron*. **1583** *Rates of Customs* D vij b, *Plane Irons for Carpenters the dozen xiid. **1831** J. HOLLAND *Manuf. Metal* I. 321 In the manufacture of the lighter sorts of edge-tools, and especially in plane-irons. **1800** *New Ann. Direct. Lond.* 108 Higgs, James, *Plane-maker, 8 Little College-street, Westminster. **1815** J. SMITH *Panorama Sc. & Art* I. 31 Experienced plane-makers..use files to smooth their wood-work. **1611–12** *Knaresb. Wills* (Surtees) II. 34 Three playnes and ij *playne stockes. **1703** MOXON *Mech. Exerc.* 218, I..make a Plain-Stock with my intended Molding on the Sole of it. **1875** SIR T. TRUESTON *Fret Cutting* 83 Lay the edge of the plane-stock occasionally across the board in various parts.

plane (pleɪn), *sb.*[3] [ad. L. *plān-um* a flat surface, sb. use of neut. sing. of *plānus* adj., flat, introduced in 17th c. to express the geometrical and allied uses, which had been from the 16th c. (and were often down to the 18th) expressed by the historical form PLAIN. In F. *plan* had been similarly introduced *c* 1550. Cf. PLANE *a.*]

1. a. A plane superficies; in *Geom.*, a surface such that every straight line joining any two points in it lies wholly in it, or such that the intersection of two such surfaces is always a straight line; the simplest kind of geometrical surface, corresponding among surfaces to the straight line among lines. Hence, in *general* use, An imaginary superficies of this kind in which points or lines in material bodies lie; esp. a horizontal plane of such a kind, a level, as in 'clouds at various planes of elevation'.

Often (esp. in scientific use) with *of*, denoting the plane in which a particular figure, etc. is situated, or in or on which some process takes place; e.g. the plane of a circle, ellipse, etc., of the ecliptic, the equator, the horizon, a planet's orbit; a plane of denudation, of freezing, etc.; ***plane of projection***, a plane upon which points, lines, or figures are projected. (See also below.) Also with defining adjs., as *cyclic plane*, *diagonal p.*, *diametral p.*, *osculating p.*, *polar p.*, *tangent p.*, *vertical p.*, etc.: see these words.

[**1570**: see PLAIN *sb.*[1] 4 a.] **1646** SIR T. BROWNE *Pseud. Ep.* 156 This doth happen when the axis of the visive cones, diffused from the object, fall not upon the same plane. **1656** tr. *Hobbes' Elem. Philos.* (1839) 179 A plane or a plane superficies, is that which is described by a strait line so moved, that all the several points thereof describe several strait lines. **1665** G. HAVERS *P. della Valle's Trav. E. Ind.* 183 The pavement of the porch was also something rais'd above the plane of the Court. **1715** tr. *Gregory's Astron.* I. 92 The Intersection of the Plane of any Planet, with the Plane of the Earth's Orbit, is the Line of the Nodes of that Planet. **1765** A. DICKSON *Treat. Agric.* II. v. (ed. 2) 171 The plane of the beam must be so far raised above the plane of the head, that, when the plough is going at its proper depth, the beam may not be incommoded by any thing on the surface. **1796** H. HUNTER tr. *St.-Pierre's Stud. Nat.* (1799) II. 276 The mists, dispersed through the air, repeated on different planes the lustre of his rays in rainbows of purple, and parhelions of dazzling radiance. **1815** J. SMITH *Panorama Sc. & Art* I. 563 These satellites move in a plane nearly perpendicular to the plane of the planet's orbit, and contrary to the order of the signs. **1853** SIR H. DOUGLAS *Milit. Bridges* (ed. 3) 278 A cable should be stretched across the river, on each side of the bridge, in the plane of its floor. **1860** TYNDALL *Glaciers* II. § 11, I requested Mr. Hirst to fix two stakes in the same vertical plane, &c. **1867** DENISON *Astron. without Math.* 38 The equinoctial points, where the planes of the equator and ecliptic cross each other are of great importance in astronomy. **1875** BENNETT & DYER *Sachs' Bot.* 88 The guard-cells may, when mature, lie in one plane with those of the epidermis.

b. A material surface (approximately) of this nature; a flat or level surface of a material body. (In quot. 1796 = flatness of surface.) ***inclined plane***: see INCLINED *ppl. a.* 1. ***true plane***: see quot. 1875.

[**1571**: see PLAIN *sb.*[1] 4 b.] **1715** CHEYNE *Philos. Princ. Relig.* I. 8 Did not..the Ruggedness of the Plane, on which they move, stop their Motion. **1796** C. MARSHALL *Garden.* xi. (1813) 132 Too much plane is to be guarded against. **1823** F. CLISSOLD *Ascent Mt. Blanc* 11 A precipitous declivity, which shelved down,..in one plane of smooth rock, to the depth of 1000 feet. **1837** WHEWELL *Hist. Induct. Sc.* (1857) I. 186 The property of the inclined plane. **1875** KNIGHT *Dict. Mech.* 1725/1 A 'true plane' is a gage or test of flatness. The 'true' planes exhibited by Whitworth at the Paris Exposition were polished metallic surfaces of 100 inches area... The error is said not to have exceeded the millionth of an inch. **1885–94** R. BRIDGES *Eros & Psyche* Jan. iv, Poising the crystal bowl with fearful heed, Her eyes at watch upon the steadied plane.

c. *Dialling.* The plane surface (vertical, horizontal, or inclined) on which a dial is drawn; the surface of a dial, upon which the shadow falls.

1674 MOXON *Tutor Astron. & Geog.* (ed. 3) v. 137 Of the several Kinds of Dyal Plains... A Plane in Dyalling is that flat whereon a Dyal is described. **1703** —— *Mech. Exerc.* 311 The South Erect Plane, declining more or less towards the East or West. **1727–51** CHAMBERS *Cycl.* s.v. *Dialling*.

d. *Perspective.*

directing plane: see DIRECTING *ppl. a.* ***geometrical plane***, a plane parallel to the horizon below the line of sight, on which the object is supposed to be situated. ***horizontal plane***, a plane parallel to the horizon and passing through the eye of the spectator. ***objective***, ***original***, or ***primitive plane***, any plane situated in the object itself. ***perspective plane***, a transparent plane, usually perpendicular to the horizon, supposed to be interposed between the object and the eye, and intersected by straight lines passing from one to the other, which determine the points of the drawing: also called ***plane of delineation*** or ***plane of the picture*** (which terms may also be applied to the actual surface on which the drawing is made). ***vertical plane***, a plane perpendicular to the horizon, passing through the eye of the spectator, and intersecting the perspective plane at right angles.

1704 J. HARRIS *Lex. Techn.* I, Plane Geometrical,.. Horizontal,..Vertical. **1815** J. SMITH *Panorama Sc. & Art* II. 708 The situation of the eye..must be laid down upon the paper, on which the perspective drawing of an object is to be made, unless we propose to look at the object itself as through a transparent plane. **1823** P. NICHOLSON *Pract. Build.* 540 A primitive plane is that which contains a point, a line, or a plane surface, of a given object. **1871** DICKSEE *Perspective* 24 Properly speaking the transparent plane should be understood to mean that vertical plane which is always assumed to be interposed between the spectator and the object to be represented... On the other hand, by the plane of the picture, which is frequently termed the plane of delineation, is meant the surface on which the perspective drawing is made. **1878** ABNEY *Photogr.* (1881) 244 One of the essential suppositions of perspective is, that the picture plane should be vertical and the line of sight horizontal.

e. *Optics.*

focal plane: see FOCAL 3. ***plane of the horopter***: see quot. 1704. ***plane of incidence***: see INCIDENCE 4. ***plane of polarization***, in polarized light, the plane which passes through the incident ray and the (reflected or refracted) polarized ray, and is perpendicular to the plane of vibration of the ether in the polarized ray. ***plane of reflection, of refraction***, the plane passing through the reflected or refracted ray and the normal to the surface (which always coincides with the plane of incidence).

1704 J. HARRIS *Lex. Techn.* I, *Plane of the Horopter*,..is that which passeth thro' the Horopter, and is perpendicular to the Plane of the two Optical Axes. *Ibid.*, Plane of Reflection,..of Refraction. **1831** BREWSTER *Optics* i. 5 The plane in which these two lines lie, is called the plane of incidence, or the plane of reflexion. *Ibid.* xviii. 159 A beam of common light..consists of two beams of polarised light whose planes of polarisation or whose diameters of similar properties are at right angles to one another. **1865** WATTS *Dict. Chem.* III. 653 The plane in which a polarised ray is most easily reflected is called the plane of polarisation; it coincides with the plane of reflection (or of incidence).

f. *Cryst.* and *Min.* Each of the natural faces of a crystal; also, an imaginary plane surface related to these in some way.

plane of cleavage (or *cleavage-plane*), *composition p.*, *diametral p.*, *lateral p.*, *terminal p.*, *twinning p.*: see these words.

1800 tr. *Lagrange's Chem.* I. 225 This salt has the form of a prism of six planes, terminated by pyramids with six faces. **1805–17** R. JAMESON *Char. Min.* (ed. 3) 164 These planes would pass at the same time through the equilateral triangles. **1823** H. J. BROOKE *Introd. Crystallogr.* 3 The planes of a crystal are said to be similar when their corresponding edges are proportional, and their corresponding angles equal. **1830** KATER & LARDNER *Mech.* ii. 15 There are certain planes called planes of cleavage, in the directions of which natural crystals are easily divided. **1883** *Encycl. Brit.* XVI. 347/1 The external planes of a crystal are called its 'natural planes'; the flat surfaces obtained by splitting a crystal are called its 'cleavage planes'.

g. *Anat.* Any one of certain imaginary plane surfaces used as standards of reference for the positions of bodily organs, or (in *Craniometry*) of parts of the skull.

e.g. *alveolo-condylean plane, horizontal p. of Camper, plane of mastication, median p., nuchal p., occipital p., palatine p. of Barclay, sagittal p., temporal p.*, etc.: see these words, and quot. 1895.

1830 R. KNOX *Béclard's Anat.* 30 Their organs of sensation and motion are disposed in pairs on the two sides of an axis, or a median plane. **1895** *Syd. Soc. Lex., Plane occipital, Craniom.*, term for that part of the external surface of the *squama occipitis* which lies above the superior curved line. *Ibid., P[lane]s of body*, certain imaginary plane surfaces used in Anatomy as standards of reference in describing the portions [? positions] and relations of organs. There are five such planes drawn as tangents to the surfaces of the body, namely, an anterior, a posterior, an inferior, and two lateral planes... *P. of mastication, Craniom.*, that plane which forms a tangent with the masticatory surface of the upper teeth. (Barclay.).. *P., palatine, of Barclay* (*Craniom.*), that plane which forms a tangent with the palatine arch, drawn along the middle line.

h. *Fortif.*

plane of comparison, a horizontal plane passing through the highest or lowest part of a fortification or its site. ***p. of defilade***, a plane passing through the interior crest or the highest point of a work, and parallel to the plane of site. ***p. of site***, or ***regulating p.***, a plane coinciding approximately with that of the ground occupied by a work.

1834–47 J. S. MACAULAY *Field Fortif.* (1851) 283 A horizontal plane supposed to pass below, or ten yards above all the ground contained in the plan, and which is called the plane of comparison. *Ibid.* 289 The plane of site, or regulating plane. *Ibid.* 295 Suppose those five points are required to be placed in the same plane of defilade, or the five corresponding points of the sub-crests in the same plane of site, tangent to the exterior surface.

i. A relatively thin structure used to produce an upwards or downwards (†or sideways) force by the flow of the surrounding air or water over its surface. Orig. a flat surface (PLANE *sb.*^{3} 1 b) proposed as a source of lift for heavier-than-air machines and used to direct the ascent and descent of balloons; later designed with a slight camber and used as the wing of an aeroplane or as a hydrofoil on a boat or seaplane. Cf. AEROFOIL, AEROPLANE 1, HYDROFOIL 1, HYDROPLANE *sb.* 1.

Not now a common word exc. in the sense of HYDROPLANE *sb.* 1, and in combinations and derivatives (e.g. BIPLANE, *diving-plane*, INTERPLANE *a.*).

For the spelling *plain* (quots. *a* 1802, 1804) cf. PLAIN *sb.*^{1} 4.

[*a* **1802** G. CAYLEY *Aeronaut. & Misc. Note-bk.* (1933) 10 In estimating the mechanical power which a given plain [*transcribed as* plane] will exert when exposed in any position to a current of fluid, two things are necessary. **1804** *Ibid.* 22, I made the following experiments upon the resistance of air to a surface of a foot sq, carried round with an horizontal motion upon an arm suspended upon a delicate hinge... The angles which the plain made with the horizon were measured.] **1809** —— in *Jrnl. Nat. Philos.* XXIV. 171 It is perfectly indifferent whether the wind blow against the plane, or the plane be driven with an equal velocity against the air. **1815** *Phil. Mag.* XLVI. 323 On October 2, 1815, another experiment.. was made with a balloon six feet in diameter, having a square plane whose side was 7·5 feet, and a triangular rudder in proportion. **1816** *Ibid.* XLVII. 82 My object was to leave out the unwieldy bulk of balloons altogether, and to make use of the inclined plane propelled by a light first mover. **1842** W. S. HENSON *Brit. Pat. 9478* The first part of my Invention consists of an apparatus so constructed as to offer a very extended surface or plane.., which will have the same relation to the general machine which the extended wings of a bird have to the body when the bird is skimming in the air. *Ibid.*, The surface of the planes on either side of the car will measure four thousand five hundred square feet. **1848** *Chambers's Jrnl.* 6 May 301/1 When it attained the highest point, the edge of the plane would be reversed, and the balloon would descend thus. *Ibid.* 303/1 The wings are to be formed of long and narrow silk planes. **1866** *Ann. Rep. Aëronaut. Soc.* 25 A simple narrow blade, or inclined plane, propelled in a direct course ..is.. the only means of giving the maximum amount of supporting power with the least possible degree of 'slip'. *Ibid.* 36 To obtain the necessary length of plane.. the surfaces may be superposed, or placed in parallel rows, with an interval between them. **1891** S. P. LANGLEY *Exper. in Aerodynamics* 58 The planes whose spread is largest in comparison with their extent from front to back.. are therefore to be considered as being.. the most favourable for mechanical flight. **1907** *Engineering* 4 Oct. 457/2 The boat is provided with hydroplanes only at its stem and stern. The planes at the bow are arranged in the manner of a **V**. **1908** *Aëronaut. Jrnl.* XII. 45/2 However sound in theory the single plane aëroplane may be, every serious accident yet recorded has occurred with this type. **1908** H. G. WELLS *War in Air* iii. 82 He found the missing drawings of the lateral rotating planes, on which the whole stability of the flying-machine depended. **1910** [see AEROPLANE 2 b]. **1912** M. KERR in S. W. Murray *Poetry of Flight* (1925) 53 The tips of the planes appear and disappear As you madly drive along through the mist enladen'd air. **1915** A. FAGE *Aeroplane* iv. 31 The rudder, a vertical plane capable of rotation about a vertical axis, partially controls the yawing or turning of the machine. **1917** A. W. JUDGE *Properties of Aerofoils* iii. 51 The inclined cambered plane differs from the inclined flat plane, in conforming better with the upward trend of the air about the leading edge. **1920** G. C. BAILEY *Compl. Airman* viii. 59 The incidence of the tail plane can be varied. **1920** [see HYDROFOIL 1]. **1938** E. W. C. WILKINS *Aeroplane Design* ii. 22 In the orthodox aeroplane, the main planes, or wings, are fixed. **1966** *McGraw-Hill Encycl. Sci. & Technol.* XIII. 212/2 Each set.. may be tilted through an angle of 25° in either direction from the horizontal to develop a vertical force on the planes and thus on the submarine. **1972** J. B. ICENHOWER *Submarines* 9 At the bow and stern of a submarine are flat devices somewhat like the fins of a big fish. They are known as the *forward* and *after* hydroplanes... The diving planesmen tilt the forward planes down and the after planes up.

j. *Computers.* One of the flat, usu. square arrays of magnetic cores or other elements in a memory, each of which contains the corresponding bits of all the words held in the arrays.

1959 E. M. MCCORMICK *Digital Computer Primer* viii. 107 In a magnetic core used to store, say, 4096 words of 36 binary bits each, there would be 36 sets (planes) of cores, and each plane would contain 4096 cores arranged with 64 on each side of a square. **1964** *IBM Jrnl. Res. & Devel.* VIII. 171/2 Figure 2 shows such a memory plane containing 50 tubes centered at intervals of 0·070 in. and 100 bit lines centered at intervals of 0·030 in. **1969** [see CORE *sb.*^{1} 10 b]. **1976** 'ABD-ALLA & MELTZER *Princ. Digital Computer Design* I. ix. 329 The planes are stacked into a three-dimensional array. The *x* lines of each plane are connected in series with the same *x* line on the two adjacent core planes.

†**2.** = PLAN *sb.* 1. *Obs.* [Cf. F. *plan* = plane and plan.]

1639 in Hearne *Collect.* (O.H.S.) III. 129 He drew the Planes of them. **1682** WHELER *Journ. Greece* I. 33 Signior Marmero.. hath given a Plane of the old City. **1693** *Paris Rel. Batt. Landen* 24 The Plane of the Battel. **1706** PHILLIPS, *Plane* or *Plan*, (in Fortification) a Draught representing a Work as it would appear on the plain Field, were it cut off level with the Ground... See *Ichnography*.

3. *Mining.* Any main road in a mine, inclined or level, along which coal, etc. is conveyed in cars or trucks.

1877 BURROUGHS *Taxation* 137 Machinery for raising cars up the planes. **1881** RAYMOND *Mining Gloss., Plane*, an incline, with tracks, upon which materials are raised in cars by means of a stationary engine, or are lowered by gravity. **1890** *Daily News* 14 Nov. 3/4 The importance of travelling roads distinct from engine planes was fully recognised, and it was agreed that in all collieries where there are engine planes, travelling roads should be made for the safety of the men.

4. *fig.* (from a horizontal plane in sense 1) in reference to immaterial things, as thought, knowledge, moral qualities, social rank, etc.: Higher or lower level, grade, degree. *spec.* in *Theosophy.* (In quot. 1850, a metaphor from an inclined plane.)

1850 GROTE *Greece* II. lvi. VII. 160 Thucydidês, just before he gets upon the plane of this descending progress, makes a halt. **1873** M. ARNOLD *Lit. & Dogma* (1876) 154 They are on altogether another plane from Jesus. **1875** H. C. WOOD *Therap.* (1879) 649 Evidently the organism was constructed to run upon a certain plane of heat. **1884** *Trans. London Lodge Theosoph. Soc.* June 7 In considering the action of the law of Karma it is better to divide man into three planes; the physical, mental, and spiritual. **1885** CLODD *Myths & Dr.* I. ii. 18 The superstitious man is on the same plane as the savage. **1889** H. P. BLAVATSKY *Key to Theosophy* III. 45 That which is true on the metaphysical plane must be also true on the physical. **1892** —— *Theosoph. Gloss.* 255 Plane. From the Latin *planus*.. an extension of space or of something in it, whether physical or metaphysical, *e.g.* a 'plane of consciousness'. **1922** JOYCE *Ulysses* 139 A. E. the master mystic? That Blavatsky woman started it... A. E. has been telling some yankee interviewer that you came to him in the small hours of the morning to ask him about planes of consciousness. *Ibid.* 183 The Christ with the bridesister,.. departed to the plane of buddhi. **1951** 'Novo' *Notes on Theosophy* 13 We believe that beyond, yet interwoven with, physical matter, are other planes of such a tenuous nature that they are not apparent to the human eye. **1974** *Encycl. Brit. Macropædia* XVIII. 277/2 Most modern theosophists subscribe to a rather elaborate cosmogony... There are, it is believed, seven worlds or planes through which the universe evolves. In ascending order these are the physical plane; the emotional, or astral, plane; the mental plane; the intuitional, or Buddhic, plane; the spiritual, or Atmic, plane; the monadic, or Anupadaka, plane; and the divine, or Adi, plane. **1977** 'L. EGAN' *Blind Search* i. 6 It was reasonable to suppose that he still was, and still concerned with the people who'd meant something to him here—planes or levels of vibration or whatever.

†**plane**, *sb.*^{4} *Obs. rare*$^{-1}$. [f. PLANE *v.*^{2}] An act of 'planing', i.e. soaring with the wings extended and motionless.

1622 DRAYTON *Poly-olb.* xx. 16 Which when the Falkoner sees, that scarce one plane they make.

plane (pleɪn), *sb.*^{5} Also **'plane.** [f. AERO)-PLANE.] = AEROPLANE 2 b.

1908 *Aëronaut. Jrnl.* Apr. 45/1 The aëroplane was then taken to the Longchamps end of the field, and as soon as the propeller had been set in motion the apparatus dashed off towards Neuilly. After running along the ground for about a hundred mètres the plane lifted, and.. rushed through the air for 150 mètres or thereabouts. **1908** *Times* 1 June 6/1 Mr. Wright refused to give any details on the propeller employed, but on the general construction of the plane he said it was full of movable diversely articulated parts. **1909** KIPLING *With Night Mail* 69 Low-flying planes often 'glue up' when near the Magnetic Pole. **1909** LLOYD GEORGE in *Daily Chron.* 23 Aug. 1/1, I have not yet crossed the Financial Channel with my Budget 'plane. **1910** *Daily Mail* 27 July 6/5 To the builders of aeroplanes he cries: 'Construct me planes capable of the maximum speed.' **1920** *Blackw. Mag.* June 762/1 A plane which came from Palestine. **1931** *Daily Mirror* 27 Aug. 2/2 The 'plane struck the water. **1932** *Daily Express* 27 June 8/2 The first ape and the comic sergeant are deserting to Switzerland in a bombing 'plane. **1942** R. HILLARY *Last Enemy* I My plane had been fitted out with a new cockpit hood. **1958** 'CASTLE' & 'HAILEY' *Flight into Danger* ii. 30 There was a brief shudder as the plane freed herself from a wall of cloud. **1965** *Movie* Summer 3/2 Charlotte and Robert talk and make love in the hour before his 'plane leaves. **1976** *Daily Tel.* 7 Oct. 1/6 All 73 passengers and crew of a Cuban DC-8 airliner were believed lost when the plane plunged into the Caribbean.

2. *attrib.* and *Comb.*, as ***plane crash*** sb. (and vb. intr.), ***fare, journey, -load, park,*** †***pilot, -ride, -spotter, ticket***; **planeside** *U.S.*, an area beside an aeroplane; also *attrib.*; **plane time**, the time of departure of an aircraft on a scheduled flight.

1946 *Time* 14 Oct. 69/1 Four years before Knute Rockne *plane-crashed to death in Kansas, Irishman Frank Leahy came to Notre Dame. **1957** P. WORSLEY *Trumpet shall Sound* x. 200 These movements soon spread further into the Highlands, thriving on the.. alarm created by the war:.. plane-crashes and so on. **1972** J. AIKEN *Butterfly Picnic* i. 13 Her parents had been killed in a plane crash. **1969** B. MALAMUD *Pictures of Fidelman* iii. 69 I'll need *plane fare. **1973** 'E. MCBAIN' *Let's hear It* v. 68 The Puerto Ricans came, and some of them stayed only long enough to earn plane fare back to the island. **1974** E. AMBLER *Dr. Frigo* II. 84, I.. have no trouble at all with long *plane journeys... I always sleep soundly. **1951** R. MALKIN *Boxcars in Sky* 25 A French schoolhouse was able to be rushed to completion in record time following the flight of a *planeload of components of a prefabricated school manufactured in England. **1969** C. BOOKER *Neophiliacs* x. 261 Planeloads of American gamblers flying in to.. 'the European Las Vegas' [*sc.* London]. **1976** *Evening Standard* 29 Dec. 26/5 Representatives of the emerging nations descend by the plane-load. **1936** 'J. BEYNON' *Planet Plane* 41 The crowds began to pour from the *'plane-parks and car-parks. **1916** 'BOYD CABLE' *Action Front* 132 The *'plane pilot.. was well out of range. **1953** DYLAN THOMAS *Let.* 22 June (1966) 408, I almost liked the *plane-ride, though. **1973** *Black Panther* 4 Aug. 15/2 Nixon,.. in a plane ride from Mobile to Birmingham in 1971 with Wallace, had persuaded the charismatic Alabaman to run as a Democrat. **1968** *N.Y. Times* 28 Mar. 3 In a *planeside interview, General Abrams said [etc.]. **1968** *Sat. Rev.* (U.S.) 31 Aug. 6, I walk from planeside to a taxi. **1976** *6,000 Words* 156 Speaking briefly at planeside. **1978** *Fortune* 4 Dec. 101 (*heading*) To planeside by bus. **1960** *Guardian* 12 Mar. 6/5 The prowess of London Airport's *plane spotters is likely to become comparable with the best of the train spotters. **1975** S. JOHNSON *Urbane Guerilla* III. 152 A crowd of sightseers and plane-spotters. **1977** *Daily Mirror* 21 Mar. 13/2 Five plane spotters serving jail terms in Greece will get a spot of home comfort today. **1967** M. DRABBLE *Jerusalem the Golden* viii. 204 Her *plane ticket.. was booked from Le Bourget. **1974** D. WESTHEIMER *Olmec Head* ii. 18 Plane tickets, hotel rooms already set. **1962** L. DEIGHTON *Ipcress File* v. 30 The typewritten sheet gave *plane times. **1973** 'B. MATHER' *Snowline* ix. 112 I'll be able to get you an air ticket... You had better stay here until plane time. **1976** K. BONFIGLIOLI *Something Nasty in Woodshed* ix. 96, I slept until 'plane-time this morning.

plane (pleɪn), *a.* [ad. L. *plān-us* flat, level; or, more properly, a refashioning (late in 17th c.) of PLAIN *a.*, in certain senses, after the original L. word, so as to differentiate these senses from those now expressed by *plain*. Cf. the learned F. adj. *plan, plane* (16th c.), similarly substituted in learned or technical use for the popular *plain, plaine*.]

1. a. *Geom.* Of a surface: Perfectly flat or level, so that every straight line joining any two points in it lies wholly in it (see PLANE *sb.*^{3} 1 a). Hence applied to an angle, figure, or curve which lies wholly in such a surface.

[**1570–1727** see PLAIN *a.*^{1} 1 c.] **1704** J. HARRIS *Lex. Techn.* I, *Plane Surface*, is that which lies even between its bounding Lines; and as a Right Line is the shortest Extension from one Point to another, so a *Plane Surface* is the shortest Extension from one Line to another. **1828** J. H. MOORE *Pract. Navig.* (ed. 20) 7 To make Plane Angles; and first a Right Angle, containing 90 Degrees. **1852** SALMON (*title*) Treatise on the Higher Plane Curves. **1859** CAYLEY *Coll. Math. Papers* IV. 207 The tangent is a line passing through two consecutive points of a plane curve. **1868** LOCKYER *Elem. Astron.* vii. 241 If all three sides are on the same plane, the triangle is called a plane triangle.

b. *transf.* Relating to or involving plane surfaces or magnitudes (and no higher or more complex ones).

plane function = PLANIMETRIC function. † ***plane number*** (obs.): a number formed by the multiplication of two (prime) factors, and therefore capable of being represented by a plane (rectangular) figure whose sides represent the factors: cf. LINEAR 3, quot. 1706, and the analogous uses of *square* and *cube*. ***plane problem***: see quot. 1704.

1704 J. HARRIS *Lex. Techn.* I, *Plane Number*, is that which may be produced by the Multiplication of two Numbers one into another. *Ibid., Plane Problem*, in Mathematicks, is such an one as cannot be solved Geometrically, but by the Intersection either of a Right Line and a Circle; or of the Circumferences of two Circles. **1706** W. JONES *Syn. Palmar. Matheseos* 279 The various Uses of Plane Trigonometry. **1747** SIMPSON (*title*) Elements of Plane Geometry. **1807** HUTTON *Course Math.* II. 1 Plane Trigonometry treats of the relations and calculations of the sides and angles of plane triangles. **1854** MOSELEY *Astron.* xxxvii. (ed. 4) 126 It is the object of.. Plane Astronomy.. from the apparent motions of the heavenly bodies to educe their true motions.

2. Of a material surface (also, of a body, having such a surface): Flat, level; not convex or concave.

1666 J. SMITH *Old Age* 91 As age enfeebleth the eye, the form and figure of it becomes more plane and depressed than it was before. **1760** J. LEE *Introd. Bot.* I. xiii. (1765) 31 Plane, flat. **1796** KIRWAN *Elem. Min.* (ed. 2) II. 525 Whitehaven Coal.. Fracture plane foliated. **1815** J. SMITH *Panorama Sc. & Art* I. 274 On a surface perfectly plane, hard, and smooth, a ball also perfectly hard and smooth, as well as globular, would be carried perhaps five hundred yards, by the same force that would scarcely carry it twenty yards upon the rough pavement. **1829** *Nat. Philos.* I. iii. 7 (Usef. Knowl. Soc.) A plane glass.. has two plane surfaces parallel to one another. **1831** BREWSTER *Nat. Magic* v. (1833) 117 The representation of objects in perspective upon a plane surface. **1866** *Treas. Bot.*, *Plane*, flat or perfectly level; as in many leaves. **1869** PHILLIPS *Vesuv.* x. 272 A crystal of 24 plane sides trapezoidal in form. **1899** *Allbutt's Syst. Med.* VIII. 798 Plane spots or patches of various sizes and shapes.

3. Combinations and special collocations; **plane ashlar** (see quot.); **plane chart** († *plain chart*), a chart on which the meridians and parallels of latitude are represented by equidistant straight lines (cf. PLANE-SAILING); **plane-parallel** *a.*, both plane and parallel; **plane-plane** *a.*, having the two opposite surfaces parallel and both plane, as a glass (opp. to *plano-convex*, *plano-concave*, *concavo-convex*, etc.); **plane-polarized** *a.*, of light, polarized so that all the ethereal vibrations take place in one plane; so ***plane polarization***; **plane scale** († *plain scale*), a scale or ruler marked with lines denoting chords, rhumbs, sines, tangents, secants, etc., formerly used in mathematical operations, esp. in navigation. Also in compound adjs. denoting a combination of a plane form with another, as ***plane-convex*** (= PLANO-CONVEX); or an approximation to the plane form, as ***plane-umbilicate*** (= flatly umbilicate). See also PLANE-SAILING, PLANE-TABLE.

1823 P. NICHOLSON *Pract. Build.* 329 If the work be so smoothed as to take out the marks of the tools by which the stones were first cut, it is called *plane-ashlar. **1625** N. CARPENTER *Geog. Del.* I. vii. (1635) 167 The Geographicall Mappe is twofold: either the *Plaine Chart or the Planispheare. **1669** STURMY *Mariner's Mag.* II. 46 The making the plain Sea-Chard, and the true Sea-Chard. **1696** PHILLIPS (ed. 5), *Plane Chart*, a Plat or Chart that Seamen sail by, whose Degrees of Longitude and Latitude are made of the same Length. **1867** SMYTH *Sailor's Word-bk.*, *Plane-chart*, one constructed on the supposition of the earth's being an extended plane, and therefore but little in request. **1668** *Phil. Trans.* III. 631 The Telescope.. with four Glasses, whereof the three Ocular ones, *Plane-convexe,.. and the fourth a Sphericall Object-glass. **1903** *Amer. Jrnl. Sci.* XVI. 114 A rock-mass possessing the *plane-parallel structure. **1958** *Newnes Compl. Amat. Photogr.* 97 In order not to disturb the lens correction filter glasses have to be plane-parallel and optically finished. **1962** CORSON & LORRAIN *Introd. Electromagn. Fields* iv. 148 (*caption*) Grounded, plane-parallel electrodes terminated by a plane electrode at potential V_0. **1865** WATTS *Dict. Chem.* III. 659 If the two systems [of light-waves] are polarised in planes making an oblique angle with one another, a difference of phase equal to 0 or $m\frac{\lambda}{2}$ produces rectilinear or *plane polarisation, while every other difference produces elliptical polarisation. *a* **1853** PEREIRA *Pol. Light* (1854) 116 *Plane-polarized light reflected from metals becomes elliptically polarized. **1881** MAXWELL *Electr. & Magn.* II. 401 The disturbance will correspond to a plane-polarized ray of light. **1659** J. COLLINS (*title*) Navigation by the Mariners *Plain Scale new plain'd. **1701** MOXON *Math. Instr.* 15 *Plain Scale*, made of box, a foot long, with a double Diagonal Scale, Sines, Tangents, Secants, Chords, Rhombs, Leagues, Longitudes and Equal parts: used by Seamen to solve their questions in Plain Sailing and to save their Gunter. **1828** HUTTON *Course Math.* II. 58 Of plane scales, there should be several sizes, as a chain in 1 inch,.. a chain in ½ an inch, &c. **1887** W. PHILLIPS *Brit. Discomycetes* 126 *Hymenoscypha tuba*... Cup campanulate, disc *plane-umbilicate.

plane (pleɪn), *v.*[1] Forms: α. 4– plane, (4 plaan). β. 4–7 playn(e, 4–5 pleyne, 6–7 plaine, 6–8 plain. [a. F. *plane-r* (12th c. in Littré), = Pr. *planar*, It. *pianare*:—L. *plānāre* to make flat, level, smooth, f. *plān-us* PLANE, PLAIN; from 14th to 18th c. also spelt *playne*, *plaine*, *plain*, in agreement with PLAIN *a.*[1], but now employed only in uses which are associated with the action of a carpenter's *plane*, and so spelt. See PLANE *sb.*[1]]

I. In general sense.

1. *trans.* To make (a surface) plain, even, or smooth; to level, to smooth; †also, to spread out evenly or smoothly (*obs.*). Also *fig.* (Now chiefly in the archaic phr. *to plane the way*, or as a fig. use of sense 3.)

α. *c* **1320** *Cast. Love* 678 He stont on heiȝ Roche and sound, And is i-planed in-to þe ground. **13..** *E.E. Allit. P.* B. 310 A cofer closed of tres, clanlych planed. **1382** WYCLIF *Deut.* x. 1 Plaan to thee two stonen tables, as the rather weren. *c* **1400** *Lanfranc's Cirurg.* 336 Take þerof as miche as þou wolt, & plane it vpon leþer or vpon lynnen clooþ, & leie vpon þe place. **1513** DOUGLAS *Æneis* XII. xii. 188 Bot tho the stok of this tre doun was rent.. To that entent to plane the batale place. **1653** H. COGAN tr. *Pinto's Trav.* lxix. 280 Pioners, whom he had sent before to plane the passages and ways. **1711** P. H. *View two last Parlts.* 239 This plan'd the Way to lay Addresses. **1768–74** TUCKER *Lt. Nat.* (1834) II. 346 Let us.. exert our abilities.. to plane the way for his passage. **1847** TENNYSON *Princ.* IV. 296 What student came but that you planed her path To Lady Psyche, younger, not so wise, A foreigner?

β. **1398** TREVISA *Barth. De P.R.* XVI. lxxv. (Tollem. MS.), Stones beþ.. hewe, playnid, and squared. **1412–20** LYDG. *Chron. Troy* I. vi. (1555), And floures.. Upon their stalkes gan playn theyr leues wide. *c* **1420** *Pallad. on Husb.* II. 91 Pare al the dichis euen, playn the brinke. **1512** *Helyas* in Thoms *Prose Rom.* (1828) III. 82 He playned lovingli theyr fethers. **1579** LYLY *Euphues* (Arb.) 134 It is.. discreete demeanour that playneth the path to felicitie. **1579–80** NORTH *Plutarch* (1676) 436 He had.. Pyoners.. to plain ways. **1598** BARRET *Theor. Warres* V. i. 128 The.. field without the Citie ought to be razed or plained a thousand pases round about. **1601** HOLLAND *Pliny* II. 596 The pauement thus laid is to be plained and polished diligently with some hard stone. **1642** H. MORE *Song of Soul* I. I. xx, Such as their Phyllis would, when as she plains Their Sunday-cloths. **1703** MAUNDRELL *Journ. Jerus.* (1732) 36 An Inscription engraven on a Table plain'd in the side of the natural Rock. **1768–74** TUCKER *Lt. Nat.* (1834) II. 230 Honest Inquiry and sober Freedom are the pioneers to plain the way before thee. **1824** J. JOHNSON *Typogr.* II. 521 The pressman.. next examines his form, to see that it is properly locked up and plained down.

†**b.** *fig.* To smooth over, excuse, explain away.

13.. *Cursor M.* 26583 (Cott.) Noght wit wordes fayr and slight Agh þou for to plane þi plight. *c* **1412** HOCCLEVE *De Reg. Princ.* 4373 But if releef a-way my sorowe plane. **1494** FABYAN *Chron.* VI. ccxii. 228 They planed or excused the sharpenesse of theyr mysse lyuynge.

†**c.** To clear *away* (writing) by smoothing the surface of the tables. *Obs.*

c **1386** CHAUCER *Sompn. T.* 50 He planed awey the names euerichon That he biforn had writen in his tables.

†**d.** To level *with* the ground, to raze *to* the earth. *Obs.*

1562 J. SHUTE tr. *Cambini's Turk. Wars* 4 Leaving them [cities] desert and plained to the grounde. **1600** FAIRFAX *Tasso* I. lxxxix, The Suburbs first flat with the Earth he plained. *c* **1611** CHAPMAN *Iliad* XII. 42 All with the earth were plain'd.

†**2.** *fig.* To make plain or intelligible; to show or state plainly: to explain, display, show. *Obs.*

α. *c* **1450** HOLLAND *Howlat* 850 The pure Howlatis appele completly was planyt. **1567** *Gude & Godlie B.* (S.T.S.) 87 Quha trewlie traistis in thy Godlie name, Sall never die Eternallie, I plane. **1573** *Satir. Poems Reform.* xl. 349 To syle the suith, and sunȝe, I will plane ȝow.

β. *c* **1374** CHAUCER *Troylus* v. 1230 But al for nought he nolde his cause pleyne. **1563** *Ressoning Crosraguell & Knox* 26 b, In this manner of speaking, I will plaine my industrie. **1581** *Satir. Poems Reform.* xliii. 166, I dar not pen the speciallis, I do plaine ȝow. *c* **1590** GREENE *Fr. Bacon* ii. 18 By Æromancy, to discouer doubts, To plaine out questions, as Apollo did. **1659** [see *plane scale*, PLANE *a.* 3].

II. To smooth with a plane (the tool).

3. *trans.* To dress with a plane or planing-machine; to smooth down the surface of (wood, metal, etc.) with or as with a plane. Also *fig.*

α. **1398** TREVISA *Barth. De P.R.* XVII. clxii[i]. (Bodl. MS.), Bordes and tables.. beþ araied and hewe and planed. **1452** in Willis & Clark *Cambridge* (1886) I. 282 The selyng boord .. shalbe.. clene planed, and the sparres shalbe planed also. **1496** *Naval Acc. Hen. VII* (1896) 167 For planyng of the same orys xij[d]. **1530** PALSGR. 659/2, I plane, as a joyner or carpenter dothe his tymber or bordes with a plane or rabatte. **1622** PEACHAM *Compl. Gent.* xiii. (1634) 130 First, for your table.. plane it very even, and with Size.. white it over. **1703** MOXON *Mech. Exerc.* 68 You must turn your Stuff to Plane it the contrary way. **1837** GORING & PRITCHARD *Microgr.* 23 Get three pieces of brass planed perfectly flat. **1838–9** FR. A. KEMBLE *Resid. in Georgia* (1863) 26 White pine wood planed as smooth as marble. **1875** KNIGHT *Dict. Mech.* 1729/2 The earliest machine for planing metal was invented by Joseph Moxon... The machine was employed for planing brass mouldings. **1878** HUXLEY *Physiogr.* 183 Eating away the margin of the coast and planing it down, to a depth of perhaps 100 fathoms.

β. **1535** COVERDALE *Isa.* xliv. 13 The carpenter.. playneth it, he ruleth it, and squareth it. **1570** LEVINS *Manip.* 200/23 To Playne a bourd, *polire*. **1667** PRIMATT *City & C. Build.* 61 For plaining the boards, and shooting them for a Square, two shillings. **1703** MOXON *Mech. Exerc.* 64 To lay Boards .. against, whilst they are Trying or Plaining. **1726** LEONI *Alberti's Archit.* I. 27/2 Wood that is easily plain'd.

b. *to plane away, off*: to remove by or as by planing.

1726 LEONI *Alberti's Archit.* I. 10/2 The Summit of a Hill .. made level by plaining away the Top. **1873** J. RICHARDS *Wood-working Factories* 57 In our American shops from two to four times as much wood is planed off as in Europe. **1902** LUBBOCK *Scenery Eng.* (ed. 3) 115 The projections of rock being planed off and the hollows filled up by the waves.

4. *intr.* To use or work with a plane.

1703 MOXON *Mech. Exerc.* 68 You must begin at the hinder end of the Stuff.. and Plane forward. **1858** RAMSAY *Remin.* iv. (1870) 80 He.. taught us to saw, and to plane. **1866** G. MACDONALD *Ann. Q. Neighb.* iv. (1878) 51 But the man was again silent, planing away at half the lid.

Hence **planed** *ppl. a.*

1382 WYCLIF *Gen.* vi. 14 Make to thee an ark of planed trees. **1571** DIGGES *Pantom.* I. xxii. G ij b, A cleane foure square planed boarde. **1627–77** FELTHAM *Resolves* I. lxii. 96, I care not for the planed Stoic, there is a Sect between him and the Epicure. **1887** MOLONEY *Forestry W. Afr.* 27 Planed timber and flooring.

plane (pleɪn), *v.*[2] [a. F. *plane-r* (16th c., Rab.), f. *plan* plane, because a bird when soaring extends its wings in a plane.] **1.** *intr.* Of a bird: To soar on outspread motionless wings. (In mod. use with the idea of an aeroplane's flight.)

1611 COTGR., *Planer*,.. to plane, as a bird that flies, or houers, without mouing her wings. **1775** TWISS *Trav. Port. & Sp.* 65, I observed many eagles planing over head. **1862** W. STORY *Roba di R.* ix. (1864) 177 Sometimes.. far up in the blue height, an eagle planing over it on wide-spread motionless wings. **1941** I. L. IDRIESS *Great Boomerang* i. 2 A black dot appeared in the brazen sky. It grew, planed down and alighted on the needlewood-tree beside the first crow. **1953** R. LEHMANN *Echoing Grove* 22 A shape of silence, planing stealthily from nowhere, crossed the churchyard: a huge cream-coloured owl. **1953** J. CARY *Except the Lord* lxii. 286 A few gulls planed high overhead but made no sound. **1955** *Times* 3 Aug. 10/2 As he [*sc.* a marsh harrier] began to plane down over the water two members of his young family raced each other to meet him in the air. **1978** R. LEWIS *Uncertain Sound* vi. 154 The herring gulls planed among the bobbing masts of the fishing fleet. **1979** G. HAMMOND *Dead Game* ix. 107 Another [goose].. had gone on away over the sands, first planing and then running.

2. *intr.* To travel in an aeroplane; †to glide.

1908 *Daily Mail* 10 Aug. 5/4 Safety would reside in high flight; it would always be possible to 'plane' to earth, and in 'planing' the machine would progress many more feet than it would fall. **1909** *Westm. Gaz.* 9 Aug. 5/1 Mr. Orville Wright has stated that he and his brother are completing the perfecting of their aeroplane... With this apparatus he says one will be able to 'plane' to one's heart's content. **1909** *Daily Chron.* 26 Aug. 1/2 His engine began to show signs of distress. The aviator was seen to slow down, and then he 'planed gracefully to the earth. **1912** S. F. WALKER *Aviation* viii. 66 He can plane down. Planing down is merely gliding. **1940** *Daily Progress* (Charlottesville, Va.) 13 Aug. 1/4 Little Carolyn.. will plane out for the movie capital from the nation's capital on Thursday morning, accompanied by her mother. **1967** J. P. CARSTAIRS *No Thanks for Shroud* ii. 28, I had planed into the large air terminal at Los Angeles.

3. *intr.* Of a seaplane, boat, etc.: to skim the surface of a body of water as a result of lift produced hydrodynamically.

1913 [see HYDROPLANE *sb.* 2]. **1914** *Techn. Rep. Advisory Comm. Aeronaut. 1912–13* 243 The position of the centre of buoyancy when the float is at rest is far ahead of the centre of pressure when it is 'planing' and the machine about to fly. **1919** A. W. JUDGE *Handbk. Mod. Aeronaut.* xix. 943 Hollow Vee sections keep the spray down, cut the water more easily and cleanly, plane better, [etc.]. **1942** *R.A.F. Jrnl.* 13 June 8 There is great danger in.. level ditchings where the nose strikes first. The nose is neither shaped nor strong enough to plane along the surface. **1954** K. C. BARNABY *Basic Naval Archit.* (ed. 2) 318 When a hard chine hull is planing correctly, only the under body below the chines is in direct and constant contact with the water. **1963** J. T. ROWLAND *North to Adventure* i. 15 It was a big sail for a ten-foot punt. She seemed to leap out of the water; I believe she planed. **1972** C. MUDIE *Motor Boats* 48 A fast boat on the verge of planing or actually planing builds up a pressure on the under surfaces of the hull which, like walking on harder ground compared with bog, increases the firmness of the footing and hence the stability. **1972** R. ABBOTT *Sci. of Surfing* iii. 52 The technique of modern surfing is based on the fact that boards plane easily and efficiently. Planing is the term used to describe the way in which a surfboard rises onto the water surface and skims along at high speed. **1974** *Encycl. Brit. Macropædia* II. 1171/1 Because the displacement hull.. can never plane on the surface no matter how much power is applied, the efforts of designers were directed toward the development of hulls.. that at speed would rise to the surface and skim across the water, thus reducing.. the friction and resistance.

4. *trans.* In Surfing, to ride (a wave) with the hands protecting the face. *Austral.*

1963 B. HUTCHINGS in J. Pollard *Swimming—Austral. Style* 122/1 To 'plane' a wave, you hold your hands together in front of your head and take off in this position as the wave nears... The trick is to arrange the spear formed by the hands in such a way that the water passes along the side of the face and torso and not into the face.

Hence **'planing** *vbl. sb.*[2] and *ppl. a.* (chiefly in sense 3 of the vb.).

1908 [see AVIATE *v.*]. **1914** *Techn. Rep. Advisory Comm. Aeronaut. 1912–13* 243 Its most obvious defect was a certain slowness in rising to the planing position. **1919** A. W. JUDGE *Handbk. Mod. Aeronaut.* xix. 944 The bottom abaft the step should rise strongly, as this favours a steepening of the planing bow before suction is eliminated. **1920** *Flight* XII. 301/1 Other types of 'planing' boats. *Ibid.* 591/1 The angle of the planing bottom at the keel, forward of the step, should be 1½ degrees to the datum line. **1937** *Jrnl. R. Aeronaut. Soc.* XLI. 273 Improvements have been made recently in the shape of afterbody of the planing bottom with the object of obtaining better aerodynamic efficiency. **1967** *Jane's Surface Skimmer Systems 1967–68* 110/1 The hull.. has a hard chine.. and planing hull form. **1972** R. ABBOTT *Sci. of Surfing* iii. 52 For planing speed to be maintained and so that the wave can be ridden along its length it is necessary to turn fairly soon. **1972** C. MUDIE *Motor Boats* 48 A planing boat has a quite remarkable stability when running fast. **1974** J. KEATS *Of Time & Island* xii. 191 When you pushed forward on a throttle.. the boat mounted onto its planing step and you flew over the river. **1976–7** *Sea Spray* (N.Z.) Dec./Jan. 78/1 This is no more evident than in the development of power craft, the rise of the planing hull and the steady move over the past few years into tunnel-hulls, hydrofoils, hovercraft and so on.

planeful, 'planeful ('pleɪnfʊl). [f. PLANE *sb.*[5] + -FUL.] As much or as many as an aeroplane will hold.

1958 *Times* 14 Aug. 9/4 There is no reason why a 'planeful of them [*sc.* monkeys] should be any different. **1967** M. DAVIS *Strange Corner* (1968) vii. 58 A planeful of new guests.

planeness ('pleɪnnɪs). [f. PLANE *a.* + -NESS.] The quality or condition of being plane; flatness, levelness.

1656 tr. *Hobbes' Elem. Philos.* (1839) 202 Every strait line is like every other strait line, and every plane like every other plane, when nothing but planeness is considered. **1896** *Jrnl. Geol.* IV. 955 Overwash plains may sometimes depart from planeness by taking on some measure of undulation. **1906** CHAMBERLIN & SALISBURY *Geol.* III. xix. 345 Neither planeness nor unevenness can be ascribed exclusively to the stratified nor to the unstratified drift. **1942** F. TWYMAN *Prism & Lens Making* ix. 124 The departures from planeness of the wave front.. will give rise to a contour map of the corrections which have to be applied to the lens. **1975** D. G. FINK *Electronics Engineers' Handbk.* IX. 26 Since the periphery of the grid is colder than the center, thermal stresses tend to cause buckling or departure from planeness.

planer (ˈpleɪnə(r)). Also 6–8 plainer. [f. PLANE *v.*[1] + -ER[1].]

1. One who makes level or levels down.

1560 WHITEHORNE *Arte Warre* 68b, It is conueniente to haue plainers and labourers afore, who may make thee the waie plaine. **1883** in *Chicago Advance* 20 Sept., We may now regard our familiar earthworm as..a 'planer of the mountain-side, a maker of fertile, alluvial corn lands'.

2. One who planes; a worker with a plane.

1598 FLORIO, *Dolatore*, a planer of boords. **1648–60** HEXHAM *Dutch Dict.*, *Een schaver*, a Shaver, a Planer, or a Smoother. **1818** TODD, *Planer*, one who smooths with a plane. **1865** I. T. F. TURNER *Slate Quarries* 16 To calculate the wages due to the sawyers, planers, and raspers.

†**3.** An instrument for smoothing something, e.g. the surface of salt for the table, etc. *Obs.*

To this may belong quot. 1413, in which the word denotes a utensil belonging to a brewer.

1413 *E.E. Wills* (1882) 22 Y be-quethe to..Ion, I graners, an a flot, an a planer. **1513** *Bk. Keruynge* in *Babees Bk.* (1868) 266 Than loke your salte be whyte and drye, the planer made of Iuory, two inches brode & thre inches longe.

4. A tool or instrument for planing wood; formerly, a plane (? sometimes, a chip-axe or adze); now, a planing-machine.

1596 THOMAS *Lat. Dict.*, *Dolabra*, a carpenters axe, or.. a great plainer. **1601** HOLLAND *Pliny* I. 493 A man shall see the fine shavings thereof run alwaies round and winding,.. as the Ioyner runneth ouer the painels and quarters with his plainer. **1615** CHAPMAN *Odyss.* v. 314 A great axe, first she gave that two ways cut;..A plainer then. *a* **1691** BOYLE *Hist. Air* ii. (1692) 5 Shavings of Wood (that Carpenters and Joiners are wont to take off with their Plainers). **1864** [see 6]. **1883** INGERSOLL in *Harper's Mag.* Jan. 208/2 To them are attached planers, shingle machines..and so on. **1900** *Engineering Mag.* XIX. 670 There will be..heavy planers, boring mills, and other large tools.

5. *Printing.* A block of wood with a strip of leather at the top, which is struck with a mallet to beat down projecting types in a form.

1858 SIMMONDS *Dict. Trade*, *Planer*..a flat square-made piece of wood, used by the compositor for forcing down the type in the form, and making the surface perfectly even. **1880** *Print. Times* 15 Feb. 30/1 The appliances..consist of brushes for moulding..mallet, planer, blanket. **1896** T. L. DE VINNE *Moxon's Mech. Exerc.*, *Printing* 408 The 'Dressing-block' is now known as the planer.

6. *attrib.* (in sense 4), as ***planer-bar***, ***-centre***, ***-chuck***, ***-knife***, ***-knife-grinder***, ***-vice***, parts of a planing-machine; **planer-head**, the slide-rest of a planing-machine; **planer-miller** = *plano-miller* s.v. PLANO-[1]; **planer tool**, a tool used for planing.

1864 WEBSTER, *Planer-head*, the slide-rest of a planing machine, or planer. **1873** J. RICHARDS *Wood-working Factories* 108 For planer-knives, have a coarse grain soft stone..not less than 40 inches in diameter when new. **1875** KNIGHT *Dict. Mech.*, *Planer-bar*, a device attached to a planer for the purpose of effecting in part the work of a slotting or shaping machine. **1884** *Workshop Receipts* Ser. III. 274/2 There is..a great difference of opinion with regard to..tempering..in the case of planer tools for iron. **1943** J. R. CONNELLY *Technique Production Processes* iii. 85 (*caption*) Planer-miller. A good case of comb[in]ing the features of several standard tools for special work. **1971** C. R. HINE *Machine Tools & Processes* xiii. 308 The planer-miller is a hybrid of the two machines, but because of its size and construction (with a crossrail) it can rightfully be classified as a planer.

planerite (ˈplænəraɪt). *Min.* [Named 1862 after its discoverer D. J. Planer, mine director: see -ITE[1] 2b.] A hydrous phosphate of aluminium, allied to wavellite, found in quartz.

1868 DANA *Min.* (ed. 5) 576 *Planerite.* Under this name Hermann has described..a mineral from the copper mines of Gumeschefsk, in the Ural. It occurs in thin, subcrystalline, botryoidal layers in the cavities of a quartz rock. .. Color on fresh surface verdigris-green, passing to olive-green on exposure to the air.

ˈ**planer-tree.** [From the surname of I. J. Planer, a German botanist, whence the genus has its mod.L. name *Planera*.] A small, deciduous tree, the water elm, *Planera aquatica*, belonging to the family Ulmaceæ and native to south-eastern parts of the United States.

1810 F. A. MICHAUX *Hist. Arbres Forestiers de l'Amérique Septentrionale* I. 39 *Planer tree*, nom de la personne à laquelle cette espèce a été consacrée. **1819** A. L. HILLHOUSE tr. *Michaux's N. Amer. Sylva* III. 100, I have more particularly observed the Planer Tree in the large swamps on the borders of the river Savannah in Georgia. **1832** D. J. BROWNE *Sylva Amer.* 246 The planer tree is of the second order, and is rarely more than 35 or 40 feet high. **1884** MILLER *Plant-n.*, *Planera aquatica* and other species, Planer-tree. **1887** *Nicholson's Dict. Gardening*, *Planera* (named in honour of I. J. Planer, a German botanist, who published a Flora of Erfurt, in 1788)... *P. aquatica*.. Planer-tree... Southern United States, 1816. **1930** W. R. MATTOON et al. *Forest Trees Oklahoma* 62 The water elm or planer tree is found on the low wet flood plains of the larger streams of the eastern part of the state. **1976** *Hortus Third* (L. H. Bailey Hortorium) 882/2 Planer tree, water elm... A deciduous elmlike tree, native to N[orth] Amer[ica].

plane sailing. In 7–8 plain s. [f. PLANE *sb.*[3], formerly *plain*.] In *Navigation*, The art of determining a ship's place on the theory that she is moving on a plane, or that the surface of the earth is plane instead of spherical; navigation by a *plane chart*: see PLANE *a.* 3.

This is a simple and easy method, approximately correct for short distances, esp. near the equator.

1699 DAMPIER *Voy.* II. I. 90, 2 Dollars..which I had gotten..by teaching some of our young Seamen Plain Sailing. **1756** ROLT *Dict. Trade*, *Plain Sailing*, in navigation, is the art of working the several cases and varieties in a ship's motion on a plain chart. **1815** BURNEY *Falconer's Dict. Marine*, *Plane Sailing*..is that which is performed by means of a plane chart; in which case, the meridians are considered as parallel lines, the parallels of latitude are at right angles to the meridians, the lengths of the degrees on the meridians, equator, and parallels of latitude, are every where equal. **1867** SMYTH *Sailor's Word-bk.*, *Plane-sailing*, that part of navigation which treats a ship's course as an angle, and the distance, difference of latitude, and easting or westing, as the sides of a right-angled triangle. The easting or westing is called departure. **1890** *Cent. Dict.* s.v., In plane-sailing, the principal terms made use of are the course, distance, departure, and difference of latitude, any two of which being given the others can be found.

b. *fig.* A course so simple as to leave no room for mistakes. In this sense now commonly spelt PLAIN SAILING, q.v.

1858 GEN. P. THOMPSON *Audi Alt. Part.* I. liv. 212 The motion at first looks as if it was all what sailors call plane sailing. **1867** SMYTH *Sailor's Word-bk.* s.v., Plane-sailing is so simple that it is colloquially used to express anything so easy that it is impossible to make a mistake.

planeshear (ˈpleɪnʃɪə(r)), **planksheer** (ˈplæŋkʃɪə(r)). Forms: 8 plansheer, -shire, 9 planeshear, -sheer, plankshear, -sheer. [A corruption of PLANCHER *sb.*, by imagined connexion with PLANE, PLANK, and SHEER *sb.*] A continuous planking, covering the timber-heads of a wooden ship, in men-of-war forming a shelf below the gunwale; = *covering-board* (COVERING *vbl. sb.*[1] 3); also loosely applied to the gunwale.

1711 W. SUTHERLAND *Shipbuild. Assist.* 75 Great Rail at the After End, besides the Planshire Fore and Aft. *Ibid.* 162 Plansheers; the finishing part at the Top of the Shipside. **1832** MARRYAT *N. Forster* xvii, He was on the planesheer of the brig. **1833** —— *P. Simple* l, We discharged our ten muskets, into the boat, but this time we waited until the bowman had hooked on the planeshear with his boat-hook, and our fire was very effective. **1851** G. COGGESHALL *Voy.* iii. 40 The force of the sea broke one of the top timbers or stancheons, and split open the plank-sheer. **1869** SIR E. J. REED *Shipbuild.* xii. 238 A continuous angle-iron, which also serves to receive the fastenings of the wooden planksheer.

So, in same sense, **plank-sheering**.

a **1687** PETTY *Treat. Naval Philos.* I. i, Between the Plank-sheering, and the Keels.

planet (ˈplænɪt), *sb.*[1] Forms: 3–6 planete, (4–6 -ette, 5 -ett, *Sc.* -ait, 6 *Sc.* -eit, 7 plannet(t), 5– planet. [ME. a. OF. *planete* (F. *planète*), ad. late L. *planēta* or *planētēs* (cited only in pl. *planētæ* = cl. L. *stellæ errantes*), a. Gr. πλανήτης wanderer, hence, in *pl.* (ἀστέρες) πλανῆται wandering stars, planets, f. πλανᾶν to lead astray, in *passive* to wander. (Another Gr. form was πλάνης, -ητος, in pl. πλάνητες ἀστέρες, L. *planētes*.)]

†**1. a.** *Old Astron.* A heavenly body distinguished from the fixed stars by having an apparent motion of its own among them; each planet, according to the Ptolemaic system, being carried round the earth by the rotation of the particular sphere or orb in which it was placed. *Obs.*

The seven planets, in the order of their accepted distance from the Earth, were the Moon, Mercury, Venus, the Sun, Mars, Jupiter, and Saturn.

[*c* **1050** *Byrhtferth's Handboc* in *Anglia* (1885) VIII. 320 þa steorran þe man hæt planete on lyden.] *a* **1300** *Cursor M.* 1550 (Cott.) þe planetes all ar went again O þair first making in to þe state. *c* **1400** *Destr. Troy* 4366 Venus the worthy.. of planettes of prise has hor pure nome. *c* **1420** LYDG. *Assembly of Gods* 1695 The seuyn planettys Haue her propre names by astronomers. *c* **1470** HENRY *Wallace* XI. 500 Quhill day began to peyr; A thyk myst fell, the planet was not cleyr. **1481** CAXTON *Myrr.* I. xx. 60. A way that is comune to the vii planetes. **1600** NASHE *Summer's Last Will* D j, Resplendent Sol, chiefe planet of the heauens. **1621** BURTON *Anat. Mel.* I. ii. I. ii. (1651) 45 Gregorius Tholosanus makes seven kindes of ætherial spirits or angels, according to the number of the seven Planets, Saturnine, Jovial, Martial. **1687** tr. *Marana's Turkish Spy* I. xii. 35 It is a great while since we have had any Commerce here with the Sun; there being forty nine Days since this beauteous Planet appeared to us. **1727** BAILEY vol. II. s.v., There is none of the Planets, except the Sun that shines with his own Light. **1766** PORNY *Heraldry* (1787) 19 Arms..are blazoned..by Planets, when they belong to Sovereign Princes, Kings, and Emperors.

b. *esp.* in *Astrol.*, said with reference to the supposed 'influence' or quality of any one of these bodies in affecting persons and events; in later usage said vaguely or allusively of an occult controlling fateful power.

c **1290** *St. Michael* 431 in *S. Eng. Leg.* I. 312 þe planetes ne doth non oþur bot ȝiuez in mannes wille, To beon luþur oþur guod ase heore uertue wole to tille. *c* **1391** CHAUCER *Astrol.* I. §21 Whan the planetes ben vnder thilke signes, þei causen vs by hir influence operaciouns & effectes lik to the operaciouns of bestes. *c* **1400** MAUNDEV. (Roxb.) xviii. 81 þai dwell vnder a planett þat es called Saturnus. **1568** GRAFTON *Chron.* II. 616 The wittie Captaynes..thought it necessary to take the tyme while their good planet reigned. **1570** GOLDING *Justin* XIX. 99 Sodainly by the influence of a pestilent planet, [he] lost all his men of warre. **1670** MILTON *Hist. Eng.* II. Wks. 1851 V. 93 Blind, astonish'd, and strook with superstition as with a Planet. **1738** SWIFT *Pol. Conversat.* 82, I was born under a Threepenny Planet, never to be worth a Groat. **1837** MRS. SHERWOOD *Henry Milner* III. ix. 176 One of us poor creatures who are born under a three-halfpenny planet.

c. ***to rain***, etc., ***by planets, in planets*** (*dial.*): see quots. ***to rule a planet***, said †(*a*) of the zodiacal sign in which the planet is (*obs.*), (*b*) of a person, To calculate a horoscope, practise astrology. *dial.*

c **1470** HENRY *Wallace* VII. 175 That wykked syng so rewled the planait; Saturn was than in till his heast stait. **1670** RAY *Eng. Prov.* 45 *It rains by planets*, this the Countrey people use when it rains in one place and not in another; meaning that the showers are governed by the Planets. **1807** STAGG *Poems* 22 Heavier now the tempest musters, Down in plennets teems the rain. *a* **1825** FORBY *Voc. E. Anglia* s.v., In changeable weather the rain and sunshine come and go by planets. A man of unsteady mind acts by planets; meaning much the same as by fits and starts. **1882** in Lucas *Stud. Nidderdale* 206 That no two floods in Nidderdale are alike in effect, which is locally accounted for by saying, 'that the rain falls in planets'. **1886** ELWORTHY *W. Somerset Word-bk.* s.v., To 'rule the planets' is to practise rustic astrology. **1903** *Eng. Dial. Dict.* s.v., 'He's getten his planet ruled.'

2. *Mod. Astron.* The name given to each of the heavenly bodies that revolve in approximately circular orbits round the sun (***primary planets***), and to those that revolve round these (***secondary planets*** or SATELLITES).

The primary planets comprise the ***major planets***, of which nine are known, viz., in order of distance from the sun, Mercury, Venus, the Earth, Mars, Jupiter, Saturn, Uranus, Neptune, and Pluto, and the ***minor planets*** or ASTEROIDS, the orbits of most of which lie between those of Mars and Jupiter.

1640 WILKINS (*title*) A Discovrse concerning a New Planet. Tending to prove, That 'tis probable our Earth is one of the Planets. **1664** POWER *Exp. Philos.* III. 163 Who can imagine that any of the primary Planets were wholly designed for the service of Us and our Earth? **1704** J. HARRIS *Lex. Techn.* I. s.v., We now number the Earth among the Primary Planets, because we know it moves round the Sun, ..and that in a Path or Circle between Mars and Venus. **1710** *Ibid.* II. s.v., The Motions of the Secondary Planets or Satellites round their Primary ones. **1815** J. SMITH *Panorama Sc. & Art* I. 510 The primary planets are again distinguished into superior and inferior. The superior planets are those farther from the sun than our Earth..and the inferior planets are those nearer the sun. **1836** MACGILLIVRAY tr. *Humboldt's Trav.* xix. 279 The waters have scooped a great hollow..in the ancient revolutions of our planet. **1850** TENNYSON *In Mem.* Concl. 138 The man, that with me trod This planet. **1878** HUXLEY *Physiogr.* xxi. 371 Astronomers are acquainted with 182 bodies called planets.

3. *fig.* In various obvious senses: e.g. a source of influence; a luminary; (***rogues'*** *cant*) a candle.

1423 JAS. I *Kingis Q.* xcix, Hye quene of lufe! sterre of beneuolence! Pitouse princes, and planet merciable! **1596** DRAYTON *Legends* ii. 237 Those two bright Planets, cleerer then the Seven, That with their Splendor, light the World to Heaven. **1790** J. ADAMS *Wks.* (1854) IX. 571 What the conjunctions and oppositions of two such political planets may produce, I know not. **1840** LONGF. *Sp. Stud.* III. v, As soon as you see the planets are out, in with you.

4. A planet wheel.

1912 R. W. A. BREWER *Motor Car Construction* xii. 154 If one sun wheel is held, the whole of the planets with their star piece move bodily in a circle when the other sun wheel is revolved. **1928** V. W. PAGÉ *Mod. Aircraft* xi. 474 Various methods of compounding plain epicyclic gears have been tried, but the best type is undoubtedly that combining double planets, an annulus driven from the crankshaft, and a sun fixed to the engine casing. **1962** D. W. DUDLEY *Gear Handbk.* iii. 15 With some ratios it has been possible to squeeze in as many as twenty planets. **1970** *A.A. Bk. of Car* 110/1 In the simple epicyclic gear, a pair of planets revolve on spindles supported by the U-shaped planet carrier, which is mounted on the same shaft as the sun wheel.

5. *attrib.* and *Comb.*, as ***planet-making***, ***-prognosticator***, ***-ruler*** (cf. 1c), ***-sphere***; also ***planet-blazoned***, ***-crested***, ***-like***, ***-producing***, ***-spotted*** adjs.; **planet-book**, a book professing to tell fortunes by means of the planets; **planet cage**, a cylindrical form of planet carrier; **planet carrier**, the frame on which the planet wheels are mounted in a planetary gear; **planet earth** (without *the*, and usu. with one or both initials capitals), the earth as the particular planet on which man lives; **planet-gear**, a system of gearing in which planet-wheels are introduced; a mechanical combination for converting power into speed; a planet wheel; also **planet-gearing**; **planet pinion**, a planet wheel, esp. one smaller than the sun wheel; **planet shower**, a local shower (cf. PLANET *sb.*[1] 1c); **planet stirrer** = *planetary stirrer* s.v. PLANETARY *a.* and *sb.* A. 1f; **planet-wheel**, the exterior wheel which revolves round the central or sun wheel, in the SUN-AND-PLANET motion; **planet-wide** *a.*, occurring all over the planet, as extensive as the planet. See also PLANET-STRICKEN, -STRUCK.

1839 BARHAM tr. *Grotius' Adamus Exul* 43 This vast and *planet-blazoned universe. **1677** *Rosamond* in Evans *Old Ballads* (1784) I. 72 Go fetch me down my *planet-book,.. For in the same I mean to look, What is decreed my doom. **1908** *Planet cage [see *planet pinion* below]. **1947** *Jrnl. R. Aeronaut. Soc.* LI. 100/1 This usually leads to the adoption of an epicyclic gear with its associated problems of planet cage design and high centrifugal loadings. **1956** MOLLOY & LANCHESTER *Automobile Engineer's Ref. Bk.* XII. 60 The short planet gears rotate round the internal ring gear, in the same direction as the input shaft, thus rotating the *planet carrier and attached output shaft at a reduced speed. **1976** LEEMING & HARTLEY *Heavy Vehicle Technol.* vi. 117/2 If the planet carrier is braked and the sun wheel driven, the annulus is driven in a reverse direction—the planet wheels being idler wheels only—and reverse ratio is obtained. **1965** J. H. JACKSON *Pictorial Guide to Planets* v. 34 (*heading*) *Planet earth. **1976** L. DEIGHTON *Twinkle, Twinkle Little Spy* viii. 80 We should simply seek to make a mark in the universe.. that some other civilization will detect and so know there is.. sophisticated life on planet Earth. **1978** *Listener* 12 Jan. 54/1 The hopeful television producers.. who have invaded planet earth. **1979** *Guardian* 18 Aug. 10/8 The SF buff.. believes that Planet Earth is done for... He wants more money spent on space. **1916** J. E. HOMANS *Automobile Handbk.* iii. 42 As soon as the engine starts—there being no clutch necessary on a car with such apparatus—the two spurs keyed to the main shaft.. rotate with it, driving the '*planet' gears in mesh with them. **1956** [see *planet carrier* above]. **1971** B. SCHARF *Engin. & its Lang.* xii. 161 The planet gears are mounted on pins attached to a common frame, the planet carrier. **1581** SIDNEY *Apol. Poetrie* (Arb.) 72 If.. you be borne so neere the dull making Cataphract of Nilus, that you cannot heare the *Plannet-like Musick of Poetrie. **1715** CHEYNE *Philos. Princ. Relig.* I. 74 The Sun and fixt Stars are only Planet-like Bodies, vehemently heated. **1839** BAILEY *Festus* xxiv. (1848) 303 Oh! let not a planet-like eye Imbeam its tale on thine. **1908** *Daily Chron.* 14 Nov. 8/6 Greater attention is being paid to the elimination of internal friction from these devices, as in the provision of ball bearings for the *planet pinions in the Sturmey Archer gears, and roller bearings for the planet cage in the Armstrong. *a* **1935** [see BACK-LASH a]. **1966** *McGraw-Hill Encycl. Sci. & Technol.* X. 273/2 The number of teeth on the planet pinion of a simple planetary gear does not enter into the equations for speed ratio because the pinion engages both sun and ring gears. **1652** GAULE *Magastrom.* 23 Away.. with all superstitious hearkning to weather-wizzards, *planet-prognosticators, and fortune-spellers! **1894** *Spectator* 17 Feb. 231 She went to consult a *planet-ruler (the name now given to white witches) in Bristol. **1853** MAYNE REID *Rifle Rangers* (rev. ed.) lvii. 288 We were treated each day to some five or six hours of a '*planet' shower. **1880** W. H. PATTERSON *Gloss. Words Antrim & Down* 78 *Planet showers*, short heavy showers. **1925** E. SITWELL *Troy Park* 39 Not medicines *planet-spotted like fritillaries For country sins and old stupidities. **1902** C. SALTER tr. *G. von Georgievics's Chem. Technol. Textile Fibres* 249 Stirring is effected by so-called *planet stirrers. **1827** J. FAREY *Treat. Steam Engine* I. vi. 449 The link causes the centre of the *planet-wheel to travel in a circular orbit.. when it revolves round the sun-wheel. **1875** KNIGHT *Dict. Mech.* 1727 The latter sleeve has an arm carrying a planet-wheel. **1912** R. W. A. BREWER *Motor Car Construction* xii. 153 The large bevel wheel is bolted to a casing, which holds firmly a star piece having four arms on each of which runs a planet wheel... These four planet wheels engage with two sun wheels. **1976** Planet-wheel [see *planet carrier* above]. **1969** *Listener* 14 Aug. 215/2 It is now evident that on Mars, the craters are *planet-wide. **1974** *Icarus* XXII. 239 (*heading*) Martian planetwide crater distributions.

Hence †'**planet** *v. Obs. rare* (with *it*), to divine by the planets; '**planeted** *ppl. a.*, placed in a planet; '**planeting** *vbl. sb.*, the (fabled) singing or music of the planets.

1596 NASHE *Saffron-Walden* Wks. (Grosart) III. 121 A singular Scholler,.. set vpon it, and answered it in Print.. demonstrating what a lying Ribaden, and Chinklen Kraga it was, to constellate and plannet it so portentously. **1742** YOUNG *Nt. Th.* IX. 777 Tell me, all Ye Starr'd, and Planeted, Inhabitants! What is it? **1635** B. JONSON *Sad Sheph.* III. ii, Tempering all The jarring spheres, and giving to the world Again his first and tuneful planetting.

planet ('plænɪt), *sb.*[2], ‖**planeta** (plə'niːtə). [ad. med.L. *planēta* (633, Fourth Council of Toledo) a chasuble, orig. a name of the *pænula*, *infula*, *casula*, a large cloak or mantle worn by travellers; perh. from Gr. πλανήτης a wanderer.] A chasuble, esp. in its primitive form of a large loose mantle covering the whole body.

α. **1602** *Archpriest Controv.* (Camden) II. 28 A supplication for me to have a planet, chalice, and crucifix. *a* **1746** LEWIS in Gutch *Coll. Cur.* II. 178 This garment [the priest's chasuble] was likewise called a Planet, to distinguish it, I suppose, from the Chesible worn by the Deacon. **1885** DIXON *Hist. Ch. Eng.* III. 190 They bore on their left arm a folded planet or chasuble. **1894** REICHEL in *Trans. Exeter Archit. & Archæol. Soc.* I. 37 Neither deacons nor subdeacons wear the neckcloth, but walk in white albs and planets.

β. **1848** MRS. JAMESON *Sacr. & Leg. Art* (1850) 403 The planeta, which was a mantle made of a wide circular piece of cloth with an aperture in the middle for the head to pass through. **1867** C. WALKER *Ritual Reason Why* 179 The planeta or planet, so called because from being folded back it presented the appearance of a star when partially eclipsed.

'**plane-,table**, *sb.* Also 7–9 plain-table. [f. PLANE *a.* + TABLE *sb.*] A surveying instrument used for measuring angles in mapping, consisting of a circular drawing-table mounted horizontally on a tripod, and having an alidade pivoted over its centre.

1607 NORDEN *Surv. Dial.* III. 127 Two principall instruments, fit.. for the plotting of grounds,.. a plaine table, and the Theodolite which sometimes I use. **1766** *Complete Farmer* s.v. *Surveying*. To explain, in a very easy and concise manner, the use of the plain table. **1828** HUTTON *Course Math.* II. 76 In surveying with the plain table, a field-book is not used. **1871** PROCTOR *Light Sc.* 274 The plane-table is a flat board turning on a vertical pivot.

'**plane-,table**, *v.* [f. prec. sb.] *trans.* To survey with the plane-table. Also *intr.*, to work with a plane-table.

1883 H. H. GODWIN-AUSTEN et al. *Hints to Travellers* (ed. 5) i. 109 There is no measuring, no counting of paces or noting of time by a watch, no anxiety about the record, when Plane-Tabling. **1886** *Athenæum* 3 July 21/2 Major Holdich with his assistants, Capts. Gore and Talbot, have plane-tabled an extent of 15,000 square miles.

Hence '**plane-,tabler**, a surveyor using a plane-table; '**plane-,tabling**, the employment of a plane-table; surveying by means of the plane-table.

1871 PROCTOR *Light Sc.* 274 The principle of plane-tabling enters so largely into Indian surveying, that our notice would be incomplete without a brief account of this simple and beautiful method. **1888** *Min. Proc. Inst. Civil Engin.* XCII. 190 When a triangulation exists of the country to be mapped, the plane-tabler makes immediate use of these established points. **1923** D. CLARK *Plane & Geodetic Surveying* II. vi. 238 Plane tabling is the most extensively used method for the survey of topography. **1950** J. CLENDINNING *Princ. & Use of Surveying Instruments* vii. 166 Plane-tabling is a graphical method of survey in which the map is rough-drawn in the field as the survey proceeds. **1965** *Textbk. Topogr. Surveying* (Min. of Defence) (ed. 4) xi. 205 The trigonometrical framework will have been surveyed... The plane tabler then proceeds to break down from this framework using methods similar to those employed by the triangulator. **1971** R. J. P. WILSON *Land Surveying* viii. 164 In the past plane tabling was the method used for supplying topographical detail for maps at scales of 1:10 000 to 1:250 000, but its use in this respect has largely .. been superseded by air survey.

'**planetal**, *a. rare.* [f. PLANET *sb.*[1] + -AL[1].] Of or belonging to the planets, planetary.

1624 DARCIE *Birth of Heresies* xxii. 104 The body it self of the planetall Sunne remaines and continues in his sphericall Orbe. **1908** *Encycl. Relig. & Ethics* I. 187/1 The planetal series of our days of the week places Sunday before Monday.

planetarian (plænɪ'tɛərɪən), *a.* and *sb. rare.* [f. late L. *planētāri-us* PLANETARY + -AN.]

A. *adj.* Belonging to or connected with a planet or planets; planetary.

1652 GAULE *Magastrom.* 275 They refused to worship (the planetarian god) the sun. **1811** SOUTHEY in *Q. Rev.* VI. 337 The planetarian temple is well imagined.

B. *sb.* †**1.** An astrologer. *Obs.*

1652 GAULE *Magastrom.* 85 Dreams of later planetarians, or magicall astrologians.

2. An inhabitant of a planet.

1829 J. MILLER *Sibyl's Leaves* I. 217 Are your planetarians long or short, biped or decemped? **1855** B. POWELL *Ess.* 179 The most plausible image we can conjure up of the nature and appearance of lunarians or planetarians.

planetarily ('plænɪtərɪlɪ), *adv.* [f. PLANETARY *a.* + -LY[2].] After the manner of a planet; *fig.* with uncertain recurrence.

1610 HEALEY *St. Aug. Citie of God* 274 Under the Sun is the bright star Venus mooving diurnally and planetarily. *a* **1631** DONNE *Lett.* (1651) 27 That friendship which is not moved primarily by the proper intelligence, discretion,.. returns to the true first station and place of friendship planetarily, which is uncertainly and seldome.

‖**planetarium** (plænɪ'tɛərɪəm). [mod.L., f. *planētārius* PLANETARY: see -ARIUM.]

a. A machine illustrating by the movement of its parts the motions of the planets; an orrery.

1734 J. T. DESAGULIERS *Course Exper. Philos.* I. 430 A short Description of my Planetarium, an Instrument.. to shew the Motion of the heavenly Bodies. **1774** J. ADAMS *Diary* 27 Aug., Wks. 1850 II. 356 Here we saw.. an orrery or planetarium, constructed by Mr. Rittenhouse, of Philadelphia. **1805** H. K. WHITE *Rem.* I. 170, I have constructed a planetarium, or orrery, of a very simple kind. **1849** NOAD *Electricity* i. (ed. 3) 35 A little arrangement usually called the electrical planetarium.

b. A plan, model, or structure, representing the planetary system.

1860 HOLLAND *Miss Gilbert* i. 15 The mystery of the chalk planetarium was solved. **1901** *Daily News* 23 Feb. 6/3 Stonehenge has been variously.. called a temple of the sun, and of serpent worship, a shrine of Buddha, a planetarium, a gigantic gallows on which defeated British leaders were solemnly hung in honour of Woden.

c. The planetary system. *rare.*

1835 CHALMERS *Nat. Theol.* I. II. i. 219 It is passing marvellous that we should have more intense evidence for a God in the construction of an eye than in the construction of the mighty planetarium.

d. A device for projecting an image of the night sky at various times and places on to the interior of a dome for public viewing; a building housing this. Also *attrib.* and *fig.*

1929 *Encycl. Brit.* XVII. 1000 Planetarium is the name given to an arrangement made by Zeiss of Jena, for producing an artificial sky. By optical methods images of the sun, moon, planets and stars are projected on a large hemispherical dome and by mechanical and electrical means the apparatus can be revolved so as to show the principal motions. **1950** *Engineering* 21 July 63/1 A planetarium.. building will have.. the dome representing the sky.. diameter 60 feet. The simulation of the sun, moon, planets and stars.. projected on the 'sky' will have great educational value. **1958** *New Scientist* 20 Mar. 6/3 Zeiss Planetaria have been operated in 32 cities. **1958** [see ASTRONAVIGATION]. **1963** V. NABOKOV *Gift* iii. 166 Now on the [chess] board there shone, like a constellation, a ravishing work of art, a planetarium of thought. **1973** C. SAGAN *Cosmic Connection* viii. 60 Several million people visit planetariums in North America and Britain each year.

planetary ('plænɪtərɪ), *a.* and *sb.* [ad. late L. *planētārius*, prop. adj. 'belonging to a planet or planets', but only recorded as sb., an astrologer (Augustine). So F. *planétaire*. (The normal L. adj. would be *planētāris*: cf. *stellāris*.)]

A. *adj.* **1. a.** Belonging to, or connected with, a planet or planets; of the nature of, or resembling a planet; having some attribute of a planet.

planetary electron, an electron bound to an atom and 'in orbit' round its nucleus; *planetary ellipsoid*: see quot. 1881; *planetary engineering* (see quots. 1951, 1964); *planetary nebula*: see quot. 1854; *planetary precession*: see PRECESSION 3 a; *planetary system*, the system comprising the sun and planets, the solar system; also *fig.* a system of correlated parts; *planetary year*: see YEAR[1].

1610 GUILLIM *Heraldry* III. ii. (1611) 85 Of Starres some are fixed, and some are planetary or wandering. *a* **1652** J. SMITH *Sel. Disc.* v. 141 As the sun in the firmament is said to walk from one planetary house to another. *a* **1680** BUTLER *Rem.* (1759) I. 11 To stretch our Victories beyond Th' Extent of planetary Ground. **1715** tr. *Gregory's Astron.* I. 425 The Inclination of any Planetary Orbit to the Plane of the Ecliptic. **1785** *Phil. Trans. R. Soc.* LXXV. 266 A very bright, planetary nebula, about half a minute in diameter, but the edges are not very well defined. **1802** [see NEBULA 3]. **1815** W. H. IRELAND *Scribbleomania* 299 *note*, Lilly.. was universally reputed for his supposed planetary knowledge. **1816** PLAYFAIR *Nat. Phil.* II. 289 They proved, that the planetary system is stable. **1837** WHEWELL *Hist. Induct. Sc.* (1857) I. 169 The determination of the Planetary Orbits. **1854** BREWSTER *More Worlds* xi. 173 Planetary nebulae, or such as resemble planets from their discs being round or slightly oval. **1869** tr. *Pouchet's Universe* (1871) 511 All the stars are, according to Kepler, only suns like ours, each of which has its planetary system. **1881** MAXWELL *Electr. & Magn.* I. 221 Ellipsoids of this kind, which are figures of revolution about their conjugate axes, are called planetary ellipsoids. **1921** *Phil. Mag.* XLII. 305 Consider the nucleus alone, and not the surrounding system of planetary electrons. **1927** N. V. SIDGWICK *Electronic Theory of Valency* i. 10 The other planetary electrons would be distributed between these limits. **1951** A. C. CLARKE *Exploration of Space* 118 The greatest technical achievements of the next few centuries may well be in the field of what could be called 'planetary engineering'— the reshaping of other worlds to suit human needs. **1956** I. ASIMOV *Inside Atom* ii. 31 The number of planetary electrons in an ordinary atom is equal to the number of protons in the nucleus. **1960** *Analog Science Fact/Fiction* Oct. 34/1 We are coming off Mass-Time to go on planetary drive. **1964** *Listener* 15 Oct. 575/1 It will be possible to modify the climates and atmospheres of at least some of the planets, so that we can live on them... This technique of the future has been called 'planetary engineering'. **1971** *Nature* 3 Dec. 246/2 Why should planetary scientists suggest that a spacecraft costing nearly $100 million should be destroyed by taking it so close to Jupiter?

b. esp. in *Astrol.* with reference to the supposed 'influence' of a planet.

1607 SHAKS. *Timon* IV. iii. 108 Be as a Plannetary plague, when Ioue Will o're some high-Vic'd City, hang his poyson In the sicke ayre. **1613** MARKHAM *Eng. Husbandman* II. II. iv. (1635) 53 By Thunder, Lightning, or other planetarie stroakes. **1687** DRYDEN *Hind & P.* III. 472 Casting schemes by planetary guess. **1706** E. WARD *Wooden World Diss.* (1708) 92 The Captain.. perceiving him, by I know not what private Planetary Marks, to be an Engine form'd.. for his Use. **1843** PRESCOTT *Mexico* (1850) I. 102 The astrological scheme of the Aztecs was founded less on the planetary influences than on those of the arbitrary signs they had adopted for the months and days. **1861** C. W. KING *Ant. Gems* (1866) 459 Planetary rings, to which wonderful virtues were ascribed in the Middle Ages, were formed of the gems assigned to the several planets, each set in its appropriate metal.

c. *planetary hour*, the twelfth part of the natural day or night; called also *unequal hours* because they vary in length: see HOUR I.

In *Astrol.* supposed each to be ruled by a planet, the first and eighth by that after which the day is named, the others by the other planets in succession, the order being from Saturn to the Moon.

1593 FALE *Dialling* 43 Which may shew the place of the Sunne in every Signe, and likewise the planetary or vnequall houres. **1643** SIR T. BROWNE *Relig. Med.* II. § 11, I was born in the Planetary hour of Saturn. **1674** MOXON *Tutor Astron.* IV. iii. (ed. 3) 130 The first of these Planetary Hours takes its denomination from the Planetary Day; and the rest are named orderly from that Planet according to the succession of the Planetary Orbs. As if it be Munday, that is the Moons day.. the Planet reigning the first Hour shall be ☽, the Planet ruling the second Hour shall be ♄. **1697** DRYDEN *Virg. Georg.* III. 444 This, gather'd in the Planetary Hour, With noxious Weeds, and spell'd with Words of Pow'r. **1697** POTTER *Antiq. Greece* III. viii. (1715) 74 By Astronomers term'd unequal and Planetary Hours.

d. *Her.* Relating to the use of the names of planets for tinctures.

1661 MORGAN *Sph. Gentry* III. iv. 37 The planetary part of blazon doth well become persons that are above the vulgar.

e. Involving, being, or forming part of a sun-and-planet gear, usu. having (in addition to the sun and planet wheels) an internally geared

annulus coaxial with the sun wheel and with which the planet wheels are meshed.
1904 T. H. WHITE *Petrol Motors* II. 108 When the pinion A is revolved, and the internally toothed ring B is held from revolving, the planetary pinions C are caused to run around the ring B and carry the plate D with them. **1910** [see *band clutch* s.v. BAND *sb.*² III]. **1934** *Jrnl. R. Aeronaut. Soc.* XXXVIII. 738 This specification describes a planetary reduction gear for aero engines in which an internally toothed annulus is driven by the engine, the propeller is driven by the planetary ring, [etc.]. **1948** [see EPICYCLIC *a.*]. **1956** A. HUXLEY *Adonis & Alphabet* 127 The simple planetary gears, by means of which conventional turntables can be used for slow-playing disks. **1969** *Jane's Freight Containers 1968–69* 583/3 Torque converter is standard. All drive wheels planetary drive powered. **1975** *Sci. Amer.* Dec. 120/2 The upper end of the larger planetary gear engages a spur gear fixed to a turntable.

f. *Engin.* Characterized by the circular motion of a part about a point outside it.
planetary mill, a heavy rolling mill for reducing hot strip in a single pass, the strip being forced between two large rolls each of which has a number of smaller work rolls around its circumference, the former being rotated in the direction of feed so that the latter rotate against the strip; ***planetary mixer*** or ***stirrer***, one in which paddles are rotated about an axis which itself is moved in a circular path.
1917 T. R. SHAW *Precision Grinding Machines* ii. 28 Grinding machines with planetary spindles, specially adapted to the requirements of locomotive building. **1949** S. E. RUSINOFF *Manuf. Processes* x. 405, (*A*) of Fig. 17 illustrates the principle by which holes are ground in a locomotive side rod on a planetary grinder. A gyratory motion is imparted to the grinding wheel spindle so that the wheel sweeps the bore of the workpiece. **1950** KIRK & OTHMER *Encycl. Chem. Technol.* V. 705 In a planetary stirrer, the paddle rotates and at the same time the axis about which it rotates follows a circular orbit. *Ibid.* 707 Small-scale laboratory and pilot-plant models of planetary mixers ..are available. **1953** *Engineer* 23 Oct. 526/2 The first commercial installation of a new design of hot strip rolling mill..has been installed at the works of Ductile Planetary Mills, Ltd., of Willenhall, Staffs. *Ibid.*, The slabs have to be pressure fed into the rolls..by pinch or feed rolls, which are mounted in the same housing as the planetary assemblies. *Ibid.* 527/2 Immediately following the planetary mill is a two-high planishing mill. **1963** F. H. HABICHT *Mod. Machine Tools* xi. 166 Planetary grinding is usually limited to large or awkward work-pieces that cannot be conveniently rotated. **1967** IRVING & SAXTON in Uhl & Gray *Mixing* II. viii. 214 Vertical-shaft mixers..include planetary mixers and Pony mixers, as well as heavier duty, twin-shaft machines. **1968** R. N. PARKINS *Mech. Treatm. Metals* iv. 213 The great advantage of the planetary mill is that it can reduce a hot slab directly to strip, thereby replacing the three or four roughing mills and the six-stand finishing mill. **1971** C. R. HINE *Machine Tools & Processes* xiv. 330 The planetary miller is unique in that the work is held stationary while the revolving cutter or cutters move in a planetary path to finish a circular surface on the work, either internally or externally.

2. Belonging to this planet; terrestrial, mundane.
1831 *Blackw. Mag.* XXIX. 769 The Latin language has a planetary importance; it belongs not to this land or that land, but to all lands. **1901** F. W. H. MYERS *Human Personality* §320 I. 96 That..response to our surroundings which forms not only the planetary but the cosmic history of all our race.

3. *fig.* Wandering like a planet; erratic.
1607 J. KING *Serm. 5 Nov.* 26 Other planetary, cursorie, moueable from place to place, as Gerard, Tesmond, Hammond, Hal, with the like. **1636** SAMPSON *Vow-Breaker* I. i. B ij, Weomens minds are planetary, and amble as fast as Virginalls Iackes. **1655** FULLER *Ch. Hist.* IX. vii. §68, I am credibly informed he..disliked his own erratical and planetary life. **1710** NORRIS *Chr. Prud.* iii. 116 Such wandring, unprincipled, Planetary men as these. **1900** *Daily News* 22 Jan. 4/7 Readers..must have been struck with his planetary career over the face of the globe.

B. *sb.* †**1.** An astrologer, star-gazer. *Obs.*
1625 T. GODWIN *Moses & Aaron* (1641) 172 As if the Originall signified properly a Planetary, or Starre-gazer. **1652** GAULE *Magastrom.* 142 Now is the planetary more malignant or malefick..than are all the planets themselves. *a* **1716** SOUTH *Serm.* (1744) XI. 103 Which sufficiently prove the greatest pretenders to it [astrology] to be indeed but mere planetaries; that is, as we may well interpret it from the force of the word, such as use to err and to be deceived.

2. A planetary body.
1819 *Metropolis* I. 221 You are a fixed star in the firmament of attraction, around which we minor planetaries revolve with delight.

3. *ellipt.* for *planetary nebula.*
1903 A. M. CLERKE *Probl. in Astrophysics* II. i. 175 Spectroscopically, they [*sc.* Novae] simulate minute 'planetaries'. **1974** *Nature* 31 May 430/1 The precise details of the evolutionary history of the planetaries are uncertain.

4. *ellipt.* for *planetary gear* or ***wheel*** (= *planet-gear, -wheel*).
1941 *Electronic Engin.* XIV. 166/1 The planetary of the differential is connected to a gear-reduction train. **1962** D. W. DUDLEY *Gear Handbk.* iii. 21 Bevel planetaries can be made to handle a range of ratios.

planetesimal (plænɪˈtɛsɪməl), *a.* and *sb. Astr.* [f. PLANET *sb.*¹ + INFINIT)ESIMAL *sb.* and *a.*]

A. *adj.* Pertaining to, involving, or composed of planetesimals; applied *esp.* to the hypothesis that the planets were formed by the accretion of a vast number of planetesimals in a cold state.
1904 T. C. CHAMBERLIN in *Carnegie Inst. Year Bk.* II. 263 This led to studies upon alternative hypotheses. Among these is the conception that the earth, instead of descending from a gaseous spheroid, may have been built up by the gradual ingathering of its material from a scattered meteoroidal or planetesimal condition. **1904** *Amer. Geologist* XXXIII. 95 The planetesimal hypothesis..seems much better to explain both the astronomical and geological phenomena. **1906** *Athenæum* 18 Aug. 191/1 For the last ten years Prof. Chamberlin, aided by Dr. Forest R. Moulton, of Chicago, has been developing what is called the Planetesimal Theory of the earth's origin. **1937** WOOLDRIDGE & MORGAN *Physical Basis Geogr.* i. 5 The earth..grew from small beginnings by the addition of planetesimal matter. **1969** *Nature* 19 July 259/1 When planetologists meet to discuss the surface of the Moon they separate into those favouring the dominance of planetesimal (meteoric) impact and those who advocate volcanic activity.

B. *sb.* A small solid body following a planetary orbit; a miniature planet.
1904 *Amer. Geologist* XXXIII. 95 The new hypothesis holds..that the globular planets were formed by the slow accretion or infalling of cold, discrete bodies or particles ('planetesimals'). **1906** CHAMBERLIN & SALISBURY *Geol.* II. ii. 94 The planetesimals originated, by hypothesis, from gaseous matter shot forth from the ancestral sun. **1952** H. C. UREY *Planets* vii. 219 Planetesimals probably formed simultaneously with the protoplanets and accumulated into larger objects. **1971** *Sci. Amer.* Oct. 52/3 *Apollo 14* landed on the Fra Mauro formation, believed to be a blanket of ejecta thrown out by the giant meteorite or planetesimal that excavated the basin of Mare Imbrium. **1973** *Nature* 21/28 Dec. 451/3 Courten believes a planetesimal 'between 80 and 500 miles in diameter' moves in an orbit about 0·1 AU from the Sun. **1977** *Ibid.* 8 Dec. 506/1 Accumulation and fragmentation of planetesimals may have competed in the planetary accretion process, and a planetesimal which could survive catastrophic destruction may have become a planet.

planetfall (ˈplænɪtfɔːl). [f. PLANET *sb.*¹ + *-fall* as in LANDFALL.] A landing upon a planet after a journey through space.
1954 'J. CHRISTOPHER' *22nd Cent.* 98 The *Lucas* did not normally make planet-falls. *Ibid.* 123 Smoking was strictly prohibited from take-off until planet-fall. **1960** K. AMIS *New Maps of Hell* (1961) i. 19 A few writers..arrange for their travellers to put themselves into..deep freeze until just before planetfall. **1974** M. CAIDIN (*title*) Planetfall.

ˈplanethood. *nonce-wd.* [f. PLANET *sb.*¹ + -HOOD.] The condition or rank of a planet.
1674 N. FAIRFAX *Bulk & Selv.* 90 That which claws away world from about them, would, 'tis like, wring out their Planethood from within them.

†**plaˈnetic,** *a. Obs.* [ad. late L. *planētic-us*, a. Gr. πλανητικός wandering, f. πλανήτης: see PLANET *sb.*¹ and -IC.] Erratic, erring, extravagant.
1654 Z. COKE *Logick* a j, By it are confuse things made Distinct; Abstruse, Obvious:..the Planetick thoughts to act Concentrick, and in its Sphere. **1716** M. DAVIES *Athen. Brit.* II. 242 The Weather-Cock Brains of a Restless and Planetick Arian. **1858** in MAYNE *Expos. Lex.*

†**plaˈnetical,** *a. Obs.* [f. as prec. + -AL¹.]
1. Of or pertaining to the planets; planetary.
1585 LUPTON *Thous. Notable Th.* (1595) Pref. A iij b, Because the Planeticall power and effect in theyr howres.. should not be hidde or vnknowne. **1646** SIR T. BROWNE *Pseud. Ep.* IV. xiii. 228 Conjunctions and oppositions Planeticall. **1672** —— *Lett. Friend* §6 To make an end of all things on earth, and our planetical system of the world, He need but put out the Sun.

2. Wandering, roving, vagrant.
1657 FULLER *Best Employment* 17 Such, who..must have a whole province or principality for the circuit of their Planeticall preaching.

plaˈneticose, *a. nonce-wd.* [f. as prec + -OSE.] Given to wandering.
1849 LYTTON *Caxtons* XIII. i, Is there no mission in thy native land, O planeticose and exallotriote spirit?

planetismal (plænɪˈtɪzməl), *a.* and *sb. Astr.* [Alteration of PLANETESIMAL *a.* and *sb.*] = PLANETESIMAL *a.* and *sb.*
1910 *Westm. Gaz.* 16 Apr. 12/3 He accepts what is known as the 'planetismal hypothesis', which is, in his opinion, the most positive advance in natural science which has been made for a very long time. **1938** *Nature* 5 Nov. 843 The planetismal hypothesis is the parent of the more recent tidal theories. **1970** *Sci. Jrnl.* May 32/1 This theory has it that the Moon formed out of the coagulation of a 'sediment-ring' of planetismals which originally circled the Earth.

†**ˈplanetist.** *Obs. rare.* [See -IST.] One who consults the planets, a star-gazer, an astrologer.
1509 BARCLAY *Shyp of Folys* (1874) II. 19 Ye planetystis and wytches, and other of this sort. **1626** MINSHEU *Ductor* (ed. 2) 554 *Planetist*, an obseruer of the Planets.

planetkin (ˈplænɪtkɪn). *nonce-wd.* [f. PLANET *sb.*¹ + -KIN.] A small planet.
1832 CARLYLE *Reminisc.* (1881) I. 44 A temporary fraction of this planetkin, the whole round of which is but a sandgrain in the all.

ˈplanetless, *a.* [See -LESS.] Void of planets.
1817 SHELLEY *Rev. Islam* III. xxii, A shoreless sea, a sky sunless and planetless.

planetocentric (ˌplænɪtəʊˈsɛntrɪk), *a. Astr.* and *Astronautics.* [f. PLANET *sb.*¹ + -O + -CENTRIC.] Referred to, measured from, or having a planet as centre (usu. a planet other than the earth.)
1960 BAKER & MAKEMSON *Introd. Astrodynamics* xii. 264 The regions in space where one would expect the vehicle to be in a predominantly geocentric, heliocentric, or planetocentric field, can be delineated by calculating the ratio of the perturbative accelerations to the two-body acceleration. **1971** S. HERRICK *Astrodynamics* I. v. 106 A similar consideration of the planetocentric velocity at the Mars or Venus end of the trajectory..indicates that it is desirable to have the tangency at Mars's aphelion or at Venus's perihelion. **1972** *Nature* 11 Aug. 325/2 The heliocentric orbital longitude of Mars η, and the planetocentric longitude of the Sun are approximately related by $\eta = L_3 + 85°$.

planeˈtography. [f. Gr. πλανήτης PLANET *sb.*¹ + -GRAPHY.] A description of the planets.
1730–6 BAILEY (folio) Pref., *Planetógraphy*..a Treatise or Discourse of the Planets. **1735** B. MARTIN *Philos. Gram.* 119 (*heading*) Of planetography, or the philosophy of the planets. **1960** *Analog Science Fact/Fiction* Oct. 33/1 Got to know enough about it through an elementary planetography.

planetoid (ˈplænɪtɔɪd), *sb.* (*a.*) [f. PLANET *sb.*¹ + -OID. So F. *planétoïde.*] A body resembling a planet; a name sometimes given to the minor planets or asteroids (see ASTEROID B. 1).
1803 *Edin. Rev.* I. 430 Why may we not coin such a phrase as *Planetoid*? **1803** HERSCHEL in *Phil. Trans.* XCIII. 339 It is not in the least material whether we call them asteroids, as I have proposed; or planetoids, as an eminent astronomer, in a letter to me, suggested. **1863** H. SPENCER *Ess.* II. 46 With respect to the asteroids, or planetoids, as they are otherwise called. **1892** *N. & Q.* 8th ser. I. 15/2 [Term discussed]. **1899** *Daily News* 17 Jan. 7/3 The new 'planetoid' was discovered by Herr Witt, of the Urania Observatory of Berlin.

B. *adj.* (or *attrib.*). Of or belonging to the asteroids. So **planeˈtoidal** *a.*, in same sense.
1862 SIR H. HOLLAND *Ess.* 280 *note*, Nearly seventy now (1862) stand in our catalogues..the heathen mythology has been invoked in vain to furnish names for this planetoid throng. **1881** PROCTOR *Poet. Astron.* x. 362 Jupiter's action on the planetoidal ring.

planetokhod (ˈplænɪtəkɒd, -xɒd). Also **Planetokhod.** [a. Russ. *planetokhód*, f. *planéta* PLANET *sb.*¹ (after LUNOKHOD).] A Russian self-propelled vehicle for transmitting information about another planet as it travels over its surface.
1970 *Times* 18 Nov. 1 The vehicle is called Lunokhod-1. .. Soviet scientists are predicting that other such vehicles, named Planetokhod or Marsokhod, will eventually move over the surface of the Planets. **1973** *Nature* 23 Mar. 219/2 His remarks relating to the possible 'planetokhod' exploration of Venus and the outer planets seem highly speculative.

planetolatry (plænɪˈtɒlətrɪ). *rare.* [f. PLANET *sb.*¹ + -LATRY, -OLATRY.] Idolatrous worship of the planets.
1964 C. S. LEWIS *Discarded Image* v. 104 Despite this careful watch against planetolatry the planets continued to be called by their divine names.

planetology (plænɪˈtɒlədʒɪ). *Astr.* [f. PLANET *sb.*¹ + -OLOGY.] The study of the planets and their evolution.
1907 P. LOWELL in *Century Mag.* Nov. 113 Planetology we may call this science of the making of worlds, since it concerns itself with the life-history of planetary bodies from their chemically inert beginning to their final inert end. **1959** *Wall St. Jrnl.* 25 July 8/2 'We believe lunar science, or planetology, is here to stay,' he says. **1973** *Nature* 18 May 121/1 Planetology, with several tens of papers on the Moon, Mars and the Allende Meteorite, profited particularly this year.

Hence **planetoˈlogic, planetoˈlogical** *adjs.*, of or pertaining to planetology; **planeˈtologist**, an expert or specialist in planetology.
1908 *Century Mag.* Feb. 505/1 This gives us a most instructive glimpse into one planetologic process. **1933** *O.E.D.* Suppl., Planetologist. **1966** *Ann. N.Y. Acad. Sci.* CXL. 289 For the planetologist, it seems very important to be able to measure, even approximately, the relative amounts of oxygen, silicon, and aluminum in the surface layers of the planets. **1969** [see PLANETESIMAL *a.* and *sb.* A]. **1975** *Nature* 7 Aug. 455/3 The development of a cratering chronology was one of the principal challenges to comparative planetologists studying impact bombardment of the terrestrial planets. **1976** *Ibid.* 22 Jan. 176/1 G. Wetherill's..time scale and planetological-geological framework for the early Precambrian seemed generally accepted.

plane-tree (ˈpleɪntriː). [f. PLANE *sb.*¹ + TREE.]
a. A tree of the genus *Platanus*: = PLANE *sb.*¹ 1.
14.. *Nom.* in Wr.-Wülcker 716/30 *Nomina arborum*..*Hec plantacius*, a plantre. **1483** *Cath. Angl.* 283/1 A Playn tree, *platanus.* **1562** TURNER *Herbal* II. 95 b, I haue sene the leues of that Platanus that groweth in Italy, and two very yong trees in England which were called there Playn trees..It is doutles that these two trees were ether brought out of Italy, or of som farr countre beyound Italy. **1578** LYTE *Dodoens* VI. lxxiv. 755 The Plane tree groweth in many places of Greece ..it is vnknowen in this Countrie. **1616** SURFL. & MARKH. *Country Farme* 306 The Plane tree..I remember, that I haue seene one at Basil. **1731–3** MILLER *Gard. Dict.* s.v. *Platanus*, The Plane-Tree..hath an amentaceous Flower,.. the Embryo's of the Fruit..are turgid, and do afterwards become large spherical Balls. **1856** STANLEY *Sinai & Pal.* ii. (1858) 120 The plane-trees which once shaded the bare landscape of Attica.
attrib. **1786** POLWHELE tr. *Theocritus*, etc. (1792) II. Notes 37 We will weave for thee a garland of lotus, and hang it on the plane-tree branches.

b. *Sc.* and *north. Eng.* = PLANE *sb.*¹ 2.
1778 LIGHTFOOT *Flora Scot.* 639 *Acer pseudo-platanus.* The great Maple, or Bastard Sycomore. The Plane-Tree, *Scottis.* **1866** *Treas. Bot.* 900 Plane-tree, Mock, or Scotch, *Acer Pseudo-Platanus.* **1902** BUCHAN *Watcher by Threshold* 157 Some large plane-trees grew near the house.

ˈplanet-ˌstricken. *a.* Also 7 -stro(o)ken, -strucken. = next.
1600 DEKKER *Olde Fortunatus* Wks. 1873 I. 116 If your wits be not planet strucken, if your braines lie in their right

place. **1611** Speed *Hist. Gt. Brit.* IX. xxiv. §352 Some..who thought they might presume best of her fauour, haue been so suddenly daunted and Planet-stricken, that they could not lay downe their griefe thereof, but in their graues. *a* **1613** Overbury *A Wife*, etc. (1638) 76 An Amorist is a man blasted or planet-strooken. **1615** Brathwait *Strappado* (1878) 114 The Planet-stroken Albumazar, Shaues the Muses like a razor. **1643** *Plain English* 25 How could I.. drop spirit and vigour into the hearts of my plannet-stricken Country-men? **1819** Wordsw. *P. Bell* III. xxx, Like planet-stricken men of yore, He trembles, smitten to the core.

Hence **'planet-strike** *v. trans.* (*rare*$^{-0}$), to strike as a malignant influence, to blast.

1611 Florio, *Assideratione*..a blasting or planetstreeking. **1659** Torriano, *Assideráre*, to Planet-strike, to blast as trees doe through great heat and drought.

'planet-struck, *a.* Also 7 -strook(e. [f. planet *sb.*[1] 1 b + pa. pple. of strike *v.* Cf. *moonstruck, lunatic.*] Stricken by the supposed malign influence of an adverse planet; blasted; sometimes said in reference to paralytic or other sudden physical affections; hence, Stricken with sudden fear or amazement, panic-stricken; terrified, bewildered, confounded.

1614 Markham *Cheap Husb.* I. xi. (1668) 49 Cold flegmatick humors..sometimes weakening but one member only, then it is called Planet-strook. **1658** Bromhall *Treat. Specters* I. 102 They being affrighted (as it were Planet-struck) and confounded with shame. **1667** Milton *P.L.* x. 414 The blasted Starrs lookt wan, And Planets, Planet-strook, real Eclips Then sufferd. **1708** *Brit. Apollo* No. 28. 1/2 Reading the last Weekly Bill of Mortality, I saw one among the Casualities Planet-struck. **1726** *Dict. Rust.* (ed. 3), *Planet-struck*, or *Shrew-Running* (in Horses) is a deprivation of Feeling or Motion. **1799** Sickelmore *Agnes & Leonora* II. 12 The Count became planet-struck as he listened to the grossness of this retort. **1865** Kingsley *Herew.* xli, I shall be overlooked—planet-struck. **1925** A. Huxley *Sel. Poems* 48 Let me..Dream planet-struck.

'planetule. *rare.* [f. L. type **planētula*, dim. of *planēta*.] A diminutive planet.

1846 in Worcester (citing Conybeare). **1850** *Fraser's Mag.* XLI. 297 The rotation of the planetule on its axis. *Ibid.* 299 Heydon, too, had only described one of these planetules in his account of the Holy Island.

planform ('plænfɔːm). Also **plan-form, plan form.** [f. plan *sb.* + form *sb.*] The shape or outline of an aircraft wing in plan. Also *transf.*

1908 F. W. Lanchester *Aerodonetics* x. 319 When the author's standard combination of parabolic grading and elliptical plan form is used, it is a property of the resulting aerofoil that [etc.]. **1913** *Aeronaut. Jrnl.* XVII. 83 In advocating this plan-form he does not appear to have had stability in his mind at all. **1942** T. P. Faulconer *Introd. Aircraft Design* i. 18 The choice of a wing plan form and thickness is governed in general by the range requirements. **1958** *Engineering* 21 Mar. 363/1 The main building has an interesting planform of a question mark. **1965** *Times* 11 Sept. 7/6 Where opinions differ is on the wing planform for take-off, for approach and for landing. **1967** *Jane's Surface Skimmer Systems 1967–68* 2/1 The Aeromar A-1 is a gas turbine powered craft with a circular planform. **1975** L. J. Clancy *Aerodynamics* xvi. 538 Consider a wing whose planform is represented..by the sketch.

planful ('plænfʊl), *a. rare.* [f. plan *sb.* + -ful.] Full of plans, devices, or schemes.

1877 Blackie *Wise Men* 6 By planful wisdom overawed. **1905** G. T. Ladd in *Child & Relig.* iii. 133 The active planful imagination which develops so early in the child.

plange, obs. form of planch *sb.*

plangency ('plændʒənsɪ). [f. L. type **plangentia*, f. *plangent-em*: see next and -ency.] The quality of being plangent.

1858 Carlyle *Fredk. Gt.* v. vii. (1872) II. 117 Friedrich Wilhelm's words, in high clangorous metallic plangency.. fall hotter and hotter. **1882** Stevenson *New Arab. Nts.* II. xii. 192 Her voice had charm and plangency. **1900** W. Raleigh *Milton* 54 The hurt he had suffered..gives eloquence and plangency to his divorce pamphlets. **1923** C. Mackenzie *Parson's Progress* xvi. 222 All the regret..was expressed in the plangency of the violin speaking of the individual's grief. **1928** Kipling *Limits & Renewals* (1932) 18 It's not a bad couplet in itself. Did you see how he admires the 'plangency' of it? **1972** *Times Lit. Suppl.* 25 Aug. 991/3 The Dreyfus affair..had an unusual public plangency. **1977** *N.Y. Rev. Bks.* 29 Sept. 6/4 The strain of plangency and nostalgia, combined with indignation, is Irish.

plangent ('plændʒənt), *a.* [ad. L. *plangent-em*, pr. pple. of *plang-ĕre* to strike noisily, beat the breast, lament aloud. (Cf. plain *v.*)]

1. Making the noise of waves breaking or beating on the shore, etc.

1822 G. Darley *Errors of Ecstacie* 26 The mighty deep, Shaking the firm strand with its plangent waves. **1858** Farrar *Eric* xiii, The mingled scream of weltering tempest and plangent wave. **1880** Swinburne *Birthday Ode* 256 With pulse of plangent water like a knell.

2. Loud-sounding, striking the ear powerfully; applied sometimes to a metallic, sometimes to a loud thrilling or plaintive sound. Also *fig.*

1858 Carlyle *Fredk. Gt.* IV. iii. (1872) I. 285 This rugged young King, with his plangent metallic voice. **1871** Morley *Crit. Misc., Byron* 272 That universal protest which rings through Byron's work with a plangent resonance. **1888** Howells *Annie Kilburn* xxv, The bell on the orthodox church called the members of Mr. Peck's society together.. with the same plangent, lacerant note that summoned them to worship on Sundays. **1901** *Athenæum* 8 June 720/2 How fine..the plangent union of accent and quantity throughout the line. **1928** Kipling *Limits & Renewals* (1932) 14 The freshness, the fun, the humanity, the fragrance of it all, cries—no, shouts—itself as Dan's work. Why 'Daiespringe mishandled' alone stamps it from Dan's mint. Plangent as doom, my dear boy—plangent as doom! **1936** [see facture 4].

plangently ('plændʒəntlɪ), *adv.* [f. plangent *a.* + -ly[2].] In a way that beats strongly or distressingly on the mind or feelings.

1927 R. L. Mégroz *Three Sitwells* 9 We are driven inwards because the external reality we have created is plangently ugly. **1928** *Observer* 19 Feb. 9/2 Nothing is here to make us beat the breast. The old matchless rhythms are no less plangently certain. **1963** *Times* 12 June 13/3 The theme of African unity so plangently struck at the Addis Ababa conference.

†**plan'giferous**, *a. Obs. rare*$^{-1}$. [irreg. f. L. *plangĕre* (see plangent *a.*) + -ferous.] Producing or accompanied by the noise of beating.

1620 Dekker *Dreame* (1860) 32 Toss'd too and fro By gusts implacable, able downe to throw Rampires of brasse, which still beat out the braines, And still renewde them with plangiferous paines.

†**plangor.** *Obs. rare*$^{-1}$. [a. L. *plangor* noisy beating, loud lamenting, f. *plangĕre*: see plangent.] A loud or piercing lamentation.

1598 Meres *Pallad. Tamia* 280 b, Euery one mourneth when hee heareth of the lamentable plangors of Thracian Orpheus for his dearest Euridice.

plangorous ('plæŋgərəs), *a.* [f. as prec. + -ous.] Characterized by loud lamentation.

1593 Nashe *Christ's T.* (1613) 55 From vnder the Altar there issued penetrating plangorus-howlings. **1647** R. Baron *Cyprian Acad.* 8 He suddenly heard such a plangerous and lamentable cry. *a* **1693** *Urquhart's Rabelais* III. xxiii. 193 The grievously plangorous howling and lowing of Devils. **1892** E. Gosse *In Mem. Miss Anne Clough*, It tolls and tolls with plangorous tongue, For empty lives and hearts unbless'd.

plangstee, obs. form of planxty.

‖**planh** (plaɲ). Also **planc.** [Provençal, f. L. *planctus* planctus.] A mournful troubadour song. Cf. planctus.

1843 *Penny Cycl.* XXV. 307/2 Their 'Planhs', or songs on the death of a mistress. **1878** F. Hueffer *Troubadours* I. xiii. 134 Two minor branches of the *sirventes*..are the *planh* or complaint, and the crusader's song,..the former belonging more especially to the personal..class of poems.. The *planh* is a poem written on the death of a mistress, a friend, or a protector. **1909** E. Pound *Exultations* 46 (*title*) Planh for the Young English King. **1923** H. J. Chaytor *Troubadours & England* ii. 92 The troubadour Austorc de Segret in a *planh* upon the death of St. Louis, written between 1270 and 1274, refers to the problems before Edward. **1964** 'E. Queen' *Four Men called John* (1976) xiv. 154 A number of twelfth-century secular manuscripts. There are: six *planhs*, apparently the work of Bertran de Bon, [etc.]. **1970** W. Apel *Harvard Dict. Mus.* (ed. 2) 461/2 A late 12th-century troubadour *planc* (*planh*) by Gaucelm Faudit deplores the death of Richard the Lion-Hearted.

plani- (pleɪnɪ), combining form of L. *plānus* level, flat, smooth, used chiefly in scientific terms.

planicaudate (-'kɔːdət) *a. Zool.* [L. *cauda* tail], having a flat tail, as certain reptiles (Mayne *Expos. Lex.* 1858). **planicipital** (-'sɪpɪtəl) *a. Zool.* [L. *caput* head: cf. *occipital*, etc.], having a flat head, as an insect; flat-headed. **planidorsate** (-'dɔːsət) *a. Zool.* [L. *dorsum* back], having a flat back (*Cent. Dict.*). †**plani'folious** *a. Bot. Obs.* [L. *folium* leaf], having or consisting of flat leaves; applied to composite flowers consisting wholly of ligulate florets. **planiform** ('pleɪnɪfɔːm) *a.*, having a flattened shape; *spec.* in *Anat.* said of a joint in which the surfaces of the bones are nearly or quite plane (= arthrodial). †**pla'niloquent** *a. Obs. rare*$^{-0}$ [after L. *plāniloquus* (Plautus)], plain-speaking; so †**pla'niloquy** *Obs. rare*$^{-1}$, plain speaking. **planipennate** (pleɪnɪ'pɛnət) *a. Zool.* [L. *pennātus* winged], (*a*) having flat wings; (*b*) *spec.* in *Entom.* belonging to the suborder *Planipennia* of neuropterous insects, characterized by flat wings not folded when at rest; so **planipennine** (-'pɛnaɪn), *a.* = planipennate (*b*); *sb.* a planipennine insect. **planipetalous** (-'pɛtələs) *a. Bot.*, having flat petals. **planirostral** (-'rɒstrəl), **planirostrate** (-'rɒstrət), *adjs.* [L. *rostrum* beak], having a broad flat beak. **planispiral** (-'spaɪərəl) *a.*, of a flat spiral form: applied to the proboscis of lepidopterous insects, and to certain shells, as in the genus *Planorbis*.

1686 *Phil. Trans.* XVI. 285 Those that have a perfect *planifolious Flower. **1727–41** Chambers *Cycl.* s.v. *Flower*, Planifolious Flowers, those which are composed of plain Flowers, set together in circular rows, round the center, and whose face is usually indented, notched, uneven, and jagged. **1830** R. Knox *Béclard's Anat.* 282 The close and *planiform diarthrosis..is that in which the surfaces are superficial, the ligaments strong and tight, the motions obscure and confined to sliding. **1858** Mayne *Expos. Lex.*, *Planiformis*, applied..to a Family..of the *Coleoptera*, comprehending those that have the body much depressed; flat-shaped: planiform. **1881** Mivart *Cat* 122 Such joints are termed Planiform or Arthrodia. **1656** Blount *Glossogr.*, **Planiloquent*.., that speaks his mind plainly and freely. **1658** Phillips, **Planiloquy*, (lat.) plain, and free speech. **1783** Lemon *Eng. Etymol.* s.v. *Haunch*, Such planiloquy is fit only for the large, open, yawning mouth of a Dutchman. **1858** Mayne *Expos. Lex.*, *Planipennis*,..having flat wings: *planipennate. **1730–6** Bailey (folio), **Planipetalous Flower* .., flat leaved, as when these small flowers are hollow only at the bottom, but are flat upwards, as in Dandelion, Succory, &c. **1895** *Syd. Soc. Lex.*, **Planirostral*, having a flat beak. **1858** Mayne *Expos. Lex.*, *Planirostris*, having the beak or the snout flat: *planirostrate. **1895** *Syd. Soc. Lex.*, **Planispiral*, spiral, with the coils lying..in one plane. **1945** M. F. Glaessner *Princ. Micropalaeont.* iv. 69 Perfectly planispiral coiling produces bilaterally symmetrical tests. **1975** *Nature* 3 Apr. 419/1 Sinistral..and planispiral.. coiling are uncommon among gastropods.

planigale ('plænɪgeɪl, plænɪ'geɪliː). *Austral.* [mod.L. (E. Le G. Troughton 1928, in *Rec. Austral. Mus.* XVI. 282), f. plani- + *Phasco*)*gale*, the name of a closely related genus.] A flat-skulled marsupial mouse of the genus so called, belonging to the family Dasyuridæ and native to Australia and New Guinea.

1946 E. Troughton *Furred Animals of Australia* (ed. 3) 29 (*heading*) Planigales or Flat-skulled Marsupial-Mice. **1966** *New Scientist* 20 Jan. 130/2 The little planigales or flat-skulled 'mice' found in Australia and New Guinea. **1970** W. D. L. Ride *Guide to Native Mammals of Austral.* 119 David Fleay has kept Ingram's Planigales in captivity. **1974** *Courier-Mail* (Brisbane) 15 Apr. 10/3 (*caption*) Planigale mother with some of her clinging brood of babies.

planigraph ('plænɪgrɑːf, -æ-). [ad. F. *planigraphe*, f. plani- + Gr. -γραφος: see -graph.] An instrument (invented by Marmet, of Versailles) for reducing or enlarging drawings.

It consists of a rule fitted with two scales having graduations of different magnitude, placed end to end in opposite directions, and turning about a pivot at the point of junction; it is provided with a number of different scales for different degrees of reduction.

1884 in Knight *Dict. Mech.* Supp.

‖**planilla** (pla'niʎa). [Sp. Amer. dim. of *plana* a level.] A cleaning-floor at a Californian mining-station.

1877 Raymond *Statist. Mines & Mining* 5 Sheds over planillas at Day tunnel and Deep Gulch tunnel. *Ibid.* 7 A much larger quantity of waste vein-matter..has to be examined and passed over the planillas or cleaning-floors.

planimeter (plə'nɪmɪtə(r)). Also **-metre.** [ad. F. *planimètre*, f. plani- + *-mètre*, -meter.] An instrument for mechanically measuring the area of an irregular plane figure.

1858 in Simmonds *Dict. Trade.* **1872** F. J. Bramwell in *Rep. Brit. Assoc.* 401 Amsler's Planimeter..for measuring the area of any figure, however irregular, by the mere passage of a tracer round about its perimeter. **1875** Darwin *Insectiv. Pl.* xv. 355 The area of all the leaves together with their footstalks, was found by a planimeter. **1898** *Engineering Mag.* XVI. 115/1 The area enclosed was measured by a planimeter.

planimetric (pleɪnɪ'mɛtrɪk), *a.* [f. as prec. + -ic: cf. Gr. μετρικός of measuring.] Belonging or relating to planimetry. So **plani'metrical** *a.*

planimetric function (*Math.*), 'a function expressing one of the relations between the areas of the three triangles formed by joining a variable point in a plane to the vertices of a fundamental triangle': also called *plane function*.

1727 Bailey vol. II, *Planimetrical*, pertaining to the Mensuration of plain Surfaces. **1802–3** tr. *Pallas's Trav.* (1812) I. p. xvi, Planimetrical delineation of Mount Burgussan..which appears to have been formerly a fortified place. **1828–32** Webster, Planimetric, Planimetrical. **1906** *Q. Rev.* Jan. 122 A group of individual objects in 'planimetric' relation.

planimetrically (pleɪnɪ'mɛtrɪkəlɪ), *adv.* [f. planimetric *a.*: see -ically.] By means of, or with regard to, planimetry. (In quot. 1944, 'in the plane'.)

1944 *Burlington Mag.* Dec. 296/1 The essential difference lies elsewhere: previously border decoration was planimetrically designed, whereas in the new style the border ornament lives in the space above the page. The illusion is created that branches, flowers, insects and birds etc. have been dropped on the page, loosely dispersed, casting their shadow on the coloured foil. **1948** Lysholm & Bull in J. W. McLaren *Mod. Trends Diagnostic Radiol.* xxiv. 322 The composite pneumographs have also been measured planimetrically in relation to the corresponding brain cross-sections. **1959** *Trans. & Papers Inst. Brit. Geogr.* No. 26. 31 A planimetrically correct landform map has been constructed from an existing contour map..for a mountainous area in Colorado. **1969** G. C. Dickinson *Maps & Air Photographs* xi. 166 The profiles are truly 'lines on the ground' and must therefore be in their correct position planimetrically, so that detail can be traced directly from the map and will fit the profiles.

planimetry (plə'nɪmɪtrɪ). Also 4 **planemetrie**; 7 **planametrie, -ye**; 8–9 **plano-.** [Ultimately f. L. *plān-us* flat + *-metria*, -metry, on L. type *plānimetria*; the ME. *planemetrie* prob. represents an OF. form; but F. *planimetrie* appears only as of 1520 in Godef. *Compl.*, and med.L. *planimetria* is cited only from 16th c., though prob. used much earlier. *Planametry* and *planometry* are formed on less correct analogies.] The measurement of plane surfaces; the geometry of plane surfaces, plane geometry.

1390 GOWER *Conf.* III. 134 Ful many a worthi clerc ther is, That writen upon this clergie The bokes of Altemetrie, Planemetrie and eke also. 1603 OWEN *Pembrokeshire* i. (1892) 4 The miles beinge multiplied together and reduced to Planametrie, the onlye meanes to knowe the contente of anye thinge. 1674 *Phil. Trans.* IX. 85 In Planimetry, the Measuring of Triangles with and without a Perpendicular. *a* 1696 SCARBURGH *Euclid* (1705) 94 In this 35th Proposition Euclide makes an entry into the Doctrine of Planometry. 1795–8 T. MAURICE *Hindostan* (1820) I. I. xii. 439 From planimetry, or the mensuration of surfaces, they soon proceeded to the more complicated science of stereometry, or the mensuration of solids. 1884 tr. *Lotze's Metaph.* 227 They would have been able to add the geometry of the newly discovered direction to the Planimetry which they possessed without having to change anything in their previous perceptions.

planing ('pleɪnɪŋ), *vbl. sb.*¹ [-ING¹.]

1. The action of PLANE *v.*¹

c 1440 *Promp. Parv.* 403/1 Planynge, *levigacio.* 1580 HOLLYBAND *Treas. Fr. Tong, Applanissement*, a planing. 1703 MOXON *Mech. Exerc.* 68 So continue your several lays of Planeing. 1825 J. NICHOLSON *Operat. Mechanic* 560 Planing..by which wood is reduced to a smooth and uniform surface, by means of an instrument called a plane.

†**2.** *concr.* A piece planed off; a shaving. *Obs.*

1598 FLORIO, *Piallure*, shauings, chips, or planings of timber. 1676 WORLIDGE *Cyder* (1691) 162 Thin shavings or planings of beech. 1707 MORTIMER *Husb.* (1721) II. 313 Put into your Vessel the plaining, or Chips of green Beech.

3. *attrib.* and *Comb.*, esp. in the names of tools, etc., used in planing, as ***planing-axe***, ***-iron***, ***-steel***, ***-table***, ***tool***; **planing machine**, a machine (of various kinds) for planing wood or metal; **planing-mill**, = planing-machine; also, a workshop where planing is done.

1545 *Rates Customs* C ij b, Playninge tabels the dossen iiiis. 1630 B. JONSON *New Inn* IV. ii, You Will carry your goose about you still, your planing-iron! Your tongue to smooth all! 1693 Plaining axe [see CHIP-AXE]. 1840 *Civil Eng. & Arch. Jrnl.* III. 172/2 The 'planing tool', an instrument made of steel, somewhat in the form of a hook, with the point so inclined as to present itself towards the surface of the metal to be planed. 1840 *Digest of Patents U.S., 1790–1839* 346 Planing machine... June 1, 1805. 1844 *Knickerbocker* XXIV. 184 The uplifted arm of Labor..meets his eye in the ..planing mill. 1851 C. CIST *Sk. Cincinnati in 1851* 227 Planing machines..made..by B. Bicknell. 1858 SIMMONDS *Dict. Trade, Planing-machine, Planing-mill*, a facing-machine for smoothing boards, etc. 1875 KNIGHT *Dict. Mech.* 1729/1 The *cylinder planing-machine.* This is now the usual machine. It has cutters on a drum rotating on a horizontal axis over the board which passes beneath. 1897 P. WARUNG *Tales Old Regime* 183 A many-sided man, the majority of whose facets were, unfortunately..shaped by the planing-steel of the System. 1902 *Westm. Gaz.* 1 Dec. 2/1 Magnets..will lift from the planing-table a casting of 32 cwt.

planing, *vbl. sb.*² and *ppl. a.*: see PLANE *v.*²

†'**planir**, *a. Obs. rare*⁻¹. [ad. OF. *planier* (*planeir*, Chron. Turpin):—late L. *plānārius* flat, level, f. *plānus* level; see -ARY¹.] Flat, level.

a 1400–50 *Alexander* 4138 Quare nouthire holtis was ne hilles ne no hiȝe [h]eggis, Bot all as planir & as playn as a playn table.

planish ('plænɪʃ), *v.* [f. obs. F. *planiss-*, lengthened stem of *planir* (in Palsgr.) to smooth (F. *aplanir*), f. *plan* level, flat: see -ISH².]

1. *trans.* To make level or smooth; to level.

1580 HOLLYBAND *Treas. Fr. Tong, Esplanade, faire des esplanades*, to planish and make euen the way. 1816 KIRBY & SP. *Entomol.* xv. (1828) I. 497 Then entering the cell, [they] place it at the angles and sides, &c. which they had previously planished.

b. *spec.* To flatten (sheet-metal or metal-ware) on an anvil by blows of a smooth-faced hammer, or by rubbing a flat-ended tool over the surface; to flatten and reduce in thickness; to condense (an engraver's copper-plate, etc.) by hammering; to reduce (coining-metal) to the required thickness by passing between rollers; to polish (paper, etc.) by means of a roller. Cf. PLANISHER, PLANISHING.

1688 R. HOLME *Armoury* III. 150/2 *Planish the Plate*, is to beat it on a smooth Anvile, with a broad, smooth faced Hammer. 1825 J. NICHOLSON *Operat. Mechanic* 725 The silver..is planished, and then scraped on the surface to be fitted on the copper. 1831 J. HOLLAND *Manuf. Metal* I. 333 Saws are manufactured..of iron, which is hammer-hardened, or planished on an anvil. 1884 KNIGHT *Dict. Mech.* Suppl. 688/2 Saw blades are planished to straighten them. Buckling is removed by planishing.

†**2.** To remove by planing, to plane *away*. *Obs.*

1622 MABBE tr. *Aleman's Guzman d'Alf.* II. 274 Those thinne shauings which your joyners planish away with their plainers when they shaue their wainscoat.

Hence '**planished** *ppl. a.*

1683 MOXON *Mech. Exerc., Printing* ii. ¶2 Neal'd thick Brass..will never come to so good and smooth an Edge as Planish't Brass will. 1819 H. BUSK *Vestriad* IV. 156 The even temper of the flowing mass, Had left no speck to blur the planish'd glass. 1884 in *Century Mag.* Dec. 266/2 Planished copper, and enameled iron tubs.

planisher ('plænɪʃə(r)). [f. prec. vb. + -ER¹.]

1. A person who planishes.

1858 SIMMONDS *Dict. Trade, Planisher*..a workman who smooths or planes.

2. A tool or instrument used for planishing, in various applications, *esp.*

a. A flat-ended tool for smoothing metal-work; a tool used by silver-chasers. **b.** An instrument for smoothing or glazing the surface of photographs, engravings, cards, writing paper, etc. **c.** A contrivance for flattening sections cut by the microtome for microscopic examination.

1858 SIMMONDS *Dict. Trade, Planisher*, a tool used by turners for smoothing brass work. 1895 *Model Steam Engine* 90 It is..2nd, smoothed with a planisher; 3rd, polished with a fine file, or with oil and rotten-stone.

'**planishing**, *vbl. sb.* [f. as prec. + -ING¹.] The action of the verb PLANISH, in various senses.

1688 R. HOLME *Armoury* III. 259/2 Planishing, to make it [the metal] smooth [in goldsmith's work]. 1873 H. SPENCER *Stud. Sociol.* xi. 271 An artizan practised in 'planishing'. 1884 KNIGHT *Dict. Mech.* Suppl. 688/2 The old mode of forming the 60 gallon copper, sugar, or soap-kettle was planishing, the parts being subsequently united by brazing. *a* 1900 W. B. SLATER *Let. to Editor*, Planishing in silver manufacture is the final hammering given to an article being made, which does not alter the shape but levels the surface.

b. *attrib.* and *Comb.*, as ***planishing anvil***, ***stake***; **planishing hammer**, a hammer with polished slightly convex faces, used for planishing sheetmetal; **planishing roller**, a roller used in planishing; *esp.* in *pl.*, the second pair of rollers, of hardened and polished iron, between which coining-metal is passed to reduce it to the proper thickness.

1688 R. HOLME *Armoury* III. xxii. (Roxb.) 270/1 He beareth Gules, a Planishing Anvile, Argent... He beareth Azure, three Planishing Hamers, Argent, handles Or. 1815 J. SMITH *Panorama Sc. & Art* I. 16 Clockmakers, tin-plate workers, and braziers, polish the face of their planishing hammers, by rubbing them upon a soft board, covered with a mixture of oil and finely washed emery. 1839 URE *Dict. Arts* 860 The plates are passed cold between these [rollers], to bring them to exactly the same thickness; whence they are called adjusting or planishing rollers. 1875 KNIGHT *Dict. Mech., Planishing stake*,..a bench stake or small anvil for holding the [copper] plate when under the action of a planishing-hammer.

planisphere ('plænɪsfɪə(r)). Also 4 **planisperie**; 6–7 **-spheare**, 7 **-sphaer**, **-sphare**. [In ME. form *planisperie*, ad. med.L. *plānisphærium*, f. L. *plān-us* flat, PLANE + *sphæra*, Gr. σφαῖρα SPHERE; in form *planisphere*, a. OF. *planisphère*.] A map or chart formed by the projection of a sphere, or part of one, on a plane; now *esp.* a polar projection of half (or more of) the celestial sphere, as in one form of the astrolabe.

[1144 *Planisphærium Ptolomæi* [*Incipit*] Rodvlphi Brvghensis ad Theodorichum Platonicum in traductionem planisphærij Claudij Ptolomæi Prefatio.] 1390 GOWER *Conf.* III. 134 Gebuz and Alpetragus eke Of Planisperie [*v.r.* palmestrie], which men seke, The bokes made. 1571 DIGGES *Pantom.* I. xxix. I ij b, Being brought to his due place the crosse diameters of the Planisphere may demonstrate the foure principall quarters of the Horizon. 1594 BLUNDEVIL *Exerc.* VI. (1636) 598 Astrolabe..is called of some a Planispheare, because it is both flat and round, representing the Globe or Spheare, having both his Poles clapt flat together. 1625 N. CARPENTER *Geog. Del.* I. vii. (1635) 174 The planispheare is a table or mappe of two faces whereon the lines are proiected circularly. 1678 *Phil. Trans.* XII. 1027, I am at present making a silver Planisphere of two foot diameter for the King; the Invention of that famous Astronomer..Mr. Cassini. 1828 W. IRVING *Columbus* (1848) I. 128 The globe or planisphere finished by Martin Behem..furnishes an idea of what the chart of Columbus must have been. 1862 SIR G. C. LEWIS *Astron. Ancients* IV. i. 208 He [Hipparchus] had drawn a planisphere according to the stereographic projection. 1905 A. B. GRIMALDI (*title*) Catalogue of Zodiacs and Planispheres, ancient and modern.

b. ***revolving planisphere***: a device consisting of a polar projection of the whole of the heavens visible in a particular latitude, covered by a card with an elliptical opening, which can be adjusted so as to show the part of the heavens visible at a given time.

1887 *Pall Mall G.* 24 Oct. 6/1 An ingenious arrangement called a Planisphere, upon which the stars for any evening of the year are, by turning a circle, brought into view. 1891 *Athenæum* 3 Oct. 457/1 An ingeniously constructed 'Revolving Planisphere.

c. ***astrolabe planisphere***: see ASTROLABE (*b*).

1872 SKEAT *Chaucer's Astrol.* Pref. 32 The term 'astrolabe'..in the sixteenth and seventeenth centuries.. was restricted to the particular kind called the 'Astrolabe Planisphere', or astrolabe on a flat surface.

Hence **planispheral** (-'sfɪərəl), **planispheric** (-'sfɛrɪk), **plani'spherical** *adjs.*, of the nature of or pertaining to a planisphere.

a 1646 J. GREGORY *Maps & Charts* Posthuma (1650) 311 In measuring the Distances of Places there is no great trust to bee had to any Planispherical Projection whatsoever. 1688 R. HOLME *Armoury* III. 373/1 A Meridian Spherical Dial [is] of some termed a Planisphearal Sun-Dial. 1856 W. H. MORLEY (*title*) Description of a Planispheric Astrolabe constructed for Sháh Sultán Husain Safawi. 1884 *Nature* 12 June 161/1 Suggestions for a planispheric representation of the cerebral convolutions.

†'**planitude**. *Obs. rare*⁻¹. [ad. late L. *plānitūdo* evenness, f. *plānus* flat: see -TUDE.] prop. = next; in quot., used as = smooth surface.

1597 A. M. tr. *Guillemeau's Fr. Chirurg.* b iij b/2 The superior planitude of the Plate, which sticketh fast to the roofe of the mouth.

planity ('plænɪtɪ). *rare*⁻¹. [f. PLANE *a.* + -ITY. (Cf. L. *plānitās* plainness, a doubtful reading in Tacitus.)] The quality of being plane.

1882 PROCTOR *Fam. Sci. Stud.* 21 The straightness of lines, the planity of surfaces and other like geometrical conceptions.

plank (plæŋk), *sb.* Also 4–5 **plaunke**, 4–7 **planke**, 5 **planc**, 6–7 **planck(e**. See also PLANCH. [ME. *planke*, a. ONF. *planke* (Tournai 1275, mod. Picard *planke*, Norm. *planque*) = F. *planche* plank, slab, little wooden bridge, measure of land; in mod.F., a narrow strip of land = Pr. *planca*, *plancha*, Cat. *planxa*, Sp. *plancha*, Pg. *prancha*, Piedm., OIt. *pianca*:—L. *planca* (post-Aug.) board, plank, slab (e.g. of marble), prob. f. root *plak-* of Gr. πλάξ, etc.]

1. a. A long flat piece of smoothed timber, thicker than a BOARD; *spec.* a length of timber sawn for building or other purposes to a thickness of from two to six inches, a width of nine inches or more, and eight feet or upwards in length.

1303 R. BRUNNE *Handl. Synne* 5259 Þe plank þat on þe bryggë was, Was as sledyr as any glas. *c* 1350 *Will. Palerne* 2778 Hent hire vp in armes, & bare hire forþ ouer-bord on a brod planke. 1393 LANGL. *P. Pl.* C. XIX. 34 And with þe ferste plaunke ich palle hym doune. 1428–9 *Rec. St. Mary at Hill* 71 Also payd for a carpenter iij dayes ij s... Also payd for a planke iiij s iiij d. 1495 *Naval Acc. Hen. VII* (1896) 154 Oken plankes of xviij fote long xij ynch brode & iiij ynch thyke. *a* 1548 HALL *Chron., Hen. VIII* 118 The Frenchmen had losed the plankes of the bridge nere a myle aboue Bray. 1653 WALTON *Angler* x. 189 Barnacles and young Goslings bred by the Suns heat and the rotten planks of an old Ship. 1794 SHERIDAN in *Sheridaniana* 154 A plank of the old stage, on which Garrick had trod. 1823 P. NICHOLSON *Pract. Build.* 159 The wood employed in Joinery is denominated Stuff; and of this there are Boards, Planks, and Battens. 1840 *Niles' Register* LIX. 157/2 At the extremity of the green [at Auburn, N.Y.],..a large platform was erected... About 40 long benches were constructed of rough planks for the ladies. 1881 YOUNG *Every Man his own Mech.* §142 Planks are pieces of wood 11 inches in width and 2½ or 3 inches thick.

transf. 1850 PRESCOTT *Peru* II. 166 They met with ten planks or bars of solid silver, each piece being twenty feet in length, one foot in breadth, and two or three inches thick.

b. Without *a* or *pl.*: Timber cut into planks; planking.

1559 in W. Boys *Sandwich* (1792) 738, xx M. elme planncke of iii and iiii ynches thicke. *Ibid.* 739. *c* 1582 T. DIGGES in *Archæologia* XI. 225 The excessiue waste of pile and plank in the Flemmyshe platte. 1665 PEPYS *Diary* 7 Aug., There comes Luellin, about Mr. Deering's business of planke, to have the contract perfected. 1720 DE FOE *Capt. Singleton* ii. (1840) 30 Want of saws to cut out plank. 1792 *Munchausen's Trav.* xxxiii. 157 The Royal George..that fine old ruin of British plank. *c* 1850 *Rudim. Navig.* (Weale) 138 *Plank*, a general name for all timber, excepting fir, which is from one inch and a half to four inches thick.

c. *fig.* esp. in reference to the use of a plank to save a shipwrecked man from drowning.

1649 G. DANIEL *Trinarch., Hen. IV* cccxxiii, The Planks Politicks make a bridge on To keepe dry Soales. 1633 P. FLETCHER *Pisc. Ecl.* IV. xvi, A thin thin plank keeps in thy vitall breath, Death ready waits. 1659 A. HAY *Diary* (S.H.S.) 123, I desired her to acquaint her father to come off upon yᵗ plank of ther setting up tolleratioun in Scotland. 1690 ABP. SHARP *Wks.* (1754) I. Serm. viii. 222 This is indeed the only plank we have to trust to, that can save us from ship-wreck. 1818 CRUISE *Digest* (ed. 2) I. 514 Though a purchaser may buy in an incumbrance, or lay hold of any plank to protect himself, yet he shall not protect himself by the taking a conveyance from a trustee, after he had notice of the trust. 1866 WHITTIER *Let. to Lucy Larcom* 29 God grant that in the strange new sea of change wherein we swim, We still may keep the good old plank, of simple faith in Him!

2. Applied to various things consisting or formed of a flat slab of wood applied to a special purpose indicated in the context; as, a narrow foot-bridge; a table or board; a hat-maker's bench or table which surrounds the 'kettle' (*Eng. Dial. Dict.*), a surf-board; also in other technical uses: see quots.

a 1400–50 *Alexander* 3740 A preue planke is at a place to pas & to entre. *c* 1430 *Pilgr. Lyf Manhode* I. xv. (1869) 11 With þi yerde þow shuldest assaye if it be to deep, or if þer neede oþer brigge or plaunke. 1480 CAXTON *Chron. Eng.* clxiii. 147 They lete come in the see barges and botes and grete plankes as many as they myght ordeyne and haue. 1599 HAKLUYT *Voy.* II. 236 The king will haue them shoote euery day at the Plancke, and so by continuall exercise they become most excellent shot. 1625 N. CARPENTER *Geog. Del.* II. v. (1635) 73 Cast on a large Table or planke, a little portion or drop of water. 1771 LUCKOMBE *Hist. Print.* 324 Before the Carriage is laid on the Ribs, [the pressman] besmears the two edges of the Plank..well with soap or grease. 1784 J. KING in Cook *Voy. Pacific Ocean* III. v. vii. 146 Whenever..the impetuosity of the surf is increased to its utmost height, they [*sc.* the natives of Karakakooa] choose that time for this amusement [riding the surf]... If by mistake they should place themselves on one of the smaller waves, which breaks before they reach the land, or should not be able to keep their plank in a proper direction on the top of the swell, they are left exposed to the fury of the next, and, to avoid it, are obliged again to dive and regain the place, from which they set out. **1855** BOOKER *Hist. Denton Chapel* (Chetham Soc. No. 37) 10 Coarse stuff hats, composed of a mixture of foreign wool and fur, the nap being laid on at the plank. **1875** KNIGHT *Dict. Mech.*, *Plank*, the frame of a printing press on which the carriage slides. **1875** *Ure's Dict. Arts* (ed. 7) II. 785 The workman..presses it [the point of a hat] down with his hand, turning it..round on its centre upon the plank, till a flat portion, equal to the crown of the hat, is rubbed out. **1888** NICHOLSON *Coal Trade Gloss.*, *Crowntree*, a plank about 2½ inches thick, and 5½ or 6 feet long, used to support the roof in coal-workings. **1890** *Cent. Dict.*, *Plank*..4 (*Ribbon-weaving*) The batten of the Dutch engine-loom or swivel-loom. **1962** *Austral. Women's Weekly* 24 Oct. (Suppl.) 3/3 Plank, any type of surfboard. **1963** *Pix* 28 Sept. 63 Five extra points if you can fit eight surfers, eight planks and a mattress in the woodie. **1967** J. SEVERSON *Great Surfing* Gloss., *Plank*, name given to heavy boards, usually referring to the redwood giants ridden prior to the 1950s.

3. †**a.** A flat slab of stone, esp. a gravestone. [So L. *planca*.] *Obs.* **b.** *Geol.* Calcareous flagstone of the Stonesfield Oolite beds.

1660 WOOD *Life* Nov. (O.H.S.) I. 345 Two stone coffins.. without planks or covers to them. *Ibid.*, Upon most of those planks or plank-stones, were engraved in them, or embossed or convexed a cross from one end to the other. **1691** —— *Ath. Oxon.* II. 384 Over his grave was soon after erected.. a monument of free stone, with a plank of marble thereon. **1871** J. PHILLIPS *Geol. Oxford* 149 We find about Sandford, in place of the 'Stonesfield slate', beds of white and yellow sand, sixteen or more feet in thickness, with irregular laminæ of calcareous sandstone, more or less blue in the centre, called 'plank'.

4. In *local* use: A piece of cultivated land longer than broad, a strip of land between two open furrows [= F. *planche*]; a regular division of land, as distinguished from the irregular ridges of the 'runrig' (*Eng. Dial. Dict.*); a more or less definite measure of land: see quots.

1814 SHIRREFF *Agric. Surv. Shetl.* App. v. 32 *Q.* Is the term plank known as applicable to lands? *A.* I..conceived it used as a term for large regular divisions, in opposition to the smaller ridges of the old *rig* and *rendal* or *runrig* divisions. **1883** R. M. FERGUSSON *Rambling Sk.* xiii. 85 The average extent of each plank was about an acre. **1892** COCHRAN-PATRICK *Med. Scot.* viii. 170 The 'plank' of land ..was generally the same in extent throughout Orkney and contained 1⅓ acre Scots or 1·32 acre English.

5. *fig.* An item or article of a political or other program. Cf. PLATFORM *sb.* (*a.*) 9 b. orig. *U.S.*

1848 LOWELL *Biglow P.* Poems 1890 II. 141 They kin' o' slipt the planks frum out th' ole platform one by one. **1848** *Boston Courier* 28 Sept. 2/2 Another plank in the platform is, no Cass or other plank to be added. **1856** *Househ. Words* XIV. 86 Every subject of the platform is spoken of as one of its planks; thus we read of 'the slavery plank', 'the tariff plank'. **1873** LD. SALISBURY in *Q. Rev.* CXXXV. 558 Neither is it necessary now to dwell on those questions which are occasionally discussed by speculative politicians, but which..are either too small or too large to be regarded as a plank in any party's platform. **1884** *Chr. World* 12 June 433/1 Another 'plank' is the restriction of Chinese immigration. **1891** *Times* 7 Oct. 10/4 It was not an admitted 'plank' in the Liberal platform, and (so far as I know) Mr. Gladstone has never promoted it or even said one word in its favour. **1894** *Liberal* 24 Nov. 42/1 They have founded a Society, the sole plank of whose platform is 'Hands off, please'. **1926** GALSWORTHY *Silver Spoon* II. i. 117 Dared he tackle the air—that third plank in the Foggart programme? **1937** *Ann. Reg. 1936* 189 Without cease the German Government protested against the alliance between Soviet Russia and France, alleging that the pact was a danger to Germany. That was one plank in the platform of German foreign policy. **1965** *Listener* 20 May 755/2 Thinkers whose ideas were fairly far removed from any of the chief party political planks. **1970** *Daily Tel.* 2 Feb. 1 The enforcement of law and order is to be one of the main planks of the Conservatives' General Election campaign. **1977** *Cornish Times* 19 Aug. 8/2 He told me that the main plank of his election campaign was going to be a policy of discrimination as advocated by an extreme political group, which was then defacing private and public buildings with stickers and misspelt slogans.

6. Phrases. † *to bring* (a gun) *to plank*: ? i.e. to the side of the ship; to run out (*obs.*). ***plank-over-plank***, with the outside planks overlapping, as in a clinker-built vessel. ***plank-upon-plank***: see quot. 1823. ***to walk the plank***, to walk blindfold along a plank laid over the side of a ship until one falls into the sea (as pirates and others are said to have made their captives do, in order to get rid of them). Also *fig.*

1557 LD. GREY in Froude *Hist. Eng.* VI. xxxiv. 493, I caused the gunners to bring up their artillery to plank, and then shot off immediately ten or twelve times. **1776** FALCONER *Dict. Marine, French Terms, Border à quein*, to plank a ship with clench-work, or plank-over-plank. **1822** SCOTT *Pirate* III. xii. 281 They deserve to be made to walk the plank for their impudence. **1823** CRABB *Technol. Dict.*, *Plank upon plank*, is when other planks are laid upon a ship's sides after she is built. **1835** J. E. ALEXANDER *Sketches in Portugal* viii. 179 The admiral..worked late and early himself, and made every body under him work, or else 'walk the plank'. **1844** MACAULAY *Barère* Misc. (1868) 262/1 It would have been necessary for Howe and Nelson to make every French sailor whom they took walk the plank. **1867** SMYTH *Sailor's Word-bk.*, *Walking a plank*, an obsolete method of destroying people in mutiny and piracy, under a plea of avoiding the penalty of murder... Also, for detecting whether a man is drunk, he is made to walk along a quarter-deck plank. **1883** STEVENSON *Treas. Isl.* I. i, Dreadful stories they were; about hanging, and walking the plank.

7. *attrib.* and *Comb.* Consisting or built of planks, as ***plank-bridge, dam, -house, -island, pile, piling, -raft, sheeting, -table, -timber, -work***; objective, as ***plank-dressing***; ***plank-built, -sided*** adjs.; **plank-bed**, a bed of boards resting on low trestles, without a mattress, used as part of the discipline of convents, prisons, etc.; **plank-buttress** [tr. G. *plankengerüst* (A. F. W. Schimper *Pflanzengeographie* (1898) III. iv. 328)], a development of a root at the base of the trunk of certain tropical trees; **plank-hook**, a pole with an iron hook at the end, used by quarrymen, miners, and others (*U.S.*); **plank-owner** *Navy slang* (chiefly *U.S.*), (*a*) a member of the original crew of a ship; a marine with long service with his ship or unit; (*b*) a marine with a light task; **plank-plant**, an Australian leguminous plant, *Bossiæa Scolopendrium*; **plank-road**, a road made of a flooring of planks laid transversely on longitudinal bearing timbers (*U.S.*); **plank steak**, steak cooked and served on a piece of plank; cf. PLANKED *ppl. a.* 2; **plank-timbering, plank tubbing**: see quots.; **plank-way**, the narrow portion of deck between the side and the frame of the hatch in a wherry, etc.

1868 FARRAR *Seekers* III. i. (1875) 265 To prefer a *plank-bed and skin and whatever else of the kind belongs to the Grecian discipline. **1887** *United Ireland* 27 Aug., To cheerfully accept the privations of the prison and its plank-bed. **1888** BERNARD *Fr. World to Cloister* v. 113 The order ..is reckoned..one of the most austere in regard to its abstinence from meat,..its plank bed, midnight office, and long hours of prayers. **1933** J. BUCHAN *Prince of Captivity* II. iv. 247 He crossed the stream by a *plank bridge. **1979** G. MITCHELL *Mudflats of Dead* iii. 35 He took to the causeway, crossed the plank bridge. **1897** MARY KINGSLEY *W. Africa* 419 An ostentatiously European *plank-built house. **1903** W. R. FISHER tr. *Schimper's Plant-Geogr.* III. i. 304 Much more frequently these buttresses assume the form of plank-like outgrowths of the base of the trunk and of the uppermost roots, and they may be termed *plank-buttresses. **1952** P. W. RICHARDS *Tropical Rain Forest* i. 4 Plank buttresses..are a highly characteristic feature of rain-forest trees. **1960** N. POLUNIN *Introd. Plant Geogr.* xiv. 467 The dominants are often of particularly massive growth and rich branching, but devoid of plank-buttresses. **1883** GRESLEY *Gloss. Coal Mining*, **Plank Dam*, a watertight stopping fixed in a heading, constructed of balks of fir placed across the passage, one upon another, sideways, and tightly wedged. **1831** JANE PORTER *Sir E. Seaward's Narr.* II. 58 David Allwood and his family had the *plank-house allotted to them. **1876** GEO. ELIOT *Dan. Der.* liv, The tiny *plank-island of a yacht. **1901** *Our Naval Apprentice* (U.S.) Aug. 14 'Patsy' is a '*Plank Owner' on 'Constellation'. **1920** *Our Navy* (U.S.) Apr. 11 Some of the plank-owners think the navy would be a great outfit if it didn't have any ships in it. **1945** *Richmond* (Va.) *News Leader* 31 May 6/3 The majority of our crew was made up of 'plank owners'—men who had been aboard the Colhoun since she..had been commissioned. **1952** A. GEER *New Breed* 6 The 'plank-owners' (any Marine not going) were subjected to a barrage of good-natured insults as they stood on the pier. **1967** M. DIBNER *Admiral* xiv. 140 He became her first gunnery officer as a 'plank owner'..at her commissioning. **1772** C. HUTTON *Bridges* 98 The piles are grooved.., and *plank piles let into the grooves. **1793** R. MYLNE *Rep. Thames* 31 A line of *Plank Piling should be run down to a little Island adjoining. **1910** *Westm. Gaz.* 24 Jan. 5/2 People..had to make use of boats or *plank-rafts. **1853** MOODIE *Life Clearings* Introd. 9 The many *plank-roads and railways in the course of construction in the province [Canada]. **1856** OLMSTED *Slave States* 365 The first plank-road in the State of New York was laid, I believe, in 1844, and in 1846 there were several in operation. **1888** *Times* 2 Oct. 11/6 Traces of old Roman plank-roads on the moor..not far from Diepholz, in Lower Hanover. **1789** W. JESSOP *Rep. Thames & Isis* (1791) 22 Instead of using Timber and *Plank Sheeting, slope the sides to an Angle of 45 degrees, and pitch them with rough flat Stones. **1897** MARY KINGSLEY *W. Africa* 563 A few steps onwards bring me in view of a corrugated iron-roofed, *plank-sided house. **1959** *Good Food Guide* 93 *Plank steak, shashlik, scampi maison, and 'nest of chicken' are among its specialities. **1972** *Vogue* Jan. 16/3 Try the spare ribs or prime plank steak. **1975** *Islander* (Victoria, B.C.) 27 Apr. 5/4 We celebrated our arrival by ordering 'plank steak'... It was juicy and tender and served on a white piece of wood. **1900** H. LAWSON *Over Sliprails* 131 A *plank-table, supported on stakes driven into the ground. **1797** *Encycl. Brit.* (ed. 3) XVIII. 659/2 The forests yield..*plank-timber, masts, and yards. **1881** RAYMOND *Mining Gloss.*, **Plank-timbering*, the lining of a shaft with rectangular plank frames. **1839** URE *Dict. Arts* 972 There are three modes of keeping back or stopping up these feeders; by *plank tubbing [etc.]. **1883** GRESLEY *Gloss. Coal Mining*, *Plank Tubbing*, shaft lining of wooden planks driven down vertically behind wooden cribs all round the shaft. **1887** W. RYE *Norfolk Broads* 48 How it did rain! The *plank-ways, parched and dry with weeks of sun, let in the water everywhere. **1889** P. H. EMERSON *Eng. Idyls* 26 Down the river..came sailing the wherry..with her plankways under water. **1890** HOSIE *W. China* 93 Rails of bamboo ran along both sides of the plank-way. **1745** *Jrnl. Siege Louisburg* in *W. Shirley's Let.* (1746) 24 The French..added to the Top of it a *Plank-work picketted, to raise it to the same Height with the rest of the Wall.

plank (plæŋk), *v.* [f. PLANK *sb.*: cf. ONF. *planquier* = OF. *planchier* to floor, plank, bridge, f. *planke, planche*.]

1. a. *trans.* To furnish, lay, floor, or cover with planks. Also with *over*.

c **1420** *Pallad. on Husb.* I. 516 Planke hit stronge ynough Vnder thin hors, that hit be lyggyng softe Ynough & harde ynough to stonde olofte. **1485** *Rec. St. Mary at Hill* 29 In the Stable a Racke & a mawnger, and it is new planked. **1580** HOLLYBAND *Treas. Fr. Tong*, *Plancher ou paver d'ais*, to floore or planke with bourdes. **1609** HOLLAND *Amm. Marcell.* 390 When he had set his ships together,..and.. planked them over in manner of a bridge, he passed over.. into the Countrey of the Quadi. **1697** DRYDEN *Æneid* II. 21 The Sides were planck'd with Pine. **1735** J. PRICE *Stone-Br. Thames* 7 These Truss Ribs, when plank'd over, will be enough. **1842** DICKENS *Amer. Notes* (1850) 143/1 The footways in the thoroughfares which lie beyond the principal street, are planked like floors.

b. To fasten or join *together*, to fasten or hold *down*, with planks.

1864 CARLYLE *Fredk. Gt.* XVII. vii, Boats planked together two and two. **1895** *Times* 5 Jan. 3/3 The ballast..does not appear to have been planked and tommed down.

2. a. To place, put, or set down; to deposit, plant. *dial.* or *slang*. **b.** To table or lay down money; to pay readily or on the spot. Const. *down, out, up*. *colloq.* (orig. *U.S.*). Also *absol.*

a. 1859 B. BRIERLEY *Day Out* (1886) 49 So we crope up th' slates, an plankt ussel' deawn ut th' top. **1886** A. G. MURDOCK *Scotch Readings* (ed. 2) 69 'Plank' it on the highest shelf in the house. **1892** [J. LUMSDEN] *Sheep-head* 205 Hastily I handed my dear Lady Matty to a seat, and planked my own huge carcase upon another one. **1894** *Sat. Rev.* 1 Sept. 234 A desire to plank down..University men in the midst of the social life of East London. **1936** J. TICKELL *See how they Run* iv. 46 How would you like to be half-starved for a bit and then planked down in a foreign school, aged twelve, and have to spend your holidays with the Geometry master? **1938** A. J. LIEBLING *Back where I came From* 182 An overstuffed chair some admirer had planked down next to the ticket booth. **1964** *Perthshire Advertiser* 13 June 14 Planking the lady into a beach chair and carrying her..to the other side.

b. 1824 *Nantucket Inquirer* 19 Apr. 2/4 His guardy was sent for, and he planked the cash. **1835** CROCKETT *Tour* 59 During the last war [he] planked up more gold and silver to lend the government than Benton ever counted. **1835–40** HALIBURTON *Clockm.* (1862) 376 Come into the iseter [= oyster] shop here, and plank the pewter. **1848** W. E. BURTON *Waggeries & Vagaries* 65 If the nigger..can plank up if he's cast, I'm darned if I don't..sue the nigger. **1887** H. FREDERIC in *Scribner's Mag.* I. 625/1 Workman would rather plank out five thousand dollars from his own pocket. **1890** 'R. BOLDREWOOD' *Miner's Right* x, He 'planks down' the dollars requisite for the purchase. **1903** SOMERVILLE & 'ROSS' *All on Irish Shore* 178 Every one squared up his books and planked ready money down on the nail. *Ibid.* 185 People began to talk then, especially as the pony's look and shape were improving each day, and after a little time every one was planking his money on one way or another. **1915** W. S. MAUGHAM *Of Human Bondage* lxxv. 389, I planked out the money to keep you. **1951** *New Yorker* 1 Dec. 63/1 (Advt.), You plank the cash on the counter for a slice of sirloin. **1966** H. KEMELMAN *Saturday Rabbi went Hungry* xxi. 127 When you ask someone to plank down a hundred and fifty-odd bucks for a lot which he doesn't think he's going to need.. it's a lot of dough. **1972** *Even. Telegram* (St. John's, Newfndl.) 5 Aug. 3/1 How could a poor man..plank down $70,000 in ready cash for a place to live in?

3. *techn.* **a.** To splice together (slivers of wool) into rovings. **b.** To harden (a hat) by felting.

1874 KNIGHT *Dict. Mech.* 362/1 Slivers of long-stapled wool are planked or spliced together. **1875** *Ibid.* 1731/2 They [hat-bodies] are planked or hardened to give them solidity, thickness, and strength. **1875** *Ure's Dict. Arts* (ed. 7) III. 1163 *Breaking-frame.*—Here the slivers are planked, or spliced together, the long end of one to the short end of another. **1902** *Brit. Med. Jrnl.* 15 Feb. 378/2 After the hat is planked it contains nothing hurtful.

4. To fix on a board (a fish that has been split open) and cook at a hot fire: see PLANKED 2. *U.S.*

1877 HOWELLS *Out of Question* (1882) 134, I suppose you plank horn-pout, here.

5. a. *intr.* To sleep on or as on a plank; to lie down on the hard ground; also *to plank it*. **b.** *trans.* To condemn to a plank-bed.

1829 B. HALL *Trav.* II. 382, I was right glad of [a berth], being wofully tired, and having no mind to plank it! **1860** DONALDSON *Bush Lays* 40 Through the day we will rough it, at night we will plank it. **1887** SIR H. CAMPBELL-BANNERMAN in *Scott. Leader* 15 Oct. 5 Who may be sent to a prison cell and planked for taking part in transactions which are as innocent and harmless as a meeting of the East Stirlingshire Liberal Association.

6. To exchange the separate strips or rigs of land of an individual owner for one compact piece of equal extent. *North. Sc. dial.*

1812 J. HENDERSON *Agric. Surv. Caithness* 268 In many cases, the arable land has been planked, or converted into distinct farms, in place of the old system of tenants occupying it in run rig, or rigg and rennal, as it was provincially termed. **1871** R. COWIE *Shetl.* II. viii. 158 The land [has been] planked or allocated in due proportion to each person.

†**plankage.** *Obs.* Also 5 plangage. [a. OF. *plancage, planchage*, f. *planke, planche*: see PLANK and -AGE.] Payment charged for the use of planks at landing-places.

1347–8 *Rolls of Parlt.* II. 212/2, Par cause de Murage ou Kayage ou Plankage. **1483** *Cal. Anc. Rec. Dublin* (1889) I. 364 Suche person and persones..that occupieth the said Watyr-bailliffes planges..shall pay for plangage to the said Water bailliffe. **1592** in Picton *L'pool Munic. Rec.* (1883) I. 70 [Various heads under which dues were claimed] Ladinge; Measuringe; Wayinge; Grondage; Ancorage;..Sea rounded groundes; Fishinges; Fowlinge; Planckage.

†**'plank-board.** *Obs.* [f. PLANK *sb.* + BOARD *sb.* See also PLANCH-BOARD.] A thick board suitable for flooring and similar purposes.

[**1394–1551**: see PLANCH-BOARD.] **1497–8** in Swayne *Sarum Churchw. Acc.* (1896) 48 Plankborde ad opus de le newe Roff. **1577–87** HOLINSHED *Chron.* III. 1139/1 The duke had prepared bridges made of planke boords..for his men to passe the ditch. **1608** WILLET *Hexapla Exod.* 605 The vsuall scantling for the thicknes of planke boord. **1707**

MORTIMER *Husb.* (1721) II. 46 'Twill make good Plank-boards and Timber.

planked (plæŋkt), *ppl. a.* [f. PLANK *v.* + -ED[1].]
1. Furnished, laid, floored, or covered with planks.
1608 SYLVESTER *Du Bartas* II. iv. IV. *Decay* 958 A flying Bridge..and planked Battlements On every story, for his Men's defence. **1651** T. DE GREY *Compl. Horseman* 21 A planked flore is warmer than a paved or pitched. **1793** R. MYLNE *Rep. Thames* 27 Both the side Streams should be shut up, with low planked Weirs. **1873** J. H. BEADLE *Undevel. West* xxxvi. 769 As one result of their smooth planked streets, much attention is given to fine turn-outs. **1956** R. W. ANDREWS *Glory Days of Logging* 23 (*caption*) Planked road of A. & M. Logging Co. Ltd...shown running from timber to log dumps. **1979** S. SMITH *Survivor* vi. 75 The planked roof of the barn.
2. Of fish, meat: Cooked by being split, fastened on a board, and held to the fire. Also, served on a piece of plank. *U.S.*
1855 *Sun* (Baltimore) 30 Apr. 4/1 Did you ever eat a 'plank'd shad'? **1877** HOWELLS *Out of Question* (1882) 134 One's ideas of planked Spanish mackerel. **1885** *Science* V. 426 The principal dish was 'planked' shad. By this process four fish are fastened to a board, and held towards a hot fire. Whilst cooking, the fish are constantly basted with a preparation made of butter, salt, and other ingredients. **1906** *N.Y. Globe* 27 Apr. 7 The planked chicken was served on the plank. **1910** *Chambers's Jrnl.* July 430/2 In the restaurants the British visitor will invariably be confronted with the possibilities contained in..'planked steak',..and so on. **1947** WODEHOUSE *Full Moon* iv. 83 An order of planked steak. **1969** R. & D. DE SOLA *Dict. Cooking* 177/1 *Planked steak*, restaurant term for a steak broiled and served on a well-seasoned plank and garnished with a border of mashed potatoes, mushroom caps, tomato slices, and sometimes julienned carrots. **1978** *Lancashire Life* Nov. 170/1 The dish in question, one of the popular specialities of the house, was described as planked steak: a reasonably substantial T-bone, prepared on that slab of oak, and accompanied by broccoli, mushrooms, tomatoes, fried onion rings and the most delicious Duchesse potatoes imaginable.

planker ('plæŋkə(r)). [f. PLANK *v.* + -ER[1].] A workman who planks or kneads hat-bodies in the process of felting them.
1902 *Brit. Med. Jrnl.* 15 Feb. 378/1 In hand-planking the 'form' is dipped in boiling water acidulated with vitriol, and then folded and vigorously kneaded by the planker's hand.

planking ('plæŋkɪŋ), *vbl. sb.* [f. as prec. + -ING[1].] The action of PLANK *v.*
1. Furnishing, flooring, or covering with planks.
1495 *Naval Acc. Hen. VII* (1896) 155 Laboryng & workyng abought Cowchyng plankyng & laying of the seid grete Rokes Stone & Gravell. **1663** GERBIER *Counsel* (1664) 70 Manger, Rack, and Planking of a Stable is eight shillings per foot in length. *c* **1850** *Rudim. Navig.* (Weale) 138 *Planking*, covering the outside of the timbers with plank; sometimes quaintly called 'skinning'. **1887** MRS. DALY *Digging & Squatting* 110 Port Darwin possessed no suitable wood for planking purposes.
2. *concr.* Planks in the mass; plank-work; the planks of a structure; *spec.* those forming the outer shell and inner lining of a ship.
1751 LABELYE *Westm. Br.* 29 The Carpenters were at Work on the Grating and Planking for the Caisson. **1842** DICKENS *Amer. Notes* ii, The planking of the paddle-boxes had been torn sheer away. **1871** HOWELLS *Wedd. Journ.* (1892) 295 The promenaders..paced back and forth upon the planking. **1904** A. GRIFFITHS *50 Yrs. Public Service* iii. 28 There was little enough comfort for us subalterns—a few feet of planking on the orlop deck.
3. The lagging or 'cleading' of a steam-cylinder.
1875 in KNIGHT *Dict. Mech.* 1732/1.
4. In technical senses of the verb.
1855 BOOKER *Hist. Denton Chapel* (Chetham Soc. No. 37) 11 For bowing, basining, boiling and planking [hat-bodies], he received in 1805, eight shillings per dozen. **1883** *Century Mag.* Aug. 549/2 Cleaning the shad for planking. **1884** *Chesh. Gloss.*, *Planking*,..the felting of hat bodies by rolling them on a plank, and frequently immersing them in acidulated water. **1902** [see PLANKER].
†**5.** Harrowing or rolling of land with a plank.
1814 M. BIRKBECK *Notes on France* 59 They then sow annual trefoil, which they cover very slightly by planking, that is, drawing a plank, on which a boy rides, over the land.
6. *attrib.* and *Comb.*, as **planking-clamp, -screw**: see quots.; **planking-machine**: see quot.
1875 KNIGHT *Dict. Mech.*, *Planking-clamp*,..an implement for bending a strake against the ribs of a vessel and holding it until secured by bolts or treenails. *Ibid.*, *Planking-machine*, a machine in which hat-bodies, after being formed, are rubbed, pressed, and steamed to give them strength and body. *Ibid.*, *Planking-screw*, an implement for straining planks against the ribs of vessels.

'plankless, *a.* [f. PLANK *sb.* + -LESS.] Having no planks; void or stripped of its planks.
1837 LONGF. *Drift-Wood* Prose Wks. 1886 I. 317 Vikings sitting gaunt and grim on the plankless ribs of their pirate ships. **1865** CARLYLE *Fredk. Gt.* XXI. iv. (1872) X. 40 The Peasant-Noble..clattered with his wooden slippers upon the plankless floor of his hut.

plankshear, -sheer, variants of PLANESHEAR.

plankter ('plæŋktə(r)). *Biol.* [f. PLANKT(ON + -ER[1].] = PLANKTONT.
1938 J. R. CARPENTER *Ecol. Gloss.* 208 *Plankt, plankter*, individual organisms comprising plankton. **1957** G. E. HUTCHINSON *Treat. Limnol.* I. xvii. 899 The only autotrophic truly open-water plankter so far encountered that requires accessory organic substances other than vitamin B_{12}, the marine diatom *Ditylum*. **1973** *Nature* 21/28 Dec. 521/1 This mechanism augmented by a rapid turnover in biomass, especially of small plankters, could account for the low residue concentrations in Gulf plankton following periods of light precipitation.

planktology (plæŋk'tɒlədʒɪ). [a. G. *planktologie* (E. Hæckel 1891, in *Jenaische Zeitschr. f. Naturwiss.* XXV. 240): see PLANKTO(N and -OLOGY.] The study of plankton. So **plankto'logical** *a.*, of or pertaining to this study; **plank'tologist**, one engaged in this study.
1893 G. W. FIELD tr. *Hæckel's Planktonic Stud.* in *Rep. U.S. Comm. Fisheries 1889–91* 571 The whole science which treats of this important division of biology is briefly called planktology. **1896** *Proc. Acad. Nat. Sci. Philadelphia* 280 Without undervaluing in any way the counting methods at present employed by planktologists, I desire here to call attention to an apparatus..by means of which one may make a large number of plankton estimations in a single day. **1912** *Rep. Brit. Assoc. 1911* 422 The Kiel planktologists have had to seek another source of food for the zooplankton. **1926** *Kongel. Danske Vidensk. Selsk. Skr.* 8th Ser. XI. 157 Those who have followed the history of planctological [*sic*] work during the last twenty years will know that it is really along these three lines that limnologists have especially worked in this area of exploration. **1947** *Nature* 4 Jan. 10/2 The technical difficulties of this type of work, particularly in planktology, are not belittled. **1967** *Oceanogr. & Marine Biol.* V. 231 A brief historical summary is necessary in order to understand the obstacles which Mediterranean planktology has had to overcome. *Ibid.* 248 This instrument becomes of questionable planktological value. **1972** *Nature* 7 Apr. 295/1 This information..will also be of help to physical oceanographers and planktologists.

plankton ('plæŋktən). *Biol.* [a. G. *plankton* (V. Hensen 1887, in *Ber. Kommission der wissenschaftlichen Untersuchung der deutschen Meere in Kiel* V. 1), a. Gr. πλαγκτόν, neut. of πλαγκτός vbl. adj., drifting, f. πλάζεσθαι to wander, roam, drift.] **1.** A collective name for all the forms of floating or drifting organic life found at various depths in the ocean, or, by extension, in bodies of fresh water. Also *attrib.*
1891 *Jrnl. R. Microsc. Soc.* 326 'Plankton' was originally defined by Hensen as including those animals which drift in the sea. **1892** E. J. BLES in *Jrnl. Marine Biol. Assoc.* II. 340 Variations of the floating fauna and flora, or plankton, of the Plymouth Waters. **1894** *Q. Rev.* Apr. 372 When the recent German expedition set out to study the Plankton or floating life of the Atlantic. **1899** *Nature* 15 June 157/1 Rich collections of plankton were made at all stations. **1908** *Jrnl. Marine Biol. Assoc.* VIII. 269 (*title*) Plankton studies in relation to the western mackerel fishery. **1921** [see BENTHOS]. **1947** *Sci. News* IV. 98 The vast bulk of life in the open sea is composed not of active creatures such as fish or whales, but of microscopic plants, and small animals which drift with the water. They are known collectively as plankton. **1956** A. HARDY *Open Sea* I. xv. 297 The herring snaps at the little plankton animals individually. **1973** *Nature* 16 Nov. 128/2 The existence of a vast aerial plankton of insects and other arthropods extending up into the sky for at least 14,000 foot is well established.
2. *Comb.* **plankton feeder**, an animal whose diet includes plankton; **plankton indicator**, an apparatus that is towed behind a ship with a filtering device by means of which the concentration of plankton can be estimated; **plankton net**, a very fine net used to collect samples of plankton or other very small organisms; **plankton recorder**, a modification of the plankton indicator in which the filter is in the form of a continuously moving roll.
1956 A. HARDY *Open Sea* I. xv. 303 Mackerel are *plankton-feeders for about half the year. **1975** C. F. HICKLING *Water as Productive Environment* vii. 65 The species of *Alestes*..came to dominate the surface waters as plankton feeders. **1925** A. C. HARDY in *Fishery Investigations* 2nd Ser. VIII. VII. 2 The present paper..describes investigations by means of an instrument which has been called the *Plankton Indicator. **1936** *Jrnl. Marine Biol. Assoc.* XXI. 148 Preliminary experiments were begun in 1922 and 1923 with a torpedo-shaped instrument called the Plankton Indicator. **1953** *Bull. Marine Ecol.* IV. 19 The small Plankton Indicator..has been used..during an ecological survey of the herring off the north-east coast of Scotland. **1952** J. CLEGG *Freshwater Life Brit. Is.* xviii. 293 Some form of pond-net is almost essential. Probably the type of most general utility is that known as a *plankton-net. .. The bag part is made of fine-mesh material, and carries at its base a tube or bottle into which the organisms descend. **1963** G. E. & R. C. NEWELL *Marine Plankton* ii. 17 There are several patterns of plankton net in common use today. **1972** F. G. STEHLI et al. in T. J. M. Schopf *Models in Paleobiol.* vi. 119 The mesh of the plankton nets used was large. **1926** A. C. HARDY in *Nature* 30 Oct. 631/1 Whilst on the *Discovery* expedition I have been experimenting with such an instrument, which I am calling the Continuous *Plankton Recorder... It is a development of the simple Plankton Indicator.., but in place of the silk netting discs, which had to be reloaded for each sample, I have substituted a long continuously moving roll operated by a propellor turned by the water through which it is towed. **1936** *'Discovery' Rep.* XI. 457 The first Continuous Plankton Recorder was used on the R.R.S. 'Discovery' in the years 1925–7. **1975** D. H. CUSHING *Marine Ecol. & Fisheries* viii. 166 The plankton recorder survey..is based on monthly samples from fixed merchant ship lines across the North Sea.

planktonic (plæŋk'tɒnɪk), *a.* and *sb. Biol.* [a. G. *planktonisch* (E. Hæckel 1891, in *Jenaische Zeitschr. f. Naturwiss.* XXV. 240): see PLANKTON and -IC.] **A.** *adj.* Of, pertaining to, or characteristic of plankton.
1893 G. W. FIELD tr. *Hæckel's Planktonic Stud.* in *Rep. U.S. Comm. Fisheries 1889–91* 571, I adopt the term Plankton in place of '*Auftrieb*', and derive from it the adjective planktonic. **1899** *Proc. Zool. Soc.* 1029 Most, if not all, *Globigerinæ*, are essentially planktonic organisms. **1905** MARR in *Q. Jrnl. Geol. Soc.* LXI. Proc. 74 Planktonic. **1930** *Times Educ. Suppl.* 22 Mar. (Home & Classroom Suppl.) p. iv/1 Quantities of nektonic and planktonic life are being caught daily. **1963** *Times* 19 Feb. 10/4 Sediments of past ages..contain a boundary clearly defined by changes in their content of fossilized planktonic remains. **1974** *Nature* 8 Feb. 393/2 Herbivorous zooplankton can graze on planktonic algae, bacteria and detrital particles.
B. *sb.* A microfossil of a foraminifer included in the plankton.
1959 *Bull. Amer. Paleontol.* XXXIX. 84 These assemblages of agglutinated forms..occur several times and are separated by assemblages of calcareous forms, often with abundant planktonics, suggestive of a depositional depth between 200 and 600 metres. **1964** *Micropaleontology* X. 3/2 The coiling characteristics of planktonics can be most useful in correlating strata from different basins and with entirely different benthic biofacies. **1976** *Ibid.* XXII. 420/1 The total number of planktonics, benthics, and fragments was counted.

planktonology (ˌplæŋktə'nɒlədʒɪ). [f. PLANKTON + -OLOGY.] = PLANKTOLOGY. So **planktono'logical** *a.*
1896 *Jrnl. R. Microsc. Soc.* 470 Dr. C. S. Dolley referring to the work of Hensen, Haeckel, and others on planktonology, explains the importance of a quantitative determination of the primitive food-supply of marine animals. **1960** *Biol. Abstr.* XXXV. 2290/1 (*title*) The new systematics and planktonology. **1961** *Ibid.* XXXVI. 284/2 (*title*) Results of planktonological research. **1975** *Jrnl. Fish. Res. Bd. Canada* XXXII. 2231 Narrower fields of specialization, such as planktonology, fisheries ecology, or studies on the benthic habitat, should be integrated. **1976** *Biol. Abstr.* LXI. 2576/1 (*title*) Physical-chemical and planktonological studies of the Great Lake of Laffrey.

planktont ('plæŋktɒnt). *Biol.* [f. PLANKT(ON + Gr. ὄν, ὀντ- being: see ONTO-.] An individual organism of the plankton.
1897 *Science* 3 Dec. 830/1 The struggles of the imprisoned organisms and the pressure of the filtering water also materially assist the escape of planktonts through the yielding meshes of silk. **1926** *Kongel. Danske Vidensk. Selsk. Skr.* 8th Ser. XI. 152 Some of the freshwater planctonts [*sic*]..were made to serve as a support for the theories of heredity. **1931** *Jrnl. Ecology* XIX. 246 Multiplication of the littoral planktonts in the open water will naturally only take place if the latter contains an adequate amount of mineral nutriment. **1935** P. S. WELCH *Limnology* ix. 205 The term planktont of the older literature should be abandoned because of its faulty word structure. **1948** *New Biol.* V. 21 Blue-green planktonts are generally most abundant..in summer and late autumn.

planktotrophic (ˌplæŋktəʊ'trɒfɪk), *a.* [f. PLANKTO(N + TROPHIC *a.*] Feeding on plankton. So **plank'totrophy**, behaviour of this type.
1946 G. THORSON in *Medd. Komm. Danmarks Fiskerei Ser. Plankton* IV. I. 476 Planktotrophic larvae with long pelagic life..originate from small eggs poor in yolk. **1963** R. P. DALES *Annelids* viii. 171 Most planktotrophic larvae develop from small eggs. **1973** *Amer. Naturalist* CVII. 348 Planktotrophy is the most common pattern in shallow-water tropical invertebrates. **1978** *Nature* 5 Jan. 56/2 Most of the commoner species of coral reef asteroids..produce many small, planktotrophic, pelagic larvae.

'plankways, 'plankwise, *adv.* [f. PLANK *sb.* + -WAYS, -WISE.] In the manner or direction of a plank; lengthways.
1815 J. SMITH *Panorama Sc. & Art* I. 90 When cut plankwise, boxwood is extremely apt to warp, unless very well seasoned. **1881** HASLUCK *Lathe Work* 35 For turning the surface of wood chucked plankways the same tools are used.

planky ('plæŋkɪ), *a.* [f. PLANK *sb.* + -Y.] Of the nature of or composed of planks.
c **1611** CHAPMAN *Iliad* XII. 442 He came before the planky gates, that all for strength were wrought. **1718** ROWE tr. *Lucan* III. 735 Darts, Fragments of the Rock, and Flames they throw, And tear the planky Shelter fix'd below.

planless ('plænlɪs), *a.* [f. PLAN *sb.* + -LESS.] Without a plan; not planned; unsystematic.
1800 COLERIDGE *Piccolom.* IV. iv. 40 Every planless measure, chance event..Will they connect, and weave them all together Into one web of treason. **1852** BLACKIE *Stud. Lang.* 11 Where not stupid, how often careless, aimless, and planless! **1887** HISSEY *Holiday on Road* 69 All England was before us; ours was a planless expedition. **1937** 'G. ORWELL' *Road to Wigan Pier* iv. 51 Little brick houses..festering in planless chaos. **1942** J. STEINBECK *Moon is Down* ii. 25 Fine weapons and fine planning against unarmed, planless enemies. **1957** [see CONTRACT *v.* 2 d].
Hence **'planlessly** *adv.*, **'planlessness**.
1894 *Scott. Leader* 8 Mar. 3 That large..school whose method seems to be to begin writing and go planlessly ahead. **1906** *Hibbert Jrnl.* Jan. 408 The planlessness of moral instruction in schools. **1932** *Times Lit. Suppl.* 1 Sept. 609/2 It has the merit, certainly, that almost any plan has over planlessness. **1944** I. ORIGO *Diary* 13 Feb. in *War in Val d'Orcia* (1947) 140 It is odd how used one can become to uncertainty for the future, to a complete planlessness. **1962** *Punch* 30 May 844/1, I have already let several valuable years slip planlessly by. **1976** *Sunday Times* (Lagos) 7 Nov. 12/2 The planlessness of the flashes should take us to the

most unlikely place where the story should begin, the epilogue.

planned (plænd), *ppl. a.* [f. PLAN *v.* + -ED[1].] Designed, projected, arranged, etc.: see the verb. ***planned economy***: an economy in which industrial production and development, etc. are determined by an overall national plan; ***planned obsolescence***: obsolescence of manufactured goods due to deliberate changes in design, cessation of the supply of spare parts, use of poor-quality materials, etc.

1770 C. CHAUNCY *Repl. Chandler's Appeal Defended* (title-p.), Objections against the planned American Episcopate. **1884** BLACK *Jud. Shaks.* xii, There had been a planned meeting. **1894** H. NISBET *Bush Girl's Rom.* 256 It must have been a planned-out affair. **1931** *Economist* 18 July 111/2 The tendency in the world is towards some or other form of planned economy. **1936** *Discovery* Sept. 295/1 Can present human motives work a planned society? **1942** *N.Y. Times* 6 Mar. 23/7 The Planned Parenthood Federation of America, Inc., is the new corporate name of the Birth Control Federation of America, Inc., according to announcement yesterday by the organization's board of directors. **1943** J. S. HUXLEY *TVA* xiii. 115 The transition from a *laissez-faire* to a planned economy. **1947** *Sun* (Baltimore) 20 Sept. 1/2 The Senator's attack on what he calls the Truman Administration's policy of 'planned inflation'. **1960** I. BENNETT *Delinquent & Neurotic Children* ix. 444 *History*: a planned baby. Both parents wanted a girl. **1965** B. PEARCE tr. *Preobrazhensky's New Economics* 159 The further abolition of the law of value..will proceed along the path of planned socialist organization of the economy in countries which make an end of the capitalist régime. **1966** *Punch* 20 July 96/3 The planned-obsolescence men won't miss *this* one. **1969** A. CAIRNCROSS in *Advancement of Sci.* XXVI. 64/2 It is possible to argue that there is no essential difference between a managed economy and a planned economy, and that planning is simply a rather inflexible form of management. **1977** *National Observer* (U.S.) 1 Jan. 10/3 Things settled down into a buyer's market again, so the businessmen came up with another new gimmick. It was called planned obsolescence. Come out with a new model every year. Put a few new gadgets on it... Don't worry about the quality, it will be obsolete in three years anyway, besides, it's cheap. **1977** J. AIKEN *Last Movement* i. 17 Dru had been a planned child, whereas I was an unexpected.. afterthought. **1977** *Spare Rib* May 20/2 On Ash Wednesday ..a newly opened Planned Parenthood Clinic in St Paul was fire bombed.

plannee (plæ'niː). [f. PLAN *sb.* or *v.* + -EE[1].] A person for whom something is planned.

1943 J. S. HUXLEY *TVA* xv. 119 He must not think of the people in his region as his subject plannees, but as participating co-planners. **1946** A. HUXLEY *Science, Liberty & Peace* (1947) I. 28 A highly organized and regimented society..is felt by the planners, and even..by the plannees to be more 'scientific', and therefore better, than [etc.].

planner ('plænə(r)). [f. PLAN *v.* + -ER[1].]

a. One who plans or makes a plan; a deviser, arranger; a projector, schemer; *spec.*, a person who plans the development or reconstruction of an urban area, or who engages in economic planning. Also (*Sc.*), a landscape gardener.

1716 COWPER in Ld. Campbell *Chancellors* (1857) V. cxvi. 305 This exempts you from the charge of being the planners of the treason. **1801** tr. *Gabrielli's Myst. Husb.* IV. 164 Having been for many years a planner of fashions, [she] had an air of smartness. **1850** T. MCCRIE *Mem. Sir A. Agnew* ii. (1852) 27 He procured the services of Mr. John Hay, late planner in Edinburgh. **1897** *Daily News* 15 Jan. 6/4 The original planner of this stupendous enterprise. **1935** *Economist* 11 May 1075/1 It is true to say that the task of the planner is the more effective mobilisation of all economic resources. **1961** L. MUMFORD *City in Hist.* vii. 185 Aristotle's position..is sounder than that of most of our present-day planners, who have not yet arrived at a functional definition of a city. **1962** *Listener* 3 May 758/2 If the French planners could prove..that their efficient techniques and the understanding with the heads of industry have proved to be the answer to all problems of economic growth [etc.]. **1973** *Times* 13 Dec. 19/2 There is an absolute shortage of planners. **1976** *Encounter* June 93/2 At present, the experts and polymaths, the thinkers and highly skilled professions, the essential organisers and planners, have no collective voice.

b. A list, table, or similar device giving information which enables one to plan.

1971 *Homes & Gardens* Sept. 99/3, I will send you a copy of our Do-It-Yourself diet planner and a calorie counter, so that you can organise a diet to suit your needs.

plannet, -ett, obs. forms of PLANET *sb.*[1]

planning ('plænɪŋ), *vbl. sb.* [f. PLAN *v.* + -ING[1].] **a.** The action of the verb PLAN; the action or work of a planner; the forming of plans; the making or delineation of a plan or diagram; scheming, designing, contriving.

1748 *Anson's Voy.* Introd. 3* Actual surveys of roads and harbours,..require a good degree of skill both in planning and drawing. **1842** J. AITON *Domest. Econ.* (1857) 127 Let there be no want of thrift: let there be both planning and plenty. **1897** RHOSCOMYL *White Rose Arno* 60 He was deep in sober discussions and plannings. **1935** *Economist* 30 Mar. 725/1 Since private enterprise has manifestly failed to bring about the necessary adjustments in industry, 'planning' must be tried. **1941** *New Statesman* 15 Feb. 151 If we are to rebuild our cities aright, we ought to plan them; and planning is inconsistent with rebuilding on the old sites. **1959** *Cambridge Rev.* 25 Apr. 429/2 The ancient City could survive if Town and University were enclosed together within a ring of traffic roads and could not be entirely traversed except on foot or bicycle... These are all matters of what is drolly called 'Planning'. **1962** *Listener* 1 Mar. 363/1 Planning, if one must risk a description, is a method of introducing more coherence, more purpose, into an economic system. *Ibid.* 364/2 The planning of private industry.

b. *attrib.*, as ***planning appeal, application, authority, blight, committee, consent, consultant, control, engineer, officer, permission.***

1971 *Reader's Digest Family Guide to Law* 174 In some *planning appeals cases..the inspector has powers to make the decision without referring the matter to the Minister. *a* **1974** R. CROSSMAN *Diaries* (1975) I. 615, I found when I arrived that eight or nine months was accepted as a reasonable time for a planning appeal to wait in the Ministry before a decision. **1976** *S. Wales Echo* 25 Nov. 2/4 Over lunch reference was made to their particular *planning application. It was obvious they knew what the planning officer's recommendation was. **1934** *Act 23 & 24 Geo. V* c. 58 s. 20 (1) '*Planning authority' means..the authority having power to control the development..of..land. **1950** *Chambers's Encycl.* XIII. 705/2 Extensive powers for the compulsory purchase of land..have also been made available to planning authorities. **1962** L. GOLDING *Dict. Local Govt.* 301 '*Planning blight'..arises when property becomes virtually unsaleable by its owner or saleable only at a low price because of a threat of development. **1976** *Liverpool Echo* 23 Nov. 7/3 The people of Garston have suffered far too long from the planning blight that has caused serious deterioration in the area affecting housing, shops and the environment in general. **1942** *Country Life* 9 Oct. 692/2 That is the London revealed as it would be by the *Planning Committee of the Royal Academy. **1964** *Oxf. Jun. Encycl.* X. 457/1 Applications are submitted to the planning committee, and only when permission has been given can work proceed. **1970** *Financial Times* 13 Apr. 25/2 Ambitions for a 2,000-room palace of tourism in West London foundered on the rocks of *planning consents. **1977** *Lancs. Life* Nov. 82/2 You could find yourself in trouble for demolishing, adding to or altering property without planning consent. **1944** J. S. HUXLEY *On Living in Revol.* xi. 115 The services of *planning consultants and a resident planning engineer. **1961** E. A. POWDRILL *Vocab. Land Planning* ii. 10 *Planning control arises from the fact that persons, groups of persons, and organisations wish to initiate some form of development. **1944** *Planning engineer [see *planning consultant* above]. **1961** H. W. DODDS in *56th Ann. Rep. Carnegie Foundation for Advancem. of Teaching* 22 A plan must therefore be brought up to date periodically, possibly with the assistance of a permanent *planning officer. **1965** in P. Jennings *Living Village* (1968) 103 Planning permission had already been given, the Planning Officer being convinced that they were a brilliant architectural achievement. **1976** *Liverpool Echo* 23 Nov. 10/5 Mr. Len Ward, planning officer for Ellesmere Port Council, is urging the highways committee to take immediate action over the cottages. **1947** *Act 10 & 11 Geo. VI* c. 51 s. 119 (1) '*Planning permission' means the permission for development which is required by virtue of section twelve of this Act. **1965** Planning permission [see *planning officer* above]. **1977** *Undercurrents* June–July 4/1 The Windscale Public Enquiry into British Nuclear Fuel Limited's..application for planning permission to build an uranium-oxide processing plant begins on June 14th.

plano ('pleɪnəʊ), *a.* [f. PLANO-[1].] Of a surface of a lens: flat.

1950 *Jrnl. Optical Soc. Amer.* XL. 523/1 The plano surfaces can introduce central coma by being tilted. **1962** L. S. SASIENI *Princ. & Pract. Optical Dispensing* x. 268 Many modern trial cases are made with plano-convex and plano-concave spheres... The powers are engraved sometimes on the plano side of the convex and on the concave side of the concave.

plano-[1] (pleɪnəʊ), used as combining form of L. *plānus* flat, smooth, level; in scientific or technical adjectives, denoting (*a*) flatly, in a flattened manner, with modification of a specified form in the direction of a plane, as ***plano-compressed, -conical, -hemispherical, -obconical, -orbicular, -patellate, -rotund, -subcucullate***; (*b*) a combination of a plane with another surface, esp. plane on one side, and of another surface on the other, as PLANO-CONCAVE, -CONVEX, etc. Also **plano-cylindric, -ical**, plane on one side and of a cylindrical form on the other; **plano-horizontal**, having a plane horizontal surface or position; **plano-miller, plano(-)milling machine**, a milling machine built in the manner of a planer and used esp. for heavy work, having a flat bed to carry the workpiece and a sliding cross-piece that carries rotating cutters as in an ordinary milling machine, rather than a planing tool; †**plano-solid** *Arith. Obs.*, applied to a number compounded of a 'plane' and a 'solid' number, i.e. of 5 prime factors; **plano-subulate**, of a flat awl-shaped form.

1839 LINDLEY *Sch. Bot.* viii. 183 Seeds *plano-compressed or winged at the apex. **1681** GREW *Museum* I. iv. 75 Some few are *Plano-Conical, whose Superfice is in part level between both ends. **1846** DANA *Zooph.* (1848) 553 Corallum firm; cells..quite shallow, plano-conical. **1727** SWIFT *Art Polit. Lying* Wks. 1755 III. I. 114 He supposes the soul to be of the nature of a *plano-cylindrical speculum ..the plain side was made by God Almighty, but that the devil afterwards wrought the other side into a cylindrical figure. **1846** DANA *Zooph.* (1848) 327 Cespitose, *plano-hemispherical. **1760** J. LEE *Introd. Bot.* II. xx. (1765) 116 *Vexillum*, the Standard; a Petal covering the rest..*plano-horizontal. **1906** J. G. HORNER *Mod. Milling Machines* v. 130 *Plano-Millers or Slabbing Machines.—This is a name that seems most appropriate to designate that large and growing group of machines which is built on the model of the common planing machine, with bed, table, housings, and cross rail. **1963** *Gen. Engin. Workshop Practice* (ed. 3) vi. 218/2 The plano-miller is a milling machine, but designed to execute certain work formerly confined to the planer. **1905** T. R. SHAW *Machine Tools* vii. 478 Universal *plano-milling machines are now constructed of any size with either one or two saddles carrying spindles on the cross-slide, just as with the tool-boxes of planing machines. **1964** S. CRAWFORD *Basic Engin. Processes* vi. 154 A plano milling machine possesses several advantages as compared with the planing machine, including the reduction of non-cutting time, wider range of operations in one setting, and increased rate of production. **1846** DANA *Zooph.* (1848) 453 With a solid *plano-obconical base. **1887** W. PHILLIPS *Brit. Discomycetes* 175 Gregarious, suberumpent, sessile, waxy, *plano-patellate. **1846** DANA *Zooph.* (1848) 347 Subcylindrical, ..*plano-rotund at top. **1662** HOBBES *Seven Prob.* Wks. 1845 VII. 67 There be some numbers called plane, other solids, others *plano-solid. **1846** DANA *Zooph.* (1848) 336 Very broad explanate, and often *plano-subcucullate. **1760** J. LEE *Introd. Bot.* II. xviii. (1765) 110 The Claws *plano-subulate.

plano-[2] (plænəʊ), before a vowel or *h* **plan-**, combining form of Gr. πλάνος wandering, used in a few scientific terms; see PLANOBLAST, PLANODIA, PLANOGAMETE, PLANURIA.

planoblast ('plænəʊblæst). *Zool.* [f. PLANO-[2] + Gr. βλαστ-ός sprout, shoot.] The free-swimming generative bud or gonophore of certain Hydrozoa, usually a craspedote medusa or medusoid. Hence **plano'blastic** *a.*, of or pertaining to a planoblast.

1871 ALLMAN *Monogr. Gymnoblastic Hydroids* I. Introd. 15 Planoblast... A generative bud with a structure fitting it for a free locomotive life when detached from the hydrosome. *Ibid.*, Umbrella, the gelatinous bell of a medusiform planoblast.

ˌplano-'concave, *a.* [f. PLANO-[1] + CONCAVE.] Having one surface plane and the opposite one concave, as a lens.

1693 E. HALLEY in *Phil. Trans.* XVII. 961 Whether the Lens be..Plano-Convex or Plano-Concave. **1807** HERSCHEL *ibid.* XCVII. 183 The plain side of a plano-concave, or plano-convex lens. **1881** LE CONTE *Sight* 34 And one with excess of dispersive over refractive power for our plano-concave lens.

ˌplano-'convex, *a.* [f. as prec. + CONVEX.]

1. Having one surface plane and the opposite one convex: chiefly of lenses; also of natural formations, as parts of plants or animals, or other objects.

1665 HOOKE *Microgr.* Pref. fj, I fixt also with wax a pretty large plano Convex Glass. **1693, 1807** [see prec.]. **1810** D. STEWART *Philos. Ess.* II. I. vii. 330 In wooded scenes, the plano-convex mirrour, which was Mr. Gray's companion in all his tours, has a pleasing effect. **1830** LINDLEY *Nat. Syst. Bot.* 75 Cotyledons plano-convex. **1884** F. J. BRITTEN *Watch & Clockm.* 102 Achromatic glass with two plano-convex lenses.

b. Of a crystal: Having some faces plane and others convex.

1805–17 R. JAMESON *Char. Min.* (ed. 3) 209 Plano-convex ..when the faces are partly straight and partly uneven, as in the diamond.

2. Having a flattened convex form.

1843 J. G. WILKINSON *Swedenborg's Anim. Kingd.* I. i. 21 The tongue's upper surface is plano-convex. **1845** LINDLEY *Sch. Bot.* vi. (1858) 83 Receptacle plano-convex, paleaceous.

‖**planodia** (plə'nəʊdɪə). *Surg.* and *Path.* [f. PLANO-[2] + Gr. ὁδός way.] (See quot.)

1858 MAYNE *Expos. Lex.*, *Planodia*, term for a false passage, as may be made in stricture of the urethra in treating by a bougie, sound, or catheter.

planogamete ('plænəʊgəˌmiːt). *Biol.* [f. PLANO-[2] + GAMETE.] A motile gamete or conjugating cell: also called *zoogamete*. Hence **planoga'metic** *a.*

1886 [see GAMETE]. **1950** E. A. BESSEY *Morphol. & Taxon. Fungi* i. 6 The two gametes may both be..motile (planogametes), as in the..Chytridiales. **1971** P. H. B. TALBOT *Princ. Fungal Taxon.* vii. 91 A planogamete is a motile gamete, or sex cell, and planogametic conjugation.. is the fusion of two gametes, one or both of which may be motile.

planographic (pleɪnəʊ'græfɪk), *a.* [f. PLANO-[1] + -GRAPHIC.] Of, pertaining to, or produced by a process in which printing is done from a plane surface.

1897 SINGER & STRANG *Etching* 121 The relief print has no plate mark, the intaglio print has one quite clear and distinct, the planographic one has a very slight mark. **1914** E. H. RICHTER *Prints* 10 The last group to be considered, planographic processes, is based entirely upon chemical and physical action. **1946** H. WHETTON *Pract. Printing & Binding* xxv. 287/1 Planographic is the term used to describe a printing surface on the same level as the plate. **1967** V. STRAUSS *Printing Industry* i. 35/2 Offset lithography.. dominates the field of planographic printing. **1972** *Physics Bull.* Sept. 532/3 The printing surface is virtually planographic and the action of development is to render the image areas oliophilic.

planography (plə'nɒgrəfɪ). [f. L. *plān-um* PLANE + -GRAPHY.] **1.** The art of drawing plans; *spec.*: see quot. *rare.*

1847 J. DWYER *Hydraulic Engineering* 131 Planography is another description of section introduced by..Sir John Macneil,..which required that a vertical section..should be laid down on the line of direction marked on the plan, and having the Cuttings and Embankments plotted on opposite sides.

2. Printing from a plane surface, in contrast to processes in which the areas to be printed are in relief or intaglio.

1914 H. J. RHODES *Art of Lithography* i. 1 The term Planography..has been much in evidence of late, and there is no reason why it should not be generally adopted to denote all processes of printing from flat surfaces. **1937** *Discovery* Oct. 297/2 Lithography is..a misnomer, though attempts to replace it by planography have not found favour. **1960** G. A. GLAISTER *Gloss. Bk.* 317/1 Planography..refers to methods of printing from flat surfaces other than stone.

Hence **pla'nographist**, one who draws a plan or map; a map-maker.

1859 W. M. THOMSON *Land & Book* v. xli. (1867) 627 All planographists of the Holy City agree that [etc.].

planometer (plə'nɒmɪtə(r)). [f. as prec. + -METER.] An accurately made flat plate, usually of cast iron, used as a standard gauge for plane surfaces; a surface-plate. So **pla'nometry**, the use of a planometer; the measurement or gauging of plane surfaces.

1864 WEBSTER, *Planometer*. **1875** KNIGHT *Dict. Mech.* 1726/2 Plane-surfaces are produced by the planing-machine, by the file, and by grinding... For the purpose of verifying their accuracy, the planometer was devised by Whitworth.

planometry, irreg. form of PLANIMETRY.

planont ('plænənt). *Biol.* [f. PLANO-[2] + Gr. ὀντ-: see ONTO-.] A motile spore, whether sexual, asexual, or a zygote; *esp.* the motile stage of certain microsporidian protozoans or phycomycetes.

1914 FANTHAM & PORTER *Some Minute Anim. Parasites* xi. 217 This amœbula [of *Nosema apis*] gives rise, by division, to daughter forms, each possessing one nucleus and capable of wandering about over the epithelium of the gut. Such forms are called planonts, or wanderers. **1943** F. K. SPARROW *Aquatic Phycomycetes* 406 In *A[llomyces] javanicus*..the planonts emerging from the resting spores..gave rise upon germination to sexual plants. **1961** R. D. MANWELL *Introd. Protozool.* xxiii. 478 At first they [*sc. Nosema* spores] remain in the gut, but they soon begin to wander and are now called 'planonts'.

‖**Planorbis** (plə'nɔːbɪs). *Zool.* [mod.L., f. *plānus* PLANE *a.* + *orbis* ORB.] A genus of freshwater snails (pond-snails), characterized by a flat rounded spiral shell.

1833 LYELL *Princ. Geol.* III. 238 We find in the marls and limestones the shells of the Planorbis, and other lacustrine testacea. **1876** *Beneden's Anim. Parasites* 38 A gasteropod mollusc, similar to a Planorbis, which lives as a messmate in the body of an annelid.

Comb. **1878** BELL *Gegenbaur's Comp. Anat.* 81 The planorbis-like shells of the Milliolidæ represent the simplest condition of these forms.

Hence **pla'norbiform**, **pla'norboid** *adjs.*, resembling, or having the form of a *Planorbis*; of a flat rounded spiral shape; **pla'norbine** *a.*, belonging to, or having the characters of, the subfamily *Planorbīnæ*, of which *Planorbis* is the typical genus; **pla'norbite**, a fossil shell belonging or allied to this genus; **pla'norbuline** *a.*, of or belonging to *Planorbulīna*, a genus of *Foraminifera* having shells of a planorboid form.

1856 WOODWARD *Mollusca* III. 398 The Achatinellæ are elongated..and the Helices planorboid and multispiral. **1879** CARPENTER in *Encycl. Brit.* IX. 380/1 Remarkable modifications of the planorbuline type. **1895** *Cambr. Nat. Hist.* III. 413 Shell very small, planorbiform.

planosol ('pleɪnəʊ-, 'plænəʊsɒl). *Soil Sci.* [f. PLANO-[1] + -SOL.] An intrazonal soil having a thin, strongly leached surface horizon overlying a compacted hard-pan or clay-pan, and occurring on flat uplands with poor drainage. Hence **plano'solic** *a.*

1938 M. BALDWIN et al. in *U.S. Dept. Agric. Yearbk.* 991 The term 'Planosol' is being proposed to cover those soils with claypans and cemented hardpans not included with the Solonetz, Ground-Water Podzol, and Ground-Water Laterite. Families of Planosols correspond to associated normal zonal soils. **1965** B. T. BUNTING *Geogr. of Soil* vi. 71 Inward from these marginal sites, on plateaux, developed zonal soils occur, of considerable age, and hydromorphic or planosolic variants may exist in the central, poorly drained parts of the widest crestal plateaux. *Ibid.* xi. 133 Planosols are widespread on level plateau surfaces or broad gentle slopes on loess, till or wide alluvial terraces in central USA. **1972** C. B. HUNT *Geol. of Soils* ix. 206 In southern Ohio, Indiana, and Illinois..are flat, poorly drained uplands covered partly by loess and partly by Illinoian till... The comparatively thin modern soils on the surface of the old weathered deposits are Planosols with light-colored surface layers and deeper layers mottled brown and reddish brown.

planospiral (pleɪnəʊ'spaɪərəl), *a.* [f. PLANO-[1] + SPIRAL *a.*] = *planispiral*: see PLANI-.

1858 in MAYNE *Expos. Lex.* 973/1.

planospore ('plænəʊspɔə(r)). *Bot.* [f. PLANO-[2] + SPORE.] A motile zoospore.

1950 E. A. BESSEY *Morphol. & Taxon. Fungi* i. 5 The motile naked zoospores..may be called planospores. **1970** J. WEBSTER *Introd. Fungi* i. 68 The zoospore is sometimes termed a planospore.

planscheour, **planschour**, **planseour**, **planshar(e**, obs. ff. PLANCHER.

plansheer, **planshire**, obs. forms of PLANESHEAR.

plansifter ('plænsɪftə(r)). [f. PLAN *sb.* + SIFTER.] A machine consisting of a mechanically agitated set of superimposed flat sieves of differing mesh, used in flour milling for separating and grading the broken grain.

Registered in the U.S. as a proprietary name.

1905 *Official Gaz.* (U.S. Patent Office) 26 Dec. 2502/1 Shaking-Bolts. Barnard & Leas Manufacturing Company, Maline, Ill. Plansifter. **1908** *Engineering* 2 Oct. 429/2 Flour was dressed through long reels, called 'bolters', some of which were about 20 ft. long. These cumbersome machines ..have given way in this country to the more adaptable centrifugal dresser, and on the Continent to the plansifter. **1936** J. H. SCOTT *Flour Milling Processes* ix. 200 The type of plansifter used..in this country is the free-swinging, balanced crank pattern, driven by a central vertical shaft. **1964** M. PYKE *Food Sci. & Technol.* iii. 43 In a modern mill, the broken grain from the plan-sifter associated with the first break roll will be passed to a second break roll where a little more flour will be sifted out.

planster ('plænstə(r)). [f. PLAN *sb.* + -STER.] A planner: used only with derogatory connotations.

1945 J. BETJEMAN *New Bats in Old Belfries* 34 The planster's vision. **1964** *Listener* 9 Jan. 71/1 Such destruction has been launched on the face and form of England by witless plansters and lethally unimaginative local authorities. **1978** *N.Y. Rev. Bks.* 23 Feb. 8/4 Does aesthetic sense in the end atrophy if it is desiccated by the continual use of this type of programmed reasoning? Is it replaced by what Betjeman called the Planster's Vision?

plant (plɑːnt, -æ-), *sb.*[1] Forms: 1 **plante**, 4–7 **plante**, (4–5 **plonte**, 5 **plantte**, **plaunte**, **plounte**, *Sc.* **playnt**, 6 **plaunt**), 5– **plant.** [In sense 1, OE. *plante* fem., ad. L. *planta* sprout, slip, cutting, graft, whence also OHG. *pflanza*, ON. *planta*. Later senses are affected by med. or mod. uses of L. *planta*, and by F. *plante*, or are direct derivatives of PLANT *v.*, or a. F. *plant* action of planting, plants collectively for planting out, f. *planter* to plant.]

I. 1. a. A young tree, shrub, or herb newly planted, or intended for planting; a set, cutting, slip; a sapling. *Obs.* or *dial.* (In local use the name for seedling vegetables at this stage, as 'healthy cabbage plants', 'plants at sixpence a hundred', etc.)

c **825** *Vesp. Psalter* cxliii. 12 Ðeara bearn swe swe niowe plant[e] steaðelunge ȝesteaðulfestad from ȝuȝuðe. *c* **897** K. ÆLFRED *Gregory's Past. C.* xlix. §2. 381 On æppeltunum, ðonne hie wel begað hira plantan and hiera impan, oð hie fulweaxne beoð. **13..** *E.E. Allit. P.* A. 104 Þe fyrre in þe fryth þe fei[r]er con ryse þe playn, þe plonttez, þe spyse, þe perez. *c* **1386** CHAUCER *Wife's Prol.* 763 Yif me a plante of thilke blissed tree; And in my gardyn planted it shal bee. *c* **1400** MAUNDEV. (Roxb.) vii. 26 Men take plantes or slyfynges þeroff and sett þam in oþer placez. *c* **1440** *Alphabet of Tales* 1, & þou sett in my garthyn a yong plante of a tre. **1526** TINDALE *Matt.* xv. 13 All plantes [Gr. πᾶσα φυτεία, Vulg. *omnis plantatio*] which my hevenly father hath nott planted shalbe plucked vppe by the rotes. **1535** COVERDALE *Ps.* xlvii. 2 The hill of Sion is like a fayre plante [LUTHER 'Der Berg Zion ist wie ein schön Zweiglein']. **1573–80** BARET *Alv.* P 467 A plant, the slip of a tree that was planted in the earth. **1600** SHAKS. *A.Y.L.* III. ii. 378 There is a man haunts the Forrest, that abuses our yong plants with caruing *Rosalinde* on their barkes. **1688** R. HOLME *Armoury* II. 86/2 Plants are young Trees fit to be set. **1719** DE FOE *Crusoe* (1840) II. ix. 196 Some plants of canes.

b. A young tree or sapling used as a pole, staff, or cudgel. Now chiefly *dial.*

1377 LANGL. *P. Pl.* B. XVI. 50 Þanne *liberum arbitrium* laccheth þe thridde plante. *c* **1450** *Merlin* 493 He caught a plante of an appell tre..and toke the barre in bothe handes, and seide he wolde make hem to remeve. *c* **1600** DAY *Begg. Bednall Gr.* v. (1881) 109 An ashen plant, a good Cudgell, what sho'd I call it? **1697** DRYDEN *Virg. Georg.* III. 638 Take, Shepherd, take a plant of stubborn oak And labour him with many a sturdy stroke. **1712** ADDISON *Spect.* No. 335 ¶2 Sir Roger's Servants..had..provided themselves with good Oaken Plants, to attend their Master upon this occasion. **1732** ELIZA HEYWOOD *Belle Assemblée* II. 121 This magnanimous Spaniard..having under his Habit, a good Sword, and a strong Oaken-Plant. **1900** MCILROY *Craiglinnie* v. 54 (Ulster) The country people came pouring in—each man carrying his ash 'plant'.

c. *fig.* Anything planted or springing up; a scion, offshoot, nurseling; a young person; a novice. Now *rare*.

1362 LANGL. *P. Pl.* A. I. 137 Loue is þe leuest þing þat vr lord askeþ, And eke þe playnt [*v. rr.* plante, plaunte, plonte] of pees. **1435** MISYN *Fire of Love* 5 Fyer of fraward lufe, þe whilk wastis burionyng of verteu, & norrysches þe plantes of all vyce. **1500–20** DUNBAR *Poems* lxxxvii. 30 Gret Gode ws graunt that we have long desirit, A plaunt to spring of thi successioun. **1648** GAGE *West Ind.* 175 The Inquisition.. considering them to be but new plants useth not such rigour with them. **1706** PHILLIPS, *Plant*, figuratively a young Man or Maid. **1812** *Sporting Mag.* XXXIX. 188 A plant from Bristol, a youth of tremendous power.

2. a. A member of the lower of the two series of organized living beings, i.e. of the vegetable kingdom; a vegetable; generally distinguished from an animal by the absence of locomotion and of special organs of sensation and digestion, and by the power of feeding wholly upon inorganic substances. (= mod.L. *planta* in botanical use.) Often popularly restricted to the smaller, esp. herbaceous plants, to the exclusion of trees and shrubs.

1551 TURNER *Herbal* I. A ij, Yᵉ Knowlege of plantes, herbes, and trees. **1567** MAPLET *Gr. Forest* 26 b, Plants be sorted and deuided into three parts: the first is the Herbe: the seconde the Shrub: the third the Tree. **1696** PHILLIPS (ed. 5), *Plant*, a Natural Body that has a vegetable Soul. **1704** J. HARRIS *Lex. Techn.* I. s.v., The Learned and Experienced Botanist, Mr. John Ray, gives us the following Characteristick Notes of the Chief Kinds of Plants. **1748** GRAY *Alliance* 1 Sickly Plants betray a niggard Earth. **1776** WITHERING *Brit. Plants* (1796) II. 180 Betula. Flowers male and female on the same plant. **1830** J. G. STRUTT *Sylva Brit.* 36 The original dimensions of this venerable plant. **1884** J. TAIT *Mind in Matter* (1892) 81 Plants, because it is their nature to produce leaves, may, by an over-plus of food, produce nothing else.

b. *fig.*

1594 SHAKS. *Rich. III*, IV. iv. 395 The Parents liue, whose Children thou hast butcher'd, Old barren Plants, to waile it with their Age. **1844** EMERSON *Lect., Yng. Amer.* Wks. (Bohn) II. 300 Government has been a fossil; it should be a plant. **1869** LECKY *Europ. Mor.* II. i. 41 Christianity alone was powerful enough to tear this evil plant from the Roman soil.

c. Sometimes applied to the leafy or herbaceous part of a vegetable.

1693 EVELYN *De la Quint. Compl. Gard.* II. 144 Leeks.. Replanted in the Month of May, very deep in the Earth, to make their Stalks and Plants thick and white.

II. Chiefly from PLANT *v.*

3. a. *collect.* A growth of something planted or sown; a crop.

1832 *Veg. Subst. Food* 199 To insure a good crop of barley and a kind plant of clover. **1846** *Jrnl. R. Agric. Soc.* VII. II. 288 The promising plant of wheat which covered it was laid ..by the rough weather. **1898** RIDER HAGGARD in *Longm. Mag.* Oct. 513 There was a very full plant of swedes, which would have produced a fine crop.

b. *abstr.* Growth. ***in plant***, growing, in leaf; ***to lose plant***, to die off, dwindle away; ***to fail in*** or ***miss plant***, to fail to spring from seed.

1844 *Jrnl. R. Agric. Soc.* V. I. 4 Clover..if sown oftener it is apt to fail in plant; and even when in plant it is not very productive unless highly manured. **1847** *Ibid.* VIII. II. 291 The spaces in the..turnips, which have missed plant, are filled up with transplanted swedes. **1852** *Ibid.* XIII. I. 58 The wheat often loses plant in the spring.

c. = *plant-cane* s.v. PLANT *sb.*[1] 11 e.

1866 'MARK TWAIN' *Lett. fr. Hawaii* (1967) xix. 209 Almost everywhere on the island of Hawaii sugarcane matures in twelve months, both ratoons and plant. *Ibid.* xxiii. 258 This year the 'plant' crop on the Wailuku plantation averages 8,000 [pounds per acre].

4. The way in which any one plants himself or is planted; footing, foothold, pose.

1817 *Sporting Mag.* L. 2 The wide area between his feet, when in a standing position, gave him so firm a 'plant', if I may so say. **1889** *Macm. Mag.* Mar. 277/1 There was doggedness and obstinacy in the plant of the figures.

5. A deposit of fish-spawn, fry, or oysters; *ellipt.* an oyster which has been bedded or is intended for bedding, as distinguished from a native. *U.S.*

6. a. The fixtures, implements, machinery, and apparatus used in carrying on any industrial process; the premises and fixtures of a business or (chiefly *U.S.*) of an institution; a place where an industrial process is carried on; also, a single machine or large piece of apparatus. Also *transf.*, the workers employed at a plant.

1789 MRS. PIOZZI *Journ. France* I. 133 The ground was destined to the purposes of extensive commerce, but the appellation of a plant gave me much disturbance, from my inability to fathom the meaning. **1838** *Civil Eng. & Arch. Jrnl.* I. 239/2 There was very little possibility of transferring these implements (technically called the Plant) from one contract to another. **1867** W. W. SMYTH *Coal & Coalmining* 110 In Durham and Northumberland a single 'plant' of pits and engines will work the ground for a mile or two on each side. **1882** *Engineer* 24 Feb. 133/2 The plant includes one steam crane, three steam travelling cranes, a steam fire-engine, a steam pump, two steam hammers, seven steam engines, three boilers, and a few hundred nail-making machines. **1894** *Westm. Gaz.* 30 Apr. 5/1 Six plants in the coke region of Pennsylvania are now in operation. **1904** W. T. MILLS *Struggle for Existence* III. xvii. 216 The great steel plants maintain great laboratories. **1922** *Managem. Engin.* Feb., 86/2 No more time is lost by having all the plant out on strike for a week than in having a tenth of the force absent for 10 weeks. **1925** *Scribner's Mag.* July 31/2 (Advt.), Irving School for boys... Modern plant, complete equipment. **1927** *Brit. Med. Jrnl.* 3 Sept. 374/1 To those American investigators a school meant buildings, equipment, and machinery, or 'plant' as they themselves would say. **1930** J. BUCHAN *Castle Gay* xii. 194 He made his way round to the back regions, which had once been stables and coach-houses, and housed now the electric plant and a repairing shop for cars. **1939** D. L. SAYERS *In Teeth of Evidence* 9 They all want to..play with the apparatus. One of them got loose last time and tried to electrocute itself on the X-ray plant. **1949** *Sat. Rev. Lit.* 21 May 4/3 Its guiding genius.. has seen this school grow from an abstract idea to a two-million-dollar plant. **1957** J. H. ARNISON *Pract. Road Constr.* iii. 52 The shafts for the manholes may be cut out by manual labour, and the main trench by mechanical plant. **1958** *Engineering* 14 Mar. 322/2 Most of the plants benefiting from this influx of dollars are in the Glasgow area. **1958** *Times Lit. Suppl.* 10 Oct. 569/2 The new church 'plant' ..is one of the most impressive and novel signs of the boom atmosphere. Mormons, Catholics, Methodists, Seventh

Day Adventists, all flourish, to judge by the ecclesiastical building boom. **1960** *Washington Post* 16 Nov. A 16 The institution has almost never received adequate funds, is understaffed, has an inadequate and deteriorating physical plant and is 'on its way to becoming a second rate municipal zoo'. **1963** *Times Rev. Industry* Mar. 51/2 Mr. Justice Pennycuick..said that 'plant', in its ordinary sense, 'includes whatever apparatus is used by a businessman for carrying on his business' . **1971** B. SCHARF *Engin. & its Language* xvii. 245 Examples of mobile earthmoving plant are bulldozers, graders and scrapers. **1972** J. MOSEDALE *Football* xi. 150 Workers at the meat packing plants. **1973** *Times* 16 Nov. 20/8 At plant level, the [German] philosophy is the shared responsibility of capital and labour for the growth of the enterprise. **1977** *Jrnl. R. Soc. Arts* CXXV. 300/2 With the reduction of teacher training the amount of surplus 'plant' becoming available would eliminate capital construction costs.

b. *fig.* The instrumentalities employed in carrying on spiritual or intellectual work.

1861 LD. LINDSAY *Scepticism* 341 We must take stock here, likewise, of our spiritual plant, our intellectual capital. **1881** *Nation* (N.Y.) XXXII. 437 The college is to him a sort of industrial enterprise,..and the professors are part of the plant. **1887** *Ch. Times* 21 Jan. 54/3 The policy of increasing the plant of the Roman Catholic body here..is still pursued.

c. *Austral.* The equipment, stock, vehicles, etc., of a drover, a farm, a road-mending team, etc.

1901 H. LAWSON *Prose Wks.* (1948) 427 Andy had charge of the 'droving-plant' (a tilted two-horse wagonette, in which we carried the rations and horse-feed). **1903** 'T. COLLINS' *Such is Life* 7 Soon we became aware of two teams coming to meet us... Victorian poverty spoke in every detail of the working plant. **1928** 'BRENT OF BIN BIN' *Up Country* xvii. 290 Charlotte was to have her cows and poultry, so that when the diggings were played out there would be a grazier's plant to fall back upon. **1934** *Bulletin* (Sydney) 31 Jan. 32/2 Although he knew our standard of horsemanship so well, he is so ignorant of our calling as to refer to my plant as my 'herd'. **1954** B. MILES *Stars my Blanket* xxiv. 211 He..was then about to return to Elsey with his 'plant'—a drover's 'plant' being his spare horses and packs. **1963** A. LUBBOCK *Austral. Roundabout* 42 'That'll be Dan Daley with his droving plant,' said Barney, shading his eyes. 'Plant?' I queried. 'Outfit—we call it "plant" here.'

7. a. [f. PLANT *v.* 8.] A hoard of stolen goods; also the place where they are hidden. Also, a hiding-place for people or goods; the people or goods so hidden; *spec.* (a hiding-place for) drugs or equipment used by a drug-addict. *slang.*

1785 *Sessions Papers of Central Criminal Court* Apr. 582/1 He opened a place in the wainscot, which is called 'a plant', it was a secret cupboard. **1796** *Grose's Dict. Vulg. T.* (ed. 3), *Plant*, the place in the house of the fence, where stolen goods are secreted. **1812** J. H. VAUX *Flash Dict.* s.v., Any thing hid is called, *the plant*,..such article is said to be *in plant*; the place of concealment is sometimes called *the plant*, as 'I know of a fine plant'; that is a secure hiding-place. To *spring a plant*, is to find any thing that has been concealed by another. To *rise the plant*, is to take up and remove any thing that has been hid, whether by yourself or another. **1829** H. WIDOWSON *Present State of Van Diemen's Land* xi. 118 The slabs were very loose; on pulling them up, the plant was sprung and mutton in abundance was discovered stowed away in a large barrel. **1837** J. D. LANG *New S. Wales* II. 52 He had found, to his astonishment and disappointment, that some person had *sprung the plant*—a cant phrase for discovering and carrying off property which another person has stolen and concealed. **1846** [see DUNNY *sb.*[2] 1]. **1874** HOTTEN *Slang Dict.* 256 *Plant*, a hidden store of money or valuables. To 'spring a plant' is to unearth another person's hoard. **1926** J. BLACK *You can't Win* xii. 160 The sack contained his 'plant', an eye dropper with a hypodermic needle soldered to it, and a small paper of morphine. *Ibid.* xx. 314, I could lift the plant and be far away before daylight. **1967** S. LLOYD *Lightning Ridge Bk.* iii. 8 Gibson never located this plant of opal again.

b. A person who, or thing which, has been 'planted' (see PLANT *v.* 2 c). *slang.*

1926 *Amer. Speech* I. 436/2 *Plant*, a member of an act planted in the audience or the orchestra pit who performs his share of the act from there, or who comes upon the stage from the audience to take part in the performance as a supposed non-member of the profession. **1949** *Newsweek* 3 Oct. 36/3 Fifteen government witnesses, a half-dozen of them FBI 'plants' who infiltrated the Communist Party, had taken the stand. **1952** KOESTLER *Arrow in Blue* IV. xxiii. 191 One of her favourite pastimes was to fabricate apocryphal news items... One of the most successful of her plants ran something as follows. **1969** *TV Times* (Austral.) 15 Oct. 10/3 One Press agent made an interesting slip of the tongue when he commented: 'The first thing any publicist does in the morning is to read the plants, I mean the trades.' **1978** G. VAUGHAN *Belgrade Drop* ii. 15 'Heroin!' the detective shouted... Yardley had never seen the package before... He said: 'That stuff's a plant.' **1978** M. WALKER *Infiltrator* iv. 48 If she was a plant... I would have to take her along, ..and find out who had planted her and why.

8. A scheme or plot laid to swindle or defraud a person; an elaborately planned burglary or other form of theft or robbery. (The notion appears to be that of a trap or snare carefully planted or laid in the ground and covered up.) *Sharpers' slang.*

1825 C. M. WESTMACOTT *Eng. Spy* I. 241 A regular plant to clear me out. **1836** DICKENS *Sk. Boz, Greenwich Fair*, The 'plant' is successful, the bet is made, the stranger of course loses. **1837** —— *Pickw.* xlviii, 'It's a conspiracy', said Ben Allen. 'A regular plant', added Mr. Bob Sawyer. **1860** GEN. P. THOMPSON *Audi Alt.* III. cxliii. 124 When the classes who live by warfare with society, lay a deliberate scheme by which an honest man's house is to be entered, or his property carried off, it takes at the Police Offices the title of a 'plant'. **1884** *Pall Mall G.* 20 Feb. 4 He..charges.. Blackburn with having, in language, which has recently become parliamentary, 'put up a plant' on his innocent young friend.

9. [f. PLANT *v.* 2 c.] A spy, a detective; a picket of detectives. *slang.*

1812 *Sporting Mag.* XXXIX. 210 He sold forged notes to a plant [*note* A person sent for the purpose of detecting him] which led to his untimely end. **1880** *Daily Tel.* 26 Nov., At Shepperton Lock the keeper..cautioned the defendant as he was going through the lock to take care, as there was a 'plant' out that night. *Mod.* A plant set to detect motorists travelling at illegal speed.

10. *Billiards, Snooker*, etc. In a situation where two balls (usu. reds) are touching: a shot whereby the cue-ball strikes one of them so as to pot the other; the result of this shot.

1884 W. COOK *Billiards* xxiv. 132 There are circumstances under which..the smash becomes..the undoubted game, and this is when there is a 'plant' on. **1896** W. BROADFOOT et al. *Billiards* iii. 106 The plant is still possible when the line through the centres falls slightly to the right or left of the pocket. **1937** H. LINDRUM *Billiards & Snooker* 103 B is called a 'dead plant'. The two reds are touching and in a line with middle of pocket. **1954** *Billiards & Snooker* ('Know the Game' Ser.) 32/2 *Set* or *Plant*. The two terms have become practically synonymous... They apply to a position in which two balls (invariably reds) are touching one another. In such a position it is possible to pot one or other of the balls by contacting..the ball nearer the pocket, or..the further one... Correct contact on the ball further from the pocket gives the necessary direction to the one nearer the pocket. **1985** *Guardian* 29 Apr. 27/5 Taylor ..preferring a speculative plant to the middle pocket to an open red playing onto a low value colour for safety.

III. *attrib.* and *Comb.*

11. a. Simple attrib., as ***plant-centre***, ***-covering***, ***-disease***, ***-egg***, ***-ferment***, ***-fetish***, ***-form***, ***-growth***, ***hire***, ***-kingdom***, ***-life***, ***-movement***, ***-name***, ***-ornament***, ***pot***, ***-remains***, ***-species***, ***-spirit***, ***-stand***, ***-wealth***, ***-world***. **b.** Appositive, as ***plant-ancestor***. **c.** Objective and obj. gen., as ***plant-dispersal***, ***-dropper***, ***-eater***, ***-eating***, ***-forcer***, ***-growing***, ***-hirer***, ***-hunting***, ***-naming***, ***-worship***, ***-worshipper***; ***plant-bearing***, ***-feeding***, ***-stimulating***, ***-sucking*** adjs. **d.** Instrumental, as ***plant-clothed***, ***-grown*** adjs.

1876 H. SPENCER *Princ. Sociol.* I. xxiii. §181 Now if an animal regarded as original progenitor, is therefore reverentially treated; so..may we expect the *plant-ancestor will be. **1894** *Geol. Mag.* Oct. 473 The Carboniferous *plant-bearing strata of Roberts' valley. **1894** *Board Agric. Circular* x. 4 These traps..should be placed close to the [hop] hills or *plant-centres. **1880** A. R. WALLACE *Isl. Life* 250 Fruits eaten by birds afford a means of *plant-dispersal. **1862** H. SPENCER *First Princ.* II. xiv. §110 Among animals the flesh-eaters cannot exist without the *plant-eaters. **1905** V. L. KELLOGG *Amer. Insects* xii. 252 (*Plant-eating beetles.) Tribe Phytophaga. **1941** J. S. HUXLEY *Uniqueness of Man* vi. 157 The best-analysed cases concern..plant-eating insects adapted to different food plants. **1973** W. S. ROMOSER *Science of Entomology* vii. 186 Phytophagous means literally 'plant eating'. **1684** T. BURNET *Th. Earth* I. 197 This is not necessary in *plant-eggs or vegetable seeds. **1778** [W. MARSHALL] *Minutes Agric.* 23 Oct. an. 1775, The manure is..equally incorporated with the *plant-feeding stratum. **1899** *Daily News* 22 Feb. 6/3 The belief in *plant-fetishes, wherein the informing spirit or ghost occupies the place of natural property. **1875** BENNETT & DYER *Sachs's Bot.* 130 In the same manner, from a morphological point of view, stems, leaves, hairs, roots, thallus-branches, are simply members of the *plant-form. **1902** *Daily Chron.* 29 Apr. 3/3 The wild *plant-grown embankments of railway cuttings. *Ibid.* 10 July 3/4 Means.. for restraining injurious *plant-growth or for disposing of an insect pest. **1976** 'L. BLACK' *Healthy Way to Die* xi. 118 There were thirty-five companies ranging from a merchant bank to..a *plant-hire outfit. **1978** J. SHERWOOD *Limericks of Lachasse* xi. 133 Get on to that plant hire place..and get them to have an excavator up here..to dig up the car park. **1973** *Times* 11 May 19/5 *Plant hirers are able to offer such machines. **1878** HOOKER & BALL *Marocco* 346 Ball enjoyed a capital day's *plant-hunting at Tangier. **1884** R. FOLKARD *Plant Lore* (title-p.) Folk-Lore of the *Plant-Kingdom. **1862** H. SPENCER *First Princ.* II. viii. §70 *Plant-life is all directly or indirectly dependant on the heat and light of the sun. **1894** *Persian Pict.* 183 A luxuriant plant-life covered every stem and log. **1594** *La Primaud. Fr. Acad.* II. 134 A name [*Zoophyta*], which in our language signifieth as much as *plant-liuing creatures. **1878** BRITTEN & HOLLAND (*title*) A Dictionary of English *Plant-names. **1898** M. A. BUCKMASTER *Elem. Archit.* 26 The acanthus..was the favourite *plant-ornament with the Greeks and Romans. **1963** *Times* 21 Jan. 15/1 The Italian company..plans to make *plant pots for the horticultural trade. **1975** D. CLARK *Premedicated Murder* iv. 52 They both said yes together, like plant-pot men. **1977** G. SCOTT *Hot Pursuit* vii. 68 The shelves were filled with files and papers and plant pots. **1880** A. R. WALLACE *Isl. Life* 195 Proofs of a mild Arctic climate, in the abundant *plant-remains of East Siberia and Amurland. **1876** H. SPENCER *Princ. Sociol.* I. xxiii. §182 No explanation of the conceived shape of the *plant-spirit. **1862** *Catal. Internat. Exhib., Brit.* II. No. 6070, Ornamental wire *plant-stands, model rosery, and verandah. **1903** K. D. WIGGIN *Rebecca* 247 She buried her face in the blooming geraniums on Miss Maxwell's plant-stand. **1974** *Trafford Catal.* Spring/Summer 591/2 Pedestal plant stand..with six variable position pot holders. **1908** *Westm. Gaz.* 30 May 7/3 There are very few who realise the enormous number of species that in reality make up this mischievous group of *plant-sucking parasites. **1969** *New Scientist* 2 Oct. 19/1 The Australian plantsucking psyllid bug..lives on eucalyptus leaves. **1936** E. SITWELL *Sel. Poems* 12 The ethereal quality of the *plant-world. **1876** H. SPENCER *Princ. Sociol.* I. xxiii. §183 *Plant-worship,..like the worship of idols and animals, is an aberrant species of ancestor-worship. **1883** *Century Mag.* Sept. 720/2 The ornament which we have derived from Chaldean *plant-worshippers.

e. Special Combs.: **plant-bed**, (*a*) a stratum containing fossil plants; (*b*) *U.S.*, a bed of earth prepared for the germination of seeds and the growth of young plants, esp. of tobacco seedlings; **plant-beetle**, a beetle of the family *Chrysomelidæ*, feeding on plants, a leaf-beetle; **plant-breeder**, one who cultivates plants with the object of improving existing varieties, or producing new ones; also **plant-breeding** *vbl. sb.*; **plant-cane**, a sugar-cane of one year's growth; **plant-cover(ing)**, vegetation spreading over the surface of the earth; **plant-cutter**, (*a*) a passerine bird of the S. American genus *Phytotoma*, having the habit of biting off the shoots of plants; (*b*) *U.S. Hist.*, (*pl.*) rioters in early times in Virginia, who systematically cut down the tobacco plants; **plant-feeder**, any animal that feeds upon plants; **plant-food**, a substance, or the substances collectively, on which plants feed; the food of plants; **plant geographer** = PHYTOGEOGRAPHER; **plant geography** = PHYTOGEOGRAPHY; **plant hormone** = HORMONE 2, PHYTOHORMONE; **plant-house**, (*a*) a greenhouse or conservatory; (*b*) a building containing industrial plant; **plant-marker**, a small tablet of wood, zinc, terra-cotta, etc., set in the ground beside a plant, and bearing its name; **plant-of-gluttony**, rendering of Gael. *lus-a-chraois*, name for the dwarf cornel, *Cornus suecica*, the berries of which are reputed to stimulate the appetite (*Treas. Bot.* 1866 s.v. *Cornus*); **plant pathology** = *phytopathology* (*a*) s.v. PHYTO-; so **plant pathologist**; **plant physiology**, the scientific study of the normal functions and phenomena of plants; so **plant physiologist**; † **plant-plot**, a nursery for young plants; **plant-tin**, a tinned vessel for carrying plants, a botanical case or vasculum; **plant-wax**, wax obtained from plants.

1833 *Niles' Reg.* XLIV. 411/1 He is clearing new grounds; preparing and burning *plant-beds. **1881** *Rep. Geol. Explor. N. Zealand* 48 The Mataura series in the Hokanui Hills overlying the plant-beds. **1907** *St. Nicholas* May 651/1 A 'running' board was put around the base and a plant bed about a foot wide made within this. **1966** *Publ. Amer. Dial. Soc.* XLV. 20 We put cotton canvas over the plant bed. **1816** KIRBY & SP. *Entomol.* xxiii. (1818) II. 321 The beautiful tribe of *plant-beetles (*Chrysomela*, F.). **1906** *Chambers's Jrnl.* 28 July 556/2 The experiments open up a new and interesting field for the *plant-breeder. **1929** T. THOMSON tr. *Büsgen's Structure & Life of Forest Trees* xiv. 403 The expert eye of the plant breeder is able to discover them [*sc.* individual differences between plants]. **1970** R. GORER *Development of Garden Flowers* i. 26 To the plant breeder, the importance and interest of germ cell formation lies in the first stage of meiosis. **1908** *Westm. Gaz.* 28 Mar. 6/2 Few who are making a study of the fundamental principles of *plant-breeding are unfamiliar with the name and the results achieved by Luther Burbank. **1926** J. S. HUXLEY *Essays in Pop. Sci.* ii. 10 There has sprung into being a new science, of animal- and plant-breeding. **1970** R. GORER *Development of Garden Flowers* i. 21 The essential basis of plant breeding is selection. **1790** W. BECKFORD *Descr. Account Island of Jamaica* I. 161 It is a common practice, where corn will grow, to plant it with the canes... Among *plant-canes, I do not conceive it of consequence. **1793** EDWARDS *W. Indies* II. v. i. 210 Plant-canes in this soil.. have been known in very fine seasons to yield two tons and a half of sugar per acre. **1853** *Harper's Mag.* Nov. 757 The 'growing crop' in Louisiana consists of three kinds of cane: the first is technically called 'plant cane' and is that which springs directly from the 'seed cane'. **1949** *Caribbean Quarterly* I. I. 5 A cane field was not ripe for its first harvest (the 'plant cane') until the second winter after its planting. **1943** J. S. HUXLEY *TVA* 17 Forests and *plant cover were stripped. **1976** *Field* 18 Nov. 976/3 Where the vegetation has been worn away, the shade of the plant cover lost.., evaporation from the bare surface proceeds apace. **1911** W. G. SMITH in A. G. Tansley *Types Brit. Vegetation* xiii. 312 The *plant covering is distinctly xerophilous in response to frequent dry periods. **1946** *Nature* 2 Nov. 605/1 Nomadism ..a mode of life, indeed, in which defacement of the plant-covering by ploughing or digging is the worst of economic offences. **1802** LATHAM *Gen. Synops. Birds* Supp. II. 212 *Plant-cutter. **1894** in NEWTON *Dict. Birds* 730. **1869** *Rep. U.S. Comm. Agric. 1868* 396 Such *plant-food as rain-water and the atmosphere supply. **1887** MOLONEY *Forestry W. Afr.* 101 Virgin forest soil is considered best..because it contains sufficient plant-food. **1902** *Westm. Gaz.* 17 June 12/2 There is no substance so rich in plant-food as the carcass of an animal. **1939** LAWRENCE & NEWELL *Seed & Potting Composts* ii. 23 These chemical compounds absorbed by the plant..we shall refer to as 'plant foods'. **1976** J. BERRISFORD *Backyards & Tiny Gardens* viii. 59 Such a growing medium contains no plant foods, so fertilizers must be added before planting. **1913** *Jrnl. Ecology* I. 27 This character [*sc.* the physiognomy of vegetation] is unjustly regarded as merely superficial..by many modern *plant-geographers. **1973** P. A. COLINVAUX *Introd. Ecol.* ii. 27 On the grand-scale, maps of climate based on the plant geographer's boundaries were useful. **1903** W. R. FISHER tr. *Schimper's Plant-Geogr.* p. vi, The connexion between the forms of plants and the external conditions at different points on the earth's surface forms the subject-matter of oecological *plant-geography. **1934** H. GILBERT-CARTER tr. *Raunkiaer's Life Forms of Plants* iv. 111 The units of floristic plant geography are the same as those of systematic botany. **1977** *Sci. Amer.* May 99/1 Specimens were collected and filed in herbaria for later investigation by new techniques ranging from cytology and physiology to plant geography and ecology. **1935** *Biol. Rev.* X. 429 Other *plant hormones, such as the wound hormones of Haberlandt, we need not discuss, since less quantitative knowledge is available on the subject. They apparently also act by diffusion from cell to cell. **1951**, etc. [see HORMONE 2]. **1959** L. J. AUDUS *Plant Growth Substances* i. 18 Plant hormones are substances which regulate..some aspect of plant growth and which are produced by the organism itself. They may be growth hormones, flowering hormones, and so forth. **1974** *Physiologia Plantarum* XXXII. 369 (*heading*) Effect of abscisic acid and other plant hormones on growth of apical and lateral buds of seedlings. **1863** *Horticulturist* XVIII. 306 We again have the satisfaction of presenting two examples of *Plant Houses; one a *Green-house*, and the other a *Cold Grapery*. **1881** *Encycl. Brit.* XII. 221/2 Plant houses must be as far as possible impervious to wet and cold air from the exterior. **1909** *Westm. Gaz.* 6 May 5/3 A plant-house is being erected outside the south wall of the provincial capital. **1909** B. M. DUGGAR *Fungous Diseases of Plants* 3 There was a bright prospect for controlling many of the fungous diseases of plants, and there developed..an immediate need for *plant pathologists. **1977** *Daily Tel.* 6 July 2/1 Dr Alan Walker, Ministry Plant Pathologist, said that cereal diseases which could cut yield by up to 15 per cent. were minimal this year. **1895** *Jrnl. Chem. Soc.* LXVIII. 11 (*heading*) Chemical investigations in *plant pathology. **1908** P. T. DONDLINGER *Bk. of Wheat* ix. 148 Studies in plant pathology of any great practical bearing or importance are..modern and recent. **1935** *Discovery* Oct. 294/1 The intimate relationships between plant pathology.. and other branches of botany. **1973** *Nature* 27 Apr. 595/2 Plant pathology..is to plants what the whole of medicine and veterinary science is to man and animals. *Ibid.* 596/1 Is it right that any comprehensive book on the principles of plant pathology should dismiss viruses and mycoplasmata with thirty-six pages and an apology? **1931** W. O. JAMES *Introd. Plant Physiol.* i. 2 The methods used by *plant physiologists..are mainly derived from various branches of chemistry and physics. **1898** S. A. MOOR tr. *W. Detmer's Pract. Plant Physiol.* p. vii, *Plant physiology is now of.. far-reaching significance for students of Natural Science, Agriculture, Forestry, and Medicine. **1937** W. H. SAUMAREZ SMITH *Let.* 10 July in *Young Man's Country* (1977) ii. 80, I was interested to see the place where all his [*sc.* Tagore's] disciples are following out the lines of research suggested by his highly original work in plant-physiology. **1968** F. C. STEWARD *Growth & Organization in Plants* p. iii, The author's, and indeed a customary, approach to plant physiology is deeply ingrained in the study of cells, their membranes and particulate inclusions, their metabolism and responses to stimuli. **1610** HOLLAND *Camden's Brit.* (1637) 100 Tributes also were imposed..for Corne-grounds, *plant-plots, groves or parks. **1611** SPEED *Theat. Gt. Brit.* xxiii. (1614) 45/2 From Creekelad a towne in Wiltshire, the Academie was translated unto Oxford, as unto a plant-plot, both more pleasing and fruitfull. **1896** *Daily News* 12 Dec. 6/2 In the winter there is no occupation for *plant-tin or insect-net. **1924** J. A. THOMSON *Science Old & New* xviii. 101 There are *plant-waxes as well as animal-waxes.

†**plant**, *sb.*² *Obs.* Also 4–6 **plaunte**, 5–6 **plante**. [ME. *pla(u)nte*, a. F. *plante*:—L. *planta* sole of the foot.] The sole of the foot.

1382 WYCLIF *Acts* iii. 7 Anoon the groundis and plauntis [*gloss* or solis] of him ben saddid to gidere; and he lippinge stood, and wandride. **1483** CAXTON *Gold. Leg.* 15/2 Fro the plante of his foot vnto the toppe of his heed was none hole place. **1580** SIDNEY *Ps.* XVIII. x, My heeles and plants Thou didst from stumbling slip sustaine. **1610** B. JONSON *Masque of Oberon* Wks. (Rtldg.) 584/2 Knotty legs, and plants of clay, Seek for ease, or love delay. **1655** tr. *Com. Hist. Francion* XII. 24 Before you put the Iron to the plant of his Feet, give me a cord.

†**plant**, *sb.*³ *Obs. rare.* [a. F. *plant*, in obs. use 'the ground-plant of a building; also, the foundation, or ground-worke of a building; also, a planting' (Cotgr.), f. stem of *planter* to plant. Cf. It. *pianta* a ground-plan.] A ground-plan.

1624 WOTTON *Archit.* in *Reliq.* (1651) 256 Much less upon a bare *Plant* thereof, as they call the Schiographia or Ground lines. **1665** J. WEBB *Stone-Heng* (1725) 20 The outward Circle of Mr. Jones his Plant No. 6 of the Ruins. *Ibid.* 25 The Plant of the main Structure is in Diameter, one third Part of the Diameter of the whole Extent, or Circumvallation.

plant (plɑːnt, -æ-), *v.* Forms: α. 1 **plantian, plontian**, 2–4 **plant(i)en**, 4–5 **plau-, plawnte(n**, 4–6 **plante**, 5 **plonte, plaunt**, (5 *Sc.* **playnt**, 8 **plaint**), 5– **plant**. [OE. *plantian*, ad. L. *plantāre* to plant, fix in place: cf. PLANT *sb.*¹ The sense-development agrees in the main with that of F. *planter* (12th c.) (:—L. *plantāre*).]

I. To plant a thing in or on a place.

1. a. *trans.* To set or place in the ground so that it may take root and grow (a living tree or herb, a shoot, cutting, root, bulb, or tuber; sometimes, a seed; also, by extension, a crop, a bed of flowers, a garden, vineyard, orchard, forest, or other collection of plants). Also *absol.*

c **825** *Vesp. Psalter* lxxix. 9 [lxxx. 8] Wingeard of Ægyptum ðu afirdes awurpe ðeode & plantades hie. *c* **897** K. ÆLFRED *Gregory's Past. C.* xl. 292 He underfeng ða halgan ȝesamnunga to plantianne & to ymbhweorfanne, swæ se ceorl deð his ortȝeard. *c* **1000** ÆLFRIC *Gen.* xxi. 33 Abraham þa plantode ænne holt. *c* **1200** *Vices & Virtues* 51 Ys ȝeplanted an iblesced treu amidde ðare hali chereche. *a* **1300** *Cursor M.* 8239 (Cott.) All frutes he plantede in þat place. *c* **1380** WYCLIF *Sel. Wks.* III. 91 Plaunt þou a vine. *c* **1400** MAUNDEV. (Roxb.) xxx. 137 He gert plant þerin all maner of erbez. **1526** TINDALE *1 Cor.* iii. 6–7, I have planted; Apollo watred..Nether is he that planteth eny thynge nether he that watreth. **1697** DRYDEN *Virg. Georg.* IV. 25 Plant..Wild Olive Trees, or Palms, before the busie Shop. **1752** HUME *Ess. & Treat.* (1777) I. II. v. 334 There are many edicts of the French king, prohibiting the planting of new vineyards. **1849** LYTTON *Caxtons* II. iii, You can plant a very extensive apple-orchard on a grand scale. **1868** Q. VICTORIA *Life Highl.* 19 Each of us planted two trees, a fir and an oak. **1893** B. MITFORD *Gun-Runner* iv. 34 Along the banks of this [watercourse] the careful Jeremiah had planted and sown. **1896** *Forum* July 515 Our forefathers..came to work, to plant, to reap, where they might worship God with freedom. **1961** *Atlanta Constitution* 17 Aug. 5 The people who try to raise and can meat, to plant, grow vegetables, and put them up. **1979** *Verbatim* Summer 8/1 In South Australia a farmer *seeds*,..and in Queensland he *plants*.

b. To introduce (a breed of animals) into a country; to deposit (young fish, spawn, oysters) in a river, tidal water, etc.; to naturalize.

1899 *19th Cent.* Sept. 405 Brought from the Pacific and 'planted' in the Great Lakes, these steel-heads are the most prized of all the Salmonidae. **1903** *Daily Chron.* 25 Mar. 7/2 Mr. Henry Herman Kater..in 1839 chartered the Euphrates for the purpose of planting blood horses in Australia.

c. ***plant out***, to transfer from a pot or frame to the open ground; to set out (seedlings) at intervals, so as to afford room for growth; also, to arrange plants or trees in a piece of ground. Also *transf.* and *fig.* (cf. sense 6).

1664 J. EVELYN *Kalendarium Hortense* 60 Now also plant out your Colly-flowers to have early. **1793** *Trans. Soc. Arts* (ed. 2) V. 54 When they [plants] are planted out, after once hoeing, they will take care of themselves. **1846** J. BAXTER *Libr. Pract. Agric.* (ed. 4) I. 323 The more tender kinds should not be thinned till some time after they have been planted out. **1858** GLENNY *Gard. Every-day Bk.* 179/1 Plant out all the sorts and sow once or twice others to succeed. **1901** *Year-bk. U.S. Dept. Agric. 1900* 373 Each orchardist will no doubt develop some method of his own in planting out the orchard. *a* **1910** 'MARK TWAIN' *Autobiogr.* (1924) I. 274 They would often plant out eleven columns of new ads on a standing galley. **1917** P. S. ALLEN *Let.* 8 July (1939) 139 So many of your books are here 'on deposit'... I wonder if you recognised what was in my mind..when I wrote of Rud. Agricola's 'planting out his books in friends' houses as pledges of return'. **1927** KIPLING *Limits & Renewals* (1932) 170, I was planting out plants from my garden. **1962** *Times* 19 May 11/4 Every partridge-rearing system encounters its critical phase when the birds are 'planted out'. **1972** *Shooting Times & Country Mag.* 4 Mar. 24/3 'Unfed fry' [*sc.* trout]..are ready to be planted out to start off their natural lives in the sidestreams and the river. **1975** B. DOUGHERTY *Green Gardener* x. 115 Avoid touching their [*sc.* tomatoes'] stems when planting out, holding them only by the leaflets.

d. *intr.* Of seed: To grow into or form plants.

Cf. PLANT *sb.*¹ 3, from which this is perh. directly taken.

1849 *Jrnl. R. Agric. Soc.* X. I. 55 The seed was put in precisely the same as [in] the preceding year, but it never planted so well.

2. a. To insert, set, or place firmly, to fix *in* or *on* the ground or any other body or surface; to set *down* or *up* in a firm position; to put or fix in position; to post, station.

1382 WYCLIF *Ps.* xciii. [xciv.] 9 He that plauntide the ere, shal he not heren? *c* **1450** *Two Cookery-bks.* 98 Make faire lowe coffyns, and couche þis stuff there-in, And plonte pynes aboue. *c* **1470** *Gol. & Gaw.* 312 Thai plantit doun ane pailyeoun. **1598** BARRET *Theor. Warres* III. i. 36 Hee is to be taught how to plant his pike on the ground. **1687** A. LOVELL tr. *Thevenot's Trav.* III. 26 The Banners which the Banians had planted on the top and highest Branches of it. **1712** J. JAMES tr. *Le Blond's Gardening* 89 In the..Point of Intersection, plant the Stake H. **1714** *Lond. Gaz.* No. 5248/2 He planted the British Colours on the Castle. *a* **1719** ADDISON *Rosamond* II. vi, Or this right hand performs its part, And plants a dagger in thy heart. **1849** MACAULAY *Hist. Eng.* ix. II. 485 As soon as the prince had planted his foot on dry ground he called for horses. **1853** KANE *Grinnell Exp.* xi. (1856) 82 To plant an ice-anchor, a hole is cut obliquely to the surface of the floe. **1874** BURNAND *My time* xv. 127 Planting her elbows on her knees. **1892** E. REEVES *Homeward Bound* 263 As the bull passes him, he has to plant these two darts at the same time in the back, and jump aside.

b. To put or place (artillery) in position for discharging. † *to plant a siege*, to lay siege.

1560 DAUS tr. *Sleidane's Comm.* 401 b, Plantyng your ordenaunce here and there on your walles and Bulwarkes. **1568** GRAFTON *Chron.* II. 748 The Capitaines..planted a strong siege, and enuironed it round about. **1604** E. GRIMSTONE *Hist. Siege Ostend* 214 The siege being planted before Escluse. **1688** R. HOLME *Armoury* III. xviii. (Roxb.) 140/2 Plant a peece, is to order it for it discharging that it may do service or execution. **1748** *Anson's Voy.* III. viii. 382 Four swivel guns..were planted at the mouth of each funnel. **1862** CARLYLE *Fredk. Gt.* XIII. iii. (1872) V. 39 Cannon with case-shot planted themselves in all the thoroughfares.

fig. **1650** FULLER *Pisgah* I. i. 1 This cavill is not planted particularly against my indevours.

c. To station (a person); *esp.* (in slang or vulgar use) to place for a surreptitious or unavowed purpose; to post as a spy or detective. Now esp., to conceal (stolen goods, incriminating evidence, etc.) with a view to misleading a later discoverer. Also (not *slang*), to introduce (a character, scene, etc.) into a play, film, etc., for some specified purpose.

1693 EVELYN *De la Quint. Compl. Gard.* II. 16 The Person must be dispos'd and planted near his Tree, in such a manner as to stand firm. **1706** J. DRAKE *Secret Mem. Earl of Leicester* Pref., The guard of his own creatures, spies and dependants which he had planted about her. **1764** FOOTE *Patron* III. Wks. 1799 I. 353 Intelligent people are planted, who will bring me..a faithful account of the process. **1777** WATSON *Philip II* (1793) I. VIII. 333 He planted strong guards along the banks of the river. **1842** COBDEN in Morley *Life* ix. (1902) 31/1 He was planted (to use a vulgar phrase) upon me by his party. **1865** J. H. A. BONE *Petroleum & Petroleum Wells* (ed. 2) 153 Frauds are not infrequently perpetrated by 'planting' oil in dry wells. **1892** ZANGWILL *Bow Mystery* 151 You plant one in my house to tell my secrets to Wimp, and you plant one in Wimp's house to tell Wimp's secrets to me. **1930** *Times Lit. Suppl.* 1 May 373/1 The nephew..sought to clinch the available, and misleading, evidence by planting the victim's dental plate on the spot. **1933** H. J. LEE *Eagle Police Manual* 152 *Plant*, to place incriminating evidence in a man's pocket or elsewhere. **1939** E. S. GARDNER *D. A. draws Circle* (1940) 200 Someone is planting evidence. *Ibid.* 203 It had been planted on him. **1948** A. HUXLEY *Let.* 16 Jan. (1969) 578, I have been trying to put this question to the general and specialized publics for the last year or two—even succeeding in planting it in the *Bulletin of the Atomic Scientists*. **1950** *Ibid.* 16 Feb. 619 We have to plant the business of the currants, so that we are forced to show them lunching. **1958** *Listener* 30 Oct. 704/3 The man was 'planted' as a nervous stammerer, but to be nervous is not necessarily to be a nitwit. **1969** *It* 11–24 Apr. 10/1 Everyone was searched and told to stay clear of the area under the threat of being planted. **1970** G. F. NEWMAN *Sir, You Bastard* 261 Planting microphones was easier. **1974** *Howard Jrnl.* XIV. 43 [The police] are now seen by many West Indians..as racist 'enemies', who taunt, intimidate, assault, plant and 'trump up' charges. **1978** S. BRILL *Teamsters* i. 18 Government investigators..had planted an informant among organized-crime figures in California.

d. *refl.* To place, station, post, fix oneself; to take up one's position.

1703 ROWE *Ulyss.* III. i. 1362 Remember well to plant thee at that Door. **1754** CHATHAM *Lett. Nephew* v. 34 Open your chest, place your head upright, and plant you well upon your legs. **1819** SCOTT *Ivanhoe* iii, One grisly old wolf-dog alone ..had planted himself close by the chair of state. **1871** L. STEPHEN *Playgr. Eur.* (1894) iii. 84 [They] persisted in planting themselves steadily in some safe nook.

3. a. To found, establish, institute (a community or society, esp. a colony, city, or church).

c **897** [see sense 1]. **1555** EDEN *Decades* 160 That they myght in this prouince plant a newe colonie or habitation. **1601** R. JOHNSON *Kingd. & Commw.* (1603) 146 This hapeneth by meanes of the Grimme Tartar, that will neither himselfe plant townes to dwell in..nor suffer the Russie.. to people those partes. *c* **1656** BRAMHALL *Replic.* iii. 153 Planting and ordering schools for the education of youth. **1676** I. MATHER *K. Philip's War* (1862) 40 In three and twenty Towns, there were Indian Christian Churches Planted. **1700** PRIOR *Carmen Seculare* 441 Let him unite his Subjects Hearts, Planting Societies for peaceful Arts. **1745** *De Foe's Eng. Tradesman* (1841) II. xli. 134 Planting colonies in New Jersey, Pennsylvania, and Carolina. **1878** MACLEAR *Celts* v. (1879) 88 They planted monasteries under abbot-bishops.

b. To settle (a person) in a place, establish as a settler or colonist. (Cf. PLANTATION 4.)

a **1300** *Cursor M.* 8033 (Cott.) Passed war a thousand yere, Sin þai war planted in þat place. *c* **1375** *Sc. Leg. Saints* ii. (*Paulus*) 452 Sut[h]faste hirdis, þat has þe playntit in hewine reme to be bettir and happliare. *c* **1425** *Eng. Conq. Irel.* 24 He, as largh man & good prynce..owr lond folke wyll setten & planten stydfastly yn þys lond, nowe & euer. **1535** COVERDALE *2 Sam.* vii. 10, I wyll appoynte a place, and wyll plante them, that they maye remayne there. *a* **1568** *Satir. Poems Reform.* xlvii. 89 In ȝour tolbuth sic presoun eris to plant. **1607** R. TINDALL in *Capt. Smith's Wks.* (Arb.) Introd. 38 Wee are safelye arryued and planted in this Contreye [Virginia]. **1672** PETTY *Pol. Anat.* (1691) 44 In some Counties, as in Kerry,..few English were ever planted. **1719** DE FOE *Crusoe* (1840) I. ix. 156 My being planted so well in Brazil. **1870** FREEMAN *Norm. Conq.* (ed. 2) I. ii. 11 Teutonic soldiers planted as colonists by the Roman government.

c. *refl.* To establish oneself, settle.

1560 DAUS tr. *Sleidane's Comm.* 98 b, To sette and plante himselfe there. **1699** BENTLEY *Phal.* 152 The Zanclæans invited the remainder of the Milesians to come and plant themselves in Sicily. **1871** FREEMAN *Norm. Conq.* (1876) IV. xviii. 230 Benedict, a monk of Auxerre, who planted himself in solitude among the wild forests by the Ouse.

†**d.** *absol.* or *intr.* To form a colony or colonies; to colonize; to settle. *Obs.*

1535 STEWART *Cron. Scot.* II. 459 How King Gregoure with his Power passit in Fyffe..and plantit and pleneist as he passit. **1555** W. WATREMAN *Fardle Facions* I. iii. 36 Thei ..made themselues cotages, and began to plante in plompes one by another. **1625** BACON *Ess., Plantations* (Arb.) 534 If you Plant, where Sauages are, doe not onely entertaine them with Trifles, and Gingles; But vse them iustly, and gratiously. **1725** DE FOE *Voy. round World* (1840) 159 It seems they are resolved to plant there.

4. To put, set, or place *in* some local position; to locate, situate; in *pa. pple.* situated. Also *fig.*

1558 *Act 1 Eliz.* c. 14 §4 Faire large townes..as well planted for cloth making as the sayd towne of Goddelmine or better. **1576** FLEMING *Panopl. Epist.* 110 In them I plant my chiefest pleasure. **1624** WOTTON *Archit.* in *Reliq.* (1651) 205 A Town..finely built, but foolishly planted. **1650** FULLER *Pisgah* I. ii. 5 Some perchance will place their scorn, where they ought to plant their wonder. **1856** STANLEY *Sinai & Pal.* iv. (1858) 226 If Neby-Samwil be the high place of Gibeon, then Mizpeh which Dr. Robinson planted there, must be sought elsewhere.

5. Various *fig.* uses derived from prec. senses.

a. To implant, cause to take root and spring up or grow; to introduce, e.g. an idea or sentiment in the mind.

1415 HOCCLEVE *To Sir J. Oldcastle* 68 Plante in thyn herte a deep contricioun. **1529** MORE *Dyaloge* I. Wks. 145/2 God ..euer shall kepe in his church the right faith and righte beleue by the helpe of his owne hande that planted it. **1538** STARKEY *England* I. i. 14 Thes vertues..by the bunfyte and powar of nature in hys hart are rotyd and plantyd. **1709** STEELE *Tatler* No. 77 ¶2 That noble Thirst of Fame and Reputation which is planted in the Hearts of all Men. **1878** MACLEAR *Celts* v. (1879) 78 It was his great aim to plant the truth in the minds of his hearers.

b. To fix, settle, establish firmly, as a principle, opinion, doctrine, religion, practice, or the like.

1529 MORE *Dyaloge* I. Wks. 159/1 Now were..ye pointes of Christes faith..knowen, as I saye and planted before. **1570–6** LAMBARDE *Peramb. Kent* (1826) 167 At variaunce with that opinion which Leland would plant. **1638** JUNIUS *Paint. Ancients* 309 If the history doth but once beginne to plant her image in our imagination. **1726** DE FOE *Hist. Devil* I. i. (1840) 5 [They] planted religion in those countries. **1857** LIVINGSTONE *Trav.* vi. 115 Christianity, as planted by modern missions.

c. To establish or set up (a person or thing) in some position or state.

a **1562** G. CAVENDISH *Wolsey* (1893) 230 Sir, ye do entend to delyver them [the keys]..and to plant an other in my rome. **1577** *F. de L'isle's Legendarie* G iv b, Therof ensued the order..established in the Kings council..wherein the Queene mother was planted vpright. **1588** SHAKS. *L.L.L.* I. i. 165 A man in all the worlds new fashion planted. **1593** —— *Rich. II*, v. i. 63 Thou which know'st the way To plant vnrightfull Kings. **1622** FLETCHER & MASS. *Span. Curate* II. i, He would entreat your care To plant me in the favour of some man. **1622** MISSELDEN *Free Trade* 97 They do what in them lyeth to plant their owne Draperies, and to supplant ours. **1874** S. COX *Pilgr. Ps.* i. 10 Planting himself on his habit of crying unto God in his distresses.

d. *intr.* for *refl.*

1580 SIDNEY *Ps.* XXV. vii, Such as keep His covenaunt, And on His testimonys plant. **1594** WILLOBIE *Avisa* XLV. v, No reason rules, where sorrowes plant.

II. With the place, etc., as object.

6. a. To furnish or stock (a piece of land) with growing plants. Also with *to*.

1585 T. WASHINGTON tr. *Nicholay's Voy.* I. xvi. 17 b, The earth is carried into it and planted with all sorts of excellent fruteful trees. **1600** J. PORY tr. *Leo's Africa* VIII. 303 The citie of Bochin..is now planted with date-trees. **1697** DRYDEN *Virg. Georg.* IV. 171 With wild Thyme and Sav'ry, plant the Plain. **1799** T. R. MALTHUS *Diary* 16 July (1966) 159 There are many grounds about the town planted to potatoes. **1838** DICKENS *Nich. Nick.* ii, It is not supposed that they were ever planted, but rather that they are pieces of unreclaimed land, with the withered vegetation of the original brick-field. **1901** *Year-bk. U.S. Dept. Agric. 1900* 373 The land should be planted to a crop for at least a year or two before setting out the trees. *a* **1907** *Mod.* He enclosed a piece of the common and planted it with firs. **1941** E. P. O'DONNELL *Great Big Doorstep* 92 She reached a field planted to okra, the stalks rising taller than she. **1949** E. HYAMS *Not in our Stars* xvi. 195 A four-acre field..which Drover had planted to cherries in the previous season. **1976** *National Observer* (U.S.) 12 June 9/1 Grapevines are now found..creeping into fields once planted to pears and apples.

b. To furnish or provide *with* a number of things set or disposed over the surface.

a **1400–50** *Alexander* 3146 þe sepulture of a sire..Was of an athill amatist..Plantid full of palmetres & many proud fowles. *c* **1470** HENRY *Wallace* VI. 345 Thai playntyt thar feild with tentis and pailȝonis. **1588** SHAKS. *Tit. A.* II. iii. 62 Thy Temples should be planted presently With Hornes. **1638** SIR T. HERBERT *Trav.* (ed. 2) 113 The Portugall..built a strong castle here, planted it with seventeene cannon..and a thousand musquets. **1711** ADDISON *Spect.* No. 159 ¶8 A vast Ocean planted with innumerable Islands. **1849** MACAULAY *Hist. Eng.* v. I. 556 A battery was planted with some small guns taken from the ships.

c. To furnish a district *with* settlers or colonists; to colonize or settle; to stock *with* inhabitants, cattle, etc.

c **1608** in *Buccleuch MSS.* (Hist. MSS. Comm.) I. 75 The necessity of planting Leitrim with the greater part of British. *a* **1677** HALE *Prim. Orig. Man.* II. vii. 195 He..grants that Iceland, and some part of Groenland were visited and planted by Ericus Ruffus. **1762** *Gentl. Mag.* 101 We cannot spare people to plant those islands. **1869** RAWLINSON *Anc. Hist.* 31 Planted it [Media] with cities. **1904** *Dundee Advert.* 5 July 6/3 The other 23 States being..thinly 'planted' with horned animals.

†**d.** To furnish (a vacant church) *with* a minister. *Sc. Obs.*

1574 in Row *Hist. Kirk* (Wodrow Soc.) 50 That vackand Kirks be planted, and stipends assigned to them. **1583** STUBBES *Anat. Abus.* II. (1882) 87 Most churches are planted and fraught with single reading ministers. **1721** WODROW *Hist. Ch. Scot.* I. iii. 119 The Bishops are appointed to plant the Kirks which have vaiked since the Year 1637.

III. Colloquial uses, of slang or vulgar origin.

7. a. To deliver (a blow, stroke, thrust) with a definite aim; to cause to alight or fall. (So F. *planter un soufflet sur...*) *Pugilistic slang.*

1808 *Sporting Mag.* XXXII. 76 Gully made play, and planted two other blows on his adversary's head. **1829** MARRYAT *F. Mildmay* xxvi, I planted a stomacher in his fifth button. **1883** F. M. PEARD *Contrad.* xxii, You know how to plant a straight blow just where it is most telling.

b. *fig.*

1847–8 H. MILLER *First Impr.* xix. (1857) 337 He finds every Highlander..adroit of fence, in planting upon him as many queries as can possibly be thrust in. **1882** STEVENSON *New Arab. Nts.* (1884) 96 The thin tones of Lady Vandaleur planting icy repartees at every opening.

8. To hide, to conceal; esp. stolen goods. orig. *Thieves' slang*; now esp. *Australian.*

1610 ROWLANDS *Martin Mark-all* E iij b, *To Plant*, to hide. *a* **1700** B. E. *Dict. Cant. Crew, Plant*, to lay, place, or hide. **1785** in GROSE *Dict. Vulg. Tongue.* **1812** J. H. VAUX *Flash Dict.* s.v., To hide, or conceal any person..is termed planting him. **1827** P. CUNNINGHAM *N.S. Wales* II. xxi. 60 'Pa! Bill has planted it' (hid it). **1837** J. D. LANG *N.S. Wales* II. 51 They..observed the robbers plant or conceal a quantity of the property, of which they had just plundered the cottage. **1840** *Sydney Herald* 10 Feb., Conveying horses out of the way, or *planting* them, as it is technically called, until a reward is offered for their restoration. **1902** *Daily Chron.* 29 Dec. 5/2 The plunder was 'planted' under the floor of a restaurant in Geelong.

9. a. To place (gold dust, ore, etc.) in a mining claim in order to give a false impression of its productiveness; to 'salt'. *Gold-digging slang.*

1850 READE *Gold* IV. i, *Levi.* This dust is from Birmingham, and neither Australian or natural. *Rob.* The man planted it for you. **1886** P. CLARKE *New Chum* vi. 72 A 'salted claim', a 'pit' sold for a £10 note in which a nugget worth a few shillings had before been 'planted'.

b. To plan or 'get up' by fraudulent methods; to devise as a 'plant' or fraudulent scheme.

1892 *Daily News* 27 May 3/4 Mr. Keay maintained that the affair was 'planted' between the two brothers, the Indian resident having..opportunities to carry out that object.

10. To abandon. [Cf. F. *planter là.*]

[**1814** SCOTT *Wav.* liii, And so he glided off and left me *planté là.*] **1821** BYRON *Juan* III. iv, But one thing's pretty sure: a woman planted (Unless at once she plunge for life in prayers) After a decent time must be gallanted. **1852** HOSKYNS *Talpa* 18 Here I was, fairly planted, at the first onset. **1858** HOGG *Life Shelley* II. 399 For some six years..he makes her a most exemplary husband; and then, all at once, he plants her; plants her at once and for ever.

11. To bury (a dead person). *slang* (orig. *U.S.*).

1855 *Harper's Mag.* Dec. 37/1 Let it [*sc.* yellow fever] catch hold of a crowd of 'Johnny come latelys', and it plants them at once. **1866** 'MARK TWAIN' *Lett. fr. Hawaii* (1967) 242 It's about the orneryest thing for a monument I've ever struck yet... If I was planted under it, I'd highst it. **1888** [see FLAMDOODLE]. **1927** C. A. W. MONCKTON *Some Experiences of New Guinea Resident Magistrate* 2nd Ser. i. 16 There's Alligator Jack and Red Bill..planted here, and Gawd, 'E knows whether they have rested easy. **1931** GALSWORTHY *Maid in Waiting* ii. 10 'Is he to be planted here?' 'I expect in the Cathedral, but Father will know.' **1967** C. ROUGVIE *When Johnny Died* iii. 66 It was raining when we planted him, and I thought he'd get out of his coffin. **1974** R. JEFFRIES *Mistakenly in Mallorca* xv. 143 The funeral must be fixed up at once. Where did non-Catholics get planted?

plantable ('plɑːntəb(ə)l, -æ-), *a.* [f. PLANT *v.* + -ABLE. (Cf. It. *piantabile.*)] Capable of being planted (in various senses of the verb); fit for planting or cultivation.

1675 EVELYN *Terra* (1729) 14 Roots of any plantable Fruit. **1699** DAMPIER *Voy.* II. II. 58 The Land as you go farther from the Sea..becomes of a more plantable Mould. **1707** MORTIMER *Husb.* (1721) II. 17 Taking of such up as are of a plantable size from Hedge-rows and Woods.

plantad ('plæntæd), *adv. Anat.* [f. L. *planta* the sole of the foot + *-ad*: cf. DEXTRAD.] Towards the sole of the foot.

1808 BARCLAY *Muscular Motions* 448 A general surface that is concave poplitead or plantad, and another surface that is convex rotulad. *Ibid.*, The motion poplitead or plantad, commonly called flexion.

†**'plantage.** *Obs.* [a. F. *plantage* plantation (1427 in Godefroy *Compl.*), f. *planter* to plant: see PLANT *v.* and -AGE.]

1. The cultivation of plants; planting.

1632 LITHGOW *Trav.* I. 14 There are neither Cornes, nor Wines, nor Village, Plantage, or Cultivage. **1688** R. HOLME *Armory* IV. viii. (Roxb.) 328/2 All such as trade in tillage of Land, pasturage, or feeding of cattle or plantage in orderings of orchards and Gardens.

2. Plants in the mass; vegetation, herbage.

1606 SHAKS. *Tr. & Cr.* III. ii. 184 As true as steele, as plantage to the Moone: As Sunne to day: as Turtle to her mate. **1825** SOUTHEY *Tale Paraguay* III. 22 To clear a circle there, And trample down the grass and plantage round.

plantaginaceous (ˌplæntədʒɪ'neɪʃəs), *a. Bot.* [f. mod. Bot. L. *Plantaginaceæ*: see -ACEOUS.] Of or pertaining to the natural order *Plantaginaceæ* or *Plantagineæ* of herbs, of which the typical genus is *Plantago*, PLANTAIN[1].

Mod. Littorella is a plantaginaceous genus.

planta'gineous, *a. Bot.* = prec.

1858 in MAYNE *Expos. Lex.* 973/1.

plantain[1] ('plæntɪn, -tɪn). Forms: 3 **plauntein,** 4 **-eyne, -oyne,** 5 **-eyn;** 4–5 **plawnteyn(e;** 4 **planteine,** 4–6 **-ayn(e,** 5–6 **-eyne,** 6–7 **-an, -(a)ine,** 6–9 **-ane,** 7 **-in, -en,** 7– **plantain;** also 6 **playntayne,** 8 **plaintain.** [ME. a. OF. *plantain, -ein*:—L. *plantāgin-em* (nom. *plantāgo*) plantain, app. from the root of *planta* sole of the foot, in reference to its broad prostrate leaves: cf. the OE. name *Wegbrāde*, OHG. *wegbreita*, WAYBREAD or -BREDE (f. *brād*, Ger. *breit* broad).]

1. a. A plant of the genus *Plantago*, esp. the Greater Plantain, *P. major*, a low herb with broad flat leaves spread out close to the ground, and close spikes of inconspicuous flowers, followed by dense cylindrical spikes of seeds.

[*c* **1265** *Voc.* in Wr.-Wülcker 559/27 *Arnoglosa*, plauntein.] *c* **1386** CHAUCER *Can. Yeom. Prol. & T.* 28 His forheed dropped as a stillatorie Were ful of plantayne [*v. rr.* -eyne, -eyn, -ayn, pleintein] and of paritorie. **1390** GOWER *Conf.* III. 131 The tenthe sterre is Almareth..His Ston is Jaspe, and of Planteine He hath his herbe sovereine. *c* **1400** *Lanfranc's Cirurg.* 351 Distempere it wiþ þe iuys of lactuce & plaunteyn. *c* **1440** *Promp. Parv.* 403/1 Planteyne, or plawnteyn, herbe, *plantago.* **1516** *Grete Herbal* cccxliv, Plantayne or weybrede..is an herbe that ye greke call arnoglosse. It is called also..grete plantayne, and groweth in moyst places & playne feldes. **1577–87** HOLINSHED *Chron.* I. 9/2 A kind of herbe like vnto plantine. **1588** SHAKS. *L.L.L.* III. i. 74 Or sir, Plantan, a plaine Plantan. **1612** *Two Noble K.* I. ii. 61 These poore sleight sores Neede not a plantin. **1617** MORYSON *Itin.* III. 51 Those of Paduoa [are said] to love women with little brests, which makes their women use the juyce of Plantane to keep them from growing. **1736** BAILEY *Househ. Dict.* s.v., The leaves of plantain are good for all sorts of ulcers, and for cicatrizing such as are old. **1872** OLIVER *Elem. Bot.* II. 222 The Seeds of Greater Plantain are a favourite food of cage-birds.

b. With defining words distinguishing species and varieties.

The chief are *greater plantain* (see above); *broad-leaved p.*, *Plantago maxima*; *hoary p.*, *P. media*; *buck's-horn* or *hartshorn p.* (Star of the Earth), *P. Coronopus*; *rose p.*, *P. major* var. *rosea*; *seaside p.*, *P. maritima*; *long, narrow-leaved*, or *ribwort p.*, *P. lanceolata*.

1516 *Grete Herbal* cccxlv, *Delanceolata*... Longe plantayne is good agaynst fystales, yf the iuce be put in them dyuers dayes, it healeth and sleeth them. **1578** LYTE *Dodoens* I. lxiii. 92 We call the fourth [kind]..Sea Plantayne. *Ibid.* lxiv. 95 We may also call it Hartes horne Plantayne, Bucke-horne Plantayne, or Coronop Plantayne. **1629** PARKINSON *Paradisi* lxxxv. 352 *Plantago Rosea.* Rose Plantane..is in all things like vnto the ordinary Plantane or Ribworte..but..hath..a thicke long spike of small greene leaues vpon short stalkes. **1741** *Compl. Fam.-Piece* II. i. 325 That Herb which is called Rose Plantane, or by some, Star Plantane. **1742** SHENSTONE *Schoolmistr.* 103 And plaintain ribb'd, that heals the reaper's wound. **1861** MISS PRATT *Flower. Pl.* IV. 259 Plantago media (Hoary Plantain)..The leaves make a good astringent lotion. **1895** *Syd. Soc. Lex., Plantago virginica*, the white plantain or ribwort.

2. Applied with defining words to other plants resembling the plantain: as **bastard plantain,** *Limosella aquatica*; **water plantain,** *Alisma Plantago*; **lesser water plantain,** *A. Ranunculus*; **least water plantain,** ? = *bastard plantain*; **white plantain,** (?) *Gnaphalium americanum.*

1538 TURNER *Libellus*, Alisma dioscoridæ..officinis & herbariis plantago aquatica..nostratibus water plantane or water waybrede. **1579** LANGHAM *Gard. Health* (1633) 496 Falling euill, drink the leaues, roots or buds of water Planten. **1597** GERARDE *Herbal* II. xciv. 343 *Holosteum*..is also called..Spanish hairie small Plantaine, or flowring sea Plantaine. **1687** J. CLAYTON in *Phil. Trans.* XLI. 145 They use also the *Gnafalium Americanum*, commonly called there White Plantain. **1760** J. LEE *Introd. Bot.* App. 323 Plantain, Least Water, *Limosella. Ibid.*, Plantain, Star-headed Water, *Alisma.* **1806** *Gazetteer Scotl.* (ed. 2) 360/1 *Alisma ranunculoides*, or lesser water plantain. **1861** MISS PRATT *Flower. Pl.* IV. 134 Common Mudwort..is sometimes called Bastard Plantain.

3. *attrib.* and *Comb.*, as ***plantain leaf***, hence ***plantain-leaved*** adj.; **plantain lily** = FUNKIA, HOSTA; **plantain shoreweed,** *Littorella lacustris*; **plantain-water,** a decoction made from the plantain.

1592 SHAKS. *Rom. & Jul.* I. ii. 52 *Romeo.* Your *Plantan leafe is excellent for that. *Ben.* For what I pray thee? *Romeo.* For your broken shin. **1747** WESLEY *Prim. Physic* (1762) 37 A spoonful of the juice of Nettles and Plantane leaves. **1789** J. PILKINGTON *View Derbysh.* I. 395 *Plantain-leaved Sandwort. **1882** *Garden* 9 Sept. 225/1 This *Plantain Lily should be grown by everyone as a pot plant. **1894** W. ROBINSON *Wild Garden* (ed. 4) xiv. 170 The Plantain Lilies are plants for the wild garden. **1927** [see FUNKIA]. **1957** C. LLOYD *Mixed Border* vi. 60 Among plantain lilies..the prevalence of slugs and snails is all too likely. **1976** B. SWAIN *Commonsense of Gardening* v. 207/2 The charming Plantain Lilies..have often disappointed because of unsuitable conditions. **1879** PRIOR *Plant-names* (ed. 3), **Plantain-Shoreweed*, a weed of the plantain tribe found beside lakes and ponds. **1597** A. M. tr. *Guillemeau's Fr. Chirurg.* 25/2 They washe it with *Plantine-water.

plantain[2] ('plæntɪn, -tɪn). Now *Obs.* or *rare.* Forms: 6 **plantayne, -in, -yne,** 7– **plantain.** [a. obs. F. *plantain* (16th c. in Godef.), *plantoine*, used beside *platane*, ad. L. *platanus* plane-tree, PLATAN, of which there was also a med. or early mod.L. by-form *plantanus*: cf. PLANTAIN[3].] The Plane (*Platanus orientalis*). Also *attrib.*, as ***plantain leaf, tree.***

1535 COVERDALE *Ecclus.* xxiv. 14, I am exalted like as a plantayne tre [Vulg. *platanus*] by the water syde. **1553** BRENDE *Q. Curtius* L viij, The riuer was shadowed ouer wyth Plantyne and Pople trees [*platani quoque et populi*]. **1608** TOPSELL *Serpents* (1658) 711 To Plantain-leaves [*platani ramis*] the Sparrow did her young commit. **1791** GILPIN *Forest Scenery* I. 291 In Turkey it is common to see inferior buildings raised around the bole of a large plantain. **1843** BORROW *Bible in Spain* xliv, In the streets of Aranjuez, and beneath the mighty cedars and gigantic elms and plantains which compose its noble woods.

plantain[3] ('plæntɪn, -tɪn). Forms: 6 **platan,** 6–8 **plantane,** 7–8 **-an, -aine, -ine,** 7– **plantain,** (7–8 **plaintain**). [In 16th c. *platan, plantan(e*, ad. Sp. *plátano, plántano*, in same sense, identical in form with *plátano, plántano* plane-tree: see PLANTAIN[2], PLATAN, PLANE *sb.*[1]

There is no similarity of aspect or nature between the plane-tree and the plantain (a fact noted already by D'Acosta in 1590), so that no reason appears for a transfer of the name from the former to the latter. It has therefore been suggested that in this sense *plátano* was a corruption of some native name. And, in fact, the plantain or banana appears in Ant. Biet's Galibi Dictionary of 1664, and again in that of 1763, as *palatana*, in Raymond Breton's Carib Dict. of 1665 as '*Balátana*, grosses bananes', and in the Arawak lang. as *prátane*. But there appears to be no material for determining whether these are native words, or merely corruptions of the Spanish. The Tupi name of the fruit is *pacova.*]

1. A tree-like tropical herbaceous plant (*Musa paradisiaca*) closely allied to the Banana (*M. sapientum*), having immense undivided oblong leaves, and bearing its fruit, for which it is extensively cultivated, in long densely-clustered spikes.

Musa paradisiaca and *M. sapientum* (the Banana), if really distinct species, are very closely allied, and some of their numerous varieties are scarcely distinguishable. The names *plantain* and *banana* are also imperfectly differentiated. In the West Indies, Western Africa, etc., *banana* is applied to the forms with a purple-spotted stem, and a smaller and more delicate fruit, which is eaten raw; while the name *plantain* is given to those with larger and coarser fruit, which is cooked as a vegetable; but in India this usage is reversed, *plantain* being the general name: see Yule *Hobson-Jobson*. In French, *banane* is the general name for both; so *bananier* a banana- or plantain-tree.

[**1555** EDEN *Decades* II. 197 (tr. of Italian version, 1534, of Oviedo's Spanish, 1526) There are also certeine plantes which the christians caul Platani. **1589** PARKE tr. *Mendoza's Hist. China* (Hakl. Soc.) II. 330 Orange trees, siders, limas, plantanos, and palmas. **1640** PARKINSON *Theat. Bot.* XVI. lxix. 1497 They of Brassile call the tree Paquouere and the fruit Pacova, Oviedus and Acosta call it Platanus, for what cause is not knowne. **1760–72** tr. *Juan & Ulloa's Voy.* (ed. 3) I. 74 The most common of all are, the *platanos*... These are of three kinds. The first is the banana,..the second..are the dominicos... The third are the quincos.] **1604** E. G[RIMSTONE] *D'Acosta's Hist. Indies* IV. (Hakl. Soc.) I. 241 The first that shall be needefulle to treate of is the Plantain, or Plantano, as the vulgar call it... The reason why the Spaniards call it platano (for the Indians had no such name) was, as in other trees, for that they have found some resemblance of the one with the other, even as they called some fruites prunes, pines, and cucumbers, being far different from those which are called by those names in Castille. **1615** G. SANDYS *Trav.* 121 Plantains, that haue a broad flaggy leafe, growing in clusters, and shaped like cucumers. *Ibid.* 289 A groue of Plantines. **1657** LIGON *Barbadoes* 81 The Bonano differs nothing from the Plantine, in the body and leaves, but only this, that the leaves are somewhat lesse, and the bodie has here and there some blackish spots... This fruit is of a sweeter taste then the Plantine..we find them as good to stew, or preserve as the Plantine... This tree wants a little of the beauty of the Plantine. **1697** DAMPIER *Voy.* (1699) 316. **1698** FRYER *Acc. E. India & P.* 19 Lower than these, but with a Leaf far broader, stands the Curious Plantan. **1777** G. FORSTER *Voy. round World* I. 254 They handed up to us a green stem of a plantane. **1852** TH. ROSS *Humboldt's Trav.* I. vi. 205 An acre planted with plantains produces nearly twenty times as much food as the same space sown with corn. **1882** *Garden* 22 July 65/2 A large specimen of this fine Plantain is now flowering in the Victoria house at Kew.

2. The fruit of this plant, a long, somewhat pod-shaped or cucumber-like, fleshy fruit (botanically a berry); it forms a staple food of a considerable part of the human race within the tropics.

1555 EDEN *Decades* 197 This cluster owght to bee taken from the plant, when any one of the Platans begynne to appere yelowe. **1628** *World Encomp. by Sir F. Drake* (Hakl. Soc.) 142 Fruit which they call *Figo*.., but it is no other than that which the Spaniards and Portingalls have named Plantanes. **1634** SIR T. HERBERT *Trav.* 183 Bananas or Plantanes. **1697** DAMPIER *Voy.* (1729) I. 311 The Plantain I take to be the King of all Fruit. **1698** FRYER *Acc. E. India & P.* 40 Bonanoes, which are a sort of Plantain, though less, yet much more grateful. **1740** JOHNSON *Life Drake* Wks. IV. 418 Ripe figs, cocoes, and plantains. **1777** G. FORSTER *Voy. round World* I. 343 Loads of horse-plantanes, a coarse sort, which grows almost without cultivation. **1860** E. B. COWELL in *Life & Lett.* (1904) 167, I generally keep to plaintains, which are like a very poor pear, grafted on a potato. **1875** J. THOMSON *Straits Malacca* 8 Of the pisang or plantain.. there are over thirty kinds of which the *Pisang-mas*, or golden plantain,..though one of the smallest, is nevertheless, most deservedly prized. **1897** MARY KINGSLEY *W. Africa* 38 Along the Coast, and in other parts of Africa, the coarser, flat-sided kinds of banana are usually called plantains, the name banana being reserved for the finer sorts, such as the little 'silver banana'.

3. Applied with defining words to other plants allied to or resembling the plantain; as **bastard plantain** (see quot. 1866); **wild plantain**, (*a*) the Indian Shot or Plantain-shot (*Canna indica*); (*b*) the Manilla Hemp plant (*Musa textilis*).

1756 P. BROWNE *Jamaica* 365 Wild Plantane Tree. This beautiful plant grows wild in most of the cooler mountains of Jamaica. **1866** *Treas. Bot.*, Bastard Plantain, *Heliconia Bihai*. **1885** LADY BRASSEY *The Trades* 181 Even the hardy wild-plantain (*Canna indica*) with its brilliant yellow stem and scarlet flowers..was reduced to a bare stem and branches.

4. *attrib.* and *Comb.*, as ***plantain-drink***, ***-garden***, ***-leaf***, ***-stalk***, ***-tree***; **plantain-cutter**, **plantain-eater**, a bird of the genus *Musophaga* or of the family *Musophagidæ*, a TURACO; **plantain-meal**, the powdered substance of the dried fruit of the plantain; **plantain-shot**, a name given to *Canna indica*, the Indian Shot (see quot. 1750); **plantain-walk**, a plantation of plantains.

1663 BOYLE *Usef. Exp. Nat. Philos.* II. ii. 100 In the Barbada's they have many Drinks unknown to us; such as are *Perino*, the *Plantane-drink [etc.]. **1801** LATHAM *Synops. Birds* Suppl. II. 104 *Plantain-eater... This beautiful bird is found on the plains near the borders of rivers in the province of Acra, in Guinea, and is said to live principally on the fruit of the plantain. **1886** OWEN *Vertebr. Anim.* II. 12 *Musophagidæ*..Touraco or Plantain-eater. **1697** DAMPIER *Voy.* (1699) 167 These wild Indians have..good *Plaintain-Gardens; for Plantains are their chiefest food. **1681** R. KNOX *Hist. Ceylon* 37 He eats on a green *Plantane-Leaf. **1859** LANG *Wand. India* 305 Portions..were distributed on plantain leaves to each guest by the Brahmins. **1871** KINGSLEY *At Last* xvi, Why should not *Plantain-meal be hereafter largely exported for the use of the English working classes? **1750** G. HUGHES *Barbadoes* 168 The flowers are succeeded by small capsulæ, each inclosing a round black hard seed, as big as swan-shot. From these, and the make of its leaves, they derive the name of *Plantain-shot. **1613** PURCHAS *Pilgrimage* (1614) 700 The Ganga..with *Plantaine stalkes hitteth euery one. **1640** PARKINSON *Theat. Bot.* XVI. lxix. 1495 *Musa arbor.* The Indian Figge or *Plantaine tree. **1769** E. BANCROFT *Guiana* 29 The Plantin Tree is natural to America. **1660** HICKERINGILL *Jamaica* (1661) 25 The *Plantane-Walks are usually made choice of, for such Nurseries. **1812** S. ROGERS *Columbus* Poems (1839) 44 Thro' plantain-walks where not a sun-beam plays.

plantal ('plæntəl), *a.* Now *rare.* [f. PLANT *sb.*[1] + -AL[1], after *animal*.] Pertaining or relating to a plant; vegetable; used by Henry More and other Platonists to translate Gr. φυτικός, applied to the lowest and simplest kind of life in living beings: see quots.

1642 H. MORE *Song of Soul* II. i. II. xv, When to plantall life quick sense is ti'd. *Ibid.* II. iii. I. ix, Three centres hath the soul; One plantall hight. **1656** —— *Enthus. Tri.* 3 A man differs in them little from a Plant, which therefore you may call the Vegetative or Plantall faculties of the Soul. **1659** —— *Immort. Soul* III. i. 328 The same..made him surmise that the most degenerate Soules did at last sleep in the bodies of Trees, and grew up meerly into Plantal life. **1678** CUDWORTH *Intell. Syst.* Pref. 10 A fourth atheistick form.. concluded the world not to be an animal,..but onely one huge plant or vegetable, having an artificial, plantal, and plastick nature. **1736** H. BROOKE *Univ. Beauty* III. 273 Wide o'er the bank the plantal reptile bends, Adown its stem the rooty fringe depends. **1789** T. TAYLOR *Proclus' Comm.* II. 288 A plantal nature, and a power of acting on body, which is denominated φυτικοι, when it enters the lunar globe. **1816** —— in *Pamphleteer* VIII. 461 Wholly changed..into a plantal condition of being. **1889** N. S. SHALER in *Chautauquan* Oct. 19 Some forms range through a great variety of physical and plantal conditions.

plant-'animal. Now *rare.* [a. early mod.L. *plantanimal*, invented by Budé (Budæus, 1508 in *Annot. in Pandectas*) to render Gr. ζωόφυτον. Cf. G. *pflanzenthier*.]

1. A zoophyte or 'animal plant'.

1646 SIR T. BROWNE *Pseud. Ep.* 134 Though plant animalls doe multiply, they doe it not by copulation, but in a way analogous unto plants. **1651** J. F[REAKE] *Agrippa's Occ. Philos.* 188 In Elements there are five kinds of mixt bodies, viz. Stones, Metals, Plants, Plant-Animals, Animals. [*a* **1677** HALE *Prim. Orig. Man.* I. ii. 47 Animals..that are almost in the nature of Plants, called *Zoophyta* or *Plant animalia*.] **1707** *Curios. in Husb. & Gard.* 87 A Zoophyte, that is, a Plant-Animal. **1853** *Zoologist* II. 4054 The plant-animals of the sea are revealed to us in all their loveliness. **1879** tr. *Haeckel's Evol. Man* I. viii. 196 Plant animals (Zoophyta).

†**2.** A plant-like animal growth. *Obs. nonce-use.*

1663 BOYLE *Usef. Exp. Nat. Philos.* II. App. 346 Hartshorn..grow's to a considerable bulk like a Vegetable, and is (unlike most other Hornes of Animals) at certain set Periods of time, deciduous..this Plant-Animal (if I may so call it) does [etc.].

†**3.** *fig.* A dull, inert, or stupid person. *Obs.*

1673 *S'too him Bayes* 40, I suppose Trans does not think himself a plant-animal. **1687** M. CLIFFORD *Notes Dryden* i. 4 If thou art not the dullest Plant-Animal that ever the Earth produced, all [etc.]. **1706** HEARNE *Collect.* 25 Oct. (O.H.S.) I. 298 He being but a degree from a Natural, and upon y[t] Account..stiled the Plant Animal.

plantar ('plæntə(r)), *a. Anat.* [ad. L. *plantāris* adj., f. *planta* sole of the foot.] Pertaining or relating to the sole of the foot.

1706 PHILLIPS, *Plantar*, belonging to the Sole of the Foot. **1741** A. MONRO *Anat. Nerves* (ed. 3) 69 The two plantar Nerves. **1831** *Encycl. Brit.* (ed. 7) III. 10/2 It is well known that the horse supports himself on the plantar surface of the coffin bone only. **1872** HUMPHRY *Myology* 18 The dorsal and plantar aspects of the limb. **1951** *Chambers's Jrnl.* Aug. 507/1 'You've been grousing for months about the corn you picked up last tour, foot-slogging round Masailand.'.. 'It's not a corn, it's a plantar wart,' I said indignantly. **1976** *Muir's Text-bk. Path.* (ed. 10) 985 The histology of the vulgar wart usually seen on the hands and knees is essentially similar to the plantar wart found on the soles of the feet.

‖**plan'tarium.** *Obs. rare.* Also anglicized as **'plantary.** [L. *plantārium* (Plin.), f. *planta* a slip, young plant.] A nursery ground; also *fig.*

1637 BASTWICK *Litany* I. 19 Seminaryes and plantaryes of pride and luxury. **1664** EVELYN *Sylva* (1776) 38 A very small Plantarium or Nursery, will in a few years, stock a vast Extent of Ground.

plantation (plæn'teɪʃən). [ad. L. *plantātiōnem* planting, transplanting, n. of action f. *plantāre* to plant; see -ATION. Cf. F. *plantation* (1486).]

1. a. The action of planting, the placing of plants in the soil so that they may grow. Now *rare.*

c **1450** *Mirour Saluacioun* 1065 Aarons ȝerde fructified without plantacioune. **1612** CAPT. SMITH *Map Virginia* 16 In Aprill they begin to plant, but their chiefe plantation is in May. **1667** MILTON *P.L.* IX. 419 In Bowre and Field he sought, where any tuft Of Grove or Garden-Plot more pleasant lay, Thir tendance or Plantation for delight. **1724** SWIFT *Drapier's Lett.* Wks. 1755 V. II. 129 The manifest defects in the acts concerning the plantation of trees. **1816** T. TAYLOR in *Pamphleteer* VIII. 469 She instructed the Eleusinians in the plantation of corn.

b. *fig.* The action of establishing or founding anything, e.g. a religion; the implanting (*of* a quality); †the laying out (of wealth).

1605 BACON *Adv. Learn.* I. vi. §13 Those instruments, which it pleased God to use for the plantation of the faith. **1620** E. BLOUNT *Horæ Subs.* 327 The place where holinesse, and religion, aymed to haue their principall plantation. **1654** tr. *Scudery's Curia Pol.* 183 Heaven and Nature concur in the plantation of that quality [fortitude] in the hearts of men. **1795** HORSLEY *Serm.* (1811) 247 The plantation of churches and the propagation of the gospel.

c. The settlement of persons in some locality; *esp.* the planting of a colony; colonization.

1586 J. HOOKER *Hist. Irel.* Ep. Ded., Not for anie religion or plantation of a Commonwealth. **1610** T. BLENERHASSET (*title*) A Direction for the Plantation in Ulster. **1610** (*title*) A true and sincere Declaration of the Purpose and Ends of the Plantation begun in Virginia. **1625** N. CARPENTER *Geog. Del.* II. xiii. (1635) 213 The first plantation of Inhabitants immediately after the Deluge. *a* **1645** HABINGTON *Surv. Worc.* in *Worc. Hist. Soc. Proc.* II. 317 Before theyre plantation in Worcestershire they weare of Rageley. **1672** PETTY *Pol. Anat.* vii, The old protestants of Queen Elizabeth and King James's plantation..did not much love the new English, who came over since 1641. **1788** PRIESTLEY *Lect. Hist.* III. xvi. 143 Before the discovery of America and the plantation of our colonies, the interest of money was generally twelve per cent. all over Europe. **1870** *Athenæum* 23 July 110/2 Plantation meant the establishment of Englishmen as landowners in Ireland, the extermination of native proprietors, and the reduction of the inhabitants at large to slavery.

2. a. An assemblage of growing plants of any kind which have been planted.

1569 *Reg. Privy Council Scot.* II. 32 Destroy and put away ..all biggingis, munitionis, plantationis and commoditeis within and about the same. **1649** BLITHE *Eng. Improv. Impr.* (1653) 157 So thou must go on throughout thy whole Plantation. **1658** SIR T. BROWNE *Gard. Cyrus* i, Which was no ordinary plantation, if..it contained all kindes of Plants. **1741** *Compl. Fam.-Piece* II. iii. 404 Make Plantations of the Suckers or Cuttings of Goosberries, Currants, and Rasberries. **1766** *Compl. Farmer* s.v. *Onion*, About October all their leaves die away, which has occasioned some to think all the plantation [*i.e.* onion-bed] lost. **1846** J. BAXTER *Libr. Pract. Agric.* (ed. 4) I. 71 Culture, &c. of the Common Artichoke... I also prefer one single row to a regular plantation or bed, on account of the better admission of light and air.

b. Now, *esp.*, a wood of planted trees.

1669 STURMY *Mariner's Mag.* V. iv. 15 You will have the true Plott of your Ground, or Park, or Wood-land, or Plantation. **1739** GRAY *Let.* Poems (1775) 71 On either hand vast plantations of trees, chiefly mulberries and olives. **1806** *Gazetteer Scotl.* (ed. 2) s.v. *Lhanbryd*, A plain..covered with corn, grass, or plantations. **1846** M[c]CULLOCH *Acc. Brit. Empire* (1854) I. 546 During the last half century, many very large additions have been made to the plantations of Scotland... The total woodland must, at this moment.. considerably exceed 1,000,000 acres.

†**3.** *fig.* **a.** That which has been planted, founded, or settled, as an institution, a mission station. *Obs.*

1570 FOXE *A. & M.* (ed. 2) 1053/1, I take it [auricular confession] for a plantation, not planted by God in his worde. **1653** E. CHISENHALE *Cath. Hist.* 83 The Apostles amongst themselves were equall, and their severall plantations coordinate and equal. **1704** NELSON *Fest. & Fasts* vii. (1739) 90 Both [were] sent down by the Apostles to Samaria, to settle the Plantations Philip had made.

b. An oyster-bed: see PLANT *v.* 1 b.

1891 W. K. BROOKS *Oyster* 127 Before the bottom was laid out in private plantations, there were very few persons living there.

4. a. A settlement in a new or conquered country; a colony. Also *transf. Obs.* exc. *Hist.* (Cf. 1 c.)

Chiefly those formed in the New World, and on the forfeited lands in Ireland; also, the ancient colonies of Greece, etc.

1614 SYLVESTER *Bethulia's Rescue* I. 385 (Bees) Else-where to plant their goodly Colonies; Which keep, still constant, in their new Plantation. **1622** CAPT. SMITH (*title*) New Englands Trials... With the present estate of that happie Plantation, begun by but 60 weake men in the yeare 1620. **1635** PAGITT *Christianogr.* I. ii. (1636) 86 In America, there be diverse Plantations of the English, Dutch, and French. *a* **1656** USSHER *Ann.* VI. (1658) 169 Heraclea, a plantation of the city of Megara. *a* **1687** PETTY *Pol. Arith.* Pref., Ireland and the Plantations in America..are a Burthen to England. **1769** *Junius Lett.* i. (1820) 6 A new office is established for the business of the plantations. **1800** COLQUHOUN *Comm. Thames* xi. 328 All goods of the produce of Ireland, and the British Plantations. **1865** MERIVALE *Rom. Emp.* VIII. lxiii. 42 Roman plantations, and possibly military stations also reached even to the Dniester.

†**b.** A company of settlers or colonists. *Obs.*

1647 STAPYLTON *Juvenal* 231 Ascanius..carrying forth a plantation of men,..found a white sow with 30 pigges sucking her. **1651** HOBBES *Leviath.* II. xxiv. (1839) 239 Those we call plantations, or colonies..are numbers of men sent out from the commonwealth, under a conductor, or governor, to inhabit a foreign country, either formerly void of inhabitants, or made void then by war. *a* **1715** BURNET *Own Time* (1823) II. 321 (*an.* 1682) This revived among them [the gentry] a design..of carrying over a plantation to Carolina.

c. ***to send*** (prisoners, etc.) ***to the plantations***, i.e. to penal service or indentured labour in the colonies, 'a method of treating criminals of all kinds much in favour during the 17th century' (C. H. Firth in *Eng. Hist. Rev.*, 1889, 335).

As the labour was chiefly on the plantations in sense 5, the phrase tended to be associated with that sense.

1650 *Acts Parl. Scot.* (Recd. ed.) VI. II. 745 b, To deliver unto Mr Samuel Clarke, to transport to Virginia, 900 prisoners of the Scots [taken at Dunbar]..according to such desires as shall bee made by anie who will carrie them to plantations not in enmity to this Commonwealth. 1655 *Mercurius Politicus* 24-31 May, Divers persons..who were in the late rebellious insurrection, were to be sent away to the foreign plantations. c1664 in Burnet *Own Time* II. (1724) I. 209 If his Majesty had any such intention, he would rather choose to be sent to a plantation. 1760 BURKE *Corr.* (1844) I. 73 Will the law suffer a felon sent to the plantations, to bind himself for life? 1849 MACAULAY *Hist. Eng.* v. I. 660 Some of them had been hanged:..and the rest should be sent to the plantations.

5. An estate or farm, esp. in a tropical or subtropical country, on which cotton, tobacco, sugar-cane, coffee, or other crops are cultivated, formerly chiefly by servile labour: see PLANTER 4.

1706 PHILLIPS, *Plantation*, a Spot of Ground in America for the planting of Tobacco, Sugar-canes, &c. 1719 DE FOE *Crusoe* (1840) I. xi. 180, I had..two plantations in the island. 1818 CRUISE *Digest* (ed. 2) VI. 85 A person..devised to trustees..a plantation in the island of Grenada, upon trust. 1837 HT. MARTINEAU *Soc. Amer.* II. 143 They were seized upon by two slaves of the neighbouring plantation. 1898 BESANT *Orange Girl* II. xxv, In Virginia every estate is a plantation..with its servants and slaves.

†**6.** That on which any structure is planted; a base, a foundation, a platform. *Obs. rare.*

a1680 BUTLER *Rem.* (1759) I. 352 You had better undertake to find out a Plantation for Archimedes his Engines to move the Earth. 1688 CAPT. J. S. *Fortification* 69 Platforms..are the Plantations where the Guns are laid.

7. *attrib.* and *Comb.*, as (in senses 1, 2) ***plantation-hoe, -making; plantation-like*** adj.; (sense 4) ***plantation-aloe, †-cause, †clerk, †-land, -sugar; plantation-built*** adj.; (sense 5) ***plantation-coolie, -dance, -house, manners, -mansion, -Negro, -slave, style, -worker;*** †**plantation-acre**, an acre in plantation-measure; = the Irish acre; **plantation creole**, a creolized language arising amongst a transplanted and largely isolated Negroid community; **plantation crepe** *U.S.*, used *attrib.* of a variety of crêpe-rubber sole on footwear; †**plantation-measure**, the variety of land-measure formerly used in the plantations of Ireland, in which the acre contained 7840 sq. yards; **plantation-mill**, a mill suitable for use on a plantation, for crushing oats, etc.; † **Plantation Office**, early name of the Colonial Office; **plantation song**, a song of the kind sung by Negroes on the American plantations.

1771-2 *Irish Act 11 & 12 Geo. III*, c. 21 §5 Any bog of less dimensions than ten *plantation acres. 1766 *Compl. Farmer* s.v. *Purging*, The Succotrine aloes should always be preferred to the Barbadoes, or *plantation aloes. 1709 *Lond. Gaz.* No. 4541/3 The Ship Rolland.., *Plantation-built. c1744 in Hanway *Trav.* (1753) II. I. xii. 68 Any other British or plantation-built ship. a1715 BURNET *Own Time* III. (1724) I. 298 There was..a *Plantation-cause at the Council board. 1684 E. CHAMBERLAYNE *Pres. St. England* II. (ed. 15) 241 Ricard Savage, *Plantation Clerk. 1938 *Social Forces* Oct. 114/2 The *plantation creole tongues are true *Sklavensprachen.* Although they owe something to the sailors' trade jargons, they began essentially as a makeshift means of communication between masters and field hands. 1978 *Verbatim* Feb. 10/1 Both authors hold to..the Creolist theory, which traces the present-day Black English vernacular to a Plantation Creole, to a plantation-maritime pidgin, to an African origin. 1967 *New Yorker* 7 Oct. 109/2 (Advt.), Clark's original Desert ® Boots..with *plantation crepe soles. 1969 *Sears, Roebuck & Co. Catal.* Spring-Summer 454/2 Durable, buoyant, plantation crepe rubber sole and heel. 1969 E. WILSON *Hist. Shoe Fashions* xx. 258 A plantation crepe sole was one of the many soft soles which added to its comfort. a1860 ALB. SMITH *Lond. Med. Stud.* (1861) 10 He was about to practise his *plantation-dance upstairs, and..the ceiling might come down. 1766 *Compl. Farmer* s.v. *Lucern*, Before that time the flat *plantation-hoe may be used. 1722 DE FOE *Col. Jack* (1840) 283, I came to the *plantation-house. 1831 J. M. PECK *Guide for Emigrants* II. 55 All the plantation houses are surrounded with rich and beautiful groves. 1973 *Advocate-News* (Barbados) 2 Feb. 15/4 (Advt.), Besides the plantation house there is available the plantation manager's house. 1974 *Country Life* 3-10 Jan. 18/1 The Virginian plantation houses of the 18th century, such as Carter's Grove, Westover and Shirley. 1639 *Irish Act 15 Chas. I*, sess. II. c. 6 §2 Towns, villages, hamlets, lands,..usually called *plantation lands, in or neere the territories of Cloncolman. 1897 MARY KINGSLEY *W. Africa* 642 He did his utmost to try and get the natives to embark on *plantation-making, ably seconded by Mr. Billington, the botanist. 1854 THOREAU *Walden* 165 Men of almost every degree of wit called on me in the migrating season. Some who had more wits than they knew what to do with; runaway slaves with *plantation manners, who listened from time to time, like the fox in the fable, as if they heard the hounds a-baying on their track. 1897 *Congress. Rec.* 31 Mar. 548/2 When I was a boy,..I used to read a great deal about what the early Republicans called 'plantation manners'. 1642 *Act 18 Chas. I*, c. 36 (*Ireland*) *Plantation measure,..every Acre thereof shall consist of eightscore Pearches or Poles..of one and twenty foot. 1771-2 *Irish Act 11 & 12 Geo. III*, c. 21 §2 No greater quantity of such bog shall be so set to any one person than fifty acres, plantation measure. 1771 in *Maryland Hist. Mag.* (1919) XIV. 135 My people..do not live so well as our House negroes, But full as well as any *Plantation negroes. 1866 A. FLINT *Princ. Med.* (1880) 511 Among the plantation negroes of the Southern States. 1956 G. P. KURATH in A. Dundes *Mother Wit* (1973) 108/1 Recreational dances of plantation Negroes commenced with a prayer. 1753 *De Foe's Tour Gt. Brit.* (ed. 5) II. 104 Where formerly was kept the Office of the Secretary of State for Scotland, now abolished, is the *Plantation-office. 1871 DE VERE *Americanisms* 116 The Negro-minstrel is the artist who blackens his face, adopts the black man's manner and instrument, and recites his field and *plantation songs. 1896 HUNGERFORD *Lonely Girl* xiii. 127 Singing plantation songs to the..banjo. 1957 P. WORSLEY *Trumpet shall Sound* viii. 148 *Plantation-workers were convinced by Runovoro's ability to write meaningless works. 1976 *Honolulu Star-Bull.* 21 Dec. A-8/2 Approximately 175 Molokai Dole plantation workers..lost their jobs last year because of foreign competition.

Hence **plan'tationer**, one who took part in the plantation of Ulster; †**plan'tationite**, a colonist.

1756 *Monitor* No. 71 II. 184 Hear ye men of Britannia! give ear ye..Plantationites! and such as dwell on the continent of America. 1888 J. HARRISON *Scot in Ulster* iv. 56 The 'plantationers' came accompanied by clergymen.

†**plan'tator.** *Obs. rare.* [a. late L. *plantātor* (Augustine) a planter, transplanter, f. *plantāre* to plant; see -ATOR.]

1. One who transplants something, e.g. a custom.

1632 LITHGOW *Trav.* x. 438 Can you draw from them [i.e. the French]..a greater draught, then they draw from the Italian, for first they be Imitators; next, Mutators; thirdly, Temptators; and lastly, your Plantators, in all the varieties of vanity.

2. A settler, colonist, 'planter'.

1632 LITHGOW *Trav.* x. 411 A great discouragment for our collonizd plantators there. 1654 H. L'ESTRANGE *Chas. I* (1655) 123 This year the protestants and English plantators in Ireland, began to grow into some discontent.

plant-bug. [f. PLANT *sb.*[1] + BUG *sb.*[2]] Any one of various hemipterous insects (esp. of the family *Capsidæ*) that infest, and feed upon the juices of, plants. Cf. PLANT-LOUSE.

1864 *Reader* No. 97. 572/1 Aphides, or plant-bugs.

Planté ('plɑːnteɪ, -æ-). *Electr.* The name of R. L. Gaston *Planté* (1834–89), French physicist, used *attrib.* to designate lead-acid accumulator plates formed by a process which he invented, cells containing such plates, and the process itself.

1881 *Electrician* 3 Sept. 249/2 A Planté cell that has been long in use gives a better result than one that has been freshly constructed. 1889 G. W. DE TUNZELMANN *Electr. in Mod. Life* xiv. 195 The original Planté accumulator has been considerably improved by Faure and others. 1923 GLAZEBROOK *Dict. Appl. Physics* II. 76/2 Owing to its high cost the original Planté process is no longer employed. *Ibid.* 77/1 Planté negatives are not generally used, as their advantages are not compensated by the additional weight of lead... Planté positives are employed extensively in stationary batteries. 1959 *Times* 11 Sept. 9/2 The field in which the new cell is designed to replace current Planté types is a very wide one. 1964 G. SMITH *Storage Batteries* ii. 21 These do not have quite the same long life as the Planté battery. 1970 C. L. MANTELL *Batteries & Energy Systems* xiii. 112 Planté plates are prepared from lead blanks which have been cast, rolled, cut, and stamped.

planted ('plɑːntɪd, -æ-). *ppl. a.* [f. PLANT *v.* + -ED[1].]

1. Set in the ground, as a plant; fixed in the ground, set up, established, etc.; placed surreptitiously or misleadingly; hidden esp. so as to deceive the discoverer: see PLANT *v.*

14.. *Voc.* in Wr.-Wülcker 590/4 *Insitus*, planted or graffed. c1440 *Promp. Parv.* 403/1 Plantyd, *plantatus.* a1625 JAS. I *Ps.* i. 3 Hee shall be like a planted tree. 1685 BAXTER *Paraphr. N.T.* Acts xv. 36 Converted Souls and Planted Churches, must be further visited. 1804 J. GRAHAME *Sabbath* (1839) 23/2 The planted standard falls Upon the heaving ground. 1864 WEBSTER. *Planted* (Joinery), fixed in place, as a projecting member or molding, after having been first wrought on a separate piece of stuff. 1963 *TV Times* (Austral.) 18 Apr. 10/2 *Planted*, hidden. 1972 *Jrnl. Social Psychol.* Dec. 301 When the class was asked if anyone wanted to make a statement to the 'teacher', a planted student responded with a standard complaining, corrective request. 1973 M. WOODHOUSE *Blue Bone* x. 93 'He said..that he was quite happy where he was.' 'In answer to a planted question, yes, he did.' 'You're fairly sure it was planted?'..'Of course... This whole thing was just a put-up job... So that Karel could state for the record that he was fine where he was.' 1977 G. V. HIGGINS *Dreamland* xiv. 169 We're even bigger suckers for a planted story..if we really had to scout around for it. 1978 J. GARDNER *Dancing Dodo* xxxix. 324 It's a greater threat than a planted nuclear device.

2. a. Furnished with plants, trees, etc.

14.. *Voc.* in Wr.-Wülcker 598/32 *Obsitus*,..by-set a bowte, or plantyd a bowte. 1719 DE FOE *Crusoe* (1840) I. vii. 118 It looked like a planted garden. 1849 MACAULAY *Hist. Eng.* ii. I. 219 In the newly planted alleys of Versailles.

†**b.** *Sc.* Of a church or congregation: Supplied with a minister, settled. *Obs.*

1699 T. BOSTON *Art of Man-Fishing* (1900) 75 When thou goest to preach in planted Congregations.

†**plantein.** *Obs. rare*[−1]. In 4 plauntein. [? a. OF. *plantin* or ? *planton* young plant, deriv. of *plante* PLANT.] A young plant.

c1400 *Lanfranc's Cirurg.* 232 Take a litil plauntein of a note [*paruam plantam nucis*] & take it vp of þe ground wiþ alle hise rotis.

planteous, variant of PLAINTEOUS *Obs.*

planter ('plɑːntə(r), -æ-). [f. PLANT *v.* + -ER[1].]

I. Of persons.

1. One who sets plants in the ground to grow, or who sows seed; hence, a cultivator of the soil, a farmer, an agriculturist.

1382 WYCLIF *Jer.* xxxi. 5 Plaunte shul plaunteres [*Vulg.* plantabunt plantantes]. c1475 *Pict. Voc.* in Wr.-Wülcker 809/32 *Hic plantator*, a plantor. 1575 FENTON *Gold. Ep.* (1577) 99 Fruites returne seedes to their planter. 1667 MILTON *P.L.* IV. 691 Chos'n by the sovran Planter, when he fram'd All things to mans delightful use. 1726 W. HAMILTON *To C'tess of Eglintoun w. Gentle Sheph.*, Or with th' industrious planter dost thou talk, Conversing freely in an ev'ning walk? 1846 J. BAXTER *Libr. Pract. Agric.* (ed. 4) I. 393 Planter of hops not obliged to give more than twenty-four hours' notice of his intention to weigh. 1856 EMERSON *Eng. Traits, Aristocr.* Wks. (Bohn) II. 78 The virtues of pirates gave way to those of planters, merchants, senators, and scholars.

2. *fig.* One who plants a church, religion, institution, or the like, which takes root and grows.

1632 SANDERSON *Serm.* I. 287 St. Peter, and St. Paul, the two chiefest planters of the churches. 1710 PRIDEAUX *Orig. Tithes* ii. 36 The Ministers of the Gospel who were to be sent out to be the first Planters of it. 1870 E. ARBER *Ascham's Scholem.* Introd. §5 These Planters of the ancient Literature in England hoped well of their Mother Tongue.

3. a. One of the persons who 'plant' or found a colony; an early settler, a pioneer; a colonist; in Ireland, one of the English or Scotch settlers planted on forfeited lands in the 17th c. *Hist.*

1620 E. BLOUNT *Horæ Subs.* 533 They seuerally giue different orders, and customes, according to the intent and purpose of the first Planters. 1630 *R. Johnson's Kingd. & Commw.* 641 A new Colony and plantation... The Planters sustaine themselves by what God and Nature affords them for their labour upon the place. 1657 CROMWELL *Sp.* 21 Apr., We have settled almost all the affairs in Ireland; the rights and interests of the soldiers there, and of the planters and adventurers. a1677 HALE *Prim. Orig. Man.* 197 Where the Accessions [to a Colony] are but thin and sparing, and scattered among the Natives of the Country where they come..it falls out that the very first Planters do soon degenerate in their Habits, Customs and Religion. 1699 BENTLEY *Phal.* 334 The Planters were the Phocæans, who were driven out of Asia by Harpagus. 1807 G. CHALMERS *Caledonia* I. II. vi. 306 The law of Gavil-kind, which the original planters had carried with them from Britain. 1868 E. EDWARDS *Ralegh* I. xxi. 479 The written records of.. Ralegh's persistent labours as a planter are numerous.

b. In Ireland, in 19th c., A person settled in the holding of an evicted tenant.

1890 *Daily News* 18 June 3/5 Mr. McCarthy gave..the reason for this refusal to sanction sales under the Ashbourne Act to the planter or emergency tenants who replaced the old tenants. 1892 *Pall Mall G.* 22 Sept. 4/3 'If the Government don't put 'em (the planters) out, we will', said one of the men to me. 1894 *Daily News* 20 Apr. 4/7 What does Mr. Morley propose to do with the man who is settled on the farm—the 'planter', as he is called, a name of historical memory in Ireland?

4. a. The proprietor or occupier of a plantation or cultivated estate, orig. in the W. Indies and the southern colonies of N. America; now used generally of such persons in tropical and subtropical countries. Often in Comb., as ***coffee-, cotton-, indigo-, sugar-, tobacco-planter.***

1647 WARD *Simp. Cobler* (1843) 4 The Sub-planters of a West-Indian Island. 1660 HICKERINGILL *Jamaica* (1661) 19 Another singular benefit to the Planter, is the large numbers of wild Horses. 1706 PHILLIPS, *Planter*,..also a Master, or Owner of a Plantation in the West-Indies. 1725 DE FOE *Voy. round World* (1840) 220 One of the Spanish Prisoners was a planter, as it is called in the West Indies, or a farmer, as we should call it in England. 1858 J. B. NORTON *Topics* 269 A planter of the Sheveroy Hills wrote to me that he had detected some women stealing his coffee. 1879 *Cassell's Techn. Educ.* IV. 209/2 Before leaving the hands of the planter, the cotton is subjected to a rough cleaning process.

b. ***planter's*** (or ***planters'***) ***punch***: a cocktail containing rum.

1924 A. MACMILLAN in *Land of Abiding Sunshine*, A 'swizzle' or 'a planter's punch' would very welcome be. 1935 S. LEWIS *It can't happen Here* iv. 38 His reputation for research among planters'-punch recipes..might cause his defeat by the church people. 1958 G. GREENE *Our Man in Havana* v. ii. 198 Have a planter's punch. They are good here. 1971 'D. HALLIDAY' *Dolly & Doctor Bird* viii. 108, I don't suppose Beltanno has tasted planter's punch. 1978 G. GREENE *Human Factor* v. iii. 285 What about a Planter's Punch? They do them OK here, so I'm told.

5. One who forms, owns, or maintains oyster-beds.

1892 *Law Times* XCII. 177/2 Mr. Williamson, a very large oyster planter and dealer in oysters.

6. *Austral. slang.* One who steals and hides cattle: see PLANT *v.* 8.

1890 'R. BOLDREWOOD' *Col. Reformer* xxv. III. 54 What's a little money..if..your children grow up duffers [*sc.* cattle-duffers] and planters?

7. *Newfoundland.* The owner of fishing or shipping 'plant': see quots.

1860 BARTLETT *Dict. Amer.* (ed. 3), *Planter*,..in Newfoundland, a person engaged in the fishery. 1883 SIR A. SHEA *Newfoundland Fisheries* 10 (Fish. Exhib. Publ.) The sailing vessels were in a large degree the property of resident 'planters', whose earnings helped to swell the common wealth. 1895 R. G. TABER in *Outing* (U.S.) XXVII. 19/2 Over one-half of these Labrador-going fishermen are what are termed 'planters, sharesmen and crews'... A 'planter' may either be the owner of a 'plant', speculating on his own account, or an agent in charge of a merchant's plant.

II. Of things or beasts.

8. a. An implement or machine for planting or sowing seeds: often in Comb., as ***corn planter, cotton-seed planter, potato planter.***

1850 *Rep. U.S. Comm. Patents 1849* I. 151 Having thus fully described my improved grain and seed planter. **1856** *Engineer* I. 14/1 The accompanying engravings represent.. improvements in hand corn planters. **1874** KNIGHT *Dict. Mech.* 25/1 Seed-planter..Sugar-cane planter. **1939** W. FAULKNER *Wild Palms* 65 For seven years now he had run his plough and harrow and planter within the very shadow of the levee. **1950** [see BAGGER b].

b. A pot, tub, or other container for growing or displaying plants. orig. *U.S.*

1959 in WEBSTER Add. **1966** 'L. HOLTON' *Out of Depths* viii. 72 The brick planters facing the ocean were gay with blossoms. **1968** *Washington Post* 3 July A24/8 (Advt.), Distinctive redwood planter at savings! **1969** *Islander* (Victoria, B.C.) 5 Oct. 3/3 On the foundations of the cabin there is now a summer patio with brick planters made from the cabin chimney. **1973** *Center City Office Weekly* (Philad.) 9 Oct. 10/4 Cream scuttle... Can be used as a planter, or for artificial flowers.

9. *U.S.* A snag formed by a tree-trunk embedded in a more or less erect position in a river.

1802 A. ELLICOTT *Journal* (1803) 123 From the mouth of the Ohio..it is not safe to descend the river in the night, unless the boat be uncommonly strong, on account of the sawyers and planters. **1812** BRACKENRIDGE *Views Louisiana* (1814) 43 In time, the trees thus fallen in, become sawyers and planters; the first..named from the motion made by the top when acted upon by the current, the others are the trunks of trees of sufficient size to resist it. **1860** BARTLETT *Dict. Amer.* (ed. 3), *Planter*,..the most dangerous among the 'snag and sawyer' family, to which vessels navigating the Western rivers are exposed. **1884** T. W. HIGGINSON in *Harper's Mag.* June 125/1 Their talk was of the dangers of the river; of 'planters and sawyers'.

10. *Pugilistic slang.* A blow planted, a well-directed blow: cf. PLANT *v.* 7.

1821 *Sporting Mag.* VIII. 234 Smith put in a dreadful planter on Powell's throat.

11. *colloq.* A horse that has the habit of refusing to move.

1864 TREVELYAN *Compet. Wallah* (1866) 140 Mofussil horses..are incorrigible planters, considering it essential to their dignity to stand perfectly still for ten minutes after they have been put between the shafts.

Hence **ˈplanterdom**, the class or social order of planters or owners of plantations in America, the West Indies, etc.; **ˈplanterly** *a.*, befitting a planter (in sense 4); **ˈplantership**, the office or condition of a planter.

a **1603** T. CARTWRIGHT *Confut. Rhem. N.T.* (1618) 379 That God should bestow the grace of Apostleship and Plantership upon him rather then upon Apollo. **1797** *Encycl. Brit.* (ed. 3) XV. 793/1 He [James Ramsay] stood, in opinion, a rebel against the interest and majesty of plantership. **1827** LD. BROUGHAM in *Life & Lett. Z. Macaulay* (1900) 445 That heathenly and planterly and almost slave-trading speech. **1838** *Encycl. Brit.* (ed. 7) XVII. 778/2 In the West Indies, plantership denotes the management of a sugar plantation. **1861** RUSSELL *Diary North & S.* (1863) I. 186 Meeting only two or three vehicles containing female planterdom on little excursions of pleasure or business.

[**ˈplanticle**, error for PLANTULE, q.v.]

plantie-cruive. Also **planta-, planti-, planty-, -crew, -crü.** *dial.* (*Shetl.* and *Orkn.*) [f. Sc. *plantie*, dim. of PLANT *sb.*[1] + CRUIVE.] A kitchen-garden enclosure.

1814 J. SHIRREFF *Agric. Surv. Orkn.* 80 *note*, The plants are raised from seed sown in little enclosures of turf,.. called, in Orkney, planta crews. **1814** SCOTT *Diary* 4 Aug. in *Lockhart*, Some dozen of these little enclosures about twenty or thirty feet square are in sight at once. They are called planty-cruives. **1822** —— *Pirate* xxx. **1876** [see CRUIVE 3]. **1898** CLARK *N. Gleams* 166 (E.D.D.) Robbing a bee's nest in the wall of his planti-crü.

†**planˈtigenous**, *a. Obs. rare.* [f. L. type **plantigen-us* (f. *planta* plant + *-gen-us* born: cf. *terrigenus*) + -OUS.] Generated or sprung from plants.

1671 *Phil. Trans.* VI. 3004 That the divers races of Ichneumons are generated by their respective Animal-parents, and particularly that those, which the divers Excrescencies of Vegetables produce, are not plantigenous.

plantigrade (ˈplæntɪgreɪd), *a.* (*sb.*) *Zool.* [a. F. *plantigrade* (Geoffroy and Cuvier 1795), in mod.L. *plantigradus* walking on the sole of the foot, f. L. *planta* sole + *-gradus* going, walking.]

Walking upon the soles of the feet (opp. to DIGITIGRADE); also said of the feet, or of the walk, of an animal. (In this general sense, man is a plantigrade animal.) Commonly restricted to the former tribe *Plantigrada* of carnivorous mammals, comprising several quadrupeds now distributed in various families, as the bear, wolverene, badger, racoon, etc.

1831 *Encycl. Brit.* (ed. 7) III. 10/2 The animals distinguished by the name of Plantigrade are believed to support themselves on the entire foot. **1836-9** *Todd's Cycl. Anat.* II. 978/2 The hinder feet in the whole of this order are plantigrade. **1875** SIR W. TURNER in *Encycl. Brit.* I. 830/1 The human foot, therefore, is a pentadactylous, plantigrade foot. **1877** COUES *Fur Anim.* vii. 188 They are terrestrial animals,..the walk is plantigrade.

b. In reference to human beings: Placing the whole sole of the foot upon the ground at once in walking; flat-footed.

1837 C. LE GRICE in *Lamb's Wks.* (1876) I. 7 His [Lamb's] step was plantigrade, which made his walk slow and peculiar. **1861** RUSSELL *Diary North & S.* (1863) I. 384 He [the negro] is plantigrade and curved as to the tibia.

c. *transf.* Of or belonging to a plantigrade animal, as a bear.

1853 KANE *Grinnell Exp.* xl. (1856) 362 A hirsute, bearded fellow, with the true plantigrade countenance. **1860** O. W. HOLMES *Elsie V.* iv, The black bear alone could have set that plantigrade seal.

B. *sb.* A plantigrade animal; *esp.* one of the former order *Plantigrada*: see above.

1835 KIRBY *Hab. & Inst. Anim.* II. xvii. 212 The Plantigrades are so called because they walk, like man, upon the whole foot. **1859** DARWIN *Orig. Spec.* i. (1872) 7 With the exception of the plantigrades or bear family.

Plantin (ˈplæntɪn). The name of Christophe *Plantin* (1514–89), printer, of Antwerp, used to designate a family of old-face types, based on a 16th-century Flemish original, the first of which was designed by F. H. Pierpont for the Monotype Corporation in 1913.

1914 *Monotype Recorder* July 68 (*caption*) First showing of light face Plantin O.S. **1919** J. P. THORP *Printing for Business* viii. 81 The headlines, section numbers and little acorn ornaments are in vermilion, the text in 12-point Plantin. **1929** F. MEYNELL *Typogr. Newspaper Advertisements* 28 Plantin (particularly the Monotype face) declares in its strength and straightness that it stands for the machine-seller. **1951** S. JENNETT *Making of Books* xv. 262 Types like Times and Plantin, which are so large on the body that they are unpleasant when set solid, become useful and legible when they are suitably leaded. **1967** J. B. LIEBERMAN *Types of Typefaces* 89/2 Plantin..is based on 16th century forms.

ˈplanting, *vbl. sb.* [f. PLANT *v.* + -ING[1].]

1. a. The action of the vb. PLANT, in various senses.

c **1000** *Ælfric's Voc.* in Wr.-Wülcker 149 *Propaginatio*, wintwiga plantung. **1426** LYDG. *De Guil. Pilgr.* 21791 But thow shalt ageyn retourne Toward the heggh off hyr plauntyng. **1585** T. WASHINGTON tr. *Nicholay's Voy.* I. xvii. 20 [They did] aduaunce their trenches and approaches for planting of their ordinance. **1625** BACON *Ess., Plantations* (Arb.) 530 Planting of Countries, is like Planting of Woods; For you must make account to leese almost Twenty yeeres Profit, and expect your Recompence, in the end. **1649** *Proc. Commiss. Gen. Assembly* (1896) 285 Recommende to the Presbyterie the planting of that Kirk with diligence. **1702** C. MATHER (*title*) Magnalia Christi Americana: or, the Ecclesiastical History of New-england, from Its First Planting in the Year 1620. unto the Year..1698. **1818** in Willis & Clark *Cambridge* (1886) I. 573 The planting of Clare Hall walk..with Ivy.

†**b.** Position, situation. *Obs.*

1585 T. WASHINGTON tr. *Nicholay's Voy.* I. xvii. 20 A hill, from whence we might easily see..the planting of their campe and their approches.

2. Concrete and collective uses.

†**a.** A slip, cutting, young plant, of a vine, etc.

c **1000** *Ags. Gosp.* Matt. xv. 13 Ælc plantung þe min heofenlica fæder ne plantode byþ awurt-walod. **1382** WYCLIF *Ps.* cxliii. 12 Whos sones; as newe plauntingis in ther ȝouthe. —— *Dan.* xi. 7 A plauntyng shal stonde of the buriownyng of hir rootis.

b. A clump or bed of things planted; *esp.* a clump or wood of planted trees; a plantation. Chiefly *Sc.* and *north. dial.*

1632 LITHGOW *Trav.* x. 498 The delectable planure of Murray.., inriched with Cornes, Plantings, Pastorage. **1719** DE FOE *Crusoe* (1858) 385 If they offered to..destroy any of the corn, plantings, buildings. **1720** *Lond. Gaz.* No. 5866/3 A considerable Quantity of well advanc'd Forest Planting. **1725** RAMSAY *Gentle Sheph.* v. iii, Busy gardeners shall new planting rear. **1812** SIR J. SINCLAIR *Syst. Husb. Scot.* I. 44 Hedges are often accompanied with hedge-rows, and sometimes by what are called belts of planting. **1854** H. MILLER *Sch. & Schm.* (1858) 205 When the day was fine, I used to spend it by the side of a mossy stream..or in a neighbouring planting. **1891** T. E. KEBBEL *Old & New Eng. Country Life* 48 In the woods and plantings trees are being felled.

3. *attrib.* and *Comb.*, as ***planting district, produce, season, work***; **planting-attorney**, in the West Indies, the manager of a plantation or estate; **planting-ground**, (*a*) a place where crops are planted; (*b*) 'a place where oysters are sown or planted' (*Cent. Dict.*); **planting-plough**: see quot. 1832; **planting-stick**, a dibble.

1552 HULOET, Plantynge stycke or debyll, *pastinum*. **1707** MORTIMER *Husb.* (1721) II. 269 Being cut off about the beginning of Planting-season, it will grow. **1719** LONDON & WISE *Compl. Gard.* 215 We make with a planting-stick, holes about four Inches deep. **1769** E. BANCROFT *Guiana* 369 He recurs to his planting-ground for his future provision. **1832** *Planting* 56 in *Libr. Usef. Knowl., Husb.* III, For the preparation of heath soils, incumbent on sand or loose gravel, an improved paring plough, which we call Fyshe Palmer's planting plough, is a valuable implement. **1878** J. INGLIS *Sport & W.* xvii. 222 Let him leave the planting districts, and go up to the wastes of Oudh. **1953** *Caribbean Q.* III. III. 142 The planters and planting-attornies were worried about the continuation of estate labour after the slaves should be apprenticed. **1956** H. G. DE LISSER *Cup & Lip* i. 19 Arthur was earnest at his work as his uncle's planting attorney.

ˈplanting, *ppl. a.* [f. PLANT *v.* + -ING[2].] That plants.

1827 STEUART *Planter's G.* (1828) 1 A 'Planting Nation', or, to speak with more correctness, a 'Nation of Planters'.

b. Owning or cultivating plantations (in colonies or semi-tropical countries).

1856 OLMSTED *Slave States* 272 From the beginning the planting aristocracy had merely been living on its capital. **1884** *Pall Mall G.* 27 May 2/2 On behalf of the Queensland planting community. **1893** *Westm. Gaz.* 25 Sept. 3/1 Those who in the seventeenth century brought slavery into the planting colonies.

c. Cattle-stealing (*Austral.*): see PLANT *v.* 8.

1890 'R. BOLDREWOOD' *Col. Reformer* xx. II. 152 That planting rascal Joe.

†**ˈplantisoun.** *Obs. rare*[−1]. [a. OF. *planteisun, -eson* (12th c.):—L. *plantātiōn-em.*] A plant.

c **1400** tr. *Secreta Secret., Gov. Lordsh.* 92 Anoþer plantisoun ys sayd for collodioun þat engendrys [hate and contempt].

plantivorous (plænˈtɪvərəs), *a.* [f. mod.L. *plantivorus* plant-eating + -OUS.] Devouring plants.

1890 in *Cent. Dict.* (citing Westwood).

plantless (ˈplɑːntlɪs, -æ-), *a.* [f. PLANT *sb.*[1] + -LESS.] Destitute of plants; without vegetation.

a **1846** *Edinb. Rev.* cited in WORCESTER.

ˈplantlet. [f. PLANT *sb.*[1] + -LET.] **a.** An embryo or undeveloped plant. **b.** A diminutive or tiny plant.

1816 KEITH *Phys. Bot.* II. 17 At the end of the ninth day the plantlet had wholly escaped from its integuments. **1877** FR. HEATH *Fern W.* 10 This plantlet or embryo consists of two principal organs united to each other. **1878** —— *Woodland Trees* 23 Temporary abiding places of the plantlets. **1899** [see DAMPING *vbl. sb.* 2]. **1935** A. F. HORT *Garden Variety* IV. 226 Here [*sc.* in a box] the plantlets..will remain for weeks or months. **1946** D. C. PEATTIE *Road of Naturalist* i. 18 For a seed is not just part of a plant; detached it is a complete plant, with a plantlet folded inside, a supply of food, an infinitesimal supply of moisture. **1970** *Nature* 19 Sept. 1265/2 Anthers from entirely white shoots gave rise to white plantlets.

plantlike (ˈplɑːntlaɪk, -æ-), *a.* [f. PLANT *sb.*[1] + -LIKE.] Resembling a plant or that of a plant.

1567 MAPLET *Gr. Forest* 26 So long is he plantlike. **1844** MARG. FULLER *Wom. 19th C.* (1862) 114 His song tended to reinstate a plant-like gentleness in the development of energy. **1888** ROLLESTON & JACKSON *Anim. Life* Introd. 20 Nutrition becomes holophytic or completely plantlike.

ˈplantling. [f. PLANT *sb.*[1] + -LING.] A little or young plant; a plantlet.

1766 *Museum Rust.* VI. 53 The plantlings, transplanted to a proper close bed. **1861** W. BARNES in *Macm. Mag.* June 126/2 A pea is planted, and there spring from it a rootling and a plantling.

plant-louse (ˈplɑːntlaʊs, -æ-). **a.** Any small hemipterous insect that infests plants; *esp.* an aphis.

1805 PRISCILLA WAKEFIELD *Dom. Recreat.* iv, It is called the aphis, puceron, vine-fretter, or plant-louse. **1815** KIRBY & SP. *Entomol.* iii. (1818) I. 67 Hemiptera, consisting of Bugs, Cicadæ,..Plant-lice. **1822-34** *Good's Study Med.* (ed. 4) IV. 2 In the aphis (puceron or green-plant louse) through all its divisions. **1840** J. & M. LOUDON tr. *Köllar's Treatise on Insects* II. 149 The plant-lice are especial enemies to various sorts of culinary vegetables. **1899** B. S. CRAGIN *Our Insect Friends & Foes* 228 Family Aphididæ. These are the Plant-lice, some with wings and some without. **1932** E. STEP *Wasps, Ants & Allied Insects Brit. Isles* 79 Like that of most of the other Black Wasps, its special prey is the Plant-louse (*Aphis*). **1968** R. LOWELL *Notebook* (1969) 48 The lily pads bright as mica, swarming with plant-lice. **1973** W. S. ROMOSER *Science of Entomology* xi. 346 Especially significant families are Psyllidae, jumping plant lice,..Aphididæ, aphids or plant lice, [etc.].

b. *Comb.* **plant-louse-lion** [after ANT-LION], an 'aphis-lion', which preys on aphides, the larva of various *Hemerobiidæ*, or lace-winged flies.

1805 PRISCILLA WAKEFIELD *Dom. Recreat.* iv, An insect called the plant-louse-lion.

plantmilk (ˈplɑːntmɪlk, -æ-). [f. PLANT *sb.*[1] + MILK *sb.*] A synthetic milk substitute prepared from vegetable matter.

1959 *Oxford Mail* 19 Mar. 4/5 It is estimated that the plantmilk which will soon be available to the general public will cost a few pence more than cows' milk. **1959** *New Scientist* 1 Oct. 596/1 Plantmilks based on soya are being used in America to treat milk allergies in infants. **1962** *Guardian* 27 Aug. 2/3 A plantmilk, made from cereals and pulses, has been on sale for some years. **1965** *Times* 1 Sept. 6/6 Drinka pinta milka day but make it plantmilk, Dr. Alan Stoddard advised delegates at the International Vegetarian Union's world congress at Swanwick, Derbyshire, today.

planˈtocracy. [irreg. f. PLANT(ER + -OCRACY, after *aristocracy*, etc.] A dominant class or caste consisting of planters (in the W. Indies, etc.).

a **1846** *Eclectic Rev.* cited in WORCESTER. **1865** *Morn. Star* 12 Dec., In the midst of a fierce conflict with the plantocracy in British Guiana. **1889** J. J. THOMAS *Froudacity* 254 The irritation and rancour seething in the breast of the new plantocracy.

†**plantoun.** *Obs. rare.* Also plaunt-. [a. OF. *planton* a young shoot, deriv. of *plante* PLANT *sb.*[1]] A plant or ? young plant.

c **1400** tr. *Secreta Secret., Gov. Lordsh.* 92 Of þe kynde of plauntouns ys oon þat engendrys langour,.. whos floures er whit, ouerpassant þe leuys. *Ibid.*, Anoþer ys of þe maner of plantouns þat ys helefull.

'plantsman. [f. *plants'*, possessive case of PLANT *sb.*[1] + MAN *sb.*[1]] An expert gardener; a connoisseur of plants. Hence **'plantsmanship**, a desire to display knowledge of unusual or especially rare plants.

1881 *Gard. Chron.* XVII. 770 A picture the plantsman.. is not likely soon to forget. **1900** *Nature* 5 Apr. 537/2 Long experience..often enables the plantsman to make conjectures which afterwards prove to be correct. **1952** *Archit. Rev.* CXII. 343/1 None of these plants remain in that environment for long as they are serviced and maintained by fully competent plantsmen. **1962** *Amateur Gardening* 21 Apr. 21/1 *Actinidia polygama*..has fruit of unpleasant flavour, but this should not..deter those who practise plantsmanship from planting a 'bower of bliss' with a few prominently labelled specimens. **1963** *Times* 3 June 1/7 Some of the best garden spurges are described by a plantsman contributor. **1978** W. BLUNT *In for Penny* xxi. 155 This lovely blue orchid [*sc. Vanda cœrulea*] had become a status symbol for rich plantsmen. **1979** J. HARVEY in J. Harris *Garden* 8/1 The abbeys, priories and hospitals were particularly concerned with plantsmanship, cultivation and improvement.

‖**plantula** ('plæntjʊlə). *Entom.* [mod.L. dim. of *planta* sole of the foot.] An accessory lobe or process occurring between the claws in various insects. Hence **'plantular** *a.*, pertaining to the plantula.

1826 KIRBY & SP. *Entomol.* III. 386 *Pseudonychia*... Two stiff claw-like bristles, that terminate the Plantula. **1895** *Camb. Nat. Hist.* V. 105 Between the claws there is frequently a lobe or process,..varied in different Insects, called empodium, arolium, palmula, plantula, pseudonychium, or pulvillus.

plantu'lation. *Bot. rare.* [a. F. *plantulation* (Richard 1808), n. of action f. assumed L. **plantulāre*, f. *plantula*: see next.] The development of the rudimentary plant from the embryo; germination.

1819 LINDLEY tr. *Richard's Obs. Fruits & Seeds* 68 We call germination that first spontaneous action... Perhaps it might..be called Plantulation, since the formation and developement of a little plant is the result. **1858** MAYNE *Expos. Lex., Plantulatio*,..term by L. C. Richard for the developement of the embryo during germination: plantulation.

plantule ('plæntjuːl). *Bot.* ? *Obs.* [ad. mod.L. *plantula*, dim. of *planta* a shoot, slip.] An embryonic or rudimentary plant.

[**1706** PHILLIPS, *Plantula Seminalis*, (among Herbalists) is the little Herb that lies as it were an Embryo in miniature in every Seed.] **1733–40** TULL *Horse-hoeing Husb.* Add. 264 'Tis as unreasonable to suppose a Power in an animal or vegetable Body to produce Animalcles or Plantules from inorganical Matter by Secretions of the Aliment. **1766** *Compl. Farmer* s.v. *Seed*, The rest of the seed serves to feed the young plant, or plantule. **1791** E. DARWIN *Bot. Gard.* I. Notes 106 After fecundation a body begins to appear.. which in process of time proves to be two lobes containing a plantule. **1865** *Reader* No. 143. 355/2 The production of amyliferous plantules.

‖**planula** ('plænjʊlə). *Zool.* Pl. -æ. [mod.L., a little plane, dim. of *plānus* PLANE *a.*] The flat-shaped ciliated free-swimming embryo of certain Hydrozoa; hence extended to a similar embryo in Cœlenterates generally.

1870 NICHOLSON *Man. Zool.* 89 The embryo is a free-swimming, oblong, ciliated body, termed a planula. **1877** HUXLEY *Anat. Inv. Anim.* iii. 146 In most Hydrophora the ciliated, locomotive, planula becomes elongated and fixed by its aboral pole. **1878** BELL *Gegenbaur's Comp. Anat.* 98 Developed, just like the Hydroid-Polyps, from a planula, which is at first free, and which afterwards becomes fixed. *attrib.* **1887** SOLLAS in *Encycl. Brit.* XXII. 425/2 The history of the second or planula type [of development] has been thoroughly worked out by Schulze in a little incrusting Tetractinellid sponge (*Plakina monolopha*, Schulze).

So **'planulan**, a planula; **'planular** *a.*, (*a*) of flattened form; (*b*) pertaining to or of the nature of a planula; **'planulate** *a.*, of a flattened form; **'planuliform** *a.*, of the form of a planula; **'planuloid** *a.*, resembling a planula.

1886 GEDDES in *Encycl. Brit.* XX. 420/2 The passage from Protozoa to Metazoa was, according to Bütschli, effected neither by *planulan nor gastrula but by a disk-like 'placula'. **1858** MAYNE *Expos. Lex., Planularis*, applied by Lamarck to a section (*Planulares*) of soft worms having flat bodies: *planular. **1895** *Syd. Soc. Lex., Planular*, pertaining to a Planula. **1846** DANA *Zooph.* (1848) 570 The cells are nearly circular, contiguous, or *planulate. **1877** HUXLEY *Anat. Inv. Anim.* viii. 459 In the fresh-water Polyzoa, the impregnated ovum gives rise to a saccular *planuliform embryo. **1895** *Syd. Soc. Lex.*, **Planuloid*, the same as *Planuliform.*

†**'planure.** *Obs. rare.* [a. obs. F. *planure* = It. *pianura* plain, f. L. *plān-um* level ground: see -URE.] A flat or level district, a plain. Hence †**'planured** *a.*, situated in a plain.

1632 LITHGOW *Trav.* I. 40 The Territo[r]y of Venice..in the planure is narrow, but stripeth larger among the hills and lakes. *Ibid.* VIII. 367 The two Hills on both sides the planur'd Citty..are ouer-cled with streetes and houses. *Ibid.* x. 498 The delectable planure of Murray.

‖**planuria** (plə'njʊərɪə). *Path.* Also in anglicized form **planury** ('plænjʊərɪ). [f. Gr. πλάνο-ς wandering, straying + -URIA, f. οὖρον urine.] Discharge of urine through an abnormal channel, e.g. a fistula.

1853 DUNGLISON *Med. Lex., Planuria*, discharge of urine through unwonted ways. **1858** MAYNE *Expos. Lex., Planuria*,..planu'ry. **1895** *Syd. Soc. Lex., Planuria*, the passage of urine through a fistulous opening. *Plan'ury*, the same as *Planuria.*

planxty ('plæŋkstɪ). *Irish Music.* Also 8 **plangstee, plansty.** [Derivation unknown. App. not native Irish, see Petrie, *Ancient Music of Ireland* (1855) 13–15. (Some suggest its formation in some way from L. *plangĕre* to strike, beat.)] 'A harp tune of a sportive and animated character, moving in triplets. It is not intended for or often adaptable to words, and is slower in pace than the jig' (Stainer and Barrett).

1790 J. WILLIAMS *Shrove Tuesday* (1794) 6 I'd make him chaunt a solemn *drimmundub* Or jocund plangstee, pæan or quaint air. **1807** *Edin. Rev.* X. 47 He..leaves at every hospitable mansion..a planxty, celebrating the virtues, charms, or high descent of the hostess. **1825** T. C. CROKER *Fairy Leg.* 288 He could play jig and planxty without end. **1842** S. LOVER *Handy Andy* xix, Dick Dawson was whistling a planxty and eyeing his man. **1855** G. PETRIE *Anc. Music Irel.* 13 Of the Planxty and the Pleraca..the difference seems to me to be only in names which are convertible... In a collection of Irish tunes, chiefly of Carolan's composition, published..in 1810, the term Planxty [is] given as the English name, and Pleraca as the Irish one of the same tune. .. The tunes called Planxties, as well as those called Pleracas, owe their origin, if not, as I believe, their names to Carolan [died 1738]. **1904** *Daily Chron.* 17 Mar., All last night they danced in Caxton Hall..—slip jigs, reels, and planxties, and never a foreign dance among them!

plap (plæp), *v.* [Onomatopœic: cf. for beginning *plash*, for end *flap*, *slap*. See also PLOP.] *intr.* To come down or fall with a flat impact, and with the sound that this makes. Also as *sb.* or *adv.*, in phr. ***to play plap.***

1846 THACKERAY *Cornhill to Cairo* x, Constantinople beauties..waddling and plapping in their odious yellow papooshes. **1855** —— *Newcomes* lxvi, Hark, there is Barnes Newcome's eloquence still plapping on like water from a cistern. **1860** —— *Round. Papers, Christmas Tree* 109 The white bears winked their pink eyes, as they plapped up and down by their pool. **1894** CROCKETT *Raiders* 231 The rain drops played 'plap' on my naked skin.

plapper ('plæpə(r)), *v.* [imit.: see S.N.D.] *intr.* To make sounds with the lips.

1866 W. GREGOR in *Trans. Philol. Soc.* 127 *Plapper*,..to make a noise with the lips. **1922** JOYCE *Ulysses* 258 She took no notice while he read by rote a solfa fable for her, plappering flatly.

plaque (plɑːk, ‖plak). [F. *plaque*: see PLACK.]

1. a. An ornamental plate or tablet of metal or porcelain, of quadrangular, round, oval, or other regular form, either plain or decorated with figures, intended to be hung up as a wall-decoration, or to be inserted in a piece of furniture, etc. Also, an inscribed plate identifying a monument or building, etc.

1869 C. SCHREIBER *Jrnl.* (1911) I. 13 A large plaque of Smalto glass, with landscape in brown. **1870** *Ibid.* I. 68 We saw..a very fine Terra Cotta plaque, by Clodion, 3 to 4 feet long. **1875** MASKELL *Ivories* 41 The plaques have borders with foliated ornaments; birds and animals, flowers and fruits, filling the intermediate spaces. **1875** FORTNUM *Maiolica* iii. 23 A votive plaque preserved in the museum of the hôtel Cluny, at Paris. **1879** J. J. YOUNG *Ceram. Art* 38 Picture-painting on the flat surface of porcelain plaques. **1884** MRS. C. PRAED *Zéro* xix, The brazen plaques above the mantel-piece resembled menacing heads. **1956** A. J. CRONIN *Crusader's Tomb* III. ix. 195 At the base of the pediment was a time-worn plaque defining the intention of the founder to tend the sick. **1968** *Guardian* 19 Sept. 18/3 In a few days Britain will have two fish and chip shops, each proclaiming itself by plaque to be the oldest..in the world. **1969** M. PUGH *Last Place Left* xxiii. 175 Why don't you wait fifty years or so? I imagine there will be a plaque outside his house. **1971** *Times* 19 Apr. 12/5 Mrs. Pankhurst's house in Clement's Inn is being demolished and the Women's Liberation movement is concerned lest the blue plaque from the house..should disappear. **1979** ATTERBURY & IRVINE *Doulton Story* 20 Probably the best known Doulton commemoratives are the plaques made for the LCC and other bodies to mark places associated with famous people and events.

b. A small ornamental tablet worn as a badge of high rank in an honorary order.

1848 THACKERAY *Van. Fair* xlix, A nobleman tightly girthed, with a large military chest, on which the *plaque* of his order shone magnificently. *Ibid.* lxiv, Men with *plaques* and *cordons*. **1860** RUSSELL *Diary India* II. 239 In front of his turban there was a plaque of diamonds and emeralds.

c. A counter used in gambling. Cf. CHIP *sb.*[1] 2 d.

1904 A. BENNETT *Great Man* xxv. 281 A croupier counted out..sundry..gold *plaques* of a hundred francs each. **1964** A. WYKES *Gambling* xii. 288 The big bets are placed with rectangular colored chips, called plaques. **1972** D. LEES *Zodiac* 47 Françoise picked up the plaques from the table in front of her. **1973** 'R. MACLEOD' *Burial in Portugal* vi. 117 Deliberately, Salvador used a one thousand escudo plaque to scratch along his small moustache.

d. *Mus.* A thin metal plate inserted into the separated tip of the double reed of a wind instrument while the reed is being scraped.

1940 J. ARTLEY *How to make Double Reeds* 13/1 Insert the plaque between the blades of the reed. *Ibid.* 14/1 While working on the lay with the knife, use the plaque at all times. **1953** E. ROTHWELL *Oboe Technique* vi. 48 *Tongue, or plaque*, for inserting into the reed while scraping. Small flat piece of metal, oval shaped with pointed ends. *Ibid.* 53 In order to avoid any confusion between the human tongue and the metal one, I shall, throughout this chapter, refer to the latter as the *plaque*, the alternative word used little in England but almost exclusively in America. **1957** A. BAINES *Woodwind Instruments & their Hist.* iii. 82 The *tongue* (or *plaque*, fig. 11, *t*) is a thin, oval steel plate about 40 × 15 millimetres, and it is always placed between the blade tips while scraping after the tips have been separated. **1962** E. C. MOORE *Oboe & its Daily Routine* iv. 13/1 Few tools are needed..a plaque to slip between the blades of the reeds, [etc.].

2. a. *Path.* A patch of eruption or the like.

1876 BARTHOLOW *Mat. Med.* (1879) 311 Before the exudation has spread and consolidated into membranous plaques. **1899** *Allbutt's Syst. Med.* VIII. 658 The eruption of hydroa gestationis..consists of erythematous patches, some of which are rounded plaques. *Ibid.* 809 Plaques like those of lichen ruber planus may be seen.

b. *Anat.* A small flat discoidal formation, as a hæmatoblast or blood-plate.

1895 *Syd. Soc. Lex., Plaque*, a plate. A French word adopted of late by medical writers meaning either a small disc-like object, as a blood-platelet, or a rounded patch.

c. *Med.* A patch of fibrous tissue or of fatty matter on the wall of an artery; the substance of which such a patch is formed.

1891 *Trans. Assoc. Amer. Physicians* VI. 182 The nodular form of arterio-sclerosis is due to circumscribed dilations of the arteries and a new formation of connective tissue which exactly fills out the dilated area. When such arteries are examined after having been injected with paraffine.., the raised plaques which are so prominent in the uninjected vessels have entirely disappeared, leaving a smooth intima. **1943** *Physiol. Rev.* XXIII. 188 The atherosclerotic lesions.. were classified as fatty plaques, fibrous plaques, calcified plaques, and atheromatous ulcers. **1972** *Daily Colonist* (Victoria, B.C.) 4 May 2/1 As the years pass, the walls of our arteries thicken and accumulate a certain amount of plaque, or fatty deposits. **1975** *Daily Tel. Mag.* 5 Dec. 20/4 These so-called plaques, and the attached clots, build up and obtrude upon the bore of the vessel. **1978** *Time* 3 July 54/1 Tests showed that his left main coronary artery was clogged with cholesterol-laden plaque.

d. *Dentistry.* A patch of deposit that contains bacteria and adheres firmly to the surface of a tooth; the substance of which such patches are composed.

1898 G. V. BLACK in *Dental Cosmos* XL. 448 Leptothrix threads..are found..clinging in and upon gelatinous microbic plaques upon the teeth. **1921** RYAN & BOWERS *Teeth & Health* xi. 154 In caries, or dental decay, placques or films of saliva form on the tooth surfaces, in combination with particles of carbohydrates. **1959** WILKINS & MCCULLOUGH *Clin. Pract. Dental Hygienist* ii. 109 Dental plaque is a thin, tenacious, film-like deposit made up principally of microorganisms and mucinous substances from the saliva. It is removed by polishing procedures. Plaque is the most commonly found of all tooth deposits. *Ibid.*, Dental plaques vary in thickness, degree of adherence to the tooth surface, and percentage composition. **1971** *Daily Tel.* 24 Aug. 5 (Advt.), The toothbrush is undoubtedly the most effective weapon in the fight against bacterial plaque. Plaque produces the harmful acids and chemicals that cause tooth decay and discoloration. **1976** J. J. MURRAY *Fluorides in Caries Prevention* xii. 185 Dental plaque is a soft, tenacious bacterial deposit suspended in a protein matrix which forms on the surface of teeth. It also contains varying amounts of extracellular polysaccharide and desquamated bacterial cells.

e. *Biol.* A relatively clear area in a culture of micro-organisms or other cells produced by the inhibitory or lethal effect of a virus or other agent.

D'Herelle used *plage*, not *plaque*, in Fr. (*Le Bactériophage* (1921) i. 13).

1924 *Jrnl. Bacteriol.* IX. 397 These lytic areas, or plaques, are usually circular and may vary in size from pits of microscopic dimensions to eroded fields possessing a diameter of 18 to 20 mm. **1930** G. H. SMITH tr. *F. D'Herelle's Bacteriophage & its Clin. Applic.* i. 12 Each bare spot, which I have termed a *plaque*, represents a colony of bacteriophage particles. **1952** *Proc. Nat. Acad. Sci.* XXXVIII. 747 (*heading*) Production of plaques in monolayer tissue cultures by simple particles of an animal virus. **1963** *Science* 26 Apr. 405/1 Distinct plaques, each of which is due to the release of hemolysin by a single antibody-forming cell, are revealed by complement after incubation, in an agar layer, of a mixture of sheep red cells and lymphoid cells from a rabbit immunized with sheep red cells. **1970** T. D. BROCK *Biol. Microorganisms* x. 260 Since the agar prevents the new virus particles from moving too far away, a localized area of lysis develops that contains no bacteria but many virus particles... This local area of lysis is called a plaque..and represents the end result of a chain of events initiated by one virus particle.

3. *Med.* A flat applicator designed to contain radium or one of its salts, formerly applied to the surface of the body over cancerous tissue for the curative effect of the radiation.

1919 [see *radium plaque*]. **1922** F. E. SIMPSON *Radium Therapy* xii. 110 The best type of metal applicator is made of silver, the radium salt being spread uniformly over a glazed surface which forms the face of the applicator. Lead free glass must be used. Plaques of this type are known as glazed radium applicators. **1931** G. E. BIRKETT *Radium Therapy* xi. 150 Superficial sclerosing type [of rodent ulcers].—In the early stages these may be successfully treated by the application of an unscreened radium plaque. **1950** Walter & Miller *Short Textbk. Radiotherapy* viii. 195 A beta-ray applicator is an example of a plaque. The one illustrated in Fig. 82 is made of brass, has an area of 4 sq. cm. and contains 5 mgm. of radium per square cm. It is covered by a filter of 0·1 mm. of monel metal.

plaquet, obs. form of PLACCATE.

‖**plaquette** (pla'kɛt). [F. dim. of *plaque*: see -ETTE.]

1. A small plaque or ornamental tablet.

1888 *Academy* 8 Dec. 377/1 The work of another North Italian worker in bronze,..from an examination of several plaquettes from his hand. **1894** *Times* 20 Feb. 3/1 In bronze there are statuettes, medals, and plaquettes in great numbers. **1903** *Westm. Gaz.* 1 Dec. 7/2 At the reception.. each British M.P. was presented with a beautiful silver plaquette representing England and France fraternising.

2. *Anat.* = PLAQUE 2 b.

1883 *Smithsonian Rep.* 735 G. Hayem insists that the elements of the blood, to which he gave the name of hematoblasts, are identical with the 'plaquettes', or corpuscles, described by Bizzozero.

plas, plasce, plase, obs. forms of PLACE.

plash (plæʃ), *sb.*[1] Forms: 1 plæsc, plesc; 4 plasch, 5 plaisshe, playche, 5–6 plasche, 6 plasshe, 5– plash, (6, 9 *dial.* plesh, 9 *dial.* plosh). [OE. *plæsc*, ME. *plasch*, cognate with MDu., Flem. *plasch* pool, also MDu., Du., MLG., LG. *plas*, LG. *plasse*; app. of the same origin as PLASH *v.*[2], prob. onomatopœic: cf. FLASH *sb.*[1] From the LG. came also OF. *plasquier*, *plasquis*, *plassis* a marsh (Froiss.), *plascq* a damp meadow (Tournai 1443).] A shallow piece of standing water, a pool made by inundation or by the rain; a marshy pool; a puddle.

963 *Grant by K. Eadgar* in Birch *Cart. Sax.* III. 355 In duobus locis quæ sic vocitantur Plesc et Eastun. *Ibid.* 356 Ærest of plæsc in þone broc..of mæne leʒe to þam broce, of þam brocæ þæt æft in plesc. ?*a* **1400** *Morte Arth.* 2799 Betwyx a plasche and a flode, appone a flate lawnde. *c* **1400** *Laud Troy Bk.* 6226 Eche stede stod ful, bothe plasch & polk, Of mennes blode that died there. *c* **1440** *Promp. Parv.* 403/1 Plasche, or flasche, where reyne watyr stondythe. *c* **1475** *Pict. Voc.* in Wr.-Wülcker 799/40 *Hec lacuna*, a playche of water. **1523** Ld. Berners *Froiss.* I. cccxcviii. 691 Before them there was a great plasshe of standynge water. **1590** Spenser *F.Q.* II. viii. 36 The red blood flowed fresh, That underneath his feet soone made a purple plesh. **1605** Bacon *Adv. Learn.* II. xxiii. §41 Two frogs..consulted when their plash was drie whither they should go. **1648–78** Hexham *Dutch Dict.*, *Plas, Plasch*, Plash of water. **1773** *Gentl. Mag.* XLIII. 539 When crossing any plash of water, she lifted him over. **1868** J. C. Atkinson *Gloss. Cleveland Dial.* 385 *Plosh* sb., puddle, liquid mire, like the sloppy mud on a road after much rain. **1871** Tennyson *Last Tourn.* 420 Many a glancing plash and sallowy isle. **1895** J. Thomas *Randigal Rhymes* 22 Nor don't ee lag, or stag yourself By stanking through the plosh. **1930** H. Walpole *Rogue Herries* III. 495 He found himself in the little dark wood,.. his feet in plosh and mire.

Comb. **1621** G. Sandys *Ovid's Met.* VI. (1626) 116 With shrubby osiers, and plash-loving reeds.

plash, *sb.*[2] (*adv.* or *int.*) Also plosh. [Goes with PLASH *v.*[2], being (though known earlier) app. the sb. naming the act. In sense it is more directly akin to the vb. than to PLASH *sb.*[1]]

The noise made when any body strikes the surface of water so as to break it up, or plunges into or through it; an act accompanied by this noise; a plunge, a splash.

1513 Douglas *Æneis* IX. xiii. 82 Than at the last, al suddanly, with a plasch, Harnes and all togiddir..[he] lap into the flude. **1582** Stanyhurst *Æneis* I. (Arb.) 21 Doune the pilot tumbleth wyth plash round soommoned headlong. **1808** Scott *Marm.* VI. xxxiv, Tweed's echoes heard the ceaseless plash, While many a broken band, Disordered, through her currents dash, To gain the Scottish land. **1840** Thirlwall *Greece* VII. liv. 34 The plash of numberless oars. **1866** Geo. Eliot *F. Holt* vii, Mr. Christian here let a lemon slip from his hand into the punch-bowl with a plash which sent some of the nectar into the company's faces. **1876** C. C. Robinson *Gloss. Dial. Mid-Yorks.* 103/2 *Plosh* is much more heard than 'plodge', and, as a substantive, bears relation to an object as well as an action. *Plosh* is anything of the nature and consistency of a puddle, into which, if a hasty foot be placed, or a stick let fall, there results a *plosh*. **1882** Mrs. Riddell *Pr. Wales' Garden-Party* 65 There was the plash of a water-fowl in the stream. **1893** Leland *Mem.* I. 12 The mighty sturgeon..falling on his side with a plash. **1928** Blunden *Undertones of War* 138 The plosh of the whizzing fuse-top into the muck. **1935** S. Desmond *African Log* xlii. 208 'To listen to the silence of the forest', to hear the plosh in the dried herbage of the grasshoppers.

b. The like noise produced when water or other liquid is dashed against or falls upon a body, or when masses of water dash against each other; an act producing this noise.

1808 Scott *Marm.* II. xviii, The mildew drops fell one by one With tinkling plash upon the stone. **1814** —— *Ld. of Isles* III. xxviii, The short dark waves, heaved to the land, With ceaseless plash kissed cliff or sand. **1837** Disraeli *Venetia* I. xii, The plash of the troubled and swollen lake. **1851** Helps *Comp. Solit.* ix. (1874) 155 The only noise was a plash of the water against a jetty.

c. A heavy fall of rain. *Sc.* and *north. dial.* [Cf. Du. *plasregen*, Ger. *platzregen*, Da. *plaskregn* (*pladsregn*).]

1820 *Blackw. Mag.* May 158/1 The thunder-rain, in large drops, came plash after plash on the blanket roof. **1887** Ruskin *Præterita* II. 162 Penthouses..to keep the plash of heavy rain from the house windows. **1894** *Weather Saw* in Heslop *Northumb. Gloss.*, If the oak before the ash, Then we're sure to have a plash.

d. A splash of colour, or *fig.* of light, thrown upon a surface.

1848 Lowell *Fable for Critics* (ed. 2) Introd., The tall grove of hemlocks, with moss on their stems, like plashes of sunlight.

†**e.** *transf.* (?) A liquid perfume for the face.

1649 Lovelace *Poems* 146 No Cabinets with curious Washes, Bladders and perfumed Plashes.

f. *attrib.* † **plash-breach**, the breaking of waves against the shore.

1582 Stanyhurst *Æneis* III. (Arb.) 83 Theese shoars were sundred by the plash breache, fame so doth vtter... Swift the sea with plasshing rusht in.

B. *adverbially* or *int.* With a plash: cf. CRASH.

1842 J. Wilson *Chr. North* I. 31 Plash, plash, through the marsh, and then on the dry furze beyond..away fly hare and hounds towards the mountain. **1866–7** Livingstone *Last Jrnls.* (1873) I. vii. 172 We go plash, plash, plash, in the lawn-like glade. **1897** *Outing* (U.S.) XXX. 354/2 Plash, plash, the great drops pelted down furious and fast.

†**plash**, *sb.*[3] *Obs.* or *dial.* [f. PLASH *v.*[1]] A plashed bough or bush; a plashed thicket.

1638 Brathwait *Spir. Spicerie*, etc. 427 The fresh fragrant flowers of Divine Poesie..could not like to be removed nor transported to those thorny places and plashes of the Law. **1707** Mortimer *Husb.* (1721) I. 11 Avoid the laying of them too high, which draws all the Sap into the Plashes. **1827** *Nat. Hist.* in *Ann. Reg.* 522/1 There will be one plash for every interval between the stems of the plants. You must..lay the plashes with their points all one way.

plash (plæʃ), *v.*[1] Forms: 5–6 plashe, 6 plasche, plasshe, 6, 8 plach, 7 plaish, 6– plash, (9 *dial.* plesh, plush). See also PLEACH. [a. OF. *plaiss(i)er*, *plai(s)cier*, *plassier*, *pless(i)er* (3 sing. pres. *plaisse*, *plaisce*):—late L. type **plectiāre*, f. **plectia* twined or plaited hedge (whence OF. *plaisse*, *plesse* hedge), f. L. *plectĕre* to plait, interweave, twine. (Med.L. *plessa* (1215 = *virgulta implexa*, Du Cange) and *plessare* were f. OF. *plesse*, *plesser*.) Cf. the cognate PLEACH, found somewhat earlier.]

1. *trans.* To bend down and interweave (stems half cut through, branches, and twigs) so as to form them into a hedge or fence; = PLEACH *v.* 1.

1495 [see PLASHING *vbl. sb.*[1]]. **1523** Fitzherb. *Husb.* §127 At euery two fote, or .iii. fote, to leaue one set growyng not plasshed; and the toppe to be cut of foure fote hygh..to stande as a stake..and to wynd the other that be pleched about them. **1523** —— *Surv.* xxv. 43 Take a great boughe of a tree, and plasshe the bowes abrode. **1563** Golding *Cæsar* (1565) 54 b, Cutting yong trees half a sunder and bowyng downe theyr toppes to the grounde, and plasshyng the boughes that growe thicke oute of the sydes wyth bushes and thornes betwene them, they brought to passe that their hedges were as good a defence to them as a wal. **1595** *Drake's Voy.* (Hakl. Soc.) 15 Some of our men..came to the trees which they [the Spaniards] had plasshed to make theyr palizadoe. **1629** Parkinson *Paradisus* iii. 7 Some againe plant Cornell Trees, and plash them..to forme them into an hedge. **1712** J. James tr. *Le Blond's Gardening* 59 Arbors made of the Trees plashed one over the other. **1844** Stephens *Bk. Farm* II. 571 The hedger plashes down the stems he left standing.

†**b.** To bend down, break down (trees, bushes, or plants) for other purposes. *Obs.*

1625 Lisle *Du Bartas, Noe* Past. Ded. 5 Plash thistles and presumptuous thorns That neare the way grow up among the corns. **1630** Lennard tr. *Charron's Wisd.* II. vii. (1670) 279 Too much plenty plasheth down the corn! **1684** Bunyan *Pilgr.* II. (1847) 233 Christiana's Boys..being pleas'd with the Trees, and with the Fruit that did hang thereon, did Plash them, and began to eat. **1727** Bradley *Fam. Dict.* s.v. *Hart*, Let him plash down small Twigs, some above and some below.

†**c.** To interlace (a fruit-tree in trellis-work); to support or train against a trellis or a wall. *Obs.*

[*c* **1420**: see PLEACH *v.* 1.] ?*c* **1600** *Distracted Emp.* III. i. in Bullen *O. Pl.* III. 210 Our pore retyred famylie must..not be plashd Or propt agaynst the walls of pallaces. **1613** Markham *Eng. Husbandman* I. II. xx. (1635) 226 As you use to plash a Vine against a wall. **1648** *Hunting of Fox* 6 It cannot stand unles it be propped up, or plashed against a Wall. **1676** Worlidge *Cyder* (1691) 39 It is usual with some to plash them to poles, to make a pallisade-hedge.

†**d.** To intertwine, interweave, like plants in a thicket. *Obs.*

1653 H. Cogan tr. *Pinto's Trav.* xxiii. (1663) 84 Stuck every where with most fragrant Roses and Violets all plashed so close together that we could not see the Rowers. **1657** Austen *Fruit Trees* I. 66 Trees..kept (by cutting and plaishing one branch within another) from growing very large. **1735** Somerville *Chase* IV. 63 Thread the Brake With Thorns sharp-pointed, plash'd, and Bri'rs inwoven.

2. a. To make, dress, or renew (a hedge) by cutting the stems partly through, bending them down, and interlacing stems, branches, and twigs, so as to form a close low fence, which will in time grow in height; to lay (a hedge); = PLEACH *v.* 2.

1523 Fitzherb. *Husb.* §127 To plasshe or pleche a hedge. **1577** B. Googe *Heresbach's Husb.* II. (1586) 50 The common hedge made of dead wood, well staked and thicke plashed, or railde. **1616** Surfl. & Markh. *Country Farme* 20 If any of your Hedges were left vnplasht in the Spring, plash them now, for it is an excellent Season. **1787** W. Marshall *Norfolk* I. 101 The practice of plashing, or laying hedges, is in a great degree, unknown in this district. **1891** T. Hardy *Tess* 9/1 The lanes are white, the hedges low and plashed.

†**b.** To treat (a wood, or place full of trees or underwood) in the same way, in order to obstruct a pass or entrance, or defend a fastness; to form hurdles, weirs, etc. by such interweaving.

1586 J. Hooker *Hist. Irel.* in *Holinshed* II. 7/2 They..did fell downe trees, plashed the wood, cast great trenches and ditches round about, and made it so strict, narrow, crooked, and strong, that there was no passage nor entrie for the enimie. **1633** T. Stafford *Pac. Hib.* II. xiv. (1810) 376 In a strong Fastnesse of Bogg and Wood, which was on every quarter plashed. **1796** W. Marshall *W. England* I. 81 To plash the sides (or outer brinks of the mounds), and shovel out the ditches. **1875** Knight *Dict. Mech.*

Hence **plashed** *ppl. a.*

1602 *Burford Reg.* (Hist. MSS. Comm.) *Varr. Collect.* I. 164 Makinge of plaished hedge and other fensed hedge. **1615** W. Lawson *Orch. & Gard.* (1623) 20 The plasht bough lying on the ground. **1621** G. Sandys *Ovid's Met.* XII. (1626) 242 Plashed bowres at sundrie tables plac't. **1844** Stephens *Bk. Farm* II. 571 The plashed stem is cut over, of the length required for the particular gap. **1858** R. S. Surtees *Ask Mamma* lxv, A well drained wheat stubble, with a newly plashed fence.

plash (plæʃ), *v.*[2] [Known from *c* 1580; but the accompanying PLASH *sb.*[2] goes back to *c* 1500. Agreeing more or less in form with MLG., LG. *plasken*, *plaschen*, LG. *platsken*, MDu., Du., LG. *plassen*, early mod.Du. *plasschen* ('int water plasschen, *poteliner en l'eau*', Plantijn 1572), Ger. *platschen*, *plätsche(r)n*, *plan(t)schen*, Da. *pla(d)ske*, Sw. *plaska* to splash, dabble; all app. closely related to PLASH *sb.*[1] See also PLASH *sb.*[2], and SPLASH *v.*, which last appears to be a derivative from this.]

1. *trans.* To strike the surface of (water) so as to break it up; to plunge into (water or other liquid) or drive it against any body or against itself with commotion and noise; to splash.

1582 Stanyhurst *Æneis* II. (Arb.) 50 Two serpents monsterus ouglye Plasht the water sulcking to the shoare moste hastelye swinging. **1694** tr. *Milton's Lett. State* Wks. 1851 VIII. 403 Unless they lay themselves down to be trampl'd under foot, plash'd like Mortar, or abjure their Religion. **1859** Geo. Eliot *A. Bede* v, We must go and plash up the mud a little. **1861** Mrs. Norton *Lady La G.* (1862) 61 The summer rain, That..plashed the azure of the river's flow.

b. To dash with breaking water or other liquid so as to wet; to splash. Also *absol.*

1602 Warner *Alb. Eng.* x. lvii. (1612) 251 Where Massacres haue plashed, there is spread a triple breede. **1608** T. Morton *Preamble Encounter* 1 My Aduersarie.. hath plashed me, as it were, with these aspersions. **1706** Phillips, To *Plash*, to dash with Water. **1791** J. Learmont *Poems* 59 (E.D.D.) He..coaches owr the dubs to plash him. **1856** G. Henderson *Rhymes Berwick* 74 The floor all plashed with blood. **1884** W. C. Smith *Kildrostan* 90 Had I but such a Naiad..To plash her large limbs in the waves for me!

c. To dash (a wall) with wet matter, so as rapidly to colour or cover it; to splash.

1864 Webster, *Plashing*,..the dashing or sprinkling of coloring matter on the walls of buildings, as an imitation of granite, and the like.

2. *intr.* **a.** To strike and break the mass of water with commotion and noise; to dash, rush through, or tumble about in water with the like noise; to splash.

1650 T. Bayly *Herba Parietis* 129 Every strooke that plashed upon those waters of life gave both life and music. **1718** Ramsay *Christ's Kirk Gr.* III. xix, Thro' thick and thin they scour'd about, Plashing thro' dubs and sykes. **1840** Thackeray *Catherine* viii, The fish were jumping and plashing. **1857–8** Sears *Athan.* vii. 58 He plashes in the brooks. **1872** Black *Adv. Phaeton* xv, The two long oars plashed in the silence. **1898** G. W. Steevens *With Kitchener to Khartum* 304 We plashed through the water.

b. Of water or other liquid: To dash against or upon any body; to tumble about in agitation, with the characteristic noise of breaking water.

1665 Sir T. Herbert *Trav.* (1677) 392 The salt water plashes and froaths to see it self so suddenly resisted. **1828** Hawthorne *Fanshawe* viii, Plashing continually upon one spot, the fount has worn its own little channel of white sand. **1855** Longf. *Hiaw.* XVI. 245 Far below him plashed the waters.

fig. **1841** H. Ainsworth *Old St. Paul's* VI. vii, Another fiery cascade..flooding the aisles and plashing against the massive columns.

3. *Comb.* **plash-wheel** = *dash-wheel*: see DASH *v.*[1] 16.

1882 Ogilvie (Annandale).

'**plasher**. *local.* [f. PLASH *v.*[1] + -ER[1].]

a. A bough or sapling with which a hedge is plashed or intertwisted. **b.** A hedger who plashes hedges.

a **1722** Lisle *Husb.* (1757) 436 That the cattle may not come at the shoots of the plashers, and browse them, and kill them. **1886** *S.W. Linc. Gloss.*, *Plasher*, a labourer employed in laying hedges. **1886** Elworthy *W. Somerset Word-bk.*, *Plusher*, the layer, or horizontal stick crooked down in making a hedge. **1904** *19th Cent.* Sept. 229 [He] chooses with care the likeliest growing wood for 'plashers'.

'**plashet**. Now *dial.* Also 6 -ette. [ad. OF. *plassiet*, *plaschiet* (Froiss.) marsh, dim. of *plascq* damp meadow; see PLASH *sb.*^{1} and -ET^1.] A little plash or marshy pool.

1575 TURBERV. *Falconrie* 191 Some water plashet or pitte where wylde fowle lye, as Teales or suche lyke. 1578 LYTE *Dodoens* v. lxviii. 633 This herbe [arsesmart] groweth also in moyst marrishe places, and alongst the water plasshettes. 1880 PEARD *Mother Molly* xv. 189 Let's run down here, there's a plashet at the bottom.

†**'plashful**, *a. Obs. rare*$^{-1}$. [f. PLASH *sb.* (^{1} or ^{2}) + -FUL.] Plashy, splashy.

1638-48 G. DANIEL *Eclog.* v. 132 To which our notes Would sound more harsh then plash-full marish throats.

plashily ('plæʃılı), *adv. rare.* [f. PLASHY *a.*^{2} + -LY^2.] With a plashing noise.

1926 R. MACAULAY *Crewe Train* III. i. 240 Going away, going away, going away. The waves plashily said it over.

'plashing, *vbl. sb.*^{1} [f. PLASH *v.*^{1} + -ING^1.] The action of PLASH *v.*^{1} in various senses. Also *concr.* A piece of plashed hedge or thicket.

1495 *Trevisa's Barth. De P.R.* XVII. cxliii. (W. de W.), By plashynge [*MS.* plechinge] shredynge and parynge a wylowe is thycker in bowes and braunches. 1511 *MS. Acc. St. John's Hosp., Canterb.*, Payd for plaschyng off a heg. 1600 DYMMOK *Ireland* (1843) 35 The passag..was very difficult..for plashin[g] made that morninge by yᵉ rebell. 1669 WORLIDGE *Syst. Agric.* (1681) 268 This is the only time for plashing of Quick-sets, and a very good season for the shrouding or lopping of Trees. 1844 STEPHENS *Bk. Farm* II. 571 What is termed *plashing*, that is, laying down a strong and healthy stem across an opening..in the hedge. 1904 *19th Cent.* Sept. 229 A wren..hiding out of sight behind the old level plashing upon the bank.

b. *attrib.*, as *plashing-bill*, *-tool*.

1813 in Marshall *Rev. Agric.* (1817) V. 27 The plashing system is carried on to the greatest extent. 1890 *Cent. Dict.*, *Plashing-tool*, a knife used in plashing hedges; a hedging knife. 1899 *Jrnl. R. Agric. Soc.* Mar. 104 The hedge assumes under the plashing-bill the triangular shape.

'plashing, *vbl. sb.*^{2} [f. PLASH *v.*^{2} + -ING^1.] The action of PLASH *v.*^{2} in various senses; the dashing of water, splashing; noisy plunging; etc.

1582 STANYHURST *Æneis* III. (Arb.) 83 Swift the sea with plasshing rusht in. 1602 HEYWOOD *Woman killed w. Kindn.* Wks. 1874 II. 103 Himselfe all spotted And stain'd with plashing. 1814 SCOTT *Wav.* viii, Everything around..would have been silent, but for the continued plashing of the fountain. 1882 O'DONOVAN *Merv Oasis* I. 315 The silence was broken only by the plashing of the oars.

'plashing, *ppl. a.* [f. PLASH *v.*^{2} + -ING^2.] That plashes like dashing or falling water; that dashes against water; also *fig.* said of the sound.

1813 SCOTT *Rokeby* I. i, Hears..by fits the plashing raindrop fall. 1814 —— *Ld. of Isles* v. xiii, The dazzled sea-fowl..Dropp'd from their crags on plashing wave. 1869 TOZER *Highl. Turkey* I. 337 The plashing fountain at the further end of the court. 1871 R. ELLIS *Catullus* lxiv. 273 Light surges a plashing silvery laughter.

b. *transf.* of ground, etc. on which heavy rain dashes.

1837 LYTTON *E. Maltrav.* I. ii, He heard steps without upon the plashing soil. 1841 —— *Nt. & Morn.* v. ii, Through the plashing streets. 1894 CROCKETT *Raiders* 302 It was the plashing wet evening of a September day.

Hence **'plashingly** *adv.*, with plashing.

1881 *Daily News* 15 July 5/4 Some heavy raindrops fell plashingly.

'plashment. *rare*$^{-1}$. [f. PLASH *v.*^{2} + -MENT.] Plashing.

1876 LANIER *Clover* 38 Lakes Pout gentle mounds of plashment up to meet Big shower-drops.

'plash-mill. *Sc.* [f. PLASH *v.*^{2} + MILL; in Du. *plasmolen*.] A fulling-mill.

1868 G. MACDONALD *R. Falconer* I. 240 The plash-mill, or, more properly, wauk-mill—a word Robert derived from the resemblance of the mallets to two huge feet, and of their motion to walking—with the water plashing and squirting from the blows of their heels.

Hence **'plash-ˌmiller**, a fuller.

1822 *Dundee Advertiser* 19 Dec. (Jam.), John Young, plash-miller at East Mill, was drowned in the river Esk. 1897 W. LINDSAY in *Bards of Angus & Mearns* 282 Then I turned a plashmiller and wrought at that.

†**'plashoote.** *Obs. rare.* [Syncopated from *plash-shoot*, f. PLASH *sb.*^{3} + SHOOT *sb.*] A shoot from a plashed hedge.

1602 CAREW *Cornwall* 25 Almost euerie hedge serueth for a Roade, and euerie Plashoote for Springles to take them.

†**'plash-pole.** *Obs.* [f. PLASH *v.*^{1} or *sb.*^{3} + POLE.] A space, a pole or less in width, surrounding a wood, reserved for the purpose of making plashed hedges.

1613 MARKHAM *Eng. Husbandman* II. I. ii. (1635) 45 A pole or halfe pole..you shall preserue..to repaire the ring-fences of your Wood:..and this amongst Woodwards is called Plash-pole. 1664 EVELYN *Sylva* (1776) 468 Remember..to preserve sufficient plash-pole about the verge and bounds of the copse for fence and security.

plashy ('plæʃı), *a.*^{1} [f. PLASH *sb.*^{1} + -Y. So LG. *plassig* swampy.] Abounding in shallow pools or puddles; marshy, swampy, boggy; wet and sloppy; full of plashes of rain.

*a*1552 LELAND *Itin.* II. 37, 3. litle Bridges of Wood, wher under wer plaschy Pittes of Water of the overflowing of Tame Ryver. 1599 NASHE *Lenten Stuffe* Wks. (Grosart) V. 211 Those slymie plashie fieldes of Gorlstone. *a*1656 USSHER *Ann.* VI. (1658) 736 The field was very plashy by reason of much rain that fell. 1770 GOLDSM. *Des. Vill.* 130 Yon widow'd, solitary thing, That feebly bends beside the plashy spring. 1786 W. GILPIN *Lakes Cumberld.* (1808) I. vii. 99 The fen is a plashy inundation, formed on a flat. 1857 HUGHES *Tom Brown* I. iii, The two..jogged along the deep-rutted plashy roads. 1862 R. PAUL in *Mem.* xviii. (1872) 237 Such a plashy and untoward month of March.

b. Growing in plashes or wet places.

1822 HAZLITT *Table-t.* Ser. II. vii. (1869) 149 A stream, skirted with willows and plashy sedges.

c. Of watery consistence and taste.

*a*1653 GOUGE *Comm. Heb.* xiii. 1 Love is as salt, which infuseth a savoury and wholesom taste into such things as would otherwise be fresh and plashy.

'plashy, *a.*^{2} [f. PLASH *sb.*^{2} + -Y.]

1. That plashes; that dashes or falls with a plash, as water; that splashes the water.

1582 STANYHURST *Æneis* III. (Arb.) 76 Vp swel thee surges, in chauffe sea plasshye we tumble. 1794 BURNS *Jockey's ta'en the Parting Kiss* i, Plashy sleets and beating rain! 1820 W. IRVING *Sketch Bk, Leg. Sleepy Hollow*, A plashy tramp by the side of the bridge caught the sensitive ear of Ichabod. 1859 HOLLAND *Gold F.* xxiv. 273 Repeat the music of the rain, at the feet of plashy waterfalls.

2. Marked as if splashed with colour. *rare.*

1820 KEATS *Hyper.* II. 45 Creüs was one;..Iäpetus another; in his grasp, A serpent's plashy neck.

-plasia (-'pleızıə), a word-forming element (f. Gr. πλάσις moulding, conformation (πλάσσειν to form, mould) + -IA^1) used in medical and biological terms in the sense 'growth, development (of tissue)', as DYSPLASIA, HETEROPLASIA. Occas. anglicized as **-plasy**.

plasm (plæz(ə)m). Also 7 **plasme**. [ad. late L. *plasma*: see next.]

†**1.** A mould or matrix in which something is cast or formed; the cast of a fossil. Also *fig. Obs.*

1620 T. GRANGER *Div. Logike* 165 Certaine it is that the name Adam expresseth the nature of his plasme or vessell. 1695 WOODWARD *Nat. Hist. Earth* v. (1723) 256 The Shells served as Plasms or Moulds to this Sand. 1764 PLATT in *Phil. Trans.* LIV. 46 *note*, The Plasm or mould of the Belemnite. *Ibid.* 47 *note*, The parts are carried away and lost in the interstices of the earth, and a mould or plasm is left, which Steno calls an aërial shell.

b. Something moulded or formed, an image. *humorously pedantic nonce-use.*

1877 BLACKMORE *Cripps* II. viii. 125 His outward faculties ..rendered to his inward and endiathetic organs a picture, a schema, a plasm—the proper word may be left to him—such as would remain inside, at least while the mind abode there.

†**2.** = PLASMA 2. *Obs. rare.*

1747 DINGLEY in *Phil. Trans.* XLV. 503 The Stone.. most frequently found next is the Plasm or prime Emerald; and then the Hyacinth or Jacinth. *Ibid.*, The Plasm or prime Emerald is green.

3. *Phys.* = PLASMA 3.

1876 tr. *Schützenberger's Ferment.* 131 A series of gaseous diffusions from the red globules to the plasm of the blood.

4. *Biol.* The living matter of a cell, protoplasm; sometimes *spec.* the general body of protoplasm as distinct from the nucleus.

1864 WEBSTER, *Plasm*...2. (*Physiol.*) The same as *Plasma*. 1877 O'MEARA in *Encycl. Brit.* VII. 170 [In Diatoms] There is first what Pfitzer designates the plasm-sac, consisting of a fine colourless plasm forming a closed sac of the same shape as that of the cell. 1899 *Allbutt's Syst. Med.* VIII. 334 Functional and formative plasm must progress. 1905 *Brit. Med. Jrnl.* 25 Feb. 442 The relative masses of nucleus and plasm.

plasma ('plæzmə). [Late and eccl. L. *plasma* a thing formed or moulded, an image, a. Gr. πλάσμα, fr. πλάσσειν to form, mould.]

†**1.** Form, mould, shape. *Obs. rare.*

1712 *H. More's Antid. Ath.* I. v. §3 *schol.*, They act upon the Matter and form it into this or that Plasma or Fashion. 1824-9 LANDOR *Imag. Conv., Southey & Porson* ii. Wks. 1846 I. 83/2 A great portion of his compositions is not poetry, but only the plasma or matrix of poetry. *Ibid. Alfieri & Salomon* 190/1 We Italians sometimes fall into what.. you may call the plasma of witticism, by mere mistake, and against our genius.

2. A subtranslucent green variety of quartz, allied to chalcedony and heliotrope, anciently used for ornaments.

1772 tr. *Cronstedt's Min.* 81 Plasma or mother of the emerald. 1839 URE *Dict. Arts* 208 Under it [calcedony] may be grouped..chrysoprase, plasma,..and sard. 1861 C. W. KING *Ant. Gems* (1866) 14 Plasma..sometimes written Prasma..is merely Calcedony coloured green by some metallic oxide, probably copper or nickel. 1864 —— *Gnostics* 76 This amulet, which is always cut in Plasma, the Jasper par excellence of the ancients.

attrib. 1900 A. S. MURRAY in *Brit. Mus. Ret.* 64 Green plasma scaraboid, with intaglio of a warrior.

3. *Phys.* The colourless coagulable liquid part of blood, lymph, or milk, in which the corpuscles (or, in milk, oil-globules) float; also, the similar liquid obtained from fresh muscle.

1845 G. E. DAY tr. *Simon's Anim. Chem.* I. 114 The plasma of living blood exists as a clear fluid, in which the corpuscles are seen to float. 1855 HOLDEN *Hum. Osteol.* (1878) 19 The nutrient fluid, or 'plasma' of the blood. 1873 RALFE *Phys. Chem.* 118 The muscular plasma is obtained by injecting the muscles of a freshly killed animal with a 1 per cent solution of sodium chloride. 1876 tr. *Wagner's Gen. Pathol.* (ed. 6) 230 Normal lymph consists of a colorless plasma and lymph-corpuscles. 1895 in *Syd. Soc. Lex.*

4. *Biol.* = PLASM 4.

1864 WEBSTER, *Plasma*..2. (*Physiol.*) The viscous material of a cell from which the new developments take place. 1867 J. HOGG *Microsc.* I. iii. 223 For certain delicate organisms, as the Desmidaceae and Diatomaceae, whose plasma may be affected by too dense a medium. 1872 BEALE *Bioplasm* i. §14 As the germ of every living thing consists of matter having the wonderful properties already mentioned, I have called it germinal matter; but the most convenient and least objectionable name for it is living plasma or bioplasm. 1876 LANKESTER tr. *Haeckel's Hist. Creat.* I. 185 The entire body..consists..of shapeless plasma, or protoplasm.

5. *Pharm.* A name for glycerite or starch.

1890 in *Cent. Dict.* 1895 in *Syd. Soc. Lex.*

6. *Physics.* A gas in which there are positive ions and free negative electrons, usu. in approximately equal numbers throughout and therefore electrically neutral; *esp.* one exhibiting phenomena due to the collective interaction of the charges. Also, any analogous collection of charged particles in which one or both kinds are mobile, as the conduction electrons in a metal or the ions in a salt solution.

Electrical neutrality and collective phenomena are often made necessary characteristics of a plasma (e.g. quot. 1967^2).

1928 I. LANGMUIR in *Proc. Nat. Acad. Sci.* XIV. 628 It seemed that these oscillations must be regarded as compressional electric waves somewhat analogous to sound waves. Except near the electrodes..the ionized gas contains ions and electrons in about equal numbers so that the resultant space charge is very small. We shall use the name *plasma* to describe this region containing balanced charges of ions and electrons. 1930 *Physical Rev.* XXXVII. 1467 The plasma used in this investigation was the positive column of a mercury arc. 1941 MILLMAN & SEELY *Electronics* x. 307 The largest portion of a glow discharge is the plasma. *Ibid.* 309 In addition to the electrons and ions that exist in equal concentrations, a plasma contains many gas molecules. 1958 *Engineering* 31 Jan. 134/2 The stable plasma reaches the high temperatures, of the order of 5 million deg. K., necessary for producing thermonuclear reactions. 1960 *Soviet Physics Doklady* V. 363 At a distance from the earth of 4 earth radii, a plasma with a temperature of not more than tens of thousands of degrees was detected. 1966 *McGraw-Hill Encycl. Sci. & Technol.* X. 386/1 If the over-all dimensions of a region containing a plasma are small compared to λ_D, only simple collisional or single-particle behavior is to be expected, the plasma will behave as an ordinary low-density gas, and collective processes will not be important. 1967 L. K. BRANSON *Introd. Electronics* ix. 315 The plasma consists of a mixture of positive, negative, and neutral particles and ..in any given volume-element there are equal numbers of ions and electrons. Further, the plasma..fills the entire volume between anode and cathode except for a narrow region at the cathode called the sheath. 1967 CONDON & ODISHAW *Handbk. Physics* (ed. 2) IV. xi. 188/1 The phenomena that occur in a plasma and distinguish it from any arbitrary collection of charged particles are the near equality of positive and negative charges throughout the plasma volume and the ability of the charges to participate in plasma oscillations. 1969 STEELE & VURAL *Wave Interactions in Solid State Plasmas* i. 4 In a metal like copper, the free electrons comprising the plasma are electrically compensated by the positively ionized copper atoms. 1971 E. NASSER *Fundamentals of Gaseous Ionization & Plasma Electronics* xiv. 427 Liquid plasmas exist in salt solutions where the positive and negative ions move separately. 1974 R. C. DAVIDSON *Theory of Nonneutral Plasmas* p. xi, Nonneutral plasmas exhibit collective properties that are qualitatively similar to those of neutral plasmas. For example, in klystrons and traveling-wave tubes, the collective oscillations necessary for microwave generation and amplification are excited even under conditions in which the electron beams..are unneutralized. 1974 *Nature* 5 Apr. 494/2 In a cold plasma (which is a good approximation for most of the magnetosphere away from the equatorial region) there are two wave modes. 1976 T. BEER *Aerospace Environment* i. 16 The solar wind is a plasma of hydrogen ions (protons) and electrons travelling at speeds that range from 300 km s^{-1} to 1000 km s^{-1}, depending on solar activity.

7. *Soil Sci.* (See quots.)

1958 I. W. CORNWALL *Soils for Archaeologist* xvii. 190 Intergranular spaces and conducting channels may be filled, or partly filled, with colloids and precipitates, conveyed and deposited..by percolating moisture. This is the soil-plasma, which constitutes in part the cement between adjacent grains and in part mere filling of available voids. 1976 COURTNEY & TRUDGILL *Soil* ii. 17/2 In thin sections under a microscope the soil plasma can be recognized... It is an amorphous combination of humus, clays and chemical compounds (e.g. iron oxide), and is produced by the secondary weathering processes..and by the incorporation of organic matter. *Ibid.*, The presence of mineral matter in the plasma distinguishes it from the overlying purely organic horizons.

8. a. *attrib.*, as *plasma cloud*; **plasma arc**, a very hot plasma jet produced by passing a noble gas through a nozzle that is one electrode of an electric arc, used in plasma torches; **plasma-corpuscle**, name given to a type of cell found in connective tissue; **plasma-current**, **-layer**, **-zone** = PLASMATIC *current*, etc.; **plasma dynamics** (also as one word), the science of the dynamical properties and behaviour of gaseous plasmas; so **plasma-dynamic**, **-dynamical** adjs.; **plasma engine**, a form of jet engine that produces and ejects plasma; **plasma frequency**, the natural resonant frequency of a plasma oscillation, which is also the minimum frequency of electro-magnetic waves that can travel through the plasma without attenuation and is approximately 8920 $\sqrt{n}$ Hz, where *n* is the number of free electrons per cc.; **plasma jet**, a high-speed stream of plasma (ionized gas) ejected from a plasma engine or plasma torch; **plasma membrane** *Biol.* = PLASMALEMMA; also, a similar membrane around an intracytoplasmic vacuole; **plasma oscillation**, a collective oscillation of the electrons in a plasma; **plasma physics**, the physics of plasmas such as ionized gases; hence **plasma physicist**; **plasma probe**, any device that is inserted or immersed in an ionized gas to investigate its physical properties; **plasma propulsion**, propulsion of a vehicle by means of a plasma engine; **plasma sheath**, a thin layer of space charge covering a surface in an ionized gas; **plasma torch**, a small device that produces a very hot plasma jet for use in cutting solids or coating them with refractory material.

1958 *Iron Age* 4 Dec. 136/1 Thanks to the development of the new *plasma arc torch, a brand new method for fabricating shapes and applying ultra-high-temperature coatings is now a reality. **1963** H. R. CLAUSER *Encycl. Engin. Materials & Processes* 480/2 The cost of depositing the high-melting-point coatings with the plasma-arc process is comparable with that of the flame-sprayed coatings. **1973** *Materials & Technol.* VI. i. 60 A number of unconventional methods of cutting wood have been examined, largely with the object of reducing waste. These include the use of the plasma arc, which produces very high temperatures with a nozzle of very small diameter. **1869** KIRBY in *Q. Jrnl. Microsc. Sci.* IX. 31 Naked *Plasma-bodies without nuclei. **1960** *Aeroplane* XCVIII. 610/1 It appears that *plasma clouds emitted from the Sun run up against the Earth's magnetic field, causing it to release previously trapped particles into the atmosphere. **1967** M. KENYON *Whole Hog* xviii. 181 Along comes space which everyone had thought was empty, a void, but it turns out it's not, it's filled with radiation belts and plasma clouds and solar winds. **1969** *Monthly Not. R. Astron. Soc.* CXLV. 328 In the Ryle-Longair model, plasma clouds formed by a strong explosion within a galaxy expand..until their dimensions exceed galactic dimensions, at which time they are ejected from the parent galaxy and henceforth evolve independently. **1964** E. STUHLINGER *Ion Propulsion* vi. 277 The heat energy absorbed by the coolant in the reactor may be used to heat ..the plasma in a *plasmadynamic converter, or the working fluid in a thermodynamic converter. **1959** *Astrophysical Jrnl.* CXXIX. 217 We are interested in the distance in which a stream of tenuous plasma, directed against another oppositely moving stream of tenuous plasma, is brought to rest as a consequence of *plasma dynamical interaction. **1960** *Aeroplane* XCIX. 837/2 Such subjects as magneto-hydrodynamics, MHD mechanics, and *plasmadynamics. **1970** *New Scientist* 5 Feb. 273/2 Plasma dynamics is a subject with applications in many branches of physics and technology..—space physics and the quest for thermo-nuclear fusion being but two examples. **1958** *S.A.E. Jrnl.* Apr. 93/2 Another phase of our investigations ..is the development of a *plasma engine, in which small amounts of plasma are ejected at extremely high velocities. **1967** *Electronics* 6 Mar. 8/2 He directed work on plasma engines and space suits. **1974** HAWKEY & BINGHAM *Wild Card* xv. 131 The propulsion pack was okay for the demonstration... We plan to replace it with a small plasma engine. [**1929** *Physical Rev.* XXXIII. 198 Thus the lower frequency limit for long waves coincides with the plasma-electron frequency.] **1949** *Ibid.* LXXV. 1852/1 For a typical density of 10^{12} electrons per cm^3, the *plasma frequency is about 10^{10} c.p.s. **1964** D. B. NEWMAN *Space Vehicle Electronics* iv. 225 Above the plasma frequency the plasma has dielectric properties... Well below the plasma frequency, the plasma acts like a conductor. **1971** FERRY & FANNIN *Physical Electronics* vii. 96 For a metal, where the electron concentration is about 10^{28} m^{-3}, the plasma frequency is found to be about $5·6 \times 10^{15}$ Hz, or in the ultraviolet region. **1957** G. M. GIANNINI *Plasma Jet & its Applications* (U.S.A.F. Office Scientific Res. Techn. Note 57–520) 22 The '*plasma jet' can be used for many of the purposes described... The jet is very hot, highly ionized, has a high velocity. **1960** *Aeroplane* XCVIII. 610/2 Because of the low thrust produced, the plasmajet cannot be employed for rocket-launching from Earth. It must be carried into orbit by a more powerful chemical rocket and started in the weightless environment of space. **1964** *Sci. News Let.* 12 Sept. 163 Plasma jets, the white-hot streams of gas used for such tasks as cutting and welding, may soon have yet another use, 'steering' satellites through space. **1972** D. G. SHEPHERD *Aerospace Propulsion* viii. 202 The arc jet or plasma jet utilizes the very high temperatures in arcs to heat the propellant. **1876** tr. *Wagner's Gen. Pathol.* (ed. 6) 178 The *plasma-layer..disappears in the smaller arteries and veins. **1900** *Ann. Bot.* XIV. 352 The entire structure, antheridium, tube, and oogonium, have in reality become for a time a single cell bounded by a single continuous *plasma-membrane. **1922** W. STILES in *New Phytologist* XXI. 141 The term plasma-membrane will be used to denote a surface layer of protoplasm which behaves as a membrane surrounding the bulk of the protoplasm, and which may exhibit different degrees of permeability to different substances... The membrane bounding the outside of the protoplast, and so in contact with the cell wall, will be called the external plasma-membrane, and that bounding the vacuole, the internal plasma-membrane. **1948** *New Biol.* V. 40 The plasma membrane is highly permeable to substances which are soluble in fats and in fat solvents. **1965** BELL & COOMBE tr. *Strasburger's Textbk. Bot.* 13 The inner plasma membrane surrounding the vacuole is known as the tonoplast, and that adjacent to the cell wall as the plasmalemma. **1968** R. RIEGER et al. *Gloss. Genetics & Cytogenetics* 341 In some cells (bacteria, plants), a cell wall ..is universally recognized as a structure separate from the plasma membrane. **1970** AMBROSE & EASTY *Cell Biol.* viii. 258 The outer cell membrane, or plasma membrane (sometimes known as the cell membrane, or plasmalemma), has a unique role, since the cell interacts with its environment through it. **1928** I. LANGMUIR in *Proc. Nat. Acad. Sci.* XIV. 629 *Plasma Oscillations.—If..we change the concentration of electrons by some transient external means, the resulting electric fields act..to equalize the concentration, but the potential energy of these fields is converted into kinetic energy of the electrons so that oscillations occur, and electric waves may result. **1970** W. A. HARRISON *Solid State Theory* iii. 288 Physically these plasma oscillations correspond to soundlike compression waves in the electron gas. **1972** AKASOFU & CHAPMAN *Solar-Terrestrial Physics* vii. 472 While the plasma cloud is streaming through the solar atmosphere it induces plasma oscillations there. These oscillations are observed at the earth as a Type II radio burst. **1968** *New Scientist* 24 Oct. 186 To bring about nuclear fusion..plasma with a density of 10^{14} nuclei per cu. cm. must be held together for about one second. To bring this about is the dream of *plasma physicists. **1976** T. BEER *Aerospace Environment* i. 2 The plasma physicist can use the Earth's upper atmosphere as a gigantic laboratory to study the behaviour of a large-scale plasma being acted upon by the Earth's magnetic field. **1958** C. C. ADAMS *Space Flight* 345 Some scientists think that controlled fusion may be with us in 20 years or so, and if so we may completely bypass fission... Work in *plasma physics will have to be carefully watched, and it is through research in this area that eventual success is expected. **1963** *Wall St. Jrnl.* 22 Jan., Kirtland researchers are delving into plasma physics—the study of partially ionized gases—to determine to what extent high-level nuclear blasts are likely to disrupt vital communications. **1970** G. K. WOODGATE *Elem. Atomic Structure* i. 3 Quantitative calculations of the behaviour of free atoms are required for the less well-defined fields..of, for example, solid-state physics, plasma physics, and..astrophysics. **1961** *Flight* LXXIX. 462/2 Valuable information had been transmitted from the rubidium vapour magnetometer, two fluxgate magnetometers and the *plasma probe. **1965** K. W. GATLAND *Spacecraft & Boosters* II. 87/2 The radio-frequency plasma probe consisted of a pair of grid-like electrodes through which a radio-frequency electric field was applied to a small region near the satellite. **1977** *Sci. Amer.* Mar. 39/3 The first data available from the Ames Research Centre's plasma probe on *Pioneer 10* as it traversed interplanetary space were the hourly values of the speed of the [solar] wind. **1958** C. C. ADAMS *Space Flight* 54 A new Astronautics Research Laboratory with propulsion, astrophysical, and materials sections to study very high-energy fuels, including *plasma propulsion systems. **1969** BOYD & SANDERSON *Plasma Dynamics* v. 107 Space research has given a great impetus to the development of plasma propulsion since it has important potential advantages over conventional propellants, especially for long-range missions. **1961** *Aeroplane* C. 462/2 During hypersonic flight on the return from orbit, an ionized '*plasma sheath' will envelop the glider, impeding the reception and transmission of radio signals. **1969** M. A. KASHA *Ionosphere* iii. 48 A spacecraft is generally surrounded by some form of plasma sheath. This means that it is very difficult to measure..the electrical potential of the space plasma. **1959** *Welding Engineer* Feb. 50/2 Two 600-amp units power a 50-kw *plasma torch, and voltage requirements are being set by the gas being used. **1961** *Jrnl. Appl. Physics* XXXII. 821/1 This article describes a plasma torch based on inductive coupling to an ionized gas... Conventional plasma torches require electrodes to carry energy to the gas. **1968** *Observer* 22 Dec. 4/5 The plasma torch, another torch device in industrial use, can virtually disintegrate material at a temperature of 36,000 degrees C.

b. Used *attrib.* to designate (the concentration of) substances in blood plasma.

1891 W. D. HALLIBURTON *Text-bk. Chem. Physiol. & Path.* xv. 238 The globulin pre-existent in the blood plasma ..may be termed plasma-globulin. **1927** [see PLASMAPHERESIS]. **1941** *Amer. Jrnl. Path.* XVII. 360 The question whether increase of the plasma protein concentration would protect against heavy metal poisoning. **1956** *Nature* 4 Feb. 238/1 The amino-acid pattern of the urine from this cystinuric dog is.., apart from threonine, identical with that found in cases of human cystinuria, while the finding of a low plasma-cystine points to a similar etiology. **1961** *Lancet* 22 July 171/2 Because of the diurnal variation in plasma-cortisol (hydrocortisone) concentration, all blood samples were drawn between 9 A.M. and 10 A.M. **1969** E. KELEMEN *Physiopath. & Therapy Human Blood Dis.* i. 105 About 80–90% of plasma proteins, i.e. fibrinogen, albumin, and certain globulins, including most of the plasma coagulation factors, are formed in the liver. **1975** J. W. LINMAN *Hematol.* v. 183/1 Plasma fibrinogen is increased in persons with valvular prostheses or homografts.

plasmablast, var. PLASMOBLAST b.

'plasma cell. *Histology.* Also **plasma-cell.** [tr. G. *plasmazelle* (W. Waldeyer 1875, in *Arch. f. mikrosk. Anat.* XI. 189; also P. G. Unna 1891, in *Monatschr. f. prakt. Dermatol.* 1 Apr. 304): see PLASMA and CELL *sb.*[1]] †**a.** A name given to a type of cell found in connective tissue. *Obs.* **b.** A cell now recognized as the chief source of antibodies which is found in lymphoid tissue and at sites of chronic inflammation, and which has a strongly basophilic cytoplasm containing an extensive rough-surfaced endoplasmic reticulum and a usually eccentric nucleus. Cf. PLASMACYTE.

1888 ROLLESTON & JACKSON *Anim. Life* 115 Edible Snail. .. The connective tissue consists of plasma-cells, a matrix, and fibrils. **1895** *Jrnl. R. Microsc. Soc.* 613 Waldeyer's plasma-cells correspond in staining reactions to Ehrlich's *Mastzellen*, but not to Unna's 'plasma-cells', and Waldeyer proposes to give up his use of the term as applied to normal elements of connective tissue. The cells he described as 'plasma-cells' are Ehrlich's *Mastzellen* and eosinophilous cells. **1904** *Brit. Med. Jrnl.* 10 Sept. 586 In addition to these, we have the so-called plasma cells. **1906** *Jrnl. Amer. Med. Assoc.* 20 Oct. 1272/2 The intimæ of the smaller arteries are lifted or completely dissected off by an exudate composed chiefly of cells of the lymphocyte series, among which are examples of the typical plasma cell. **1929** *Amer. Jrnl. Ophthalm.* XII. 731/1 In 1875 Waldeyer applied the name of plasma cell to a poorly differentiated type of wandering cell which he found in chronically inflamed connective tissue. **1940** *Acta Med. Scand.* CIII. 569 When Waldeyer..used the term plasma cell in 1875, he elected to do so not because he thought these cells secreted part of the plasma, but because of the abundant protoplasm. He made use of the term plasma cell to designate a number of different cells rich in protoplasm, but in subsequent works, especially those of Unna..and Marschalko.., the use of the name was restricted to the cell that is now known as the plasma cell: a cell rich in protoplasm, with eccentrically placed nucleus, relatively small, round or oval, with five to eight bands of chromatine extending from the centre like the spokes of a wheel; around the nucleus is a lighter zone, whilst the abundant protoplasm is otherwise dark, basophile. **1960** *New Biol.* XXXI. 100 Absolute proof that plasma cells make antibody was furnished by an ingenious and elegant technique devised by Dr. A. H. Coons. **1968** PASSMORE & ROBSON *Compan. Med. Stud.* I. xvi. 5/1 Plasma cells are found where foreign proteins are likely to gain entrance to the body, e.g. beneath the epithelial membranes lining the respiratory and alimentary tracts. **1975** *Lancet* 3 May 1031/2 The plasma-cell is one of the effector cells of the B-lymphocyte system.

Hence **plasma-celled** *a.*, composed of plasma cells; **plasma'cellular** *a.* (also **plasmo-** and as two words), of or pertaining to plasma cells.

1929 *Jrnl. Path. & Bacteriol.* XXXII. 293 (*heading*) Two cases of myelomatosis: (1) Diffuse plasma-celled (2) with tumour-like nodules and visceral lesions. **1947** *Nature* 12 Apr. 499/1 (*heading*) Plasma cellular reaction and its relation to the formation of antibodies *in vitro*. **1948** R. A. WILLIS *Path. Tumours* l. 787 The multi-nucleated cells of plasma-celled and other myelomas are of no special histogenetic significance. **1957** *Jrnl. Amer. Med. Assoc.* 4 May 20/2 In the broadest sense of the term this plasmocellular barrier may be called an immune process. **1971** *Biol. Abstr.* LII. 6201/2 The ultrastructure of plasmacellular paracrystalline inclusions, detected in the sternal marrow of a patient with type k micromolecular myeloma was studied.

plasmacyte ('plæzməsaɪt). *Histology.* Also **plasmo-**. [f. PLASMA + -CYTE.] = PLASMA CELL b.

1941 I. N. KUGELMASS *Blood Disorders in Children* xiii. 498 Accumulation of plasmacytes is probably due to migration from the blood stream and subsequent multiplication by fission. **1961** *Lancet* 16 Sept. 639/2 We must think of the effective (abnormal) cells in the spleen as plasmacytes which have taken on the character of low-grade tumour cells. **1976** *Ann. Rev. Microbiol.* XXX. 591, B cells were being transferred to the local granuloma as the site of antigen, and were then transferring to antibody-producing plasmacytes.

So **plasma-, plasmocytic** (-'saɪtɪk, -'si:tɪk) *a.*, of, pertaining to, or composed of plasmacytes; **plasma-, plasmo'cytoid** *a.*, resembling (that of) a plasmacyte.

1932 *Jrnl. Path. & Bacteriol.* XXXV. 545 Histologically the tumour was plasmocytic and there were many cells of giant size. **1959** M. BURNET *Clonal Selection Theory of Acquired Immunity* iv. 61 Active proliferation to produce plasmacytoid cells and lymphocytes with active antibody-liberating capacity. **1970** R. T. SILVER *Morphol. Blood & Marrow in Clin. Pract.* ix. 111 In other cases, the lymphocyte..may assume a plasmacytoid shape while still retaining the nuclear configuration of a lymphocyte. **1972** *Acta Med. Scand.* CXCII. 291/2 The morphological investigations have,..in most of the cases, revealed the presence of an infiltration in the lympho-reticular organs of plasmocytoid cells of varying maturity, probably responsible for the production of the monoclonal immunoglobulin. **1974** *Immunol.* XXVI. 486 The development of giant cells, epithelioid tubercles and plasmacytic infiltrates.

plasmacytoma (plæzməsaɪ'təʊmə). *Path.* Also **plasmo-**. Pl. **-omas, -omata.** [mod.L., ad. G. *plasmocytom* (H. Boit 1907, in *Frankfurter Zeitschr. f. Path.* I. 172): see prec. and -OMA.] A myeloma composed largely of plasma cells.

1907 *Index Medicus* V. Index 173/1 Plasmocytoma. **1931** *Amer. Jrnl. Med. Sci.* CLXXXI. 171 There appear in the literature cases of both extra-osseous and intra-osseous plasmocytomata. *Ibid.* 178 There is no very sharp line of demarcation between localized, benign plasmocytomata on the one hand, and the malignant, fatal multiple myelomata on the other. **1940** *Acta Med. Scand.* CIII. 569 There is no increase of globulin in a number of plasmocytoma cases. **1961** [see MYELOMATOSIS]. **1972** [see MULTIPLE *a.* and *sb.* A. 3 d]. **1973** *Jrnl. Bone & Joint Surg.* A. LV. 1749 Most solitary plasmocytomas eventually become classic multiple myelomas if they are followed long enough. **1976** *Lancet* 6 Nov. 1003/2 Bone-resorbing factors have also been identified in cultured human tumour cells, including those from plasmacytomas.

plasmacytosis (plæzməsaɪ'təʊsɪs). *Path.* Also **plasmo-**. Pl. **-cytoses.** [f. as prec. + -OSIS.] The presence of more plasma cells than usual in a tissue.

1930 *Q. Cumulative Index Med.* VII. 1278/1 Uterine plasmocytoma and plasmocytosis. **1959** *New Engl. Jrnl. Med.* 5 Nov. 954/2 Multinucleate and atypical forms are observed in both the neoplastic and non-neoplastic plasmocytoses. **1963** *Lancet* 19 Jan. 125/2 In several cases there was bone-marrow plasmacytosis. **1968** *Amer. Jrnl. Clin. Path.* L. 304/1 Cytologically, all cases of plasmacytosis were characterized by proliferation of mature looking plasma cells in addition to more primitive lymphoreticular forms.

plasmagel ('plæzmədʒɛl). *Biol.* Also **plasma gel.** [f. PLASMA + GEL *sb.*] Gelatinous cytoplasm, such as surrounds the plasmasol in an amœboid cell. Cf. PLASMASOL.

1923 S. O. MAST in *Proc. Nat. Acad. Sci.* IX. 258 By careful observations on Amœba proteus in motion the following structures can clearly be differentiated: (1) A central elongated fluid portion; (2) A solid layer surrounding the fluid portion; (3) A very thin elastic surface layer or membrane. The first I shall designate the *plasmasol*, the second the *plasmagel* and the third the *plasmalemma*. **1939** W. B. YAPP *Introd. Animal Physiol.* iv. 131 *Amœba* consists of three layers. On the outside there is a thin plasmalemma, which can be lifted off with needles and is of a dough-like consistency. Inside this is the plasmagel, which is solid, and includes the classical ectoplasm and some endoplasm; inside this again is liquid plasmasol. **1942** G. H. BOURNE *Cytol. & Cell Physiol.* iii. 97 Streaming in [the aquatic plant] *Elodea* cells is associated with gelation, and..is abolished by application of sufficient hydro-static pressure to liquefy the cortical plasmagel. **1970** AMBROSE & EASTY *Cell Biol.* xi. 360 The plasma gel is located near the plasma membrane; it is generally free from granules and other inclusions. **1973** N. ADRESEN in K. W. Jeon *Biol. of Amœba* iv. 102 The large pseudopodia..may contain several parallel streams of plasmasol, each running in its own tube of plasmagel.

plasmagene (ˈplæzmədʒiːn). *Genetics.* [f. PLASMA + GENE.] A supposed cytoplasmic entity having genetic properties.

1939 C. D. DARLINGTON *Evol. Genetic Systems* xx. 121 The particles in the nucleus are genes; those in the plastids and cytoplasm may perhaps be treated more rigorously if we also think of them as genes—plastogenes and plasmagenes. **1952** [see PLASMID]. **1963** E. MAYR *Animal Species & Evolution* vii. 172 Like the chromosomal genes, plasmagenes seem to consist of nucleic acid molecules (including possibly RNA). **1965** STERN & NANNEY *Biol. of Cells* xix. 529 The concept of the plasmagene, a gene-like cytoplasmic element capable of differential assortment and replication during development, provided a possible means of rationalization. .. Nevertheless, this interpretation was never generally accepted with enthusiasm. *Ibid.*, The episomes of bacteria ..on occasion behave like plasmagenes. **1974** A. T. SOLDO in W. J. Van Wagtendonk *Paramecium* 377 When kappa particles were first discovered they were generally regarded as cytoplasmic units of hereditary or 'plasma-genes'.

Hence **plasmaˈgenic** *a.*, of, pertaining to, or being a plasmagene.

1950 *Heredity* IV. 17 The existence of plasmagenic sub-units in any one of the self-duplicating, cytoplasmic structures has not yet been established. **1968** J. A. SERRA *Mod. Genetics* III. xix. 37 Probably infection is produced by a particle of the plasmagenic type.

plasmal (ˈplæzməl). *Biochem.* [a. G. *plasmal* (coined with PLASMALOGEN): see PLASM and -AL².] An aldehyde formed by the hydrolysis of a plasmalogen; chiefly used *attrib.* in **plasmal reaction**, a modification of the Feulgen reaction for detecting plasmalogens and aldehydes in tissue.

1925 *Chem. Abstr.* XIX. 1156 Plasmal is an aldehyde, a solid at ordinary temp. *Ibid.*, In accordance with its aldehyde nature, plasmal quickly takes a violet color when stained with H_2SO_3 fuchsin... This staining process is termed the plasmal reaction,..and the presence of plasmal, or its precursor plasmalogen, in frozen sections of tissues can be shown microscopically. **1949** *Stain Technol.* XXIV. 19 The plasmal reaction is here modified so that it is made specific for acetal lipids alone. **1966** *McGraw-Hill Encycl. Sci. & Technol.* X. 397/2 The Feulgen test for plasmalogens depends on the liberation of plasmal, principally palmitaldehyde and stearaldehyde, from these lipids by the action of mercuric chloride and acetic acid. **1969** *Acta Histochem.* XXXII. 425 (*heading*) Application of the plasmal reaction to suspensions.

plasmalemma (ˈplæzmələmə). *Biol.* Pl. **-lemmas, -lemmæ.** [f. PLASMA + LEMMA².] The thin membrane immediately surrounding the cytoplasm of a cell, which restricts the passage of molecules into it.

1923 [see PLASMAGEL]. **1931** J. Q. PLOWE in *Protoplasma* XII. 202 Mast (1924) has given us the term 'plasmalemma'. .. It has seemed permissible..to extend its use to the botanical world, and to employ it to denote a distinct, differentiated layer on the outer surface of the plant protoplast. **1965** K. ESAU *Plant Anat.* (ed. 2) ii. 15 Surface membranes delimit the cytoplasm from the wall (plasma membrane, plasmalemma, or ectoplast) and from the vacuole (vacuolar membrane, or tonoplast). **1965, 1970** [see *plasma membrane* s.v. PLASMA 6 a]. **1970** *Austral. Jrnl. Bot.* XVIII. 285 Host plasmalemmae are invaginated by invading hyphae, and encapsulations are formed. **1971** *Proc. R. Soc.* B. CLXXVIII. 195 (*caption*) The plasmalemmas.. of the two cells. **1976** *Nature* 9 Sept. 158/2 We report..a gradual increase in microviscosity of protoplast plasmalemma from petals of ageing rose flowers.

Hence **ˈplasmalemmal** *a.*, of, pertaining to, or formed from a plasmalemma.

1968 *Jrnl. Cell Biol.* XXXVII. 252 (*caption*) Grazing section of the endothelium in a blood capillary of rat myocardium showing the large accumulation of plasma-lemmal vesicles..on the tissue front. **1975** *Ibid.* LXIV. 505/2 After fixation by immersion, the plasmalemmal membranes limiting the endothelial and epithelial cells were heavily delineated by the reaction product.

plasmaˈlemmasome. *Cytology.* Also -lemmo-. [f. prec. + -SOME⁴.] A plant or microbial cell organelle formed by invagination of the plasma membrane and composed of tissue derived from it.

1962 M. R. EDWARDS in *Abstr. 8th Internat. Congr. Microbiol.* 31/1 The ingrowths of the plasmalemma may branch repeatedly and anastomose to give rise to a complicated honeycomb-like organelle. This organelle may be termed a plasmalemmosome in view of its origin from the plasmalemma. **1968** *Ann. Bot.* XXXII. 468 In higher plants, at least some of the plasmalemmasomes appear to have granular or fibrillar contents within well-defined vesicles. **1973** *Protoplasma* LXXVI. 235 The morphology of plasmalemmasomes in the species examined is variable and ranges from vesicles or tubules within the plasmalemma invagination to parallel arrays of membrane lamellae. Plasmalemmasomes thus appear to be primarily excess plasma membrane that has accumulated, perforce, endocellularly.

plasmalogen (plæzˈmælədʒən). *Biochem.* [a. G. *plasmalogen* (Feulgen & Voit 1924, in *Pflügers Arch. f. ges. Physiol.* CCVI. 399): see PLASMAL and -OGEN.] Any of a class of phospholipids that yield an aldehyde on mild hydrolysis and are now regarded as having an unsaturated ether linkage in place of one of the fatty acid ester linkages.

1925 *Chem. Abstr.* XIX. 1155 Throughout the protoplasm of animal tissues there is to be found, very widely disseminated, a substance of lipoid character, insol. in water but sol. in org. solvents and extractable by alc., termed plasmalogen. When subjected to acids..this substance is split into undetd. components termed plasmal. **1964** A. WHITE et al. *Princ. Biochem.* (ed. 3) v. 75 Plasmalogens without a nitrogenous base, *i.e.*, α, β-unsaturated ethers of phosphatidic acid, have also been reported in animal tissues, *e.g.*, liver. **1964** [see CEPHALIN²]. **1968** PASSMORE & ROBSON *Compan. Med. Stud.* I. x. 5/1 The plasmalogens have an unsaturated ether group, rather than an ester group, on the α position [of the glycerol molecule]. Those of ethanolamine and choline form a big proportion of the phospholipids of brain and heart.

Hence ˌ**plasmaloˈgenic** *a.*

1939 *Chem. Abstr.* XXXIII. 8635 This fraction contg. plasmalogenic acid (I) increases with the time of alk. hydrolysis. **1962** *Compar. Biochem. & Physiol.* V. 220 (*caption*) The arrow..points out the phosphatidic acid plasmalogen (plasmalogenic acid) characteristic of blood-fed leeches. **1970** R. W. MCGILVERY *Biochem.* xxiv. 600 The vinyl ether group [in plasmalogens] is believed to be formed by reduction of a diglyceride... The resultant plasmalogenic diglyceride reacts..to form phosphatidal-choline..in the same way that ordinary diglycerides react in the formation of the phosphatidylcholines.

plasmapause (ˈplæzməpɔːz). [f. PLASMA + PAUSE *sb.*] The outer limit of a plasmasphere, marked by a sudden change in the plasma density and lying wholly within the magnetosphere (in the case of the earth extending up to several earth radii from its centre at equatorial latitudes).

1966 [see PLASMASPHERE]. **1971** *New Scientist* 1 July 8/2 The time at which Io crosses the plasmapause [of Jupiter] and sets off a burst of radio emission therefore depends on the Sun's activity. **1976** T. BEER *Aerospace Environment* vi. 113 At around fifty-five degrees geographic latitude the plasmapause is in the F region and it is almost vertical. *Ibid.* vii. 137 We can expect a plasmapause on Mars somewhere above 400 km.

plasmapheresis (plæzməˈfɛrɪsɪs, -fəˈriːsɪs). *Med.* Also **-phoresis, †-pharesis.** [f. PLASMA + APHÆRESIS; *plasmaphoresis* by alteration (cf. -PHORESIS).] The removal of blood plasma from the body by the withdrawal of blood, its separation into plasma and cells in a centrifuge, and the reintroduction of the cells suspended in a harmless medium.

1920 G. H. WHIPPLE et al. in *Amer. Jrnl. Physiol.* LII. 99 Bleeding a dog from a large artery and a simultaneous replacement of a red blood cell Locke's solution mixture may be called 'plasma depletion' or 'plasmapharesis'. **1927** M. BODANSKY *Introd. Physiol. Chem.* vii. 168 Reduction of the plasma proteins by plasmapharesis..results in a condition of shock. **1935** H. SOBOTKA in Harrow & Sherwin *Textbk. Biochem.* iv. 144 Experimental anemia produced by repeated withdrawal of blood or plasma (plasmaphoresis). **1943** *Jrnl. Immunol.* XLIV. 112 Rabbits whose protein-reserves have been reduced by plasmapheresis and a low-protein diet (carrots) show a definitely lessened capacity to produce antibodies. **1971** *Nature* 27 Aug. 629/2 Before and during corticosteroid-induced labour large samples of plasma..were obtained by plasmaphoresis from chronically implanted catheters. **1974** PASSMORE & ROBSON *Compan. Med. Stud.* III. li. 16/2 The donation of blood by plasmapheresis is now a major part of blood transfusion practice. The main purpose is to procure large amounts of plasma rich in specific immunoglobulins..and blood grouping reagents.

plasma sheet (ˈplæzmə ʃiːt). Also **plasma-sheet.** [f. PLASMA + SHEET *sb.*¹] A layer of plasma in the magnetotail which lies in the equatorial plane of the earth some distance beyond the plasmapause and has two branches that diverge to reach the earth in polar latitudes.

1966 *Physical Rev. Lett.* XVI. 138 (*heading*) Electrons in the plasma sheet of the earth's magnetic tail. **1970** V. M. VASYLIUNAS in G. Skovli *Polar Ionosphere* II. 27 Intense fluxes of electrons extend across the entire magnetotail, forming the plasma sheet, first detected by the Luna 2 space probe in 1959. **1974** *McGraw-Hill Yearbk. Sci. & Technol.* 276/2 The plasmasheet plays a key role in the development of the magnetospheric sub-storm.

plasmasol (ˈplæzməsɒl). *Biol.* Also **plasma sol.** [f. PLASMA + SOL *sb.*⁶] Cytoplasm in the form of a sol, such as exists in the middle regions of amœboid cells. Cf. PLASMAGEL.

1923, etc. [see PLASMAGEL]. **1951** [see GELATE *v.*]. **1970** AMBROSE & EASTY *Cell Biol.* xi. 360 The relative viscosity of the plasma sol is quite low, being about two to ten times greater than that of water; on the other hand the gel is a moderately rigid structure which shows elasticity and breaks on application of a critical force.

plasmasome, erron. f. PLASMOSOME.

plasmasphere (ˈplæzməsfɪə(r)). [f. PLASMA + SPHERE *sb.*] The roughly toroidal region surrounding the earth at latitudes away from the poles in which there is a relatively dense plasma of low-energy electrons and protons that is thought to rotate with the earth; an analogous region around another planet. Cf. PLASMAPAUSE.

1966 D. L. CARPENTER in *Jrnl. Geophysical Res.* LXXI. 695/1 With regard to nomenclature, the word 'plasma-pause' will be used when the three-dimensionality of the knee phenomenon is emphasized... The word 'plasma-sphere' will be used to indicate the dense region inside the plasmapause, and 'plasma trough' to indicate the tenuous region outside. **1971** *New Scientist* 1 July 8/1 The work..led to this detection of the Jovian plasmasphere from the now well-known modulation of Jupiter's radio emission caused by Io. **1974** *McGraw-Hill Yearbk. Sci. & Technol.* 345/2 The characteristic changes in size and shape of the plasmasphere which are observed by satellites and by ground-based vlf measurements have a direct effect on the dynamics of the F region of the ionosphere and on the location of regions of wave turbulence in the outer magnetosphere.

Hence **plasmaˈspheric** *a.*

1974 *Nature* 29 Mar. 401/1 He II λ303 Å emissions will be incident on the night-time upper atmosphere, arising from resonance scattering of the solar helium lines..by plasmaspheric He^+ ions. **1978** *Ibid.* 26 Jan. 310/2 Inside the plasmasphere the characteristic emission is a featureless 'plasmaspheric hiss' which effectively fills the high density region but is believed to be generated by cyclotron resonant interactions with > 30 keV electrons near the outer edge of the plasmasphere.

†**ˈplasmate,** *v. Obs. rare*⁻¹. [f. ppl. stem of Chr. L. *plasmāre* (Tertull., Vulg.) to form, etc., f. PLASMA.] *trans.* To form, mould; to create.

a **1608** DEE *Relat. of Spir.* I. (1659) 371 Now if this Power, this Plasmating, if this Taking, which was the Word, become man, perfect man; then followeth it, that man was and is, God creating and created.

plasmatic (plæzˈmætɪk), *a.* [ad. Gr. πλασματικ-ός imitative; but taken as the adj. corresponding to PLASMA: see -ATIC.] Relating to the plasma, esp. of the blood.

plasmatic cell = PLASMA CELL. ***plasmatic current, layer, stream***: 'the part of the blood-stream in the small arteries which lies between the column of red corpuscles in mid-channel (*axial current*) and the wall of the vessel' (*Syd. Soc. Lex.*).

1828–32 WEBSTER, Plasmatic, Plasmatical. **1864** *Ibid.* s.v., The plasmatic fluid. **1870** *Q. Jrnl. Microsc. Sci.* X. 79 Plasmatic circulation in connective tissue. **1876** tr. *Wagner's Gen. Pathol.* (ed. 6) 150 In the so-called Plasmatic Canals—spaces of the smallest size found in connective tissue. **1898** *Allbutt's Syst. Med.* V. 497 In ordinary cases..the plasmatic elements of the blood seem to be sufficient for vegetative growth. **1899** *Ibid.* VI. 245 The distinction between axial and plasmatic current is obliterated.

†**plasˈmatical,** *a. Obs. rare*⁻¹. [f. Gr. πλασματικός (see prec.) + -AL¹.] Having the quality of moulding, or giving shape or form; formative.

1647 H. MORE *Song of Soul* Notes 342 Psyche..working ..by her plasmaticall Spirits or Archei, all the whole world into order and shape.

†**plasˈmation.** *Obs.* [a. OF. *plasmacion*, or ad. Chr. L. *plasmātiōn-em* (Jerome), n. of action f. *plasmāre*: see PLASMATE.] Moulding, forming, fashioning; creation.

1388 *Pol. Poems* (Rolls) I. 275 They bere a newe fascion, *humeris in pectore tergo*; Goddes plasmacion *non illis complacet ergo*. **1432–50** tr. *Higden* (Rolls) I. 29 The iiij. ages of the world, from the plasmacion of Adam vn to the incension of the temple of the Iewes. **1568** GRAFTON *Chron.* I. 6 Neuerthelesse, the plasmation or creation of Adam is reconed among the generations. *a* **1608** DEE *Relat. Spir.* I. (1659) 371 The wisedome of the Father, in love, created and made man... But how? By Plasmation. For it is written, Let us make man. *a* **1677** HALE *Prim. Orig. Man.* IV. iii. 309 Not as if God Almighty used any Manual or Physical Plasmation of a Man, as the Statuary makes his Statue.

plasmatoparous (plæzməˈtɒpərəs), *a. Bot.* [f. Gr. πλάσμα, πλασματο- (see PLASMA) + L. *-parus* producing (see -PAROUS).] Applied to a mode of germination in certain fungi: see quot.

1887 GARNSEY & BALFOUR *De Bary's Fungi* Explan. Terms 498/1 In Peronosporeae: forms are plasmatoparous when in germination the whole protoplasm of a gonidium issues as a spherical mass which at once becomes invested with a membrane and then puts out a germ tube.

†**ˈplasmator.** *Obs.* Also 6 *Sc.* -our. [ad. OF. *plasmateur* (13th c. in Godef.), ad. Chr. L. *plasmātor* (Tertull.) former, creator (applied to God), agent-n. f. *plasmāre*: see PLASMATE.] He who forms or fashions; a maker, creator.

? *a* **1500** in *York Myst.* 514 Fader eternall, Parfite plasmator and god omnipotent. **1513** DOUGLAS *Æneis* x. Prol. 1 Hie plasmatour of thingis vniuersall. **1549** *Compl. Scot.* iii. 27 The supreme plasmator of hauyn ande eird. **1653** URQUHART *Rabelais* II. viii, The Soveraign Plasmator God Almighty, hath endowed and adorned humane Nature at the beginning.

†**ˈplasmature.** *Obs.* [a. early mod.F. *plasmature*, ad. L. type *plasmātūra, f. *plasmāre*:

see PLASMATE, and -URE.] Form, mould; *concr.* (*collect.*) things formed in moulds, cast ware.

1610 W. FOLKINGHAM *Art of Survey* I. vii. 14 Tonnel or Conduit-pipes, Glasse, Purslane, and other Plasmature. **1653** URQUHART *Rabelais* II. viii, That so stately frame and Plasmature, wherein the man at first had been created.

plasmic ('plæzmɪk), *a.* [mod. f. PLASM or PLASM-A + -IC.] Pertaining to or consisting of plasm; protoplasmic.

1875 LANKESTER in *Phil. Trans.* CLXV. 43 The stages of the [molluscan] egg's nutrition may be thus grouped:—1st stage, Plasmic [etc.]. **1904** *Brit. Med. Jrnl.* 15 Oct. 968 This plasmic environment could not vary excessively without causing death to parent and germ and sperm cell alike.

plasmid ('plæzmɪd). *Biol.* [f. PLASM + *-id* (cf. ID, CHROMATID).] Any genetic structure in a cell that can replicate independently of the chromosomes; *esp.* one in the cytoplasm of a bacterium.

1952 J. LEDERBERG in *Physiol. Rev.* XXXII. 403, I propose *plasmid* as a generic term for any extrachromosomal hereditary determinant. *Ibid.*, The taxonomic classification of plasmids as viruses, symbionts, or plasmagenes should not obscure careful descriptions of their function, hereditary or pathological, or both. *Ibid.* 414, *κ*, a plasmid in *Paramecium aurelia*. *Ibid.* 425 This review has contrasted the various forms of plasmid: the hereditary parasites as against the functionally coordinated plasmagenes, with the mutualistic endosymbionts somewhere between. **1964** *Daily Mirror* 24 July 8/2 The Rogue Bug's real name is RTF plasmid—R.T.F. stands for Resistance Transfer Factor. It is a tiny particle that appears to move from one bacterial cell to another, carrying with it a built-in resistance to new drugs. **1969** A. M. CAMPBELL *Episomes* i. 13 Episomes are thus distinguished from chromosomal genes on the one hand and obligately cytoplasmic elements (plasmids) on the other. **1973** R. G. KRUEGER et al. *Introd. Microbiol.* xv. 421/1 There are.. transmissible plasmids or sex factors like the F factor, which promote their own transfer to recipient bacteria, and there are nontransmissible plasmids which are incapable of transferring themselves to recipient cells. **1975** *Sci. Amer.* July 25 It has been called plasmid engineering, because it utilizes plasmids to introduce the foreign genes... Because of the method's potential for creating a wide variety of novel genetic combinations in microorganisms it is also known as genetic engineering. **1977** *Time* 18 Apr. 48/1 They possess much smaller closed loops of DNA, called plasmids —which consist of only a few genes.

plasmin ('plæzmɪn). *Chem.* [ad. F. *plasmine*, f. PLASM-A + *-ine*, -IN[1].] †**1.** A proteid substance obtained from the plasma of the blood, soluble in water, the solution coagulating into fibrin. *Obs.*

1866 WATTS *Dict. Chem.* IV. 662 *Plasmin*,.. applied by Denis (Compt. rend. lii. 1239; Jahresb. 1861, p. 725) to a constituent of the blood to which he supposes the property of spontaneous coagulation to be due... It is soluble in water... The solution.. solidifies after a few minutes to a colourless transparent jelly, which by pressure between paper is converted into fibres of fibrin. **1876** FOSTER *Phys.* I. i. (1879) 15 The coagulation of blood is the result of the conversion of plasmine into fibrin. **1895** *Syd. Soc. Lex.*, *Plasmine*.. is a mixture of at least two bodies, *paraglobulin* and *fibrinogen*.

2. *Physiol.* A proteolytic enzyme which destroys blood clots by attacking fibrin.

1945 CHRISTENSEN & MACLEOD in *Jrnl. Gen. Physiol.* XXVIII. 581 Under this scheme the activated enzyme may be termed 'plasmin' in comformity [*sic*] with common usage for proteases, where the prefix indicates the source of the enzyme, followed by -in... The inactive enzyme as it occurs in serum and plasma may be designated as 'plasminogen' to indicate its source, the plasma, and also to indicate that it is in an inactive, precursor state... The term 'plasmin' has been used in the past to designate a fraction of blood obtained by a special salting-out procedure. This usage, however, has become obsolete and the possibility of confusion with the proteolytic enzyme system is remote. **1962** [see *fibrinolysin* s.v. FIBRINO-]. **1968** PASSMORE & ROBSON *Compan. Med. Stud.* I. xxvi. 16/1 The active enzyme in this system, plasmin, is proteolytic but possesses a preference for fibrin as substrate. It is formed from an inactive soluble blood protein precursor, plasminogen, by the action of plasminogen activator. **1976** *Nature* 22 Jan. 235/2 Plasminogen is the plasma proenzyme which, on conversion to its active form, plasmin, is considered responsible for lysis of fibrin deposits resulting from physiological or pathological activation of the coagulation cascade.

plasminogen (plæz'mɪnədʒən). *Physiol.* [f. prec. + -OGEN.] The inactive precursor, present in blood, of the enzyme plasmin.

1945 [see prec.]. **1962** *Lancet* 27 Jan. 191/1 The presence of plasminogen activator in tissue suggests that it may have a role in the removal of unwanted fibrin. **1968**, **1976** [see prec.].

plasmo-, before a vowel **plasm-**, combining form of Gr. πλάσμα, πλασματ- plasm, in various scientific terms. (The fuller form is *plasmato-*.)

plasmoblast ('plæzməʊblɑːst, -æ-). *Histology.* [f. PLASMO- + -BLAST.] The precursor of a plasmacyte. †**a.** (See quot.; cf. PLASMOCYTE a.) *Obs.*

1897 G. EISEN in *Proc. Calif. Acad. Sci.* (*Zool.*) I. 16 The polar accumulations must, therefore, be considered as something entirely separate from the balance of the cytoplasm; they, in fact, give rise to the plasmocytes, and may, therefore, appropriately be called plasmocytoblasts, or for the sake of brevity, plasmoblasts.

b. Also **plasmablast**. [a. G. *plasmoblast* (S. Moeschlin 1940, in *Helv. Med. Acta* VII. 231).] An immature plasma cell. Cf. PLASMACYTE.

1942 *Amer. Jrnl. Anat.* LXX. 485 Moeschlin believes that some of the youngest lymphoid reticular cells begin to assume plasma cell characters, and that beginning with this 'plasmoblast' there is a developmental sequence of stages leading to the mature plasma cell, and that this sequence is probably independent of the lymphocytic line. **1949** *Jrnl. Exper. Med.* XC. 165 Maturation of plasmoblasts to plasma cells was associated.. with reduction in the size of the nucleus and disappearance of the PNA [*sc.* pentose nucleic acid] in the nucleolus. **1959** M. BURNET *Clonal Selection Theory of Acquired Immunity* vii. 113 In lymph nodes the first small foci of plasmoblasts appeared in a perivascular situation near the arterioles of the medullary cords. **1973** R. I. WEED tr. *M. Bessis's Living Blood Cells & their Ultrastructure* vii. 521/1 Plasmablast. On a smear, this cell measures 15 to 20 microns in diameter. Its principal characteristic is the profound basophilia of its cytoplasm.

Hence **plasmo'blastic** *a.*

1970 *Jrnl. Nuclear Med.* XI. 599/2 EH was a 54-year-old W.F. with plasmoblastic multiple myeloma with widespread skeletal involvement, [etc.]. **1975** *Biol. Abstr.* LIX. 6033/1 In lymphoblastic and plasmoblastic acute leukemias pathological cells were capable of synthesizing various Ig classes.

plasmocellular, var. PLASMACELLULAR *a.*

Plasmochin ('plæzməkɪn). *Pharm.* [f. PLASMODIUM + G. *chin*(*in* QUININE.] A proprietary name for PAMAQUIN. Cf. PLASMOQUINE.

1926 *Trade Marks Jrnl.* 17 Mar. 631 Plasmochin... Chemical substances prepared for use in medicine and pharmacy. Bayer Products, Limited,.. London,.. merchants and manufacturers. **1926** *Lancet* 16 Oct. 825/2 The great merits of plasmochin are that it is cheaper than quinine, tastes better, and gives rise to less unpleasant secondary effects. **1926** *Official Gaz.* (U.S. Patent Office) 26 Oct. 715/1 I. G. Farbenindustrie Aktiengesellschaft.. Germany. Filed Aug. 14, 1926. Plasmochin.. Preparation for the Treatment of Malaria. Claims use since about December, 1925. **1948** J. H. BURN *Lect. Notes Pharmacol.* 90 Pamaquin was introduced by the Germans as plasmochin; it is a quinoline derivative. **1962** —— *Drugs, Med. & Man* xx. 197 Domagk was working in the Bayer fabrik in Elberfeld in Germany, where the advances had been made which led to the discovery of the antimalarial agents plasmochin and later atebrin.

plasmocyte ('plæzməʊsaɪt). *Histology.* [f. PLASMO- + -CYTE.] †**a.** (See quots.) *Obs.*

1897 G. EISEN in *Proc. Calif. Acad. Sci.* (*Zool.*) I. 4 A new corpuscle, which I have termed *plasmocyte*. *Ibid.* 13 (*heading*) Plasmocytes.—I apply this name to a hitherto undescribed element in the blood, first described by me in the blood of Batrachoseps. **1897** *Jrnl. R. Microsc. Soc.* 271 The plasmocyte may be defined as a corpuscle, generally without a cell-wall, always without a nucleus, consisting of the archosome and three spheres of cytoplasm. It shows power of growth, movement, phagocytosis, &c. **1900** E. B. WILSON *Cell* (ed. 2) i. 52 Eisen ('97) asserts that in the blood of a salamander.. the attraction-sphere.. containing the centrosomes may separate from the remainder of the cell (nucleated red corpuscles) to form an independent form of blood-corpuscle or 'plasmocyte', which leads an active life in the blood.

b. var. PLASMACYTE.

plasmocytoma, **plasmocytosis**, variants of PLASMACYTOMA, -CYTOSIS.

plasmodesma (plæzməʊ'dɛzmə). *Bot.* Also anglicized as **'plasmodesm** (-dɛz(ə)m). Pl. **plasmodesmata**; also **-desmæ**, ‖**-desmen**, **-desms**; (erron.) **-desma**. [a. G. *plasmodesma*, pl. *plasmodesmen* (E. Strasburger 1901, in *Jahrb. f. wissensch. Bot.* XXXVI. 503 (sing. form on p. 607)): see PLASMO- and DESMA.] A narrow thread of cytoplasm that passes through cell walls and affords communication between plant cells.

1905 *Amer. Naturalist* XXXIX. 220 A new point of view was introduced into the discussion by the very important paper of Strasburger, in 1901. He considered the protoplasmic connections as sufficiently clearly differentiated structures to rank as organs of the cell and proposed for them the name plasmodesmen. **1925** E. B. WILSON *Cell* (ed. 3) i. 103 It is probable that an important part in the coördination of the cell-activities is played by direct protoplasmic connections between cells ('cell-bridges', 'plasmodesms'). **1927** FRITSCH & WEST *Treat. Brit. Freshwater Algae* (ed. 2) 40 The pit-membrane in such cases is probably traversed by plasmodesmae. **1931** *Stain Technol.* VI. 127 (*heading*) A technic for demonstrating plasmodesma. **1934** L. G. LIVINGSTONE in *Amer. Jrnl. Bot.* XXI. 707 The only way to arrive at a satisfactory understanding of the true nature of plasmo-desmata in the living plant is to study the cell walls in an unaltered state. **1935** —— in *Ibid.* XXII. 75 The word plasmodesma is proposed for the singular, to designate an individual structure, and plasmodesmata is used in the plural sense. **1941** *Bot. Rev.* VII. 254 Plasmodesmata generally run straight from cell to cell, and only in the neighborhood of intercellular spaces or pit membranes of narrow pits are the outer plasmodesmata curved. **1951** F. DROUET in G. M. Smith *Man. Phycol.* viii. 163 Species of *Stigonema* have trichomes which in age become multiseriate throughout; the spherical or depressed-spherical cells are connected by strands of protoplasm usually considered to be plasmodesmen. **1966** *Protoplasma* LXI. 82 In longitudinal sections of the plasmodesms the real continuity of the cytoplasmic membranes can be observed. **1975** *Ann. Rev. Plant Physiol.* XXVI. 13 Despite other suggestions, the word plasmodesma has continued to be used to describe a protoplasmic connection. *Ibid.* 14 Plasmodesmata have been described in angiosperms, gymnosperms, pteridophytes, bryophytes, and many algae.

Hence **plasmo'desmatal** *a.*, of, pertaining to, or being plasmodesmata.

1961 in WEBSTER. **1964** J. HESLOP-HARRISON in H. F. Linskens *Pollen Physiol. & Fertilization* II. 41 The peripheral archesporial cells show plasmodesmatal links with the tapetal cells, and these in turn with the cells of the inner wall layer of the anther. **1975** *Ann. Rev. Plant Physiol.* XXVI. 15 There are considerable technical difficulties involved in obtaining reliable estimates of plasmodesmatal frequency.

‖**plasmodium** (plæz'məʊdɪəm). *Biol.* Pl. **-ia**. Rarely anglicized **plasmode** ('plæzməʊd). [mod.L. (1863, Cienkowski in Pringsheim *Botanik* III. 400), f. PLASMA + *-odium*: see -ODE[1].]

1. A mass or sheet of naked protoplasm, formed by the fusion, or by the aggregation, of a number of amœboid bodies (***true*** or ***fusion-plasmodium***, ***pseudo-*** or ***aggregation plasmodium***), and having an amœboid creeping movement.

First observed as one stage in the life-history of the *Myxomycetes* or *Mycetozoa*, the position of which as vegetable or animal organisms is disputed; also in certain groups of *Protozoa*, and other simple animal forms.

1875 *Encycl. Brit.* III. 693/2 The formation of the plasmodium is a kind of complex conjugation. **1875** BENNETT & DYER *Sachs' Bot.* 276 Myxomycetes... The swarm-spores cease dividing and unite, two or more of them coalescing—after they have gone over into the Amœba form —into a homogeneous protoplasmic substance, also endowed with an Amœba-like motion, the Plasmodium. **1875** ALLMAN in *Phil. Trans.* CLXV. 561, 571. **1877** HUXLEY *Anat. Inv. Anim.* ii. 81 A certain number of the myxopods unite together, and become fused into an active plasmodium, which exhibits no trace of their primitive separation. **1880** GEDDES in *Proc. Royal Soc.* XXX. 252 On the coalescence of Amœboid cells into Plasmodia. *Ibid.* 254 The formation of plasmodia was at first supposed to be peculiar to the Myxomycetes, but several Rhizopods have been described in which a more or less complete cell-fusion has been observed... All the evidence points to the conclusion that the power of coalescing with its fellows, under favourable circumstances, to form a plasmodium, is ..a very widely spread, if not a general property of the amœboid cell. **1882** VINES *Sachs' Bot.* 263. **1888** ROLLESTON & JACKSON *Anim. Life* 912 Fusion to form *plasmodia* recurs in some Proteomyxan *Monadineæ*, as to the animal nature of which there can be no doubt. **1890** *Cent. Dict.*, *Plasmode*, same as *plasmodium*.

2. Name given to certain parasitic organisms found in the blood of patients with recent malaria, and quartan and tertian ague.

Discovered by Laveran (1880), and named by him, as a vegetable organism, *Oscillaria malariæ*; referred by Marchiafava and Celli to the animal kingdom, and called by them (1885) *Plasmodium malariæ*; more recently distinguished as belonging to two genera of Protozoa, *Laverania* and *Plasmodium*. (Minchin in Ray Lankester *Treatise on Zoology* I. ii. 243 (1903).)

1895 in *Syd. Soc. Lex.* **1897** *Allbutt's Syst. Med.* II. 724 Marchiafava and Celli described with great accuracy the intra-corpuscular amœboid form, to which they gave the name plasmodium. **1898** P. MANSON *Trop. Diseases* i. 2 *note*, The malaria parasite is not a plasmodium in the zoological meaning of the word. **1899** *Allbutt's Syst. Med.* VI. 595 The most careful examination of the blood during the paroxysms showed no evidence of plasmodia.

attrib. and *Comb.* **1898** P. MANSON *Trop. Diseases* ii. 37 It has been considered advisable to expunge the term remittent fever as indicative of a distinct species of plasmodium disease. *Ibid.* 49 The plasmodium-infected corpuscles. *Ibid.* iii. 86 A protective, plasmodium-destroying agency inherent in the human body. *Ibid.* vi. 116 Plasmodium-like organisms.

Hence **plas'modial**, **plasmodic** (-'ɒdɪk) *adjs.*, pertaining to, of the nature of, or arising from, a plasmodium; **plas'modiate** *a.*, having or characterized by plasmodia, as the *Mycetozoa*; **plas'modiate** *v. intr.*, to become fused into a plasmodium; **plasmodi'ation**, formation of a plasmodium; **plas'modiocarp** [Gr. καρπός fruit], an irregular-shaped fructification occurring in the *Myxomycetes* (hence **plas,modio'carpous** *a.*).

1892 J. A. THOMSON *Outl. Zool.* 109 The *plasmodial stage in the cycle is predominant. **1896** *Allbutt's Syst. Med.* I. 542 Malaria (which is due to plasmodial infection and is not a bacterial disease). **1882** A. S. WILSON in *Gard. Chron.* XVII. 671 The application of moisture to a spore.. is directly seen to cause it either to give birth to a zoospore, or to *plasmodiate, retaining its contents. *Ibid.*, A manure.. of a hygrorsorptive character is just the very manure to promote the *plasmodiation of these spores, and render them fit to be absorbed in the form of a fluid plasm by the roots of the plants. **1877** M. C. COOKE *Myxomycetes Gt. Britain* 30 (Contrib. to *Mycologia Britann.*) *Plasmodiocarp. **1899** *Knowledge* 1 May 116/1 Plasmodiocarp is a term applied to the spore-bearing part when it is sessile and irregular in form, sometimes like a cushion, sometimes like.. a long tube.

plasmogamy (plæz'mɒgəmɪ). *Biol.* [ad. G. *plasmogamie*: see PLASMO- and -GAMY.] The fusion of the cytoplasm of two or more cells.

1912 E. A. MINCHIN *Introd. Study Protozoa* viii. 128 In many cases, union of distinct individuals can be observed which have nothing to do with syngamy, since no fusion takes place of nuclei, but only of cytoplasm. Such unions are distinguished as plastogamy (or plasmogamy) from true syngamy. **1932** L. A. BORRADAILE et al. *Invertebrata* ii. 26 The union of nuclei is karyogamy: in most cases of syngamy it is accompanied by plasmogamy or the fusion of cytoplasm... Plastogamy..is plasmogamy without karyogamy. **1958** *Ibid.* (ed. 3) ii. 40 Here may be mentioned the union of individuals by fusion of their cytoplasm, the nuclei remaining distinct, which is practised by the Mycetozoa..and in some other cases. This process, which is not syngamy, is known as plasmogamy, and its product as a plasmodium. **1969** F. E. ROUND *Introd. Lower Plants* iv. 60 In most of the higher terrestrial fungi, plasmogamy, which is the fusion of small masses of cytoplasm containing the nuclei, is separated in time from karyogamy.

plasmogen (ˈplæzməʊdʒɛn). *Biol.* [f. PLASMO- + -GEN.] The chemically highest or most elaborate form, stage, or part of protoplasm, which by its vital activity forms the tissues or other organic products; true or formative protoplasm; bioplasm.

1888 E. R. LANKESTER in *Encycl. Brit.* XXIV. 817/1 Physiologists have come to use the word 'protoplasm' for *one* of the chemical substances of which Schultze's protoplasm is a structural mixture—namely, that highest point in the chemical elaboration of the molecule which is attained within the protoplasm, and up to which some of the chemical bodies present are tending... This 'critical' substance, sometimes called 'true protoplasm', should assuredly be recognized by a distinct name 'plasmogen'.

plasmogeny (plæzˈmɒdʒɪnɪ), **-gony** (-gənɪ). *Biol.* [f. PLASMO- + -GENY. The variant *plasmogony* is ad. Ger. *plasmogonie* (Haeckel) with suffix repr. Gr. -γονία begetting, generation: cf. *cosmogony*.] Name for a mode of spontaneous generation: see quot., and cf. AUTOGENY.

1876 E. R. LANKESTER tr. *Haeckel's Hist. Creat.* I. 339 We call spontaneous generation *plasmogeny* when the organism arises in an *organic formative fluid*, that is, in a fluid which contains those requisite fundamental substances dissolved in the form of complicated and fluid combinations of carbon. **1904** MCCABE tr. *Haeckel's Wond. Life* xv. 369, I distinguished two principal stages—*autogony* (the formation of the first living matter from inorganic nitrogenous carbon-compounds) and *plasmogony* (the formation of the first individualised plasm; the earliest organic individuals in the form of monera).

plasmoid (ˈplæzmɔɪd). *Physics* and *Astr.* [f. PLASM(A + -OID.] A coherent mass of plasma (PLASMA 6).

1956 W. H. BOSTICK in *Physical Rev.* CIV. 292/1 The plasma is emitted not as an amorphous blob, but in the form of a torus... We shall take the liberty of calling this toroidal structure a plasmoid, a word which means plasma-magnetic entity. The word plasmoid will be employed as a generic term for all plasma-magnetic entities. [*Note*] The term 'plasmon' (in line with the term 'geon' used by Wheeler) was originally proposed. However, David Pines (of Princeton University) has pointed out that the term 'plasmon' should be reserved for a quantum of plasma-oscillation energy. He kindly proposes the term 'plasmoid', which we adopt. **1962** RILEY & SAILOR *Space Systems Engin.* v. 129 Techniques have been developed..whereby doughnut-shaped 'blobs' of plasma or plasmoids can be projected by magnetic forces at speeds exceeding 10^7 cm/sec. **1971** S. SINGER *Nature of Ball Lightning* viii. 119 Spherical plasmoids of relatively small dimensions, such as those reported for ball lightning or involved in experimental work, have presented greater difficulty for theoretical analysis. **1976** *Nature* 12 Feb. 451/1 As the galaxy ploughs through a dense intracluster gas at supersonic speed, it is envisaged to eject pairs of plasmoids in opposite directions, as commonly assumed for 'normal' double radio galaxies.

plasmology (plæzˈmɒlədʒɪ). [f. as PLASMOGENY + -LOGY.] (See quots.)

1888 E. R. LANKESTER in *Encycl. Brit.* XXIV. 803/2 *Plasmology.*—The study of the ultimate corpuscles of living matter. **1889** *Athenæum* 12 Jan. 47/2 Prof. Lankester assigns ..to 'Plasmology' the study of the cell in its widest sense. **1895** *Syd. Soc. Lex.*, *Plasmology*, histology.

‖**plasmolysis** (plæzˈmɒlɪsɪs). *Biol.* [mod. (De Vries, 1877) f. PLASMO- + Gr. λύσις loosing, setting free.] Contraction of the protoplasm of a vegetable cell with separation or freeing of the lining layer from the cell-wall, due to the withdrawal of liquid by exosmosis when the cell is placed in a liquid of greater density than the cell-sap. Hence ˌ**plasmolysaˈbility**; ˈ**plasmolysable** *a.*, capable of undergoing plasmolysis; ˈ**plasmolyse** (-laɪz) *v.* [cf. *analyse*], to subject to plasmolysis, cause plasmolysis in; ˈ**plasmolysed, -lysing** *ppl. adjs.*; **plasmolytic** (-ˈlɪtɪk) *a.*, pertaining to, showing, or causing plasmolysis; **plasmoˈlytically** *adv.*, by means of plasmolysis.

1883 *Q. Jrnl. Microsc. Sci.* XXIII. 151 (*heading*) On plasmolysis and its bearing upon the relations between cell wall and protoplasm. *Ibid.* 152 The protoplasmic body would appear to separate with a 'smooth surface' from the cell wall on treatment with the plasmolysing solution. *Ibid.* 153 Naegeli..described strings of protoplasm which connect the contracted protoplasmic body with the cell wall in plasmolysed cells. **1885** GOODALE *Physiol. Bot.* (1892) 390 Such substances [as cause contraction of the protoplasm] are termed plasmolytic agents. **1886** VINES *Lect. Physiol. Plants* iii. 39 Turgid cell..in 10 per cent. solution, shewing complete plasmolysis. *Ibid.* 44 When the cells of the Beet-root are placed in syrup they become plasmolytic. **1888** HUXLEY & MARTIN *Elem. Biol.* xi. 404 In order to see the primordial utricle better, plasmolyse the cell by running in 10 p.c. salt solution. **1891** DARWIN in *Rep. Brit. Assoc.* (1892) 672 As the plasmolysing agent continues to act, a reverse movement takes place. *Ibid.*, In different stages of plasmolysis. **1896** *Jrnl. Linnean Soc.: Bot.* XXXI. 370 A few of the younger leaves and leaf-cells are found to be living and plasmolysable, but show no assimilation. **1903** *Science* 1 May 706/2 A reduction of temperature gave rise to parthenogenetic spore formation.., as was also the case when water was plasmolytically withdrawn from the cells. **1955** P. J. KRAMER in W. Ruhland *Encycl. Plant Physiol.* I. II. 212 Errors in the plasmolytic method include adhesion of the cytoplasm to the wall, penetration of the plasmolyzing solute, and difficulty in measuring cell volume. **1960** L. PICKEN *Organization of Cells* iii. 77 The plasmolysability of the cells implies that the cell wall cannot contract below a certain area. **1964** J. LEVITT in D. W. Newman *Instrumental Methods Exper. Biol.* xiii. 420 These very cells, with which the incipient plasmolysis method leads to difficulties, cannot have their osmotic potentials determined in any other way, and at least approximate values may be obtained plasmolytically. **1971** *Nature* 16 July 159/2 Attempts to fix and section plasmolysed sieve tubes have not so far yielded supporting evidence.

plasmolyte (ˈplæzməʊlaɪt). *Physiol.* [f. PLASMO- + Gr. λυτ-ός loosed, soluble (f. λύειν to loosen), or f. G. *plasmolytikum* PLASMOLYTICUM.] = next.

1927 *Biol. Abstr.* I. 238/2 The increase in volume after full plasmolysis is due to penetration of the plasmolyte. **1935** *Plant Physiol.* X. 119 That concentration of a harmless non-permeable plasmolyte which at osmotic equilibrium causes the protoplasm to recede ever so little from the cell wall. **1939** *Ibid.* XIV. 132 As a rule a minimal area form is not assumed during the process of plasmolysis but is reached either on standing in the plasmolyte, or at least after a slight degree of subsequent deplasmolysis. **1964** J. LEVITT in D. W. Newman *Instrumental Methods Exper. Biol.* xiii. 419 Potassium nitrate was the plasmolyte used by many of the earlier investigators.

plasmolyticum (plæzməʊˈlɪtɪkʌm). *Physiol.* Pl. -lytica. [mod.L. (ad. G. *plasmolytikum*), f. PLASMO- + Gr. λυτικ-ός able to loosen (f. λύειν to loosen).] A substance used to produce plasmolysis.

1943 *Ann. Bot.* VII. 269 In experiments on rates of plasmolysis or deplasmolysis one would expect to find the wall-resistance exercising an effect when sucrose is used as the plasmolyticum. **1946** *New Phytologist* XLV. 7 The plasmolysis form taken up in any plasmolyticum, sucrose and KCl included, is much influenced by the distance of the cell from the cut edge of the strip of epidermis. **1973** COCKING & EVANS in H. E. Street *Plant Tissue & Cell Culture* v. 100 Irreversible, damaging effects on the viability of isolated protoplasts readily result from the use of plasmolytica of either too high or too low an osmotic potential. **1974** A. J. PEEL *Transport of Nutrients in Plants* x. 189 The sections were irrigated with plasmolytica composed of 0·5–2·0 M solutions of glucose or fructose.

plasmoma (plæzˈməʊmə). *Path.* Pl. **plasmomata.** [f. PLASM(A + -OMA.] = PLASMACYTOMA.

1901 L. P. HAMBURGER in *Johns Hopkins Hosp. Bull.* XII. 43/1 Recently, Wright has described a myeloma in detail... The tumor elements, according to his research, really form a variety of plasma cells. A myeloma does not originate in the marrow cells as a whole, but in only one of its elements, the plasma cell. Following the results of this important contribution, the tumor may be classed as a plasmoma. **1931** *Amer. Jrnl. Med. Sci.* CLXXXI. 170 In our series of cases extra-osseous involvement occurred in..one of the plasmomata primary in a lymph node. **1961** *Arch. Path.* LXXI. 229 (*heading*) Extramedullary plasmacytoma of gastrointestinal tract with a case report of plasmoma of the rectum.

plasmon (ˈplæzmɒn). [f. PLASM(A + -ON[1] (in sense 1 an arbitrary ending).] †**1.** Also **Plasmon.** A proprietary name of a soluble proteinaceous extract of milk; used *attrib.* to designate various foodstuffs made with this, as ***Plasmon biscuit, chocolate, cocoa.*** *Obs.*

1900 *Daily Express* 31 July 2/6 Plasmon is nothing more or less than milk dried after removing the cream and sugar. *Ibid.*, The writer has found Plasmon chocolate a most useful preparation in cycling. **1901** *Daily Tel.* 18 Mar. 11/6 (Advt.), Why Plasmon cocoa is a nourishing food. *Ibid.*, Plasmon is the albumen of pure fresh milk in the form of a dry, soluble, granulated white powder. **1906** *Trade Marks Jrnl.* 4 Apr. 477 *Plasmon...* Substances used as food or as ingredients in food. International Plasmon, Limited,.. London,..food manufacturers. **1912** G. W. E. RUSSELL *Afterthoughts* xvi. 157 Miss Larkins sups on strong coffee and a cigarette, and Meakin on hot milk with a plasmon biscuit. **1915** GALSWORTHY *Freelands* xxxvii. 335 Open your mouth and let me pop in one of these delicious little plasmon biscuits. They're perfect after travelling. **1921** R. WHYMPER *Cocoa & Chocolate* (ed. 2) xxiv. 359 Plasmon cocoa..a powder containing added matter in the form of dried milk solids (approximately sixty parts milk solids to forty parts cocoa powder). *Ibid.* 360 Plasmon, which was regarded as a soluble form of milk proteid, is rendered to some extent insoluble when added to cocoa. **1922** [see HOOSH *sb.*]. **1935** E. A. KNOX *Reminisc. Octogenarian* x. 194 One of our side stole out during the debate, and fetched some 'Plasmon' biscuits. **1946** O. SITWELL *Scarlet Tree* III. iii. 48 He had..altogether lost touch with his teeth, being confined by his doctor to a total diet of Plasmon biscuits, a health food.

2. *Genetics.* Also **-one.** [a. G. *plasmon* (F. von Wettstein 1927, in *Nachr. von der Ges. der Wissensch. zu Göttingen* (*Math.-Physik. Klasse*) 259).] The totality of cytoplasmic, or of extra-nuclear, genetic factors.

1932 *Proc. 6th Internat. Congr. Genetics* II. 281 The abnormal development of chlorophyll (pale color) may be caused by a non-Mendelian nuclear or cytoplasmic factor or by a certain state of the genome or plasmon. **1954**, **1965** [see PLASTOME]. **1970** T. DOBZHANSKY *Genetics Evolutionary Process* x. 345 The plasmon of *E*[*pilobium*] *luteum* has retained its properties despite having carried an *E. hirsutum* genome for several generations. **1973** K. MATHER *Genetical Structure of Populations* ii. 6 Together with the nuclear genotype, the plasmon can play its part in the process of adaptation especially..in the building up of barriers to crossing. **1976** BELL & COOMBE tr. *Strasburger's Textbk. Bot.* 401 Plastome and plasmone mutations have been insufficiently studied..but their importance for evolution should not be underestimated.

3. *Astr.* and *Physics.* = PLASMOID.

1955 W. BOSTICK *Anat. of Plasmons* (U.S. Atomic Energy Comm., Rep. UCRL-4530) 2 Plasmons (plasma-magnetic entities) are toroidal packages of plasma wrapped up in their own magnetic fields. **1963** *Soviet Astron.—AJ* VI. 471/2 If the 'plasmons' ejected by the 'active' nuclei of radio galaxies experience no deceleration, the age of sources similar to Centaurus A and Fornax A will not exceed 10^8 years. **1971** R. C. HAYMES *Introd. Space Sci.* xv. 447 The jet [of the galaxy M87] appears to be composed of a group of irregular concentrations of plasma, called 'plasmons' by some. **1974** *Nature* 23 Aug. 629/2 Christiansen has shown that a plasmon can travel a distance $D = M/(\pi \times 1{\cdot}67 \times 10^{-24}\, n, r^2)$ before dispersing. Here M is the mass of the plasmon, r its radius and n, the number density of the gas surrounding the component.

4. *Physics.* The quantum or quasiparticle associated with a collective oscillation of charge density.

1956 D. PINES in *Rev. Mod. Physics* XXVIII. 184/1 The valence electrons in the solid..are capable of carrying out collective oscillations at a high frequency... The valence electron collective oscillations resemble closely the electronic plasma oscillations observed in gaseous discharges. We introduce the name 'plasmons' to describe the quantum of elementary excitation associated with this high-frequency collective motion. **1966** C. KITTEL *Introd. Solid State Physics* (ed. 3) viii. 233 It is possible to excite a plasmon by passing an electron through a thin metallic film ..or by reflecting an electron from the film. The reflected or transmitted electron will show an energy loss equal to integral multiples of the plasmon energy. **1972** F. WOOTEN *Optical Properties of Solids* ix. 220 The bulk plasmons we have considered so far are purely longitudinal. They cannot couple to transverse electromagnetic waves. However, at the surface of a solid an oscillation of surface charge density fluctuations is possible. These surface plasmons exist in a number of modes. **1976** J. KLECZEK *Universe* ii. 71 A plasmon is a quantum of plasma waves, just as photons are quanta of electro-magnetic radiation.

Plasmoquine (ˈplæzməkwɪn, -kwiːn). *Pharm.* Also **-quin.** [f. PLASMO(DIUM + QUIN(IN)E.] A proprietary name for PAMAQUIN. Cf. PLASMOCHIN.

1926 *Trade Marks Jrnl.* 22 Dec. 2757/1 Plasmoquine... Chemical substances prepared for use in medicine and pharmacy. Bayer Products, Limited,..London,.. merchants and manufacturers. **1927** *Proc. R. Soc. Med.* XX. 920 The detailed formula for plasmochin (plasmoquine), as it is now known, has not as yet been definitely stated. **1938** *Times* 22 Mar. 17/4 The striking success of acriflavine..is another case in point, and so also are..atebrin and plasmoquin used in malaria. **1945** *New Biol.* I. 102 Atebrin (mepacrine) and plasmoquine are the most useful of the synthetic anti-malarial drugs. **1963** F. HAWKING in Schnitzer & Hawking *Exper. Chemotherapy* I. xix. 693 Experiments in rabbits have been carried out by Pols..who tried..chlortetracycline, babesin,..and plasmoquine without significant results.

ˈ**plasmosome** (-səʊm). *Biol.* Also *erron.* **plasma-.** [f. PLASMO- + Gr. σῶμα body.] 'A separate particle of protoplasm, such as certain particles observed in cell-nuclei' (*Syd. Soc. Lex.*).

1889 *Q. Jrnl. Microsc. Sc.* XXX. II. 168 The out-wandering plasmasomes form the so-called 'paranuclei' (Nebenkerne), which take so important a share in the regeneration of cells. **1900** E. B. WILSON *Cell* (ed. 2) 34 The so-called true nucleoli or plasmosomes.

plasmotomy (plæzˈmɒtəmɪ). *Biol.* [ad. G. *plasmotomie* (F. Doflein 1898, in *Zool. Jahrb.* (*Abt. für Anat. und Ontogenie*) XI. 317): see PLASMO- and -TOMY.] A mode of reproduction in certain protozoans, in which the organism divides into two or more multinucleate daughter cells.

1902 *Encycl. Brit.* XXXII. 817/2 Cohn and Döflein have discovered cases of plasmotomy, in which a kind of protoplasmic bud of ectosarc and endosarc containing some nuclei becomes detached. **1947** *Jrnl. Morphol.* LXXX. 96 Finally, the organism undergoes plasmotomy into from 2 to 6 individuals. **1973** M. A. SLEIGH *Biol. Protozoa* iv. 72 Division of a cell is normally preceded by nuclear division, by either mitosis or meiosis, although in some multinucleate forms fission and nuclear division are not linked, so that for example new individuals may be formed by plasmotomy in which the body is simply separated into multinucleate masses—at any time some nuclei may be found in mitosis in such organisms.

Hence **plasmoˈtomic** *a.*

1949 *Jrnl. Morphol.* LXXXV. 164 Plasmotomic division into two daughter individuals does not results [*sic*] in a 50:50 distribution of the nuclei.

plasome (ˈplæsəʊm). *Biol.* [a. G. *plasom* (Wiesner), shortened from his original term *plasmatosom*, f. Gr. πλάσμα, πλασματ- plasm + σῶμα body.] (See quots.)

1895 *Syd. Soc. Lex.*, *Plasome*,..a term used by Brüche and Wiesner for hypothetical minute vital particles, made up of a group of protoplasmic molecules, and constituting the smallest units which can exhibit the primary vital [functions]. They correspond [to a certain extent] to Weismann's 'biophors', and to the 'pangenes' of de Vries. **1902** E. A. MINCHIN in *Encycl. Brit.* XXXII. 41/1 In other cases the assumption of invisible protoplasmic units has been inspired by a desire..to explain the general vital and animative powers of protoplasm, as, for example, the 'micellæ' of Nägeli and the 'plasomes' of Wiesner.

plass(e, obs. form of PLACE.

plasson (ˈplæsən). *Biol.* [a. G. *plasson* (Haeckel), a. Gr. πλάσσων, -ον, pres. pple. of πλάσσειν to mould, form.] Name for the homogeneous protoplasm of hypothetical primitive organisms, not yet differentiated into nucleus and general cell-substance, or for that of non-nucleated cells or cytodes.

1879 tr. *Haeckel's Evol. Man* I. vii. 182 The vital activities of each cell form a sum of mechanical processes, which depend radically on movements of the smallest 'life-particles', the molecules of the living substance. If we call this active substance the Plasson, and the molecules the Plastidules, we may say that the individual physiological character of each cell depends on the molecular movement of its plastidules. **1904** MCCABE tr. *Haeckel's Wond. Life* vii. 163 On the first view, which I hold, the plasm, or living matter, of the earliest organisms on the earth..was a homogeneous plasson or archiplasm—that is to say, a plasma-compound that was not yet differentiated into outer cytoplasm and inner caryoplasm.

Hence **plaˈssonity** (*humorous*, after *paneity*, etc.), the quality of being 'plasson'.

1882 COUES *Biogen* (1884) 33 The original arch-amœba is as much of a mystery as ever; we know not where he came from, how he got there, or in what the essence of his plassonity subsists.

-plast, combining element repr. Gr. πλαστός formed, moulded, in various terms, chiefly scientific, as *bioplast*, *endoplast*, *protoplast*.

plaste, obs. var. of *placed*: see PLACE *v.*

plaster, † **plaister** (ˈplɑːstə(r), -æ-), *sb.* Forms: α. 1, 4- **plaster**, 3–5 **plastre**, 4 **-tir**, 5 **-tere**, **-tyr**, **plaaster**, **platster**. β. 4 **plaistre**, 5 **playstir**, **-tyr**, **-tre**, 5–7 **playster**, 5–9 **plaister**. [The form *plaster* occurs in sense 1 in OE., ad. pop. L. *plastrum* (med.L. in Du Cange), shortened from *emplastrum* a plaster (medical and in grafting), a. Gr. ἔμπλαστρον (Galen), var. of ἔμπλαστον plaster, salve, f. ἐμπλαστός vbl. adj. 'daubed on or over'. Cf. OHG. *pflastar*, Ger. *pflaster*, also from pop. L. In ME. reinforced by OF. *plastre* (13th c. in Littré, but the deriv. vb. *plastrir* in 12th c.), mod.F. *plâtre*, only in branch II below (for which also med.L. *plastrum* (1233) is cited by Du Cange). Thus the medical sense was from med.L., the builder's sense through French. The collateral form *plaister*, which has been current since 14th c., and has sometimes been more common (as a written form) than *plaster*, occurs also in 14th c. in OF. (*plaistre*), but it was not the normal OF. form even in Norman or Picard, and its history is obscure. Although still frequent in the 18th c., and found in Dr. Johnson's writings, it was not recognized by him in his Dictionary. In mod. dial. *plaister* (ˈplestər) is the form in Sc. and north. Eng.]

I. 1. a. *Med.* An external curative application, consisting of a solid or semi-solid substance spread upon a piece of muslin, skin, or some similar material, and of such nature as to be adhesive at the temperature of the body; used for the local application of a medicament, or for closing a wound, and sometimes to give mechanical support. See also COURT-P., MUSTARD-P., STICKING-P.

α. *a* **1000** *Be Dômes Dæge* (E.E.T.S.) 80 Hwi ne bidst ðu ðe beþunga and plaster? *c* **1000** *Sax. Leechd.* I. 304, ȝenim þas ylcan wyrte wyrc to plastre; leȝe to ðære wunde. *c* **1290** *S. Eng. Leg.* I. 360/54 Leie it..ase þei hit a plastre were. **13..** *Seuyn Sag.* (W.) 1572 He laide a plastre under his ribbe. *c* **1400** *Lanfranc's Cirurg.* 60 Take schepis talow & buttere, & make a plaster. **1579** LANGHAM *Gard. Health* (1633) 90 A plaster of sowre bread boyled in wine, draweth sores passing well. **1785** BURNS *Holy Fair* xiii, O how they fire the heart devout, Like cantharidian plasters. **1804** ABERNETHY *Surg. Obs.* 231 On the third day the plasters were removed from the wound. **1856** KANE *Arct. Expl.* II. vi. 71 One of the many who stick to me like a plaster.

β. **1413** *Pilgr. Sowle* (Caxton) I. xxxi. (1859) 35 A very fool may he be clepid that leith a plaister corosyf to a wounde. **14..** *Stockh. Med. MS.* 87 For to make trete þat ys callyd playster of plomb. **1535** COVERDALE *Isa.* xxxviii. 21 And Esay sayde: take a plaster of fyges [1611 a lumpe of figges ..for a plaister], and laye it vpon the sore. **1682** BUNYAN *Holy War* 318 It was a plaister to the brave Captain Credence his wound. **1758** J. S. *Le Dran's Observ. Surg.* (1771) 43 Slips of Linen,..spread with an Agglutinative Plaister. **1874** MOTLEY *Barneveld* I. ii. 115 An aged lackey with a plaister over one eye.

b. *fig.* A healing or soothing means or measure.

α. *a* **1310** in Wright *Lyric P.* xxx. 89 Of penaunce in his plastre al. **1340** *Ayenb.* 148 þe plastres of zuete warningges. **1560** DAUS tr. *Sleidane's Comm.* 17 To heale the wounde with a plaster of reconciliation. *a* **1628** PRESTON *Breastpl. Faith* (1630) 104 Adversity is not a Plaster or a Medicine, but a poyson to him.

β. **1450–1530** *Myrr. our Ladye* 163 Thow haste made a playster of penaunce to sorowfull peple. **1625** SANDERSON *Serm.* I. 126 The breath of the people being but a sorry plaister for a wounded conscience. **1647** N. BACON *Disc. Govt. Eng.* I. lxiv. (1739) 133 The most part of those Laws were little other than plaisters applied to particular botches of those times.

c. ***burglar's plaster***, see quot. 1905. ***poor man's plaster***, a plaster composed of tar, resin, and yellow wax.

1845 COL. HAWKER *Diary* (1893) II. 257 Shipped lots of poor man's plaster and went afloat. **1860** WARTER *Seaboard* II. 287 Before the attack came on,..I put a poor man's plaister on the nape of her neck. **1905** *Daily Chron.* 29 Aug. 6/7 A 'burglar's plaster'..is the technical name for a piece of brown paper covered with treacle and used to deaden the sound of breaking glass.

II. 2. a. A composition of a soft and plastic consistency, which may be spread or daubed upon a surface, as of a wall, where it afterwards hardens; *spec.* a mixture of lime, sand, and (generally) hair, used for covering walls, ceilings, etc.

α. **13..** *E.E. Allit. P.* B. 1549 þe lettres bileued ful large vpon plaster. **1382** WYCLIF *Deut.* xxvii. 2 Thow shalt arere greet stonus..and with plastre thow shalt dawbe hem. **1591** PERCIVALL *Sp. Dict.*, *Açotéa*, a flat roofe couered with lead, or plaster. **1715** PRIOR *Down-Hall* 152 Why 'tis plaster and lath. **1839** E. D. CLARKE *Trav. Russia* 103/1 They form cylinders, by scooping out almost all except the bark; and then, closing their extremities with plaster or mud.

β. *c* **1440** *Promp. Parv.* 402/2 Playstyr for wallys..*gipsum, litura, plastrum.* **1472–3** *Rolls of Parlt.* VI. 51/2 Howses and walles of stone and plaister. **1585** T. WASHINGTON tr. *Nicholay's Voy.* II. iii. 33 Walles..made of grauen stone without morter or playster. **1660** BOYLE *New Exp. Phys. Mech.* ix. (1682) 39 The Plaister was made of quick lime. **1756–7** tr. *Keysler's Trav.* I. 458 The floor is made of plaister.

b. *transf.* A sticky mass.

1599 HAKLUYT *Voy.* II. 223 They eate it made in plaisters with the lime made of Oistershels. **1655** tr. *Com. Hist. Francion* IV. 12 This goodly Musician that playes with me hath beaten me into plaister. **1728** RAMSAY *Monk & Miller's Wife* 138 Think ye..his gentle stamock's master To worry up a pint of plaister Like our mill-knaves?

3. Sulphate of lime, gypsum: **a.** †(*a*) in its natural state; (*b*) powdered, but not calcined; used as a ground for painting and gilding, or for work in relief; (*c*) calcined; = PLASTER OF PARIS.

α. **1391** *Earl Derby's Exp.* (Camden) 79 Et pro plastre et lapide ibidem emptis. **1393** *Mem. Ripon* (Surtees) III. 120 In xviij carectatis de plaster emp. pro quodam novo domo. **1428** *Surtees Misc.* (1888) 6 Blended plaster or lyme among his alom. **1481** in *Ripon Ch. Acts* (Surtees) 345 Ad quandam querruram de plaster vocatam Sparre stone. **1483** *Cath. Angl.* 283/1 Plastere, *gipsus.* *a* **1552** LELAND *Itin.* I. 40 Plentiful Quarres of Alabaster, communely there caullid Plaster. **1756–7** tr. *Keysler's Trav.* (1760) III. 340 Eight statues..made of plaster, by the celebrated Barbarigo. **1793** SMEATON *Edystone L.* §194 *note*, Plaster or Gypsum..is an earthy salt composed of calcareous matter dissolved in the acid of Vitriol. **1813** J. C. EUSTACE *Class. Tour Italy* II. i. 2 The plaster, or stucco, is extremely hard, and in a climate so dry may equal stone in solidity and duration. **1859** GULLICK & TIMBS *Paint.* 142 Plaster, strictly speaking, is the Italian *gesso*,..and in old books on art, plaster casts are commonly called 'gessos'.

β. **1387** TREVISA *Higden* (Rolls) I. 271 Bysides Parys is greet plente of a manere stoon þat hatte gypsus and is i-cleped white plaistre [**1432–50** playster, HIGDEN *album plastrum*]. **1555** EDEN *Decades* 161 They beate the playster into fyne floure. **1661** J. CHILDREY *Brit. Baconica* 120 This Shire yieldeth Flax and Alabaster, and Plaister. **1785** JEFFERSON *Corr.* Wks. 1859 I. 403 It was thought proper to take a model of his bust in plaister. **1808** H. HOLLAND *Surv. Cheshire* 28 The workmen distinguish..the sulphate of lime by that [name] of plaister.

b. *U.S.* Plaster of Paris, formerly used as a top-dressing for soils.

1787 G. WASHINGTON *Diary* 10 June (1925) III. 222 Where the Plaister had been spread the white and red clover was luxuriant. **1816** U. BROWN *Jrnl.* 6 June in *Maryland Hist. Mag.* (1915) X. 264 A poor Hill Country well watered & adapted to Plaster. **1839** J. BUEL *Farmer's Compan.* xxii. 213 Districts..in which clover and plaster..were first introduced..have unquestionably made the most rapid strides in agricultural improvement. **1880** *Harper's Mag.* June 67/2 Another glance detects the..farmer sowing his load of plaster across the whitening field.

III. 4. *attrib.* and *Comb.*, as (sense 1) ***plaster-bandage***, ***-box***; (sense 2) ***plaster groining***, ***wall***; ***plaster-fronted*** adj.; (sense 3) ***plaster-kiln***, ***mould***, ***-sieve***, ***-stuff***; also ***plaster-like*** adj. and adv.; **plaster bill**, a bird, the surf-duck or surf-scoter of N. America, *Œdemia perspicillata*; **plaster-bronze**, a plaster cast covered with bronze dust, to resemble a bronze; † **plaster-clover** (*plaister-claver*, Syd. Soc. Lex.), the sweet clover, *Melilotus officinalis*, which was formerly used in ointments; † **plaister-faced** *a.*, having the face plastered with a composition to hide the wrinkles; **plaster-jacket**, in orthopædic surgery, a body casing or bandage stiffened with plaster of Paris, for correcting curvature of the spine, etc.; **plasterman**, a moulder in plaster of Paris; **plaster-mill**, a mill for grinding the materials for making plaster, as gypsum or lime, also old plaster; a mortar-mill; **plaster-mull**, **-muslin**, a plaster consisting of a thin sheet of gutta-percha, backed with mull or muslin, and spread on the inner side with a medicated and adhesive substance; **plaster-rock**, **plaster-stone**, raw gypsum; **plaster saint**, a virtuous person; freq. in ironical use, a person who makes a show of virtue; a hypocrite.

1803 *Med. Jrnl.* IX. 113 The *Plaster-Bandage is adapted to almost every species of ulcer. **1685** COOKE *Mellif. Chirurg.* I. i. (ed. 4) 2 With Needles, Lint, *Plaister-box, Salvatory furnished. **1722** DE FOE *Col. Jack* (1840) 67 The surgeon's plaster-box..was..full of silver instruments. **1898** *Daily News* 19 July 3/2 An excellent bust, coming out ..much better in plain plaster than in the *plaster-bronze. **1628** BP. HALL *Righteous Mammon* Wks. 720 Heare this, ye *plaister-faced Iezabels! **1900** *Century Mag.* LIX. 491/1 One..quaint *plaster-fronted house. **1815** J. SMITH *Panorama Sc. & Art* I. 163 There does not seem to be any wooden inner roofs, except *plaster groining. **1879** *St. George's Hosp. Rep.* IX. 616 The *plaster-jacket precludes the use of the cold douche. **1825** J. NICHOLSON *Operat. Mechanic* 482 The clay is boiled on a *plaster-kiln. **1611** SPEED *Hist. Gt. Brit.* v. ii. 6 [Rocks] chalky, or of a *plaster-like substance. **1676** WORLIDGE *Cyder* (1691) 67 Pat it smooth with the back of your spade plaster-like. **1895** *Daily News* 25 Oct. 6/4 'The pimple' had evidently been put on by some keen-witted *plasterman who knew the tendency of the human mind to dwell upon trifles. *c* **1790** IMISON *Sch. Art* II. 9 To prepare a *Plaster Mould, so as to take a Brimstone or Wax Impression from it. **1899** *Allbutt's Syst. Med.* VIII. 787 Salicylic acid, in the form of the *plaster-mull. *Ibid.* 521 The *plaister-muslins (mulls), introduced by Unna, are intermediate between ointments and surgical plasters. **1835–40** HALIBURTON *Clockm.* (1862) 153 A water privilege to put into the market, or a *plaister rock to get off, or some such scheme. **1890** KIPLING *Barrack-Room Ballads* (1892) 8 Single men in barricks [*sic*] don't grow into *plaster saints. **1898** G. B. SHAW *Philanderer* IV, in *Plays Unpleasant* 148 You fraud! You humbug! You miserable little plaster saint! **1934** —— *On Rocks* II, in *Too True to be Good* 260 Theyd be sent back to Parliament by working class constituencies as if they were plaster saints. **1938** W. B. YEATS *New Poems* 13 My father upon the Abbey stage, before him a raging crowd: 'This Land of Saints,' and then as the applause died out, 'Of plaster Saints.' **1964** 'S. WOODS' *This Little Measure* vi. 78 It's no good my setting up as a plaster saint..but I do think I'd draw the line at poison. **1965** *New Statesman* 30 Apr. 690/1 The total effect is that Tchaikovsky as plaster saint becomes a monster who couldn't have created anyone's music, let alone his own. **1751** J. HILL *Hist. Mat. Med.* 256 *Plaister Stone,..the white, glittering hard Kind [of Gypsum], which resembles fine Sugar,..generally known under the Name of Plaister of Paris Stone. **1765** BOWLES in *Phil. Trans.* LVI. 231 These mountains are formed of sand-stone, lime-stone, plaster-stone (or gypsum) and emery-stone. **1799** G. SMITH *Laboratory* I. 202 To make the *plaster-stuff come off the easier. **1424** *Mem. Ripon* (Surtees) III. 152 Pro renovacione (?) *plastyrwal. **1887** W. PHILLIPS *Brit. Discomycetes* 105 Growing on ashes, burnt ground, plaster walls, and damp paper.

plaster, † **plaister**, *v.* Forms: see prec. sb. [f. PLASTER *sb.*, or a. OF. *plastrer* (15th c. in Littré) to plaster (a wall), mod.F. *plâtrer*. OF. had *plastrir* in 12th c. (Hatz.-Darm.).]

1. a. *trans.* To overlay, daub, or cover with builder's plaster, or any material used for a similar purpose.

α. *a* **1300** *Cursor M.* 1674 Wit pike..Plaster [*v. rr.* plastir, plastre] it wel wit-oute and wit-In. **1483** *Cath. Angl.* 283/1 To Plastere, *gipsare.* **1548** UDALL, etc. *Erasm. Par. Acts* vii. 26 b, He was cast out in a twigge basket or hamper, plastered ouer with lyme, into the ryuer of Nilus. **1555** EDEN *Decades* 344 Cotages made of bouwes of trees plastered with chauke. **1719** DE FOE *Crusoe* (1840) II. xiv. 285 It was plastered with the earth that makes China Ware. **1863** RUSKIN *Munera P.* (1880) 164 Why could he not plaster the chinks? **1865** LUBBOCK *Preh. Times* xvi. (1878) 599 By plastering them on the outside with clay.

β. *c* **1440** *Promp. Parv.* 402/2 Playstryn wallys, *gipso.* **1577** B. GOOGE *Heresbach's Husb.* IV. (1586) 169 b, The Douehouse..must be well pargetted and plaistred without. **1611** BIBLE *Deut.* xxvii. 2 Thou shalt set thee vp great stones, and plaister them with plaister [COVERD. playster them with playster]. **1625** K. LONG tr. *Barclay's Argenis* I. v. 13 In the Entrance, a little way was playstered, that it might be adorned with Letters and Pictures. **1796** MORSE *Amer. Geog.* I. 205 On the inside, plaistered with mud. **1808** A. PARSONS *Trav.* v. 123 These baskets are quite circular, plaistered over with bitumen on the outside.

b. *transf.* To bedaub, besmear, coat, cover with any adhesive substance; to overspread, overlay (often implying excessive or vulgar adornment).

α. **1585** T. WASHINGTON tr. *Nicholay's Voy.* II. xx 57 The inner part of the temple is altogether plastered and couered with great tables of Porphyre. **1766** GOLDSM. *Vic. W.* iv, Their hair plastered up with pomatum. **1860** THACKERAY *Round. Papers, Ribbons* (1876) 18 The Great Duke (the breast of whose own coat was plastered with some half-hundred decorations). **1898** *Allbutt's Syst. Med.* V. 93 By the second or third day [of pneumonia] the tongue is thickly plastered with white fur.

β. *c* **1420** *Pallad. on Husb.* IV. 104 Plaister it with moolde, eke in the roote. **1680** MORDEN *Geog. Rect., Turkey* (1685) 335 Walls of rough Stone, plaistered over with little pointed Battlements on the Top. **1732** POPE *Ep. Bathurst* 90 With all th'embroid'ry plaister'd at thy tail. **1774** *Westm. Mag.* II. 95 Bills plaister posts, songs paper ev'ry wall.

c. *fig.* To cover, load to excess, e.g. with praise; also, to hide, gloze over, palliate; to patch, botch, mend or restore superficially. Also with *over*, *up*.

α. **1602** MARSTON *Antonio's Rev.* II. v, Thou art made as durt, To plaster up the bracks of my defects. **1813** *Examiner* 22 Mar. 187/1 They plaster the memory of that intriguing politician with unbounded praise. **1858** S. M. SCHMUCKER

Public & Private Hist. Napoleon III x. 154 In an hour every prominent place in the capital was plastered over with proclamations. **1865** *Sat. Rev.* 5 Aug. 169/2 To plaster his friends with praise in order that he in turn may be similarly beplastered. **1907** G. B. SHAW *John Bull's Other Island* III. 54 Ive seen them in that office, telling my father what a fine boy I was, and plastering him with compliments. **1924** A. HUXLEY *Let.* 29 Apr. (1969) 229 From Parma, which is a superb town, fairly plastered with Corregio's paintings, we went..to Mantua. **1953** *John o' London's Weekly* LXII. 3/4 They show two maps of middle England plastered with the names of remote villages and towns associated with the Lollard rising of 1413–14.

β. **1546** BALE *Eng. Votaries* I. 20 Se here the conueyaunce of these spyrytuall gentylmen in Playsterynge vp their vnsauerye sorceryes. **1599** NASHE *Lenten Stuffe* (1871) 3 With light cost of rough cast rhetorick, it may be tolerably plaistered over. **1683** KENNETT tr. *Erasm. on Folly* 43 A second Prometheus, to plaister up the decayed image of Mankind.

2. a. To treat medically with a plaster; to apply a plaster to. Also *absol.*

α. **1377** LANGL. *P. Pl.* B. xx. 308 Lettres þei sent, ȝif any surgien were [in] þe sege þat softer couth plastre. *Ibid.* 312 More of phisyke bi fer and fairer he plastreth. **1768** FOOTE *Devil* III. Wks. 1799 II. 275 Full power..to pill,..plaster, and poultice, all persons. **1843** LYTTON *Last Bar.* I. iv, She bound the arm, plastered the head.

β. *c* **1440** *Promp. Parv.* 402/2 Playstryn sorys, *cataplasmo.* **1593** R. HARVEY *Philad.* 18 She thought it no reason, to plaister one bodie for an other bodies sores.

b. *fig.* To apply a remedy to, soothe, alleviate; hence, humorously, to give compensation for.

1377 LANGL. *P. Pl.* B. XVII. 95 Bathed in þat blode,..And þanne plastred with penaunce, and passioun of þat babi. **1393** *Ibid.* C. xx. 89 And ȝut be plastred with pacience, when fondynges hym prykieþ. **1649** G. DANIEL *Trinarch., Rich. II* cxlix, A promis'd Parliament can plaster ore This Gash. **1891** T. HARDY *Tess* 78/1 Clare..did what he usually did in such cases, gave the man five shillings to plaster the blow.

3. a. To mix or pound into a soft tenacious mass; in *Sporting slang*, to shatter (a bird) with shot. In other sports, to defeat utterly, to trounce.

14.. *Med. Receipts* in *Rel. Ant.* I. 53 Tak the white of .iij. egges..and whete flour, and erth of an oven, and playster al-to-gider. *c* **1450** *ME. Med. Bk.* (Heinrich) 224 Tak mosse of aþorn, and seþ hyt in red wyn, and playstre hyt þer to. **1883** BROMLEY-DAVENPORT in *19th Cent.* Dec. 1097 The plasterer, whose plastering often arises from jealousy, will plaster—i.e. blow the pheasant into a pulp. **1919** J. MASEFIELD *Reynard the Fox* 30 He could plaster All those who boxed out Tencombe way. **1951** *Amer. Speech* XXVI. 230/2 Normal *plasters* Western. **1958** F. C. AVIS *Boxing Ref. Dict., Plaster*, to hit an opponent hard and often.

b. *intr.* To form a plastery mass, to cake.

1812 SIR J. SINCLAIR *Syst. Husb. Scot.* I. 215 Any rain that falls, so impregnates the soil with moisture, that if worked, it plasters, and the north-east winds harden it like stone.

c. *trans.* To shell or bomb (a target) extensively or heavily.

1915 'I. HAY' *First Hundred Thousand* xviii. 262 The German front-line trenches had been 'plastered' from end to end. **1925** FRASER & GIBBONS *Soldier & Sailor Words* 224 *Plaster*,..to shell heavily, *e.g.* 'The village was plastered badly last night'. **1941** *Hutchinson's Pict. Hist. War* 14 May–8 July 224 At night there is a concentrated attack on Bremen; the shipyards there and at Vegesack are plastered with bombs. **1942** E. WAUGH *Put out More Flags* iii. 243 The bombers were not aiming at any particular target; they were plastering the ground in front of their cars. **1945** *Penguin New Writing* XXIV. 32 They've started firing... Here they come again. They're plastering the other side. **1957** 'N. SHUTE' *On Beach* vi. 185 You'd think with Boeing as the target all this area would have been well plastered. **1971** B. W. ALDISS *Soldier Erect* 249 Our gunners back at Zubza and Jotsoma kept plastering the heights from which the Japs plastered us.

4. To apply, affix, or stick (something) like plaster (or a plaster) upon a surface. Also *fig.*

1864 HAWTHORNE *Dolliver Rom.* (1879) 80 The name that they caused the clergyman to plaster indelibly on the poor little forehead at the font. **1876** MOZLEY *Univ. Serm.* iii. (ed. 2) 46 It is always easy for the originator of a new Philosophy to plaster any amount of high morals upon it. **1879** STEVENSON *Trav. Cevennes* (1886) 80 Black bricks of firwood were plastered here and there upon both sides. **1889** *Spectator* 14 Dec. 842 The mosquito—the best thing is to fling forth an indignant hand and plaster him to the wall.

5. a. To treat (wine) with gypsum or sulphate of potash with the object of neutralizing excessive acidity, etc. **b.** To dust (vines) with gypsum in order to prevent rot or mildew of the berries. **c.** To treat (land, a crop) with plaster of Paris.

1814 J. TAYLOR *Arator* 155 [Bird-foot clover] among the plastered wheat will be three or four fold more luxuriant, than among the adjoining unplastered. **1819** [see PLASTERED]. **1852** *Trans. Mich. Agric. Soc.* III. 171 As soon as the corn came up, it was plastered on the hill. **1886** *Standard* 14 May, Sherry..brandied to make it keep, and plastered with sulphate of lime to kill the tartar which makes it over acid. **1905** H. D. ROLLESTON *Dis. Liver* 183 Sulphate of potash, with which wines in Paris were formerly largely 'plastered'.

Hence **'plastered, † plaistered** *ppl. a.*, (*a*) covered with, treated with, or formed of plaster; (*b*) *slang*, highly inebriated; drunk.

α. **1388** WYCLIF *Amos* vii. 7 Lo! the Lord stondinge on a wall plastrid. **1535** COVERDALE *ibid.*, Beholde, the Lorde stode vpon a plastered wall. **1735** SOMERVILLE *Chase* IV. 169 O'er clogging Fallows, o'er dry plaster'd Roads. **1819** W. FAUX *Mem. Days in America* (1823) 139 Plaster of Paris..is found to operate on land by attracting dew. More dew is always seen in plants and grains growing on plastered fields. *a* **1859** MACAULAY *Hist. Eng.* xxiii. (1861) V. 70 That ugly old labyrinth of dingy brick and plastered timber. **1912** *Dialect Notes* III. 585 *Plastered*,..very drunk. **1924** WODEHOUSE *Bill the Conqueror* xv. 242 Freddy had got so plastered and tried to play the trap-drums. **1931** —— *Big Money* xiii. 309 You would have expected something better from a business man like J. B. Hoke, even if he had been getting steadily plastered all the afternoon. **1934** E. WAUGH *Handful of Dust* iii. 110 The old boy's plastered. **1939** J. B. PRIESTLY *Let People Sing* iii. 71 He's gone to cool off. He's very bottled, fairly plastered. **1942** E. WAUGH *Put out More Flags* iii. 182 'If it had been anyone else but Angela, I should have thought she was tight.' 'Darling, she was plastered.' **1946** E. O'NEILL *Iceman Cometh* II. 118 Hanging around here getting plastered with you, Mac, is pleasant, I won't deny, but the old booze gets you in the end, if you keep lapping it up. **1953** L. HOBSON *Celebrity* iii. 29 'My God,' he confided to the ceiling, 'I'm plastered.' **1958** [see HONKERS *a.*]. **1964** N. MARSH *Dead Water* iii. 75 He's overdone it to-night. Flat out in the old bar parlour..he was plastered. **1966** J. BETJEMAN *High & Low* 66 You're barmy or plastered, I'll pass you, you bastard. **1979** G. HAMMOND *Dead Game* xiv. 180 'I'll probably get plastered.'.. Keith carried his pint over to Constable Murchy.

β. ? *a* **1400** *Morte Arth.* 3043 Paysede and pelid downe playsterede walles. **1413** *Pilgr. Sowle* (Caxton 1483) IV. xxx. 80 A feyned hede formed of playstred clothe. **1626** T. H[AWKINS] *Caussin's Holy Crt.* 127 All the plaistered pretending sectes..are quite vanished. **1776** WITHERING *Brit. Plants* (1796) IV. 146 On the sides of caverns in limestone rocks, and on plaistered walls in vaults.

plasterboard ('plɑːstəˌbɔəd, -æ-). Also **plaster board, plaster-board.** [f. PLASTER *sb.* II + BOARD *sb.* I.] A light-weight building board made of gypsum plaster with a reinforcing or strengthening material, now usu. thick paper bonded to both sides of a plaster core. Also *attrib.* and *fig.*

1906 *Sci. Amer. Suppl.* 29 Sept. 25703/1 Thin plaster boards are nailed on the rafters. **1914** *Chem. Abstr.* VIII. 2620 Plastic composition for making 'plaster board', boxes, etc., formed of straw pulp. **1919** *Ibid.* XIII. 1916 A mixt. for the manuf. of plaster-board is formed of calcined gypsum.., ground tan bark.., a 'hastener'..and about 30 lbs. H_2O for each 100 lbs. of the other ingredients. **1929** W. C. HUNTINGTON *Building Constr.* xiv. 464 Plaster board consists of a gypsum plaster core and surfaces of fibrous felt sheets pressed together. **1936** *Archit. Rev.* LXXX. 192 On the inside this is sound-proofed with wood rock, plaster board and American rock-wool in blanket form. **1946** *Times* 9 Sept. 15/6 Plasterboard partitions in existing buildings would serve to provide married quarters. **1956** *Builders' & Decorators' Ref. Bk.* VI. 24 Plaster boards should be fixed with 1½-in. galvanized French wire nails No. 12 W.G. **1965** G. MCINNES *Road to Gundagai* xi. 197 Almost as well known as the actors were the props:..the 'ruin' of doric plasterboard which was Ninny's Tomb, Cleopatra's palace and Henry V's tent. **1973** A. ROSS *Dunfermline Affair* 72 Our separate rooms had once been one... The wall would probably be less solid than the others, perhaps even only plaster-board. **1974** *Times Lit. Suppl.* 22 Mar. 281/4 He dithers between the historical figure, who cannot fail at this stage to have some life in him, and the plasterboard Schuyler and his tedious sex life.

plaster-cast ('plɑːstəˌkɑːst, -æ-). Also **plaster cast, plastercast.** [f. PLASTER *sb.* + CAST *sb.*] A reproduction in plaster made from a mould. Also *attrib.* and *fig.* and as *v. trans.* Hence **plaster-casting** *vbl. sb.* and *ppl. a.*

1825 J. NICHOLSON *Operat. Mechanic* 616 A back-ground ..of plaster-cast to the ornament or figure. **1842** *Knickerbocker* XX. 468 The head of Miss Jewett is a portrait, taken from a plaster cast. **1856** MRS. STOWE *Dred* I. 18 Bronzes and plaster-casts..gave evidence of artistic culture. **1859** *Handbk. Turning* p. xxvii, The wonderful discovery of voltaic electricity, by which copper plates, plaster casts, wood engravings, and medals may be copied. **1912** D. H. LAWRENCE *Phoenix II* (1968) 271 The method of translation, we are told, is the 'plaster-cast': that is, the outward form is strictly preserved. **1919** 'W. N. P. BARBELLION' *Jrnl. Disappointed Man* 163 A plaster-cast mask of Voltaire when first hung up made him chuckle with indecent laughter. **1922** JOYCE *Ulysses* 411 Plastercast reproductions..such as Venus and Apollo. **1959** P. & L. MURRAY *Dict. Art & Artists* 248 Plaster Casting is an intermediate stage in the production of a piece of sculpture which is often the last process actually to be carried out by the sculptor himself. **1970** *Oxf. Compan. Art* 879/2 Plaster casts of limbs..may also be made direct from the human body and then used as models by the stone-carver. *Ibid.* 880/1 The Vienna Academy..had a plaster-casting workshop of its own and devoted a whole floor of its palatial building to its collection of casts. **1977** 'M. YORKE' *Cost of Silence* xv. 115 Footprints..were very distinct, and a detective was making a plaster cast of one of the sharpest.

'plasterer, † plaisterer. [f. PLASTER, PLAISTER *v.* + -ER[1].]

1. One who works with or in plaster.

a. One who plasters buildings.

α. **1393** *Mem. Ripon* (Surtees) III. 120 In solucione facta Ricardo Plasterer et fratri suo in parte salarii ejus pro parietibus..plastrandis. **1415** in *York Myst.* Introd. 19 Ordo paginarum ludi Corporis Cristi..Plasterers. *a* **1548** HALL *Chron., Hen. VI* 97 Against the excessiue takyng of Masons, Carpenters, Tilers, Plasterers and other laborers. **1704** *Lond. Gaz.* No. 4050/4 Any Plasterers desirous to Perform the Work in the Great Hall. **1847** SMEATON *Builder's Man.* 118 The Plasterer..His duty is to cover the naked timbers and brickwork in ceilings and walls.

β. **1350–1** *Rolls of Parlt.* II. 234/1 Item, plaisterers & autres ouverours des mures d'argill. **1548** *Act 2 & 3 Edw. VI*, c. 15 §4 Any..Bricklayer, Plaisterer, Joyner, Hardhewer, Sawyer. **1593** SHAKS. *2 Hen. VI*, IV. ii. 140 Villaine, thy Father was a Playsterer. **1751** JOHNSON *Rambler* No. 161 ¶4 The plaisterer having..obliterated, by his white-wash, all the smoky memorials which former tenants had left. **1822** J. MACDONALD *Mem. J. Benson* 468 The existence of that Chapel is..owing to William Beacock, a plaisterer.

b. One who moulds or casts figures in plaster.

α. **1615** W. GEDDE (*title*) Booke of Sundry Draughtes, principally serving for Glasiers, and not impertinent for Plasterers and Gardiners. **1624** WOTTON *Archit.* in *Reliq.* (1651) 294 *Plastique* is not only under Sculpture, but indeed very Sculpture itself: but with this difference; that the Plasterer doth make his Figures by Addition. **1823** P. NICHOLSON *Pract. Build.* 376 The plasterers of the present day cast all their ornaments in Plaster of Paris.

β. **1668–9** PEPYS *Diary* 10 Feb., To the plaisterer's at Charing Cross, that casts heads and bodies in plaister.

c. *Sporting slang.* (See PLASTER *v.* 3.)

1883 [see PLASTER *v.* 3].

2. Name of a S. African digger-wasp: see quot.

1857 LIVINGSTONE *Trav.* xxvii. 539 A hymenopterous insect called the plasterer (*Pelopœus Eckloni*) which in its habits resembles somewhat the mason-bee. It..may be observed coming into houses, carrying in its forelegs a pellet of soft plaster about the size of a pea.

'plastering, † plaistering, *vbl. sb.* [-ING[1].]

1. The action of the verb PLASTER.

a. Working or covering with or as with plaster.

α. **1453** *Mem. Ripon* (Surtees) III. 160 Johanni Plastr' pro plasteryng muri aulæ. **1598** in Willis & Clark *Cambridge* (1886) II. 252 Places wher plasteringe is needefull. **1703** MOXON *Mech. Exerc.* 249 Names and Uses of Tools relating to Plastering. **1880** MISS BRADDON *Just as I am* iv, Doing an odd job of plastering.

β. *c* **1440** *Promp. Parv.* 402/2 Playstrynge of wallys, *litura, gipsatus.* **1663** GERBIER *Counsel* 79 Playstering upon Lath. **1667** PRIMATT *City & C. Build.* 67 For Lathing and Plaistering against Ceelings and Partitions.

b. Application of a curative plaster.

c **1440** *Promp. Parv.* 402/2 Playsterynge of sorys, *cataplasmacio.* **1591** PERCIVALL *Sp. Dict., Emplastradura*, plaistering, *fomentatio.* **1641** 'SMECTYMNUUS' *Answ.* (1653) 68 The plaistring or palliating of these rotten members. *a* **1716** SOUTH *Serm.* (1744) VIII. ii. 55 In spight of all our plaisterings and dressings of it 'twill prove incurable.

c. Formation of a sticky mass.

1812 SIR J. SINCLAIR *Syst. Husb. Scot.* I. 215 That dry friable porous surface..upon which, if rain falls, no plastering ensues.

d. The treatment of wines with gypsum.

1872 THUDICHUM & DUPRÉ *Treat. Origin, Nature & Var. Wine* iv. 119 (*heading*) Plastering of wine and must. *Ibid.* 121 Diminution of yield is..not the only drawback connected with the plastering of wine. **1873** J. L. W. THUDICHUM *On Wines, their Production, Treatment & Use* ii. 16/1 Sherry.. if properly treated, does not require either plastering, or the addition of..boiled must. **1895** S. P. SADTLER *Handbk. Industr. Org. Chem.* (ed. 2) 204 Of the methods of 'improving' wines, as it is termed, that known as 'plastering' is probably most largely practised. **1959** W. JAMES *Word-bk. Wine* 145 It is said that plastering was given a bad name in England by whisky distillers jealous of sherry's growing popularity. **1967** A. LICHINE *Encycl. Wines & Spirits* 405/1 *Plastering*, addition of plaster of Paris (gypsum or calcium sulphate) to low-acid musts to induce the necessary degree of acidity.

2. *concr.* Plastered work; a coating of plaster, or of anything plastered or daubed on.

α. **1580** HOLLYBAND *Treas. Fr. Tong* s.v. *Enduit*, The plastring of a house. **1703** MOXON *Mech. Exerc.* 249 They.. brish over their new Plastering when they set, or finish it. **1847** SMEATON *Builder's Man.* 17 When plastering is laid and set hard on bricks which are not perfectly dry. **1899** *Westm. Gaz.* 14 Dec. 2/2 Those stiff plasterings of guipure lace on coat collars and revers lost favour with the chic.

β. **1538** ELYOT, *Tectorium*, the playstrynge or pariettynge of a house. *a* **1661** HOLYDAY *Juvenal* 122 After that she has taken-off the plaistering of steeped bread and asses milk. **1726** LEONI *Alberti's Archit.* II. 14/2 The middle coat, which we call plaistering, is to prevent any faults or defects in..the other two.

3. *attrib.*, as *plastering-work.*

1538 ELYOT, *Tectorium opus*, perietting or plastring wark. **1576** FLEMING *Panopl. Epist.* 227 Plastering worke, and earthly mixture. **1726** LEONI *Alberti's Archit.* I. 35/2 River-sand..is more tractable and better for Plastering-work. **1765** *Museum Rust.* IV. 80 Plaistering-lath, 1*s.* 5*d.* per bunch.

† 'plasterish, 'plaisterish, *a. Obs. rare*[−1]. [f. PLASTER *sb.* + -ISH[1].] = PLASTERLY, PLAISTERLY *a.*

1610 HOLLAND *Camden's Brit.* I. 24 Fracastorius.. supposeth that this Iland gat the name Albion of the said plasterish [**1637** plaisterish] soile.

plasterless ('plɑːstəlɪs, -æ-), *a.* [f. PLASTER *sb.* + -LESS.] Of a building, structure, etc.: not provided with plaster; lacking plaster.

1866 'MARK TWAIN' *Lett. from Hawaii* (1967) 101 A huge gridiron of plasterless lathing droops from above. **1919** J. MASEFIELD *Battle of Somme* 29 A few skeleton sheds of plasterless woodwork. **1926** *Public Opinion* 26 Mar. 310/1 A plasterless brick house would be preferable to a plasterless steel house.

† 'plasterly, 'plaisterly, *a. Obs. rare*[−1]. [f. as PLASTERISH, PLAISTERISH *a.* + -LY[1].] Of the nature of plaster.

1655 FULLER *Hist. Camb.* vii. §36 Others looked for it [cause of sweating-sickness] from the earth, as arising from an exhalation in moist weather out of Gipsous or plaisterly [*ed.* 1840 plasterly] ground.

plaster of Paris. Also 6 Paris plaster. [See PLASTER *sb.* 3.] **a.** A fine white plaster, consisting of gypsum rendered anhydrous by calcination, which swells and rapidly sets when mixed with water, and hence is used for making moulds and casts, as a cement, etc.; so called because prepared from the gypsums of Montmartre, Paris.

α. *c* **1462** *Wright's Chaste Wife* 86 The chambyr he lett make fast, Wyth plaster of parys þat wyll last. **1577** HARRISON *England* II. xii. (1877) I. 235 Parget of fine alabaster burned, which they call plaster of Paris. **1579** PUTTENHAM *Partheniade* in *Eng. Poesie* III. xix. (Arb.) 251 Her bosome sleake as Paris plaster, Helde vp two balles of alabaster. **1787** M. CUTLER in *Life*, etc. (1888) I. 279 There are several Casts, done in Plaster of Paris. **1894** *Labour Commission* Gloss., *Plaster of Paris*, a composition of several species of gypsum dug near Montmartre, near Paris... This term is, however, frequently applied to plaster stone, or to any species of gypsum.

β. [**1387**: see PLASTER *sb.* 3 β.] **1516** *Maldon, Essex, Liber B.* lf. 84 b, Paied for iii busshellis of playster of paris price the busshell viii*d.* **1658** W. SANDERSON *Graphice* 80 The quality of this plaister of Paris, is to bind the Colours together. **1705** HEARNE *Collect.* 15 Oct. (O.H.S.) I. 56 Wood's Head [is] taken in Plaister de Paris. **1803** *Med. Jrnl.* X. 72 The drawing was taken from a cast in plaister of Paris.

attrib. **1753** HOGARTH *Anal. Beauty* x. 108 It was drawn from a plaster-of-Paris figure cast off nature. **1831** BREWSTER *Optics* ii. 17 A plaister of Paris statue strongly illuminated. **1879** *St. George's Hosp. Rep.* IX. 615 The limb was then bandaged to a splint, and enclosed in a plaster-of-Paris case.

b. *U.S.* Formerly used as a top-dressing for soils.

1787 G. WASHINGTON *Diary* 10 June (1925) III. 222 We rid to the farm of one Jones, to see the effect of the plaister of Paris, which appeared obviously great. **1810** W. THORNTON *Let.* 22 June in J. Steele *Papers* (1924) II. 627 Salt can be brought up the river in sufficient quantity, & plaister of paris if necessary to give a good coat of white clover on the soil.

† **ˈplasterwise, plaisterwise,** *adv. Obs.* [f. PLASTER *sb.* + -WISE.] In the manner of a plaster; of the consistency of a plaster.

c **1540** in *Vicary's Anat.* (1888) App. ix. 221 Allwayes styrring it vntill it be plaster-wyse. **1541** R. COPLAND *Guydon's Formul.* X j, Somtyme is a lytell hony put therto and medled playsterwyse. **1671** SALMON *Syn. Med.* 432 Mustard..plaisterwise helps the Epilepsy, &c. **1747** WESLEY *Prim. Physic* (1762) 76 Spread it thick Plaister-wise.

ˈplasterwork. Also **plaster-work, plaster work.** [f. PLASTER *sb.* + WORK *sb.*] The surface of a wall or other builders' work executed in plaster. Hence **ˈplasterworker,** = PLASTERER.

1600 J. PORY tr. *Leo's Africa* v. 236 Pictures..artificially carued vpon the plaister-work and timber. **1797** J. WOODFORDE *Diary* 3 Nov. (1931) V. 77 My Back-Kitchen.. almost all taken down of the Stud and Plaister Work. **1845** *Gloss. Terms Archit.* (ed. 4) 272 In the market-place at Newark is a wooden house with small figures and canopies over them in plaster-work. **1897** W. MILLAR *Plastering Plain & Decorative* i. 34 From 1750 to 1780 A. Wilton did some fine plaster work at Cambridge. **1908** G. P. BANKART *Art of Plasterer* vii. 97 Exeter is rich in examples of seventeenth-century plasterwork. **1926** M. JOURDAIN *English Decorative Plasterwork of Renaissance* i. 6 The names of the plasterworkers that have so far come down to us are English. **1959** M. S. BRIGGS *Conc. Encycl. Archit.* 252 Apart from its normal function of providing a smooth external or internal surface for walls and ceilings, plaster-work has often reached a high level of artistic excellence. **1977** *New Yorker* 4 July 66/2 The plasterwork inside the hall itself blossoms with Manueline exuberance.

plastery (ˈplɑːstərɪ, -æ-), *sb.* [f. PLASTER *sb.* + -Y[3].] Plastered work; plastering.

1842 *Amer. Pioneer* I. 207 The stone work and plastery was done by major William Rutledge, a soldier of the revolutionary war.

ˈplastery, *a.* Also 6 **plastry,** 6–7 **plaistrie.** [f. PLASTER *sb.* + -Y.] **a.** Of the nature of or like plaster; viscid, tenacious.

1533 ELYOT *Cast. Helthe* (1541) 8 b, Fleume plastry, whiche is very grosse, and as it were chalky. **1600** SURFLET *Countrie Farme* III. lxi. 567 Hauing gotten by long space.. a plasterie crust or hardnes ouer all the parts of it. **1849** CLOUGH *Let. to his Mother* 18 Apr., St. Peter's disappoints me; the stone of which it is made is a poor plastery material; and, indeed, Rome in general might be called a rubbishy place.

b. Built with plaster, or in a manner suggestive of plaster.

1862 'G. HAMILTON' *Country Living* 6 To move from this tumble-down old house..into a..plastery, shingly, stary, new one. **1907** *Daily Chron.* 18 Sept. 4/4 Plastery little red and white cottages and villas set at all angles among cabbage-plots.

Hence **ˈplasteriness.**

1661 J. CHILDREY *Brit. Baconica* 126 Fracastorius attributes this sweating sickness to the Plaistriness of the soil.

plastic (ˈplæstɪk, ˈplɑːstɪk), *a.* and *sb.*[3] Also 7–8 **-tick, -tique,** (8 **plaistic**). [ad. L. *plastic-us* (Vitr.), a. Gr. πλαστικός that may be moulded, belonging to moulding or modelling, plastic, f. πλαστ-ός formed, moulded, f. πλάσσειν to mould, form. So F. *plastique* (1556 in Hatz.-Darm.).]

A. *adj.* **I.** In active sense.

1. a. Characterized by moulding, shaping, modelling, fashioning, or giving form to a yielding material, as clay or wax; capable of shaping or moulding formless matter.

plastic art (†*art plastic*), the art of shaping or modelling; any art in which this is done, as sculpture or ceramics.

1632 B. JONSON *Magn. Lady* IV. iii, Not..as we were to mould every scene anew; that were a mere plastic or potter's ambition. *a* **1637** —— *Discov., De Progress. Picturæ*, The art plastic was moulding in clay, or potters earth anciently. **1677** PLOT *Oxfordsh.* 251 He [John Dwight] has so far advanced the Art Plastick, that 'tis dubious whether any man since Prometheus have excelled him. **1728** POPE *Dunc.* I. 101 So watchful Bruin forms, with plastic care, Each growing lump, and brings it to a bear. **1741** WARBURTON *Div. Legat.* II. 554 God, the great plastic Artist. **1745** J. G. COOPER *Power of Harmony* I. 21 As o'er the rock the plastic chissel moves. **1852** tr. *Müller's Archæol. Art* 65 The plastic talent which creates material forms cannot certainly fail to be recognized even as early as Homer.

b. In surgery: Concerned with remedying a deficiency of structure; reparative of tissue; as ***plastic surgery, a plastic operation.*** So ***plastic surgeon,*** one skilled in plastic surgery.

1839 *Brit. & Foreign Med. Rev.* VII. 388 We are, therefore, willing to confine ourselves, with our German author [*sc.* Zeis], to the use of the simple expression 'Plastic surgery', which is sufficient to imply generically all we mean. *Ibid.* 393 Syphilis, lupus, scrofula, &c. have made cases whereon to exercise the ingenuity of the plastic operator. **1853** J. ERICHSEN *Sci. & Art of Surg.* xlviii. 665 By plastic or reparative surgery is meant those processes by which mutilations are repaired, and loss of structure replaced. **1879** *St. George's Hosp. Rep.* IX. 379 There were 2 plastic operations. **1883** HOLMES & HULKE *Syst. Surg.* (ed. 3) III. 681 Plastic Operations on the Cheek (Meloplasty). **1897** W. ANDERSON *Lupus* 14 The raw surface may be covered in partially or completely by gliding portions of detached integument from an adjacent part, or other resources of plastic surgery may be employed. **1911** F. S. KOLLE *Plastic & Cosmetic Surg.* i. 8 The successful plastic surgeon has become an imitator of nature's beauty to-day. **1935** W. DE LA MARE *Early One Morning* 271 Even if he could delete the scar of a wound of this kind which time has healed, how many of us would hasten to consult the plastic surgeon? **1941** *Ann. Surg.* CXIII. 642 The title of Eduard Zeis' (1807–1868) book, published in 1838, was Handbuch der Plastischen Chirurgie, and he says: 'As far as I know I was the first to use the words "plastic surgery".' **1972** *Daily Tel.* 18 July 3/3 After the accident she had plastic surgery, but found fashion jobs hard to get because of her scars. **1974** J. GRADY *Six Days of Condor* 83 The plastic surgeons had done a marvelous job on his ear.

2. Causing the growth or production of natural forms, esp. of living organisms; formerly, in a quasi-philosophical sense, as an attribute of an alleged principle, virtue, or force in nature; formative, procreative; creative.

1646 SIR T. BROWNE *Pseud. Ep.* 117 The plastick or formative faculty, from matter appearing homogeneous and of a similary substance erecteth bones, membranes, veynes and arteries. **1658** —— *Gard. Cyrus* iii, In what diminutives the plastick principle lodgeth is exemplified in seeds. *a* **1677** HALE *Prim. Orig. Man.* II. vii. 192 Those that think that these *Conchæ* or Petrified Shells were no other than the *Lusus naturæ*, the Effects of the Plastick power of the Earth. **1732** BERKELEY *Alciphr.* III. § 14 He is positive as to the being of God; and that not merely as a plastic nature, or soul of the world. **1794** COLERIDGE *Sonn. to Bowles*, Like that great Spirit, who with plastic sweep Moved on the darkness of the formless deep. **1830** LYELL *Princ. Geol.* I. 23 The absurdity of having recourse to a certain 'plastic force', which it was said had power to fashion stones into organic forms. **1875** E. WHITE *Life in Christ* I iv. (1878) 30 The creation of groups by successive acts of divine power, or..by successive acts of the plastic force of nature.

3. *fig.* in reference to immaterial things, conditions, or forms, æsthetic or intellectual conceptions, literary productions, etc.

1662 STILLINGFL. *Orig. Sacr.* III. i. § 4 The great enquiry then is, how far this Plastick Power of the understanding, may extend its self in its forming an Idea of God. **1756–82** J. WARTON *Ess. Pope* (ed. 4) I. iii. 113 The genuine poet, of a lively plastic imagination. **1783** JUSTAMOND tr. *Raynal's Hist. Indies* VI. 29 He considered the sign of wealth, as the plastic and preserving principle of political strength. **1837** SIR W. HAMILTON *Metaph.* xlv. (1870) II. 500 Imagination creates nothing..it only builds up old materials into new forms; and..ought, therefore, to be called, not the productive or creative, but the plastic. **1871** R. H. HUTTON *Ess.* I. 133 There is a formative plastic power that is ever urging us towards our truest life. **1877** DOWDEN *Shaks. Prim.* v. 59 The compression of the large and rough matter of history into dramatic form demanded vigorous exercise of the plastic energy of the imagination.

II. In neuter and passive sense.

4. a. Pertaining, or connected with, or characteristic of moulding or modelling; produced by moulding, modelling, or sculpture, as distinguished from that which is drawn on a surface. ***plastic merit,*** merit as a piece of moulding or sculpture.

1726 LEONI *Alberti's Archit.* I. 32/2 This sort of Works, which are call'd Plastic [*che si chiamano lavori di Terra*]. **1841** W. SPALDING *Italy & It. Isl.* I. 217 Four Bronze Horses..more noted for their adventures and undoubted antiquity than for their plastic merit. **1863** MARY HOWITT *F. Bremer's Greece* I. vii. 238 The Greeks have an abhorrence of any plastic images of the saints.

b. Pertaining to, characterized by, or utilizing an ability to be permanently changed in shape, without fracture or rupture, by temporary pressure or tension; esp. in ***plastic deformation*** or ***flow.***

1877 *Jrnl. Franklin Inst.* CIV. 228 (*heading*) Plastic flow. **1879** *Encycl. Brit.* IX. 240/2 More shapely bricks are thus produced than by plastic moulding. **1888** W. C. UNWIN *Testing of Materials of Construction* i. 18 When a body is subjected to the action of external forces, it undergoes a deformation which is either a deformation which disappears if the load is removed (elastic deformation), or a deformation which remains after the load is removed (plastic deformation). **1923** GLAZEBROOK *Dict. Appl. Physics* V. 395/1 Associated with plastic strain in many metals is the occurrence or formation of 'twinned' crystals. *Ibid.* 400/1 A viscous, under-cooled liquid, may..undergo deformation of a 'plastic' (*i.e.* non-elastic) nature. **1925** *Jrnl. Iron & Steel Inst.* CXII. 451 A consideration of the laws of plastic deformation of hot material during rolling and working. **1940** *New Statesman* 16 Mar. 360/1 In its simplest form we see plastic extrusion as combs or as cosmetic boxes, where the resin has been forced into a mould, with instantaneous cooling. **1951** *Gloss. Terms Plastics Industry* (*B.S.I.*) 24 *Plastic yield*, non-elastic deformation. **1963** E. S. HILLS *Elements Structural Geol.* xii. 355 Plastic deformation of wall-rocks is exhibited around the Bald Rock batholith, California. **1967** M. CHANDLER *Ceramics in Mod. World* ii. 63 Shaping methods..include..plastic pressing, and extrusion. **1968** A. H. COTTRELL *Introd. Metallurgy* xxi. 387 This leads to a plastic instability in which all subsequent deformation becomes concentrated in one short section.. which stretches excessively and forms a narrow neck. **1968** R. W. FAIRBRIDGE *Encycl. Geomorphol.* 1191/2 Plastic flow will occur when an ice body attains a thickness of 100–150 feet. **1976** *Physics Bull.* Oct. 459/1 Most of part one is concerned with the elastic, plastic and fracture behaviour of minerals and rocks.

5. a. Susceptible of being moulded or shaped; capable of taking a new form when subjected to pressure (as clay); readily assuming a new shape.

plastic crystal, a variety of Portland cement of remarkable plasticity (see also sense 5 g). ***plastic sulphur,*** an allotropic form of sulphur: see quot. 1868.

1791 E. DARWIN *Bot. Gard.* I. 85 Etruria! next beneath thy magic hands Glides the quick wheel, the plastic clay expands. **1797** GODWIN *Enquirer* I. iii. 12 How unformed and plastic is his body! **1811** A. T. THOMSON *Lond. Disp.* (1818) p. cxiii, Kneading the coating material, so as to render it very plastic. **1860** TYNDALL *Glac.* II. xxii. 349 The ice..was plastic to pressure but not to tension. **1868** WATTS *Dict. Chem.* V. 531 Plastic sulphur..is obtained by heating melted sulphur to the temperature 260–300°, and then cooling it suddenly by pouring it in a very thin stream into cold water. It is thus obtained as a soft, yellowish-brown, semitransparent mass, capable of being drawn out into fine elastic threads possessed of considerable tenacity. **1881** *Engineering* 20 May 513/3 (*heading*) Richards' plastic metal. *Ibid.*, 'J. Richards' Plastic Metal' is being made by the J. Richards' Plastic Metal Company, of Charlotte-street, Birmingham. In general outward appearances it resembles ..other varieties of white metal so largely used for lining bearings... Its special feature..is its great affinity for other metals..enabling it to be readily 'pasted on'. **1907** *Chem. Abstr.* I. 1077 Process of manufacturing a plastic material suitable for the production of fibers, pellicles, blocks, or plates, consisting in mixing together phenol, 17, casein, 40, pressing, heating..and pressing again, then adding glycerol to give plasticity. **1908** L. DESVAUX *Brit. Pat.* 9313 A plastic product for the manufacture of combs, molded objects of any kind and similar applications, composed of a mixture in variable proportions of nitrocellulose and camphor,..and of the food product extracted from maize by treating this substance with higher alcohols. **1921** *Chem. Abstr.* XV. 1770 A description of the classes of com. materials falling under the category of plastic masses. B. divides the important and most useful products into 6 classes, (1) glues, (2) papier maché, (3) wood products, (4) cellulose products, (5) egg white and casein, and (6) resins. The criterion for plastics is the condition of the raw material or of the final product... B. takes exception to the older classification of plastics based on some temporary condition during manuf.

b. ***plastic clay*** (*Geol.*), a name given (after the F. *argile plastique* of Cuvier and Brongniart) to the middle group of the Eocene beds, immediately underlying the London clay, now called the Woolwich and Reading series. [tr. F. *argile plastique* (Cuvier & Brongniart 1808, in *Jrnl. des Mines* XXIII. 432).]

1812 T. WEBSTER *Let.* 2 Aug. in H. C. Englefield *Description Isle of Wight* (1816) 210 The clay connected with this sand is frequently fit for the potter, and hence has been called the plastic clay. **1813** R. JAMESON in R. Kerr tr. *Cuvier's Essay on Theory of Earth* 227 The fundamental rock or basis of the [Paris] district is chalk. This chalk is covered with plastic clay, and what is termed coarse marine limestone. **1832** DE LA BECHE *Geol. Man.* (ed. 2) 229 Above these beds, to which, strictly speaking, the term 'plastic clay' is alone applicable, there is often another clay, separated from the former by a bed of sand. **1833** LYELL *Princ. Geol.* III. 244 Plastic clay and sand. **1885** *Lyell's Elem. Geol.* 229 Woolwich and Reading series.—..formerly called the Plastic clay, as it agrees with a similar clay used in pottery, which occupies the same position in the French series. **1929** P. G. H. BOSWELL in Evans & Stubblefield *Hand-bk. Geol. Gt. Brit.* 417 The lowest Eocene deposits are therefore the Reading Beds..which..consist of mottled clays ('Plastic Clay') and sands with a glauconitic bed at the base. **1955** G. G. WOODFORD tr. *M. Gignoux's Stratigr. Geol.* ix. 477 Mammalian remains are present..at the base of the plastic clay. **1961** B. KUMMEL *Hist. Earth* 8/2 Of the strata above the Purbeck beds and below the Plastic clay, the most conspicuous unit is the Chalk.

c. ***plastic explosive,*** an explosive of putty-like consistency that can be shaped by hand and so placed in intimate contact with its target; so ***plastic bomb,*** one containing plastic explosive; ***plastic-bomb*** vb. trans., ***-bombing*** vbl. sb.

1906 C. E. BICHEL *Brit. Pat.* 16,882 Add to the trinitrotoluol liquid resins..in such wise that..the crystalline trinitrotoluol with or without warming is worked in suitable mixing machines into a plastic explosive that detonates well. **1946** T. C. OHART *Elements of Ammunition* ii. 37 A plastic explosive known as RDX-composition C is formed by mixing about 88% cyclonite with 12% plasticizer. **1955** G. GREENE *Quiet American* III. i. 185 That day all over Saigon innocent bicycle-pumps had proved to be plastic bombs and gone off at the stroke of eleven. **1961** *Times* 12 July 10/3 Bombs made with plastic explosive were discovered not far from the entrance to the Simplon. **1961** *Economist* 25 Nov. 777/1 One farmer has threatened to plastic-bomb the line. **1962** *Spectator* 23 Feb. 229/1 The imported disease of plastic-bombing the home of your adversary at the risk of maiming or killing his wife and children. **1962** *Daily Tel.* 14 June 14 Casual and indiscriminate plastic-bombing, in Paris as well as in Algeria, has been followed by attacks on a hospital.. and on an oil-well. **1963** *Ann. Reg. 1962* 236 In France there were plastic bomb attacks, directed mainly against liberal politicians and journalists. **1976** N. FREELING *Lake Isle* xv. 113 A couple of cops stayed for a search. They got back.. with an old army revolver, two-thirds of a kilo of plastic explosive, and a lot of gold coins.

d. ***plastic bronze***, bronze containing a high proportion of lead, which is used for bearings on account of its softness.

1907 G. H. CLAMER in *Chem. Engineer* Aug. 93 This alloy is largely sold under the name of 'plastic bronze'. **1939** [see LEADED *ppl. a.* e]. **1954** *Kempe's Engineer's Yearbk.* I. 633 'Plastic' bronze Cu 73 Sn 7 Pb 20.

e. ***plastic wood***, a mouldable material that hardens to resemble wood and is used for filling knot holes, crevices, and the like.

1921 *Engineering* 9 Dec. 785 This material.. is named by the firm 'Plastic Wood'. It is a collodion preparation made with very fine wood meal, and as supplied ready for use is of the consistency of soft putty. **1938** A. DURST *Wood Carving* 16 Knot-holes and blemishes of a like nature can be filled with plastic wood. This is a quickly-drying preparation of cellulose and wood pulp. **1974** J. MELVILLE *Nun's Castle* ix. 205 The old wooden door frame had shrunk... The door around the lock had been built up with.. plastic wood.

f. ***plastic paint***, paint which is sufficiently thick and coarse when applied for it to retain a texture given to it with the aid of a brush, spatula, or the like.

1925 *Amer. Paint Trade Buyer's Guide* 208/2 Plastic Paint —*see* Plastic Relief Compositions. **1955** *Mod. Building Encycl.* 492/2 In addition to the excellent proprietary materials available, plastic paints may be prepared from equal parts of distemper and plaster-of-paris. **1974** E. MCGIRR *Murderous Journey* 28 A room painted with a dark shade of plastic paint.

g. ***plastic crystal***, a soft substance in which the molecules occupy the points of a regular crystal lattice but have freedom of rotation about those points. (See also sense 5 a.)

1961 *Physics & Chem. of Solids* XVIII. 8/2 In liquid crystals, by heating, the fluidity comes first, but in plastic crystals, the isotropy comes first. **1968** A. BONDI *Physical Properties of Molecular Crystals* vi. 140 The very small expansions of plastic crystals at their melting point generally result from the fact that a much larger expansion took place at a first-order transition of the crystal at some lower temperature. **1974** P. A. WINSOR in Gray & Winsor *Liquid Crystals & Plastic Crystals* I. ii. 48 Plastic crystals separate in the crystal forms of the cubic system (rarely hexagonal) and to this extent resemble ordinary solid crystals. However, they show unusually low yield points. The most plastic.. will flow under their own weight and although the majority are less soft, they may readily be cut with a knife or extruded through a small hole.

6. a. Of immaterial things and conditions: Capable of being moulded, fashioned, modified, or impressed; impressionable, pliable; susceptible to influence; pliant, supple, flexible.

1711 SHAFTESB. *Charac.* (1737) I. IV. iii. 146 Such is Poetical, and such (if I may so call it) Geographical or Plastick Truth. **1816** BENTHAM *Chrestom.* 133 Of all known languages, the Greek is assuredly in its structure the most plastic and most manageable. **1842** BARHAM *Ingol. Leg.* Ser. II. *Babes in Wood*, While his mind's ductile and plastic, I'll place him at Dotheboys Hall. **1875** JOWETT *Plato* (ed. 2) V. 67 Plato.. fancies that the life of the state is as plastic.. as that of the individual.

b. *Biol.* Pertaining to or (of an organism) exhibiting an adaptability to environmental changes.

1905 F. E. CLEMENTS *Research Methods in Ecol.* iii. 103 The amount of response to a stimulus is proportional to the intensity of the factor concerned. This does not mean that the same stimulus produces the same response in two distinct species, or.. in two plants of one species. In these cases the rule holds only when the plants or species are equally plastic. *Ibid.* 146 Stable plants are less susceptible of evolution than plastic ones. **1930** *Jrnl. Ecol.* XVIII. 376 The broad-leaved plantain has proved, even within five months, exceedingly plastic. **1965** *Adv. Genetics* XIII. 133 The species that are plastic for leaf shape, that are able to produce both sorts of leaf, are all typically species of shallow water. *Ibid.* 137 Plastic response is able to provide adaptation to directional selection in some populations which in others is provided by genetic change.

7. *Biol.* and *Path.* Capable of forming, or being organized into, living tissue, as ***plastic lymph, a plastic exudation***; pertaining to or accompanied by such a process, as ***plastic bronchitis***.

1834 J. FORBES *Laennec's Dis. Chest* I. (ed. 4) 61 The inflammatory affections of the mucous membrane of the bronchi, may be divided into the catarrhal, the plastic or crusty, and the ulcerous. **1851** CARPENTER *Man. Phys.* (ed. 2) 375 It gives origin to similar changes in the effused fibrine, which it converts from a plastic or organizable deposit, into an aplastic or unorganizable one, namely, pus. **1877** ROBERTS *Handbk. Med.* (ed. 3) I. 376 Plastic or Croupous Bronchitis is almost always chronic. **1886** FAGGE & PYE-SMITH *Princ. Med.* (ed. 2) I. 66 In speaking of 'plastic lymph' as undergoing development into connective tissue and vessels, one means not the fibrin itself but the cells that are included in it.

III. 8. absol. ***the plastic***: †**a.** The plastic principle or virtue (*obs.*); **b.** plastic art, plastic beauty.

1661 GLANVILL *Van. Dogm.* 214 To the knowledge of the poorest simple, we must first know its efficient, the manner, and method of its efformation, and the nature of the Plastick. **1682** H. MORE *Annot. Glanvill's Lux O.* 238 All Souls are indued with the Plastick whether of Brutes or Men. **1881** H. JAMES *Portr. Lady* xxxvi, His appreciation.. was based partly on his fine sense of the plastic.

IV. [Partly deriving from the sb. used attrib.]

9. a. Made of plastic; of the nature of a plastic, or containing plastic as an essential ingredient.

1909 *Chem. Abstr.* III. 724 Artificial plastic materials industry... An interesting account.. giving descriptions of the process for artificial rubber, leather, and substitutes; celluloid, viscoid, etc.; plastics obtained from cellulose and its compounds; and plastics from casein, maisin, albuminoids, and gelatins. **1911** E. C. WORDEN *Nitrocellulose Industry* II. xiv. 630 Formation of plastic rods and tubes was first successfully made by the patented process of I. and J. Hyatt. *Ibid.* 708 The manufacture of plastic cuffs and shirt bosoms. **1912** *Sci. Amer. Suppl.* 20 Apr. 246/1 The term 'plastic materials' is here employed in a restricted sense, including only such materials as celluloid and its numerous substitutes, which can easily be shaped by cutting and grinding, as well as by molding, and excluding artificial textile fibers and India rubber and its imitations. **1931** *Brit. Plastics Year Bk.* 17 We have pleasure in presenting to the Plastics Industry the first Year Book.. dealing exclusively with Plastic Materials. **1940** *Economist* 29 June 1108/2 Plastic structural material has been introduced into the aircraft industry. **1943** *Times Weekly Ed.* 10 Feb. 17/1 Plastic bearings were going into the heaviest engineering applications. **1949** E. COXHEAD *Wind in West* ii. 36 His wife, in a thin.. plastic raincoat, looked perished with cold. *Ibid.* 41 Little Mrs. Turner, who had gone nearly as blue as her plastic mackintosh. **1951** A. BARON *Rosie Hogarth* 60 She.. hung plastic curtains in his bedroom. **1957** *Daily Mail* 5 Sept. 11/5 Pre-cooked hamburgers.. in their little frozen transparent plastic bags. **1958** *Engineering* 14 Mar. 349/1 Acid wastes are disposed of through plastic pipes. **1958** *Observer* 6 July 9/4 The light plastic mac, easily stuffed into pocket or bag, comes into its own during the British summer. **1961** *Ann. Reg. 1960* 510 Growers of flowers complained that imports of plastic flowers, mainly from Hong Kong, were having an adverse effect. **1966** 'G. BLACK' *You want to die, Johnny?* x. 193 There were.. plastic tiles on the floor. **1969** W. R. R. PARK *Plastics Film Technol.* vi. 147 With the current proliferation of.. plastics films, the growing interest in and use of plastic laminates may seem somewhat surprising. **1972** *Guardian* 16 Oct. 9/4 Furtive gestures by elderly men in plastic macs. **1975** *New Yorker* 29 Sept. 43/1 The couch and the armchairs are protected by plastic covers. **1977** B. PYM *Quartet in Autumn* xiii. 109 A plastic bag lying on the kitchen table.

b. *fig.* Artificial; superficial, insincere.

1963 *Daily Tel.* 22 May 16 The plan's promoters must not take it amiss if, winking an eye, some of our elder oysters inquire whether plastic houses might not connote plastic people. **1967** *Harper's* Aug. 19 Now that so many of the young seem to wear their hearts on their sleeves, it is hard to tell which ones are real and which ones are plastic. **1970** *Observer* (Colour Suppl.) 15 Feb. 24/1 Sinister influences are at work to turn Fiji into another Hawaii, that plastic paradise further along the route. **1974** *Times Lit. Suppl.* 1 Mar. 219/5 The characters are by no means badly drawn and the girl in particular is notably less plastic than usual. **1977** *Daily Tel.* 16 Apr. 16 The flabby, chalky, doughy slabs of our unpalatable plastic muck which masquerades as bread.

c. Special collocations. ***plastic bullet***, a type of projectile made of PVC, which is fired from a riot-gun and is used esp. by security forces in riot-control (see quot. 1976 and ***rubber bullet*** s.v. RUBBER *sb.*[1] 12 a); ***plastic money*** (orig. *U.S.*), plastic credit cards and similar items considered as a form of money or as a means for making purchases.

1972 *News Let.* (Belfast) 11 Aug. 5/2 New devices for riot control, including a *plastic bullet, have been issued to the Army in Northern Ireland. **1976** *New Scientist* 16 Dec. 672/1 The grim news from Belfast focused attention for the first time on the plastic bullet, the sleeper among the new generation of British anti-riot weapons. Basically it is rather shorter than a rubber bullet and made of PVC. A cylinder 1½ inches in diameter and rather over four inches long, it looks like a thick white lump of candle. **1986** *N.Y. Times* 10 May 1. 32/5 Dr. Gross was awarded the Medal for Merit in 1948 for his invention of a plastic bullet for gunnery training in World War II. **1974** *Time* 29 Apr. 93/3 About 503 million credit cards are in use in the U.S. today—proof enough that '*plastic money' is replacing the folding kind. **1977** *New Scientist* 17 Feb. 398/1 Plastic money is taking on a new form that seems sure to make it even more widespread on the British banking scene. **1985** R. MACLEOD *Cut in Diamonds* iv. 86 He paid by credit card... Luckily, we've a reasonable relationship with most of the plastic money people.

B. *sb.*[3] **I. 1.** A plastic material. **a.** A solid substance that can be readily moulded or shaped.

1905 E. H. ANGLE in E. C. Kirk *Amer. Text-bk. Oper. Dentistry* (ed. 3) xxiv. 720 Models sufficiently perfect cannot be made from impressions taken in modelling compound or other of the plastics. **1921** [see A. 5]. **1923** *Blackw. Mag.* June 722/2 In the evenings Roupin constructed in plastic.. a complete model of Haidar Pasha. **1933** L. F. RAHM *Plastic Molding* ii. 19 The molding properties of rubber are such as to make it one of the simplest plastics to handle. **1936** L. M. T. BELL *Making & Moulding of Plastics* i. 13 Dental uses of plastics... Stabalite [composed of china clay, rubber, sulphur, etc.] is used very largely for artificial palates. **1944** E. C. JAHN in L. E. Wise *Wood Chem.* xxiii. 820 In 1942.. wood and lignin plastics are still largely in the developmental stage.

b. Any of a large and varied class of substances which are polymers of high molecular weight based on synthetic resins or modified natural polymers and may be obtained in a permanent or rigid form following moulding, extrusion, or similar treatment at a stage during manufacture or processing when they are mouldable or liquid; see also ***laminated plastic, reinforced plastic***. Also used generically (without *a* and *pl.*): material of this kind.

In techn. usage the term is usu. held to exclude the synthetic rubbers (elastomers), and sometimes also any plastic in the form of fibres.

1909 L. H. BAEKELAND in *Jrnl. Industr. & Engin. Chem.* Mar. 156/2 As an insulator.. it [*sc.* Bakelite] is far superior to hard rubber, casein, celluloid, shellac and in fact all plastics. *Ibid.* 157/1 It can be used for similar purposes like knobs, buttons, knife handles, for which plastics are generally used. **1911** E. C. WORDEN *Nitrocellulose Industry* II. xiv. 691 Pyroxylin plastic is extensively used for the bits of pipe stems, and consists of ordinary plastic containing.. dyestuffs, picric acid, [etc.]. **1915** J. E. CRANE in A. Rogers *Industr. Chem.* (ed. 2) xliv. 914 Pyroxylin plastics, variously called celluloid, xylonite,.. viscoloid, and other names consist of a mixture or solid solution of cellulose nitrate and camphor. **1928** *Chem. Abstr.* XXII. 4209 Plastics are defined as materials that are horny and elastic at ordinary temp. but can be molded at higher temp. They include (1) cellulose plastics, (2) artificial resins and (3) protein plastics. **1935** *Economist* 7 Dec. 1140/1 The use of plastics in the motor accessory field will undoubtedly increase... Already the fitting of wireless sets as standard equipment on several cars has opened up a.. new field for their application. **1941** *Electronic Engin.* XIV. 482 A large percentage of.. plastics have good insulation properties, while at the same time the materials are available in a wide variety of forms.. from lacquers.. through rubber-like materials to the hard and rigid bakelite-type resins. **1945** *Daily Mirror* 27 Sept. 3/1 British-made women's shoes in 'patent leather' plastics may be on sale next summer. **1953** KIRK & OTHMER *Encycl. Chem. Technol.* X. 798 When the resin itself is capable of being shaped into a finished article without a plasticizer.., as polystyrene, the terms resin and plastic are interchangeable for that material. **1955** *Observer* 13 Nov. 3/3 Nearly all plastics—except nylon stockings—crept into the house by the back door, disguised as 'cheap' substitutes for the real thing—china, glass, wood, metal, silk or wool. Now they have their own status, either as alternatives.. or as new materials, to do a new job. **1963** H. R. CLAUSER *Encycl. Engin. Materials & Processes* 486/2 Silicones are unique among plastics, in that they are semiorganic, i.e., the molecular spine has alternating silicon and oxygen atoms with organic groups attached to the silicon. **1968** KIRK & OTHMER *Encycl. Chem. Technol.* (ed. 2) XV. 790 Nylon and poly(ethylene terephthalate) are used both as fibers and plastics. **1973** *Materials & Technol.* VI. viii. 499 Twenty years later [*sc.* about 1890], casein plastics prepared by reacting together milk protein and formaldehyde were developed in Germany. **1973** *Sci. Amer.* Aug. 107/1 This container can be a baking pan made of sheet metal or plastic.

2. Plastic explosive.

1966 M. R. D. FOOT *SOE in France* xi. 367 Though they had no plastic, they could get unlimited dynamite from the mines. **1968** D. LAMPE *Last Ditch* vii. 75 Plastic is a form of cyclonite,.. and is still today the standard military sabotage high explosive. **1973** D. LEES *Rape of Quiet Town* vii. 119 The bank manager type who'd been playing with the plastic had stayed behind. **1978** T. ALLBEURY *Lantern Network* ix. 112 Parker.. showed them how to wire the plastic so that a whole length of track was taken out in a single explosion.

II. 3. *attrib.* in sense 1 b.

1911 E. C. WORDEN *Nitrocellulose Industry* II. xiv. 578 The general principles of plastic manufacture. *Ibid.* 660 The entire field of plastic molding. **1931** *Brit. Plastics Year Bk.* 69 The plastic trade consumes 1,200 tons of wood dust per annum for mouldings. **1956** A. H. COMPTON *Atomic Quest* 326 Paper, plastic, and textile plants. **1960** I. WALLACH *Absence of Cello* 16 He was a trouble-shooter.. for a large plastic corporation. **1969** T. C. THORSTENSEN *Pract. Leather Technol.* xiv. 235 The increased 'plastic look' in leather may, in the long run, harm the marketing position of leather in its competition with synthetic materials.

4. Used *attrib.* in *pl.*, often to avoid possible confusion with branches I and II of the adj.

a. Of, pertaining to, or concerned with plastics; = sense 3.

1925 *Plastics* Oct. 7/1 The plastics industry. **1935** *Economist* 4 Mar. 1042/2 Their interest in the plastics industry, through Mouldrite, Limited, continued to make progress. **1957** J. BRAINE *Room at Top* 61 He owned a plastics factory, a tannery, a bodywork builders.

b. = sense 9 of the adj.

1934 H. READ *Art & Industry* II. 90 The wireless cabinet is an example of the encroachment of new plastics materials, such as bakelite, on a province hitherto reserved for wood. **1958** *Engineering* 7 Mar. 320/2 Various tools with plastics handles. **1971** *Daily Tel.* 15 Feb. 4/8 Plastics windows to protect passengers from stone-throwing are being installed in trains in the New York area. **1974** *Brit. Standard 4998* (*title*) Moulded plastics dustbins.

5. *Comb.* Instrumental, as ***plastic-coated, -covered, -lined, -tiled, -topped, -wrapped*** (so ***-wrap*** vb.) adjs. Parasynthetic, as ***plastic-macked, -mackintoshed***.

1960 *Farmer & Stockbreeder* 23 Feb. 69/1 The cab framework is constructed of precision steel tubing and the weatherproof roof of plastic-coated nylon fabric. **1977** D. MACKENZIE *Raven & Kamikaze* iv. 56 The wire was plastic-coated and copper, the sort of thing used on a radio. **1961** *House & Garden* June 136/2 Even a neat, plastic-covered plunge is not exactly a joy to behold. **1973** R. LEWIS *Blood Money* viii. 125 There's a plastic-covered card identifying the dead man. **1969** *Jane's Freight Containers 1968–69* 239/3 The walls are of plastic-lined plywood plates. **1979** *Tucson Mag.* Apr. 64/2 Another alternative is a plastic-lined pool. **1964** *Guardian* 9 Sept. 5/8 Plastic-macked parents and hordes of soggy children. **1973** J. WAINWRIGHT *Devil you Don't* 25 A plastic-mackintoshed young woman. **1962** *Listener* 10 May 831/3 Plastic-tiled and similar floors also need damp-washing. **1957** *Observer* 13 Oct. 1/2 The Queen and the Duke.. walked to a plastic-topped limousine which drew away to drive to Government House. **1973** D. FRANCIS *Slay-Ride* xiii. 159 We sat at a plastic topped table amid travellers with untidy hand luggage. **1968** *Economist* 11 May 69/3 The meat is cut, quick-frozen and plastic-wrapped under contract to supermarkets and to restaurant chains. **1975** M. BRADBURY *Hist. Man* ix. 148 Contemporary, plastic-wrapped food. **1978** B. NORMAN *To nick Good Body* xvi. 132 A lump of plastic-wrapped, processed Cheddar.

plastic (ˈplæstɪk), *sb.*[1] Now *rare*. Also 6–7 plastick(e, 7 plaistique, plastique. [ad. F. *plastique*, ad. L. (*ars*) *plastica*, *plasticē*, a. Gr. πλαστική (τέχνη) the plastic art, fem. of πλαστικός PLASTIC *a*. So Ger. *plastik*.] The art of modelling figures: primarily, in clay, wax, etc.; also, in wider sense, in a harder material by sculpture. Also *fig.* †*a. sing. Obs.*

1598 R. HAYDOCKE tr. *Lomazzo* I. 7 Painting, Carving and Plasticke are all but one and the same arte. **1624** WOTTON *Archit.* in *Reliq.* (1651) 293 *Plastique* is not only under Sculpture, but indeed very Sculpture it self. **1684** tr. *Agrippa's Van. Arts* xxv. 70 Of Statuary and Plastick.

β. In *pl.* form.

1686 PLOT *Staffordsh.* 272 How dame Nature came thus to mis-carry in her plastics. **1850** LEITCH tr. *C. O. Müller's Anc. Art* §20 (ed. 2) 7 The living plastics of the gymnic games and choral dances were afterwards..exalted in a surprising manner by sculpture in stone and brass.

†**plastic**, *sb.*[2] *Obs.* [ad. late L. *plasticus* moulder, sculptor, a. Gr. πλαστικός adj.: see PLASTIC *a*.] A modeller, moulder, sculptor; *fig.* a former, fashioner, creator.

1644 BULWER *Chiron.* 58 It is impossible for any Painter, or Carver, or Plastique to give right motions to his works or Hand. **1661** RUST *Origen* in *Phenix* (1721) I. 75 The beautiful Idea, according to which the Plastick works. **1661** GLANVILL *Van. Dogm.* 128 'Tis education is our Plastick. **1694** R. BURTHOGGE *Reason & Nat. Spirits* 247 For in this Terrestrial World, as to the several Regions of it, the Animal, the Vegetable, and the Mineral, it is as certain, that all had but one Plastic, as that the Body of a Man, or any other particular Animal, had not more. **1837** CARLYLE *Fr. Rev.* (1872) I. I. ii. 6 Ours is a most fictile world; and man is the most fingent plastic of creatures.

plastic, *sb.*[3]: see PLASTIC *a*. B.

-plastic, *suffix*. [f. -PLAST(Y or Gr. πλαστ-ός formed + -IC.] Forming adjectives that correspond to sbs. in *-plasty* (Gr. -πλαστία, f. πλαστός formed) or *-plasia* (Gr. πλασία, πλάσις formation).

†ˈ**plastical**, *a. Obs.* [f. L. *plastic-us* (see PLASTIC *a*.) + -AL[1].] = PLASTIC *a*.; formative.

1615 CROOKE *Body of Man* 429 The Plasticall or formatiue faculty of the wombe. *a* **1646** J. GREGORY *Serm.* Posthuma (1649) 70 At the last Daie, a kinde of Plasticall Dew shall fall down upon the Dead, and ingender with Luz, the little Bone spoken of before. **1653** H. MORE *Conject. Cabbal.* (1713) 14 The Plastical Power of the Souls that descend from the World of Life, did faithfully and effectually work those wise contrivances of Male and Female. **1681** GLANVILL *Sadducismus* I. (1726) 96 The Subdivision of Spirits, into meerly Plastical and Perceptive, supposing there are Spirits that are meerly Plastical.

ˈ**plastically**, *adv.* [f. as prec. + -LY[2]: see -ICALLY.] In a plastic manner, in various senses of the adj.; according to plastic art; by moulding or modelling; as a plastic substance.

1835 *Southern Lit. Messenger* Dec. 43/2 Pictorially, or graphically, or as a German would say plastically. **1840** *Fraser's Mag.* XXII. 149 Thou..hast not always had materials for thy prodigious brain to wield and plastically build up. **1856** DE QUINCEY *Confess.* Wks. V. 42 The command over a language, the power of adapting it plastically to the expression of your own thoughts, is almost exclusively a gift of nature. **1876** SYMONDS *Grk. Poets* Ser. II. xi. 358 Both persons and situations are plastically treated —subjected, that is to say, to the conditions best fulfilled by sculpture. **1886** —— *Renaiss. It., Cath. React.* (1898) VII. xiv. 237 Humanity moves like a glacier, plastically. **1957** G. E. HUTCHINSON *Treat. Limnol.* I. vii. 532 A slow fall in temperature apparently permits the ice to flow plastically over the lake surface without cracking. **1966** C. R. TOTTLE *Sci. Engin. Materials* vii. 158 Many materials show only a very short elastic range and begin to deform plastically at comparatively low stresses. **1972** J. G. DENNIS *Structural Geol.* vi. 109 'Brittle' rocks could yield plastically.

plasticate (ˈplæstɪkeɪt), *v.* [f. PLASTIC *a*. + -ATE[3], prob. after *masticate*.] **1.** *trans.* To change (particles of rubber or thermoplastic) into a homogeneous plastic (mouldable) mass by passing it through a suitable extruder and usu. simultaneously heating it.

1929 W. A. GORDON *Brit. Pat.* 334,509 (*title*) Machines for plasticating materials. **1934** *Industr. & Engin. Chem.* Mar. 349/1 Rubber, plasticated in the Gordon machine, which gives the same y_5 value..as a sample of mill-massed rubber, appears much stiffer in factory processing operations. **1968** *Encycl. Polymer Sci. & Technol.* IX. 8 Machines are either single-stage, in which plastication and injection are done by the same cylinder, or double-stage, in which the material is plasticated in one cylinder and fed to a second for injection into a mold. **1975** *Mod. Plastics Internat.* Nov. 25/2 In the twin-screw section, powder PVC or other material is plasticated at low shear with close control over temperature.

2. [ad. F. *plastiquer*.] *trans.* To blow up or destroy with a plastic bomb.

1962 *Guardian* 3 Jan. 7/4 Paris butchers are now using plastic bombs against colleagues... One butcher's shop.. was 'plasticated' early this morning. **1965** D. FRANCIS *Odds Against* (1967) xix. 222, I couldn't get hold of Radnor on account of the office phones being plasticated.

Hence ˈ**plasticated** *ppl. a.*, ˈ**plasticating** *vbl. sb.* and *ppl. a.*

1934 *Industr. & Engin. Chem.* Mar. 349/1 There is need of a method for detecting the difference..between the plastic properties of plasticated and mill-massed rubber. **1953** *Ibid.* May 970/2 The combined operation of melting and extruding is called 'plasticating extrusion'. **1959** J. B. PATON in E. C. Bernhardt *Processing of Thermoplastic Materials* iv. 228 In the design of an extruder used for processing thermoplastic materials, the complex operations of plasticating, compacting, and conveying..must also be considered. **1970** TADMOR & KLEIN *Engin. Princ. Plasticating Extrusion* i. 8 Today's plasticating extruders operate mostly in the speed range of 20–200 rpm.., extruding up to 3500 lb/hr of polymer.

plastication (plæstɪˈkeɪʃən). [f. prec. + -ATION.] The action of plasticating.

1939 *Ann. Rep. Progr. Rubber Technol.* II. 116 Knowledge of the mechanism of plastication has been carried a stage further by a study of mastication in an internal mixer at various temperatures. **1968** [see PLASTICATE *v*. 1].

plasticator (ˈplæstɪkeɪtə(r)). [f. as prec. + -OR.] An extruder for plasticating rubber or thermoplastic particles, usu. by subjecting them simultaneously to pressure and heat.

1934 *Industr. & Engin. Chem.* Mar. 349/1 Two distinctly different types of masticating machines are employed in modern rubber plants, mills, and plasticators. **1968** *Encycl. Polymer Sci. & Technol.* IX. 48 The most widely used contemporary machines [for molding plastics] include: (a) the ram injection-molding machine..; (b) the plunger- or screw-type plasticator..; and (c) the reciprocating-screw injection machine. **1972** P. W. ALLEN *Natural Rubber & Synthetics* vii. 196 In place of the standard [masticating] machines shown..some factories use a 'plasticator' which fulfils essentially the same function.

plastician (plæˈstɪʃən). [f. PLASTIC *a*. + -ICIAN.] An expert or specialist in plastic art, plastic surgery, etc.

1928 T. E. LAWRENCE *Let.* 16 Apr. (1938) 591 So many plasticians seem to admit to their notice the outside of machinery, and to exclude its purposefulness. **1933** *Archit. Rev.* LXXIII. 266/2 As a complement to the elaborate laboratory researches into the nature of thermoplastic.., there is need of research and experiment directed to the proper development of design... It [*sc.* Lethaby's *Art and Workmanship*] should be in the hands of every 'plastician'. **1934** *Punch* 26 Dec. 718/2 And, by marvellous plasticians in mysterious robes arrayed, Faces are most wonderfully and most fearfully remade.

Plasticine (ˈplæstɪsiːn, ˈplɑːst-). [f. PLASTIC *a*. + -INE[4].] Proprietary name for a composition capable of remaining plastic for a long time, used in schools, etc. as a substitute for modelling clay. Also *Comb.* and quasi-*adj.* (in *fig.* use).

1897 W. HARBUTT (*title*) Harbutt's plastic method and the use of Plasticine. **1903** H. G. WELLS in *Fortn. Rev.* Jan. 184 Some one of the plastic substitutes for modelling clay now sold by educational dealers, plasticine for example. **1926** R. MACAULAY *Crewe Train* II. vii. 152 She..idled about with toy soldiers or plasticine or meccano. **1935** H. G. WELLS *Things to Come* xiii. 124 A nursery of children. Anno 2055. They play with plasticine, draw on sheets of paper.., build with bricks or run about after each other. **1958** *Spectator* 4 July 12/1 He was so pliant, so plasticine,..so insidiously seeing it all the other chap's way. **1967** H. PORTER in *Coast to Coast 1965–6* 177 The sugar..infesting their plasticine-like texture tasted of garlic. **1976** *Times* 28 Jan. 1/3 The Russians..would respect us more if we were led by an iron lady rather than a Plasticine man.

plasticism (ˈplæstɪsɪz(ə)m). [f. PLASTIC *a*. + -ISM.] **a.** The doctrine of the plastic principle of nature. **b.** The practice of the plastic art.

1858 MAYNE *Expos. Lex.*, *Plasticismus*..term for the plastic force or power; plasticism. **1864** *Gd. Words* 403/1 Are we quite sure that this eclectic plasticism will always be kept within the limits of congruity?

plasticity (plæˈstɪsɪtɪ). [f. PLASTIC *a*. + -ITY; so F. *plasticité* (1785 in Hatz.-Darm.).] **a.** The quality of being plastic, in various senses of the adj.; *spec.* Capacity for being moulded or undergoing a permanent change in shape.

1782–3 W. F. MARTYN *Geog. Mag.* I. 325 Inclining to plasticity, (or easiness of impression). **1793** SMEATON *Edystone L.* §218 *note*, The lime will receive the most sand in that way, without losing its plasticity. **1801** W. TAYLOR in *Monthly Mag.* XII. 588 Moulded into metaphors, or carved into comparisons, with marvellous plasticity. **1859** BAIN *Emotions* II. ix. §20. 519 Some natures are distinguished by plasticity or the power of acquisition, and therefore realize more closely the saying that man is a bundle of habits. **1867** V. OTTOLINI et al. *Terracotta Archit. N. Italy* 5 Plasticity and homogeneity of ingredients are the two conditions essential to the composition of any ceramic paste. **1878** STEWART & TAIT *Unseen Univ.* iii. §108 Effects of the extraordinary plasticity of glacier-ice. **1933** L. F. RAHM *Plastic Molding* ii. 24 In molding, shellac compounds are generally preheated to sufficient plasticity to require no further heat from the mold. **1935** G. E. DOAN *Princ. Physical Metallurgy* v. 109 If deformation is continued until the temperature of the object is below the recrystallization temperature.., the plasticity of the metal may be insufficient and the object may crack in the operation. **1968** W. J. PATTON *Materials in Industry* iii. 61 Most forming operations during manufacture require plasticity for their execution. **1971** B. SCHARF *Engin. & its Lang.* i. 2 Ductility, malleability and plasticity are closely related properties.

b. *Biol.* Adaptability of an organism to changes in its environment.

1868 CLIFFORD *Lect.* (1879) I. 102 The race must at a certain time have a definite amount of plasticity, that is, a definite power of adapting itself to altered circumstances by changing in accordance with them. **1908** J. A. THOMSON *Heredity* iii. 72 It is certain that many unicellular organisms are very plastic, and it seems reasonable to suppose that as differentiation increased, restrictions were placed on the primary plasticity, while a more specialised secondary plasticity was gained in many cases, where the organisms lived in environments liable to frequent vicissitudes. **1951** *Jrnl. Ecol.* XXXIX. 217 Ecological plasticity..may be defined as the potentialities of expression of physiological characters that determine what factors of the environment shall limit the distribution of a species or other taxon. **1976** BELL & COOMBE tr. *Strasburger's Textbk. Bot.* 401 The wild strawberry..reproduces vegetatively by vigorous runners.. and each clone can only develop the desirable genetic plasticity by means of stepwise somatic mutations (bud sparts). **1978** *Nature* 14 Sept. 140/2 The potential for plasticity of the developing mammalian visual system has been the subject of several investigations.

plasticization (plæstɪsaɪˈzeɪʃən). [f. PLASTIC *a*. + -IZATION.] The process of rendering (more) plastic or mouldable; *spec.* (*a*) addition of a plasticizer to a synthetic resin; (*b*) = PLASTICATION.

1927 *Chem. Abstr.* XXI. 2535 The diff. methods of plasticization of a no. of natural and artificial plastics are discussed. **1937** A. JONES *Cellulose Lacquers* iv. 54 Plasticisation has long been studied in metallurgy in the production of soft alloys like solder and type metals. **1946** F. MARCHIONNA *Butalastic Polymers* xiii. 414 Plasticization [of Buna-S] may also be effected by first masticating the sheet and then subjecting it to thermal softening. **1953** KIRK & OTHMER *Encycl. Chem. Technol.* X. 773 The most important classes of thermoplastic resins requiring plasticization are the vinyls and the cellulosics. **1969** M. A. WHEELANS in W. S. Penn *Injection Moulding of Elastomers* ix. 84 Plasticization by screw is quicker, more controllable and gives a more homogeneous distribution of heat and viscosity than that given by a simple plunger system. **1972** *Nature* 21 Apr. 405/1 A number of other insecticide chemicals also caused plasticization of the abdominal cuticle.

plasticize (ˈplæstɪsaɪz), *v.* [f. PLASTIC *a*. + -IZE.] **1.** *trans.* To render plastic (mouldable); to produce or promote plasticity in (a substance), e.g. by addition of a plasticizer or by plastication.

1927 *Chem. Abstr.* XXI. 2535 Mech. and chem. methods for plasticizing such modern plastics as rubber, cellulose products, galilith [*sic*], phenol-formaldehyde resins, etc. **1931** *Engineering* 2 Jan. 26/1 The scrap [rubber] was then plasticised by treatment with steam in a horizontal heater. **1945** A. T. BIRKBY *Phenolic Plastics* viii. 92 Any attempt to plasticize a large mass of thermo-setting material at one time to a condition suitable for extrusion through a die in a continuous process would fail. **1957** H. R. SIMONDS *Conc. Guide to Plastics* iii. 111 Most resins are plasticized by heat, solvents, or plasticizers. **1969** M. A. WHEELANS in W. S. Penn *Injection Moulding of Elastomers* ix. 84 The rubber is heated and plasticized as it progresses along a retractable screw. **1971** *Nature* 9 July 88/2 Textile fibres which are in bulk production are usually used. These are..usually copolymers containing a proportion of a second molecule to plasticize the fibre and to allow it to be spun and handled more easily. **1972** *Ibid.* 21 Apr. 405/1 The acetone-treated insects neither became paralysed nor was their abdominal cuticle plasticized.

2. *trans.* To treat or make with plastic.

1940 *New Statesman* 16 Mar. 361/1 An enterprising silk manufacturer..'plasticised' gold lace so that it became a permanent table-cloth when used as a table-surface. **1970** *Daily Tel.* 13 Jan. 15/6 Walls and ceiling are covered with a check fabric..and it is specially plasticised to resist condensation. **1977** *Austral. House & Garden* Jan. 49/1 (*caption*) Atel's modular kitchen units have an Italian Parawood teak veneer surface that has been plasticised for easy care.

Hence ˈ**plasticizing** *vbl. sb.* and *ppl. a.*

1925 *Paint, Oil & Chem. Rev.* 22 Jan. 10/2 The resin 'may or may not have been treated with..a plasticizing agent'. **1927** *Chem. Abstr.* XXI. 2535 (*heading*) The influence of plasticizing on the mechanical-elastic properties of natural and artificial plastics. **1948** DALZELL & TOWNSEND *Masonry Simplified* I. i. 13 In order to yield a mortar, the lime or lime putty must exert a certain minimum plasticizing effect on the mortar. **1953** *Industr. & Engin. Chem.* May 989/1 A plasticizing extruder whose job is to transform the cold feed into a hot, formable melt. **1973** *Materials & Technol.* VI. viii. 606 For the plasticizing of the more polar cellulose nitrate the low-molecular phthalates are preferred.

plasticized (ˈplæstɪsaɪzd), *ppl. a.* [f. prec. + -ED[1].] **1.** Rendered (more) plastic; treated with a plasticizer.

1943 *Industr. & Engin. Chem.* May 383/2 Paper and cloth coated with the plasticized esters may be crumpled without cracking the coating. **1971** *Nature* 3 Dec. 254/2 Plastic coatings may be applied to metals by dipping the preheated metal part into either a fluidized bed of polymer powder or into a liquid plastisol. The former process is applicable to polyethylene, nylon and unplasticized PVC, whereas the latter is applicable only to plasticized PVC compounds.

2. Treated or made with plastic.

1945 *Richmond* (Va.) *News-Leader* 26 July 27/2 Sheer originality is seen in the new plasticized beaver fur coat which will not mat or curl in the stormiest weather. **1972** *Daily Tel.* 7 Jan. 13 The cover-ups in plastic or plasticised cotton are good for sploshy activities like painting, attempts at cooking.

3. *fig.* = PLASTIC *a*. 9 b.

1974 *Globe & Mail* (Toronto) 12 Oct. 8/1 The CEGEPs are huge, modern, plasticized education factories of as many as 5,000 students with little discipline, relaxed standards and the best equipment money can buy. **1975** R. H. RIMMER *Premar Experiments* (1976) ii. 156 A simpler world of man experiencing man instead of machines and a plasticized environment?

plasticizer ('plæstɪsaɪzə(r)). [f. PLASTICIZE *v.* + -ER[1].] Any substance which when added to another makes it (more) plastic or mouldable; *spec.* one (usu. a solvent) added to a synthetic resin to produce or promote plasticity and flexibility and to reduce brittleness.

1925 *Paint, Oil & Chem. Rev.* 29 Jan. 10/3 In order that the film may remain flexible..plasticizers—inert liquids of low vapor tension—are incorporated in the lacquer. **1943** H. R. FLECK *Plastics* vii. 160 Poly-vinyl chloride as formed is a hard brittle amorphous white powder which is useless for moulding purpose until plasticizer is added. **1947** J. C. RICH *Materials & Methods of Sculpture* xi. 342 Films of lacquer tend to harden and to become brittle as they age. For this reason plasticizers must be added to a lacquer formula. **1948** DALZELL & TOWNSEND *Masonry Simplified* I. i. 16 In cement concrete, lime functions as a plasticizer. **1962** A. NISBETT *Technique Sound Studio* 248 Direct-cut disc... These are made of cellulose nitrate (which contains a castor oil plasticizer to soften it for easy cutting) but are often referred to as 'acetates'. **1967** M. CHANDLER *Ceramics in Mod. World* iv. 132 Most steatite electrical products..are most commonly shaped by dust-pressing, but because the body contains little clay the ceramist adds artificial plasticizers such as waxes or polyvinyl alcohol. **1971** *Materials & Technol.* II. v. 253 The so-called plasticisers which are added to mortars improve their working properties by causing air to be entrained into them at the time of gauging the mortar. **1972** *Ibid.* V. xxii. 844 Hairsprays nearly always include an important minor ingredient called a 'plasticizer' which softens the resin film and prevents it flaking on the hair.

plasticky ('plæstɪkɪ), *a.* Also **plasticy**. [f. PLASTIC *sb.*[3] + -Y[1].] Suggestive of or resembling plastic.

1972 *Oxford Times* 12 May 20/4 His elder daughter Julie, 9, 'smelt plasticky fumes'. **1972** *Daily Tel.* 21 June 13/3 The interior [of the car] is rather 'plasticy' and the seats became hot in the sunshine. **1979** R. RENDELL *Make Death love Me* xvi. 144 The gun..was a toy, as you could tell really by the plasticky look of it.

† **'plasticly**, *adv. Obs. rare*[−1]. [f. PLASTIC *a.* + -LY[2].] = PLASTICALLY.

1678 CUDWORTH *Intell. Syst.* I. v. 668 The true and proper Cause of Motion..is not the Matter itself organized; but the Soul either as cogitative or plastickly self active..ruling over it.

plasticware ('plæstɪkwɛə(r)). [f. PLASTIC *a.* + WARE *sb.*[3]] Articles made of plastic.

1972 *Science* 2 June 1039/2 We used plasticware or siliconized glassware..throughout the experiments. **1975** *New Yorker* 24 Nov. 102/2 D/R has imported a collection of opaque plasticware, in yellow, red, green, or white, from the firms of the celebrated English designer Terence Conran.

plasticy, var. PLASTICKY *a.*

plastid ('plæstɪd), *sb.* (*a.*) [a. Ger. *plastid* (Haeckel), f. Gr. πλαστός (see -PLAST) + *id*, after Gr. -ιδιον, dim. suffix.]

1. *Biol.* An individual mass or unit of protoplasm, as a cell or unicellular organism.

1876 E. R. LANKESTER *Adv. Sc.* (1890) 283 Haeckel's useful term 'plastid' for a corpuscle of protoplasm. **1877** DAWSON *Orig. World* 377 If we reduce organized beings to their ultimate organisms—cells or plastids. **1878** BELL *Gegenbaur's Comp. Anat.* p. viii, Our knowledge of the nucleus of organic cells or plastids.

2. *Bot.* A differentiated corpuscle or granule occurring in the protoplasm of a vegetable cell; e.g. a chlorophyll-granule, a chromoplastid, or a leucoplastid.

1885 GOODALE *Physiol. Bot.* (1892) 287 As the cells which develop from the growing point assume the different characters which fit them for special services..[so] their plastids may likewise assume special characters.

B. *adj.* Having the character of a plastid.

1890 in *Cent. Dict.* **1895** in *Syd. Soc. Lex.*

Hence ˌ**plastidoge'netic** *a.*, producing plastids.

1899 *Natural Science* Dec. 458 The respiratory trees of Holothuroids have four functions—respiratory, hydrostatic, plastidogenetic, and excretory.

plastidome ('plæstɪdəʊm). *Cytology.* [a. F. *plastidome* (P. A. Dangeard 1918, in *Compt. Rend.* CLXVI. 440), f. *plastide* PLASTID *sb.* 2, after *chondriome, chromosome*, etc.] The plastids of a cell collectively.

1926 *Science* 18 June 620/2 Following..the non-committal terminology of the Dangeards, the components demonstrated are as follows: (1) Spindle fibers and cytoplasmic network... (2) Plastidome... (3) Spherome... (4) Vacuome. **1971** W. STUBBE in J. Reinert et al. *Origin & Continuity of Cell Organelles* 77 We assume that the division of the plastidome into a number of lentil-shaped chloroplasts and the consequent increase in surface may be the reason for the prevalence of this type among higher plants.

plastidule ('plæstɪdjuːl). *Biol.* [a. Ger. *plastidul* (Haeckel), dim. of *plastid*: see -ULE.] A hypothetical molecule or ultimate particle of protoplasm, constituting a vital unit, and forming an element or constituent of a plastid or cell.

1877 DAWSON *Orig. World* 377 And with Spencer and Haeckel suppose these to be farther divisible into still smaller particles or plastidules. **1878** tr. *Virchow's Freedom of Science* 23. **1879** [see PLASSON]. **1905** *Academy & Lit.* 28 Jan. 82 Haeckel claims priority for his notion of the plastidule, though this and numerous variants with other names are notoriously none other than the 'physiological unit' of Spencer, which preceded them all.

attrib. **1877** *Nature* 4 Oct. 492/2 The speaker [Virchow] then criticised somewhat severely Prof. Haeckel's theory of the plastidule soul and of the animated cell.

Hence **pla'stidular**, **plasti'dulic** *adjs.*, pertaining to a plastidule.

1878 tr. *Virchow's Freedom of Science* 24, I am unable to admit that we should be at all justified in importing the 'plastidulic soul' into the course of our education. **1884** A. LAMBERT in *19th Cent.* June 954 The theory of a 'plastidulic soul'.

plastifier ('plæstɪfaɪə(r)). [f. as next + -ER[1].] = PLASTICIZER.

1919 H. DREYFUS *Brit. Pat. 160,225*, This invention has reference..to the manufacture of celluloid-like masses of any kind having a basis of cellulose ac[e]tate wherein high boiling solvents, called plastifiers, for the cellulose acetate, are incorporated with the mass in conjunction with one or more volatile liquids or diluents. **1971** *Materials & Technol.* II. ii. 111 Plastifiers and air-entraining agents. These materials improve the workability of concrete mixture.

plastify ('plæstɪfaɪ), *v.* [f. PLASTIC *a.* + -IFY.] = PLASTICIZE *v.* 1, 2. Hence **'plastifying** *vbl. sb.*

1919 H. DREYFUS *Brit. Pat. 160,225*, The solvent action on the cellulose acetate increases so that this is more and more dissolved and plastified until..only very little volatile diluent remains. **1963** H. R. CLAUSER et al. *Encycl. Engin. Materials & Processes* 348/1 A reciprocating plunger.. forces the material into the plastifying cylinder. An equal quantity of fluid plastic is thus forced out of the front of the cylinder..into the mold. **1963** *Engineering* 13 Sept. 330/2 The concrete..is 'plastified' and remixed intensively by vibration. **1972** *Buenos Aires Herald* 4 Feb. 14/2 (Advt.), Floors polished, scraped, repaired, plastified.

plastigel ('plæstɪdʒɛl). [f. PLASTI(C *a.* + GEL *sb.*] A plastisol thickened to a putty-like consistency so that it retains its shape when heated.

1952 *Mod. Plastics* Jan. 99/1 Plastigels may be handled by many of the conventional methods of fabricating plastics but the pressures required are lower, leading to lower machine and mold costs. **1954** *Plastics Engin. Handbk.* x. 283 The control over the flow which is obtained with plastigels makes it possible to coat open-weave cloth or porous surfaces without excessive penetration. **1969** *Encycl. Polymer Sci. & Technol.* X. 246 With certain plasticizers or with modified paste resins the plastisol may become a gelatinous mass, or plastigel, under controlled conditions.

plastimeter, var. PLASTOMETER.

plastin ('plæstɪn). *Biol.* [f. Gr. πλαστός (see -PLAST) + -IN[1], after *chromatin*.] A viscous substance found in the nucleus of a cell.

1889 *Q. Jrnl. Microsc. Sc.* July 169 Besides the 'nuclein', ..Reinke and Rodewald..have found 'plastin', and Kossel ..'histon' and 'adenin'.

Comb. **1905** *Brit. Med. Jrnl.* 25 Feb. 442 The Karyosome ..contains eight chromatin elements surrounded by a coloured plastin-like substance.

‖**plastique** (plastik). [F., sb. use of *plastique* adj., plastic.] **1.** A name given to a plastic composition for modelling.

[**1803** SARRETT *New Pict. London* 80 The ornaments are plastick, a composition something like plaster of Paris.] **1903** *Daily Mail* 7 Sept. 7/4 Modelling may be done in wax, clay, or plastique.

2. Statuesque poses or slow graceful movements in dancing; the art or technique of these.

1893 G. B. SHAW *Music in London 1890–94* (1932) III. 111 The unhappy students had been taught 'plastique' until they dared not call their arms and legs their own. The plastique professor..is almost as fatal a person as the harmony professor. **1897** —— *Our Theatres in Nineties* (1932) III. 146 Her interest in life and character will be supplanted by an interest in plastique and execution. **1947** *Ballet Ann.* I. 56 *Romeo and Juliet*..does contain both the passionate, lyrical dancing and strong, dramatic *plastique* demanded by the tragedy. **1960** *Times* 15 Mar. 6/1 Jive and an expressionistic development of *plastique* give more to these ballets than footwork. **1977** *New Yorker* 16 May 79/2 True to the 'Oriental' plastique of the period, the steps are all turned in.

3. Plastic explosive; a plastic bomb. Also *attrib.*

1968 L. W. ROBINSON *Assassin* (1969) xvi. 199 He planted another bomb... Bomb squad says it's made of *plastique*. **1969** E. AMBLER *Intercom Conspiracy* (1970) vi. 136 They had no trouble..fixing the *plastique*, the bomb. **1974** *Publishers Weekly* 11 Feb. 64/2 To hold hostage a TV studio audience with a human plastique bomb.

‖**plastiqueur** (plastikœr). [Fr.] A person who plants or detonates a plastic bomb. Also *fig.*

1961 *Economist* 4 Nov. 435/1 Professor Palmer is the last and not the least of the *plastiqueurs*, as readers of the press learned not long ago, when he alleged that Evans had misstated some of his evidence in support of his pet theories. That explosion in the press was what gunners call a premature, and did Professor Palmer's discovery little good. **1962** *Times* 23 Apr. 9/2 The *plastiqueurs* were daily at work in metropolitan France. **1971** *Guardian* 17 July 9/4 The plastiqueurs were..soundly committed to private enterprise.

plastisol ('plæstɪsɒl). [f. PLASTI(C *a.* + SOL *sb.*[6]] A dispersion of particles of a synthetic resin in a non-volatile liquid consisting chiefly or entirely of plasticizer, which can be converted into a solid plastic simply by heating (cf. ORGANOSOL).

1946 *Mod. Packaging* Mar. 262/2 It is possible to prepare these dispersions without any volatile carrier. Such 100% solids dispersions are known as plastisols. **1954** [see *hot dipping* (HOT *a.* 12)]. **1963** H. R. CLAUSER *Encycl. Engin. Materials & Processes* 489/1 One of the most dramatic applications of plastisols is as a lining for kitchen dishwashers. **1971** [see PLASTICIZED *ppl. a.* 1]. **1980** *Daily Tel.* 17 Jan. 11 (Advt.), A major manufacturer of PVC resins, compounds and plastisols.

plastochron ('plæstəkrɒn). *Bot.* Also **-chrone** (-krəʊn). [a. G. *plastochron* (E. Askenasy 1878, in *Verhandl. des Natur-hist.-med. Vereins zu Heidelberg* II. II. 76), f. Gr. πλαστό-ς formed, moulded (see -PLAST) + χρόν-ος time.] The interval of time between consecutive formations of leaf primordia (or of pairs of such primordia) in a growing shoot apex of a plant.

1929 *New Phytologist* XXVIII. 41 These differences may partly be accounted for by the fact that an interval elapses —called by some authors the 'plastochron'—between the initiation of successive primordia. **1938** PRIESTLEY & SCOTT *Introd. Bot.* xiii. 173 In the ⅜ system it will be noted..that each primordium is three plastochrones removed from its one neighbour, two from the other. **1957** *Amer. Jrnl. Bot.* XLIV. 298/1 A plastochron is conventionally defined as the time interval between initiation of two successive leaves. It might be more broadly defined as the interval between corresponding stages of development of successive leaves, and one might choose initiation, maturity, or any intermediate stage of development as the stage of reference. **1960** *Ibid.* XLVII. 707/1 This plastochron, averaging 3 wk. in length, delimits the 2 developmental stages of the heterophyllous shoot.

b. Special Combs.: **plastochron index**, an index of the developmental age of a shoot, being the number of leaves that are not less than some stated length, plus a fractional adjustment so calculated that the value of the index changes smoothly as the shoot grows; **plastochron ratio** (see quot. 1948).

1955 F. J. MICHELINI (*title of Ph.D. Dissertation, Univ. Pennsylvania*) The use of the plastochron index in studies of morphological and physiological development in *Xanthium italicum* Moretti. **1973** R. MAKSYMOWYCH *Anal. Leaf Development* i. 5 The leaf plastochron index (LPI) can be used in developmental studies limited specifically to only one leaf. **1948** F. J. RICHARDS in *Symp. Soc. Exper. Biol.* II. 226 The differences between the various orders of phyllotaxis have been referred to differences in the ratio of the distances of two successive primordia from the apical centre... The ratio will be referred to as the 'plastochrone ratio'. **1968** C. W. WARDLAW *Morphogenesis in Plants* ix. 231 As the several systems..in Fibonacci phyllotaxis have closely comparable divergence angles, i.e. about 137·5°, the essential differences between them are due to their plastochrone ratios. As the *P.R.* approaches unity, the phyllotaxis rises.

Hence **plasto'chronic** *a.*

1953 K. ESAU *Plant Anat.* v. 104 The changes in the morphology of the shoot apex occurring during one plastochron may be referred to as plastochronic changes. **1957** *Amer. Jrnl. Bot.* XLIV. 302/1 Much would be gained by determining the precise plastochron age of each apex, rather than..judging the plastochronic phase subjectively.

plastocyanin (plæstəʊ'saɪənɪn). *Biochem.* [f. CHLORO)PLAST + -O + CYANIN.] A blue copper-containing protein (differing slightly from species to species) which is found in the chloroplasts of green plants and in certain bacteria, and is involved in photosynthesis.

1961 KATOH & TAKAMIYA in *Nature* 25 Feb. 665/2 In view of its localization in the chloroplasts and its characteristic blue colour in the oxidized form, the name 'plastocyanin' is proposed for this copper protein. **1966** *Plant Physiol.* XLI. 1641/1 From its absorption spectrum, the plastocyanin of *C. reinhardi* resembles the plastocyanin of spinach. **1974** *Sci. Amer.* Dec. 74/1 (*caption*) The electron is passed through a series of carrier molecules including..plastoquinone..and cytochrome *f*.., to plastocyanin. **1976** *Nature* 27 May 344/2 The 'small blue proteins'—azurins from bacteria, plastocyanins from photosynthetic cells.

plastogamy (plæ'stɒgəmɪ). *Biol.* [f. Gr. πλαστ-ός moulded + -γαμία marriage.] The fusion of the protoplasm of two or more cells or unicellular organisms, as in the formation of a plasmodium. Hence **plasto'gamic** *a.*, pertaining to plastogamy.

1891 HARTOG in *Nature* 17 Sept. 483/2 Plastogamy: the fusion of cytoplasta into plasmodium, the nuclei remaining free. **1901** G. N. CALKINS *Protozoa* 218 Thus cytotrophy, leading first to contiguity, may result in plastogamy, or the fusion of cell-plasms. *Ibid.*, Four individuals may be found in plastogamic union.

† **'plastograph**. *Obs. rare*[−0]. [Cf. Gr. πλαστογράφος adj. 'forging, falsifying' (Liddell & Scott), f. πλαστός moulded, forged + γράφειν to write.]

1658 PHILLIPS, *Plastograph*, (Greek) counterfeit writing.

plastography (plæ'stɒgrəfɪ). *rare*[−0]. [In sense 1, ad. Gr. πλαστογραφία, f. πλαστογράφος: see prec. In sense 2, f. Gr. πλαστός moulded + -GRAPHY (erroneously used).]

† **1.** (See quot.) *Obs.*

1656 BLOUNT *Glossogr.*, *Plastography* (*plastographia*), a counterfeiting or false writing.

¶ **2.** 'The art of forming figures in plaster' (Maunder *Treas. Knowl.* 1830).

plastome ('plæstəʊm). *Genetics.* Also **plastom.** [a. G. *plastom* (O. Renner 1929, in *Handb. d. Vererbungswissenschaft* IIA. 32), f. *plastid* PLASTID *sb.* 2, after *genom* GENOME.] The sum-total of the genetic factors or information in the plastids of a cell.

1954 P. MICHAELIS in *Adv. Genetics* VI. 290, I propose.. with Renner (1929) to include all extranuclear hereditary elements of the cell in the term plasmon, and to subdivide this into (1) the cytoplasmon, that is, the elements of the cytoplasm, and (2) the plastom, that is, the hereditary elements of the plastids, etc. **1965** WETTSTEIN & ERIKSSON in S. J. Geerts *Genetics Today* xvi. 594 In higher plants two non-chromosomal genetic systems controlling chloroplast structure and function—the plastome and the plasmone—have long ago been recognized from the different modes of inheritance of certain chloroplast defects. **1967** KIRK & TILNEY-BASSETT *Plastids* ix. 277 There are as many as five genetically different plastoms within the subgenus *Euoenothera.* **1976** [see PLASMON 2].

plastometer (plæ'stɒmɪtə(r)). Also **pla'stimeter.** [f. PLAST(ICITY + -OMETER.] An instrument for measuring the plasticity of a substance. Hence **pla'stometry.**

1919 BINGHAM & GREEN in *Proc. Amer. Soc. Testing Materials* XIX. II. 645 As we wish, in a sense, to measure the 'plasticity' of a paint the apparatus for making the measurements has been called a 'plastometer'. **1922** E. C. BINGHAM *Fluidity & Plasticity* 319 (*heading*) Practical plastometry. **1933** *Physics* IV. 285/1 The theory of parallel-plate plastometry. **1940** *Brit. Standard Methods testing Latex* (*B.S.I.*) 26 Compress the pellet between thin sheets of paper under a load of 5 kg. in a parallel plate plastimeter. **1946** *Nature* 14 Sept. 371/1 The original type of plastometer, devised by Bingham, is still in use, with slight modifications, in many laboratories to-day. **1958** *New Scientist* 5 June 112/1 (*caption*) This machine.. is a capillary plastometer.. and is particularly suitable for studying the flow properties of semi-solid materials. **1971** J. A. C. HARWOOD in C. M. Blow *Rubber Technol. & Manuf.* iii. 59 The elastic recovery is measured by the height of the sample a fixed time after removal from the plastimeter.

plastoquinone (plæstəʊ'kwɪnəʊn). *Biochem.* [f. CHLORO)PLAST + -O + QUINONE.] Any of a homologous series of compounds which have a quinone nucleus with a terpenoid sidechain, and which occur in the chloroplasts of plants; *spec.* one having the formula $C_{48}H_{72}O_2$.

1958 F. L. CRANE in *Plant Physiol.* XXXIV. 547/1 It is proposed that Q_{254} should be called plastoquinone... This name will serve to emphasize the localization in chloroplasts and possibly other plastid structures. **1968** *New Scientist* 25 Jan. 189/1 Terpenoids in chloroplasts of green leaves include.. plastoquinone. **1973** *Biochim. & Biophys. Acta* CCCI. 36 Several homologues of plastoquinone.. have been detected in algae and chloroplasts of higher plants... The detailed chemical structure of plastoquinones B and C is not known yet. **1975** D. JARVIS tr. *D. Hess's Plant Physiol.* 41 Another important redox system which is engaged in electron transport in photosynthesis is plastoquinone. **1978** *Sci. Amer.* Mar. 111/3 The two electrons that cross the membrane from P-680 are picked up at the outer surface by a hydrogen carrier similar in structure to ubiquinone but called plastoquinone, or PQ.

'plastral, *a.* [f. next + -AL[1].] Of or pertaining to a plastron.

1889 *Brit. Mus. Cat. Chelonians* 25 Plastral shields subject to great variations. **1890** in *Cent. Dict.*

plastron ('plæstrən). Also 6 **plasteroun.** [a. F. *plastron* breast-plate, also in other senses as in Eng., ad. It. *piastrone*, augment. of *piastra* breast-plate, prop. plate of metal; see PIASTRE, PLASTER.]

1. a. A steel breast-plate formerly worn beneath the hauberk. *Obs.* exc. *Hist.*

1506–7 *Acc. Ld. High Treas. Scot.* III. 367 Item, for ane hebreschoun.., and ane plasteroun to the samyn. **1834** PLANCHÉ *Brit. Costume* 87 In later times we shall find the plastron called the gorget. **1837** H. AINSWORTH *Crichton* II. 392 The point of his lance glanced off the sharp gorget of the plastron. **1853** JAMES *Agnes. Sorel* (1860) I. 45, I should be thrown on one side like a rusty plastron.

b. A leather-covered wadded shield or pad, worn by professional fencers over the breast.

1693 DRYDEN *Juvenal* vi. (1697) 134 Against the Post their wicker Shields they crush, Flourish the Sword, and at the Plastron push. **1706** PHILLIPS, *Plastron*, a Fencing-Master's quilted Breast-Leather, which serves for his Scholars to push at. **1893** MCCARTHY *Red Diamonds* I. 261 Endeavouring to plant her foil on the leather plastron of the fencing-master's chest.

transf. *a* **1648** DIGBY *Closet Open.* (1677) 162 Laying under it a thick Plastron of Beef-Suet.

fig. **1755** CHESTERF. *Let. to Bp. Chevenix* 15 Dec., The several situations, which I have been in, having made me long the *plastron* of dedications, I am become as callous to flattery, as some people are to abuse.

c. Applied to an ornamental plaque worn on the breast.

1883 D. H. R. GOODALE in *Harper's Mag.* July 242/2 That plastron of steel ornaments is effective.

2. a. In women's dress, A kind of ornamental front to a bodice, introduced in the latter half of the 19th c.; extended to a loose front of lace, or of some light fabric edged with lace, embroidery, etc.

1876 *Echo* 30 Aug. (*Fashions*). **1881** *Truth* 31 Mar. 446/1 The low satin bodice has a plastron embroidered in purple and gold jet. **1883** *Cassell's Fam. Mag.* Sept. 619/1 Occasionally the waistcoat or plastron is made full. **1886** J. K. JEROME *Idle Thoughts* (1889) 152, I shall wear my plum-coloured body.. with a yellow plastron. **1893** *Lady* 10 Aug. 146/3 The vest or plastron is of silk covered with lace. **1903** *Daily Chron.* 28 Mar. 8/4 The stock.. is usually made to fasten at the back, so that the front part may be decorative, and is seen, as well, with a little overhanging plastron or wedge-shaped front, or a deep point, edged with open-work or coloured embroidery. **1906** *Advertisement*, Real Irish crochet lace Plastron.. Real Bruges lace Plastron.

b. In men's dress, A starched shirt-front; esp. of the kind without pleats.

1890 *Athenæum* 7 June 745/3 The one restraining influence upon the civilized man is the 'plastron', otherwise the shirt front of evening dress. **1900** *Daily News* 24 Mar. 6/4 The light from the lamp.. shows a curious and useful reflection on the plastron of the white shirt.

3. *Zool.* **a.** (After Cuvier.) The ventral part of the shell of a tortoise or turtle.

1831 tr. *Cuvier's Anim. Kingd.* IX. 67 The plastron, or breast-plate [of the Order Chelonia] is yellowish and flat, truncated,.. and covered with twelve scaly plates. **1835–6** *Todd's Cycl. Anat.* I. 201/2 This plastron is the sternum, or ..the union of several sternums. **1870** GILLMORE tr. *Figuier's Reptiles & Birds* 158 Terrestrial Tortoises are distinguished by their short, oval and convex bodies, covered by carapace and plastron.

b. Applied to the analogous part in various other animals, as in the extinct labyrinthodon (an amphibian), the glyptodon (allied to the armadillos), certain fossil fishes, and certain existing echinoderms (e.g. *Spatangus*): see quots.

1854 H. MILLER *Sch. & Schm.* xxiv. (1858) 528 The extraordinary form of *Pterichthys*.. with its arched carapace and flat plastron restored before me. **1888** ROLLESTON & JACKSON *Anim. Life* 557 As to the interambulacral plates, they become much expanded near the peristome of *Spatangidæ*... The whole structure constitutes a raised plastron. **1890** *Cent. Dict.* s.v. *Glyptodon*, They are all distinguished from the living armadillos.. by possessing a ventral shield or plastron.

c. *Ent.* [a. Fr. (F. Brocher 1912, in *Ann. Biol. Lacustre* V. 141).] In certain aquatic insects, a type of external gill formed by a patch of cuticle covered with hairs which retain a thin layer of air under water. Also *attrib.*

1947 THORPE & CRISP in *Jrnl. Exper. Biol.* XXIV. 227 (*title*) Studies on plastron respiration. *Ibid.* 229 The volume of gas in the plastron is negligible. **1959** SOUTHWOOD & LESTON *Land & Water Bugs Brit. Is.* 367 The air film is self-renewing: oxygen continually diffuses in and out, the whole forming a plastron, or external gill. **1969** R. F. CHAPMAN *Insects* xxiv. 481 The volume of the plastron is constant and usually small since it does not provide a source of air but acts as a gill. **1976** H. E. HINTON in H. R. Hepburn *Insect Integument* xxv. 482 In *Ptyopteryx*..the only diffraction lines are those formed by the plastron on the ventral surface of the abdomen.

4. *Ornith.* A coloured area on the breast or belly of a bird, like or likened to a shield.

1890 *Cent. Dict.* cites COUES. **1895** in *Syd. Soc. Lex.*

5. *Anat.* The sternum together with the costal cartilages, the part removed in post-mortem examinations.

1890 in *Cent. Dict.* **1895** in *Syd. Soc. Lex.*

plastry, obs. form of PLASTERY.

† **'plasture, plaisture.** Erroneous form of PLASTER *sb.*, the ending confused with -URE.

c **1550** LLOYD *Treas. Health* Kj, Hete al together, and make a plasture of it beyng hote. **1589** GREENE *Tullie's Loue* Wks. (Grosart) VII. 132 For so deepe a wound the Lady Cornelia bringeth in a lenitiue plaisture. *Ibid.* 165 Apply them not as outward plastures, but as inward potions. **1608** HIERON *Defence* II. 72* His laste plasture for this cure maketh the soare to run out wyder.

-plasty, combining element, repr. Gr. -πλαστία, f. πλαστός formed, moulded, used in sense 'moulding, formation' in technical terms, chiefly of surgery, as *dermatoplasty, hypoplasty, osteoplasty.*

plat, *sb.*[1] *Obs.* exc. *dial.* Forms: 1 plætt, 5–6 *Sc.* platt, plat. [OE. *plætt* buffet, smack; cf. MLG. *plat* smack, MHG. *platz, blatz*, Ger. *platz, plotz* resounding blow, bang, crash. Goes with PLAT *v.*[1], both being app. of onomatopœic origin.

(But cf. PLAT *a.* flat; a buffet is struck with the flat palm.)]

A flat blow; a smack, slap.

c **1000** ÆLFRIC *Hom.* II. 248 Drihten soðlice us sealde hælu þurh ðam ear-plættum, and ece alysednysse. *c* **1500** *Rowlis Cursing* 122 in Laing *Anc. Poet. Scotl.*, With skulȝeoun clowttis and dressing knyvis, Platt for plat on thair gyngyvis. **1513** DOUGLAS *Æneis* XII. iv. 203 Syne with hys kne him possit with sic ane plat, That on the erd he spaldit him all flat. **1535** LYNDESAY *Satyre* 855 Sapience, thow servis to beir a plat. *c* **1900** (*Conversation in Co. Donegal*), 'Did the "old gentleman" ever set foot on this Island (St. Patrick's in Lough Derg)?' 'A few plats of the Prior 'ud soon make him lave.' (H. Chichester Hart.)

plat (plæt), *sb.*[2] *arch.* or *dial.* Forms: 4- plat, (5–7 platte, 6–9 platt); *pl.* plats: in 3 platen, 5–7 plattes, 6 plates. [app. a. OF. *plat* flat surface or thing, dish, etc., sb. use of the adj. *plat, plate* flat: see PLAT *a.* Cf. Ger. *platte* plate (of iron, etc.), slab.]

I. A flat thing, part, or surface.

† **1. a.** A flat piece, a plate (of metal); a thin slab of anything; a sheet, slice. *Obs.*

In early instances, esp. in the plural, not separable from PLATE *sb.* I.

[*c* **1290**: see PLATE *sb.* I.] *c* **1375** *Sc. Leg. Saints* xxviii. (*Margaret*) 552 þane wes of Irne mony plat Layd til hyr sydis, brynnand hat. *Ibid.* xxxvii. (*Vincencius*) 287, & yrne platis brynnand hat Wes laid on hyme to mak hym mat. **1420** *E.E. Wills* (1882) 46, I. bord mausure.., wyth a prent in þe myddylle, and a grypp amyde, and a narow plat be þe syddys, with iij lyonis of syluer, and ouerguld. **1526** TINDALE *Matt.* xxvii. 3 The xxx plattes off sylver. **1560** DAUS tr. *Sleidane's Comm.* 178 Thinne plats of leade of the same breadth. **1581** W. STAFFORD *Exam. Compl.* ii. (1876) 60, I had as liefe haue smal gadds or plats of Siluer and Gold, without any coyne at al to go abroade from man to man for exchaunge. **1593** in Willis & Clark *Cambridge* (1886) I. 29 [Not only do we find a charge for.. the.. stage on which the book-cases were to stand, but] platts [for the shelves are bought].

† **b.** A flat ornament of gold or other precious material. *Obs. rare*[−1].

1604 E. G[RIMSTONE] *D'Acosta's Hist. Indies* IV. xiv. 250, I have not knowen that.. they have found any of the form and bignesse of the platt or iewel they have at Genes.

† **c.** A flat leaf, a blade. *Obs. rare*[−1].

1716 *Lond. Gaz.* No. 5416/4 The Plat or Leaf of the Palmetor-Tree.

2. The flat part or side of anything; † **a.** The flat of a sword, as opposed to the edge (*obs.*); † **b.** The sole of the foot (*obs.*); **c.** The mould-board of a plough (*dial.*).

c **1386** CHAUCER *Sqr.'s T.* 154 To stroke hym with the plat [*v.r.* platte] in that place Ther he is hurt. **1426** LYDG. *De Guil. Pilgr.* 2664 Ther grevous woundys to allegge, Bet ys the platte than the egge. **1574** WITHALS *Dict.* 64/1 The platte [*ed.* 1566 plant] of the foote, *planta.* **1616** J. LANE *Cont. Sqr.'s T.* xi. 99 Tho touchd his woundes with the platt of thilke swoord, Which closd all vp, and instantlie recurd. **1765** *Univ. Mag.* XXXVII. 33/2 The plat, or earth-board, turned most of the carrots out of the ground. **1843** *Jrnl. R. Agric. Soc.* IV. I. 284 As soon as it leaves the mould-board, or, as we call them in Norfolk, the plats.

3. a. Anything placed in a flat or horizontal position: see quots. *Obs.* exc. *dial.*

? *a* **1400** *Morte Arth.* 2478 Pyghte pauyllyons of palle, and plattes in seegge. **1847–78** HALLIWELL, *Plat*,.. anything flat or horizontal, as a piece of timber so laid in building.

† **b.** A platform. *Obs.*

1558–9 *Passage Q. Eliz.* D iij, A stage.. and in the same a square platte rising with degrees.

4. A small bridge, a foot-bridge. (Also in form plot.) *Obs.* exc. *dial.*

1652 *Manch. Crt. Leet Rec.* (1887) IV. 73 Richard Haworth.. shall repaire and make good A Bridge or Plott in the Milgate. *Ibid.* 84 Should repaire and make good a Platt in the Millngate. **1670** in Picton *L'pool Munic. Rec.* (1883) I. 277 The.. pulling downe of the said bridge or platt.. is adjudged to be an act done for the good of the Corporation. **1835** *Act 5 & 6 Will. IV*, c. 50 §67 The said Surveyor.. shall ..make and lay such trunks, plats, or bridges as he shall deem necessary. **1869** *Lonsdale Gloss.*, *Plat*, a small foot-bridge.

5. A flat country, a plateau or table-land. *U.S.*

1788 J. BACKUS *Jrnl.* in W. W. Backus *Genealogical Mem. Backus Family* (1889) 20 A beautiful platt of a considerable extent. **1812** BRACKENRIDGE *Views Louisiana* (1814) 107 There are many fine tracts, and extensive platts. **1836** W. IRVING *Astoria* (1849) 248 These lofty plats of table-land seem to form a peculiar feature in the American Continents.

6. *Mining.* A widened space in a level, near the shaft, where trucks may cross, or ore is collected for hoisting, etc.

1874 J. H. COLLINS *Metal Mining* (1875) 40 Where the level meets the shaft, an enlargement is usually made; this is called a 'plat'. It is most useful as a place of deposit for the ore previous to its being sent up 'to grass'. **1897** *Daily News* 3 Nov. 9/5 As soon as the 200 feet level is reached, the intention is to open out and cut plats on both sides of the shaft.

II. A surface or place generally.

† **7.** A surface in general (whether plane or not).

[**1513** DOUGLAS *Æneis* VIII. iii. 96 This Electra gret Atlas begat, That on his schuldir beris the hevynnis plat.] **1535** COVERDALE *1 Kings* vii. 36 On the plat of the same sydes and ledges, he caused to carue Cherubins, lyons and palme trees. **1545** ASCHAM *Toxoph.* (Arb.) 124 Yf there be any whirlynge plat in the water, the mouynge ceasethe when it commethe at the whyrlynge plat. **1551** RECORDE *Pathw. Knowl.* I. Defin., A plaine platte is that, whiche is made al equall in height, so that the middle partes nother bulke vp, nother shrink down more then the bothe endes. For whan the one parte is higher then the other, then is it named a Croked platte. *Ibid.*, And the two poyntes that suche a lyne maketh in the vtter bounde or platte of the globe, are named polis. **1593** FALE *Dialling* 45 b, The making of an Horizontall Sphericall or hollow Diall... Prepare your Sphere or plat perfectly hollow, of what quantity you will.

8. a. A place, spot, point of space; a locality or situation. (Cf. PLAT *sb.*[3] I.) *Obs.* exc. *dial.*

1558 PHAER *Æneid* VII. T ij b, She seeth Æneas glad, and plattes vprise for men to dwell. **1560** INGELEND *Disob. Child* in Hazl. *Dodsley* II. 297 They need.. to sit still, or stand in one plat. **1608** WILLET *Hexapla Exod.* 731 They had stayed 40. daies in a plat. **1662** GURNALL *Chr. in Arm.* verse 18. I. liii. 419/1 He turns himself on his bed.. not an easie plat that he can find in it. **1770** LANGHORNE *Plutarch* (1879) I. 528/2 Whereas the academy before was a dry and unsightly plat, he brought water to it, and sheltered it with groves. **1828**

Craven Gloss. (ed. 2), *Plat*, place, situation..as 'I steud at that time i this vara plat'.

†**b.** A 'place' or part of a surface, as of the body; cf. PLOT *sb.* 1. *Obs.*

1642 ROGERS *Naaman* 35 And did cause each face to waxe pale, and each hand to be on the pained plat. **1658** GURNALL *Chr. in Arm.* verse 14. II. xviii. (1669) 68/2 If there be but one sore plat.

plat (plæt), *sb.*[3] Also (6 plate), 6–7 platt(e. [A collateral form of PLOT *sb.*, which arose early in the 16th c., app. under the influence of PLAT *sb.*[2]

The chronology appears to show that *plat* in sense 1 originated as a variant of PLOT *sb.* sense 2, assimilated to PLAT *a.* and *sb.*[2] through association of sense, a *plot* of ground being usually a *plat* or flat area. Hence also, through the notion in sense 2 of 'a plan on the flat', arose senses 3–5. But sense 1 being indifferently *plot* or *plat*, the same vacillation of form extended to these senses, so that they also varied with *plot*, giving rise to senses 3–6 of PLOT *sb.* Thus, in sense 1, *plat* is a variant of *plot*, but, in senses 2–5, *plot* appears to be a variant of *plat*. Both forms still survive in senses 1 and 2; in senses 3–5 *plat* has yielded to *plot*.]

I. = PLOT *sb.* 2 (which is found earlier).

1. A piece or area of ground (usually) of small extent; a patch. Often with a word defining its nature or character, as ***grass-plat, plat of grass***.

1517 *Domesday Inclos.* (1897) I. 256, ij acres of arrable ground lieng in seuerall plattes in Asseby. **1539** BIBLE (Great) *Acts* i. 18 A plat [1526 TINDALE plott] of grounde. **1557** RECORDE *Whetst.* N ij, I must multiplie .210. by it self, and so haue I the iust platte of grounde of .44,100. foote. **1565–73** COOPER *Thesaurus*, *Cepetum*, an onion bed: a plat of onions. **1573** L. LLOYD *Marrow of Hist.* (1653) 144 A certain plat of ground, almost two hundred acres. **1611** BIBLE *2 Kings* ix. 26. **1632** MILTON *Penseroso* 73 Oft on a Plat of rising ground, I hear the far-off Curfeu sound. **1667** —— *P.L.* IX. 456 This flourie Plat, the sweet recess of Eve. **1703** MAUNDRELL *Journ. Jerus.* (1732) 39 A large Quadrangular plat of ground. **1825** COBBETT *Rur. Rides* 17 Digging up their little plats of potatoes. **1885–94** R. BRIDGES *Eros & Psyche* June v, The grassy plat 'Midst of her garden, where she had her seat.

II. = PLOT *sb.* 3–6 (in which *plat* is earlier).

2. A plan or diagram of anything; *esp.* a ground-plan of a building or of any part of the earth's surface; a draught, design, map, chart; = PLOT *sb.* 3. †*to set down in plat*: to map down, make a plan of (*obs.*). Now only *U.S.*

1511–12 in Willis & Clark *Cambridge* (1886) I. 478 They can..vawte the church..after the fourme of a platte therfor devised. *a* **1517** *Reg. Vetus Coll. Merton.*, [Contract for a farme place to be bilded at Holiwell] acording to a plate drawonne for the same. **1552** HULOET, Platte for a buyldynge, *orthographia*. **1571** GOLDING *Calvin on Ps.* Ep. Ded. 1 Some description of the platte of the whole Earth. **1574** BOURNE *Regiment for Sea* xix. (1577) 49 For the making of plats or cards, as touching Hydrographia commonly called sea cards. **1598** HAKLUYT *Voy.* I. 437 To note all the Islands, and to set them downe in plat. **1659** MOXON *Tutor to Astron.* (1686) Pref., Globes, Maps, Platts, and Sea-drafts of New discoveries. **1669** STURMY *Mariner's Mag.* IV. xv. 196 To prick the same down in a Blank Chart or Mercator's Plat. **1740** *Hist. Jamaica* vii. 227 Every Surveyor shall return Two Plats upon every Survey to the Patent-Office. **1756** ROLT *Dict. Trade, Plat*, a popular term, among mariners, &c. for a sea-chart. **1893** *Scribner's Mag.* June 695/1 We ordered from the State Land Offices plats, showing the lands subject to entry. **1954** *Ann. Assoc. Amer. Geographers* XLIV. 248 Areal boundaries on the congressional township plats do not always clearly differentiate the several areal units such as marshes, prairies, wet prairies, swamps, and timberlands. **1974** *Sumter* (S. Carolina) *Daily Item* 24 Apr. 15A/4 A plat showing where the land is located must also be submitted before any transfer of land can be made. **1977** *Sci. Amer.* Sept. 184/1 (*caption*) The computer-held data in turn can be fed to a plotter that will automatically convert days of field observations into a standard surveyor's plat.

†**3.** *fig.* A plan or scheme of the actual or proposed arrangement of anything; an outline, a sketch; also, arrangement, disposition. Cf. PLOT *sb.* 4. *Obs.*

1525 *St. Papers Hen. VIII*, VI. 415 Knowing a plat and likelihode of thEmperours mynde. **1556** ROBINSON *More's Utop.* (Arb.) 167 Yea like, or rather more likely Platoes platte to excell and passe. For what Platoes penne hathe platted briefely..The same haue I performed fully. **1568** V. SKINNER tr. *Montanus' Inquisition* 48 My meaning in this place is, onely to make a platte with out any order or fashion. **1598** HAKLUYT *Voy.* I. 9 No easier, readier, or perfecter plat and introduction, is..come to my imagination. **1721** STRYPE *Eccl. Mem.* II. II. ii. 257 He desired of the said Duke to have a plat or a scheme of the said new discipline.

†**4.** A plan of action or proceeding in some undertaking; a scheme, design; = PLOT *sb.* 5. *Obs.*

1574 SIR T. SMITH in Ellis *Orig. Lett.* Ser. II. III. 39 Yt is high tyme som conclusion were made, and some plat drawen to be folowed in that enterprice of Ulster. **1584** *Reg. Privy Council Scot.* III. 681 A plat and meane quhairby his Majestie..may import a greit proffeit. **1596** HARINGTON *Metam. Ajax* (1814) 115 What think you, no Platt? is there not here a good plat laid. *a* **1656** USSHER *Ann.* vi. (1658) 264 He saw that plat fit to serve for a bridle in the mouths of the neighbouring nations.

†**5.** The plan or scheme of a work of fiction, a drama, poem, etc.; = PLOT *sb.* 6. *Obs.*

1589 PUTTENHAM *Eng. Poesie* III. xxv. (Arb.) 312 Our maker or Poet is..first to deuise his plat or subiect, then to fashion his poeme. **1602** MARSTON *Ant. & Mel.* III. Wks. 1856 I. 38 Here might be made a rare Scene of folly, if the plat could beare it.

III. in *Scottish Eccl. Hist.*

†**6. a.** The scheme for the territorial organization of the reformed church in Scotland on a presbyterian system, and for the provision and modification of stipends. Hence **b.** The body in charge of this, the Commission under the Great Seal of 1573 empowered to carry out the scheme.

1580 in *Bk. of Univ. Kirk of Scotl.* (1840) 470 It is considderit and thocht meitt, that my Lord Clerk of Register sould be requeestit to concurre with the Laird of Dun, Mrs. Robert Pont..and Johne Duncanson, or any thrie or four of them, to lay [doun] and devyse a Platt of the Presbytries and Constitutiouns therof as best appeirit be thair judgement, to be reportit be them againe the nixt Generall Assemblie. **1581** *Ibid.* 524 The Assemblie ordeaned a Platt of their Kirks to be exhibit the morne to be consulted on. **1581** *Ibid.* 535 Who sall awaite upon the platt for modifieing of the Ministers stipends. **1597** *Ibid.* 940 It was reportit be the Commissioners of the Generall Assemblie, that the constant Platt for planting of euery particular kirk, was hindred be the taksmen who hes the haill teinds in their hands, and refuseth to condiscend to any substantiall ordour anent the planting of the Ministrie. **1602** *Ibid.* 999 That command be givin to the modifiers of the platt of this instant ȝeir to assigne out of the saids pensiouns for planting of kirks. **1627** *Rep. Parishes Scotl.* (Bann.) 1 The kirk of Prestone is vnyted to the kirk off Bonckell..be the plate ordeaned to be haldin For the provisione of kirkis vnprovydit. **1637–50** ROW *Hist. Kirk* (Wodrow Soc.) 167 Everie Presbyterie is to choise one fittest to attend the Platt, with a full information of all that concerns that Presbyterie, and all the kirks therein contained. **1672** *Rec. of Inverness Presbyt.* (S.H.S.) 9 The Mod[r] asked the minister if he had ane decree of plat. **1693** WALLACE *Orkney* ix. 52 By an act of platt, dated at Edinburgh the 22 of November [1615], the several Dignities and Ministers, both in the Bishoprick and Earldom [of Orkney], were provided to particular maintainances.

plat (plæt), *sb.*[4] *Obs.* or *dial.* Also 6 plate, 8–9 platt. [A collateral form of PLAIT *sb.*, going with PLAT *v.*[3] (The spelling *plate* was prob. for *plat*, but may sometimes have been for *plait*.)]

1. A contexture of interlaced hair, straw, etc.; = PLAIT *sb.* 2. (In last quot. = *straw-plait*.)

1535 COVERDALE *Song Sol.* vii. 5 The hayre of thy heade is like the kynges purple folden vp in plates [*R.V.* tresses]. **1597** SHAKS. *Lover's Compl.* v, Her haire nor loose nor ti'd in formall plat. **1753** in *6th Rep. Dep. Kpr.* App. II. 127 Leghorn Hats..and the Platts whereof the same are made. **1837** WHITTOCK, etc. *Bk. Trades* (1842) 419 Wholly a rural business in its preparatory state, as *straw platt*. *c* **1880** *Bedfordsh. Dial.*, She wraps the plat round her arm as she makes it and stands at her door half the day.

2. *Naut.* (See quots.)

1678 PHILLIPS (ed. 4), *Plats* [*ed.* **1706** *Platts*], (in Navigation) are certain flat Ropes, by which the Cable in the Hause, is preserved from Galling. **1704** J. HARRIS *Lex. Techn.* I. *Platts* in a Ship, are flat Ropes made of Rope-yarn, and weaved one over another; their Vse is to save the Cable from Galling in the Hause, or to wind about the Flukes of the Anchors to save the Pendant of the Fore-sheet from galling against them. **1709** FALCONER *Dict. Marine* (1776) Cccb, *Lever la fourrure du cable*, to take the plat, or other service, off from the cable. **1841** DANA *Seaman's Man.* 118 *Plat*, a braid of foxes.

†**3.** A fold; a pleat; = PLAIT *sb.* 1. *Obs. rare.* (Only in spelling *plate*.)

1503 *Acc. Ld. High Treas. Scot.* II. 203 For ane elne lynnyne to the platis uptaking of the crammesy cote, xiiij d. **1530** PALSGR. 255/2 Plate of a garment, *plat, ply*. **1563** SHUTE *Archit.* Bj b, They also fashioned the body of the pilloure, and filled it with Canalicoli, and Striges, as thoughe it were the plates of her garmentes.

†**plat**, *sb.*[5] *Obs.* Forms: 5–6 playte, 6 plate, 7 plat. [a. F. *plate* (in 15th c. *plet(t)e, pleyte*) fem., also *plat* masc. (Godef.), sb. use of *plat, plate* adj., flat. Cf. It. *piatta* a barge.] A flat-bottomed boat, used for fishing, etc. (Cf. FLAT *sb.*[3] 9 a.)

1443 in Rymer *Fœdera* XI. 44 Duas Naves vocatas Playtes, quandam Navem vocatam a Cogship. **1558–9** *Act 1 Eliz.* c. 13 §3 No Hoye or Plate..from any Porte Creek or Place of this said Realme of Englande..shall trauers or crosse the Seas. **1577** HOLINSHED *Chron.*, *Hist. Scot.* 113/2 They bestowed them aborde in .xxx. hulkes, hoyes, and playtes. **1669** STURMY *Mariner's Mag.*, *Penalties & Forfeitures* 4 If any Hoy or Plat cross the Seas.

‖**plat** (pla), *sb.*[6] [F. *plat* dish: see PLATE *sb.*]

a. A dish.

1763 SMOLLETT *Trav.* vii. (1766) I. 118 The petit maitre ate of fourteen different *plats*, besides the desert. **1824** BYRON *Juan* XV. lxxiii, The simple olives,..Must I pass over ..? I must, although a favourite 'plat' of mine. **1882** ANNIE EDWARDES *Ballroom Repent.* I. 295 These suave, serious parties, with their wines and *plats*.

b. ***plat du*** (erron. ***de***) ***jour***: dish of the day; one of a restaurant's specialities on any particular occasion; also *fig.* and *ellipt.* as *plat*.

1906 W. J. LOCKE *Beloved Vagabond* (1907) vi. 71 The placarded list of each day's *plat du jour*. **1934** I. STONE *Lust for Life* v. xi. 374 The man scanned the menu, ordered a *plat du jour*, and within a moment was scooping up his soup with a large spoon. **1953** WODEHOUSE *Performing Flea* 213 We formed up in a queue, each man with a porcelain bowl for the *plat de jour* and a plate or a tin or a cigar-box for the potatoes. **1960** *Guardian* 3 Feb. 8/7 On Thursday the plat du jour will be paella. **1975** R. ROSTAND *D'Artagnan Signature* (1976) xxxvii. 210 Davis ordered the *plat du jour* and a full *pichet* of *vin rosé*. **1979** *Guardian* 26 Feb. 10/6 The Poetry Society seems to have achieved some success... The main plat du jour was the announcement of the winner of its new £1,000 prize. **1979** B. PETERSON *Peripheral Spy* vi. 147 A menu..informed him that the *plat* today was *tendrons de veau*, a favourite of his.

plat (plæt), *a.* and *adv.* *Obs.* exc. *dial.* Also 4–6 platt(e, 5 plate, *Sc.* playt, 9 *Sc.* plet. [a. F. *plat* (11th c. in Littré):—late pop.L. **plattus* adj., flat, smooth (whence also It. *piatto*, Prov. *plat*, Sp., Pg. *chato*, also Ger. *platt*, Du. *plat* flat); of uncertain history, but perh. from Gr. πλατύς broad, flat. Cf. PLACE, PLATE.]

A. *adj.* †**1.** Flat, level: plane; plain. *Obs.*

(In the first example *plat* may be considered an adv.; in the second it may possibly be a sb., 'plane plat' = level spot: cf. PLAT *sb.*[2] 8.)

[**13..** *Cursor M.* 16684 Abouen his hefd, als i yow tell, a bord was festen plate [*v.r.* plat]. **13..** *E.E. Allit. P.* B. 1379 Stalled..Prudly on a plat playn, plek alþer fayrest.] **13..** *K. Alis.* 2001 (Bodl. MS.) Platte feet & longe honde, Nas fairer body in a londe. *c* **1386** CHAUCER *Sqr.'s T.* 156 Ye moote with the plat [*v.r.* platte] swerd ageyn Strike hym in the wounde. *c* **1400** MAUNDEV. (Roxb.) xxii. 100 In anoþer ile is a maner of folk þat has a platte face, withouten nese or eghen;..þai hafe a platte mouth, lippless. *c* **1448** HEN. VI in Willis & Clark *Cambridge* (1886) I. 367, .j. cours of platt Yorkschire stone. **1456** SIR G. HAYE *Law Arms* (S.T.S.) 49 Hanyball was in the plate placis of Lumbardy. **1546** *St. Papers Hen. VIII*, XI. 76 They cannot be able in dede to resiste the Frenche menn, soo sodenly passing the plat countrie. **1570** *Wills & Inv. N.C.* (Surtees) I. 337 One dos' ½ of potendiches xviij[s]. Twoo dos' ½ of plattrenchers x[s]. **1578** *Reg. Privy Council Scot.* III. 32 All sortis of gold and sylvir, ayther in plat werk or cunyie. **1584** R. NORMAN *Safeguard of Sailors* 6 The east side is shallow and plat.

†**2.** *fig.* 'Flat', plain, blunt, straightforward, downright, unqualified; esp. in phrase ***plat and plain***. *Obs.*

c **1375** *Sc. Leg. Saints* xxx. (*Theodera*) 106 For-þi of þat thing spek nomare! For playt na [*i.e.* plat 'no'] sal be þi ansuere. *Ibid.* xli. (*Agnes*) 120 Bot scho plat nay ay said hym til. *c* **1386** CHAUCER *Knt.'s T.* 987 My wyl is this for plat conclusion With outen any repplicacion..That [etc.]. **1533** MORE *Apol.* xxiii. 141 They speke openly platte and playne heresye. **1559–60** *MS. Cott., Caligula* B. ix, Gods providence [hes] sa altered the case, ȝea changed it to the plat contrary. **1560** D. COLE *Lett. to Jewell* i, A plat and plain answer. [**1891** *Cornh. Mag.* Mar. 231 (temp. Edw. III) Let things be plat and plain between us.]

B. *adv.*

†**1.** Of position: In or into a flat position, flatly, flat; level or even with the ground or any surface.

(Some would consider *plat* an adj. in these instances.)

13.. *Cursor M.* 17709 þai fell..Gruflinges dun to erth plate [*v.r.* plat]. *Ibid.* 25045 (Fairf.) If þou plat hit lais on grounde. *c* **1400** *Rom. Rose* 1734 Whan I was hurt thus in [that] stounde, I fel doun plat unto the grounde. **1483** CAXTON *Gold. Leg.* 52/1 Alle they to gydre fille doun platte to the ground. **1549** *Compl. Scot.* vii. 70 Lyand plat on his syde on the cald eird.

2. Of manner: Flatly, bluntly, plainly, straightforwardly, without circumlocution or qualification. Often ***plat and plain***. Now *Sc.* and *north. dial.*

c **1386** CHAUCER *Monk's T.* 768 Thus warned hym ful plat and ful pleyn, His doghter. **1390** GOWER *Conf.* III. 229 Seie unto the poeple plat,..The leste finger of thin hond It schal be strengere overal Than was thi fadres bodi al. *c* **1420** HOCCLEVE *Jereslaus's Wife* 810 Be nat aferd but tell on plein & plat. **1513** DOUGLAS *Æneis* VI. vi. 6 With sic busteous wordis he thaim grat, And..gan thame chiding thus plat. **1596** DALRYMPLE tr. *Leslie's Hist. Scot.* x. 295 The Gouernour denyes and platt refuses the condicioune. **1597–8** BP. HALL *Sat.* IV. i. 53 But single out, and say once plat and plaine That [etc.].

3. Of degree: Entirely, quite, absolutely. Now only *Sc. dial.*

13.. *E.E. Allit. P.* B. 83 So þat my palays plat ful be pyȝt al aboute. **1390** GOWER *Conf.* I. 92 Thei myhte noght acorde plat; On seide this, an othre that. **1481** CAXTON *Reynard* xxxix. (Arb.) 105 Tho [= then] wende the wulf to haue ben plat blynde. **1513** DOUGLAS *Æneis* IV. vii. 59 The damecellis fast to thar lady thringis, That was in deidlie swoun plat for dispair.

4. Of direction: Directly, exactly, due, straight. Now only *Sc. dial.*

1483 CAXTON *Gold. Leg.* 395/1 Fourty dayes and fourty nyghtes after they saylled platte eest. **1511** GUYLFORDE *Pilgr.* (Camden) 69 The wynde fell platte ayenste vs. **1584** J. MELVILL *Let.* in *Diary* (Wodrow Soc.) 212 Plat contrar to the word of Chryst. **1597** BRUCE in Wodrow *Life* (1843) 179 Tended not all their speeches to end plat contrary? **1825** JAMIESON, Plet south, plet north. (Aberdeen.)

†**plat**, *v.*[1] *Obs.* Forms: 1 plættan, 4 platte, plette. *Pa. t.* 1 plætte, 4 plat, plette. *Pa. pple.* 4 plat. [OE. *plættan* to buffet, smack, f. *plætt*, PLAT *sb.*[1] So MDu. *platten*, Ger. *plätzen* to smack, MHG., Ger. *platzen* to crash, bounce, strike noisily. Cf. the frequent. Du. *pletteren* to bruise, crush, MHG. *blatren, platren* to strike noisily.]

1. *trans.* To buffet, slap, smack; to strike, knock.

c **1000** *Ags. Gosp.* John xix. 3 Hi plætton hyne mid hyra handum. *c* **1300** *Havelok* 2626 With þe swerd so he him grette, þat his heued of he plette. *Ibid.* 2755 Hwan he hauede him so shamed, His hand of-plat, and yuele lamed. **13..** *E.E. Allit. P.* B. 1542, & he with plattyng his paumes displayes his lers. *a* **1400** *Langl.'s P. Pl.* C. XIX. 50 *note*, Thenne palle [*v.r.* platte] ich a-downe þe pouke with þe þridde shoryere.

2. *intr.* To hurry, rush; (?) to move noisily (Skeat).

c **1300** *Havelok* 2282 þat he ne come sone plattinde, Hwo hors ne hauede com gangande. *Ibid.* 2613 To armes al so swiþe plette, þat þei wore on a litel stunde Greithed.

plat (plæt), *v.*[2] *Obs.* exc. *dial.* Pa. t. 4 **platte,** 6 **platt,** 6–7 **plat.** [ME. *platte*, f. PLAT *a.* Cf. Du. *pletten*, Ger. *platten, plätten* to flatten, smooth; also OF. *plat(t)ir* (f. *plat* adj.) to flatten, throw down flat (Chr. de Pisan), lie flat.]

I. 1. *trans.* To lay, throw, or cause to fall flat (on the ground, on one's face, back, knees, etc.); to spread flat, smooth, or even; to press flat.

1362 LANGL. *P. Pl.* A. v. 45 Pernel proud-herte platte hire to grounde. **1513** DOUGLAS *Æneis* IX. ix. 117 And he his hand plat to the wound in hy. **1530** PALSGR. 660/1, I platte, I stryke a thyng upon another as clay, or butter, or saulve *je saulue*... He platteth his butter upon his breed with his thombe, as it were a lytell claye. *a* **1572** KNOX *Hist. Ref.* Wks. 1846 I. 59 At which wordis, he..platt him self upoun his knees, and..burst furth in these wourdis. **1903** *Eng. Dial. Dict.* (West Cornw.), Your hair is rough; plat it down with your hands. When our mangle was broken we platted down the sheets with the iron.

†**2.** *intr.* To become flat. *Obs.*

c **1430** *Pilgr. Lyf Manhode* II. cxlvii. (1869) 134 The more men smyten it the lasse it platteth, and the more men heten it the hardere it waxeth.

†**3.** *intr.* To lie, sink, or fall down flat. *Sc. Obs.*

1500–20 DUNBAR *Poems* xxxii. 58 This wylie tod plat doun on growf. **1513** DOUGLAS *Æneis* III. ii. 52 And we plat law gruffillingis on the erd [*submissi petimus terram*]. *a* **1578** LINDESAY (Pitscottie) *Chron. Scot.* (S.T.S.) I. 222 Mr Patrick..plat on his kneis befoir the king.

II. †**4.** *trans.* To clap (*into* a place); to place, set. *Obs.* [Perh. a different word.]

1529 LYNDESAY *Complaynt* 135 Thay tuke that ȝoung Prince frome the sculis,..And haistelie plat in his hand The gouernance of all Scotland. **1567** *Satir. Poems Reform.* vi. 102 Syne plat me godly men into thair place. **1568** T. HOWELL *Arb. Amitie* (1879) 11 As Horace first his trifling toyes, in booke did place and plat. **1639** R. BAILLIE *Lett.* (1775) I. 160 Leith fortifications went on speedily; above 1000 hands, daily employed, plat up towards the sea, sundry perfect and strong bastions.

plat, *v.*[3] Also 5–7 **plate.** Pa. t. and pple. **platted;** contr. pa. t. 4 **platte,** pa. pple. 6 *Sc.* **plat(t.** [A parallel form of PLAIT *v.*, going with PLAT *sb.*[3]

The spelling *plate* appears to belong here, but in later instances (cf. quot. 1687) may sometimes stand for *plait.*]

1. *trans.* To intertwine, intertwist; to plait (hair, straw, etc.); to form (hats, etc.) by plaiting; = PLAIT *v.* 2. Now a less usual spelling than PLAIT (which, however, in this sense, is usually pronounced *plat*).

1382 WYCLIF *Exod.* xxxix. 3 He made hem into thredes, that thei myȝten be plattid with the weft of the rather colours. —— *Judith* x. 3 And she wesh hir bodi, and oyntide hirself with the beste myrre, and she platte the her of hir hed. **1483** *Cath. Angl.* 283/1 To Plate, *implicare, intricare*. *c* **1532** DU WES *Introd. Fr.* in *Palsgr.* 956 To plat heres, *trescher*. *a* **1578** LINDESAY (Pitscottie) *Chron. Scot.* (S.T.S.) I. 301 His hair was lang lyke wemens and plat in ane heid lace. **1578** T. N. tr. *Conq. W. India* 30 In wars they use their haire platted and bound about their foreheads. **1582** N. T. (Rhem.) *John* xix. 2 The souldiars platting [**1611** platted, 1881 plaited] a crowne of thornes. **1627** DRAYTON *Quest Cynthia* xix, A Fountain..Whose brim with pinks was platted. **1687** RANDOLPH *Archip.* 39 They have their hair plated [cf. *ibid.* which serves for a pettycoat..being plaited very thick]. **1687** A. LOVELL tr. *Thevenot's Trav.* I. 239 They ..plat all their Hair in Tresses. **1691** RAY *Creation* I. (1692) 124 Pieces of Rose or other Leaves which she [a bee]..plats and joyns close together by some glutinous Substance. **1773** G. FITZGERALD *Acad. Sportsman* 12 The baffled Sportsman ..Each Bush explores, that plats the Hedge with Pride. **1836** *Encycl. Brit.* (ed. 7) XII. 7/1 Hexagon mesh, formed of three flax threads twisted and platted to a perpendicular line or pillar. **1855** HT. MARTINEAU *Autobiog.* (1877) I. 26, I platted bonnets at one time.

†**2.** To fold, gather in folds; = PLAIT *v.* 1, PLEAT *v. Obs. rare.*

1687 A. LOVELL tr. *Thevenot's Trav.* III. 36 Silk breeches ..so long that they must be plated upon the Leg.

plat, *v.*[4] [In origin, a collateral form of PLOT *v.*[1]: cf. PLAT *sb.*[3]]

†**1.** *trans.* To plan; to sketch. ***to plat forth***, to sketch out a plan of (something to be made). *Obs.*

1556 ROBINSON *More's Utop.* (Arb.) 167 What Platoes penne hathe platted briefely In naked wordes,..The same haue I perfourmed fully. **1579** J. STUBBES *Gaping Gulf* C v b, Henry of Lancaster..during the time that he platted thys enterprise, founde hospitalitye in Fraunce. **1581** MULCASTER *Positions* vi. (1887) 49, I must..plat forth the whole place of exercising the bodie, at ones for all ages. **1585** ABP. SANDYS *Serm.* xii. (Parker Soc.) 222 It is not for nothing that God was so curious in platting forth the tabernacle. **1609** HOLLAND *Amm. Marcell* 387 Plotting and platting as long examinations as possibly they can to protract the time.

†**b.** To plan *to do* or *have* something; = PLOT *v.*

1596 NASHE *Saffron Walden* Wks. (Grosart) III. 85 They shuld plat (what euer their other cheere were) to haue a salt eele..continuallye seru'd in to their tables.

†**2.** To arrange or lay out on some plan. *Obs.*

1577–87 HOLINSHED *Chron.* III. 907/1 The court was platted in tables and benches in manner of a consistorie.

3. To make a plan of, to lay down on a plan or chart; to draw to scale, so as to calculate distances, area, etc.; = PLOT *v.*[1] 3. Now only *U.S.*

1751 C. GIST *Jrnls.* (1893) 61, I platted down our Courses and I found I had still near 200 M Home upon a streight Line. **1766** *Compl. Farmer* s.v. *Surveying*, So that any person, of a common capacity,..may be able to survey and parcel out land, plat it, and give up its content. **1840** CALHOUN *Wks.* (1874) III. 539 About three fourths have been surveyed and platted. **1893** *Harper's Mag.* Apr. 712/2 Professional 'boomers'..invaded the State, bought and platted additions, which they sold at exorbitant prices.

plataleiform (plə'teɪliːɪfɔːm), *a. Ornith.* [f. L. *platalea* the spoonbill (a bird) + -FORM.] Like a spoonbill in form or structure. So **plataleine** (plə'teɪliːaɪn) *a.* [-INE[1]], related to the genus *Platalea*, including the spoonbills.

platan ('plætən). Also 6- **platane.** [ad. L. *platan-us* plane-tree. See OF. *platan*, F. *platane*. Cf. PLANE *sb.*[1], PLANTAIN[2].] The Oriental plane-tree (*Platanus orientalis*): = PLANE *sb.*[1] 1.

1387 TREVISA *Higden* (Rolls) II. 303 Iacob took grene ȝerdes of populers of almand trees and of platans. **1581** T. WATSON *Centurie of Loue* Ep. Ded., I humbly make request, that..these my little ones may shrowde them selues vnder the broad leafed Platane of your Honours patronage. **1590** SPENSER *F.Q.* I. i. 9 The fruitfull Olive; and the Platane round. **1667** MILTON *P.L.* IV. 477, I espi'd thee, fair indeed and tall, Under a Platan. **1834** LD. HOUGHTON *Mem. Tour Greece* 78 The glorious platans, whose boughs uniting with those of the other side of the stream lead it on under one continual bower. **1885–94** R. BRIDGES *Eros & Psyche* Aug. ix, A forest thick and dark With heavy ilexes and platanes high.

b. *attrib.* and *Comb.*, as ***platan leaf, table, tree.***

1382 WYCLIF *Ezek.* xxxi. 8 Platan trees weren not euen to his bouwis. **1593** R. BARNES *Parthenophil & P.* Madr. iv. in Arb. *Garner* V. 347 To draw My Mistress' portrait; which, on platane table, (With nature, matching colours), as he saw Her leaning on her elbow. **1638–48** G. DANIEL *Eclog.* iii. 190 See the mad Roman, who to make more fine His Platan trees, drencht them in Showers of wine. **1851** TRENCH *Stud. Words* ii. 42 To compare the shape of this region [lower Greece] to platane leaf.

So **pla'taneous, 'platanine** *adjs.*, of or pertaining to the genus *Platanus.*

1858 MAYNE *Expos. Lex.* 974/2 Plataneous. **1656** BLOUNT *Glossogr.*, *Platanine*..of or belonging to a Plane-tree. **1658** PHILLIPS, *Platanine*, belonging to a Platane, or Planetree.

platanna (pla'tana). *S. Afr.* Also **platana, plathander.** [Afrikaans, f. PLAT *a.* + *-hander* HANDER[2].] The clawed frog or toad, *Xenopus lævis*, belonging to the family Pipidæ and native to South Africa.

1898 *Empire* 24 Sept. (Pettman), It's a platana, one of them web-footed, flat-backed, smooth-skinned, yeller frogs, with a mouth that goes all round its neck. **1911** J. D. F. GILCHRIST *S. Afr. Zool.* 224 The..Plathander (flat hand) or Clawed toad..occurs in most pools of water. **1949** *Cape Times* 21 Sept. 13/4 Two hundred female platanna frogs.. left Stellenbosch yesterday on an adventurous journey to Canada. **1961** D. M. COCHRAN *Living Amphibians of World* 52/1 The three inner toes of the platanna's hind foot..bear the short black claws. **1971** C. A. DU TOIT in D. J. Potgieter et al. *Animal Life S. Afr.* 267/2 Just over thirty years ago physiologists in Cape Town, using the platanna as a test animal, discovered and perfected the first reliable test for pregnancy.

‖**platanus** ('plætənəs). Also 8–9 **plantanus.** [L., a. Gr. πλάτανος: see PLANE *sb.*[1]]

1. = PLATAN. Also ***platanus-tree***. Now *rare.*

1398 TREVISA *Barth. De P.R.* XVII. cxix. (Bodl. MS.), Platanus..haþ þat name for þe leues þerof ben playne brode and large. **1683** EVELYN *Diary* 16 Aug., He shewed me the zinnar tree or platanus. **1707** MORTIMER *Husb.* (1721) II. 55 The Plantanus is a very beautiful Tree, and grows very well in England. **1808** SCOTT *Autobiogr.* in Lockhart *Life* I. i. 38 Beneath a huge platanus-tree..in the garden I have mentioned.

2. *Bot.* The name of a genus of trees constituting the N.O. *Platanaceæ* and consisting of from 6 to 9 species, of which *P. orientalis, P. occidentalis*, and *P. acerifolia*, are among the best known. See PLANE *sb.*[1]

platband ('plætbænd). [a. F. *platebande* (1547 in Hatz.-Darm.), f. *plate* fem., flat + *bande* band. (The French word has many senses.)]

1. *Arch.* **a.** A flat rectangular moulding or fascia, the projection of which is less than its breadth. **b.** The list or fillet between the flutings of a column.

1696 PHILLIPS (ed. 5), *Platband*, a square Member which terminates the Architecture of the Doric Order, and passes under the Triglyphs. **1723** CHAMBERS tr. *Le Clerc's Treat. Archit.* I. 105 The Plat-Band..terminating the first Story, and shewing where the second commences. *Ibid.* 107 'Tis usual to have Windows much less adorn'd; and..a Plat-Band around them. **1727–41** CHAMBERS *Cycl.*, *Plat-band*, in architecture, is any flat, square moulding, whose height much exceeds its projecture. *Ibid.*, *Plat-bands* of flutings, the lists or fillets between the flutings of columns. **1807** NICHOLS *Progr. Q. Eliz.* (1823) III. 121 *note*, Sutton Place.. furnished with a double sculptured platband of a yellowish brick earth running round it. **1854** CNT. DE WARREN tr. *De Saulcy's Round Dead Sea* II. 224 Two fillets, separated by a torus, and surmounted by an ogee and plat-band.

c. (See quots.)

(These are doubtfully English: cf. senses of F. *plate-bande* in Littré.)

1727–41 CHAMBERS *Cycl.*, *Plat-band* of a door or window, is used for the lintel, where that is made square, or not much arched. These plat-bands are usually crossed with bars of iron, when they have a great bearing. **1828** HUTTON *Course Math.* II. 175 To point out the construction..of the plat-band, or 'flat arch', as it is sometimes called. **1842** *Civil Eng. & Arch. Jrnl.* V. 251/2 Straight Arch, or Plat Band, with joints converging to a common centre.

2. *Hort.* A narrow bed of flowers or strip of turf forming a border.

1725 BRADLEY *Fam. Dict.*, *Plat-band*, a Term used concerning a Bed of Earth which borders an Alley. **1727–41** CHAMBERS *Cycl.* s.v. *Alley*, It has platbands of turf run across it from space to space. *Ibid.*, *Plat-band*, in gardening, a border, or bed of flowers, along a wall, or the side of a parterre. **1839** MRS. GORE in *Tait's Mag.* VI. 650 To content myself with the narrow limits and formal platbands of Sancta Benedicta.

platch, *v.* Chiefly *dial.* [prob. onomatopœic.]

1. *intr.* To fall in large wet spots.

1853 TAUTPHŒUS *Cyrilla* I. vi. 79 Heavy drops of rain began to platch into the half-melted snow.

2. *trans.* To besmear or splash with large wet spots.

1903 in *Eng. Dial. Dict.*

plate (pleɪt), *sb.* Forms: 3- **plate;** also 5 **plaate,** 5–6 **platt, playt(e, pla(y)the,** 5–7 **plaite, plaitt,** 5–8 **plat, plait,** 6 (*Sc.*) **pleit, plet.** [ME. *plate*, a. OF. *plate* (*c* 1175 in Littré) thin plate, lamina of metal, etc. (in form = Pr., Sp. *plata*, Pg. *prata*, It. *piatta*), in origin the fem. form of F. *plat*, *plate*:—late and med.L. *plattus, -a, -um* adj. 'flat': see PLAT *a.* (In Sp. and Pg., from the sense 'plate or disk of metal' (quasi **plata d'argento* plate of silver, coin), *plata, prata* developed that of 'silver, money', in which sense it has superseded *argento.*) Senses 13 and 14 are orig. from OF., but were reinforced in 16th c. from Sp. *plata*. In sense 15, *plate* represents OF. *vaisselle en plate*, orig. vessels (dishes, plates, etc.) of a single piece of metal (not made up of pieces), particularly of silver or gold, mod.F. *vaisselle plate* = (silver) plate. Branch III might be considered a distinct word; it represents OF. *plat* (14th c. in Littré) 'a platter or great dish; also, a dish of meat' (Cotgr.) = It. *piatto*, 'a platter, a dish, a charger, a plate'; also 'a messe or dish of meat' (Florio), med.L. *plat(t)um*, in origin the masc. or neuter form of the same adj. (quasi-late L. **vas plattum* flat vessel). But in Eng. it has run together with the senses from OF. *plate*, and is more or less associated with senses 15, 17. From the OF. *plate*, or its Romanic equivalent, came also MLG., MDu., LG. *plāte*, Du. *plaat*, MHG. *plate, blate*, Ger. *platte* a plate.]

I. A flat sheet of metal, etc.

1. A flat, comparatively thin, usually rigid sheet, slice, leaf, or lamina of metal or other substance, of more or less uniform thickness and even surface. **a.** Of metal.

In early instances, esp. in the pl., not separable from PLAT *sb.*[2] 1.

c **1290** *S. Eng. Leg.* I. 187/79 He let nime platus of Ire sum del þunne and brode..And on þe berninde plates him casten. **1382** WYCLIF *2 Kings* xviii. 16 Ezechias brake the doris of the temple of the Lord, and the platis of gold, the whiche he hadde affitchide. *c* **1400** *Lanfranc's Cirurg.* 195 Take whete & leie bitwixe two platis of iren hoot. *c* **1400** MAUNDEV. (Roxb.) xxi. 94 Þe walles within er couerd with plates of gold and siluer; and in þose platez er storys of kynges and knyghtes and batales. **1533** *Acc. Ld. High Treas. Scot.* VI. 84 For xx plaitis of quhite irne to be ane skons to the chymnay in the Kingis chalmer. **1641** WILKINS *Math. Magick* II. i. (1648) 153 A leaden bullet shot from one of these gunnes..will be beaten into a thinne plate. **1878** HUXLEY *Physiogr.* 75 A plate of polished iron or steel.

b. Of other substances.

1665 *Phil. Trans.* I. 64 Getting Plates of glass thick and broad enough. **1758** REID tr. *Macquer's Chym.* I. 292 The Sedative Salt begins to make its appearance in little, fine, shining plates, floating on the surface of the liquor. **1807** T. THOMSON *Chem.* (ed. 3) II. 613 The crystals are brilliant plates. **1831** BREWSTER *Optics* xii. 102 The method used by Sir Isaac Newton for producing a thin plate of air. **1860** TYNDALL *Glac.* I. vii. 54, I could with ease obtain plates of it [glacier ice] a quarter of an inch thick. **1900** J. HUTCHINSON in *Arch. Surg.* XI. No. 41. 17 The congestion is attended by conspicuous loosening of the epidermis from the derma in plates of greater or less size.

c. *Anat., Zool.*, and *Bot.* A thin flat organic structure or formation. ***blood-plate*** = HÆMATOBLAST a.

1658 ROWLAND *Moufet's Theat. Ins.* 985 The Bruchus... The Male..from the back to the tail it is set out with six leek coloured plates running across from the back to both sides. **1664** POWER *Exp. Philos.* I. 23 The Gloworm..the broad flat cap or plate which covers her head. **1842** H. MILLER *O.R. Sandst.* iii. (ed. 2) 73 A strong armour of bony plates. **1870** ROLLESTON *Anim. Life* 145 The ambulacral plates [of Echinoderms]. **1899** *Allbutt's Syst. Med.* VI. 597 Nor were there any blood-plates. *Ibid.* VIII. 894 The growths [of Xanthoma] occur either as thin flat plates..or as nodules or lumps.

d. A number of animal skins sewn together, for making up into fur coats or for linings, trimmings, etc.

1910 *Encycl. Brit.* XI. 354/2 A very great feature of German and Russian work is the fur linings called rotondes, sacques or plates. **1957** M. B. PICKEN *Fashion Dict.* 256/1 *Plate*,..2. Skins sewn together, but not completely fitted or finished, for fur linings; also used to make garments or trimmings. **1972** *Guardian* 11 Aug. 7/8 The [import] ban did not include 'plates'—sections of fur coats ready to be made up. **1974** *Encycl. Brit. Macropædia* VII. 816/1 Theless costly skin-on-skin method consists of sewing one full skin adjacent to another in a uniform alignment. This method is sometimes employed to sew the leftovers of full skins such as paws and flanks, into blanket-like 'plates' that are then fashioned into garments.

e. *Geol.* Each of the several nearly rigid pieces of lithosphere which are thought to make up the whole of the earth's surface and to be moving slowly relative to one another, the boundaries between adjacent ones being identified with well-defined belts of seismic, volcanic, and tectonic activity.

[**1904** H. B. C. SOLLAS tr. *Suess' Face of Earth* I. II. xxii. 600 Towards the north [of North America], however, a very extensive 'plate' without folding appears, which stretches nearly to the Arctic archipelago. **1910** *Bull. Geol. Soc. Amer.* XXI. 191 As Suess says, we do not know the character of the platforms upon which lie the seas behind island arcs; . . the platforms may be composed of ancient, crystalline rocks which moved as 'plates' without parallel foldings.] **1965** J. T. WILSON in *Nature* 24 July 343/1 Many geologists have maintained that movements of the Earth's crust are concentrated in mobile belts, which may take the form of mountains, mid-ocean ridges or major faults... This article suggests that these features are not isolated, that few come to dead ends, but that they are connected into a continuous network of mobile belts about the Earth which divide the surface into several large rigid plates. **1969** *Jrnl. Geophysical Res.* LXXIV. 4298/2 In the New Guinea mainland the zone of southerly dipping earthquakes can be associated with the northern edge of the Australian continent meeting the Pacific 'plate' and creating an overthrust zone of mountain building. **1972** *McGraw-Hill Yearbk. Sci. & Technol.* 305/1 Lithospheric plates are . . segments of upper mantle and crust, varying in thickness from approximately 5 km at ridges to 150 km under central areas of continents, that are generated by growth of crust and mantle at oceanic ridges . . and consumed in trenches. **1976** M. A. KHAN *Global Geol.* viii. 147 The lower boundary of the plates is the base of the rigid lithosphere which moves over the plastic convecting asthenosphere. The plates are therefore often referred to as lithospheric plates.

2. As a material: Metal beaten, rolled, or cast into sheets.

c **1380** *Sir Ferumb.* 1330 Þe celynge with-inne was siluer plat & with red gold ful wel yguld. **1497** *Naval Acc. Hen. VII* (1896) 88 Doubles of plate for charging ladelles. **1567** MAPLET *Gr. Forest* 10 Vpon a Stith with a Mallet it [gold] is brought into most thin leafe or plate. **1703** MOXON *Mech. Exerc.* 25 Take care when you elect this thin Piece of Plate, that it be broad enough for the Ward. **1870** RUSKIN *Wks.* (1872) III. 153 When metal is beaten thin, it becomes what is technically called 'plate'. **1881** RAYMOND *Mining Gloss.*, *Black-plate*, sheet iron before tinning.

3. a. One of the thin pieces of steel or iron composing plate-armour. **b.** (without *a* or *pl.*) Armour composed of these pieces fastened together or upon leather or some strong woven material; plate-armour: often *attrib.*: see also 20. Cf. BREAST-PLATE, etc. Now *Hist.* or *arch.*

13.. *Coer de L.* 375 For plate, ne for acketton. **13..** *Gaw. & Gr. Knt.* 2017 Boþe his paunce & his platez, piked ful clene. *c* **1386-** [see BREAST-PLATE 1]. *a* **1400-50** *Alexander* 1213 Grathed in playthes [*MS. A.* armed in plates]. *c* **1420** LYDG. *Sege Thebes* 1864 He . . armed hym in Mayle and sure platys. **1517** *Test. Ebor.* (Surtees) V. 83 Meam tunicam præliariam, quæ dicitur a cott of plait. **1594** CAREW *Tasso* (1881) 15 Playted lockes pressing with cap of plate. **1602** in Burns & Nicholson *Westmld.* (1777) 595 To be armed with jack, steel cap, plaite sleeves, plaite breeches, plaite socks. **1667** MILTON *P.L.* VI. 368 Mangl'd with gastly wounds through Plate and Maile. *a* **1674** —— *Hist. Mosc.* i. Wks. 1851 VIII. 478 Thir Armour is a Coat of Plate, and a Scull on thir Heads. **1808** SCOTT *Marm.* I. vi, Well was he armed from head to heel In mail and plate of Milan steel. **1874** BOUTELL *Arms & Arm.* x. 195 A gorget of plate at times was worn about the neck.

4. A flat piece or slab of metal, wood, or other substance, forming or adapted to form part of a piece of mechanism, etc.;

e.g. **a.** each of the parallel sheets of metal forming the back and front walls of a lock, or of a watch or clock; **b.** the circular piece of glass in an electrical machine, which generates a current when rubbed between cushions; **c.** a stiffening piece of metal on each side of the lock of a fire-arm; **d.** the flat slab for the reception of the bait in a spring trap; **e.** one of the sheets of metal of which ships' armour, steam-boilers, etc., are composed, or a similar sheet forming the bed or roof of a furnace; **f.** (*Dentistry*) the portion of a denture which fits to the mouth and holds the teeth; also, a similar portion of any orthodontic appliance; by extension, the whole denture or other appliance; **g.** a CENTRE-BOARD.

c **1391** CHAUCER *Astrol.* I. §3 The moder of thin Astrelabie is þe thikkeste plate, perced with a large hole. **1485** in Sharp *Cov. Myst.* (1825) 189 Payd for revettyng of þe plats, & for þe iiij boultes *xs.* ob. **1682** *Lond. Gaz.* No. 1768/4 He had a Case of Holster-Pistols, with *R. Silke* Engraven on the Plate of the Lock. **1703** MOXON *Mech. Exerc.* 24 To every Ward on the Plates, you must make a Slit, or Ward in the Bit of the Key. **1823** P. NICHOLSON *Pract. Build.* 219 The blade of a saw is generally called the plate. **1839** G. BIRD *Nat. Philos.* 183 When the plate or cylinder of the machine is turned, the rubber communicating to the earth by a metallic chain, if a brass knob, or a knuckle be held towards the prime conductor, a vivid spark darts between them. **1845** *Looking Unto Jesus* 17 It was then found necessary to have a plate made and fitted on her front teeth. **1863** P. BARRY *Dockyard Econ.* 231 The plate and angle-bar mills are capable of turning out 20,000 tons of plates and angle-bars annually, for ships, boilers, or bridges. **1880** CARNEGIE *Pract. Trap.* 35 The traps if baited will require about twenty grains of corn to be placed on the plate. **1884** F. J. BRITTEN *Watch & Clockm.* 199 The plates of a watch are the discs of brass which form the foundation of the movement... The plates of a clock are the two pieces of brass which receive the pivots of the train. **1895** *Outing* XXVI. 488/2 Her draft will be 7 inches, and she will carry a dagger plate of $\frac{3}{16}$ bronze. **1902** *Westm. Gaz.* 4 Nov. 8/2 The four fire-boxes will want new crown plates. **1932** E. BOWEN *To North* v. 44 Her confirmation . ., the fixing-in of a plate to correct prominent teeth, . . had all been reported to him. **1973** M. AMIS *Rachel Papers* 162, I had been coming down from Oxford about six times a year since I was ten so that he could put in and take out all the lousy braces and plates and other crap with which he tried to tame my mouth. **1977** B. PYM *Quartet in Autumn* v. 52 He had to visit the dentist, to adjust his new plate and to practise eating with it.

h. *Electr.* A metal plate that acts as a charge-storing electrode in a capacitor.

1782 *Phil. Trans. R. Soc.* LXXII. p. xxvii, An ample conductor, weakly electrified, imparts a considerable quantity of electricity to the metal plate of our condenser. **1801** *Encycl. Brit.* Suppl. I. 591/1 The mode of accumulating great quantities of fluid by means of parallel plates. **1887** P. BENJAMIN *Age of Electricity* xi. 259 The condenser will be charged with a quantity of electricity depending upon . . the surface of the plates opposed to each other, and . . the number of plates in the respective sets. **1923** E. W. MARCHANT *Radio Telegr. & Teleph.* ii. 15 A condenser can be charged by supplying positive electricity to one plate and negative electricity to the other. **1963** A. F. ABBOTT *Ordinary Level Physics* xxxv. 460 A parallel-plate capacitor is set up as shown . ., one plate being earthed and the other . . charged.

i. *Electr.* A metal electrode in a cell or battery, esp. one in the form of a plate or grid.

[**1801** H. DAVY in *Phil. Trans. R. Soc.* XCI. 397, I have found that an accumulation of galvanic influence, exactly similar to the accumulation in the common pile, may be produced by the arrangement of single metallic plates, or arcs, with different strata of fluids.] **1807** —— in *Ibid.* XCVII. 15 The strong action of a battery of 150 pairs of plates of 4 inches square. **1828** F. WATKINS *Pop. Sk. Electro-Magnetism* 15 Batteries of this construction usually consist of ten or twelve pairs of plates. **1923** GLAZEBROOK *Dict. Appl. Physics* II. 71/1 The container [of a dry cell] is made of zinc and this is used as the zinc plate. **1963** A. F. ABBOTT *Ordinary Level Physics* xxxvi. 474 In modern commercial practice the plates [of a lead-acid cell] are made of grids of a lead-antimony alloy filled with paste... Red lead (Pb_3O_4) is used for the positive plates and litharge (PbO) for the negative plates. **1970** *AA Bk. Car* 82/4 When the surfaces of both plates have turned completely to lead sulphate, the battery is flat.

j. *Electronics.* The anode of a thermionic valve.

1905 J. A. FLEMING in *Proc. R. Soc.* LXXIV. 477 It is preferable to use a metal plate carried on a platinum wire sealed into the glass bulb, the plate being bent into a cylinder which surrounds both the legs of the carbon loop. *Ibid.* 479 The resistance of these valves . . may be anything from a few hundred ohms up to some megohms, depending on the state of incandescence of the filament . ., as well as upon the size of the filament and the plate. **1915** *Electrician* 21 May 244/2 The plate of the pliotron oscillator is then connected to one of the terminals of the condenser. **1948** A. L. ALBERT *Radio Fundamentals* vi. 178 The plate usually surrounds the cathode in high-vacuum diodes. **1975** D. G. FINK *Electronics Engineers' Handbk.* VII. 21 The collector element for the electron flow is the anode, or plate.

5. a. A smooth or polished plate of metal, etc. (as in sense 1) for writing or engraving on.

1388 WYCLIF *Job* xix. 24 With an yrun poyntil, ethir with a plate of leed; ethir with a chisel be grauun in a flynt. **1571** DIGGES *Pantom.* I. xxvi. H ij b, Ye shall vppon some plaine borde, plate, or suche like, drawe a straight line. **1576** FLEMING *Panopl. Epist.* 85 Which also you haue imprinted in the tables of your remembrance, and ingrauen in the plates of your deep understanding. *c* **1595** CAPT. WYATT *R. Dudley's Voy. W. Ind.* (Hakl. Soc.) 33 Another plate of lead with her Majesties armes drawne on it.

b. Such a plate of metal, etc., bearing a name or inscription, for affixing to anything, as BRASS *plate*, COFFIN-*plate*, DOOR-PLATE, NAME-*plate*.

letter plate, a plate with a slot through which letters may be dropped, for attaching to a door.

1668 P. FISHER (*title*) The Catalogue of Most of the Memorable Tombes, Grave-stones, Plates, Escutcheons, or Atchievements in the . . Churches of London. **1807** WORDSW. *Wh. Doe* VII. 345 Plate of monumental brass Dim-gleaming among weeds and grass. **1840** DICKENS *Old C. Shop* xxxiii, Of no greater importance than the plate, 'Brass, Solicitor', upon the door. **1881** YOUNG *Every Man his own Mechanic* §1044 Letter Plates, from 1/- to 15/- each. **1894** HALL CAINE *Manxman* v. vi, A line of houses having brass plates.

c. *Photogr.* A thin sheet of metal, porcelain, or (now usually) glass, coated with a film sensitive to light, on which photographs are taken.

A ***whole-plate*** measures $8\frac{1}{2} \times 6\frac{1}{2}$ inches; ***half-plate*** (English) $6\frac{1}{2} \times 4\frac{3}{4}$ inches; (U.S.) $5\frac{1}{2} \times 4\frac{1}{4}$ inches; ***quarter-plate***, $4\frac{1}{4} \times 3\frac{1}{4}$ inches. ***dry plate***: see DRY *a.* C. 3.

1840 *Penny Cycl.* XVIII. 113/2 Thus prepared, the plate is next placed within a camera-obscura . . and the delineation of the object is then effected. **1855** HARDWICH *Man. Photogr. Chem.* 13 We are indebted to Sir John Herschel for the first use of glass plates to receive sensitive Photographic films. **1876** ABNEY *Instr. Photogr.* (ed. 3) 61 With dry plates, and on some occasions with wet plates, there is another system . . of calling forth the invisible image, and this . . is known as the 'alkaline development'. **1901** *Westm. Gaz.* 23 Feb. 8/1 He planned and built a mammoth camera to secure on a single plate a picture $4\frac{1}{2}$ ft. by 8 ft., three times as large as the largest plate ever before exposed.

d. The number plate of a motor vehicle. Chiefly in *pl.*

1950 J. D. MACDONALD *Brass Cupcake* (1955) iii. 23 She's got a grey Chevvy business coupé with Massachusetts plates. **1970** *Globe & Mail* (Toronto) 28 Sept. 27/4 (Advt.), 2 door sedan, 3 cylinder, 2 cycle. Not certified, no plates. **1973** R. LEWIS *Blood Money* vi. 67 That car . . ended in some garage with a bent mechanic stripping it, respraying it, changing the plates. **1975** *Drive* New Year 98/1 Secondhand plates are not expensive but they can be difficult to obtain.

6. a. A polished sheet of copper or steel engraved to print from; hence **b.** an impression from this; an engraving. Also short for BOOK-PLATE.

1655 MRQ. WORCESTER *Cent. Inv.* §100 All . . of these Inventions . . shall be printed by Brass-plates. **1663-** [see COPPER-PLATE 2, 3]. **1681** RAY *Corr.* (1848) 130 To imitate Dr. Plukenet, . . and thrust many species into a plate. **1762** H. WALPOLE *Catal. Engravers, List Vertue's Wks.* (1765) 19 Plate to put in lady Oxford's books. **1832** BABBAGE *Econ. Manuf.* xi. (ed. 3) 70 An artist will sometimes exhaust the labour of one or two years upon engraving a plate. **1863** LYELL *Antiq. Man* ii. 19 A series of most instructive memoirs, illustrated with well-executed plates, of the treasures in stone, bronze and bone. **1866** G. MACDONALD *Ann. Q. Neighb.* ix. (1878) 146, I am sorry to find that one of the plates is missing from my copy. **1880** WARREN *Book-plates* i. 4 Some plates possess interest for their heraldry alone, some for their topography.

c. A stereotype or electrotype cast of a page of composed movable types, from which the sheets are printed.

1824 J. JOHNSON *Typogr.* II. xxii. 657 All the plates of the Bible and Common Prayer were sent to the Chiswell Street Foundry, and there melted down. *Ibid.* 659 Stereotype plates must always be done at iron presses, on account of the vast power required to bring them off. **1839** *Encycl. Brit.* (ed. 7) XVIII. 565/1 The plates of the *Encyclopædia Britannica*, . . the most extensive work ever stereotyped. **1875** KNIGHT *Dict. Mech.*, *Plate*, a page of type, stereotype, or electrotype, for printing.

7. *Arch.* A horizontal timber at the top or bottom of a framing; often supporting other portions of a structure. Usually with defining word, as ***ground, roof, wall, window plate.***

1449 in *Calr. Proc. Chanc. Q. Eliz.* (1830) II. Pref. 54 The platez of þe same hous shullen be in brede x inchis and in thiknes viij inches. *Ibid.* 55 To all the which hous . . Thomas shall fynde plates, postes, punchons, somers, byndynges, gistes, gurdynges. **1663** GERBIER *Counsel* 72 Rafters ten and seven inches, . . Plates the same. **1703** MOXON *Mech. Exerc.* 163 *Plate*, a piece of Timber upon which some considerable weight is framed... Hence Ground-Plate, . . Window-plate, &c. **1729** DESAGULIERS in *Phil. Trans.* XXXVI. 199, AT, the upper Piece of the Crane, is an horizontal Situation, call'd the Plate of the Crane. **1731-3** MILLER *Gard. Dict.* s.v. *Stoves*, Upon the Top of this Brick-work in Front must be laid the Plate of Timber, into which the Wood-work of the Frame is to be fasten'd. **1901** *J. Black's Illustr. Carp. & Build., Home Handicr.* 68 The plate is regarded as the weakest part of a greenhouse, as it is so situated as to be almost constantly moist or alternately wet and dry. Never should a plate be left with its upper surface flat.

8. A wheel-track consisting of a flat strip of iron or steel with a projecting flange to retain the wheels, on which colliery trams are run: an early form of railroad; also ***plate-rail.*** Locally retained for a rail on an ordinary railway: cf. ***plate-layer.***

1825 J. NICHOLSON *Operat. Mechanic* 644 Bars of cast iron . . known . . by the denomination of the plate-rail, tram-way plate, barrow-way plate... The first we shall distinguish by the name of the edge railway; the second, by that of the plate railway. **1887** P. MᶜNEILL *Blawearie* 41 Pringle . . had made his way off at the far side of the cage, crossed the plates, leapt from the embankment over into the field. **1894** *Northumb. Gloss.*, *Plates*, sometimes called *tram-plates*, the rails on which colliery trams are run. The rails used on our railway lines are still known by the workmen as plates.

9. A light shoe worn by race-horses when racing.

1836 *Spirit of Times* 20 Feb. 6/2 Having the misfortune to break the plate on her left hind foot on one side, . . she was withdrawn after the first heat. **1840-70** BLAINE *Encycl. Rur. Sports* (ed. 3) §1238 Racing plates for the feet [of horses] are of two kinds, the full and the three-quarter... The plate must not be put on nearer the end of the horse's heels than there is sound horn for it to rest upon. **1937** E. RICKMAN *On & off Racecourse* vi. 130 If a horse is to be relieved of the considerable weight of these shoes, during a race they must be replaced by light plates made of aluminium or other suitable alloy. **1965** D. FRANCIS *Odds Against* viii. 119 Horses race in thin light shoes called plates... Blacksmiths change them before and after, every time a horse runs.

†10. A confection or sweetmeat made in a flat cake. *Obs.*

1355-6 *Durham Acc. Rolls* (Surtees) 555 Una libr. de plate, pr. iiij s. ij d. *c* **1440** *Anc. Cookery* in *Househ. Ord.* (1790) 455 And then take sugre plate or gynger plate, or paste royale. *a* **1483** *Ibid.* 81 In the makinge of confections, plates, gardequinces. *Ibid.*, Plaates. **1533** in Rogers *Agric. & Prices* III. 537/4 Comfits . . 1 box of plate /7.

11. *Mining.* Shale, thin slaty rock: see quots.

1794 W. HUTCHINSON *Hist. Cumbld.* I. 48 Strata of plate between the coal. **1828** *Craven Gloss.* (ed. 2), *Plate*, shale. **1839** URE *Dict. Arts* 748 It is rare in the rock called plate (a solid slaty clay) for the [lead] vein to include any ore. **1859-65** PAGE *Geol. Terms*, *Plate*, a north of England mining term for compact beds of shale, which, when exposed to the weather, break up into thin plates or laminæ. **1895** J. W. ANDERSON *Prospector's Handbk.* (ed. 6) 163 Plate—Black shale; a slaty rock.

12. The thin part of the breast or brisket of beef; also ***plate-rand.*** Cf. RAND *sb.*[1] 2.

1854 MISS BAKER *Northampt. Gloss.*, *Plate-rand*, the flat ribs of beef. **1884** G. P. KEESE in *Harper's Mag.* July 299/1 [Chicago] Plates are cut into five pieces. *Ibid.*, The division [of the carcasses] is made into . . loins, ribs, mess, plates, chucks, rolls, rumps [etc.]... 'Extra mess' is composed of chucks, plates, rumps, and flanks.

13. *Baseball* and *Softball.* A flat piece of metal or stone marking the home base; the home base itself. Also *fig.*

[**1857** *Spirit of Times* 28 Feb. 420/3 The home base and pitcher's point to be each marked by a flat circular iron plate, painted or enamelled white.] 1867 *Ball Players' Chron.* 5 Sept. 5/1 Thorne..pitched slow, 'drop' balls, many of which struck outside of 'the plate'. 1886 H. Chadwick *Art of Pitching & Fielding* 43 When the Umpire indicates the height of the ball required, the pitcher should send it in at once at the height required, but *not* over 'the plate'. 1902 *Encycl. Brit.* XXVI. 161/2 This corner is marked by a white plate a foot square, sunk level with the ground, and called the home base. 1917 C. Mathewson *Sec. Base Sloan* 172 Ellis walked to the plate and faced Chase grimly determined to get a hit. 1931 D. Runyon *Guys & Dolls* (1932) x. 224 Jo-jo squares away at the plate. 1936 *N.Y. Herald Tribune* 4 Oct. ii. 2/1 The Democrats have scored in their half of the last inning, but the Republicans still have a chance to bat. Alfred E. Smith has just come up to the plate for them. 1952 B. Malamud *Natural* (1963) 70 When Roy came up with Wonderboy, he hugged the plate too close to suit Fowler who was in there anyway only to help the batters find their timing. 1967 C. Potok *Chosen* i. 16, I went up to home plate for some batting practice. 1973 C. Sagan *Cosmic Connection* xv. 112 If he swings and misses—or, more likely, if the ball is wide of the plate—he can then go home for a two-hour nap, returning with his catcher's mitt to catch the ball. 1977 *Guernsey Weekly Press* 21 July 8/6 Rangers pushed five runs over the plate before going one down, but errors..were mainly responsible.

II. A thin piece of silver or gold; silver or gold utensils.

†14. A piece of (silver) money, a silver coin: usually in full ***plate of silver, silvern plate***; *spec.* from 16th c. the Spanish coin *real de plata*, the eighth part of a piastre or Spanish dollar. *Obs.*

c1250 *Gen. & Ex.* 2370 Fif weden best bar beniamin, ðre hundred plates of siluer fin. a1300 *Judas* in *Rel. Ant.* I. 144 Judas,..thritti platen of selver thou bere upo thi rugge. 1382 Wyclif *Jer.* xxxii. 9 Ten siluerne platys. —— *Matt.* xxvi. 15 Thei ordeyneden to hym thritti platis of seluer. c1430 Lydg. *Min. Poems* (Percy Soc.) 50 His lyneng derk, there were no platis bright, Only for lak of plate and of coyngnage. 1526 Tindale *Matt.* xxvii. 3, xxx plattes of silver. *Ibid.* 9 They toke the xxx silver plates. c1592 Marlowe *Jew of Malta* ii. ii, And if he has, he is worth three hundred plates. 1606 Shaks. *Ant. & Cl.* v. ii. 92 Realms & Islands were As plates dropt from his pocket.

15. a. Precious metal; bullion: from 16th c. usually silver, after Sp. *plata*. Now only *Hist.*

a1400-50 *Alexander* 3673 All pargeste of plate, as pure as þe noble. c1430 [see prec. sense]. 1559 Morwyng *Evonym.* 78 Some vse..a pipe of white plate or other metall, very longe, writhen into many boughtes and tourninges. 1621 G. Sandys *Ovid's Met.* ii. (1626) 219 Assumed viands straight Betweene his greedie teeth conuert to plate. 1671 tr. *Palafox's Conq. China* xxxii. 567 The buttons are ordinary of Plate, either Silver or Gold. 1702 Luttrell *Brief Rel.* (1857) V. 185 The Spanish governours..are resolved not to suffer any plate to be brought thence to Europe. 1740 tr. *Barba's Metals, Mines & Min.* 59 And find Abundance of Plate in them, which can be attributed to nothing but to the perpetual Generation of Silver.

†b. Standard of value of Spanish silver coins, as in ***old plate, new plate***, etc. *Obs.*

1676 Lady Fanshawe *Mem.* (1830) 215, 8550 ducats, plate, which is about £2000 pounds sterling. 1748 *Earthquake of Peru* i. 30 Thirteen Chests of Ryals of Plate. 1788 Rees *Chambers' Cycl.* s.v. *Coins*, Maravedis of Madrid, etc., new plate... Maravedis of Barcelona, etc., old plate. 1811 P. Kelly *Cambist* II. 188 Silver coins..Spain..Real of Mexican Plate (1775)..6¼d... Real of new plate (1795)..5d.

c. See quot. 1746. (Cf. bullion[4] 2.)

1746 Miles in *Phil. Trans.* XLIV. 161 Instead of common Thread, I used Silver and Gold Twist, or what, I think, the Ladies call Plate. 1880 L. Higgin *Handbk. Embroidery* i. 9 *Plate* consists of narrow plates of gold or silver stitched on to the embroidery by threads of silk. 1881 C. C. Harrison *Woman's Handiwork* i. 54 Bullion, passing, plate and spangles are employed in silk embroidery.

16. *Collective sing.* Utensils for table and domestic use, ornaments, etc.: a. originally of silver or gold.

c1400 *Destr. Troy* 9504 Bassons full brode, & other bright vessell; Pesis of plates plentius mekyll. 1454 *Rolls of Parlt.* V. 255/2 To ley in plege all my grete Jowellys, and the most partie of my Plate. 1489 Caxton *Faytes of A.* i. xxi. 67 A grete quantyte of plate bothe of golde and of syluere. 1530 Palsgr. 255/2 Plate sylver vessel, *uaysselle dargent*. 1583 *Rates of Customs* D vij b, Plate gilt the vnce *vs.* Plate parcel gilt ye vnce iiijs. *vid.* Plate white the vnce iiijs. 1600 Holland *Livy* xxxiv. lii. 882 Many vessels of plate of all sorts, and most engrauen. 1662 Pepys *Diary* 27 Apr., A salt-cellar of silver,..one of the neatest pieces of plate that ever I saw. 1711 Addison *Spect.* No. 15 ¶4 Whether they keep their Coach and six, or eat in Plate. 1773 *Lond. Chron.* 7 Sept. 248/3 Sacramental plate. 1846 Landor *Imag. Conv.*, *Southey & Landor* Wks. 1853 II. 73/1 The rich cupboards of embossed plate. 1885 *Law Times* LXXIX. 175/1 A service of plate bequeathed by a baronet to devolve with his baronetcy.

b. Extended to plated ware, and to other kinds of metal: usually with distinctive additions, as ***pewter plate, British plate, electro-plate***, etc.

1545 *Rates of Customs* c ij b, Plate white or blacke double or syngle hundreth pounde, *xs.* 1662 R. Mathew *Unl. Alch.* §89 Take a large Funnel of Crooked-lane plate, or of thin Brass. 1777 Sheridan *Sch. Scand.* v. i, The silver ore of pure charity is an expensive article..; the sentimental French plate..makes just as good a show, and pays no tax. 1861 M. Pattison *Ess.* (1889) I. 45 Round the apartment..was displayed..silver and pewter plate. 1889 Besant *Bell St. Paul's* III. 263 Spoons and forks of real silver, not trumpery plate.

†c. Table-ware; plates (see 19), dishes, etc. *Obs.*

1623 Lisle *Ælfric on O. & N. Test.* Pref. §4 And who but would earnestly desire that cleere and hammerable glasse of old, for plate and other utensils. 1698 Fryer *Acc. E. India & P.* 30 Their Tables, which are strewed liberally with Dainties served up in Plate of China.

d. As a non-collective *sb.*: A thin coating of metal, esp. one applied electrolytically.

1915 *Chem. News* 10 Dec. 288/1 Plates on various stock pieces satisfactorily withstood the various bending, hammering, and burnishing tests. 1946 *Trans. Electrochem. Soc.* LXXXIX. 384 The nickel-cobalt plate is whiter, harder and more corrosion-resistant than nickel deposits. 1959 T. M. Rogers *Hand-bk. Pract. Electroplating* 14 The work is..given a thin plate of Rochelle copper. 1974 P. D. Groves *Electrochem.* xii. 92 A mixture of nickel (II) sulphate and nickel (II) chloride together with a boric acid buffer and a wetting agent..produces a good plate which resists wear and abrasion, even at high temperatures.

17. *Her.* A roundel representing a flat piece of silver with a plain surface; a roundel argent.

1562 Leigh *Armorie* 150 These are called plates, because they are of Siluer, and haue no simylitude on them, but plaine round, as though they were shaped to ye coygne. 1592 Wyrley *Armorie, Ld. Chandos* 87 In cheefe three plats of siluer standen plaine. 1704 J. Harris *Lex. Techn.* I, *Balls* or *Bullets*..are never called so in Heraldry, but according to their several Colours have the following Names; *Besants*, when the Colour is Or. *Plates*, when 'tis Argent [etc.]. 1882 Cussans *Her.* iv. (ed. 3) 74 The Bezant, Plate, and Fountain are always to be represented flat.

18. Originally, in *Horse-racing*, a prize consisting of a silver or gold cup or the like given to the winner of a race; now extended to prizes in other contests; loosely, a contest in which the prize is a plate. Also *fig.*

selling plate, a horse-race the condition of entry to which is that the winner must be sold at a price previously fixed.

1639 R. Verney *Let.* in F. P. Verney *Memoirs* (1892) I. viii. 185 'My Lord Carlile's white nagg,' says Ralph, 'hath beaten Dandy, and Sprat woone the cup, and Cricket the plate.' 1675 *Lond. Gaz.* No. 1012/4 The Plate at Rowell Slade, in the County of Northampton, will be continued on the first Thursday of September, and will be worth about Forty pound. 1698 *Bodl. Charters, Norfolk* No. 533, Article 14 Every owner of any horse that starteth for this plate shall be obliged to sell such horse..for thirty Guineys, the Contributers present shall throw dice who shall be the Purchaser. 1713 Steele *Guard.* No. 6 ¶5 Not to be particular, he puts in for the Queen's plate every year. 1725 *Newcastle Courant* 28 Aug., The Lady's Plate of fifteen pounds' value by any horse, &c. Women to be the riders: each to pay one guinea entrance, three heats. 1758 Johnson *Idler* No. 62 ¶10, I had a chesnut horse..who won four plates. 1888 *Times* 26 June 4/5 He said Success was a good horse for a selling plate. 1902 *Even. Standard* 5 June, The Riddlesdown Plate of 200 sovs: winner to be sold for 200 sovs. 1910 *Encycl. Brit.* XIII. 728/2 In 1739 an act was passed to prevent racing by ponies and weak horses,..which also prohibited prizes or plates of less value than £50. 1939 Joyce *Finnegans Wake* (1964) i. 39 The classic Encourage Hackney Plate was captured by two noses in a stablecloth finish, ek and nek. 1955 *Times* 5 Aug. 4/1 Magic Key may be favourite to open the card at Lewes in the selling race. He has been placed in his last three races, being unlucky enough to come up against horses above the average for selling plates. 1979 K. Bonfiglioli *After you with Pistol* v. 22 A diet of beefsteak, oysters and Guinness would soon lift me out of the selling-plate class.

III. A shallow vessel.

19. a. A shallow, usually circular vessel, originally of metal or wood, now commonly of earthenware or china, from which food is eaten. Often with preceding word noting special use or purpose, as ***dessert-, dinner-, fruit-, soup-plate***. Also in colloq. phrases: ***to hand*** (something to someone) ***on a plate*** and varr.: to give (something to someone) without his asking or seeking or without requiring any effort or return from him; to present in ready-to-use form; ***to have a lot (enough,*** etc.) ***on one's plate***: to have a lot (enough, etc.) to worry about or cope with.

a1450 *Knt. de la Tour* (1868) 11 She drowe oute of a donghille a plater of siluer..and there come a voys to her and saide, score so longe on this plate tille ye haue hadde awey alle the blacke spottis. 1485 *Naval Acc. Hen. VII* (1896) 51 Trayes..v, Plates of tree..iij dd. 1684 *Bucaniers Amer.* iii. v. 47 The Pirats,..without any..Napkins, or Plates, fell to eating very heartily the..pieces of Bulls and Horses Flesh. 1697 Dryden *Æneid* vii. 159 Ascanius this observ'd, and, smiling, said, See, we devour the plates on which we fed. 1700 R. Sinclair in *Leisure Ho.* (1883) 205/2 Putre plats and trenchers. 1853 Mrs. Gaskell *Cranford* (1892) 61 Miss Pole..left them on one side of her plate untasted. 1894 *Cassell's Univ. Cookery Bk.* 1255 One [rack] to hold a dozen plates and three dishes. 1922 Joyce *Ulysses* 135 Gave it to them on a hot plate, Myles Crawford said, the whole bloody history. 1928 *Daily Express* 4 July 9/2 Can you tell me how many times in all she has forbidden you the house?—No, sir. Half a dozen times?—It might have been. I cannot say. I have a lot on my plate... Mr. Justice Horridge: A lot on your plate! What do you mean? Elton Pace: A lot of worry, my lord. 1935 Wodehouse *Right Ho, Jeeves* ii. 27 He can't get action when he's handed the thing on a plate. 1945 *Penguin New Writing* XXIV. 32 We haven't time to worry about D though, we shall probably have enough on our own plate any minute now. 1946 R. G. Collingwood *Idea of Hist.* 256 If anyone else..hands him on a plate a ready-made answer to his question, all he can do is to reject it. 1957 *Listener* 11 July 72 It is not often that radio is presented on a plate with such a fine natural script as these extracts made. 1959 'R. Simons' *Houseboat Killings* xiv. 142 I'll leave you at it. I've got plenty on my plate at the moment. 1960 L. Cooper *Accomplices* i. vi. 67 That was an easy one—Steyne had handed it to us on a plate. 1963 T. Parker *Unknown Citizen* iii. 78 Duggie's got a lot on his plate just now, I didn't want to worry him. 1970 *Manch. Guardian Weekly* 11 July 4 If New Zealand has the EEC door slammed in her face..car factories of Japan..would have a new market handed to them on a plate. 1973 'P. Malloch' *Kickback* xii. 78 You make that kind of mistake you're handing it on a plate to the cops. *Ibid.* xxiii. 145 The police..[have] got enough on their plate. We pull our job tomorrow while they're trying to tidy up their own mess.

b. *transf.* That which is placed on a plate; *spec.* †(*a*) a supply of food; eating and drinking (*obs.*); (*b*) a dish or course.

1577 *Reg. Privy Council Scot.* II. 634 That scho haif..siclyke assignatioun of money and victuallis for the support of hir plate as of befoir. 1686 tr. *Chardin's Coronat. Solyman* 82, I may be able to entertain him with a Plate of Pelo. 1745 Pococke *Descr. East* II. i. 11 The European pilgrims..are well served with three or four plates. 1886 Kipling *Departmental Ditties* (ed. 2) 13 Who can raise a two-plate dinner off eight paltry 'dibs' a day? a1907 *Mod.* They shared a plate of strawberries. 1971 'D. Shannon' *Ringer* (1972) viii. 138 'Oh—the low-calorie plate,' as the waiter came up. 1972 J. Wambaugh *Blue Knight* (1973) i. 19, I promised to come back Friday for the De luxe Businessman's Plate. 1974 D. E. Westlake *Help* (1975) xlii. 246 The man..recommended the roast beef plate..and the woman..said the turkey diet plate was first-rate.

c. A similar vessel of metal or wood used for taking the collection at places of worship, etc.

1779 Johnson *Prayers & Medit.* 4 Apr., I gave two shillings to the plate. 1837 McKerrow *H. Belfrage* i. 3 *note*, A plate or collection-box is placed at the entry to the place of worship, to receive the voluntary offerings of the people. 1872 Besant & Rice *Ready Money Mort.* xi, The plate came round, and caught him unprepared.

d. ***plates of meat***: feet; freq. ellipt. as ***plates***; †***plate of meat***: a street (*obs.*). *Rhyming slang.*

1857 'Ducange Anglicus' *Vulgar Tongue* 15 *Plate of meat*,..street. 1887 *Referee* 6 Nov. 7/3 As she walked along the street With her little 'plates of meat'. 1889 J. S. Farmer *Americanisms* 425/2 *Plate of meat* (Cant),..in America does duty as the name, among thieves, for a street or highway. a1896 A. R. Marshall in Farmer & Henley *Slang* (1902) V. 224/2 He is rocky on his plates, for he has forced them into 'sevens'. 1898 J. D. Brayshaw *Slum Silhouettes* 85 If a peeler heaves in sight..they'll..take a rise out of 'im with a chorus of 'Boots!' alluding to his 'plates o' meat', as they calls 'em. 1917 W. Muir *Observations of Orderly* xiv. 222 To get your 'plates of meat' frostbitten wasn't such a 'cushy wound' as it was cracked up to be. 1948 C. Day Lewis *Otterbury Incident* ii. 17 'Your clodhopping feet.' 'Plates of meat,' murmured Dick Cozzens, who is an expert in slang. 1951 P. Branch *Lion in Cellar* ix. 105 He..took off his shoes. 'Heaven!' he sighed. 'My plates have been quite, quite killing me.' 1975 P. G. Winslow *Death of Angel* xii. 229 Gawd, I wore out my plates of meat.

e. *Biol.* and *Med.* A shallow vessel, usu. a Petri dish, used to contain a medium for the cultivation of micro-organisms; freq. used inclusively of this medium.

1886 E. M. Crookshank *Introd. Pract. Bacteriol.* v. 68 The glass plates are sterilised by filling the iron box..and placing it in the hot-air steriliser, at 150° C., from one to two hours. 1896 G. M. Sternberg *Text-Bk. Bacteriol.* viii. 72 By Koch's famous 'plate method' we obtain colonies of any particular microörganism which we desire to study. 1934 A. T. Henrici *Biol. Bacteria* xii. 203 The colonies which develop upon agar or gelatine plates exhibit specific characters by which one may often identify the organism of which they are composed. 1973 R. G. Krueger et al. *Introd. Microbiol.* xiv. 388/2 On mixed indicator plates phages that are wild type for the host range character (h+) form turbid plaques because they can only lyse one of the two kinds of bacteria in the mixture, whereas the h mutants, since they lyse both kinds of bacteria equally well, form clear plaques.

f. *U.S.* A place at a formal meal or banquet, for which one subscribes.

1925 L. S. Dunway in B. A. Botkin *Treas. S. Folklore* (1949) ii. iii. 278 The committee on arrangements called on Jeff Davis at his office and wanted to know if the governor would like to have a plate at the banquet, the cost of which was $5. 1941 B. Schulberg *What makes Sammy Run?* xii. 288 They gave Sidney a testimonial dinner at the Ambassador at ten dollars a plate. 1964 Mrs. L. B. Johnson *White House Diary* 9 Apr. (1970) 105 The luncheon took place before an audience of twenty-eight hundred, who had paid $12·50 a plate. 1974 *News & Reporter* (Chester, S. Carolina) 24 Apr. 8-A/1 Tickets, priced at $3.50 per plate, are on sale with any members of the sponsoring Chester Girls Club and the Diversity Study Club.

g. *U.S. slang.* A gramophone record.

1935 *Vanity Fair* (U.S.) Nov. 38/1 None of these plates will be senders. 1937 *Amer. Speech* XII. 100 Behind the microphone they [*sc.* gramophone records] are referred to variously as *discs, E.T.'s, plates, platters, wax* and *cuts*. 1942 Berrey & Van den Bark *Amer. Thes. Slang.* §581/2 *Phonograph record*,..plate.

h. *N.Z.* and *Austral.* A plate of cakes, sandwiches, or the like contributed by a participant towards the catering at a social gathering.

1953 M. Scott *Breakfast at Six* viii. 70 Gents half-a-crown, ladies a plate... Larry explained what 'a plate' meant in the backblocks. 1962 S. Gore *Down Golden Mile* 110 We might start by having some sort of social. Nothing elaborate, you know. Just perhaps all the ladies could bring a plate. 1966 G. W. Turner *Eng. Lang. in Austral. & N.Z.* iii. 48 Newcomers to New Zealand country districts have been embarrassed by a failure to detect this semantic development [*sc.* metonymy] in the advertisements for country dances, used to ensure that the right amount of supper will be provided and the hire of the hall paid—'Gents 2/-—Ladies a plate'. Since New Zealand countrywomen are renowned for their cooking of fancy cakes, an empty plate shows up rather poorly.

IV. *attributive* and in *Combination*.

20. a. attributive (in various senses), as ***plate armour, -book, -box, -brass, -brush, -bush, -chest, -closet, -copper, -dish, -frame, furnace, -glove, -guide, -hoe, -iron, -jack*** (jack *sb.*[2]), ***-pile, -rand*** (see 12), ***-sleeve, washer, work, worth***;

(sense 1 e) ***plate boundary***; (sense 4 j) ***plate circuit, current, voltage***; (sense 13) ***plate umpire***.

1802 Bingley *Anim. Biog.* (1813) I. 127 The body of the Armadillo is covered with a kind of *plate armour. **1874** Boutell *Arms & Arm.* x. 188 Armour worn in England since the Norman conquest.. 1. First—Mail Armour... 2. Second—Mixed Mail and Plate Armour: from about 1300 to about 1410. 3. Third—Plate Armour: from about 1410 to about 1600. **1971** I. G. Gass et al. *Understanding Earth* xix. 263/1 We distinguish between a *plate boundary, the surface trace of the zone of motion between two plates, and a plate margin, the marginal part of a particular plate. **1979** C. Kilian *Icequake* v. 70 It looks now as if the ice sheet put a strain..on a series of faults on the far side of the Queen Maud Range. Tim and I are pretty sure the faults mark the edge of a plate boundary. **1683** Moxon *Mech. Exerc., Printing* xii. ¶6 A piece of *Plate-Brass. **1875** Knight *Dict. Mech.*, *Plate-brass*, rolled brass. Latten. **1868** Joynson *Metals* 120 Apply this..with a soft *plate-brush. **1844** Stephens *Bk. Farm* III. 927 A journal, which has its bearing in a close brass *plate-bush or socket. **1849** E. B. Eastwick *Dry Leaves* 173 When one is a mere depositary—a sort of animated *plate-chest. **1919** J. A. Fleming *Thermionic Valve* 224 In general the external E.M.F. required in the *plate circuit of a very hard valve is 100 volts, or even more, to produce a plate current of 3 or 4 milliamperes with the grid at zero potential. **1974** *Encycl. Brit. Macropædia* VI. 688/1 Many of these secondary electrons are attracted to the screen grid and flow in its circuit, rather than in the plate circuit, where the output should flow for greatest circuit efficiency. **1900** *Spectator* 22 Dec. 923/2, I do intend to have my cellar and my *plate-closet put under proper rules. **1766** Sharp in *Phil. Trans.* LVII. 87 Wood, and *plate-copper. **1915** *Electrician* 21 May 243/1 (*diagram*) *Plate current. **1966** T. Korneff *Introd. Electronics* vi. 198 The plate current is a function of the screen grid voltage and does not depend too much on the plate voltage. **1624** Heywood *Gunaik.* vii. 331 A Basin and Ewre with other *Plate-dishes. **1861** Fairbairn *Iron* 48 This *plate furnace in not only perfectly secure, as regards the expansion and contraction, but it is found to be economical and to answer every purpose in common with the large stone and iron-bound furnaces. *a* **1598** Rollock *Lect. 2 Thess.* (1606) 128 He wil get on a croslet and *plateglufe. **1890** *Anthony's Photogr. Bull.* III. 176 In the diagram, the heavy lines show the cut in lower board,..the light lines the upper board or *plate-guide aperture. **1881** Whitehead *Hops* 46 This space is hoed with an ordinary *plate-hoe to remove the weeds. **1703** Moxon *Mech. Exerc.* 3 Used when the work is..flat, and generally for all *Plate Iron. **1862** *Catal. Internat. Exhib.* II. x. 6 Carried on cross girders between pairs of plate-iron girders. *c* **1720** *Bewick & Graham* xxii. in Child *Ballads* vii. (1890) 147/1 He put on his back a good *plate-jack, And on his head a cap of steel. **1802** Scott *Eve St. John* iii, His plate-jack was braced, and his helmet was laced. **1879** *Cassell's Techn. Educ.* ii. 80/2 Into these grooves large plates of iron, which the engineer calls *plate-piles, are fitted and driven down. **1578–9** *Reg. Privy Council Scot.* III. 107 They..spuilyeit him of his jak, *plaitslevis, his pistolet, his belt [etc.]. **1624** *Burgh Rec. Peebles* (Rec. Soc.) 364 Ordanis to haue ane lans, ane steill bonnet and ane pair of pletsleuis and ane hagbuit. **1967** *Boston Herald* 1 Apr. 17/4 The area around home plate was especially soft and with two sinker ball pitchers working, *plate umpire Larry Nap had a terrible time. **1922** *Encycl. Brit.* XXXII. 1027/2 The *plate voltage of the oscillating valve is not supplied by a high voltage battery but at most by a few cells. **1966** Plate voltage [see *plate current* above]. **1874** Thearle *Nav. Archit.* 134 A hexagonal *plate washer. *a* **1400–50** *Alexander* 3223 Polischid all of pure gold & of *plate werkis. **1654** Whitlock *Zootomia* 355 This Touchstone of solid and *plate worth (as I may tearm it).

b. Objective, instrumental, simulative, etc., as ***plate-bender, -keeper, -lifter, -roller, -warmer; plate-collecting, -glazing, -making, -printing, -tossing; plate-bending, -buttoned, -cutting, -encased, -formed, -glazed, -like, -rolling, -shaped*** adjs.

1884 Knight *Dict. Mech.* Suppl., **Plate Bender*, a round bitted pincers, for bending dental plates without showing the pinch marks. **1875** *Ibid.* 1737/1 **Plate-bending Machine*, a machine for bending plates of metal to any required curve for boilers, water-wheel buckets, etc. **1727** Somerville *Bowling-Green* Poems 68 Attorneys spruce, in their *Plate-button'd Frocks. **1898** *Westm. Gaz.* 19 Apr. 10/1 The earliest reference to *plate collecting dates from 1835, when the Rev. Daniel Parsons wrote a short article on book-plates. **1861** Fairbairn *Iron* 117 At the Paris Universal Exhibition ..a *plate-cutting machine was exhibited. **1854** H. Miller *Sch. & Schm.* xxiv. (1858) 526, I could find in our recent fishes..no such *plate-encased animals as the various species of *Coccosteus* or *Pterichthys*. **1597** A. M. tr. *Guillemeau's Fr. Chirurg.* cj b/1 A *Plate-formed Cauterye, to cauterize the bone and the fleshe, and the whole parte. **1915** J. Southward *Mod. Printing* (ed. 3) II. xxx. 258 *Plate-glazed Paper is finished by being placed sheet by sheet between copper or zinc plates... The pile is pressed through powerful rollers. **1911** *Encycl. Brit.* XX. 734/2 The *plate-glazing process is adopted mainly for the best grades of writing-papers, as it gives a smoother, higher and more permanent gloss than has yet been imitated by the roll-calender. **1962** F. T. Day *Introd. Paper* iv. 47 Plate glazing is carried out by passing the paper between zinc plates and pressing it to give the desired finish. **1888** *Pall Mall G.* 24 Apr. 1/2 His employment was one of great trust, he being the *platekeeper of the Guards' mess at St. James's Palace. **1862** G. P. Scrope *Volcanos* 139 Thin *plate-like crystals of felspar. **1901** *Westm. Gaz.* 28 Feb. 3/2 The other very low and broad plate-like hats of the Louis Quinze and Louis Seize periods. **1939** R. R. Karch *Printing & Allied Trades* (ed. 2) xviii. 180 (*heading*) Offset *Plate Making. **1967** E. Chambers *Photolitho-Offset* iii. 31 A good reproduction proof..becomes copy and is photographed in the normal way for plate-making. **1839** Ure *Dict. Arts* 706 The shingling and *plate-rolling mill. **1837** Thackeray *Ravenswing* vii, Under the sideboard stands..a..*plate-warmer. **1875** Knight *Dict. Mech.*, *Plate-warmer*, a small cupboard standing in front of a fire and holding plates to warm.

21. Special Combinations: **plate-basket**, (*a*) a baize-lined basket in which silver spoons, forks, etc. are kept; (*b*) a metal-lined basket for removing plates and the like which have been used at table; **plate-black**: see quot.; **plate-bolt**, (*a*) a bolt which slides on a flat plate; (*b*) a bolt having a wide flat head; **plate-bone**, (*a*) ? cf. buckler *sb.*[2] 3; (*b*) the shoulder-blade; **plate-bulb**, a thickened edge in an iron plate, having a cross-section of mushroom form; **plate camera**, a camera designed to take photographs on coated glass plates rather than film; **plate-clutch**, a form of clutch in which the engaging surfaces are flat metal plates; † **plate-coat**, a coat of mail of plate; **plate count**, an estimate of cell density in milk, soil, etc., made by inoculating a plate (sense 19 e) with a suitably diluted sample and counting the number of colonies that appear; **plate-cultivation, -culture** (of micro-organisms): see quot. 1895; **plate cylinder**, in a rotary printing press, the cylinder to which printing plates are attached; **plate-day**, the day of the race for a plate; **plate electrical machine**: see *plate machine* (*a*); **plate-gauge**, a gauge consisting of a plate with edges notched in progressive order, for measuring the thickness of metal plates; **plate girder**, a girder formed of a plate or plates of iron or steel; **plate-hat**, a hat having a nap of finer material than the body (*Cassell's Encycl. Dict.* 1886); **plate-holder** *Photogr.*, a frame impervious to light in which sensitized plates are contained; **plate-horse** = plater 3; **plate-kiln**, a form of malt-kiln; **plate-knee**, a metal knee consisting of two flat plates giving an extended surface for the bolts; † **plate-lace**, silver or gold lace: cf. sense 15 c; **plate-lap** *Shipbuild.*, the overlapping of the plates covering the sides of a ship; **plate-lead**: see platine, quot. 1797; **plate-leather**, wash-leather for rubbing and polishing silver plate, etc.; **plate-line** = plate-mark 2; **plate-lock**, a lock having the outer case of wood, commonly used on outside doors; also, a lock in which the works are pivoted on an iron plate; **plate machine**, (*a*) a machine for producing electricity, in which a cushion rubs against a revolving plate of glass; (*b*) a variation of the potter's wheel adapted for making table-ware, plates, dishes, etc.; **plate-matter**, stereotype matter for newspapers such as is sometimes supplied from a central establishment to local journals; **plate metal**, (*a*) see quot. 1861; (*b*) = *plate pewter*; **plate mill**, a rolling mill for metal plates; **plate mundic, plate-nail, plate-of-wind** (in an organ): see quots.; **plate-painter**, one who paints decorative designs on china, etc.; **plate-paper**, paper of fine quality on which engravings are printed; **plate pewter**, the hardest variety of pewter, used for plates and dishes; **plate pie** (see quot. 1946); **plate-piece of eight** = piece of eight (see sense 14, and piece *sb.* 13 c); **plate-powder**, a polishing powder for silver plate and silver ware generally; **plate-printer**, a workman who prints from plates; **plate-rack**, a rack or frame in which plates are placed to drain, or in which they are usually kept; (on board ship) a closed cupboard in which plates are kept; also, a grooved frame for draining photographic plates; **plate-rail** = 8; so **plate-railway**; **plate-rock, plate-shale** *Mining* = 11; **plate-roll**, a smooth roller for rolling metal plate or sheet; **plate-room**, (*a*) a room for keeping plate (sense 16); (*b*) = *plate-safe*; **plate-safe** (see quot.); **plate-shears**, strong hand-shears for cutting sheets of metal; also, a powerful machine for cutting boiler- or armour-plates, etc.; **plate-ship**, a vessel carrying silver, a ship of the plate fleet; **plate-shy** *a. Baseball* (see quots.); † **plate silver** = silver plate; **plate tectonics** *Geol.*, a theory of the earth's surface based on the concepts of moving plates (plate *sb.* 1 e) and sea-floor spreading, used to explain the distribution of earthquakes, mid-ocean ridges, deep-sea trenches, and orogenic belts; hence **plate-tectonic** *a.*, **plate tectonicist**; **plate tracery** *Arch.*: see quots.; **plate-way**, a plate-railway; **plate-wheel**, a wheel in which the hub is connected with the rim by a plate, instead of by spokes; **plate-worker**, † (*a*) one who works in gold or silver (*obs.*); (*b*) a worker in sheet-metal. Also plate fleet, plate-glass, plate-layer, etc.

1838 Dickens *O. Twist* xxviii, I..seized the loaded pistol that always goes up-stairs with the *plate-basket. **1870** Miss Bridgman *Rob. Lynne* I. xiii. 220, I shouldn't care to leave any of them alone with my plate-basket. **1889** *Cent. Dict.* s.v. *Black*, **Plate-black*, a combination of lampblack and bone-black..used in plate-printing. **1703** T. N. *City & C. Purchaser* 33 *Plate, and Spring-bolts..to fasten Doors and Windows. **1839** *Encycl. Brit.* (ed. 7) XIX. 290/2 One of the most perfect securities for a beam-end..is the plate-bolt... The extreme end of the beam is tied downward by bolts. *a* **1648** Digby *Closet Open.* (1677) 126 Take any bones..as the Ribs, the Chine bones, the buckler *Plate-bone. **1693** *Phil. Trans.* XVII. 975 The lateral Fins..being excarnated, are like the whole Arm, with a Plate-bone, Shoulder-bone. **1874** Thearle *Naval Archit.* 110 This method is also sometimes employed in forming the arms of *plate bulb beams, but in this case the end of the beam must be heated and cut, and the lower part bent. **1937** *Discovery* June 177/2 Really good second-hand *plate-cameras can be bought quite cheaply. **1956** *Focal Encycl. Photogr.* 868/1 Plate cameras are generally larger than film cameras. **1977** *Times* 31 Aug. 10/4 A man peering through a large plate camera at them. **1906** *Plate clutch [see *disc-clutch* s.v. disc *sb.* 8 f]. **1960** *Farmer & Stockbreeder* 5 Jan. 95/2 Power..is transmitted via an independent plate-clutch. **1542** Udall *Erasm. Apoph.* ii. 277 b, An helmet & a Jacke or *platecote hideth all partes of a manne sauyng the legges. **1677** *Lovers Quarrel* 278 in Hazl. *E.P.P.* II. 264 Thou'st have the horse with all my heart, And my Plate Coat of silver free. **1901** *Jrnl. Hygiene* I. 301 The effect of the ice-packing upon the number of colonies appearing in the ordinary *plate count has been already discussed. **1928** *Jrnl. Bacteriol.* XVI. 270 The manner of making plate counts which prevails in public-health and other laboratories where daily counts are made on a number of samples of milk. **1956** *Nature* 4 Feb. 221/1 The time of soaking and shaking the leaves before plating influenced the plate-count. **1972** *Ann. Rep. Freshwater Biol. Assoc.* XL. 41 Bacterial numbers as shown by plate counts. **1886** Klein *Microorganisms & Disease* (ed. 3) 41 One of the best methods for isolation is that of *plate cultivation introduced by Koch [1883] in connection with the choleraic comma bacilli. **1895** *Syd. Soc. Lex.*, *Plate-cultivation, Plate-culture*, term for the method of cultivating micro-organisms in nutrient media spread out on glass plates... The term is also used for the colonies thus grown. **1886** Biggs tr. *Hueppe's Methods of Bacteriol. Investig.* 140 An enormous number of germs can in this way be certainly separated from one another in a single *plate culture. **1899** *Allbutt's Syst. Med.* VIII. 900, 6799 colonies developed in a plate culture by the end of two days. **1932** Place & Clunes in W. Atkins *Art & Practice of Printing* II. xi. 192 The *plate-Cylinder is made to carry the curved plates; plate-Cylinders have to be very accurately ground. **1973** J. Moran *Printing Presses* xiii. 198 It [*sc.* the plate] was then placed in a bending box, where it received the appropriate curvature to enable it to lie on the plate cylinder. **1704** *Lond. Gaz.* No. 4000/4 Galloways..to be kept in Ipswich..till the *Plate-day. **1849** Noad *Electricity* (ed. 3) 25 The *Plate Electrical Machine..consists of a circular plate of thick glass, revolving vertically by means of a winch between two uprights [etc.]. **1849** W. Fairburn *Acct. Construction Britannia & Conway Tubular Bridges* i. 176 Is there anything new in this application of wrought-iron *plate girders? **1891** *Notes Building Construction* iv. viii. 154 The web of a plate girder being very thin can bear but a very small part of the direct stresses. **1950** *Engineering* 8 Dec. 465/3 Mr. Dean, in his report on metal under-bridges, concluded that plate girders are the most economical and satisfactory form of construction for the main girders. **1875** Knight *Dict. Mech.* 1738/2 Inside frames..are used within the *plate-holder for making small negatives. **1894** *Outing* (U.S.) XXIV. 63/1 A waterproof carrier, which contained my camera-top, plate-holders and plates. **1810** *Sporting Mag.* XXXVI. 158 He afterwards was a very capital *plate horse. **1851** Nimrod *Road* 14 He had been a fair plate horse in his time. **1743** *Lond. & Country Brew.* iii. (ed. 2) 173 The *Plate-Kiln, and the Tile-Kiln, which are full of small Holes, were invented to dry brown Malts, and to save Charges. **1839** *Encycl. Brit.* (ed. 7) XIX. 290/2 Robert's *plate-knee is a very strong method of fastening [a beam-end to the side of a ship]. **1600** in Nichols *Progr. Q. Eliz.* (1823) III. 510 Garnished with buttons and loopes, of *plate lace of Venice silver. **1890** W. J. Gordon *Foundry* 62 The *plate-laps, ribbands, stringers, and deck-beams. **1782** *Encycl. Brit.* (ed. 2) IX. 6711/1 The high-lisses, or lists, are a number of long threads, with platines, or *plate-leads, at the bottom. **1797** [see platine]. **1931** A. Esdaile *Student's Man. Bibliogr.* v. 151 All intaglio engravings will show a '*plate-line'; the paper which is pressed by the plate is smooth and sunk, while beyond the edge of the plate it keeps its natural surface; the resulting line is called the plate-line. **1961** T. Landau *Encycl. Librarianship* (ed. 2) 281/1 *Plate line*, a characteristic mark in intaglio printing, especially of engravings, due to the great pressure exerted by the engraving press on the paper. **1365–6** in *Archæol.* (1857) XXXVII. 25 Stock-locks, *plate-locks,..clykett-locks. **1485** *Rec. St. Mary at Hill* 29 Ther is, for the postern gate, a plate locke with a bolte, yryn, & ij keyes. Also v plate lockes with v cleket keyes. **1891** *N. & Q.* 7th Ser. XI. 313/2 Plate lock is still the trade term in Wolverhampton and elsewhere for a stock lock, i.e., a lock of which the outer case is wood, usually oak. **1789** Nicholson in *Phil. Trans.* LXXIX. 269 *Plate machines do not collect more electricity than cylinders..do with half the rubbed surface. **1849** Noad *Electricity* (ed. 3) 83 Five turns of a two feet plate-machine ..were sufficient to produce a bubble of gas on the negative point. **1887** Z. L. White in *Westm. Rev.* CXXVIII. 862 This '*plate-matter' became at once so popular with country publishers that new features were from time to time introduced... Today one of these 'plate-matter' manufacturing firms has branch offices and foundries in New York, Boston..Chicago..San Francisco... It furnishes matter for almost every department of a newspaper except editorial articles and local news. **1668–9** in C. Welch *Hist. Worshipful Co. Pewterers* (1902) II. 140 It is..agreed..that..every person that taketh Hollow-ware of any workman & returneth not him for the same ½ *plate mettle and ½ London Trifles, shall pay unto such workman [etc.]. **1831** J. Holland *Manuf. Metal* I. 84 The quantity of plate metal put into the furnace at once varies, according to circumstances. **1861** Fairbairn *Iron* 90 From the refinery the metal is run out into large moulds, and is then broken up into what is technically distinguished as 'plate metal'. **1867** *Engineering* 4 Jan. 1/2 In the reversing *plate mill at the London and North-Western Steel Works..the reversal of the motion of the rolls is effected by reversing the..engines. **1964** *Recent Progr. Metal Working* ii. 39 Automatic control of a plate mill entails..control of gauge in the last cross-rolling and last finishing pass. **1797** *Encycl. Brit.* (ed. 3) XII. 126/1 Iron..mixed.. With arsenic; called *mispickel* by the Germans, and *plate mundic in Cornwall. **1851** GREENWELL *Coal-trade Terms Northumb. & Durh.* 39 **Plate Nails*, used, in laying tramway, to nail the plates to the sleepers. **1894** *Northumb. Gloss.* s.v., A plate-nail is driven through a hole in the plate, which is countersunk to receive the head of the nail. **1875** KNIGHT *Dict. Mech.*, **Plate-of-wind*, in the construction of organ-pipes, a thin aperture whence a sheet of air issues, impinging upon the lip of the mouth and receiving a vibration which is imparted to the column of air in the pipe. **1875** W. CORY *Lett. & Jrnls.* (1897) 379 Do not Minton's *plate-painters enjoy the same freedom of invention as middle-age stone-carvers? **1879** *Print. Trades Jrnl.* XXIX. 6 Printed on superfine *plate-paper. **1839** URE *Dict. Arts* 952 The *plate pewter has a bright silvery lustre when polished. **1911** *Encycl. Brit.* XXI. 339/1 Plate pewter (100 parts of tin, 8 of antimony, 4 of copper and 4 of bismuth). **1946** F. M. MCNEILL *Recipes from Scotland* 13 A *plate-pie, *i.e.*, with pastry above and below the filling. **1975** *Times* 19 July 11/4 Rhubarb plate pie. **1673** TEMPLE *Ess. Irel.* Wks. 1731 I. 111 In 1663, when the *Plate-pieces of Eight were raised three Pence in the Piece. **1786** J. WOODFORDE *Diary* 24 Apr. (1926) II. 241 For some *plate Powder at Chases p^d 0. 1. 0. **1877** J. H. EWING in *Aunt Judy's Mag.* 146 The over-bearingness of the butler,..the inferior quality of the new plate-powder. **1883** *Chambers's Encycl.* VII. 585/1 A plate-powder is..sometimes made by levigating quicksilver with twelve times its weight of prepared chalk [etc.]. **1976** *Century of Trade Marks* (Patent Office) 44 There is no longer any general need for such things as plate powder, polishing paste and blacking. **1889** *Cent. Dict.*, *Plate-printer. **1902** *Encycl. Brit.* XXXIII. 414/2 Plate Printers' Union of United States, National Steel and Copper. **1921** *Dict. Occup. Terms* (1927) §529 *Printer, plate*, prints from copper or steel plates, on which design or lettering is sunk below surface of plate, instead of being raised as in letterpress work. **1807–8** SYD. SMITH *Plymley's Lett.* v. Wks. 1859 II. 153/2 Making a gallant defence behind hedge-rows, and through *plate-racks and hencoops. **1862** C. P. SMYTH *Three Cities in Russia* II. 140 Furnished in the corners with towering plate-racks, holding a number of gold and silver dishes. **1825** *Plate-rail, plate-railway [see sense 8]. **1839** URE *Dict. Arts* 982 The rails [in a coal-mine] are called tram-rails, or plate-rails, consisting of a plate from 3 to 4 inches broad, with an edge at right angles to it of about two inches and a half high. **1900** A. ADDERLEY in *Speaker* 29 Dec. 349/1 Much of the land being nothing but *plate rock. **1861** W. FAIRBAIRN *Iron* 111 The cylindrical part B, for *plate-rolls should be slightly concave. **1930** *Engineering* 7 Nov. 579/2 (*heading*) Plate-roll finishing machine. **1888** *Plate room [see *plate-safe*]. **1931** *N. & Q.* 10 Oct. 262/2 The plate-room..is a strong steel and fireproof apartment. **1888** *Encycl. Brit.* XXIII. 710/1 The *plate-safe or plate-room is the repository of the stereo and electro plates. **1881** RAYMOND *Mining Gloss.*, **Plate-shale*, a hard argillaceous bed. **1599** A. M. tr. *Gabelhouer's Bk. Physicke* 112/1 With a greate payre of *platesheares cut the same of such a longitude as you desire to have it. **1861** FAIRBAIRN *Iron* 116 Before the introduction of the plate shears, they were used to cut boiler plates. **1884** *Sat. Rev.* 14 June 770/2 The Spanish Government also might..sell a concession to raise the *plate-ships sunk in Vigo Bay. **1912** C. MATHEWSON *Pitching* iv. 90 For a long time, 'Josh' Devore, the Giant's left-fielder was '*plate shy' with left-handers—that is, he stepped away. **1942** BERREY & VAN DEN BARK *Amer. Thes. Slang* §677/37 *Plate-shy*, afraid to stand close to the plate. **1756** C. LUCAS *Ess. Waters* II. 20 [It] sticks to the surface of *plate silver and tarnishes it. **1972** *Sci. Amer.* May 59/1 According to the *plate-tectonic view, continents and oceans are rafted along by the same crustal conveyor belt. **1976** *Nature* 9 Sept. 118/1 In the plate tectonic model, the Himalaya is considered to be the classic example of a continent-continent collision system. **1973** *Ibid.* 30 Nov. 263/1 They are in disagreement with the views of some *plate tectonicists who wish to have the whole 500 km shift take place after mid-Miocene. [**1966** *Bull. Geol. Soc. Amer.* LXXVII. 707 The folds and faults mapped at the surface [near the San Andreas fault] are attributed to raft tectonics whereby a passive surficial plate is deformed as it rides coupled to a moving under-mass.] **1969** *Sci. Jrnl.* Aug. 40/2 *Plate tectonics..has shown its ability to predict, amongst other things, the direction of the movement accompanying earthquakes. **1972** *Observer* (Colour Suppl.) 13 Feb. 12/1 During the past five years, there has been a revolution in the Earth Sciences, involving a theory called plate tectonics. **1976** *McGraw-Hill Yearbk. Sci. & Technol.* 314/1 The widespread acceptance by the earth sciences community of plate tectonics has had a revitalizing effect on many research fields, but none more so than paleobio-geography, the study of the factors controlling the distribution of fossil organisms. **1855** STREET *Brick & Marble* xii. 264 The tracery commonly called *plate tracery ..only calls attention to the piercings here and there in the large block of stone or marble. **1875** PARKER *Gloss. Archit.* s.v. *Plate*, Plate tracery is..that kind of solid tracery which appears as if formed by piercing a flat surface with ornamental patterns. **1876** GWILT *Archit.* III. iii. 958 The only tracery which can be properly executed in brick is in fact the simplest plate tracery. **1825** J. NICHOLSON *Operat. Mechanic* 547 The bars or plates of metal of which railways and *plate-ways are composed. **1882** *Society* 28 Oct. 8/2 Liverpool..is for constructing a special and novel form of a road called a 'plateway', along which lorries and ordinary carts may be drawn in a string by a traction engine or by horses. **1835** URE *Philos. Manuf.* 275 The axis of the *plate-wheel lies in a curvilinear slot. **1884** W. S. B. MCLAREN *Spinning* (ed. 2) 139 The bottom cone is in gear..with the main wheel of the differential motion called the 'crown wheel', or sometimes the 'plate wheel'. **1670** *Canterb. Marriage Licences* (MS.), Samuel Kannon, civitatis Cant', *plateworker. **1773** in *Reliquary* Jan. 26 An Account of the Number of Goldsmiths, Silversmiths, and Plateworkers,.. within the Town of Newcastle-upon-Tyne. **1906** *Athenæum* 20 Jan. 70/3 The Wire-workers, who were closely associated, if not indeed identical, with the Plate-workers, appear to have remained..a branch of the Girdlers' Company at least as late as..1685.

plate (pleɪt), *v.* [f. PLATE *sb.*, or (?) a. OF. *plater* to plate (Godef.).

Late OE. had app. a vb. *platian* to make into thin plates (cf. sense 3), evidenced by the vbl. sb. *platung* and pa. pple. *aplated* (gold) beaten into thin plate; derived from late L. or early med.L. *platum* (sc. *aurum*) gold in thin plate; but this has app. no historical connexion with *plated* in Chaucer.

a **1000** *Aldhelm Gloss.* (Napier) 450 *Obrizum*, aplatad. *Ibid.* 2118 *Obrizo*, aplatedum. *Ibid.* 3534 *Obrizum, .i. aurum optimi coloris*, smæte gold, platum. *a* **1000** *Ags. Gloss.* in Wr.-Wülcker 196/24 *Brateolis, laminis*, platungum.]

1. *trans.* **a.** To cover or overlay with plates of metal, for ornament, protection, or strength; in late use, to cover (ships, locomotives, etc.) with armour-plates.

c **1384** CHAUCER *H. Fame* III. 255 Flore and roof and alle Was plated half a foote thikke Of gold. **1533** *Acc. Ld. High Treas. Scotl.* VI. 81 Ane harnes doublat, platit upoun the gardeis. **1622** MABBE tr. *Aleman's Guzman d'Alf.* (1623) 60 The Rivers plated with silver streames..may much cheere and glad thy heart. **1776** G. SEMPLE *Building in Water* 95 They are to be dovetailed and plaited with half flat Bar-iron. **1862** W. H. RUSSELL in *Times* 27 Mar., Paddlewheel merchant steamers which have been plated. **1889** HENTY *With Lee in Virginia* (1890) 128 The *Merrimac*, a steamer which the Confederates had plated with railway iron.

b. *Surg.* To treat (a fracture) by fixing a metal plate to both the fractured parts so as to hold them together; to attach a plate to (a bone).

1910 *Brit. Med. Jrnl.* 8 Oct. 1064/2 It..did the progress of surgery a disservice to suggest that to plate a fracture was a matter lightly to be undertaken. **1948** [see FIXATION 3 c]. **1959** A. G. APLEY *Syst. Orthopaedics & Fractures* xi. 110 When a fracture has been plated, the technique of 'delayed splintage' is of great value. *Ibid.* xxi. 256 If closed reduction of a radius and ulna has failed.. the bones should..be plated.

2. a. To cover with a thin coating or film of metal; *esp.* to cover articles made of the baser metals with gold or silver; also iron with tin. Also *fig.*

a **1704** T. BROWN *Sat. Quack* Wks. 1730 I. 63 The beast was thinly plated with the man. **1706** PHILLIPS, To *Plate*, to cover with a thin Plate of Gold, or Silver; as To Plate Brass-Money. **1760** H. WALPOLE *Let. to G. Montagu* 1 Sept., One man there [at Sheffield] has discovered the art of plating copper with silver. **1839** URE *Dict. Arts* 999 In plating copper wire, the silver is first formed into a tubular shape. **1855** *Mechanics Mag.* 7 July 4/1 A patent has recently been obtained..for an improved process for plating or coating lead, iron, or other metals with tin, nickel, or alumina. **1879** FROUDE *Cæsar* x. 111 The oars of the galleys of their [buccaneers'] commanders were plated with silver. **1919** *Rep. Progr. Appl. Chem.* IV. 255 A lead anode is employed when plating with lead. **1929** *Ibid.* XIV. 322 Automobile parts..to be plated with nickel or chromium. **1940** A. MORGAN *Things a Boy can do with Electrochem.* xii. 177 It is an easy matter to plate iron, steel, and brass articles with copper or nickel. **1966** *McGraw-Hill Encycl. Sci. & Technol.* IV. 531/2 Chromium plating is conducted from solutions containing chromic acid and sulfuric acid... For irregular shapes, auxiliary anodes must be used to plate the surface completely. **1968** *Rep. Progr. Appl. Chem.* LIII. 68 Smith and Lewis..successfully plated toughened polystyrene.

b. with *on, upon*, and construction reversed. Also, to deposit as a coating, esp. electrolytically.

1790 KEIR in *Phil. Trans.* LXXX. 367 Among the manufactures at Birmingham, that of making vessels of silver plated on copper is a very considerable one. **1878** GLADSTONE *Prim. Homer* 134 We are told of the rare artificer, instructed by Hephaistos and Athenè, who plated gold upon silver, and so produced beautiful works. **1919** *Rep. Progr. Appl. Chem.* IV. 255 Nickel can be plated directly on aluminium. **1947** *Electronic Engin.* XIX. 161/3 The chemical reduction method of plating nickel on steel is too expensive to replace electrodeposition. **1959** T. M. ROGERS *Hand-bk. Pract. Electroplating* 218 Nickel is normally plated from an acid solution. **1972** I. ASIMOV *Asimov's Guide to Science* (1975) I. v. 291 Attempting to plate a silicon layer on a platinum surface... The expected plating did not occur. **1979** *Sci. Amer.* May 71 (Advt.), Man has been plating chromium for over a century.

3. To make or beat (metal) into plates. *rare*$^{-0}$.

1706 PHILLIPS, *Plate*,..to bring any Metal into Plates or thin Pieces. **1755** in JOHNSON; and in mod. Dicts.

4. To make a stereotype or electrotype plate of (type) for printing. Cf. PLATE *sb.* 6 c.

a **1907** *Mod.* Page 227 has been plated and the type distributed.

5. To shoe (a horse) with plates (PLATE *sb.* 9).

1674 *Rutland MSS.* (1905) IV. 551 Francis Smith's charges at Lenton, for plateing Robin, 1*s.* **1755** J. SHEBBEARE *Lydia* (1769) II. 440 We shall accurately search into..the true manner of plating horses, and of jockying, at these celebrated places. **1840–70** BLAINE *Encycl. Rur. Sports* (ed. 3) §1237 Plate such horses as may have good sound feet ..the evening prior to their running.

6. *Biol.* and *Med.* To inoculate (cells or infective material) *into* or *on to* a plate (PLATE *sb.* 19 e), esp. with the object of purifying a particular strain or estimating viable cell numbers. Freq. with *out*.

1892 A. C. ABBOTT *Princ. Bacteriol.* xviii. 181 Again, 0·25 c.c. of this dilution is plated and we find 180 colonies on the plate. **1901** *Jrnl. Hygiene* I. 202 In order to isolate the organisms, one c.c. of each of the liquid stools was diluted 1-10,000 and 1-100,000 with distilled water, and $\frac{1}{10}$ c.c., $\frac{1}{4}$ c.c., and $\frac{1}{2}$ c.c. of these dilutions were plated out in gelatine. **1905** *Ibid.* V. 342 The resulting cultures were plated and re-plated to ensure pure growths. **1930** [see BROTH *sb.* 1 c]. **1971** *Nature* 10 Sept. 121/1 When these strains were plated on various drug agar plates..we obtained the growth pattern given in Table 1. **1972** *Ibid.* 18 Feb. 368/2 Rat lymph node cells are plated out onto mouse fibroblast monolayers *in vitro*.

7. To examine or test the distribution of shot from (a shot-gun) by firing at a pattern plate set at a suitable distance.

1904 *Kynoch Jrnl.* Oct.–Dec. 189 You can plate your gun with your favourite charge. **1932** G. BURRARD *Mod. Shotgun* III. 80 No record of such a thing has ever been noted on any pattern plate since the plating of guns first began.

8. To provide (a book) with a book-plate.

1906 [see PLATING *vbl. sb.* 1 g]. **1930** *Publishers' Weekly* 1 Mar. 1095/2 After the latter book had been punched and plated, one of our catalogers discovered that..it was an exact duplicate of the former. **1941** *Amer. Speech* XVI. 311 Verbs are made from nouns, for instance *to plate*.., to furnish with bookplates.

9. *trans.* and *intr.* To practise fellatio or cunnilingus (on). *slang.*

1961 PARTRIDGE *Dict. Underworld* Add. 807/1 *Plate, v.* This and *french, go down, nosh*, are prostitutes' (esp. London) verbs, both transitive and, less commonly, intransitive, for 'to gamâruche' a man: C. 20. **1969** FABIAN & BYRNE *Groupie* i. 10, I wondered whether I should plate him. I hadn't done much of that, but I knew guys on the scene liked it because Nigel had told me so. **1969** B. PATTEN *Notes to Hurrying Man* 27 Guitarist from Mike's group Taught her how to plate correctly. **1971** J. MANDELKAU *Buttons* vii. 99 The various chapter prospects were showing everyone how well they could screw and plate her.

10. *trans.* To provide (a goods vehicle) with a plate recording particulars of weight, etc., according to government regulations.

1968 [see PLATING *vbl. sb.* 1 j]. **1970** *Times* 29 Jan. 26/6 All trailers manufactured before January 1 last year should have been tested and plated by the Ministry within 12 months. **1972** [see PLATING *vbl. sb.* 1 j]. **1976**, etc. [see PLATED *a.* 6]. **1977** 'D. RUTHERFORD' *Return Load* ii. 32, I see it's plated at 43·3 tons. That's more than ten in excess of the UK limit.

11. *trans.* To put on a plate; to serve upon a plate.

1970, etc. [implied in PLATED *a.* 5]. **1976** *Times* July 10/6 Dishes are plated in the kitchen, and mistiming is common. **1977** *Guernsey Weekly Press* 21 July 2/8 Mr Nugent said that when the policemen arrived the meals were ready and plated.

plate, obs. form of PLAT *sb.*, *a.*, and *v.*

‖**platea** (plə'tiːə). *Medieval Drama.* Also **placea**; pl. **plateæ**. [L., street; (late L.) courtyard, square; f. Gr. πλατεῖα.] An area before a raised stage, providing additional acting space as well as accommodation for the audience.

1831 J. P. COLLIER *Hist. Dramatic Poetry* II. 154 A castle and a ship were introduced [in the Digby Miracle-play of Mary Magdalen]. The 'place', termed *placea*, and a *mons* are also mentioned in the stage-directions. **1903** E. K. CHAMBERS *Mediaeval Stage* II. III. xx. 80 The *diabolus* thinks he is prevailing upon Adam. He joins the other demons and make [*sic*] sallies about the *plateae*. **1957** R. SOUTHERN *Medieval Theatre in Round* 235 The *platea* developed not into the stage of our modern theatre, but into the pit-and-stalls. **1978** *Amer. N. & Q.* Apr. 118/1 The Digby *Mary Magdalen* has the most complete stage directions in medieval drama, directions that provide several precise technical dramatic terms which distinguish exits from moves within and about the *platea*.

† '**plateasm**. *Obs.* [ad. Gr. πλατειασμ-ός (Quintil.) a broad Doric pronunciation, f. πλατειάζειν to pronounce broadly, f. πλατεῖα, fem. of πλατύς broad.] (See quots.)

1656 BLOUNT *Glossogr.*, *Plateasm*, a fault in speech, when it is over-broad and full. **1678** PHILLIPS (ed. 4), *Plateasm*, (Greek) a broad speaking, a pronouncing words in an over-broad tone. **1727** *Art of Speaking in Publick* 62 Persons.. affected with another vice, which the Greek Rhetoricians call Plateasm: That is to say; a Broad way of Speaking, with the mouth wide open. [**1753** CHAMBERS *Cycl. Supp.*, *Platiasmos*, a word used by many authors to express a fault in pronunciation, owing to a person's opening his mouth too wide, and thence speaking indistinctly.]

plateau (plə'təʊ, 'plætəʊ), *sb.*[1] Pl. **plateaux, -eaus** (-əʊz). [a. F. *plateau*:—OF. *platel* (12th c.) flat piece of metal, wood, etc., dim. of *plat*: see PLAT *a.*]

1. a. *Geog.* An elevated tract of comparatively flat or level land; a table-land.

1796 *State Papers* in *Ann. Reg.* 262/2 The summits, *plateaux* (flat tops of hills), mountains, and other places. **1807** *Ibid.* 11 A rising ground or flattish hill, which, in the military phraseology of the French, is called a *plateau*. **1830** LYELL *Princ. Geol.* I. 375 On the chalk of Berkshire, extensive plateaus, six or seven miles wide, would again be formed. **1834** PRINGLE *Afr. Sk.* ix. 293 A sort of plateau or table-land, rising abruptly from the plains..in immense buttresses of naked rock. **1880** HAUGHTON *Phys. Geog.* iv. 168 The great Central tableland of Asia, culminating in the lofty plateau of Thibet. **1898** BULLEN *Cruise of Cachalot* 91 The grassy plateau on which the village stands.

b. *transf.* A level elevation in a sphygmographic tracing of the pulse; hence, the form of pulse which shows this. More widely, a more or less level portion of a graph adjacent to a lower sloping portion; a condition or period that can be so represented, when there is neither an increase nor a decrease in something.

1894 W. EWART *Pulse-Sensations* IV. xiii. 277 In the cardiogram..this point occurs in the line of descent—or else in the 'plateau'. **1898** *Allbutt's Syst. Med.* V. 470 In the systolic plateau two minor undulations of pressure are seen. *Ibid.* 934 This feature of the pulse and its long plateau would set aside that extremely rare affection pulmonary stenosis.

1943 J. D. WHITE in H. L. Mencken *Amer. Lang.* Suppl. I. (1945) 416 Plateaus are the thing now. War production is on a plateau, meaning that it is way up and has been up long enough to establish a plateau in the curve of production figures. **1948** *Manch. Guardian Weekly* 30 Dec. 9 The men on the Stock Exchange modestly allow they will be content with 'a plateau'. **1959** *Listener* 1 Jan. 18/1 The Ionians..had already reached a high plateau of civilization. **1961** *Ann. Reg. 1960* 474 Although industrial production in aggregate was seemingly on a plateau, the fortunes of particular industries showed marked variations. **1969** H. PERKINS *Key Profession* v. 208 The post-1947 decline in the birth-rate would be succeeded by a further upturn, rising to a higher and more permanent 'plateau' from about 1960 onwards. **1976** *Nature* 8 July 83/2 The world total of annual military expenditure..has remained on a plateau of 210,000 million US dollars (at 1970 prices) for seven years now. *Ibid.* 146/1 Fig. 1*b* shows a large current with a plateau at around +0·8 V.

c. *Psychol.* A stage in learning when no apparent progress is made.

1897 BRYAN & HARTER in *Psychol. Rev.* IV. 52 All agree that just below the ability to understand what is spoken, there is a long discouraging plateau where many give up [learning telegraphy] in despair. **1936** *Brit. Jrnl. Psychol.* XXVI. 218 The occurrence of breathing-places and plateaux in the learning process has usually been attributed ..to the gradual formation of low and high habits... A plateau means that the lower order habits are approaching their maximum development, but have not become sufficiently automatic to leave attention free to attack the higher order habits. **1964** P. M. FITTS in A. W. Melton *Categories of Human Learning* 265 The present writer knows of no evidence contrary to Keller's (1958) conclusion that a true plateau in skill learning has not been demonstrated, and that when such effects occasionally are reported they are artifacts. **1972** P. BACH-Y-RITA *Brain Mechanisms* iv. 77 Acquisition of a predominantly perceptual skill..and acquisition of a motor skill..are remarkably similar processes. Each is slow, and has several plateaus.

d. *Physics.* The range of applied voltage over which the counting rate of a Geiger counter remains approximately the same, for a given intensity of radiation.

1937 *Physical Rev.* LI. 1027/1 Reliable counting characteristics and long plateaus were obtainable only with counters whose cathode surfaces were completely cleaned.. previous to filling. **1953** H. H. STAUB in E. Segrè *Exper. Nucl. Physics* I. I. iv. 149 A good counter shows a plateau of 160 volts over which the counting rate should not increase by more than 3 percent. **1973** J. YARWOOD *Atomic & Nucl. Physics* xiv. 396 Well designed counter tubes have a plateau slope of about 2 per cent. increase in count rate for an operating voltage increase of 100 V. This flat plateau is valuable since it means that the operating voltage is not critical.

e. The second of four recognized stages of sexual intercourse (see quot. 1960), in which there is an intense sexual excitement lasting a variable but usually short time following a longer phase of increasing excitement and succeeded either by orgasm or by a longer period of decreasing excitement. Usu. *attrib.*, esp. in ***plateau phase.***

1960 W. H. MASTERS in *Western Jrnl. Surg., Obstetr. & Gynecol.* LXVIII. 58 The four phases of the human female's sexual response cycle are in order of their development: (1) the excitement phase; (2) the plateau phase; (3) the orgasmic phase; and (4) the resolution phase. *Ibid.*, This plateau phase of sexual response is the base line from which the individual climbs with relative ease and rapidity to orgasm. **1966** MASTERS & JOHNSON *Human Sexual Response* i. 7 Some physiologic reactions..may be confined to one particular phase of the cycle. Examples are the plateau-phase color changes of the minor labia in the female and the coronal engorgement of the penis in the male. **1972** *Encycl. Love & Sex* 1. 8/2 One of the most common of all sexual problems occurs when the man's plateau phase is short,..so that he reaches his climax too soon to satisfy his partner. **1974** H. S. KAPLAN *New Sex Therapy* i. 9 During plateau, the local vasocongestive response of the primary sex organ is at its peak in both genders. *Ibid.* 21 The retarded ejaculator becomes excited, reaches the plateau, may experience the intense urge to proceed to orgasm which is characteristic at this time, but cannot ejaculate despite vigorous and effective stimulation. **1976** B. GOLDSTEIN *Human Sexuality* ix. 157 If sexual motivation is maintained by adequate erotic stimulation, the excitement phase accelerates to the plateau phase.

2. a. An ornamented tray or dish for table-service. **b.** A decorative plaque.

1791 WASHINGTON *Lett.* Writ. 1892 XII. 53 The plateaux which you had the goodness to procure for me arrived safe. **1796** LD. COLCHESTER *Diary* (1861) I. 34 The middle of the table was filled with a painted plateau ornamented with French white figures and vases of flowers. **1800** in *Spirit Pub. Jrnls.* IV. 11 An elegant platteau, and a silver epergne. **1831** J. HOLLAND *Manuf. Metal* I. 136 The plateau sufficiently large to hold the entire tea equipage of a numerous party. **1861** *Times* 6 June, The Grocers..have secured a lasting record of their commercial adventures in the shape of a gorgeous silver plateau, comprising four massive pieces, each representing a scene in the progress of a trading caravan through the Desert.

3. *transf.* A style of woman's hat with level top.

1900 *Daily News* 21 July 6/5 Merely a burnt-straw plateau with a cluster of flowers under the raised brim at the left side. **1901** *Lady's Realm* X. 650/1 Yet again have I seen the double plateau look perfectly charming in all-black.

4. *attrib.* and *Comb.*, as (in sense 1) ***plateau air, -ice, land, region, state, valley; plateau-like*** adj.; (in sense 1 b) ***plateau length, level, slope, value***; (in sense 3) ***plateau hat***; **plateau basalt**, basaltic lava extruded from fissures and forming sheets that cover many square miles; in *Petrol.* freq. used with the implication of a tholeiitic or, formerly, an alkalic nature; **plateau gravel**, gravel occurring in a sheet on hilltops or a plateau, at a height that suggests it has been raised by earth movement since its deposition.

1888 *Proc. R. Soc. Edin.* XV. 347 In Antrim bosses of trachyte and pitchstone rise through the *plateau-basalts. **1933** *Amer. Jrnl. Sci.* CCXXV. 241 Olivine-Basalt Magma-Type... Many of the Patagonian plateau basalts appear to be of this type and some, at least, of the Siberian Traps. *Ibid.* 242 The Deccan Traps and the majority of the plateau basalts which have been studied are of tholeiitic composition. **1944** A. HOLMES *Princ. Physical Geol.* xx. 458 Plateau basalts covering areas of 200,000 square miles or more occur in the Columbia and Snake River region of the north-western United States. **1972** G. A. MACDONALD *Volcanoes* xi. 255 The basaltic lava flows that built the plains have commonly been called pleateau basalts. **1977** A. HALLAM *Planet Earth* 20/3 The materials of cratered plains [on the moon] resemble terrestrial plateau basalts. **1872** WOOD & HARMER in S. V. Wood *Suppl. Monogr. Crag Mollusca* p. xxvi. (*heading*) The *Plateau gravel. **1873** J. GEIKIE *Gt. Ice Age* (1894) 559 The deposition of the plateau-gravels was succeeded by a long period of valley-erosion. **1881** *Proc. Geologists' Assoc.* VI. 33 On the top of Crawley (Portesbury) Hill..the plateau-gravel, with its overlying loam (loess) and its ferruginous layers, is well seen in the railway-cutting. **1970** R. J. SMALL *Study of Landforms* vii. 234 In the New Forest.., the Tertiary sands and clays are overlain at many points by thick plateau gravels of Quaternary age. **1856** KANE *Arct. Expl.* I. xxv. 336 The surface of the *plateau-ice, the *mer-de-glace* of the island. **1897** MARY KINGSLEY *W. Africa* 638 The great park-like *plateau lands. **1965** *Wireless World* Aug. 382/2 This is particularly useful for Geiger tubes, as they tend to have individual working points and sometimes, if aged, a limited *plateau length. **1957** G. E. HUTCHINSON *Treat. Limnol.* I. xii. 744 The absolute concentration..fell rapidly, reaching a *plateau level which represents about 10 per cent of the original amount added. **1863** MARY HOWITT *F. Bremer's Greece* I. i. 7 The Acropolis..is a rock, which, *plateau-like, rises directly from the plain. **1962** *Newnes Conc. Encycl. Nucl. Energy* 296/1 A good counter is one which has a low *plateau slope, e.g. less than 5 per cent increase in count-rate for 100 V increase in applied voltage. **1964** L. WILETS *Theories Nucl. Fission* i. 3 As a function of excitation energy, the probability of fission frequently assumes the form of a barrier transmission curve.., rising to some *plateau value.

5. *Med.* (Passing into adj.) Of the pulse: having a plateau (sense 1 b) in the rising portion of the sphygmomanometric tracing.

1923 W. D. REID *Heart in Mod. Practice* xviii. 231 If the pulse is anacrotic and plateau in type, the diagnosis [of aortic stenosis] obtains strong support. **1936** S. A. LEVINE *Clin. Heart Dis.* iv. 77 The plateau form of radial pulse is fairly characteristic of aortic stenosis. *Ibid.*, This will counteract the plateau character. **1972** PASSMORE & ROBSON *Compan. Med. Stud.* III. xvi. 6/1 The plateau pulse..is due to the slow ejection of blood from the left ventricle through the narrowed orifice.

Plateau ('plætəʊ, ‖plɑto), *sb.*[2] *Math.* The name of J. A. F. *Plateau* (1801–83), Belgian physicist, used *attrib.*, in the possessive, and with *of* to designate the problem of finding the surface of smallest area bounded by any given closed curve.

1911 *Encycl. Brit.* XXVI. 123/2 The problem of finding a minimal surface to pass through a given curve in space, known as Plateau's problem, possesses an exceptional interest. **1927** *Bull. Amer. Math. Soc.* XXXIII. 259 This paper reduces the Plateau problem to a system of two integral equations. **1930** *Math. Zeitschr.* XXXII. 765 The problem of Plateau and the problem of least area have a common solution. **1976** *Sci. Amer.* July 82/3 In his honour an entire range of mathematical questions that deal with the geometry of soap-bubble-like and soap-film-like surfaces is referred to as Plateau's problem.

plateau ('plætəʊ, plə'təʊ), *v.* [f. PLATEAU *sb.*[1]] *intr.* To enter a period of stability or stagnation; to cease increasing or progressing, to level *out*. So **'plateaued (or pla'teaued)** *ppl. a.*; **'plateauing (or pla'teauing)** *vbl. sb.*

1952 *Proc. Soc. Exper. Biol. & Med.* LXXIX. 584/2 In each experiment 10 'plateaued' female rats of the Long-Evans strain were used. **1966** *Electronics* 3 Oct. 23 Many companies have diversified their activities or extended their product lines, after having been scared by the plateauing of business in 1962 and 1963. *Ibid.*, U.S. electronic companies have bitten deeply into local markets, causing the sales of European firms to plateau or slide on their home grounds. **1967** *Economist* 16 Sept. 1009/1 There is an ominous lull in military cargoes which the shipping companies believe is temporary but which the military expect to be permanent and which they describe as 'the pipeline plateauing out'. **1969** D. CLARK *Nobody's Perfect* ii. 60 The hope that some graph will plateau higher up the scale. **1973** *Maclean's Mag.* Aug. 63/1 Kids get into swimming and they have a lot of initial success and then they plateau—they stick at the same level for a long period, maybe six months. **1975** *Harvard Business Rev.* LIII. 30/3 We found a large number of managers who, in the judgment of their organization, have 'plateaued'. That is, there is little or no likelihood that they will be promoted. **1976** *New Scientist* 26 Aug. 439/2 The counts from radioactive carbon dioxide rose rapidly and then plateaued. **1978** *Jrnl. R. Soc. Arts* CXXVI. 483/2 Petroleum supply will peak or plateau at the end of the century.

plate-basket to **-cutting:** see PLATE *sb.* 20, 21.

plated ('pleɪtɪd), *a.* [f. PLATE *sb.* or *v.* + -ED.]

1. a. Overlaid, covered, or strengthened with a plate or plates of metal for ornament or defence; (of persons) wearing plate-armour; (of ships, trains, etc.) protected by armour-plate.

1483 *Cath. Angl.* 283/1 Plated (*A.* Playted), *squamatus.* **1590** SPENSER *F.Q.* I. xi. 9 Like plated cote of steele, so couched neare That nought mote perce. *a* **1661** FULLER *Worthies* (1840) II. 516 Where he lieth buried under a fair plated stone in the Chancel. **1671** MILTON *Samson* 139 Old Warriors turn'd Thir plated backs under his heel. **1760–72** H. BROOKE *Fool of Qual.* (1807) IV. 117 They laid his remains in a plated coffin. **1870** *Standard* 19 Dec., A plated locomotive went along the railway as far as that place to-day. **1874** BOUTELL *Arms & Arm.* vii. 109.

b. *transf.* of animals, etc.: Having a defensive covering of scales or bony plates.

1562 PHAER *Æneid.* VIII. Bb iij, Wt serpent skales beset, & fyne wt gold Were dragons drawen in wrethes, and poolisht pure in plated fold. **1837** M. DONOVAN *Dom. Econ.* II. 67 The Pangolin..is a kind of ant-eater,..plated over with bright sharp scales, shaped like a muscle-shell.

c. *Surg.* Of a fracture: see PLATE *v.* 1 b.

1916 E. W. H. GROVES *Mod. Methods Treating Fractures* vi. 198 In so many plated fractures removal of the plates and screws is required. **1959** A. G. APSLEY *Syst. Orthopædics & Fractures* xxi. 256 If..a patient walks with a recently plated tibia unprotected by plaster, the plate will break.

2. a. Covered or overlaid with a thin film of gold or silver. Also used with reference to metals other than gold and silver; ***plated wire***, a wire of a non-magnetic metal such as copper having a thin coating of a magnetic alloy, used as an element in some computer memories. Cf. *chromium-plated* ppl. adj. s.v. CHROMIUM 2.

1686 tr. *Chardin's Trav. Persia* 8 Pieces of Five Sous.. which were only Copper plated over. **1781** H. NEWDIGATE *Let.* 8 Oct. in A. E. Newdigate-Newdegate *Cheverels* (1898) iii. 42 All were well pleas'd to find we were only ten miles from Sheffield... We got there..and saw the Plated Manufactory through all its branches. **1789** E. SHERIDAN *Jrnl.* (1960) 182 The plated candlesticks will also be very useful to us. **1798** *Hull Advertiser* 4 Aug. 2/2 A neat light gig, with plated harness. **1874** BLACKIE *Self-Cult.* 65 Plated work will never stand the tear and wear of life like the genuine metal. **1881** *Athenæum* 17 Dec. 822/3 The objects found consist of..several plated [*mispr.* plateal] brass coins, mostly effaced. **1899** J. W. URQUHART *Electro-Plating* (ed. 4) 222 The advantages of a thick deposit of nickel are that it can be manipulated by the polisher with confidence and the 'life' of the plated article is..greatly increased. **1931** E. F. BENSON *Mapp & Lucia* viii. 205 A magenta carpet and a nickel-plated mantelpiece. **1960** T. R. LONG in *Jrnl. Appl. Physics* XXXI. Suppl. 124S/2 After rinsing the plated wire, it is passed through a mercury ground contact and then through small testing coils. These coils..allow a continuous monitor of the nondestructive readout signal. **1967** *Times Rev. Industry* Feb. 104/2 (Advt.), UNIVAC 9000 Series computers utilize a plated-wire memory, basically a thin film electroplated on an extremely fine wire. **1967** *Engineering* 24 Feb. 306/3 Plated plastics parts can replace metal components in many domestic, industrial and automobile applications. **1976** M. WELLS *Computing Systems Hardware* ii. 49 Plated wire stores are substantially faster than ferrite core stores of the same capacity.

b. Having an outer surface or nap of finer material than the body. Also, produced by plating (sense 1 h).

1846 MCCULLOCH *Acc. Brit. Empire* (1854) I. 763 Plated hats..Stuff ditto..Silk ditto..Wool felts. **1882** BECK *Draper's Dict.* s.v., A plated hat was one in which the body was of lamb's-wool, and the plate, or nap, of musquash or neutria; and plated hosiery stockings had an outside face of silk upon a ground of cotton. *c* **1890** *American Mail Order Fashions* (1961) 12 Ladies' Outsize Plated Silk Hose, black, ..1.50. **1926** J. CHAMBERLAIN *Hosiery, Yarns & Fabrics* vi. 131 Innumerable colour designs are produced on a plated principle on plain and rib fabrics. **1963** A. J. HALL *Textile Sci.* iii. 152 Thus using cotton and wool yarns it can be arranged that the front of the fabric appears to be made of cotton with the back made of wool. Such fabrics are known as *plated* fabrics. **1968** J. IRONSIDE *Fashion Alphabet* 245 A knitted fabric which has a different kind of yarn as the face and back, is said to be plated.

3. Consisting of, beaten or rolled into plates.

a **1674** MILTON *Hist. Mosc.* v. Wks. 1851 VIII. 516 A great Chain of plated Gold about his Neck. **1790** KEIR in *Phil. Trans.* LXXX. 367 Cutting out the rolled plated metal into pieces of the required forms and sizes. **1796** KIRWAN *Elem. Min.* (ed. 2) II. 19 Fragments [Slaty Alum] Trapezoidal, or plated.

4. Applied as a thin coating on another material.

1925 *Rep. Progr. Appl. Chem.* X. 301 Piersol finds plated chromium superior to any other metal for reflectors. **1966** *McGraw-Hill Encycl. Sci. & Technol.* IV. 533/1 The thickness of a plated coating is the most important factor in its protective value.

5. In which food is ready-served on a plate.

1970 *Drive* Spring 43/1 Plated service means that your meal arrives complete, on the plate. Semi-plated service is when the principal component of the meal arrives on the plate; vegetables are served from silver dishes. **1976** *Liverpool Echo* 23 Nov. 10/6 Some patients at Clatterbridge Hospital enjoy a plated meals service which gives them advance choice of menu and portion size. **1977** *Lancet* 16 July 130/1 Plated meals were packed in charcoal heated containers and dispatched at 11 A.M.

6. Of a goods vehicle: see PLATE *v.* 10.

1976 *Liverpool Echo* 22 Nov. 11/4 (Advt.), Two Leyland Boxer Vans, plated,..M.O.T. until February 1977. **1977** *Horse & Hound* 14 Jan. 44/2 (Advt.), Bedford T.K. petrol, 2/3 horses, good box, very reliable, plated till January 1977. **1978** *Taxi* 16 Feb. 19/1 (Advt.), For Sale: 'J' reg. auto. Just rebored. Excellent condition, plated till July. **1980** *Daily Tel.* 6 Mar. 2 (Advt.), It's a big truck all right. But its plated weight is only 7·38 tons GVW.

plate fleet. *Hist.* [f. PLATE *sb.* 15.] The fleet which annually brought the produce of the American silver mines to Spain.

1625 in *Crt. & Times Chas. I* (1848) I. 68 The rest of the fleet would stay awhile to watch the Plate fleet not yet come home. **1663** COWLEY *Verses Sev. Occas., Adv. of Five Hours,* As when our Kings (Lords of the spacious Main,) Take in just wars a rich Plate Fleet of Spain. **1763** W. ROBERTS *Nat. Hist. Florida* 90 Treasure out of the wreck, where the galleons, or plate-fleet, were cast away.

plateful ('pleɪtfʊl). [f. PLATE *sb.* + -FUL.] The quantity (*of* anything) with which a plate is filled.

1766 ALEXANDER in *Phil. Trans.* LVII. 67, I..swallowed down a plate-ful of the broth. **1852** HAWTHORNE *Blithedale Rom.* xvi, Let me have a plateful of that pork!

plate-gauge, etc.: see PLATE *sb.* 21.

plate-glass ('pleɪtglɑːs, -æ-). [f. PLATE *sb.* + GLASS *sb.*] **a.** A fine quality of thick glass, cast in plates, used for mirrors, shop-windows, or in any position where an undistorted view, great strength, or the exclusion of sound, is desired. Also *attrib.*

1727–41 CHAMBERS *Cycl.* s.v. *Glass,* It is from this adulteration that those threads and other defects in plate glass arise. **1766** ENTICK *London* IV. 398 The other remarkable places..are..a plate glasshouse, a bottle glasshouse. **1795** *Gentl. Mag.* LXV. II. 961 Mr. Harman's seat..had a great number of plate-glass windows broke. **1807** T. THOMSON *Chem.* (ed. 3) II. 508 The plate glass is poured melted upon a table covered with a sheet of copper. The plate, as cast, is about an inch thick; but it is ground down to the proper..thinness, and then polished. **1860** *All Year Round* No. 67. 397 The partition which separated my own office from our general outer office,..was of thick plate-glass.

b. *spec.* (also with capital initial) used *attrib.* to denote any of the new British universities founded in the 1960s; also passing into adj., of or pertaining to such a university.

1968 M. BELOFF *Plateglass Universities* i. 20 The self-confident and colourful character of the Plateglass universities reflects the spirit of the high Macmillan age. **1968** —— in *Encounter* May 14/1 The New University explosion of the last decade has an element of illusion about it... Only seven..are new institutions... The difference between the Plateglass Universities and both their predecessors and upgraded successors was that in them alone was there the opportunity for pure experiment. **1968** *Economist* 1 June 47/1 Of the non-Oxbridge successful candidates, only four came from the new generation of plate-glass universities. **1971** C. DRIVER *Exploding University* I. iv. 187 Some time ago a Plate-glass professor suggested that a new university's potential for innovation fades after about three years. **1973** J. H. M. SCOTT *Dons & Students* ii. 17 Though the new universities have been dubbed 'plate-glass'..they have no monopoly of that material. **1979** *Times Higher Educ. Suppl.* 23 Nov. 27/5 Among universities, such labels as Oxbridge, Red Brick, Green Field and Plate Glass define origins and location rather than reputations.

Hence **plate-'glasser,** a student or graduate of one of the new British universities.

1968 *Economist* 1 June 47/1 A man from Aberystwyth got into the Foreign Service, along with two plate-glassers, one red-brick man, one Dubliner, nine from Oxford and eleven from Cambridge.

plate-hat to **-lap:** see PLATE *sb.* 20, 21.

plate-layer ('pleɪtˌleɪə(r)). *orig.* One who lays, keeps in order, and renews the plates (see PLATE *sb.* 8) on a tramway or railway; hence, a man employed in fixing and keeping in order the rails, metals, or permanent way of a railway. So **'plate-ˌlaying.**

1836 *Newcastle Courant* 24 Dec. 1/1 *Advt.,* To Plate-layers and others. The Directors of the Stanhope and Tyne Railroad Company wish to receive Proposals for the Upholding of their Road. **1857** H. SPENCER in *Westm. Rev.* Apr. 482 Sundry new occupations, as those of drivers, stokers, cleaners, plate-layers. **1862** *Rep. Directors E. Ind. Railw. Comp.* 27 Progress..limited by the supply of sleepers, the want of which has since arrested platelaying.

plate-lead, -leather, etc.: see PLATE *sb.* 21.

plateless ('pleɪtlɪs), *a.* [f. PLATE *sb.* + -LESS.] Without a plate or plates.

1874 T. HARDY *Far fr. Madding Crowd* I. xv. 171 Breakfasting off bread and bacon..eaten on the plateless system.

platelet ('pleɪtlɪt). [See -LET.] **1.** A small or minute plate. ***blood-platelet,*** a minute colourless disk-shaped corpuscle which exists in large numbers in the blood of all mammalia; usu. simply *platelet* [(*blood-*)*platelet* tr. G. (*blut*)*plättchen* (G. Bizzozero in *Centralbl. für die med. Wissensch.* (1882) I. 17, 18), F. *petite plaque* (*du sang*) (*idem* in *Arch. ital. de Biol.* (1882) I. 1, 16)].

1895 *Syd. Soc. Lex., Platelets, blood-,* the same as blood-plates. **1895** in *Daily News* 13 Aug. 6/1 The armour of these strange animals consisted of either circular or many-sided plates, encircled by a rim of smaller polygonal platelets. **1898** *Allbutt's Syst. Med.* V. 400 A minute spindle-shaped body, the hæmatoblast, not unlike a blood platelet. **1910** H. W. ARMIT tr. *P. Ehrlich's Anæmia* iv. 203 He then determined the relative proportions of the platelets to the blood corpuscles. **1955** *Sci. News Let.* 14 May 320/3 Platelets, tiny cell fragments found in the blood, arrest bleeding by sticking to the edge of the wound and to each other until they pile up into a little cork that fills the hole. **1970** *Physics Bull.* July 322/1 The crystal..is then sliced into platelets 50 μm or so thick. **1978** *Detroit Free Press* 5 Mar. B4/1 Blood clots that block arteries are formed by platelets, the body's first line of defense against injury.

2. platelet count, the number of platelets in a stated volume of blood; a calculation of this.

1909 *Jrnl. Exper. Med.* XI. 542 In the experiments careful erythrocyte and leukocyte counts have been made and then the platelet count obtained by the indirect method, *i.e.,* by ascertaining their number relative to that of the red blood cells in fresh preparations and checking this result by the relative number in carefully made stained smears. *Ibid.* 544 In an animal which had received repeated doses of saponin intravenously..there was a high platelet count (1,400,000 per cubic millimeter). **1966** *Lancet* 24 Dec. 1384/1 The platelet-count gradually recovered after the drugs had been stopped.

plate-machine, etc.: see PLATE *sb.* 21.

'plate-ˌmaker. [f. PLATE *sb.* + MAKER.]

†**1.** A maker of plate-armour. *Obs. rare.*

1297 *Coram Rege Roll* (1898) 143 Johannem le Platemaker.

2. One who makes plates of various kinds; e.g. a manufacturer of photographic plates.

1772 J. WEDGWOOD *Let.* 22 July (1965) 127, I have ordered another sett of plate makers to work, and will if possible have a *sufficient stock* of those *every day* Articles. **1863** *1st Rep. Children's Employment Commission* 3 in *Parl. Papers* XVIII. 1 *Flat pressers*... It includes dishmakers, platemakers, saucermakers, and cup and bowl makers. **1889** *Anthony's Photogr. Bull.* II. 182 A plate-maker issuing developing formulæ for his plates. **1905** *Westm. Gaz.* 21 Jan. 14/2 The plate-maker..is constantly increasing the sensitiveness of his wares.

3. One who casts or prepares plates for engraving or printing.

1904 *Athenæum* 21 May 645/1 We feel pleasure in congratulating..the publisher and the editors, and including the printers, plate-makers, and binders.

plateman ('pleɪtmən). [f. PLATE *sb.* + MAN.]

1. ? = PLATE-MAKER 1.

1435 *Maldon, Essex, Liber A.* lf. 27b, Johannes Wytte, Playteman, receptus est in libertatem. **1437** *Maldon, Essex, Court-Rolls* (Bundle 23, no. 1v), Johannes Whitte, playteman, queritur versus Johannem Vowle..skynner.

2. A man who has the custody of silver plate.

1861 *Times* 8 July, Porter, or Plateman in a club, family, or commercial hotel.

'plate-mark. [f. PLATE *sb.* + MARK *sb.*[1]]

1. A name for the various marks legally impressed on gold and silver plate for the purpose of indicating maker, degree of purity, hall or place of assay, date, etc.; also called HALL-MARK.

These consist of (1) the maker's initials or mark; (2) the mark of the particular assay-office; (3) the assay-mark or sovereign's mark; (4) a letter indicating the date. Plate made between 1784 and 1890 also bore (5) the duty-mark, being the head of the reigning sovereign.

1858 SIMMONDS *Dict. Trade, Plate marks,* special marks.. stamped on gold or silver plate. **1883** *Chambers' Encycl.* VII. 585 There can be no deception, if the public understand the plate-marks.

2. The impression left on the margin of an engraving by the pressure of the plate.

1889 *Anthony's Photogr. Bull.* II. 62 If a plate mark is wanted it can be easily put on when the mat is partly dry by using the edge of a blunt chisel-shaped piece of hard wood, with a ruler as a guide. **1903** *Daily Chron.* 28 Dec. 3/4 It has ..been alleged that the plate mark has been added to the prints subsequently.

Hence **'plate-marked** *a.,* having a plate-mark.

1902 *Westm. Gaz.* 7 May 12/2 Portraits..printed..on handsome plate-marked boards, with gold bevelled edges.

plate-matter to **-mundic:** see PLATE *sb.* 21.

platen ('plætən, -(ə)n), *sb.* Forms: 5 **plateyne,** 6 **-tyne,** 6–9 **plattin,** 7 **plataine,** 7–9 **platin,** 8 **platine,** 7–9 **platten,** 8– **platen.** [ME. *plateyne,* a. OF. *platine* (13– 14th c.) flat piece, metal plate, also a popular alteration of *patene* PATEN, from its form; in mod.F. a tabular portion of a machine, e.g. of a printing-press; f. *plat* adj.: see PLAT *a.* and -INE[4].]

1. †**a.** A flat plate of metal for various purposes. *Obs.*

1541 COPLAND *Guydon's Quest. Chirurg.* P iv b, Take your platyne or quyl and apply them all colde, but ye must nat let them lye long, and than gyue the cauteres to the workeman that shall applye them all hote and very flamynge. **1597** LOWE *Chirurg.* I. (1634) 6 To put..a platten in the roofe of the mouth, which is needfull to those who..have the roofe of the mouth falling. **1702** W. J. *Bruyn's Voy. Levant* x. 40 Some wear upon their Heads a *Kalpak,* or Fur Cap; others a large round Platine, after the Fashion of the Jewish women. **1813** J. THOMSON *Lect. Inflam.* 273 They heated red hot their actual cauteries, of which some were shaped like a button, others like an olive, and a third sort like a platin; they applied them red-hot to the orifices of the vessels as soon as the member was separated.

b. *Engin.* The movable table of a planing or milling machine.

1908 S. H. MOORE *Mech. Engin.* xiii. 298 Horizontal milling machines..resemble in a way the conventional planer with its deep bed and long platen or table. **1950** C. R. HINE *Machine Tools for Engineers* viii. 122 The worktable, or platen, moves back and forth on the bed ways and carries the work past the tool.

†**2.** = PATEN 1 (cf. etymol.). *Obs.*

c **1450** LOVELICH *Grail* xvii. 49 There lefte he up the plateyne anon That vppon this glorious vessel was don. **1607** R. C[AREW] tr. *Estienne's World of Wonders* 189 Had his challice and plattin stolne by one which holpe him to say Masse. **1624** DARCIE *Birth of Heresies* xvii. 71 The Priest must lift the vaile ouer the Chalice, and release it from the Plataine, to represent the rent vaile..at Christs death.

3. *Printing.* **a.** An iron (formerly wooden) plate in a printing-press, which presses the paper against the inked type so as to secure an impression; hence *spec.* a flat metal surface by means of which pressure is applied in a press. Also applied to a similar part in other machines.

1594 R. ASHLEY tr. *Loys le Roy* 22 He maketh the traine of the presse to roule..till it come vnder the vice or spindle, vnto which the plattin is fastned. **1683** MOXON *Mech. Exerc., Printing* ii. ¶2 Brass Rules,..if they be but a little too high,..will bear the Plattin off the Letters that stand near them. **1706** PHILLIPS, *Platen* or *Platine,* the Plate of a Printer's Press. **1790** *Bystander* 158 That part which is called the platen is found to be insufficient to bring off an even impression. **1824** J. JOHNSON *Typogr.* II. xv. 513 The face of the plattin must be perfectly level and smooth. **1873** E. SPON *Workshop Receipts* Ser. I. 310/1 Place the board or side upon which the stamp is placed, upon the platen of the stamping-press. **1894** *Brit. Jrnl. Photogr.* XLI. 48 From the plates breaking so frequently, we suspect that the platten of the press is not perfectly true. **1927** KNIGHT & WULPI *Veneers & Plywood* xx. 210 The platens are alternately squeezed together to flatten the veneer, and opened up to allow the moisture to escape from the wood surfaces. **1936** H. W. ROWELL *Technol. of Plastics* xv. 97 The simple up-stroke hydraulic press with steam or electrically heated platens..is a cheap and economical machine. **1963** H. R. CLAUSER et al. *Encycl. Engin. Materials & Processes* 347/2 Two mold halves, which..combine to form one or more negative forms of the article to be molded, are tightly clamped between the platens of an injection-molding machine. **1964** B. LATHAM *Wood* xiii. 159 A modern hot press may have ten, twelve, or even twenty platens, so enabling up to twenty sheets of plywood to be manufactured at each pressing operation. **1975** A. D. DEUTSCHMAN et al. *Machine Design* iv. 170 Laminating... It is possible to produce shapes other than flat sheets by using shaped molding dies between the forming press platens.

b. In a typewriter, the surface against which the paper is held and the type strikes (a cylindrical roller in most machines). Freq. *attrib.*

1890 A. E. MORTON *Type-Writing & Type-Writers* 12 The paper-carriage is much smaller, and the platen or cylinder differs from that of other machines in that it presents a flat surface for the types to strike against. **1899** J. WARDLE *Universal Typewriter Man.* 45 *Platen knob,* for turning the Platen..either backward or forward. *Ibid., Platen roller,* for the paper to rest upon when printing. **1907** F. H. BURNETT *Shuttle* xxiii. 227 The platen roller is easily removed without a long mechanical operation. **1909** G. C. MARES *Hist. Typewriter* i. 45 The platen cylinder is supported in a carriage that slides on a rod. **1928** M. CROCKS *Touch Typewriting for Teachers* xvii. 125 The student can be trained to get the right amount of 'flick' with the platen knob to enable the paper to enter the machine up to whatever writing point is desired. **1962** *Which?* Dec. 354/1 The bail bar, which should hold the paper against the platen, was thin and bent easily. **1976** J. FRASER *Who steals my Name?* x. 122 He pressed the activate key, and..paper began to spew from the platen, printed in neat lines at the rate of ten words a second.

4. *attrib.* and *Comb.,* as **platen-cord,** one of the cords by which the platen was suspended from the hose, in old presses; **platen-gauge:** see quot. (also called lay-gauge); **platen-machine, platen printing-machine,** a press having a platen, as opposed to a rotary or cylinder-press; **platen-pan,** in old presses, a metal socket in which the toe of the spindle works; **platen-plate,** a square iron plate let into the upper side of the platen, in the centre of which the platen-pan was fixed; **platen press,** a platen machine (not necessarily a printing-machine).

1683 MOXON *Mech. Exerc., Printing* xi. ¶14 If the *Plattin-Cords are too loose. **1878** HALLECK in *Sci. Amer.* XXXIX. 338/1 A New *Platen Gauge..applied to the platen of a printing press for holding and guiding the paper that is printed upon. **1888** JACOBI *Printer's Voc.* 101 **Platen machine,* printing machines which have a flat impression, not a cylindrical one. **1683** MOXON *Mech. Exerc., Printing* xi. ¶18 Into this square Frame is fitted the Stud of the *Plattin Pan. **1824** J. JOHNSON *Typogr.* II. 513 To receive the stud of the circular brass plattin pan. **1683** MOXON *Mech. Exerc., Printing* xi. ¶18 In the middle of the upper-side [of the Platen] is let in..an Iron Plate called the *Plattin-Plate. **1888** *Encycl. Brit.* XXIII. 704/2 We may say that of *platen presses there are the hand-press, the treadle platen press, and the steam or other power-driven press. **1927** KNIGHT & WULPI *Veneers & Plywood* xxvi. 294 Pressing plywood singly, even in the multiple platen presses,..is a slow and expensive process. **1967** V. STRAUSS *Printing Industry* vi. 278/1 Platen presses are the smallest and least complex of all widely used letterpress printing machines. **1873** CURWEN *Hist. Booksellers* 468 In 1867 he introduced a *platten printing machine.

platen, obs. f. PLATTEN *v.,* to flatten.

plate number. **1.** *Philately.* (See quot. 1912.)

1912 *Gloss. Philatelic Terms* 19 *Plate Numbers,* numbers inserted in the margins of plates from which stamps are printed, indicating (in the case of British and British Colonial stamps) the order in which the plates for those particular values were made. **1934** *Neuphilologische Mitteilungen* XXXV. 130 Stamp-collecting..*plate number*

'number appearing in the margin of certain stamps'. **1971** D. POTTER *Brit. Eliz. Stamps* v. 63 In complete sheets all Bradbury Wilkinson printings bear a plate number, in the lower margin to the right; this consists of a number or a number and letter.

2. A serial number on the pages of some engraved music, which can indicate the chronological place of the score in the publisher's output.

1940 *Papers Amer. Musicological Soc. 1938* 114[Hoffmeister] made arrangements in 1784 with the publisher..to do the engraving for him... Work issued during this period either had no plate number engraved at the foot of the plates, or else used as an identifying device the opus number of the composition. **1942** *Music Library Assoc. Notes* Dec. 1 Mathias Artaris..generally adds the initials 'M.A.' to his plate numbers. **1946** O. E. DEUTSCH *Music Publishers' Numbers* 7 This list..is..only a preliminary compilation of titles and plate-numbers known to the authors. **1965** NEIGHBOUR & TYSON (*title*) English music publishers' plate numbers in the first half of the nineteenth century. **1966** J. H. DAVIES *Musicalia* xv. 139 The dating of music by publishers' plate-numbers and paper-makers' watermarks begins to achieve some degree of accuracy.

3. The registration number of a motor vehicle, exhibited on a plate.

1973 'D. SHANNON' *No Holiday* (1974) iv. 64 Hackett.. got the plate number of the truck.

plate-painter to **-powder**: see PLATE 20, 21.

plater ('pleɪtə(r)). [f. PLATE *v.* and *sb.* + -ER[1].]

1. One who coats or plates articles with a film of metal, usually of silver or gold; often in Comb., as ***electro-plater***, ***tin-plater***.

1777 *Birmingham Directory* 5 Bewhouse, Thomas, Plater. **1798** W. HUTTON *Autobiog.* App. E. 132 A buckle-plater sued O and M for a guinea. **1830** N. S. WHEATON *Jrnl.* 404, I went to the platers, where every species of silver and plated ware is produced. **1884** *Brit. Alm. & Comp.* 123 A working-man..employed as a silver plater.

2. A man engaged in the manufacture or application of metal plates, esp. in iron shipbuilding.

1864 *Daily Tel.* 11 Aug., Upon Shoeburyness..the gunners and the armour-platers have pitched their camp. **1869** SIR E. J. REED *Shipbuild.* x. 194 The fitting, marking, and fixing of the outside plating are performed by a party of workmen known as platers. **1892** *Labour Commission* Gloss., *Platers*, skilled mechanics..who mark, shear, roll, flange, bend, shape, punch.., set, fit, and fix in place..the steel plates..&c., for the outside and inside and hull of a ship, or for boilers and bridges.

3. *Horse-racing.* A horse that competes chiefly in plate or prize races (see PLATE *sb.* 18); an inferior race-horse. Also *fig.*

1859 LEVER *Davenport Dunn* xxxi. 261 You might have guessed, Master Grog, that she never could be a 'Plater'. **1864** ADMIRAL ROUS in *Edin. Rev.* July 124 The form of the best race-horse in 1750 is inferior to those of the commonest plater of the present day. **1886** *Sat. Rev.* 6 Mar. 327/2 A veteran selling-plater who has passed through some ten or a dozen stables.

4. A machine for calendering paper: see quot.

1884 KNIGHT *Dict. Mech.* Suppl., *Plater*, a paper calendering machine... The paper is packed between smooth plates of zinc or copper, and passed between the rolls back and forth till the desired finish is obtained.

plater, obs. form of PLATTER.

plate-rack: see PLATE *sb.* 21.

plateresque (plætə'rɛsk), *a.* [ad. Sp. *plateresco*, f. *platero* a silversmith, goldsmith (f. *plata* silver) + *-esco*: see -ESQUE.] Resembling silver work: applied to a rich grotesque style of decoration, etc.

1842–76 GWILT *Archit.* §599 Diego de Rianno..in that year [1530] designed and executed..the plateresque or renaissance *sacristia mayor*. **1882** *Harper's Mag.* LXV. 219 The expensively adorned plateresque Chapel. **1886** *Sat. Rev.* 24 Apr. 585/1 'Vegetable forms' are..the chief characteristic of the superb Spanish plâteresque embroideries, in silver and gold thread, of the sixteenth and seventeenth centuries.

plate-rock to **-room**: see PLATE *sb.* 21.

†'**platery.** *Obs. rare.* [f. PLATE *v.* + -ERY.] The work of a PLATER; plating. Hence †'**platerer** *Obs.* = PLATER (sense 1).

1664 PEPYS *Diary* 8 Apr., What I have done in the contract with the platerer. *Ibid.* 9 Apr., From my being over-concerned with Stanes's business of the platery of the navy.

pla'tessiform, *a. Ichth.* [f. L. *platessa* plaice + -FORM.] Resembling the plaice, or the genus *Platessa*, in form or structure.

platetrope ('plætɪtrəʊp). *Anat.* [f. Gr. πλάτος, πλατε- breadth, width + τρόπος turning.] (See quot.)

1882 WILDER & GAGE *Anatom. Technol.* 32 Two similar organs, one upon each side, are lateral in position, and called *paired organs*. Each such paired organ may be called the *platetrope* of the other, or its *lateral homologue*, or the *fellow of the opposite side*.

Hence **platetropy** ('plætɪtrəʊpɪ), bilateral symmetry.

1890 in *Cent. Dict.*

†**plate-vein.** *Obs.* Also 7–9 **plat-**, 8 **plait-**. The cephalic vein in the horse.

1607 TOPSELL *Four-f. Beasts* (1658) 294 Let him [the horse] bloud on both sides abundantly in the plat veins, and then give him this drink. **1610** MARKHAM *Masterp.* II. cxxvii. 428 They will also stop the blood, which is in the principall veines, called the plat veines. **1730** BURDON *Pocket Farrier* (1735) 25 Then bleed him in the plait Vein. **1831** YOUATT *Horse* 181 The *plate* vein, which comes from the inside of the arm, and runs upwards directly in front of it towards the jugular, may be opened. **1841** *Encycl. Brit.* (ed. 7) XXI. 632/1 Occasionally there is inflammation of the jugular from bleeding, and more rarely, of the plate and saphena vein.

plate-way, -work, etc.: see PLATE *sb.* 20, 21.

platfond, obs. form of PLAFOND.

†**platfoot**, *a.* and *adv.* *Sc. Obs.* [f. PLAT *a.* + FOOT *sb.* So Du. *platvoet* 'ayant les pieds larges' (Plantin), MHG. *blatevuoz*, Ger. *plattfuss*.] **a.** *adj.* Flat-footed. **b.** *adv.* Flat-footedly. In quotations, the name of a dance-tune.

1530 LYNDESAY *Test. Papyngo* 88 To lerne hir language artificiall, To play platfute, and quhissill fute before. *a* **1550** *Christis Kirke Gr.* I. vi, Platfute he bobbit vp with bendis, For Mald he maid requeist.

platform ('plætfɔːm), *sb.* (*a.*) Forms: 6 **platte-**, 6–7 **platt-**, 6– **plat-**; 6–7 **-fo(u)rme**, 6– **-form**. In 6–8 often as two words, or hyphened. *β.* 6–7 **plotform(e**. [a. F. *plateforme* (in 1433 *platte fourme*), *lit.* 'flat form', 'plane figure', representation on the flat, ground-plan, 'a plot, modell, or draught of a building; also, the foundation thereof' (Cotgr.): see PLAT *a.* and FORM *sb.* The *β* forms arose from the running together of *plat* and *plot*: see PLAT *sb.*[3]]

A. *sb.* **I.** A plane surface; a plan on the flat.

†**1.** *Geom.* A plane figure (as a triangle, quadrilateral, circle, etc.); also, a plane surface, a plane, and, in wider sense, any surface. *Obs.*

1551 RECORDE *Pathw.* I. Defin., Of platte formes some be plain, and some be croked, and some partlie plaine, and partlie croked. *Ibid.*, In a dye (whiche is called a cubike bodie) by geometricians..there are .vi. sides, whiche are .vi. platte formes, and are the boundes of the dye. *Ibid.* II. Introd., Two right lines make no platte forme. **1574** BOURNE *Regiment for Sea* xviii. (1577) 49 The most parte of the seamen make their account as though the earth were a platforme. **1674** JEAKE *Arith.* (1696) 181 A Diametral Number may have more parts then be apt for the Sides of the Platform or Rectangle Figure it represents.

†**2.** A plan or representation on the flat (*of* any structure existing or projected); a ground-plan; a topographical plan, chart, map; a plan or draught to build by. *Obs.*

[Kington Oliphant cites *platform* 1513–25 from State Papers, which may be in this sense or 4.]

1551 ROBINSON *More's Utop.* II. (1895) 131 They sat that kyng Vtopus himself..appointed, and drew furth the platte fourme of the city. **1579–80** NORTH *Plutarch* (1676) 456 [They] were every one occupied about drawing the Platform of Sicilia. **1639** HORN & ROB. *Gate Lang. Unl.* xlviii. §525 The master-builder, having first drawne out the plot, buildeth according to that draught (modell or plat-forme) with other work-men helping him. **1665** G. HAVERS *P. della Valle's Trav. E. India* 8 Captain Woodcock..shew'd me a Chart or Plat-form of the whole Streight of Ormuz, made by himself. **1763** GRAY *Let.* 15 Jan., I conclude with a rude draught of the platform [of York Cathedral] according to my idea, but without any mensuration. **1774** JOHNSON *Journ. N. Wales* 17 Aug., All the walls remain, so that a complete platform, and elevations, not very imperfect, may be taken.

β. **1606** HOLLAND *Sueton.* 14 He..viewed, and considered the plotforme according to which he was about to build a Schoole of swordfencers.

II. Figurative uses derived from sense 2 (*plan*).

†**3. a.** A plan, design; something intended or taken as a pattern, a model. *Obs.*

1574 R. SCOT (*title*) A Perfite Platforme of a Hoppe Garden, and necessarie instructions for the making and mayntenaunce thereof. **1575** GASCOIGNE *Making of Verse* Wks. T iv, Many wryters when they haue layed the platforme of their inuention, are yet drawen sometimes (by ryme) to forget it. **1586** A. DAY *Eng. Secretary* I. (1625) 1 To lay downe a platforme or method for writing of Epistles. **1693** J. EDWARDS *Author. O. & N. Test.* 105 This garden was the platform of those before mentioned. *a* **1703** BURKITT *On N.T.* Luke xi. 1 The Lord's prayer is..a pattern and platform, according to which all our prayers ought to be framed. **1775** BURKE *Corr.* (1844) II. 3 You will naturally follow the platform of the London petition, and can be at no loss in the wording. **1827** HALLAM *Const. Hist.* (1842) II. 522 This noble design was not altogether completed according to the platform.

β. **1591** R. HICHCOCK in *Garrard's Art Warre* A iv b, Ample and fine drawne plots, goodly plotformes, needfull inuentions. **1615** W. LAWSON *Country Housew. Gard.* (1626) 17 The Plot-forme being laid, and the Plot appointed where you will plant euery Set in your Orchard.

†**b.** A written outline or sketch; a scheme; a description. *Obs.*

1596 SPENSER *State Irel.* Wks. (Globe) 633/1 Ane affectation of Irish captaynrye, which in this plattforme I endevour specially to beate downe. **1647** TRAPP *Comm. Rom.* ii. 19 A platform of wholsome words, a systeme, a method artificially moulded, such as Tutours and Professours of Arts and Sciences have, and do read over again and again to their Auditours. **1680** N. LEE *Cæsar Borgia* I. i, Thus have I drawn the platform of their Fates. **1716** M. DAVIES *Athen. Brit.* III. *Dissert. Physick* 56 The solid Platforms of the Astrological and Hydrological Branches of Physick shall be set down next. **1727** J. ASGILL *Metamorph. Man* I. 141 The two Records in the Thessalonians and Corinthians, left us as a Platform of the first Resurrection.

†**4. a.** A plan of action; a scheme, design, device. *Obs.*

1550 GARDINER *Let. to Ld. Protector* in Foxe *A. & M.* (1583) 1342/1 If my Lord of S. Dauides, or such others haue theyr head combred with any new platforme. **1577–87** HOLINSHED *Chron.* I. 132/2 His destruction intended by queene Quendred, hir platforme of the practise to kill him. **1649** BLITHE *Eng. Improv. Impr.* (1653) 64 A good method, or plat-form to advance each mans labour to the best furtherance of a work. **1686** F. SPENCE tr. *Varillas' Ho. Medicis* 137 Those who had drawn up the platform of the Pazzi's conspiracy. **1815** J. ADAMS *Wks.* (1856) X. 140 A magnificent confederation, association, platform, or conspiracy, call it what you will, of three great personages to separate all South America from Spain.

β. ? *a* **1600** *Grim the Collier* in Hazl. *Dodsley* VIII. 423 A sudden plotform comes into my mind, And this it is.

b. *spec.* A plan or draught of church government and discipline; a scheme of principles or doctrines, made by or on behalf of a religious party, church, or sect. Now *rare*.

1573 CARTWRIGHT *Repl. Answ. Whitgift* 13 A true and perfect patern or platforme of reforming the church. *c* **1589** *Theses Martinianæ* 8 That the platforme of gouernment by Pastors, Doctors, Elders, and Deacons was not deuised by man, but by our Sauiour Christ himselfe. **1644** (*title*) The Platforme of the Presbyterian Government with the Forme of Church Worship, &c. Published by Authority. **1674** HICKMAN *Hist. Quinquart.* (ed. 2) 92 How it can be proved, that..the Belgick Churches did first embrace Religion according to the Lutheran, and not the Calvinian platform? *a* **1732** ATTERBURY *Serm.* (1737) IV. 24 They imposed the platform of their doctrine..as divine. **1759** ROBERTSON *Hist. Scot.* III. Wks. 1813 I. 194 The first book of discipline.. contains the model or platform of the intended policy. **1835** HALIBURTON *Clockm.* Ser. I. 47 Under what Church platform? *a* **1881** STANLEY in A. Elliot *State & the Church* (1882) 26 No existing Church can find any pattern or platform of its government in those early days. **1882** J. H. BLUNT *Ref. Ch. Eng.* II. 406 Nothing in the Church could be 'pure', in their estimation, unless it conformed itself to the Genevan 'platform'.

†**c.** A plan or scheme of government or administration; a plan of political action. *Obs.* (Cf. 9 b.)

1598 GRENEWEY *Tacitus' Ann.* XIII. i. (1622) 179 Then he [Nero] laid downe a platforme of his future regiment. **1610** HEALEY *St. Aug. Citie of God* III. xvi. (1620) 122 This was the yeare wherein Rome deuised her platforme of new gouernment. **1625** in *Debates in Ho. Comm.* 6 Aug. (Camden) App. 140 Sir Robert Philips commended the platforme of Sir Nathaniel Rich, and sayd that wee were beholding unto him for shewing us the way. **1757** BURKE *Abridgm. Eng. Hist.* Wks. (1812) 8 A violent and ill-considered attempt was made, unjustly, to establish the platforms of the Government.

III. The surface or area on which anything stands; esp. a raised level surface.

†**5. a.** The area occupied by any structure; the site of a group of buildings, a fort, camp, etc. *Obs.*

1598 HAKLUYT *Voy.* I. 436 With your instrument, for trying of distances, obserue the platforme of the place. **1664** EVELYN tr. *Freart's Archit.* etc. 122 The Area or Floor, by Artists often called the Plan or Plat-forme. **1671** S. PARTRIDGE *Double Scale Proportion* 37 If the platform were a piece of land, 30 perches broad, and 183 perches long. **1726** LEONI *Alberti's Archit.* I. 2/1 Under the Title of Platform, we..include all those Spaces of the Buildings, which in walking we tread upon with our Feet. **1739** CIBBER *Apol.* (1756) I. 301 The area or platform of the old stage projected about four foot forwarder in a semi-oval figure. **1796** H. HUNTER tr. *St.-Pierre's Stud. Nat.* (1799) III. 70, I was sitting by the platform of these cottages, and contemplating their ruins.

b. *fig.* The ground, foundation, or basis *of* an action, event, calculation, condition, etc. Now *rare*.

1625 *Gonsalvio's Sp. Inquis.* To Rdr., Which is so farre off from any figuratiue speech, as it is knowne to be the very Platforme and foundation of all these broyles and troubles. **1698** FRYER *Acc. E. India & P.* 12 All the Seasons of the Year being undergone.., we may begin to calculate our Ephemeris afresh; and as a fit Platform, Easter Holy-days bring with them such Weather as is essential to Christide [at the Cape]. **1724** tr. *Pliny's Epist.* I. Life 18 Probably the first Platform of his future Industry and Application was laid in an habitual Care to oblige [his uncle]. **1829** SOUTHEY *Sir T. More* II. 174 A new government has been constituted in a new country,..and consequently upon a different platform. **1832** *Niles' Register* 1 Sept. XLIII. 1/2 Fifteen per cent. being the 'platform' on which certain interests would agree to protect the national industry!!!

c. *fig.* ***the platform***, or more fully ***the equal dividend platform***, in the Free and United Free Churches of Scotland, the position or general level of churches drawing an equal dividend from the Sustentation Fund, as opposed to embryo or merely mission churches not yet 'on the platform'.

1862 *Proc. of Free Ch. Scot.* 168 Charges formed out of Home Mission efforts and not yet admitted on the equal dividend platform.

d. *fig.* A plane or level *of* action, thought, etc.

1870 EMERSON *Soc. & Solit., Clubs* Wks. (Bohn) III. 95 Conversation in society is found to be on a platform so low as to exclude science, the saint, and the poet. **1875** HELPS *Soc. Press.* ix. 129 The platform of thought upon which each generation finds itself placed, is a platform of a very different kind from that of the preceding thirty years.

6. A raised level surface or area.

a. A level place constructed for mounting guns in a fort or battery.

1560 Whitehorne *Ord. Souldiours* (1588) 18 b, That which shall haue either caualiers or platformes. **1571** Digges *Pantom.* i. xxx. I iv, Suche as shall haue committed to their charge any platfourme with ordinaunce. **1602** Shaks. *Ham.* i. ii. 252 Fare ye well: Vpon the Platforme twixt eleuen and twelue, Ile visit you. **1704** J. Harris *Lex. Techn.* I, *Platform*, in Fortification, is a Place prepared on the Ramparts for the raising of a Battery or Cannon; or it is the whole Piece of Fortification raised in a re-entring Angle. **1814** Wellington in Gurw. *Desp.* XI. 564 To construct the battery, with its traverses, platform and magazines in one night. **1827** Roberts *Voy. Centr. Amer.* 179 Twelve pieces of Cannon..mounted..on a wooden platform of great thickness.

β. **1575** Gascoigne *Noble Art Venerie* Wks. 1870 II. 304 Patterns..Of Plotformes, Loopes, and Casamats, deuisde by warlike men. **1626** Capt. Smith *Accid. Yng. Seamen* 33 If she [a piece] be well mounted, vpon a leuell plot-forme.

†**b.** An open walk or terrace on the top of a building or on a wall. *Obs.*

1580–1 *Reg. Privy Council Scot.* III. 364 The haill tymmer of the bak platfurme and bartesing. **1687** A. Lovell tr. *Thevenot's Trav.* ii. 142 A great wall of blackish stones four Foot thick, which supports a large Platform or Terrass. **1691** T. H[ale] *Acc. New Invent.* 107 Lead which was first laid on about twelve Years since upon two Platforms at my House there. **1704** J. Harris *Lex. Techn.* I, *Platform*, in Architecture, is..a kind of Terrass Walk, or even Floor on the Top of the Building; from whence we may take a fair Prospect of the adjacent Gardens or Fields.

c. A natural or artificial terrace, a flat elevated piece of ground; a table-land, a plateau. *spec.* in *Geol.* and *Physical Geogr.*: (i) A level or nearly level strip of land at the base of a cliff close to the water-level; occas., a similar terrace away from a body of water but thought to have been formed by the sea in such a situation.

1813 Scott *Trierm.* iii. xiv, The brave De Vaux Began to scale these magic rocks, And soon a platform won. **1832** Lyell *Princ. Geol.* II. 40 The great platform [in Mexico] which is the scene of sport is at an elevation of about nine thousand feet above the level of the sea. **1838** *Murray's Hand-bk. N. Germ.* 351 The *Brockenhaus* is the name of the inn on the platform of bare rock which forms the summit of the Brocken. **1841** C. Lyell *Elem. of Geol.* (ed. 2) I. vi. 150 The sea is advancing upon the land, and removing annually small portions of undermined rock. By this agency a submarine platform is produced on which we may walk for some distance from the beach in shallow water, the increase of depth being very gradual, until we reach a point where the bottom plunges down suddenly. This platform is widened with more or less rapidity according to the hardness of the rocks, and when upraised it constitutes an inland terrace. **1860** Tyndall *Glac.* ii. x. 284 The station chosen..was on a grassy platform. **1862** Stanley *Jew. Ch.* (1877) I. vi. 120 The loftier and still loftier regions of the mountain platform. **1865** J. Fergusson *Hist. Archit.* I. i. ii. iv. 172 The buildings we..find on the platform at Persepolis. **1901** *Bull. Geol. Soc. Amer.* XII. 212 A looped bar or ridge of gravel and sand formed on an old wave-cut platform. **1922** E. M. Ward *Eng. Coastal Evol.* ii. 34 There must come a time when further coast retreat would involve the total exhaustion of wave energy in crossing the shallow water of a wide wave-cut platform. **1944** A. Holmes *Princ. Physical Geol.* xiv. 289 As the cliffs are worn back a wave-cut platform is left in front.., the upper part of which is visible as the rocky foreshore exposed at low tide. **1964** W. C. Putnam *Geol.* xiv. 387/2 Where the platform is mantled with sand, it is the beach. *Ibid.* 388/1 These coasts may be bordered by a whole flight of terraces, which are elevated wave-cut platforms. **1975** R. V. Ruhe *Geomorphol.* ix. 178/2 There are five marine terraces in Santa Cruz, California; each platform was cut during rising sea level, and its cover of marine sediments was deposited during falling sea level.

(ii) ***continental platform***: see continental *a.* 1 d.

(iii) A former erosion surface or plateau represented by the common surface or summit level of neighbouring hills or other land forms.

1908 *Q. Jrnl. Geol. Soc.* LXIV. 384 Of the older topography..partly destroyed by post-Pliocene denudation, the most striking feature in the higher part of the area is presented by two well-marked high-level platforms, one at 750 feet above the sea, and the other may be called the 1000-foot platform, although it is really a little below this altitude. The latter was first recognized on Davidstow Moor,..but traces of it are to be seen on the surrounding high land in all directions. **1938** A. K. Wells *Outl. Hist. Geol.* xvii. 226 In a few localities on the Chiltern dip slope remnants of the Lenham platform form a gently inclined shelf above the 400-feet platform. **1954** J. F. Kirkaldy *Gen. Princ. Geol.* ix. 96 Accordance of summit levels or the presence of platforms at lower levels can be inferred from the layout of the contours. **1966** J. I. Clarke in G. H. Dury *Ess. Geomorphol.* 257 In Britain..there is a marked tendency to attribute platforms to marine erosion.., while in Australia..and elsewhere it is often held that uplift and rejuvenation of ancient surfaces are possible. *Ibid.* 270 Sparsely-distributed height-values rarely give..a good indication of erosion-platforms.

(iv) The part of a kratogen (craton) where the basement complex, elsewhere exposed as a shield, is overlain by a layer of more recent, relatively flat and undisturbed strata that are mainly sedimentary.

1908 tr. *Suess's Face of Earth* III. iv. ix. 376 The pre-Cambrian platform. In front of the Urals there extends the vast Russian plain. Its ancient foundation is not visible till we proceed a considerable distance to the west and south-west. **1923** L. D. Stamp *Introd. Stratigr.* iii. 36 The whole area of S.E. England consists of a blanket of Mesozoic Rocks resting on an eroded surface of Palæozoic rocks called the Palæozoic Platform. **1958** L. P. Smirnow in L. G. Weeks *Habitat of Oil* 1168 (*heading*) Oil-bearing basins on eastern edge of the Russian platform. **1968** C. R. Twidale *Geomorphol.* iii. 49 The Australian continent is built of a Shield, a Platform and an Orogen. **1972** B. B. Brock *Global Approach to Geol.* iv. 35 The Russian platform, with a moderate thickness of flat-lying rocks covering the basement, brings the Baltic shield up to the normal size.

7. †**a.** A division of the orlop of a man-of-war, between the cock-pit and the main-mast. *Obs.*

1667 *Lond. Gaz.* No. 159/4 The Lieutenant succeeding in the command, was about half an houre after wounded in both leggs, and carried down to the Platforme. **1704** J. Harris *Lex. Techn.* I, *Platform*, or *Orlop*, in a Man of War, is a Place on the Lower Deck of her, abaft the Main Mast, and round about the Main Capstan, where, in the Time of Service, Provision is to take care of the Wounded Men; 'tis between the Main Mast and the Cock-pit. **1727–41** Chambers *Cycl.* s.v. *Ship*, Plate, The Platform or Orlop.

b. In a small boat or yacht: a light deck.

1950 R. Moore *Candlemas Bay* i. 47 Otherwise she'd have come up and drained her platform through the scuppers, as soon as she floated. **1961** F. H. Burgess *Dict. Sailing* 161 *Platform*, floor boards laid over the floors in small yachts to make a walking space.

8. A raised level surface formed with planks, boards, or the like.

a. *generally*, as used for standing, sitting, walking, for seeing or being seen, or for any purpose for which such an arrangement is useful.

In a glass-furnace, the bench on which the pots are placed (Knight *Dict. Mech.* 1875). ***feeding platform***, in *Pisciculture*, a platform fixed in a trout-pond, a few inches from the bottom, on which food is thrown for the fish.

1727 A. Hamilton *New Acc. E. Ind.* II. iii. 255 The Teytocks Chair..was raised on a plat Form of Deals, with three Steps of Ascent. **1761** *Ann. Reg.* 218/2 (*Coronation of Geo. III*) A platform was erected from the upper end of Westminster Hall..to the west door of the abbey. **1777** W. Dalrymple *Trav. Sp. & Port.* ix, At night we were provided with clean beds and platforms. **1792** A. Young *Trav. France* 194 Cross the Po by a most commodious ferry; a platform on two boats. **1820** *Ann. Reg.* ii. 1372/2 It resembles the platforms used on land for weighing waggons. **1826** Hone *Every-Day Bk.* I. 1182 There were fifteen hundred variegated illumination-lamps disposed over various parts of this platform [in front of a theatre at a fair]. **1827** *Hull Advertiser* 14 Dec. 4/1 In this order they went..over the temporary Bridge..and passed down an inclined platform..to the bottom of the South or Humber Dock Pit. **1831** *Fraser's Mag.* IV. 374 The Queen..advanced in procession to the platform [on which the coronation ceremony was to take place]. **1864** Lowell *Fireside Trav.* 153 He laid the bags upon a platform of alders, which he bent down.

b. A horizontal stage or piece of flooring resting on wheels, as in a railway carriage, truck, or tram-car; Colonial and U.S. *esp.* the open portion of the floor at the end of a railway car.

1832 *Penny Mag.* I. 275 Fixed on a moveable platform, having four wheels; these wheels move along an iron railway which is itself fixed on another platform. **1846** *Hull & Lincoln Railw. Bill* 11 Conveyed on a truck or platform. **1892** Stevenson *Across the Plains* 34 The platform of the car. **1896** *Daily News* 10 Nov. 2/1 (Lord Mayor's Show) Upon the platform-on-wheels officially billed as 'England and her Heroes' were men..representing the uniforms of the Buffs at the beginning of the century,..the Black Watch,..and a couple of antique Jack Tars. **1903** *Westm. Gaz.* 4 Mar. 12/1 A passenger..warned not to ride on the platform of a car which was speeding at the rate of fifty miles an hour. **1931** H. F. Pringle *Theodore Roosevelt* i. xv. 205 On the special train..a bugler appeared on the rear platform to sound the cavalry charge. **1932** *Atlantic Monthly* Apr. 437/2 As the train pulled out I saw from the back platform my two men. **1971** *Power Farming* Mar. 48/4 Illustrated recently in the trade press was a foot-propelled backward-travelling strawberry picking platform used in Israel. **1971** M. Tak *Truck Talk* 119 *Platform*, a flat bed trailer, a trailer that has a deck (or platform) on which cargo rests but no sides. **1978** R. L. Hill *Evil that Men Do* (1979) xx. 244 An early 'fifties flatbed farm truck sat beside the shack, its stacked platform serving as a temporary pen for two enormous sows. **1979** P. Theroux *Old Patagonian Express* xviii. 286 We were supposed to have been in Mainara for three minutes... I sat on the steps of the platform and smoked my pipe.

c. A raised walk or floor along the side of the line at a railway station, for convenience in entering and alighting from the trains. (See also quot. 1900.)

1838 F. W. Simms *Public Wks. Gt. Brit.* 2 On the opposite side an arrival stage or platform is erected. **1846** *Fraser's Mag.* XXXIV. 522 The platform of an extensive railway station. **1878** F. S. Williams *Midl. Railw.* 216 The Citadel Station..in 1860 consisted of a single platform for both up and down trains. **1900** *Engineering Mag.* XIX. 703 The movable platform, or traveling sidewalk [at the French *Exposition*]. *Ibid.*, In large machine works..time now lost in passing from one part to another might be saved by a travelling platform. *Mod.* Subway to platforms 1, 2, 3, and 4.

d. A structure which is designed to stand on the bed of the sea (or a lake) and to provide a stable base above water level from which a number of offshore oil or gas wells can be drilled or regulated.

1938 *World Petroleum* May 76/3 The coast line..is exposed to strong winds and rough seas during six months of the year, so that a very substantial platform has to be provided when underwater drilling is to be done. **1955** *Rev. Petroleum Technol.* XIV. 24 Fixed-well platforms, unless capable of multiple-well work, are uneconomical 'at sea'. **1973** *Guardian* 23 May 13/1 In Scotland today the word platform means..a production unit weighing perhaps a quarter of a million tons, going up to 700 feet high..for use in the North Sea oilfields. **1974** *Esso Mag.* Summer 7 The next generation of platforms, now under construction, are concrete structures, in which a massive concrete cellular base, which doubles as oil storage, supports the towers which carry the production platform. **1975** *Sunday Times* 25 May 4/5 Britain's gas supplies are unlikely to be affected, even if some platforms have to stop production temporarily.

e. A gyroscopically stabilized mounting which is isolated from the angular motion of the craft carrying it and provides an inertial frame for the accelerometers of an inertial guidance system; the gyroscopes, accelerometers, and other instruments associated with this.

1946 Wells & Glenny in M. Davidson *Gyroscope* iii. i. 174 The gyroscope and the magnetic compass assemblies are supported on platforms attached to a rectangular frame. **1954** *Aviation Age* Oct. 21/1 Gyros, by virtue of their ability to maintain a fixed direction in inertial space, provide a ready means for stabilizing the accelerometer platform against angular motion of the vehicle. **1964** C. F. O'Donnell *Inertial Navig.* i. 20 To aid in platform stabilization, servos are used, with their input signals coming from pick-offs mounted on the precession or output axis of the gyroscopes. **1970** *Time* 27 Apr. 15 He charged up *Odyssey's* small re-entry batteries..and transferred the precise alignment of the command module's 'platform'—its complex of navigational gyroscopes and accelerometers—to a similar platform in the lunar lander. **1977** *Sci. Amer.* Feb. 21/2 A long-range cruise missile employs an inertial-guidance system consisting essentially of three or more accelerometers mounted on gyroscope-stabilized platforms, to guide it along a preassigned course.

f. A rigid diving-board fixed at any of a series of standard heights varying from 3 to 10 metres above the surface of the water; also, in a diving contest, the highboard event.

1971 L. Koppett *N.Y. Times Guide Spectator Sports* ix. 169 Off the platform, some dives are made from a handstand. **1973** *Tucson* (Arizona) *Daily Citizen* 21 Aug. 61/7 Finneran is a [*sic*] Olympic veteran, finishing fifth in the three-meters last year in Munich and ninth in the platform. **1974** *Encycl. Brit. Macropædia* XVII. 863/2 When diving first became part of the Olympic program in 1904, it was little more than plain high diving from five- and ten-metre fixed platforms. **1974** *Rules of Game* 202 Competitive diving... Highboard diving platforms and springboards are provided at the heights shown.

9. a. *spec.* A temporary (or sometimes permanent) piece of raised flooring in a hall, or in the open air, from which a speaker addresses his audience, and on which the promoters of a meeting sit; hence, *transf.* or allusively, in reference to public speaking or discussion on a platform, the making of political or other speeches, platform oratory; also, the body of supporters who appear on a platform, as 'an influential' or 'representative platform'. Also *fig.*

c **1820** [Said to have been in use]. **1836** *Hull Observer* July, Ample arrangements had been made on the ground by the erection of hustings for the spectators and a platform for the speakers. **1840** *Niles' Register* 7 Mar. LVIII. 4/3 On the platform above the officers of the convention a beautiful transparency had been placed, representing general Harrison in uniform. **1853** A. Prentice *Hist. Anti-Corn Law League* I. 12 On Thursday August 2nd [1832] Mr. Loyd appeared on a platform on the Clarendon Inn bowling green. **1857** W. Collins *Dead Secret* ii. i, He was quite incapable of finding his way to the platform of Exeter Hall. **1868** M. Pattison *Academ. Org.* 6 So much of it [the question] as could be brought upon the platform, was made into a party topic. **1874** Blackie *Self-Cult.* 25 To go to the pulpit or platform with a thorough command of his subject. **1885** H. N. Oxenham *Short Stud. Eth. & Relig.* x. 86 Foolish and erroneous..notions are fostered by the periodical press, but the same might be said of the pulpit and the platform. **1886** J. Bright in G. C. Brodrick *Mem. & Impress.* (1900) 230, I have quitted the platform, and no longer feel the warm interest which is required to make me speak. **1901** *Daily Chron.* 11 Dec. 3/4 He lamented the growth of the platform. He ignored the Press. His one concern was to be a capable official. **1964** E. B. White *Let.* 21 Feb. (1976) 517 A man is privileged to say anything he wants to about the magazine, but..he can't use one of my books as a platform. **1966** 'W. Haggard' *Power House* vii. 72 *The Freeman* was important to him since it provided him with a platform. **1977** *It* May 29/4 Aims... To act as a platform for people with radical ideas and opinions.

b. *fig.* A basis on which persons unitedly take their stand and make their public appeal; *spec.* in U.S. politics, a public declaration of the principles and policy on which a political party proposes to stand; now *esp.* such a declaration issued by the representatives of the party assembled in convention to nominate candidates for an election. Also *transf.*

This *fig.* use was developed in U.S. between 1844 and 1848; in early instances, as well as in the phrase 'a plank of the platform' (cf. plank *sb.* 5), it is associated directly with the material platform on which persons meet and publicly speak (a sense known in U.S. from 1840). Although to some extent approaching senses 4 b, 4 c, 5 b, this in its origin had no direct connexion with these.

1803 *Massachusetts Spy* 27 Apr. (Th.), The platform of Federalism. **1837** *Liberator* 15 Dec. 203/3 We care not who is found upon this broad platform of our common nature. **1838** *Congress. Globe* 11 Jan. App. 73/1 We wanted no platform on which to stand, save the Constitution of our country. **1844** *Address Democr. State Convent. Virginia* 3 Feb. in *Niles' Register* LXV. 408/1 These are our doctrines—this the broad platform on which we stand. Here is our confession of faith..old as the constitution—old as the days of our fathers. **1845** C. Sumner in *Mem. & Lett.* (1893) III. 104 S. C. Phillips and W. B. Calhoun..will labor to bring the Whig party of Massachusetts to the antislavery platform. **1847** S. P. Chase in *Ann. Rep. Amer. Hist. Assoc. for 1902* II. 123, I care nothing for names. All I ask for is a platform and an issue. **1847** W. Lumpkin *Ibid. for 1899* II. 1138 The passage of the Wilmot resolutions by Congress, I believe..will enlarge the platform on which we stand. **1848** *N.Y. Herald* 6 May 4/1 We hope that the coming convention will..solemnly re-affirm our old party position, by adopting, as its platform of action, the general resolutions of 1844. *Ibid.*, The whigs, whether on the Lexington platform, or some other non-committal platform, will be and must be at once known and doomed as the party that opposed their country. **1848** Lowell *Biglow P.* viii. 154 It gives a Party Platform, tu, jest level with the mind Of all right-thinkin', honest folks thet mean to go it blind. **1853** Cobden 1793 & 1853 iii. 87 The advocates of peace have found in the peace congress movement a common platform, to use an Americanism, on which all men who desire to avert war..may co-operate. **1862** T. Hughes in J. M. Ludlow *Hist. U.S.* 379 The platform on which Abraham Lincoln came in. **1864** Knight *Passages Work. Life* II. vi. 124 A cordial union of men of very different persuasions..who have met upon a common platform. **1878** *N. Amer. Rev.* CXXVII. 103 A Western Democrat on a soft-money platform. **1882** *Sydney Slang Dict.* 7/1 *Platform*, a standpoint, as 'Home rule's my platform'. Originally an Americanism. **1883** *Standard* 28 Apr. 5/4 The platform of the Convention [of the Irish Nationalists] occupies a column of small type in the papers. **1888** Bryce *Amer. Commw.* II. III. lxx. 549 *note*, The nearest English parallel to an American 'platform' is to be found in the addresses..issued at a general election by the Prime Minister..and the leader of the Opposition. **1891** [see plank *sb.* 5]. **1909** 'O. Henry' *Roads of Destiny* x. 166 He leaned on the desk and declared his platform to the clerk. He said he had come to Elmore to look for a location to go into business. **1924** H. G. Wells *Dream* 142, I adopted Votes for Women as the first plank of my political platform. **1926** A. Conan Doyle *Hist. Spiritualism* I. ii. 25 The broad platform upon which his beliefs were constructed. **1937** [see plank *sb.* 5]. **1964** Gould & Kolb *Dict. Social Sci.* 484/2 The party platform is adopted before the candidates for President and Vice-President are nominated and..it can happen that the candidate and the platform disagree in important particulars. **1976** *Survey* Spring 87 The Communist Party of the United States of America..has held conventions to..discuss its strategy and approve a platform.

10. = *platform sole*. Also short for *platform shoe*.

1945 Webster Add., *Platform*,..an outsole a half inch or more thick, made of wood, cork, etc., and usually covered with leather. **1946** *Sun* (Baltimore) 2 Nov. 3 (Advt.), Picture-Pretty Platforms... Two flattering styles to choose from..both mounted on black faille platforms. **1960** D. Lessing *In Pursuit of English* vii. 229, I could not keep my eyes off her shoes... The soles were platforms two inches deep. **1970** *New Yorker* 31 Oct. 125/1 A boot with a small platform in a contrasting color. **1973** *Times* 7 Nov. 18/3 An office manager wearing 4½ inch..platforms said 'they give you a masculine walk because you walk heavy'. *Ibid.* 18/4 He wore them to catch up with his girl friend's six inch platforms. **1977** C. McFadden *Serial* (1978) v. 17/2 A woman in..eight-inch platforms that reminded him of the moon shot.

†**B.** *adj.* Of flat form, flat. *Obs. rare*$^{-1}$.

1632 Lithgow *Trav.* v. 208 The tectures of her Houses..being platforme.

C. *attrib.* and *Comb.*, as ***platform-framer***, ***-lead***, ***-pavilion***; (sense 8 b) ***platform body***; (sense 8 c) ***platform foreman***, ***inspector***, ***official***, ***track***; (sense 8 d) ***platform leg***, ***operator***; (sense 8 f) ***platform diving***; (sense 9) ***platform appeal***, ***campaign***, ***denunciation***, ***eloquence***, ***engagement***, ***-maker***, ***man***, ***manner(s)***, ***orator***, ***oratory***, ***plank***, ***point***, ***reply***, ***speaker***, ***speaking***, ***woman***; ***platform-proud***, ***-ridden*** adjs.; (sense 10) ***platform-wearer***; **platform-bridge**, in *U.S.* a gangway between the platforms of two railway-carriages; **platform-car** (*U.S.*), **platform-carriage**, a low four-wheeled wagon or truck without sides, for transporting mortars and other heavy articles; **platform-crane**, a crane mounted on a railway-truck; **platform machine** = *platform scale*; **platform-mud** *Geol.*, an elevated deposit of mud with level surface; **platform paddle tennis** = *platform tennis*; **platform party**, the group of officials or distinguished persons who sit on the platform at a ceremony or a meeting; **platform rocker** orig. *U.S.*, a rocking chair constructed with a fixed stationary base; **platform sandal**, a sandal with a platform sole; **platform scale**, a weighing-machine with a platform on which the object to be weighed is placed; **platform shoe**, a shoe with a platform sole; **platform sole**, a very thick outer shoe-sole; also *attrib.*; hence ***platform-soled*** adj.; **platform-spring**: see spring *sb.*; **platform stage** *Theatr.* (see quots. 1951) (cf. *apron stage* s.v. apron *sb.* 4 j); **platform tennis**, a form of paddle tennis (see paddle *sb.*[1] 12) played on a platform, usu. of wood, enclosed by a wire fence; **platform ticket**, a ticket admitting a non-traveller to a railway station platform; **platform tree** *poet. nonce-use*, a tree with a wide-spreading, flat-topped crown; **platform truck**, a road transport vehicle having a platform body; **platform-wagon** = *platform-carriage*; **platform yard**, a yard where oil platforms are built.

1959 *Times* 18 June 13/2 Dame Christabel [Pankhurst]..deliberately based her '*platform appeal' on charm rather than logic. **1973** *Amer. Speech 1969* XLIV. 207 **Platform body*, truck or trailer body with a floor but no sides or roof. **1977** *Horse & Hound* 14 Jan. 44/2 (Advt.), A 16 ft horse box frame, for Bedford T.K. platform body, rear ramp with springs. **1909** *Daily Chron.* 9 Feb. 1/7 The National Passive Resistance League is organising a *platform campaign against the House of Lords. **1843** E. H. Derby *Two Months Abroad* (1844) 20/1 By this, with the aid of a winch, diligences and private carriages are..lifted, with their passengers and baggage, from the wheels and axles, and transferred to *platform cars. **1900** *Westm. Gaz.* 23 Oct. 8/1 An order for..several steel platform cars of forty tons capacity. **1850** Robertson *Serm.* Ser. III. i. (1872) 7 *Platform denunciations. **1971** L. Koppett *N.Y. Times Guide Spectator Sports* xx. 249 *Platform and three-meter springboard diving. **1966** *Listener* 24 Nov. 783/3 Mr. Sandford's work was a ferocious contemporary indictment. .. *Cathy Come Home* may have done more in its hour and a quarter than the *platform eloquence of half a year. **1907** G. Ade *Let.* 3 June (1973) 41, I have no hankering to undertake any *platform engagements as long as I can get money doing something else. **1897** *Daily News* 29 Dec. 5/1 *Platform foreman at Euston Station. **1901** *Q. Rev.* July 55 These by-gone *platform-framers and 'leaders of revolts'. **1703** T. N. *City & C. Purchaser* 190 Sometimes *Platform-lead is near ⅛ of an Inch thick. **1975** *Offshore* Aug. 51/2 Divers can be employed to hand risers or lead pipeline ends up into *platform legs when lines are pulled. **1922** G. A. Owen *Treat. Weighing Machines* x. 134 *Platform machines and weighbridges..are used in the main for weighing above 1 cwt., and are distinguishable by a goods platform. **1969** T. J. Metcalfe *Weighing Machines* I. x. 99 Platform machines may be portable or dormant. **1928** *Daily Tel.* 12 June 14/7 To-day the '*platform-makers' of both parties were trying to frame an election programme. **1903** Morley *Gladstone* III. x. v. 433 *Platform-men united with pulpit-men in swelling the whirlwind. **1969** B. Turner *Circle of Squares* iii. 23 Anyone who was suspicious of Hirst's *platform manner would be disarmed by that bulldozing statement. **1947** *Penguin Music Mag.* Sept. 34 As if Chopin was a puppet worked by a skilled ventriloquist of charming *platform-manners. **1863** Lyell *Antiq. Man* xvi. 336 Deposits of '*platform mud', as it has been termed in France, might be extensively formed. **1975** *BP Shield Internat.* May 1/3 A relatively new breed of oilman will be required. These are the *platform operators, the men responsible for the day-to-day running of the platforms. **1866** J. C. Patteson *Let.* in C. M. Yonge *Life J. C. Patteson* (1874) II. x. 207 Let no *platform orator divulge the great secret. **1979** W. J. Fishman *Streets of E. London* 117/2 Eleanor Marx-Aveling['s]..remarkable qualities as teacher, platform orator and organiser. **1879** Froude *Cæsar* vi. 55 He had no turn for *platform oratory. **1935** in F. S. Blanchard *Paddle Tennis* (1944) III. v. 56 The following rules..are the officially approved rules for *Platform Paddle Tennis. **1959** —— (*title*) Platform paddle tennis: the official guide to platform tennis. **1967** O. H. Durrell *Official Guide to Platform Tennis* i. 3 Originally called paddle tennis, it later became platform paddle tennis and was finally shortened to platform tennis although most old timers..still refer to it as paddle. **1967** O. Wynd *Walk Softly, Men Praying* xii. 186 You can come with us. As one of the *platform party. **1976** C. Bermant *Coming Home* II. iii. 143 The platform party enters, preceded by a mace bearer, and behind him..the Chancellor. **1931** H. F. Pringle *Theodore Roosevelt* I. xii. 161 He borrowed many a *platform plank from the man he professed to hold in contempt. **1976** *National Observer* (U.S.) 28 Aug. 4/5 They swallowed platform planks calling for Constitutional amendments to bar abortions and school busing for racial balance. **1949** *Economist* 15 Oct. 825/2 His [*sc.* Lord Beaverbrook's] *platform points are pure chauvinism. **1926** R. Frost *Let.* 11 Feb. (1964) 178 You should get so *platform proud as to be undealable with. **1904** G. B. Shaw *Common Sense of Municipal Trading* x. 89 One of the keenest grievances of the commercial man who sees profitable branches of his own trade undertaken by the municipality is that it is competing against him 'with his own money', meaning that it forces him to pay rates, and then uses the rates to ruin him in his business. The effective *platform reply to this is that the profitable municipal trades, far from costing the ratepayers anything, actually lighten their burden. **1969** J. Gloag *Short. Dict. Furnit.* (rev. ed.) 564 A revolutionary design, invented in America about 1870, was the *platform rocker. **1970** *Globe & Mail* (Toronto) 26 Sept. 45/7 (Advt.), Walnut platform rocker. **1958** *Times* 17 Oct. 17/1 Ivan is first shown wearing four-inch *platform sandals. **1967** *Vogue* June 98 White patent platform sandals, 18 gns. **1834** *Mechanics' Mag.* 25 Oct. 248/2 E. & J. Fairbanks, a Concentrated *Platform Scale—a diploma. **1851** C. Cist *Sk. Cincinnati in 1851* 227 Factories in which platform scales are made. **1948** D. M. Considine *Industr. Weighing* iv. 67 The portable platform scale consists essentially of a rugged cast iron base mounted on four rubber tired wheels. **1969** T. J. Metcalfe *Weighing Machines* I. x. 105 The compound lever machine shown..is properly described as a 'low pattern steelyard platform scale'. **1969** T. C. Thorstensen *Pract. Leather Technol.* xv. 248 Open-toed and *platform shoes are more easily made by sliplasted procedures. **1977** D. Watkin *Morality & Archit.* 12 An unhappy example of this [*sc.* public unconcern with what planners would deem practical] in costume would be the craze for 'platform shoes'. **1939** M. B. Picken *Lang. Fashion* 113/3 **Platform sole*, thick shoe sole, usually from ½ inch to 3 inches in depth; often of cork or wood. **1941** *Amer. Speech* XVI. 98 The advertising writer reserves his best efforts for the finished products... Fine figures include..a platform sole about as thick as the wafer you get with your malted milk. **1960** R. P. Jhabvala *Householder* iii. 154 She would wear her platform-sole shoes and jasmine in her hair. **1977** *Monitor* (McAllen, Texas) 28 Mar. 7A/2 High platform soles..are being phased out although still available for young customers. **1973** *Woman's Own* 6 Jan. 61 Today's fashions, with their high-heeled, *platform-soled shoes and long, straight trousers can easily make you look taller. **1974** 'G. Black' *Golden Cockatrice* ix. 142 She was short even with platform-soled shoes. **1903** *Westm. Gaz.* 18 Mar. 1/1 An admirable *platform speaker. **1895** G. B. Shaw *Our Theatres in the Nineties* (1932) I. 189 The modern pictorial stage is not so favorable to Shakespearean acting and stage illusion as the *platform stage. **1951** *Oxf. Compan. Theatre* 218/2 Before English actors had any settled homes they played chiefly in inn-yards.., and their first permanent buildings..were wooden structures, roughly circular, with a raised platform stage backing on to the wall and jutting out into the open space, still called a 'yard'. *Ibid.* 236/2 The success of Davenant's playhouse..laid the foundations of the new style, and the Elizabethan platform stage was henceforth out of fashion. **1961** Bowman & Ball *Theatre Lang.* 261 *Platform stage*, a stage using an acting area which extends into the auditorium without a proscenium picture frame. **1955** *N.Y. Times* 14 Mar. 31/2 *Platform tennis..is one of the fastest growing and most enjoyable of American sports. **1967** *Time* 3 Mar. 45 Platform tennis, more commonly called paddle tennis, is not only the newest addition to the family of tennis-type court games: it is unique in that it is played primarily in winter and always outdoors. **1972** *N.Y. Times* 27 Feb. v. 6 More than 250 players on 128 teams will gather at the 'home of platform tennis', the Fox Meadow Tennis Club in Scarsdale, N.Y., on Friday to compete in the 38th annual United States men's doubles championship. **1977** *Club Tennis* Mar. 13 (*title*) Platform tennis—the game of the 80's paddling its way to success. **1901** *Railway Engineer* XXII. 68/2 In Berlin, at all the railway stations, no one is allowed on the platform unless actually going by train or provided with a '*platform ticket'. **1929** *Station Accounts Instruction Bk.* (Gt. Western Railway) 4 Passengers travelling from Platform Ticket Stations without Railway Tickets must surrender their Platform Tickets, and excess fares be charged accordingly. **1935** C. Winchester *Railway Wonders of World* I. 241/3 At the outset no charge was made for platform tickets by the English railways, but to-day a charge of one penny or thereabouts is usual. **1975** S. Briggs *Keep Smiling Through* 92/2 The Government had never intended the Tubes to be used permanently as shelters... However, there was nothing illegal in your buying a platform ticket for 1½d and not travelling. **1925** E. Sitwell *Troy Park* 67 All day in the limp helpless breeze Beneath the empty *platform trees He sits with Brobdignagian asses. **1925** *Proc. Inst. Production Engineers* V. 144 If trucking is resorted to then use a *platform truck. **1967** *Jane's Surface Skimmer Systems 1967–68* 7/1 *Accommodation*. It is available in three versions: a platform truck with a payload of 2,500 to 3,000 kg; or as a coach or bus with seats for twenty passengers and a driver. **1977** *Grimsby Even. Tel.* 14 May 8/5 (Advt.), 1969 Ford D800 platform truck (no test). **1866** Brande & Coxe *Dict. Sci.* etc. II. 929 **Platform Waggon*, in Artillery, a carriage on four wheels, fitted for the transport of guns, mortars, traversing platforms, or other heavy stores. **1876** T. Hardy *Ethelberta* (1890) 276 These stage and *platform women have what they are pleased to call Bohemianism so thoroughly engrained with their natures that [etc.]. **1901** *Westm. Gaz.* 24 Aug. 8/1 She is not a 'platform woman' in the common acceptation of the phrase. **1973** A. Price *October Men* ix. 128 He's got a rig of his own... He's built a *platform yard of his own at Hartlepool. **1977** *Offshore Engineer* Apr. 9/3 An end-of-contract bonus payment dispute flared up..at Highlands Fabricator's Nigg platform yard, where the steel platform for Chevron's Ninian field..is being completed.

Hence (chiefly *nonce-wds.*) **'platformally** *adv.*, in the manner of a platform speaker; **'platformish** *a.*, resembling that of a platform speaker; **'platformism**, the making of (political) platform speeches; **'platformist**, a platform speaker; **platfor'mistic** *a.*, characteristic of or suitable to platform speaking; **'platformless** *a.*, lacking a platform; **'platformy** *a.* = *platformish*.

1870 Dickens *E. Drood* xvii, 'The Commandments say, no murder, sir!' proceeded Honeythunder *platformally pausing. **1892** *Daily News* 3 Feb. 6/6 A manner described..as a trifle too *platformish for the House of Commons. **1866** Visct. Strangford *Selections* (1869) II. 323, I venture to think that the time for *platformism is past, even in this platform-ridden country. *Ibid.* I. 79 [A] true Liberal—as opposed to a technical or *platformistic Liberal. **1892** Kipling in *Times* (weekly ed.) 25 Nov. 13/2 The railway..a *platformless, regulationless necessity. **1893** *Daily Tel.* 22 Mar. 5/3 Mr. Fowler's speech in introducing the measure was..a trifle *platformy in style.

'platform, *v.* [f. platform *sb.*]

†**1.** *trans.* To plan, outline, sketch, draw up a scheme of. *lit.* and *fig. Obs.*

1592 G. Harvey *Four Lett.*, *Sonn.* xiv, Vertues all, and Honours all inflame Braue mindes to platfourme, and redoubted handes To doe such deedes. **1593** —— *Pierce's Super.* Wks. (Grosart) II. 186 Conceit, that buildeth Churches in the Ayer, and platformeth Disciplines without stayne, or spott. **1602** Fulbecke *2nd Pt. Parall.* Ded., To platforme a consummate and exemplarie Parallele or Trinomion. **1641** Milton *Ch. Govt.* I. i. 29 To grant that church discipline is platformed in the Bible.

†**2.** To furnish (a building) with a platform: see platform *sb.* 6 b. *Obs.*

1616 *Aberdeen Regr.* (1848) II. 341 The said Thomas sall ..platforme and mack watterthicht the haill heid of the hous with fyne aisler. **1632** Lithgow *Trav.* VIII. 365 The houses ..are all builded with mudde, and platformed on their tops. **1796** Morse *Amer. Geog.* II. 483 Houses, two stories high, platformed at the top for walking.

3. To place on or as on a platform.

1793 Smeaton *Edystone L.* §167 Every course must not only be tried singly together upon the platform,..but it must have the course next above it put upon it,..and this.. amounted to the platforming of every course twice. **1844** Mrs. Browning *To Flush* xii, Platforming his chin On the palm left open. **1844** —— *Drama of Exile* 602 Platformed in mid air.

4. *intr.* To speak on a platform.

1859 Lincoln in *Voice* (N.Y.) 11 June (1896) 4/1 The point of danger is the temptation in different localities to 'platform' for something that will be popular just there. **1892** H. Jephson *Platform* II. 543 On the 18th September two Conservative ex-Ministers 'platformed'. **1897** *Westm. Gaz.* 23 Apr. 2/1 She has never appeared on any platform, in any cause—to 'platform' betrays, in a woman, a high stomach.

Hence **'platforming** *vbl. sb.*[1]

1594 C[AREW] *Huarte's Exam. Wits* viii. (1616) 108 In platforming, and building, which belong to the imagination. **1640** T. WARMSTRY *Addr. to Two Houses* in *Sighs Ch. & Commonw. Eng.* 2 For the right and just platforming of your designs and undertakings. **1793** [see sense 3]. **1892** H. JEPHSON *Platform* I. 556 Its attendant meetings and Platformings.

ˈplatformed, *a.* [f. PLATFORM *sb.* + -ED[2].] Formed as a platform, level-topped; elevated as on a platform or plateau; furnished with a platform.

1632 LITHGOW *Trav.* VI. 267 A platformd rocke, all couered with..siluer. *Ibid.* x. 498 The second soyle for pleasure, is the platformd Carse of Gowry. **1883** *American* VI. 265 An engine and one platformed car.

ˈplatformer[1]. [f. PLATFORM *v.* + -ER[1].]

† **1.** One who designs or devises a 'platform'; a schemer, contriver, plotter. *Obs.*

1592 G. HARVEY *Four Lett.* Wks. (Grosart) I. 223 The Ringleaders of leaud Licentiousnes, are more pestilent, then the Platformers of vaine Fantasticallity. **1593** BILSON *Govt. Christ's Ch.* Pref. 2 It was..a ridiculous oversight in our new platformers. **1606** G. W[OODCOCKE] *Lives Emperors* in *Hist. Ivstine* Lliv, These Iesuites..are the common platformers for the Romish Church to poison all the commonwealths of Christendome.

2. One who speaks on a public platform.

1892 H. JEPHSON *Platform* II. p. ix, Popular Platformers. *Ibid.* p. xi, Bright on the Chartist Platformers.

platforming, *vbl. sb.*[1]: see PLATFORM *v.*

Platforming (ˈplætfɔːmɪŋ), *vbl. sb.*[2] Also **platforming.** [f. PLAT(INUM + RE)FORMING *vbl. sb.*] A proprietary name for a process for reforming petroleum using a platinum catalyst. Freq. *attrib.* Hence **ˈplatformate** [after *distillate, filtrate*, etc.], the end product of the process; **ˈplatformer**[2], an installation for Platforming.

1949 E. F. NELSON in *Oil & Gas Jrnl.* 7 Apr. 95/1 Our [*sc.* Universal Oil Products'] research and development departments have become so used to referring to the process as 'platforming' that we have decided that at this time we would officially christen it. *Ibid.* 100/2 The platformate has an end point slightly above that of the charge. **1952** *Official Gaz.* (U.S. Patent Office) 29 Jan. 1178/2 Universal Oil Products Company, Chicago..Platforming. For solid catalyst. Claims use since Aug. 29, 1947. **1954** *Ibid.* 19 Jan. 609/1 Platforming. For apparatus in the nature of a plant for the treatment of hydrocarbons. **1954** *Wall St. Jrnl.* 16 Aug. 5/3 Sunray Oil Corp., Tulsa, completed a new 5,000 barrel a day platforming unit at its Sunray Village refinery in Duncan, Okla. **1955** *Times* 8 June 9/4 The extension and modernization of the Suez refinery (including a 'platformer' to improve the quality of the motor benzine). **1957** *Trade Marks Jrnl.* 8 May 470/1 Platforming... Catalysts. Universal Oil Products Company.., Des Plaines, Illinois, United States of America; manufacturers. **1959** *Petroleum Handbk.* (ed. 4) 216 Platformate is used as a component in motor and aviation gasoline blends. **1973** S. A. BERRIDGE in Hobson & Pohl *Mod. Petroleum Technol.* (ed. 4) xi. 410 The Universal Oil Products Company has combined the Udex process with its Platforming process in an operation called Rexforming... The highly paraffinic raffinate from the Udex plant is recycled to the Platformer. **1978** *Trends in Oil & Gas Refining* (Shell Internat. Petroleum Co.) 5 In catalytic reforming..there has been 20 years of Shell experience in the design, development and operation of platformer units.

plat-ful, erron. for *plat ful*: see PLAT *adv.*

plathander, var. PLATANNA.

plathelminth: see PLATYHELMINTH.

platic (ˈplætɪk), *a. Astrol.* [ad. late and med.L. *platicus* (Firmicus, 4th c.) broad, general, ad. late Gr. πλατικός, -ικός broad, diffuse, f. πλατύς broad: see -IC.] Of an aspect: Not exact or within a degree, but within half the sum of the 'orbs' of the two planets: opp. to PARTILE 2.

a **1625** FLETCHER *Bloody Bro.* IV. ii, Mars out of the self same house, (But another Sign) here by a Platique aspect Looks at the Hilege. **1792** SIBLY *Occult Sc.* I. 144 By a platic aspect we are to understand two planets so posited, as to admit half the degrees of each of their own rays or orbs. **1819** WILSON *Dict. Astrol.* s.v. *Familiarities*, There are two kinds of approximation in familiarities: partile and platic. **1896** J. M. MANLY in *Harvard Studies* V. 112 *note*, Venus and Mars ..are in platic conjunction when less than six or eight degrees apart.

Hence **ˈplaticly** *adv.*, with a platic aspect.

1686 GOAD *Celest. Bodies* III. i. 394, ♂ among the rest, platiquely opposing ♄.

platie (ˈpleɪtɪ). *Sc.* [dim. of PLATE *sb.*: see -IE.] A little plate.

1786 BURNS *Twa Dogs* 223 Owre the wee bit cup an platie.

† **plaˈtilla.** *Obs.* Also 7 -illo, 8 -ille (?). [a. Sp. *platilla* 'a sort of Silesia linen'; ? dim. of *plata* silver.] (See quot. 1858.)

(App. the name in the Spanish colonies; cf. quot. 1699.)

1699 DAMPIER *Voy.* II. II. 110 Thus far Ships come to bring goods, especially European Commodities; viz. Broadcloth, Serges,..Ghentins, Platilloes, Britannias, Hollandilloes, Iron-work. **1740** *Hist. Jamaica* xiii. 336 The chief saleable Goods are.., Silks, Platilloes, all Sorts of Iron-ware. **1800** *Hull Advertiser* 3 May 2/2, 124½ Platilles, containing 1364 ells. **1858** SIMMONDS *Dict. Trade*, *Platillas*, a white linen fabric made in Silesia for export to America.

platin, platen, platina, alleged name of an alloy of copper and zinc: see quots.

1790 W. RICHARDSON *Chem. Princ. Met. Arts* 167 Platina, eight ounces of brass, and five ounces of spelter. **1884** C. G. W. LOCK *Workshop Receipts* Ser. III. 16/2 For button brass, an alloy of 8 parts of copper and 5 of zinc is commonly used by the Birmingham makers, under the name of 'platin'.

¶ Investigation has shown that no alloy is, or has been within memory, known in Birmingham under this name, unless it was a workman's pronunciation of *plating* (metal); the composition given is merely that of ordinary brass.

platin- (ˈplætɪn), combining form of PLATINUM before a vowel, in names of chemical compounds, as ***platinamine***, an amine of platinum; ***platinammonium***, a compound of platinum and ammonium; PLATINIRIDIUM.

1856 W. A. MILLER *Elem. Chem.* II. 1066 Salts of Platinamine. **1873** WATTS *Fownes' Chem.* (ed. 11) 349 Platinum tetrachloride absorbs four molecules of ammonia, forming platinammonium chloride.

platina (ˈplætɪnə, pləˈtiːnə). Now *rare* or *Obs.* [a. Sp. *platina* (plaˈtina) platinum, dim. from *plata* silver: see -INE[4].] The earlier name of PLATINUM.

1750 *Phil. Trans.* XLVI. 584 Several Papers concerning a new Semi-Metal, called Platina. **1754** LEWIS *ibid.* XLVIII. 638 The substance brought into England under the name of platina appears a mixture of dissimilar particles. **1786** JEFFERSON *Writ.* (1859) I. 505 You have often heard of the metal, called platina, to be found only in South America. **1815** J. SMITH *Panorama Sc. & Art* II. 91 Platina is the heaviest body known to exist. **1840** *Penny Cycl.* XVIII. 230/2 *Platina* or *Platinum* an important metal. [In the article *platina* is the only form used.] **1865** *Pall Mall G.* 28 June 7 The prisoner denied that he had ever stolen any platina, and said he was innocent of the charge.

b. *attrib.* (usually = Consisting or made of platinum) and *Comb.*

1794 PEARSON in *Phil. Trans.* LXXXIV. 388 A small piece of purified white lac, in a platina spoon. **1819** CHILDREN *Chem. Anal.* 375 Held in a pair of platina pincers. **1825** J. NICHOLSON *Operat. Mechanic* 356 He..determined to try to draw platina-wire. **1883** *Hardwich's Photogr. Chem.* (ed. Taylor) 307 To have it [an enlargement] made on a more stable and permanent base than silver, hence carbon and platina printing find most favour for such a purpose.

platina: see PLATIN.

platinate (ˈplætɪnət), *sb. Chem.* [f. PLATIN-UM + -ATE[1] 1 c.] A salt derived from platinic oxide, in which platinum is tetravalent.

1858 MAYNE *Expos. Lex.*, *Platinate*, term for a combination in which platinic oxide plays the part of an acid. **1866** WATTS *Dict. Chem.* IV. 669 A compound of platinic chloride with platinate of calcium.

platinate (ˈplætɪneɪt), *v.* [f. PLATIN-UM + -ATE[3].] *trans.* = PLATINIZE.

1889 *Philos. Mag.* Dec. 454 The plates were next platinated by a process given in Gore's 'Electro-metallurgy' under the name of 'Roseleur's Process'. *Ibid.*, To prepare the plates for platinating.

† **ˈplatine.** *Weaving. Obs.* [a. F. *platine*; see PLATEN.] A plate-lead: see quot. 1797.

1688 R. HOLME *Armoury* III. xxi. (Roxb.) 252/1 The Platines are Lead of a halfe round forme, hung in strings (as pack thrid) which pass between two cross sticks; these strings goe to pullaces fix in the top castle and so to the Tradles and are called Lames vnder the workmans feet, so that by the riseing and falling of the Tradles, these play vp and down. **1797** *Encycl. Brit.* (ed. 3) XVI. 230/1 The plate-leads, or platines, are flat pieces of lead, of about six inches long, and three or four inches broad at the top, but round at the bottom; some use black slates instead of them: their use is to pull down those lisses which the workman had raised by the treddle, after his foot is taken off.

plating (ˈpleɪtɪŋ), *vbl. sb.* [f. PLATE *v.* + -ING[1].]

1. The action of the verb PLATE in various senses.

a. The making or application of metal plates; *spec.* in *Surg.*: cf. PLATE *v.* 1 b.

1831 J. HOLLAND *Manuf. Metal* I. 139 The operation of plating..in the manufacture of spades and shovels. **1890** W. J. GORDON *Foundry* 67 When it comes to the plating—the 'shell plating', as it is called—the hand-hammer has still to be brought into play. **1914** A. P. C. ASHHURST *Surgery* xii. 313 It is better not to plate a recent compound fracture.., but to postpone the plating until the soft parts have healed. **1971** W. J. W. SHARRARD *Paediatric Orthopaedics & Fractures* xx. 985 (*heading*) Sound union of both fractures 8 weeks after plating.

b. The process of coating with a thin adherent layer of precious metal or other, *spec.* by means of electrolysis.

1825 J. NICHOLSON *Operat. Mechanic* 725 Copper may likewise be plated by heating it, and burnishing leaf-silver upon it; so may iron and brass. This process is called French Plating. **1869** BOUTELL *Arms & Arm.* ii. (1874) 29 The decorative processes of plating, gilding, and enamelling. **1872** *Jrnl. Chem. Soc.* XXV. 1134 Plating with aluminium cannot be effected. **1946** *Trans. Electrochem. Soc.* LXXXIX. 384 In a recent cost analysis..on the plating of an electric flatiron, it cost $0·46 to apply nickel and chromium. **1966** *McGraw-Hill Encycl. Sci. & Technol.* IV. 531/1 It is difficult to apply zinc coatings thinner than about 0·002 in. by hot dipping... For many articles, thinner coatings are adequate and are applied by plating. **1968** R. W. BERRY *Thin Film Technol.* v. 266 In vapor plating, a volatile compound of the substance to be deposited is vaporized, then thermally decomposed at the substrate to yield the desired deposit. **1972** [see PLATE *v.* 2 b].

c. See quot., and cf. PLATED 2 b.

1844 G. DODD *Textile Manuf.* vi. 197 A process termed 'plating' which..consists in putting a coating of silk on a substratum..of cotton.

d. The shoeing of a horse with plates or racing-shoes. Also *attrib.*

1840–70 BLAINE *Encycl. Rur. Sports* §1237 In the plating of race-horses, much caution is required in the selection of a proper smith. *Ibid.* §1238 Either of these varieties of plating shoes. **1951** E. RICKMAN *Come racing with Me* viii. 63 Principal items are veterinary charges, shoeing (or 'plating' as it is called).

e. Plate-racing.

1865 *Daily Tel.* 7 Nov. 5/2 Frittering away its money in minor and unseasonable plating. **1875** 'STONEHENGE' *Brit. Sports* II. I. v. § 1. 429. **1888** *Illustr. Sport. & Dram. News* 21 Jan. 511/1 Will they [young race-horses] descend to the depths.., and after a career of plating turn up some day in a selling hurdle-race, winner to be sold for £50?

f. *Biol.* and *Med.* The preparation of a culture on a plate (see PLATE *v.* 6).

1898 *Public Health* (Papers & Rep. Amer. Public Health Assoc.) XXIII. 81 The technical difficulties in the way of successful 'plating' in agar are considerable. **1916** *Jrnl. Bacteriol.* I. 513 Eight different samples of raw and heated soil were selected for this examination, some samples being plated immediately, others being incubated at 37°C. for 48 hours before plating. **1934** A. T. HENRICI *Biol. Bacteria* xii. 201 The procedure most commonly used for obtaining pure cultures from mixtures of microbes is the process of plating introduced by Koch. *Ibid.* 203 Plating may be used also to measure or estimate the number of bacteria in a given substance. **1969** M. R. DROOP in Norris & Ribbons *Methods in Microbiol.* III B. xi. 276 The sample for isolation will usually require a considerable degree of dilution before plating.

g. The furnishing of a book with a book-plate.

1906 *Daily Chron.* 10 Aug. 3/2 'Plating'..would appear to be the process of affixing the book-plate to the inside of the first cover of the volumes. **1938** L. M. HARROD *Librarians' Gloss.* 116 Plating, the process of pasting labels in library books.

h. *Machine knitting.* (See quot. 1946.)

1946 A. J. HALL *Standard Handbk. Textiles* iii. 140 It is possible to run two threads at once into the knitting machine and arrange that one of these predominates in the back of the fabric whilst the other is mostly seen on the front... This method of knitting is known as plating. **1954** *Textile Terms & Defs.* (Textile Institute) 30 Plating usually involves the knitting of two yarns of different colour, different lustre, or different composition, so that only one of these yarns is visible on the face of the stitch.

i. = FELLATIO, CUNNILINGUS. *slang.*

1965 W. YOUNG *Eros Denied* xiv. 137 *Gamming*, from the French *gamahucher*, or *blowing*, or *plating*, or *noshing*. **1969** FABIAN & BYRNE *Groupie* ii. 16 Why do you think plating is perverted? Everyone I know does it.

j. With reference to a goods vehicle: see PLATE *v.* 10.

1968 *Economist* 27 Jan. 61/2 All three firms have had a couple of prosperous years recently, benefiting from the rapid transition from rigid lorries to articulated vehicles and by the introduction of 'plating' and other new inspection requirements. **1972** *Police Rev.* 10 Nov. 1463/1 The Minister's approval certificate..will eventually obviate the necessity of attending the testing station for plating.

2. *concr.* The result or product of this action.

a. An external layer or sheath of plates; sheathing-plates collectively.

1843 CARLYLE *Past & Pr.* II. iii, St. Edmund's Shrine glitters..with a plating of wrought gold. **1891** KIPLING *Light that Failed* (1900) 277 The narrow-gauge armoured train... Two bogie trucks running before the locomotive were completely covered in with plating. **1895** *Outing* (U.S.) XXVI. 381/1 There are five strakes of this plating from deck to garboard.

b. The surface of precious metal with which copper, etc. is plated. Also, any metal coating. Also *fig.*

1833 T. HOOK *Widow & Marquess* viii, She..dreaded that the appearance might be deceitful—if it were so, the plating was extremely thick. **1839** URE *Dict. Arts* 998 Were it to remain a very little longer, the silver would become alloyed with the copper, and the plating be thus completely spoiled. **1870** LOWELL *Study Wind.* (1886) 61 The plating of Anglicism rubs off. **1901** B. BLOUNT *Pract. Electro-Chem.* v. 268 Nickel plating is harder and more brittle than the metal in massive form. **1946** *Trans. Electrochem. Soc.* LXXXIX. 409 (*heading*) Plating deposited from nickel-cobalt chloride solution. **1962** *Engineering* 7 Sept. 321/3 (*heading*) Mirror surface on copper plating.

c. *Biol.* and *Med.* A culture on a plate (PLATE *sb.* 19 e).

1901 *Jrnl. Hygiene* I. 298 Platings from this broth have then been made in litmus-lactose-agar. **1928** *Jrnl. Bacteriol.* XVI. 272 Platings were made of each sample of milk immediately after it was received.

3. *attrib.* and *Comb.*, 'occupied or used in plating'; as ***plating liquid, mill, trade***; **plating bar**, a bar made from special pig-iron for making into plate-iron; **plating bath**, a bath containing the metallic solution in which articles to be plated are immersed; **plating certificate**, a certificate stating that a goods vehicle has had a plating examination; **plating examination**, a legally-required inspection of a goods vehicle to establish weight, roadworthiness, etc.; **plating hammer**, (*a*) a heavy hammer for clinching; (*b*) a steam-hammer for working on armour-plate, etc.

1892 *Daily News* 13 June 2/7 There is a fair enquiry for *plating bars. **1895** *Westm. Gaz.* 24 Oct. 5/2 Purchasing bar silver for the purpose of strengthening their *plating bath.

1968 *Goods Vehicles (Plating & Testing) Regulations* (601) Reg. 2 'Ministry plate' means a plate issued by the Minister for a goods vehicle following the issue or amendment of a *plating certificate. **1978** *Highway Code* 64 Before driving, make sure that..you have a current plating certificate for your goods vehicle. **1973** J. Duckworth *Kitchin's Road Transport Law* (ed. 16) 94 The first examination consists of a *plating examination in which the vehicle's axle and gross weights are assessed and recorded on a plate, followed by a test of roadworthiness. **1543** *Richmond Wills* (Surtees) 43, ij nalyng hamers ij[d]. Item a hake hamer with a *platyng hamer, ij[d]. c **1865** G. Gore in *Circ. Sc.* I. 225/1 A good *plating liquid should contain one equivalent of..cyanide of potassium. **1877** Raymond *Statist. Mines & Mining* 358 In 1750..Parliament..prohibited the erection in America of slitting, rolling, or *plating mills, or steel furnaces.

platini- (ˈplætɪnɪ), *Chem.*, combining form of PLATINUM, denoting compounds in which it has its higher valency (cf. PLATINIC).

1887 A. M. Brown *Anim. Alkaloids* 73 Chloride of platinum gives with chlorohydrate of betaine a platinichloride in yellow crystals. **1890** Webster, *Platinichloric*.

platinic (pləˈtɪnɪk), *a. Chem.* [f. PLATIN-UM + -IC. So F. *platinique*.] Applied to those compounds of platinum in which it exists in its higher degree of valency, i.e. as a tetrad; as ***platinic oxide***, PtO_2; ***platinic chloride***, $PtCl_4$. Opposed to PLATINOUS. (Cf. FERRIC, and see -IC 1 b.)

1842 Parnell *Chem. Anal.* (1845) 95 The conversion of the platinous oxide compounds into the platinic oxide. **1866** Watts *Dict. Chem.* IV. 665 Platinum forms two series of compounds, the platinous compounds in which it is diatomic, *e.g.* $PtCl_2$, PtO, etc., and the platinic compounds in which it is tetratomic, *e.g.* $PtCl_4$, PtO_2, etc. *Ibid.* 668 Tetrachloride of Platinum or Platinic Chloride, $Pt^{iv}Cl_4$.

platiniferous (plætɪˈnɪfərəs), *a.* [f. PLATIN-UM + -FEROUS.] Bearing or yielding platinum.

1828–32 Webster s.v., Platiniferous sand. *Dict. Nat. Hist.* **1853** Th. Ross *Humboldt's Trav.* III. xxxii. 312 On its western slope lies the famous auriferous and platiniferous land. **1896** *Educ. News* (Philad.) 25 Apr. 270 One bed of platiniferous lead ore is a mile long.

platiniridium (ˌplætɪnɪˈrɪdɪəm). *Min.* Also **platino-iridium.** [f. PLATIN-UM + IRIDIUM.] A native alloy of platinum and iridium, occurring in small grains or cubes with truncated angles, of a white colour.

1848 J. D. Dana *Man. Mineral.* vi. 309 A similar platin-iridium has been obtained at Ava in the East Indies. **1888** *Encycl. Brit.* XXIV. 480/1 The new standard of the International Metric Commission is a line-standard of platino-iridium, 40 inches long. **1908** *Practitioner* Sept. 485 The best needle to use is one of platino-iridium, since it can be rendered absolutely sterile in the flame of a spirit lamp. **1965** G. J. Williams *Econ. Geol. N.Z.* x. 154/2 Farquharson (1910) quoted earlier reports on the occurrence of 'osmiridium' and 'platiniridium' in the Tertiary auriferous quartzose conglomerates..in north-western Nelson.

platinite (ˈplætɪnaɪt). [f. PLATIN-UM + -ITE[1] 4 b.] **1.** *Chem.* A salt derived from platinous oxide, in which platinum has its lower valency.

1866 Watts *Dict. Chem.* IV. 671 Platinous Oxide..when recently precipitated..dissolves in potash and in soda, forming salts called platinites, which appear also to be formed when metallic platinum is heated with caustic alkalis. **1878** Abney *Photogr.* (1881) 157 A solution of 'chloroplatinite' of potassium.

2. *Metallurgy.* Also **Platinite.** An alloy of iron with 42 to 50 per cent nickel which has the same coefficient of expansion as platinum and has supplanted that metal in various electrical applications, esp. for metal-to-glass contacts in lamps.

1918 *Nature* 15 Aug. 471/1 The Germans..have found that for certain purposes an alloy of nickel and iron may replace platinum. The alloy—called 'platinite'—may be used in electric lamps. **1923** *Engineering* 23 Nov. 651/3 The iron-nickel alloy known as 'Platinite', containing 46 per cent. of nickel and about 0·15 per cent. of carbon, had practically the same coefficient of expansion as glass. **1929** [see ELINVAR]. **1965** A. D. Merriman *Conc. Encycl. Metallurgy* 731 Platinite..is used for lead-in wires in electric-lamp bulbs.

platinize (ˈplætɪnaɪz), *v.* [f. PLATIN-UM + -IZE.] *trans.* To coat with platinum. Hence **ˈplatinized** *ppl. a.*, **ˈplatinizing** *vbl. sb.*; also **platiniˈzation**, the action or process of platinizing.

1825 J. Nicholson *Operat. Mechanic* 721 Porcelain and other wares may be platinised, silvered, tinned, and bronzed. **1842** *Mech. Mag.* XXXVI. 461 The platinized silver battery invented by Mr. Smee. **1878** Abney *Photogr.* (1881) 138 This toning may consist of gilding the silver image, platinising it, or substituting some other metal for it.

platino- (ˈplætɪnəʊ), combining form of PLATINUM; *spec.* in *Chem.* denoting compounds in which it is divalent (Watts *Dict. Chem.* IV. 665.); **platinoˈcyanide**, any of a series of fluorescent salts which contain the anion $Pt(CN)_4^{2-}$; **platino-iridium**, var. PLATINIRIDIUM.

1845 W. Gregory *Outl. Chem.* II. 306 The platinocyanides of barium, strontium, and calcium..crystallise readily in beautiful greenish yellow colour. **1873** Watts *Fownes' Chem.* (ed. 11) 346 The acid tartrate and the platinochloride being among the least soluble. **1884** *Chamb. Jrnl.* 1 Mar. 141/1 The platino-barium cyanide, becomes highly luminous when inclosed in a tube and traversed by the electric current. **1899** Cagney tr. *Jaksch's Clin. Diagn.* vii. (ed. 4) 298 For ferrocyanide of potassium, platinocyanide of potassium may be substituted. **1926** *Sunday at Home* 677/2 The luminous paint..consists..of a mixture of some radium or thorium salt with some photosensitive substance like barium platinocyanide. **1974** *Sci. Amer.* Mar. 96/1 The screen would consist of a thin, translucent disk of mica, coated with a phosphor such as barium platinocyanide or zinc silicate.

platinode (ˈplætɪnəʊd). *Electr.* [f. PLATIN-UM + Gr. ὁδός path, as in *anode*, *cathode*, *electrode*, etc.] The negative plate or pole (cathode) of a voltaic cell (often consisting of platinum). Opp. to ZINCODE.

1839 Noad *Electricity* (1849) 162 The phenomenon of the transfer of the charcoal from one electrode to the other..was abundantly apparent; taking place from the zincode (or positive pole) to the platinode (or negative pole). c **1865** J. Wylde in *Circ. Sc.* I. 194 The pole or terminal,..proceeding from, and ending the wire of the copper or platina plate of a battery, has been termed the platinode, or anode.

platinoid (ˈplætɪnɔɪd), *a.* and *sb.* [f. PLATIN-UM + -OID.] **A.** *adj.* Resembling platinum.

1864 in Webster. **1886** in *Cassell's Encycl. Dict.*

B. *sb.* [Cf. *metalloid*.]

1. *Chem.* Any metal of the class comprising platinum and those commonly found in association with it and resembling it in several properties, viz. iridium, osmium, palladium, rhodium, and ruthenium. Also called *platinum metals*.

1882 in Ogilvie.

2. Name for an alloy of nickel, zinc, copper, and tungsten, of a silvery white colour, and resembling platinum in non-liability to tarnish, etc.

1885 *Engineering* 3 July 17 Platinoid is practically German silver with from 1 to 2 per cent. of tungsten in it. **1892** *Pall Mall G.* 21 Mar. 3/1 Very fine wires of 'platinoid', or some other convenient alloy.

platiˈnoso-, combining form of mod.L. *platinōsus* PLATINOUS.

1858 Mayne *Expos. Lex.*, *Platinoso-*, a prefix employed by Berzelius in compound terms or epithets of double salts which result from the combination of a platinous salt with another metallic salt, as *Platinoso-ammonicus*, etc. **1866** Watts *Dict. Chem.* IV. 667 A dark brown solution supposed by Magnus to contain platinoso-platinic chloride.

platinotype (ˈplætɪnəʊtaɪp). *Photogr.* [f. PLATINO- + TYPE.] A process of photographic printing by which prints in platinum-black are produced, the paper being prepared by coating with a solution of chloro-platinite of potassium, K_2PtCl_4 (commonly called platinum chloride) and ferric oxalate, and developed in a hot solution of potassic oxalate. Also *attrib.*

1880 *Times* 5 Oct. 6/6 There is now a Platinotype Company, as there has long been a Woodburytype and an Autotype. **1881** *Athenæum* 18 June 817/3 The Earl of Rosse ..presented to the Society photographic copies of the drawings made by the platinotype process. **1884** *Pall Mall G.* 5 Dec. 2/2 A print in platinotype which will not fade, can be had.

b. A print produced by this process.

1884 *Sat. Rev.* 12 July 58/2 Mr. Keene's illustrations..a great many of which are 'platinotypes'..are very good. **1892** *Times* 20 Oct. 14/1 The 210 platinotypes..constitute an exhibition of much beauty and interest.

platinous (ˈplætɪnəs), *a. Chem.* [f. PLATIN-UM + -OUS c.] Applied to those compounds of platinum in which it exists in its lower degree of valency, i.e. as a dyad. Opposed to PLATINIC.

1842 [see PLATINIC]. **1858** Mayne *Expos. Lex.*, Berzelius terms *Oxydum platinosum* the first degree of oxidation of *platina*; *Sulphur platinosum* the first degree of sulphuration; *Sales platinosi* the combinations of platinous oxide with the oxacids. **1866** Watts *Dict. Chem.* IV. 667 Dichloride of Platinum or Platinous Chloride, $PtCl_2$. *Ibid.* 671 Platinous Oxide is obtained as a hydrate, $Pt''O.H_2O$ or $Pt''H_2O_2$, by digesting platinous chloride in a warm solution of potash and washing the precipitate. **1890** Abney *Photogr.* (ed. 6) 171 A platinous salt..was mixed with a ferric oxalate.

platinum (ˈplætɪnəm). [mod.L., altered by Bergman (followed by Davy), from PLATINA, in conformity with the names of other metals in *-um*.]

1. a. A somewhat rare metal (at first named PLATINA), of a white colour like silver but less bright, very heavy, ductile, and malleable, unaffected by all simple acids, and fusible only at an extremely high temperature; used chiefly in chemical and other scientific processes. Chemical symbol Pt.

1812 Sir H. Davy *Chem. Philos.* 448 The ores of platinum are very rare; they have been found only in South America and in Spain. *Ibid.* 449 Platinum was first described as a peculiar metal by Dr. Lewis, in 1754. **1827** N. Arnott *Physics* I. 10 Platinum can be drawn into wire much finer than human hair. **1832** Babbage *Econ. Manuf.* xiv. (ed. 3) 123 In Russia platinum has been employed for coin. **1838** J. L. Stephens *Trav. Russia* 83/1 The largest piece of platinum in existence, from the mines of Demidoff, weighing 10 pounds, is here also [Hotel des Mines, St. Petersburg]. **1866** Watts *Dict. Chem.* IV. 665 The unalterability of platinum at high temperatures, and its power of resisting the action of most chemical agents, render it extremely useful for the construction of crucibles, evaporating dishes, forceps for blowpipe experiments, etc.

b. A greyish white colour like that of platinum.

1923 *Daily Mail* 1 Aug. 2 In the following colours: Black, White,..Suede, Platinum and Champagne. **1951** E. Paul *Springtime in Paris* xvi. 313 Looking pensively down at the moving river surface, ebony and indigo. The moon, coming out thinly.., contributed platinum. **1976** *Milton Keynes Express* 11 June 38/2 (Advt.), 1974, 'M' Vauxhall Victor 2300 Auto Saloon. Finished in platinum, fitted wing mirrors, radio.

c. = *platinum fox*, sense 2 c below.

1948 A. L. Rand *Mammals Eastern Rockies* 105 Various other 'varieties' [of red fox] have been developed on fur farms, including the platinums and various white-spotted phases.

2. *attrib.* **a.** Made or consisting of platinum.

1840 *Penny Cycl.* XVI. 40/1 Heated in a platinum spoon it [balsam of Peru] burns with a white smoke. **1842** Parnell *Chem. Anal.* (1845) 330 Heated to redness in an open platinum crucible. **1849** Noad *Electricity* (ed. 3) 22 The experiment was made with a platinum wire. **1899** Cagney tr. *Jaksch's Clin. Diagn.* vi. (ed. 4) 206 A particle..of the cultivation from agar is taken on a platinum point.

b. Of, related to, containing, or combined with platinum; as ***platinum compounds***, ***platinum ore***, ***platinum salts***; with names of other metals, denoting alloys, as ***platinum-iridium***, ***-steel***; also **platinum-black**, a black powder resembling lampblack, consisting of platinum in a finely-divided state; **platinum-blue** [tr. G. *platinblau* (Hofmann & Bugge 1908, in *Ber. d. Deut. Chem. Ges.* XLI. 312)], any of a class of dark blue polymeric complexes, a number of which have antitumour activity, which are formed by divalent platinum with amide ligands; orig. *spec.* one formed with acetamide; **platinum-lamp**, an incandescent lamp having the filament made of platinum; **platinum metals**, name for the class of metals comprising platinum and certain others associated with it (see PLATINOID B. 1); **platinum sponge**, a grey amorphous form of platinum which is obtained as spongy masses on heating ammonium chloroplatinate and is used as a catalyst; **platinum-zinc** *a.*, formed of plates alternately of platinum and zinc, as a voltaic cell.

1854 J. Scoffern in *Orr's Circ. Sc.*, *Chem.* 511 The substance termed *platinum black furnishes the metal in a condition of still more minute division. **1878** Abney *Photogr.* 157 The prints produced by this [platinum] process are exceedingly beautiful, and, as platinum black forms the image, they may be considered as being far more permanent than a silver print. **1908** *Jrnl. Chem. Soc.* XCIV. I. 141 (*heading*) *Platinum-Blue. **1964** *Ibid.* 2835 Platinum Blue is very soluble in water, methanol, and dimethylformamide from which it can be crystallised by the addition of dichloromethane. **1975** *Cancer Chemotherapy Rep.* I. LIX. 296/1 We tentatively conclude from these early results that the 'platinum blues' may have activity against a broad spectrum of tumors. **1976** *Cancer Res.* XXXVI. 3822/1 Platinum-uracil blue and platinum-thymine blue are prototype examples of platinum-blue complexes which have been shown to have a higher therapeutic index against ascites Sarcoma 180. **1866** Watts *Dict. Chem.* IV. 669 All *platinum-compounds are reduced to spongy platinum in the inner flame [of the blowpipe]. **1901** *Brit. Med. Jrnl.* No. 2095 Epit. Med. Lit. 32 The author recommends electrolysis with a *platinum-iridium needle. **1865** Watts *Dict. Chem.* III. 974 Ruthenium and osmium differ from the other *platinum-metals in the degree of their oxidisability. **1849** D. Campbell *Inorg. Chem.* 247 Analysis of *platinum ore, containing, besides platinum, ruthenium,..osmium,..iridium,..palladium,..rhodium,..copper, and iron. **1866** Watts *Dict. Chem.* IV. 671 From most *platinum-salts alkalis throw down basic double salts. **1826** W. Henry *Elem. Exper. Chem.* (ed. 10) I. vii. 355 Into a mixture of carbonic oxide with a larger proportion of the explosive mixture, the *platinum sponge cannot be introduced without causing detonation. **1894** G. S. Newth *Text-bk. Inorg. Chem.* III. xiv. 644 This action is more rapid in the case of platinum sponge, when a larger surface is brought into play, and a fragment of this material introduced into a detonating mixture of oxygen and hydrogen at once determines its explosion. **1968** A. A. Baker *Unsaturation in Org. Chem.* ix. 125 In 1838 Frederic Kuhlmann produced ammonia by heating a mixture of nitric oxide and hydrogen in the presence of platinum sponge. **1875** Knight *Dict. Mech.*, **Platinum-steel*, steel alloyed with $\frac{1}{110}$ part of platinum. It is said not to be quite so hard as silver steel, but tougher. **1878** Abney *Photogr.* (1881) 157 Pictures may be obtained by means of *platinum tetrachloride, mercuric chloride, and potassium dichromate, &c., though greater exposure with these is necessary. **1849** Noad *Electricity* (ed. 3) 263 As copper is a better conductor of Electricity than platinum, a copper-zinc circuit ought to be more efficacious than a *platinum-zinc circuit, which is contrary to fact.

c. Platinum or platinum-blonde (see below) in colour, as ***platinum hair***, ***lace***; esp. of animals or their fur, as ***platinum coney***, ***fox***, ***mink***; also ***platinum-grey***; **platinum blond(e)** *a.*, (of the hair) silvery-blonde in colour; (of a person) having silvery-blonde hair; also as *sb.*, a person, esp. a woman, with platinum-blonde hair.

1931 *Daily Express* 15 Oct. 19/5 (*caption*) Miss Binnie Barnes, who appears as a *platinum blonde in 'Cavalcade', is seen here as a brunette. Nature gave her auburn-red hair. **1934** R. Ferguson *Celebrated Sequels* 264 A costly platinum-blond young man from a famous night-club. **1934**

F. STARK *Valleys of Assassins* ii. 187 It was a blue stream, as vivid in that thirsty solitude as a platinum blonde in a monastery. **1942** A. CHRISTIE *Body in Library* ii. 24 She had scarlet lips, blackened eyelashes, and a platinum-blonde head. **1966** J. S. COX *Illustr. Dict. Hairdressing & Wigmaking* 118/1 *Platinum blonde*, a very fair, silvery hued colour popularized by Jean Harlow, the late curvaceous American film star. **1977** *Transatlantic Rev.* LX. 53 From ten to eleven, no one checked in except a commercial salesman with three suitcases of samples and a middle-aged gent with a platinum blonde. **1923** *Daily Mail* 14 Aug. 1 The wide collar and side panels..are made of the richest pulled *Platinum Coney. **1946** A. CHRISTIE *Hollow* viii. 77 The *platinum foxes that swathed her shoulders. **1908** *Westm. Gaz.* 25 Apr. 13/2 Such a suit is a very pleasant idea for the summer. I saw one the other day in a *platinum-grey. **1951** WODEHOUSE *Old Reliable* xv. 171 This miserable creature, who has probably got *platinum hair and a lisp. **1978** D. FRANCIS *Trial Run* i. 11 Her fine-boned face and thick platinum hair. **1923** *Daily Mail* 20 June 8 In a *platinum lace gown and cape. **1949** R. CHANDLER *Little Sister* xviii. 117 No big money,..no *platinum mink, no name in neons. **1950** 'S. RANSOME' *Deadly Miss Ashley* i. 12 She was wearing a fur piece... It was platinum mink.

d. Designating a framed platinum gramophone record presented to a popular musician or group whose record has sold at least one million copies. Applied chiefly *attrib.* and as *adv.* (*to go platinum*) to a record which achieves such sales. Cf. GOLD[1] 8a. orig. *U.S.*

1971 *New Yorker* 21 Aug. 22/3 'The 'Paranoid' album will be awarded a platinum disc very shortly!' 'What's a platinum disc?' we shouted. 'When you sell a million units of an album, you get a platinum disc!' **1977** *New Musical Express* 12 Feb. 3/1 They will also feature their Platinum album 'Fleetwood Mac', one of the top U.S. sellers of 1976. **1978** *Time* 18 Sept. 81/3 The Austin sound—redneck rock or progressive country—began crossing over from country to pop charts and racking up sales once scarcely dreamed of in the country field. In the past two years, three such albums have gone platinum, in trade parlance (*i.e.*, sold 1 million copies). **1984** *Southern Rag* No. 22. 13/1 It proceeded to sell two million! Even *I* didn't see that coming. *Year Of The Cat* was platinum or gold all over the world. **1985** *Times* 14 Feb. 10/7 Despite a BBC ban Frankie go to No. 1 and stay there for five weeks, going platinum (over a million sales) in March.

platitude ('plætɪtjuːd). [a. F. *platitude* (Dict. Acad. 1694), f. *plat* PLAT *a.*, on analogy of *latitude*, *altitude*, etc.: see -TUDE.]

1. Flatness, dullness, insipidity, commonplaceness (as a quality of speech or writing).

1812 *Edin. Rev.* XIX. 276 With all the brevity and platitude imaginable. **1818** *Q. Rev.* XIX. 120 Such abundance of platitude and inanity. *a* **1850** ROSSETTI *Dante & Circ.* I. (1874) 12 A repartee..which has all the profound platitude of mediæval wit.

2. A flat, dull, or commonplace remark or statement; esp. one uttered or written with an air of importance or solemnity.

1815 SIMOND *Tour Gt. Brit.* I. 100 Every species of improbability and platitudes. **1833** SARAH AUSTIN *Charac. Goethe* II. 212 *note* 36 A Philister..may, I think, be paraphrased a man of common places—a pompous dealer in identicalisms and platitudes. **1888** BRYCE *Amer. Commw.* II. xlv. 191 It is one of those platitudes which are constantly forgotten or ignored.

plati'tudinal, *a. rare.* [As if f. L. **plātitūdo, -din-* + -AL[1]; cf. LATITUDINAL.]

= PLATITUDINOUS.

1870 O. LOGAN *Before Footlights* xxiii. 288 At the risk of uttering truisms and being altogether a platitudinal truist, I may mention that it requires a pretty strong organic construction to stand the ravages of an eight months' tour in the land of fast eaters. **1885** J. COLEMAN in *Longm. Mag.* VII. 76 'Junius' failed..because it was a platitudinal play upon an unsavoury subject. **1900** *Daily News* 17 Oct. 4/6 His remarks do not seem to us wholly free from a modern kind of 'platitudinal stodge', as he calls it, and we fear that 'platitudinous' would, of the two, be more correct.

platitudinarian (ˌplætɪtjuːdɪˈnɛərɪən), *sb.* and *a.* [f. as prec., after LATITUDINARIAN.]

A. *sb.* One who utters or deals in platitudes.

1855 *Tait's Mag.* XXII. 531 To expose such showy platitudinarians as Tupper. **1876** GEO. ELIOT *Dan. Der.* xxii, A political platitudinarian as insensible as an ox to everything he can't turn into political capital. **1890** *Cornh. Mag.* Dec. 580 A man of words rather than of action, a platitudinarian.

B. *adj.* Characterized by platitude; addicted to the use of platitudes.

1866 *Contemp. Rev.* I. 164 Of all forms of cant and platitude, probably the most unreal and platitudinarian. **1884** *Chr. Commw.* 23 Oct. 20/3 All our colleges together manufacture only platitudinarian pulpiteers.

Hence **platitudi'narianism**.

1887 A. J. GORDON in *Missionary Herald* Sept. 367 As much need to be on their guard against platitudinarianism as against latitudinarianism. **1892** J. B. ALLEN in *Academy* 23 Jan. 84/2 One of the most tiresome of the minor faults to which novelists are liable is platitudinarianism.

platitudinary (plætɪ'tjuːdɪnərɪ), *a.* [As if f. L. **platitudo, -din-* + -ARY[1]; cf. LATITUDINARY *a.*] = PLATITUDINARIAN *a.*

1920 *Glasgow Herald* 2 Apr. 6 At a song-recital..the critic is again troubled by Elgar—this time by a 'tawdry catch-penny ballad'... At a Queen's Hall Concert the Elgar of the Second Symphony is 'platitudinary and tedious'. **1933** DYLAN THOMAS *Let.* Sept. (1966) 24 Wordsworth was..the humourless, the platitudinary reporter of Nature in her dullest moods.

plati'tudinist. *rare.* [f. PLATITUDINIZE *v.* + -IST.] A person who utters platitudes; a platitudinizer.

1905 W. J. LOCKE *Usurper* xx. 243 Jasper..was not sorry when the kind-hearted platitudinist had gone. **1905** —— *Morals of Marcus Ordeyne* ii. 22 If there is one platitudinist I dislike more than another, it is Marcus Aurelius.

platitudinize (plætɪ'tjuːdɪnaɪz), *v.* [f. as PLATITUDINARIAN *sb.* and *a.* + -IZE.] *intr.* To utter platitudes. Hence **platitudini'zation** (in quot. as if from a *trans.* sense 'to impart a character of platitude to'); **plati'tudinizer**, **plati'tudinism**.

1885 *Sat. Rev.* 7 Feb. 191/2 A diplomatist..is a man who retains the tradition and faculty of respectable platitude. Many men now platitudinize, but not as a rule respectably. **1888** *Ibid.* 18 Feb. 179/1 The platform platitudinizers. **1893** *Pall Mall Mag.* II. 351/2 He moves platitudinising and attitudinising through a play. **1895** ZANGWILL *Master* 441 Art—the last of the rebels against the platitudinisation of life. **1897** *Strand Mag.* Aug. 179 He has a rich gift of what an eminent American calls 'platitudinizing'. The word..is most effective as indicating a constant ever fed supply of pointless words, wrapped up in cotton woolly sentences. **1903** *Ch. Times* 12 June 747/2 The Archbishop of Canterbury departed a little from the area of platitudinism, when..he alluded to the 'passive resistance' movement.

platitudinous (plætɪ'tjuːdɪnəs), *a.* [f. as prec. + -OUS; cf. *multitudinous*.] Characterized by or of the nature of a platitude; full of platitudes; of a person, uttering or writing platitudes.

1862 *Illustr. Lond. News* 11 Jan. 51/1 The bulk of the speech is somewhat platitudinous. **1874** L. STEPHEN *Hours in Library* I. 232 Schiller's excellent but remarkably platitudinous peasants in 'William Tell'. **1882** TRAILL *Sterne* v. 56 The Sermons are..of the most commonplace character, platitudinous with the platitudes of a thousand pulpits.

Hence **plati'tudinously** *adv.*, **plati'tudinousness**.

1858 *Sat. Rev.* 28 Aug. 201/1 The consequences are.. an extreme tenuity of thought and an excessive platitudinousness of expression. **1892** *Daily News* 21 May 2/2 His orations are enormously, portentously, platitudinously dull.

†**'platlings**, *adv. Obs.* [f. PLAT *a.* + *-lings*: see -LING[2].] Flat, flatly, flatlings.

1447 BOKENHAM *Seyntys* (Roxb.) 69 He home went on to his plas And fel down platlyngys sorwyng hevely. **1535** STEWART *Cron. Scot.* III. 329 Sic ane straik vpoun him sone scho set, Quhill that scho feld him platlingis on that plane.

†**'platly**, *adv. Obs.* [f. PLAT *a.* + -LY[2].] In a plat manner; flatly, bluntly, plainly, directly.

c **1374** CHAUCER *Troylus* III. 737 (786) This Troylus right platly for to seyn Is þurgh a goter, by a preuy wente Into my chambre ycome. *c* **1386** —— *Pars. T.* ¶948 þou must tell it platly be it neuer so foul ne so horrible. *c* **1407** LYDG. *Reson & Sens.* 1480 For ther is platly non that may Disobey[e]n hir byddyng. **1549** HOOPER *Declar. 10 Commandm.* vi. Wks. (Parker Soc.) I. 325 A great number, that say, not platly and plainly, 'there is no God'; but by certain circumlocutions and paraphrases. **1567** TURBERV. *Ovid's Epist.* 26 b, Of so noble fame, as platly doth appeare.

†**'platness.** *Obs.* [f. PLAT *a.* + -NESS.] Flatness, plainness.

1530 PALSGR. 255/2 Platnesse, *plattevr.*

platode ('plætəʊd), *a. Zool.* [irreg. f. Gr. πλατύς broad + -ODE[1], after *cestode*, etc.] = next.

platoid ('plætɔɪd), *a. Zool.* [f. as prec. + -OID, after *cestoid*, *trematoid*, etc.] Of a flattened form, as the worms of the group *Platyhelminthes*.

1894 W. S. WINDLE in *Pop. Sc. Monthly* XLIV. 454 Besides larvae, numerous adult forms, as..platoid worms.. are collected.

platometer (plə'tɒmɪtə(r)). [f. Gr. πλάτος breadth + -METER.] An instrument for measuring areas: = PLANIMETER.

1852 SANG in *Trans. Scot. Soc. Arts* IV. 119 Description of a platometer, an instrument for measuring the areas of figures drawn on paper. **1865** BALFOUR *Ibid.* VII. 198 A new form of platometer.

†**pla'tometry.** *Obs. rare.* [f. as prec. + -METRY.] The art of measuring the breadth of some (distant or inaccessible) object.

1570 DEE *Math. Pref.* aiij b, It informeth the measurer, how Broad any thing is, which is in the measurers vew: so it be on Land or Water: and may be called Platometrie.

Pla'tonian, *sb.* and *a.* [f. Gr. Πλάτων Plato + -IAN.]

†**A.** *sb.* = PLATONIST. *Obs.*

1569 J. SANFORD tr. *Agrippa's Van. Artes* 68 b, Whiche was the Platonians opinion. **1611** A. STAFFORD *Niobe* 80 The Platonians were so enamoured of this amiable goddess.

B. *adj.* = PLATONIC *a.* 1. *rare*.

1942 B. BERENSON *Jrnl.* 28 Feb. in *One Year's Reading for Fun* (1960) 30 Aristides speaks in the Platonian *Theages*.

Platonic (plə'tɒnɪk), *a.* and *sb.* [ad. L. *Platōnicus*, a. Gr. Πλατωνικός, f. Πλάτων Plato: see -IC. Cf. F. *Platonique* (16th c. in Godef.).]

A. *adj.*

1. a. Of or pertaining to Plato, a famous philosopher of ancient Greece (B.C. *c* 429–*c* 347), or his doctrines; conceived or composed after the manner of Plato.

1533 ELYOT (*title*) Of that Knowledge, whiche maketh a wise Man. A disputation Platonike. **1638** WILKINS *New World* I. (1684) 173 'Twas an Old Platonick Principle, that there is in some part of the World such a place where Men might be Plentifully Nourished, by the Air they Breath. **1697** EVELYN *Numism.* vii. 235 More like a Platonic Notion. **1833** J. H. NEWMAN *Arians* I. iii. (1876) 39 That comprehensive philosophy, which was reduced to system about the beginning of the third century, and then went by the name of the New Platonic, or Eclectic. **1875** JOWETT *Plato* (ed. 2) I. 240 The Ion, like the other earlier Platonic Dialogues. **1884** tr. *Lotze's Logic* 435 The Platonic expression Idea is usually rendered Universal conception.

b. Of a person: Holding or maintaining the doctrines of Plato; that is a follower of Plato.

a **1654** SELDEN *Table-T.* (Arb.) 53 The first Christians many of them were Platonick Philosophers. **1831** I. TAYLOR *Pref. Ess. to Edwards' Freed. Will* iii. 50 Commencing with the Platonic fathers, and ending with the last writers on both sides of the Calvinistic controversy.

c. Appositive, as ***Platonic-Christian*** adj., both Platonic and Christian, of or pertaining to Christianity influenced by or fused with Platonism.

1933 A. N. WHITEHEAD *Adventures of Ideas* iii. 40 In the hands of theologians..the Platonic-Christian tradition leant heavily towards its mystical religious side. **1948** L. SPITZER *Linguistics & Lit. Hist.* 55 To Dante, all dialects appeared as inferior..realizations of a Platonic-Christian ideal pattern of language. **1960** *Encounter* Feb. 49/1 This is at the root of the Platonic-Christian (or religious) tradition.

2. a. Applied to love or affection for one of the opposite sex, of a purely spiritual character, and free from sensual desire. Also of affection for one of the same sex. Hence in various allusive applications. (Now usu. with lower-case initial.)

[*Amor platonicus* was used synonymously with *amor socraticus* by Ficinus (the Florentine Marsilio Ficino, 1433–99), president of Cosmo de' Medici's *Accademia Platonica*, to denote the kind of interest in young men with which Socrates was credited: cf. the last few pages of Plato's *Symposium*. As thus originally used, it had no reference to women. (Prof. I. Bywater.)]

1631 JONSON *New Inne* III. ii. sig. E5[v], Most Socratick Lady! Or, if you will Ironick! gi' you ioy O' you Platonick loue here. **1636** DAVENANT (*title*) The Platonic Lovers. *c* **1645** HOWELL *Lett.* (1650) VI. 203 The Court affords little news at present, but that ther is a love, call'd Platonick love, which much swayes there of late. It is a love..[that] consists in contemplation and idæas of the mind, not in any carnall fruition. **1651** STANLEY (*title*) A Platonick Discourse Upon Love. Written in Italian by John Picus Mirandula. **1678** NORRIS *Coll. Misc.* (1699) 355 Platonic Love is the Love of Beauty abstracted from all sensual Applications, and desire of Corporal Contact. **1741** RICHARDSON *Pamela* (1824) I. lxxviii. 438, I am convinced, and always was, that Platonic love is Platonic nonsense. *c* **1805** JANE AUSTEN *Lady Susan* (1954) x. 258 We are advancing now towards some kind of confidence, and in short are likely to be engaged in a kind of platonic friendship. **1857** LEWES *Biograph. Hist. Philos.* 195 Love is the longing of the Soul for Beauty; the inextinguishable desire which like feels for like, which the divinity within us feels for the divinity revealed to us in Beauty. This is the celebrated Platonic Love, which, from having originally meant a communion of two souls, and that in a rigidly dialectical sense, has been degraded to the expression of maudlin sentiment between the sexes. **1862** GEN. P. THOMPSON in *Bradford Advertiser* 8 Mar. 6/1 As well might be said that Tories of the olden time only fought for..a Platonic love for rotten boroughs. **1905** 'A. CAMBRIDGE' (*title*) A platonic friendship. *Ibid.* v. 67 What is known as a platonic friendship is generally nothing of the kind. **1919** G. B. SHAW *Heartbreak House* II. 87 *Hector*... What do you get by it? Are you her lover? *Randall*. You must not misunderstand me. In a higher sense— *Hector*. Psha! Platonic sense! She makes you her servant; and when pay-day comes round, she bilks you: that is what you mean. **1924** 'W. FABIAN' *Sailors' Wives* vii. 94 'You're taking a lot of notice of that dangerous young person, old bean,' remarked Dorr lightly. 'Platonic, purely. Couldn't well be anything else for a man with my prospects.' **1925** C. CONNOLLY *Let.* 14 May in *Romantic Friendship* (1975) 78, I think I care more for Maurice than anyone else here—and the fact that such affection can be nothing but platonic enhances it, if anything. **1928** A. HUXLEY *Point Counter Point* xiii. 232 He had such a pure, childlike and platonic way of going to bed with women, that neither they nor he ever considered that the process really counted as going to bed. **1957** J. BRAINE *Room at Top* vii. 64 'Teddy wouldn't understand. Our relationship is strictly platonic.' 'Yes, I understand,' Teddy said, putting his arm round June's waist. 'I'm trying to take June on a platonic weekend. Of course, it'll be too bad if she has a platonic baby.' **1975** A. PRICE *Our Man in Camelot* v. 76 'Sharing a bedroom with a strange man in the line of duty. Kind of special relationship.' 'Special *platonic* relationship.'

b. Feeling or professing platonic love.

1650 BULWER *Anthropomet.* 163 The Mother-in-Law of Forestus, a fruitfull woman, would not match her daughters to Platonique men. **1709** STEELE *Tatler* No. 32 ¶3 This Order of Platonick Ladies are to be dealt with in a peculiar Manner from all the rest of the Sex. **1872** MORLEY *Voltaire* 43 She had ridiculed the pedantical women and platonic gallants of the Hôtel Rambouillet as the Jansenists of love.

3. a. ***Platonic bodies*** (Geom.): a name for the five regular solids (tetrahedron, cube, octahedron, dodecahedron, icosahedron). Now also called ***Platonic solids***.

[**1571**: see PLATONICAL 3]. *a* **1696** SCARBURGH *Euclid* (1705) 282 The five Platonick Bodies, so much fam'd, Pythagoras first found, Plato explain'd; Euclide on them Immortal Glory gain'd. **1704** J. HARRIS *Lex. Techn.* I, *Platonick Bodies*. See *Regular Bodies*. **1745** E. STONE *Euclid's Elements* (ed. 2) II. p. xxiv, The thirteenth, fourteenth and fifteenth Books entertain us with curious and useful Speculations, relating to the five regular or platonick Bodies, in Regard to which, as Proclus tells us, Euclid compiled the whole Body of the Elements, the Platonicks having had them in wonderful Esteem. **1873** J. Booth *Treat. Some New Geom. Methods* I. p. xi, That the principle of Duality should not have been discovered by the great geometers of Ancient Greece is the more remarkable, as the five regular solids, the Platonic bodies as they were called, were with them a favourite subject of speculation. **1917** H. E. Dudeney *Amusements in Math.* 70/2 The icosahedron is another of the five regular, or Platonic, bodies having all their sides, angles, and planes similar and equal. **1952** Cundy & Rollett *Math. Models* iii. 70 The so-called Platonic solids.. form the first and simplest group of polyhedra. **1952** G. Sarton *Hist. Sci.* I. xvii. 439 If the regular solids are restricted to five, those five bodies (later called the Platonic bodies) must each have some definite meaning. **1971** M. J. Wenninger *Polyhedron Models* i. 19 The dodecahedron is in some ways the most attractive of the five Platonic solids.

b. ***Platonic year***: a cycle imagined by some ancient astronomers, in which the heavenly bodies were supposed to go through all their possible movements and return to their original relative positions (after which, according to some, all events would recur in the same order as before); sometimes identified with the period of revolution of the equinoxes (about 25800 years: see precession).

1639 Fuller *Holy War* v. xxviii. 278 Except the Platonick yeare, turning the wheel of all actions round about, bring the spoke of his Holy warre back again. **1658** Phillips, *Platonick Year, i.* the space of 36000 years. **1684** T. Burnet *The. Earth* ii. 149 Call'd the Platonick year, as if Plato had been the first author of that opinion; but that's a great mistake. **1727–41** Chambers *Cycl.*, *Platonic year*, or the *great year*, is.. the space wherein the stars and constellations return to their former places, in respect of the equinoxes. The Platonic year, according to Tycho Brahe, is 25816; according to Ricciolus 25920; according to Cassini 24800 years. **1867–77** G. F. Chambers *Astron.* Voc. Defin. 919. **1922** W. B. Yeats *Seven Poems* 23 Are not those who travel in the whirling dust also in the Platonic Year?

B. *sb.* [Cf. F. *Platonique* (1486 in Godef. *Compl.*).]

†**1.** A follower of Plato: a Platonist. *Obs.*

1605 Timme *Quersit.* i. ii. 6 The Platonicks called the same the soule of the worlde. **1609** Bible (Douay) *Comm.* II. 1001 Platonikes or Academikes conceived more of God, and pure spirites, but thought both corporal and spiritual creatures were coeternal with God. **1707** in Hearne *Collect.* 13 June (O.H.S.) II. 20 The Primitive Fathers were Platonicks in their comments upon the Scriptures. **1758** Eliz. Carter tr. *Epictetus* Introd., The Platonics.. do yet, with the Stoics, constantly maintain fate.

2. A platonic lover (see A. 2b). ? *Obs.*

a **1658** Cleveland *Gen. Poems*, etc. (1677) 157 Sure at this Grate those Chrisom Lovers, call'd Platonicks, had their first Training. **1712** Arbuthnot *John Bull* i. viii, Very pretty, indeed! A wife must never go abroad with a Platonic to see a play or a ball! **1757** Mrs. Griffith *Lett. Henry & Frances* (1767) II. 291 Till they dwindle into that stage of life, when, and when only, lovers become Platonics indeed.

3. (Usually *pl.*) Platonic love; the acts or doings of a platonic lover.

1800 Mar. Edgeworth *Belinda* xvii, Are they out o' the horn-book of platonics yet? **1836** F. Mahony *Rel. Father Prout* (1859) 76 That was attributed to a sort of Platonic he felt for the fascinating Donna Maria da Gloria. **1923** R. Macaulay *Told by Idiot* i. 11 To Vicky a young man *was* a young man, and no platonics about it. **1937** 'M. Innes' *Hamlet, Revenge!* ii. vi. 173 It is one of those affairs that are laced with long-term platonics.

Pla'tonical, *a.* ? *Obs.* [f. as prec. + -al[1].]

1. = Platonic A. 1.

1561 T. Norton tr. *Calvin's Inst.* i. xiv. (1634) 69 Let us therefore forsake that Platonicall philosophy. **1642** H. More (*title*) A Platonical Song of the Soul. **1758** Eliz. Carter tr. *Epictetus* Introd., There is no real difference betwixt the Platonical and Stoical philosophy, in the opinion of fate, and the freedom of human actions. **1845** Maurice *Mor. & Met. Philos.* in *Encycl. Metrop.* (1847) II. 612/1 The attempt to divide matter from substance and look upon things sensible as not sensible, has led to all the Pythagorean and Platonical inventions, which he regards with so much dislike.

2. = Platonic A. 2.

1636 Davenant *Platonic Lovers* Wks. (1673) 414 Since not.. amongst you all He can find one will prove Platonical. **1823** Byron *Juan* ix. lxxvi, The noblest kind of love is love Platonical.

3. = Platonic A. 3.

1571 Digges *Pantom.*, *Math. Disc.* Pref., I haue thought good to adioyne this Treatise of the 5 Platonicall bodies. *Ibid.*, The fiue bodyes Regulare or Platonicall. **1656** Blount *Glossogr.*, *Platonical year* (*annus platonicus*) is every 36000th. year, when some Philosophers imagined, all persons and things should return to the same state as now they are.

Hence **Pla'tonicalness**.

1668 G. C. in H. More *Div. Dial.* Pref. i. (1713) 6 Which therefore agrees well with the Platonicalness of Cuphophron's Genius.

pla'tonically, *adv.* Also Platonically. [f. Platonic *a.* + -al[1] + -ly[1]; in early use perh. f. Platonical *a.*] In a Platonic (platonic) manner: see Platonic *a.* 1, 2.

1636 Davenant *Platonic Lovers* Wks. (1673) 404 The Turk! Is he platonically given? *a* **1639** Wotton *Life Dk. Buckingham* in *Reliq.* (1651) 77 To mould him as it were Platonically to his own Idea. **1826** *Q. Rev.* XXXIV. 432 Madame de Montesson was platonically jealous. **1901** Conrad & Hueffer *Inheritors* iii. 39 Gurnard I disliked platonically; perhaps because his face was a little enigmatic—a little repulsive. **1941** J. D. Carr *Case of Constant Suicides* iii. 34 There is nothing like spending the night with a girl, even platonically, to remove a sense of constraint. **1972** *Nature* 17 Mar. 92/1 It would be convenient if there were such a platonically ideal chemistry. **1973** *Listener* 6 Sept. 312/1 They stood in tasteful tableaux, their hands platonically resting on one another's nether regions.

†**Plato'nician.** *Obs.* [ad. F. *platonicien* (Oresme 14th c.), f. L. *Platonic-us* Platonic: see -ian: cf. *mechanician.*] = Platonist.

1741 tr. *D'Argens' Chinese Lett.* xxxviii. 289 The Platonicians suppose that God and Matter were the Principles of all Beings. **1776** Gibbon *Decl. & F.* xiii. I. 399 The new Platonicians.. exhausted their strength in the verbal disputes of metaphysics. **1829** K. Digby *Broadst. Hon.* I. *Godefridus* 157 Philo a celebrated philosopher among the Platonicians.

Platonicism (plə'tɒnɪsɪz(ə)m). *rare.* [f. Platonic + -ism.] = Platonism 3.

a **1678** H. Scougal *Wks.* (1765) 333 Many naughty affections do shelter themselves under the plausible title of Platonicism. **1741** Richardson *Pamela* (1824) I. lxxvii. 435 She little depended upon Platonicism in him.

†**Pla'tonicker.** *Obs. rare*$^{-1}$. [f. Platonic + -er[1].] = Platonist.

1582 N.T. (Rhem.) *John* i. 1 *note*, This first sentence of the Gospel not only the faithful but the Platonickers did so admire.. that they wished it to be written in gold.

Platonism ('pleɪtənɪz(ə)m). [ad. mod.L. *platonism-us*, f. Gr. *Πλάτων* Plato: see -ism. So mod.F. *platonisme* (Dict. Acad. 1762).]

1. The philosophy or doctrine of Plato, or of his followers.

1570 Levins *Manip.* 146 Platonisme, *Platonismus*. **1642** H. More *Song of Soul* ii. Pref., Those that are rightly acquainted with Platonisme, will accept of that small pains. **1782** Priestley *Corrupt. Chr.* I. i. 11 That.. was introduced from the principles of platonism afterwards. **1806** Knox & Jebb *Corr.* I. 283 Thinking as I do, that platonism was prepared providentially, not only as preliminary to Christian piety, but as a kind of fermenting principle, to act occasionally in reinvigorating it. **1856** R. A. Vaughan *Mystics* (1860) I. 52 Platonism in Philo does for Judaism what it was soon to do for Christianity.

2. (with *pl.*) A doctrine or tenet of Platonic philosophy; a saying of, or like those of, Plato.

1610 Healey *St. Aug. Citie of God* 400 He overthrowes one great Platonisme. *Ibid.* 694 A philosopher came to him and expounded certaine Platonismes unto him. **1845** R. Choate *Amer. Bar* in *Addresses* (1878) 165 Hear the striking platonisms of Coleridge.

3. The doctrine or practice of platonic love. (Cf. Platonicism.)

1782 Alexander *Hist. Women* I. vii. 233 The Troubadour.. was not always satisfied with pure platonism, and frequently debauched the virgin or the wife whom he attended. **1893** Saltus *Madam Sapphira* 59 For that reason.. platonic affection, or, more exactly, reciprocal platonism, is discoverable only among married people.

Platonist ('pleɪtənɪst). [ad. med.L. *platanista* (1286 in *Catholicon*), f. Gr. *Πλάτων* Plato: see -ist.] A follower of Plato; one who holds the doctrines or philosophy of Plato.

1549 Latimer *6th Serm. bef. Edw. VI* (Arb.) 166 He [St. Augustine] became of a Maniche and of a platoniste a good christian. **1570** Levins *Manip.* 147 Platoniste, *Platonista*. **1626** Bacon *Sylva* §944 As for Love, the Platonists, (some of them,) go so farre as to hold that the spirit of the Lover, doth passe into the spirits of the Person Loved. **1678** Cudworth *Intell. Syst.* Pref. 36 Vpon which Occasion we take notice of a Double Platonick Trinity; the One Spurious and Adulterated, of some latter Platonists; the Other True and Genuine, of Plato himself, Parmenides, and the Ancients. **1787** Sir J. Hawkins *Johnson* 542 Dr. Henry More, of Cambridge, he did not much affect: he was a platonist, and, in Johnson's opinion, a visionary. **1847** Emerson *Repr. Men, Plato* Wks. (Bohn) I. 310 Hamlet is a pure Platonist.

b. A platonic lover. Also *attrib.*

1756 (*title*) Memoirs of a Young Lady of Quality, a Platonist. **1895** *Westm. Gaz.* 6 July 3/3 The author has endeavoured to give a sympathetic view of a warm-hearted woman in her relations with a platonist husband.

Hence **Plato'nistic** *a.*, pertaining to or characteristic of the Platonists or of Platonism; **Plato'nistically** *adv.*

1859 W. Key *Lect. on St. August.* 12 He was speaking with an aged Christian about some Platonistic books. **1953** M. H. Abrams *Mirror & Lamp* i. 29 Shelley's Platonistic 'Defence of Poetry'. **1957** G. Ryle in C. Mace *Brit. Philos. in Mid-Cent.* 263 The difficulty is to steer between the Scylla of a Platonistic and the Charybdis of a lexicographical account of the business of philosophy and logic. **1959** P. F. Strawson *Individuals* viii. 234 No doubt some philosophers have deluded themselves with myths, have invested non-particulars with a character they do not really possess. There is Platonistic zeal as well as nominalistic zeal. But zeal of either kind is out of place. **1977** G. W. H. Lampe *God as Spirit* iv. 108 The Platonistically conceived Second Person of the Trinity in the classical formulations of the fourth and fifth centuries.

Platonize ('pleɪtənaɪz), *v.* [ad. Gr. *πλατωνίζειν* (Origen), f. *Πλάτων* Plato: see -ize. So F. *platoniser* (*a* 1587 in Godefroy).]

1. *intr.* To follow the doctrine of Plato; to philosophize after the manner of Plato; to be a Platonist.

1608 Hieron *Defence* ii. 157* Aust. did platonize a little, we maie saie, the D. doth platonize a greate deale more. **1610** Healey *St. Aug. Citie of God* 649 Philo either Platonized or Plato Philonized. **1678** Cudworth *Intell. Syst.* i. iv. §27. 457 Macrobius plainly Platonized, asserting a Trinity of Archical or Divine Hypostases. **1833** J. H. Newman *Arians* i. iii. (1876) 40 The grave imputation.. of considering the Son of God inferior to the Father, that is, of Platonizing or Arianizing.

2. To act as platonic friends. *nonce-use.*

1821 *New Monthly Mag.* III. 119 If I could venture to invent a word.. I would say, that we will 'platonize' together, under the constant guidance of nature and philosophy.

3. *trans.* To give a Platonic character to; to render Platonic.

1850 Grote *Greece* ii. lxviii. VIII. 556 Of the ethical dialogues much may be probably taken to represent Sokrates more or less platonized. **1871** Blackie *Four Phases* i. 148 The record of this conversation, no doubt.. largely Platonized.

Hence **'Platonized, 'Platonizing** *ppl. adjs.*; also **Platoni'zation**, the action of Platonizing or condition of being Platonized (in quot., in sense 2); **'Platonizer**, one who Platonizes, a Platonist.

1843 *Fraser's Mag.* XXVIII. 277 Their passion for the *danseuse* having, in the meantime, metempsychosed itself into a *platonisation. **1845** Maurice *Mor. & Met. Philos.* in *Encycl. Metrop.* (1847) II. 638/1 The warrior lived on through the days of Julian, lived to see the utmost done that could be done for *Platonized paganism. **1734** A. Young *Idolatrous Corrupt.* I. 109 Philo the Jew, who was a great *Platonizer, calls the Stars Divine Images, and incorruptible and immortal Souls. **1701** Norris *Ideal World* i. v. 241 The second Hypostasis whom the Platonists called the *νοῦς*, and the *Platonizing Apostle the *λόγος*. **1827** Moore *Epicur.* xvii, The platonising refinement of Philo. **1885** W. Wallace in *Encycl. Brit.* II. 267/2 The materials of the work.. are conceived in a Platonising spirit.

†**Pla'tonne.** *Obs. nonce-wd.* [Formed as a F. fem. of *Platon* Plato: cf. *baron*, *baronne.*] *lit.* A female Plato: in quot. a female adherent of the doctrine of Platonic affection.

1709 Swift *Tatler* No. 32 ¶2, I am fallen desperately in Love with a profess'd Platonne, the most unaccountable Creature of her Sex.

platoon (plə'tu:n), *sb.* Forms: 7–8 **plotton**, 8 **plat-**, **plottoon**, 8– **platoon**. [ad. F. *peloton* (15th c. in Hatz.-Darm., *pron.* plɔtɔ̃) little ball, platoon, dim. of *pelote*: see pellet *sb.*[1] and -oon.]

1. a. *Mil.* A small body of foot-soldiers, detached from a larger body and operating as an organized unit; variously applied: see quots. (*obs.*); *spec.* half a company, a squad, a tactical formation preserved in some armies for purposes of drill, etc. Revived in the British army for an organizational unit (usu. a quarter) of a company of infantry. Also used for comparable organizational units in other armies.

Formerly volley-firing was done by platoons: cf. b.

1637 Monro *Exped.*, etc. ii. *Abridgm. Exerc.* 184 Eight Corporall-ships of Musketiers, being thirty-two Rots divided in foure Plottons, every Plotton being eight in front, led off by a Captaine. **1704** J. Harris *Lex. Techn.* I, *Plattoon*.. is a small Square Body of Musketeers, such as is usually drawn out of a Battalion of Foot, when they form the Hollow Square to strengthen the Angles. **1727–41** Chambers *Cycl.*, *Plattoon*, or *Plottoon*, in war, a small, square body of 40 or 50 men, drawn out of a battalion of foot, and placed between the squadrons of horse, to sustain them; or in ambuscades, streights, and defiles, where there is not room for battalions or regiments. **1734** tr. *Rollin's Anc. Hist.* (1827) II. v. 254 Platoons which consisted of four and twenty men each. **1788** M. Cutler in *Life*, etc. (1888) I. 420 Just as we got up with them, they began to fire by platoons. **1846** *Hist. Rec. 1st Regiment of Foot* 130 The street contained only a platoon abreast, so the first platoon fired their 24 rounds, and then filed off, and were succeeded by the next and following platoons. **1853** Stocqueler *Mil. Encycl.*, *Platoon*, a subdivision or small body of infantry. The word is obsolete, except in the term 'manual and platoon exercise'. **1875** tr. *Ct. de Paris' Hist. Civ. War in Amer.* I. 272 The recruits must go through a series of exercises and evolutions.. first singly, then by platoons, by battalions next, and finally by brigades. **1913** *Army Order* No. 323. 16 Sept. §4 A company will be divided into four platoons, each commanded by a subaltern... Each platoon will be sub-divided under regulations to be issued later. **1915** D. O. Barnett *Let.* 18 Jan. 40 I've bought A. Coy. No. 4 Platoon. **1917** J. M. Barrie *Old Lady shows her Medals* 72 You have knitted enough things already to fit up my whole platoon. **1929** *Encycl. Brit.* XVIII. 64/2 In the U.S. cavalry a troop is divided into four platoons. **1938** 'I. Hay' *King's Service* xiv. 245 The number of platoons in a rifle company has been reduced from four to three. **1945** H. P. Samwell *Infantry Officer with Eighth Army* iv. 33 We had agreed that he should bring up Company H.Q. and the reserve platoon behind, while I led the forward platoons. **1948** N. Mailer *Naked & Dead* (1949) i. ii. 25 What a bunch of good old boys there were in the platoon, he told himself. **1964** H. D. Chaplin *Queen's Own Royal W. Kent Regiment 1951–1961* ii. 45 Four platoons under Major Crumplin spent Christmas and the New Year festival in the jungle. **1964** Clough & Cash tr. *Gorbatov's Years off my Life* x. 161, I told Kostevich to send a platoon from each battalion to man the line. **1965** I. Adamson *Forgotten Men* i. 15 Working with Animal Transport Platoons had been part of their training in the Bush Warfare School. **1971** E. Luttwak *Dict. Mod. War* 153/2 *Platoon*, an army formation subordinate to the battalion and comprising a number of squads or sections. Normally the smallest unit with an organizational identity, it varies in size from the 12 men of a Soviet army tank platoon to the 40 plus men of a U.S. army infantry platoon. **1972** J. Strawson *Battle for Ardennes* vi. 90 The critical feature was occupied.. by a weak platoon numbering some eighteen men of the 394 US Infantry Regiment of 99th Division.

b. *transf.* A number of shots fired simultaneously by a platoon or body of men; a volley.

1706 FARQUHAR *Recruiting Officer* III. ii, I tell you what, I'll make love like a platoon. **1747** *Gentl. Mag.* 317 The Welsh fuzileers fired two platoons upon the Dutch. **1817** M. WILKS *Hist. Sk. S. India* (1869) II. xxxiii. 145 Threw in a regular platoon on the flank which killed the officer commanding. **1889** DOYLE *Micah Clarke* 298 These can fight in line and fire a platoon as well as one could wish to see.

fig. **1775** SHERIDAN *St. Patr. Day* I. i, 2 *Sol.* We'll argue in platoons. 3. *Sol.* Ay, ay, let him have our grievances in a volley.

†**c.** Short for *platoon exercise. Obs.*

1796 *Instr. & Reg. Cavalry* (1813) 251 After the manual and platoon, the battalion remains formed at close order, and the major returns to his post in the rear. **1816** 'QUIZ' *Grand Master* II. 50.

2. *transf.* and *fig.* **a.** A squad; a company or set of people.

1711 *Acc. Last Distemper of T. Whigg* II. 44 Tom.. danc'd away the Hays with them in regular Plattoons. **1790** BURKE *Fr. Rev.* Wks. V. 100 To love the little platoon we belong to in society, is the first principle (the germ as it were) of publick affections. **1837** W. IRVING *Capt. Bonneville* (1849) 376 This is played by two parties drawn out in opposite platoons before a blazing fire. **1841** EMERSON *Lect., Times* Wks. (Bohn) II. 250 If you speak of the age, you mean your own platoon of people.

b. *Amer. Football.* A group of players trained to act together as a single unit of attack or defence and usu. sent into or withdrawn from the game as a body.

1941 *Charlottesville* (Va.) *Daily Progress* 14 Jan. 11 They [*sc.* football teams] can still send in as many players—platoons included—while the clock is stopped. **1948** *N.Y. Times* 28 Sept. 36/6 Eleven men may be sent in at a time now, even with the clock running.. but Lou [Little] is opposed to this unlimited substitution rule in theory. Maj. Joel Stephens, of West Point,.. said that Army has the 'two-platoon' system now. **1949** *Sun* (Baltimore) 2 Dec. 17/7 Schweder is one of the unusual football players of the 'platoon age' in that he plays on both offense and defense.

c. *Baseball.* (See quot.)

1976 *Webster's Sports Dict.* 318/2 *Platoon.. Baseball*, two or more players who alternate at the same position. The players who make up a particular platoon are usually average players who are adequate fielders but who are not outstanding hitters.

3. *attrib.*, as ***platoon commander***, ***corporal***, ***drill***, ***exercise***, ***fire***, ***firing***, ***leader***, ***officer***, ***sergeant***, ***-training***; also humorously ***platoon swearing*** (= utterance of a 'volley' of oaths, quot. 1793).

1917 W. OWEN *Let.* 23 Nov. (1967) 509 Interesting work but hardly 'lighter' than a *Platoon Commander's. **1920** J. C. CHASE *Soldiers All* 57 He received orders to proceed to Hill 182... He sent runners to notify his platoon commanders. **1974** G. BLAXLAND *Queen's Own Buffs* iii. 21 There was to be similar pairing of platoon commanders and platoon sergeants. **1941** A. COTTERELL *What! No Morning Tea?* 29 After breakfast there was a joint lecture by our two *platoon corporals on what to call the various parts of the rifle. **1935** I. MILLER *School Tie* xv. 290, I could never get the hang of anything more evolutionary than *platoon-drill. **1796** *Instr. & Reg. Cavalry* (1813) 251 The major closes rear ranks for the *platoon exercise. **1818** SCOTT *Hrt. Midl.* li, Nature seems to expect the thunder-burst, as a condemned soldier waits for the *platoon-fire which is to stretch him on the earth. **1899** *Allbutt's Syst. Med.* VI. 514 The discharging [of neurons] may take place by *platoon firing or by company firing, or by desultory rank firing.. the general opinion is in favour of platoon firing. **1952** T. J. MULVEY *These are your Sons* iv. 85 He's got three rifle *platoon leaders and one weapons platoon leader. **1923** KIPLING *Irish Guards in Great War* I. 24 A newly appointed *platoon-officer.. admonished them unofficially. **1915** D. O. BARNETT *Lett.* 41, I like the men awfully, especially my *platoon sergeant. **1965** BROPHY & PARTRIDGE *Long Trail* 224 The Staff.. were known only by occasional glimpses. The platoon-sergeant, whatever his defects, was visible and human. **1974** Platoon sergeant [see *platoon commander*]. **1793** LAW in E. A. Bond *Trial Warren Hastings* (1860) III. 266 After having tried his hand to hit the mark twice alone, then he indulged in *platoon swearing. **1923** KIPLING *Irish Guards in Great War* II. 138 These Somme officers were accordingly told that most of their time should be given to *platoon-training. **1942** E. WAUGH *Put out More Flags* ii. 125 After the stand-easy they fell in for platoon training.

pla'toon, *v.* [f. prec. sb.]

†**1.** *intr.* To fire a volley; also *fig. Obs.*

1706 FARQUHAR *Recruiting Officer* III. ii, I'll kneel, stoop, and stand, faith; most ladies are gained by platooning. **1780** S. J. PRATT *Emma Corbett* (ed. 4) II. 46 The veteran Carbines, after having platooned and pioneered it for a number of years.., could keep the field no longer.

2. *trans.* To dispose in platoons.

1961 in WEBSTER s.v., The advantages from platooning students in smaller schools.

3. *Baseball.* **a.** *trans.* To alternate (a player) with another in the same position. **b.** *intr.* To interchange with another player in the same position. Hence **pla'tooning** *vbl. sb.*

1967 WEBSTER Add., *Platoon..*, to alternate (one player) with another player in the same position (as on a baseball team). **1969** *Time* 5 Sept. 52 Hodges decided to 'platoon' him by playing him only against lefthanded pitchers. **1971** L. DUROCHER in *Webster* Add. s.v., If I can't play him every day, I'll platoon him in left field. **1971** *Ibid., Platoon..*, to alternate with another player in the same position. **1972** *N.Y. Times* 4 June v. 2/7 Buckner also shares first base with Wes Parker and Crawford platoons with Manny Mota in left field. *Ibid.* 3 Nov. 45/6 He might junk the platooning system used rigidly by Williams.

platopic (plə'tɒpɪk), *a. Craniom.* [irreg. f. Gr. πλατύς broad + ὤψ, ὠπ- face + -IC.] = *platyopic* (the etymological form): see PLATY-.

1885 *Jrnl. of Anthrop. Inst.* 156 The cranial characters of the Yahgans.. platopic, mesoprosopic, and mesognathous.

pla'tos-, pla'toso-. *Chem.* Formative, shortened from PLATINOS(O-, forming names of compounds in which platinum is bivalent, as **pla'tosamine**, NH_2Pt, the ammonia-base supposed by Gerhardt to exist in the ammonio-platinous compounds (Watts); **platosa'mmonium**, the group Pt. $2NH_3$ (as in ***platosammonium chloride***, Pt. $2NH_3Cl$), **platosodia'mmonium**, the group Pt. $2N_2H_6$ (as in ***platosodiammonium chloride***, Pt. $2N_2H_6Cl$).

1856 MILLER *Elem. Chem.* II. 1066 Salts of Platosamine (Reiset's second base).. Hydrochlorate of platosamine (yellow) $PtH_3N.Cl$. **1857** *Ibid.* III. 260 The two platinum bases from pyridine are:—Platinopyridine.. Platosopyridine. **1865** MANSFIELD *Salts* 455 'Reiset's second Platinum base'.. is supposed by Gerhardt to contain a body which he calls an alkali, 'Platosamine', NH_2Pt. **1873** WATTS *Fownes' Chem.* (ed. 11) 349 Platinum dichloride absorbs 2 molecules of ammonia, forming platosammonium chloride.

†**plat-roof.** *Obs. rare*$^{-1}$. In 4 *pl.* **platrowes.** [f. PLAT *a.* + ROOF *sb.*] A flat roof.

c **1380** WYCLIF *Serm.* Sel. Wks. I. 194 þei shulden preche opinli upon platrowes of housis.

platt, platte, obs. forms of PLAT.

Platt: see next.

Plattdeutsch (plæt'dɔɪtʃ). Also **Platt-Deutsch.** [G., ad. Du. *Platduitsch* Low German, f. *plat* flat, low + *Duitsch* German.] The collective name of those dialects of Germany which are not High German (see GERMAN *sb.*[2] 2 b). Also *attrib.* Also *ellipt.* as **Platt.**

1814 H. WEBER *Illustr. North. Antiq.* 217 As the fragment [sc. *Hildebrandslied*] is evidently written in the dialect of the northern parts of Germany, now denominated Plat-t, or Low German, which was once nearly identical with the Anglo-Saxon, a great number of the words have been rendered into such as, with little variation, existed in the old English and Scottish. *a* **1834** COLERIDGE *Table Talk* (1835) I. 119 Originally.. in the *Platt-Deutsch* of the north of Germany there were only two definite articles. **1867** J. MACGREGOR *Rob Roy on Baltic* xix. 239 What a linguist this critic must be before he attempts a voyage such as we have described! First he must learn Norwegian, then Swedish,.. then Platt (on the Elbe), [etc.]. **1886** STRONG & MEYER *Outl. Hist. German Lang.* 67 New-Low-German, or *Plattdeutsch*, so called from being spoken in the *platte land* or the low country. **1908** T. G. TUCKER *Introd. Nat. Hist. Lang.* 220 The Saxonic dialects, under the name of *Nieder-Deutsch* or *Platt-Deutsch* are still in regular use among the populace of North Germany. **1939** L. H. GRAY *Found. Lang.* 349 Lower Franconian is essentially Low Teutonic of the type represented by Flemish, Frisian, Old Saxon, and Plattdeutsch. **1942** *Amer. Pol. Sci. Rev.* XXXVI. 537 At present, the speakers of the Lower Saxon, Plattdeutsch vernacular of Gelderland, of Frisian in Friesland, and of genuine Lower Frankish, Dutch dialects are all united in using Dutch as the language of school and church and as the medium of their common national allegiance. **1953** *Trans. Philol. Soc.* 1952 135 The Plattdeutsch forms require discussion. **1970** L. DEIGHTON *Bomber* xxiv. 349 [He was] trying to understand Voss's fast guttural *Plattdeutsch*, as much like Dutch as German. **1973** *Word* 1970 XXVI. 44 All informants felt that it was a loanword... A few said it was not good *Platt*, while others felt that it [*sc. hauptsächlich*] was thoroughly acceptable. **1977** *Trans. Philol. Soc.* 1975 187 At first sight North Frisian seems to have more in common with the Plattdeutsch spoken in Schleswig than with other forms of Frisian, and so the question arises as to what justification there is for not considering Frisian to be a variety of local Platt.

'platted, *ppl. a.* [f. PLAT *v.*[3] + -ED[1].] Formed into or made of plaits; = PLAITED 2.

1483 *Cath. Angl.* 283/1 Plattyd, *jmplicatus, jntricatus.* **1597** SHAKS. *Lover's Compl.* ii, A plattid hiue of straw. **1609** HOLLAND *Amm. Marcell.* 255 Shields,.. made of platted oysiers. **1784** COWPER *Task* VI. 239 Who wore the platted thorns with bleeding brows. **1885** MISS BRADDON *Wyllard's Weird* II. 142 A head crowned with masses of platted hair.

‖**platteland** ('platəlant). *S. Afr.* Also with capital initial and hyphened (**platte-land**). [Afrikaans, f. Du. *plat* flat + *land* country.] The rural areas of South Africa. Also *attrib.* Hence **plattelander** ('platəˌlandər), a native or inhabitant of a rural area.

1933 C. J. UYS *In Era of Shepstone* vii. 199 Like a leaven the discontent spread from town to town—leaving the *platteland* unaffected—while the Cape and Natal journals magnified the danger out of all proportion. **1934** *Sunday Times* (Johannesburg) 13 May, It is useless to take the platteland youngster and to teach him to enter a college or university. **1934** E. A. WALKER *Gt. Trek* ii. 46 Generally speaking the plattelanders were healthy, as they had need to be if they were to survive. **1935** N. GILES *Dark Border* II. i. 171 The cattle return to-morrow to the *platteland* and you will go with them. **1943** J. Y. T. GREIG *Language at Work* 106 Political discussions.. take place on the stoep or in the bar-parlour of a hotel in some dorpie of the platteland. **1954** W. K. HANCOCK *Country & Calling* vi. 173 Some idealists of the Dutch Reformed Church have recently deduced from *apartheid* the necessity of an immense economic investment in the Native Reserves. It is improbable that voters on the *platteland* will recognize the same necessity. **1955** J. H. WELLINGTON *Southern Afr.* II. III. xv. 215 The larger urban populations have no great sympathy with what they often regard as the reactionary and parochial attitudes of the platte-landers. **1958** A. JACKSON *Trader on Veld* 20 The idea of leaving the comfort and relative sophistication of Port Elizabeth held no terrors for me, and when my Uncle mentioned that he might fix me up on the Platteland, I was eager to hear more. **1960** *Economist* 7 May 505/2 The prime minister's escape from assassination—an escape regarded by the platteland mentality as providential in a more than political sense. **1967** 'L. BLACK' *Two Ladies in Verona* ii. 28 She told him of her childhood in the platte-land of South Africa. **1971** *Progress* (Cape Town) May 9/5 The Provincial Executive would.. value any.. contact which the plattelanders might make. **1971** *Rand Daily Mail* 4 Sept. 8/4 Platteland towns are being encouraged to join in the great property development game which has been largely confined until now to the bigger South African centres. **1977** *Time* 21 Nov. 10/2 'Man,' he shouted, 'this [*sc.* B. J. Vorster] is the man! This is the Churchill of the *platteland*!'

platten ('plæt(ə)n), *v.* Also 7 **platen.** [f. PLAT *a.* + -EN[5].]

†**1.** *trans.* To make flat, to flatten. *Obs.*

1688 R. HOLME *Armoury* III. xiv. (Roxb.) 19/2 Thatchers Termes... Platen the sids down.

2. To rivet or clinch a nail, by turning down the point. *Sc.*

1903 in *Eng. Dial. Dict.*

3. To form into a plate.

1875 KNIGHT *Dict. Mech., Plattening Glass*, the operation of forming glass into sheets or plates.

platter[1] ('plætə(r)). Forms: 4–6 **plater,** 5 **platere,** (6 *Sc.* **plaitter**), 6– **platter.** [ME. *plater* a. AF. *plater* (Bozon), deriv. of *plat* dish.] **1. a.** A flat dish or plate for food; in later usage often a wooden plate. Now chiefly *arch.*

13.. *Coer de L.* 1490 Bye us vessel gret plente, Dysschys, cuppys and sawsers, Bolles, treyes, and platers. *c* **1330** *Arth. & Merl.* 2270 Alder-next his side he sat, And of his dische and plater at. **1382** WYCLIF *Matt.* xxiii. 25 Woo to ȝou, scribis and Pharisees, ipocritis, that maken clene that thing of the cuppe and plater, that is with outforth. *c* **1400** MAUNDEV. (Roxb.) xxxiv. 153 þe grettest prelate.. lays it apon a grete plater of siluer. **1474** CAXTON *Chesse* 26 Ete his mete out of platers and dysshes of tree and of wode. **1512** *Act 4 Hen. VIII*, c. 7 §7 Untrue.. Workmanship.. in Platters, Chargers, Dishes. **1526** TINDALE *Matt.* xiv. 8 Geve me here John baptistes heed in a platter. **1571** *Satir. Poems Reform.* xxviii. 118 Plaitter nor pois we neuer left ane plak. **1655** MOUFET & BENNET *Health's Impr.* (1746) 235 Fish coming out of a Pan is not to be covered with a Platter, lest the Vapour congealed in the Platter drop down again upon the Fish. **1764** GOLDSM. *Trav.* 196 While his lov'd partner .. Displays her cleanly platter on the board. **1824** W. IRVING *T. Trav.* I. 58 Half a dozen great Delft platters, hung.. by way of pictures. **1851** LAYARD *Pop. Acc. Discov. Nineveh* vii. 123 The girls.. returned, each bearing a platter of fruit which they placed before me.

b. In colloq. phr. ***to hand*** (something to someone) ***on a (silver) platter*** = ***to hand on a plate*** s.v. PLATE *sb.* 19 a; ***platters of meat*** (Rhyming slang) = *plates of meat* s.v. PLATE *sb.* 19 d; also *ellipt.* as ***platters.***

1918 T. WOLFE *Let.* 18 Feb. (1958) 8 You don't get anything handed to you on a silver platter. **1923** J. MANCHON *Le Slang* 227 *Plates of meat,..* = *feet.* On dit aussi *platters of meat.* **1945** L. SHELLY *Jive Talk Dict.* 16/1 *Platters..*, big feet. **1960** J. FRANKLYN *Dict. Rhyming Slang* 108/2 *Platters of meat*, feet. 20 C., a form of *plates*.. and not used in Cockney circles. **1960** G. SANDERS *Mem. Professional Cad* I. vii. 55, I was otherwise engaged at the time building a telescope in my back garden and being, by vocation, a dilettante, this interested me far more than the golden future which Mr. Mayer was going to offer me on a silver platter. **1968** J. UPDIKE *Couples* iii. 229 It's *you* who want to keep them down, to give them on a platter everything everybody else in this country has had to work for. **1970** C. MAJOR *Dict. Afro-Amer. Slang* 92 *Platters*, feet. **1973** *New Yorker* 3 Feb. 49/1 Other things are handed to you on a platter.

c. *attrib.* and *Comb.*, as ***platter-case***, ***-mat***, ***-mouth***, ***-plate***; ***platter-shaped*** adj.; **platter-face**, a broad, round, flat face; so **platter-faced** *a.*; **platter-foot** *dial.*, a flat foot; **platter pull**, a type of ski-lift (see quots.).

1793 SMEATON *Edystone L.* §303 In the kitchen.. were two settles with lockers, a dresser with drawers, two cup-boards, and one *platter case. **1621** BURTON *Anat. Mel.* III. ii. IV. i. (1651) 519 Though she.. have a swoln Juglers *platter face, or a thin, lean, chitty face. **1675** COTTON *Scoffer Scoft* 116 Her pale, full moon, platter face. **1922** JOYCE *Ulysses* 374 Some good matronly woman.. to mother him. Take him in tow, platter face and a large apron. **1533** UDALL *Flowres Lat. Sp.* 199 b, That reed heeded, grey eyed, *platter-faced, and hawkenosed wenche. **1707** J. STEVENS tr. *Quevedo's Com. Wks.* (1709) 391 The Platter-fac'd Deity Bacchus. **1834** SIR F. B. HEAD *Bubbles Brunnen* 7 Holland is but a platter-faced .. country, after all. **1897** F. T. JANE *Lordship, Passen & We* xix. 213 She.. set out as brave a *platter-foot as a man could wish for to see. **1567** GOLDING *Ovid's Met.* xv. (1593) 360 At his nostrils and His *platter mouth did puffe out part of sea upon the land. **1871** G. MEREDITH *H. Richmond* xv, He and the dog took alternate bites off a *platter-shaped cake. **1951** *Amer. Ski Ann. & Skiing Jrnl.* 1952 30 (Advt.), Belleayre Mountain.. Chair Lift Rope Tow *Platter Pull Lifts. **1953** *Ibid.* 1954 117/2 The J- and T-bar are a form of seat. Later .. came.. the platter pull, a platter-shaped seat. These lifts are basically the same and tow the skier from an overhead cable. **1963** *Amer. Speech* XXXVIII. 206 *Platter pull,..* a kind of pull transporting skiers uphill. The skier places between the thighs a rubber or plastic disk which is suspended, usually on a bar, from a rope or a cable permanently fixed to the lift cable. **1970** M. BENNETT *How to ski just a Little Bit* ii. 87 A platter pull, sometimes also called a poma, looks as if you took a T-bar, bent it a little, cut the crosspiece off, and attached instead a flat, slightly oval disc approximately six inches in diameter.

2. *slang*. A gramophone record. Cf. PLATE *sb.* 19 g.

1931 H. MUTSCHMANN *Gloss. Americanisms* 46/2 *Platter*, a gramophone record. **1935** *Vanity Fair* (N.Y.) Nov. 38/1 There ought to be a hot coupling on every platter. **1943** H. A. SMITH *Putty Knife* 163, I bought a couple of Crosby platters. **1960** *Master Detective* July 83/2 Rock and Roll, that's what I'm good at. I got a terrific collection of platters. **1967** 'T. WELLS' *Dead by Light of Moon* xviii. 184, I went into Fink Roth's pad and found treasures. Good old platters and stamps. I sold them. Got a good price for the records. The stamps were only so-so. **1977** *Sounds* 9 July 18/1 'Starz'—as the premier platter was called—was hardly the strongest product ever to find its way on to the record racks.

3. The metal disc of a turntable unit, on which the record is placed for playing.

1975 *Gramophone* Jan. 1297 (Advt.), With the heavy platter and extra thick turn-table mat, our final figures are impressive. **1975** *Hi-Fi Answers* Feb. 66/1 Trouble was experienced with ferrous platters inducing a high level of hum.

platter[2]. [f. PLAT *v.*[3] + -ER[1].] One who or that which plats or plaits; a plaiter.

1818 TODD, *Platter*. 2 [from *To plat*.] One who plats or weaves. Hence **1828** in WEBSTER; and in mod. Dicts.

'platterful. [f. PLATTER[1] + -FUL.] As much as a platter will contain.

1611 COTGR., *Platelée*, a platterfull, or dish full. *a* **1693** *Urquhart's Rabelais* III. xiv. 114 There have you a large Platter-full of Dreams.

platting ('plætɪŋ), *sb. dial.* [f. PLAT *sb.*[2] 4, small bridge, plank-bridge + -ING[1] 1 g.] A small foot-bridge: cf. PLAT *sb.*[2] 4.

1600 *Manch. Crt. Leet Rec.* (1885) II. 156 So that the water maye passe vnder John Gee his plattinge. **1634** *Ibid.* III. 216. **1653** *Ibid.* IV. 106 To fence and sufficiently to amend the dangerous plattinge over against the land lately his. *c* **1890** HALLAM *Derbysh. Gloss.* (MS.), *Platting*.

'platting, *vbl. sb.* [f. PLAT *v.*[3] + -ING[1].]

1. The action of PLAT *v.*[3]; plaiting.

1483 *Cath. Angl.* 283/2 A Plattynge, *jntricatura*. **1862** BURTON *Bk. Hunter* (1863) 401 The skilful platting of withes.

2. Plaited straw, grass, palmetto, or the like, in ribbon-like strips, for making hats, bonnets, etc.

1725 BERKELEY *Proposal for College Bermuda* Wks. 1871 III. 222 Bermuda hats are worn by our ladies' they are made of a sort of mat, or..platting made of the palmetto-leaf. **1812** J. SMYTH *Pract. of Customs* (1821) 183 Platting is the slips of Cane, Straw, or Chip, woven or platted into pieces, for making Hats. **1887** MOLONEY *Forestry W. Afr.* 461 Paper, Textiles, Platting, Basket-work, Clothing.

'plattnerite. [Named (by Haidinger 1845) after its describer K. F. Plattner: see -ITE[1].] Native dioxide of lead (PbO_2) occurring in violet black concretions.

1849 J. NICOL *Min.* 418 Plattnerite..[is] hexagonal but dimensions unknown. **1892** DANA *Min.* (ed. 6) 239.

plature ('plætjʊə(r)). *Ornith.* [ad. mod.L. *Platūrus*, for **Platyūrus*, a. Gr. πλατύουρος, f. πλατύ-ς broad, flat + οὐρά tail.] A humming-bird of the genus *Platurus*, characterized by a broad tail. So **platurous** (plə'tjʊərəs) *a.*, broad-tailed (cf. *platyurous* PLATY-).

1858 MAYNE *Expos. Lex.*, *Platurus*, having a broad tail.. platurous. **1890** *Cent. Dict.*, *Plature*.

platy ('pleɪtɪ), *a.* [f. PLATE *sb.* + -Y.]

†**1.** Consisting or formed of plates; plate-like.

1533 ELYOT *Cast. Helthe* IV. x. (1541) 88 b, Some groundes or residences [in urine] bee lyke vnto plates..and may be named platy resydence, in latyne *Laminea*. **1612** W. PARKES *Curtaine-Dr* (1876) 27, I [Satan] keepe the best that euer nation bred, Within my Kingdome in a platy bed.

2. *Geol.* Consisting of or easily separating into plates; flaky.

1806 FORSYTH *Beauties Scotl.* IV. 271 The small fissures of the rock contain the like [lead] ore, but platy, and of a less firm cohesion. **1829** *Nat. Philos.* I. *Optics* xiii. 33 (Usef. Knowl. Soc.) Mica, a thin platy mineral. **1879** RUTLEY *Study Rocks* xiii. 258 Sometimes a platy or tabular structure is developed in basalt. **1894** *Northumbld. Gloss.* s.v. *Plate*, Sandstone, when intermixed with shale beds or partings, is called platy freestone or platy post.

platy- (plætɪ), a. Gr. πλατυ-, comb. form of πλατύς broad, flat, entering into numerous scientific terms. Among these are the following: **platybasic** (-'beɪsɪk) *a. Craniom.*, having a broad base: applied to a skull in which the occipital angle of Daubenton exceeds 80°; **platybrachycephalic** (-brækɪsɪ'fælɪk) *a. Craniom.*, (of a skull) both platycephalic and brachycephalic, i.e. flat, and short in proportion to its breadth; **platybregmate** (-'brɛgmət), **-bregmatic** (-brɛg'mætɪk) *adjs. Craniom.*, having a broad bregma (*Syd. Soc. Lex.*); so **platybregmete** (-'brɛgmiːt), a broad bregma, as in Mongolian skulls (*Cent. Dict.*); **platycarpous** (-'kɑːpəs) *a. Bot.* [Gr. καρπός fruit], having broad fruit; **platycephalic** (-sɪ'fælɪk), **-cephalous** (-'sɛfələs) *adjs.* [Gr. κεφαλή head], having a flat or broad head; *spec.* in *Craniom.* applied to a skull of flattened form, having a vertical index of less than 70; so **platycephaly** (-'sɛfəlɪ), the condition of having a platycephalic skull (*Cent. Dict.*, *Syd. Soc. Lex.*); **platycercine** (-'sɜːsaɪn) *Ornith.* [Gr. κέρκος tail], *a.*, belonging to the subfamily *Platycercinæ* or broadtailed parakeets; *sb.* a bird of this subfamily; **platycnemic** (-'kniːmɪk) *a. Anat.* [Gr. κνήμη tibia], of the tibia, broad and flat; also, of a person, having such tibiæ; so ‖**platy'cnemia** [mod.L.], **-'cnemism**, **-'cnemy**, platycnemic condition; **platycœlian** (-'siːlɪən); **cœlous** (-'siːləs) *adjs. Anat.* [Gr. κοῖλος hollow], flat in front and concave behind, as the centrum of a vertebra (= OPISTHOCŒLIAN, -CŒLOUS); **platy'cranial** *a.*, broad-skulled; **platycrinid** (-'krɪnɪd, -kraɪ-), **-'crinite**, **'crinoid**, an encrinite or fossil crinoid of the genus *Platycrinus* or family *Platycrinidæ*, having broad flat radial and basal plates; **platydactyl** (-'dæktɪl) *Zool.* [Gr. δάκτυλος digit], *a.*, having broad flat toes; *spec.* belonging to the division *Platydactyla* or *Discodactyla* of batrachians; *sb.* a platydactyl batrachian (= DISCODACTYL: opp. to OXYDACTYL); so **platy'dactylous** *a.*, flat-toed; **platydolichocephalic** (-ˌdɒlɪkəʊsɪ'fælɪk) *a. Craniom.*, (of a skull) both platycephalic and dolichocephalic, i.e. flat, and long in proportion to its breadth; **platy'gastric** *a.*, having broad gastric cavities; also, allied to the genus *Platygaster* of parasitic hymenopterous insects; **platy'glossal**, **-'glossate**, **-'glossous** *adjs.* [Gr. γλῶσσα tongue], having a broad tongue; **platyhieric** (-'haɪərɪk) *a. Anat.* [Gr. ἱερὸν (ὀστέον) = L. (*os*) *sacrum*], having a broad sacrum, or one whose breadth exceeds its height; **platymesaticephalic** (-ˌmɛsətɪsɪ'fælɪk), **-ˌmesoce'phalic** *adjs. Craniom.*, (of a skull) both platycephalic and mesati- (or meso-) cephalic, i.e. flat, and of medium breadth; **platymeter** (plə'tɪmɪtə(r)) *Electr.* [-METER], an apparatus for measuring the inductive capacity of different dielectrics in the form of plates or disks; **platy'notal** *a. Zool.* [Gr. νῶτον back], broad-backed; *spec.* belonging to the group *Platynota* of lizards, also called *varanoid*; so **'platynote**, *a.* = prec.; *sb.* a platynotal or varanoid lizard; **platyodont** ('plætɪəʊdɒnt) *Zool.* [Gr. ὀδούς, ὀδοντ- tooth], *a.* broad-toothed; *sb.* a broad-toothed animal; **platyopic** (-'ɒpɪk) *a. Craniom.* [Gr. ὤψ, ὠπ- face], having a broad or flat face (see quot.); so **'platyope** (-əʊp), a platyopic person, animal, or skull; **platy'pellic** *a. Anat.* [Gr. πέλλα bowl, taken as = pelvis], having a flat pelvis (see quot.); **platypetalous** (-'pɛtələs) *a. Bot.*, having broad petals; **platyphylline** (-'fɪlɪn, -aɪn), **-phyllous** (-'fɪləs) *adjs. Bot.* [Gr. φύλλον leaf, φύλλινος of leaves], broad-leaved, or resembling a broad leaf; **platypygous** (plætɪ'paɪgəs) *a. Zool.* [Gr. πυγή rump], having broad buttocks; **platyrhynchine** (-'rɪŋkaɪn), **-rhynchous** (-'rɪŋkəs) *adjs. Ornith.* [Gr. ῥύγχος beak], having a flat or broad bill; *spec.* belonging to the genus *Platyrhynchus* or subfamily *Platyrhynchinæ* of American fly-catchers; **platyscopic** (-'skɒpɪk) *a.* [Gr. σκοπός looker, σκοπεῖν to view], trade-name for a lens or combination of lenses giving a wide field of view; **platysome** ('plætɪsəʊm) *Entom.* [Gr. σῶμα body] a beetle of Latreille's division *Platysomata* (= the modern family *Cucujidæ*), characterized by a flat body; **platy'somid**, *sb.* a fish of the extinct family *Platysomidæ*; *a.* belonging to this family; **platysternal** (-'stɜːnəl) *a. Zool.*, having a broad flat sternum or breast-bone, as a ratite bird; **platystomous** (plə'tɪstəməs) *a. Zool.* [Gr. στόμα mouth], having a broad mouth or opening; **platyurous** (-'(j)ʊərəs) *a. Zool.* [Gr. οὐρά tail], having a broad or flat tail. Also PLATYHELMINTH, etc. q.v.

1878 BARTLEY tr. *Topinard's Anthrop.* v. 177 The second [deformity] has been called plastic by Mr. B. Davis,..and *platybasic by M. Broca. **1813–26** PRICHARD *Phys. Hist. Man.* (ed. 2) I. 174, I propose to divide the varieties of the skull into three classes... 1. The first..may be termed the mesobregmate... 2. Stenobregmate... 3. *Platybregmate. Section of the vertex widened, and assuming a square figure, the cheek-bones projecting considerably beyond the outline of this section. **1858** MAYNE *Expos. Lex.*, *Platycarpus*, having large fruit,..*platycarpous. **1861** *Sat. Rev.* 7 Sept. 253 A *platy-cephalic skull belonged to the skeleton of an old man in the same barrow. **1878** BARTLEY tr. *Topinard's Anthrop.* v. 176 Platycephalic, with the vault of the skull flattened, elliptical. **1846** SMART Suppl., **Platycephalous*, broad-headed,—epithet of a species of the asaphus, a trilobite. **1858** MAYNE *Expos. Lex.*, *Platycephalus*, *Bot.* applied to a mushroom having a flat head,..platycephalous. **1902** *Platycephaly [see *brachycranial* adj. s.v. BRACHY-]. **1946** *Nature* 28 Sept. 428/1 Many of the skull characters are remarkably simian, including heavy projecting supra-orbital ridges, retreating forehead, marked platycephaly and massive jaws. **1899** *Cambr. Nat. Hist.* IX. 362 At the base is generally a large swollen cere..in the *Platycercine group this is very small. **1878** BARTLEY tr. *Topinard's Anthrop.* II. iv. 299 The character which the tibia sometimes presents, and which bears the name of *platycnemia. **1902** J. BEDDOE in *Jrnl. Roy. Inst. Cornwall* XV. 168 There is very little tendency to platyknemia in the Harlyn Bay bones. **1863** LYELL *Antiq. Man* vii. (1873) 144 The tibia or shin bone was somewhat *platycnemic or flattened. **1874** DAWKINS *Cave Hunt.* v. 155 These remains..present the peculiar character of *platycnemism. **1888** *Athenæum* 26 May 666/2 M. Manouvrier's memoir on *platycnemy in man and the anthropoids is a complete analysis of all observations made upon the shape of the tibia. **1854** R. OWEN *Skel. & Teeth* in *Orr's Circ. Sc.* I. *Org. Nat.* 202 This '*platycœlian' type.. we find in the dorsal and caudal vertebræ of the.. cetiosaurus. **1902** *Biometrika* I. 462 Brachycephaly is associated with *platycranial characters in both races. **1846** SMART Suppl., **Platycrinite*, a lily-shaped animal with a broad flat scapula. **1864** WEBSTER, *Platycrinite* (*Paleon.*), a kind of encrinite, the body of which is stout, and made up of a few large plates. **1895** *Syd. Soc. Lex.*, **Platydactyl*, having flat, broad digits. **1858** MAYNE *Expos. Lex.*, *Platydactylus*,.. having the hind feet expanded in form of oars: *platydactylous. *Ibid.*, *Platyglossate... *Platyglossous. **1855** PROF. W. THOMSON in *25th Rept. Brit. Assoc.*, *Trans. Sections* 22 Electroplatymeter. **1886** W. TURNER in *Jrnl. Anat. & Path.* XX. 317 The following descriptive terms may conveniently express these differences in the relative length and breadth of the sacrum. As the Greek word ἱερὸν is the equivalent of the Latin sacrum; the term *dolichohieric* would signify a sacrum in which the length exceeded the breadth, whilst **platyhieric* would signify a sacrum in which the breadth exceeded the length. **1895** *Syd. Soc. Lex.*, *Platyhieric*, with broad sacrum. Epithet applied to species or individuals in whom the sacral index (breadth × 100 ÷ height) exceeds 100. Nearly all females of whatever race are platyhieric, but amongst males few black races come under this head. *a* **1892** (*Scientific Jrnl.*) For small capacities [of electricity and magnetism] Sir W. Thomson's *platymeter and sliding condenser may be used. **1843** *Penny Cycl.* XXVI. 125/2 *Varanidæ*, a family of Lizards, designated..as *Platynote or Broad-backed Saurians. **1885** O. THOMAS in *Jrnl. Anthrop. Inst.* XIV. 334 Individual skulls or races having indices below 107·5 might be named **platyopic* or flat faced; from 107·5 to 110·0 *mesopic*. **1885** *Athenæum* 31 Jan. 156/1 The terms *pro-opic*, *mesopic*, and *platyopic* were suggested for skulls or races showing various degrees of development in this respect. **1885** W. TURNER in *Jrnl. Anat. & Path.* XX. 128, I..shall make three divisions, two of which will represent extreme forms in opposite directions, whilst the third will be intermediate. I shall express these divisions in terms derived from the Greek, so that the nomenclature in pelvic classification may be as far as possible on the same lines as the well-known divisions of crania... By *dolichopellic* is to be understood a pelvis in which the conjugate diameter of the brim is either longer than the transverse or approaches closely to it: by **platypellic* a pelvis in which the transverse diameter of the brim greatly exceeds the conjugate; by *mesatipellic* a pelvis in which the transverse diameter is not so greatly in excess of the conjugate. **1895** *Syd. Soc. Lex.*, *Platypellic*, term applied by Turner to pelves having a brim-index under 85. **1966** Platypellic [see MESATIPELLIC *a.*]. **1882** TUCKERMAN *N. Amer. Lichens* I. 74 Thallus sub-membranaceous, stellate, appressed, *platyphylline. **1858** MAYNE *Expos. Lex.*, *Platyrhynchous. **1881** *Nature* 8 Sept. p. cxxxviii, A new *Platyscopic Lens of lower power and a larger field than.. previously made. **1893** G. ALLEN in *Westm. Gaz.* 27 June 2/1 Six months in the fields with a platyscopic lens would teach them strange things about the world around them. **1842** BRANDE *Dict. Sci.* etc., **Platysomes*,..species with a wide and much depressed body. These insects are found under the bark of trees. **1900** *Nature* 20 Sept. 507/1 It has the *platysomid head contour and a long-based dorsal. **1858** MAYNE *Expos. Lex.*, Platysternal..*Platystomous, ..*Platyurous.

platycodon (plætɪ'kəʊdən). [mod.L. (A. de Candolle *Monographie des Campanulacées* (1830) 125), f. PLATY- + Gr. κώδων bell.] A herbaceous perennial plant of the monotypic genus so called, belonging to the family Campanulaceæ, native to China and Japan, and bearing blue or white bell-shaped flowers; = *balloon-flower* s.v. BALLOON *sb.*[1] 10 c.

1844 J. W. LOUDON *Ladies' Flower-Garden Ornamental Perennials* II. 52 The Large-flowered platycodon. **1905** H. R. ELY *Another Hardy Garden Bk.* v. 141 By the third year the Platycodons become large, strong plants. **1937** DUNBAR & MAHONEY *Gardener's Choice* 139 The best way of increasing the Platycodon is from seed. **1959** *Times* 3 Jan. 9/5 The platycodon makes a fine pot plant for a cool greenhouse. **1977** J. JEFFREYS *Perennials for Cutting* II. 160 In a suitable site this platycodon is fully hardy and long-lived.

platyhelminth (plætɪ'hɛlmɪnθ). *Zool.* Also **plathelminth**. [f. mod.L. pl. *Platyhelmintha*, *-thes*, f. PLATY- + Gr. ἕλμινς (ἑλμινθ-) worm: see HELMINTH.] An animal of the group *Platyhel'mintha* or *Platyhel'minthes*, comprising the nemertean, trematode, cestode, and turbellarian worms (with other classes in some classifications); a flat-worm.

[**1878** BELL *Gegenbaur's Comp. Anat.* 129 In most Platyhelminthes the mouth is some distance from the head.] **1890** *Cent. Dict.*, Plathelminth. **1897** *Allbutt's Syst. Med.* II. 1091 Bilharzia..hæmatobia is a trematode platyhelminth, inhabiting the veins of man, monkeys, and probably also of cattle and dogs. **1901** *Daily Chron.* 30 Oct. 3/4 The Platyhelminthes include 'liver flukes' and 'tape-worms', besides [other] non-parasitic creatures devoid of a vernacular name.

platykurtic (plætɪ'kɜːtɪk), *a. Statistics.* [f. PLATY- + Gr. κυρτ-ός bulging + -IC.] Of a frequency distribution or its graphical representation: having less kurtosis than the normal distribution.

1905 [see LEPTOKURTIC *a.*]. **1937** YULE & KENDALL *Introd. Theory Statistics* (ed. 11) ix. 165 Platykurtic curves, like the platypus, are squat with short tails. Leptokurtic curves are high with long tails like the kangaroo—noted for 'lepping'! **1952** [see KURTOSIS]. **1966** S. BEER *Decision & Control* xiii. 334 Moreover, the distributions may be either leptokurtic or platykurtic—that is, either too peaked or too flattened to be Gaussian. **1979** *Nature* 25 Jan. 297/1 Platykurtosis is not sufficient to demonstrate bimodality, but bimodal distributions are platykurtic.

Hence **ˌplatyˈkurtosis** [KURTOSIS], the property of being platykurtic.

1939 A. E. TRELOAR *Elem. of Statistical Reasoning* ii. 34 Positive (or lepto-) kurtosis, mesokurtosis (that of the 'law of error' or normal curve), and negative (or platy-) kurtosis mean simply that the clustering at the center is respectively greater than, equal to, or less than that of the normal curve. **1949** [see LEPTOKURTOSIS]. **1979** [see above].

platymeria (plætɪˈmɪərɪə). *Anat.* Also anglicized as **platymery** (ˈplætɪmɪərɪ). [ad. F. *platymèrie* (L. Manouvrier 1899, in *Compt. rend. Congr. internat. d'Anthropol. et d'Archéol. préhist.* (1891) 363), f. Gr. μηρία thigh bones: see PLATY-, -IA[1], and -Y[3].] The condition of a femur of which the antero-posterior diameter of its shaft is unusually small relative to the corresponding transverse diameter. Also **ˈplatymerism**, in the same sense. Hence **platyˈmeric** *a.*, of, pertaining to, or displaying platymery; esp. as ***platymeric index***, the quotient of these diameters, multiplied by 100.

1895 *Proc. Soc. Antiquaries Scotland* V. 415 Dr Manouvrier of Paris.. describes.. femora from.. neolithic burials.. which showed the antero-posterior flattening in a very marked form, and to this condition he has given the name platymery (flat femur). *Ibid.* 416 The platymeria was very strongly marked. *Ibid.* 417 A platymeric femur is not necessarily associated with the squatting attitude. **1896** *Jrnl. Anat. & Pathol.* XXXI. 14 By far the most remarkable feature of this bone was its Platymeric index, which was almost as low as that of the lowest Maori indices. **1904** W. L. H. DUCKWORTH *Morphol. & Anthropol.* xiii. 313 Platymeria implies flattening in two regions of the femoral shaft, viz., in an upper region, immediately below the level of the lesser trochanter, and in a lower region about 40 mm. above the highest level of the external portion of the anterior aspect of the condylar articular surface. **1934** J. CAMERON *Skeleton of Brit. Neolithic Man* x. 159 The author wishes to mention.. that the platymeric condition he is about to describe is that affecting the upper third of the femoral shaft. Platymeria involving the popliteal area at the lower end of the femur has also been described. *Ibid.* 165 A group of characteristic features that are more or less regularly present as concomitant phenomena of platymerism. **1971** *Nature* 6 Aug. 383/2 The flattening (platymeria) of the upper end [of the shaft of the femur] is exaggerated by the presence of a marked lateral expansion at the level of the gluteal tuberosity. **1972** J. T. ROBINSON *Early Hominid Posture & Locomotion* x. 143 If SK 97 belonged to a male, then it is not improbable that SK 82 belonged to a female since it has a smaller head, a smaller angle of the neck, a less robust shaft, and a lower platymeric index than has SK 97. **1976** *Nature* 17 June 575/1 The long slender platymeric shaft is unexpected and provides intriguing evidence for the possible variation of the femur in this genus.

platypod (ˈplætɪpɒd), *a.* and *sb.* *Zool.* [f. Gr. πλατύπους, πλατυποδ- flat-footed: cf. next.]

a. *adj.* Having broad or flat feet; *spec.* belonging to the group *Plaˈtypoda* of monotrematous mammals (typical genus *Platypus*: see next), or to the group *Platypoda* of gastropod molluscs, having a broad flat foot adapted for crawling; also in *Orinth.* having the toes joined so as to form a broad sole, syndactyl. **b.** *sb.* A broad-footed animal; one belonging to any of these groups.

1846 SMART Suppl., *Platypod*, a broad-footed animal. **1864** in WEBSTER.

‖**platypus** (ˈplætɪpəs). *Zool.* [mod.L. (Shaw 1799), a. Gr. πλατύπους flat-footed, f. πλατύς flat + πούς foot. Orig. the generic name, but, having already been given to a genus of beetles, it was in 1800 changed for *Ornithorhynchus*.] A name of the ORNITHORHYNCHUS or DUCK-MOLE of Australia.

1799 SHAW *Naturalist's Misc.* X. Pl. 385 *Explan.*, The Duckbilled Platypus. **1832** BISCHOFF *Van Diemen's Land* iii. 52 The skins of the.. oppossum, tiger-cat, and platthypus, or ornythorhyncus paradoxus, are exported. **1878** R. B. SMYTH *Aborigines of Victoria* I. 251 The duck-billed platypus makes no nests, but lives in holes on the banks of rivers.

attrib. **1893** *Scribner's Mag.* June 792/2 Platypus hunting requires as quick an eye and hand as shooting woodcock in close cover. *Ibid.* 794/1 Platypus shopping-bags and purses are not disdained by the fair who crowd the marts.. in Melbourne, or.. in Sydney.

platypussary (ˈplætɪpəsərɪ). *Austral.* Also **platypusary, platypussery.** [f. PLATYPUS + -ARY[1].] An enclosure or building in which platypuses are kept.

1945 BAKER *Austral. Lang.* xiv. 242 *Platypussary* has made its appearance only in recent years. **1960** —— *Drum* 135 Platypussery: A pen or specially prepared area in which platypuses are kept. Also, platypussary. **1966** G. DURRELL *Two in Bush* v. 161 David's pair were housed in his specially designed Platypusary.

platyrrhine, platyrhine (ˈplætɪraɪn), *sb.* and *a.* [ad. mod.L. *Platyrrhini* (E. Geoffroy 1812, in *Ann. Mus. Hist. Nat.* XIX. 104), f. Gr. πλατύ-ς PLATY- + ῥίς, ῥιν- nose.]

1. a. *sb.* *Zool.* A monkey belonging to the infraorder Platyrrhini of the order Primates, distinguished by a flattened nose with widely separated nostrils facing outwards and including most of the New World monkeys. **b.** *adj.* Of or pertaining to this group of monkeys.

1842 BRANDE *Dict. Sci.*, etc., *Platyrhines*,.. these monkeys are peculiar to the New World. **1857** WHEWELL *Hist. Induct. Sc.* (ed. 3) III. 565 Remains of an extinct platyrhine monkey. **1862** DANA *Man. Geol.* 422 *note*, They include.. the Platyrrhines, peculiar to South America, having the nostrils subterminal and wide apart. **1877** HUXLEY *Anat. Inv. Anim.* i. 74 The great armadillos, anteaters and platyrrhine apes of the caves of South America. **1894** H. O. FORBES *Hand-bk. Primates* I. 127 The New World Monkeys ..have the nose flat and the opening of their nostrils directed outwards, and the one nostril separated from the other by a broad cartilaginous septum, and they are therefore designated Platyrrhine Monkeys. **1920** *Proc. Zool. Soc.* 91 The observations recorded in this paper are based mainly upon the Platyrrhine Monkeys that have died in the Zoological Gardens during the past ten years. **1930** *Ann. & Mag. Nat. Hist.* VI. 387 In the more primitive Platyrrhines the brain is relatively small and has few sulci. **1934** W. E. LE GROS CLARK *Early Fore-runners of Man* vii. 177 In the Platyrrhine monkeys the nostrils are relatively wide apart. **1957** W. C. O. HILL *Primates* III. 91 The only platyrrhine monkey whose total musculature has been systematically studied is the Common Marmoset. **1957** I. T. SANDERSON *Monkey Kingdom* viii. 80/1 All the living New World primates used to be called the Platyrrhines. **1967** J. R. & P. H. NAPIER *Handbk. Living Primates* i. 15 In the majority of Cebidæ the nostrils are wide apart (platyrrhine condition). **1978** *Nature* 11 May 173/3 The separation between the New World monkeys (platyrrhines) and the Old World monkeys and apes (catarrhines) is an ancient one.

2. *Anthropol.* **a.** Having the nose, or the nasal bones, flat or broad; having a nasal index of from 51 to 58. **b.** as *sb.* A platyrrhine person or skull.

1885 *Jrnl. R. Anthropol. Inst.* XIV. 71 Nasal Index... Leptorhine 47·0 and under. Mesorhine 47·1 to 51·0. Platyrhine 51·1 to 58·0. Hyperplatyrhine 58·1 and over. **1886** J. DALLAS in *Jrnl. Anthrop. Inst.* 305 The nose is platyrrhine. **1976** *Lancet* 25 Dec. 1394/2 The special features of the upper respiratory tract.. in platyrrhine peoples.

So **platyr(r)hinian** (plætɪˈrɪnɪən) *a.* and *sb.* = PLATYRRHINE (in either sense); **platyr(r)hiny** (ˈplætɪraɪnɪ), the condition of being platyrrhine.

1878 BARTLEY tr. *Topinard's Anthrop.* II. ii. 257 The platyrrhinians, with the nasal skeleton wide. **1895** *Syd. Soc. Lex.*, *Platyrrhinian*, platyrrhine; also, in *Anthropol.*, having flattened, broad nasal bones.. *Platyrrhiny*, the condition of being platyrrhinian. **1897** *Jrnl. Anthrop. Inst.* Nov. 283 Platyrhiny, elongated narrow palate, and large teeth.. are exaggerated in the Akka. **1902** [see *chamæconchy* s.v. CHAMÆ-]. **1957** W. C. O. HILL *Primates* III. 85 The nasal opening in the skull gives little indication of the characteristic external platyrrhiny. **1970** F. SNOWDEN *Blacks in Antiquity* i. 7 The platyrrhiny of the Ethiopian, like his color and his hair, was the norm for anthropological comparisons.

‖**platysma** (pləˈtɪzmə). [mod.L., a. Gr. πλάτυσμα flat piece, plate, flat cake, f. πλατύνειν to widen, f. πλατύ-ς broad, flat.]

†**1.** *Med.* (See quot.) *Obs.* (or never in Eng. use.)

1693 *Blancard's Phys. Dict.* (ed. 2), *Platisma*, a broad Linnen-cloth put upon Sores. **1704** in J. HARRIS *Lex. Techn.* I. **1895** in *Syd. Soc. Lex.*

2. *Anat.* (In full, ***platysma myoides*** or ***myodes***: see MYOID.) A thin broad layer of muscular fibres just beneath the skin on each side of the neck in man, extending from the shoulder and collar-bone to the face; corresponding to the *panniculus carnosus* (see PANNICLE 1) of some quadrupeds.

1693 *Blancard's Phys. Dict.* (ed. 2), *Platysma Myodes.* **1804** ABERNETHY *Surg. Obs.* (1827) 52 A man.. had a large tumour on the side of his neck, beneath the *platysma myoides*. **1840** G. V. ELLIS *Anat.* 70 The facial artery.. is covered, at first, by the platysma. **1899** *Allbutt's Syst. Med.* VII. 290 The fits began with spasm in the right platysma, and were frequently confined to this muscle.

platytera (plætɪˈtɛərə). *Iconography.* [ad. Gr. πλατυτέρα she who is wider, compar. of πλατύς wide.] A type of icon of the Incarnation, also known as the Icon of the Sign, depicting the Mother of God, *orant*, and in front of her the Child, each usu. surrounded by a mandorla. Cf. ORANS.

1911 O. M. DALTON *Byzantine Art & Archaeol.* xii. 674 The *orans* type holding the Christ-medallion over the breast ..is sometimes described as Blacherniotissa, while that in which the Virgin stands and the medallion is unsupported is known as *Platytera*. **1943** C. DE TOLNAY *Michelangelo* I. 158 The idea of placing the Christ Child between the knees of His mother is exceptional. Michelangelo seems to approach in this, as well as in the severe vertical axis of the position, an artistic conception of the Middle Ages—the Platytera, or Virgin who carries the Child in her bosom. In the ordinary Platytera type the Child is surrounded by a mandorla... We may note the seated Platytera which occurs in the Etchmiadzin Gospels. **1944** *Burlington Mag.* July 176/1 Its form is derived from the 'platytera', showing the child as an abstract symbol affixed to but not inside the body of the mother... The 'platytera' proper appears in Byzantine art as early as the fifth or sixth century.. and in many adapted forms spreads over Europe during the Middle Ages. **1963** VON HERZFELD & RICE tr. *Onasch's Icons* 345/2 This older type shows the Virgin [*sc.* as *orans*] without a medallion before her, the later type represents her with it. This later type is called in Greek 'Platytera', the Ample One, with reference to a hymn: 'He made your womb more ample than the heavens'. In Russian icon painting it is called the 'Virgin of the Sign' (Znamenie).

plaud (plɔːd), *sb.* Now *rare* or *Obs.* [f. PLAUD *v.*: cf. APPLAUD *sb.*] Applause; praise.

c **1590** MARLOWE *Faust.* Chorus 9 The form of Faustus' fortunes, good or bad: To patient judgements we appeal our plaud, And speak for Faustus in his infancy. **1719** D'URFEY *Pills* II. 315 Tho' he toil with Pains And fights, and flys, his Head small Plaud it gains. **1836** *Pulpit Treasury* July 201 (Cent. Dict.) While a poor widow's hard-earned gains May win the plaud 'More than they all'.

plaud, *v.* Now *rare* or *Obs.* [ad. L. *plaud-ĕre* to applaud, prop. to strike, clap the hands. So obs. F. *plaudir* intr., to applaud.] *trans.* To applaud; to praise.

1598 CHAPMAN *Blinde Begger* ad fin., That at our banquet all the Gods may tend, Plauding our victorie and this happie end. **1642** H. MORE *Song of Soul* I. III. xxxix, But you.. false to God, his tender sonne do gore, And plaud your selves. **1764** CHURCHILL *Candidate* 301 Thy Friends.. Plaud thy brave bearing. **1824** in *Spirit Pub. Jrnls.* (1825) 180 Ye of Surrey raise the ready hand To 'plaud a brother.

†ˈ**plaudable,** *a.* *Obs. rare.* [irreg. f. prec. + -ABLE.] Deserving of applause or favourable reception; = PLAUSIBLE 2.

1566–7 Q. ELIZ. *Sp. Parl.* Jan. in D'Ewes *Jrnls.* (1682) 116 These things being so plaudable [*so in orig. MS.*], as indeed to all men they are.

†ˈ**plaudiat(e.** *Obs. rare.* [? erroneous form of PLAUDIT.] = next.

1589 WARNER *Alb. Eng.* Prose Add. 154 Oportunitie the chiefe Actresse in al attempts, gaue the Plaudiat [*ed.* 1592 Plaudiate, 1612 Plaudite] in Loue his Comedie. **1601** YARINGTON *Two Lament. Trag.* v. ii. 123 b, To store her with the thundring furniture, Of smoothest smiles, and pleasing plaudiats.

plaudit (ˈplɔːdɪt), *sb.* Also 7 -ite. [Shortened from PLAUDITE.] An act of applauding; a round of applause; a clapping of the hands, or other audible expression of approval or praise; hence, any emphatic expression of approval.

1624 QUARLES *Job* Prop. Wk., Div. Poems (1630) 171 Expect the Plaudit, when the Play is done. *a* **1668** DENHAM *Poems, Of Old Age* IV. 44 True Wisdom must our Actions so direct, Not only the last Plaudite to expect. **1739** 'R. BULL' tr. *Dedekindus' Grobianus* 59 Happy! tho' all dislike, if still you find The Plaudit of your own impartial Mind. **1838** DICKENS *Nich. Nick.* xxv, The Romeo was received with hearty plaudits. **1883** S. C. HALL *Retrospect* II. 247 Preferring the noisy plaudits of the pit and gallery to the silent.. approval of the cultivated few.

Hence ˈ**plaudit** *v.* (*rare*), also 7 **-ite**, to applaud.

1640 YORKE *Union Hon.*, *Commend. Verses*, He that has Wit To flash a line, and friends to plaudite it May weare the Laurell. **1906** H. SUTCLIFFE in *Westm. Gaz.* 22 Mar. 2/3 The world should hear my song, And warlike men and striplings Should plaudit high and long.

plaudite (ˈplɔːdɪtiː). Also 6 **plaudetie -ytie,** 6–7 **-itie, -ity.** [a. L. *plaudite* applaud (ye)! 2 pl. imperative of *plaudĕre* to applaud; the customary appeal for applause made by Roman actors at the end of a play. The ending was early confounded with that of sbs. in -ITY; later the final *-e* became mute, giving rise to PLAUDIT.]

1. An appeal for applause at the conclusion of a play or other performance. (Now only as Latin.)

1567 DRANT *Horace, Art of Poetry* A v, That when the Epilogue is done we may with franke intente, After the plaudite stryke vp our plausible assente. **1606** HOLLAND *Sueton.* 84 He adioyned with all this finall conclusion, for a Plaudite,.. Now clap your hands and all with ioy resound a shout. **1880** SHORTHOUSE *J. Inglesant* xxvi. 363 A theatre built in a mausoleum, and pantomime airs and the 'plaudite' heard amid the awful silence of the grave.

†**2.** *transf.* A round of applause. *Obs.* (Now PLAUDIT.)

[The request put for the thing requested: cf. *to grant a petition, request*, etc.]

1573 G. HARVEY *Letter-bk.* (Camden) 129 A Plaudite and Deo Gratias for so happy an euente, And then to borrowe a nappe, I shalbe contente. **1575** *Gammer Gurton* v. ii, For Gammer Gurtons nedle sake, let vs haue a plaudytie. **1623** I. M. *To Mem. Shaks.* in *S.'s Wks.*, That's but an Exit of Mortalitie; This, a Re-entrance to a Plaudite. **1711** STEELE *Spect.* No. 248 ¶5 The House passed his Account with a Plaudite.

ˈ**plauditor.** *rare*[−1]. [irreg. f. PLAUDIT + -OR, or f. L. *plaudĕre* to applaud (*plaudit-* being erron. taken as ppl. stem) + -OR; cf. *auditor.*] One who applauds. So ˈ**plauditory** *a.*, applauding, applausive, laudatory.

1813 COLERIDGE *Lett.* II. 604 No dramatic author ever had so large a number of unsolicited, unknown, yet predetermined plauditors in the theatre, as I had. *a* **1845** HOOD *Lit. & Literal* xiv, Her sister auditory All sitting round, with grave and learned faces, Were very plauditory. **1847** SIR H. TAYLOR *Poems, Heroism in Shade* i, A thousand journals teem with good report And plauditory paragraph.

plaunche, plauncher(e, -our(e, obs. ff. PLANCH, PLANCHER.

plaunflet, obs. erron. f. PAMPHLET.

plaunke, obs. f. PLANK.

plaur, var. PLAV.

†**plause.** *Obs. rare.* [ad. L. *plaus-us* (*u-* stem), vbl. sb. f. *plaudĕre* to applaud.] Applause.

c **1540** tr. *Pol. Verg. Eng. Hist.* (Camden No. 29) 188 So desyrus was he to prowle after vaine plause and congratulation. *a* **1662** HEYLIN *Laud* II. 396 To gain to themselves the popular plause of meekness and mildness.

plausibility (plɔːzɪˈbɪlɪtɪ). [f. L. *plausibilis* (see PLAUSIBLE) + -ITY. So F. *plausibilité* (1725).] The quality of being plausible.

†**1.** Readiness to applaud or approve. *Obs.*

1598 HAKLUYT *Voy.* I. 287 He..was conducted through the Citie of London with great admiration and plausibilitie of the people running plentifully on all sides. **1644** BULWER *Chiron.* 106 Although the ancient Oratours received this token of approbation from the hands of the their auditors yet they never exhibited upon any occasion such Manuall plausibilitie to the people.

†**2.** The quality of deserving applause or approval; agreeableness of manner or behaviour, affability; with *pl.*, an instance of this, something worthy of applause; a praiseworthy quality or trait, an agreeable or courteous act. (Cf. PLAUSIBLE *a.* 2.) *Obs.*

1596 NASHE *Saffron-Walden* Wks. (Grosart) III. 69 What's the saluation of Dauid Gorge? A Nullitie... What the plausibilitie of Martin? A Nullitie. **1611** SPEED *Hist. Gt. Brit.* VI. xxiii. 113 Hoping by such his plausibility and indulgences to purchase to himselfe their best concurrence for the obtaining of the Empire. **1673** VAUGHAN *Life & Death Jackson* in *J.'s Wks.* (1844) I. p. xlv, [He] carried on his dignity with that justice, modesty, integrity, fidelity, and other gracious plausibilities, that in a place of trust he contented those whom he could not satisfy. **1681** GLANVILL *Sadducismus* Pref., He must study the little plausibilities, and accomodate the humour of the Many.

3. As a quality of an argument, statement, or the like: Seeming worthiness of acceptance; appearance of reasonableness; speciousness.

1649 MILTON *Eikon.* 100 Using the plausibility of large and indefinite words to defend himself. *a* **1745** SWIFT (J.), The last excuse..was allowed indeed to have more plausibility, but less truth. **1748** HARTLEY *Observ. Man* II. ii. 72 The Circumstances which gave some Plausibility to the Fiction. **1824** L. MURRAY *Eng. Gram.* (ed. 5) I. 174 The analogy of other languages..gives plausibility to the conjecture. **1830** LYELL *Princ. Geol.* I. 39 He had the art to throw an air of plausibility over the most improbable parts of his theory.

b. (with *pl.*) An instance of this; a plausible argument, statement, or the like.

1660 JER. TAYLOR *Duct. Dubit.* I. ii, Nothing but a heap of probable inducements, plausibilities, and witty entertainments. **1881** MORLEY *Cobden* xiv. (1902) 50/1 Political plausibilities will reconcile men to everything, save the deprivation of their property.

c. As a quality of a person: Capacity of putting forward plausible statements; fair-spokenness.

1754 FIELDING *Jon. Wild* II. iii, A certain plausibility in his voice and behaviour would have deceived any. **1856** FROUDE *Hist. Eng.* (1858) II. vii. 233 His plausibility long enabled him to explain away his conduct.

†ˈ**plausibilize,** *v.* *Obs.* *rare*⁻¹. In 7 plausiblelize. [f. next + -IZE.] *trans.* To render 'plausible' or acceptable; to ingratiate.

1655 FULLER *Ch. Hist.* IV. iv. §7 By erecting and endowing of Religious Houses; so to plausiblelize himself, especially among the Clergy.

plausible (ˈplɔːzɪb(ə)l), *a.* (*sb.*) Also 6 **-able, -eble, -yble,** *Sc.* **plausabill, plawsable,** 6–7 **plaucible, plawsible.** [ad. L. *plausibilis* deserving applause, acceptable, f. *plaus-*, ppl. stem of *plaudĕre* to applaud: see PLAUD *v.* and -IBLE. Cf. F. *plausible* (1552).]

A. *adj.* †**1.** Deserving of applause or approval; praiseworthy, laudable, commendable. *Obs.*

1561 T. NORTON *Calvin's Inst.* III. 216 To me it should not be very laborsom, and yet very plausible to bewray to their great shame those things that thei haue heretofore bosted vpon as mysteries. **1592** G. HARVEY *Four Lett.* iii. Wks. (Grosart) I. 185 The plausible examples of..diuers such vertuous Romanes, and sundry excellent Greekes. **1637** R. HUMPHREY tr. *St. Ambrose* I. 106 Those exercises which they thinke more plausible. **1711** SHAFTESB. *Charac.* (1737) II. III. ii. 401 Is there a fair and plausible Enthusiasm, a reasonable Extasy and Transport allow'd to other Subjects?

†**2. a.** Such as to be received with favour; acceptable, agreeable, pleasing, gratifying; winning public approval, generally acceptable, popular. *Obs.* (Common in late 16th and 17th c.)

1541 PAYNEL *Catiline* viii. 13 b, Nothynge was so plausyble to the people as perswasion agaynst the lawe Agraria. **1605** STOW *Ann.* 1426 This change was very plawsible or well pleasing to the Nobility and Gentrye. **1730** in *Swift's Lett.* (1768) IV. 249 Which..you will allow to be a desperate crisis under any party of the most plausible denomination. **1828** D'ISRAELI *Chas. I*, I. iii. 30 An invective against royal pedantry would always be plausible.

†**b.** Of persons, or their manners, etc.: Affable, agreeable, ingratiating, winning. *Obs.* (Cf. 3 b.)

1577–8 *Reg. Privy Council Scot.* II. 667 The said souirteis requirit the saidis officiaris with plausabill wordis to desist. **1624** HEYWOOD *Gunaik.* II. 102 His aspect more plaucible and his countenance more amiable than the former. **1633** BP. HALL *Hard Texts, N.T.* 20 The Sonne of Man came in a kinde, affable, and plausible manner. *a* **1704** T. BROWN *Praise of Wealth* Wks. 1730 I. 87 A plausible poetaster. **1841** LYTTON *Nt. & Morn.* I. ii, Robert, you are a careful, sober, plausible man.

3. a. Having an appearance or show of truth, reasonableness, or worth; apparently acceptable or trustworthy (sometimes with implication of mere appearance); fair-seeming, specious. (Chiefly of arguments or statements.)

1565 *Reg. Privy Council Scot.* I. 369 Undir pretence of that plausabill argument to draw eftir thame a large tale of ignorant personis. **1588** *Ibid.* IV. 281 The narrative..hes ane plawsable face to cullour the..pretendit forme thairof. **1682** DRYDEN *Medal* 111 A Tempting Doctrine, plausible and new. **1711** ADDISON *Spect.* No. 90 ¶7 They told me such a plausible Story, that I laughed at their Contrivance. **1838** THIRLWALL *Greece* IV. xxxii. 259 According even to the avowed doctrines of Protagoras and Gorgias, no truth could claim any higher value than that of a plausible opinion. **1876** PAGE *Adv. Text-bk. Geol.* ii. 48 Little aided by conjecture, however plausible. **1933** *Oxf. Eng. Dict.* Suppl. 403/2 One of the most plausible suggestions of etymology is F. *gâchette*. **1952** G. SARTON *Hist. Science* I. xi. 280 If Hippocrates actually wrote the first textbook of geometry, which is not only possible but plausible. **1969** *Daily Tel.* 17 Oct. 16/3 Something seriously missing here—the older actress, perhaps, needed to play this part, and certainly some more plausible explanation of the lady's behaviour. **1976** *Nature* 29 Apr. 813/3 Some ideas which have been suggested to explain this unexpected finding are plausible.

b. Of persons: Characterized by presenting specious arguments, etc.; fair-spoken (with implication of deceit).

1846 MRS. GORE *Eng. Char.* (1852) 29 So is it with the Plausible. By dint of strenuously pretending to be good, wise, or zealous, they contract almost the form and pressure of virtue and wisdom. **1860** EMERSON *Cond. Life, Fate* Wks. (Bohn) II. 327 A swindler.., then a quack, then a smooth, plausible gentleman. **1875** A. R. HOPE *Schoolboy Friends* 221 He was a plausible, cunning kind of fellow.

†**4.** In active sense: Expressive of applause or approbation; plausive, applausive. *Obs.*

1542 BECON *Pathw. Prayer* ix. E vj b, Now I wyll haste to declare of what vertue & strength the true and Christen prayer is, yᵗ men..may wᵗ yᵉ more plausible & ioyful mindes delyght in it. **1567** [see PLAUDITE 1]. **1600** HOLLAND *Livy* XXXIX. l. 881 For a while there was a plausible noise heard among them as they approued his words. **1622** C. FITZ-GEFFRY *Elisha* 1 A plausible Acclamation, The Chariot of Israel, and the Horse-men thereof.

B. *absol.* or as *sb.* That which is plausible; a plausible argument or statement.

1654 WHITLOCK *Zootomia* 162 Having ensnared the silly vulgar, by the dazle of their fame, (in some plausible or other). **1670** *Moral State Eng.* 101 To discourse or argue plausibles. **1831** J. S. MILL in *Examiner* 6 Feb. 83/2, I mean the really profound and philosophic inquirers into history in France and Germany, not the Plausibles, who in our own land of shallowness and charlatanerie, babble about induction without having ever considered what it is. **1833** CARLYLE *Misc., Diderot* (1857) III. 226 The plausiblest Plausible on record.

C. *Comb.*, as *plausible-looking*.

1841 LEVER *C. O'Malley* xcv, With a very plausible-looking tray.

ˈ**plausibleness.** Now *rare.* [f. prec. + -NESS.] The quality of being plausible; plausibility.

1598 R. BERNARD tr. *Terence, Andria* I. i. (1629) 9 Now a dayes, plausiblenesse gaines friends, and truth gets foes. **1681** TEMPLE *Mem.* III. Wks. 1731 I. 350 The Generality of the House of Commons were carried..with the Plausibleness of the Thing. **1705** S. CLARKE *Dem. Being God* ix. 139 It might have Objected with much more Plausibleness, that the Supreme Cause cannot be Free.

plausibly (ˈplɔːzɪblɪ), *adv.* [f. as prec. + -LY².] In a plausible manner.

†**1.** With applause; approvingly. *Obs.*

1581 MULCASTER *Positions* xli. (1887) 240 His iudgement is so often, and so plausibly vouched by the curteouse maister Askam. **1593** SHAKS. *Lucr.* 1854 The Romans plausibly did give consent To Tarquin's everlasting banishment. **1646** SIR T. BROWNE *Pseud. Ep.* v. xxi. 272 We hope they wil plausibly receave our attempts, or candidely correct our misconjectures.

†**2. a.** So as to deserve applause, commendably. **b.** So as to win approval; acceptably, agreeably; affably. *Obs.*

1612 BP. HALL *Contempl., O.T.* I. iv, Who can hope to liue plausibly and securely among so many Cains? **1631–2** *High Commission Cases* (Camden) 253 If you preach for applause plausibly there is temporall punishment to be inflicted on you heere. **1651** HOBBES *Leviath.* II. xxx. 179 Having the Faculty of discoursing readily, and plausibly.

3. With an appearance of truth or trustworthiness; in a way that seems true or right; with fair show; speciously.

1648 *Hunting of Fox* 37 They might more plausibly induce the common People..to come down to Whitehall. **1789** BELSHAM *Ess.* I. iii. 48 Mr. Hume..plausibly apologizes for Charles I. **1846** MRS. GORE *Eng. Char.* (1852) 26 In England, you may do what you like, provided you do it plausibly. Cant your way through life, with the seven deadly sins in your train. **1884** DUNCKLEY in *Manch. Exam.* 26 May 6/1 The objection might be urged more plausibly if the question..were now heard of for the first time.

plausive (ˈplɔːsɪv), *a.* Now *rare.* [f. L. *plaus-*, ppl. stem of *plaudĕre* (see PLAUD *v.*) + -IVE.]

1. Having the quality of applauding; expressive of approval by or as by applause; applausive.

1600 HEYWOOD *If you know not me* Wks. 1874 I. 202 Those plausiue shouts, which giue you entertaine. **1621** BRATHWAIT *Nat. Embassie* (1877) 7 When Pandora had made this plausiue Oration. **1753** L. M. *Accomplished Woman* II. 4 They who have a good voice sing where there is an echo, with a better grace, because the plausive sound makes them more sprightly. **1819** WORDSW. *Malham Cove* 8 No mightier work had gained the plausive smile Of all-beholding Phoebus! **1870** EMERSON *Soc. & Solit., Work & Days* Wks. (Bohn) III. 69 The young graduate..would..find the air faintly echoing with plausive academic thunders.

†**2. a.** = PLAUSIBLE 1 or 2. *Obs.*

1601 SHAKS. *All's Well* I. ii. 53 His plausiue words He scatter'd not in eares, but grafted them To grow there and to beare. **1602** —— *Ham.* I. iv. 30 By some habit, that too much o'er-leavens The form of plausive manners.

†**b.** = PLAUSIBLE 3. *Obs.*

1601 SHAKS. *All's Well* IV. i. 29 What shall I say I haue done? It must bee a very plausiue inuention that carries it. **1767** *Antiq.* in *Ann. Reg.* 145/1 The plausive arguments of false reasoners. **1820** R. POLWHELE *Introd. Lavington's Enthus. Meth. & Papists* Cj, All this under the plausive pretext of Toleration.

plaustral (ˈplɔːstrəl), *a. rare.* [f. L. *plaustr-um* wagon + -AL¹.] Pertaining to a cart or wagon.

1762 GOLDSM. *Cit. W.* lxxxvi, Whether the grand jury, in council assembled, had gloriously combined to encourage plaustral merit, I cannot take upon me to determine. **1885** RUSKIN *Pleas. Eng.* 138 The carter..is convinced of the truth of a plaustral catastrophe at first incredible to him.

†ˈ**plaustrary.** *Obs. rare.* [ad. L. *plaustrārius* belonging to a wagon, as sb. a wagoner; f. *plaustr-um* wagon: see -ARY.] A carter, a wagoner.

1592 R. D. *Hypnerotomachia* 56 b, These two Nymphes plaustraries, did take them downe [the contents of the 'repositorie or cupbord on wheels'] and deliver them..to the wayters. *Ibid.*, The first Table beeing chaunged, euerie thing was brought backe agayne to the plaustraries.

plautine (ˈplɔːtaɪn), *a.* [ad. L. *Plautīnus* of or belonging to Plautus.] Pertaining to, characteristic of, or in the style of the Roman comic poet Plautus (died B.C. 184).

1881 *Athenæum* 5 Feb. 199/3 The 'Miles'..contains much critical matter, not to speak of the Plautine verses which the author has included in his preface. **1882** A. S. WILKINS in *Encycl. Brit.* XIV. 330/2 It is needless to dwell further upon the details of Plautine scansion.

‖**plav** (plav). Also **plaur** (ˈplaʊə(r)). [a. Romanian *plav*, regional synonym of *pláur*.] One of the floating mats of reeds on the Danube, or the material of which it is composed.

1916 *Jrnl. Linnean Soc.* (*Bot.*) XLIII. 234 In Rumania, Plav is practically confined to the delta of the Danube. *Ibid.* 264 Reed of any size may in the delta of the Danube form an entire Plav, or portion of a Plav, from the base upwards. **1924** J. A. HAMMERTON *Countries of World* XVI. 1653/1 Many creatures perish, while such as do escape..eke out a desperate existence on floating islands of plaur or marsh weeds, so thickly matted and intertwined as to furnish a secure footing for both man and beast. **1961** *Times* 28 Oct. 9/7 We clambered out on to the *plaur*, the floating mass of decayed reeds.

plaw, plawe, obs. forms of PLAY.

plawncher, obs. form of PLANCHER *sb.*

play (pleɪ), *sb.* Forms: α. 1 **pleȝa,** *Angl.* **plæȝa,** 3 **pleȝe, plæȝe, pleay, pleiȝe,** 3–7 **pley,** 4 **plei(e,** 4–5 **pleye;** 4 **plai,** 5–7 **playe,** 6 **plaie,** 4– **play.** β. 1 *Merc.* **plaȝa,** 3 **plaȝe, plahe,** 3–7 **plawe,** 4 **plau,** 5 **plaw.** γ. 3 **pleoi, pleowe, ploȝe, plohe.** [OE. *pleȝa* (*plæȝa, plaȝa*), wk. sb. from root of *pleȝ(e)an, -ian, plæȝian, plaȝian* to PLAY, q.v. As in the verb, the phonology is difficult; the OE. forms vary in the vowel: the usual WSax. *pleȝa* and Anglian *plæȝa* have given the mod. *play*; the Anglian *plaȝa* gave ME. *plahe, plawe,* and *plau.* The 13th c. γ forms appear to mix the two types *ple(o)ȝe* and *plawe.*]

I. Exercise, brisk or free movement or action.

†**1. a.** Of living beings: Active bodily exercise; brisk and vigorous action of the body or limbs, as in fencing, dancing, leaping, swimming, clapping of the hands. *Obs.* or merged in other senses.

c **725** *Corpus Gloss.* 1477 *Palestra*, plaeȝa. *a* **900** CYNEWULF *Crist* 743 þa wearð burȝwarum, eadȝum, ece ȝefea Æþelinges pleȝa. *a* **1000** *Guthlac* 1334 Lagu-mearȝ snyrede ȝeblæsted to hyðe, þæt se hærn-flota æfter sund-pleȝan sond-lond ȝespearn. *a* **1000** *Cædmon's Gen.* 1989 þær wæs heard pleȝa, wælgara wrixl, wiȝcyrm micel, hlud hildesweȝ. *c* **1050** *O.E. Chron.* an. 1004 (MSS. C. & D.) þæt hi næfre wyrsan hand pleȝan on Angel cynne ne ȝemetton þonne Ulfcytel him to brohte. *c* **1050** *Gloss.* in Wr.-Wülcker 414/14 *Gesticulatio*, pleȝa. *c* **1200** *Trin. Coll. Hom.* 211 C[h]orea ceruisia forum monasterium..þat on is pleȝe, þat oder [sic] drinch, þe þridde chepinge, þe ferðe chirche. *Ibid.*, At pleȝe he teldeð þe grune of idelnesse, for al hit is idel þat me at pleȝe bihalt..þih and shonkes and fet oppieð, wombe gosshieð. *a* **1290** *St. Eustace* 280 in Horstm. *Altengl. Leg.*

(1881) 217 þere nes non at þare plawe Wiþ sheld and spere out i-drawe þat hoere dunt atstode.

b. The gestures made by cock birds to attract the hens.

1875 'STONEHENGE' *Brit. Sports* I. I. iv. § 1. 72 The 'play' of the capercaillie is very remarkable; it is confined to the males, who indulge in it in order to astonish and excite the hens.

c. The action of lightly and briskly wielding or plying (as a weapon in a contest). Also in combinations, as ***buckler-play, sword-play***.

Beowulf 2039 Oð ðæt hie forlæddan to ðam lindplegan swæse gesiðas. *c* **850** *Kentish Gloss., Libera tuta [tua] pelta*, gefria ðine plægsceldæ. *a* **1000** *Waldere* 13 Ðy ic ðe gesawe æt ðam sweordplegan.. wig forbugan oððe on weal fleon. **1670** STAPYLTON *Juvenal* 48 [see SWORD-play]. **1839** LONGF. *Black Knight* ii, In the play of spears, Fell all the cavaliers. **1860** DICKENS *Uncomm. Trav.* vii, Some of the sword play being very skilful. **1899** E. J. CHAPMAN *Drama Two Lives, Fir-tree* 78, I thrust him to earth, and he lay there, For all his boasted play. **1901** *Daily Chron.* 21 Oct. 8/6 The latter's play being very correct, and his parries both neat and effective.

2. a. Of physical things: Rapid, brisk, or light movement, usually alternating or fitful; elusive change or transition (of light or colour); light motion about or impact upon something.

a **1628** F. GREVIL *Mustapha* Chorus ii. Wks. (1633) 116 A play of Sunne-motes from mans small World come. **1801** SOUTHEY *Thalaba* VI. viii, Alternate light and darkness, like the play Of sunbeams on the warrior's burnish'd arms. **1805** W. SAUNDERS *Min. Waters* 494 This operation always admits the play of air upon the feverish body. **1850** BRYANT *Saw-Mill* Poet. Wks. (1903) 370 The saw, with restless play, Was cleaving through a fir-tree Its long and steady way. **1875** DAWSON *Dawn of Life* ii. 13 Iridescent play of colours. *a* **1878** SIR G. G. SCOTT *Lect. Archit.* (1879) I. 224 This gives.. great play of light and shade.

b. Short for *play of light* or *colour* (as above).

1698 FRYER *Acc. E. India & P.* 214 You may set it upon full scraped Ivory, which graceth the Play of the Stone. **1825** J. NICHOLSON *Operat. Mechanic* 715 The intention of foils is either to increase the lustre or play of the stones, or more generally improve the colour, by giving an additional force to the tinge. *Ibid.* 716 To stones or pastes, that have some share of play, it gives a most beautiful brilliance.

†**3.** (In form *plaw*.) A boiling up, ebullition. *Obs.*

c **1440** *Promp. Parv.* 403/2 Plaw, or plawynge, *bullicio, ebullicio*. **1601** HOLLAND *Pliny* XIV. xvii, Boile them al together at a soft fire, until they haue had ten plawes or walmes.

4. *fig.* and *gen.* **a.** Action, activity, operation, working: often implying the ideas of rapid movement or change, variety, etc. (Now almost always of abstract things, as feeling, fancy, thought, etc.; formerly of persons.)

1599 SHAKS. *Hen. V*, IV. viii. 114 Without stratagem, But in plaine shock, and euen play of Battaile. **1649** J. E[LLISTONE] tr. *Behmen's Epist.* vi. § 44 God hath made all things in his Divine pley or operation out of his Spiration. **1800** tr. *Lagrange's Chem.* I. 312 There will be a play of double affinity, and a double decomposition will take place. **1837** DISRAELI *Venetia* III. ii, That enchanting play of fancy which had once characterized her. **1874** L. STEPHEN *Hours in Library* (1892) I. vi. 232 The play of evil passions gives infinite subjects for dramatic interests. **1875** JOWETT *Plato* (ed. 2) I. p. xviii, The lively play of fancy.

b. Phr. †*in play*: actively engaged or employed; so ***out of play***, unoccupied, out of employment or office (*obs.*). ***in full play***: in full action or operation, acting with its full force.

1661 PEPYS *Diary* 2 Sept., There are endeavours to get my Lord out of play at sea. **1669** *Ibid.* 26 Jan., My Lord Privy Seale, whom I never before knew to be in so much play, as to be of the Cabinet. **1719** SWIFT *To Yng. Clergyman* Wks. 1755 II. II. 19 Men who were impatient of being out of play, have been forced to.. reconcile their former tenets with every new system of administration. **1844** ALB. SMITH *Adv. Mr. Ledbury* xviii, The usual bustle was in full play. **1873** LYTTON *Coming Race* v, There was a huge engine in the wall which was in full play.

c. ***to hold*** or ***keep*** (a person, etc.) ***in play*** (orig. ***to hold*** or ***keep*** (a person) ***play***): to keep exercised, occupied, or engaged; to give (a person) something to do (usually in the way of self-defence or delay, as in a contest). Also, to keep (something) in exercise or practice (quot. 1809).

a **1548** HALL *Chron., Hen. VIII* 37 b, The Capitayn.. prayed God that the Kynge of Scottes woulde come wyth hys puyssaunce, for he woulde kepe hym playe tyll the tyme that the Kynge of Englande came oute of Fraunce. **1582** MUNDAY *Eng. Rom. Life* 10 They must war within, while other holds them playe with out. **1600** HOLLAND *Livy* XXVII. xlvi. 662 [He] had by all the devises and policies of warre, mocked him and kept him play. *c* **1645** T. TULLIE *Siege of Carlisle* (1840) 12 Forest was the only man who held the Cavalliers in play. **1648** GAGE *West Ind.* 30 To overcome them, or else to hold them play. **1714** SWIFT *Pres. St. Affairs* Wks. 1755 II. I. 207 A struggling faction kept them continually in play. **1809** MALKIN *Gil Blas* v. i. ¶7 To keep my devotion and my wind in play by the rehearsal of an anthem or two. **1842** MACAULAY *Lays, Horatius* xxix, I, with two more to help me, Will hold the foe in play. **1851** J. RICHARDSON in *Harper's Mag.* Jan. 234/2 Nothing that we have fallen in with.. could hold her play.

d. ***to come into*** (†***in***) ***play***: to come into action or operation, become active (formerly of persons: cf. b). So ***to bring*** or ***call into play***: to begin to exercise, bring into action, make active.

1650 WELDON *Crt. Jas. I* 41 Salisbury liking not that any of Essex his faction should come into play. **1691** LOCKE *Lower. Interest* Wks. 1727 II. 54 Today your new Coin comes in play, which is 5 per Cent. lighter. **1706** BAYNARD in Sir J. Floyer *Hot & Cold Bath.* II. 336 A Distemper in England almost worn out, but now it begins to come in Play again. **1799** HAN. MORE *Fem. Educ.* (ed. 4) I. 115 Those societies in which their kind of talents are not likely to be brought into play. **1842** A. COMBE *Physiol. Digestion* (ed. 4) 124 The muscular fibres of the stomach.. next come into play. **1865** M. ARNOLD *Ess. in Crit.* ii. 81 The intelligence and judgment of Mr. Ruskin.. are brought into play. **1874** CARPENTER *Ment. Phys.* I. i. § 3 The reaction of his brain upon the impressions which called it into play.

e. ***to make play***: in *Racing* and *Hunting*, to exercise pursuers or followers; in *Pugilism*, to deliver blows actively or with effect; hence *gen.* to act effectively, produce an effect; to hasten or hurry on. (In quots. 1813, 1889, to keep an adversary engaged: cf. c.)

1799 E. DU BOIS *Piece Family Biog.* I. 152 A pause having succeeded.. Mr. Burley thought it a fit time (in the jockey-term) to make his play. **1808** *Sporting Mag.* XXXII. 76 Gully made play, and planted two other blows on his adversary's head. **1809** *Ibid.* XXXIII. 89 The fox.. made play towards Mr. Thellusson's. **1813** *Ibid.* XLII. 243 A young bull of great game, made play for no less than nine-and-twenty dogs. **1824** BYRON *Juan* XVI. lxxviii, But I'm too late, and therefore must make play. **1857** HUGHES *Tom Brown* II. v, There he goes in, making play with both hands. **1883** *Scotsman* 11 July 10/1 Fontenoy made play to the distance, where the favourite took the lead. **1889** DOYLE *Micah Clarke* 75, I trust that the Duke will muster every man he can, and make play until the royal forces come up.

5. a. Free or unimpeded movement (usually from or about a fixed point); the proper motion of a piece of mechanism, or a part of the living body.

1653 WALTON *Angler* ii. 53 Give him [the chub] play enough before you offer to take him out of the water. **1733** TULL *Horse-Hoeing Husb.* xxii. 326 Now the Distance between these Two Marks, is the Measure.. of the Tongue's Play at the place of pressure. **1778** JOHNSON in *Mme. D'Arblay's Diary* Aug., Such a.. restless, fatiguing play of the muscles. **1794** *Rigging & Seamanship* II. 270 The great length.. is an obstacle to the play of the rudder. **1856** AYTOUN *Bothwell* II. vii, And felt once more The pulse's stirring play. **1897** *Pall Mall Mag.* Aug. 526 The girl.. was an arch, ogling person, with.. a great play of shoulders.

b. Freedom or room for movement; the space in or through which anything (esp. a piece of mechanism) can or does move.

1659 LEAK *Waterwks.* 18 The two Buckets.. have about three feet play, rising and falling. **1703** MOXON *Mech. Exerc.* 30 Square Staples, just fit to contain the Bolt with an easie Play. **1793** HERSCHEL in *Phil. Trans.* LXXXIII. 217 The shake, or play, of the screw is less than 3-tenths of a division. **1858** G. MACDONALD *Phantastes* (1878) II. xxi. 142 The overlappings in the lower part [of the armour] had more play than necessary. **1860** *Merc. Marine Mag.* VII. 113 Taking care to allow at least an inch of play. **1876** J. ROSE *Compl. Pract. Machinist* xix. 359 Suppose, for instance, there was even a trifling amount of play in the eccentric or any of the bolts.

c. *fig.* and *gen.* Free action; freedom, opportunity, or room for action; scope for activity.

1641 MILTON *Reform.* II. Wks. 1851 III. 37 Yet to give them play front, and reare, it shall be my task to prove that Episcopacy.. is not only not agreeable, but tending to the destruction of Monarchy. **1711** ADDISON *Spect.* No. 160 ¶9 They.. form themselves altogether upon Models, without giving the full Play to their own natural Parts. **1787** J. WHITAKER *Mary Q. of Scots Vind.* I. i. § 3. 24 Those scenes.. where he might have a play for his activity in cunning. **1837** SIR W. HAMILTON *Metaph.* xliv. (1870) II. 477 All pleasure, thus, arises from the free play of our faculties and capacities. **1857** BUCKLE *Civilization* I. viii. 543 Their comprehensive minds would, in that state of society, have found no play. **1888** BRYCE *Amer. Commw.* II. lii. 325 To allow the fullest play to the Sentiment of State independence.

d. Attention or patronage; a show of interest; publicity. *slang* (orig. *U.S.*).

1929 D. RUNYON in *Hearst's International* July 57/1 Everybody goes to the Chicken Club now and then to give Tony Bertazzola, the owner, a friendly play. **1931** F. L. ALLEN *Only Yesterday* viii. 189 The insignificant Gray-Snyder murder trial got a bigger 'play' in the press than the sinking of the *Titanic*. **1935** J. O'HARA *Appointment in Samarra* 46 The Apollo [*sc.* a hotel] got a big play from salesmen who had their swindle sheets to think of. **1959** *Wall St. Jrnl.* 20 Nov. 17/2 Du Pont Co.'s nylon 501, brought out late last year, is getting a big play this fall from James Lees & Sons Co. and E. T. Barwick Mills, Inc., and other mills have nylon 501 carpets in production. **1970** *Washington Post* 30 Sept. B2/2 Asked her opinion on the 'youth revolt', she replied: 'I think it's such a minority—it gets far too much play.'

II. Exercise or action for amusement or diversion; and derived uses.

6. a. Exercise or action by way of recreation; amusement, diversion, sport, frolic. (In early use sometimes in bad sense: Vicious or profligate indulgence, revelling.) ***at play***, engaged in playing.

c **1200** *Trin. Coll. Hom.* 55 Vte we.. al þese.. dages forleten blisfulle songes, and plege, and leden clenliche ure lif. **13..** *E.E. Allit. P.* B. 1502 In þe poynt of her play he poruayes a mynde. *a* **1400** *Pistill of Susan* 53 Whon þeos perlous prestes perceyued hire play. *a* **1450** *Knt. de la Tour* (1868) 155 That is my play and my gladnesse to be aboute hym, and forto do hym seruice unto his ease and plesaunce. **1523** FITZHERB. *Husb.* § 153 It is conuenient for euery man.. to haue playe & game accordynge to his degre. **1562** ROWBOTHUM *Cheasts* A j, Most men are geuen rather to play then to studye. **1667** MILTON *P.L.* IV. 404 A Tiger, who by chance hath spi'd In some Purlieu two gentle Fawnes at play. **1712** ARBUTHNOT *John Bull* I. iii, John naturally loved rough play. **1818** BYRON *Ch. Har.* IV. cxli, But where his rude hut by the Danube lay There were his young barbarians all at play, There was their Dacian mother. *Proverb*, All work and no play makes Jack a dull boy.

β. *c* **1430** *Hymns Virg.* 111 Ceesse, & seie to hir no sawe To make hir for to synne assent, Ne please hir not with no nyce plawe, But kepe weel cristis comaundement.

γ. *c* **1205** LAY. 20844 þan voxe þenne he bið baldest.. & hafeð his fulle plose [*c* **1275** pleay] & fugeles inoge.

†**b.** Enjoyment, pleasure, joy, delight; a source of delight. *Obs.*

1340 *Ayenb.* 92 Hi nemeþ and useþ þe lostes ulessliche and þe pleges þet be þe vif wyttes comeþ. **1362** LANGL. *P. Pl.* A. XII. 90 þat þi play be plentevous in paradys with aungelys. *c* **1460** *Towneley Myst.* xvi. 363 Alas! and walo-way! my child that was me lefe! My luf, my blood, my play, that neuer dyd man grefe! **1503** DUNBAR *Thistle & Rose* 181 Our peax, our play, our plane felicite.

β. *c* **1400** *Laud Troy-bk.* 15358 Achilles than & his ffelawe Rode so forth with mochel plawe.

c. Amorous disport; dalliance; sexual indulgence. Now *rare* or *Obs.*

a **1000** *Riddles* xxi. 28 (Gr.) Ic wið bryde ne mot hæmed habban, ac me þæs hyhtplegan geno wyrneð. *c* **1400** *Rom. Rose* 4876 The pley of love, for-ofte seke. *a* **1425** *Cursor M.* 9247 (Trin.) Mathan gat Iacob in pleye, Iacob Ioseph soþ to seye. **1565** RANDOLPH in Tytler *Hist. Scot.* (1864) III. 215 He knoweth himself that he hath a partaker in play and game with him. **1667** MILTON *P.L.* IX. 1045 Till dewie sleep Oppress'd them, wearied with their amorous play.

β. *c* **1250** *Gen. & Ex.* 537 Wapmen bi-gunnen quad mester, bi-twen hem-seluen hun-wreste plage.

7. a. Jest, fun, sport (as opp. to *earnest*); trifling. Often in phr. ***in play***.

a **1300** *Cursor M.* 2816 Bot al þat loth to þaim can sai, þam thoght it was not bot in plai. *c* **1386** CHAUCER *Clerk's T.* 974 Grisilde quod he as it were in his pley, How liketh thee my wyf and hire beautee? *c* **1420** LYDG. *Assembly of Gods* 1662 Chaunge from ernest in to mery play. **1500–20** DUNBAR *Poems* xxxiii. 27 To sum man thair it was no play The preving of his sciens. **1513** MORE *Rich. III* (1883) 60 The king.. made her answer part in ernest, part in play merely. **1613** PURCHAS *Pilgrimage* (1614) 367. I desire not sacrifices and inwards, these are plaies. *a* **1907** *Mod.* Don't be offended; I only said it in play. (More commonly *in fun*.)

β. *a* **1300** *Cursor M.* 18167 (Cott.) Hell and ded.. O þair pride thoght þam litel plau And gaf a cri wit mikel au. *c* **1320** *Sir Tristr.* 3101 Aski sche wil in plawe, And say þou comest fro me. *c* **1325** *Spec. Gy Warw.* 15 If þu louest more worldes god þan god him-sel[e] in þi mod, þu shalt hit finde an yuel plawe.

b. ***play of words***: a playing or trifling with words; the use of words merely or mainly for the purpose of producing a rhetorical or fantastic effect. ***play on*** or ***upon words***: a sportive use of words so as to convey a double meaning, or produce a fantastic or humorous effect by similarity of sound with difference of meaning; a pun. See also WORD-PLAY.

1739 HUME *Hum. Nat.* (1874) I. II. ii. 339 To confess.. that human reason is nothing but a play of words. **1798** FERRIAR *Illustr. Sterne*, etc. *Genius* 278, I cannot suspect so excellent a poet of Buchanan, of any intentional play on the words ingenium and genius. **1810** D. STEWART *Philos. Ess.* iii. 123 A childish play upon words, quite foreign to the point at issue. **1850** ROBERTSON *Serm.* Ser. III. ix. 114 It was.. no mere play of words which induced the apostle to bring these two things [fulness of the Spirit and fulness of wine, Eph. v. 18] together. **1871** FREEMAN *Norm. Conq.* IV. xviii. 174 To a Latin or French speaker the name of Urse might have suggested an easy play upon words. **1881** JOWETT *Thucyd.* I. Introd. 14 The Speeches of Thucydides everywhere exhibit the antitheses, the climaxes, the plays of words.. of the rhetorician.

8. a. (with *pl.*) A particular amusement or diversion; a game, a sport. Now *rare* or *Obs.*

a **700** *Epinal Gloss.* 577 *Ludi litterari(i)*, staebplegan. **971** *Blickl. Hom.* 99 Heora bliss & heora plegan wæron swiðe genihtsume. **13..** *Guy Warw.* (A.) 812 He þat best doþ þat day, þer he schal winne þat play. **13..** *Cursor M.* 28146 (Cott.) Caroles, iolites, and plaies. *c* **1400** MAUNDEV. (1839) iii. 17 For joustynges, or for other pleyes and desportes. *a* **1533** LD. BERNERS *Huon* liii. 178, I shall cause thee to be assayed at yᵉ playe of the chesse. *a* **1533** —— *Gold. Bk. M. Aurel.* (1546) C vij b, Dyuers persounes were assembled in the hygh mountayne Olimpius, to celebrate the playes. **1588** SHAKS. *L.L.L.* IV. iii. 78 All hid, all hid, an old infant play. **1659** D. PELL *Improv. of Sea* 418 When the Sea was calm, they were at their sports and playes. **1728** T. SHERIDAN *Persius* iii. (1739) 44 The Boys had a Play of pitching Nuts into a narrow-mouth'd Vessel. **1798** JANE AUSTEN *Northang. Abb.* i, She was fond of all boy's plays. **1841–4** EMERSON *Ess., Experience* Wks. (Bohn) I. 178 The plays of children are nonsense, but very educative nonsense.

β. *a* **1225** *Leg. Kath.* 106 Ne luuede ha nane lihte plahen [*v.r.* plohen]. *c* **1250** *Gen. & Ex.* 3575 Moyses cam ner and sag ðis plages, And ðis calf, and ðis ille lages.

b. A country pleasure-fair or wake. *dial.*

1847–78 HALLIWELL, *Play*.. a country wake. *Somerset.* **1886** STEVENSON *Kidnapped* xxii, Like people lifting weights at a country play.

†**9.** *transf.* **a.** An act or proceeding, esp. of a crafty or underhand kind; manner of action, method of proceeding; a trick, dodge, 'game'. *Obs.* (exc. as in 12).

a **1300** *Cursor M.* 16898 þar bes an iuel plai. **1481** CAXTON *Reynard* iii. (Arb.) 7 Maister reynard.. bygan to playe his olde playe [orig. *hi speelde sijn oude speel*], ffor he had caught kywaert by the throte. **1572** *Satir. Poems Reform.* xxx. 183 3it was the pepill puneist for sic playis. **16..** LOCKE (J.), The answerer on his side makes it his play to distinguish as much as he can. **1702** *Eng. Theophrast.* 184 When a man has any notable defect about him, 'tis the best of his play to try the Humour, if he can turn it into a fashion. **1746** *Rep. Cond. Sir*

J. Cope 151 In case they keep only to their strong Passes, which hitherto has been their 'Play'.

β. **1297** R. Glouc. (Rolls) 5906 Vpe þin owe heued it ssal come þi moderes luþer plawe þoru ssedinge of þi broþer blod þat þus is ybroȝt of dawe.

†**b.** A device of magic, a trick of conjuring, or the like. *Obs.*

1426 Lydg. *De Guil. Pilgr.* 3803 Yiff I now made a newe pley, ffor to take the sonne away. *c* **1450** *Merlin* 362 Than seide the mayden, that he sholde make yet a-nother pley that neuer myght faile.

10. a. The carrying on or playing of a game.

a **1450** Myrc 336 Bal and bares and suche play. *a* **1550** *Christis Kirke Gr.* i. i, Nowthir at Falkland on the grene, Nor Peblis at the play. **1610** Shaks. *Temp.* v. i. 186 What is this Maid, with whom thou was't at play? **1673** Temple *Observ. United Prov.* Wks. 1731 I. 76 No Man at Play sees a very great Game..unexpectedly lost, but he is apt to consider, whether it could have been saved. **1736** Gray *Statius* i. 32 Phlegyas the long-expected play began. **1736** in Waghorn *Cricket Scores* (1899) 17 The weather proving very rainy, they were forced to give over play. **1882** *Daily Tel.* 24 June, Play was very slow,..twenty minutes being consumed in getting ten runs.

β. **13..** *Guy Warw.* (A.) 3176 Michel y desire þi loue to haue. Go we togider wiþ game & plawe.

b. Manner or style of playing; skill in playing.

1531 Elyot *Gov.* i. xxvi, If fortune brynge alwaye to one man iuell chaunces, whiche maketh the playe of the other suspected. **1773** in Waghorn *Cricket Scores* (1899) 91 The match of cricket,..showing great play on both sides. **1824** Scott *St. Ronan's* xviii, Lord Etherington seemed at first indolently careless and indifferent about his play. **1850** 'Bat' *Cricket. Man.* 101 His 'forward play' is..peculiar. **1883** G. A. MacDonnell *Chess Life-Pictures* 166 Eliciting his opponent's best play.

c. A point in playing, a special device in a game. (Cf. 9.)

1778 C. Jones *Hoyle's Games Impr.* 41 If you win that Trick, your next Play is, to throw out the Queen of Trumps.

d. *in play*: said of a ball, etc. = being played with, being used in the course of the game. So *out of play*. Hence *play*, transf. (in *Cricket* and *Football*), that part of the ground within definite boundaries in which the game, or the chief part of it, is carried on.

c **1788** *Laws of Cricket* §14, The Striker is out..if, in striking, or at any other time while the ball is in play, both his feet are over the popping-crease, and his wicket put down. **1816** W. Lambert *Instr. & Rules Cricket* 34 Always endeavour to hit the Ball on the same side on which it is bowled, and not draw it across the play. **1849** in 'Bat' *Cricket. Man.* (1850) 56 If the striker touch..the ball while in play. *Ibid.* 60 The fieldsman must return the ball so that it shall cross the play between the wicket and the bowling stump. **1857** T. Hughes *Tom Brown's School Days* i. v. 109 As soon as the ball gets past them, it's in touch, and out of play. **1882** *Australians in England* 22 He got half way up the play, and just reached the ball with one hand. **1900** *Westm. Gaz.* 12 Dec. 7/2 Walton tried another big kick, but the ball fell in play, and was well returned by Strand-Jones. **1976** *South Notts Echo* 16 Dec. 7/3 The ball bounced across the goal line and into play.

e. Phr. † *ball play* (obs.), *boy's play*, *child's play*: applied to anything that involves very little trouble, or is of very little importance; a very easy or trifling matter. (See ball *sb.*[1] 21, boys'-play, child *sb.* 18.) Formerly also with *a* (see 8).

a **1225** *Ancr. R.* 184 Al nis bute ase bal pleowe [*MS. C* ploȝe]. *c* **1386**, etc. [see child *sb.* 18]. *c* **1450** tr. *De Imitatione* iii. xxxvii. 107 Lorde, þis is not o. days werke ner children pley, but, þat more is, in þis shorte worde is includid all perfeccioun of Religiose folke. **1560** Daus tr. *Sleidane's Comm.* 179 The persecution of thys yere was but a balle playe in comparison of that. **1579** Tomson *Calvin's Serm. Tim.* 246/1 To make this allegorie, is but a boyes play. **1849** Macaulay *Hist. Eng.* iii. I. 322 Elderly gentlemen who had seen service which was no child's play. **1850** Scoresby *Cheever's Whalem. Adv.* v. (1859) 74 This towing of captured whales is no boy's play.

†**f.** In the game of Beast: see quot. *Obs.*

1674 Cotton *Compl. Gamester* xxv. 153 They make three heaps, the King, the Play, and the Triolet... He that wins most tricks takes up the heap that is called the Play.

g. An attempt to achieve or gain something; a move, manœuvre, or venture; *spec.* (*a*) *U.S. Sports*, an attacking move in a team game; an action that advances one's team's interest; (*b*) an attempt to attract or impress a person of the opposite sex; freq. in phr. *to make a play* (*for*). *slang* (orig. *U.S.*).

1868 H. Chadwick *Game of Base Ball* 46 A 'treble play' is made when three players are put out after the ball is hit, before it is pitched to the bat again. **1905** 'H. McHugh' *Get Next!* 75 His intentions are honorable and he wishes to prove them so by shooting his lady love if she renigs when he makes a play for her hand. **1906** H. Green *At Actor's Boarding House* 87 She had once made a play for the Swede, but he couldn't see her. **1912** C. Mathewson *Pitching* 174 Most clubs try to keep an umpire feeling hostile toward the team because, even if he means to see a play right, he is likely to call a close one against his enemies, not intending to be dishonest. **1930** *Amer. Mercury* Dec. 457/1 We make a play on their plant, but don't score. **1939** E. S. Gardner *D.A. draws Circle* ii. 26 Stall the thing along, make it casual, and be sure to back my play. **1943** D. Powell *Time to be Born* vi. 132 If you were twenty years younger I'd make a play for you, no fooling. **1961** P. Field *Rattlesnake Ridge* xiv. 170 It's the second time War Ax hands made a play for their money. **1961** *Dallas Morning News* 10 Oct. ii. 2 Gannon contributed saving plays on the Falcons' aerial thrusts in the late stages. **1966** Wodehouse *Plum Pie* i. 26 Grab the girl while the grabbing's good, because..your nephew Bertram is making a heavy play in her direction. **1969** *Official Baseball Rules* 13 A double play is a play by the defense in which two offensive players are put out as a result of continuous action. **1972** *Newsweek* 10 Jan. 30/2 In the U.S., a guard is supposed to handle the ball and set up plays. **1973** N. Moss *What's the Difference?* 45/1 *Play, n*, a team's action in American football, hence a strategic move towards a goal. **1973** E. Page *Fortnight by Sea* viii. 88 She'd been certain he would make a play for her the moment Lockwood took himself off. **1978** S. Brill *Teamsters* ii. 60 The attempt that finally worked was the play by Giacalone, to get Hoffa to a peace meeting.

11. *spec.* The playing of a game or games for money or other valuable stakes; gaming, gambling.

a **1300** *Floriz & Bl.* 376 Ȝerne he wule þe bidde and preie þat þu legge þe cupe to pleie. *a* **1580** in *Stanyhurst's Æneis*, etc. (Arb.) 153 By losse in play men oft forget Thee duitye they dooe owe. **1683** Evelyn *Mem.* (1857) II. 194 He has lost immense sums at play. **1710** in *Lond. Gaz.* No. 4754/4 William Bradbury, Esq.; Deputy Groom-Porter, will open his House..to Morrow.., to keep Play for all Persons of Quality and Gentlemen, being the only Person authorized so to do. **1769** *Junius Lett.* i. (1820) 4 A young nobleman,.. ruined by play. **1845** McCulloch *Taxation* ii. viii. (1852) 325 During the carnival, when, from the excitement of the season, the extent of play is always the greatest.

12. In phrases *fair play*, *foul play*: rarely *lit.* (in sense 10); usually *fig.* (in sense 9) action, conduct, dealing: see fair *a.* 10 c, foul *a.* 14 b. So †*false play*, treacherous dealing (*obs.*). *while the play is good* (*Sc.*), before the situation becomes serious, dangerous, or unpleasant.

c **1440** *Gesta Rom.* lx. 248 (Harl. MS.) Tristing..that the lion wolde have I-made a foule pleye withe þe lorde & withe þe lady. **1567** Maplet *Gr. Forest* 84 He is good in finding out false play or adulterie done. *a* **1586** Sidney *Arcadia* ii. (1590) 181 b, To preuent any foule play that might be offered vnto me. **1595**, etc. [see fair *a.* 10 c]. **1610**, etc. [see foul *a.* 14 b]. **1678** Butler *Hud.* iii. ii. 1068 We threw the Box and Dice away, Before y'had lost us at foul Play. **1770** C. Jenner *Placid Man* vi. iv, She endeavoured..to give both sides fair play. **1816** Scott *Old Mort.* xxxvi, Come, laddie, speak while the play is good; you're too young to bear the burden will be laid on you else. **1853** Lytton *My Novel* i. xii, In strict truth, it was hardly fair play—it was almost swindling. **1888** *Daily News* 14 Feb. 3/4 His hat and bag being missing has given rise to the conjecture of foul play. *Mod. Sc.* Stop now while the play is good; you have gone far enough.

13. [from the notion of recreation, sense 6] Cessation or abstinence from work; the condition of being idle, or not at work (as of workmen on strike, or out of employment); *the play* (Sc.), holiday from school.

1601 Shaks. *All's Well* i. i. 23 A father..whose skill.., had it stretch'd so far, would haue made nature immortall, and death should haue play for lacke of worke. **1723** Wodrow *Corr.* (1843) III. 33 There was never a schoolboy more desirous to have the play than I am to have leave of this world. **1772** Mrs. Montagu in Doran *Lady Last C.* vii. (1873) 173 The doctor allowed me to ask a play for the boys, which made them very happy. **1826** J. Wilson *Noct. Ambr.* Wks. 1855 I. 150 You micht hae gien him the play the day, I think, sir, you micht hae gien him the play. **1845** Disraeli *Sybil* (1863) 116 When miners and colliers strike they term it going to play. **1866** Ruskin *Crown Wild Olive* 20 Down in the black north country, where 'play' means being laid up by sickness. **1892** *Daily News* 26 Feb. 5/7 The question of 'play' [is] to be discussed at the next conference [which] will settle the question how long the cessation of work is to last. **1900** Strain *Elmslie's Drag-net* 281 It was Saiterday mornin'—they get the play frae the school.

III. Mimic action, dramatic performance.

14. a. A mimic representation of some action or story, as a spectacle upon the stage, etc., a dramatic or theatrical performance. †Rarely without article, Dramatic performance, acting (quot. *c* 1325). Esp. in phr. *as good as a play*: very entertaining or amusing; *a play within a play*: a play acted as part of the action of another play (also with *the*, usu. with reference to Shakespeare's *Hamlet*).

c **893** K. Ælfred *Oros.* vi. ii. §2 Wearþ eft Godes wracu Romanum, þa hie æt hiora theatrum wæron mid heora plegan. *c* **1325** *Poem Times Edw. II* 285 in *Pol. Songs* (Camden) 336 Hii ben degised as turmentours that comen from clerkes plei. *c* **1380** Wyclif *Wks.* (1880) 429 As men seyen in þe pley of ȝork. *c* **1400** *Destr. Troy* 2923 Hit is wondur to wit of wemen dissyre, þat..prese vnto playes pepull to beholde. **1556** *Chron. Gr. Friars* (Camden) 12 This yere beganne a gret pley from the begynnyng of the worlde.., that lastyd vij. dayes contynually. **1601** J. Manningham *Diary* (Camden) 18 Wee had a play called Twelve Night. [**1638** J. Taylor *Bull, Beare, & Horse* sig. C7, It was as good as a Comedy to him to see the trees fall.] **1672** Marvell *Rehearsal Transpros'd* 53 It was grown almost as good as a Play among us. **1767** *Woman of Fashion* I. 96, I went to the Play, as they call it—Play, indeed! Faith, Brother, I think it was past a Joke. **1827** T. Creevey *Let.* 22 Nov. in *Creevey Papers* (1963) xiii. 232 This morning after breakfast he has been as good as a play. **1868** Helps *Realmah* xvii. (1876) 475 Give me some good plays to go to, played by great players. **1871** Mrs. H. Wood *Dene Hollow* xx, The tale that Master Jarvis told was as good as a play. **1875** [see good *a.* 11 b]. **1925** A. Huxley *Those Barren Leaves* ii. iii. 111 He is the life and soul of Miss Carruthers's establishment... To see him with Fluffy—it's as good as a play. **1952** W. Plomer *Museum Pieces* xviii. 160 His eager account of the play was itself 'as good as a play'. **1975** D. M. Davin *Closing Times* vi. 129 'He's as good as a play,' my own parents would have said of him, had they known him.

1883 *Oxf. Mag.* 17 Oct. 308/1 He knew that the play within the play was meant for the conscience of the king. **1918** *Mod. Lang. Rev.* XIII. 151 The idea of having a play within the play is a famous one. **1935** *Ibid.* XXX. 433, I believe that in the circumstances surrounding the death of Francesco Maria I della Rovere, Duke of Urbino, we may well see the ultimate origin, not only of the play within the play, but of other elements in the plot of *Hamlet*. **1937** G. Rawson tr. *Schücking's Meaning of Hamlet* i. 3 The main action..reaches its apogee in the 'play within a play', a device that richly entertains both eye and ear. **1961** *Times* 24 Jan. 13/3 A play-within-a-play..convinces the audience that the actors are real addicts. **1973** *Listener* 26 Apr. 563/1 As a variation on the play-within-a-play we had the documentary-within-a-play.

b. *transf.* A performance, proceeding, piece of action (in real life).

1581 Pettie *Guazzo's Civ. Conv.* iii. (1586) 172 b, The Count saide nothing to it, but..attended the ende of the play. **1849** Thackeray *Pendennis* xlv, This little play being achieved, the Marquis of Steyne made..two profound bows ..and passed on.

15. A literary composition in the form of dialogue, adapted for performance on the stage with appropriate action, costume, and scenery, in imitation of real events; a dramatic piece, a drama.

c **1440** *Promp. Parv.* 404/1 Pley..þat begynnythe wythe myrthe, & endythe wythe sorowe, *tragedia*. **1530** Palsgr. 255/2 Playe an enterlude, *farce*. *Ibid.*, Playe of sadde matters, *moralité*. **1542–3** *Act 34 & 35 Hen. VIII*, c. 1 By.. balades, plaies, rimes, songes, and other phantasies, subtilly and craftely instructing his highnes people. **1602** *2nd Pt. Return fr. Parnassus* iv. v. (Arb.) 58 Few of the vniuersity pen plaies well, they smell too much of that writer Ouid,.. and talke too much of Proserpina and Iuppiter. **1712** Steele *Spect.* No. 266 ¶2 A Scene in one of Fletcher's Plays. **1806** R. Cumberland *Mem.* (1807) I. 203, I had no expectation of my play being accepted. **1892** Tennyson in *Mem.* (1897) II. 423, I have just had a letter from a man who wants my opinion as to whether Shakespeare's plays were written by Bacon. I feel inclined to write back, 'Sir, don't be a fool'.

IV. 16. a. Performance on a musical instrument. *rare.* ? *Obs.* (Usually *playing*.)

1297 R. Glouc. (Rolls) 5514 Þere he harpede so wel þat he payde al the route... After mete þo hii nolde nammore of is pley Hii ȝeue him siluer uor is gle, & lete him go is wey. *c* **1407** Lydg. *Reson & Sens.* 1762 In his lifte honde A flowte he helde..Ther with to pipe and make play. **1642** Tasman *Jrnl.* in *Acc. Sev. Late Voy.* i. (1694) 133 The play which they heard was much like that of a Jews-Trump. **1755** Johnson, *Play, n.s.*..8. Act of touching an instrument.

b. The act of playing a gramophone record. *colloq.*

1961 in Webster. **1963** *Guardian* 15 June 3/7 The juke boxes each achieve 800 'plays' a week. **1967** *Melody Maker* 29 Apr. 10/4 It's nice party dance music..but the attention tends to wander after a few plays. **1974** *Listener* 3 Jan. 28/1 About eight records are played on each edition of *Top of the Pops*. That makes for four thousand 'plays' in ten years. **1978** *Oxford Times* (City ed.) 13 Jan. 15 A catchy tune with a sprightly arrangement that might make a hit if it gets enough plays on the radio.

V. 17. *attrib.* and *Comb.*, as (in senses 6–11) *play-activity*, *-area*, *-bell*, *-centre*, *-clothes*, *-form*, *-garden*, *-hole*, *-hour*, *-impulse*, *-instinct*, *-lady*, *-language*, *-matter*, *-park*, *-place*, *-sack*, *-season*, *-shed*, *-song*, *-space*, *-spell*, *-task*, *-theory*, *-toy*, *-world*, *-yard*; † *play idle*, *-ruined*, *-wearied* adjs.; (in senses 14 and 15) *play-conceit*, *-fable*, *-folk*, *-gull*, *-haunter*, *-judger*, *-lover*, *-opera*, *-poem*, *-poet*, *-producer*, *-reader*, *-reading*, *-story*, *-taster*, *-wrecker*, *-writer*; *play-producing* adj.; *play-writing* sb. and adj.; **play-act** *v. intr.*, to act in a play; to be suitable for acting in a play; also *trans.*, to act (a scene, part, etc.); freq. *fig.*, to pretend, make-believe; to behave theatrically or insincerely; **play-acting**, the acting of a play or plays, dramatic performance; also *fig.* and as *ppl. a.*; also (*Sc.*) **play-actor**, an actor of plays, a dramatic performer (= actor 4, player[1] 4); hence **play-actorism**, action or manner characteristic of a play-actor, theatrical or affected style or performance; **play-actoring** *ppl. a.*; **play-actress**, a female actor of plays (= actress 2); **play-bird**, a tame bird used as a decoy for catching wild birds in a net, in connexion with a *play-line* and *play-stick*; **play-bone**, a bone played with: = knuckle-bone 2 b; **play-box**, a box in which a child, esp. at a boarding-school, keeps toys, books, and other personal possessions; also *transf.* and *fig.*; † **play-boy**, a school-boy actor; **playbroker** orig. *U.S.*, an agent who serves as an intermediary between playwrights and managers or actors; **playbus**, a bus adapted for children to play in; **play-by-play** *a.*, denoting a running commentary on a game; also *ellipt.* as *sb.*; **play-card**, (*a*) = play-bill; (*b*) repr. non-standard pronunc. of placard *sb.* 2; **play-club** (*Golf*), a wooden-headed club used in playing the ball off from the tee, a driver; **play-debt**, a debt incurred at play, a gaming debt; **play-doctor**, a professional improver of other people's plays; **play-dough** orig. *U.S.*, a child's modelling clay; † **play-dresser**, one who arranges plays for acting; † **play-end**, an end of a speech from a play, a 'tag'; **play face**, an expression seen in apes or monkeys at play, in which the mouth is open but the teeth are hidden; **play-field**, †(from 14) a field in which a play is acted; (from 10) a field for playing in, a playground; **playfight**, a fight in play; hence **play-fighting** *sb.* and *a.*; **play-green** ? *Obs.*, a piece of land suitable for children to play on; **play-jobber**, a writer of plays for hire; **playland**, an area suitable for recreation; **play-leader**, an adult who leads or helps with children's play; the leader of, or a helper at, a play-group; so **play-leadership**; **play-line**, a line or cord attached to a *play-bird* (q.v.), by means of which it is 'played' or caused to flutter so as to entice other birds into the net; **play-lunch** *Austral.* and *N.Z.*, a snack taken by children to school for eating at playtime; **play-map**, a dissected map for playing with, a puzzle-map; **play-mare** (*Sc.*) = HOBBY-HORSE *sb.* 2; **play-material**, (*a*) material used by children at play; (*b*) (see quot. 1969); **play-method** = *play-way*; **playmobile**, (*a*) (with capital initial) the proprietary name of a type of toy motor vehicle; (*b*) a vehicle containing facilities for a play-group; **play-money**, money won by play or gaming; **play-monger**, a dealer in, i.e. writer of, plays; **play-night**, (*a*) a night on which a play is performed; (*b*) in Jamaica, a night of entertainment in connection with a funeral; **play-party**, (*a*) a party at which a play or plays are performed; (*b*) *U.S. dial.*, a party at which games are played, esp. dancing-games without music; also *attrib.*; **play-pen**, an enclosure in which a young child may play in safety; **play-pretty** *U.S. dial.*, a toy, plaything; **play-right**, the author's proprietary right of performance of a musical or dramatic composition; **playscheme**, a local project offering play facilities for children, esp. during school holidays; **play school**, a nursery-school or kindergarten (orig. *U.S.*); **play-seer**, one who (habitually) sees plays, a playgoer; **play-stick**, a stick upon which a *play-bird* (q.v.) is tied by a loose knot; **play-street**, a street closed to traffic so that children can play in it; **play suit**, (*a*) an actor's costume (*obs. rare*); (*b*) a light, casual outfit; **play-table**, a gaming-table; **play therapy** *Psychol.*, therapy in which emotionally disturbed children are encouraged to act out and express their fantasies and feelings through play, aided by the therapist's interpretations; hence **play therapist**; **play-way**, an educational method which seeks to utilize play; **play-white** *S. Afr.* (see quot. 1956); **playwrite** *v. trans.*, to write in the form or style of a play; **playwriter** = PLAYWRIGHT; **playwriting** *vbl. sb.* See also PLAY-BILL, -BOOK, etc.

1896 G. B. SHAW *Let.* 6 Sept. (1965) I. 650, I always cut myself to the bone, reading the thing over and over until I have discovered the bits that can't be made to *playact anyhow. **1901** N. MUNRO *Doom Castle* iv. 39 Very well pleased at the chance your coming gave him of play-acting the man of war. **1915** F. M. HUEFFER *Good Soldier* III. i. 140 She wished to appear like the heroine of a French comedy.. she was always play-acting. **1938** S. V. BENÉT *Thirteen O'Clock* 321 They had to play-act whatever happened. **1962** I. MURDOCH *Unofficial Rose* xv. 149 Or they might cold-bloodedly have play-acted the scene together, laughing about it afterwards. **1969** *Listener* 5 July 28/2 She wanted more dirty experience: could he not play-act a rapist? **1974** A. PRICE *Other Paths to Glory* II. vi. 190 Most of us were play-acting—pretending to be soldiers. **1857** TROLLOPE *Barchester T.* I. x. 138 Did you ever.. hear anything so like *play-acting as the way in which Mr. Harding sings the litany?.. There must be no more play-acting here. **1873** SYMONDS *Grk. Poets* vii. 184 The habit of play-acting.. never wholly expired. **1875** P. PONDER *Kirkumdoon* 142 Gettin' a vain play-actin' cretur to be oor minister. **1896** E. TERRY *Let.* 4 Dec. in *Ellen Terry & Shaw* (1931) 133 Why don't you both come round after the play up to my room? Mayhap she doesnt like playacting folk? **1903** *Daily Chron.* 16 Oct. 5/2 Elizabeth Inchbald, beloved of playgoers in her day both for her play-writing and her play-acting. **1938** M. ALLINGHAM *Fashion in Shrouds* xi. 175 Georgia was doing no play-acting for Val. They were equals coming down to essentials. **1954** J. R. R. TOLKIEN *Fellowship of Ring* 183 You might be a play-acting spy, for all I can see, trying to get us to go with you. You might have done in the real Strider and took his clothes. **1972** J. BLACKBURN *For Fear of Little Men* iii. 45, I don't give a damn what you do, but I'm tired of play-acting. **1890** W. JAMES *Princ. Psychol.* II. xxiv. 429 The immense extent of the *play-activities in human life is too obvious to be more than mentioned. **1927** G. A. DE LAGUNA *Speech, Its Function & Development* iv. 72 It was the adaptation of the play-activity to the needs of social coordination that was the essential agency in the process [of developing human speech]. **1633** PRYNNE *Histriomastix* **vij b, If any *Play-Actors or Spectators thinke themselves injured by any censure I have here past upon them. **1893** F. F. MOORE *I Forbid Banns* 138 We are more or less play-actors. **1836** J. M. WILSON *Tales of Borders* III. 29 Pittin sic daft-like notions intil a bairn's head as to read *play-actorin books an' novels. **1851** CARLYLE *Sterling* II. vii. 156 Sterling's view of the Pope.. doing his big *play-actorism under God's earnest sky. **1867** —— *Remin.* (1881) II. 187 Our main revenue three or four (?) years now was lectures; .. Detestable mixture of prophecy and play-actorism. **1822** COBBETT *Weekly Reg.* 30 Mar. 773 To those daughters.. he gave a late *play-actress for mother-in-law! **1857** W. COLLINS *Dead Secret* I. i, Did you ever hear that our mistress was a play-actress when our master married her? **1968** *Punch* 13 Mar. 388/3 The day is not far off when all that will be left of unspoilt countryside will be designated '*Play Areas', with good parking and litter facilities and a free issue of blinkers to see what is left of the view. **1979** *Lore & Lang.* Jan. 1 Built before the turn of the century, the two tarmac play areas would nowadays be considered cramped. **1878** M. BROWNE *Pract. Taxidermy* ii. 26 An important actor in the performance is the '*playbird', which is a bird braced by a peculiar knot or 'brace'.. on an arrangement called the playstick. *Ibid.* 27 Directly birds appear, the playline is smartly pulled, which has the effect of jerking the playbird upwards, while at the same time it flutters its wings to regain its perch. This motion is mistaken by the wild birds as a natural proceeding; they accordingly alight around the playbird. **1865** *Boy's Own Mag.* VI. 72/2, I had withdrawn from the school-room to 'the loft',.. a long room above the school, where *play-boxes were deposited. **1882** F. ANSTEY *Vice Versa* v. 103 Let every boarder go down into the box-room and fetch up his playbox, just as it is, and open it here before me. **1909** (*title*) The play-box, a picture reading book for little folks. **1923** GALSWORTHY *Captures* 56, I had taken them out of my playbox, together with the photographs of my parents and eldest sister. **1929** W. DEEPING *Roper's Row* viii. 80 At her aunt's in Vane Street she had an attic which she called her studio, a young woman's play-box, and all that she knew she had taught herself by drawing things and yet more things. *Ibid.* xxi. 234 For, to Ruth Avery, No. 7 Roper's Row was a child's play-box, and much more than that—for it was the first playbox of her very own that she had possessed. **1949** I. COMPTON-BURNETT *Two Worlds & their Ways* iv. 143 Here is the key of your playbox, Bacon. **1972** *Even. Telegram* (St. John's, Newfoundland) 23 June 3/1 When they tolerate a bunch of dandies sitting in that fancy playbox on.. New Gower Street? **1630** B. JONSON *New Inn* I. i, Pretty boy! Goes he to school?.. He prates Latin, An it were a parrot, or a *play-boy. **1910** *N.Y. Dramatic Mirror* 12 Mar. 9/4 Practically all of the new playwrights have been discovered by *play-brokers. **1929** *Evening News* 9 Jan. 11/2 Major James Clare, a leading playbroker, who is also a dramatist. **1975** *Village* Winter 85 This interesting *playbus experiment in Cumbria... The provision of holiday play facilities for village children. **1976** *Ann. Rep. Manpower Services Comm. 1975–76* iii. 23/2 On Merseyside, young people are working with craftsmen to convert buses into playbuses. **1927** *Amer. Speech* II. 241/2 The football extra, containing a '*play by play' story of all but the last few minutes, is locked on the press with a hole left in the plate. **1931** F. L. ALLEN *Only Yesterday* viii. 207 Thousands more sat in warm living-rooms to hear the play-by-play story over the radio. **1966** J. BALL *Cool Cottontail* (1967) x. 101 He turned on the radio and listened to a play-by-play of the California Angels. **1976** *Times Lit. Suppl.* 2 Jan. 13/3 The bulk of the book is given over to what looks like a play-by-play account of Hegel's thought. **1976** *Billings* (Montana) *Gaz.* 17 June 1-H/4 Announcers Lane Saunders and Bernie Lustig will provide the color and play-by-play, and a variety of guests will be lined up for half-time interviews. **1979** D. ANTHONY *Long Hard Cure* ix. 89, I began giving him a play by play of the events of Friday night. **1881** P. FITZGERALD *World behind Scenes* IV. 268 The Court Theatre, the Princesses, and the St. James have adopted square cards of a pale blue tint—an abnormal and inconvenient form. In the instance of the first-named house it is folded diagonally, it is a *play card, and no longer a bill. **1934** T. S. ELIOT *Rock* i. 40 On Christmas Day we can organize a Anti-God procession.. with playcards an' ex'ibitions exposin' all the dope o' Christianity. **1908** *Westm. Gaz.* 1 Feb. 7/3 The *play-centres, far from tending to diminish the influence of home life, actually made the children appreciate it more. **1914** *Encycl. Relig. & Ethics* VII. 363/2 The 'play-centre', where, outside school hours, children who have no play-ground but the street, are taught organized games. **1936** G. M. YOUNG *Victorian England* ix. 60 The Mechanics' Institutes.. sank into play-centres for serious clerks. **1973** *Daily Tel.* 6 July 2/1 More than 80 London play centres are to be opened during the school summer holidays where children can play games, watch television, paint or read. **1919** *Ladies' Home Jrnl.* Mar. 62 Turn kids out in.. *Play Clothes—and let them play. **1959** *Times* 26 Jan. 11/1 Wit in styling, good fabrics and lovely colours are what the designers of 'play' clothes usually offer. **1971** *Times Lit. Suppl.* 20 Aug. 990/2 Japanese are not the only ones to feel irritation when they see elderly American tourists in gaudy 'play clothes' cavorting in Tokyo as if it were another Honolulu. **1857** *Chambers' Inform. People* II. 693/2 The *play-club is for swiping off the tee, and is further used throughout the green if the ball is lying fair, and the distance more than a full drive from the hole you are approaching. **1673** [R. LEIGH] *Transp. Reh.* 22 This we took for a *play-conceit ill transpros'd. **1712** ADDISON *Spect.* No. 295 She has several *Play-debts on her Hand, which must be discharged very suddenly. **1760** FOOTE *Minor* I. Wks. 1799 I. 241 They wou'd as soon now-a days pay a tradesman's bill, as a play debt. **1887** *Spectator* 8 Oct. 1333 Agreements .. they would regard as Englishmen regard play-debts. **1922, 1938** *Play doctor [see DOCTOR *sb.* 6 c]. **1967** P. MCGERR *Murder is Absurd* ii. 32 A play doctor was brought in to rework Rex's unfinished script. **1978** I. B. SINGER *Shosha* vii. 128 In America we have men who are called play doctors. They can't write a line themselves, but somehow they know how to rearrange a piece and make it right for the stage. **1959** J. FOSTER *Educ. in Kindergarten* (ed. 3) xi. 176 Clay, plasticine, *play dough, sawdust and paste,.. all afford the child the opportunity to make a three-dimensional impression of one sort or another. **1969** B. RYAN *Your Child & First Year of School* iii. 56 Play dough, if it is made from scratch from salt, flour, water, and perhaps a little alum powder as a preservative, gives an even broader experience of chemistry before little fingers begin to manipulate it. **1970** G. R. TAYLOR *Doomsday* vi. 126 Asbestos powder mixed with water is even given to children, in some schools, as play-dough. **1977** C. MCFADDEN *Serial* xi. 29/2 She was standing at the sink digging the play-dough out of her demitasse cups. **1601** B. JONSON *Poetaster* v. iii. 225 Arraigned vpon the Statute of Calumny.. by the name of Demetrivs Fannivs, *play-dresser and plagiary. [Cf. III. iv. 339 One Demetrivs, a dresser of plaies about the towne.] **1599** —— *Cynthia's Rev.* IV. i, Letting this gallant expresse himselfe.. with *play-ends and pittifull verses. **1868** MILMAN *St. Paul's* xi. 313 The indecencies of their heathenish and idolatrous *play-fables. **1962** J. A. R. A. M. VAN HOOFF in *Symp. Zool. Soc.* No. 8. 120 (*heading*) The Play Face. *Ibid.* 121 Suddenly one of the partners may.. show the *play face in the direction of the other who will immediately react by resuming the play. **1966** R. & D. MORRIS *Men & Apes* vi. 213 The play face.. is performed by a number of species during vigorous bouts of playful wrestling and tumbling and is particularly obvious in young chimpanzees. **1971** J. VAN LAWICK-GOODALL *In Shadow of Man* ix. 99 He opened his mouth in the play-face or chimpanzee smile. **1973** *Observer* (Colour Suppl.) 16 Dec. 32/2 Certain facial expressions are also used [by monkeys to establish friendship with one another], such as the 'playface'—a smile with teeth covered. **1977** SAVAGE & RUMBAUGH in D. M. Rumbaugh *Language Learning by Chimpanzees* xvi. 300 A playface given with vocal laughter and head-covering can be used as a signal to continue tickling. **1568** *Bannatyne Poems* (Hunter. Cl.) 463 Heir begynnis the Proclamatioun of the Play, made be Dauid Lynsayis, of the Month, Knicht in the *Playfeild. **1883** BESANT *All in Garden Fair* (1886) 22 This forest play-field. **1922** JOYCE *Ulysses* 442 An armless pair of them flop wrestling, growling, in maimed sodden *playfight. **1932** S. ZUCKERMAN *Social Life Monkeys & Apes* xvii. 277 The *play-fighting activities and bodily examinations continued intermittently. **1953** *Psychological Rev.* LX. 293/1 Among the social interactions there were a few instances of serious aggression, many occurrences of bluffing or exhibitionistic behavior, a great deal of play-fighting, wrestling, [etc.]. **1764** FOOTE *Patron* III. Wks. 1799 I. 354 The words the *playfolk were talking. **1911** J. A. THOMSON *Biology of Seasons* II. 224 For the endless task of finding out about the world has its *play-form—which is obviously one of the roots of science. **1963** G. J. MCCALL in A. Dundes *Mother Wit* (1973) 425 As has happened with so many play-forms of games.. it has become a 'multi-situated game', requiring a vast proliferation of goals, roles, and strategies. **1916** A. S. NEILL *Dominie Dismissed* xiii. 153 The attraction of a *play-garden school with its charms of social intercourse. *c* **1650** *Lillumwham* in Hales & Furnivall *Bishop Percy's Folio MS.* (1867) *Loose & Humorous Songs* 98 Other three on won *play greene. **1800** M. EDGEWORTH *Parent's Assistant* (ed. 3) II. 178 All the children.. were assembled in the play-green. **1812** —— *Absentee* in *Tales Fashionable Life* VI. ix. 131 He went to the village school—a pretty, cheerful house, with a neat garden and a play-green. **1610** *Histrio-m.* II. 308 Give your *play-gull a stool, and my lady her fool, And her Usher potatos and marrow. **1634** *Documents agst. Prynne* (Camden) 49 It speakes onely of the expenses of common *play-haunters at publike playes and theatres. **1880** CARNEGIE *Pract. Trap.* 8 The traps will have to be set in the runs and about the *play-holes (*i.e.*, burrows only used, as their name implies, for playing or for use during the day). **1741** RICHARDSON *Pamela* IV. lxiv. 454 The Misses at their Books too, or their Needles; except at their *Play-hours, when they were never rude, nor noisy. **1857** HUGHES *Tom Brown* Pref. (1871) 11 His play-hours are occupied in fagging. **1925** BLUNDEN *English Poems* 19 And blushed for pride when other girls and boys Laughed at us sweethearts in the playhour's noise. **1890** W. JAMES *Princ. Psychol.* II. xxiv. 427 The sexes differ somewhat in their *play-impulses. **1927** W. E. COLLINSON *Contemp. Eng.* 127 The English play-impulse has certainly produced some remarkable forms. **1896** W. JAMES *Will to Believe* (1897) 23 Mephistophelian scepticism.. will satisfy the head's *play-instincts much better than any vigorous idealism can. **1897** T. RIBOT *Psychol. of Emotions* II. 198 The play-instinct, if we use this word to designate the tendency to expend superfluous activity.. is a stock which puts forth several branches. **1899** *Westm. Gaz.* 4 Sept. 2/1 Melodrama written by the most adroit *play-jobber of our times. **1672** LACY *Dumb Lady* Prol., Though such things pass on those that sermons hear, It will not do with *play-judgers, I fear. **1966** *New Statesman* 24 June 923/3 There is a '*play lady'.. who spends her whole time seeing to the personal interests and difficulties of the children in the wards. **1976** *Amer. Speech 1973* XLVIII. 208 At RT, he will meet *play ladies*, not to be confused with those in peds, but ones specially trained to teach physical activities. **1946** *Sun* (Baltimore) 26 Apr. 11/4 Baltimore is to be tied into schedules into the *playland of Michigan, bringing PCA flights out of the local airport to fourteen daily. **1974** *Sat. Rev. World* (U.S.) 2 Nov. 8/2 Cyprus.. would be.. a Mediterranean playland. **1977** *Time* 4 July 28/2 Remembering the rapacious play-lands of the past, where gambling, boozing and whoring were as rife as popcorn and pizza, most theme parks promote soft drinks and fast foods. **1934** O. JESPERSEN *Language* 149 Children.. at first employ *play language for its own sake. **1907** *Westm. Gaz.* 29 Aug. 3/1 A pressing need is for trained *play-leaders who know how to play games and to organise the interests of children in ways that build the body and character as well. **1953** Play leader [see *adventure playground* s.v. ADVENTURE *sb.* 10]. **1970** *Guardian* 14 May 11/4 Two mothers volunteered to take a play-leaders' course. **1975** *New Society* 18 Sept. 632/2 The Chells adventure playground, which is very large and has three full-time playleaders. *Ibid.* 13 Nov. 393/2 (Advt.), The successful applicant will be required to give general assistance within the *Playleadership service. **1977** *Time Out* 28 Jan.–3 Feb. 53/1 (Advt.), Applicants, male or female, should be able to demonstrate experience in these areas, preferably within playleadership. **1878** *Play-line [see *play-bird*]. **1962** *N.Z. Listener* 27 July 39/1 Children like to take the special little packets [of raisins and sultanas] to school for their *playlunch. **1963** E. SPENCE *Green Laurel* ix. 109 She was not hungry enough to go back for her play-lunch, and to stay close to the class-room appeared to be the safest thing to do. **1974** *Age* (Melbourne) 12 Oct. 12/5 *Play lunch*, emergency rations for morning recess, usually being a piece of fruit, cake or some chocolate crackles. **1825** COLERIDGE *Aids Refl.* (1848) I. 16 Draw lines of different colours round the different counties.. and then cut out each separately, as in the common *play-maps that children take to pieces and put together. **1820** SCOTT *Abbot* xiv, Here one fellow.. performed the celebrated part of the hobby-horse, so often alluded to in our ancient drama. *Note*, This exhibition, the *play-mare of Scotland, stood high among holyday gambols. **1943** H. READ *Educ. through Art* v. 158 For example, in analysing the quantitative differences in the kinds of *play-material used by children of age groups from 4 to 8, Dr. van Wylick found that.. the use of human beings could not be related to the progressive age-groups. **1969** E. AMBLER *Intercom Conspiracy* (1970) ii. 39 'Play material' was the jargon phrase used to describe the low-grade classified information fed back to the enemy through double agents.

1971 D. O'Connor *Eye of Eagle* xxii. 154 There'll be stretches on this tape with nothing on them but a lengthy silence. You could fill them in, if you wanted, with play material. 1581 Sidney *Apol. Poetrie* (Arb.) 67, I haue lauished out too many wordes of this *play matter. 1914 H. C. Cook (*title*) First-fruits of the *play method in prose. 1961 in *Amer. Speech* (1964) XXXIX. 79 *Playmobile. 1963 *Official Gaz.* (U.S. Patent Off.) 21 May TM 148/1 DeLuxe Reading Corporation, Newark, N.J. *Playmobile* for toy miniature automobiles. First use Feb. 20, 1961. 1971 *Guardian* 16 Dec. 11/1 A children's playgroup in a converted double-decker bus?.. The Playmobile will penetrate the drab streets of slumland. 1973 *Times* 25 July 13/2, I feel we should also provide the opportunity for the community to have far greater involvement in concern for others. Involvement such as taking playmobiles round to all our caravan sites. 1979 *Trade Marks Jrnl.* 4 July 1134/1 *Playmobil*... Toys having movable parts. Geobra Brandstätter GmbH & Co. K.G...Zirndorf..Germany; manufacturers and merchants.—17th March 1978. 1705 Vanbrugh *Confed.* I. iii, *Play-money..amongst people of quality, is a sacred thing, and not to be profaned. 1593 G. Harvey *Pierce's Super.* Wks. (Grosart) II. 132 A professed iester, a Hick-scorner, a scoff-maister, a *playmunger, an Interluder. 1885 *Manch. Exam.* 9 Apr. 5/4 A miserable poverty of invention on the part of the playmonger. 1755 C. Charke *Life* 103 Those Assailants of Liberty..constantly attended every *Play-Night there. 1786 J. Woodforde *Diary* 6 Apr. (1926) II. 238 It being Play Night we went to the Theatre. 1849 *Theatrical Programme* 2 July 43/1 His Majesty [*sc.* George II]..was pleased to order that the Guards should in future do duty every playnight, which custom has not yet been dispensed with. 1961 D. De Camp in R. B. Le Page *Creole Language Studies* II. iv. 72 Plie-nait. 1937 *Sun* (Baltimore) 12 Apr. 5/3 'The Second Hurricane' is neither grand nor light opera, and somebody had to think up a name for it. This turned out to be '*play opera'. 1954 *Grove's Dict. Music* (ed. 5) VIII. 125/2 The two other works of this period are the ballet-pantomime 'Schlagobers'.., and the autobiographical play-opera 'Intermezzo', for which Strauss wrote his own libretto. 1971 P. Young in J. Spencer *Eng. Lang. W. Afr.* 183 The dramatised version of *The Palm Wine Drinkard* was published in English originally, but performed as a play-opera in Yoruba at Ibadan. 1962 *Guardian* 31 Oct. 6/5 The *playparks are a welcome addition to the other nursery facilities. 1964 *Ibid.* 30 Oct. 6/6 The number of play parks where children can 'let off steam' is to be increased after the Greater London Council takes over next year. 1977 *Cork Examiner* 6 June 1/8 In the past proceeds have gone to specific projects such as the building of a social room, gymnasium facilities, play park and equipment etc. 1879 L. Troubridge *Jrnl.* June in J. Hope-Nicholson *Life amongst Troubridges* (1966) 152 Met Amy and had quite a gay visit to Abbey Lodge, doing lots of plays. Uncle Hay failed us for a *play party. 1902 *Dialect Notes* II. 241 *Play-party*, a party at which old-fashioned games are played. 1912 I. S. Cobb *Back Home* 44 Strict church members..wouldn't let their children..go to any parties except play parties. 1926 M. D. Lake in J. F. Dobie *Rainbow in Morning* (1965) 109 Parties of various kinds were indulged in at Christmas... Dominoes, candy pulls, corn poppings, play-parties, and dancing furnished additional amusement. 1937 B. A. Botkin *Amer. Play-Party Song* I. i. 16 The play-party..was a rural American social gathering for playing games, distinguished by the manner in which it was 'got up', by the age of its participants, and by the character of the games played. 1938 [see caller *sb.* 1 e]. 1968 P. Oliver *Screening Blues* i. 31 It might be said..that the blues singer rejoices in his folk-songs—his dance songs, play-party and game songs, ballads and stomps. 1973 Schafer & Riedel *Art of Ragtime* i. 13 This 'play-party' country ragtime style is of great age and hardiness. 1931 *Daily Express* 21 Sept. 7/5 (Advt.), Well built *play-pens in best hard-wood. 1940 J. Betjeman *Old Lights for New Chancels* 47 White o'er the play pen the sheen of her dress. 1967 N. Freeling *Strike Out* 81 A child's playpen stood folded against the wall. 1972 J. Wilson *Hide & Seek* ii. 35 Jean picked Jamie out of the playpen and sat with him on her lap. 1976 W. H. Canaway *Willow-Pattern War* xiii. 136 A set of beads on wires, a bit similar to the set I'd had on my play-pen when I'd been smaller. 1781 Cowper *Charity* 538 Perhaps the man..had no other *play-place for his wit. 1884 J. Colborne *Hicks Pasha* 188 The river and its banks are the play-place of the crocodile. 1625 Bacon *Ess., Envy* (Arb.) 512 It must needs be, that he taketh a kinde of *plaie-pleasure, in looking vpon the Fortunes of others. 1907 *Daily Chron.* 17 May 3/7 A soulful little French *play-poem, Coppée's 'Le Passant'. 1928 V. Woolf *Writer's Diary* 7 Nov. (1953) 137 Yes, but *The Moths*? That was to be an abstract mystical eyeless book: a playpoem. 1977 *Times Lit. Suppl.* 4 Feb. 123/1 Virginia Woolf described *The Waves* as a 'playpoem'. She was conscious of the hazards of poetic fiction, the dangers of uncontrolled fantasy, and wanted to minimize these by assimilating to prose fiction the structural tightness and compression of drama. 1633 Prynne *Histriomastix* (title-p.), Wherein it is..evidenced..that the profession of *Play-poets, of Stage Players; together with the penning, acting, and frequenting of Stage-playes, are unlawfull, infamous and misbeseeming Christians. 1905 *Dialect Notes* III. 90 The children want some *play-pretties for Christmas. 1929 W. Faulkner *Sound & Fury* 36 Aint you shamed of yourself. Taking a baby's play pretty. 1935 R. Bass in A. Dundes *Mother Wit* (1973) 395 On the graves of little children are placed some play-pretties, little doll heads, small cups, or toy animals. 1942 J. Thomas *Blue Ridge Country* 160 The children's play-pretties—the poppet, a make-believe corn-shuck doll. 1976 *Publ. Amer. Dial. Soc. 1973* LX. 17 One..called it [*sc.* a toy] *a pretty*, another *a play-pretty*. 1913 *Writer's Mag.* Dec. 253/1 For we are now in an era wherein the *play-producer is on the alert for the young and virile writer. 1908 *Daily Chron.* 19 May 1/6 Several uncommercial *play-producing societies..had done..good work recently. 1968 *Daily Tel.* 4 Nov. 9/5 And so we come back to the independent, unsubsidised play-producing companies. 1711 Shaftesb. *Charact.* (1737) III. 289 To do justice to our *play readers, they seldom fail to humour our poets in this respect. 1922 Play-reader [see doctor *sb.* 6 c]. 1969 L. Hellman *Unfinished Woman* v. 53, I worked as a play reader for Anne Nichols,..who wanted to become a producer. 1913 F. H. Burnett *T. Tembarom* xix. 244 On still another evening they tried Shakespeare. He found *play-reading difficult and Shakespearian language baffling. 1935 N. Mitchison *We have been Warned* II. 154 The next pupil was late... 'Sorry,' he said, 'it was the play-reading society.' 1968 J. Haythorne *None of us cared for Kate* 61 We do try in our small way to keep the torch of culture flickering. Are you fond of play-reading? 1972 D. H. Laurence *Bernard Shaw: Coll. Lett. 1898–1910* 4 [Shaw]..joined Grant Allen and other neighbours in a play-reading society. 1891 Martineau in *Law Times* XC. 250/1 A musical composition, the copyright and *play-right of which had expired by effluxion of time. 1696 *Pol. Ballads* (1860) II. 55 For converts and bullys, And *play-ruin'd cullys. 1970 *Daily Progress* (Charlottesville, Va.) 21 Mar. c2/5 If the age group is 4 to 10,..*playsacks..are imaginative animal costumes that slip on easily. 1972 *Where* Apr. 104/2 There were in fact something over 400 playschemes in England and Wales last summer. 1975 *Village* Winter 83 You would have been looking at Cumbria's first mobile playscheme. 1935 *Sun* (Baltimore) 15 July 7/3 Three children's '*play schools' scheduled here were canceled. 1959 C. V. Good *Dict. Educ.* (ed. 2) 402/2 *Play school*,..an organized experience usually lasting for a short time to provide opportunities for high school and college students to observe and work with a small group of young children in a supervised situation. 1964 S. Bellow *Herzog* 267 I'm picking June up at noon tomorrow. She goes to a play school, half-days. 1973 *Times* 7 Mar. 10/3 Whoever coined the term 'play school' captured perfectly the ideal concept for the young child. 1977 D. MacKenzie *Raven & Kamikaze* iv. 49 The babble of children came from the open windows of the play school. 1713 Addison *Guard.* No. 120 ⁋3 The day lies heavy upon her until the *play-season returns. 1637 J. Rutter *Cid* To Rdr. (1650) 4 This age consists of such *Play-seers. 1906 *Macmillan's Mag.* Nov. 19 Rooms for the teachers and for the permanent staff, a covered *play-shed, and all the outside accessories. 1932 *Times Educ. Suppl.* 20 Aug. 318/1 Playsheds can as a rule be omitted, but inexpensive bicycle sheds may be advisable and serve as shelters for the children against rainstorms. 1898 J. C. Harris *Tales of Home Folks in Peace & War* 19 The negroes made the night melodious with their *play-songs. 1924 G. Parkes in M. W. Beckwith *Jamaica Anansi Stories* 110 Massah, me kyan' stop him singing, because it mus' of been his little play-song what he have singing. 1959 I. & P. Opie *Lore & Lang. Schoolch.* i. 3 The same continuity obtains in their games and play songs. 1958 *Times* 30 Aug. 7/4 The whole of the underside of the tall block is planned as a covered paved *play space. 1959 [see bed-sitting-room]. 1974 *Listener* 7 Mar. 296/3 Families..live around courtyards, half of which serve..as play-spaces for children. 1976 *Ilkeston Advertiser* 10 Dec. 10/3 The parents..told Broxtowe District Council about the lack of play space for children on Broad Oak Drive estate. 1845 S. Judd *Margaret* II. i. 186 And her own *play-spell comes, if, indeed, her whole life were not a play-spell. 1861 L. L. Noble *Icebergs* 295 Allowed a play-spell, perhaps a long yellow holdiay. 1878 *Play-stick [see *play-bird*]. 1858 Lytton *What will he do* I. iii, He contrived to cut up that *play-story. 1937 C. V. Godfrey *Roadsense for Children* viii. 64 Closing certain lesser thoroughfares to vehicular traffic and reserving them for the exclusive use of children..is how *Play Streets came into being. 1968 *Guardian* 25 Apr. 7/6 Some local authorities label streets as play streets when they have not enough money for playgrounds. 1977 *Wandsworth Borough News* 7 Oct. 14/5 It was a 'playstreet' with bollards to prevent all traffic, where children could safely play under the eyes of their parents. 1609 T. Dekker *Guls Horne-Booke* vi. 29 By sitting on the stage, you may..examine the *play-suits lace. 1908 *Sears, Roebuck Catal.* 529/1 Play Suits. 1936 *New Yorker* 7 Mar. 64/1 Crisp, wearable and washable shirt-waist dresses, play suits, shorts, slacks, and skirts. 1942 *Capital* 3 Feb. 5/6 (*caption*) Ilyana Yankwich wearing a California-made playsuit; it's in vivid green and brown tones with a gay leaf motif. 1959 *New Statesman* 26 Sept. 384/2 Unguents, oils, special sun-bathing attire, bikinis and play-suits..have become big business. 1963 Playsuit [see Garbo¹]. 1848 Thackeray *Van. Fair* lxv, The day after the meeting at the *play-table. 1905 *Macm. Mag.* Dec. 102 The enormous extent of Fox's transactions at the play-tables is of course recorded. 1925 I. A. Richards *Princ. Lit. Crit.* 233 The objection to the *Play Theory..lies in its suggestion that the experiences of Art are in some way incomplete, that they are substitutes. 1960 C. Winick *Dict. Anthropol.* 535/2 *Play theory*, the theory that fine art is produced independently of the struggle for existence and that the imagination is exercised for the sake of the sense of freedom (Schiller), or power (Groos), or for conscious self-deception (Lange). 1942 *Brit. Jrnl. Psychol.* Jan. 262 A direct interpretation given to the child of the meaning of his play should be undertaken only..by the experienced *play therapist. 1963 A. Heron *Towards Quaker View of Sex* 49 The child may have treatment with a play therapist. 1939 *Psychol. Abstr.* XIII. 111/1 The author believes that active *play therapy offers rapid diagnostic and therapeutic assistance in the emotional problems of childhood. 1948 L. Kanner *Child Psychiatry* (ed. 2) xvii. 244 'Play therapy' thus becomes a form of participation, a means to an end, rather than an isolated technique. 1961 A. Huxley *Let.* 8 Jan. (1969) 903 One can imagine a genuinely realistic treatment of the mentally ill..by work and play therapy. 1978 M. T. Erickson *Child Psychopathol.* x. 225 Traditional clinicians have offered an array of treatments to children with learning disabilities: psychoanalysis,..play therapy, and group therapy. 1935 Z. N. Hurston *Mules & Men* 19 I'll put this *play toy in his hand, and he will seize it and go away. Then I'll say my say and sing my song. 1914 H. C. Cook *First-Fruits of Play Method* 52 The boys do not object to learning anything, so long as they may do it in the *Play way. 1920 T. P. Nunn *Education* viii. 92 Members of a rapidly growing company of pioneers..are all busily engaged in exploring the 'play-way' of teaching the several subjects of the curriculum. 1973 *Times* 13 Jan. 12/3 Nephew X, proud of himself for being tough with his daughter over the cello lessons, dismisses all this 'play-way' approach to education as a lot of soft nonsense. 1832 [R. Cattermole] *Beckett*, etc. 191 Sunk to rest Like a *play-wearied child. 1956 A. Sampson *Drum* xv. 205 Harry was only one of thousands of '*play-whites', as they call the light-skinned Coloureds who 'pass for white' and break away from the Coloured world. 1909 *Daily Chron.* 13 Dec. 3/4 Nature's kingdom is not all a reign of tooth and claw, but a *play-world also. 1915 D. H. Lawrence *Rainbow* xi. 264 The religion, which had been another world for her, a glorious sort of play-world. 1962 W. Nowottny *Lang. Poets Use* iv. 89 This realization is articulated most clearly at the climax of the passage..and so too is the sense of the irruption into his play-world of intractable segments of reality. 1978 I. B. Singer *Shosha* vii. 135 There is no reason why hedonism, the cabala, polygamy, asceticism, even our friend Haiml's blend of eroticism and Hasidism could not exist in a play-city or play-world. 1901 *Chambers's Jrnl.* Aug. 545/2 Organised *play-wreckers, who without uttering a word or an unseemly laugh have succeeded in destroying whatever chance of success a play may have had. 1949 *Sat. Rev. Lit.* (U.S.) 24 Dec. 24/3 One of the unique and beckoning characteristics of his plays was that they were written no less than *playwritten. 1644 Milton *Educ.* Wks. (1847) 101/1 This would make them..perceive what despicable creatures our common rhimers and *playwriters be. 1766 Fordyce *Serm. Yng. Wom.* (1767) I. iv. 155 The common herd of Play-writers. 1872 W. L. Collins *Aristophanes* iii. 41 To win the verdict of popular applause, which was the great aim of an Athenian play-writer, he must above all things hit the popular taste. 1903 W. B. Yeats *Let.* 27 July (1954) 408, I suppose every playwriter finds out the methods that suit him best. 1809 Malkin *Gil Blas* vii. xiii. ⁋9 [He] exercised his genius at one time in sonnets or ballads, at another in *play-writing. 1898 G. B. Shaw *Plays Unpleasant* Pref. p. v, I made a rough memorandum for my own guidance that unless I could produce at least half a dozen plays before I was forty, I had better let playwriting alone. 1935 *Discovery* May 130/2 Historical playwriting has had considerable vogue. 1959 *Times* 24 Oct. 9/2 *Pursue the Dry Stubble*, the winning entry in the playwriting competition organized by the Tower Theatre, was given the first of six performances there last night. 1976 *Radio Times* 27 Mar.–2 Apr. 37/1 Sir Terence Rattigan looks back over 40 years of playwriting from *French without Tears* to *Cause Celèbre*. 1960 J. J. Rowlands *Spindrift* iii. 186 One particularly important question was whether the *play-yard in Heaven was equipped with an old dory with a mast and sail. 1973 *Jrnl. Genetic Psychol.* Sept. 160 Assertive behavior is a relatively stable characteristic of the preschool child, a characteristic which he brings to many situations and which can be seen even in 15 minutes in the play yard.

play (pleɪ), *v.* Forms: α. 1 pleᵹ(i)an, (pleoᵹ-), *Angl.* plæᵹian; 2–5 pleie, 3 plaiȝen, plæie, 3–5 pleiȝe, pleyȝe, 3–6 pley(e, 4–7 plai(e, playe, 4– play, (6 plee). β. 1 *Angl.* plaᵹian, pleaᵹ(i)an, 3 plaȝe, 4–6 plaw(e, 6 *Sc.* pla, 7–9 *dial.* plaw. γ. 2–3 ploȝe(n, 3 pleoȝe, pleowe, pleuwe. Pa. t. and pple. played: pa. t. 1 pleᵹode, -ede, -ade, pleoᵹede; plaᵹade, pleaᵹade; plæᵹde, plæᵹede. Pa. t. and pa. pple. often contracted; pa. t. 3–5 pleide, 4–5 pleyde, *Sc.* plait, 4–8 plaid, 6 playd, pled, *Sc.* plade, 7 plaide; pa. pple. 4 pleide, 6–7 playd, 6–8 plaid. [OE. *pleᵹan, -ean, -ian, plaᵹian, plæᵹian*, corresp. to MDu. *pleyen, pleien, playen* to dance, leap for joy, rejoice, be glad (Verwijs and Verdam). As to its relation to OS. *plegan*, Du. *plegen*, Ger. *pflegen* 'to have the care of, take charge of, attend to, cultivate', 'to be in the habit of, to be wont or accustomed to', see below. The OE. verb is recorded in several diverging forms, so that it is difficult to determine its original type and the conjugation to which it belonged. The usual WSax. form *pleᵹian* gave ME. *pleie(n*, later *plaie(n, play*; the OE. *plaᵹian* in Anglian texts gave the northern *plawe, plaw*. The γ forms in 2–3 *pleoȝe, ploȝe, pleowe, pleuwe* appear to mix the two.

The primary senses under each of the following branches were already in OE., and the order of their development is more or less inferential; but all the uses of 'play' are seen to arise naturally from a primary notion 'to exercise, bestir, or busily occupy oneself', the line of development having been here determined by the recreative or divertive purpose of the exercise. In the miners' 'play', the sense of exercise or busy occupation disappears, and the word (sense 15; cf. play *sb.* 13) comes to mean 'to cease work, to be idle'. The same primary notion, developed in quite a different line, accounts for the continental senses of *plegen, pflegen*, 'to have care of, take kindly charge of, cultivate', and 'to be in the practice or habit of', notions which evidently imply occupying oneself busily about a thing or person, and habitually exercising oneself in an action.]

I. To exercise oneself, act or move energetically; actuate, exercise (a craft, etc.).

†**1. a.** *intr.* To exercise or occupy oneself, bestir one's self, be busily engaged; to act, operate, work. *Obs.* exc. with allusion to other senses.

*c*960 *Laws Edgar* c. 64 (Thorpe *Laws* II. 258) We læraþ ðæt preost ne beo hunta ne hafecere ne tæflere ac pleᵹe on his bocum. 971 *Blickl. Hom.* 85 Þis is se ilca þe þu longe for his deaþe pleᵹodest. 1377 Langl. *P. Pl.* B. iii. 307 Eche man to pleye with a plow pykoys or spade. 1481 Caxton *Myrr.* ii. xxiv. 116 [The air] susteyneth the byrdes fleeyng that so playe with their wynges and meue them so moche al aboute therin that they disporte them..therin. 1484 —— *Fables of Æsop* v. v, Now shalle we see who shalle playe best for to preserue and saue hym self. 1581 Savile *Tacitus, Agricola* (1622) 194 Agricola hauing vnderstood by spies what way the enemies had taken..commandeth the lightest horsemen and footmen to play on their backes and maintaine the skirmish. *a*1586 Sidney *Ps.* xlii. i, So my soul in panting playeth, Thirsting on my God to look. 1646 Sir T. Browne *Pseud. Ep.* i. x. (1686) 28 There is an invisible Agent,..who plays in the dark upon us. 1677 Temple *Wks.* (1731) II. 453 Thus I believe that Affair plays at present. 1883 Romanes *Ment. Evol. Anim.* iii. 34 There is no doubt that the hemispheres are able to 'play down' upon these ganglia as upon so many mechanisms.

†**b.** To clap with the hands; also *trans.* to clap (the hands). *Obs.*

*c*825 *Vesp. Psalter* xlvi. 2 Alle ðiode plaᵹiað mid hondum [*omnes gentes plaudite manibus*]. *Ibid.* xcvii. 8 Flodas plæᵹiað mid hondum [*flumina plaudent manibus*]. *a* **1000** *Elene* 806 (Gr.) He mid bæm handum eadiȝ and æȝleaw upweard pleȝade. *a* **1300** *E.E. Psalter* xcvii[i]. 8 Stremes sal plaie handes, samen. *a* **1325** *Prose Psalter* xlvi[i]. 1 ȝe alle folk, plaieþ wyþ hondes; gladeþ to God in voice of ioie. *a* **1340** HAMPOLE *Psalter* xlvi. 1 All genge playes with hend.

c. To strut, dance, or otherwise display itself, as a cock bird before the hens. Also ***play up***.

1765 *Treat. Dom. Pigeons* 4 Cocks will often play to, and disturb the others as they sit. *Ibid.*, Allowing eighteen inches between shelf and shelf, that powters may not be under the necessity of stooping for want of height, for in that case they would contract an habit of playing low, which spoils their carriage. **1768** G. WHITE *Selborne* xvi. (1853) 68 In breeding time the snipes play over the moors, piping and humming. **1892** *Cornh. Mag.* July 37, I have put black-cock up here many years ago, one of my woodland friends having invited me over to see them play up.

2. a. *intr.* Of living beings: To move about swiftly, with a lively, irregular, or capricious motion; to spring, fly, or dart to and fro; to gambol, frisk; to flit, flutter.

a **900** *Andreas* 370 (Gr.) Hornfisc pleȝode, glæd ȝeond garsecg. *a* **1000** *Cædmon's Gen.* 724 (Gr.) Swa hit him on innan com, hran æt heortan, hloh þa & pleȝode bode bitre ȝehuȝod. *c* **1200** *Trin. Coll. Hom.* 127 Þat child on his blisse witeȝede; for hit floxede, and pleide to-ȝenes hire. *a* **1225** *Ancr. R.* 94 Auh ancren..schulen..lihture beon & swifture & ine so wide scheakeles pleien ine heouene. *c* **1275** LAY. 26941 And hit gan to daȝeȝe And þe deor to pleoye. *a* **1300** *Cursor M.* 23342 On sunni dai To se fixs in a water plai. *a* **1310** in Wright *Lyric P.* xiv. 45 In May hit murȝeth when hit dawes, In dounes with this dueres plawes. **1611** BIBLE *Job* xl. 20 Surely the mountaines bring him foorth foode: where all the beasts of the field play. **1667** MILTON *P.L.* VII. 410 On smooth the Seale And bended Dolphins play. **1767** G. WHITE *Selborne* 9 Sept. (1853) 29 Bats drink on the wing ..by sipping the surface, as they play over pools and streams. **1869** THIRLWALL *Lett.* (1881) II. 209 He played about them like a bee, only to take in honey for his art-cell.

b. *trans.* To get or bring *into* something by playing or fluttering.

1657 tr. *De Imitatione* p. ix, Larkes..play themselves into the Fowlers net.

3. a. *intr.* Of things: To move briskly or lightly, especially with alternating or irregular motion, as lightning, flame, leaves in the wind, etc.; to change or alternate rapidly, as colours in iridescence or prismatic refraction; to pass gently around, or strike lightly upon, something, as waves, wind, light, etc.; to dance, flutter, flicker, glitter, ripple, vibrate, sway lightly, etc. Also *fig.*

1590 SPENSER *F.Q.* I. i. 34 Thereby a christall streame did gently play, Which from a sacred fountaine welled forth alway. **1591** SHAKS. *1 Hen. VI*, v. iii. 62 As playes the Sunne vpon the glassie streames, Twinkling another counterfetted beame. **1638** JUNIUS *Paint. Ancients* 18 The inward Imaginations that doe continually stirre and play in our mindes. **1664** POWER *Exp. Philos.* Pref. cj, The Magnetical Atoms continually playing about them. **1697** DRYDEN *Virg. Georg.* IV. 432 When Western Winds on curling Waters play. **1726** SHELVOCKE *Voy. round World* 418 You'll see in the night a sort of faint light'ning, flashing and playing..in that part of the Horizon. **1797** MRS. RADCLIFFE *Italian* i, Her fine hair was negligently bound up in a silk net, and some tresses that had escaped it played on her neck. **1827** WILLIS *Healing Daughter Jairus* 33 The breaking waves play'd low upon the beach. **1847** EMERSON *Repr. Men, Shaks.* Wks. (Bohn) I. 364 Shakespeare, Homer, Dante, Chaucer, saw the splendour of meaning that plays over the visible world. **1851** MAYNE REID *Scalp Hunt.* xlii, The tempest still played around us. **1859** TENNYSON *Geraint & Enid* 1537 A splendid silk..Where like a shoaling sea the lovely blue Play'd into green. **1869** HUGHES *Alfred Gt.* xxiii. 296 Alfred allows his fancy to play round the idea. **1871** H. AINSWORTH *Tower Hill* I. v, No smile ever played upon her thin lips.

b. *transf.* To exhibit a play of light or colour.

1698 FRYER *Acc. E. India & P.* 214 A Rose Diamond that is very thick, it's good to set it close upon the Ivory, and it will play very well.

c. To keep moving to and fro. *rare.*

1513 SIR E. HOWARD in Ellis *Orig. Lett.* Ser. II. I. 217 Barges..to play up and down betwen Dover & Caleys. **1716** B. CHURCH *Hist. Philip's War* (1865) I. 79 The other Canoo play'd off to see the event, and to carry tydings if the Indians should prove false.

4. a. *intr.* To bubble and roll about as a boiling liquid; to boil. *Obs.* exc. *dial.*

(In this sense *plaw* is frequent dialectally, even where *play* is used in other senses.)

a **1400** *Sir Beues* (MS. E) 3455 Þoo hit dede seþe and playde ffaste. *c* **1400** *Sloane MS.* 3548 lf. 16 b, Put it ynne a cowdrun ful of water, and layt yt play longe þerin. **1513** DOUGLAS *Æneis* VI. iii. 120 Sum spedis to graith haite wattir besely In caldrouns playing on the fire fast by. **1721** KELLY *Sc. Prov.* 106 Fair words will not make the Pot play. **1813** PICKEN *Now-a-days* Misc. Poems I. 124 Their wealth..Will ne'er gar Simon's pat play brown.

β. *c* **1440** *Promp. Parv.* 403/2 Plawyn, as pottys, *bullio, ferveo.* *a* **1450** *Stockh. Med. MS.* I. 56 in *Anglia* XVIII. 296 Take a porcioun of whete-bren, And as it plawyth, cast þer in. *c* **1460** *Play Sacram.* 664 In to the Cawdron I wylle yt Cast, I shalle..putt yt down that yt myght plawe. **1674** RAY *S. & E.C. Words* 74 To *Play*, spoken of a pot, kettle or other vessel full of liquor, i.e. to boil... In Norfolk they pronounce it *plaw*.

b. *trans.* To cause to boil; to boil. Now *dial.*

a. *c* **1420** *Liber Cocorum* (1862) 42 Fyrst play þy water with hony and salt. **14..** *Noble Bk. Cookry* (1882) 100 Sett it down and play it up with cow mylk till yt be enoughe. **1533** *Test. Ebor.* (Surtees) VI. 42 A lesser lede to play growte in.

β. *a* **1450** *Stockh. Med. MS.* I. 54 in *Anglia* XVIII. 296 Tak and plaw it ouer þe fyir. *a* **1825** FORBY *Voc. E. Anglia*, *Plaw*, to parboil.

5. *intr.* To move, revolve, or oscillate freely (usually within a definite space); to have its proper unimpeded movement, as a part of any mechanism, or of the living body; to have free play.

1595 SHAKS. *John* III. iv. 132 Warme life playes in that infants veines. **1614** B. JONSON *Bart. Fair* II. ii, You should get this chayre let out o' the sides, for me, that my hips might play. **1627** CAPT. SMITH *Seaman's Gram.* ii. 12 The Tiller playeth in the Gunroome. **1664** POWER *Exp. Philos.* I. 24 You may see their heart play, and beat very orderly for a long time together. **1669** STURMY *Mariner's Mag.* VII. x. 16 [Hold] the Instrument..Horizontally as neer as you can, that the Needle may have liberty to play to and fro. **1715** DESAGULIERS *Fires Impr.* 130 Two Iron Eyes for the ends of Axis to play in. **1741** MONRO *Anat. Bones* (ed. 3) 151 The Condyles..play in the Cavity. **1825** J. NICHOLSON *Operat. Mechanic* 670 The engines..have a cogged wheel, playing in a rack, which is laid as one of the rails of the road. **1881** *All Year Round* XXVII. 294 The molars..play vertically on each other like a pair of scissors. **1888** BRYCE *Amer. Commw.* II. xliv. 145 To inquire how the organs of government which have been described play into one another in practice.

6. *trans.* To cause to play; to ply.

a. To wield (something) lightly and freely; to keep in motion or exercise; to actuate, operate, work (any instrument). ***to play (a good) knife and fork***, to eat (well or heartily): see KNIFE AND FORK 1; so ***to play a good stick***, to fence well.

1589 R. HARVEY *Pl. Perc.* (1590) 3 Thy late Customers, which play more sacks to the mill, haue brought greists or iests at least wise to be ground. **1713** STEELE *Guard.* No. 50 ¶2 The dexterity..consists in playing the razor, with a nimble wrist, mighty near the nose without touching it. **1727–41** CHAMBERS *Cycl.* s.v. *Organ*, One of these hydraulic organs; with two men..seeming to pump the water which plays it. **1748** SMOLLETT *Rod. Rand.* (1812) I. 47 You hear he plays a good [fiddle-]stick. **1788** J. MAY *Jrnl. & Lett.* (1873) 88 Five hands at work... Two playing the whipsaw. ? *a* **1800** in *Daily News* 11 July (1892) 2/5 If..he is a tolerable good boxer, can play a good stick. **1848** THACKERAY *Van. Fair* xliii, The Colonel plays a good knife and fork at tiffin. **1885** *Illustr. Lond. News* 28 Nov. 548/1 The dining-hall.. where the occupants..played 'knife and fork'.

†**b.** To deal with; to treat. *Obs.*

1491 CAXTON *Vitas Patr.* (W. de W. 1495) I. cxii. 153 b/1, I haue done many offences to my god, the whyche he playeth mekely, in yeuynge vnto me example. **1584** LODGE *Alarum agst. Usurers* 12 The vsurer that playes all this rie, will yet be counted an honest and well dealing man. **1597** J. KING *On Jonas* (1618) 619 It is a great mastery, saith Seneca, to play a man kindely.

c. To discharge, fire, let *off* (artillery, etc. (*on* or *upon* persons or things), also fireworks); to cause (a fountain or the like) to play. Also *fig.* In quot. 1881, to fire upon (an enemy).

1595 SHAKS. *John* II. i. 385 Their battering Canon charged to the mouthes... I'de play incessantly vpon these Iades. **1670** COTTON *Espernon* I. IV. 156 [He] plai'd so many Cannon-shot into the Town, that not a man durst appear. **1682** BUNYAN *Holy War* xii, The gate from the top of which the captains did play their slings at the enemies. **1712** J. JAMES tr. *Le Blond's Gardening* 197 To play a Spout still bigger,..there must be a large Pipe. **1713** ADDISON *Guard.* No. 152 ¶6 She played upon him so many smiles and glances, that she quite weakened and disarmed him. **1721** G. ROUSSILLON tr. *Vertot's Rev. Portug.* 83 There should be fireworks ready to be play'd off. **1759** *Chron.* in *Ann. Reg.* 62/2 Playing their hand-grenades and swivels to excellent purpose. **1790** *Laws of Harvard Coll.* 25 If any Scholar.. shall make bonfires..or play off fireworks. **1799** G. SMITH *Laboratory* I. 25 Avoid..a damp, foggy, rainy or windy night, to play your rockets. **1804** NICHOLL in Owen *Wellesley's Desp.* (1877) 530 They opened a battery, which they continued playing until 3 o'clock. **1881** CLARK RUSSELL *Ocean Free Lance* I. iv. 154 We kept playing the enemy with round-shot.

†**d.** To toss *off*, to finish (liquor). *Obs. slang.*

1596 SHAKS. *1 Hen. IV*, II. iv. 18 When you breath in your watering, then they cry hem, and bid you play it off. **1607** DEKKER *Iests to make Merie* Wks. (Grosart) II. 350 He requested them to play off the sacke and begon.

e. *Angling.* To give play to (a fish); to allow (it) to exhaust itself by pulling against the line. Also *fig.*

1741 RICHARDSON *Pamela* (1824) I. 69, I..soon hooked a lovely carp. Play it, play it, said she: I did, and brought it to the bank. **1787** BEST *Angling* (ed. 2) 40 He seldom breaks his hold, if your tackle is strong and you play him properly. **1856** KANE *Arct. Expl.* I. xxx. 414 The victim..is played like a trout by the angler's reel. **1895** *Pall Mall Mag.* Nov. 367 But where would be the sport of playing the fish? **1900** MRS. H. WARD *Eleanor* 97 Eleanor had played her with much tact, and now had her in her power.

f. To cause to move or pass lightly, flutter, glitter, etc. (see 3); to exhibit with brilliant effect; to draw lightly upon a surface.

a **1716** SOUTH *Serm.* (1744) X. 357 When the allurement of any sinful pleasure or profit plays itself before him. **1742** YOUNG *Nt. Th.* v. 903 Tho' Fortune too (our third and final Theme), As an Accomplice, play'd her gaudy Plumes. **1746–7** HERVEY *Medit.* (1818) 127 She plays her lovely changes, not to enkindle dissolute affections, but to display her Creator's glory. **1812** R. H. in *Examiner* 25 May 329/1 The lines are played over the forms with..freedom and taste. **1843** E. JONES *Sens. & Event* 54 Should prudes blame my dress, oh! all beautiful braid, Yellow, crimson, and green over it shall be play'd. **1892** *Electr. Engineer* 16 Sept. 285/2 The search-light began to play a dazzling ripple along their line from end to end.

7. a. *intr.* To operate artillery, to fire (*on* or *upon* persons or things); also said of the artillery, or of a mine, etc.: To be discharged or fired.

1601 R. JOHNSON *Kingd. & Commw.* (1603) 56 They never cease playing with their Ordinance, till they have laide all levell with the ground. *a* **1627** HAYWARD *Four Y. Eliz.* (Camden) 55 The artillerie plaied and the footemen skirmished most part of the daie. **1628** DIGBY *Voy. Medit.* (1868) 23 All this while the fortes played vpon the boates and our shippes. **1633** STAFFORD *Pac. Hib.* I. ix. (1810) 116 When wee looked that the Cannon should begin to play. *a* **1649** DRUMM. OF HAWTH. *Idea* Wks. (1711) 221 The mine going straight, there lacked nothing but some match to make it play. **1709** STEELE *Tatler* No. 53 ¶11 The Cannon on each Side began to play. **1748** in G. Sheldon *Hist. Deerfield, Mass.* (1895) I. 564, I played away with our cannon and small arms for an hour and ¾. **1777** WATSON *Philip II* (1839) 515 His cannon had hardly begun to play upon it, when Vidossan, the governor, retired with the garrison into the castle. **1894** LD. WOLSELEY *Life Marlborough* II. 181 Another battery..which Marlborough erected to play upon the south-eastern bastion.

fig. **1709** HEARNE *Collect.* 11 Nov. (O.H.S.) II. 306 He.. playd particularly [in his sermon]..upon the Bp. of Sarum.

b. Of a firework: To be fired, to go *off* (*fig.* in quot.).

1762 GOLDSM. *Cit. W.* li, Yet it [a farce] played off, and bounced, and cracked, and made more sport than a firework.

8. *intr.* Of a fire-engine, fountain, etc.: To emit a jet of water, to spout. Also said of the water, or of the person, e.g. of a fireman.

1666 BOYLE in *Phil. Trans.* I. 233 The Cock would play altogether on that side. **1687** A. LOVELL tr. *Thevenot's Trav.* I. 9 A great many Fountains, where the Water-works, playing very high, render the place altogether delightful. **1711** ADDISON *Spect.* No. 5 ¶3 There are several Engines filled with Water, and ready to play at a Minute's warning. **1855** MACAULAY *Hist. Eng.* xii. III. 166 The fountains played in his honour. **1860** DICKENS *Uncomm. Trav.* iv, The fire-engine maker..having brought out the whole of his stock to play upon its last smouldering ashes. **1889** *Century Mag.* Apr. 929 The firemen were not permitted to play on the flames.

9. a. *trans.* To practise, perform, do (some action); †to ply, exercise (a craft) (*obs.*); to perform, execute (a movement); usually (influenced by II), to perform or practise in the way of sport, deceit, etc. (a trick, prank, joke, etc.: const. *on*, *upon*, or with simple dative). In mod. use also with *off* (? expressing complete or successful action: see OFF A. 5).

c **1391** CHAUCER *Astrol.* ii. §40 Yif thow wolt pleie this craft with the arisyng of the Mone, loke thow rekne wel her cours howre by howre. *c* **1400** *Gamelyn* 307 Whan Gamelyn the yonge thus hadde pleyd his play. *c* **1425** *Cursor M.* 16623 (Trin.) And siþen in his honde þei sett: a muchel greet rede And to him pleiden a bobet. **1562** *Jack Juggler* in Hazl. *Dodsley* II. 138, I know that he playeth you many a like prank. **1603** SHAKS. *Meas. for M.* II. ii. 121 Man..Plaies such phantastique tricks before high heauen, As makes the Angels weepe. **1660** F. BROOKE tr. *Le Blanc's Trav.* 17 For fear he should play me some trick, I dissembled. **1782** COWPER *Gilpin* 134 Thus all through merry Islington These gambols he did play. **1815** W. H. IRELAND *Scribbleomania* 190 *note*, The hoax played off some years back, by the late commentator Steevens. **1890** W. A. WALLACE *Only a Sister* 201 Only something very important would have made you play this game.

b. *Sc. colloq.*

1826 J. WILSON *Noct. Ambr.* Wks. 1855 I. 134 See ane [tiger] play spang upon you..and gar ye play tapsalteerie ower a precipice.

II. To exercise oneself in the way of diversion or amusement.

10. a. *intr.* To employ or exercise oneself in the way of amusement or recreation; to amuse or divert oneself; to sport, frolic. (Formerly in wider sense than now, including any kind of recreation, e.g. dancing.)

c **897** K. ÆLFRED *Gregory's Past.* C. I. 391 We..wiernað urum cildum urra peninga mid to pleȝianne. *c* **950** *Lindisf. Gosp.* Matt. xi. 17 We sungun iuh & ne plæȝde ȝe. *c* **1175** *Lamb. Hom.* 7 Þa children ploȝeden in þere strete heriende ure drihten. *a* **1300** *Cursor M.* 12275 Iesus went him for [*v.r.* forth] to plai Wit childir on an halidai. *c* **1330** R. BRUNNE *Chron. Wace* (Rolls) 3845 Elydour þorow a wode schold wende, ffor to pleye by o ryuer. *c* **1386** CHAUCER *Frankl. T.* 169 Hire freendes..schopen for to pleyen somwher elles. *c* **1491** *Chast Goddes Chyld.* 14 A louynge moder listeth to play with her souking childe. **1576** E. DE VERE *Fayre Fooles* Poems (Grosart) 72 To playe with fooles, oh, what a foole was I. **1632** MILTON *L'Allegro* 97 And young and old com forth to play On a Sunshine Holyday. **1742** GRAY *Eton* 52 Regardless of their doom The little victims play! **1840** J. H. NEWMAN *Par. Serm.* (1842) V. iii. 35 To make professions is to play with edge tools. **1856** FROUDE *Hist. Eng.* (1858) I. ii. 151 The gardens of the Alhambra, where she had played as a child.

†**b.** To enjoy oneself, be joyful or merry, rejoice; esp. in reference to the bliss of heaven. *Obs.*

c **1230** *Hali Meid.* 41 Ah schulen ai bifore þe pleien in heuene. *a* **1272** *Luue Ron* 133 in *O.E. Misc.* 97 Alle heo schule wyþ engles pleye some and sauhte in heouene lyhte. *c* **1374** CHAUCER *Anel. & Arc.* 321 For nowe I pleyn and now I playe. **1377** LANGL. *P. Pl.* B. XVI. 256, I loked on his lappe, a lazar lay þere-inne Among patriarkes and profetes pleyande togyderes.

c. To sport amorously; *euphem.* to have sexual intercourse. Cf. PLAY *sb.* 6 c. Now *rare* or *Obs.*

a **1000** *Riddles* xliii. 2 (Gr.) Ic seah wyhte wrætlice twa undearnunga ute pleȝan hæmedlaces. *c* **1250** *Gen. & Ex.* 2016 His wif..One and stille ðoȝt hire gamen Wið ioseph speken and plaiȝen samen. *c* **1320** *Sir Tristr.* 2617 Tristrem wiþ Ysoude lay..And wok And plaiden ay bitvene. **1375** BARBOUR *Bruce* v. 542 Throu vomen that he vald with play. **1483** CAXTON *G. de la Tour* F j, Which for a lytel syluer made her to synne and playe with a pryour. **1592** SHAKS. *Ven. & Ad.* 124 Be bold to play, our sport is not in sight. **1667**

MILTON *P.L.* IX. 1027 Now let us play.. For never did thy Beautie.. so enflame my sense With ardor to enjoy thee.

d. ***to play around***: to amuse oneself; to behave in a playful or irresponsible manner; *spec.* to have a sexual relationship *with* (a person or persons of the opposite sex), esp. casually or extra-maritally. *colloq.* (orig. *U.S.*).

1929 D. HAMMETT *Red Harvest* xi. 109 Max was up there with a girl he used to play around with. **1932** G. GREENE *Stamboul Train* IV. iv. 248 You mean you killed him.. just because he'd played around with your daughter? **1934** J. O'HARA *Appointment in Samarra* ii. 46 He played around a little, but Al knew Helene was the only one he really cared for, and Helene really cared for him. **1960** *Sunday Express* 14 Aug. 14/6, I went to all the parties; I played around. **1963** D. GRAY *Murder in Mind* xv. 83 And if I found you were playing around, I'd give you a damned good hiding. **1973** S. DOBYNS *Man of Little Evils* (1974) iii. 31 Ralph played around with other women but he liked one.

†**11. a.** *refl.* To amuse or disport oneself: = 10.

c **1290** *S. Eng. Leg.* I. 349/148 þat þis child scholde wende an hontingue, to pleiȝen him. *a* **1300** *Cursor M.* 3025 Þir breþer þam plaijd samen. *c* **1386** CHAUCER *Melib.* ¶2 He for his desport is went into the feeldes hym to pleye. *c* **1430** *Pilgr. Lyf Manhode* IV. ix. (1869) 181 A crooked staf me lakketh.. and a bal to pleye me with. *c* **1440** *York Myst.* xvii. 212 Go we.. To playe vs in som othir place. *c* **1530** LD. BERNERS *Arth. Lyt. Bryt.* (1814) 37 Arthur.. humbly requyred both hys fader and moder.. to giue hym licence to go play hym a season out of that countrey. **1646** E. F[ISHER] *Marrow Mod. Divin.* (ed. 2) 171 We may go play us then, and work no working at all. **1651** BAXTER *Inf. Bapt.* 182 When you have plaid your self with your own absurd fictions.

†**b.** *trans.* To furnish with the means of playing; to amuse. *Obs. rare.*

1570 *Durham Depos.* (Surtees) 192 Some of the leves of the said bookes the said wyffes toke away with them, to play their children withall.

c. To bring *into* some condition, etc. by playing or sport.

1642 FULLER *Holy & Prof. St.* IV. xix. 337 He playeth himself into Learning before he is aware of it.

12. *intr.* ***play with***: To amuse oneself with, sport with; to touch or finger lightly, or move slightly with the hand (a material object) by way of frivolous amusement; to treat (anything) lightly or frivolously; to dally, trifle, or toy with. In quot. 1827, to do what one will with, to manage according to one's pleasure. (See also 13 b, 14.) ***to play with fire***: see FIRE *sb.* A. 3 g.

c **1200** *Vices & Virtues* 135 Ne lat hie nawht ðe hande pleiȝende mid stikke. *c* **1205** LAY. 17335 þus þe vnwise king plaȝede [*c* **1275** pleoyde] mid worden. *a* **1225** *Ancr. R.* 76 Ȝe þat pleieð mit te worlde, nulich ou nout iheren. **1340** HAMPOLE *Pr. Consc.* 1307 When welthe of þe worlde with þe plays, Sek þan gude consayl wyth-alle. *c* **1400** *Laud Troy Bk.* 6248 When he his cosyn ded saw, Him lyked noght with Ector plaw. **1529** MORE *Dyaloge* I. Wks. 161/1 Than will he call it no scripture, as he plaith with the pystle of sainct Iames. **1650** BAXTER *Saints' R.* III. v. §5 (1651) 95 As children, we play with our meat when we should eat it. **1782** COWPER *Table Talk* 505, I play with syllables, and sport in song. **1827** HALLAM *Const. Hist.* (1876) II. x. 263 It required a dexterous management to play with the army. **1870** J. H. NEWMAN *Gram. Assent* II. viii. 304 Montaigne.. could thus afford to play with life, and the abysses into which it leads us. **1945** *Tee Emm* (Air Ministry) V. 52 This will give you a little to play with and allow for a drop in barometric pressure. **1965** V. CANNING *Whip Hand* iii. 33, I like a girl who doesn't play with her food or drink. **1976** SCOTT & KOSKI *Walk-In* (1977) xxiii. 237 He was sweating now, all right. And is he playing with me? he wondered. Is the bastard playing with me? **1978** *Lancashire Life* Sept. 76/3 How could they possibly build docks when they had merely £60,000 to play with.

b. ***to play with*** (someone): to masturbate; usu. *refl. colloq.*

1922 JOYCE *Ulysses* 552 You can apply your eye to the keyhole and play with yourself while I just go through her a few times. **1954** H. K. FINK *Long Journey* 14, I was going with girls.. and I didn't feel the urge to play with myself. **1966** L. H. FARBER *Ways of Will* iii. 58 This opening scene of a faceless woman silently playing with herself.. sets the tone. **1967** A. WILSON *No Laughing Matter* II. 65 That kind of thinking can easily land you in the loony bin. It's worse than playing with yourself. **1969** H. MILLER *Sexus* (1970) viii. 166 'Play with it a bit while I finish this.' 'You're filthy,' she said, but she did as I told her. **1971** 'V. X. SCOTT' *Surrogate Wife* 54 He played with me. And little by little.. I played with him. *Ibid.* 114 In bed, we played with each other. **1974** E. TIDYMAN *Dummy* xv. 199 I'd glance over at Donald and he'd be playing with himself in the courtroom.

13. a. *intr.* To do something which is not to be taken seriously, but merely as done in sport or frolic; to trifle *with*.

1382 WYCLIF *Gen.* xix. 14 And he was seen to hem as pleiynge to speke. —— *Prov.* xxvi. 19 The man that gilendeli noȝeth to his frend, and whan he were caȝt, shal sey Pleiende I dide [**1388** Y dide pleiynge]. **1484** CAXTON *Fables of Æsop* v. xv, Loke hyther, callest thow this a playe.. now I shalle shewe to the how thow oughtest not to playe so with thy lord. **1545** ASCHAM *Toxoph.* (Arb.) 97 The lacke of teachynge to shoote in Englande, causeth very manye men to playe with the kynges Actes. **1842** MARRYAT *Perc. Keene* x, I'd recommend you not to play with 'post captains', said Captain Bridgman.

b. ***play on*** or ***upon*** (†***with***) ***a word*** or ***words***: to make playful use of a double meaning of a word, by way of sport or jest; to pun. Also *trans.* in causative sense: see quot. 1865.

1593 SHAKS. *Rich. II*, II. i. 84 Can sicke men play so nicely with their names? **1596** —— *Merch. V.* III. v. 48 How euerie foole can play vpon the word. **1683** D. A. *Art Converse* 125 They play often upon words. **1861** WRIGHT *Ess. Archæol.* II. xxiii. 231 The wit or ingenuity of our Anglo-Saxon forefathers was chiefly exerted in playing upon words. **1865** BUSHNELL *Vicar. Sacr.* III. v, A practice on words that plays them into inferences not contained in their meaning. **1876** TREVELYAN *Macaulay* I. iii. 134 He did not play upon words as a habit.

†**c.** ***play upon***: to return or recur fancifully to (a phrase, etc.); to dwell upon by repetition; to harp on. *Obs.*

1605 CAMDEN *Rem.* 14 Giraldus Cambrensis.. played vpon these verses. **1646** SIR T. BROWNE *Pseud. Ep.* I. ix. (1686) 26 Playing much upon the simile.

14. a. *intr.* To make sport or jest at another's expense; to mock. ***play with*** (†*at*, †*on*, †*upon*): to make sport of, make fun of, ridicule, mock at; to befool, delude. Now *rare* or merged in 12. (Cf. also 30 a.)

c **1000** ÆLFRIC *Gen.* xxi. 9 Sarra beheold hu Agares sunu wið Isaac pleȝode. *c* **1205** LAY. 16554, & þet þine hired-childeren pleien [*c* **1275** pleoye] mid þissen hunde scotien mid heore flan & his cun scenden anan. **1382** WYCLIF *Isa.* lvii. 4 Vp on whom pleiden ȝee? [1388 On whom scorneden ȝe?] *a* **1533** LD. BERNERS *Gold. Bk. M. Aurel.* (1546) K k viij b, All ye togyther there present played, and gested on me. *c* **1550** CHEKE *Matt.* ii. 16 Then Herood seing yᵗ he was plaied withal bi yᵉ wiseards. *c* **1586** C'TESS PEMBROKE *Ps.* LXXXIX. xiii, Of all his haters none, But boasts his wrack and at his sorrow plaieth. **1611** TOURNEUR *Ath. Trag.* I. ii, That same heartlesse thing That Cowards will be bold to play upon. **17..** POPE (J.), I would make use of it rather to play upon those I despised, than to trifle with those I loved. **1844** MRS. BROWNING *Lay of Brown Rosary* I. vi, In a sternness quoth she, 'As thou play'st at the ball art thou playing with me?'

†**b.** *refl.* with *of*: To make fun of, mock at. *Obs.*

c **1489** CAXTON *Blanchardyn* xxiii. 75 But iapeth & playeth her self of theym that ben amerouse.

c. *trans.* To make sport of. *colloq.*

1891 E. KINGLAKE *Australian at H.* 117 Those who pass their lives in the bush generally have their heart in the right place, though they do love to play a new chum.

15. *intr.* To abstain from work; to take a holiday. [A special development of sense 10.] Now *dial.* (esp. of workmen on strike or out of work).

1377 LANGL. *P. Pl.* B. Prol. 20 Some putten hem to þe plow, pleyed ful selde. **1430–40** LYDG. *Bochas* I. ix. (1554) 19 b, A conuencion By enterchangyng, yᵗ eche should reigne a yere The other absent to play & cum no nere. **1542** RECORDE *Gr. Artes* (1575) 443 A Mason.. played 12 dayes and wrought 28 dayes. **1568** GRAFTON *Chron.* II. 889 They neuer gaue their enemies one day to rest or play be the space of .xx. dayes. **1581** J. BELL *Haddon's Answ. Osor.* 132 b, Surely where nothyng is blameworthy their Pardon may goe play. **1598** SHAKS. *Merry W.* IV. i. 12 Master Slender is let the Boyes leaue to play. **1800** *Hull Advertiser* 24 May 4/2 The men will often play on a Monday. **1806** HUTTON *Course Math.* I. 139 A workman was hired for 20 days, at 3*s.* per day, for every day he worked; but with this condition, that for every day he played, he should forfeit 1*s.* **1892** *Spectator* 16 Apr. 529/1 This Yorkshire idiom means to cease work from any cause whatever. A man ill with rheumatism told me that he had been 'playing' eight weeks. **1894** *Daily News* 13 July 7/7 Of the 70,000 men 'playing' 40,000 are non-unionists.

III. To engage in a game; and derived senses.

16. a. *trans.* To exercise or employ oneself in, engage in, practise (a game or definite form of amusement). Also in various figurative expressions: see GAME *sb.* 5, also BO-PEEP, DUCK AND DRAKE, FAST AND LOOSE, HANDY-DANDY, etc.

c **888** K. ÆLFRED *Boeth.* xxxvi. §5 [6] Ða cild.. maniȝfealde pleȝan pleȝiaþ ðær hi hyriað ealdum monnum. *c* **1250, 1297** [see GAME *sb.* 5, 3 b]. *a* **1300** *Cursor M.* 16623 (Cott.) And wit him þai plaid sitisott, And badd þat he suld rede Quilk o þaim him gaf þe dint. *c* **1369** CHAUCER *Dethe Blaunche* 618 For fals Fortune hath pleyd a game Atte ches with me. *c* **1440** *Promp. Parv.* 404/2 Pleyyn buk hyde, *angulo*. **1576** FLEMING *Panopl. Epist.* 350 The common games plaide and practised at Olympus. **1635** JACKSON *Creed* VIII. xxxi. §7 As the proverb is, by-standers sometimes see more than they who play the game. **1679** *Establ. Test* 6 The After-game they had to play.. was to be managed with .. Skill. **1796** *Chron.* in *Ann. Reg.* 33/1 Next morning the match was played out. **1838** DE MORGAN *Ess. Probab.* 111 We are entitled to conclude that.. the games played were each not less than 3 to 2 in favour of the bank. **1866** MRS. GASKELL *Wives & Dau.* xiii, He taught young ladies to play billiards on a wet day. **1885** *Times* (weekly ed.) 13 Feb. 16/4 The young men played fives against the tower.

b. ***to play the game***: i.e. according to the rules, fairly; hence to 'play fair', act honourably. *colloq.*

1889 [see GAME *sb.* 4 c]. **1898** KIPLING *Days' Work* 248 (*Maltese Cat*) 'Play the game, don't talk', the Maltese Cat whickered. **1904** *Daily Chron.* 2 May 4/5 Men do not talk about their honour nowadays—they call it 'playing the game'.

c. To represent or imitate in sport; to make pretence of: to practise or deal with in a trifling way or as if for amusement, not seriously. Also with *obj. cl.* to pretend, make believe (*that...*) for sport or amusement.

c **1386** CHAUCER *Shipman's T.* 233 Or elles that we pleye A pilgrymage, or goon out of the weye. **1821** LAMB *Elia* Ser. I. *Old & New Schoolmaster*, The noises of children, playing their own fancies. **1875** LOWELL *Spenser* Prose Wks. 1890 IV. 324 Children who play that everything is something else. **1890** *St. Nicholas Mag.* Oct. 1007 We played that we were gypsies. (Cf. 19.)

d. ***to play politics***: to act on an issue for personal or political gain rather than from principle. orig. *U.S.*

1863 W. PHILLIPS *Speeches* vi. 113 We do not play politics. **1907** *Springfield* (Mass.) *Weekly Republican* 13 May 6 Mr. Balfour has seized the opportunity to play politics, and has apparently come out squarely in favor of trade preference. **1931** H. F. PRINGLE *Theodore Roosevelt* II. vii. 343 Roosevelt .. was playing politics in his own behalf. **1962** *Listener* 15 Nov. 798/1 It has been fashionable to claim that Mr Gaitskell.. was deliberately playing politics with the Common Market issue. **1963** *Times* 11 Feb. 11/3 If it is too much to ask any Government to stop playing politics with the economy, the Opposition can at least be urged not to abet it in doing so. **1976** *Punch* 16 June 1070/2 There are a few people who find it disturbing that we are now the most heavily indebted nation in the industrial world—but as the Government would wish me to point out, they are just playing politics.

e. ***to play the dozens***: to engage in a bout of verbal insults and ridicule with one or more other people: used of a ritualized form of dialogue customary among American Blacks.

1933 E. CALDWELL *God's Little Acre* x. 142 If you want to play the dozens, you're at the right homestead. **1939** J. DOLLARD in *American Imago* Nov. 6 One asked the other, 'Do you want to play the Dozens?' The other boy said, 'Yes.' *Ibid.* 7 These reactions of concealment and shame convinced me that playing the Dozens is not an orgy of licentious expression for lower-class Negroes; all know that the themes treated are in general forbidden, some refuse to play the game and still others are very resentful and defensive at the mere thought of it. **1942** Z. N. HURSTON in A. Dundes *Mother Wit* (1973) 24/1 The bookless may have difficulty in reading a paragraph in a newspaper, but when they get down to 'playing the dozens' they have no equal in America. **1962** R. D. ABRAHAMS in *Ibid.* 298/1 'Playing the dozens' is one of the most interesting folkloristic phenomena found among contemporary Negroes. **1970** H. E. ROBERTS *Third Ear* 11/1 Playing the dozens, making derogatory.. remarks about another's mother, parents. **1973** *Black World* Aug. 58/2 Could play the dozens for days, talk about your momma bad enough to make you cry. **1973** A. DUNDES *Mother Wit* 141/2 A sample of some of the special techniques and forms of extended word play should convince even the most adamant sceptic that no black child who can signify or play the dozens can rightly be called lacking in verbal skills.

f. ***to play pussy*** (Aeronaut.): to fly under cover in order to avoid detection by another aircraft, etc. *slang.*

1942 *We speak from Air* 30, I wondered if he was playing pussy and intending to jink away. **1942** *Gen* 1 Sept. 14/1 Waiting in the air.. he 'snakes about' or 'plays pussy' in the clouds. **1943** HUNT & PRINGLE *Service Slang* 52 *Play pussy*, to take advantage of cloud cover, jumping from cloud to cloud to shadow a potential victim or avoid recognition. **1948** PARTRIDGE *Dict. Forces' Slang* 143 *Play pussy*, to speed from one cloud to another in order to escape detection or to pounce upon a shadowed enemy aircraft.

17. a. *intr.* To engage or take part in a game. In *Cricket* said esp. of the batsman.

c **1205** LAY. 8134 Summen pleoden on tæuelbrede [*c* **1275** Somme pleoide mid tauel]. *c* **1320** *Sir Tristr.* 310 A cheker he fond bi a cheire, He asked who wold play. **1484** CAXTON *Fables of Avian* xxi, The euylle.. whiche doo no thynge but playe with dees and cardes. *a* **1548** HALL *Chron.*, *Hen. V* 41 b, The Dolphyn.. sent to hym [Henry V] a tunne of tennis balles to plaie with. **1562** J. HEYWOOD *Prov. & Epigr.* (1867) 163 He pleyth best that wins. **1687** A. LOVELL tr. *Thevenot's Trav.* I. 34 Though they play for nothing, yet they take great pleasure at play. **1750** CHESTERF. *Lett.* (1792) II. 334 A man may play with decency; but if he games he is disgraced. **1866** *Routledge's Every Boy's Ann.* 355 The batsman must play with additional care. **1884** H. C. BUNNER in *Harper's Mag.* Jan. 305/1 Well played, sir! **1884** BLIGH in *Lillywhite's Cricket Ann.* 3 The last named.. playing in his best style.

b. *spec.* To play for stakes, esp. for the sake of gain; to game, gamble.

1511 *Churche of Yuell Men* (Pynson) E vij, They that make, sell, bye.. the dyce, the cardes, the tables... They that serue the players.. they yᵗ lende them money for to play. **1599** SHAKS. *Hen. V*, III. vi. 119 When Lenitie and Crueltie play for a Kingdome, the gentler Gamester is the soonest winner. **1615** STEPHENS *Ess. & Char.*, *Gamester* (1857) 169 If he plaies upon Ticket, he knowes you are.. not able to exact, though hee resolves to pay nothing. **1789** CHARLOTTE SMITH *Ethelinde* (1814) I. 13 He has had the character of playing monstrous deep. **1809** MALKIN *Gil Blas* VII. xii. ¶8 Playing for his last stake. *a* **1832** BENTHAM *Deontol.* ii. (1834) II. 125 Every gamester who plays upon equal terms, plays to a disadvantage.

c. imper. ***play!*** In *Cricket*, said by the umpire to the whole of the players at the beginning of an innings or session of play (formerly also, by the bowler as a call to the batsman immediately before the delivery of the ball); also in *Lawn Tennis* by the server at the beginning of each service.

1787 in Waghorn *Cricket Scores* (1890) p. xiii, When the umpire shall call 'play', the party refusing to play shall lose the match. **1837** DICKENS *Pickw.* vii, 'Play', suddenly cried the bowler. **1869** *Routledge's Every Boy's Ann.* 639 'Play' again called, we commenced our innings.

d. *transf.* In *Cricket*, said of the ground or 'wicket', in reference to the effect of its condition upon the play.

1866 *Routledge's Every Boy's Ann.* 355 The ground will afterwards play as differently as possible. **1881** *Daily News* 9 July 2 The wicket did not seem to play particularly well.

e. ***play or pay***: a sporting phrase meaning that, if one party to a race or other match fails to 'play' or engage in the match, his backers have to pay as if he had lost. Hence ***play or pay bet***, a bet holding good whether the horse runs or not.

1821 *Sporting Mag.* IX. 55 A man gammons himself most truly, if he makes play or pay bets. **1877** H. SMART *Play or*

Pay viii, I got a letter to say that the regiment had been wild enough to back me, run or not—play or pay, as it is termed, which means that they will have to pay their money even if I don't run.

f. ***to play back, backward(s)***: in *Cricket*, said of the batsman: to move back before striking the ball; ***play forward***: to move forward in making a stroke; ***play through***: in *Golf*, to continue playing, passing other players who have agreed to suspend their game for this purpose.

1816 W. LAMBERT *Instr. & Rules Cricket* 27 [This] will direct him to play forward at the..bowling. *Ibid.* 29 If at these [short] kind of balls the Striker plays back about two feet behind the popping crease..it will afford him a little more time to judge how the Ball is coming. **1851** W. CLARKE in W. Bolland *Cricket Notes* 135 It is the ball that catches him in two minds, so that he does not know whether to play forward or backward. **1899** W. G. GRACE *Cricketing Reminiscences* x. 288 If a boy has once learned to play forward confidently he will soon adapt himself to playing backwards at balls that demand it. **1934** W. J. LEWIS *Lang. Cricket* 198 *Play back*,..to step back with the right foot towards the wicket, playing the ball behind the popping crease. *Ibid.* 199 *Play forward*,..to reach forward, advancing the left foot and the bat, in making a stroke. **1967** M. GREEN *Art of Coarse Golf* x. 110 The general rule of etiquette in Coarse Golf seems to be that solo players have right of way over all matches. It is not normally necessary for them to ask permission to play through—they simply pound on round the course. **1970** H. TAYLOR *Golf Dict.* 159 If a ball is lost and cannot be found, the player with the consent of the other players signals to those following to 'play through'. **1973** A. MACVICAR *Painted Doll Affair* viii. 89 The strangers came and putted... Duncan told them we were in no hurry and suggested they should play through. **1975** *Times* 29 Aug. 6/4 In breach of the game's etiquette, one fourball, finding itself behind the other at the second hole, attempted without invitation or request to 'play through' the slower group.

g. To co-operate, comply, agree; to do what is required of one; freq. in negative contexts. *colloq.*

1937 M. ALLINGHAM *Case of Late Pig* viii. 59 'Mr. Whippet,' she began breathlessly, 'he's gone! The body's gone! What shall we do?'..I was glad to see she wasn't playing, either. 'The body's gone,' she repeated. **1940** J. REITH *Diary* 17 Jan. (1975) v. 238 To see Attlee... Went over past troubles between his party and the Ministry of Information... I think I can make him play but of course he is weak. **1947** 'N. BLAKE' *Minute for Murder* x. 223 Charles comes here to fetch Alice. He tells her Nita won't play. They decide to put their plan into operation. **1958** 'A. BRIDGE' *Portuguese Escape* ix. 146 Tell me what's happened? Did the Duque play? **1961** E. WAUGH *Unconditional Surrender* III. i. 218 The Air Force aren't playing until they know what's going on over there. **1967** 'F. CLIFFORD' *All Men are Lonely Now* I. ii. 30 'I've had another word with the Minister.' 'Will he play?' 'He's promised to do everything he can.' **1973** 'M. INNES' *Appleby's Answer* III. xi. 105 Miss Pringle didn't want to play. She choked off her friend.

18. *fig.* or *gen.* To act, behave, conduct oneself (in some specified way); chiefly in special phrases.

Cf. also 16, 34.

1555 LATIMER *Wks.* (Parker Soc.) II. 441 They think that other, hearing of such men's going to mass, do see or inquire of their behaviour there; and thus they play wilily, beguiling themselves. **1599** B. JONSON *Cynthia's Rev.* IV. i, If she have play'd loose with me, I'll cut her throat.

a. ***to play fair***: to play according to the rules of the game, without cheating; also, by extension, to do the thing regularly, to act justly or honourably.

c **1440** *York Myst.* xxix. 365 Playes faire in feere, and I schall fande to fest it With a faire flappe, and þer is one and þer is ij. **1603** SHAKS. *Meas. for M.* III. i. 141. **1763** C. JOHNSTON *Reverie* I. 153 They will imagine that you do not play fair. **1866** MRS. GASKELL *Wives & Dau.* vi, He'll get a ..fellowship if they play him fair.

b. ***to play false, foul, foully***; also ***to play*** (a person) ***false***: to cheat in a game or contest; to deceive, betray.

1579 LYLY *Euphues* (Arb.) 98 Venus played false. **1590-** [see FALSE B. 3]. **1605** SHAKS. *Macb.* III. i. 3 Thou hast it now, King, Cawdor, Glamis, all As the weyard Women promis'd, and I feare Thou playd'st most fowly for't. **1680** OTWAY *Orphan* IV. iii. 1420, I fear the Priest has plaid us false. **1775** SHERIDAN *Rivals* II. ii, You play false with us, madam. **1884** *Times* (weekly ed.) 3 Oct. 13/3 Appearances might play them false. **1893** *N. & Q.* 8th Ser. IV. 534/1 If my memory does not play me false, I have also seen the paper in the *Gent. Mag.*

c. ***to play into the hands of*** (formerly also ***to play*** something ***into the hands of***): to act so as to give an advantage to (another, either partner or opponent).

1705 tr. *Bosman's Guinea* 32 If the Enemies themselves had not seasonably plaid an Opportunity into our Hands. **1753** HANWAY *Trav.* (1762) I. VI. lxxxv. 393 Whatever we play into their hands, is a losing game to this country. **1809** MALKIN *Gil Blas* VII. xv. ¶4, I suspect the clerk of the kitchen and my steward of playing into one another's hands. **1878** H. H. GIBBS *Ombre* 24 He will hold the balance between his friend and the Ombre; playing into the hand of one or the other so as to divide the tricks equally between them. **1879** FROUDE *Cæsar* iii. 29 The powers which he had played into the hands of the mob to obtain.

d. ***to play it on*** (cf. 9): to play a trick upon, take in, cheat; so ***to play*** (***low***) ***down on*** to take a mean or unfair advantage of. (*slang* or *colloq.*) So † ***to play on*** (or ***with***) ***both hands*** (see HAND *sb.* 40); ***to play on*** or ***upon the square*** (see SQUARE).

1871 B. HARTE *Heathen Chinee* iii, Yet he played it that day upon William And me in a way I despise. **1894** *Outing* (U.S.) XXIV. 288/1 This played it on our pursuers very neatly. **1904** MARIE CORELLI *God's Gd. Man* xxi, I always do my best not to play down on a woman.

e. ***to play favourites***: to show favouritism. *colloq.* (orig. *U.S.*).

1902 H. L. WILSON *Spenders* 201, I mustn't 'play favourites', as those slangy nephews of mine put it. **1905** R. E. BEACH *Pardners* i. 31 Not wishing to play any favourites, I'd picked up a basket of tomatoes, a gunny-sack of pineapples, and a peck of green plums. **1973** *Black Panther* 7 July 7/2 The foreman plays favorites and only likes Blacks that act the way they want Blacks to act. **1974** 'S. WOODS' *Done to Death* 132, I decline to think that Lizzie—sorry, I'm not allowed to play favourites, am I?

f. ***to play for safety, to play safe***: to act in such a way as to avoid risks (for orig. use in Billiards see SAFETY 1 g); ***to play for time***: to try to gain more time for oneself; to postpone an action or decision.

1906 KIPLING *Puck of Pook's Hill* 212 The habit of playing for time sticks to a man! **1911** *Conc. Oxf. Dict.* 750/2 *Play for safety*, avoid risks in game or fig[uratively]. **1911** H. B. WRIGHT *Winning of Barbara Worth* xxviii. 395 Greenfield is playing for time so that the strikers will make trouble. **1919** F. HURST *Humoresque* 54 'Oh, anybody that plays as safe as you—' He raised his voice, shoving back his chair. **1919** R. W. LARDNER *Real Dope* iv. 105 Its best to play safe..and see what comes off. **1930** *Engineering* 11 July 56/3 Consequently in 'playing for safety' in getting the casting through the machine shop the foundryman has tended towards using softer materials which give open and sometimes porous structures in the heavier sections. **1931** W. R. INGE *More Lay Thoughts* 85 A young man, we will suppose, is rather deficient in natural sympathy and has no expensive tastes. He is also of an anxious temperament and disposed to play for safety. **1942** M. B. LOWNDES *Let.* 2 Apr. (1971) 229 He said he had come to the *Times* office last week hoping they would make a row, but of course they played for safety. **1944** 'G. GRAHAM' *Earth & High Heaven* (1945) 134 All she could do was to go on playing for time, trying to keep Marc from finding out what her family really thought of him, until, after a while, they thought a little better. *Ibid.* 268 The people who play safe don't change anything, they just sit tight and wait for someone else to change it. **1950** E. H. GOMBRICH *Story of Art* xxvii. 421 No artist can always 'play safe'. **1966** G. N. LEECH *Eng. in Advertising* ix. 88 One of their functions is a non-communicative one—that of 'playing for time' under the pressure of extempore performance. **1975** S. LAUDER *Killing Time on Corvo* iv. 41 'What are they doing out there?.. Playing for time?' I was inclined to say that they were playing for the gallery. **1976** *Southern Even. Echo* (Southampton) 11 Nov. 16/4 Mrs. Phillis Babey thought she was playing safe when she telephoned a hospital before leaving home to make sure there was a bed waiting for her.

g. Used with impersonal *it* as object, together with an adj., adv., or advb. phr., to denote a particular manner of behaviour; to deal with (something) in a specified way; esp. ***to play it close to one's chest***: see CHEST *sb.*[1] 9 c; ***to play it cool***: to behave in a relaxed or unemotional manner (see COOL *a.* 4 e); ***to play it low*** (***down***): to behave meanly or despicably; ***to play it safe*** = ***to play for safety*** (see sense 18 f above).

1873 *Winfield* (Kansas) *Courier* 24 July 3/1 The horses attached to [the] hack which runs between this place and Wellington, one day last week concluded to 'play it alone'. **1882** B. HARTE *Flip* ii, It's playing it rather low down on the old man. **1901** CONRAD & HUEFFER *Inheritors* i. 7 'Oh, come', I expostulated, 'this is playing it rather low down. You walk a convalescent out of breath and then propound riddles to him.' **1919** R. W. LARDNER *Real Dope* iv. 117, I thought I would show them to Capt. Seeley and play it safe. *a* **1921** G. H. GIBSON in *Penguin Bk. Austral. Ballads* (1964) 207 It's playin' it low on William, but perhaps he'll buckle-to. **1941** F. & R. LOCKRIDGE *Murder out of Turn* vi. 72 It's worth playing it that way until we find out different. **1951** *Manch. Guardian Weekly* 17 July 15 The Republicans are playing it safe. **1955** W. C. GAULT *Ring around Rosa* vi. 77 Most gamblers I've met would play it cooler than that. **1960** L. COOPER *Accomplices* II. i. 73 Edwardes tried to play it just a bit too clever and that's what did him in. **1960** *Encounter* Nov. 30/2 My concern is that young people to-day, by 'playing it cool' and fearing to be thought 'squares', may create a style of life, not only in work but in every dimension of existence, which is less full, less committed, less complex, and less meaningful than mid-century opportunities allow. **1963** J. PRESCOT *Case for Hearing* x. 163 Let's wait until he's gone too far to draw back, and then we can produce our evidence and shoot him down in flames. That's how I'd like to play it. **1971** C. BONINGTON *Annapurna South Face* ix. 108 John Edwards dived for cover, but Jonathan Lane, the camera-man, played it cool, pausing to switch on the camera before getting out of the way. **1972** D. CRAIG *Double Take* xii. 149 Everyone knows we've got to play it your way, Mick. **1973** 'D. JORDAN' *Nile Green* i. 11, I let him play it his way. He was my boss. **1977** *Time* 10 Oct. 17/3 You have to follow your hunch. You can't play it safe.

19. ***play at***: **a.** To engage or take part in (a specified game or diversion: also *fig.*): = 16.

1297 R. GLOUC. (Rolls) 3965 Wiþ pleyynge [*v.rr.* pleynde, pleiȝinge] atte tables oþer atte chekere. *a* **1300** *Floriz & Bl.* 344 Þenne he wule..bidde þe pleie at þe escheker. *c* **1440** *Promp. Parv.* 404/2 Pleyyn at the bal, *pililudo*. *a* **1548** HALL *Chron., Hen. VIII* 98 b, On saterday the kyng & the Emperor playd at tennice at the Bayne. **1560** DAUS tr. *Sleidane's Comm.* 290 To passe away the time, the Lantgrave playeth at the cardes. **1596** SHAKS. *Merch. V.* II. i. 32 If Hercules and Lychas plaie at dice Which is the better man. **1613** PURCHAS *Pilgrimage* (1614) 742 Our men plaied at foot-ball with them of the Iland. **1728** MORGAN *Algiers* II. ii. 232 His Majesty..really never appeared better pleased than when playing at Loggerheads, provided there was a Prospect of his being a Gainer. **1853** LYTTON *My Novel* I. xi, There, two can play at that game! **1884** *Illustr. Lond. News* Christmas No. 22/1 'I'm afraid, doctor, we are playing at cross questions and crooked answers', said Fred.

b. To represent in sport; to amuse oneself with an imitation of: = 16 c.

1840 MACAULAY *Clive* Ess. (1887) 527 There is still a Mogul, who is permitted to play at holding courts and receiving petitions. **1832-8** WARREN *Diary Physic.* (1844) II. iii. 175 'I'll play you for a hundred pounds, Doctor!' said Sir Henry; 'and give you a dozen!' **1899** *Tit-Bits* 8 Apr. 21/1 Charles Dawson, who has just been playing John Roberts for the championship [in billiards].

1849 —— *Hist. Eng.* v. I. 613 In their childhood, they were accustomed to play on the moor at the fight between King James's men and King Monmouth's men. **1895** MISS SYMONDS *Stud. Prejudices* vii, Though she had often played at sentiment, no man had ever touched her heart.

20. *trans.* with personal object. **a.** To play against; to contend against in a game.

c **1430** *Batayle of Egyngecourte* 281 in Hazl. *E.P.P.* II. 104 We will play them euerychone, These lordes of Englande, at the tenys. **1832-8** WARREN *Diary Physic.* (1844) II. iii. 175 'I'll play you for a hundred pounds, Doctor!' said Sir Henry; 'and give you a dozen!' **1899** *Tit-Bits* 8 Apr. 21/1 Charles Dawson, who has just been playing John Roberts for the championship [in billiards].

b. *Cricket*, etc. To employ (a person) to play; to employ in a match; to include in a team or company of players.

1751 in H. T. Waghorn *Cricket Scores* (1899) 49 The Earl of Sandwich playes..eleven gentlemen of Eton College against any other eleven gentlemen in England which the Earl of March shall chuse. **1846** W. DENISON *Cricket* 65 He has..long been played alone for his batting. **1887** *Daily News* 8 Dec. 3/4 Let the county committees stamp it out.. simply by not playing the offenders. **1892** *Pall Mall G.* 4 Aug. 5/2 The day of bowlers who are played for their bowling only is over. **1894** *Times* 22 June 8/2 Surrey played the eleven which has done so well for them in their other matches.

21. a. To stake or wager in a game; to hazard at play. Also *fig.*

1483 CAXTON *Cato* B iv b, A player [at dice] demaunded of hym [St. Bernard] yf he wolde playe his hors ageynst his sowle. **1575** in *10th Rep. Hist. MSS. Comm.* App. v. 441 Neither shall he plaie his said maisters goodes at tables, dyce, tennies, or any other unlawfull games. **1589** *Hay any Work* A iij b, Our brother Westchester had as liue playe twentie nobles in a night, at Priemeero on the cards. **1601** SHAKS. *Twel. N.* II. v. 207 Shall I play my freedome at tray-trip, and becom thy bondslaue? **1870** BURTON *Hist. Scot.* (1873) V. liii. 11 It gave the ruler of Scotland a stake which he might play against the English Government.

b. ***play away*** (†***off***): to lose in gambling; *fig.* to waste, squander, throw away recklessly.

1562 *Jack Juggler* in Hazl. *Dodsley* II. 115 He hath no money but what he doth steal, And that he doth play away every deal. **1647** WARD *Simp. Cobler* (1843) 67 They will play away..Knights, Rooks,..and all. **1693** LUTTRELL *Brief Rel.* (1857) III. 5 The King..at night..plaid off 200 guineas, according to custome. **1721** RAMSAY *Rise & Fall of Stocks* 52 Some lords and lairds sell'd riggs and castles, And play'd them aff with tricky rascals. **1879** DOWDEN *Southey* iv. 112 Southey could not afford to play away his health at hazard.

c. To play for, or in order to gain (something); to gain by playing: in phr. ***to play*** BOOTY, ***to play a*** PRIZE (see these words).

d. To bet or gamble at or on (races, cards, etc.); to take chances with. *colloq.* (orig. *U.S.*).

1858 D. C. PETERS *Life of Kit Carson* 354 He'd bin playin' the papers (meaning gambling) and had lost every-thing. **1902** G. H. LORIMER *Lett. Self-Made Merchant* 115 When he chooses a father-in-law who plays the bucket shops, he needn't be surprised if his own son plays the races. **1925** E. WALLACE *King by Night* vi. 21 We never say 'played the races' here; we say 'go racing'. **1932** WODEHOUSE *Hot Water* i. 25, I was a rich man myself at the time of our wedding. But unfortunately I played the Market. **1958** BLESH & JANIS *They all played Ragtime* iii. 61 With ten to twenty a night in tips, a piano-player had more than he could spend so long as he didn't gamble or play the ponies. **1973** 'R. MACLEOD' *Burial in Portugal* iv. 73 He plays the stock market.

22. To move or throw (a piece, etc., with which a game is played), as an item in the playing of the game. **a.** *Chess*, etc. To move (a man) to another square on the board.

1562 ROWBOTHUM *Cheasts* B iv b, Thou shalt playe thy Queenes Paune as farre as he may go. **18..** WALKER in *Mod. Hoyle* (1870) 45 When you touch a piece with the *bonâ fide* intention of playing it. **1870** *Ibid.* 48 To open the game well, some of the Pawns should be played out first.

b. *Cards.* To take (a card) from one's 'hand' and lay it face upwards on the table, in one's turn. Also *transf.*, said of a 'hand', in reference to its effect upon the game; *fig.* to bring forward, or deal with in some way (a thing or person) for one's own advantage; ***to play one's cards well***, to make good use of one's resources or opportunities (cf. CARD *sb.*[2] 2 d).

1680 COTTON *Compl. Gamester* (ed. 2) 82 That he [your Partner] may either Trump them, or play the best of that suit on the Board. You ought to have a special eye to what Cards are play'd out. **1753** FOOTE *Eng. in Paris* I. i, If Lucinda plays her Cards well, we have not much to fear from that Quarter. **1809** MALKIN *Gil Blas* VII. ii. ¶10 After this, if you do not play your cards, it is your own fault. **1879** 'CAVENDISH' *Card Ess.*, etc. 163 He played a false card. **1891** T. HARDY *Tess* I. vii, She ought to make her way with 'en, if she plays her trump card aright. **1964** N. SQUIRE *Bidding at Bridge* ii. 23 The hand may play better in either Spades or no-trumps. **1977** *Homes & Gardens* Feb. 17 Work out how the above hand would play opposite this typical Three Diamond opening.

c. In games with balls, as cricket, tennis, golf, billiards, bowls, etc.: To strike (the ball) with the bat, racket, stick, cue, etc., or to deliver it with the hand, so as to send it in a particular direction or place it in a particular position.

1756 *Gentl. Mag.* XXVI. 489/1 From the Parthian steed, Not more unerring flew the barbed reed Than rolls the ball, with vary'd vigour play'd. **1816** W. LAMBERT *Instr. & Rules Cricket* 33 The Striker should move his right-foot back at the moment of hitting, playing the Ball between his left-leg and the wicket. **1850** F. T. FINCH in 'Bat' *Cricket. Man.* 95 Cricket ne'er shall be forgot while we can play a ball. **1882** *Daily Tel.* 27 May, In the first innings the Antipodeans experienced some difficulty in playing the bowling of Jones. **1891** W. G. GRACE *Cricket* 233 If you can keep up your wicket and play the ball hard away from you, runs are sure to come. **1901** H. MCHUGH *John Henry* 67 'Play the round ball!' suggests Shine.

d. ***play on*** (*Cricket*): of a batsman, to play the ball on to his own wicket, putting himself 'out'.

1858 *Bell's Life* 26 Sept. 7/4 Mr M'Dougall and Grundy caused a total of 20, when the latter 'played on'. **1882** *Daily Tel.* 19 May, When only half-a-dozen had been scored, Butler played on, and he had to make way for Barnes. **1894** *Times* 10 July 11/2 Mr. Mordaunt was out in [Brockwell's] first over, for, after cutting and driving the ball for four, he played on. **1963** *Times* 7 Feb. 3/3 Sir Donald Bradman hit one straight drive for four before playing on to Statham. **1977** *Times* 2 Dec. 10/5 Another [wicket] to the left arm spin bowler Iqbal Qasim when Willis played on, completed England's misery.

23. To bring into some condition by playing; e.g. ***to play oneself in***, to get into form for, or adapt oneself to the conditions of, play; also *fig.*; ***to play time out***, to extend the play until the end of the appointed time.

1869 *Routledge's Ev. Boy's Ann.* 639 Their players had strict injunctions to 'play time out'. **1894** *Times* 10 July 11/2 Mr. Jackson came in with Dr. Grace, and, although a little uncomfortable at starting, soon played himself in. **1900** W. J. FORD *Cricketer on Cricket* xii. 144 If he would only play himself in quietly..he would get 'lashings' of runs. **1928** A. PHILIPS *Boy at Bank* I. i. 13 The cricket was slow to begin with; while the batsmen 'played themselves in' carefully. **1969** 'J. FRASER' *Cock-pit of Roses* vii. 132 'Of course, the first day's always difficult.' 'Question of playing yourself in?' **1971** D. AYERST *Guardian* xxx. 461 He was tied to the Manchester office and given little opportunity to play himself in as a public figure. **1974** A. LASKI *Night Music* 122 'We'll start with the Mozart, play ourselves in.'..He took the violin out of its case. **1975** *Times* 25 Aug. 9/3 He..went in in the second innings with no time to play himself in.

24. *fig.* **a.** To use or treat as a counter or plaything, to manage or use for one's own ends (like chessmen or cards in a game). Also, to fool, swindle; ***to play*** (someone) ***for a sucker***: to treat (a person) as a dupe; to make a fool of; to cheat. Cf. sense 6 e

1656 COWLEY *Pind. Odes, Destinie* ii, Some Wisemen, and some Fools we call, Figures, alas, of Speech, for Destiny plays us all. **1879** 'MARK TWAIN' *Let.* 12 Nov. (1917) I. 369 You could have played him on a stranger for an effigy. **1886** *Lantern* (New Orleans) 20 Oct. 3/2 Some blokes can never see when they are being played for suckers. **1892** KIPLING *Many Inventions* (1893) 168 We've played 'em for suckers so often that when it comes to the golden truth—I'd like to try this on a London paper. **1901** CONRAD & HUEFFER *Inheritors* vi. 95 It seemed to me that she was playing me with all this nonsense—as if she..were fooling me to the top of her bent. **1931** E. LINKLATER *Juan in America* II. xv. 167, I told him what would happen if he tried to play me for a sucker. **1938** *New Statesman* 8 Jan. 39/2 The 'steamer' (the victim) after being 'steered' (picked up) by one performer and 'played' (told the tale) by another, [etc.]. **1941** A. CHRISTIE *Evil under Sun* viii. 146 Crazy about the woman, idealising her, suddenly finding out he'd been played for a sucker. **1959** T. S. ELIOT *Elder Statesman* I. 27 Stay out of politics, and play both parties: What you don't get from one you may get from the other. **1966** R. STOUT *Death of Doxy* ii. 14 If the errand I had tackled for Orrie had been on the level, if he hadn't been playing me,..there would be fur flying soon. **1967** *New Yorker* 18 Mar. 50 Wise up. They're playing you for a bunch of saps! **1973** 'D. JORDAN' *Nile Green* xxxiv. 166 She's a fraud... She's working for the Russians... She's played me for a sucker.

b. To set in opposition, oppose, pit (one person, thing, or party ***against*** another), esp. for one's own advantage. In mod. use frequently ***play off***. Also in phr. ***to play both ends against the middle***.

1643 *Plain English* (1690) 9 They could play one Party of Protestants against another. **1732** BERKELEY *Alciphr.* VI. §24 An ingenious Free-thinker may..play one absurdity against another. **1807** *Ann. Reg.* 4/2 He played off France against the world, and the world against France. **1835** LYTTON *Rienzi* X. iv, The folly is mine, to have played against the crafty Tribune so unequal a brain as thine. **1885** *Manch. Exam.* 6 Aug. 5/1 The Sultan likes to play off one Power against another. **1938** E. WAUGH *Scoop* II. iv. 211 The President kept his end up pretty well—played one company off against the other for months. **1950** O. NASH *Family Reunion* (1951) 46 The wise child handles father and mother By playing one against the other. **1965** *Listener* 10 June 852/1 Their deep African fear of a relapse into subordination makes them play off Eastern and Western contributors. **1972** T. P. MCMAHON *Issue of Bishop's Blood* v. 62 He would be the first member of the FBI who played both ends against the middle to get a personal belief buttressed. **1974** J. STUBBS *Painted Face* xiv. 192 Natalie.. played one against the other for a few days, and reconciled them the following weekend. **1978** M. PUZO *Fools Die* xxv. 285 He was trying to play both ends against the middle, doing his friend the favor and yet trying to warn the reader off the book with an ambiguous quote.

c. ***play off***: to cause (a person) to exhibit himself disadvantageously.

1712 STEELE *Spect.* No. 497 ¶3 His whole Delight was in finding out new Fools, and, as our Phrase is, playing them off, and making them shew themselves to advantage. **1713** ADDISON *Guard.* No. 71 ¶5 He would now and then play them off, and expose them a little unmercifully. **1864** MISS YONGE *Trial* ix, She knew that he was playing the widow off, and that, when most smooth and bland in look and tone, he was inwardly chuckling.

d. To pass ***off*** as something else; to palm ***off***.

1768 H. WALPOLE *Hist. Doubts* 99 Her preparing the way for her nephew, by first playing off and feeling the ground by a counterfeit. **1867** R. GIFFEN in *Fortn. Rev.* Nov. 620 The trick of playing off Jacobite effusions as the national literature of Scotland had already been found out.

e. ***to play the field***: see FIELD *sb.* 10 d.

IV. To exercise oneself or engage in sword-play, fighting, or fencing.

25. a. *intr.* To exercise oneself or contend with weapons; *spec.* to contend for exercise or pastime with swords, rapiers, or sticks; to joust, tourney; to fence. In quot. *a* 1300, ? to contend (in general sense). *Obs.* or *arch.*

c **1205** LAY. 8145 Þeos tweien cnihtes bi-gunnen mid sceldes to scurmen, ærst heo pleoweden [*c* **1275** pleoiden] and seoððe pliht makeden. *c* **1275** *Ibid.* 8126 And pleoiden in þan feldes mid sceaftes and mid scealdes. *a* **1300** *K. Horn* 186 Us he dude lede Into a galeie, Wiþ þe se to pleie,.. Wiþute sail and roþer. *c* **1440** *Gesta Rom.* liv. 235 (Harl. MS.) Cornelius..come with the aduersarijs ayenste the Emperour, the whiche wolde play. **1553** T. WILSON *Rhet.* 7 b, I maie commende hym for plaiyng at weapons. **1602** SHAKS. *Ham.* v. ii. 206 He sends to know if your pleasure hold to play with Laertes. **1692** SIR W. HOPE *Fencing-Master* (ed. 2) 137 Whither you be to play with Blunts or Sharps. **1792** in Southey *Life A. Bell* (1844) I. 440 The officers..passed the whole day in the Sun, playing at long bullets.

†**b.** *trans.* with the bout or contest as object; as, ***to play a play***, ***to play a touch*** (also *fig.*; see TOUCH *sb.*). *Obs.*

1470–85 MALORY *Arthur* VIII. xxxix. 333 Goo thou to yonder pauelione and arme the of the best thou fyndest there, and I shalle playe a merueillous playe with the. **1562** *Jack Juggler* in Hazl. *Dodsley* II. 114, I care not much At the bucklers to play with thee one fair touch. **1598** R. BERNARD tr. *Terence, Heauton.* II. iii, See you play no wild touch [L. *Vide sis, ne quid imprudens ruas*].

V. To perform instrumental music.

26. a. *intr.* To perform upon a musical instrument. Const. *on, upon* (†*at*, †*of*).

(In quot. *c* 825, the vb. seems to be intr. with *timpanan* in the instrumental case, as the trans. const. with the instrument as obj. is not otherwise known before the 18th c.; but the meaning may also be 'to actuate, operate', 6.)

c **825** *Vesp. Psalter* lxvii. 26 Plæȝiendra [*c* **1000** *Ags. Ps.* (Spelm.) pleȝyndra] timpanan [L. *tympanistriarum*]. *a* **1240** *Ureisun* 28 in *Cott. Hom.* 193 Murie dreameð engles biuoren þin onsene. Pleieð, and sweieð, and singeð, bitweonen. *c* **1275** LAY. 20315 His harpe he wende..And gan þare to pleoye And moche game makie. *c* **1384** CHAUCER *H. Fame* III. 111 Ther herd I pleyen vpon an harpe..Orpheus ful craftely. *c* **1400** MAUNDEV. (Roxb.) xxv. 115 Mynstrallez, playand on diuerse instrumentes of music. **1553** T. WILSON *Rhet.* (1580) 133 He can speake the tongues well, he plaies of Instrumentes, fewe men better. **1578** *Nottingham Rec.* IV. 177 Man that pled on the drum. **1673** RAY *Journ. Low C.* 395 All of them cannot paint or play on music. **1743** POCOCKE *Descr. East* I. 82 Three Mahometans sung Arab songs, beating time with their hands, and playing on a tambour. **1816** JANE AUSTEN *Emma* II. vi. 106 'Did you ever hear the young lady..play?'..'She plays charmingly.' **1821** SHELLEY *Epipsychidion* 65 A Lute, which those whom love has taught to play Make music on. **1894** HALL CAINE *Manxman* IV. xiv, There came the sound of a band playing at a distance. **1907** G. B. SHAW *Major Barbara* I. 207 *Undershaft.* Do you play, Barbara? *Barbara.* Only the tambourine. **1920** D. H. LAWRENCE *Lost Girl* 17 She even taught heavy-handed but dauntless colliers, who were seized with passion to 'play'. *a* **1953** E. O'NEILL *Long Day's Journey* (1956) III. 89, I couldn't play with such crippled fingers, even if I wanted to. *Ibid.* IV. 151, I play so badly now. I'm all out of practice. **1974** *Encycl. Brit. Macropædia* X. 1035/1 In March 1831 he [*sc.* Liszt] heard Paganini play for the first time.

b. Said of the instrument or the music itself.

1588 SHAKS. *L.L.L.* v. ii. 216 The musicke playes, vouchsafe some motion to it. **1660** WOOD *Life* 11 Nov. (O.H.S.) I. 347 The canons and students of Ch. Ch...began to weare surplices and the organ playd. *a* **1706** R. SEMPLE *Piper of Kilbarchan* vi, His pipe play'd trimly to the drum. **1860** DICKENS *Uncomm. Trav.* v, Hear this instrument that was going to play. *a* **1907** *Mod.* Just then the music began to play.

27. a. *trans.* To perform (music, or a piece of music) on an instrument.

1509 HAWES *Past. Pleas.* xvi. (Percy Soc.) 70 Where that Musyke, wyth all her minstralsy, Dyvers base daunces moost swetely dyd playe. *c* **1600** SHAKS. *Sonn.* cxxviii, When thou, my music, music play'st, Upon that blessed wood. **1676** DRYDEN *Aurengz.* II. Stage Direct., Betwixt the Acts, a Warlike Tune is plaid. **1727** GAY *Begg. Op.* Introd. (1729) 2 Play away the ouverture. **1882** MISS BRADDON *Mt. Royal* II. x. 218 Christabel played a *Capriccio* by Mendelssohn. **1891** *Blackw. Mag.* CL. 862/2 The band played a republican air.

b. To express or describe by music played on an instrument. Chiefly *poet.*

1603 KNOLLES *Hist. Turks* (1621) 830 Certain Turkish minstrels..plaied them up many a homely fit of mirth. **1697** DRYDEN *Virg. Past.* v. 134 This tuneful Pipe; the same That play'd my Corydon's unhappy Flame.

28. a. To play or perform on (a musical instrument); to cause (it) to sound.

1727–41 CHAMBERS *Cycl.*, *Flute*, an instrument of musick ..played by blowing in it with the mouth. **1755** JOHNSON, *To Play* v.a...2. To use an instrument of musick. [*Todd adds*: as, he plays the organ, fiddle, etc.] **1868** MISS BRADDON *Dead Sea Fr.* (Tauchn.) II. vi. 97 Accompanying herself on the guitar, which she played with a rare perfection. **1879** GROVE *Dict. Mus.* I. 701/1 He [*sc.* Johann Michael Haydn] played the violin and organ. **1885** *Times* (weekly ed.) 14 Aug. 6/1 We have..to play the same fiddle as they played, but we..are not going to play the same tune. **1925** F. SCOTT FITZGERALD *Great Gatsby* v. 114 'Klipspringer plays the piano,' said Gatsby, cutting him off. 'Don't you, Ewing, old sport?' **1946** E. O'NEILL *Iceman Cometh* II. 141 She was beautiful and she played the piano beautifully and she had a beautiful voice. **1959** 'E. MCBAIN' *'Til Death* xii. 162 My kid sister plays piano. **1973** *Publishers Weekly* 14 May 39/2 Cooke would be shown wandering around historical sites —playing piano in a former brothel in New Orleans, for instance. **1976** S. BRETT *So much Blood* v. 69 He plays guitar too?

b. To cause (a gramophone record or a tape) to reproduce what is recorded on it; ***to play back***, to play (a recording) after having made it; also *fig.*

1903 *Talking Machine News* Oct. 103/2 Each machine should play three records. **1907** [see *gramophone needle* s.v. GRAMOPHONE 2]. **1932** *Times Educ. Suppl.* 1 Oct. 372/4 The record was 'played back' to him, and an expression of amazement dawned on his face. **1934** *B.B.C. Year-Bk.* 419 The ability to play-back a wax before processing is of great assistance in making records of running commentaries. **1939** *Electronics & Television* XII. 172/1 Automatic record changers..enable records to be played for almost three-quarters of an hour without attention. **1956** R. E. B. HICKMAN *Magn. Recording Handbk.* v. 124 A tape which has been in storage for some length of time should be re-spooled a short while before it is due to be played. **1957** *Technology* June 132/3 Magnetic tape is fed to a control unit associated with the machine tool. When played back the servomechanisms..carry out the demanded movements. **1958** *Listener* 4 Dec. 921/1 Having read what history books have to say about this person..he can play back as much of it as suits him as *The Confessions of*—for example—*Judas Maccabaeus*. **1962** A. NISBETT *Technique Sound Studio* i. 19 Even with a single microphone, it is still possible to make direct comparison tests by recording short snatches of the various music balances and playing them back. **1962** G. LAWTON *John Wesley's English* 199 Many a time Wesley plays back to his readers..the common observations of familiar speech. **1973** 'H. HOWARD' *Highway to Murder* xiii. 150 I've said no already. If you like I'll put it on tape and you can play it back to yourself. **1974** [see PLAY *sb.* 16 b]. **1978** S. BRILL *Teamsters* xii. 290 Barkett paused, as if to play back what he had just said.

c. *intr.* Of a gramophone record or a tape: to reproduce sound (esp. for a specified period).

1903 *Talking Machine News* Aug. 66/1 Most phonos finish the records almost as soon as one begins to enjoy them, but yours plays quite a long time. *Ibid.* Dec. 150/1 A record will play..without being screwed down. **1952** GODFREY & AMOS *Sound Recording & Reproduction* vi. 163 When running at full speed, a reel of tape which plays for 21 minutes can be rewound in about 2 minutes. **1966** 'R. GARIOCH' *Sel. Poems* 28 What a time a reel of tape can play!

d. ***to play the piano*** (see quot. 1933). *Austral.* and *N.Z. slang.*

1933 L. G. D. ACLAND in *Press* (Christchurch, N.Z.) 18 Nov. 15/7 *Play the piano*, to run the fingers over the sheeps' backs in order to find the softest and easiest to shear. **1966** BAKER *Austral. Lang.* (ed. 2) iii. 55 An old hand at shearing can spot such a defect in a moment by what is known as *playing the piano*.

29. With adverbial extension (*in, out, off, down, up*, etc.): To lead, dismiss, or accompany (persons) with instrumental music. Also, to pass (time) in playing.

1674 HEAD & KIRKMAN *English Rogue* III. xi. 136 Mine Host..causing them [*sc.* the 'fidlers'] to cease their playing ..said..If you have played away my Guests, you shall pay their reckoning. **1823** *Spirit of Public Jrnls.* (1825) 354 Handel being once in a country church, asked the organist to permit him to play the people out. **1844** W. H. MAXWELL *Sports & Adv. Scotl.* xxxiv. (1855) 275 The Frasers..were played off the ground by their pipers. **1883** in *Standard* 22 Mar. 3/3 The Hampshire Artillery Band will play all the Artillery past the saluting point. **1884** J. HATTON *Henry Irving's Impressions of America* I. III. 94 It is customary in American theatres for the orchestra to play the audience out as well as in. **1897** HALL CAINE *Christian* x, A band in yellow and blue uniform sat playing the people in. **1898** BESANT *Orange Girl* II. iii, The small band..played the company into the supper-room. *Mod.* The organist was playing the congregation out. **1902** A. MACHRAY *Night Side London* xiii. 196 When you go upstairs, you find more members up here playing the wee sma' 'oors away.

30. In figurative expressions.

a. ***play on*** or ***upon***: To make use of, or take advantage of (some quality or disposition of another person); to practise upon.

1602 SHAKS. *Ham.* III. ii. 380 You would play vpon mee; you would seem to know my stops. *Ibid.* 387–9. **1697** COLLIER *Ess.* II. (1703) 74 To flatter the vanity, and play upon the weakness of those in power. **1775** SHERIDAN *Rivals* II. i. (1798) 32 You rely upon the mildness of my temper —you do, you Dog! you play upon the meekness of my disposition! **1809** MALKIN *Gil Blas* v. i. ¶35 We fancied that he meant to play upon our fears. **1870** ROGERS *Hist. Gleanings* Ser. II. 116 It is..natural that shrewd politicians should play on the credulity of their dupes.

b. ***to play first*** or ***second fiddle***: see FIDDLE *sb.* 1 b. So ***to play second***, to take a subordinate part.

1809 MALKIN *Gil Blas* x. xi. ¶10, I am..to play second fiddle in all your laudable enterprises. **1822, 1862** [see FIDDLE *sb.* 1 b]. **1884** *Manch. Exam.* 9 May 5/5 The Union will..have to play second to the Central Committee.

VI. To perform dramatically; and derived senses. [Cf. OE. *pleȝan* sb. pl. = L. *ludi* (see PLAY *sb.* 14); *pleȝhús*, PLAYHOUSE, theatre.]

31. a. *trans.* To represent in mimic action; to perform as a spectacle upon the stage, etc.; to act (a pageant, drama, etc.). Also *intr.*, to be performed; to take a specified time to be performed. Also *fig.*

c **1380** WYCLIF *Serm.* Sel. Wks. II. 15 Alle þer garmentis ..ben atier taken of þe fend, to playe þer pagyn among men. **1457, 1468** [see PAGEANT *sb.* 1]. **1528** TINDALE *Obed. Chr. Man* Wks. (Parker Soc.) I. 340 Mark what pageants have been played, and what are yet a playing, to separate us from the emperor. **1542–3** *Act 34 & 35 Hen. VIII*, c. 1 If ani.. person..play in enterludes, sing or rime, any matter contrarie to the saide doctrine. **1548** UDALL, etc. *Erasm. Par. Matt.* vi. 44 Like as players on the stage do playe theyr playe. **1589** PUTTENHAM *Eng. Poesie* I. xvii. (Arb.) 51 The old comedies were plaid in the broad streets vpon wagons or carts vncouered. **1602** SHAKS. *Ham.* III. ii. 93 The whil'st this Play is Playing. **1809** MALKIN *Gil Blas* II. vii. ⁋25 The doctor..had not the least suspicion of the farce that was playing. **1869** *Punch* 9 Jan. 10/2 Mr. Burnand's new Burlesque, now playing at the Haymarket, is called *The Frightful Hair.* **1883** *Manch. Exam.* 22 Nov. 5/3 'Our Boys' was played at Guy's Hospital for the amusement.. of the nurses and patients. **1896** *Pall Mall Mag.* Feb. 234 He was alone in the world, with his life half played. **1929** *Radio Times* 8 Nov. 388/2 *Typhoon* plays for about an hour. **1935** E. WAUGH *Edmund Campion* ii. 75 In 1577 a tragedy of his ..was produced..before..the widow of Charles IX of France; it played for six hours. **1958** *Spectator* 31 Jan. 135/1 The new symphony plays for an hour. **1972** *New Yorker* 8 Apr. 32/2 Mr. Zeffirelli watched the action from the back of the auditorium, and he told us that, except for a few small details, the scene was playing well.

b. *play off*: to show off or exhibit by imitation. (Cf. *take off.*) ? *Obs.*

1789 MME. D'ARBLAY *Diary* 21 Jan., He took up a fan.. and began playing off various imitative airs with it. **1809** MALKIN *Gil Blas* VII. vii. ⁋16 Phenicia..was playing off the amiable and unaffected simpleton.

c. To perform a play or the like in (a specified town, theatre, etc.); to appear as a performer or entertainer at (a particular place). orig. *U.S.*

1896 *N.Y. Dramatic News* 29 Aug. 11/3 A troup of barnstormers..are playing the smaller towns in this vicinity. **1933** P. GODFREY *Back-Stage* xvi. 206 He writes for lodgings to the next town he is playing. **1936** N. COWARD *'Red Peppers'* in *To-night at 8.30* I. 103 'I'll see you don't play this date any more.'..'I'd sooner play Ryde Pier in November.' **1959** *Manch. Guardian* 26 Feb. 8/7 Sir John Gielgud is back in London after a tour of Canada and the United States... He played sixty towns and gave 81 performances. **1965** *Listener* 18 Nov. 801/1 The trouble with Freud and his theory of economy of psychic endeavour is that Freud never played Glasgow Empire second house on a Friday night, and I have. **1973** *Times* 27 Jan. 11/8 It's my greatest dream, to play the Palladium. **1975** *New Yorker* 26 May 30/3 The Bolshoi Ballet, now visiting New York en masse for the first time in nine years, is a younger and considerably more experimental version of the company that played the old Met back in 1966.

32. a. *trans. play out*: to perform to the end; *fig.* to bring to an end; *refl.* to come to an end, become obsolete or effete.

1596 SHAKS. *1 Hen. IV*, II. iv. 531 Out you Rogue, play out the Play. **1854** MRS. AUSTIN *Germany*, etc. 344 The great heroic tragedy which was now being played out on the world's stage. **1867** H. CONYBEARE in *Fortn. Rev.* Nov. 513 The classical and pointed styles each ran their course from prime to decadence—in fact, 'played themselves out' completely. **1884** J. QUINCY *Figures of Past* 21 This burlesque..gradually played itself out, and came to an end.

b. *intr.* for *refl.* or *pass.* Also, to become worn out or extremely weak.

1835 BROWNING *Paracelsus* IV. 680 As though it mattered how the farce plays out, So it be quickly played! **1872** *Rep. Vermont Board Agric.* I. 79 The old native fruit of our country is about playing out, as the saying is. **1885** HOWELLS *Silas Lapham* (1891) I. 61 Gentlemaning as a profession has got to play out in a generation or two. **1924** R. J. FLAHERTY *My Eskimo Friends* III. ii. 93 The dogs almost played out before we reached the crest. **1964** MRS. L. B. JOHNSON *White House Diary* 15 July (1970) 178 A little past one my enthusiasm played out and I put my head in the pillow.

c. pa. pple. *played out*: performed to the end; brought to an end, ended, finished, over and done with; also, exhausted, used up, effete, worn out. (Cf. 16, 22 b, and PLAYED *ppl. a.* 2.)

1864 BURTON *Scot. Abr.* I. iv. 183 The drama is not yet entirely played out. **1870** B. HARTE *Further L. fr. Truthful James* i, Is our civilization a failure? Or is the Caucasian played out? **1887** *Westm. Rev.* June 272 About twelve or fifteen years ago he was decidedly of opinion that Mr. Gladstone was played out. **1888** LEES & CLUTTERBUCK *B.C.* 1887 xxix. (1892) 325 Today they had made forty miles over this awful trail, and their horses were not unnaturally quite played out.

33. To represent (a person or character) in a dramatic performance; to act the part of.

c **1386** CHAUCER *Miller's T.* 198 Somtyme to shewe his lightnesse and maistrye He [Absolon] pleyeth Herodes vp on a Scaffold hye. **1513** MORE *Rich. III* (1883) 79 In a stage play all the people know right wel that he that playeth the sowdayne is percase a sowter. **1590** SHAKS. *Mids. N.* I. ii. 31 Yet my chiefe humour is for a tyrant. I could play Ercles rarely. *a* **1631** DONNE *To Sir H. Wotton* Poems (1654) 146 Courts are Theaters, where some men play Princes, some slaves. **1825** J. NEAL *Bro. Jonathan* I. 92, I do not go to see the characters of the Bible played. *a* **1845** BARHAM *Ingol. Leg.* Ser. III. *Marie Mignot*, Miss Kelly plays Marie.

34. Hence *fig.* in real life: To sustain the character of; to perform the duties or characteristic actions of; to act as if one were, act or behave as or like, act the part of. (Almost always with *the* before the object; rarely with adj. absol. as obj.). Esp. in various phrases, as *to play the* DEUCE, *the* DEVIL, *the* FOOL, *the* MAN, *the* MISCHIEF, POSSUM, REX, TRUANT, etc.: see the sbs.

c **1374** CHAUCER *Troylus* II. 1191 (1240) But ye han pleyed tyraunt neigh to longe, And hard was it your herte for to grave. **1426** AUDELAY *Poems* (Percy Soc.) 29 Thai play not the fole, Contenuali thai go to scole. **1433** LYDG. *St. Edmund* II. 381 Among sarseynes he pleied the lioun. *c* **1530** H. RHODES *Bk. Nurture* in *Babees Bk.* 84 Auoyde murther, saue thy selfe, play the man, being compelde. **1550** CROWLEY *Way to Wealth* A viij b, With extreme crueltie ye haue plaied the lordes ouer them. **1581** SIDNEY *Apol. Poetrie* (Arb.) 20 Will they now play the Hedgehog that..draue out his host? *a* **1603** J. RAYNOLDS *Proph. Obadiah* iii. (1613) 38 Play the good fellowes your selues with the world. **1662** BP. HOPKINS *Fun. Serm.* (1685) 93 Chess-men that on the board play the King and Queen, but in the bag are of the same materials, and rank with others. **1790–1811** COMBE *Devil on Two Sticks* (1817) I. 274 It is an act of prudence to let a woman play the fool, for fear she should play the devil. **1823** LOCKHART *Reg. Dalton* VIII. i, But we must not play sad now, my dear, I hope you will be happy here. **1896** *Pall Mall Mag.* May 5 It was gall to me to play jackal to Dan, or to any one else.

35. To sustain, represent, act (*a part, the part of*), *lit.* in dramatic performance, or *fig.* in real life: see PART *sb.* 9, 9 b.

c **1470** HENRY *Wallace* I. 165 King Herodis part thai playit in to Scotland. **1548, 1584, 1590, 1600** [see PART *sb.* 9, 9 b]. **1655** CULPEPPER *Riverius* Printer to Rdr., The friends of the Sick must play their part, or all will not be well. **1672** [H. STUBBE] *Rosemary & Bayes* 12 Though this expression of taking upon him the person [= *personam induere*]..may not be culpable enough..and therefore the case must be aggravated with *playing a part*; truly, the words of *playing the part* are too light and unbecoming. **1711** ADDISON *Spect.* No. 89 ⁋4 She ought to play her Part in haste, when she considers that she is suddenly to quit the Stage. **1855** MACAULAY *Hist. Eng.* xix. IV. 310 The parts which she was in the habit of playing, and..the epilogues which it was her especial business to recite. **1881** GARDINER & MULLINGER *Introd. Stud. Eng. Hist.* I. xi. 195 In the final struggle.. England played her part well.

36. a. *intr.* To act a drama, or a part in a drama; to perform; = ACT *v.* 8. Also *fig.*

1580 in W. H. Turner *Select. Rec. Oxford* (1880) 408 No Mayor..shall geve leave to any players to playe within the guilde hall. **1602** SHAKS. *Ham.* III. ii. 104 *Ham.* My Lord, you plaid once i th' University, you say? *Polon.* That I did my Lord, and was accounted a good Actor. **1700** DRYDEN *Pal. & Arc.* III. 889 Even kings but play, and when their part is done, Some other, worse or better, mount the throne. **1838** DICKENS *Nich. Nick.* xxiii, Did you ever play at Canterbury? **1880** MCCARTHY *Own Times* IV. lxiv. 434 He showed that he was resolved to play on a vaster stage.

b. *play up to* (*Theatrical slang*): to act in a drama so as to support or assist another actor; hence, to support, back up; to flatter, toady.

1809 MALKIN *Gil Blas* VI. i. ⁋8 You want two good actors to play up to you. **1827** HONE *Every-day Bk.* II. 323 He [a performing elephant] was 'played up to' by the celebrated columbine, Mrs. Parker. **1826** DISRAELI *Viv. Grey* II. xv, There is your Playing-up toady, who, unconscious to its feeder, is always playing up to its feeder's weaknesses. **1894** *Times* 5 Mar. 14/1 The windows here are designed, like the others, to play up to the mosaics, and are not intended to be too visible in profile. **1907** J. H. ELDER-DUNCAN *House Beautiful & Useful* ii. 18 Many of our leading architects and decorative artists..'play up to', or subordinate everything to one feature in a room. **1927** CHESTERTON *Secret Fr. Brown* i. 40 There was something downright creepy about that little goblin with the yellow hair, that seemed to play up to the impression. **1929** KIPLING *Limits & Renewals* (1932) 358 His mother did social small-talk without daring to stop, and Wilkie played up to her. **1972** J. MOSEDALE *Football* x. 142 While the pros proved that wasn't literally true, Trippi played up to the spirit of the comment.

c. *to play down to*: to lower one's standard, quality, etc., to suit the tastes or demands of (one's public); to bring oneself down to (a low standard, level, etc.).

1889 G. B. SHAW *London Music in 1888–9* (1937) 234 When a theatre has been playing down as nearly as possible to the music-hall level. **1906** BEERBOHM *Around Theatres* (1924) II. 215 No dramatist, moreover, ever yet achieved popularity by deliberately 'playing down to' the public. **1930** *Cambridge Daily News* 24 Sept. 8/1 Let us avoid playing down to the public, lest it ask us for a better article than we can provide. *a* **1936** KIPLING *Something of Myself* (1937) viii. 218 Never play down to your public.

d. *to play* (a person) *off the stage*: to act much better than (another actor); to dominate the stage at the expense of (another person). Also *fig.*

1895 G. B. SHAW *Let.* 9 Mar. (1965) I. 494 Our actor managers have a not unnatural reluctance to be played off their own stages by their leading ladies. **1905** BEERBOHM *Around Theatres* (1924) II. 144 He played all the other people off the stage, figuratively. Literally, they remained there, I regret to say. **1920** G. B. SHAW *Let.* 22 Dec. in *B. Shaw & Mrs. Campbell* (1952) 216 You played Hackett off the stage, and made only a few blunders. **1979** P. MASON *Skinner* xi. 78 Perron was rather surly, a peasant..who is being played off the stage by a man with style.

e. *to play for laughs* (or *a laugh*): to try to arouse laughter in one's audience; also *trans.*, to depict or use (something) with the aim of arousing laughter.

In quot. 1905 used as *attrib.* phr. (without *to*).

1905 G. B. SHAW *Let.* 2 Oct. (1972) II. 565 The sooner we get John Bull off, the better... An abominable, coarse, play-for-laughs, third class suburban performance. **1906** BEERBOHM *Around Theatres* (1924) II. 256 Mr. Shaw was not merely 'playing for a laugh'. He was trying to reproduce a thing that exists in life. **1963** *Listener* 14 Mar. 468/1 Joan Littlewood sensibly lets this plot look after itself. Her concern is to play for laughs. **1965** *New Statesman* 9 Apr. 580/3 Mr Donleavy..plays the genre for sad laughs.

VII. With adverbs.

37. play along. a. *intr.* = sense 17 g above; also, to pretend to agree or co-operate. Freq. const. *with. colloq.* (orig. *U.S.*).

1929 D. HAMMETT *Red Harvest* xi. 112 If the dick would play along, the hole in Tim's head from his own gun..would smooth everything over pretty. **1935** S. LEWIS *It can't happen Here* xix. 214 All we desire is for you to play along with us in your paper. **1947** J. STEINBECK *Wayward Bus* 45 There were only two things for Ernest to do—to laugh at her or play along. **1959** B. KOPS *Hamlet of Stepney Green* II. ii. 50, I have no choice. I'll have to play along with him. **1965** *New Statesman* 23 Apr. 638/1 The Labour Party should stand no nonsense from the House of Lords. Although the Tory leadership there is still playing along, defeats of government business inflicted by gangs of Tory backwoodsmen could amount to a deliberate policy of obstruction. **1974** M. BIRMINGHAM *You can help Me* iv. 102 She seemed a little surprised at our enthusiasm for literature... But she was ready to play along with us.

b. *trans.* To deceive or tease (a person); to 'string *along*'. *colloq.*

1965 D. FRANCIS *Odds Against* ii. 23, I smiled at him, and he guessed that I'd been playing him along. **1974** 'J. LE CARRÉ' *Tinker, Tailor* vi. 51 'Wait till Percy sees that,' I tell her—playing her along, like.

38. play down. To minimize; to try to make (something) appear smaller or less important than it really is; to make little of.

1930 *New Statesman* 27 Dec. 351 They accused the Washington departments of being in league with the large employers to 'play down' the number of the unemployed and so encourage the too-ready optimism which continues to assert that prosperity is, once again, just round the corner. **1934** J. O'HARA *Appointment in Samarra* x. 295, I heard the boss tell you to play down the story. **1956** E. M. FORSTER *Marianne Thornton* 29 Personal immortality today may not be denied by orthodoxy but it is played down, it is felt to be self-centred and anti-social. **1958** *Listener* 18 Sept. 428/2 This impression is much diluted in the Arts Council's exhibition, a timid selection which tends to play down the more extreme and remarkable developments of Bomberg's art. **1973** 'E. FERRARS' *Foot in Grave* x. 186 She might have ..given the pair an exaggerated idea of their importance. She had been sure that Henry had been right to play the incident down. **1977** *Sunday Tel.* 4 Dec. 3/6 He accuses church leaders of playing down or disregarding these views and making those who hold them feel 'guilty and almost unchristian'.

39. play up. a. *intr.* To behave in a boisterous, unruly, or troublesome manner; to misbehave; *spec.* of a horse: to jump or frisk about. orig. *dial.*

1803 G. COLMAN *John Bull* II. iii. 23 (*Voices behind.*) *Bur.* They are playing up old Harry below; I'll run and see what's the matter. **1866** J. E. BROGDEN *Provincial Words in Lincolnshire* 151 He came home beery, and playing-up, broke the dolly. **1877** E. PEACOCK *Gloss. Words Manley & Corringham, Lincolnshire* 195/1 They're still enif when ther faather's at hoam, but they do play up when they're to their sens. **1886** R. E. G. COLE *Gloss. S.-W. Lincolnshire* 112 This pony does not play up at the trams as the other did. **1888** 'R. BOLDREWOOD' *Robbery under Arms* II. iii. 42 He could do more with a horse than any man I ever saw. They never seemed to play up with him. **1909** J. SWIRE *Anglo-French Horsemanship* 25 The secret of remaining on a horse when he 'plays up' is to drop the hands, press the heels down, [etc.]. **1931** L. A. G. STRONG *Garden* 41 Paddy was always resentful of strangers, and played up with a redoubled vigour if he saw that they were afraid of him. **1968** [see GET *v.* 70 m]. **1973** K. GILES *File on Death* iv. 108 Cucumber generally played up with the Chief Inspector. **1976** J. SNOW *Cricket Rebel* 66 Back in England, before he had time to bid for a place against Australia, his left elbow started playing up and he was ordered to rest.

b. To behave manfully or heroically; to act in a helpful or co-operative manner. Cf. sense 36 b.

1897 H. NEWBOLT *Vitaï Lampada* in *Admirals All* 21 Play up! play up! and play the game! **1899** E. WHARTON *Greater Inclination* viii. 249, I was in fact the only one of the three who did n't instantly 'play up'; but such virtuosity was inspiring, and by the time Vard had thrown off his coat and dropped into a senatorial pose, I was ready to pitch into my work. **1904** R. FRY *Let.* 9 Jan. (1972) I. 216 It is interesting to find that America is playing up so well and I can quite understand it if B.B. transfers his centre of gravity..to Boston. **1924** G. L. MALLORY *Let.* 27 May in E. F. Norton *Fight for Everest: 1924* (1925) II. 236, I look back on tremendous effort and exhaustion... And yet there have been a good many things to set on the other side. The party has played up wonderfully. **1966** B. KIMENYE *Kalasanda Revisited* 42 The other members played up nicely by expressing them-selves as completely horrified. **1979** D. GURR *Troika* vii. 42, I had to sound sensible. Adult... To hide the secret voice of the schoolboy yelling from the side lines to play up, play up.

c. *trans.* To make the most of; to emphasize; to exploit or trade upon, esp. in journalism and advertising. orig. *U.S.*

1909 R. BEACH *Silver Horde* 106 It is a good newspaper story and I'll play it up. **1926** *Publishers' Weekly* 22 May 1687/1 Let us play up the habits, the appearance, the likes and dislikes, let us sell authors to our public. **1933** E. O'NEILL *Ah, Wilderness!* (1934) I. 23 *Richard* (coming forward—seizing on the opportunity to play up his pre-occupation..). **1945** [see EASE *v.* 8 b]. **1961** *Los Angeles Times* 4 Aug. III. 4 The West Berlin crisis is being played up artificially because it is needed by the United States to justify its arms drive. **1973** 'D. JORDAN' *Nile Green* xi. 49 Guy always plays up the limey accent when he's in the States.

d. To tease, annoy, or irritate (someone); to make sport with; to give trouble to.

1924 GALSWORTHY *White Monkey* II. iv. 151 Did she choose that he should go away, thinking that she had 'played him up' just out of vanity? **1927** *Daily Express* 10 Dec. 1 The girls thought they had got hold of a soft-hearted fool, and they began to play me up. **1934** L. A. G. STRONG *Corporal Tune* 138 His body was frightened of what it had undergone..; and now, having succeeded in making Ignatius aware of it, it played him up, throwing him into something approaching panic. **1964** A. CHRISTIE *Caribbean Mystery* xxii. 223 That's the sort of thing you feel like when your husband's playing you up and you're terribly fond of him. **1974** J. MITCHELL *Death & Bright Water* vi. 55 He wasn't in the mood for throwing, not with his back playing him up like it was. **1977** J. AIKEN *Last Movement* xi. 230 They are trying to play me up. They believe that..I lose control. **1979** 'M. HEBDEN' *Death set to Music* xv. 163 His stomach was playing him up again.

play, obs. form of PLEA *sb.* and *v.*

playa ('plaɪə). orig. *U.S.* [a. Sp. *playa* shore, beach, coast, f. late L. *plagia*: cf. PLAGE[1].]

1. a. A flat silt- or sand-covered area, free of vegetation and usu. salty, that lies at the bottom of a desert basin and after rain becomes a temporary lake (***playa lake***). **b.** A playa lake.

1854 J. R. BARTLETT *Pers. Narr. Explorations* I. 246 The playas..seemed to have an extent of twenty-five or thirty miles. **1856** in *Publ. S. Calif. Hist. Soc.* (1928) XIV. 124 We ..stopped 1½ hours at the wagon & took breakfast & then pushed on to the playa & went ahead to hunt for water. **1885** I. C. RUSSELL in *Monogr. U.S. Geol. Survey* XI. 10 Other lakes, which indicate still more pointedly the contrast between an arid and a humid climate, we may call playa lakes. These are sheets of shallow water, covering many square miles in winter season, but evaporating to dryness during the summer, their beds becoming hard, smooth mud-plains or playas. **1939** P. G. WORCESTER *Textbk. Geomorphol.* ix. 246 Ancient playas which have not been covered with water for many years are likely to have quite irregular surfaces. *Ibid.* 247 Two types of sloping plains usually connect the borders of desert basins with the flat central playa plains. These are bajadas and pediments. **1945** J. L. MARSHALL *Santa Fe* 188 In the *playas*—saucerlike depressions in the desert—were beds of glistening salt and gypsum. **1957** G. E. HUTCHINSON *Treat. Limnol.* I. i. 6 The lakes of southern Oregon and northern California already mentioned are shallow playas. **1969** TWIDALE & FOALE *Landforms Illustrated* xvi. 110/1 Salts crystallise out and form a distinct layer covering the bed of the playa, which is called a saltpan... All the large playas of South and Western Australia are salty. **1975** MCALESTER & HAY *Physical Geol.* x. 330 In arid regions..intermittent playa lakes are formed by infrequent downpours and quickly dry up, leaving an accumulation of evaporites.

2. A beach.

[**1855** in *Publ. S. Calif. Hist. Soc.* (1934) XVI. 59 La Playa (the beach) is that part of the city nearest the mouth of the harbor.] **1856** 'J. PHOENIX' *Phoenixiana* 202 Three other small buildings,..a fence, and a grave-yard, constitute all the 'improvements' that have been made at the 'Playa'. **1857** in *Amer. Speech* (1941) XVI. 265 The following is a list of words and phrases frequently used in English conversation in California, and not unfrequently quoted in California newspapers:..*Playa*, beach. **1924** *Chambers's Jrnl.* Aug. 581/1 They turned eastward..keeping to the *playas*, or little beaches. **1934** R. MACAULAY *Going Abroad* i. 14, I think I shall go down to the playa and bathe. **1964** S. BLANC *Yellow Villa* (1965) 12 The South Seas setting that has made land along the northern *playa* so very expensive. **1966** M. STEEN *Looking Glass* viii. 160 Little lights of fishing boats far away down on the *playa* [in Málaga].

3. (See quot. 1972.)

1898 R. T. HILL *Cuba & Porto Rico* v. 48 Occasionally a few acres of *playa*, or low alluvial land, may be found around the harbors, but the rivers are free from wide bottoms, and the land as a whole stands well above the sea. **1972** *Gloss. Geol.* (Amer. Geol. Inst.) 548/1 *Playa*, a flat, alluvial coastland, as distinguished from a beach.

playable ('pleɪəb(ə)l), *a.* [f. PLAY *v.* + -ABLE.]

† **1.** Given to play, playful, sportive. *Obs.*

1483 *Cath. Angl.* 282/2 Playabylle, *ludibundus, ludicris, ludicer, ludibilis.*

2. Capable of being played: in various senses.

1860 READE *8th Commandm.* 30 There were passages in 'Le Château Grantier' not playable in England. **1873** BENNETT & CAVENDISH *Billiards* 480 Any ball or balls behind the baulk-line,..are not playable if the striker be in baulk. **1875** M. PATTISON *Casaubon* 154 The part of chaplain-man-of-the-world, a part often played, and still playable. **1887** GURNEY *Tertium Quid* II. 57 Old Scotch tunes playable on the black keys of a piano. **1898** *Daily News* 5 May 5/2 The maestro laid the instrument down with an evident air of contempt, but he declared it to be playable.

b. Of a cricket or football ground or the like: Admitting of or fit for playing on.

1872 *Daily News* 15 July, The play did not commence.. until half-past 11, when the ground was rendered 'playable' by the copious use of sawdust. **1881** *Sportsman* 31 Jan. 4/5 Football at Oxford..the ground will hardly be playable until the end of this week.

Hence **playa'bility**, the quality of being playable.

1881 STEVENSON *Virg. Puerisque* 259 Bound up with the subject of play, and the precise amount of playfulness, or playability, to be looked for in the world. **1977** *Early Music* Apr. 151 It would be a useful piece of work if someone were to collect and analyse them [*sc.* wind instruments depicted in medieval manuscripts] according to types and theoretical playability.

play-actor, -actress, etc.: see PLAY *sb.* 17.

playback ('pleɪbæk). Also play-back. [f. vbl. phr. *to play back*: PLAY *v.* 28 b.] **1. a.** The reproduction of a recording, esp. soon after it has been made. Also *fig.* and *attrib.*

1929 *Photoplay* Apr. 110/2 *Play-back*,..the immediate playing of the sound record after the taking of a scene in order that actors and directors may hear how it all sounds. .. The play-back is only possible from disc recording,..as in film recording the film must be developed before the sound can be heard. **1931** N. H. SLAUGHTER in L. Cowan *Recording Sound for Motion Pictures* iv. 61 Disc recording permits play-backs, often a boon to the director and cast. **1934** *B.B.C. Year-Bk.* 419 For immediate play-backs the Blattner system requires a little time to rewind the tape before running off again. **1940** *N.Y. Times* 19 May IX. 10/2 As future generations listen to play-backs of the uses to which radio was put for propaganda purposes..they, too, may be amazed. **1941** B. SCHULBERG *What makes Sammy Run?* xi. 282 He felt he had to justify himself. He insisted upon giving me a play-back of that historic interview. **1949** *Sun* (Baltimore) 5 Feb. 7 A courtroom playback of the broadcasts..brought out that Nazi propaganda was inserted between the GI's messages. **1949** *Electronic Engin.* XXI. 149/3 The recording and play-back heads are so arranged that two tracks of recording can be stored on the standard tape. **1957** C. MACINNES *City of Spades* II. v. 140 On and on she went, like a playback from a tape recorder. **1957** W. H. WHYTE *Organization Man* 133 A young man's idle dream? It is a playback only mildly exaggerated of a vision of the future. **1959** *News Chron.* 25 Aug. 3/5 Visitors to the Radio Show..will be able to see how TV shows are recorded ready for immediate playback. **1970** N. ARMSTRONG et al. *First on Moon* ix. 203 We've been looking at your systems data on playback and everything is looking good. **1976** *Gramophone* Oct. 532 (Advt.), Pickering's exclusive new design development also makes it superior to other cartridges in the playback of stereo records. **1978** G. MCDONALD *Fletch's Fortune* x. 65 The playback volume was too high.

b. *Cinemat.* A technique of recording the voice of a singer for the soundtrack of a film as a substitute for that of an actor or actress when songs are called for. ***playback singer***, a singer whose voice is so used; also *ellipt.*

1952 R. SPOTTISWOODE *Film & its Techniques* 351 The technique of prescoring and playback with singer and orchestra. **1962** *Times* 26 Jan. (Survey of India) p. xiii/2 The well-loved singers of prewar days were displaced by a strange new tribe known as 'play-backs'. **1963** BARNOUW & KRISHNASWAMY *Indian Film* 164 A Cine Writers Association and a Playback Singers Association had been launched but had ceased activity because of lack of support. **1966** R. P. JHABVALA *Star & Two Girls* in *Experience of India* (1971) 74 A playback singer rendered a love-song with.. feeling. **1971** *Sunday Nation* (Nairobi) 11 Apr. 31/4 The best male playback singer trophy.

2. An apparatus for playing recordings.

1930 PITKIN & MARSTON *Art of Sound Pictures* 271 *Play-back*, a device which repeats the voices, recorded on a wax record. **1936** E. S. BESINGER tr. *London's Film Music* IV. 114 The American 'play back' invention has the advantage of less danger, and accuracy more easily attained. **1945** L. A. G. STRONG *Othello's Occupation* 44 It's a recording unit, with a play-back and ordinary controls for loud-speaker. **1960** *Aeroplane* 15 July 51 (Advt.), Permanent radar records with the AEI radar recorder and playback.

play-bill ('pleɪbɪl). A bill or placard announcing a play and giving the names of the actors to whom the various parts are assigned.

1673 [R. LEIGH] *Transp. Reh.* 1 Having posted up a playbill for the title of his book..being prefer'd from writing of bills for the play-houses. **1759** JOHNSON *Idler* No. 47 ¶ 10 His first care in the morning is to read the play-bills. **1875** LOWELL *Wks.* (1890) IV. 376 Theatrical critiques as ephemeral as play-bills.

play-book ('pleɪbʊk). Also without hyphen, as one word, or two. [f. PLAY *sb.* + BOOK *sb.* 3.]

1. A book of plays or dramatic compositions.

1535 *Cov. Corp. Chr. Plays* App. II. 107 Payd for makyng of the playe-boke vs. **1624** MASSINGER *Parl. Love* II. iii, Comparing of these eyes to the fairest flowers,..And such hyperboles stolen out of playbooks. **1727** GAY *Begg. Op.* I. x, Those cursed Play-books she reads have been her ruin. **1856** EMERSON *Eng. Traits, Aristocr.* Wks. (Bohn) II. 80 'Tis an old sneer, that the Irish peerage drew their names from playbooks.

2. A book of games and pastimes for children.

1694 (*title*) A play-book for children. **1761** A. BARCLAY (*title*) Tom Thumb's play book. **1886** (*title*) The golden playbook.

3. *Football.* A book containing various strategies and systems of play. *U.S.*

1967 *Time* 6 Jan. 64 On the field, Plimpton did the calisthenics and learned the playbook cold, but when the test came during an intra-squad scrimmage before a large crowd,..every play was botched. **1969** *Sunday Times* 28 Sept. 22 They spend most of their time watching films of their next opponents or studying the 'play-book' which sets out the dozens of moves they have to learn before the next match. **1972** J. MOSEDALE *Football* v. 57 He absorbed the fundamentals..out of a playbook more than 300 pages long.

playboy ('pleɪbɔɪ). *colloq.* Also play-boy. [f. PLAY *sb.* + BOY *sb.*[1]] A man, esp. a wealthy man, who sets out to enjoy himself; a selfish pleasure-seeker (in quot. 1898 used of the devil). Also as *v. intr.* Hence **'playboyish** *a.*, **'playboyishness**, **'playboyism**.

Cf. also the obsolete sense s.v. PLAY *sb.* 17.

1829 G. GRIFFIN *Collegians* viii. 161 The pretty Syl repeatedly told him that he was 'a funny gentleman' and 'a great play-boy'. **1898** J. MACMANUS *Bend of Road* 107 The divil sittin cheek be jowl with him in his own chimbley corner!..an' himself an' the playboy shoughed out o' the same pipe! **1907** J. M. SYNGE (*title*) The playboy of the western world. *Ibid.* II. 51 You're the walking playboy of the western world. **1926** C. DAY LEWIS in *Oxford Poetry* 20 Proud Playboy of his own complacency. **1926** *N.Y. Times* 11 Oct. 24/2 The playboy of baseball might have heard his name go ringing down the corridors of baseball as a man who won a series game with a home run. **1933** J. CARY *Amer. Visitor* 226 Jukes used to say all these officials were playboys moved by some impractical notion or other. **1936** M. DE LA ROCHE *Whiteoak Harvest* xi. 160 No matter how hard I worked I was looked on as a sort of playboy who couldn't do a man's job. **1939** JOYCE *Finnegans Wake* (1964) I. 183 The house..was the worst, it is hoped, even in our western playboyish world for pure mousefarm filth. **1952** E. O'NEILL *Moon for Misbegotten* I. 55 He is not the blatantly silly, playboy heir to millions whose antics make newspaper headlines. **1954** N. COWARD *Future Indefinite* I. 4 Beneath a glittering veneer of..playboyishness, I had managed..to retain a few normal human instincts. **1959** M. CUMBERLAND *Murmurs in Rue Morgue* xvii. 105 What's the matter with this age?.. Its bitterest insults are to call people playboys, pleasure-lovers, hedonists. **1960** WODEHOUSE *Jeeves in Offing* vi. 60 A New York playboy, accustomed from his earliest years to pursue blondes like a blood-hound. **1962** *Times* 28 Feb. 5/1 The elder boy, who has gone in for playboyism in a big way. **1963** V. CANNING *Limbo Line* xvi. 218 Who wanted money? Amadeo to playboy around? **1973** 'D. JORDAN' *Nile Green* xx. 76 The Lebanese ladies..lusted after the trim, brown-tanned Beirut playboys. **1976** BOTHAM & DONNELLY *Valentino* xi. 86 Wearing tails as the Paris playboy, he was dancing his way into cinema history.

playcart, obs. f. PLACARD.

playce, obs. f. PLAICE.

playche, obs. f. PLEACH, PLASH *v.*[1]

playd, -e, obs. ff. PLAID, PLEA, PLEAD.

play-day ('pleɪdeɪ). **1. a.** A day given up to play; a day exempted from work; *esp.* a school holiday.

1601 HOLLAND *Pliny* I. 555 Worse than either of these is he, who doth that vpon work days which should haue bin don on play-daies or idle holidaies. **1655** in *Nicholas Papers* (Camden) II. 334 He wrote of the sending of Maynard, Windham and Twisden to the Towre; he said it was a strange playdaye. *a* **1716** SOUTH *Serm.* (1724) VI. x. 343 The Soul's Play-day is always the Devil's working Day, and the idler the Man, still the busier the Tempter. **1768** WESLEY *Wks.* (1872) XIII. 285 We have no play-days (the school being taught every day in the year but Sundays). **1876** GRANT *Burgh Sch. Scotl.* II. v. 172 In 1763 the play-days at the grammar school of Kinghorn were fixed as the afternoons of every Wednesday and Saturday.

attrib. **1747** W. DUNKIN in Francis *Horace, Ep.* II. ii. 299 Or, wanting Prudence, like a Play-day Boy Blindly rush on, to catch the flying Joy.

b. A week-day on which miners or others do not work: cf. PLAY *sb.* 13, *v.* 15.

1892 *Daily News* 12 Apr. 6/4 With reference to the weekly 'playday' being fixed for Saturday the agent advised the men to accept this,..it was decided unanimously to take a ballot whether the playday shall be Monday, Thursday, or Saturday. **1901** *Daily Mail* 7 Nov. 3/4 The miners obeyed their leaders as implicitly as they did on..the three previous 'play-days'.

2. *Theatr.* A day on which a play is performed.

1761 in G. C. D. ODELL *Annals of N.Y. Stage* (1927) I. iv. 83 Those ladies who would have places kept in the boxes will please to send a sensible servant to the theatre at three o'clock on every play-day. **1888** G. O. SEILHAMER *Hist. Amer. Theatre* I. xi. 111 Mr. Allyn's benefit took place on Saturday, instead of the regular play-day.

play-down, playdown ('pleɪdaʊn). orig. *Canad.* [f. PLAY *v.* + DOWN *adv.*] (See quot. 1939.)

1939 WEBSTER Add., *Playdown*, one of a series of play-offs, as among the winning teams from different leagues or localities. *Canada.* **1970** *Globe & Mail* (Toronto) 28 Sept. 21/2 Senior hockey in Canada may abandon the Allan Cup playdowns in favor of an annual tournament with six to eight teams participating. **1973** *Courier & Advertiser* (Dundee) 26 Feb. 9/1 The north district play-down in the Scottish Curling championship was concluded at Perth Ice Rink yesterday.

† **playe**, *v. Obs. rare.* [a. Of. *pleiier*, in 3 sing. pres. *pleie* (mod.F. *plier* and *ployer*) to fold:—L. *plicāre.* A doublet of PLY *v.*] *trans.* To fold.

c **1450** *Bk. Curtasye* III. 818 in *Babees Bk.* 326 Be-fore þo lorde and þe lady..Dowbelle he playes þo towelle þere.

playe, plaȝe, obs. forms of PLAY.

played (pleɪd), *ppl. a.* [f. PLAY *v.* + -ED[1].]

1. That has been played.

1833 J. CAIRNIE *Ess. Curling* 61 Every stone shall be reckoned as played, if the player part with the handle. **1877** *Encycl. Brit.* VI. 713/2 If a played stone rolls over, or stops, on its side or top, it shall be put off the ice. **1892** J. BROWN *Man. Bowling* (ed. 2) 76 As soon as the last played bowl stops, the control of the rink is transferred to the other party. **1969** R. WELSH *Beginner's Guide to Curling* xvi. 102 If a curler touches a played stone belonging to his side, he himself will remove it from the ice.

2. a. ***played-out***: see PLAY *v.* 32 c.

1863 HOLLAND *Lett. Joneses* xvi. 239 One remains, here and there, a played-out man.

b. Exhausted, worn out; passé, finished. *U.S. colloq.*

1872 *Republican Rev.* 16 Mar. 2/4 The days of forked sticks for plows is about played. **1883** 'MARK TWAIN' *Life on Mississippi* xliii. 439 That *used* to be, but that's all played now; that is, in this particular town. The Irish got to piling up hacks so, on their funerals, that a funeral left them ragged and hungry for two years afterward; so the priest pitched in and broke it all up. **1897** *Outing* XXIX. 421/2 He's about played.

3. ***played-down***: see PLAY *v.* 38.

1960 G. CHARLES in J. Pudney *Pick of Today's Short Stories* 45 He would have liked to have dropped a modest, played-down remark or two on his standing in his own community. **1973** J. WAINWRIGHT *Touch of Malice* 109 The deliberately played-down tone of his talk.

player[1] ('pleɪə(r)). Forms: 1 pleȝere, 4 pleier, 5 pleyar(e, 5–6 pleyer, 5–7 plaier, (6 plear), 5– player. [OE. *pleȝere*, f. *pleȝan*, PLAY *v.* + -ER[1].]

I. One who plays.

1. In general sense. (The OE. instance appears to be a mistranslation by the glossator.)

c **1000** ÆLFRIC *Voc.* in Wr.-Wülcker 108/9 *Gimnosophista*, nacod pleȝere. **1382** WYCLIF *Jer.* xv. 17, I sat not in counseil of pleieres [Vulg. *ludentium*], and gloriede fro the face of thin hond. *c* **1440** *Promp. Parv.* 404/1 Pleyare, *lusor*. *Ibid.*, Pleyare, þat alwey wyl pley, *ludibundus*. **1552** HULOET, Player at all games, pastymes, and sportes, *ludio*. **1604** SHAKS. *Oth.* II. i. 113 You are Pictures out of doore.. Wilde-Cats in your Kitchens.. Players in your Huswiferie. **1755** JOHNSON, *Player*, an idler; a lazy person. *Mod.* A player at farming.

2. a. One who engages in some game, usually specified in the context, e.g. chess, draughts, cards, tennis; one who is practised or skilful in some game.

c **1420** LYDG. *Assembly of Gods* 1232 Well he shalbe taught As a pleyer [? at chess] shuld to drawe another draught. *c* **1440** *Promp. Parv.* 404/2 Pleyar, at the bal, *pililudius*. *a* **1500** *MS. Ashm.* 344 (Bodl.) lf. 20 b, If ye be a great plaier [at chess] & can well defende your game. **1562** ROWBOTHUM *Cheasts* A iij, The by standers (whiche commonlye see more then the plaiers). **1630** *R. Johnson's Kingd. & Commw.* 180 Let us doe as Players at Tennis, be judged by all the lookers on. **1778** C. JONES *Hoyle's Games Impr.* 25 Suppose I play the Ace of a Suit of which I have Ace, King, and three small ones; the last Player does not chuse to trump it, having none of the Suit. **1867** *Rugby School Football Laws* 19 Any player obtaining a ball in a maul, must have it down as soon as possible.

b. One who plays for stakes; a gambler.

1483 [see PLAY *v.* 21]. **1511** *Churche of Yuell Men* (Pynson) B vj, Oft my players shall say, by the deth such one was a nimble player, for when he came to the play he had but .v.s. & wan .x.s. *c* **1515** *Cocke Lorell's B.* (Percy Soc.) 11 Gardeners, and rake fetters; Players, purse cutters, money baterers. **1755** JOHNSON, *Players*.. a gamester.

c. A professional player (at cricket, golf, etc.). Also *transf.*

1806, etc. [see GENTLEMAN 4 a]. **1884** *Lillywhite's Cricket Ann.* 29 The two matches between the Gentlemen and Players. **1891** W. G. GRACE *Cricket* 210 Every player selected by the Committee to play against the Gentlemen is paid at the rate of £10 per match. **1895** *Daily News* 1 Aug. 6/2 England has generally the better of Scotland, both in the Amateur and Player [Golf] Championships. **1976** W. GREATOREX *Crossover* 31 Meade.. seemed to like having a Player like Calder in among the Gentlemen of the section. **1978** B. LEVIN in K. Gregory *First Cuckoo* 12 We are all, gentlemen and players alike, engaged in the business.. of expressing our views to thousands, or even millions, of people who have not invited us to do so. **1979** L. MEYNELL *Hooky & Villainous Chauffeur* viii. 106 That's how cricket was run in those days; it was gentlemen and players then.

†**3.** One who plays or performs tricks to amuse others: a juggler; an acrobat. *Obs.*

c **1430** *Pilgr. Lyf Manhode* IV. xlvii. (1869) 199 He maketh of þilke þat pleyen with hem, and doon it, hise principal pleyeres, and hise special jogeloresses. **1530** PALSGR. 255/1 Player or goer upon a corde, *batelleur*.

4. One who acts a character on the stage; a dramatic performer, an actor. (In earlier use, one who played in an interlude.)

1463-4 *Rolls of Parlt.* V. 505/2 That.. Pleyers in their Enterludes, be not comprised in this Acte. **1466** *Mann. & Househ. Exp.* (Roxb.) 325 And the sonday nexte after the xij. day, I ȝafe to the pleyeres of Stoke, ij. s. *a* **1533** LD. BERNERS *Gold. Bk. M. Aurel.* (1546) G viij, Counterfaityng plaiers of farces and mummeries. **1539** in *Vicary's Anat.* (1888) App. xii. 240 To y[e] quenes pleyers for pleyng before y[e] king this Cristemas iiij li. **1569** *Nottingham Rec.* IV. 132 A reward gevyn to Ser John' Beron plears. **1600** SHAKS. *A.Y.L.* II. vii. 140 All the world's a stage, And all the men and women, meerely Players. *a* **1680** CHARNOCK *Self-Exam.* Wks. (1849) 175 A player is not a prince, because he acts the part of a prince. **1742** H. WALPOLE *Lett. Mann* (1834) I. 146 All the run is now after Garrick, a wine-merchant who is turned player at Goodman's-fields. **1868** HELPS *Realmah* xvii. (1876) 475 Give me some good plays to go to, played by great players.

5. One who plays on an instrument of music.

1463 in *Bury Wills* (Camden) 18 Y[e] pleyers at y[e] orgenys ij d. **1539** BIBLE (Great) *1 Sam.* xvi. 16 A man, that is a connyng player with [*Geneva* vpon] an harpe. **1608** WILLET *Hexapla Exod.* 198 The singers and players of instruments. **1837** *Encycl. Brit.* (ed. 7) XV. 615/1 The safest compass for ordinary players [of the serpent] is the two first of these octaves.

II. That which plays.

†**6.** A metal pendant to a horse's bit. *Obs.*

1598 FLORIO, *Saliuéra*,.. among riders the plate whereat the players that hang in the mids of a port are fastned. **1607** MARKHAM *Caval.* VI. (1617) 57 He shall haue Snaffles of all shapes.. with small rings in the midst, and sundry sort of small players fastned to those ringes, which to a trauelling horse breedes pleasure. **1611** COTGR., *Babillons*, the players that hang to the port of a bitt.

†**7.** *pl.* The antennæ or palpi of an insect. *Obs.*

1747 GOULD *Eng. Ants* 5 Each Horn [of an Ant's Mouth] has several little Joints, by which means it plays to and fro with great facility... These Players are of particular Use to the Ants both in feeding themselves and also their Young.

8. *Billiards, Croquet.* (See quot.)

1868 W. J. WHITMORE *Croquet Tact.* 9 The term 'player' is borrowed from billiards in the game of pool, and means the ball which, after you have finished your break, will play on you.

9. A record-player.

1948 *Mod. Plastics* Mar. 84 (*heading*) Unique design of portable player, molded in phenolic, matches polystyrene record carrier. **1953** E. T. CANBY *Home Music Systems* vi. 91 The greatest reason for using a manual player is to achieve better sound quality. **1963** J. FOWLES *Collector* II. 167 G.P. jumped up and turned off the player. **1968** 'E. TREVOR' *Place for Wicked* i. 3 Alec said if music wasn't good enough to listen to without talking it wasn't worth putting on the player. **1976** J. DRUMMOND *Funeral Urn* xxv. 127 Margot found him.. listening to a recording by Led Zeppelin. He switched off the player and beckoned Margot in.

III. 10. *attrib.* and *Comb.* (chiefly *appositive*, in sense 4), as ***player-devil***, ***-girl***, ***-man***, ***-woman***, etc.; also **player-coach**, one who plays a game and also coaches his fellow-players; similarly, **player-manager**, **-trainer**; **player-like** *a.*, like or befitting a player or actor; **player-piano**, a piano having a mechanical apparatus by which it can be played automatically.

1948 *Sporting Mirror* 21 May 11/1 Bobby Baxter, former Scottish international and *player-coach to Leith Ath., has been appointed team manager to the Edinburgh speedway team. **1961** *Times* 12 May 4/7 The decision of the Toulston Club to engage an Argentine as player-coach. **1972** J. MOSEDALE *Football* ii. 21 Strictly functional equipment modeled by player-coach George Halas. **1596** LODGE *Wits Miserie* 40 They say likewise there is a *Plaier Deuil, a handsome sonne of Mammons. **1837** H. AINSWORTH *Crichton* I. 197, I can scarce comprehend how a *player-girl like this can occasion him so much trouble. **1548** UDALL, etc. *Erasm. Par. Mark* iv. 24 b, Farre from all manour of *playerlyke ostentation. **1641** PRYNNE *Antip.* 123 Pageants, Theaters, Sceans, and Player-like representations, in making a puppet-play. **1675** WYCHERLEY *Country Wife* II. i, She chid me just now for liking the *playermen. **1771** SMOLLETT *Humph. Cl.* 2 Apr., Miss Liddy had like to have run away with a player-man. **1905** *Daily Chron.* 5 Apr. 7/2 The *player-manager is a rarity. **1951** *Sport* 16–22 Mar. 3/1 He was.. inundated with player-manager offers from non-League sides. **1977** *Western Morning News* 30 Aug. 12/4 On the eve of Exeter City's glamour second round Football League Cup-tie player-manager Bobby Saxton anxiously waits this morning for the latest fitness reports to know if he can field his strongest side to challenge the might of Cup holders Aston Villa. [**1901** *Everybody's Mag.* Oct. 490/1 In the section devoted to musical instruments one can hear hourly concerts by mechanical piano-players.] **1907** *Strand* Nov. 103 It.. is.. the most remarkable achievement in *player-piano construction. *Ibid.* 105 Melody Stops.. distinguish the 'Autopiano' from all.. player-pianos. **1913** [see *music-roll* s.v. MUSIC *sb.* 13 d]. **1922** S. GREW *Art of Player-Piano* 1 The player-piano, like the pianoforte and the organ, is a musical instrument. **1946** R. BLESH *Shining Trumpets* II. xi. 243 He made an unknown quantity of player-piano rolls. **1973** *Times* 25 Oct. 38/7 (Advt.), Steinway and Sons.. are prepared to purchase or take part exchange pianos of their own or other makes except player pianos. **1956** *People* 13 May 13/6, I have had several offers to join clubs in Germany as player-coach or *player-trainer.

Player[2] ('pleɪə(r)). Also **Players**, **Player's**. The proprietary name of a cigarette made by the John Player Company. Also *Comb.*

[**1885** *Trade Marks Jrnl.* 9 Dec. 1196 Player's Rough & Ready Mixture... John Player,.. Nottingham; manufacturer. **1889** *Ibid.* 20 Mar. 285 Player... Manufactured tobacco, except snuff. The firm trading as John Player,.. Nottingham, tobacco manufacturers.] ? **1932** DYLAN THOMAS *Sel. Lett.* (1966) 6 I've got a large Players, and my shoes are off. **1943** *R.A.F. Jrnl.* Aug. 29 'Why was that, Flight?' the Corporal asked, taking a packet of Players from his pocket and selecting one. The Flight Sergeant reached over and helped himself. 'In my days.. corporals couldn't afford expensive fags like these.' **1945** DYLAN THOMAS *Let.* 28 Aug. (1966) 283, I raise one Player-coloured aspen hand to salute and supplicate. **1960** *Tobacco* June 37 A new Player pack... Player's Medium Navy Cut cigarettes, the big sellers, are now introduced in a new modernised pack. **1977** R. BARNARD *Death on the High C's* xiii. 144 He.. puffed his way through a third of his Player's. **1978** D. BLOODWORTH *Crosstalk* vii. 54 She.. lit a Player with a book match.

'**playeress.** *rare.* [f. PLAYER[1] + -ESS.] An actress.

1830 in Cobbett *Rur. Rides* (1885) II. 334 Many playeresses had become peeresses.

† '**playerly**, *a. Obs. rare.* [f. as prec. + -LY[1].] Of the nature or character of an actor; befitting an actor.

1618 BOLTON *Florus* II. xiv. (1636) 132 Whereby they.. were overcome in battell, not by true, and very kings, but this phantastike and playerly one. **1633** PRYNNE *Histriomastix* II. II. i. 852 The Satyricall invectiues of Iuuenall and others against this infamous Playerlie Emperor. *Ibid.* IV. i. 939 Poeticall streines of wit and Playerly eloquence.

Playfair ('pleɪfɛə(r)). The name of Lyon *Playfair*, 1st Lord Playfair (1818–98), British chemist and administrator, used *attrib.* and *absol.* to designate a cipher in which successive pairs of letters are replaced by pairs chosen in a prescribed manner from a matrix of 25 letters, usu. arranged in accordance with a key-word.

1922 J. C. H. MACBETH *Langie's Cryptography* iv. 166 M. Langie has omitted to give any reference to the 'Playfair' cipher, which has been extensively used for military purposes. This cipher is one of the substitution variety, and may be operated with one or more key-words. **1932** D. L. SAYERS *Have his Carcase* xxvi. 344 Here's a cipher message. Probably Playfair. **1966** M. R. D. FOOT *SOE in France* iv. 105 As simple as a Playfair code based on a single word. **1974** *Encycl. Brit. Micropædia* X. 643/3 He [*sc.* Sir Charles Wheatstone].. invented the Playfair cipher, which is based on substituting different pairs of letters for paired letters in the message. **1979** *Listener* 18 Jan. 131/1, I see that I have to encipher my answers to other [crossword] clues in Playfair without knowing the keyword... I have a friend who could solve two Playfair squares before breakfast.

playfellow ('pleɪˌfɛləʊ). [f. PLAY *sb.* + FELLOW.] A companion in play or amusement: usually said of children or young people.

1513 MORE *Rich. III* (1883) 36, I pray God send them both better playfelowes than hym. **1590** SHAKS. *Mids. N.* I. i. 220. **1633** HEYWOOD *Eng. Trav.* I. Wks. 1874 IV. 10 My wife and you, in youth were play-fellowes. **1790** COWPER *Lett.* 27 Feb., Mrs. Hewitt.. was my playfellow at Berkhamstead. **1838** DICKENS *Nich. Nick.* i, At times, a recollection of his old playfellow broke upon him through the haze in which he lived.

†**playfere** ('pleɪfɪə(r)). *Obs.* Forms: 3 **plaȝe iuere**, **pleiuere**, 3–4 **pleifere**, 4 **plaw-**, **plowe-**, **pleyefere**, 4–7 **pleyfere**, 5–8 **playfere**, (5 **-uere**, **fer**, 5–7 **-feer**, **-feere**, 6 **-fiere**, **-feir**, **-feare**, 7 **-pheer(e**; 5 **pleyfer**, **playefere**, 6 **-feere**, **plaifere**, **-feere**, **-fiere**, **-faier**). [f. PLAY *sb.* + FERE *sb.*[1], companion, comrade.] A companion at play, a playfellow, playmate; a companion generally, or in any action or course.

c **1205** LAY. 15631 Ifunden Mærlin & his plaȝe-iueren [*c* **1275** pleiueres] mid him. *a* **1225** *Juliana* 56 Þi sari gast schal wið þe schucke pleiferen pleien in helle. *c* **1305** *St. Edmund Conf.* 64 in *E.E.P.* (1862) 72 Wiþ þe ic go in eche stede.. & þi pleyfere ic am. *a* **1310** in Wright *Lyric Poetry* xv. 49 Glotonie mi glemon wes,.. Prude wes my plowe fere. **1388** WYCLIF *Judg.* xi. 38 Whanne sche hadde go with hir felowis and pleiferis [**1535** COVERD. playefeeres], sche biwepte hir maydynhed in the hillis. *a* **1400** *Transl. N.T.*, *Acts* xiii. 1 (Paues 157) Manaen þat was þo plawfere [Vulg. *collactaneus*] of Herowde þo Tetrarke. *c* **1470** HARDING *Chron.* CLXXVIII. vi, Roger Mortymer.. was that tyme the quenes playfeer. *a* **1548** HALL *Chron.*, *Hen. V* 33 One of his wanton mates and vnthriftie plaifaiers. **1612** *Two Noble K.* IV. iii. 79 Learne what maides haue beene her companions and play-pheeres. *a* **1765** *Jew's Daughter* ii. in Child *Ballads* (1888) III. 244/1, I winna cum in, I cannae cum in, Without my play-feres nine.

fig. **13..** *E.E. Allit. P.* C. 45 Thus pouerté & pacyence are nedes play-feres.

play-field, **-folk**, etc.: see PLAY *sb.* 17.

playful ('pleɪfʊl), *a.* [f. PLAY *sb.* + -FUL.] Full of play, frolicsome, sportive; also, showing a sportive or sprightly humour, pleasantly humorous or jocular, jocund, merry.

a **1240** *Lofsong* in *Cott. Hom.* 205 Tovel spac and slow to Godd.. sumehwile to pleiful, to drupi oðer hwiles. *a* **1568** ASCHAM *Scholem.* (Arb.) 64, I was neuer, either Stoick in doctrine, or Anabaptist in Religion to mislike a merie, pleasant, and plaifull nature. *a* **1719** ADDISON (J.), He is scandalized at youth for being lively, and at childhood for being playful. **1798** BLOOMFIELD *Farmer's Boy*, *Autumn* 340 Loud the Scream Of Geese impatient for the playful Stream. **1807** CRABBE *Par. Reg.* III. 849 His scorn, his love, in playful words he spoke. **1874** L. STEPHEN *Hours in Library* (1892) II. vii. 208 The playful humour which immortalised John Gilpin.

'**playfully**, *adv.* [f. prec. + -LY[2].] In a playful or sportive manner; jokingly.

1791 BOSWELL *Johnson* 15 May an. 1776, I mentioned a scheme.. of making a tour to the Isle of Man..; and that Mr. Burke had playfully suggested as a motto, 'The proper study of Mankind is Man'. **1845** FORD *Handbk. Spain* I. 87 *Picaro, picara*, rogue (may be used playfully). **1875** JOWETT *Plato* (ed. 2) IV. 59 We playfully threatened that you should not be allowed to go home until the question was settled.

'**playfulness.** [f. as prec. + -NESS.] The quality of being playful; sportiveness.

1795 SOUTHEY *Lett. fr. Spain* (1799) 96 With all the baby playfulness of love. **1823** W. SCORESBY *Jrnl. Whale Fish.* 17 The [auroral] arch extending across the zenith, showed an uncommon playfulness of figure and variety of form. **1880** L. STEPHEN *Pope* iv. 84 His playfulness was too near deadly earnest for the comedy of common life.

'**play-game.** A game of play; a piece of sport; an amusement, a sport; a plaything.

1598 BARCKLEY *Felic. Man* I. (1603) 62 They esteeme this our life to be but a play-game. **1632** J. HAYWARD tr. *Biondi's Eromena* 30 A small Barke.. that had beene rob'd by Pirates, and left as a play-game to the windes. **1697** DAMPIER *Voy. round World* (1699) 496, I had been in many eminent Dangers before now,.. but the worst of them all was but a Play-game in comparison with this. **1972** *Evening Telegram* (St. John's, Newfoundland) 24 June 3/1, I won't be spending such a week as the one just past. All jokes aside, it has been no playgame. **1973** *Shooting Times & Country Mag.* 7 July 21/1 To my way of thinking, anything easy to acquire is never valued for long and, compared to what it was in my younger days, fishing is now almost a playgame.

playg(e, **playght**, obs. ff. PLAYOCK, PLAIT.

playgirl ('pleɪgɜːl). *colloq.* Also **play girl**, **play-girl**. [f. PLAY *sb.* + GIRL *sb.*] A woman who sets out to enjoy herself; a good-time girl. Cf. PLAYBOY.

1934 *Sun* (Baltimore) 9 Oct. 7/3 Colletta.. had better be good or she will be sent to a reformatory, her mother.. warned today as the Pittsburgh (Pa.) playgirl arrived in Manila. **1935** *Mademoiselle* May 15 Just trick yourself out in your wildest clothes and turn playgirl for one evening. **1935** A. J. POLLOCK *Underworld Speaks* 89/1 *Play girl*, a promiscuous female who goes out for a good time. **1939** F. SCOTT FITZGERALD *Let.* 4 Jan. (1964) 283 She has tendencies toward being a play-girl and has been put on probation. **1942** *Time* 16 Feb. 64/2 Victor Mature.. announced the breakup of his eight-month marriage to Martha Stephenson Kemp, complained that she was a 'playgirl'. **1963** I. FLEMING *On H.M. Secret Service* v. 55 The worm of self-destruction.. behind the wild, playgirl façade, was eating away.. her soul. **1964** *Punch* 8 Jan. 66/3 A rich American playgirl. **1977** *Spare Rib* Jan. 41/3 And more and more they will try to con us into believing that, for playgirls as well as playboys, a taste for porn is a proof of liberation.

playgoer ('pleɪˌgəʊə(r)). [f. PLAY *sb.* + GOER; cf. *church-goer*.] One who (habitually) goes to the play; a frequenter of the theatre.

1822 LAMB *Elia* Ser. I. *Artif. Comedy Last Cent.*, The present generation of playgoers. **1857** MRS. MATHEWS *Tea-Table Talk* II. 313 Night after night I revelled in delights known only to the play-goer of those times.

So **'play-ˌgoing** *sb.* and *a.*

1780 T. DAVIES *Mem. Garrick* (1808) II. 48 (Jod.) By these means drawing all the playgoing people to Drury Lane. **1896** *Daily News* 28 Jan. 6/6 It has been said that the play-going of a man of the world is one of the most cherished of his memories.

'playground. A piece of ground used for playing on, esp. one attached to a school; hence, a place of recreation however extensive. Also *transf.*, *fig.*, and *attrib.*

1780 A. YOUNG *Tour in Ireland* 104 The school is a building of considerable extent..with..a spacious play-ground walled in. **1794** SOUTHEY *Retrospect* 79 Much of the easy life the scholars led, Of spacious play-ground and of wholesome air, The best instruction and the tenderest care. **1798** *Hull Advertiser* 16 June 1/2 Seminary at Thorp-Arch. .. Adjoining are extensive Play Grounds, for the recreation of the young gentlemen. **1857** MRS. MATHEWS *Tea-Table Talk* I. 4 A Magazine is..an actual playground of indulgence to young authors. **1871** L. STEPHEN (*title*) The playground of Europe. **1874** SYMONDS *Sk. Italy & Greece* (1898) I. i. 6 Our travellers..have made of Switzerland an English playground. **1878** STUBBS *Const. Hist.* III. xxi. 595 The neighbouring villages were the play-ground and sporting-ground of the townsmen. **1901** *Expositor* July 47 Science has found the problem no playground. **1910** *Westm. Gaz.* 31 Jan. 1/3 The 'playground' England, the England of great country houses, of game preserves, [etc.]. **1916** A. HUXLEY *Let.* 7 Sept. (1969) 111 They tell me..you are returning to..England. Or else pacifically to what the Editor of *Truth* would call the *playground of Europe*. **1929** A. E. FORD *My Minnesota* iv. 194 Like hundreds of others we wish our vacation would never end, and we know now why Minnesota has become the 'Playground of the Nation'. **1963** W. SOYINKA *Dance of Forests* 2 Ogun, they deify, for his playground is the battle field. **1968** *Listener* 19 Dec. 819/2, I gave midnight nudie bathing parties from my private yacht moored at the millionaires' playground of Grimsby. **1970** G. GREER *Female Eunuch* 271 The most telling playground for feelings of rejection about women is the joke department. **1971** 'D. HALLIDAY' *Dolly & Doctor Bird* vii. 89 Great Harbour Cay is an island..undergoing transformation into a luxurious international playground for tropical sport. **1975** M. SIMPSON *Chrome Connection* ii. 10 A reminder about.. playground duty. **1976** H. NIELSEN *Brink of Murder* iii. 26 Simon sent off ten cables to ten European playgrounds where Jack Keith might be holidaying. **1977** *Wandsworth Borough News* 16 Sept. 15/1 Planning Proposals... St. Faith's School, Smardale-road, Wandsworth—erection of playground shelter.

play group ('pleɪgru:p). orig. *U.S.* [f. PLAY *sb.* 6 + GROUP *sb.* 3 a.] **a.** *Sociol.* A group formed naturally by young children in a neighbourhood for play and companionship.

1909 C. H. COOLEY *Social Organization* (1913) iii. 24 The most important spheres of this intimate association and coöperation.. are the family, the play-group of children, [etc.]. *Ibid.*, Nor can any one doubt the general prevalence of play-groups among children. **1939** F. J. BROWN *Sociology of Childhood* 177 Miss S. Wisletzky was able to distinguish three factors in the formation of play groups. **1947** —— *Educ. Psychol.* x. 220 The first play group is small,..of a transitory character, formed only to carry on a specific activity of the moment. *Ibid.*, The activity itself is the basis for the organization of the play group. **1954** J. A. C. BROWN *Social Psychol. of Industry* v. 129 Cooley gave as typical examples of primary groups the family, the play-groups of children, and the neighbourhood group of elders in the village community. **1964** GOULD & KOLB *Dict. Social Sci.* 281/1 The dividing line between a clique or a play group and a gang is by no means clear and in practice such a group is whatever the researcher chooses to call it.

b. A group, freq. one organized informally by parents of pre-school children, formed with the object of providing supervised companionship for children. Also *attrib.*

1942 C. LANDRETH *Educ. Young Child* I. i. 17 For this group probably the best immediate solution under 1942 conditions is parents' cooperative backyard play groups. **1962** *Guardian* 6 Nov. 18/3 A pre-school play group which a group of mothers are organising. **1968** D. LAWTON *Social Class, Lang. & Educ.* iii. 24 Linguistic handicaps could be alleviated by separating the twins into different play-groups. **1969** *Times* 5 Nov. 13/4 Three years ago there were many Members of Parliament who thought playgroups had something to do with drama. **1973** B. CROWE *Playgroup Movement* v. 79 In some areas..the groups have not been allowed to start unless the play-group leader is 'suitably qualified'. **1975** H. JARECKI *Playgroups* 10 Vivid pictures of children and their parents in the playgroup setting.

'playhouse. **1. a.** A house or building in which plays are acted; a theatre.

a **1000** *Aldhelm Glosses* (Napier) 1752 *Cęlestis theatri*, þæs heofenlican pleghuses. **1599** SHAKS. *Hen. V*, II. Chorus 36 The Scene Is now transported (Gentles) to Southampton, There is the Play-house now, there must you sit. **1623** in *N. Shaks. Soc. Trans.* (1885) 504 Att the play howse called the Cockpitt in Drurie Lane. **1666** PEPYS *Diary* 27 Oct., The playhouses begin to play next week. **1733** SWIFT *Lett.* Wks. 1841 II. 697 The comedy (which our poor friend [Gay] gave to the playhouse the week before his death). **1809** KENDALL *Trav.* I. xiv. 164 There is no play-house in Harford, nor in any other place in Connecticut. **1851** D. JERROLD *St. Giles* iv. 30, I was born a lady..though I do sell fruit in the playhouse. **1892** [see PLAYLET].

fig. **1705** WYCHERLEY *Let. to Pope* 5 Nov., You may see.. the two great Play-houses of the Nation, those of the Lords and Commons, in dispute with one another.

b. *attrib.* †**playhouse pay** (see quot. 1794). *Obs.*

1673 DRYDEN *Marr. à la Mode* Prol. 16 The women.. swore they would be true;..But..they were made of playhouse flesh and blood. **1700** T. BROWN *Amusem. Ser. & Com.* iv. (1709) 45 A Play-house Wit is distinguish'd by wanting Understanding. **1761** (*title*) A New Academy of Compliments..With a collection of the newest Play-house Songs. **1790** T. WILKINSON *Mem.* I. 146 The theatre being for the first month opened three nights in a week, my salary was only fifteen shillings as play-house pay, and when got to four nights, merely twenty shillings. **1794** C. MATHEWS *Let.* 19 June in A. Mathews *Mem. Charles Mathews* (1838) I. v. 90 Most of the salaries are what they call 'play-house pay'; that is, payment only each night they play; so that a man engaged at three pounds a-week, if he performs three times a-week only, has only half his salary. **1845** *Bentley's Misc.* June 600 In the year 1728 a first-rate singer, according to play-house pay, which means the actual nights of performance, could command no more than *forty-five pounds* annually. **1896** KIPLING *Seven Seas* (Tauchn.) 54 Like playhouse-scenes, the shore slid past our sleepy eyes.

2. a. (Freq. *play-house*.) A house, usu. small, in or with which children may play.

1792 A. YOUNG *Trav. France* I. 108 These cases of models ..have so much the air of children's playhouses, that I would not answer for my little girl..not crying for them. **1857** M. J. HOLMES *Meadow-Brook* xxv. 317 At a short distance from the house was a tall cypress..where now was a play-house. **1908** G. JEKYLL *Children & Gardens* ii. 11 A good play-house..is a little house somewhere in garden or shrubbery, consisting of a kitchen and a sitting-room. **1916** *Daily Colonist* (Victoria, B.C.) 13 July 8/3 She makes all sorts of toys; animals and dolls, rocking horses and play houses. **1965** *Guardian* 20 Nov. 3/8 (Advt.), Playhouse... 59/6... Takes 4/5 children. **1968** *Sunday Times* 16 June 61 The Peter Murray play house..is big enough to hold several children at once. **1978** *Detroit Free Press* 16 Apr. F11/1 (Advt.), 4 bdrm house,..att gar, play house for kids on 2 acres.

playing ('pleɪɪŋ), *vbl. sb.* [f. PLAY *v.* + -ING[1].]

1. a. The action of the verb PLAY, in various senses.

a **1310** in Wright *Lyric P.* xxx. 88 As y me wende omy pleyȝyng, on mi folie y thohte. *c* **1320** *Sir Tristr.* 1744 Sche þouȝt..Tristrem and y boaþe Beþ schent for our playing. *c* **1420** *Chron. Vilod* ccxx, Edgar rode ouȝt on his pleyeng, In to a fforest neyȝt to his place. **1535** COVERDALE *Ecclus.* xlix. 1 Swete as hony.., and as the playenge of Musick. **1561** T. HOBY tr. *Castiglione's Courtyer* I. (1577) Cvb, Some in ryding, some in playing at fence. **1601** BP. W. BARLOW *Serm. Paules Crosse* 60 They call it the playeing of the Bit in the horse mouth. **1691** T. H[ALE] *Acc. New Invent.* p. lxiii, A playing of the Tide too and fro. **1711** in *10th Rep. Hist. MSS. Comm.* App. v. 148 The action..mostly consisted in the playeing of the artillery. **1712** J. JAMES tr. *Le Blond's Gardening* 193 Conveying the Water..for the playing of Jets. **1885** *Athenæum* 14 Nov. 645/2 First-class orchestral playing.

†**b.** (In form *plawing*.) Boiling. *Obs.*

1465 in *Paston Lett.* III. 435 A grete lede to brew v. comb malte with one plawyng. **1683** PETTUS *Fleta Min.* II. 14 Antiently Boyling was called Plawing.

2. *attrib.* and *Comb.*, as ***playing day, garment, gear, -life, place, -time, week***; †**playing-board**, a board for playing some game on, e.g. a dice-board or chess-board; **playing-croft** (*Sc.*), a playground; †**playing-fere**, a playfellow (= PLAYFERE); **playing-field**, a field or piece of ground for playing in; applied esp. to the playgrounds at Eton; **playing-house, -passage**, in quots. applied to the 'bower' constructed by bower-birds; †**playing-stock**, a butt for jests, a laughing-stock; †**playing-table** = *playing-board*; †**playing-thing** = PLAYTHING. See also PLAYING-CARD.

1398 TREVISA *Barth De P.R.* XVII. clxii. (Bodl. MS.), And in anoþer manere table is a *pleyinge borde þat men pley one atte dies and oþer games. **1804** W. TAYLOR in *Ann. Rev.* II. 370 If both sexes have separate *playing-crofts. **1575** *Recorde's Gr. Artes* II. Ee vij b, Then woulde the quotient declare the true number of the working dayes, and not of *playing dayes. **1598** SHAKS. *Merry W.* IV. i. 9 'Tis a playing day I see: how now Sir Hugh, no Schoole to day? **1387** TREVISA *Higden* (Rolls) I. 357 He loueþ somdel her norice and here *pleieng feres. *c* **1450** *Cov. Myst.* (Shaks. Soc.) 115 Ffarewel, Goddys sustyr, and his pleynge fere. **1583-4** in Willis & Clark *Cambridge* (1886) I. 464 (Eton Coll. Acc.) Trees..aboute the *playinge fildes. **1736** H. WALPOLE *Corr.* (1820) I. 6 The playing fields at Eton. **1898** J. A. GIBBS *Cotswold Village* 28 Pass on to Eton... Mark well the playing fields. *c* **1440** *Promp. Parv.* 404/2 *Pleyynge garment, *ludix*. **1531** in Sharp *Cov. Myst.* (1825) 44 The seid pagyaunt, with the implements and *playng geire belongyng to the same. **1840** GOULD in *Proc. Zool. Soc.* 94 They are used by the birds as a *playing-house or 'run', as it is termed. **1957** *Records & Recording* Nov. 20/1 If it is already tracking properly, a sapphire should have a *playing life of about 50 hours. **1871** DARWIN *Desc. Man* I. I. ii. 63 The Bowerbirds..tastefully ornamenting their *playing-passages with gaily-coloured objects. *c* **1350** *Will. Palerne* 750 þat preui *pleyng place..Ioyned wel iustly to meliors chamber. **1556** OLDE *Antichrist* 87 b, The plaieng place, which they call *Theatrum Colosseum*. **1852** W. J. BRODERIP *Leaves Notebk. of Naturalist* 152 On visiting the cedar-brushes of the Liverpool range, he discovered several of these bowers or playing-places. **1579-80** NORTH *Plutarch* (1676) 748 To make him a *playing stock in common playes. **1519** HORMAN *Vulg.* 282 b, I haue bought a *pleyeng tabull: with .xii. poyntis on the one syde: and chekers on the other syde. **1639** in *Bury Wills* (Camden) 180, I give vnto my sonne-in-law..my inlaid playeing tables. *c* **1440** *Promp. Parv.* 404/2 *Pleyynge thynge, or thynge þat menn or chyldyr pley wythe. **1577** T. WHITE *Sermon* (1578) sig. C viii *verso*, If it [*sc.* the Theatre] be not suppressed..it will make such a Tragedie, yt all London may well mourne..for it is no *playing time..but time to pray rather. **1949** FRAYNE & WOLFE *Elements of Sound Recording* xxix. 600 Magnetic materials can be erased and reused..and..reasonable fidelity can be obtained with extremely long playing time. **1951** *Sport* 16-22 Mar. 2/1 Installation of large playing-time clocks on all major league grounds. **1961** *Jazz Monthly* Mar. 27/2 It doesn't amount to much qualitatively, or quantitatively in 36 minutes playing time. **1966** *Jrnl. Canad. Operational Res. Soc.* 117 *Ratio, playing time*, the ratio of playing time to combat time for an event or series of events. **1523-4** *Rec. St. Mary at Hill* 322 Mr parson gave to them a *playng weke to make mery. **1892** *Daily News* 2 Nov. 6/4 The desirability or otherwise of a 'playing' week at Christmas.

'playing, *ppl. a.* [f. as prec. + -ING[2].] **a.** That plays, in various senses: see the verb. **playing trick** *Cards* (see quots. 1959, 1964).

a **1000** in Cockayne *Shrine* 32 An pleȝende cild arn under wænes hweowol. *c* **1374** CHAUCER *Boeth.* III. met. ii. (Addit. MS.), þe pleiyng [*ludens*] besines of men. **1575** CHURCHYARD *Chippes* (1817) 152 For to plant, some playing pieces there A mount was raysd, which kept the foe in feare. **1701** EVELYN *Diary* Apr. (1819) II. 74 A lively playing boy. **1871** RUSKIN in *Daily News* 24 Feb. (1898) 6/2 Turner has put the only piece of playing colour in all the picture into the reflections in this. **1899** SOMERVILLE & 'ROSS' *Some Experiences Irish R.M.* iv. 90 We were in the first game..and I was holding a very nice playing hand. **1959** REESE & DORMER *Bridge Player's Dict.* 166 Playing tricks are tricks that a hand may reasonably be expected to take when playing in its own best trump suit. **1964** *Official Encycl. Bridge* (Amer. Contract Bridge League) 430/2 *Playing trick*, an expected trick if the holder or his partner buys the contract. **1976** 'TREVANIAN' *Main* ii. 24 He has a fair playing hand but no meld to speak of.

†**b.** Boiling. (Also in form *plawing*.) *Obs.*

c **1400** *Sege Jerus.* 671 Hote playande picche amonge þe peple ȝeten. *c* **1420** *Liber Cocorum* (1862) 37 In playand water þou kast hit schalle To harden. **1552** HULOET, Bubble, lyke plawing water,..*scateo*.

'playing-card. Each card of a set or 'pack' used in playing various games: = CARD *sb.*[2] 1.

1543 tr. *Act 3 Edw. IV*, c. 4 No marchant..shal bryng.. into this realme..chessemen, playeng cardes [*orig.* cardes a Juer]. **1684** *Lond. Gaz.* No. 1925/4 Making of Playing Cards in England, (wherein many hundred Poor People are imployed). **1816** SINGER (*title*) Researches into the History of Playing Cards.

'playingly, *adv. rare.* [f. PLAYING *ppl. a.* + -LY[2].] In the way of play or recreation.

1680 AUBREY *Brief Lives* (1898) I. 2, I doe it playingly. This morning..I writt two lives.

'playless, *a.* [f. PLAY *sb.* + -LESS.] Devoid of play or plays (in different senses).

a **1834** COLERIDGE cited in WEBSTER (1864). **1882** C. S. in *Society* 14 Oct. 11/1 Is not France in the same deplorable playless condition? **1889** *Daily News* 28 May 5/2 The playless playgrounds of French schools.

'playlet. [f. as prec. + -LET.] A diminutive or short dramatic play.

1884 B. MATTHEWS in *Century Mag.* XXVIII. 916 In these beautiful and witty playlets there is but the ghost of an action. **1892** *Welsh Rev.* I. 751 The modern playhouse..has become the home, not of the play, but the playlet.

play-list ('pleɪlɪst). Also **playlist**. [f. PLAY *sb.* + LIST *sb.*[6]] **1.** A list of theatrical plays to be performed.

1962 *Times* 23 Jan. 13/3 The classical play-list consists of *Ruy Blas*,..*Amphitryon*, and *L'Homme à la Main de Fer*.

2. A shortlist of musical records that may be broadcast by a radio station in a given period. Also *attrib.*

1975 *Listener* 26 June 848/1 Radio 1 severely limits the number of records it plays... By and large you will hear only the few that are put on the mysterious 'play-list' each week. **1976** *New Musical Express* 17 Apr. 17/1 It makes most of the present Radio One playlist shrivel into insignificance. **1977** *Sounds* 1 Jan. 4/1 Stephen Bishop will triumph. Top of the Pops producers and BBC playlist folks be prepared.

†**'playlome, -loom.** *Obs. rare*[−1]. [f. PLAY *sb.* + ME. *lome*, LOOM.] An instrument of play: in quot. applied to a club.

a **1400** *Sir Perc.* 2013 Go reche me my playlome, And I salle go to hym sone..Ane iryne clobe takes he; Agayne Percevelle the fre He went than fulle right.

'play-ˌmaker. Also **playmaker**. **1.** A maker, composer, or writer of plays; a dramatic author. Now *rare*.

1530 PALSGR. 255/1 Playe maker, *facteur, factiste*. **1581** SIDNEY *Apol. Poetrie* (Arb.) 44 Perchance it is the Comick, whom naughtie Play-makers and Stage-keepers, have iustly made odious. **1691** WOOD *Ath. Oxon.* II. 261 He retired to the Metropolis, lived in Greys Inn, and set up for a playmaker. **1812** *Dramatic Censor 1811* 182 This may be what our modern playmakers call *light* and *shade*. **1903** *N. & Q.* 9th Ser. XI. 201/2 He insults Greene, Elderton, Tarleton, and all play-actors and play-makers. **1953** *Scrutiny* XIX. 204/3 The Restoration playmakers did not exercise their classical imitation by ordering *any* general issues into *any* pattern.

2. A player in a team game, esp. basketball, who leads an attack, or brings other players on his side into a position to score. Hence **playmaking** *a.* orig. *U.S.*

1942 BERREY & VAN DEN BARK *Amer. Thes. Slang* §662/2 Hockey... *Playmaker*, a player who does not attempt to score but puts the puck in place for the scorer. **1951** *Sun* (Baltimore) 12 Jan. 14/4 Bill Kelso, Patterson's playmaker at guard, is expected to be back in action tonight after missing the game against Southern. **1961** *Look* 15 Aug. 84 In high school..he was better known as a basketball playmaker than as a pitcher. **1967** *Boston Sunday Herald* 26 Mar. II. 1/5 Jones, the playmaker, turned gunner Saturday night... The Celtics went up 2-0 on New York in their best-of-five first-round Eastern Division playoffs. **1972** *N.Y. Times* 4 June 6/1 Ford, a playmaker on the varsity basketball team, is the son of Doug Ford. **1974** *Anderson* (S. Carolina) *Independent* 23 Apr. 7A/5 Little Ernie DiGregorio, the Buffalo Braves' playmaking guard, and big Ron Behagen, the Kansas City-Omaha Kings' brawny forward, were unanimous choices on the National Basketball Association's All-Rookie team for the 1973–74 season. **1975** *New Yorker* 7 Apr. 94/3 He was just the man the Bucks had wanted—an experienced ball handler and playmaker who would give the team the steadiness it needed in the backcourt. **1979** *Guardian* 26 Apr. 22/4 The Austrians could offer nothing in attack, where their elegant playmaker, Prohaska, continually dwelt on the ball.

playman (ˈpleɪmən). *nonce-wd.* A man addicted to play, a gamester.

1844 THACKERAY *B. Lyndon* xi, She knew that as a playman I had never failed in my word.

playmate (ˈpleɪmeɪt). [f. PLAY *sb.* + MATE *sb.*[2]] A companion in play, a playfellow. Also *fig.*

1642 H. MORE *Song of Soul* II. iii. III. lviii, The lovely playmates of pure verity. **1798** COLERIDGE *Frost at Midnight* 43 My play-mate when we both were clothed alike! **1828** CARLYLE *Misc.* (1857) I. 213 Brother and playmate to all Nature. **1859** HELPS *Friends in C.* Ser. II. II. i. 14 Hunger and dirt for his playmates. **1879** MEREDITH *Egoist* vi, She had been taken by playmate boys in her infancy to peep into hedge-leaves.

Hence **ˈplaymating** *sb.*, the being playmates, companionship in play.

1888 G. W. CABLE in *Library Mag.* (N.Y.) May 21 Nor [is there] a tenth as much..playmating of white and colored children as there was in the days of slavery.

play-money, monger: see PLAY *sb.* 17.

playn, -e, obs. ff. PLAIN, PLANE.

playnchour, -shore, variants of PLANCHER *sb.*[1]

playner, obs. var. PLENAR.

playnt, obs. f. PLAINT, PLANT.

playntain, -tein, -teyne, obs. ff. PLANTAIN.

playntie, obs. Sc. form of PLENTY.

playock, plaik, plaig (ˈpleːək, pleːk, pleːg). *Sc.* Forms: α. 5 playok, 8– *dial.* **plack**, 9 **playock, -ick, playke, plaik.** β. 6 **playg**, 6– **plaig, (plague).** [f. PLAY *v.* or *sb.*: second element uncertain: ? *-ock* diminutive.] A plaything, toy.

c **1425** WYNTOUN *Cron.* IX. vi. 588 Westymentis, bukis, and othir ma Plesand playokis, he gave alsua. **1508** *Acc. Ld. High Treas. Scot.* IV. 137 For mending of the Princis playg of silvir. **1595** DUNCAN *App. Etymol.* (E.D.S.), *Crepundia*, bairnes plagues. **1711** WODROW *Corr.* (1843) I. 227 Send me word..what placks to buy for Mary. **1820** *Blackw. Mag.* VIII. 395 Put half a crown in the hand of each of the poor weans for a playock. **1821** CARLYLE *Early Lett.* I. 349 Forsaking the switch and quizzer and other plaiks invented by French barbers. *Mod. Sc.* Bring in your plaigs, it's gaun to rain. [See *Eng. Dial. Dict.*]

ˈplay-off, playoff. [f. PLAY *v.* + OFF *adv.*] **a.** An additional game or match played to decide a draw or tie; a replay. **b.** *N. Amer.* A series of games or matches played to decide a championship, etc. Also *transf.*, *fig.* and as *v. intr.*

1895 *Outing* June 50/2 In the play-off for the championship of the city, the Sodality team won a bitterly contested game. **1906** *Liverpool Even. Express* 9 Mar., The play-off resulted in a win. **1915** *Literary Digest* (N.Y.) 21 Aug. 361/1 The race with the Cubs was a tie at the end of the season and a play-off game was necessary to decide the pennant. **1932** *Sun* (Baltimore) 6 Sept. 14/2 The play-off for the Middle Atlantic League baseball title will start Wednesday. **1939** *Beaver* June 25/2 He had a son with the St. Boniface Seals and..was very interested in the fact that they were in the Dominion Junior Hockey Championship play-offs. **1947** A. P. GASKELL *Big Game* 12 He spoke for a while about the traditions of the [Rugby] club and then about the honour of playing off for the championship. **1959** *Times* 29 May 5/2 P. Gill..won the..first prize..after a six holes play-off. **1969** *John Edwards Mem. Foundation Quarterly* V. IV. 145 Guthrie Meade is presently studying fiddling contests... Many of the contests involved preliminary play-offs. **1970** G. F. NEWMAN *Sir, You Bastard* vii. 190 He'd use the man in his play-off with Manso. **1973** *Courier & Advertiser* (Dundee) 1 Mar. 13/2 The six rinks who have qualified for the finals of the 1973 Scottish curling championships will play-off, on a league basis, for the right to represent Scotland at the world championship. **1978** *Morecambe Guardian* 14 Mar. 11/6 The third division could have to go to a play-off, depending upon the result of the..match, still to be played.

play-right: see PLAY *sb.* 17.

play-room (ˈpleɪruːm). Also **play room, playroom.** [f. PLAY *sb.* + ROOM *sb.*[1]] A room used for children to play in; a nursery. Also *attrib.*

1819 M. WILMOT *Let.* 31 Oct. (1935) 25 The children's Nursery and play room are lovely. **1838** *Knickerbocker* XI. 12 One Saturday afternoon when seated with two or three other children in my little play-room. **1840** H. COCKTON *Valentine Vox* xi. 82 He nevertheless contended within himself, that they were games which ought strictly to be confined to the play-room. **1847** J. H. NEWMAN *Let.* 26 Jan. (1962) XII. 26 At Christmas..we find him in the playrooms (cameratas) with the little boys about him, they dressed up as the Magi. **1865** MRS. STOWE *House & Home Papers* 45 Charlie and Jim..detesting the dingy lonely play-room, used to run the city streets. **1890** O. WILDE *Pict. Dorian Gray* viii, in *Lippincott's Monthly Mag.* July 61 He had used it first as a playroom when he was a child and then as a study. **1895** KIPLING *Day's Work* (1898) 365 The two rooms..that had been his nursery and his play-room. **1905** F. H. BURNETT *Little Princess* iii. 32 Is it true that you have a play-room all to yourself? **1909** *Westm. Gaz.* 22 Apr. 2/3 We will wander hand in hand, Like a boy and girl in a playroom land. **1927** *Ladies' Home Jrnl.* Dec. 12/1 Jessica's song and the children's noise, every sound in the play room, broke off short. **1932** *New Yorker* 23 July 22/2 My quarters would inevitably be under the play room, where my host's little ones would indulge in matutinal exercises. **1957** J. MASTERS *Far, Far the Mountain Peak* 105 Her brother..who..stands in a lordly manner in front of the play-room fire. **1966** *New Statesman* 13 May 691/3 There can be no denying that the most obvious method of bettering the circumstances of these working-class mothers is to improve their housing and to raise their standard of living, so that they have gardens or playrooms where the children may run loose. **1973** *Country Life* 14 June Suppl. 1 (Advt.), Georgian house..3 reception rooms..Playroom. Outside studio. **1979** G. ST. AUBYN *Edward VII* ii. 114 Alix..doted on her son. All her instincts were to keep him in the playroom, while his wife tried to interest him in serious matters.

plays, obs. f. PLACE.

plays(e, -sce, -sse, obs. ff. PLAICE.

playsance, -ant, obs. ff. PLEASANCE, -ANT.

playse, playsir, -e, obs. ff. PLEASE, PLEASURE.

play-seer: see PLAY *sb.* 17.

playsome (ˈpleɪsəm), *a.* Now chiefly *dial.* [f. PLAY *sb.* + -SOME.] Inclined to play; playful.

1612 SHELTON *Quix.* I. III. iii. 137 All pleasant folke, wellminded, malicious, and playsome. **1711** SHAFTESB. *Charac.* (1737) III. Misc. II. iii. 117 Not asham'd of expressing any Extasy of Joy or playsom Humour. **1755** HUME *Nat. Hist. Relig.* Ess. 1817 II. 451 The playsome whimsies of monkeys. **1870** VERNEY *Lettice Lisle* 305 He always said he [the horse] were only playsome and that 'tweren't vice.

Hence **ˈplaysomely** *adv.*, **ˈplaysomeness.**

a **1643** LD. FALKLAND, etc. *Infallibility* (1646) 56 He that were playsomely disposed. **1676** GLANVILL *Seasonable Reflect.* 108 How much slightness and playsomeness in speaking of serving God. **1884** BROWNING *Ferishtah, Camel-driver* 60 My playsomeness had pleased thee.

playstead (ˈpleɪstɛd). ? *local.* [f. PLAY *sb.* + STEAD.] A place for play, a playground.

c **1251** *Bittlesden Chartulary* lf. 121 (B.M.), Et in campo orientali vna dimidia acra super playstude iuxta terram Roberti le deuenes. **1889** *Boston Even. Traveller* July, The fortunate children of Boston..go there [Franklin Park]..and engage in games over the playstead.

playster, -ir, obs. forms of PLASTER.

ˈplaystow. *local.* Forms: 1 **pleᵹstów**, 3 **pleystow**; now (as place-name) **Plaistow, Plestor.** [OE. *pleᵹstów* a place of play, a gymnasium, f. *pleᵹ*, PLAY *sb.* + *stów* place.] A place of play, a playground; now surviving in names of English villages (*Plaistow* in Sussex and Essex), and in *Plestor*, name of an open space of about one third of an acre near the church at Selborne, Hants.

10.. *Sax. Leechd.* III. 206 [þonne man] On pleᵹstowe oððe on wafung stowe andbidian hine ᵹesihð styrunge sume ᵹetacnað. *c* **1050** *Cott. Cleopatra Glosses* in Wr.-Wülcker 411/45 *Gymnasio* on pleᵹstowum. *Ibid.* 465/40 *Palestrarum*, ᵹestrynga, pleᵹstowa. **1789** WHITE *Antiq. Selborne* x, Sir Adam Gurdon..in conjunction with his wife Constantia, in the year 1271, granted to the prior and convent of Selborne all his right and claim to a certain place, *placea*, called *La Pleystow*, in the village aforesaid, '*in liberam, puram, et perpetuam elemosinam*'. This *Pleystow, locus ludorum*, or play-place, is a level area near the church of about forty-four yards by thirty-six, and is known now by the name of the *Plestor*. **1875** MORT. COLLINS *Thoughts in Gard.* (1880) II. 109 There is also to be a cross to his [Gilbert White's] memory... Is there no sculptor who could adorn that cross which is to be erected on the plaistor with a flying swallow in marble of Sicily?

playsur(e, -yr(e, obs. ff. PLEASURE.

playt, -e, obs. ff. PLAIT, PLAT, PLATE, PLEA, PLEAD.

ˈplay-the-ball. *Rugby League.* Also **play the ball.** [PLAY *v.*] A move restarting play after a tackle, in which the tackled player kicks or heels the ball from the ground, with opponents in specified positions in front of him and a member of his team behind.

1959 *Observer* 13 Sept. 32/2 Some of their habits at the play-the-balls were suspiciously close to being offside. **1974** *Rules of Game* 158/5 The team in possession is allowed three successive play-the-balls (five in Britain and Australia). **1976** *Liverpool Echo* 6 Dec. 17/9 Midway through the period Les Gorley sneaked a smart try from a play-the-ball. **1978** *Times* 20 Nov. 9/2 In the first half Peponis nipped over from a play the ball, and Cronin kicked two penalties.

plaything (ˈpleɪθɪŋ). [f. PLAY *sb.* + THING.] A thing to play with, a toy.

1675 TRAHERNE *Chr. Ethics* 450 Say he delighteth in armies and victories, and triumphs, and coronations: these are great in respect of playthings; but all these are feeble and pusillanimous to a great soul. **1690** LOCKE *Hum. Und.* I. iii. (1695) 14 A Child knows his Nurse and his Cradle, and by degrees the Play-things of a little more advanced Age. **1738** SWIFT *Pol. Conversat.* 29 A Child would have cry'd half an Hour before it would have found out such a pretty Plaything. **1856** KANE *Arct. Expl.* II. xxi. 207 Strange that these famine-pinched wanderers of the ice should rejoice in sports and play-things like the children of our own smiling sky.

b. *fig.* A man, animal, or thing, treated as a thing to be played with.

1680 OTWAY *Caius Marius* I. i, Sylla too, a Boy, a Woman's Play-thing. **1779–81** JOHNSON *L.P.*, *Akenside* Wks. IV. 289 A physician in a great city seems to be the mere play-thing of Fortune. **1868** FREEMAN *Norm. Conq.* II. vii. 75 The Empire..had now become the plaything of a worthless woman.

c. *attrib.* (Chiefly *appositive.*)

1781 COWPER *Hope* 543 Yet charge not heavenly skill with having planned A play-thing world, unworthy of his hand. **1811** W. R. SPENCER *Poems* Ded., Fancy bestow'd a plaything-lyre. **1851** H. D. WOLFF *Pict. Span. Life* 186 His plaything sword is quivering in the bully's heart.

playtime (ˈpleɪtaɪm). [f. PLAY *sb.* + TIME *sb.*]

1. A time for play or recreation.

1661 COWLEY *Prop. Adv. Exp. Philos.*, *School*, Upon Festivals and Play-times they should exercise themselves in the Fields by..Mustering and Training after the manner of Soldiers. **1844** MRS. BROWNING *Cry of Children* i, They are weeping in the playtime of the others. **1874** BURNAND *My Time* iv. 37, I had come to the end of my play-time.

2. The time for the performance of a play. Also, the time during which a play is being performed.

1616 JONSON *Epicœne* IV. ii, in *Wks.* 572 Who will..inuite vs to the cock-pit, and kisse our hands all the play-time? **1749** SMOLLETT tr. *Le Sage's Gil Blas* IV. XII. i. 179, I waited impatiently for play-time, that I might go to the theatre. **1809** MALKIN *Gil Blas* XII. i. ¶5, I waited with impatience for play-time.

ˈplayward, *a. dial.* [f. as prec. + -WARD: cf. *wayward.*] Given or inclined to play; playful.

1882 T. HARDY *Two on Tower* I. I. 26 The maid was a..playward piece o' flesh when he married her. **1887** —— *Woodlanders* I. iv. 62 It seems no time ago that she was a little playward girl.

playwoman (ˈpleɪˌwʊmən). (?) *nonce-wd.* A woman who acts in plays; an actress.

1889 DOYLE *Micah Clarke* 256 The brat of a wandering playwoman.

play-work (ˈpleɪwɜːk).

1. Work of the nature of play; an easy or trifling occupation.

1824 MISS MITFORD *Village* Ser. I. (1863) 216 It was delightful to observe her enjoyment of this play-work. **1877** SYMONDS *Renaiss. Italy* 450 Cultivation of Latin poetry was no mere play-work to Italian scholars.

2. Work at plays or dramatic performances.

1901 *Westm. Gaz.* 21 Nov. 12/1 At the Vaudeville, fourteen boys and sixteen girls are already mingling arithmetic and history with their play-work on the stage.

playwright (ˈpleɪraɪt). [f. PLAY *sb.* + WRIGHT.] A professional maker or author of plays; a dramatist.

1687 M. CLIFFORD *Notes Dryden* iv. 16 Wherein you may ..thrive better, than at this damn'd Trade of a Play-wright. **1715–16** POPE *Let. to Blount* 21 Jan., Horace's rule for a play may as well be applied to him as a Play wright. **1877** DOWDEN *Shaks. Prim.* v. 49 Shakspere's powers as a rising playwright must have been recognised.

Hence **ˈplaywrightess** (*nonce-wd.*), a female dramatist; **ˈplaywrighting, ˈplaywrightry** (*nonce-wd.*), the action or occupation of a playwright.

1831 CARLYLE in Froude *Life* (1882) II. viii. 171 Various playwrightesses and playwrights. **1851** *Fraser's Mag.* XLIV. 624 What is this but play-wrightry? **1896** *Godey's Mag.* Feb. 186/2 Literary feeling is not everything in playwrighting. **1928** *Publishers' Weekly* 16 June 2445 Francis Brett Young, not content with writing distinguished novels and poems, has turned his attention to playwrighting. **1966** *Punch* 10 Aug. 230/1 Those grand old ample days of playwrighting when plots were clear and motives required no hard brainwork. **1973** E. BULLINS *Theme is Blackness* 12 In the area of playwrighting, Ed Bullins, at this moment in time, is almost without peer in America.

plaza (ˈplɑːzə, formerly ˈplɑːθa, ˈplɑːsa). [Sp.:—pop. L. *plattia:—L. *platea*: see PLACE *sb.*] In a Spanish-speaking country, A market-place, square, public place. Also *U.S.*, a public square or open space; in extended uses (orig. and chiefly *N. Amer.*), a large paved area surrounded by or adjacent to buildings, esp. as a feature of a shopping complex. Also *attrib.*

1683 SALGADO (*title*) A Description of the Plaza or Sumptuous Market-Place of Madrid. **1826** F. B. HEAD *Pampas* 176 In the centre of the town there is a Plaza or great square. **1844** J. GREGG *Commerce of Prairies* II. 77 Two or three miles above the plaza there is a dam of stone and brush. **1850** PRESCOTT *Peru* II. 129 The Spanish soldiery assembled by torch-light in the *plaza* to witness the execution of the sentence. **1852** *Knickerbocker* XL. 197 The spirit-stirring fife and drum, and the roar of cannon on the plaza [at New Orleans], announce the hour for morning parade. **1856** G.

H. Derby *Phoenixiana* 126 Every citizen..was aroused at 2 A.M. by the soul-stirring and tremendous report of the Plaza Artillery. **1884** Sweet & Knox *Through Texas* xxiii. 307 Old Gen. Ignacio Barterra 'cussed' a forty-foot steeple on the old church on the plaza. **1907** S. E. White *Arizona Nights* iii. 47 A freight outfit brought him to Tucson and dumped him down on the plaza. **1948** *Sun* (Baltimore) 20 Nov. 14 (*caption*) All tolls for travel across the Chesapeake Bay Bridge will be paid at booths on the 1000-foot toll plaza on the Western Shore approach to the bridge. **1957** *Times* 2 Dec. 13/1 Shopping..is simplified [in Canada] by the presence of suburban shopping plazas..an enormous parking lot encircled by branches of the down-town stores. **1959** *Ottawa Citizen* 11 July 21/7 Two plazas with parking facilities and offices for Customs and Immigration..are to be built. **1961** L. Mumford *City in Hist.* Note to plate 62, Ossip Zadkine's sculpture..placed on a plaza fronting the inner Harbor of Rotterdam. **1966** T. Pynchon *Crying of Lot 49* v. 103 She came..into a plaza teeming with corduroy, denim, bare legs,..students in nose-to-nose dialogue. **1969** *Guardian* 15 July 10/6 There is no place nearer to hell than the all-under-one-roof shopping 'plaza'. **1969** *Parade* (N.Y.) 14 Dec. 18/3 It is not at all uncommon..to see hippies and Indians sitting together in the town's main plaza, sharing a canteen of water or a pack of cigarettes. **1974** *Sci. Amer.* Feb. 99/3 Bending and shear forces are maximum at the plaza (ground floor) level. **1975** *N.Y. Times* 16 Oct. 43/6 Scheduled for completion in one year, it will have 24 tennis courts, 14 tennis 'alleys' for practice,..and a 13,000-square-foot covered plaza, including an arcade, between 56th and 57th Streets.

‖**plaza de toros** ('plaθa, 'plaza de 'toros). [Sp.: see PLAZA.] In a Spanish-speaking country: a bull-ring. Also *fig.*

1846 R. Ford *Gatherings from Spain* xxi. 296 All the world crowds to the *Plaza de toros*. **1910** *Encycl. Brit.* IV. 789/2 Before the introduction of railways there were comparatively few bull-rings (*plazas de toros*) in Spain... At the present day nearly every larger town and city in Spain has its *plaza de toros*. **1922** J. Hergesheimer *Bright Shawl* (1923) 70 At the Plaza de Toros..she was seated on an upper tier..over the entrance for the bulls. **1934** A. Huxley *Beyond Mexique Bay* 285 A temporary *Plaza de Toros* had been built..a circular fence with a precarious grandstand on the shadier side. **1965** C. D. Eby *Siege of Alcázar* iii. 58 Toledo was converted into a noisy *plaza de toros*, but the matador was never in danger of being gored by his victim. **1973** *Sat. Rev.* (U.S.) 25 Sept. 29/1, I remember clearly the first bullfight I ever saw, in Barcelona... The *plaza de toros* was packed.

plazolite ('plæzəʊlaɪt). *Min.* [f. Gr. πλάζ-ειν to perplex + -ITE[1].] A calcium aluminosilicate that occurs as small, colourless to pale yellow, dodecahedral crystals with a vitreous lustre, and is probably a variety or impure form of hibschite.

1920 W. F. Foshag in *Amer. Mineralogist* V. 183 Included in some material collected by the writer near Riverside, California, were several specimens of vesuvianite associated with small colorless dodecahedrons. The latter proved to be distinct from any known species and the writer proposes the name plazolite from the greek *plazo*, to perplex, in allusion to the difficulty in interpreting its composition. **1941** *Amer. Mineralogist* XXVI. 451 Hibschite and plazolite are very much alike in their properties. Chemically, plazolite differs only by a small and rather variable content of CO_2, and geometrically by the form of its crystals. **1962** W. A. Deer et al. *Rock-Forming Minerals* I. 104 Plazolite originally was thought to contain essential CO_2, but this has been shown to be due to contamination and plazolite must be regarded as being similar to hibschite. **1968** *Mineral. Abstr.* XIX. 139/2 The so-called skarns accompanying some ore deposits in the western region of Honshu Island are revealed to be composed of many veinlets which contain hydrous silicate. The most remarkable..are scawtite, hillebrandite, plazolite, [etc.].

ple, early form of PLEA; erron. f. PLEASE *v.*

plea (pliː), *sb.* Forms: α. 3 **plaid, playd** (see also PLEAD *sb.*). β. 3–4 **plait, playt,** 5 **pleet,** 5–6 **plete, 7 pleyt.** γ. 3 **plai,** 3 (6 *Sc.*) **play,** 3–6 **ple,** 4–6 **plee, pley,** (5 *pl.* **place**), 6– **plea**; (*Sc.* 6 **plei, plie,** 6– **ply,** 7 **pleie, pleye),** 7–8 **pley).** As to *common place* for COMMON PLEAS, see the latter. [ME. *plaid, plai,* a. OF. *plaid* (842 in Strasburg oath), agreement, decision, decree, lawcourt, suit, action, in Anglo-Norm. *plai* (*c* 1170 in *Horn*), *play*, law-suit, action:—**playid-*, **plagid-*:—L. *placit-um* that which pleases or is agreed upon, a decision, decree, etc., in 9th c. (in phrases *placita habēre, tenēre*), an assembly for discussion and decision of matters of state; sb. use of pa. pple. neut. of L. *placēre* to please: see PLACIT. The β forms agree with the OF. variant *plait* (11th c.), *plet, plaict* (Godef.), Prov. *plait*, Sp. *pleito*, Pg. *preito*, It. *piato*, early med.L. *plaitum* (Du Cange) from *placitum.*]

I. In Law.

1. a. A suit or action at law; the presentation of an action in court. Now *Hist.* and *Sc.* (esp. in phr. ***a law-plea***).

α. *a* **1250** *Owl & Night.* (Cott.) 5 Þat plait [*Jesus MS.* playd] was stif & starc & strong. *Ibid.* 1737 An lateþ dom þis plaid [*Jesus MS.* playd] tobreke.

β. *c* **1290** *Beket* 601 ȝif ani plait [R. Glouc. (Rolls) 9704 play] to chapitle were i-drawe And ani man made ani apel. **1340** *Ayenb.* 39 To þise zenne belongeþ al þet barat, alle ualshedes, and alle gyles þet comeþ ine plait. *c* **1400** *Apol. Loll.* 79 In þe court of pleet. **1510–20** *Compl. too late maryed* (1862) 7 To daye I had peas, rest, and unyte, To morowe I had plete and processe dyvers. **1622** Malynes *Anc. Law-Merch.* 470 For the tenth time, the pleyte or suite, with all the records, goeth out of that Iudges court to a higher court.

γ. [**1292** Britton I. xvi. §4 Si soit le plé del princepal suspendu [let the plea against the principal be suspended]. *Ibid.* II. xv. §5 Si le play soit meu, et en plé pledaunt soit le bref trové vicious [if the plea be opened, and in the course of pleading the writ be found defective].] *c* **1290** *Beket* 576 in *S. Eng. Leg.* I. 123 Þe king wolde þat In his court þat plai [*v.r.* ple] scholde beon i-driue. *c* **1380** Wyclif *Eng. Wks.* (1880) 89 He meynteneþ most synne bi preuylegies, exempcions & longe plees. *c* **1440** Lydg. *Hors, Shepe & G.* 1 Controuersies pleys & discordis Atween persones were it too or thre. *c* **1450** *Godstow Reg.* 303 William Fitz Petir called into plee Moolde Vpton, Abbesse of Godestowe, and the Covent of the same place, in a plee of dette in the Courte of Mighell of Meldon. **1463–4** *Plumpton Corr.* (Camden) 9 Be the place of the detinue for a chalise shold be lent to you; also the writts were out. *c* **1470** Henryson *Tale of Dog* 45 It is..perrilous Till enter in pley befoir ane juge suspect. **1487** *Sc. Acts Jas. III* (1814) II. 177/2 That all Ciuile accionis questionis and pleyis..be determytt & decidit befor the Iuge ordinaris. **1535** Coverdale *2 Sam.* xv. 4 O..that euery man which hath a plee or matter to do in yᵉ lawe, might come to me. **1557** Grimalde *Mans Life* in *Tottell's Misc.* (Arb.) 109 The courts of plea, by braul, and bate, driue gentle peace away. **1570** Buchanan *Chamæleon* Wks. (1892) 46 [He] socht to mak ane other change of court, and set vp new play agane. *c* **1575** *Balfour's Practicks* (1754) 53 All mutes and pleyis quhilk happinis to rise within burgh, sould be pleadit and determinat within the samin. **1577** Harrison *England* II. ix. (1877) I. 202 These cases are otherwise called plees or action, wherof there are two sorts, the one criminall and the other ciuill. **1591** Lambarde *Archeion* (1635) 16 No man ought to sue out of the Countrey, or to draw his Plea from thence. **1609** Skene *Reg. Maj.* I. 8 To compeir, and answere..vpon the principall pleie..touching the lands vnjustlie occupied be him. **1637–50** Row *Hist. Kirk* (Wodrow Soc.) 174 The Session charged with buying of pleyes, delaying of justice and bryberie. *a* **1735** Arbuthnot *John Bull* (1755) 14 A plea between two country esquires about a barren acre upon a common. **1822** Galt *Provost* xxvii, This gave rise to many pleas, and..bickerings, before the magistrates. **1862** McGilvray *Poems* 75 (E.D.D.) You won the plea.

b. Phrases. ***to hold pleas*** (= med.L. *tenere placita*), to try actions at law, to have jurisdiction; ***to hold a plea***, to try an action.

1477 *Rolls of Parlt.* VI. 187/2 That..no Styward..hold plee uppon any Action, atte sute of any persone. **1494** Fabyan *Chron.* VII. 344 Syr Hugh Bygotte, iustyce,..kepte his courte at Seynt Sauyours, & helde there the plees callyd Itinerii, the whiche is to meane, the traueylynge, or the waye plees. **1531** *Dial. on Laws Eng.* II. xxxvi. (1638) 127 For else it were a thing in vaine for him to hold plee of Advowsons. **1570–6** Lambarde *Peramb. Kent* (1826) 182 Having a court ..in which they hold plea of all causes and actions, reall and personall, civill and criminall. **1620** J. Wilkinson *Coroners & Sherifes* 46 By a writ of Justicies out of the chancery, which is a commission to the Sherif to hold plea of any summe whatsoever. **1768** Blackstone *Comm.* III. vii. 112 This writ may issue..to the county courts or courts-baron, where they attempt to hold plea of any matter of the value of forty shillings. **1874** Stubbs *Const. Hist.* I. iii. 46 The count ..is still allowed to hold pleas.

c. ***common pleas***: originally, legal proceedings on matters over which the Crown did not claim exclusive jurisdiction; later, actions at law brought by one subject against another, identified with *civil actions*, and sometimes called † ***civil pleas*** (*obs.*). Often short for *Court of Common Pleas*: see COMMON PLEAS.

c **1215–1550** [see Common Pleas]. **1591** Lambarde *Archeion* (1635) 20 [see d]. *Ibid.* 21 Courts of Law, that have Jurisdiction of Civill or Common Pleas arising betweene our owne subjects. *a* **1634** Coke *2nd Inst.* 21 Common or civil pleas are divided into real, personall, and mixt. **1768–1844** [see Common Pleas]. **1895** Pollock & Maitland *Eng. Law* II. 571 Trespass *vi et armis*, even when..it had become as civil an action as civil could be, was still not for every purpose a Common Plea, for, despite Magna Carta, it might 'follow the King'.

d. ***Pleas of the Crown*** (*placita Coronæ*): originally, legal proceedings on matters over which the Crown claimed an exclusive jurisdiction, as being breaches of the king's peace; later, in England including all criminal proceedings, as opposed to common pleas or civil proceedings (*obs.*); in Scotland limited to four of the gravest kinds of action: see quot. 1607.

[**1215** *Magna Carta* c. 17 Nullus vicecomes constabularius coronatores uel alii balliui nostri teneant placita corone nostre.] **1529** Rastell *Pastyme, Hist. Brit.* (1811) 183 The plees of the crowne were holden in the towre. **1591** Lambarde *Archeion* (1635) 20 The Courts of Law doe either hold civill, or criminall Causes (more anciently tearmed Common Pleas, and Pleas of the Crowne). **1607** Cowell *Interpr.* s.v., Pleas of the Crowne in Scotland be 4, roberie, rape, murder, and wilfull fire.., with vs they be all suites in the Kings name against offences committed against his Crowne and dignitie.., or against his Crowne and peace. **1651** Hobbes *Leviath.* (1839) 296 The pleas according thereunto called public, *judicia publica*, Pleas of the Crown; or Private Pleas. **1769** Blackstone *Comm.* IV. i. 2 The code of criminal law; or, as it is more usually denominated with us in England, the doctrine of the pleas of the crown. **1895** Pollock & Maitland *Eng. Law* II. 571 More native to our law was the distinction between Pleas of the Crown and Common Pleas, which was often supposed to coincide with, though really it cut, the more cosmopolitan distinction [i.e. between civil and criminal].

2. a. A pleading; an allegation formally made by a party to the Court; an argument or reason urged by or on behalf of a litigant or party to a suit, in support of his case. ***to make plea***, to plead. Still in Sc. Law: see quots. 1825, 1861.

c **1381** Chaucer *Parl. Foules* 485 Of al myn lyf syn that day I was born So gentil ple in loue or othir thyng Ne herde neuere no man me be-forn. **1390** Gower *Conf.* III. 154 Ther was with him non advocat To make ple for his astat. **1467** *Mann. & Househ. Exp.* (Roxb.) 402 Item, [paid] for a nother wrytte..Item, for makenge of a ple for the same, v.s. **1607** Cowell *Interpr., Plea*..signifieth in our common lawe, that which either partie alleadgeth for himselfe in court. **1825** *Act 6 Geo. IV.* c. 120 §9 Each of the Parties shall ..lodge with the Clerk, previous to the final Adjustment of the Record, a short and concise Note, drawn and signed by Counsel, of the Pleas in Law on which the Action or Defence is to be maintained. **1861** W. Bell *Dict. Law Scot.* 636/1 Pleas in law, as a distinct portion of a record, were introduced by the Judicature Act, 6 Geo. IV. c. 120, §9. *Ibid.* 636/2 The pleas are in general so framed as to ground any legal argument which the facts may warrant. *Ibid.* 637/1 The panel's plea must either be *guilty* or *not guilty*.

b. A formal statement, written or oral, made by or on behalf of a prisoner or defendant, alleging facts either in answer to the indictment, or to the plaintiff's declaration, bill, or statement of claim, or showing cause why the prisoner or defendant should not be compelled to answer.

In civil process, since 1875, technically superseded by *defence. declinatory, dilatory, foreign, peremptory*, etc. *plea*: see the adjectives.

[**1337** *Year-Bk. 11 Edw. III* (1883) 5 Il nad nulle cause par quei cesti ple girreit en vostre bouche de pleder en barre.] **1449** *Rolls of Parlt.* V. 169/1 To plede any plee or plees in barr of the accyon, or in abatement of the bille. *a* **1531** in *Dial. Laws Eng.*, etc. (1886) 360 In an action of debt upon a prompt, it is no plea to say, that he receiveth the money in contestation of his obligation. **1607** Cowell *Interpr.* s.v., Then is there a Forein plea, whereby matter is alleadged in any court that must be tried in another. **1769** Blackstone *Comm.* IV. xxvi. 326 We have now to consider the plea of the prisoner or defensive matter alleged by him on his arraignment. **1818** Cruise *Digest* (ed. 2) II. 222 On debate the plea was allowed by Lord Keeper Bridgeman. **1875** *Judicature Act* O. xix. r. 13 No plea or defence shall be pleaded in abatement.

c. ***special plea***. In civil and criminal law, a plea either in abatement or in bar of an action or prosecution, alleging some new fact, and not merely disputing the ground of action or charge: opposed to *the general issue*. Cf. *plead specially*, PLEAD *v.* 7 b (also Coke *On Litt.* 282 b). Also, ***plea-in-bar*** (without *special*). (In quot. 1847 *fig.*)

1699 in Ld. Raymond *Reports* (1790) I. 393 A rule was made by consent that the defendant should waive the special plea, and plead the general issue. **1729** G. Jacob *New Law-Dict.* sig. L 1 *verso*, A Plea in Bar, not giving a full Answer to all the Matter contained in the Plaintiff's Declaration, is not good. *Ibid.*, If the Plea in Bar be to the Action it self, and the Plaintiff is barred by Judgment, &c. it is a Bar for ever in Personal Actions. **1768** Blackstone *Comm.* III. xx. 305 When he meant to distinguish away or palliate the charge, it was..usual to set forth the particular facts in what is called a special plea. *Ibid.*, Pleas that totally deny the cause of complaint are either the general issue, or a special plea in bar. *Ibid.* 306 A justification is likewise a special plea in bar. **1769** *Ibid.* IV. xxvi. 329 Special pleas in bar; which go to the merits of the indictment, and give a reason why the prisoner ought not to answer it at all, nor put himself upon his trial for the crime alleged. These are of four kinds: a former acquittal, a former conviction, a former attainder, or a pardon. **1817** W. Selwyn *Law Nisi Prius* (ed. 4) II. 692 Special pleas, either in bar or abatement, are seldom pleaded to this action [Ejectment]. **1847** Dickens *Dombey* (1848) xxiii. 229 A plea in bar that they would have valuable consideration for their kindness. **1963** *Times* 9 May 17/5 Connelly said yesterday that he wished to withdraw that plea of Not Guilty and to enter a plea-in-bar on the grounds of *autrefois acquit*.

d. *ellipt.* for 'a plea of guilty', *spec.* in *U.S.* slang phr. ***to cop a plea***, to plead guilty, usu. as part of a bargain or agreement with the prosecution. Also *transf.* in Black English (see quot. 1970[1]).

1927 *Amer. Speech* II. v. 281/1 *Cop a plea*, to tell the truth. **1929** Hostetter & Beesley *It's a Racket!* 222 *Cop a plea*, to plead guilty to a lesser crime than the one originally charged. **1941** J. Smiley *Hash House Lingo* 19 *Cop a plea*, acknowledge a complaint. **1959** Jowitt *Dict. Eng. Law* II. 1350/2 The word 'plea' is used colloquially to mean a plea of guilty. **1963** J. Prescot *Case for Hearing* viii. 123 As for the trial itself, I don't give it more than half a day. It's bound to end up in a plea. **1970** *Daily Tel.* (Colour Suppl.) 6 Mar. 19/2 The majority of accused pleaded guilty—the case then being known to practitioners as a 'plea' as distinct from a 'fight'—and for pleas there was no legal aid. **1970** C. Major *Dict. Afro-Amer. Slang* 41 *Cop a plea*, to be verbally evasive. **1970** J. Cole in A. Chapman *New Black Voices* (1972) 495 The street life style is the cool world... It is here we see the greatest development of stylized talking, sounding,.. copping a plea and whupping game. **1972** J. L. Dillard *Black English* i. 4 Characteristic ghetto uses of language like ..'coppin' a plea', and 'the dozens', are now fairly familiar. **1974** *Telegraph* (Brisbane) 4 June 14/7 Today he did what Americans call copped a plea, in return for pleading guilty to the least serious charge against him, all the other charges of involvement in Watergate and the burglary of Daniel Ellsberg's psychiatrist were dropped.

II. Extended and figurative uses.

3. Controversy, debate, contention, quarrel, strife. In later usage chiefly, now only, *Sc.*

a **1250** [see 1 α]. *c* **1320** *Cast. Love* 1078 'A! Ich am bitrayȝed,' qᵈ þe fend þo, 'Nou Ich am þorw ple over-comen so.' **1382** Wyclif *Isa.* lviii. 4 Lo! to ples and to striues ȝee fasten, and smyten with the fist vnpitously. **1387–8** T. Usk *Test. Love* II. v. (Skeat) I. 22 Wherof cometh plee, debat, thefte, begylinges, but richesse to winne. **1483** Caxton *Gold. Leg.* 305/1 He also had a grete plee and altercation with the deuylle for the body of Moyses. **1560** A. L. tr.

Calvin's Foure Serm. Songe Ezech. i, He entreth not into plea with God. **1596** DALRYMPLE tr. *Leslie's Hist. Scot.* x. 316 Sum captanis fra baith pairtes, sped with speid to stanche this pley, and mitigate this controuersie. *Ibid.* 433 Tha suld returne But plie [L. *sine armorum strepitu*]. *a* **1774** FERGUSSON *Hallowfair* Poems (1845) 16 Pleys that bring him to the Guard And eke the Council Chammer. *a* **1810** TANNAHILL *Poems* (1846) 11 His wife and him are at some family plea. **1872** MICHIE *Deeside Tales* xiv. 120 There was like to be a ply between them an' the Forbeses.

4. That which is pleaded, maintained, or urged in justification or excuse; a pleading, appeal, argument, claim; an apology, pretext, excuse.

a **1550** *Vox Populi* 423 in Hazl. *E.P.P.* III. 283 Thei are dryven to theire plea. **1568** GRAFTON *Chron.* II. 612 The Capitaine perceiuing his dilatorie ple, by force tooke him from the officers. **1589** NASHE *Pref. Greene's Menaphon* (Arb.) 14, I had rather referre it, as a disputatiue plea to diuines. **1638** *Penit. Conf.* vii. (1657) 127 Their best plea is from the words of Christ. **1667** MILTON *P.L.* IV. 394 So spoke the Fiend, and with necessity, The tyrant's plea, excused his devilish deeds. **1754** RICHARDSON *Grandison* III. xviii. 152 No plea is too weak for folly and self-interest to insist upon. **1771** HORNE in *Junius Lett.* li. (1772) II. 197, I admit the plea. **1838** THIRLWALL *Greece* xxxvii, V. 5 He obtained leave to decline the command on a plea which can scarcely have been more than a pretext. **1877** FROUDE *Short Stud.* (1883) IV. I. i. 4 The privilege and authority of bishops and clergy was Becket's plea for convulsing Europe.

†**5.** *transf.* That which is demanded by pleading; a claim. *Obs. rare.*

1588 SHAKS. *L.L.L.* II. i. 7 The plea of no lesse weight Than Aquitaine. **1596** —— *Merch. V.* IV. ii. 284 But none can driue him from the enuious plea Of forfeiture, of iustice, and his bond. *Ibid.* IV. i. 198, 203.

†**6.** A proposal, offer. *Obs.*

c **1450** *Merlin* 365 And yet shall I make to yow a feire plee: com with me to Bredigan..and do hym homage..and I shall yelde yow the castell all quyte. *Ibid.* 366, I sente hym to wite that I wolde he make no pleet, ne noyse to no man of his companye.

7. *attrib.* and *Comb.*: (in sense 2) *plea-roll*; **plea-bargaining** *vbl. sb.* (orig. *U.S.*), a practice whereby a defendant in criminal proceedings agrees to plead guilty to a charge in exchange for the prosecution's cooperation in securing a more lenient sentence or some other mitigation; hence (as a back-formation) **plea bargain** *sb.* and *v. intr.*; **plea-house** *Sc.*, a court of law; **plea-side**, the civil side of a court having both civil and criminal jurisdiction.

1969 *Northwestern Reporter* 2nd Ser. CLXV. 528/1 Court has proper role of discreet inquiry into propriety of settlement whereby defendant as a result of *plea bargain agrees to plead guilty to lesser degree of offense than that with which he was charged. **1974** *Harper's Mag.* Jan. 8 The vast majority of criminal sentences in the United States.. are the result of 'plea bargains' in which the defendant 'waives' his constitutional right to trial in exchange for a 'good deal'. **1974** *Newsweek* 28 Jan. 14/2 Jaworski was plea-bargaining with a number of the principals—'dealing up' with reduced charges in return for their testimony against their betters. **1976** *National Observer* (U.S.) 22 May 3/3 That attitude, shared by some other judges here, is yet another reason for the sharp increase in jury trials. So is Connick's refusal to plea bargain with defendants in all but a relative handful of cases. **1978** *Globe & Mail* (Toronto) 2 Feb. 15/1 In a plea bargain, Polanski pleaded guilty Aug. 8 to one count of unlawful sexual intercourse with a minor. Five other counts were dismissed. **1964** *Univ. Pennsylvania Law Rev.* CXII. 865 Some prosecuting attorneys object to the use of the phrase '*plea bargaining'. One prosecutor indicated that 'by labelling the procedure "plea bargaining" you tend to make the procedure sound unethical and improper'. **1967** *Atlantic Reporter* 2nd Ser. CCXXIII. 703/1 Plea bargaining between the prosecution and the defense is a frequently resorted to technique. In exchange for a guilty plea, the prosecutor may agree to recommend a lighter sentence, to accept a plea to a lesser included offense, or to dismiss other pending charges. **1970** *Guardian* 25 Aug. 1/1 The Lord Chief Justice, Lord Parker, yesterday banned 'plea bargaining', where a court agrees to impose a lighter sentence if the accused pleads guilty. **1972** *N.Y. Times* 3 Nov. 18/3 Two-thirds of the addicts now in the program were admitted after being found guilty, usually in plea-bargaining situations in Criminal Court. **1973** *Reader's Digest* Nov. 169/1 They'll tell you that plea bargaining—in which a youngster pleads guilty to a lesser offense in return for a lighter sentence—is possible. **1975** P. MOYES *Black Widower* xii. 146 What about plea-bargaining?.. Suppose you told Martin that the police would only ask for a nominal fine on the streaking charge..if in return Martin would talk to me. [**1459**: see PLEAD *sb.* 4.] **1818** SCOTT *Hrt. Midl.* v, He's seldom at hame when there's ony o' the *plea-houses open. **1873** A. C. EWALD *Our Public Records* 37 The *Plea Rolls contain the general proceedings in causes, but are very defective, owing to the neglect of attorneys to bring the records in. **1886** [see *issue roll* s.v. ISSUE *sb.* 16]. **1936** *Oxoniensia* I. 140 It is impossible to make intelligent use of a plea roll or a pipe roll without fully understanding the governmental machinery that produced it. **1959** JOWITT *Dict. Eng. Law* II. 1567/2 In the old common law practice the steps in every action were entered on a roll, which was called the plea roll, the issue roll, or the judgment roll, according to the stage which the action had reached. **1978** *Bodl. Libr. Rec.* X. 30 Chief clerks of the Court of Common Pleas were responsible for keeping the plea rolls. **1768** BLACKSTONE *Comm.* III. iv. 42 *On the plea-side, or civil branch.

plea, *v. Sc.* and *north. dial.* Forms: 5 play, pleye, 5–6 pley, 6 plie, 7– plea. [f. PLEA *sb.*]

1. *intr.* = PLEAD *v.* 1–3.

c **1440** *Alphabet of Tales* 28 On a day he come in to þe cowrte & pleyd with þe men of cowrte & þe judgies & ouer come þaim. *Ibid.* 208 Gude angels stude on þe toder syde & playid agayns þaim. *c* **1470** HENRYSON *Mor. Fab.* XII. (*Wolf & Lamb*) viii, Yaa, quod the wolf, yit pleyis thow agane. **1599** in R. M. Fergusson *Hume* (1899) 222 *note*, The Magistrats..sall rather accept voluntarlie ten bolls mault ȝeirlie..then to pley for ye said Landis. **1700** Z. HAIG in J. Russell *Haigs* xi. (1881) 335 He advised me in general to quit two or three thousand merks rather then plea. *c* **1817** HOGG *Tales & Sk.* V. 155 Another great acquisition of property, for which I had pleaed. **1868** J. SALMON *Gowodean* II. i. 41 Scorn the love of whilk sae mony plea.

2. *trans.* = PLEAD *v.* 4–7.

1581 *Satir. Poems Reform.* xliii. 160 It was the Dowglassis douchtaly them dang, And pleit ȝour proces in that parliament. **1596** DALRYMPLE tr. *Leslie's Hist. Scot.* I. 116 Athir ar thay preistes seruieng the kirk; or men of law to plie a cause, or men of weir to fecht. **1816** SCOTT *Old Mort.* xlii, The estate was sair plea'd between Leddy Margaret Bellenden and the present Laird. **1887** MISS M. R. LAHEE *Traits Lanc. Flk.* 9 (E.D.D.) Aw'm like to plea poverty.

plea, erron. obs. f. PLEASE *v.*

†**'pleable**, *a. Sc. Obs.* In 6 pleyable, -bill. [f. PLEA *v.* + -ABLE.] That may be the subject of litigation; debatable.

1533 BELLENDEN *Livy* III. xxv. (S.T.S.) II. 49 Quhen þe tribunis war finalie callit, þai Iugit þe pleyabill landis to pertene to romanis. **1553** *Reg. Privy Council Scot.* I. 150 Upoun the severall ground of Scotland, nother pleyable nor debatable, ane gret way within the peceable marche of Scotland.

pleace, obs. var. PLEASE *v.*

pleach (pliːtʃ), *sb.* [f. PLEACH *v.*] Interlacing, intertwining; intertwinement of boughs; *spec.* a flexible branch or stake or an intertwined arrangement of these, forming a hedge.

1819 WIFFEN *Aonian Hours* (1820) 45 His nest, the pleach Of many a wilding bough in the next giant beech. **1823** E. MOOR *Suffolk Words & Phrases* 283 *Pleach*, is described to be a branch of whitethorn brought down and laid horizontally in a fence to thicken a weak part. It is notched (or snotched) at the point of tact with the earth which is loosened to encourage the pleach to strike root. **1920** E. POUND *Umbra* 114 Come buds on bough and spalliard pleach. **1941** [see HEADER 5 d]. **1968** J. ARNOLD *Shell Bk. Country Crafts* xx. 244 Stakes of cleft ash or chestnut..is [*sic*] driven into the ground, to form a rough 'weave' or pleach, depending on the flexibility of the stems. **1976** *Countryman* LXXXI. I. 56 The hedges have been carefully layered and made stock-proof by the use of horizontal 'pleaches', the wide bottoms providing shelter for a variety of wild life.

pleach (pliːtʃ), *v.* Forms: 5–6 pleche, 6 pleissh(e, *Sc.* pleich, 7 plesh, plish, 7– pleach. [ME. *pleche*, a. OF. **plechier* (mod.F. dial. *plécher*), dial. form of OF. *plessier*, *plaissier* PLASH *v.*[1]]

1. *trans.* To interlace or intertwine (the bent down or half-cut stems and branches of young trees and brushwood) so as to form a fence or the like; = PLASH *v.*[1] 1.

1398 TREVISA *Barth. De P.R.* XVII. cxliii. (Bodl. MS.), The wiþie..is þikker in bowes & spraies bi pleching schredinge and paringe. *c* **1420** *Pallad. on Husb.* III. 330 Nowe husbondrie his olde vines plecheth. *Ibid.* 418 Bende as a bowe, or vynes that men pleche. **1523** FITZHERB. *Husb.* §127 Let the toppe of the tree lye ouer the rote of an other tree, and to pleche downe the bowes of the same tree, to stoppe the holowe places. *Ibid.* [see PLASH *v.*[1] 1]. **1818** KEATS *Endym.* III. 934 Plunder'd vines..pleach'd New growth about each shell and pendant lyre. **1893** STEVENSON *Catriona* xxiii. The trees meeting overhead; some of them trimmed, some pleached.

b. To layer (a shoot, e.g. of a vine).

c **1420** *Pallad. on Husb.* IV. 648 At October in luke lond plecheth [L. *propagat*] he.

2. To make, dress, or renew (a hedge or the like) by the above process; = PLASH *v.*[1] 2.

1523 [see PLASH *v.*[1] 2]. **1635** SIR E. VERNEY in *Mem. Verney Fam.* (1892) I. 129 The Gardner shall pleach noe Hedge this yeare. **1825** BROCKETT *N.C. Gloss.*, *Pleach*, to bind a hedge. **1874** SYMONDS *Sk. Italy & Greece* (1898) I. xiii. 280 The low broad arches of the alleys pleached with vines. **1886** *Cornh. Mag.* July 32 The banks of the.. hedgerows, which were seldom cut or pleached.

3. *generally.* To entwine, interlace, tangle, plait.

1830 TENNYSON *Poems* 125 Pleached with her hair, in mail of argent light Shot into gold, a snake her forehead clips. **1861** F. METCALFE *Oxonian in Irel.* 96 The earth, being pleached together by the roots of dwarf willows and grass, has defied the pelting storm. **1865** SWINBURNE *Poems & Ball.*, *At Eleusis* 209 Poppied hair of gold Persephone Sadtressed and pleached below her brows.

Hence **'pleaching** *vbl. sb.* and *ppl. a.*

1398 [see sense 1]. **1504** *Nottingham Rec.* III. 314 For pleisshing at the coppy [= coppice]. **1804** J. GRAHAME *Sabbath* (1839) 18/1 Tangled so thick with pleaching brambleshoots, With brier and hazel branch, and hawthorn spray. **1889** *Boy's Own Paper* 21 Dec. 178/3 The pleaching [of the hedges] ended at the foot of a rise in the ground.

pleached (pliːtʃt, *poet.* 'pliːtʃɪd), *ppl. a.* [f. PLEACH *v.* + -ED[1].]

1. Of boughs: Interlaced, intertwined, tangled; *transf.* of the arms, folded together.

1606 SHAKS. *Ant. & Cl.* IV. xiv. 73 Would'st thou..see Thy Master thus with pleacht Armes, bending downe His corrigible necke? **1896** *Field* 1 Dec. 828/2 The pleached laurels near the house. **1897** MARY KINGSLEY *W. Africa* 280 It was hedged with thickly pleached bushes.

2. Formed by the pleaching or intertwisting of boughs and twigs; fenced, bordered, or overarched with pleached boughs, as a garden-alley or arbour. Now chiefly as a Shaksperian expression revived by Scott.

1599 SHAKS. *Much Ado* I. ii. 10 The Prince and Count Claudio walking in a thick pleached alley in my orchard. *Ibid.* III. i. 7 Bid her steale into the pleached bower, Where hony-suckles ripened by the sunne, Forbid the sunne to enter. **1822** SCOTT *Nigel* x, He..proposed..that they should take a turn in the pleached alley. **1829** *Anniversary*, *Beatrice* 232 She couches in the pleached bower Which tasselling honeysuckles deck. **1861** WHYTE MELVILLE *Tilbury Nogo* 240 An occasional grass field, enclosed by high rotten banks and 'pleached' fences.

'pleacher. *local.* [f. PLEACH *v.* + -ER[1].] = PLASHER: **a.** A bough with which a hedge is pleached. **b.** A hedger.

1882 MISS JACKSON *Shropsh. Word-bk.*, *Pleachers* same as *Layers*, the quick-thorn shoots which are laid down to form the hedge. **1889** *Portfolio* Dec. 231/2 The topiarius, or pleacher, was kept actively at work in trimming the hedges and trellis walks.

†**plead**, *sb.* Chiefly *Sc. Obs.* Forms: (3 plaid), 5–6 (*Sc.*) pled, plede, pleid, 6 (*Eng.*) plead, -e, (*Sc.*) plaid. [f. PLEAD *v.*; perh. in part a reminiscence of OF. and early ME. *plaid*, rare byform of *plait*: see PLEA *sb.*]

1. A suit or action at law; a controversy, dispute; = PLEA *sb.* 1, 3.

[*a* **1250** Plaid: see PLEA *sb.* 1.] **14..** *Wyntoun's Cron.* VIII. iv. 440 Quhare thar is in pleid [*v.r.* pley] twa men Askand the Crowne off a kynrike. *c* **1470** HENRY *Wallace* x. 104 He.. maid Stewart with hym to fall in pled. *c* **1470** HENRYSON *Mor. Fab.* VI. (*Sheep & Dog*) xiii, And thair began the pleid. **1561** T. HOBY tr. *Castiglione's Courtyer* IV. (1577) Y iij, Bycause the pleade betweene you maye happen bee to long. **1567** *Gude & Godlie B.* (S.T.S.) 149, I fand the loste from blis, Throuch Adamis sin and pleid. **1581** MARBECK *Bk. of Notes*, 269 The matter..is in plead.

2. A plea, allegation, claim.

1456 SIR G. HAYE *Law Arms* (S.T.S.) 208 To ask resoun and move plede before him..suld be small redress, and bot ane unprouffitable plede. **1560** ROLLAND *Crt. Venus* III. 863 Quhairthrow we all was quite of Plutois pleid. **1560** DAUS tr. *Sleidane's Comm.* 307 The foundation of your pleade is so fallen, yt I nede not to answere thy protestation.

3. Pleading, harangue, speech, talk, discussion.

c **1450** HOLLAND *Howlat* 818 The barde held a grete pleid In the hie hall. **1500–20** DUNBAR *Poems* xlvi. 115 Thir birdis ..Singing of lufe amang the levis small, Quhois ythand pleid ȝit maid my thochtis grene. **1535** STEWART *Cron. Scot.* II. 494 Thus endit scho that first begouth that pleid. **15..** *Freiris of Berwik* 256 in *Dunbar's Poems* (S.T.S.) 294 Ga fill the stowp, hald me no mair in pleid, For I am verry tyrit, wett and cauld. **1573** *Satir. Poems Reform* xl. 197 How he suld fend from furie and thair fead, Syne leaue this lyfe with list for all thair plaid.

4. *attrib.*, as **plead-house** = *plea-house*: see PLEA *sb.* 7.

1459 SIR G. HAYE *Law Arms* (S.T.S.) 270 A plede that is maid before a juge ordynare in a plede hous.

plead (pliːd), *v.* Forms: α. 3–4 plaide(n, plaid-i, 3–6 playde, 4 plede(n, 4–7 plede (5 pledde, plide, 5–7 pled), 6 pleade (pleed), 6–7 *Sc.* pleid, 6– plead. *Pa. t.* and *pple.* **pleaded**: contracted 5 pladde, (9 *dial.* plad), 5– pled (orig. *Sc.* and *dial.*), 7–9 **plead**. β. 4 **pleit-y, pleyte, playt-y, playte, pleten, -yn,** 4–6 **plete,** 5–6 **pleete,** 6 **pleate.** [In ME. form *plaiden*, *plaidi*, a. OF. *plaid-ier* (Roland, 11th c.) to go to law, sue, plead, f. OF. *plaid*: see PLEA *sb.*; parallel to med.L. *placitāre*, to hold pleas, to litigate (*c* 800 in Du Cange), f. *placitum* PLEA; thence AF. *pleder*, ME. *plêde(n*, *plead*. ME. *plaiten*, *plaity*, *plêten*, *plete* was a secondary form, corresp. to OF. *plaitier* (14th c. in Godef.): cf. also med.L. *plaitāre* (9th c. in Du Cange) from *placitāre*, and OF. and ME. *plait* sb., for *plaid*, PLEA. Cf. the later PLEA *v.*]

I. Intransitive uses.

†**1. a.** To raise or prosecute a suit or action, to go to law, to litigate. *Obs.*

α. [**1292** BRITTON III. i. §1 La manere de pleder, coment chescun pleyntif deit repurchacer sa seisine de fraunc tenement.] **1442** *Rolls of Parlt.* V. 45/1 Able to purchace Londes..and also plede and be empleded. **1523** FITZHERB. *Surv.* xi. (1539) 17 Shall nat plede nor be impleded of their tenementes.

β. *c* **1380** WYCLIF *Sel. Wks.* III. 348 Freris..moven londis to bateilis, and pesible persones to plete. *a* **1400–50** *Alexander* 78 He..sawe two men of þe same towne bifore a iuge pletyng. *a* **1500** in *Arnolde's Chron.* 34 Ye shal not pleete wt noo freman of the Cite wtout the cite. **1529** MORE *Dyaloge* II. Wks. 184/1 Rather than thei shoulde pleate and striue in the law before the infidels. *a* **1550** *Merch. & Son* 42 in Hazl. *E.P.P.* I. 135 Thou schalt be pletyd with, when y am gon.

†**b.** In extended and fig. use: To contend in debate; to wrangle, argue *with*, *against*. Also *to plead it*. *Obs.*

α. *a* **1250** *Owl & Night.* 184 We mawe bet..Wiþvte cheste and bute vyhte Playde [*v.r.* plaidi] mid soþe & mid ryhte. **1500–20** DUNBAR *Poems* lix. 5 Sen he plesis with me to pleid, I sall him knawin mak hyne to Calyss. **1557** N.T. (Genev.) *Rom.* ix. 20 Who art thou which playdest against God? **1560** ROLLAND *Crt. Venus* II. 306 Quhat than, gif thay of my craft with me pleid? **1593** G. HARVEY *Pierce's Super.* Wks. (Grosart) II. 42 Come..you that loue to pleade it out inuincibly at the barre of the dunghill, and will rather loose your liues, then the last word.

β. *c* **1315** SHOREHAM *Poems* vii. 723 Ich schal makye contekhede By-tuyce þyne and wyues sede, And moche to pleity. **1388** WYCLIF *Judg.* xxi. 22 Whanne the fadris and britheren..bigynne to pleyne and plete [1382 chiden] aȝens ȝou. **1535** COVERDALE *Job* xvi. 21 Though a body might pleate with God, as one man doth with another.

2. a. To address the court as an advocate on behalf of either party; to maintain or urge the claim, or state the case, of a party to a suit.

α. *c* **1305** *St. Kath.* 77 in *E.E.P.* (1862) 92 Gret schame.. An Emperour to siche aboute:..After maistres, to plaidi aȝen a ȝung wenche. *c* **1380** WYCLIF *Wks.* (1880) 24 Sendynge of men..of lawe..bi here owen persones for to plede. **1455** *Cal. Anc. Rec. Dublin* (1889) I. 288 No man of lawe schold pled befor Mayre and Baylyfys of the sayde citte. **1581** MULCASTER *Positions* xxxix. (1887) 202 The first and chiefe..in law among lawyers though he do not pleade. **1596** SPENSER *F.Q.* v. ix. 43 And with him..came Many grave persons that against her pled. **1651** HOBBES *Leviath.* II. xxvi. 145 Sentences..to be taken by them that plead, for Lawes in that particular case. **1776** GIBBON *Decl. & F.* xvi. (1869) I. 397 He had pleaded with distinction in the tribunals of Rome.

β. **1377** LANGL. *P. Pl.* B. VII. 39 Men of lawe..þat pleteden for Mede. **1387** TREVISA *Higden* (Rolls) III. 201 þat day þat he pletede to fore a inge. **1480** CAXTON *Chron. Eng.* ccxxxii. (1482) 248 It was ordeyned that men of lawe fro that tyme forth shold plete in hir moder tonge. **1502** *Ord. Crysten Men* (W. de W. 1506) III. iii. 160 He pleated by thre yeres in the grete assyse in the cyte of Bourgeys.

b. In extended and fig. use: To urge a suit or prayer; to make an earnest appeal, entreaty, or supplication; to beg, implore. Const. *with* the person appealed to; *for* the thing desired, or the person in whose interest one speaks; also *against*.

α. **1390** GOWER *Conf.* III. 155 Bot thogh him lacke forto plede, Him lacketh nothing of manhede. **1624** QUARLES *Job* xi. 60 Let me, a while, with my Accusers plead [*rime* dead]. **1662** in *Cosin's Corr.* (Surtees) II. 313 My Lord hath been ..pled with for something for him to keepe him here. **1721** RAMSAY *Content* 374 My mind, indulgent, in their favour pled. **1757** SMOLLETT *Reprisal* II. v, Tho' silent his tongue, he will plead with his eyes. **1757** HOME *Douglas* III, We search'd his clothes, And found these jewels, whose rich value plead Most powerfully against him. **1837** WHITTIER in *Life* (1894) I. 199 We have caucused in season and out of season, threatened and coaxed, plead and scolded. **1838** LYTTON *Alice* I. x, Do not scorn to plead for me. **1869** FREEMAN *Norm. Conq.* III. xii. 158 All Roger's services could not plead against this ill-timed tenderness to a foe. **1871** *Ibid.* IV. xvii. 42 His skill doubtless pleaded for him. **1882** J. H. BLUNT *Ref. Ch. Eng.* II. 197 It does not appear that any one pleaded for his pardon except himself. **1932** E. WILSON *Devil take Hindmost* xii. 126 Irma went to his boss and pled with him. **1932** 'J. ASTON' *They winter Abroad* xii. 192 The shades of Rugby and Caius, or wherever it was that he had been bred to be a Hawk, pled against him mutely. **1941** E. R. EDDISON *Fish Dinner* vii. 103 Should a been unlorded long since,..but the Vicar pled for him. **1943** S. LEWIS *G. Planish* xxxi. 407 I've pled with them.

β. **1340** *Ayenb.* 99 Loke hou..Iesu crist..þe tekþ wel to playty. *c* **1374** CHAUCER *Troylus* II. 1419 (1468) Be [ye] nought war how fals Polyphete Is now abowte eft soones for to plete. *c* **1380** WYCLIF *Serm.* Sel. Wks. I. 114 Medefulli plete wiþ men.

3. To put forward a plea. Cf. PLEADING *vbl. sb.* 3.

a. To put forward any allegation or formal statement forming part of the proceedings in an action at law. (Cf. PLEA *sb.* 2 a.) ***plead over***: see quots. 1872, 1890.

1444 *Rolls of Parlt.* V. 112/1 Yef.. the Defendauntz or Pleintifs in suche foreign Plees plede to issue. **1683** GRIMSTONE *Croke's Rep.* (1791) III. 651 (Case 20 Jac. I, 1623) His plea in bar is not answered when he doth rely upon it, but pleads over in bar. **1824** H. J. STEPHEN *Princ. Pleading* (1843) 160 Faults in pleading are, in some cases, aided by pleading over. **1872** *Wharton's Law Lex.* 739/1 *Plead over*, to follow up an opponent's pleading by replying, etc., so overlooking some defect to which exception might have been taken. **1875** *Judicature Act* O. xxvii. r. 5 When any party has amended his pleading under rule 2 or 3 of this Order, the other party may apply..for leave to plead or amend his former pleading. **1890** *Cent. Dict.*, *Pleading over*, going on to respond by pleading, after a previous pleading has been judged insufficient, or has been withdrawn.

b. *esp.* To put forward an answer or objection on the part of the defendant to the plaintiff's bill. (Cf. PLEA *sb.* 2 b.)

14.. *Rolls of Parlt.* V. 396/1 Provided also that that Act stop not ne conclude the said Thomas..to answer or plede to eny matier abovesaid. **1477** *Ibid.* VI. 187/2 They may answere and plede to the action, or in abatement of the pleyntes. **1490-1** *Cal. Anc. Rec. Dublin* (1889) I. 371 To pledde to a quest in lyke wise in ther owne persones. **1681** DRYDEN *Span. Friar* v. ii, He will not hear me out!.. Was ever criminal forbid to plead? **1727** *Wodrow Corr.* (1843) III. 299 The Assembly desired him to propound what he had to say against their being his judges... Then his two lawyers, Mr Grant and Mr Murray, pled upon that head. **1796** BURKE *Let. Noble Ld.* Wks. VIII. 8, I ought to be allowed a reasonable freedom,..and no culprit ought to plead in irons. **1824** H. J. STEPHEN *Princ. Pleading* (1885) 50 If the defendant does not demur, his only alternative method of defence is, to oppose or answer the declaration by matter of fact. In so doing he is said to plead.

II. Transitive uses.

†**4.** To go to law with, sue (a person). *Obs. rare.*

β. **1382** WYCLIF *Isa.* lviii. 3 Alle ȝoure detoures ȝee pleten [1388 ȝe axen [Vulg. *repetitis*] alle ȝoure dettouris]. *a* **1500** in *Arnolde's Chron.* 5 b, We haue graunted to our citezens of london that none of them pleete [*pr.* pletee] othor wythout the wallis of london.

5. To maintain (a plea or cause) by argument in a court of law. Also *transf.*

α. [**1292** BRITTON I. i. § 7 Qe des pletz pledez devaunt eux ..eynt record. *Ibid.* § 8 A pleder communs pletz.] **1482** *Monk of Evesham* (Arb.) 77 He was to many that pledyd her causis of god consciens a vyolent oppressur. **1551** ROBINSON tr. *More's Utop.* II. vii. (1895) 235 They thinke it most mete that euery man shuld pleade his owne matter, and tell the same tale before the iudge, that he would tel to his man of lawe. **1560** DAUS tr. *Sleidane's Comm.* 235 The Prince sent two of his counsellours..to playde the case. *c* **1586** C'TESS PEMBROKE *Ps.* LXXIV. xxi, Rise, God, pleade thyne owne case. **1675** PRIDEAUX *Lett.* (Camden) 36 Our law case is not yet ended; four advocates come down from Drs Commons to plead it next term. **1777** W. CAMERON in *Sc. Paraphr.* XVII. vi, Plead the widow's cause. **1814** SCOTT *Ld. of Isles* IV. xiv, Anxious his suit Lord Ronald pled. **1929** R. S. LYND *Middletown* II. x. 122 It is not intended here to take the conventional forms under which divorce cases are pled as anything more than very roughly suggesting.

β. *c* **1450** *Godstow Reg.* 100 One acre of mede..whereof hit was I-pleted bitwene them in the forsaid Courte. **1484** CAXTON *Fables of Alfonce* ix, They remytted the cause to be discuted or pleted before the Juge. **1539** BIBLE (Great) *Job* xxiii. 3 O that I myght come before his seate, to pleate my cause before him. **1550** BALE *Image Both Ch.* 85 It is Christes onely office to receyue all complayntes to pleate them and to iudge them.

6. To sue for in a court of law. Also *transf.* to beg, entreat for. In later use chiefly *Sc.*

α. **13..** *Gaw. & Gr. Knt.* 1304, I schal kysse at your comaundement, as a knyȝt fallez, And fire lest he displese yow, so plede hit no more. **1594** MARLOW & NASHE *Dido* I. ii, That crave such favour..As poor distressed misery may plead. **1637-50** ROW *Hist. Kirk* (Wodrow Soc.) 190 If a minister throw povertie be not able to plead his gleeb and manse, that the rest assist him by contributing till he evict it. **1711** ADDISON *Spect.* No. 46 ¶6 The Misery of my Case, and great Numbers of such Sufferers, plead your Pity and speedy Relief. **1811** CHALMERS *Diary* in *Life* (1850) I. 231 Had been apprized..that my augmentation was to be pled on the 18th.

β. *c* **1500** *New Not-br. Mayd* 66 Mercy I pleate.

7. a. To allege formally in the course of the pleadings. (Cf. PLEA *sb.* 2 a.)

α. *c* **1460** *Godstow Reg.* 120 A Charter of Stephyn Agothe, I-pleyd in the kyngis Courte, for a tenemente in Irelandes lane. **1491** *Act 7 Hen. VII*, c. 2 §1 Courtes where the seid proteccions shalbe pleded or leyed for any of the seid persons in all plees, plees of Dowre..except. **1765** BLACKSTONE *Comm.* Introd. 76 All other private customs must be particularly pleaded. **1890** *Law Reports 24 Q.B.D.* 630 The paragraph was properly pleaded and ought not to be struck out.

β. **1480** CAXTON *Chron. Eng.* VII. (1520) 83/1 That no letter nor commaundement that came from Rome shold be receyued nor pleted in Englande.

b. To allege formally as a plea (PLEA *sb.* 2 b). ***plead specially***, to allege as a special plea (PLEA *sb.* 2 c).

1531 *Dial. on Laws Eng.* II. liii. (1638) 159 If the defendant ..in any action plead a plee that amounteth to the general issue. **1602** FULBECKE *1st Pt. Parall.* 72 This ple he was enforced to pled by the court. **1659** H. L'ESTRANGE *Alliance Div. Off.* 22 St. Augustine plead it in bar to Celer's action of unkindnesse against him. **1756** HUME *Hist. Eng.* (1812) II. xxxvi. 286 The counsellors pleaded constraint as an excuse for their treason. **1768** BLACKSTONE *Comm.* III. xx. 305 Every defence which cannot thus be specially pleaded may be given in evidence upon the general issue at the trial. **1769** *Ibid.* IV. xxvi. 336 A pardon may be pleaded in bar. **1817** W. SELWYN *Law Nisi Prius* (ed. 4) II. 753 An executor may plead the same plea in bar, that his testator might have pleaded. **1828** SCOTT *F.M. Perth* xxxii, Ramorny, pale as death,..pled his knighthood, and demanded the privilege of dying by the sword. **1863** H. COX *Instit.* I. v. 30 It would be vain to plead..the king's command to do an unlawful act. **1875** *Judicature Act* O. xix. r. 15 No defendant in an action for the recovery of land who is in possession..need plead his title.

c. In extended and fig. use: To allege or urge as a plea, esp. in defence, apology, or excuse, or as extenuating an offence. Freq. with direct speech as object.

1601 HOLLAND *Pliny* XVIII. xxvii. 593 Thou shouldest not either plead ignorance, or neglect the same. **1621** T. WILLIAMSON tr. *Goulart's Wise Vieillard* 101 Old age is miserable, that can plead nothing else for Antiquitie, but the wrinckles of the face and the white haires. **1671** MILTON *Samson* 833 If weakness may excuse, What Murtherer,.. Incestuous, Sacrilegious, but may plead it? **1709** POPE *Ess. Crit.* 166 And have, at least, their precedent to plead. **1733** BERKELEY *Th. Vision* §3 If I am mistaken, I can plead neither haste nor inattention. **1820** W. IRVING *Sketch Bk.* I. 256, I can only plead my inexperience in this branch of literature. **1910** E. M. FORSTER *Howards End* xxvii. 235 'Don't you worry,' he pleaded. 'I can't bear that. We shall be all right if I get work. If I could only get work—something regular to do.' **1952** M. LASKI *Village* xiii. 187 'I'm really sorry,' pleaded Margaret contritely. **1955** W. GADDIS *Recognitions* I. v. 198 Is your name really Adeline? he pled. **1974** E. S. GRUEN *Last Generation Roman Republic* viii. 327 Gabinius pled that his Egyptian adventure was in the interests of state. **1976** B. FREEMANTLE *November Man* viii. 108 'Stop it, Hannah,' he pleaded urgently.

d. Phrase. ***to plead not guilty*** (in civil and criminal law), to deny liability or guilt: in Law-French, *plaider de rien coupable*. So ***to plead guilty***; also *fig.* to confess to an accusation or imputation. Also *ellipt.* ***plead***, in sense 'to plead guilty'.

to plead guilty appears later, and evidently arose in imitation of *plead not guilty*. *Guilty* is technically not a *plea*, but a confession. Blackstone *Comm.* IV. 324, 332, 399, never uses *plead guilty*, but writes of the prisoner confessing the fact.

[**1344** *Year Bk. 18 Edw. III* 4 Et quant a les bienz..il pleda de rien coupable.] **1454** *Rolls of Parlt.* V. 239/2 In the Court of th' Eschequer..the seid Thomas..to the said Bille and Action aunswered and pleted not gylty. **1681** *Trial S. Colledge* 6 *Cl. of Cr.* You must plead to the Court, Guilty or not Guilty. **1802-12** BENTHAM *Ration. Judic. Evid.* Wks. 1843 VI. 473 Where it happens to a prisoner to answer in the affirmative—in appropriate language, to plead guilty—if he insists on it, the general understanding seems to be that he has a right to have such his plea recorded: in which case there is a necessary end of the trial, and the verdict follows of course. **1806** *Med. Jrnl.* XV. 60, I may..be represented as discouraging experiments. To this I must, in some measure, plead guilty. **1875** *Judicature Act* O. xix. r. 16 Nothing in these Rules contained shall affect the right of any defendant to plead not guilty by statute. **1892** 'D. DONOVAN' *In Grip of Law* 58 When called upon to plead, she pled not guilty in a firm clear voice. **1959** JOWITT *Dict. Eng. Law* II. 1352/1 The word 'plead' is used colloquially to mean plead guilty. **1963** J. PRESCOT *Case for Hearing* vii. 109 The reek of spirits..met me like a wave... Dr. Depree depressed his right thumb. 'You'll have to plead to this one.' *Ibid.* viii. 119, I'll stake my pension on a conviction. In fact, if the lad's any sense he'll hold up his hand and plead. **1970** P. LAURIE *Scotland Yard* vi. 137 Said he'd plead, then when he got in the box he gave you a grin and said, 'Not guilty'.

†**8.** To argue or dispute upon in a court of law; to practise (the law). *Obs.*

1362 LANGL. *P. Pl.* A. Prol. 86 Seriauns..to seruen atte Barre; Pleden [*v.r.* pleten] for pons and poundes þe lawe. **1529** MORE *Dyaloge* I. Wks. 158/1 Thei..that longed to lerne the lawe. Not to plete it and for glory to dispute it, but to teche it agayne mekely. **1577** HARRISON *England* II. i. (1877) I. 28 The canon law..which is dailie pleaded.

Hence **'pleaded** *ppl. a.*, uttered or alleged in pleading; ***pleaded-for***, defended by pleading.

1668 H. MORE *Div. Dial.* IV. xxxi. (1713) 380 Do you see, Cuphophron, whither your pleaded-for Impostures carry, even to savage Murther and Blood-shed? **1725** POPE *Odyss.* I. 321 She seems attentive to their pleaded vows. **1754** RICHARDSON *Grandison* V. xiv. 105 We shall now see what the so often pleaded for dignity of your sex, will enable you to do. **1850** J. S. B. MONSELL *Parish Musings* (1871) 40 Yield to thine own pleaded word.

pleadable ('pliːdəb(ə)l), *a.* Also 5-7 pled-, 6 pleade-. [ME. a. AF. *pledable* (1292 Britton) = OF. *plaidable*, f. *plaidier* to PLEAD: see -ABLE.]

1. That may be pleaded.

a. Of a cause: That may legally be maintained or defended in a court of law.

[**1292** BRITTON II. i, La fourme et la manere de pleder personels pletz pledables par attachementz de cors.] **1576** FLEMING *Panopl. Epist.* 256 As cases of lawe, pleadable in courtes of assise &c. **1643** *Virginia Stat.* (1823) I. 262 That all monie debts made since the 26th day of March 1642.. shall not be pleadable or recoverable in any court of justice vnder this government. *c* **1645** HOWELL *Lett.* (1688) IV. 455 A Forrest hath her Courts of Attachments..where Matters are as pleadable..as at Westminster Hall. **1707** E. CHAMBERLAYNE *Pres. St. Eng.* II. xv. (ed. 22) 196 Real Actions are pleadable in no other Court.

b. That may be alleged formally in the course of the pleadings, or urged as a plea, in a court of law.

[**1312** *Rolls of Parlt.* I. 284/2 Bref en Chauncellerie pledable en Baunk le Roi.] **1455** *Ibid.* V. 326/1 Such plees as in lawe were pledables. **1531** *Dial. on Laws Eng.* II. ii. (1638) 62 If an Obligation beare date out of the realme..[it is] not pleadable at the Common law. **1660** R. SHERINGHAM *King's Suprem. Asserted* ii. (1682) 8 The words of a Statute..are pleadable in their usual and grammatical sense to all purposes. **1688** SIR G. TREBY in *Collect. Poems* 263 No Pardon to be pleadable to an Impeachment in Parliament. **1884** *Law Times Rep.* 16 Feb. 773/2 The allegations in question are properly pleadable..being allegations of matters which may be given in evidence at the trial.

c. *gen.* That may be pleaded, claimed, urged, or alleged in behalf of a cause.

1565 CALFHILL *Answ. Treat. Crosse* 46 b, Your comparison is not pleadeable: eche part conteyneth some peece of vntruth. **1680** ALLEN *Peace & Unity* 70 If this were not so, their case would not be so pleadable as now it is. **1786** A. GIB *Sacr. Contempl.* 289 Bequeathing to his people..a pleadable interest in all his services and sufferings for their Salvation. **1862** RUSKIN *Unto this Last* iv. 161 Meat! perhaps your right to that may be pleadable; but other rights have to be pleaded first.

†**2.** ***pleadable brief***, Sc. Law: see BRIEVE. ***pleadable day***: a day on which pleadings can take place.

1471 *Sc. Acts Jas. III* (1814) II 101/2 Quhen ony brefis pledable hapnis to be folowit before quhatsumeuer Juge. **1609** SKENE *Reg. Maj.*, *Stat. Rob. I* 24 Na man sould be ejected furth of his free tenement, quherein he alledges him to be vested and saised as of fee; without the kings pleadable briefe, or the like briefe.

[**1292** BRITTON I. xii. §5 Chescune simayne une foiz en tens pledable (*tr.* in time pleadable).] **1601** HOLLAND *Pliny* II. 457 For his better aduancement he opened vnto him the whole course of dayes pleadable and not pleadable, exhorting..him withal, to publish that secret and mysterie.

Hence **'pleadableness**, the quality of being pleadable.

1774 A. GIB *Present Truth* II. 141 The pleadableness thereof at the bar of Law and Justice.

†**'pleadant, 'pledant.** *Obs. rare*$^{-1}$. [a. F. *plaidant* plaintiff, also advocate who pleads: sb. use of pres. pple. of *plaider* to PLEAD.] A plaintiff.

1599 R. LINCHE *Anc. Fiction* K iv, Giue wrongfull iudgement vpon the truth-inferring pledant.

pleader[1] ('pliːdə(r)). Forms: α. as PLEAD *v.* α. + 3 -ur, 4 -or, 4–5 -our, -ere, 5 -are, 5– -er, 6 *Sc.* -ar. β. 4 playtour, -ere, 5–6 pleter, -ar(e, 6 pleater. [α. ME. *playdur, -our*, a. OF. *plaideor* (13th c. in Hatz.-Darm.), F. *plaideur*, agent-n. f. OF. *plaidier, plaider* to PLEAD; with subsequent change of suffix: see -OUR, -ER[1]. β. after the collateral form *playte, plete, pleat* of the vb.]

1. One who pleads in a law-court; an advocate.

α. *c* **1275** *Sinners Beware* 133 in *O.E. Misc.* 76 Þeos playdurs beoþ wel kene. *c* **1380** WYCLIF *Serm.* Sel. Wks. II. 252 Þus seien pleders and pursueris, þat þei done þus al for love. **1390** GOWER *Conf.* I. 274 The pledour and the plee schal faile, The sentence of that ilke day. **1430–40** LYDG. *Bochas* I. xviii. (MS. Bodl. 263) 76/1 Plederes [*ed.* 1554 pleters], which for lucre & meede, Meyntene quarelis, and questis doon enbrace. **1514** BARCLAY *Cyt. & Uplondyshm.* (Percy Soc.) 32 Yet is in the cyte a nombre incurable, Pleders & brokers, a foule & shamefast rable. **1629** MASSINGER *Picture* II. ii, The tradesman, merchant, and litigious pleader, And such-like scarabs bred in the dung of peace. **1772** *Junius Lett.* lxviii. (1820) 338 The learning of a pleader is usually upon a level with his integrity. **1871** R. ELLIS *Catullus* xxxix. 3 The bench.. Where stands a pleader just prepar'd to rouse our tears.

β. **1303** R. BRUNNE *Handl. Synne* 8746Þyr was a man þat hyghte Valentyne, Playtour he was, and ryche man fyne. **1340** *Ayenb.* 44 To þise zenne belongeþ þe zenne of ualse domesmen and of ualse playteres. **1474** CAXTON *Chesse* III. iii. 3, I suppose that in alle cristendom are not so many pletars attorneys and men of the lawe as been in Englond onely. **1545** BRINKLOW *Compl.* 2 That all iudges and pleaters at the barre may lyue of a stypend.

†**b.** In opprobrious sense. Cf. SPECIAL PLEADER.

1382 WYCLIF *Isa.* iii. 12 My puple his pleteres [*gloss* or wrong axers] spoileden. *a* **1400–50** *Alexander* 1731 Þat wickidly þou haues.. Purvayd þe pletours [L. *latrunculos*] oure partis to ride. *c* **1440** *Gesta Rom.* iii. 8 (Harl. MS.) Advocatis, and pletouris, þe which by sotilte and wickidnesse getithe þe goode of þis wordle.

†**c.** A suitor. *Obs. rare.*

1653 URQUHART *Rabelais* I. xx. 89 Pleaders are miserable; for sooner shall they attain to the end of their lives, then to the final decision of their pretended rights.

2. *gen.* One who pleads, entreats, or intercedes.

1607 SHAKS. *Cor.* v. i. 36 But sure if you Would be your Countries Pleader, your good tongue... Might stop our Countryman. *a* **1635** SIBBES *Confer. Christ & Mary* (1656) 47 We have a pleader in heaven, that will take our part against the accuser of our brethren. **1712** BERKELEY *Pass. Obed.* §33 One great principle which the pleaders for resistance make the ground-work of their doctrine. **1884** MAX MÜLLER in *19th Cent.* June 1016 We know how able, how persuasive a pleader Darwin could be.

3. See SPECIAL PLEADER.

†'**pleader**[2]. *Obs. rare. Law.* Also 5 pletere. [a. F. *plaider*, AF. *plaiter, pleter*, infinitive used as sb.: see PLEAD *v.* and -ER[4].] Pleading.

c **1450** *Merlin* 18 This was Merlynes pletere for his moder. **1698** SIR G. TREBY in *Mod. Rep.* XII. 229 Testator took out a writ against the defendant.., and died during the pleader.

pleading ('pliːdɪŋ), *vbl. sb.* Forms: see PLEAD *v.* [f. PLEAD *v.* + -ING[1].] The action of the verb PLEAD, in various senses.

†**1.** The carrying on of a suit in a court of law, litigation; hence, a law-suit, action, legal process; a controversy. *Obs.*

1297 R. GLOUC. (Rolls) 9662 In playdinge & in asise..& in Iugement also. *c* **1374** CHAUCER *Boeth.* III. pr. iii 55 (Camb. MS.) Whennes comyn elles alle thyse foreyne compleyntes or quereles of pletynges. **1483** CAXTON *Gold. Leg.* 431 b/1 Doubtyng that the stryf accions and pletynges of the poure shold come onely to the presence and knowlege of hys counceyllours. **1556** *Aurelio & Isab.* (1608) K iij, That they be juges, parties, and advocates of one selfe pletinge.

2. The advocating of a cause in a court of law; the art of drawing pleadings; the body of rules and usages constituting this art.

1377 LANGL. *P.Pl.* B. III. 294 Shal no seriaunt.. were.. no pelure in his cloke for pledyng atte barre. *c* **1386** CHAUCER *Pars. T.* ¶92 Ther ne shal no pledynge [*Hengwrt MS.* pletynge] auaille ne sleighte, we shullen yeuen rekenynge of euerich ydel word. **14..** *Pol., Rel. & L. Poems* (1866) 96 Ther charter helpys þe not þat dey, Ther pletyn is not worth an hawe. **1522** SKELTON *Why not to Court* 315 In pletynge of theyr case At the Commune Place. **1552** HULOET, Pleadynge, *actitatio, aduocatio.* **1766** ENTICK *London* IV. 34 The terms, or times for pleading and ending of causes in the Civil Courts. **1875** MAINE *Hist. Inst.* ix. 255 The proceedings included a series of assertions and reassertions of right by the parties, and this formal dialogue was the parent of the Art of Pleading.

3. A formal allegation, now generally a written document (formerly, an oral statement) setting forth the cause of action or the defence; in pl. *pleadings*, the formal statements on both sides; in strict use, excluding the count or declaration.

1531 ELYOT *Gov.* I. xiv, The pleadynge used in courte and Chauncery called motes. **1540** *Act 32 Hen. VIII*, c. 30 §1 Replycacyons, reioynders, rebutters, ioynyng of issues, and other pleadynges. **1596** BACON *Max. & Use Com. Law* I. iii. (1636) 22 Pleadings must be certain, because the adverse party may know wherto to answer. **1768** BLACKSTONE *Comm.* III. xx. 293 Pleadings are the mutual altercations between the plaintiff and defendant; which at present are set down and delivered into the proper office in writing. **1825** *Act 6 Geo. IV*, c. 120 §10 The Record of the Pleadings as adjusted shall be authenticated by the Lord Ordinary by his Signature; and the Record so made up and authenticated shall be held as foreclosing the Parties from the Statement of any new Averments in point of Fact. **1883** H. H. S. CROFT *Elyot's Gov.* I. 152 *note*, The pleadings down to the time of Edward III were *vivâ voce*, and those who pleaded orally would no doubt pursue the method first recommended by Quintilian in his Institutes, and afterwards adopted by later Rhetoricians. **1885** *Law Rep. 29 Ch. Div.* 451 The Court is entitled to look at the pleadings in the Irish action.

4. *gen.* Intercession, advocacy, supplications, earnest entreaty.

c **1430** *Hymns Virg.* 97 'What', quod þe synner, '..Canst þou neuere of þi pletinge blynne?' **1526** *Pilgr. Perf.* (W. de W. 1531) 243 Makyng (as saynt Paule sayth) interpellacyon & pletynge for vs before yᵉ father of heuen. *a* **1758** RAMSAY *Adieu for while* ii, Thou dost not obey The pleading of love. **1791** MRS. RADCLIFFE *Rom. Forest* i, The beauty.. of Adeline, united with the pleadings of humanity in her favour. **1874** GREEN *Short Hist.* viii. §5.511 'Comus'.. rises into an almost impassioned pleading for the love of virtue.

5. See SPECIAL PLEADING.

6. *attrib.* and *Comb.*, as ***pleading-house, -place***, etc.

c **1440** *Promp. Parv.* 405/1 Pletynge howse, or place, *placitorium.* **1656** COWLEY *Pind. Odes, 34th Chapter Isaiah* v, Then shall the Market and the Pleading-place Be Choakt with Brambles and oregrown with grass. **1888** LD. HERSCHELL in *Law Rep.*, *Ho. Lords* XIII. 9 As a pleading point, this would have been good.

'**pleading**, *ppl. a.* [f. as prec. + -ING[2].] That pleads; entreating, beseeching, imploring.

1818 SHELLEY *Rosalind & H.* 870 What avail.. the knit soul that pleading and pale Makes wan the quivering cheek? **1880** MISS BRADDON *Just as I am* vi, He noticed that tender pleading glance at the time. *Mod.* His pleading tones move compassion.

Hence '**pleadingly** *adv.*, in a pleading manner; '**pleadingness**, the quality of pleading.

1847 WEBSTER, *Pleadingly*, by pleading. **1865** E. C. CLAYTON *Cruel Fortune* I. 227 She looked so pleadingly, so beseechingly,.. that Lady Charington relented. **1866** NONA BELLAIRS *Wayside Fl.* iii. 27 Cry.. of a little child... Its intense pleadingness haunted me. **1868** GEO. ELIOT *Sp. Gipsy* III. 293 She spoke tenderly, pleadingly.

†'**pleaful**, *a. Obs.* [f. PLEA *sb.* + -FUL.] That pleads powerfully, persuasive.

1625 LISLE *Du Bartas' Noe* 12 So from his pleafull tongue falls cheering dew and aire.

†'**pleament.** *Obs. rare*$^{-1}$. In 5 plement. [f. PLEA *v.* + -MENT. Cf. OF. *plaidement* (*a* 1400 in Godef.).] A pleading; an action at law.

1480 CAXTON *Chron. Eng.* ccxxxv, In a certain plement he [Earl of Pembroke] stode & was ayenst the riȝtes and fraunchises of holy chirche.

pleasable ('pliːzəb(ə)l), *a.* Now *rare.* Also 4 plesable, 6 pleasible. [ME. *plesable*, a. OF. *pleisable* (*c* 1185 in Godefroy), *plaisable* agreeable, f. *plaisir* (= *plaire*) to please; see PLEASE and -ABLE.]

1. Capable of being pleased; placable, mild.

1382 WYCLIF *Gen.* xliii. 14 And my God Almyȝti make hym plesable to ȝow [*Vulg.* Deus.. faciat vobis eum placabilem]. **1552** NORTHUMBERLAND in Tytler *Edw. VI* (1839) II. 148, I love not to have to do with men which be neither grateful nor pleasable. **1570** LEVINS *Manip.* 2/23 Pleasable, *placabilis, e.* **1839** LADY GRANVILLE *Lett.* 21 June, As good-humoured and pleasable as it is possible to be.

†**2.** Acceptable, pleasing, agreeable. *Obs.*

1382 WYCLIF *Isa.* lx. 7 Thei shul ben offrid vpon my plesable [1388 acceptable] auter. *Ibid.* lxi. 2, I shulde.. prechen a ȝer plesable to the Lord [*Vulg.* Annum placabilem Domino]. **1554** KNOX *Godly Let.* A iij b, I haue ben compelled to speake in your presens.. such thinges as were not pleasable to the eares of men.

Hence '**pleasableness**, placability.

1553 GRIMALDE *Cicero's Offices* I. (1558) 39 There is nothing more seemely for a great.. man than pleasablenes and mercy.

pleasance[1] ('plɛzəns). Forms: 4– pleasance, (-aunce); also 4–7 plesaunce, 4–7 (9) -ance, 5 -auns, -awns, pley-, playsaunce, -aunse, plezeauns, 5–6 pleasauns, (*Sc.*) plesans, -ence, 7 (9) plaisance. [ME. a. OF. *plaisance* (*a* 1296 in Littré) pleasure, delight, in 16th c. place of delight, f. *plaisant* pleasing, *plaisir* to please; so med.L. *placentia*, It. *piacenza*: see -ANCE.]

1. The condition or feeling of being pleased; enjoyment, delight, pleasure, joy. *arch.* and *poet.*

c **1374** CHAUCER *Troylus* IV. 1071 (1099) In þe des right as þere fallen chaunces, Right so in loue þere com and gon plesaunces. *c* **1385** —— *L.G.W.* 1150 (*Dido*) Thus is this quyen in plesaunce & in Ioye. **1490** CAXTON *Eneydos* xviii. 67 Yf thou euer toke playsance in ony thyng that by me cam. **1523** LD. BERNERS *Froiss.* I. cclix. 384 The Englysshemen toke great pleasaunce at theyr valiant dedes. **1710** PHILIPS *Pastorals* ii. 97 Untoward Lads, who Pleasance take in Spite. **1812** BYRON *Ch. Har.* II. lxxviii, Some days of joyaunce are decreed to all, To take of pleasaunce each his secret share. **1830** TENNYSON *Lilian* ii, When my passion seeks Pleasance in love-sighs. **1866** LONGF. *Flower-de-luce* iii, Beautiful lily, ..born to joy and pleasance, Thou dost not toil nor spin. **1876** J. ELLIS *Caesar in Egypt* 59 All sights and sounds of pastime and plaisance.

†**2.** The action of pleasing; the disposition to please; complaisance; agreeable or pleasing manners or behaviour, courtesy. *Obs.*

c **1386** CHAUCER *Pard. T.* 81 Som for plesance of folk and flaterye To ben auanced by ypocrisye. *c* **1412** HOCCLEVE *De Reg. Princ.* 3083 Good plesaunce is of swich beneuolence, þat what gode dede he may in man espie, He preysith it, and rebukith folye. *c* **1475** *Rauf Coilȝear* 907 To tell him as I haue tauld the, Withoutin plesance. **1568** GRAFTON *Chron.* II. 398 Manye Noble men were compelled to pay vnto the king great sommes of money, which was called Pleasaunce, to please the king withall [cf. BENEVOLENCE 3, 4]. **1599** B. JONSON *Ev. Man out of Hum.* IV. viii, Content: good Sir, vouchsake vs your pleasance.

b. A sprightly or pleasing trick; a pleasantry. *Obs.* exc. *poet.*

1681 GLANVILL *Sadducismus* II. (1726) 452 Fancy may be permitted its plaisance and inoffensive Raileries. **1681–6** J. SCOTT *Chr. Life* (1700) I. 284 Those little plaisances and inoffensive railleries of fancy which are sometimes requisite to sauce our conversation. **1873** E. BRENNAN *Witch of Nemi*, etc. 178 Isis, she Who with her myriad plesances and wiles Chafes the unbloomed desire of Egypt's maids.

†**3.** That which pleases one; pleasure, desire wish, will. *Obs.*

c **1340** HAMPOLE *Prose Tr.* 21 In the turnynge of thi wille enterely to his seruyce and his plesaunce. *c* **1412** HOCCLEVE *De Reg. Princ.* 1345 To the plesaunce of God thou the conforme. ? **1461** *Paston Lett.* II. 67, I shall doo your pleasauns as moche as in me is. **1530** *Compend. Treat.* in *Rede me*, etc. (Arb.) 180 To doo his office to the plesaunce of god.

4. Pleasure-giving quality; pleasantness. *Obs.* exc. *poet.*

c **1386** CHAUCER *Frankl. T.* 189 The odour of floures and the fresshe sighte, Wolde han maked any herte lighte.. So ful it was of beautee and plesance. *c* **1485** *Digby Myst.* (1882) III. 1304, A, welcum masenger of grett plezeavns! **1503** DUNBAR *Thistle & Rose* 39 For to discryve the Ross of most plesance. **1590** SPENSER *F.Q.* I. iv. 38 With pleasaunce of the breathing fields yfed. **1611** SPEED *Hist. Gt. Brit.* IX. viii. (1623) 554 Deseruedly for the pleasance of the place named Beaulieu. **1748** THOMSON *Cast. Indol.* I. xxvii, It was a fountain of Nepenthe rare, Whence, as Dan Homer sings, huge pleasaunce grew. **1830** TENNYSON *Recoll. Arab. Nts.* x, Thence thro' the garden I was drawn—A realm of pleasance.

b. That which awakens or causes pleasure; that in which one delights; an (objective) pleasure or delight. *Obs.* exc. *poet.*

1485 CAXTON *Paris & V.* 53 Oute of al joyes and playsaunces worldly. **1619** W. SCLATER *Exp. 1 Thess.* (1630) 301 As when.. a father [shows] nuts and such like pleasances to his child. **1812** BYRON *Ch. Har.* I. xxiii, How Vain are the pleasaunces on earth supplied.

5. A pleasure-ground, usually attached to a mansion; sometimes a secluded part of a garden, but more often a separate enclosure laid out with shady walks, trees and shrubs, statuary, and ornamental water. (Now sometimes surviving as the name of a street or 'place', as the Pleasance in Edinburgh, Falkirk, etc. In *Sc.* ('plizəns).)

1585 T. WASHINGTON tr. *Nicholay's Voy.* IV. xxiii. 139 Diuers gardens and pleasaunces, planted with Orange trees. *a* **1600** *Hist. James the Sext* (1825) 94 The gunnis war transportit to a fauxburg of the toun [Edinburgh] callit Pleasands. **1821** SCOTT *Kenilw.* xxvi, The window.. commanded a delightful view of what was called the Pleasance; a space of ground inclosed and decorated with arches, trophies, statues, fountains, and other architectural monuments. **1847** E. WARWICK (*title*) The Poets' Pleasaunce or Garden of all sorts of pleasant Flowers. **1888** HARE *Story my Life* (1900) VI. xxv. 161 A charming old pleasaunce with bowling-green and long grass walks.

¶From the final *s* sound this word was formerly, esp. by Scotch writers, often taken as a plural, and written *plesandis, -antis, pleasands, -ants*, with a pseudo-singular in *-ant*. (But *-antis* may sometimes be a misreading for *-ancis*.)

c **1375** *Sc. Leg. Saints* vii. (*Jacobus*) 497 Þare-fore suld god mare plesandis hafe In til his blud þan al þe lafe. *c* **1449** PECOCK *Repr.* v. vii. 523 The othere plesauntis and eesis of the religiosis persoones. *c* **1485** *Digby Myst.* (1882) III. 648 Seyth.. al þe plesawnt of your mynd. *a* **1600** [see 5]. **1824** GALT *Rothelan* II. xiv, She rose and went down into the pleasants of the castle.

†'**pleasance**[2]. *Obs.* Forms: 5 ples-, 6 pleasa(u)nce, pleasauntes, -antes, -ants. [app. a. F. *Plaisance*:— L. *Placentia*, whence It. *Piacenza*, a city of Emilia, now an important seat of textile industry (silk, cotton, etc.).] A fine kind of lawn or gauze; in *a* 1548 identified with LUMBERDYNE.

c **1420** LYDG. *Assembly of Gods* 299 A kerchyef of plesaunce stood ouer hys helme ay. **1440** *Paston Lett.* I. 40 A Knyght out of Spayne, wyth a kercheff of plesaunce i-wrapped aboute hys arme; the qwych Knyght wyl renne a cours wyth a sharpe spere for his sovereyn lady sake. **1473** *Acc. Ld. High Treas. Scot.* I. 72 Item vj elne of plesance, price elne iiij s. *a* **1548** HALL *Chron., Hen. VIII* 7 [1509] Two ladyes.. in kyrtels of Crymosyne.. and ouer their garmentes were rochettes of pleasantes,.. their heades rouled in pleasauntes and typpets lyke the Egipcians, enbroudered with golde. Their faces, neckes, armes & handes, couered in fyne pleasaunce blacke: Some call it Lumberdynes, which is marueylous thine, so that the same ladies semed to be nygrost [*sic*] or blacke Mores. **1577–87** HOLINSHED *Chron.* III. 849/1. **1594** MARLOWE & NASHE *Dido* I. i, Whenas I.. held the cloth of pleasance whiles you drank. **1801** STRUTT *Sports & Past.* III. ii. 147 *note*, Pleasaunce was a fine thin species of gauze, which was striped with gold.

†'**pleasancy.** *Obs.* [f. as PLEASANCE[1]: see -ANCY.]

a. Pleasing character, pleasantness. **b.** Gaiety, pleasantry.

1545 JOYE *Exp. Dan.* iii. 31 b, The amenite & pleasancy of the place. **1684** I. MATHER *Remark. Provid.* (1856) 141 It is reported that one of the Popes, in way of pleasancy, saying to a parrat, 'What art thou thinking of?' the parrat immediately replied, 'I have considered the dayes of old, the years of antient times'. **1702** C. MATHER *Magn. Chr.* III. II. xvi. 435 He had a certain pleasancy in conversation.

pleasant ('plɛzənt), *a.* (*adv.*) Forms: α. 4-7 **ples-**, 5 **plays-**, **pleys-**, 5-8 **plais-**, 6 *Sc.* **pleis-**, 6- **pleas-**; 4- **-ant**, (4-7 **-ante**, **-aunt(e**, 5 **-awnt**, 7 *Sc.* **-ent**). β. (chiefly *Sc.*) 4-6 **plesand**, 5-6 **pleasand**, **-ande**, (5 **-aund**, **-ond**, **plessand**, 6 **pleis-**, **pleysand**). [ME. a. OF. *plais-*, *pleisant* (12th c. in Littré, Hatz.-Darm.), prop. pr. pple. of *plaisir* = mod.F. *plaire* to please; see PLEASE *v.* In the β forms identified with the north. and Sc. pr. pple. in -AND[1], and thus really a northern variant of PLEASING *ppl. a.*]

A. *adj.* **1.** Having the quality of giving pleasure; originally synonymous with PLEASING, but now used more vaguely: Agreeable to the mind, feelings, or senses; such as one likes.

1375 BARBOUR *Bruce* I. 10 And suth thyngis that ar likand Tyll mannys heryng, ar plesand. *Ibid.* 208 Horse, or hund, or othir thing, That plesand war to thar liking. **1390** GOWER *Conf.* III. 42 And thus what thing unto his pay Was most plesant, he lefte non. **1460** CAPGRAVE *Chron.* (Rolls) 27 Pilgrime ful rich was he [Abraham] and plesaunt to God. **1483** *Cath. Angl.* 283/2 Plesande, *acceptus, gratus.* **1484** CAXTON *Fables of Æsop* I. i, This fayre and playsaunt book. **1509** FISHER *Fun. Serm. C'tess of Richmond* Wks. (E.E.T.S.) 305 A pleasaunt & a swete lyfe..a lyfe full of ioye & pleasure. **1552** ABP. HAMILTON *Catech.* (1884) 3 Na thing culd be to God mair plesand. **1576** FLEMING *Panopl. Epist.* 252 It is vnto mee the pleasauntest thing in the world vniuersall. **1639** in *Proc. Soc. Antiq.* Ser. II. XIV. 373 The other 2 [marble pillars]..very pleasaunt and strounge. **1762** KAMES *Elem. Crit.* ii. § 6 (1833) 59 Pleasant and painful are qualities of the emotions we feel. **1863** KINGSLEY *Water-Bab.* i, The pleasantest time of all the twenty-four hours.

2. Of persons or their attributes: Having pleasing manners, demeanour, or aspect; agreeable, cheerful, good-humoured.

1560 DAUS tr. *Sleidane's Comm.* 347 b, Jhon Cardinall of Lorayne..had bene all his life time a most pleasaunt gest and companion. **1604** T. WRIGHT *Passions* v. §4. 239 Our Lord loveth a pleasant giver. **1642** H. MORE *Song of Soul* I. II. cxlii, A jolly Swain Methought he was; meek, chearfull, and pleasant. **1705** STANHOPE *Paraphr.* I. 115 Content and even pleasant under Hardships. **1831** SIR J. SINCLAIR *Corr.* II. 385 One of the liveliest and pleasantest men I ever met with, was the Marquis del Campo. **1873** BLACK *Pr. Thule* ii, A clever woman is always a pleasanter companion than a clever man.

†**3. a.** Humorous, jocular, facetious; merry, gay. ***to make pleasant***, to be festive, make merry. *Obs.*

1530 PALSGR. 321/1 Pleasante propre, *galliarde.* **1545** *Primer Hen. VIII* in *Three Primers* (1848) 502 Arise, Lord.., let..the righteous and Christ's disciples make pleasant and merry. **1555** EDEN *Decades* 134 When the pleasaunt wanderer perceaued that the Christians ceased to pursue hym. **1581** PETTIE *Guazzo's Civ. Conv.* I. (1586) 45 Which kinde of men, a pleasant writer scoffing at, sayth, That that meate is vnpleasant in tast, which smelleth of the smoake. *c* **1670** HOBBES *Dial. Com. Laws* (1681) 24 All..the Contentments and Ease which some pleasant men have related of the land of Cocquany. **1710** STEELE *Tatler* No. 246 ¶9 Dick Reptile, who does not want Humour, is very pleasant at our Club when he sees an old Fellow touchy at being laughed at for any Thing that is not in the Mode. **1782** COWPER *Gilpin* 169 Now Gilpin had a pleasant wit.

b. Hilarious or excited from drink; tipsy. *rare.*

1596 RALEIGH *Discov. Gviana* 55 Some of our captaines garoused of his wine till they were reasonable pleasant, for it is very strong with pepper. **1680** BURNET *Rochester* (1692) 12 The natural heat of his fancy being inflamed by wine made him..so extravagantly pleasant that [etc.]. **1853** 'C. BEDE' *Verdant Green* iv, He comes home pleasant at night from some wine-party.

†**4.** Amusing, laughable, ridiculous, funny. *Obs.*

1583 STOCKER *Civ. Warres Lowe C.* I. 15 With such other like pleasant iestes. **1604** E. G[RIMSTONE] *D'Acosta's Hist. Indies* I. xiv. 47 From our Peru..they might well bring gold, silver, and pleasant monkies. **1688** PENTON *Guard. Instruct.* (1897) 43 It was pleasant to see how my Son trembled to see the Proctour come in. **1716** ADDISON *Freeholder* No. 9 ¶13 The most pleasant Grievance is still behind. **1760** FOOTE *Minor* II. Wks. 1799 I. 260 They took him off at the play-house some time ago; pleasant, but wrong. Public characters shou'd not be sported with.

5. *Comb.*, chiefly parasynthetic, as ***pleasant-faced***, ***-featured***, ***-looking***, ***-mannered***, ***-minded***, ***-natured***, ***-sounding***, ***-spirited***, ***-spoken***, ***-tongued***, ***-witted*** adjs.

1586 W. WEBBE *Eng. Poetrie* (Arb.) 67 Which all I will referre to the consideration of euerie pleasant headded Poet in their proper gifts. **1597** HOOKER *Eccl. Pol.* v. lxxiv. §3 It is no great disgrace though they suffer pleasant witted men, a little to intermingle with zeale scorne. **1599** SHAKS. *Much Ado* II. i. 355 By my troth a pleasant spirited Lady. **1653** R. SANDERS *Physiogn.* 279 This various, yet pleasant relisht Doctrine. **1685** DRYDEN *Daphnis* Misc. Poems II. 119 A pleasant sounding name's a pretty thing. **1843** DICKENS *Christmas Carol* 145 He is the pleasantest-spoken gentleman. **1853** MRS. GASKELL *Cranford* viii. 153 Lady Glenmire..who had been very pretty in the days of her youth, and who was even yet very pleasant-looking. *c* **1863** T. TAYLOR in M. R. Booth *Eng. Plays of 19th Cent.* (1969) II. 93 Ah, there's a pleasant looking party yonder. **1873** 'MARK TWAIN' & WARNER *Gilded Age* xx. 187 Senator Dilworthy was..a pleasant spoken man, a popular man with the people. **1877** MRS. FORRESTER *Mignon* I. 2 There is one pleasant-faced, cheery mannered Divine. **1896** *Peterson Mag.* Jan. 97/1 He is very pleasant-spoken, and invited me to come and spend the night with him. **1959** T. S. ELIOT *Elder Statesman* I. 22 A foreign person By the looks of him. But talks good English. A pleasant-spoken gentleman. **1978** R. LUDLUM *Holcroft Covenant* xiv. 162 He was in his early thirties, Noel guessed, and pleasant-looking.

†**B.** as *adv.* = PLEASANTLY. *Obs.*

1553 T. WILSON *Rhet.* (1580) 140 More..then the pleasant disposed man is willyng fullie to set forthe. **1604** E. G[RIMSTONE] *D'Acosta's Hist. Indies* II. xiv. 115 They might live at the Indies very pleasant and happily. **1609** BIBLE (Douay) *Exod.* xx. *Comm.*, How pleasant eloquent is that Gregorie, called the great.

†'**pleasant**, *sb. Obs.* Also 7 **plaisant**. [a. F. *plaisant* (16th c.), sb. use of *plaisant* PLEASANT *a.*] A jester, fool, clown.

1595 DUNCAN *App. Etym.* (E.D.S.), *Morio*, a pleasand, a playfoole. **1606** HOLLAND *Sueton.* 250 Whereupon one of these plaisants [*quidam urbanorum*] came out with a pretie conceit. **1617** in *3rd Rep. Hist. MSS. Comm.* 409/1 Archibald Armstrong his Majesties pleasant quha come to this burght with the Inglishe Knichtis. **1632** HOLLAND *Cyrupædia* 42 Why should not they more truely be called, merry conceited Pleasants rather than Boasters?

'**pleasant**, *v. rare.* [In trans. use f. PLEASANT *a.*; in intr. ad. F. *plaisanter* to jest, f. *plaisant* PLEASANT.]

†**1.** *trans.* To please by indulgence; to indulge.

1627-77 FELTHAM *Resolves* I. xiii. 20 He sings, and reuels, and pleasants his spleen.

†**2.** To spend in pleasure. *Obs.*

1633 EARL MANCH. *Al Mondo* (1636) 83 Some pleasant their lives, as if the world should alwayes laugh upon them.

3. *intr.* To joke, indulge in pleasantry.

1845 *Bachelor Albany* (1848) 263 Adelaide had that very night been pleasanting with Laura on the subject of the bachelor.

†'**pleasantable**, *a. Obs. rare.* [irreg. f. PLEASANT *a.* + -ABLE.] = PLEASURABLE.

1619 CHAPMAN *Two Wise Men* II. i. 16 Mee thinkes this praying in a Church among those of high degree is nothing pleasantable, and blushing takes away my devotion.

pleasantish ('plɛzəntɪʃ), *a.* [f. PLEASANT *a.* + -ISH[1].] Somewhat pleasant.

1832 *Fraser's Mag.* V. 97 His eye has a pleasantish twinkle.

pleasantly ('plɛzəntlɪ), *adv.* [f. PLEASANT *a.* + -LY[2].] In a pleasant manner.

1. In a way that pleases or gratifies; pleasingly, agreeably.

c **1380** WYCLIF *Wks.* (1880) 3 þei myȝten lyue as plesandeli to god & as moche profit to holi chirche. *c* **1420** LYDG. *Assembly of Gods* 1689 That they should sowne To the eares of hem the more plesauntly. **1529** *Supplic. to King* (E.E.T.S.) 48 Castelles, pleasauntely set abowte with parckes. **1687** A. LOVELL tr. *Thevenot's Trav.* II. 93 All the women of Persia are pleasantly apparelled. **1776** LD. HAILES in Boswell *Johnson* 30 Aug., Dr. Johnson's *Suasorium* is pleasantly and artfully composed. **1875** JOWETT *Plato* (ed. 2) V. 193 On our way we can pass the time pleasantly in talking.

2. In a manner showing pleasure or contentment; cheerfully, goodhumouredly.

1388 WYCLIF *Ps.* l[i]. 21 Thanne thou schalt take plesauntli the sacrifice of riȝtfulnesse. **1540** HYRDE tr. *Vives' Instr. Chr. Wom.* II. x. (1557) 105 b, That they [servants] do their duty diligently, mekely, and buxomly, yea and merily to, and pleasantly. **1655** STANLEY *Hist. Philos.* III. (1701) 94/2 He gave him the Cup, Socrates took it chearfully,..and looking pleasantly upon him, demanded whether he might spill any of it in libation. **1866** GEO. ELIOT *F. Holt* (1868) 12 The young brown eyes seemed to dwell on her pleasantly.

†**3.** By way of pleasantry; humorously, facetiously, jocosely. *Obs.*

1551 T. WILSON *Logike* (1580) 48 b, Many wittie men take occasion to reason pleasantly upon the interpretation of a worde. **1617** MORYSON *Itin.* I. 259 They will giue you a head of Garlick rosted in the ashes, and pleasantly call it a pigeon. **1787** G. WHITE *Selborne* iv. (1789) 10 This embellishment..has occasioned strangers sometimes to ask us pleasantly, 'whether we fastend our walls together with tenpenny nails?'

pleasantness ('plɛzəntnɪs). [f. PLEASANT *a.* + -NESS.] The quality of being pleasant (in various senses: see the adj.).

1530 PALSGR. 255/2 Plesantnesse, *plaisance.* *Ibid.*, Plesantnesse, *amenité.* **1555** EDEN *Decades* 25 The Lieuetenaunt beinge entysed by the pleasantnes of the kynges syster. **1610** A. WILLET *Hexapla Dan.* 261 Italie..is for pleasantnes and fruitfulnesse farre beyond other regions. **1611** BIBLE *Prov.* iii. 17 Her wayes are wayes of plesantnesse: and all her pathes are peace. **1685** tr. *Gracian's Courtiers Orac.* 76 There is nothing more unpleasant than a continual pleasantness... Some minutes are to be allowed to mirth, and the rest to seriousness. *a* **1715** BURNET *Own Time* (1766) I. 373 He had a pleasantness in his conversation that took much with the king. **1815** ELPHINSTONE *Acc. Caubul* (1842) I. 99 The influence of the rains of Hindoostaun..had cooled the air, and given it a peculiar softness and pleasantness. **1877** TENNYSON *Harold* IV. i. 14 She hath won upon our people thro' her beauty And pleasantness among them.

pleasantry ('plɛzəntrɪ). Also 8-9 **plaisanterie**. [a. F. *plaisanterie*, OF. *plesanterie* (13th c. in Godef.), f. *plaisant* PLEASANT, jocose; see -RY.]

1. a. A pleasant and sprightly humour in conversation; jocularity, fun, facetiousness; good-humoured ridicule, raillery.

1655 tr. *De Parc's Com. Hist. Francion* 23 Ravished with the pleasantry of the severall passages he had heard. **1693** DRYDEN *Juvenal* Ded. (1697) 60 There can be no Pleasantry where there is no Wit. **1734** tr. *Rollin's Anc. Hist.* (1827) I. 115 Ridicule, or to express the same word by another, pleasantry. **1763** C. JOHNSTON *Reverie* I. 256 Pumping his brain for pleasantry, and labouring for wit to entertain the sneering crowd around him. **1827** CARLYLE *Misc., Richter* (1857) I. 14 That light matter which the French call pleasantry. **1849** MACAULAY *Hist. Eng.* iii. I. 328 A species of simony, which furnished an inexhaustible subject of pleasantry to three or four generations of scoffers.

b. With *a* and *pl.* A humorous passage, action, or (now, esp.) speech: a joke, a jest.

1701 *Stanley's Hist. Philos.* Biog. 6 Many other Pleasantries of the same Kind are mention'd in their Place. **1711** ADDISON *Spect.* No. 31 ¶2 The several Woods in Asia ..will give the Audience a Sight of Monkies dancing upon Ropes, with many other Pleasantries of that ludicrous Species. **1716** M. DAVIES *Athen. Brit.* II. To Rdr. 3 With their Censorious Plaisanteries upon the greatest of Authors and Worthies. **1809** SYD. SMITH *Serm.* I. 235 They..think that a few silly pleasantries, and slender arguments, are a sufficient preparation to decide on these proofs of a future life. **1880** MCCARTHY *Hist. Own Times* III. xlvii. 431 He seldom indulged in any pleasantries that could wound or offend.

2. †**a.** Pleasure, pleasantness, enjoyment. *Obs.*

1741 RICHARDSON *Pamela* II. 253 To take up the good Company's Attention now, will spoil their Pleasantry. **1780** BURKE *Let. to T. Burgh* Wks. 1842 II. 409 Lord North was either wholly out of the house, or engaged in other matters of business or pleasantry, in the remotest recesses of the West Saxon corner.

b. An instance of pleasantness or enjoyment; a pleasurable circumstance.

1790 G. WALKER *Serm.* II. xxi. 109 We lose the relish for the thousand pleasantries of life. **1925** T. DREISER *Amer. Tragedy* (1926) I. I. iii. 17 A nerve plasm palpitation, that spoke loudly for all the seemingly material things of life, not for the thin pleasantries of heaven. **1959** *Kentucky Folklore Rec.* V. 118 The consumption of large quantities of watermelons during the day... With all these pleasantries, it is surprising that the afternoon [church] services are well attended.

'**pleasantsome**, *a. rare*[−1]. [f. PLEASANT *a.* + -SOME.] Somewhat pleasant.

1836 F. MAHONY *Rel. Father Prout, Songs Hor.* I. (1859) 389 Some..find Larissa pleasantsome Or Sparta deem seductive.

please (pliːz), *v.* Forms: 4-5 (*Sc.* 6-8) **pleis(e**, 4-6 **pleys** (*Sc.* **pleyss**), **plese** (*Sc.* **ples**, 4 **pleece**), 5 **plaise**, **plase**, **place**, 5-6 **playse** (*Sc.* **pleiss**, **pless**, *erron.* **ple**), 5- **please**, (6 **pleace**, **pleas**, **plise**, *Sc.* **plaiss**). [ME. *plaise*, *pleise*, *plese*, a. OF. *plais-ir* (3 pl. pres. *plaise-nt*) = Pr. *plazer*, Sp. *placer*, Pg. *prazer*, It. *piacere*:—L. *placēre* to be pleasing or agreeable, f. root *plac-* in *placidus* gentle, mild, peaceful, *placor* contentment, satisfaction, *plācāre* to calm, soothe, still. The mod.F. infinitive *plaire* (12th c. in Littré) is a collateral form, repr. a pop. L. *placĕre*, *plac're*.]

I. †**1. a.** *intr.* To be agreeable; to give pleasure or satisfaction. Const. *to* = F. *plaire à*, L. *placēre* with dative; *with*, etc. *Obs.*

a **1325** *Prose Psalter* lii. 7 [liii. 5] For God wasted þe bones of þem þat plesen to men. *c* **1350** *Will. Palerne* 4729 In what maner þat i miȝt mest with þe plece. **1375** BARBOUR *Bruce* I. 198 That Scottis men mycht do na thing That euir mycht pleyss to thar liking. **1382** WYCLIF *1 Thess.* iv. 1 As ȝe han resceyued of vs how it bihoueth ȝou for to go and plese to God. —— *1 Sam.* xviii. 26 The word pleside in the eyen of Dauyd. *c* **1400** *Prymer* (1895) 50 þat we mowe serue to þee wiþ chast bodi, & plese to þee wiþ clene herte.

†**b.** ***to please to oneself***, to take pleasure, be well pleased. *Obs.*

1382 WYCLIF *Isa.* xlii. 1 Al plesede to hym in hym my soule [1388 my soule pleside to it silf in hym]. **1382** —— *Wisd.* vi. 3 Ȝiueth eres, ȝee that holden togidere multitudis, and plesen to ȝou [1388 plesen ȝou] in cumpanyes of naciouns.

2. a. *trans.* To be agreeable to; to gratify, satisfy, delight.

The vb. was here orig. *intr.* as in 1, the object being a dative; but this not being formally distinct from an accusative or direct object, the vb. came at length to be viewed as transitive, and to have a passive voice (see 4). (It has no passive in Fr.)

c **1330** R. BRUNNE *Chron.* (1810) 68 þe meyne in alle þing plesed him next the king. *c* **1350** *Will. Palerne* 188 Bliþe was eche a barn ho best miȝt him plese. **1388** WYCLIF *1 Thess.* iv. 1 Hou it behoueth ȝou to go and to plese God [1382 to God]. **1398** TREVISA *Barth. De P.R.* VIII. i (1495) 296 We shall fle the worlde though he playse [*Bodley MS.* please] vs wyth welthe. *Ibid.* XVIII. xiv. 774 An oxe herde plasyth the oxen wyth whystlynge and wyth songe. *c* **1483** CAXTON *Dialogues* 5/6 *Mais sil vous plaist aulcune chose Que ie puisse fayre*: But if you plaise ony thyng That I may doo. *c* **1500** *Melusine* 9 The king said to them 'That playseth me'. *c* **1560** A. SCOTT *Poems* (S.T.S.) x. 38 Is not in erd I cure, Bot pleiss my lady pure. **1611** BIBLE *Esther* ii. 4 The thing pleased the king, and he did so. **1639** S. DU VERGER tr. *Camus' Admir. Events* 85 Imagining..that all was lawfull that pleased his humour. **1748** SMOLLETT *Rod. Rand.* xl, But she was resolved to please her eye, if she should plague her heart. **1837** ARNOLD *Let.* 21 Apr. in Stanley *Life* II. 81 Jacob Abbott's last work ..will, I think, please you very much.

b. *absolutely.* (At first perh. *intr.* = 1.)

1390 GOWER *Conf.* III. 158 For thei that cunnen plese and glose, Ben..the norrices Unto the fostringe of the vices. **1484** CAXTON *Fables of Æsop* I. xvii, The vnwyse displeseth there where as he supposeth to please. *c* **1530** *Pol., Rel. & L. Poems* (1866) 31 Pleace with thi dedys rathir than with thy clothis. **1681** DRYDEN *Abs. & Achit.* 747 Two names, that always cheat, and always please. **1747** JOHNSON *Prol. Opening Drury-Lane* 54 The drama's laws, the drama's patrons give, For we that live to please, must please to live. *a* **1849** H. COLERIDGE *Ess.* (1851) I. 356 Men and writers, if they please at all, must please by doing their best in their own way. **1877** FURNIVALL *Leopold Shaks.* Introd. 120 The revived doctrine that the main object of poetry is to please, seems to me too contemptible to be discusst.

c. *refl.* To gratify or satisfy oneself. Also *colloq.* To do as one likes, take one's own way.

c **1586** C'TESS PEMBROKE *Ps.* XLIX. vii, Please they them selves, and think at happiest stay Who please them selves. **1600** SHAKS. *A.Y.L.* v. iv. 78 If I sent him word..it [his beard] was not well cut, he wold send me word he cut it to please himselfe: this is call'd the quip modest. **1608** —— *Per.* IV. i. 101 Perhappes they will but please themselues vpon her, not carrie her aboord. **1620** T. GRANGER *Div. Logike* A iij, I purposed not so much to please my selfe, and a few, as to be beneficiall. **1779–81** JOHNSON *L.P., Pope* Wks. IV. 67 Warburton..had, in the early part of his life, pleased himself with the notice of inferior wits. **1855** MACAULAY *Hist. Eng.* xiii. III. 334 The clans which took no part in the insurrection..pleased themselves with the hope that they should easily make their peace with the conquerors.

3. *Impersonally*, with formal subject *it* (the real subject being a following infinitive or clause, expressed or understood): To seem good to one; to be one's will or pleasure. (Equivalent in sense to 'will', 'choose', 'think proper', etc., with the person as subject: cf. 4 b.)

Formerly usual in deferential phrases of address or request, as *and, an, if it please you*, etc., *may it, will it please you, your honour*, etc.; ellipt. *please it* (corruptly *pleaseth*) *you*, etc.; also (with omission of *it*), *so please you, please you*, and still in *please your honour, please God, please the pigs*, etc.

†**a.** Const. with *to* (= F. *à*, L. dative). *Obs.*

a **1325** *Prose Psalter* xxxix. 18 [xl. 13] Plese it, Lorde, to þe, þat þou defende me. **1382** WYCLIF *Esther* i. 19 If it plese to thee [Vulg. *si tibi placet*], go ther out a maundement. *c* **1434** *Paston Lett.* I. 36 Plese it to Commines of the present Parlement, that William Paston..takyth diverse fees [etc.]. *a* **1450** *Knt. de la Tour* (1868) 90 But she was paied, as it plesed to God, atte the laste.

b. Const. with simple object (orig. a dative). †*please it you*, may it please you; also in *arch.* use as *sb.*

(A following infinitive often lost its *to* in 16–17th c.)

1388 WYCLIF *Esther* ix. 13 If it plesith the kyng [1382 If to the king it plese, Vulg. *si regi placet*], power be 3ouun to the Jewis. **1406** HOCCLEVE *La male regle* 416 If it thee lyke & plese. **1423** *Rolls of Parlt.* IV. 249 Please it your full wyse discretions, to consider the matier. *c* **1460** *Play Sacram.* 73 And yt place yow. **1478** *Paston Lett.* III. 221 Withouth it ple vow to send oon of yowr men to me. **1503** *Rolls of Parlt.* VI. 553/1 Pleas it nowe your Highnesse..to ordeyn. **1509** in *Mem. Hen. VII* (Rolls) 433 And hyt ple your grace..that [etc.]. **1568** GRAFTON *Chron.* II. 350 Pleaseth you also to remember how many Lords, noble men, and good commons ..died in thoss warres. *c* **1590** MARLOWE *Faust.* Wks. 121/2 Please it your Holiness, I think it be some ghost. **1591** SHAKS. *Two Gent.* I. ii. 140 Come, come, wilt please you go? **1594** —— *Rich. III*, IV. iv. 488 Pleaseth [*Qos.* please it] your Maiestie to giue me leaue, Ile muster vp my friends. **1598** —— *Merry W.* I. i. 275 Wil't please your worship to come in, Sir? *Ibid.* II. ii. 37 Not so, and 't please your worship. **1602** *2nd Pt. Return fr. Parnass.* II. vi. (Arb.) 32 Not a word more sir ant please you. **1611** BIBLE *Acts* xv. 34 It pleased Silas to abide there still. **1646** *Hamil on Papers* (Camden) 117 May it please your Grace. **1822** B'NESS BUNSEN in Hare *Life* I. vi. 196 Wherefore he follows this plan it has never pleased him to explain. **1881** 'MARK TWAIN' *Prince & Pauper* xii. 138 With never a by-your-leave or so-please-it-you, or anything of the sort.

c. With omission of *it*; in †*please you*, †*so please you*, may it (so) please you; *please your honour*, *please God*, etc.

c **1440** *Alphabet of Tales* 72 Me pleis [= pleises] not at nowder of þies sulde be sent þis message. **1600** SHAKS. *A.Y.L.* IV. iii. 37 *Ros.* Will you heare the letter? *Sil.* So please you, for I neuer heard it yet. **1611** —— *Cymb.* II. ii. 1 *Imo.* Who's there? My woman: Helene? *Lady.* Please you Madam. **1738** SWIFT *Pol. Conversat.* 69 An please your Honour, there's a Man below wants to speak to you. **1794** MRS. RADCLIFFE *Myst. Udolpho* vi, 'Please your honour, he may be a robber', said Michael. **1834** LYTTON *Pompeii* II. ii, To-morrow night, please the gods, we will have then a snug carousal.

4. a. *Passive. to be pleased*: To be gratified, delighted, or agreeably satisfied. Const. *with*.

1387 TREVISA *Higden* (Rolls) VIII. 149 Þe pepil was i-plesed wiþ his faire speche. **1426** AUDELAY *Poems* 3 Therwith he is both plesud and payd. **1535** COVERDALE *Ps.* l[i]. 19 Then shalt thou be pleased with the sacrifice of rightuousnesse. **1718** *Free-thinker* No. 61. 40 Every One is pleased with such an Occasion of shewing the Superiority of his Understanding. **1850** MCCOSH *Div. Govt.* II. ii. (1874) 213 Nor can God be pleased with the perverted adoration.

b. (*a*) with *infinitive* (or *clause*), expressing the subject of satisfaction. Also, (*b*) To have the will or desire, to be moved; (*c*) To think proper, vouchsafe, choose; to have the kindness, be so obliging as; *sarcastically*: to have the humour. *pleased to meet you*: a formula used in reply to an introduction. Cf. MEET *v.* 4.

(This is the passive of the impersonal construction: *I was pleased to see* = *it pleased me to see*.)

c **1400** *Rom. Rose* 3008, I was wel plesed..To see the botoun fair and swote, So fresshe spronge out of the rote. **1595** SHAKS. *John* II. i. 246 Be pleased then To pay that dutie which you truly owe. **1610** —— *Temp.* III. ii. 44 Wilt thou be pleas'd to hearken..to the suite. *Ibid.* III. iv. 161 If you be pleas'd, retire into my Cell, And there repose. **1611** BIBLE *Transl. Pref.* 10 The tongues wherein God was pleased to speake to his Church by his Prophets and Apostles. —— *Ps.* xl. 13 Be pleased, O Lord, to deliuer me. **1680** SIR C. LYTTELTON in *Hatton Corr.* (Camden) 239 He was pleased to tell mee the King sayd it was for his service. *c* **1680** BEVERIDGE *Serm.* (1729) I. 60 To persecute..persons that he is pleas'd to call heriticks. **1697** DRYDEN *Virg. Georg.* III. 459 Pleas'd I am, no beaten Road to take. **1712** HEARNE *Collect.* (O.H.S.) III. 424 He was pleas'd to mention the Controversy between D^r. Kennett and me. **1759** FRANKLIN *Ess.* Wks. 1840 III. 405 The governor is pleased to doubt our having such letters as we mentioned. **1826** DISRAELI *Viv. Grey* II. vi, My dear Sir! you are pleased to be amusing this morning. **1871** FREEMAN *Norm. Conq.* IV. xvii. 67 A noble and powerful city, inhabited by rich, daring, and he is pleased to add faithless, citizens. **1914** C. MACKENZIE *Sinister Street* II. III. xv. 802 Doesn't it make you shiver? It's like the 'Pleased to meet you', of Americans and Tootingians. **1916** 'TAFFRAIL' *Pincher Martin* vii. 102 Pleased ter meet yer, miss. **1934** A. CHRISTIE *Murder on Orient Express* II. iv. 97 Mrs. Hubbard murmured: 'Pleased to meet you, I'm sure.' **1955** M. ALLINGHAM *Beckoning Lady* v. 68 Pleased to meet you... I thought I'd just step across..and touch my cap, so to speak. **1966** J. CLEARY *High Commissioner* iii. 41 'Lady Porthleven, may I present Mr. Malone?' 'Pleased to meet you,' said Malone. 'Oh, really?' Lady Porthleven looked surprised: no one had ever actually *told* her he was pleased to meet her. **1974** A. PRICE *Other Paths to Glory* III. vi. 185 'Mr.—Hayhoe?' Mitchell thrust out his hand... 'Pleased to meet you.' Hayhoe nodded easily... There was room neither for deference nor condescension in the greeting.

5. *trans.* To appease, pacify, satisfy. *Obs.* or *dial.*

1382 WYCLIF *Lev.* i. 3 A maal with outen wemme he shal offre..to plese to hym the Lord [1388 to make the Lord plesid to hym, Vulg. *ad placandum sibi dominum*]. —— *Ps.* xlviii. 8 [xlix. 7] He shal not 3iue to God wher of he be plesid [1388 to God his plesyng, Vulg. *placationem suam*]. **1563** *Homilies* II. *For Gd. Friday* II. (1859) 420 He could do nothing that might please God's wrath. **1565–73** COOPER *Thesaurus* s.v. *Pio*, *Delicta plare*..to please god for sinne. **1828** *Craven Gloss.* (ed. 2), *Pleease*, to satisfy, to make an equivalent. 'I'll pleease you for 't.'

II. 6. a. *intr.* To be pleased, to like; to have the will or desire; to have the humour; to think proper. (In sense, exactly = the passive in 4, 4 b.)

The history of this inverted use of *please* (observed first in Scottish writers) is obscure. But exactly the same change took place in the 14th c. in the use of the synonymous verb LIKE, where the impersonal 'it liked him', 'him liked', became 'he liked' *c* 1430. It may therefore be assumed that 'I please' was similarly substituted for 'it pleases me', 'me pleases' (*c* 1440 in 3 c). Cf. also Malory's 'me ought', in alliterative *Morte Arthure* 'me aughte', with Wyclif's 'Y awȝte', later 'I ought'. The remarkable thing in the case of *please* is that the sense was already logically expressed by the passive *to be pleased* (sense 4), and that the new idiom was therefore not needed, 'he pleases' being simply = 'it pleases him', and 'he is pleased'. Shakspere uses the three forms indifferently. Indeed, all the constructions of the vb., exc. 6 c, are richly exemplified in his works: see Schmidt.

1500–20 DUNBAR *Poems* lxxxi. 38 3our melody he pleissis nocht till heir. **1513** DOUGLAS *Æneis* IX. vii. 5 From Lawrentum..War horsmen sent to Turnus, for to se Quhat he plesyt. **1530** [see b]. **1535** COVERDALE *Ps.* cxxxiv. [cxxxv.] 6 What so euer ye Lorde pleaseth, y^t doth he in heauen & in earth. [Elsewhere C. has always 'pleaseth the Lord', which also stands here in the Great Bible and Geneva.] **1581** N. BURNE *Disput.* in *Cath. Traciates* (S.T.S.) 122 Lauch alsmekle als ye pleiss. **1581** PETTIE *Guazzo's Civ. Conv.* I. (1586) 2 b, This your anguish of mind, or melancholie, as you please to tearme it. **1588** GREENE *Perimedes* Ep. Ded., If he [Perimedes] please I have my desire. **1601** SHAKS. *All's Well* III. v. 71 This yong maid might do her A shrewd turne if she pleas'd. **1612** *Two Noble K.* II. ii. 59, I see two comforts rysing, two meere blessings, If the gods please. **1638** SIR T. HERBERT *Trav.* (ed. 2) 140 They..single what beast they please to fight with. **1649** HOWELL *Pre-em. Parl.* 3 The Book you pleased to send me. **1651** HOBBES *Leviath.* II. xxvi. 138 He may when he pleaseth, free himselfe from that subjection. **1660** F. BROOKE tr. *Le Blanc's Trav.* 21 He travels a foot with his whole Court, yet his Courtiers go as they please. **1665** BOYLE *Occas. Refl.* IV. xvii. (1848) 270, I can make her speak to me, just what I please. **1684** BUNYAN *Pilgr.* II. 81 That he will please to let me know all therein. **1713** ADDISON *Guard.* No. 160 ¶7 You may make what use of it you please. ? **1800** W. B. RHODES *Bomb. Fur.* i. (1830) 7 What will your Majesty please to wear? **1885** *Law Rep.* 29 *Ch. Div.* 488 The plaintiff..has a right to have the trial where he pleases.

b. *if* (†*and, an*) *you please*: if it please you, if you like, if it is your will or pleasure: a courteous qualification to a request, the acceptance of an offer, etc.; also (parenthetically), a sarcastic way of emphasizing any surprising statement, as if asking leave to make it. (So F. *s'il vous plaît*. Cf. *by your leave*: see LEAVE *sb.*[1] 1.)

Here *you* may have been originally dative, as in 3 b (i.e. if (it) please you, = L. *si vobis placet*, F. *s'il vous plaît*, Ger. *wenn es Ihnen gefällt*), as in quot. 1483 in 2; but it is now taken as nominative (i.e. if you are pleased, if you like, if it is your will or pleasure): cf. *if he pleases*; *if they please*, above (in 6); and 'if ye please' here in 1530. Shakspere has both *if you be pleased* (4 b), and *if you please*.

1530 *Jyl of Brentford's Test.* (Ballad Soc.) 15 But tary, I pray you all, Yf ye please. **1588** SHAKS. *L.L.L.* I. i. 50 Let me say no, my Liedge, and if you please. **1596** —— *Merch. V.* I. i. 147 If you please To shoote another arrow that selfe way. **1601** —— *Twel. N.* III. iv. 355 Pray sir, put your sword vp if you please. **1621** ELSING *Debates Ho. Lords* (Camden) 58, I wyll goe, and you please. *a* **1653** BINNING *Serm.* (1845) 419 Ye need not be made miserable, but if you please. *a* **1907** *Mod.* Will you take another cup? If you please. (*To child*) Say 'If you please', and you shall have it.

1816 JANE AUSTEN *Emma* I. xii. 214 South End is prohibited, if you please. **1848** THACKERAY in *Scribner's Mag.* I. 391/1, I heard of the father and son in the other regiment.., the Slashers if you please, being carried up drunk to bed. **1879** *Cornh. Mag.* XL. 558 He wants to pay his addresses, if you please, to Ursula! *a* **1907** *Mod.* He must travel first class, if you please, like his betters. **1951** J. CORNISH *Provincials* 57 In the winter the heating system was always going on the blink and then the headmistress would scurry round *opening* windows, if you please. **1973** *Math. Teacher* May 479/1 To a monotonous degree, then, each aspect of the operation of the Council is in the hands of the mathematics educators—the *teachers*, if you please. **1979** 'M. YORKE' *Death on Account* xi. 110 He's gone away for the weekend, if you please.

c. *please!* (imperative or optative) was app. originally short for *please you* (3 c) = 'may it (or let it) please you'; but it is now usually taken as = 'Be pleased' (imperative of 6), or as short for 'if you please' (6 b).

This use of *please* appears to have been unknown to Shakspere, whose shortest form is *please you* (3 c).

When parenthetical, or without construction, *please* is = may it please you, if it please you, if you please; e.g. Please, may I go out? May I come in, please? Come here, please; Give me my hat, please; Please, Sir, did you call? Shall I ring the bell? Yes, please. Will you, please, take a message for me?

But when followed by an infinitive, it is = Be pleased: e.g. Please to excuse my keeping you waiting; Please to return the book soon; Please not to lose it.

[**1622** F. MARKHAM *Bk. War* v. vii. 185 Please then my Lord to read this Epistle.] **1667** MILTON *P.L.* v. 397 Heav'nly stranger, please to taste These bounties which our Nourisher,.. To us for food and for delight hath caus'd The Earth to yeild. **1875** JOWETT *Plato* (ed. 2) I. 90 Please then to take my place. **1891** KIPLING *Light that Failed* (1900) 226 'Then I'll tell the boys...' 'Please not, old man.' **1898** G. B. SHAW *Plays* II. *You never can tell* 309 Yes, sir. Please, who are you?

d. *as you please*, in comparative phrases.

1928 'BRENT OF BIN BIN' *Up Country* xvi. 273 The native-born maids were as pretty and perky as you please. **1964** MRS. L. B. JOHNSON *White House Diary* 23 Jan. (1970) 60 Lynda Bird got up..and said she had just come from the University of Texas where we had the Number One football team..to the house where she could listen to the Number One people of the nation.., just as poised as you please.

†**7.** *trans.* To be pleased with, take pleasure in; to like. *Sc. Obs.*

1578 *Ps.* li. in *Scot. Poems 16th C.* (1801) II. 119 Gif thou had pleased sacrifice I suld have offered thee. **1616** J. HAIG in J. Russell *Haigs* vi. (1881) 139 Gif they pleasit not his wark when they saw it, he should correct it. *a* **1665** GUTHRIE *Chr. Gt. Interest* I. viii. (1766) 119 You wonder that any man should not please the device of salvation by Christ. **1719** *Wodrow Corr.* (1843) II. 470, I please what you term the demy [paper], but I think it's thin.

†**please**, *sb. Sc. rare.* [f. prec.] Pleasing, pleasure.

a **1550** *Freiris of Berwik* 428 in *Dunbar's Poems* (S.T.S.) 299 Bot all thair sport, quhen thay wer maist at eiss, Vnto our deme it wes bot littill pleiss.

pleased (pliːzd), *ppl. a.* [f. PLEASE *v.* + -ED[1].] Affected by feelings of satisfaction or pleasure; contented, gratified, in good humour; †appeased.

1382 WYCLIF *Ps.* lxxvii. 38 He forsooth is merciful, and plesid [1388 merciful] shal be maad to the synnes of hem. **1493** *Festivall* (W. de W. 1515) 58 Therwith he helde hym pleased. **1530** PALSGR. 321/1 Pleased, *content.* **1593** SHAKS. *2 Hen. VI*, I. ii. 55 Nay be not angry, I am pleas'd againe. **1596** —— *Merch. V.* III. ii. 182 Among the buzzing pleased multitude. **1657** AUSTEN *Fruit Trees* I. 25 The spirits are refreshed, and in a pleased temper and condition. **1782** MISS BURNEY *Cecilia* VIII. vii, I am not quite pleased with your looks. **1873** BLACK *Pr. Thule* vi, A pleased smile appeared on her face.

pleasedly ('pliːzɪdlɪ), *adv.* [f. prec. + -LY[2].] In a pleased manner; with pleasure or satisfaction.

1651 JER. TAYLOR *Holy Dying* i. §3 (1719) 26 He..that can look upon another Man's Lands evenly and pleasedly as if they were his own. **1661** FELTHAM *Resolves* II. xl. 262 He that would be pleasedly innocent, must refrain from the tast of offence. **1867** *Contemp. Rev.* IV. 417 [She] would have lingered pleasedly.

pleasedness ('pliːzd-, 'pliːzɪdnɪs). [f. as prec. + -NESS.] The condition of being pleased; pleasure, satisfaction.

1665 BOYLE *Occas. Refl.* (1848) 69 It may put him in mind of the pleas'dness and alacrity, with which a charitable person should set himself to the doing of good. **1680** BAXTER *Cath. Commun.* iii. (1684) 16 Pleasedness, and Displeasedness are in the Passions, and signify Joy and Trouble. **1828** J. BALLANTYNE *Exam. Hum. Mind* III. ix. 323 That pleasedness, if it be in a considerable degree, is the very same with the affection of joy or delight.

†**'please-God**, *a. Obs. rare.* [f. PLEASE *v.*] That pleases God.

1606 SYLVESTER *Du Bartas* II. iv. II. *Magnificence* 3 Salomon: His (please-God) Choice of Wisdom, wins him Honor.

†**'please-man.** *Obs. rare.* [f. PLEASE *v.*] One who tries to please men, a man-pleaser.

1588 SHAKS. *L.L.L.* v. ii. 463 Some carry-tale, some please-man, some slight Zanie.

pleaser ('pliːzə(r)). [f. PLEASE *v.* + -ER[1].] One who or that which pleases or aims at pleasing.

1526 TINDALE *Col.* iii. 22 Not with eye service as men pleasers. **1591** HARINGTON *Orl. Fur.* Pref. ¶iij b, A bitter inuectiue against Poets and Poesie..That it is a nurse of lies, a pleaser of fooles. **1656** *Artif. Handsom.* 190 A pleaser of all men..that he might gaine some. **1861** J. BROWN *Horæ Subs.* (1882) 308 If it be a great pleasure to see others pleased, and a greater to be the pleaser.

†**'please-time.** *Obs. rare.* [f. PLEASE *v.*] One who tries to please the time, a time-server.

1606 WARNER *Alb. Eng.* lxxxi. 341 Live ever..in this Forehead of our Song by Please-times now forgot.

pleaship ('pliːʃɪp). *rare.* [f. PLEA *sb.* + -SHIP.] The condition of being at law; litigation.

1824 SCOTT *Redgauntlet* Let. xiii, Peter Peebles and Paul Plainstanes entered into partnership... But..*societas est mater discordiarum*: partnership oft makes pleaship.

pleasing ('pliːzɪŋ), *vbl. sb.* [-ING¹.]

1. The action of the vb. PLEASE; the giving of pleasure or satisfaction; the fact of being pleased or satisfied.

†*to have pleasing to*: to take pleasure in; *to do* (one) *pleasing*: to give pleasure to (*obs.*).

1362 LANGL. *P. Pl.* A. III. 237 Preostes and Persones þat plesyng desyreþ, And taketh Meede and moneye for Massen þat þei syngen. *a* **1450** *Knt. de la Tour* (1868) 48 Whi loue ye or haue more plesinge to ani man than to youre husbonde? *Ibid.* 67 To make her selff the fayrer to the plesinge of the worlde. **1596** RALEIGH in *Four C. Eng. Lett.* (1880) 36 Preferringe your plesinge before myne own desire. **1611** BIBLE *Col.* i. 10 That yee might walke worthy of the Lord vnto all pleasing, being fruitfull in euery good worke. **1895** CLIVE HOLLAND *Jap Wife* (ed. 11) 78 She is a graduate in the art of pleasing.

†**b.** Appeasing, pacification, blandishment.

c **1380** *Antecrist* in Todd *3 Treat. Wyclif* 123 þei disceyven þe hertis of innocentis be swet wordis & plesyngis & oþer feyned signes. **1382** WYCLIF *1 Macc.* i. 47 Sacrifices and plesyngis for to be don in the temple of God. *c* **1400** *Harrow. Hell* 977 (Add. MS.) A lettre þai wrote all of plesynge.

†**2.** One's liking, pleasure, desire, will. *Obs.*

c **1430** *Hymns Virg.* 2 Tota pulcra þou art to my plesynge, My moder, princes of paradijs. *c* **1485** *Digby Myst.* (1882) III. 1480 That wold I lerne; Ittis my plesyng. **1527** *Prose Life St. Brandan* (Percy Soc.) 40 Therfore our Lorde hath set us here..in full grete joye and myrth, after his pleasynge, here to serve hym.

†**3.** A source of pleasure; an object of delight. *Obs. rare.*

c **1386** CHAUCER *Man of Law's T.* 613 They moste take in pacience at nyght Swiche manere necessaries as been plesynges To folk þat han ywedded hem with rynges.

†**4.** = PLEASINGNESS. *Obs.*

1581 SAVILE *Tacitus' Agric.* (1622) 184 The sweetnesse and pleasing of idlenesse, and of doing nothing, creepeth into our sences. **1594** SHAKS. *Rich. III*, I. i. 13 He capers nimbly in a Ladies Chamber, To the lasciuious pleasing of a Lute.

'pleasing, *ppl. a.* [f. PLEASE *v.* + -ING².]

1. That pleases; that gives pleasure or satisfaction; agreeable, grateful.

c **1380** WYCLIF *Serm.* Sel. Wks. II. 19 However þis ende comeþ beste, is moost plesing to God. *c* **1440** *Jacob's Well* 191 Plesyd wyth fayre woordys & plesyng speche. **1563** *Mirr. Mag., Hastings* lvi, The pleasyngst meanes boade not the luckiest endes. **1592** WARNER *Alb. Eng.* VIII. xli. (1612) 200 The teares did wash her pleasing face. **1621** LADY M. WROTH *Urania* 327 What is pleasinger then varietie, or sweeter then flatterie? **1702** POPE *Dryope* 19 Her smiling babe (a pleasing charge) she prest Within her arms. **1741** RICHARDSON *Pamela* (1824) I. 9 He has reconciled the pleasing to the proper. **1877** MRS. FORRESTER *Mignon* I. 15 No longer a young man, yet not too old to be pleasing to women.

†**2.** Willing, approving. *Obs. rare.*

1652 HOWELL *Giraffi's Rev. Naples* II. 81 Whereunto Don John gave no pleasing ear.

pleasingly ('pliːzɪŋlɪ), *adv.* [f. prec. + -LY².]

1. In a pleasing manner; so as to please; pleasantly.

c **1400** *Lanfranc's Cirurgie* 8 Be he trewe..& plesynglyche bere he hym-self to hys pacientis. **1593** NASHE *Christ's T.* (1613) 129 No Orator was euer more pleasingly perswasiue. **1779** FORREST *Voy. N. Guinea* 256 An island, where I spent my time so pleasingly. **1869** TOZER *Highl. Turkey* II. 190 There is..very little variety, nor are the different objects pleasingly arranged.

†**2.** With pleasure; = PLEASANTLY 2, PLEASEDLY. *Obs.*

c **1410** LOVE *Bonavent. Mirr.* xxxiii. 62 (Gibbs MS.) Oure lord iesu accepted more plesyngly & preferred þe priuy contemplacyoun of marye. **1591** LAMBARDE *Archeion* (1635) 89 If one that hath a judiciall place..shall pleasingly heare the proofes of the one partie, and peremptorily cut off the other. **1612** W. MARTYN *Youth's Instruct.* 77 Neither doe you relish too pleasingly your owne actions. **1682** NORRIS *Hierocles* Pref. 19 That can look upon another man's Lands evenly and pleasingly as if they were his own. [Cf. PLEASEDLY, quot. 1651.]

pleasingness ('pliːzɪŋnɪs). [f. as prec. + -NESS.]

a. Pleasing quality; agreeableness, pleasantness. †**b.** Pleasedness, pleasure (*obs.*).

a. *a* **1586** SIDNEY *Arcadia* (1622) 55 Time..seeming..short..in the pleasingnesse of such presence. **1662** STILLINGFL. *Orig. Sacr.* I. iv. §2 (ed. 3) 59 The novelty and pleasingness of musick and poetry. **176.** WESLEY *Husb. & Wives* iii. Wks. 1811 IX. 62 The Effects of Nuptial Love are three, Pleasingness, Faithfulness, Helpfulness. **1832** L. HUNT *Sir. R. Esher* (1850) 234 Warts and wrinkles..inimical to pleasingness of aspect.

b. **1649** EARL MONM. tr. *Senault's Use Passions* (1671) 53 One might..see pleasingness take the same place in his countenance, which Choler had possest.

pleasura'bility. *rare.* [f. next + -ITY.] The quality of being pleasurable.

1813 L. HUNT in *Examiner* 12 Apr. 227/1 He..talks as if he were all pleasurability or dignity.

pleasurable ('plɛʒərəb(ə)l), *a.* [f. PLEASURE *sb.* + -ABLE, after *comfortable.*]

1. Affording, or capable of affording, pleasure; agreeable, pleasant.

1579 E. K. in *Spenser's Sheph. Cal.* Ep. Ded. §4 These my present paynes if to any they be pleasurable, or profitable. **1695** J. EDWARDS *Perfect. Script.* 223 Recreating and pleasurable entertainments. **1810** D. STEWART *Philos. Ess.* III. i. 225 When the mind is strongly influenced, either by pleasurable or painful sensations. **1855** BAIN *Senses & Int.* II. iv. §20 (1864) 288 Exercise is pleasurable only when we are expending surplus energy.

†**2.** Devoted to or engaged in pleasure; pleasure-seeking, pleasure-loving. *Obs.*

1599 B. JONSON *Ev. Man out of Hum.* v. ii, O, sir, you are very pleasurable. **1618** S. WARD *Jethro's Justice* (1627) 41 Idle pleasurable gentlemen. **1709** STEELE *Tatler* Ded., The manners of the Pleasurable, as well as the Busie Part of Mankind.

'pleasurableness. [f. prec. + -NESS.] Pleasurable quality; pleasantness, delightfulness.

a **1660** HAMMOND *Serm. Isa.* i. 5 Wks. 1684 IV. 533 Could he but..espy the whole sweetness and pleasurableness of it secretly let out. **1713** M. HENRY *Wks.* (1853) I. 168 To screw up the delights of sense to a greater degree of pleasureableness. **1865** M. ARNOLD *Ess. Crit.* viii. (1875) 326 A sympathy with intellectual activity for its own sake, and for the sake of its inherent pleasurableness and beauty.

pleasurably ('plɛʒərəblɪ), *adv.* [f. as prec. + -LY².] In a pleasurable manner; in or with pleasure, pleasantly, agreeably.

1633 BP. HALL *Hard Texts, Amos* vi. 1 Woe to those that live securely, and pleasurably in Zion. *a* **1822** SHELLEY *Pun. Death* Ess. & Lett. (Camelot ed.) 65 The mind..will be painfully or pleasurably affected. **1830** MACKINTOSH *Eth. Philos.* Wks. 1846 I. 25 Prudence..teaches that we cannot live pleasurably without living justly and virtuously, nor live justly and virtuously without living pleasurably.

†**'pleasurance.** *Obs. rare*⁻¹. [f. PLEASURE *v.* + -ANCE, or ? error for *pleasance.*] Pleasure.

c **1400** *Destr. Troy* 3471 Playnond with pytie, no pleasurance at all, With sykyng & sorow [she] said on this wise.

pleasure ('plɛʒ(j)ʊə(r), 'plɛʒə(r)), *sb.* Forms: see below. [ME. *plesir, plaisir* a. OF. *plesir, plaisir* (12th c. in Littré), + Pr. *plazer*, Sp. *placer*, Pg. *pracer*, It. *piacere*, Com. Romanic substantival use of the vb. infin.:—L. *placēre* to please. By 1400, *ple'sīr* had become (in prose) *'plēsir, 'plēser*, and its unstressed ending being confounded with that of words etymologically in *-ure*, e.g. *measure*, it was corruptly spelt and pronounced *plesure, pleasure*. The dialects have retained more eytmological forms in *pleezer, plezzer* ('pliːzə(r), 'plɛzə(r)).]

A. Illustration of Forms.

α. 4–5 **plesir,** 5 **plesyr, -yre, -ire, -ier, -yer; plaisir, playsir, -ire, -yr, -yre; pleasir, -ire, -ier, -yr, -er; pleeser;** 5–6 **pleser, -ere;** 6 **pleasire;** 9 *dial.* **pleezer, plezzer.**

1390 GOWER *Conf.* II. 144 Sche scholde thanne afore his ye Schewe al the plesir that sche mihte. *c* **1420** LYDG. *Assemb. Gods* 197 Ye shall haue all your plesere [*rime* here = hear]. *c* **1430** —— *Min. Poems* (Percy Soc.) 35 A yong rotour, redy to hir pleasier. **1450** Q. MARGARET in *Four C. Eng. Lett.* (1880) 8 To be disposed to our pleasir. *c* **1450** *Merlin* 1 At his plesier. **1463** *Bury Wills* (Camden) 27 To the pleeser of Almighty God. **1466** *Cal. Anc. Rec. Dublin* (1889) I. 322 Juncte or severell at his plesyre. ? *c* **1470** *Paston Lett.* III. 302 Sythe with your partyng, depertyd my plesyer [*rimes* desyer, fyer]. **1470–85** MALORY *Arthur* VII. xxii. 248 To doo hym alle the pleasyr that I can. **1474** CAXTON *Chesse* 14 For his solas and plaisir. **1481** —— *Myrr.* I. xiii. 39 Without his playsir nothyng may endure. **1482** MARG. PASTON in *P. Lett.* III. 289 To the most pleaser of God. **1484** CAXTON *Fables of Æsop* v. x, I praye the that one playsyre thow wylt do to me. **1485** —— *Chas. Gt.* 1 To reduce for his playsyr somme hystoryes. **1488** *Act 4 Hen. VII*, c. 7 §1 At the Kynges plesire. *a* **1500** *Flower & Leaf* 113 Wherof I had so inly greet plesyr. *c* **1500** *Melusine* 31 That I shall euer doo youre playsire. **1536** R. BEERLEY in *Four C. Eng. Lett.* (1880) 34 All fowlows our owne sensyaly and pleser. **1828** *Craven Gloss.* (ed. 2), *Plezzer*, pleasure.

β. 5 **plaisur, playsur, -ure;** 5–6 **plesur; pleasur, -our** (–7 *Sc.*); 5–7 **plesure;** 5– **pleasure;** 6 **plesour, -oure, -owre, -ewre; pleasor,** *Sc.* **pleisour, -ure, pleissour, plessour, -uir,** 7 **pleaceur,** *Sc.* **pleassour, plessor.**

c **1440** *Generydes* 144 For his plesur trowly ther lakkyd noght. *c* **1450** tr. *Higden* (Rolls) V. 373 [He] entrenge in..hade his pleasure. **1484** CAXTON *Fables of Alfonce* vi, For to take his desporte and playsure. **1486** *Certificate* in *Surtees Misc.* (1888) 47 God preserve you to His pleasour. *c* **1489** CAXTON *Sonnes of Aymon* 50 Where your plaisur shalle be to sette vs vnto. **1490** —— *Eneydos* xxvii. 98, I myghte..haue doon wyth theym after my playsur and wyll. **15..** *Sir J. Mandeville & Gret Souden* 75 in Hazl. *E.P.P.* (1864) I. 157 He that hase most plesure is best. **1514** BARCLAY *Cyt. & Uplondyshm.* (Percy Soc.) p. xlviii, Now judge, Coridon, if herein be pleasour. **1529** *Test. Ebor.* (Surtees) VI. 21 To be paid at the pleasor of my sone. **1530** PALSGR. 255/2 Pleasure, *commodité.* *c* **1540** J. HEYWOOD *Wit & Folly* (Percy Soc.) 16 The sewrte of plesewre eternall. **1552** ABP. HAMILTON *Catech.* (1884) 7 How we suld observe the commandis to the plesour of God. **1554–9** *Songs & Ball.* (1860) 1 Farewell my joye and plesure to. **1556** OLDE *Antichrist* 65 b, To mayntene their pleasur and idlenesse. **1588** A. KING *Canisius' Catech.* (S.T.S.) 213 To take pleissour. **1596** DALRYMPLE tr. *Leslie's Hist. Scot.* I. 7 Pleisour; 43 pleisure; 94 plesour; 152 pleasour. **1611** SIR W. MURE *Misc. Poems* (S.T.S.) I. 34 Pleasoures: 51 pleasour; 80 pleassour. **1640–1** *Kirkcudbr. War-Comm. Min. Bk.* (1855) 35 That they be baithe committit to warde, presentlie, during thair plessor.

B. Signification.

1. a. The condition of consciousness or sensation induced by the enjoyment or anticipation of what is felt or viewed as good or desirable; enjoyment, delight, gratification. The opposite of *pain*.

1390 [see A. α]. **1490** CAXTON *Eneydos* Prol. 1 In whiche booke I had grete playsyr. **1546** J. HEYWOOD *Prov.* (1867) 27 Flee pleasure, and pleasure will folowe thee. **1601** SHAKS. *Twel. N.* III. iii. 2 Since you make your pleasure of your paines, I will no further chide you. **1651** HOBBES *Leviath.* I. vi. 25 Pleasure..(or Delight) is the apparence or sense of Good. **1685** *Roxb. Ball.* (1886) VI. 122 What in pleasure begins too oft endeth in pain! **1690** LOCKE *Hum. Und.* II. vii. (1695) 56 By Pleasure and Pain I would be understood to signifie, whatsoever delights or molests us. **1721** MORTIMER *Husb.* (ed. 5) II. 197 I..shall next proceed to the Garden of Pleasure or Flower-Garden. **1732** BERKELEY *Alciphr.* II. §14 You admit, therefore, three sorts of pleasure:—pleasure of reason, pleasure of imagination, and pleasure of sense. **1756** BURKE *Subl. & B.* I. ii, Pain and pleasure are simple ideas, incapable of definition. **1757** GRAY *Bard* 74 Youth on the prow, and Pleasure at the helm. **1831** SIR J. SINCLAIR *Corr.* II. 120 The two former I had the pleasure of finding in Paris. **1881** W. H. MALLOCK *Rom. 19th Cent.* II. 243 Her face flushed with pleasure. **1894** SIR E. SULLIVAN *Woman* 88 'Pleasure is to the mind, what good food is to the stomach.' Pleasure is what all creatures desire; pain what they all avoid.

b. In unfavourable sense: Sensuous enjoyment as a chief object of life or end in itself. Opp. *business*. Sometimes personified as a female divinity.

1526 TINDALE *1 Tim.* v. 6 But she [a widow] that liveth in pleasure, is deed even yet alive [**1611** is dead while she liueth]. **1675** WYCHERLEY *Country-Wife* II. 32 Go, go, to your business, I say, pleasure, whilst I go to my pleasure, business. **1710** SHAFTESB. *Charac.* (1737) I. III. ii. 309 When we follow Pleasure merely, we are disgusted, and change from one sort to another. **1735** POPE *Ep. Lady* 215 Men, some to Bus'ness, some to Pleasure take; But every Woman is at heart a Rake. **1767** T. HUTCHINSON *Let.* 30 Sept. (1883) I. v. 243 Pleasure should always give way to business. **1768–74** TUCKER *Lt. Nat.* (1834) II. 683 Pleasure and interest are two great deceivers we must warn men against, as continually leading them astray. **1784** COWPER *Task* III. 51 Thou art not known where Pleasure is adored, That reeling goddess with the zoneless waist And wandering eyes. **1790** BURNS *Tam o' Shanter* 59 But pleasures are like poppies spread, You seize the flower, the bloom is shed. **1802** W. CUTSPEAR *Dram. Rights* 47 Pleasure is the business of the great. **1804** M. EDGEWORTH *Pop. Tales* III. 30 Business was his aversion; pleasure was his business. **1819** BYRON *Juan* I. cxix, O pleasure! you're indeed a pleasant thing, Although one must be damn'd for you, no doubt. *Mod.* Men who made pleasure the business of their lives. Wearied votaries of pleasure. A life given up to pleasure. **1837** C. G. F. GORE *Stokeshill Place* III. vi. 99 'Business before pleasure' is a golden rule which most of us regard as iron. **1853** R. S. SURTEES *Handley Cross* xxii. 158 Business first, and pleasure afterwards. **1857** [see BUSINESS 13]. **1934** *Law Rep.* 27 Mar. 238 In my judgment, the word 'pleasure' is used in this policy in contradistinction to 'business'. **1941** F. GRUBER *Hungry Dog* xv. 183 Pleasure before business. **1943** P. CHEYNEY *Farewell to Admiral* x. 238, I never believe in mixing business with pleasure. **1976** HOOKER & BUTTERWORTH *M.A.S.H. goes to San Francisco* (1977) xiii. 170 Oh, how nice! And I think about *you*, too. But business before pleasure, as I always say.

c. In strictly physical sense: The indulgence of the appetites; sensual gratification.

c **1450** [see A. β]. **1562** *Child-Marriages* 75 He wold have had his pleasure of her. **1611** BIBLE *Gen.* xviii. 12 Therefore Sarah laughed within her selfe, saying, After I am waxed old, shall I haue pleasure, my lord being old also? **1725** LADY M. W. MONTAGU *Lett., to C'tess Mar* (1887) I. 363 Dying as he had lived, indulging his pleasures. **1877** MRS. OLIPHANT *Makers Flor.* xii, The vileness which calls itself pleasure was paralyzed.

d. The condition or fact of being pleased or satisfied, the negation of which is displeasure (DISPLEASURE 1); satisfaction, approval. *rare.*

1568 GRAFTON *Chron.* II. 734 [He] was not the best pleased, but pleasure or displeasure, there was no remedie.

e. *Psychol.* Used *attrib.* (esp. in ***pleasure principle***) and as first element with *-pain* to denote the theory that the drives to achieve pleasure and to avoid pain are basic motivating forces in human and animal life; in psychoanalysis, the theory that the tension set up by unpleasure or the desire to achieve a pleasurable result forms the chief source of mental activity and is part of the life instinct, though frequently opposed by the reality-principle. Also in more general use.

1894 CREIGHTON & TITCHENER tr. *Wundt's Human & Animal Psychol.* xiv. 211 The reference of feeling to a subjective condition of pleasure-pain. **1897** H. G. WELLS *Under Knife* in *Plattner Story* 107 It occurred to me that the real meaning of this numbness might be a gradual slipping away from the pleasure-pain guidance of the animal man. **1912** *Amer. Jrnl. Psychol.* XXIII. 134 The sex impulses find no outlet before puberty. Until that time they remain under the control of the subconscious (pleasure principle). **1925** J. RIVIERE tr. *Freud's Papers on Metapsychology* in *Coll. Papers* IV. 14 It is called the pleasure-pain (*Lust-Unlust*) principle, or more shortly the pleasure-principle. **1951** S. F. NADEL *Found. Social Anthropol.* xi. 306 Emotions, sentiments, even the elementary pleasure-pain reactions, possess their dynamic properties..because they are the concomitants of instinctive tendencies. 1957 N. Frye *Anat. Criticism* ii. 75 In literature..the reality-principle is subordinate to the pleasure-principle. 1968 A. Laski *Keeper* xi. 133 Ralph's whole working life had been devoted to the pleasure principle. 1971 *Listener* 2 Sept. 299/1 Freud responded to the First World War by positing a death instinct beyond the pleasure principle. 1976 *Vogue* Jan. 5/2 The small son of the house witnesses Sigmund Freud looking askance at the pleasure principle embodied in Coney Island.

2. With possessive pronoun, or sb. in possessive relation: How one is pleased or wills in reference to any action contemplated; that which is agreeable to one or in conformity with one's wish or will; one's will, desire, choice.

?c1368 (16th c. MS.) Chaucer *Compl. to his Lady* 126 As is your most plesure, so doth by me. c1420 Lydg. *Assembly of Gods* 577 The goddes hygh plesure to fulfyll, Performe my desyre. 1485 Caxton *St. Wenefr.* 2 Whiche..aroos & humbly demaunded hym what was his playsir. 1543–4 *Act 35 Hen. VIII*, c. 1 It is in the only pleasure and will of almighty God, how longe his highnes..shall lyue. 1568 Grafton *Chron.* II. 120 When his good pleasure shall be. 1591 Shaks. *Two Gent.* II. iv. 117, I wait vpon his pleasure: Come Sir Thurio, Goe with me. 1669 Marvell *Corr.* Wks. (Grosart) II. 275 So expecting your pleasure, I remaine, Gentlemen, [etc.]. 1761 Hume *Hist. Eng.* II. xxxvi. 289 They were determined not to submit..to her will and pleasure. 1849 Macaulay *Hist. Eng.* x. II. 549 They would submit to William's authority, and would, till his pleasure should be known, keep their men together.

3. a. That which gives pleasure, or in which one delights; a source or object of pleasure or delight. (*it is, was*, etc.) ***my pleasure***: a colloq. dismissal of thanks.

c1495 *Plumpton Corr.* (Camden) 107 Therin you wil do,.. that may be plesur to you & my contry. 1517 Torkington *Pilgr.* (1884) 18 They Caryed with them Riches and pleasurs, As clothe of gold and Crymsyn velvett. 1585 T. Washington tr. *Nicholay's Voy.* I. xvi. 17b, This place excelleth all others in pleasures and dainties. 1639 N. N. tr. *Du Bosq's Compl. Woman* I. 11 Is there a greater pleasure, then to be present at the birth and ruin of Empires, and Monarchies? 1715 De Foe *Fam. Instruct.* I. v. (1841) I. 101 These are the very things your sister calls the pleasure of her life. 1858 Earl of Aberdeen in *G. C. Lewis's Lett.* (1870) 352 Your..love of truth renders this a duty as well as a pleasure. 1950 L. Kaufman *Jubel's Children* xxi. 259 Think nothing of it. My pleasure. 1963 [see not at all]. 1975 R. Lewis *Double Take* i. 26 'I enjoyed the evening, Mr Hood.' 'It was my pleasure, Miss Stevens.'

†**b.** A pleasure-ground. *Obs.*

1485 *Rolls of Parlt.* VI. 293/1 Tennements,..thanne lyinge nie to the said late Lord Herbert, and to hys plesure. 1494 Fabyan *Chron.* VII. cliv, In the xxi. yere of hys reygne Kynge Henry [I] made yᵉ parke of Wodestoke besyde Oxenforde, with other plesures to the same. 1633 Ford *Broken H.* I. iii, None have access into these private pleasures, Except some near in Court. [Cf. 1721 in sense 1.]

c. As name of a locality.

1666 Wood *Life* 18 June (O.H.S.) II. 80, June 18, M., Oliver Craven, B.A. of Trinity Coll. drowned at Patten's Pleasure. 1692 *Ibid.* III. 399.

4. The quality which gives pleasure; pleasurableness.

c1530 *Crt. of Love* vi, To her be all the pleasure of this book. 1626 Bacon *Sylva* §475 The Shining Willow which they call Swallow-Tail because of the Pleasure of the Leaf. 1732 Berkeley *Alciphr.* II. §14 Consequently the pleasures perfective of those acts are also different. 1869 Tozer *Highl. Turkey* I. 149, [I] realised what I had never felt before—the pleasure of pale colours.

5. Phrases.

†**a.** ***at pleasure***: with pleasure, pleased. *Obs.*

1579 Tomson *Calvin's Serm. Tim.* 294/2 The Papistes (of whom we speake not so at pleasure). 1595 Daniel *Civ. Wars* I. ii, Whilst Fraunce, to see they spoyles, at pleasure stood!

b. ***at* (*one's*) *pleasure, at pleasure***: as or when one pleases; at will, at discretion. ***during* (*one's*) *pleasure***: while one pleases.

1442 *Rolls of Parlt.* V. 44/1 Lifte up and close the seid lef att their pleser. 1484 Caxton *Fables of Æsop* II. xvii, I drynke and ete at my playsyr. 1523 Ld. Berners *Froiss.* I. cxv. 137, I shall make you amendes at your pleasures. 1566 *Reg. Privy Council Scot.* I. 460 He being absent at the plesour of God. 1617 Moryson *Itin.* I. 8 We had freedome to leaue the coach at our pleasure. 1634 W. Tirwhyt tr. *Balzac's Lett.* (vol. I) 132, I am not able to do any thing but at the Physitians good pleasure. 1669 Sturmy *Mariner's Mag.* I. ii. 33 Draw two Right Lines, making any Angle at pleasure. 1816 Scott *Old Mort.* xiii, Whom the.. housekeeper..huffed about at her pleasure. 1885 *Act 48 & 49 Vict.* c. 61 §2 A Secretary..who shall hold office during Her Majesty's pleasure. 1885 *Law Rep.* 15 *Q. Bench Div.* 360 The belts..could be slipped off the drum..at pleasure.

c. ***to do or †show* (*one*) (*a*) *pleasure***: to perform an acceptable service, do a favour; to please, gratify. (In quot. 1685 used *ironically*.)

c1460 Fortescue *Abs. & Lim. Mon.* vii. (1885) 124 Such as do, or shall do to hym seruice, or oþer maner off pleasures. 1472 *Paston Lett.* III. 54 To do my Lord a plesur. 1526 Tindale *Acts* xxiv. 27 Felix, willynge to shewe the Jewes a pleasure, lefte Paul in preson bounde. 1560 Daus tr. *Sleidane's Comm.* 364 The citezens shewed them what pleasure they could. 1685 R. Burton *Eng. Emp. Amer.* ii. 50 One..who to do the Spaniards a pleasure gave them [the English] information of a great Ship called the St. Anna expected from the Philippine Islands,..which..they took within a few days after. 1871 Browning *Balaust.* 2359 But certainly Thou dost thy friend no pleasure in the act. a1907 *Mod.* Do me the pleasure of dining with me. I will do myself the pleasure of calling on you.

d. ***man* (*woman*) *of pleasure***: one who is devoted to the pursuit of sensual pleasure; a licentious person, a profligate. † ***lady, woman of pleasure***: a wanton, a courtesan (*obs.*).

1623 Webster *Duchess of Malfi* v. ii, We that are great women of pleasure..join the sweet delight And the pretty excuse together. 1637, c1645, 1708 [see lady *sb.* 4e]. 1667 Evelyn *Diary* 27 Aug., He [Clarendon] had enemies at Court, especially the buffoones and ladys of pleasure. 1673 *Essex Papers* (Camden) I. 72 These men of Pleasure (yᵉ very Pest and ruine of all Courts). 1732 Berkeley *Alciphr.* II. §3 Thus in our Dialect a vicious Man is a Man of Pleasure. 1742 Young *Nt. Th.* VIII. 793 A Man of Pleasure is a Man of Pains. 1849 Macaulay *Hist. Eng.* v. I. 635 Kirke was also, in his own coarse and ferocious way, a man of pleasure.

† **e.** ***to pleasure, to* (*one's*) *pleasure***: so or such as to please; to one's liking. *Obs.*

1470–85 Malory *Arthur* II. xiv. 92 There were brought hym robes to his pleasyr. 1819 Keats *Lamia* II. 192 When in an antechamber every guest Had felt the cold full sponge to pleasure press'd..upon his hands and feet.

f. ***to take* (*a*) *pleasure***: to be pleased, to enjoy oneself, to delight (*in*, *to do* something, etc.).

1538 Elyot *Dict.*, *Teneri ludo*, to take pleasure in game. 1590 Marlowe *2nd Pt. Tamburl.* IV. i, I take no pleasure to be murderous. 1611 Bible *Ps.* cii. 14 Thy servants take pleasure in her stones. 1727 A. Hamilton *New Acc. E. Ind.* I. xix. 231 Was drowned..by a Pinnace's oversetting, in which he and his Lady had been taking a Pleasure on the Water. 1734 tr. *Rollin's Anc. Hist.* (1827) II. IV. 211, I took a pleasure of informing myself of his birth. 1858 Hawthorne *Fr. & It. Note-Bks.* II. 48 Were taking their pleasure in our neighborhood.

g. ***pleasures of the table***: see table *sb.* 6c.

6. *attrib.* and *Comb.* **a.** simple attrib., 'of or for pleasure', as ***pleasure-barge, -brake, -car, -carriage, -cart, -chariot, -cottage, -craft, -cruise, -cruiser, -cruising, -day, -dome, -driving, -economy, -excursion, -farming, -feast, -fleet, -garden, -gardener, -horse, -land, -navy, -park, -party, -path, -plane, -plat, -resort, -ship, -sleigh, -steamer, -traffic, -train, -travel, -traveller, -trip, -vehicle, -vessel, -visit, -voyage, -walk, -yacht***. **b.** objective, obj. genitive, instrumental, etc., as ***pleasure-hater, -hunter, -taker, -taking***; ***pleasure-bound, -crazed, -crowded, -feeling, -giving, -greedy, -loving, -mad, -minded, -tired, -trading, -wasted, -yielding*** adjs.

1775 *Chron.* in *Ann. Reg.* 216/1 *Pleasure-barges.. moored in the river. 1873 E. Brennan *Witch of Nemi* 223 *Pleasure-bound and peace-inspiring days. 1908 *Westm. Gaz.* 12 Aug. 8/3 She was cycling along the Bromley-road when a *pleasure-brake..turned out of a side-street. 1833 *Amer. Railroad Jrnl.* II. 481/3 A *pleasure car has been flying between this town and the river. 1960 C. Achebe *No longer at Ease* ii. 14 [In Lagos] if you don't want to walk you only have to wave your hand and a pleasure car stops for you. 1802 W. Priest *Trav. U.S.A.* 31 There are 806 two and four wheeled machines entered at the office, and pay duty, as *pleasure carriages.* 1844 Pleasure-carriage [see fiesta]. 1789 J. Woodforde *Diary* 27 Nov. (1927) III. 156 My Brother went in my little *pleasure Cart with Briton. 1797 *Hist. Mr. Fantom* (Cheap Repos. Tracts) 8 That multitude of coaches ..stages, pleasure-carts and horses. 1865 J. H. Ingraham *Pillar of Fire* (1872) 69 Besides their war-chariots, the Egyptians possess a small number of *pleasure-chariots. a1828 D. Wordsworth *Jrnl.* (1941) II. 247 A charming spot for a *pleasure-cottage. 1906 Conrad *Mirror of Sea* 38 Their striving for victory..has elevated the sailing of *pleasure craft to the dignity of a fine art. 1943 J. S. Huxley *TVA* ix. 63 Nearby is a public lodge and a boat-house and dock for pleasure craft. 1932 *New Yorker* 23 July 12/2 It is not your idea..of a mad night on *pleasure-crazed Broadway. 1906 B. von Hutten *What became of Pam* I. x. 73 The time that had seemed so long to her had quite naturally seemed to him, with his *pleasure-crowded days, very short. 1926 *Scribner's Mag.* Aug. 12 (Advt.), Start planning now for pleasure-crowded days on cool, blue waters. 1909 *Daily Graphic* 26 July 2/1 (Advt.), P. & O. cheap return tickets *pleasure cruises and round the world tours. 1976 H. MacInnes *Agent in Place* xxvi. 277 'Where are we going?' 'For a pleasure cruise.' 1926 *Daily Chron.* 13 May 3/6 (*heading*) *Pleasure Cruisers on and off the rocks. 1945 Koestler *Yogi & Commissar* I. iii. 35 For he is a captain of a warship, not of a pleasure-cruiser. 1950 *Oxf. Jun. Encycl.* IX. 382/1 It was not..until the early 1920's that modern pleasure cruising with its carefully planned itineraries really became established. a1828 D. Wordsworth *Jrnl.* (1941) II. 292 The buoyancy of spirits felt in the earlier part of a *pleasure-day's journey. 1797 Coleridge *Kubla Khan* 2 In Xanadu did Kubla Khan A stately *pleasure-dome decree. 1957 *Observer* 3 Nov. 19/2 The triumphal renaissance, last Thursday night, of the New Shakespeare Theatre in Liverpool. This lambent pleasure-dome..was built in the eighties. 1973 G. Beare *Snake on Grave* xvi. 93 It's a kind of floating pleasure dome, they have a restaurant, night-club, casino. 1977 *Time* 19 Dec. 41/1 Macy's.., the basement where women..battled with umbrellas for lingerie markdowns has become one of New York City's great gastronomic pleasure domes. 1910 W. James in *McClure's Mag.* Aug. 467 A permanently successful peace-economy cannot be a simple *pleasure-economy. 1833 L. Ritchie *Wand. by Loire* 225 Agatha..prepared..for her *pleasure-excursion to Nantes. 1891 Kebbel *Old & New Eng. Country Life* 132 The age of *pleasure-farming—of work and play combined..is gone for ever. 1890 Donisthorpe *Individualism* xi. 378 A larger sum-total of *pleasure-feeling sentient beings. 1890 *Nature* 4 Sept., Electric coaling-stations for the river *pleasure-fleet. 1712 J. James tr. *Le Blond's Gardening* (title-p.) Fine Gardens, commonly called *Pleasure-Gardens. 1961 L. Mumford *City in History* xiii. 379 Such pleasure gardens were popular everywhere that court life was visibly on parade: the famous Tivoli Gardens in Copenhagen still bears witness to this. 1779 J. Meader (*title*) The Planter's Guide: or *Pleasure Gardener's Companion. 1824 Coleridge *Lett.*, *to T. Gillman* (1895) 731 You will have received another,..more amusing, at least *pleasure-giving Scripture from me. 1879 H. Spencer *Data of Ethics* vi. §33. 83 Sentient existence can evolve only on condition that pleasure-giving acts are life-sustaining acts. 1860 Adler *Fauriel's Prov. Poetry* xii. 263 Corrupt and *pleasure-greedy set of men. 1940 Auden *Another Time* 42 As a rule It was the *pleasure-haters who became unjust. 1817 T. L. Peacock *Melincourt* (1875) 211 The keeping of *pleasure-horses. 1974 *Greenville* (S. Carolina) *News* 23 Apr. 11/3 The pleasure horse class will give spectators a chance to see the finest of the American saddlebred pleasure horses in competition. 1833 J. S. Mill in *Monthly Repos.* VII. 660 Few persons among the crowds of *pleasure-hunters have diverged from the beaten track of the Rhine, Switzerland, and Italy. 1850 Robertson *Serm.* Ser. III. ii. (1872) 24 The mere giddy pleasure-hunter of the hour. 1927 *Daily Tel.* 13 Sept. 12/2 Thirty years ago Piccadilly had still to establish its claim to be regarded as the centre of *pleasure-land. 1818 Lady Morgan *Autobiog.* (1859) 94 We were all young, enterprising, and *pleasure-loving. 1925 *Scribner's Mag.* Oct. 373 It was exactly the kind of crowd which a dour philosopher might have described as typical of '*pleasure-mad America'. 1907 *Daily Chron.* 12 Oct. 4/7 Allah forfend, my *pleasure-minded love, That aught shall harm thee in the Desert Lands. 1873 'Vanderdecken' *Yachts & Yachting* xxix. 247 There are not a few sea-lawyers to be met with amongst the *pleasure navy Jacks. 1904 R. J. Farrer *Garden of Asia* 70 Here we may fancy known beings resting in this *pleasure-park of necessity. 1835 *Southern Lit. Messenger* IV. 303/1 *Pleasure-parties to and from the Springs..were dashing along the well graded road. 1873 Leland *Egypt. Sketch-Bk.* 21 The Afreet chose the season of the Equinoctial for their pleasure-party. c1806 D. Wordsworth *Jrnl.* (1941) I. 351 It is not easy to see the use of a *pleasure-path leading to nothing. 1911 *Chambers's Jrnl.* Jan. 57/1 The aspect of the heavens will be wonderfully changed when the *pleasure-plane of the air has arrived. 1856 Mrs. Browning *Aur. Leigh* VI. 699 It is not wholesome for these *pleasure-plats To be so early watered by our brine. 1883 'Mark Twain' *Life on Miss.* xli. 427 Modern-style *pleasure resorts. 1891 E. Kinglake *Australian at H.* 64 The children are taken to some pleasure resort. 1869 Mark Twain *Innoc. Abr.* lvii. 609 When I travel again, I wish to go in a *pleasure ship. 1977 *New Scientist* 24 Mar. 707/2 The foundering of a pleasureship. 1774 'J. H. St. John de Crevecœur' *Sk. 18th-Cent. Amer.* (1925) 146 The *pleasure-sleigh..can easily carry six persons. 1827 Pleasure-sleigh [see fiddle *sb.* 1b]. 1798 Sotheby tr. *Wieland's Oberon* (1826) II. 24 Amanda scarce believes her *pleasure-sparkling eye. 1872 B. Jerrold *London* iv. 43 The river..bright with the trifles of cockleboats and *pleasure-steamers. 1948 *Brit. Birds* XLI. 314, I was on a pleasure steamer at the time. 1855 J. R. Leifchild *Cornwall Mines* 34 Strange sightseers, and uproarious *pleasure-takers. 1827 Moir *Contadina* iv, Beside thee sleep or play Thy loveliest children, *pleasure-tired, in the blue light of day. 1805 *Mod. London* 458 It is by no means so prolific in its raree shews as the *pleasure-trading Paris. 1861 *Times* 22 Aug., The *pleasure traffic was materially deranged..by the cheerless weather. 1871 Howells *Wedd. Journ.* (1892) 163 The season of *pleasure-travel. 1846 Dickens *Pictures from Italy* 150 *Pleasure-travellers through life. 1936 *Discovery* Aug. 247/2 An area that is not well known to the general run of pleasure-travellers. 1833 *Chambers's Edin. Jrnl.* II. 285/2 The individuals who make *pleasure-trips along the railway. 1926 *Daily Chron.* 13 May 3/6 The 20,000 ton R.M.S. steamer Otranto struck a rock on the way to the port of Athens... The Otranto is on a pleasure trip. 1906 Conrad *Mirror of Sea* 33 The writer praises that class of *pleasure vessels, [*sc.* 52-foot linear raters] and I am willing to endorse his words. 1926 D. H. Lawrence *David* xiv. 103 My lord Jonathan comes too early for a *pleasure visit. 1906 Conrad *Mirror of Sea* 39 For racing, a cutter; for a long *pleasure voyage, a schooner; for cruising in home waters, the yawl. 1763 Smollett *Trav.* (1766) I. x. 161 The ground is agreeably laid out in *pleasure-walks, for the recreation of the inhabitants. 1847 Dickens *Dombey* (1848) xxiii. 238 As many spars and bars and bolts..as you'd want an order for on Chatham-yard to build a *pleasure-yacht with. 1879 H. Spencer *Data of Ethics* xiii. §89. 334 The sum of pleasures, or of *pleasure-yielding things.

pleasure (ˈplɛʒ(j)ʊə(r), ˈplɛʒə(r)), *v.* [f. prec. sb.]

1. a. *trans.* To give pleasure to; to please, gratify; *spec.* to gratify (someone) sexually; to have sexual intercourse with.

Revived in recent use.

c1559 R. Hall *Life Fisher* lf. 34b, He ment to give definitive sentence against her to pleasure the kinge withall. 1563 *Homilies* II. *Almsdeeds* I. (1859) 387 [He] is both able to pleasure and displeasure us. c1616 R. C. *Times' Whistle* (1871) 90 Silvius doth shew the citty dames brave sights, And they for that doe pleasure him a nightes. 1652 Culpepper *Eng. Physic.* 9 All Apples..pleasure the stomach by their coolness. 1764 Foote *Patron* II. i, I am no churl, I love to pleasure my friends. 1837 Dickens *Pickw.* vi, The wall must be crumbled, the stone decayed, To pleasure his dainty whim. 1895 Crockett *Men of Moss-Hags* xxii, 'Walter, will you not pleasure us with your company to-night?' 1968 J. R. Ackerley *My Father & Myself* xii. 124 We entered together, quickly unbuttoned and pleasured each other. 1973 *Observer* 29 July 26/7 The rest of the treatment takes place in a hotel bed. Couples are first instructed to 'pleasure' each other by caressing, and not to attempt intercourse until they have learnt to recognise each other's body signals that express delight. 1975 *Times Lit. Suppl.* 9 May 503/1 Her first love, who took her to tea-dances..and pleasured her regularly at home on the brocade couch. 1977 *Observer* (Colour Suppl.) 27 Feb. 17/1 The brown Chippewa girl who was the first female he had ever pleasured.

b. *refl.* To take one's pleasure; *spec.* to obtain sexual gratification.

a1619 Fletcher, etc. *Q. Corinth* III. i, One that hath As people say, in forraigne pleasur'd him. 1908 C. W. Wallace *Children of Chapel at Blackfriars* ix. 112 Elizabeth intended the establishment of the Children of her Chapel as actors at Blackfriars..to pleasure herself and entertain the Court. 1938 M. K. Rawlings *Yearling* x. 89 'I'll bet we kin ketch us a cattywampus in one o' them ponds.' 'We kin sure pleasure ourselves tryin'.' 1947 *N.Y. Herald Tribune Weekly Bk. Rev.* 2 Mar. 10/3 Mordaunt Fitzmaurice Godolphin..has left Virginia because he pleasured himself with a married lady and then killed her husband in a duel. **1972** *Time* 17 Apr. 66/3 Pauline Tabor was smart enough to open up a house of her own. 'Pauline's' became a Kentucky institution—politicians went to pleasure themselves there.

c. In impersonal construction with *it* as subject (cf. PLEASE *v.* 3).

1937 R. S. MORTON *Woman Surgeon* xxxi. 346 A young carpenter said to me, 'It would not pleasure me if I could not see the cypress greening in the spring.' **1949** R. K. MARSHALL *Little Squire Junior* 249 Little Squire borrowed somethin of mine, and it pleasured me no end. **1951** L. CRAIG *Singing Hills* xiii. 124 It pleasures us a sight that you would come to see us. **1970** *New Yorker* 12 Sept. 109/3 It pleasured him to see the smoke.

2. a. *intr.* To take pleasure, to delight. Const. *in*, or *to* with *infin.*

1538 in *Lett. Suppress. Monasteries* (Camden) 172 Surely his predecessours plesured moche in odoryferous savours. **1581** RICHE *Farewell* (Shaks. Soc.) 28 The Duke greately pleasuryng to heare the pretie aunswere of the childe, replied in this wise. **1621** LADY M. WROTH *Urania* 557 What others gloryed and pleasured in, tortured her. *a* **1810** TANNAHILL *Poems* (1846) 79 Brutes are but brutes, let men be men, Nor pleasure in cock-fighting. **1882** LD. COLERIDGE in *Fortn. Rev.* 1 Feb. 234 There are some sports which appear to me so cruel and so unmanly, that I wonder very much how any one can pleasure in them.

b. *colloq.* To go out for pleasure, take a holiday: chiefly in vbl. sb. PLEASURING.

Hence **'pleasured** *ppl. a.*, filled with pleasure. Also as *pa. pple.* (const. *up*).

1606 J. CARPENTER *Solomon's Solace* xiv. 60 Though a man bee neuer so rich,..and pleasured in this life: yet shall he not carry away any of those riches. **1813** T. BUSBY *Lucretius* II. 441 Milk kindly greets The pleasured palate with nutritious sweets. **1930** D. RUNYON in *Collier's* 13 Sept. 8/2 They get all pleasured up over what he has to say. **1968** 'J. WELCOME' *Hell is where you find It* iv. 61 He was wearing..the look of a pleasured tom-cat.

'pleasure-boat. A boat constructed or used for pleasure, as distinguished from one for business. So **'pleasure-,boating** *sb.* and *a.*

1661 PEPYS *Diary* 16 Apr., We went on board the King's pleasure boat. **1712** J. JAMES tr. *Le Blond's Gardening* 75 Gondolas and Pleasure-Boats. **1817** J. EVANS *Excurs. Windsor*, etc. 398 Having embarked in a neat Pleasure-boat. **1891** *Pall Mall G.* 28 July 3/1 It is absurd to think that the interests of pleasure-boating may be left to take care of themselves.

'pleasuredrome. [f. PLEASURE *sb.* + -DROME.] An amusement centre.

1959 *Spectator* 9 Oct. 467/1 The possibility of turning the Isle of Wight into some vast pleasuredrome (cf. Fr. *Baisodrome*). **1966** *Punch* 13 Mar. 392/2 He might bring his millions here and make West Hove the pleasuredrome of the Western world. **1973** *Daily Tel.* (Colour Suppl.) 18 Apr. 19/2 One corporation, which already operated 'pleasuredromes' in Dallas, Atlanta, and St. Louis, is.. negotiating to open a park in New Jersey.

pleasureful ('plɛʒəfʊl), *a.* [f. PLEASURE *sb.* + -FUL.] Full of or fraught with pleasure; pleasing, delightful.

1553 GRIMALDE *Cicero's Offices* II. (1558) 100 For so rashnesse be auoyded, liberalitie is very pleasurefull. **1617** ABP. ABBOT *Descr. World* (1634) 113 Reputed alwayes very commodious and pleasureful Country. **1802** MRS. RADCLIFFE *Gaston de Blondeville* Posth. Wks. 1826 I. 95 It was a pleasureful sight, to behold that vision of light. **1884** J. SHARMAN *Hist. Swearing* iii. 39 The habit owes its.. source of delight to some soothing and pleasureful qualities.

'pleasure-ground. A ground or piece of land laid out and ornamented for purposes of pleasure or amusement, or naturally adapted to such use.

1768 HOLDSWORTH *On Virgil* 200 The Romans seem..to have used the word Tempe, as the Greeks did Παράδεισοι.. for any very pleasing place; or pleasure-grounds, as our gardeners of late call them. **1855** MACAULAY *Hist. Eng.* xii. III. 242 A beautiful pleasure-ground, situated on a woody promontory which overlooks Lough Erne. **1886** W. J. TUCKER *E. Europe* 101 Isn't it grand—a park of this size? It's fully fifty acres, and all pleasure-ground, too!

'pleasurehood. *nonce-wd.* [f. PLEASURE *sb.* + -HOOD.] The condition of living in or for pleasure.

1842 MRS. BROWNING *Grk. Chr. Poets* 39 That words may flourish Of which mine enemy would spoil me, Using pleasurehood to foil me!

'pleasure-house. [f. PLEASURE *sb.* + HOUSE: cf. Ger. *lusthaus.*] A house used for purposes of pleasure or recreation; a summer-house.

1590 H. WOTTON *Let.* in L. P. Smith *Life & Lett. H. Wotton* (1907) I. 247 The plot of his Majesty's pleasure-house shall in convenient time be provided. **1688** *Lond. Gaz.* No. 2376/3 The Elector being lodged in the Pleasure-house without the Town, which was purposely built for Sultan Mahomet. **1756** NUGENT *Gr. Tour, Italy* III. 325 Fiorenzola, where the great duke has a pleasure-house. **1830** TENNYSON *Pal. Art* 1, I built my soul a lordly pleasure-house, Wherein at ease for aye to dwell. **1904** R. J. FARRER *Garden of Asia* 106 How few of the many Europeans who visit Japan, ever see the real pleasure-houses of the country! **1908** *Daily Chron.* 12 Dec. 4/6 The ballroom of a notorious eighteenth-century pleasure-house kept by a Mme. Cornelys. **1936** A. W. CLAPHAM *Romanesque Archit.* iii. 55 The actual court of Palermo leaned heavily towards the Moslem element and the pleasure-houses and palaces of the Favara, Menani (Roger II), la Ziza (William I) and la Cuba (William II) were almost purely Moslem both in form and decoration.

pleasureless ('plɛʒəlɪs). [f. PLEASURE *sb.* + -LESS.] Devoid of pleasure; joyless.

1814 in *New Brit. Theatre* III. 254 He might have become penitent, and deplored the enormity of his pleasureless vices. *a* **1851** MOIR *Chr. Musings* vi, I told how life all pleasureless would be. **1872** GEO. ELIOT *Middlem.* lxxix, He himself was sliding into that pleasureless yielding to the small solicitations of circumstance.

Hence **'pleasurelessly** *adv.*

1873 MISS BROUGHTON *Nancy* II. 35, I wander objectlessly, pleasurelessly about with Vick.

'pleasurement. *rare.* [f. PLEASURE *v.* + -MENT.] Indulgence in pleasure; taking of enjoyment; = PLEASURING 2.

1843 LYTTON *Last Bar.* VIII. iii, I..have your royal interests too much at heart to while an hour in my pleasurement.

'pleasure,monger. [See MONGER.] One who makes pleasure his business.

1616 W. FORDE *Serm.*, etc. 47 As did those pleasure-mungers, who, though they lived, [etc.]. **1654** WHITLOCK *Zootomia* 396 The Power-mongers, Wealth-mongers, and Pleasure-mongers of the World. **1888** *Boston* (Mass.) *Jrnl.* 23 June 6/3 The youthful pleasuremonger has lived on excitement all winter..and cannot settle down.

pleasurer ('plɛʒərə(r)). [f. PLEASURE *sb.* or *v.* + -ER[1].] A pleasure-seeker; a holiday-maker.

1833 L. RITCHIE *Wand. by Loire* 182 These pleasurers [earn] their enjoyments by the sweat of their brow. **1836** DICKENS *Sk. Boz, Lond. Recreations*, Let us turn now to another portion of the London population..we mean the Sunday pleasurers. **1876** MRS. WHITNEY *Sights & Ins.* xxii, Parties of pleasurers returning from their day's excursions.

'pleasure-,seeker. One who seeks pleasure; *spec.* a holiday-maker.

1825 HONE *Every-day Bk.* I. 438 Pleasure-seekers at sixpence per head. **1846** *Swell's Night Guide* 14 At all hours of the night, the pleasure-seeker may gain admission. **1852** MUNDY *Our Antipodes* (1857) 17 Select parties of pleasure-and-oyster seekers may be seen proceeding by water or land. **1894** HALL CAINE *Manxman* v. vi, Coaches, choked full with pleasure-seekers from Port Erin.

So **'pleasure-,seeking** *sb.* and *a.*

1886 J. G. MATTESON *Hist. Sk.* 63/1, I found the people in Norway far more religiously inclined than those in Denmark; they..are not so much given to pleasure-seeking. **1888** BARRIE *When a Man's Single* xv, Dowton's whole existence has been devoted to pleasure-seeking. **1896** MRS. CAFFYN *Quaker Grandmother* 12 That lady watched the pleasure-seeking vagaries of her charge, with a painful and discriminating interest. **1936** *Discovery* Oct. 301/1 Only a slight ripple on the normal pleasure-seeking surface of Blackpool was caused by the arrival and departure of the British Association.

pleasuring ('plɛʒərɪŋ), *vbl. sb.* [See -ING[1].] The action of the vb. PLEASURE.

1. The giving of pleasure; pleasing, delectation.

1575 CHURCHYARD *Chippes* (1817) 34 [To write] for passing of the time, and pleasuring of his friends. **1897** GUNTER *Ballyho Bey* iii. 41 She is a sybarite in the pleasuring of her senses.

2. The taking of pleasure; pleasure-seeking; going on a pleasure excursion; taking a holiday.

1598 MARSTON *Pygmal.* xxxvi. 133 When all things fit for loues sweet pleasuring Inuited him to reape a Louers blisse. **1748** RICHARDSON *Clarissa* (1811) IV. xlii. 275 A little trim vessel, which shall sail a pleasuring backward and forward to Portsmouth. **1825** LAMB *Elia* Ser. II. *Superann. Man*, Expressing the hollowness of a day's pleasuring. **1869** MISS MULOCK *Woman's Kingd.* III. 218 Who refused, year after year, to take her autumn pleasuring..because her husband would only have to work the harder for it.

3. *attrib.*, designating things designed for, used for, or devoted to pleasure.

1869 *Daily News* 16 July, Nor is this practice..confined to pleasuring vans. **1872** *U.S. Statutes* XVII. 32 A public park or pleasuring ground for the benefit and enjoyment of the people. **1895** *Westm. Gaz.* 9 Nov. 3/2 A pleasuring tour to some distant part of the States.

pleasurist ('plɛʒərɪst). [f. PLEASURE *sb.* + -IST.] **a.** A devotee of pleasure, a voluptuary. **b.** A pleasure-seeker.

1682 SIR T. BROWNE *Chr. Mor.* III. §23 The Delights wherein mere Pleasurists place their Paradise. **1851** F. WALPOLE *Ansayrii* II. 326 Pilgrims and pleasurists from all nations. **1855** ZIMMERMAN *Solitude* II. i. 240 The wearied pleasurist..flies to scenes of public gaiety.

'pleasurous, *a. nonce-wd.* [f. as prec. + -OUS.] Characterized by pleasure; joyous; voluptuous.

1839 BAILEY *Festus* xvi. (1852) 182 Begin we, then, our sweet and pleasurous sway.

pleat (pliːt), *sb.* Also 5 plete, 6–7 pleate. [A collateral form of PLAIT *sb.* (app. akin to the β forms there): cf. OF. *plet* a fold (in Godef.).

This form of the sb. appears to have become obsolete in the 17th c.; it is absent from the 17th, 18th, and early 19th c. dictionaries, and reappears only in those of the late 19th c. (e.g., Annandale's Ogilvie, Cassell) with a cross-reference to *Plait.* But as a spoken word it was in use in the 18th c., for Walker 1791 s.v. *Plait* says 'There is a corrupt pronunciation of this word, as if written *plete*, which must be carefully avoided'. This pronunciation has not only asserted itself, but in the latter part of the 19th c. caused the restoration of the spelling *pleat* in sense 1.]

1. A fold of cloth or drapery; now *esp.* one of a series of folds by which the edge of a skirt or other loose drapery is regularly and symmetrically taken in, so as to be attached to a band or the like, while the unattached part hangs full; = PLAIT *sb.* 1. *box-pleat*: see BOX *sb.*[2] 24.

1581 DERRICKE *Image Irel.* II. E iij b, Their shirtes..With pleates on pleates thei pleated are, as thicke as pleates maie lye. **1625** PURCHAS *Pilgrims* II. IX. xix. 1658 They carrie it ..alwaies about in the pleats of their Girdle. **1681** W. ROBERTSON *Phraseol. Gen.* (1693) 617 A fold or pleat, *plica.* **1688** R. HOLME *Armoury* III. 194/2 Doctor John Bridgman late Bishop of Chester..wore his Bishops Hat all covered in pleats with Taffaty, from whence he was vulgarly termed John with the Taffaty Hat. **1883** [see BOX *sb.*[2] 24]. **1884** G. ALLEN *Philistia* I. 49 The peacock-blue [dress] with the satin box-pleats. **1887** J. ASHBY STERRY *Lazy Minstrel* (1892) 28 A snowy skirt, all frill and pleat.

fig. **1593** SHAKS. *Lucr.* 93 Hiding base sin in pleats of Maiestie. **1902** CORNISH *Naturalist Thames* 178 The water ..forms a ripple above each ridge; and from the everlasting throb of these pleats of running water the sunlight flashes as if from a moving river of diamonds.

†**2.** A plait of hair or cord: = PLAIT *sb.* 2. *Obs.* (or ? *dial.*)

1495 *Trevisa's Barth. De P.R.* v. lxvi. 183 The pletes [*Bodley MS. c* 1450 plettes] of wymmens heer ben knytte and bounde wyth laces. **1605** DRAYTON *Man in Moone* 77 Her Hayre tuck'd up in many a curious pleate. **1613** W. BROWNE *Brit. Past.* II. v, She pinckes the hayre, and working them in pleat [etc.].

Hence **'pleatless** *a.*, without pleats, unpleated.

1898 *Blackw. Mag.* Jan. 28/1 Tartans with..pleatless kilts on them. **1898** *Westm. Gaz.* 11 Nov. 2/2 The upper skirt.. with its circular cut, fitting pleatless round the hips.

pleat (pliːt), *v.* Also 4–6 plete, (4 pleit). [A collateral form of PLAIT *v.* (app. akin to the β forms there), going with PLEAT *sb.*

Like the sb. PLEAT, the vb. appears to have become practically obs. by 1700, after which the only examples are dialectal in sense 2, till late in the 19th c., in which the vb., like the sb., was restored in sense 1. Like the sb., it was certainly much earlier in spoken use in this sense, and although ignored in the dictionaries may have been current from the 17th c. onward.]

1. *trans.* To fold (cloth, etc.); now *esp.* to gather (loose or flowing drapery) into pleats or regular folds fixed in position at the edge; = PLAIT *v.* 1.

1362 LANGL. *P. Pl.* A. v. 126, I..Brochede hem with a pak-neelde and pletede [*v.r.* pleit; *B.* plaited, playte, plytyd, plyghted] hem togedre. **1547** BOORDE *Introd. Knowl.* ix. (1870) 149 Theyr mantles of say, gadryd & pleted mouch like after nonnes fashyon. **1570** B. GOOGE *Pop. Kingd.* II. 26 A linnen vesture wondrous white, and pleated here and there. **1632** J. HAYWARD tr. *Biondi's Eromena* 52 A gown.. pleated and crisped about the necke. **1687** A. LOVELL tr. *Thevenot's Trav.* II. 92 The sleeves..are much longer, and therefore they pleat them that they may not hang over the Wrists. **1864** WEBSTER, *Pleat*, to plait or double in narrow folds. See *Plait.* **1879** SALA *Paris herself again* (1880) II. xii. 181 A pretty young Dutchwoman who could not pleat her.. ruff to her satisfaction.

fig. **1605** SHAKS. *Lear* I. i. 283 (Qo.) Time shall vnfold what pleated [1623 *Fol.* plighted] cunning hides. **1714** C. JOHNSON *Country Lasses* IV. ii, Verily thou hast well unfolded thy message: now pleat it up carefully again. **1900** DOYLE *Gt. Boer War* xv. 253 The ground in front of him was pleated into long folds.

2. To plait (hair, a garland, etc.): = PLAIT *v.* 2. *Obs.* exc. *dial.*

1483 *Cath. Angl.* 284/1 To Plete, *jntricare*,..*plectere.* **1575–85** ABP. SANDYS *Serm.* (Parker Soc.) 310 The hair, which before had been..coloured, pleated, and bordered. **1658** SIR T. BROWNE *Gard. Cyrus* ii, The Triumphal.. Crowns..were pleated after this order. *c* **1704** PRIOR *Henry & Emma* 606 I'll weave Her Garlands; and I'll pleat Her Hair. **1897** CALDER *Poems* (Berwicksh.) 91 (E.D.D.) We pleated wreaths o' varied hues, to bind our lassie's hair. (In dialects from Cumbld. to E. Yorksh.: see E.D.D.)

Hence **'pleated** *ppl. a.*; **'pleating** *vbl. sb.*

accordion-pleated, pleated (by machinery) with very fine equal single pleats; ***knife-pleated***, pleated by hand with a blade of a knife (or by a machine producing the same result).

1483 *Cath. Angl.* 284/1 Pletyd, *jntricatus*, *jnvolutus.* *Ibid.*, A Pletynge, *jntricatura.* **1605** [see 1. *fig.*]. **1881** *Truth* 19 May 686/2 The train is of pleated sky-blue satin. **1895** *Outing* (U.S.) XXVI. 52/2 A greyhound's stomach almost equals an accordian pleated skirt in expansiveness. **1904** *Daily Chron.* 23 Sept. 8/3 Pipings, and pleatings of velvet. **1905** *Ibid.* 29 May 8/5 In the case of a linen gown..it would be as well to do without the knife-pleated frills.

pleat, -e, obs. ff. PLEAD *v.*

pleater ('pliːtə(r)). [f. PLEAT *v.* + -ER[1].] (See quot. 1921.)

1921 *Dict. Occup. Terms* (1927) §428 *Pleater*, pleats or folds material in pleats, by hand or by pleating machine. **1970** *Classification of Occupations* (Office of Population Censuses and Surveys) 66/2 Pleater.

pleay, obs. f. PLAY *sb.*

pleaze, obs. irreg. f. PLACE *sb.*

pleb (plɛb). *slang.* [Abbreviation of *plebeian.*] **A.** *sb.* A plebeian, one of the common people or lower classes: *spec.* (*a*) see quot. 1902; (*b*) = PLEBE 2 (*U.S.*). See also PLEBS.

1865 MRS. NEWBY *Common Sense* (1866) II. ii. 23 The well-dressed boy, who was so unlike a pleb. **1878** P. ROBINSON *In Indian Gard.* II. 82 The muggur [broad-snouted crocodile] is a gross pleb, and his features stamp him low-born. **1883** W. BLAIKIE in *Harper's Mag.* Nov. 908/1 At West Point, no matter how stooped the entering pleb, he is soon taught to carry himself..erect. **1902** FARMER & HENLEY *Slang, Pleb...* (Westminster School).—A tradesman's son. **1911** H. G. WELLS *New Machiavelli* I. iv. 104 They're Plebs and they know it. They haven't the Guts to get hold of things. **1922** *Dialect Notes* V. 189 At Annapolis, the natives are *crabs*, the freshmen *plebs*, the sophomores *youngsters*. **1928** A. HUXLEY *Point Counter Point* ix. 138 'A bit of a pleb, wasn't he?' put in the military friend. **1939** JOYCE *Finnegans Wake* (1964) I. 175 The pleb was born a Quicklow and sank alowing till he stank out of sight. **1960** *Guardian* 29 Sept. 9/7 It all ends happily, with the squire and the pleb firm friends. **1973** *Nation Rev.* (Melbourne) 31 Aug. 1441/6 The YLA executive sat at a head table while the plebs and proles were strewn together en masse. **1977** J. WAINWRIGHT *Nest of Rats* I. xii. 92 You were..an aristocrat... And you turned pleb. Like grandfather.

B. *attrib.* or as *adj.* = PLEBEIAN *a.* b. *colloq.*
1972 *Daily Tel.* 12 Feb. 11/2 Basically the situations, pursuit of boy friends, anxiety about the landlord, are identical, only here the background is pleb rather than deb. **1972** J. SYMONS *Players & Game* xxvi. 196 'What *was* his name? Barber?' 'No, some other pleb occupation. Taylor?' **1974** *New Statesman* 17 May 698 Orwell darkened the picture: Bowling is frankly pleb, Comstock descends from a line of sexless scrimpers.

Hence **'plebbie, 'plebby** *a.*
1962 'J. LE CARRÉ' *Murder of Quality* i. 9 Mrs. Rode's quite decent..in a plebby sort of way: doyleys and china birds. **1977** J. MCCLURE in *Winter's Crimes* 9 80 Portland Bill..all coach parties and orange peel... It does tend to be a bit plebbie.

†**'plebal,** *a. Obs. rare*$^{-1}$. [f. L. *pleb-s* (see PLEBS) + -AL[1].] Plebeian.
1606 WARNER *Alb. Eng.* XIV. lxxxv. 352 And former Popularity, whereto Ambition weads, Hath furnisht him of plebale Friends, a Beast of many heads.

†**'pleban.** *Sc. Obs. rare.* [ad. med.L. *plēbān-us*, f. *plēbs, plēbēs* diocese, parish, parish church (Du Cange). So OF. *plebain* (Valenciennes, 1347), It. *piovano* rural dean.] A rural dean.
1481 *Peebles Charters* (1872) 188 Chaplanis and serwandis at the paroche alter, in Sant Andros kyrk, as pleban and curat of the parochanaris. *Ibid.* 189 The said Gylbert.. constitut..the saidis plebane curat and chaplanis and thair successoris..to be kepparis to the archidenis place. [**1706** PHILLIPS, *Plebanus*, a Rural Dean, so call'd because the Deaneries were commonly united to the Plebaniæ, or chief Mother-Churches within a particular District.]

‖**plebania** (pliːˈbeɪnɪə, plɪ-). [med.L., f. *plēbānus* PLEBAN.] (See quots.) Hence †**ple'banian** in same sense.
1631 WEEVER *Anc. Fun. Mon.* 180 Questionlesse these Plebanians were like our side-wasted Parishes in Lanchishire, whose extensure is so large, that..one of those Parish Churches hath fourteene Chappels of ease..within.. her limits. **1706** PHILLIPS, *Plebania* or *Plebanalis Ecclesia*, (in old Latin Records) a Mother-Church, which has one or more subordinate Chappels. **1902** W. S. CROCKETT *Scott Country* xii. 247 It was the plebania or mother-church of the district.

'plebbish, *a. slang.* Also **plebish.** [f. PLEB + -ISH[1].] Of plebeian character; caddish. Hence **'plebbishness.**
1860 MAYNE REID *Wild Huntress* xxxii, It [Mormonism] appeals neither to reason nor romance. The one is insulted by the very shallowness of its chicanery, while its rank *plebbishness* disgusts the other. **1928** A. HUXLEY *Point Counter Point* xxi. 388 This is the sort of thing that really does make me feel rather pleb-ish. **1942** BERREY & VAN DEN BARK *Amer. Thes. Slang* §147/1 *Ungentility; plebeianism*,.. plebishness. *Ibid.* §147/5 *Plebeian; commonplace*,..plebish.

plebe (pliːb). [In sense 1 app. a. F. *plèbe* (in 14th c. *plebe*), ad. L. *plēb-s, plēbem*: see PLEBS. In sense 2 app. shortened from PLEBEIAN: cf. PLEB.]
†**1.** The Roman Plebs; by extension, the commonalty of any other nation. *Obs.*
1612 HEYWOOD *Apol. for Actors* II. 35 All other roomes were free for the plebe or multitude. **1614** SYLVESTER *Bethulia's Rescue* III. 391 But still the Plebe, with thirst and fury prest, Thus roaring, raving, 'gainst their Chiefs contest. **1635** HEYWOOD *Hierarch.* VI. Dial. 363 The Plebe with the motion seem'd content, Proserpine smil'd and Cerb'rus howl'd consent.

2. a. *U.S. colloq.* A member of the lowest class at a military or naval academy; a newly entered cadet, a freshman. Also **PLEB.** Also *attrib.*
1833 in *Mil. & Naval Mag.* (U.S.) (1834) Oct. 85 My drill master, a young stripling, told me I was not so '*gross*' as most other pleibs, the name of all new cadets. **1834** in *Ibid.* June 281, I was reckoned, already, as one of a class of cadets. To be sure, it was the 'plebe class'; but what of this? **1860** in *Amer. Hist. Rev.* (1928) XXXIII. 601 In most of our tents the cadets and plebes live together, 2 cadets, and 2 plebes to wait on them generally. **1884** ROE *Nat. Ser. Story* ii, You could see a squad of 'plebes' drilling. **1896** *Peterson Mag.* VI. 266/2 Although he was only a 'plebe', as the newly entered cadet was termed, even the hazers respected the native dignity and modesty that marked his demeanor. **1947** *Newsweek* 6 Oct. 78/2 The 'plebe' system which gives upper classmen authority over newcomer midshipmen filled Smith with revulsion. **1948** MENJOU & MUSSELMAN *It took 9 Tailors* 26 New arrivals are called plebes and a plebe is the dirt beneath an upperclassman's shoes; but to add insult to injury, a plebe has to clean and polish the shoes while he is being stepped on. **1970** N. ARMSTRONG et al. *First on Moon* vii. 156 Buzz ranked number one in his class at the end of his plebe year. **1973** H. GRUPPE *Truxton Cipher* iii. 31 Pozo was given to salting his speech with naval maxims left over from his days as a plebe. **1977** *Time* 19 Sept. 39/3 That summer, it [*sc.* West Point] enrolled its first women plebes—and now has 177 female cadets.

b. *Comb.* **plebeskin** (*U.S. slang*) civilian dress.
1888 *New York World* 22 July (Farmer), West Point, N.Y., July 21. The fourth class entered camp on Monday, but are still wearing their plebeskins. They will don their dress coats the first week in August, when they enter the battalion.

†**ple'beiall,** *a. Obs. rare*$^{-1}$. [f. L. *plēbēi-us* (see next) + -AL[1].] = PLEBEIAN *a.*
1594 T. BEDINGFIELD tr. *Machiavelli's Florentine Hist.* (1595) 77 We will call the one populer, the other plebeiall.

plebeian (pliːˈbiː(ɪ)ən, plɪˈbiːən), *sb.* and *a.* Forms: 6 *Sc.* **plebeane,** 6–7 **-eyan,** 6–9 **-ian,** 7 **-ean,** 6– **-eian.** [f. L. *plēbēi-us* belonging to the PLEBS + -AN; cf. F. *plébéien* (14th c.) By Shakspere sometimes stressed '*plebean.*]
A. *sb.* **a.** A member of the Plebs of ancient Rome; a Roman commoner, as opposed to the patricians, senators, and knights.
1533 BELLENDEN *Livy* IV. ii. (S.T.S.) II. 57 Na plebeane will tak þe dochter of ane patriciane but hir consent. **1557** NORTH *Gueuara's Diall Pr.* (1582) 35 She was none of the Senatours wiues, but a Plebeian, as much to say as a craftes woman, and no gentlemans daughter borne. **1607** SHAKS. *Cor.* I. ix. 7 The dull Tribunes, That with the fustie Plebeans, hate thine Honors. **1781** GIBBON *Decl. & F.* xvii. II. 29 The proudest and most perfect separation which can be found in any age or country, between the nobles and the people, is perhaps that of the Patricians and the Plebeians, as it was established in the first age of the Roman republic. **1850** MERIVALE *Rom. Emp.* i. I. 8 The patricians and plebeians of Rome represent, at this early period, two races of different origin.

b. In general, A person not of noble or privileged rank, one of the common people, a commoner.
a **1586** SIDNEY *Wanstead Play* in *Arcadia*, etc. (1629) 619 Hath not the pulchritude of my vertues protected me from the contaminating hands of these Plebeians? **1611** COTGR., *Roturier*, a Yeoman, or Plebeyan;..any lay man that is no Gentleman. *a* **1687** PETTY *Pol. Arith.* iv. (1691) 80 Whether the Plebeians of England (for they constitute the Bulk of any Nation) do not spend a sixth part more than the Plebeians of France? **1792** BURKE *Let. to Sir H. Langrishe* 13 The nobles have the monopoly of honour. The plebeians a monopoly of all the means of acquiring wealth. **1888** BRYCE *Amer. Commw.* II. lviii. 408 In some cantons [in Switzerland] the old families have so completely withdrawn..from public office..that it would be assumed that a politician was necessarily a plebeian.

c. *fig.* In various depreciatory applications.
1668 H. MORE *Div. Dial.* II. xiv. (1713) 133 If the Philosophers themselves be such fools, what are the Plebeians? **1791** COWPER *Iliad* II. 234 What plebeian base soe'er he heard. **1835** LYTTON *Rienzi* II. iv, To the brave, there is but one sort of plebeian, and that is the coward.

B. *adj.* **a.** Of or belonging to the Roman Plebs; that was a plebeian.
1566 PAINTER *Pal. Pleas.* I. 15 To what purpose be the plebeian magistrates ordained? **1841** W. SPALDING *Italy & It. Isl.* I. 51 His plebeian colleague Decius Mus..crowned a worthy life by devoting himself to death for the state in conformity with a national superstition. **1874** BANCROFT *Footpr. Time* i. 88 Rutilius, the first plebeian dictator at Rome.

b. Of low birth or rank; of or pertaining to the common people; belonging to or connected with the commons or populace; popular.
1600 W. WATSON *Decacordon* (1602) 301 Priuate person or plebian multitude. *c* **1620** MORYSON *Itin.* IV. v. iii. (1903) 477 Setting vp maypooles, daunsing the morris with hobby horses,..and like Plebean sportes. **1641** MILTON *Reform.* I. Wks. 1851 III. 23 The Prelates..comming from a meane, and Plebeyan Life on a sudden to be Lords of stately Palaces. **1698** FRYER *Acc. E. India & P.* 394 The Plebean Woman walk without Doors. **1795** BURKE *Let. to R. Burke* Wks. 1842 II. 458 To cut off (perhaps) three millions of plebeian subjects..from all connexion with the popular representation of the kingdom. **1886** RUSKIN *Præterita* I. vi. 178 For the abashing of plebeian beholders.

c. Having qualities, mental or physical, attributed to the lower classes; commonplace, undistinguished; vulgar or vulgar-looking, low, ill-bred, coarse, mean, base; ignoble. Also *fig.*
1615 *Val. Welshm.* (1663) B j, For to Plebean wits, it is as good, As to be silent, as not understood. **1651** HOBBES *Leviath.* II. xxxi. 192 That Prayers and Thanksgiving, be made in Words and Phrases, not sudden, nor light, nor Plebeian. **1676** DRYDEN *Aurengz.* V. i. 2472 A Queen, and own a base Plebean Mind. **1838** DICKENS *Nich. Nick.* xxi, An important gentleman..of rather plebeian countenance. **1853** C. BRONTE *Villette* vii, Their dress implied pretensions to the rank of gentlemen, but, poor things! they were very plebeian in soul. **1858** O. W. HOLMES *Aut. Breakf.-t.* xi, There are certain patches of ground, which..Nature..has covered with hungry plebeian growths [of weeds].

Hence **ple'beianly** *adv.*; **ple'beianness.**
1659 GAUDEN *Serm.*, etc. (1660) a ij b, An age pittifully and plebeianly Antiepiscopal. **1831** *Examiner* 809/2 Patriot Kings who walk about with umbrellas under their arms, prepared to be plebeianly rained upon, instead of royally reigning. **1840** *New Monthly Mag.* LX. 513 While I have a voice, sir, I will uplift it against such low-bred vulgarity and plebeianness.

ple'beiance. *rare.* [Irreg. f. L. *plēbēi-us* PLEBEIAN + -ANCE.] Plebeian condition or action.
1621 *Summary Du Bartas* To Rdr., Hauing extinguished all the distinctions betwixt Nobilitie and Plebeiance. **1896** *Godey's Mag.* (U.S.) Apr. 363/1 Such amazing verisimilitude, and such fascinating plebeiance, that the audience takes her into its heart of hearts.

ple'beianism. [f. PLEBEIAN + -ISM. So F. *plébéianisme* (Babœuf, *a* 1796).] Plebeian character or style.
1775 STERNE *Sent. Journ.* IV. 230 The young fellow was dressed very genteelly, with a sword, and carried no marks of plebeianism about him. **1828** *Blackw. Mag.* XXIII. 372 A prig who..can never cease for a moment to betray his plebeianism. **1882** *Athenæum* 22 Apr. 505 Her mother's kin ..were..tainted with a worse stain than that of honest plebeianism.

ple'beianize, *v.* [f. PLEBEIAN + -IZE.] *trans.* To make plebeian, reduce to plebeian rank; to make common, popular, or vulgar.
1844 *Blackw. Mag.* LV. 45 The new art, which, by plebeianizing knowledge and enlightening the mass, deprived the law and the prophets of half their terrors. **1849** *Tait's Mag.* XVI. 256/1 She dropped the *de*, and thus plebeianised her name. **1882** *Fraser's Mag.* XXVI. 343 It [an inn] took to billiards, and became gradually plebeianised.

†**ple'beious,** *a. Obs. rare.* [f. L. *plēbēi-us* plebeian + -OUS.] Of plebeian character or rank.
1610 W. FOLKINGHAM *Art of Survey* IV. iii. 82 They [sports] are either Generous, as Hunting and Hawlking: Or Plebeious, as Fishing and Fowling. **1657** TOMLINSON *Renou's Disp.* 595 No Tonsor so plebeious, but he was a Laudanister.

†**ple'beity.** *Obs. rare.* Also 7 **plebeyity.** [f. L. *plēbēi-us* plebeian + -ITY: cf. *laity, nobility*, etc.; L. had *plēbitās* *plebity.]
1. The lower or plebeian class; the commonalty.
1618 WOTTON in *Reliq.* (1651) 190 The Plebeyity (whose supream Object is Bread) cried in all corners, *Viva Donato.* **1656** BLOUNT *Glossogr.*, *Plebeity*, the commonalty, the vulgar people.
2. Plebeian rank or birth.
1679 *Jenison's Popish Plot* Pref. 7 That..his Extraction may advance him above the common exceptions of Lowness and Plebeity, which inferiour Testimonies are subject to.

plebeskin: see PLEBE 2 b.

ple'bicolar, *a. rare*$^{-1}$. [f. L. *plēbicola* one who courts the common people, (f. *plēbs* + *-cola* cultivator) + -AR[1].] That courts the common people. So **ple'bicolous** *a.*, in same sense; **ple'bicolist** *sb.*
[**1626** in Rushw. *Hist. Coll.* (1659) I. 356 Eightly, Merchants and Citizens, who deceive the King of Custom. Ninethly, Innovators, Plebicolæ.] **1656** BLOUNT *Glossogr.*, *Plebicolist*, a favorer of the common people. **1820** COLERIDGE *Lett.*, etc. I. 118 These Answers of the Queen's, conjointly with her plebicolar (or plebicolous) Clap-Trappines in the live puppet show of Wicked Punch and his Wife.

plebifi'cation. *rare.* [n. of action f. PLEBIFY.] A making or rendering plebeian; vulgarization.
1809–10 COLERIDGE *Friend* (1818) III. 132 You begin with the attempt to popularize learning and philosophy; but you will end in the plebification of knowledge. **1830** —— *Ch. & State* vii. 71. **1885** H. N. OXENHAM *Short Stud.* xv. 127 What is practically meant by the plebification of opinion..is, when put in its extremest form, the tyranny of unintelligent or half-intelligent mobs.
So **'plebificate** *v. rare.* = next.
1893 *Nation* (N.Y.) 6 Apr. 258/1 Religion, to adapt Coleridge's apothegm, was to be not only popularized but plebificated.

plebify (ˈpliːbɪfaɪ), *v. rare.* [f. L. *plēb-em* (PLEBS) + -FY.] *trans.* To make or render plebeian; to vulgarize.
1890 in *Cent. Dict.* **1894** MACCUNN *Ethics Citizenship* viii. 165 The best and greatest things on earth, in being popularised, may be plebified.

†**'plebile,** *a. Obs. rare*$^{-1}$. [f. L. type **plēbīl-is* (cf. *civīlis*), f. *plēb-em* (PLEBS): see -ILE.] = PLEBEIAN.
1606 G. W[OODCOCKE] *Lives Emperors* in *Hist. Ivstine* E e iv, He..had the loue of the Plebile sedition, and the hatred of Silla.

plebiscitarian (pliːbɪsɪˈtɛərɪən, plɪ-), *a.* and *sb.* [f. as PLEBISCITARY + -AN.]
A. *adj.* = PLEBISCITARY.
1870 *Daily News* 20 Sept., Now that she [France] is a plébiscitarian monarchy, the utmost that can be done..is to resort once more to the plébiscite. **1883** *Pall Mall G.* 13 Feb. 1/1 Regular political councils 'of senators, deputies, and politicians attached to the plebiscitarian cause'.
B. *sb.* An advocate or supporter of a plebiscite.
1888 *Times* 5 Sept. 5/1 All the remaining Cæsarians and Plebiscitarians had enrolled themselves under a new leader.

ple'biscitarism. *rare*$^{-1}$. [ad. F. *plébiscitarisme*, f. *plébiscitaire* (see next) + -ISM.] The principle or practice of appealing to a plebiscite.
1888 *Times* 17 Apr. 5/3 The..*Etoile Belge* says that neither speeches nor objurgations can stem the rising flood of plebiscitarism.

plebiscitary (pliːˈbɪsɪtərɪ, plɪ-), *a.* [ad. F. *plébiscitaire*, f. *plébiscite* (see next).] Relating to, based on, favouring, or of the nature of a plebiscite.
1870 *Daily News* 22 Apr., The following is the Plebiscitary manifesto, signed by 17 deputies of the Extreme Left and the committee of seven journalists associated with

them. **1881** *Standard* 17 June 4/8 The Plebiscitary Vote which is to decide whether the Prince is to be retained as a Ruler. **1898** Bodley *France* II. III. iii. 161 French advocates of the referendum disclaim its plebiscitary tendency.

plebiscite, -it ('plɛbɪs(ɑ)ɪt, ‖plebisit). Also (6 *Sc.* plebescit), 9 ‖**plébiscite.** [a. F. *plébiscite* (14th c. in Littré in sense 1), ad. L. *plēbiscītum.*]

1. *Rom. Hist.* = PLEBISCITUM 1.

1533 Bellenden *Livy* III. xxiii. (S.T.S.) II. 41 We sufferit ..þe plebescitis to be vsit in maner of lawis abone þe faderis. **1602** Fulbecke *Pandectes* 31 By plebiscite or popular determination to be quitted and freed. **1658** Phillips, *Plebiscite* (lat.), a decree, statute, or law, made by the common people. **1875** Poste *Gaius* I. §3 A statute is a command and ordinance of the people: a plebiscite is a command and ordinance of the commonalty. **1880** Muirhead *Gaius* I. §3 A *lex* is a law enacted and established by the whole body of the people; a plebiscit, one enacted and established by its plebeian members.

†**b.** *transf.* A popular decree or maxim. *Obs.*

1637 Pocklington *Altare Chr.* 148 Principles so full of spawne..as this feracious and pregnant Plebiscite, that what is by law, custom, prescription..appointed and settled, shall not be allowed, or practised.

2. In modern politics, A direct vote of the whole of the electors of a state to decide a question of public importance, e.g. a proposed change in the constitution, or the ratification or rejection of a measure approved by the legislature (see REFERENDUM); also by extension, a public expression, with or without binding force, of the wishes or opinion of a community.

In French, applied by Voltaire, 1776, to such a vote as used in some of the Swiss cantons (Littré); in the First French Republic used in connexion with the *coup d'état* of 18th Brumaire (9 Nov. 1799) and other acts, including that by which the consulate and imperial power were conferred on Napoleon I; in 1852 applied to the ratification of the *coup d'état* of Dec. 1851, and conferring of the imperial crown upon Napoleon III. It was in connexion with the last of these that the word became familiar in English.

1860 *Times* 7 Mar. 9/6 The decree summoning Tuscany to give on the 11th and 12th inst. a plebiscite, by universal suffrage, and by ballot, for the annexation, or for a separate kingdom. **1863** Kinglake *Crimea* I. xiv. 211 He [Louis Napoleon] knew how to strangle a nation in the night-time with a thing he called a 'Plebiscite'. **1870** *Daily News* 23 Apr., It is expected that the proclamation of the Emperor respecting the plebiscite will be issued on Saturday. **1884** H. Spencer *Man versus State* 14 If people by a *plébiscite* elect a man despot over them, do they remain free because the despotism was of their own making?

Hence **plebi'scitic** *a.* (*rare*), of, pertaining to, or established by a plebiscite.

1892 *Contemp. Rev.* Aug. 153 It [monarchy] had recently been humbled on the field by a plebiscitic adventurer.

‖**plebiscitum** (pliːbɪ'saɪtəm). *Pl.* **-a.** [L. *plēbiscītum* (also *plēbis scītum, plēbi scītum,* lit. an ordinance of the plebs), f. *plēbis,* genitive of *plēbs* the commons + *scītum* ordinance, decree, sb. use of pa. pple. of *sciscĕre* to approve, vote for.]

1. In ancient Roman History, A law enacted by the Plebs assembled in the *comitia tributa.*

a **1577** Sir T. Smith *Commw. Eng.* I. vii. (1584) 6 The Emperours claime this tyrannicall power by pretence of that Rogation or *plebiscitum,* which Caius Cæsar or Octauius obtained. **1704** Hearne *Duct. Hist.* (1714) I. 372 Within this period the Plebeians procured the *Plebiscita* to pass into Laws and to bind the Patritians, which was confirmed by Q. Hortentius the Dictator and from him called Lex Hortentia. **1774** Bp. Hallifax *Rom. Law* 7.

2. = PLEBISCITE 2.

1864 *Spectator* 443 Physical force is not all on the side of the tyrants, nor does a plebiscitum invariably sanction only a crime. **1869** *Pall Mall G.* 4 Aug. 2 If Louis Napoleon means to give the Liberal empire a fair trial, he will..'go to the country', not by the outworn and exploded device of a plebiscitum, but by a general election, conducted under the auspices of public liberty.

b. *fig.* An expression of popular opinion.

1859 Kingsley *Misc., Raleigh* I. 105 A terrible plebiscitum has been passed in the West country against the betrayer of its last Worthy.

‖**plebs** (plɛbz). [L. *plēbs* (earlier *plēbēs*).] In ancient Rome, The commonalty, originally comprising all citizens that did not belong to one of the patrician *gentes,* to which privileged order were afterwards added the *equites* or knights.

1835 Lytton *Rienzi* I. ii, All the insolent and unruly turbulence which characterised the *Plebs* of the Ancient Forum. **1845** Graves *Rom. Law* in *Encycl. Metrop.* II. 756/1 There were several co-operating causes which..rendered the *plebs* anxious to obtain a body of revised and written laws. **1882** *Athenæum* 21 Oct. 524/3 The two offices which by the close of the Republic had thrown all others into the background, those of the tribunes of the plebs in Rome and of the proconsuls in the provinces.

b. In transferred use, The common people; the populace, the mob. See also PLEB A.

1647 G. Daniel *Poems* Wks. (Grosart) II. 131 'Tis an Easier Thing To make Trees Leape, and Stones selfe-burthens bring..Then stop the giddie clamouring of *Plebs* [*rime* Thœbes]. **1866** J. Martineau *Ess.* I. 132 We..take our place with the plebs who believe [etc.]. **1890** *Cincinnati Chr. Advocate* 5 Feb. 10/2 Whether the plebs hoot or not.

pleck (plɛk). Now *dial.* Forms: α. 4 **plek,** 5 pleke, 5–8 plecke, (8 plack), 7– pleck. β. 4 plecche. [ME. *plecche, plecke, plek,* repr. an OE. **plecce,* cognate with MDu. and early mod.Du. *plecke* piece of ground, plot, spot, speck, stain, blemish, Du. *plek* spot, LG. *plek* piece of ground, place. (Thought by some to be related to MLG. *plack,* LG. *plak, plakke* patch, spot, rag, Du. *plak* slice, flat piece.) Not connected with Old Northumbrian *plæce, plætse,* ad. L. *platea* (see PLACE *sb.*).]

1. A small piece or spot of ground; a plot or plat; a small enclosure.

13.. *E.E. Allit. P.* B. 1379 Prudly on a plat playn, plek alþer-fayrest. *c* **1410** *Master of Game* (MS. Digby 182) xxxiv, If he see þat þe hare hath be at pasture in grene corne, or in eny oþer plecke. *c* **1440** *Promp. Parv.* 405/1 Plecke, or plotte, *porciuncula.* **1485** in *Descr. Cat. Anc. Deeds* (1890) I. 358 A howse to kepe there wod dry yn wt a gardyn pleke. **1575** *Nottingham Rec.* (1889) IV. 160 Payd for a locke for the medow plecke yate iijd. **1638** in Harwood *Lichfield* (1806) 484 An hedge betwixt Collin's pleck and the orchard. **1793** *Trans. Soc. Arts* (ed. 2) IV. 17 Planted at the same time on two distinct placks with Peas and magazan Beans. **1855** *Chamb. Jrnl.* III. 281 Cultivation is daily claiming, acre by acre, rushy moor and newdried pleck and plash.

†**2.** A (discoloured) spot or patch; a stain, a blemish. *Obs.*

c **1315** Shoreham *Poems* IV. 327 Oþere souche plecches Scheweþ wat onde deþ. **1535** Coverdale *Lev.* xiii. 4 Eny whyte plecke in the szkynne of his flesh.

3. 'A square bed of dried grass' (*E.D.D.*).

1688 R. Holme *Armoury* III. 72/2 [At Haymaking] Plecks is to make it, or turn it into square Beds.

4. A place; a town, village, or the like. *dial.*

1674 Ray *N.C. Words* 37 A *Pleck,* a Place. *c* **1746** J. Collier (Tim Bobbin) *View Lanc. Dial.* Wks. (1862) 51 His Gronny's alive an wooans..e Grinfilt, at Pleck where his nown Mother coom fro. *c* **1860** Staton *Rays fro' th' Loomenary* ii. 33 He neer knocks;..he comes into th' pleck withe-awt axin' leave.

†**plecked,** *a. Obs.* [f. prec. + -ED[2].] Speckled, spotted.

1387 Trevisa *Higden* (Rolls) I. 429 In þe welmes ofter þan ones Is y-founde reed splekked [*v.r.* plekked] stones. **1527** *Trevisa's Higden* I. xxii. 20 Shep that drynke of that one [river] shall wexe blacke and sheep that drynke of ye other wexe whyte..And yf they drynke of bothe they shall wexe plecked [1482 Caxton splekked] of dyuers coloure.

plecolepidous (plɛkəʊ'lɛpɪdəs), *a. Bot.* [f. Gr. πλέκος wickerwork, πλέκ-ειν to plait, twist + λέπις, λεπιδ- scale + -OUS.] Of Composite plants: Having the bracts of the involucre coherent.

1858 Mayne *Expos. Lex., Plecolepidus,*..applied by H. Cassini to the periclinium of the *Synanthereæ* when the scales are intergrafted or grown together at the base: plecolepidous. **1890** in *Cent. Dict.*

plecopterous (plɪ'kɒptərəs), *a.* [f. as prec. + Gr. -πτερος winged + -OUS.]

1. *Entom.* Of or pertaining to the *Plecoptera,* a group of pseudo-neuropterous insects, comprising the single family *Perlidæ,* having the reticulated wings folded in repose. So **ple'copter, ple'copteran,** an insect of the group *Plecoptera.*

1890 in *Cent. Dict.*

2. *Ichthyol.* Of or pertaining to the *Plecoptera* of Duméril, a family of Cartilaginous fishes, 'having the *Catopi* united under the pectoral fins'.

1858 in Mayne *Expos. Lex.*

plecotine ('plɛkəʊtaɪn), *a. Zool.* [f. mod.L. *plecōt-us* (f. as prec. + Gr. οὖς, ὠτ- ear) + -INE[1].] Of or pertaining to the genus *Plecōtus* of long-eared bats of the family *Vespertilionidæ,* having imperfect nasal appendages.

1891 Flower & Lydekker *Mammals* 660 The various genera may be conveniently grouped into the Plecotine, Vespertilionine, Miniopterine, and Thyropterine divisions.

plectellarian (plɛktɪ'lɛərɪən), *a. Zool.* [f. mod.L. *Plectellāria* (f. **plectella,* dim. of *plecta* interwoven border + *-aria,* -ARY[1]) + -AN.] Of or pertaining to the *Plectellaria,* a suborder of radiolarians without a shell, or having an incomplete latticed shell. **b.** *sb.* A radiolarian of this order.

1890 in *Cent. Dict.*

†**'plectile,** *a. Obs. rare.* [ad. L. *plectil-is* plaited, f. *plectĕre* to plait, weave: see -IL, -ILE.] Plaited, woven.

a **1682** Sir T. Browne *Tracts* ii. Wks. 1852 III. 204 The crowns and garlands of the Ancients..were made up after all ways of art, compactile, sutile, plectile.

plectognath ('plɛktəgnæθ), *a.* and *sb. Ichthyol.* [f. mod.L. *Plectognathi,* f. Gr. πλεκτός plaited, twisted + γνάθος jaw.] **a.** *adj.* Of or pertaining to the *Plectognathi,* a suborder of teleostean fishes, having the upper jaw attached to the cranium, and the skeleton imperfectly ossified. **b.** *sb.* A fish of this suborder. So **plectognathian** (-'gneɪθɪən) *a.* and *sb.,* **plectognathic** (-'gnæθɪk), **plectognathous** (-'ɒgnəθəs) *adjs.* = sense above.

1835 Kirby *Hab. & Inst. Anim.* II. xxi. 391 Plectognathian Fishes. Gill-covers concealed under a thick skin. Ribs rudimental. Ventral fins wanting. **1841** E. Scudamore *Nomenclature, Plectognathic,*..fishes with fixed jaws, as the sun-fish, &c. **1858** Mayne *Expos. Lex., Plectognathus,* knitted or connected cheeks..from a peculiar arrangement of the jaw and palatine arch: plectognathous.

plectonemic (plɛktəʊ'niːmɪk), *a. Biol.* [f. Gr. πλεκτός twisted + νῆμα thread + -IC.] Of, pertaining to, or designating two or more like helices coiled together side by side in such a way that they cannot be fully separated unless they are unwound. Opp. PARANEMIC *a.*

1941 A. H. Sparrow et al. in *Canad. Jrnl. Res.* C. XIX. 325 Kuwada..describes two types of double-stranded spirals: (1) orthospirals, which are formed when the two threads being coiled have one end free so that internal twisting does not occur; (2) anorthospirals, which result when two strands with both ends fixed are coiled together and in consequence have a twist compensating for each gyre of the spiral... Orthospirals are interlocked and cannot be separated without untwisting; anorthospirals are independent and can readily be pulled apart or fitted into each other... The term 'paranemic' (*para* = beside) instead of anorthospiral will be used here since it is simpler and its implications are clear. Instead of orthospiral 'plectonemic' (*plektos* = twisted) will be used as this has the advantage of indicating the relationship of the strands. **1950** [see PARANEMIC *a.*]. **1953** Watson & Crick in *Cold Spring Harbor Symp. Quant. Biol.* XVIII. 129/2 We therefore believe that if a helical structure is present [in DNA], the relationship between the helices will be plectonemic. **1971** *Nature* 22 Jan. 241/1 Tropocollagen..consists of three protein chains with similar, specific and very characteristic amino-acid compositions, twisted into a plectonemic triple helix of about 100 turns. **1974** [see PARANEMIC *a.*].

Hence **plecto'nemically** *adv.*

1953 *Cold Spring Harbor Symp. Quantitative Biol.* XVIII. 128/2 Apart from breaking the chains there are only two sorts of ways to separate two chains coiled plectonemically. **1966** Mahler & Cordes *Biol. Chem.* iv. 140 DNA in its B lattice configuration..consists of two right-handed helical polynucleotide chains of opposite polarity, plectonemically coiled around the same axis to form a double helix. **1979** *Nature* 26 Apr. 780/3 Sasisekharan *et al.*..have..proposed that the two strands of DNA do not coil plectonemically round one another.

plectospondyl (plɛktəʊ'spɒndɪl), *a.* and *sb. Ichthyol.* [f. mod.L. *Plectospondyli,* f. Gr. πλεκτός (see PLECTOGNATH *a.* and *sb.*) + σπόνδυλ-ος vertebra.] **a.** *adj.* Belonging to or having the characters of the *Plectospondyli,* teleostean fishes having some of the vertebræ co-ossified. **b.** *sb.* A fish of this order. So **plecto'spondylous** *a.*

plectre ('plɛktə(r)). *rare.* [a. F. *plectre* (14th c. in Godef.), ad. L. *plectrum.*] = PLECTRUM.

1603 Holland *Plutarch's Mor.* 1348 For an instrument and plectre (as it were) to set it aworke, we allow a spirit or winde. **1840** Browning *Sordello* II. 740 He'd strike that lyre adroitly—speech, Would but a twenty-cubit plectre reach.

plectropterine (plɛk'trɒptəraɪn), *a.* [f. mod.L. *Plectropter-us* (f. Gr. πλῆκτρο-ν cock's spur + πτερόν wing) + -INE[1].] Of or pertaining to the genus *Plectropterus,* the spur-winged goose of Africa, having a sharp bony spur on the radial carpal bone.

1890 in *Cent. Dict.*

‖**plectrum** ('plɛktrəm). Pl. **-a.** [L., a. Gr. πλῆκτρον anything to strike with, esp. an instrument for striking the lyre; also, a spear-point, cock's spur, etc.; f. πλήσσειν to strike.]

1. A small instrument of ivory, horn, quill, or metal, with which the strings of the cithara or lyre were plucked; now used for playing wire-strung instruments, as the zither, guitar, or mandolin.

1626 Bacon *Sylva* § 102 The Sound is not created between the Bow or Plectrum, and the String; But between the String and the Aire. **1763** J. Brown *Poetry & Mus.* v. 69 *note,* On the first rude Formation of Instruments, the Plectrum would give the more clear and effectual Stroke. **1806** Moore *Genius of Harmony* ii, A liquid chord is every wave that flows, An airy plectrum every breeze that blows! **1875** Jowett *Plato* (ed. 2) I. 52 To take up the lyre and tune the notes, and play with the fingers, or strike with the plectrum.

2. *Anat., Ornith.,* and *Ent.*: see quots.

1826 Kirby & Sp. *Entomol.* IV. xlvi. 339 *Plectrum,*..a marginal bristle stronger than the rest, observable about the middle of the costa and standing out from it. Ex. Many *Muscidæ.* **1842** Dunglison *Med. Lex., Plectrum,* the styloid process of the temporal bone. Also, the uvula and the tongue. **1895** *Syd. Soc. Lex., Plectrum..Ornith.,* a spur on the wing or foot.

3. *attrib.,* as ***plectrum banjo, guitar, lute*** (LUTE *sb.*[1] 1 a).

1954 *Grove's Dict. Mus.* (ed. 5) I. 401/2 The banjo played with the fingers is referred to as the 'finger-style' banjo, to distinguish it from the instrument (called the '*plectrum banjo') which is played with a plectrum. **1961** A. Birch in A. Baines *Mus. Instrum. through Ages* 182 The standard instrument is the 'finger-style' banjo with five gut or nylon strings tuned *d′, b, g, c, g′,* i.e. with the highest string on the left of the bass (and with its peg midway along the neck.) The 'plectrum banjo' omits this half-length string. **1956** I. Mairants in S. Traill *Play that Music* ix. 94 The *plectrum guitar with wire strings for dance music and jazz. **1961** A. Birch in A. Baines *Mus. Instrum. through Ages* 182 In the early days of jazz, the banjo was replaced by the '*plectrum guitar*'... The plectrum guitar has metal strings fastened not usually to the bridge..but to a tailpiece screwed to the end of the instrument. **1970** P. Oliver *Savannah*

Syncopators 109 *Kambreh*, *plectrum lute played widely in the Savannah regions.

pled, plede, pledde: see PLEAD *sb.* and *v.*

pledge (plɛdʒ), *sb.* Forms: 4–6 plege, plegge, 6 pledg, 5– pledge (6 *Sc.* pladge, plage, plaige, pleage, 7 pleg). [Late ME. a. OF. *plege* (Roland, *c* 1080, and Anglo-F.), *pleige, plaige, plo(i)ge*, etc., mod.F *pleige* hostage, security, bail, pledge:—early Frankish L. *plevium, plibium, plebium, a* 600 in *Pact. Childeb. & Chlot.* 10 (Hessels, *Salic Law* 417), med.L. *plivium* (?*a* 1200, Barcelona) in Du Cange; app. deriv. sb. (on type of *gaudium, odium, colloquium*) from med.L. *plevīre, plebīre* (*a* 800 in *Lex Romana Rætica Curiensis* IX. i. [4], *plivīre* (1080 Aquitaine, Du Cange), Pr. *plevir* (pres. ind. *pliu*), OF. *plevir* (Roland), *pleivir*, early mod.F. *plevir, pleuvir*, F. dial. *pluvir* Godef.), to warrant, assure, undertake for, engage (Cotgr.): cf. PLEVIN, REPLEVIN. See Note below.]

1. *Law* and *gen.* **a.** A person who becomes surety for another; a bail; a surety; a member of a frank-pledge or frithborh (mod.L. *plegius*). *Obs.* exc. *Hist.*

[**1224** *Bracton's Note Bk.* (1887) II. 176 Amerciauerunt eum..et Iordanum de Treuergan plegium suum..ad unam marcam. **1292** BRITTON I. ii. §10 Celui volums nous qe soit pris,..et lessez par plege jekes a nostre venue en le pays..et qe le Corouner face enbrever lour nouns et les nouns des pleges. **1314–15** *Rolls of Parlt.* I. 293/2 De ceo qe les chief plegges a le Letes, & al Tourn de Visconte, presentent fausement gentz estre copables.] *c* **1386** CHAUCER *Melib.* ¶860 Thanne Melibee..receyued hire obligacions and hir boondes by hire othes vp-on hire plegges and borwes. **1467** in *Eng. Gilds* (1870) 382 Also yf eny mans wyf becom dettor or plegge. **1502** *Ord. Crysten Men* (W. de W. 1506) I. iv. 45 And in as moche the godfader and godmoder ben pledges and maketh good for hym. *a* **1548** HALL *Chron., Hen. IV* 12 b, Thou knowest wel inough that I am thy pledge borowe and mayneperner, body for body. **1562** *Reg. Privy Council Scot.* I. 221 To entir as plege and souerte for his said fadder. **1581** LAMBARDE *Eiren.* I. iii. (1602) 14 Borowhead, Borsholder, and Tythingman..signifie, The chiefe man of the free pledges within that Borowe, or Tything. **1596** SHAKS. *Tam. Shr.* I. ii. 45 Petruchio patience, I am Grumio's pledge. **1647** N. BACON *Disc. Govt. Eng.* I. xxvi. (1739) 43 Each one being pledge for others good abearing. **1874** STUBBS *Const. Hist.* (1875) I. v. 87 Each association (*frithborh*) has a headman, a 'capital pledge', *borhs-ealdor* or *frith-borge-head*, to manage the business of the ten. Thus constituted, they are standing sureties for one another. **1895** POLLOCK & MAITLAND *Hist. Eng. Law* I. II. iii. §4. 558 The chief pledge seems to have exercised a certain authority over his subordinate pledges.

†**b.** A hostage. *Obs.*

1387 TREVISA *Higden* (Rolls) III. 129 Seleucus..somtyme plegge and prisoner at Rome. **1535** COVERDALE *1 Macc.* ix. 53 He toke also the chefest mens sonnes in the countre for pledges, and put them in the castel at Ierusalem to be kepte. **1597** JAMES VI in *3rd Rep. Hist. MSS. Comm.* 422/2 Burdynit with the keiping of the pleges and broken men reteinit for gude ordour on the bourdouris. **1633** T. STAFFORD *Pac. Hib.* I. vii, And also take himselfe Prisoner, and the fower English Pledges.

2. a. Anything handed over to or put in the possession of another, as security for the performance of a contract or the payment of a debt, or as a guarantee of good faith, etc., and liable to forfeiture in case of failure (med.L. *plegium*).

[**1164** *Constit. Clarendon* v. in Stubbs *Sel. Charters* (1895) 138 Excommunicati..debent dare..tantum vadium et plegium standi judicio ecclesiae, ut absolvantur.] *c* **1489** CAXTON *Sonnes of Aymon* xxii. 471 Yf he wolde not graunte me peas wyth hym, I promyse you he sholde leve his hede for a pledge. **1513–14** *Act 5 Hen. VIII*, c. 1 He shall..bring in sufficient gage and plegge to the verey value of the contentes of the same writtyng obligatorie. **1535** COVERDALE *Job* xxii. 6 Thou hast taken the pledge from thy brethren for naught, and robbed the naked of their clothinge. **1593** SHAKS. *3 Hen. VI*, III. iii. 240 What Pledge haue we of thy firme Loyalty? **1667** MILTON *P.L.* VIII. 325 The Tree.. which I have set The Pledge of thy Obedience and thy Faith, Amid the Garden by the Tree of Life. **1696** PHILLIPS, *Pledges*, in Common Law are sureties either Real or Personal which the Plaintiff finds to prosecute his Sute. **1818** CRUISE *Digest* (ed. 2) V. 577 The lord did not become entitled to a fine on these surrenders, because they were only intended as a pledge for securing the repayment of the money advanced. **1838** THIRLWALL *Greece* IV. xxvii. 9 They therefore sent seven galleys..as a pledge of their loyalty.

b. *spec.* A thing put in pawn.

1800 *Act 39 & 40 Geo. III*, c. 99 §2 Any time during which the said pledge shall remain in pawn. **1859** TENNYSON *Geraint & Enid* 220, I do not doubt To find, at some place..arms On loan, or else for pledge. **1863** GEO. ELIOT *Romola* iv, Hold the ring..as pledge for a small sum far beneath its value. **1878** STUBBS *Const. Hist.* III. xviii. 106 The crown, which had been kept by bishop Beaufort as a pledge, was placed in the custody of the treasurer.

c. A gage of battle; = GAGE *sb.*[1] 2.

1590 SPENSER *F.Q.* I. iv. 43 He..threw his gauntlet, as a sacred pledge, His cause in combat the next day to try. **1814** SCOTT *Ld. of Isles* III. vi, The honour'd pledge you gave In every battle-field shall wave Upon my helmet-crest.

d. *fig.* Applied to a child, as a token or evidence of mutual love and duty between parents, or as a hostage given to fortune.

1590 SPENSER *F.Q.* I. x. 4 But faire Charissa to a lovely fere Was lincked, and by him had many pledges dere. **1613** PURCHAS *Pilgrimage* (1614) 91 Yeerely sacrifice of the deerest pledges of Nature to Saturne. **1651** DAVENANT *Gondibert* I. ix, No male Pledge, to give a lasting name, Sprung from his bed. **1726** SWIFT *Gulliver* II. viii, I could never forget those domestic pledges I had left behind me. **1856** KANE *Arct. Expl.* II. vi. 71 Exulting over the first pledge of their union, a fine little girl.

3. Something given or taken as a sign or token of favour or the like, or as an earnest of something to come.

1526 *Pilgr. Perf.* (W. de W. 1531) 13 b, Innumerable.. benefytes and consolacyons he hathe gyuen vs, as very pledges and sure tokens of loue. **1548–9** (Mar.) *Bk. Com. Prayer, Communion*, He hath lefte in those holy Misteries, as a pledge of his loue..his owne blessed body, and precious bloud. *a* **1653** BINNING *Serm.* (1845) 240 Christ's rising is the pledge and pawn of the second resurrection. **1792** BURKE *Corr.* (1844) III. 447 The exertion of one virtue is always a pledge for the exertion of another. *a* **1839** PRAED *Poems* (1864) II. 438 A precious pledge that, wander where he will, One heart will think and dream about him still.

4. An assurance of allegiance or goodwill attested by drinking in response to another; the drinking of a health to a person, party, etc.; a toast.

1635 HEYWOOD *Philocothonista* 12 [Alexander] dranke healths to every man round, and pledged them severally againe;..Calistenes [when] the King offered him a deepe quaffing-bowle, which he modestly refused,..said aloud. I desire not, Oh Alexander, to receive a pledge from thee; by taking which, I shall be presently inforced to inquire for a Physition. **1715** LADY M. W. MONTAGU *Town Ecl., St. James' Coffee-Ho.*, A certain duke one night my health begun; With chearful pledges round the room it run. **1816** SCOTT *Old Mort.* i, Old Mortality was..prevailed upon to join his host in a single glass of liquor,..on condition that he should be permitted to name the pledge.

5. a. A solemn engagement to do or refrain from doing something; a promise, vow.

1814 CARY *Dante, Paradise* v. 67 Yet not bent, as Jephthah once..to redeem his pledge By doing worse. **1828** D'ISRAELI *Chas. I*, I. vi. 170 [The] oath of allegiance..was a pledge for civil, and not for religious purposes. **1844** H. H. WILSON *Brit. India* II. 376 The greater number adhered to their pledge. **1855** BREWSTER *Newton* II. xv. 82 He obtained them..under the pledge of secrecy. **1883** *Manch. Exam.* 30 Oct. 5/5 The measure was introduced..in defiance of the most solemn pledges of the British Government.

b. *the (temperance, total abstinence) pledge*: a solemn engagement to abstain from intoxicating drink. Phrases: *to take, sign, keep the pledge.*

1833 *New Engl. Mag.* (Boston) Aug. 137 The Temperance Pledge. *Ibid.* 141 Has he signed the pledge? **1840** *Southern Lit. Messenger* VI. 325/1, I have signed the pledge, and since it is done I will make a virtue of necessity. **1843** in M. Miliband *Observer of 19th Cent.* (1966) 161 Father Mathew ..called upon those who wished to take the 'pledge' to kneel down... About 3,000 persons took the pledge... From the appearance of many of them, we should say the total abstinence pledge was very necessary. **1846** W. E. FORSTER in Reid *Life* (1888) I. vi. 183 As to the temperance pledge, I find many men [in Ireland] still keeping it, but..a large proportion have broke. **1860** WARTER *Sea-board* II. 436 More than one case has come to my knowledge in which the pledge has been of service. **1864** *Soc. Sci. Rev.* 259 When a man is a drunkard, and can still respect and keep an oath, by all means let him take the pledge. **1914** G. B. SHAW *Fanny's First Play* III. 214, I dont want any whisky and soda. I'll take the pledge if you like. **1922** JOYCE *Ulysses* 348 Had her father only avoided the clutches of the demon drink, by taking the pledge or those powders the drink habit cured in Pearson's Weekly, she might now be rolling in her carriage, second to none. **1930** G. B. SHAW *Apple Cart* I. 43 Though none of us doubted that he would sign the pledge, we were not equally certain that the infirmities of his nature would allow him to keep it. **1970** J. H. GRAY *Boy from Winnipeg* 126 It was only when bootleg beer became openly available in the downtown hotels after 1920 that he gradually slipped from the pledge.

c. *U.S. college slang.* A student who has promised to join a fraternity or sorority. Also *transf.*

1901 *Univ. of Chicago Weekly* 1 Aug. 1087/1 Still if the Kappas are as bad as you say—you say they lifted two pledges last year. **1930** *Randolph Enterprise* (Elkins, W. Virginia) 18 Dec. 1/1 [They]..have been announced as two of five pledges chosen by the University Dramatic club at Morgantown. **1945** W. MAXWELL *Folded Leaf* 52 Shortly after seven o'clock the pledges appeared, one at a time, in the hotel lobby. **1949** *Reader's Digest* Aug. 71/1 The chapter might..keep Tom as a sort of permanent pledge. **1972** M. MEAD *Blackberry Winter* viii. 98 For one thing, I had no dates; these were all arranged through commands to the freshman pledges of certain fraternities to date the freshman pledges of certain sororities.

6. The condition of being given or held as a pledge; the state of being pledged: in the phrases *to be, lay, put in pledge, to give, have, lay, put to pledge, to take out of pledge*, etc.

1382 WYCLIF *1 Macc.* i. 11 The sone of Antiochi kyng, that was at Rome in seegyng [*gloss* or plegge; 1388 in ostage]. *c* **1430** *Syr Gener.* (Roxb.) 3158 My life to plegge shal he haue. **1516** *Life St. Bridget* in *Myrr. our Ladye* p. liii, Take my two sones and lay them in plegge to your credytours. *a* **1529** SKELTON *El. Rummyng* 293 Some layde to pledge Theyr hatchet and theyr wedge. **1567** *Gude & Godlie B.* (S.T.S.) 23 And gaif thy self to plaige. **1665** MANLEY *Grotius' Low C. Warres* 485 He..to meet and stop out want, had put to pledge, and pawned most of his own Houshold-stuff. **1818** CRUISE *Digest* (ed. 2) II. 86 If he doth not pay, then the land which is put in pledge, upon condition for the payment of the money, is taken from him for ever. **1862** MRS. H. WOOD *Mrs. Hallib.* T. I. xxii, Pressed for a sum of money..he had put his Sunday coat in pledge. **1901** *Daily Chron.* 14 May 7/7 Mr. Cardwell's scheme..abolished purchase in the Army, took the Army out of pledge, as the reform was wittily described.

7. *attrib.* and *Comb.*, as *pledge-cup* (sense 4), *-form, -jewel, -mania* (sense 5 b), *-office, -ring, -room*; (sense 5 c) *pledge-master, pin, week*; objective and instrumental, as *pledge-breaker* (so *pledge-breaking* vbl. sb. and ppl. adj.), *pledge-keeper, -taker; pledge-making, -mongering, -signing* vbl. sbs.; *pledge-bound, -free* adjs.; **pledge card**, (*a*) a card on which one may sign a temperance pledge; (*b*) *N. Amer.* a card on which one expresses willingness to contribute to a fund, sponsor a charity event, etc.; †**pledge-chamber, -house**, a chamber or house for the confinement of sureties or debtors (*Sc. obs.*).

1900 *Westm. Gaz.* 20 Oct. 4/3 An absolute united *pledge-bound party returns to represent Ireland at Westminster. **1887** *Pall Mall G.* 23 May 5/2 Suggestive of the *pledge-cards issued by Bands of Hope. **1958** *Times Lit. Suppl.* 10 Jan. 15/1 'Pledge' (temperance) cards and 'Decision' (conversion) cards interpolated their small crises. **1967** *Boston Sunday Herald Mag.* 26 Mar. 19/2 In 1960 Msgr. Leonard launched an $800,000 fund drive and more than 400 volunteers distributed pledge cards throughout the parish of about 3,000 families. **1970** *Toronto Daily Star* 24 Sept. 17/5 Pledge cards for the walk are available at any Dominion store while anyone wishing to enter a team in the skatathon can call 889-3967. **1578** *Reg. Privy Council Scot.* Ser. I. III. 24 Put in ward within the *pledge chalmer of the burgh of Drumfreis. **1629** *Ibid.* Ser. II. III. 12 They derned thameselffes in commodious parts ewest to the pledge chamber. **1851** D. WILSON *Preh. Ann.* (1863) II. IV. ix. 489 The *pledge cup and wassail bowl. **1721** WODROW *Hist. Suff. Ch. Scot.* I. II. xiii. §6 Mr. Webster and his two Friends ..removed to the *Pledge-house, where Debtors used to be put. **1850** GOSSE *Rivers of Bible* (1878) 48 The *pledge-jewels of Jesus' love. **1552** HULOET, *Pledge keper, *depositarius.* **1832** MILL *Let.* 17 Sept. in *Wks.* (1963) XII. 121, I should say that the *pledge-mania had been abated. **1949** *Sun* (Baltimore) 9 May 1/2 Santarelli..is *pledge-master for Phi Theta Upsilon Fraternity at the Northern Illinois College of Optometry. **1944** *Chicago Daily News* 28 Oct. 1 After the incident, Soik turned in his *pledge pin. **1891** *Daily News* 21 Sept. 7/2 The defendant..told her that he had had a fire in the *pledge room, and her cloak was burnt. **1552** HULOET, *Pledge taker, *pignerator.* **1949** *Time* 21 Mar. 47/2 As a finale to Brown's *pledge week, fraternity men had made the rounds of chapter houses to 'congratulate' each other. **1964** *Amer. Speech* XXXIX. 193 The social affairs that are a major concern for most students, such as..pledge and rush weeks.

[*Note.* Many attempts have been made to find a Latin derivation of the med.L. and OF. words: see Diez (s.v. *Plevir*), Littré (s.v. *Pleige*), Körting; all (including Diez's own suggestion, *plēbium* from *præbium* from *præbēre fidem*), unsatisfactory. The prevalent opinion now is that *plevēre, -īre*, was of Germanic derivation, and represented some form of WGer. *plehan* (OE. *pleon*), *plegan*, or Goth. **plaihwan*, in sense 'to incur risk or responsibility for, become responsible for' (see PLIGHT *sb.*[1]), which suits the sense of the med.L. and Romanic words exactly, though not free from difficulty phonologically: see Mackel *Franz. Studien* VI. I. 78. Med.L *plegium, plegius, plegiare*, It. *pieggio*, were from French.]

pledge (plɛdʒ), *v.* Forms: see PLEDGE *sb.* [Late ME. *plege, plegge*, f. PLEDGE *sb.*, or a. OF. *plegier*, mod.F. *pleiger* to guarantee, bail, f. *pleige*, pledge; so med.L. *plegiāre* (France, 1191 in Du Cange).]

†**1. a.** *trans.* To become surety for, make oneself responsible for (a person, thing, or statement). *Obs.*

c **1450** *Merlin* 35 Ye haue plegged me vpon youre lyves that I shall haue no drede of deth. **1474** CAXTON *Chesse* 37 His felawe pledgyd hym and was seurte for hym.

†**b.** *intr.* To become surety. *Obs. rare.*

1574 *Reg. Privy Council Scot.* II. 422 To caus all his freindis or servandis within Annanderdaill not ellis plegit for, to entir under plegis.

†**c.** *trans. to pledge out*: to redeem (a thing) from pawn or pledge; to ransom or bail (a person) out of prison, etc. *Obs.*

1464 *Mann. & Househ. Exp.* (Roxb.) 266 Delyveryd to Mechegod to plege owt Brokys salatt, xij.d. **1503** in *Test. Vetusta* II. 454 Such pledges as she hath of mine, I woll they be pledged out by William, and he to have them. **1523** LD. BERNERS *Froiss.* I. xl. 56 So [they] brought hym to the lorde Beaumonde who incontynent dyde pledge hym out fro his maisters handes. **1530** PALSGR. 660/1, I pledge, or borowe one out of prison or captyvyte, or redeme a thyng out of pledge, *je pledge.* To my great coste and charge I have pledged hym out of prison.

2. a. To deliver, deposit, or assign as security for the repayment of a loan or the performance of some action; to pawn.

1515 BARCLAY *Egloges* i. (1570) A v b, His sworde and buckler is pledged at the bere. **1586** T. B. *La Primaud. Fr. Acad.* I. (1594) 221 My estates and dignities are as it were in sequestration, and my life as it were laid in pawne and pledged vnto me. **1686** *Lond. Gaz.* No. 2105/4 If already sold or pawn'd,..the money [shall be] return'd for what they are pledg'd for. **1818** CRUISE *Digest* (ed. 2) II. 86 In the reign of Henry II. two modes of pledging lands were in use, which are fully described by Glanville. **1833** HT. MARTINEAU *Manch. Strike* x. 112 The..son pacing slowly to the pawnbroker's to pledge his aged mother's last blanket. **1877** GREEN *Hist. Eng. People* I. II. ii. 139 Normandy and been pledged to him by his brother Robert.

b. *fig.* as in *to pledge the future*; also, to plight or stake (one's life, honour, troth, word, etc.).

1775 SHERIDAN *Rivals* II. i, My vows are pledged to her. **1797** MRS. RADCLIFFE *Italian* ii, I now pledge you that honourable word that Ellena is innocent. **1841** JAMES *Brigand* xxv, To this I pledge my honour. **1871** R. ELLIS *Catullus* lxiv. 182 A loyal lover, a hand pledg'd surely, shall ease me. **1890** *Spectator* 4 Oct. 434/1 To pledge the future to the hilt is a temporary and evanescent joy.

3. a. To put (a person, or oneself) under a pledge; to bind by or as by a pledge. Also *refl.*

1571 *Satir. Poems Reform.* xxviii. 97 Be justice airis I pledgit all the pepill, Than spairit nane thocht thay wer Innocent. **1771** *Junius Lett.* lxv. (1820) 328, I pledge myself, before God and my country..to make good my charge against you. **1801** ELIZ. HELME *St. Marg. Cave* II. 175, I here pledge myself, by all my hopes of happiness hereafter. **1827** LYTTON *Falkland* I. 12 All eager for my commands, and all pledged to their execution. **1836** DICKENS *Let.* ? 19 Nov. (1965) I. 198 He could not..pledge himself whether it would appear this season, or whether they would begin with it, at the opening of the next. **1850** HT. MARTINEAU *Hist. Peace* II. v. vi. 295 The two millions whom he had in a few months pledged to temperance. **1883** *Manch. Exam.* 1 Dec. 5/1 A resolution..pledging the House to deal with the subject at the first fitting opportunity.

b. *trans.* and *intr.* To enrol (a new student) in a college society. Of a student: to undertake to join a college society; to enrol in (a society). *U.S.*

1871 L. H. BAGG *Four Years at Yale* 62 They are very attentive to his wants and do not leave him until he is 'pledged'. **1887** *Lippincott's Mag.* Nov. 741 If as a result of several such interviews he is approved, he is asked to 'pledge', that is, to promise to join the society. **1901** *Munsey's Mag.* Feb. 734/2 The time and manner of pledging members to the fraternities vary with different colleges. **1949** *Reader's Digest* Aug. 69/1 The rushing season, during which freshmen are pledged to the various houses, was in full swing. **1977** *Rolling Stone* 19 May 67/2 Even though Hamilton went to the University of Georgia and pledged Phi Delta Theta, his exuberant intelligence wouldn't allow him to be satisfied with conformity.

4. a. To guarantee or assure the performance of. **b.** To solemnly promise, or undertake to give.

1593 SHAKS. *3 Hen. VI*, III. iii. 250 Yes, I accept her, for she well deserues it, And heere to pledge my Vow, I giue my hand. **1869** FREEMAN *Norm. Conq.* III. xiii. 288 Their own personal service they pledged at once.

c. To promise solemnly (*to* do something).

1928 *Sunday Dispatch* 2 Sept. 1/3 On my pledging not to disclose his name..he promptly handed over another cheque for £10,000.

5. To give assurance or promise of friendship or fidelity to (any one) by or in the act of drinking. Also *absol.*, or with the drink as obj.

†**a.** To drink in response to another; to drink to a health or toast which has been proposed. *Obs.* **b.** To drink to the health of, drink a toast to; to toast.

1546 J. HEYWOOD *Prov.* II. iv. (1874) 104, I drinke, (quoth she). Quoth he, I will not pledge. **1568** GRAFTON *Chron.* II. 116 He dranke a great draught, the king pledging him. **1590** SPENCER *F.Q.* I. iii. 31. **1592** NASHE *P. Penilesse* 22 b, You do me the disgrace if you do not pledge me as much as I drunke to you. **1602** ROWLANDS *Tis Merrie when Gossips meete* 17 This to you both, Cousse Grace, and mistresse Besse; A full Carowse, Ile haue you pledge no lesse. **1616** B. JONSON *Forest* ix. *To Celia* i, Drink to me, only with thine eyes, And I will pledge with mine. *a* **1627** HAYWARD in Spurgeon *Treas. Dav.* Ps. lxix. 10 God handleth thee no otherwise.. than he handled his only Son, who hath pledged thee in this bitter potion. **1706** POTTER *Antiq. Greece* II. IV. xx. 396 Alexander..is reported to have drank a Cup containing two Congii,..to Proteas, who commending the king's Ability, pledg'd him, then call'd for another Cup of the same Dimensions, and drank it off to him. The king, as the Laws of good Fellowship requir'd, pledg'd Proteas in the same Cup. **1727** SWIFT *Poisoning E. Curll* Wks. 1755 III. I. 149 Mr. Pope..very civilly drank a glass of sack to Mr. Curll, which he as civilly pledged. **1773** GOLDSM. *Stoops to Conq.* II. i, Will you be so good as to pledge me, sir? **1802** MAR. EDGEWORTH *Moral T.* (1816) I. xix. 171 Pledge him in a bumper of port. **1855** KINGSLEY *Heroes* II. v. (1868) 169 In his hand a sculptured goblet, as he pledged the merchant kings. **1870** BRYANT *Iliad* I. IV. 104 From cups of gold They pledged each other.

Hence **pledged** (plɛdʒd) *ppl. a.*, given or put in pledge; pawned, plighted; bound by a pledge; '**pledging** *vbl. sb.*

1538 ELYOT, *Pigneratio*, a pledgynge or gagynge. **1552** HULOET, Pledged, *pigneratus*. **1579** *Reg. Privy Council Scot.* III. 164 His plege,..contenit in the buke of plegeing. **1628** PRYNNE (*title*) Healthes: Sicknesse. Or, a Compendiovs and briefe Discourse; prouing the Drinking, and Pledging of Healthes, to be Sinfull. **1860** MILL *Repr. Govt.* (1865) 64/1 A strong inducement..not to confine themselves to pledged party men. **1887** *Daily News* 21 July 6/1 The calling-in of loans on pledged property. **1893** F. ADAMS *New Egypt* 186 We believe..absolutely in the pledged word, the pledged honour of England. **1929** *Old Oregon* June 10 They went through rushing, pledging, moving, 'open house', freshman duties, in a cycle which at that time seemed to move ponderously over each event. **1959** *Ann. Reg. 1958* 152 At a special pledging conference in October 35 governments promised $27½ million for the Agency's work. **1964** *Amer. Speech* XXXIX. 194 The vocabulary of pledging, rushing.

pledgeable ('plɛdʒəb(ə)l), *a.* [f. PLEDGE *v.* + -ABLE.] That can be pledged or pawned.

1865 *Brit. Workman* 52, I pledged my coat, I pledged my bed, I pledged in short everything that was pledgable. **1901** *Dundee Advertiser* 12 Apr. 4 The revenues pledgeable, like tribute rice, the Manchu allowances, &c.

pledgee (plɛ'dʒiː). [f. PLEDGE *v.* + -EE.] **1.** One with whom a pledge is deposited; a pawnee.

1766 BLACKSTONE *Comm.* II. xxv. 396 In case of goods pledged or pawned upon condition, either to repay money or otherwise; both the pledgor and pledgee have a qualified, but neither of them an absolute, property therein. **1800** *Acc. Bks.* in *Asiat. Ann. Reg.* 59/2 The whole amount due to the pledgee must be paid before the pledge can be demanded. **1869** *Smith's Dict. Gr. & Rom. Antiq.* 917/1 The pledger could also sell the thing pledged,..but such sale did not affect the right of the pledgee. **1875** [see PLEDGER 1].

2. One who takes a pledge, *spec.* = PLEDGE *sb.* 5 c.

1937 (heard by Prof. A. L. Hench, Univ. of Virginia) 24 Nov., I needn't worry so long as I'm a pledgee. **1942** BERREY & VAN DEN BARK *Amer. Thes. Slang* §825/34 Pledge, pledgee,..a prospective fraternity member who has promised to join.

'**pledgeless**, *a.* [f. PLEDGE *sb.* + -LESS.] Without a pledge.

1846 WORCESTER, *Pledgeless*, having no pledges. *Qu. Rev.*

pledger ('plɛdʒə(r)). Also (in legal use, opposed to *pledgee*) **-eor, -or** (plɛ'dʒɔː(r)). [f. PLEDGE *v.* + -ER[1], -OR. Cf. OF. *plegeour* (13th c. in Godefroy).]

1. One who deposits something as a pledge; a pawner.

1766 [see PLEDGEE 1]. **1875** POSTE *Gaius* II. §64 This..may be said to rest on the assent of the pledgor..which empowered the pledgee to sell in default of payment. **1883** *Q. Rev.* Jan. 120 Bulky articles may now be deposited if the pledgers will pay for their storage. **1906** *Daily Chron.* 19 Feb. 4/3 There are..people in the poorer districts of London who make a living by pawning articles for other persons. Sometimes these 'professional pledgers' are women.

2. One who drinks in response to, or to the health of, another. Also *fig.* Cf. PLEDGE *v.* 5.

1576 GASCOIGNE *Del. Diet for Drunkards* (1789) 20 If the Pledger bee inwardlie sicke or have some infyrmitie, whereby too much drinke..doo empayre his health. **1617** RICH *Irish Hvbbvb* 24 The cup being newly replenished..he that is the pledger must now begin his part, and thus it goes round throughout the whole company. **1663** DRYDEN *Wild Gallant* III. i, This fellow is onely the Sollicitor of a quarrel ..and will leave the fighting part to the Curteous pledger.

3. One who pledges himself or takes a pledge.

1837 HT. MARTINEAU *Soc. Amer.* III. 204 The bond of Temperance societies is a pledge or vow respecting the personal conduct of the pledger.

†'**pledgery**. *Obs. rare*[−0]. [a. OF. *plegerie* (12th c. in Godef.); thence med.L. *plegeria*.]

1706 PHILLIPS, *Pledgery* or *Pleggery*, Suretiship, an Undertaking, or Answering for. **1775** in ASH.

pledget ('plɛdʒɪt). Forms: 6 **plagette, pleggat,** 7 **plageat, (plegant, -ent, pleagant, -eant),** 7–8 **plaget, pleget,** 7–9 **pledgit,** 7– **pledget.** [Known from 16th c.: origin and early history of obscure.

The divergent spellings in 16–17th c. leave uncertain the original form, and even the sound of the *g*, and the nature of the ending (in which *-ette, -et* suggest a Romanic diminutive). On the supposition that the *g* was hard, the derivation has been sought in *plug*, and in MDu. *plagge, plagghe* patch of cloth, rag, wrapper, covering, Du. *plagge* turf, tan-cake, MLG. and LG. *plagge* tangled or matted mass, turf, patch, rag. Others have thought of a diminutive from L. and Romanic *plāga* wound, F. *plaie*, or a deriv. from PLEACH *v.*: cf. Prov. *plecha 'no plago* to bandage a wound. But all these suggestions present difficulties.]

A small compress or flattened mass of lint or other soft absorbent material (often steeped in some medicament), for applying over a wound, sore, etc.; see also quot. 1892.

c **1540** *Pract. Cyrurgyons* Aj, Stupes, or plagettes made of lynte, Cotten or other lyke stuped or dypped in hote Oyles. **1575** TURBERV. *Falconrie* 258 Spread of this vpon a pleggat of linnen cloth. **1612** WOODALL *Surg. Mate* Wks. (1653) 92 With plegents of lint drie fil up the orifice. **1615** MARKHAM *Eng. Housew.* II. i. (1668) 35 Take *Unguentum Aurum*, and lay it upon a pleagant of lint. **1616** SURFL. & MARKH. *Country Farme* 48 Apply it vnto the teates vpon plageats as hot as may be endured. **1643** J. STEER tr. *Exp. Chyrurg.* vi. 20 It may be spread on little pleggets and applyed. **1737** BRACKEN *Farriery Impr.* (1757) II. 240 Spread upon Pieces of Lint, or what we call Pledgets of Lint. **1741** *Compl. Fam. Piece* I. i. 88 To be apply'd..with Plagets and other Helps. **1812** J. J. HENRY *Camp. agst. Quebec* 75 He drew a pledget of linnen quite through the wound. **1892** *Photogr. Ann.* II. 49 Be sure to go over the face of the plate with a wet pledget of cotton wool.

plee, pleen, obs. ff. PLAY, PLEA, PLY, PLAIN *v.*

pleep (pliːp). *slang* (? *obs.*). [? Echoic: see quot. 1948.] (See quots.)

1942 *Gen* 1 Sept. 14/2 A Heinkel pilot who shoots too soon or runs for home is definitely a 'poor type' or just a 'pleep'. **1943** HUNT & PRINGLE *Service Slang* 52 *Pleep*,..a Hun pilot who turns tail. **1948** PARTRIDGE *Dict. Forces' Slang* 144 *Pleep*, an enemy pilot that refuses aerial combat. Echoic of a timorous young bird.

pleeser, pleezer, obs. and dial. ff. PLEASURE.

pleet, -e, obs. ff. PLEA, PLEAD *v.*

pleg, plege, plegg(e, obs. ff. PLEDGE.

plegant, -ent, -et, obs. ff. PLEDGET.

-plegia, formative element, f. Gr. πληγ-ή blow, stroke (f. πλήσσειν to strike) + -IA[1], used with the sense 'paralysis', as in HEMIPLEGIA, PARAPLEGIA, *iridoplegia* s.v. IRIDO-.

†'**plegnic**, *a.* (*sb.*) *Obs. rare.* [app. arbitrarily f. Gr. πληγή blow, stroke + -IC.] Acting by a blow or stroke, as a hammer; also as *sb.*: see quots.

1612 STURTEVANT *Metallica* 37 Plegnicks..performe their opperation and effect, by their dexterous and artificiall ioynt-mooving... There is a great vse of the Plegnick instruments for the making of Eumechanick and reformed Milnes and Bellowses. **1664** J. WILSON *Projectors* III. 36 From the Pestle and Mortar [came] all sort of Mills, whether Horizontal, or Plegnick; Horse, Hand, Wind, Water, or otherwise.

plegometer (plɪ'gɒmɪtə(r)). *rare.* [f. Gr. πληγή stroke + -(O)METER.] **a.** An instrument for measuring and recording the force of blows. **b.** = PLEXIMETER.

1839 URE *Dict. Arts* 535 The balls were fired against Austen's recoiling target, a very delicate plegometer. **1857** DUNGLISON *Dict. Med.*, *Plegometer*, pleximeter.

plei, pleie, obs. forms of PLAY, PLEA.

Pleiad ('plaɪəd). *Pl.* **Pleiads**; more commonly in Lat. and Gr. form **Pleiades** ('plaɪədiːz); also 4 **Pliades,** 5 **Plyades.** [a. L. *Plēïas, Plējas, Plīas*, pl. *Plēïades* etc., a. Gr. Πλειάς, pl. -άδες, Ion. Πληιάς: see -AD; so F. *Pléiade*, pl. *Pléiades*.]

Astron. In *pl.*, A close group or cluster of small stars in the constellation Taurus, commonly spoken of as seven, though only six are visible to the average naked eye. (Good eyes on a clear night can make out about nine, while the telescope shows a great number.)

According to Greek Mythology, the Pleiades were the seven daughters of Atlas and Pleione, the eldest of whom, Electra, was 'the lost Pleiad', and not represented by a star. The seven names, with those of the parents, have since Ricciolo (1665) been individually applied to the nine brightest stars; of these Alcyone is of the third magnitude, Electra and Atlas of the fourth, Merope, Maia, and Taygete of the fifth, Pleione, Celeno, and Asterope, between the sixth and the seventh. Some think that the name was actually derived from πλεῖν to sail, because the season of navigation began with their heliacal rising.

1388 WYCLIF *Job* xxxviii. 31 Whether thou schalt mowe ioyne togidere schynynge sterris Pliades [*marg.* that is, the seuen sterris; 1382 The shynende seue sterres]. **1555** EDEN *Decades* 162 The goynge downe of the seuen starres cauled *Vergiliae* or *Pleiades*. **1560** BIBLE (Genev.) *Job* xxxviii. 31 Canst thou restraine the sweete influences of yᵉ Pleiades? or loose the bands of Orion? **1667** MILTON *P.L.* VII. 374 The gray Dawn, and the Pleiades before him danc'd, Shedding sweet influence. **1788** GIBBON *Decl. & F.* xliii. IV. 323 The fable of Electra the seventh of the Pleiads. **1817** BYRON *Beppo* xiv, Whose course and home we knew not, nor shall know, Like the lost Pleiad, seen no more below. **1842** TENNYSON *Locksley Hall* 9 Many a night I saw the Pleiads, rising thro' the mellow shade, Glitter like a swarm of fire-flies tangled in a silver braid. **1868** LOCKYER *Astron.* §71 The Pleiades..The six or seven stars visible to the naked eye become 60 or 70 when viewed in the telescope.

b. *fig.* (*sing.*) A brilliant cluster or group of persons or things, especially of seven, as the group of poets of the French Renaissance, called in French *La Pléiade*, and including Ronsard and Du Bellay.

1822–56 DE QUINCEY *Confess.* (1862) 54 Donne, Chillingworth, Sir T. Browne, Jeremy Taylor, Milton, South, Barrow, form a *pleiad*, a constellation of seven stars, such as no literature can match. **1838–9** HALLAM *Hist. Lit.* II. II. i. §5. 5 Dorat..was also one of the celebrated pleiad of French poets. **1882** *Illustr. Lond. News* 7 Oct. 371 Noriac was one of the brilliant pleiad of writers who formed the staff of the original weekly *Figaro*.

pleid, obs. f. PLAID, PLEAD.

pleide, obs. pa. t. of PLAY *v.*

pleight, obs. f. PLAIT.

pleign(e, plein(e, pleinly, obs. ff. PLAIN, -LY.

‖**plein-air** (also plain-air), from the Fr. phrase *en plein air* (ɑ̃ plɛ̃nɛr) 'in the open air' (lit. 'in full air'): used attrib. to denominate certain impressionist schools and styles of painting, which originated in France about 1870, and aimed at the representation of effects of atmosphere and light that cannot be observed in the studio. Also used to designate work painted out of doors, or representing out-door scenes.

1894 *Nation* (N.Y.) 14 June 444/2 Mysticism has misled M. Rochegrosse into a plein-air problem, in which the meaning of his 'Chevalier aux Fleurs' is less puzzling than his ignoring of all values. **1898** *Daily News* 15 Feb. 8/5 Another of the plain-air painters of this show. **1902** L. BÉNÉDITE in *Encycl. Brit.* XXXII. 443/1 The 'plein-air', or open-air, school. **1930** *Observer* 6 Apr. 13 The giant Constable, the first of the plein air moderns. **1947** [see IMPRESSIONISTIC *a.*]. **1970** *Daily Tel.* 9 July 12 Dame Laura never succeeded in liking town life. It was the wind and the sun and wild places that were her real loves and it was as a *plein air* painter of sunlight on landscapes and seascapes that she first succeeded. **1970** *Oxf. Compan. Art* 822/1 The expression '*plein air*'..implies a style of painting which emphasizes the impression of the open and of spontaneity and naturalness. On the other hand it also indicates an actual technique of painting, which involved more than working in the open direct from nature instead of the older practice of composing a finished picture in the studio from rough sketches done on the spot. **1974** *Country Life* 6 June 1436/2 The impact of these *plein air* (in effect if not in fact) pictures.

Also **plein-'airish** *a.*, resembling or characteristic of the *plein-air* school of painting; **plein-airism, -isme** (-ism), the theories and practices of the plein-airists; **plein-airist**, a painter of the 'plein-air' school; **plein-airiste** (-ist) = *plein-airist.*

1891 *Academy* 6 June 544/3 'Impressionists', 'tâchistes', 'plein airistes', and 'pointillistes', to use the jargon of the day. **1893** *Sketch* 6 Sept. 321/1 Admirers may..get a glimpse of the great pleinairist as he passes. **1897** *Daily Tel.* 10 Feb. 9/6 These pretty illustrations, from the designs of the well-known French *plein-airiste* and figure painter, Raphaël Collin, are delicate and graceful even to the verge of effeminacy. **1900** *Edin. Rev.* July 193 The English plein-airists are too well known to need special mention. **1931** A. HUXLEY *Music at Night* 65 Bernini is, spiritually speaking, a *plein-airiste.* **1932** *New Statesman & Nation* 23 Jan. 93/1 Finally, with the emulation of his pleinairish friends, Manet loses not only his distinction of rhythm, but a great deal of his feeling for colour. *Ibid.*, It [*sc.* the Demoiselles au bord de la Loire].. marks the beginning of the long and triumphant development of pleinairism. **1946** *Penguin New Writing* XXVIII. 142 To imagine now an art of landscape into which plein-airisme had never intruded..it is impossible. **1959** *Listener* 9 Apr. 633/2 Go careful with the washing tub And do not spill the crystal slops Lest any of the escaping drops Should water down the *pleinairiste* Delights of Lady Tristram's feast! **1961** *Ibid.* 12 Oct. 571/2 It was necessary at the time..to talk about *plein airism* as though it was nothing else but a campaign against the time-worn clichés of the academic tradition. **1969** R. MAYER *Dict. Art Terms & Techniques* 299/2 The artists specifically called *pleinairistes* were a group of Impressionists of the 1880's and 1890's, notably Camille Pissaro.., Claude Monet.., Alfred Sisley.., and Pierre Auguste Renoir. **1972** D. SUTTON *Lett. Roger Fry* I. 9 Fry was suspicious of Impressionism, by which he meant (I suspect) the watered-down *pleinairisme* of Bastien-Lepage, so popular in England, or the fragile pastiches of Whistler's followers. **1974** *Country Life* 28 Feb. 421/3 The historical emphasis..is on *plein air-ism* and the freshness and spontaneity of handling it produced. **1978** *Times* 17 Oct. 10/6 Some really wonderful paintings by the *plein-airists* of the 1880s on, whether it be McTaggart..or Guthrie.

pleiner, obs. f. PLENAR.

pleing(i)e, -ȝie, obs. ff. PLAIN *v.*

‖**plein jeu** (plẽ ʒø), *adv. phr.* and *sb. Mus.* [Fr. 'full play'.] **A.** *adv. phr.* As a direction: with full power; *spec.* in organ playing: without reeds.

1837 J. A. HAMILTON *Dict. 2,000 Terms* (ed. 4) 54 *Plein jeu*.., full organ. **1938** *Oxf. Compan. Mus.* 670/2 *Plein jeu*, French for 'Full to Mixtures' (without reeds). *Ibid.* 739/1 *Plein jeu* (Fr.) 'full play', i.e. the whole power of the organ (or harmonium). **1954** *Grove's Dict. Mus.* (ed. 5) VII. 102/1 In the course of a piece it [*sc.* the term *organo pleno*] means the same as the French term *plein jeu.* **1960** *Times* 26 Apr. 16/2 The emotional stops are playing *plein jeu* in *Erwartung.* **1968** A. NILAND *Introd. Organ* vi. 93 Bach writes at the beginning of several pieces, *pro organo pleno* (for full organ). This was undoubtedly the equivalent of the French *plein jeu.*

B. *sb.* A type of mixture stop on the organ; music written for the full organ. Also *fig.*

1855 E. J. HOPKINS in Hopkins & Rimbault *Organ* II. 328 The Madelaine [*sic*], at Paris... Clavier du Grand Orgue, 12 Stops... Plein-Jeu, X ranks. **1880** GROVE *Dict. Mus.* II. 601/1 The scheme of Ducroquet's French organ stood as follows:—Great Organ. 10 stops... Bourdon..Prestant.. Plein jeu. **1898** J. MATTHEWS *Handbk. Organ* II. 29 Such compound stops are variously termed, Full, Grave, Acute or Sharp Mixture,.. Fourniture, Plein Jeu, Cymbal, etc. **1919** G. A. AUDSLEY *Organ of 20th Cent.* iii. 87 The largest Plein-Jeu known to us is that of ten ranks in the Grand division of the Organ in the Madeleine, Paris. **1944** W. APEL *Harvard Dict. Mus.* 588/1 *Plein-jeu*.., full organ. Also name for pieces written for the full organ. **1952** W. L. SUMNER *Organ* x. 297 The plein-jeu is a large true mixture with sub-unison and unison ranks in the treble. **1958** *Times* 30 Sept. 3/5 He begins to draw out more stops in Siegfried..though reserving his *plein jeu*, so to speak, for a later date. **1963** CLUTTON & NILAND *Brit. Organ* i. 38 Unlike the Germans, the French did not use their 'plein jeux' much for polyphonic music. **1975** *New Yorker* 28 Apr. 133/1 In addition, further pistons can bring on or silence the mixtures, the reeds, the *Plein Jeu*, the *Grand Jeu*, and 'Tutti'. **1978** *Gramophone* June 90/1 By the nature of the organs, many of the most effective pieces are dialogues between a group of reeds (the trompeteria) and the *plein jeu.*

pleintith, obs. Sc. f. PLENTY.

pleio-, plio- (plaɪəʊ), **pleo-** (pliːəʊ), combining forms of Gr. πλείων (poet. πλέων), πλεῖον, more, compar. of πολύς, -ύ, much; see POLY-. *Plio-*, which follows Latin spelling, is chiefly used in generic names and their derivatives, as *Pliosaurus, Pliosaurian.*

‖**pleiochasium** (-'keɪzɪəm) *Bot.* [mod.L., irreg. f. Gr. χάσις separation, after DICHASIUM], a cymose inflorescence having three or more lateral axes, a multiparous cyme. ‖**pleiomastia** (-'mæstɪə), pleo-, *Anat.* [mod.L., f. Gr. μαστός breast, mamma], the condition of having more than one nipple upon the mamma. ‖**pleiomazia** (-'meɪzɪə), pleo-, *Anat.* [mod.L., f. Gr. μαζός, dial. var. of μαστός: see above], the condition of having more than the normal number of mammæ. **pleiomerous** (plaɪ'ɒmərəs) *a. Bot.* [Gr. μέρος part], having (as a floral whorl) more than the normal number of parts; so **plei'omery**, pleiomerous condition. **pleiophyllous** (-'fɪləs) *a. Bot.* [Gr. φύλλον leaf]. **'pleiophylly**: see quots. **pleiosporous** (plaɪ'ɒspərəs, plaɪəʊ'spɔərəs) *a. Bot.* [Gr. σπόρος seed], having more than the usual number of spores. **'pleiotaxy** (-tæksɪ) *Bot.* [Gr. τάξις arrangement: cf. *phyllotaxy*], the condition of having more than the usual number of floral whorls, as in 'double' flowers. **pleiothalamous** (-'θæləməs) *a. Bot.* [Gr. θάλαμος chamber], having more than the usual number of chambers or receptacles. ‖**pleiotrachea** (-trə'kiːə) *Bot.* [mod.L.: see TRACHEA], a vessel containing a spiral band composed of a number of fibres. See also words in PLEO-, PLIO-.

1850 J. BIRKETT *Dis. Breast* 206 *Pleiomastia... There are examples..of the existence of supernumerary nipples... They may be situated near together, and possess an areola in common, or they may be separated and encircled by an areola distinctly defined. **1895** in *Syd. Soc. Lex.* **1850** J. BIRKETT *Dis. Breast* 23 *Pleiomazia..signifies numerical excess beyond the usual complement of the mammæ. **1895** *Syd. Soc. Lex.*, *Pleomazia.* **1898** tr. *Strasburger's Bot.* II. ii. 453 The origin of a *pleiomerous whorl from one consisting of fewer members is equally well shown in the flowers of Tilia. **1895** *Syd. Soc. Lex.*, **Pleiomery*,..due either to the branching of one member at an early stage or to an original development of two members in place of one. **1898** tr. *Strasburger's Bot.* II. ii. 453 Multiplication of the members of a whorl (pleiomery) occurs most often in the andrœcium. **1832** LINDLEY *Introd. Bot.* I. ii. 46 By some writers nodi, upon which buds are obviously formed, are called compound, or artiphyllous; and those in which no apparent buds are discoverable, are named simple, or *pleiophyllous. **1858** MAYNE *Expos. Lex.*, *Pleiophyllus*, applied to a plant which bears a great number of leaves without a branch at the axilla, as the *Linum, Abies*, and *Taxus*: pleiophyllous. **1895** *Syd. Soc. Lex.*, **Pleiophylly*, a condition of abnormal increase in the number of leaves growing from a certain point, or in the number of leaflets of a plant. **1890** *Cent. Dict.*, *Pleiosporous. *Ibid.*, *Pleiotaxy. **1895** in *Syd. Soc. Lex.* **1890** *Cent. Dict.*, *Pleiothalamous. **1876** BALFOUR in *Encycl. Brit.* IV. 86/1 The spiral in such cases is called compound, and the vessels **pleiotracheæ.*

pleiocene, pleiohippus: see PLIO-.

pleiomorphy ('plaɪəmɔːfɪ). [f. PLEIO- + Gr. μορφή form + -ια, -Y.] (See also PLEOMORPHY, etc.) In *Bot.* **a.** The occurrence of more than one distinct stage or form in the life-cycle of a species, as in certain heterœcious fungi, which pass through two or three stages. **b.** The state of a flower which is usually irregular, but becomes regular by the multiplication of its irregular elements, so as to form a whorl; = PELORIA. Hence **pleio'morphic** *a.*, exhibiting or characterized by pleiomorphy; **pleio'morphism** = pleiomorphy (sense a).

1890 in *Cent. Dict.* **1895** in *Syd. Soc. Lex.*

pleione (plaɪ'əʊniː). Also **Pleione.** [mod.L. (D. Don *Prodromus Floræ Nepalensis* (1825) 36), f. Gr. Πληιόνη, the name of the mother of the Pleiades.] An orchid of the genus so called, belonging to the family Orchidaceæ, native to mountainous regions of northern India, Burma, and China, and bearing white, pink, or purple flowers, with plicate leaves which, in most species, fall before flowering begins.

1851 LINDLEY & PAXTON *Paxton's Flower Garden* II. 5 The spotted Pleione has long been known to botanists as a species belonging to that Alpine group of so-called Cœlogynes. **1890** W. WATSON *Orchids* li. 424 Pleiones are distinguished by their fleshy pseudo-bulbs, which are only of annual duration. **1930** T. W. BRISCOE *Orchids for Amateurs* iv. 96 Pleiones are deciduous, and the leaves usually fall when the growths are matured. **1961** *New Statesman* 19 May 808/2 Cymbidiums..and pleiones..are cool-house plants. **1975** A. M. COATS *Treasury of Flowers* pl. 117 (*caption*) The Pleiones..are familiar to many gardeners, as they are both beautiful and easy to grow. **1979** *Country Life* 18 Jan. 158/4 Recently taxonomists have lumped together all the omnifarious pleione species under the aggregate specific epithet *P. bulbocodioides.*

pleiotropic (plaɪəʊ'trɒpɪk, -'trəʊpɪk), *a. Genetics.* [f. as next: see -IC.] Pertaining to, displaying, or being pleiotropy. Hence **pleio'tropically** *adv.*

1938 *Proc. R. Soc.* B. CXXV. 138 The analysis of the pathological symptoms given above allows us to bring some order into the multitude of 'pleiotropic' effects produced by our lethal factor. **1956** C. AUERBACH *Genetics in Atomic Age* 104 The gene for waltzing in the mouse acts pleiotropically on behaviour and hearing. Most or all genes have pleiotropic effects, often on such general characteristics as size, fertility, and longevity. **1964** *New Scientist* 17 Dec. 779/3 The streptomycin resistance is 'pleiotropic'—it brings about simultaneously one or more metabolically unrelated nutritional requirements. **1973** B. J. WILLIAMS *Evolution & Human Origins* ii. 30/1 A gene is said to have pleiotropic effects if it affects more than one phenotypic trait. **1974** *Jrnl. Gen. Microbiol.* LXXXI. 165 Mutants in a gene..in *Aspergillus nidulans* pleiotropically affect the utilization of many nitrogen sources.

pleiotropism (plaɪ'ɒtrəpɪz(ə)m). *Genetics.* [f. as next: see -ISM.] = PLEIOTROPY.

1927 *Zeitschr. für Induktive Abstammungs- und Vererbungslehre* XLIII. 331 Plate..proposed the term 'pleiotrop'... Some of the highest authorities in the field of genetics have come to the conclusion that the pleiotropism of the genes is not an exception but rather the general rule. **1943** *Jrnl. Genetics* XLV. 6 A distinction has been made between genuine and spurious pleiotropism. **1970** T. DOBZHANSKY *Genetics of Evolutionary Process* vii. 210 Correlated responses due to pleiotropisms (physiological correlations) may make it impossible to endow a breed.. with combinations of characteristics that would be desirable to man. **1973** B. J. WILLIAMS *Evolution & Human Origins* ii. 30/1 Pleiotropism does not interfere with a Mendelian analysis of inheritance. **1977** *Lancet* 29 Oct. 925/1 Gardner described such a family (no. 109) who also had extracolonic benign growths (fibromas, sebaceous and epidermal inclusion cysts, osteomas) which showed pleiotropism.

pleiotropy (plaɪ'ɒtrəpɪ). *Genetics.* [ad. G. *pleiotrop* (L. Plate 1910, in *Festschr. für R. Hertwig* II. 597), f. Gr. πλείων (see PLEIO-) + τροπή turn, turning: see -Y[3].] The production by a single gene of two or more apparently unrelated phenotypic effects; an instance of this.

1939 C. H. WADDINGTON *Introd. Mod. Genetics* vii. 162 (*heading*) Multiple effects of a factor or pleiotropy. **1957** —— *Strategy of Genes* 208 The more detailed the analysis, the more pleiotropy will be uncovered. **1973** *Nature* 21/28 Dec. 499/2 True pleiotropies of blood group genes are impossible to identify with the relatively crude characterisation of blood group specificities presently available. **1974** *Ibid.* 7 June 528/2 The suppression and temperature sensitivity characteristics were not separable, thus confirming that in each strain a single mutation was responsible for the pleiotropy. **1977** *Lancet* 9 Apr. 786/1 Genes always have more than one effect—a property known as pleiotropy.

pleiotypic (plaɪəʊ'tɪpɪk), *a. Biol.* [f. PLEIO- + TYP(E *sb.*[1] + -IC.] Pertaining to the process whereby a single stimulus can elicit multiple unrelated responses from a living cell.

1971 *Nature New Biol.* 7 Apr. 162/1 Gordon Tomkins has proposed that mammalian cells may have a 'pleiotypic' control system to coordinate changes in the overall levels of synthesis and degradation of RNA and proteins. *Ibid.* 163/2 Dr. G. M. Tomkins (University of California, Medical Center, San Francisco) drew attention to a possible similarity between what he terms pleiotypic effects in mammalian cells and stringent control exhibited by bacteria deprived of nutrients. **1972** *Science* 5 May 486/1 The processes which have thus far been found to be under pleiotypic control are uridine uptake.., RNA synthesis.., polysome formation [etc.].

pleisand, obs. f. PLEASANT.

pleise, obs. f. PLAICE, PLEASE.

pleisour, -ssour, -sure, pleiss, obs. ff. PLEASURE, PLEASE.

Pleistocene ('plaɪstəsiːn), *a.* (*sb.*) *Geol.* [f. Gr. πλεῖστος most (superl. of πολύς much) + καινός new, recent.] Epithet applied at first to the newest division of the Pliocene or Upper Tertiary formation (as containing the greatest number of fossils of still existing species), also called Newer Pliocene; afterwards to the older division of the Post-tertiary or Quaternary, also called Post-Pliocene. Also applied to the animals, etc., of either of these periods. Also *ellipt.* as *sb.* = pleistocene division or formation.

1839 LYELL in *Mag. Nat. Hist.* New Ser. III. 323 In the Appendix to the French translation of my 'Elements of Geology', I have proposed, for the sake of brevity, to substitute the term *Pleiocene* for *Older Pleiocene*, and *Pleistocene* for *Newer Pleiocene.* **1854** BREWSTER *More Worlds* iii. 46 The superficial deposits, or Pleistocene group, viz. all diluvial and alluvial deposits of gravel and other materials. **1861** GEIKIE *E. Forbes* ix. 256 He states..that even the pleistocene, which is a subdivision of the pliocene, needs to be partitioned into a newer and older series. **1873** J. GEIKIE *Gt. Ice Age* xxx. 423 The pleistocene hippopotamus. **1874** LYELL *Elem. Geol.* x. 123 In former editions of this work I divided the Post-tertiary deposits into Recent and Post-pliocene, but this latter term has many inconveniences... I have, therefore, determined for the future to adopt the name of 'Pleistocene', proposed by me in 1839 as a synonym for Newer Pliocene, but which, having been used by the late Edward Forbes as the equivalent of Post-pliocene, has now passed into general use with that signification.

pleistodox ('plaɪstədɒks), *a. nonce-wd.* [f. Gr. πλεῖστος most + δόξα opinion, after *orthodox.*] Holding the opinion of the majority.

1814 COLERIDGE *Lett. to J. P. Estlin* (1884) 109 His proper language as an orthodox, or (if I might coin a more modest expression), a pleistodox..man.

pleistoseist ('plaɪstəsaɪst). [f. Gr. πλεῖστ-ος most + σειστός shaken, σειστής earth-shaker, from σεισμός shock, earthquake.] (See quot.)

1886 MILNE *Earthquakes* i. 10 The isoseismic area in which the greatest disturbance has taken place is called the 'meizoseismic area'. Seebach calls the lines enclosing this area 'pleistoseists'.

pleit, -e, obs. ff. PLAIT, PLATE *sb.*, PLEAD.

plek, pleke, obs. forms of PLECK.

†**ple'mmirrulate**, *a. Obs. rare*[−1]. [ad. It. *plemmirulato* ppl. adj., perh. f. Gr. πλημμυρεῖν to rise like a flood-tide, overflow.] ? Overflowing.

1592 R. D. *Hypnerotomachia* 51 b, An edging of Orient Pearle..euer pressing hir plemmirrulate trammels of hayre [*plemmyrulati supprimeua*].

plemy'rameter. [f. Gr. πλήμυρα = πλήμμυρις flood-tide + -METER.] An instrument for measuring variations of the level of water; *spec.* that devised by Prof. Forel of Lausanne for measuring those of the Lake of Geneva.

1898 G. H. DARWIN *Tides* ii. 22 Having studied seiches with a plemyrameter for some time, Forel used another form of apparatus.

† **'plenal,** *a. Obs. rare.* [ad. med.L. *plēnāl-is*, f. L. *plēn-us* full: see -AL[1].] Full, complete, plenary.

1624 R. DAVENPORT *City Night-cap* III. (1661) 32 Upon the plenal and approv'd report Of your integrity and upright dealing. **1648** EARL OF WESTMORELAND *Otia Sacra* (1879) 77 By which plenall satisfaction, The Vials of his Fathers wrath were stopt.

Hence † **'plenally** *adv.*, fully; † **'plenalty,** fullness.

1631 HEYWOOD *2nd Pt. Fair Maid of West* Ep. Ded., Yours plenally devoted, Thomas Heywood. **1636** —— *Loves Mistris* Addr. to Rdr., Better pleased, or more plenally satisfied. **1660** BURNEY Κέρδ. Δῶρον (1661) 30 The Supream Jewell of the Crown, their Plenitudinem Potestatis, the plenalty of their power.

† **'plenar, plener,** *a. Obs.* (or *arch.*) Forms: 3–6 plener, (4–5 -ere, 5 -air, -or, 5–6 -are, -yer, 7 -eere), 4–6 (9) plenar. (Also 4 pleiner, 4–5 pleyner, *Sc.* planer, 5 planar, 6 playner.) [ME. a. AF. *plener* = OF. *plenier* (Roland), *plener*, *planier* etc., mod.F. *plénier*:—late L. *plēnār-is* (med.L. in Du Cange) complete, f. L. *plēnus* full; see -AR[1]. So also Pr. *plen(i)er*, Sp. *llenero*.]

1. Of an assembly: Composed or consisting of the full number of members; = PLENARY 2; of the place of assembly: Filled, full; of the members: Fully assembled, in full assembly.

c **1290** *Edmund Conf.* 445 in *S. Eng. Leg.* I. 444 Þe chapitle at salesburi i-holde was plener; Alle þe chanouns of þe ordre þudere come fer and ner. *c* **1330** R. BRUNNE *Chron. Wace* (Rolls) 11171 When Arthures court was plener, & alle were comen, fer and ner. **1377** LANGL. *P. Pl.* B. XI. 108 And whan þe peple was plenere comen þe porter vnpynned þe ȝate. **1467–8** *Rolls of Parlt.* V. 623/1 Be cause they were then present more plener in nombre. *c* **1475** *Partenay* 2751 Thys fest plener And ryght delectable.

2. Complete, entire, perfect; = PLENARY 1, FULL *a.* 7.

13.. *Cursor M.* 26164 He þat pouste has al plener. *c* **1385** CHAUCER *L.G.W.* 1603 *Hipsiph. & Medea*, [He] coude of loue al the craft & art pleyner. *c* **1400** *Beryn* 787 Constantynys sone, & of plener age, Was Emperour I-chose. **1430–40** LYDG. *Bochas* VII. ii. (MS. Bodl. 263) 344/2 Bi Augustus plener [*ed.* 1554 plenair] commyssioun. *c* **1440** *York Myst.* xx. 127 And poure haue playnere & playne to say. **1536** *Act 28 Hen. VIII*, c. 7 §9 Full and plenar power and auctoritie. **1614** W. BROWNE *Sheph. Pipe* I. B vij b, To her words credence he gaue pleneere [*rime* cheere]. **1839** BAILEY *Festus* xx. (1854) 333 The spirit takes the plenar vows of truth.

plenargyrite (plɪ'nɑːdʒɪraɪt). *Min.* [mod. (F. v. Sandberger 1882) f. L. *plēn-us* + Gr. ἄργυρος silver + -ITE[1]; cf. MIARGYRITE.] A sulphide of silver and bismuth found near Schapbach in Baden; said to contain more silver than *miargyrite*.

plenarily ('pliːnərɪlɪ), *adv.* [f. PLENARY *a.* + -LY[2].] In a plenary manner: completely, fully.

1596 [see PLENARLY 2, quot. 1570]. **1615** SIR E. HOBY *Curry-combe* iii. 125 Neither do we fully and plenarily receiue the benefit and effect thereof. **1667** WATERHOUSE *Fire Lond.* 23 With more charge, more difficulty, less constantly, less plenarily. **1883** *Manch. Exam.* 7 Nov. 5/3 The priest employed..may not be plenarily inspired.

'plenariness. [f. as prec. + -NESS.]

1727 BAILEY vol. II, *Plenariness*,..fulness.

plenarium (plɪ'nɛərɪəm). Pl. plenaria. [ad. med.L. *plēnārium* in same sense, f. *plēnārius* complete: cf. PLENARY *a.* (*sb.*)] A book or manuscript containing a complete set of sacred writings, e.g. all the gospels or all the epistles.

1908 W. G. COLLINGWOOD *Scandinavian Britain* 243 Bishop Patrick set forth to Iceland 'with wood for building a church, and a plenarium, and an iron bell'. **1911** F. MERSHMAN in *Cath. Encycl.* XII. 164 Plenarium or Plenarius (*Liber*) is any book that contains completely all matters pertaining to one subject otherwise found scattered in several books... The entire mortuary office..is called Plenarium. A complete copy of the four gospels was called an 'Evangelium plenarium'... Some Plenaria gave all the writings of the New Testament, others, those parts of the Sacred Scriptures that were commonly read in the Divine service and bore the name 'Lectionarium plenarium'. **1929** E. C. THOMAS *Lay Folks' Hist. Liturgy* I. xvii. 87 In the form for Consecrating a Church we find..a form for the consecration of a stole and of the Plenarium or Four Gospels as part of the Rite.

† **'plenarly, -erly,** *adv. Obs.* [f. PLENAR, PLENER + -LY[2].]

1. In full assembly, in full number.

c **1290** *Beket* 1502 in *S. Eng. Leg.* I. 149 Þo þe chapitle plenere was, þudere þe king sende to þe Abbotus alle plenereliche. **1390** GOWER *Conf.* I. 21 Nought only upon ten ne twelve Bot plenerliche upon ous alle. **1494** FABYAN *Chron.* VII. 485 In the whiche counsayll it was plenerly determyned that the kynge myght nat gyue ouer the sayd soueryntie without great peryll of his soule.

2. Fully, completely, entirely, perfectly.

1303 R. BRUNNE *Handl. Synne* 11712 He solde hys gode plenerlye. *c* **1325** *Chron. Eng.* 734 (Ritson) So hy dude treweliche Thre yer plenerelyche. *c* **1400** MAUNDEV. (1839) v. 42 Of his ryalle estate & of his myghte I schalle speke more plenerly, whan I schalle speke of the lond & of the contree of Ynde. **1523** SKELTON *Garl. Laurel* 6 Whan Lucina plenarly did shyne. **1570** FOXE *A. & M.* (ed. 2) 1346/2 To assoyle them plenarely [*so edd.* 1576–83; *ed.* 1596 plenarilie] from all their sinnes.

plenarty ('pliːnətɪ). Also 5 -erte, 7–8 -artie. [Late ME. a. AF. *plenerte*, OF. *plenierete* fullness, abundance, f. *plenier*, *plener* complete: see PLENAR and -TY.]

1. *Eccl. Law.* Of a benefice: The state of being full or occupied. Opp. to VACANCY.

1425 *Rolls of Parlt.* IV. 291/1 Hit be lefull to his Patron to make newe Presentation not withstondyng the plenerte of hyme be VI moneths. *a* **1625** SIR H. FINCH *Law* (1636) 197 But against the King plenartie is accounted from the time of induction, and not before. **1791** *Blackstone's Comm.* (ed. 11) III. xvi. 243 When the clerk was once instituted (except in the case of the king, where he must be inducted) the church became absolutely full: so the usurper by such plenarty, arising from his own presentation, became in fact seised of the advowson. **1889** *Dublin Rev.* Oct. 324 The Archbishop ..sent one of his clerks to govern the vacant see and receive all the fees which during the plenarty had been paid to the clerks of the bishop deceased.

† **2.** Completeness, fullness. *Obs. rare.*

1660 WATERHOUSE *Arms & Arm.* 27 All ages and people by a plenarty of consent. **1720** WELTON *Suffer. Son of God* I. v. 88 In the Body of Christ..dwells the whole Plenarty and Fulness of the Godhead.

plenary ('pliːnərɪ), *a.* (*sb.*) Also 6 -ari, 6–7 -arie, 7 -iary. [ad. late L. *plēnāri-us* complete (*plenarium, consilium*, 4th c. in Augustine *Ep.* xliii), f. *plēn-us*: see PLENAR and -ARY[1].]

A. *adj.* **1.** Complete, entire, perfect, not deficient in any element or respect; = FULL *a.* 7; absolute, unqualified: as ***plenary indulgence, power, remission. plenary inspiration***: see INSPIRATION.

1517 TORKINGTON *Pilgr.* (1884) 31 And ther ys Plenarie Remission. **1532–3** *Act 24 Hen. VIII*, c. 12 §1 One supreme head and kynge..institute and furnysshed..with plenari, whole, and entier power. **1630** PRYNNE *Anti-Armin.* 94, I shall adde the concurrent, plenary, and copious attestation of Mr. William Tyndall. **1652** EARL MONM. tr. *Bentivoglio's Hist. Relat.* 161 Hee assured him..of a plenary pardon for all that was past. **1675** tr. *Machiavelli's Prince* (Rtldg. 1883) 245 The Pope might be supplicated..for a plenary indulgence. **1877** FROUDE *Short Stud.* (1883) IV. I. v. 53 A legate..sent with plenary powers to hear the cause.

2. Of an assembly, etc.: Composed of all the members: fully constituted, fully attended: = PLENAR 1.

1532 *Festivall* 191 b, In eche quarter of the yere ones, whan the people is moost plenary in holy chyrche. **1614** T. ADAMS in Spurgeon *Treas. Dav.* Ps. ii. 12 Lord grant..that we may come to the plenary wedding supper hereafter. **1646** BP. MAXWELL *Burd. Issach.* 48 The next plenarie Generall Assembly may *derogare, abrogare, obrogare*, &c. **1662** GUNNING *Lent Fast* 62 Those things..are retained..from plenary, (i.e. general) councils. **1855** MILMAN *Lat. Chr.* IX. v. (1864) V. 290 The King sullenly consented to convoke a plenary Court of his nobles. **1885** *Daily Chron.* 12 Sept. 5/4 Both the sittings were plenary, that is, consisted of the members of all the sections and subsections. **1894** *Daily News* 27 June 5/6 A caucus or plenary meeting of the Democratic groups of the Senate and the Chamber was held.

3. Possessing full powers or authority. *rare.*

1861 *Sat. Rev.* 30 Nov. 547 International law would be a nullity if every commander of a man-of-war were to constitute himself in the first instance a plenary judge, and condemn as contraband whatever he might like to seize on.

4. *Law.* See quot. 1848.

1726 AYLIFFE *Parergon* 152 The Cause is hereby made a Plenary Cause, and ought to be determin'd Plenarily. **1848** WHARTON *Law Lex.*, *Plenary*, full, complete; an ordinary proceeding through all its gradations; opposed to *summary*.

B. *ellipt.* as *sb.* **1.** = Plenary indulgence. *rare.*

1826 SOUTHEY *Vind. Eccl. Angl.* 496 A plenary may be gained every first Sunday of the month for confessing and communicating.

2. *in plenary*: of an assembly, etc.: fully constituted or attended.

1969 D. WIDGERY in Cockburn & Blackburn *Student Power* 122 The infrequency of Council Sessions..and its unwieldy size in plenary means that the Executive alone takes the fundamental decisions about policy implementation and initiation.

3. Anglicized form of PLENARIUM.

1909 *Encycl. Relig. & Ethics* II. 609/1 There were the select passages for Sunday in the so-called Plenaries, Postils, and Books of the Gospels and the Epistles. **1920** M. DEANESLY *Lollard Bible* xii. 318 Of the three late fourteenth century English 'plenaries', or gospels and homilies, one is certainly Wycliffite.

¶ The sense 'Decisive procedure', given by Johnson, and copied in later Dicts., is without foundation. In the quot. which J. cites from Ayliffe *Parergon* 301 'Institution without induction does not make a plenary against the king, where he has a title to present', *plenary* is a misprint for *plenarty*, which Ayliffe has in the correct spelling on the same page and elsewhere; cf. quot. 1791 in PLENARTY 1.

plencher, plensher, var. PLANCHER *sb.*[1]

plene (pliːn), *a. rare*[−1]. [ad. L. *plēnus* full. Cf. PLAIN *a.*[2] of which *plene* was a common form in 15–17th c.] Complete.

1882–3 *Schaff's Encycl. Relig. Knowl.* II. 1430 Rules were laid down concerning..the plene and defective writings.

plene, plenȝe, plenye, obs. ff. PLAIN *v.*

‖ **plene administravit** ('pliːniː ədmɪnɪs'treɪvɪt). *Law.* [L., 'he has fully administered'.] (See quot. 1959.)

1729 G. JACOB *New Law-Dict.* s.v. *Executor*, If an Executor sued by several Creditors, pleads *Plene Administravit* to all at the same Time; and that he hath no Assets *præter* to pay one or two, he will make himself liable to all the debts. **1790** in Durnford & East *Rep. Cases King's Bench* III. 693 If an executor may plead *plene administravit* and neglect to do so, I see no difference between such a case and one where he does so plead and the plea is found against him. **1924** G. S. BOWER *Res Judicata* I. vi. 108 Where a defendant, sued in the character of executor or administrator, omits to plead *plene administravit*. **1959** JOWITT *Dict. Eng. Law* II. 1354/2 *Plene administravit* (he has fully administered), a defence by an executor or administrator that he has fully administered all the assets which have come to his hands.

plener, -e, -ly: see PLENAR, -LY.

plenicorn ('pliːnɪkɔːn, 'plɛnɪ-), *sb.* and *a.* [f. L. *plēnus* full + *cornu* horn.] **a.** *sb.* A quadruped having solid horns; formerly, (in *pl.*) name of a division of ruminants. **b.** *adj.* Having solid horns.

1842 BRANDE *Dict. Sci.* etc., *Plenicorns*, the name of a tribe of Ruminants, including those which have horns composed of an uniform solid osseous substance as the antlers of deer.

pleniloquence (plɪ'nɪləkwəns). *rare*[−1]. [f. L. *plēn-us* full + *loquentia* talking.] Fullness of talk, excessive speaking.

1838 EMERSON in *Corr. Carlyle & E.* (1883) I. xxvi. 174 Though I hate American pleniloquence I cannot easily say no to young men who bid me speak also.

plenilune ('pliːnɪl(j)uːn, plɛnɪ-). Chiefly *poet.* [ad. L. *plēnilūnium*: see below. Cf. It. *plenilunio*.] **a.** The time of full moon. **b.** A full moon.

1432–50 tr. *Higden* (Rolls) VI. 103 Unto the tru knowlege of the kepynge of Ester thre thynges ar to be attendide,..the equinoccialle of ver, the perfite plenilune or fullenesse of the moone, and Sonneday. **1599** B. JONSON *Cynthia's Rev.* v. iii, Whose glory, like a lasting plenilune, Seems ignorant of what it is to wane. *c* **1600** *Timon* IV. i. (Shaks. Soc.) 61 Look to thy braines, least in the plenilune Thou waxe more madde. **1878** SWINBURNE *Poems & Ball.*, *Vis. Spring*, Large nightfall and imperial plenilune.

Hence **pleni'lunal, pleni'lunar, pleni'lunary** *adjs.*, belonging to or resembling the full moon.

1882 E. FITZGERALD *Lett.* (1889) I. 486, I shall try and pay you my *plenilunal due. **1767** A. CAMPBELL *Lexiph.* (1774) 25 A ruddy *plenilunar resplendent countenance. **1845** DE QUINCEY *Coleridge & Opium-eating* Wks. 1859 XII. 92 The wrath of Andrew, previously in a crescent state, actually dilated to a plenilunar orb. **1646** SIR T. BROWNE *Pseud. Ep.* IV. xiii. 228 If we adde the two Ægyptian daies in every moneth, the interlunary and *plenilunary exemptions, the Eclipses of Sunne and Moon.

‖ **pleni'lunium.** *Obs.* [L. *plēnilūnium* full moon, prop. adj. of the full moon (sc. *tempus* time), f. *plēnus* full + *lūna* moon.] = PLENILUNE.

1658 A. FOX tr. *Würtz' Surg.* III. xxii. 287 Piony root.. must be digged in Aprill,..at a plenilunium before the rising of the Sun. **1686** GOAD *Celest. Bodies* I. xviii. 116 The New ☽ brings more such Days than the Plenilunium.

plenipo ('plɛnɪpəʊ), *sb.* Colloquial shortening of PLENIPOTENTIARY.

c **1687** DRYDEN *Let. to Etherege* 12 And both to wives and husbands show The vigour of a plenipo. **1713** STEELE *Englishm.* No. 36. 230 His Envoys and Plenipoes come over publickly. **1823** BYRON *Juan* VI. xcv, Without the aid of prince or plenipo. **1858** O. W. HOLMES *Ant. Breakf.-t.* xi, I would, perhaps, be Plenipo,—But only near St. James.

Hence **'plenipo** *v. intr.*, to act as plenipotentiary.

1890 SARAH J. DUNCAN *Soc. Departure* (1891) 120 A certain foreign minister who returned from special plenipoing.

plenipotence (plɪ'nɪpətəns). *rare.* [f. as next + -ENCE.] Full power or authority.

1649 MILTON *Eikon.* vi, A whole parliament..endued with the plenipotence of a free nation, to make laws, not to be denied laws. **1761–2** HUME *Hist. Eng.* (1806) III. xlviii. 743 Such a plenipotence as none of their ancestors..had ever pretended to. **1884** *Manch. Exam.* 22 Mar. 5/1 What plenipotence we fancied ourselves to possess.

ple'nipotency. *rare.* [f. L. type **plēnipotentia* (prob. in med. or mod.L.), f. *plēnipotens*: see next and -ENCY; cf. POTENCY.] The quality of being plenipotent; full authority.

1624 *Brief Inform. Affairs Palatinate* 52 His Maiestie.. caused a plenipotency or full power to be dispatched by his said Embassadour. **1755** CARTE *Hist. Eng.* IV. 87 This was arrogating plenipotency to themselves.

plenipotent (plɪ'nɪpətənt), *a.* (*sb.*) *rare.* [ad. late L. *plēnipotens, -potent-em* (Priscian *c* 500), f. L. *plēn-us* full + *potens* POTENT.] Invested with or possessing full power or authority.

1658 J. ROBINSON *Endoxa* i. 18 A company of faithful.. may, with a plenipotent Octroy or Concession, claim priviledge. **1667** MILTON *P.L.* x. 405 My Substitutes I send ye, and Create Plenipotent on Earth, of matchless might

Issuing from mee. **1795** SOUTHEY *Let. to G. C. Bedford* 22 Aug., And now will you permit me..to be corrector plenipotent? **1839** J. ROGERS *Antipopopr.* xiii. §1. 284 Convinced that they have God's plenipotent commission.

b. as *sb.* A person possessing full authority; a plenipotentiary.

1818 MILMAN *Samor* 93 Before the assemblage proud Speaks frank and bold that gray Plenipotent.

ˌplenipoˈtential, *a. rare.* [f. as PLENIPOTENCY + -AL[1]: cf. *potential.*] Of or belonging to a plenipotentiary; possessed of full authority.

1663-4 MARVELL *Corr.* Wks. (Grosart) II. 140, I having a plenipotential Letter from his Royal majesty. **1829** SOUTHEY *Sir T. More* II. 349 The chosen and plenipotential committee of literature. **1894** *Q. Rev.* Apr. 479 They had no plenipotential powers.

Hence †**ˌplenipotentiˈality,** the quality of being plenipotential or plenipotentiary.

1650 B. *Discolliminium* 45 All the variations, interpretations, reservations,..evasions, possessions, plenipotentialities and fedifractions, that I..can devise or possibly imagine.

plenipotentiary (ˌplɛnɪpəʊˈtɛnʃərɪ), *a.* and *sb.* [ad. med. and law L. *plēnipotentiārius*, f. **plēnipotentia*: see PLENIPOTENCY and -ARY[1]. So F. *plénipotentiaire* sb. and adj. (Balzac *a* 1654).]

A. *adj.* Invested with full power, esp. as the deputy, representative, or envoy of a sovereign ruler; exercising absolute power or authority.

Often, after French usage, placed after its sb., as *ambassador, envoy, minister plenipotentiary.*

c **1645** HOWELL *Lett.* (1650) II. xliv. 58, I hear the peace twix't Spain and Holland is absolutely concluded by the plenipotentiary Ministers at Munster. **1713** *Lond. Gaz.* No. 5144/6 Thomas Earl of Strafford,..One of Her Majesty's Ambassadors-Plenipotentiary at the Congress at Utretch. **1796** MORSE *Amer. Geog.* I. 332 One of the ministers plenipotentiary of the United States. **1844** H. H. WILSON *Brit. India* I. 223 He was..nominated his Majesty's envoy extraordinary and plenipotentiary.

b. Of or belonging to a plenipotentiary (see B.); absolute, full, unlimited.

1648 *Hamilton Papers* (Camden) 199 Giveing Sir Tho. Fairfax a plenipotentiary comission of the Militia to raise what number and secure and impres on what persons he pleased. **1663** COWLEY *Verses & Ess., Ode Restauration* i, Nor whilst around the Continent, Plenipotentiary beams ye sent. **1793** JEFFERSON *Writ.* (1830) IV. 479 It was given in as plenipotentiary a form as held by any sovereign. **1880** TROLLOPE *Duke's Children* III. ii. 19 A liberal party, with plenipotentiary power, must go on..to the logical conclusion of its arguments.

B. *sb.* A person invested with full, unlimited, or discretionary powers or authority, *esp.* in regard to a particular transaction, as the conclusion of a peace or treaty; an envoy or ambassador deputed by his sovereign to act at his own discretion.

1656 BLOUNT *Glossogr., Plenipotentiaries,* ambassadors.. from their King..sent, to treat and conclude with an enemy or other person upon all or such points as are contained in their Commisssion, etc. **1668** TEMPLE *Let. to Ld. Arlington* Wks. 1731 II. 94, I know not why the Character of Plenipotentiary may not agree with that of Envoy Extraordinary on all Hands. *a* **1715** BURNET *Own Time* (1766) I. 17 The States General..act only as Plenipotentiaries of the several provinces. **1877** FREEMAN *Norm. Conq.* (ed. 3) I. App 643 A document..which..gives ..the names of the plenipotentiaries on both sides.

b. *transf.* and *fig.*

a **1711** KEN *Sion* Poet. Wks. 1721 IV. 328 To chuse some fit Plenipotentiary: Of sacred Hymn I strait made choice. **1850** ROBERTSON *Serm.* Ser. III. v. 71 Not as a plenipotentiary supernaturally gifted to convey a mysterious benefit.

Hence †**ˌplenipotentiˈarian,** a plenipoteniary; **plenipoˈtentiarly** *adv.*, in a plenipotentiary manner; **plenipoˈtentiarize** *v. intr.*, to act as a plenipotentiary; **plenipoˈtentiaryship,** the office of a plenipotentiary.

1654 tr. *Martini's Conq. China* 48 When the Emperour had perused the Treatie, he presently found his *Plenipotentiarian had sold him. **1649** *Bounds Publ. Obed.* 13 Persons plenipotentiarily deputed to conclude for the publique good of the people,..sit at Westminster. **1841** *Fraser's Mag.* XXIV. 737 The other continued to *plenipotentiarise till he..forced his government to dismiss him in disgrace. **1800** SOUTHEY *Let. to Coleridge* 1 Apr., Should you be in Bristol, of course the *plenipotentiaryship is vested in you.

†**pleni-power.** *Obs. rare.* [f. L. *plēnus* full + POWER: prob. rendering a foreign expression, e.g. L. *plēnipotentia*, F. *plein pouvoir*, Ger. *vollmacht.*] Full power or authority.

1700 RYCAUT *Hist. Turks* III. 561/2 That the Proclamation being made in both the Emperors Names, no Passports should be delivered, either from the Germans to the Turks, or from the Turks to the Germans; but that a Pleni-power should be given to the Mediators to grant Passports.

plenish (ˈplɛnɪʃ), *v.* Chiefly *Sc.* Forms: 5 **plenys(s, plennes, 6 planish, -eis, -es, plenisch, -ishe, -iss, 6–7 plenniss, 6– plenish.** [ad. OF. *pleniss-*, lengthened stem of *plenir* (Langtoft *c* 1300) to fill, f. stem *plen-*:—L. *plēnus* full.]

1. *trans.* To fill up, furnish, supply, stock; to replenish. Orig. *Sc.* and *north. dial.*; also general Eng. in 19th c.

c **1470** HENRY *Wallace* VII. 1024 Thai..Plenyst the toune agayne with Scottis blud. **1513** DOUGLAS *Æneis* IV. Prol. 42 Thow plenest paradise, and thow heriet hell. **1528** LYNDESAY *Dreme* 682 This part of Asia, Weill planesit with Cieteis, towris, and townis. *c* **1560** A. SCOTT *Poems* (S.T.S.) xxvi. 9 ȝit thay ar planeist and repleit Of falset and dissait thair sell. **1829** *Examiner* 756/2 The doctor..drew the tureen near to his plate, which he plenished and replenished. **1844** STEPHENS *Bk. Farm* II. 178 On the return of the horses to the stable..they find their mangers plenished with corn. **1854** S. DOBELL *Balder* xxiii. 107 So comes Morn, Plenishes all things, and completes the world.

b. *spec.* To furnish (a house, a farm, etc.). *Sc.* and *north. dial.*

a **1578** LINDESAY (Pitscottie) *Chron. Scot.* (S.T.S.) I. 171 The landis was so waistit..that na thing was plenischit wntill Edinburgh. **1663** SIR G. MACKENZIE *Religious Stoic* xii. (1685) 111 He had plenished his house abundantly. **1680** in A. Laing *Lindores Abbey* xx. (1876) 252 Resolves to plenish a room. ? *a* **1700** in P. Walker *Remark. Passages* (1727) 16 (Jam.), I told you to take no more rooms at Martinmas, than ye will plenish at Whitsunday. **1822** SCOTT *Let. to D. Terry* 10 Nov. in *Lockhart*, Your kind and unremitting exertions..will soon plenish the drawing room. **1825** BROCKETT *N.C. Gloss., Plenish* or *Plennish*, to furnish a house.

†**2.** *absol.* or *intr.* To spread abroad; to fill a vacant space. *Sc. Obs.*

1457 *Sc. Acts Jas. II* (1814) II. 51/2 That na man mak ȝardis nor heggis of dry staikis..nor ȝit of na hewyn wode bot allanerly of lyffand wode þe quhilk may grow & plenyss. **1535** STEWART *Cron. Scot.* II. 87 He rode..Withoutin stop ay on to Tynismouth, And planeist had that tyme ouir all that place.

Hence **ˈplenished** *ppl. a.*, furnished, stocked.

1586 *Reg. Privy Council Scot.* IV. 92 Laying of grite plennist boundis waist. **1856** MERIVALE *Rom. Emp.* V. xlii. 56 Behind so well-plenished an equipage.

ˈplenishing, *vbl. sb.* Chiefly *Sc.* [f. PLENISH *v.* + -ING[1].]

1. The action of filling up or furnishing.

1477 *Charter Jas. III* in Maitland *Hist. Edin.* I. i. (1753) 8 For the Honoure of oure said Burgh and Plennesing of voide Places within the samyn.

2. That with which anything is plenished; equipment, gear, stock, furniture; *esp.* household furniture.

1561 *Reg. Privy Council Scot.* I. 170 The best of the gudis and the plennissing thairof. **1567** *Ibid.* 565 With the haill munitionis, artaillierie, pulder, and uther plenissing being thairin. **1629** RUTHERFORD *Lett.* (1862) I. 45 Ye have to rejoice that ye have now some plenishing up in heaven. **1773, 1814** [see OUTSIGHT[2]]. **1814** SCOTT *Wav.* xviii, Insight plenishing is cumbrous to carry. **1830** MISS MITFORD *Village* Ser. IV. (1863) 223 He settled him in the Pond Farm, with a decent though scanty plenishing. **1876** W. WHITE *Holidays in Tyrol* xxxviii. 279 A chest or two, and a big stool, complete the plenishing.

b. The outfit of a bride, her contribution to setting up house. ***plenishing-wain*** = BRIDE-WAIN.

1876 *Whitby Gloss., Bride-wain*, or *Plenishing-wain*, a waggon loaded with household goods, to be conveyed from the house of the bride's father, to that of the bridegroom. **1877** MRS. OLIPHANT *Makers Flor.* iv, The big *cassone*.. rudely painted, in which..[she] brought home her plenishing when she married. **1888** BLACKIE *Burns* 115 She came bringing her beautiful self along with cartloads of plenishing.

[**plenishing-nail:** see PLANCHING *vbl. sb.* c.]

ˈplenishment. *Sc.* [f. PLENISH *v.* + -MENT.] Plenishing, outfit.

1823 GALT *R. Gilhaize* II. xvi. 157 Sarah's father.. bestowed on us seven rigs, and a cow's grass,..as the beginning of a plenishment to our young fortunes. **1879** W. SYNGE *Tom Singleton* II. viii. 140 A plenishment of new teeth.

plenisphere (ˈplɛnɪsfɪə(r)). *rare*$^{-1}$. [f. L. *plēnus* full + SPHERE *sb.*] A perfect sphere.

1912 E. POUND tr. *Calvacanti's Sonnets & Ballate* 99 Light I do see within my Lady's eyes And loving spirits in its plenisphere.

plenist (ˈpliːnɪst). [f. L. PLEN-UM + -IST.] An adherent of the theory that all space is full of matter, and that there is no such thing as a vacuum: see PLENUM 1.

1660 BOYLE *New Exp. Phys. Mech.* xvii. 122 The Plenists (if I may so call them) do not prove that such spaces are replenish'd with such a subtle Matter as they speak of. **1682** CREECH *Lucretius* Notes (1683) 14 And this Mr. Hobs, a great Plenist, freely confesseth would follow. **1708** *Brit. Apollo* No. 8. 1/2 Cou'd the Plenists prove their plenum. **1899** *Dublin Rev.* Oct. 326 This harmless vacuum was a great thorn in the side of some of the later plenists.

†**ˈpleni-ˌtide.** *Obs. rare.* [irreg. f. L. *plēni-* (in PLENILUNE) + TIDE.] A full tide; a flood-tide.

159. *Greene's Groats-w. Wit, Epitaph* (1617) G iv, Let rowling Teares in pleni-tides oreflow, For losse of Englands second Cicero.

plenitude (ˈplɛnɪtjuːd). Also 5–6 **plenytude.** [a. OF. *plenitude*, ad. L. *plēnitūdo* (Pliny), f. *plēnus* full: see -TUDE.]

1. The condition of being absolutely full in quantity, measure, or degree; fullness, completeness, perfection. (In first two quots. from the Vulgate.)

1432-50 tr. *Higden* (Rolls) IV. 257 The seyenge of thapostle, 'When the plenitude of tyme schalle comme.' **1483** CAXTON *Gold. Leg.* 308/2 Pawle sayth the plenytude of the lawe is loue and charyte. **1570-6** LAMBARDE *Peramb. Kent* (1826) 149 The Pope loosed them..by the plenitude of his Apostolike power from allegiance to their Prince. **1669** GALE *Crt. Gentiles* I. I. i. 2 From [God]..al things at first flow, as from the Plenitude of Being. **1856** DOVE *Logic Chr. Faith* VI. 347 God in the full plenitude of majesty has spoken to man. **1873** SYMONDS *Grk. Poets* xii. 405 That death in the plenitude of vigour is desirable.

b. *Her.* Fullness (of the moon).

1864 BOUTELL *Her. Hist. & Pop.* xi. 71 The Moon is in her Complement, or in her Plenitude, when at the full. **1882** CUSSANS *Her.* 102 When full-faced and shining, it is described as In her Complement or Plenitude.

c. Comparative fullness; amplitude, plentifulness, abundance.

1653 H. MORE *Conject. Cabbal.* I. 206 That there may be the greater plenitude of life in the whole man. **1794** MRS. PIOZZI *Synon.* II. 299 Plenitude of incident without confusion, and of adventure without gross improbability. **1893** C. HODGES in *Reliquary* Jan. 3 The plenitude of stone in the northern counties generally..led to a more frequent use of stone..than in the rest of the country.

2. The condition of being filled, fully occupied, or full of something; fullness; †*spec.* in *Physics* = PLENUM 1 (*obs.*).

1662 HOBBES *Seven Prob.* Wks. 1845 VII. 17 How does the difficulty of separation argue the plenitude of all the rest of the world? **1728** PEMBERTON *Newton's Philos.* 143 A prevailing opinion,..that where no sensible matter is found, there was yet a subtle fluid substance by which the space was filled up; even so as to make an absolute plenitude. **1857** BULLOCK *Cazeaux' Midwif.* 67 The ovaries vary in size.. from the plenitude or vacuity of the uterus.

†**b.** *Bot.* Doubleness of a flower. *Obs.*

1760 J. LEE *Introd. Bot.* I. xx. (1765) 54 The Plenitude, Fullness, is occasioned by the Stamina running into Petals. *Ibid.* 55 Plenitude is chiefly incidental to polypetalous Flowers. **1766** *Compl. Farmer* s.v. *Larkspur*, In order to continue their plenitude, all plants with single flowers should be destroyed so soon as they appear.

†**3.** *Med.* Animal fullness; repletion; plethora.

1533 ELYOT *Cast. Helthe* III. vii, Wherefore the lettynge of bloude is..expedient..also for them, in whom, without plenitude, callyd fulness, inflammations begyn to be in their bodies. **1696** PHILLIPS (ed. 5), *Plenitude*, in Physick, when a Man has too much blood, or abounds with ill humours. **1767** GOOCH *Treat. Wounds* I. 321 Pain or disorder in his head, with symptoms of plenitude. **1802** *Med. Jrnl.* VIII. 67 That in the act of vomiting, the state of the brain is rather that of depletion than plenitude.

†**4.** The condition of being fully supplied with everything; affluence. *Obs.*

1631 R. H. *Arraignm. Whole Creature* xiii. §4. 220 He accounted his best plenitude and plenty without God.. extreame penurie. **1782** MISS BURNEY *Cecilia* VIII. viii, Perverse repining of ungrateful plenitude!

5. Fullness of dress. *humorous nonce-use.*

1837 W. IRVING *Capt. Bonneville* III. 260 Pantaloons of the most liberal plenitude.

Hence **ˌplenitudiˈnarian** = PLENIST; **pleniˈtudinary** *a.*, characterized by plenitude, full; **pleniˈtudinous** (-ˈtjuːdɪnəs) *a.*, well-filled; stout, portly. All *rare.*

1710 SHAFTESB. *Charac.* (1733) I. III. 301 The *Plenitudinarian..brings his Fluid in Play and joins the Idea of Body and Extension. **1647** N. BACON *Disc. Govt. Eng.* I. lviii. (1739) 108 A strange kind of Government.. wherein..a Subject shall have a *plenitudinary power beyond that which his Lord and King had. **1812** L. HUNT in *Examiner* 11 May 289/1 Six-bottle Ministers and *plenitudinous Aldermen. **1840** —— in *Vaubrugh's Wks.*, Miss Hoyden, without delay or 'mistake', is for consolidating everything into the tangible and plenitudinous.

†**ˈplenity.** *Obs.* [ad. OF. *plenité, pleineté*, ad. L. *plēnitās* (Vitruv.).] Fullness, plenitude.

a **1622** AINSWORTH *Annot. Song Sol.* v. 12 Washing in milke, sitting in plenity. **1623** COCKERAM, *Plenitie*, fulnesse. **1678** CUDWORTH *Intell. Syst.* I. ii. 75 [The] Hypothesis of some modern Atomists..that supposes a Plenity.

†**pleˈnorderly,** *adv. Obs. nonce-wd.* [f. L. *plēn-us* full + ORDER + -LY[2].] By all the orders (or estates of the realm).

1650 B. *Discolliminium* 27 That this power is plenipotentiarily deputed: Ergo. But that is not Nationally nor plenorderly deputed: Ergo... Because of the old forme of King, Lords, and Commons, is ceased.

plenshing-nail: see PLANCHING *vbl. sb.* c.

plente, plentee, obs. forms of PLENTY.

plenteous (ˈplɛntɪəs), *a.* (*adv.*) Now chiefly *poetic.* Forms: α. 4–5 **plentifous, -efous, -evous,** 5 **-yfous, -ivous(e, -yvows.** β. (*u* for *v*) 4 **-euus,** 4–5 **-euous(e, -iuous(e, -yuous,** 5 **-euose.** γ. 4 **plentwis,** 5–6 **-uous(e,** 6 **-uus.** δ. 4 **plenteus,** 5– 6 **-ius, -ious(e, -yous, -iose,** 6 **-yus, -eouse,** 6– **plenteous.** (Also 5–6 **plaint-.**) [ME. *plentifous, -ivous*, a. OF. *plentivous* (*c* 1220 in Godef.), *plentevous, -veus, -vious*, extended forms of *plentif*, f. *plenté* PLENTY: see -IVE, -OUS. Reduced through the successive stages *plentivous, -evous, -euous, -uous*, to *-ious, -eous.* Cf. BOUNTEOUS.]

1. Present or existing in plenty or in full supply; abundant, plentiful, copious.

a **1340** HAMPOLE *Psalter* xci. 14 Þai sall be multyplyed in plentifous elde. *Ibid.* cxxix. 7 At him plentevous bying. **1340** —— *Pr. Consc.* 4618 We haf pees and welthe plenteuus. *c* **1375** *Sc. Leg. Saints* xxvii. (*Machor*) 1067 Thru plentwis gyft of goddis grace. **1388** WYCLIF *Ps.* cxxix. [cxxx.] 7 Plenteous redempcioun is at hym. *c* **1400** *Destr. Troy* 341 In yche place of the playne with plentius stremes. *Ibid.* 3153 þere pepull are so plaintiose & placis of strenght. **1526** *Pilgr. Perf.* (W. de W. 1531) 169 b, With the plenteous infusyon of grace. **1540** HYRDE tr. *Vives' Instr. Chr. Wom.* (1592) C c iij, More plentuous advantage shal come hereof. **1554–9** *Songs & Ball.* (1860) 4 A plentyus newe yeres gyfft. **1715–20** POPE *Iliad* VIII. 634 The flaming piles with plenteous fuel raise. **1830** COLERIDGE *Ch. & St.* (1839) 277 A plenteous crop of such philosophers and truth-trumpeters. **1868** LYNCH *Rivulet* CXLVI. iii, He bears the plenteous living grain.

2. Bearing or yielding abundantly; fertile, prolific, productive. Const. *in*, *of*.

1297 R. GLOUC. (Rolls) 531 In god contreie & plentiuous. *c* **1374** CHAUCER *Boeth.* I. metr. ii. 4 The plentyuos Autompne. **1388** WYCLIF *Ps.* lxiv. [lxv.] 14 The..valeis schulen be plenteuouse of wheete. *c* **1400** MAUNDEV. (Roxb.) xii. 51 þe flum Iordan..es riȝt plentifous of fisch. *c* **1400** *Beryn* 1496 So plentivouse this world is of iniquite! **1535** JOYE *Apol. Tindale* (Arb.) 37 John..beyng so plentuouse in telling one thing so ofte and so many ways. **1541** BELLENDEN *Descr. Alb.* ix. in *Cron. Scot.* B vj b, This firth [of Forth] is rycht plentuus of coclis, osteris, muschellis, selch, pellok, merswyne and quhalis. **1603** SHAKS. *Meas. for M.* I. iv. 43 Her plenteous wombe Expresseth his full Tilth, and husbandry. **1682** R. BURTON *Admirable Curios.* 8 The Soil plenteous of Corn, Cattle, Waters, and Woods. **1863** GEO. ELIOT *Romola* xxi, The seasons had been plenteous in corn.

†**3.** Possessing or having abundance; abundantly provided or supplied; rich. *Obs.*

a **1340** HAMPOLE *Psalter* xi. 8 Here as helples & pore bot in heuen as plentefous & riche. *c* **1491** *Chast. Goddes Chyld.* 19 Yf they can thenne well gader togider frute and herr j 6bes of vertues than shall thei be plenteous. **1581** W. STAFFORD *Exam. Compl.* i. (1876) 19 We be not so plentious as we haue bene, the first fruits and tenthes are deducted of our liuings. **1643** PRYNNE *Sov. Power Parl.* II. 55 It had beene long evill ruled by evill Officers, so that the Land could not be plenteous neither with Merchandize, chaffer, nor riches.

†**4.** Giving abundantly; generous, liberal, bountiful. *Obs.*

1377 LANGL. *P. Pl.* B. x. 80 Ne beth plentyuous to be pore as pure charite wolde. **1531** ELYOT *Gov.* III. iv, Be a man neuer so valiaunt, so wise, so liberall or plentuous. **1617** FLETCHER *Valentinian* v. viii, From thy plenteous hand divine, Let a river run with Wine. **1697** DRYDEN *Virg. Georg.* III. 604 With plenteous Hand Bring Clovergrass. *a* **1700** DRYDEN *Hymn, 'Creator Spirit, by whose Aid'* iii, Plenteous of Grace, descend from high, Rich in thy Sevenfold Energy!

†**B.** *adv.* = PLENTEOUSLY. *Obs. rare.*

c **1400** *Destr. Troy* 9504 Pesis of plates plentius mekyll. *Ibid.* 11492 The grekes Were of pepull & pouer plaintius mony.

plenteously (ˈplɛntɪəslɪ), *adv.* Now chiefly *poet.* [f. prec. + -LY².] In a plenteous manner; abundantly, copiously; †bountifully.

1340 *Ayenb.* 51 Uor þet þet me eth and dryngþ to-uore time..Oþer to plentyuousliche. *c* **1350** *Will. Palerne* 180 Briddes & smale bestes wiþ his bow he quelles so plenteousliche. *c* **1400** MAUNDEV. (Roxb.) xvii. 76 Men findez manna mare plentifously and better þan in any oþer place. **1535** COVERDALE *Tobit* iv. 8 Yf thou hast moch, geue plenteously. **1551** TURNER *Herbal* I. B j, This herbe groweth plenteously in my lordes gardyne at Syon. **1667** MILTON *P.L.* VII. 392 Each Soul living, each that crept, which plenteously The waters generated by thir kindes. **1702** YALDEN *Æsop at Court* XIII. iii, He shook his sides, and wish'd them gone, Whilst plenteously they fed. **1855** LYNCH *Rivulet* XVIII. iii, So shall thy good fruits plenteously Hang ripening for us.

plenteousness (ˈplɛntɪəsnɪs). Now chiefly *poet.* [f. as prec. + -NESS.] The quality or condition of being plenteous; abundance, plentifulness; fertility, fruitfulness.

c **1375** *XI Pains of Hell* 47 in *O.E. Misc.* 212 Hou dredful is hel..In þe wych of wepyng is gret plenteuesnes. *c* **1400** [see PLENTEOUSTE]. **1535** COVERDALE *2 Chron.* xi. 23 He gaue them plenteousnes of fode. **1638** JUNIUS *Paint. Ancients* 226 Our cheerfull minde..might..offend rather in too much plenteousnesse. **1785** PALEY *Mor. Philos.* (1818) I. 244 The Supreme Proprietor..who has filled the world with plenteousness. **1864** TENNYSON *En. Ard.* 558 Set in this Eden of all plenteousness.

†ˈ**plenteouste.** *Obs.* In 4 plentuuste, plenteuouste, -owste, 5 plentefoste. [a. OF. *plantuoussete* (Godef.), f. *plentivous* PLENTEOUS: see -TY.] Plenteousness, plentifulness.

a **1340** HAMPOLE *Psalter* xxxv. 9 þai sall be drokynd of þe plentuuste of þi hows. **1382** WYCLIF *Deut.* xxx. 9 God shal make thee to be plenteuous in alle the werkis of thin hoondis, ..in plenteuowste of thin erthe. *c* **1400** *Lanfranc's Cirurg.* 58 þe whiche discrasye þou schalt helpen..with plentefoste [*MS. A.* plenteuousnes] of gode mete.

plenteth, -eythe, -i(e, -ieth, obs. ff. PLENTY.

plentethnes: see PLENTINESS.

plentiful (ˈplɛntɪfʊl), *a.* (*adv.*) [f. PLENTY *sb.* + -FUL.]

1. Full of plenty; furnished with or yielding abundance; copiously supplied; opulent. Now *rare.*

1470–85 MALORY *Arthur* VII. xxxv. 269 Ther is plentyful countrey. **1526** *Pilgr. Perf.* (W. de W. 1531) 225 Plentyfull of al good thynges. **1622** R. HAWKINS *Voy. S. Sea* (1847) 149 The Shore plentiful of Fish and good for refreshing. **1626** BACON *Sylva* § 580 If it be a long winter, it is commonly a more plentiful year. **1646** J. BENBRIGGE *God's Fury* 22 The Scripture is plentifull in avouching this truth. **1726** SHELVOCKE *Voy. round World* 294 There were Inhabitants who lived in a plentiful manner on the product of that Island. **1838** LYTTON *Alice* II. ii, His table plentiful, but plain.

2. Present or existing in great plenty; abundant; copious, ample.

c **1510** *Gesta Rom., Add. Stories* v. 439 Ye..shall fynde yᵉ mercy of God plentefull. **1563** HYLL *Art Garden.* (1593) 6 A fat and loose ground, which..yeeldeth also plentifullest and greatest fruite. **1602** SHAKS. *Ham.* II. ii. 202 They haue a plentifull lacke of Wit. **1695** WOODWARD *Nat. Hist. Earth* IV. (1723) 190 A plentifull Admixture of Sulphur. **1711** STEELE *Spect.* No. 79 ⁋ 3, I have a plentiful Fortune. **1893** R. WILLIAMS in Traill *Soc. Eng.* I. i. 30 There is a plentiful supply of materials. **1898** J. ARCH *Story of Life* x. 254 The 'Thank yous' we got for our pains were not as plentiful as blackberries [cf. PLENTY *a.* 1, quot. 1596].

†**3.** Liberal, generous, profuse, lavish. *Obs.*

1568 GRAFTON *Chron.* II. 626 Which things daylie more and more encreased, by his abundant liberalitie, and plentifull house keeping. **1625** BACON *Ess., Expence* (Arb.) 117 A Man had need, if he be Plentifull, in some kinde of Expence, to be as Sauing againe, in some other... For he that is Plentifull in Expences of all Kindes, will hardly be preserved from Decay.

†**B.** as *adv.* = next. *Obs.*

1563 HYLL *Art Garden.* (1574) 12 By that meanes, dothe the ground yealde the plentifuller.

plentifully (ˈplɛntɪfʊlɪ), *adv.* [f. prec. + -LY².]

1. In plentiful measure or number; abundantly, copiously; in or with abundance.

1553 EDEN *Treat. Newe Ind.* (Arb.) 14 *Lacha* groweth there more plentifully then in any other countre. **1611** BIBLE *Luke* xii. 16 The ground of a certaine rich man brought foorth plentifully [TINDALE, *Geneva*, plenteously]. **1683** DRYDEN *Life Plutarch* 30 He liv'd tho not splendidly yet plentifully. **1727** DE FOE *Syst. Magic* I. iv. (1840) 115 This sort of wise men, of whom the age is plentifully stored at this time. **1849** MACAULAY *Hist. Eng.* vii. II. 229 Money was plentifully contributed to build a meeting house for him.

Comb. **1894** H. NISBET *Bush Girl's Rom.* 196 A well-wooded and plentifully-watered glen.

†**2.** With fullness of treatment or expression; fully, in detail. *Obs.*

1560 DAUS tr. *Sleidane's Comm.* 372 Which shal treat al thinges more plentifully. **1659** PEARSON *Creed* (1839) 161 The second part of the argument..the Scriptures manifestly and plentifully assure us.

plentifulness (ˈplɛntɪfʊlnɪs). [f. as prec. + -NESS.] The state or condition of being plentiful.

1. The condition of having or yielding abundance; affluence; abundant productiveness. Now *rare.*

1537 tr. *Latimer's Serm. bef. Convoc.* A v, What man hath any thynge I praye you, but he hath receiued it of his plentyfulnes? **1585** T. WASHINGTON tr. *Nicholay's Voy.* II. vi. 36 Through the plentifulnesse of the yeere they do deliuer more. **1603** KNOLLES *Hist. Turks* (1638) 153 To breake into Thessaly, with the plentifulnesse thereof to relieue their wants. **1795** J. SULLIVAN *Hist. Maine* 38 There is none which..exceeds it in plentifulness of fish.

2. Abundance, copiousness, plenty.

1555 EDEN *Decades* 266 This sea..poureth furth his plentifulnesse. **1848** MILL *Pol. Econ.* I. xii. § 2 The plentifulness of land seems to me the true explanation. **1905** *Edin. Rev.* July 197 Evident from the very plentifulness of these remains.

plentify (ˈplɛntɪfaɪ), *v.* [f. PLENTY + -FY.]

†**1.** *trans.* To make plenteous; to enrich; to fertilize (soil). *Obs.*

1555 W. WATREMAN *Fardle Facions* II. iii. 123 Wherewith thei so plentifie their grounde, that thei communely receiue two hundred busshelles for a busshell. **1605** SYLVESTER *Du Bartas* II. iii. I. *Abraham* 1145 God his own with blessings plentifies. **1608** R. JOHNSON *Seven Champions* A iij b, After this the land was plentified with Citties.

2. *intr.* To become plentiful. *dial.*

1901 GWENDOLINE KEATS *Tales Dunstable Weir* (*Devon. dial.*) 208 Wi' the coming o' warmer weather and the plentifying o' eggs he would be hiszulf agin.

†ˈ**plentily,** *adv. Obs. rare.* In 4 plenteliche. [f. PLENTY *a.* + -LY².] = PLENTIFULLY *adv.*

1340 *Ayenb.* 105 þe more þe zaule onderuangþ plenteliche þise þri ȝefþes of god.

†**plentiness.** *Obs.* [f. PLENTY *a.* + -NESS. Wyclif's *plentethnes* was either formed irreg. on *plenteth*, early form of PLENTY *sb.*, or (?) an error for **plentifnes*.] = PLENTIFULNESS.

1382 WYCLIF *Gen.* xli. 30 Seuen ȝeres..of greet plente.. whom shulen folwe othere seuen ȝeer of as greet bareynes, that to forgetyng be takun al the bihynd plentethnes [*v.r.* plentenes]. *Ibid.* 47 And plentithnes cam of the seuen ȝeer. **1511** in *10th Rep. Hist. MSS. Comm.* App. v. 394 Corne or grayne..shall be sold and ratiffied acording the plentines of the yere. **1582** STANYHURST *Æneis*, etc., *Ps.* I. iii, Yeelding abundant plentines Of fruict, in harueſt seasoned.

plentious(e, -ius, obs. ff. PLENTEOUS.

plentith(e, -nes, obs. ff. PLENTY, PLENTINESS.

plentitude (ˈplɛntɪtjuːd). Erroneous form of PLENITUDE, influenced by PLENTY *a.* (Prob. in some cases a misprint.)

1615 T. ADAMS *Spir. Navig.* 3 A happy and excellent knowledge given to the saints, and that in a wonderfull plentitude. **1768–74** TUCKER *Lt. Nat.* (1834) II. 22 The plentitude of the universe. **1824** SCOTT *Redgauntlet* ch. i, They were met..by..Peter Peebles, in his usual plentitude of wig and celsitude of hat. **1939** JOYCE *Finnegans Wake* (1964) II. 241 A plentitude of house torts. **1944** AUDEN *For Time Being* (1945) 47 It was therefore only necessary for you to presuppose one genius, one unrivalled I to wish these wonders in all their endless plentitude and novelty. **1978** *Dædalus* Summer 197 This 'natural man' enjoys a plentitude of being.

†**plentive,** *a. Obs. rare*⁻¹. In 4 plentyue. [a. OF. *plentif, -tive* adj., plentiful, f. *plenté* PLENTY: see -IVE.] Yielding abundance, fertile.

c **1330** R. BRUNNE *Chron. Wace* (Rolls) 6444, Y ne sey nere ..A fairer lond, ne more plentyue.

plentivos, -ivous(e, -ues, -uis, -uous(e, etc., obs. ff. PLENTEOUS.

plentuuste, variant of PLENTEOUSTE *Obs.*

plenty (ˈplɛntɪ), *sb.* (*a.*, *adv.*) Forms: see below. [ME. *plenteð, plenteth, plenté*, a. OF. *plentet* (12th c. in Oxf. Ps.), *plented, plenté, -teit*, nom. *-tez, pleynte*, mod.F. dial. *plenté, pleinté*:—L. *plēnitāt-em* fullness, f. *plēn-us* full: see -TY.]

A. Illustration of Forms.

α. 3 plenteð, 4–6 plenteth, 4–7 -ith, 5 -eythe, pleintith, 6 plentieth. β. 4 plentez, -es.

c **1250** *Gen. & Ex.* 3709 Ðes .xii. ðider hem hauen broȝt Of ðe plenteð ðe god ðor gaf. **13..** *Cursor M.* 1359 (Cott.) Quen þe plentez [*Fairf.* plentes] sal cum o time. **1382** WYCLIF *Gen.* xli. 31 To spille the greetnes of plentithe. *c* **1420** *Chron. Vilod.* cxxx, Plenteythe of fysshe. **1461** Plenteth [see B. 2]. **1464** *Rolls of Parlt.* V. 511/1 Shewyng unto hym..the pleintith of his good Lordship. **1542** UDALL *Erasm. Apoph.* 308 b, Yet ye haue holes plentieth in your eares. **1555** Plenteth; *a* **1603** Plentith [see B. I. 2].

γ. 3–6 plente, 4–6 -ee, 5–7 -ie, 6 -i, -ye, 5– -y.

a **1225** *Ancr. R.* 194 Plente of worldliche þinges. *c* **1400** MAUNDEV. (Roxb.) xiv. 63 Grete plentee of wylde bestes. *c* **1440** *Anc. Cookery* in *Househ. Ord.* (1790) 440 Put therto gode plentie of pynes. **1483** *Cath. Angl.* 283/2 Plenty, *abundancia*. **1525** LD. BERNERS *Froiss.* II. 259 They had wynes to drynke plentye. **1550** J. COKE *Eng. & Fr. Heralds* iii. (1877) 57 Fraunce hath of them plente. **1573** G. HARVEY *Letter-bk.* 9 Plenti to furnish up a trim tragedi. **1638** JUNIUS *Paint. Ancients* 228 Plentie..must have a meane.

δ. *Sc.* 4–6 pleynte, plaintie, playntie.

c **1375** *Sc. Leg. Saints* xxvii. (*Machor*) 1488 þai wane froyt of land & se..in gret pleynte. **1500–20** DUNBAR *Poems* xxxiv. 93 Fair claithis and gold plaintie. **1514** BARCLAY *Cyt. & Uplondyshm.* (Percy Soc.) 8 Some man hath pleynte of cunnynge. *a* **1550** *Freiris of Berwik* 369 in *Dunbar's Poems* (S.T.S.) 297 And ȝe sall haif playntie.

B. Signification. **I.** *sb.*

1. a. The state of abounding or being in abundance; plentifulness, abundance. *in plenty*: plentiful, abundant; in abundance, plentifully, abundantly.

1382 [see A. α]. **1551** TURNER *Herbal* I. D ij, Camomyle groweth..in mooste plenty of al, in hunsley hethe. **1600** J. PORY tr. *Leo's Africa* III. 140 Onix-stones..are brought hither in great plentie. **1622** MISSELDEN *Free Trade* (1623) 117 By reason of the plenty of money. **1634** W. WOOD *New Eng. Prosp.* (1865) 107 In the Summer..when Lobsters be in their plenty and prime. **1786** H. TOOKE *Purley* 68 They [abbreviations] have been introduced, in different plenty, and more or less happily, in all Languages. **1852** MISS YONGE *Cameos* II. xxix. 307 Compliments passed in plenty.

†**b.** The state of having abundance. *Obs. rare.*

c **1290** *S. Eng. Leg.* I. 230/402 Heore procratour to hem cam, and was euere in plente, he brouȝte heom mete and drinke i-nouȝ, as he hadde er i-do.

†**c.** Liberality. *Obs. rare.*

c **1410** *Sir Cleges* 24 His mete was fre to euery man, That wold com and vesite hym than: He was full of plente.

†**d.** Full or complete state; fullness, completeness, perfection; = FULLNESS 2 b, 3. *Obs.*

13.. [see A. β]. *c* **1374** CHAUCER *Boeth.* v. pr. vi. 135 (Camb. MS.) Of the whiche lyf it ne myhte nat enbrace the plente in dwellynge. **1382** WYCLIF *Ps.* xxiii. 1 Off the Lord is the erthe, and the plente of it. *c* **1400** *Apol. Loll.* 30 He holdiþ not þe plente ne þe perfeccoun þat falliþ to his consecracoun.

e. In proverbial phrases.

c **1449** PECOCK *Repr.* 184 Experience wole weel schewe that plente is no deinte, and ouermyche homelines with a thing gendrith dispising toward the same thing. **1533** BELLENDEN *Livy* III. i. (S.T.S.) I. 241 Plente generis contemptioun. **1542** RECORDE *Gr. Artes* B ij, Plentie is no deintie, as the common saieyng is. **1600** HOLLAND *Livy* III. i. 88 But plentie, as the manner is, soone caused lothing.

2. a. A full or abundant supply; as much as one could desire; a large quantity or number; abundance *of* something. Also, a large amount, a great deal.

a **1225** [see A. γ]. **1297** R. GLOUC. (Rolls) 139 In þe contrey of kanterbury mest plente of fiss is. **1388** WYCLIF *Acts* xxii. 6 At myddai sudeynli fro heuene a greet plente of liȝt schoon aboute me. *c* **1400** *Destr. Troy* 3433 Gret plenty of pepull, —all the place full. **1555** BONNER *Homilies* 2 That multitude and plenteth of preachers. *a* **1603** T. CARTWRIGHT *Confut. Rhem. N.T.* (1618) 725 By this plentith and overflow of Gods blessings. **1632** LITHGOW *Trav.* v. 184 Scarcity of water, and too much plenty of scorching heate. **1756** T. in *Connoisseur* No. 105 ⁋ 3 He was in a fine open country with plenty of foxes. **1857** MAURICE *Ep. St. John* i. 5 A treatise containing plenty of errors. **1885** FARGUS *Slings & Arrows* 192 We were in plenty of time. **1939** R. STOUT *Some buried Caesar* xiv. 164 The bill was $66.20, which was plenty. **1973** M. YORKE *Grave Matters* I. vi. 35 He must have paid plenty for the place, besides what they're going to shell out in alterations.

b. with *a*: an abundance (*of*). Now chiefly *U.S.*

1627–77 FELTHAM *Resolves* I. xi. 17 If euer I should wish a plenty; it should be for my friends, not me. **1628** FORD *Lover's Mel.* III. ii, That freedom Which heaven hath with a plenty made you rich in. **1726** SHELVOCKE *Voy. round World*

401 This soil produces a plenty of wood. **1787** M. CUTLER in *Life*, etc. (1888) I. 274 The river, where a plenty of several kinds of fish may be caught. **1849** LONGF. *Kavanagh* 71 Remember to let it have a plenty of gravel in the bottom of its cage. **1855** THACKERAY *Newcomes* xxvi, A plenty of smoke was delivered from the council of three. **1857** WHITNEY *Life Lang.* vii. 125.

c. Following a sb. Now *rare*. Cf. II. 1 b.

13.. *Coer de L.* 1488 Styward,.. Bye us vessel gret plenté. Dysschys, cuppys and sawsers [etc.]. *c* **1420** *Liber Cocorum* (1862) 16 Seson hit with sugur grete plenté. **1600** J. PORY tr. *Leo's Africa* VI. 270 They haue goates great plentie. **1841** *Scot. Let.* in Catlin *N. Amer. Ind.* (1844) I. iv. 25 There are cattle a plenty on that spot [cf. b above].

3. a. Abundance of the necessaries and comforts of life; a condition of general abundance; a time of abundance. ***horn of plenty*** = CORNUCOPIA.

1377 LANGL. *P. Pl.* B. VI. 165 Worth neuere plente amonge þe poeple þer-while my plow liggeth. **1393** *Ibid.* C. XVIII. 93 Ther sholde be plente and pees perpetuel for euere. *c* **1430** LYDG. *Min. Poems* (Percy Soc.) 6 To regne in pees, plente, and plesaunce. *c* **1586, 1707**, etc. Horn of plenty [see HORN *sb.* 12 b]. **1601** SIR W. CORNWALLIS *Ess.* II. xlviii. (1631) 305 Profit is divided into the obtaining peace and plentie. **1750** GRAY *Elegy* 63 To scatter plenty o'er a smiling land. **1818** BYRON *Ch. Har.* IV. xlviii, Plenty leaps To laughing life, with her redundant horn. **1855** MACAULAY *Hist. Eng.* xvi. III. 680 Here, therefore, was a plenty unknown in any other part of Munster.

†**b.** *concr.* in *pl.* Things that constitute 'plenty'; the necessaries and comforts of life; provisions; possessions. *Obs.*

1599 SHAKS. *Hen. V*, v. ii. 35 Peace, Deare Nourse of Arts, Plentyes, and ioyfull Births. **1614** C. BROOKE *Epithal. Dinner*, The board being spread, furnisht with various plenties. **1671** BARROW *Serm. Ps.* cxii. 9 Wks. 1687 I. 456 Can we with any content taste our dainties, or view our plenties, while the poor man stands in sight pining with hunger? **1723** DK. WHARTON *True Briton* No. 52 II. 456 The exuberant Plenties of a most beneficent Climate.

4. *attrib.* and *Comb.*, as ***plenty-monger***, ***plenty price*** (cf. *famine price*); ***plenty-scanting*** adj.

1593 NASHE *Christ's T.* Wks. (Grosart) IV. 215 Great plenty-scanting calamities, art thou to await, for wanton disguising thy selfe against kind. **1654** WHITLOCK *Zootomia* 56 Plentymongers (that wanton away their own or Husbands Moneys). **1681** T. JORDAN *London's Joy* 12 My Name Fructifera, The Plenty-Governess of India. **1860** GEN. P. THOMPSON *Audi Alt.* III. cxxix. 88 That corn merchants in a famine ought to sell their corn at plenty price.

II. *adj.* or quasi-*adj.* [app. an idiomatic use of the sb.]

1. a. In predicate. Existing or present in ample quantity or number; in plenty, in abundance; abundant, plentiful, numerous. Now chiefly *colloq.*

a **1300** *Cursor M.* 23460 (Cott.) All oþerkin blisses þat mai be, All þire in þe sal be plente. *c* **1440** *Ipomydon* 1364 There lordis were grete and plente. **1525** LD. BERNERS *Froiss.* II. cxxvi. [cxxii.] 357 At this siege euery thynge was plenty. **1577** NORTHBROOKE *Dicing* (1843) 23 As for sermons, they are not daintie, but very plentie. **1596** SHAKS. *1 Hen. IV*, II. iv. 265 If Reasons were as plentie as Blackberries, I would giue no man a Reason vpon compulsion. **1656** H. PHILLIPS *Purch. Patt.* (1676) 6 Where money is plenty, and land scarce. **1722** DE FOE *Plague* (1756) 100 Where they could not find such, for they were not very plenty. **1779** H. COWLEY *Who's Dupe?* I. 1 When flowers are plenty, no body will buy 'em. **1794** N. PARRY in *Reg. Kentucky Hist. Soc.* (1936) XXXIV. 390 Though much broken with Limestone, which is very plenty through these places. **1803** SYD. SMITH *Wks.* (1850) 32 In the one, land is scarce, and men plenty; in the other, men are scarce, and land is plenty. **1847** LE FANU *T. O'Brien* 84 Wherever kicks and cuffs are plentiest. **1850** *New England Farmer* II. 123 The gopher.. is very plenty on the west side of Mississippi. **1869** 'MARK TWAIN' *Innoc. Abr.* xxxiv. 368 Mosques are plenty, churches are plenty, graveyards are plenty, but morals and whisky are scarce. **1870** LOWELL *Study Wind.* (1886) 22 Poets would be plentier. **1883** R. L. STEVENSON *Silverado Squatters* 235 It is the same, they say, in the neighbourhood of all silver mines; the nature of that precious rock being stubborn with quartz and poisonous with cinnabar. Both were plenty in our Silverado.

b. Following a sb.: = In plenty, in large quantity. *Obs.* exc. *dial.* Cf. I. 2 c.

13.. *Cursor M.* 4811 (Cott.) Bot quen þai sagh þat corn plente, Bliþer men moght neuer be. **1470–85** MALORY *Arthur* VII. xxvi. 253 Gold and syluer plente to spend. **1500–20** [see A. δ]. **1542** [see A. α]. **1614** JACKSON *Creed* III. xvi. §7 The meanest handmaid.. had infallible pledges plenty of his extraordinary calling. **1818** BENTHAM *Ch. Eng. Catech.* 420 Who has conies plenty to dispose of cheap. **1844** E. B. BROWNING *Poems* II. 181 What glory then for me In such a company?—Roses plenty, roses plenty, And one nightingale for twenty? **1922** JOYCE *Ulysses* 609, I seen icebergs plenty, growlers. **1939** —— *Finnegans Wake* (1964) II. 316 Besides proof plenty, over proof.

c. Preceding a sb. = *plenty of* (I. 2). *dial.*

1857 E. BANDEL *Diary* 28 May in R. P. Bieber *Frontier Life in Army* (1932) 138 A splendid country around us: plenty wood and water. **1878** STEVENSON *Inland Voy.* 8 Although there are plenty other ideals that I should prefer. **1899** 'S. RUDD' in Murdoch & Drake-Brockman *Austral. Short Stories* (1951) 111 The water they brought was a little thick.. but Dad put plenty ashes in the cask to clear it. *a* **1907** *Mod. Sc.* There were plenty folk ready to help. I know of plenty places to go to. **1934** D. L. SAYERS *Nine Tailors* 219 There's plenty farms now with the big brewing coppers still standing. **1939** JOYCE *Finnegans Wake* (1964) III. 443 Pretty knocks, I promise him with plenty burkes for his shins. **1942** 'M. INNES' *Daffodil Affair* II. 47 I've known plenty men turn queer there. **1969** G. GREENE *Travels with my Aunt* I. ix. 93 Leopard Society in Sierra Leone. They kill plenty people. **1973** *Sunday Express* (Trinidad) (Suppl.) 1 Apr. 12/3 When all dem fellas gambling and heap up plenty money, we.. bawl out 'Police!'

†**2.** Characterized by or having abundance; abundantly supplied. *Obs. rare.*

1570 *Henry's Wallace* VIII. 990 *note*, Schir, be ye gydyt be me, The bowndandest [*v.r.* plentiest] part off Ingland ye sall se. **1583** STUBBES *Anat. Abus.* II. (1882) 4 Is this country fruitfull, and plenty of all things, or barren, and emptie?

3. Excellent. *slang.*

1933 *Fortune* Aug. 47/1 In sum, Mr. Brown plays *plenty trombone* or, as his friend suggested, a *gang o'horn.* **1941** R. P. SMITH *So it doesn't Whistle* 53 When they want to say a man's good, they say he plays plenty sax or plenty drums. **1970** C. MAJOR *Dict. Afro-Amer. Slang* 92 *Plenty*, good, excellent.

III. quasi-*adv.* Abundantly. *colloq.*

1842 J. AITON *Domest. Econ.* (1857) 331 A leaden collar for the stick, with the hole in the collar plenty large enough. **1884** H. COLLINGWOOD *Under Meteor Flag* 87 They're plenty large enough. **1908** M. H. MORGAN *How to dress Doll* (1973) xii. 85 Cut the hood.. making it plenty large enough to slip on easily over Dolly's head. **1934** J. M. CAIN *Postman always rings Twice* vi. 53, I was plenty blue around the gills. **1939** JOYCE *Finnegans Wake* (1964) II. 311 And plenty good enough, neighbour Norreys, every bit and grain. **1945** *Sun* (Baltimore) 13 June 8-O/7 Pavot just had the speed and the stamina, and turned it on plenty. **1956** B. HOLIDAY *Lady sings Blues* (1973) iii. 35 Benny Goodman came around plenty, too, and eventually he asked me to make my first record with him. **1970** *New Yorker* 3 Oct. 32/1 You are wrong—but plenty. **1973** *Times* 27 July 8 It was not my business. I was plenty busy with other things. **1974** R. M. PIRSIG *Zen & Art of Motorcycle Maintenance* III. xxvi. 306 This notebook gets plenty grease-smeared and ugly.

plentyfous, -y(o)us, -yvous(e, -yvows, obs. ff. PLENTEOUS.

‖**plenum** (ˈpliːnəm). [L., neut. of *plēnus* adj. full (sc. *spatium* space): cf. *vacuum* empty (space).]

1. a. *Physics.* A space completely filled with matter; *spec.* the whole of space regarded as being so filled; opposed to VACUUM *sb.*

1678 CUDWORTH *Intell. Syst.* I. i. 9 Leucippus and his Companion Democritus make the first Principles of all things to be *Plenum* and *Vacuum* (Body and Space). **1714** *Let. fr. Layman* (ed. 2) 7 A Government can't rightfully restrain a Man's professing the Belief of a *Vacuum* or a *Plennum.* **1727–41** CHAMBERS *Cycl.* s.v., The Cartesians adhere firmly to the doctrine of an absolute *plenum.* **1747** FRANKLIN *Lett.* Wks. 1840 V. 191 Here we have a bottle containing at the same time a *plenum* of electrical fire, and a *vacuum* of the same fire. **1822** R. HALL *Serm.* Wks. 1833 VI. 13 In a perfect *plenum*, motion would be impossible. **1827** J. FAREY *Treat. Steam Engine* I. vi. 447 There is.. a plenum of steam in one compartment, and a vacuum, or exhaustion in the other. **1876** C. SLAGG *Sanitary Wk.* IX. 102 The motion of the pan.. disturbs the equilibrium between the air-pressure in the receiver and the outside, causing at times a partial vacuum and at other times a plenum of air in the receiver. **1887** *Encycl. Brit.* XXII. 565/1 From the astronomers the Stoics borrowed their picture of the universe,—a *plenum* in the form of a series of layers or concentric rings, first, the elements, then the planetary and stellar spheres, massed round the earth as centre. **1956** E. H. HUTTEN *Lang. Mod. Physics* iii. 90 In Newton's theory it [*sc.* the aether] plays no rôle save to help visualisation: the victory of the Cartesian conception of space as a plenum as against the Aristotelian void. **1972** *Sci. Amer.* Apr. 115/2 It is not the ether as a medium that is denied by Einstein... We can deny only the Newtonian properties of the ether, in particular the linear addition of velocities. Quantum electrodynamics builds a real plenum in space.

b. *transf.* A condition of fullness; a full place.

1795 SOUTHEY *Lett. fr. Spain* (1799) 6 This.. was followed by some excellent chocolate, and I soon established a plenum in my system. **1878** GEO. ELIOT *Coll. Breakf. P.* 117 An ache, a need That spaceless stays where sharp analysis Has shown a plenum filled without it. **1949** E. POUND *Pisan Cantos* lxxvii. 61 Mind come to plenum when nothing more will go into it.

2. A full assembly; a meeting of a legislative body, conference, association, etc., at which all the members are expected to be present; *spec.* a meeting of all the members of a communist party committee; †in Sweden, a meeting of one of the legislative chambers (*obs.*).

1772 *Town & Country Mag.* 50 Stokholm Dec. 6 In the plenum held yesterday, the inferior orders made no alteration in the resolution they had taken of adopting the royal capitulation with the projected changes. **1772** *Hartford Merc.* Suppl. 18 Sept. 3/3 The Marshal of the Diet opened the Plenum of the Nobility with a long panegyric upon the King. **1885** LD. LOFTUS in *Pall Mall G.* 6 May 2/1 All colonial questions in common to the empire would be discussed by the Plenum, but would have to be sanctioned by the Imperial Parliament before receiving the Queen's sanction. **1899** *Daily News* 12 June 9/1 Germany.. will.. only give her final decision when the Pauncefote scheme, with the inevitable amendments, comes before the plenum. **1948** J. TOWSTER *Political Power in U.S.S.R.* x. 189 The plenums of the village and city soviets electing their own executive organs. **1950** D. W. BROGAN *Era of Franklin D. Roosevelt* xv. 315 [The American Communist] regional party meetings had the strange title of 'plenums'. **1956** *Ann. Reg. 1955* 234 The Third Plenum of the Central Committee of the P.Z.P.R., held in Warsaw from 21 to 24 January. **1965** *New Statesman* 9 Apr. 566/2 At the recent Plenum, the first since Mr K was ousted, Ilyichev was booted upstairs as Deputy Foreign Minister. **1966** *Ibid.* 29 July 158/1 Ten years ago the man who failed Mao over the speed of collectivisation simply did not get promoted; today's failures suddenly find themselves dismissed and denounced, apparently without even the 'due process' of a central committee plenum. **1974** T. P. WHITNEY tr. *Solzhenitsyn's Gulag Archipelago* I. I. x. 417 Bukharin.. willingly assured the Plenum of his repentance, and immediately abandoned his hunger strike.

3. a. *attrib.*, as ***plenum method***, ***system***, a system of artificial ventilation in which fresh air, forced into the building to be ventilated, drives out the vitiated air. Also applied to things connected with this method (which is used also for heating and air-conditioning).

1844 D. B. REID *Illustr. Theory & Pract. Ventilation* II. iii. 121 Plenum ventilation.. can be sustained only by the constant use of machinery. **1888** J. A. EWING in *Encycl. Brit.* XXIV. 160/2 A broad distinction may be drawn between what are sometimes called vacuum and plenum methods of artificial ventilation. **1894** J. KEITH *Houses of Parl.: Rep. Heating & Ventilation* 3 The action of the Plenum fan.. in blowing in the fresh air upwards through the grated floor of the Chamber. **1903** *Architect* 24 Apr. 276/2 The ventilation of the hospital was secured by natural, as opposed to artificial, means, such as that usually called the Plenum system. **1934** H. M. VERNON *Princ. Heating & Ventilation* ix. 177 A comparison of some thousands of observations made in factories ventilated by plenum air and by natural means showed very little defect of humidity in the plenum factories. **1948** T. BEDFORD *Basic Princ. Ventilation & Heating* xii. 198 In most of the plenum installations found in industry the air is untreated except that it is warmed in cold weather. **1967** W. P. JONES *Air Conditioning Engin.* xvi. 428 The primary air delivered by the nozzles escapes from the room through a plenum relief grille. **1968** *New Scientist* 7 Mar. 517/1 This [underwater] tunnel was driven by traditional methods, and the 'plenum' method (using compressed air behind the tunnelling shield) was not then known. **1978** LD. DROGHEDA *Double Harness* xiii. 143 We had allowed for proper air conditioning... Instead we installed a horrible thing called plenum ventilation, which warmed the air in winter, filling the offices with smuts.. but failing to cool it in summer.

b. (Not *attrib.*) = *plenum chamber* (*a*).

1940 W. H. CARRIER et al. *Mod. Air-Conditioning* xviii. 425 The fan.. is permitted to discharge into a plenum of section area at least ten times that of the fan discharge. **1970** *Toronto Daily Star* 24 Sept. 40/1 (Advt.), Humidifier... Coated pans fit sloped/vertical plenums. **1975** CROOME-GALE & ROBERTS *Airconditioning & Ventilation of Buildings* vii. 272 There are three sources of pressure change within the plenum which must be kept under control to ensure uniform plenum pressure.

4. Special Combs.: **plenum chamber**, (*a*) in some plenum systems, an enclosed space into which the outside air is forced (after any conditioning) and from which ducts lead to the various outlets inside the building; (*b*) any analogous enclosure in which the pressure is maintained above that of the atmosphere by the forcing in of air, as in some air-cooled engines, a ram-jet, or a hovercraft; **plenum space** = *plenum chamber* (*a*).

1908 A. G. KING *Pract. Steam & Hot Water Heating* xxi. 227 Separate ducts may be arranged to connect the main hot-air supply with the rising flues, or the heated air.. may be discharged under a slight pressure into a *plenum chamber with which all supply pipes or warm-air ducts are connected. **1949** *Aircraft Engin.* Nov. 346/2 A disadvantage is that the pressure of the combustion chambers raises the temperature of the air in the plenum chamber, with a slight loss of power. **1959** *Motor* 30 Sept. 236/1 The entire engine, enclosed in the pressed-steel plenum chamber, is exposed to the cooling air, which escapes through vents below and behind. **1965** D. HERBERT *How to design & install Warm Air Heating* iii. 47 A concrete or brick foundation should be laid to provide a flat and level base for the plenum chamber, which is that part of the heater to which the ducts are connected. **1967** *New Scientist* 31 Aug. 435/1 The cushion of air on which a hovercraft rides is created continuously by a flow of air delivered through ducts, which empty themselves into the plenum chamber by nozzles equally spaced around its edge. **1975** M. J. NUNNEY *Automotive Engine* v. 175 The cooling air flow entering the plenum chamber from the fan is directed downwards over the cylinders and cylinder heads. **1916** C. L. HUBBARD *Ventilation Hand Bk.* ix. 154 The flues connecting the *plenum space with the registers are.. concealed in the leg of the pew. **1975** CROOME-GALE & ROBERTS *Airconditioning & Ventilation of Buildings* vii. 278 The ventilated ceiling system is an all-air system which delivers supply air through .. ductwork to a plenum space over a suspended ceiling, so that a relatively small plenum pressure may be used to evenly distribute the air through the ventilated ceiling to the room below.

pleny-: see PLENI-.

pleny(e, -yie, -ȝie, obs. Sc. ff. PLAIN *v.*; hence **plenyhand, plenȝeand** *pr. pple.*: see PLAINAND.

plenyie, plenȝie, *sb. Sc.* [f. *plenȝie*, Sc. form of PLAIN *v.*] Complaining, grumbling.

1819 W. TENNANT *Papistry Storm'd* (1827) 107 He spak, and instant a' the senzie Did ratifie it without plenzie.

pleo, obs. erron. form of PILAU.

pleochroic (pliːəʊˈkrəʊɪk), *a. Cryst.* [f. *pleo-*, PLEIO- + Gr. χρώς complexion, colour, -χρο-ος coloured + -IC: cf. DICHROIC.] Showing different colours when viewed in two or in three different directions (*dichroic* or *trichroic*), as certain double-refracting crystals. ***pleochroic halo***, each of a series of concentric dark-coloured circles seen in sections of certain minerals and having a radioactive inclusion at their centre; usu. *pl.*

1864 WEBSTER, *Pleochroic.* **1868** DANA *Min.* (ed. 5) 212 Epidote... Var.. 3. Withamite. Carmine-red to straw-yellow: strongly pleochroic; the colour as seen through in one direction, deep crimson, in another transverse, straw-yellow. **1894** *Naturalist* 68 Pleochroic haloes, surrounding minute zircon crystals, are seen in both micas. **1909** F. P. MENNELL *Introd. Petrol.* ix. 57 'Pleochroic halos'.. often occur round crystals so small as otherwise to pass unnoticed. **1926** R. W. LAWSON tr. *Hevesy & Paneth's Man. Radioactivity* xxvi. 216 (*heading*) Age determination from the intensity of coloration of pleochroic haloes. **1972** M. H. BATTEY *Mineral. for Students* iii. 93/2 Small crystals of zircon, containing thorium, embedded in biotite, may by their α-radiation produce an intensely pleochroic halo round the zircon grain.

So **pleochroism** (pliːˈɒkrəʊɪz(ə)m), the quality of thus exhibiting different colours; dichroism or trichroism; **pleochroitic** (-krəʊˈɪtɪk) *a.* [irreg., after *dendritic*, etc.], of or pertaining to pleochroism: **pleochroˈmatic** *a.* [see CHROMATIC] = *pleochroic*; **pleoˈchromatism** = *pleochroism*; **pleochroous** (pliːˈɒkrəʊəs) *a.* = *pleochroic*.

1857 WHEWELL *Hist. Induct. Sc.* (ed. 3) III. 542 Experiments on the *pleochroism of minerals. **1886** *Builder* 24 Apr., Dichroism, or pleochroism, practically never occurs in crystals belonging to the cubic system. **1879** RUTLEY *Stud. Rocks* vii. 58 Determining the position of the *pleochroitic maxima. **1864** WEBSTER, **Pleochromatic* ..**Pleochromatism*..**Pleochroous*.

pleocytosis (pliːəʊsaɪˈtəʊsɪs). *Path.* [f. *pleo-*, PLEIO- + -CYT(E + -OSIS.] The presence of abnormally many cells, *spec.* of lymphocytes in the cerebro-spinal fluid.

1911 STEDMAN *Med. Dict.* 681/1 *Pleocytosis*, lymphocytosis in the cerebrospinal fluid in syphilitic and parasyphilitic diseases of the central nervous system. **1924** BROWNING & MACKENZIE *Recent Methods in Diagnosis & Treatment of Syphilis* (ed. 2) xvi. 304 Pleocytosis is found in practically all acute and chronic inflammatory processes affecting the meninges. **1976** *Lancet* 4 Dec. 1222/1 The cerebrospinal fluid in patient 3 showed pleocytosis (23 mononuclear cells/mm).

pleodont (ˈpliːədɒnt), *a.* (*sb.*) *Zool.* [f. Gr. *πλέος, -ως* full + *ὀδούς, ὀδοντ-* tooth.] Solid-toothed, as certain lizards: opp. to *cœlodont*. **b.** *sb.* A solid-toothed lizard.

1840 *Penny Cycl.* XVIII. 252/1 The Pleodonts are divided into two.. groups: the first with a compressed tail.. as in the Crocodiles; the other with the tail perfectly conical.

pleoi, obs. form of PLAY.

pleomastia, -mazia: see PLEIO-.

pleomorphic (pliːəʊˈmɔːfɪk), *a.* [f. *pleo-*, PLEIO- + Gr. *μορφή* form + -IC.] Having more than one form: (*a*) *Biol.*, exhibiting different forms at different stages of the life-history, as certain bacteria and parasitic fungi; pleiomorphic; (*b*) *Chem.* and *Min.* crystallizing in two or more fundamentally different forms; polymorphic. So **pleoˈmorphism**, the fact or condition of thus exhibiting a plurality of forms: (*a*) = pleiomorphism; (*b*) = polymorphism; **pleoˈmorphist**, an advocate of a theory of pleomorphism; **pleoˈmorphous** *a.* = *pleomorphic*; **ˈpleomorphy** = *pleomorphism*.

1886 E. R. LANKESTER in *Nature* 4 Mar. 413/2, I gave the name *Bacterium rubescens* to this *pleomorphic, or, as I termed it, 'Protean', species. **1864** WEBSTER, **Pleomorphism*, the property of crystallizing under two or more distinct fundamental forms,.. said of various substances, as carbon, which occurs in octahedral and related forms in the diamond, and in hexagonal prisms in graphite. **1876** tr. *Wagner's Gen. Pathol.* (ed. 6) 86 Upon this depends the so-called pleomorphism. **1884** *Nature* 4 Sept. 433/2 The then recent discoveries of Pleomorphism and the reproductive organs.. were leading mycologists to suspect that a reproductive process exists in the case of all the higher Fungi. **1887** *Athenæum* 6 Aug. 184/3 When De Bary discovered and demonstrated the wonderful fact of heterœcism.. it is not astonishing that many saw in this the way to crown the wildest conjectures of the *pleomorphists of the day. **1864** WEBSTER, **Pleomorphous*, having the property of pleomorphism. **1882** VINES *Sachs' Bot.* 232 The erroneous theory of so-called *Pleomorphy among Fungi was the result of a defective perception of the true nature of the different kinds of reproductive organs on which the common name of Spore had been bestowed.

‖**pleon**[1] (ˈpliːən). *Zool.* [Arbitrarily f. Gr. *πλέων*, pr. pple. of *πλεῖν* to swim, sail: cf. PEREION.] A name for the abdomen in Crustacea, as bearing the swimming limbs (see PLEOPOD). Also applied by Owen to the tail-spine or telson in the king-crab, etc., considered as representing the abdomen.

1855 C. SPENCE BATE in *Rep. Brit. Assoc.* (1856) 27 Abdominal segments (or pleon). (*Note*), From *πλέω*, navigo: pleon, part which supports the swimming legs. **1873** OWEN *Anat. King Crab* 9 The tail-spine ('pleon' and 'telson'..) nearly equals in length the two antecedent divisions. *Ibid.* 44 In the development of *Limulus*, the pleon or tail-spine (= pygidium) was the last to appear. **1888** *Challenger Rep.* XXIX. I. 652 The feeble structure of the mouth-organs and of the after-part of the pleon.

Hence **ˈpleonal**, **ˈpleonic** *adjs.*, pertaining to the pleon (in quots. the telson of the king-crab).

1873 OWEN *Anat. King Crab* 26 The posterior or 'pleonic' artery.. has more definite tunics and holds a longer course. *Ibid.* 48 Pleonic plexus.. Pleonic artery.. Pleonal nerve, or continuation of neural cord.

pleon[2] (ˈpliːən). *Bot.* [a. Gr. *πλέον, -ων*, neuter of *πλέος, -ως* full: cf. L. PLENUM.] A term proposed by Nägeli for an aggregate of molecules which cannot be increased or diminished in size, without changing its chemical nature.

1882 VINES *Sachs' Bot.* 664 *note* 1 It will be noted that the Atom, Molecule, and Pleon are chemical ideas, whereas the Micella and Micellar Aggregate are purely physical. **1885** GOODALE *Physiol. Bot.* (1892) 212 The terminology now proposed by Nägeli applies the word *pleon* to those aggregates of molecules which cannot be increased or diminished without changing their chemical nature.

pleonasm (ˈpliːənæz(ə)m). Formerly in Lat. form **pleoˈnasmus**. [ad. L. *pleonasmus* (Mart.), a. Gr. *πλεονασμός*, f. *πλεονάζειν* to be superfluous or redundant, also in Gram. to add superfluously, f. *πλέον* more, compar. of *πολύ* much. Cf. F. *pléonasme* (1613).]

1. *Gram.* and *Rhet.* The use of more words in a sentence than are necessary to express the meaning; redundancy of expression (either as a fault of style, or as a figure purposely used for special force or clearness); with *a* and *pl.*, an instance of this, or the superfluous word or phrase itself.

1586 A. DAY *Eng. Secretary* II. (1625) 82 *Pleonasmus*, where, with words seeming superfluous, we doe increase our reasons, as thus, With these eares I heard him speake it. **1589** PUTTENHAM *Eng. Poesie* III. xxii. (Arb.) 264 The first surplusage the Greekes call *Pleonasmus*, I call him (too full speech) and is no great fault. **1610** HEALEY *St. Aug. Citie of God* (1620) 15 Some thinke the preposition *επί* to be here a Pleonasme.. and that *σκοπος* and *ἐπίσκοπος* is all one. **1621** BURTON *Anat. Mel.* Democr. to Rdr. 12, I require a favourable censure of all faults omitted, harsh compositions, pleonasms of words, tautological repetitions, &c. **1681** R. WITTIE *Surv. Heavens* 28, I take it to be a Pleonasm, a Figure frequently used in Scripture. **1741** WARBURTON *Div. Legat.* II. 556 The genius of the Hebrew tongue, which so much delights in pleonasms. **1860** GEN. P. THOMPSON *Audi Alt.* III. cxiv. 45 What the energetic pleonasm of our ancestors denominated 'a false lie'.

†**b.** *Gram.* The addition of a superfluous (or apparently superfluous) letter or syllable to a word. *Obs. rare.*

1678 PHILLIPS (ed. 4), *Pleonasm*, in Grammar it is the adding of a Letter or Syllable, either to the beginning of a word, and is then called Prosthesis, or to the middle, and is then called Epenthesis, or to the end, and is then called Paragoge. **1763** SWINTON in *Phil. Trans.* LIV. 131 A pleonasmus or redundancy of מ having not been antiently uncommon.

2. *gen.* Superfluity, redundancy, excess; something superfluous or redundant. In mod. use only *fig.* from 1.

1617 PURCHAS *Pilgrimage* (ed. 3) 609 If it come short of the Turke in Geometricall dimension of ground, it is with a great pleonasme supplyed by the fertilitie of his Soyle, and in the vnion of all his Territories. **1673** *Indulgence not to be Refused* 3 It is but a pleonasme or overflow of that great kindness. **1836–7** SIR W. HAMILTON *Metaph.* (1877) I. xix. 369 This hypothesis is not only a psychological solecism, it is, likewise, a psychological pleonasm; it is at once illegitimate and superfluous. **1855** MISS COBBE *Intuit. Mor.* 19 This great school of souls would be a superfluity, a pleonasm in creation.

b. *Anat.* and *Path.* A growth or formation in excess of the normal, in size or number of parts.

1858 MAYNE *Expos. Lex.*, *Pleonasmus. Med.*, *Pathol.*, *Physiol.*, term for a faulty formation, with a stronger growth, or an over-number or over-quantity of parts: a pleonasm. [**1895** *Syd. Soc. Lex.*, *Pleonasmus.*]

†**pleoˈnasmic**, *a.* *Obs. rare.* [ad. F. *pléonasmique* (Cotgr.), f. *pléonasme*: see -IC.]

1656 BLOUNT *Gl.*, *Pleonasmick*, superfluous, redundant.

So †**pleoˈnasmical** *a.*

a **1693** *Urquhart's Rabelais* III. xxxviii, Pleonasmical fool.

pleonast (ˈpliːənæst). *rare*$^{-1}$. [f. Gr. type **πλεοναστής*, agent-n. f. *πλεονάζειν*; see PLEONASM.] One who uses pleonasm.

1863 READE *Hard Cash* II. xxv. 120 The mellifluous pleonast.. oiling his paradox with fresh polysyllables, to make it slip into the Banker's narrow understanding.

pleonaste (ˈpliːənæst). *Min.* Also **pleonast**. [a. F. *pléonaste* (Haüy 1801), ad. Gr. *πλεοναστός* abundant, f. *πλεονάζειν*; see PLEONASM.] A synonym of CEYLONITE, a variety of spinel.

(From the multitude of faces of the crystal, each solid angle of the octahedron being often replaced by four faces.)

1804 R. JAMESON *Syst. Min.* I. 79 The ceylanite of La Metherie or pleonast of Haüy. **1831** BREWSTER *Optics* xvi. 139 Black pleonaste and obsidian afford examples of solid substances which absorb all the colours of the spectrum proportionally. **1897** *Edin. Rev.* Oct. 342 The almost black pleonaste.. is used sometimes for mourning jewellery.

pleonastic (pliːəˈnæstɪk), *a.* [f. Gr. type **πλεοναστικ-ός*, f. *πλεοναστ-ός*: see prec. So F. *pléonastique.*] **a.** *Gram.* Characterized by pleonasm; using more words than are necessary (as a sentence, a speaker, or writer); constituting pleonasm, superfluous, redundant (as a word or phrase).

1778 BP. LOWTH *Transl. Isaiah* (ed. 12) Notes 390 A pleonastic pronoun. **1797** *Monthly Mag.* III. 11 *Μη*..not; after verbs of contradicting, or denying, it is pleonastic. **1879** FARRAR *St. Paul* I. 519 *note*, A mere pleonastic phrase for 'in the direction of the sea'. **1898** H. SWEET *New Eng. Gram.* II. 54 The pleonastic genitive, as in *he is a friend of my brother's*, is generally partitive = 'one of the friends of my brother'. **1947** [see INTERLINGUISTICS]. **1951** E. H. STURTEVANT *Compar. Gram. Hittite Lang.* (ed. 2) ii. 23 Pleonastic Vowels. In Akkadian, vowels are frequently written double (*U-UL* 'not', *BEE-EL* 'lord'). **1972** W. LABOV *Language in Inner City* iv. 146 The general nonstandard rule which operates here can be written as a simple pleonastic transformation.

b. *gen.* or *fig.* Done to excess or superfluity.

1876 E. MELLOR *Priesth.* iv. 164 If.. the priests who both eat the wafer and drink the cup have not two full and perfect sacraments.. if they have and derive any benefit from such a pleonastic sacrament. **1894** A. BIRRELL *Ess.* xvi. 177 His bonâ-fide character.. has been roughly condemned as pleonastic.

So †**pleoˈnastical** *a.* = prec.; **pleoˈnastically** *adv.*, in a pleonastic manner, with pleonasm.

1653 ASHWELL *Fides Apost.* 17 They esteemed it essentiall to these, but pleonasticall unto those. **1657** J. SMITH *Myst. Rhet.* 187, 1 Joh. I. i, We have seen with our eyes... These Pleonastical inculcations are not vain, but serve to work things the better upon our hard hearts. **1725** BLACKWALL *Sacr. Classics* (1727) I. 142 The noblest classics use this particle pleonastically. **1881** *St. James's Gaz.* 1 Apr. 11 People who are ignorant of the good old word 'mere' have taken to talking pleonastically of Windermere Lake.

pleonectic (pliːəˈnɛktɪk), *a.* [ad. Gr. *πλεονεκτικός* disposed to take too much, greedy, f. *πλεονέκτης* one who has or claims more than his share, f. *πλέον* more + *ἔχειν* to have.] Of or pertaining to *pleonexia*; covetous, greedy, grasping.

1858 in MAYNE *Expos. Lex.* **1882** *Pall Mall G.* 15 Sept. 3 The pleonectic spirit which prompted this practice will no doubt be chastened into greater accordance with the principles of distributive justice.

‖**pleonexia** (pliːəˈnɛksɪə). [a. Gr. *πλεονεξία* greed, assumption, f. as *πλεονέκτης*: see prec.] Covetousness, avarice, greed.

1858 MAYNE *Expos. Lex.*, *Pleonexia*, term for greediness, grasping selfishness, overbearing temper or arrogance, regarded as mental disease. **1892** *Daily News* 4 Nov. 5/3 Competitive, grasping fellows, cursed with the vice of pleonexia, of wanting more than their share.

pleophony (pliːˈɒfənɪ). *Linguistics.* [f. *pleo-*, PLEIO- + *phony* after HOMOPHONY, etc.] Vowel duplication; epenthesis of a vowel which harmonizes with that in the preceding syllable. Hence **pleoˈphonic** *a.*

1949 *Archivum Linguisticum* I. 165 The East Slavonic languages.. present the curious and striking phenomenon of pleophony or double vowelling. **1966** H. BIRNBAUM in Birnbaum & Puhvel *Anc. Indo-Europ. Dial.* 162 One such feature is 'pleophonic' /ToroT/ as a reflex of P[roto] Sl[avic] /TorT/. *Ibid.* 167 This change must have preceded in time the /TorT/>/ToroT/modification ('pleophony') mentioned above.

pleopod (ˈpliːəpɒd). *Zool.* [f. as PLEON[1] + Gr. *πούς, ποδ-* foot.] One of the swimming limbs attached to the *pleon* or abdomen in Crustacea: see PLEON[1]. Also **pleopodite** (pliːˈɒpədaɪt). Cf. *pereiopod*, *-podite*, s.v. PEREION.

1855 C. SPENCE BATE in *Rep. Brit. Assoc.* (1856) 38 Pleopoda or swimming feet are attached to.. the pleon. **1877** *Encycl. Brit.* VI. 635/2 The next six somites bear each a pair of swimming-feet (or *pleopodites*). **1893** STEBBING *Crustacea* iv. 45 The first five of these segments frequently have appendages that are really natatory and may properly be called pleopods, swimming-feet.

pleoptics (pliːˈɒptɪks), *sb. pl.* (const. as *sing.* or *pl.*). *Ophthalm.* [ad. G. *pleoptik* (A. Bangerter 1953, in *Wiener klin. Wochenschr.* 20 Nov. 966/2), f. *pleo-*, PLEIO- + *optik* OPTICS.] A method of treatment for amblyopia and eccentric fixation employing the selective dazzling of parts of the retina in order to stimulate the use of the fovea and render it more sensitive.

1955 *Q. Cumulative Index Med.* LVIII. 1517/1 (*heading*) Pleoptics and orthoptics. **1962** J. W. HENDERSON in G. M. Haik *Strabismus* v. 111 For the eccentric fixator over 5 years of age, pleoptics rather than occlusion are thought to be the most acceptable method [of treating amblyopia] . **1964** A. SCHLOSSMAN in A. Sorby *Mod. Ophthalm.* III. 141 Pleoptics, which was initiated by Bangerter of St-Gallen, Switzerland, has its greatest value in the treatment of the large number of patients with eccentric fixation who cannot be managed by any other form of therapy. **1975** M. M. PARKS *Ocular Motility & Strabismus* xi. 98/1 An eccentrically fixating eye in some older children has been restored to central fixation using pleoptics after occlusion therapy has failed.

So **pleˈoptic** *a.*

1960 *Amer. Orthoptic Jrnl.* X. 7/1 The development of pleoptic methods and their therapeutic application preceded the discovery of some hitherto unknown characteristics of amblyopia. **1964** S. DUKE-ELDER *Parsons' Diseases of Eye* (ed. 14) XXX. 482 If eccentric fixation is well established, it is often well to occlude the affected eye for some weeks and then to stimulate the macula by special pleoptic methods (flashing devices, the production of after-images, etc.). **1967** J. L. C. MARTIN-DOYLE *Synopsis Ophthalm.* (ed. 3) 188 Pleoptic treatment is arduous and the instruments expensive. **1975** M. M. PARKS *Ocular Motility & Strabismus* xi. 98/1 The final result in the majority of amblyoptic patients is the same whether.. simple occlusion therapy is used exclusively or if pleoptic exercises are used.

pleowe, pleoȝe, obs. forms of PLAY *sb.* and *v.*

plereme ('pli:ri:m). *Linguistics.* [f. Gr. πλήρ-ης full: see -EME.] **a.** = *full word.* **b.** A unit of meaning. Hence **plere'matic** *a.*, **plere'matically** *adv.*, **plere'matics** *sb. pl.*

1939 [see GLOSSEMATIC *sb. pl.* and *a.*]. **1939**, etc. [see KENEME]. **1949** C. E. BAZELL in E. P. Hamp et al. *Readings in Linguistics II* (1966) 209 No fusion in the expression of plerematic units is here involved. **1950** S. POTTER *Our Language* 87 *Sememes* (including *pleremes* and *kenemes*). **1957** —— *Mod. Linguistics* vii. 143 Operators are sometimes called *kenemes* by those describing Chinese, as opposed to ..*pleremes.* **1958** C. F. HOCKETT *Course in Modern Linguistics* lxiv. 575 Here the terms 'phonological' and 'grammatical' make too direct a reference to human language; it will be better to introduce two new terms for general applicability: *cenematic* and *plerematic.* The cenematic structure of language is phonology; the plerematic structure of language is grammar. Phonemes are linguistic *cenemes*; morphemes are linguistic *pleremes. Ibid.* 576 Productivity implies that some messages in the system ..are *plerematically complex*: that they consist of an arrangement of two or more pleremes, instead of each consisting of a single indivisible plereme. If one starts with a system with no plerematic complexity, then there is only one variety of analogy by which a new message can be coined: *blending.* **1959** W. A. C. H. DOBSON *Late Archaic Chinese* i. 14 Undistributed, a plerematic word might be said to represent a notion undifferentiated by grammatical quality. **1961** F. W. HOUSEHOLDER in Saporta & Bastian *Psycholinguistics* 25/2 They [*sc.* distinctive features] may also be considered as 'cenemes' of which 'plerematic' phonemes are composed. **1967** C. L. WRENN *Word & Symbol* 4 The names of things, qualities or acts..are the words which linguists of the Danish school used to term *pleremes* (words of full or complete significance). **1969** *Word* 1967 XXIII. 469 My observations apparently support the structuralist separation of cenetics and plerematics. *Ibid.* 471 In addition to their two cenetic and two plerematic systems, bilingual children naturally have to master two sets of form-to-meaning relationships. **1978** *Amer. Speech* LIII. 275 A communicative system has *duality of patterning*..if its meaningful signals (pleremes) are built out of some convenient stock of meaningless but differentiating pieces (cenemes). *Ibid.* 276 Some special sort of discourse in which there is a planned regularity of recurrence of cenematic features independent of their plerematic role.

pleresye, obs. form of PLEURISY.

plerocephalic (plɪərəʊsɪ'fælɪk), *a. Path.* [f. Gr. πλήρης, πληρο- full + κεφαλή head + -IC.] Of œdema: caused by increased intracranial pressure.

1927 H. M. TRAQUAIR *Introd. Clin. Perimetry* ix. 115 Plerocephalic œdema (œdema due to increased intracranial pressure)... As 'Papillœdema' and 'choked disc' refer to ophthalmoscopic appearances which may occur in local optic nerve disease this term has been chosen to indicate œdema of the disc due to increased intracranial pressure. **1976** *Proc. R. Soc. Med.* LXIX. 455/2 In the following 12 cases varying degrees of optic atrophy occurred in space-occupying lesions of the brain in children because of the development of plerocephalic œdema.

plerocercoid (plɪərəʊ'sɜ:kɔɪd). *Zool.* [f. Gr. πλήρης, πληρο- full + κέρκος tail + -OID.] A larval form of certain tapeworms, in which the body is solid, lacking a bladder. Also *attrib.* or as *adj.*

1906 P. FALCKE tr. *Braun's Animal Parasites of Man* 219 Human beings, like other hosts, can only acquire the broad tapeworm by ingesting its plerocercoids. **1928** *Jrnl. Amer. Med. Assoc.* 30 June 2081/1, I found the plerocercoids in pike. **1961** SWELLENGREBEL & STERMAN *Animal Parasites in Man* xiii. 241 The plerocercoids have been recovered from various internal organs. **1962** J. D. SMYTH *Introd. Anim. Parasitol.* xix. 222 The lycophora..develops into a procercoid and later a plerocercoid larva. **1973** T. C. CHENG *Gen. Parasitol.* xiv. 488/2 Procercoids develop into solid, wormlike plerocercoids, each with one invaginated scolex at one end.

‖**pleroma** (plɪ'rəʊmə). [a. Gr. πλήρωμα that which fills, a complement, f. πληροῦν to make full, f. πλήρης full.]

1. Fullness, plenitude; **a.** in Gnostic theology, The spiritual universe as the abode of God and of the totality of the Divine powers and emanations.

1765 MACLAINE tr. *Mosheim's Eccl. Hist.* I. ii. II. v. (1833) 62/2 He placed in the *pleroma* (so the Gnostics called the habitation of the Deity) thirty æons. **1831-3** E. BURTON *Eccl. Hist.* iii. (1845) 58 One of these later emanations passed the boundaries of the Pleroma, which was the abode of the Deity, and there coming in contact with matter created the world. **1875** LIGHTFOOT *Comm. Col.* (1886) 100 For this totality [of the Divine powers] Gnostic teachers had a technical term, the *pleroma* or *plenitude.*

b. Used in reference to Colossians ii. 9, where the Eng. versions from 1388 have 'fullness':

Ὅτι ἐν αὐτῷ κατοικεῖ πᾶν τὸ πλήρωμα τῆς θεότητος σωματικῶς Wyclif 1388, 'For in hym dwellith bodilich al the fulnesse [1382 al plente, *Vulg.* plenitudo] of the Godhed'.

1875 LIGHTFOOT *Comm. Col.* 329 The ideal church is the pleroma of Christ, and the militant church must strive to become the pleroma. **1883** SCHAFF *Hist. Ch.* II. XII. xcv. 777 The pleroma of the Godhead resides in Christ corporeally: so the pleroma of Christ, the plenitude of his graces and energies, resides in the church as his body.

2. *Bot.* = PLEROME. *rare*$^{-0}$.

1890 in *Cent. Dict.* **1895** in *Syd. Soc. Lex.*

Hence **pleromatic** (plɪərəʊ'mætɪk) *a.*, pertaining to the pleroma.

1858 MAYNE *Expos. Lex.* 977/2 The *pleromatic kingdom* was the name given by Stockenstrand to the whole powers which animate the world and the stars which fill the celestial space. **1879** SCHAFF *Person of Christ* 56 The completeness or pleromatic fulness of the moral and religious character of Christ.

plerome ('plɪərəʊm). *Bot.* [ad. Ger. *plerom* (Hanstein 1868), ad. Gr. πλήρωμα a filling: see prec.] The innermost layer of the primary tissue or meristem at a growing-point, which develops into the fibrovascular tissue, or into this and the pith. (Cf. DERMATOGEN, PERIBLEM.)

1875 BENNETT & DYER *Sachs' Bot.* 127 If no pith is formed, as in many roots and some shoots.., the whole of the plerome is developed into procambium. **1884** BOWER & SCOTT *De Bary's Phaner.* 7 As Hanstein has shown, the young embryo of the Angiospermous Phanerogams separates, while still consisting of few cells,..into three layers, or groups of cells, which differ in their arrangement and direction of division; these were termed by their discoverer, Dermatogen, Periblem, and Plerome.

b. *attrib.*, as ***plerome-body, -cylinder, -sheath.***

1882 VINES *Sachs' Bot.* 166 The origin of lateral roots in a mother-root is always on the outside of its axial fibrovascular or plerome-cylinder. *Ibid.* 167 These mother-cells of the lateral roots lie in the plerome-sheath.

pleromorph ('plɪərəʊmɔ:f). *Min.* [mod. f. Gr. πλήρης, πληρο- full + μορφή form: introduced (in Ger.) by A. Kenngott 1859.] A form produced by the filling of a cavity left by the removal of a crystal with another mineral substance.

1890 in *Cent. Dict.* **1906** H. A. MIERS *Let. to Editor*, A pleromorph is a natural cast of a crystal in some other mineral substance.

plerophory (plɪ'rɒfərɪ). Now *rare.* [ad. Gr. πληροφορία (Heb. vi. 11, x. 22, etc.) fullness of assurance, f. *πληροφόρος bringing satisfaction, f. πλήρης full, satisfied + -φόρος bearing; cf. πληροφορεῖν to bring full measure, satisfy fully.] Full assurance or certainty. (Common in 17th c. in theological use.)

1605 A. WOTTON *Answ. Pop. Articles* 90 Not one of many thousands attaines to that plerophorie or full perswasion. **1647** TRAPP *Comm. 1 Tim.* iii. 13 The peace of a good conscience, and the plerophory of faith. **1745** WESLEY *Answ. Ch.* 22 The other is, such a Plerophory or full Assurance that I am forgiven, and so clear a Perception, that Christ abideth in me; as utterly excludes all Doubt and Fear. **1893** F. HALL in *Nation* (N.Y.) 13 Apr. 275/2 To forbear, in some measure, that plerophory of cocksureness with which he habitually dogmatizes.

plerotic (plɪ'rɒtɪk), *a. Med. rare*$^{-0}$. [ad. Gr. πληρωτικ-ός filling up (Dioscorides), f. πληροῦν to fill.] Having the property of supplying or restoring lost flesh or tissue.

1858 MAYNE *Expos. Lex.*, *Plerosis*, old term for repletion and refection,..used by Hippocrates..*Pleroticus*, applied to medicines...of or belonging to *Plerosis*: plerotic.

ples, plese, plesance, -aunce, plesant, -aunt, pleser(e, etc. obs. ff. PLEASE, PLEASANCE, PLEASANT, PLEASURE.

plesh, obs. or dial. f. PLASH, PLEACH.

plesiadapid (pli:zɪ'ædəpɪd), *sb.* and *a. Palæont.* [f. mod.L. family name *Plesiadapidæ*, f. the generic name *Plesiadapis* (P. Gervais 1877, in *Jrnl. Zool.* VI. 76), f. PLESIO- + *Adapis*, generic name of another fossil primate + -ID^{3}.] **A.** *sb.* A primitive, extinct primate belonging to the family Plesiadapidæ, known from Palæocene fossil remains found in North America and Europe. **B.** *adj.* Of, pertaining to, or resembling an animal of this kind.

1945 A. S. ROMER *Vertebr. Paleontol.* (ed. 2) xviii. 343 The plesiadapids have been thought to be aberrant lemurs or tree shrews. **1949** W. E. LE GROS CLARK *Hist. Primates* 50 We know little as yet about the limb bones of the plesiadapids. **1963** E. L. SIMONS in J. Buettner-Janusch *Evolutionary & Genetic Biol. Primates* I. ii. 79 The anterior teeth of plesiadapids were enlarged and procumbent. **1970** [see LORISID *sb.* and *a.*]. **1975** *Nature* 10 Jan. 111/2 Five plesiadapid lineages are known, at least two of which were common to both Europe and North America.

plesiadapoid (pli:zɪ'ædəpɔɪd), *sb.* and *a. Palæont.* [f. mod.L. name of suborder *Plesiadapoidea*, f. the generic name *Plesiadapis* (see prec.) + -OID.] **A.** *sb.* A primitive, extinct primate belonging to the suborder Plesiadapoidea. **B.** *adj.* Of, pertaining to, or resembling an animal of this kind.

1966 A. S. ROMER *Vertebr. Paleontol.* (ed. 3) xviii. 217/2 (*heading*) Plesiadapoids. **1973** *Nature* 24 Aug. 518/1 The dental characteristics distinguishing primitive Early Eocene adapids and omomyids from other Eocene mammals are present in primitive plesiadapoids. **1974** B. J. STAHL *Vertebrate History* ix. 471 The plesiadapoids..became extinct without issue before the close of the Eocene. *Ibid.* 472 A change in the climate is implicated in the failure of the plesiadapoid primates to survive.

Plesianthropus (pli:zɪ'ænθrəpəs). *Palæont.* [mod.L. (R. Broom 1938, in *Nature* 27 Aug. 377/1), f. PLESI(O- + Gr. ἄνθρωπος man.] An African fossil hominid of the genus formerly so called, now usually included in the species *Australopithecus africanus.*

1941 *Nature* 5 July 11/1 Plesianthropus..has a skull somewhat like that of the chimpanzee in size. **1948** A. L. KROEBER *Anthropol.* (rev. ed.) iii. 91 Australopithecus and Plesianthropus came to light in quarrying operations. **1960** E. WINICK *Dict. Anthropol.* 421/1 *Plesianthropus*, an African man-like ape fossil from the Pleistocene period. **1977** G. W. HEWES in D. M. Rumbaugh *Language Learning by Chimpanzee* i. 40 As for the Australopithecines (based on casts of the Sterkfontein individual formerly called 'Plesianthropus') no articulate language would have been possible for them.

plesiaster (pli:sɪ'æstə(r)). *Zool.* [f. PLESIO- + ASTER.] In sponges, A form of spicule with a very short straight axis: see quot.

1888 SOLLAS in *Challenger Rep.* XXV. p. lxiii, The plesiasters are always much larger when fully grown than the metasters,..and the metasters are larger than the spirasters; the three forms present a perfect gradational series.

plesier, obs. form of PLEASURE.

plesio-, comb. form from Gr. πλησί-ος near, used in scientific terminology.

plesiomorphous (,pli:sɪəʊ'mɔ:fəs), *a. Cryst.* [f. PLESIO- + Gr. μορφή form + -OUS.] Very near in form; crystallizing in forms closely resembling but not identical with each other. So **,plesio'morphic** *a.* in same sense; **,plesio'morphism**, the fact or condition of being plesiomorphous.

1833 *Rep. Brit. Assoc. 1831, 1832* 429 Plesiomorphism.—As the differences between the angles of the carbonates and sulphates above quoted cannot be accounted for by any accidental causes.., some crystallographers have been led to reject the term *isomorphous* as applied to such crystallized compounds, and to substitute in its place the term *plesiomorphous.* **1837** WHEWELL *Hist. Induct. Sc.* III. 222 It has since been proposed to call such groups plesiomorphous. **1845** *N. Brit. Rev.* II. 314 The term plesiomorphous (nearly of the same shape) is generally substituted. *Ibid.*, Plesiomorphism serves to remove the difficulties. **1850** DAUBENY *Atom. The.* vi. (ed. 2) 175 It has been proposed to employ the term *plesiomorphism*, where the resemblance between two bodies in external form is not regarded as complete. **1890** *Cent. Dict.*, *Plesiomorphic*, same as *plesiomorphous.*

‖**plesiosaurus** (,pli:sɪəʊ'sɔ:rəs). *Palæont.* Pl. -i. [mod.L. generic name (Conybeare 1821) f. PLESIO- + Gr. σαῦρος lizard: see quot. 1825.] A genus of extinct marine reptiles, having a long neck, a small head, a short tail, and four large paddles; from the Lias and neighbouring formations; a reptile of this genus.

1825 W. D. CONYBEARE in *Philos. Mag.* LXV. 420 The name I have originally [in 1821] given to this animal, *Plesiosaurus* (approximate to the Saurians), may appear rather vague in this state of our knowledge. **1833** SIR C. BELL *Hand* (1834) 113 The ichthyosaurus and plesiosaurus ..inhabited the sea; their remains are found low in the lias deposit. **1854** F. C. BAKEWELL *Geol.* 49 Some of the plesiosauri must have been 20 feet long.

fig. **1876** LOWELL *Among my Bks.* Ser. II. 137 Fortunately Scotland was not yet annexed, or the poem [Polyolbion] would have been even longer, and already it is the plesiosaurus of verse.

Hence **plesiosaur** ('pli:sɪəʊ,sɔ:(r)), a reptile of the extinct genus *Plesiosaurus* or order *Plesiosauria*; **,plesio'saurian** *a.*, belonging to the order *Plesiosauria*; *sb.* a reptile of this order; **,plesio'sauroid** *a.*, resembling or allied to the *Plesiosaurus* (in quot., characteristic of the *Plesiosaurus*).

1839 *Civil Eng. & Arch. Jrnl.* II. 148/2 The ichthyosaur, or fish-lizard, and its ally the *plesiosaur. **1860** OWEN *Palæont.* 223 Cuvier deemed the structure of the Plesiosaur ..to have been the most singular, and its characters the most anomalous that had been discovered amid the ruins of a former world. **1858** MAYNE *Expos. Lex.*, *Plesiosaurius*, ..*plesiosaurian. **1896** LYDEKKER *Roy. Nat. Hist.* V. 103 The skeleton of the Lariosaur, a small plesiosaurian. **1860** OWEN *Palæont.* 229 The slight indication of the sacral vertebræ; the non-confluence of the caudal hæmapophyses with each other, are all '*plesiosauroid'.

plesir(e, -our(e, -owre, etc., obs. ff. PLEASURE.

plessigraph ('plɛsɪgrɑ:f, -æ-). *Med.* [ad. F. *plessigraphe*, f. Gr. πλήσσειν to strike: see -GRAPH.] (See quot. 1895.)

1870 GEE *Auscult. & Percuss.* I. iv. 63 *note*, There is a description of sundry 'plessigraphs' which have been contrived of late. **1895** *Syd. Soc. Lex.*, *Plessigraph*, a special form of Pleximeter, invented by Peter, a colleague of Trousseau, designed to reduce the percussed surface to a minimum so that the user may be able to map out more exactly the limits of any organ or dull area.

plessimeter (plɛ'sɪmɪtə(r)). [ad. F. *plessimètre.*] = PLEXIMETER. So **plessi'metric** *a.* = PLEXIMETRIC; **ple'ssimetry** = PLEXIMETRY; **plessor** = PLEXOR.

1857 DUNGLISON *Dict. Med. Sc.*, *Plesser*, Plexor. *Plessimeter*, Pleximeter. **1858** MAYNE *Exp. Lex. Plessimeter*, ..an instrument..used to receive the strokes of the *plesser* in percussion. **1861** T. J. GRAHAM *Pract. Med.* 161 The best plessimeter will be found to be the first, or first and second, fingers of the left hand. **1870** GEE *Auscult. & Percuss.* I. iv. 62 From time to time divers plessors have been contrived.

1895 *Syd. Soc. Lex.*, *Plessimeter, Plessimetry.* 1898 *Allbutt's Syst. Med.* V. 981 In some cases I have found on plessimetric percussion that the right border of dulness does not meet the line which indicates the upper border of the liver at a right angle.

plessiur, -or, -our, plesyr(e, etc., obs. ff. PLEASURE.

plet, *sb.*[1] Chiefly *Sc.* and *north. dial.* [Collateral form of PLAIT *sb.*, going with PLET *v.*] = PLAIT *sb.*

c1450 *Trevisa's Barth. De P.R.* v. lxvi. (Bodl. MS.), þe plettes of wommanes heere bene ykutte and ybounde with laces. 1595 Duncan *App. Etymol.* (E.D.S.), *Lacinia*, a plet, or rag. 1641 Best *Farm. Bks.* (Surtees) 16 Fold-hankes or hankinges..which is as thicke againe as plough-string, being a loose kinde of two plettes. 1828 *Craven Gloss.* (ed. 2), *Pletts*, folds or gathers of linen. *Ibid.*, *Plet*, work performed by platting.

‖**plet** (plɛt), *sb.*[2] Also **plete, plitt.** [a. Russ. *plet*^{i} scourge, whip.] A three-thonged whip loaded with lead, formerly used for flogging in Russia.

1864 Webster, *Plitt*, an instrument of punishment or torture resembling the knout, used in Russia. 1870 'W. M. Cooper' *Flagellation & Flagellants* xxvi. 259 The plêt is a whip made of strips of raw hide, and having three lashes tipped with small leaden balls. 1885 A. Griffiths in *Encycl. Brit.* XIX. 762/2 There is another flagellator,..called the *plete*, a whip of twisted hide,..retained at a few of the most distant Siberian prisons.

plet, *v.* Chiefly *Sc.* and *north. dial. Pa. t.* **plet(t, plat;** *pa. pple.* **plet(t;** also **pletted.** [Collateral form of PLAIT *v.*, going with PLET *sb.*[1]]

1. *trans.* To intertwine (strands) so as to form one combined texture; = PLAIT *v.* 2; also to form (a garland, band, or the like) by this process; = PLAIT *v.* 2 d. Also in *mod. dial.* to cross (the legs); = PLAIT *v.* 3.

c1450 *Trevisa's Barth. De P.R.* v. lxvi. (Bodl. MS.), Wymmenes heere is..ipletted [*W. de W.* 1495 pleted] and ybounde with laces. c1450 *Mirour Saluacioun* 4619 A corovne of sharpest thornes mayde thyne Enemys plettyng. c1470 Henryson *Mor. Fab.* viii. (*Preach. Swallow*) xlii, The feind plettis his nettis scharpe and rude. 1513 Douglas *Æneis* ix. ii. 64 The wyld wolf..Abowt the bowght, plet all of wandis tyght, Bayis and gyrnis. a1600 Montgomerie *Misc. Poems* xix. 5 A garland properly sho plets, To set vpon hir heid. 1600 Fairfax *Tasso* xiv. lxviii, Of woodbines, lillies, and of roses sweete,..All pletted fast, well knit, and ioyned meete. 1725 Ramsay *Gentle Sheph.* ii. iv, For thee I plet the flow'ry belt and snood. 1828 *Craven Gloss.* (ed. 2), *Plet*, to plat. 1839 J. M. Wilson *Tales of Borders* V. 251/2 He plets his legs, and passes his hand along his leg. 1903 In E.D.D. from Shetland to North Lincolnsh.

†**2.** To fold; to fold in one's arms. *Obs.*

c1425 Wyntoun *Cron.* ix. xxvii. 3258 Wyth blyth chere thare he hym plet In [his] armis so thankfully. 1513 Douglas *Æneis* xiii. xi. 4 Bayth hir armys abowt hys feit [scho] plet, Enbrasyng thame and kyssand reuerently. 1536 Bellenden *Cosmogr.* xi, Thir salmond..spawnis, with thair wamis plet to uthir. c1560 A. Scott *Poems* (S.T.S.) xxviii. 8 Quhen þat I went with þat sweit may,..And oft tymes in my armis plet hir.

†**3.** To bind, tie up, make fast. *Obs.*

1560 Rolland *Crt. Venus* iv. 364 To se his handis into ane cord thus plet. 1585 James VI *Ess. Poesie* (Arb.) 37, I had farr rather Babell tower forthsett, Then the thre Grecian hilles on others plett.

4. *mod. dial.* To fold, to wrinkle.

1861 Quinn *Heather* (1863) 123 Care in wan wrinkles deeply plettin' Nell's bonnie face.

Hence **plet** *ppl. a.*, plaited, intertwined.

1503 *Acc. Ld. High Treas. Scot.* II. 231 Vj elne braid ribanes to be ane plet suord belt to the King. 1508 Dunbar *Tua Mariit Wemen* 15 Throw pykis of the plet thorne I presandlie luikit.

plet, obs. f. PLATE.

-plet (plɛt), the ending of *triplet, multiplet*, etc., used with a prefixed numeral to denote a multiplet having the specified number of members.

1973 L. J. Tassie *Physics Elementary Particles* xiii. 173 Taking the neutron and proton as members of the *SU*(6) 56-plet yields the ratio of their magnetic moments as..–3/2 which is close to the experimental value of –1·46. 1975 *Physics Bull.* Apr. 180/3 The octet of mesons is now part of a 15plet which groups together one octet and one singlet with no charm, and two triplets with charm 1 and –1, respectively.

plete, early var. PLEA *sb.*, secondary form of PLEAD *v.*, obs. f. PLEAT.

plether: see PLETHRON.

plethora ('plɛθərə, plɪ'θɔərə). Also (after F.), 6 **pletore,** 7 **plethor.** See PLETHORY. [a. med.L. *plēthōra*, a. Gr. πληθώρη fullness, repletion, f. πλήθειν to become full. In F. *pléthore* (16th c.). Bailey 1731 has the etymological pronunciation *ple'thōra*; ed. 1742 and J. 1755 have *'plethora.*

plethora and *plethory* were app. sometimes viewed as derived from L. *plētūs* filled, *plētūra* repletion, plethora.]

1. *Path.* A morbid condition, characterized, according to the older writers, by over-fullness of blood or of any other humour (or of juices in a plant); according to later writers, by an excess of red corpuscles in the blood.

1541 R. Copland *Galyen's Terap.* Civ, The superhaboundaunce of humours..that the Grekes cal Plethora. *Ibid.* G iv, Of cacomye y^t is coniunct w^t the vlcere, or of Pletore, or of phlegmon. 1671 Salmon *Syn. Med.* i. xliv. 99 The Antecedent Cause of Diseases is twofold, the one is called a Plethor or Plenitude. 1673 Grew *Anat. Roots* ii. §16 Lest the Barque, being spongy, should suck it up too fast, and so the Root should be, as it were, surcharged by a Plethora. 1777 Sheridan *Sch. Scand.* iv. iii, Your character at present is like a person in a plethora, absolutely dying from too much health. 1851 Carpenter *Man. Phys.* (ed. 2) 317 When they [red corpuscles] are present in an amount much above the average, they seem concerned in producing the condition termed Plethora..which borders upon various diseases. 1877 Roberts *Handbk. Med.* I. 17 The redness and turgidity of plethora.

2. *fig.* Over-fullness in any respect, superabundance; any unhealthy repletion or excess.

[1597 Howson *Serm.* 24 Dec. 44 That πληθώρα, fulnes of blood in our Bishopricks. a1640 Jackson *Creed* xi. xxxiv. §4 We are all subject to that πληθώρα whereof the Lord so often forewarned Israel.] 1700 Bp. Patrick *Comm. Deut.* xxxii. 15 This was the lamentable effect of their plethora or fullness. 1835 Marryat *Olla Podr.* xvii, We are..suffering under a plethora of capital. 1868 Farrar *Seekers* i. ii. (1875) 27 A plethora of words.

†**pletho'retic,** *a. Obs. rare*$^{-0}$. [f. prec., after *theoretic*, etc.] = PLETHORIC. So **pletho'retical.**

1727 Bailey vol. II, *Plethoretick*: whence in Johnson. Webster 1864, etc. 1882 Ogilvie (Annandale), *Plethoretic, Plethoretical.* 1886 in *Cassell's Encycl. Dict.* etc.

plethoric (plɪ'θɒrɪk, 'plɛθərɪk), *a.* [ad. med.L. *plēt(h)ōricus* (Du Cange), a. Gr. πληθωρικός (Galen), f. πληθώρη PLETHORA. Prob. immed. from F. *pléthorique* (Paré c1550), whence the stressing *'plethoric*: cf. *'catholic.*]

1. *Path.* Characterized by plethora, of a full habit of body.

1620 Venner *Via Recta* viii. 172 Such as haue plethoricke and full bodies. 1764 Goldsm. *Trav.* 144 The nation found, with fruitless skill, Its former strength was but plethoric ill. 1803 *Med. Jrnl.* X. 51 A young man,..of a plethoric habit. 1846 J. Baxter *Libr. Pract. Agric.* (ed. 4) II. 131 Cattle are very subject to sudden determination of blood to the head. They are naturally plethoric.

†**b.** *absol.* as *sb.* A plethoric person. *Obs.*

1707 Floyer *Physic. Pulse-Watch* 191 If the Pulse be too full, as in Plethorics, we must use some general Evacuations.

2. *fig.* Full to excess, overstocked, overloaded; swollen, inflated, turgid.

1644 Bulwer *Chiron.* 114 This happens to some by reason of a certain Plethorique wit. 1800 *Hist. India* in *Asiat. Ann. Reg.* 3/2 That plethoric opulence with which the merchants of Alexandria sunk into idleness. 1848 Lowell *Biglow P.* Ser. i. Introd., The pockets, plethoric with marbles round, That still a space for ball and pegtop found. 1864 Burton *Scot Abr.* II. i. 126 Plethoric volumes which slumber in decorous old libraries.

†**ple'thorical,** *a. Obs.* [f. as prec. + -AL[1].] = prec. 1.

1603 Holland *Plutarch* Explan. Words, *Plethoricall plight*,..that state of the body, which being full of blood and other humours, needeth evacuation. 1625 Hart *Anat. Ur.* ii. viii. 99. 1676 T. Garencieres *Coral* 74 Unless the body be extraordinarily plethorical.

ple'thorically, *adv.* [f. prec. + -LY[2].] In the manner of a plethoric person; with plethora.

1800 Lamb *Lett., to Wordsw.* (1837) I. v. 170, I am not plethorically abounding in cash at this present. 1837 Carlyle *Fr. Revol.* I. ii. i, When such Institution plethorically says to itself, Take thy ease, thou hast goods laid up. 1871 Le Fanu *Tenants of Malory* iv. 15 They have ..grown plethorically robust.

plethorous ('plɛθərəs), *a. rare.* [f. PLETHORA + -OUS.] = PLETHORIC *a.* 1.

1906 J. P. Barry *At Gates of East* p. vii, But the book.. may do good in a practical way, if it weans the wearied, the plethorous and the valetudinarian from the Cult of the Spas.

plethory ('plɛθərɪ), *sb.* (*a.*) Now *rare.* Also 7 **pletory.** [irreg. from PLETHORA; or perh. deduced from *plethoric*, on analogy of *historic, history, allegoric, allegory*, etc.]

1. = PLETHORA 1.

1625 Bp. Hall *Serm. Thanksgiving* 29 Jan. 47 Hee saw that in this common Plethorie it was fit for vs to bleed. 1651 Jer. Taylor *Serm. f. Year* i. v. 59 The appetite..ready to burst with putrifaction and an unwholsome plethory. 1708 *Brit. Apollo* No. 102, 2/1 A Plethory or fulness of Blood. 1835 Henslow *Princ. Bot.* ii. iii. 206 Less sap is exhaled.. and the tree attains a state of plethory.

2. *fig.* = PLETHORA 2.

1624 Bp. Hall *Heaven upon Earth* xiii, Perhaps thou labourest of some plethorie of pride. a1677 Hale *Prim. Orig. Man* ii. x. 228 A Plethory or excess of Numbers of Men, sometimes..cause Wars. 1778 Johnson 9 Apr. in *Boswell*, It is..owing to a plethory of matter that his style is so faulty. 1843 *Blackw. Mag.* LIII. 522 The king [Louis XVI] whose plethory was cured by that sharp remedy.

†**B.** *adj.* = PLETHORIC *a. Obs. rare.*

a1643 J. Shute *Judgem. & Mercy* (1645) 29 To have a pletory fulnesse of Crude, and raw humours in his Stomach.

Hence †**'plethoriness.** *rare*$^{-1}$.

1665 J. Fraser *Polichronicon* (S.H.S.) 345 His plethoriness came to such a hight that from spitting it flowed to vomiting of blood.

‖**plethron** ('plɛθrən). Pl. **-a.** Also (after F.), 7 **plether.** [a. Gr. πλέθρον. In F. *plèthre.*] An ancient Greek measure of length, containing a hundred Greek, or about 101 English feet; also a square measure, the side of which is a linear plethron, in extent slightly below an imperial rood.

1623 Bingham *Xenophon* p. iii, The necke of land, that ioyneth to the Continent, is at least foure plethers in bredth. 1706 Phillips, *Plethron.* 1797 *Encycl. Brit.* (ed. 3) II. 711/2 A square of four plethra, or 400 feet, on each side. 1875 Browning *Aristoph. Apol.* 2215 Nobody now can say 'this plot is mine, Though but a plethron square'.

ple'thysmogram. *Physiol.* [f. as next + -GRAM.] The record produced by a plethysmograph.

1894 W. Ewart *Heart Stud.* I. 181 The need for a separate study of shape, volume, and velocity of the pulse is rendered obvious by the difference between the three curves, which may be termed respectively the sphygmogram, the plethysmogram, and the tachogram, obtained by means of the three instruments bearing corresponding names. *Ibid.* 231 The plethysmogram (volumpuls) of the forearm.. shows an increase in the size of the oscillations. 1929 *Proc. Soc. Exper. Biol. & Med.* XXVI. 711 (*heading*) A photographic method of recording plethysmograms. 1971 *Nature* 1 Oct. 340/2 Burton has ascribed the slow fluctuations..seen in human digital plethysmograms to the action of the thermoregulatory system.

plethysmograph (plɪ'θɪzməgrɑːf, -æ-). *Physiol.* [f. Gr. πληθυσμός enlargement (f. πληθύνειν to increase, f. πληθύς fullness) + -GRAPH, after It. *pletismografo.*] An instrument, invented by Mosso of Turin c1870, for recording and measuring the variation in the volume of a part of the body, esp. as due to the changes in the circulation of the blood produced by emotion, etc.

It consists of a closed vessel surrounding the part of the body, filled with water, air, or other fluid, and connected with a means of measuring its displacement.

1872 *Sci. Amer.* July 403/1 By using two plethysmographs, Dr Mosso has obtained pen traces representing..valuable physiological data leading to the demonstration of the most important phenomena of the blood vessels. 1882 Hardaker in *Pop. Sci. Monthly* XX. 578 The plethismograph..measures the amount of blood sent to the brain in any particular process of thought, and records the exact time for each process. 1896 *Allbutt's Syst. Med.* I. 343. 1957 *Clin. Sci.* XVI. 103 (*heading*) Venous collection in forearm and hand measured by the strain-gauge and volume plethysmograph. 1964 *Times* 5 Sept. 12/3 A small electronic instrument called a plethysmograph used for measuring changes of blood volume in the body's circulation. 1972 *English Studies* LIII. 76 Measurements were made..of the variations in volume of the air in the lungs. This..involved the use of a plethysmograph, a rigid airtight container enclosing the subject entirely except for head and neck.

Hence **ple,thysmo'graphic** *a.*, belonging to, or obtained by, the plethysmograph; **ple,thys'mographically** *adv.*, by means of a plethysmograph; **plethy'smography,** the use of the plethysmograph.

1886 *Medical News* XLIX. 276 In experiments made with the plethysmographic method..it was found that..a constriction..may be produced by an electric stimulation of the sciatic nerve. 1890 Webster, *Plethysmography.* 1897 *Jrnl. Exper. Med.* II. 334 The striking effect of such stimuli upon the volume of a limb when measured plethysmographically. 1898 *Jrnl. Physiol.* XXII. 380 A few experiments on intestinal plethysmography were made by Bayliss. 1899 *Allbutt's Syst. Med.* VII. 745 Plethysmographic observations on the cutaneous circulation. 1930 *Amer. Jrnl. Physiol.* XCI. 717 That the abdominal venous reservoirs empty (into the chest) during systole can be demonstrated by abdominal plethysmography. 1970 *Nature* 18 July 276/2 The volume of the foot was measured plethysmographically before injection of carrageenin. 1977 *Lancet* 9 July 66/1 Strain-gauge plethysmography is probably an appropriate method for demonstrating arterial insufficiency in this condition.

pleting, pletour, ME. ff. PLEADING, PLEADER.

plette, obs. pa. t. of PLAT *v.*[1]

†**'pletter,** *v. Obs. rare.* [ad. Du. *pletteren* to bruise, crush (Kilian), f. stem *platt* blow (Franck).] *trans.* To bruise, crush.

1597 A. M. tr. *Guillemeau's Fr. Chirurg.* ('truelye translated out of Dutch into Englishe') 2/1 The vaynes, the arteryes, or the sinneus themselves, come to be squised and plettered. *Ibid.* 2b/1 Those woundes which come by crushinge or pletteringe are farre worse then those which are onlye hewede. *Ibid.* 13/1 The sownde bone which is next vnto the plettered bone.

pleu, pleuch-e, pleugh, Sc. ff. PLOUGH.

‖**pleura** ('plʊərə). *Anat.* and *Zool.* Pl. **-æ.** [med.L., a. Gr. πλευρά side of the body, rib.]

1. One of the two serous membranes, right and left, which line the thorax and envelop the lungs in mammals; each is reflected on itself so as to form a closed sac, one side or layer of which (*pulmonary pleura*) invests the lung, while the other (*costal* or *parietal pleura*) is attached to the inner wall of the chest.

Sometimes applied to the upper part of the common membranous lining of the thorax and abdomen in vertebrates below mammals (*peritoneum* or *pleuroperitoneum*).

1664 Power *Exp. Philos.* i. 40 The Heart in this Animal [lamprey] is..cemented and glewed as it were on all sides to the Pleura, or innermost skin of the Thorax. **1748** HARTLEY *Observ. Man* I. i. 96 The Vibrations excited in the Pleura and Peritonaeum. **1876** BRISTOWE *The. & Pract. Med.* (1878) 454 Malignant disease of the lungs and pleuræ.

2. In invertebrates: **a.** Name for a part of the body-wall on each side in arthropods; in insects, the part to which the lower wings are attached. (Cf. PLEURON.)

1826 KIRBY & SP. *Entomol.* III. 380 (The Pleuræ). The space behind the scapulars, on which the lower organs of flight are fixed. *Ibid.* 574 *Pleura.* By this name I would distinguish the part which laterally connects the metathorax and postpectus. It includes in it the socket of the secondary wings.

b. In molluscs, The region on each side of the rachis of the lingual ribbon of the odontophore.

1851 WOODWARD *Mollusca* I. 28 The teeth on the pleuræ are termed *uncini*; they are extremely numerous in the plant-eating gasteropods. **1866** TATE *Brit. Mollusks* iii. 50 The lateral areas are called the pleuræ. **1872** NICHOLSON *Palæont.* 163 The pleuræ are in one piece with the axis, but are separated from it by a more or less pronounced groove, the 'axal furrow'.

pleura, plural of PLEURON, PLEURUM.

pleuracanth (ˈplʊərəkænθ). *Palæont.* [ad. mod.L. *Pleuracanthus*, f. Gr. πλευρά side + ἄκανθα spine, thorn.] A fish of the extinct genus *Pleuracanthus* or family *Pleuracanthidæ*, characterized by having a row of sharp hooks or spines along each side. Also *attrib.* So **pleuraˈcanthid**, a fish of the family *Pleuracanthidæ*; **pleuraˈcanthoid** *a.*, resembling or belonging to the family *Pleuracanthidæ*; *sb.* = *pleuracanthid.*

1900 *Nature* 20 Sept. 505/1 Assuming that the Pleuracanth form originated from one..of simple parallel rods.

pleural (ˈplʊərəl), *a.*[1] [f. PLEURA + -AL[1]; so F. *pleural.*] Of or pertaining to the pleura.

1843 R. J. GRAVES *Syst. Clin. Med.* xx. 242 The accumulated fluid in the pleural cavity. **1846** G. E. DAY tr. *Simon's Anim. Chem.* II. 498 The exudation in the pleural sac. **1884** M. MACKENZIE *Dis. Throat & Nose* II. 47 Pleural inflammation..affecting the base of the left lung.

ˈpleural, *a.*[2] [f. PLEURON + -AL[1].] Of or pertaining to the pleuron or side of the body, or (in arthropods) of a somite; costal; lateral.

1887 SOLLAS in *Encycl. Brit.* XXII. 417/2 Now broaden out the prora on the eggshell into oval lobes (*proral pteres*); and from each pole draw a lobe midway between the prora and the tropis (*pleural pteres*). **1888** ROLLESTON & JACKSON *Anim. Life* 491 The somite..may consist of a dorsal plate, the tergum, and a ventral plate, the sternum, connected laterally by a soft pleural membrane.

‖**pleuralgia** (plʊˈrældʒɪə). *Path.* [mod.L., f. Gr. πλευρά side + -αλγία, f. ἄλγος pain.] Pain in the side; pleurodynia. Hence **pleuˈralgic** *a.*, pertaining to or affected with pleuralgia.

1822–34 *Good's Study Med.* (ed. 4) I. 679 That acute pain which is often complained of in the head or the side: in the latter case sometimes amounting to pleuralgia.

‖**pleurapophysis** (plʊərəˈpɒfɪsɪs). *Comp. Anat.* Pl. **-yses** (-ɪsiːz). [mod.L., f. Gr. πλευρά side + APOPHYSIS.] Owen's term for each of the lateral processes of a typical vertebra, forming part of the hæmal arch (cf. HÆMAPOPHYSIS); represented in the thoracic region, and sometimes in other parts of the trunk, by the ribs.

1854 OWEN *Skel. & Teeth* in *Orr's Circ. Sc.* I. *Org. Nat.* 168 The hæmal arch is formed by a pair of bones called 'pleurapophyses'. **1871** T. R. JONES *Anim. Kingd.* (ed. 4) 657 At the sides of the centrum,..a canal is circumscribed by the pleurapophysis, or costal process.

Hence **pleurapophysial** (ˌplʊərəpəʊˈfɪzɪəl) *a.*, pertaining to or of the nature of a pleurapophysis.

1854 OWEN *Skel. & Teeth* in *Orr's Circ. Sc.* I. *Org. Nat.* 203 This intermediate pleurapophysial appendage is called the 'ilium'. **1872** HUMPHRY *Myology* 8 This..indicates a serial correspondence with the skeletal formations in the sternal rather than with those in the vertebral ('pleurapophysial') region of the visceral wall.

pleuratic, -etic: see PLEURITIC.

pleurecbolic (plʊərɛkˈbɒlɪk), *a. Zool.* [f. Gr. πλευρά side + ἔκβολ-ος cast out, put out, f. ἐκβάλλειν to cast out + -IC.] Capable of being protruded by eversion of the sides, as the tentacies of some molluscs and worms. So **pleuremˈbolic** *a.* [Gr. ἔμβολ-ος thrown in, f. ἐμβάλλειν to throw in, insert], capable, when protruded, of being retracted by inversion of the sides.

1883 LANKESTER in *Encycl. Brit.* XVI. 652/1 If we start from the condition of full eversion of the tube and watch the process of introversion, we shall find that the pleurecbolic variety is introverted by the apex of the tube sinking inwards. *Ibid.* 652/2 The Gastropod's introvert is pleurembolic (and therefore acrecbolic).

‖**pleurenchyma** (plʊˈrɛŋkɪmə). *Bot.* Also in anglicized form **pleuˈrenchym.** [mod.L., f. Gr. πλευρόν rib, πλευρά side + ἔγχυμα infusion, after *parenchyma*, etc.] 'The woody tissue, consisting of tough slender tubes, out of which the woody parts are mainly formed' (*Treas. Bot.*). Hence **pleurenchymatous** (-ɛŋˈkɪmətəs) *a.*, of the nature of pleurenchyma.

1842 WILLSHIRE in *Ann. Nat. Hist.* IX. 85 The long pleurenchymatous cells surrounding the first-formed vascular bundles are carried along with the latter to the centre of the plant. **1848** LINDLEY *Introd. Bot.* (ed. 4) II. 173 Pleurenchym is apparently destined for the conveyance of fluid upwards or downwards,..and for giving firmness and elasticity to every part. **1876** *Encycl. Brit.* IV. 85/2 Under the term *pleurenchyma* is included tissue composed of such elongated prosenchymatous, flexible, thickened cells, as are found in the bast or phloëm layers of ordinary trees.

pleuric (ˈplʊərɪk), *a. rare.* [f. PLEURA + -IC; cf. late L. *pleuricus* at the side, lateral (Front.), Gr. πλευρικός of or for the ribs (Schol. Ar.).] = PLEURAL *a.*[1]

1858 MAYNE *Expos. Lex.*, *Pleuricus*, of or belonging to the *pleura*: pleuric. **1903** *Daily Chron.* 16 July 5/3 To prevent the pleuric liquid..from remaining in the thorax.

pleurisy (ˈplʊərɪsɪ). Forms: 5 pluresy, (pleresye), 6 pluresye, -sie, pleuritie, plewrisie, -osy, plurice, 6–7 plurisie, pleuresie, 6–8 -isie, 7 -esy, plurasie, 7–8 -isy; 6– pleurisy. Also β. 6 in L. forms pl(e)uresis, plurisis. [a. OF. *pleurisie* (13th c.), *-esie* (mod.F. *pleurésie*), f. late L. *pleurisis* (Prudent. *c* 400), mod.L. *pleuresis*, substituted for *pleurītis*, a. Gr. πλευρῖτις pleurisy: see PLEURITIS. Sense 2, and the forms in *plu-*, are partly due to a supposed derivation from L. *plūs*, *plūr-* more (cf. med.L. *plūritās* multitude), as if pleurisy were due to an excess of humours.]

1. *Path.* Inflammation of the pleura, with or without effusion of fluid (serum, pus, blood, etc.) into the pleural cavity; a disease characterized by pain in the chest or side, with fever, loss of appetite, etc.; usually caused by chill, or occurring as a complication of other diseases (scarlatina, rheumatic fever, phthisis, etc.). Formerly often with *a* and *pl.*

dry pleurisy, (formerly) pleurisy without expectoration; (now) pleurisy without effusion. So ***humid*** or ***moist pleurisy.***

1398 TREVISA *Barth. De P.R.* v. xxxi. (Bodl. MS.), Sommetyme aposteme is ibrad þerein as it fareþ in pleresye and is ybrad and comeþ of aposteme þat is þe tendrenes of þe ribbes wiþin. *Ibid.* VII. xi. (1495) 231 Pluresy is a postume on the rybbes wythin. **1534** MORE *Comf. agst. Trib.* III. Wks. 1256/2 And they y^t lye in a plewrosy, thinke that euery time they cough, they fele a sharpe sweorde swap them to the heart. **1547** BOORDE *Brev. Health* cclxxxv. 94 A plurice the which is an impostume in the cenerite of the bones. **1562** BULLEYN *Bulwark, Bk. Simples* 52 The seede drunke, is good against the pleuritie. **1579–80** NORTH *Plutarch* (1676) 370 The disease whereof he died, which was a Pleurisie. **1676** WORLIDGE *Cyder* (1691) 194 Apples..are good against melancholy and the pleuresie. **1709** *Lond. Gaz.* No. 4513/1 Many have died during the Severity of this Winter of Plurisies. **1862** H. W. FULLER *Dis. Lungs* 171 Pleurisy..is one of the commonest diseases.

β. **1527** ANDREW *Brunswyke's Distyll. Waters* D ij b, Good for the sekenes named pleuresis. *a* **1548** HALL *Chron., Hen. V* 82 His chamberlain affirmeth that he [Hen. V] died of a Plurisis. **1568** GRAFTON *Chron.* II. 938 He sickened of a disease, called Pluresis.

2. *fig.* Now *rare* or *Obs.*; formerly almost always in sense 'superabundance, excess' (due to a mistaken etymology: see above).

a **1550** *Vox Populi* 655 in Hazl. *E.P.P.* III. 290 Suppresse this shamfull vsurye, Comonlye called husbondrye: For yf there be no remeadye,..Yt wyll breade to a pluresye. **1597** HOWSON *Serm.* 44 For feare of a Pleurisie by impropriations, customes and compositions. **1602** SHAKS. *Ham.* IV. vii. 118 For goodness, growing to a plurisy, Dies in his own too much. **1642** FULLER *Holy & Prof. St.* II. xiii. 101 Long since had this land been sick of a plurisie of people, if not let blood in their Western Plantations.

3. *attrib.* **pleurisy-root**, name for *Asclepias tuberosa*, also called Butterfly-weed, the root of which is a popular remedy for pleurisy.

1785 T. JEFFERSON *Notes on State of Virginia* 63 Pleurisy root, Asclepias decumbens. **1831** J. DAVIES *Man. Mat. Med.* 238 Pleurisy-root. Fluxroot, &c... A perennial plant, growing all over the United States of America, in gravelly and hilly grounds. **1932** J. B. HARVEY *Wild Flowers Amer.* 55 Butterfly Weed or Pleurisy Root..bears brilliant orange flowers, arranged in flat, terminal clusters.

pleurite (ˈplʊəraɪt). *Zool.* [f. Gr. πλευρά side + -ITE[1] 3.] The side or lateral portion of each somite or segment of the body in arthropods. (Correlated with *tergite* and *sternite.*)

1868 PACKARD *Guide Study Insects* 9 The typical ring or segment..consists of an upper (tergite), a side (pleurite), and an under piece (sternite). **1895** in *Syd. Soc. Lex.*

pleuritic (plʊˈrɪtɪk), *a.*[1] (*sb.*) Forms: 6 pleureticke, -itique, 7 -etick, 8–9 -etic, (*erron.* 7 pluratick, 8 pleuratic), 7–8 pleuritick, 8– pleuritic. [a. F. *pleurétique* (OF. *pleuretic*, 13th c.), or ad. L. *pleuriticus* (Plin.), later *pleureticus*, a. Gr. πλευριτικός, f. πλευρῖτις PLEURITIS.]

1. Affected with or suffering from pleurisy.

1570 LEVINS *Manip.* 121/36 Pléureticke, *pleureticus.* **1572** J. JONES *Bathes of Bath* Pref. 2 Some Pleuritique, Hydropique, some with Ptisique. **1628** A. LEIGHTON in *Camden Misc.* VII. p. ix, They are like pleuretick patients that cannot spit. **1744** BERKELEY *Siris* §78 Having known some pleuritic persons cured without bleeding. **1845** G. E. DAY *Simon's Anim. Chem.* I. 266 The buffy coat is particularly characteristic, and seldom absent in pleuritic blood.

2. Of or pertaining to pleurisy; characteristic or symptomatic of pleurisy.

1652 BENLOWES *Theoph.* I. xliii, By opening Veins Death's sluc'd out, and pleuretick Pains. **1689** MOYLE *Sea Chyrurg.* III. vi. 108 These carry away a great deal of wind and Pluratick matter. **1732–3** MRS. DELANY in *Life & Corr.* (1862) 402 She is confined to her bed with a pleuratic disorder. **1843** R. J. GRAVES *Syst. Clin. Med.* xvii. 197 Fixed pains of a pleuritic character. **1883–4** *Med. Ann.* 47/1 Almost immediately the pleuritic effusion disappeared.

b. Characterized by or liable to cause pleurisy.

1744 ARMSTRONG *Preserv. Health* III. 490 The pleuritic spring Glides harmless by.

B. *sb.* A person affected with pleurisy. *rare.*

[**1398** TREVISA *Barth. De P.R.* VII. xxx. (Bodl. MS.), Pleuretici þat haue aposteme vponne the ribbes inward.] **1768–74** TUCKER *Lt. Nat.* (1834) I. 45 The pleuretic lying on his left side does not expect pleasure by turning to the other; he has no more in view than a diminution of pain.

pleuˈritic, *a.*[2] *Zool.* [f. PLEURITE + -IC.] Pertaining to a pleurite; lateral: = PLEURAL *a.*[2]

1890 in *Cent. Dict.* **1895** in *Syd. Soc. Lex.*

†**pleuˈritical**, *a. Obs.* [See -ICAL.] = PLEURITIC *a.*[1] Hence †**pleuˈritically** *adv.*

1615 CROOKE *Body of Man* 247 By which way also the matter or pus of pleuriticall and Peripneumonicall, or Empyicall patients descendeth. *a* **1625** BP. HALL *Contempl., N.T.* IV. xi, One is sicke..of the pleuriticale stitches of envie. **1733** DOVAR in *Allbutt's Syst. Med.* (1897) III. 20 The blood does not appear more pleuritical or sizey in any distemper than this. **1674** R. GODFREY *Inj. & Ab. Physic* 99 A Physician..when he came found her Pleuritically affected.

‖**pleuritis** (plʊˈraɪtɪs). *Path.* [L. *pleurītis* (Vitr.) a. Gr. πλευρῖτις (Hipp.), f. πλευρά side, rib; see -ITIS.] Inflammation of the pleura; more usually called PLEURISY.

1693 *Blancard's Phys. Dict.* (ed. 2), *Pleuritis*, a Pleurisie, an Inflammation of the Membrane Pleura, and the intercostal Muscles. **1745** W. THOMPSON *Sickness* ii, Pleuritis bending o'er its side in pain. **1822–34** *Good's Study Med.* (ed. 4) I. 505 Pleuritis. **1868** DARWIN *Anim. & Pl.* I. iii. 97 The Leicester sheep were so rapidly destroyed by pleuritis.

pleuro. Chiefly *Austral.* Colloquial abbreviation of PLEUROPNEUMONIA. Also *attrib.*

1885 R. C. PRAED *Austral. Life* 244 Pleuro is very bad our way. I don't believe much in inoculation—do you? **1890** *Daily News* 16 Oct. 2/7 Pleuro has broken out afresh in Cheshire on the farms..near Winsford. **1897** 'R. BOLDREWOOD' *My Run Home* xx. 176 'Do you ever have any pleuro among your cattle?' said I; 'I heard something about it in England.' **1902** H. LAWSON *Children of Bush* 244 Jack started coughing again, like an old cow with the pleuro. **1917** A. B. PATERSON *Three Elephant Power* 42 Providence sends the pleuro, and big strong beasts slink away by themselves. **1944** W. E. HARNEY *Taboo* (ed. 3) 40 One day..a pleuro bullock chased him. **1965** *Bulletin* (Sydney) 13 Feb. 40/3 They used their weapons on the local pleuro bull which was the only large, live target they had a chance to assail. **1975** *Sunday Mail* (Brisbane) 20 July 10/5 Today he looks back with pride at the successful eradication of the killer disease 'pleuro' which threatened the cattle industry in 1970.

pleuro- (plʊərəʊ), before a vowel **pleur-**, combining form of Gr. πλευρά side, PLEURA, πλευρόν rib; used in various scientific terms, chiefly in the senses of 'side' and 'pleura', occasionally in that of 'rib'. (See the more important of these in their alphabetical places.)

pleuroblastic (-ˈblæstɪk) *a. Bot.* [Gr. βλαστός germ], see quot. ‖**pleurobranchia** (-ˈbræŋkɪə), also anglicized as **ˈpleurobranch** (-bræŋk), *Zool.*, a pleural branchia or gill, i.e. one attached to the epimeron of a thoracic somite, in Crustacea. **pleuroˈbranchial** *a.*, of or pertaining to a pleurobranchia. **pleuroˈbranchiate** *a.*, having pleurobranchiæ, as a crustacean; having gills along the sides, as a gastropod mollusc of the order *Pleurobranchiata.* **pleuro-bronˈchitis**, *Path.*, inflammation of the pleura and bronchi; pleurisy with bronchitis. **ˈpleurocele** (-siːl), *Path.* [Gr. κήλη tumour], hernia of the pleura. ‖**pleuroˈcentrum** (pl. **-a**) *Anat.*, each lateral half of the centrum of a vertebra, a hemicentrum; hence **pleuroˈcentral** *a.*, pertaining to a pleurocentrum. **pleuroˈcerebral** *a.*, connecting a pleural with a cerebral ganglion: applied to a nerve-cord in certain invertebrates. **ˈpleurocœle** (-siːl) *Zool.* [Gr. κοῖλος hollow], each lateral chamber of the hinder part of the visceral cavity in a brachiopod. **pleurocolic** (-ˈkɒlɪk) *a. Anat.*, having relation to the ribs and the colon: applied to a ligament or fold of the peritoneum (= COSTOCOLIC). **ˈpleuroconch** (-kɒŋk) *Zool.*, a lamellibranchiate mollusc of the division *Pleuroconcha*, characterized by inequivalve shells. **pleurodiran** (-ˈdaɪərən) *Zool.* [Gr. δειρή neck], *a.* applied to those tortoises which bend the neck sideways in the shell (opp. to *cryptodirous*); *sb.* a pleurodiran tortoise. **pleuroˈdirous** *a.* = prec. adj. **pleuroˈdiscous** *a. Bot.*, 'growing on the sides of the disk' (*Treas. Bot.*, 1866). **pleurogenic** (-ˈdʒɛnɪk), **pleurogenous** (-ˈɒdʒɪnəs) *adjs., Path.* [see -GEN, -IC, -OUS], originating in the pleura. **pleurogynous** (-ˈɒdʒɪnəs) *a. Bot.* [see -GYNOUS], applied to stamens or petals when inserted on the sides of the ovary. **pleurogyrate** (-ˈdʒaɪərət) *a. Bot.* [see GYRATE] (see quot.). **pleurohepatitis** (-hɛpəˈtaɪtɪs) [see HEPATITIS], inflammation involving the pleura and the liver (Billings *Med. Dict.* 1890). **pleuropathy** *Path.* [Gr. -πάθεια, πάθος suffering], disease of the pleura (Mayne *Expos. Lex.* 1858). **pleuroˈpedal** *a. Zool.* [see PEDAL *a.*[1]], applied to a nerve-cord connecting a pleural with a pedal ganglion, in molluscs (*Syd. Soc. Lex.* 1895). **ˌpleuro-periˈcardial** *a.*, belonging to the pleura and the pericardium: applied to a friction-sound heard in auscultation in cases of pleurisy. **ˌpleuro-pericarˈditis**, *Path.*, inflammation involving the pleura and pericardium. **pleuroperiˈpneumony**, ‖ **-periˈpneuˈmonia** (now *rare* or *Obs.*) [see PERIPNEUMONY] = PLEURO-PNEUMONIA. **pleuro-ˈpulmonary** *a.* [see PULMONARY], pertaining to the pleura and the lungs. **pleurorhizal** (-ˈraɪzəl) *a. Bot.* [Gr. ῥίζα root], having the radicle placed laterally against the cotyledons (i.e. having the cotyledons accumbent), as in the embryo of some crucifers; so **pleuroˈrhizeous** *a.*, belonging to the tribe *Pleurorhizeæ* (De Candolle) of *Cruciferæ*, characterized by this arrangement in the embryo; **pleuroˈrhizous** *a.* = *pleurorhizal*. ‖**pleurorhœa** (-ˈriːə) *Path.* [Gr. ῥοία flow], effusion of fluid into the cavity of the pleura (Dunglison 1853). **ˌpleurosponˈdylian** *a. Zool.* [Gr. σπόνδυλος, σφόνδυλος vertebra], having the ribs rigidly fixed to the vertebræ, as the group *Pleurospondylia* of Reptiles, comprising the turtles and tortoises; of or belonging to this group. **ˈpleurospasm** *Path.*, cramp in the side (Billings *Med. Dict.* 1890). ‖**pleuˈrosteon** (pl. -ea) *Zool.* [Gr. ὀστέον bone], a lateral part on each side of the sternum in birds (in young birds forming a separate bone), to which the ribs are attached; hence **pleuˈrosteal** *a.*, pertaining to or of the nature of a pleurosteon. **pleuˈrotomy**, *Surg.* [Gr. τομή a cutting], 'incision into the pleura' (Billings 1890). ‖**pleuˈrotonus** *Path.* [Gr. τόνος stretching, tension] = PLEUROTHOTONOS; hence **pleuroˈtonic** *a.* **ˈpleurotribe** *a. Bot.* [Gr. τρίβειν to rub], applied to flowers having stamens and styles so placed as to rub against the sides of insects that frequent them, thus ensuring cross-fertilization; so **pleuroˈtribal** *a.* in same sense. **pleuro-ˈtyphoid** *a. Path.*, typhoid (fever) accompanied with pleurisy. **pleurovisceral** (-ˈvɪsərəl) *a. Zool.*, of a nerve-cord or loop: connecting a pleural and a visceral ganglion in certain invertebrates.

1887 tr. *De Bary's Fungi* 498/1 In Peronosporeæ: forms producing vesicular lateral outgrowths serving as haustoria are *pleuroblastic. **1892** THOMSON *Outl. Zool.* xiii. 240 There remain three *pleurobranchs, one on the epimeron of the fifth large limb, and two quite rudimentary on the two preceding segments. **1880** HUXLEY *Crayfish* ii. 79 From this mode of attachment [to the sides of the thorax, above the joint] it is distinguished from the other [branchiæ] as a *pleurobranchia. **1898** *Allbutt's Syst. Med.* V. 25, I have long been in the habit of using the name '*pleuro-bronchitis' to suggest something more than an accidental coincidence. **1842** DUNGLISON *Med. Lex.*, *Pleurocele, hernia of the pleura. **1889** NICHOLSON & LYDEKKER *Palæontology* II. 1031 According to Dr. Fritsch's restoration.., the *pleurocentra belonging to this vertebra would be on the anterior side. **1885** DAVIDSON in *Trans. Linn. Soc.* Ser. II. IV. *Zool.* 210, I propose to give the name *pleurocœles to these spaces [in *Lingula*] simply from their position as side chambers. **1890** BILLINGS *Med. Dict.*, *Pleurocolic ligament, phrenocolic ligament. **1862** DANA *Man. Geol.* 500 Of the integripallial Mesozoic species, one half were *Pleuroconchs (species having unequal valves). **1887** *Athenæum* 9 July 58/3 A *pleurodiran chelonian of terrestrial and herbivorous habits. **1901** *Ibid.* 16 Mar. 343/3 In late Secondary and early Tertiary times the Pleurodiran chelonians were almost cosmopolitan. **1890** *Cent. Dict.*, *Pleurogenic. **1895** *Syd. Soc. Lex.*, *Pleurogenic*, the same as *Pleurogenous. **1905** H. D. ROLLESTON *Dis. Liver* 175 Cases of interstitial pneumonia secondary to chronic pleurisy (pleurogenous pneumonia). **1819** LINDLEY tr. *Richard's Obs. Fruits & Seeds* 58 The genus *Nymphæa*, in which the insertion of the petals and stamina is *pleurogynous. *Ibid.* 86 *Pleurogynous (insertion)*; on the body itself of an *ovarium superum*. **1866** *Treas. Bot.* 905 *Pleurogyrate, a term employed for those ferns whose spore-case has a ring carried round the sides. **1876** tr. *von Ziemssen's Cycl. Med.* VI. 595 This sound is called the extra-pericardial.. or *pleuro-pericardial friction sound. **1890** BILLINGS *Med. Dict.*, *Pleuropericarditis, pleuritis with pericarditis. **1738** STACK in *Phil. Trans.* XL. 434 The distinctive Characteristics of the true Pleurisy and Peripneumony, and..of the frequent Combination of both, or *Pleuro-Peripneumony. **1782** KIRKLAND in *Med. Commun.* I. 23 *note* 27 A pleuro-peripneumony finished his life. **1898** *Allbutt's Syst. Med.* V. 64 Setting up a proliferative irritation in the *pleuro-pulmonary connective tissue. **1886** *Cassell's Encycl. Dict.*, *Pleurorhizal. **1858** MAYNE *Expos. Lex.*, *Pleurorhizeous. **1875** NEWTON in *Encycl. Brit.* III. 720/1 In *Turnix* there are two more centres, mesiad of the *pleurostea, these are the *coracostea*. **1895** *Syd. Soc. Lex.*, *Pleurosteon... In young birds this can be seen to be a separate bone, one being on each side of the lophosteon or median bone. **1899** *Allbutt's Syst. Med.* VII. 332 This general *pleurotonic spasm instantly ceases when the electrodes are transferred [from the free nucleus caudatus] to the surface of the optic thalamus. *Ibid.* 524 We have once seen the opisthotonos accompanied by left-sided *pleurotonus. **1901** OSLER *Princ. & Pract. Med.* i. 28 It [i.e. pleurisy] may occur at the outset —— *pleuro-typhoid —— or slowly during convalescence.

pleurocarpous (plʊərəʊˈkɑːpəs), *a. Bot.* [mod. f. PLEURO- + Gr. καρπ-ός fruit + -OUS.] Of mosses: Bearing the fructification on the sides of the branches; lateral-fruited. Cf. ACROCARPOUS.

1863 BERKELEY *Brit. Mosses* iii. 14 In Pleurocarpous Mosses.. true ramification constantly takes place. **1866** —— in *Treas. Bot.* 766 The same genus [of mosses] has acrocarpous and pleurocarpous species.

pleurodont (ˈplʊərədɒnt), *sb.* and *a. Zool.* [f. PLEURO- + Gr. ὀδούς, ὀδοντ- tooth.]

a. *sb.* A lizard having teeth fixed to the side of the jaw-bone. **b.** *adj.* (*a*) Belonging to the *Pleurodontes*, a group of lizards having this character; (*b*) applied to such teeth or their attachment.

1840 *Penny Cycl.* XVIII. 260/2 The maxillary teeth of the species composing the Pleurodonts have their summit.. more or less trilobated. **1862** DANA *Man. Geol.* 346 In others (Pleurodonts) the teeth are implanted in a groove, the outer border of which projects more than the inner. **1872** MIVART *Elem. Anat.* vii. 256 We may find a development of a bony alveolar plate on one side.., to which the teeth may become attached by actual bony growth..as in the Iguanian Lizards. Such a form of attachment is termed *pleurodont*.

‖**pleurodynia** (plʊərəʊˈdɪnɪə). *Path.* Also †**pleurodyne** (-ˈɒdɪniː), **pleurodyny** (-ˈɒdɪnɪ). [mod.L., f. PLEURO- + Gr. -οδυνία in comb. f. ὀδύνη pain; in F. *pleurodynie*.] Pain in the side caused by rheumatism in the muscles of the chest.

1802 HOOPER *Quincy's Med. Dict.*, Pleurodynia. **1808** *Med. Jrnl.* XIX. 187 Account of Diseases in London... Pleurodyne. **1822–34** *Good's Study Med.* (ed. 4) I. 505 The last genus of diseases..under the present order, is that which has been usually denominated pleurodyne. **1852** T. THOMPSON *Ann. Influenza* 378 Tightness of chest and pleurodiny are the result. **1878** A. M. HAMILTON *Nerv. Dis.* 428 Pleurodynia is often mistaken for pleurisy.

pleuroid (ˈplʊərɔɪd). *Anat.* [f. PLEURO- + -OID.] Baur's name for either element of the pleural arch of a typical vertebra; a pleurapophysis.

1887 *Amer. Nat.* Oct. 945 The spines connected with the neuroids ought to be called, as before, *neural spines*; those connected with the pleuroids, *pleural spines*.

pleurolepidal (-ˈlɛpɪdəl), *a. Palæont.* [f. mod.L. *Pleurolepis* (f. Gr. πλευρόν rib + λεπίς scale) + -AL[1].] Having rows of scales with bony processes like ribs, interlocking with each other, as the fishes of the extinct genus *Pleurolepis* or family *Pleurolepididæ*; consisting of such scales. So **pleuroˈlepidid**, **pleuroˈlepidoid** *adjs.*, belonging to the family *Pleurolepididæ*.

1880 GÜNTHER *Fishes* 366 Body..covered with rhombic scales arranged in decussating pleurolepidal lines.

‖**pleuron** (ˈplʊərən). *Anat.* and *Zool.* Pl. **pleura**. [a. Gr. πλευρόν rib, side.] The lateral part of the body-wall, the side; *spec.* in Arthropoda, the lateral part of each somite or section of the body (in insects, of each thoracic somite).

1706 PHILLIPS, *Pleuron*, a Side or Rib. **1872** NICHOLSON *Palæont.* 146 A plate which is called the pleuron, or pleura. **1880** HUXLEY *Crayfish* iii. 96 Where these two join, a broad plate is sent down on each side, which overlaps the bases of the abdominal appendages and is known as the pleuron.

pleuronect (ˈplʊərənɛkt). *Ichthyol.* [ad. mod.L. *Pleuronectēs*, f. Gr. πλευρά side + νήκτης swimmer.] A fish of the genus *Pleuronectes* or family *Pleuronectidæ*; a flat-fish. So **pleuroˈnectid**, **pleuroˈnectoid**, *sb.* a fish of the family *Pleuronectidæ*; *a.* belonging to this family.

[**1774** GOLDSM. *Nat. Hist.* (1862) II. III. i. 299 The Pleuronectes or Flat-fish.] **1849–52** *Todd's Cycl. Anat.* IV. 849/2 The eyes of the pleuronects are of different sizes. **1894** *Athenæum* 12 May 617/3 The *recessus orbitalis*, an accessory visual organ of the pleuronectid fishes.

pleuro-peritoneal, -æal (ˌplʊərəʊpɛrɪtəʊˈniːəl), *a. Anat.* [f. PLEURO- + PERITONEAL, or f. next + -AL[1].] Of or belonging at once to the pleuræ and the peritoneum, or the pleuro-peritoneum.

1872 MIVART *Elem. Anat.* vi. 218 The heart and the roots of the great vessels which proceed from it are..placed within the inner wall of this pleuro-peritoneal cavity. **1875** HUXLEY & MARTIN *Elem. Biol.* (1877) 165 As this cavity answers to those of the pleuræ and of the peritoneum in the higher animals, it is termed the pleuroperitoneal cavity; and the soft smooth membrane which lines it and covers the contained viscera is the pleuroperitoneal membrane. **1898** *Allbutt's Syst. Med.* V. 152 A general chronic inflammation with thickening of the whole pleuro-peritoneal cavity.

‖**ˌpleuro-peritoˈneum, -ˈnæum.** *Anat.* [mod.L., f. PLEURO- + PERITONEUM.] The serous membrane lining the body-cavity and enveloping the viscera in vertebrates below mammals: corresponding to the pleuræ and peritoneum in mammals. Also called simply PERITONEUM.

1875 HUXLEY & MARTIN *Elem. Biol.* (1877) 201 Note the smooth moist membrane (pleuroperitoneum) lining the inside of the body-cavity and covering the outside of the contained viscera. **1897** *Allbutt's Syst. Med.* III. 680 The possibility of a development of true carcinoma in connection with the pleuro-peritoneum is at once obvious.

‖**pleuro-pneumonia** (ˌplʊərəʊnjuːˈməʊnɪə). Also without hyphen, and in anglicized form **pleuro-ˈpneumony**. Also **pleuri-**. [mod.L., f. PLEURO- + PNEUMONIA. So F. *pleuropneumonie* (16th c.).] *Path.* Inflammation involving the pleura and the lung; pneumonia complicated with pleurisy; *esp.* a contagious febrile disease peculiar to horned cattle.

1725 N. ROBINSON *Th. Physick* 117 By several Authors of good Credit, both these Diseases are express'd by one compound Term, viz. *Pleuripneumonia*, or a Pleuripneumony. **1843** GRAVES *Syst. Clin. Med.* xxi. 252 A man, after fever, gets an attack of pleuro-pneumonia. **1856** *Farmer's Mag.* Nov. 442 Pleuro-pneumonia, or lung disease, having broken out in several parts of the county. **1880** *Manch. Guard.* 6 Dec., In the cargoes [of cattle] landed last year very few cases of pleuro-pneumonia were detected.

b. *Biol.* ***pleuropneumonia-like organism***: = MYCOPLASMA. Abbrev. *PPLO* s.v. P II.

1935 E. KLIENEBERGER in *Jrnl. Path. & Bacteriol.* XL. 93 (*heading*) The natural occurrence of pleuropneumonia-like organisms in apparent symbiosis with *Streptobacillus moniliformis* and other bacteria. **1951** *Jrnl. Bacteriol.* LXI. 395 A characteristic of the parasitic pleuropneumonialike organisms (PPLO) is the requirement of serum or ascitic fluid for growth *in vitro*. **1964** *New Scientist* 19 Nov. 497/1 The workers in Glasgow have grown pleuropneumonia-like organisms from cell cultures containing leukaemia 'virus'. **1973** *Nature* 9 Mar. 83/1 Mycoplasmas, which used to be known as pleuropneumonia-like organisms, are the smallest free-living organisms.

Hence **pleuro-pneumonic** (-ˈnɒnɪk) *a.*, of, pertaining to, or affected with pleuro-pneumonia.

1898 *Allbutt's Syst. Med.* V. 71 The influence of pleuro-pneumonic fibrosis.

pleurostict (ˈplʊərəʊstɪkt), *a. Entom.* [ad. mod.L. *Pleurosticta* neut. pl., f. PLEURO- + Gr. στικτός, vbl. adj. f. στίζειν to prick.] Belonging to the division *Pleurosticta* of scarabæid beetles, characterized by having the abdominal spiracles (except the anterior ones) pleural, or situated on the dorsal part of the abdominal segments.

1882 *Amer. Nat.* XXII. 951 The views of the late Dr. Le Conte of the position of [Pleocoma], which he insisted was a Laparostict, and not a Pleurostict Lamellicorn.

‖**pleurothotonos** (plʊərəʊˈθɒtənɒs), **-us** (-əs). *Path.* Often erron. **pleurosth-** (after *emprosthotonos, opisthotonos*). [mod.L., f. Gr. πλευρόθεν from the side (f. πλευρά side) + -τονος stretched, stretching.] Tetanic bending of the body to one side.

1822–34 *Good's Study Med.* (ed. 4) III. 263 The pleurosthotonos of authors of a later date. **1842** DUNGLISON *Med. Lex.*, *Pleurothotonos*. **1874** CARPENTER *Ment. Phys.* App. (1879) 715 An immediate *pleurosthotonos*, or bending of the body to one side. **1878** tr. *von Ziemssen's Cycl. Med.* XIV. 318 To this original division Boenecken afterwards added another form pleurothotonos (or tetanus lateralis).

pleurotomarioid (ˌplʊərəʊtəʊˈmɛərɪɔɪd), *a.* and *sb. Zool.* [f. mod.L. *Pleurotomāri-a* (f. *pleurotoma* see next) + *-āria* (see -ARY 1) + -OID.] **a.** *adj.* Resembling the genus *Pleurotomaria* of gastropod molluscs, having top-shaped shells with a deep cleft in the outer lip; found (living) in deep tropical seas, and (extinct) in many formations from the Silurian onward. **b.** *sb.* A gastropod of the family *Pleurotomariidæ*.

pleurotomid (plʊˈrɒtəmɪd). *Zool.* [ad. mod.L. *Pleuroˈtomidæ* pl., f. *Pleuˈrotoma*, name of the typical genus, f. Gr. πλευρά side + τομή cutting: see -ID.] A gastropod mollusc of the family *Pleurotomidæ*, having shells usually spindle-shaped, with a notch in the outer lip. So **pleuˈrotomine** (-maɪn) *a.*, belonging or related to the genus *Pleurotoma*; **pleuˈrotomoid**, *a.* resembling *Pleurotoma*, or belonging to the *Pleurotomidæ*; *sb.* a mollusc of this family.

‖**pleurum** ('pluərəm). *Zool.* Pl. **pleura.** [mod.L. variant of PLEURON, made to correspond with *tergum* and *sternum.*] = PLEURON in the specific sense, as applied to Arthropoda.

1898 PACKARD *Textbk. Entomol.* 87 Each segment consists of the *tergum, pleurum*, and *sternum.*

†**pleven-plait.** *Obs. Sc.* Also **plaven plait, planeplait** (? plauen*plait). [? f. PLEVIN assurance, warranty + PLATE *sb.* 3 b.] ? Plate armour of proof, warranted armour.

1535 STEWART *Cron. Scot.* (Rolls) I. 140 And pleven plait with mony riall rufe, With courtlie cast of cot-armour abufe. *Ibid.* 402 And pansis proude of plaven plait of pryde. *Ibid.* II. 39 Ane greit power, in planeplait of steill.

plever, obs. form of PLOVER.

†**plevin.** *Law. Obs.* Also 5 **plevyne.** [a. OF. *plevine* pledge (12th c. in Godef.), = med.L. *plevīna*, f. *plevīre*, in F. *plevir* to warrant; see PLEDGE.] Pledge, assurance, warrant.

(Frequent in AF. legal use; in Eng. law-books since 16th c.; rare in ME., quot. *c* 1400 not legal.)

[**1275** *Act 3 Edw. I*, c. 17 (*Stat. Westm.*) Le Visconte ou le Baillif,.. voyst asayer de fere la plevine des avers a celui qe pris les avera. **1292** BRITTON III. vi. §6 Et si le pleintif soit si povere qe il ne puse suerté trover, suffit la plevine par sa fey [*tr.* And if the plaintiff be so poor that he cannot find security, the pledging of his own faith shall be sufficient].] *c* **1400** *Ywaine & Gaw.* 1253 Thar wedded Ywaine in plevyne The riche lady Alundyne. **1543** *transl. of quot.* 1275 The same shyryffe or baylyffe.. do assay to make pleuyn of the beastes from him that toke them. **1607** in COWELL *Interpr.* **1704** J. HARRIS *Lex. Techn.* I, *Plevin*, in Common Law, signifies a Warrant or Assurance. See *Replevin.* **1727–41** CHAMBERS *Cycl., Plevin, Plevina*, in law, a warrant or assurance; the same with *Pledge.*

†'**plevisable**, *a.* *Law. Obs. rare.* [a. OF. *plevisable*, f. *plevir* to warrant.] = BAILABLE *a.*[2] 1.

[**1292** BRITTON I. xxii. §3 Qi..ount lessé les nent plevisables prisouns par meynprise, et les plevisables detenuz [*tr.* Have let to mainprise prisoners who were not bailable, and have detained others who were bailable].] **1670** *Tryal W. Penn & W. Mead* App. in *Phenix* I. 329 By the antient Law of England, it was Felony to detain a man in Prison, after sufficient Bail offer'd, where the Party was plevisable; every Person was plevisable, but he that was appeal'd of Treason, Murder, Robbery or Burglary.

plew (plu:). [Canadian F. *pélu*, = F. *poilu* hairy, f. *poil* hair.] The skin of a beaver.

1851 MAYNE REID *Scalp Hunt.* xviii, The beaver skins have fallen, according to their phraseology, to '*plew a plug*'. **1899** *Blackw. Mag.* Jan. 40/1 Each beaver-plew of full-grown animal or 'kitten' fetched six to eight dollars overhead.

plew, -e, plewch, plewgh, Sc. and north. ff. PLOUGH.

plewme, plewrisie, -osy, obs. ff. PLUME, PLEURISY.

†**plex**, *sb. Obs. rare*⁻¹. [? ad. L. *plex-us* plaiting, braid.] A plait or braid (of hair).

1460 *Lybeaus Disc.* 128 Hys berd was yelow as ony wax, To hys gerdell henge the plex, I dar well say yn certe.

plex (plɛks), *v. rare*⁻⁰. [f. L. *plex-*, ppl. stem of *plectĕre* to plait, interweave: cf. *perplex.*] *intr.* To form a plexus. Hence **plexed** (plɛkst) *ppl. a.*, formed into or like a plexus, plexiform.

1890 in *Cent. Dict.*

plexal ('plɛksəl), *a. rare*⁻⁰. [irreg. for **plexual*, f. PLEXUS + -AL[1]: cf. *sexual, gradual.*] Of or pertaining to a plexus.

1890 in *Cent. Dict.* **1895** in *Syd. Soc. Lex.*

†,**plexi-chro'nometer.** *Obs. rare*⁻¹. [ad. F. *plexichronomètre*, f. Gr. πλῆξις a striking (? taken in sense 'beat') + *chronomètre* chronometer, metronome; see CHRONOMETER.] An instrument for timing the beats in music; a metronome.

1786 JEFFERSON *Writ.* (1859) I. 504 They have ordered all music which shall be printed here, in future, to have the movements numbered in correspondence with the plexichronometer.

plexicose ('plɛksɪkəʊs), *a. rare*⁻¹. [irreg. f. PLEXUS + -IC + -OSE, app. after *bellicose.*] Of the nature of a plexus, or composed of plexuses.

1847–9 *Todd's Cycl. Anat.* IV. 301/2 The lymphatics from the different organs.. form plexicose chains.

plexiform ('plɛksɪfɔːm), *a. Anat.* [mod. f. PLEX-US + -FORM. So F. *plexiforme.*] Of the form of a plexus; forming a plexus or plexuses. ***plexiform layer*** [tr. F. *couche plexiforme (externe, interne)* (S. Ramón y Cajal 1893, in *La Cellule* IX. 132)], either of two layers of the retina separated by the inner nuclear layer, the outer one of which contains synapses between the rods and cones and the neurones of the nuclear layer, whilst the inner one contains synapses between these neurones and ganglion cells; = *molecular layer* (*a*) s.v. MOLECULAR *a.* 5.

1828 WEBSTER, *Plexiform*, in the form of network; complicated. *Quincy.* **1830** R. KNOX *Cloquet's Anat.* 463 Of these portions the outer and larger, which is plexiform, triangular and flattened, comes from the Gasserian ganglion. **1894** *Quain's Elem. Anat.* (ed. 10) III. III. 41 (*heading*) Inner molecular or inner plexiform layer, neurospongium. **1900** *Brit. Med. Jrnl.* No. 2040. 248 Its papilla is covered with a plexiform mesh of dilated vessels. **1911** *Ophthalmoscope* IX. 437 The external plexiform layer remains very narrow. **1959** W. ANDREW *Textbk. Compar. Histol.* xv. 604 The ten layers in order, from without in, i.e. toward the vitreous humor, are: (1) the pigmented epithelium, (2) the layer of rods and cones,..(5) the outer plexiform layer, (6) the inner nuclear layer, (7) the inner plexiform layer,..and (10) the inner limiting membrane. **1972** THORPE & GLICKSTEIN in tr. *S. Ramón y Cajal's Structure of Retina* p. viii, The dendritic trees of the ganglion cells spread at different levels within the inner plexiform layer and form associations with the processes of the amacrine and bipolar cell processes, thereby creating the distinct laminar appearance of this layer so clearly described by Cajal.

Plexiglas ('plɛksɪglɑːs, -æs). Chiefly *U.S.* Also **Plexiglass**, and with lower-case initial. A proprietary name for the substance also sold under the names of PERSPEX and LUCITE. Freq. *attrib.*

1935 *Trade Marks Jrnl.* 10 Apr. 451 Plexiglass... Glass. Röhm & Haas, Aktiengesellschaft.., Darmstadt, Germany; manufacturers. *Ibid.* 31 July 968/2 Plexiglass... Glass substitutes made from artificial resins. Röhm & Haas Aktiengesellschaft.., Darmstadt, Germany; manufacturers. **1936** *Official Gaz.* (U.S. Patent Office) 30 June 999/1 Röhm and Haas Company, Philadelphia. *Plexiglas* for sheets of solid transparent resinous material to be used as a glass substitute. Claims use since June 5, 1935. **1936** *Jrnl. Aeronaut. Sci.* Nov. 13/1 For smaller aircraft, Plexiglas, Glyptal, and Vinylite are available in sheet form. **1941** *Product Engin.* May 267/3 Area of windows is 20 sq. ft., hence lighter Plexiglass instead of plate glass. **1943** J. STEINBECK in *N.Y. Herald Tribune* 31 Aug. 17/4 The sergeant had carved the handles of his gun from the plexiglass from the nose of a bomber. **1951** *Archit. Rev.* CX. 222/1 (*caption*) Roof, tar and gravel with plexiglass skylights. **1954** *Trade Marks Jrnl.* 15 Dec. 1264/2 Plexiglas... Chemical products used in industry, science and photography; fire extinguishing compositions, soldering preparations.., adhesives.., and synthetic resins. Röhm & Haas Gesellschaft mit beschränkter Haftung.., Darmstadt, Germany; manufacturers. **1955** *Ibid.* 13 April 387/1 Plexiglas... All goods..made of glass or of glass substitutes made from plastics. Röhm & Haas Gesellschaft. **1957** *Economist* 19 Oct. 229/2 The ceremonial drive in an open landau..or the neighbourhood tour in a grey Cadillac with plexiglas top. **1965** ZIGROSSER & GAEHDE *Guide Coll. Orig. Prints* vii. 115 Plexiglas is sometimes used for framing because it is unbreakable. The Plexiglas should be coated with an antistatic to eliminate its tendency to attract dust. **1970** HARARI & HAYWARD tr. *A. Amalrik's Involuntary Journey to Siberia* iv. 56 This door had a small panel of plexiglass. **1976** *S9* (N.Y.) Feb. 30/2 The large full-feature backlighted digital clock has buzz signal alarm. All encased in a modern smoked plexiglas front panel. **1977** *Time* 31 Jan. 15/2 Cairo's flying squads of riot police with their Plexiglas face masks, shields and staves were in control.

pleximeter (plɛk'sɪmɪtə(r)). *Med.* Also (irreg.) **plexometer.** See also PLESSIMETER. [f. Gr. πλῆξις stroke, percussion (f. πλήσσειν to strike) + -METER (the suffix being loosely used, and with the sense of 'estimating' rather than 'measuring').] A small thin plate of ivory or other substance, which is placed firmly upon some part of the body and struck with a PLEXOR in medical percussion. Also applied to anything used for the same purpose.

1842 in DUNGLISON *Med. Lex.* **1843** SIR T. WATSON *Lect. Princ. & Pract. Physic* xlvii. II. 10 Many persons..use no other pleximeter than the fingers of the left hand. **1853** MARKHAM *Skoda's Auscult.* 2 The pleximeter renders percussion much less irksome to the patient, and the sounds more distinct;..we are able, by its aid, to recognize differences in sound, which are not otherwise perceptible. **1882** OGILVIE, *Pleximeter, Plexometer.* **1882** *Standard* 13 Dec. 5/5 The pleximeter, the stethoscope,..the laryngoscope, the ophthalmoscope,..could scarcely have been familiar to the..doctor.

Hence **pleximetric** (plɛksɪ'mɛtrɪk) *a.*, pertaining to a pleximeter or the use of it; **pleximetry** (plɛk'sɪmɪtrɪ), the use of a pleximeter.

1858 MAYNE *Expos. Lex., Pleximetric.* **1895** *Syd. Soc. Lex., Plessimetry*, see *Pleximetry.*

plexor ('plɛksə(r)). *Med.* See also PLESSOR. [irreg. f. Gr. πλῆξι-ς or πλήσσ-ειν (see PLEXIMETER) + -OR, after *flexor*, etc.] A small hammer or other instrument used (with a PLEXIMETER) in medical percussion; a percussion-hammer.

1844 in DUNGLISON *Med. Lex.* **1895** *Syd. Soc. Lex., Plexor*, a striker; used specifically of that which strikes in Medical percussion. This may be either a hammer or the fingers of the physician.

plexure ('plɛksjʊə(r)). *rare.* [f. L. type **plexūra* a plaiting, f. *plectĕre, plex-* to plait, interweave.] A plaiting or interweaving; something plaited or interwoven. In quot. 1671 = PLEXUS 1.

1671 GREW *Anat. Plants* I. ii. §14 'Tis most probable, that none of their Fibres are truly inosculated, saving perhaps, in the Plexures. **1736** H. BROOKE *Univ. Beauty* III. 297 Their social branch the wedded plexures rear. **1832** J. P. KENNEDY *Swallow B.* iv, An intruding rose has stolen a nest among the plexures of the vine.

plexus ('plɛksəs). Pl. **plexuses** (in 8 plexus's), rarely **plexus.** [a. L. *plexu-s* (*u*-stem), pl. *plexūs*, f. *plectĕre, plex-* to plait, interweave.]

1. *Anat.* A structure in the animal body consisting of a bundle of minute fibres or tubes, as nerves, blood-vessels, or lymphatics, closely interwoven and intercommunicating; a network of fibres or vessels.

Usually named from its relation to or situation in some part or organ, or from its form, as *brachial p., cardiac p., carotid p., choroid p., cœliac p., coronary p., gastric p., hepatic p., lumbar p., mesenteric p., pampiniform p., pelvic p., pulmonary p., sacral p., solar p., splenic p.*, etc.

1682 T. GIBSON *Anat.* 19 Fallopius will have it to proceed from the superiour and inferiour plexus of Nerves of the Abdomen. **1702** J. PURCELL *Cholick* (1714) 13 If these Animal Spirits or Recrements can continue their Motion down the minute Channels of the little Nerves, into these Plexus's, Why should they stop there? **1727–41** CHAMBERS *Cycl., Plexus*,..a name common to several parts in the body, consisting of bundles of little vessels interwoven in form of net-work. *Ibid.*, Several branches both from the hepatic and splenic plexus..form the mesenteric plexus. **1872** HUXLEY *Phys.* xi. 271 Great net-works, or plexuses.

2. *gen.* Any intertwined or interwoven mass; a complex body, collection, or set of things (material or immaterial); a web, network, complication.

1769 E. BANCROFT *Guiana* 33 Their footstalks are inclosed in a strong reticular web-like plexus, which is the cloathing this tree has been said to afford. **1863** H. SPENCER *Ess.* III. 24 Relations each of which has for its terms a complete plexus of antecedents and a complete plexus of consequents. **1875** MAINE *Hist. Inst.* iv. 106 A dissolution of the plexus of mutual rights and a partition of the family property. **1891** J. W. POWELL in *Scribner's Mag.* Oct. 465 The partial channels sometimes interlock so as to form a plexus over the area of the delta.

3. *Math.* (See quot.)

1860 CAYLEY *Coll. Math. Papers* IV. 603 Such a system of equations, or generally the system of equations required for the complete expression of the relations existing between a set of quantities (and which are in general more numerous than the relations themselves) is said to be a *Plexus.*

†**pley.** *Obs. rare.* [ad. Sp. *playa* coast of the sea, or of a river;—L. *plāga.*]

a **1500** in Arnolde *Chron.* (1811) 233 Walkyng..by the pley of the ryuer of this said towne [San Lucas de Berrameda].

pley, -e, obs. ff. PLEA.

pleyde, obs. pa. t. of PLAY *v.*

pley-e, pleyȝe, pleȝe, obs. ff. PLAY.

pleyght, pleyt, -e, obs. ff. PLAIT.

†**pleykstare**, variant of BLEYKSTER, bleacher.

c **1440** *Promp. Parv.* 525/2 Why(t)stare, or pleykstare (*H.* plykstare, *P.* whytstar or blykstar), *candidarius, candidaria. Ibid.* 404/1.

pleyn(e, pleynaunt, obs. ff. PLAIN, PLAINANT.

pleys(e, pleyss, pleysa(u)nce, -and, -a(u)nt: see PLEASE, PLEASANCE, -ANT.

pleyt: see PLEA *sb.* and *v.*

plezeauns, obs. f. PLEASANCE.

pliability (plaɪə'bɪlɪtɪ). [f. PLIABLE *a.*: see -ILITY.] The quality or property of being pliable.

a. Of material things: see PLIABLE *a.* 1.

1795 HERSCHEL in *Phil. Trans.* LXXXV. 402 To preserve the pliability of the ropes. **1802** PALEY *Nat. Theol.* viii. (1819) 103 The suppleness and pliability of the joints. **1815** J. SMITH *Panorama Sc. & Art* I. 4 [To] give the steel pliability without diminishing its hardness. **1899** *Allbutt's Syst. Med.* VIII. 670 The normal pliability of the skin.

b. Of mind or character: see PLIABLE *a.* 2.

1768 STERNE *Sent. Journ.* (1778) II. 74 Sweet pliability of man's spirit, that can at once surrender itself to illusions! **1834** *Oxf. Univ. Mag.* I. 123 Pliability was the peculiar characteristic [of the constitution of 1688]. **1860** W. COLLINS *Wom. White* I. vi, Those feminine attractions of gentleness and pliability.

pliable ('plaɪəb(ə)l), *a.* [a. F. *pliable* (15th c. in Godef.), f. *plier* to bend: see PLY and -ABLE.]

1. Easy to be bent or folded; flexible, supple, yielding; †easily moulded or shaped, plastic.

1483 *Cath. Angl.* 284/1 Plyabylle (*A.* Pliabylle), *flexuosus, flexibilis.* **1494** FABYAN *Chron.* VI. cxlvii. 133 Lyke as the hamer makyth all metallys plyable, so Charlis made his foos or enmyes plyable to his hestis. **1578** LYTE *Dodoens* I. lv. 80 Round, tough, and pliable braunches. **1599** HAKLUYT *Voy.* II. II. 91 That earthen or pliable matter commonly called porcellan. **1646** SIR T. BROWNE *Pseud. Ep.* 105 To walke on ropes..requireth not only a broad foot, but a plyable flexure of joynts. *c* **1790** IMISON *Sch. Art* I. 91 Two slender and pliable wires..are to be fastened. **1879** *Cassell's Techn. Educ.* III. 150/2 Leather..is soaked in water to make it pliable.

2. *fig.* Flexible in disposition or character; that is easily inclined, disposed, or influenced; ready to yield, docile; adaptable. Sometimes in

1494 [see 1]. **1526** *Pilgr. Perf.* (W. de W. 1531) 144 b, That a soule be plyable to the inspiracyons of the holy goost. **1561** T. NORTON *Calvin's Inst.* I. 12 Very few of them do geue themselues pliable to learne of the word of God. **1624** BEDELL *Lett.* vii. 109 The Scholler if he be of a plyable disposition,..yeelds himselfe to his Teacher. **1720** OZELL *Vertot's Rom. Rep.* II. XIV. 332 Agree with Antony; you'll find him more pliable since his Defeat. **1844** LD. BROUGHAM *Brit. Const.* xv. (1862) 237 The members were far from being very pliable to his wishes. **1863** H. COX *Instit.* I. v. 24 Pliable judges were previously chosen. **1876** M. COLLINS *From Midnight to Midn.* II. ii. 233 The girl's voice was remarkably clear and pliable.

†**3.** [Aphetic for APPLIABLE.] Applicable, pertinent, agreeable, conformable. *Obs.*

1596 HARINGTON *Metam. Ajax* (1814) 36 A distichon that is very pliable to my purpose. *a* **1638** MEDE *Wks.* (1672) 62 How pliable the Analogy of Water is to typifie the Spirit. **1641** *Argts. agst. Bowing at Name of Jesus* 14 This is most plyable to the meaning of the Canon.

pliableness (ˈplaɪəb(ə)lnɪs). [f. prec. + -NESS.] The quality of being pliable; pliability. **a.** *lit.*

1581 W. STAFFORD *Exam. Compl.* ii. (1876) 58 If yee prayse the Gold for his weight or plyablenes. **1748** HARTLEY *Observ. Man* I. iii. 410 The Perfection and Pliableness of their vocal Organs. **1825** J. NICHOLSON *Operat. Mechanic* 639 This varnish is destined for articles which require durability, pliableness, and transparency.

b. *fig.* (Often in sinister sense.)

1562 T. NORTON *Calvin's Inst.* Table of Contents Tttvij b, The pliablenesse or weake power of Freewill, whiche was in the fyrst man. **1613** R. CAWDREY *Table Alph.*, *Buxomnesse*, plyablenesse. **1683** *Apol. Prot. France* iv. 38 This Jesuitical pliableness and malice. **1834** J. BROWN *Lett. Sanctif.* iv. 272 An inward pliableness to divine influence.

ˈpliably, *adv.* [f. as prec. + -LY².] In a pliable manner; flexibly; yieldingly, docilely.

1629 DONNE *Serm., Matt.* vi. 21 (1660) III. 223 That I come into the hands of my God as pliably, as ductily, as that first clod of earth of which he made me in Adam. **1692** WOOD *Ath. Oxon.* II. 583/1 Those lukewarm irreligious Temporizers, who had learn'd..pliably to tack about, as still to be ready to receive whatever revolution and turn of affairs should happen.

pliades, obs. form of PLEIADES.

†**ˈpliance.** *Obs. rare*⁻¹. [f. PLIANT *a.*: see -ANCE; cf. *compliance*.] Compliance, yielding.

1643 HAMMOND *Loyal Convert* (1644) 4 If a good King, he must have our praise and our plyance; If an evill King, he must have our Prayers and our Patience.

pliancy (ˈplaɪənsɪ). [f. PLIANT *a.*: see -ANCY.] The quality of being pliant; flexibility.

a. Of material things: see PLIANT *a.* 1.

1711 ADDISON *Spect.* No. 115 ¶5 Giving such an Activity to the Limbs, and such a Pliancy to every Part. **1787** JEFFERSON *Writ.* (1859) II. 97 The difficulty was..to give to old wood the pliancy of young. **1835** JAMES *Gispy* ii, The agile pliancy of youth.

b. *fig.* Of the mind, etc.: see PLIANT *a.* 2.

1789 BP. WATSON *Anecd.* (1817) 225 To be overlooked for want of political pliancy, is a circumstance I need not blush to own. **1810** FOSTER in *Life & Corr.* (1846) I. 424 Social dexterity and pliancy of mind. **1879** B. TAYLOR *Stud. Germ. Lit.* 210 A very little tact and pliancy of nature might have greatly advanced his fortunes.

pliant (ˈplaɪənt), *a.* Forms: 4 **pleaunt, plyande,** 5–6 **pli-, ply-, -aunt(e, -awnt,** 5–8 **plyant,** 6– **pliant.** [a. F. *pliant* (13th c.), pr. pple. of *plier* to bend, PLY.] Bending, yielding.

1. Bending; capable of being bent or folded with ease; supple, lithe, flexible; †ductile, plastic.

13.. *E.E. Allit. P.* C. 439 Hit watz playn in þat place for plyande greuez, For to schylde fro the schene. **1382** WYCLIF *Gen.* iii. 24 He sette cherubyn..and a flawmynge swerde & pleaunt to the waye of the tree of liif to be kept. **1398** TREVISA *Barth. De P.R.* XVI. c. (Tollem. MS.), [Glass] is so plyaunt, þat it fongeþ ful sone diuerse and contrary schappes, by blaste of þe glasier. *Ibid.* XVII. cxliii. (Bodl. MS.), Some weþies..beþ..so pliaunte þat þei brekeþ nought. **1519** HORMAN *Vulg.* 109 The elephante hath a long nose lyke a troumpe, pliant hither and thither. **1601** DONNE *Poems* (1650) 301 The free inhabitants of the plyant ayre. **1699** DAMPIER *Voy.* II. I. 43 These Hats are as stiff as boards, and sit not plyant to their heads. **1774** GOLDSM. *Nat. Hist.* (1776) VI. 397 [Tortoise shells] are easily cast into what form the workman thinks proper, by making them soft and pliant in warm water, and then screwing them in a mold, like a medal. **1880** L. MORRIS *Ode of Life* 25 The fisher, with his pliant wand.

2. *fig.* **a.** Easily bent or inclined to any particular course; readily influenced for good or evil; yielding, compliant; accommodating, complaisant.

c **1400** *Rom. Rose* 4386 Haue herte as hard as dyamaunt, Stedefast, and nought pliaunt. *c* **1530** H. RHODES *Bk. Nurture* 129 in *Babees Bk.* (1868) 85 A plyaunt seruaunt gets fauour to his great aduauntage. **1612** BRINSLEY *Lud. Lit.* ii. (1627) 10 This first age is that wherein they are most pliant. **1701** ROWE *Amb. Step-Moth.* IV. i. 1792 'Twill..make his Youth more plyant to my Will. **1766** FORDYCE *Serm. Yng. Wom.* (1767) II. ix. 75 Men..pliant to good advice. **1860** MOTLEY *Netherl.* I. vii. 405 A committee thus instructed was likely to be sufficiently pliant. **1877** FROUDE *Short Stud.* (1883) IV. I. ii. 25 The king would find some other prelate who would be more pliant in his hands.

b. = FLEXIBLE 4.

1635–56 COWLEY *Davideis* I. 776 Thrice in glad Hymns.. The pliant voice on her seven steps they raise. **1665** BOYLE *Occas. Refl.* (1848) 36 He may..attain to so pliant a style, that scarce any thought will puzzle him to fit words to it. **1882** COX *Expositor* IV. 197 It should be pliant to or leave room for the discoveries of widening science.

c. That lends itself to some purpose; apt, adaptable, suitable. *rare.*

1604 SHAKS. *Oth.* I. iii. 151 Which I obseruing, Tooke once a pliant houre, and found good meanes To draw from her a prayer. **1861** J. PYCROFT *Ways & Words* 60 Noble companions of many a pliant hour.

3. *Comb.*, as ***pliant-bodied, -necked***, etc.

1798 LANDOR *Gebir* VII. 139 Swans pliant-necked. **1870** BRYANT *Iliad* XII. I. 383 Like pliant-bodied wasps or bees.

ˈpliantly, *adv.* [f. prec. + -LY².] In a pliant manner; supply, accommodatingly.

a **1638** MEDE *Wks.* (1672) 118 [The words] yield the sense I speak of pliantly enough. **1672** DRYDEN *Assignation* I. i, You bow so pliantly! **1862** LYTTON *Str. Story* II. 152 Whether it was that..my mind could more pliantly supple itself to her graceful imagination.

pliantness (ˈplaɪəntnɪs). Now *rare.* [f. as prec. + -NESS.] = PLIANCY.

1398 TREVISA *Barth. De P.R.* XVIII. ix. (Bodl. MS.), þat doþ serpentes wiþ bendinge and wigelinge and pliauntnes of þe bodie. **1530** PALSGR. 255/2 Plyantnesse, *ploiantevr*. **1602** CAREW *Cornwall* 72 To your lymmes I yeelde active plyantnesse. **1654** GAYTON *Pleas. Notes* IV. iv. 197 Shee was gentle as a Lamb or a Cow..and this pliantnesse she had partly by Nature and partly by example of her mother. **1725** BRADLEY *Fam. Dict.* s.v. *Orange Tree*, He will perceive when the Tree is dry, by handling its Leaves, if they feel soft,.. and yet this Softness and Pliantness is not always a Sign of it.

‖**plica** (ˈplɪkə, ˈplaɪkə). Pl. **plicæ**: see also sense 4. [med.L. *plica* plait, fold, f. *plicāre* to fold: see PLY. In F. *plique*; also, in sense 1, *plica*.]

1. *Path.* (More fully **ˈplica poˈlonica.**) A matted filthy condition of the hair due to disease; Polish plait (PLAIT *sb.* 2 c).

1684 BOYLE *Porousn. Anim. Bodies* vii, That disease, which, from the country it most infests, is called the *Plica Polonica*. **1693** *Blancard's Phys. Dict.* (ed. 2), *Plica*, an epidemical Disease in Polonia, when their Hairs grow together like a Cow's Tail. **1731** MORTIMER in *Phil. Trans.* XXXVII. 51 The Plica has been always..thought to be a Distemper. **1843** R. J. GRAVES *Syst. Clin. Med.* xxx. 383 The phenomena of plica polonica,..establishes the vitality of the hair. **1893** *Nation* (N.Y.) 23 Mar. 217/1 The terrible disease of the hair, the *plica polonica*, is said to have entirely disappeared.

2. A fold or folding of any part, as of the skin or a membrane. In *Entom.* a fold-like ridge or carina; *spec.* an elytral ridge in Coleoptera.

1706 PHILLIPS, *Plica*, (Lat.) a Pleat, Fold or Wrinkle. **1754–64** SMELLIE *Midwif.* I. 95 The internal membrane of the neck and *Fundus*, which is likewise full of *plicæ*. **1828** STARK *Elem. Nat. Hist.* II. 131 (*Annelides*) The plicæ lamellar, close, waved, vertical. **1849** [see PLICATION 2].

3. *Bot.* (See quot.)

1866 *Treas. Bot.* 906 *Plica*, an excessive multiplication of small twigs, instead of branches.

4. *Medieval Mus.* (Also with pl. **plicas.**) A notational symbol, variously interpreted but now usu. considered to represent a type of ornament; the ornament indicated. Also *attrib.*

1782 C. BURNEY *Gen. Hist. Mus.* II. iii. 188 Few of the musical terms in the tract of Franco, are more difficult to comprehend or define than the word *Plica*, which he calls 'a note of *division* of the same sound, ascending or descending.' **1801** T. BUSBY *Dict. Mus.* s.v., *Plica*, the name formerly given to a kind of ligature used in the old music as a sign of hesitation, or pausing. **1881** GROVE *Dict. Mus.* III. 4/1 *Plica* ..a character, mentioned by Franco of Cologne, Joannes de Muris, and other early writers, whose accounts of it are not always very easily reconciled to each other. Franco describes four kinds... Joannes de Muris describes the Plica as a sign of augmentation, similar in effect to the Point. Franco tells us that it may be added at will to the Long, or the Breve; but to the semibreve only when it appears in Ligature. Some other writers apply the term 'Plica' to the tail of a Large, or Long. The Descending Plica is sometimes identified with the Cephalicus. **1903** C. F. A. WILLIAMS *Story of Notation* vi. 101 In the sixth chapter Franco treats of the Plica. **1940** G. REESE *Music in Middle Ages* (1941) III. x. 283 Another type of ornament was notated by the *plica*. This was attached to either single notes..or ligatures... When it was applied to single notes, usually two parallel strokes of unequal length were added to the note-head. These strokes, enfolding the head, gave the *plica* its name. **1942** W. APEL *Notation of Polyphonic Music, 900–1600* (1944) III. iii. 234 The *plica* is a passing tone which is indicated..by a downward or upward dash attached to the right of a note. In modal notation, the *plica* appears preferably in connection with ligatures. *Ibid.* 235 We shall carefully distinguish between *plica*-note and *plica*-tone. The former term refers to the written note to which the *plica*-dash is attached; the latter to the extra tone called for by the dash. **1954** *New Oxf. Hist. Music* II. 325 The *plica*.. is a short stroke which modifies the single square note, leading either upwards or downwards. *Ibid.*, The instructions of the medieval theorists most often quoted are those of the Anonymus of Paris, who in his *Quædam de arte discantandi* tells us that 'it should be formed in the throat with the epiglottis', and of Lambert, who wrote under the pen-name of Aristotle: 'The *plica* is made in the voice by compressing the epiglottis, combining it neatly with a repercussion of the voice.' *Ibid.*, The second, semi-vocal, note of the plica is not an ad libitum ornament..but has a time-value of its own, one-third or one-half of that which would belong to the parent note if it were not plicated. **1957** C. PARRISH *Notation of Medieval Music* (1958) v. 130 Plicas are used sparingly. **1979** *Early Music* Apr. 189/1 The *plica* is a note with stems on *both* sides of the note head and is meant to be sung as two pitches, the first one specified by the position of the note head, the second one unspecified, but lying above or below the first note, depending on the direction of the stems.

†**ˈplicable**, *a. Obs. rare.* [f. L. type **plicābilis*, f. *plicāre* to fold, bend, PLY.] Flexible.

c **1407** LYDG. *Reson & Sens.* 6813 Whos herte harder ys to grave, Touching her honour, than ys glas... Men kan nat maken yt plicable Nor forge yt to be Malliable. **1548–77** VICARY *Anat.* v. (1888) 39 The Nose is a member.. somewhat plicable, because it shoulde the better be clensed.

plical (ˈplaɪkəl), *a.* [f. med.L. *plica* (see PLICA) + -AL¹.] Pertaining to or of the nature of a plica.

1890 *Cent. Dict.*, *Plical*, in *Bot.*, of or pertaining to plica. **1895** MEYRICK *Brit. Lepidopt.* 617 Stigmata raised, blackish, first discal somewhat before plical.

plicate (ˈplaɪkət), *a.* [ad. L. *plicāt-us*, pa. pple. of *plicāre* to fold.] Folded, pleated.

a. *Bot.* (See quots.)

1760 J. LEE *Introd. Bot.* I. xii. (1765) 28 Corolla..Plicate, folded, as in *Convolvulus*. **1870** HOOKER *Stud. Flora* 75 Geranium, Crane's-bill..cotyledons plicate or convolute. **1880** GRAY *Struct. Bot.* iv. (ed. 6) 133 Leaves are as to the mode of packing, Plicate or Plaited, when folded on the several ribs, in the manner of a closed fan. *Ibid.* 139 Plicate or Plaited, applied to the flower-bud as a whole. —— The term is used for the plaiting of a tube or cup, composed of a circle of leaves combined into one body.

b. *Zool.*, *Geol.* (See quots., and cf. PLICA 2.)

1819 G. SAMOUELLE *Entomol. Compend.* 154 Genus 45. *Abax*..elytra united, their shoulders carinate plicate. **1826** KIRBY & SP. *Entomol.* IV. xlvi. 334 Plicate (*Plicata*). When they have two or three contiguous abbreviated furrows which exhibit the appearance of folds. **1831** R. KNOX *Cloquet's Anat.* 629 Mucous..Membrane... Thin, reddish, and plicate in the direction of its length. **1849** DANA *Geol.* App. I. (1850) 687 Surface longitudinally plicate..; plications smooth.

plicate (ˈplaɪkeɪt, plɪˈkeɪt), *v.* [f. ppl. stem of L. *plicāre* to fold: see -ATE³.] **1.** *trans.* To fold, pleat. (Chiefly in passive.)

1698 B. ALLEN in *Phil. Trans.* XX. 377 The Belly plicated as other Beetles. **1841** T. R. JONES *Anim. Kingd.* 677 Its lining membrane is loose and much plicated. **1880** *Specif. U.S. Patent* No. 229479 (*title*) Machine for plicating fabrics. **1904** *Edin. Rev.* Jan. 230 The Lias and Oolites themselves.. were plicated and subjected to sub-aerial denudation.

2. *Medieval Mus.* To add a plica to. (Chiefly as ppl. adj.)

1903 C. F. A. WILLIAMS *Story of Notation* vii. 120 An imaginary dialogue dated 1326..shows a 'plicated' semibreve when three semibreves are used with one syllable. **1927** *Grove's Dict. Mus.* (ed. 3) IV. 210/1 Besides longs and breves, semibreves could be plicated when in ligature. **1954** [see PLICA 4]. **1977** *Early Music* Apr. 199 The neum..is assumed to be the plicated equivalent of the *pressus*.

plicated (ˈplaɪkeɪtɪd, plɪˈkeɪtɪd), *ppl. a.* [f. as prec. + -ED¹.]

1. *Anat.*, *Bot.*, *Geol.* Folded, plicate.

1753 CHAMBERS *Cycl. Supp.* s.v. *Leaf*, *Plicated leaf*, one from the base of which there run [ribs] which extend themselves to the extreme sides, and..raise and..depress the disk..in an alternate order, making acute angles. **1835–6** *Todd's Cycl. Anat.* I. 304/2 The..marsupium..is a plicated vascular membrane. **1882** GEIKIE *Text Bk. Geol.* IV. VIII. §3. 584 A highly plicated and crumpled condition.

†**2.** Complicated. *Obs. rare.*

1666 J. H. *Treat. Gt. Antidote* 9 The more Disease is plicated, the longer is required.

3. *Medieval Mus.* (See PLICATE *v.* 2.)

ˈplicately, *adv.* [f. PLICATE *a.* + -LY².] In a plicate manner; in or with folds.

1846 DANA *Zooph.* (1848) 708 Suberect plicately aggregated laminæ. **1881** BENTHAM in *Jrnl. Linn. Soc.* XVIII. 339 Leaves usually larger, more coriaceous, or plicately ribbed than in the other subtribes.

plicatile (ˈplɪkətɪl, -aɪl), *a.* [ad. L. *plicātilis* (Pliny), f. *plicāre* to fold. So in F.]

†**1.** Capable of being folded or convoluted. *Obs.*

1653 H. MORE *Antid. Ath.* x. App. (1662) 169 Whether these images or impresses consist in a certain posture or motion of the plicatile fibres or subtile threds of which the brain consists.

2. *Entom.* (See quot.)

1826 KIRBY & SP. *Entomol.* IV. xlvi. 336 *Plicatile*... When the wings at rest are folded in one or more longitudinal plaits.

plication (plɪ-, plaɪˈkeɪʃən). [a. OF. *plication*, *-acion* (Godef.), n. of action f. L. *plicāre* to fold.]

1. The action of folding; folded condition.

c **1400** *Lanfranc's Cirurg.* 23 It is necessarie some lymes to han a sustentacioun & a plicacioun, þat is a foldynge. **1854** WOODWARD *Mollusca* II. 285 The smallness of the space for the branchiæ may have been compensated by deep plication of those organs. **1886** W. ANDERSON *Pict. Arts Japan* 202 An artist of the Chinese school..may accentuate folds of drapery by a kind of shadow beneath the plication.

2. *concr.* A folding, a fold.

1748 RICHARDSON *Clarissa* lxxiii. (1811) VI. 345 The folds, as other plications have done, opened of themselves to oblige my curiosity. **1766** PARSONS in *Phil. Trans.* LVI. 209 This bird has a plication of the aspera arteria. **1824** SCOTT *Redgauntlet* Let. i, Thy juridical brow expanding its plications. **1849** DANA *Geol.* App. I. (1850) 710 There are 14 to 16 plications in half an inch; and the plicæ are smooth. **1874** CARPENTER *Ment. Phys.* I. ii. §87 (1879) 94.

3. *Geol.* The bending or folding of strata; a fold in a stratum.

1859 MURCHISON *Siluria* xvii. (ed. 3) 450 The plications of the strata in Belgium. **1865** GEIKIE *Scen. & Geol. Scot.* ix. 232 Plications following each other from top to bottom of the cliff. **1882** *Nature* XXVI 241/1 These crystalline masses underwent enormous plication and subsequent denudation.

plicato- (plɪ-, plaɪˈkeɪtəʊ-), combining adv. form from L. *plicātus* plicate, prefixed to other adjs. in the sense 'plicately—', 'plicate and—', as ***plicato-contorted*** (plicately contorted), ***plicato-cristate*** (with plicate crests), ***plicato-lacunose***, ***plicato-lobate*** (with plicate lobes), ***plicato-papillose*** (papillose with plications or wrinkles), ***plicato-undulate***.

1846 DANA *Zooph.* (1848) 141 Upper margin sublobate or plicato-undulate. *Ibid.* 152 Margin plicato-lobate. *Ibid.* 410 Frond.. often variously plicato-contorted. *Ibid.* 500 In part plicato-cristate, rising into crests more or less plicate. **1887** W. PHILLIPS *Brit. Discomycetes* 4 Pits elongated, narrow, plicato lacunose.

plicator, -er (plɪ-, plaɪˈkeɪtə(r)). [agent-n. from PLICATE *v.*, or L. *plicāre* to fold.] A folder; an apparatus for folding fabrics.

1880 *Specif. U.S. Patent* No. 229479 The table projects, apex forward, from the frame and I have named it the 'plicater'. **1884** KNIGHT *Dict. Mech.* Suppl., *Plicator*, a mechanical device for making a plait or fold, as in some sewing-machine attachments, for instance.

plicatulate (plɪˈkætjʊlət), *a. Nat. Hist.* [f. L. type **plicātul-us* (f. *plicāt-us* PLICATE: cf. *barbātul-us, līmātul-us*) + -ATE[2].] Minutely plicate.

1849 DANA *Geol.* App. I. (1850) 697 Palleal impression faint, anteriorly plicatulate.

plicature (ˈplɪkətjʊə(r)). [ad. L. *plicātūra* a folding, f. *plicāre* to fold.] Folding, mode of folding; a fold; = PLICATION.

1578 BANISTER *Hist. Man* VII. 96 Into this plicature.. are immitted two Arteries named Carotides. *a* **1652** J. SMITH *Sel. Disc.* i. 10 They unfold the plicatures of truth's garment, but they cannot behold the lovely face of it. **1671** *Phil. Trans.* VI. 3038 Leaves, intended for the said Trunk, and foulded up in the same plicature, wherein, upon the Bean's sprouting, they do appear. **1767** GOOCH *Treat. Wounds* I. 271 The *Pia Mater*.. investing the brain, in all its convolutions or plicatures. **1830** LINDLEY *Nat. Syst. Bot.* 18 Divisions have been founded upon the nature of the plicature of the cotyledons.

plicht, Sc. f. PLIGHT; †short for PLICHT-ANKER.

a **1515** DUNBAR *Poems* lxxxv. 31 Haile, plicht, but sicht! Haile, mekle of mycht! **1567** *Gude & Godlie B.* (S.T.S.) 15 Quhair Purgatorie and pardonis will not sell, And gude intent, thair Pylat plycht and leid.

†**plicht-anker.** *Sc. Obs.* Also 6 **plycht-**. [ad. LG. *plicht-anker*, Du. *plechtanker* 'the principall or chief anchor that houlds a ship' (Hexham 1678); in Da. *pligt-anker*.

The Du. and LG. word is usually referred to MLG., LG. *plicht*, MDu., Du. *plecht*, a small fore (or after) -deck of an open boat, OHG. *phlihta*, MHG. *pflihte*, Da., Sw. *pligt*; Doornkaat-Koolman (*Ostfr. Wbch.*) prefers derivation from *plicht* responsibility: see PLIGHT *sb.*[1]]

The main anchor of a ship; in quots. *fig.*: cf. *sheet-anchor*.

1508 DUNBAR *Gold. Targe* 187 Scho tuke Presence plicht ankers of the barge,.. And Cherising for to complete hir charge. *a* **1520** —— *Poems* xi. 46 Thy Ransonner, with woundis fyve, Mak thy plycht anker and thy steiris, To hald thy saule with him on lyve. **1552** ABP. HAMILTON *Catech.* (1884) 153 Lat this faith be thi plycht ankir, and doutless thow sall be saiffit fra all the dangeir of syn.

plicidentine (plɪsɪˈdɛntɪn). [f. med.L. *plica* fold, pleat + DENTINE.] A form of dentine in which it is folded on a series of vertical plates, causing the surface of the tooth to be fluted.

1854 OWEN *Skel. & Teeth* in *Orr's Circ. Sc.* I. *Org. Nat.* 273 With reference to the main and fundamental tissue of tooth, we find.. six leading modifications in fishes.. Vasodentine.. Plicidentine.. Dendrodentine. **1866** BRANDE & COX *Dict. Sc.* etc. II. 935/2 The basal part of the teeth of the Wolf-fish, of the *Lepidosteus oxyurus*, and of the *Ichthyosaurus*, affords examples of plicidentine.

pliciferous (plɪ-, plaɪˈsɪfərəs), *a.* [f. med.L. *plica* fold + -FEROUS.] Having or bearing plicæ or folds: in *Entom.* said of elytra having an internal plica, also of beetles having such elytra.

1858 in MAYNE *Expos. Lex.*

pliciform (ˈplɪsɪ-, ˈplaɪsɪfɔːm), *a.* [f. as prec. + -FORM.] Having the form of a plica, fold, or plait.

1858 in MAYNE *Expos. Lex.*

plide, plie, obs. forms of PLEAD, PLEA, PLY.

‖**plié** (plie). *Ballet.* Also **plier**. [Fr., f. *plier* to bend.] A movement in which the dancer lowers the body, bending the knees outwards in line with the out-turned feet. Also as *v. intr.*, to execute such a movement.

1892 E. SCOTT *Dancing as Art & Pastime* vi. 76 The foot passes from the *fourth rearward position* to the *fourth in front* with a very decided *plié de genoux* as it comes into the *first position*. *Ibid.* 77 A movement consisting of two *pliés* in advancing and three forward steps. **1913** C. D'ALBERT *Dancing* 125 *Plié*,.. flexion or bending of one or both knees in preparation for any step. **1920** *Dancing Times* July 793 The Russians take the grands battements at the end of the side practice instead of immediately after the 'plier'. **1922** BEAUMONT & IDZIKOWSKI *Man. Classical Theatr. Dancing* II. i. 37 The *plié*, or bend, may be small (*plié à quart*).. medium (*plié à demi* or *demi-plié*).. or large (*grand plié*). **1930** CRASKE & BEAUMONT *Theory & Pract. Allegro in Classical Ballet* 16 An *assemblé* is said to be *soutenu* when the knees are straightened and another *plié* is made before executing the next *pas*. **1949** A. CHUJOY *Dance Encycl.* 376/1 It is said that the entire technique of ballet consists in knowing when and how to do a plié. **1958** *Observer* 14 Sept. 14/7 Beautifully musical, he can turn a double *tour en l'air* into a deep *plié en arabesque* as trimly as if it were a phrase in a Mozart sonata. **1971** 'D. HALLIDAY' *Dolly & Doctor Bird* xi. 146 Krishtof would raise me.. while I stood up. He would then plié round me. **1977** *New Yorker* 19 Sept. 43/1 The marble-floored reception area alone, on the ground floor, is vast enough to accommodate the entire corps de ballet of four or five major ballet companies, all doing their pliés and entrechats.

Pliensbachian (pliːnzˈbɑːkɪən), *a. Geol.* [ad. G. *Pliensbachien* (A. Oppel 1858, in *Jahresh. des Vereins f. vaterlandische Naturkunde in Württemberg* XIV. 249), f. *Pliensbach*, name of a locality near Boll, a village near Göppingen in Baden-Württemberg, W. Germany: see -IAN.] Of, pertaining to, or designating a stage of the Lower Jurassic in Europe comprising the Middle Lias and part of the Lower Lias. Freq. *absol.*

1903 *Q. Jrnl. Geol. Soc.* LIX. 455 In some districts—East Gloucestershire for instance—only a few feet of Toarcian are found separating the Inferior Oolite (Aalenian) from the Middle Lias (Pliensbachian). **1955** E. NEAVERSON *Stratigr. Palaeont.* (ed. 2) xii. 440 Pliensbachian brachiopods are most abundant in the limestone facies of Somerset. **1975** A. HALLAM *Jurassic Environments* ii. 13 No zonal subdivision for the Pliensbachian of southern Europe as a whole has yet been satisfactorily achieved. **1978** *Nature* 13 July 131/1 The initial Jurassic transgression here took place in the Pliensbachian.

plier (ˈplaɪə(r)). Also 6 **plyar**, 7–9 **plyer**. [f. PLY *v.* + -ER[1]. Cf. F. *plieur* folder.]

1. One who plies: in various senses of the verb.

1673 R. HEAD *Canting Acad.* 147 Going into a sinning-house.. she found a young Plyer there. *a* **1700** B. E. *Dict. Cant. Crew*, *Plyer*, a Crutch. **1725** *New Cant. Dict.*, *Plyer*..; also a Trader. **1827** HONE *Every-day Bk.* II. 57 The companies alight,.. without the aid of attendant pliers. **1872** JEAFFRESON *Brides & Bridals* (1873) II. 143 Solicited by a 'plier' to accompany him to a convenient tavern.

2. In *pl.* Pincers, usually small, having long jaws mostly with parallel surfaces, sometimes toothed; used for bending wire, manipulating small objects, etc.

1568–9 in Swayne *Sarum Churchw. Acc.* (1896) 283 Paier of plyars, 6d. **1587** MASCALL *Govt. Cattle, Hogges* (1627) 271 With a paire of plyers bow and turne the points of the wyar into the holes of his nostrils. **1634** PEACHAM *Gentl. Exerc.* I. xxvii. 94 Take it forth againe with a paire of pliers or small tongs, and light it at the fire. **1677** MOXON *Mech. Exerc.* i. 6 Plyers are of two sorts, Flat Nos'd and Round Nos'd. Their office is to hold and fasten upon all small work, and to fit it in its place. **1833** J. HOLLAND *Manuf. Metal* II. 318 The pliers commonly used for cutting wire.

plig (plɪg). *U.S. dial.* [Shortening of POLYGAMIST.] A polygamist, used esp. with reference to the practice of polygamy attributed to the Mormon Church.

1977 *Washington Post* 8 Aug. A14 Many citizens in Utah show an uncomfortable dualism toward polygamists, derisively calling them 'pligs'. **1978** *Observer* (Colour Suppl.) 12 Mar. 33/4 Polygamy.. has made a surprising comeback of late. 'The Pligs are sprouting like weeds,' said a county sheriff.

plight (plaɪt), *sb.*[1] Forms: 1–4 **pliht**, (4 erron. **plith**), 3 **plihht**, **pliȝht**, 3–5 **pliȝt**, 4–5 **plyȝt**, 4–6 **plyght**, 5 **plyȝht**, 5–6 *Sc.* **plycht**, 5– *Sc.* **plicht**, 4– **plight.** *β.* ? 4 **plyt**, 4–5 **plit**, **plite**, 5 **plyte**. [OE. *pliht* danger, risk, = OFris. *plicht* danger, concern, care; cf. MDu. *plicht*, *plecht* responsibility, obligation, duty, Du. *pligt*, *plicht*, MLG., LG. *plicht* obligation, duty; OHG., MHG. *phliht*, *pfliht* obligation, duty, office, concern, care of or for, Ger. *pflicht* duty, etc.; f. stem *pleh-*, *pleg-* of OE. *pleón* (with genitive) to risk the loss of, expose to danger, or WGer. *plegan*, in OS. and OHG. (Notker) with genitive, to take the risk or responsibility of (an act), to be reponsible for, answer for (a thing or person). Cf., from same root, OE. *pleoh* (:—**pleh*) danger, hurt, peril, risk, responsibility, OFris. *ple*, *pli* danger; OHG. *pfligida* risk, danger. The continental langs. show the sense-gradation from 'danger, risk', through 'responsibility, duty', to 'office, concern, care', etc. See Franck in *Kuhn's Zeitshr.* XXXVII. 132.

Already in the 14th c., in some dialects, *h*, *ȝ*, or *gh* was lost in the combination *-ight*, leaving *-īt*, whence the occasional *β* spellings above, *plīt*, *plīte*, *plyt*, and the modern pronunciation. *Plight* being thus identified in pronunciation, and sometimes in spelling with ME. *plīt* from AF., the two words ran together in the form *plight*: see PLIGHT *sb.*[2]]

†**1.** Peril, danger, risk. *Obs.*

c **825** *Vesp. Psalter* cxiv. 3 Ymbsaldun mec sar deðes & plihtas helle [*pericula inferni*] ȝemoettun mec. *c* **1000** ÆLFRIC *Colloq.* in Wr.-Wülcker 96 Ic hit toȝelæde eow hider mid micclan plihte ofer sæ. *c* **1205** LAY. 8132, & summe heo gunnen pleien. pliht com on ueste. **1303** R. BRUNNE *Handl. Synne* 7279 Also falle men yn plyght, þat sytte vp þe þursday at night. **13..** *Gaw. & Gr. Knt.* 266 þat I passe as in pes, & no plyȝt seche. *c* **1440** *York Myst.* xxxii. 162 þe perill and þe plight is thyne. **1503** HAWES *Examp. Virt.* vii. 12 Full often he brought theym to the plyght. **1572** *Satir. Poems Reform.* xxxii. 104 Blaming thy tressoun, the caus of all our plicht. *c* **1630** DRUMM. OF HAWTH. *Poems* 107 That thou shouldst.. die for those deserv'd eternall plight.

β. *c* **1400** *Destr. Troy* 8019 Priam.. Wold haue put hym to þe plit for perell of all. *c* **1412** HOCCLEVE *De Reg. Princ.* 1221, I haue had habundance Of welfare ay; and now stond in þe plite Of scarsetee. *c* **1450** *St. Cuthbert* (Surtees) 2575 For to dy scho semed in plyte.

†**2.** Sin, offence; guilt, blame. *Obs.*

c **1200** ORMIN 10213 Forr grediȝnesse is hæfedd plihht, & follȝheþþ helless bisne. **13..** *Cursor M.* 5077 (Cott.) Mi breþer dere, Your plight [*v.r.* gilt] i haue for-giuen yow. *c* **1330** R. BRUNNE *Chron.* (1810) 131 þe kyng suld haf no plight, þat Thomas so was dede. *c* **1375** *Sc. Leg. Saints* xxvi. (*Nycholas*) 932 Quhy suld he sa be dycht For þare mysded & þar plicht.

β. **13..** *E.E. Allit. P.* B. 1494 þe lorde þat þe lyfte ȝemes Displesed much at þat play in þat plyt stronge.

3. Undertaking (of a risk or obligation); pledge (under risk of forfeiture); engagement, plighting.

(After ME., perh. a new formation from the vb.)

c **1250** *Gen. & Ex.* 1269 He bad him maken siker pliȝt Of luue and trewðe, in frendes riȝt. **1303** R. BRUNNE *Handl. Synne* 1494 þat man þat demeþ alle to þe ryȝt, Of mercy get he no plyȝt. *c* **1320** *Sir Tristr.* 888 Crounes þai gun crake Mani, ich wene, apliȝt [= in plight]. *c* **1430** *Syr Tryam.* 767 Thus they justyd tylle hyt was nyght, Then they departyd in plyght, They had nede to reste. **1605** SHAKS. *Lear* I. i. 103 Happily when I shall wed, That Lord, whose hand must take my plight, shall carry Halfe my loue with him. *a* **1700** DRYDEN *Song*, '*What shall I do?*' Not pray for a smile, And not bargain for plight. **1891** G. MEREDITH *One of our Conq.* I. iv. 58 An engagement,.. a mutual plight of faith.

β. **13..** *St. Erkenwolde* 285 in Horstm. *Altengl. Leg.* (1881) 272 Nas I a paynym vnpreste þat neuer þi plite knewe Ne þi mesure of þi mercy ne þi mecul vertue?

4. *Comb.* **plight-ring**, an engagement-ring.

1877 W. JONES *Finger-ring* 241 A sacred plight-ring was considered almost as impassable a barrier as the veil itself, against the marriage of the wearer.

plight (plaɪt), *sb.*[2] Forms: *α.* 4–5 **plit**, **plyt**, 5–6 **plite**, **plyte**, (5 **plyet**). *β.* 4–5 **pliȝt**, **plyȝt**, 5–6 **plyght**, **-e**, 5– **plight**. [ME. *plit*, *plyt*, a. Anglo-F. *plit* (in Gower and Law French), for ONF. **pleit*, OF. *ploit* fold, act or manner of folding; also, manner of being, trim, condition, state (13th c. in Godef.): see PLAIT *sb.*[1] (of which this is in origin a doublet). The *β* forms are taken over from PLIGHT *sb.*[1]; when that word was (in some parts of England, already in 14th c.) reduced to *plīt*, *plīte*, and thus indentified in pronunciation and sometimes in spelling with this, this began in turn to be spelt *plyght*, *plight*, which superseded *plite* in 16th c. This spelling appears first in branch II, and perh. there was association of sense, peril (PLIGHT *sb.*[1] 1) being a kind of 'evil plight' (4 b below). In 16–17th c. the *gh* was often extended to the synonym PLAIT, written *pleight*, *plaight* (but for this there were also other possible models in *eight*, *weight*, *straight*, riming with *plait*, *wait*).]

I. Fold; manner of folding; plait.

†**1.** A fold, in drapery or the like; a pleat; = PLAIT *sb.* 1 a. *Obs.*

α. **1399** LANGL. *Rich. Redeles* III. 156 And if pernell preisid the plytis bihynde, The costis were acountid paye whan he myȝth. *c* **1430** *Pilgr. Lyf Manhode* II. x. (1869) 79 Come forth clerk,.. vndo þese letteres out of plyt. *a* **1568** ASCHAM *Scholem.* (Arb.) 100 To clothe him selfe with nothing els, but a demie bukram cassok, plaine without plites.

β. *c* **1460** J. RUSSELL *Bk. Nurture* 242 Now fold ye alle there at oonys þat a pliȝt passe not a fote brede alle way. **1547** BOORDE *Introd. Knowl.* xviii. (1870) 169 Theyr rayment.. is made.. wyth two wrynckkles and a plyght. **1697** tr. *C'tess D'Aunoy's Trav.* (1706) 229 She is drest.. with a short Gown without any plights.

†**b.** A fold in a natural structure, a convolution, a bend; = PLAIT *sb.* 1 b. *Obs.*

α. **1594** T. B. *La Primaud. Fr. Acad.* II. 350 These foldings, plites, and windings [of the ileon or folded gut].

β. **1543** TRAHERON *Vigo's Chirurg.* I. i. 2 b, In the plyghte of the arme. **1607** TOPSELL *Four-f. Beasts* (1658) 554 This [horn of unicorn].. is neither light nor hollow,.. revolved into many plights, sharper than any dart. **1671** FLAVEL *Fount. Life* i. Wks. 1731 I. 2/1 It is of many Sorts and Forms, of many Folds and Plights.

†**c.** *fig.* (Cf. PLAIT *sb.* 1 c.) *Obs.*

1387–8 T. USK *Test. Love* III. ix. (Skeat) I. 77 In this boke be many privy thinges wimpled and folde; unneth shul leude men the plites unwinde.

†**2.** A plait of hair or the like; = PLAIT *sb.* 2.

1601 WEEVER *Mirr. Mart.* B ij b, Diuides each haire, each plight vndresses. **1617** MORYSON *Itin.* III. 129 A taile.. very woolly and fat, and close wouen in many plights. **1800** COLERIDGE *Christabel* II. 33 Geraldine.. Puts on her silken vestments white, And tricks her hair in lovely plight.

†**b.** *fig.* A contexture of conditions. (Cf. sense 4.) *Obs. rare.*

1674 N. FAIRFAX *Bulk & Selv.* 74 It seems then, that the thing that calls us up is Morningness, or that woof and plight that the whole ticklish frame of worldly beings are wheel'd into at such a tide of day.

†3. A recognized length or 'piece' of lawn. (? Orig. the length into which it was folded. See Beck *Draper's Dict.* 178 *note.*) *Obs.*

1415 *Test. Ebor.* (Surtees) I. 382, j plite [*printed* plice] de lawnd. **1452** *Will of Britte* (Somerset Ho.), Vnum plyte de lawne. **1463** *Act 3 Edw. IV*, c. 5 Coverchiefs del price dun plite de cynqe souldz. **1463–4** *Rolls of Parlt.* V. 505/1 Eny Kerchef, wherof the price of a plyght shall excede the some of iiis. iiiid. *Ibid.*, Kerchiefs, of the price of a plyte of vs. **1483, 1502** [see LAWN *sb.*[1] 1]. **1535** *Rutland MSS.* (1905) IV. 277 For vj plightes of fyne lawne for sleves for the Quene. [**1607** COWELL *Interpr., Plite of Lawne...* Seemeth to be a certaine measure, as a yard or an elle, etc.]

II. Manner of being; condition, state. (Cf. *complexion.*)

4. Condition, state, trim. **a.** *orig.* neutral or good.

a. **13..** *E.E. Allit. P.* B. 111 With peple of alle plytez þe palays þay fyllen. *c* **1386** CHAUCER *Can. Yeom. Prol. & T.* 399 The nexte tyme I shal fonde To bryngen oure craft al in another plite. **1387–8** T. USK *Test. Love* II. i. (Skeat) l. 8 Chaunging of the lift syde to the right halve tourneth it so clene in-to another kynde, that never shal it come to the first plyte in doinge. *c* **1440** *Promp. Parv.* 405/1 Plyte, or state, ..*status.* **1530** PALSGR. 255/2 Plyte or state, *poynt.* **1570** LEVINS *Manip.* 151/6 Plite, plight, *habitudo.*

β. *c* **1350** *Will. Palerne* 5373 But heriȝed be þe hiȝe king ȝou þus haþ holpe, & pult ȝou to þis pliȝt fram pouert euermore! **1534** MORE *Treat. Passion* Wks. 1288/2 And [to] lyue here in suche pleasaunt plight as we shuld haue lyued if Adam had not synned. **1596** DRAYTON *Leg.* iv. 214 Being in so excellent a plight. **1652–62** HEYLIN *Cosmogr.* I. (1682) 269 The Town remaining in as good plight..for Trade and Buildings, as most Towns do which want a navigable River. **1768** BLACKSTONE *Comm.* III. i. 9 Nothing shall be distreined for rent, which may not be rendered again in as good plight as when it was distreined. **1838–9** FR. A. KEMBLE *Resid. in Georgia* (1863) 124 It is a happy and hopeful plight for us both. **1851** GALLENGA *Italy* 251 Not in the best plight or order.

b. Now generally qualified as evil.

a. **13..** *E.E. Allit. P.* C. 114 Now hatz he put hym in plyt of peril. **13..** *Gaw. & Gr. Knt.* 733 Þus in peryl, & payne, & plytes ful harde. **1390** GOWER *Conf.* III. 200 In sori plit and povere he lay. **1470–85** MALORY *Arthur* IV. xxiii. 152 She shalle be in as euyl plyte as he is or it be long to.

β. **13..** *E.E. Allit. P.* A. 1074 Þe planetez arn in to pouer a plyȝt. **1490** CAXTON *Eneydos* l. 142 Turnus..knewe well thenne that he was deceyued,..sore an-angred he was, whan he founde hym selfe in that plyght. *c* **1586** C'TESS PEMBROKE *Ps.* CVII. iii, They cry'd to him in woefull plight. **1632** J. HAYWARD tr. *Biondi's Eromena* 56 We cannot be in worse plight than we are. **1664** BUTLER *Hud.* II. i. 31 We forget in what sad plight We lately left the captiv'd Knight. **1766** GOLDSM. *Vic. W.* xiii, He was now in a woful plight. **1863** P. BARRY *Dockyard Econ.* 23 Dockyard administration is in a sorry and almost hopeless plight.

†**c.** Manner, fashion, way. *Obs. rare.*

c **1460** J. RUSSELL *Bk. Nurture* 434 Pecok, Stork, Bustarde, & Shovellewre, ye must vnlace þem in þe plite of þe crane prest & pure. **1581** J. BELL *Haddon's Answ. Osor.* 8 b, We deny all, in the same plight as you have set them downe.

5. Bodily or physical condition; state as to health; now esp. of cattle.

1390 GOWER *Conf.* II. 47 Thus was the hors in sori plit. *c* **1410** *Master of Game* (MS. Digby 182) xii, Also þe scabbe cometh to hem, for to hye plyet, when þei abyde in her kenel to longe and goth not on huntynge. **1551** TURNER *Herbal* I. K iij, Blake Ciche..taken wyth beanes..maketh a good plyte and fatt fleshe. **1586** A. DAY *Eng. Secretary* I. (1625) 125 The woman also in very good plight too. *a* **1649** WINTHROP *New Eng.* (1853) I. 37 Some horses came over in good plight. **1792** COWPER *Let.* 29 July, Mary..is in pretty good plight this morning, having slept well. **1855** HT. MARTINEAU *Autobiog.* II. 35 Another of our neighbours admitted the fine plight of my cows.

b. *absol.* Good or proper condition, health.

c **1450** *St. Cuthbert* (Surtees) 3823 Þai wald noȝt bring þe childe in plyte [*i.e.* to health]. **1573** TUSSER *Husb.* xxxvi. (1878) 85 Use cattle aright, to keepe them in plight. **1704** SWIFT *T. Tub* xi, When a traveller and his horse are in heart and plight. **1760–72** H. BROOKE *Fool of Qual.* (1809) III. 84 [Of a ship] Though she had been in plight, we had not hands left sufficient to work her. **1866** FELTON *Anc. & Mod. Gr.* I. I. vii. 119 [Of a dog] His strength, his plight, his speed so light, You had with wonder viewed.

†**6.** State of mind, mood, esp. *to do* something.

[**1376–9** GOWER *Mirour de l'omme* 10661 Comment q'il plourt, comment q'il rit, Toutdis se tient en un soul plit.] *c* **1400** *Destr. Troy* 545 [To] put you in plite your purpos to wyn. **1513** MORE in Grafton *Chron.* (1568) II. 773 Thinketh he that I would send him hence, which is neyther in the plight to sende out? **1632** MILTON *Penseroso* 57 'Less Philomel will daign a Song, In her sweetest, saddest plight. **1726** SHELVOCKE *Voy. round World* 27 He coming in a very humble plight, asking my pardon.

7. State or position from a legal point of view.

a. Of an enactment, privilege, use, etc.

1540 *Act 32 Hen. VIII*, c. 16 §11 The same proclamacion shal abide, be, and remain in the same plight and strength that it is, and as if this acte had neuer bene made. **1570–6** LAMBARDE *Peramb. Kent* (1826) 243 As touching this privilege.., although it continue not altogither in the same plight, yet some shadowe thereof remaineth even to this day. **1818** CRUISE *Digest* (ed. 2) II. 443 The statute of uses executes the possession to the use, in the same plight as the use was limited.

b. Of a person, etc.: Legal status.

[*a* **1481** LITTLETON *Tenures* §306 III. iv. (1516) D iv b, Est en tiel plite sicomme il que auoit droit.] **1663** *Act 15 Chas. II*, c. 6 §7 Whether Persons prohibited to preach by the said Act are in the same Plight as to Punishment, with Persons disabled by the said Act to preach. **1769** BLACKSTONE *Comm.* IV. xxx. 392 The effect of falsifying, or reversing, an outlawry is that the party shall be in the same plight as if he had appeared upon the *capias.*

8. Attire, array, dress. *rare.*

1590 SPENSER *F.Q.* III. xii. 8 Like as the sunburnt Indians do aray Their tawney bodies in their proudest plight. **1743** J. DAVIDSON *Æneid* VII. 192 Three hundred of them stood shining and in full plight. **1821** JOANNA BAILLIE *Metr. Leg., Ld. John* xii, In reveller's plight, he is bedight.

plight (plaɪt), *v.*[1] Now chiefly *poet.* or *rhet.* Pa. t. and pple. **plighted.** Forms of inf.: see PLIGHT *sb.*[1] *Pa. t.* 4 **pliȝt, plyghte,** 4–7 **plight,** 5 **plyght, plyȝt,** 6 *Sc.* **plicht,** 8– **plighted.** *Pa. pple.* 3–5 **pliȝt,** 3 **i-pluht,** 4 **y-plight, y-pliȝt, y-plyȝt,** 4, 7– **plight,** 5 **i-pleyht,** 6 **plyght** (*Sc.* **plicht**), **plyted,** 6– **plighted.** [OE. *plihtan*, f. *pliht* danger, damage: see PLIGHT *sb.*[1] Cf. OHG. *phlihten* refl. to engage one's self, MDu. *plichten* to guarantee.]

†**1.** *trans.* To cause to incur danger, bring danger upon; to endanger; to compromise (life, honour, etc.). With *dat.* (OE.)

a **1016** *Laws Æthelred* v. c. 28 (Schmid) Plihte him sylfum and ealre his are. *Ibid.* VI. c. 36 Þonne plihte hi heora æhton, butan hit frið-benan sindan.

2. *trans.* To put (something) in danger or risk of forfeiture; to give in pledge; to pledge or engage (one's troth, faith, oath, promise, etc.).

a **1225** *Ancr. R.* 208 Al so as dusi biheste, oðer folliche ipluht trouðe, & longe beon unbishoped..þeos, & alle swuche beoð iled to slouhðe. *c* **1386** CHAUCER *Wife's T.* 153 Plight me thy trouthe heere in myn hand quod she The nexte thyng that I requere thee Thou shalt it do. *c* **1450** *Godstow Reg.* 517 To this couenaunte to be holde truly and with-out gyle, bothe perties plight ther trowthes. **1554–9** in *Songs & Ball.* (1860) 2 To fullfyll the promys he had plyght. *c* **1560** A. SCOTT *Poems* (S.T.S.) ii. 75 William his vow plicht to the powin, Ffor favour or for feid. **1567** *Satir. Poems Reform.* iii. 64 Off hir finger fals she threw ane Ring, And said, 'my Lord, ane taikin I ȝow plycht'. **1582** STANYHURST *Æneis* II. (Arb.) 46 My faith I plight heere, to relate thee veritye soothlye. **1607** TOPSELL *Foure-f. Beasts* 353 Truely her troath She him plight, That she would not come within the night. **1700** DRYDEN *Pal. & Arc.* I. 291 Have we not plighted each our holy oath, That one should be the common good of both? **1813** SCOTT *Rokeby* I. xv, Hast thou kept thy promise plight, To slay thy leader in the fight? **1855** MACAULAY *Hist. Eng.* xxi. IV. 685 They came in multitudes ..to plight faith to William, rightful and lawful King.

b. esp. in reference to betrothal or marriage: cf. TROTHPLIGHT.

a **1300** *Cursor M.* 8386 (Cott.) Well i wat þat þou me hight, Ar þou to spouse me trouth plight. *c* **1386** CHAUCER *Frankl. T.* 600 And in myn hand youre trouthe plighten ye To loue me best. **1398** TREVISA *Barth. De P.R.* VI. xiii. (Bodl. MS.), In contract of wedding [he] pliȝte[þ] his trowith and obligeþ hym selfe to lede his life with his wyfe and to pay here dettes. **1548–9** *Bk. Com. Prayer, Matrimony*, And therto I plight thee my trouth. **1653** WALTON *Angler* i. 24 What is said of Turtle Doves;..that they silently plight their troth and marry. **1841** JAMES *Brigand* vii, I told him..that my heart was given and my hand plighted to another.

†**c.** Phrase. ***I thee (you) plight*** (*sc.* my word): I warrant or assure you, I promise you. *Obs.*

c **1400** *Sowdone Bab.* 318, I shal have an othere, I you plighte, Like to this every dele. *c* **1485** *E.E. Misc.* (Warton Cl.) 50 The old man sayd 'Y the plyȝte, Thou schalt have as y the hyght'. *a* **1500** *Sir Beues* 2154 (Pynson) In that caue they were al nyght Wythout mete or drynke, I you plyght.

†**3.** To pledge or bind oneself to do or give (something); to promise. *Obs.*

c **1205** LAY. 13071, & þu wulle me an hold plihten; þat ich hit scal al dihten. *c* **1250** *Gen. & Ex.* 2677 Or haue he hire pliȝt & sworen, Ðat him sal feið wurðful ben boren. **14..** in *Tundale's Vis.*, etc. (1843) 145 Heyle godly lady in the was plyght Tho joy of man bothe all and sum. **1526** *Pilgr. Perf.* (W. de W. 1531) 239 b, Than doest thou all that thou hast plyght. **1587** *Misfort. Arth.* III. iv. in Hazl. *Dodsley* IV. 313 The quiet rest that princely palace plights.

4. To engage or bind (oneself); *pass.* to be engaged or bound *to* some one.

1362 LANGL. *P. Pl.* A. I. 46 Pilgrimes and Palmers Plihten hem to-gederes For to seche Seint Ieme and seintes at Roome. **1377** *Ibid.* B. v. 202, I..was his prentis ypliȝte, his profit to wayte. *c* **1380** *Sir Ferumb.* 1045 Y til him am trewe y-pliȝt, & haue myn oþ y-swered. **1832** HT. MARTINEAU *Irel.* iv. 72 So you have plighted and pledged yourself to your band since you swore you would wed me only. **1870** E. PEACOCK *Ralf Skirl.* III. 116 His daughter was plighted to the very man he would have chosen for her.

†**plight,** *v.*[2] *Obs.* Forms: see PLIGHT *sb.*[2] [ME. *plite*, etc., collateral form of PLAIT *v.*; later *plight*, going with PLIGHT *sb.*[2]]

1. *trans.* To fold, to pleat; = PLAIT *v.* 1, PLEAT *v.* 1; also, to contract into folds or wrinkles.

c **1374** CHAUCER *Troylus* II. 1155 (1204) Now goode Nece be it neuere so lyte, Yif me þe labour it to sowe and plyte. *c* **1374** —— *Boeth.* I. Pr. ii. 5 (Camb. MS.), With the lappe of hir garment Iplitid in a frounce sche dryede myn eyen. **1530** PALSGR. 660/2, I plyght a gowne, I set the plyghtes in order, *je plye.* *a* **1548** HALL *Chron., Hen. VIII* 76 The garment was large, and plited verie thicke. **1627** tr. *Bacon's Life & Death* (1651) 8 Things, which by Heat are not onely wrinkled, but ruffled and plighted. **1658** ROWLAND tr. *Moufet's Theat. Ins.* 973 The wings are of a decayed purple colour passing to a lively blue, and all plighted severally.

b. To fold (in the arms), embrace.

c **1440** *York Myst.* xli. 81 And in his armes he shall hym plight. **1596** R. L[INCHE] *Diella* (1877) 76 Diego..Came running forth, him in his arms to plight.

c. *fig.*

c **1374** CHAUCER *Troylus* II. 648 (697) What to done best were, & what eschue, That plitede she ful ofte in many folde. **1640** J. STOUGHTON *Def. & Distrib. Divinity* ii. 78 So long as these Divine truths are folded and plighted together in these few divisions, there is no lustre or light sparkles from them.

2. To intertwine or interweave into one combined texture; = PLAIT *v.* 2; to knit, to tie in a knot.

1589 GREENE *Menaphon* (Arb.) 76 Hir lockes are pleighted like the fleece of wooll. *c* **1590** —— *Fr. Bacon* vi. 127 I'll plight the bands and seal it with a kiss. **1590** SPENSER *F.Q.* II. vi. 7 Sometimes her head she fondly would aguize With gaudy girlonds..or rings of rushes plight. **1633** P. FLETCHER *Purple Isl.* VII. xxiii, A long love-lock on his left shoulder plight.

Hence **'plighted** *ppl. a.* (also **plited, plight**), plaited, pleated, folded, involved; **'plighting** *vbl. sb.*, pleating, folding, wrinkling.

1502 *Ord. Crysten Men* (W. de W. 1506) II. v. 95 Sleues with syde lappes or plyted. *c* **1530** *Crt. of Love* 1102 The nonnes, with vaile and wimple plight. **1601** WEEVER *Mirr. Mart.* C vij b, This all-affrighting Comet I haue heard To be the plighted tresse of Meropes. **1627** tr. *Bacon's Life & Death* (1651) 8 Contraction by the Fire..causeth Plighting. **1670** MILTON *Hist. Eng.* II. Wks. 1851 V. 62 She [Boadicea] wore a plighted garment of divers colours, with a great gold'n Chain. **1693** tr. *Emilianne's Hist. Monast. Ord.* 152 A black plited cloak.

plight, obs. form of PLIGHTED *ppl. a.*[1] and [2].

plightage ('plaɪtɪdʒ). *rare*[−1]. [f. PLIGHT *v.*[1] + -AGE.] The fact or state of being plighted or betrothed.

1908 HARDY *Dynasts* III. v. iv. 442 These vile tricks, to pluck you from Your nuptial plightage..Make me belch oaths!

plighted ('plaɪtɪd), *ppl. a.*[1] Also 3 **ypliȝt,** 4 **pliht,** 5 **plight.** [f. PLIGHT *v.*[1] + -ED[1].]

1. Of a thing: Pledged, given in pledge or assurance, solemnly promised.

1297 R. GLOUC. (Rolls) 3819 Sikernesse & treuþe ypliȝt of þis voreward hii nome. **1567** TURBERV. *Ovid's Epist.* 156 b, I broken haue my plighted hest. **1697** DRYDEN *Virg. Georg.* I. 688 Perfidious Mars long plighted Leagues divides. **1794** SOUTHEY *Wat Tyler* III. i, The King must perform His plighted promise. **1867** FREEMAN *Norm. Conq.* I. iv. 218 His plighted faith went for as little as the plighted faith of a deliberate perjurer.

2. Of a person: Bound by pledge; engaged.

1362 LANGL. *P. Pl.* A. v. 116, I..was his pliht prentys his profyt to loke. *c* **1450** *St. Cuthbert* (Surtees) 1044 Þou haly bischop and preste plight. **1849** MISS MULOCK *Ogilvies* xii, Unless they were plighted lovers. *a* **1861** MRS. BROWNING *Parting Lovers* x, Many a plighted maid and wife.

†**plighted,** *ppl. a.*[2]: see under PLIGHT *v.*[2]

'plighter. *rare.* [f. PLIGHT *v.*[1] + -ER[1].] One who or that which plights or pledges.

1606 SHAKS. *Ant. & Cl.* III. xiii. 126 My play-fellow, your hand; this Kingly Seale, And plighter of high hearts.

'plightful, *a.* Also 4 **plihtful.** [f. PLIGHT *sb.*[1] + -FUL.] †**1.** Perilous; sinful, guilty, blameworthy. *Obs.*

c **1325** *Metr. Hom.* (1862) 29 Thaim birð lef thair plihtful play. **13..** *Cursor M.* 6614 (Cott.) Þat plightful folk thoght þan na plai. *Ibid.* 29154 Qua dos heui plightful dede Of heuy penance has he nede.

2. Grievous; fraught with suffering. *rare.*

1906 HARDY *Dynasts* II. VI. v. 304 The tears that lie about this plightful scene Of heavy travail in a suffering soul.

†**'plightless,** *a.* *Obs. rare.* Also 4 **plihtles, ply3tles.** [f. PLIGHT *sb.*[1] + -LESS.] Blameless.

13.. *Cursor M.* 28945 (Cott.) Til him þat has bene hauand,..And falles in-to state o nede, Plight-les for his aun dede. **13..** *St. Erkenwolde* 296 in Horstm. *Altengl. Leg.* (1881) 273 Adam, oure alder, þat ete of þat appulle þat mony a plyȝtles pepul has poysned for euer.

†**'plightly,** *a.* *Obs. rare.* In 3 **plihtliche.** [f. PLIGHT *sb.*[1] + -LY[1].] Perilous, of grave import.

c **1205** LAY. 23528 Þa weoren inne Paris Plihtliche spelles ful iwis [*c* 1275 sori tidynge foliwis].

†**'plighty,** *a.*[1] *Obs. rare.* [f. PLIGHT *sb.*[1] + -Y. So MDu., MLG. *plichtich* liable, responsible.] Responsible, guilty.

13.. *Cursor M.* 6689 (Cott.) Qua smites his thain wit a wand, And he be deid vnder his hand, He sal be plighty for þe sin. *Ibid.* 8112 Til all plighti þair pardun [sal rise].

†**'plighty,** *a.*[2] *Obs. rare.* [f. PLIGHT *sb.*[2] + -Y.] Full of folds, wrinkled, rugose.

1615 CROOKE *Body of Man* 110 The other proper coate is on the inside in the small guts rugous or plightie.

plihht, pliht, obs. forms of PLIGHT *sb.*[1]

plim (plɪm), *v.* Chiefly *dial.* [Known only from 17th c.; connected with the root of PLUM *v. Plim* adj. 'filled out' is used in dialects from Rutland to Devon.]

a. *intr.* To swell, fill *out*, grow plump.

1654 GAYTON *Pleas. Notes* II. vi. 62 Yet plimming by a generous heat, That always by one Pulse did beat. **1691** LOCKE *Lower. Interest* Wks. 1727 II. 38 [He] first discovered himself to be out of his Wits..by boiling a great Number of Groats with a Design, as he said, to make them plim, i.e. grow thicker. *a* **1722** LISLE *Husb.* (1752) 147 The barley-straw..broke off..before the grain was full plimmed. **1883** G. ALLEN in *Nature* XXVII. 442/2 The leaves..plim out at once into a larger rounded type. **1891** T. HARDY *Tess* (1892) 22 Don't that make your bosom plim?

b. *trans.* To swell, inflate.

1881 G. ALLEN *Evolutionist at Large* xv. 149 The wings [of a butterfly] are by origin a part of the breathing apparatus, and they require to be plimmed by the air before the insect can take to flight. **1881** —— *Vignettes fr. Nat.* iv. 32, I saw an orange-tip plimming its unexpanded wings and displaying its beautiful markings on a blade of grass.

ˈplimsoll (ˈplɪmsɒl, -səl). [The name of S. Plimsoll, M.P. for Derby, to whose agitation the Merchant Shipping Act of 1876 was due.]

1. (With capital initial). In ***Plimsoll line*** (LINE *sb.*[2] 7), ***mark***, also called ***Plimsoll's mark*** (see MARK *sb.*[1] 12), the load-line required to be placed upon the hulls of British ships. Also *fig.* ***Plimsoll's pancake*** = *Plimsoll line.*

1881 [see MARK *sb.*[1] 12]. **1884** *Chr. World* 13 Mar. 185/3 On the vessels in our docks and harbours may now be seen the 'Plimsoll mark'. **1894** *Westm. Gaz.* 17 Oct. 1/2 The only question in dispute is where to affix this Plimsoll line of respectability. **1896** *Nautical Mag.* Jan. 17 'Plimsoll's pancake' will ruin the colonial carrying trade. **1912** R. W. SERVICE *Rhymes of Rolling Stone* (1913) 78 Loaded to the Plimsoll mark With God's sunshine was that boy. **1920** P. L. WALDRON *Afloat & Ashore* 57 The ship was loaded down to 'Plimsoll's pancake'. **1957** R. CAMPBELL *Portugal* 29 It.. will pierce a crocodile if shot on the 'Plimsoll-line' between back and belly. **1961** *John o' London's* 18 May 567/1 Wearing towel..and not wearing that a millimetre more than the censor demands either below or above the cheesecake plimsoll-line. **1964** C. WILLOCK *Enormous Zoo* iv. 59 Big bull elephants..stand up to their plimsoll lines in the lake. **1972** *Author* Winter 187/2 The secondary school performance was worse—only 9 'good' and 13 'reasonable', with 140 below the Plimsoll line. **1976** *National Observer* (U.S.) 31 July 15/2, I tried to teach my wife, Lila, to fish, but with only a mud turtle, a rusty bucket, and a two-inch bluegill to show for standing three hours up to her Plimsoll line in cold water, she became an incorrigible dropout. **1978** T. DE V. WHITE *My Name is Norval* i. 15 She had..[a] formula for..the restraining of male advances: a Plimsoll mark below which she was theoretically in danger.

2. Also (through association with SOLE *sb.*[1] 2) ***plimsole***. A kind of rubber-soled canvas shoe. Usu. *pl.* Also *attrib.*

1907 *Yesterday's Shopping* (1969) 326/1 The Plimsoll or Sand Shoes. **1922** *Times* 27 Dec. 7/7 When Seabrook appeared in court he was wearing white plimsolls. **1927** W. DEEPING *Kitty* xii. 148 These stealthy affairs..made him think of sneaking out in plimsolls and kidding some 'cop'. **1930** W. PETT RIDGE *Miss Collingwood* i. 12 She kicked off her plimsolls, and walked about in stockinged feet. **1936** G. POLLET *Song for Sixpence* xi. 89 For two pleasant days I have been holidaying it in plimsolls whilst my shoes have been upon the rack. **1939** JOYCE *Finnegans Wake* (1964) II. 397 Their blankets and materny mufflers and plimsoles. **1965** D. FRANCIS *Odds Against* xii. 163 Chico had made a plimsole-shod inspection. **1968** J. IRONSIDE *Fashion Alphabet* 131 *Canvas shoes*..are usually 'plimsoll' or espadrille shape for sports, beach or leisure. **1973** 'D. JORDAN' *Nile Green* xxxvi. 181 She came in through the door like a commando in plimsolls.

Hence **ˈplimsol(l)ed** *a.*, wearing plimsolls.

1955 E. BLISHEN *Roaring Boys* iv. 183 Dancing on plimsolled toes like a boxer. **1959** F. BAINES *In Deep* 29 Moses and I put on plimsolls and slipped down the alley-way. **1963** 'R. EAST' *Pin Men* iii. 62 He lifted his plimsolled foot. **1974** C. FREMLIN *By Horror Haunted* 157 The wary, plimsoled footstep.

pling (plɪŋ), *v. U.S. slang.* [Origin unknown.] *intr.* and *trans.* To beg; to beg from (someone); ***pling the stem*** (see quot. 1927[2]). Hence **ˈplinger**, a beggar; **ˈplinging** *vbl. sb.*

1913 L. LIVINGSTON *Trail of Tramp* vii. 55 The other one will make a good assistant for me in plinging. *Ibid.* 56 It meant for James McDonald that he had become an apprentice for Kansas Shorty, the Plinger—a begging tramp. **1915** *N.Y. World* 9 May (Suppl.) 14/3 *Plinging*, to reach out for 'handouts'; to beg. **1927** *Amer. Speech* II. 390/1 A street is..a *stem*... Dinging the stem is known as *mooching, stemming* and *plinging*. *Plinging 'em right and left* is an arduous occupation, calling for gall, tact and sharp eyes. **1927** *Dialect Notes* V. 459 *Pling the stem*, to beg money on the street. **1931** G. IRWIN *Amer. Tramp & Underworld Slang* 148 *Pling*, to beg on the street, probably a corruption of 'pillinge'.

Plinian (ˈplɪnɪən), *a.* and *sb.* [ad. L. *Plīniānus*, f. *Plīnius* Pliny (see also sense A.2). In B, a. Ger. *plinian*.]

A. *adj.* **1.** Belonging to or named after Pliny, esp. Pliny the elder, C. Plinius Secundus, the naturalist (A.D. 23–79).

1649 OGILBY tr. *Virg. Georg.* II. (1684) 79 *note*, Salmasius (in his Plinian Exercitations) takes it for a Fable. **1962** D. HARDEN *Phoenicians* xi. 154 The Plinian tradition that glass was invented in Phoenicia.

2. Also **plinian**. Applied to (the stage of) a volcanic eruption in which a narrow blast of gas is ejected with great violence from a central vent to a height of several miles before it expands sideways. [In this sense ad. It. *Pliniano* (A. Stoppani *Corso di Geologia* (1871) I. II. v. 310); so called because the eruption of Vesuvius in A.D. 79, which killed Pliny the Elder and was described by his nephew the younger Pliny, was of this kind.]

Quots. 1884, 1897 refer specifically to the eruption of A.D. 79.

[**1884** H. J. JOHNSTON-LAVIS in *Q. Jrnl. Geol. Soc.* XL. 37 Some authors have supposed that the principal part of the Vesuvian cone was thrown up by the eruption which destroyed Pompeii... Let us imagine the condition of affairs towards the termination of the Plinian eruption. **1897** I. C. RUSSELL *Volcanoes N. Amer.* i. 16 Following the Plinian eruption Vesuvius became quiet once more.] **1903** A. GEIKIE *Text-bk. Geol.* (ed. 4) I. 278 Three phases of its [*sc.* Vesuvius'] energy are recognised... In the third and most vigorous phase, which has been termed Plinian,..large volumes of steam, dust, ashes, scoriæ, bombs and blocks are expelled with great violence high into the air and fall around the crater, while occasionally streams of lava issue from rents in the cone. **1944** A. HOLMES *Princ. Physical Geol.* xx. 466 Four days after the paroxysm [of Vesuvius in 1906]—the Vesuvian phase—began, it culminated in a mighty uprush of gases—the Plinian phase..—which continued for the greater part of a day,..tearing away the upper portions of the cone, and reaching a height of 8 miles. **1965** R. FURNEAUX *Krakatoa* iii. 37 Its occasional 'Plinian' outbursts bring Vesuvius within the same classification as Krakatoa. **1975** FIELDER & WILSON *Volcanoes of Earth, Moon & Mars* iv. 47/2 The pyroclastic blanket could easily be generated by a lunar plinian eruption. **1976** P. FRANCIS *Volcanoes* iii. 114 Probably the best modern example of a Plinian eruption was that of the Bezymianny volcano in Kamchatka.

B. *sb. Min.* Name given by Breithaupt (1846) to a supposed monoclinic variety of cobaltiferous arsenopyrite.

1868 DANA *Min.* (ed. 5) 80 Arsenopyrite, or Mispickel... Plinian. **1896** CHESTER *Dict. Min., Plinian...* A syn. of arsenopyrite, the new name being given because it was supposed to be monoclinic.

plink (plɪŋk), *v.* [Imit.] **a.** *intr.* To emit a short sharp metallic or ringing sound; to play a musical instrument in this manner.

1941 E. P. O'DONNELL *Great Big Doorstep* 194 A frog plinked, squirmed out, snapped open and away. **1945** B. MACDONALD *Egg & I* (1946) xii. 144 The berries..had begun to plink into the..buckets. **1976** *Gazette* (Montreal) 19 July 3/3 (*heading*) Pianist plinking for Canada. **1979** G. HAMMOND *Dead Game* v. 77 A bullet at full speed plinks like somebody leaned on the lid of a biscuit-tin.

b. *intr.* and *trans.* To shoot a gun *at* a target; to hit (a target) with a shot from a gun.

1966 R. THOMAS *Spy in Vodka* x. 94 It was an ugly gun, [not] designed..for plinking at rabbits. **1975** G. V. HIGGINS *City on Hill* vi. 160 The back was full of rats... I bought an air-pistol..and I'd plink at them. **1976** L. DEIGHTON *Twinkle, twinkle, Little Spy* iv. 41 Goddamned weather... I would have plinked him but for that damned patch of ice.

So **ˈplinking** *ppl. a.* and *vbl. sb.*

1961 *Guns & Hunting* Dec. 11/2 You may therefore convert the gun into a small-game and plinking arm. **1965** *Listener* 30 Sept. 507/3 On summer Wednesdays we have supped full of horrors with heartbeats down the corridors, creaking boards, plinking music and plenty of the consequences of over-tidiness, over-mothering, and all that suppressed sex. **1977** J. CLEARY *High Road to China* iv. 139 The General practising his banjo..the plinking of the strings. **1977** R. E. HARRINGTON *Quintain* xiv. 162 Quintain heard a brittle plinking sound that went from a high tone to a low tone. **1978** *Detroit Free Press* 2 Apr. 8E/1 Say you owned a handgun and wanted to take it out for plinking or target practice.

plink (plɪŋk), *sb.* [f. the vb.] The sound or action of plinking; a sharp metallic noise. Also quasi-*adv.* and as *int.*

1954 J. R. R. TOLKIEN *Two Towers* viii. 153 And plink! a silver drop falls. **1961** *Amer. Speech* XXXVI. 305 The smaller pebble goes *plink*, the larger, *plunk*. **1971** *Daily Tel.* (Colour Suppl.) 3 Dec. 7/1 No wonder..that the first plink of those conciliatory ping-pong balls produced rapturous applause. **1974** *Times* 7 Mar. 12/4, I cannot dance to electronic music, because I simply do not know how to hear those plinks and plonks and bumps.

plinth (plɪnθ). [ad. L. *plinthus* plinth (Vitruv. in senses 1 a, 2 a), a. Gr. πλίνθος tile, brick, stone squared for building. Cf. F. *plinthe*. The L. form *plinthus* was at first used.]

1. a. 'The lower square member of the base of a column or pedestal' (Gwilt).

[**1563** SHUTE *Archit.* C iv b, The antiques haue made three Plinthus, one aboue an other, the occasion wherof is this, that the earthe should not ouer growe the Base of the Pedestale. *Ibid.* D iij b, The Abacus hangeth ouer more then the Plinthus of the Base of the pillor.] **1611** COTGR., *Plinthe*, a Plinth, or Slipper; a flat, and square peece of Masonrie, &c., placed sometimes aboue, sometimes below, the footstall (but euer the first of the Basis) of a piller, &c. **1688** R. HOLME *Armoury* III. 459/1 The Plinth, or Plinthus. **1727** CHAMBERS *Cycl.* s.v., The plinth is..that flat square table, under the mouldings of the base and pedestal..seeming to have been originally intended to keep the bottom of the primitive wooden pillars from rotting. *a* **1849** POE *Coliseum* iv, These ivy-clad arcades..These mouldering plinths. *a* **1878** SIR G. G. SCOTT *Lect. Archit.* (1879) I. 151 In earlier instances the plinth and sub-plinth are both square in plan.

b. A block of stone, etc., serving as a base or pedestal to a statue, bust, vase, etc.; also, the squared base of a piece of furniture.

1712 J. JAMES tr. *Le Blond's Gardening* 216 Upon the Stone Coping, are Plinths to set Vases and Flower-Pots on. **1832** GELL *Pompeiana* I. vi. 109 These figures..stand upon little square plinths.

c. The projecting part of a wall immediately above the ground. Also, a course of bricks or stones in a wall, above ground level, by which the part of the wall above is made to be set back in relation to the part below; = *plinth course* s.v. sense 4 below. Also *attrib.*, as ***plinth-stone***.

1823 P. NICHOLSON *Pract. Build.* 312 A Plinth, in masonry, is the first stone inserted above the ground. **1842–76** GWILT *Archit.* Gloss. 1298 In a wall the term *plinth* is applied to two or more rows of bricks at the base of it, which project from the face. **1845** PARKER *Gloss. Archit.* 292 *Plinth*, the plain projecting face at the bottom of a wall immediately above the ground. **1878** McVITTIE *Christ Ch. Cath.* 66 Springing from a plinth which runs round the building. **1968** W. G. NASH *Brickwork* II. v. 112 The golden rule to remember when setting out the bonding for plinth courses and the walling below is to set out the neat work immediately above the plinth course first and let the bonding below the plinth be bonded to suit the neat work. In other words, always bond downwards from the face-work and *not* upwards from the work below the plinth courses.

d. *fig.* A plinth-like base or foundation.

1803 REPTON *Landscape Garden.* (1805) 86 A terrace.. forms a base line or deep plinth. **1897** MARY KINGSLEY *W. Africa* 405 Its surrounding plinth of rock shows in places at low water. **1904** R. J. FARRER *Garden of Asia* xvi. 150 That glorious cone towering up into the sky from its plinth of hills. **1935** 'E. QUEEN' *Spanish Cape Mystery* ix. 187 Ellery was sprawled on his side in an uncomfortable position, his eyes glued to a plinth of light.

2. †**a.** After Vitruvius, The abacus of the capital of a column. *Obs.*

[**1563** SHUTE *Archit.* C j b, The Capital..hath vpon Echinus a littel edge, which seteth forth Plinthus with a more beautiful Proiecture.] **1611** COTGR., *Abaque*, a Plinth, or flat square Stone, on the Capitell of a pillar. **1726** LEONI *Alberti's Archit.* II. 45/2 Over the Capitals of their Columns another Abacus or Plinth. **1727–41** CHAMBERS *Cycl.* s.v., Vitruvius also calls the Tuscan abacus, *plinth*, from its resembling a square brick.

b. The uppermost projecting part of a cornice or of a wall. See also quot. 1727–41. Now *rare.*

1613 CHAPMAN *Maske Inns Court* a j, A..Temple..whose Pillars..bore vp an Architraue, Freese, and Cornish: Ouer which stood a continued Plinthe; whereon were aduanc't statues of siluer. **1727–41** CHAMBERS *Cycl., Plinth of a wall* .. in the general, for any flat high moulding, serving in a front wall to mark the floors; or to sustain the eaves of a wall, and the larmier of a chimney. **1863** PATERSON *Hist. Ayr.* I. 216 The plinth at the top of the walls was composed of the same material.

3. A shallow wooden cabinet in which a record deck is mounted.

1963 *Hi-Fi Year Bk.* 35 Both the GL58 and GL70 are now available on plinths. **1975** *Gramophone* Sept. 537/2 The model BDS80 is the first of the new BSR Belt Drive Series of transcription turntables; the unit under review was delivered already mounted in a plinth. **1976** *Southern Even. Echo* (Southampton) 2 Nov. 9/2 (Advt.), Pioneer SA5300 amplifier 2 × 12 watts RMS plus Garrard 125SB belt drive turntable, plinth, cover, fitted with Shure M75/6/SM magnetic cartridge.

4. *Comb.* as ***plinth-like***, ***plinth-shaped*** adjs.; **plinth block**, a block sited on the floor and forming part of the base of the moulding of a door or window; **plinth course** = sense 1 c above.

1893 J. P. ALLEN *Pract. Building Construction* xviii. 293 *Plinth blocks or bases..are often put at the bottom of architraves..for the skirting to run up against, as well as for appearance. **1932** F. L. WRIGHT *Autobiogr.* II. 138 The whole exterior was bedeviled..with corner-boards, panel-boards, window-frames, corner-blocks, plinth blocks, rosettes, fantails, ingenious and jigger work in general. **1873** F. ROGERS *Specifications Pract. Archit.* II. xxv. 375 All *plinth courses, jambs of doors and windows, and window-sills, strings, and chimney-cappings to be in red moulded bricks. **1968** Plinth course [see 1 c above]. **1905** *Harper's Mag.* July 195/1 Those short, stubbed girls and women.. were of *plinthlike bigness up and down.

Hence **ˈplinthiform** *a.*, having the form of a plinth; **ˈplinthless** *a.*, without a plinth.

1845 PALEY *Goth. Mouldings* 64 An interposed square edge, or plinthiform member. **1898** J. F. CURWEN *Hist. Descr. Levens Hall* 13 The square plinthless but embattled tower.

plinthite (ˈplɪnθaɪt). *Min.* [Named by T. Thomson 1836, f. Gr. πλίνθος brick + -ITE[1].] A brick-red clay occurring among the trap rocks of Antrim and the Hebrides.

1836 T. THOMSON *Min.* I. 323 Sp. 8 *Plinthite.* I give this name to a mineral which occurs in the County of Antrim, from its brick red colour. **1843** PORTLOCK *Geol.* 217 Plinthite is not an uncommon mineral, occurring in the softer varieties of the trap rocks. **1883** *Athenæum* 30 June 833/3 Saponite, plinthite, Thomsonite..were found [near Stainchol, Skye].

ˈPlinyism. *rare.* [f. *Pliny* (see PLINIAN) + -ISM.] A statement of dubious correctness, such as some found in Pliny's Natural History.

1702 C. MATHER *Magn. Chr.* III. II. iii. (1852) 368 Of which 'twill be no Plinyism to observe..that it flowers the first of all trees. *Ibid.* xix. 442 There is frequently..much likeliness between a Plinyism and a fable.

Pliocene (ˈplaɪəsiːn), *a.* (*sb.*) *Geol.* Also Pleiocene. [f. Gr. πλείων, -ον more (see PLEIO-) + καινός new, recent.] **a.** Epithet applied to the newest division of the Tertiary formation, distinguished from EOCENE and MIOCENE as containing a larger proportion of fossil shells of still existing species; called also Upper Tertiary. Also applied to animals, etc., of this period. **b.** *absol.* as *sb.* = Pliocene division or formation.

1831 [see EOCENE *a.* 1]. **1833** LYELL *Princ. Geol.* III. v. 53 We derive the term Pliocene from πλειων, *major*, and καινος, *recens*, as the major part of the fossil testacea of this epoch are referrible to recent species. **1866** BRANDE & COX *Dict. Sc.*, etc. II. 935/2 The pliocene rocks of England..include the red crag and coralline crag of the eastern counties. **1900** *Athenæum* 21 July 93/1 Years afterwards French anthropologists also found Pliocene man.

Pliofilm (ˈplaɪəʊfɪlm). Also pliofilm. A proprietary name for a type of transparent, waterproof membrane made of rubber hydrochloride and widely used for packaging, waterproofing, etc. Freq. *attrib.*

1934 *Official Gaz.* (U.S. Patent Office) 20 Nov. 537/2 Goodyear Tire & Rubber Company, Akron, Ohio. Filed Sept. 22, 1934. Pliofilm... Claim use since June 28, 1934. **1936** *Trade Marks Jrnl.* 19 Feb. 223/1 Pliofilm... Material in sheets, strips and films manufactured from a composition consisting principally of a derivative of india-rubber. The Goodyear Tire & Rubber Company.., Akron, Ohio, United States of America; manufacturers. **1938** *India Rubber World* XCVIII. III. 47/1 Pliofilm..is being used in direct contact with many food and pharmaceutical items. **1949** *Times* 26 Feb. 3/1 Aero engines and delicate instruments..were contained in Pliofilm envelopes during shipment. **1956** H. Gold *Man who was not with It* xxxii. 310 Shoppers..wearing rubber or pliofilm galoshes on their shoes. **1961** L. Mumford *City in History* xvii. 546 A world in which he is insulated by glass, cellophane, pliofilm from the mortifications of living. **1969** J. H. Stickelmeyer in W. R. R. Park *Plastics Film Technol.* i. 7 'Pliofilm' is produced by adding hydrogen chloride gas to a special grade of natural crude rubber in benzene solution. **1974** H. McCloy *Sleepwalker* v. 73 All these furs were..in dry cleaner's pliofilm bags.

‖**Pliohippus** (plaɪəʊˈhɪpəs). *Palæont.* Also Pleio-. [mod.L., f. *plio-* in Pliocene + Gr. ἵππος horse.] An extinct genus of horses, the fossil remains of which are found in the Pliocene and Miocene strata of N. America.

1874 O. C. Marsh in *Amer. Jrnl. Sc.* Ser. 3 VII. 252 *Pliohippus.* A new genus of solipeds, allied to *Equus*..found in Pliocene strata, Nebraska. **1876** *Times* 7 Dec., In the recent strata was found the common horse; in the Pleiocene, the Pleiohippus and the Protohippus or Hipparion.

‖**Pliolophus** (plaɪˈɒləfəs). *Palæont.* [mod.L., f. Gr. πλεῖον more + λόφος crest: see quot. 1857.] A genus of fossil perissodactyl hoofed quadrupeds, whose remains are found in the Middle and Lower Tertiary strata. Hence **ˈplioloph**, an animal of this genus; **pliˈolophoid** *a.*, resembling this genus, or belonging to the *Pliolophoidea* or *Pliolophidæ*, of which it is the type; *sb.* a pliolophoid animal.

1857 Owen in *Q. Jrnl. Geol. Soc.* XIV. 55 A new genus and species of perissodactyle pachyderm, for which I propose the name of *Pliolophus vulpiceps*, or Fox-headed Plioloph. *Note.* By it [the term *Pliolophus*] I..mean that it is more near to the Lophiodont type than its close ally the Hyracotherium. **1859** Page *Handbk. Geol. Terms*, *Pliolophus*, a small *lophiodont* mammal, whose remains have been found in eocene and miocene tertiaries.

Plio-Pleistocene (ˌplaɪəʊˈplaɪstəsiːn), *a. Geol.* [f. Plio(cene *a.* (*sb.*) + Pleistocene *a.* (*sb.*).] Of or pertaining to the end of the Pliocene and the beginning of the Pleistocene epochs, or the Pliocene and Pleistocene epochs together. Also *absol.*

1929 *Q. Jrnl. Geol. Soc.* LXXXV. 520, I am the more inclined to look on the remarkable conglomerate of Wadi Abu Nefukh..as of the late Pliocene or Plio-Pleistocene age. **1946** F. E. Zeuner *Dating the Past* v. 135 Reasons have been given..for fixing the Plio-Pleistocene boundary just before the Early Glaciation. **1957** J. K. Charlesworth *Quaternary Era* xl. 1087 The exchange of plants between Asia and North America and the spread of the horse and camel-llama from North America to Asia about the Plio-Pleistocene transition. **1975** *Nature* 4 Dec. 395/1 Plio-Pleistocene lacustrine and fluvial strata exposed along the east side of Lake Rudolf, Kenya, now known as 'East Rudolf', have been under study since 1969. **1977** *Offshore Engineer* May 37/3 Plio-Pleistocene sedimentation could not keep pace, and layers are very thin. **1978** *Nature* 17 Aug. 662/2 In the Plio-Pleistocene of East Africa, the various species of hippo are most common in river channel and lake margin sediments.

‖**Pliosaurus** (plaɪəʊˈsɔːrəs). *Palæont.* Also pleio-. [mod.L., f. Gr. πλεῖον more, pleio- + σαῦρος lizard; so called because more near to the saurian type than the ichthyosaurus.] A genus of fossil marine reptiles, resembling *Plesiosaurus*, but with shorter neck, larger head, and stronger jaws and teeth; their remains are found in the Upper Oolite. Also anglicized as **ˈpliosaur**. Hence **plioˈsaurian** *a.*, of or belonging to the genus *Pliosaurus*.

1851 Richardson *Geol.* (1855) 300 The Pliosaurus was a gigantic reptile, intermediate between the two preceding genera. We know two species from the Oxford and Kimmeridge clays. **1859** Owen in *Encycl. Brit.* (ed. 8) XVII. 148/2 This short-necked and big-headed amphicœlian Pliosaur. **1888** R. Lydekker in *Q. Jrnl. Geol. Soc.* XLV. 50 Further indications of Pliosaurian affinities.

pliotron (ˈplaɪətrɒn). *Electronics.* [f. Gr. πλείω-ν more (see pleio-) + -tron.] A high-vacuum thermionic valve with one or more grids.

1915 I. Langmuir in *Electrician* 21 May 242/2 The term 'Pliotron' has been adopted to designate a Kenotron, in which a third electrode has been added for the purpose of controlling the current flowing between the anode and the cathode. **1918** *Wireless World* July 230 The characteristics of the pliotron depend upon the length of filament used. **1945** Cooke & Markus *Electronics Dict.* 278/2 *Pliotron*, a high vacuum thermionic tube in which one or more electrodes (grids) are employed... All amplifier tubes in radio sets are pliotrons, but the term has never gained extensive use. **1971** G. M. & R. D. Chute *Electronics in Industry* (ed. 4) x. 167 A third element, called the grid, is placed between the anode and cathode to form a high-vacuum type of triode (also called the pliotron).

plip-plop (ˈplɪpˈplɒp). [Imit.] A representation of a rhythmically regular sequence of sounds. Hence **ˈplip-plopping** *a.*

1953 *John o' London's Weekly* 23 Jan. 75/3 Several percussion players produced delicate plip-plops, and three sopranos murmured the vocal line. **1961** *Countryman* Autumn 514 Plip-plop went the donkey's decorously pointing toes. *Ibid.* 516 Then a 'plip-plop'... The donkey..was tittupping round the dustbin. **1979** J. Barnett *Backfire is Hostile!* xiv. 165 Rain began to fall slowly, in large separate plip-plopping drops.

‖**plique à jour** (plik a ʒur). [Fr.] A technique in enamelling in which small areas of translucent enamel are fused into the spaces of a wire framework to give an effect similar to stained glass.

1878 J. H. Pollen *Anc. & Mod. Gold & Silver Smiths' Work* p. clxii, French writers give this kind of [transparent] enamel the name of 'plite' or 'plique à jour'. **1899** H. Cunynghame *Art-Enamelling* iv. 95 By plique-à-jour we mean filigree-work executed in gold or silver, and filled up with transparent enamels. **1959** *Times* 9 Feb. 10/5 Her work in *cloisonné*, *plique-à-jour* and *champlevé* won medals and certificates in several countries. **1964** H. Hodges *Artifacts* iii. 63 To do this type of work, plique-à-jour, the areas for the enamel were fretted and given a temporary backing of sheet mica or some similar material to which the enamel would not adhere. **1973** *Country Life* 26 July 250/2 A gold filigree cup with a band of enamel in the exacting technique of *plique-à-jour*. **1975** *Times* 1 Aug. 17/6 A gold, *pliqué* [sic] *à jour* enamel and crystal kaleidoscope jewel made £750... It is an outstanding piece of French nineteenth-century craftsmanship.

plise, obs. variant of please *v.*

plisky (ˈplɪskɪ), *sb.* (*a.*) *Sc.* and *north. dial.* [Origin unknown.] A mischievous trick; a frolic.

1786 Burns *Earnest Cry & Prayer* xvi, Deil na they never mair do guid, Play'd her that pliskie! **1816** Scott *Antiq.* xli, I can hae nae reason to play an ill pliskie t'ye in the day o' your distress. **1887** P. McNeill *Blawearie* 154 Get them fu', and we'll soon play them a plisky.

b. An awkward plight.

1829 Hogg in R. Chambers *Sc. Songs* (1829) I. 136 Ye little ken what pains I prove, Or how severe my pliskie, O! **1847** E. Brontë *Wuthering Heights* xiii, I nobbut wish he may catch ye i' that plisky.

B. *adj.* Tricky, mischievous. *rare.*

1887 J. Service *Dr. Duguid* I. iv. (ed. 3) 27 Auld Habkin o' the Pethfit, who was a pliskie body.

plissé (plise), *sb.* and *a.* [Fr., pa. pple. of *plisser* to pleat.] **A.** *sb.* A piece of fabric shirred or gathered into narrow pleats; a gathering of pleats. Also in *Comb.*

1873 *Young Englishwoman* June 286/1 The front width of the skirt is trimmed with a blue plissé, headed with a deep flounce. **1880** [see gold[1] 8 b]. **1920** *Glasgow Herald* 13 Nov. 4 Plissé is the last word in style, and the latest knitted frocks have wide borders done in ribbed work that spring out into plissés. **1954** *Sun* (Baltimore) 8 May 5 (Advt.), Glamour gown... Made of Strat-o-Sheer plisse. **1969** *Sears Catal.* Spring/Summer 11 Cool, comfortable Plissé-textured Pajamas of 80% cotton, 20% polyester.

B. *adj.* Formed into small pleats.

1875 [see *elbow-sleeve* s.v. elbow *sb.* 5]. **1895** *Montgomery Ward Catal.* Spring & Summer 12/2 Printed plisse silk, 20 inches wide. This is the newest idea in gauffre or crinkled silks... It is a small, crinkly stripe pattern in white grounds over which is printed..floral designs. **1928** *Times* 9 May 10/6 A train of lime green and silver tissue, lined with plissé chiffon. **1962** J. T. Marsh *Self-Smoothing Fabrics* iv. 40 Combinations of various factors are capable of disguising creases, as in crepes, seersuckers and plissé fabrics, but other combinations may accentuate the crease. **1967** Singha & Massey *Indian Dances* xv. 130 Over these they wore plissé skirts made of stiff material in three tiers the longest of which reached several inches above the knee.

plit. *Agric.* [Invented by W. Marshall: see quot. 1778.] The slice of earth turned over by a ploughshare.

1778 [W. Marshall] *Minutes Agric.* 13 May an. 1775, Each furrow.., and the fresh-formed surface of each *plit*, may lie..wholly exposed to the weather. [*Ibid.*, *note*, A spade-full is called a *Spit*, and, by analogy, a plow-full a *Plit.*] **1812** Sir J. Sinclair *Syst. Husb. Scot.* I. 156 Where the land is excessively steep, it is often necessary to plough directly across, throwing the plits or furrow slices all down hill. **1813** R. Ker *Agric. Surv. Berwick* 150 At its fore part it is an exceedingly sharp wedge, so as to insinuate between the fastland and the plit, or furrow slice.

plit, plite, obs. forms of plight.

†**plitch**, *v. Obs.* Forms: 1 *plycc(e)an, 5 plycche. *Pa. t.* 4 plight(t)e, (pleightte), 5 plyȝte, plyghte. *Pa. pple.* 4 plyȝt, 5 plight, 6 plyghte. [OE. 2 sing. subj. and imper. *plyce*, *plice*, irreg. forms from **plycc(e)an*:—WGer. type **plukkja-* pluck (whence also Du. *plucken*, LG. *plücken*, MHG., Ger. *pflücken*): see pluck *v.*] *trans.* To pluck, pull, snatch.

? *a* **1000** in *Techmer's Intern. Zeitschr. Sprachw.* (1885) II. 122 Đonne þu setræȝel habban wille, þonne plice þu ðine aȝene ȝeweda mid twam fingrum. *Ibid.* 127 þæt þu strece forð þin wenstre handstoc and plyce innan mid þinre wynstran hande. **13..** *Guy Warw.* (A.) 2401 His swerd of stiel he haþ up pliȝt. *c* **1320** R. Brunne *Medit.* 626 Fersly here swete sone ys from here plyȝt. *c* **1374** Chaucer *Troylus* II. 1071 (1120) He seyd here þus and out þe lettre plighte. *c* **1380** *Sir Ferumb.* 3029 He..plyȝte him of is sadel with mayn. *c* **1386** Chaucer *Man of Law's Prol.* 15 And sodeynly he plighte his hors aboute.

Hence †**ˈplitching** *vbl. sb.*, plucking, carping.

c **1440** *Jacob's Well* 294 þe synnes of þi mowth arn.. plycchyng at loue & charyte.

plith, obs. f. plight *sb.*[1]

plo, obs. f. plough.

ploat, plote (plot), *v. Sc.* and *north. dial.* [a. Fl. and Du. *ploten* (in Kilian only as Fl.) to pluck the wool off; in meaning identical with *blooten*, but connexion is uncertain.] *trans.* To pluck, to strip of feathers, wool, etc.; *fig.* to rob, plunder fleece.

1825 Brockett *N.C. Gloss.*, *Plote*, to pluck, to chide vehemently, 'See how she plotes him'. **1855** Robinson *Whitby Gloss.*, *To Ploat*, to pluck the feathers off a fowl... 'They'll ploat him', fleece him. **1863** Robson *Bards of Tyne* 431 The geese 'ill niver feel ye ploat.

Hence †**ˈploater, plotter** [see -er[1]; cf. Du. *ploter* white leather-dresser, 'vellerum siue lanarum tonsor' (Kilian).] *Obs.*

1601 in Cochran-Patrick *Med. Scot.* iii. (1892) 40 Ayr took three of them—George Baert, 'plotter and comber'; James Claers, weaver; and Arane Janson, 'scherar'.

‖**ploc.** *rare*$^{-0}$. [F. *ploc* in same and other senses (1567 in Hatz.-Darm.).] (See quot.)

1858 Simmonds *Dict. Trade*, *Ploc*, a mixture of hair and tar for covering a ship's bottom. **1864** in Webster; and in later Dicts.

‖**ploce** (ˈplɒsiː). *Rhet.* Also 6 ploche, 7 ploke (ˈplɒkiː). [Late L. *plocē* (Mart. Capella), the rhetorical figure, a. Gr. πλοκή plaiting, f. πλέκειν to plait.] The repetition of a word in an altered or more expressive sense, or for the sake of emphasis.

1586 A. Day *Eng. Secretary* II. (1625) 86 *Ploche*, when by an Emphasis, a word is either in praise or disgrace reiterated or repeated. **1589** Puttenham *Eng. Poesie* III. xix. (Arb.) 211 Ploche, or the Doubler. **1657** J. Smith *Myst. Rhet.* 109 *Ploce*,..A figure when a word is by way of Emphasis so repeated, that it denotes not only the thing signified, but the quality of the thing. **1678** Phillips (ed. 4), *Ploce*,..a Rhetorical figure of Elocution,..as, In that great victory Cæsar was Cæsar. **1711** Addison *Spect.* No. 61 ⁋3 He generally talked in the Paranomasia,..he sometimes gave into the Plocè. **1859** tr. *Bengel's Gnomon* I. 356 Ὁ ποιήσας ἐποίησεν (He who made, made), is a striking example of Ploce.

ploch, variant of plotch *sb. Obs.*

plock (plɒk), *sb.* [Imit.] A sharp click or report, as of one hard object striking another.

1936 C. Day Lewis *Friendly Tree* xii. 173 The cries of the boys, the curt shouts of the masters, the plock as bat met ball—all these sounds were somehow unsynchronized. **1969** H. R. F. Keating *Inspector Ghote plays Joker* xvi. 210 From the lit table there came the soft double plock of one of the balls striking the other two. **1976** G. Ewart *No Fool* 11. 61 The plock of bat on ball penetrates out-fields, calming to the mind.

plock (plɒk), *v. rare.* [Imit.: cf. prec.] *intr.* To make a sound as of taut fabric being pierced.

1931 V. Sackville-West *All Passion Spent* II. 161 Sitting down by her, as her needle plocked in and out of her embroidery, he would gaze fondly at her bent head.

plod (plɒd), *v.* Also 7–8 *dial.* plad. [Known from *c* 1560; app. of onomatopœic origin. (ME. *plodder* seems to be unconnected.)

Some would connect it with ME. *plod* (*plodde*), plud, a puddle, a pool, taking the original sense as 'to wade in a puddle, to splash through water or mud'; but no special reference to puddles or wading appears in the use of the word, which seems rather to suggest the dull sound of labouring steps on moderately firm ground.]

1. *intr.* To walk heavily or without elasticity; to move or progress laboriously, to trudge. Also *plod on. lit.* and *fig.*

a **1566** R. Edwards *Damon & Pithias* in Hazl. *Dodsley* IV. 27, I like not this soil, for as I go plodding, I mark there two, there three, their heads always nodding, In close secret wise. **1589** R. Harvey *Pl. Perc.* (1860) 3 Plodding through Aldersgate..with a quarter Ashe staffe on my Shoulder. **1601** Shaks. *All's Well* III. iv. 6 Bare-foot plod I the cold ground vpon. **1610** W. Folkingham *Art of Survey* I. x. 27 Wee plod-on in the common Road of habituated husbandry. **1766** Fordyce *Serm. Yng. Wom.* (1767) I. i. 31 Plodding along through a tasteless existence. **1821** Joanna Baillie *Metr. Leg.*, *Wallace* i, If such there be still let him plod On the dull foggy paths of care. **1888** Burgon *Lives 12 Gd. Men* I. III. 340 We plodded along in profound silence.

b. *trans.* To trudge along, over, or through (a road, etc.); to make (one's way) by plodding.

1750 Gray *Elegy* 3 The plowman homeward plods his weary way. **1816** Byron *Ch. Har.* III. iii, The journeying years Plod the last sands of life. **1896** A. E. Housman *Shropshire Lad* xlvi, Nor plod the winter land to look For willows in the icy brook. **1903** R. D. Shaw *Pauline Epist.* 176 In obedience to a dream..Augustus plodded the streets of Rome and gathered coppers as a beggar.

2. *intr.* To work with steady laborious perseverance; to toil in a laborious, stolid, monotonous fashion; to drudge, slave. Const. *at*, *on*, *upon.*

1562 J. Heywood *Prov. & Epigr.* (1867) 91 What thing is it..in your brain ploddyng. **1594** Carew *Huarte's Exam. Wits* (1616) 170 If such a one wax obstinat in plodding at the Lawes, and spend much time in the Schooles. *a* **1633**

AUSTIN *Medit.* (1635) 66 The dull Christian sitts often fruitlesly plodding on the Booke, nay heares the Prophesies often preached to no purpose. **1706** PHILLIPS, *Plod*, to labour earnestly in Business, to have one's Head full of it. **1768–74** TUCKER *Lt. Nat.* (1834) II. 686 We may suppose the possessor of it argued..'It is not worth while to plod with a single talent, for sake of the slender profit that may be made of it by the best management'. **1879** G. MEREDITH *Egoist* xii, There you have the secret of good work—to plod on and still keep the passion fresh.

†**b.** *trans.* ***plod out***: To spend (time) in plodding. *Obs. rare.*

1749 CHESTERF. *Lett.* (1792) II. 294 To plod out the evenings..at home over a book.

†**3.** Of hounds: see quot. 1688. *Obs.*

1575 TURBERV. *Venerie* 36 If there be any yong hounde which woulde carie or hang behind, beyng opinionate..and ploddyng by himselfe. *Ibid.* 240 Hounds do cal on, bawle, bable, crie, yearne, lapyse, plodde, baye and such like other noyses. **1688** R. HOLME *Armoury* III. 76/1 They plod, is when Hounds hang behind, and beat too much upon the scent in one place.

¶**4.** Confused with or influenced by PLOT *v.* in various senses. *Obs.* (Cf. PLOT *v.*³ = plod.)

1631 J. TAYLOR (Water P.) *Turn Fort. Wheel* Pref., Which makes our foes complot consult and plod, How and by what means they may warr with God. **1663** R. BLAIR *Autobiog.* iii. (1848) 54 Yet gave I not over plodding to obstruct my settling there. **1712** STEELE *Spect.* No. 450 ⁋4, I fell a plodding what Advantages might be made of the ready Cash I had. **1775** ADAIR *Amer. Ind.* 240 They were plodding mischief for twenty years before we forced them to commit hostilities.

plod (plɒd), *sb.*¹ [f. PLOD *v.*] **a.** An act or spell of plodding; a heavy tiring walk. Also *fig.* Also with alliterative reduplication, as ***plod-plod***.

1880 *Daily News* 3 Nov. 5/8 We accepted an ankle-deep plod through filth indescribable and treacherous boulders. **1890** R. BRIDGES *Shorter Poems* III. 13 Only life's common plod: still to repair The body and the thing which perisheth. **1899** N. B. TARKINGTON *Gentleman from Indiana* xv. 266 What was there left but the weary plod, plod, and dust of years? **1926** *Blackw. Mag.* Apr. 519/2 The angles of the rungs become very painful under the slow plod-plod of the horse's movement. **1972** *Times Lit. Suppl.* 9 June 654/2 This plod-plod of approach and application isn't novel. **1975** M. BRADBURY *Hist. Man* ix. 148 The agenda has grown longer..a routine plod through matters of budgets..and examinations. **1979** *Guardian* 23 Oct. 15/8 Those who found the book a bit of a plod but hoped the screen might set it up.

b. The sound of a heavy dull tread or the like; tramp, thud.

1902 *Westm. Gaz.* 23 June 1/3 What is the voice of London? Is it not the plod, plod, dumping plod of the horses' hoofs?

plod (plɒd), *sb.*² *Austral.* [perh. PLOP *sb.* influenced by PLOT *sb.*: see PLOD *v.* 4.]

a. A (particular) piece of ground worked by a miner. Also, a work sheet with information relevant to this.

1941 BAKER *Dict. Austral. Slang* 55 *Pitching the plod*, 'the exchange of words' between miners 'on the state of the ground when coming on or going off shifts'. **1948** K. S. PRICHARD *Golden Miles* 72 He had to go to the office for his plod—the card on which he filled in particulars of the work he was doing, its position in the mine, and the hours he was working.

b. A story or yarn; an excuse.

Plod is entered in the *Eng. Dial. Dict.* as a Cornish word meaning 'a short or dull story; a lying tale'.

1945 G. CASEY *Downhill is Easier* 136 'I suppose he told you the whole plod?' I sneered. **1954** T. A. G. HUNGERFORD *Sowers of Wind* 241 That's the plod he put up, anyway. **1975** X. HERBERT *Poor Fellow my Country* III. xxi. 1126 Put in a plod for me, mate.

plod, plodan, plodden, obs. ff. PLAID, -ING.

plod, plodde, obs. forms of PLOUD, PLUD.

†**ploddall.** *Obs. rare*⁻¹. [? = *plod-all*: cf. *save-all*, etc.] A plodder.

16.. *MS. Bodl.* 30 lf. 13 b, Our Schollers..verie ploddalls of Art.

†**ploddeill.** *Obs. rare*⁻¹. [Origin and sense obscure: the radical part is prob. as in PLODDER¹, the ending perh. = F. *-aille* collective] ? A company or band of thrashers or cudgellers. (*Contemptuous.*)

c **1425** WYNTOUN *Cron.* VIII. 4998 (Wemyss MS.), I vow to God scho beris hir swell The Scottis wenche with hir ploddeill; For, cum I airly, cum I lait, I fynd ay Annes at the 3ait.

†**plodder**¹. *Obs.* [Origin and sense uncertain: perh. f. 16th c. Fr. (and mod.Norm. dial.) *plauder* for *pelauder* 'to thwack, swindge, belabour..cudgell..; to vse roughly..handle rudely' (Cotgr.).] ? One who belabours or handles roughly.

c **1400** *Destr. Troy* 12862 Pilours and plodders, piked þere goodes, Kyld of þe comyns, & myche care did. *a* **1475** *Wyntoun's Cron.* VII. 4998 (Royal MS.), I vow to God scho mais grete stere The Scottis wenche ploddere. [Cf. prec.]

plodder² (ˈplɒdə(r)). [f. PLOD *v.* + -ER¹.] One who plods. **a.** Usually, One who works slowly and laboriously; a persevering toiler, a drudge.

1588 SHAKS. *L.L.L.* I. i. 86 Small haue continuall plodders euer wonne, Saue base authoritie from others Bookes. **1691** WOOD *Ath. Oxon.* I. 312 Being an indefatigable plodder at his book [he] took the degree of M. of Arts. **1760** JOHNSON *Idler* No. 95 ⁋13 Wealthy plodders were only purveyors for men of spirit. **1850** S. DOBELL *Roman* v, Shall I..Work first and be paid after, like the plodder In yonder field?

b. One who trudges in walking. *rare.*

1832 W. STEPHENSON *Gateshead Local Poems* 35 Old harmless..Deborah Dick, Thro' thick and thin a Plodder.

Hence †ˈ**plodderly** *adv.*, after the manner of a plodder; laboriously, clumsily.

c **1605** BEAUMONT (Sloane MS. 1709) in *Athenæum* 27 Jan. (1894) 115/1 Pronunciation of vile speeches in vile plotts..in the most plodderly plotted shew of Lady Amity.

ˈ**plodding,** *vbl. sb.* [-ING¹.] The action of the verb PLOD; walking heavily, trudging; toiling or striving with laborious industry.

1588 SHAKS. *L.L.L.* IV. iii. 305 Vniuersall plodding poysons vp The nimble spirits in the arteries. **1645** MILTON *Tetrach.* Wks. 1851 IV. 155 No worthy enterprise can be done by us without continuall plodding and wearisomnes to our faint and sensitive abilities. **1820** L. HUNT *Indicator* No. 24 (1822) I. 190 Between the plodding of a sexton through a Church-yard, and the walk of a Gray, what a difference! **1891** *Athenæum* 9 May 602/3 After laborious plodding through page after page of the letters.

So **plod-plodding**, designating a continuous thudding sound.

1881 BLACK *Sunrise* III. iv. 74 They had by this time grown quite accustomed to the plod plodding of the train.

plodding (ˈplɒdɪŋ), *ppl. a.* [f. PLOD *v.* + -ING².] That plods; walking or working slowly and laboriously; diligent without brilliancy; persevering.

1589 NASHE *Anat. Absurd.* Wks. (Grosart) I. 37 Let the indifferent Reader diuine what deepe misterie can be placed vnder plodding méeter. **1599** B. JONSON *Cynthia's Rev.* II. iii, A dull, plodding face, still looking in a direct line. **1628** EARLE *Microcosm.* (Arb.) 72 A Plodding Student Is a kind of alchymist or Persecutor of Nature. **1686** GOAD *Celest. Bodies* II. iv. 198 The Plodding Countryman overlooks such Vicissitudes of Nature. **1702** YALDEN *Æsop at Court* x. iv, A solemn plodding Ass that graz'd the plain. **1822** HAZLITT *Table-t.* Ser. II. xii. (1869) 250 The English are considered as comparatively a slow plodding people.

Hence ˈ**ploddingly** *adv.*, ˈ**ploddingness**.

1592 NASHE *P. Penilesse* (ed. 2) 13 For his hire any handy craft man..wil ploddingly do his day labor. **1880** GREEN *Hist. Eng. People* IV. IX. i. 223 Grenville was ploddingly industrious. **1882** H. E. MERIVALE *Faucit of B.* I. I. xi. 185 Out of the dulness and the ploddingness.

plodge (plɒdʒ), *v.* Chiefly *dial.* Also **pludge**. [Onomatopœic; allied to PLOD, but with expressive change of final consonant; perh. influenced by *plunge*.] *intr.* To wade or walk heavily in water, soft ground, or anything in which the feet sink.

1825 BROCKETT *N.C. Gloss.*, *Plodge*, to wade through water, to plunge. **1855** ROBINSON *Whitby Gloss.*, To *Plodge*, to plunge up and down in water with the feet. **1863** ROBSON *Bards of Tyne* 27 To see the folks a' duckin; men an' wives together pludg'd. **1885** *Fortnt. in Waggonette* 63 What work to plodge through it [heather] for hour after hour!

†**plod-shoe.** *Obs.* [f. PLOD *v.* + SHOE.] A strong clumsy shoe, in which one walks heavily.

1697 VANBRUGH *2nd Pt. Æsop* iii. 151 Because I han't a pair of plod shoes, and a dirty shirt, you think a woman won't venture upon me for a husband. **1705** —— *Confed.* I. ii. 64 How like a dog will you look, with a pair of plod shoes, your hair cropp'd..and a bandbox under your arm.

plog(g, plogh(e, ploh, obs. ff. PLOUGH.

ploȝe, plohe, obs. forms of PLAY *sb.* and *v.*

-ploid (plɔɪd), the ending of HAPLOID *a.* (and *sb.*) and DIPLOID *a.*, used to form analogous terms referring to the number of chromosome sets in a cell or organism (as EUPLOID, HEXAPLOID, *hyperploid* s.v. HYPER- IV. *adjs.*); occas. used with prefixed arabic number as 16-*ploid*. [*haploid*, *diploid* f. Gr. ἁπλόος single (also ἁπλοΐς, -ΐδος and ἁπλο-ειδής, f. εἶδος form), διπλόος double; the *-id* in these words Strasburger (*Progresses Rei Bot.* (1907) I. 137), their coiner, connected with *id*, *idant*, and *idioplasm* (f. Gr. ἰδιο-: see IDIO-).]

1928 *Hereditas* X. 245 Lately Blackburn.., investigating chromosome numbers in *Silene*, has described two races of *Silene ciliata* differing in chromosome number, the one being tetraploid (as compared with most other *Silene*-species), the other 16-ploid.

ploidy (ˈplɔɪdɪ). *Biol.* [f. HA)PLOIDY, POLY)PLOIDY, etc.] The number of homologous sets of chromosomes in a cell, or in each cell of an organism.

1947 *Genetics* XXXII. 512 A state of indefinite 'ploidy'. **1953** *Jrnl. Gen. Microbiol.* VIII. 101 Another possibility is that there is a different degree of effective ploidy of the F+ and F− gametic cells, the F− gametic cell having a higher degree of ploidy (or, possibly, more nuclei) than the F+. **1961** *Lancet* 5 Aug. 318/1 All metaphases have been analysed. When an exact account was impossible the ploidy level has been estimated. **1970** *Watsonia* VIII. 140 As most of our counts are approximate the ploidy level rather than the chromosome number is given. **1976** *Nature* 29 Apr. 785/2 To confirm the ploidy, both strains were grown axenically and their chromosomes were stained.

ploïmate (ˈpləʊɪmət), *a.* *Zool.* [f. mod.L. *Ploïma*, neut. pl. (C. J. Hudson, 1884) (f. Gr. πλώϊμος fit for sailing, seaworthy, f πλώειν, πλεῖν to sail) + -ATE².] Of or pertaining to the *Ploïma*, a division of *Rotifera* or wheel-animalcules, having no foot, and progressing only by swimming.

ˈ**ploiter,** *v.* *dial.* [Akin to PLOUTER.] *intr.* To work in an ineffective way; to potter; to dawdle.

1848 DE QUINCEY *Sortilege & Astrol.* Wks. 1858 IX. 269 She shifted her hand, and 'ploitered' amongst the papers for full five minutes. **1895** IAN MACLAREN *Brier Bush* VII. i, What are ye ploiterin' aboot here for?

plok(ke, plom, plomage, obs. forms of PLUCK, PLUM, PLUMAGE.

†**plomayle.** *Obs.* *rare*⁻¹. [a. OF. *plumail* (*Monstrelet Chron.* 14..) a plume; cf. L. *plūmālis* feathered.] Plumage.

1399 LANGL. *Rich. Redeles* II. 32 þey plucked the plomayle ffrom þe pore skynnes.

plomb, var. PLOMBE.

plombage (plɒmˈbɑːʒ). *Surg.* [a. F. *plombage* filling of teeth, f. *plomber* to fill, apply lead to (f. *plomb* lead: see PLUMB *sb.*) + *-age* -AGE.] The introduction of plombe into the cavity of the chest; treatment with plombe.

1933 *Tubercle* XV. 97 (*heading*) The operation of plombage in pulmonary tuberculosis. *Ibid.* 98 Before plombage could be considered it was necessary that extrapleural thoracoplasty..should reach a stage of technical efficiency. **1957** P. DUFAULT *Diagnosis & Treatment of Pulmonary Tuberculosis* (ed. 2) xix. 352 Plombage for the purpose of collapsing a limited area in mid-lung has been replaced by wedge resection. **1975** *Amer. Rev. Respiratory Dis.* CXI. 270/1, 13 animals..underwent left pneumonectomy with wax plombage.

plombe (plɒm). *Surg.* Also **plomb**. [a. G. *plombe* seal, filling (of tooth), plombe, f. F. *plomb* lead, lead weight (see PLUMB *sb.*).] (A mass of) soft material inserted into a bone cavity or into the cavity of the chest around a collapsed lung.

1904 *St. Thomas's Hosp. Rep.* XXXII. 433 The material used for bone-plugging (iodoform-knochen plombe).. consists of a mixture of 60 parts of the finest pulverised iodoform and 40 parts each of spermaceti and oil of sesame. **1905** GOULD *Dict. New Med. Terms* 423/2 *Plomb...P., iodoform* (of Mosetig-Moorhof), an antibacillary agent for filling bone-cavities after operations for tuberculosis or osteomyelitis. **1909** H. PRINZ *Dental Materia Medica & Therapeutics* III. 436 The material advocated by Mosetig.. is known in general surgery as 'bone plombe'. *Ibid.*, The plombe must completely fill the cavity. **1931** *Surg., Gynecol. & Obstetr.* LII. 738/2 (*heading*) Sketches showing the effects of paraffin filling (plombe) on a cavity of the left lung. **1956** *Jrnl. Chronic Dis.* IV. 623 The material used in the plomb has varied over the years; currently the most popular material is methyl methacrylate (Lucite) spheres sealed in a polyethylene bag, or folded polyethylene sheets. The plomb is placed between the lung and periosteum centrally and the deperiostealized ribs peripherally. **1965** JENKINS & WOLINSKY in G. L. Baum *Textbk. Pulmonary Dis.* viii. 195/1 Stabilizing the subperiostally freed and collapsed chest wall with some type of plomb.

plombe, plombette, obs. ff. PLUMB, PLUMMET.

‖**plombgomme** (plɔ̃gɔm). *Min.* [F., lit. gummy lead, f. *plomb* lead + *gomme* gum.] = PLUMBOGUMMITE.

1839 URE *Dict. Arts* 746 *Plomb-gomme.* This lead ore..is of a dirty brownish or orange-yellow. **1866** WATTS *Dict. Chem.* IV. 685 *Plombgomme*, syn. with Plumboresinite. **1868** DANA *Min.* (ed. 5) 577 S. Tennant (who died in 1815) is said to have first analyzed plombgomme and made it a combination of oxyd of lead, alumina, and water.

plombière (plɒmbɪˈɛər). [f. F. *Plombières-les-Bains*, name of a village in the Vosges Department of eastern France.] A kind of dessert made with ice cream and glacé fruits. Freq. *attrib.* or as *adj.*

1846 A. SOYER *Gastron. Regenerator* 573 Prepare..the.. plombière ice... Make a border of patisserie d'amande.. upon your dish, in the centre of which put a little of the plombière. **1849** THACKERAY *Pendennis* I. xxiv. 233 The ice was brought in—an ice of *plombière* and cherries. **1907** [see CROÛTE]. **1958** W. BICKEL tr. *Hering's Dict. Classical & Mod. Cookery* 724 *Plombière*, vanilla ice cream mixed with salpicon of candied fruit macerated in kirsch, filled in parfait mould alternately with apricot jam. **1962** S. BECK et al. *Mastering Art French Cooking* x. 549 (*heading*) Plombières with Fresh Strawberries or Raspberries.

plombierite (ˈplɒmbɪəraɪt). *Min.* [f. Plombières, France: see -ITE¹ 2 b.] (See quots.)

1866 WATTS *Dict. Chem.* IV. 685 *Plombierite*, a hydrated silicate of calcium..formed by the action of a hot mineral spring at Plombières on an old Roman mortar. **1868** DANA *Min.* (ed. 5) 802 *Plombierite*,..a gelatinous substance, which hardens in the open air, formed from the thermal waters of Plombières.

plome, plomet(e, -ette, -it, plomp, obs. forms of PLUM, PLUME, PLUMBET, PLUMMET, PLUMP.

†**plone.** *Obs. rare*⁻¹. App. an alteration of an orig. *plane*, PLANE *sb.*¹

(*Plum* has been suggested, but appears to be formally impossible.)

13.. *Minor Poems fr. Vernon MS.* liii. 70 Þe palme and þe poplere, þe pirie, þe plone [*rimes* Ione, lone, *for orig.* Iane, lane], Þe Iunipere ientel, Ionyng bi-twene.

plong, plonge, obs. forms of PLUNGE.

plonge (plɒndʒ), *sb. Fortif.* [After F. *plongée.*] 'The superior slope given to the parapet' (Stocqueler *Milit. Encycl.* 1853); = PLUNGE *sb.* 6.

†**plonge** (plɒndʒ), *v. Obs.* [var. of PLUNGE.] *trans.* To cleanse (an open drain or sewer) by stirring up the mud at the bottom so that the outward flow may carry it off.

1851 MAYHEW *Lond. Labour* (1861) II. 425/1. *Ibid.* 427/1 'When we go plonging', one man said, 'we has long poles with a piece of wood at the end of them, and we stirs up the mud.. while the tide's a going down.. and lets out the water, mud, and all, into the Thames'.

plongeon, variant of PLUNGEON, *Obs.*

‖**plongeur** (plɔ̃ʒør). [Fr.] A boy who is employed as a menial in a restaurant or hotel.

1933 'G. ORWELL' *Down & Out in Paris & London* iv. 32 The whole staff, from the manager down to the *plongeurs*, was working twenty-one hours a day. **1954** J. ATKINS *George Orwell* iv. 94 Why does the *plongeur* exist if his work is largely useless? **1964** *Punch* 1 Apr. 494/1 He'd have to become a dish-washer, or perhaps even a *plongeur*. **1967** G. WOODCOCK *Crystal Spirit* II. v. 100 The world of common lodging-houses.. as different from his [*sc.* Orwell's] life among the *plongeurs* as England is different from France. **1976** *Observer* 22 Feb. 22/3 It is over 40 years since George Orwell described a *plongeur's* life in 'Down and Out in Paris and London'. **1977** *Daily Tel.* 18 Mar. 18 Titles are nice but surely the Dorchester is going a little too far advertising for a 'Supervisor Plongeur' to head the washing up department.

plonk (plɒŋk), *v. dial.* and *colloq.* [Imit.: cf. PLUNK *v.*] **1. a.** *trans.* To hit or strike with a plonk. Chiefly *dial.*

1874 in A. Easther *Gloss. Dial. Almondbury & Huddersfield* (1883) 103 There were three fighting when you plonked Wells in the face. **1883** A. EASTHER *Ibid.* 102 *Plonk*, to hit plump. Used especially of marbles, when the one shot strikes the other before touching the ground. **1891** *Leeds Mercury Weekly Suppl.* 3 Jan. 8/6 I'll plonk tha. **1896** *Ibid.* 21 Mar. 3/8 Plenk him one o' t'noase if he doesn't shut up. **1903** in *Eng. Dial. Dict.* IV. 549/2 I'll plonk tha, if I get hod on tha. **1925** FRASER & GIBBONS *Soldier & Sailor Words* 225 *Plonk*, to shell. Suggested by the sound of the impact and burst. **1941** *London Opinion* May 64/1, I plonked him good and hearty on the beak.

b. *intr.* To emit or cause something to emit an abrupt vibratory sound, *spec.* in playing a musical instrument. Freq. with *away*.

1927 *Melody Maker* May 489/2 Can you imagine.. a saxophone section playing a nice ligato movement and the banjo plonking away for all he is worth.. and killing the good work of the saxes. **1976** D. HEFFRON *Crusty Crossed* i. 8 By age three I was plonking away at the piano on my own. **1979** *Stand* XX. iv. 34/1 The band plonks away at sad, slow French and Italian numbers.

2. a. *trans.* To set or drop (something) in position with a heavy or clumsy gesture; to put *down* firmly. Also (with a person or object), to set (someone) abruptly in a particular place or set of circumstances; to seat (someone) hurriedly or unceremoniously. Cf. PLANK *v.* 2 a, PLUNK *v.* 3 b.

1941 BAKER *Dict. Austral. Slang* 55 *Plonk down*, to put down. Also, 'plonk one's frame into a chair': to sit down. **1946** F. COOZE *Ten Bob Each Way* 22 So next time I plunged I forgot the tip And plonked my all on my own little pick. **1959** *Woman* 16 May 23/2 An officious nurse plonked down a gas and air mask on my face. **1959** *Sunday Times* 17 May 20/4 Jones has been plonked down in Gagland where the jokes are separate from the action and so has small chance of coming out strong as the comic actor we know him to be. **1967** *Spectator* 29 Sept. 358/2 A nasty-looking structure will be plonked down in front of King's Cross, thus ruining its two magnificent archways. **1972** G. DURRELL *Catch me Colobus* vii. 145 Then you'd lead her [*sc.* a piglet] carefully to the pan and she'd plonk both her stubby front feet into it, little hooves wide-spread, and dig her nose in and guzzle. **1976** P. CAVE *High Flying Birds* ii. 20 A litre bottle of red wine was plonked down on to the counter under my nose. Plonked plonk, in fact. **1977** *Sounds* 9 July 10/4 The 150 press-persons present were ushered into a darkened room, plonked on rows of chairs, told to put headphones on and left to listen.

b. *refl.* and *absol.* To sit (oneself) down heavily or unceremoniously.

1946 U. KRIGE *Way Out* v. 64 Handing them two cigarettes each, I plonked down beside them to tell them the whole story. **1976** M. SPARK *Takeover* xii. 178 Walter now plonked himself, tired from his walk, on the sofa. **1979** *Guardian* 9 Aug. 22/8 They would plonk themselves down, undress.. to encourage support for local naturists.

Hence '**plonking** *ppl. a.*, (*a*) *dial.* large; (*b*) that plonks; *spec.* (see quot. 1950); '**plonking** *vbl. sb.*; '**plonkingly** *adv.*

1896 *Leeds Mercury Weekly Suppl.* 21 Mar. 3/8 What a plonkin' hoile tha hes fer a bedrahm. Little Jimmy hes a plonkin' wife. **1903** in *Eng. Dial. Dict.* IV. 550/1 A gurt plonkin' cat. **1950** S. POTTER *Lifemanship* iii. 44 If you have nothing to say, or, rather, something extremely stupid and obvious, say it, but in a 'plonking' tone of voice—i.e. roundly, but hollowly and dogmatically. *Ibid.* 45 'Plonking' of a kind can be made by the right use of quotation or pretended quotation. **1957** *Economist* 5 Oct. 21/2 India, entangled in its own frontier troubles and engrossed with the problem of borrowing from abroad, has lately sounded a little less plonking in its pronouncements on international affairs. **1959** S. CLARK *Puma's Claw* xv. 181 Delivered with a gruff, passionate intensity (Potter would certainly call them plonking) those words always announced our arrival on a summit. **1965** *New Statesman* 19 Mar. 426/2 These reports, so far from being accurate, have been described by one member of the shadow cabinet as 'absolute poppycock', and by another even more plonkingly, as 'balls'. **1969** D. FRANCIS *Enquiry* ii. 31 'The bet was struck,' Gowery said plonkingly, pointing to the ledger. **1977** *Listener* 5 May 591/1 Presented with an argument that.. he intended to ignore, Lord Reith would say in a matter-of-fact way: 'I hear you.' It was an admirably plonking rhetorical device. **1977** *Chainsaw* Sept./Oct. 8/2 The singer is accompanied only by electric organ, regular drum beats, and plonking bass.

plonk (plɒŋk), *sb.*[1] [Imit.: cf. prec. and PLUNK *sb., adv., int.*] The sound of or as of one hard object hitting another; a heavy thud. Also as *adv.*, with a plonk, directly, and as *int.* So **plonk-plonk**.

1903 WODEHOUSE *Tales of St. Austin's* 9 There was a beautiful, musical *plonk*, and the ball soared to the very opposite quarter of the field. **1914** *Picture Fun* 26 Dec. 2 He unfortunately pinched it just as the waiter was passing with a tray of ices, and plonk came that kangaroo's hind paws,.. bang agin the old chap's tummy! **1920** *Punch* 10 Mar. 199/2 A befogged Zeppelin laid a couple of bombs plonk into the homestead. **1928** *Manch. Guardian Weekly* 15 June 474/1 A patois that sounds like the plonk-plonk of ping-pong balls on a hard table. **1943** H. PEARSON *Conan Doyle* iii. 46 'Plonk' went the gun [*sc.* an airgun], and down went the medal. **1960** *Oxf. Mag.* 28 Apr. 248 (Advt.), The satisfying plonk of *The Observer* falling on the doormat. **1978** M. BIRMINGHAM *Sleep in Ditch* 118, I feel as if I'd thrown off an enormous weight. I hope it hasn't landed plonk on you.

plonk (plɒŋk), *sb.*[2] *colloq.* (orig. *Austral.*). [prob. a corruption of *blanc* in Fr. *vin blanc.*] Cheap wine, or wine of poor quality. Also *attrib.*

Various popular and humorous etymologies, such as that suggested in quot. 1967, are without foundation. Although it may be argued that the word denotes red wine more commonly than it does white wine, the etymology given above is attested by the earliest sources.

[**1919** W. H. DOWNING *Digger Dialects* 52 *Vin blank*, white wine. *Ibid.*, Von blink, a humorous corruption of vin blanc.] **1930** H. WILLIAMSON *Patriot's Progress* iv. 137 Nosey and Nobby shared a bottle of plinketty plonk, as *vin blanc* was called. **1933** *Bulletin* (Sydney) 11 Jan. 12 The man who drinks illicit brews or 'plonk' (otherwise known as 'madman's soup') by the quart does it in quiet spots or at home. **1940** A. L. HASKELL *Waltzing Matilda* 37 Fortified red wine of the kind that inebriates with speed and economy is 'pinky' or 'plonk'. **1941** K. TENNANT *Battlers* ix. 104 'Keep off the plonk,' Thirty-Bob said in an undertone to the Stray. 'They just spilt some on my boot and it burnt a hole.' **1946** D. STIVENS *Courtship of Uncle Henry* 72 Jessie's been on the plonk again... Goes round the wine bars at the Cross. **1949** *Here & Now* (N.Z.) Oct. 9/1 Rows of gaudily-labelled bottles of local 'plonk' stacked on shelves behind the bar. **1950** 'N. SHUTE' *Town like Alice* 322 He asked me if I would drink tea or beer or plonk. 'Plonk?' I asked. 'Red wine,' he said. **1953** A. UPFIELD *Murder must Wait* viii. 76 Mother gallivants about to plonk parties.. plonk being Alice McGorr's designation of a sherry party. **1965** *New Statesman* 3 Dec. 873/3, I do not eat in restaurants, travel first-class, or buy fillet steak. But there are cheaper cuts of meat, and wine, though mostly poor plonk stuff in the South, is cheap enough. **1967** *Daily Tel.* 15 Nov. 21/8 Surely the word 'plonk' is onomatopoeic, being the noise made when a cork is withdrawn from the bottle? **1968** *Listener* 1 Aug. 134/3 Over the numerous bars were texts urging moderation and adverts pushing the cheapest and most potent plonk in Britain. **1970** *Times* 23 Mar. 25/5 Sales of his newly introduced Vin Plonque, or 'plonk' in the British vernacular, are soaring. **1973** E. MCGIRR *Bardel's Murder* ii. 29 A Miss Traylor, aged seventy, intelligent and given to plonk. **1976** *Scotsman* 24 Dec. (Weekend Suppl.) 3/6 The author is particularly scathing about Sainsbury's Spanish plonk, but does not mention the same chain's better-than-average range of Hocks and Moselles. **1977** *Time Out* 21 Jan. 3/3 Your review of 'party plonk'.. misses out the largest 'chain' of off-licences in London, the independents who belong to no chain. **1979** *Globe & Mail* (Toronto) 25 Aug. 10/6 The only other customer was a construction worker who was buying a bottle of white plonk for about $1.40.

plonk (plɒŋk), *sb.*[3] *R.A.F. slang.* [Origin uncertain.] An aircraftman second class.

1941 *New Statesman* 30 Aug. 218/3 *A.C. Plonk*—Lowest in the R.A.F., aircraftman 2nd class. **1943** C. H. WARD-JACKSON *Piece of Cake* 10 A/C Plonk, aircraftman 2nd class. In 1914–1918 'plonk' was Flanders slang for 'mud'. Hence, an A/C Plonk is an aircraftman literally in the mud or at the bottom—that is, lowest classification of the lowest rank in the R.A.F. **1946** *Slipstream* 62 Another synonym for an A.C.2 is A.C.Plonk. **1949** J. R. COLE *It was so Late* 61, I was only an A.C. plonk at the time.

plonked (plɒŋkt), *a. slang.* [f. PLONK *sb.*[2] + -ED[2].] Intoxicated, drunk.

1943 *Life* 30 Aug. 70/2 A few badly plonked soldiers blearily unaware of just where they were. **1949** 'THE SARGE' *Excuse my Feet!* 42 George was difficult and Herbert was slightly *plonked*.

plonker ('plɒŋkə(r)). *dial.* and *slang.* [f. PLONK *v.*] **1. a.** Something large or substantial of its kind. *dial.*

1861 C. C. ROBINSON *Dial. Leeds* 386 'A plonker' is an article having extraordinary substance. A piece of woven material unusually thick is 'a plonker'. **1885** *Pudsey Almanack & Hist. Reg.* Mar., Sitha Bill at that young woman's improver, isn't it a plonker? **1898** B. KIRKBY *Lakeland Words* 114 Noo that's a plonker. **1903** *Eng. Dial. Dict.* IV. 550/1 That turnip's a plonker.

b. A shell. *Austral.*

1941 BAKER *Dict. Austral. Slang* 55 Plonker, a shell. Diggers' slang. **1961** PARTRIDGE *Dict. Slang* Suppl. 1226/1 *Plonker*, a (cannon) shell: Australian soldiers': 1939 +.

2. (See quot. 1970). *slang.*

1966 J. GASKELL *All Neat in Black Stockings* 72 If she'd been my daughter in fact I'd never have let her go out with an obvious plonker like myself. **1970** *Sunday Truth* (Brisbane) 13 Sept. 36/2 Do you know what a plonker is? —It's a chap who shares his ladyfriends with his mate.

plonket, plonte, obs. forms of PLUNKET, PLANT.

plonko ('plɒŋkəʊ). *Austral. slang.* [f. PLONK *sb.*[2] + -O[2].] One who is addicted to 'plonk'.

1963 A. MARSHALL *In Mine Own Heart* 187 You end up a plonko with bells ringing in your head. **1965** W. DICK *Bunch of Ratbags* 69 We could go and see if there's any plonkos under Martin's Bridge and chuck rocks at 'em.

ploo, obs. form of PLOUGH.

plook, plooky, etc.: see PLOUK, PLOUKY.

ploot, var. PLUTE.

plop (plɒp), *sb.* and *adv.* [Echoic: cf. PLUMP.] **A.** *sb.* The sound made by a smooth object dropping into water without splashing, by water falling in a small mass, or by bursting bubbles in boiling liquid; the act of falling with this sound. Also in *transf.* and extended uses.

1833 M. SCOTT *Tom Cringle* ix, We tugged at the sable heroine, and first one leg came home out of the tenacious clay, with a plop. **1863** BARING-GOULD *Iceland* 212 The plop plop of the little mud pools. **1886** G. ALLEN *Life Darwin* i. 9 The wave of thought and feeling.. stirred on the unruffled pond of eighteenth century opinion by the startling plop of Buffon's little pebble. **1892** LOWNDES *Camping Sk.* 85 We threw tiny stones into the water, at the quick plop of which the angler would hurry to the spot. **1941** *Sun* (Baltimore) 4 Nov. 10/7 'Plops', the sound heard when 'p' or 'b' is spoken too loudly. **1965** *Wireless World* Aug. 379/2 Another effect is the possibility of a 10W 'plop' when switching on the power supply. **1967** P. A. PINCKNEY *Painting in Texas* v. 77 They might even hear the plop of acorns or pecans falling from trees along the creek. **1969** A. GLYN *Dragon Variation* vi. 171 The gas fire went out with a plop. **1974** HARVEY & BOHLMAN *Stereo F.M. Radio Handbk.* v. 104 The system is arranged so that the audio mute is activated before the i.f. mute and this staggering of the two muting levels reduces the edge-of-station 'plop'. **1979** W. NELSON *Minstrel Code* ix. 77 The automatic.. was so silent that even the characteristic 'plop' of a silencer had been eliminated.

B. *adv.* or *int.* With a plop.

1844 THACKERAY *Wand. Fat Contrib.* ii, She advances backwards towards the coming wave, and as it reaches her —plop! she sits down in it. **1863** KINGSLEY *Water-Bab.* iii, A few great drops of rain fell plop into the water.

C. As first element in various alliterative combinations, as ***plop-plop, plop-plump***, etc. Chiefly as *adv.* or *int.*

1893 'A. HOPE' in *Westm. Gaz.* 9 Dec. 2/1 Miss Phaeton flicked Rhino, and the groom behind went plop-plop on the seat. **1921** *Blackw. Mag.* Feb. 198/2 There is something peculiarly gratifying in the sound of the plop-plump of your naked feet in the round shallow pools of muddy water. **1922** JOYCE *Ulysses* 552 Whispering lovewords murmur liplapping loudly, poppysmic plopslop. **1928** J. M. BARRIE *Peter Pan* III. 75 There are many mermaids here, going plop-plop, and one might attempt to count the tails.

plop (plɒp), *v.* [Echoic: cf. prec., and PLUMP *v.*] **1.** *intr.* To fall with or as with a plop; to drop flat *into* or *upon*; to plump, flop. ***to plop up***: To rise with a plop, as a bubble, etc. Also *trans.* in causative sense, and *refl.* (and with *down*). Also *fig.*

1821 CLARE *Vill. Minstr.* II. 16 The brook, which I have .. watch'd with joy till bursting off it plopt In running gushes of wild murmuring groans. **1839** THACKERAY *Catherine* vii, An apple plops on your nose, and makes you a world's wonder and glory. **1897** KIPLING *Captains Courageous* iii, The released lead plopped into the sea far ahead. **1900** E. GLYN *Visits Eliz.* 66, I do hate to see a great hand.. plopping a dish down.. in the middle, so that one has to look at the next course all the time one is finishing the last one. **1960** V. NABOKOV *Invitation to Beheading* iii. 37 Emmie was gazing after them, while she lightly plopped the glossy red and blue ball in her hands. **1971** *Angling Times* 10 June 6/2, I plopped that lot under a bridge.. and cheerfully expected to net every eel that passed downriver that night. **1975** A. BERGMAN *Hollywood & LeVine* vi. 71 She plopped herself comfortably onto the couch. **1975** *New Yorker* 28 July 8 (Advt.), Something happens at The Biltmore that just doesn't happen in those plasti-glass, modular hotels that have plopped themselves down in every city in the country.

2. *intr.* To emit a sound or series of sounds suggestive of plopping.

1927 C. CONNOLLY *Let.* 4 Jan. in *Romantic Friendship* (1975) 207, I got very depressed on Sunday evening and thought of.. gas mantles plopping in evening chapel. **1972** R. ADAMS *Watership Down* III. xxxviii. 316 All the surface of the river was winking and plopping in the rain.

Hence '**plopping** *vbl. sb.* and *ppl. a.*

1827 CLARE *Sheph. Cal.* 84 The plopping gun's sharp, momentary shock. **1893** J. A. BARRY *S. Brown's Bunyip*, etc. 218 Ploppings and splashings as of many small swimmers. **1897** *Blackw. Mag.* Nov. 589/2 The plopping of the waves against the wall.

†'**plorabund,** *a. Obs. rare*$^{-0}$. [f. L. type **plōrabund-us*, f. *plōrāre* to weep.]

1623 COCKERAM, *Plorabunde*, one that weepeth much.

ploration (plɒˈreɪʃən). *rare.* [ad. L. *plōrātiōn-em*, n. of action from *plōrāre* to weep.] Weeping. So **ˈploratory** *a.*, weeping, mournful.

1828 *Blackw. Mag.* XXIII. 596 Philanthropists..pour out their plorations on the fate of 'Afric's swarthy sons'. **1858** MAYNE *Expos. Lex.* 982 The shedding of tears; ploration. **1831** *Crayons fr. the Commons* 48 In dismal doleful ploratory strain He explicates th' amount of loss and gain.

†**plore**, *v. Obs. rare*⁻⁰. In 5 plowre. [ad. L. *plōrāre*, F. *pleurer.*] *intr.* To weep, wail.

c **1440** *Promp. Parv.* 405/2 Plowryn, or wepyn, *ploro, fleo. Ibid.*, Plowrynge, or wepynge, *ploratus.*

plosh, dial. form of PLASH *sb.*¹

plosh, var. PLASH *sb.*²

‖**ploshchadka** (plɒʃˈtʃadka). *Archæol.* Pl. **ploshchadki.** [Russ., = ground, area, platform.] In Ukrainian sites of the Neolithic period, a raised area or platform, *spec.* one formed of burnt clay from the debris of collapsed buildings.

1913 E. H. MINNS *Scythians & Greeks* vii. 134 The first finds were made about the village of Tripolje on the Dnêpr forty miles below Kiev, whence this is called the Tripolje culture. The remains consist of so-called 'areas' (*ploshchádka*). **1923** *Nature* 26 May 726/1 The painted pottery comes either from large rectangular structures of wattle and daub called *ploshchadky* or from huts partly hollowed out in the earth. **1928** C. DAWSON *Age of Gods* iii. 56 The clay figures..are found in Russia chiefly on the site of the curious buildings or platforms known as 'ploshchadki', which seem to have had a religious object. **1940** C. F. C. HAWKES *Prehist. Foundations of Europe* vi. 236 The Kiev region, where the peasants..made also..rectangular structures ('ploshchadki') whose remains are always found burnt, without as yet any agreed explanation. **1957** V. G. CHILDE *Dawn Europ. Civilization* (ed. 6) viii. 137 The houses of later phases are represented by the celebrated *ploščadki*, areas of baked clay resulting from the burning and collapse of walls and floors.

plosion (ˈpləʊʒən). *Phonetics.* [f. EX)PLOSION.] The eruption of breath involved in uttering a plosive. Hence **ˈplosional** *a.*, of or pertaining to plosion.

1918 D. JONES *Outl. Eng. Phonetics* viii. 37 (*heading*) Faucal Plosion... Lateral Plosion. **1932** G. E. FUHRKEN *Standard Eng. Speech* vi. 71 Nasal plosion is avoided if awkward combinations of consonants would result. **1935** B. TRNKA *Phonol. Analysis Present-Day Stand. Eng.* 6 In the system of English consonantal phonemes there are two correlations, namely those of 1. voice and 2. plosion. **1946** [see ARTICULATOR 4]. **1961** L. F. BROSNAHAN *Sounds of Lang.* viii. 185 Consonants, produced primarily by plosional, frictional, or vibratory interference with the air stream. **1964** [see ALVEOLARITY].

plosive (ˈpləʊzɪv), *sb.* and *a. Phonetics.* [f. EX)PLOSIVE *a.* and *sb.*] **A.** *sb.* A consonantal sound in the formation of which the passage of air is completely obstructed and then suddenly released. **B.** *adj.* Of or pertaining to a plosive.

1899 W. RIPPMANN tr. *Vietor's Elem. Phonetics* 12 The passage may be completely closed. The breath is stopped for a moment..; but then it bursts through the obstacle with a little explosion. The result is a (voiced or voiceless) *stop* (or plosive or explosive). **1902** E. W. SCRIPTURE *Elem. Exper. Phonetics* xxix. 445 The *Association Phonétique Internationale* classifies and represents the consonants in the following way... Plosive [etc.]. **1909** D. JONES *Pronunc. of Eng.* 65 When we try to pronounce a breathed plosive, e.g. p, by itself, it is generally followed by a short breathed sound h. *Ibid.*, The explosion of a plosive consonant is formed by the air as it rushes out at the instant when contact is released. **1933** L. BLOOMFIELD *Language* vi. 97 If we place the tongue or the lips (or the glottis) so as to leave no exit, and allow the breath to accumulate behind the closure, and then suddenly open the closure, the breath will come out with a slight pop or explosion; sounds formed in this way are *stops* (*plosives, explosives*), like our unvoiced [p, t, k] and our voiced [b, d, g]. **1961** *Amer. Speech* XXXVI. 220 Influence of preceding consonants negligible; that of following consonants, considerable. Vowels shorter before voiceless consonants than before voiced counterparts, before plosives than before fricatives. **1968** W. S. ALLEN *Vox Graeca* 2 If the speech-organs form a complete closure, during which air is prevented from passing until the closure is released, the resulting sound is termed a 'stop'. Stops are further subdivided into 'plosives' and 'affricates'. **1968** CHOMSKY & HALLE *Sound Pattern Eng.* 321 Thus of the three nonnasal types with plosive efflux, one is aspirated and the other two are nonaspirated. **1968** J. LYONS *Introd. Theoretical Linguistics* iii. 104 If the obstruction in the air passage is complete, the resulting sounds are described as *stops* (or plosives). **1973** *Studies in Eng. Lit.: Eng. Number* (Tokyo) 20 The plosive sound in 'priest' in the third line is repeated in the succession of plosives, 'bound, brave, peril, doomed', in the fourth line. **1976** *Archivum Linguisticum* VII. 19 The Basque is not geminated, so if we wish to postulate that *sapo* had become a Castilian word before the intervocalic plosives had generally voiced, we might even be reduced to calling it 'culto'.

plot (plɒt), *sb.* Also 5–7 plotte, 6–7 plott. [Appears in late OE. (see sense 2), if indeed the single instance belongs to this word, and then not till late 14th c.; in senses 3–7 not before 16th c. Origin unknown. See also the collateral form *plat* (PLAT *sb.*³), which arose in the 16th c., and was for two centuries or more common in all senses exc. 1 and 7. Senses 3–6 are found earlier in *plat.* For the relations between the two, see PLAT *sb.*³ As to sense 7 see the note under branch III.]

I. †**1.** A small portion of any surface (e.g. of the skin, a garment) differing in character or aspect from the rest of the surface; a patch, spot, mark. *Obs.*

1377 LANGL. *P. Pl.* B. XIII. 275–6 He hadde a cote of crystendome..Ac it was moled in many places with many sondri plottes, Of pruyde here a plotte, and þere a plotte of vnboxome speche. *c* **1440** *Promp. Parv.* 405/1 Plecke, or plotte, *porciuncula. Ibid.*, Plot, *idem quod* plek. **1583** LYLY *Epist.* in T. Watson *Centurie of Loue* (Arb.) 29, I could finde nothing but..loose stringes, where I tyed hard knots: and a table of steele, where I framed a plot of wax. **1598** HAKLUYT *Voy.* I. 98 The men shaue a plot four square vpon the crownes of their heads. **1607** TOPSELL *Four-f. Beasts* (1658) 325 The horse will be..full of scabs and raw plots about the neck. **1686** *Lond. Gaz.* No. 2143/4 A daple gray Mare,..a Plott chafed upon the side of her Cheek. **1822–34** *Good's Study Med.* (ed. 4) IV. 490 Very minute pustules, forming circular plots of a brown, or reddish hue.

2. a. An area or piece (of small or moderate size) of ground, or of what grows or lies upon it; *esp.* one used for some special purpose, indicated by the context; a patch, spot. Cf. PLAT *sb.*³ 1.

? *a* **1100** (*Charm*) in Liebermann *Gesetze der Angels.* 400 Ic agnian wylle to agenre æhte ðæt ðæt ic hæbbe & næfre ð[em]yntan ne plot ne ploh, ne turf ne toft, ne furh ne fotmæl, ne land ne læse. **1463** in *Mann. & Househ. Exp.* (Roxb.) 461 An acre of medew in a noder plotte. **1490** CAXTON *Eneydos* xxxvi. 125 We requyre onely..a lytyll plotte of grounde where we maye dwelle in peas. *a* **1500** *Flower & Leaf* lxxii, And why that some did reverence to the tree, And some unto the plot of floures fair? **1573** TUSSER *Husb.* (1878) 213 In Cambridge then, I found agen, a resting plot. **1590** SHAKS. *Mids. N.* III. i. 3 This greene plot shall be our stage. **1598** FLORIO *Ital. Dict.* Ep. Ded. 2 What pleasure in a plot of simples. **1624** MIDDLETON *Game at Chess* III. i. 127 Poor countrymen have but one plot To keep a cow on. **1660** *Season. Exhort.* 20 Youth, who are the seed plot of future woe or weal. **1669** STURMY *Mariner's Mag.* I. ii. 24 We call any plain Superficies, whose Sides are unequal..a Plot, as of a Field, Wood, Park.., and the like. **1722** WOLLASTON *Relig. Nat.* vii. 146 The little plots, which the several families possess, and cultivate. **1820** W. IRVING *Sketch Bk., Rural Life Eng.* ¶9 The trim hedge, the grass plot before the door. **1891** *Law Rep.* Weekly Notes 82/2 A land company..afterwards sold the adjoining land in building plots.

†**b.** The place on which a building, town, city, etc. is situated; site, situation. *Obs.*

1548 W. PATTEN *Exped. Scot.* A iij b, The plot of this Castell standeth so naturally strong. **1551** ROBINSON *More's Utop.* II. i. (1895) 119 Cities..in all poyntes fashioned a lyke, as farfurth as the place or plotte suffereth. **1587** FLEMING *Contn. Holinshed* III. 1549/1 He likewise began..the strengthening of Athelon with gates and other fortifications, the foundation and plot of the bridge of Caterlagh. **1601** HOLLAND *Pliny* I. 114 They who founded it..were so blind as that they could not choose it for the plot of Chalcedon. **1603** T. M. *Progr. to London of Jas. I* C iij, He bestowed this day in surueying of the plots and fortifications [of Berwick].

II. In the following senses *plat* occurs earlier; see PLAT *sb.*³

3. a. A ground-plan of a building, city, field, farm, or any area or part of the earth's surface; a map, a chart: = PLAT *sb.*³ 2.

1551 RECORDE *Pathw. Knowl.* II. Pref., To drawe the plotte of any countreie that you shall come in, as iustely as maie be. **1579–80** NORTH *Plutarch* (1676) 439 Hannibal..drew a plot of a City..and caused it to be built and inhabited. **1628** DIGBY *Voy. Medit.* (1868) 50 Our English plottes are verie ill made, and the land wrong drawne where wee haue litle trade. **1669** STURMY *Mariner's Mag.* V. ii. 11 How to take the Plott of a Field at one Station. **1706** PHILLIPS, To *Prick a Plot* (among Sailers), is..to make a small Prick in the Plot or Chart in that Latitude and Longitude, where the Ship is suppos'd to be at that time. **1775** JOHNSON *West. Islands* Wks. X. 339 The ruins of the cathedral of Elgin... Its whole plot is easily traced. **1881** *Scribner's Mag.* Apr. 835 It will be seen on reference to the plot of the place. **1899** MIDDLETON & CHADWICK *Treat. Surveying* I. iv. 146 It is often desirable to make a preliminary plot, as work progresses, to see how the work comes in. **1931** M. HOTINE *Surv. from Air Photogr.* ix. 159 The minor control plot is the foundation of all subsequent detail plotting and will repay time and care spent on its construction. **1942** *R.A.F. Jrnl.* 13 June 11 Frequent advice from the plot was called for as to the safe course to steer. **1962** *Times* 22 Mar. 14/7, I had no idea where I was as there was no automatic plot in my ship and we had been too busy to keep an accurate reckoning. **1971** R. J. P. WILSON *Land Surveying* ii. 45 Once the pencil plot has been completed and checked the chain survey network of lines..is inked in. **1973** H. GRUPPE *Truxton Cipher* xv. 154 Is it not standard procedure for the Combat Information Center to keep a plot of the ship's movements?

†**b.** *fig.* The type or representation *of* something. *Obs. rare.*

1597 MIDDLETON *Wisd. Solomon* ii. 24 Blotted by him that is the plot of evil, Undone, corrupted, vanquish'd by the devil.

c. *Theatr.* A scheme or plan indicating the disposition and function of lighting and stage property in a particular production.

1883 D. COOK *On Stage* I. x. 219 The property-maker is duly furnished with a 'plot' or list of articles required of his department. **1949** T. RATTIGAN *Harlequinade* 56 The lighting for this scene has gone mad. This isn't our plot. There's far too much light. *Ibid.* 57 Check your plot, please. **1959** W. C. LOUNSBURY *Backstage from A to Z* 91 *Plot*, a floor plan or cue sheet or both, indicating location of lights, furniture, props, etc. Light plots, furniture plots, and prop plots should be made by the person responsible for each field, and notations of cues and changes should be clearly indicated.

d. A diagram showing the relation between two variable quantities each measured along one of a pair of axes usu. at right angles; = GRAPH *sb.*¹ 2.

1912 *Jrnl. Amer. Chem. Soc.* XXXIV. 462 And reading from this plot by extrapolation to $C\Lambda = 0$, the value of $1/\Lambda_0$. **1947** E. E. WAHLSTROM *Ign. Minerals & Rocks* viii. 240 (*caption*) Harker plot of analyses in Table 6. **1953** E. R. PECK *Electricity & Magnetism* ix. 279 Sometimes it is of interest not only to use the ratio B/H, but to plot in detail the B-H curve. Such plots are basic in the discussion of ferromagnetism. **1971** *Physics Bull.* Feb. 86/1 A ln σ against $1/T$ plot should, at the temperature of conversion, exhibit a change of slope.

e. *R.A.F. slang.* A group of enemy aircraft as represented on a radar screen.

1943 P. BRENNAN et al. *Spitfires over Malta* 44 We warned the new boys to be careful, as it was probably a big plot coming in and they would be certain to bomb Ta-kali. **1959** R. COLLIER *City that wouldn't Die* vii. 109 Every radar station reported a mass plot and the planes flew too high for visual checks.

†**4.** *fig.* A sketch or outline of a literary work. Cf. PLAT *sb.*³ 3. *Obs.*

1548 PATTEN *Exped. Scot.* Pref. D ij b, Least I mai woorthely be doubted by the plot of my Prologe, to haue made the foorme of my booke lyke the proportion of saainct Peters man, I will here leaue of further proces of Preface. **1554** LD. DARNLEY in Ellis *Orig. Lett.* Ser. II. II. 249 It haith pleased your moste excellente Maiestie laitlie to accepte a little Plote of my simple penning, which I termed *Vtopia Nova.* **1605** BACON *Adv. Learn.* II. Ded. §15 Such a plotte made and recorded to memorie; may..minister light to any publique designation. *a* **1626** MIDDLETON *Women Beware Women* V. i. 170 Why, sure, this plot's drawn false; here's no such thing.

†**b.** ? A device, a design. *Obs. rare.*

1602 MARSTON *Ant. & Mel.* V. Wks. 1856 I. 60 Hee..makes six plots of set faces, before he speakes one wise word.

†**5.** A plan or scheme for the constitution or accomplishment of anything; a purpose, device, design, scheme: = PLAT *sb.*³ 4. *Obs.* (exc. as in 7).

1587 FLEMING *Contn. Holinshed* III. 1397/1 That the kalendar once reformed according to this plot, need neuer hereafter either to be altered or amended. **1596** SPENSER *State Irel.* Wks. (Globe) 609/1 There have beene divers good plottes devised, and wise counsells cast alleready about reformation of that realme. **1607** T. SPARKE *Brotherly Persuasion* B ij, I neuer yet could bee brought..to thinke that forme and plot of Church gouernment so much admired and magnified as the perpetuall and onely fit gouernment for Christes Church..fitting for such a Monarchye as this is. *a* **1652** J. SMITH *Sel. Disc.* vii. 310 This is the great design and plot of the gospel. **1678** CUDWORTH *Intell. Syst.* I. iv. 269 A design or policy of the Devil..to counter-work God Almighty in the plot of christianity.

6. The plan or scheme of any literary creation, as a play, poem, or work of prose fiction. Cf. PLAT *sb.*³ 5.

1649 LOVELACE *Poems* 78 Th'other [Comedy] for the Gentlemen oth' Pit, Like to themselves all Spirit, Fancy, Wit In which plots should be subtile as a Flame. **1677** W. HUGHES *Man of Sin* III. iii. 62 The Plots of the best Poets may sometimes have a hole pick'd in them. **1732** BERKELEY *Alciphr.* VI. §16 To censure the plot of a play. **1759** GOLDSM. *Misc. Wks.* (1837) III. 495 The whole plot of these five cantos is no more than a young lady happening to prick her finger with a needle. **1852** LEWIS *Meth. Reason. Politics* v. §5. 118 In every narrative, there is a certain connexion of events..which, in a work of fiction, is called a plot. **1878** GLADSTONE *Prim. Homer* ii. 28 In the plot of the Odyssey, symmetry is obvious at first sight: in the plot of the Iliad, it has to be sought out.

III. Probably influenced by COMPLOT.

[*Complot* was used in Fr. from the 14th c., and occurs in Eng. *c* 1575. It might be even more correct to view *plot* in this sense as short for *complot* under the influence of the sense 'plan, scheme, or device', already present in 5. The usage probably became widely known in connexion with the 'Gunpowder Plot'.]

7. A plan or project, secretly contrived by one or more persons, to accomplish some wicked, criminal, or illegal purpose; a conspiracy; also in later use, *humorously* for a sly plan, an innocent scheme.

1594 SHAKS. *Rich. III.* I. i. 32 Plots haue I laide, Inductions dangerous,..To set my Brother Clarence and the King In deadly hate. **1617** VICARS (*title*) Mischeefes Mysterie: or, Treasons Master-peece, The Powder-plot. Inuented by hellish Malice. *a* **1634** CHAPMAN *Alphonsus* V. iv, He only knew All Plotts, and complots of his villanie. **1681** DRYDEN *Abs. & Achit.* 83 Plots, true or false, are necessary things To raise up commonwealths, and ruin kings. **1683** EVELYN *Diary* 18 June, The Popish Plot also..began now sensibly to dwindle, thro' the folly, knavery, impudence, and giddiness of Oates. **1769** ROBERTSON *Chas. V*, III. Wks. 1813 V. 336 The author of this dangerous plot was Charles, duke of Bourbon. **1838** THIRLWALL *Greece* IV. xxx. 127 They could not..have suspected the plots which were laid for their destruction. **1849** MACAULAY *Hist. Eng.* ii. I. 267 There were two plots..The object of the great Whig plot was to raise the nation in arms against the government. The lesser plot, commonly called the Rye House plot,..had for its object the assassination of the king and of the heir presumptive.

IV. 8. *attrib.* and *Comb.*, as (in sense 2) *plot-holder, -owner, -place*; (in sense 3 e) *plot-room*; (in sense 6) *plot-building, -construction, -formula, -interest, -seller, -source, -spinning, -structure*; (in sense 7) *plot-caster, -mad* (see MAD *a.* 4 c), *-maker, -master, -monger, -night, weaver*; **plot-divided** *a.*, divided into plots;

plot-line, (*a*) the main features of a plot or story; a summary; (*b*) (see quot. 1961); **plot-proof** *a.*, proof against plots; **plot-ratio**, a ratio representing the density of building in a specified area of land (see quot. 1971).

1901 *Scribner's Mag.* XXIX. 505/2 The fault [found] with the average successful American novel is that its workmanship is inferior; inferior to its *plot-building and invention. **1600** W. WATSON *Decacordon* (1602) 4 The first *plotcasters of their innocent brethrens ruines. **1612** T. JAMES *Jesuits' Downf.* 62 [He] then tooke vpon him with his Iesuiticall Plotcasters, to be an Actor, an orator or a broker. **1885** H. O. FORBES *Nat. Wand. E. Archip.* 170 Rice, which they grew..on the wet system, in *plot-divided terraces. **1957** N. FRYE *Anat. Criticism* 52 We may think of our romantic, high mimetic and low mimetic modes as a series of *displaced* myths, *mythoi* or *plot-formulas. **1881** *Philad. Press* 8 June 2 The *plotholders in the Easton Cemetery held their annual meeting Monday night. **1865** *Fortn. Rev.* 15 Dec. 354 The distinctive element in Fiction is that of *plot-interest. The rest is vehicle. **1866** H. SIDGWICK in A. & E. M. Sidgwick *Henry Sidgwick* (1906) 143 The plot-interest does not turn entirely on amativeness. **1961** M. MCCARTHY *On Contrary* (1962) 290 The chief plot interest in these books is to try to find out what happened before the book started. **1965** K. GRAHAM *Eng. Criticism of Novel* iv. 99 By 1883..his [*sc.* Wilkie Collins's] brand of plot-interest was..out-moded. **1957** J. D. SALINGER *Zooey* in *New Yorker* 4 May 33/3 The *plot line [*sc.* of 'a sort of prose home movie'] ..is largely the result of a rather unholy collaborative effort. **1961** BOWMAN & BALL *Theatre Lang.* 267 *Plot line*, usually in the plural: Dialogue essential to the unfolding of the plot of a dramatic piece. **1962** *John o' London's* 12 Apr. 363/1 Its [*sc.* a film's] plot-line has the same grotesque implausibility. **1972** P. H. KOCHER *Master of Middle-Earth* iv. 57 Like Greek drama or Miltonic epic which begin late along their plot lines, *The Lord of the Rings* begins just before the climax of Sauron's efforts to subdue the West. **1976** S. HYNES *Auden Generation* viii. 294 The main plot-line concerns an indigent painter..whose only completed picture..is seized by bailiffs. **1867** G. MEREDITH *Vittoria* xxxvii. III. 83 She saw that he was *plot-mad, and she set him at work on a stupendous plot. **1961** *Encounter* Apr. 71/1 Either Querry is right, or God is a *plot-maker, working through his inferior priests,..ready to use any degree of absurdity..to get His own way. **1611** SPEED *Hist. Gt. Brit.* IX. xiv. (1623) 771 The chiefe *plot-master, the Earle. **1721** AMHERST *Terræ Fil.* No. 11 (1754) 56 He is no *plot-monger, as a less conjurer than you..might have easily seen. **1818** *Edin. Rev.* XXX. 175 Deluded by the fabrications of our plot-mongers. **1900** *N. & Q.* 9th Ser. VI. 509/1 Light-coloured 'parkin' or '*plot-night' (Guy Fawkes) treacle or gingerbread made of ordinary household flour. **1907** *Daily Chron.* 3 June 3/6 An association of..*plot-owners has been formed for the purpose of improving their position. **1611** SPEED *Theat. Gt. Brit.* xxxi. (1614) 61/1 The Grey Friars..whose suppression hath suppressed the *plot-place of his grave. **1611** SHAKS. *Wint. T.* II. iii. 6 The harlot-King Is quite beyond mine Arme, out of the blanke And leuell of my braine: *plot proofe. **1956** *Archit. Rev.* CXIX. 46 The main area of the site is developed according to the *plot-ratio of 5:1 laid down by the City Corporation. **1958** *Listener* 23 Oct. 642/2 Plot ratios and daylight factors are now everyday tools at the disposal of the designer; only a decade ago such logical aids did not exist. **1971** P. GRESSWELL *Environment* 81 The density of business and commercial areas is usually expressed by total floor space of buildings divided by the area of the site, called 'floor space index' when local access roads are included, and *plot ratios* when they are not. **1973** *Geo. Abstr.* F. 65 The development of secondary dwelling areas should be subordinated to an overall objective for total land use intensity and the relation between gross and net plot ratios, together with the proportion of open space that is derived from this. **1978** *N.Y. Rev. Bks.* 23 Feb. 4/2 Leslie Martin, the most influential architectural teacher,..has for years pointed out that a far more effective use of a plot ratio can be devised than tower blocks. **1947** *Times* 3 Feb. 6/6 Below in the *plot rooms radar engineers checked their screens for the position of the Home Fleet and exchanged bearings with the navigating officers. **1938** O. SITWELL *Trio* 60 The well-known *plot-seller, Mr. X. Y. Z., is at present planning a new financial coup. **1885** J. O. HALLIWELL-PHILLIPPS *Outl. Life Shakes.* (ed. 5) 566 The subtle devices ..some of which..may be equally observed..in the original *plot-sources of his dramas. **1962** *Times* 24 Apr. 14/7 Passages of *plot-spinning conversation. **1957** N. FRYE *Anat. Criticism* 207 The source of tragic effect must be sought..in the tragic mythos or *plot-structure. **1962** *Punch* 11 July 65/1 A good film..can hide even the most elaborate plot-structure by superficial casualness and naturalism. **1977** *Dædalus* Fall 107 Work on plot structure, the goal of which is a grammar of plots, has been carried out in many countries. **1897** *Dublin Rev.* Apr. 303 The most successful.. of all these *plot-weavers was..the Secretary Cecil.

plot (plɒt), *v.*[1] [f. PLOT *sb.*]

1. a. *trans.* To make a plan, map, or diagram of (an existing object, as a portion of the earth's surface, a building, etc.); to draw to scale; to lay down on a map (as the position of a place, a ship's course); to represent by a plan or diagram (the course or result of any action or process). ***to plot*** (one quantity) ***against, versus***, etc. (another): to draw a graph in which ordinates (*y*-coordinates) represent values of the first quantity and abscissas (*x*-coordinates) represent those of the second. Also with *down*. Also *fig.*

1590 GREENE *Francescos Fortunes* To Rdrs., Wks. (Grosart) VIII. 118 You may see plotted downe many passions full of repentant sorrowes. **1602** CAREW *Cornwall* To Rdr., Reckon therefore..that this treatise plotteth downe Cornwall, as it now standeth. **1669** STURMY *Mariner's Mag.* v. iv. 16 How to Plot a Field by the Rule before-going. **1766** *Compl. Farmer* s.v. *Surveying*, All closes, or parcels of land, are either such as need not be plotted for finding their true measure..or such as cannot be conveniently measured without plotting or protraction. **1859** BACHE *Discuss. Magn. & Meteorol. Observ.* I. 18 If we plot the disturbance curve on the same scale. **1860** *Merc. Marine Mag.* VII. 236 The Commander..had so plotted the rock upon his chart. **1880** W. C. ROBERTS *Introd. Metallurgy* 34 The results, tabulated or plotted into curves ..form permanent records of the greatest value. **1883** *Century Mag.* Oct. 944/1 Plotting down this position on the chart, it appeared that Cape Rivers, on the island of Celebes, was the nearest land, bearing S. by E. 125 miles. **1910** *Jrnl. Amer. Chem. Soc.* XXXII. 1015 The method of procedure employed has been to plot the values obtained by each observer for $\Delta t/N$ as ordinates against those of log N as abscissas. **1934** *Proc. R. Soc.* A. CXLV. 576 This would be shown clearly if the density were plotted against the logarithm of exposure, as is usually done for photographic plates. **1952** J. P. CASEY *Pulp & Paper* II. xvi. 825 Stress-strain curves can be plotted as load scale reading versus angular deflection. **1976** *Sci. Amer.* Dec. 93/1 Data from spectrophotometry..enable one to plot the supernova's change in radius with respect to time.

b. To make or draw by plotting.

1863 H. S. MERRETT *Pract. Treat. Sci. Land & Engin. Surveying* II. 124 For practical purposes, surveys should never be plotted to a less scale than three or four chains to the inch. **1886** H. S. BROWN *Autobiog.* vii. (1887) 30 They were busy plotting their maps. **1906** BREED & HOSMER *Princ. & Pract. Surveying* I. xv. 397 The field maps of the U.S. Coast and Geodetic Survey are usually plotted on a scale of 1/10000. **1923** D. CLARK *Plane & Geodetic Surveying* II. vi. 244 In plotting the map, the distances and elevations required must be obtained from the perspective dimensions on the photographs. **1963** W. K. KILFORD *Elem. Air Survey* xi. 240 The radial-line plotter makes it possible to plot a map from the model formed in an ordinary mirror stereoscope. **1976** J. B. GARNER et al. *Surveying* ii. 21 When the survey has been plotted it should, if possible, be checked visually on the ground.

2. a. To make a plan of (something to be laid out, constructed, or made, as a city, fortress, garden, railway). Also with *out* and *fig.*

1588 SPENSER *Virg. Gnat* 652 He gins to fashion forth a place; And squaring it in compasse well beseene, There plotteth out a tombe by measured space. **1590** GREENE *Royal Exchange* Ep. Ded., Our Cittie of London..plotted and erected by Brute. **1649** BLITHE *Eng. Improv. Impr.* (1653) 155 When thou wouldest plot out thy Land thou designest to plant. **1887** LOWELL *Old Eng. Dram.* (1892) 40 His tragedy of 'Dido, Queen of Carthage', is also regularly plotted out. **1898** *Allbutt's Syst. Med.* V. 486 Unless the line of the smaller curvature be plotted out. **1915** W. HOLT *Beacon for Blind* xiv. 140 When a proposed party was being plotted out he would say, 'Oh, don't ask the So-and-so's, they are such frumps'. **1928** *Oxford Poetry* 9 And, a week later, still, by plotting out The course of all the roadways round about 'In these some score of places he may be'. **1969** D. WIDGERY in Cockburn & Blackburn *Student Power* 130 The next period is worth some examination to plot out the Executive's responses to a fluid situation.

b. To lay *out* (land) in plots.

1889 C. D. WARNER *Stud. South & West* xv. 384 There is not level ground for a large city, but what there is is plotted out for sale.

c. *Theatr.* To plan or devise (a stage production); to arrange lighting and stage property for (a production). (See PLOT *sb.* 3c.)

1933 P. GODFREY *Back-Stage* iv. 44 The amount of work [for the stage-manager] involved in organizing and plotting the complete stage arrangements for a simple play with a few changes of scene is considerable. **1974** *Times* 28 Dec. 7/3 At read-throughs and when you're plotting it [*sc.* a play], you stand there trembling..behind your script.

3. a. To plan, contrive, or devise (something to be carried out or accomplished); to lay plans for. Now always in evil sense.

1589 GREENE *Menaphon* Wks. (Grosart) VI. 117 Who listning not a little to this counsaile, that was neuer plotted for his aduantage. **1600** E. BLOUNT tr. *Conestaggio* 10 He had first plotted a warre against the Indians. **1631** GOUGE *God's Arrows* III. §94. 360 They..plotted the..mercilesse, devilish, and damnable gunpowder-treason. **1638** ROUSE *Heav. Univ.* x. (1702) 150 Then do not think it safe to rob God of His Glory which he hath thus plotted and contrived. **1712** STEELE *Spect.* No. 263 ¶1 The good Man and Woman ..who used to sit and plot the Welfare of us their Children. **1841** LANE *Arab. Nts.* I. 83 Therefore, I will plot his destruction with my wit and reason, like as he hath plotted with his cunning and perfidy. **1868** E. EDWARDS *Ralegh* I. xx. 451 A..protestation that whatsoever he had foolishly plotted, he had never plotted treason.

b. With *infinitive* or *clause*.

1594 SHAKS. *Rich. III*, III. v. 38 The subtill Traytor This day had plotted..To murther me. **1601** B. JONSON *Ev. Man in Hum.* (Qo.) II. ii. 3 My labouring spirit..can embrace no rest Till it hath plotted by aduise and skill How to reduce him from affected will To reasons manage. **1671** *Charente's Let. Customs* 28 They plotted to go in the day time and build them a Hutt. **1762** H. WALPOLE *Vertue's Anecd. Paint.* (1765) I. vi. 137 Had he plotted to dethrone a princess who had delivered him from a prison and offered him a throne. **1841** LANE *Arab. Nts.* I. 91 And plot with thee to destroy him.

4. *intr.* To form a plan, device, or plot (in modern use, always for some evil, reprehensible, or hostile end); to scheme, lay plans, contrive, conspire. ***to plot it***, to do the plotting.

1607 J. CARPENTER *Plaine Mans Plough* 1 Wel he beginneth and soundly he plotteth, who..beholdeth his face. **1611** BIBLE *Ps.* xxxvii. 12 The wicked plotteth against the iust. *a* **1720** SEWEL *Hist. Quakers* (1795) I. Pref. 18 For the Quakers, so called, have not plotted against the government. **1870** BRYANT *Iliad* I. I. 29 Oh crafty one, with whom, among the gods, Plottest thou now? **1897** RHOSCOMYL *White Rose Arno* 206 We've had about enough of your plots: I'll plot it from now on.

5. *trans.* To devise the plot or story of (a literary work). Also *absol.*

1596 NASHE *Saffron Walden* Wks. (Grosart) III. 196 Hee subscribing to me in anie thing but plotting Plaies, wherein he was his crafts master. *c* **1650** DENHAM *On T. Killigrew's Ret. fr. Venice* ii, Having plotted and penned Six plays. **1943** *Writer* V. 99/1 Plotting problems are usually the chief difficulties fiction-writers have to face. **1951** F. BROWN *Murder can be Fun* x. 138 There's a big difference in plotting soap operas and plotting magazine stories. **1962** *Listener* 30 Aug. 311/2 In *A Burnt Out Case* he [*sc.* Graham Greene] had kept the plotting simple, but it seemed somehow too strong all the same; 'perhaps it would have seemed less plotted if there had been more plot.' **1973** *Daily Tel.* 15 Mar. 8/5 The story is confusingly plotted. **1977** *Ibid.* 10 Sept. 7/2 Mrs Robins plots better but relies a bit much on coincidence.

plot (plɒt), *v.*[2] [ad. F. *peloter* (p(ə)lɔte), to form into a ball (*pelote*): see PELLET[1], and cf. PLATOON.] To solidify (soap paste) by pressure in a mortar (*peloteuse*). Hence **'plotting** *vbl. sb.*; **plotting-machine**, a machine for solidifying soap.

1885 W. L. CARPENTER *Soap & Candles* vii. 200 The soap is ready for the final operation, known as 'plotting' (from the French, *pelotage*), in which the paste is subjected to enormous pressure..to form it into cakes, or..bars... Such a machine..will 'plot' 200 lb. at each operation.

†plot, *v.*[3] *Obs.* Erron. form of PLOD *v.*

1621 S. WARD *Happiness of Practice* 15 If the gaine of practice did not sweeten it, few would plot vpon Ployden.

plot, *v.*[4], variant of PLOTE *v.*

†plotch, *sb. Obs.* Also 6 ploche. [Origin uncertain; possibly related to BLOTCH *sb.*, which is later. Cf. also PLOT *sb.* 1.] A botch or blotch; in quots. applied to the spots of leprosy.

1548 UDALL *Erasm. Par. Luke* v. 55 Abhorred & lothed of all men for the foule ploches of the leprie. **1612** tr. *Benvenuto's Passenger* I. i. 69 A person..who stood at the Temple gate demanding of almes, with certaine counterfait plotches of a leaper [*Ital.* con macchie artificiate di lepra].

plotch (plɒtʃ), *v. rare*[−1]. [Perh. f. PLOTCH *sb.*, or imit.] *trans.* To splash on to, to mark.

1922 JOYCE *Ulysses* 745 All the mud plotching my boots.

†plotcock. *Sc. Obs.* [app. a perversion of *Pluto*, in accordance with some popular etymology.] Pluto; in later popular use, the devil.

a **1578** LINDESAY (Pitscottie) *Chron. Scot.* (S.T.S.) I. 260 Thair was a cry hard at the marcat crose of Edinburgh at the houre of midnight..nameit and callit be the proclamer thairof the sowmondis of Plotcok, quhilk desyrit all men to compeir..withtin the space of xl. dayis befoir his maister. *c* **1587** MONTGOMERIE *Sonn.* xxi, The tym sall come vhen ȝe sall be accusit, And syn compeld at Plotcok to appeir. **1725** RAMSAY *Gentle Sheph.* II. ii, And seven times does her prayers backwards pray, Till Plotcock comes with lumps of Lapland clay, Mixt with the venom of black taids and snakes.

plote, plot (ploːt), *v. Sc.* and *north. dial.* Also ploat, plooat, plout, plott, etc.: see *Eng. Dial. Dict.* [Origin uncertain. In S.E. Sc. and north. Eng. the *o* is long, as in *mote*.]

1. *trans.* To scald, to parboil; to plunge into boiling water.

1724 RAMSAY *Tea-t. Misc.* Dec. vii, E'en while the tea's filled reeking round, Rather than plot a tender tongue, Treat [etc.]. **1824** MACTAGGART *Gallovid. Encycl.*, *Plotted*, boiled, or ratherly plunged in boiling water. **1829** BROCKETT *N.C. Gloss.*, *To plote a pig* is to pour scalding water upon it, which causes the hair to come off. **1882** J. WALKER *Jaunt to Auld Reekie* 223 The water scaudin' hot To plot thy skin.

2. To scorch, burn.

1785 W. FORBES *Dominie Depos'd* 4, I never sooner siller got, But a' my pouches it wou'd plot, And scorch them sair, it was sae hot. **1814** W. NICHOLSON *To Tobacco* xvii, Let Welchmen plot an' toast their cheese. **1881** PAUL *Aberdeen.* 68 I'm like to be plotted wi' heat.

plote, plotform: see PLOAT, PLATFORM.

plotful ('plɒtfʊl), *a. rare*[−1]. [f. PLOT *sb.* + -FUL.] Full of plots; scheming.

1732 FIELDING *Cov. Gard. Trag.* I. i, Not so the statesman scrubs his plotful head.

Plotinian (pləʊ'tɪnɪən), *a.* [f. L. *Plōtīnus*, a. Gr. *Πλωτῖνος*, proper name.] Of or pertaining to Plotinus (A.D. *c* 204–270), the most noted philosopher of the Neo-Platonic school, the doctrines of which he taught at Rome. So **Plo'tinic, Plo'tinical** *adjs.*, in same sense; **'Plotinism**, the system or teaching of Plotinus; **'Plotinist**, a follower of Plotinus; **'Plotinize** *v. intr.*, to imitate, or philosophize in the manner of, Plotinus.

1678 CUDWORTH *Intell. Syst.* 4 It must needs fall under one or other of those two General Heads in the Plotinical Distribution last mentioned. *Ibid.* 152 Which Plotinick Doctrine, may well pass for a Commentary upon Empedocles. **1791** W. ENFIELD *Hist. Philos.* II. III. ii. 69 We shall trace the progress of the Plotinian, or Eclectic, school. **1864** WEBSTER, *Plotinist*. **1871** J. S. MILL in *Fortn. Rev.* X. 524 A heap of useless and mostly unintelligible jargon, not of his own [*sc.* Berkeley's] but of the Plotinists. **1879** MCCLINTOCK & STRONG *Encycl. Bibl. Lit.* VIII. 296/2 Creuzer condenses his summary of the Plotinian doctrine into three theses. **1882–3** *Schaff's Encycl. Relig. Knowl.* II. 1854 They Plotinized even more than they Platonized in their religious philosophy. **1906** W. M. MACINTYRE in *Expositor* Feb. 162 According to the Plotinist, mental prayer

..has this office committed to it, to elevate the sense-life into the life of reason. **1969** T. F. TORRANCE *Theol. Sci.* i. 18 This was the Augustinian doctrine of the sacramental universe, combining Plotinian and Ptolemaic notions in a 'Christian' cosmol

plotless ('plɒtlɪs), *a.* [f. PLOT *sb.* + -LESS.]

1. Without a plot or story; having no plot. **1704** *Faction Displ.* x, Van's Bawdy, Plotless Plays were once our Boast. **1882** *Standard* 25 Mar. 5 The curious plotless story called 'Kavanagh'. **1926** in C. Bailey *Mind of Rome* I. 167 Semi-dramatic productions, improved on the formal side but still plotless, became an established diversion. **1971** *Homes & Gardens* Sept. 134/1 Her story reads like a charming but plotless novel. **1979** A. CHISHOLM *Nancy Cunard* viii. 76 *Antic Hay*..is a deliberately plotless picture of..amusing, erratic, fundamentally desperate characters.

2. *Ecol.* Of a method of ecological sampling: not based on a defined unit of area. **1957** P. GREIG-SMITH *Quantitative Plant Ecol.* ii. 46 Considerable attention has recently been paid to a method of plotless sampling, particularly adapted to forest vegetation, where there are practical difficulties in delimiting the relatively large quadrats necessary for sampling trees. **1974** MUELLER-DOMBOIS & ELLENBERG *Aims & Methods of Vegetation Ecol.* vii. 99 Plotless sampling means sampling without such a prescribed area unit. Plotless methods are available for all three commonly used quantitative parameters.

Hence '**plotlessness**. **1823** J. LACY in *Lond. Mag.* Dec. 648/1 The plotlessness ..of modern plays.

† '**plotmeal**, *adv. Obs. rare*$^{-1}$. [f. PLOT *sb.* I + -MEAL.] A piece at a time, piece by piece. *c* **1412** HOCCLEVE *De Reg. Princ.* 2053 [Aristotle's] booke of governaunce Of which, and eek of Gyles of regyment Of princes, plotmel thynke I to translate.

† '**plotment.** *Obs. rare*$^{-1}$. [f. PLOT *v.*[1] + -MENT.] ? An allotment, apportionment. **1634-5** *Stat. Irel.* (1765) II. 169 All which the poore people dare not deny them..and therefore..doe make cuts, levies and plotments upon themselves to pay them.

Plott (plɒt). The surname of Jonathan *Plott* (fl. 1750-80) and his descendants, used *attrib.* in **Plott hound** to designate a hunting dog belonging to a breed developed by this family from hounds brought from Germany to North Carolina in 1750, characterized by a smooth, dark brown coat, often with a black saddle or white feet, and large, drooping ears; it has long been used for bear and boar hunting in North Carolina and Tennessee, and recently the breed has become more widely known. **1945** C. L. B. HUBBARD *Observer's Bk. Dogs* 202 Plott Hound. Although this breed is not yet given official status by the American Kennel Club, it is fairly popular among sporting men in the U.S.A... Mr. Geo. L. Gilkey of Wisconsin is piloting the modern Plott to popularity. **1949** H. P. DAVIS *Modern Dog Encycl.* 466/2 The present demand for Plott Hound stock is far in excess of the supply. **1969** E. H. HART *Encycl. Dog Breeds* 257 The Plott Hound differs from all other hounds in colouring for he is a brindle dog with a black saddle. **1976** E. M. SCHULER *Dog Lover's Answer Bk.* II. 358 The Plott hound is a heavy-set, well-muscled dog with large ears.

plott, obs. f. PLOT; var. PLAT *sb.*[2] (sense 4).

plottable (plɒtəb(ə)l), *a.* [f. PLOT *v.*[1] + -ABLE.] That may be plotted, in the various senses of the verb. **1968** A. L. ALLAN et al. *Pract. Field Surveying & Computations* ix. 456 The misclosure of a tacheometric traverse should always be within the plottable error of the plan and no adjustment is permitted. **1972** C. MUDIE *Motor Boats & Boating* 116 Voyages out of sight of land only extend the distances between plottable positions and it is quite difficult nowadays to get out of range of the radio navigation beacons. **1976** S. R. SIMPSON *Land Law & Registration* viii. 145 The boundaries could only be replaced to the plottable accuracy of the map.

plottage ('plɒtɪdʒ). [f. PLOT *sb.* + -AGE.]

1. Phr. ***a mess of plottage***, used disparagingly of theatrical productions (by analogy with *a mess of pottage*: see MESS *sb.* 2 a). **1937** *Sun* (Baltimore) 7 Aug. 4/1 '*The Big Shot*', now showing at the Hippodrome Theater, is just another mess of plottage that some RKO Radio writers sold their birthrights for. **1958** *Spectator* 22 Aug. 249/3 The London Studio cast manage to make the whole mess of plottage taste mouldier even than it is.

2. The size or value of a specified piece of land, regarded in terms of the area accumulated from its constituent plots. Usu. in ***plottage increment*** (see quot. 1965). **1939** in WEBSTER Add. **1952** 'VIGILANS' *Chamber of Horrors* 100 *Plottage*, the area of a plot of land. (The deplorable result of an illicit union between *plot* and *acreage*.) **1961** R. U. RATCLIFF *Real Estate Analysis* iii. 52 This value increment resulting from the assembly of a tract [of land] of sufficient size for a more intensive use is termed *plottage*. **1965** L. E. DAVIDS *Dict. Insurance* 162 *Plottage increment*, the increase or appreciation of the unit value resulting from the joining together of smaller lots, parcels, or land units into one large single ownership, the resulting total value being larger than the individual unit values. **1973** *N.Y. Law Jrnl.* 2 Aug. 11/3 A plottage increment of 10 per cent is allowed for an appraised land area of 12,322 square feet.

plotted ('plɒtɪd), *ppl. a.* [f. PLOT *v.*[1] + -ED[1].]

1. Planned, premeditated, pre-arranged by a plot. **1607** BP. HALL *Ps.* vii, Back to his own head shall rebound His plotted mischiefe. **1625** K. LONG tr. *Barclay's Argenis* v. vii. 351 With wondrous confidence..he begun his plotted Tale. *a* **1701** SEDLEY *Tyrant of Crete* IV. iii, By miracle I scap'd thy plotted Mischiefs. **1899** MACKAIL *Life Morris* I. 171 They [Greeks] slip out of the [Trojan] horse, and take their plotted ways.

2. Laid down or delineated on or in a plan or chart. **1612** SELDEN *Illustr. Drayton's Poly-olb.* vi. 98 Plowshares for describing the content of plotted Cities. **1895-6** *Cal. Univ. Nebraska* 134 A plotted chart of measurements is furnished to each student desiring it, at the cost of the price of the chart.

3. Constructed or furnished with a plot. Freq. with advs. **1704** D'URFEY *Tales* Pref. a j b, The plotted Drama. **1970** *Daily Tel.* (Colour Suppl.) 11 Aug. 5/2 In our time it has become meaningless to produce a strongly plotted short story like Maupassant's *The Necklace* or a strongly plotted novel like *David Copperfield*. **1978** *Broadcast* 28 Aug. 8/1 Plays which were both tightly plotted and eminently actable. **1979** F. KERMODE *Genesis of Secrecy* v. 113 We are more likely to remember a plotted narrative.

plottee (plɒ'tiː). *nonce-wd.* [f. PLOT *v.*[1] + -EE; correlative to PLOTTER 3.] One who is plotted against. **1832** HT. MARTINEAU *Ella of Gar.* ix, Both moralized on the beauty of sincerity..till the supposed plotter but real plottee yawned.

plotter ('plɒtə(r)). [f. PLOT *v.*[1] + -ER[1].]

1. One who makes a plan or map; one who plots points on a map. **1593** NORDEN *Spec. Brit., M'sex* I. 12 Many Surueyours and plotters of land seem to haue a speciall curiositie in obseruing this variation of the compasse. **1908** *Geogr. Jrnl.* XXXI. 536 Some central organization at home would be required for plotting the results. This could be done..by a plotter and plotting machine attached to any existing photographic establishment. **1943** 'T. DUDLEY-GORDON' *Coastal Command at War* ii. 17 At a long table sits a W.A.A.F. officer, writing and making calculations. She is the 'plotter'... As the signals pour in..she translates the data into positions and..pin-points the chart, drawing pencil lines which 'lay off' courses of ships and aircraft. **1958** 'P. BRYANT' *Two Hours to Doom* 48 Teams of plotters were at work, drawing in..the X points and target routes of the 843rd Wing. **1976** J. B. GARNER et al. *Surveying* i. 7 The spacing of grid lines should be chosen so that it assists the plotter without becoming predominant on the completed sheet. **1978** *Daily Tel.* 19 Aug. 13 (*caption*) Mrs Vera Shaw, who was a Waaf plotter during the Battle of Britain.

2. One who plans or devises anything; a planner, schemer; one who invents or constructs a dramatic or literary plot. Now *rare*. **1589** NASHE *Martins Months Minde* Wks. (Grosart) I. 181 These gambols..are not fit for Church plotters, nor common wealth casters, such as wee are. **1598** F. MERES *Pallad. Tamia* 283 Anthony Mundye our best plotter. **1606** in Nichols *Progr. Jas. I* (1828) III. 68 In so short a time to be accomplished, a most statelie Pageant, the workmen and plotters thereof having not past twelve dayes of respit after their first warning. **1748** RICHARDSON *Clarissa* (1811) I. iv. 25 A great plotter, and a great writer.

3. *spec.* One who contrives or joins in a mischievous or wicked plot; a conspirator. **1606** *Proc. agst. Late Traitors* 108, I will name it the Jesuites treason..they were the proprietaries, plotters and procurers of it. **1624** CAPT. SMITH *Virginia* III. iv. 54 Plotters of those villanies. **1685** EVELYN *Diary* 10 Apr., Amongst the plotters for poisoning the late King. **1738** WARBURTON *Div. Legat.* I. 230 The baffled Plotter who died on a Gibbet. **1821** BYRON *Sardan.* I. ii. 308 Not for all the plotters That ever shook a kingdom!

4. a. An instrument or machine for making plots; *spec.* one for drawing maps or automatically plotting points on them. [**1908** *Geogr. Jrnl.* XXXI. 544 A stereo-plotter.. combines the offices of the stereo-comparator and plotting board.] **1926** R. M. ABRAHAM *Surveying Instruments* x. 174 When the region to be mapped is rugged or mountainous the stereo method in conjunction with a suitable plotter is undoubtedly superior to all others. **1943** A. L. HIGGINS *Elem. Surveying* viii. 102 [With the plane table] angles are not observed in magnitude, as in the case of any goniometer, ..such as the compass..and theodolite, but instead are constructed directly, so that the instrument is a goniograph, or angle plotter. **1948** *Rev. Sci. Instruments* XIX. 647/2 (*caption*) An automatic [electric] field plotter. **1959** *Engineering* 27 Feb. 262/2 The additional information derived from the true motion type of presentation is obtained from the movement of a target vessel across the PPI screen... This is not entirely satisfactory so a tube face reflection plotter..was developed. With its aid, true plots of own and several target vessels can be easily kept by the navigator. **1963** [see PLOT *v.*[1] I b]. **1972** *Sci. Amer.* Mar. 2/2 (Advt.), Our 745 flatbed plotter will scribe lines equal to the tolerances and standards of the most skilled mapmaker's hand.

b. An instrument for automatically plotting a graph. **1956** *Proc. Eastern Joint Computer Conf.* 73/2 The Ballistic Research Laboratories have for some time been concerned with the development of a digital plotter capable of absorbing the output of..digital computers used in processing of missible ballistic data. **1970** O. DOPPING *Computers & Data Processing* xi. 172 In some simple plotters, the paper is continuously fed in one direction, while a printing device, directly controlled by the computer, moves at right angle [*sic*] to the direction of paper motion. **1975** *Nature* 16 Oct. 559/2 Engineers, on the other hand, might well set up a mathematical model for a bridge—or an aircraft wing—and use the minicomputer to display on a visual display unit or graph plotter the consequences of certain input data (loading, sizes of beams, or whatever).

5. One who owns a plot of land, a plot-holder. **1927** *Smallholder* 20 Mar. 106/3 Every plotter should pull his weight, not only for his own sake but for the good of the national cause. **1976** D. G. HESSAYON (*title*) Vegetable plotter.

'**plottery.** *nonce-wd.* [f. PLOTTER: see -ERY.] The action of a plotter; plotting, scheming. **1823** BYRON *Juan* XIII. lxxxii, I've seen..a so-so matron boldly fight Her way back to the world by dint of plottery.

plotting ('plɒtɪŋ), *vbl. sb.*[1] [-ING[1].] **a.** The action of PLOT *v.*[1] in various senses. **1593** NASHE *Christ's T.* Wks. (Grosart) IV. 45 Without any care, fore-cast, or plotting on thy part..I shall bee to thee all in all. **1607** J. NORDEN *Surv. Dial.* III. 127 Two principall instruments, fit indeede for the plotting of grounds,..a plaine table, and the Theodolite. **1672** DRYDEN *Def. Epil.* Wks. 1883 IV. 229 Our admired Fletcher.. neither understood correct plotting, nor that which they call 'the decorum of the stage'. **1683** *Roxb. Ball.* (1885) V. 329 But Heaven, I hope, will all Plotting disclose, And the Laws of the Nation shall punish the Foes. **1831** LYTTON *Godolphin* ii, Like Lysander, he loved plotting. **1842** *Penny Cycl.* XXIII. 329/2 The term 'plotting' is applied to the process of laying down on paper the plan of the ground which has been surveyed. **1893** *Athenæum* 17 June 760/2 The initial plotting and construction necessary..should have occupied less time..than the trivialities which have been allowed to take their place.

b. *Comb.* in sense 'used in plotting or drawing to scale', as ***plotting-book, -paper, -scale, sheet***; in sense 'forming plots', as ***plotting-school***. **plotting board**, (*a*) a form of drawing board on which the positions or courses of objects may be plotted; (*b*) = PLOTTER 4 b; **plotting machine**, a machine for automatically plotting maps; **plotting rod**, a long rod made for moving the counters on a plotting table; **plotting table**, (*a*) a large table bearing a small-scale map of a region on which the positions of enemy aircraft may be represented by movable counters or the like; (*b*) = PLOTTER 4 b. **1903** *Jrnl. U.S. Artillery* Nov.-Dec. 253 A location of a fixed target is thus plotted, the corrections for atmospheric conditions and drift are determined by the ballistic board, the range and azimuth for the gun are determined by relocation on the *plotting board, and transmitted to the gun by the gun telautograph. **1908** *Geogr. Jrnl.* XXXI. 544 The position in plan and height of any object can be plotted from readings of the three scales..and corresponding settings on a detached plotting-board. **1957** C. S. FORESTER *Naval War of 1812* 36 There had been exercises with a plotting-board in the Tripoli prison. **1961** S. FIFER *Analogue Computation* II. ix. 300 The Autograf..is an example of a cylindrical plotting board. In this case the pen is controlled, as before, by one variable, but the moving carriage is replaced by a rotating drum which is driven by the second variable. **1879** *Cassell's Techn. Educ.* IV. 92/1 The *plotting-book is a simple rectangular note-book. **1908** *Plotting machine [see PLOTTER I]. **1963** W. K. KILFORD *Elem. Air Survey* xi. 269 Some firms produce special plotting machines in which the relative orientation is already set for use with a particular pair of short-base cameras. **1977** J. M. SMITH in P. G. J. van Sterkenburg et al. *Lexicologie* 243 Graphical output devices, based on the principles of plotting machines, can be used too. **1883** *Harper's Mag.* July 165/2 A..speculator whose imagination is let loose upon a *plotting paper. **1948** T. E. WINSLOW *Forewarned is Forearmed* i. 19 The size of a plotting table depends also on the 'stretch' of a plotter provided with a *plotting rod. **1963** N. D. SMITH *Royal Air Force* vi. 66 Plotters, using long-handled plotting rods, moved coloured magnetic counters on the large table map. **1842** BRANDE *Dict. Sc.*, etc., **Plotting scale*, a mathematical instrument used in plotting, or setting off lengths of lines in surveying. **1681** T. FLATMAN *Heraclitus Ridens* No. 31 (1713) I. 200 May he too come To have my Doom That first set up this *Plotting-school. **1926** *Blackw. Mag.* Dec. 830/2 By degrees there appeared on the *plotting sheet a series of tiny needle-pricked marks. **1971** R. J. P. WILSON *Land Surveying* viii. 165 The plane table, essentially a drawing board,..carries the plotting sheet. **1943** P. F. M. FELLOWES *Britain's Wonderful Air Force* xiii. 303 At each centre there is a centre room, with a *plotting table on which is fitted a squared map. **1960** ROGERS & CONNOLLY *Analog Computation in Engin. Design* ii. 47 When it is desired to plot one variable against another, an *XY* plotting table is used. This unit employs a double servo system to drive a pen along an arm proportional to *Y*, and the arm along the plotting table proportional to *X*. **1968** *Listener* 15 Aug. 196/3 But it was all right to have mixed anti-aircraft batteries, with women tracking the target, and an ATS officer at the plotting table calculating the exact moment to shout the order 'Fire'. **1973** 'A. HALL' *Tango Briefing* xviii. 224 The whole of this area was on the plotting table at the Bureau. **1977** *Navy News* June 8 (*caption*) Prince Philip and Rear-Admiral D. W. Haslam (Hydrographer of the Navy) take a close look at the computer linked automatic plotting table being described by the commanding officer of H.M.S. Hecate.

plotting, *vbl. sb.*[2]: see PLOT *v.*[2]

plotting ('plɒtɪŋ), *ppl. a.* [f. PLOT *v.*[1] + -ING[2].] That plots, scheming. **1676** D'URFEY (*title*) A Fond Husband, or the Plotting Sisters: a Comedy. **1748** RICHARDSON *Clarissa* (1811) IV. xxiii. 125 Have I not called thine the plottingest heart in the universe? **1849** MACAULAY *Hist. Eng.* iv. I. 476 The burgesses of Wigan assured their sovereign that they would defend him against all plotting Achitophels and rebellious Absaloms.

Hence '**plottingly** *adv.*

1742 Richardson *Pamela* IV. 106 There never..could be a Gentleman, so foolishly tender, yet so plottingly cruel, to his Lady. **1864** Lowell *Fireside Trav.* 31 Frederick the Great, with head drooped plottingly.

plotton, -oon, obs. forms of PLATOON.

plotty ('plɒti), *sb. Sc.* Also plot(t)ie. [f. PLOTE, PLOT *v.* + -Y.] A hot drink, composed of wine or spirits with hot water and spices.

1824 Scott *St. Ronan's* xxviii, Get us a jug of mulled wine—plottie, as you call it. *Ibid.*, Your plottie is excellent, ever since I taught you to mix the spices in the right proportion. **1857** J. Stewart *Sk. Scottish Char.*, etc. 114 (E.D.D.) Arise, an' tak' your morning plotty.

plotty ('plɒtɪ), *a.* [f. PLOT *sb.* + -Y.] Connected with a plot or intrigue. Also, of a novel, play, or the like: having an elaborate or complicated plot.

1897 'S. Grand' *Beth Bk.* xl. 405, I would not write plotty-plotty books either. **1898** E. Pugh *Tony Drum* ix. 120 Novels of a common type, plotty and passionate, but gilt-edged with the proprieties. **1901** *Literature* 1 June 457/1 It is a relief to recall the 'plotty' incident at the inn in connexion with this statement. **1934** E. Bowen *Cat Jumps* 112 So plotty, so damned smart, so careful no one would see us who would remember, a different place every time. **1959** *Times Lit. Suppl.* 25 Sept. 546/5 His Phrygian Slave in the *Orestes*—admittedly a problem—talks a hair-raising amalgam of Wardour Street and hill-billy vernacular. 'God darn him dead For plotty sneaks,' this surprising menial observes at one point. **1973** L. Hellman *Pentimento* (1974) 197 What I thought was bite they [*sc.* theatre critics] thought sad, touching, or plotty and melodramatic. **1974** *Times* 18 Apr. 7/5 The basic plot is a bit plotty.

'plotwise, *adv.* [f. PLOT *sb.*[1]: see WISE *sb.*[1] II.] As regards or in terms of a plot (in sense 6 of the sb.).

1955 *Times* 26 May 11/4 We gave what was, plotwise, a perfectly coherent rendering of *Romeo and Juliet* in 20-odd minutes.

plotz (plɒts), *v. U.S. slang.* [ad. Yiddish *platsen*, f. G. *platzen* to burst; in sense 1 influenced by G. *platz* place, seat.] **1.** *intr.* To sit down wearily, to flop; to slouch, loaf (*around*). Also *trans.* in causal sense.

1941 A. Kober *My Dear Bella* 199 At the end of a day I'm just like a wet rag... All I'm good for is to *plotz* in a chair. **1960** J. Kirkwood *There must be Pony* vi. 43 He just kind of plotzed around waiting to fall into some sort of a cushy job. **1976** *National Observer* (U.S.) 30 Oct. 20/1, I find there is still little to justify a parent plotzing his offspring in front of the tube for long hours on Saturday morning. **1978** R. Condon *Bandicoot* xv. 91 We are plotzing one night and I bring out a whole miniature roulette layout.

2. *intr.* To burst; usu. in *fig.* senses, esp. to 'explode' with frustration or annoyance, to demonstrate one's anger.

1967 P. Welles *Babyhip* iii. 46 'You're not smoking that filthy thing in here. I'll *plotz*,' Mrs Green said. **1968** L. Rosten *Joys of Yiddish* 292 So Pincus broke into a run, and he ran and he ran until he thought his heart would *plotz*. **1970** L. M. Feinsilver *Taste of Yiddish* 367 A recent ad for a Yiddish revue read: 'In Miami they're plotzing'—meaning, 'they're still howling over the preview'. **1978** J. Krantz *Scruples* vii. 214 She came back to pick them up today and *plotzed* for joy all over the studio.

plotzed (plɒtst), *a. slang.* [f. as prec. + -ED[2].] Intoxicated, drunk.

Not clearly associated with the senses of PLOTZ *v.*

1962 J. D. MacDonald *Key to Suite* (1968) ii. 16 If one of our boys gets plotzed, we run him off the team fast before any damage is done. **1974** 'M. Allen' *Super Tour* v. 175 Mimi got drunk that night..but something more than liquor knocked her off base... She was so loaded I had to put her to bed, and I know from my own experience that when I am plotzed I go out for the night.

†**ploud.** *Sc. Obs.* Also 6 plod. [Derivation unknown.] A green sod, a turf.

1535 *Aberdeen Regr.* XV. (Jam.), xij laid of elding, half pettis, half plodis. *Ibid.*, ix[xx] layd of elding, peittis & ploddis. **1793** *Statist. Acc. Scot.* VI. 218 They are supplied with turf and heather from the muirs, and a sort of green sods, called plouds, which they cast in the exhausted mosses.

plough, plow (plaʊ), *sb.*[1] Forms: see below. [Late OE. *plóh* (*plóȝ*), = ON. *plógr* (in Rígsmál 10–11th c.); so Sw. *plog*, Da *ploug*, *plov*; in OFris. *plōch* (EFris. *plōg*, NFris. *pluwge*), MLG. *plōch*, *plūch*, MDu. *ploech* (Du. *ploeg*), OHG. *pfluog* (MHG. *pfluoc*, Ger. *pflug*):—Teut. type *plôgo- or *plôho-, whence also Lombard Lat. *plo(v)um*, *-us* (Du Cange), Lomb. *piò*, Tirol. *plof* plough. The regular OE. inflexion of *plóh* would have dat. *ploȝe*, gen. *ploȝes*, nom. pl. *ploȝas*, giving in early ME. *ploh*, *ploȝe*, *ploȝes*, later *plouh*, *plowh*, *plowgh*, pl. *plowes*; whence, by form-levelling, *plough*, *ploughs*, or *plow*, *plows*; the former the accepted spelling in England since 1700, the latter usual in U.S. In pronunciation, the final guttural was lost in some districts in 14th c., and has quite disappeared not only in the standard language, but in all dialects south of the Peak of Derbyshire; it remains in Scotland as (x) (*pleuch*, *pluich* = (pløx, plʏx)), and in the north of England is represented by f (*pleuf*, *plewf*, *pluif*, *pluf*, *pleaf*, *plif*, etc.: see *Eng. Dial. Dict.* s.v.). In PLOUGH *v.* (q.v.) neither *gh* nor *f* is pronounced.

As with *path*, *penny*, and other early *p*-words in Teutonic, the origin of *plôȝ*, *plôh*, is involved in obscurity. Apparently the word was of late appearance. It is not found in Gothic, which used *hôha*, nor in OE. which used *sulh*, still retained dialectally, esp. in s.w., where *plough* is not used in this sense: see SULL *sb.*, and cf. *Eng. Dial. Dict.* In Norse, also, the earlier name appears to have been *arðr*, cognate with OS. *erida*, f. vbl. root *ar-* to till, plough (see EAR *v.*), which survives in Norwegian as *ar* a small plough, perh. an earlier and simpler implement than the *plógr*. The name is also found in Lith. *pliugas*, and in the Slavonic langs. generally, OSlav., Serv., Russ. *plugŭ*, Pol. *plug*, Boh. *pluh*; but is there admittedly from German.]

A. Illustration of Forms.

1. *sing.* α. 1–4 ploh, 2 ploȝ, 3–4 plouh, plouȝ, 3–5 plogh, 4–5 plowȝ(-e), 4–7 plowgh, 4– plough, (5 ploghe, plowghe, plowh(-e), 5–6 ploughe).

a **1100** *Sax. Leechd.* III. 286 Ne plot ne ploh. *c* **1200**, *a* **1225** Ploh [see B. 1]. *a* **1250** *Prov. Ælfred* 95 in *O.E. Misc.* 108 þat..þe cheorl beo in fryþ..And his plouh beo i-dryue to vre alre bihoue. *a* **1300** *Cursor M.* 12388 (Cott.) Plogh [*Tr.* plowȝe] and haru cuth he dight. **1362** Langl. *P. Pl.* A. vii. 95 His pilgrym atte plouȝ. *Ibid.* 118 For oure plouh. *c* **1386** Chaucer *Knt.'s T.* 29 Wayke been the Oxen in my Plough [*rime* ynough]. *c* **1400** Maundev. (1839) xvii. 183 Callynge on oxen in the plowgh [*Roxb.* plugh]. *c* **1425** *Voc.* in Wr.-Wülcker 665/42 *Hoc aratrum*, plogh. **1426** Lydg. *De Guil. Pilgr.* 11400 Carte & plowh, they ber vp al. *c* **1450** Lovelich *Grail* liii. 310 Good Inowhe, Of londes and Rentes, Oxen And plowhe. **1483** *Cath. Angl.* 284/2 A Ploghe (*A.* Plughe), *aratrum*. **1530** Palsgr. 256/1 Ploughe, *chareve*. **1532** in Weaver *Wells Wills* (1890) 65 Half my plowȝthe the viz. iij oxen. **1573** Tusser *Husb.* (1878) 54 Mad braine, too rough, Marres all at plough.

β. 4 plou, 4–5 plo, 4–7 plowe, 5 ploo, 4– plow.

13.. *E.E. Allit. P.* B. 68 To see hem pulle in þe plow. *c* **1460** *Towneley Myst.* ii. 459, I shall hang the apon this plo [*rimes* do, lo]. **1466** *Paston Lett.* II. 286 They shuld hold the plowe to the tayle. **1607** Norden *Surv. Dial.* iv. 181 A dayes worke of a plowe. **1702** Addison *Dial. Medals* ii. (1727) 93 And does the plow for this my body tear? **1718** Rowe tr. *Lucan* i. 48 Fields unknowing of the plow [*rime* low]. **1828** Webster, Plow. **1902** *Ibid.*, Plow, Plough.

γ. *Sc.* and *north.* 4–5 plugh, 5 pluȝe, plughe, pleuche, (plucht), 6 plewgh(-e), plewch(-e), pluch(-e), pluiche, plwch, (pluchet), 6–8 plewch, 5– pleuch, 8– pleugh; 4 plue, 5 plwe, 5–6 plewe, 6 pleu, 4– plew; 9 *dial.* pluff, pleuf, pleaf, pliff, etc.

c **1375** *Sc. Leg. Saints* xxviii. (*Margaret*) 70 Sic as men wynnis of erd & pleuch. *Ibid.* xl. (*Ninian*) 132 In goddis ȝard to set plucht [*rime* Inuch]. *c* **1400** Maundev. (Roxb.) xviii. 85 þe ox will drawe in þe plugh. *c* **1420** *Avow. Arth.* xlix, God hase a gud pluȝe. **1456** Sir G. Haye *Law Arms* (S.T.S.) 240 The ox may nocht wele drawe in the pleuche bot gif he have a falowe. **1513** Douglas *Æneis* xiii. x. 7 First gan he mark and cirkill with a plewch. **1535** *Aberdeen Regr.* XV. (Jam.), Ane pluchet furnest with gair tharto. **1535** Stewart *Cron. Scot.* III. 273 That men sould leve thairout baith da and nycht Thair plew yrnis. *a* **1568** *Wowing Jok & Jynny* vi. (Bann. MS.), Withouttin oxin I haif a pluche. **1721** Ramsay *Richy & Sandy* 70 Thomas has loos'd his ousen frae the pleugh. **1786** Burns *Twa Dogs* 201 A country fellow at the pleugh. **1825** Brockett *N.C. Gloss.*, *Pluff, pleugh*, a plough.

2. *pl.* 2 ploȝes, 3 plouis, 4–5 plowȝes, 4–7 plowes, 5 ploes, plogges, 5–7 ploughes, 6 *Sc.* plewis, 6– plows, 7– ploughs.

1131 *O.E. Chron.* an. 1131 On þa tun þa wæs tenn ploȝes oðer twelfe gangende, ne belæf noht an. *a* **1275** *Prov. Ælfred* 95 in *O.E. Misc.* 109 His plouis to driuin. *c* **1330** R. Brunne *Chron. Wace* (Rolls) 2785 To hem þat at plowes ȝede. **1387** Trevisa *Higden* (Rolls) VI. 165 Here plowȝes ȝede nouȝt aryȝt. *c* **1400** Maundev. (1839) xxiii. 250 Cartes, plowes, and waynes. *c* **1420** *Anturs of Arth.* xii. (Irel. MS.), Of palas, of parkes, of poundes, of ploes [*rime* cloes = cloughs]. **1449** *Maldon, Essex, Court-Rolls* (Bundle 29 No. 3), Nullus habeat plogges. **1523** Fitzherb. *Husb.* §1 Howe a plough shulde be made. §2 There be plowes of dyuers makynges. **1566** *Reg. Privy Council Scot.* I. 493 Oxin to serve and labour in his plewis. **1632** Heywood *1st Pt. Iron Age* i. i. Wks. 1874 III. 272 So many Hatchets, Hammers, Plowes and Sawes Were thither brought. **1765** A. Dickson *Treat. Agric.* (ed. 2) 156 There are no less than an hundred different ploughs in England.

B. Signification.

1. a. An agricultural implement, used to prepare the soil for sowing or planting, by cutting furrows in it, and turning it up, so as to expose a fresh surface to the action of the air. Often used as the symbol of agriculture, esp. in such expressions as *to be at the plough*, *to follow* or *hold the plough*.

It consists essentially of a cutting blade (in primitive types a pointed stick) fixed in a frame drawn by oxen or horses (or in recent times by mechanical power, as steam), and guided by a man.

c **1200** Ormin 15902 þatt all swa summ þe nowwt i ploh þe turrnenn erþe & tawwenn. *a* **1225** *Ancr. R.* 384 ȝif..þe spade ne dulue, ne þe suluh [*MS. T.* ploh] ne erede, hwo kepte ham uorte holden? *c* **1400** *Plowman's T.* 1042 Had they ben out of religioun, They must have honged at the plow. **1515** Barclay *Egloges* iv. (1570) C iv/1 Some for the charet, some for the cart or plough, And some for hakneyes, if they be light and tough. **1568** Grafton *Chron.* II. 390 Few or none of them were Gentlemen, but taken from the plough and cart, and other craftes. **1577** B. Googe *Heresbach's Husb.* (1586) 21 The partes of the Plowe, are the Tayle, the Shelfe, the Beame, the Foote, the Coulter, the Share, the Wheeles, and the Staffe. **1601** Cecil in Sir S. D'Ewes *Jrnl. Ho. Lords & Comm.* (1693) 674, I do not dwell in the Country, I am not acquainted with the Plough: But I think that whosoever doth not maintain the Plough, destroys this Kingdom. **1718** Rowe tr. *Lucan* i. 323 Foreign Tenants reap the harvest now, Where once the great Dictator held the Plow. **1756–7** tr. *Keysler's Trav.* (1760) IV. 481 The celebrated Mr. Vareinge, professor of mathematics, followed the plough till he was eight and twenty years of age. **1822** Scott *Pirate* iv, The heavy cart-load of timber, called the old Scots plough.

b. With prefixed words, denominating peculiarities of structure or purpose: e.g.

double plough, a plough with two shares, one by which two furrows can be turned at once; also, a reversible plough; *hand-p.*, a small light garden plough drawn or pushed by hand; *seeding-p.*, a plough which also scatters seed in the furrow; *side-hill p.*, one adapted for ploughing across a steep slope; *skeleton-p.*, one in which certain parts are in skeleton form; *straddle-p.*, one with two shares for running on each side of, and covering in, a line of seed; also *double mould-board p.*, *drain-p.*, *mole-hill p.*, *reversible p.*, *steam-p.*, *subsoil-p.*, etc. Others, of which the meaning is not self-evident, will be found under their first element, or in their alphabetical place; e.g. BREAST-, DRAY-, GANG-, HOE-, ICE-, MOLE-, SHIM-, SNOW-, TURN-WREST-, WHEEL-PLOUGH, etc.

1653 Blithe *Eng. Improv. Impr.* 202 The Double Plough ploughing two Furrows at one time. **1704** *Dict. Rust.* s.v., The Double-wheeled Plough, constantly used in Hartfordshire and elsewhere... The One-wheeled plough, which may be almost used in any sort of Land. **1721** J. Edmonds in Mortimer *Husb.* I. 101 He says likewise, that he improved some of the same sort of Land by plowing of it up with a Breast-plough. **1741** *Compl. Fam.-Piece* iii. 416 Plough up your Mole-hills, &c. with a Mole-hill Plough. **1836** *Penny Cycl.* V. 307 In Brabant..They use the excellent Flemish swing plough, which they call a foot plough, as it is also called in some parts of England, in contradistinction to a wheel plough. At the same time they also retain the old and heavy turn wrest plough. **1874** Knight *Dict. Mech.* 728 The double-plow, in which a shallow share preceded the deeper-running, longer plow, originated in England, where it is known as the *skim-coulter plow*. *Ibid.* 940 The originator of the double plow seems to have been Lord Somerville, who devoted much attention to the practical details of agriculture (1799). His plow..he called a *double-furrow* plow.

c. In various *fig.* applications: e.g. †(*a*) as the instrument or means of earning one's livelihood (*obs.*); (*b*) in reference to its breaking up hard ground; etc.

(*a*) *c* **1375** *Sc. Leg. Saints* xxxiv. (*Pelagia*) 57 þat wynnyng wes lang hir plucht. *c* **1386** Chaucer *Shipman's T.* 288 But o thyng is..Of Chapmen that hir moneie is hir plogh. *a* **1400** *Isumbras* 397 þay bade hym swynke,..'Hafe we none oþer ploghe'.

(*b*) **1526** *Pilgr. Perf.* (W. de W. 1531) 23 Our hertes, whiche we eare & breke with the plough of abstynence. **1668** R. Steele *Husbandman's Calling* vi. (1672) 142 He puts in the plough of mortification. **1781** Cowper *Hope* 234 Their mind a wilderness through want of care, The plough of wisdom never entering there.

d. Phrases. (*a*) ***to put*** (***lay, set***) ***one's hand to the plough*** (after *Luke* ix. 62), to undertake a task; to enter upon a course of life or conduct.

1382 Wyclif *Luke* ix. 62 No man sendynge [1388 that puttith] his hond to the plouȝ, and biholdinge aȝen, is able to the rewme of God. **1526** Tindale *ibid.*, No man that putteth hys honde to the plowe, and loketh backe is apte to the kyngdom of god. **1596** Dalrymple tr. *Leslie's Hist. Scot.* iv. 253 Quhen he had put hand to the pluiche, to receiue yairof proffite and gude fructe. **1632** Sanderson *Serm.* 417 Reach foorth thine hand towards this spirituall Plow. **1718** Hickes & Nelson *J. Kettlewell* i. xxiii. 47 It was Time..to set his Hand to the Plow in good Earnest. **1886** Mrs. Lynn Linton *P. Carew* xxv, He had put his hand to the plow, and he was not the man to turn back.

†(*b*) ***to put the plough before the oxen***, to reverse the natural or proper order: cf. CART *sb.* 5. *Obs.*

[**1340** *Ayenb.* 243 Moche uolk of religion zetteþ þe zuolȝ beuore þe oksen.] **1571** *Satir. Poems Reform.* xxix. 9 That makis..The plewche befoir the oxin go, the best the man to gyde. **1653** Urquhart *Rabelais* i. (Farmer), He would put the plough before the oxen, and claw where it did not itch.

(*c*) ***under the plough***: (of land), in cultivation.

1836 *Penny Cycl.* V. 225 There are actually under the plough 307,800 [acres].

2. a. *Sc.* A team of horses (or oxen) harnessed to a plough.

[Cf. quot. 1131 in A. 2.] **1575–6** *Reg. Privy Council Scot.* II. 501 Arthour Grahame..cruellie..cuttit the plewis, dang and straik his servandis to the greit effusioun of thair blude. **1786** Burns *To Auld Mare* xv, My pleugh is now thy bairn-time a', Four gallant brutes as e'er did draw. **1809** Bawdwen *Domesday Bk.* 101 Earl Alan has now in the demesne six ploughs, and 14 villanes and 6 bordars with four ploughs. There is a church and a priest with half a plough.

b. Chiefly *s.w. dial.* A team of draught beasts harnessed to a wagon; sometimes including the wagon.

1505 *Liber Ruber Wells Cath.* lf. 123 b, Departed unto God by a mysfortune of his ploughe by reson whereof [etc.]. *c* **1630** Risdon *Surv. Devon* §328 (1810) 337 He took harts..and made of them a plow to draw timber thence to build a church. **1669** Worlidge *Syst. Agric.* (1681) 330 A Plough, a term used in the Western parts for a Team of Horse or Oxen. **1762** Borlase in *Phil. Trans.* LII. 507 The driver of a plough,..laden with tin, for Penzance coinage,..found himself and the plough, on a sudden, surrounded by the sea. **1813** T. Davis *Agric. Wilts* Gloss. s.v., A waggon and horses, or cart and horses together, are called plough in South Wilts. **1873** Williams & Jones *Somerset Gloss.*, *Plough*, a team of horses; also a waggon and horses, or a waggon and oxen.

†**3. a.** = PLOUGH-LAND 1. *Obs.*

a **1100** [see A. 1 *a*]. *c* **1400** *Gamelyn* 57 Iohn my eldest sone shal haue plowes fyue That was my fadres heritage while he was on lyue. *Ibid.* 358 þou hast hade..xv. plowes of lond þis sixtene ȝere. *c* **1450** *Oseney Cart.* 163/25 (E.E.T.S.), j. mese with ij. croftes..In the towne of Edburbury, and j. plowe of londe In the feldes of þe same towne. **1483** *Cath. Angl.* 284/2 A Ploghe of lande, *carrucata*. **1597** Skene *De Verb. Sign.*,

Hida terræ, ane pleuch of land. **1761** HUME *Hist. England* I. xix. 443 The ecclesiastical revenues, which..contained eighteen thousand four hundred ploughs of land. **1791** NEWTE *Tour Eng. & Scot* 237 A plough of land in the Highlands..is, on an average, about fifteen Scotch, or twenty English acres of arable land, besides a certain extent of hilly, or pasture land.

b. Ploughed land. (Chiefly *hunting slang.*)

1861 WHYTE MELVILLE *Mkt. Harb.* 18 It makes no odds to him, pasture or plough. **1883** *Pall Mall G.* 21 Dec. 4/2 It is by his permission..that the gaily-decked squadrons..go thundering across the pasture and ploughs of middle and southern England. **1884** *Graphic* 18 Oct. 410/1 The scent [of the fox] on the plough is cold.

4. *transf.* (With capital initial.) The group of seven prominent stars, also called Charles's Wain, in the constellation of *Ursa Major*; also, that constellation as a whole.

Cf. L. *Triones* (lit. plough-oxen), the Great and Little Bears (Virg. *Æn.* III. 516 *geminos Triones*).

1513 DOUGLAS *Æneis* VIII. Prol. 151 The pleuch, and the polys, the planettis begane, The son, the sevin sternis, and the Charll wane. **1868** LOCKYER *Elem. Astron.* §341. 154 One of the most striking circumpolar constellations is Ursa Major.., the Plough, or Charles's Wain. **1893** K. GRAHAME *Pagan Papers* (1894) 104 High and dominant amidst the Population of the Sky..hangs the great Plough.

5. Applied to various instruments, parts of machinery, etc., resembling a plough in shape or action.

a. An instrument or machine for cutting or trimming the edges of books; the knife of a plough-press or cutting-press.

1688 R. HOLME *Armoury* III. 360/2 Plow, or cutting Knife by which the leaves of Books are cut even. **1771** LUCKOMBE *Hist. Print.* 409 The..parts of the paper whose Margin is adjusted..are subject to the Bookbinder's Plough. **1873** E. SPON *Workshop Receipts* Ser. I. 395/2 Upon one of the cheeks [of the cutting press] are two guides, or small raised rails, for the plough to work in.

b. A plane for cutting rabbets or grooves.

1678 MOXON *Mech. Exerc.* iv. 68–9 The Plow..is a narrow Rabbet-Plain,..The Office of the Plow is to plow a narrow square Groove on the edge of a Board. **1815** J. SMITH *Panorama Sc. & Art* I. 111. **1881** YOUNG *Every Man his own Mechanic* §396 The plough is necessary in such work as making drawers.

c. An instrument for cutting the flushing parts of the pile or nap of fustian.

1875 in KNIGHT *Dict. Mech.*

d. A knife used for 'ploughing' mackerels, etc.: see PLOUGH *v.* 7 c and MACKEREL-*plough*.

†**e.** An instrument for taking the altitude of a heavenly body. *Obs.*

1690 LEYBOURN *Curs. Math.* 617 There are other Instruments for taking of the Altitude of the Sun and Stars; as the Plough, the Astrolabe, the Demi-Cross, the Bow. **1710** J. HARRIS *Lex. Techn.* II, *Plow*, an Ancient Instrument, tho' now not much used at Sea.

f. A narrow shovel with which the barley is turned over in malting.

1875 URE *Dict. Arts* II. 188 When turning only is required, he uses what is called the 'plough'; this is a long-handled tool, in shape very much resembling the scull of a boat, and in using it is made to pass through the grain, precisely as a scull is made to do in the water.

g. In an electric tramcar on the conduit system: The rod maintaining contact with the live rail.

1903 *Daily Chron.* 16 Mar. 5/2 They are..fitted..with the underground trolleys which make contact with the feeding conductors by means of a 'plough' lowered into the slotted conduit.

h. Any of various implements for deflecting (e.g. off a conveyor belt or a railway track) material against which they move, or which moves against them; in quots. 1860, 1975, a snow-plough.

1860 CLARK & COLBURN *Rec. Pract. Locomotive Engine* 68/2 In heavy snows, a plough of large size is fitted in front of the engine, to clear the line. *a* **1884** KNIGHT *Dict. Mech.* Suppl. 173/2 Dowling's plow for unloading platform gravel-cars, is a V-shaped implement which has two flaring wings. **1901** M. M. KIRKMAN *Building & Repairing Railways* viii. 333 The Rodgers ballast car dumps the ballast in the center of the track, the last car in train of ballast cars having a plow for cleaning and flanging the track. **1922** F. V. HETZEL *Belt Conveyors & Belt Elevators* viii. 159 In some European boiler houses the bunker is served by a flat belt which runs through a movable carriage equipped with a V-point plow and a two-way chute. **1953** W. W. HAY *Railroad Engin.* xxii. 316 A spreader-type plow follows the unloading operation to spread the ballast where it is needed. **1971** B. SCHARF *Engin. & its Language* xvi. 235 A plough (movable gate) may be provided across the belt so that the conveyor can be unloaded at that point or in order to deflect the material on to another conveyor. **1975** D. PITTS *Target Manhattan* (1976) xxviii. 117, I want your team of plows at Broadway and West 14th.

i. *Coal Mining.* A machine with cutting blades that remove a thin strip of coal when it is hauled along a coal face.

1950 *Trans. Inst. Mining Engineers* CIX. 273 The coal seams in this country are too hard to allow of the plough being successfully used. **1952** *Times* 16 Sept. 3/2 In his report for 1951, published to-day, Mr. G. Hoyle, North-Western Divisional Inspector of Mines, refers to revolutionary developments in mining technique... He instances the use of the plough and stripper for coal getting. **1964** A. NELSON *Dict. Mining* 335 Normally, on a wide face, and working 6 hr, a plough will produce 800 tons and more of coal in a 3 ft thick seam. **1971** *Daily Tel.* 20 Oct. 13/1 Machines, with strange names like Anderton shearers, trepanners, rapid ploughs or Huwood slicers, have replaced men underground.

6. An antler or branch on the horn of a caribou.

1892 W. PIKE *North. Canada* 45 The perfect double plough is more often seen in the smaller specimen, the larger animal being usually provided with only one, or with one plough and a spike.

7. *attrib.* and *Comb.* (some of which may belong to the verb). **a.** attrib., 'of or pertaining to a plough or ploughing', as ***plough-beast, -chain, -clevis, -collar, -coulter, -culture, -feast, -field, -folk, -furrow, -garran*** (GARRON), ***-ground, -harness, -horse, -jade, -mark, -neat, -ox, -rein, -rip, -rope, -servant, -service, -shaft, -sock, -tackling, -team, -timber, -time, -track, -upland, -wheel, -woman, -work***; **b.** objective and obj. genitive, as ***plough-holder, -maker***; **c.** instrumental, etc., as ***plough-bred, -cloven, -torn*** adjs.; **d.** similative, as ***plough-shaped*** adj.

1454 in Ellis *Orig. Lett.* Ser. II. I. 120 Toke all the *plow-bestes and other bestes of the said villages. **1788** E. PICKEN *Now-a-days* Poems 61 Ilk *plow-bred wight wad gang, dear safe us! **1897** CROCKETT *Lad's Love* xxix, I'll..send the men up wi' *pleuch-chains and cairt-rapes. **1875** KNIGHT *Dict. Mech.*, **Plow-clevis*, the stirrup-shaped piece on the nose of a plow-beam, having three loops, in either of which the open ring of the double-tree may be placed, according to the depth of furrow desired. **1871** SWINBURNE *Songs bef. Sunrise, Hertha* 37 The *plough-cloven clod. **1908** *Sears, Roebuck Catal.* 137/4 A Southern *Plow Collar. Made of heavy cotton duck with leather chafes on the side where the chain or trace attaches to the hame. **1942** W. FAULKNER *Go down, Moses* 255 Plowlines and plow-collars and hames and trace-chains. **1937** R. H. LOWIE *Hist. Ethnol. Theory* viii. 114 Thus was conceived the antithesis of primitive 'hoe-culture' and '*plough-culture', the latter being the exclusive mark of higher civilizations. **1961** L. MUMFORD *City in Hist.* i. 27 Where hoe culture supported hamlets, plow culture could support whole cities and regions. **1607** TOPSELL *Four-f. Beasts* (1658) 66 The Athenians had three several *plow-feasts which they observed yearly. **1805** *Sporting Mag.* XXV. 315 My landlady's two sons were arrived from the *plough field. **1577** tr. *Bullinger's Decades* (1592) 273 If the *plough-folks do idlely wast their maisters substance. **1844** STEPHENS *Bk. Farm* I. 490 Deeper than the *plough-furrow. **1687** *Irish Proclam.* 24 Sept., *Plow-Garrans and other small horses. **1640** in H. Bond *Hist. Watertown, Mass.* (1855) II. 998 Ordered that the hither Plain, being subdivided into several Lotts for *Plow-ground, shall be made a common field. **1895** W. RAYMOND *Smoke of War* vii. 84 Like a rook in a plough-ground. *c* **1386** CHAUCER *Miller's T.* 576 A smyth,..That in his forge smythed *plough harneys. **1886** T. HARDY *Mayor Casterbr.* iv, Plough-harness at the saddler's. **1613** MARKHAM *Eng. Husbandm.* iii. B iij, A stay and aide to the *Plough houlder. **1539** WYATT *Let.* in R. W. Bailey *Early Mod. English* (1978) 233/1 And I w[i]t[h] much ado apon *plow horse In the diepe and fowle way gatt afore that nyght late to loshes. **1573** T. TUSSER *Five Hundreth Points Good Husbandry* xviii, Sedge couers for plow horse, for lightnes of neck. **1744** W. ELLIS *Mod. Husbandman* Jan. xxi. 56, I feed my Plough Horses with these green Thetches. **1817** SCOTT *Rob Roy* II. xiii. 280 There may be pasture aneugh for pleugh-horses, and owsen, and forty or fifty cows. **1880** *Harper's Mag.* Aug. 356/2 The next day the two girls, mounted on the plough horse and mare, followed an old Indian trail. **1911** R. D. SAUNDERS *Col. Todhunter* ix. 118 A wall-eyed plow-horse with his tail full o'cuckle-burs. **1955** W. MOORE *Bring Jubilee* i. 5 He would lay the reins on the plough-horse's back. **1561** DAUS tr. *Bullinger on Apoc.* (1573) 214 The pampered Palfreyes which eate away the prouender from the leane *plough Iades. **1600** HEYWOOD *2nd Pt. Edw. IV*, Wks. 1874 I. 122 That sike bonny men sud be hampert like plu-jades. **1812** SIR J. SINCLAIR *Syst. Husb. Scot.* II. App. 38 Apprentice to a country carpenter and *ploughmaker. **1930** W. FAULKNER *As I lay Dying* 125 After a while she went on, stumbling a little on the *plow-marks. **1963** *Field Archaeol.* (Ordnance Survey) (ed. 4) 56 A recent excavation has shown round huts ..closely associated with plough-marks in underlying sand. **1973** *Nature* 23 Nov. 191/2 Further ambiguity was introduced by the presence of iceberg plough marks around the Rockall bank and evidence of ice-rafted deposition. **1552** HULOET, *Ploughe neate or oxen, *triones.* **1503** DUNBAR *Thistle & Rose* 111 Lat no bowgle, with his busteous hornis, The meik *pluch ox oppress. **1906** KIPLING *Puck of Pook's Hill* 237 Down would come the King's Officers, and take our plough-oxen to haul them [*sc.* guns] to the coast. **1946** E. LINKLATER *Private Angelo* xx. 257 Two pairs of matched plough-oxen arrived in Pontefiore. **1844** STEPHENS *Bk. Farm* I. 619 The ploughman guides the horses with *plough-reins, made of rein-rope. **1536** *MS. Acc. St. John's Hosp., Canterb.*, Payd for ij par' of *plowgh ryppis iiij d. *c* **1586** C'TESS PEMBROKE *Ps.* CXXIX. ii, Thou Hast their *plow-ropes cutt in two! **1733** TULL *Horse-Hoeing Husb.* xi. 124 Villainies of English *Plow-Servants. **1766** BLACKSTONE *Comm.* II. vi. 80 Our common lawyers..derive it from *soca*, an old Latin word denoting (as they tell us) a plough:..that, in memory of it's original, it still retains the name of socage or *plough-service. **1878** BELL *Gegenbaur's Comp. Anat.* 435 The '*plough-shaped bone' forms the terminal portion of the vertebral column. **1695** J. TELFAIR in Nicholson *Hist. & Trad. Tales* (1843) 16 It cast a *plough-sock at him. **1814** SCOTT *Wav.* l, Plough-socks, shuttles, candlesticks, and other ordinaries. **1695** J. EDWARDS *Perfect. Script.* 114 The Gordian knot was but *plough-tackling hamper'd in a knot. **1799** J. ROBERTSON *Agric. Perth* 324 Formerly, four horses a-breast was the *plough team of the highlands, and is still in use. **1896** M. T. PEARMAN *Hist. Manor Bensington, Oxon.* 10 The quantity of land a plough-team will turn up in a year varies according to the soil. **1626** BACON *Sylva* §658 Some are best for *Plough-Timber: as Ash. **1607** SHAKS. *Timon* IV. iii. 193 Dry vp thy Marrowes, Vines, and *Plough-torne Leas. **1844** STEPHENS *Bk. Farm* I. 490 The black mould immediately under the *plough-track had been compressed. **1730** *N. Jersey Archives* XI. 226 There is also 100 Acres of *Plough-Upland in very good Order. **1733** TULL *Horse-Hoeing Husb.* xxv. 414 In plowing miry Clays, where *Plow Wheels cannot go. **1860** G. H. K. in *Vac. Tour.* 164 The *plough-woman dropped her cras-crom in the scratch that did duty for a furrow. **1880** *Dorothy* p. xvi, The two Yorkshire girls were..both..excellent ploughwomen.

8. Special Combs.: †**plough-bat** = PLOUGH-STAFF; †**plough-beetle** = PLOUGH-MELL; **plough-bird, -bolt**: see quots.; †**plough-boon**, in ME. *ploȝbone*, ploughing done as a service by a tenant for his lord; **plow-breast** = BREAST *sb.* 9 b; **plough-bullock**, (*a*) a bullock used in ploughing; (*b*) one of the mummers in the Plough-Monday festivities; also **plough-bullocker**; so **plough-bullocking** *vbl. sb.*; †**plough-chip** = PLOUGH-HEAD 1; **plough-cleaner**: see quot.; †**plough-clout**, an iron plate nailed to the frame of a plough at the side: cf. CLOUT *sb.*[1] 2; †**plough-cock** = COCK *sb.*[1] 14; **plough-cutter** = *plough-press*; **plough-day**, (*a*) a day on which the tenant was bound to plough for his lord; (*b*) = PLOUGH-MONDAY; **plough-diamond**, a kind of glass-cutter: see quot.; †**plough-ear**, a piece of iron attached to the right side of the plough-beam, to which the harness was attached: = *plough-cock*; **plough grinding** *Cotton Spinning*, a way of grinding the wires of a cotton card (see quots.); so **plough-ground** *a.*; **plough-jag** (*local*) = *plough-bullock* (*b*); hence **plough-jagging**, acting as a plough-jag, mumming; †**plough-jobber** = PLOUGH-JOGGER; **plough-knife**, the knife of a bookbinder's plough-cutter; **plough-light**: see quot.; **plough-line**, (*a*) the line marking the limit of ploughed land; (*b*) cord used for the traces or reins of a plough; also (usu. *pl.*), the reins themselves; also *fig.*; †**plough-master**: see quot; †**plough-meat**, cereals; **plough-medal**, a medal given as a prize at a ploughing-match; **plough-money**, † (*a*) money paid for the right of ploughing; (*b*) money collected by plough-boys on Plough-Monday; **plough-paddle, -pattle, -pettle**, a plough-staff: = PADDLE *sb.*[1] 1, PATTLE, PETTLE *sb.* 1; **plough pan** *Agric.* [PAN *sb.*[1] 8], a compacted layer in cultivated soil resulting from repeated ploughing; **plough-path**: see quot.; †**plough-penny**, (*a*) = PLOUGH-ALMS; (*b*) *nonce-use*, a penny gained by ploughing; **plough-pillow** = PILLOW *sb.* 4 d; †**plough-pin**, a pin or bolt used in connexion with the collar of a plough: see COLLAR *sb.* 13; **plough-plane** = sense 5 b; **plough-point**, the point of a plough-share; often detachable = SLIP-POINT; *U.S.*, the first (usu. detachable) share at the front of a plough; †**plough-pote**: see PLOUGH-FOOT; **plough-press**, in bookbinding, a press in which a book is held while the edges are cut or 'ploughed' (also called *cutting-press*); †**plough-rest, -ryst** = REEST *sb.*; †**plough-shackle**, the clevis of a plough; **plough-sheath**, †**plough-silver**: see quots.; **plough-soil**, soil that has been thrown up by ploughing; **plough-spade** = PLOUGH-STAFF; †**plough-spindle**: see quot.; †**plough-star** = sense 4, or ? Arcturus; **plough-stock**, the iron or metal frame of a plough; **plough-stot** = *plough-bullock*; †**plough-string**, one of the traces of a plough; **plough-stuff**, the timber used for a wooden plough; †**plough-throck** = PLOUGH-HEAD 1; †**plough-till, -tilth** = PLOUGH-LAND 1; **plough-tree**, a plough-handle; **plough-trench** *v.*, to trench with a plough; **plough-truck**, a riding attachment to a plough; †**plough-ware**, beasts employed in ploughing; **plough-witch, -witcher** (*dial.*), a Plough-Monday mummer; **plough-witching**, the performance of the plough-witchers. Also PLOUGH-ALMS, PLOUGH-LAND, etc.

1362 *Plowbat [see *plough-pote*]. **1530** PALSGR. 256/1 *Ploughe betyll, *mailliet de charve.* **1573** TUSSER *Husb.* (1878) 37 A plough beetle, ploughstaffe, to further the plough. **1707** MORTIMER *Husb.* (1721) I. 366/1 Plough Staff and Beetle. **1888** *Ibis* 45 The local name of this bird [*Sterna Antarctica*] in the neighbourhood of Cape Kidnappers, is 'The *Plough Bird', or 'Plough Boy', given on account of its habit of following the farmer's plough. **1884** KNIGHT *Dict. Mech.* Suppl., **Plow Bolt*, a bolt for securing the share, landside, or mold-board to the stock. **1438** *Rental of Guiseley co. York* in *Add. Roll* 41659 Ob. et quadrans for *plogbone. **1884** *Implement & Mach. Rev.* 1 Dec. 6716/2 A horned *plough-breast..is recommended for ploughing after sheep. **1762** *Gentl. Mag.* Dec. 568/2 *note*, Plough-Monday... On this day the young men yoke themselves, and draw a plough about with musick, and one or two persons, in antic dresses, like jack-puddings, go from house to house, to gather money to drink... We call them [in Derbyshire] the *Plough-Bullocks. **1766** *Compl. Farmer* s.v. *Turnip*, To my plough bullocks I allow the same quantity of turnips. **1899** A. NUTT in H. Lowerison *Field & Folklore* 63 Certain players, distinguished by scarlet jackets, and known as plough-bullocks or boggins. **1905** *Eng. Dial. Dict.* IV. 552/1 *Plough..-bullockers,..-bullocking.* **1923** E. C. PULBROOK *Eng. Country Life* xiii. 194 At Whitby, the young men come in to celebrate the Plough Stots as of old, and the Plough Bullockers occasionally drive their decorated plough through the villages of Derbyshire, to the detriment of those who refuse largesse. **1838** W. Howitt *Rural Life of Eng.* II. III. 144 Maying, guising, *plough-bullocking, morris-dancing, were gone before.. Methodism appeared. **1649** Blithe *Eng. Improv. Impr.* xxviii. (1653) 190 Some call them the Plough-throck, some the *Plough-chip, &c. I shall retain the term of Plough-head. **1875** Knight *Dict. Mech.*, **Plow-cleaner*, a long-handled thrusting implement by which the plowman may rid the plow of choking weeds, or the share of accumulated soil. **1376–7** *Durham Acc. Rolls* (Surtees) 386 In uno moldebredclot et ij *plueclot empt... xvd. **1485** in *Ripon Ch. Acts* (Surtees) 373, ij plogh clowtes. **1866** Rogers *Agric. & Prices* I. xxi. 537 Flat plates of iron nailed to the wooden frame are called plough-clouts. **1688** R. Holme *Armoury* III. 333/2 The *Plow Cock is the Iron to tye the Oxen to the Plow. **1550** in *7th Rep. Dep. Kpr. Irel.* 94 [From every husbandman] vi *ploughe daies, vi cart daies, iii men for a daie to repp corne in harvest. **1616** Surfl. & Markh. *Country Farme* 20 From Plow-day, which is euer the Munday after Twelfth-day, till S. Valentines day. **1825** J. Nicholson *Operat. Mechanic* 636 *Plough diamonds have a square nut on the end of the socket, next the glass, which, on running the nut square on the side of the lath, keeps it in the cutting direction. **1523** Fitzherb. *Husb.* §3 The *ploughe-eare is made of thre peces of yren, nayled faste vnto the ryght syde of the plough-beame. *Ibid.* §4 Somme plowes have a bende of yron tryanglewise, sette there as the plough-eare shulde be, that hath thre nyckes on the farther syde. **1892** J. Nasmith *Students' Cotton Spinning* iv. 135 The usual solution of the difficulty is found in the formation of a tooth with a chisel or knife edge, which is presented to the action of the cotton. This is usually obtained by what is called '*plough grinding'—that is, a method of passing between the teeth of the clothing a thin emery disc, which 'ploughs' deeply between them and grinds them on each side until they present a sharp edge to the cotton. **1923** T. Thornley *Adv. Cotton Spinning* (ed. 3) ii. 77 The plough grinding of the wire works is really side grinding carried to its most perfect degree, and producing a bevelled effect on each tooth from point to knee. **1965** W. G. Byerley et al. *Man. Cotton Spinning* III. vi. 108 In addition to surface- and side-grinding, reference must be made to 'plough-grinding'. This process was devised and patented by an English firm in 1880... The process.. was superseded by the side-grinding process. **1896** W. S. Taggart *Cotton Spinning* I. vi. 176 A is the *plough-ground wire, and is formed by grinding the sides away, almost to the bend, by special emery discs. **1923** T. Thornley *Adv. Cotton Spinning* (ed. 3) ii. 76 The plough ground tooth is obtained at the wire-making establishment by grinding away the sides of the teeth down to the knee or bend. **1870** E. Peacock *Ralf Skirl.* III. 230 What the mummer is to some other parts of England, the *plough-jag is to Lincolnshire. *Ibid.* 229 *Plew-jaggin' is for lads and young men.. not for a chap like me, that's just a-goin' to be married. **1683** Kennett tr. *Erasm. on Folly* 126 Why an Ass, or a *Plough-Jobber shall sooner gain it than a Wise man. **1719** D'Urfey *Pills* (1872) I. 25 Lye safe at home and our Plowjobbers rule. **1825** Hone *Every-day Bk.* I. 73 Anciently, light called the **Plough-light*, was maintained.. before images in some churches, and on Plough Monday they.. went about with a plough.. to get money to support the Plough-light. **1777** *New Jersey Gaz.* 17 Dec. 3/3 *Plough-lines, Bed-Lacings,.. Sold by Edward Pole,.. Burlington. **1852** C. W. Hoskins *Talpa* 119 The plough-line steals up the mountain-side. **1886** F. T. Elworthy *W. Somerset Word-Bk.* 582 *Plough-lines*, or *plough-guides*,.. the cords used as reins. **1895** *Rep. Educ. Scot.* in *Westm. Gaz.* 25 June 8/1 Hung by a loop of what is known on farms as plough-line. **1935** Z. N. Hurston *Mules & Men* (1970) I. ii. 54 Y'all lady people ain't smarter *than* all men folks. You got plow lines on some of us, but some of us is too smart for you. **1940** W. Faulkner *Hamlet* i. 8 One afternoon he was in the store, cutting lengths of plow-line from a spool. **1969** G. E. Evans *Farm & Village* xi. 126 There they made rope for the plough-lines, the reins or *cords*, as the horsemen invariably called them. **1642** in *Linc. N. & Q.* July (1888) 86 [In the old Churchwardens' Book of Waddington there is.. 1642, the appointment of 4] *Plowmeisters.. [These plough masters had in their hands certain monies called plough money, which they undertook to produce on plough day.] **1573** Tusser *Husb.* (1878) 102 Som cuntries lack *plowmeat, and som doe want cowmeat. **1844** Stephens *Bk. Farm* I. 648 The *plough medals.. have.. excited a spirit of emulation among ploughmen. *a* **1600** Owen *Baronia* in *Pembrokeshire* (1892) 195 *note*, Within Eglosserow onely Arian Eredig, or *Plowe monye, for right of ploughing. **1828** *Craven Gloss.* (ed. 2), **Plough-paddle*,.. called also a *plough-staff*. **1404** *Plogh pattyl, **1786** Pleugh-pettle [see pattle, pettle 1]. **1820** Scott *Monast.* xiii, 'He will take to the pleugh-pettle, neighbour', said the good dame. **1883** W. T. Lawrence *Princ. Agric.* I. 30 By repeatedly ploughing at about the same depth, their downward progress [*sc.* that of roots] is checked by the formation of a hard bottom called a *plough-pan. **1924** Watson & More *Agric.* v. 86 Sub-soiling is absolutely necessary where a plough-pan has been formed. **1960** *Farmer & Stockbreeder* 19 Jan. 74/1 (*caption*) Years of cultivation at constant depth have resulted in some plough pan. Once this is broken up the crops will have a better chance of establishment. **1873** Williams & Jones *Somerset Gloss.*, **Plough-path*, bridle-path. **1547** *Mem. Ripon* (Surtees) III. 45 Et de x s. vj d. de redditibus vocatis *Plowe pence accidentibus hoc anno. **1608** Armin *Nest Ninn.* (1842) 33 Enuy.. makes them sterril of all good manners, as the lawyer the poore clyant's plow pence, the cittie the country commodities. **1707** Mortimer *Husb.* (1721) I. 46 The *Plough-pin and Collar-links.. the *Plough-pillow and Boulster. **1823** P. Nicholson *Pract. Build.* 248 The *Plough-Plane.. is used for sinking a groove in a board, by taking away a solid in the form of a rectangular prism. **1856** in G. N. Jones *Florida Plantation Rec.* (1927) 478 Paid Mr. Lem Jones 50 cts. on account of '54 maid by J. Evans for 2 *Plow points. **1875** Knight *Dict. Mech.*, *Plow-point*, a detachable share at the extreme front end of the plow-body. **1891** C. Roberts *Adrift Amer.* 39, I made two or three unsuccessful attempts to get the plough point into the hard frozen ground. **1942** W. Faulkner *Go down, Moses* 168 The boy first remembered himas sitting in the door of the plantation black-smith shop, where he sharpened plow-points and mended tools. **1362** Langl. *P. Pl.* A. vii. 96 Mi *plouh-pote [*v.r.* plowbat, *B.* ploughwes foot, plow-pote, *C.* ix. 64 plouh-fot, plowbat] schal be my pyk and posshen atte Rootes, And helpe my coltre to kerue and close pe vorwes. *c* **1350** *Nominale Gall.-Angl.* 148 (E.E.T.S.) Man doth a *plou-reste in the bem. **1613** Markham *Eng. Husbandm.* iii. B iij b, The Plough-rest.. is a small peece of woode, which is fixt at one end in the further nicke of the Plough head, and the other end to the Ploughs right-hand hale. **1552** Huloet, *Ploughe ryst [*printed* ryft], *bura, buris.* **1483** *Cath. Angl.* 284/2 A *Plughe schakille. **1523** Fitzherb. *Husb.* §3 The *ploughe sheth is a thyn pece of drye woode, made of oke, that is set fast in a morteys in the plough beame, and also in to the sharebeame, the whiche is the keye and the chiefe bande of all the plough. **1465** *Norfolk Deed* (Anct. Deeds, P.R.O. IV. 68 No. 6678) *Plowsilver. **1675** W. Jones *Reports* 280 In some places they have Plough-silver and Reap-silver, which is Socage Tenure now turned into Money. **1809** Tomlins *Law Dict.*, *Plow-silver*, in former times, was money paid by some tenants, in lieu of service to plough the lord's lands. **1967** *Antiquaries Jrnl.* XLVII. 166 Today, the bank and the ditch.. have been largely either ploughed flat or masked by comparatively modern accumulations of *plough-soil. **1976** C. Thomas in P. H. Sawyer *Medieval Settlement* II. xii. 149 Site XX is a field bounded by a ditch... Its date of use can be fixed by the dated broken pot sherds, part of the extensive domestic manure incorporated in the plough-soil. **1978** R. Bradley *Prehist. Settlement of Britain* 41/2 His argument was based on the foreign stones incorporated in the ploughsoil. **1844** Stephens *Bk. Farm* II. 493 This the ploughman does with his plough-staff, or shaft of his *plough-spade. **1613** Markham *Eng. Husbandm.* iii. B iij, The *Plough spindels,.. are two small round peeces of woode, which coupleth together the hales. **1558** Phaer *Æneid.* III. H ij b, The wayne, the *plowstar, and the seuen that stormes and tempests poures [*Æn.* III. 516 Arcturum pluviasque Hyadas geminosque Triones]. **1582** Stanyhurst *Æneis* III. (Arb.) 87 Thee lights starrye noting in globe celestial hanging: Thee seun stars stormy, twise told, thee plowstar eke Arcture. **1786** G. Washington *Diary* 9 Jan. (1925) III. 5 [I] directed them to get me.. scantling for *Plow stocks. **1865** *Oregon State Jrnl.* 28 Oct. 4/2 Plow Stocks etc., made to order, on short notice. **1940** W. Faulkner *Hamlet* I. ii. 35 Ab.. had snuck the wagon out the back way with the plow stocks and the sorghum mill in it. **1944** T. D. Clark *Pills, Petticoats & Plows* 276 Centre and rear passageways were blocked with piles of iron plows.. plow stocks.. and axes. **1820** *Sporting Mag.* VI. 283 Youth dragging a plough, who, as they officiate for oxen, are called *plough-stots. **1893** *Whitby Gaz.* 8 Dec. 2/5 It would seem as though the spirit of the Plough Stots is waning and that for some reason or other they are losing interest in their annual excursions into the town. *c* **1350** *Nominale Gall.-Angl.* 858 (E.E.T.S.) *Lapparayle pur charue*.. *Plowestryngges. **1649** *Plough-throck [see *plough-chip*]. **1494** Fabyan *Chron.* VII. ccxxii. (1516) 143/2 *margin*, A knyghts fee shuld welde clx. acres, and that is demed for a *ploughe tyll in a yere. **1597–1602** *Transcript W. Riding Sessions Rolls* 104 Every person occupying a *plough-tilth of land. **1869** Blackmore *Lorna D.* lxxiv, I.. held my *plough-tree just the same as if no King or Queen had ever come to spoil my.. hand. **1707** Mortimer *Husb.* (1721) I. 56 It may be done by one Plough making of a deep Furrow, and another following in the same Furrow, or by *Plough-trenching, which is for a Plough to make a deep Furrow, and to have eight or ten Men with Spades to follow the Plough, and making the Trench a spit deeper. **1765** *Museum Rust.* IV. 174 Instead of digging it with the spade, I plough-trenched it at least eighteen inches deep. **1465** Marg. Paston in *P. Lett.* II. 183 He had a plowe goyng in your lond in Drayton, and ther your seyd servaunts.. toke hys *plowe ware, that ys to say ij marys. *Ibid.* 184 Ther was taken a playnt ayenst hem.. for takyng of the forseyd plowarre at Drayton. **1827** Clare *Sheph. Cal.* 156 On *Plough-witch-Monday, I was in the barn. **18..** E. Smith *MS. Collect. Warwicks. Words* (E.D.D.), Down to 1874.. the plough witches presented themselves on the evening of Plough Monday, with faces painted white, and marked out hideously in red or black lines. **1860** *N. & Q.* 2nd Ser. IX. 381/2 The mummers are called '*Plough-witchers', and their ceremony '*Plough-witching'.

plough, *sb.*[2] *slang.* [f. Plough *v.* 8.] The act or fact of rejecting a candidate in an examination.

1863 Reade *Hard Cash* ii. I. 52 It is only out of Oxford a plough is thought much of. **1897** *Westm. Gaz.* 3 1 Nov. 10/1 In the.. Bar examination, the percentage of ploughs is.. 9 per cent... ploughed in Roman Law, and 20 per cent. in Constitutional History. **1899** *Ibid.* 1 June 10/1 There has been the usual plough in the final of about 36 per cent.

plough, plow (plaʊ), *v.* Forms: 5–6 plowghe (5 *north.* plugh(e), 5–7 plowe, 6– plow (*Sc.* plew), (6–7) 8– plough. (Erron. pa. pple. 6 plowen.) [f. plough *sb.*[1] So MDu., Du. *ploegen*, MLG., LG. *plogen*, MHG. *phluogen*, Ger. *pflügen*, ON. *pløgja*. In 16–17th c. the sb. was normally *plough* and the vb. *plow(e*, repr. ME. types *ploh*, *ploȝen* or *plowen* (cf. *enough*, *enow* = OE. *ȝenóh*, *ȝenóȝe*); so mod.Sc. *pleuch* sb., *pleuw* vb.; but the spelling *plough* occurs also for the verb in 16–17th c., and became usual in England during the 18th c., when sb. and vb. were levelled in form; in U.S. they have both become *plow*.]

1. a. *trans.* To make furrows in and turn up (the earth) with a plough, especially as a preparation for sowing; also *absol.* to use a plough.

c **1420–40** Plowynge [see ploughing *vbl. sb.* 1]. *c* **1460** *Towneley Myst.* ii. 54 That we had ployde [? ploȝde] this land. **1483** *Cath. Angl.* 284/2 To Plowghe (*A.* Plugh), *arare.* **1523** Fitzherb. *Surv.* 2 It is conuenyent that they be plowen and sowen. **1530** Palsgr. 660/2, I wyll ploughe all the lande I have in your towne to yere. **1607** Norden *Surv. Dial.* IV. 181 As much as 2. oxen could plow. **1611** Cotgr., *Charruë*, a Plough. *Charruër*, to till, eare, plow. *Charrué*, tilled, plowed. **1707** *Curios. in Husb. & Gard.* 133 Once Ploughing the Land.. will.. be sufficient. **1759** tr. *Duhamel's Husb.* I. vii. (1762) 17 It is plowed into high ridges with a strong plough. **1796** H. Hunter tr. *St.-Pierre's Stud. Nat.* (1799) I. 361 As much land as a yoke of oxen could plough in one day. **1816** W. Smith *Strata Ident.* 12 When wet and fresh plowed. **1816** Scott *Old Mort.* vii, I am no clear if I can pleugh [*error for* plew] ony place but the Mains and Muckle-whame. **1880** *Scribner's Mag.* 215 They have plowed and fitted for grain-growing 3,000 acres.

b. With resultant object: To make (a furrow, ridge, line) by ploughing. Also *fig.*

1589 *Pasquil's Ret.* C j b, God shall.. punish euery forrow they haue plowed vpon his backe. **1797** *Encycl. Brit.* (ed. 3) I. 286/2 By casting, that is, by ploughing two ridges together beginning at the furrow that separates them. **1810** Amos *Ess. Agric. Mach.* ii. 18 [A machine] for ploughing Furrows nine by five inches square. **1901** Ld. Rosebery in *Times* 20 July 15/5, I must proceed alone. I must plough my furrow alone. **1936** E. White *Wheel Spins* iii. 29 She always ploughed a straight furrow, right to its end. **1977** *Dædalus* Summer 149 In the United States, George Sarton had been plowing a lonely furrow at Harvard's Widener Library for about twenty-five years. **1978** *Lancashire Life* Nov. 39/2 No easy task, with everybody else ploughing the same furrow.

2. a. *intr.* (or *absol.*) To use the plough, work as a ploughman, till the ground.

1535 Coverdale *Prov.* xx. 4 A slouthfull body wyl not go to plowe for colde. **1607** Shaks. *Cor.* III. i. 71 The Cockle of Rebellion, Insolence, Sedition, which we our selues haue plowed for, sow'd. **1611** Bible *Job* i. 14 The oxen were plowing [Coverdale a plowinge], and the asses feeding beside them. —— *1 Cor.* ix. 10 That hee that ploweth, should plow in hope. **1685** Baxter *Paraphr. N.T.* 2 Tim. ii. 6 The Husbandman must labour (plow, sow, &c.) before he reap and gather the Fruit. **1847** L. Hunt *Jar of Honey* (1848) 197 Twenty-three pair of oxen were ploughing together within a square of thirty acres. **1868** Ruskin *Arrows of Chace* (1880) II. 199 A man taught to plough, row or steer well,.. [is] already educated in many essential moral habits.

b. *intr.* in pass. sense (of land): To bear or stand ploughing (easily, well, etc.); to prove (tough, etc.) in the ploughing.

1762 Mills *Syst. Pract. Husb.* I. 152 It ploughed very tough, and the cattle mired in some places. **1847** *Jrnl. R. Agric. Soc.* VIII. II. 571 The land generally ploughs up in a friable state. **1864** *Ibid.* XXV. II. 528 The clover-lands.. ploughed remarkably well.

3. a. *trans.* By extension: To furrow as by ploughing; to gash, tear up, scratch (any surface). Often *plough up*: see 9 e.

1588, etc. [see 9 e]. **1740** Somerville *Hobbinol* II. 84 Th' insidious Swain.. Fell prone and plough'd the Dust. **1784** Cowper *Task* v. 50 His dog.. snatches up the drifted snow With ivory teeth, or ploughs it with his snout. **1856** J. H. Newman *Callista* i. 2 The Bagradas.. ploughed the rich and yielding mould with its rapid stream.

b. With resultant object, as *course*, *line*.

1831 Scott *Cast. Dang.* iii, The course which the river had ploughed for itself down the valley. **1855** Kingsley *Glaucus* 14 It was.. the stones fallen from Snowdon peak into the half-liquid lake of ice above, which ploughed those furrows. **1873** Hamerton *Intell. Life* II. i. (1875) 51 The line-engraver.. month after month, ploughs slowly his marvellous lines.

c. *intr.* To move through soft ground, snow, etc., furrowing it.

1847 Le Fanu *T. O'Brien* 209 Drenched in inky slime.. Miles Garrett ploughed and floundered to the other side. **1876** A. H. Green *Phys. Geol.* iv. §5 (1877) 160 Icebergs which after they had run aground and ploughed into the bottom [of the deposits of boulder clay]. **1894** Fenn *In Alpine Valley* II. 246 Deane came ploughing through the snow up to the window.

4. *fig.* Of a ship, boat, swimming animal, etc.: To cleave the surface of the water. Chiefly *poet.*

a. *trans.*

1607 Shaks. *Timon* v. i. 53 'Tis thou that rigg'st the Barke, and plow'st the Fome. **1633** P. Fletcher *Purple Isl.* I. xxxvi, Vain men.. who plough the seas, With dangerous pains, another Earth to finde. **1698** Fryer *Acc. E. India & P.* 24 Once again committing ourselves to the Sea, we ploughed deeper Water. *a* **1732** Gay *Fables* II. viii. 25 When naval traffic plows the main. **1782** Cowper *Loss Royal George* x, He and his eight hundred Shall plough the wave no more. **1836** Macgillivray tr. *Humboldt's Trav.* xvi. 216 The river was ploughed by porpoises, and the shore crowded with aquatic birds.

b. With resultant object, as *course*, *way*.

1696 Prior *To the King* 56 On.. Britain's joyful sea, Behold, the monarch ploughs his liquid way. **1780** Cowper *Table-t.* 522 Give me the line [of verse] that plows its stately course Like a proud swan, conquering the stream by force. **1856** Kane *Arct. Expl.* I. xviii. 228 Ploughing its way with irresistible march through the crust of an investing sea. **1873** Black *Pr. Thule* ii, The steamer.. ploughed her way across the blue and rushing waters of the Minch.

c. *intr.*

1850 Lyell *2nd Visit U.S.* II. 154 These streams.. spread out into broad superficial sheets or layers, which the keels of vessels plough through. **1867** *Good Cheer* 2 He had 'ploughed over many a stormy sea'. **1897** *Outing* (U.S.) XXX. 117/1 A few tugs plowing up stream left behind them wakes.

5. *trans. fig.* To furrow (the face, brow, etc.) deeply with wrinkles; also with resultant object.

1725 Ramsay *Gentle Sheph.* v. iii, Has fifteen years so plew'd A wrinkled face that you have often view'd. **1742** Pope *Dunc.* IV. 204 Before them march'd that awful Aristarch; Plough'd was his front with many a deep Remark. **1818** Byron *Ch. Har.* IV. xlii, Italia!.. On thy sweet brow is sorrow plough'd by shame. **1837** Wheelwright tr. *Aristophanes* I. 56 *note*, Her face.. rough, and ploughed with wrinkles. **1857** Holland *Bay Path* xix. 218 Jealousy and pride.. ploughed no furrows across her brow.

b. To obliterate by ploughing wrinkles.

1818 Byron *Mazeppa* v, A port, not like to this ye see, But smooth, as all is rugged now; For time, and care, and war, have plough'd My very soul from out my brow.

6. a. In various figurative applications of the primary and transferred senses.

1535 COVERDALE *Job* iv. 8 Those that plowe wickednesse . . and sowe myschefe, they reape yᵉ same. **1576** FLEMING *Panopl. Epist.* 342 The soyle of his inuention, memorie, and iudgement, is so ordinarily ploughed with practise and experience. **1606** SHAKS. *Ant. & Cl.* II. ii. 233 Royall Wench: She made great Cæsar lay his sword to bed, He ploughed her, and she cropt. **1607** —— *Cor.* v. iii. 34 Let the Volces Plough Rome, and harrow Italy. **1608** —— *Per.* IV. vi. 154. **1609** BIBLE (Douay) *Ecclus.* vii. 13 Plowe not a lie [Vulg. *noli arare mendacium*] agaynst thy brother. **1624** FORD *Sun's Darling* II. i, Beckon the rurals in; the country-gray Seldom ploughs treason: **1652** MILTON *Sonn. Cromwell*, Cromwell . . who through a cloud . . To peace and truth thy glorious way hast plough'd. **1838** EMERSON *Addr. Camb. Mass.* Wks. (Bohn) II. 193 Jesus . . whose name is not so much written as ploughed into the history of this world. **1884** MISS F. P. COBBE in *Contemp. Rev.* Dec. 805 Out of hearts ploughed by contrition spring flowers.

b. *intr.* To proceed laboriously or doggedly *through*, to labour, to plod.

1891 C. T. C. JAMES *Rom. Rigmarole* 40 He never ceased speaking. . . In a monotonous tone, he ploughed solemnly onward, oblivious. **1897** FLANDRAU *Harvard Episodes* 30 He could . . fancy himself ploughing doggedly in self-defence through an incredible number of courses in history. **1952** C. BARDSLEY *Bishop's Move* xi. 119, I almost said 'plough through' the Bible. **1959** *Daily Tel.* 23 July 1/6 The Prime Minister . . gave the House the impression that he was ploughing, with as much force and gaiety as he could muster, through an almost impenetrable bog. **1978** P. BOARDMAN *Worlds of P. Geddes* xi. 408 One ploughs through the often complicated sentences of P.G.'s writings of 1926–30.

c. *intr.* Of a road vehicle, train, aeroplane, or the like: to move clumsily or laboriously, usu. at speed; to advance out of control *into* (or *through*, etc.) an obstacle.

1972 *Daily Tel.* 29 Dec. 2/5 A three-coach train was derailed . . when it ploughed into a herd of cattle at 60 mph. **1973** *Times* 31 Dec. 5/5 The airliner . . ploughed to a halt on the runway. **1976** *Southern Even. Echo* (Southampton) 11 Nov. 16/5 A Southampton lorry driver suffered only cuts and bruises last night when his lorry ploughed through a bridge and plunged 15 feet into a field at Wimborne. **1977** *Evening Gaz.* (Middlesbrough) 11 Jan. 1/9 Police in Cleveland are hunting the driver of a sports car which forced another car to plough into four people.

7. Applied to mechanical processes: cf. PLOUGH *sb.*¹ 5. **a.** *Bookbinding.* To cut with a 'plough' or plough-press.

1873 E. SPON *Workshop Receipts* Ser. I. 395/2 The cutting press stands on a hollow frame . . which . . receives the paper shavings as they are ploughed off.

b. *Carpentry.* To cut or plane (a groove, rabbet) with a 'plough'. Also *intr.*

1805 [see PLOUGHING 1 b]. **1866** G. MACDONALD *Ann. Q. Neighb.* xiii, The carpenter . . was ploughing away at a groove. **1875** *Carpentry & Join.* 104 A groove being ploughed under the over-hanging edge to cause the rain to drip clear of the wall.

c. To cut or gash (mackerel, etc.) so as to give it a better appearance: cf. CRIMP *v.*¹ 4. *U.S.*

1890 in *Cent. Dict.*

d. *Coal Mining.* To cut (coal) by means of a plough; to push (coal so obtained) away from the face by means of a plough.

1950 *Trans. Inst. Mining Engineers* CIX. 256 The first train of thought was to plough machine-cut coal on to a face conveyor. **1951** H. F. BANKS in E. Mason *Pract. Coal Mining* (ed. 2) I. viii. 123/2 This device carries steel blades which shear or plane off the coal to a limited depth and ploughs it on to the face conveyor. **1964** A. NELSON *Dict. Mining* 335 Hard anthracite is being ploughed with only water infusion to soften the coal.

e. *trans.* To clear (an area) of snow using a snow-plough.

1961 'E. LATHEN' *Banking on Death* (1962) xii. 99 'Don't know why they can't plow these streets,' he muttered as he pulled into the single lane left by the piles of snow. **1978** *Times* 23 Jan. 12/7 There was . . slush and compacted snow on roads the ploughs had not reached. It says much for the authorities in West Virginia . . that they had ploughed all but about 40 miles of my route. **1979** J. VAN DE WETERING *Maine Massacre* ii. 12 They may not have plowed the strip . . last time. . . I had to circle while they pushed the old plow around.

8. *Univ. slang.* To reject (a candidate) as not reaching the pass standard in an examination: a slang substitute for *pluck* in this sense (PLUCK *v.* 7).

1853 'C. BEDE' *Verdant Green* II. xi, It's impossible for them to plough me. **1863** READE *Hard Cash* Prol. 16 That . . adds to my chance of being ploughed for smalls. . . 'Ploughed' is the new Oxfordish for 'plucked'. **1883** *Times* 1 June 4 My young friend was undeservedly ploughed.

9. With *advbs.*; mostly *trans.*

a. ***plough around***: *lit.* in reference to stumps left in cultivated land; *fig.*, to make tentative approaches, feel one's way. *U.S. political slang.*

1888 BRYCE *Amer. Commw.* II. III. lxx. 557 The more skilful leaders begin (as it is expressed) to 'plough around' among the delegations of the newer . . States.

b. ***plough down***: to throw or thrust down by ploughing. Also *fig.*

1765 A. DICKSON *Treat. Agric.* (ed. 2) 126 On a part of a field where whins were plowed down. **1877** BLACK *Green Past.* xxix, Any of which would be ploughed down by this huge vessel.

c. ***plough in, plough into the land***: to embed or bury in the soil (manure, vegetation, etc.) by ploughing. Also *fig.*

1764 *Museum Rust.* II. 172 When a farmer intends to plow in his vetches, I would . . advise him to do it some weeks before he sows his wheat. **1847** *Jrnl. R. Agric. Soc.* VIII. I. 62 Others spread the dung on the surface and plough it in. **1895** B. SEDGWICK in *Westm. Gaz.* 12 Sept. 4/3 He ploughed his capital into the land, and it never came out.

d. ***plough out***: to dig or thrust out (of the ground) with the plough; hence, to disinter, dig out; to root out, eradicate, cast out, tear out, remove with violence; also, to excavate or hollow out by or as by ploughing (cf. 3 b).

1643 MILTON *Divorce* II. xx. Wks. 1851 IV. 118 God loves not to plow out the heart of our endeavours with over-hard and sad tasks. *a* **1645** HABINGTON *Surv. Worc.* in *Worc. Hist. Soc. Proc.* III. 504 Ploughed out of obscure antiquities I will now use the true name. **1863** LYELL *Antiq. Man* xiv. (ed. 3) 266 A third period when the marine boulder drift formed in the middle period was ploughed out of the larger valleys by a second set of glaciers. **1886** A. WINCHELL *Walks Geol. Field* 54 These North-American rivers have plowed out channels whose deep walls rise as high as the smoke from the steamers.

e. ***plough up***: to break up (ground) by ploughing; to throw or cast up, eradicate (roots, weeds) with the plough; to cut up roughly, excavate, furrow or scratch deeply, by any similar action.

1588 SHAKS. *Tit. A.* IV. ii. 87 Sooner this sword shall plough thy bowels vp. **1601** BP. W. BARLOW *Serm. Paules Crosse* 45 For he . . hath plowed vp my hart. **1606** SHAKS. *Ant. & Cl.* IV. xii. 38 Let Patient Octavia plough thy visage vp With her prepared nailes. **1718** LOWTH *Comm. Jer.* iv. 3 The Prophet . . exhorts them to Repentance and Reformation under the Metaphor of Plowing up their fallow Ground. **1774** GOLDSM. *Nat. Hist.* (1776) III. 172 The wild boar plows it [the earth] up like a furrow, and does irreparable damage in the cultivated lands. **1817** W. SELWYN *Law Nisi Prius* (ed. 4) II. 1245 If . . the owner of a close over which there is a right of way plough up the way, and assign a new way. *a* **1895** LD. C. E. PAGET *Autobiog.* i. (1896) 8 Her decks were literally ploughed up with grape shot.

f. ***plough under***: to bury in the soil by ploughing.

1900 *Year-Bk. U.S. Dept. Agric.* 379 If crimson clover is grown, it should be plowed under rather early in the spring to get the best results. **1979** *Country Life* 6 Dec. 2141 The express way will bypass the old road . . ploughing under landmarks that meant much to people.

g. ***plough back***: to invest (income or profit) in the enterprise from which it emanates.

1930 *Economist* 24 May 1172/2 The extensive resort of American managements to the practice of 'ploughing back earnings into the business' further emphasises this tendency. **1945** *Richmond* (Va.) *Times-Dispatch* 25 Oct. 6/3 The proposed act would limit the annual dividends of such corporations to 6 per cent, requiring that all additional profits would have to be 'plowed back' into redevelopment. **1949** *Sun* (Baltimore) 26 Jan. 12/3 Profits are being plowed back into industry at unprecedented rates. **1955** *Times* 1 July 17/3 The profits that have accrued from this company have been largely ploughed back for further development and expansion. **1965** *Listener* 23 Dec. 1023/1 It was not long before we had functioning money-raising sweet shops, bargain stores—and the 'Green Dragon'. Profits were all ploughed back. **1970** *Physics Bull.* Mar. 99/2 For the services it renders the Centre charges small fees which are ploughed back into its operations. By this means it is planned to be selfsupporting within three years. **1974** N. FREELING *Dressing of Diamond* 96 We ploughed every penny back for ten years. **1976** *Milton Keynes Express* 30 July 11/4 He would not consider ploughing some of the £4 million back into the services and said he hoped the kitty would increase.

10. Phrases. **a.** ***to plough with any one's heifer*** (*ox, †calf*) after *Judges* xiv. 18. See also HEIFER 1 b. (In quot. 1632, app. to be yoked together with.)

1535 COVERDALE *Judg.* xiv. 18 Yf ye had not plowed with my calfe [1611 heifer], ye shulde not haue founde out my ryddle. **1584** G. B. *Beware the Cat* Ded., I doubt whether M. Stremer will be contented that other men ploughe with his oxen. **1632** MASSINGER *City Madam* II. iii, I will undertake To find the north passage to the Indies sooner Than plough with your proud heifer.

b. ***to plough the sands***: a frequent type of fruitless labour. Also ***to plough the air***.

1590 GREENE *Never too late* Wks. (Grosart) VIII. 166 With sweating browes I long haue plowde the sands . . Repent hath sent me home with emptie hands. **1647** JER. TAYLOR *Lib. Proph.* Ep. Ded. 5 That I had as good plow the Sands, or till the Aire, as perswade such Doctrines, which destroy mens interests. **1775** WESLEY *Jrnl.* 15 Nov., I preached at Dorking. But still I fear we are ploughing upon the sand: we see no fruit of our labours. **1894** ASQUITH *Sp. at Birmingham* 21 Nov., All our time, all our labour, and all our assiduity is as certain to be thrown away as if you were to plough the sands of the seashore, the moment that the Bill reaches the Upper Chamber.

Hence **ploughed, plowed** *ppl. a.*: also, (in sense 9 g) ***ploughed-back***; ***ploughed-out***, obscured or destroyed by ploughing; (in sense 9 e) ***ploughed-up*** (in quot. *fig.*). Also (in sense 9 g) ***ploughing-back*** *vbl. sb.*

1535 COVERDALE *Jer.* iv. 26 The plowed felde was become waist. **1665** BOYLE *Occas. Refl.* IV. ii. (1848) 173 We began to traverse certain plow'd Lands. **1759** B. MARTIN *Nat. Hist. Eng.* II. *Herts.* 15 The Surface of every Plowed Field. **1815** J. SMITH *Panorama Sc. & Art* II. 619 When ploughed lands are to be laid down for meadow or pasture. **1920** J. MASEFIELD *Enslaved* 120 From these ploughed-up souls the spirit brings Harvest at last. **1931** *Economist* 18 July 128/1 Reserves against remote contingencies, and those representing the 'ploughing back' of earnings into the business, should be set aside openly. **1944** J. S. HUXLEY *On living in Revol.* xii. 130 This compulsory ploughing-back of any excess profits is essential if the development of the area is to proceed at a reasonable rate. **1950** *Oxoniensia* XV. 7 Ploughed-out field-systems appear on air-photographs as a network of white lines which can often be recognized to some extent on the ground by bands of broken chalk and flints. **1957** *Times* 12 Dec. 18/1 Additional capital . . has been injected into the business . . in the form of ploughed-back profits. **1958** *Spectator* 18 July 117/3 It is finding about 85 per cent. of its capital through ploughed-back profits. **1959** *Manch. Guardian* 7 Aug. 1/2 The suggestion that a reduction in selling prices might, in present circumstances, take precedence over the ploughing back of profits. **1974** C. TAYLOR *Fieldwork in Medieval Archaeol.* iv. 74 The discovery of Iron Age and Roman sherds scattered on a spur above the River Nene near Irthlingborough, Northamptonshire, led to the identification of ramparts round this spur as part of a ploughed out 'hill fort'. **1977** *Interim* IV. iv. 4 Then the light marks over ploughed-out walls or banks . . provide . . an accurate deliniation of landscape elements.

'ploughable, 'plowable, *a.* [f. PLOUGH *v.* + -ABLE.] Capable of being ploughed; arable.

1570 LEVINS *Manip.* 3/10 Plowable, *arabilis.* **1611** COTGR., *Arable*, earable, ploughable, tillable. **1778** [W. MARSHALL] *Minutes Agric., Digest* 25 Light Soils are plowable at a small expence. **1864** CARLYLE *Fredk. Gt.* xv. xii. (1872) VI. 87 There may be patches ploughable for rye.

'plough-,alms, plow-alms. Now *Hist.* [f. PLOUGH *sb.*¹ + ALMS; repr. OE. *sulh-ælmessan.*] A church-due in Old English times and later, consisting of one penny per annum for each plough or plough-land.

[*a* **1000** *Laws of Edmund* I. c. 2 (Schmid) Be teoðungum and ciric-sceattum. Þeoðunge we bebeodað ælcum cristenum men be his cristendome, and cyric-sceat, and Romfeoh, and sulh-ælmessan.] **1291–2** in Dugdale *Monast. Angl.* (1682) I. 256 De qualibet caruca juncta inter Pascha et Pentecostem unum denarium, qui dicitur ploualmes. **1647** N. BACON *Disc. Govt. Eng.* I. xi. (1739) 20 Another Income arose from the Plough, and under the name of Plough-Alms. **1844** LINGARD *Anglo-Sax. Ch.* (1858) I. iv. 174 *Plough-alms*, a penny from every land, which was yearly offered, &c.

'plough-back, plow-. *Econ.* Also as one word. [f. *to plough back*: see PLOUGH *v.* 9 g.] Investment of income or profit in the enterprise from which it emanates; the capital so invested.

1946 *Sun* (Baltimore) 28 Mar. 19/2 After payment of . . taxes and . . dividends, the company showed a plow-back of $64.90 a share. **1961** *Times Lit. Suppl.* 6 Jan. 2/2 Less socialist-minded politicians . . taxed such 'plough-backs' into companies' own coffers more heavily. **1966** *Economist* 26 Mar. 1264/2 Borax would have to justify itself by giving an assurance on the future flow of dollar dividends from the American ploughback. **1970** *Daily Tel.* 2 Jan. 14 Some new Government, if well advised, will be in a position to let the private sector have more of its head in . . plough-backs, investment and profits. **1974** M. B. BROWN *Economics of Imperialism* v. 123 The 7 per cent or so of Britain's national income, which was invested in the decades before the 1830s had . . to be found almost entirely from the ploughback of profits.

'plough-beam, 'plow-. The central longitudinal beam or bar of timber or iron in a plough, to which the other principal parts are attached.

14 . . *Voc.* in Wr.-Wülcker 569/21 *Burris*, the plowebeme. **14 . .** *Nom.* ibid. 724/27 *Hec buris*, a plughbeme. **1523** FITZHERB. *Husb.* §3 The ploughe beame, is the longe tree aboue, the whiche is a lytel bente. **1613** MARKHAM *Eng. Husbandm.* iii. B ij, The first member thereof, as being the strongest and most principallest peece of timber belonging to the same, is called the Plough-beame, being a large long peece of timber much bending. **1727** BRADLEY *Compl. Body Husb.* 41 The plough-beam, about seven foot long, and five inches square, from the tail . . to the coulter . . , and then tapers to three inches and half. **1884** *Longm. Mag.* Feb. 403 An elm . . to fashion into a plough-beam.

fig. **1607** J. CARPENTER *Plaine Mans Plough* 206 The Plough Beame of Impietie is, the repletion of bread . . and luxurie.

'ploughbote, ploughboot, plow-. *Hist.* [f. PLOUGH *sb.*¹; see BOOT *sb.*¹ 5 b.] In *Old Law*, The wood or timber which the tenant had a right to cut for making and repairing ploughs and other agricultural implements.

1531 in Weaver *Wells Wills* (1890) 193 My dwyllyng house . . wyth sufficyent housebote, heybote, fyrebote, plough-bote growyng upon any growne belonging unto the said house. **1567** in F. J. Baigent *Crondal Rec.* (1891) 166 Wood . . for ploughe-boote, hedge-boote, fyar-boote, . . and harrowe-boote. **1669** WORLIDGE *Syst. Agric.* (1681) 285 Fell Trees for Mechanick uses; as Plough-boot, Cart-boot, &c. **1766** BLACKSTONE *Comm.* II. iii. 35 Plough-bote and cart-bote are wood to be employed in making and repairing all instruments of husbandry.

'plough-boy, 'plow-boy. A boy who leads the team of oxen or horses that draw a plough; hence, a boy of the rustic labouring class.

1569 *Lanc. Wills* (1857) II. 254 To every ploughe boy and other boyes servinge within my house sixe shillinges eighte pence. **1724** WATTS *Logic* I. vi. §4 A ploughboy, that has . . seen nothing but thatched houses, and his parish church, is naturally led to imagine that thatch belongs to the very nature of a house. **1818** COBBETT *Pol. Reg.* XXXIII. 255 If I do not, by the means of that Grammar, enable any Plough-Boy of sound mind to write English as correctly in one year [etc.]. **1903** *Spectator* 28 Nov. 903/2 The plough-boy figures on the prehistoric rock carvings of the Maritime Alps, . . using the goad, while the ploughman guides the plough. . . With the use of horses the ploughboy has disappeared, except where the land is so heavy that he has to lead the extra horse.

ˈplough-ˌdriver, ˈplow-. [Cf. Da. *plov-driver.*] One who drives the beasts drawing a plough.
1483 *Cath. Angl.* 284/2 A Ploghe dryfer, *stigarius.* **1552** HULOET, Ploughe dryuer, *iugarius.* **1603** DEKKER *Wonderfull Yeare* Wks. (Grosart) I. 115 Those misbeleeuing Pagans, the plough-driuers. **1679** O. HEYWOOD *Diaries*, etc. (1881) II. 262 The plow-holder left the plow.. the plow-driver at last came to them. **1812** SIR J. SINCLAIR *Syst. Husb. Scot.* I. 343 Horses.. were herded.. on the pasture land, by the boys then employed as plough drivers.

plougher, plower (ˈplaʊə(r)). [f. PLOUGH *v.* + -ER[1]. In ON. *plógari*, LG. *ploger*, Du. *ploeger*, Ger. *pflüger.*] One who ploughs; a ploughman. Also in *transf.* and *fig.* senses.
c **1515** *Cocke Lorell's B.* 10 Parchemente makers, skynners, and plowers. **1535** COVERDALE *Ps.* cxxviii. [cxxix.] 3 The plowers plowed vpon my backe, & made longe forowes. **1548–9** LATIMER *Ploughers* (Arb.) 17 Now I shal tel you who be the plowers. **1791** COWPER *Iliad* XVIII. 685 Ploughers not few, There driving to and fro their sturdy teems. **1869** *Daily News* 30 Aug., The ploughers of dangerous seas, or the occupiers of troubled frontiers. **1880** *Dorothy* 34 Now was the autumn come, and ploughers went forth to their ploughing.

b. *Comb.* †**ˈplougher-band**, some part of the harness of a plough.
1404 *Durham Acc. Rolls* (Surtees) 398, iij plogherbandis.

†**ˈplough-foot, ˈplow-.** *Obs.* [Cf. Norw. dial. *plog-fot.*] In a wheelless plough, an adjustable piece of wood or iron, attached to the front of the beam, regulating the depth of the ploughing: see quots.
It is doubtful however whether the *plow-fote* in Piers Plowman had this meaning; the variant reading *plow-bat* and the context point rather to its identity with *plough-staff*.
1377 LANGL. *P. Pl.* B. VI. 105 My plow-fote shal be my pyk-staf and picche atwo þe rotes, And helpe my culter to kerue and clense þe forwes [*v.rr. A.* plouh-pote, plowbat; *B.* plow-pote, ploughwes foot; *C.* plouh-fot, plowbat]. **1523** FITZHERB. *Husb.* §3 The plough fote is a lyttell pece of wodde, with a croked ende set before in a morteys in the ploughe beame, sette fast with wedges, to dryue vppe and downe, and it is a staye to order, of what depenes the ploughe shall go. **1613** MARKHAM *Eng. Husbandm.* iii. B iv b, Plough foote,.. the vse of it is to giue the Plough earth, or put it from the earth, as you please. **1707** W. BAXTER *Gloss. Antiq. Rom.* etc. (1731) 406 Tho' our Translation.. makes Samgar to have slain six hundred Men with an Ox-goad: The LXX say it was ἐν τῷ ἀροτρόποδι, which.. is *Dentale*, or the Plow-foot.

†**ˈplough-gang.** *Sc. Obs.* [f. PLOUGH *sb.*[1] + GANG *sb.*[1] (app. a late formation on analogy of *ox-gang*).] A measure of arable land; by Jamieson taken as a synonym of *plough-gate.*
(The statements of its extent differ widely, and may point to different local uses: quot. 1793 makes it 13 acres, i.e. one eighth of a carucate or plough-land, and so = ox-gang; quot. 1748 makes it half a carucate; Jamieson, if his 'one plough' means the original plough and team of eight oxen, identifies it with the carucate; but he may have meant a modern two-horse plough. See next for a fourth value.)
1748 W. CULLEN *Let.* in *Life* (1832) I. 69 As much [ground] as may employ four horses or what we call a plough-gang. **1793** *Statist. Acc. Scotl., Perth.* V. 56 The number of plough-gangs, in the hands of tenants, is about 141½,.. reckoning 13 acres of arable land to each plough-gang. **1808** JAMIESON, *Pleuch-gang, Plough-gang*, as much land as can be properly tilled by one plough... We also use the phrase a *pleuch* of land in the same sense. [Apparently an erroneous statement.]

plough-gate, plow- (ˈplaʊgeɪt). *north. Eng.* and *Sc.* Now only *Hist.* [f. as prec. + GATE *sb.*[2]; cf. *ox-gate.*] Originally, perhaps the same as PLOUGH-LAND (and hence commonly used by Scottish antiquarian writers to render *carrucata*); but in later times apparently applied to a much smaller quantity of land.
Jamieson says: 'A plough-gate or plough-gang of land is now [1825] understood to include about forty Scots acres [= 50⅝ Imperial acres] at an average. Fife.'
1565 *Wills & Inv. N.C.* (Surtees) I. 235, I bequyethe vnto my said Wyfe during hir Lyfe naturall my toure in Brankston wt the two plewegait of Land And all other comoditts theirto belongyng. **1789** PILKINGTON *View Derby.* II. 77 The charter of Edward II.. grants the canons at Calke possession of a plough-gate of land in Leke. **1791** *Statist. Acc. Scotl.* I. 121–2 There are 56 plough-gates and a half in the parish [Innerwick]. **1799** J. ROBERTSON *Agric. Perth* 392 A number of plough-gates in one village, or several tenants about one plough, having their land mixed with one another, is a great bar to the improvement of any country. **1806** *Gazetteer Scot.* (ed. 2) 412/1 The island [Papa Westray].. is divided into 24 ploughgates of land, and contains about 240 inhabitants. **1818** SCOTT *Hrt. Midl.* xii, The defences proposed say, that *non constat* at this present what is a plough-gate of land, whilk uncertainty is sufficient to elide the conclusions of the libel. **1872** E. W. ROBERTSON *Hist. Ess.* 135 The agricultural measurement in Scotland upon which the *regium gildum* was levied.. was the Ploughgate, or carucate of 104 acres.

ˈplough-gear, plow-. [f. as prec. + GEAR *sb.*] The appurtenances of a plough: = next.
1418–19 in *Cal. Proc. Chanc. Q. Eliz.* (1827) I. Introd. 16 The abbot and the convent.. ledeth a wey from his parsonage his plogh yren and his plogh and his plogh gere. **1523** FITZHERB. *Husb.* §5 It is necessarye for hym, to lerne to make his yokes, oxe bowes, stooles, and all maner of plough geare. **1566** *Wills & Inv. N.C.* (Surtees) I. 263 All my Waynes and wayneger all my plewes and plewgeire to be dewyded equalle betwyxt them. **1584** *Knaresborough Wills* (Surtees) I. 145 Plowes and plowe geare. **1644** *Archives Maryland* (1887) IV. 279 The ploughgeare sent of Engl[and]. *a* **1815** M. LONSDALE *Love in Cumberland* in *Westmoreland & Cumberland Dial.* (1839) 211 Thy plew-geer's aw liggin how-strow. **1885** 'C. E. CRADDOCK' *Prophet Gt. Smoky Mts.* i. 15 The girl's hand trembled violently as she stepped swiftly to his horse and took off the plough-gear. **1940** W. FAULKNER *Hamlet* iii. 64 He would give them credit for food and plow-gear when they needed it. **1952** *Oxf. Jun. Encycl.* VI. 243/1 Plough gear is generally simpler than chain gear; it has a transverse backband supporting the chains, and sometimes a loose bellyband.

plough-graith (ˈplaʊgreɪθ). *Sc.* [f. as prec. + GRAITH *sb.*] The harness and equipment of a plough.
1569 *Reg. Privy Council Scot.* II. 62 Tuke away his plewch grayth. **1597** *Sc. Acts Jas. VI*, c. 82 (heading) Destroyers of pleuch-graith [*body of act* pleuchgeire]. **1822** SCOTT *Pirate* iv, There was not a corner of the farm fit for any thing but to break plough-graith, and kill cattle. **1828** —— *F.M. Perth* ii, Locks and bars, plough-graith and harrow-teeth!

ˈplough-ˌhandle, plow-. [Cf. Da. *plov-handel.*] One of the two handles or stilts of a plough.
Some forms of plough had only one handle, esp. where the soil was light.
1483 *Cath. Angl.* 284/2 A Ploghe handylle, *stiua.* **1530** PALSGR. 256/1 Plowe handell, *manche.* **1853** J. STEVENSON tr. *Ch. Historians Eng.* I. 611 Directing the plough-handle, or working iron.

plough-head, plow. [f. PLOUGH *sb.*[1] + HEAD *sb.*[1] Cf. OHG. *pflogis-houbit.*]
†**1.** The share-beam of a plough; a wooden frame to which the share was fixed. *Obs.*
1453–4 *Durham Acc. Rolls* (Surtees) 150, ij plogheuedez. **1483** *Cath. Angl.* 284/2 A Ploghe hede, *dentale.* **1523** FITZHERB. *Husb.* §2 In Sommersetshyre.. the sharbeame, that in many places is called the ploughe hedde, is foure or fyue foote longe, and it is brode and thynne. **1613** MARKHAM *Eng. Husbandm.* iii. B ij b, The Plough head.. is a flat peece of timber, almost three foote in length if it be for clay ground, otherwise shorter, of breadth seauen inches.
2. The front part of a plough: see quots.
1733 TULL *Horse-Hoeing Husb.* xxi. 301 The Plow-Head contains the two Wheels A, B. **1864** WEBSTER, *Plow-head, Plough-head*, the draught-iron at the end of the beam of a plow. **1875** KNIGHT *Dict. Mech.*, *Plow-head*, the *clevis* of a plow. That part to which the draft is attached.

ploughing, plowing (ˈplaʊɪŋ), *vbl. sb.* [f. PLOUGH *v.* + -ING[1].]
1. a. The action of the verb PLOUGH; the result of this, a ploughed furrow.
c **1420** *Pallad. on Husb.* II. 73 In deluyng al, or plowyng, or dichynge. *c* **1440** *Promp. Parv.* 405/2 Plowynge, or erynge, *aracio.* **1523** FITZHERB. *Husb.* §8 In all maner of plowynge, se that thy eye, thy hande, and thy fote do agree, and be alwaye redy one to serue a-nother. **1648** MILTON *Observ. Art. Peace* xxii, One [Act] prohibiting the plowing with Horses by the Tail. **1763** MILLS *Pract. Husb.* II. 197 On sounding the plowings, I found them deeper. **1864** D. G. MITCHELL *Wet Days at Edgewood* 38 Columella urges, like Cato, frequent ploughings.
b. *Carpentry.* The planing of a groove with a 'plough'; the groove so made.
1805 R. W. DICKSON *Pract. Agric.* I. 47 It is a good method to.. unite the different planks by ploughing and tonguing. **1837** WHITTOCK, etc. *Bk. Trades* (1842) 103 Grooving or ploughing, by which a narrow channel is excavated out of the thickness of the timber.
c. *Univ. slang.* The rejection of a candidate in an examination; plucking.
1882 EMMA J. WORBOISE *Sissie* xxxiv, He just escaped plucking or ploughing—I forget which Dr. Heavisides said—'by the skin of his teeth'.
2. *attrib.* and *Comb.*, as ***ploughing-team***, ***-time***; **ploughing-day**: see quot.; **ploughing-iron** = PLOUGH-IRON; **ploughing-land, ground**, arable land; **ploughing-match**, a competitive exhibition of ploughing.
1868 ATKINSON *Cleveland Gloss.*, **Ploughing-day*, the day on which the farmer who has taken a new farm asks, and receives, the assistance of his neighbours' Draughts in getting the necessary ploughing done. **1755** *N. Jersey Archives* XIX. 483 The whole is good Meadow and *Plowing Ground. **1636** MASSINGER *Bashf. Lover* I. ii, In a cause like this, The husbandman would change his *ploughing-irons To weapons of defence. **1694** *Lond. Gaz.* No. 2977/4 A Farm, containing near 160 Acres of Land,.. most *plowing Land,.. with the advantage of Commoning. **1812** SIR J. SINCLAIR *Syst. Husb. Scot.* I. 196 The original *ploughing matches were warmly patronized by Mr. Erskine of Mar. **1845** *Ainsworth's Mag.* VII. 369 Unfortunately, my lord [*sc.* a servant] got a premium at a ploughing-match. **1882** [see MATCH *sb.*[1] 7]. **1949** E. BLUNDEN *After Bombing* 41 Here was a set of anglers, there the ploughing-match. **1976** *Southern Even. Echo* (Southampton) 17 Nov. 6/5 The 1976 Hampshire County Ploughing Match will be at Upper Silkstead Farm, Poles Lane, Otterbourne, next Saturday. *a* **1715** BURNET *Own Time* (1766) II. 25 Vexed to see such waste made upon their estates, in *plowing time especially. **1896** MANNING in *Cath. Mag.* Mar. 187 The next three or four years of your life.. are like the ploughing-time and the sowing-time in the year.

plough-iron, plow- (ˈplaʊaɪən). [f. PLOUGH *sb.*[1] + IRON *sb.* So ON. *plóg-járn* plough-iron, plough-share, Da. *plov-jærn*, LG. *plōg-îsen* (Doorn.), Du. *ploeg-ijzer*, OHG. *pflug-ysen*, Ger. *pflugeisen* coulter, also ploughshare.] Any iron part of a plough, *esp.* in *pl.*, the coulter and share.
1418–19 [see PLOUGH-GEAR]. **1458** *Exch. Rolls Scotl.* VI. 425 Pro aratris, harpicis, et ferro, et factura de plwe irnys. **1523** FITZHERB. *Husb.* §2 In Buckyngham-shyre, are plowes made of an nother maner, and also other maner of ploughe-yrons. **1577–87** HOLINSHED *Chron.* I. 187/1 In passing barefooted ouer certeine hot shares or plough-irons, according to the law *Ordalium.* **1596** SPENSER *F.Q.* VII. vii. 35 Yet in his time he wrought as well as playd, That by his plough-yrons mote right well appeare. **1791** J. LEARMONT *Poems* 120 To the plough irons turn'd the hostile spear. **1844** STEPHENS *Bk. Farm* II. 397 It is.. more economical to sharpen the plough-irons every day.

ˈplough-ˌjogger, plow-. One who jogs or pushes a plough; a ploughman. (*humorous* or *contemptuous.*)
1605 ARMIN *Foole upon F.* (1880) 23 A Country Plow Jogger.. secretly stole a peece of Shoomakers waxe,.. and coming behind him, clapt him on the head. **1658** CLEVELAND *Rustic Rampant* Wks. (1687) 429 A medley.. of Botchers, Coblers,.. Draymen,.. and Plough-joggers. *c* **1787** in *Q. Rev.* Jan. (1882) 66 He was.. a plain man.. who begged to say a few words to his 'brother plough-joggers'. *a* **1852** F. M. WHITCHER *Widow Bedott Papers* (1856) xx. 207, I wanted old Dawson's wife to see't I'd got a pardner ruther above a common plow-jogger, such as hern is. **1862** *Harper's Mag.* Nov. 782/2 City folks most generally fetch along a lot of traps and finery to show off afore us plowjoggers. **1865** *Trans. Illinois Agric. Soc.* V. 255 At least the old plow jogger will be mounted on his buggy seat.

plough-land, plow-land (ˈplaʊlænd). [f. PLOUGH *sb.*[1] + LAND *sb.*[1]: cf. OE. *sullung*, a derivative of *sulh* plough, used in a similar sense in Kent and elsewhere. For the form, cf. ON. *plógs-land* (= plough's land), Sw. *plogland* an acre; and, in sense 2, Du. *ploegland*, Ger. *pflugland.*]
1. *Hist.* The name used in the northern and eastern counties of England, after the Norman Conquest, for the unit of assessment of land, based upon the area capable of being tilled by one plough-team of eight oxen in the year: corresponding to the HIDE of the south and south-west (with which it was often equated), and, like it, embracing originally the meadow and pasture-land, and other necessary appurtenances of the holding.
In Domesday Bk. and other records in Latin, this unit is expressed by *carrucata* (= AF. *carue*, ONF. *caruee*, F. *charuée*, CARUCATE) a derivative of *carruca* plough, while the *hide* is rendered *hida.* It is not possible to say whether 'plough-land' was a translation of *carrucata* or the converse; but we have no instance of the word before the end of the 13th c., and *plough* itself appears first in the 12th. The fact that the counties in which the *carrucata* was the unit of assessment are precisely those in which Danish influence prevailed, favours the theory that the plough-land was of Norse origin; but there are difficulties. ON. *plógs-land* meant an acre, the normal area ploughed in one day. The extent of the normal plough-land, like that of the hide, is usually given as 120 acres; but in numerous instances it fell short of or exceeded this; the variations being prob. due to attempts to make the areal plough-lands correspond with the traditional assessment of the manors, to the inclusion or exclusion of the appurtenances and fallow land, and to local differences in the size of the acre.
The plough-land was divided into 8 ox-gangs, as against the 4 yard-lands or virgates of the hide.
1297 R. GLOUC. (Rolls) 7676 þe king willam.. Let enqueri streitliche þoru al engelonde, Hou moni plou lond, & hou moni hiden al so, Were in euerich ssire, and wat hii were wurþ þer to. *c* **1394** *P. Pl. Crede* 169 þe pris of a plouȝ-lond of penyes so rounde To aparaile þat pyler were pure lytel. *c* **1475** *Pict. Voc.* in Wr.-Wülcker 796/6 *Hec carucata*, plowlonde. **1555** *Act 2 & 3 Phil. & Mary* c. 8. §2 Every Plow-Land in Tillage or Pasture that he shall occupy in the same Parish. **1568** GRAFTON *Chron.* II. 16 A Knightes fee should conteyne .C.lx. Acres, and that is accompted for a plough land for a yere. **1596** SPENSER *State Irel.* Wks. (Globe) 664/1 Ulster.. doth contayne nine thousand plowe-landes, everye of which plow-landes contayneth six score acres, after the rate of 21 foote to every pearche of the sayd acre. **1610** W. FOLKINGHAM *Art of Survey* II. vii. 60 A Plow-land or Carue of land (*Carucata terrae*).. is said to containe 4 Yard-land at 30 acres to the Yard-land. **1628** COKE *On Litt.* 5 Hida is all one as a plow-land, viz. as much as a plow can till. **1656** L. SMITH in Sir W. Petty *Down Survey* (1851) 96 The countrey was divided into plowlands, one plowland being great, and another small, as they were in goodness or badness, for many of the plowlands were but seaventy or eighty acres, others are two or three hundred. **1896** M. T. PEARMAN *Hist. Manor Bensington, Oxon.* 10 The hide or plough-land in Preston-Cromarsh, a part of Benson before the Conquest, consisted of one hundred acres.
2. Land, or a plot of land, under cultivation with the plough; arable land.
1530 PALSGR. 256/1 Plowe lande, *terre labouree.* **1548–9** LATIMER *Ploughers* (Arb.) 17 What sede shuld be sowen in Gods field, in Goddes plough land. **1638** in H. Bond *Hist. of Watertown, Mass.* (1855) II. 997 All the Land lying beyond the Plowland.. shalbe for a Common for Cattle. *a* **1670** SPALDING *Troub. Chas. I* (1829) 11 The marquis of Huntly, with his lady, and virgin daughter, was in the ploughlands in harvest. **1771** MRS. GRIFFITH *Hist. Lady Barton* III. 218 It consists of this cottage, a small plough-land, a close for pasture, and a little garden. **1861** W. F. COLLIER *Hist. Eng. Lit.* 122 Soft woodland.. and rolling plough land.

ploughman, plow- (ˈplaʊmən). [Cf. MDu. *ploegh-man.*] **a.** A man who follows and guides the plough; often used generically for a farm-labourer or rustic.

1271 *Recds. Leicester* (1899) I. 137 Joh. Carucario (le caruer) Plouman. *c* **1290** *S. Eng. Leg.* I. 425/182 Huy comen..plouȝ-Man with his Aker-staf, Archer mid bouwe and knyue. **1362** LANGL. *P. Pl.* A. VII. 3 Quaþ perkyn þe plouȝmon..'I haue an half Aker to herie bi þe heiȝe weye'. *c* **1386** CHAUCER *Prol.* 529 With hym ther was a Plowman was his brother That hadde ylad of dong ful many a fother. *c* **1440** *Alphabet of Tales* 214 Hurde-men & plew-men rescowid his childer fro þis lyon & þis wulfe. **1535** COVERDALE *1 Sam.* viii. 12 To be plowemen to tyll his londe and to be reapers in his haruest. **1548–9** LATIMER *Ploughers* (Arb.) 19 Because I lyken preachyng to a ploughmans laboure and a prelate to a ploughman. **1750** GRAY *Elegy* i, The plow-man homeward plods his weary way. **1807** CRABBE *Par. Reg.* II. 321 Unletter'd swains and ploughmen coarse they slight. **1879** SHAIRP *Burns* i. 34 Now [1786] persons of every rank were anxious to become acquainted with the wonderful Ayrshire Ploughman.

b. *attrib.* and *Comb.* (*a*) appositional, as ***ploughman lad***, etc.; (*b*) with possessive, **ploughman's fee**: see quot. 1885; **ploughman's lunch**, a cold snack, usu. including bread, cheese, and pickle, and freq. served in a public house at lunch-time; also *ellipt.*, as ***ploughman's***; **ploughman's spikenard**, a plant: see SPIKENARD.

(*a*) **1608** TOPSELL *Serpents* (1658) 694 They are found.. among the Pastoral or Plow-men Africans. **1786** BURNS *Scotch Drink* xi, The braunie, bainie, ploughman chiel. **1834** A. CUNNINGHAM *Brit. Lit.* 19 Songs..written by a ploughman-lad.

(*b*) **1885** C. I. ELTON in *Encycl. Brit.* XIX. 735/1 The strict English primogeniture as applied to the rustic holdings, sometimes called *fiefs de roturier* or 'ploughman's fee'. [**1837** J. G. LOCKHART *Mem. Life W. Scott* IV. v. 161 The surprised poet swung forth to join them, with an extemporized sandwich, that looked like a ploughman's luncheon, in his hand.] **1970** R. TREHANE in B. H. Axler *Cheese Handbk.* p. iii, English cheese and beer have for centuries formed a perfect combination enjoyed as the Ploughman's Lunch. **1971** *Oxford Mail* 27 Oct. 1/8 The loaf is to be cut into 200 pieces and eaten as part of 200 ploughman's lunches. **1973** P. THEROUX *Saint Jack* v. 60 We had a ploughman's lunch in the village—beautiful old pub—and went back to London. **1975** *Times* 30 Aug. 10/2 The pubs specialize in lunchtime catering..and you can get a decent 'ploughman's' for between 20p and 30p. **1977** J. THOMSON *Case Closed* v. 73 He treated himself to a ploughman's lunch of bread, cheese and pickle..at the Red Lion.

'ploughmanship, 'plow-. [f. prec. + -SHIP.] The art of the ploughman; skill in ploughing.

1649 BLITHE *Eng. Improv. Impr.* (1653) 219 The very mystery of Ploughmanship lyeth upon the knowledge and practice of them. **1778** [W. MARSHALL] *Minutes Agric., Digest* 65 How to set a Plow is perhaps the most difficult lesson on Plowmanship. **1880** *Dorothy* p. xvi, Both he and they were proud of their ploughmanship.

†**plough-mell, plow-.** *Obs.* [f. PLOUGH *sb.*[1] + MELL *sb.*[1]] A mallet formerly carried on the plough for breaking up large clods; a plough-mallet.

a **1450** *Turn. of Totenham* 151 in Hazl. *E.P.P.* III. 89 The chefe was of a ploo mell, And the schadow of a bell. **1523** FITZHERB. *Husb.* §3 Men that be no husbandes,..that knowe not whiche is the ploughe beame, the sharebeame,..and the ploughe mal. **1765–94** PERCY *Reliques* (1845) Gloss., *Plowmell*, a small wooden hammer occasionally fixed to the plow, still used in the North; in the Midland counties in its stead is used a plow-hatchet.

Plough-Monday, Plow- ('plaʊmʌndeɪ). The first Monday after Epiphany, on which, esp. in the N. and E. of England, the commencement of the ploughing season is, or till recently was, celebrated by a procession of disguised ploughmen and boys (*plough-bullocks, -jags, -stots, -witchers*, etc.) drawing a plough from door to door.

1542 BALE *Yet a Course* 28 Than ought my lorde [Bonner] to suffre the same selfe ponnyshment..for not sensinge the plowghes vpon Plowgh mondaye. **1573** TUSSER *Husb.* (1878) 180 Plough Monday, next after that Twelftide is past, Bids out with the plough, the woorst husband is last. **1674** BLOUNT *Glossogr.* (ed. 4), *Plow-Monday*,..on which day, in the North of England, the Plowmen themselves draw a Plough from door to door, and beg Plow-money to drink. **1892** *Times* 12 Jan. 6/2 Yesterday being 'Plough-Monday', as the first Monday after the Epiphany is called.

ploughshare, plow- ('plaʊʃɛə(r)). [Cf. MFl. *ploegh-schere*, Du. *ploeg-schaar*.]

1. The large pointed blade of a plough, which, following the coulter, cuts a slice of earth, and passes it on to the mould-board; = SHARE.

c **1380** WYCLIF *Sel. Wks.* III. 136 Men schal welle hor swerde into plowgh-schares. **1535** COVERDALE *Micah* iv. 3 Of their swerdes they shal make plowshares, and sythes off their speares. **1568** GRAFTON *Chron.* I. 180 If she will go bare footed for her selfe ouer fioure ploughe shares,..brennyng and fire hote. *a* **1639** WOTTON *Descr. Countrey's Recreat.* iv. in *Reliq.* (1651) 532 Wounds are never found, Save what the Plow-share gives the ground. **1795** SOUTHEY *Joan of Arc* III. 540 O'er red-hot plough-shares make me skip to please Your dotard fancies! **1857** RUSKIN *Pol. Econ. Art* 23 A government which shall have its soldiers of the plough-share, as well as its soldiers of the sword.

fig. **1742** YOUNG *Nt. Th.* IX. 168 Final ruin fiercely drives Her ploughshare o'er creation! **1865** SWINBURNE *Atalanta* 107 Thou, I say, Althæa, since my father's ploughshare, drawn Through fatal seedland of a female field, Furrowed thy body. **1871** TYNDALL *Fragm. Sc.* (1879) I. ix. 301 It is the snout of a glacier that must act the part of a ploughshare.

2. *Anat.* The vomer; as ***ploughshare bone*** (*a*).

3. *attrib.* and *Comb.*, as ***ploughshare instinct, line, vaulting***; ***ploughshare-shaped*** adj.; **ploughshare bone** *Anat.*, (*a*) the vomer; (*b*) the pygostyle of a bird.

1831 *Encycl. Brit.* (ed. 7) II. 778/2 The *vomer* or ploughshare bone is symmetrical,..forming the posterior part of the nasal partition. **1835–6** *Todd's Cycl. Anat.* I. 291/2 The *Ischio-coccygeus*..extending..to the sides of the..ploughshare bone. **1870** ROLLESTON *Anim. Life* 18 The terminal ploughshare-shaped vertebrae. *a* **1878** SIR G. G. SCOTT *Lect. Archit.* (1879) II. 187 This twisting of the surface has received the very appropriate name of ploughshare vaulting. **1881** MIVART *Cat* 465 The caudal vertebræ do not end in a 'ploughshare bone'.

plough-shoe, plow- ('plaʊʃuː). A name variously applied, at different times or in different localities, to appliances for covering, protecting, or supporting the ploughshare: see quots.

1377–8 *Durham Acc. Rolls* (Surtees) 387 In yokys, Plushone, harows, cribris, iijs. iiijd. **1405–6** *Ibid.* 222 Pro 1 sok et plogschone, ijs. jd. **1813** BATCHELOR *Agric.* 162 (E.D.D.) Plough-shoe and ground-wrists, £0. 3s. 0d. **1893** *S.E. Worc. Gloss., Plough-shoe*, a piece of iron fastened to the side of the 'throck' to prevent its wearing away with the friction with the soil. **1901** J. T. FOWLER *Durham Acc. Rolls* Gloss., *Plushone*, plough shoes, sledges placed under ploughs so that they may be drawn along the ground without going in. **1903** *Eng. Dial. Dict., Plough-shoe*, (*a*) the ironwork upon which the sock is fixed; the casing of iron at the nose or forepart of that part of a plough which enters the ground; also in *pl.*; (*b*) a wooden frame for conveying a plough upon a road. **1906** HONE *Manor & Manorial Records* 106 A plough-shoe (or iron tip for a wooden share).

'plough-staff, 'plow-. A staff, ending in a small spade or shovel, used by the ploughman to clear the coulter and mould-board from earth, roots, weeds, etc.

1297 R. GLOUC. (Rolls) 2198 Vor ȝe beþ men bet iteiȝt to ssofle & to spade, To cartstaf & to ploustaf. **1483** *Cath. Angl.* 285/1 A Ploghe-staffe, *scudium*. **1573** TUSSER *Husb.* (1878) 37 A plough beetle, ploughstaff, to further the plough, Great clod to a sunder that breaketh so rough. **1667** O. HEYWOOD *Diaries*, etc. (1883) III. 100 He took up the plow-staff and knockt him down. **1740** SOMERVILLE *Hobbinol* II. 53 High o'er his Head His pond'rous Plough-Staff in both Hands he rais'd. **1844** STEPHENS *Bk. Farm* I. 425 Fig. 89 represents the plough-staff, another and a necessary article of the movable furniture of the plough.

†**'plough-start, plow-.** *Obs.* [f. PLOUGH *sb.*[1] + START, tail. So MDu. *ploech-staert* (*c* 1415), MFl. *ploegh-steert*, Du. *ploegstaart*.] A plough-handle, plough-tail.

c **1440** *Promp. Parv.* 405/2 Plowstert, *stiua*. **1530** PALSGR. 256/1 Plowe start, *manche*. **1552** HULOET, Ploughe starte whyche the tylman holdeth, *stiua, æ*.

'plough-stilt, plow-. *dial.* [f. as prec. + STILT *sb.*] A plough-handle.

1523 FITZHERB. *Husb.* §3 The plough stylte is on the ryghte syde of the ploughe, wher vpon the rest is set, the rest is a lyttell pece of woode, pynned fast vpon the nether ende of the stylt, and to the sharebeame in the ferther ende. **1581** *Calr. Laing Charters* (1899) 256 [The sheriff-depute] deliverit the plewch stilt in the said Davidis handis vpone the arabill grownd thairof. **1822** BEWICK *Mem.* 255 To find him so soon attempt to equal his whistling and singing master at the plough-stilts. **1824** SCOTT *Redgaunt.* Let. x, A hand that never held pleugh-stilt or pettle. **1883** *Longm. Mag.* Apr. 645 What farmers want between the plough-stilts are a pair of strong arms.

†**'plough-strake, plow-.** *Obs.* [f. as prec. + STRAKE *sb.*] A piece of hoop-iron for strengthening or repairing a plough.

1395 *Cartular. Abb. de Whiteby* (Surtees) II. 618 Pro ii dosan plewstrakys. **1428** in *Surtees Misc.* (1888) 5 He bad John Holgate mersshall make hym ploghstrakes of drosse and landyren yat he sent hym and na osmundes.

†**'plough-swain, 'plow-.** *Obs.* [f. as prec. + SWAIN.] A ploughman.

1582 STANYHURST *Æneis* I. (Arb.) 17 A labor and a trauaile too plowswayns hertelye welcoom. **1638** SIR T. HAWKINS *Odes Horace* I. iv. (ed. 4) 6 Beasts leave their stals, plough-swaines their Fires forgo.

'plough-tail, 'plow-. The rear or handles of a plough. Symbolically, the following of the plough, the place of the farm-labourer, farm-labour; as in *at, to, from the plough-tail*. Also *attrib.*

1523 FITZHERB. *Husb.* §3 The plough-tayle is that the husbande holdeth in his hande. **1600** J. PORY tr. *Leo's Africa* IV. 230 They forsooke their generall, and returned home to the plough-taile. **1697** DRYDEN *Virg.* (1721) I. *Ess. Georg.* 207 Something of a rustick Majesty, like that of a Roman Dictator at the Plow-Tail. **1712** BUDGELL *Spect.* No. 307 ¶16 A Man..who might have done his Country excellent Service at a Plough-tail. **17..** BURNS *MS. presented to Mr. Riddel* Wks. (1833) 83/2 He..was bred at a plough-tail. **1831** COL. HAWKER *Diary* (1893) II. 32 The men were all from the ploughtail. **1877** R. C. JEBB *Prim. Grk. Lit.* I. ii. 41 How should the axle-tree of a waggon be made, and what is the best wood for a plough-tail or a pole? **1912** *Chamber's Jrnl.* Sept. 564/1 No doubt the chie thought he cut a dash among the plough-tail lads.

'plough-wise, *a.* [f. PLOUGH *sb.*[1] + -WISE.] Said of writing, the lines of which run alternately from right to left and from left to right; boustrophedon.

1883 I. TAYLOR *Alphabet* II. vii. 33 This was succeeded by βουστροφηδόν, or 'plough-wise' writing.

plough-wright, plow- ('plaʊraɪt). [f. as prec. + WRIGHT.] A maker of ploughs.

1285 in W. P. Baildon *Court Rolls Wakefield* (1901) I. 195 Robertus le Plogwryth. *c* **1440** *Promp. Parv.* 405/2 Plow wryhte, *carrucarius*. **1562** *Act 5 Eliz.* c. 4 §30 The Art or Occupation of a Smith, Wheel-wright, Plough-wright, Mill-wright, Carpenter. **1649** BLITHE *Eng. Improv. Impr.* (1653) 191 A plough-wright or plow maker..cannot work true to a false foundation. **1885** W. RYE *Hist. Norfolk* 117 These Thaxters..seem to have been blacksmiths and plough-wrights for generations.

plouh, obs. form of PLOUGH *sb.*[1]

plouk, plook (pluk), *sb.* Forms: 5 **plowke**, 6 **plouke, plucke**, *Sc.* **pluik**, 6–7 **pluke**, 7– **plouk**, 9 **plook**. [Origin obscure: cf. Sc. *plouk, pluke* = PLUG *sb.* Gael. *pluc* a lump, knot, bung, tumour, pimple, appears to be from Sc.]

1. A pimple. Now *Sc.* and *north. dial.*

1483 *Cath. Angl.* 284/1 A Plowke, *pluscula*; *plusculetus*. **1562** TURNER *Herbal* II. 168 b, If they [raisins] be layd to with rue..they heale rede angri nyght ploukes and sores. **1562** —— *Baths* 9 b, This bath..is good..for scalde heades and pluckes in the heade. **1578** J. MELVILL *Diary* (Wodrow Soc.) 64 The twa men war verie read and tead-lyk faced, for ploukes and lumpes. **1579** LANGHAM *Gard. Health* 510 Head plouks and blaines, rub it with the iuice and wine. **1589** R. BRUCE *Serm. Isa.* xxxviii. 1–3 (1591) 1 b, A pestilentious byle..stryking out in many heades or in many plukes. **1804** ANDERSON *Cumbld. Ball.* 106 Aw spatter'd owre wi' reed plouks. **1855** ROBINSON *Whitby Gloss., Plooks*, small scabs or blotches.

†**2.** A small knob placed a short distance below the brim of a metal vessel for measuring liquids, to show the point of exact measure. *Sc. Obs.*

1599 *Burgh Rec. Stirling* (1887) 93 That all stoupis..sal be agriabill in mesour to the jug and stampit with the townis stamp, and that the pluik be benethe the mouth of ilk stoup as followis. **1826** GALT *Lairds* xviii. 163 *note*, Scotch pint-stoups, before the reformation of the imperial measure, were made to hold something more than the standard quantity, but at the point of the true measure a small *papilla* or plook projected, the space between which and the brim was left for an *ad libitum*.

Hence †**plouk, plook** *v.*, *trans.* to furnish (a stoup) with a plouk or measuring-knob.

1580–1 *Burgh Rec. Glasgow* (Rec. Soc.) I. 83 The treyn stoipis to be plovkit and merkit lykwys.

plouked, plooked ('plukɪd, -ɪt), *a.* *Sc.* and *north. dial.* Also 5 **pluccid**, 6 **plukkit**. [f. prec. sb. + -ED[2].] Pimpled.

c **1400** *Destr. Troy* 3837 Polidarius was pluccid as a porke fat. **1513** DOUGLAS *Æneis* VI. Prol. 23 Quhat of thir fureis, or Pluto that plukkit duke, Or call on Sibil, deir of a revin sleif? **1857** J. STEWART *Sk. Scottish Char.*, etc. 132 (E.D.D.) Drunkards and sots Wi' their red plookit noses.

plouky, plooky ('plukɪ), *a.* *Sc.* and *north. dial.* Forms: 5 **plowkky**, 6 **plowkie**, 8 **plouckie, pluggy, plucky**, 8– **plouky, plooky**. [f. PLOUK *sb.* + -Y.] Pimply, pimpled.

14.. *MS. Linc. Med.* lf. 294 (Cath. Angl. 284) For hyme that is smetyne with his awenne blode,..and waxes plowkky, and brekes owte. **1535** STEWART *Cron. Scot.* II. 361 Abhominable to ony man to se, With plowkie visage, bowdin brow and bre. **1822** GALT *Provost* xxxii. (1868) 95 His face was as plooky as a curran' bun. **1868** *Cleveland Glossary, Plooky*, having pimples or small blotches on the surface.

b. *Comb.*, as ***plouky-faced***.

17.. F. SEMPILL *Bridal* iii, Plouckie-fac'd Wat in the mill. **1719** D'URFEY *Pills* VI. 351 Pluggy fac'd Wat. **1825** BROCKETT *N.C. Gloss., Plooky-faced*, pimpled.

plounce (plaʊns), *v.* *dial.* [app. ad. OF. *ploncier*, 3rd sing. pr. *plonce* (Godef.), by-form of *plonger* to PLUNGE; cf. also FLOUNCE *v.*[1]] *trans.* and *intr.* To plunge in water or liquid mud; to duck, souse; to flounder. Hence **'plouncing** *vbl. sb.*

1631 *Min. Bks. Bor. Crt. Dorchester* 6 May (E.D.D.), Mary Tuxderry, for scoulding at the sergeants..is ordered to be plounced when the wether is warmer. **1634** *Ibid.* 23 May, [Three scolds] to be plounced thrice apiece under the water this present afternoone. **1654** GAYTON *Pleas. Notes* IV. viii. 219 Aftir halfe an houres plounsing in this Bathing-tub, you will be eas'd of your paine. *a* **1670** HACKET *Abp. Williams* II. (1692) 200 Our observation must not launch now into the whirl-pool, or rather plounce into the mudd and quagmire of the people's power and right pretended. *a* **1825** FORBY *Voc. E. Anglia, Plounce*, to plunge with a loud noise. **1883** MRS. F. MANN *Parish of Hilby* ii. 27 Wading in after the little rebellious imp, plouncing defiantly a yard or so out of reach.

plounte, obs. form of PLANT.

plousi'ocracy. *nonce-wd.* [f. Gr. πλούσιος rich + -CRACY. The regular romanized form would be *plusio-*.] The rule of the wealthy, plutocracy.

1839 SYD. SMITH *Wks.* I. Pref. 9 To say a word against..any abuse which a rich man inflicted, or a poor man suffered, was treason against the *Plousiocracy*.

plout (plaʊt), *v.* *Sc.* and *north. dial.* Also **plowt**. [Origin obscure: perh. onomatopœic: cf.

PLOUTER.] *intr.* To fall with a splash or plump; to plunge or splash in water.

1825–80 JAMIESON, *Plout*, to splash or dash, implying both sound and action. **1856** J. BALLANTINE *Dawn of Morning* v, Screaming, pouting, plouting, plashing, Tell of tiny elfins washing. **1867** W. S. PLUMER in Spurgeon *Treas. Dav.* Ps. xi. 5, 9 Behold Pharaoh.. and his horses, plouting and plunging. **1898** N. MUNRO in *Blackw. Mag.* Feb. 186/2 A linn.. where the salmon plout in a most wonderful profusion.

Hence **plout** *sb.*, a heavy fall of rain: = PLUMP *sb.*³ 3.

1823 W. TENNANT *Cdl. Beaton* IV. iii. 113 We'll hae a thud o' thunner wi' a guid plout o' weet. **1905** J. G. MCPHERSON *Meteorology* 99 For short periods, the heaviest falls or 'plouts' of rain are during thunder-storms.

plouter (ˈplaʊtə(r)), *v.* Chiefly *Sc.* Also **plowter, plotter.** [app. frequentative of PLOUT *v.*

There are many similar dialect forms, as *ploiter, plodder, plother*: see *Eng. Dial. Dict.* Cf. also Du. *ploeteren*, LG. *pludern, plûdern* to splash in water, bathe with splashing.]

intr. To flounder or move about with splashing in water or mire; to dabble or work in anything wet or dirty; also, to work ineffectually, to potter.

1808 JAMIESON, *Plouter*, to make a noise among water,.. to be engaged in any wet and dirty work. **1833** M. SCOTT *Tom Cringle* xvii. (1859) 478, I found a score of Crusanos all ploutering in the water. **1834** J. WILSON in J. Hamilton *Mem.* v. (1859) 164 We supped on our arrival at Inverness, after ploutering up stairs and sweeping the dust out of our eyes. **1847** E. BRONTË *Wuthering Heights* ix, Miss's pony has trodden down two rigs o' corn, and plottered through, raight o'er into t' meadow. **1861** G. H. KINGSLEY *Sport & Trav.* (1900) 250 He.. saw them plowthering about in the moss-hags as if they had been looking for a wounded stag. **1899** CROCKETT *Kit Kennedy* 297 Your mither has dune naething but plowter aboot the hoose.

Hence **ˈploutering** *vbl. sb.*, also **ˈplouter** *sb.*, the action of this verb, floundering in water; splashing, the sound of splashing.

1806 R. JAMIESON *Pop. Ball.* I. 294 For mony a foul weary plouter She'd cost him through gutters and glaur. **1826** J. WILSON *Noct. Ambr.* Wks. 1855 I. 142 Sometimes playin plouter into a wat place up to the oxters. **1862** NAPIER *Life Dundee* II. 68 There was so much petting and plunging, praying and ploutering, piking in, and pulling out. **1893** STEVENSON *Catriona* xiv. 152 The sea was extremely little, but there went a hollow plowter round the base of it [the Bass].

ploutocracy, -cratic, var. PLUTOCRACY, -CRATIC.

plover (ˈplʌvə(r)). Forms: α. 4 **pluwer,** 4–6 **pluuer,** 4–7 **plouer,** 5 **plouier, plowere,** *Sc.* **pluwar,** 5–6 **plovere,** 6 **plower,** *Sc.* **pluvar,** 6–7 **pluver,** 4– **plover.** β. 4 **plewer,** 5–6 **pleuer,** 6 **plevar, plever, pliuer,** 7 **pluiver,** 8 **pliver.** [ME. and AF. *plover* = OF. *plovier* (*a* 1200 in Hatz.-Darm.), later *plouvier, pleuvier, pluvier*, = Pr. *pluvier*:—late L. **plovārius* belonging to rain, f. L. *pluvia* rain; in mod.L. *pluvārius, pluviārius*; cf. Sp. *pluvial* plover, ad. L. *pluviālis* rainy, also Ger. *regenpfeifer*, lit. rain-piper, and Eng. *rain-bird*.

The connexion with rain expressed in the various names has been variously explained. Belon, 1555, said the birds were so called because most easily taken in rainy weather, which modern observation contradicts. Others, because they arrive in flocks in the rainy season (Littré); according to Prof. Newton, the Golden and Grey Plovers arrive on the shores of the Mediterranean at the approach of winter. Others, because of the restlessness of the bird when rain is approaching: see R. Lubbock *Fauna of Norfolk* (1845) 61–2. Others have attributed it to the appearance of the upper plumage, as if spotted with rain-drops.]

1. The common name of several gregarious grallatorial (limicoline) birds of the family *Charadriidæ*, esp. those of the genera *Charadrius* and *Squatarola*, the former including the ***golden plover*** of Europe (*C. pluvialis*), also called ***yellow*** or ***green plover***, and the closely allied ***field*** or ***golden plover*** of North America, the latter the ***grey*** or ***Swiss plover***, *S. helvetica*; also popularly given to the Lapwing, the eggs of which are sold as 'Plovers' eggs', and in N. America to three birds of the *Scolopacidæ* or Snipe family, the Bartramian Sandpiper, *Bartramia longicauda*, and the Greater and Lesser Yellowshank, *Totanus melanoleucus* and *flavipes*.

α. **1312–13** *Durham Acc. Rolls* (Surtees) 10, l pluuers. **13..** *Coer de L.* 3526 Partrick, plover, heroun, ne swan. **1390** GOWER *Conf.* III. 33 As the Plover doth of Eir I live, and am in good espeir. ?*a* **1400** *Morte Arth.* 182 Pacockes and plovers in platers of golde. *c* **1440** *Promp. Parv.* 405/2 Plovere (bryd), *pluviarius*. ?*a* **1550** *Freiris of Berwik* 397 in *Dunbar's Poems* (S.T.S.) 298 Pertrikis and pluveris befoir thame hes scho brocht. **1594** NASHE *Unfort. Trav.* 42 As fat and plum euerie part of her as a plouer. **1661** LOVELL *Hist. Anim. & Min.* 182 Plover. *Pluvialis*... The flesh is very pleasant, and better than the green Lapwing. **1763** *Brit. Mag.* IV. 156 The wheeling plover, and the timid hare. **1810** SCOTT *Lady of L.* v. xi, Fancy.. in the plover's shrilly strain, The signal whistle heard again. **1843** YARRELL *Hist. Birds* II. 382 The Great Plover's.. shrill and ominous whistle.. is supposed to be the note.. alluded to by Sir Walter Scott in .. the *Lady of the Lake*. **1894** NEWTON *Dict. Birds* 732 The birds just spoken of [*Squatarola, Charadrius*] are those most emphatically entitled to be called Plovers; but the Dotterel, the group of Ringed Plovers.. and the Lapwing, with their allies, have, according to usage, hardly less claim to the name. *Ibid.* 733 Plovers.. must be regarded as constituting a somewhat indefinite group, for no very strong line of demarcation can be drawn between them and the Sandpipers and Snipes.

β. **1390–91** *Durham Acc. Rolls* (Surtees) 597, xviij plewers empt. iij s. **1486** *Bk. St. Albans* F vj b, A fall of Woodecockis. A Congregacion of Pleuers. **1572** *Satir. Poems Reform.* xxxiii. 396 Peirtryks and pleuers pyping on the speit. **1596** DALRYMPLE tr. *Leslie's Hist. Scot.* I. 90 Kaipounis, pliueris and vtheris sik kynd of cheir. **1728** RAMSAY *Lure* 12 Peartricks, teals, moor-powts, and plivers.

2. With defining words, applied to species of the family *Charadriidæ*, and extended to some of the allied *Thinocoridæ* and *Scolopacidæ* or Snipe family, and to the isolated genus *Dromas* (Crab Plover). The chief of these are:

bastard p., † **black p.,** the lapwing; **bishop p.,** in U.S., the turnstone, *Strepsilas interpres*; **black-bellied p.** = *grey plover* (*a*); **black-breasted p.,** in Ireland, the golden plover in its summer plumage; in U.S. = next (*b*); **black-heart p.,** (*a*) in Canada, the American dunlin, *Tringa pacifica*; (*b*) in U.S., *Philomachus spinosus*; **bull-head p.** = *grey plover* (*a*); **chattering p.**: see quot.; **cornfield p.,** *Bartramia longicauda* (see 1); **crab p.,** of the Indian Ocean, *Dromas ardeola*; **crookbilled p.,** of New Zealand, *Anarhynchus frontalis*; **dot p.,** the dotterel (Swainson); **field p.,** (*a*) the American golden plover; (*b*) *Bartramia longicauda* (see 1); **golden p.,** *Charadrius pluvialis*, and the allied American *C. dominicus* (see 1); **grass p.** = *field plover* (*b*); **great p.,** the stone curlew, *Œdicnemus scolopax* (*Œ. crepitans*); **greater p.,** the greenshank (Swainson); **green p.,** (*a*) = *golden plover*; (*b*) in Ireland, the lapwing; **grey p.,** (*a*) *Squatarola helvetica*; (*b*) in Ireland, the golden plover in its summer plumage; (*c*) in Scotland, the knot, *Tringa canutus*, in its winter plumage (Swainson); **heath p.** = *golden plover*; **Helvetian p.** = *grey plover* (*a*); **highland p.** = *field plover* (*b*); **hill p.,** in Scotland = *golden plover*; **Kentish p.,** a British ring plover, *Ægialitis cantianus*; **lark p.,** a quail-snipe of the S. Amer. genus *Thinocorys*, allied to the sheath-bills; **long-legged p.,** the stilt; **mountain p.,** in western U.S., *Podasocys montanus*; **mud p.** = *grey plover* (*a*); **noisy p.** = *chattering p.*; **Norfolk p.** = *great p.*; **oyster p.,** the oyster-catcher; **pasture p.** = *field plover* (*b*); **piping p.,** a N. Amer. ringed plover, *Ægialitis melodus*; **plain p., prairie p.** = *field plover* (*b*); **red-legged p.,** in U.S., the turnstone; **ring p., ringed p.,** one of various small species, ringed or barred about the neck, etc., mostly of the genus *Ægialitis*, esp. the British *Æ. hiaticula*; **rock p.,** in Ireland, = *grey plover* (*a*); **ruddy p.,** the adult male sanderling in summer plumage (Swainson); †**russet p.** = *golden plover*; **sand p.,** a local name for birds of the genus *Ægialitis* (Newton); **sea p.** = *grey plover* (*a*) (Swainson); **silver p.,** the knot in winter plumage; **Spanish p.,** in Jamaica, the willet, *Symphemia semipalmata*; **speckled-back p.,** in U.S., the turnstone, *Strepsilas interpres*; **spotted p.**: see quot.; **spur-winged p.,** any species of *Chettusia*; **stone p.,** (*a*) the stone curlew; (*b*) in Ireland, = *grey plover* (*a*); (*c*) = *ringed plover*; (*d*) the dotterel; (*e*) any shore plover of the genus *Æsacus*; (*f*) the bar-tailed godwit; (*g*) the whimbrel; **strand p.,** in Ireland, = *grey plover* (*a*) (Swainson); **streaked-back p.,** in U.S., the turnstone; **swallow p.,** any species of pratincole (*Glareola*); **Swiss p.** = *grey plover* (*a*); **upland p.** = *field plover* (*b*); **variegated p.,** the turnstone; **whistling p.,** (*a*) = *golden plover*; (*b*) = *grey plover* (*a*) (Swainson); (*c*) the stone curlew; **wry-billed p.** = *crook-billed plover*; **yellow p.,** in Scotland, = *golden plover*; **yellow-legged p.,** in U.S., either species of yellowshanks (*Totanus*): see 1.

1552 HULOET, Plouer called *bastarde plouer, or blacke plouer, *vpupa*. **1839** STONEHOUSE *Axholme* 67 The pee-wit or bastard plover still hovers around its accustomed haunts. **1538** ELYOT *Dict.*, *Vpupa*, a lapwynk or *blacke plouer. **1743** EDWARDS *Nat. Hist. Birds* I. 47 The *Black-breasted Indian Plover.. is something bigger than the Lapwing. **1754** CATESBY *Nat. Hist. Carolina* III. Catal. 2. 71 The *Chattering Plover.. *Charadrius vociferus*. **1893** NEWTON *Dict. Birds* 109 *Crab-plover, the Anglo-Indian name for a curious bird of wide range, frequenting the east coast of Africa from the Red Sea to Natal, as well as the northern.. shores of the Indian Ocean, the Bay of Bengal,.. *Dromas ardeola*. **1785** LATHAM *Synopsis Birds* III. I. 193 *Golden Plover. **1797** BEWICK *Brit. Birds* I. 330 The Golden Plover is common in this country, and all the northern parts of Europe. **1834** MCMURTRIE *Cuvier's Anim. Kingd.* 146 *Charadrius pluvialis*.. (The Golden Plover).. is the most common of all, and is found throughout the whole globe. **1797** BEWICK *Brit. Birds* I. 321 The *Great Plover. Thick-knee'd Bustard, Stone Curlew, Norfolk Plover. **1843** YARRELL *Hist. Birds* II. 381 The Great Plover.. is.. much more numerous in the southern and south-eastern counties of England than far to the west, or to the north. **1678** RAY *Willughby's Ornith* 298 *Greater Plover of Aldrovand: the Venetian Limosa of Gesner. **1590** R. PAYNE *Descr. Irel.* (1841) 7 Heathcocks, Plovers, *greene and gray. **1624** CAPT. SMITH *Virginia* v. 171 Many sorts of Fowles, as.. the gray and greene Plouer, some wilde Ducks. **1678** RAY *Willughby's Ornith.* 308 The green Plover, *Pluvialis viridis*. **1828** SCOTT *Tales Grandf.* Ser. II. l. (1841) 228/2 That beautiful bird the Green-plover, in Scottish called the Peese-weep. *a* **1549** in *Gentl. Mag.* May (1813) 427/1 Plovers *grey the dosen, iij *s.* **1674** RAY *Words, Water Fowl* 91 The Grey-plover, *Pluvialis cinerea*. **1838** *Encycl. Brit.* (ed. 7) XVI. 617/2 The gray plover (*Charadrius squatarola*) .. distinguished.. by a very small hind toe. **1885** SWAINSON *Provinc. Names Birds* 195 Knot (*Tringa canutus*)... But the sober tints of its feathers in winter have caused it to be called .. Grey plover (Scotland). **1828** STARK *Elem. Nat. Hist.* I. 288 *C. Cantianus*... The *Kentish Plover. **1768** PENNANT *Zool.* II. 380 The *long-legged plover.. is the most singular of the British birds. **1840** *Penny Cycl.* XVIII. 285/1 *Himantopus melanopterus*... This is.. the Stilt Plover, Long-legged Plover, and Longshanks of the modern British. **1785** PENNANT *Arct. Zool.* II. 484 *Noisy Plover... Inhabits New York, Virginia and Carolina. **1797** *Encycl. Brit.* (ed. 3) IV. 341/2 The [*Charadrius*] *Vociferus*, or Noisy Plover.. has black streaks on the breast, neck, forehead, and cheeks. **1768** PENNANT *Zool.* II. 378 The *Norfolk Plover. **1797** BEWICK *Brit. Birds* I. 334 The Ring Dotterel, *Ring Plover, or Sea Lark (*Charadrius Hiaticula* [etc.])... These birds.. migrate into Britain in the spring, and depart in autumn. **1785** PENNANT *Arct. Zool.* II. 486 *Ruddy Plover with a black strait bill. **1634** *Althorp MS.* in Simpkinson *Washingtons* (1860) App. p. xxiii, For a *sea plover 00 01 00. **1750** EDWARDS *Nat. Hist. Birds* III. 140 The *Spotted-Plover. **1797** *Encycl. Brit.* (ed. 3) IV. 341/2 The [*Charadrius*] *Apricarius*.. is the spotted Plover of Edwards .. a native of Canada. **1785** LATHAM *Synopsis Birds* III. I. 213 Plover. *Spur-winged. Size of the Golden Plover. **1840** *Penny Cycl.* XVIII. 284/2 The Spur-winged Plovers.. are very numerous and exceedingly noisy. **1893** NEWTON *Dict. Birds* 507 Allied to the Lapwing are several forms .. *Hoplopterus spinosus*, the Spur-winged Plover. **1678** RAY *Willughby's Ornith.* 292 The Godwit, called in some places .. the *Stone-Plover. **1768** WALES in *Phil. Trans.* LX. 117 We shot a few birds, much about the size, colour, and make of a woodcock: these they call here stone-plover. **1840** *Penny Cycl.* XVIII. 279/2 The Couriers.. are closely united to the *Pratincoles*, or *Swallow-Plovers, forming the genus *Glareola*. **1682** S. WILSON *Acc. Carolina* 12 On the grassy plaines the *whistling Plover and Cranes.

† **3.** *Old Cant.* **a.** A 'pigeon', a dupe, a victim. **b.** A courtesan. *Obs.*

1614 B. JONSON *Bart. Fair* IV. v, Here will be Zekiell Edgworth, and three or foure gallants, with him at night, and I ha' neither Plouer nor Quaile for 'hem. **1626** —— *Staple of N.* II. iii, Who's here?.. what Plouer's that They haue brought to pull? *Bra.* I know not, some green Plouer. I'le find him out. **1631** CHAPMAN *Cæsar & Pompey* II. i. Wks. 1873 III. 142 Thou art a most greene Plouer in policy, I Perceiue.

4. *attrib.* and *Comb.*, as ***plover-folk, -net, -shooting***; ***plover-haunted*** adj., ***plover-like*** adj. and adv.; **plover-billed turnstone** *U.S.*, the surf-bird, *Aphriza virgata*; **plover-quail,** any species of *Pedionomus*; **plover-snipe,** any bird of the *Pressirostres*; **plover's provider** = PLOVER-PAGE.

1904 H. SUTCLIFFE in *Westm. Gaz.* 31 May 2/4 Wide wastes of sky and wind, Of hawk and *plover-folk! **1869** T. W. HIGGINSON *Army Life* (1870) 197 Some lonely ride.. on the *plover-haunted barrens. **1873** TRISTRAM *Moab* xii. 217 The sand-grouse,.. *plover-like, kept skimming past in flocks large and small. **1895** *Pop. Sci. Monthly* Apr. 766 We have the pratincoles.. curious little ploverlike birds. **1404** *Nottingham Rec.* II. 22, j. *plover nett, xij d. **1551** *Richmond Wills* (Surtees) 71 To Thomas Parwyne on plower nett with all geyr pertenyng to it. **1874** J. W. LONG *Amer. Wild-fowl* iii. 74 Others, who understand *plover-shooting better than wild-fowling, say, 'Wait for them to double'. **1892** DICKINSON *Cumb. Gloss.* 380 *Sea moose*,.. Plover's page, *Plover's provider.

plover-page, plover's page. *Sc.* [f. prec. + PAGE *sb.*¹] The dunlin (*Tringa alpina*), which is said to attend or follow the golden plover; applied also to other species of *Tringa*, and to the Jack Snipe (*Limnocryptes gallinula*).

1837 R. DUNN *Ornith. Orkney & Shetl.* 86 *Scolopax Gallinula*... Plover Page. Jack Snipe. Judcock. **1861** *Zoologist* XIX. 7342 All the Tringas are called locally 'plover pages'. **1887** A. C. SMITH *Birds Wilts.* 438 It is.. said that a solitary Dunlin will attach itself to a solitary Golden Plover: and this strange notion has extended to the Hebrides, where from its habit of associating with those birds, it is called the 'Plover's Page'.

plovery (ˈplʌvərɪ), *a.* [f. PLOVER + -Y.]

a. Abounding in or frequented by plovers.

1887 STEVENSON *Underwoods* (1894) 30 The plovery forest and the seas That break about the Hebrides. **1903** W. B. YEATS *Celtic Twilight* 136 There is no more ready shortcut to the dim kingdom than this plovery headland.

b. Of, characteristic of, or reminiscent of a plover.

1932 J. JOYCE *Let.* 1 Jan. (1966) III. 239, I would be engaging you with my plovery soft accents.

plow, another spelling of PLOUGH *sb.*¹ and *v.*

plowe, plowgh, -e, plowh, -e, ploy(e, obs. ff. PLOUGH.

plowmb, plowme, obs. ff. PLUM.

plowmpe, obs. form of PLUMP *sb.*¹

†**ploy**, *sb.*[1] *Obs.* Also 6 ployе. [a. OF. *ploi* m. or *ploie* f.:—late L. **plica* a fold. Cf. MDu. *plôie*, Du. *plooi*, MLG. *ploy* a fold, also from Fr.] ? A ply or fold.

1550–1600 *Customs Duties* (B.M. Add. MS. 25097), Henego cloth in longe ploye, the pece xxiiij s. **1662** *Stat. Irel.* (1765) II. 411 Elbing or Dansk cloth double ploy.

†**ploy**, *sb.*[2] *Sc. Obs.* [ad. F. *ploit* (Burguy) = *plait*, *plai*, PLEA.] 'An action at Law' (Jam.).

c **1575** *Balfour's Practicks* (1754) 240 Gif ony persoun being in veritie bastard.. deceissis befoir ony ploy, or clame, or pley, be intentit aganis him be the richteous air.

ploy (plɔɪ), *sb.*[3] orig. *Sc.* and *north. Eng.* [Of uncertain origin.

Some uses suggest an aphetic form of EMPLOY *sb.* 3, 'that on which one employs oneself, or finds occupation'; but evidence is wanting.]

1. Anything in which one personally engages; a piece of action, a proceeding, esp. one in which one amuses himself; a personal enterprise or pursuit, a hobby, a piece of amusement; a game, pastime, or sport; a frolic or escapade; a trick.

1722 W. HAMILTON *Wallace* x. iv. (1774) 205 John was a cliver and auldfarrand boy, As you shall hear by the ensuing ploy. **1768** ROSS *Helenore* II. 84 Says Colen, for he was a sicker boy, Neiper, I fear this is a kittle ploy. **1796** MACNEILL *Will & Jean* II. xxvi, Think o' nought but rural quiet, Rural labour! rural ploys! **1814** SCOTT *Wav.* lxiv, Twa unlucky red-coats were up for black-fishing, or some siccan ploy. **1818** —— *Hrt. Midl.* xviii, One woman is enough to dark the fairest ploy that ever was planned. **1881** *Blackw. Mag.* Apr. 530 They gathered from great distances to such ploys as the sheep-shearing or the sheep-washing. **1900** L. HUXLEY *Life Huxley* I. xviii. 253 He went off for a ploy with Tyndall.. into Derbyshire. **1916** E. F. BENSON *David Blaize* xi. 208, I think you're rather an ass, unless you prefer writing out the 'Æneid' to any other ploy. **1926** R. MACAULAY *Crewe Train* II. viii. 159 Whatever ploy she had on hand at the moment, such as lead casting, table tennis, or naval battles in the bath. **1930** *Times* 16 Apr. 15/4 Training in domestic ploys such as household work. **1936** A. CHRISTIE *Cards on Table* xviii. 175 You'd gone off on your own ploys with the boy friend. **1936** 'J. TEY' *Shilling for Candles* xxiii. 257 Smuggling Edward Champnels might descend to, as a ploy, a mere bit of excitement. **1953** J. TRENCH *Docken Dead* ii. 27 He's obviously gone off on some ploy of his own. **1959** 'M. NEVILLE' *Sweet Night for Murder* xi. 106 'Did you ever accompany her while she was shopping for clothes?'.. 'I wouldn't be much good at that sort of ploy... She didn't need anyone to help her choose what to wear.' **1979** *Country Life* 8 Nov. 1687/1 The search for the alternative life style is.. a new rationalisation of a ruralising ploy.

2. A move or gambit suggested by particular circumstances and made in order to gain a calculated advantage, esp. self-advancement or the frustration of an opponent's intentions; a planned device or manœuvre.

1950 S. POTTER *Lifemanship* 15 Each one of us can, by ploy or gambit, most naturally gain the advantage. *Ibid.* 90 P. Lewis, expert in Oxford Undergraduateship, has set it down as basic to this ploy that, where the Layman would concentrate on his subject, the Gamesman *concentrates on his tutor*. **1955** *Times* 24 June 10/3 Apart from claiming possible support in London and Glasgow and assuring the men that there would be 'important developments during the next 48 hours'—a ploy with which the strikers are becoming a little disillusioned—the speakers had nothing to offer. **1957** *Listener* 13 June 967/3 It is a common 'ploy' of reviewers to take the opportunity of a review to air their own views. **1957** *Economist* 5 Oct. 69/1 Conventional East-West political ploys that took the form of proposing, and rejecting rather more sharply than usual, the suggestion that non-members of the United Nations, such as Red China, should be admitted as observers. **1958** A. WILSON in *Times Lit. Suppl.* 15 Aug. p. viii/2 Whatever the ingenious and at times embarrassing ploys with which English novelists periodically assert their amateur, their unintellectual or their purely entertaining status.. they are.. concerned always to be serious. **1960** 'W. HAGGARD' *Closed Circuit* viii. 105 For suspects there is a standard ploy. You test them. **1966** *Listener* 13 Jan. 78/3 If West held the queen of spades, as he did, it would be East's duty to guard the suit. The only way to accomplish this end was by the unusual ploy of discarding a trump on the third round of clubs. **1970** G. F. NEWMAN *Sir, You Bastard* 267 Perhaps she should cook it and leave it for him, but she recognized that thought as a ploy to delay herself, hoping that he'd return and prevent her departure.

ploy, *v.* [In sense 1, a. F. *ployer*:—L. *plicāre* to bend: see PLY *v.*; cf. MDu. *ployen*, Du. *plooijen*, MLG. *ploien*, LG. *plojen*. In sense 2 app. aphetic for *employ*; in sense 3, perh. back-formation from DEPLOY.]

†**1.** *intr.* and *trans.* To bend. *Obs.*

1481 CAXTON *Myrr.* II. xxiv. 116 Yf it fonde not thayer thycke, it shold not bowe ne ploye. **1578** LYTE *Dodoens* VI. vi. 663 Twigges lyke rushes, the whiche are easy to ploy and twist any way without breaking.

2. *trans.* To employ. *dial.*

1670 COVEL *Diary* (Hakl. Soc.) 262 At all these we ployed our wooden artillery of the spoon. **1871** JONES *Nhb.* 212 (E.D.D.) Gin ye ploy ony fair, hard-workin' lassie. *Ibid.* 263 Macduff, wha was ployed amang the flower-beds.

3. *Mil. trans.* To move (troops) from line into column. Also *intr.* said of the troops. (The opposite of *deploy*.)

1840 SIR C. NAPIER *Mil. Life* II. IV. vii. 213 There.. they acquire the art of ploying and deploying their troops. **1864** in WEBSTER.

Hence **'ployment**, formation of column from line.

1890 in *Cent. Dict.*

†**ployk, pluyk.** *Sc. Obs.* [Etymology obscure: early Sc. *ployk*, *pluyk*, for *plōk*, *plūk*, corresponds phonetically to a mod.Sc. *pluik*, and ME. **plōk*, *ploke*, mod. **plook*, OE. type **plóc*: but no trace of corresp. Eng. forms has been found. Gael. *ploc*, genitive *pluic*, block of wood, stump of a tree, club or bludgeon with a round or large head, is evidently the same word, and, if from Lowland Sc. or Eng., might represent Eng. *block*, ME. *blok*, but this with its short *o* would not give *ployk*, *pluik* in Sc.] A club, bludgeon.

c **1375** *Sc. Leg. Saints* xix. (*Cristofore*) 98 Christofore þis lef has tane, & roydly passit furth allane,.. & his pluyk in til his hand. *Ibid.* 215 In-sted of staf, a ployk [he] had, Wele nere as a perktre mad.

pluch, -e, plucht, obs. Sc. ff. PLOUGH *sb.*[1]

pluck (plʌk), *sb.*[1] Forms: see PLUCK *v.*; also 5 ploke, 7 (? *pl.*) plux. [f. PLUCK *v.*, in a number of disconnected uses. Cf. Du., LG. *pluk*, *plukk-*, the act of plucking, that which is plucked, flock of wool, handful, LG. *plock* handful, flock.]

I. 1. a. An act of plucking; a sudden sharp pull, a tug, a jerk, a twitch, a snatch.

c **1435** *Torr. Portugal* 1624 Glad pluckys there he toke, Set sadly and sare. *a* **1450** *Fysshynge w. an Angle* (1883) 16 þe floote plumbe hym so hevy þat þe lest ploke of any fysche may pluke hym doune yn to þe watur. **1591** PERCIVALL *Sp. Dict.*, *Atenazadas*, with plucks of pincers. **1676** HOBBES *Iliad* (1677) 246 To th' ground Patroclus fetcht him with a pluck. **1691** RAY *Creation* II. (1692) 58 The Plucks and Attractions of the motory Muscles. **1782** MISS BURNEY *Cecilia* v. i, Little dog gave it a pluck; knot slipt. **1863** WOOLNER *Beautiful Lady* 92 Her breath caught with short plucks and fast, Then one hot choking strain.

b. *pluck-up*, the act of plucking up; a pull. †*pluck-up fair*, an old term for a general scramble for booty or spoil.

1573 *Satir. Poems Reform.* xxxix. 199 Than on the morne thay maid the pluk vp fair.. Vpone that spuilȝe I will spend na tyme. *Ibid.* 341 Quhar as he fand vs at the plukup fair. **1894** *Pall Mall Mag.* Nov. 380 A little lugger hanging on astern [of the tug] to get a 'pluck-up' towards home.

†**c.** *fig.* 'A turn, or set-to' (Nares); a snatch; a bout; an attempt; a 'go', 'a smack'. *Obs.*

a **1529** SKELTON *Bouge of Court* 387 (ed. 1568) Let vs laugh a plucke [*vr.* placke] or two at nale. *c* **1537** *Thersites* in Hazl. *Dodsley* I. 413 Now with my sword have at thee a pluck! *c* **1567** Q. ELIZ. in *Harington's Nugæ Ant.* (ed. Park 1804) I. 114 He, of base and basterdlye mynde that wrestells a pluck with the world's order, conceyves therof an evill opynion. **1684** BUNYAN *Pilgr.* II. 158 *margin*, They being come to By-path Stile, have a mind to have a pluck with Gyant Dispair. **1691** SHADWELL *Scourers* IV. i, Haste and lock em up again, I'll try a pluck with thee. **1762** GOLDSM. *Cit. W.* li, There is no work whatsoever but he can criticize.. even though you wrote in Chinese, he would have a pluck at you.

d. *Naut.* A pull or tow.

1918 *Yachting Monthly* Jan. 155 A pluck out of dock, a fishing permit and a light breeze. **1934** 'TAFFRAIL' *Seventy North* iii. 57 'D'ye want a rope's end, ole pal? We'll give ye a pluck home!' Sam's retort to this nautical insult was jocular but mostly unprintable. **1962** W. GRANVILLE *Dict. Sailors' Slang* 89/2 *Pluck*, a tow or tug. **1964** *Roving Commissions 1963* 176 A feeble little motor-boat gave us a half-hearted pluck and went away.

2. In a university or other examination: The act of plucking or rejecting a candidate; the fact of being plucked or of failing to pass an examination.

1852 MRS. SMYTHIES *Bride Elect* xlvi, Visions of a pluck danced before the weary eyes of tutor and pupil. **1860** JESSOPP *Middle-Class Exams.* 12 The proportion of the plucks to the passes. **1888** BRYCE *Amer. Commw.* III. 447 Nearly all American students do graduate.., the proportion of plucks in the later examinations is small.

II. Something that is plucked.

†**3.** ? A small rope attached to a bell-rope. (Cf. IMP *sb.* 7 a.) *Obs.*

1637 *Parish Acc. Wragby, Yorks.* (MS.), Itm for two bellropes and one plucke.. o. 5. 5. **1639** *Ibid.*, Itm for 5 plucks and nailes.. o. o1. 7.

†**4.** *Herring Fishery.* (See quot.) *Obs.*

1758 *Descr. Thames* 227 Fishers distinguish their Herrings into six different Sorts: As the Fat Herring..; the Meat Herring..; the Night Herring..; the Pluck, which has received some Damage from the Nets; the Shotten Herring..; and the Copshen.

5. *Spinning.* (See quot.)

1825 J. NICHOLSON *Operat. Mechanic* 389 In hand-spinning, the pluck, that is, the portion plucked from the sliver or combed wool, was placed across the fingers of the left hand and from the thick part of it, the fibres were drawn, and twisted, as the hand was withdrawn from the end of the spindle, to which it had been previously attached.

III. 6. a. The heart, liver, and lungs (sometimes with other viscera) of a beast, as used for food.

1611 COTGR., *Ventresque*,.. th'offals.. of an (edible) creature; as a calues pluck. **1661** LOVELL *Hist. Anim. & Min.* 23 It may be boiled as that of other beasts, and eaten with butter and vineger; so the plux. *a* **1756** MRS. HAYWOOD *New Present* (1771) 19 The pluck contains the heart, liver, lights, melt, and skirt. **1832** W. STEPHENSON *Gateshead Local Poems* 95 For to make us some pottage, There'll be a sheep's head and a pluck. **1904** *Edin. Even. News* 28 June 3 The Sheriff inquired the meaning of the word 'pluck'. The prosecutor explained that it referred to the internal organs which could be removed at one pull or pluck, the liver, lungs, and heart.

b. In reference to human beings.

c **1710** in J. Ashton *Soc. Life Q. Anne* (1882) I. xviii. 234 [There were the purl houses, where] Tradesmen flock in their Morning gowns, by Seven, to cool their Plucks. **1710–11** SWIFT *Jrnl. to Stella* 16 Mar., It vexes me to the pluck that I should lose walking this delicious day. **1764** T. BRYDGES *Homer Travest.* (1797) II. 369 Boaking as if I'd bring my pluck up. **1897** MARY KINGSLEY *W. Africa* 467, I saw.. five unpleasant-looking objects stuck on sticks. They were the livers and lungs, and in fact the plucks, of witch-doctors.

†**c.** *fig.* The inward part, essence. *Obs.*

1674 N. FAIRFAX *Bulk & Selv.* 57 You must not pull out the pluck of it, and make it quite another thing from number.

7. a. *colloq.* (orig. app. *pugilistic slang.*) The heart as the seat of courage; courage, boldness, spirit; determination not to yield but to keep up the fight in the face of danger or difficulty.

1785 GROSE *Dict. Vulg. T.* s.v., *He wants pluck*, he is a coward. **1808** *Sporting Mag.* XXXII. 34 Inferior in science, and what is technically called *pluck*, to no one. **1813** SIR R. WILSON *Priv. Diary* in *Life* (1862) II. 446 If the enemy have the pluck and force which I expect to find. **1819** *Metropolis* I. 240 He was.. lauded, in the highest terms, by the mob, for what they, very genteelly, called his pluck. **1821** CARLYLE *Early Lett.* (1886) I. 359, I have no pluck in me for such things at present. **1827** SCOTT *Jrnl.* 4 Sept., What is least forgiven.. is want of that article blackguardly called *pluck*. **1835** DISRAELI *Corr. w. Sister* 9 May, All men agree I have shown pluck. **1856** EMERSON *Eng. Traits, Manners* Wks. (Bohn) II. 45 The one thing the English value is pluck. **1879** SALA in *Illustr. Lond. News* 1 Nov. 406/1 Yes! the British word 'pluck' is the word to use. 'Courage', 'bravery', 'heroism' are all too feeble.

b. *Photogr. slang.* 'Boldness' or distinctness of effect: cf. PLUCKY 1 b.

1889 *Anthony's Photogr. Bull.* II. 253, I also saw other negatives of the same scenes developed with potash; they.. gave pictures of greater snap, what some call 'pluck'. **1894** *Brit. Jrnl. Photogr.* XLI. 49 The image will have more pluck and a larger range of gradation.

c. Wine. *U.S. Black slang.*

1964 *N.Y. Times Mag.* 23 Aug. 64/2 *Pluck*, wine. **1967** *Trans-Action* Apr. 8/1 The dudes 'rap' and 'jive' (talk), gamble, and drink their 'pluck' (usually a cheap, sweet wine). **1969** H. R. BROWN *Die Nigger Die!* ii. 24 We went and got some 'pluck' (wine) and I told him I was in college. **1973** *Black World* July 55/1 We want some pluck man, got any scratch? *Ibid.* 56/1 We was gittin away from the broke pluck bottles.

IV. 8. A two-pronged fork with the teeth at right angles to the shaft, for moving dung, etc.

1825 in JAMIESON. **1858** in SIMMONDS *Dict. Trade*, etc.

V. 9. Special Comb.: **pluck side** *Physical Geogr.*, the rough, 'downstream' side of a roche moutonnée from which rock has been plucked by a glacier.

1905 *Jrnl. Geol.* XIII. 6 We will no longer call the two sides of a *roche moutonnée* 'push side' and 'lee side', but we prefer the expressions 'scour side' and 'pluck side' introduced by Shaler. **1942** C. A. COTTON *Climatic Accidents Landscape-Making* xviii. 244 The lee side is termed also the 'pluck' side.

pluck, *sb.*[2] *Sc. dial.* [Origin obscure; cf. Gael. *ploc*: see PLOYK.] A fish, *Agonus cataphractus*.

1810 NEILL *List Fishes* 9 (Jam.) *Cottus Cataphractus*, Pogge or Armed Bullhead; Pluck... This is often taken in oyster-dredges, and herring-nets, but is detested by the fishermen.

pluck (plʌk), *v.* Forms: α. 1 pluccian, 4–6 plukke, pluk(e, 4–7 plucke, 6 pluc, 6– pluck. β. 1 ploccian, 2 plockien, 4 plokke(n. [Common WGer.: late OE. *ploccian*, *pluccian*, cognate with MLG. *plucken*, MDu., MG. *plocken*, Flem. *plokken*; also ON. *plokka*, *plukka* (*c* 1200) to pluck fowls, Sw. *plocka*, Da. *plukke*. These suppose a WGer. type **plokkôn*. Beside these stands ME. *plicchen*, OE. type **plycc(e)an* (PLITCH) = MDu. *plucken*, Du. *plukken*, LG. *plükken*, MHG., Ger. *pflücken* (not in OHG., and still absent from Oberdeutsch dialects), which indicate an umlauted type from **plukkjan*. These words are thought by some to be derived from a popular L. **piluccāre*, inferred from It. *piluccare* to pluck (hair, feathers, grapes), Pr. *pelucar* to pluck (a fowl). OF. *peluchier* (Marie de France, *c* 1180), ONF. *pelukier*, *plusquier*, mod.Norm. and Picard *pluquer* to pick, also clean, peck, Walloon *ploki* to pick (grain); also with *ex-*, Romansch *spluccar* to pluck out, F. *éplucher* to pick, sift; all from a popular L. sb. **pilucca* tuft of hair, deriv. of *pilus* hair, widely represented in the Romanic languages: see PLUSH, PERUKE. (See Diez, Körting, s.v. *piluccare*, Kluge s.v. *pflücken*)

It has been suggested that the late L. or Romanic word was taken into Low German in connexion with the trade in down and feathers on the coasts of the North Sea; but, in spite of the close similarity of form and sense, there are chronological, historical, and phonetic difficulties, which are increased by the entire lack of evidence of the occurrence of either the Teutonic or the Romanic word before the 10th c. Cf. Franck s.v. *plukken*.]

1. a. *trans.* To pull off (a flower, fruit, leaf, hair, feather, etc.) from where it grows; to pick off or out; to pick, cull, gather. Also *intr.* for *pass.*

a **1000** *Ags. Voc.* in Wr.-Wülcker 200/6 *Carpunt, uellint,* plucciaþ. *Ibid.* 222/40 *Discerpit, lacerat,* toslit, i. *deuorat, carpit,* ploccaþ. *c* **1000** ÆLFRIC *Hom.* (Th.) I. 212 þa lareowas an Godes cyrcan, þe pluccia𝔡 þa cwydas 𝔡æra apostola. *c* **1000** *Ags. Gosp.* Matt. xii. 1 Hiȝ ongunnun pluccian [*c* **1160** *Hatton G.* plockien] þa ear & ætan. *c* **1350** *Nominale Gall.-Angl.* 228 (E.E.T.S.) Man of walnote-tre plukith note. **1362** LANGL. *P. Pl.* A. VI. 72 Loke þou plokke no plonte þer, for peril of þi soule. *c* **1380** *Antecrist* in Todd 3 *Treat. Wyclif* 137 þei.. leten here shep perishen, and taken of hem and plucken a wey þe wolle as non herdis. *c* **1440** *Promp. Parv.* 405/2 Plukkyn, or pulle frute, *vellico, avello.* **1567** *Gude & Godlie B.* (S.T.S.) 165 Thay can nocht pluk ane lytill hair Furth of our heid, nor do vs deir. **1591** SHAKS. *1 Hen. VI,* II. iv. 30 Let him.. From off this Bryer pluck a white Rose with me. **1611** BIBLE *Gen.* viii. 11 In her mouth was an Oliue leafe pluckt off. **1704** ADDISON *Italy* 2, I pluck'd above Five different Sorts.. as Wild-Time, Lavender, Rosemary, Balme and Mirtle. **1871** PALGRAVE *Lyr. Poems* 139 Plucking the plumes of the Spanish pride. **1945** H. J. MASSINGHAM *Wisdom of Fields* viii. 163 It plucked dead ripe.

absol. **1779** J. DUCHÉ *Disc.* (1790) I. xv. 293 He plucks and eats but still remains unsatisfied. **1868** H. LAW *Beacons of Bible* (1869) 18 She lusted and plucked.

b. *Geol.* Of a glacier: to break loose (pieces of rock) by the mechanical action of ice which has formed around projections and in cavities in the rock; to erode (rock) by this process. Occas. also used of water (see quot. 1930). Freq. with advbs., esp. *out.*

1893 *Bull. Mus. Compar. Zoöl. Harvard Coll.* XVI. 209 The pits which were left where masses of the rock were plucked out and borne away by the moving ice. **1915** L. V. PIRSSON *Text-bk. Ecol.* I. v. 124 The ice at the bottom of the névé fields being frozen into cracks and cavities and around projections in its stony bed, when motion begins, 'plucks' or quarries masses of rock and takes them forward with it. **1930** C. R. LONGWELL *Outl. Physical Geol.* iv. 43 In a stream flowing over horizontal layers of rock, corrasion along joints loosens large blocks, which are then torn or 'plucked' away by the current. In some situations this plucking action is much more important than wear by simple rasping. **1955** M. HOLLANDER tr. *Kuenen's Realms Water* iv. 152 The glacier will from time to time pluck out large blocks from the lower part of the protuberance. **1971** I. G. GASS et al. *Understanding Earth* xv. 220/2 Rocks have been plucked into characteristic glacial shapes.

c. *Printing.* Of ink: to detach and remove the surface of paper during printing. Also *intr.* for *pass.*

1960 G. A. GLAISTER *Gloss. Bk.* 321/1 *Plucking,* a printing fault which is caused by the ink plucking the surface of the paper and leaving irregular white patches in printed areas. **1967** E. CHAMBERS *Photolitho-Offset* i. 6 If 'washing-out' were omitted, the resin would cause trouble by causing the paper to 'pluck', owing to the resin sticking to the paper when printing.

2. a. To pull or draw with a forcible effort; to drag; to snatch. With various adverbs and prepositions: to pull *away, in, out, off, on, up,* etc. *arch.* (Now usually expressed by *pull.*) See also 8.

1377 LANGL. *P. Pl.* B. XI. 109 þe porter vnpynned þe ȝate, And plukked in *panci* priueliche and lete þe remenaunt go rowme! *c* **1440** *Gesta Rom.* ii. 5 (Harl. MS.) þey sawe fully the toode sitting on his brest; And none of hem might pluk it awey with no crafte. **1526** TINDALE *Matt.* v. 29 Yf thy right eye offende the plucke hym out and caste him from the. **1553** T. WILSON *Rhet.* (1580) 170 Giue hym leaue first to plucke of your spurres, ere he meddle with your bootes. **1560** DAUS tr. *Sleidane's Comm.* 295 They plucke vp the drawe bridge immediatlye. **1561** T. HOBY tr. *Castiglione's Courtyer* III. (1577) Q ij b, When shee came to the ryuer.. she fayned to plucke on her shoe. *a* **1591** H. SMITH *Serm.* (1637) 3 Sampson pluckt the house on his own head. **1594** KYD *Sp. Trag.* II. v. 1 (Wks., 1901, 31), What out-cries pluck me from my naked bed. **1611** BIBLE *John* x. 29 No man is able to pluck them out of my Fathers hand. **1698** FRYER *Acc. E. India & P.* 176 He plucked off his own Coat,.. and gave it him. *a* **1713** ELLWOOD *Autobiog.* (1714) 237 Then pressing.. to the place where Morgan stood, he plucked him from thence. **1877** TENNYSON *Harold* v. ii, Pluck the dead woman off the dead man, Malet! **1881** 'MARK TWAIN' *Prince & Pauper* xv. 163 He is the stranger that plucked Giles Witt out of the Thames. **1975** *New Yorker* 19 May 120/2 After the war, the son got a job at the American Embassy, and one day in 1948 was plucked off the street and taken to prison.

b. With *down*: To 'pull down' or demolish (a building). *arch.*

1531 *Dial. on Laws Eng.* II. lv. 158 Yf a man plucke downe hys howse & sellyth yt. **1551** ROBINSON tr. *More's Utop.* I. (1895) 52 They plucke downe townes; and leaue nothing stondynge. *a* **1661** FULLER *Worthies, Surrey* 78 Otherwise (being now plucked down) the form and fashion thereof [Palace of Richmond] had for the future been forgotten. **1847** TENNYSON *Princ.* IV. 395 A rampant heresy.. which might well deserve That we this night should pluck your palace down. **1878** SIMPSON *Sch. Shaks.* I. 8 He.. ordered the church of Notre Dame of Boulogne to be plucked down, and a monument erected in its place.

c. To pull or tear *asunder, in pieces,* etc. Now *rare* or *Obs.*

1526 TINDALE *Acts* xxiii. 10 Lest Paul shuld have bene pluckte asondre off them. **1530** PALSGR. 661/1, I prayed you to stretche it out a lytell, but nat to plucke it in peces. **1599** HAKLUYT *Voy.* II. I. 213 At Feluchia the marchants plucke their boats in pieces. **1674** RAY *Collect. Words, Notes Husb.* 132 Take a Rook and plucking it limbe from limbe, cast the several limbes about your field.

d. *absol.* or *intr.* To draw or drag; to snatch or take by force, to steal; †to draw cards from the pack (*obs.*). Cf. PICK *v.*[1] 9 b.

1340–70 *Alex. & Dind.* 296 Ne sette solow on þe feld ne sowe none erþe, In ony place of þe plow to plokke wiþ oxen. **1494** FABYAN *Chron.* VI. cxcvii. 204 Eueryche of theym was constrayned to plucke & stele from other. **1570** *Satir. Poems Reform.* xvi. 3 And euerie man dois pluke and pow, And that the pure may finde. **1606** *Choice, Chance,* etc. G j, He that wil not pluck for a card, is not worthie of a prime. *a* **1625** FLETCHER & MASS. *Cust. Country* I. i, Would any man stand plucking for the ace of harts, With one pack of cards, all days on's life?

3. *fig.* **a.** *trans.* To pull, draw, or snatch something intangible, or something from or into a state or condition; to bring (disaster, etc.) *upon* a person; to snatch, rescue *from* danger, etc. Now *rare.*

1387–8 [see PLUCKING *vbl. sb.* 1]. **1534** TINDALE *Matt.* xi. 12 The kyngdome of heven suffreth violence, and they that go to it with violence pluck [1526 pull] it vnto them. **1535** COVERDALE *Amos* iii. 11 Thy strength shalbe plucte from the, and thy palaces robbed. **1549** COVERDALE, etc. *Erasm. Par. Rom.* 18 Fleashly luste pluckyng to euyll. **1563** WINȜET *Wks.* (S.T.S.) II. 54 Thai nocht content.. euir ar desyrous to eik sum thing to religioun, to change, or to pluk fra it. **1570** BILLINGSLEY *Euclid* I. def. vii. 2 You must conceiue them in mynde, plucking them by imagination from all matter. **1607** SHAKS. *Cor.* I. iii. 8 When yet hee was but tender-bodied..; when youth with comelinesse pluck'd all gaze his way. **1673** *Ess. Educ. Gentlewom.* 27 One Athaliah, married to Joram, plucks ruine upon the House of Jehosaphat. **1719** YOUNG *Busiris* v. i, I leave a mark behind, Shall pluck the shining age from vulgar time. **1842** TENNYSON *Two Voices* 118 'Hard task, to pluck resolve', I cried, 'From emptiness and the waste wide Of that abyss, or scornful pride!' **1865** DICKENS *Mut. Fr.* III. ix, The grim life out of which she had plucked her brother.

†**b.** With *down* or some equivalent: To bring down, bring low; to humble, humiliate; to 'pull down' (in strength). *Obs.*

to pluck down a side: i.e. with which a person plays.

1545 ASCHAM *Toxoph.* (Arb.) 19 Other that neuer learned to shote,.. wyll be as busie as the best, but suche one commonly plucketh doune a syde. **1555** BRADFORD in Strype *Eccl. Mem.* (1721) III. App. xlv. 131 Other men in Ingland, whose stoutnes must be plucked lowe. **1567** *Trial Treas.* (1850) 42 This gere I suppose will plucke downe your fleshe. **1611** BEAUM. & FL. *Maid's Trag.* II. i, She will pluck down a side. **1628** LAUD *Diary* 30 Sept., Tuesday, Septemb. ult., I was sore plucked with this sickness. *c* **1672** WOOD *Life* 9 Apr. an. 1659 (O.H.S.) I. 277 A tertian ague.. pluck'd downe his body much.

c. In phr. *to pluck a rose*: of women, to visit the lavatory; to urinate or defecate. *slang.*

1613 BEAUMONT & FLETCHER *Knight of Burning Pestle* 11, Then up and ride, Or if it will please you walke for your repose, Or sit or if you will go plucke a rose. **1730** SWIFT *Panegyrick on the D—n* in *Miscellanies* V. (1735) 139 The bashful Maid, to hide her Blush; shall creep no more behind a Bush; Here unobserv'd, she boldly goes, As who should say to pluck a Rose. **1745** in J. R. Hetherington *Selina's Aunt* (1965) 21/1 Those ladies, who are so proud and lazy, that they will not be at the Pains of stepping into the Garden to pluck a Rose, but keep an odious Implement, sometimes in the Bedchamber itself.. which they make Use of to ease their worst Necessities. **1768** STERNE *Sentimental Journey* I. 203 Grieve not, gentle traveller, to let Madame de Rambouliet p-ss on—And, ye fair mystic nymphs! Go each one *pluck your rose.* **1785** F. GROSE *Classical Dict. Vulgar Tongue, To pluck a rose,* an expression said to be used by women, for going to the necessary house, which in the country usually stands in the garden. **1800** in *Proc. Amer. Antiquarian Soc.* (1897) XII. 248 Mrs. M. having occasion to pluck a rose as is usual with delicate women after a ride of 22 miles. **1937** PARTRIDGE *Dict. Slang* 641/1 *Pluck a rose,* to visit the privy.

d. *U.S. Mil. slang.* To cashier or retire (an officer).

1941 *Sun* (Baltimore) 5 Aug. 11/3 There are numerous retirements under way. However, it is highly unlikely that the army will make announcement of the officers who are being 'plucked' under the recent act permitting the Secretary of War to retire those whom a board has decreed to be 'unsuited for further active duty'. **1942** BERREY & VAN DEN BARK *Amer. Thes. Slang* §888/5 *Pluck,* to retire an officer.

4. a. To give a pull at; to pull abruptly or with a jerk; to twitch; to sound (the strings of a musical instrument) by doing this, to twang. Also, to pull (a person or animal) *by* some part of the body or dress.

to pluck the Proctor's gown, the means formerly used (and understood to be still usable) to challenge the granting of a degree to a person, notwithstanding his having passed the requisite examinations. See J. Wells *Oxford Degree Ceremony* (1906) 5, 9–10; also *N. & Q.* 9th ser. VI. 74.

14.. *Erasmus* in Horstm. *Altengl. Leg.* (1878) 202 (Bedf. MS.), [Passion] xxvi[ti] was plukkyng his flesshe withe fullers combes. *a* **1450** *Knt. de la Tour* (1868) 23 They.. plucked eche other bi the here of the hede. **1577** B. GOOGE *Heresbach's Husb.* III. (1586) 154 b, To make them feerce and curst, you must plucke them by the eares. **1605** SHAKS. *Lear* III. vii. 36 By the kinde Gods, 'tis most ignobly done To plucke me by the Beard. **1653** H. COGAN tr. *Pinto's Trav.* xxiii. 85 Some of his friends pluckt him two or three times by the surplis for to make him give over. **1770** GOLDSM. *Des. Vill.* 184 Children.. pluck'd his gown. **1879** STAINER *Music of Bible* 52 Strings which, when the keys were pressed down, were plucked by quills. **1879** F. TAYLOR in Grove *Dict. Mus.* II. 7/1 In the so-called Musical Box.. a series of metal tongues are plucked by pins or studs fixed in a revolving barrel.

1846 [see sense 7]. **1853** 'C. BEDE' *Verdant Green* I. xi. *note,* The proctor then walks once up and down the room, so that any person who objects to the degree being granted may signify the same by pulling or 'plucking' the proctor's robes. **1900** T. FOWLER in *N. & Q.* 9th Ser. VI. 74, I believe.. that I was the last proctor who was the subject of this ceremony. During my procuratorial year [1862–3].. the 'pen-wiper', a small piece of folded silk which is attached to the back of the proctor's gown (not 'the proctor's sleeve'..) was duly plucked on each successive degree day, the college dean.. informing me in a whisper to which candidate he objected.

b. *intr.* To pull sharply or forcibly, to tug (*at* something). Also, to make a sudden movement in order to lay hold of something; to snatch *at.*

c **1410** HOCCLEVE *Mother of God* 20 þat with his handes tweye, And his might, plukke wole at the balance. **1481** CAXTON *Reynard* viii. (Arb.) 15 He [the bear] wrastled and plucked so harde and so sore that he gate out his heed. **1597** SHAKS. *2 Hen IV,* IV. i. 208 Plucking to vnfixe an Enemie, Hee doth vnfasten so, and shake a friend. *c* **1672** WOOD *Life* 14 May an. 1657 (O.H.S.) I. 219 However he plucked at them [bell-ropes] often with some of his fellow-colleagues for recreation sake. **1864** TENNYSON *En. Ard.* 366 But when the children pluck'd at him to go, He laugh'd, and yielded readily to their wish.

c. *trans.* To disentangle and straighten (wool) by means of a PLUCKER.

1695 J. EDWARDS *Perfect. Script.* 258 Those who deal about combing or plucking the wool.

5. a. To pull off the feathers, hair, fruit, etc. from; to strip or make bare; *esp.* to strip (a bird) of feathers by pulling them off.

a crow to pluck: see CROW *sb.*[1] 3 b.

1377 LANGL. *P. Pl.* B. XII. 249 So is possessioun payne.. To alle hem þat it holdeth, til her taille be plukked. *c* **1440** *Promp. Parv.* 405/2 Plukkyn bryddys, *excatheriso.* *a* **1450** *Knt. de la Tour* (1868) 70 That ye plucke no browes, nother temples, nor forhed. **1560** BIBLE (Genev.) *Ps.* lxxix. [lxxx.] 12 All thei, whiche passe by the waie, haue plucked her. **1598** SHAKS. *Merry W.* v. i. 26 Since I pluckt Geese, plaide Trewant, and whipt Top. **1692** R. L'ESTRANGE *Fables* vii. 6 If you dispute [the matter].. we must e'en Pluck a Crow about it. **1841** H. AINSWORTH *Old St. Paul's* II. 300 He had just.. commenced plucking one of the geese. **1860** READE *Cloister & H.* lv, These monks would pluck Lucifer of his wing feathers. **1890** [see PLUCKED *ppl. a.* 2].

b. To shape or thin (the eyebrows) by removing hairs.

c **1450** *Bk. of Knight of La Tour-Landry* (1868) 67 She hadde.. plucked her browes, front, and forehed, to haue awey the here, to make her selff the fayrer to the plesinge of the worlde. **1926** F. SCOTT FITZGERALD *Great Gatsby* ii. 35 Her eyebrows had been plucked and then drawn on again at a more rakish angle. **1932** S. GIBBONS *Cold Comfort Farm* xxii. 291 You shall not find me plucking my eyebrows, nor dieting. **1935** C. ISHERWOOD *Mr. Norris changes Trains* ix. 147 He spent ten minutes.. thinning his eyebrows with a pair of pincers. ('Thinning, William: *not* plucking'). **1974** *Times* 22 Jan. 11/6 Whether you pluck your eyebrows depends on your type of looks.

6. *fig.* To rob; to plunder; to swindle, fleece.

to pluck a pigeon: see PIGEON *sb.* 3 b.

c **1400** *Rom. Rose* 5989 He shal, in a fewe stoundes, Lese alle his markes & his poundes.. Our maydens shal eek plukke him so. **1569** *Reg. Privy Council Scot.* II. 70 To pluk and use piracie upoun the trew marchandis. **1604** DEKKER *Honest Wh.* Wks. 1873 II. 169, I did pluck those Ganders, did rob them. **1805** *Sporting Mag.* XXVI. 55 Her amiable companion.. instead of helping to pluck her grace, never played for a guinea in the course of her life. **1816** *Ibid.* XLVIII. 218 A noble Duke or Lord, would have as little scruple in plucking a pigeon as their inferiors. **1843** LE FEVRE *Life Trav. Phys.* III. III. x. 210 To allow a fair profit to the proprietor without plucking the traveller.

7. To reject (a candidate) as not reaching the required standard in his examination; usually *pass. to be plucked,* to fail to pass in an examination. Also *transf.* (Originally in the universities, whence generally.)

The origin of this is doubtful; originally a candidate might be plucked or refused his degree on other grounds than an unsatisfactory examination. See quot. 1846, and the note under sense 4.

1713 HEARNE *Collect.* (O.H.S.) IV. 172 Dr. Lancaster, when Batchelor of Arts, was pluck'd for his Declamation. **1721** AMHERST *Terræ Fil.* No. 50 (1754) 273 Mr. Scurlock, A.B. fellow of Jesus-college, and a member of the constitution-club was pluck'd, (i.e. disgraced, and forbid to proceed in performing his exercise) for mentioning the word king in his declamation. **1772** NUGENT tr. *Hist. Fr. Gerund* I. 538 Notwithstanding his having been plucked three times in the examination for the subdiaconate. **1820** *Gentl. Mag.* XC. I. 32/2 To expend vast sums in the education of sons, who when they apply for degrees, are *plucked* (as failure upon Examination is denominated). **1846** MCCULLOCH *Acc. Brit. Empire* (1854) II. 338 Those who fail in showing such an amount of proficiency as, in the opinion of the examiners, entitles them to their degree, are said, in the language of the place, to be 'plucked'; a phrase which originates in an ancient custom by which any one, who objected to a degree about to be conferred in congregation, notified his dissent by plucking the sleeve of the proctor's gown. **1885** E. W. HAMILTON *Diary* 10 June (1972) II. 880 Several Baronetcies are to be made. One or two claims were put aside; those who were not to the fore in the Division List on Monday were 'plucked', e.g. Mr. Palmer, which I regret because he has at other times rendered good service. **1886** STUBBS *Lect. Med. & Mod. Hist.* xvii. 386, I have never plucked a candidate.. without giving him every opportunity of setting himself right. **1894** SALA *London up to Date* ii. 31 If you had to pass an examination for the post.. you would in all probability be plucked.

8. pluck up. (See also 2.) **a.** *to pluck up* (*one's*) *heart, spirits, courage,* etc.: to summon up courage, take courage, rouse one's spirits, cheer up.

13.. *Sir Beues* (A.) 632 þo his bodi be-gan to smerte, He gan plokken vp is hertte. **13..** *Seuyn Sag.* (W.) 2325 Pluk up thi cher. **1562** PILKINGTON *Expos. Abdyas* Pref. 9 Let us therefore pluck vp stomackes, and pray with S. Augustine. **1596** SHAKS. *Tam. Shr.* IV. iii. 38 Plucke vp thy spirits, looke cheerfully vpon me. **1719** DE FOE *Crusoe* (1840) I. xii. 210 Plucking up my spirits as well as I could. **1775** SHERIDAN *Duenna* II. i, I'll pluck up resolution. **1867** FREEMAN *Norm. Conq.* I. v. 376 Æthelred seems now to have plucked up a little heart. **1869** TROLLOPE *He Knew* lv, She could not pluck up courage to speak a word in Italian.

b. To pull up; to pull (something) out of the ground or place in which it is planted or set; to uproot, eradicate; to raze, demolish. Also *fig.* Now *rare* or *arch.*

1484 CAXTON *Fables of Æsop* I. xx, [The swallow said] Come with me ye al & lete vs plucke vp al this [flax]. **1490** —— *Eneydos* iv. 18 To arache or plucke vp a gretter tree. **1535** COVERDALE *Eccl.* iii. 1 There is a tyme to plant, and a tyme to plucke vp the thinge, yᵗ is planted. **1568** GRAFTON *Chron.* II. 158 All fortresses and defences by them there made, were plucked vp and destroyed. **1596** DALRYMPLE tr. *Leslie's Hist. Scot.* IV. 205 Vnto the tyme quhen hæresie pluked vpe al monumentes of pietie in Scotland. **1680** *New Hampshire Prov. Papers* (1867) I. 391 Whosoever shall willfully pluck up, remove or deface any Landmark or bound betweene propertie and propertie. **1759** tr. *Duhamel's Husb.* II. i. (1762) 110 He plucked up..some of the most thriving plants. **1844** MRS. BROWNING *Lady Geraldine's Courtship* lxxiv, I plucked up her social fictions.

c. *intr.* or *absol.* To recover strength or vigour; to 'pick up' (PICK *v.*[1] 21 o). Also, to get new courage, to take heart again. (Cf. 3 b.)

1841 H. AINSWORTH *Old St. Paul's* II. 305 Her better health..Heaven be praised! she has plucked up a little since we came here. **1842** DICKENS *Amer. Notes* I. ii. 20 Even those passengers who were most distrustful of themselves plucked up amazingly. **1890** W. C. RUSSELL *Marriage at Sea* I. i. 10 But she had plucked up as she drew towards the close of her letter. **1901** G. B. SHAW *Caesar & Cleopatra* III. 153 He eats another date, and plucks up a little.

9. In phrasal combinations: †**pluck at the crow** (*Sc.* **craw**): name of an old sport, in which a person appears to have been pulled about by the rest; †**pluck-buffet**, app. a competition between archers, in which he who missed or failed 'caught' a buffet from his competitor; †**pluck-crow** *a.*, got by plucking a crow; †**pluck-penny**, name of some gambling game.

1563 WINȜET *Wks.* (S.T.S.) II. 81 Gif thai..imagin thame to rug of his clathis, as thai war playng with him,—*pluk at the craw. **1570** *Satir. Poems Reform.* xxii. 58, I traist in God that anis sall cum the day, Pluk at the Craw quhen barnis sall with yis bird. *c* **1510** *Gest Robyn Hode* VIII. 27 And they shote *plucke-buffet, As they went by the way And many a buffet owr kinge wan of Robin Hode that day. **1593** G. HARVEY *Pierce's Super.* Wks. (Grosart) II. 18 Shrew Prose, thy *pluckcrow implements addresse, And pay the hangman pen his double fee. **1643** [HEYLIN] *Theeves, Theeves* 2 He that is once so skilled in the Art of gaming, as to play at *Pluck-penny, will quickly come to Sweep-stake.

'pluckable. *nonce-wd.* [f. PLUCK *v.* + -ABLE.] Capable of being plucked. Hence **plucka'bility**.

1841 *Tait's Mag.* VIII. 8 The guilelessness of the dove, the pluckability of the pigeon.

pluckage ('plʌkɪdʒ). *nonce-wd.* [f. PLUCK *v.* + -AGE.] The action or process of plucking.

1835 BECKFORD *Recoll.* vi. 63 He..plucked off his beard by handfuls... The details of this frantic pluckage are to be found in a letter.

plucked (plʌkt), *a. colloq.* [f. PLUCK *sb.*[1] + -ED[2].] **a.** Having pluck or courage; usually in Comb., as ***good-plucked***, ***rare-plucked***, ***well-plucked***; so ***bad-plucked***, deficient in courage.

1846 *Swell's Night Guide* 79 At a set to, he is a Dick Curtis the second; and an out and out plucked one. **1848** THACKERAY *Van. Fair* xxxvii, What a good plucked one that boy of mine is! **1857** HUGHES *Tom Brown* I. vii, The bad plucked ones thinking that after all it isn't worth while to keep it up. **1873** *Routledge's Yng. Gentl. Mag.* Feb. 137/2 'You see I'm a plucked'un', he said. **1916** F. M. FORD *Let.* 23 Aug. (1965) 69 George V..really was in some danger... Still he gave the impression of a 'good plucked 'un'.

b. ***hard-plucked***, hard-hearted, wanting in tenderness.

1857 KINGSLEY *Two Y. Ago* iv, A very sensible man,..but a terrible hard-plucked one.

plucked (plʌkt), *ppl. a.* [f. PLUCK *v.* + -ED[1].] In various senses of the verb.

1. a. Picked off; pulled sharply, twitched, etc.

1552 HULOET, Plucked in sunder, *distractus*. **1821** BYRON *Sardan.* I. ii. 605 So let me fall like the pluck'd rose! **1881** BROADHOUSE *Mus. Acoustics* 197 The tone of plucked cat-gut strings..is..much less tinkling than that of metal strings.

b. *Textiles.* (See quot. 1940.)

1799 G. SMITH *Laboratory* I. 197 Fine short plucked cotton. **1940** *Chambers's Techn. Dict.* 654/2 *Plucked*.., the term used to denote uneven thickness in a top, roving, or yarn, generally caused by excessive draft. **1974** H. MCCLOY *Sleepwalker* v. 72 A short coat of plucked nutria.

2. a. Denuded of feathers or hair.

1508 DUNBAR *Tua Mariit Wemen* 382, I thoght my self a papingay, & him a plukit herle. **1886** W. J. TUCKER *E. Europe* 44 [She] sold live geese, and plucked geese on the market here. **1890** *Cent. Dict.*, *Plucked, p.a.*, having the long stiff hairs removed: said of the pelt of a fur-seal.

b. ***plucked wool***: wool from a dead sheep.

1911 in WEBSTER. **1932** E. MIDGLEY *Technical Terms in Textile Trade* II. 156 *Plucked wool*, wool plucked from a sheep which has been dead a few days. Sometimes this term is applied to skin wool. **1957** M. B. PICKEN *Fashion Dict.* 258/1 *Plucked wool*, wool from dead sheep.

c. Of eyebrows: shaped or thinned by plucking out hairs.

1928 R. HALL *Well of Loneliness* xlviii. 449 A handsome young man with severely plucked eyebrows. **1935** R. STOUT *League of Frightened Men* xvii. 237 Her face..with its broad flat nose and plucked eyebrows. **1938** L. MACNEICE *I Crossed Minch* ii. 25 A few signpost details such as plucked eyebrows and lipstick. **1962** M. BARRETT *Return of Cornish Sailor* ii. 15 The plucked eyebrow lifted. **1974** *Times* 26 Oct. 8/8 The corny peroxide blondes with their plucked eyebrows.

3. Rejected in a university or other examination.

1827 *Blackw. Mag.* XXI. 895 Of the three classes of Predicamentists, the fiercest are the Plucked. **1853** 'C. BEDE' *Verdant Green* II. ii, 'I have been examined', observed Mr. Pucker, with the air of a plucked man.

4. *Physical Geogr.* Eroded or broken off by plucking. (Cf. PLUCK *v.* 1 b.)

1893 *Bull. Mus. Compar. Zoöl. Harvard Coll.* XVI. 210 The plucked out material carried away in the form of boulders amounts to as much as one fifth of that removed in the other forms of erosion. **1942** C. A. COTTON *Climatic Accidents Landscape-Making* xvii. 245 Shorn hills may.. present somewhat steep lee sides, perhaps plucked. **1957** J. K. CHARLESWORTH *Quaternary Era* I. xi. The 249 boundary between abraded and plucked surfaces is sometimes that between different kinds of rock.

Hence **'pluckedness**.

1867 *Gd. Words* 657/2 The abject nakedness—more than nakedness—pluckedness of his body.

pluckee (plʌ'kiː). *nonce-wd.* [f. PLUCK *v.* + -EE[1].] One who or that which is plucked.

1831 *Blackw. Mag.* XXX. 339 'It might be safe to pluck it up.' Safe to whom? To the plucker or the pluckee?

plucker ('plʌkə(r)). [f. PLUCK *v.* + -ER[1].]

1. One who plucks, in various senses: see the verb. Often with adverb, as ***plucker away***, ***down***, ***up***. Also †***plucker-at***, one who pulls sharply at, or (*fig.*) carps at, or attacks, another (quot. 1463).

c **1450** *Oseney Reg.* (E.E.T.S.) 15 Of this owre confirmacion agayne-sayers and pluckers a-waye. **1463** G. ASHBY *Prisoner's Refl.* 193 Yef thow be ryght welthy for the seson, Many pluckers-at thow mayst haue. **1495** *Act 11 Hen. VII*, c. 5 The plukkers uppe and takers awey of the seid weares and engynes. **1593** SHAKS. *3 Hen. VI*, II. iii. 37 Thou setter vp, and plucker downe of Kings. **1707** MORTIMER *Husb.* (1721) I. 154 At which time let the Pluckers be nimble, and tye it up in handfuls. **1748** RICHARDSON *Clarissa* (1811) VII. xcvii. 416 Thorns..pricking the fingers of the too-hasty plucker. **1831** [see PLUCKEE]. **1902** N. MUNRO in *Blackw. Mag.* Nov. 589/1 Tales of Fingal the brave and Ossian the plucker of harps.

2. A machine for disentangling and straightening long wool to render it fit for combing: see quots.

1835 URE *Philos. Manuf.* 144 After drying, the wool is removed to a machine called the plucker. **1844** G. DODD *Textile Manuf.* iv. 125 When the wool is dried, it is passed through a machine called a 'plucker', consisting of a pair of spiked rollers fed by an endless apron.

Plückerian (plʊ'kɪərɪən), *a. Math.* [f. proper name *Plücker* (see below) + -IAN.] Applied to certain equations or formulæ expressing the relations between the order and class of a curve and the number of its singularities, investigated by the German mathematician Julius Plücker (1801–1868). ***Plückerian characteristic***, one of the quantities occurring in such equations, denoting some characteristic of the curve.

pluckily ('plʌkɪlɪ), *adv. colloq.* [f. PLUCKY *a.* + -LY[2].] In a plucky manner; bravely, courageously.

1858 TROLLOPE *Dr. Thorne* xxix, 'No', said Frank, pluckily, as he put his horse into a faster trot, 'I won't mortgage that'. **1859** SMILES *Self-Help* 20 He did not.. retire dejected,..but pluckily set himself to work.

'pluckiness. [f. as prec. + -NESS.] The quality of being plucky; pluck.

1864 in WEBSTER citing THACKERAY. **1867** MRS. WHITNEY *L. Goldthwaite* vi, Her quaint, queer expression, in which curiosity, pluckiness, and a foretaste of amusement mingled.

plucking ('plʌkɪŋ), *vbl. sb.* [-ING[1].]

1. The action of the verb PLUCK, in various senses.

1387–8 T. USK *Test. Love* II. xiv. (Skeat) I. 78 By my pluckinge was she to foryevenesse enclyned. *c* **1440** *Promp. Parv.* 405/2 Plukkynge, or pullynge of fowlys. **1560** DAUS tr. *Sleidane's Comm.* 52 The plucking downe of Images, hath procured vs no smale displeasure. **1837** MRS. SHERWOOD *H. Milner* III. xv, The cant phrase of plucking in our universities. **1868** M. PATTISON *Academ. Org.* v. 239 Let the pass-examination, with its attendant pluckings..cease. **1893** *Bull. Mus. Compar. Zoöl. Harvard Coll.* XVI. 195 The southern end of Iron Hill is so much covered with glacial waste that it is not possible accurately to determine the relative amount of plucking which went on there. **1937** WOOLDRIDGE & MORGAN *Physical Basis Geogr.* xxii. 366 Rock-masses on the floor or sides of a glacier may be frozen on to, or into, the ice and removed by 'plucking' in the onward motion of the glacier. **1952** A. VOET *Ink & Paper in Printing Process* xiv. 149 The separation of the paper-ink-plate union..occurs normally in the ink film... This phenomenon, characterized by partial or complete rupture of the paper stock, is known as 'picking' or 'plucking'. **1959** *Washington Post* 31 July 1/6 Legislation passed this week providing for the 'plucking' of some 2500 senior officers was quietly amended..to abolish 'tombstone promotions'. **1960** *Gloss. Paper, Stationery Terms* (*B.S.I.*) 11 *Plucking*, the detachment of superficial zones of the sheet when the adhesion due to an applied external force is higher than the internal cohesion of the paper. **1968** *Gloss. Formwork Terms* (*B.S.I.*) 19 *Plucking*, spalling of the concrete face due to adhesion of concrete to the form.

attrib. *a* **1548** HALL *Chron., Hen. VII* 59 b, Euery man.. hauing either lande or substaunce, was called to this pluckyng bancket. **1959** W. K. RICHMOND *Brit. Birds of Prey* xiii. 150 A cock Sparrow-hawk has several plucking-posts on his beat.

2. *concr.* Something plucked, in various senses. (Cf. PICKING *vbl. sb.*[1] 3 b.)

1648–60 HEXHAM, *Het Plucksel van lijnwaet*, the Pluckings, or loose Threads of linnen. **1823** J. BADCOCK *Dom. Amusem.* 55 Mangel wurzel..would, if permitted to run up,..afford a good plucking of potage vegetables twice a week. **1828** *Craven Gloss.* (ed. 2), *Plucking*, the quantity of worsted plucked from the end of the sliffer, or sliver, and folded over the fingers whilst turning the spinning wheel. **1901** *Scotsman* 9 Apr. 4/4 If I were a planter in Assam..I would never rest till the pluckings of my garden became the staple drink of the native artisan.

'plucking, *ppl. a.* [-ING[2].] That plucks: see the verb PLUCK.

1898 *Westm. Gaz.* 7 Sept. 1/3 Within reach of a plucking hand are the 250 varieties of heather that star the sides of Table Mountain.

pluckless ('plʌklɪs), *a.* [f. PLUCK *sb.*[1] 7 + -LESS.] Without pluck; devoid of courage or spirit. Hence **'plucklessness**.

1821 *Blackw. Mag.* X. 217 You should let those pluckless Tories know the truth. **1824** *Ibid.* XV. 92, I do care for the intense plucklessness of our party. **1832** *Ibid.* XXXI. 142/2 The fear may be great—and it is so among the pluckless—but the danger is small.

plucky ('plʌkɪ), *a. colloq.* [f. PLUCK *sb.*[1] 7 + -Y.] **1.** Characterized by pluck; showing determination to fight or struggle; brave, courageous, daring.

[**1826** DISRAELI *Viv. Grey* II. xv, He can still follow a fox, with as pluck a heart, and with as stout a voice, as any squire in Christendom.] **1842** BARHAM *Ingol. Leg.* Ser. II. *Smuggler's Leap*, If you're 'plucky', and not over-subject to fright. **1857** HUGHES *Tom Brown* I. v, The 'bravos' of the School-house attest the pluckiest charge of all that hard fought day. **1883** LD. R. GOWER *My Remin.* I. vii. 135, I do not think any account of this plucky..adventure has appeared elsewhere. **1889** 'J. S. WINTER' *Mrs. Bob* (1891) 286 You are the pluckiest little woman I ever knew.

b. *Photogr.* Of a print or negative: Bold, decided, bright, clear.

1885 C. G. W. LOCK *Workshop Receipts* Ser. IV. 352/2 It works exceedingly well, and uniformly brings out brilliant and plucky images. **1894** *Brit. Jrnl. Photogr.* XLI. 7 Negatives..strong and plucky in their contrasts.

2. *Geol.* [f. PLUCK *v.* 1 b.] 'Disposed to break away in large irregular conchoidal chips'.

1891 G. P. MERRILL *Stones for Build.* 39 Fine grained compact rocks..break into concave and convex shell-like surfaces... Such stones are called *plucky* by the workmen. **1895** in *Funk's Stand. Dict.*

plud. *Obs.* exc. *dial.* Forms: 4 plodde, 4–6 pludde, 5 (–9 *dial.*) plud, (5 plutte, 9 *dial.* plut). [Origin obscure: cf. Ir., Gael. *plod* a pool, standing water; also PUDDLE *sb.*] A pool, puddle.

1297 R. GLOUC. (Rolls) 11077 In a foul plodde [*v.r.* pludde] in þe stret suþþe me him slong. *c* **1400** *Laud Troy Bk.* 10610 To se the syght hit was delful, How euery plud of blod stode ful. **1482** *Monk of Evesham* (Arb.) 77 Now yn a stynkyng ponde, and now fowle ouerkeuryde yn fenne and plutte. **1527** *Trevisa's Higden* Dyalogue 1 This reason is worthy to be plunged in a pludde. **1781** J. HUTTON *Tour to Caves* (ed. 2) Gloss., *Plud*, a puddle. **1873** WILLIAMS & JONES *E. Somerset Gloss.*, *Plud*, the swamp surface of a wet ploughed field. **1879** MISS JACKSON *Shropsh. Word-bk.*, *Pluts*, temporary pools of water.

'plud-'pludding. Var. of *plod-plodding* (s.v. PLODDING *vbl. sb.*), perh. under influence of PLUD.

1912 W. DEEPING *Sincerity* i. 1 The grinding of wheels and the 'plud-pludding' of drenched horses drifted along the high road.

plue, obs. Sc. form of PLOUGH.

pluff (plʌf), *sb.* (*a.*, *int.*) *Sc.* [Echoic. So LG. *pluf*, Du. *plof* interj.; LG. *pluffen*, Du. *ploffen*, WFris. *ploffien* to puff, explode.]

1. A strong puff or explosive emission of air, gas or smoke (as in the firing of gunpowder), or of dust; hence, *colloq.* a shot of a musket or fowling-piece.

1663 W. SHARP in *Lauderdale Papers* (Camden) I. 131 But this, amongst other great shott, may turn to be a pluff. **1822** GALT *Steam-boat* iv. 78 He went out of the world like a pluff of powther. **1828** J. WILSON in *Blackw. Mag.* XXIII. 494 He calls..on old Ponto, and will take a pluff at the partridges. **1895** CROCKETT *Men of Moss-Hags* xlvii, We could see the soldiers running their horses and firing off white pluffs of powder.

2. A powder-puff. *Obs.* or *dial.*

1816 SCOTT *Antiq.* xxxvi, A veshell that rins ashore wi' us flees asunder like the powther when I shake the pluff, and it's as ill to gather ony o't again.

B. *adj.* Puffed up, swollen. In quot. *fig.*

1673 *Answ. to Seasonable Disc.* 11 All of you look'd as pluffe and big upon the Layty, as starch it self could make you.

C. as *int.* or *adv.* With a pluff; puff! *colloq.*

1860 RUSSELL *Diary India* I. xvi. 253 As I spoke, pluff came a spirt of smoke with red tongue in it.

pluff (plʌf), *v.* *Sc.* and *dial.* [f. as prec.]

1. *trans.* To blow out (smoke or breath) with explosive action, to puff. Also *intr.* to discharge a gun, shoot.

1629 Z. BOYD *Balm of Gilead* 84 These that spend the tyme with pluffing of reeke, which should be better employed. **1826** *Blackw. Mag.* XIX. 249 He..went pluffing disconsolately among the hills.

2. *intr.* To swell up, become puffed up.

1885 SHARLAND *Ways Devon. Village* vii. 110 Hasn't it [the pudding] pluffed (risen) up beautifully?

Hence **'pluffing** *vbl. sb.* and *ppl. a.*; also **'pluffer**, a shooter, gunner (*colloq.*).

1828 J. WILSON in *Blackw. Mag.* XXIV. 278 Is that the pluffer at partridge-pouts who had nearly been the death of poor Ponto? **1852** *Ibid.* LXXII. 220 If in Central Africa, you would suppose they were practising in a menagerie, and you conclude that there must be prime pluffing in Polito's. **1853** MRS. CARLYLE *Lett.* (1883) II. 227 She..slept a fine natural 'pluffing' sleep till one in the morning.

pluffy ('plʌfi), *a.* *dial.* [f. PLUFF *sb.* + -Y.] Having a puffed-up appearance; puffy, fleshy. Of birds, hair, etc.: Fluffy, downy.

1828 HOGG in *Blackw. Mag.* XXIV. 489 A big, dun-faced, pluffy body. **1849** ALB. SMITH *Pottleton Leg.* x. 84 A light pluffy moustache. **1853** G. H. KINGSLEY *Sport & Trav.* (1900) 469 We shall have nothing rising before us but barren pairs and pluffy cheepers [*i.e.* young partridges]. **1861** LEVER *One of Them* xiv. 104 A good-looking fellow—a thought too pluffy, perhaps.

plug (plʌg), *sb.* [app. a. MDu. and early mod.Du. *plugge* a plug, bung, stopper, Du. *plug*; so MLG., LG. *plugge*, *plügge*, LG. *plüg*, also Swed. *plugg*, *pligg*, Da. *plög*. Other types appear in MLG., LG. *plock*, *pluck*, MHG. *pfloc*, *pflocke*, Ger. *pflock*; and in NFris. *plaak*, Da. *plök*. Further history unknown. (Ir., Gael. *pluc* is from Eng.)]

1. a. A piece of wood or other solid or firm material, driven into or used to stop up a hole or aperture which it tightly fits, to fill a gap, or act as a wedge; also *transf.* a natural or morbid concretion having a similar action.

1627 CAPT. SMITH *Seaman's Gram.* ii. 10 A Hause-plug at Sea. **1648** HEXHAM *Dutch Dict.*, *Een Plugge*, a Plugge, or a wooden Pegg. **1660** BOYLE *New Exp. Phys. Mech.* To Ld. Dungarvan, Wks. I. 9 Shutting the valve with the plug,..he is to draw down the sucker to the bottom of the cylinder. **1669** —— *Contn. New Exp.* I. (1682) 161 On which was put a Wooden Plug markt with Ink. **1705** J. TAYLOR *Journ. Edinborough* (1903) 62 The Canopy is not supported by a Pillar, but by..a Pinn or Plugg plac't exactly in the Center. **1706** PHILLIPS, *Plug*, a great wooden Peg, to stop the Bottom of a Cistern or Cask. **1790** J. C. SMYTH in *Med. Commun.* II. 483 The plug or stopper of the Canula was taken out. **1825** J. NICHOLSON *Operat. Mechanic* 464 The aperture being supplied with a plug of the required form, some clay is put into the cylinder, and the piston forced down, by turning the screw, which causes the clay to protrude through the aperture in the shape required. **1845** BUDD *Dis. Liver* 143 A string of small abscesses had formed along them, separated here and there by a plug of lymph. **1861** WYNTER *Soc. Bees* 194 Instantly he drops..a plug of molten solder, which hermetically seals it. **1865** TYLOR *Early Hist. Man.* i. 1 Wooden plugs as big as table spoons put through slits in the under lip. **1899** *Allbutt's Syst. Med.* VIII. 555 Small plugs of horny epidermis can be picked out, leaving pits behind.

b. *spec.* One for temporarily stopping the waste pipe at the bottom of a sink, wash-basin, or bath.

1860 T. HAMILTON in T. L. Donaldson *Handbk. Specifications* I. 221 A neat wash-hand basin, with brass plug, socket, and chain. **1872** W. EASSIE *Healthy Houses* iv. 37 Although not long introduced the ordinary troughs and basins with plugs at the bottom and with supply taps..are sufficiently familiar as not to need any description. **1901** G. L. SUTCLIFFE *Sanitary Fittings & Plumbing* vii. 48 The plug is of the type known as 'sunk', the stud and chain-ring being in the sunk portion of the plug, so as not to project above the bottom of the sink. **1965** A. L. TOWNSEND *Plumbing Second Yr.* iii. 72 The bath will..be fitted with a waste plug and chain. *Ibid.*, The 'pop-up' plug is operated by turning a handle incorporated in the overflow fitting.

c. A device designed to be inserted into a suitable socket to establish an electrical connection; *spec.* one for connecting the lead of an appliance to an electricity supply, consisting of an insulated casing with two or three pins (or, formerly, with one pin and a ring); also (chiefly *colloq.* or as ***wall plug***), a socket fixed to or in a wall for receiving such a plug. Also *fig.* (For *to pull the plug* see sense 2 k.)

1883 J. W. URQUHART *Electric Light* (ed. 2) ix. 286 When it is required to transmit the current to a particular lamp, a metal plug is inserted at the point where the bar connected with the lamp and the bar connected with the machine intersect. *Ibid.* 296 The 'safety fusible plugs' employed in the Edison and Swan systems usually consist of a short length of lead wire. Their function is to melt..should an unduly strong current..be transmitted. **1888** D. SALOMONS *Management of Accumulators* (ed. 3) II. ii. 97 Wall plugs are most useful about a house for attaching a portable lamp or small motor at will. *Ibid.* 98 The portable lamp has a reel of twin wire at its base, with the ends of wires going to the lamp-holder and a connector respectively. This connector fits the wall plug by pushing in the two pins it carries. **1890** *Ibid.* (ed. 5) II. ii. 166 Mr. Taylor Smith's pattern of portable lamp has a reel of twin wire in its base, with the ends of the wires going to the lamp-holder and a connector plug respectively. The two pins of this plug are pushed into the wall connector..to obtain the light. **1891** F. C. ALLSOP *Telephones* vi. 97 When the plug is inserted between the two blocks.., the circuit is closed. **1892** —— *Pract. Electr.-Light Fitting* v. 72 When the plug..is inserted in the socket,..the lamp can be lighted. **1923** T. E. HERBERT *Teleph.* xiii. 316 It is particularly important that during the insertion of the plug the two springs of the jack shall not be short circuited. **1929** E. A. ROBERTSON *Three came Unarmed* vii. 111 Nonie was..stooping to fix into a wall-plug the flex of the standard lamp. **1945**, etc. [see PIN *sb.*[1] 1 m]. **1960** H. PINTER *Caretaker* II. 48 There used to be a wall plug for this electrolux. **1972** *Village Voice* (N.Y.) 1 June 5/4 The whole point of the call, her thinking I was a plug into good connections. **1976** D. PHILLIPS *Planning your Lighting* 13/1 A power point with an outcrop of plugs and flexes feeding a number of different items of equipment is still a common sight.

2. *spec.* in various technical applications; as

a. A small block of boxwood let into an engraved woodblock to replace a damaged part of the surface. **b.** *Die-sinking.* A soft steel cylinder on the end of which an impression is taken from a punch to form a die. **c.** A tapering block of wood driven into a wall between the stones or bricks so as to bear a nail. **d.** *Mining.* The iron wedge or punch which is driven between two other wedges, called feathers (FEATHER *sb.* 16 b), to split rock, coal, stone, etc. **e.** In railways, A wedge-pin driven between a rail and its chair. **f.** *Dentistry.* The filling of a hollow tooth. **g.** The part of a tap or stop-cock which passes transversely through the pipe and cuts off the water or permits it to flow. **h.** A cylindrical piece of wood used in firing a line from a gun in life-saving operations. †**i.** The plunger of a pump.

1766 CROKER, etc. *Dict. Arts*, etc. s.v. *Water*, At the end of which [levers] are jointed four rods with their forcing plugs working into four cast iron cylinders. **1836** BRANDE *Chem.* (ed. 4) 172 The piston having reached the bottom of the cylinder, the plug of the cock..shifts its position, and..the steam enters as before.., and passes in the direction of the arrows to the bottom cylinder, so as to elevate the piston. **1839** CHATTO *Wood Engrav.* 645 *note*, The 'plug' which they [Albert Dürer and his contemporaries] inserted was usually square, and not circular as at present. **1841** *Civil Eng. & Arch. Jrnl.* IV. 30/2 A long coil of rope, ¾ inch diameter, with a stout piece of wood or plug..fastened to it. This plug is intended to be put in the mouth of the gun. *Ibid.* 125/1 The carronade was fired from off the pier, which carried the plug beyond the breakers. **1842–76** GWILT *Archit.* Gloss., *Plug and Feather*, or *Key and Feather*, a name given to a method of dividing hard stones by means of a long tapering wedge called the key, and wedge-shaped pieces of iron called feathers. **1860** BARTLETT *Dict. Amer.*, *Plug*, applied by dentists to a filling of gold or other material inserted in a tooth. **1875** URE *Dict. Arts* (ed. 7) II. 31 This punch becomes an inexhaustible parent of dies, without further reference to the original matrix; for now by impressing upon it plugs of soft steel..we procure impressions from it to any amount. **1875** KNIGHT *Dict. Mech.* 1749/2 An instrument for condensing the filling or plug in a tooth by a rapid succession of strokes. **1881** YOUNG *Ev. Man his Own Mechanic* §1275 The proper manner of making or cutting a plug to drive between bricks. **1893–4** *Northumbld. Gloss.* s.v., The plug and feather was introduced into coal mining by Mr. G. C. Greenwell in 1869. It had been from early times used in lead mining.

j. *Zool.* = PISTON *sb.* 3.

1854 WOODWARD *Mollusca* II. 249 The large central impression is produced by the muscle of the plug (the equivalent of the byssal muscle in Pinna and Modiola).

k. In some old types of water-closet, a stopper which kept the water in the pan and was pulled to let the contents fall into the soil pipe. Now *Obs.* exc. *Hist.* and in phr. ***to pull the plug***, to flush the lavatory; also *fig.* and *transf.*, usu. referring to sudden release or (with allusion to sense 1 c) disconnection.

1859 F. NIGHTINGALE *Notes on Nursing* i. 13 As well might you have a sewer under the room, or think that in a water closet the plug need be pulled up but once a day. **1873** B. LATHAM *Sanitary Engin.* 331 When the handle H which lifts the plug is raised, everything in the basin is suddenly discharged into the trap below, and so into the drain. **1896** T. E. COLEMAN *Sanitary House Drainage* xiii. 97 Should a small piece of paper or other substance prevent the plug resting tightly upon its seat, the water above gradually escapes into the drain, and impure air is then free to enter the building. **1919** R. FRY *Let.* May (1972) II. 451 A real Victorian W.C. *with a pull up plug*. **1934** V. M. YEATES *Winged Victory* xix. 152 Showers of tracers..frightened him and made him pull the plug rather too soon, and..he..saw his bombs burst a long way from his target. **1935** A. J. POLLOCK *Underworld Speaks* 92/1 *Pull the plug*, to start negotiations; proceed; tell the narrative without delay. **1935** D. SAYERS *Gaudy Night* ii. 43 It was not..an agreeable drawing... She took it..into the nearest lavatory, dropped it in and pulled the plug on it. **1939** R. GODDEN *Black Narcissus* xxv. 214 I've come to mend a loose joint in your pipe... The plug won't pull till I do. **1943** C. H. WARD-JACKSON *It's a Piece of Cake* 50 *To pull the plug*, to release the bombs in one go, as distinct from playing the piano. **1943** G. GREENE *Ministry of Fear* I. iii. 60 Pull the plug... Wait till the cistern refills, then pull the plug again. **1948** *Amer. Speech* XXIII. 38/2 [Submarines] *Pull the plug*, to dive or submerge. **1949** D. SMITH *I capture Castle* (1950) iii. 31 It had a huge bath with a wide mahogany surround, and two mahogany-seated lavatories, side by side, with one lid to cover them both. The pottery parts showed views of Windsor Castle and when you pulled the plug the bottom of Windsor Castle fell out. **1961** C. COCKBURN *View from West* vii. 81 The British statesman finds its [*sic*] nearly impossible to make a simple statement..which might not inadvertently pull the plug on himself and flush him..down the drain. **1964** C. MACKENZIE *Life & Times* III. 75 'They must not hurt my seat.' He then pulled up the plug, and pushed it down again. 'Doulton you see.' **1965** *Ibid.* IV. 22 The plug in the water-closet seldom worked. **1972** *Guardian* 4 Sept. 11/1 Pauline Jones..was transferred from Holloway to open prison..and the plug was suddenly pulled out of the big public outcry over the sentence. **1973** *Houston Chron.* 21 Oct. 28 For the first time data are at hand on when to 'pull the plug' on an unconscious patient being sustained artificially. **1974** *Observer* 18 Aug. 11/4 Any prudent banker would have pulled the plug on Court Line long ago. **1977** *Spare Rib* Sept. 12/2 The older lady pulled the plug on her tormentors by prudently using the vibrator.

l. *Geol.* (i) A cylindrical mass of solidified lava occupying the vent of a volcano. Cf. NECK *sb.*[1] 12 c.

1882 A. GEIKIE *Text-bk. Geol.* 256 If the tuff of a cone.. were swept away, we should find a central lava plug or core resembling the volcanic 'heads'..of Germany. **1900** *Q. Jrnl. Geol. Soc.* LVI. 221 Mount Kenya is an ancient much-eroded volcano; the highest peak is formed of the rocks of the central plug. **1944** A. HOLMES *Princ. Physical Geol.* xx. 456 Later, the plug of the conduit was forced bodily upwards, through the dome, thus forming the celebrated 'spine' of Mont Pelée. **1976** P. FRANCIS *Volcanoes* iii. 123 The vent may well become blocked with a slow-moving or stationary plug of lava.

(ii) A mass of rock, esp. salt, which has been forced upwards by tectonic pressures, lifting overlying strata into the form of a dome.

1906 *Prof. Papers U.S. Geol. Survey* No. 46. 67 Lee Hager ..has suggested a hypothesis which explains the origin of these..domes..by the upthrust of an igneous plug. **1918** *Econ. Geol.* XIII. 452 The intrusion or formation of the salt plug has produced a sharp local doming or quaquaversal structure. **1944** *Nat. Geogr. Mag.* Jan. 16/2 Those 'salt domes' or 'plugs' that yield oil may also yield sulphur. **1970** W. G. ROBERTS *Quest for Oil* iii. 30 Salt..flows relatively easily under the high pressures exerted by earth movements, and can be forced into a plug or dome.

m. A sparking plug.

1886 D. CLERK *Gas Engine* viii. 204 The igniting points.. consist of porcelain plugs. **1890** W. ROBINSON *Gas & Petroleum Engines* vii. 225 The igniter..consists of a brass tube..screwed into the end covers at the top of cylinder. This tube contains a plug of porcelain..to insulate the points of the platinum wires. **1902** J. E. HUTTON in A. C. Harmsworth *Motors & Motor-Driving* viii. 151 An English firm has recently introduced a plug which contains no breakable insulators. **1922** J. BUCHAN *Bk. Escapes* viii. 151 They had flown all the way to Egypt without cleaning their plugs! **1948** A. MORGAN *Boys' Bk. of Engines* ix. 110 When a spark jumps across the plug points it ignites the petrol-air mixture in the cylinder. **1973** F. PETERSON *Hand-bk. Lawn Mower Repair* iii. 52 You can clean the old plug with a wire brush, then make sure the electrodes are set the proper distance apart.

3. The cock upon a public water-pipe to which a hose is attached to obtain water for a fire-engine and other purposes; a fire-plug.

1727 BRADLEY *Fam. Dict.* s.v. *Building*, One Leather Pipe and Socket of the same Size as the Plug or Fire-Cock, to the intent the Socket might be put into the Pipe, to convey the Water clean into the Engine. **1812** H. & J. SMITH *Rej. Addr.*, *T. Drury Lane*, Before the plug was found. **1833** *Act 3 & 4 Will. IV*, c. 46 §97 The said commissioners may provide one or more fire engines and fire cocks or plugs. **1875** KNIGHT *Dict. Mech.*, This pipe is closed by a cap or plug, which is removed..when the hose is to be attached.

4. a. Tobacco pressed into a flat oblong cake or stick. **b.** A piece of cake or twist tobacco cut off for chewing, etc.

1728 SWIFT *Past. Dial.* vi, The dean threw me this tobacco plug: A longer ha'p'orth never did I see. **1841** CATLIN *N. Amer. Ind.* II. xlii. 66 Offering him a few plugs of tobacco. **1844** DICKENS *Mart. Chuz.* xxi, Cutting a quid or plug from his cake of tobacco. **1898** *Allbutt's Syst. Med.* V. 853 The tobacco being generally twist or plug.

5. A blow of the fist; a punch, a knock. *slang.*

1798 PITT in Ld. Rosebery *Life* (1891) 208 The bill is to be read a second time tomorrow, and, in spite of many Plugs from Sir W. Pulteney, will certainly pass. **1898** M. DAVITT *Life & Progr. Australia* xxxv. 192 If he hits a man in fighting That is what he calls a 'plug'.

6. a. Applied to a horse: with various connotations. *U.S.*, *Austral.*, and *N.Z. slang.*

Explained in American Dicts. as 'a horse past his prime', 'an old horse worn down by hard work'; a New Zealander knows it as a horse which is 'a good sort'; an Australian authority, as applied to a horse of 15 hands or 15·1, of a good steady ambling character, working well but not fast.

1860 in A. H. Oldroyd *Lincoln's Campaign* (1896) 171 There's an old plow 'hoss' whose name is 'Dug'... He's short and thick and a regular 'plug'. **1872** 'MARK TWAIN' *Innoc. Abr.* xxvii. 208 We bought two sorry-looking Mexican 'plugs'. **1885** HORNADAY *2 Yrs. in Jungle* xxiv. 284 The horses were large and rather raw-boned Australian 'plugs', well qualified for the work they had to do. **1888** *Brooklyn Daily Eagle* 22 Apr. (Farmer *Amer.*), In the first race a plug named Cator was the favorite, but another plug named Battledore won. **1930** V. PALMER *Men are Human* xxi. 195 There would be a moral rot and everyone would be looking for an old plug to ride. **1948** *Chicago Tribune* 12 Dec. (Grafic Mag.) 5/5 He was a hopeless plug and never ran in the money. **1972** *Dict. Contemp. & Colloq. Usage* (Eng.-Lang. Inst. Amer.) 22/3 *Plug*,..a worn-out old horse; a nag.

b. *transf.* An incompetent or undistinguished person. Also, a bloke, a fellow. Also *attrib.*

1848 *Ladies' Repository* VIII. 316/2 *Plug*,..a nickname for a homely man. **1863** in J. D. Billings *Hardtack & Coffee* (1887) 72 Next came General Meade, a slow old plug, For he let them away at Gettysburg. **1899** 'J. FLYNT' *Tramping* II. iv. 278 I'm always willing to be square to a square plug (fellow). *Ibid.* IV. 396 *Plug*, a fellow; synonymous with 'bloke' and 'stiff'. **1900** *Dialect Notes* II. 49 *Plug*... 2. A hard student... 3. A slow, disagreeable person. 4. A short, thick-set person. **1904** 'No. 1500' *Life in Sing Sing* 251/1 *Plug*, a fellow. **1920** S. LEWIS *Main St.* 308 You figure I'm just a plug general practitioner. **1921** [see GEE *sb.*[4]]. **1935** N. ERSINE *Underworld & Prison Slang* 58 *Plug*, a working stiff, an ox. **1948** *Redbook Mag.* (Chicago) Mar. 48/2 You—you broken reed! You doormat! Old steady, unimaginative, dumb *plug*!

c. A book which does not sell well, and becomes bad stock.

1889 *Cent. Dict.* (1890) VI. 4565/1 *Plug*,..a shelf-worn book. **1901** *Dialect Notes* II. 145 *Plug*, a book left on author's or publisher's hands. N.Y. City. **1928** *Publisher's Circular*

21 July 59/2 Out of the vast number of publications issued, some must, indeed, turn out to be plugs. **1930** *Publisher's Weekly* 15 Mar. 1546/1 The so-called plugs are weeded out ..making room for new titles. **1948** H. L. MENCKEN *Amer. Lang.* Suppl. II. xi. 739 *Plug*, a good book that no one wants. **1970** R. K. KENT *Lang. Journalism* 104 *Plug*. 1. (a) a book sold at a reduced price by a publisher after sales have fallen off: in plural, also *remainders*.

d. A steady plodding course. (Cf. PLUG *v.* 4.)

1903 *Eng. Dial. Dict.* IV. 557/2 *Plug*,..a long-continued pull. **1909** *Daily Chron.* 16 Sept. 3/4 The story is of the quiet plug of the prosaic Henry and the meteoric flight of the splendid Len. **1911** A. CHERRY-GARRARD *Jrnl.* 17 Dec. in *Worst Journey in World* (1922) II. x. 359 It was a hard plug up the waves.

7. Short for *plug-hat*: see 11. *U.S. slang.*

1848 *Ladies' Repository* VIII. 316/2 *Plug*, a hat. **1864** WEBSTER, *Plug*,..a gentleman's silk hat; so called from its cylindrical form. (*Colloq.* and *low.*) **1891** E. KINGLAKE *Australian at H.* 6 The reign of the 'stove pipe', or as the Americans have it, 'the plug', is as secure in Australia as anywhere. **1891** KIPLING *City Dreadf. Nt.* 9 He steps into the brougham and puts on—a top hat, a shiny black 'plug'.

8. A draught of beer. *slang.*

1816 'QUIZ' *Grand Master* VII. 184 Come, Sir, another plug of malt.

9. An advertisement; an instance of publicity; a method of drawing attention to (a product, an entertainment, etc.). *colloq.* (orig. *U.S.*).

1902 G. ADE *Girl Proposition* 50 They were friendly to the prosperous Bachelor and each one determined to put in a few quiet Plugs for Sis. **1929** *Variety* 10 July 1/5 Everything gets a Wrigley plug, for the benefit of his gum. **1937** [see CREDIT *sb.* 13 d]. **1946** *Sat. Rev. Lit.* 30 Nov. 5/1 Dale gets in a neat plug for the publisher's blurb on the dust jacket. **1953** *Recorder* 17 Nov. 4/5 Why do you give them [*sc.* Selfridges] a free plug? **1957** *Time* 2 Sept. 27/1 The policy emerged mostly as a clearly reasoned plug for the kind of development job private capital and U.S. aid have been doing in Latin America. **1958** *Spectator* 13 June 762/1 Nobody will be a penny the better off for the debate except Mr. Noel-Baker, whose new book on disarmament..got a series of plugs that not even a film programme on BBC television could rival. **1965** N. GULBENKIAN *Pantaraxia* xiv. 288 It was to give a 'plug' to Jack Barclay..and.. Panelcraft..that I agreed to appear in 'Tonight'. **1973** *Nation Rev.* (Melbourne) 31 Aug. 1442/5 The *Observer* more than compensated..in the same edition as the pious editorial and the color plug. **1978** *Jrnl. R. Soc. Arts* CXXVI. 418/1, I was interested in Sir Monty's plug for engineers to be involved as managers in top management.

10. *Angling.* A lure with one or more hooks attached.

1932 *Kansas City Times* 13 May 22 There is some balm for the fellow who thinks he is paying too much for his plugs, flies and other equipment. **1944** 'N. SHUTE' *Pastoral* i. 5 To take his new rod and his new reel and his new plugs. **1960** M. SHARCOTT *Place of Many Winds* v. 100 These beaches have been known to yield many valuable articles, the best of which are probably the fishing lures, or plugs as fishermen call them. **1967** *Daily Tel.* 21 Oct. 14/6 Orange-coloured plugs are the most killing for late evening. **1976** *Norwich Mercury* 19 Nov. 9/5 Jeremy Epton and Anthony Raywood, 11, were having no success at all dipping a plug into the nearby River Wensum hoping for a pike.

11. *attrib.* and *Comb.*, as ***plug-bat***, ***-bolt***, ***-bullet***, ***-finisher*** (sense 2 f), ***-machine***, ***-point***, ***-pony*** (sense 6), ***-shot***; ***plug-like*** adj.; (sense 9) ***plug number***, ***schedule***, ***song***; **plug-arbor** , an arbor or mandril in a lathe on which a drill chuck is mounted (Knight *Dict. Mech.* Suppl. 1884); **plug-assist**, a heated plunger used in the vacuum moulding of plastics which forces the plastic partially into the mould cavity before the vacuum is applied; the technique of using this device; freq. *attrib.*; hence **plug-assisted** *a.*, using a plug-assist; **plug-bait** = PLUG *sb.* 10; **plug-basin**, a wash-hand basin having a plug-hole for letting the water out; †**plug-basket** (*Brewing*), ? the depression at the bottom of the mash-tun into which the plug drops; **plug-bayonet**, the original form of bayonet, which was fixed in the muzzle of the gun; **plug-board** (*Electr.*), a switch-board in which the connexions are made by inserting plugs (*Cent. Dict.* 1890); also, a similar piece of equipment used with data-processing apparatus, in which receptacles can be interconnected by lengths of wire with a plug at each end, and which is usually made to be removable to facilitate changes of program or function, the receptacles making electrical contact with fixed terminals on the machine when it is in place; **plug-box** (*Mining*), a wooden pipe to carry off water while putting the watertight casing to a shaft; **plug-centre-bit**: see quot.; **plug-cock**, (*a*) a tap having a perforated plug through which the liquid flows when turned on; (*b*) see quot.; **plug-draining**, a system of draining heavy clay land, in which plugs or blocks of wood are placed at the bottom of the cutting to keep the channel open, and are withdrawn after the cutting has been filled up; **plug-drawer**, one who took part in the *plug-riots*, q.v.; **plug flow**, flow of a body of ice or other viscous fluid *en bloc*, with no shearing between adjacent layers; **plug-frame**, a contrivance attached to the beam of a steam-engine, for opening and closing the valves of the cylinder; **plug fuse** *Electr.*, a fuse that is screwed into a socket; **plug gauge**, a gauge in the form of a plug which is used for measuring the diameter of a hole; **plug-hat**, (*a*) (*U.S. slang*), a silk, 'top', or 'chimney-pot' hat [some say, because the head fits in it like a plug]; (*b*) *Austral.*, a bowler-hat; hence **plug-hatted** *a.*; **plug-hole**, an aperture fitted with a plug by which it can be closed; also in *fig.* phrases (cf. DRAIN *sb.* 1 e); **plug horse** *N. Amer.* = sense 6; **plug-joggle** (*Masonry*), a joggle of the character of a plug; **plugman**: see quots.; **plug nozzle**, in a rocket or jet engine, a nozzle containing a central plug that diverges towards the exit and then converges, so that the gas is expelled in a converging annular stream; also *attrib.*; **plug-riots**, a name given to certain riotous proceedings *c* 1842, when cotton mills in Lancashire were stopped from working by the removal or 'drawing' of a few bolts or 'plugs' in the boilers so as to prevent steam from being raised; **plug-rod**, (*a*) see quot. 1858; (*b*) = *plug-frame*; **plug-switch** (*Electr.*), a switch in which connexion is made by inserting a metal plug; **plug-tap**, a cylindrical tap for cutting the threads of female screws or of screw-plates; **plug tobacco** = sense 4; **plug-tree** = *plug frame*; **plug-valve**: see quot.

1958 *Brit. Plastics* XXXI. 20/2 Almost immediately the heated *plug-assist is lowered into the bubble. **1958** *Times Rev. Industry* Aug. 57/2 This machine uses deep-draw, drape, Airslip, and drop-form plug assist techniques either individually or in combination. **1958** *Brit. Plastics* XXXI. 352/2 Drape and *plug-assisted techniques are particularly suitable. **1965** L. A. H. EASTMAN tr. *Thiel's Princ. Vacuum Forming* iv. 41 For single mouldings plug-assisted forming seldom offers any advantage over air-slip forming. **1955** *Plug-bait [see IRONMONGERY 1 d]. **1743** *Lond. & Country Brew.* IV. (ed. 2) 267 Flour of all Malt, especially if it is ground very small, is apt to wash to the *Plug-Basket, and thereby cause a foul Wort to run off. **1837** *Civil Eng. & Arch. Jrnl.* I. 44/2 A hole of two inches diameter having been ..made in each side of the stone, and *plug bats..inserted. **1883** *4th Meeting U.S. Nat. Telephone Exchange Assoc., 1882* 38 Switchboards are generally classified as 'cord' or '*plug' boards. *Ibid.* 39 The plug boards were the favorites. **1946** *Ann. Computation Lab. Harvard Univ.* I. 21 The out-relay,..through which the product is read out of the multiply unit, connects to the buss through a plugboard provided to fix the decimal point relation between the product counter and the buss. **1957** D. D. MCCRACKEN *Digital Computer Programming* 231 A number of the small machines are controlled by a removable plugboard... There are ordinarily many of them with each machine, one for each recurring problem. **1970** O. DOPPING *Computers & Data Processing* xv. 231 In older computers, the distribution of input card fields over different parts of memory was often effected with plugboards as in conventional punched card machines. **1977** *Sci. Amer.* Sept. 155/1 Hardware prototyping mechanisms commonly include wire-wrap breadboard models, plugboard setups or printed-circuit prototypes. **1838** *Ibid.* 258/2 A form of *plug bolt peculiarly adapted for mooring and warping up rapids. **1883** GRESLEY *Coal Mining Gloss.*, **Plug Box*, a wooden water-pipe used in coffering. **1858** GREENER *Gunnery* 390 'Wobbling', a principle inherent in all *plug bullets after leaving the muzzle. **1875** KNIGHT *Dict. Mech.*, **Plug-center Bit*, a bit having a cylinder instead of a point, so as to fit within the hole around which a countersink or enlargement is to be made. **1884** *Ibid.* Suppl., **Plug Cock*, a faucet which is simply driven into a barrel, not screwed in. **1833** *Encycl. Brit.* (ed. 7) VIII. 139/2 *Plug draining..is exclusively confined to the draining of tenacious clay, and chiefly practised on pasture land. **1888** F. PEEL (*title*) The Risings of the Luddites, Chartists, and *Plugdrawers. **1884** KNIGHT *Dict. Mech.* Suppl., **Plug Finisher*,..a fine file for finishing the surfaces of tooth fillings. **1951** *Proc. R. Soc.* A. CCVII. 560 There is then no relative movement except in the lowest layer and the block simply slides downhill as a rigid body... (The corresponding motion in a block between rough plates has been called '*plug flow'.) **1972** B. W. SPARKS *Geomorphology* (ed. 2) xiii. 382 Temperate glaciers in summer are likely to be the most effective agents of erosion especially if they are sliding over their beds and undergoing plug flow. **1974** D. K. SMITH in P. L. Moore et al. *Drilling Practices Manual* xvi. 437 This readily converts to a maximum pump rate in order to remain in plug flow. **1763** FITZGERALD in *Phil. Trans.* LIII. 152 The *plug frame, which is a piece of timber moved by the leaver through a wooden groove, by which the steam valve, and injection cock are opened and shut alternately. **1824** R. STUART *Hist. Steam Engine* 71 In the perpendicular working beam, called by Beighton [? *c* 1720] the plug-frame, there is a slit which is contrived so that its pins work on the fore part, middle, and back part, to raise and depress the levers..that move the iron axle. **1905** *Jrnl Inst. Electr. Engineers* XXXV. 365 The earliest form of Edison *plug fuse dates from 1880. *Ibid.* 405 Enclosed or cartridge fuses..have been developed from the Edison plug fuse. **1971** W. N. ALERICH *Electr. Construction Wiring* xi. 283 (*heading*) Plug fuse designed to pass safely 15 amps. **1895** *Appleby's Illustr. Handbk. Machinery* IV. 129 The *plug gauges above 2 inch are cored out for lightness. **1905** [see LAP *v.*⁴]. **1971** B. SCHARF *Engin. & its Language* vii. 49 Plug gauges (plain, tapered or pin gauges) are used for checking holes, mainly in order to ensure that they are not too narrow at any point. **1863** in J. D. Burn *Three Yrs. Working Classes U.S.* (1965) 223 Fancy a ragged man..with a gun, a knapsack, a butcher's knife and a *plug hat. **1881** *Philad. Record* (U.S.) No. 3455/6 The plug hat is virtually a sort of social guarantee for the preservation of peace and order. **1899** MORROW *Bohem. Paris* 138 A dizzy whirl of skirts, feathers, plug hats, and silken stockings. **1941** BAKER *Dict. Austral. Slang* 55 *Plug hat*, a bowler hat. **1947** Plug-hat [see COW-HIDE *sb.* 4]. **1977** *Time* 14 Mar. 30/1 He chuckled over the memory of seeing Tammany Democrats dressed in their long coats and plug hats but so broke they could not pay their hotel bills. **1891** KIPLING *City Dreadf. Nt.* 4 An austere, *plug-hatted redskin. **1773** *Gentl. Mag.* XLIII. 497 To prevent the steam from coming out at the *plug-hole.. or lid. **1823** J. BADCOCK *Dom. Amusem.* 60 A vessel, having a plug-hole at bottom. **1898** *Westm. Gaz.* 10 Sept. 2/3 While the Post Office..provides and maintains the fire alarm, the County Council undertake to supply the necessary telephones and to make plug-holes in the alarm posts. **1968** *Listener* 22 Feb. 243/1 May I ask..whether the anonymity demanded by the ethics of the 'profession' is now to be regarded as having..gone down the plug-hole? **1973** *Guardian* 28 Mar. 10/6 Nothing escaped so completely as Warhol himself. A positive plug hole of a man around which the bath water swirled. **1973** *Times* 17 May 12/5 That [term] went down the plughole of progress. **1887** *Courier-Jrnl.* (Louisville, Ky.) 4 Feb. 3/5 Wanted—40 *plug horses and mares at Lum Simon's Stables. **1969** N. W. PARSONS *Sagebrush Harp* xviii. 97 Later, Papa bought another plug horse, giving a note due the following fall. **1791** SMEATON *Edystone L.* 194/2 The central *plug joggle, fixed in place.. ready for the reception of the center stone of the next Course. **1875** HUXLEY & MARTIN *Elem. Biol.* (1877) 61 The two [cells]..subdivide and ultimately form a *plug-like, cellular, mass, which imbeds itself firmly in the substance of the prothallus. **1875** KNIGHT *Dict. Mech.*, **Plug-machine*, a machine for making wooden plugs for faucet-holes of.. barrels. **1852** *Mining Gloss.* (in *Northumb. Gloss.*), **Plugman*, the man in charge of a pit pumping engine. **1862** SMILES *Engineers* III. 27 George [Stephenson]'s duty as plugman was to watch the engine, to see that it kept well in work, and that the pumps were efficient. **1883** GRESLEY *Coal Mining Gl.*, *Plugman*, an old term for engineman. **1960** *Astronautics* Apr. 100/2 There are many ways in which such combustors can be combined with a nozzle..to form attractive propulsion system configurations. One possible configuration is a segmented annular combustor with a '*plug nozzle'. **1970** A. V. CLEAVER in N. H. Langton *Rocket Propulsion* II. iv. 136 There would be..appreciable savings in the length and weight of interstage vehicle structures if plug-nozzle engines were used in the upper stages; on the other hand,..the small performance gains would be associated more with the use of plug nozzles on bottom stages. **1933** P. GODFREY *Backstage* xiv. 173 In pursuance of his theory of the value of reiteration de Courville instituted the feature of the '*plug number'. **1884** BOURKE *Snake Dance Moquis* xxix. 315 Our mules and Nahi-vehma's *plug pony stampeded. **1849** COBDEN *Speeches* 90 In 1842, when the country was disturbed by the great *plug riots, not a thread was disturbed from a spindle. **1888** F. PEEL *Risings of Luddites*, etc. xxxix. 338 Trade in 1842, the year of the plug riots, was worse than ever. **1858** SIMMONDS *Dict. Trade*, **Plug-rod*, an air-pump rod. **1875** KNIGHT *Dict. Mech.*, *Plug-rod*, (Steam-engine) *a.* A rod attached to the working-beam of a condensing-engine, for the purpose of driving the working-gear of the valves. Sometimes called the plug-tree. *b.* The air-pump rod. **1878** THURSTON *Growth Steam-Engine* 121 A similar pair of tappets on the opposite side of the plug-rod move the valves. **1947** *Time* 24 Nov. 74/3 Music publishers and recording companies were getting together on '*plug schedules' to ration out the hits. **1901** G. DOUGLAS *Ho. w. Green Shutters* 138 He..ground them [his words] out like a labouring mill, each word solid as *plug shot. **1939** *Melody Maker* 3 June 1/2 Each band..will be playing in any programme of ten items, no less than eight *plug songs. **1952** B. ULANOV *Hist. Jazz Amer.* (1958) xiv. 159 The plug songs of the moment. **1815** J. SMITH *Panorama Sc. & Art* I. 39 When it is cylindrical, it is called a *plug tap. **1861** CAMPIN *Hand-turn.* v. 111 A plug-tap has the full depth of screw-thread all along its length. **1891** *Cent. Dict.* s.v. *Tap*, Taps are usually made in sets of three..the third, called the plug-tap or finishing tap, is always cylindrical, with the first two or three threads tapering off. **1814** in *Deb. Congress U.S.* (1855) 17th Congress 2 Sess., App. 1218 *Plug tobacco manufactured at Columbia, one shilling and three pence per pound. **1897** *Westm. Gaz.* 20 May 2/3 The tax on..plug and smoking tobacco is to be permanently raised. **1899** *New Cent. Rev.* V. 133 Passable cigars are obtainable, and the plug tobacco is bad. **1825** J. NICHOLSON *Operat. Mechanic* 169 Mr. Henry Beighton, of Newcastle,..invented the part called the *plug-tree, for opening and shutting the valves. **1842** *Penny Cycl.* XXII. 476/2 As the plug-tree moved up and down with the beam, the tappets struck the ends of bent levers or cranks, which raised or depressed the valves in proper succession. **1875** KNIGHT *Dict. Mech.*, **Plug-valve*, a tapering valve, fitting into a seat like a faucet.

plug (plʌg), *v.* [f. PLUG *sb.*; or immediately a. early mod.Du. *pluggen* (Plantin), f. *plugge* PLUG *sb.* So MLG. *pluggen*, LG. *plüggen*, Norw. *plugga* to plug.]

1. a. *trans.* To stop, close tightly, or fill (a hole or aperture) with or as with a plug; to drive a plug into. Chiefly with *up*.

1630 *R. Johnson's Kingd. & Commw.* 6 Neere unto the North pole men thinking to draw in their breaths, are in danger to have their throats pluggd up with an Isicle. **1665** MANLEY *Grotius' Low C. Warres* 213 Divers of their Ships being shot through with great Bullets, for that they could neither plug up the Holes or Breaches, nor free them from Water by their Pumps, were swallow'd up in the devouring and merciless Waves. **1776** G. SEMPLE *Building in Water* 42 We found it advisable to plug up the Pipe. **1833** J. HOLLAND *Manuf. Metal* II. 183 In some instances, the holes admit of being plugged with bits of metal. **1849** CLARIDGE *Cold Water-cure* 147 Sometimes when a tooth is plugged, the pressure on the nerve renders it insupportable. **1878** HOLBROOK *Hyg. Brain* 39 When a clot of blood plugs up an artery.

b. In wood-engraving: see PLUG *sb.* 2 a.

1839 CHATTO *Wood Engrav.* 645 If a small part be badly engraved, or the block has sustained an injury, the defect may be repaired by inserting a small piece of wood and re-engraving it: this..is technically termed 'plugging'.

c. To insert a wooden peg or block into (a wall, etc.) to afford a hold for a nail or screw. Also, to insert a fibre or plastic tube or cylinder for the same purpose.

1881 Young *Ev. Man his Own Mechanic* §743 When fixed to a brick wall, the wall must be plugged to take the nails. *Ibid.* §1275 Due provision having been made for this by 'plugging' the wall.

d. To insert as a plug; to drive (something) in.

1857 Holland *Bay Path* xxiv. 281 It goes by wind..and it'll plug a bullet right into a man. **1952** Dylan Thomas *Let.* 21 July (1966) 375 Now it's up to me & him to plug in lots more expenses. **1976** *National Observer* (U.S.) 17 Jan. 14/1 (Advt.), There's no need to rip out your old grass. Plug in Amazoy Zoysia Grass and let it spread into beautiful turf that never needs replacement.

e. (i) *trans.* To insert (electrically a plug or the like) *into* a socket; to connect electrically (an appliance or apparatus) by inserting a plug *into* a socket; also ***to plug in*** (trans.), to connect electrically in this way. Also *absol.*, *transf.*, and *fig.*

1923 T. E. Herbert *Teleph.* xiii. 347 The operator plugs in with the service plug, restores the indicator, and ascertains the number required. **1925** P. J. Risdon *Crystal Receivers & Circuits* 15 A complete set of such coils will thus enable a big range of wave-lengths to be efficiently covered, by plugging in a coil most nearly corresponding to the wave-length required. **1925** *Scribner's Mag.* July 54/2 He wandered in to his radio, lighted the tubes and plugged in the ear phones. **1932** *Pictorial Weekly* 19 Mar. 201/1 Rescue vessels can 'plug in' to this buoy, and talk to the men below. **1934** *Archit. Rev.* LXXV. 108/3 (*caption*) A portable fire that can be 'plugged in' to a gas point in bedroom or bathroom. **1948** F. Thompson *Still glides Stream* i. 10 One here and there of her pupils had shown the sudden gleam of comprehension..which..she had referred to..as 'plugging in', or 'taking the bait'. **1960** *Farmer & Stockbreeder* 15 Mar. 143/1 A large range of implements can be 'plugged-in' for doing a number of other jobs. **1965** *Daily Tel.* 1 June 15/8 Extract this Danish machine and plug it into an AC power point. **1970** *Atlantic Monthly* July 88 Five children were plugged into a tape recorder, listening to a story and following it in the books in front of them. **1971** [see Jack *sb.*[1] 15 d]. **1971** J. H. Smith *Digital Logic* ii. 18 A power supply ..with facilities for plugging at least ten modules into it at any one time. **1972** *Sci. Amer.* Apr. 13/1 (Advt.), The most advanced automotive check-up in the world today... Your car will actually be plugged into a computer. **1972** *National Observer* (U.S.) 27 May 22/3 They tell us that to be entirely into the new literary life, one must in some way be plugged into films. **1972** *Sci. Amer.* July 105/1 All 10 digits are plugged into the expression ABC × DE = FGH × IJ. **1977** *Ibid.* Aug. 80/3 The placental embryo..is plugged into the maternal blood supply for nourishment.

(ii) *intr.* To be, or to be capable of being, plugged *in* or *into*. Also *fig.*

1956 T. E. Ivall *Electronic Computers* iv. 45 When the unit is put into the patch panel it also plugs into a d.c. amplifier at the rear. **1963** *Which?* Dec. 378/2 The *Timac* plugged directly into the mains socket. **1974** *Physics Bull.* Sept. 401/1 This assembly plugs into a choice of sockets dependent upon the position in which the instrument is to be used.

1903 *Westm. Gaz.* 20 Jan. 9/2 Directly the sub-stations shut down, the Battery-room attendant 'plugs in' and takes the load for lighting purposes, for driving fans for ventilation purposes.

f. *trans.* To cut a cylindrical core from. Also *absol.* *U.S.*

1874 'Uncle Bob' *Lett. to Children* 19, I used to be a great hand to go into the patch, plug 'em before they were ripe, and then turn the cut side down. *a* **1910** 'Mark Twain' *Autobiogr.* (1924) I. 111, I know how to tell when it [*sc.* a watermelon] is ripe without 'plugging' it. **1948** *Chicago Tribune* 25 June 11. 3/3 The safest and best way to tell quality is to 'plug' the melon. **1969** *Times* 22 July (Moon Suppl.) p. i/1 It's a very soft surface, but here and there where I plug with the contingency sample collector, I run into a very hard surface.

g. *slang.* To copulate with.

1901 Farmer & Henley *Slang* V. 231/1 *Plug*,..to copulate. **1977** *Amer. Speech* 1975 L. 64 'I plugged her last night.' (male use).

h. ***to plug off*** or ***back***: to seal off (an oil well or a rock formation) by inserting a plug. Also *absol.*

1919 *Summary of Operations Calif. Oil Fields* (Calif. State Mining Bureau) V. I. 9 *Plugged off.* Describes the condition existing when fluid encountered in a lower part of a well has been excluded from a higher part of the well by placing an effective plug between the two places. **1924** L. C. Uren *Textbk. Petroleum Production Engin.* ix. 276 It will be important..to estimate carefully the volume of that part of the well which it is desired to plug off. **1938** C. P. Parsons in A. E. Dunstan et al. *Sci. of Petroleum* I. ix. 472/2 The amount of cement left in the bottom of the tubing depends upon the amount of hole to be plugged back. **1938** Wilde & Moore in *Ibid.* xi. 573/2 Having located the water, it is important to plug off the water sand. **1976** L. St. Clair *Fortune in Death* i. 8 We've wasted enough time fishing drill pipe out of this hole. Let's plug back and slant-drill.

2. *trans.* To put a bullet into, to shoot. Also, to fire (a bullet) *into* (example *fig.*). *slang.*

1870 J. C. Duval *Adv. Big-Foot Wallace* xix. 99 Just at that instant Jeff plugged him with a half-ounce bullet. **1882** E. W. Hamilton *Diary* 27 Aug. (1972) I. 326 He has had a narrow escape of losing an eye, having been plugged in the face by Newport while grouse driving at Wharncliffe's. **1888** 'R. Boldrewood' *Robbery under Arms* xxxi, If that old horse they put you on had bobbed forward..you'd have got plugged instead. **1891** 'Mark Twain' in 'Twain' & Howells *Mark Twain—Howells Lett.* (1960) II. 635, I will plug into you at short range the first chapter of my new book. **1900** *Westm. Gaz.* 10 Jan. 8/2, I got plugged a few yards in front of the line, and two of my fellows pulled me back, as I could not walk. **1901** *Munsey's Mag.* XXV. 340/1 'I'll wait till I get within twenty yards of the beggar,..Then I'll plug 'im!' **1904** [see lam *sb.*[3]]. **1924** [see frame *sb.* 2]. **1936** G. Greene *Gun for Sale* i. 22 Don't say a word or I'll plug you... I don't care a damn if I plug one of you. **1969** C. Burke *God is Beautiful, Man* (1970) 28 They told their old man..if they didn't bring Ben back Simon would get plugged. **1973** W. M. Duncan *Big Timer* xxi. 137 That Carver packed a wallop, didn't he? I should have plugged him sooner.

3. *trans.* To strike with the fist. Also, with a missile. *slang.*

1875 P. Ponder *Kirkcumdoon* 86 (E.D.D.) Great uproar, and cries of 'Sit doon, Matthy!' 'Plug him!' 'Stick in, Matthy!' **1891** *Athenæum* 28 Nov. 713/2 'To plug a man in the eye' is a common enough piece of slang. **1971** Wodehouse *Much obliged, Jeeves* xvi. 169 Sidcup got a black eye. Somebody plugged him with a potato.

4. *intr.* **a.** To 'stick to it', keep on persistently or doggedly; to plod. Freq. const. with advbs. **b.** To labour with pistonlike strokes against resistance. *slang.*

a. *c* **1865** (Remembered on the river at Oxford) 'Plug, you fellows, plug!' 'We plugged for all we were worth'. **1897** *Outing* (U.S.) XXX. 476/1 The crews have rowed in wretched form,..their ability to plug has enabled them to hang on to the leaders in bulldog fashion. **1900** G. Ade *More Fables* 44 Any Husband could..get up every Morning ready to Plug for a Renaissance of their Early love. *Ibid.* 146 You take a Man who is Plugging along on a Salary. **1911** E. Ferber *Dawn O'Hara* vii. 99 Lots of us are pluggin' an' savin' in the hopes that some day we'll have money enough to get back at some people we know. **1947** K. Tennant *Lost Haven* (1968) vi. 88 He was a mug to plug away at yet another new boat. **1953** Wodehouse *Performing Flea* 58, I am plugging along with *Hot Water* and have done 60,000 words. **1954** A. Huxley *Let.* 16 Sept. (1969) 711 Lacking the ability to write a text book, I have to plug on at these other, more precarious forms of literature. **1973** *Philadelphia Inquirer* 7 Oct. 19 Ronnie's not a quitter. He really plugs. **1977** *World of Cricket Monthly* June 11/1 Australia's bowlers plugged away, with Max Walker breaking through when Surrey were 2 wickets down for 147, and snaring 3 quick wickets for only 6 runs.

b. **1898** G. W. Steevens *With Kitchener to Khartum* 310 The steamers..plug-plugged their steady way up the full Nile. **1898** —— *Egypt* xix. 216 We are plugging past a twenty-foot river bank, semaphored with miles of water-hoists. **1898** *Cycling* vi. 27 When a beginner attempts to cycle up-hill at anything like a fast pace, he invariably develops a plugging action.

5. To prevent (a person) from carrying out a project by anticipating him or depriving him of his opportunity; to block (an action or design). *U.S.*

1880 *Scribner's Mag.* 492/2 One fisherman 'plugs' another when he puts out from shore and casts in ahead of him. **1896** G. Ade *Artie* xii. 110, I wouldn't like to start in and plug his game.

6. *intr.* (for *refl.*). To stick or jam; to become obstructed.

1902 S. E. White *Blazed Trail* xlviii. 338 Several times the jam started, but always 'plugged' before the motion had become irresistible. **1964** M. Gowing *Britain & Atomic Energy 1939–1945* viii. 222 The membranes must not 'plug', that is, get blocked.

7. a. *trans.* To popularize (a song) by having it played many times; to present (something) repeatedly; to publicize, emphasize, draw attention to. *colloq.* (orig. *U.S.*).

1906 H. Green *At Actors' Boarding House* 68, I ain't got any music, so you kin plug any publisher's stuff an' play what you wanter. **1927** *Daily Express* 9 Nov. 9/4, I..thought it would encourage them to plug my songs. **1930** [see cut *v.* 55 f]. **1940** *Brit. Jrnl. Psychol.* Oct. 118 The technique of 'plugging' trivial news about important personages. **1959** *Elizabethan* June 27/2, I gather from John that the other papers have plugged the crisis for all they're worth. **1967** *Wall St. Jrnl.* 12 Jan. 1/4 Mrs. Glick..now plugs Excedrin on television. **1970** G. F. Newman *Sir, You Bastard* i. 21 I'm obliged to listen to clients plugging their virility as relevant facts. **1975** C. James *Fate of Felicity Fark* v. 45 She found the concentration of rehearsal More challenging by far than plugging *Persil.*

b. *intr.* ***to plug for***: to act in support of; to make favourable statements about. *U.S. colloq.*

1927 *Amer. Speech* II. 256/1 'Pluggers' or 'rooters', 'plug' or 'root' for their side or for their favorite players. **1929** D. Runyon in *Hearst's Internat.* July 58/1 Miss Missouri Martin keeps plugging for Dave the Dude with Miss Billy Perry. **1932** *Sun* (Baltimore) 27 Apr. 1/1 The secret subsidizing of newspaper financial writers to 'plug' for stocks in process of manipulation upward. **1943** *Amer. Speech* XVIII. 249 Judge James A. Chase, a Cashmere citizen, who had visited the Vale of Kashmir, plugged for the new name and won. **1974** *News & Courier* (Charleston, S. Carolina) 7 Apr. A-14/3 At present he is plugging for a written history of Dillon County.

pluggable ('plʌgəb(ə)l), *a.* [f. plug *v.* + -able.] Suitable for or capable of being plugged. **a.** Of a song or recording (see plug *v.* 7 a).

1930 *Punch* 9 Apr. 414 One good rousing 'pluggable' air, 'The March of the Musketeers'. **1977** *Time* 19 Dec. 54/1 The first film..features a sound track overcrowded with highly pluggable Bee Gees songs.

b. Of an electrical device (see plug *v.* 1 e).

1946 *Ann. Computation Lab. Harvard Univ.* I. 251 The L10 counter has a pluggable read-out from the counter into the buss. **1954** *Jrnl. Assoc. Computing Machinery* I. 13/2 Converting..consists principally of adding magnetic heads and pluggable units. **1977** *New Yorker* 12 Sept. 93/2 (Advt.), These remarkable, pluggable, portable 4-band radio-cassette recorders give you the wide sound of stereo FM.

plugged (plʌgd), *ppl. a.* [f. plug *v.* + -ed[1].] **1.** Stopped up, closed, or filled with or as with a plug. Of a shell: Having a plug in place of the fuze.

1872 *Routledge's Ev. Boy's Ann.* 184/2 A plugged shell of 105 lb. **1884** *Mil. Engineering* (ed. 3) I. ii. 104 The instructor will cause each man to throw both land and sea service plugged hand grenades. **1899** *Allbutt's Syst. Med.* VII. 603 A plugged vein on each side..was peculiarly prominent.

2. *U.S.* Of coins: having a portion removed and the space filled with base material.

1888 *Texas Siftings* 3 Nov., Ticket Agent—Can't sell you a ticket for that quarter; it's plugged. **1890** B. Hall *Turnover Club* 207 The first speaker..paid the price of his folly with a plugged quarter. **1909** 'O. Henry' *Options* 312 Mr. Hinkle told me..you'd never taken in a lead silver dollar or a plugged one. **1912** *Pearson's Mag.* (Amer. ed.) XXVII. 691/2 For a plugged peso I'd stay with you! **1923** C. E. Mulford *Black Buttes* 265 He says..he'll see us both in hell before he'll pay a plugged peso. **1936** C. Sandburg *People, Yes* 63 He seems to think he's the frog's tonsils but he looks to me like a plugged nickel. **1946** E. O'Neill *Iceman Cometh* (1947) iv. 210 Listen, you cockeyed old bum, for a plugged nickel I'd——. **1974** Hawkey & Bingham *Wild Card* viii. 81 If as much as a whisper gets out..none of our lives are going to be worth a plugged nickel.

3. plugged-in, electrically connected by means of a plug (see plug *v.* 1 e); also *fig.*

1957 V. Nabokov *Pnin* i. 14 His devoutly plugged-in clock would make nonsense of his mornings after a storm in the middle of the night had paralyzed the local power station. **1970** E. McGirr *Death pays Wages* vi. 126 A box with a plugged-in pair of earphones. **1975** *Wentworth & Flexner's Dict. Amer. Slang* Suppl. 732/1 *Plugged-in* adj. = turned-on. **1977** M. Herr *Dispatches* (1978) 32 After a year I felt so plugged in to all the stories..that even the dead started telling me stories.

plugger ('plʌgə(r)). [f. plug *v.* + -er[1].] **a.** One who or that which plugs; *spec.* in *Dentistry*, an instrument for driving in and consolidating the filling material in the cavity of a carious tooth.

1867 C. A. Harris *Dict. Med. Terminol.* 86/1 *Automatic plugger*, a dental instrument which is operated by pressing the point upon the gold in the cavity, in the manner of an ordinary hand-plugger. **1872** L. P. Meredith *Teeth* (1887) 109 A sidelong blow on the end of the plugger may throw the point to one side..and break off or crack a portion of the tooth. **1905** *Daily Chron.* 1 July 4/4 The boat-club captain's eye has been upon those valiant pluggers in the 'fours'.

b. See quot.

1897 *Westm. Gaz.* 1 Dec. 2/3 Elaborate precautions were taken against 'pluggers', as impersonators are called in Canada. The Conservatives, in their anxiety to prevent 'plugging' (or personation), armed their scrutineers with the kodak.

c. One who extols or publicizes. Cf. plug *v.* 7 b. orig. *U.S.*

1913 *Writer's Bulletin* Oct. 127/2 Publishers spend thousands..in order to attract the attention of out-of-town performers with whom, neither they nor their 'pluggers' ever come in contact. **1921** *Cleveland* (Ohio) *Enterprise* 4 June 1/3 Everybody out here is a booster and plugger for one common purpose. **1927** [see plug *v.* 7 b]. **1958** [see *A. and R.* (A III)]. **1972** P. Black *Biggest Aspidistra* I. iii. 29 The pluggers kept the initiative by inventing the request item. This was..almost impossible to identify as a proven plug.

d. *Angling.* One who fishes with a plug (sense 10).

1967 *Daily Tel.* 21 Oct. 14/7 Many successful bass pluggers work on the principle that it is a fish with an easily aroused temper. So they use a 'teaser'.

plugging ('plʌgɪŋ), *vbl. sb.* [f. plug *v.* + -ing[1].] **1.** The action of the verb plug in various senses.

1708 J. C. *Compl. Collier* (1845) 14 Pluging will stop any Bore-hole Feeder I dare affirm. **1797** *Deb. Congress U.S.* 13 Dec. (1851) 718 They knew the silver coin circulated by tale, the gold by weight; the value of the latter had actually diminished by various means, such as sweating, plugging, clipping, &c. **1841** *Florist's Jrnl.* II. 266 The form is almost perfect, with great depth of petals, and an excellent rising centre, such as cannot be imitated by any of the usual plugging and trickery sometimes played off, or at least attempted, at exhibitions; and thus it is an excellent show Dahlia. **1842** Dunglison *Med. Lex.* (1855), *Plugging*.., the introduction of a plug of lint or rag into a wound or natural cavity..to arrest hemorrhage; or of some substance into a carious tooth to prevent tooth-ache. **1897** *Outing* (U.S.) XXX. 475/2 One quality..observable in Pennsylvania crews of late years is that of 'plugging'. **1897** [see prec.]. **1899** *Allbutt's Syst. Med.* VII. 490 An extensive plugging of small vessels. **1908** *Animal Managem.* 211 Piece by piece the straw is wetted and forced into the body of the collar... This process is termed 'plugging'. **1908** K. McGaffey *Show-Girl* 109 Is it considered au fait for a bride-about-to-be to do a little plugging for wedding presents this early in the game? **1921** A. J. Empey *Madonna of Hills* xviii. 130 Plugging means to push the sale of songs by singing them in cabarets and places. **1926** Whiteman & McBride *Jazz* viii. 169 While plugging is important, the publishers contended recently that there can be too much of any good thing. **1934** *Evening News* 13 July 6/5, I wonder, by the way, whether Uncle Andre, in view of his hour tonight, has been asked to reduce the amount of 'plugging' in it. **1957** *Listener* 10 Oct. 583/1 This plugging of his plays, early and late, successful and otherwise. **1969** E. W. Hildick *Close Look at Advertising* 31 Some of the celebrities have been known to collect very large sums of money for 'letting slip' just such recommendations. It is known as plugging. **1974** G. S. Ormsby in P. L. Moore et al. *Drilling Practices Manual* vi. 167 Underflow plugging is usually caused either by a dry beach or by solids over-load.

2. *concr.* Plugs collectively: see plug *v.* 1 c.

1875 Knight *Dict. Mech.*, *Plugging*, pins driven into the joints of brick or stone walls to receive the nails whereby battens are fastened to the walls.

3. *attrib.*, as ***plugging-forceps***, ***-instrument***.

1867 C. A. Harris *Dict. Med. Terminol.*, *Plugging-Instruments*, dental instruments for introducing and consolidating fillings. **1875** Knight *Dict. Mech.*, *Plugging-forceps*, a dentist's instrument used in compressing a filling into an excavated hole in a carious tooth. **1929** *Melody Maker* Feb. 124/3 The listener is often served with all kinds of tripe songs, reiterated *ad nauseam*, at the dictates of the wire pullers over an extensive plugging period. **1932** *Sun* (Baltimore) 27 Apr. 15/7 Checks..were indentified..as payments for stock 'plugging' publicity. **1959** *Punch* 10 June 766/3, I suspect it may be a new plugging gimmick, a form of filibustering.

'pluggy, *a. dial.* [f. PLUG *sb.* + -Y.] **a.** Short and stumpy. *colloq.* **b.** Stiff, as clay.

a **1825** FORBY *Voc. E. Anglia*, *Pluggy*, short, thick, sturdy. **1861** AGNES STRICKLAND *Old Friends* Ser. II. ii. 33 Betty, Molly, and the cook..united..in describing Martin..as 'a short, pluggy (thick) man, with a pug nose'. **1892** H. HUTCHINSON *Fairway Isl.* 8 The crumbly ploughed land did not hold the clean impression as the pluggy clay had done.

plugh, -e, obs. forms of PLOUGH.

'plug-in, *a.* and *sb.* [f. vbl. phr. *to plug in* (PLUG *v.* 1 e).] **A.** *adj.* Designed to be plugged into a socket (esp. an electrical one); of or pertaining to such devices.

1922 *Wireless World* 8 July 458/1 One sees so many makeshift plug-in devices..in amateur sets. **1926** R. W. HUTCHINSON *Wireless* 187 The aerial inductance L_1 and the reaction coil L_2 are of the plug-in type. **1954** *Sun* (Baltimore) (B ed.) 19 June 15/1 Portable plug-in telephones with conveniently located outlets offer a modern convenience where a telephone is desired on a part-time basis in certain rooms. **1965** *Wireless World* Sept. 464/2 An encapsulated version..for plug-in applications is available. **1966** 'A. YORK' *Eliminator* iv. 57 A mahogany-boxed erinoid plug-in chess set lay on the coffee table. **1968** R. PETRIE *MacLurg goes West* viii. 67 The hotel manager was knocking at MacLurg's door, followed by a porter with a plug-in telephone. **1968** B. TURNER *Sex Trap* v. 28 His kitchen boasted one cup and a plug-in percolator. **1971** J. H. SMITH *Digital Logic* ii. 18 A very easy method of construction is to use one of the commercially available rack construction systems with plug-in units. **1977** WARNER & BELL in D. M. Rumbaugh *Language Learning by Chimpanzee* vii. 144 Purchasing the computer, its plug-in modules and peripherals proved to be a wise decision.

B. *sb.* A plug-in device or unit.

1950 *Sun* (Baltimore) 31 Aug. 8/7 The refrigerator units will operate either from car batteries or 110-volt or 220-volt plug-ins for use where electricity is available. **1955** *IRE Trans. Electronic Computers* IV. 3/1 One standard plug-in contains four flip-flops and eight cathode-followers for isolation. **1965** *Wireless World* July 54 (Advt.), Three new instruments..have all the in-built virtues of the original plug-ins. **1967** *Electronics* 6 Mar. 2 (Advt.), Sweep Oscillators with RF and marker plug-ins meet virtually all of your swept frequency testing requirements. **1971** C. FICK *Danziger Transcript* (1973) 171, I heated some coffee on my plug-in and we lit cigars. **1972** 'G. BLACK' *Bitter Tea* (1973) xiii. 212 The jacks for the phone plug-ins. **1975** *Sci. Amer.* Mar. 11/1 (Advt.), Priced at $800 for the main-frame and $110 to $250 for the plug-ins, the 5150A is easily the new price/performance leader in instrumentation recorders.

plugless (ˈplʌglɪs), *a.* [f. PLUG *sb.* + -LESS.] Having no plug or stopper.

1830-6 O. W. HOLMES *Daily Trials* 23 Women, with tongues Like polar needles, ever on the jar; Men, plugless word-spouts, whose deep fountains are Within their lungs.

plugola (plʌˈgəʊlə). orig. *U.S.* [f. PLUG *sb.* 9 + -OLA.] Incidental or surreptitious promotion of a person or product, esp. on radio or television; a bribe for this. Also *attrib.* and *transf.*

1959 *Washington Post* 7 Dec. A12/4 The nasty charges of fees collected for plugola. **1963** R. I. MCDAVID *Mencken's Amer. Lang.* 213 *Plugola*, a subspecies [of payola]—payments to disk jockeys in return for frequently playing a record company's new recordings—was also disclosed during these scandals. **1972** *Times Lit. Suppl.* 29 Sept. 1138/2 If the garret doesn't get you, the plugola circuit will. **1972** *Guardian* 20 Dec. 4/5 Mr Whitehead spoke of 'ideological plugola' and went on: 'Station licensees have final responsibility for news balance.' **1977** *National Observer* (U.S.) 1 Jan. 2/2 The Federal Communications Commission said it will hold hearings next year into alleged 'payola' and 'plugola' by broadcasters. The FCC said it had received information that illegal payments had been made to disc jockeys for playing certain records and to broadcasters for mentioning products.

plug-ugly (plʌgˈʌglɪ). *slang* (orig. and chiefly *U.S.*). [Origin obscure: see quots.] A city ruffian or rowdy. More widely, a man of violence, one who adopts intimidatory methods. Also *attrib.* and as *adj.*

1856 *Butte Rec.* (Oroville, Calif.) 29 Nov. 3/7 The..Plug Uglies..went to Philadelphia on election day..to fight off and whip the democracy from the polls. **1857** *Lawrence* (Kansas) *Republican* 30 July 2 Only a pitiful minority of the actual voters of Kansas, cast their votes for delegates to the plug ugly convention. **1860** BARTLETT *Dict. Amer.* (ed. 3), *Plug Ugly*, a term assumed by a gang of rowdies in Baltimore. It originally belonged to certain fire companies. **1861** [see *blood-tub* (BLOOD *sb.* 21)]. **1865** *Reader* 19 Aug. 203 In order the better to deal with the rowdies and plug-uglies of the more turbulent wards. **1876** in *Times* 4 Nov. 9/6 'Plug-Uglies'... Several years ago I was in Baltimore, where the class of rowdies who originated this euphonious name abounded, and was told it was derived from a short spike fastened in the toe of their boots, with which they kicked their opponents in a dense crowd, or, as they elegantly expressed it, 'plugged them ugly'. **1884** *Pall Mall G.* 17 July 4/1 His friends were alternately the 'plug-uglies' of Sixth Avenue and the dudes of Delmonico's. **1909** *Dialect Notes* III. 358 *Plug-ugly*, an ugly person or thing, especially an ugly horse. **1915** *Ibid.* IV. 187 *Plug ugly*, adj. phr. Said of a very ugly man, not genteel. (Applied more commonly to an 'ugly customer'.—*Ed.*) **1923** WODEHOUSE *Adventures of Sally* xiv. 176 After he'd paid these two pluguglies their guarantees..he was just about cleaned out. **1935** *Punch* 13 Nov. 550/2 Readers who have led sheltered lives will think of plug-uglies, and I hope the cleaner kinds of plug-ugly will think of baths. **1953** [see *lunatic fringe* s.v. LUNATIC *sb.* 1 c]. **1956** D. KARP *All Honorable Men* 18 The plug-uglies on the Right and the Left are the only people who don't give a damn about the opposing argument, and I don't count myself among them. **1972** K. BONFIGLIOLI *Don't point that Thing at Me* ii. 12 'Yes, Sir.' said Plug Ugly II. **1975** *New Yorker* 1 Dec. 136/2 When a director like Sam Peckinpah puts a group like his Wild Bunch on the screen, the men are so alive that the last thing that would ever come into your head is that some of them are plug-uglies. **1978** N. MARSH *Grave Mistake* ii. 62 Verity thought, I've..drunk their champagne so now I turn plug-ugly and refuse.

plum (plʌm), *sb.* Forms: *α.* 1 plúme, (in comb.) plúm-, 4–5 plowme, 5 plowmbe, 6 ploume, 8–9 *north dial.* ploum, ploom. *β.* 4–6 plome, 4–7 plom, 5 (in comb.) plomb-, 5–6 plomme; 4–7 plumbe, 5–7 plumme, 6–9 plumb, 4– plum. [OE. *plúme* fem. plum (earlier *plúmæ*, *-ę*, plum, fruit and tree) corresp. to OLG. **plûma*, MLG. *plûme* (LG. *plumme*, EFris. *plûme*, *plûm*), ON. *plóma* f. (? from OE.); OHG. **phlûma* fem. plum (*pflûmo* m. plum-tree), MHG. *pflûme*, Ger. *pflaume*; variants of OHG. *phrûma*, *pfrûma* f., OLG. **prûma*, MLG., LG. *prûme*, MDu. *prûme*, Du. *pruim* f.; the forms in *pr-* being the original, a. late L. or Romanic *prūna* f., for L. *prūnum* neut., a. later Gr. προῦνον, for cl. Gr. προῦμνον plum. (Cf. L. *prūnus* fem., Gr. προύμνη, προύνη plum-tree.) The late L. *prūna* gave also Pr. *prūna*, F. *prune* plum: see PRUNE. The shortening of the vowel in Eng. is found from the 14th c., but the long vowel occurs in Levins 1570, and is still repr. by north. Eng. and Sc. (plaʊm, plum); cf. Eng. *thumb*, OE. *þúma*, north. Eng. and Sc. *theaum*, *thoum*, *thoom*; the vowel is shortened also in LG. *plumme*, Sw. *plommon*, Da. *blomme*. The form *plýme* given in OE. glosses as = *prunus* and *prunum* is explained by Pogatscher from L. *prūneus*: cf. It. *prugna* plum, *prugno* plum-tree.

The change of *pr-* to *pl-* is found only in the Teutonic forms, or in med.L. written in England, etc.: see *plunas* (? *plunus*), *plumum* in Corpus Gl., *plumnus* (Wr.-Wulcker 269/30). The Celtic forms, Cornish *pluman*, Ir. *pluma*, Gael. *plumbais*, *-bas*, are evidently from Eng. The change of *n* to *m* in *prūna*, *prūma* is attributed by Kluge and Franck to the influence of the preceding labial; Meyer-Lübke suggests derivation from Gr. προῦμνον. *Prume* in south-east French dialects may be influenced by German.]

1. a. The fruit of the tree *Prunus domestica*, a roundish fleshy drupe of varying size and colour, covered with a glaucous mealy bloom, and having a somewhat flat pointed stone and sweet pulp.

α. *c* **725** *Corpus Gloss.* 1600 in *O.E.T.*, *Plumum*, plumæ. *c* **1000** ÆLFRIC *Gram.* vii. (Z.) 20 *Hoc prunum*, seo plyme [*v.r.* plume]. ? *a* **1366** CHAUCER *Rom. Rose* 1375 Medlers, plowmes, perys, chesteyns. **1483** *Cath. Angl.* 284/1 A Plowmbe (*A.* Plowme), *prunum*. **1570** LEVINS *Manip.* 219/35 A Ploume, *prunum*. **1828** *Craven Gloss.* (ed. 2), *Ploum*, a plum. *a* **1907** *Mod. Sc.* Soor plooms.

β. **1393** LANGL. *P. Pl.* C. XIII. 221 As pees-coddes and pere-Ionettes, plomes and chiries. **14..** *Voc.* in Wr.-Wülcker 647/30 *Hoc prunum*, plumme. **14..** *Nom.* ibid. 715/20 *Hoc prunum*, a plum. **1484** CAXTON *Fables of Æsop* I. vi, Men sayen that it is not good to ete plommes with his lord. **1523** FITZHERB. *Husb.* §140 As for cheryes, dampsons, bulleys, plummes, and suche other. **1570** B. GOOGE *Pop. Kingd.* 44 b, Here haue they peares, and plumbs. **1577** —— *Heresbach's Husb.* II. (1586) 97 There are sundry sortes of Plomes. **1578** LYTE *Dodoens* VI. xlvii. 720 The fruite is called ..in Englishe, a Plumme or Prune. **1601** HOLLAND *Pliny* XV. xiii. 436 To come now to Plums, there is a world of them: some of sundrie colours, others blacke, and some againe white. **1697** DRYDEN *Virg. Georg.* IV. 215 He knew to..tame to Plumbs the Sourness of the Sloes. **1809** PINKNEY *Trav. France* 222 In every hedge..were medlars, plumbs, cherries and maples. **1870** YEATS *Nat. Hist. Comm.* 182 Dried plums, under the names of prunes and French plums, form an important article of commerce.

†**b.** Phrase. *the bloom* or *blue of the plum*: delicate freshness, charm: cf. BLOOM *sb.* 4 b. *Obs.*

1727 A. HAMILTON *New Acc. E. Ind.* II. xlix. 215 The Maids keep their Teeth very white, till they have lost the blue of their Plumb, and then they dye them as black as Jet. **1738** SWIFT *Pol. Conversat.* 90 She has quite lost the Blue on the Plumb.

2. The tree bearing this fruit, *Prunus domestica* (N.O. *Rosaceæ*).

P. domestica, the cultivated or garden plum in its many varieties, and the European wild plum or BULLACE, *P. insititia*, are now considered to be specifically identical with the Blackthorn or SLOE-bush, *P. spinosa*, the three forms being referred to a single species, *P. communis*.

a **700** *Epinal Gloss.* 822 in *O.E.T.*, *Prunus*, plumæ. (So *Erfurt Gl.*) *c* **725** *Corpus Gloss.* 1664 *Prunus*, plume. *c* **1350** *Nominale Gall.-Angl.* 681 (E.E.T.S.) Bolas plumbe and cirne. *c* **1420** *Pallad. on Husb.* XII. 247 In peche Is graffid plomme. **1657** AUSTEN *Fruit Trees* I. 66 It is the custome (of late) to make..hedges of Quodlings, Plums, and vines. **1718** J. CHAMBERLAYNE *Relig. Philos.* (1730) II. xxiii. §32 If an Abricot be grafted upon a Plumb. **1785** MARTYN *Rousseau's Bot.* vii. (1794) 75 The genus plum, comprehending the apricot and cherry. **1899** NORA HOPPER in *Westm. Gaz.* 1 Mar. 10/1 Blossom on the plum,..Leaves upon the cherry.

3. With qualifying words. **a.** Applied to many species (and varieties) of the genus *Prunus*: **beach p.** of the Atlantic coast of U.S., *P. maritima*; **Canada p.**, *P. americana* (Miller *Plant-n.*); **cherry** or **myrobella p.**, *P. Myrobalana*; **chickasaw p.** of N. America, *P. Chicasa* (*Treas. Bot.*); **damascene**, †**damasco**, **damask**, or **damson p.**: see DAMASK, DAMSON; **Japanese p.**, *P. japonica*; see also b; **Morocco p.**, ? = DAMSON; †**muscle p.**, a purple variety of the plum; **wild p.**, in Britain, *P. insititia* or *spinosa*; in N. America, *P. americana* and *P. subcordata* (*Treas. Bot.* and Miller *Plant-n.*); see also b. See also HORSE-PLUM, PEAR-*plum*, etc.

1796 MORSE *Amer. Geog.* I. 188 *Beach Plumb (*Prunus maritima*). **1856** WHITTIER *Ranger* x, Where the purple beach-plum mellows. **1866** *Treas. Bot.* 933 *P*[*runus*] *myrobalana*, which is named *Cherry Plum, probably from its colour, is a species from Canada. **1904** *Westm. Gaz.* 9 Jan. 8/1 This year there are fresh cherry-plums from Argentina on sale. **1657** AUSTEN *Fruit Trees* I. 57 The *Damasco Plum is a good fruit, and the trees beare well. **1707** MORTIMER *Husb.* (1721) II. 298 The black Damascen, the *Morocco, the Barbary, the Myrobalan, the Apricock Plumb, a delicate Plumb that parts clean from the Stone. **1626** BACON *Sylva* §509 All your dainty Plummes, are a little dry, and come from the Stone; As the *Muscle-Plumme. **1709** J. LAWSON *New Voy. Carolina* 105 The *wild Plums of America are of several sorts. **1838** E. FLAGG *Far West* II. 177 Endless thickets of the wild plum..were to be seen. **1863** R. HENNING *Let.* 26 Nov. (1966) 146 We sat down under the shade of a wild-plum tree. *Ibid.*, They are not bad, those wild plums; they are about the size of a medlar, quite black in colour, and when ripe they taste very like sloes. **1902** CORNISH *Naturalist Thames* 244 Low mounds... Some are covered with wild-plum bushes. **1925** Z. A. TILGHMAN *Dugout* 56 Fan being gone after some wild plums down the creek. **1951** W. FAULKNER *Requiem for Nun* III. 213 A mere dusty widening of the trace, trail, pathway in a forest of oak and ash and..wild plum.

b. Extended to many trees resembling the plum, esp. in fruit:

American black p. ? = *cocoa p.*; **Assyrian p.** = *sebesten p.* (Miller *Plant-n.* 1884); **Australian p.** or **black p. of Illawarra**, *Cargillia australis*, N.O. *Ebenaceæ* (ibid.); **blood p.** of Sierra Leone, *Hæmatostaphis Barteri*, N.O. *Anacardiaceæ* (*Treas. Bot.*); **Brazilian p.**, species of *Spondias*, N.O. *Anacardiaceæ* (Lee 1760); **cocoa p.** of tropical America and Africa, *Chrysobalanus Icaco* (Lee 1760); **Darling p.**, the Red Ironwood of W. Indies and Florida, *Reynosia latifolia*; **East Indian p.**, *Flacourtia cataphracta*, and *F. Ramontchi* (Miller); **grey p.** or **Guinea p.**, of Sierra Leone, *Parinarium excelsum*, N.O. *Chrysobalanaceæ*; of Australia, *Cargillia arborea*; **Jamaica p.**, a species of Hog-plum, *Spondias lutea*; **Japan** or **Japanese p.** the Loquat; **mountain p.**, *Ximenia americana*, N.O. *Olacaceæ*; **Port Arthur p.**, of Tasmania, *Cenarrhenes nitida*, N.O. *Proteaceæ* (*Treas. Bot.*); **Queensland p.**, *Owenia venosa*, N.O. *Meliaceæ*; **sapodilla p.** of West Indies, *Sapota Achras*; **sebesten p.**, *Cordia Myxa* and *C. latifolia*, N.O. *Boraginaceæ*; **Spanish p.** of W. Indies and S. Amer., *Spondias purpurea* (*Treas. Bot.*); also in the Antilles, *Mammea humilis*, N.O. *Clusiaceæ* (Miller); **tamarind p.**, a leguminous tree of E. Indies, *Dialium indum*; **Tasmanian p.** = *Port Arthur p.* (Miller); **urucuri p.**, a S. Amer. palm, *Attalea excelsa*; **wild p.** of S. Africa, *Pappea capensis*, N.O. *Sapindaceæ*; of N.S. Wales, *Sideroxylon australis*, N.O. *Sapotaceæ*; **yellow (Spanish) p.** of W. Indies = *Jamaica p.* See also DATE-*plum*, GINGERBREAD-*plum*, HOG-PLUM, OLIVE-*plum*, PERSIMMON-*plum*, etc.

1866 *Treas. Bot.* 223 The *Black Plum of Hiawarra (*Cargillia australis*)..is a slender tree..; the fruits are the size of a large plum, and of dark purple colour. *Ibid.*, The *Grey Plum (*Cargillia arborea*) grows to a height of fifty or a hundred feet. *Ibid.* 846 The fruit of *P*[*arinarium*] *excelsum* is about the size of an Imperatrice plum, covered with a rough skin of a greyish colour, and commonly called the Rough-skin or Grey Plum. **1756** P. BROWNE *Jamaica* 229 The yellow or *Jamaica Plumb Tree... The fruit is much esteemed by some people. **1889** J. H. MAIDEN *Usef. Native Plants* 49 *Queensland Plum, Sweet Plum. This plant bears a fine juicy red fruit with a large stone. **1866** *Treas. Bot.* 1018/2 S. Achras yields an edible fruit called in the West Indies the *Sapodilla plum. **1866** BRANDE & COXE *Dict. Sc.*, etc. II. 937/2 *Sebesten-plum is the fruit of *Cordia*. **1866** *Treas. Bot.* 397 The *Tamarind Plum of the East Indies, *D*[*ialium*] *indum*, has a delicious pulp resembling that of the Tamarind, but not quite so acid. **1863** BATES *Nat. Amazon* x. (1864) 297 The fruit of this palm ripens on the upper river in April,..similar in size and shape to the date... Vicente shook his head when he saw me one day eating a quantity of the *Urucuri plums. **1880** SILVER & CO. *S. Africa* (ed. 3) 139 The..*Wild Plum is the fruit of *Pappea Capensis*, a tree pretty common in Kaffirland. **1887** MOLONEY *Forestry W. Afr.* 305 Hog Plum or *Yellow Spanish Plum of Jamaica, *Spondias lutea*.—Large tree.

4. a. A dried grape or raisin as used for puddings, cakes, etc.

This use probably arose from the substitution of raisins for dried plums or prunes as an ingredient in *plum-broth*, *-porridge*, etc. with retention of the name 'plum' for the substituted article. Quotations 1725–1733 prob. belong here.

a 1660 [Mock sermon: see PLUM-PIE] p. 6 But there is your Christmas pye and that hath plums in abundance... He that discovered the new Star in Cassiopeia..deserves not half so much to be remembered, as he that first married minced meat and Raisins together. 1725 WATTS *Logic* I. vi. §6 A grocer is a man who buys and sells sugar, and plumbs, and spices, for gain. 1727–41 CHAMBERS *Cycl.*, *Plumb*, or *Plum*, in matters of spicery. See *Currans* and *Raisins*. 1733 FIELDING *Don Quix.* I. vi, 'Tis not only plumbs that make a pudding. 17.. *Hist. Jack Horner* [see PLUM-PIE 1]. 1755 JOHNSON, *Plum*,..2. Raisin; grape dried in the sun. 1768–74 TUCKER *Lt. Nat.* (1834) II. 686 Children, to whom you give a pill wrapped up in a raisin, will suck the plum and spit out the medicine. 1804 ANN & JANE TAYLOR *Poems Inf. Minds*, *Plum-cake*, While fingers and thumbs, for the sweetmeats and plums, Were hunting and digging beside. *a* 1845 HOOD *Son & Heir* v, A Grocer's plum might disappoint. 1884 DOWELL *Hist. Taxat.* IV. I. vii. 37 The dried grapes..we term simply raisins when used for eating uncooked, and plums when they form an ingredient in the famous English plum pudding.

b. = SUGAR-PLUM. (First quot. doubtful.)

1694 CONGREVE *Double Dealer* III. iv, So when you've swallowed the potion, you sweeten your mouth with a plum. 1790 COWPER *My Mother's Pict.* 61 Thy morning bounties ere I left my home, The biscuit, or confectionary plum.

c. *fig.* A stone or mass of rock embedded in a matrix of later origin; a pebble in a conglomerate; also, a stone embedded in concrete.

a 1817 T. DWIGHT *Trav. New Eng.*, etc. (1821) II. 355 The plums, or stones, embosomed by the matrix, are exactly of the same kinds, which are found everywhere in the earth adjacent. 1894 *Times* 22 Sept. 13/3 The interior was filled in with concrete deposited in layers of nine inches, while large single stones, technically called 'plums', weighing, as a rule, about three-and-a-half tons, were placed as close together as possible and bedded in mortar.

d. *fig.* A 'good thing', a tit-bit; one of the best things to be found in a book or article; one of the best or choicest things among situations or appointments; one of the 'prizes' of life; also, the pick or best of a collection of things, animals, etc.; the best part of a musical work.

1825 MAR. EDGEWORTH *Harry & Lucy, Concluded* IV. vii. 167 It is only the stupid parts of books which tire one. All that is necessary is to pick out the plums. 1853 LYTTON *My Novel* VIII. i, Much too old a world to allow any Jack Horner to pick out its plums for his own personal gratification. 1876 GEO. ELIOT *Dan. Der.* II. xvi, To fight it away for the sake of getting some sort of plum that he might divide with his mother and the girls. 1887 in G. Stimpson *Bk. about Amer. Politics* (1952) 258 The boys enjoying the plums will support anybody who is good for him or them. 1888 'R. BOLDREWOOD' *Robbery under Arms* v, There were some real plums among the horses. 1889 *Academy* 2 Nov. 280 The reviewer who picks all the 'plums' out of a book is a person who is regarded with reasonable terror and resentment by both authors and publishers. 1901 *Scotsman* 5 Sept. 4/8 The posts named are justly regarded as plums of the Indian Civil Service. 1937 W. H. SAUMAREZ SMITH *Let.* 16 Oct. in *Young Man's Country* (1977) ii. 94 It [*sc.* the job] is definitely one of the three plums for the young civilian. 1967 *Boston Herald* 8 May 24/5 José has played his cards just right, and a rich little plum named Lucy falls into his outstretched arms. 1973 *Times* 20 Oct. 13/6 Its slow movement is its 'plum', a glorious, unbroken song. 1978 *Time* 3 July 42/2 Center directors receive only $11,000 a year, but Mendel offers them a plum: their kids can attend free.

5. a. The sum of £100,000. *slang.* Now *rare.*

1689–1702 EARL OF AILESBURY *Mem.* (1890) 499 Those even that had nothing at the Revolution had the reputation after of being worth one hundred, and others two hundred thousand pounds. The first sum was christened one plum, and the last, two. *Ibid.* 634 In King William's time..the tally trade alone brought in to some a hundred thousand pounds, which they then called a plum. 1709 PRIOR *Ladle, Moral*, The Miser must make up his Plumb, And dares not touch the hoarded sum. 1710 STEELE *Tatler* No. 244 ¶6 An honest Gentleman who..was worth half a Plumb. 1789 J. BELKNAP in *M. Cutler's Life*, etc. (1888) II. 252 The revenue is now about £90 plum, to be increased by funding. 1818 *Gentl. Mag.* LXXXVIII. 201/2 Though the personal effects do not exceed 140,000*l.* there are real estates sufficient to complete the second plumb. 1898 BESANT *Orange Girl* I. v, The only son of Sir Peter Halliday..the heir to a plum.

†**b.** *transf.* One who is possessed of £100,000.

1709 ADDISON *Tatler* No. 100 ¶3 Several who were Plumbs, or very near it, became Men of moderate Fortunes. 1746 FIELDING *True Patriot* No. 11 Wks. 1775 IX. 322 A thing highly eligible by every good man, i.e. every Plumb. 1774 *Westm. Mag.* II. 238 Warm Citizens with the insolence of a plumb in their countenances.

6. = *plum-colour.*

1878 *Trans. Illinois Dept. Agric.* XIV. 210 [Siamese Swine] varied in color from deep rich plum to dark slate and black. 1895 *Montgomery Ward Catal.* 3/1 Cashmere... All the fashionable colors..golden brown, medium plum, heliotrope. 1940 GRAVES & HODGE *Long Week-End* xvi. 278 Victorian colours—plum, maroon, and violet—were in favour. 1970 *Guardian* 5 June 9/2 She has featherweight car rugs in brushed wool in plum and purple at a modest three guineas each.

7. *attrib.* and *Comb.* **a.** attrib., as ***plum-bloom***, ***-blow*** (BLOW *sb.*[3]), ***brandy***, ***-culture***, ***-flower***, ***-frumenty***, ***-gum***, ***-juice***, ***-lea***, ***-loaf***, ***-moth***, ***-pattern***, ***-season***, ***-stock***, ***-stone***, ***-tart***, ***-trade***, ***-weevil***, ***wine***. **b.** objective, similative, etc., as ***plum-feeder***, ***-gathering***, ***-holder***, ***-seller***; ***plum-dark***, ***-purple***, ***-rich***, ***-round*** adjs.; ***plum-like*** adj. **c.** parasynthetic, as ***plum-coloured***, ***-necked***, ***-stained***, ***-tinted*** adjs. **d.** Special comb.: **plum-bird**, **-budder**, local names of the bullfinch; **plum-colour**, a shade of purple; so **plum-coloured** *a.*; **plum-fir**, a tree, *Podocarpus andina*, N.O. *Taxaceæ*; **plum-gouger**, a weevil (*Coccotorus scutellaris*); **plum-in-the-mouth** *a.* (*colloq.*), indistinctly articulated, esp. in a manner associated with the British upper classes (of speech, etc.); **plum-pockets**, a disease of plums in which the fruit grows hollow, without a stone (cf. *pocket-plum* s.v. POCKET *sb.*); **plum pox** [tr. Bulgarian *sharka na slivite* (D. Atanasoff 1932, in *Godishnik na Sofiĭskiya Universitet Agronomski Fakultet* XI. 49)], a virus disease of plum trees characterized by yellow blotches on the leaves and pockets of dead tissue in the fruit; also known as *sharka*; **plum rains** [tr. Jap. *bai-u*] = BAI-U; applied also to the corresponding rains in southern China. See also PLUM-BROTH, PLUM-CAKE, etc.

1879 MISS JACKSON *Shropsh. Word-bk.*, **Plum-bird*, the Bullfinch. *Ibid.*, **Plum-budder.* 1897 *Daily News* 12 June 6/2 Other fashionable colours for gloves are Liberty green,..salmon pink, coral red, sky blue, *plum-bloom. 1868 WHITMAN *Singing in Spring* 23 in *Sel. Poems* 390 Stems of currants, and *plum-blows, and the aromatic cedar. 1950 *Chambers's Encycl.* IV. 326/1 Plums are grown as fresh fruit and for jam, though some are distilled into *slivovice* (*plum brandy). 1958 A. L. SIMON *Dict. Wines, Spirits & Liqueurs* 147/1 Slivovitz..is very similar to the Alsatian Plum Brandy called Quetsch. 1977 H. FAST *Immigrants* 11 The husband of the Polish woman..hoarded plum brandy. 1882 *Garden* 30 Sept. 288/3 Flowers which change from white to *plum colour. 1898 G. B. SHAW *You never can Tell* III. 274 The wall decoration of Lincrusta Walton in plum color and bronze lacquer. 1960 S. PLATH *Colossus* (1967) 21, I squat.. Counting the red stars and those of plum-colour. 1820 M. EDGEWORTH *Let.* 8 June (1970) 160 Fannys *plum colored [*sic*] and Harrets lilac tabbinets. 1840 BARHAM *Ingol., Jackd. Rheims*, The Cardinal drew Off each plum-colour'd shoe. 1902 *Daily Chron.* 5 July 5/2 *Plum-culture is a lottery: for plums either fruit too lightly or they break the tree and glut the market. 1887 *Nicholson's Dict. Gard.* III. 168/2 The *Plum Curculio (*Conotrachelus nenuphar*) is about ⅙ in. long,..and has on each wing-case, in the middle, a black, shining hump. 1957 L. DURRELL *Bitter Lemons* 103 *Plum-dark mountain roses. 1958 —— *Balthazar* i. 13 A single plum-dark sail, moist, palpitant. 1963 *Glamour* Sept. 146 Plum-dark wool frames the soft blue silk collar of the coat, worn over a matching plum-dark flared skirt. 1866 *Treas. Bot.* 496 *Plum Fir, *Prumnopitys elegans*, [a name proposed by Philippi for *Podocarpus andina*]. 1887 *Nicholson's Dict. Gard.* III. 172/2 P[*odocarpus*] *andina*.., Plum Fir, fr[uit] resembling in form and size the berry of an ordinary White Grape, but in structure that of a Cherry. 1763 *Brit. Mag.* IV. 170 The *plum-firmity and mellow ale at sheep-shearing dwindled into small-beer, and roasted apples. 1928 C. DAY LEWIS *Country Comets* 25 At the time of *plum-gathering When the hedge is plumy With Traveller's Joy. 1887 *Nicholson's Dict. Gard.* III. 168/2 The second species [of Plum-weevil] (*Coccotorus scutellaris*) is popularly called the *Plum Gouger. 1730 BURDON *Pocket Farrier* (1735) 82 Take one Ounce of *Plumb Gum beaten very small. 1897 W. C. HAZLITT *Ourselves* 30 The *plum-holders, instead of sharing with their poorer brethren, ask the public to make up the deficiency. 1926 D. H. LAWRENCE *Plumed Serpent* vi. 118 She spoke rapidly, a rather *plum-in-the-mouth Spanish. 1934 S. R. NELSON *All about Jazz* vii. 163 The lukewarm, plum-in-the-mouth style of some of the white vocalists. 1900 J. HUTCHINSON in *Arch. Surg.* XI. No. 41. 73 A red *plum-juice colour. 1866 *Treas. Bot.* 844 Its fruit..is called Wilde Pruime (i.e. Wild Plum) from its *plum-like eatable flesh. 1879 SIR E. ARNOLD *Lt. Asia* II. (1882) 45 The *plum-necked parrots swung from fruit to fruit. 1895 *Daily News* 29 Nov. 2/3 An oviform jar and cover of *plum-pattern. 1891 *Cent. Dict.*, *Taphrina*, a genus of parasitic discomycetous fungi... *T. Pruni* [causes] the disease of plums known as '*plum-pockets'. 1933 *Rev. Applied Mycol.* XII. 230 The disease, which the author [*sc.* D. Atanasoff] terms *plum pox, was proved to be readily transmissible to healthy trees by grafting. 1943 *Bull. Min. Agric. & Fish.* CXXVI. 64 A single tree bearing foliage with symptoms corresponding to those of Plum Pox..was observed early in August 1934 at East Oakley, Hants. 1952 E. RAMSDEN tr. *Gram & Weber's Plant Diseases* II. 204/2 A disease called plum pox, well known in Bulgaria, probably occurs as far north as Bohemia and Holland. 1976 *Nature* 12 Feb. 499/2 The Ministry of Agriculture reported that at least 150 acres of plums have some levels of infection with plum pox (sharka) virus, an aphid-borne virus. 1862 G. M. HOPKINS *Vision of Mermaids* (1929), *Plum-purple was the west. 1882 *Garden* 4 Nov. 396/1 The rich-shaded, plum-purple pips. 1922, 1945 *Plum rains [see BAI-U]. 1968 G. R. RUMNEY *Climatol. & World's Climates* xii. 235/1 The cloudiness, humidity, and generally oppressive conditions accompanying the start of the warm season's heavy rains in southern Japan combine to create a period of depressing, gloomy weather called here, as in south China, the plum rains (*Bai-u*). 1971 *Handbk. Aviation Meteorol.* (Meteorol. Office) xxiii. 378 In May, tropical air begins to advance northwards and is heralded by cyclonic activity and the widespread 'plum' rains of China and Japan. 1932 AUDEN *Orators* I. 3 The *plum-rich red-earth valley of the Severn. 1581 C. T. in Farr *S.P. Eliz.* (1845) 395, I will not maserate, Saith he, my *plum-round physnomie. 1670 EACHARD *Cont. Clergy* 30 An ordinary cheesemonger or *plum-seller. 1922 JOYCE *Ulysses* 564 Two trickies Frauenzimmer *plum-stained from pram falling bawling. 1699 EVELYN *Kal. Hort.* (ed. 9) 132 [Graft] Plums, on *Plum-stocks. 1707 MORTIMER *Husb.* (1721) II. 251 Plumb-stocks and Cherry-stocks may be raised from Suckers as well as from Stones. 1770 J. WOODFORDE *Diary* 12 Oct. (1924) I. 102, I gave them for dinner a..*Plumb Tart and an Apple Tart. *c* 1900 *Beeton's Every-day Cook. Bk.*, *Plum Tart*..Seasonable, with various kins of plums, from the beginning of August to the beginning of October. 1887 *Nicholson's Dict. Gard.* III. 168/1 The flowers and fruits are attacked chiefly by the *Plum Weevil (*Rhynchites cupreus*) and the Plum Tortrix (*Carpocapsa funebrana*). 1728 E. SMITH *Compl. Housewife* (ed. 2) 208 To make *Plum-wine. Take twenty pound of Malaga raisins..water..damson juice..at 4 or 5 months bottle it. 1976 'M. DELVING' *China Expert* i. 11 The guest list included..Chinese and Westerners, all..eager to sample the stuffed, glazed chicken and fish in plum wine sauce.

e. passing into *adj.* = *plum-coloured* adj.

1922 JOYCE *Ulysses* 551 In a flunkey's plum plush coat and kneebreeches, buff stockings and powdered wig. 1930 V. SACKVILLE-WEST *Edwardians* v. 229 Buttoned into her plum velvet bodice, like the wife of any British tradesman. 1975 J. MCCLURE *Snake* x. 133 There was a white Jaguar, a plum Datsun coupé and a..Land-Rover.

f. (sense 4 d) passing into *adj.* Choice, valuable, coveted.

1958 *Listener* 21 Aug. 277/1 Was the promotion of Chiappe to the plum governorship an easy method of shedding a dangerous man in a key position? 1959 *Economist* 2 May 455/2 While the aircraft industries of Britain and France are declining for lack of military orders, a plum military contract has been won by a company making its first serious venture into aircraft design since the war. 1966 *Listener* 26 May 746/2 After the Nationalists had come to power, they felt that they had to admit some Afrikaners to their boards and directorates. These were plum appointments and the Boers had been longing for them for years. 1970 *Financial Times* 13 Apr. 10/6 Europe (the present plum client in the German Railways advertising service). 1976 BOTHAM & DONNELLY *Valentino* xi. 85 The director..congratulated him on winning the plum role. 1977 *Time* 3 Jan. 50/2 The leader of L.D.P.'s largest faction, whose intellect had won him plum jobs in the Ministry of Finance before he turned to politics in 1952, has probably done exactly that.

plum (plʌm), *a.* Also 6 plumme, 7–9 plumb. [app. f. same root as PLUM *v.*]

1. = PLUMP *a.*[1] 3. Now *dial.*

1570 NORTH *Doni's Philos.* II. 50 This Tenche was so plumme and fatte that shee might well serue him for a good meale. *Ibid.* III. 69 Hee is rounde, plumme, fatte, and as full as an Egge. 1591 HARINGTON *Orl. Fur.* VII. xiv, Her necke was round, most plum and large her brest. 1594 NASHE *Unfort. Trav.* 42 A pretie rounde faced wench..as fat and plum euerie part of her as a plouer.

2. *dial.* Soft and elastic, as a cushion; well-raised and light, as bread.

1847–78 HALLIWELL, *Plum*, light, soft. *West.* 1853 *N. & Q.* 1st Ser. VIII. 65/2 *Plum*..employed in Devonshire in the sense of 'soft', e.g. 'a plum bed': meaning a soft, downy bed. *Ibid.*, If the cake rises well in the oven, it is commonly said that it is 'nice and plum'. 1893 'Q.' [COUCH] *Delectable Duchy* 207 The cushions felt extraordinary plum.

3. *dial.* Of a rock: Soft, easily worked.

1855 J. R. LEIFCHILD *Cornwall Mines* 96 As regards granite, the miner commonly prefers the somewhat decomposed kinds, in a state to which he applies the term *plumb*—a term much in use in Cornwall to express softness combined with a fair amount of resistance. *Ibid.* 97 A plumb granite or elvan is more particularly esteemed for tin, though the cases are not rare in which large bunches of copper and tin ores are found in hard granite.

For other dial. senses see *Eng. Dial. Dict.*

4. *Comb.*

1598 FLORIO, *Puttotta*, a good handsome, plum-cheekt wench or lasse. 1603 —— *Montaigne* I. xxiv. 63 Insteade of plum-feeding the same [mind], hee hath onely spunged it vp with vanitie. *Ibid.* I. xxxviii. 121 More plumb-cheekt, in better health and liking then I am.

plum, *v.* *Obs.* exc. *dial.* Forms: 5 plumb-y, plum-, 6 plom, 9 plum, plumb. [This and the related adj. PLUMMY are known from *c* 1400; the vb. appears to contain a root found also in PLIM *v.*, and perh. in PLUMP.]

1. *intr.* To swell up; to become light or spongy, as dough when 'rising'.

1398 TREVISA *Barth. De P.R.* XVII. ii. (Bodl. MS.), þer is clene and pure aier and moche swete humoure and þat for plumynge and holes þat drawiþ and fongeth swete humoure. *Ibid.* XIX. iv, Moiste mater ipressed and ifonge [*ed.* 1495 take] is araied & made to plumby & to sprede [*humidum compressum paratur ad sparsionem et partium separationem*]. 1853 *N. & Q.* 1st Ser. VIII. 65/2 There is also a verb *to plum*... Dough, when rising under the influence of heat and fermentation, is said to be *plumming* well. 1875 M. G. PEARSE *Dan. Quorm* 32 Why there was the pan of bread set down before the fire to 'plumb'.

2. a. *trans.* To make plump; to render soft and springy: = PLUMP *v.*[2] 1.

1594 PLAT *Jewell-ho.* III. 27 How to plom vp a horse, and to make him fatte and lustie. 1903 *Eng. Dial. Dict.* (Cornwall), To 'plum up' the bed or pillow, i.e. to render them soft.

b. To fill or stuff *up* (a person) with false information.

1921 *Chambers's Jrnl.* May 323/1 He ain't to know no different but what Jack's got prairie fever. Mind you plum him up stiff. 1927 *Observer* 20 Nov. 26/5 He has recently returned from Upper Silesia..and promptly puts into writing all that his clever German friends have been 'plumming' him up with.

plum, variant of PLUMB *sb.*, *a.*, and *v.*

plumaceous (plu:ˈmeɪʃəs), *a.* *rare*⁻⁰. [f. mod.L. *plūmāce-us*, f. L. *pluma* plume: see -ACEOUS.] Feathery, having the character of a contour-feather.

1858 MAYNE *Expos. Lex.*, *Plumaceus*,..pertaining to a feather; feathery; plumaceous.

pluˈmach, pluˈmash. *Obs.* exc. *Hist.* [a. F. *plumache* (now only dial.) = It. *piumaccio* a plume or bunch of feathers; f. L. *plūma* feather

+ suffix repr. L. *-aceus, -um*.] A plume. Cf. PLUMASSE.

1494 in *Lett. Rich. III & Hen. VII* (Rolls) I. 400 Foure balde horsses, well barded and like crestes on theyr heddys as wer on theire tentes stondyng be twen ij. great and high plumashis of whit. *a* **1684** LAW *Mem.* (1818) 162 Plumashes above, and gramashis below, Its no wonder to see how the world doth go. **1687** A. LOVELL tr. *Thevenot's Trav.* I. 86 Having on their Heads their Caps of Silver guilt, with Plumaches of Feathers. *c* **1689** in Napier *Dundee* (1862) II. 11 He wore a white plumach that day. **1904** A. LANG *Hist. Scot.* xi. 335 He was the more conspicuous as the only wearer of a white plumach.

† **plu'maciol.** *Med. Obs.* Also 6 **-aciolle, -aceole.** [ad. med.L. *plūmāciolus*, dim. from late L. *plūmācium* down pillow (Ambrose, Cassiod.), f. *plūma* soft feather, down. Cf. OF. *plumaceole*, and *plumacel* (in Godef.) in similar sense.] A pledget or small pad used in surgery.

c **1400** *Lanfranc's Cirurg.* 13 Brynge þou þe parties of þe wounde togidere þoruȝ sowynge, or wiþ plumaciols—þat ben smale pelewis—or wiþ byndynge, if þat sewynge be nouȝt nessessarie. **1597** A. M. tr. *Guillemeau's Fr. Chirurg.* 11 b/2 With lint, and with little plumaceoles therof being made. *Ibid.* 18 b/2 A flatte plumaciolle or tent made of linte.

† **plu'made.** *Obs. rare.* [app. corrupt. of *plumard*: cf. *cockade*. (Palsgr. has 'Busshe of oystrisshe fethers, *plumart*', f. *plume* + *-art*, -ARD.)] A mourning plume for a horse.

1722 *Lond. Gaz.* No. 6084/4 A Mourning Horse covered with black Cloth,..with Plumades before and behind. **1736** LEDIARD *Life Marlborough* III. 418 The second Mourning-Horse, covered with black Cloth, caparisoned with the same Arms.., with Plumades, led by a Groom on Foot.

plumage ('plu:mɪdʒ). Also 5 **plomage,** 7 **plummage.** [a. OF. *plumage* (14th c., *plumaige*, in Littré), f. *plume* PLUME: see -AGE.]

1. Feathers collectively; the natural covering of a bird.

1481 CAXTON *Myrr.* II. xvi. 102 The pecock..is moche prowde of his fair fethers and plumage. **1486** [see MAIL *sb.*[1] 5]. **1630** DRAYTON *Noah's Flood* Wks. (1748) 467/1 Pruning his plumage, cleansing every quill. **1678** PHILLIPS (ed. 4), *Plumage*, a term in Hawking for the Feathers under a Hawks Wing. **1742** GRAY *Spring* 47 No painted plumage to display. **1801** STRUTT *Sports & Past.* II. i. 54 We are not..to conclude, that the goose alone afforded the plumage for the arrows. **1859** DARWIN *Orig. Spec.* i. (1873) 16 The period at which the perfect plumage is acquired varies.

fig. **1852** MRS. STOWE *Uncle Tom's C.* xvi, While she was thinking what to say, Marie gradually wiped away her tears, and smoothed her plumage in a general sort of way.

† **b.** *spec.* in *Falconry.* Feathers given to a hawk as a casting (CASTING *vbl. sb.* 3 c). *Obs.*

1486 *Bk. St. Albans* A iij b, Euer fede hir with vnwassh meet and looke that hir castyng be plumage. **1575** TURBERV. *Falconrie* 117 Giue hir casting or plumage agayne according as hir state dothe require. **1633** LATHAM *Falconry* Words Art Expl., *Plummage* are small downy feathers which the Hawke takes, or are giuen her for casting.

2. *fig.* **a.** In reference to the use of plumes.

1805 WORDSW. *Prelude* VI. 296 All the strength and plumage of thy youth. **1823** SCOTT *Peveril* xii, This expression of liberality and trust..gave full plumage to Mistress Deborah's hopes. **1862** GOULBURN *Pers. Relig.* ix. (1873) 327 The false plumage of an expiation.

b. Jocularly applied to dress.

1895 RASHDALL *Univ. Europe* I. 22 The Doctor of Music, who in spite of his gorgeous plumage is not a member of Convocation.

3. A bunch or tuft of feathers used as an ornament; a plume. Now *rare.*

1656 BLOUNT *Glossogr.*, *Plumage*, feathers or a bunch of feathers. **1677** *Lond. Gaz.* No. 1206/1 Having Scarlet, and other fine Coats, all richly laced, and bearing very rich Plumages, Scarfs, and Embroidered Belts. **1738** GLOVER *Leonidas* I. 400 The purple plumage nods. **1858** CARLYLE *Fredk. Gt.* IX. x. (1872) III. 174 Nothing of the soldier but the epaulettes and plumages.

4. *attrib.* and *Comb.*, as **plumage-stitch** (*Embroidery*), a stitch or arrangement of stitching designed to imitate plumage; **plumage-work**: see quot. 1886.

1886 LADY ALFORD *Needlework as Art* vi. 207 The 'Opus Plumarium' is one of the most ancient groups, and includes all flat stitches... I propose to restore its original title of plumage work. **1901** L. F. DAY & MARY BUCKLE *Art in Needlework* vii. (ed. 2) 62 [Feather-stitch] is not to be confounded with what is called 'plumage-stitch', which..is a version of satin-stitch. *Ibid.* x. 100 The worker adapts.. the length of the stitch to the work to be done, directing it also according to the form to be expressed, and so arrives,.. by way of satin-stitch, at what is called plumage-stitch.

plumaged ('plu:mɪdʒd), *a.* [f. prec. + -ED[2].] Furnished with or as with plumage, feathered; having plumage.

1820 KEATS *Cap & Bells* v, On they swim With the sweet princess on her plumag'd lair. **1837** H. AINSWORTH *Crichton* I. 297 Parrots, and other gaily plumaged birds. **1865** ALEX. SMITH *Summ Skye* (1880) 287 Every knoll plumaged with birches. **1874** COUES *Birds N.W.* 302 They..became very finely plumaged by the fall. **1895** MRS. B. M. CROKER *Village Tales* 87 Flocks of bright-plumaged water-fowl.

plumagery ('plu:mɪdʒrɪ). [f. as prec. + -RY.] (See quot.)

1879 *Cassell's Techn. Educ.* III. 204/2 The Chinese are now very skilful and ingenious in the art of plumagery or feather-working.

plumash: see PLUMACH.

plumasite ('plu:məsaɪt). *Petrogr.* [f. the name of *Plumas* Co., California, where it was first found + -ITE[1].] A coarse-grained, under-saturated, dike-rock consisting essentially of crystals of corundum in an oligoclase matrix.

1903 A. C. LAWSON in *Bull. Dept. Geol. Univ. Calif.* III. 228 This particular type of rock magma does not appear to have been as yet recognized among the known occurrences of rocks, and it is, therefore, proposed to name it, for convenience in reference, *Plumasite*, from Plumas county to which it occurs. **1949** F. H. HATCH et al. *Petrol. Ign. Rocks* (ed. 10) III. iii. 262 Dioritic rocks of unusual composition include plumasite. **1972** *Jrnl. Geol. Soc. India* XIII. 198 Investigations in the present case have proved that plumasite is a result of the local enrichment of alumina in the magma due to the reaction of the acid magma of the Peninsular gneissic period with the older magnesian country.

† **plu'masse.** *Obs. rare.* [a. obs. F. *plumasse* (1505) a great plume, f. *plume* PLUME + augment. suffix *-asse*:—L. *-ācea*, adj. suffix.] = PLUMACH.

1494 in *Lett. Rich. III & Hen. VII* (Rolls) I. 396 Therll of Suffolkes..crest..was a lion of gold, the taille fourched, sett in maner of a curnalles with plumasses whit and grene.

† **plu'massery.** *Obs. rare*[−0]. [a. OF. *plumasserie* ornament of feathers (Godef.), f. *plumasse*: see prec., and cf. next.]

1656 BLOUNT *Glossogr.*, *Plumassery*, a plume or bunch of feathers. [So 1775 in ASH; and in subseq. Dictionaries.]

plumassier (plu:mə'sɪə(r)). Also 6 **-asier.** [a. F. *plumassier* (1480), f. *plumasse*: see above and -IER.] One who works or trades in feathers or plumes for ornamental purposes.

1598 HAKLUYT *Voy.* I. 250 The couerings of his tent..are all of gold..with the curious workemanship of plumasiers. **1812** MOORE *Post-bag* (heading) Anacreontic to a Plumassier. **1846** MRS. GORE *Eng. Char.* (1852) 46 Lady Downingstreet must take care that her Royal Highness's court plume come home in due time from the plumassier. **1894** *Spectator* 20 Jan. 80/1 The plume of egret's feathers, or 'ospreys', as the plumassiers..chose to call them.

plumate ('plu:mət), *a. Entom.* [ad. L. *plūmāt-us*, pa. pple. of *plūmāre* to cover with feathers.] Feathered, covered with plumose down.

1826 KIRBY & SP. *Entomol.* IV. xlvi. 324 *Plumate*..when the awn is feathered. **1890** *Cent. Dict.*, *Plumate antenna*, an aristate antenna with the arista covered with fine hairs, as in many flies.

† **'plumatile,** *a. Obs. rare.* [ad. L. *plūmātilis* (Plautus) embroidered like feathers, f. *plūma* feather.] Made of feathers.

1715 tr. *Pancirollus' Rerum Mem.* II. i. 279 That plumatile kind of Work..brought to us from the utmost Parts of the West Indies.

† **plu'mation.** *Obs. rare*[−1]. [n. of action from L. *plūmāre* to feather: see -ATION.] An application of a feather or of down to a sore, etc.

1597 LOWE *Chirurg.* (1634) 206 Sometimes the tumor is so malignant, that..we are constrained to apply actuall cauters, or tents, and plumations what [? wet] in oyle of Vitreoll.

† **plumative,** *a. Obs. rare*[−0]. [f. L. *plumāt-us* feathered + -IVE.]

1623 COCKERAM, *Plumatiue*, made of feathers. [**1644** Ridiculed in *Vindex Anglicus* 5, 6.]

plumb (plʌm), *sb.* Forms: 3–7 **plumbe,** 3–9 **plum,** 4–7 **plumme,** 5 **plomme,** 5–6 **plombe,** 5–7 **plume,** 6 **plome,** 7– **plumb.** [ad. F. *plomb*:—L. *plumb-um* lead; the ME. forms *plumbe, plombe, plomme*, app. a. OF. **plombe, plomme* (1309 in Godef.) sounding lead:—late L. **plumba*, orig. pl. of *plumbum*. In sense 2 app. f. PLUMB *v.*]

1. A mass or ball of lead, used for various purposes. **a.** The weight attached to a mason's plumb-line, to secure its perpendicularity; also a weight attached for the same purpose to a quadrant.

off or *out of plumb*, out of the perpendicular.

a **1300** *Cursor M.* 2247 Wit cord and plum [*v.rr.* plumbe, plumme] þai wroght sa hei. **14..** in Halliw. *Rara Math.* (1841) 58 Til..þe threde whereon þe plumbe henges falle vpon þe mydel lyne of þe quadrant. *c* **1440** *Promp. Parv.* 405/2 Plumbe, of wryhtys or masonys (*K.*, *P.* plumme..), *perpendiculum.* **1530** PALSGR. 256/1 Plumbe for a carpenter, *riglet.* **1769** WALES in *Phil. Trans.* LX. 151 The spirits of wine, in which the plumb of the quadrant is immersed. **1858** W. ARNOT *Laws fr. Heaven* Ser. II. xv. 128 They suspend their plumb, not from the middle, but from one edge of the rule. **1891** *Pall Mall G.* 2 Mar. 3/2 The column is seriously off plumb. **1906** *Expositor* Feb. 180 It is not level .., and therefore, being out of plumb, must sooner or later fall.

b. A sounding-lead, a mariner's plummet; also a plummet used by anglers to measure the depth of a stream or pond. Also *fig.*

[Cf. **1309** JOINVILLE *Vie de S. Louis* cxxii. (Godef.), Giete ta plomme.] *c* **1440** LOVELICH *Merlin* 4564 He Sank a-down lik a plom of led. **1530** PALSGR. 256/1 Plumbe for a shyppeman, *plomb de sonde.* *a* **1653** G. DANIEL *Idyll.* ii. 8 For once that word had weight, a whineing Man Hangs to the Plumme. **1863** COWDEN CLARKE *Shaks. Char.* xi. 276 His mind intellectual plumb hath never yet sounded.

c. In other senses (chiefly *obs.*), as: a small piece of lead with which a scourge or rod is loaded; a weight of a clock or of a similar instrument; a small weight attached to a fishing-line below the float, to keep the latter in an upright position; a ball or bullet of lead as a missile; a kind of dumb-bell.

a **1350** *St. Laurence* 191 in Horstm. *Altengl. Leg.* (1881) 110 With staues he bad þai suld him bete And pelt on him with plumes of lede. *c* **1440** CAPGRAVE *St. Kath.* v. 1133 Bete hir and rende hir with Iern and plummes of leed! *a* **1450** *Fysshynge w. an Angle* (1883) 16 þe next plume to the hoke schall be ther from a large fote & more and euery plumbe of quantite to þe gretnes of the lyne. **1463** *Bury Wills* (Camden) 28 To..wynde vp the peys and the plummys as ofte as nede is. **1496** *Acc. Ld. High Treas. Scot.* I. 293 Lede to ȝet the plumbis. *Ibid.* 295 To cary the plumbis of lede fra the Abbay to the clos cartis. **1601** DENT *Pathw. Heaven* 281 The plumbe of a clocke, being the first moouer, doth cause all the other wheeles to mooue. **1625** *Vestry Bks.* (Surtees) 296 For a rope for the great plumbe of the clocke, 2s. 6d. **1681** CHETHAM *Angler's Vade-m.* iv. §14 (1689) 46 The least weight of Plumb or Lead you can. **1867** J. B. ROSE tr. *Virgil's Æneid* 211 They..hurled from slings the deadly plumb of lead.

2. *Sc.* and *north. dial.* 'A deep pool in a river or the sea; a perpendicular fall' (E.D.D.). (Usually spelt *plum.*)

1819 in R. Ford *Harp Perth.* (1893) 208 (E.D.D.) Yon fause stream, that near the sea, Hides monie a shelve and plum. **1835** J. WILSON *Noct. Ambr.* Wks. 1856 IV. 235 Tak tent you dinna droon me in some plum. **1895** OCHILTREE *Redburn* xv. 144 The 'plums' were the only parts of its narrow channel that showed signs of water.

3. *Comb.*: † **plumb-right** *a.*, exactly vertical; † **plumb-wise (plim-wise)** *adv.*, in the manner of a plumb-line, perpendicularly.

1532 MORE *Confut. Tindale* Wks. 826/2 Wyth a strynge by the halfe keepe them plume right vnder. **1552** HULOET, Plummeryght downe, *perpendicularis.* **1613** M. RIDLEY *Magn. Bodies* vii. 26 The Waight *C* is attracted plim-wise to the Axis *A.B.*

plumb, plum (plʌm), *a.* and *adv.* Forms: 5 **plom,** 6 **plome, plum(m)e,** 6–7 **plumbe,** 5– **plum,** 7– **plumb** (9 **plomb**). [f. PLUMB *sb.*]

A. *adj.* **1.** Vertical, perpendicular.

c **1460** *Towneley Myst.* iii. 520 The water, syn she [the dove] com, Of depnes plom, Is fallen a fathom. **1519** HORMAN *Vulg.* 240 All wallis..muste be made leuell and plumme. **1613** M. RIDLEY *Magn. Bodies* 142 A waight.. fastned at the bottome to hold this ring plumbe and steady. **1715** LEONI *Palladio's Archit.* (1742) I. 1 The care of erecting the Walls very plum. **1897** BAILEY *Princ. Fruit-growing* 245 Necessity for staking and tying the trees to keep them plumb.

2. a. Downright, thorough-going; sheer.

1748 RICHARDSON *Clarissa* (1810) IV. xi. 259 Neither can an opposition, neither can a ministry, be always wrong. To be a plumb man, therefore, with either is an infallible mark, that the man must mean more and worse than he will own he does mean. **1894** *Chicago Advance* 6 Sept., Nothing but pests—just plum pests. **1904** C. MARRIOTT *Genevra* vi. 106 Addling their brains with plum trash about love and all.

b. *Cricket.* Of the wicket: Level, true.

1902 *Daily Chron.* 29 July 3/2 To witness a modern first-class match on a 'plumb' wicket. **1903** LD. HAWKE in *Westm. Gaz.* 13 Mar. 9/2, I believe there are counties who go into the field on a day when, we will say, there is a plumb wicket, and say 'we shall be here until half-past six'.

B. *adv.* [Cf. F. *à plomb* straight down.]

1. Of motion or position: Vertically, perpendicularly; straight *down*; rarely, straight *up*.

c **1400** *Laud Troy Bk.* 1833 Hit was diked doun plum, That no man myȝth ther-ouer com. *a* **1548** HALL *Chron.*, *Hen. VIII* 24 Diches..so brode and so plume [*ed.* **1550** plum, GRAFTON plumme] stepe yᵗ was wondre to behold. **1601** HOLLAND *Pliny* I. 8 When the Sunne shineth directly plumbe ouer mens heads, and causeth no shadow. **1640** G. ABBOT *Job Paraphr.* 252 The eagle is so strong as to mount plum up..to an infinit height. **1667** MILTON *P.L.* II. 933 Fluttring his pennons vain plumb down he drops. **1755** YOUNG *Centaur* v. Wks. 1757 IV. 240 Shall we rush, as down a precipice, and leap plumb into the jaws of extempore death? **1843** CARLYLE *Past & Pr.* II. xiii, The Abbot, starting plumb up..answered [etc.]. **1849** RUSKIN *Sev. Lamps* iv. §11. 103 Drapery..fell from their human forms plumb down.

2. *transf.* and *fig.* **a.** Exactly, directly, precisely.

1601 HOLLAND *Pliny* XVIII. xxxiv. 609 The wind Septentrio that bloweth plumbe North, is far more daungerous and mischievous. **1701** CIBBER *Love Makes Man* II. ii, Lay your Lips softly, softly, close and plum to hers. **1748** RICHARDSON *Clarissa* (1810) III. lvi. 303 Her daughter..imagined herself plumb against me. **1851** MAYNE REID *Scalp Hunt.* xx. 147 Most of them [Delawares] can hit 'plumb centre' with any of their mountain associates. **1871** MORLEY *Crit. Misc.* Ser. I. 246 The famous diatribe against Jesuitism in the Latter-Day Pamphlets..points plumb in the same direction.

b. Immediately, directly, straight.

a **1734** NORTH *Exam.* I. iii. §144 (1740) 216 If the Lords had come plumb upon their Trial, and..had been acquitted, the politic Crisis had been at an End.

c. As an intensive: Completely, entirely, absolutely, quite. Chiefly *U.S. slang.*

1587 *Misfortunes of Arthur* (1828) II. iv. *Chorus* 41 Then rowles and reeles and falles at length plum ripe. **1787** GROSE *Provinc. Gloss.*, *Plum pleasant*, very pleasant. **1846** S. F. SMITH *Theatr. Apprenticeship* 213 Long before the time arrived..the house was plum, chock full—full to overflowing. *a* **1861** T. WINTHROP *John Brent* xxviii. 296 When we got here, I paid their tickets plum through to York out of my own belt. **1882** Burdett *Life Penn* v. 83 Penn.. wrote his wife and children a long letter.. which filled them plumbfull of good advice. **1893** *Harper's Weekly* Christmas 1211/1 'You're plumb crazy', she remarked, with easy candor. **1897** Kipling *Captains Courageous* 21 You've turned up, plain, plumb providential for all concerned. **1901** F. Norris *Octopus* I. iii. 121 'I'll get plumb out of here,' he trumpeted. 'I won't stay here another minute.' **1926** 'R. Crompton' *William—the Conqueror* v. 89 Poor woman! She's sure plumb crazy! **1934** A. Christie *Murder on Orient Express* II. ix. 136 'You are sure of that, M. Hardman?' 'I'm plumb certain.' **1967** G. F. Fiennes *I tried to run a Railway* vii. 76 In his presence I was tense, tongue-tied and often plumb stupid. **1973** E. Lemarchand *Let or Hindrance* xiv. 182 They must both be plumb crazy.

plumb (plʌm), *v.* Also 4 **plumben**, 5 **plome**, 5–7 **plumbe**, 6 **plombe**, 6–9 **plum**. [f. plumb *sb.* and *a.*, in various unconnected senses; partly perh. after F. *plomber* (1539 in Hatz.-Darm.).]

I. 1. *intr.* To sink or fall like a plummet; to fall or plump straight down. *rare.*

c **1380** Wyclif *Serm.* Sel. Wks. II. 186 þer hertis ben so hevy þat þei plumben doun to helle. **1940** *Sat. Even. Post* 6 Apr. 17/3 [He] rolled down [from a house-top] & plumbed into the yard.

II. 2. a. *trans.* To sound (the sea, etc.) with a plummet; to measure (the depth) by sounding.

a **1568** *Satir. Poems Reform.* xlvi. 29 Plum weill the grund quhat evir ȝe doo. **1580** Hollyband *Treas. Fr. Tong*, *Plomber*, to plombe or sounde the depth of a thing. **1708** J. Chamberlayne *St. Gt. Brit.* I. I. iii. (1737) 10 Poole's-Hole .. has been plumbed to the Depth of 800 Fathom, and yet no Bottom found. **1726** Swift *Gulliver* I. v, I consulted the most experienced seamen upon the depth of the channel, which they had often plummed. **1867** F. Francis *Angling* ii. (1880) 71 The depth having been carefully plumbed.

b. *fig.* To sound the depths of; to fathom, to reach the bottom of.

1599 *Broughton's Let.* xii. 40 Though Plato and Hermes haue plumbd it deeply, must wee reach no further, then their shallow sounding? **1847** Lytton *Lucretia* ii, Silently she looked down, and plumbed them all [infirmities]. **1849** Clough *Amours de Voy.* v. 151 So I plumb the deeps of depression.

c. *to plumb a track* (*U.S. colloq.*), to trace or follow out a road.

1844 Mrs. Houston *Yacht Voy. Texas* II. 205 Plumbing the track, the Texan term for tracing a road, is, at all times, a slow and tedious operation. **1892** J. L. Lawless in *Country Church* (Buckland, Mass.) 16 Mar., I.. always noticed that when Old Rover took one track and plumbed it through, he holed the game.

III. 3. To render vertical, to adjust or test by a plumb-line. Also *fig.*

1711 W. Sutherland *Shipbuild. Assist.* 162 To *Plum*, to hew any Piece downright, or perpendicular. **1795** *Phil. Trans.* LXXXV. 448 Slender staffs were.. made upright, by being plumbed in directions at right angles to each other. **1874** Thearle *Naval Archit.* 23 They are valuable aids in plumbing the frames and keeping the side of the ship fair.

4. a. To place vertically above or below.

1838 *Civil Eng. & Arch. Jrnl.* I. 235/1 Above will be elegant sheds and powerful cranes, to plumb the hold. **1875** Bedford *Sailor's Pocket Bk.* vii. (ed. 2) 264 The shears should be so placed that a boat.. may come under them, or be 'plumbed' from their heads when sloped.

b. *intr.* To hang vertically.

1867 Smyth *Sailor's Word-bk.*, *To plumb*, to form the vertical line. **1882** Nares *Seamanship* (ed. 6) 121 The purchase [will] plumb clear of the ship's side.

IV. †5. *trans.* (?) To solder with lead. [Cf. Cotgr. '*Plomber*, to lead, or tinne; also, to soulder, or colour with lead,' etc.] *Obs.*

c **1479** *Paston Lett.* III. 271 A standing cuppe with a cover therto plommed.

6. To weight with lead.

a **1450** *Fysshynge w. an Angle* (1883) 16 Your lynys must be plomed with leyd. **1616** Surfl. & Markh. *Country Farme* 512 After your hooke is thus fastened, you shall plumbe your line; which is to fasten certain pieces of lead.. about it. **1669** Worlidge *Syst. Agric.* (1681) 243 Stake this Net athwart the River; the bottom being plumbed, that it may sink about six inches. **1811** W. Taylor in *Monthly Rev.* LXVI. 464 The oars are plumbed in the handle, so as to balance on the edge of the boat.

7. To seal (luggage) with a leaden seal.

1756 Nugent *Gr. Tour, France* IV. 20 When your luggage has been searched, you had better have your trunk plumbed with a leaden stamp for Paris. **1788** Jefferson *Writ.* (1859) II. 473, I shall have the whole corded and plumbed by the Custom house here. **1820** Mrs. Starke *Direct. Trav. on Cont.* ii. 36 We had our trunks plumbed, in order to secure them from examination [by the custom-house officers].

V. [Back-formation from *plumber*.]

8. *intr.* To work in lead as a plumber. Also *trans.* (*colloq.*)

1889 W. S. Gilbert *Foggerty's Fairy*, etc. (1892) 217, I am a plumber... I have plumbed in the very best families. **1901** *Speaker* 30 Mar. 703/1 There was once a perfect being who did actually plumb. *Mod. newspaper*, The house has been duly plumbed, painted, and whitewashed.

9. *trans.* To connect (a domestic appliance or the like) permanently to the water supply and the drain. Usu. with *in.*

1963 *Which?* 6 Feb. 46/2 The Easiclene [dishwashing machine] would normally be plumbed in, but could be used with hoses from a tap and into a sink. **1976** I. Chanarin et al. *Blood & its Dis.* ix. 79 Automatic equipment using potentially toxic reagents should be plumbed-in. **1976** *Star* (Sheffield) 20 Nov. 10/7 (Advt.), Abbey Plumbing Emergency Service. Bursts and leaks, washing machines plumbed, gas fitting and alterations.

Hence **'plumbing** *ppl. a.*, doing plumbers' work.

1896 *Daily News* 1 Feb. 3/1 Even the plumbing fraternity cannot grumble. It is a mistake.. to suppose that a very rigorous winter is the best for plumbers.

plumb: see plum.

plumbagin (plʌm'beɪdʒɪn). *Chem.* [ad. F. *plombagine*, f. L. *plumbāgo* (see plumbago) + *-ine*, -in[1].] The acrid principle of the root of *Plumbago europæa.* (See plumbago 3.)

1830 *Amer. Jrnl. Sc.* XVII. 385 *Plumbagine*, a new vegetable substance... M. Dulong has obtained a particular vegeto-principle from the roots of the *Plumbago Europæa.* **1838** T. Thomson *Chem. Org. Bodies* 767 Plumbagin.. was discovered by M. Dulong d'Astafort, in the root of the *plumbago Europæa*, in 1828. **1866** Watts *Dict. Chem.* IV. 685 *Plumbagin*.. crystallises in delicate needles or prisms often grouped in tufts; has a styptic saccharine taste, with acrid biting after-taste.

† plum'bagine. *Obs.* Also **plomb-**. [ad. F. *plombagine* (1572 in Godef.), ad. L. *plumbāgo, -inem*: see plumbago.]

1. See quots. (Perh. never in Eng. use.)

[**1611** Cotgr., *Plombagine*, f., pure lead turned almost into ashes by the vehemence of the fire: This is th'artificiall *Plombagine*, and comes of lead put into a furnace with gold, or siluer oare, to make them melt the sooner... There is also a naturall, or minerall *Plombagine*, which (as Mathiolus thinketh) is no other then siluer mingled with lead-stone, or oare.] **1656** Blount *Glossogr.*, *Plumbagin* [quoting Cotgr. verbatim]. **1658** Phillips, *Plumbagin* [**1706** -ine], silver mingled with lead stone, or oar. **1730–6** Bailey (folio), *Plumbagine*, lead naturally mingled with silver.

2. = plumbago 2.

1802 Playfair *Illustr. Hutton. The.* 304 In the banks of the same river [Ayr] some miles higher up, he [Dr. Hutton] found a piece of coal.. involved in whinstone, and extremely incombustible. It consumed very slowly in the fire, and deflagrated with nitre like plumbago. This he considered as the same fossil which has been described under the name of *plombagine.* **1811** Pinkerton *Petralogy* I. 552 Anthracite seems to have been first observed by Dolomieu; but Born.. has classed it under graphite, which he calls *plombagine*, or carburet of iron. **1854** J. Scoffern in *Orr's Circ. Sc., Chem.* 384 Crystallized carbon is.. found naturally.. as a mineral species known by the appellation plumbagine. **1857** Birch *Anc. Pottery* (1858) I. 245 Vauquelin takes it to be a carbonaceous matter, such as plumbagine or black-lead.

plumbaginous (plʌm'bædʒɪnəs), *a.* [f. L. *plumbāgo, -in-em* plumbago + -ous.] Of the nature of or pertaining to plumbago or graphite.

1796 Kirwan *Elem. Min.* (ed. 2) II. 184 Plombaginous, or micaceous iron ore. **1820** Faraday *Exp. Res.* xvi. (1859) 77 It.. considerably resembles the plumbaginous powder.. obtained by the action of acid on cast iron. **1845** Lyell *Trav. N. Amer.* I. 249 In the plumbaginous anthracite of Worcester the proportion of volatile matter is about 3 per cent. **1862** Dana *Man. Geol.* v. 77 The variety plumbaginous schist contains plumbago in its layers.

plumbago (plʌm'beɪgəʊ). Also 7 **plumbage**, 8 **plombago**. [a. L. *plumbāgo* a species of lead ore, also a plant, leadwort, fleawort (Pliny): in both senses rendering Gr. μολύβδαινα of Dioscorides, deriv. of μόλυβδος lead. For the original meaning and complicated history of the word, see note below.]

†1. Applied to the yellow oxide of lead (litharge); also sometimes to the sulphide (galena); and (in quot. 1612) app. to minium or red oxide of lead, obtained from litharge by further oxidation. *Obs.*

1612 Woodall *Surg. Mate* Wks. (1653) 77 Plumbago, or red lead, hath the force of binding. **1661** Lovell *Hist. Anim. & Min.* 38 Plumbage [L.] *Plumbago.* P[lace] It sticks to the furnace in the purifying of silver or gold. M[atter] of Silver or Gold purified with lead. N[ame] Μολύβδαινα Molybdæna ..it's like litharge in vertue. **1669** Rowland tr. *Schroder's Med.-Chem. Pharmacop.* xix. 245–6 Molybdena or Plumbago. It is natural or artificial: the first is Lead Ore or that mixed with silver. The artificial is a kind of Litharge, that sticks to the bottom of the Furnace [etc.].

2. *Min.* Black lead or graphite; one of the allotropic forms of carbon: used for pencils, also, mixed with clay, for making crucibles; and for many other purposes.

'Black lead' is the popular, and 'graphite' the strictly scientific name; but the term 'plumbago' is largely used in the arts, esp. in mining.

1784 Kirwan *Elem. Min.* 158 Plumbago, *Reissbley.. Blyertz* of the Swedes... In a strong heat and open fire it is wholly volatile. **1786** tr. *Scheele's Chem. Ess.* 243 The black lead or plumbago which is generally known in commerce, is very different from molybdæna. *Ibid.* 250 Hence I am convinced, that plumbago is a kind of mineral sulphur or charcoal; the constituent parts of which are aerial acid and a considerable quantity of phlogiston. **1788** *Cronstedt's Min.* (ed. 2) II. 451 Black lead or plumbago is a fossil substance extremely black. **1795** Pearson in *Phil. Trans.* LXXXV. 335 The black matter was therefore a compound of iron and carbon, or, as some chemists term it, plumbago; and which in the new system is denominated a carburet of iron. **1796** Kirwan *Elem. Min.* (ed. 2) II. 58 Plumbago. Graphite of Werner.. carbon combined with one tenth or one eighth of its weight of malleable iron. **1799** —— *Geol. Ess.* 191 Probably because the iron.. had absorbed too great a quantity of carbon, and was thus converted into plombago. **1808** Henry *Epit. Chem.* (ed. 5) 242 Another combination of iron and carbon, which is a true carburet of iron, is the substance called plumbago, or black-lead, used in fabricating pencils, and in covering iron to prevent rust. [So **1815** (ed. 7) II. 120.] **1843** Humble *Dict. Geol.* (ed. 2) 32/1 Anthracite resembles and appears to pass into plumbago. **1846** McCulloch *Acc. Brit. Empire* (1854) I. 619 That very rare mineral called black lead, plumbago, or wad, is found in Borrowdale, in Cumberland. The mines in this place have been wrought since the days of Queen Elizabeth, and furnish the very best material hitherto discovered for making pencils. **1869** Roscoe *Elem. Chem.* (1871) 82 Graphite, or Plumbago, crystallizes in six-sided plates.

3. *Bot.* A genus of herbaceous plants, inhabiting Southern Europe, Asia, Africa, and America, having spikes of subsessile flowers, with a tubular five-parted calyx; leadwort: so called from the colour of the flowers. [Pliny's name (rendering Gr. Μολύβδαινα), adopted as generic name by Tournefort, 1700.] Also *attrib.*

[**1601** Holland *Pliny* II. 336 There groweth commonly an herbe named in Greeke Molybdæna, that is to say in Latine, *Plumbago*, euen vpon euery corne land.] **1747** Wesley *Prim. Physic* (1762) 42 Infusion of Leaves of Plumbago in Olive Oil. **1776** Lee *Introd. Bot.* App. (ed. 3) 337 Leadwort, *Plumbago.* **1877** J. A. Chalmers *Tiyo Soga* vi. 53 He distributed twigs from the plumbago plant to be worn round the neck. **1903** *Contemp. Rev.* Mar. 346 Pale blue plumbagos, yellow canariensis.

[*Note.* In Dioscorides, μολύβδαινα, f. μόλυβδος lead, was applied to a mineral substance (v. 97, 100), and a plant. The former was yellow oxide of lead (PbO), esp. the litharge produced in the extraction of gold and silver from ores containing lead. By Pliny this is latinized as *molybdæna*, also once (xxxiv. 18. 50) by *plumbāgo*, which, as well as *galēna*, were applied by him to the yellow oxide, but prob. included as an inferior variety the sulphide (PbS), called by Dioscorides μολυβδοειδὴς λίθος, 'lead-like stone', the modern galena. For the plant Pliny always uses *plumbago*. In the French transl. (1572) of Matthioli's Commentary on Dioscorides, μολύβδαινα = *plumbago* is rendered *plombagine*, in It. *piombaggine*, and is stated to be identical with litharge; but other ores may have been included. Thence the explanations of the word in Cotgrave and other English writers down to Bailey: see plumbagine, and sense 1 above. In Holland's *Pliny*, *plumbago* is rendered *litharge*. In the 16th c., to Agricola and others in Germany practically interested in mining, *plumbago* mainly meant the sulphide of lead, but also included other substances similar to this in appearance, and in the property of staining the fingers and marking paper, esp. the native sulphides of antimony and molybdenum, stibnite (Sb_2S_3) and molybdenite (MoS_2), and the mineral graphite. In 1567 Christoph. Enkel (Encelius) of Saalfeld, while identifying Pliny's *molybdæna*, *galēna*, and *plumbāgo*, distinguished the 'productive' species (i.e. the oxide and sulphide of lead) from the 'barren' (*sterilis*), which yielded no lead, and was mainly graphite; the latter was described by Ferrante Imperato in 1599 as employed in the *grafio piombino*, 'leaden pencil'. In 1779 Scheele found that certain samples of the 'barren' plumbago, on being burnt, were dissipated into carbonic acid gas, and that in fact they consisted of carbon: see quot. 1786 in sense 2. In 1789 Werner and Karsten proposed the name graphite instead of the ambiguous 'plumbago'. But its composition was still disputed. An analysis, made by French chemists in 1786, had given, after volatilization, a residue of iron, and plumbago was pronounced a carburet of iron (see quot. 1795). This view prevailed until Karsten in 1826 and Sefström in 1829 proved that the iron was only an impurity in the specimens analysed, and that graphite or plumbago was, as Scheele had said in 1779, really a mineral form of carbon. (See paper by Dr. John W. Evans, F.G.S., in *Trans. Phil. Soc.* 1907.)]

plum'bagoed, *a.* [f. prec. + -ed[2].] Covered with plumbago, black-leaded.

1860 Alex. Watt *Electro-Metallurgy* 58 A solution of nitrate of silver.. will answer well for depositing on plumbagoed surfaces.

plum'ballophane. *Min.* [See plumbo-.] 'A variety of allophane containing a little lead' (Chester *Dict. Min.* 1896).

plumbane. *Chem.* [f. L. *plumb-um* lead + -ane 2.] **†1.** Davy's proposed name for chloride of lead, horn-lead. *Obs.*

1812 Sir H. Davy *Chem. Philos.* 397 One combination only of lead with chlorine is known.. called horn lead by the old chemists... The name proposed for it is plumbane.

2. [-ane 2 b.] **a.** Any of the alkyl compounds of lead or the hypothetical series of saturated lead hydrides (analogous to the alkanes) from which they are formally derived; freq. as a formative element in names of such compounds. **b.** *spec.* Lead tetrahydride, PbH_4, an extremely unstable gas.

1920 *Chem. Abstr.* XIV. 2182 The mol. wt. indicates that it has the double formula $[(C_8H_9)_3Pb]_2$ so that it might be considered as hexa-*p*-xylyldiplumbane. **1950** N. V. Sidgwick *Chem. Elements & Compounds* I. 554 Lead hydride, plumbane, presumably PbH_4.. was prepared by Paneth in 1920. *Ibid.* 596 The diplumbane formed may change further into lead tetra-aryl and metallic lead. **1964** A. Rochow *Organometallic Chem.* i. 4 The system [of nomenclature] is so useful that it has been extended.. even to tin and lead (..$(C_6H_5)_2PbCl_2$, diphenyldichloroplumbane), although the older inorganic names like diphenyllead dichloride still persist to a considerable extent. **1967** P. L. Pauson *Organometallic Chem.* iii. 78 The rather unstable plumbanes have only been obtained by direct reduction of the halides with suitable hydrides. **1971** Wiberg & Amberger *Hydrides Elements of Main Groups I–IV* x. 757 Similar attempts to obtain plumbane, PbH_4,.. were unsuccessful. *Ibid.* 760 Trimethylplumbane, Me_3PbH, and triethylplumbane, Et_3PbH, decompose according to kinetics that are first-order for $[R_3PbH]$. **1973** J. J. Lagowski *Mod. Inorg. Chem.* xi. 368 Plumbane has been prepared in only trace amounts from the reactions which yield the hydrides of the other elements in this family.

† **'plumbary.** *Obs. rare.* [ad. L. *plumbārius*, f. *plumbum* lead.] Lead ore, galena.

1657 TOMLINSON *Renon's Disp.* 428 Lead..is extracted also out of a certain Plumbary, effoded out of Mynes, which stone they call Molybdoides; the Lead thus secerned and melted, is poured into water, while hot, till it leave its dross.

plumbat, obs. Sc. form of PLUMMET.

† **'plumbate,** *sb.*[1] *Obs.* Also 7 (?) plumbet. [app. ad. late L. *plumbātæ* leaden balls, also (Cod. Theodos.) a scourge to which leaden balls were attached, f. *plumbāre* to make of lead; but cf. PLUMMET *sb.* 4.] In *pl.* The leaden balls with which a scourge was loaded.

1570 FOXE *A. & M.* (ed. 2) 94/1 Then Decius moued with anger commaunded hym to be beaten with plumbattes (which is sayth Sabellicus, a kinde of scourging). **1609** HOLLAND *Amm. Marcell.* 330 Sericus and Asbolius..he caused to be killed with the mightie pelts of plumbets.

'plumbate, *sb.*[2] *Chem.* [f. L. *plumb-um* lead + -ATE[1] 1 c; first formed as F. *plombate* (E. Fremy 1843, in *Jrnl. de Pharm.* III. 32).] Any of various (salts of) oxyanions or hydroxyanions of quadrivalent lead, which are formed esp. by the action of alkalis on lead dioxide. Now also extended occas. to (salts of) any oxyanion of lead, the oxidation state being specified in brackets.

1851 H. WATTS tr. *Gmelin's Handbk. Chem.* V. 160 (*heading*) Plumbate of potash. **1865** WATTS *Dict. Chem.* III. 555 The solution of plumbate of potassium forms with metallic salts precipitates of analogous composition. **1889** I. REMSEN *Inorg. Chem.* xxx. 645 Other salts derived from the acid $PbO(OH)_2$ are known, and are called plumbates. **1950** N. V. SIDGWICK *Chem. Elements & Compounds* I. 603 Plumbic hydroxide, $Pb(OH)_4$. This..gives a series of salts, the plumbates, of various types, such as Ca_2PbO_4 and Na_2PbO_3. **1958** *Engineering* 21 Feb. 242/1 The manufacture, properties and applications of..rust-inhibiting calcium plumbate paint were outlined. **1959** *Nomencl. Inorg. Chem.* (I.U.P.A.C.) 32 By dissolving, for example, Sb_2O_3, SnO, or PbO in sodium hydroxide an antimonate(III), a stannate(II), a plumbate(II), *etc.*, is formed in the solution. **1962** COTTON & WILKINSON *Adv. Inorg. Chem.* xix. 364 Crystalline alkali metal stannates and plumbates can be obtained as trihydrates, for instance, $K_2SnO_3{\cdot}3H_2O$... Such materials..contain the anions $Sn(OH)_6^{2-}$ and $Pb(OH)_6^{2-}$. **1974** G. I. BROWN *Introd. Inorg. Chem.* xviii. 210 Tin(II) and lead(II) oxides..form salts with acids and stannates(II) and plumbates(II) with alkalis. *Ibid.* 211 Both oxides react with caustic alkalis to form stannates(IV) or plumbates(IV).

plumbate ('plʌmbeɪt), *a.* and *sb.*[3] [f. L. *plumb-um* lead + -ATE[2].] Of or pertaining to a type of glazed and usu. lead-coloured pottery made in pre-Columbian central America. Also *absol.* as *sb.*

1926 S. K. LOTHROP *Pottery of Costa Rica & Nicaragua* I. i. iv. 116 The vitrified surface of the Plumbate Ware did not lend itself to painted decoration. **1936** —— *Zacualpa* 39 The typical vessel of pure plumbate clay is hard, well fired and has a glossy surface. **1940** J. E. S. THOMPSON in *Maya & their Neighbours* 129 The absence of plumbate and typical fine orange pottery, turquoise, and gold..hint that these sites are not contemporaneous with the Mexican Period of Yucatan. **1948** A. O. SHEPARD *Plumbate* 1/2 Plumbate effigies in particular show a fascinating versatility coupled with a tendency to follow fixed types. **1962** G. KUBLER *Art & Archit. Anc. Amer.* ix. 205 A few 'glazed sherds' found during excavation: if these were plumbate, a Toltec Maya date would be in order. **1971** L. A. BOGER *Dict. World Pottery & Porcelain* 345/2 Two outstanding types of pottery made in large quantities and traded wherever Toltec influence was evident are Fine Orange ware..and Plumbate. *Ibid.* 346/1 Plumbate ware dates from around 1000.

‖**plum'bator.** [med.L. *plumbātor*, f. L. *plumbāre* to solder with lead.] In the Papal service, A custodian of the leaden seal.

1677 W. HUGHES *Man of Sin* II. xii. 229 Innocent 8... His new office of Plumbators..brought him in 26000 crowns.

plumb-bob ('plʌm,bɒb). The leaden bob, usually conoidal, forming the weight of a plumb-line.

1835–40 HALIBURTON *Clockm.* (1862) 16 If he is found here after twenty-four hours, they'd make a carpenter's plumb-bob of him, and hang him outside the church steeple. **1879** *Cassell's Techn. Educ.* IV. 190/1 A spirit level is laid upon its edge, or a plumb-bob is dropped from its middle point.

† **'plumbean,** *a. Obs.* [f. L. *plumbe-us* leaden + -AN.] Resembling lead; leaden; lead-coloured.

1656 BLOUNT *Glossogr.*, *Plumbean, Plumbeous*, of the colour and property of lead; leaden; also dull, blunt. *a* **1688** CUDWORTH *Immut. Mor.* I. iii. §7 To make wisdom..to be..regulated by such a..'plumbean and flexible rule' as that is, is quite to destroy the nature of it. **1783** POTT *Chirurg. Wks.* II. 312 He had..a pale plumbean countenance.

plumbeous ('plʌmbiːəs), *a.* [f. L. *plumbe-us* leaden (f. *plumb-um* lead) + -OUS.]

1. Made of or resembling lead, leaden; lead-coloured. Chiefly in *Zool.*

1623 COCKERAM, *Plumbeous*, full of lead, heauie. **1658** PHILLIPS, *Plumbeous*, leaden, of the colour of lead; also blunt, or dull. **1826** KIRBY & SP. *Entomol.* IV. 284. **1867** A. L. ADAMS *Wand. Nat. India* 115 Another and smaller species, the plumbeous or sooty redstart. **1874** COUES *Birds N.W.* 321 Feathers..plumbeous at base and brown at tip.

b. *Ceramics.* Lead-glazed.

1875 FORTNUM *Maiolica* i. 4 Glazed and enamelled wares ..plumbeous or lead glazed. **1879** J. J. YOUNG *Ceram. Art* 63 Silicious, or glass-glazed, and plumbeous, or lead-glazed, both of which are transparent.

† **2.** *fig.* Heavy, dull, ponderous, leaden. *Obs.*

1578 SIDNEY *Wanstead Play* in *Arcadia*, etc. (1629) 622 Attend and throw your eares to mee..till I haue endoctrinated your plumbeous cerebrosities. *c* **1645** HOWELL *Lett.* (1650) II. 30 The motion of Saturn,..plumbeous, long, and heavy. **1686** GOAD *Celest. Bodies* II. ix. 284 Whether he be such a Plumbeous Blew-nosed Planet as Antiquity marks him.

plumber ('plʌmə(r)). Forms: 4 **plomber**, 4–8 **plummer**, 5 **plomere**, **plommer**, **plumbar**, 5–6 **plomer**, 5–7 **plumer**, 6 **plommar**, *Sc.* **plummair**, 5– **plumber**. [a. OF. *plummier* (1266), *plommier*, mod.F. *plombier*:— L. *plumbārius* a plumber, f. *plumbum* lead.] **1. a.** An artisan who works in lead, zinc, and tin, fitting in, soldering, and repairing the water and gas pipes, cisterns, boilers, and other work executed in these metals in the construction of a dwelling-house or other building. Originally applied to a man who dealt and worked in lead. In mod. use, a workman who installs and repairs piping and fittings to do with water supply, sanitation, and drainage.

1385–6 [see b]. **1399** *Mem. Ripon* (Surtees) III. 129 In salario Willelmi Bettys, plummer, operanti super corpus ecclesiæ. *c* **1440** *Promp. Parv.* 406/1 Plumber, or plomere, *plumbarius*. **1477** *Paston Lett.* III. 212 Vyncent the plomer is a nothir that chal bere the dawnger. **1548** *Act 2 & 3 Edw. VI*, c. 15 §4 Any..Brick-maker, Tile maker, Plummer or Labourer. **1584** *Vestry Bks.* (Surtees) 17 Item given to the plumer for mendinge the leades, xiij s. iiij d. **1610** B. JONSON *Alch.* II. i, And, early in the morning, will I send To all the plumbers, and the pewterers, And buy their tin, and lead vp. **1663** GERBIER *Counsel* 47 Sauder, wherewith an unconscionable Plummer can ingrosse his Bill. **1706** PHILLIPS, *Plummer*, one that deals, or works in Lead. **1847** SMEATON *Builder's Man.* 130 Within the last four years, zinc has been extensively employed instead of lead, and the plumber has undertaken the execution of such works. **1887** *Spectator* 29 Oct. 1445 All the tradesmen employed, down even to the plumber.

b. *attrib.* and *Comb.*, as ***plumber-house, -work***; ***plumber's force-pump, furnace*** (see quots.).

1385–6 *Durham Acc. Rolls* (Surtees) 391 Pro punctura x rod' et dimid. de Wrigthous et le Plomberhous. **1844** STEPHENS *Bk. Farm* I. 195 Of the specifications of plumber-work..done after the carpentry. **1875** KNIGHT *Dict. Mech.*, *Plumber's force-pump*, a pump used by plumbers for testing pipe or withdrawing obstacles from a gorged pipe. **1884** *Ibid.* Suppl. *Plumbers' furnace*, a portable soldering furnace.

2. *transf.* **a.** *Services' slang.* An armourer or engineering officer. **b.** *slang.* During the administration of United States President Richard M. Nixon (1969–74), a member of a White House special unit for investigating leaks of government secrets, which came to public notice after it was discovered that they had engaged in illegal practices, including the installation of concealed microphones; also *transf.*

a. 1941 D. MASTERS *So Few* xix. 224 The plumbers—the name by which the armourers are generally known in the service. **1943** C. H. WARD-JACKSON *It's a Piece of Cake* 48 *Plumber*, the Engineering Officer. **1946** G. HACKFORTH-JONES *Sixteen Bells* I. vii. 106 To the average 'Plumber' the word Engine is synonomous [*sic*] with steam. **1962** *Flight* 11 Nov. 605/2, I am not an engineer (or 'plumber', as the Royal Air Force equivalent is unofficially called). **1970** *Navy News* Feb. 2/1 It would be of great help in this project if, among your readers, there were a few ex-Keyham 'plumbers' who would be prepared to turn out their photographs of those times for us to borrow.

b. 1972 *Time* 28 Aug. 24/2 The intelligence squad grew out of a team of so-called 'plumbers', originally recruited by the Administration to investigate leaks to the media. **1973** *Times* 15 May 7/1 President Nixon sent a personal letter to Mr J. Edgar Hoover, then Director of the Federal Bureau of Investigation (FBI), in June, 1971, telling him that Mr Egil Krogh had been put in charge of a special White House task force on national security and asking for FBI cooperation with it. The group later became known as 'the plumbers' because it tried to plug leaks of information. **1974** *Times* 9 Jan. 5/6 The investigating magistrate in the case of *Le Canard Enchaîné* questioned for two hours today a counter-espionage agent who has been allegedly identified as one of the 'plumbers' in the attempted bugging of the satirical weekly magazine. **1976** *Billings* (Montana) *Gaz.* 6 July 3A 1 Ehrlichman is now appealing a five-year sentence following his conviction for obstruction of justice for his part in the break-in of the office of Daniel Ellsberg's psychiatrist by the now-infamous 'plumbers'. **1977** *Time* 24 Jan. 52/1 He found a band of 'plumbers' busily installing listening devices.

Hence **'plumbership**, the office of plumber.

1455 *Rolls of Parlt.* V. 316/2 Th' office of Plummership of the Castels of Carnarvan, Beaumares and Hardlagh.

plumber-block: see PLUMMER-BLOCK.

plumbery ('plʌmərɪ). Also 5 **plomerye**, 6 **plombmery**, **plumery**. [ME. a. OF. *plommerie* (1304), *plomberie* lead-work, plumber's workshop, f. *plommier* plumber; in med.L. *plumbāria*; cf. L. *plumbārius* of or belonging to lead, *plumbārium* a place to keep leaden vessels in.]

1. A plumber's workshop.

14.. *Voc.* in Wr.-Wülcker 603/34 *Plumbaria*, a plomerye. *c* **1544** in *Wiltsh. Archæol. & Nat. Hist. Mag.* (1867) X. 79 To cary the leed outh of the halle to the plombmery. **1649** in Nichols *Progr. Q. Eliz.* (1823) II. 416 One room, called the Plummery, and several other rooms and lodgings belonging to the Clerk of the Works. **1823** *Mechanic's Mag.* No. 13. 205 Stating that a plumbery had been burnt at Dover, and that the fire was occasioned by..workmen permitting some lead to boil over. **1896** ST. JOHN HOPE in *Proc. Soc. Antiq.* Ser. II. XVI. 164 The room..was formerly the plumbery, and has in the centre a large table for casting sheets of lead.

2. Plumber's work, plumbing.

1464 *Rolls of Parlt.* V. 547/2 Th' office of Serjeaunt of oure Plumbery within this our Reaume. **1703** T. N. *City & C. Purchaser* 228 *Plumbery*..the Art of Working in Lead. **1823** P. NICHOLSON *Pract. Build.* 403 The Art of Plumbery comprehends the practice of casting and laying sheet-lead. **1853** TURNER *Dom. Archit.* II. i. 18 The jurors found that..plumbery was needed to the value of 20 marks.

† **plumbet.** *Obs.* Also 6 **plumet**, **plommett**, **plomet**, **-it**. [app. a deriv. of F. *plomb* lead, PLUMB *sb.*, perh. in reference to its colour, and thus practically a parallel form of PLUNKET, of which it appears to be a synonym. Note the alteration of *plumbet* to *plumket* in the later edition of Udall.] A woollen fabric; app. the same as PLUNKET. Also *attrib.*

1533 UDALL *Floures Lat. Spekynge* 199 b, *Cæsius*,..and *glaucus*, is blew or grey, as the sky is when it hath litle speckes of grey clowdes in a faire day, as it were a plumbet [*ed.* 1560 plumket] colour. **1590** *Lanc. & Chesh. Wills* III. 68 My best cloke my jirkine and breeches of stript plumet. **1661** PEACHAM *Compl. Gent.* (ed. 3) 156 Plumbet colour, i.e. like little Speks of gray clouds in a fair day. **1720** STRYPE *Stow's Surv.* II. v. ix. 180/1 The sorts of this new Drapery [time of Q. Eliz.] were various. They were Bays,..Rash or Stannet,..Serche,..Plomets, Carells, Fustians of Naples. *Ibid.* 181/1 Plomits, wrought with Silk, or otherwise. **1882** BECK *Draper's Dict.*, *Plommetts, pommetts*, stuffs mentioned in 1592 as being in pieces of fourteen yards each, of four pounds weight, and valued at £1.

plumbet, var. PLUMBATE; obs. f. PLUMMET.

plum'bethyl. *Chem.* [See PLUMBO- and ETHYL.] A compound of lead with molecules of ethyl, as *plumbotriethyl*, $Pb_2(C_2H_5)_6$, the *methplumbethyl* of Löwig, a yellowish mobile oil; *plumbotetrethyl* $Pb(C_2H_5)_4$, diethylide of lead, a transparent colourless liquid.

1857 MILLER *Elem. Chem.* III. 214 Oxide of Plumbethyl (hydrated). **1865** MANSFIELD *Salts* 291 Löwig has more recently described another metallothylic base... This is his Plumbethyl.

plumbian ('plʌmbɪən), *a. Min.* [f. L. *plumb-um* lead + -IAN 2.] Of a mineral: having a (small) proportion of a constituent element replaced by lead.

1930 W. T. SCHALLER in *Amer. Mineralogist* XV. 571 Lead—plumbian. **1944** C. PALACHE et al. *Dana's Syst. Min.* (ed. 7) I. 804 *Var.* Ordinary. Calcium and uranium... Plumbian... With PB:U = 3:8 (anal. 1). Titanian. With Ti:Cb + Ta:Fe³ = 9:3:1 (anal. 6). **1968** I. KOSTOV *Mineralogy* II. ii. 169 The following varieties are recognized: (*a*) of tetrahedrite—ordinary, zincian, ferroan,..plumbian, nickelian, etc.

plumbic ('plʌmbɪk), *a.* [f. L. *plumb-um* lead + -IC. Cf. F. *plombique*.] Of or pertaining to lead.

a. *Chem.* Combined with lead; applied to compounds in which lead has its higher valency (quadrivalent), as ***plumbic acid***, dioxide of lead, PbO_2. Formerly also applied by some writers to compounds of bivalent lead (cf. PLUMBOUS *a.* 2).

plumbic ochre, lead ochre, massicot.

1799 SIR H. DAVY in Beddoes *Contrib. Phys. & Med. Knowl.* (1799) 119 The plumbic phosoxyd evidently contains oxygen and light. **1854** J. SCOFFERN in *Orr's Circ. Sc., Chem.* 465 Three combinations are known of oxygen with lead... The latter [the binoxide] is sometimes denominated plumbic acid. **1854** R. D. THOMSON *Cycl. Chem.* 328/1 Binoxide, Peroxide, Deutoxide, Brown or puce oxide, Plumbic acid.—PbO_2. **1865** WATTS *Dict. Chem.* III. 555 With bases, peroxide of lead unites more readily than with acids, behaving towards alkalis like a weak acid, and may therefore be called plumbic acid. **1868** W. A. MILLER *Elem. Chem.* (ed. 4) II. xviii. 717 Lead oxide, plumbic oxide, or protoxide of lead (PbO = 223)... This oxide is well known under the name of litharge. *Ibid.* 719 Plumbic dioxide, or peroxide of lead (PbO_2= 239). **1873** WATTS *Fownes' Chem.* (ed. 11) 593 Plumbic Ethide is produced by the action of plumbic chloride on zinc ethide. **1900** W. A. SHENSTONE *Elem. Inorg. Chem.* xxix. 439 Plumbic oxide (PbO) is known as litharge or massicot. **1921** J. R. PARTINGTON *Text-bk. Inorg. Chem.* xliv. 925 A yellow liquid, which is lead tetrachloride, or plumbic chloride, $PbCl_4$, is deposited. **1935** *Chambers's Encycl.* VI. 564/1 Plumbic Oxide (monoxide of lead, massicot, litharge), PbO. .. Plumbic Peroxide..PbO_2... Plumbic Chloride (chloride of lead), $PbCl_2$. **1950** N. V. SIDGWICK *Chem. Elements & Compounds* I. 587 The change from the plumbous alkyls to the plumbic is less easy with the heavier alkyls. **1962** P. J. & B. DURRANT *Adv. Inorg. Chem.* xviii. 641 A list of certain alkyl and aryl compounds of lead in the plumbic condition. *Ibid.* 644 Lead tetra-acetate (plumbic acetate), $Pb(CH_3COO)_4$, is made by saturating hot glacial acetic acid with red lead.

b. *Path.* Due to the presence of lead.

1875 H. C. WOOD *Therap.* (1879) 38 Plumbic renal degeneration is evidently the result of a long-continued irritation. **1897** *Allbutt's Syst. Med.* II. 979 Occasionally in plumbic paralysis a small indolent swelling on the back of the wrist is noticed.

plumbicon ('plʌmbɪkɒn). *Television.* [f. L. *plumb-um* lead + *-icon*, after VIDICON.] A type of television camera tube similar to a vidicon but in which the photoconductive layer of the signal plate is of lead monoxide.

1962 E. F. DE HAAN in *Philips Technical Rev.* XXIV. 58/1 The photoconductive layer consists of vapour-deposited lead monoxide, PbO, and we have therefore called this tube the 'Plumbicon'. **1971** *Physics Bull.* Aug. 457/1 The other is the plumbicon colour TV tube now used in practically all colour TV cameras all over the world. **1976** *Wireless World* June 75/3 A camera based on three 2/3-in. Plumbicons with built-in image enhancement.

plum'biferous, *a.* [f. L. *plumb-um* lead + -FEROUS. Cf. F. *plombifère*.] Containing lead.

1796 KIRWAN *Elem. Min.* (ed. 2) II. 222 The Plumbiferous Silver Ore also contains 48 per cent. of Lead. **1839** URE *Dict. Arts* 748 The total thickness of the plumbiferous formation. **1879** J. J. YOUNG *Ceram. Art* 56 Transparent glaze may be plumbiferous or alkaline.

†**'plumbine**, *a. Obs. rare.* [f. L. *plumb-um* lead + -INE[1].] Of leaden colour.

1597 LOWE *Chirurg.* (1634) 17 The Melancholicke which is..of colour, livide, & plumbine.

plumbing ('plʌmɪŋ), *vbl. sb.* [-ING[1].] **a.** The action of the vb. PLUMB, in various senses; now *esp.* the work of a plumber.

1666 BOYLE in *Phil. Trans.* I. 335 What methods the mine-men use in following the Vein, and tracing their passages under ground (which they call Plumming and Dyalling) according to the several exigencies? **1711** W. SUTHERLAND *Shipbuild. Assist.* 162 *Plummet*, a Weight hanging by a Line to prove the Plumming. **1884** CHANDLER in *Pall Mall G.* 24 July 11/2 Three years ago..a plumbing law was passed, which placed the control of plumbing and drainage in all new houses in the hands of the Board of Health. **1886** *York Herald* 3 Aug. 7/6 'Plumbing' was largely indulged in, top fishing being abandoned except in a few cases.

b. *concr.* That which is made by this action; lead-sealing; plumber's work. Also *transf.* in various senses: (*a*) *colloq.*, a system of pipes, tubes, or ducts in an engine or other complicated apparatus or installation; (*b*) *Jazz slang*, a trumpet, trombone, or similar wind instrument; (*c*) *spec.* a lavatory; lavatory installations (*colloq.*); (*d*) *slang*, fillings in teeth; (*e*) *joc.*, the excretory tracts, the urinary system.

1756 NUGENT *Gr. Tour, France* IV. 33 As soon as you enter Paris, you will be stopt in your chaise, and your pass and plumbings, and every corner of the whole chaise will be examined. **1899** *Westm. Gaz.* 23 Oct. 2/3 They tore down gas-pipes, water-pipes, and electric wires from the walls, demolished the fixtures, wrenched the plumbing apart.

a. *a* **1929** in V. W. Pagé *Mod. Aviation Engines* (1929) II. xl. 1593 Courtney's flight, Franco's flight and the Polish flight were all three terminated by what is popularly known as 'plumbing' trouble... The engines stopped through failure of the feed lines. **1938** —— *Airplane Servicing Man.* xxii. 758 Aircraft space is limited, and..complicated plumbing must be installed in very close quarters. **1950** J. L. NAYLER *Mod. Aircraft Design* v. 78 Pumps and their connections have to be installed in places where they can be inspected and 'plumbing' is accordingly a big factor in their installation. **1955** *Sci. Amer.* Oct. 34/3 New materials—e.g., liquid sodium as the coolant, beryllium as the moderator, zirconium for the 'plumbing'..—may open the way for reactors..needing only a modest investment of fissile fuel. **1959** *New Scientist* 12 Feb. 359/2 The wave-guide, or 'plumbing' as the radar engineer calls it, is simply a metal tube down which radio waves will travel. **1971** H. E. ENNES *Telev. Broadcasting: Equipment, Syst. & Operating Fund.* xii. 548 Fig. 12-11 illustrates typical microwave plumbing.

b. **1935** *Vanity Fair* (N.Y.) Nov. 71/3 *Plumbing* or *piston* for trumpet. **1951** *Cosmopolitan* July 85 Hap said, 'You with the plumbin', what's your name?' **1955** *Vogue* 15 Sept. 124 Kai Winding and J. J. Johnson (above) pair their spruce, understated trombones ('just plumbing') against a backing of bass, drums and piano.

c. **1950** *Publ. Amer. Dial. Soc.* XIV. 50 *Outside plumbing*, euphemism for no plumbing, a privy. **1971** *Countryman* Winter 118 The house is progressing at last. We have bought a mountain of building supplies—pink plumbing and all. **1978** S. ALLAN *Inside Job* i. 18, I expect she wants to wash... Don't be obtuse... I want to show her the plumbing.

d. **1955** J. THOMAS *No Banners* xiv. 117 The fillings in his teeth had been removed and replaced by unmistakable French 'plumbing'.

e. **1960** in Wentworth & Flexner *Dict. Amer. Slang* 398/1 This mild little medicine will fix your constipation, your stomach, your plumbing. **1963** M. MCCARTHY *Group* v. 103 Helena had known about sex from a very early age but treated it as a joke, like what she called your plumbing. **1972** G. BELL *Villains Galore* iii. 31 Excuse me, Albert, but I must see to the plumbing. Won't be a minute.

c. *attrib.*, as **plumbing-line**, **-rope**, a lead-line, sounding line.

1688 BOYLE *Final Causes Nat. Things* iv. 136, I do not find that mens..plumming lines have reached above one mile of that great number. **1693** OLIVER in *Phil. Trans.* XVII. 908 Fastening our Bottle to our Plumbing-rope.

plumbism ('plʌmbɪz(ə)m). *Path.* [f. L. *plumb-um* lead + -ISM.] Lead-poisoning.

1876 BARTHOLOW *Mat. Med.* (1879) 227 In prescribing the preparations of lead for internal use, the danger of producing plumbism should not be overlooked. **1878** A. M. HAMILTON *Nerv. Dis.* 410 The tremor from lead is attended usually by colic and other symptoms of plumbism. **1901** *Speaker* 16 Nov. 174/1 It is the solubility of the lead when taken into the system that causes plumbism.

,plumbi'solvent, *a.* Erron. plumbo-solvent. [f. L. *plumb-um* lead + SOLVENT: for the form cf. L. *tergiversans*, *velivolans*, *bellipotens*, etc.] Acting as a solvent on lead, capable of dissolving lead. Hence **plumbi'solvency**, capacity of dissolving lead.

1892 M. MACKENZIE in *Youth's Comp.* 31 Mar. 162 (Funk) Lead is a fruitful source of disease in certain districts.. where the water has what is termed a plumbo-solvent quality. **1897** *Allbutt's Syst. Med.* II. 965 Occasionally it is necessary to test the 'plumbo-solvency' of a suspected water. *Ibid.* 966 Water..may..dissolve lead by a true plumbo-solvent action.

plumbite ('plʌmbaɪt). *Chem.* [ad. F. *plombite* (E. Fremy 1843, in *Jrnl. de Pharm.* III. 31), f. *plomb* lead: see -ITE[1].] Any of various (salts of) oxyanions or hydroxy anions of bivalent lead, which are formed esp. by the action of alkalis on lead(II) hydroxide and are freq. represented as PbO_2^{2-}; applied also to certain mixed oxides of bivalent lead and another metal.

1851 H. WATTS tr. *Gmelin's Hand-bk. Chem.* V. 158 (*heading*) Plumbite of ammonia. **1903** H. C. JONES *Princ. Inorg. Chem.* xl. 480 Lead hydroxide..has..acid properties dissolving readily in strong bases. The salts have the composition M_2PbO_2 and are known as plumbites. **1927** J. W. MELLOR *Comprehensive Treat. Inorg. & Theoret. Chem.* VII. xlvii. 665 The plumbites all appear to be salts of a monobasic acid analogous with the corresponding stannites and germanites. *Ibid.* 669 Grube obtained a mixture, $2MgO.PbO.3H_2O$, or magnesium plumbite, by the oxidation of magnesium hemiplumbide in the presence of moisture. **1950** N. V. SIDGWICK *Chem. Elements & Compounds* I. 603 It is possible to make a plumbate by atmospheric oxidation of a plumbite. **1968** K. M. & R. A. MACKAY *Introd. Mod. Inorg. Chem.* xv. 223/1 Addition of alkali to lead II solutions gives a precipitate of the hydrated oxide, which dissolves in excess alkali to give plumbites.

'plumb-joint. [For *plumbed joint*: cf. PLUMB *v.* 5.] A lap-joint in sheet-metal in which one of the edges to be joined is laid flat over the other and soldered down; a soldered lap-joint.

1875 in KNIGHT *Dict. Mech.* 1751.

plumbless ('plʌmlɪs), *a.* [f. PLUMB *v.* + -LESS.] That cannot be plumbed; fathomless.

1651 OGILBY *Æsop* (1665) 209 May..quaff If he had twenty Plumbless Oceans. **1854** DICKENS *Hard T.* xv, The moment shot away into the plumbless depths of the past. **1946** W. DE LA MARE *Traveller* 29 Into a plumbless deep of sleep he sank. **1960** C. ACHEBE *No Longer at Ease* iii. 26 For the first time since they had left Liverpool, the sea became really blue; a plumbless blue set off by the gleaming white tops of countless wavelets.

plumb-line ('plʌmlaɪn), *sb.* Also 7 plim-.

1. A line or cord having at one end a metal bob or plummet, for testing or determining vertical direction; sometimes = PLUMB-RULE.

1538 ELYOT *Dict. Perpendiculum*, a plumlyne, such as masons and carpenters haue, with leadde at the ende. **1609** BIBLE (Douay) *Isa.* xxxiv. 11 A measure shal be stretched out upon it, to bring it to nothing and a plumme line unto destruction. **1611** COTGR., *Aniveller*, to..square by plumbe-line, or plumbe-rule. **1613** M. RIDLEY *Magn. Bodies* 43 A plim line fastened to one end of the diamiter. **1706** PHILLIPS, *Plumb-Line, Plumb-Rule*, or *Plummet*, an Instrument us'd by Carpenters, Masons, Bricklayers and others, to find whether a Pillar, Wall, etc. stand upright. **1815** J. SMITH *Panorama Sc. & Art* I. 277 The attraction of a lofty mountain is found to draw a plumb-line..a little out of the perpendicular.

b. *fig.* A means of testing or judging; a standard.

1570 T. NORTON *Nowel's Catech.* (1853) 182 To be directed and tried by the most precise rule, and, as it were, by the plumbline of God's law and judgment. **1666** SANCROFT *Lex Ignea* 18 We have no Plumb-line of Reason.

†**2.** *Geom.* A vertical or perpendicular line; a straight line at right angles to another. *Obs.*

1551 RECORDE *Pathw. Knowl.* I. Defin., When one line lyeth flatte (whiche is named the ground line) and an other commeth downe on it, and is called a perpendiculer or plumme lyne. **1570** BILLINGSLEY *Euclid* I. x. 3 A perpendicular line, commonly called among artificers a plumbe lyne. **1704** J. HARRIS *Lex. Techn.* I, *Plumb-Line*, the same with Perpendicular.

3. A mariner's sounding-line; also *fig.* something with which to fathom intellectual or moral depths.

1648 C. WALKER *Hist. Independ.* I. 116 This is an unsoundable Gulfe, here any plumb-line faileth me. **1864** *Spectator* 7 May 527/2 This truth..that degrees of guilt are so utterly beyond the fathoming powers of our plumb-lines without a knowledge of the moral opportunities and antecedents of every life. **1884** J. TAIT *Mind in Matter* Pref. (1892) 6 The plumbline of human degradation surely never touched a lower depth.

Hence **'plumb-line** *v.*, to sound, or determine, as by a plumb-line.

1846 MRS. GORE *Eng. Char.* (1852) 3 The moment a presumptuous individual acts or thinks an inch out of the plumb-lined perpendicularity exacted by the formalities of society. **1875** LEWES *Probl. Life & Mind* II. II. §78. 90 Some unattainable depth to be postulated, but not plumb-lined.

plumbly ('plʌmlɪ), *adv. rare.* [f. PLUMB, PLUM *a.* + -LY[2].] Vertically downwards.

1931 J. C. GREGORY *Short Hist. Atomism* 7 The atoms that fell plumbly through the void were still restless.

plumbo-, before a vowel plumb-, used as combining form of L. *plumbum* lead, forming chemical and mineralogical terms.

plumbo'calcite *Min.*, an isomorphous mixture of the carbonates of lead and calcium, $Pb''CO_3.32Ca''CO_3$, occurring in rhombohedral forms at Leadhills and Wanlockhead (Watts). **plumbo'cuprite** *Min.* = CUPRO-PLUMBITE (Chester). **plumbo'gummite** *Min.* [f. F. *plombgomme* + -ITE[1]], a hydrous phospho-aluminite of lead resembling gum. **plumbo'jarosite** *Min.* [JAROSITE], a basic sulphate of lead and ferric iron, $PbFe_6(SO_4)_4(OH)_{12}$, that occurs as brown hexagonal crystals, esp. as a secondary mineral in lead ores in arid regions. **plumbo'manganite** *Min.*, a sulphide of lead and manganese, $PbS.3MnS$. **plumbo'methyl** *Chem.*, a compound of lead with molecules of methyl, as ***plumbotrimethyl*** $Pb(CH_3)_3$; ***plumbotetramethyl*** $Pb(CH_3)_4$, a colourless mobile liquid (Watts *Dict. Chem.* III. 563). **plumbo'resinite** *Min.* = *plumbogummite*. **plumbo'stannite** *Min.* [L. *stannum* tin], sulphantimonide of tin, lead, and iron (Chester). **'plumbostib**, **-'stibnite** *Min.* [L. *stibium* antimony] = BOULANGERITE.

1834 *Amer. Jrnl. Sc.* XXVI. 386 *Plumbocalcite.. described by Johnson as a mineral found at Wanlockhead in Scotland. **1892** DANA *Min.* (ed. 6) 855 *Plumbogummite. **1902** *Plumbojarosite [see *natrojarosite* s.v. NATRO-]. **1938** *Jrnl. R. Soc. W. Australia* XXIV. 112 This appears to be the first occasion on which either beudantite or plumbojarosite has been found in Australia. **1959** *Mineral Abstr.* XIV. 275/2 Plumbojarosite is found as compact and powdery aggregates of flaky crystals in the Akatuev deposit in eastern Transbaikal region. **1877** J. B. HANNAY in *Mineralog. Mag.* 149 *Plumbomanganite. **1866** WATTS *Dict. Chem.* IV. 685 *Plumboresinite, *Plombgomme*. **1868** DANA *Min.* (ed. 5) 99 **Plumbostib* is also from Nertschinsk. It consists, according to Plattner, of antimony, arsenic, sulphur, a little iron, with 58·8 p.c. of lead; and appears to be boulangerite.

plumbo-solvent, erron. f. PLUMBISOLVENT.

plumbous ('plʌmbəs), *a.* [ad. L. *plumbōs-us* full of lead: see -OUS. Cf. F. *plombeux*.]

†**1.** Leaden; *fig.* dull; = PLUMBEOUS. *Obs.*

1685 H. MORE *Illustration* 336 Such a senseless conceit, that nothing can be more wooden or plumbous. **1737** G. SMITH *Curious Relations* I. iv. 550 To be of a plumbous or leaden Temper and Colour.

2. *Chem.* Applied to compounds in which lead is bivalent; as in ***plumbous acid*** 'term for *plumbi oxidum* in combination with potassium and other bases' (*Syd. Soc. Lex.*). Cf. PLUMBIC a. Formerly also applied by some writers to substances in which lead was thought to be univalent (cf. PLUMBIC *a.* a).

1854 R. D. THOMSON *Cycl. Chem.* 327/2 Protoxide of Lead. Yellow Oxide, Massicot, Litharge, Plumbous Acid. PbO. **1868** W. A. MILLER *Elements of Chemistry* (ed. 4) II. xviii. 721 When heated in closed vessels, part of the sulphur is expelled, and a subsulphide, or plumbous sulphide (Pb_2S) is left. **1883** C. L. BLOXAM *Chem.* (ed. 5) 373 Oxide or protoxide of lead (plumbous oxide) is prepared on a large scale by heating lead in air. **1884** FRANKLAND & JAPP *Inorg. Chem.* xxxix. 699 Plumbous oxide, 'Pb'_2O, is best prepared by heating plumbic oxalate to 300° with exclusion of air... It is a black powder. **1892** MORLEY & MUIR *Watts' Dict. Chem.* (rev. ed.) III. 128/2 Lead protoxide PbO. (Plumbous oxide. Litharge. Massicot.) **1900** W. A. SHENSTONE *Elem. Inorg. Chem.* xxix. 439 Plumbous oxide (Pb_2O). When oxalate of lead is heated to 300° out of contact with air, it leaves a grey residue which absorbs oxygen with avidity. This is the suboxide. **1926** P. C. L. THORNE tr. *Ephraim's Text-bk. Inorg. Chem.* xv. 359 When red lead, Pb_3O_4 (*i.e.* $2PbO.PbO_2$), is treated with nitric acid, the plumbous portion of this compound dissolves, leaving PbO_2 as a brown powder. **1950** [see PLUMBIC *a.* a]. **1962** P. J. & B. DURRANT *Adv. Inorg. Chem.* xviii. 638 Plumbous nitrate, $(Pb(NO_3)_2$, is made by dissolving lead, lead oxide, or lead carbonate in dilute nitric acid... Concentrated sodium hydroxide solution dissolves plumbous chromate.

†**plum-broth.** *Obs.* A kind of thick broth or soup made of beef, prunes, raisins, currants, white bread, spices, wine, sugar, and other ingredients; formerly a Christmas dish. Probably dried plums or prunes were the original characteristic.

a **1613** OVERBURY *Charact., Puritan*, Good bits he holds breed good positions, and the Pope he best concludes against, in plum-broth. **1652** COLLINGES *Caveat for Prof.* xxx. (1653) 118 He hath more mind to the plum-broth then the devotion of the day. **1713** *Queen's Royal Cookery* (Nares) To make plumb-broth. Take a leg of beef, and a piece of the neck..two pound of currans..three pound of raisins of the sun, three pound of prunes well stew'd..have a two-penny white loaf grated, mix it with some of the broth, and put the pulp of the prunes to it..garnish the dish with some of the stew'd prunes, some raisins and currans out of the broth. **1724** POPE *Lett.* (1735) I. 283 A thing call'd Christian Chearfulness, (not incompatible with Christmas Pyes and Plum-broth). [**1864** *Chambers' Bk. Days* II. 755/2 Plum-broth figures in Poor Robin's Almanac for 1750, among the items of Christmas fare.]

plumb-rule ('plʌmruːl). [f. PLUMB *sb.* + RULE *sb.*] An instrument used by builders, masons, carpenters, etc., for ensuring or testing the verticality of an erection; consisting of a plummet and line attached to and swinging freely on the surface of a narrow straight-edged board, marked with a longitudinal line which, when its position is vertical, coincides with the string.

c **1391** CHAUCER *Astrol.* II. §38 Set thy pyn by a plomrewle euene vpryht. **1578** COOPER *Thesaurus*, *Ad perpendiculum*, to trie by the plumbe rule. **1663** GERBIER *Counsel* 27 Brick-layers.. to use often their line, and plumrule. **1879** *Cassell's Techn. Educ.* III. 140/2 *note*, A plumbrule is a straight piece of wood, to which is attached a string with a plummet or lump of lead.

† **'plumby**, *a. Her. Obs.* [ad. OF. *plomé* (*a* 1449 in Godef.) lead-coloured:—L. *plumbātus*, pa. pple. of *plumbāre* to make of lead.] Lead-coloured. In quot. 1586 app. confused with PLUMMY *a.*[2], as if it meant 'plum-coloured'.

1486 *Bk. St. Albans, Her.* aiij, The iiij. stone is calde a Margarete a clowdy stone, plumby hit is calde in armys. **1586** FERNE *Blaz. Gentrie* 246 Purple was called Plumby.

plum-cake. A cake containing raisins, currants, and often orange-peel and other preserved fruits. As to the name, cf. PLUM-BROTH.

1635 [GLAPTHORNE] *Lady Mother* III. ii. in Bullen *O. Pl.* II. 148 Your Schoolefellow With whome you usd to walk to Pimblicoe To eate plumbe cakes and creame. **1664** BUTLER *Hud.* II. ii. 798 And cramm'd 'em.. With Cawdle, Custard, and Plum-cake. **1774** WARTON *Hist. Eng. Poetry* lxi. (1840) III. 396 The splendid iceing of an immense historic plumbcake, was embossed with a delicious basso-relievo of the destruction of Troy. **1859** W. COLLINS *Q. of Hearts* ii, Hadn't we better begin.. by getting her a plum-cake?

plum-coloured, -curculio: see PLUM *sb.*

plum-'damas, -'damis. *Sc.* Also 6 plumdamus, 7 plum(be)-dames, plomdaimes, (8 erron. plumdanes). [f. PLUM *sb.* + OF. *Damas* Damascus; see DAMASK, DAMSON I, 3 (damson plum).] A (? dried) damson plum; a prune.

1565 *Reg. Privy Council Scot.* I. 360 Wyne, vennagir, plumdamas, buttir, cheise. **1577** *Ibid.* II. 645 Ane hundrith pund wecht of plum damus. **1621** *Sc. Acts Jas. VI* (1816) IV. 626/2 Feggis Raisingis plumdames almondis and vther vnconfected fruittis. **1675** in Hunter *Biggar & Ho. Fleming* vi. (1862) 61 A quarter of pund of plomdaimes. **1692** *Scotch Presbyt. Eloq.* (1738) 138 Lord, feed them with the Plumdanes and Raisins of thy Promises. *a* **1780** SHIRREFS *Poems* (1790) 210 Guid barley broth.. Wi' raisins and plumdamis mixt. **1828** MOIR *Mansie Wauch* ii. 25 The table was covered with dishes full of jargonelles and pippins,.. shell-walnuts, and plumdamases.

plum-'duff. Also -dough. [f. PLUM *sb.* 4 + DUFF *sb.*[1]] Plain flour pudding with raisins or currants in it, boiled in a cloth or bag.

1840 R. H. DANA *Bef. Mast* viii. 18 This day was Christmas.. The only change was that we had a 'plum duff' for dinner. **1851** MAYHEW *Lond. Labour* I. 197/2 Plum dough is one of the street-eatables. **1883** STEVENSON *Treas. Isl.* (1886) 241 Alive, and fit, and full of good plum-duff.

Hence **plum-'duffer**, a seller of plum-duff.

1851 MAYHEW *Lond. Labour* I. 198/1, I have ascertained .. that take the year through, six 'plum duffers' take 1s. a day each.

plume (pluːm), *sb.* Also 6 plome. [a. OF. *plume*:—L. *plūma* a small soft feather, down.

OE. had (*a* 1050 in *Lib. Scintill.*) *plūm-feðer*, down, from L. *plūma*; but this has no historical connexion with the ME. and mod. word.]

1. a. A feather; now chiefly *poet.* and *rhet.*; also, a large or conspicuous feather, such as are used for personal adornment, as a plume of an ostrich or egret; in *Ornith.* a contour-feather, as distinguished from a plumule.

1399 LANGL. *Rich. Redeles* III. 49 Thanne cometh.. Anoþer proud partriche.. And sesith on hir sete, with hir softe plumes. **1513** DOUGLAS *Æneis* XI. vi. 113 My feris lost, with plumys in the ayr As thame best lykis ar fleand our alquhair. **1552** HULOET, Plume, *pluma, et plumula*, a very yonge fether. **1601** SHAKS. *Twel. N.* II. v. 37 Contemplation makes a rare Turkey Cocke of him, how he iets vnder his aduanc'd plumes. **1667** MILTON *P.L.* v. 286 Like Maia's son he stood, And shook his Plumes. **1754** GRAY *Poesy* 22 With ruffled plumes and flagging wing. **1851** *Times* 3 Sept. 7/2 The *Trogon resplendens* clad in golden iridescent green, with long lax flowing plumes. **1893** NEWTON *Dict. Birds* 241 The dorsal plumes of the Egrets.

b. *fig.* With various reference to the feathers of birds as used in flight, displayed in pride, raised or ruffled in excitement, or borrowed in pretentious display (as the peacock's plumes assumed by the jackdaw in the fable).

1591 SHAKS. *1 Hen. VI*, III. iii. 7 Let frantike Talbot triumph for a while, And like a Peacock sweepe along his tayle, Wee'le pull his Plumes, and take away his Trayne. **1606** *Sir G. Goosecappe* I. iv. in Bullen *O. Pl.* III. 22 Farre above the pitch of my low plumes. **1641** J. JACKSON *True Evang. T.* I. 4 They stole them out of holy Writ, and pride themselves in the plumes of a Prophet indeed. **1642** R. CARPENTER *Experience* III. iv. 20 If we but glaunce upon the knowledge of our selves, our plumes fall, and we begin to be humble. **1649** BLITHE *Eng. Improv. Impr.* xxvi. (1653) 185 Let him that flatters himself to raise good Clover upon barren heathy Land.. pull down his Plumes after two or three years experience, unless he devise a new way of Husbandry. **1802** *Med. Jrnl.* VIII. 268 In the process of his examination, he is stripped of his borrowed plumes. **1850** KINGSLEY *Alt. Locke* xxxii, My soul.. in the rapid plumes of song Clothed itself sublime and strong.

2. a. Downy plumage, down; plumage generally.

† *of a plume*: cf. *of a feather*, FEATHER *sb.* 2 c.

1552 HULOET, Thystle toppe, whych is lyke plume, *pappus*. **1601** HOLLAND *Pliny* I. 280 A second commoditie that Geese yeeld.. is their plume and downe. For in some places their soft feathers are pluckt twice a yeare. **1633** LATHAM *Falconry* Words Art Expl., *Plume* is the generall colour or mixtures of feathers in a Hawke, which sheweth her constitution. **1654** H. L'ESTRANGE *Chas. I* (1655) 21 To interdict him with the Earls of Somerset, Middlesex, Bristow, (all of an inclination, though not all of a plume). **1667** MILTON *P.L.* XI. 186 The Bird of Jove.. Two Birds of gayest plume before him drove. **1812** J. WILSON *Isle of Palms* III. 600 Vaunt not, gay bird! thy gorgeous plume. **1870** YEATS *Nat. Hist. Comm.* 312 The lower barbs in feathers are usually loose, and form the down, which is called the 'accessory plume'.

b. The web or vane of a quill; the feathering of an arrow.

1808 PIKE *Sources Mississ.* II. (1810) 150 They buried the arrow to the plume in the animal. **1883** D. C. MURRAY *Hearts* III. 38 Carroll held a quill pen in his hand... The hand looked steady, but the quivering plume told how tense the nerves were.

3. a. An ornament, usually symbolizing dignity or rank, consisting of a large feather or bunch of feathers, or a waving feather-like tuft or bunch of hair, etc.; esp. when attached to a helmet, hat, or other head-dress as an aigrette or crest, or worn in the hair, as the ***court plume*** of ostrich feathers; also borne in processions and used at funerals.

† *plume of feathers*: see FEATHER *sb.* 8 b.

1530 PALSGR. 256/1 Plome of oystrydge fethers, *plummart*. *a* **1548** HALL *Chron., Hen. IV* 12 One parte had their Plumes all white, another had them all redde. **1607** SHAKS. *Cor.* III. iii. 126 Your Enemies, with nodding of their Plumes Fan you into dispaire. **1711** ADDISON *Spect.* No. 42 ¶1 The ordinary Method of making an Hero, is to clap a huge Plume of Feathers upon his Head. **1822** BYRON *Werner* v. i, We will lay Aside these nodding plumes and dragging trains. **1832** TENNYSON *Lady of Shalott* II. iv, A funeral, with plumes and lights And music. **1845** DISRAELI *Sybil* II. ii, His hat white with a plume of white feathers. **1848** W. H. KELLY tr. *L. Blanc's Hist. Ten Y.* I. 335 The grenadiers flung away their black plumes.

b. *fig.* (Cf. *a feather in one's cap.*)

1605 CAMDEN *Rem.* 3 It was accounted one of the fairest and most glorious Plumes in the triumphant Diademe of the Roman Empire. **1667** MILTON *P.L.* VI. 161 Well thou comst Before thy fellows, ambitious to win From me som Plume. **1848** DE QUINCEY *Pope* Wks. 1858 IX. 14 An error in which Pope himself participated, that his plume of distinction from preceding poets consisted in correctness.

c. Self-satisfaction, triumph. *rare.*

1910 W. DE MORGAN *Affair of Dishonour* iv. 66 He wanted .. to choose his time, as a nobleman might then do.. not only without shame or remorse, but even with some sense of plume or strut.

4. *transf.* Anything resembling the down of feathers or a feather, in form or in lightness.

1601 HOLLAND *Pliny* II. 239 The plume or downe which it beareth,.. cureth the inordinat flux of waterish humors into the eies. **1810** SOUTHEY *Kehama* IV. iv, The shadow of the Cocoa's lightest plume Is steady on the sand. **1859** G. MEREDITH *R. Feverel* xx, The plumes of the woodland are alight. **1870** SWINBURNE *Ess. & Stud.* (1875) 357 A boy's figure,.. with a curling plume of hair.

b. *Bot.* (*a*) A plumose pappus or other appendage of a seed, by which it floats away; †(*b*) = PLUMULE I (*obs.*).

1578 LYTE *Dodoens* I. xxiv. 36 Which [flowers] at length do turne into downe, or Cotton, and the plume is carried away with the winde. **1671** GREW *Anat. Plants* i. §14 The Plume is that Part which becomes the Trunk of the Plant. *Ibid.*, These three Parts, sc. the Main Body, the Radicle, and the Plume, are concurrent to the making up of a Seed. **1688** J. CLAYTON in *Phil. Trans.* XVII. 947 If gleamy Weather happen at that time, it breeds a small Flie, which consumes the Plume of the Plant. **1766** *Compl. Farmer* s.v. *Malt*, Malt which has not had a sufficient time to shoot, so that its plume, or acrospire as the adepts in malting call it, may have reached to the inward skin of the barley, remains charged with too large a quantity of it's unattenuated oils. **1813** SIR H. DAVY *Agric. Chem.* iii. (1814) 70 In every seed there is to be distinguished 1. the organ of nourishment. 2. the nascent plant or the plume.

c. *Zool.* A plumose or feather-like part or formation, as a plumate hair of an insect, a ciliated or branchiate organ of a crustacean or mollusc, a plume-like tuft of zoophytes, etc.

1834 MᶜMURTRIE *Cuvier's Anim. Kingd.* 487 There is a double range of numerous tentacula on the mouth, curved into a half moon, forming a plume of that figure. *Ibid.*, The species are very numerous in fresh water... They form bushes, arbuscles, plumes, &c. &c. **1846** PATTERSON *Zool.* 19 A single plume of a species found upon our shores has been estimated to contain 500. **1880** HUXLEY *Crayfish* ii. 78 This stem [on the gills] divides into two parts, that in front, the plume, resembling the free end of one of the gills. **1888** ROLLESTON & JACKSON *Anim. Life* 182 The stem of the branchia bends at right angles to this base and divides into an apical plume and a lamina. The free extremity of the plume is simple and filiform.

d. *Astron.* A plume-like projection of the solar corona.

1887 LOCKYER *Chem. Sun* 441 There is an exquisite tracery curved in opposite directions, consisting of plumes or panaches. **1902** MRS. W. MAUNDER in *Knowledge* Feb. 33 In an eclipse like that of May 1901 the polar regions are left absolutely free [of synclinal rays] except for the beautiful and regular tufts of light which have earned for themselves the appropriate name of 'plumes' or ' panaches'.

†**e.** *Confectionery.* One of the degrees in boiling sugar; = FEATHER *sb.* 13. *Obs.* [F. *plume.*]

1658 SIR T. MAYERNE *Archimag. Anglo-Gall.* §156. 107 Seeth your sugar untill the plume or skin appear.

f. (i) A long streamer of smoke, vapour, or other fluid issuing from a localized source in the same or a different fluid and spreading out as it travels, esp. one with a degree of buoyancy in the ambient medium.

1878 STEVENSON *Edinburgh* (1889) 25 The long plume of smoke over the plain. **1947** *Q. Jrnl. R. Meteorol. Soc.* LXXIII. 428 Smoke plumes from factory chimneys. **1955** *Trans. Amer. Soc. Mech. Engineers* LXXVII. 1/1 Under favorable weather conditions the plume from a smoke-stack will rise gradually as it flows downwind and the gases will be dispersed until only a negligible concentration prevails in the atmosphere. **1969** *Ann. Rev. Fluid Mech.* I. 30 Turbulent plumes (like jets) have a sharp boundary between the turbulent buoyant fluid and the surroundings; they increase their width through.. entrainment of external fluid across this boundary by large eddies. **1970** *Nature* 7 Nov. 545/2 Ball lightning does not rise like hot air nor is it disrupted by convection into a thermal plume as are hot fireballs. **1975** *New Yorker* 12 May 70/3 At discharge, how fast should it come out, and at what level? Would fish die in the thermal plume? **1975** J. L. PAVONI et al. *Handbk. Solid Waste Disposal* iii. 127 Water vapor plumes are caused when the relative humidity of the effluent gas stream is significantly higher than the relative humidity of the ambient air around an incinerator chimney. **1977** *Daily Tel.* 25 Apr. 1/1 The awesome plumbing job.. involves stuffing a 12 inch rubber plug into an 18-inch diameter well to staunch a plume of oil and gas sprouting 200 ft into the air.

(ii) *Geol.* A column of magma rising from the lower mantle and spreading sideways on reaching the base of the lithosphere, proposed as an explanation of the motion of lithospheric plates and of sites of volcanic activity away from plate margins.

1971 W. J. MORGAN in *Nature* 5 Mar. 42/2, I now propose that these hotspots are manifestations of convection in the lower mantle which provides the motive force for continental drift. In my model there are about twenty deep mantle plumes bringing heat and relatively primordial material up to the asthenosphere and horizontal currents in the asthenosphere flow radially away from each of these plumes. **1975** *Sci. Amer.* Mar. 62/1 According to this argument, all upward movement of mantle material is confined to about 20 plumes, each plume a few hundred kilometers in diameter, rising from the core-mantle boundary. **1976** P. FRANCIS *Volcanoes* i. 49 The plume effectively burns a hole through the overlying crustal plate .. and a volcano results.

5. Short for *plume-moth*: see 6.

1819 G. SAMOUELLE *Entomol. Compend.* 409 *Pterophorus pentadactylus.* The large white Plume. **1832** J. RENNIE *Butterflies & Moths* 231 The Six-cleft Plume (*Alucita hexadactyla*, Haworth).

6. *attrib.* and *Comb.*, as ***plume-feather***, ***-maker***, ***-trade***; ***plume-bearing***, ***-crowned***, ***-decked***, ***-dressed***, ***-embroidered***, ***-fronted***, ***-soft***, ***-uplifting***, ***-waving*** adjs.; **plume alum**, a pseudo-alum crystallizing in tufts of silky fibres: see ALUM *sb.* 4; **plume-bearer** = *plume-holder*; **plume-bird**, a bird with conspicuous plumes, such as are used for ornament; *spec.* a bird of paradise of the subfamily *Epimachinæ*; **plume-bouquet**, a loosely constructed, spray-shaped bouquet; **plume-dark** *a.*, dark with the feathers of flying birds; **plume-grass**, a grass of the genus *Erianthus*, having a plume-like inflorescence, a Woolly Beard-grass; **plume-holder**, that which holds a plume, *spec.* a small tube attached to a helmet for that purpose; **plume-hunter**, a man who kills wild birds to supply the plume trade; **plume-moth**, any species of the family *Pterophoridæ* (*Alucitidæ*), small moths whose wings are divided into feathery lobes; **plume-nutmeg**, a tree of the N.O. *Atherospermaceæ* (see quots.); *esp.* the Tasmanian Sassafras, *Atherosperma moschata*; **plume-plucked** *a.*, stripped of plumes, humbled: see 3 b; **plume-stick**, a small stick surmounted by a feather, used in religious rites by certain American Indians; † **plume-striker**: see quot.; **plume-thistle**, a thistle having a feathery pappus, as *Carduus lanceolatus* and the genera *Cirsium* and *Cnicus*.

[*c* **1530** *Hickscorner* in Hazl. *Dodsley* I. 178 He.. privily spake To a prentice.. for a halfpenny worth of *alum plumb.] **1780** J. T. DILLON *Trav. Spain* (1781) 378 The white stone called plume alum, or *pseudo asbestus.* **1812** J. SMYTH *Pract. of Customs* (1821) 21 Plume Alum is a kind of natural Alum, composed of a sort of threads or fibres, resembling feathers, whence it has its name. **1730–46** THOMSON *Autumn* 869 Infinite wings! till all the *plume-dark air And rude-resounding shore are one wild cry. **1857** G. THORNBURY *Songs Cavaliers & Roundheads* 300 Two crones.. Stood by a *plume-decked bed. **1591** SPENSER *M. Hubberd* 210 Upon his head an old Scotch cap he wore, With a *plume feather all to peeces tore. **1876** PLANCHÉ *Cycl. Costume* I. 402 *Plume-holder. **1894** *Daily News* 1 Jan. 5/6 The armet having been strained to close it over a plume-holder above the nape of the neck. **1898** *Nat. Science* June 369 The most destructive agencies are sportsmen, *plume-hunters, boys after eggs. **1819** G. SAMOUELLE *Entomol.*

Compend. Index, *Plume moth. **1857** Henfrey *Bot.* 365 The nuts are enclosed in the tube of the perianth, and the persistent styles grow out into feathery awns, whence the plants are called *Plume-nutmegs. **1866** *Treas. Bot., Atherospermaceæ* (Plume Nutmegs). A small natural order of trees from Australia and Chili, deriving their English name from their aromatic nuts being furnished with a permanent style, clothed with long hairs. **1593** Shaks. *Rich. II*, iv. i. 108, I come to thee From *plume-pluckt Richard, who with willing Soule Adopts thee Heire. **1812** W. Tennant *Anster F.* iii. v, They turn their *plume-soft bosoms to the morn. **1882** *N.Y. Tribune* 5 Mar., The prayers..were addressed directly to the *plume-sticks, which were placed one by one in the bottom of the hole, the feathers standing upright. **1658** Phillips, A **Plumestriker*, a parasite, or flatterer, so called from pulling hairs, or feathers off from other mens Cloakes. **1844** Stephens *Bk. Farm* III. 942 In pastures, the biennial spear *plume-thistle, *Cnicus lanceolatus*, is prevalent. **1882** J. Hardy in *Proc. Berw. Nat. Club* IX. No. 3. 468 The melancholy plume thistle (*Carduus heterophyllus*) was very prevalent. **1819** Shelley *Prometh. Unb.* ii. ii. 53 A *plume-uplifting wind. **1848** Buckley *Iliad* 99 But him, *plume-waving Hector answered not.

plume (plu:m), *v.* Also 4–5 **plewme**, 5 **plomme**. [a. OF. *plumer* to pluck (a bird) (12th c. in Godef.), to pull out (hair), pillage, f. *plume* plume *sb.* In branch II, f. plume *sb.* or ad. L. *plūmāre* to cover with feathers, embroider, intr. to become fledged.]

I. † **1.** *intr.* In *Falconry*: To pluck the feathers of its prey, as a hawk; const. *upon*, *on*. *Obs.*

1399 Langl. *Rich. Redeles* ii. 163 Than bated he boldeliche, as a bird wolde, To plewme on his pray þe pol ffro þe nekk. *c* **1430** *Bk. Hawkyng* in *Rel. Ant.* I. 297 While the hawke plumyth on the pertrich. **1486** *Bk. St. Albans* C viij, She plommyth when she pullith federis of ony fowle or of any thyng and castys hem from her. **1575** Turberv. *Falconrie* 125 Lette hir grype and seaze the praye at hir pleasure, and lette hir also plume thereupon as long as she will. **1667** Dryden *Maiden Queen* iii. i, Look, how he peeps about, to see if the coast be clear; like an hawk that will not plume, if she be looked on.

fig. **1570–6** Lambarde *Peramb. Kent* (1826) 312 One of these at the Sea in a Navie of common vessels, being able to make havocke, to plume, and to pray upon the best of them at her owne pleasure. **1577** Fenton *Gold. Epist.* 164 Beeing so possest by straunge women, where they haue no possibilitie to marry with you, they will plume vpon you, till they haue left you neyther fether nor flesh.

2. *trans.* To pluck, 'case' (a bird); hence, to strip, bare. Now *rare*.

1599 T. M[oufet] *Silkwormes* 21 No Caterpillers..To rauish leaues, or tender buddes to plume. **1602** Heywood *Woman killed w. Kindness* Wks. 1874 II. 98 *Char.* [*to the Falconer*]. Now she hath seis'd the Fowle, and gins to plume her, Rebecke her not. **1616** B. Jonson *Devil an Ass* iv. iv, Madame, you take your Hen, Plume it, and skin it, cleanse it o' the inwards. **1706** Phillips, *To Plume*, to pick, or pluck the Feathers off. **1828** Scott *F.M. Perth* xii, I will so pluck him as never hawk plumed a partridge. **1852** R. F. Burton *Falconry in Valley of Indus* vi. 67 *note*, A few victims..which she is allowed to..tire and plume as much as she pleases.

† **b.** To pluck (feathers) from a bird. Also *fig.*

1524 J. Clerk in Ellis *Orig. Lett.* Ser. ii. I. 309 Ther shold be fownd manye ryght mean powars in Italy that wold plume his fethers. **1681** Dryden *Abs. & Achit.* i. 920 A numerous faction..In Sanhedrins to plume the regal rights.

† **c.** *fig.* To 'pluck', despoil, rob, plunder. *Obs.*

1571 *Satir. Poems Reform.* xxviii. 82 Without respect to God or feir of faith, Plumand, but pietie I did oppres the pure. **1622** Bacon *Hen. VII* 111 To say 'That the King cared not to plume his Nobilitie and People, to feather himselfe'. **1667** Dryden *Maiden Queen* ii. i, One whom instead of banishing a day, You should have plum'd of all his borrow'd honours. **1760** *Impostors Detected* iii. v, One of the ladies who had the day before so finely plumed our missionaries.

II. 3. *trans.* To furnish or cover with plumes, feathers, or plumage; to fledge, feather; to adorn with a plume or plumes. Also *fig.*

1423 Jas. I *Kingis Q.* xciv, With wingis bright, all plumyt, ..There sawe I sitt the blynde god Cupide. **1588** Greene *Pandosto* (1607) 10 Report is plumed with times feathers. **1627** tr. *Bacon's Life & Death* (1651) 10 The Swan..is a Bird excellently plumed. **1754** Mrs. Delany in *Life & Corr.* (1862) 285 How many girls, that have plumed, and tiffed, perhaps turned down their hats, for him, will be disappointed! **1801** Strutt *Sports & Past.* ii. i. 54 It was necessary..to have several arrows.., plumed with feathers from different wings, to suit the diversity of the winds. **1832** Tennyson *Œnone* 205 My dark tall pines, that plumed the craggy ledge High over the blue gorge.

b. To set or place as a plume. *rare.*

1667 Milton *P.L.* iv. 989 His stature reacht the Skie, and on his Crest Sat horror Plum'd.

4. *refl.* **a.** Of a bird: To dress its feathers. **b.** To dress oneself with borrowed plumes. Chiefly *fig.*

1702 S. Parker tr. *Cicero's De Finibus* v. 293 The Masters of the Porch..have plum'd themselves from the Peripateticks and Academicks, that is, they have taken their Sense of Things to themselves, and impos'd new Turns of their own Devising. **1707** Mortimer *Husb.* (1721) I. 264 Swans..being a large Fowl, must not be kept in a strait place,..but in some inclosed Pond where they may have room to come ashore and plume themselves. **1744** Parsons *Muscular Motion* i. 12 in *Phil. Trans.* XLIII, Authors.. who, by pluming themselves with his Feathers, had monopolized much..Attention. **1763** C. Johnston *Reverie* II. 144 When he has plumed himself in the merit of them for a while, I'll strip the gawdy daw of his stolen feathers. **1865** Dickens *Mut. Fr.* i. xi, Like a veritable cock of the walk literally pluming himself in the midst of his possessions.

c. *fig.* Usually with *on*, *upon* (†*for*, †*in*, †*over*, †*with*): To take credit to oneself, pride oneself, congratulate oneself, show self-satisfaction, esp. regarding something trivial, ridiculous, or unworthy, or to which one has no just claim.

1643 Sir T. Browne *Relig. Med.* ii. §8, I have seen a Grammarian towr and plume himself over a single line in Horace, and shew more pride in the construction of one Ode, than the Author in the composure of the whole book. **1699** Bentley *Phal.* 388 Admiring and pluming himself for that glorious Emendation. **1715** South *Serm.* VI. 118 Pluming and praising himself, and telling fulsome stories in his own commendation. **1756** C. Lucas *Ess. Waters* II. 58 Some gentlemen..have plumed themselves upon introducing a more frequent use of sea water. **1760** Hooper in *Priv. Lett. Ld. Malmesbury* (1870) I. 83, I am told the Duke of Bedford plumes himself with hopes of great support. **1775** S. J. Pratt *Liberal Opin.* cvi. (1783) IV. 17, I see nothing wherein to plume ourselves, as to that prerogative. **1823** Jefferson *Writ.* (1830) IV. 265 The atheist here plumes himself on the uselessness of such a God. **1884** J. Payn *Lit. Recoll.* 25 N. plumed himself on his judgment of sheep.

† **5.** *intr.* = 4c. *Obs.*

1707 Hearne *Collect.* 30 Aug. (O.H.S.) II. 39 A certain Gent..plumes a little. **1715** M. Davies *Athen. Brit.* I. 140 Our modern Arians plum'd also upon the unnecessary Heats of two English Doctors. **1753** Mrs. Delany in *Life & Corr.* (1861) III. 221 Mrs. C. plumes extremely upon it.

6. *trans.* To preen, trim, or dress (the feathers or wings); to prepare for flight. Also *fig.*

1821 Byron *Heav. & Earth* iii. 222 The winds, too, plume their piercing wings. **1859** G. Meredith *R. Feverel* xii, Pluming a smile upon his succulent mouth. **1867** 'Ouida' *C. Castlemaine* (1879) 17 Herons plumed their silvery wings by the water-side. **1874** Motley *Barneveld* I. v. 273 And calumny plumed her wings for a fresh attack. **1878** M. A. Brown *Nadeschda* 26 She sits there..Pluming daintily her feathers.

plume, obs. form of plumb.

‖**plumeau** (plymo). [Fr.] A duvet.

1892 C. A. M. Fennell *Stanford Dict.* 637/1 *Plumeau*,.. a thick quilt stuffed with feathers. **1931** E. Sackville-West *Simpson* iii. 250 Childeric was lying on his bed, half buried in the voluminous *plumeau*. **1967** T. La Chard *Sailor Hat* iii. 59, I subsided in sleep under my vast crimson *plumeau*, a towering feather bed gleaming through its white crochet covering.

plumed (plu:md, *poet.* 'plu:mɪd), *ppl. a.* [f. plume *v.* + -ed[1].]

† **1.** Plucked; stript of plumes or feathers. *Obs.*

1573 Twyne *Æneid* xi. (1584) R viij b, The goarie blood, and fethers plumed flit the ayer about. **1647** N. Bacon *Disc. Govt. Eng.* i. xvi. (1739) 31 Kings were not then like unto plumed Eagles, exposed to the charity of the Fowls for food. **1730** *Hist. Litteraria* I. 31 He opened a Salamander's Mouth, and endeavoured to make it bite a young plumed Chicken.

2. Furnished with a plume or plumes; feathered.

1526 Skelton *Magnyf.* 479 Your Counterfet Countenaunce is all of Nysyte, A plummed partrydge all redy to flye. **1590** Spenser *F.Q.* ii. vi. 31 Quite it clove his plumed crest in tway. **1616** R. C. *Times' Whistle*, etc. (1871) 132 When Dædalus his plumed bodie brings Safe to the shore. **1805** Priscilla Wakefield *Dom. Recreat.* vi. (1806) 89 The bell-flower animal, or, as some term it, the plumed polype. **1814** Scott *Ld. of Isles* vi. xi, The plumed bonnet and the plaid By these Hebrideans worn. **1882** 'Mark Twain' *Innoc. at Home* ii. *Roughing It*, etc. 272 The plumed hearse,..the flags drooping at half-mast.

3. Special collocations: **plumed serpent**, a mythical creature depicted as part bird, part snake; *spec.* (freq. with capital initials) any of various deities in the religions of ancient Mesoamerica having this form, esp. Quetzlcoatl, the Aztec deity of vegetation and fertility; also *attrib.*

1915 *Amer. Anthropologist* XVII. 480 (*caption*) (*a*), Pelican design; (*b*), plumed serpent design; from La Bermuda. Collection [of pottery] of Señor Alberto Imery. *Ibid.* 481 Two bowls in the Imery collection..bear upon the outside an interesting representation of the plumed serpent. **1926** D. H. Lawrence (*title*) The Plumed Serpent. **1935** *Discovery* Sept. 270/1 A flint dagger, 8¼ inches long, with a handle fashioned to represent the body and head of the Plumed Serpent. **1937** *Burlington Mag.* July 55/1 Another point of far-reaching significance is brought out in the discussion of the symbol of the plumed serpent... In China a bird is given the emphasis and the serpent appears on its wings..while among the Mayas the serpent dominates but has the wings and feet of a bird. **1959** C. S. Chinchilla in Kidder & Chinchilla *Art of Ancient Maya* 29 They do not worship Gukumatz (the plumed serpent) and Balau (the tiger) as animals, but as the deities that they embody under these forms. **1972** *Funk's Stand. Dict. Folklore* 915/1 *Quetzalcoatl*. The feathered or plumed serpent god: known over all Middle America, and surviving in mythology to this day. **1979** P. Theroux *Old Patagonian Express* iii. 47 The Indians liked him [*sc.* Maximilian] because he was blond, like Quetzalcoatl—Cortez enjoyed the same bizarre notoriety for his resemblance to the Plumed Serpent.

plumeless ('plu:mlɪs), *a.* [f. plume *sb.* + -less.] Destitute of plumes or feathers.

1608 Sylvester *Du Bartas* ii. iv. iv. *Decay* 277 Hence, plume-less wings. **1655** tr. *Com. Hist. Francion* ii. 38 The Plumelesse Pigeon..addressed multitudes of supplications to him that was intrusted as his guard. **1804** J. Grahame *Sabbath*, etc. (ed. 6) 65 To her plumeless brood Bears off the prize. **1873** Symonds *Grk. Poets* x. 314 Her dragons..fold their plumeless wings.

plumelet ('plu:mlɪt). [f. plume *sb.* + -let.]

† **1.** *Bot.* = plumule 1. *Obs.*

1816 Keith *Phys. Bot.* II. 17 The plumelet was still enveloped in the seminal leaves. *Ibid.* II. 224 But the fluid, which has been thus conducted to the radicle,..ascends..to the plumelet through the..tubes of the alburnum.

2. A minute plume.

1850 Tennyson *In Mem.* xci, When rosy plumelets tuft the larch. **1883** *Cornh. Mag.* Jan. 57 The plumelets of the butterfly's wing.

Hence **'plumeletage** (*nonce-wd.*), small delicate plumage.

1855 Bailey *Spirit. Leg.* in *Mystic*, etc. 97 Bright humming-bird of gem-like plumeletage, By western Indians living sun-beam named.

'plume-like, *a.* [f. plume *sb.* + -like.] Like or resembling a plume; feathery.

1847 Longf. *Ev.* ii. ii. 15 Green islands where plumelike Cotton-trees nodded their shadowy crests. **1851** Woodward *Mollusca* i. 62 The respiratory organs consist of two or four plume-like gills. **1883** G. Allen in *Knowledge* 8 June 336/1 Tufted flowers hanging loose in graceful plume-like panicles.

ˌplumeo'picean, *a. humorous nonce-wd.* [f. L. *plūme-us* feathery + *pice-us* pitchy + -an.] Composed of tar and feathers: alluding to the practice of tarring and feathering an obnoxious person.

1843 Syd. Smith *Let. Amer. Debts* ii. Wks. 1859 II. 331/2, I will appear on my knees at the bar of the Pennsylvanian Senate in the plumeopicean robe of American controversy. **1861** *Sat. Rev.* 7 Dec. 573 Those whom it proposed to teach would destroy the types, and invest the compositors with the plumeopicean robe of the republican Nemesis.

plumeous ('plu:mi:əs), *a. rare.* [f. L. *plūme-us* downy + -ous: see -eous.] Of the nature of down or fine feathers; feathery.

1657 Tomlinson *Renou's Disp.* 401* The last is often called plumeous Alome. **1664** Power *Exp. Philos.* i. 8 The Butter-Fly..Nature having imp'd her wings (for her better flight) with those plumeous excrescences.

† **plumer**[1]. *Obs. rare.* [ME., prob. AF., corresp. to an AF. or OF. **plumier*, L. *plūmārius*, f. *plūma* plume. Cf. plumier.] A dealer in plumes or feathers.

1282 in *Cal. Let. Bk. A Lond.* (1899) 46 John de Cestrehunte 'plumer'. [Cf. *Ibid.* 57 Fethermongere.]

† **'plumer**[2]. *Obs. rare*[−1]. ? A bird having plumes; a fully fledged bird.

14.. *Voc.* in Wr.-Wülcker 603/29 *Plumacius*, a plumere, *avis est*.

‖**Plumeria** (plu:'mɪərɪə). *Bot.* Also **Plumieria**. [mod.L.; named by Tournefort, 1700, after the botanist C. Plumier (*Plumerius*).] A tropical genus of trees (N.O. *Apocynaceæ*), having large fragrant salver-shaped flowers, white, yellow, or purplish, in terminal cymes. There are about forty species, among them the *red jasmine tree*, *nosegay-tree*, and *pagoda-tree* of the West Indies.

1753 Chambers *Cycl. Supp.* s.v., The plumeria with a rose-coloured and very sweet flower [etc.]. **1785** Martyn *Rousseau's Bot.* xvi. (1794) 215 Plumeria or Red Jasmine has two reflex follicles, with the seeds flat, winged, and imbricate. **1836** Macgillivray *Humboldt's Trav.* xiv. 168 Arborescent ferns, more than twenty-seven feet high, heliconias, plumerias, browneas,..palms, and other plants. **1882** *Garden* 9 Sept. 225/1 The most beautiful Plumieria we have seen.

plumery ('plu:mərɪ). *rare.* [f. plume *sb.* + -ery.] Plumes collectively, mass of plumes.

1805 Southey *Madoc in Azt.* xxv, Twice ten thousand feathered helms, and shields, Glittering with gold and scarlet plumery. **1810** —— *Kehama* x. xx, The bird of gorgeous plumery. **1829** Landor *Imag. Conv., Marvel & Bp. Parker* Wks. 1853 II. 112/2 Before there strutted under a triumphal arch of curls, and through a Via Sacra of plumery, Lewis the fourteenth.

plumery, obs. form of plumbery.

plumet ('plu:mɪt). *rare.* [a. F. *plumet* (15th c.) a small plume: see plume *sb.* and -et[1].] A small plume.

1585 T. Washington tr. *Nicholay's Voy.* iii. ix. 84 b, Certain common plumets of Eastrige feathers. **1895** *Daily News* 13 Nov. 5/4 The newest thing took the shape of the plumet or feathery tuft in the képis of the chasseurs-à-pied of the Empire. **1902** J. Conrad *Youth*, etc. (1903) 192 He.. brushed the oil painting..with a plumet kept suspended from a small brass hook by the side of the heavy gold frame.

plumet, var. plumbet *Obs.*; obs. f. plummet.

‖**plumetis** (plymәti). [F. *plumetis* (1495 in Littré), f. *plumeté* adj. (in Heraldry) sprinkled with spots like bunches of feathers.] Tambour-work.

1850 *Harper's Mag.* I. 720 The lower part of the body.. is round and stiffened, from which descends a *chatelaine*, formed by a wreath of *plumetis*. **1904** *Daily Chron.* 3 May 8/1 The new Plumetis batistes, in which floral designs in variegated tones are worked upon white, cream or buff ground.

plumetty ('plu:mɪtɪ), *a.* and *sb. Her.* Also 5 **plomte**; **plumeté**. [ad. F. *plumeté*: see plumetis.]

(A heraldic device) with a motif of feathers (see quots.).

a **1500** in *Ancestor* (1903) Oct. 193 Gold and purpull plomte. **1780** J. EDMONDSON *Compl. Body Heraldry* II. Gloss., *Plumetty*. When the field is divided into fusils, filled with the ends of feathers, depicted in metal and colour alternately, such field is said to be *Plumetty*. **1892** WOODWARD & BURNETT *Treat. Heraldry* I. iii. 71 Two curious forms of *Vair* occasionally met with in Italian or French coats are known as '*Plumeté*' and '*Papelonné*'. *Ibid.* 72 In *Plumeté* the field is apparently covered with feathers. **1929** *N. & Q.* 2 Nov. 317/2 'Papelonny'..and its analogue, 'plumetty',..are represented in English heraldry. Homologous in their tricking, the diapering of the one takes the form of fish scales; of the other, of the breasts of birds. **1969** FRANKLYN & TANNER *Encycl. Dict. Heraldry* 261/2 *Plumetty*, a field..of feathers.., a form that did not survive, and of which the few examples preserved from the feudal period contradict each other in appearance: one form is semé ..of feathers; another consists of barwise rows of feathers conjoined laterally; yet a third displays a field totally covered with overlapping feathers.

'plumicome. *Zool.* [mod. f. L. *plūma* feather + *coma* the hair of the head.] In sponges, Lendenfeld's name for a hexaster, the rays of which terminate in a number of plumose branches. Hence **plu'micomous** *a.*, having the character of a plumicome.

1886 VON LENDENFELD in *Proc. Zool. Soc.* 562 *Plumicome.* Rays terminated with a number of plumose branches.

'plumicorn. *Ornith.* [f. L. *plūma* PLUME, feather + *cornu* horn.] One of the pair of horn-like or ear-like feathers on the head of several species of owl, often called horns or ears.

1884 COUES *Key N. Amer. Birds* (ed. 2) 503 Bubo... [Generic characters]..Plumicorns highly developed.

plumier ('pluːmɪə(r)). *rare.* [f. PLUME: cf. F. *plumier* feather-dealer, and PLUMER[1].] A featherer of arrows.

1887 E. GILLIAT *Forest Outlaws* 295 The booths of the vintners, the fletchers, the plumiers, and wymplers.

,plumifi'cation. *rare.* [n. of action f. L. type **plūmificāre*, f. *plūma* PLUME: see -FICATION.] The action of feathering or fact of being feathered.

1819 *Blackw. Mag.* VI. 75 If Leigh Hunt had ever had the misfortune to have been tarred and feathered, he would have written a sonnet on his plumification. **1834** MUDIE *Brit. Birds* (1841) I. 313 The relation between the economy of nest and the progress of plumification.

plumiform ('pluːmɪfɔːm), *a. Zool.* [f. L. *plūma* PLUME + -FORM.] Feather-shaped.

1834 McMURTRIE *Cuvier's Anim. Kingd.* 247 Their branchiæ, composed of plumiform lobes, are situated on the hind part of the back. **1852** DANA *Crust.* I. 227 A dense villous coat, the hairs of which are plumiform.

Hence **'plumiformly** *adv.*, in the manner of a feather.

1798 MITCHELL tr. *Karsten's Min. Leskean Museum* 329 Plumiformly streaked Native Bismuth.

† plumi'formar, *a. Anat. Obs. rare.* [irreg. f. as prec.] Feather-shaped; penniform, pennate.

1718 J. CHAMBERLAYNE *Relig. Philos.* (1730) I. x. §17 These Muscles are called plumiformar, because the moveable Tendon has inserted into it, on both Sides, a great Number of carnous Fibres, all which, like the single Feathers of a Quill, run parallel to each other.

plumigerous (pluː'mɪdʒərəs), *a. rare.* [f. L. *plūmiger* feather-bearing (f. *plūma* PLUME + *gerĕre* to bear) + -OUS.] Plume-bearing; relating to the wearing of plumes.

1656 BLOUNT *Glossogr., Plumigerous*, that beareth feathers. **1721** in BAILEY. **1827** SYD. SMITH *Wks.* (1850) 475 Military colleges, with thirty-four professors, educating seventeen ensigns per annum,..with every species of nonsense, athletic, sartorial, and plumigerous.

† 'pluminary. *Obs. rare*$^{-1}$. [irreg. f. PLUME: cf. med.L. *plūmināre* (Du Cange from *Modena Chron.* 1329) a pillow stuffed with feathers.] ? A worker or dealer in feathers.

a **1631** DONNE *Paradoxes*, etc. (1652) 59 Embroiderers, Painters and such Artificers of curious Vanities, which the vulgar call Pluminaries.

'pluminess. *rare.* [f. PLUMY *a.* + -NESS.] Plumy or feathery quality or condition.

1802 COLERIDGE *Lett.* (1895) 410 Even the Scotch firs luxuriate into beauty and pluminess.

'pluming, *vbl. sb.* [f. PLUME *v.* + -ING[1].] The action of the verb PLUME, in various senses.

1583 STUBBES *Anat. Abus.* I. (1879) 71 Againste whiche daie she made greate preparation, for the plumyng of her self in gorgious arraie. **1633** LATHAM *Falconry* Explan. Words, *Plumming*, is when a Hawk ceaseth [= seizeth] a fowle, and pulleth the feathers from the body. **1801** STRUTT *Sports & Past.* II. i. 54 The feathers..he thought were preferable to any others for the pluming of an arrow.

'plumiped, *a. rare.* [ad. L. *plūmipēs, -pedem* feather-footed, f. *plūma* PLUME + *pēs, ped-* foot.] Having plumed or winged feet.

1727 BAILEY vol. II, *Plumipede*, having feathered feet. *a* **1890** R. F. BURTON tr. *Catullus, Carmina* lv. 25 Not if with Pegasèan wing I sped, Or Ladas I or Perseus plumiped.

plumist ('pluːmɪst). *rare.* [f. PLUME *sb.* + -IST.] A maker of plumes, a feather-dresser.

1812 MOORE *Anacreontic to Plumassier* 2 Fine and feathery artisan, Best of Plumists (if you can With your art so far presume) Make for me a Prince's Plume. *Ibid.* 24 Bravo, Plumist!—now what bird Shall we find for Plume the third?

plumket: see PLUNKET.

plumless ('plʌmlɪs), *a.* Without plums.

1835 *Fraser's Mag.* XI. 618 Here we have the plumless plumpudding.

plummer, obs. form of PLUMBER.

plummer-block ('plʌməblɒk). *Mech.* Also 9 plomer-, plumber-. [Second element BLOCK *sb.* 6; first uncertain. No evidence of any connexion with PLUMBER *sb.* ? From a personal surname.] A metal box or case for supporting a revolving shaft or journal, having a movable cover secured by bolts, so as to admit of the bearings being tightened when required; = *pillow-block* (PILLOW *sb.* 6).

1814 R. BUCHANAN *Ess. Millwork* (1823) 547 Hence the term pillow block, and sometimes, corruptly, Plumber Block. In Manchester they are called Pedestals. **1825** J. NICHOLSON *Operat. Mechanic* 373 This trough is firmly fixed by means of a plumber block..which has the top coupling screwed down fast, and the trough is supported at the other end by means of a cylindrical pin, which works in a hole in the cap. **1839** R. S. ROBINSON *Naut. Steam Eng.* 91 The plomer blocks are sockets, in which all the shafts or axes, used in the engine, revolve. **1875** J. W. BENSON *Time & Time-Tellers* (1902) 126 By means of a contrivance, known to engineers as plumber blocks, any part of the mechanism may be removed without disturbing the remainder. **1894** *Daily News* 28 July 6/4 In connection with the gigantic wheel at the exhibition at Earl's Court..the axle of the wheel was hoisted to its position on the plummer blocks on top of the towers.

Plummer-Vinson ('plʌmə 'vɪnsən). *Path.* The names of H. S. *Plummer* (1874–1936), U.S. physician, and P. P. *Vinson* (1890–1959), U.S. surgeon, used *attrib.* to designate a syndrome characterized by dysphagia, glossitis, and iron-deficiency anæmia.

1926 A. F. HURST in *Guy's Hospital Rep.* LXXVI. 426 *(heading)* The Plummer-Vinson syndrome (spasm of the pharyngo-œsophageal sphincter with anæmia and splenomegaly). **1958** TERRACOL & SWEET *Dis. Esophagus* xiii. 302 The Plummer-Vinson syndrome occurs predominantly in women in the proportion of approximately four to one. *Ibid.* 303 The Plummer-Vinson syndrome is a clinical complex, the cause of which though still not clearly understood has to do with avitaminosis, endocrine disturbances, and lack of available iron. *Ibid.* 306 There is strong clinical evidence to suggest that the mucosal changes characteristic of the Plummer-Vinson syndrome are of a precancerous nature. **1971** *Brit. Med. Bull.* XXVII. 34/1 The Paterson-Kelly or Plummer-Vinson syndrome was first described in 1919.

plummet ('plʌmɪt), *sb.* Forms: 4–7 plomet, 5 plomm-, plombette, 5–6 plom-, plummette, *Sc.* plumat, 5–7 plumet, 6 plom-, plumbete, plomm-, plumet)e, *Sc.* plumbat, plummett, 6–8 plumbet, 6– plummet. [ME. a. OF. *plommet, plombet, plummet* ball of lead, plummet, dim. of *plomb* lead: see PLUMB *sb.* and -ET[1].]

1. A ball or piece of lead, or other weight, attached to a line, and used for determining the vertical; a plumb-bob.

a. The bob of a plumb-line used by masons, builders, carpenters, etc.; also, the whole instrument, consisting of bob, line, and board.

1388 WYCLIF *Zech.* i. 16 Myn hous schal be bildid in it,.. and a plomet [1382 an hangynge lyne] schal be streiȝt out on Jerusalem [Vulg. *et perpendiculum extendetur super Ierusalem*]. *c* **1391** CHAUCER *Astrol.* II. §23 A plomet hanging on a lyne heyer than thin heued on a perche. **1398** TREVISA *Barth. De P.R.* II. iv. (1495) b iij/1 Hangynge plometes and mesures. **1553** T. WILSON *Rhet.* (1580) 159 The Carpenter hath his squire, his rule, and his plomette. **1703** MAUNDRELL *Journ. Jerus.* (1732) 77 No Architect with Levels and Plummets could build a Room more regular. **1793** SMEATON *Edystone L.* §97 As we were..exposed to fresh gales of wind ..there was no trusting to the perpendicularity of Threads and Plumbets. **1870** BRYANT *Iliad* II. I. 7 The plummet showed Their height the same.

b. A similar appliance attached to a scientific instrument, as a quadrant.

1571 DIGGES *Pantom.* I. viii. Dj, Conuey the left side of your quadrant Geometricall towarde the Sunne, the threade and Plummet hauing their free course. **1625** N. CARPENTER *Geog. Del.* I. vi. (1635) 157 The line and plummet falling on the Basis shall make right Angles with it. **1707** MORTIMER *Husb.* (1721) II. 99 Hold your Quadrant so as that your Plummet may fall on 45 Degrees. **1866** R. M. FERGUSON *Electr.* (1870) 22 A small plummet hangs down from the object-glass of the theodolite.

c. *fig.* A criterion of rectitude or truth.

1553 BALE *Gardiner's De vera Obed.* 5 By the perfect line and plummet of Gods word. **1587** GOLDING *De Mornay* xviii. (1592) 293 That he may holde the Plommet of his minde steddy without shaking or stirring. **1677** GILPIN *Demonol.* III. xvii. 140 Lay all to the Line and Plummet of the written Word.

d. A suspended weight used as a metronome.

1844 *Regul. & Ord. Army* 140 The Music for Slow and Quick Time is to be practised..with the plummet, until the prescribed cadence has been acquired.

2. A piece of lead or other metal attached to a line, and used for sounding or measuring the depth of water; a sounding-lead.

1382 WYCLIF *Acts* xxvii. 28 The whiche sendinge doun a plomet, founden twenty pasis of depnesse. **1555** EDEN *Decades* 121 He coulde at no tyme touche the grounde with his soundynge plummet. **1610** SHAKS. *Temp.* III. iii. 101 Therefore my Sonne i'th Ooze is bedded; and I'le seeke him deeper then ere plummet sounded. **1713** YOUNG *Last Day* I. 300 Where plummet never reach'd, he draws his breath. **1860** MAURY *Phys. Geog. Sea* (Low) xiii. §574 The greatest depths at which the bottom of the sea has been reached with the plummet are in the North Atlantic Ocean.

fig. **1632** MARMION *Holland's Leaguer* II. ii, Your politicians with their..plummets of wit, sound the depth of me. **1742** YOUNG *Nt. Th.* IX. 1860 Man's science is the culture of his heart; And not to lose his plumbet in the depths Of nature, or the more profound of God. **1849** LYTTON *Caxtons* I. iii, Certainly there were deeps in his nature which the plummet of her tender woman's wit had never sounded.

† 3. The pommel or knob on the hilt of a sword (sometimes weighted with lead). *Sc. Obs.*

c **1425** WYNTOUN *Chron.* III. i. 46 His suerd at he baire prevely [He] put it in his wambe sa fast Till it in to þe plomat past. **1513** DOUGLAS *Æneis* XII. xii. 97 Quhen that he saw hys rycht hand wapynles, And persauyt the plummet was onknaw. **1587** *Reg. Privy Council Scot.* IV. 205 The plumbattis or gairdis of ane of thair swerdis. ? *a* **1600** *Dick o' the Cow* xl. in Scott *Minstr. Scott. Bord.* (1869) 124 Dickie could na win at him wi' the blade o' the sword, But fell'd him wi' the plummet under the e'e.

† 4. a. A ball or lump of lead used for various purposes; e.g. as a missile, fastened to a line, as a weapon or instrument of scourging, etc. *Obs.*

1481 CAXTON *Myrr.* I. xvii. 53 Yf one threwe a stone or an heuy plomette of leed that wel weyed. **1483** —— *Gold. Leg.* 171/1 Thenne dyd he doo bete Saynt Urbane wyth plommettys. **1494** FABYAN *Chron.* VII. 596 They toke stonys & plummettes of lede, & trussyd them secretely in theyr sleuys & bosomys. **1579–80** NORTH *Plutarch* (1676) 769 They themselves were also hurt by them with their Darts and Plummets of Lead. **1612** DEKKER *If it be not good*, etc. Wks. 1873 III. 269 Wey down his loftiest boughes With leaden plomets.

b. *fig.* That which presses or weighs down, like a dead weight.

a **1625** FLETCHER & MASS. *Laws Candy* IV. i, When sad thoughts perplex the mind of man, There is a plummet in the heart that weighs, And pulls us, living, to the dust we came from. **1672** SIR T. BROWNE *Let. Friend* §45 Hang early Plummets upon the Heels of Pride. **1874** in Spurgeon *Treas. Dav.* Ps. cxix. 25 Earthly cares and sins have..attached a leaden plummet to the wings of a soul which..would fain soar upwards.

5. *spec.* **† a.** A leaden weight used in gymnastic exercises; a weight enclosed in a cestus. *Obs.*

1533 ELYOT *Cast. Helthe* (1541) 49 b, The plummettes, callid of Galen Alteres, being of equall weight and accordyng to the strength of him that exerciseth,..holdynge in euery hande one plummet, and lyftyng them on high, and bringing them downe with moche vyolence. **1538** ELYOT, *Cæstus*, a weapon hauyng great plummates hangyng at the ende of a clubbe. **1572** J. JONES *Bathes Buckstove* 12 b, Plumbetes..one borne in eche hand vp and downe the stayers..may bee a good and profitable exercise. **1616–61** HOLYDAY *Persius* 322 The cæstus..some describe to have been a kind of club, having plummets of lead fastned to it, which some call a whorle-bat.

† b. A weight of a clock; also *fig.* a motive force, spring of action. *Obs.*

1594 NASHE *Terrors Nt.* Wks. (Grosart) III. 233 Such is our braine oppressed with Melancholly, as is a clocke tyed downe with two heauie weights or plummets. **1628** WITHER *Brit. Rememb.* VIII. 2561 The Clock, whose plummets are not weight, Strikes sometimes one for three, and sixe for eight. **1679** J. GOODMAN *Penit. Pard.* II. ii. (1713) 185 Let us now see what are the springs or plummets that set this great engine on work. **1697** *Davies' Immort. Soul* Pref. bj b, Remarking how one part moves another,..from the first Springs and Plummets, to the very Hand that points out the visible and last Effects.

c. In angling, a small piece of lead attached to a fishing line, as a weight to keep the float in an upright position, as an anchor in ledger fishing, or as a sounding lead to measure the depth.

1616 SURFL. & MARKH. *Country Farme* 512 You shall vnderstand, that your first plummet would be a foot from the hooke, the rest not aboue an ynch one distant from another, & not being aboue fiue or seuen at the most. **1651** T. BARKER *Art of Angling* (1653) 3 Feeling the Plummet running on the ground..plumming my line according to the swiftnesse of the stream. **1653** WALTON *Angler* vii. 155 If you would have this ledger bait to keep at a fixt place..then hang a small Plummet of lead, a stone, or piece of tyle. **1741** *Compl. Fam.-Piece* II. ii. 332 A Piece of thin Sheet-lead rolled up, of about an Ounce or better, makes the best Plummet.

† 6. A pencil of lead, formerly used to rule lines; a lead-pen. *Obs.*

1634 J. B[ATE] *Myst. Nat.* 104 Then with your blacke chalke or blacke lead plummets, draw it as perfectly..as you can. **1669** STURMY *Mariner's Mag.* v. iv. 16 You must rule your Paper or Parchment with an obscure plummet. **1811** *Self Instructor* 26 A leaden plummet or pencil to rule lines. **1828** WEBSTER, *Plummet*..a piece of lead used by schoolboys to rule their paper for writing.

7. *Comb.*, as *plummet-line*; *plummet-deep, -like, -measured, -shaped* adjs.; *plummet-wise* adv.; **plummet-level:** see quot. 1875.

1598 SYLVESTER *Du Bartas* II. ii. IV. *Columnes* 747 Pale Phlegm, moist Autumn, Water moistly-cold, The Plummet-like-smooth-sliding Tenor hold. **1863** HAWTHORNE *Our Old Home* (1879) 122 Shakespeare has surface beneath surface..adapted to the plummet-line of every reader. **1875** KNIGHT *Dict. Mech., Plummet-level*, that form of a level having a suspended plummet in a standard at right angles to the base-piece. A mason's level. **1895** K. GRAHAME *Golden Age* (1904) 18 On the blue ocean of air, a hawk hung ominous; then, plummet-wise, dropped to the hedgerow. **1899** *Daily News* 20 June 5/5 A piece of turned steel.. with a plummet-shaped head sharply pointed. **1938** W. DE LA MARE *Memory* 38 Fleeter than Nereid, plummet-deep, Enticed by some long-sunken ship, She [*sc.* Memory] ..laughs out to see The treasure she retrieves for me. **1939** W. B. YEATS *Last Poems* 16 And pressed at midnight in a public place Live lips upon a plummet-measured face.

Hence **'plummetless** *a.*, unfathomable.

1893 *Nat. Observ.* 11 Mar. 413/2 There is no deep so plummetless.

'plummet, *v.* [f. PLUMMET *sb.*]

†**1.** *trans.* To fathom, sound. *Obs. rare.*

1626 T. H[AWKINS] *Caussin's Holy Crt.* 221 Depths are plummeted.

†**2.** To let fall or draw (a vertical line) by means of a plummet. *Obs. rare.*

1711 W. SUTHERLAND *Shipbuild. Assist.* 67 Strike the streight Line 4. 3. 1. 5. and plummet that Line down at the Ends of your Piece.

3. *intr.* To fish with a line weighted with a plummet: cf. PLUMMET *sb.* 5 c, DRAIL *sb.* 1. *rare.*

1888 GOODE *Amer. Fishes* 180 It is not known when the custom of drailing for mackerel was first introduced,..it is [the common method] in the present day in England, under such names as 'whiffing', 'railing', 'drailing' or 'plummeting'.

4. a. *trans.* To cause to drop rapidly, to hurl down. **b.** *intr.* To drop or fall rapidly, to plunge *down.* Also *fig.*

1933 *Sun* (Baltimore) 11 Apr. 1/1 The U.S.S. Akron had reports that the weather was unfavorable for her purpose when she took off last Monday on the fatal flight that plummeted her into the sea from lightning-swept skies. **1939** WEBSTER Add., *Plummet, v.i.*, to drop or plunge straight down. **1944** F. LEIBER in D. Knight *100 Yrs. Sci. Fiction* (1969) 93 'I'm glad to see the last of that fellow,' he muttered,..as they plummeted toward the roof. **1953** A. MOOREHEAD *Rum Jungle* vii. 96 They [*sc.* gulls] plummeted down with their beaks wide open. **1958** B. NICHOLS *Sweet & Twenties* x. 132 Even worse, waists plummeted nine inches, to remain suspended somewhere below the navel. **1959** *Daily Tel.* 21 Nov. 1/6 Capt. Kittinger plummeted towards the earth until his parachute opened automatically at 10,000 feet. **1961** *Time* (Atlantic ed.) 23 June 26 The price of new potatoes plummeted to 1¢ a pound. **1963** C. L. COOPER *Black* x. 153 Twice I stumbled over the garbage cans lining the walk, rising,..to plummet on, not daring to imagine the scene I might find in the apartment. **1972** G. DURRELL *Catch me a Colobus* ix. 186 Great gouts of water plummeted down from the sky so that the road, which was an earth one, was immediately turned into a dangerous mire. **1978** D. BLOODWORTH *Crosstalk* xi. 91 Rumours that Mao's health is failing have sent the Hong Kong stock exchange plummeting. **1979** *Amer. N. & Q.* Apr. 127/1 The *Phillipe, Count of Darkness* stories..plummeted his [*sc.* F. Scott Fitzgerald's] story-asking price from $3000 to $300.

Hence **'plummeting** *vbl. sb.* and *ppl. a.*

1952 *Chambers's Jrnl.* May 262/1 The stone-like plummeting before the 'chute opens, the gentle floating in space, the enormous thud with which you hit the ground —these combine to give an experience unparalleled elsewhere. **1957** *Economist* 2 Nov. 380/2 The most calamitous thing..would be a world depression with plummeting prices. **1958** *Times Rev. Industry* Dec. 78/1 Spending..led to a rise of £80m. in the Union's imports, and the plummeting of the South African foreign exchange reserves.

†**'plummy**, *a.*[1] *Obs. rare.* [f. stem of PLUM *v.* + -Y.] Loose in texture, spongy, porous.

1398 TREVISA *Barth. De P.R.* XVII. lxiii. (Tollem. MS.), The tre [beech] is not ful sad and faste in substaunce, but plummy [*ed.* 1535 pory] and ful of holes [*orig.* Non est autem [fagus] in substantia arbor multum solida sed rara potius et porosa].

Hence †**'plumminess**[1], sponginess, porousness.

1398 TREVISA *Barth. De P.R.* XVII. ii. (Bodl. MS. lf. 189 b/2), Aristotel seiþ þouȝe somme tree ne haue prikkes, þat comeþ nouȝt of þe entente of kinde þat gendreþ þe tree, but happeþ of plumines [*MSS. and ed.* 1495 plummes] of þe tree, þat draweþ colde humoure þat is litel digeste, and passeþ out atte plumines [*MSS. and ed.* plummes] of the tree, and is iharded into a prik oþer a þorne bi heete of þe sonne. [*Orig.* Sed accidit ex raritate arboris siue plante per quam attrahitur humor frigidus parum coctus & exiens per illam arboris raritatem a calore solis in spinam coagulatur.]

plummy ('plʌmɪ), *a.*[2] [f. PLUM *sb.* + -Y.]

1. Consisting of, abounding in, or like plums.

1759 MISS TALBOT in *Eliz. Carter's Lett.* (1808) I. 448 You have been all your life in a great error in eating that strange jumble of substantives, *plumb-cake*, when the adverb *plumby* is plainly the right thing. **1861** GEN. P. THOMPSON *Audi Alt.* III. clvii. 164 They do not want the cake to be shorn of its plums. It would not do, to have the 'plummy stuff' taken out. **1885** L. F. DAY in *Art Jrnl.* 213/1 The ground of a plummy brown.

2. *fig.* **a.** Of the nature of a 'plum'; rich, good, desirable. *slang* or *colloq.*

1812 J. H. VAUX *Flash Dict.*, *Plummy*, right; very good; as it should be: expressing your approbation of any act, or event. **1876** GEO. ELIOT *Dan. Der.* II. xvi, Signing one's self over to wickedness for the sake of getting something plummy. **1890** *Tablet* 10 May 729 So far from getting anything plummy by becoming Catholics, Anglican clergymen have often to make great sacrifices.

b. Of the voice, then of sound gen.: thick-sounding, rich, 'fruity'; indistinct; with bass predominating.

1881 *Punch* 23 July 25/2 The same aged lover was bidding, with rather a 'plummy' voice, the More-than-Middle-Aged Heroine 'good bye for ever'. **1947** *Jrnl. Inst. Electrical Engin.* XCIV. IIIA 446/1 Such distortions can be tolerated.. without serious loss of articulation, though the speech will usually sound rather 'plummy' and unnatural. **1951** K. HARRIS *Innocents from Abroad* 199 The rich, plummy voice of [actor] Edward Arnold. **1955** *Times* 3 May 14/4 A disc which sounds plummy and muffled in tone. **1965** G. MCINNES *Road to Gundagai* xi. 197 His voice..was wonderfully plummy and Edwardian. **1970** *Daily Tel.* 1 Sept. 9/5 All India Radio—modelled..on the BBC, even down to the plummy accents of its announcers. **1975** *City Press* 1 May 16/5 Her duchess on the make is a finely pointed performance, the plummy vowels contrasting splendidly with consonants periodically marred by the lack of false teeth. **1977** *Early Mus.* Oct. 549/3 The plummy..tone [of Flemish virginals] is evidently more popular than the musically versatile but astringent Italian virginal. **1978** *Gramophone* Feb. 1439/1 His tone is mellow, but again, as in the Waltzes..the sound sometimes seems a bit plummy and close.

3. *Comb.*, as ***plummy-voiced*** adj.

1972 *Jazz & Blues* Oct. 8/3 His smooth, plummy-voiced style. **1978** *Times* 21 Jan. 14/7 The plummy-voiced announcers.

Hence **'plumminess**[2]; **'plummily** *adv.*

1927 J. MASEFIELD *Midnight Folk* 208 You haven't got such a thing as a seedless raisin about you?.. It's a real treat ..to taste a bit of plumminess. **1953** *John o' London's Weekly* 13 Mar. 208/4, I was not persuaded at the première by his 'young Octavius', who had a curious plumminess. **1955** *Times* 31 Aug. 5/4 The creamy richness—free from all 'plumminess'—of her contralto voice is a constant delight. **1958** *Listener* 25 Dec. 1092/2 It was all splendidly true to type, and plummily theatrical. **1962** *Ibid.* 8 Feb. 268/3 The plumminess of the normal Wagnerian baritone. **1972** A. ROSS *London Assignment* 17 'Go ahead, old boy,' he said plummily, 'He's all yours.'

plumose (pluːˈməʊs), *a.* [ad. L. *plūmōsus* covered with down (f. *plūma* PLUME): see -OSE.] Furnished with feathers or plumes, feathered; feathery; resembling a feather or plume in having two series of fine filaments on opposite sides: esp. in *Zool.*, *Bot.*, and *Min.*

1727 BAILEY vol. II, *Plumose*, full of feathers.

a. in *Zoology.*

plumose anemone, a sea anemone, *Actinoloba dianthus.*

1752 J. HILL *Hist. Anim.* 361 The cuneiform-tailed Psittacus, with naked temples, and plumose lines. **1826** KIRBY & SP. *Entomol.* IV. xlvi. 324 *Plumose*... Antennæ feathered on all sides with fine long hair. **1852** DANA *Crust.* I. 227 One of the plumose hairs of the villous coat. **1871** DARWIN *Desc. Man* xiii. (1883) 385 The barbs of the feathers ..are filamentous or plumose.

b. in *Botany.*

1760 J. LEE *Introd. Bot.* I. xiv. (1765) 37 *Plumose*, feathery. **1831** J. DAVIES *Manual Mat. Med.* 271 Fruits elongate, surmounted by a plumose pappus. **1872** OLIVER *Elem. Bot.* App. 310 Stigmas plumose.

c. in *Mineralogy*, etc. ***plumose alum***, feather or plume alum: see ALUM *sb.* 4.

1796 KIRWAN *Elem. Min.* (ed. 2) II. 34 Sal Ammoniac... Its Crystals are plumose. **1802** *Edin. Rev.* I. 58 Crystals of gypsum and plumose alum. **1826** HENRY *Elem. Chem.* I. 467 Plumose branches of ice dart from the sulphuret to the bottom of the vessel, and the whole water is suddenly frozen. **1834** BAIRD in *Proc. Berw. Nat. Club* I. No. 2. 49 Mixed with the 'comoid' variety of 'cirrus',..accompanied with some specimens of the 'plumose' variety.

Hence **pluˈmoseness.**

1730–6 in BAILEY (folio).

plumosite (ˈpluːməsaɪt). *Min.* [ad. Ger. *plumosit*, named by Haidinger 1845, f. L. *plūmōsus* downy + *-it*, -ITE[1], after the older Ger. name *federerz* 'feather-ore'.] = JAMESONITE.

1864 in WEBSTER. **1881** *Academy* 7 May 341 The recent discovery of plumosite which is a double sulphide of lead and antimony.

plumosity (pluːˈmɒsɪtɪ). *rare.* [f. as PLUMOSE + -ITY.] Feathery or feathered condition.

1656 BLOUNT *Glossogr.*, *Plumosity* (*plumositas*), fulness of feathers. **1730–6** BAILEY (folio), *Plumoseness, Plumosity*,..a being full fledg'd. **1782** LEMON *Diss. Shooting Flying* 15 Before the birds are ripe in plumosity.

plumous (ˈpluːməs), *a. rare.* [ad. L. *plūmōsus*, F. *plumeux*: see PLUMOSE and -OUS.] Feathery, downy.

1822 T. TAYLOR *Apuleius* x. 254 What was intended also to be our genial bed,..was tumid with a plumous heap, and florid with a silken coverlet. **1858** MAYNE *Expos. Lex.*, *Plumosus*.., plumous.

plump (plʌmp), *sb.*[1] Now *arch.* and *dial.* Forms: 5 plomp, plowmpe, 5–6 plompe; 5–7 plumpe, 6– plump (6–7 ? plumb(e). [Of uncertain origin.

There appears to be no corresponding or related sb. in the other langs. In English, the only apparently earlier word of the *plump* group is PLUMP *v.*[1], with which this can hardly be directly connected. If the original notion were that of an unshaped or irregular assemblage or cluster, it might conceivably be connected with the MLG. and MDu. *plump* adj. in the sense 'massive, unshapen', whence the later Eng. PLUMP *a.*[1] But cf. also the words *lump* and *clump* in allied senses; sense c below is exactly = CLUMP *sb.* 2.]

A compact body of persons, animals, or things; a band, troop, company; a flock; a cluster, bunch, clump.

a. Of persons. *Obs.* exc. in archaic phrase ***a plump of spears***, a band of spearmen (revived by Scott).

?*a* **1400** *Morte Arth.* 2199 Thane..þe riche kynge.. Presede in-to þe plumpe, and with a prynce metes. *c* **1400** MAUNDEV. (1839) 252 Whan thei will fighte, thei wille schokken hem to gidre in a plomp. **1489** CAXTON *Faytes of A.* I. xxv. 80 Take hede that thyn enemyes make not a plowmpe of theyre folke to entre and breke thy batayile. *a* **1548** HALL *Chron., Hen. VIII* 32 b, The kynges speres passed and skyrmyshed wyth the plumpe of speres that Sir Jhon spake of. **1568** GRAFTON *Chron.* II. 46 So vpon a plumbe going together as neere as they might, escaped. *a* **1600** *Flodden F.* I. (1664) 9 A Knight of the North Country, Which leads a lusty plumpe of Spears. **1618** BOLTON *Florus* (1636) 36 Comming in an huge plumpe from the utmost coasts of the earth. *Ibid.* 171 They [Cimbrians] came rolling down upon Italy in plumbs. **1808** SCOTT *Marm.* I. iii, And soon appears O'er Horncliff-hill, a plump of spears. **1826** HOR. SMITH *Tor Hill* (1838) I. 42 We are too old skirmishers to be frightened by a few plumps of spears.

b. Of animals that go in flocks.

1591 G. FLETCHER *Russe Commw.* (Hakl. Soc.) 11 The manner of the seals is..to gather all close together in a throng or plumpe. **1697** DRYDEN *Æneid* XII. 374 A plump of Fowl he spies, that swim the Lakes. **1834** H. MILLER *Scenes & Leg.* xvii. (1857) 250 They saw a plump of whales blowing and tumbling. *Ibid.* 251 The plump had gone high up the frith. **1854** THOREAU *Walden, Spring* (1863) 334 A 'plump' of ducks rose at the same time.

c. Of trees, shrubs, or plants: = CLUMP *sb.* 2.

1470–85 MALORY *Arthur* I. xvi. 60 [The knights] tooke newe sperys and sette them on theire thyes and stode stille as hit had ben a plompe of wood. **1575** TURBERV. *Venerie* 73 They go to the plumpes and tufts of coleworts or of hasill nuts or grene corne. **1615** G. SANDYS *Trav.* 203 We laid vs downe in the bottome vnder a plump of trees. **1707** MORTIMER *Husb.* (1721) II. 24 In Hedge-rows and Plumps they will thrive very well. **1868** LOWELL *Invitation* x, Plumps of orchard-trees arow. **1903** *Eng. Dial. Dict.* (Aberdeen to Lincolnsh.).

d. Of other things, material and ideal.

1553 T. WILSON *Rhet.* 70 b, Many conjectures and great presumptions..heapyng them al into one plumpe whiche before were sparpled abrode. **1568** T. HOWELL *Newe Sonets* (1879) 157 O plumpe of paines, O endles woes, O man infortunate. **1624** BACON *Consid. War w. Spain* Wks. 1879 I. 542/2 England, Scotland, Ireland, and our good confederates the United Provinces, lie all in a plump together, not accessible but by sea, or, at least, by passing of great rivers. **1659** in *Burton's Diary* (1828) IV. 279 Let us not admit them [resolutions] in a plump. **1893** *Nat. Observer* 23 Dec. 135/1 The little plump of yachts cast anchor.

†**plump**, *sb.*[2] *Obs.* Also 6 plompe, (plummpe), 6–7 plumpe. [A collateral form of PUMP *sb.*, found also in LG. *plumpe* and vb. *plumpen* to pump. Perh. due to association with PLUMP *v.*[1] and its cognates, from the plumping or plunging action of the piston.] An obsolete by-form of PUMP. Also in *Comb.*

1477 NORTON in Ashm. *Theat. Chem.* 83 In Plomps.. Where heavie Water ariseth after Ayre. *a* **1490** BOTONER *Itin.* (Nasmith 1778) 268 Unius plump-maker villæ Bristolliæ. **1505–6** *Oriel Coll. Treas. Acc.* 509 Item, primo die Maii pro reparacione ly plumpe xij[d]. *c* **1515** *Cocke Lorell's B.* 12 Some the anker layde, some at the plompe a sayll swepe. **1517** *Yatton Churchw. Acc.* (Som. Rec. Soc.) 136 Payd..for drawyng up y[e] plummpe to y[e] welle, j[d]. **1551** RECORDE *Cast. Knowl.* (1556) 112 Manye drawe water at a plompe, that knowe not the cause, why the water dothe ascend. **1663** WOOD *City of Oxford* (O.H.S.) I. 477 Opposite to the two fact [= faced] plumpe.

plump (plʌmp), *sb.*[3] Also 5 plumbe, 9 plomp. [f. PLUMP *v.*[1]]

1. An act of plumping (see PLUMP *v.*[1] 1); the fall of a solid body into water, mud, etc., with little or no splash; an act of dropping flat on the ground; an abrupt plunge or heavy fall. *familiar.*

a **1450** *Fysshynge w. Angle* 18 Kepe hym euer [under] þe rod..So þat ȝe may susteyne hys lepys & plumbes [cf. 1496 in PLUNGE *sb.* 3]. **1596** DALRYMPLE tr. *Leslie's Hist. Scot.* II. 161 With a plumpe he fercelie fallis in al kynde of mischeife. **1694** R. OVERTON *Defiance of Act Pardon* 7 A mighty stone fell..and gave a mighty plump. **1760** C. JOHNSTON *Chrysal* (1822) III. 295 The waggon came into a deep hole, with such a plump. **1884** G. M. BARKER *Tea Planter's Life in Assam* viii. 208, I heard..a 'plomp' as he made a hole in the water. **1896** J. LUMSDEN *Poems* 169, I will lichten an' brichten As weel as plumps in Tyne.

†**2.** A firm blow. *slang. Obs.*

1763 C. JOHNSTON *Reverie* I. 135 Challenging him to fight, and before he can be on his guard, hitting him a plump in the bread-basket, that shall make him throw up his accounts. **1785** GROSE *Dict. Vulg. T.* s.v., I'll give you a plump in the bread-basket..I'll give you a blow in the stomach.

3. A sudden heavy fall of rain. Chiefly *Sc.*

1822 GALT *Steam-boat* xi. 261 The thunder plump that drookit me to the skin. **1857** COL. K. YOUNG *Diary & Corr.* (1902) 273, I wish it would come down a good plump of rain. **1878** STEVENSON *Inland Voy.* 74 The whole day was showery, with occasional drenching plumps.

plump (plʌmp), *a.*[1] Forms: 5–6 plompe, 6–7 plumpe, 6– plump. [In senses 1 and 2 corresp. to MDu. *plomp* blunt, in both senses 'not pointed' and 'not sharp', Du. *plomp* blunt, obtuse (of weapons), thick (as a nail), coarse, clumsy, also rude, clownish, blockish, dull, MLG. *plump*, *plomp* massive, unshapen, obtuse, blunt, stumpy, LG. *plump* coarse, clumsy. The later Eng. senses appear to belong to the same word, passing through the sense 'blunt, rounded, not sharp or angular', into a eulogistic sense (? possibly through some association with PLUM *a.*

and *v.*). In MLG. Schiller & Lübben quote *Vocab. Engelh.* for 'corpulentus, *plumpich*'.

From LG. come also Da., Sw. *plump* rude, coarse, clumsy, unfashioned, unpolished, clownish. The ulterior origin is obscure. Doornkaat-Koolman takes the original notion as 'cut off short or suddenly, docked', and connects it with the echoic int. and adv. *plump, plumps*, expressing sudden action: cf. PLUMP *int.* and *adv.*]

I. †**1.** Blunt (in manners); not 'sharp' in intellect; dull, clownish, blockish, rude. *Obs.*

1481 CAXTON *Reynard* xxxiv. 100 But rude and plompe beestis [*orig.* ruyde ongheuallighen beesten] can not vnderstonde wysedom. *c* **1620** MORYSON *Itin.* (1903) 370 The Hollanders have of old beene vulgarly called *Plumpe*, that is blunt or rude.

†**2.** Of an arrow-head: Blunt and broad (? rounded). *Obs.*

1545 ASCHAM *Toxoph.* (Arb.) 137 There be dyuerse kyndes, some be blonte heades, some sharpe, some both blonte and sharpe. The blont heades men vse bycause they perceaue them to be good, to kepe a lengthe wyth all.. bycause a man poulethe them no ferder at one tyme than at another. For in felynge the plompe ende alwayes equallye he may lowse them.

II. 3. Of full and rounded form; sufficiently fleshy or fat to show no angularity of outline; chubby; having the skin well filled or elastically distended. **a.** Of persons, animals, or parts of the body; **b.** also of fruit, grain, etc., and *transf.* of a well-filled bag or purse, a springy cushion, etc.

a. **1545** [implied in PLUMPNESS¹]. **1569** *Reg. Privy Council Scot.* II. 46 Riche Grahame callit the Plump. **1592** SHAKS. *Ven. & Ad.* 142 My flesh is soft and plump. **1634** HEYWOOD & BROME *Witches Lanc.* IV. i. Wks. 1874 IV. 223 You may see by his plump belly.. he [a horse] hath not bin sore travail'd. **1687** T. BROWN *Saints in Uproar* Wks. 1730 I. 78 Having so jolly plump lasses under your care. **1728** POPE *Dunc.* II. 41 All as a partridge plump, full-fed, and fair. **1756–7** tr. *Keysler's Trav.* (1760) III. 342 In his other pictures.. all his figures are very plump. **1784** COWPER *Task* IV. 595 The plump convivial parson. **1837** M. DONOVAN *Dom. Econ.* II. 209 The Arabians, Caffres, and Hottentots, consume vast quantities of locusts when they are plump. **1866** GEO. ELIOT *F. Holt* i, Harold lifted his arm and spread out his plump hand.

b. **1599** B. JONSON *Ev. Man out of Hum.* I. iii, To see how plumpe my bags are, and my barnes. **1601** HOLLAND *Pliny* I. 417 After they [dried grapes] be well drenched and infused in some excellent wine vntill they be swelled and plumpe, they presse them. **1771** LUCKOMBE *Hist. Print.* 322 To keep the Ball-Leathers plump the longer. **1794** J. ROBERTSON *Agric. Perth* (1799) 208 It produces excellent crops of plump grain. **1845** MRS. CARLYLE *Lett.* I. 339 He.. looked as plump as a pincushion.

c. Of coins: Of full size and weight, not clipped.

1867 SIR C. BLACKBURN in *Law Rep., Queen's Bench* II. 175, I do not believe that the coins in actual currency at that time were 'plump'. I think it probable that they were much clipped and sweated.

d. *fig.* (with various shades of meaning): 'Fat', rich, abundant; well-supplied; full and round in tone; great, big; complete, round. *familiar.*

1635 QUARLES *Embl.* II. iii. 74 Will no plump Fee Bribe thy false fists, to make a glad Decree? **1641** MILTON *Reform.* I. Wks. 1851 III. 18 What a plump endowment to the.. mouth of a Prelate. *a* **1700** B. E. *Dict. Cant. Crew, Plump-in-the-pocket*, flush of Money. **1775** MME. D'ARBLAY *Early Diary, Lett.* 10 June, Such a powerful voice!.. her shake—so plump—so true, so open! **1827** POLLOK *Course T.* III. 153 The stripling youth of plump unseared hope. **1857** TROWBRIDGE *Neighbor Jackwood* ix, I hold not a very plump opinion of them.

e. *Comb.*, as ***plump-bellied, -cheeked, -faced, -thighed, -uddered*** adjs.

1684 OTWAY *Atheist* III. i, You Plump-cheek'd, merry-ey'd Rogue. **1712** STEELE *Spect.* No. 431 ¶3 A plump-fac'd, hale, fresh-colour'd Girl. **1891** C. T. C. JAMES *Rom. Rigmarole* 22 The stubble fields were tented thick with sheaves of plump-faced wheat. **1916** JOYCE *Portrait of Artist* iii. 127 Thrust it out of men's sight into a long hole in the ground, into the grave, to rot, to feed the mass of its creeping worms and to be devoured by scuttling plump-bellied rats. **1922** —— *Ulysses* 537 A nannygoat passes, plumpuddered, buttytailed, dropping currants.

plump, *a.*²: see PLUMP *int.*

plump (plʌmp), *v.*¹ [A Common LG. verb. = MLG., LG. *plumpen*, MDu., Du. *plompen* to fall or plunge into water with the characteristic sound, EFris. *plumpen* to make a hollow sound as water when anything falls into it, to fall with such a sound; thence, Ger. *plumpen* to fall plump or abruptly, also to beat water with a heavy stick, Da. *plumpe* to plunge, Sw. *plumpa* to plump, to fall with impact. Prob. of echoic origin, expressing a sound and action akin to those of PLOP *v.*, but with more distinct expression of the liquid 'gulp' made by water when a body falls into it.

Cf. numerous more or less echoic or onomatopœic words in *-ump*, as *bump, dump, mump, stump, thump, tump*. Some have compared L. *plumbāre* to cover with lead, later prob. to throw the lead-line, whence It. *piombare*, Pr. *plombar* to plunge (see PLUMB *v.*, PLUNGE *v.*); but the approach of form between *plombar* and the LG. *plump-, plomp-* group seems merely fortuitous.]

1. *intr.* To fall, drop, sink, plunge, or impinge, with abruptly checked movement, as when a solid body drops, **a.** into water, etc., or **b.** upon a surface; to fall, plunge, or come down (or against something) flatly or abruptly (usually implying 'with full or direct impact').

a. **13..** *K. Alis.* 5760 (Bodl. MS.) Þo hij seiȝe þat folk i wys Hii plumten doune as an doppe In þe water at on scoppe Þoo hij plumten þe water vnder þe folk had of hem grete wonder. **1749** FIELDING *Tom Jones* IV. iii, The poor lad plumped over head and ears into the water. **1803** *Edin. Rev.* II. 279 The tradesman plumps into a pond. **1827** MONTGOMERY *Pelican Isl.* v. 112 The heavy penguin, neither fish nor fowl,.. Plump'd stone-like from the rock into the gulf. **1892** STEVENSON & L. OSBOURNE *Wrecker* (ed. 2) 305 The rain still plumped like a vast shower-bath.

b. **1712** STEELE *Spect.* No. 492 ¶2 It will give you a Notion how Dulcissa plumps into a Chair. **1786** MME. D'ARBLAY *Diary* 13 Aug., Others.. plumped down on both knees, and could hardly get up again. **1844** THACKERAY *Wand. Fat Contrib.* i, I removed to the next seat.. He plumped into my place. **1857** DUFFERIN *Lett. High Lat.* 86 A vast cavern into which the upper crust subsequently plumped down. **1888** LD. WOLSELEY in *Fortn. Rev.* Aug. 287 The horror of hearing bullets plump into the bodies of their comrades with a horrible thud.

c. *transf.* and *fig.* To come plump, i.e. all at once (into some place or condition); to plunge, burst (*in* or *out*). *familiar.*

1829 LAMB *Lett., to Procter* (1888) II. 219 Lest those raptures.. should suddenly plump down.. to a loathing and blank aversion. **1835** MRS. CARLYLE *Lett.* I. 27 Through them we have plumped into as pretty an Irish connection as one would wish. **1843** —— *Let. to Carlyle* 11 July, For God's sake do not let John plump in upon me in my present puddlement. **1874** LISLE CARR *Jud. Gwynne* I. vii. 212 With a convulsive gurgle, out plumped the words. **1884** HUXLEY in *Life* (1900) II. vi. 84 We.. plumped into bitter cold weather.

2. *trans.* To drop, let fall, throw down, plunge abruptly (into water, etc., or upon a flat surface); to pay *down* at once and in one lot; *refl.* to 'let oneself fall', drop down abruptly and heavily.

c **1420** *Liber Cocorum* (1862) 51 Fyrst sly thy capon over tho nyȝght Plump hym in water wher he is dyȝt. **1573** TUSSER *Husb.* (1878) 53 Seeith water and plump therein plenty of sloes. **1728** POPE *Dunc.* II. 405 As what a Dutchman plumps into the lakes, One circle first, and then a second makes. **1840** THACKERAY *Paris Sk.-bk.* i. (1872) 3 The sun has plumped his hot face into the water. **1849** ALB. SMITH *Pottleton Leg.* vii. (1856) 35 A.. man brought in some.. bags, and plumped them down in a corner. **1869** TOZER *Highl. Turkey* II. 27 [He] plumped himself down on the grass, and declared he would go no further. **1888** *Ch. Times* 24 Aug. 720/1 We may as well plump a shot or two into him. **1892** ZANGWILL *Bow Mystery* 79 She plumped down the money and walked out.

3. *transf.* and *fig.*: esp. in reference to speech: To utter abruptly, to blurt *out*. [Cf. *to say, utter, blurt out plump* in PLUMP *adv.* 3.] *familiar.*

1579 FULKE *Heskins' Parl.* 96 This is a verie peremptorie sentence, plumped downe of you. **1861** HUGHES *Tom Brown at Oxf.* ix, I plumped out that St. Paul's was the finest cathedral in England. **1865** DICKENS *Mut. Fr.* I. viii, 'If, it ain't a liberty to plump it out', said Mr. Boffin, 'what do you do for your living?' **1890** *Pall Mall G.* 6 Sept. 7/1 When you must plump the question square at a man and simply get a cold and passionless reply.

†**4.** *slang.* To give (one) a blow; to shoot. *Obs.*

1785 GROSE *Dict. Vulg. T.* s.v., Plump his peepers, or daylights, give him a blow in the eyes; he pulled out his pops [= pistols] and plumped him.

5. *intr.* [Short for *to vote plump* or *give a plumper.*] To vote at an election *for* one candidate alone (when one is entitled to vote for two or more). Also *transf.* More widely, to opt *for*. Also, to decide or vote *against*.

The original sense was app. to give a direct, straight, unqualified, or absolute vote *for* a person; this implied no weakening or qualifying of it by voting for any other. See PLUMP *adv.* 4, *a.*² 2, PLUMPER² 2.

1806 in *Acc. Elect. Liverpool Nov.* 1806, For Tarleton, a plumper, let's vote one and all,.. We'll plump for Tarleton, to prove we are free. **1813** W. TAYLOR in *Monthly Mag.* XXXV. 427 (*heading*) Plumping at Elections. **1848** THACKERAY *Bk. Snobs* xxviii, Friendship.. induces me to plump for St. Michaels. **1866** GEO. ELIOT *F. Holt* xi, I'll plump or I'll split for them as treat me the handsomest and are the most of what I call gentlemen. **1890** BARRÈRE & LELAND *Dict. Slang* II. 140/2 *Plump, to...* (Racing), to lay one's money on one single horse. But I shall *plump* for Lord R. Ch.'s L' Abbesse de Jouarre, who has been well tried. —*Truth.* **1894** [see VOTRESS²]. **1903** *Sat. Rev.* 4 Apr. 415/2 The method of voting.. is that of the 'general ticket'. Each voter would be required to vote for as many candidates as there were vacancies, and no voter would be allowed to give more than one vote to any candidate. This secures against the danger of 'plumping' in any form. **1929** C. CONNOLLY *Let.* in *Romantic Friendship* (1975) 325, I have plumped against England. **1934** *Discovery* June 176/1 The more one knows.. the less one is inclined to 'plump' for one particular solution rather than another. **1963** *Ann. Reg. 1962* 17 The largest union.. had plumped two-to-one against a strike. **1966** *Observer* 3 Apr. 10/5 A large section of the electorate plumped for the Liberals. **1972** *Nature* 25 Feb. 424/3 The consultants recommend three road crossing schemes but plump for a Flint-Burton crossing with a coast road. **1976** *Which?* May 100/3 We don't think now is the best time to invest in equipment. Better to wait until one of the systems appears to be winning the battle and then plump for that.

Hence **ˈplumping** *vbl. sb., ppl. a.*

c **1829** H. MILLER *Lett. on Herring Fish.* iv, They [herrings].. sunk with a hollow plumping noise. **1878** STEVENSON *Edinburgh* (1889) 2 Among bleak winds and plumping rain.

plump, *v.*² [f. PLUMP *a.*¹ 3.

(But the first quot. is somewhat earlier than any found for the corresponding sense of the adj.)]

1. a. *trans.* To make plump; to cause to swell; to fill *out*, dilate, distend; to fatten *up*. *spec.* of pillows, cushions, and other upholstery.

1533 J. HEYWOOD *Play of Weather* Plays (1905) 115 For springing and plumping all manner corn Yet must ye have water or all is forlorn. **1631** CHETTLE *Hoffman* IV. Hj, Art not thou plumpt with laughter my Lorrique? **1661** BOYLE *Spring of Air* (1682) 93 These particles [of air] so expanding themselves, must necessarily plump out the sides of the bladder.. and so keep them turgid. **1704** *Phil Trans.* XXV. 1621 If the.. Grain were well soakt and plumpt up with Water. **1775** JOHNSON *Journ. West. Isl., Coriatachan*, Fowls.. not like those plumped for sale by the poulterers of London. **1848** THACKERAY *Van. Fair* xxxvii, Dolly.. plumping and patting the pillows of the bed. **1848** DICKENS *Dombey & Son* lvii. 571 Mrs. Miff resumes her dusting and plumps up her cushions. **1852** *Fraser's Mag.* XLVI. 469 The oil.. has plumped his cheeks.. and expanded his whole form. **1883** R. HALDANE *Workshop Receipts* Ser. II. 371/1 The hide is unhaired by being placed in a liquid, which.. plumps the hide. **1960** M. SPARK *Ballad Peckham Rye* viii. 168 She turned and plumped out the cushion behind her. **1962** A. SEXTON *All my Pretty Ones* 43 The houseboy, A quick-eyed Filipino.. plumping up The down-upholstery. **1972** M. J. BOSSE *Incident at Naha* i. 13 The bed, made with.. carefully plumped-up pillows. **1975** L. GILLEN *Return to Deepwater* iv. 68 The cushions on the settee freshly plumped.

b. *fig.*

1628 FELTHAM *Resolves* II. [I.] x. 27, I will.. plumpe my ioyes by letting them surprize mee. **1655** FULLER *Ch. Hist.* II. iii. §17 Which made them.. 'to plump up the Hollownesse of their History with improbable Miracles'. **1691** WOOD *Ath. Oxon.* II. 671 The godly faction [was] then plump'd up with hopes to carry on their diabolical designes. **1887** G. MEREDITH *Ballads & P.* 109 Heaven! 'tis heaven to plump her [England's] life.

2. *intr.* To become plump; to swell *out* or *up*.

1602 MARSTON *Antonio's Rev.* II. v, Swell, plump, bold heart; For now thy tide of vengeance rowleth in. **1612** R. DABORNE *Chr. turn'd Turke* 1498 You Manticora, that plumpe vpon raw flesh. **1693** EVELYN *De la Quint. Compl. Gard.* II. 166 Their Fruit begins to plump at the full Moon. **1843** LADY GRANVILLE *Lett.* (1894) II. 358 He [a dog] is plumping up, his coat glossy. **1882** *Fraser's Mag.* XXV. 687 Her cheeks had plumped out.

Hence **ˈplumping** *vbl. sb.*

1593 NASHE *Christ's T.* (1613) 145 They shew the swellings of their mind, in the swellings and plumpings out of their apparrayle. **1700** FLOYER *Hot & Cold Bath.* I. 36 Hot Baths.. cause the plumping up of the Habit of the Body. **1890** LE GALLIENNE *G. Meredith* 85 That plumping of her exquisite proportions on bread and butter.

plump, *v.*³ [f. PLUMP *sb.*¹]

†**1.** *intr.* To form plumps; to mass or crowd together. *Obs.*

1530 PALSGR. 661/2 What meane yonder men to plompe togyder yonder,.. *qui sarroutent aynsi?* **1535** COVERDALE *Exod.* xv. 8 The depes plomped together in yᵉ myddest of the see.

†**b.** ***to plump out***, to come out in a mass. *Obs.*

1555 W. WATREMAN *Fardle Facions* I. vi. F viij, The barel now broken, the swarme plomped out.

2. *trans.* To sow (seed) in plumps or clumps.

1844 STEPHENS *Bk. Farm* III. 750 The plumping mode, as this method of sowing by intervals is termed.

†**plump**, *v.*⁴ An obsolete by-form of PUMP *v.* Cf. PLUMP *sb.*²

1589 RIDER *Bibl. Schol.* 1112 To Plumpe, v. pumpe.

plump (plʌmp), *int., adv.*, and *a.*² [app. the onomatopœic stem of PLUMP *v.*¹ used to express the manner of the action, or the echoic imitation of the sound of the act.]

A. †*int.* Imitative of the sound made by a heavy body falling into water.

[Cf. LG. *plump*, 'an interjection which expresses the sound made by anything heavy when it falls into water' (*Bremisches Wbch.*).]

1597 BEARD *Theatre God's Judgem.* (1612) 121 [They] threw them peecemeale into a deepe well, to heare them crie plumpe.

B. *adv.* (Mostly *familiar.*)

1. With a sudden drop or fall into water.

1610 B. JONSON *Masque Oberon* Wks. (Rtldg.) 583/1, I would fain.. to some river take 'em, Plump; and see if that would wake 'em. *c* **1614** FLETCHER, etc. *Wit at Sev. Weap.* I. i, The art of swimming, he that will attain to 't Must fall plump, and duck himself at first. **1713** STEELE *Guard.* No. 50 ¶4 The lover, with much amazement, came plump into the river. **1850** SCORESBY *Cheever's Whalem. Adv.* iii. (1859) 40 But no sooner was the last fold of blubber.. hoisted in,.. than it [the carcase] sank plump down.

2. With a sudden or abrupt fall or sinking down; with sudden direct impact, flat upon or against something; with a sudden or unexpected encounter.

1594 CAREW *Tasso* (Grosart) 9 There hence againe, to pastures of Tortose, Plump downe directly leuels he his flight. **1778** MISS BURNEY *Evelina* (1791) II. ix. 69 As we were a-going up Snow-Hill, plump we comes against a cart. **1806–7** J. BERESFORD *Miseries Hum. Life* (1826) x. vi, Sitting plump on an unsuspected cat in your chair. *a* **1845** BARHAM *Ingol. Leg.* Ser. III. *Marie Mignot*, Her Ladyship found Herself plump on the ground. **1865** DICKENS *Mut. Fr.* III. i, I took a shot at him and brought him down plump.

3. *fig.* Directly, at once, straight, without hesitation or circuitous action; *esp.* in reference to a statement or question: Directly, without circumlocution or concealment, in plain terms, bluntly, flatly.

a **1734** NORTH *Lives* (K.O.), Refuse plump. **1779** MME. D'ARBLAY *Lett.* Dec., The shortest way of doing this is by coming plump upon the question. **1809** Malkin *Gil Blas* xii. vii. ¶4 If you must have it plump, I was born to live and die a poet. **1811** *Minutes Evid. Berkeley Peerage* 202, I question whether I ever said plump Miss Tudor, I said Ma'am. **1840** Thackeray *Catherine* iv, Hayes first said no, plump. **1888** 'R. Boldrewood' *Robbery under Arms* xlviii, He told us, plump and plain, that he wasn't going to shift. **1898** *Pall Mall Mag.* Nov. 368, I lied.. plump and pat, I will confess.

†**4.** ***to vote plump***, to vote 'straight' or without any qualification. *U.S. Obs.*

1776 J. Adams *Wks.* (1854) IX. 398 New Jersey has dethroned [Govr. William] Franklin, and in a letter, which is just come to my hand from indisputable authority, I am told that the delegates from that colony 'will vote plump!' [*sc.* for the Declaration of Independence.]

C. *adj.* **1. a.** Descending directly, vertical, sheer. **b.** Directly facing in position.

1611 Cotgr., *Escore*,.. plumpe, or straight down, in depth. **1890** *Anthony's Photogr. Bull.* III. 287 In buildings, plump views are objectionable; they should always be taken at an angle.

2. *fig.* Of statements, etc.: Direct, blunt, straight-spoken, downright, unqualified, 'flat'. *familiar.*

1789 Mme. D'Arblay *Diary* Dec., She.. made the most plump inquiries into its particulars, with a sort of hearty good humour. **1803** Mar. Edgeworth *Belinda* xvii, I hate qualifying arguers; plump assertion or plump denial for me! **1828–32** Webster s.v., A plump lie. **1840** Lady C. Bury *Hist. Flirt* i, She gave a plump decline, and said something about his morals. **1872** H. Lawrenny in *Fortn. Rev.* Mar. 321 Neither man nor woman would dare to answer with a plump No.

3. Plumped down; paid down at once.

1865 Dickens *Mut. Fr.* iii. xiii, Paying up in full, in one plump sum.

plumpen ('plʌmpən), *v. rare.* [f. plump *a.*[1] + -en[5].] *trans.* To make plump, swell out. Also *intr.*, to grow plump. Hence **'plumpening** *vbl. sb.* the action or process of making or becoming plump.

1687 A. Lovell tr. *Bergerac's Com. Hist.* i. 13 As if it were likely that the Sun.. had only been kindled to ripen their Medlars, and plumpen their Cabbage! **1853** G. J. Cayley *Las Alforjas* I. 121 They shall go plump into our book, line for line, and word for word, and serve to plumpen the two voluminous volumes. **1926** *Sectator* 1 May 801/2 The plumpening of cherries on lichened wall. **1966** P. V. Price *France* 307 The chickens.. wander about the roads in the Bresse plain, plumpening visibly.

plumper[1] ('plʌmpə(r)). [f. plump *v.*[2] + -er[1].] That which plumps or makes plump.

a. A small light ball or disk sometimes carried in the mouth, for the purpose of filling out hollow cheeks.

1690 *Songs Costume* (Percy Soc.) 189 And that the cheeks may both agree, Plumpers to fill the cavity. **1697** tr. *C'tess D'Aunoy's Trav.* (1706) 120 With one blow of her fist she not only made several of her Teeth leap out of her Mouth, but also two little Cork plumpers, which served to fill out her hollow Jaws. **1710** Steele *Tatler* No. 245 ¶2 Two Pair of brand-new Plumpers, Four Black-lead Combs, Three Pair of fashionable Eye-brows. **1755** *Connoisseur* No. 77 ¶1 Vamped up for show with paint, patches, plumpers, and every external ornament that art can suggest. **1905** *Dial* 16 Feb. 116/2 She.. was charged by some of the ladies at the summer boarding house where we met with wearing 'plumpers' in her cheeks.

†**b.** A contrivance for expanding the skirts; a bustle or hoop, a pannier. *Obs.*

1749 Mrs. E. Montagu *Lett.* (1813) III. 86 Old Mrs. Ashley has added a yard of whalebone to her plumpers merely on his account.

c. A preparation for causing hides to plump.

1903 L. A. Flemming *Pract. Tanning* xxii. 375 Quebracho is not a good plumper, and for this reason some material is necessary to plump the leather. *Ibid.* 376 Quebracho, being a sweet tan, is not of itself a plumper.

plumper[2] ('plʌmpə(r)). [f. plump *v.*[1] or *adv.*]

1. a. An act of plumping, as into water, or to the ground; a fall from a horse.

1810 *Splendid Follies* II. 138, I had such a plumper off the old mare the first time I went out! *Ibid.* III. 79 After my plumper, the animal made for the woods.

†**b.** *slang.* A heavy blow. *Obs.*

1764–72 T. Brydges *Homer Travest.* 378 (Farmer) Gave me a plumper on the jaw, And cry'd: Pox take you! **1796** *Sporting Mag.* VIII. 145 Which was immediately followed by a plumper just under the right eye.

2. a. [Cf. plump *a.*[2] 2, and plump *adv.* 4.] A vote given solely to one candidate at an election (when one has the right to vote for two or more). Also attrib. ***plumper vote***.

1785 Grose *Dict. Vulg. T.* s.v. *Plump*, A *plumper*, a single vote at an election. **1813** W. Taylor in *Monthly Mag.* XXXV. 427 C, who splits none of his votes, will have seven supporters. The majority falls to the lot of the candidate [C] whose adherents give plumpers. **1843** Le Fevre *Life Trav. Phys.* I. i. v. 95 They shall not have my vote..; you shall have a plumper. **1853** Lytton *My Novel* xi. xiii, If canvassing for yourself alone, you could not carry a sufficient number of plumper votes. **1894** J. K. Fowler *Recoll. Old Co. Life* i. 8 An old printed document.. giving.. the number of plumpers, or single votes, polled for each candidate.

b. A voter who 'plumps'. *rare.*

1818 in Todd Suppl. **1832** Geo. Eliot in Cross *Life* I. 28 The numerous plumpers.. being constantly interrupted in their endeavours to go to the hustings.

3. a. A downright lie. (Cf. *cracker*, *whacker*, etc.) *vulgar.* ? *Obs.*

1812 *Salem* (Mass.) *Gaz.* 26 Nov. 3/3 A Plumper.—The Gazette.. states [etc.]... A more barefaced falsehood never was published. *a* **1814** *He must be married* i. i. in *New Brit. Theatre* IV. 234, I will propose you to him—I shall tell him a few plumpers. **1828–32** Webster, *Plumper*,.. a full unqualified lie. (*In vulgar use.*) Hence in mod. Dicts.

b. *colloq.* An unusually large example of its type; a whopper. ? *Obs.*

1881 *Punch* 1 Oct. 155/1 Lovers of England.. can hardly do better than help to fill that Purse, which Mr. Punch hopes will prove a 'plumper'.

4. *attrib.* **plumper line**, a rope used by divers in making their descent.

1896 *Strand Mag.* XII. 349/1 The [pearl-divers'] descent is made by means of a rope called the plumper line. **1896** *Daily News* 14 Nov. 6/7 Three or four of these [descents] were spent in restoring the plumper-line, which Diver May finally secured to the ring of the trap-door of the specie tank.

'plumper[3]. [f. plump *sb.*[1] or *v.*[3]] A machine for sowing seed in 'plumps' or clumps.

1844 Stephens *Bk. Farm* III. 788 The drill-sowing machines.. are designated in Scotland plumpers, from their dropping their gifts on one point. **1854** *Jrnl. R. Agric. Soc.* XV. i. 110 They are.. dibbled by a machine called a plumper or sown in shallow drills by the hand.

plum-pie. [f. plum *sb.* 1, 4 + pie.]

†**1.** A pie containing raisins and currants; esp. a mince-pie. *Obs.*

a **1660** [Mock sermon] *Brewerton Ch.* cxix. *Ver.* xxxi, '*And they did eat their Plum-pies, and rejoiced exceedingly*', (Bodl. Lib.) p. 6, Here now we are to consider what sort of Plum-pye this was, and how many sorts of plum pyes there are... There is your Christmas pye and that hath plums in abundance, that is your Metropolitan plum pye, tis the cream of all plum pyes, and in brief there is no plum pye like it... Mark but the ingredients.. Minced pyes are beset with plums and spice... Your Neat's tongue.. your Currants.. your raisins. [Cf. **17..** *Hist. Jack Horner* i. 4, Jack Horner, in the Corner, Eats good Christmas Pye, And with his Thumbs pulls out the Plumbs, And said, Good Boy am I.]

2. A pie containing plums or prunes.

1830 Maunder *Dict.*, *Plumpie*, a pie with plums in it. **1846** in Worcester. **1847** in Webster. **1880** Ruskin *Hortus Inclusus* (1887) 70, I lunched with Cardinal Manning, and he gave me such a plum pie.

'plumping, *ppl. a. colloq.* [f. plump *v.*[2] + -ing[2].] Very large, unusually big.

1903 'A. McNeill' *Egregious English* 91 You win by the skin of your teeth or with a plumping majority, as the case may be. **1978** *Guardian Weekly* 2 Apr. 20/3 The Master Builder is a sexless play in which a plumping girl with an alpenstock invades the home of an elderly architect.

'plumpish, *a.* [f. plump *a.*[1] + -ish[1].] Somewhat plump. Hence **'plumpishness**.

1758 J. Clubbe *Misc. Tracts* (1770) I. Pref. 11 My body.. which was once plumpish, and inclined to be fat upwards. **1942** W. Faulkner *Go down, Moses* 226 The boy standing there looking down at the short plumpish grey-haired man. **1977** M. Hinxman *One-Way Cemetery* i. 7 She was nice, plumpish, friendly. **1979** 'G. Black' *Night Run from Java* iii. 27 Don't forget the plumpish redundancy payments they all want to collect. **1979** 'J. Ross' *Rattling of Old Bones* ii. 14 Plumpish.. and a sensual plumpishness at that.

plumply ('plʌmplɪ), *adv.*[1] [f. plump *a.*[1] + -ly[2].] To a plump degree, with plumpness.

1611 Cotgr., *Rondement*, roundly, circularly, orbicularly; fully, plumply. **1860** Lever *One of Them* xiv, A long silk purse, plumply filled. **1895** *Harper's Weekly* Feb. 337/2 One of those plumply mellow quadrigenarious bodies.

'plumply, *adv.*[2] *familiar.* [f. plump *a.*[2] + -ly[2].]

1. Directly, without hesitation or circumlocution, plainly, flatly: = plump *adv.* 3.

1786 Mme. D'Arblay *Diary* 8 Aug., I proposed it myself. The offer was plumply accepted. **1822** *New Monthly Mag.* V. 144 The last I contradict plumply. **1874** Lisle Carr *Jud. Gwynne* I. iv. 130 It's out at last plainly and plumply.

2. With direct impact; full against something: = plump *adv.* 2.

1846 Joyce *Sci. Dial.* i. xiii. 34, I have sometimes shot my white alley against another marble so plumply, that [etc.].

plumpness[1] ('plʌmpnɪs). [f. plump *a.*[1] + -ness.] The quality or condition of being plump; fullness and roundness of form; fatness, fleshiness.

1545 Raynold *Byrth Mankynde* (1564) 18 b, In softnes of skin and plumpnes of the body. **1660** Boyle *New Exp. Phys. Mech.* Exp. iv, This plumpness of the bladder proceeded from.. the stronger spring of the air remaining in the bladder. **1704** Newton *Opticks* (1721) 13 For those Convex glasses supply the defect of plumpness in the Eye... And the contrary happens in short-sighted Men whose Eyes are too plump. **1885** *Truth* 28 May 850/1 Plumpness sheathes the nerves and gives an impression of good humour.

'plumpness[2]. *familiar.* [f. plump *a.*[2] + -ness.] Directness or bluntness of statement.

1780 Mme. D'Arblay *Diary* Apr., She.. speaks her opinion.. with a plumpness of honesty.. that both pleases and diverts me. **1879** Howells *L. Aroostook* v, 'Yes, Maria, I be', returned her father, with uncommon plumpness. **1906** *Daily News* 22 Jan. 6 Sometimes the more simple-minded apologists.. put the thing with astonishing plumpness and plainness.

†**'plum-'porridge.** *Obs.* Porridge containing prunes, raisins, currants, etc.; formerly in favour as a Christmas dish. Probably, as in *plum-broth*, the dried plums or prunes were the original characteristic, and gave the name.

1591 Lyly *Endym.* v. ii. 69 A great platter of plum-porridge of pleasure wherein is stued the mutton of mistrust. **1608** Heywood *Rape Lucrece* iii. Wks. 1874 V. 200 My Lords, the best plumporedge in all Rome cooles for your honours. **1698** W. King tr. *Journ. London* 5 Prunes.. they have not had enough to lay round their Plum-porridge at Christmas. **1712** Arbuthnot *John Bull* iii. v, Plum-porridge and minced pies. **1808** Scott *Marm.* vi. Introd. 67 There the huge sirloin reeked; hard by Plumb porridge stood, and Christmas pye. **1901** *Daily Chron.* 25 Dec. 5/1 The plum-pudding may be said to be a work of evolution, and to have supplanted entirely the older dish of plum-porridge, with its congeners the December and Christmas pies.

†**'plum-'pottage.** *Obs.* ? = prec.

1573 Baret *Alv.* P 555 Plumme potage, or potage made thicke with meate or crummes of bread, *puls, pultis.* **1658** J. Harrington *Prerog. Pop. Govt.* Wks. (1700) 297 We, who have bin us'd to our Plumpottage, are like enough to make faces (as did the King of Pontus) at the Lacedemonian black broth. **1682** Wheler *Journ. Greece* i. 43 Christmas pies, Plum-potage, Cake and Puddings. **1864** *Chambers' Bk. Days* II. 755/2 In old times plum-pottage was always served with the first course of a Christmas dinner. It was made by boiling beef or mutton with broth, thickened with brown bread; when half-boiled, raisins, currants, prunes, cloves, mace and ginger were added.

plumptitude ('plʌmptɪtju:d). *joc.* ? *Obs.* Also **plumpitude.** [f. plump *a.*[1] + *-titude* after *altitude*, *aptitude*, etc.: see -tude.] Plumpness.

1828 F. Kemble in G. Macpherson *Mem. Life Anna Jameson* (1878) ii. 44 To behold her sitting on a sofa in a very becoming state of blooming *plumpitude.* **1850** *Godey's Lady's Bk.* XLI. 180/2 At every pore I'm oozing—(I'm 'caving in' to-day)—My plumptitude I'm losing, And dripping fast away. **1854** G. Greenwood *Haps & Mishaps* ii. 43 The lord chancellor having formally announced that parliament stood prorogued until the 20th of August, Her Majesty rose as majestically as could be expected of one more remarkable for rosy plumptitude than regal altitude. **1890** *Daily News* 19 Aug. 3/1 Our own countrymen and countrywomen are more prone to a condition of 'blooming plumptitude', which too much sugar is likely to increase unduly.

plum pudding, plum-pudding (plʌm'pʊdɪŋ). A pudding containing plums.

a. (= *Christmas plum-pudding*) *spec.* A boiled pudding now composed of flour, bread-crumbs, suet, raisins, currants, and other fruits, with eggs, spices, etc., sometimes flavoured with brandy or other spirit, eaten at Christmas; also, an ordinary suet pudding with raisins.

1711 *Vind. Sacheverell* 75 This is just as proper as I had a good Plumb Pudden to day with a Mixture of Flower and Raisins. **1725** De Foe *Voy. round World* (1840) 302, I gave the cook order to make every mess a good plum-pudding. **1772** Mackenzie *Man World* ii. xi. (1823) 478 A plumb-pudding of a very uncommon circumference was raised conspicuous in the middle. **1797** *Lond. Complete Art Cookery* 69 An excellent Plumb-Pudding. **1901** *Daily Chron.* 25 Dec. 5/2 Plum-pudding gradually came into the bills of fare in the early years of the eighteenth century.

b. A pudding of fresh plums contained in a crust.

1813 W. Taylor in *Monthly Mag.* XXXV. 233 Little Jack Horner, we fear, misapplies the word *plum*, when he calls a dried raisin, or currant, by that name. The bullace pudding, the prune pudding, and the damascene pudding, are better entitled to be called plum-puddings than the currant, or raisin, puddings, which have usurped that appellation. *c* **1900** *Beeton's Every-day Cook. Bk., Plum Pudding.* (Fresh Fruit.).. Seasonable with various kinds of plums, from the beginning of August to the beginning of October.

c. (*a*) *attrib.* and *Comb.* (esp. in names of things resembling a plum pudding in shape or mottled appearance), as ***plum-pudding head***, ***horse***; (*b*) **plum-pudding breed, -dog**, the Dalmatian or Spotted Coach breed of dog; **plum pudding mahogany**, mahogany with a mottled finish; **plum-pudding stone** (*Geol.*), a term applied orig. to a conglomerate of flint pebbles embedded in a siliceo-calcareous matrix; now, *loosely*, to any conglomerate; **plum-pudding voyage**, a short voyage for which a supply of fresh provisions is carried (*slang*).

(*a*) **1776** Foote *Capuchin* i. Wks. 1799 II. 385 Wictuals! Lord help your roast beef and plum-pudding soul! **1899** *Westm. Gaz.* 24 June 8/1 Mademoiselle has probably by this time mastered the art of plum-pudding making. **1900** *Ibid.* 14 Feb. 8/1 'Mr. Goodnight' is a plum-pudding horse with a brain as near that of a human being as it is permitted for a four-footed creature to possess. **1902** *Little Frolic* 36 Greedy.. saw two grinning little men with plum-pudding heads.

(*b*) **1897** *Westm. Gaz.* 11 Feb. 4/1 The '*plum-pudding' breed, as the Dalmatian or carriage dog is commonly termed, is so well represented as to make it obvious that this breed is rapidly coming to the front again. **1881** *Daily News* 1 Sept. 5/2 The Dalmatian pointer, commonly known as a *plum-pudding dog. **1924** G. O. Wheeler *Old English Furniture* (ed. 3) xii. 278 The plum mottle.. signifies the spotted and mottled wood known as '*plum-pudding' mahogany. **1968** *Canad. Antiques Collector* Nov. 8/2 (Advt.), Sheraton style 'Plumb [*sic*] Pudding' Mahogany cabinet.. circa 1790. **1976** *Country Life* 26 Feb. (Suppl.) 24c/1 An unusual Chippendale period supper table with two tier top. The table is of 'Plum pudding' mahogany, with carved detail. **1739** Labelye *Short Acc. Piers Westm. Bridge* 53 Stones commonly call'd *Plumb-pudding Stones. **1813** Sir H. Davy *Agric. Chem.* iv. (1814) 195 Plum pudding stone (a secondary rock) consisting of pebbles cemented by a ferruginous or siliceous cement. **1851** H. Melville *Whale* xvii. 94 Some sailors who had just come from a *plum-pudding voyage as they called it.

d. (See quots.)

1851 H. Melville *Moby Dick* III. viii. 64 Plum-pudding is the term bestowed upon certain fragmentary parts of the whale's flesh. **1904** *Sci. Amer. Suppl.* 5 Mar. 23551/3 A muscular, fibrous substance known as 'plum pudding' permeates the blubber of the tongue of these two species of whales.

e. *Mil. slang.* A type of trench mortar shell.

1925 Fraser & Gibbons *Soldier & Sailor Words* 225 *Plum pudding*, the name for a type of trench mortar shell; suggested by its size and shape. **1928** Blunden *Undertones of War* 51 Now more serious and immediate omens of ordeal appeared in the mounds of trench mortar bombs—'plum puddings' or 'footballs', steely and shining.

Hence **plum-'puddinger**, a whaling ship employed in short voyages; cf. *plum-pudding voyage*; also, a member of the crew of such a ship.

1851 H. Melville *Moby Dick* I. xvii. 137 After listening to these plum-puddingers till nearly eleven o'clock, I went up stairs to go to bed. **1874** C. M. Scammon *Marine Mammals* II. iv. 241 Provincetown has ever been foremost with her numerous fleet of plum-puddingers,.. which are small vessels employed on short voyages in the Atlantic Ocean. **1934** F. R. Dulles *Lowered Boats* iv. 45 Only the little 'plum-pud'ners' of Rhode Island remained wholly true to the Greenland whale.

plumpy ('plʌmpɪ), *a.* [f. plump *a.*[1] + -y.] Characterized by plumpness; plump.

1606 Shaks. *Ant. & Cl.* II. vii. 121 Come thou Monarch of the Vine, Plumpie Bacchus, with pinke eyne. **1755** J. Shebbeare *Lydia* (1769) I. 13 Her mouth was little, encircled by the plumpy lip. **1862** Trollope *Orley F.* I. 9 That mild-eyed, soft, round, plumpy prettiness gives way beneath such a weight as that.

plumrock, -rose, Sc. corrupt ff. primrose.

1787 Burns *Let. W. Nicol* 1 June, A new blawn plumrose in a hazle shaw. **1789** D. Davidson *Seasons* 1 Hail, lovely Spring! thy bonny lyart face, And head wi' plumrocks deck'd, bespeak the sun's Return.

† **'plumster.** *Obs.* [f. as *plummer*, plumber, with suffix -ster: cf. *brewster*, etc.] A plumber.

c **1440** *Nom.* in Wr.-Wülcker 686/33 *Hic plummarius*, a plumstere.

plum-tree ('plʌmtriː). The tree which bears plums; = plum *sb.* 2. Also *fig.*, the source of the spoils of political office; esp. in phr. ***to shake the plum tree*** (*U.S.*). Also *attrib.*

c **1000** *Sax. Leechd.* II. 310 Nim plum treowes leaf, wyl on wine, & swile mid þone muþ. *c* **1325** *Gloss. W. de Bibbesw.* in Wright *Voc.* 162 Asch, brom, plum-tre. *c* **1350** *Nominale Gall.-Angl.* 649 (E.E.T.S.) Plumtre, bolastre and hookus [Fr. *Pruner, creker, et chene*]. **1362** Langl. *P. Pl.* A. v. 16 Piries and Plomtres were passchet to þe grounde. **1483** *Cath. Angl.* 284/1 A Plowmbe tre garthe, *prunetum*. **1552** Huloet, Plumbe tree, *prunus, spinus*; *prunetum, spinetum*, the place wher plumme trees growe. **1657** Austen *Fruit Trees* I. 57 The Violet and Premorden Plum-trees are very great bearing trees. **1756–7** tr. *Keysler's Trav.* (1760) III. 4 An ever-green, with leaves resembling those of a pear or plumb-tree. **1905** D. G. Phillips *Plum Tree* ii. 24, I mentally called the roll—wealth, respectability, honor, all on their knees before Dominick, each with his eye upon the branch of the plum tree that bore the kind of fruit he fancied. **1906** U. Sinclair *Jungle* xxvii. 340 Those golden hours when he, too, had a place beneath the shadow of the plum tree. **1922** Joyce *Ulysses* 668 The name on the label is Plumtree. A plumtree in a meatpot, registered trade mark. **1933** *Sun* (Baltimore) 23 May 14/1 The thought uppermost in everybody's mind at the gathering at which James was the guest of honor was: When will you shake the plum tree? **1952** G. Stimpson *Bk. about Amer. Politics* 258 While he [*sc.* Matthew Stanley Quay] was State treasurer (1885–1887) he placed large sums of State money in the People's Bank of Philadelphia and used it to buy stocks on margin. On one occasion Quay and his associates piled up orders for the stock of the Metropolitan Railroad of New York until only about $10,000 was left in the bank. John S. Hopkins, the cashier, became frightened and protested to the political boss. Quay sent the cashier the message: 'Buy and carry a thousand Met for me and I will shake the plum tree.' **1959** *Chambers's Encycl.* X. 804/1 Pruning of standard plum trees simply means cutting out branches which intercross or thinning out overcrowded branches.

‖**plumula** ('pluːmjʊlə). *Bot.* [L. *plūmula* (Colum.), dim. of *plūma* plume.] = plumule 1.

1760 J. Lee *Introd. Bot.* I. vii. (1765) 15 *Plumula*, a scaly Part of the Corculum, which ascends. **1830** Lindley *Nat. Syst. Bot.* 253. **1846** J. Baxter *Libr. Pract. Agric.* (ed. 4) I. 85 The plumula begins to grow; and when this has grown to a certain extent within the grain, the further germination is checked by exposing the grain on a kiln.

plumulaceous (pluːmjuː'leɪʃəs), *a.* [f. L. *plūmula* (see prec.) + -aceous.] Of the nature of or resembling a plumule, downy.

1879 in Webster Suppl. **1890** Coues *Gen. Ornith.* 139 The ventral feathers are usually more largely plumulaceous, and less flat and imbricated.

plumular ('pluːmjʊlə(r)), *a.* [f. L. *plūmula* (see above) + -ar.] Of or pertaining to a plumule.

1881 F. O. Bower in *Jrnl. Microsc. Sc.* Jan. 18 The size and form of the plumular leaves.. may be gathered from figs. 7 and 8. **1895** in *Syd. Soc. Lex.*

Plumularia (ˌpluːmjuː'lɛərɪə). *Zool.* [mod.L.; f. *plūmula* (see above).] A genus of hydroids having a plume-like form. Hence **plumu'larian**, *a.*, of or pertaining to *Plumularia*, or the family of which it is the type; *sb.*, a member of this family.

1859 Kingsley *Glaucus* (ed. 4) 74 Mingled with them are Plumulariæ, always to be distinguished from Sertulariæ by polypes growing on one side of the branch, and not on both. **1872** Allman *Gymnobl. Hydroids* 156 The beautiful plumularian group represented by the genus *Aglaophenia*. **1888** Rolleston & Jackson *Anim. Life* 765 The colonies [of *Hydroidea*].. occasionally attain a great height, e.g. a Plumularian in the Pelew Islands that of a man.

'plumulate, *a. Bot.* [f. L. *plūmul-a* + -ate[2] 2.] Minutely plumate or plumose.

1890 in *Cent. Dict.*

plumule ('pluːmjuːl). [ad. L. *plūmula* (see above), or perh. a. F. *plumule*.]

1. *Bot.* The rudimentary shoot, bud, or bunch of undeveloped leaves in a seed; the stem of the embryo plant.

1727–41 Chambers *Cycl.*, *Plume* or *Plumule*,.. a little member of the grain or seed of a plant; being that which in the growth of the plant becomes the stem, or trunk thereof. **1805** Knight in *Phil. Trans.* XCV. 262, I have never been able to satisfy myself that all the buds were eradicated without having destroyed the base of the plumule. **1875** Bennett & Dyer *Sachs Bot.* 560 The shoot which developes from the plumule becomes the primary stem of the plant.

2. A little feather; *spec.* in *Ornith.*, a down-feather. Also *fig.*

1847 Emerson *Poems, Monadnoc* Wks. (Bohn) I. 439 Fled the last plumule of the Dark, Pants up hither the spruce clerk. **1856–8** W. Clark *Van der Hoeven's Zool.* II. 380 Nostrils not covered by plumules. **1867** Tegetmeier *Pigeons* 8 The whole of the feathers of the pigeon are destitute of the small second feather or accessory plumule.

b. *transf.* The plumose pappus of a seed.

1894 Crockett *Lilac Sunbonnet* 46 The plumules were blowing off freely now.

3. *Entom.* **a.** A little plume-like organ or ornament. **b.** One of the peculiar obcordate scales found on the wings of certain lepidopterous insects, as *Pieridæ*.

1890 in *Cent. Dict.* **1895** *Syd. Soc. Lex.*, *Plumule*,.. 2. *Entom.* A plume-like appendage.

plumuliform ('pluːmjʊlɪfɔːm), *a.* [f. L. type **plūmuliform-is*, f. plumula: see -form.]

1858 Mayne *Expos. Lex.*, *Plumuliformis*,.. having the appearance of a small feather: plumuliform. **1895** in *Syd. Soc. Lex.*

plumulose ('pluːmjʊləʊs), *a.* [ad. mod.L. *plūmulōs-us*, f. plumula: see -ose.] (See quots.)

1826 Kirby & Sp. *Entomol.* IV. xlvi. 276 *Plumulose*,.. when the hairs branch out laterally like feathers. **1858** Mayne *Expos. Lex.*, *Plumulosus*,.. having or full of plumes; plumulose. *Entomol.* having the form of a small plume, as the hair of the *antennæ* of the *Phyllis plumulosa*. **1895** in *Syd. Soc. Lex.*

plumy ('pluːmɪ), *a.* (*sb.*) [f. plume *sb.* + -y.]

† **1.** Composed of down, downy. *Obs.*

1582 Stanyhurst *Æneis* IV. (Arb.) 101 What feathers plumye she beareth, So manye squint eyebals shee keeps.. So manye tongues clapper. **1649** Lovelace *Poems* 54 But whilst a plumy curtaine she doth draw, A Chrystall Mirror sparkles in thy breast. **1700** Dryden *Pygmalion* 56 Her head did on a plumy pillow rest.

2. Characterized by or abounding in plumes or feathers; feathery; feathered.

1597–8 Bp. Hall *Sat.*, *Defiance to Envie* 37 Or would we loose her plumy pineon. **1715–20** Pope *Iliad* XXIV. 363 Let the strong sovereign of the plumy race Tower on the right of yon ethereal space. **1807** Crabbe *Par. Reg.* I. 642 What plumy people sing in every grove! **1855** T. R. Jones *Anim. Kingd.* (ed. 2) 737 It causes their plumy covering to repel moisture.

3. Adorned or decked with a plume or plumes.

1700 Dryden *Pal. & Arcite* III. 452 Crested morions, with their plumy pride. **17..** Beattie *To Lady C. Gordon* iii, The plumy helmet. **1891** Atkinson *Last Giant-killers* 186 He saw the horses and the plumy black wain.

4. Plume-like, feathery.

c **1611** Chapman *Iliad* XII. 158 When a drift wind shakes Blacke clouds in peeces, and plucks snow in great and plumie flakes. **1798** Bloomfield *Farmer's Boy, Summer* 136 When the first sheaf its plumy top uprears. **1890** *Harper's Mag.* July 200/1 Great plumy bunches of asparagus.

5. *Comb.* as ***plumy-crested***, ***-pounced***, ***-varnished***.

1599 Marston *Sco. Vill.* II. vii. 203 Drawn through the eare with Ribands, plumy crested. **1726** Pope *Odyss.* XIX. 36 Ulysses bears The plumy-crested helms. **1812** W. Tennant *Anster F.* VI. lix, Two doves of plumy-varnish'd throat.

† **B.** *sb.* A person wearing a plume. *Obs.*

1687 Mrs. Behn *Emperor of Moon* I. i, I have been at the Chapel, and seen so many Beaus, such a number of Plumeys.

plunder ('plʌndə(r)), *sb.* [f. plunder *v.*[2] (Not from Ger. *plunder* trash, lumber, obs. Du. *plunder* household stuff (Plantin), to which however the American sense 3 may be immediately due.)]

1. a. The action of plundering or taking as spoil; *spec.* as practised in war or a hostile incursion; pillage, spoliation, depredation. Now *rare* or *Obs.*

1643 Prynne *Sov. Power Parlt.* IV. 29, I abhorre all violence, plunder, rapine, and disorders in Souldiers. **1650** R. Stapylton *Strada's Low C. Warres* v. 125 The Merchants, fearing an universall plunder, shut their doors, and barricadoed them. **1726** Leoni *Alberti's Archit.* I. 15/2 After the plunder and spoiling of the Temple. **1839** Thirlwall *Greece* xlix. VI. 187 This was a signal for indiscriminate plunder. **1845** S. Austin *Ranke's Hist. Ref.* II. 331 The English should.. advance as far as possible into the heart of the kingdom, carefully abstaining from plunder.

b. *transf.* The acquisition of property by violent, questionable, or dishonest means; spoliation.

1672 South *Serm.* (1727) V. vi. 243 Those Reforming Harpies, who, by Plunders and Sequestrations, had scraped together three or four Thousand a Year. **1841** Cobden *Let.* 4 Mar. in *Westm. Gaz.* 4 June (1904) 13/1 It is a dishonour to the name and character of Englishmen to submit to such a system of aristocratic plunder as the Corn Law is now proved to the world to be. **1881** Froude *Short Stud.* (1883) IV. II. i. 180 The wretched novice was an object of general plunder till he had learnt how to take care of himself.

2. a. Goods taken from an enemy by force; spoil, booty, prey, loot.

1647 Ward *Simp. Cobler* 59, I would not speake thus.. for all the plunder your plunderers have pillaged. **1694** tr. *Milton's Lett. State* 27 Apr. an. 1650, The most certain Fairs for the Sale of their Plunder. **1726–31** Tindal tr. *Rapin's Hist. Eng.* (1743) II. XVII. 146 Being impatient to return with his plunder to England. **1844** H. H. Wilson *Brit. India* III. 428 The instigator of the depredations.. sharing in the plunder.

b. *transf.* Property acquired by illegal or questionable means; also (*slang*), profit, gain.

1790 Burke *Fr. Rev.* Wks. V. 224 They would not hear of transferring the whole plunder of the kingdom to the stock-holders in Paris. **1851** Mayhew *Lond. Labour* I. 175 I'll get more for it in the cavaldry.. there's better plunder there. (*Plunder*, I may explain, is a common word in the horse trade to express *profit*.) **1865** Holland *Plain T.* v. 188 A set of men.. actuated by no higher motive than a love of plunder and of place.

3. Personal belongings or household goods; luggage, baggage. *U.S. local.* Also *fig.* and in occas. wider use.

1805 M. Lewis in *Lewis & Clark Exped.* (1904) II. 220, I dispatched Sergt. Ordway with 4 Canoes and 8 men to take up a load of baggage as far as Capt. Clark's camp and return for the remainder of our plunder. **1817** J. K. Paulding *Lett. fr. South* I. 38 We accordingly set forth on horseback, carrying our *plunder* (as the Virginians call baggage) in a light Jersey wagon. **1822** J. Flint *Lett. Amer.* 286 Are you pedling? Is it goods or plunder that you have got? *Note*, Plunder is a cant term used in the western country, signifying travelling baggage. **1827** F. Cooper *Prairie* I. ii. 31 You seem to have but little plunder, stranger, for one who is so far abroad. **1873** *Lynch Law in Sucker State* (Farmer), Two long dug-outs, loaded with plunder, stopped at the cabin... This was the family and property of Hank Harris. **1941** E. P. O'Donnell *Great Big Doorstep* 119 Your father puts on more every time he tells that there story. The plunder that man's got in his head! The plunder! **1948** E. N. Dick *Dixie Frontier* 113 Mules and a hardy tough breed of Indian and Spanish horse.. were used to carry the money and plunder. **1962** W. Stegner *Wolf Willow* (1963) III. ii. 160 He gathers together his plunder and he hightails her off the mountain. **1972** O. Frederickson *Silence of North* viii. 64 We didn't have much plunder, and with only two grown-ups, a baby, and a pair of sled dogs on board, it rode high.

4. *Comb.*, as ***plunder-master***; ***plunder-fed*** adj.

1646 *Querela Cantabrigiensis* 13 They have constituted a decay'd Hatter, Plunder-master Generall. **1767** A. Campbell *Lexiph.* 19 On a vicinary bench, sate a plunder-fed soldier.

† **'plunder,** *v.*[1] *Obs.* [A variant of blunder *v.*, to confuse, confound, distract: the phonetic change is unexplained.] *trans.* To confuse, confound, distract, muddle. Hence † **'plundered** *ppl. a.*: cf. blundered; † **'plundering** *vbl. sb.*

1601 Dent *Pathw. Heaven* 255 Howsoeuer they might by wit and learning shuffle it ouer, and in a plundred sort, speake reason: yet had they no feeling of that which they said. **1611** Cotgr., *Academié*,.. besotted, puzled, or plundered, with too much skill or studying. **1641** J. Jackson *True Evang. T.* III. 228 Our peace both of Church and Common-wealth hath beene a little plundered and perplexed. **1642** Jer. Taylor *Episc.* xl. 282 But for all their plundering, and confounding, their bold pretences have made this discourse necessary.

plunder ('plʌndə(r)), *v.*[2] [a. Ger. *plündern* (also †*blündern*), late MHG., MLG., LG. *plünder(e)n*, *plünnern* (early mod.Du. and Du. *plunderen*, also †*plonderen*, Kil.) to pillage, sack, lit. to rob of household effects, f. MG., MHG. *blunder*, *plunder* bed-clothes (14th c.), clothing, household stuff, whence obs. Du. *plunder*, *plonder* household stuff (Plantin, in Kil. 'vetus, Germ.'); in mod.Ger. *plunder* lumber, trash. Cf. MLG., MDu. *plunde*, *plunne*, in LG. also *plünde*, *plünne*, household stuff, clothes, often depreciatory, 'duds', rags, Du. *plunje* clothes, baggage. (In Swiss dial. *plündern* is 'to remove or "flit" with one's household goods' (Grimm).)

The word was much used in Germany during the Thirty Years' War, in reference to which it was current in England from *c* 1630; here, word and thing became familiar on the outbreak of the Civil War in 1642, being especially associated with the proceedings of the forces under Prince Rupert.]

1. *trans.* To rob (a place or person) of goods or valuables by forcible means, or as an enemy; esp. as done in war or a hostile incursion; to pillage, rifle, ransack, spoil; to rob systematically. Also *fig.*

1632 *Swedish Intelligencer* II. 179 The Swedish Dragoones .. plundered the Townes of Wurtbach and Waldsee, neere unto Weingarten. *Ibid.* 180 Both [Bishoprics] are plundered and disarmed, and the best Ordnance sent to Auspurg. **1642** (Nov. 24) *Relation of King's Army at Braintford* (in *Exact Collection* (1643) 761), The Kings Army upon Saturday the twelfth of November after they had possessed themselves of [Braintford], they plundered it without any respect of persons. **1643** PRYNNE *Sov. Power Parlt.* IV. 28, 29, I think the Parliament never yet approved the plundering (or in plain English, robbing) of any man, by any of their forces; they having plundered no places taken by assault, for ought I hear; though the Kings forces on the contrary, have miserably plundered all the Kingdom almost. **1647** MAY *Hist. Parl.* III. i. 3 Many Townes and Villages he [Prince Rupert] plundered, which is to say robb'd, for at that time first was the word plunder used in England, being borne in Germany. **1684** *Scanderbeg Rediv.* v. 119 Twelve Thousand Persons made Prisoners, and the Town first plundred and then Burnt. **1725** DE FOE *Voy. round World* (1840) 323 Searching about for gold in the brooks and small streams, .. and that after they had as it were plundered them at the first discovery. **1769** *Junius Lett.* xxxv. (1820) 161 The people of Ireland have been uniformly plundered and oppressed. **1838** THIRLWALL *Greece* IV. xxxiii. 308 The royal troops plundered the camp of all that fell in their way. **1840** *Penny Cycl.* XVIII. 12/1 The church of S. Francesco was plundered of the 'Descent from the Cross', .. by Paul V., and the picture is now in the Borghese Gallery. **1855** MACAULAY *Hist. Eng.* xiv. III. 424 A crowd of negligent or ravenous functionaries .. plundered, starved, and poisoned the armies and fleets of William. **1896** A. BEARDSLEY *Let.* 29 Oct. (1970) 193 How abominably she [*sc.* George Sand] has been plundered by everyone since. **1961** H. ADAMS in *Webster* s.v., Shakespeare and his fellow-dramatists plundered the Church legends. **1964** T. M. ANDERSSON *Probl. Icelandic Saga Origins* v. 90 *Eiríks saga rauða* and *Grettis saga* combine to show that when *Landnáma* was used, it was plundered wholesale and not plucked for an occasional name.

2. *trans.* To take (goods, valuables, etc.) with illegal force, or as an enemy; to appropriate wrongfully, embezzle; to take by robbery, steal.

1645 FEATLY *Dippers Dipt* (1646) 131 The graces of the Spirit, which cannot be plundered. **1651** USSHER *Lett.* (1686) 543 Those .. I can by no means find, and do much fear that they were plundred, among my other Books and Papers, by the rude Welch in Glamorganshire. *a* **1774** GOLDSM. *Hist. Greece* II. 235 The inhabitants .. were determined to plunder Darius's treasures. **1869** F. W. NEWMAN *Misc.* 151 If they feed themselves honestly, and neither steal men or plunder their goods. **1883** J. W. SHERER *At Home & in India* 141 Wrecking a village .., unroofing the houses and plundering the sweetmeats and grain.

3. *absol.* or *intr.* To commit depredations.

1638 DRUMM. OF HAWTH. *Irene* Wks. (1711) 167 Impiety is no Zeal, Cruelty no Valour, .. open and violent Oppression and Robberies, or your Plundering, no fair Stratagems. **1693** *Mem. Cnt. Teckely* IV. 57 The Imperialists on their side plundered upon the Turks. **1845** S. AUSTIN *Ranke's Hist. Ref.* III. 447 When the Hungarians .. pushed on .. westward, plundering and laying waste by the way. **1849** JAMES *Woodman* x, You will find it so to your cost, .. if you attempt to plunder here.

Hence **'plundered** *ppl. a.*, **'plundering** *vbl. sb.* and *ppl. a.*

1638, 1643 [see 3, 1]. **1649** *Comm. Adv. Money* (1888) II. 1127 Divers plundering officers and soldiers of the late King. **1656** EARL MONM. tr. *Boccalini's Advts. fr. Parnass.* I. lxxxvii. (1674) 117 The ruines, plundrings, affronts, and .. desolations which she had received. **1663** COWLEY *Cutter Coleman St.* v. i, I shall ha' some plunder'd Plate, I hope, to entertain my Friends with. **1693** G. STEPNEY in *Dryden's Juvenal* VIII. (1697) 201 The Plundred still have Arms. **1856** EMERSON *Eng. Traits, Aristocr.* Wks. (Bohn) II. 78 Henry VIII .. gave him a large share of the plundered church lands. **1859** R. F. BURTON in *Jrnl. Geog. Soc.* XXIX. 116 A place of comparative plenty when the plundering Wahumba do not interfere.

'plunderable, *a.* [f. PLUNDER *v.*[2] + -ABLE.] That can be plundered or subjected to spoliation.

1802–12 BENTHAM *Ration. Judic. Evid.* (1827) II. 334 Persons in whose purses any considerable quantity of plunderable matter was seldom to be found. **1825** [see next].

plunderage ('plʌndərɪdʒ). [f. PLUNDER *v.*[2] + -AGE.] The action of plundering; pillage, spoliation; *spec.* in *Maritime Law*, 'embezzling goods on shipboard' (Wharton 1848–83); *concr.* spoil obtained by such means.

1796 COLQUHOUN *Treat. Police Metrop.* 427 That Wharfingers should be liable for plunderage of Goods. **1816** *Chron.* in *Ann. Reg.* 142/1 Some plunderage took place by the negroes. **1825** BENTHAM *Offic. Apt. Maximized, Indications* (1830) 26 As plunderable matter increases, so will plunderage. **1831** *Examiner* 139/2 Plunderage of the Chancery Suitors. **1861** SMILES *Engineers* II. VIII. vii. 363 To form another system of docks at Wapping, .. with the view of saving lighterage and plunderage, and bringing the great mass of commerce so much nearer to the heart of the City.

plunderbund ('plʌndərbʊnd). *U.S. colloq.* [f. PLUNDER *sb.* + G. *bund* alliance, league.] A corrupt alliance of political, commercial, and financial interests engaged in exploiting the public

1914 *Voice of People* (New Orleans) 8 Jan. 1/1 The whole force of the Texan plunderbund .. are howling at the heels of the dauntless army of workers. **1933** *Sun* (Baltimore) 27 Apr. 8/6 The .. unemployed, .. the losers in banks, stocks, homes, .. and business people .. are forever through with this systematic plunderbund. **1949** *Chicago Tribune* 2 Sept. 12/6 Hello, suckers who voted for the continuation of chaos and corruption and the plunderbund last November.

plunderer ('plʌndərə(r)). [f. PLUNDER *v.*[2] + -ER[1]. Cf. obs. Du. *plunderer* (Plantin), G. *plünderer.*] One who plunders; a pillager, spoiler, robber.

1647 [see PLUNDER *sb.* 2]. **1649** PRYNNE *Demurrer to Jews' Remitter* 73 One of them formerly a Trooper and Plunderer in Prince Ruperts army. **1675** COCKER *Morals* 34 Learning, not Gold, defies the Plunderer. **1741** MIDDLETON *Cicero* II. vi. 417 The plunderer of all Temples, houses, and the whole City. **1821** CLARE *Vill. Minstr.* I. 169 So dont ye [mice] drive your jokes too far, Ye cupboard-plunderers as ye are. **1855** MACAULAY *Hist. Eng.* xii. III. 214 Of the [Irish] Roman Catholic peasantry .. the majority had enlisted in the army or had joined gangs of plunderers.

Hence **'plunderess,** a female plunderer.

1835 *Blackw. Mag.* XXXVII. 214 The royal plunderess thought that she could thus .. procure a warm addition to her nest.

'plunderless, *a. nonce-wd.* [See -LESS.] Characterized by no plunder or wrongful profit.

1808 SYD. SMITH *Plymley's Lett.* (ed. 11) 130 A lean and plunderless integrity.

plunderous ('plʌndərəs), *a.* [f. PLUNDER + -OUS.] Given to or characterized by plundering.

1845 CARLYLE *Cromwell* (1871) I. 110 Royalism and plunderous Rupertism. **1865** —— *Fredk. Gt.* XX. vii. (1872) IX. 147 A foolish love for their horses makes them astonishingly plunderous of forage. **1881** HENFREY in *Antiquary* Apr. 181/2, I think it very likely .. that the owner of this little hoard buried his money on the approach of the King's army, and Rupert's plunderous troopers, in September 1642. **1973** *Freedomways* XIII. 8 With the plunderous taxes .. a large section of the people .. are being returned to the bread lines. **1976** *Times* 30 Sept. 8/3, I would jot down all the best jokes from *Take It From Here* and write a new plot round them... So I can't really jibe when the writer of that Jimmy Edwards classic has the same kind of plunderous notion for making a book. **1977** *Evening News* 4 June 5/4 William Palmer .. made a plunderous visit to the treasury.

plung (plʌŋ). *rare.* [Echoic.] A resonant noise as of a tennis racket striking a ball.

1952 J. BETJEMAN *First & Last Loves* ii. 13 So that the real Bournemouth is all pines and pines and pines and flowering shrubs, lawns, begonias, azaleas, bird-song, dance tunes, the plung of the racket and creak of the basket chair. **1954** —— *Few Late Chrysanthemums* 69 'Oh! Plung!' my tauten'd strings would call, 'Oh! Plung! my darling, break my strings.'

plunge (plʌndʒ), *sb.* [f. PLUNGE *v.*]

I. 1. a. A place where one plunges or may plunge; a deep pool, a depth. *Obs.* exc. *dial.*

a **1400–50** *Alexander* 5546 In at a wicket he went, & wynly it speris; Princes pointid it with pik, & he þe plunge entres [L. *descendit in profundum maris*]. **1500–20** DUNBAR *Poems* xxxiii. 113 And he lay at the plunge evirmair, Sa lang as any ravin did rair. **1847–78** HALLIWELL, *Plunge*, a deep pool. *Somerset.*

b. = *plunge bed* (see sense 8 below).

1973 *Times* 22 Sept. 13/2 If we have .. an Indian summer, water the 'plunge' regularly.

2. An act of plunging; a sudden downward or head-foremost movement into water or the like; a dive, dip; also *fig.* Esp. in phr. *to take* (less frequently *make*) *the plunge*, to take a decisive first step, to commit oneself irrevocably to a course of action.

1711 ADDISON *Spect.* No. 94 ¶9 After his first Plunge into the Sea. **1845** DICKENS *Let.* 20 Oct. (1977) IV. 412 The venture is quite decided on; and I have made the Plunge. **1848** THACKERAY *Pendennis* (1849) I. vi. 61 The poor boy had taken the plunge. Trembling with passionate emotion, .. poor Pen had said those words which he could withhold no more. **1863** E. V. NEALE *Anal. Th. & Nat.* 113 Descartes .. was preserved by his strong sense of personal activity, from sinking his individuality in the ocean of being. But .. the plunge was made by Malebranche and Spinoza. **1873** BLACK *Pr. Thule* x, Her first plunge into the pleasures of civilized life. **1876** TROLLOPE *Prime Minister* IV. x. 162 'You would not wish to live all your life in terror of seeing Arthur Fletcher?' 'Not all my life.' 'Take the plunge and it will be over.' **1883** STEVENSON *Treas. Isl.* III. xiii, The plunge of our anchor sent up clouds of birds wheeling and crying over the woods. *a* **1911** [see LIMIT *sb.* 2 h]. **1915** W. OWEN *Let.* 15 Jan. (1967) 316 If I could devote myself to training in Music or Painting, I would take the plunge, were I never to read a book more. **1965** *New Statesman* 23 Apr. 630/3 At present only one local Co-op .. is affiliated to Transport House, though London is thought to be contemplating taking the plunge. **1977** C. MCCULLOUGH *Thorn Birds* xviii. 460, I think she's terrified of committing herself to .. marriage... At least he's got the sense to wait until she's ready to take the plunge. **1979** G. WAGNER *Barnardo* xi. 183 Samuel Smith .. finally persuaded Barnardo to take the plunge and set up his own emigration scheme.

3. *transf.* **a.** A sudden and heavy or violent pitching forward of the body.

1496 *Bk. St. Albans, Fishing* 20 Kepe hym [the fish] euer vnder the rodde .. : soo that your lyne may susteyne and beere his lepys and his plungys [*a* 1450 plumbes: see PLUMP *sb.*[3] 1]. **1589** NASHE *Pasquil's Ret.* Wks. (Grosart) I. 123 Like a furious beast wrapt in the cordes .. after many a vayne plunge which he giues to breake away. **1889** R. S. S. BADEN-POWELL *Pigsticking* 106 By directing the animal's plunges judiciously I got him also on *terra firma.*

b. A heavy downward blow.

1836 E. HOWARD *R. Reefer* xiii, Two boys fight .. ; one of them gets a plunge on the nose.

4. The fall or breaking of a wave; a heavy downpour of rain (*rare*).

1781 *Gentl. Mag.* LI. 616 The weight of the former [water spout], by heavy plunges raised the sea into mountains. *c* **1841** CARLYLE in *Atlantic Monthly* (1898) LXXXII. 450/2 Before that it was as bad as weather at any time need be: long continued plunges of wet [etc.]. **1862** MRS. CARLYLE *Lett.* III. 96 Then walk or ride three hours under a plunge of rain. **1862** LONGF. *Wayside Inn* I. *Prel.* 264 The plunge of the implacable seas.

II. 5. The point of being plunged or overwhelmed in trouble, difficulty, or danger; a critical situation, crisis, pinch, stress, strait; a dilemma; esp. in phr. *at* (*in*) *a plunge*, *to put to* or *into the plunge* or *plunges*. *Obs.* exc. *dial.*

1535 FISHER *Wks.* (E.E.T.S.) I. 415 When a person hath deserued a great open shame, & is broght euen to the plunge of the matter, and yet by the meanes of helpe he is deliuered. **1542** UDALL *Erasm. Apoph.* 186 To bee putte to the plounge or makynge or marryng & .. to wynne al, or to lese al. **1553** *Short Catech.* in *Liturgies*, etc. (Parker Soc.) 522 We beseech our Father, that he bring us into no such hard escape and peril, nor leave us in the very plunge of danger. **1579** TOMSON *Calvin's Serm. Tim.* 900/2 Or if it bee the deuill that worketh by the inchaunters hands, will not men say that God is put to his plunges to ouercome Satan? **1611** COTGR. s.v. *Breviaire, Il est au bout de son breviaire*, he is at a plunge, or nonplus; he hath no more to say. *c* **1656** SIR H. CHOLMLEY *Mem.* (1870) 28 When I was in the greatest plunge for money. **1687** A. LOVELL tr. *Thevenot's Trav.* I. 264 The Captain demanding payment of his Money, put the Prince to a great plunge. **1740** WARBURTON *Div. Legat.* VI. vi. III. 670 As he had no great Stock of Argument, .. at a Plunge any Thing would be acceptable that came to his Relief. **1780** HARRIS *Philol. Enquiries* Wks. (1841) 454 At length, after various plunges and various escapes, it [the Eastern empire] was totally annihilated in the fifteenth century. **1854** MISS BAKER *Northampt. Gloss.*, *Plunge*, a strait, a difficulty. 'I was put to a plunge'. **1884** *Upton-on-Severn Gloss.*, *Plunge*, a falling into, or going under trouble or sickness.

III. 6. = PLONGE.

1859 F. A. GRIFFITHS *Artil. Man.* (1862) 260 The top [of the parapet] is formed with a slight declivity towards the country, which is called the superior slope, or plunge.

7. *Geol.* The angle a fold axis or linear feature makes with the horizontal, measured in a vertical plane. Cf. PITCH *sb.*[2] 24 b.

1913 W. LINDGREN *Min. Deposits* xi. 142 The plunge[1] .. of an ore-body is the vertical angle between a horizontal plane and the line of maximum elongation of the body. In lenticular ore-bodies in metamorphic rocks which have undergone strong mechanical deformation, the plunge is an important factor, and often it is determined by the direction of the cleavage or schistosity. [*Note*] [1]Called 'pitch' or 'rake' by many authors. **1932** *Bull. Amer. Assoc. Petroleum Geologists* XVI. 209 The type of fold is an overturned anticline in which the plunge increases from a comparatively low degree until it becomes vertical and finally overturns. **1936** C. M. NEVIN *Princ. Structural Geol.* (ed. 2) iii. 43 The angle of dip of the axial line [of a fold] is called the pitch or plunge. **1962** [see PITCH *sb.*[2] 24 b]. **1976** B. E. HOBBS et al. *Outl. Structural Geol.* iv. 177 The orientation of the hinge line or, since the fold is cylindrical, its axis, is expressed by its plunge and direction of plunge... The orientation of a line can also be expressed by means of its pitch... For pitch to be meaningful the orientation of the plane must be known.

IV. 8. *attrib.* and *Comb.*, as (in sense 'done by or used with a plunge') ***plunge-bath***, ***-net***; **plunge basin** *Physical Geogr.*, a deep basin excavated at the foot of a waterfall by the action of the falling water; **plunge bed**, a flower-bed, often containing peat or other moisture-retaining material, in which plants in pots can be sunk; **plunge-board** *rare*, a diving board; **plunge-churn**, a simple form of churn consisting of an upright wooden cask in which a plunger is worked up and down; **plunge cut** *Engin.*, a cut made by feeding a grinding wheel into the work-piece in the plane of rotation, without any traverse; usu. *attrib.* in ***plunge-cut grinding*** (= *plunge grinding*); so **plunge cutting**; **plunge grinding** *Engin.*, grinding by means of a wheel with no traverse of the work; **plunge neck, neckline** = *plunging neckline* s.v. PLUNGING *ppl. a.* e; hence **plunge-necked** *a.*; **plunge-pole**, the hollow pump-rod of a pumping-engine (Ogilvie, 1882); **plunge pool**, (*a*) *Physical Geogr.*, a plunge basin, or the water occupying one; freq. *attrib.*; (*b*) a cold-water pool, forming part of the equipment of a sauna bath.

1905 *Bull. Geol. Soc. Amer.* XVI. 24 A river can excavate a *plunge-basin at the foot of a cataract. **1939** A. K. LOBECK *Geomorphol.* vi. 195 There are several other plunge basins along the course of this former stream. **1966** J. WYCKOFF *Rock, Time, & Landforms* x. 231 Today there is likely to be a waterfall at the mouth of the hanging trough, and beneath the fall perhaps a plunge basin or an alluvial cone or fan. **1856** KANE *Arct. Expl.* I. ix. 99 Submitting ourselves to a succession of *plunge-baths as often as we trusted our weight on the ice-capped stones above the surface. **1896** *Pall Mall Mag.* May 37 Taking headers into the large plunge bath there [at Marylebone Gardens]. **1871** S. HIBBERD *Amateur's Flower Garden* xiii. 242 The question now is about the formation of the *plunge beds. **1935** A. G. L. HELLYER *Practical Gardening* xxx. 193 (*caption*) A useful plunge bed for pot plants. **1973** *Times* 22 Sept. 13/2 Pot them the same day if possible, and put them in their peat 'plunge bed'. **1908** *Daily Chron.* 15 Feb. 8/5 When a man wants to take a second plunge into the water he has to get out and remount the *plunge-board. **1815** *Pennecuik's Wks.* 84 *note*, A wooden armed chair .. a few stools .. and a *plunge churn, completes the inventory of household furniture. **1844** STEPHENS *Bk. Farm* III. 899 The old-fashioned upright hand plunge-churn is now confined chiefly to the use of small farmers and cottars. **1935** O. W. BOSTON *Engin. Shop Practice* II. v. 268 An automatic in-feed mechanism ..

is contained in the saddle... This is used for *plunge cuts and is independent of the traverse in-feed mechanism. **1937** COLVIN & STANLEY *Grinding Practice* i. 7 The wheel in this instance is fed into within 0·001 to 0·0015 in. of size, using the plunge cut and making as many plunges as are necessary to cover each section ground. **1941** F. D. JONES *Engin. Encycl.* II. 971 *Plunge-cut grinding*, this term has been applied to grinding which is done by directly feeding into the work a wheel, the face of which is sufficiently wide to cover the entire surface being ground. **1964** S. CRAWFORD *Basic Engin. Processes* vii. 190 The wheel is fed slowly into the work while the latter is oscillated a very slight amount to equalise the wheel wear. This method is known as plunge-cut grinding. **1972** E. N. SIMONS *Dict. Machining* 142 **Plunge cutting*, a method of grooving parts to close limits of size with an accurately-positioned brazed carbide tool. **1974** *Sci. Amer.* Jan. 35/3 A process known as plunge cutting is employed to cut holes in a metal casting. **1935** O. W. BOSTON *Engin. Shop Practice* II. v. 265 When the wheel face is as wide as the length of the surface being ground or when it is impracticable to traverse the work, the wheel may be fed in with no traverse of the wheel or work. This is called *plunge grinding. **1958** *Times Rev. Industry* May 34/3 The workpiece is then released, so that it can be rotated by means of the control wheel while plunge-grinding is being carried out. **1967** *Industr. Diamond Rev.* XXVII. 437/2 In plunge grinding, the whole depth of profile is normally ground in one pass. **1951** *Sunday Times* 28 Oct. 11/3 Some [spencers], sleeveless and with a *plunge neck, give never a sign of their comforting presence beneath cocktail dresses and chiffon blouses. **1959** *Woman's Own* 20 June 17/4 She was wearing a *plunge-necked dress of some white material. **1949** *Sun* (Baltimore) 28 Jan. 4 (Advt.), *Plunge neckline wool jersey glamour blouse. **1959** 'O. MILLS' *Stairway to Murder* v. 50 Its plunge neckline was so low that Geoff was almost driven for safety to the handwoven wool and Fair Isle cardigan. **1977** M. HINXMAN *One-Way Cemetery* xv. 112 Daphne delved into her deep plunge neckline and retrieved a gold chain. **1883** F. DAY *Indian Fish* 64 (Fish. Exhib. Publ.) *Choba.*—A *plunge-net, used chiefly in shallow water to capture fish which lay half-concealed in the mud. From Poona. **1917** *Scientific Monthly* V. 559 *Plunge pools are potholes, in general, of large size, occurring at the foot of a vertical or nearly vertical waterfall... In most plunge pools the water is much deeper than it is in the stream channel on their downstream side. **1932** *Jrnl. Geol.* XL. 333 By recession of the falls the plunge-pool hole is elongated upstream, forming the deeper part of the channel of a gorge, the upper part of which is produced by a caving in process as the plunge-pool undercuts the face of the fall. **1957** G. E. HUTCHINSON *Treat. Limnol.* I. i. 111 The most impressive of such plunge-pool lakes are on that part of the former course of the Columbia River that now forms the Grand Coulee in the state of Washington. **1970** MACDONALD & ABBOTT *Volcanoes in Sea* xix. 367 (*caption*) Vertical valleys being cut by plunge-pool action of waterfalls. **1973** *Times* 21 Nov. 18/8 There is a plunge pool with two massage jets. **1976** 'D. HALLIDAY' *Dolly & Nanny Bird* ix. 116 It was time for the plunge pool with the hydrojet massage.

plunge (plʌndʒ), *v.* Forms: 4– **plunge**, 5 **plownge**, 5–6 **plounge**, 5–7 **plonge**, (6 **plong**, 6–7 **plundge**). *β.* 5 **plonchyn, plounch, plunch(e.** [ME. *plunge(n, plonge, plonche*, a. OF. *plunjer* (Oxford Psalter, *a* 1140), *plung(i)er, plong(i)er, ploncier, ploncher, plungher*, F. *plonger*, OPicard *plonkier*, Picard dial. *plonquer* to plunge, dive, (according to Diez):—late L. **plumbicāre* to heave the lead, f. *plumbum* lead.]

1. a. *trans.* To put violently, thrust, or cast *into* (or †*in*) a liquid, a penetrable substance, or a cavity; to immerse, to submerge; in quot. *c* 1380, †to baptize by immersion (*obs.*).

c **1380** *Sir Ferumb.* 1085 And het him sone þat he wer diȝt, To blessy þe holy fanston,.. þe prelat dide al so he hiȝt, & plungede him sone þer-on. **1483** CAXTON *Gold. Leg.* 431/1 Other there wende that the shyppe shold haue broken and be plonged in the see. **1542** BOORDE *Dyetary* xxxviii. (1870) 300 To plounge the eyes in colde water in the morenyng. **1569** J. SANFORD tr. *Agrippa's Van Artes* 15 The riuer Mosa ..plungeth him selfe, not in the ocean, but in the Rhene. **1590** SPENSER *F.Q.* I. xii. 64 Sometimes the one would lift the other quight Above the waters, and then downe againe Her plong. **1617** HIERON *Wks.* (1619–20) II. 371 If thou be not mercifull vnto me, I shall eternally be plundged into the nethermost hell. **1711** ADDISON *Spect.* No. 94 ¶8 The holy Man bid him plunge his Head into the Water. **1800** tr. *Lagrange's Chem.* I. 24 Plunge a thermometer into the mixture, and its temperature will be found to be two degrees. **1856** KANE *Arct. Expl.* II. xv. 163 The lance is plunged into the left side. **1878** HUXLEY *Physiogr.* 77 You have only to plunge a lighted taper into it.

β. *c* **1440** STAUNTON *St. Patr. Purg.* (1900) 71 Fendes takyng þilk bisshop.. and plunchyng him in þat blak water. **1447** BOKENHAM *Seyntys* (Roxb.) 87 Of cursyd custum plounchyd in the myre.

†**b.** *plunge up*, to heave up, pump up. *Obs.*

1567 in Turberville *Epitaphs* 78 b, Plunge vp a thousande sighes, for griefe your trickling teares distill.

2. *fig.* To thrust, force, or drive *into* (or †*in*) some thing, condition, state, or sphere of action.

c **1374** CHAUCER *Boeth.* III. pr. ii. 51 (Camb. MS.) And many folk.. wenen þat it be ryght blysful thyng to plowngen hem in voluptuos delit. *c* **1407** LYDG. *Reson & Sens.* 6762 Y-plonged in ful gret distresse. **1567** *Satir. Poems Reform.* iv. 51 Quhomlit in sorow and plungeit in cair. **1641** MILTON *Prel. Episc.* Wks. 1851 III. 75 The Councels themselves were fouly corrupted with ungodly Prelatisme, and.. plung'd into worldly ambition. **1686** tr. *Chardin's Coronat. Solyman* 87 The young Prince having plundg'd himself into the excesses of Wine and Women. **1796** H. HUNTER tr. *St.-Pierre's Stud. Nat.* (1799) III. 181 Violent passions always plunge the soul into contrary extremes. **1838** THIRLWALL *Greece* xxii. III. 227 The commotion, which.. agitated Syracuse, and threatened to plunge it into a civil war. **1875** JOWETT *Plato* (ed. 2) IV. 373 We are plunged at once into philosophical discussions.

β. *c* **1440** LYDG. *Compleynt* 376 in *Temple of Glas*, etc. (1891) 64 Now canst thow sette men aloft, And now hem plonchyn ful vnsoft, Doun from hegh felycyte.

†**3.** *fig.* To overwhelm, overpower, esp. *with* trouble or difficulty; to put to straits, embarrass.

c **1485** *Digby Myst.* (1882) IV. 462 This womans harte is plungid with payn. **1513** BRADSHAW *St. Werburge* I. 888 Plonget with sorowe, syghynge day and nyght. **1600** ABP. ABBOT *Exp. Jonah* 191 What is all this to plunge his abilitie who can do everie thing. **1643** SIR T. BROWNE *Relig. Med.* I. §21 [He] was so plunged and gravelled with three lines of Seneca, that all our Antidotes.. could not expel the poyson of his errour. **1681** *Relig. Clerici* 188, I am more and more plunged and puzled in this point.

4. *Gardening.* To sink (a pot containing a plant, less usually, a plant itself) in the ground.

1664 EVELYN *Sylva* (1679) 13 Plunge it [the branch] half a foot under good mould. **1825** *Greenhouse Comp.* I. 132 Chrysanthemum indicum might be introduced when in bloom, and plunged in the borders as if growing there. **1851** *Beck's Florist* 87, I would recommend plunging the pots, but be sure you have a dry bottom. **1869** P. HENDERSON *Pract. Floricult.* xxix. 200 (Funk) These pots should be planted, or, as we term it, 'plunged' to the rim, or level with the surface. **1935** A. G. L. HELLYER *Pract. Gardening* xxix. 183 It is an excellent plan to plunge the pots to their rims in a bed of ashes to reduce the necessity for frequent watering. **1965** *Sunday Mail Mag.* (Brisbane) 26 Sept. 15 You may read of pots being plunged. This refers to the burying of a pot up to its rim.

5. a. *intr.* To throw or hurl oneself *into* water or the like; to dive head-foremost; to fall or sink (involuntarily) *into* a deep place (as a pit or abyss); also, to penetrate impetuously *into* a crowd, a forest, or any thing or place in which one is submerged or lost to view.

1375 BARBOUR *Bruce* II. 355 For the best, and the worthiest.. Plungyt in the stalwart stour, And rowtis ruyd about thaim dang. *c* **1380** *Sir Ferumb.* 5784 How þat þys water ys arayed, þat y schal plungy on. *a* **1450** *Knt. de la Tour* (1868) 112 A yonge childe.. that wente forto bathe hym, and happed to plonge and to fall in a depe pitte withinne the ryuer. **1470–85** MALORY *Arthur* VII. xx. 243 Many tymes his hors and he plonged ouer the hede in depe myres. **1601** SHAKS. *Jul. C.* I. ii. 105 Accoutred as I was, I plunged in, And bad him follow. **1697** DRYDEN *Virg. Past.* VIII. 84 From yon high Cliff I plunge into the Main. **1789** W. BUCHAN *Dom. Med.* lv. (1790) 633 It is now fashionable for persons of all ranks to plunge into the sea, and drink the mineral waters. **1840** DICKENS *Barn. Rudge* lix, He plunged into the thickest portion of the little wood. **1860** TYNDALL *Glac.* I. 58 Saw the stream plunge into a shaft.

β. *c* **1400** tr. *Secreta Secret., Gov. Lordsh.* 96 þe sawle shall plunche into þe depnes of helle.

b. *transf.* To enter impetuously or abruptly *into* (a place). Also with *upon*. Also, to emerge or come *out* or *out of* (a place) impetuously or abruptly.

1834 L. RITCHIE *Wand. Seine* 110 We.. plunged into the high road leading to Duclair. **1841–71** T. R. JONES *Anim. Kingd.* (ed. 4) 341 Others [tubes] without any vesicular enlargement, plunge at once into different textures, and supply the viscera and internal organs. **1885** *Manch. Exam.* 22 Jan. 5/2 Under a well-organised fire from the works, the Arabs plunged forth upon the square. **1891** KIPLING *Light that Failed* (1000) 202 He stumbled across the landing and plunged into Torpenhow's room. **1891** C. GRAVES *Field of Tares* IV. vi. 241 The Norwich Express, plunging out of Liverpool Street Station. **1892** R. BUCHANAN *Come live with Me* xxiii. 256 Finally.. he plunged out into the darkness and disappeared. **1896** C. M. SHELDON *His Brother's Keeper* viii. 226 They plunged right out of a great hole.

c. *transf.* To descend abruptly and steeply; to dip suddenly (as a road or stratum). *spec.* in *Geol.*, of a fold: to have an axis that slopes or dips downwards, whether at a large or a small angle; also said of the axis.

1854 MURCHISON *Siluria* ii. 31 They are seen to fold over and plunge to the east-south-east. **1882** B. HARTE *Flip* i, The stage-road that plunged from the terrace.. into the valley below. **1905** CHAMBERLIN & SALISBURY *Geol.* I. viii. 488 If the axis of a fold is not horizontal, that is, if it 'plunges'. **1932** *Bull. Amer. Assoc. Petroleum Geologists* XVI. 210 At this time all of the folds plunged consistently eastward at a low angle. **1942** M. P. BILLINGS *Structural Geol.* iii. 46 In the southwest corner, the anticline plunges 15 degrees to the southwest. **1965** A. HOLMES *Princ. Physical Geol.* (ed. 2) ix. 210 The axes of folds are not infrequently found to be tilted instead of horizontal; the folds are then said to pitch or plunge.

6. *intr.* To enter impetuously or determinedly *into* some state, condition, or affair; to involve oneself deeply.

a **1694** TILLOTSON (J.), He could find no other way to conceal his adultery, but to plunge into the guilt of a murther. **1714** ADDISON *Cato* I. i, Bid me for honour plunge into a war Of thickest foes. **1771** BURKE *Corr.* (1844) I. 252 The character of their party is to be very ready to plunge into difficult business. **1791** MRS. RADCLIFFE *Rom. Forest* i, It was only to plunge into new errors. **1875** JOWETT *Plato* (ed. 2) V. 5 We plunge abruptly into the subject of the dialogue.

7. *transf.* **a.** *intr.* To fling or throw oneself violently forward, esp. with a diving action: said of a horse (opposed to REAR *v.*[1] 15 b); of a ship: = PITCH *v.*[1] 19 b; of the chest: to expand with falling of the diaphragm.

1530 PALSGR. 661/2, I plunge, as a horse doth, *je plonge*. **1633** HEYWOOD & ROWLEY *Fort. by Land & Sea* III. i. Wks. 1874 VI. 392 Our teems.. plunge in pain. **1735** SOMERVILLE *Chase* III. 334 Wounded, he rears aloft, And plunging, from his Back the Rider hurls Precipitant. **1802** MAR. EDGEWORTH *Moral T.* (1816) I. xvi. 137 He taught Sawney to rear and plunge, whenever his legs were touched by the broom. **1817** *Sporting Mag.* L. 17 Dick kept plunging with his favourite right-handed hits. **1836** MARRYAT *Midsh. Easy* xxvi, The frigate.. no longer jerked and plunged as before. **1860** *Merc. Marine Mag.* VII. 115 The water came in every time the ship plunged. **1898** *Allbutt's Syst. Med.* V. 287 The chest may plunge, but there is no expansion of the thoracic cavity.

b. *trans.* With complement: To make oneself (weary, etc.) by plunging.

1607 MARKHAM *Caval.* II. (1617) 95 They will, after they haue plunged themselues weary, fall downe.

c. Of a horse: To throw or pitch by plunging.

1603 KNOLLES *Hist. Turks* (1621) 66 At the farther side of the river [he] was plunged by his horse, at his landing, that he was taken up for dead.

†**8.** *trans.* To penetrate by plunging, diving, or digging; to plunge into or through. *Obs. rare.*

a **1649** DRUMM. OF HAWTH. *Poems* Wks. (1711) 1 Vaunt not, rich pearl, red coral, which do stir A fond desire in fools to plunge your ground. **1724** RAMSAY *Health* 313 He'll plunge the deep, And with expanded arms the billows sweep.

9. *absol.* Of artillery: To send shot downwards from a higher level. Cf. *plunging fire* in PLUNGING *ppl. a.* c.

1815 SCOTT *Paul's Lett.* (1839) 123 Our artillery on the ridge were brought to plunge into it.

10. a. *intr.* To spend money or bet recklessly; to speculate or gamble deeply; to run into debt. *slang.*

1876 BESANT & RICE *Gold. Butterfly* xxxviii, They plunged as regarded hansoms, paying whatever was asked with an airy prodigality. **1883** MISS BRADDON *Phant. Fort.* xliv, She has been plunging rather deeply. **1886** *Fortn. Rev.* Mar. 319 'Plunging' was the order of the day, and lansquenet was the game at which most of this.. was done.

b. *trans.* To bet or speculate (a sum of money).

1922 JOYCE *Ulysses* 320 Boylan plunged two quid on my tip *Sceptre* for himself and a lady friend.

11. *trans.* or *absol.* *Railways.* To release (signals or points, etc.) by depressing a plunger. Cf. PLUNGER 2 g.

[**1923** J. F. GAIRNS *Railways for All* xviii. 179 Sykes' 'Lock and Block' instruments.. are operated by pressing a knob or plunger, hence the term 'plunging' used to describe their working by the signalmen.] **1926** C. J. ALLEN *Iron Road* xii. 180 Then the signalman in the next box cannot 'plunge' on his instrument until he has put his own starting signal lever back to danger in the lever frame behind the last preceding train. **1940** *Railway Signalling & Communications* iii. 93 All facing points unprotected by track circuit must be provided with a locking bar in addition to the plunger, and the points must be plunged before the signal reading over them can be cleared.

Hence **plunged** *ppl. a.*

1581 T. HOWELL *Deuises* (1879) 177 The plunged state, wherein I lyue and dwell. **1767** BEVIS in *Phil. Trans.* LVII. 378 Depending on the relation of the height *a* to the plunged part.

'**plungeon.** [a. F. *plongeon* (OF. *plongon*, Flor. et Blanc.) a diver, a bird of genus *Colymbus*, f. *plonger* to dive, PLUNGE + *-eon*:—L. *-iō(nem*: cf. PIGEON.] †**1.** A diving bird; a diver. *Obs.*

1480 CAXTON *Ovid's Met.* XI. xxii, Because he plongeth contynuelly in such manere, he is called Plongeon or Dyvar. **1589** RIDER *Bibl. Schol.* 1704 A Plungeon: a kinde of water fowle with a long reddish bill, *Phalacrocorax*. **1601** HOLLAND *Pliny* I. 296 Among the Alps: where also the Plungeons [L. *mergi*] or bald Rauens be, which heretofore were thought proper and peculiar to the Baleare Islands. **1706** PHILLIPS, *Plungeon* or *Diver*, a sort of water-fowl. Hence **1730–6** in BAILEY (folio); **1755** in JOHNSON.

2. *south-west. dial.* A ford across a rhine (RHINE[1]).

c **1685** A. PASCHALL *Let.* in S. Heywood *Vindication of Mr. Fox's Hist.* (1811) p. xl, The horse, which the Lord Grey led marched towards the upper Plungeon. *Ibid.*, Whether Sir Francis were there.. or came to the Plungeon afterwards.. we do not know. **1894** LD. WOLSELEY *Life Marlborough* I. xxxix. 314 They [*sc.* the Somerset 'rhines'] could only be crossed, even by single horsemen, at fords, called by the peasantry 'plungeons' or 'steanings'. **1933** W. S. CHURCHILL *Marlborough* I. xii. 216 Grey's cavalry would branch off and .. cross the Bussex Rhine at one of the plungeons to the east of the royal camp. **1955** *Hist. Today* V. 57/2 There were two easy crossings for cavalry, known as the upper.. and lower 'plungeons'. **1969** C. C. TRENCH *Western Rising* x. 209 He [*sc.* Feversham] ordered the reserve cavalry in the village.. to cross the Bussex Rhine by the upper plungeon. *Ibid.*, Similarly three troops of horse and one of dragoons crossed the lower plungeon.

plunger ('plʌndʒə(r)). [f. PLUNGE *v.* + -ER[1].]

I. 1. a. One who plunges; a diver. (So F. *plongeur*.)

1611 COTGR., *Plongeur*, a plunger, ducker, diuer. **1730–6** BAILEY (folio), *Plunger*, a diver. **1848** CLOUGH *Bothie* III. 46 Here, the pride of the plunger, you stride the fall and clear it; Here,.. into pure green depth drop down from lofty ledges. **1893** *Tablet* 18 Feb. 272 Would the plunger hold his own in the vortex of troubled waters?

†**b.** A diving bird; *spec.* the Black Gull. *Obs.*

1655 MOUFET & BENNET *Health's Impr.* (1746) 194 White Gulls, Grey Gulls, and Black Gulls (commonly termed by the Name of Plungers and Water-Crows).

c. *N. Amer.* A type of sailing boat (see quot. 1948).

1860 *North-West* (Port Townsend, Wash.) 12 July 3/1 The following craft were entered for the stakes:—Sloop H. L. Tibbals, Port Townsend;.. and the plunger Star of the South. **1892** *Outing* Mar. 467/1 Yachting on the Pacific coast dates from about 1869, when the first club.. was organised, though a few small plungers and sloops had long been owned on the bay. **1948** R. DE KERCHOVE *Internat. Maritime Dict.* 541/2 *Plunger*, name given to various sailing craft employed in the Pacific coast oyster fisheries for transportation... Also called oyster sloop. Most of them are built with flush deck and a large central cockpit divided by a centerboard. The larger type is keel built... All are cat-rigged. **1969** *Islander* (Victoria, B.C.) 23 Mar. 4/2 The next day [24 Dec. 1860] a plunger brought a quantity of salvaged goods to Victoria, mostly in the form of cases of Old Tom gin.

2. In various technical applications, an instrument or part of a mechanism which works with a plunging or thrusting motion.

a. Any solid piston, as that of a force-pump, *esp.* the piston of a Cornish pump; a hollow piston forming the bucket of a lift-pump. **b.** The dasher of a churn. **c.** The firing pin in some breech-loading firearms; also, a bolt sliding in a groove on the breech for securing the barrel in firing position. **d.** A metallic cylinder or plug for regulating an electric current. **e.** *Pottery.* A vessel in which clay is beaten to paste or slip. **f.** Short for *plunger-brake* (see 5). Also in other applications: see quots.

1777 MACBRIDE in *Phil. Trans.* LXVIII. 115 Stirring it [the leather] up with the utensil called a plunger, which is nothing more than a pole with a knob at the end of it. **1822** J. IMISON *Sc. & Art* I. 457 Plungers are pistons that nearly fill the working barrel. **1831** LARDNER *Pneumat.* vi. 312 A heavy beam, or plunger, suspended from a chain, and capable of descending by its own weight in water. **1837** *Flemish Husb.* 62 in *Libr. Usef. Knowl., Husb.* III, Sometimes..a dog walks in a wheel, which turns the machinery by which the plunger is moved up and down [in churning]. **1839** R. S. ROBINSON *Naut. Steam Eng.* 83 It is ..very usual to see two plungers attached, one on each side of the cross-head of the air pump; one works a bilge pump, the other the feed pipe. **1866** *Cornh. Mag.* Sept. 355 The barrel is closed by a sliding plunger or bolt, which can be pushed forward against the barrel, or withdrawn for the admission of the cartridge. **1870** *Daily News* 31 Aug. 2 The cartridges fall into slots in the barrels, and are gradually pushed into the firing position by 10 plungers or pistons. **1875** KNIGHT *Dict. Mech.* 1778/2 The clays are..prepared by mixing them in a plunger containing a large wheel, by which they are, with the addition of water, converted into a mass of the consistency of cream. **1878** F. S. WILLIAMS *Midl. Railw.* 424 Hydraulic power is obtained by a 40-horse engine, pumping the water into two upright cylinders, fitted with solid plungers.

g. *Railways.* Applied to various knobs or buttons used to operate signalling mechanisms and points; *esp.* (*a*) one with which a signalman operates an electric relay which releases locked signals or points, freq. in an adjacent block section; (*b*) a tapping key on a block instrument.

1881 *Daily News* 7 Sept. 2/5 Uxbridge..signalled a couple of 'beats' to the West Drayton box, when the officer there in charge replied with four beats, pressed the 'plunger' and took off the lock at Uxbridge signals. **1897** W. E. LANGDON *Applic. Electr. Railway Working* (new ed.) v. 103 The block instrument is fitted with a bell key or 'plunger'. **1899** J. PIGG *Railway Block Signalling* iv. 214 For the lines converging at the junction the plunger used to liberate the signal at the rear cabin of any one of the converging sections is arranged to be free for use only when the points have been set for a train coming from that direction. **1926** C. J. ALLEN *Iron Road* xii. 173 Below the instrument box is..a plunger or a 'tapper'..by the use of which the signalman exchanges the prescribed code of bell signals with his neighbour. *Ibid.* 180 Only the action of 'accepting' the train by the box next in advance—that is, of giving 'Line Clear' by means of the special plunger on the signalling instrument—will free the lock on the lever, and allow it to be pulled over. **1963** KICHENSIDE & WILLIAMS *Brit. Railway Signalling* v. 44 If Mottingham can accept the train the signalman there acknowledges the 'Is line clear?' code and presses the plunger on his home signal instrument. This...unlocks Lee's starting signal and places the block indicator at Lee in the raised position. **1967** G. F. FIENNES *I tried to run Railway* iv. 46 As soon as he put his signals back and took the hook off his Sykes plunger Crowlands offered him the Mail and gave him On Line at once.

h. *Jazz slang.* A plunging device, resembling the type used by plumbers to clear blocked pipes, used as a mute for a trumpet or trombone. Freq. *attrib.* and *Comb.*

1936 L. & E. DOWLING *Panassié's Hot Jazz* i. 15 Some players..use a regular mute and place over it a rubber plunger—of the sort used by plumbers—which is manipulated by hand to produce 'wa-wa' effects. **1946** MEZZROW & WOLFE *Really Blues* 340 The trumpet got different tonal effects by using plungers and other home-made devices. **1949** L. FEATHER *Inside Be-Bop* III. 93 Took a couple of plunger solos on Decca. **1958** S. DANCE in P. Gammond *Decca Bk. Jazz* xxiii. 293 Cootie at first found Miley's growl legacy altogether too strange... He had always previously played open horn, but since Duke had engaged him to fill Miley's chair, he felt bound to experiment with the plunger style. **1961** *John o' London's* 6 July 55/1 Booty Wood's melancholy plunger-muted trombone. **1966** *Crescendo* Jan. 6/1 A slow opening with Tricky Sam style plunger trombone (sounding here very much like a human voice).

II. 3. *Mil. slang.* A cavalry man.

1854 THACKERAY *J. Leech's Pict.* 82 He used rather to laugh at guardsmen, 'plungers', and other military men. **1857** KINGSLEY *Two Y. Ago* xvi, It's an insult to the whole Guards, after refusing two of us, to marry an attorney, and after all to bolt with a plunger.

4. *slang.* One who bets, gambles, or speculates rashly or recklessly.

1876 *World* V. No. 115. 4 The prince of plungers, with hat jauntily cocked over one eye. **1877** BESANT & RICE *Son of Vulc.* I. i, Plungers in baccarat, badminton, loo, and opera-dancers. **1892** JESSOPP *Stud. by Recluse* vi. (1893) 192 He took to the turf,..was a regular plunger, and got deeply into debt.

III. 5. *attrib.* and *Comb.*, as ***plunger-button***, ***-case***, ***-pole***, ***-rod***; **plunger-brake**: see quots.; **plunger-bucket**, **plunger-lift**, in a pump, a bucket having no valve; also = *plunger-piston* (*b*); **plunger mute** = sense 2 h; **plunger-piston**, (*a*) a solid cylindrical piston used in a plunger-pump; (*b*) a similar piston used in a pressure-gauge, steam-indicator, etc.; **plunger-pump**, one with a solid piston, as a force-pump; **plunger-valve**, a valve having a plunging action.

1898 *Westm. Gaz.* 13 July 3/2 With my *Plunger brake I rode down every inch of the descent from the top of the Grimsel Pass to the Rhone Glacier. [**1898** *Cycling* ix. 52 [A brake] actuated by means of a lever attached to the handle bar, which is connected by a hinged joint with a plunger.] **1875** KNIGHT *Dict. Mech.*, **Plunger-bucket*, one without a valve. **1947** I. LANG *Jazz in Perspective* vii. 90 Miley was the pioneer and master of a new style of trumpet-playing—a powerful and strangely moving 'growl' obtained by the use of a rubber *plunger mute. **1965** *New Yorker* 27 Feb. 123/1 Rudd, a former Dixieland trombonist,..uses the plunger mute effectively. **1977** *Ibid.* 20 June 95/1 Another muted passage (this time using a plunger mute), in which he mumbled funny gibberish through his instrument, all the while using his slide and seeming to blow out the words. **1840** *Civil Eng. & Arch. Jrnl.* III. 41/1 Motion is given to the piston, bucket, or *plunger-pole of the pump. **1882** *Rep. to Ho. Repr. Prec. Met. U.S.* 147 Stationary double *plunger pumps. **1898** *Engineering Mag.* XVI. 52 The water is taken out of the mines by means of two Rittinger telescopic plunger pumps, placed at the present lowest level, one hundred and eighty feet below the adit. **1839** URE *Dict. Arts* 187 There is also a rack and toothed sector, with a balance weight connected to the inclined plane at the top of the *plunger-rods. **1844** STEPHENS *Bk. Farm* III. 929 The very unfavourable position in which a man applies his force directly to the plunger-rod of this churn. **1908** *Westm. Gaz.* 2 Jan. 4/1 The crank-case, into the cover of which the cam-shaft and *plunger-valves are built. **1931** *Engineering* 2 Oct. 5 (Advt.), Being a combination of a plunger valve with a mushroom valve, they possess a greater efficiency than is possible with either of these types alone.

plunging ('plʌndʒɪŋ), *vbl. sb.* [-ING[1].] **a.** The action of the verb PLUNGE in various senses; *spec.* †immersion in baptism (*obs.*).

a **1450** MYRC 609 Whenne thou comest to the plungynge. **1532** FRITH *Mirror* (1829) 234 The sign in baptism, is the plunging down in the material water, and lifting up again. **1607** MARKHAM *Caval.* II. (1617) 93 A mare..which..was naturally giuen to the vice of plunging. **1865** CARLYLE *Fredk. Gt.* XVIII. vii. (1872) VII. 221, I could..leave Fortune to her whirlings and her plungings. **1883** MRS. BISHOP in *Leisure Ho.* 143/1 At times..came huge plungings, with accompanying splashings.

b. *attrib.* and *Comb.*, as ***plunging bath***, ***-hole***, ***-material***, ***-pit***, ***system***; **plunging-battery** (*Electr.*), a battery in which the plates may be plunged into or withdrawn from the fluid, when the battery is or is not in use (Knight *Dict. Mech.* 1875); **plunging-siphon**, a small tube with open ends, used to draw a small quantity of liquor by plunging it into the bulk, and stopping one end with the finger (Dunglison, 1857).

1843 SIR C. SCUDAMORE *Med. Visit Gräfenberg* 70 Neither plunging bath nor douche were used. **1871** S. HIBBERD *Amateur's Flower Garden* xiii. 238 The object of the plunging system is to keep up a rich display of flowers or leaves on the same spot the whole year round. **1882** *Garden* 21 Jan. 49/2 Plants of two or three sorts should be selected from the cold plunging pits. **1885** ELDER in *Our Corner* V. 177 Cocoanut fibre may be put on as a plunging material into which pots, seed-pans, or boxes can be plunged.

'plunging, *ppl. a.* [-ING[2].] That plunges. **a.** Of a horse or its action, a wave, a ship, etc.: Diving; rushing or falling forward or downward; pitching; sinking steeply.

1538 ELYOT, *Sternax*, a steerynge or ploungynge horse. **1548** *Ibid.*, *Sternax equus*, a plungyng hors that casteth his ridar. **1818** BYRON *Mazeppa* xvii, The steeds rush on in plunging pride. **1840** BROWNING *Sordello* I. 172 Richard, light-hearted as a plunging star. **1875** H. JAMES *Passionate Pilgr.*, etc. 236 She sat on an ivied stone, on the edge of a plunging wall. **1885** BLACK *White Heather* v, In the darkened and plunging waters.

b. *fig.* in various senses: see the verb.

1568 T. HOWELL *Arb. Amitie* (1879) 37 Most greedy gripes with plunging paines, do pierce my ruthfull hart. **1794** MATHIAS *Purs. Lit.* (1798) 442 His unbridled licence of language, and his plunging desperate doctrines.

c. ***plunging fire***, artillery or rifle fire directed downwards from a higher level. Cf. PLUNGE *v.* 9.

1875 KNIGHT *Dict. Mech.*, *Plunging-fire*,..shot fired at an angle of depression below point-blank. **1891** G. W. BAIRD in *Century Mag.* July 357 The Indians held the sharp crests of the steep hills, and were delivering a plunging fire into the troops.

d. *Geol.* Of a fold (see PLUNGE *v.* 5 c).

1905 CHAMBERLIN & SALISBURY *Geol.* I. viii. 483 Fig. 403 shows a doubly plunging anticline; that is, an anticline the axis of which dips down at either end. **1942** M. P. BILLINGS *Structural Geol.* iii. 44 Although the larger plunging folds cannot be directly observed, they are easily recognized from their outcrop pattern. **1968** [see PITCHING *ppl. a.* 1].

e. ***plunging neckline***, a very deep-cut neckline on a woman's garment.

1949 *Sun* (Baltimore) 18 Nov. 14/2 Will you please express your opinion about the good taste of women wearing the so-called 'plunging necklines' to their business offices. **1959** *Sunday Express* 22 Nov. 6/6, I do wish Mr. Braine could tear his eyes away from girls' provocative, plunging necklines. **1973** 'D. JORDAN' *Nile Green* xxxiv. 162 A temp with a plunging neckline and shaky shorthand.

Hence **'plungingly** *adv.*

1872 GEO. ELIOT *Middlem.* iii, Fred hesitated an instant, and then went on plungingly.

plungy ('plʌndʒɪ), *a. rare.* [f. PLUNGE + -Y.] Causing or coming in plunges; bringing heavy showers, rainy (*obs.* or *dial.*).

c **1374** CHAUCER *Boeth.* I. met. iii. (Camb. MS.), The fyrmament stant dirked by wete plowngy [*v.r.* ploungy] clowdes. *Ibid.* III. met. i, The sterres shynen more agreablely whan the wynd nothus leteth hise plowngy blastes. **1566** DRANT *Horace, Sat.* VII. F iij b, Pufte up with pleasures plungie puffes.

plunk (plʌŋk), *v. colloq.* [In senses 1 and 2 app. echoic; sense 3 may be the same, or an altered form of *plump*: cf. also northern Fr. *plonquer* to plunge. Sense 4 may be from PLUNK *sb.* Sense 5 is of obscure origin: cf. early mod.Du. *plencken* 'vagari, divagari, palari, errare' (Kilian). There may be two or three different words here.]

I. 1. a. *trans.* To pluck (a string) so as to cause an abrupt vibratory sound; to twang sharply. Also, to play (a note) or pick *out* (a melody) on a stringed instrument.

1805 A. SCOTT *Poems* (1808) 229 Let Europe plunk her fiddle strings, Till them to unison she brings. **1898** *Chicago Advance* 31 Mar. 436/1 Robert marched out plunking the banjo, Charles rattling the bones. **1952** B. ULANOV *Hist. Jazz in Amer.* (1958) xx. 254 She reached her majority plunking two bass notes with her left hand. **1973** *Time* 25 June 94/3 Hungate got to tinkering at the piano one day and in 15 minutes plunked out a ditty he calls *Down at the Old Watergate.*

b. *intr.* To make a plunking sound.

1903 *Cosmopolitan* Sept. 484 Street pianos plunk away unweariedly. **1929** [see GUBBLE *v.*]. **1946** D. C. PEATTIE *Road of Naturalist* iii. 35 Into southern Utah they came trekking, with fine fat oxen, with meal sacks under the seats, and banjos plunking. **1978** G. VIDAL *Kalki* vi. 153 Deafening was what H. V. W. would call the din from the rock stars' dressing rooms where electric guitars whined, drums rattled, sitars plunked.

2. *intr.* To croak or cry as a raven. *Sc.*

? *a* **1800** *Scotch Song* (Jam.), The corpie plunkin' i' the bog, Made a' my flesh turn cauld.

II. 3. a. *intr.* To plump, to drop down abruptly.

1808 JAMIESON, *Plunk*, v.n., to plunge with a dull sound, to plump. **1888** E. MOTT in *Chicago Herald* (Farmer), B' that time the ol' man had plunked inter a bar'l. **1891** J. H. PEARCE *Esther Pentreath* I. i. 15 He 'plunked-down' all-of-a-heap on a neighbouring balk of timber.

b. *trans.* To place or set *down* heavily. Also *refl.* to 'let oneself fall'. Cf. PLUMP *v.*[1] 2.

1899 G. W. PECK *Peck's Uncle Ike & Red Headed Boy* (1903) xxii. 194 The old man plunked down two dollars.. and they went and got seats on the bleachers. **1936** R. LEHMANN *Weather in Streets* I. 222 The woman..plunked a great unappetising tray on my bed. **1943** A. RANSOME *Picts & Martyrs* v. 46, I say, Dot, when you've plunked the roses in her room... Some on the dressing-table. **1963** *New Statesman* 11 Jan. 38/1 A pair of steel nuts that another worker inadvertently plunks on a plate. **1976** D. HEFFRON *Crusty Crossed* xi. 85, I went into the bedroom and plunked myself down on our bed. **1977** *Time* 29 Aug. 24/1 He [*sc.* Elvis Presley] had wandered into Sun Records with his guitar, two summers before, plunked down $4 to sing a couple of tunes to his mother.

c. *intr.* To opt *for*. Cf. PLUMP *v.*[1] 5.

1948 A. H. VANDENBERG *Let.* 6 Dec. in Vandenberg & Morris *Private Papers of Senator Vandenberg* (1953) xxi. 414 We should smack down the Russkies more effectively in our speeches in the UN Council and Assembly... I plunk with you for 'curt decisiveness' mixed with 'derision'.

III. 4. a. *trans.* To drive or propel with a sudden push (? like a cork from a bottle).

1884 A. A. PUTNAM *Ten Yrs. Police Judge* v. 29 The especial bull's-eyes which the rocks of reform were aimed to hit, and, as it were plunk out. **1893** KIPLING *Many Invent.* 104 The moving galley's bow was plunking them [oars] back through their own oar holes. **1899** J. COLVILLE *Scott. Vernacular* 11 (E.D.D.) Whin and broom pods plunkt their peas on ruddy cheeks.

b. *trans.* To hit, wound, shoot. *slang* (orig. *U.S.*).

1888 *Texas Siftings* 21 Apr. 12 (*caption*) He'd jest swallerd brother Bill afore I plunked him. **1891** *Outing* Nov. 138/2, I would plunk the big gobbler I could distinguish from where I lay. **1896** [see OUTASIGHT *a.*]. **1916** C. J. DENNIS *Songs of Sentimental Bloke* 42 Romeo..Plunks Tybalt through the gizzard wiv 'is sword. **1916** H. L. WILSON *Somewhere in Red Gap* 120 Darned if he didn't up with this here air gun..and plunk me with a buckshot it carried. **1937** D. & H. TEILHET *Feather Cloak Murders* xvi. 286, I wish you'd killed Jeff instead of plunking him in the leg. **1978** L. PRYOR *Viper* iii. 41 We..plunked about five hundred clay birds a day.

IV. 5. *intr.* and *trans.* To play the truant; to be a truant from. *Sc.*

1808 JAMIESON, To *Plunk*,..to play the truant. **1870** J. NICHOLSON *Idylls* 36 Shinties to fung the fleeing bool, An' aiblins gar me plunk the schule. **1898** *N. Brit. Daily Mail* 28 Oct. 2 He and his brother 'plunked' the school frequently, and were afraid to go home.

Hence **'plunking** *vbl. sb.* and *ppl. a.*

1941 W. C. HANDY *Father of Blues* xviii. 246, I had been everlastingly at the piano, forever picking out notes and chords for *Long Gone* but never playing anything consistently. A victim of all this plunking had been her parrot. **1952** B. ULANOV *Hist. Jazz in America* (1958) vi. 65 With this considerable rhythmic skill, however, went something less engaging, a plunking insistence on the beat. **1973** 'B. MATHER' *Snowline* x. 123 The plunking of an out-of-tune guitar. **1979** G. HAMMOND *Dead Game* vi. 77 A bullet that's been deflected by passing through something.. may make a plunking sort of sound.

plunk, *sb.*, *adv.*, *int.* Chiefly *dial.* [f. PLUNK *v.*]

A. *sb.* **1.** The action of the verb PLUNK; the resonant sound of a heavy blow, or of a plunge; the blow or plunge itself; also, the sound made by the drawing of a cork, etc.

1809 T. BATCHELOR *Anal. Eng. Lang.* 140 *Pelsy, Plungk*, a blow. **1813** G. BRUCE *Poems* II. 166 In his guid naig's fat rump it [a dirk] stuck: Whilk nae being us'd to sic a plunk, Gae suddenly a fearfu' funk. **1822** *Blackw. Mag.* Sept. 313/1 The King's name, and the plunk of corks drawn to drink his health, resounded in every house. **1834** L. RITCHIE *Wand. by Seine* 167 We hear..the pistol-like report of beer, and the more soberly alluring plunk! of wine-corks. **1900** *Westm. Gaz.* 29 Dec. 2/1 Suddenly there was a plunk! splash! Haw-haw-ooof! **1901** G. DOUGLAS *Ho. w. Green Shutters* 59 Swipey..planted a gob of mud right in the middle of his brow... Beneath the wet plunk of the mud John started back.

2. *slang.* †**a.** A large sum, a fortune. *Obs.* **b.** A dollar. *U.S.*

1767 JOSIAH WEDGWOOD in *Life* x. (1894) 102 He is in no danger of making a Plunk, or what would be esteemed a Fortune by any other than a little country manufacturer. **1891** J. MAITLAND *Amer. Slang Dict.* 207 *Plunk* (Am.), a dollar. **1901** H. McHUGH *John Henry* 12 Sarah Bernhardt at five plunks a chair. **1909** W. G. DAVENPORT *Butte & Montana beneath X-Ray* 56 Make it 25 plunks and let it go at that. **1929** WODEHOUSE *Gentleman of Leisure* xiii. 107 Dere's a loidy here..dat's got a necklace of jools what's worth a hundred t'ousand plunks.

B. *adv.* and *int.* With a plunking noise; plump.

1892 'MARK TWAIN' *Amer. Claimant* xix. 196 Feel my pulse: plunk—plunk—plunk. **1894** [W. D. LATTO] *Tammas Bodkin* xxx, Afore ye cud hae said sax the train played plunk into Moncrieff Tunnel. **1895** 'IAN MACLAREN' *Brier Bush* v. 188 They slip aff sudden in the end, and then they juist gang plunk. **1897** *Outing* (U.S.) XXX. 114/2 He poised on the edge of the pier. Then he went down—plunk—and came up in a moment. **1897** CROCKETT *Lad's Love* v. 52 [Peas] are a' vera weel in broth, but if ye got them plunk on the jaw wi' a strong chairge o' powder ahint them, they might bring the water to your e'en. **1936** A. RANSOME *Pigeon Post* xxvii. 292 They heard the noise up in the top of the wood... Plunk, plunk, plunk, and the rhythmic scraw of a saw.

Also redup. **'plunkety-'plunk**; also *attrib.*

1884 'MARK TWAIN' *Huck. Finn.* viii. 63, I hear a *plunkety-plunk, plunkety-plunk*, and says to myself, horses coming. **1960** *Twentieth Cent.* Dec. 556 The plunkety-plunk banjo sound.

†**'plunket**, *sb.*[1] and *a. Obs.* Forms: 4 **plunkett**, 4–7 **plonket**, 5 **-ete, -eut, -ett, plounkette**, 5–6 **ploncket**, 5–8 **plunket**, (6 **plumket, pluncket**). [ME. *plonket, plunket*, app. derived from OF. *plunkié* (1254), *plonquié* lead-coloured, lead-grey, also a kind of grey cloth (pa. pple. of *plonquier* to cover with lead:—late L. **plumbicāre*, f. *plumbum* lead: see PLUNGE *v.*).

The ending *-et* may be the earlier form of *-é*; but cf. other names of coloured fabrics, as BLANKET, BLUET, BURNET, RUSSET, WATCHET. See also BLUNKET (app. an alteration of this, perh. associated with *blanket*); also PLUMBET.]

A. *sb.* A woollen fabric of varying texture, app. of a grey or light blue colour. Cf. BLUNKET *sb.*

1375–6 *Durham Acc. Rolls* (Surtees) 582 Pro xij uln. de plunkett. **1377–8** *Ibid.* 586, xiij uln. de Plonket empt. pro tunicis, pro pagettis xiij s. **1466** *Mann. & Househ. Exp.* (Roxb.) 493 My master delyverd..xviij. yerdes of fyne plonket..to dye into fyne morrey engreyned. **1483** *Act 1 Rich. III*, c. 8 §4 That this Acte..extende not..to the makynge..of eny clothe called Vervise, otherwise called Plounkettes Turkyns or Celestrines, with broade Lists. *a* **1548** HALL *Chron., Hen. VIII* 22 Sodainly the Mount opened, and out came sixe ladies all in Crimosin satin and plunket, enbroudered with Golde and perle. **1616** BULLOKAR *Eng. Expos.*, *Plonkets*, a kind of wollen cloth. **1721** C. KING *Brit. Merch.* II. 96 What is become of our noble Manufacture of Plunkets, Violets, and Blues, formerly made in Suffolk? **1876** PLANCHÉ *Cycl. Costume* I. 402.

B. *adj.* Of a greyish blue colour; light blue. Cf. BLUNKET *a.*

c **1440** *Promp. Parv.* 406/1 Plunket (*K. P.* coloure), *jacinctus*. **1465–6** *Mann. & Househ. Exp.* (Roxb.) 329, xxiij. narow clothes called statutes, of the..color of red viij., and of the colour of plonkeut xv. **1496** *Bk. St. Albans, Fishing* (1883) 10 Lete woode your heer in an woodefatte a lyght plunket colour. **1543** GRAFTON *Coutn. Harding* 596 In two or thre places the saied sleues were cut, and fastened together againe with a plunket ryband. *a* **1548** HALL *Chron., Hen. VIII* 50 The Duke of Vaudosme and his bende in clothe of golde, and pluncket veluet. **1560** Plumket [see PLUMBET, quot. 1533].

Plunket ('plʌŋkɪt), *sb.*[2] *N.Z.* The name of Lady *Plunket*, wife of the Governor-General of New Zealand 1904–10 (see quot. 1938), used *attrib.* and *absol.* (with reference to the *Plunket Society*, a popular name for the Royal New Zealand Society for the Health of Women and Children), to designate a nurse trained in the methods of child feeding and care advocated by this society, a baby reared according to these methods, or a clinic following them.

1909 *Ann. Rep. Soc. for Promotion of Health of Women & Children* No. 1. 9 The doctor was pleased to have the assistance of the Plunket nurse, and at once consented to the children being fed on humanised milk. **1938** H. C. D. SOMERSET *Littledene* vii. 69 The Royal New Zealand Society for the Health of Women and Children..commonly called the Plunket Society from the name of its first president, Lady Plunket, was founded by Dr. Truby King in 1907. **1941** S. J. BAKER *N.Z. Slang* vi. 58 No record..would be complete without reference to the famed organization, the Plunket Society. For the past twenty years or more it has been known as the Plunket. **1944** F. L. W. WOOD *Understanding N.Z.* iv. 48 The town will have..Plunket rooms (baby clinics). *Ibid.* ix. 130 Nearly three-quarters of the children born in New Zealand become 'Plunket babies'. **1945** R. M. BURDON *N.Z. Notables* II. ii. 41 By 1913.. twenty-seven trained Plunket nurses were working from their appointed centres. **1958** *N.Z. News* 11 Mar. 3/1 In 1912, the Government gave him [*sc.* Truby King] six months' leave of absence to preach the movement throughout the country, and the number of 'Plunket' nurses rapidly multiplied. **1960** S. ASHTON-WARNER *Incense to Idols* 80 Organize societies for crippled children and the intellectually handicapped, Plunket for the babies, Heritage for the care of War Orphans. **1966** G. W. TURNER *Eng. Lang. in Austral & N.Z.* viii. 173 A New Zealander is likely to begin life as a 'Plunket baby'. His mother is visited periodically by the Plunket nurse from the Plunket Society, founded by Sir Truby King as an early experiment in socially supervised child care and named after the wife of the then Governor-General.

plunther ('plʌnðə(r)), *v. dial.* [Akin to PLUNDER *v.*[1]] *intr.* To flounder.

1839–41 S. WARREN *Ten Thous. a Year* ix. I. 274 The little doctor was plunthering on, ankle-deep in snow, towards the vicarage. **1849** *Fraser's Mag.* XXXIX. 51 We went plunthering along, sinking deeply at every step.

plup (plʌp). [Echoic: cf. PLOP *sb.* and *adv.*] The sound of or as of a body falling on a hard surface, into liquid, etc. Also *fig.*

1911 R. BROOKE in E. Marsh *Rupert Brooke* (1918) p. lxvii, The 'quaint' remarks fall all round one during meal times, with little soft plups like pats of butter. **1926** *Chambers's Jrnl.* Dec. 847/1 The surge of the water down below, and the *plup* of 'escape' above the roof, were but soft sounds. **1931** E. A. ROBERTSON *Four Frightened People* v. 144 Gas bubbles rose with a soft 'plup-plup'-ing.

pluperfect (ˌpluːˈpɜːfɪkt, ˈpluːˌpɜːfɪkt), *a.* (*sb.*) Also plus-. [Contracted from *plus-quam-perfect*, ad. L. (*tempus præteritum*) *plus quam perfectum* '(past tense) more than perfect', transl. Gr. (χρόνος) ὑπερσυντελικός. Cf. F. *plus-que-parfait* (1521).

400 MACROBIUS *De different. Verb.* 7 In Græcis verbis quæ in Ω exeunt omne perfectum tempus mutat in fine *A* in *EIN* et facit plusquam perfectum quod illi ὑπερσυντελικὸν vocant. *c* **500** PRISCIAN 805 (Putsch) Praeteritum plusquam-perfectum, in quo iampridem res perfecta ostenditur.]

1. *Gram.* Applied to that tense of the verb which expresses a time or action completed prior to some past point of time, specified or implied. Also *absol.* or as *sb.*, *ellipt.* for *pluperfect tense*.

1530 PALSGR. 88 The Preter Pluperfit Tens. *Jauóye parlé*, I had spoken. *Ibid.* 113 Verbes actives circumlocute theyr preterperfit and plus perfit tenses throughe all theyr modes, ..with the tenses of *je ay* and the participle preterit. **1599** MINSHEU *Span. Gram.* (1623) 22 Indicatiue moode. Pres. Imperfect. First preterperfect. Second perfect. Pluperfect tense. **1824** L. MURRAY *Eng. Gram.* (ed. 5) I. 124 The Pluperfect Tense represents a thing, not only as past, but also as prior to some other point of time specified in the sentence: as, 'I had finished my letter before he arrived'. **1837** G. PHILLIPS *Syriac Gram.* 52 By means also of the auxiliary verb two other tenses are defined; namely, the imperfect and plusperfect. **1879** ROBY *Lat. Gram.* IV. xvii. §1487 The Pluperfect denotes an action in past time, done before another past action.

2. *gen.* More than perfect; in quot. 1802 misused for 'superfluous'; *spec.* in *Mus.* (rarely) applied to an augmented (as distinguished from a perfect) fourth or fifth. Also (*slang*), used as an intensive.

1802 W. TAYLOR in *Monthly Mag.* XIII. 12 Junius had a dislike to the letter *k*..: it would have been more rational to indulge an antipathy against *c*, which is a very pluperfect letter, and represents sometimes *k*, sometimes *s*, and sometimes *ts*. **1856** *Leisure Ho.* 31 Jan. 74 It will happen in all binderies..that on examination certain volumes are found imperfect or pluperfect, either wanting a sheet, or having a sheet too much. **1876** STAINER & BARRETT *Dict. Mus. Terms* s.v. *Interval*, Intervals greater than major or normal have been termed (besides *augmented*) extreme, sharp, superfluous, pluperfect. **1876** HULLAH *ibid.* s.v. *Nomenclature*, Imperfect as applied to the exceptional fifth. As an antonym to this I have long used the epithet pluperfect, which has been very largely adopted. **1889** *Virginia University Mag.* Dec. 186 So take a drink, oh, Phæon, dear, we'll raise pluperfect Cain. **1917** 'CONTACT' *Airman's Outings* 204, I fully expect that we of the air service will lead the armies of pursuit and make ourselves a pluperfect nuisance to the armies of retreat. **1928** A. PHILIPS *Boy at Bank* I. v. 49 Mrs. Fravalton, one of those mothers who believe their children pluperfect. **1933** E. CALDWELL *God's Little Acre* x. 145 What in the pluperfect hell have you boys got to fight about so much, anyhow? **1977** *New Society* 5 May 238/2 They have done it with such bureaucratic precision... The erudition and workmanship are as impeccable, and absolutely deathly, as this kind of pluperfect reconstruction must always be.

†**'pluracie.** *Sc. Obs.* [irreg. f. L. *plūs, plūr-* more: cf. med.L. *plūritās*.] = PLURALITY.

1581 *Sc. Acts Jas. VI* (1814) III. 211/1 It being found maist difficill, That in þe charge of pluracie [*ed.* 1597 pluralitie] of kirkkis ony ane minister may instructe mone [1597 monie] flokis.

plural ('plʊərəl), *a.* (*sb.*) Also 4–5 **plurel**, 5–6 **-ell(e**, 5–7 **-all.** [a. OF. *plurel* (12th c.), or ad. L. *plūrālis* (Quint.), f. *plūs, plūr-* more: see -AL[1].]

A. *adj.* **1.** *Gram.* Applied to the form of a word which denotes more than one (or, in languages having a dual form, more than two): opposed to *singular*.

1377 LANGL. *P. Pl.* B. x. 237 Three propre persones ac nouȝt in plurel noumbre, For al is but on god. **1387** TREVISA *Higden* (Rolls) II. 171 He moste be i-cleped Argi in þe plural nombre. **1483** *Cath. Angl.* 285/1 Plurelle, *pluralis*. **1530** PALSGR. 4 The thyrde parsonnes plurelles of verbes actyves in the frenche tonge..ende in *ent*. **1631** GOUGE *God's Arrows* III. §72. 320 Nor is it [*Jehovah*] declined: nor hath it the plurall number. **1764** W. PRIMATT *Accentus Redivivi* 111 Provided they were third persons plural. **1844** LD. BROUGHAM *Brit. Const.* ix. §1 (1862) 113 They speak in the plural number, and the reader is utterly deceived. **1845** STODDART *Gram.* in *Encycl. Metrop.* (1847) I. 28/1 Quintilian..observes, that there were some writers..who contended that the dual number, in the third person plural of verbs, was properly marked by the termination *e*; as *consedere* if two persons sate together, *consederunt* if more than two; but, adds he, this rule is observed by none of our best writers.

2. More than one in number; consisting of, containing, pertaining to, or equivalent to, more than one. ***plural community***, a community made up of culturally different ethnic groups; ***plural democracy*** (see quots.); ***plural economy***, the economy of a plural society within which the different ethnic groups keep, to a great extent, their own economic systems; ***plural livings***: see PLURALITY 3; ***plural marriage*** (see MARRIAGE 1 d); ***plural society***, a society composed of different ethnic groups or cultural traditions; a society in which ethnic differences, etc., are reflected in the political structure (see quot. 1971); ***plural vote***, the right of giving more than one vote, or of voting in more than one parliamentary constituency; hence ***plural voter***, ***voting***.

1591 SHAKS. *Two Gent.* v. iv. 52 Better haue none Then plurall faith, which is too much by one. *a* **1631** DONNE *Serm.* vii. 66 God is a plurall God, and offers himselfe to all collectively; God is a singular God, and offers himselfe to every man distributively. **1860** MILL *Repr. Govt.* (1865) 73/1 Until there shall have been devised..some mode of plural voting which may assign to education, as such, the degree of superior influence due to it, and sufficient as a counterpoise to the numerical weight of the least educated class. **1869** *Utah Mag.* 18 Sept. 310/1 The Mormon proposition is not to make plural marriage obligatory on the world, but to declare its necessity and legitimacy under certain circumstances. **1895** *Daily Chron.* 6 Dec. 6/7 One of the few beneficed clergymen holding plural livings. **1897** *Westm. Gaz.* 10 Aug. 8/1 In spite of the law which forbids it, polygamy still prevails in Utah... In Salt Lake City they don't call it polygamy, but 'plural marriage'. **1906** I. ZANGWILL in *Times* 29 Oct. 10/5 In another leader on the very same page you defend plural voting on the ground of the necessity of 'the representation of local interests'. **1922** JOYCE *Ulysses* 480 Dragging a lorry on which are..plaster figures..representing the new nine muses, Commerce, Operatic Music,..Plural Voting, Gastronomy. **1939** J. S. FURNIVALL *Netherlands India* xiii. 446 One finds a plural society also in independent states, such as Siam, where Natives, Chinese and Europeans have distinct economic functions, and live apart as separate social orders. *Ibid.*, Some Dutch writers use the term dual or plural economy.. to connote the co-existence within the same political community of two or more distinct sets of different economic principles. **1947** *Sun* (Baltimore) 26 Nov. 5/2 Eighteen Utah residents..were charged with conspiring to advocate plural marriage. **1952** B. DAVIDSON *Rep. Southern Afr.* I. vii. 79 They hold in their hands the saving—or the sinking—of a plural society in South Africa. *Ibid.* II. vii. 138 Clearly confronted with the fact of a plural community, they steadfastly refuse to recognize the plurality. **1963** W. N. STEPHENS *Family in Cross-Cultural Perspective* (1964) ii. 33 This chapter will deal with the last three forms: polygyny, polyandry, and group marriage, the forms of plural marriage. **1965** *New Statesman* 19 Nov. 796/2 The common theme..is the theory of the West Indies as 'plural societies', that is, societies lacking institutions, traditions and habits common to all members. **1966** JACOBS & ZINK *Mod. Govt.* (ed. 3) I. vi. 70 Plural voting..resulted from the British belief that a person should be allowed to vote in every district where he was qualified... The Representation of the People Act of 1948 eliminated it completely. **1971** *Race* XII. 462 It appears theoretically useful, then, to partition the universe of culturally diverse societies into: (1) 'plural societies', in which politics tends (exclusively) to follow ethnic lines, and (2) 'pluralistic societies', in which politically relevant issues and actions do not always coincide with ethnic groups. **1977** *Time* 21 Nov. 12/1 What is at stake, ultimately, is whether the government will be able to carry on with the Afrikaners' grand scheme of apartheid—also known as 'separate development' and more recently as 'plural democracy'. **1978** *Guardian Weekly* 4 June 7/3 Apartheid—which has since [1948] undergone minor ideological mutations and several changes in name... Plural democracy, as apartheid is now known.

B. *sb.* **a.** *Gram.* The plural number. **b.** The fact or condition of there being more than one.

plural of excellence or ***majesty***, ***plural intensive***, terms applied in Hebrew Grammar to a plural sb. used as the name of a single person; the typical example being *ĕlōhīm*, lit. gods, deities, used as the name of (the one) God.

1398 TREVISA *Barth. De P.R.* XVII. cxxxiii. (Bodl. MS.), Porrum..is hoc Porrum in þe singuler & hij porri in þe plurel. **1655** FULLER *Ch. Hist.* II. ii. §56 If respect be had to the severall Arts there professed, Sigebert founded Schools in the plurall. **1756** F. GREVILLE *Maxims* 27 We confess our faults in the plural, and deny them in the singular. **1770** LANGHORNE *Plutarch* (1879) I. 202/2 The number three, as being the first of plurals. **1835** *Court Mag.* VI. 186/1 This literary fashion of speaking in the plural, sadly puzzles an old gentleman unused to composition, like myself. **1837** G. PHILLIPS *Syriac Gram.* 103 A *plural of excellence* the Syrians have not. *c* **1860** *Gesenius's Heb. & Chaldee Lex.* 30/2 The plural of majesty, [*ĕlōhīm*]; occurs more than two thousand times. **1898** F. BROWN *Heb.-Eng. Lex.* 43 Pl. intensive. **1875** JOWETT *Plato* (ed. 2) I. 277 Do not make a singular into a plural, as the facetious say of those who break a thing.

‖**plurale tantum** (plʊəˈreɪlɪ ˈtæntəm). *Gram.* Pl. **pluralia tantum.** [med.L. *plūrāle* the plural f. *plūrālis* PLURAL *a.* + L. *tantum* only.] A noun which, in any particular sense, is used only in plural form.

1930 T. SASAKI *Lang. R. Bridges' Poetry* II. iii. 57 The so-called 'pluralia tantum' (e.g. breeches, dregs). **1940** A. H. GARDINER *Theory of Proper Names* viii. 27 Here a *plurale tantum* has been resolved into its component individual members, each of whom is thus represented as a bearer of the proper name in question. **1957** R. W. ZANDVOORT *Handbk. Eng. Gram.* II. 95 Some nouns never occur without a plural suffix; they are known as *pluralia tantum* (sing. *plurale tantum*). Such are *riches, thanks, tongs. Ibid.* 340 Most of the *pluralia tantum* in Kruisinga's lists may also occur without *-s*, if usually in another sense: *compasses* 'instrument for describing circles', but *compass* 'instrument showing magnetic meridian'..*colours* 'flag', but *colour* 'hue'. **1969** *Language* XLV. 239 A collective is precisely to be expected in a word for 'clothes'; cf. the English plurale tantum as well as Gk. *heímata*, only as neuter plural in Homer. **1976** *Archivum Linguisticum* VII. 105 Because these so-called 'uncountable' nouns are in fact to be found in plural form, I dub them *pseudo-uncountables* to distinguish them from true uncountables like *thunder* and *heat*, and pluralia tantum like *scissors*.

pluralism (ˈplʊərəlɪz(ə)m). [f. PLURAL + -ISM, after PLURALIST.] The character of being plural; the condition or fact of being a pluralist.

1. *Eccl.* **a.** The system or practice of more than one benefice being held at the same time by one person. **b.** The holding of two or more offices of any kind at one time.

1818 BENTHAM *Ch. Eng., Catech. Exam.* 248 Obtainment on false pretences, as proved by Non-Residence, Pluralism, and Sinecurism. *a* **1882** SIR R. CHRISTISON *Life* (1885) I. 411 Pluralism was at this period [1822] in the ascendant in the Scottish Church. **1892** J. C. BLOMFIELD *Hist. Heyford* 68 The last [century]..so sadly notorious for the pluralism and non-residence of the parochial clergy. **1904** *Daily Chron.* 24 Nov. 6/2 (*heading*) Justice Buckley on Pluralism in Directorships. *Ibid.*, It did not follow..that a rich man was the best administrator, but if the system of payment he suggested were adopted there should be an end of pluralism.

2. *Philos.* A theory or system of thought which recognizes more than one ultimate principle: opposed to MONISM. Also, the theory that the knowable world is made up of a plurality of interacting things.

1882 W. JAMES *Let.* 6 Dec. in R. B. Perry *Tht. & Char. W. James* (1935) I. 686 After all, pluralism and indeterminism seem to be but two ways of stating the same thing. **1884** T. H. GREEN tr. *Lotze's Metaphysic* I. vi. 125 The Pluralism with which our view of the world began has to give place to a Monism, through which the 'transeunt' operation, always unintelligible, passes into an 'immanent' operation. **1887** BOWNE *Philos. Theism* i. (1902) 62 We replace..the pluralism of spontaneous thought by a basal monism. **1904** *Contemp. Rev.* Sept. 416 Philosophically this is neither Pluralism nor out-and-out Monism. It is not the former because ultimately no other source of being but God, no principle of life but the Divine, is recognised. **1905** *Athenæum* 11 Feb. 170/2 Thus we reach a pluralism. It is, however, the pluralism, not of Leibnitz, but of Lotze. The monads are not absolute, but interact. **1919** *Mind* XXVIII. 57 For pluralism, the living experience of the subject consists actually in his interaction with other subjects. **1955** R. CARNAP in *Internat. Encycl. Unified Sci.* I. 49 It seems doubtful whether we can find any theoretical content in such philosophical questions as discussed by monism, dualism, and pluralism. **1969** N. RESCHER *Many-Valued Logic* iii. 214 There is no balking the fact of *pluralism* in logic. *Ibid.*, Faced with the fact of pluralism, the step to relativism or conventionalism might seem short and easy. **1972** K. R. POPPER *Objective Knowledge* iv. 153 Some philosophers have made a serious beginning towards a philosophical pluralism, but pointing out the existence of a *third world*.

3. *Pol. Sci.* **a.** A theory which opposes monolithic state power and advocates instead increased devolution and autonomy for the main organizations that represent man's involvement in society. Also, the belief that power should be shared among a number of political parties.

1919 H. J. LASKI in *Philos. Rev.* XXVIII. 568 The monistic state is an hierarchical structure in which power is ..collected at a single centre. The advocates of pluralism are convinced that this is both administratively incomplete and ethically inadequate. **1941** H. M. MAGID *Eng. Political Pluralism* i. 8 If we deny the inevitability of totalitarianism, we may discover in pluralism..an attempt to analyze the problem of freedom in the light of modern world conditions. **1954** B. & R. NORTH tr. *Duverger's Pol. Parties* II. i. 257 As a 'party system' the single party is obviously different from the multi-party system or 'pluralism'. **1969** M. BROADY in *Architectural Assoc. Quarterly* I. 67 Political pluralism is concerned essentially with the relationship between the State and other kinds of social organization, and it draws attention to the limitations of State power in order to assert the importance in a democratic society of alternative and independent sources of power and foci of interest. **1977** M. WALKER *National Front* i. 16 Britain is historically accustomed to one form or another of coalition government, which is the essence of pluralism.

b. The existence or toleration of diversity of ethnic or cultural groups within a society or state, of beliefs or attitudes within a body or institution, etc.

1933 *Sociol. & Social Research* XVIII. 103 (*title*) Social pluralism. **1956** H. M. KALLEN *Cultural Pluralism* 46 'Cultural Pluralism' is a controversial expression. *Ibid.* 51 This pluralism is the kind always and everywhere characterizing men's undertakings. **1965** *New Statesman* 19 Nov. 796/2 The relevance of this 'pluralism' to Caribbean politics is plain. Analysis of social problems in simple economic terms..will not do. **1969** *Guardian* 20 Sept. 4/4 A good deal of discussion at the conference..has been about pluralism as opposed to assimilation. **1971** *Deb. House of Commons Canada* 8 Oct. 8580/2 Ethnic pluralism can help us overcome or prevent the homogenization and depersonalization of mass society. **1976** *Times* 7 Aug. 14/4 To be in favour of pluralism is to declare that one does not intend to hound or persecute theologians or catechists whose expression of faith differs from your own. **1977** F. YOUNG in J. Hick *Myth of God Incarnate* ii. 42 The future seems to lie with pluralism in christology.

pluralist (ˈplʊərəlɪst), *sb.* (and *a.*) [f. PLURAL + -IST.]

1. a. *Eccl.* One who holds two or more benefices at the same time. Also *attrib.*

1626 in *Crt. & Times Chas. I* (1848) I. 82 A bill is also talked of for pluralists to allow their curate, of the benefice they reside upon, £50 per annum. **1692** WASHINGTON tr. *Milton's Def. Pop.* M.'s Wks. 1738 I. 456 Branded with the odious Names of Pluralists and Non-residents. **1760** JORTIN *Erasm.* II. 188 He seems to have had in view..Cardinal Wolsey, who had been a scandalous pluralist. **1804** *Ann. Rev.* II. 217/1 The Rev. James Hook..had..taken up the gauntlet in favour of his pluralist and non-resident brethren. **1859** GEO. ELIOT *A. Bede* v, A pluralist at whom the severest Church-reformer would have found it difficult to look sour.

b. In extended use, One who combines two or more offices, professions, or conditions. Also *attrib.*

1818 T. BROWN *Brighton* II. 181 This long pole is but a walking stick to the magical wand of old Hurlothrumbo, the pluralist, who can fill so many places. **1842** R. BURNS *Mem. Rev. Dr. MacGill* i. 14 The idea of a pluralist, he could not ..endure; and in his instant declinature of the tempting proposal [of the Chair of History at St. Andrews, when he already had a small country parish] we discover the germ of [his] opposition..to the pluralising system. **1851** RUSKIN *Stones Ven.* I. App. v. 354 Patriots rather than pluralists. **1865** *Pall Mall G.* 24 Oct. 13 M. Doré is, in fact, a pluralist in point of styles, and he has given us at least three or four distinct and separate ones in this work. **1869** *Ibid.* 11 Oct. 2 Mr. White is a pluralist in treasurerships. **1891** *Daily News* 30 Dec. 5/1 The whole land will soon be too hot to hold the pluralists of matrimony [practisers of 'plural marriage']. **1901** *Daily Chron.* 18 May 7/4 Mr. Bowles..never heard of a private secretary who received £300 a year under one vote, and £800 a year under another... He objected strongly to these pluralist appointments.

2. *Philos.* One who holds the theory of

1885 W. JAMES *Lit. Remains of H. James* 116 Their most serious enemy will be the *philosophic* pluralist. **1895** in *Funk's Stand. Dict.* **1919** C. A. RICHARDSON *Spiritual Pluralism* i. 12 The above is but a broad outline of the pluralist argument as applied to the inorganic world. **1919** *Mind* XXVIII. 58 The pluralist..recognizes that the fundamental fact from which the start must be made, is not a dualism of matter and mind, but the unity of the individual experience, which comprises a duality of subject and object. **1966** F. J. COPLESTON *Hist. Philos.* VIII. x. 250 The idea of God has the benefit of increasing the pluralist's confidence in the significance of finite existence.

3. *Pol.* and *Sociol.* One who upholds pluralism and is opposed to monolithic state power or to policies of cultural or ethnic assimilation. Also *attrib.* or as *adj.*, designating a system based on pluralism.

1920 *Amer. Pol. Sci. Rev.* XIV. 407 The all important fact, so consistently overlooked by the pluralist, that the truly federal state is a unitary state. *Ibid.*, The pluralist doctrine is timely in that it calls attention to the present bewildering development of groups within the body politic. **1957** M. P. FOGARTY *Christian Democracy* I. iii. 29 A certain 'solidarist' conception of the individual's responsibility to and for the society around him, and, following from this, a 'federalist' or 'pluralist' ideal of the structure of society and the processes which go on within it. **1964** GOULD & KOLB *Dict. Social Sci.* 244/2 Today attention is frequently paid to the difficulties of maintaining a pluralist society under the impact of mass society and culture. *Ibid.* 563/2 Pluralists define public opinion in terms of controversy. **1972** *Times Lit. Suppl.* 4 Feb. 115/2 The cheerful belief that the Negro was entering mainstream pluralist politics became incredible after Watts, Newark and Detroit. **1975** *N.Y. Times* 9 Oct. 3/3 The Market withheld similar aid in July for the Gonçalves Government on the ground that it did not represent a 'pluralist democracy'. **1977** M. WALKER *National Front* i. 16 The great strength of the British pluralist system of channelling political allegiance into one of two wide coalitions is that many citizens who sympathize with totalitarian objectives are encouraged to stay within the political mainstream.

pluralistic (plʊərəˈlɪstɪk), *a.* [f. prec. + -IC: see -ISTIC.] Of or belonging to a pluralist or to pluralism, in any sense; *spec.* in *Philos.* recognizing more than one ultimate principle in ontology: opposed to MONISTIC; in *Pol.* and *Sociol.* (see PLURALISM 3); ***pluralistic ignorance*** (see quot. 1970).

1854 *Edin. Rev.* XCIX. 360 Even the 'pluralistic' marriage service has been published [by the Mormons]. The following is an extract from this novel rubric. **1877** WINCHELL *Sci. & Rel.* ii. (1881) 40 The later Eleatics were pluralistic—holding to the distinction of matter and spirit. **1884** *Lotze's Metaph.* I. 443 What I looked for in vain in other statements of the pluralistic hypothesis. **1891** F. C. S. SCHILLER *Riddles of Sphinx* 403 The pluralistic answer given to the ultimate question of ontology. **1909** W. JAMES (*title*) Pluralistic universe. **1919** H. J. LASKI in *Philos. Rev.* XXVIII. 562 (*title*) The pluralistic state. **1920** *Amer. Jrnl. Sociol.* XXV. 388 Pluralistic behavior, in distinction from individual behavior, has its own conditions, forms, and laws. **1933** *Sociol. & Social Research* XVIII. 107 The pluralistic conception of society carries with it the principle of functionalism. **1950** T. M. NEWCOMB *Social Psychol.* xvi. 608 We have a condition for which F. H. Allport.. suggested the term pluralistic ignorance. Everyone assumes that everyone except himself accepts the norms uncritically. **1963** F. COPLESTON *Hist. Philos.* VII. II. xii. 252 A pluralistic metaphysics which calls to mind the atoms of Democritus and the monads of Liebnitz. **1964** T. B. BOTTOMORE *Elites & Society* vi. 119 Aron, when he urges the importance of the diffusion of power in the pluralistic democracies does not invoke only the principal elites. **1970** G. A. & A. G. THEODORSON *Mod. Dict. Sociol.* 301 *Pluralistic ignorance*, a situation in which individual members of a group believe incorrectly that they are each alone..in believing or not believing in particular values. **1971** [see *plural society*]. **1972** *Times Lit. Suppl.* 18 Feb. 195/2 We are now living in a morally pluralistic society;.. attempts by one group to impose its morality on another are futile. **1975** *N.Y. Times* 10 Sept. 20/7 Mr. Kissinger added that the United States was 'working in closest harmony with our European allies' on the problem of encouraging 'the emergence of a pluralistic system' in Portugal. **1976** P. DONOVAN *Relig. Lang.* viii. 95 Apologists for the Baha'i World Faith appeal to the reasonableness of a syncretistic faith in today's pluralistic world. **1977** M. WALKER *National Front* i. 15 The pluralistic kind of society has agreed to permit its citizens to differ about the society's objectives.

Hence **pluraˈlistically** *adv.*

1880 *Athenæum* 25 Dec. 851/3 [Julius Bahnsen's] philosophy..defines the 'Ding an sich' of Schopenhauer, the Will, pluralistically, and not, as Hartmann does, monistically.

plurality (plʊˈrælɪtɪ). [a. OF. *pluralite* (14th c.), ad. late L. *plūrālitās* (Ambrose), f. *plūrāl-is* PLURAL.]

I. Related in sense to *plural.*

1. The state of being plural; the fact or condition of denoting, comprising, or consisting of more than one.

1398 TREVISA *Barth. De P.R.* XVIII. xxxii. (MS. Bodl.), Pluralite of hornes folowiþ þe clifte of fote [in four-footed beasts]. **1563** *Homilies* II. *Of Cert. Places of Script.* I. (1859) 374 The plurality of wives was by a special prerogative suffered to the fathers of the Old Testament. **1624** GATAKER *Transubst.* 183 To shew how in one nature there may be a plurality of persons. **1727–41** CHAMBERS *Cycl.* s.v., A plurality of worlds is a thing which Mr. Huygens has endeavoured to prove in his Cosmotheoros. **1781** GIBBON *Decl. & F.* xviii. II. 103 Many of the Armenian nobles still refused to abandon the plurality of their gods and of their wives. **1869** TOZER *Highl. Turkey* I. 27 The..question of the unity or plurality of authorship of the poem. **1898** J. R. ILLINGWORTH *Divine Immanence* (1904) vii. 86/2 The fact that there is plurality, triune plurality in God.

b. The fact of there being many; numerousness; hence, a large number or quantity; a multitude.

1432–50 tr. *Higden* (Rolls) I. 27, I haue studiede that hit schal be called *Policronicon* of the pluralite of tymes whom it dothe conteyne. **1533** BELLENDEN *Livy* I. Prol. (S.T.S.) I. 7 In sic pluralite of writaris my fame is obscure and of litill estimatioun. **1535** STEWART *Cron. Scot.* II. 445 Pluralitie of meit and drink siclike, Forbiddin wes bayth for puir and ryke. **1609** B. JONSON *Sil. Wom.* IV. iii, Doe you count it lawfull to haue such pluralitie of seruants? **1664** POWER *Exp. Philos.* I. 37 Through a good Microscope, he may easily see..variety in the plurality, paucity, and anomalous Situation of eyes. **1859** MILL *Liberty* iii. (1865) 42/2 Europe is, in my judgment, wholly indebted to this plurality of paths for its progressive and many-sided development. **1866** ROGERS *Agric. & Prices* I. xx. 512 The money-chest was also secured by a plurality of locks.

2. *Eccl.* **a.** The holding of two or more benefices or livings concurrently by one person. **b.** A benefice or living held concurrently with another or others; *pl.* two or more benefices held together.

1362 LANGL. *P. Pl.* A. XI. 197 Dewid he is also, And haþ possessions & pluralites for pore menis sake. *c* **1440** *Jacob's Well* 18 Alle þey bene acursed, þat receyvin & holdyn pluralyte of cherchys. **1551** CROWLEY *Pleas. & Pain* 533 Geue ouer your pluralities..betake you to one benifice. **1642** MILTON *Apol. Smect.* Wks. 1851 III. 325 Who ingrosse many pluralities under a non-resident and slubbring dispatch of soules. *a* **1715** BP. BURNET *Own Time* VII. (1823) VI. 646 The scandalous practices of non-residence and pluralities. *Ibid.*, I do not reckon the holding poor livings that lie contiguous, a plurality, where both are looked after, and both afford only a competent maintenance. *a* **1817** T. DWIGHT *Trav. New Eng.*, etc. (1821) II. 50 There are two congregations in North-Haven: a Presbyterian, and an Episcopal. The latter is a small plurality, under the care of a neighbouring minister. **1877** FREEMAN *Norm. Conq.* (ed. 3) II. vii. 83 This holding of sees in plurality..was by no means uncommon at the time.

c. *transf.* of offices or positions generally.

1678 LADY CHAWORTH in *12th Rep. Hist. MSS. Comm.* App. v. 47 Some mention the laying sums upon all pluralities of qualities, dignities, and offices. **1850** LYELL *2nd Visit U.S.* II. 82 Some wealthy slave-owners of Alabama have estates in Mississippi. With a view of checking the increase of these 'pluralities', a tax has recently been imposed on absentees. **1893** *Law Times* XCIV. 452/1 There is a growing feeling that plurality in the matter of directorships is dangerous and to be deprecated.

II. Related in sense to L. *plus* more.

Etymologically, these are improper uses, being in form derivatives of *plural*, while in sense they are derivatives of *plūs, plūr-*. On the analogy of *major-ity, minor-ity, superior-ity*, etc., the etymological form is PLURITY.

3. The greater number or part; more than half of the whole; = MAJORITY 3. [At first Scotch, from F. *pluralité*.]

1578 *Bk. Univ. Kirk of Scotl.* (Bann. Cl.) 412 For electioun of ane Moderatour, Mrs Johne Row, David Fergusone and Johne Duncansone was proponit in leits, and be pluralitie of votes Mr Johne Row [Minister at Perth] was chosin Moderatour. **1581** *Ibid.* 522 The said Mr Johne, be pluralitie of votes, was chosin Moderator hac vice. **1600** E. BLOUNT tr. *Conestaggio* 228 The pluralitie of voices refusing to accept the armes. **1651** HOBBES *Leviath.* (1839) 528 To bring the people together, to elect them by plurality of votes. **1654** FULLER *Comm. Ruth* (1868) 37 Verity consisteth not in the plurality of voices. **1683** EVELYN *Mem.* (1857) II. 187 The plurality of the younger judges and rising men judged it otherwise. **1703** DUKE OF QUEENSBERRY in Ellis *Orig. Letters* Ser. II. IV. No. 394. 227 This was thrown out by a great plurality. **1794** *Hist.* in *Ann. Reg.* 91/1 The plurality.. of their chiefs endeavoured in vain to stem the torrent of disobedience. **1823** *Niles' Register* XXIV. 217/2 At the late election..[in Maine], only three gentlemen were chosen... Neither of the others had a plurality of the whole number of votes. **1875** JOWETT *Plato* (ed. 2) I. 74 Socrates would rather not decide the question by a plurality of votes.

4. *U.S. Politics.* An excess of votes polled by the leading candidate in an election above those polled by the one next to him, in cases where there are three or more candidates; as distinguished from *majority*, which in such cases is applied to an absolute majority of all the votes given.

(The earlier sense (3) was in use in 1823: see above.)

1828 WEBSTER s.v., In elections, a plurality of votes is when one candidate has more votes than any other, but less than half of the whole number of votes given. **1846** WORCESTER s.v., A candidate, in an election, receives a plurality of votes, when he receives more than any other candidate; and he receives a majority of votes, when he receives more than all others. **1864** WEBSTER s.v., *Plurality of votes*, the excess of votes cast for one individual over those cast for any other of several competing candidates. **1884** *Manch. Exam.* 8 Nov. 4/7 Governor Cleveland had a thousand plurality in New York State, and was elected President. **1885** *Pall Mall G.* 31 Mar. 8/2 He ran again last fall, and had a plurality over the Republican candidate; but as it requires in that State [Connecticut] a majority over all to elect, the Legislature elected his Republican competitor.

III. 5. *attrib.* and *Comb.*

1642 MILTON *Apol. Smect.* Wks. 1851 III. 307 The non-resident and plurality-gaping Prelats, the gulphs and whirle pooles of benefices. **1899** *Allbutt's Syst. Med.* VIII. 863 The differences on which the plurality hypothesis is founded.

pluralize (ˈpluərəlaɪz), *v.* [a. F. *pluraliser*: see PLURAL and -IZE.]

1. a. *trans.* To make plural; to attribute plurality to; to express in the plural.

1803 *Monthly Mag.* XV. 3 We cannot well avoid the use of many ancient words unaltered, as English nouns; but I would lay it down as a rule, never to pluralize them by inflection, but simply by the addition of the *s* or *es.* **1854** *Blackw. Mag.* LXXVI. 520 Gulliver, to magnify present times, pluralises them all and each. **1864** *Mattie, a Stray* II. 251 'Perhaps it serves *us* right', said Mattie, pluralizing the case after her old fashion. **1871** EARLE *Philol. Eng. Tongue* §382 Those words which we have adopted from Latin or Greek..unaltered, have usually been pluralised according to Greek and Latin grammar.

b. *intr.* Of a word or phrase: To become plural; to assume plural form.

1871 EARLE *Philol. Eng. Tongue* §599 Any part of speech will assume in compounding the substantive character, and will pluralise as such.

c. *intr.* To express or form the plural.

1964 *Language* XL. 135 The way in which speakers of English pluralize.

2. *intr.* To hold more than one benefice (or office) at one time; to be or become a pluralist.

1842 [see PLURALIST 1 b]. *a* **1875** [see PLURALIZED].

Hence ˈ**pluralized** *ppl. a.*, ˈ**pluralizing** *vbl. sb.* and *ppl. a.*; also **plurali'zation**, the act of pluralizing.

1813 W. TAYLOR in *Monthly Rev.* LXXI. 475 The pluralizing formulas [in language]. **1836** G. S. FABER *Prim. Doctr. Election* I. ix. 133 Clement, by his use of a pluralising phraseology in the first person, shews us [etc.]. *a* **1875** R. S. HAWKER *Prose Wks.* (1893) 169 A pluralised clergyman of the days of the Georges. **1878** H. SPENCER in *Pop. Sc. Monthly* July 300 'Inferiors invariably use the third person plural in addressing their superiors': a form which, while dignifying the superior by pluralization, increases the distance of the inferior by its relative indirectness. **1970** *English Studies* LI. 395 Participles used as adjectival modifiers were also disregarded, as were those used nominally (with actual or potential determiners, pluralisation, or government by a preposition). **1972** *Language* XLVIII. 356 All these authors, characteristically, regard the rules of Spanish pluralization as phonological ones. **1978** *Amer. Speech* LIII. 35 Personal singular *you* similarly takes what is formally a plural verb form (*are, were*), as do French *vous*, German *Sie*, and Russian *vy*; as with singular *they—themself*, this 'pluralization' of singular *you* can be said to follow reflexivization (whence a plural verb but a singular reflexive *yourself*).

ˈ**pluralizer**, *sb.* [f. PLURALIZE *v.* + -ER[1].] 1. = PLURALIST 1 (Webster 1864).

2. *Gram.* a. A pluralizing affix, inflexion, or word. b. A noun that may appear in plural form.

1933 *Times Lit. Suppl.* 16 Nov. 798/2 *Shang* is one of the six pluralizers. **1951** *Archivum Linguisticum* III. 66 Suffix: *-naka* ~ *-nak-* '(noun) pluralizer'. **1961** R. B. LONG *Sentence & its Parts* ii. 39 The basic forms of pluralizer nouns are most often used as heads within nounal units, since they generally require determiners. *Ibid.*, Quantifiables such as *courage, fun,..machinery,* and *furniture* are not made plural, though it is true that some quantifiables have pluralizer status also. **1965** *Canad. Jrnl. Linguistics* Spring 172 The pluralizer *qə-* of Position 4. **1971** [see INTENSIFIER].

plurally (ˈpluərəlɪ), *adv.* [f. PLURAL + -LY[2].] In the plural number; so as to express or imply more than one; in a plural manner.

c **1380** WYCLIF *Sel. Wks.* II. 345 Whan God bihiȝte Abraham þat he shulde ȝyve þat lond to him and to his seed, he seid not pluraliche, þat he shulde ȝyve it to his seedis. **1552** LATIMER *1st Serm. Lord's Prayer* Wks. (Parker Soc.) II. 5 Mark that he saith, *advocatum, non advocatos.* He speaketh singularly, not plurally. *a* **1666** C. HOOLE *Accidence* (1671) 3 Nouns be declined with six Cases, Singularly and Plurally. **1685** BAXTER *Paraphr. N.T.* 1 Cor. xi. 23, 24 That Christ gave it them together plurally. **1860** RUSKIN *Mod. Paint.* V. VII. iv. §27. 152 'The heavens' when used plurally..remained expressive of the starry space beyond. **1904** *Daily Chron.* 5 Mar. 4/6 Mormons who were (plurally) married before polygamy was made illegal.

pluranimity. *rare.* [f. L. *plus, plūr-* more, substituted for *un-* in UNANIMITY.] Diversity of opinions.

1907 W. DE MORGAN *Alice-For-Short* ix. 95 Whatever innate ideas on the subject of oil-painting he possessed, had been disorganised and carefully thrown out of gear by the want of unanimity, or presence of pluranimity, in his instructors.

† **plu'ranimous,** *a. Obs. nonce-wd.* [f. L. *plūs, plūr-* more + *animus* mind + -OUS; after *unanimous.*] Not unanimous.

1650 B. *Discolliminium* 28, I could demonstrate it to be Heterogeneous, Heterodoxous,..Omnigenous, Pluranimous.

† ˈ**plurar,** *a. Obs. rare.* [f. L. *plūs, plūr-* more + -AR; = OF. *plurier* plural: app. after *singular*, F. *singulier.*] = PLURAL.

a **1613** OVERBURY *A Wife*, etc. (1638) 93 To bee briefe he is a Heteroclite, for hee wants the plurar number.

plurasie, -esie, -esy, obs. forms of PLEURISY.

plurative (ˈpluərətɪv), *a.* [ad. L. *plūrātīvus* adj. (Gell.) plural, f. L. *plūs, plūr-* more, after grammatical terms in *-ātīvus*, as *nōminātīvus, comparātīvus, indicātīvus*, etc. So obs. F. *pluratif* (E. Deschamps in Godef.).]

† 1. *Gram.* = PLURAL *a.* 1. *Obs. rare.*

1585 FOXE *Serm. on 2 Cor.* v. 6 This nominative (*Nos*) in the plurative number, is not here to be expounded after the stile of Rome.

2. *Logic.* (See quots.)

1849 W. THOMSON *Laws of Thought* (ed. 2) II. 174 The judgment—'Most men are prejudiced' cannot..be considered as particular, for it implies not only that *some* men, but *more than the half* of mankind are prejudiced. These are termed *plurative* judgments. **1867** ATWATER *Elem. Logic* 102 Plurative Judgments are those in which more than half, but not all of the subject is taken. **1870** JEVONS *Elem. Logic* xxii. 191 The name of Plurative propositions has been proposed for all those which give a distinct idea of the fraction or number of the subject involved in the assertion.

pluri- (pluərɪ), combining form of L. *plūs, plūr-* more, pl. *plūr-ēs* several, as in the following:

pluri'capsular *a.*, having several capsules, as a radiolarian. **pluri'cellular** *a.*, composed of several cells. **pluri'central** *a.*, having more than one centre or nucleus. **pluri'cipital** *a. Bot.* [L. *caput, -cipit-* head], having more than one head, as a root-crown (*Syd. Soc. Lex.* 1895). **pluri'cuspid** *a.*, having several cusps, as a tooth. **pluri'dentate** *a.*, having several tooth-like processes or appendages (*Syd. Soc. Lex.*). **pluri'disciplinary** *a.*, having or consisting of several disciplines or branches of learning; = INTERDISCIPLINARY *a.* **pluri'flagellate** *a. Zool.*, having many flagella (*Syd. Soc. Lex.*). **pluri'florous** *a.* [L. *flōs, flōr-* flower], many-flowered (*ibid.*). ˈ**pluriform** *a.*, existing in many different forms; multiform; hence **pluri'formity. plurifœ'tation,** the conception of more than one fœtus at once. **pluri'foliate** *a. Bot.* [L. *folium* leaf], having many leaves (*Syd. Soc. Lex.*). **pluri'foliolate** *a. Bot.* [L. *foliolum* leaflet], having many leaflets, as a compound leaf (Webster 1864). **pluri'guttulate** *a. Bot.* [L. *guttula* droplet, f. *gutta* drop], containing many drops or drop-like bodies (*Syd. Soc. Lex.*). **pluri'lingual** *a.* and *sb.* = MULTILINGUAL *a.* and *sb.*, POLYGLOT *a.* and *sb.*; hence **pluri'lingualism. pluri'literal** *Heb. Gram.* [L. *littera* letter], *a.* containing more than three letters in the root; *sb.* a root consisting of more than three letters: cf. BILITERAL, TRILITERAL. **pluri'locular** *a. Biol.* [L. *loculus* little place], containing many cavities or cells. **pluri'mammate** *a. Zool.* [L. *mamma* pap], having more than two paps (*Syd. Soc. Lex.*). **pluri'modal** *a.*, consisting of or involving more than one mode (in various senses). **pluri'nominal** *a.* [L. *nōmen* name], consisting of or involving more than one name; *spec.* in *Nat. Hist.*, applied to a system of nomenclature or a name not confined to two terms; polynomial. **pluri'nucleate** *a.*, having several nuclei; so **pluri'nucleated** *a.* (*Syd. Soc. Lex.*). **pluri'partite** *a.*, deeply divided with numerous incisions (Mayne *Expos. Lex.* 1858): cf. PARTITE. **pluri'septate** *a.*, having several septa or partitions (*Syd. Soc. Lex.*). **pluri'serial** *a.*, consisting of several series or rows; hence **pluri'serially** *adv.* **pluri'seriate** *a.*, arranged in several series. ˈ**plurisetose** *a. Bot.* and *Zool.*, having many setæ or bristles (*Syd. Soc. Lex.*). **pluri'spiral** *a.*, having many spiral coils (*ibid.*). **plu'risporous** *a.*, having more than one spore (*ibid.*). **pluri'syllable,** a word of two or more syllables; hence **plurisy'llabic** *a.* ˈ**plurivalve** *a. Bot.* and *Zool.*, having several valves or appendages of valve-like form; multivalve (*ibid.*). **plu'rivorous** *a.* [L. *-vorus* devouring], living or feeding on hosts belonging to widely differing families, as a fungus.

1890 *Cent. Dict.*, *Pluricapsular. **1895** in *Syd. Soc. Lex.* **1884** BOWER & SCOTT *De Bary's Phaner.* 61 Among the branched forms,..those described under the unicellular hairs recur as *pluricellular. **1902** *Brit. Med. Jrnl.* 12 Apr. 908 Cancers either started from one centre (unicentral or monocentral), or from many centres (multicentral or *pluricentral). **1880** GÜNTHER *Fishes* 194 A jaw-like bar with *pluricuspid teeth. **1970** *Guardian Weekly* 14 May 12/1 The substitution of medium-sized *pluri-disciplinary universities for the existing monstrous faculties. **1972** *Science* 12 May 621/3 They would also be 'pluridisciplinary' which meant..that the universities would 'associate wherever possible arts and letters with sciences and technics'. **1979** *Guardian* 12 June 8/7 This is a pluri-disciplinary show—which means that all the arts are being covered. **1890** BILLINGS *Nat. Med. Dict.*, *Plurifetation. **1973** *Times* 28 May 9/6 The remarks regarding churchmanship can only be described as naive; most Anglicans know their Church to be *pluriform. **1974** *Times Lit. Suppl.* 22 Mar. 229/2 To say that all religions are equally true amounts to saying that all are equally false. But are not some more equal than others? Or is there a case for saying that truth can be pluriform? *Ibid.* 5 July 732/3 The New Testament writings are to be seen as pluriform. They were not composed..to produce a volume on a theme previously agreed. **1975** *Caribbean Contact* Feb. 4/3 One effective way of developing a pluriform approach in the context of the many needs of any single community is through the team ministry approach. **1947** *Theology* L. 419 The *pluriformity of the churches is undoubtedly a sin of Christendom. **1975** *Church Times* 21 Feb. 14/2 No small part of his achievement has been the fundamental preservation of orthodoxy, despite the extensive adoption of pluriformity in forms of worship. **1976** *Times* 21 Feb. 15/6 We, like our Latin brothers, have come to accept pluriformity in belief as much as in cultural tradition. **1938** I. GOLDBERG *Wonder of Words* p. vii, It was the curiosity born of this *pluri-lingual heritage that led me..to..a special interest in language. **1956** *Publ. Amer. Dial. Soc.* XXVI. 9 Strictly speaking, a bilingual..is one who knows two languages, but will here (as commonly) be used to include also the one who knows more than two, variously known, as a *plurilingual*, a *multilingual*, or a *polyglot.* **1962** Y. MALKIEL in Householder & Saporta *Probl. Lexicogr.* 11 Pluri-lingual dictionaries, which patently mark an increase in coverage. **1976** *Word 1971* XXVII. 407 The period of language 'acquisition' for plurilingual children is claimed to be longer than the period for monolingual children. **1971** *Incorporated Linguist* X. 42/1 Languages involved in societal systems of *plurilingualism tend to stabilize their roles on a basis of complementary distribution—either spatially, functionally, or both. **1828–32** WEBSTER, *Pluriliteral [*adj.* and *sb.*]. **1831** LEE *Hebr. Gram.* (1832) 221 On these pluriliteral verbs [etc.]. **1839** PAULI *Analecta Hebr.* xxviii. 209 It does not belong to the province of this book to trace the Pluri-literals..to their original roots. **1819** LINDLEY tr. *Richard's Obs. Fruits & Seeds* 83 Having the appearance of being *plurilocular, but proceeding from an unilocular ovarium. **1902** D. H. CAMPBELL *Univ. Text-bk. Bot.* v. 129 In many of the Phæosporeæ..there are formed the plurilocular sporangia. **1961** R. W. BUTCHER *New Illustr. Brit. Flora* I. 19 Sometimes several carpels..are united along the flat sides, so forming a plurilocular ovary of 2—many cells. **1969** F. E. ROUND *Introd. Lower Plants* iii. 44 Plurilocular sporangia may also occur on the sporophyte. **1949** WELLEK & WARREN *Theory of Lit.* iii. 25 The alternative to these seems some bi-modal or *pluri-modal truth. **1951** G. S. CARTER *Animal Evolution* i. 26 If for the specimens collected at one horizon we plot a variability curve.., the curve..should have an apex for each of the mixed populations (pluri-modal) if the population consists of distinct but mixed elements. **1976** *Word 1971* XXVII. 195 Verbal expression, however, is only one facet of the plurimodal (multichannel) process of interpersonal communication. **1881** *Times* 12 Mar. 11/2 M. Gambetta.. is thought to be anxious to return to the *plurinominal system of voting..while M. Grévy..adheres to the uninominal system. *Ibid.*, According to the alternative system of *scrutin de liste*, or plurinominal method of voting, the department is taken as the electoral unit. **188.** COUES in *Auk* VI. 320 (Cent. Dict.) Perceiving sundry objections to binomial, etc., some have sought to obviate them by using binominal, uninominal, plurinominal, etc. **1887** GÜNTHER in *Encycl. Brit.* XXII. 190/1 Small and *pluriserial on the upper parts of the body and tail, large and uniserial on the abdomen, and generally biserial on the lower side of the tail. **1884** BOWER & SCOTT *De Bary's Phaner.* 521 In general so arranged that the sieve-tubes form single, biseriate, or *pluriseriate, tangential rows. **1924** J. S. KENYON *Amer. Pronunc.* 30 A *Plurisyllable is a word of more than one syllable. **1934** WEBSTER 1897/3 Plurisyllable..plurisyllabic. **1965** *Amer. Speech* XL. 12 There is also *tsetse*..and a fair number of other plurisyllables. *Ibid.* 13 *Sclaff*..is less well known than plurisyllabic *sclerosis*..and *sclerotic.* **1899** *Nat. Sci.* Dec. 389 Professor Dietal..considers the question of their descent from one or more *plurivorous forms—forms, that is, which inhabited indifferently hosts belonging to the most different families of flowering plants.

pluriarc ('pluərɪɑːk). [a. Fr. (G. Montandon *La Généalogie des Instruments de Musique* (1919) 52), f. PLURI- + ARC.] A West African musical instrument made of a wooden resonator to which several curved rods holding taut strings are attached.

1961 A. BAINES *Musical Instruments* i. 46 When played it [*sc.* the bow lute] is held like a harp, giving it the impression of being a harp in which each string has a separate neck... The French word *pluriarc*..expresses this well. **1970** *Western Folklore* XXIX. 237 It must be considered possible that the..American instruments of more than one string derive from pluriarcs and trough zithers.

plurice, obs. form of PLEURISY.

‖**pluries** ('pluərɪiːz). *Law.* In full pluries capias. [L. = '(thou mayest take) several times': late L. *plūriēs* oftentimes, frequently, f. *plūs*, *plūr-* more, several.] The name given to a third writ of attachment, issued when the first (see CAPIAS) and second (see ALIAS *sb.* 2) prove ineffectual; so called from the Latin phrase *pluries capias* occurring in the first clause.

1444 *Rolls of Parlt.* V. 109/2 To award and directe the seide Writts of Pluries Capias and Exigent, to the Shiref. **1465** MARG. PASTON in *P. Lett.* II. 217 Your councell thynketh it were well don that ye gete an *allias* and a *pluries* that it myght be sent don to the scheryf and than he can mak non excuse. **1544** tr. *Littleton's Nat. Brev.* 19 If he make [nat] execution, then shal there go out a sicut alias..and after that one pluries. **1607** MIDDLETON *Phœnix* II. iii. F ij b, For all your *Demurres*, *Plures*, *Sursurarers*, which are all Longswords: that's Delaies: al the comfort is, in nine yeares a man may overthrowe you. **1769** BLACKSTONE *Comm.* IV. xxiv. 314 If he cannot be taken upon the first *capias*, a second, and a third shall issue, called an *alias* and a *pluries capias*.

† **pluri'farious**, *a. Obs. rare*$^{-0}$. [f. L. *plūrifārius* manifold, various (f. *plūs*, *plūr-* more: cf. *multifārius*) + -OUS.] Manifold, multifarious.

1656 BLOUNT *Glossogr.*, *Plurifarious*, of divers fashions.

† '**plurified**, *ppl. a. Obs.* [pa. pple. of a vb. *plurify, a. obs. F. *plurifier* (14th c. in Godef.), ad. med.L. *plūrificāre* to multiply, increase, f. *plūs*, *plūr-* more: see -FY.] *lit.* Made more than one, multiplied, multiple; hence *Eccl.* Holding a plurality of livings.

1590 [J. GREENWOOD] *Confer.* iii. 57 Endowed Curats.. are but the Parsons substitutes to help a dumbe or plurified Parson. **1603** H. CROSSE *Vertues Commw.* (1878) 85 What do they with these plurified liuings? **1604** H. JACOB *Reasons*, etc. 29 Plurified men may haue their 2 Benefices neare togither.

pluriparous (plʊ'rɪpərəs), *a.* [f. mod.L. *pluripar-us* (f. *plūs*, *plūr-* more + *-parus* bearing) + -OUS.]

1. *Zool.* Bringing forth two or more at a birth.

1882 OGILVIE cites H. SPENCER.

2. Being the mother of two or more children.

1890 in *Cent. Dict.* **1895** in *Syd. Soc. Lex.*

Hence **pluri'parity**, pluriparous state.

1890 in *Cent. Dict.* **1895** in *Syd. Soc. Lex.*

pluripotency (pluərɪ'pəʊtənsɪ). *Biol.* [ad. G. *pluripotenz*: see PLURI- and POTENCY.] The property of being pluripotential; = PLURIPOTENCE, PLURIPOTENTIALITY.

1927 *Biol. Abstr.* I. 217/1 The term pluripotency is used to describe the virtual ability possessed by every organism, under certain conditions, to strike out upon developmental paths deviating from the type. **1942** J. NEEDHAM *Biochem. & Morphogenesis* ii. 100 This condition of multiple potency of the parts of the early egg-cell has been termed pluripotency. **1974** *Cell* II. 166/1 To study the relationships between tumorigenicity, pluripotency, and growth control in vitro, eleven subclones of SIKR [*sc.* a cell line] were isolated in parallel.

pluripotent (pluərɪ'pəʊtənt), *a. Biol.* [f. PLURI- + POTENT *a.*[1] and *sb.*[2]] = next. Hence **pluri'potence** = PLURIPOTENCY.

1942 J. NEEDHAM *Biochem. & Morphogenesis* ii. 228 The retention of pluripotence through many cleavages, followed by separation of blastomeres. *Ibid.* iii. 435 They are at first pluripotent or relatively undetermined. **1963** J. W. LASH in M. Locke *Cytodifferentiation & Macromolecular Synthesis* 257 Even embryonic systems involving so-called 'pluripotent' reacting tissues are equational to the systems discussed in this paper. **1977** *Lancet* 26 Mar. 680/1 If we assume that the intrathymic stem-cells are really pluripotent and that their capacity to differentiate into various tissues is genetically controlled, this pattern of autoimmune pathogenesis need not be restricted to synaptic autoantigens and myasthenia.

pluripotential (pluərɪpəʊ'tɛnʃəl), *a. Biol.* [f. PLURI- + POTENTIAL *a.* and *sb.*] Of a cell, tissue, or organism: capable of developing in any of various directions; = *multipotential* s.v. MULTI- 1 a.

1925 *Arch. Neurol. & Psychiatry* (Chicago) XIII. 468 Phylogenetically considered, this structure is a pluripotential organ, which in some of the vertebrates has become differentiated as an eye. **1939** *Nature* 27 May 903/1 The lymphocyte may be regarded as a pluripotential element capable of differentiation along several lines, the particular one followed being dependent upon the individual requirements. **1962** *Lancet* 27 Jan. 207/1 Many have regarded it [*sc.* the small lymphocyte] as a mature cell which could not become anything else, while others have regarded it as a temporarily resting stage of a primitive pluripotential cell capable of active development under suitable conditions. **1974** *Nature* 11 Oct. 518/2 We have recently proposed that the proliferative compartment of foetal epidermis is built up by 'pluripotential' stem cells which are replaced by 'committed' stem cells during adolescence.

Hence ˌ**pluripotenti'ality** = PLURIPOTENCY.

1956 R. W. EVANS *Histol. Appearances of Tumours* xi. 165 The question of the pluripotentiality and transmutation of lymphocytes into other cells is considered by many authors to be concerned with the enigmatic disappearance of lymphocytes. **1971** *Jrnl. Immunol.* CVII. 1583 (*heading*) The pluripotentiality of mouse spleen lymphocytes.

pluripresence (ˌpluərɪ'prɛzəns). [f. L. *plūs*, *plūr-* more + PRESENCE.] Presence in more than one place at the same time.

1773 JOHNSON 7 May in *Boswell*, (*Toplady*) Does not their invocation of saints suppose omnipresence in the saints? (*Johnson*) No Sir, it supposes only pluri-presence. **1849** MACAULAY *Hist. Eng.* iv. I. 496 What was more impolitic than to reject the services of good soldiers, seamen, lawyers, diplomatists, financiers, because they hold unsound opinions about the number of the sacraments or the pluripresence of saints? **1865** LECKY *Ration.* I. i. 80 The miracle of trans-substantiation seems to destroy all the improbability of the pluri-presence of a human body.

plurisegmental (ˌpluərɪsɛg'mɛntəl), *a.* [f. PLURI- + SEGMENTAL *a.*] **1.** *Physiol.* That involves nerves from more than one segment of the spinal column.

1898 C. S. SHERRINGTON in *Phil. Trans. R. Soc.* B. CXC. 151 It follows..that the reflex centrifugal discharge of the spinal cord is pluri-segmental. **1924** *Amer. Jrnl. Physiol.* LXIX. 649 The data indicate for the frog a plurisegmental innervation such as Agduhr..has shown to exist in cats and rabbits. **1969** J. P. SWAZEY *Reflexes & Motor Integration* v. 95 It is the pluri-segmental character of the motor nucleus, as expressed by reciprocal innervation, which gives the limb its functional solidarity.

2. *Linguistics.* = SUPRASEGMENTAL *a.*

1964 R. H. ROBINS *Gen. Linguistics* 107 The most important features that must be treated as plurisegmental.. are stress, pitch, and general voice quality. **1965** *Language* XLI. 309 The Firthian distinction of phonematic units (with 'unisegmental..relevance'..) and prosodies (with 'plurisegmental relevance') is probably more acceptable to some old-fashioned Americans than the Chomsky-Halle treatment of all features as equal.

Hence ˌ**pluriseg'mentally** *adv.*

1930 *Jrnl. Physiol.* LXX. 210 Frogs which have been kept in the tank for several months and whose muscles are much atrophied, are likely to show a very low proportion of plurisegmentally innervated fibres. **1960** *Jrnl. Compar. Neurol.* CXV. 47/2 The neurons..occur plurisegmentally.

plurisie, -sy, obs. forms of PLEURISY.

plurisign ('pluərɪsaɪn). [f. PLURI- + SIGN *sb.*] A 'sign' or word used with more than one meaning simultaneously: opp. MONOSIGN. Hence **plurisig'nation**, **pluri'signative** *a.*, **pluri'signatively** *adv.* Also ˌ**plurisignifi'cation**.

1940 *Kenyon Rev.* II. 266 The atomic ingredient of poetic language tends to be the plurisign. *Ibid.* 268 We may distinguish three types of simultaneous plurisignation. *Ibid.* 282 There is also a third important dimension, which may be called the dimension of *plurisignative fullness*, or *poetic richness*. *Ibid.* 504 The realm of poetry-connotation-plurisignification. **1954** P. WHEELWRIGHT *Burning Fountain* iv. 61 The poetic symbol tends.. to be plurisignative. *Ibid.* vi. 106 In plurisignation, a single verbal expression carries two or more meanings simultaneously. *Ibid.* vii. 149 A serious metaphoric pun, a poetic plurisign. *Ibid.* x. 217 The directions of mythic reference which..make a tragic action plurisignatively meaningful. **1964** J. STONE *Legal System & Lawyers' Reasonings* i. 34 (*heading*) 'Law properly so-called' and plurisignation of words. **1965** *Encycl. Poetry* 760/1 The depth symbol tends to be *plurisignative*; which is to say, its intended meanings are likely to be more or less multiple, yet so fused as to produce an integral meaning which radically transcends the sum of the ingredient meanings.

‖**pluris petitio** ('pluərɪs pɪ'tɪʃɪəʊ). *Sc. Law.* [L. *petitio* asking, *plūris* of more.] The asking more judicially than is truly due.

1760 LD. KAMES *Equity* I. I. (1767) 226 It is admitted that where the *pluris petitio* is occasioned by an innocent error.. the adjudication ought to be supported as a security for what is justly due. **1838** W. BELL *Dict. Law Scot.* s.v., Where an adjudication is led for a larger sum than what is actually due to the adjudging creditor, it is said to be a *pluris petitio*. **1902** *Scotsman* 3 Jan. 7/3 It is not, I am afraid, a mere matter of pluris petitio. For it brings up at once a difficulty which goes to the substance of the demand.

† '**plurity**. *Obs. rare.* [ad. med.L. *plūritās*, f. *plūs*, *plūr-* more: see -ITY.] *prop.* Moreness (cf. PLURALITY II): but in quot. = PLURALITY 2.

1600 THYNNE *Epigrams* xiii. 1 Pruritie of wemenn.. Seekes pluritie of men to worke satisfaction.

plurivalent (pluərɪ'veɪlənt, pluə'rɪvələnt), *a.* [f. PLURI- + L. *valēnt-em*, pr. pple. of *valēre* to be worth.] = MULTIVALENT *a.*, *spec.* sense 2.

1905 E. B. WILSON in *Jrnl. Exper. Zoöl.* II. 374 In the case of compound or plurivalent chromosomes..McClung's term 'chromatid' may conveniently be applied to each of their univalent constituents. **1952** *Archivum Linguisticum* IV. 169 The sorting out of plurivalent words like G. *Preis* between 'prize' and 'price'. **1976** *Nature* 1-8 Jan. 57/1 Aggregation of the minute somatic single chromosomes to large plurivalent chromosomes prevents mistakes in meiotic distribution.

pluri-valued (pluərɪ'væljuːd), *a. Logic.* Also **plurivalued**. [f. PLURI- + VALUED *ppl. a.*] Of a system of logic: using truth values in addition to those of true and false; many-valued.

1939 R. CARNAP *Found. Logic & Math.* in *Internat. Encycl. Unified Sciences* I. III. §12. 28 The systems of plurivalued logic as constructed by Lukasiewicz and Tarski, etc. **1949** A. PAP *Elements Anal. Philos.* v. 105 Is it possible to construct a logic which does not assume that every proposition is either true or false ('pluri-valued logic')? **1969** N. RESCHER *Many-Valued Logic* i. 10 Two interesting procedures for creating new pluri-valued logics out of old ones—the methods of system *extension* and of forming the *product* of two systems—have been devised by Stanislaw Jaśkowski. *Ibid.* ii. 83 The prospect remains that two-valued logic is somehow fundamental to the construction of all systems of pluri-valued logic in general.

plurocentral, erron. f. *pluricentral*: see PLURI-.

plurry ('plʌrɪ), *a.* and *adv. Austral.* and *N.Z. slang.* [Maori corruption of BLOODY *a.* and *adv.*] = BLOODY *a.* 10, *adv.* 2.

1900 H. LAWSON *Verses, Pop. & Humorous* 227 And their language that day, I am sorry to say, Mostly consisted of 'plurry'. **1916** *Anzac Book* 137 By this time, being the twelfth month of the same year, it waxed 'plurry' cold, even unto a fall of snow. **1933** H. G. WELLS *Bulpington of Blup* vi. 239 Gawd save us from any plurry mucking pushes. *Ibid.* 242 You're plurry well doing too much with your mouth... *Shut* it! **1938** R. D. FINLAYSON *Brown Man's Burden* 31 It's all right for Pakeha's to spout about Maori art but it won't help me to get manure for my plurry cow farm. **1959** *News Chron.* 6 July 4/2 'You watch your plurry step, man,' he said. 'We know your plurry kind.' **1966** G. W. TURNER *Eng. Lang. in Austral. & N.Z.* x. 200 The literary convention of Maori English interlarded with *plurry*..belongs to the language of journalists rather than the language of Maoris. **1977** *Sunday Times* 3 July 28/7 I'll bowl a plurry sight faster if they'd let me take my boots off.

plus (plʌs). [a. L. *plūs* more. As in the case of MINUS (q.v.), the quasi-prepositional sense 1 did not exist in Latin, but the words *plus* and *minus* were used by Leonardo of Pisa in 1202 for the excess and deficiency in the results of two suppositions in the Rule of Double Position.

The signs + and − are used, app. as well-known signs, in the *Behende und hübsche Rechnung auf allen Kauffmannschafft* of Joh. Widmann 1489 (and subseq. edd. to 1526); but while he refers to the latter as *minus*, the former is said to stand for *mer* (i.e. *mehr*) 'was − ist, das ist minus, und das + ist das mer'. So far as yet collected, English examples of *plus* do not occur so early as those of *minus*.

As to the origin of the symbol +, various conjectures have been made; perhaps the most likely is that it originated in the MS. abbreviation of the L. *et* 'and' (which Leonardo always uses in his additions). Cantor *Vorlesungen über Geschichte der Mathematik* (1899) II. 230–1, from which these facts are mainly taken, cites, from mathematical MSS. of the beginning of the 15th c., and a non-mathematical MS. of the beginning of the 14th, a form of & = *et* which might easily pass into +.]

1. a. quasi-*prep.* Placed between two expressions of number or quantity to indicate that the second is to be added to the first. In mathematical use only as the oral rendering of the symbol +. Hence, in non-technical use: With the addition of; with... besides. (Opp. to MINUS 1.)

1668 [see 4]. **1674** PETTY *Disc. Dupl. Proportion* 58 Four like Rowers shall move the same Vessel.. 12000 feet, in 1800 seconds *plus* 360 seconds, or in all 2160 seconds. **1727–41** CHAMBERS *Cycl.* s.v. *Character*, It [+] is also the sign of addition, and is read *plus*, or *more*; thus 9 + 3 is read 9 *plus* 3, or 9 more 3; that is, 9 added to 3, or the sum of 9 and 3, equal to 12. **1823** J. KEBLE *Let.* in G. Battiscombe *John Keble* (1963) iv. 71 A deaf handmaid, and a clerk-plus-gardener-plus-groom by no means dumb. **1848** MILL *Pol. Econ.* II. xii. §4 (1872) 224/1 Wages plus the allotment. **1850** GROVE *Corr. Phys. Forces* (ed. 2) 86 A compound of one equivalent of hydrogen plus two of oxygen. **1891** *Law Rep.*, *Weekly Notes* 58/1 The same sum as that stated in the balance order, *plus* further interest. **1922** JOYCE *Ulysses* 642 A cup of Epp's cocoa and a shakedown for the night plus the use of a rug or two and overcoat doubled into a pillow. **1961** B. FERGUSSON *Watery Maze* xiv. 348 No. 1 Special Service Brigade under Lovat had one Marine and three Army Commandos, plus Lovat's personal piper. **1966** *Oxf. Univ. Gaz.* 23 Dec. 430/1 Just a reference from one meeting of Congregation to another slightly different meeting of Congregation, plus a few alumni. **1974** E. AMBLER *Dr Frigo* III. 190 There..was a..plane waiting plus an army scout car and a guard of soldiers. **1975** N. LUARD *Travelling Horseman* xiv. 247 That meant me plus Billy to drive me. It was a two-part job.

b. *predicatively.* †(*a*) Abundantly supplied *with*, containing an excess of something (*obs. rare*$^{-1}$); (*b*) *colloq.* Having (something) in addition, having gained (opp. to MINUS 1 b).

1807 VANCOUVER *Agric. Devon* (1813) 462 In all chalky soils, and such as are plus with the calcareous principle. **1856** KANE *Arct. Expl.* I. xii. 132 Bonsall was minus a big toe-nail, and plus a scar upon the nose.

c. *ellipt.* Placed after a round number or a whole number to indicate a smaller or fractional amount more; with a positive amount added; or more, but not less. Also to indicate a slightly higher grade, as ***beta plus*** (β+). Also *colloq.* after other sbs. to indicate with extra qualities, better than usual.

[**1902**: see ALPHA 4.] **1916** A. HUXLEY *Let.* 19 Mar. (1969) 94 Beta double plus is quite adequate for language. **1927** *Rep. Consultative Comm. Educ. Adolescent* 185 Raising the school age to 15 plus must lead either to the building of new schools or to the remodelling of existing schools. **1928** *Oxford Mag.* 25 Oct. 40 Till the University finds some benefactor willing to give '£100,000 plus' (to use modern phraseology). *a* **1930** D. H. LAWRENCE *Collier's Friday Night* i. 20, I generally get an alpha plus. That's the highest, you know, mater. **1951** WODEHOUSE *Old Reliable* x. 120 You were right in mid-season form. It was battling plus. **1958** L. VAN DER POST *Lost World Kalahari* vi. 104 'This,' I thought before sleeping, 'is Alpha Plus.' **1962** *Listener* 18 Jan. 112/2 To put forward a positive conception of coexistence—we might call it coexistence 'plus'—which includes as its principal ingredient the central idea..of *ideological* coexistence. **1962** *Guardian* 5 Dec. 6/4 Everything you could possibly want in make-up plus, for 1s 6d a time. **1966** *Listener* 30 June 951/2 Many of these can now be walled off, but not Garrincha of Brazil, who on his day is Stanley Matthews plus. **1972** J. MOSEDALE *Football* ii. 21 The $225-plus material worn by Kansas City tackle Buck Buchanan. **1973** P. MOYES *Curious Affair of Third Dog* i. 10 The Second World War, an unbelievable thirty-plus years ago. **1978** *Jrnl. R. Soc. Arts* CXXVI. 617/2 It will be a hundred years plus before we have a significant contribution.

d. quasi-*conj.* And in addition. *colloq.* (chiefly *N. Amer.*).

1968 N. GIOVANNI in W. King *Black Short Story Anthol.* (1972) 26 If, on the other hand, a tom tells you to get off the streets and you don't..plus if you can encourage him in a physical way to come on over to your side, then you've made a friend. **1972** C. L. COOPER in *Ibid.* 210 There was rain on the roof, and I was poor. Plus my mother was sick. **1973** *Black World* Jan. 63/2 All the ladies brought pies and cakes. .. Plus they had coffee and tea and punch. **1974** *Sci. Amer.* Jan. 1/1 (Advt.), Initial cost of our centerline design (WX 200) is $200K instead of the $600K of equivalent current models, plus it will deliver 100 hours MTBF (mean time between failures). **1974** *Maclean's Mag.* Dec. 16/2 But after all is said and done, take away the football game itself from the Grey Cup and what have you got? An early start home, for one thing. Plus you save maybe $30 on tickets. **1977** *Ripped & Torn* vi. 8/2, I was stereotyped as nothing but a drag act. Plus I was tired of doing it. **1978** *Daily Tel.* 9 Feb. 2 (Advt.), W. H. Smith have big names at big savings. Plus you get one year manufacturer's guarantee. **1978** *Detroit Free Press* 2 Apr. 6E/4 Plus they've added pitchers Rudy May and Ross Grimsley.

2. a. As the oral rendering of the sign + in its algebraical use to denote a positive quantity, as + *x*, read *plus x*. Hence *attrib.* or *adj.* in ***plus quantity***, a quantity having the sign + prefixed (or not having the sign −), a positive quantity. (Only as opp. to MINUS 2, 2 b.)

1579 [see MINUS 2]. **1975** *Times* 15 Jan. 20/4 A 230-volt standard for electrical supplies throughout Europe was agreed yesterday... The new level has a tolerance of plus or minus 10 per cent.

b. *Electr.* (*a*) *adv.* Positively. (*b*) *adj.* Positive; positively electrified. (Opp. to MINUS 2 d.)

1747 [see MINUS 2 d]. **1789** NICHOLSON in *Phil. Trans.* LXXIX. 279 When the one ball was electrified *plus* and the other *minus*, the signs of both electricities appeared. If the interval was not too great, the long zig-zag spark of the *plus* ball struck to the strait flame of the *minus* ball. **1849** NOAD *Electricity* (ed. 3) 112 The small residuary charge will be *plus.* **1854** J. SCOFFERN in *Orr's Circ. Sc., Chem.* 225 Electrified + or plus.

3. a. *adj.* Additional, extra.

1756 AMORY *Buncle* (1770) II. 79 When they are abroad, it is at a plus-expense. **1869** *Daily News* 19 May, Somehow or other no Bill securing the tenant the plus-value added to the land by his labour and industry has yet been passed. **1891** *Labour Commission* Gloss., *Plus System*, also called 'bonus' system, is one by which a certain proportion of wages, called 'subsistence money', is paid every day, and the remainder on the completion of the job or contract. This remainder is called the *plus*, or 'contingent money'. **1894** *Westm. Gaz.* 3 May 5/1 After a ship was discharged, there was generally 8s. or 9s. for the men to receive as 'plus' money. **1897** *Ibid.* 18 Feb. 8/1 The disposal of the 'plus values', that is, surplus of the revenues assigned to the service of the debt. **1928** *Publishers' Weekly* 30 June 2598 The material for the plus sale is always at hand in the book business. **1930** *Publishers' Circular* 2 Aug. 163/2 The whole book business should look on the reprint business as being *plus* business.

b. In various games, having an adverse handicap of a number of strokes or points.

1908 A. W. MYERS *Compl. Lawn Tennis Player* 127 It will not take him long to discover the kind of decoy that will deliver the 'plus 15.3' men into his clutches. **1909** *Westm. Gaz.* 8 Feb. 12/4 Supposing a plus 3 man is partnered with a steady player whose handicap is 8, the two as a foursome side would be handicapped at 5. **1922** J. CANNAN *Misty Valley* 203 Isn't it just like you to come up to the club-house ..and to send a plus man in to fetch me out? **1927** R. J. B. SELLAR *Play!* 32 The newly-joined member..asked if they might have a game together. 'Humph,' growled the plus player, 'perhaps. What's your handicap?'

c. Of superior quality; excellent of its kind.

1960 *Times* 10 Dec. 7/6 The country was surveyed to find 'plus trees' (superior examples of all useful species). **1968** *Globe & Mail* (Toronto) 17 Feb. 45 (Advt.), Living room, 15' dining room are plus features!

4. *sb.* in various applications. **a.** The mathematical symbol +; also ***plus sign***. Also *fig.* and in sense 4 d below. **b.** A quantity added; something additional or extra; an addition, a gain. **c.** A positive quantity (also *fig.*). Opp. to MINUS 3. **d.** An advantage.

1654 [see MINUS 3]. **1668** BRANCKER *Introd. Algebra* 3 The Sign for Addition is + i.e. *Plus*, more. **1685, 1708** [see MINUS 3]. **1727–41** CHAMBERS *Cycl.* s.v. *Addition*, The character of Addition is +, which we usually express by *plus*. [*Ibid.*, *Positive quantities* are design'd by the character + prefixed to them, or supposed to be prefixed.] **1791** H. WALPOLE *Let.* 26 July (1905) XV. 25 The villain Paine..is engaged in a controversy with the Abbé Sieyès, about the *plus* or *minus* of the rebellion. **1836** E. HOWARD *R. Reefer* xxvi, A slate-full of plusses, minusses. **1843** MILL *Logic* v. vii. §2 (1856) II. 396 *Minus* multiplied by *plus* gives *minus*, and *minus* multiplied by *minus* cannot give the same product as *minus* multiplied by *plus*. **1862** RUSKIN *Unto this Last* 131 The *plus* quantities, or—if I may be allowed to coin an awkward plural—the *pluses*, make a very positive and venerable appearance in the world. **1891** *Daily News* 7 Jan. 3/1 Representatives of the dockers watched over their interests in the matters of labour, pay, and 'plus'. **1902** W. JAMES *Varieties Relig. Exper.* 166 Peace cannot be reached by the simple addition of pluses and elimination of minuses from life. **1943** *Sun* (Baltimore) 12 Feb. 17/1 American Telephone was up 1⅞, and lesser plus signs were retained by Radio Corporation, Johns-Manville, Goodrich and United States Gypsum. **1959** *Washington Post* 20 July A 6/1 Radio city is one block from the Hotel Victoria. Other location plusses: Madison Square Garden is two blocks away, so are all subways. **1964** G. C. KUNZLE *Parallel Bars* ix. 403 Its great plus is the fact that the superior difficulty is the dismount. **1971** *Guardian* 25 Nov. 15/4 Those whom Mr Blond has published are treated as human beings... This is a major plus in his favour. **1972** *Sci. Amer.* Jan. 83/2 The superscript plus sign denotes a positive ion. **1972** *Business Week* 18 Mar. 20/2 The ability to offer assurances of such long-range supplies..is a big plus for U.S. equipment builders. **1974** T. ALLBEURY *Snowball* xviii. 104 The friction between the governments—it's a plus but it's a side issue. **1975** *Daily Tel.* 4 Jan. 10 Fiction is not on the wane, but actually registered a plus in the number of books published in 1974. **1975** *Publishers Weekly* 31 Mar. 47/1 There are items here..that will interest only a handful of people west of Manhattan. But there are compensating plusses. **1975** *Studies in Eng. Lit.: Eng. Number* (Tokyo) 44 In Table 9 the frequency of occurrence is indicated by means of figures appended to plus signs (like + 1) for constructions which are themselves rare. **1976** *Evening Post* (Nottingham) 15 Dec. 24/7 But Glaxo 383p, Fisons 288p, Tubes 290p, and GEC 163p, still showed small plus signs. **1976** *Early Music* Oct. 382/2 Could..the same reader get something from an article on..the pluses and minuses of using gut strings? **1977** *Time* 7 Mar. 49/2 The scenery and the costumes..are a dazzling plus. **1978** C. BLACK *Asterisk Destiny* (1979) v. 122 All I am..is the plus sign in a necessary equation.

‖**5.** ***plus minus*** [late L.]: more or less. *Obs.*

1615 CORYAT *Crudities*, etc. (1776) III. Lijb, The Persians [revenues are] fiue millions *plus minus.* **1650** TRAPP *Comm. Gen.* i. 1 There were two thousand years, *plus minus*, before the law.

6. Special Combs.: **plus juncture** *Linguistics* = *open juncture* s.v. OPEN *a.* 22 c; **plus word**, a word which is characteristic of its user, or is used frequently.

1951 TRAGER & SMITH *Outl. Eng. Struct.* 68 Within each phonemic phrase the constituents delimited by *plus-junctures are noted. **1964** E. BACH *Introd. Transformational Gram.* vi. 129 One can save the situation by positing a phoneme of internal open juncture ('plus-juncture'). **1972** HARTMANN & STORK *Dict. Lang. & Linguistics* 241/2 Open transition (open juncture),..often called plus juncture, which occurs at a word boundary. **1976** *Amer. Speech 1974* XLIX. 15 Predictable pitch contours are not marked here and 'plus juncture' is indicated by conventional spacing. **1959** N. N. HOLLAND *First Mod. Comedies* vi. 53 'Solid' became a '*plus' word because it suggested realness, the mass and volume the new physics could measure. **1962** A. ELLEGÅRD *Statisical Method for Determining Authorship* ii. 12 The typical, characteristic words of the writer—we shall ..call his 'plus words'. **1963** *Times Lit. Suppl.* 25 Jan. 67/2 Words and expressions that were used particularly frequently (plus-words).

plusage ('plʌsɪdʒ). Also **plussage.** [f. PLUS + -AGE.] **a.** (See quot. 1932). **b.** Something extra or added on; a bonus; a surcharge.

A word of restricted currency.—R.W.B.

1932 *N. & Q.* 30 Jan. 82/2, I have seen in print the word 'plus(s)age' used to denote a plurality of pluses in a collective sense, i.e., (15 per cent. plus 10 per cent. plus 15 per cent.) total plussage of 40 per cent. **1935** A. P. HERBERT *What a Word!* iii. 83 From a well-known London shop: 'Should your order not exceed the sum of 17/6 an additional *plusage* of 25% will be charged.' **1959** *Times* 3 Nov. 13/4 When I took up a part-time job three weeks ago I was given a card with which to 'clock in' and 'out'. Among the list of payments was a heading 'Any further plusages'. **1962** *Engineering* 10 Aug. 181 Normal day rate together with a plusage for reaching a certain level of output. **1966** *New Statesman* 22 Apr. 563/1 A woman catcher's rate on a cigarette-making machine, for instance, is about £3 a week less than a man's, although the bonus or 'plussage' for both is equal.

‖**plus ça change** (plʏ sa ʃɑ̃ʒ). In full, ***plus ça change, plus c'est la même chose.*** [Fr., 'the more it changes, the more it stays the same'.] A semi-proverbial phrase, expressing the fundamental immutability of human nature, institutions, etc. Hence **plus ça change-ness** *nonce.*

[**1849** A. KARR in *Les Guêpes* Sér. 6 (new ed.) 1859 Janv. 305 [After comment on recent political events in France] Après tant de bouleversements, de changements, il serait temps de s'apercevoir d'une chose, c'est que c'est comme au cabaret:—cachet vert, cachet rouge, etc.—On change quelquefois le prix, quelquefois le bouchon, mais c'est toujours la même piquette qu'on nous fait boire.—Plus ça change—plus c'est la même chose.] **1903** G. B. SHAW *Man & Superman* 182 The mere transfiguration of institutions, as from military and priestly dominance to commercial and scientific dominance, from commercial dominance to proletarian democracy,..are all but changes from Tweedledum to Tweedledee: *plus ça change, plus c'est la même chose.* **1955** *Times* 5 July 11/4 We have an uneasy suspicion that there is something to be said for the epic angle on history. After all, when boy met—or meets—girl, *plus ça change.* **1959** 'J. BYROM' *Take only as Directed* i. 8 'I don't like being out of date!' '*Plus ça change,*' I said. **1966** *New Statesman* 2 Sept. 306/1 Meanwhile it is a sort of lottery whether a murderer is hanged or not... Out of seven capital sentences passed at the Winter Assizes 1871/1872, *only one* was carried out. *Plus ça change. Ibid.* 312/3 Browsing in my current bedside book, *The Paston Letters*, I have been struck by the *plus ça change*-ness of the human animal. **1969** R. BLYTHE *Akenfield* 15 Where the strict village existence is concerned it is *Plus ça change, plus c'est la même chose.* **1970** W. GARNER *Puppet-Masters* i. 14 *Plus ça change*—! The present French government's simply following tradition. **1978** *Language* LIV. 383 For both theories, then, plus ça change, plus c'est la même chose; and, interestingly, the même chose of each turns out to be the même chose for both.

‖**plus-chaud,** *a. Obs.* Also **plusechaud.** [F. (plyʃo) hotter.] Extra hot.

1362 LANGL. *P. Pl.* A. vii. 299 Bote hit weore Fresch Flesch or elles Fisch I-Friȝet, Boþe chaud and pluschaud for chele of heore Mawe. *c* **1380** *Antecrist* in Todd 3 *Treat. Wyclif* 130 Metes of þe best..well diȝt wiþ spicerie chaud and plusechaud.

plus-foured (plʌs'fɔəd), *a.* [f. next + -ED².] Wearing or clad in plus fours.

1925 *N. & Q.* 28 Nov. 387/2 In *Truth* of Oct. 14 a writer ventured 'plus-foured'. **1926** *Daily Chron.* 13 May 2/2 'I'll be sorry to leave the old bus tonight,' said the plus foured pull-overed youth at the wheel of the 'General' yesterday afternoon. **1934** C. LAMBERT *Music Ho!* iv. 242 A begoggled, leather-coated and plus-foured figure. **1967** O. LANCASTER *Eye to Future* iii. 64 The hearties, grey flannel-trousered or elaborately plus-foured. **1978** *Daily Tel.* 21 Jan. 9/1 On Saturday morning he stands tweedily plus-foured beside a gate, serving as honorary secretary of the beagles.

plus fours (plʌs 'fɔəz). [f. PLUS 3 + FOUR *a.* and *sb.*, since, to produce the overhang, four inches is normally added to the length required for ordinary knickerbockers.] A distinctive style of long, wide knickerbockers, or a suit having such knickerbockers, originally much worn by golfers and associated with outdoor pursuits. Also *transf.* and *attrib.* (Also in form ***plus-four***).

1920 *Isis* 25 Feb. 6/2 (*caption*) 'Plus Fours'. *Ibid.* 12 May 10/2 The desuetude of the traditional grey flannel 'bags' of the undergraduate... 'Plus fours' have succeeded them. **1921** *Isis* 1 June p. xii, Knicker (plus four) Suits from 8½ gns. **1922** J. CANNAN *Misty Valley* 201 A tall man in plus fours and a yellow waistcoat. **1923** S. HERD *My Golfing Life* 151 The first time I saw a golfer wearing baggy 'plus 4's' I thought he looked like a lassie. **1928** *Sat. Evening Post* 10 Mar. 174/3 You can almost visualize the venerable Francis Joseph tweaking away at his plus-four whiskers. **1929** H. A. VACHELL *Virgin* ix. 154 The Major got himself up 'to kill', wearing a new suit of 'plus fours'. **1934** G. B. SHAW *Village Wooing* ii. 119 He is in hiking costume..but wears well cut breeches (not plus fours) instead of shorts. **1939** JOYCE *Finnegans Wake* (1964) i. 30 In topee, surcingle, solascarf and plaid, plus fours, puttees and bulldog boots. **1951** N. M. GUNN *Well at World's End* xix. 152 He wore a plusfour suiting of discreet checks and unpronounced bagginess. **1961** C. WILLOCK *Death in Covert* i. 13 He wore knicker-bocker trousers that..were nearly plus-fours: say, plus-threes. **1972** *Country Life* 12 Oct. 926/2 Rust battle-jacket with plus-fours in Shetland tweed. By Christian Dior Monsieur. **1974** 'P. B. YUILL' *Bornless Keeper* ii. 19 Wood-pigeons strutted like fat old squires in plus fours. **1978** G. SIMS *Rex Mundi* xxvi. 156 He was dressed in a brown plus-fours suit.

plush (plʌʃ), *sb.* and *a.* [ad. F. *pluche*, contracted form of *peluche* a hairy fabric, shag, plush = OSp. *peluza*, mod.Sp. *pelusa* down on fruit, nap on cloth, velvet, Cat. *pelussa* down on fruit (cf. It. *peluccio*, *peluzzo* a little hair, soft down, fine hair), f. late L. type **pilūceus*, *-ea*, f. L. *pilus* hair.]

A. *sb.* **1. a.** A kind of cloth, of silk, cotton, wool, or other material (or of two of these combined), having a nap longer and softer than that of velvet; used for rich garments (esp. footmen's liveries), upholstery, etc. In quot. 1633, taken as the typical livery of the 'fool' or clown.

1594 NASHE *Unfort. Trav.* 50 The trappings of his horse were pounced and bolstered out with rough plumed siluer plush. *c* **1611** CHAPMAN *Iliad* xxiv. 338 Wast coats of silke plush laying by. *a* **1626** BACON *New Atl.* (1650) 25 He sate alone, upon Cushions, of a kinde of excellent Plush, blew. **1633** SHIRLEY *Bird in Cage* v. i, All places he is free of, and fooles it without blushing At Maskes and Playes, is not the Bayes thrust out, to let the plush in. **1682** N. O. *Boileau's Lutrin* iv. 71 A fair silk Cassock, richly lin'd with Plush. **1784** COWPER *Task* i. 11 As yet black breeches were not, satin smooth, Or velvet soft, or plush with shaggy pile. **1882** BECK *Draper's Dict.* s.v., Plush may be described roughly as long-napped velvet, and any kind of stuff may be used in its manufacture—cotton, silk, wool, any kind of hair, or even swansdown.

b. *pl.* Plush breeches (as worn by footmen).

1844 J. T. HEWLETT *Parsons & W.* xxiv, A footman in green plushes and a powdered head. **1852** R. S. SURTEES

Sponge's Sp. Tour (1893) 14 His lace-bedaubed coat, gold-gartered plushes and stockings.

c. Colloq. phr. *on* (or *in*) (*the*) *plush*: in comfortable circumstances.

1930 WODEHOUSE *Very Good, Jeeves* ix. 226 He was, to all appearances, absolutely on plush. He ate well, slept well, was happily married. **1945** *Richmond* (Va.) *Times-Dispatch* 23 Mar. 20/3 Morgenthau..made it plain that the drive would be aimed chiefly against 'the boys who live in the plush' rather than the small taxpayer.

2. *transf.* A natural substance likened to the preceding.

a **1619** FLETCHER *Knt. Malta* I. i, O my black swan, sleeker than signet's plush. **1635** QUARLES *Embl.* III. xiii. (1718) 177 The proud summer-meadow, which to day Wears her green plush, and is to morrow hay. **1688** R. HOLME *Armoury* II. 117/1 Plush [is] the middle of.. Marigolds, &c., of some termed.. Thrummy heads; of others Hairy heads. **1862** JOHNS *Brit. Birds* (1874) 56 Eggs, from which emerge.. bodies enveloped in a soft plush of grey yarn.

3. *attrib.* and *Comb.* **a.** *attrib.*, usually in sense Made or consisting of plush; also, of or pertaining to plush. Also, covered or upholstered in plush. (In quots. 1629, *a* 1640. Clad in plush.)

1629 B. JONSON *New Inn, Ode to Himself*, Brave plush and velvet-men. *a* **1640** DAY *Parl. Bees* To Rdr. (1881) 9 Some Plush-Midas that can read no further But 'Bees'. *c* **1645** HOWELL *Lett.* (1650) II. 28 They unmantled him of a new plush cloak. **1787** 'G. GAMBADO' *Acad. Horsem.* (1809) 31 Riding in black plush breeches. **1848** THACKERAY *Bk. Snobs* vii, Pea-green plush inexpressibles. **1895** *Montgomery Ward Catal.* 113/1 Silk plush work box with silvered center and corner ornaments. **1926** E. O'NEILL *Great God Brown* I. iii. 89 At the left is a bald-spotted crimson plush chair. **1935** R. MACAULAY *Personal Pleasures* 135 Pointing us to seats in the middle of an eagerly gazing row of persons, past whom we push, to subside into plush chairs and eagerly gaze too. **1935** *Punch* 4 Sept. 256/2 And, what is more, though you were seeing it in comfort from a plush seat, it was nearly as good as if you had been energetic and enthusiastic enough to go to Victoria. **1976–7** *Hamley's Catal.* 66/3 A fully jointed soft plush teddy.

b. *Comb.*, as ***plush-weaver***; ***plush-bottomed***, ***-bound***, ***-capped***, ***-clad***, ***-coloured***, ***-covered***, ***-fitted***, ***-framed***, ***-lined***, ***-wearing*** adjs.; **plush-copper** (see quot.); **plush horse**, used as a symbol of ostentation and over-elaborateness; also *attrib.*; **plush-stitch**, a kind of stitch in worsted or wool work, forming projecting loops which can be cut so as to make a long nap as in plush; **plush-velvet**, a kind of plush with short nap, resembling velvet; **plush-velveteen**, a cotton plush imitating silk plush as velveteen does velvet.

1901 CONRAD & HUEFFER *Inheritors* xiii. 210, I sat on a *plush-bottomed gilded chair. **1902** CONRAD *Typhoon* xxiii. 185 She reclined in a plush-bottomed and gilt hammock-chair near a tiled fireplace. **1912** C. MACKENZIE *Carnival* xxxiv. 347 These..were now propped dismally against the overmantel, individually obscured..by a plush-bound photograph of Mr. Lloyd George. **1876** G. M. HOPKINS *Wreck of Deutschland* xiii, in *Poems* (1967) 54 How a lush-kept *plush-capped sloe Will, mouthed to flesh-burst, Gush! **1913** C. MACKENZIE *Sinister Street* I. II. vii. 259 He saw..*plush-clad children who continually dropped Sunday-school books in the mud. **1927** A. CONAN DOYLE *Case Bk. Sherlock Holmes* i. 38 A butler..handed me over to a plush-clad footman, who ushered me into the Baron's presence. **1678** T. JORDAN *Triumphs Lond.* 7 A Sky-colour'd Scarf Fringed with Silver, *Plush-colour'd Hose. **1881** RAYMOND *Mining Gloss.*, **Plush-copper*, chalcotrichite, a fibrous red copper ore. **1882** MISS BRADDON *Mt. Royal* II. iv. 58 In the spacious *plush-covered chair. **1938** L. MACNEICE *Zoo* 227 *Plush-fitted theatres. **1937** E. SITWELL *I live under Black Sun* 98 A *plush-framed photograph. **1922** S. LEWIS *Babbitt* ii. 23 Just compare a real human like you and these neurotic birds like Lucile McKelvey—all high-brow talk and dressed up like a *plush horse. **1936** J. DOS PASSOS *Big Money* 201 What I'd love more than anything in the world would be to get out and make my own living. I hate this plushhorse existence. **1946** P. LARKIN *Jill* 184 The competition is very keen, because they're very, very *plush-lined jobs. **1848** W. H. KELLY tr. *L. Blanc's Hist. Ten Y.* II. 252 The *plush-weavers..took into consideration a general stoppage of the looms.

B. *adj.* Luxurious, expensive, stylish. *colloq.*

1927 in Wentworth & Flexner *Dict. Amer. Slang* (1960) 398/2 'Plush' indicates..stylish. **1934** M. H. WESEEN *Dict. Amer. Slang* 192 *Plush*, stylish. **1944** 'P. QUENTIN' *Puzzle for Puppets* xix. 141 We had the plushest hotel suite of any married couple in San Francisco. **1946** *Richmond* (Va.) *Times-Dispatch* 30 Oct. 1/2 The recently established plush eating place. **1952** W. R. BURNETT *Vanity Row* (1953) v. 48 'Apartment address?' asked Roy. Joe gave it to him. 'H'm' said Roy. '..Pretty plush.' **1955** *Bull. Atomic Sci.* Feb. 51/2 These need not be plush or elaborate shelters. **1959** *Sunday Express* 1 Feb. 19/6 The word 'Set' in this context is an economic symbol—a plush version of what humbler people call 'The Gang'. **1959** H. HOBSON *Mission House Murder* ii. 8 The sales-minded débutante who was earning pin-money in the plush establishment. **1971** *Guardian* 28 May 8/2 It was really plush, with 25 waitresses. **1978** *New York* 3 Apr. 27/1 Plush place with excellent service, a great chef, and strolling guitarist-singer.

plush, *v.* *nonce-wd.* [f. prec. sb.] **a.** *intr.* Of velvet: To have the nap crushed or flattened by pressure or wet. **b.** *to plush it*: to wear plush, i.e. to act as footman.

1867 W. H. L. TESTER *Poems* 54 He plush'd it there for many a day. **1904** *Daily Chron.* 1 Sept. 8/5 Corduroy velvet would certainly look well, but it would be less suitable than the woollen on account of its greater weight and liability to 'plush' with damp or pressure.

plushed (plʌʃt), *a.* [f. PLUSH *sb.* + -ED².]

a. Made with a long nap like plush. **b.** Clad in plush, wearing plush. **c.** Of velvet, etc.: Having the pile crushed or flattened.

1594 NASHE *Unfort. Trav.* Wks. (Grosart) V. 171 Hidden vnder cloth rough plushed and wouen like eglantine and woodbine. **1835** *Blackw. Mag.* XXXVII. 438 The plushed poacher pursuing the ptarmigan. **1853** SOYER *Pantroph.* 368 The Latins used a sort of thick, plushed, cloth.

†**'plusher.** *dial. Obs.* [app. f. **plush* vb., in mod.Cornish dial. *plosh* to plunge or splash in water or mud; cf. *plosher* a half-grown bream.] Some kind of sea fish.

1602 CAREW *Cornwall* 34 The Pilcherd are pursued and devoured by a bigger Kinde of fish, called a Plusher, being somewhat like the Dog-fish.

plushery ('plʌʃərɪ). *U.S. Show-business slang.* [f. PLUSH *sb.* + -ERY.] (See quots.)

1951 GREEN & LAURIE *Show Biz* 570/2 *Plushery*, class joint (hotel, nitery, eatery). **1961** A. BERKMAN *Singers' Gloss. Show Business Jargon* 69 *Plushery*,..a classy restaurant or night club.

plushette (plʌ'ʃɛt). [f. PLUSH *sb.* + -ETTE: cf. *flannelette*, etc.] An inferior kind of plush.

1887 *Queen* 29 Oct. 558/2 Your plushette is a lovely colour. **1893** MRS. T. COKE *Gentlew. at Home* vi. 87 Curtains ..of Indian red plushette.

plushly ('plʌʃlɪ), *adv.* [f. PLUSH *a.* + -LY².] Richly, sumptuously, elegantly.

1951 W. SANSOM *Face of Innocence* iii. 34 In all her attitudes—stretching and crossing her long legs,..finding a green background to burn plushly behind her white profile—she was assured. **1959** *Observer* 30 Aug. 11/7 There it [*sc.* a countryside] all is, laid out so plushly for mile after mile. **1971** *Daily Tel.* (Colour Suppl.) 7 May 50/3 A lush settee and two armchairs, all plushly covered in fine green velvet.

plushy ('plʌʃɪ), *a.* [f. PLUSH *sb.* + -Y.]

a. Of the nature of or resembling plush; soft and shaggy. **b.** Covered or adorned with plush.

1611 FLORIO, *Villóso*..shaggie, plushie, or hauing a high nap. **1750** G. HUGHES *Barbadoes* 169 The top of the stalk supports a blunt-pointed conic plushy tuft. **1890** H. M. STANLEY *Darkest Africa* I. xi. 250 A variegated green of plushy texture. **1897** FLANDRAU *Harvard Epis.* 190 The horrid plushy little room.

c. Luxurious, sumptuous, elegant. *colloq.*

1923 A. HUXLEY *Antic Hay* i. 14 Over the plushy floors of some vast and ignoble Ritz slowly he walked, at ease, with confidence. **1942** *Sat. Rev. Lit.* (U.S.) 6 June 3/2 De Graff's plushy offices would lead the innocent visitor to conclude that successful publishing requires only some good titles and the organization to distribute them whole-sale. **1942** R. CHANDLER *High Window* (1943) iv. 34 Runs a plushy night-club and gambling joint. **1947** *Yale Law Jrnl.* Dec. 188 Driving Fords..rather than more plushy 'petit bourgeois' cars. **1953** W. STEVENS *Let.* 4 June (1967) 779 The picture of her in her prime was plushy, but cold. **1959** W. CAMP *Ruling Passion* 116 'This is a wee bit plushy, I must admit,' said Simon, as Paul entered his fantastically opulent-looking office. **1960** *Times* 29 Feb. 3/3 Much tongue wagging here [*sc.* Paris] from the plushier night haunts down to the homeliest *bistro*. **1970** 'D. HALLIDAY' *Dolly & Cookie Bird* i. 7 The lawyer-trustee..took me to a nice plushy lunch at the Café Royal. **1977** *Sunday Tel.* 11 Sept. 19/7 In ministerial quarters there are plenty of plushy berths to be filled.

Hence **'plushily** *adv.*, **'plushiness**.

1916 W. J. LOCKE *Wonderful Year* xiii. 183 The primly and plushily furnished salon. **1969** *Amateur Photographer* 21 May 53/1 Intimate exclusiveness, though not plushiness, is also a feature of the club cinema.

'plusquam-, L. *plus quam* more than, as in *plus quam perfectum* pluperfect, used with adjs. to form compounds, chiefly humorous nonce-wds.

1824 *Edin. Rev.* XLI. 15 By a kind of *plusquam-perfecting* operation. **1832** *Examiner* 49/2 The plusquam perfect wisdom of Legislators. **1848** CLOUGH *Bothie* i, Long constructions strange and plusquam Thucydidean. **1896** *Daily News* 6 June 5/7 Fanatics of the ultra-clerical and the plusquam-clerical type.

plussage, var. PLUSAGE.

plus twos (plʌs 'tu:z). [After PLUS FOURS.] A narrower version of plus fours. Also (in form *plus two*) *attrib.*

1967 *Daily Tel.* 24 May 26/3 (*caption*) The high-waisted winter weather coat has a Russian influence, and the country outfit a single-breasted jacket and tartan plus-twos. **1970** P. DICKINSON *Seals* vii. 136 Father in his plus-twos. **1977** *Field* 13 Jan. 68/4 (Advt.), Plus Two breeches.

Plutarchian (plu:'tɑ:kɪən), *a.* [f. L. *Plutarchius* adj. from *Plutarchus*, Gr. Πλούταρχος, proper name (lit. master of riches).] Pertaining to Plutarch, a famous Greek biographer of the first century A.D.; hence, of the class of distinguished men whose lives were written by Plutarch.

1856 GROTE *Greece* II. xcvi. XII. 512 *note*, In the next page of the very same Plutarchian life. **1899** *Daily News* 20 Apr. 6/2 Plutarchian heroes were they, in their virtues.

So **Plu'tarchic**, **-ical** *adjs.*; hence **Plu'tarchically** *adv.*, in the style or after the comparative manner of Plutarch in his 'Lives'.

1821 *Blackw. Mag.* X. 588 Comparing me most Plutarchically with Waithman.

plutarchy ('plu:tɑ:kɪ). [f. Gr. πλοῦτος wealth, riches + -αρχία rule; after *monarchy*, etc.] The rule or dominion of wealth, or of the wealthy; plutocracy.

c **1643** *Maximes Unfolded* 28 When the best in wealth and estates governe the poore, it is called Plutarchie, the Empire of riches. **1652** [see PLUTOMANIA 1]. **1834–43** SOUTHEY *Doctor* cii. (1862) 233 We had our monarchy, our hierarchy, our aristocracy,..but we had no plutarchy, no millionaires, no great capitalists to break down the honest and industrious trader with the weight of their overbearing and overwhelming wealth. **1890** A. CARNEGIE in *Pall Mall G.* 5 Sept. 7/1 It is said that in America, although we have no aristocracy, we are cursed with a plutarchy... A man who carries a million dollars on his back carries a load. He cannot be elected for anything.

plute (plu:t). *slang* (chiefly *U.S.*). Also ploot. Abbrev. of PLUTOCRAT. Hence **'plutish** *a.*, plutocratic.

1908 S. FORD *Side-Stepping with Shorty* i. 13 Then we bumps up against a really truly plute, and gets a squint at his dinner check. **1910** WODEHOUSE *Gentleman of Leisure* i. 3 He's got much more money than any man, except a professional plute, has any right to. **1922** S. LEWIS *Babbitt* ii. 23 Our little bunch has a lot liver times than all those plutes. **1923** *Daily Mail* 29 May 8 'The plutes', as he [*sc.* Henry Ford] humorously nicknames the financial and industrial interests of the country, would never permit his nomination. *c* **1926** 'MIXER' *Transport Workers' Song Bk.* 80 This plutish press condemns our class. **1931** E. POUND *Let.* 6 Oct. (1971) 235 The only person in Amurikuh who *cd.* continue your periodical is Marianne. The necessary irreproachable respectability, the that against which no lousy ploot can object on the grounds of her not bein' a lady or bein' likely to pervert the growing school child, etc... Marianne has experience—quality dear to the cautious ploot. **1932** *Randolph Enterprise* (Elkins, W. Va.) 18 Feb. 5/2 You'll hear the plutes cry out, The 'Yellow Peril' is Japan. **1955** E. POUND *Classic Anthol.* II. 106 Folk with no salary The heavens swat, while ploots can manage And the 'outs' cannot. **1959** —— *Thrones* 67 Ultramontaines Bitched France and then Austria, aristos are ignorant Plus illiteracy of the ploots.

pluterperfect (ˌplu:tə'pɜ:fɪkt), *a.* *nonce-wd.* [Poss. a corruption of Fr. *plus-que-parfait*: see PLUPERFECT *a.* (*sb.*)] = PLUPERFECT *a.* 2.

1922 JOYCE *Ulysses* 34 The pluterperfect imperturbability of the department of agriculture. *Ibid.* 412 An omnivorous being which can..pass through the ordinary channel with pluterperfect imperturbability such multifarious aliments as cancrenous females emaciated by parturition.

‖**pluteus** ('plu:tɪəs). Pl. plutei (-i:aɪ). [L. *pluteus*: see sense 1.]

1. *Rom. Antiq.*, etc. **a.** *Arch.* A barrier or light wall placed between columns. **b.** *Mil.* A kind of shed or penthouse for protection of the soldiers, sometimes movable and running on wheels. **c.** A shelf for books, small statues, busts, etc.

1832 GELL *Pompeiana* I. ii. 16 The pillars of the upper portico..stood upon a sort of *pluteus*. **1895** *Nation* (N.Y.) 9 May 359/1 The entrance and the wooden ceiling, as well as the reading-desks or *plutei*, were of Michelangelo's designing.

2. *Zool.* The larva of an echinoid or ophiuroid: known from its shape as the 'painter's easel larva'.

1877 HUXLEY *Anat. Inv. Anim.* ix. 565 Where an Echinopaedium stage exists, the larva is a Pluteus. **1888** ROLLESTON & JACKSON *Anim. Life* 569 The free swimming larva [in Ophiuroidea] is a Pluteus, and differs from the Echinoid Pluteus in possessing a pair of lateral arms.

Hence **'pluteal** *a.*, pertaining to a pluteus; **'pluteiˌform** *a.*, of the form of a pluteus (sense 2).

1877 HUXLEY *Anat. Inv. Anim.* ix. 544 The vermiform Holothurid and the pluteiform Ophiurid or Echinid larvae. **1900** E. R. LANKESTER *Treat. Zool.* III. 292 The young of Echinus..undergo metamorphosis during the development and resorption of the pluteal skeleton.

Pluto[1] ('plu:təʊ). [a. L. *Plūto*, Gr. Πλούτων, name of the god of the underworld, brother of Jupiter and Neptune.] **1.** A small planet of the solar system lying beyond the orbit of Neptune, discovered only in 1930 by C. W. Tombaugh.

1930 *N.Y. Times* 26 Mar. 10/3 'Pluto' is the provisional name that Italian astronomers have given to the new trans-Neptune planet discovered March 13 at Lowell Observatory in Flagstaff, Ariz... Hugh Rice..yesterday opposed naming the newly discovered planet 'Minerva', as has already been suggested, because an asteroid already bears that name. **1930** V. M. SLIPHER *Lowell Observatory Observation Circular* 1 May, Many names have been suggested and among them Minerva and Pluto have been very popular... Pluto seems very appropriate and we are proposing to the American Astronomical Society and to the Royal Astronomical Society, that this name be given to it. As far as we know Pluto was first suggested by Miss Venetia Burney, aged 11, of Oxford, England. [*Note*] Kindly cabled by Prof. H. H. Turner. **1930** H. H. TURNER in *Times* 28 May 17/5 A post-card from the President of the Royal Astronomical Society offered this morning 'congratulations to the suggester of the name Pluto, now adopted'. The reference is to a telegram which I had the honour of sending to the Lowell Observatory on March 15..conveying the suggestion of Miss Venetia Burney, of Oxford, made at breakfast on that day to her grandfather, who sent it on to me... It was a brother of that same grandfather who suggested the names Deimos and Phobos for the satellites of Mars. **1933** D. L. SAYERS *Hangman's Holiday* 120 Presently they had guessed among other things Miss Tomkin's mother's photograph,..the new planet Pluto,..and had failed to guess the Prime Minister's wireless speech. **1939** SKILLING & RICHARDSON *Astron.* i. 12 The length of seasons depends, of course, upon the length of time required for the planet to go around the sun—all the way from about 3 months for Mercury to 248 years for Pluto. **1953** A. F. O'D. ALEXANDER in M. Davidson *Astron. for Everyman* iv. 203 Pluto's path never crosses Neptune's.. for its orbit-plane is inclined 17° to the ecliptic plane. **1972** P. L. BROWN *Astron. in Color* ii. 86 One theory accounts for the origin of Pluto by considering that it is an ex-satellite of Neptune which somehow broke free. **1976** J. GRIBBIN *Astron. for Amateur* v. 70 Because of its elliptical orbit Pluto sometimes passes within the orbit of Neptune, and just now (until the end of this century) Neptune is the furthest planet from the Sun.

2. The name of a cartoon dog that made its first appearance in Walt Disney's *Moose Hunt*, released in April 1931; a toy dog representing this character.

1932 W. DISNEY *Adventures Mickey Mouse* II. 14 Mickey watched, and Minnie, too, And Pluto hid himself from view. **1936** —— *Mickey Mouse Fables* 3 'Now for my bone,' said Pluto, licking his lips. **1957** D. D. MILLER *Walt Disney* viii. 137 Pluto got his nose stuck to flypaper and tried to blow it off. **1962** L. DEIGHTON *Ipcress File* ii. 22 A cigarette-girl.. offered me a pink felt pluto, too. **1972** *Guardian* 21 Aug. 11/5 Ten dogs took part, plus one yellow plastic Pluto on wheels. **1973** L. MALTIN *Disney Films* iv. 267 As the 1930s wore on.. Mickey played a progressively less important role in the proceedings, some cartoons completely taken over by the character of Pluto.

'Pluto². [Acronym f. initial letters of *P*ipe *L*ine *u*nder *t*he *O*cean.] The code name for a system of pipe-lines laid in 1944 to carry petrol supplies from Britain to Allied forces in France. Also *attrib*.

1945 *News Chron.* 1 June 2/5 As in the Pluto pipeline, petrol was the basis of this secret weapon. Like Pluto the experts said at first that it could not be done. **1946** *Ann. Reg. 1945* 37 Foremost among these was the laying of a system of oil pipelines under the sea stretching across the Channel from the British coast to the Continent, and commonly known as 'Operation Pluto' (pipe line under the ocean). **1961** E. W. GLADSTONE *Army* vii. 103 Many clever inventions like the artificial 'Mulberry' harbours, and 'Pluto', the Pipe Line Under the Ocean to provide petrol, had been developed. **1978** A. WAUGH *Best Wine Last* xv. 177 The Petroleum Warfare Department.. invented 'PLUTO' (pipe line under the ocean) to carry oil across the Channel.

plutocracy (plu:'tɒkrəsɪ). Also plout-. [ad. Gr. πλουτοκρατία, f. πλοῦτο-ς wealth, riches + -κρατία power: see -CRACY. So F. *plutocratie*.]

1. The rule or sovereign power of wealth or of the wealthy.

1652 URQUHART *Jewel* Wks. (1834) 270 That poverty is an enemy to the exercise of vertue, is not unknown to any acquainted with Plutocracy, or the sovereign power of money. **1839** *Morn. Herald* 3 Sept., Of all systems of tyranny a plutocracy is the most cruel, selfish, and grinding. **1887** GLADSTONE in *19th Cent.* Jan. 17 Let us be jealous of ploutocracy, and of its tendency to infect aristocracy, its elder and nobler sister; and learn, if we can, to hold by or get back to some regard for simplicity of life. **1898** BODLEY *France* IV. ii. 359 The aggressive march of plutocracy which has transformed the character of English society.

2. A ruling or influential class of wealthy persons; a body of plutocrats.

1832 in Fonblanque *Eng. under 7 Administr.* (1837) II. 205 This infernal Bill, which.. is only to create a Plutocracy in lieu of the aristocracy, under which old England has flourished. **1878** *N. Amer. Rev.* CXXVII. 4 An ignorant proletariat and a half-taught plutocracy. **1893** F. ADAMS *New Egypt* 56 The dominant class in the one is the bureaucracy, and in the other the plutocracy.

plutocrat ('plu:təkræt). [f. prec., after *aristocrat*, *democrat*, etc.] A member of a plutocracy; a person possessing or exercising power or influence over others in virtue of his wealth.

1850 KINGSLEY *Alt. Locke* xli, When they, the tyrants of the earth,.. the plutocrats, the bureaucrats,.. are crying to the rocks to hide them. **1880** *Spectator* 3 Jan. 10 Aristocrats have a great place and plutocrats a great place in our society. **1885** *Law Times* LXXIX. 190/1 The plutocrat.. can buy as many ancestors and ancestral relics as he will.

So **plutocratic** (plu:təʊ'krætɪk) *a.*, of or pertaining to plutocrats; characterized by plutocracy.

1866 *Sat. Rev.* 21 Apr. 480/1 The Oriental empires and African kingdoms or republics (if that term can be applied to the timocratic or perhaps ploutocratic Carthage). **1883** *Fortn. Rev.* June 769 The plutocratic elements.. are, in an increasing degree, becoming detached from Liberalism. **1905** *Outlook* 11 Nov. 650/1 In Ohio and New Jersey.. democracy had been supplanted by a plutocratic despotism.

plutocratical (plu:təʊ'krætɪkəl), *a.* [f. PLUTOCRATIC *a.* + -AL¹.] = PLUTOCRATIC *a.* So **pluto'cratically** *adv.*, in a plutocratical manner.

1833 J. S. MILL *Let.* 10 July in *Wks.* (1963) XII. 166 The anomaly of a democratic constitution in a plutocratically constituted society. **1913** W. J. LOCKE *Stella Maris* xx. 238 Only the splendour.. of plutocratically owned vehicles meets the enraptured vision. **1941** E. R. EDDISON *Fish Dinner* xix. 324 An aristocratical plutocratical self-obtruding dilettante. **1978** *Country Life* 31 Aug. 589/4 In their heyday they certainly seem, plutocratically speaking, to have been a singularly unattractive lot.

plutocratizing (plu:'tɒkrətaɪzɪŋ), *vbl. sb.* [f. PLUTOCRAT + -IZE + -ING¹, after *democratizing*.] The action or process of rendering plutocratic.

1896 *Westm. Gaz.* 9 Dec. 2/3 The 'plutocratising' of the Universities was a nineteenth century movement. **1929** *New Statesman* 28 Sept. 740/1 The Americanisation and plutocratising of old England.

pluto-democracy (ˌplu:təʊdɪ'mɒkrəsɪ). Also **plutodemocracy**. [f. Gr. πλοῦτος wealth, riches + DEMOCRACY.] **1.** Plutocratic government which masquerades as democracy.

1895 in *Funk's Stand. Dict.* **1941** D. WILSON *Germany's 'New Order'* 24 German gibes at pluto-democracy. **1944** J. S. HUXLEY *On Living in Revol.* 41 Hitler has proclaimed his aims... They include.. the destruction of what he is pleased to call 'pluto-democracy'. **1970** H. ARENDT *On Violence* 72 A new system, which he [*sc.* Pareto] called 'Pluto-democracy'—a mixed form of government, plutocracy being the bourgeois regime and democracy the regime of the workers.

2. A country or state which purports to be a democracy but where power lies with the rich.

1902 *Nineteenth Century & After* July 119 If England be allowed to become a Plutodemocracy, then she has the tragic example of Venice to chasten and admonish her. **1940** *Common Sense* Aug. 6/2 The absolute power of a Stalin or a Hitler is seen to be even worse than the economic exploitation and political ineffectiveness of a 'pluto-democracy' with its checks and balances. **1942** L. B. NAMIER *Conflicts* 209 In the presence of social inequalities, parliamentary democracy without parties must inevitably result in a real 'pluto-democracy'. **1948** W. S. CHURCHILL *Second World War* I. xx. 287 The Jew Litvinov was gone, and Hitler's dominant prejudice placated. From that moment the German Government ceased to define its foreign policy as anti-Bolshevism, and turned its abuse upon the 'pluto-Democracies'.

Hence **ˌpluto-'democrat**, an adherent or advocate of pluto-democracy; **ˌpluto-demo'cratic** *a.*

1940 *Economist* 24 Feb. 328/2 German propagandists are making steady use of.. 'Britain the pluto-democrat, living in luxury on the wealth extorted from 60 million native serfs'. *Ibid.* 29 June 1102/1 German propaganda among the French troops has followed the lines of 'plutodemocratic capitalist Britain'. **1946** R. GRAVES *Poems 1938–1945* 35 By every nastier manifestation Of plutodemocratic civilisation.

plutogogue ('plu:təʊgɒg). [f. Gr. πλοῦτος wealth + ἀγωγός leading, leader, after *demagogue*.] A spokesman for the plutocrats; one who justifies or advocates the interests of the wealthy. Hence **'plutogogy**, the rule of plutogogues.

1894 *Westm. Gaz.* 17 Feb. 8/1 Mr. Williams, of Mississippi, said the opponents of the income tax are plutogogues and encouragers of plutogogy. *Ibid.*, A demagogue, he explained, appeals directly to the mob; a plutogogue appeals to the people who buy the mob. **1931** L. STEFFENS *Autobiogr.* II. III. xvi. 474 Since the plutogogues could not fasten any crime on him they fell back on the all-sufficient charge that he was a demagogue. **1937** *Sun* (Baltimore) 30 Aug. 9/4 Smith called the demagogue, plutogogue and the theogogue, 'fearful trinity, constituting the very diabolus of democracy'. **1937** *News-Week* 13 Sept. 20/2 Fascists and Communists did not strike him as any more dangerous than the man he new-named the plutogogue. The philosophy professor defined him as 'the voice of the wealthy when they can no longer speak for themselves, the successor of the plutocrat of other days'.

plutolater (plu:'tɒlətə(r)). *rare.* [f. PLUTOLATRY, after *idolater*.] One who worships wealth.

1938 S. BECKETT *Murphy* ix. 168 All the self-made plutolaters who ever triumphed over empty pockets.

plutolatry (plu:'tɒlətrɪ). [f. Gr. πλοῦτος wealth + -λατρεία (-LATRY), after *idolatry*.] Worship of wealth.

1889 LOWELL *Stud. Mod. Lang.* Latest Lit. Ess. (1891) 157 The barbarizing plutolatry which seems to be so rapidly supplanting the worship of what alone is lovely and enduring. **1895** L. F. WARD in *Forum* (U.S.) Nov. 301 Of the other sentiment,.. 'plutolatry'—the worship of wealth—even the victims show traces.

plutological (plu:tə'lɒdʒɪkəl), *a.* *rare.* [f. PLUTOLOGY + -IC + -AL.] Of or pertaining to plutology.

1920 *Edin. Rev.* July 80 The whole plutological apparatus was developed—banking, investment, partnership, joint stock companies, and even trusts. *Ibid.* 83 The economic difference between ancient, medieval and modern society is in scale, complexity and form, not in the plutological principle or the essential character of the process.

plutology (plu:'tɒlədʒɪ). *rare.* [f. as PLUTOLATRY + -LOGY.] The science of wealth; political economy. Hence **plu'tologist**, one versed in plutology.

1864 W. E. HEARN (*title*) Plutology; or the Theory of the Efforts to Satisfy Human Wants. **1874** SIDGWICK *Meth. Ethics* v. 261 As the plutologists say. **1893** *Athenæum* 1 Apr. 405/2 This ignorant peasant did not act up to certain well-ascertained laws of the 'science of wealth'. Plutology is not everything.

‖**plutomania** (plu:təʊ'meɪnɪə). Also 7 **plutomanie**. [mod.L., f. as prec. + MANIA.]

†**1.** Insane love or pursuit of wealth. *Obs.*

1652 URQUHART *Jewel* Wks. (1834) 280 A meer Plutarchy, Plutocracy, or rather Plutomanie; so madly they hale after money.

2. *Path.* A form of insanity in which the person imagines himself possessed of immense wealth.

1894 E. L. GODKIN in *Forum* (U.S.) June 394, I should conclude.. that he was laboring under the well-known hallucination called plutomania. **1895** in *Syd. Soc. Lex.*

plutomanic (plu:təʊ'mænɪk), *a.* *rare.* [f. as PLUTOMANIA + MANIC *a.*] Characterized by the insane love or pursuit of wealth.

1938 S. BECKETT *Murphy* v. 82 A colossal league of plutomanic caterers. **1963** B. S. JOHNSON *Travelling People* 159 His decision to enter the plutomanic world of commerce.

pluton ('plu:tɒn). *Geol.* [a. G. *pluton* (H. Cloos 1928, in *Fennia* L. II. 1), back-formation from *plutonisch* PLUTONIC *a.* (*sb.*)] An intrusive body of igneous rock formed beneath the earth's surface, esp. a large one.

[**1933** R. A. DALY *Igneous Rocks & Depths of Earth* vi. 75 He [*sc.* H. Cloos] states that he does not assume floors for batholiths but on the next page defines his '*Plutone*', which includes batholiths, as having visible or inferable floors.] **1936** *Proc. Geol. Soc. Amer. 1935* 67 The granite appears to have come up along the edge of the mostly consolidated Pikes Peak mass and spread in a series of plutons and sills, the mode of intrusion being largely governed by the rock invaded. **1942** M. P. BILLINGS *Structural Geol.* xv. 296 The intrusion of large plutons may be associated with orogenic movements. **1961** F. H. LAHEE *Field Geol.* (ed. 6) vi. 141 Concordant plutons include sills, laccoliths, lopoliths, and phacoliths. *Ibid.* 142 Discordant plutons include dikes, necks, chonoliths, batholiths, stocks, and bosses. **1962** [see GREISEN]. **1971** I. G. GASS et al. *Understanding Earth* v. 84/2 The observed linear relation between heat flow and heat production in granitic plutons may allow precise estimates of temperature as far down as the base of the crust. **1974** H. F. GARNER *Origin of Landscapes* iii. 130/2 Metasomatic replacement is common along borders of larger intrusive masses (plutons).

Plutonian (plu:'təʊnɪən), *a.* (*sb.*) [f. L. *Plūtōnius* (ad. Gr. Πλουτώνι-ος, f. Πλούτων Pluto, the god of the infernal regions) + -AN. So F. *plutonien*.]

1. Of or pertaining to Pluto; belonging to or suggestive of the infernal regions; infernal.

1667 MILTON *P.L.* x. 444 He.. from the dore Of that Plutonian Hall, invisible Ascended his high Throne. **1831** POE *Raven* Poems 47 Tell me what thy lordly name is on the Night's Plutonian shore. **1889** R. DOWLING *Isle of Surrey* (1891) 171 In the plutonian darkness under the bridge.

2. *Geol.* = PLUTONIC 1.

1828 WEBSTER s.v., The *Plutonian* theory of the formation of rocks and mountains is opposed to the *Neptunian*. **1860** *All Year Round* IV. 250 The moon is the object in which to study plutonian action.

B. *sb. Geol.* = PLUTONIST.

1828 WEBSTER, *Plutonian, n.* One who maintains the origin of mountains, etc. to be from fire. *Journ. of Science.*

plutonic (plu:'tɒnɪk), *a.* (*sb.*) Also **Plutonic**. [f. Gr. Πλούτων Pluto: see prec. and -IC. So F. *plutonique* (16th c.).]

1. *Geol.* **a.** Pertaining to or involving the action of intense heat at great depths upon the rocks forming the earth's crust; igneous. Applied *spec.* to the theory that attributes most geological phenomena to the action of internal heat: cf. PLUTONIST.

1796 KIRWAN *Elem. Min.* (ed. 2) I. 455 There is another system which attributes not only to basalts, but to all stony substances, an igneous origin... This may be called the *Plutonic* system. **1840** LYELL *Princ. Geol.* (ed. 6) I. I. xiii. 320 Several modern writers, without denying the truth of the Plutonic or metamorphic theory, still contend that the crystalline and non-fossiliferous formations,.. such as gneiss and granite, are essentially ancient as a class of rocks. **1847–8** H. MILLER *First Impr.* iii. (1857) 32 Both the denuding and the Plutonic agents. **1870** E. L. GARBETT in *Eng. Mech.* 11 Mar. 625/1 All this is apart from plutonic heat. **1871** HARTWIG *Subterr. W.* i. 4 Plutonic and volcanic eruptions and upheavings.. have in many places deranged .. strata deposited in horizontal layers at the bottom of the sea, or of large inland lakes.

b. *spec.* Applied to that class of igneous rocks, such as granite and syenite, which are supposed to have been formed by fusion and subsequent slow crystallization at great depths below the surface, as distinguished from *volcanic* rocks (which have been formed at or near the surface).

1833 LYELL *Princ. Geol.* III. 353 The unstratified crystalline rocks have been very commonly called Plutonic, from the opinion that they were formed by igneous action at great depths. **1849** DANA *Geol.* x. (1850) 539 Far the larger part of the land consists of ancient Plutonic and stratified rocks. **1882** GEIKIE *Text Bk. Geol.* II. II. vi. 134 Granite is thus a decidedly plutonic rock.

2. Belonging to or resembling Pluto; Plutonian.

1819 WIFFEN *Aonian Hours* (1820) 65 Winter—a Plutonic thief, Coming to claim thee for his Mourning Bride. **1857** DUFFERIN *Lett. High Lat.* 113 The Plutonic drama concluded with a violent earthquake.

B. *sb. Geol.* (*pl.*) Plutonic rocks.

1856 KANE *Arct. Expl.* II. xi. 112 The bottom series of plutonics rises to grand and mountainous proportions. **1881** R. F. BURTON in *Academy* 21 May 366/2 Here begins the new land of clayey schist and mica-slate contrasting with the plutonics of Bihé.

†**plu'tonical**, *a.* *Obs.* [f. as prec. + -AL¹.] = prec. 2.

1599 *Broughton's Lett.* xii. 39 Making Hell.. to bee nothing but that Platonicall and Plutonicall Hades of the Heathen. **1623** tr. *Favine's Theat. Hon.* II. xiii. 207 Which had so long time beene kept in that Plutonicall Mansion.

Plutonism (ˈpluːtənɪz(ə)m). *Geol.* Also **plutonism.** [f. as PLUTONIC + -ISM. So F. *plutonisme.*] The Plutonic theory: see PLUTONIC *a.* 1 a.

1847 in WEBSTER. **1910** *Encycl. Brit.* XI. 644/2 Wernerianism..rapidly declined in influence, while Plutonism came steadily to the front, where it has ever since remained. **1966** [see NEPTUNISM].

2. Geological activity associated with the formation of plutonic rocks.

1942 J. L. VAN HOUTEN tr. *Umbgrove's Pulse of Earth* iv. 66 A local thickening of the sialic crust, resulting in the formation of a 'root' of sialic material... When this root's material begins to melt and invade the surface strata as batholithic intrusions, plutonism and volcanism cannot but be strongly acid ('pacific') in character. **1949** *Q. Jrnl. Geol. Soc.* CV. 104 Plutonism does not appear to be a steady process advancing at a uniform rate, but rather one of energetic pulses interrupted by operations of diverse kinds, especially those of deformation. **1970** *Nature* 24 Jan. 315/1 After the late Mesozoic plutonism, the next phase of igneous activity in western America began in the Oligocene.

Plutonist (ˈpluːtənɪst). *Geol.* [f. as PLUTONISM + -IST. So F. *plutoniste.*] One who holds the Plutonic theory: see PLUTONIC *a.* 1 a.

1799 KIRWAN *Geol. Ess.* 336 It is in vain..that volcanists; or rather plutonists, ascribe these slips, and the disorders that accompany them, to subterraneous eruptions. **1861** BUCKLE *Civiliz.* (1871) III. v. 397 In the history of geology, the followers of Werner are known as Neptunists, and those of Hutton as Plutonists. **1882** GEIKIE *Text Bk. Geol.* III. I. iv. §2. 298 In the geological contest..between the Neptunists and the Plutonists, the two great battle cries were, on the one side, Water, on the other, Fire.

plutonium (pluːˈtəʊnɪəm). [L. *Plūtōnium*, ad. Gr. *Πλουτώνιον*, f. *Πλούτων* Pluto.] **1.** A place where there are mephitic vapours.

1775 R. CHANDLER *Trav. Asia M.* (1825) I. 292 Hierapolis was noted, besides its hot waters, for a Plutonium. *Ibid.* 294, I renewed my inquiries for the Plutonium, and an old Turk ..told me he knew the place, that it was often fatal to goats.

2. *Chem.* †**a.** = BARIUM. *Obs.*

The word was introduced in a letter to the Royal Institution dated 1 Sept. 1816, but not published until 1817 (= quot. 1817 below). Its first occurrence in print was in *Ann. de Chim. et de Physique* (Sept. 1816) III. 61 in a Fr. transl. of it. Quot. 1816 is from a letter of 5 Oct. 1816 that refers to this (then unpublished) letter.

1816 E. D. CLARKE in *Ann. Philos.* VIII. 358 The metal is in its purest state. It is the same metal for which I proposed the appellation of Plutonium; and I am glad to find the appellation generally approved. *Ibid.* 360 Plutonium, if fused in contact with platinum, always tarnishes the latter. **1817** —— in *Jrnl. Sci. & Arts* II. 120 The existence..of the metal of Barytes no longer admits of the smallest doubt... As any derivative from *βαρυς* would involve an error, if applied to a metal whose specific gravity is inferior to that of Manganese or Molybdenum, I have ventured to propose for it the appellation of *Plutonium*; because we owe it entirely to the dominion of fire.

b. A transuranic metallic element which is formed indirectly from uranium in nuclear reactors and occurs naturally in trace amounts, is chemically similar to uranium, and is very reactive; the longest-lived isotope (plutonium 244) has a half-life of 83 million years, and plutonium 239 is fissile and is produced for use in nuclear weapons and as fuel. Atomic number 94; symbol Pu. [So called from its being the next element after neptunium in the periodic table, as Pluto is the planet next beyond Neptune.]

1942 SEABORG & WAHL *Chem. Properties Elem. 94 & 93* (U.S. Office Sci. Res. & Devel. Report A-135) 17 Since such formulae are confusing when the symbols '93' and '94' are used, we have decided to use symbols of the conventional chemical type to designate these elements. Following McMillan, who has suggested the name neptunium..for element 93, we are using plutonium..for element 94. The corresponding chemical symbols would be Np and Pu. **1952** J. G. FEINBERG *Atom Story* xx. 153 On 20th December 1943 the first batch of irradiated slugs were removed from the pile for plutonium extraction. In another month the pile was turning out about one-third ton of plutonium-enriched slugs a day. **1962** J. C. WRIGHT *Metallurgy in Nucl. Power Technol.* iii. 60 The concentration of plutonium in minerals such as pitchblende is no more than one part in 10^{11}. **1964** R. L. LOFTNESS *Nucl. Power Plants* ii. 63 The maximum permissible body burden for plutonium is 0·3 microgram, and such a low limit requires the use of very efficient enclosures, or glove-boxes, for all research, development, and production work. **1968** [see NEPTUNIUM]. **1969** *Times* 22 Apr. 6/6 Scientists..claimed to have synthesized element 104..by bombarding plutonium with neon. **1970** *Daily Tel.* 23 July 3/2 The nuclear-powered pacemaker—shaped like a small bullet and powered with plutonium 238—has a life of about 10 years. **1970** tr. *Vol'skii & Sterlin's Metallurgy of Plutonium* i. 19 Pure plutonium cannot be used as a nuclear fuel because of its low melting point, poor mechanical properties, high chemical activity, and the considerable volume changes caused by phase transformations... For reactors plutonium alloys and plutonium compounds are used. **1976** *Sci. Amer.* Dec. 30/2 In addition to uranium 235 the spent fuel contains between ·7 and 1 per cent of plutonium 239, synthesized from uranium 238 by the absorption of a neutron. **1979** *Ibid.* Apr. 33/2 A Precambrian mineral, a rare-earth fluocarbonate mined for cerium in California, has yielded the all but extinct isotope of plutonium with mass 244.

3. *attrib.* and *Comb.*, as (sense 2 b) ***plutonium economy, enrichment***; **plutonium bomb**, an atomic bomb in which the fissile material is plutonium.

1948 C. PINCHER *Into Atomic Age* 53 Three days after the attack on Hiroshima..the plutonium bomb was dropped on Nagasaki. *Ibid.* 54 The 'Mark II' plutonium bomb was a definite improvement. It would have devastated the flat, round target of Hiroshima more completely than did the now obsolete uranium 'Mark I'. **1973** *Guardian* 19 Apr. 14/3 To make a plutonium bomb, with which a criminal could hold a city to ransom..one needs just 16·2 kilos of the metal. **1976** *New Yorker* 9 Feb. 44/3 Such a 'plutonium economy', in which fissionable fuel is recycled between reactor and reprocessing plant, is essential to the operation of the breeder. **1977** *Jrnl. R. Soc. Arts* CXXVI. 15/2 The distinguished Royal Commission under Sir Brian Flowers has expressed disquiet about a 'plutonium economy', but that is not to condemn all nuclear development. **1977** *Time* 7 Mar. 7/1 West German officials are further incensed over Carter's public criticism of Bonn's deal to sell a plutonium-enrichment plant and eight nuclear reactors to Brazil.

ˈplutonize, *v. nonce-wd.* [f. Gr. *Πλούτων* Pluto + -IZE.] *trans.* To make infernal.

1600 TOURNEUR *Transf. Metamorph.* iv, O who hath metamorphosed My sence? and plutoniz'd my heauenly shape?

pluˌtonometaˈmorphism. *Petrol.* [f. PLUTON(ISM + -O + METAMORPHISM.] Metamorphism that occurs at high temperatures and high pressures at great depths under the earth.

1889 A. HARKER in *Geol. Mag.* Decade III. VI. 17 We may accordingly use the term plutono-metamorphism to describe the profound changes in rocks implied in the joint influence of very elevated temperature and enormous pressure. **1950** F. H. HATCH et al. *Petrol. Ign. Rocks* (ed. 10) vii. 336 The chief problem of the eclogites concerns their origin. They are believed to be products of 'plutono-metamorphism'—to lie on the borderland between the igneous and metamorphic.

plutonomy (pluːˈtɒnəmɪ). [f. Gr. *πλοῦτος* wealth, riches + *-νομία* arrangement; after *economy*. So F. *plutonomie.*] The science of the production and distribution of wealth; political economy.

1851 J. M. LUDLOW *Chr. Socialism* 24 [Political economy] confessing its own limited nature by the mouth of its greatest exponent—by its own showing a mere *plutonomy*. **1862** T. SHORTER in *Weldon's Regr.* Aug. 9 Plutonomy, as it has been designated, is regarded by Mr. Ruskin as a base or bastard science. **1900** *Daily News* 9 Feb. 4/6 Plutonomy is a more accurate name, but the man in the street..would be apt to think it pedantic.

So **plutonomic** (pluːtəʊˈnɒmɪk) *a.*, pertaining to plutonomy, politico-economic; **plutonomist** (pluːˈtɒnəmɪst), one versed in plutonomy, a political economist.

1851 J. M. LUDLOW *Chr. Socialism* 28 Some of the worst culprits in this respect are precisely those plutonomists. **1860** —— in *Macm. Mag.* May 51 Those plutonomic doctrines which are erected into a faith for states or for individuals, and which tend to supplant everywhere duty by interest. **1888** *Pall Mall G.* 31 Mar. 2/2 Fundamental and eternal differences of plutonomic opinion forbid it [federation]. **1896** F. HARRISON in *19th Cent.* Dec. 972 The terms and dogmas of the older plutonomists.

plutonyl (ˈpluːtəʊnaɪl). *Chem.* [f. PLUTON(IUM + -YL.] The ion PuO_2^{2+}. Usu. *attrib.*

1947 B. G. HARVEY et al. in *Jrnl. Chem. Soc.* 1013 On account of the similarity between the chemistry of uranium and of plutonium in their sexavalent states, the terms 'plutonate' and 'plutonyl' have been used in the present paper to describe the sexavalent compounds of plutonium. *Ibid.*, An orange solution, which..is believed to contain plutonyl nitrate, $PuO_2(NO_3)_2$. **1961** G. R. CHOPPIN *Exper. Nuclear Chem.* xii. 192 The extent to which the internal irradiation by alpha particles causes reduction of plutonium ions to the (IV) state in an aqueous solution of PuO_2^{2+} is necessary knowledge for the inorganic chemist studying plutonyl ion chemistry. **1976** *Sci. Amer.* Dec. 33/1 In the solvents that were used hexavalent uranyl ions, $(UO_2)^{++}$, and plutonyl ions, $(PuO_2)^{++}$, together with tetravalent plutonium ions, Pu^{++}.., are soluble.

pluvial (ˈpluːvɪəl), *sb.*[1] *Eccl. Obs.* exc. *Hist.* Also pluviale. [ad. med.L. *pluviāle* (also *pluviālis*, Du Cange), prop. rain-cloak, orig. neut. of L. *pluviālis* pertaining to rain. So F. *pluvial* (12th c. in Godef.). Cf. It. *piviale, pieviale*, perhaps influenced in form by *pieve* rural deanery (*plebs*).

(But Diez takes **plēbiāle*, from *plēbs*, as the real source, and *pluvial* as due to popular etymology.)]

A long cloak worn by ecclesiastics as a ceremonial vestment; = COPE *sb.*[1] 2 (where see note); also, a similar garment used by monarchs as a robe of state.

1669 G. FOX *Arraignm. Popery* 44 They put upon the Pope a red Cope, called a Pluvial. **1690** *Lond. Gaz.* No. 2533/2 The Deputies of Nuremburg placed the Mantle or Pluviale of Charlemagne on his Shoulders. **1725** tr. *Dupin's Eccl. Hist. 17th C.* I. v. 63 The Priest had a Pluvial or Cope, besides the Habit with which he is cloath'd, when he celebrates the Mass. **1848** MRS. JAMESON *Sacr. & Leg. Art* (1850) 404 Over the whole is thrown the cope or pluviale (literally, rain-cloak) because first adopted, merely as a covering from the weather. **1886** *Athenæum* 7 Aug. 180/3 The pluvial of St. Silvester seems to her to be English.

pluvial (ˈpluːvɪəl), *a.* and *sb.*[2] [ad. L. *pluviāl-is* of or belonging to rain, f. *pluvia* rain. So F. *pluvial.*] **A.** *adj.* **a.** Of or pertaining to rain; rainy; characterized by much rain; *spec.* designating periods of relatively high average rainfall in low and intermediate latitudes during the geological past (esp. the Pleistocene) which alternated with interpluvial periods in a cycle which may be correlated with or related to the better-known cycle of glacial and interglacial periods in higher latitudes. Cf. INTERPLUVIAL, INTRAPLUVIAL *adjs.* and *sbs.*

1656 BLOUNT *Glossogr.*, *Pluvial*, of rain, like to rain, rainy, waterish. **1657** TOMLINSON *Renou's Disp.* 185 A Bath..of Sweet water, whether pluvial or fluvial. **1832** C. NICHOLSON *Ann. Kendal* iv. (1861) 157 The butter-women were exposed to the pluvial elements. **1868** A. TYLOR in *Q. Jrnl. Geol. Soc.* XXIV. 105 Many of the Quaternary deposits in all countries..are of such great dimensions and elevation that they must have been formed under physical conditions very different from our own. They indicate a Pluvial period, just as clearly as the northern drift indicates a Glacial period. **1869** PHILLIPS *Vesuv.* v. 145 Such uncommon pluvial descents may follow. **1927** PEAKE & FLEURE *Apes & Men* v. 75 He endeavoured to show that..in the valley of the Nile, there was evidence of four very wet periods, or pluvial periods. **1949** W. F. ALBRIGHT *Archaeol. Palestine* 50 The cold phases are called 'glacial periods' in northern latitudes and 'pluvial periods' in the latitude of Palestine, where there was no glaciation, but instead a greatly increased rainfall. **1954** *New Biol.* XVII. 11 There is evidence of at least two great 'Pluvial' periods of heavy rainfall in the Pleistocene when these [East African] lakes reached their maximum size and depth. **1979** *Nature* 1 Mar. 80/1 The student interested in the Pleistocene will find many discredited ideas (for example, glacial = pluvial).

b. *Geol.* Caused by rain.

1859 PAGE *Geol. Terms* s.v., We speak of the denuding or degrading effects of 'pluvial agency', just as we speak of 'atmospheric', 'fluviatile', or other similar agency. **1878** HUXLEY *Physiogr.* ix. 131 The particular kind of denudation effected by means of rain is called pluvial denudation.

B. *sb.* A pluvial period.

1929 *Nature* 6 July 9/2 A large mammalian fauna has been collected from the deposits of the various Pluvials. **1931** L. S. B. LEAKEY *Stone Age Cultures of Kenya Colony* ii. 13 The prehistoric tribes..moved down to the Rift Valley areas during the pluvials. **1959** *Bull. Geol. Soc. Amer.* LXX. 345/2 African pluvials are of great importance for climatic history, for Pleistocene correlation, and for meteorologic theory. **1970** BRAY & TRUMP *Dict. Archaeol.* 184/1 Prolonged periods of high rainfall are called pluvials, and are marked by changes in lake levels and in flora and fauna.

pluvialiform (pluːvɪˈælɪfɔːm), *a. Ornith.* [ad. mod. ornith. L. *Pluviāliformēs*, pl. of *Pluviāliformis*, f. *Pluviālis* plover: see next and -FORM.] Of or pertaining to the *Pluvialiformes*, a series of swimming and wading birds related to the plovers; having the form or character of the plover family.

1890 in *Cent. Dict.*

pluvialine (ˈpluːvɪəlaɪn), *a. Ornith.* [f. mod.L. *Pluviālēs*, the group of the plovers and allied birds, rain-birds, pl. of *pluviālis* rainy, as sb. a plover or rain-bird, whence specific name of the Golden plover, *Charadrius pluvialis*: see INE[1].] Pertaining to a plover, resembling the plovers.

1872 E. COUES *Key to N. Amer. Birds* 239 The pluvialine and scolopacine birds form the bulk of the division. **1890** in *Cent. Dict.*

pluviameter, erron. var. PLUVIOMETER.

ˈpluvian, *a. nonce-wd.* [f. L. *pluvi-us* rainy + -AN.] Rain-giving; rainy (in quot. = L. *Jupiter pluvius*).

1851 R. F. BURTON *Goa* 368 Irritated by the pertinacious viciousness of Pluvian Jove, we ride along the slippery road which bounds the East confines of the lake.

†**ˈpluviatile,** *a. Obs. rare.* [ad. L. *pluviātilis* (Cels.) belonging to rain.] Of rain, rain-(water).

1599 A. M. tr. *Gabelhouer's Bk. Physicke* 47/1 Take Hogges suet lb 6. Terebinthine which hath binne washed in pluviatile water lb *s.*

pluviograph (ˈpluːvɪəgrɑːf, -æ-). [f. L. *pluvia* rain + -GRAPH.] A self-recording rain-gauge.

1886 *Encycl. Brit.* XX. 257/1 In Beckley's 'pluviograph' a pencil, attached to a vessel which sinks as it receives the rain, describes a curve on a sheet of paper fixed round a rotating cylinder. **1895** in *Syd. Soc. Lex.*

pluviometer (pluːvɪˈɒmɪtə(r)). (Also erron. -iameter.) [f. L. *pluvia* rain + -METER. So F. *pluviomètre* (1788 in Hatz.-D.).] An instrument for measuring the rainfall; a rain-gauge.

1791 *Gentl. Mag.* LXI. I. 133 In the construction of the Pluviometer..there is a method to prevent evaporation. **1828–32** WEBSTER, Pluviameter (cites *Jrnl. Sci.*). **1834** *Nat. Philos.* III. *Phys. Geog.* 40/1 (U. Knl. Soc.), Observing the height of the water collected in a pluviometer or rain-gauge. **1863** R. F. BURTON *West Africa* I. 148 There fell in twenty-four hours 9·12 inches measured by Pluviometer, and half the island was under water.

Hence **pluvioˈmetric** *a.*, pertaining to the measurement of rainfall; ***pluviometric coefficient*** (see quot. 1917); so **pluvioˈmetrical** *a.*; whence **pluvioˈmetrically** *adv.*; also **pluviˈometry**, the measurement of rainfall.

1884 *Daily News* 2 Jan. 5/8 The Committee of the Central Meteorological Society, Switzerland, has resolved to establish..a great number of observatories, which will be known as *pluviometric stations. **1905** *Westm. Gaz.* 14 Aug. 2/1 In Indo-China alone there are 345 pluviometric stations.

1917 A. McAdie *Princ. Aërography* xv. 218 The term 'pluviometric coefficient' was introduced by Angot to indicate the ratio of the mean daily rainfall of a particular month to the mean daily rainfall of the whole year. **1944** S. Putnam tr. *E. da Cunha's Rebellion in Backlands* i. 46 Torrential rains..giving rise to higher pluviometric readings than in..fertile lands of plenty. **1959** R. E. Huschke *Gloss. Meteorol.* 428 Seen collectively, the twelve pluviometric coefficients describe the normal month-to-month distribution of the normal annual precipitation in terms of each month's 'share' of the annual amount. **1818** *Niles' Register* 17 Jan. 331/2 *Pluviometrical Observations. **1828–32** Webster, *Pluviametrical.* **1882** *Nature* XXV. 592/2 The number of pluviometrical stations in the whole of France is 1561. **1890** *Cent. Dict.*, **Pluviometrically*, **Pluviometry*.

pluvioscope (ˈpluːvɪəskəʊp). [f. as prec. + -scope.] = pluviometer.

1887 *Nature* 17 Mar. 479/1 Pluviometric observations taken at Paris during the years 1860–70 with the pluvioscope invented by the author. **1895** in *Syd. Soc. Lex.*

‖**Pluviˈose**, *sb.* [F. *Pluviôse* (plyvjoz), ad. L. *pluviōsus* rainy: see next.] The fifth month of the French revolutionary calendar, extending (in the year 1794) from 20 Jan. to 18 Feb.

1796 Burke *Let. Noble Ld.* Wks. VIII. 106 On the day which, in their gipsey jargon, they call the 5th of Pluviose.

pluviose (ˈpluːvɪəʊs), *a. rare.* [ad. L. *pluviōsus* rainy, f. *pluvia* rain: see -ose.] Rainy, watery. In quot. *fig.* tearful.

1824 *Examiner* 337/1, I was moved to vent my pluviose indignation.

pluviosity (pluːvɪˈɒsɪtɪ). *rare.* [f. L. *pluviōs-us* (see prec.) + -ity.] The quality of being rainy or of giving rain.

1845 Lowell *Lett.* (1894) I. 105 Whether in a..heavy shower, or under the artificial pluviosity of the gardener's watering-pot. **1877** Morley *Crit. Misc.* Ser. II. 110 It was at least a gain to pay homage to that faculty..which had brought the forces of nature,—its pluviosity, nivosity, germinality, and vendemiarity,—under the yoke for the service of men. [Alluding to Pluviose *sb.*]

pluvious (ˈpluːvɪəs), *a.* [a. OF. *pluvieus* (1245 in Godef.), F. *pluvieux*, or ad. L. *pluviōsus* rainy.] Of, pertaining to, or characterized by rain; full of or bearing rain or moisture; rainy.

c **1420** *Pallad. on Husb.* VI. 66 In places ouer colde And pluuyous, olyues is to done To kitte, and mosse awey be rased wolde. **1597** A. M. tr. *Guillemeau's Fr. Chirurg.* 48/2 The ayre is to moyste and pluviouse or raynye. **1646** Sir T. Browne *Pseud. Ep.* VII. iv. 346 The Rainebow..declareth a pluvious disposure in the ayre. **1844** *Blackw. Mag.* LVI. 371 The pluvious metropolis of the west. *a* **1876** M. Collins *Th. in Garden* (1880) II. 235 Dost thou not find that this pluvious weather produceth much newspaper stupidity?

Pluvius (ˈpluːvɪəs). Also with lower-case initial. [L. *pluvius* rainy, causing or bringing rain.] Used *attrib.* with ref. to the insurance of holidays, outdoor sports, entertainments, etc., against disruption by bad weather, as ***Pluvius department, insurance, policy.***

1911 *Policy* 1 Apr. 206/2 The policies will be issued in respect of weather at the resorts..for any period from May 1st to September 30th. There will be four policies, known as the Pluvius Policies A, B, C, and D. **1920** *Post Mag. & Insurance Monitor* 4 Sept. 845/1 Now that Pluvius policies have come to stay, insurance men have of necessity to take an interest in the weather. **1949** *Policy Insurance Weekly* 2 June 373 In 1911 the brokers started Pluvius insurance. **1955** *Times* 13 May 18/2 Progress has been made in the Pluvius department. Despite extremely bad weather conditions over the British Isles and Europe, the experience was satisfactory. **1958** *Times* 3 July 15/4 The most direct effects of the recent rain will be on those firms who specialize in insuring against this sort of weather risk—so-called pluvius insurance. **1960** *News Chron.* 20 July 2/1 The Pluvius Department of the Eagle Star Insurance reports that business is 25% up on last year, and claims 50% up.

plwch, plwe, obs. north. forms of plough.

ply (plaɪ), *sb.* Also 6–7 **plie**. Pl. **plies**, occas. **plys**. [a. F. *pli* (13th c. in Hatz.-Darm.) a fold, bend, altered from OF. *ploi* (12th c.), vbl. sb. f. *ployer*, later *plier*: see ply *v.*[1] Sense 4 was developed in OF., and appears in Sc. before the more literal senses.]

I. 1. a. A fold; each of the layers or thicknesses produced by folding cloth, etc.; a strand or twist of rope, yarn, or thread. Also, each of the layers that go to make up a multilayer material such as plywood or laminated plastic. ***two-ply, three-ply, four-ply***: a fold of two, three, etc., layers; used *attrib.* to designate fingering or worsted, and carpets made of two or more interwoven webs; also, material (esp. plywood) composed of that number of layers. Also ***single-ply***.

1532 *Acc. Ld. High Treas. Scot.* VI. 77 Lyning fustiane to be ane plie betwix the utir half and the lyning of the..doublat. **1539** in Pitcairn *Crim. Trials* I. 297* Blak grey to stuff þe plyise of hir goune with. **1678** A. Lovell tr. *Thevenot's Trav.* II. 92 They double it into many plies, till it be but four or five Fingers broad. **1784** J. Barry in *Lect. Paint.* iii. (1848) 121 The plies and wrinkles in the body of the Christ in Rembrandt's famous Descent from the Cross. **1883** Mrs. Bishop in *Leisure Ho.* 199/1 These pests bite through two 'ply' of silk. **1886** Stevenson *Dr. Jekyll* iv, The carpets were of many plies and agreeable in colour. **1901** *J. Black's Carp. & Build., Home Handicr.* 76 If the knife is properly sharpened..it will not be difficult to cut through the four-ply which will necessarily result from this method of folding. **1910** *Timber Trades Jrnl.* 1 Jan. p. v (Advt.), Best Russian improved waterproof 3-ply. **1919** A. W. Judge *Handbk. Mod. Aeronaut.* IV. 235 Ordinary 3-ply (⅛ to ⅟₆ in.) is used for the webs of aeroplane wing ribs. **1926** *Rep. & Memoranda Aeronaut. Res. Comm.* No. 1017. 7 The inner (gas) ply was separated for a few inches from a 2-in. strip of a three-ply rubbered balloon fabric and the single-ply gripped in the lower jaw. **1935** Dawson & Porritt *Rubber* 330/2 Sheets were calendered to produce the maximum grain in unvulcanised state and slabs built up..from plies with grain in same direction. **1936** H. W. Rowell *Technol. of Plastics* xxvii. 191 In order that all air may be expelled and the plies or laminations thoroughly consolidated, a slow curing resinoid with a long plastic stage is used. **1941** *Paper Trade Jrnl.* CXII. 33/2 In contrast to the tests in which the bonding between plies is measured normal to the sheet, there are tests that measure the force required to tear plies apart. **1944** *Chem. Abstr.* XXXVIII. 3875 (*heading*) Preparing and handling cord fabric plies in tire core manufacture. **1952** J. P. Casey *Pulp & Paper* II. xvi. 803 In laminating paper plys, it is sometimes desirable to place alternate layers of paper with their cross and machine directions at right angles. **1957** *Practical Wireless* XXXIII. 521/2 Five pieces of three-ply were used in the original. **1960** *Farmer & Stockbreeder* 15 Mar. 11/1, 1cwt 6-ply paper bags. **1970** [see *cross-ply* adj. s.v. cross- B.]. **1975** [see plywood]. **1977** *New Scientist* 6 Jan. 22/1 If the plies are set wholly radially..the tread squirms on the road far too much for acceptable roadholding. If..the plies are circumferential..the tyre..gives a harsh and unyielding ride.

b. = plywood.

1929 A. Clarke *Pilgrimage* 31, I had a painted bedpost Of blue and yellow ply. **1957** *Practical Wireless* XXXIII. 542/1 The front panel should be of ¼ in. ply or hardboard. **1974** T. R. Dennis in J. Burnett *Useful Toil* III. 348 Drinking-water was kept in a bucket..with a piece of ply over to keep dust out. **1980** *Daily Tel.* 10 Mar. 18 Roughly half will come in the form of timber products:..windows, flooring blocks, ply, hardboard and newsprint.

2. A bend, crook, or curvature; *esp.* the elbow or middle joint of a limb; *spec.* in *Falconry*, of a hawk's wing. Now *rare* or *Obs.*

1575 Turberv. *Falconrie* 267 Specially about hir heade, the plie of hir wings and hir trayne. **1597** Lowe *Chirurg.* (1634) 117 Within 8 weekes after it brake out in the ply of her arme, and under her oxter. **1678–9** Newton in Rigaud *Corr. Sci. Men* (1841) II. 409 The rays of the sun..ought..to receive a ply from the denser ether. **1688** R. Holme *Armoury* II. 237/1 The Ply, or bent of the Wing, is the middle joynt in the pinion. **1726** *Dict. Rust.* (ed. 3), *Gascoin*, the hinder Thigh of a Horse, which begins at the Stiffle, and reaches to the Ply, or bending of the Ham. **1825** Loudon *Encycl. Agric.* 918 Scurfy, scabby eruptions, affecting the back of the knee, and ply of the hock; common..in cart-horses.

3. The condition of being bent or turned to one side; a twist, turn, direction; a bent, bias, inclination, or tendency of mind or character; esp. in phrase ***to take a (the, one's) ply***. Chiefly *fig.*

1605 Bacon *Advanc. Learn.* II. xxiii. §33. 112 In some other it is..a conceite that they can bring about occasions to their plie. **1612** —— *Ess., Cust. & Educ.* (Arb.) 370 It is true that late learners cannot so well take the plie. **1673** Wycherley *Gentl. Dancing-Master* IV. i, When once they have taken the French plie (as they call it) they are never to be made so much as Englishmen again. **1707** *Reflex. upon Ridicule* II. 117 They have taken their Ply, and will never be set right. **1873** H. Rogers *Orig. Bible* viii. (1875) 356 The natural bent and ply of man's nature. **1880** Green *Hist. Eng. People* IV. VIII. iv. 107 England took a ply which she has never wholly lost.

II. 4. Plight, condition; esp. in phrases ***in*** **(†*into*)** ***ply, in good ply***: in good condition, fit; so ***out of ply***. *Sc.*

c **1470** Henryson *Mor. Fab.* II. (*Town & C. Mouse*) xxi, Quhen hir sister in sic ply hir fand, For verray pietie scho began to greit. *Ibid.* IX. (*Wolf & Fox*) viii, Kiddis, lambes, or caponis in to ply. **1508** Dunbar *Flyting w. Kennedie* 170 Thy pure pynit thrott, pelit and owt of ply. **1824** Mactaggart *Gallovid. Encycl.* (1876) 22 Few gourmands are very fat, they eat themselves out of ply. **1831** Shennan *Tales* 44 The riders mount to try If a' things be in proper ply. **1895** *Westm. Gaz.* 27 Apr. 7/2 The Carron..is one of the best spring rivers in East Ross-shire when in ply.

III. 5. Special Comb.: **ply rating**, a number indicative of the strength of a tyre casing (orig. the number of cord plies in it).

1952 E. C. Woods *Pneumatic Tyre Design* i. 5 Tyre markings now carry an indication of casing strength in the form of 'ply rating' (e.g., '8 ply rating') to serve the purpose of identifying a given tyre with its maximum recommended load. **1956** R. H. Spelman in McPherson & Klemin *Engin. Uses of Rubber* x. 299 Many standard over-the-road highway tires may be marked 10 ply rating and actually be made of 8 plies of rayon, or even of fewer plies of a stronger material, such as nylon. **1969** *Times* 12 May 16/1 Tractor tyre research is being carried out with a new mobile test rig designed to study the effects of size, ply rating, etc.

ply (plaɪ), *v.*[1] Now *rare* or *dial.* Pa. t. and pple, plied (plaɪd). [ME. *plien*, a. OF. *plier*, secondary form of *pleiier* (3 sing. pres. *plie*, Roland, 11th c.), mod.F. *plier* and *ployer*:—L. *plicāre* to fold.

In imitation of OF. *preiier*:—L. *precāre*, 3rd sing. *prie* (whence *prier*), *pleiier* took 3rd sing. *plie*, whence a secondary form *plier*, beside *pleiier*, *ploiier*, *ployer*. Cf. ploy *v.*, playe.]

1. *trans.* To bend, bow; to fold or double (cloth or the like); to mould or shape (anything plastic). Now chiefly *dial.*

c **1375** *Sc. Leg. Saints* xxiv. (*Alexis*) 343 He..plyit þat bil, ore he wald leef, & It closyt in his nefe. *c* **1386** Chaucer *Merch. T.* 186 Right as men may warm wex with handes plye. **1390** Gower *Conf.* III. 121 Whan every feld hath corn in honde And many a man his bak hath plied. **1483** *Cath. Angl.* 284/1 To Plye, *flectere*,..*vbi* to bowe. *a* **1592** Greene *George a Greene* Wks. (Rtldg.) 256/2 So have I liberty to ply my bow. **1593** Q. Eliz. *Boethius* III. metr. ii. 47 The twig drawen ons with mighty fors Bowing plies her top. **1799** G. Smith *Laboratory* I. 27 Plying the necks of the rockets at top, to the right. **1825** J. Nicholson *Operat. Mechanic* 381 With the first act of plying or doubling, which is introduced in the process of spinning. **1896** A. E. Housman *Shropshire Lad* xxxi, The gale, it plies the saplings double.

†b. *fig.* To bend in will or disposition; to bend the sense of (words); to adapt, accommodate. *Obs.*

1390 Gower *Conf.* I. 274 Ther mai no gold the Jugge plie, That he ne schal the sothe trie. **1581** J. Bell *Haddon's Answ. Osor.* 150 God leadeth and boweth..every person inwardly by his owne will, nor plyeth hee any man otherwise then voluntarily. **1639** N. N. tr. *Du Bosq's Compl. Woman* II. 27 If other Arts have their particular tearms which they ply not to accomodate themselves to such as make no profession of them. *a* **1657** Sir W. Mure *Hist.* Wks. (S.T.S.) II. 251 Haveing plyed himself much to the hwmore of the Duke of Albany.

†2. *intr.* To bend or be bent; to yield, give (*to* pressure or movement); to be pliable or yielding. *Obs.*

13.. [see *plying* below]. *c* **1386** Chaucer *Clerk's T.* 1113 The coyne..wolde rather breste atwo than plye. *c* **1407** Lydg. *Reson. & Sens.* 6810 Glas ys..Redy to breke but nat to plye. **1578** T. Proctor *Gorg. Gallery* H iij, No more then Waues..May stir the stedfast rocke, that will not ply. **1600** T. Creed tr. *Ovid's Remedie of Loue* xlv, Behold the Apple bough how it doth ply And stoope with store of fruit that doth abound. **1692** R. L'Estrange *Fables* ccxv. (1714) 233 It blew a Violent Storm. The Willow ply'd and gave way to the Gust. **1753** *Phil. Trans.* XLVIII. 29 From the coarctation of her breast, all its bones plying inwardly.

†b. To bend in reverence; to bow. *Obs.*

13.. *St. Erkenwolde* 138 in Horstm. *Altengl. Leg.* 269 þe prelate passide one þe playne: þer plied to hym lordes.

†c. To bend one's body forcibly; to twist, writhe. *Obs.*

1734 tr. *Rollin's Anc. Hist.*, Throttling, pressing in their arms, struggling, plying on all sides. **1845** T. B. Shaw in *Blackw. Mag.* LVIII. 34 'Gainst the bank, like a Wrestler, he struggleth and plyeth.

3. *fig.* To yield, give way *to*; to incline, tend; to submit, comply, consent; to be pliant or tractable. Now *rare* or *Obs.*

13.. *E.E. Allit. P.* B. 196 þat..prynce þat paradys weldez Is displesed at vch a poynt þat plyes to scaþe. **1390** Gower *Conf.* III. 227 And thanne a king list noght to plie To hiere what the clamour wolde. **1491** Caxton *Vitas Patr.* (W. de W. 1495) I. lxxxix. 125 b/1 For noo prayer he wolde not plye ne consente therto. **1587** Turberv. *Trag. T.* (1837) 18, I am content to plie unto your pleasures out of hande. *a* **1715** Burnet *Own Time* (1823) I. 426 As they never disagreed, so all plied before them. **1768–74** Tucker *Lt. Nat.* (1834) II. 615 Expecting that all things and all persons should ply to their interests and desires. **1827** Carlyle *Germ. Rom.* I. 40 With kindly indulgence plied into the daughter's will.

†4. *trans.* ***ply over***: to overlay or cover with something bent or folded. *Obs. rare.*

a **1400–50** *Alexander* 1517 He plyes ouire þe pauement with pallen webis Mas on hiȝt ouire his hede for hete of þe sone. *Ibid.* 5260 Hire palais was..Plied ouir with pure gold all þe plate-rofes.

†5. ***ply out***: to get or draw out by bending or twisting, as with pliers. *Obs. rare.*

1667 Dryden *Sir Martin Mar-all* II. i, You must..still ply out of them your advantages.

Hence **ˈplying** *ppl. a.*, bending; pliant.

13.. *E.E. Allit P.* C. 439 Hit watz playn in þat place for plyande greuez. ? *a* **1400** *Morte Arth.* 777 With pykes fulle perilous, alle plyande þame semyde. **1598** Q. Eliz. *Plutarch* xii. 10 Hither turne our witz sharpnis and pliing mind. **1710** Philips *Pastorals* v. 84 Like winds, that gently brush the plying grass.

ply (plaɪ), *v.*[2] Pa. t. and pple. **plied**. [ME. *plye*, aphetic form of ME. *aplie*, *aplye*, apply *v.*, which see for derivation and development of senses.]

I. To apply, employ, work busily at.

†1. *refl.* To apply oneself assiduously (*to*), exert oneself (*with* a weapon, etc.); = apply *v.* 14. *Obs.*

1390 Gower *Conf.* I. 265 For ay the mor that he envieth The more ayein himself he plieth. **1494** Fabyan *Chron.* VII. ccxxvi. 253 Thys Henry in his youth plyed hym to suche study yᵗ he was enstructe in the .vii. artys lyberallys. **1590** Webbe *Trav.* (Arb.) 23 The women of ye towne did plie themselues with their weapons, making a great massacre vpon our men.

†b. To address or betake oneself (*to*): = apply *v.* 27. *Obs.*

1668 Owen *Exp. Ps.* cxxx. Wks. 1851 VI. 379 He plies himself to God in Christ for pardon and mercy.

2. *intr.* To employ or occupy oneself busily or steadily; to work *at* something; to apply, attend closely *to*; = apply *v.* 15. Now *rare.*

13.. *E.E. Allit. P.* B. 1385 þe place, þat plyed þe pursaunt wythinne. **1644** Milton *Educ.* Wks. 1738 I. 137 Ere half these Authors be read (which will soon be with plying hard and daily). **1714** *Orig. Canto Spencer* xxxvi, The strugling Fly..Who still for Freedom plies both fierce and bold. **1768–74** Tucker *Lt. Nat.* (1834) II. 578 He that plies to his business finds it, when grown familiar to him, a state of satisfaction. **1825** *New Monthly Mag.* XIV. 13, I plied at Cicero and Demosthenes, I devoured every treatise on the art of rhetoric. **1849** LONGF. *Build. Ship* 182 Around the bows and along the side The heavy hammers and mallets plied.

3. *trans.* To use, handle, or wield vigorously or diligently (an instrument, tool, weapon); to employ, exert (a faculty); = APPLY *v.* 16 b.

c **1374** CHAUCER *Troylus* I. 732 Artow lyk an asse to þe harpe That hereth soun whan men þe strenges plye. **1514** BARCLAY *Cyt. & Uplondyshm.* (Percy Soc.) 25 Theyr wyt & body all hole do they ply. **1589** GREENE *Menaphon* (Arb.) 33 Lamedon so plide his teeth, that all supper he spake not one word. **1590** SPENSER *F.Q.* I. vi. 19 During which time her gentle wit she plyes To teach them truth. *c* **1595** CAPT. WYATT *R. Dudley's Voy. W. Ind.* (Hakl. Soc.) 12 The lande forces..plied their shott soe thick that our men weare forced to place all the Spanish prisoners between themselves and the shott. **1603** DRAYTON *Odes* xvii. 109 Suffolke his Axe did ply. **1620** MIDDLETON *Chaste Maid* I. ii. 112 Go to school, ply your books, boys. **1669** STURMY *Mariner's Mag.* I. ii. 20 He plies his small Shot;..Ply your Hand-Granadoes and Stink-Pots. **1718** PRIOR *Pleasure* 41 A thousand maidens ply the purple loom. *a* **1873** LYTTON *Ken. Chillingly* II. ix, Thou canst ply a good knife and fork. **1887** BOWEN *Virg. Æneid* III. 128 Together their oars they ply.

b. To apply oneself to, practise, work at (one's business, an industry, a task, etc.): = APPLY *v.* 16 a.

1494 FABYAN *Chron.* V. cxxxiv. 120 Then they plyed no thynge that was worldly, but gaue them to prechynge and techynge. **1555** W. WATREMAN *Fardle Facions* II. xii. 269 Diligently to plye the reading of holy scripture. **1616** B. JONSON *Forest* vi, When youths ply their stolne delights. *a* **1661** FULLER *Worthies* (1840) I. 442 Clothing is plied in this city with great industry and judgment. **1784** COWPER *Task* IV. 150 The needle plies its busy task. **1867** SMILES *Huguenots Eng.* vi. (1880) 97 The town in which they plied their trade.

†**c.** With indef. *it*, in various preceding senses.

1582 N. LICHEFIELD tr. *Castanheda's Conq. E. Ind.* I. lxxviii. 160 b, Also there were many Paraos and Tones,..a lading as fast as they could plye it. **1605** B. JONSON *Volpone* III. iii, A courtier would not ply it so, for a place. **1618** BOLTON *Florus* (1636) 80 They forthwith plyde it with Oare and Saile. **1666** BUNYAN *Grace Ab.* §110, I will ply it close, but I will have my end accomplished.

4. *trans.* **a.** To keep at work at, to work away at; to attack or assail vigorously or repeatedly (*with* some instrument or process). **b.** To offer something to (a person) frequently or persistently; to press (one) to take; to continue to supply *with* food, drink, gifts, etc.; = APPLY *v.* 17.

1548 PATTEN *Exped. Scotl.* Pref. a ij, Begunne, bylded, and soo well plyed in woorke, that in a fewe wekes..they wear made and left defensyble. **1576** FLEMING *Panopl. Epist.* 307 That wound neuer groweth to a skarre, which is not plyed with playsters. **1579–80** NORTH *Plutarch* (1676) 267 Marcellus plied him so..with continual alarums and skirmishes, that he brought him to a Battell. **1601** HOLLAND *Pliny* I. 544 Almond trees if they be plied with digging, will either not bloome at all, or else shed their floures before due time. **1602** ROWLANDS *Tis Merrie* 11 She ply'd him with the Wine in golden Cup. **1632** J. HAYWARD tr. *Biondi's Eromena* 11 Causing the ghing to ply the sea with their oares. **1767** T. HUTCHINSON *Hist. Mass.* II. 181 The bomb-ship..plied the French with her shells. **1856** R. A. VAUGHAN *Mystics* (1860) I. 172 To ply them more pressingly with food than with arguments.

5. To solicit with importunity or persistence; to importune, urge; to keep on at (a person) *with* questions, petitions, arguments, etc.; †*spec.* of a porter, boatman, etc.: To solicit patronage from (*obs.*); = APPLY *v.* 17.

1587 TURBERV. *Trag. T.* (1837) 149 He daily plyde her mayde, Thereby to make her graunte And yelde him his desire. **1596** SHAKS. *Merch. V.* III. ii. 279 He [Shylock] plyes the Duke at morning and at night. *a* **1639** SPOTTISWOOD *Hist. Ch. Scot.* II. (1677) 74 The Governors Brother did earnestly ply him to relinquish the English Alliance. **1678** BUTLER *Hud.* III. iii. 747 Ply her with love letters and Billets. **1725** *New Cant. Dict., Rattling Mumpers*, such [beggars] as run after, or ply Coaches. **1760** C. JOHNSTON *Chrysal* (1822) III. 292 He was overtaken by the waggon, the driver of which plied him in the usual way to take a place. **1777** *Chron.* in *Ann. Reg.* 215 One Holderness, a waterman, plied some gentlemen, and, when in his boat, asked where they were going. **1832** HT. MARTINEAU *Ireland* ii. 24 Her filial duty, religion, and love, all plied her at once in favour of an immediate marriage. **1883** EDERSHEIM *Life Jesus* (ed. 6) II. 572 In vain did he ply Christ with questions.

II. In nautical and derived uses.

6. *intr.* To beat up against the wind; to tack, work to windward. (Cf. APPLY *v.* 22.)

1556 W. TOWRSON in Hakluyt *Voy.* (1589) 110 We wayed and plyed backe againe to seeke the Hinde. *c* **1595** CAPT. WYATT *R. Dudley's Voy. W. Ind.* (Hakl. Soc.) 11 Neither might wee plie up unto that iland, the winde was soe contrarie for our course. **1697** DAMPIER *Voy. round World* (1699) 142 They always go before the Wind, being unable to Ply against it. **1748** *Anson's Voy.* II. ii. 127 Her people were ..so..weakned by sickness, as not to be able to ply up to windward. **1835** SIR J. ROSS *Narr. 2nd Voy.* iv. 52 It.. assisted us very much in plying to windward. **1867** SMYTH *Sailor's Word-bk., Ply*,..to work to windward, to beat.

b. with *about*, *off and on*, *to and again*, *up and down*, and the like.

c **1595** CAPT. WYATT *R. Dudley's Voy. W. Ind.* (Hakl. Soc.) 13 Afterwards..wee plied up and downe to finde the other carvell. **1628** DIGBY *Voy. Medit.* (1868) 7 The wind came easterly, so that wee plyed to and againe along the Spanish shore. **1670** MILTON *Hist. Eng.* Wks. 1738 II. 15 Commanded to ply up and down continually with Relief where they saw Need. **1748** *Anson's Voy.* II. v. 175 Plying on and off till the 6th of October.

fig. **1665** J. WEBB *Stone-Heng* (1725) 184 His own Testimony by plying off and on, as he hath continually done, is so little to be valued.

c. *gen.* To direct one's course (in a ship or otherwise), to steer; to move onwards; to make *towards*. Now only *poet.* = APPLY *v.* 24.

c **1595** CAPT. WYATT *Dudley's Voy. W. Ind.* (Hakl. Soc.) 4 Returninge with thease advertisements unto our Generall, wee plied for Plimworth. **1596** SPENSER *F.Q.* IV. i. 38 They chaunced to espie Two other Knights, that towards them did ply With speedie course. **1637** RUTHERFORD *Lett.* (1862) I. 207 Oh, how fair have many ships been plying before the wind that, in an hour's space, have been lying in the sea-bottom! **1779** E. HERVEY *Naval Hist.* II. 158 Returning light discovered the enemy seven leagues off Weymouth, whither the English plied, and came up with them in the afternoon. **1820** W. SCORESBY *Acc. Arctic Reg.* I. 309 We plied towards the land. *a* **1861** CLOUGH *Qua Cursum Ventus* ii, When fell the night, upsprung the breeze, And all the darkling hours they plied.

†**d.** *trans.* To use (a tide, etc.) to work a ship up a river, to windward, etc. *Obs.*

1556 S. BURROUGH in Hakluyt *Voy.* (1598) I. 279 We stopped the ebbes, and plyed all the floods to the windewards, and made our way Eastnortheast. **1673** R. HADDOCK *Jrnl.* in *Camden Misc.* (1881) 29 We wayed to plye up, and plyed the tyde to an end.

7. *intr.* Of a vessel or its master: To sail or go more or less regularly to and fro *between* certain places; also said of land-carriage.

1803 WELLINGTON in Gurw. *Desp.* (1837) II. 370 A detachment..which plies between the Godavery and camp, will keep me free from want. **1832** G. DOWNES *Lett. Cont. Countries* I. 256 A passage-boat, which plies between the hamlets of Eaux Vives and Le Paquis, situated at opposite sides of the lake. **1863** P. BARRY *Dockyard Econ.* 263 The *Richmond*, a small vessel which was built in the year 1815 and plied between London and Richmond. **1878** GLADSTONE *Primer Homer* xii. 139 We hear..of the ferryman plying between Ithaca and Cefalonia.

b. *trans.* To traverse (a river, ferry, passage) by rowing or sailing.

1700 *Col. Rec. Pennsylv.* II. 13 Ordered also That no fferryman shall be permitted to ply the River Delaware. **1812** *Chron.* in *Ann. Reg.* 115/1 James Dean..who plies the passage from Bulwell to Milford. **1897** *Daily News* 6 July 5/3 Hardy bargemen who ply Father Thames by day and night from Twickenham Ferry to the Nore.

†**8.** *trans.* To bear or bring *to* a place by journeying to and fro. *Obs. rare*$^{-1}$.

1590 GREENE *Never too late* (1600) F j, The labouring Bees ..Plied to the hiues sweet honey from those flowers.

9. *intr.* Of a boatman, porter, cabman, etc.: To wait or attend regularly, to have one's stand *at* a certain place for hire or custom.

1700 FARQUHAR *Constant Couple* III. i, Here's Tom Errand, the Porter, that plys at the Blew Posts. **1711** ADDISON *Spect.* No. 94 ¶8 He was..forced to think of plying in the Streets as a Porter. **1739** LABELYE *Short Acc. Piers Westm. Bridge* 71 Room..for the Watermen to ply for Fares. *c* **1770** DIBDIN *Song, Waterman*, And did you not hear of a jolly young waterman Who at Blackfriars Bridge used for to ply? **1885** *Chamb. Jrnl.* 1 Jan. 778, I must on no account ply for hire.

ply, var. of PLEA.

Plyades, obs. f. PLEIADES.

plyar, plyer: see PLIER.

†**plychon.** *Surg. Obs.* [? corruption of PELICAN *sb.*] (See quot.)

1688 R. HOLME *Armoury* III. xx. (Roxb.) 238/2 *A Plychon.* It is an Instrument to pull out Teeth.

plycht, plyght, ply3t, obs. forms of PLIGHT.

plyd, obs. form of PLAID.

Plyglass (ˈplaɪglɑːs, -æ-). Also **plyglass, ply glass, ply-glass.** A proprietary name for units consisting of two or more panes of glass enclosing one or more hermetically sealed spaces, which may contain dry air or be filled with a translucent material like glass fibre. Also *attrib.*

[**1949** *Trade Marks Jrnl.* 2 Mar. 191/1 *Plygloss* [sic]... Glassware.., plate glass, sheet glass, glass rods, glass tubes .., glass wool and spun glass. Plyglass Limited,..Leyton, London,..manufacturers.] **1956** *Archit. Rev.* CXIX. 46 Normal windows are of galvanized steel; panels between windows, of cantilevered section, are ply-glass. *Ibid.* CXX. 105 (*caption*) The panels between the first- and second-storey windows are of dark-green plyglass. **1958** *Engineering* 28 Feb. 276/1 Dark-blue ply glass panels are used beneath the windows on the north and south elevations. **1958** *Specification* (ed. 59) 1123/2 Uses of Plyglass diffusors are in roof lights, laylights and over-transom lights. **1960** *Trade Marks Jrnl.* 21 Sept. 1149/1 *Plyglass...* Units consisting of two or more panes of glass enclosing hermetically sealed cavities and being for use in the building industry. Plyglass Limited,..Harlow, Essex; manufacturers. **1972** *Specification* (ed. 73) II. 441/2 Plyglass thermopane insulating glass (Plyglass Ltd.) consists of two or more panes of clear glass and most types of patterned glass enclosing a layer of dehydrated and filtered air which is sealed in with Bondermetic glass to metal seal.

plying (ˈplaɪɪŋ), *vbl. sb.* [f. PLY *v.*^{2} + -ING^{1}.] The action of PLY *v.*^{2}, in various senses. *attrib.* **plying-place**, a place where a porter, hackney-carriage, or boat stands for hire (PLY *v.* 9).

1766 ENTICK *London* IV. 21 Paul's-wharf, a public plying-place for watermen and water-carriage. *Ibid.* 242 At the south extremity of Water-lane is the common plying-place and ferry.

Plym (plɪm), *sb.* [Shortened f. PLYMOUTH.]

1. *humorous.* An inhabitant of Plymouth.

1913 W. OWEN *Let.* 23 Apr. (1967) 185, I should enjoy treating at length of Plymouth and the Plyms, the charm of Devon.

2. *colloq.* A member of the Plymouth Brethren.

1953 'N. BLAKE' *Dreadful Hollow* ii. 20 Staying at a pub won't commend you to the Plyms. **1977** *Times Lit. Suppl.* 13 May 593/3 The solemn girl who turned him down, back in the 1890s, because of an apparent lack of religious conviction; she was what is known as a Plym.

†**plym, plymme**, *v. Falconry. Obs.* A parallel form of PLUME *v.* 1.

1486 *Bk. St. Albans* C v, Let hir plym vppon it as moch as she will, and when she hath plymmed Inough go to hir softely for frayng. *Ibid.* D ij, Yf she haue fownde the fowle and desire to flee ther to, let hir slee it, and plymme well vppon hir.

plymetal (ˈplaɪmɛtəl). [f. PLY *sb.* or PLY(WOOD + METAL *sb.* (and *a.*)] A construction material consisting of plywood faced on both sides with aluminium.

1927 KNIGHT & WULPI *Veneers & Plywood* xv. 139 (*heading*) Plymetal. **1936** A. F. COLLINS *Motor Car Trailers* II. 103 Where the duck joins the sheet steel bonnets of plymetal a 1" wide metal molding is used to cover the joint. **1940** BRIMM & BOGGESS *Aircraft Maintenance* 17 Plymetal is used for floorboards, baggage compartment linings, etc. **1967** *Jane's Surface Skimmer Systems 1967–68* 63/1 The frame is of ply-metal panel, consisting of 1 in. (25·4 mm) exterior grade AC plywood faced both sides with 0·050 in. (1·3 mm) mill finished 3003-H12 aluminium.

Plymouth (ˈplɪməθ). [Name of a city in Devon.]

1. a. Applied to the first hard-paste porcelain to be made in England, by a method patented in 1768 by W. Cookworthy of Plymouth (subsequently of Bristol: see BRISTOL 2 b).

1816 W. BURT *Rev. Mercantile State Plymouth* xvi. 174 The substance serving as a base for the Plymouth porcelain was a granite..composed of a reddish felspar in pieces of a tolerable size, quartz in small grains, and black scaly mica. **1857** J. MARRYAT *Hist. Pottery & Porcelain* (ed. 2) xii. 289 The Plymouth china has become very scarce. **1869** C. SCHREIBER *Jrnl.* 11 Sept. (1911) I. 36 There C.S. discovered a coloured group of Venus and Cupid..valuable as being Plymouth. **1873** H. OWEN *Two Centuries Ceramic Art in Bristol* vii. 193 The quantity of the Plymouth porcelain preserved to us, compared with the amount of Bristol manufacture in the possession of collectors, is relatively very small. **1946** F. S. MACKENNA (*title*) Cookworthy's Plymouth and Bristol porcelain. **1974** *Country Life* 28 Feb. (Suppl.) 43 Set of four Plymouth figures of the Continents, $12\frac{1}{4}$ in. high.

b. Applied to a coarse, brown and yellow earthenware manufactured at Plymouth in the 18th century.

1878 L. JEWITT *Ceramic Art Gt. Brit.* I. x. 338 (*heading*) Plymouth earthenware... The manufacture of china-ware having ceased in Plymouth in 1774 this useful and elegant art was lost to the town. Some years later rough common brown and yellow earthenware was made here. **1960** H. HAYWARD *Connoisseur's Handbk. Antique Collecting* 222/1 *Plymouth earthenware*, coarse earthenware (brown and yellow) was manufactured here in the 18th cent., but gave way about 1810 to the production of painted or printed cream colour.

2. Applied to a variety of gin orig. made in the west of England.

1864 C. TOVEY *Brit. & Foreign Spirits* iii. 118 An imitation Hollands is made by some rectifiers, and meets with a sale in Cornwall and in the West of England. Plymouth Gin is somewhat of the character of Hollands. **1885** *Encycl. Brit.* XIX. 237/2 Plymouth has few manufactures, the principal being biscuits..and the celebrated Plymouth gin. **1920** G. SAINTSBURY *Notes on Cellar-Book* vii. 104 More recent conditions, when in England and Scotland, excellent brandy cost five shillings a bottle;..and gin, whether 'squareface' or London or Plymouth, not much more than half a crown. **1951** R. POSTGATE *Plain Man's Guide to Wine* ix. 121 *Plymouth* gin.. has rather more of the distinctive flat juniper taste. **1967** J. B. PRIESTLEY *It's Old Country* iv. 43 Large pink Plymouth for me, cobber. **1968** J. D. MACDONALD *Girl in Plain Brown Wrapper* iv. 35, I took one of the big glasses and laid an impressive belt of Plymouth atop the cubes.

See also PLYMOUTH BRETHREN, PLYMOUTH CLOAK.

Plymouth Brethren. [See *Brethren* in BROTHER 3 b.] A religious body calling themselves 'the Brethren', recognizing no official order of ministers, and having no formal creed, which arose at Plymouth *c* 1830. **Plymouth brother**, a member of this body.

1842 R. M. BEVERLEY *Ch. Eng. Exam.* (1844) 1 The views of those whom he chooses to call 'the Plymouth Brethren'. **1865** *Chambers' Encycl.* VII. 614 The Plymouth Brethren reject every distinctive appellation but that of Christians. **1879** STEVENSON *Trav. Cevennes, Valley of Tarn*, He was, as a matter of fact, a Plymouth Brother.

Hence **Plymouth-brethrenism, Plymouth-brotherism;** also **Plymouth sister.**

1848 J. H. NEWMAN *Loss & Gain* viii. 197 Where else will you go? Not surely to Methodism or Plymouth-brotherism. **1860** MISS YONGE *Hopes* II. xiii. 250 She is a Plymouth sister. **1874** C. M. YONGE *Life J. C. Patteson* I. v. 161 Primitive Methodism and Plymouth Brethrenism supplied the void. **1879** CROSKERY (*title*) Plymouth Brethrenism, a refutation.

†**Plymouth cloak.** *Obs. slang.* A cudgel or staff, carried by one who walked *in cuerpo*, and thus facetiously assumed to take the place of a cloak. (For the reason of the name, see quot. *a* 1661.)

1608 DEKKER *2nd Pt. Honest Wh.* III. ii, Shall I walke in a Plimouth Cloake, (that's to say) like a rogue, in my hose and doublet, and a crabtree cudgell in my hand? **1625** MASSINGER *New Way* I. i, And I must tell you if you but aduance, Your plimworth cloke, you shall be soone instructed. *a* **1661** FULLER *Worthies, Devon* (1662) 248 *A Plimouth Cloak.* That is a Cane or a Staffe, whereof this the occasion. Many a man of good extraction, comming home from far Voiages, may chance to land here [at Plymouth], and being out of sorts, is unable for the present time and place to recruit himself with Cloaths. Here (if not friendly provided) they make the next Wood their Drapers shop, where a Staffe cut out, serves them for a covering. [**1670** RAY *Prov.* 225 adds: For we use when we walk *in cuerpo* to carry a staff in our hands, but none when in a cloak.] [*a* **1668**: see CLOAK *sb.* 5.] **1677** MRS. BEHN *Rover* III. i, Walking like the Sign of the naked Boy, with Plimouth Cloaks in our hands. *a* **1688** DENHAM *Ballad on Sir J. Mennis* vii, He being proudly mounted, Clad in cloak of Plymouth. **1855** KINGSLEY *Westw. Ho!* vii, Thou wilt please to lay down that Plymouth cloak of thine.

Plymouthism (ˈplɪməθɪz(ə)m). [See -ISM.] The system or doctrine of the Plymouth Brethren. So **'Plymouthist, 'Plymouthite,** a member of this body; also *attrib.*

1876 SPURGEON *Commenting* 61 We do not endorse the Plymouthism which pervades these notes. *Ibid.* 115 First published in the Plymouthite Magazine. **1885** *Encycl. Brit.* XIX. 238/2 French Switzerland has always remained the stronghold of Plymouthism on the Continent. *Ibid.* 239/1 There are..at least five official divisions or sects of Plymouthists.

Plymouth Rock (ˌplɪməθˈrɒk). [The spot at which the passengers of the Mayflower landed in New England in 1620.] Name of a breed of domestic fowls of American origin, characterized by large size, ashen or grey plumage barred with blackish stripes, and yellow beak, legs, and feet.

1873 in L. Wright *Bk. Poultry* (1874) 436 Our modern Plymouth Rock fowl is in no way whatever connected with the Plymouth Rock produced by Dr. Bennett some twenty-five years since, from a cross with the Asiatic fowls. **1892** J. K. FOWLER *Echoes Old Country Life* 238 Another capital race is the Plymouth Rocks bred by the Americans from, I think, a cuckoo-coloured fowl and the Cochin. **1900** *Field* 23 June 903/2 The Plymouth rock, a useful second class general utility fowl, is not as popular as it was.

†**'ply-pot.** *Obs. rare*⁻¹. [f. PLY *v.*² + POT *sb.*] One who plies the pot; one addicted to drinking.

1611 COTGR. s.v. *Gobelin, Face gobeline*, a crimzon face; the visage of a plie-pot.

plyt, -e, obs. forms of PLIGHT *sb.* and *v.*

plywood (ˈplaɪwʊd). Formerly also **ply-wood, ply wood.** [f. (*three-*, etc.) *ply wood.*] Board made of two or more thin layers of wood bonded together with the grain of adjacent layers crosswise to give increased strength and resistance to warping, there being either an odd number of layers including a thin central one or an even number sandwiching a thicker central core. Freq. *attrib.* or in *Comb.* Cf. *laminated wood* s.v. LAMINATED *ppl. a.*

1907 *Timber Trades Jrnl.* 13 Apr. 818/2 (Advt.), Agents for Swedish..wood goods..ply wood (oak, birch, alder, etc.). **1919** A. W. JUDGE *Handbk. Mod. Aeronautics* IV. 234 The ply-woods chiefly employed in aeroplane work may vary from 1/8 to 1/4 in. in thickness, and are made of ash or birch with an intermediate layer of poplar..or white-wood. **1922** W. SCHLICH *Man. Forestry* (ed. 4) I. 228 These pines..are also used for butter boxes, plywood, etc. **1926** *Glasgow Herald* 1 Oct. 5 The prosperity of the plywood industry. **1940** H. R. SIMONDS *Industr. Plastics* x. 273 Formed or molded plywood is becoming increasingly important for the manufacture of trays, shallow dishes and bowls. **1957** *Times* 12 Nov. (Canada Suppl.) p. xvi/4 A new type of express cabin cruiser..costs less than $4,000, is mostly built of plywood, and can be easily hoisted onto a trailer. **1964** B. LATHAM *Wood* xiii. 163 In the large modern plywood mills ..very little hand labour is employed. Another great plywood-producing area is the Baltic. **1969** *Jane's Freight Containers 1968–69* 523/1 The container is of welded steel frame and self-supporting plywood panel construction. **1975** W. P. K. FINDLAY *Timber* xii. 174 Thin plywood is generally made from three veneers. Multi-ply boards have an uneven number of plies so that the grain on the face and back always run in the same direction.

p.m., abbrev. of POST MERIDIEM, afternoon, q.v.

pn-, an initial combination occurring only in words from Greek; the *p* is usually mute in English.

(The *p* is pronounced in French, Spanish, Italian, German, Dutch, and other European langs.; also by Englishmen in reading Greek. It is to be desired that it were sounded in English also, at least in scientific and learned words; since the reduction of *pneo-* to *neo-*, *pneu-* to *new-*, and *pnyx* to *nix*, is a loss to etymology and intelligibility, and a weakening of the resources of the language.)

pneo- (pniːəʊ, niːəʊ), combining element from Gr. πνέ-ειν, πνεῖν to blow, breathe, used in a few rare scientific terms.

‖**pneobiognosis** (-baɪəʊˈgnəʊsɪs) [mod.L., f. Gr. βίος life + γνῶσις investigation, knowledge, after *diagnosis*], in *Medical Jurisprudence*, the test, by the presence or absence of air in the lungs, whether a child has been born alive; also called PNEUSIOBIOGNOSIS, or ‖**pneobio'mantia** [Gr. μαντεία divination]; whence **pneobio'mantic** *a.*, **pneobio'mantics. pneody'namics** [DYNAMICS], the science of the forces concerned in respiration. ‖**pneo'gaster** [mod.L., f. Gr. γαστήρ belly], term for the whole respiratory tract, considered as a specialized portion of the intestinal tract; hence **pneo'gastric** *a.* **'pneograph** [-GRAPH], (*a*) an instrument invented by Mortimer Granville for indicating the force and character of expiration by means of a light disk suspended in front of the mouth and connected with a needle which makes an automatic tracing; (*b*) = *pneometer.* **pne'ometer** [-METER], an instrument for measuring the amount of air inspired and expired, a pneumatometer, spirometer; so **pne'ometry,** the measurement of the amount of air inspired and expired, pneumatometry. **'pneoscope** [-SCOPE], an instrument for measuring the extent of movement of the thorax in respiration. (*Syd. Soc. Lex.* 1895.)

1858 MAYNE *Expos. Lex.* 984/2 Pneobiomantia. *Ibid.*, Pneobiomantics. *Ibid.*, Pneobiomantic. **1888** *Lancet* 13 Oct. 724/1 A Pocket Clinical Pneograph... The tracing of the pneograph shows the expiration by a more or less vertical line, the duration of the expiratory effort being indicated by the length of the line traced by the needle before it descends, at the moment when inspiration commences.

pneu (njuː). *colloq.* (*a*) Abbrev. of PNEUMONIA. (*b*) Abbrev. of 'pneumatic cushion'. (*c*) Abbrev. of PNEUMATIQUE. Cf. PNEUS.

1916 [see GIPPY]. **1923** A. HUXLEY *Antic Hay* i. 7 An air cushion, a delicious pneu. **1928** J. JOYCE *Let.* 19 Jan. (1966) III. 168, I got your pneu and shall follow your instructions. **1965** G. D. PAINTER *Proust* II. xvii. 362 Soon Reynaldo would come to write hurried *pneus* to Marcel's friends.

pneum, -e (pnjuːm, njuːm). *Mus.* [ad. Gr. πνεῦμα: see next.] = PNEUMA 2 b, NEUME 2.

1879 HELMORE in Grove *Dict. Mus.* I. 17/1 Accents or marks, sometimes called *pneums*, for the regulation of recitation and singing were in use among the ancient Greeks and Hebrews, and are still used in the synagogues of the Jews. **1890** *Athenæum* 26 Apr. 450/3 Twenty specimens.. selected to illustrate the gradual development of the ancient pneumes into the characters now used on a staff of lines and spaces. **1890** *Daily News* 1 May 7/5 Showing how the pneums and points gradually assumed the form of our modern notes.

‖**pneuma** (ˈpnjuːmə, ˈnjuːmə). [a. Gr. πνεῦμα wind, breath, spirit, *prop.* that which is blown or breathed, f. πνέειν, πνεῖν to blow, breathe.]

1. The Greek word for 'spirit' or 'soul', occas. used in Eng. context.

1884 W. G. STEVENSON in *Pop. Sc. Monthly* XXIV. 761 [Hippocrates] taught the existence of an 'intermediate nature', which though distinct from the mortal Soul or pneuma, was the source of vital activity. **1894** *Daily News* 25 Oct. 6/2 The pneuma, the overshadowing spirit of the new man who is sought after by Angela, the Psyche or feminine principle of aspiration and intuition.

2. *Mediæval Mus.* **a.** A long ligature or group of notes sung to one (inarticulate) syllable at the end of a plain-song melody: = NEUME 1. **b.** One of a set of signs indicating the tones of the chant: = NEUME 2, PNEUM.

1880 ROCKSTRO in Grove *Dict. Mus.* II. 691/2 The very essence of the Pneuma lies in its adaptation to an inarticulate sound. **1881** *Ibid.* III. 4/2 The Preface to the Ratisbon Gradual directs that the Pneuma shall be sung upon the vowel A.

pneumathæmia (pnjuːməˈθiːmɪə, njuː-). *Path.* [f. Gr. πνεῦμα, πνευματ- (see PNEUMA) + αἷμα blood; cf. *hyperæmia*, etc.] 'The presence of air in a blood-vessel' (*Syd. Soc. Lex.* 1895).

1876 tr. *Wagner's Gen. Pathol.* (ed. 6) 239 In the blood, pneumathæmia.

pneumatic (njuːˈmætɪk), *a.* (*sb.*) [ad. L. *pneumaticus* of or belonging to air or wind (Vitr., Plin.), a. Gr. πνευματικός of, caused by, or of the nature of wind, breath, or spirit. So F. *pneumatique* (1520 in Hatz.-Darm.).]

A. *adj.* **1.** Pertaining to, or acting by means of, wind or air. **a.** Chiefly applied to various mechanical contrivances which operate by pressure or exhaustion of air.

pneumatic cabinet, differentiation (Med.): see quot. 1895. ***pneumatic caisson***: see quot. 1875. ***pneumatic dispatch***, a system by which parcels, etc. are conveyed along tubes by compression or exhaustion of air. ***pneumatic drill***, a heavy drill for breaking stone by the rapidly repeated blows of a bit driven by compressed air. ***pneumatic engine***: formerly applied *spec.* to the air-pump. ***pneumatic paradox, railway, telegraph***: see quot. 1875.

1659 LEAK *Waterwks.* Pref. 1 Pneumatike Inventions; viz. Engins moving by the force of Air. **1667** BEALE in *Phil. Trans.* II. 425 The Pneumatick (or Rarifying) Engine of Mr. Boyle. **1713** DERHAM *Phys.-Theol.* i. 9 In a glass-receiver of the Pneumatick Engine. **1825** J. NICHOLSON *Operat. Mechanic* 375 This part of the process I call the pneumatic pressure. **1856** BREES *Gloss. Terms, Piles (pneumatic)*, hollow iron piles, driven into the ground..by withdrawing, internally, the sand or other matters filling the space in which they stand by suction. **1858** LARDNER *Handbk. Nat. Phil., Hydrost.* etc. 214 The pneumatic screw.—The screw of Archimedes..is also used for the ventilation of mines. **1863** *Illustr. London News* 28 Feb. 217/3 (*heading*) Opening of the pneumatic despatch mail service. *Ibid.*, A company was registered in 1859 for the establishment in the metropolis of lines of pneumatic tube for the more speedy and convenient circulation of despatches and parcels. **1866** BESSEMER in Joynson *Metals* (1868) 88 The metal which had been previously rendered malleable by the pneumatic process becomes less red-short. **1867** BRANDE & COX *Dict. Sc.*, etc. s.v. *Railroad*, Carried out in London by the Pneumatic Despatch Company with success. **1875** KNIGHT *Dict. Mech.*, *Pneumatic Caisson*, one which is closed at top and sunk by the exhaustion of the air within or by the weight of the masonry built thereupon as the work progresses. *Ibid.*, *Pneumatic Paradox*, that peculiar exhibition of atmospheric pressure which retains a valve on its seat under a pressure of gas, only allowing a film of gas to escape. *Ibid.*, *Pneumatic Railway*, a railroad whose rolling stock is driven by the compression or exhaustion of air in a tube laid parallel to the track. *Ibid.*, *Pneumatic Telegraph*, a telegraph used before the times of Morse and Wheatstone for communicating information by the impulse given to a column of water by pneumatic pressure. *Ibid.* 1756/2 The pneumatic dispatch-tube was started by a company in London in 1859, for conveying parcels and light goods between the Euston Square Station and the Post-Office in Evershott Street, London. *a* **1877** KNIGHT *Dict. Mech.* II. 1753/1 By the pneumatic drill, the Mt. Cenis Tunnel, seven miles in length, was bored through the Alps. *Ibid.*, *Pneumatic hammer*, a hammer in which compressed air is the agent for lifting the helve or the head. **1881** C. A. EDWARDS *Organs* 65 The pneumatic action is an ingenious arrangement by which the bulk of the pressure is taken from the key, by means of small power-bellows. **1894** W. LE QUEUX *Gt. War in Eng. in 1897* xxxi. 253 Small dynamite shells from Mackenzie's pneumatic gun had struck the car of the balloon. **1895** *Syd. Soc. Lex.*, *P[neumatic] cabinet*, name for the air-tight compartment in which a patient is placed for treatment by the inhalation of compressed air... *P. differentiation*, term for the treatment of certain lung diseases by inhalation of air either denser or less dense than that of the surrounding atmosphere. **1898** F. W. ROGERS in *Westm. Gaz.* 13 July 3/2 The pneumatic brake will do very well for Lincolnshire and Cambridgeshire. **1898** E. HOWARD *To-morrow* 48 Subways for sewerage and surface drainage,..pneumatic tubes for postal purposes, have come to be regarded as economic if not essential. **1902** *Encycl. Brit.* XXXI. 802/1 Sometimes, when only a small amount of work is to be done, pneumatic tools are brought to heavy pieces of material. *Ibid.* 803/1 The pneumatic jack..is placed below the piece to be lifted, and operates directly. **1911** *Ibid.* XXVII. 40/2 Pneumatic drills are usually worked by little motors having oscillating cylinders, by which the air and exhaust ports are covered and uncovered. **1927** *Jrnl. Amer. Med. Assoc.* 1 Oct. 1151/1 (*heading*) A pneumatic hammer for bone surgery. *Ibid.*, A light, compact, pneumatic hammer whose speed is controlled by a throttle ..on the pistol-grip handle. **1930** *Daily Express* 9 Sept. 8/7 The noise of pneumatic drills has..been found to annoy the patients in a London Hospital. **1947** J. C. RICH *Materials & Methods of Sculpture* ix. 257 The vibration of a pneumatic tool, particularly after prolonged use, apparently affects the blood vessels of the hand and arm, frequently impairing the circulation and resulting in 'white fingers' or 'pneumatic hammer disease'. **1962** L. ZELIKOV tr. *G. Kamenshchikov's Forging Practice* viii. 192 Pneumatic hammers are mainly employed for hammer forging miscellaneous work and for forging in bolster dies. **1973** 'H. CARMICHAEL' *Candles for Dead* xi. 134 Don't be quite so boisterous. Your voice has the effect of a pneumatic drill. **1978** R. JANSSON *News Caper* viii. 76 His hands were shaking as if attached to a pneumatic drill.

b. Applied to things which are inflated, or filled with compressed air, for some purpose; esp. to the tyres of the wheels of bicycles, and the like.

1862 *Catal. Internat. Exhib.* II. XII. 22 Self-righting, indestructible pneumatic life-boat. **1890** *Patent Specif.* No. 4206 Large rubber tyres..known commercially as (1) Pneumatic tyres, (2) Cushion tyres. **1891** *Bicycling News* 21 Feb., Tacagni's method of holding a Pneumatic tyre between two rims is worth more attention than it at first sight deserves. **1896** G. J. JACOBS *Addr. Inst. Brit. Carriage Manuf.*, Only six months later, June 10, 1846, he [William Thomson, C.E., of Adelphi Street, Strand] patented the india-rubber pneumatic tyre on the principle of those so much in favour to-day. **1898** *Cycling* (Ward, Lock & Co.) iv. 23 Cyclists owe much to the inventor of the pneumatic tyre.

†**c.** Of a musical instrument: Played by the breath or by compressed air; 'wind-'. *Obs.*

1695 J. EDWARDS *Perfect. Script.* 176 All other musical instruments..whether pulsative or pneumatick.

d. Belonging to or transmitted by pneumatic dispatch: see a. above.

1903 *Westm. Gaz.* 4 Mar. 2/1 Any resident within Paris may either buy at any bureau a blue pneumatic letter-card stamped with a threepenny stamp, and generally known as a *petit-bleu*, or may write an ordinary letter, weighing not more than seven grammes,..writing across the top of the envelope the word 'Pneumatic'.

e. *humorous* (*transf.* use of b). Of a woman: having a well-rounded figure, esp. a large bosom; of or pertaining to a woman having such attributes.

1919 T. S. ELIOT *Whispers of Immortality* in *Poems*, Grishkin is nice... Uncorseted, her friendly bust Gives promise of pneumatic bliss. **1926** F. M. FORD *A Man could stand Up* I. i. 17 She didn't obviously offer—what was it the fellow called it?—promise of pneumatic bliss to the gentlemen. **1932** A. Huxley *Brave New World* vi. 108 'Every one says I'm awfully pneumatic,' said Lenina reflectively, patting her own legs... 'You don't think I'm *too* plump, do you?' **1951** J. C. Fennessy *Sonnet in Bottle* I. v. 25 A pneumatic pink and yellow bathing belle. **1961** A. Wilson *Old Men at Zoo* ii. 91 He looked at her..as though searching beneath her pneumatic form for the disguised contours of some familiar, leaner enemy. **1961** P. Ustinov *Loser* ii. 46 He became aware of the pneumatic warmth of that thigh. **1974** *Publishers Weekly* 21 Jan. 88/3 Sexologist Dr. Rhona Mitchell, she of the spectacularly pneumatic proportions. **1976** *Times Lit. Suppl.* 31 Dec. 1643/2 The pneumatic barmaid at their favourite wine-bar.

2. Of, or relating or belonging to, gases. Now *rare*, exc. in ***pneumatic trough***, a trough by means of which gases may be collected in jars over a surface of water or mercury. (See hydro-pneumatic.)

1793 Beddoes *Let. to Darwin* 59 We owe to Pneumatic Chemistry the command of the elements which compose animal substances;..it is the business of Pneumatic Medicine to apply them with caution and intelligence. **1800** tr. *Lagrange's Chem.* 54 Fill a bottle with hydrogen gas, and having taken it from the pneumatic tub, immediately apply to its mouth a lighted taper. **1822–34** *Good's Study Med.* (ed. 4) I. 489 When pneumatic medicine was at the height of its popularity, much benefit was supposed to be derived from the use of oxygen and hydrogen and dilute chlorine gases [in asthma]. **1826** Henry *Elem. Chem.* I. 21 Place the jar, filled with water and inverted, over one of the funnels of the shelf of the pneumatic trough. **1836–41** Brande *Chem.* (ed. 5) 63 Priestley's entire force was directed upon Pneumatic Chemistry. **1881** Routledge *Science* xiv. 342 The 'pneumatic trough' used at the present day differs from Hales' apparatus only in having a more convenient arrangement of its parts.

3. *Zool.*, *Anat.*, and *Phys.* **a.** Pertaining to breath or breathing; respiratory. *rare.*

1681 tr. *Willis's Rem. Med. Wks.* Vocab., *Pneumatic*, windy, or belonging to wind or breath. **1826** Kirby & Sp. *Entomol.* IV. xxxviii. 37 The external respiratory organs of insects... Spiracles; Respiratory plates; and branchiform and other pneumatic appendages. **1903** *Contemp. Rev.* Jan. 43 Heart weakness, pneumatic troubles and rheumatism.

b. Containing or connected with air-cavities, as those in the bones of birds, or the swimming-bladder of some fishes.

pneumatic duct, 'a short tube by which the air-bladder communicates with the œsophagus in physostomous fishes' (*Syd. Soc. Lex.* s.v. *Ductus*).

1831 Brewster *Nat. Magic* x. (1833) 259 Those beautiful pneumatic contrivances by which insects, fishes, and even some lizards are enabled to support the weight of their bodies against the force of gravity. **1854** Owen *Skel. & Teeth* 7 A large aperture, called the 'pneumatic foramen', near one end of the bone, communicates with its interior. **1855** Holden *Hum. Osteol.* (1878) 7 In the ostrich the bones are more pneumatic than in the gulls and in the smaller song-birds. **1899** *Allbutt's Syst. Med.* VII. 604 The mastoid in children may be as pneumatic or diploetic as in adults.

c. *Hist.* Applied to a school of ancient Greek physicians (Gr. οἱ πνευματικοί, L. *Pneumatici*) who held the theory of an invisible fluid or spirit (πνεῦμα) permeating all the body, and forming the vital principle on which health and strength depended. (*Syd. Soc. Lex.* 1895, s.v. *Pneumatici*.)

1842 Dunglison *Med. Lex.*, *Pneumatic Physicians*, name given to a sect of physicians, at the head of whom was Athenæus, who made health and disease to consist in the different proportions of an element—which they called Pneuma, πνεῦμα—to those of the other elementary principles.

4. a. Belonging or relating to spirit or spiritual existence; spiritual. (Usually with direct reference to Gr. πνευματικός, esp, in N.T. and Christian use.)

1797 *Monthly Mag.* III. 525/1 This animal spirit, which blessed men have called the pneumatic soul. **1811** Jebb *Corr.* (1834) II. 50 My bodily health has..improved; my mental and pneumatic part has been..dubious. **1890** J. F. Smith tr. *Pfleiderer's Developm. Theol.* II. iv. 162 The God-man as the absolute pneumatic personality of universal spiritual power is not merely the head of men but also of angels. **1894** Swete *Apost. Creed* ii. 28 Primitive Christianity, as he [Harnack] conceives it, had two Christologies, the one pneumatic, the other adoptionist. The former regarded the Christ as a preexistent Spirit who was made Man. **1899** Stalker *Christology Jesus* i. 30 The Gospel of St. John—the pneumatic gospel, as it was called, or gospel of religious genius.

†**b.** ***pneumatic philosophy***: = pneumatology 1. So ***pneumatic philosopher***. *Obs.*

a **1744** Bolingbroke *Ess.* II. viii. Philos. Wks. 1754 II. 79 Those..may be called..by the title..of pneumatic philosophers, since their object is spirit and spiritual substances; how ridiculous soever it be to imagine spirit less an object of natural philosophy, than body. **1745** Sir J. Pringle *Let.* 19 Mar. in Bower *Hist. Univ. Edinb.* II. 294, I do hereby resign my office of Professor of ethic and pneumatic philosophy in the University of Edinburgh. **1768–74** Tucker *Lt. Nat.* (1834) I. 329 Bolingbroke.. deriding the doctrine of spiritual substance under the name of pneumatic philosophy.

5. *Comb.*, as **pneumatic-drilled** *a.* (*nonce-wd.*), resembling a pneumatic drill or its action; †**pneumatic-shod** *a.*, fitted with pneumatic tyres; **pneumatic-tyred**, (**-tired**) *a.* fitted with pneumatic tyres, as a bicycle, etc.

1947 Dylan Thomas *Let.* 14 July (1966) 316 The pick-axed and *pneumatic-drilled mosquitoes in the guest's bedroom. **1909** *Westm. Gaz.* 3 June 4/2 Although they [*sc.* motor-cars] are *pneumatic-shod, the tyres do not come into contact with the track. *Ibid.* 18 Nov. 4/2 The driving-wheels of this vehicle are fitted with Vilo wheels, in place of ordinary pneumatic-shod artillery wheels. **1895** *Daily News* 17 Dec. 6/7 The *pneumatic-tire folk are apt to despise the poor cyclist on his wretched 'old crock' and to regard him as a nuisance. **1894** L. Robinson *Wild Traits* iii. (1897) 79 A *pneumatic-tired sulky is worth several seconds in the mile to an American trotter. **1896** *Daily Tel.* 10 Feb. 5/4 A smart pneumatic-tyred roadster. **1956** *Nature* 4 Feb. 218/2 His research has covered..the dynamic instability of systems incorporating pneumatic-tyred wheels. **1967** *Gloss. Highway Engin. Terms (B.S.I.)* 34 *Pneumatic-tyred roller*, a roller in which the compacting weight is supported on wheels fitted with pneumatic tyres. The roller may be self-propelled or towed. **1979** *Guardian* 8 Nov. 22/2 A shunting locomotive with pneumatic-tyred wheels.

B. *sb.* **1.** = pneumatology 1 a. *rare*$^{-1}$.

1836–7 Sir W. Hamilton *Metaph.* (1859) I. viii. 134 *note*, The terms Psychology and Pneumatology, or Pneumatic, are not equivalents.

2. Name in Gnostic theology for a spiritual being of a high order.

1876 tr. *Hergenröther's Cath. Ch. & Chr. State* II. 293 The Church had long rejected the Gnostic distinction between pneumatics and sarcics. **1882–3** *Schaff's Encycl. Relig. Knowl.* II. 927 The Gnostics taught a transplantation of the highest order (the pneumatics) into the world of the pleroma.

3. a. A pneumatic tyre, or a cycle having such tyres.

1890 Willoughby & Lynde *Specif. Patent*, The advantages of the pneumatic are as follows. **1891** *Bicycling News* 21 Feb., Riders of solid-tyred machines, when changing to Pneumatics. **1901** *Westm. Gaz.* 24 June 10/2 Breakdowns [of motor-cars] are reported in scores; punctured pneumatics and broken wheels without number.

b. A pneumatic bellows, tube, or other part of the pneumatic action in an organ.

1890 in *Cent. Dict.*

pneu'matical, *a.* (*sb.*) Now *rare* or *Obs.* [f. as prec. + -al^1: see -ical.]

A. *adj.* †**1.** = prec. 1. *Obs.*

1609 Boys *On Ps.* xcviii. 4–6 Wks. (1629) 36 All kind of musicke, Vocall..Chordall..Pneumaticall, With trumpets. **1634** J. B[ate] *Myst. Nat.* 28 Amongst all these experiments pneumaticall, there is none more excellent than this of the Weather-Glass. **1660** Boyle (*title*) New Experiments.. Touching the Spring of the Air..Made..in a New Pneumatical Engine. *Ibid.* Experim. i, The Dilatation of the Air in Wind-Guns and other pneumatical Engines wherein the Air has been compress'd. **1696** Phillips (ed. 5) s.v., An Organ is a Pneumatical Instrument. **1815** J. Smith *Panorama Sc. & Art* II. 31 The thermometer is a chemical rather than a pneumatical instrument.

†**2.** Of the nature of air, gaseous; relating to gases (= prec. 2). *Obs.*

1626 Bacon *Sylva* §29 The Race and Period of all things, here above the Earth, is to extenuate and turn things to be more Pneumaticall and Rare. **1685** Boyle *Enq. Notion Nat.* 254 Fluids, whether Visible or Pneumatical. **1793** D. Stewart *Outl. Moral Philos.* §272 (1855) 142 The pneumatical discoveries of modern chemistry. **1794** G. Adams *Nat. & Exp. Philos.* I. xi. 431 Mr. Boyle..obtained a pneumatical fluid, answering his then only criterion of air.

3. As rendering of Gr. πνευματικός in philosophical or theological use: cf. prec. 4, 4 b.

1678 Cudworth *Intell. Syst.* 789 One of which they called, Pneumatical, or the Spirituous Body; which is weaved out as it were to it, and compounded of the Gross Sensible Body (it being the more Thin and Subtle part thereof). **1708** H. Dodwell *Nat. Mort. Hum. Souls* 46 The Psychical Body must be cloathed up with a Pneumatical Body. **1741** in Grant *Univ. Edinb.* (1884) I. 273 Professor of Pneumatical and Ethical Philosophy. **1868** *Contemp. Rev.* VII. 599 The resurrection is not that of the disembodied ψυχή at the moment of death, nor of earthly relics, but the transformation from a psychical to a pneumatical body. **1891** tr. *Sabatier's Paul* iv. §3. 90 That which for lack of another name we have called the pneumatical life, taking its rise at the point of contact between the human soul and the invisible world.

†**B.** *sb.* A gaseous substance (cf. 2 above). *Obs.*

1626 Bacon *Sylva* §98 The Spirits or Pneumaticalls, that are in all Tangible Bodies are scarce known. *Ibid.* §354 In the inferior order of pneumaticals there is air and flame; and in the superior there is the body of the star and the pure sky.

Hence **pneu'matically** *adv.* (in various senses of pneumatic or pneumatical); *spec.* (in mod. use) by means of compressed air; also *fig.*

c **1700** D. G. *Harangues Quack Doctors* 15 Hypnotically.. Pneumatically, or Synechdochically. **1800** Howard in *Phil. Trans.* XC. 216, I resolved it into these different principles, by distilling it pneumatically with nitric acid. **1904** *Daily Chron.* 17 Sept. 5/5 The Welch patents for fastening a detachable outer case to the pneumatically-tyred rim of a wheel, thus rendering rapid roadside repairs possible, finished their thorny course yesterday. **1942** *R.A.F. Jrnl.* 3 Oct. 29 Four guns were installed, harmonized and fired pneumatically. **1958** *Times* 23 June 14/3 Equipping three Russian whalers with plant for cubing whale meat and transferring it pneumatically to storage vessels at sea. **1975** *Radiol.* CXV. 222/1 (*heading*) A pneumatically operated femoral artery compressor. **1975** D. O'Sullivan in D. Marcus *Best Irish Short Stories* (1977) II. 90 'It [*sc.* beer]'s blowing me out,' said Anne pneumatically.

pneumaticity (njuːməˈtɪsɪtɪ). [f. pneumatic + -ity.] The quality or condition of being pneumatic (in quots., in sense 3 b of the adj.).

1858 Mayne *Expos. Lex.*, *Pneumaticitas*, term for that condition of the skeleton of birds into most of the bones of which the external air has the faculty of entering: pneumaticity. **1870** Rolleston *Anim. Life* 17 The greater pneumaticity which the individual bones ordinarily possess. **1882** W. K. Parker in *Nature* XXVI. 254/2 The pneumaticity of the crocodile's endocranium.

pneumatico-, combining form from L. *pneumaticus* or Gr. πνευματικός pneumatic: see quots., and pneumatic *a.* 1, 4.

1812–16 Playfair *Nat. Phil.* (1819) I. 257 The syphon is properly a pneumatico-hydraulic machine, the action of water and of air being both necessary to its effect. **1816** Bentham *Chrestom.* Wks. 1843 VIII. 90 *Pneumatico-Hedonistics*, such as have for their objects those more refined classes of pleasures which, passing through one or more of the inlets afforded by the body, find their ultimate seat in the mind.

pneu'matics. [In form, pl. of pneumatic *a.* = pneumatic treatises or matters: see -ic 2.]

1. That branch of physics which deals with the mechanical properties (as density, elasticity, pressure, etc.) of air, or other elastic fluids or gases.

[**1656** Blount *Glossogr.*, *Pneumaticks*, books treating of Spirits or the winds.] **1660** Boyle *New Exp. Phys. Mech.* Pref. 3 They may look upon these Narratives as standing Records in our new Pneumaticks. **1673** *Phil. Trans.* VIII. 6045 The whole Science of Pneumatiques. **1806** Hutton *Course Math.* II. 226 Pneumatics is the science which treats of the properties of air, or elastic fluids. **1866** Brande & Cox *Dict. Sc.* etc. 914/2 The science of pneumatics has been created entirely by modern discoveries. Galileo first demonstrated that air possesses weight. His pupil Torricelli invented the barometer.

2. = pneumatology 1 a, b. *Obs.* exc. *Hist.*

[*a* **1650** J. Prideaux (*title*) Hypomnemata, Logica, Rhetorica, Physica, Metaphysica, Pneumatica, Ethica, Politica, Œconomica.] **1695** *Evid. bef. Scott. Univ. Comm.* 1690 (1837) I. *Edinb.* App. 42 That..the pneumatics or speciall metaphysicks [be composed] by the colledge of Edinburgh. *Ibid.* III. *St. Andrews* 217 In the third year, we teach the metaphysicks and with them the Pneumaticks... We do not hold it necessary to add to the Physicks any thing *de anima*, for all questions concerning it may be discust in the Pneumaticks. **1727–41** Chambers *Cycl.*, *Pneumatics*, in the schools, is frequently used for the doctrine of spirits; as God, angels, and the human mind. **1734** *Rules made for Sir J. Pringle* in Grant *Univ. Edinb.* (1884) II. 336 The Pneumatics: that is, the being and perfections of the one true God, the nature of Angels and the soul of man, and the duties of natural religion. **1776** Adam Smith *W.N.* v. i. (1869) II. 355 What are called metaphysics or pneumatics were set in opposition to physics. **1869** *Contemp. Rev.* X. 407 It was not to be..any metaphysical pneumatics woven out of scholastic brains.

‖**pneumatique** (njuːməˈtiːk, ‖pnømatik). [Fr.; see pneumatic *a.*] The pneumatic dispatch system in Paris (see pneumatic *a.* 1 a); a letter or message sent by this system.

1924 E. Hemingway *Let.* 9 Aug. in A. Mizener *Saddest Story* (1971) xxv. 342 Ford..had stayed up all night writing pneumatiques. **1938** F. Scott Fitzgerald *Let.* July (1964) 35 A *pneumatique* might reach Nanny at 23 rue Pascal-Lecointre. **1951** R. Senhouse tr. *Colette's Chéri* 76 *Pneumatiques* of four or five lines from sponging friends. **1964** *Sunday Mail* (Brisbane) 28 June 33/4 All the letters were sent by pneumatique—the giant system of suction pipes which links all the post offices in the Paris area and allows express letters to reach their destination in the city within 60 minutes. **1973** L. Snelling *Heresy* III. ix. 191 I'll get off a *pneumatique* to his office.

'pneumatism. *rare.* [f. Gr. πνεῦμα, πνευματ- (see pneumato-) + -ism.] The doctrine of the pneumatists: see next, 2.

1884 [see next, 2]. **1890** Billings *Med. Dict.*, *Pneumatism* .., doctrine of the pneuma or special vital principle.

'pneumatist. *rare.* [f. as prec. + -ist.]

†**1.** A student or practitioner of pneumatic medicine: see pneumatic *a.* 2, quot. 1822–34. *Obs.*

1799 Sir H. Davy in Beddoes *Contrib. Phys. & Med. Knowl.* 114 The chemical principles of the most celebrated pneumatists.

2. *Hist.* A 'pneumatic physician': see pneumatic *a.* 3 c.

1884 W. G. Stevenson in *Pop. Sci. Monthly* XXIV. 761 The pneuma was deemed such an important factor in the explanation of vital phenomena, that a school called 'Pneumatists' was founded in the first century of our era... For fourteen hundred years 'pneumatism' under various forms was the accepted philosophic belief of the civilized world.

pneumatization (ˌnjuːmətaɪˈzeɪʃən). *Med.* [f. next + -ation.] The development or presence of air-filled cavities in bone or other tissue.

1934 Lake & Marshall *Surg. Anat. & Physiol.* xv. 244 Pneumatisation of mastoid process varies between extreme limits. **1959** G. E. Shambaugh *Surg. of Ear* i. 22 It is not until air enters the middle ear at birth..that pneumatization accelerates, continuing throughout infancy and early childhood. **1976** *Nature* 19 Aug. 683/2 Another unusual feature in a dinosaur is the very strong pneumatisation of the skull bones, especially those of the roof and snout.

pneumatize (ˈpnjuːmətaɪz, ˈnjuː-), *v.* [f. Gr. πνευματ- (see next) + -ize; cf. Gr. πνευματίζειν to fan by blowing.]

1. *trans.* To pass a blast of air through (molten metal) in the process of converting it into steel by the Bessemer process. *rare.*

1868 Joynson *Metals* 86 The silica which is found in Spiegeleisen has the effect of reducing the boiling or agitation of the pneumatised metal, when poured into moulds, and is therefore beneficial.

2. To furnish with air-cavities, render pneumatic: see PNEUMATIC *a.* 3 b. Chiefly as **'pneumatized** *pa. pple.* Hence **'pneumatizing** *vbl. sb.*

1890 COUES *Ornith.* II. iv. 200 Ordinarily, the greater part of the skull, and the lesser part of the trunk and limbs, is pneumatised. **1947** *Arch. Otolaryngol.* XLVI. 852 The complications of acute otitis media developed more often in temporal bones with extensive cell systems than in those that were poorly pneumatized. **1949** L. R. BOIES et al. *Fund. Otolaryngol.* i. 11 The temporal bone is pneumatized by the extension of an epithelial sac from the middle ear into the bone marrow in the region of the mastoid process. *Ibid.* 12 Any interference with.. development will cause a cessation of the pneumatizing process. **1971** *Sci. Amer.* Dec. 73/3 All birds have.. lungs, air sacs and pneumatized bones. **1976** *Nature* 19 Aug. 683/2 [In a dinosaur] the nasals, in addition to being pneumatised as a whole, each bear a large air chamber connected with the external nare.

pneumato- (pnjuːmətəʊ, njuː-), before a vowel **pneumat-**, a. Gr. πνευματο-, combining form of πνεῦμα air, breath, spirit: see PNEUMA. Used, with various senses, chiefly in scientific and other technical words; for the more important of these, see their alphabetical places. (Also contracted to *pneumo-*: see PNEUMO-, and cf. *hæmo-*, etc.)

† **ˌpneumato-'chemical** *a.*, pertaining to 'pneumatic chemistry', or the chemistry of gases; ***pneumato-chemical trough*** = *pneumatic trough* (see PNEUMATIC *a.* 2). **ˌpneumato'morphic** (-'mɔːfɪk) *a. nonce-wd.* [after ANTHROPOMORPHIC] (see quot.). **pneumatophany** (-'ɒfənɪ) *nonce-wd.* [after CHRISTOPHANY, THEOPHANY], an appearance or manifestation of the Holy Spirit. **ˌpneumatophi'losophy**, the philosophy of spirit or spiritual existence. **pneumatophobia** (-'fəʊbɪə) *nonce-wd.* [-PHOBIA], dread or abhorrence of the spiritual. **pneumatophony** (-'ɒfənɪ) [Gr. φωνή voice], 'spirit-speech', i.e. the supposed utterance of articulate sounds by disembodied spirits; hence **ˌpneumato'phonic** (-'fɒnɪk) *a.* † **ˌpneumato'pyrist** [Gr. πῦρ fire] (see quot.). **ˌpneumatothera'peutics, -'therapy** [see THERAPEUTIC], treatment of diseases, esp. of the lungs, by inhalation of compressed or rarified air (*Syd. Soc. Lex.*). **ˌpneumato'thorax** *Path.* = PNEUMOTHORAX.

1800 HENRY *Epit. Chem.* (1808) 56 The *pneumato-chemical trough, or pneumatic cistern. **1822** IMISON *Sc. & Art* II. 12 An improved pneumato-chemical apparatus. **1886** *Kernel & Husk* 62 Metaphors.. which would subtilize Him down to a thought, or a mind, or a spirit, may be called phronesimorphic, noumorphic, *pneumatomorphic. **1892** BRIGGS *Bible Church & Reason* 163 The Theophany, the Christophany, and the *Pneumatophany are the sources of the miracles of the Bible. **1847** TULK tr. *Oken's Physio-philosophy* 2 Physio- and *Pneumato-philosophy range, therefore, parallel to each other. Physio-philosophy, however, holds the first rank, Pneumato-philosophy the second; the former therefore, is the ground and foundation of the latter, for nature is antecedent to the human spirit. **1711** SHAFTESB. *Charac.* (1737) III. Misc. II. ii. 64 All Atheists (says he) are possess'd with a certain kind of Madness, that may be call'd *Pneumatophobia, that makes them have an irrational but desperate Abhorrence from Spirits or Incorporeal Substances. **1687** H. MORE *Answ. Psychop.* (1689) 107 The Psychopyrists (for so rather I call them, than *Pneumatopyrists);.. philosophers that make the essence or substance of all created spirits to be Fire. **1825** *Good's Study Med.* (ed. 2) V. 436 The pneumo-thorax of Itard and Laennec, or the *pneumato-thorax, as it is more correctly called, of Dr. John Davy.

pneumatocele ('pnjuːmətəʊsiːl, 'njuːm-). *Path.* [ad. Gr. πνευματοκήλη a flatulent tumour, f. πνεῦμα (see PNEUMATO-) + κήλη tumour. So F. *pneumatocèle.*] A tumour or hernia containing air or gas.

1693 *Blancard's Phys. Dict.* (ed. 2), *Pneumatocele*, a windy Rupture, when the Skin of the Cods is distended with Wind. **1706** PHILLIPS, *Pneumatocele* or *Physocele.* **1783** POTT *Chirurg. Wks.* II. 199 The spurious [herniæ] derive their names.. from their supposed contents, as the pneumatocele, hæmatocele, and hydrocele. **1862** *N. Syd. Soc. Year-bk. Med.* 253 Case of.. formation of a circumscribed Pneumatocele in the Neck.

'pneumatocyst (-sɪst). *Zool.* [f. PNEUMATO- + CYST.] **a.** An air-sac serving as a float in certain 'colonial' or compound Hydrozoa; the pneumatophore, or the cavity contained in this. **b.** An air-sac in the body of a bird.

1859 HUXLEY *Oceanic Hydrozoa* 6 In the adult, this sac, which I shall term the *pneumatocyst*, is sometimes open at the apex (*Physalia, Rhizophysa*), and can communicate with the exterior by a pore which traverses the ectoderm of the pneumatophore. **1861** J. R. GREENE *Man. Anim. Kingd., Cœlent.* 113 *Apolemiadæ.* Pneumatocyst small. Cœnosarc filiform. **1884** COUES *Key N. Amer. Birds* 200 The Pneumatocysts.—A bird is literally inflated with these great membranous receptacles of air, and draws a remarkably 'long breath'—all through the trunk of the body, in several pretty definite compartments. **1895** *Syd. Soc. Lex.*, *Pneumatocyst*, an air-sac, as found in birds, hydrozoa, etc.

Hence **ˌpneumato'cystic** *a.*, belonging to or of the nature of a pneumatocyst.

1890 in *Cent. Dict.*

'pneumatogram (-græm). [f. as prec. + -GRAM. (See also PNEUMOGRAM.)]

1. A diagram or tracing of the movements of the chest in respiration, obtained by a pneumograph.

1890 in *Cent. Dict.* **1895** *Syd. Soc. Lex.*, *Pneumatogram*, the graphic representation of the respiratory movements by a curved tracing.

2. [after *telegram.*] A message sent by pneumatic dispatch: see PNEUMATIC *a.* 1.

1894 STEAD *If Christ came to Chicago* v. vi, [The pneumatic tube system] began with the dispatch of pneumatograms, following the example of Paris.

'pneumatograph (-grɑːf, -æ-). [f. as prec. + -GRAPH.] = PNEUMOGRAPH.

1895 in *Syd. Soc. Lex.*

ˌpneumato'graphic, *a.* [f. prec. or next + -IC.] **a.** Pertaining to pneumatography. (*Cent. Dict.* 1890.) **b.** Pertaining to a pneumograph; pneumographic.

pneumatography (-'ɒgrəfɪ). [f. PNEUMATO- + -GRAPHY.]

1. 'Spirit-writing', i.e. writing alleged to be done directly by a disembodied spirit, without the hand of a medium or any material instrument.

1876 ANNA BLACKWELL tr. *Kardec's Medium's Bk.* xxxii. 447 *Pneumatography...* This word denotes the direct writing of spirits, without the use of the medium's hand.

2. A description of supposed spiritual beings, or of beliefs about them; the descriptive part of PNEUMATOLOGY (sense 1 a).

1881 O. T. MASON in *Smithsonian Rep.* (1883) 501.

† **pneumato'logic,** *a. Obs.* [f. mod.L. *pneumatologia* PNEUMATOLOGY + -IC: cf. F. *pneumatologique.*] Of or pertaining to PNEUMATOLOGY (1 a.).

1695 *Evid. Sc. Univ. Comm.* (1839) I. *Edinb.* App. 41 His determinationes ontologick and pneumatologick [mispr. *-ica*].

ˌpneumato'logical, *a.* [f. as prec. + -AL[1].] Pertaining or relating to pneumatology.

1802–12 BENTHAM *Ration. Judic. Evid.* (1827) V. 189 The jurisprudential operators fall far beneath the medical and pneumatological. **1841** PHILIP *Ess.* in *Bunyan's Wks.* p. xxxv, Here I apprehend is the origin of Bunyan's pneumatological Allegory. **1902** *Daily Chron.* 28 Oct. 3/1 He has laid down his own pneumatological pen for an instant, and has collected from 'the Elite' their opinions on these profound questions.

So **pneuma'tologist** [cf. F. *pneumatologiste*], one versed in pneumatology.

1800 *Hist.* in *Ann. Reg.* 227 To encourage the experimental pneumatologist to go on with his observations. **1882** OGILVIE (Annandale), *Pneumatologist*, one versed in pneumatology.

pneumatology (pnjuːmə'tɒlədʒɪ, njuː-). [ad. mod.L. *pneumatologia* (J. Prideaux *a* 1650): see PNEUMATO- and -LOGY. So F. *pneumatologie* (D'Alembert 1751).]

1. a. The science, doctrine, or theory of spirits or spiritual beings: in the 17th c. considered as forming a department of metaphysics called *Special Metaphysics* as opposed to *General Metaphysics* or ontology, and comprehending the doctrine of God as known by natural reason, of angels and demons, and of the human soul: cf. PNEUMATICS 2.

[**1695** *Evid. Sc. Univ. Comm.* (1837) II. *Glasgow* 270 That in the fourth class be taught the Speciall Physicks and the Pneumatologia.] **1678** CUDWORTH *Intell. Syst.* 26 Those atomical physiologers that were before Democritus and Leucippus were all of them incorporealists; joyning theology and pneumatology.. together with their atomical physiology. **1755** [A. GERARD] *Plan Educ. Marischal Coll. & Univ. Aberdeen*, Pneumatology or the natural philosophy of spirits, including the doctrine of the nature, faculties and states of the human mind. **1765** JOHNSON *Shaks. Wks.*, *Ham.* I. i. *note*, According to the pneumatology of that time, every element was inhabited by its peculiar order of Spirits. **1776** ADAM SMITH *W.N.* v. i. (1869) II. 356 Pneumatology, comprehending the doctrine concerning the nature of the human soul and of the Deity. **1834** S. JACKSON tr. Jung-Stilling (*title*) Theory of Pneumatology; what ought to be believed or disbelieved concerning Presentiments, Visions, and Apparitions. **1877** E. CAIRD *Philos. Kant* I. 155 Pneumatology can be nothing more than a doctrine of our necessary ignorance of a certain problematical class of beings. **1882** STALLO *Concepts & The. Mod. Physics* 128 Faith in spooks.. is unwisdom in physics no less than in pneumatology.

With the neglect of the doctrine of supernatural beings, due to the philosophical tendencies of the 18th century, pneumatology came to deal with human souls only, and to mean:

b. The science of the nature and functions of the human soul or mind, now commonly called PSYCHOLOGY.

1785 REID *Intell. Powers* Pref. (1803) 9 There are two great branches of philosophy, one relating to body, the other to mind... The branch which treats of the nature and operations of minds has by some been called Pneumatology. [HAMILTON, in note (Reid's Wks. 1846), Now properly superseded by the term *Psychology.*] **1790** BEATTIE *Moral Sc.* I. Introd. 13 The Speculative part of the philosophy of the mind has been called Pneumatology. **1814** D. STEWART *Human Mind* II. Concl. 485, I have accordingly entitled my book, Elements—not of Logic or of Pneumatology, but—of the Philosophy of the Human Mind. **1877** SHIELDS *Final Philos.* 178 Descartes.. had given the death-blow to the whole of scholastic pneumatology, with its complex series of vegetative, appetitive, sensitive souls.

2. *Theol.* The, or a, doctrine of the Holy Spirit.

1881 O. T. MASON in *Smithsonian Rep.* (1883) 507 Inasmuch as we have borrowed a specific term from the theologians to stand for the whole study of man, we may be compelled to take the word pneumatology, meaning with them the doctrine of the Holy Spirit. **1882** SCHAFF *Hist. Christ. Church* §95 II. 778 The pneumatology of Ephesians resembles that of John, as the christology of Colossians resembles the christology of John.

3. The science or theory of air or gases; pneumatics; 'pneumatic chemistry'; 'pneumatic medicine'.

1767 A. CAMPBELL *Lexiph.* 16 In a treatise on barometrical pneumatology. **1803** BEDDOES *Hygeia* IX. 15 Considerable discoveries have however been made in pneumatology. **1858** MAYNE *Expos. Lex.*, *Pneumatologia, Med., Pathol.*, term for the doctrine of air or breath: pneumatology. **1862** *N. Syd. Soc. Year-bk. Med.* 20, (1) Contributions to the Pneumatology of the Blood.

pneumatolysis (njuːmə'tɒlɪsɪs). *Petrol.* [ad. G. *pneumatolyse* (R. Bunsen 1851, as next, p. 264): see -LYSIS.] The chemical alteration of rock and formation of minerals by the action of hot magmatic gases and vapours.

1896 PHILLIPS & LOUIS *Treat. Ore Deposits* (ed. 2) I. 129 He [*sc.* Vogt] uses the word *pneumatolysis* for this action. **1905** *Rep. Board of Regents Smithsonian Inst. 1904* 335 The importance of pneumatolysis in forming ore deposits was emphasized by the discovery.. of a number of economically important deposits. **1934**, **1962** [see GREISEN]. **1966** C. A. LAMEY *Metallic & Industrial Mineral Deposits* iii. 43 Various descriptions of cassiterite deposits and wolframite deposits indicate that their formation.. was caused by pneumatolysis. **1970** R. J. SMALL *Study of Landforms* iv. 127 At many points the granite of the South-West Peninsula [of England] has been profoundly affected by the metamorphic process known as 'pneumatolysis'.

pneumatolytic (ˌnjuːmətəʊ'lɪtɪk), *a. Petrol.* [ad. G. *pneumatolytisch* (R. Bunsen 1851, in *Ann. d. Physik* LXXXIII. 238): see PNEUMATO- and -LYTIC.] Involving or formed by pneumatolysis.

1896 PHILLIPS & LOUIS *Treat. Ore Deposits* (ed. 2) I. 173 There seems no urgent reason for adopting the theory of pneumatolytic, in preference to ordinary hydrothermal action. **1903** [see FUMAROLIC *a.*]. **1909** J. P. IDDINGS *Igneous Rocks* I. vii. 276 Those minerals that appear to depend largely upon the action of gases in magmas for their presence in igneous rocks have been called pneumatolytic. **1963** D. W. & E. E. HUMPHRIES tr. *Termier's Erosion & Sedimentation* vi. 134 The minerals of rocks can be altered without exposure at the surface by pneumatolytic or hydrothermal action. **1972** *Nature* 3 Mar. 13/1 They interpreted this variation as the result of pneumatolytic and gravitative differentiation taking place in the lava column.

Hence **pneumato'lytically** *adv.*

1962 *Proc. Yorks. Geol. Soc.* XXXIII. 329 The systems of valleys which evolved would be to some extent guided by the prior existence of pneumatolytically altered zones. **1968** I. KOSTOV *Mineralogy* II. v. 362 The lithium micas are typical products of pneumatolitically [*sic*] altered acid rocks of the 'greisen' type.

Pneumatomachian (-'meɪkɪən), *sb.* and *a. Ch. Hist.* [f. late Gr. πνευματομάχος (Athanasius, A.D. 360) an adversary of the (Holy) Spirit (f. πνεῦμα spirit + μάχος fighting, fighter) + -IAN.]

a. *sb.* An adversary of the Spirit; a name applied to a sect or party (or a group of such) in the 4th century, who denied the divinity or personality of the Holy Spirit. **b.** *adj.* Belonging to such a party, or holding such a doctrine. So **Pneumatomachist** (-'ɒməkɪst) = a.; **Pneuma'tomachy**, opposition to the Spirit.

1654 BOREMAN *Triumph Faith* 5 Thus much you must know and believe against the Pneumatomachists, that this Procession of the Holy Ghost from the Father and the Sonne denotes his Communion with both in the Essence or Substance of the Deity. **1707** *Curios. in Husb. & Gard.* 297 A Heretick of Zizicum of the Sect of the Pneumatomachians. **1833** J. H. NEWMAN *Arians* IV. ii. (1876) 303 Macedonius.. passed through Semi-Arianism to the heresy of the Pneumatomachist, that is, the denial of the Divinity of the Holy Ghost, of which he is theologically the founder. **1882–3** *Schaff's Encycl. Relig. Knowl.* II. 1650 The Council of Constantinople in 381 opposed the Pneumatomachians, whose definite exclusion from the orthodox church dates from that time. **1889** C. I. BLACK (*title*) The Pneumatomachy of the Day: the Clergy and the Scriptures. **1915** *Encycl. Relig. & Ethics* VIII. 225/2 The leading doctrine of the Macedonians is found in the thesis characterized by their opponents as 'Pneumatomachian', viz. that the Holy Ghost is not to be designated Θεός. **1957** *Oxf. Dict. Chr. Ch.* 1086/2 The historians Socrates and Sozomen.. regard Macedonius as their founder, but.. his name does not occur in contemporary anti-Pneumatomachian writings.

pneumatometer (-ˈɒmɪtə(r)). [f. PNEUMATO- + -METER.] An instrument for measuring the amount of air breathed in or out at each inspiration or expiration, or for measuring the force of inspiration or expiration; a spirometer.

1834 *Good's Study Med.* (ed. 4) I. 395 *note*, Dr. Marshall Hall's..contrivance for measuring the quantity of respiration with minuteness..is named the *pneumatometer*. **1862** *Catal. Internat. Exhib.* II. x. 17 By the suitable modification of the index, it is used as a pneumatometer for measuring the capacity of the chest. **1877** HOLDEN in *Amer. Jrnl. Med. Sci.* Apr. 391 This instrument..furnishes a portable and reliable pneumatometer. **1895** *Syd. Soc. Lex.*, *P[neumatometer], Holden's*..consists of a tube..containing a syren... The variations in the note produced serve to test the individual power, both in inspiration and in expiration.

So **pneumaˈtometry**, measurement of the force or amount of breath; use of a pneumatometer.

1876 tr. *von Ziemssen's Cycl. Med.* IV. 284 Pneumatometry, recently introduced by Waldenburg, as a method of clinical exploration.

pneumatophore (ˈpnjuːmətəʊˌfɔə(r), ˈnjuː-). [f. PNEUMATO- + Gr. -φορ-ος bearing.]

1. *Zool.* In certain 'colonial' or compound Hydrozoa of the order *Siphonophora*, A specialized part or individual of the 'colony', containing an air-cavity (*pneumatocyst*) and serving as a float.

1859 HUXLEY *Oceanic Hydrozoa* 5 The float or pneumatophore is..a most remarkable and well-defined structure. **1870** NICHOLSON *Man. Zool.* 82 The large proximal dilatation of the coenosarc is termed the 'pneumatophore'. **1888** ROLLESTON & JACKSON *Anim. Life* 771 The pneumatophore or float, an air-vesicle distinctive of *Physophoridæ*, *Physalidæ*, and *Discoideæ*.

2. *Bot.* A structure having numerous lenticels, and supposed to serve as a channel for air, arising from the roots of various trees which grow in swampy places in the tropics.

1901 HENSLOW in *Gardener* 9 Mar. 1241/3 The formation of 'knees' or 'pneumatophores', i.e. air conveyers.

Hence **pneumatophorous** (-ˈɒfərəs) *a.*, of the nature of or pertaining to a pneumatophore.

1895 in *Syd. Soc. Lex.*

‖**pneumatosis** (pnjuːməˈtəʊsɪs, njuː-). [mod.L., a. Gr. πνευμάτωσις inflation.]

†**1.** *Old Physiol.* The supposed production of ANIMAL SPIRITS in the brain. *Obs.*

1693 tr. *Blancard's Phys. Dict.* (ed. 2), *Pneumatosis*, the Generation of Animal Spirits, which is performed in the barky Substance of the Brain; the little Arteries there are emptied and the Spirits distill, which after they are come as far as the middle of the Brain, they actuate and invigorate all the Nerves. **1704** in HARRIS *Lex. Techn.* I. **1706** in PHILLIPS.

2. *Path.* A morbid accumulation of gas in the bodily cavities or tissues; emphysema.

1822–34 *Good's Study Med.* (ed. 4) IV. 333 This [cellular inflation] is the pneumatosis of Sauvages and Cullen. **1858** MAYNE *Expos. Lex.*, *Pneumatosis*, windy swelling;..also termed *Emphysema*.

Hence **pneumatosic** (-ˈɒsɪk) *a.*, pertaining to or affected with pneumatosis.

1890 in *Cent. Dict.*

pneume: see PNEUM, NEUME.

pneumectomy (pnjuːˈmɛktəmɪ, njuː-). *Surg.* [f. PNEUMO- b + Gr. ἐκτομή cutting out.] (See quot. 1895.) Now usu. called *pneumonectomy* (see PNEUMONO-).

1895 *Syd. Soc. Lex.*, *Pneumectomy* (for *pneumonectomy*, from Gr. πνεύμων, a lung..), term for excision of part of the lung, an operation which has occasionally been tried in some forms of Phthisis. **1911** *Practitioner* Nov. 682 Incision and drainage of a pulmonary cavity was the first operation practised for pulmonary tuberculosis, and..it has been performed much more frequently than pneumectomy. **1932** [see LOBECTOMY].

pneumic (ˈpnjuːmɪk, ˈnjuː-), *a. rare.* [a. F. *pneumique*, erron. for *pneumonique*, f. Gr. πνεύμων lung: see -IC, and cf. PNEUMO- b.] Pertaining to the lungs, pulmonary: = PNEUMONIC 1.

pneumic acid: see quot. 1866.

1866 WATTS *Dict. Chem.* IV. 685 *Pneumic acid*, an acid existing, according to Verdeil.., in the parenchyma of the lungs of most animals. It is very soluble in water. **1895** *Syd. Soc. Lex.*, *Pneumic*, belonging to the lung. *P. acid*,..is said to be formed by the union of lactic acid and taurin.

pneumo- (pnjuːməʊ-, njuː-), combining form and verbal element, **a.** Gr. πνεῦμα wind, spirit, etc. (see PNEUMA), = the fuller form PNEUMATO- (cf. Gr. αἱμο- = αἱματο-, etc.), in various scientific terms. **b.** Short for *pneumono-*, f. Gr. πνεύμων, -μον-, lung; chiefly in terms of pathology, most of which occur also in the fuller form PNEUMONO-.

For the more important of these in either sense, see their alphabetical places.

‖**pneumocace** (pnjuːˈmɒkəsiː) = *pneumonocace*. ‖**ˌpneumocar-ciˈnoma** = *pneumonocarcinoma*. **ˈpneumocele** (-siːl) [Gr. κηλή tumour], hernia of the lung. **ˌpneumoconiˈosis** (also **-kon-**) [Gr. κόνις dust; first formed as G. *pneumonokoniosis* (F. A. Zenker 1866, in *Deutsch. Arch. f. klin. Med.* II. 171)], disease of the lungs produced by inhalation of dust; hence **ˌpneumoconiˈotic** *a.*, affected with pneumoconiosis; *sb.*, a pneumoconiotic person. **ˌpneumodyˈnamic** *a.* [DYNAMIC], acting by the force of air. **ˌpneumodyˈnamics** [after *hydrodynamics*], that branch of physics which treats of the forces exerted by air or gases (esp. in motion); pneumatics. ‖**ˌpneumo-empyˈema** *Path.* [EMPYEMA], the presence of air or gas together with pus in a cavity of the body. ‖**ˌpneumo-enteˈritis** [ENTERITIS], name introduced by Klein for 'swine-fever' (*Syd. Soc. Lex.*). ‖**ˌpneumo-ˌhæmoˈthorax**, *Path.* [cf. *hæmothorax* s.v. HÆMO-], the presence of air or gas together with blood in the pleural cavity (A. Flint *Princ. Med.* (1866–80) 152). **ˌpneumoˌhydroˈthorax**, *Path.* [cf. HYDROTHORAX], the presence of air or gas together with watery fluid in the pleural cavity (*Ibid.*). **ˈpneumolith** (-lɪθ) [Gr. λίθος stone], a stony concretion or calculus in the lung; so ‖**pneumolithiasis** (-lɪˈθaɪəsɪs), the formation of pneumoliths. **ˌpneumomyˈcosis** = *pneumonomycosis*. **ˌpneumo-peritoˈnitis** *Path.*, peritonitis caused or accompanied by the presence of air or gas in the peritoneal cavity. **ˌpneumo-ˈphthisis** *Path.*, pulmonary phthisis (Dunglison *Med. Lex.* 1853). ‖**ˌpneumo-pleuˈritis**, inflammation of the lung and pleura; pleuro-pneumonia. **ˌpneumopyoˈthorax** *Path.* [PYOTHORAX], the presence of air or gas together with pus in the pleural cavity (A. Flint). ‖**pneumorrhagia** (-ˈreɪdʒɪə), hæmorrhage in the lung, pulmonary apoplexy. **pneumoˈskeleton**, a hard external structure (exoskeleton) developed in connexion with a respiratory organ, e.g. the shell of a mollusc in connexion with the mantle; hence **pneumoˈskeletal** *a.* (*Syd. Soc. Lex.*). **pneuˈmotomy** [after *anatomy*, etc.], (*a*) dissection of the lungs; (*b*) incision into the lung. **pneumo-ˈtyphoid** *a.*, applied to typhoid fever accompanied with pneumonia. **pneumo-ˈtyphus**, (*a*) pneumo-typhoid fever; (*b*) typhus fever accompanied with pneumonia.

1862 *N. Syd. Soc. Year-bk.* 196 Traumatic *Pneumocele. **1878** T. BRYANT *Pract. Surg.* II. 41 Hernia of the lung, or pneumocele is a rare consequence of a punctured wound of the thorax. **1881** *Med. Times & Gaz.* 28 May 589/1 (*heading*) The pathology of *pneumokonioses. **1890** BILLINGS *Med. Dict.*, *Pneumoconiosis*. **1898** *Allbutt's Syst. Med.* V. 242 Pneumoconiosis, pneumonoconiosis, or ..'Dusty-lung-disease'..has attracted but little attention in this country. **1905** H. D. ROLLESTON *Dis. Liver* 85 This train of events most often follows..the pneumokonioses. **1908** T. OLIVER *Dis. of Occupation* ix. 247 There are various forms of dust diseases of the lungs, or pneumokonioses, *e.g.*, anthracosis..; chalicosis and silicosis..; and byssinosis. **1940** H. E. COLLIER *Outl. Industr. Med. Pract.* xxxix. 356 The general object of the tests has been to find a means of checking the interpretation of the X-ray appearances and thereby to provide an early method of recognizing the outset of any of the pneumoconioses before the onset of the disablement. **1953** *Jrnl. Path. & Bacteriol.* LXVI. 235 Simple pneumokoniosis..is characterised by numerous small discrete aggregations of dust in which only a little fibrosis occurs. **1969** *Daily Tel.* 5 Feb. 18 (Advt.), The Industrial Injuries Advisory Council has been asked to consider whether any change should be made in the definition of pneumoconiosis in the National Insurance (Industrial Injuries) Act 1965. The disease is at present defined in the Act as fibrosis of the lungs due to silica dust, asbestos dust or other dust, and including the condition known as dust reticulation. **1976** *S. Wales Echo* 27 Nov. 6/9 The cause of death was given as broncho-pneumonia due to recumbency following a fracture of the left femur, and pneumoconiosis. **1944** *Rep. Advisory Cttee. Treatment & Rehab. Miners in Wales Region Suffering from Pneumokoniosis* 17 The *pneumokoniotic lung, especially at the massive nodulation stage is in special degree liable to become tuberculous. **1948** *Hansard Commons* 15 Mar. 1846 Reference has been made to the..Grenfell factories in South Wales for silicotics and pneumoconiotics. **1963** K. M. A. PERRY in Perry & Sellors *Chest Dis.* I. xxxi. 566 In 1,036 pneumoconiotic lungs which he examined, he found evidence of pulmonary tuberculosis in 43 per cent. **1876** *Proc. Amer. Phil. Soc.* XVI. 286 A new telegraphic machine called a '*Pneumo-dynamic' Relay Sounder, where the local battery is replaced by compressed fluid,..condensed air. **1839** G. BIRD *Nat. Philos.* 111 General Properties of Fluids in Motion. (Hydro- and *Pneumodynamics.) **1898** *Allbutt's Syst. Med.* V. 361 In the case of *pneumo-empyema the pericardial sac may contain air, as well as pus. **1900** *Field* 1 Sept. 374/1 Swine fever, with its several names of typhoid fever of the pig, soldier, red disease, *pneumo-enteritis. **1890** BILLINGS *Med. Dict.*, **Pneumolith*, pulmonary concretion. **1898** *Allbutt's Syst. Med.* V. 250 Another peculiarity of the dust of stone is that it tends to collect in masses, forming concretions (pneumoliths). **1890** BILLINGS *Med. Dict.*, **Pneumomycosis*. **1898** *Allbutt's Syst. Med.* V. 257 Hughes Bennett in 1842, described the first example of pneumomycosis. **1895** *Syd. Soc. Lex.*, **Pneumoperitonitis*, term for the condition in which air finds entry in the peritoneal cavity. **1811** HOOPER *Dict. Med.*, **Pneumopleuritis*, an inflammation of the lungs and pleura. **1858** MAYNE *Expos. Lex.*, *Pneumopleuritis*,..(should be *Pneumonopleuritis*). **1842** DUNGLISON *Med. Lex.*, **Pneumorrhagia*, Hæmoptysis. **1866** A. FLINT *Princ. Med.* (1880) 274 Pneumorrhagia, or the extravasation of blood into the air-cells and frequently also into the interstitial tissue, is commonly known as pulmonary apoplexy. **1851** WOODWARD *Mollusca* I. 35 The shell may be regarded as a *pneumoskeleton. **1842** DUNGLISON *Med. Lex.*, **Pneumotomy*, dissection of the lungs. **1890** BILLINGS, *Pneumotomy*, incision of the lung to open a cavity. **1896** *Allbutt's Syst. Med.* I. 812 These cases are known as *pneumo-typhoid. **1890** BILLINGS, **Pneumotyphus*, typhoid fever with croupous pneumonia.

‖**pneumococcus** (pnjuːməʊˈkɒkəs, njuː-). [mod.L., f. PNEUMO- + Gr. κόκκος berry: cf. *micrococcus*.] Name for two different micro-organisms of oval form (Friedländer's and Fränkel's) which have been found in the rusty sputum of pneumonia, and supposed to be the cause of the disease. Hence **pneumococcal** (-ˈkɒkəl), **pneumococcic** (-ˈkɒksɪk), **pneumococcous** (-ˈkɒkəs), *adjs.*, pertaining to or caused by a pneumococcus.

1890 *Daily News* 11 Dec. 3/6 What is peculiar in this disease is the alliance with this bacillus of pneumococcus, which also lives in Russian marshes, river mud, and village pools. **1897** *Allbutt's Syst. Med.* IV. 518 Experiments on pneumococcal infection in rabbits. **1898** *Ibid.* V. 113 The diplococcus described by Fränkel (now often called pneumococcus, in succession to the title enjoyed for a short period by Friedländer's bacillus). *Ibid.* 27 Varieties of membrane,..described as primary diphtheritic and primary pneumococcic. *Ibid.* 348 Primary pneumococcous pleurisy is a common disease.

pneumoderm (ˈpnjuːməʊdɜːm, ˈnjuː-). *Zool.* [f. PNEUMO- b + Gr. δέρμα skin.] A gymnosomatous pteropod of the family *Pneumodermidæ* (typical genus *Pneumodermon* or *Pneumoderma*), having processes of the skin which serve as gills.

[**1878** BELL tr. *Gegenbaur's Comp. Anat.* 326 In Pneumodermon..two of these bodies are beset with suckers. **1888** ROLLESTON & JACKSON *Anim. Life* 468 The general surface of the body is respiratory in *Gymnosomata*. *Pneumodermon*, however, possesses three contractile and richly ciliated processes at the apex of the visceral dome, in and out of which the blood passes.]

ˌpneumoenˈcephalogram. *Med.* Also **pneumenˈcephalo-**. [f. as next: see -GRAM.] An X-ray taken by pneumoencephalography.

1935 *Bull. Neurol. Inst. N.Y.* IV. 261 In cases in which a septum pellucidum is present this structure forms in the anteroposterior and posteroanterior views of the pneumencephalograms a well demarcated vertical linear shadow. **1973** *Reader's Digest* Apr. 194/2 Additional tests had to be made—an angiogram and perhaps a pneumoencephalogram.

ˌpneumoencephaˈlography. *Med.* Also **ˌpneumencephaˈlo-**. [f. PNEUMO- + *encephalography* s.v. ENCEPHALO-.] Radiography following the replacement of cerebrospinal fluid by air or oxygen.

1932 *Amer. Jrnl. Roentgenol.* XXVII. 657/1 Pneumoencephalography, following withdrawal of cerebrospinal fluid and injection of air by the method of spinal puncture, permits investigation of the cisterna magna and of the subarachnoid spaces, in addition to study of the ventricles. **1935** *Bull. Neurol. Inst. N.Y.* IV. 221 It seems essential..to establish definite criteria for the diagnosis of these lesions by pneumencephalography whether ventriculography, encephalography or both are utilized in a given case. **1974** PASSMORE & ROBSON *Compan. Med. Stud.* III. xxxiv. 23/1 Pneumoencephalography visualizes the ventricular system and CSF pathways of the brain. A lumbar puncture is performed and 15 ml of air is instilled slowly into the subarachnoid space with the patient sitting upright.

Hence **ˌpneumoencephaloˈgraphic** *a.*, **-encephaloˈgraphically** *adv.*

1935 *Bull. Neurol. Inst. N.Y.* IV. 261 From the above mentioned pneumencephalographic evidence one can now diagnose the presence of a perforated septum pellucidum. **1950** DAVIDOFF & EPSTEIN *Abnormal Pneumoencephalogram* xxix. 407 A hemiplegia with a pneumoencephalographically demonstrable porencephaly. **1961** *Lancet* 9 Sept. 569/2 Myeloencephalography..confirmed the pneumo-encephalographic findings.

pneumogastric (njuːməʊˈgæstrɪk, pnjuː-), *a.* (*sb.*) *Anat.* [mod.f. PNEUMO- b + GASTRIC. So F. *pneumogastrique* (Chaussier).] Pertaining to the lungs and the stomach or abdomen; *spec.* in ***pneumogastric nerve***, name for each of the tenth pair of cerebral nerves, the most widely distributed of all these (hence also called VAGUS), which, with their branches, supply the lungs and other respiratory and vocal organs, stomach, œsophagus, spleen, liver, intestines, heart, etc.

Hence applied to connected structures, as *p. ganglion*, *p. plexus*; *p. lobule* of the cerebellum (= FLOCCULUS 2).

1831 R. KNOX *Cloquet's Anat.* 287 The lower edge.. allows the inferior laryngeal branch of the pneumo-gastric nerve to pass under it anteriorly. **1842** E. WILSON *Anat. Vade M.* (ed. 2) 384 The Pneumogastric lobule..is situated on the anterior border of the cerebellum. *Ibid.* 403 The Pneumogastric Nerve (vagus) arises by numerous filaments from the respiratory tract immediately below the glosso-pharyngeal.

B. *ellipt.* as *sb.* The pneumogastric nerve.

1874 ROOSA *Dis. Ear* (ed. 2) 66 An auricular branch from the pneumogastric. **1879** *St. George's Hosp. Rep.* IX. 608 If the trunks of the pneumogastrics had been the seat of disease, the paralysis would have been still more extensive.

pneumogram (ˈpnjuːməʊgræm, ˈnjuː-). [f. PNEUMO- + -GRAM.] **1.** A tracing taken with the pneumograph (*Syd. Soc. Lex.*): = PNEUMATOGRAM 1.

2. An X-ray photograph made by pneumography (sense 2).

1921 *Johns Hopkins Hosp. Bull.* XXXII. 74/1 (*caption*) Cerebral pneumogram..of a case of communicating hydrocephalus; air has been injected into the spinal canal. **1964** TAVERAS & WOOD *Diagnostic Neuroradiol.* 227 The straight anteroposterior pneumogram (C) reveals the forward portions of the lateral and the third ventricles outlined by gas.

ˈpneumograph. [f. as prec. + -GRAPH.] An instrument for automatically recording the movements of the chest in respiration; also called *stethograph*.

1878 FOSTER *Phys.* II. ii. §1. 258 The pneumograph of Fich is somewhat similar. **1904** *Westm. Gaz.* 11 July 4/1 The sphygmograph was followed by the cardiograph, for exploring the movements of the heart, and the pneumograph, for the study of the respiratory movements.

pneumography (pnjuːˈmɒgrəfɪ, njuː-). [f. as prec. + -GRAPHY.] **1. a.** A description of the lungs. **b.** The recording of the respiratory movements, as by a pneumograph.

1842 DUNGLISON *Med. Lex.*, *Pneumography*, the part of anatomy which describes the lungs. **1895** *Syd. Soc. Lex.*, *Pneumography*, a description of the lungs. Also, a recording of the respiratory movements.

2. *Med.* The radiography of tissues into which air or oxygen has been introduced.

1921 *Johns Hopkins Hosp. Bull.* XXXII. 70/1 The most frequent location for an obstruction in communicating hydrocephalus is in the cisternæ. This..will be seen in the results which are to follow in the patients who have been studied by cerebral pneumography. **1948** LYSHOLM & BULL in J. W. McLaren *Mod. Trends Diagnostic Radiol.* I. xxiv. 327 Subdural pneumography has proved to be valuable in the diagnosis of adhesions between brain and dura, and in subdural haematoma. **1970** *Sci. Jrnl.* Aug. 5/1 The cardiovascular system[s] of both cosmonauts were studied in detail by means of electrocardiography, seismocardiography, pneumography, [etc.].

Hence **pneumographic** (-ˈgræfɪk) *a.*, (*a*) pertaining to or of the nature of a pneumograph; (*b*) 'pertaining to pneumography' (*Syd. Soc. Lex.*); **pneumoˈgraphically** *adv.*, by means of pneumography.

1895 WOLFENDEN tr. *Joal's Respiration in Singing* 175 Scarcely revealed, except..by pneumographic instruments. **1921** *Jrnl. Amer. Med. Assoc.* 10 Dec. 1858/2 At times, it has been possible completely to remove such growths, when, except for the pneumographic record, there would have been absolutely no other way of knowing the situation of the growth. **1953** F. LINDGREN in J. W. McLaren *Mod. Trends Diagnostic Radiol.* II. xix. 291 The pneumographic diagnosis of an expanding intracranial lesion is possible because the lesion, when it has attained a certain size, affects the central fluid-filled and gas-filled space. *Ibid.* 301 These tumours cannot be demonstrated pneumographically in any way other than by encephalography. **1964** TAVERAS & WOOD *Diagnostic Neuroradiol.* 752/2 A pneumographic examination in any patient who presents a clinical syndrome that suggests a lesion in the posterior fossa. **1972** M. GADO in E. J. Potchen *Current Concepts Radiol.* xi. 261 Pneumographically differentiation between cerebellar and extra-axial masses behind the cerebellum is impossible.

†**pneuˈmology**[1]. *Obs. rare*$^{-1}$. [f. PNEUMO- a + -LOGY.] A discourse concerning spirits; = PNEUMATOLOGY 1 a.

1613 W. B. (tr. *Michaelis*) (*title*) The Admirable Historie of the Possession and Conversion of a Penitent woman, Sedvced by a Magician that made her to Become a Witch,.. wherevnto is annexed a Pnevmology, or Discourse of Spirits. **1661** BLOUNT *Glossogr.* (ed. 2), *Pneumology* (Gr.), a speaking or treating of spirits or winds.

pneuˈmology[2]. *rare.* [f. PNEUMO- b + -LOGY.] A treatise on, or the scientific description or knowledge of, the lungs.

1842 in DUNGLISON *Med. Lex.* **1895** in *Syd. Soc. Lex.*

Hence **pneumoˈlogical** *a.* (*Cent. Dict.* 1890.)

pneumolysis (njuːˈmɒlɪsɪs). *Surg.* [mod.L., f. PNEUMO- + -LYSIS.] The surgical separation of the parietal pleura either from the chest wall (*extrapleural pneumolysis*) or from the pulmonary pleura (*intrapleural pneumolysis*).

1913 *Index Med.* XI. 199/1 (Index), Pneumolysis. **1922** *Tubercle* III. 162 Since 1918, we have performed extra-pleural pneumolysis in..cases of severe unilateral pulmonary tuberculosis. **1945** KEERS & RIGDEN *Pulmonary Tuberculosis* xi. 193 Closed intrapleural pneumolysis..is the logical sequel to pneumothorax therapy where adhesion formation is preventing effective collapse of the lung. **1966** E. L. FARQUHARSON *Textbk. Operative Surg.* (ed. 3) xiv. 447 Intra-pleural pneumolysis was employed mainly as an adjunct to artificial pneumothorax.

pneumometer (pnjuːˈmɒmɪtə(r), njuː-). [f. PNEUMO- + -METER.] = PNEUMATOMETER. So **pneumometrograph** (-ˈmɛtrəʊgrɑːf, -æ-): see quot.; **pneuˈmometry** = PNEUMATOMETRY.

1857 J. MILLER *Alcohol* (1858) 79 The mercury in the animal pneumometer..does not..fall back to the old level. **1887** *Homeopath. World* 1 Nov. 527 There is an arrangement (the pneumometrograph) for measuring the amount of medicated vapour which the patient inhales. **1853** DUNGLISON *Med. Lex.*, *Pneumometry*, measurement of the capacity of the lungs for the air.

pneumonalgia, pneumonectomy: see PNEUMONO-.

pneumonia (njuːˈməʊnɪə). *Path.* Also rarely in anglicized form: 7 **pneumonie**, 9 **pneumony**. [a. medical L. *pneumonia*, a. Gr. πνευμονία (Plut.) inflammation of the lungs, f. πνεύμων, πνευμον-, lung. So F. *pneumonie* (1812 in Hatz.-Darm.).]

a. Inflammation of the substance of the lungs; a disease having many varieties, induced by cold or various other causes.

1603 HOLLAND *Plutarch's Mor.* 1012 The beginning of the Pneumonie or inflamation of the lungs. **1783** W. CULLEN *First Lines Pract. Phys.* §354 Wks. 1827 II. 56 Pneumonia, like other inflammations, often ends in suppuration. **1805** *Med. Jrnl.* XIV. 252 In consequence of imprudent exposure to a cold wind, she was seized with symptoms of pneumonia. **1828–32** WEBSTER, *Pneumonia, Pneumony.* **1846** J. BAXTER *Libr. Pract. Agric.* (ed. 4) II. 147 Pneumonia occasionally attacks all cattle, but more particularly working beasts, and those that have been driven a long way. **1853** DUNGLISON *Med. Lex.*, *Pneumony*, pneumonia. **1898** *Allbutt's Syst. Med.* V. 110 Apical pneumonia of one lung is often accompanied by basal pneumonia of the other.

b. *attrib.* and *Comb.*, as ***pneumonia patient***; **pneumonia bacillus, coccus, microbe** = PNEUMOCOCCUS; **pneumonia blouse** *colloq.*, a woman's blouse made of thin or light material and having a low neck-line.

1896 *Allbutt's Syst. Med.* I. 434 'Poultice' or 'Pneumonia jackets' are garments made of a strip of thin flannel or flannelette. **1899** CAGNEY tr. *Jaksch's Clin. Diagn.* (ed. 4) iv. 144 Some notice of the position which may be accorded to the pneumonia-coccus. *Ibid.* 146 The subject of the pneumonia-microbe needs further elucidation. **1902** in C. W. Cunnington *Eng. Women's Clothing* (1952) ii. 47 The questionable morality of the 'Pneumonia blouse'... A transparent blouse of muslin and lace with next to no collar. **1905** R. BROUGHTON *Waif's Progress* xix. 209 'Catherine had a bad cold.' 'The result of a pneumonia blouse, I suppose!' **1958** *Listener* 2 Oct. 524/1 Clergy of all denominations denounced that shocking innovation of 1914, the open-necked 'pneumonia blouse'. **1961** *Guardian* 6 Mar. 10/6 Astrakhan and felt bootees shared a narrow bench with sandals and 'pneumonia' blouse.

pneumonic (njuːˈmɒnɪk), *a.* (*sb.*) [ad. medical L. *pneumonicus*, a. Gr. πνευμονικός of the lungs, affected with lung-disease. So F. *pneumonique.*]

A. *adj.* **1.** Pertaining to the lungs; pulmonary. *rare.* ? *Obs.*

1675 *Phil. Trans.* X. 506 This Pneumonique Engin, lodged in the breast [the Lungs]. *Ibid.*, When the Blood does not duly circulate through the Heart and the Pneumonique Vessels; which may sometimes be caus'd within the right ventricle of the heart, or the Pneumonique Arteries. **1710** T. FULLER *Pharm. Extemp.* 216 It [the Hydromel]..stuffing up the pneumonic Passages, causeth an Orthopnæa.

2. Pertaining to, of the nature of, characterized by, or affected with pneumonia.

1783 S. CHAPMAN in *Med. Commun.* I. 297 The expectoration..produced by pneumonic inflammations. **1898** *Allbutt's Syst. Med.* V. 122 A pneumonic patient. **1898** *Daily News* 24 Oct. 3/3 The disease which has broken out in Vienna is not bubonic but pneumonic plague.

B. *sb.* †**a.** A person affected with lung-disease. *Obs.* **b.** A remedy for lung-disease. *rare*$^{-0}$.

1681 tr. *Willis's Rem. Med. Wks.* Vocab., *Pneumonic*, one sick of the disease of the lungs. **1727–41** CHAMBERS *Cycl.*, *Pneumonics*, medicines proper in diseases of the lungs, where respiration is affected. **1818** in TODD. **1895** *Syd. Soc. Lex.*, *Pneumonic*... 3. A remedy suitable for diseases of the lungs.

‖**pneumonitis** (pnjuːməʊˈnaɪtɪs, njuː-). *Path.* [mod.L., f. Gr. πνεύμων lung + -ITIS.] = PNEUMONIA. (See also quot. 1974.) Hence **pneumonitic** (-ˈɪtɪk) *a.* = PNEUMONIC 2.

1822–34 *Good's Study Med.* (ed. 4) I. 441 Thus it occurs to us in pleurisy, in pneumonitis. **1866** A. FLINT *Princ. Med.* (1880) 160 Pneumonia is the name commonly used: pneumonitis is the more appropriate term, being in conformity with the plan of distinguishing inflammatory affections by the suffix *-itis*. **1844** DUNGLISON *Med. Lex.*, *Pneumonitic*, of or belonging to pneumonitis, or inflammation of the lungs. **1918** *Surg. Gynecol. & Obstetr.* XXVI. 32/2 One of the most important predisposing causes of postoperative pneumonitis in patients coming into the hospital with a recent cold or free from an active cold, is the exposure to which he is subjected during the first twenty-four to forty-eight hours of his stay in the hospital. **1947** *Radiology* XLIX. 284/1 There was no opacity of the eyes, no pneumonitis. **1962** A. HUXLEY *Let.* 17 Mar. (1969) 930 A cold on the chest which..turned out in the end to be what they called pneumonitis. **1971** *Sci. Amer.* Aug. 47/3 Inhalation of cadmium oxide fumes..can produce acute damage in the lungs in the form of pneumonitis or pulmonary edema. **1974** PASSMORE & ROBSON *Compan. Med. Stud.* III. xviii. 23/2 Pneumonia is a general term meaning inflammation of the lungs; it usually refers to a clinically acute condition caused by micro-organisms but it may result from damage by one or a number of chemical or physical agents. Pneumonitis is a similar term and is sometimes used to describe mild segmental pneumonia, but it is best avoided.

pneumono- (pnjuːməʊnəʊ, njuː-), before a vowel **pneumon-**, combining form of Gr. πνεύμων, πνευμον- lung. (Often contracted to PNEUMO-.)

‖**pneumonalgia** (-ˈældʒɪə) [Gr. ἄλγος pain], pain in the lungs; **pneumoˈnectomy** = PNEUMECTOMY (*Syd. Soc. Lex.*); hence **pneumoˈnectomized** *ppl. a.*, subjected to a pneumonectomy; ‖**pneumonocace** (-ˈɒkəsiː) [Gr. κακή evil], decay or gangrene of the lung (Mayne *Expos. Lex.* 1858); ‖ˌ**pneumonocarciˈnoma** [CARCINOMA], cancer of the lung (Mayne); **ˈpneumonoˌcele** = *pneumocele*: see PNEUMO- (Dunglison *Med. Lex.* 1853); ‖ˌ**pneumonociˈrrhosis**, cirrhosis of the lung (Mayne); ‖ˌ**pneumonoconiˈosis** (also **-kon-**) = *pneumoconiosis* s.v. PNEUMO-; hence **pneuˌmonoconiˈotic** *a.* and *sb.*; ‖ˌ**pneumonoˈdynia** [Gr. ὀδύνη pain], pain in the lung (Mayne); **ˈpneumonoˌlith** (*Syd. Soc. Lex.*), ˌ**pneumonoliˈthiasis** (Mayne) = *pneumolith*, *-lithiasis*: see PNEUMO-; **pneumoˈnometer** [-METER], an instrument for measuring the capacity or strength of the lungs (= PNEUMATOMETER, PNEUMOMETER) (Mayne); ‖ˌ**pneumonomyˈcosis** [Gr. μύκης fungus], growth of a fungus in the lungs; **pneumonophorous** (-ˈɒfərəs) *a.* [Gr. -φόρος bearing], bearing or having lungs; ‖**pneumonorhagia** (-ˈreɪdʒɪə) = *pneumorrhagia*: see PNEUMO- (Mayne); **pneuˌmonoultramicroˈscopicˌsilicovolcanoconiˈosis (-koniˈosis)**, a factitious word alleged to mean 'a lung disease caused by the inhalation of very fine silica dust' but occurring chiefly as an instance of a very long word.

1857 DUNGLISON *Dict. Med. Sc.*, **Pneumonalgia.* **1895** *Syd. Soc. Lex.*, *Pneumonalgia*, pain in the lungs. A term used by Alibert for *angina pectoris*, which was the fifth genus of pulmonary diseases (*pneumoses*) in his nosology. **1939** *Brit. Jrnl. Surg.* XXVII. 411 The possibility of maintaining a permanent pneumothorax on the *pneumonectomized side is one that has not been fully investigated as yet. **1967** *Excerpta Medica*: *Radiol.* XXI. 138/2 (*heading*) Pre- and postoperative pulmonary angiography in pneumonectomized patients. **1890** *Ann. Universal Med. Sci.* III. B-27 The profession is urged by Zakharevitch to prosecute these investigations for the practice of *pneumonectomy. **1938** *Brit. Jrnl. Surg.* XXVI. 190 (*caption*) Right lung, the site of bronchial carcinoma, successfully removed by dissection pneumonectomy. **1967** [see LOBECTOMY]. **1972** T. W. SHIELDS *Gen. Thoracic Surg.* xx. 331/2 A pneumonectomy may be carried out by means of any one of the three standard thoracic positions: lateral, posterior, or anterior. **1977** *Lancet* 23 July 164/1 All the patients had a radical pneumonectomy or lobectomy. **1866** A. FLINT *Princ. Med.* (1880) 185 Under the generic name *pneumonokoniosis, proposed by Zenker, are included the various affections of the lung produced by the inhalation of dust-like particles. **1897** *Allbutt's Syst. Med.* IV. 631 Other pneumonoconioses arise in a similar manner. **1934** *Trans. Inst. Mining Engineers* LXXXVIII. 387 This pneumonoconiosis of coal-miners is a *progressive* condition, gradually passing on from its harmless early stages..to a condition of dyspnœa and breathlessness which makes work impossible. **1933** E. M. WILLIAMS *Health of Old & Retired Coalminers in S. Wales* 80 Thirty-two men..were considered on clinical grounds to be definitely *pneumonoconiotic. *Ibid.* 102 The proportion of probably tuberculous cases among these pneumonoconiotics is high. **1876** tr. *von Ziemssen's Cycl. Med.* V. 468 Vegetable Parasites [of the lungs]—*Pneumonomycosis. **1870** ROLLESTON *Anim. Life* 148 The..ambulacral vessel in all the *pneumonophorous Holothurioidea. **1936** F. SCULLY *Bedside Manna* 87 *Pneumonoultramicroscopicsilicovolcanakoniosis [*sic*], a disease caused by ultra-microscopic particles of sandy volcanic dust, might give even him laryngitis. **1966** *Word Study* Oct. 7/2 The resources of Greek have enriched the modern world as well as the ancient one. Perhaps this is most dramatically illustrated by the longest and most fantastic word now in an English dictionary (the Merriam-Webster's great Unabridged) which is forty-five letters in length: pneumonoultramicroscopicsilicovolcanoconiosis,.. meaning 'a disease of the lungs caused by extremely small particles of ash and dust'. **1973** R. MEGARRY *Second Miscellany-at-Law* 160 It has been said that 'floccinaucinihilipilification' is the longest word in the English language... The word's proud title must yield to some technical terms, such as pneumonultramicroscopicsilicovolcanokoniosis.

pneumonolysis (njuːməˈnɒlɪsɪs). *Surg.* [f. PNEUMONO- + -LYSIS.] = PNEUMOLYSIS.

1934 *Amer. Rev. Tuberculosis* XXIX. 270 We were opposed to..extrapleural pneumonolysis with paraffin filling because it is contrary to accepted surgical practice to place a foreign-body permanently in the tissues. **1975** W. L. GLENN et al. *Thoracic & Cardiovascular Surg.* (ed. 3) xi. 251/1 Pneumonolysis has..maintained a limited but definite field of usefulness.

pneumootocous (pnjuːməʊˈɒtəkəs, njuː-), *a.* *Zool.* Also **pneuˈmotocous.** [f. mod.L. *Pneumōotoca*, *Pneumōtoca* (Owen), f. PNEUMO- b + Gr. ᾠοτόκος egg-laying, oviparous.] Belonging to the *Pneumootoca*, or vertebrates that breathe air by means of lungs, and lay eggs, as birds and reptiles.

1890 *Cent. Dict.*, *Pneumoötokous . . Pneumotocous.*

ˌpneumo-periˈcardial, *a. Path.* [f. PNEUMO- b + PERICARDIAL.] Applied to a sound heard in pleurisy, attributed to the friction of the investing membrane of the lung against the pericardium: = *pleuropericardial* (see PLEURO-).

1876 tr. *von Ziemssen's Cycl. Med.* VI. 595 This sound is called the extra-pericardial, pneumo-pericardial or pleuro-pericardial friction sound.

‖**ˌpneumoperiˈcardium.** *Path.* [mod.L., f. PNEUMO- + PERICARDIUM.] The presence of air or gas in the pericardium. So ‖**ˌpneumopericarˈditis**, pneumopericardium accompanied by pericarditis (Billings *Med. Dict.* 1890).

1854 JONES & SIEV. *Pathol. Anat.* xvii. 297 A condition of the heart rarely found until after death, and termed by Laennec pneumo-pericardium, consists in an effusion of air into the sac. **1898** *Allbutt's Syst. Med.* V. 801 Pneumo-pericardium is extremely rare.

ˌpneumoperitoˈneum. *Med.* Also with hyphen. [f. PNEUMO- + PERITONEUM.] The presence of air or gas in the peritoneal cavity, whether accidentally or artificially induced.

1896 *Trans. Amer. Assoc. Obstetr. & Gynecol.* VIII. 212 Sacculated pneumo-peritoneum is frequently found in conjunction with localized appendiceal abscesses. **1934** *Amer. Rev. Tuberculosis* XXIX. 625 Therapeutic pneumoperitoneum has proved to be a technically simple and practicable treatment for intestinal tuberculosis. **1974** PASSMORE & ROBSON *Compan. Med. Stud.* III. xxviii. 3/1 A pelvic pneumoperitoneum may be induced with CO_2 and the gas used as contrast medium to define the uterus and ovaries [for radiography], but this has been largely superseded by laparoscopy.

pneumotachograph (njuːməʊˈtækəʊgrɑːf, -æ-). [a. G. *pneumotachograph* (A. Fleisch 1925, in *Pflüger's Arch. für die ges. Physiol.* CCIX. 722), f. Gr. τάχος speed: see PNEUMO- and -GRAPH.] An apparatus for recording the rate of air flow during breathing. Also shortened as **ˈpneumotach**.

1926 *Index Med.* VI. 539/2 (*heading*) Pneumotachograph. **1929** *Arch. Internal Med.* XLIV. 295 The pneumotachograph . . showed an increased respiratory rate. **1975** G. RUPPEL *Man. Pulmonary Function Testing* viii. 80 Pneumotachs utilize various physical and chemical properties to produce an electrical output that can be integrated for measurement of volumes and flows. **1975** *Nature* 4 Sept. 51/1 Forced expiratory flow-volume curves were recorded by a Fleisch No. 3 pneumotachograph connected to a differential pressure transducer . . and coupled to a carrier preamplifier.

So **pneumoˈtachogram** [A. Fleisch, *loc. cit.*, p. 718], a record produced by a pneumo-tachograph (e.g. a graph of the quantity of air expired or inspired as a function of time); **ˌpneumotachoˈgraphic** *a.*, of or pertaining to this apparatus or its use; **ˌpneumotaˈchography**.

1926 *Q. Cumulative Index to Current Med. Lit.* XI. 447/2 (*heading*) Curve of speed of human respiratory air (pneumotachogram). **1928** *Q. Cumulative Index Med.* III. 854/1 (*heading*) Pneumotachographic picture in bronchial asthma. **1929** *Arch. Internal Med.* XLIV. 293 Patients with cardiovascular and pulmonary diseases . . showed notchings of the pneumotachograms even during respiration standstill. **1930** *Jrnl. Amer. Med. Assoc.* 5 July 83/2 Pneumotachography in combination with electrocardiography is employed in the general examination of the circulation. **1955** *Jrnl. Physiol.* CXXX. 33P The method usually employed to record a pneumotachogram utilizes the pressure differences across an impedance placed in the air-flow stream. **1955** *Thorax* X. 258 (*heading*) Pneumotachographic measurement of breathing capacity. **1975** *Nature* 30 Oct. 787/2 The breathing pattern of the fish was recorded continuously by pneumotachography (Statham-Godart) and pressure measurements (Statham).

pneumothorax (ˌpnjuːməʊˈθɔəræks, njuː-). *Path.* Pl. **-thoraces, -thoraxes.** [a. F. *pneumothorax* (E. H. Itard *Dissertation sur le Pneumothorax ou les Congestions gazeuses qui se forment dans la Poitrine* (1803), f. as PNEUMO- + THORAX.] **a.** The presence of air or gas in the cavity of the thorax, i.e. of the pleura; usually caused by a wound or by perforation of the lung. Also *pneumatothorax* (see PNEUMATO-).

1821 J. FORBES tr. *Laennec's Treat. Dis. of Chest* I. II. v. 204 The disease is named by M. Itard, Pneumo-thorax. *Ibid.*, The author . . considers the pneumo-thorax as an affection always consequent to and depending on a latent phthisis. **1825** [see *pneumatothorax* s.v. PNEUMATO-]. **1843** SIR T. WATSON *Lect. Princ. & Pract. Physic* liii. II. 120 When the pleura contains air alone, the patient is said to have pneumothorax. **1894** *Pall Mall G.* 20 Dec. 7/3 It seems not improbable that the immediate cause of [Stevenson's] death may have been pneumothorax. **1974** R. J. MCCORMACK in Smith & Williams *Surg. of Lung* x. 241 All but the smallest pneumothoraces should be treated initially with intercostal water-seal drainage.

b. Pneumothorax may be induced diagnostically, or therapeutically so as to cause relaxation of a lung; it is then usu. known as ***artificial pneumothorax***.

1885 *Lancet* 16 May 894/2 Mr. Charters Symonds spoke of the induction of artificial pneumothorax as having been suggested by Dr. Mahomed in a case on which they had held a consultation. The aim of the operation was to be the arrest of phthisis. **1923** *Brit. Jrnl. Tuberculosis* XVII. 109 When inducing an artificial pneumothorax, the gas employed is usually oxygen, but after the first insufflation nitrogen or filtered air may be equally well used. **1927** H. T. LOWE-PORTER tr. *T. Mann's Magic Mountain* I. iii. 66 That was Hermine Kleefeld, she whistles with her pneumothorax. **1937** A. J. CRONIN *Citadel* IV. viii. 320 He was chary of using pneumothorax and his percentage of inductions was the lowest in the hospital. **1974** PASSMORE & ROBSON *Compan. Med. Stud.* III. xviii. 74/1 Once a mainstay of treatment for the control of tuberculous lesions, therapeutic artificial pneumothorax has now been abandoned. In modern medicine artificial pneumothorax is occasionally used as diagnostic procedure.

ˌpneumoventricuˈlography. *Med.* [f. PNEUMO- + VENTRICUL(US + -O + -GRAPHY.] The introduction of air or oxygen into the ventricles of the brain for radiographic purposes.

1918 W. E. DANDY in *Ann. Surg.* LXVIII. 6 From these and many other normal and pathological clinical demonstrations of the radiographic properties of air it is but a step to the injection of gas into the cerebral ventricles—pneumoventriculography. **1932** *Amer. Jrnl. Roentgenol.* XXVII. 657/1 Pneumoventriculography and encephalography are valuable aids in the diagnosis of cerebral lesions. **1974** PASSMORE & ROBSON *Compan. Med. Stud.* III. xxxiv. 24/1 Air may be introduced directly into the ventricle through a burr hole in the vault of the skull (pneumoventriculography).

pneus (njuːz), *sb. pl.* ? *Obs.* [Short for PNEUMATIC *sb.* 3.] Pneumatic tyres.

1902 C. N. & A. M. WILLIAMSON *Lightning Conductor* 18 On roads like these of Dieppe it would be soothing to have 'pneus', as they call them. **1907** —— in *Strand Mag.* Nov. 500/1 [The motor-car], with heated pneus, topped a commanding hill. **1908** *Westm. Gaz.* 31 Oct. 13/1 Before it [*sc.* the motor-car] can cease from injuring, . . you have to construct suitable roads, highways which it can no longer tear up with its ferocious pneus.

‖**pneusiobiognosis** (ˌpnjuːsɪəʊbaɪəʊˈgnəʊsɪs). *Med. Jurispr.* [mod.L. f. Gr. πνεῦσις a blowing, breathing + βίος life + γνῶσις investigation, knowledge.] = *pneobiognosis*: see PNEO-.

1857 in DUNGLISON *Dict. Med. Sc.*

pnicogen (ˈpnɪkəʊdʒən). *Chem.* [f. Gr. πνίγ-ειν to choke, stifle (in allusion to nitrogen) + -O + -GEN.] Any of a series of elements in group V of the periodic table, viz. nitrogen, phosphorus, arsenic, antimony, and bismuth.

1966 *Progress Sci. & Technol. Rare Earths* II. 76 The term 'pnicogen' seems to be gaining favor as a group name for the VA group of elements. **1971** *Nomencl. Inorg. Chem.* (I.U.P.A.C.) (ed. 2) 11 The use of the collective names 'pnicogen' (N, P, As, Sb and Bi) and 'pnictides' is not approved.

So **ˈpnictide** [-IDE], a binary compound of a pnicogen with a more electropositive element or radical.

1966 *Progress Sci. & Technol. Rare Earths* II. 35 (*heading*) Thermodynamic and magnetic properties of the rare earth chalcogenides and pnictides. **1973** *Physical Rev.* B. VIII. 5345 The fourth-order crystal-field parameters for the phosphides and for other rare-earth pnictides fall on a universal curve which is close to that predicted . . for the light rare earths. **1977** *Sci. Amer.* May 41/1 Removing an electron from a trigonally bonded chalcogen atom leads to a low-energy state, because the atom then becomes structurally similar to a pnictide atom in its proper configuration.

p-n-p (ˌpiːɛnˈpiː). *Electronics.* Also **pnp**, and in capitals. Designating a semiconductor device in which an *n*-type region is sandwiched between two *p*-type regions. Also *absol.*

1949 W. SHOCKLEY in *Bell Syst. Technical Jrnl.* XXVIII. 435 The principles and theory of a *p-n-p* transistor are described. *Ibid.* 474 The *p-n-p* transistor has the interesting feature of being calculable to a high degree. **1962** SIMPSON & RICHARDS *Physical Princ. Junction Transistors* iii. 51 The diffused layer forms the base, and the original material the collector, of a high-frequency *p-n-p* transistor. **1967** [see N-P-N]. **1975** D. G. FINK *Electronics Engineers' Handbk.* VIII. 26 The low current gain of a lateral *pnp* can be improved by combining it with a monolithic *npn* transistor, to form a composite transistor structure.

‖**pnyx** (pnɪks). [a. Gr. Πνύξ, *genitive* πυκνός, probably f. πυκνός packed, crowded.] Name of the public place of assembly in ancient Athens, a semicircular level cut out of the side of a little hill west of the Acropolis.

1822 T. MITCHELL *Aristoph.* I. 16 The pnyx was a public place, which derived its name from the number of stones with which it was filled. **1850** LEITCH tr. *C. O. Müller's Anc. Art* §269 (ed. 2) 320 The stage then certainly took the place of the simpler bema on the pnyx, which was in like manner constructed in the theatrical form. **1868** *Smith's Dict. Gr. & Rom. Antiq.* 146/2 Afterwards they [the ἐκκλησίαι] were transferred to the Pnyx.

†**po, poo,** *sb.*[1] *Obs.* Forms: α. 1 páuua, páwa, pawe, 5 paa, pae. β. 4–5 po, 4–6 poo. [OE. *páwa* (*pauua*) = OLG. **pâwo* (MLG. *pâwe*, LG. *pau*, Da. *paa*), OHG. *phâwo* (MHG. *pfâwe*, Ger. *pfau*), both wk. m.; WGer. a. L. *pāvo* peacock. Thence (through *pá(w)a*, *pa(we)*, ME. north. *paa*, *pa*-, midl. *pô*, *poo* (cf. OHG. *phâo*, MHG. *pfâ*). OE. had also the form *péa* from **pau* (see Sievers, ed. 3, §111 A. 2), whence ME. *pê*- in *pêcock*, *pêhenne*: see PEACOCK, etc.] A peacock. †*feathered with po*, i.e. with peacock's feathers.

α. *a* **700** *Epinal Gloss.* (O.E.T.) 826 *Pavo*, pauua. *c* **1000** ÆLFRIC *Gram.* ix. (Z.) 35 *Pauo*, pawa. *c* **1000** —— *Voc.* in Wr.-Wülcker 131/9 *Pauo, pauus*, pawe. *c* **1000** *Sax. Leechd.* II. 196 Fuȝlas þa þe heard flæsc habbað, pawa swan æned. *a* **1400–50** *Alexander* 4983 Þar bade a brid on a boghe . . Was of a port of a paa. **14..** in *Langtoft's Chron.* (Rolls) II. App. iv. 452, I beheld that litel man . . , His berd was syde ay large span, and glided als the fethere of pae.

β. *a* **1307** *Sat. Consistory Courts* in *Pol. Songs* (Camden) 159 A pruest proud ase a po, Seþþe weddeþ us bo. **1382** WYCLIF *2 Chron.* ix. 21 Thei brouȝten thennus gold, and syluer, and yuer, and apis, and poos [1388 pokokis, *v.r.* pekokis]. *c* **1400** *Laud Troy Bk.* 6961 With bowe and arwe fedred with po, He wroght amonges hem mechel wo. *c* **1500** *Three Kings' Sons* 136 Aftir thies wordes, was brought yn a Poo by ij. gentilwomen.

b. *attrib.* and *Comb.*

a **1300–1520** Pakoc, pacok, poucok, pocok, etc. [see PEACOCK *sb.* 1 β and γ]. *c* **1350** *Nominale Gall.-Angl.* 782 (E.E.T.S.), Storke pecok and pohenne. **1377** LANGL. *P. Pl.* B. XII. 257 By þe po feet is vnderstonde . . fals frendes.

†**po,** *sb.*[2] *Obs.* [Origin obscure.] (See quot. 1838.)

1678 BUTLER *Hud.* III. i. 1395 This is some Pettifogging Fiend, . . That undertakes to understand, And juggles at the second hand; And now would pass for Spirit Po, And all mens dark Concerns foreknow. [**1838** SOUTHEY *Doctor* cxxxix. V. 25 One Mr. Duke, a busy fanatic, in Devonshire in Charles II.'s days, whom old Sir Edward Seymour used to call Spirit Po, that said Po being a *petit diable*, a small devil that was *presto* at every Conjuror's nod.]

po (pəʊ), *sb.*[3] *colloq.* Pl. **poes, pos.** [ad. Fr. *pot* (*de chambre*).] A chamber-pot. Also *attrib.* and *Comb.*

1880 LONGMUIR & DONALDSON *Jamieson's Etym. Dict. Sc. Lang.* (rev. ed.) III. 517/2 *Po, s*, a matula or urinal. **1911** A. WARRACK *Scots Dial. Dict.* 420/1 *Po, n.*, a chamber-pot. **1937** PARTRIDGE *Dict. Slang* 643/1 *Po*, a chamber-pot. . . Ex the pronunciation of *pot* in Fr. *pot de chambre*. **1951** W. SANSOM *Face of Innocence* iv. 56 'In bloody pos.' 'Pose?' 'Under-the-beds. The amusing ones, roses and all get out. Bloody jerries.' **1950** G. WILSON *Brave Company* (1951) xi. 201 There was a great white china po hanging on the wall near the roof. **1961** C. WILLOCK *Death in Covert* i. 14 Do you make plastic poes? **1966** P. O'DONNELL *Sabre-Tooth* iv. 68 On her head was a po-shaped cloche hat. **1970** *Daily Tel.* 17 Oct. 6/6 And the hats—those 'po' creations had to be seen to be believed! **1974** *Punch* 27 Mar. 510/1, I kneelin' by de bed . . peein' in de smart Victorian po.

‖**p'o** (po), *sb.*[4] Also **peh, po.** [Chinese *pò*.] Soul, spirit.

1850 *Chinese Repository* Nov. 611 The Chinese philosophers . . regarded man as a microcosm, his constitution and nature formed their model. This model they conceived to consist of a body which had *hing* . . form, and of a *hwan*, . . animus, and a *peh*, anima. **1914** D. T. SUZUKI *Brief Hist. Early Chinese Philos.* 44 It is one Animal Soul (*po* . .) that becomes the drought in heaven, the metal on earth, and the animal soul in man. **1934** A. D. WALEY *Way & its Power* 28 *P'o*, which originally meant the semen, becomes the female soul, which lodges in the tomb. **1973** J. BLOFELD *Secret & Sublime* ii. 47 How they would rush about, seeking in vain some vehicle to save their *hun* and *p'o* (higher and lower souls) from gradual dissolution into nothingness! **1975** C.-Y. CHANG *Tao* x. 32 According to Ho-shang Kung, . . p'o is rendered as anima. . . Anima (p'o) is the dark yin-soul.

po' (pəʊ), *a.* Repr. a U.S. dial. pronunc. of POOR *a.* (*sb.*)

1893 H. A. SHANDS *Some Peculiarites of Speech in Mississippi* 50 Po' . . , Negro for *poor*. **1911** F. W. ROLT-WHEELER *Boy with U.S. Census* 47 The po' white . . is goin' to be only a memory like the backwoodsman o' the time o' Dan'l Boone. **1926** *Opportunity* Mar. 84/1 Dey kilt my po' daddy. **1945** *Gumbo Ya Ya* (Writers' Program, Louisiana) ii. 27, I sell to the rich, I sell to the po'; I'm gonna sell the lady Standin' in that do'. **1968** *Globe Mag.* (Toronto) 17 Feb. 18/4 Grey Owl . . was Archie Bellaney, born . . to a ne'er-do-well Englishman and . . a po' white girl from Florida.

po: see POH and next.

poa (ˈpəʊə). *Bot.* [mod.L. (Linnæus *Genera Plantarum* (1737) 20), a. Gr. πόα grass.] **a.** An annual or perennial grass of the genus so called, which is widely distributed in temperate and cold regions; = *meadow-grass* s.v. MEADOW *sb.* 4 c.

1753 in CHAMBERS *Cycl. Supp.* **1785** MARTYN *Rousseau's Bot.* xiii. (1794) 137 There are four sorts of Poa very common in most meadows. **1789** *Trans. Soc. Arts* (ed. 2) II. 57 A mixture of . . burnet, and dwarf poa. **1917** S. F. ARMSTRONG *Brit. Grasses* vii. 125 *Poa maritima*, Huds. (Sea Poa.) A somewhat creeping perennial, frequent on the shores of the British Isles. **1952** A. R. CLAPHAM et al. *Flora Brit. Isles* 1438 'Alpine Poa.' An erect, tufted perennial.

b. *Comb.* **poa-grass** (†**po-grass**), a grass of this genus; meadow-grass.

1765 *Museum Rust.* IV. xlii. 183 We have a far better grass, under the name of po-grass. **1766** *Ibid.* VI. 121, I could not distinguish the desired kind from these intruders; particularly the poa-grass. **1927** F. B. YOUNG *Portrait of Clare* VII. 762 A stone bridge spanned a chalk-stream with emerald trailing poa-grass swimming in smooth flats beneath it. **1971** *Homes & Gardens* Sept. 128/1 There is a silver-striped poa grass that shows up brilliantly anywhere, but it must not be allowed to spread.

poach (pəʊtʃ), *v.*[1] Forms: 5 pocche, 6–8 **poche**, **potch**, 7– **poach**. [a. OF. *pochier* (12th c. in Godef.), later *pocher* to enclose in a poke or bag, to bag; also in senses 1 and 2 below; f. *poche* poke, bag (Diez, Littré): see POKE *sb.*[1] The Eng. uses were adopted separately. The *o* seems to have been originally short as in Fr.]

1. *trans.* To cook (an egg) by dropping it, without the shell, into boiling water and simmering gently; to simmer or steam (an egg) in a poacher. Hence, to cook (fish, fruit, etc.) by simmering in water or another liquid. Also *absol.*

[F. *pocher*, in this sense, is usually explained as referring to the enclosure of the yolk in the white as in a bag.]

[? *c* **1390** *Form of Cury* §90. 46 Pochee. Take Ayren and breke hem in scaldyng hoot water [etc.]. *c* **1430** *Two Cookery-bks.* 24 Eyron en poche. Take Eyroun, breke hem, and sethe hem in hot Water; þan take hem Vppe as hole as þou may; þan take flowre, and melle with Mylke. *c* **1450** *Douce MS.* 55 §100 Egges pocchez.] *c* **1450** [see POACHED *ppl. a.*[1]]. **1530** PALSGR. 663/1, I potche egges, *je poche des œufs*. He that wyll potche egges well muste make his water sethe first. **1533** ELYOT *Cast. Helthe* II. xvii. (1541) 33 They [eggs] be moste holsome whan they be poched. **1598** *Epulario* L j, To poche Egges.. To poche them in milke or wine. **1626** BACON *Sylva* §53 The Yolkes of Eggs.. so they be Potched or Reare boyled. **1630** J. TAYLOR (Water P.) *Laugh & be fat* Wks. II. 76/2 This man hath played the cooke And potch'd this Ginnie Egge into thy booke. **1679** JENKINS in R. Mansel *Narr. Popish Plot* (1680) 99 She poach'd Eggs for them both. *a* **1693** *Urquhart's Rabelais* III. xx. 169 As if he had been to potch them in a Skillet with Butter and Eggs. **1742, 1889** [see POACHED *ppl. a.*[1]]. **1898** C. H. SENN *Senn's Culinary Encycl.* 74 *Poach (to)*.., to parboil or to boil slightly. Mode of cooking usually applied to eggs and quenelles of fish, meat or game. **1906** *Mrs. Beeton's Bk. Househ. Managem.* xxxviii. 1237 Put the tins in the oven, in a sauté-pan, surround them to half their depth with boiling water, and poach until the white is firm. **1907** *Yesterday's Shopping* (1969) 170/3 Steam Egg Poacher. A perfect way of poaching eggs. **1907** A. ESCOFFIER *Guide Mod. Cookery* II. xiv. 292 The poaching of fillets of sole must be effected without allowing the cooking-liquor to boil. **1940** A. L. SIMON *Conc. Encycl. Gastron.* II. 18/1 Fresh Cod.. is usually boiled, steamed or poached. **1959** *Listener* 26 Feb. 395/1 Peel and cut the pears in pieces and poach them very gently in the syrup. *Ibid.* 1 Oct. 551/2 Core the pears carefully. Poach until tender. **1963** HUME & DOWNES *Penguin Cordon Bleu Cookery* 432 Fresh peaches poached in a sugar syrup until tender. **1972** L. DAVIES *Easy Cooking* iii. 93 Very gently poach the sausages in the milk with the bay leaf, onion and seasoning, for 20 minutes.

†**2.** To sketch roughly. *Obs. rare.*

[F. *pocher*, in this sense, appears to have arisen from the obs. and dial. sense 'to make blots or blurs': cf. Cotgr. '*cet encre poche*, this Inke blurres'.]

1651 CLEVELAND *Poems* 44 Whose fervour can Hatch him, whom Nature poach'd but half a man.

poach (pəʊtʃ), *v.*[2] Forms: 6–7 **poche**, 7– **potch**, **poach**. [In 16th c. *poche*; app. in the main a palatalized collateral form of POKE *v.*[1], q.v. But sense 1 c appears to be immediately from OF. *pocher* 'to thrust or dig out with the fingers' (Cotgr.), in *pocher un œil, les yeux* (14th c. in Godef. *Compl.*) to thrust or gouge out an eye, to put out the eyes (in mod.F. to give any one 'a black eye' with a blow); itself prob. of LG. origin; and quots. 1528, 1542 in 1 b may be related to OF. *pocher* to put into a sack, to bag: see prec. The *o* was app. mostly short in 16–17th c., and *potch* is still widely spread in the dialects.]

I. 1. a. *trans.* To push or stir (anything) *with* the point of a stick, a finger, a foot, etc.; = POKE *v.*[1] 1; to stir *up* by this means; *fig.* to instigate. Now *dial.*

[*c* **1386**: see POKE *v.*[1] 1.] **1632** J. HAYWARD tr. *Biondi's Eromena* 75 Then.. tried his armour everywhere by potching it, to see if he could find any place unarmed. **1684** OTWAY *Atheist* I. i, A Woman who.. watch't her Opportunity, and poach'd me up for the Service of Satan. **1749** FIELDING *Tom Jones* v. iv, He bid him beat abroad, and not poach up the Game in his Warren. **1859** in J. Watson *Living Bards of Border* 92 (E.D.D.) We'll poach the fire, an' ha'e a crack aside the chumla lug.

b. To ram, shove, or roughly push (things) together, or in a heap. *Obs.* or *dial.*

1528 *Impeachm. Wolsey* 59 in Furniv. *Ballads fr. MSS.* I. 353 þou haste purposyd To mynester grete extorcion, By the whyche haste so furiously encrochyd, In Chestis, baggis hepyd & pochyd, Of every man Takyng A porcion. **1542** BOORDE *Dyetary* xi. (1870) 259 Mestlyng breade is made, halfe of whete and halfe of Rye. And there is also mestlyng made, halfe of rye and halfe of barly. And yll people wyll put whete and barly togyther. Breade made of these aforesayde grayne or cornes, thus poched togyther, maye fyll the gutte, but it shall neuer do good to man. **1903** *Eng. Dial. Dict.* (Warwicksh.), Potch these oddments in the corner. These things are all potched together.

c. To thrust or poke *out* (the eyes); = OF. *pocher l'œil, les yeux*. *Obs.* or *dial.*

[*c* **1380**: see POKE *v.*[1] 1.] **1584** HUDSON *Du Bartas' Judith* VI. in *Sylvester's Wks.* (1621) 752 And with their fingers poched out his eyes. **1608** SYLVESTER *Du Bartas* II. iv. IV. *Decay* 1179 O! poach not out mine eyes.

d. To strike, rap, slap. [Perh. for Ger. *pochen*.] *slang.*

1892 ZANGWILL *Childr. Ghetto* I. 87 My mother potched my face... I shall never forget that slap.

2. a. To thrust or push (a stick, a finger, a foot, etc.) into any hole or thing. Now chiefly *dial.*

1673 TEMPLE *United Prov.* i. 5 His [Charlemagne's] Horse poching one of his legs into some hollow ground, made way for the smoaking water to break out, and gave occasion for the Emperor's building that City [Aix]. **1822–56** DE QUINCEY *Confess.* (1862) 133 Lest some one of the many little Brahminical-looking cows.. might poach her foot into the centre of my face. [See *Eng. Dial. Dict.*]

b. *intr.* To poke or probe (e.g. with a stick, etc.); also, to poke, thrust oneself, intrude. Now *dial.*

a **1550** *Hye Way to Spyttel Hous* 308 in Hazl. *E.P.P.* IV. 41 One tyme to this spyttell, another to that, Probyng and pochyng to get somwhat; At euery doore lumpes of bread or meat. **1657** DAVENANT *1st Day's Entertainm. Rutland Ho.* 72 Your Bastelier.. with her long pole gives us a tedious waft, as if he were all the while poaching for Eels. **1859** in *Eng. Dial. Dict.* s.v., Eternally poachin' amang my feet.

†**3. a.** *trans.* To thrust, stab, pierce. *Obs.*

1602 CAREW *Cornwall* 31 The Flowk, Sole and Playce followe the tyde vp into the fresh riuers, where, at lowe water the Countrie people.. take them vp with their hands. They vse also to poche them with an instrument somewhat like the Sammon-speare. **1644** W. NEWPORT *Fall of Man by Sin* 4 Potch a dead man with knives, stab him with daggers, &c.

†**b.** *intr.* To make a stab or thrust *at* as in fencing. Also *fig. Obs. rare.*

1607 SHAKS. *Cor.* I. x. 15 Ile potche at him some way, Or Wrath, or Craft may get him. **1624** BACON *War w. Spain* Wks. 1879 I. 531/1 They have rather poached and offered at a number of enterprizes, than maintained any constantly.

II. 4. *trans.* To thrust or stamp down with the feet; to trample (soft or sodden ground) into muddy holes; to cut *up* (turf, etc.) with hoofs.

1677 PLOT *Oxfordsh.* 247 The Horses going.. in a string and keeping the furrow, to avoid poching the Land. **1768** EARL HADDINGTON *Forest-trees* 46 Cattle should be taken off, lest they potch the ground. **1814** SCOTT *Wav.* lxiii, The cattle of the villagers.. had poached into black mud the verdant turf. **1816** —— *Old Mort.* xv, The passage of the main body, in many instances, poached up the swamps through which they passed. **1849** STEPHENS *Bk. Farm* (ed. 2) I. 194/1 The land.. ought not to be cut up and poached by the cart-wheels and horses' feet. **1894** *Times* 18 Nov. 4/3 Pastures are soddened to an extent that must result in their being badly 'poached' where the stock cannot be taken off them.

5. *intr.* To sink (into wet heavy ground) in walking; to plod over soft ground, or through mud or mire; to tramp heavily or plungingly.

1600 NORTHBROOKE *Poore Mans Gard.* To Rdr. 2 Poching in the mire vp to the calfe of the legge. **1655** GURNALL *Chr. in Arm.* I. 88 How uncomfortable.. for a traveller in Heaven's road.. to go potching in the dark. **1686** tr. *Chardin's Trav. Persia* 176 The soyl so extreamly fat, that our Horses had much a do to poach along. **1792** A. YOUNG *Trav. France* (1794) I. 241 The hedges and ditches confine the carriages to poach through the mud. **1837** HOGG *Tales* I. *Wool-gatherer* 213 Plunging and poaching to make all the fish take into close cover.

6. *intr.* Of land: To become sodden, miry, and full of holes by being trampled.

1707 MORTIMER *Husb.* (1721) I. 15 The Chalky and Clay Lands.. have also the inconveniencies.. to burn in hot Weather, to chap in Summer, and poach in Winter. **1766** *Museum Rust.* VI. 105 Cattle unavoidably do great mischief to grass land, when it is so wet as to poach. **1807** A. YOUNG *Agric. Essex* (1813) I. 24 Strong, wet, tenacious land, poaching with rain, and sticking to the horses' legs. **1879** JEFFERIES *Wild Life in S. Co.* 378 The ground.. is still soft, and will poach under the hoofs of cattle.

7. *trans.* To soak, make sodden.

1881 *Times* 14 Apr. 10/5 As in many parts of England, along the banks of streams and rivers are considerable areas of good land, poached and scoured by frequent floods.

8. To mix with water and reduce to a uniform consistency. In *Paper-making*, to mix thoroughly (the half-stuff from the breaking-engine) with the bleach-liquor, in the poacher. (Also *potch*.)

1873 ROBERTSON *Engineering Notes* 49 The clay should be free from stones and must be well poached. **1877** W. ARNOT *Cantor Lectures* in *Jrnl. Soc. Arts* XXVI. 63/1 The breaking, poaching, and beating processes.. are all conducted in machines or engines of the same general construction. **1883** R. HALDANE *Workshop Receipts* Ser. II. 36/2 For potching half-stuffs previously gas bleached, the quantities are [etc.].

III. 9. a. *intr.* To encroach or trespass (*on* the lands or rights of another) in order to possess oneself unlawfully or unfairly of something, esp. in order to steal game; hence, to take game or fish illegally, or by unsportsmanlike devices. Also *fig.*

1611 COTGR., *Pocher le labeur d'autruy*, to poche into, or incroach vpon, another mans imployment, practise, or trade. **1682** DRYDEN & LEE *Duke of Guise* IV. iii, I scorn to poach for power. **1706** PHILLIPS, To *poach*,.. to destroy Game by unlawful means, as by laying Snares, Gins, etc. **1742** POPE *Dunc.* IV. 228 For Attic Phrase in Plato let them seek, I poach in Suidas for unlicens'd Greek. **1827** SCOTT *Jrnl.* 27 Jan., The pettish resentment that you might entertain against one who had poached on your manor. **1847** EMERSON *Repr. Men, Shaks.* Wks. (Bohn) I. 358 So keen was the hope to discover whether the boy Shakespeare poached, or not. **1855** THACKERAY *Newcomes* ix, Poaching on her lodgers' mutton. **1868** G. DUFF *Pol. Surv.* 72 A region in which the politician feels that he is poaching on the preserves of the geographer. **1885** *Standard* 20 Nov. 3/8 All the owners poached for salmon.

b. In various ball games: to enter a partner's portion of the field or court and play a ball which he normally would have played.

1889 W. M. BROWNLEE *Lawn Tennis* 167 He need not be profusely apologetic when he poaches unsuccessfully. **1928** *Daily Express* 9 July 13/3 The pretty little Australian girl.. would have won if her partner had not 'poached' and put himself out of position. **1960** *Times* 4 July 15/7 They must have noticed Osuna's swift ability to poach.

10. *trans.* **a.** To trespass on (land or water), esp. in order to kill or catch game.

1715 GARTH *Claremont* 8 They poach Parnassus, and lay snares for praise. **1807** CRABBE *Par. Reg.* I. 814 He poach'd the wood, and on the warren snared. **1858** F. E. PAGET *Curate Cumberw.* (1859) 319 A fellow who had poached lands and fished waters which Mr. Soaper himself had hired. **1885** *Field* 3 Oct. (Cassell), The Greta is not nearly so much poached as formerly.

b. To catch and carry off (game or fish) illegally; to capture by illicit or unsportsmanlike methods such as a poacher uses. Also *fig.*

1862 *Cornh. Mag.* VI. 651 Some are famished to death, and some are poached, and some get hooked. **1895** *Westm. Gaz.* 8 Nov. 1/3 You were always 'poaching' our best men. **1903** *Ibid.* 28 Mar. 2/1 She's a poacher, that woman—poaches children... Yes; poaches them;.. takes them away from other teachers who've taught in those families for years. **1955** *Times* 14 June 3/3 These are the men whom the N.A.S.D. are said to have 'poached' from the Transport and General Workers Union. **1958** *Listener* 11 Dec. 978/1 A girl doing it might later in life be tempted to poach service. **1979** *Internat. Jrnl. Sociol. of Law* VII. 176 Solicitors in the large criminal firms not only 'poach' clients, they also strive to poach each other.

c. *Racing slang.* To filch (an advantage, e.g. at the start in a race) by unfair means.

1891 *Licensed Vict. Gaz.* 20 Mar. 182/1 Seward maintained that the start was a false one, and that his opponent poached full five yards before he [Seward] moved. **1892** *Daily News* 16 May 3/5 Several [jockeys] displayed a marked desire to 'poach a bit' at the start. **1894** *Ibid.* 16 Mar. 6/5 The scratch poached the start, and gained fully half a length, rowing up to 44 to the minute against Oxford's 40.

Hence **'poaching** *ppl. a.*

1681 CHETHAM *Angler's Vade-m.* xxx. §1 (1689) 166 To be used by none but idle pouching [*sic*] fellows. **1886** C. SCOTT *Sheep-Farming* 200 In a few minutes the poaching flock is sent scampering back to their own proper walk.

poachable ('pəʊtʃəb(ə)l), *a.* [f. POACH *v.*[2] + -ABLE.] Of game or fish: that may be poached or carried off illegally; suitable for poaching.

1924 *Public Opinion* 22 Feb. 169/1 The open wood I seldom visited,—all that was poachable having been poached long before.

poached ('pəʊtʃd), *ppl. a.*[1] [f. POACH *v.*[1] + -ED[1].] **a.** Of an egg: Cooked in boiling water, without the shell. Also in extended use (see POACH *v.*[1] 1).

c **1450** *Two Cookery-bks.* 94 Potage de egges. *MS. Douce*, Pocched egges. **1528** PAYNEL *Salerne's Regim.* F j b, Poched egges are better than egges rosted hard or rere. **1620** VENNER *Via Recta* v. 84 A couple of potched [*ed.* **1650** poched] Egges. **1742** FIELDING *Jos. Andrews* I. xv, Whether a poached egg, or chicken broth. **1889** A. LANG *Prince Prigio* ii. 10 Why the king.. should have poached eggs and plum-cake at afternoon tea. **1940** A. L. SIMON *Conc. Encycl. Gastron.* II. 18/1 Fresh Cod.. may be served.. with any of the sauces which are suitable for boiled, steamed or poached Turbot. **1978** *Chicago* June 225/1 For dessert, orange-sparked chocolate mousse, poached pear with brandy and whipped-cream sauce.

b. ***poached egg***, (*a*) name of gastropod shells of genus *Ovulum*; (*b*) see quot. 1903; (*c*) *Cookery* (see quots.); (*d*) = *poached-egg flower* s.v. sense c.

1837 *Penny Cycl.* VIII. 257/1 *Ovulum*, (..commonly called Poached Eggs). **1903** *Windsor Mag.* Sept. 385/2 The ball in a stroke of this kind will assume an oval shape something like a cucumber. This stroke is called in Stické parlance 'a poached egg'. **1951** *Good Housek. Home Encycl.* 592/1 'Poached eggs' (halved and glazed peaches on rounds of sponge cake, surrounded by a ring of whipped cream). **1959** *Listener* 24 Dec. 1135/1 'Poached eggs': rounds of sponge cake, covered with a halved tinned apricot with a ribbon of whipped cream piped round the edge. **1971** *Guardian* 17 Apr. 7/8 The low-growing annual *Limnanthes douglasii*, known to children as 'Poached Eggs'.. will make a tapestry of lemon and white at the front of a sunny bed.

c. ***poached-egg flower***, ***plant***, a small annual herb, *Limnanthes douglasii*, belonging to the family Limnanthaceæ, native to California, and bearing fragrant white and yellow flowers.

1963 R. D. MEIKLE *Garden Flowers* 135 Poached-egg Flower... The cordate petals are yellow at the base and white at the apex, producing a parti-coloured effect which at once suggests (to the inartistic) the popular name. **1973** *Country Life* 30 Aug. 565/1 In Britain we call *Limnanthes douglasii* the poached-egg flower, but in America they use the much more appropriate name of meadow foam. **1977** M. ALLAN *Darwin & his Flowers* xv. 261 (*caption*) *Limnanthes douglasii*, the 'Poached Egg Plant', which Darwin found was self-pollinating. **1978** *Woman's Jrnl.* Dec. 15/4 Do consider .. the poached-egg plant called *Limnanthes douglasii*, a dwarf annual with ravishing yellow and white flowers.

poached ('pəʊtʃd), *ppl. a.*[2] [f. POACH *v.*[2] + -ED[1].] In senses of the verb: *esp.* **a.** Trodden or trampled into miry holes. **b.** Acquired by poaching; illegally captured.

1844 STEPHENS *Bk. Farm* II. 110 The cattle will soon render the whole bedding a poached mass. **1883** JEFFERIES *Nature near Lond.* 166 This very pond.. is muddy enough, and surrounded with poached mud. **1889** *Pall Mall Gaz.* 13

July 3/2 France..is made the market for English poached fish, and French poached fish find a market in England. **1955** *Times* 6 June 4/3 The union should..attempt to reach a settlement..of the dispute over 'poached' members.

c. ***poached eyes*** = F. *yeux pochés*, eyes swollen as if with a blow or weeping. [Cf. POACH *v.*[2] 1 c.]

1904 *Athenæum* 24 Sept. 408/3 Samuel re-entered with poached eyes.

poacher[1] ('pəʊtʃə(r)). Also **potcher**. [f. POACH *v.*[2] + -ER[1].]

1. a. One who poaches or trespasses in pursuit of game; one who takes or kills game unlawfully.

1667 EVELYN *Publ. Employm.* Misc. Writ. (1805) 552 The young potcher with his dog and kite, breaking his neighbours hedges, or trampling o're his corn for a bird not worth sixpence. **1668** WILKINS *Real Char.* 265 Huntsman, Hunter, Fowler, Fisher,..Game, Pocher. **1680** OTWAY *Orphan* III. i. 810 So Poachers basely pick up tir'd Game Whilst the fair Hunter's cheated of his Prey. **1774** GOLDSM. *Nat. Hist.* (1776) IV. 12 They are shot at by poachers; traced by their footsteps in the snow; caught in springs. **1863** KINGSLEY *Water-Bab.* i, A keeper is only a poacher turned outside in, and a poacher a keeper turned inside out.

transf. **1702** YALDEN *Æsop's Fables* VI. 1 Ren, an old poacher after game, Saw grapes look tempting fine. **1898** *Westm. Gaz.* 11 Feb. 10/1 To escape the jaws of the large pike, the only permitted poachers which exist at the lake.

b. ***a poacher turned gamekeeper***: one who now preserves the interests he previously attacked; conversely, ***a gamekeeper turned poacher***.

1945 *Times* 4 Aug. 5/2 Mr. Aneurin Bevan at the Ministry of Health..is conspicuously the poacher turned gamekeeper. **1977** *Times* 12 Feb. 12/6 Mr Camp has been working against the Railways Board in the interests of the unions... Is he then a poacher turned gamekeeper? **1978** *Broadbent* 27 Mar. 4/2 Stuart Wilson, former joint MD of Yorkshire Television..has been arguing with the ferocity of gamekeeper turned poacher against ITV's intended inroads into the fourth channel.

2. a. (*U.S.*) The widgeon, *Mareca americana*: said to be so called from its habit of seizing the food for which other ducks have dived. (But cf. POCHARD.)

1891 in *Cent. Dict.* **1905** C. C. TOWNSEND *Birds of Essex County, Mass.* x. 130 The Baldpate, being unable to dive, makes use of diving Ducks to obtain food in deep water, and has therefore received in some places the name of 'Poacher'. **1923** *Bull. U.S. Nat. Mus.* No. 126. 96 Such behavior has earned for the baldpate the local name of 'poacher'. **1973** *Nature West Coast* (Vancouver Nat. Hist. Soc.) 163 Some birds [*sc.* American widgeon] feed on sea-weeds, often snatching them from the bills of diving birds. Hence the popular name 'poacher'.

b. A small marine fish belonging to the family Agonidæ. Cf. *sea-poacher* s.v. SEA *sb.* 23 d.

1891 in *Cent. Dict.* **1961** E. S. HERALD *Living Fishes of World* 252/2 The cold-water marine poachers and their relatives look much like some of the South American fresh-water armored catfishes. **1978** A. WHEELER *Key Fishes N. Europe* 224 Poachers or Pogges. A small family (Agonidae) of mainly Arctic marine fishes.

3. *Paper-making.* One of the series of engines by which rags, etc., are comminuted, washed, bleached, and reduced to pulp; a poaching-engine.

1877 W. ARNOT in *Jrnl. Soc. Arts* XXVI. 91/2 The second engine is called the 'poacher', the roll of which..does little more than mix the stuff and the bleach liquor. **1883** R. HALDANE *Workshop Receipts* Ser. II. 392/1 Reduce them [rags] to half-stuff, and as soon as possible empty into the poacher..and bleach with great care. **1906** BEADLE *Papermaking* II. 65. **1906** J. CASTLE (Wolvercote Paper Mill) in *Let.*, Potcher or Poacher.

4. *attrib.* and *Comb.* (sense 1), as ***poacher-court, -herd, -work***; **poacher('s) pocket**, a large concealed pocket in a coat.

1784 BURNS *Ep. J. Rankine* viii, I..brought a Paitrick to the grun'... Somebody tells the Poacher-court The hale affair. **1834** *Tait's Mag.* I. 767/2 'It was no poacher work, Matthew', he said. **1897** CROCKETT *Lad's Love* xxii. 226 It was a portentous thing to see the poacher-herd so keen on the proprieties. **1925** [see *hare-pocket*]. **1956** G. E. EVANS *Ask Fellows who cut Hay* ii. 35 Inside the slop were two long hanging, or *poacher's*, pockets so that a shepherd could very easily conceal a couple of rabbits. **1974** *Country Life* 21 Mar. 688/2 The suit..is a three-piece garment with extremely wide lapels, poacher pockets, and baggy trousers with turn-ups. **1976** 'D. HALLIDAY' *Dolly & Nanny Bird* xviii. 247 He took up..a manilla envelope which he zipped with care into a poacher's pocket on the inner side of his waterproof jacket.

Hence **'poachery** *nonce-wd.*

1831 T. L. PEACOCK *Crotchet Castle* ix. (1887) 109 Witchery, devilry, robbery, poachery, piracy, fishery, gipsy-astrology.

poacher[2] ('pəʊtʃə(r)). [f. POACH *v.*[1] + -ER[1].] A vessel or pan for poaching eggs, usu. with shallow cup-like compartments in which an egg can be cooked over boiling water. Also, a vessel or pan in which fish, etc. can be poached (see POACH *v.*[1] 1).

1861 MRS. BEETON *Bk. Househ. Managem.* xxxiii. 827 For inexperienced cooks, a tin egg-poacher may be purchased. **1868** MARY JEWRY *Model Cookery* 82/1 The egg may also be done in a regular egg-poacher. **1884** [see *egg-poacher* s.v. EGG *sb.* 6 b]. **1895** *Montgomery Ward Catal.* Spring & Summer 433/1 Buffalo steam egg poachers. **1951** *Good Housek. Home Encycl.* 452/1 Use a wide pan..or a specially constructed egg poacher. **1975** J. BEARD et al. *Cooks' Catal.* 399 Poachers come in a range of sizes for everything from a miniature mackerel to a king-sized salmon... All poachers have a common feature—a rack that protects your fish from the direct heat source beneath and enables you to lift the whole fish from the pot intact. *Ibid.* 439 All of the so-called egg poachers on the market, however they operate, whatever they do, are not actually poaching at all. A true poached egg is cooked *in* water, not over it, and not in steam—an 'egg poacher', with its cuplike insert, actually steams an egg. **1976** *West Lancs. Evening Gaz.* 15 Dec. 1. 12/4 Two Poachers and steamer, 75p each.

poaching ('pəʊtʃɪŋ), *vbl. sb.*[1] [f. POACH *v.*[1] + -ING[1].] The action of POACH *v.*[1]

1584 COGAN *Haven Health* cxciii. (1636) 174 [Eggs] be sodden two wayes;..the first is called seething..the second poching of egges. *a* **1700** B. E. *Dict. Cant. Crew, Poching*,..an Egg Boyled in Water out of the Shell. **1907** A. ESCOFFIER *Guide Mod. Cookery* II. xiv. 292 Where the exact amount of poaching-liquor is not given, allow one-quarter pint to every four fillets. **1913** J. M. HILL *Pract. Cooking* 69 The term poaching has come to be applied to the cooking of all articles containing eggs, either in the oven or on top of the range, in dishes that are surrounded with hot water. **1956** SPRY & HUME *Constance Spry Cookery Bk.* iv. 70 *Poaching* is a term used to indicate a gentler cooking still [than simmering]. **1960** *Good Housek. Cookery Bk.* (rev. ed.) 80/2 Although this method of cooking fish is referred to as boiling, it is more accurately described as poaching, since the water should be kept only simmering, not actually boiling, while the fish is in it.

'poaching, *vbl. sb.*[2] [f. POACH *v.*[2] + -ING[1].] The action of POACH *v.*[2]

a. Trampling (of land) while in a sodden condition; becoming poachy. Also *concr.* (*poet.*), a patch of mud.

1780 A. YOUNG *Tour Irel.* I. 116 Lands..sound enough for winter feeding without poaching. **1802** C. FINDLATER *Agric. Surv. Peebles* 159 The parks were extremely subject to Winter poaching. **1879** *Amateur Poacher*, The green drive shows traces of the poaching it received from the thick-planted hoofs of the hunt when the leaves were off. **1929** J. MASEFIELD *Poems* 703 Plastered with poachings, he rode on forsaken.

b. Trespassing in pursuit of game; taking of game or fish illegally or by unsportsmanlike methods. Also *fig.*

1611 BEAUM. & FL. *Philaster* IV. i, He hunts too much in the purlues, would he would leave off poaching. **1821** EGAN *Life in Lond.* II. iv. (Farmer), You shall be admitted into the preserve; but remember no poaching. **1892** *Athenæum* 20 Aug. 246/3 He has kept free from any suspicion of..literary poaching. **1899** E. H. MILES *Lessons in Lawn Tennis* xi. 69 The man should have no false modesty..about a certain amount of poaching. **1977** *World of Cricket Monthly* June 68/3 The approach had come initially from Imran, and there was no question of poaching on the part of Sussex.

attrib. **1832** HT. MARTINEAU *Homes Abroad* i. 1 News of murderous poaching expeditions. **1899** *Westm. Gaz.* 20 Sept. 3/2 What some consider the poaching tactics of the music-halls. **1955** *Times* 27 May 11/6 He intimates that officers of the Transport and General Workers Union have been guilty of membership poaching offences.

c. *Paper-making.* See POACH *v.*[2] 8; **poaching** or **potching-engine** = POACHER[1] 3.

1877 W. ARNOT in *Jrnl. Soc. Arts* XXVI. 89/2 The bleaching or poaching engine. **1880** J. DUNBAR *Pract. Papermaker* 27 The quantities of half-stuff filled into the potching engine should at all times be as uniform as possible.

poachy ('pəʊtʃɪ), *a.* [f. POACH *v.*[2] + -Y.] Of land: Spongy, retentive of moisture, and so liable to be trampled into muddy holes; sodden, swampy.

1707 MORTIMER *Husb.* (1721) I. 56 If much Rain come upon it while it lies flat, it will make it so poachy that you cannot plow it, (especially if 'tis a wet Clay Land). **1802** C. FINDLATER *Agric. Surv. Peebles* 158 The land is put into a poachy state by every heavy shower of rain. **1844** STEPHENS *Bk. Farm* II. 45 A heavy rain may fall for some days, and render the land quite soft and poachy.

Hence **'poachiness**.

1707 MORTIMER *Husb.* (1721) I. 48 The lower Vallies, because of the poachiness of them, they keep for Grass.

poad, -e, obs. forms of PODE, POOD.

poadler, dial. var. PODLER, young coal-fish.

poak(e (pəʊk). [Origin obscure.] (See quots.)

1846 WORCESTER, *Poake*, waste arising from the preparation of skins, composed of hair, lime, and oil. *Farm. Encycl.* **1858** SIMMONDS *Dict. Trade*, *Poak*.

poak(e, poakmantie, obs. ff. POKE, POCKMANTEAU.

poale, obs. f. POLE.

Poale Zion (pəʊə'leɪ tsi:'jɒn). [Heb., 'workers of Zion'.] Name of a predominantly left-wing Zionist labour movement which first emerged in Russia about 1899.

1919 N. SOKOLOW *Hist. Zionism* II. 367 The Poale Zion was established in 1901... The programme of the organization represents a synthesis of Zionism and Socialism. **1935** A. REVUSKY *Jews in Palestine* xii. 206 The left is represented by the Poale Zion and the Communists. **1973** *Jewish Chron.* 19 Jan. 42/3 Mr Burton was a member of Poale Zion from early youth.

poan, var. POWAN.

poar, poareblind, poast, poat, obs. ff. PORE *v.*, PURBLIND, POST, POTE.

pob[1] (pɒb). *Sc.* Also *dial.* **pab**. [Origin obscure.] The refuse of flax or (more recently) jute.

1747 R. MAXWELL *Bee-master* (1750) 21 The Hive to be laid over with the Refuse of Flax, commonly called Pob-tow. **1765** *Museum Rust.* IV. 46 If the flax is to be stacked, it should be set in an airy place, upon a dry foundation, such as pob-middings or the like. **1803** *Prize Ess. Highl. Soc.* II. 10 At an old lint mill in Fife, a great heap of this refuse, or pab tow, as it is called, had been formed about 60 years ago. **1818** *Edinb. Mag.* Aug. 126/1 Observe their harness, the collars are made of straw or *pob*; (the refuse of flax when skutched). **1876** LAING *Lindores Abbey* xxvi. 389 The boys ..gathered pob, heather, and other inflammable materials in a great heap.

pob[2] (pɒb). [Echoic.] An abrupt, heavy sound as when an inelastic body strikes a hard surface.

1911 J. MASEFIELD *Jim Davis* xiii. 157 A heavy chewed slug would come 'pob' into the boat's side.

pobble, obs. or dial. var. of PEBBLE.

pobby ('pɒbɪ), *a.* orig. *dial.* [cf. POBS *sb. pl.*] Swollen, blown; also of food, pulpy, mushy.

1888 KIPLING *Phantom 'Rickshaw* 30 There are, in this land, ghosts who take the form of fat, cold, pobby corpses. **1903** *Eng. Dial. Dict.* IV. 563/1 *Pobby, adj.* Yks...., swollen, *gen.* used of a soft swelling. **1937** V. K. LIBBY *How to care for Baby* vi. 49 If you want baby to have good teeth be careful not to give a lot of 'pobby' food. Never soak the rusks in milk, etc.

‖**poblacion** (pobla'sjon, -'θjon). Also **población**. Pl. **poblaciones**. [Sp., = population; also, town, city, village.] **a.** In Spanish-speaking countries of South America: a community; a district of a town, etc. **b.** In the Republic of the Philippines: the principal community of a district; a town that is an administrative centre.

1926 J. MASEFIELD *Odtaa* xiv. 236 The hut, like the other huts of the poblacion, was, at a guess, thirty feet long by fifteen broad. **1961** WEBSTER, *Población*.., a center of a municipality in the Philippines that is usu. the barrio that gives the municipality its name and is the seat of government. **1964** A. CUTSHALL *Philippines* iii. 27 The postwar Philippine barrio and oftentimes the *poblacion*, the principal community in the municipality (county), is not appreciably different from the representative prewar village and town. **1967** M. C. BELLO in M. D. Zamora *Stud. Philippine Anthropol.* 325 The site studied is the *poblacion* which refers to a group of contiguous villages found toward the middle of the region... The poblacion settlement is situated on the top of a mountain. **1978** *Listener* 23 Nov. 668/2 The *barrio* or *poblaciones*, the shanty-towns of the poor. **1979** E. NORMAN *Christianity & World Order* iv. 47 In 1978 I visited the working class *poblaciones* around Santiago, in Chile.

‖**poblador** (pobla'dor, -'ðor). Pl. **pobladores**. [Sp.] In Spanish America, a settler, a colonist; *spec.* a country person who moves to settle or squat in a town.

1966 *Economist* 2 July 28/2 The *pobladores* (squatters) fled further up the hill. **1976** *New Yorker* 26 Apr. 122/1 Everyone seems to know precisely when his forefathers arrived—in the eighteen-fifties, as *pobladores*, or settlers, recruited..to colonize the million-acre Sangre de Cristo land grant.

pobs (pɒbz), *sb. pl. dial.* Also **pobbies**. Occas. in *sing.* (*Eng. Dial. Dict.*). A dialect and nursery name for porridge, pap, bread and milk.

1828 *Craven Gloss.* (ed. 2), Pobs, Poddish, Porridge. **1848** MRS. GASKELL *M. Barton* ix, The child..were awake, and crying for its pobbies. **1894** HALL CAINE *Manxman* VI. iv, He was ladling the pobs into the child's mouth.

†**pocalips, -yps**, obs. aphetic ff. APOCALYPSE.

1377 LANGL. *P. Pl.* B. XIII. 90 He hath dronken so depe he wil deuyne sone, And preuen it by her pocalips and passioun of seynt Auereys. *a* **1440** [see APOCALYPSE 1].

pocan ('pəʊkən). [app. native Indian name.] The Virginian Poke or Poke-weed (*Phytolacca decandra*); = POKE *sb.*[4] 2 a.

1858 SIMMONDS *Dict. Trade, Pocan-bush*, a name in the United States for the *Phytolacca decandra*. **1866** [see POKE *sb.*[4] 2 a].

pocar, pocard, poccoon, poccoson, obs. ff. POKER, POCHARD, PUCCOON, POCOSIN.

†**pocerounce, pokerounce.** *Obs. rare.* A confection mentioned in the 15th c.: see quot.

c **1430** *Two Cookery-bks.* 3 Kalendare de Leche Metys [see LEACH *sb.*[1] 2]..Pocerounce. *Ibid.* 41 *Pokerounce.* Take Hony, & caste it in a potte tyl it wexe chargeaunt y-now; take & skeme it clene. Take Gyngere, Canel, & Galyngale, & caste þer-to [etc.].

pocession, obs. form of POSSESSION.

‖**pochade** (pɔʃad). [Fr., a rough sketch, f. *pocher* to sketch in the rough, also to blur: see POACH *v.*[1] 2 and -ADE.] A rough, smudgy, or blurred sketch. Also **pochade box** (see quot. 1961).

1872 BROWNING *Fifine* xxxvi, So, any sketch or scrap, pochade, caricature, Made in a moment, meant a moment to endure, I snap at. **1959** M. STEEN *Tower* II. iv. 206 My easel had been removed, and my pochade box. **1961** M. Levy *Studio Dict. Art Terms* 88 *Pochade box*, a small portable colour-box with panels fitted into the lid for quick sketching. **1972** D. Sutton in R. Fry *Lett.* I. 90 Fry.. was usually more at ease with a *pochade* than with a finished work.

po'chaise, po'chay, pochay, colloq. contractions of POST-CHAISE.

1827 Scott *Chron. Canongate* Introd. iv, Its associations of 'pochays' and mail-coaches. **1871** G. Meredith *H. Richmond* I. 135 There was a saying in the county that to marry a Beltham you must po'chay her. *Ibid.* 158 'She's past po'chaises', Squire Gregory sighed.

pochard (ˈpəʊtʃ-, ˈpəʊkəd, ˈpɒtʃ-, ˈpɒkəd). Forms: α. 6 **pocharde**, (8 **poachard**), 7- **pochard**. β. 6-9 **pocard**, 7 **pocker, -ard**, 9 **pockard**, 7- **poker**. [Of uncertain origin: perh. augmentative of OF. and mod.F. *poche*, in mod.F. *poche-cuiller* the spoonbill: see -ARD. (But there is little likeness between the pochard and the spoonbill.) It might also be a deriv. of POACH *v.*², POKE *v.*¹ The pronunciation seems quite unfixed. Prof. A. Newton makes the *ch* = *k*; but Johnson made it as in *poacher*.] A European diving bird, *Fuligula* or *Æthyia ferina*, of the family *Anatidæ*, characterized by the bright reddish-brown colour of the head and neck; also called ***red-headed pochard***, ***poker***, ***wigeon***, ***red-eyed poker***, DUN-BIRD. Also applied to other species, as the ***African p.***, *Æthyia* or *Fuligula capensis*; the ***red-crested p.***, *F.* or *Nyroca rufina*, of India; the ***tufted p.***, *A.* or *F. cristata*, of Europe and Asia; and in U.S. to the RED-HEAD, *Anas americana*.

α. **1552** Elyot, *Boscha*, a water foule like to a ducke, but somwhat lesse: I iudge it a pocharde. **1611** Cotgr., *Albrent*, .. a Pochard. **1678** Ray *Willughby's Ornith.* III. 367 The Poker, or Pochard, or great read-headed Wigeon. **1752** J. Hill *Hist. Anim.* 431 The Anas, with grey wings, and a black rump. The Pochard. **1755** Johnson, *Poachard*, a kind of water fowl. **1820** Jodrell s.v., I know no reason, why Johnson should have.. printed this word.. differently from any other author, and spelled it 'poachard'. **1882** *Three in Norway* viii. 65 A brood of pochards under the leadership of the old duck. **1894** Speight *Nidderdale* 203 The bittern, pochard, scaup, common scoter and the tufted duck have been seen in the park. **1894** Newton *Dict. Birds* 734 *Pochard, Pockard* or *Poker*, names properly belonging to the male of a species of Duck (the female of which is known as the Dunbird).

β. **1598** Florio, *Bosca*, a bird called a pocard. **1674** Dent *Let.* in *Ray's Lett.* (1718) 21, I have put up in a Box some Water Fowl, *viz.* a Pocker, a Smew,.. a Widgeon, and a Whewer. **1678** Poker [see α]. **1706** Phillips, *Pocard*, a kind of water-fowl. **1709** Derham in *Phil. Trans.* XXVI. 466 *Anas fera fusca*... The Poker. **1768** Pennant *Zool.* II. 470 The Pochard... In London markets.. known by the name of Dun birds. **1843** Yarrell *Hist. Birds* III. 233 The Pochard, or Dun-bird, for this species is known by various names, as Red-headed Poker, and Red-eyed Poker.. is a winter visiter to this country. **1895** A. Patterson *Man & Nature* 85 We blazed away several times, pickin' up near twenty pokers (pochards).

b. *attrib.* and *Comb.*, as ***pochard-duck***; **pochard-grass**, *dial.* some water-plant, app. a species of Polygonum (Newton *Dict. Birds* 735 note).

1833 Baird in *Proc. Berw. Nat. Club* I. No. 1. 16 He had .. received.. a specimen of the pochard duck (*Anas ferina* Lin.). **1879** R. Lubbock *Fauna Norf.* 137 A particular weed, —Pochard Grass, as it is called.

poche, obs. form of POACH, POUCH.

pochette (pɒˈʃɛt). [Fr.: see POCKET *sb.*] **1. a.** A small pocket.

1913 W. de la Mare *Peacock Pie* 80 A watch.. He lifted from the hook where it was ticking And crammed in his Pochette. **1949** *Amer. Speech* XXIV. 38 The secret pockets which the conjurer is so often suspected of using are of two types, the *pochette* and the *profonde*. They differ in position and in size, the latter being the larger. **1964** *Punch* 1 Jan. 15/1 *Pochettes* in the [conjuror's] trousers.

b. A hand-bag. Also ***pochette bag***.

1923 *Weekly Dispatch* 11 Mar. 15/5 When jewels are worn in the hair the vanity-bag becomes a satin or crêpe pochette, fastened with a buckle of jewels. **1930** *Daily Tel.* 9 Apr. 9/2 If you will make yourself pochettes to match your hats, you are adding.. that extra touch of chic. **1972** *Times* 12 May 13/6 The little pochette.. slides into a bigger bag. **1973** *Country Life* 1 Feb. 302/3 A shiny PVC coat and a great flat pochette, slung on a handy shoulder strap. **1976** *Evening Post* (Nottingham) 16 Dec. 10/4 You can even get a pochette bag with the words 'Gold-Rush' as a motif. **1977** *Times* 29 Oct. 12/2 More and more men use pochettes to avoid bulging.. their trousers.

2. A small violin, supposedly once carried in the pocket by French dancing-masters; = KIT *sb.*²

1889 in *Cent. Dict.* **1976** D. Munrow *Instruments Middle Ages & Renaissance* 28/2 It was as an instrument for dancing that the small rebec survived as the *kit* or *pochette* into the eighteenth century.

‖**pochismo** (poˈtʃizmo). [Mexican Sp., f. as next + *-ismo* -ISM.] A form of slang used by speakers of Mexican Spanish and others along the border with the U.S., consisting of English words given a Spanish form or pronunciation; a word of this sort.

1944 *N.Y. Herald Tribune* 5 Aug. 10/3 The Mexican Academy has appointed a committee to eradicate 'pochismos'— that is English words and phrases used in speaking Spanish. **1946** *Mod. Lang. Jrnl.* Oct. 345 *Pochismo*, derived from *pocho*, an adjective which originally meant discolored, has now come to mean a type of popular slang in Mexico. **1966** N. S. Hayner *New Patterns in Old Mexico* xiv. 219 Students of language have a lively curiosity in the increasing use of 'pochismo', a type of popular slang, by even the most conservative of the Mexico City newspapers. **1976** F. A. & D. L. Latorre *Mexican Kickapoo Indians* ii. 29 They [*sc.* Kickapoos] have incorporated many Spanish words into their speech and many *pochismos*.. such as *lonche* ('lunch').

‖**pocho** (ˈpotʃo). [Mexican Sp., Sp. *pocho* discoloured, faded, pale.] A citizen of the United States of Mexican origin; a culturally Americanized Mexican. Also *attrib.* or as *adj.*

1944 *Newsweek* 14 Aug. 76/3 A pocho in good standing will drag his fititoes (feet) up the estrita (street). *Ibid.* Slapstick actors like Tin Tan.. who gets comic effects with pocho patter. **1960** *Time* 25 Jan. 92/2 Opium is.. smuggled .. from Mexico by special agents called 'pocho' women (generally Americans of Mexican descent) who cross the border into Mexico to shop. **1968** *Sunday Mail Mag.* (Brisbane) 25 Aug. 14/3 *Pocho*, derogatory term for American-Mexican (in U.S.A.). **1975** *Sat. Rev.* (U.S.) 8 Feb. 47/1, I was frequently labelled a *pocho*, a Mexican with gringo pretentions.

‖**pochoir** (pɔʃwar). [Fr., = stencil.] A process used in book illustration, especially for limited editions, in which a monochrome print is coloured by hand, using a series of stencils; a print made by this process. Also *attrib.*

1931 *Times Lit. Suppl.* 25 June (Salon International du Livre d'Art Suppl.) p. i/4 Emile Hazan is another publisher who has taken full advantage of the *pochoir* technique. *Ibid.* p. viii/3 Colette's 'Regarde'.. with its drawings by Mathurin Méheut coloured by *pochoir*. **1932** J. Joyce *Let.* 10 Nov. (1966) III. 266 This *pochoir* reproduction can be done only in Paris and even here only by two or three firms. **1953** *Book Collector* II. 4 The unique coloured copy of Blake's *Jerusalem*.. was recently reproduced in facsimile by the pochoir process. **1958** *Listener* 12 June 984/3 Lithographs and '*pochoirs*' by Dufy. **1965** Zigrosser & Gaehde *Guide Coll. Orig. Prints* iv. 56 In France around the 1920's,.. an expert craftsman, J. Saudé, used the straight-stencil, or *pochoir*, process as a reproductive medium for illustrating books. **1973** *Times Lit. Suppl.* 26 Jan. 103/4 French books illustrated in pochoir.. would be included. **1973** *Art Internat.* Mar. 22/2 He owned a pochoir by Gleizes and lithographs by Léger.

†**pocill.** *Obs. rare.* In 6 pocyll(e. [ad. L. *pōcillum* a little cup, dim. of *pōculum* cup.] A small cup, a phial; *transf.* a draught, a potion.

1572 J. Jones *Bathes Buckstone* 19 Take in the morninge fastinge, in pocyll whay, made with ale, to purge choller. In pocyll whay made of whyte wyne, to purge fleme. *Ibid.* 20 Of herbes for your brothes and pocylles, mallowes, cychorye, endyue, vyolettes, pacyence.

†ˈ**pocillator.** *Obs. rare.* [a. L. *pōcillātor* (Appul.), f. *pōcillum*: see prec.] A cup-bearer. So †**pociˈllation.** *Obs. rare*$^{-0}$.

1658 Phillips, *Pocillation*, the waiting on a great mans cup. **1661** Blount *Glossogr.* (ed. 2), *Pocillator* (Lat.), he that waiteth on a great persons cup, a cup-bearer. **1705** Elstob in *Hearne's Collect.* 30 Nov. (O.H.S.) I. 107 King of Pocillator's.

pocilliform (pəʊˈsɪlɪfɔːm), *a. rare.* [f. L. *pōcillum* (see POCILL) + -FORM: cf. POCULIFORM.] Of the shape of a little cup.

1846 Dana *Zooph.* 506 This species.. has pocilliform cells.

pocion, obs. form of POTION.

pock (pɒk), *sb.* Forms: 1 **poc**, 4-6 **pokke**, 4-8 **pocke**, 5 **pok**, 5-6 **poke**, 6 *Sc.* **poik**, 6- **pock**. Pl. 1 **poccas**, 4-6 **pokkes**, (5 **pocken**), 4-8 **pockes**, 6 **pocques**, 6- **pocks**; also 6-7 **poxe**, 6- **pox**: see POX. [OE. *poc*, *pocc-* pustule, ulcer, = MDu., MLG. *pocke* (*poche*), Du. *pok*, LG. *pocke*, EFris. *pok*, *pokke*, HG. dial. *pfoche*, *poche* (mod.Ger. *pocke* from LG.). So obs. F. *pocque*, *pokke*, *poxse*, *paucque* (1400-1514 in Godef.), from LG. or Eng. These continental words are all fem.; OE. *pocc* was masc. (in one place app. fem.).

Kluge and Franck refer *pocc*, *pocke* to the OTeut. vbl. stem **puh(h)-*, to swell up, blow up, whence also OE. *pohha*, *pocca* bag: see POCKET, POKE *sb.*¹]

1. A pustule or spot of eruption in any eruptive disease, esp. (since *c* 1700) in small-pox.

c **1000** *Sax. Leechd.* II. 104 Drenc wiþ poc adle wyl wæter on croccan, do huniȝ on [etc.]. *Ibid.*, Smire þær hit utslea on þone poc. *Ibid.*, Drenc wiþ poccum bisceop wyrt [etc.]. *Ibid.* III. 4 ȝif poc sy on eaȝan, nim mærc, sapan.. mid Godes fultume he sceal aweȝ. *c* **1386** Chaucer *Pard. Prol.* 30 And it is hool anon, and forthermoor Of pokkes, and of scabbe, and euery soor. **1477** Earl Rivers (Caxton) *Dictes* 97 He [Alexander] was of sangweyn colour, his face ful of pockis. **15..** *Prol. Rom.* in *N. Test. in Scots* (S.T.S.) III. 318 Ewin as anne ewill skabbe or anne poke cann not alwayis be keipit in with the violence of medicynne. **1583** Stubbes *Anat. Abus.* I. (1879) 96 It bringeth ulcerations, scab, scurf, blain, botch, pocks. *a* **1585** Montgomerie *Flyting* 316 The powlings, the palsay, with pockes like pees. **1706** Phillips, *Pock*, a Scab of the Small-Pox. **1720** Becket in *Phil. Trans.* XXXI. 56 Having great Pockes or Pustules on the Surface of their Bodies, from whence the Pox is denominated. **1760-72** H. Brooke *Fool of Qual.* (1809) IV. 40 A few of the pock appeared on his face. **1877** Roberts *Handbk. Med.* (ed. 3) I. 150 The number of spots or 'pocks' varies from a few to thousands, but as a rule from 100 to 300 are present. **1897** *Allbutt's Syst. Med.* II. 559 With the retrogression of the pock and the subsidence of the areola the local phenomena of a normal vaccination are at an end.

b. *transf.* A spot or mark like a pustule.

1894 Doyle *Mem. S. Holmes* 99 Holmes.. would.. proceed to adorn the opposite wall with a patriotic V.R. done in bullet-pocks.

2. A disease characterized by pustules or eruptive spots; *esp.* (*a*) small-pox; (*b*) 'great (French or Spanish) pox', syphilis: = POX *sb.* 1 b, e.

α. in *pl.* Now written POX. (Rarely construed with vb. in singular.)

c **1325** *Gloss. W. de Bibbesw.* in Wright *Voc.* 161 *Viroles*, pockes. **1377** Langl. *P. Pl.* B. xx. 97 Kynde come after with many kene sores, As pokkes and pestilences, and moche poeple shente. **1480** Caxton *Chron. Eng.* VII. (1520) 127 b/1 Also that tyme a sekenes that men call the pockes slewe bothe men and women through theyr infectynge. **1500-20** Dunbar *Poems* lv. 30 Quhill that thai gatt the Spanȝie pockis. **1518** Pace *Let. Wolsey* 14 July (Cal. State Papers Hen. VIII), They do die.. of the small pokkes and measels. **1529** S. Fish *Supplic. Beggers* 6 They.. that catche the pokkes of one woman, and bere theym to an other. *a* **1548** Hall *Chron., Hen. VIII* 190 Item that he hauing the Frenche pockes presumed to come and breth on the kyng. **1552** *Ordre Hosp. St. Barthol.* Pref. A v, This Hospital.. where.. there haue bene healed of the pocques, fystules.. to nombre of .viij. hundred. **1615** Sandys *Trav.* 109 The pocks is vncredibly frequent amongst them. **1681** W. Robertson *Phraseol. Gen.* (1693) 481 The disease of the Spanish Pocks.

β. in *sing.* Now *dial.* or *vulgar*.

14.. *Stockh. Med. MS.* I. 461 in *Anglia* XVIII. 306 Seint Nicasse had a pokke small. *c* **1440** *Promp. Parv.* 407/2 Pokke, sekenesse, *porrigo*. **1530** Tindale *Answ. Sir T. More*, etc. (Parker Soc., 1850) 105 If God punish the world with an evil pock, they immediately paint a block and call it Job, to heal the disease. **1530** Palsgr. 256/1 Pocke a great pocke, *la gorre, la grosse uerolle*. Pocke a small, *uerolle*. **1593** G. Harvey *Pierce's Super.* Wks. (Grosart) II. 52 Would it were not an infectious bane, or an incroching pocke. **1845** S. Judd *Margaret* II. v. (1881) 264 Glad you got through the pock so well—it takes a second time, some say. **1851** Mayhew *Lond. Labour* I. 405/2 As soon as ever the pock began to decay, it took away my eyes altogether.

†**b.** *fig.* (*sing.*) *Obs.*

1545 Brinklow *Compl.* 32 The same pock that was in the clargys wyne and clothes, hath so infected the gentylmen of the temporaltye. **1555** Eden *Decades* Pref. (Arb.) 52 Hathe not the pocke of thy licentiousnesse bruste furth in maner to thyne owne destruction? **1607** R. C[arew] tr. *Estienne's World of Wonders* A iij b, Neither can the waters.. be cured of their spirituall barrennesse, or of the Romish pock and Ægyptian scab.

†**c.** In imprecation or exclamation: see POX *sb.* 3. *Obs.*

†**3.** *sing.* and *pl.* A disease of sheep: = POX *sb.* 1 c. *Obs.*

1531 Tindale *Exp. 1 John* (1537) 30 Who dare deny saynt Anthony a flese of wol.. leste he sende the pockes amonge our shepe. **1548** Elyot, *Mentigo*, the scabbe which is among shepe, called the pockes [**1552** Huloet, pocke].

4. *attrib.* and *Comb.*, as **pock-arr** (*dial.*), **-frecken, -fret, -hole**, a scar, mark, or 'pit' left by a pustule, esp. of small-pox; **pock-arred** (*dial.*), **-broken, -eaten, -frecken, -freckled, -fret, -fretted (-fretten), -holed, -pitted (-pitten)** *adjs.*, scarred, marked, or 'pitted' with pustules, esp. of small-pox; †**pock-break**, (?) a breaking out or marking due to some form of pox; **pock-house** (*U.S. dial.*), a small-pox hospital; **pock-lymph**, the lymph of cow-pox, as used in vaccination; **pock-pit** *v. trans.*, to 'pit' or mark with pustules (in quot. *fig.*); †**pock-royal**, satirical name for a pustule of the 'great pox'; **pock-sore**, a sore caused by a pustule, or by the pox; †**pocks-rotten** *a.*: see POX *sb.* 4; **pock-stone**, local name for a hard greyish stone found in the Staffordshire coal-measures: see also *pox-stone* (POX *sb.*); †**pock-tree**: see POCKWOOD.

1611 Cotgr., *Fossetteux*,.. full of little pits, *pockars, or pock-holes. **1655, 1691** [see ARR]. **1828** *Craven Gloss.* (ed. 2), *Pock-arr, Pock-mark*, a scar or mark left by the small pox. **1825** Brockett *N.C. Gloss.*, **Pock-arred*,.. pitted with the small-pox. [See also *Eng. Dial. Dict.*] *a* **1568** Montgomerie *Misc. Poems* liv. 2 Fyndlay McConnoquhy, fuf McFadȝan, Cativilie geilȝie with ye *poik-braik. *c* **1440** *Promp. Parv.* 407/2 *Pokbrokyn, *porriginosus*. **1662** Gurnall *Chr. in Arm.* verse 17. II. xxv. §4 (1679) 322/1 What a beauty Man was, till he was pock-broken (if I may say so) by sin. **1862** Borrow *Wild Wales* xxxvii, His face was long and rather good-looking, though slightly pock-broken. *a* **1550** *Hye Way Spyttel Hous* 112 in Hazl. *E.P.P.* IV. 28 Scabby and scuruy, *pocke eaten flesh and rynde. **1530** Palsgr. 256/1 *Poke frekyns, *picquetevre* or *picquottevre de uerolle*. **1695** *Lond. Gaz.* No. 3134/4 Mary Scarlet,.. thin visage, swarthy complexion, pock frecken. **1714** *Ibid.* No. 5223/4 A spare middle-siz'd Man, *Pockfreckled and Ruddy Complexion. **1731** Medley tr. *Kolben's Cape G. Hope* II. 198 Several hairs would remain in the *pock-frets. **1744** *Boston Post-Boy* 1 Oct. 4/2 Byrn.. looks pale and *pockfret. **1693** *Lond. Gaz.* No. 2843/4 Pale-faced, and a little *Pock-fretted. *c* **1640** R. James *Poems* (1880) 213 A Virginne.. proper of all things but a pale *pock fretten face. **1840** Mrs. F. Trollope *Widow Married* i, A deal better chance that your child will be like what you see there, than to poor pock-fretten Phebe. **1552** Huloet, *Pocke hole or scarre. **1676** *Lond. Gaz.* No. 1145/4 A full set Woman with Pockholes in her face. **1708** *Ibid.* No. 4487/3 Having a thin pockhole Face. **1682** *Ibid.* No. 1722/4 He is a little broad Man, *Pock-holed. **1845** S. Judd *Margaret* II. v, A *Pock House was established, .. and a general beating up for patients was had throughout the region. **1881** Tyndall *Floating Matter of Air* 119 A quantity of matter, comparable in smallness to the *pock-lymph held on the point of a lancet. **1843** *Blackw. Mag.* LIII. 225 It becomes a plague, a moral small-pox, .. *pockpitting his small modicum of brains. **1862** Mayhew *Lond. Labour* II. 332 He was under the middle size, *pockpitted. **1864** Tennyson *Aylmer's F.* 256 Did Sir Aylmer know That great *pock-pitten fellow had been caught? **1694** Motteux *Rabelais* v. v, Embroider'd o'er the Phiz with Carbuncles, Pushes, and *Pockroyals. **1643** Prynne *Sov. Power Parl.* III. 89 Neither must the Chyrurgion dresse their wounds, or *pock-soars. **1902** C. G. Harper *Holyhead Road* ii. 33 (Wednesbury) Those foundations have an unusual interest, built as they are of the material called '*pockstone'. *c* **1532** Du Wes *Introd. Fr.* in Palsgr. 914/3 The *pocke tre, *gaiaqz ou eban.*

pock (pɒk), *v.* [f. Pock *sb.*] *trans.* To mark with pocks, or (*fig.*) with disfiguring spots. Chiefly as pa. pple. or ppl. adj.

1841 Murray *Let.* in Smiles *Mem.* (1891) II. xxxv. 474 Houses .. literally peppered and pocked from top to bottom with shot-marks. **1869** Blackmore *Lorna D.* lix, This tufty flaggy ground, pocked with bogs and boglets. **1889** *Lancet* 29 June 1314/1 The posterior parts of both lungs were pocked with tubercle in the softening stage. **1938** *Proc. Prehist. Soc.* IV. 246 The chief tombs which exhibit incised & pocked designs on their walls & roofs are New Grange, Dowth, & those at Lochcrew. **1977** *Time* 31 Jan. 42/1 On went a coat of Viacryl, a synthetic polyurethane resin meant to protect the pocked and flawed surface of the 800-year-old glass.

pock, variant Sc. spelling of Poke, bag.

Pockels ('pɒkəlz). Also erron. Pockel. The name of F. C. A. *Pockels* (1865–1913), German physicist, used, chiefly *attrib.*, with reference to an effect in certain crystals similar to the Kerr effect (sense (b)) in liquids (see quot. 1975[2]); so ***Pockels cell, constant, effect*** (cf. Kerr).

Described by Pockels in *Abhandl. der K. Ges. der Wissensch. zu Göttingen* (*Math-phys. Klasse*) (1894) XXXI. 204.

1949 *Jrnl. Optical Soc. Amer.* XXXIX. 798/2 The constants t_{ij} are .. related to Pockels' constants e_{ij}. **1957** D. E. Gray *Amer. Inst. Physics Handbk.* VI. 96 Twenty-one of the 32 crystal symmetry classes do not contain centers of symmetry, and of these, 20 may exhibit the linear Pockels effect. **1968** E. L. Steele *Optical Lasers in Electronics* v. 178 The electro-optical switches employ the photo-optical effect in a Kerr cell, Pockels cell, or Faraday rotator. **1975** D. G. Fink *Electronics Engineers' Handbk.* XI. 24 Linear Electrooptical Effect, or Pockel's Effect. Crystalline materials such as potassium dihydrogen phosphate (KDP) and lithium niobate are used.. . Metal electrodes are applied to rectangular blocks of these crystals, and the resultant structures are referred to as Pockel cells. *Ibid.* XIV. 60 In the Pockels effect the differential phase shift is linearly related to applied voltage; in the Kerr effect it is related to the voltage squared. **1976** *Nature* 22 Apr. 677/1 The emission intensities of the components parallel and perpendicular to the incident laser polarisation were determined using a Pockels cell to rotate the laser polarisation with respect to a fixed analyser.

pocker, obs. variant of Pochard.

pocket ('pɒkɪt), *sb.* Forms: 4–6 poket, 5 -ett, 5–8 pockett, 6 -ette, (pokit, 7 poccet), 6– pocket. [ME. *poket*, a. Anglo-Norman *pokete* (13th c. Godef.), mod.Norman dial. *pouquette*, dim. of ONF. *poke, poque, pouque* = F. *poche*, whence dim. *pochette*: see Poke *sb.*[1], Pouch *sb.* OF. had also a masc. form *pochet, pouchet* (1396 in Godef.), still *dial.*, also in mod.Norman dial. *pouquet.*]

1. A bag or sack. Sometimes used as a measure of quantity, varying in capacity according to the commodity contained, and the locality.

Now chiefly used for hops and wool, a pocket of wool being half a sack (in 13th c. a quarter), a pocket of hops about 168 lbs.

1280 *Memoranda Roll*, K. R. m. 13d, Venerunt coram Baronibus et recognoverunt se teneri Bonruncino et sociis suis mercatoribus de Luk' in quatuor saccis lane et uno pochetto, id est in quarta parte unius sacci. *c* **1340** *Rolls of Parlt.* II. 385/1, xx sacz & ix peres de Leyne trovez en xxiii sarplers & en i poket. **1526** in Dillon *Calais & Pale* (1892) 90 Item, for evry horseloode of pocketts iiij d. **1535** in G. Schanz *Engl. Handelspolitik* (1881) II. 385 The canvas, that goeth to the pokit with the hey and threde, that goeth to yt, weyeth about 2 nailles. **1706** Phillips, *Pocket of Wool*, the Quantity of half a Sack. See Sack of Wool and Sarplar. **1724** De Foe *Tour Gt. Brit.* I. 128 Here [at Stourbridge Fair] I saw what I have not observ'd in any other Country of England, .. a Pocket of Wool. This seems to be first call'd so in Mockery, this Pocket being so big, that it loads a whole Waggon, .. and these ordinarily weigh a Ton or 25 Hundred weight of Wool, all in one Bag. **1767** *Chron.* in *Ann. Reg.* 130/1 There were only eleven pockets of new hops, the quality of which was very bad. **1805** R. W. Dickson *Pract. Agric.* II. 755 The brightest hops, and those which have the finest colour, are put into bagging of a better quality, and termed pockets. **1809** R. Langford *Introd. Trade* 126, 147 pockets of hops, each weighing 1 cwt. 1 qr. 18 lb. **1876** *S. Kens. Mus. Catal.* §2107 Model of a hand loom .. designed to weave sacks or pockets without a seam either at the sides or end. **1907** W. H. Koebel *Return of Joe* 239 A train of pack horses, heavily laden with the weighty 'pockets' of wool, toil meekly past. **1928** E. Wallace *Gunner* xxiv. 199 Bales of silk, chests of tea, pockets of rubber. **1940** E. C. Studholme *Te Waimate* 170 Over the hills [the wool] was carried by pack horses .. each taking about 150 lbs. in what were called 'pockets'—loaf shaped packs slung one on each side of the saddle. **1953** *Word for Word* (Whitbread & Co.) 28/1 *Pocket*, a large sack made to contain roughly one and a half cwts. of dried hops.

2. a. A small bag or pouch worn on the person; *spec.* one inserted in or attached to a garment, for carrying a purse or other small articles.

c **1430** *Hymns Virg.* 62 'Apparaile þe propirli', quod Pride, 'Loke þi pockettis passe þe lengist gise'. *a* **1450** *Stockh. Med. MS.* I. 61 in *Anglia* XVIII. 296 In a poket þou it do, þat þe water may renne þer-fro. **1570** Foxe *A. & M.* (ed. 2) 192/1 He bare alwayes about hym, in hys bosome or pocket, a litle booke contayning the Psalmes of Dauid. **1596** Shaks. *1 Hen. IV*, III. iii. 61 Haue you enquir'd yet who pick'd my Pocket? *a* **1680** Butler *Rem.* (1759) II. 446 A Prodigal is a Pocket with a Hole in the Bottom. **1700** T. Brown *Amusem. Ser. & Com.* 67 Here walk'd a French Fop with both his Hands in his Pockets. **1701** Swift *Mrs. Fr. Harris' Petit.* 7 All the money I have .. I keep in my pocket, tied about my middle, next my smock. **1704** *Lond. Gaz.* No. 4072/6 Left in a .. Coach .., a white Damask Pocket. **1869** Trollope *He knew*, etc. xxvii, He carried the letter with him in his pocket. **1906** *Weldon's Ladies' Jrnl.* Sept. 90/3 This theatre pocket is a Parisian novelty, worn suspended from the waist, and is intended to hold the handkerchief, fan, opera glasses, etc.

b. *esp.* That in which money is carried; hence typically used for one's purse or stock of cash; pecuniary resources, private means. ***empty pocket***: (*transf.*) a person without money.

1717 Lady M. W. Montagu *Let. to Princess of Wales* 1 Apr., I would have paid them the money out of my own pocket. **1731** Gay in *Swift's Lett.* (1766) II. 133, I had flattered myself, your law-suit was at an end, and that your own money was in your own pocket. **1765** Foote *Commissary* I. Wks. 1799 II. 9 The bridegroom may put the purchase-money .. into his pocket. **1781** Cowper *Truth* 322 Yon cottager .. Just earns a scanty pittance, and at night, Lies down secure, her heart and pocket light. **1834** L. Ritchie *Wand. by Seine* 252 War empties the pocket; no kingdom can go to war with empty pockets. **1879** Farrar *St. Paul* I. 492 The slave-masters were touched in their pockets, and it filled them with fury. **1892** Baring-Gould *Trag. Cæsars* I. 15 Only the empty pockets and lacklands were excluded. **1894** R. Bridges *Feast of Bacchus* II. 743 A gentleman can't consider his pocket. *Mod.* One's hand has to be constantly in one's pocket here.

3. Hence, in various phrases: **a.** ***in pocket***: (*a*) Having money available; in possession of funds; (*b*) Having (so much) money left over or to profit, as 'to be ten shillings in pocket by the transaction'.

1751 *Affect. Narr. of Wager* 154 We might indeed have starved .. if Bulkeley had not happened to be somewhat in Pocket. **1755** Smollett *Quix.* (1803) IV. 143 At the end of their peregrination, they are above a hundred crowns in pocket. **1846** Jerrold *Mrs. Caudle's Curtain Lect.* xxx, If you'd a chaise of your own .. you'd be money in pocket.

b. ***out of pocket***: †out of funds (*obs.*); ***to be out of pocket***, to be a loser (by some transaction); also (*U.S.*) *transf.* to be absent or out of reach.

1693 Congreve *Old Bach.* II. i, But, egad, I'm a little out of pocket at present. **1737** Logan in Rigaud *Corr. Sci. Men* (1841) I. 319 The proprietors .. complain they are yet out of pocket by it. **1787** Nelson in Nicolas *Disp.* (1845) I. 212 If she goes soon he will still be out of pocket by the Appointment. **1837** Sir F. Palgrave *Merch. & Friar* Ded. (1844) 6, I shall be pounds out of pocket by my conscientious refusal. **1882** Miss Braddon *Mt. Royal* III. iv. 74, I am out of pocket for my expenses. **1974** *Anderson* (S. Carolina) *Independent* 20 Apr. 1A/1 If you .. have ever been sick and the only doctor is out of pocket for the weekend, then you know we need more doctors. **1978** *Internat. Herald Tribune* 24 July 14/4 Why does *out of pocket* .. mean 'out of touch'?

c. ***to put in one's pocket***: To pocket, take or keep to oneself, conceal, suppress.

1652 Collinges *Caveat for Prof.* vi. (1653) 32 You had as good have put your tongue in your pocket. **1885** W. E. Norris *Adrian Vidal* xlii, I put my pride in my pocket.

d. ***in (some one's) pocket***: (*a*) Quite close to, in close attendance upon (some one); (*b*) Under the personal control or direction of (some one); esp. in phr. ***to live in each other's pockets***: to live in excessively close proximity, to live in mutual dependence.

1812 Lady Granville *Lett.* (1894) I. 42 Lord Gower .. seemed charmed with her, sat in her pocket all the evening, both in a titter. **1851** Thackeray *Eng. Hum.* ii. (1858) 58 He was sitting with the family seat in his pocket. **1881** Mallock *Rom. 19th Cent.* IV. iii, He sits in her pocket every evening. **1959** [see grandmother *sb.* 1 c]. **1965** F. Sargeson *Memoirs of Peon* vi. 158 We lived .. in one another's pockets, so why should there be the privilege of privacy and seclusion for one and not for the other? **1978** *N.Y. Rev. Bks.* 23 Feb. 8/2 Architects and painters do not live in each other's pockets in England today.

e. ***to put one's hand in one's pocket***: to (seek to) provide money from one's own resources.

1857 C. Kingsley *Two Yrs. Ago* I. p. xxii, There are other ways of being generous, besides putting your hand in your pocket. **1878** H. James *Europeans* I. iv. 147 Robert Acton would put his hand into his pocket every day in the week if that rattle-pated little sister of his should bid him. **1948** E. Waugh *Loved One* 28 We may have to put our hands in our pockets—I don't suppose old Frank has left much.

†4. A pouch- or pocket-shaped net. *Obs. rare*⁻¹.

c **1410** *Master of Game* (MS. Digby 182) i, Elleswhere þei sle hem with smale poketes and with pursnettes, with smale nettes, with hare pipes, and with long nettes.

5. *Billiards.* One of the open-mouthed bags or pouches placed at the corners and on each side of the table, into which the balls are driven.

1754 J. Love *Cricket* (1770) 5 Or when the Ball, close cushion'd, slides askew, And to the op'ning Pocket runs, a Cou. **1801** Strutt *Sports & Past.* IV. i. §16 At the commencement of the last century, the billiard-table was square, having only three pockets for the balls to run in, situated on one of the sides. **1837** Thackeray *Ravenswing* iii, The billiard-ball eyes .. fell plump into the pocket of his heart. **1899** *Allbutt's Syst. Med.* VIII. 258 They let their adversary spot the red and take the balls out of the pockets.

6. a. *Zool.* and *Anat.* A sac-shaped or pocket-like cavity in the body of an animal; *spec.*

(*a*) A blind sac. (*b*) The cheek-pouch of some rodents, e.g. the *Saccomyidæ*. (*c*) The abdominal pouch of a marsupial. (*d*) The abdominal cavity of a halibut or other fish.

1773 *Projects* in *Ann. Reg.* 127/1 The Iceland fishermen .. beat the bone upon a block with a thick stick, till the pockets, as they term them, come out easily, and thus preserve the sounds entire. **1897** *Allbutt's Syst. Med.* III. 894 This disposition [in perityphlitic abscesses] to the formation of loculi or pockets often causes much difficulty in the healing. **1899** *Westm. Gaz.* 8 Dec. 12/1 The bullet had struck between the pocket of the arm and the shoulder-blade. **1906** *Brit. Med. Jrnl.* 13 Jan. 70 A small walled-off pocket of pus.

b. A sac-like cavity in a plant.

1862 Darwin *Fertil. Orchids* iv. 133, I found pollen masses which had their broad ends pushed by insects into this pocket.

7. a. *Mining.* A cavity in the earth filled with gold or other ore; an abruptly dilated part of a vein or lode; also, an accumulation of alluvial gold. Also (*Austral.*), an isolated body of opal or gum. **b.** A small cavity in a rock; *esp.* in *Geol.* a cavity in a rock or stratum filled up with foreign material. **c.** A subterranean cavity containing water.

a. 1850 B. Taylor *Eldorado* ix. (1862) 89 We found many persons at work .. searching for veins and pockets of gold. **1873** J. E. Tinne *Wonderland of Antipodes* 54 If a man hits on a good 'pocket' of gum. **1878** F. S. Williams *Midl. Railw.* 576 It [hæmatite iron ore] lies especially in fissures or as the miners call them 'pockets', in the rock. **1879** *Cassell's Techn. Educ.* IV. 255/2 The ores [of manganese] are rich, and are found in pockets in a schistose rock. **1896** *Pall Mall Mag.* Jan. 39 [He] had come upon a small 'pocket' of nuggets. **1910** *Lone Hand* (Sydney) Mar. 494 A dip in the seam, or some obstruction .. temporarily dammed the stream, which thickened, solidified there, and formed a 'pocket'. **1971** J. S. Gunn *Opal Terminol.* 35 *Pocket*, small cluster of opal suddenly met in one place.

fig. **1879** F. Harrison *Choice Bks.* (1886) 21 When our reading, however deep, runs wholly into 'pockets'. **1889** *Daily News* 28 Feb. 7/2 A theological romance, which turned out to be a perfect 'pocket', was not accepted by an Editor.

b. 1850 *Lit. Gaz.* 15 June 405/2 The sands which had gathered in the crevices and pockets of the rocks. **1872** Dasent *Three to One* III. 251 A great pocket of clay crops out at the edge of the Bagshot sand. **1893** *Times* 3 June 6/6 The chalk .. presents .. a precipitous front of white, unbroken except by an occasional 'pocket' of red soil from above.

c. 1852 C. W. Hoskins *Talpa* 3 Water .. without even a 'pocket' to run into for escape or concealment. **1881** Raymond *Mining Gloss.*, *Pocket .. a natural underground reservoir of water.*

8. a. A wide pit-like hollow in a cañon or fissure. **b.** A deep glen or hollow among mountains. **c.** A spot hemmed in on all sides by high ground. **d.** A hollow cut out in wood-carving.

a. 1869 Phillips *Vesuv.* ix. 250 Fissures .. open sometimes into pockets or cavities of larger area. **1884** J. G. Bourke *Snake Dance Moquis* ix. 86 The cañon widened into a pleasant little pocket.

b. 1885 Roosevelt *Hunting Trips* v. 128 In many of the pockets or glens in the sides of the hill, the trees grow to some little height.

c. 1897 Bailey *Princ. Fruit-growing* 59 The grower should avoid flat lands which are hemmed in on all sides by elevations, for these 'pockets' are nearly always frosty.

d. 1892 El. Rowe *Chip-carving* (1895) 33 A combination of triangles and diamonds all treated as sunk pockets.

9. A recess or cavity resembling a pocket in use or position, as **a.** The slot for the reception of the vertical side-pieces of a sash-frame; **b.** A receptacle in the cover of a book for a folded map, etc.; **c.** A small cabin or coal bunker on board ship; **d.** The trap of a weir in which fish are caught.

a **1817** Jane Austen *Northanger Abbey* (1818) II. xiv. 285 With so much changing of chaises .. I hope .. you have not left anything behind you in any of the pockets. **1881** Young *Ev. Man his own Mechanic* §830 A close inspection of the side of frame will show the amateur where the 'pocket' A is. **1898** *Century Mag.* Feb. 531/2 The single females are stowed in 'pockets' on both sides of the ships. **1899** F. T. Bullen *Way Navy* 95 In coaling ship the work of distributing the coal throughout the series of pockets that are plastered all around the engines and boilers is of incredible severity. **1900** *Journ. Wm. of Rubruck* (Hakl. Soc.) Contents, Map to Illustrate the Two Journeys... In pocket.

10. A baggy place, a bulge (in a sail).

1899 *Daily News* 21 Oct. 3/4 The mainsails of both yachts were glaringly faulty. There was a big pocket in the Shamrock's, pinching her to leeward.

11. a. *Racing.* The position in which a competitor is hemmed in by others and so has no chance of winning. (Cf. Pocket *v.* 1 c.)

1890 in *Cent. Dict.*

b. *Amer.* and *Canad. Football.* A shielded area formed by blockers from which a player attempts to pass; the formation itself.

1963 *Time* 18 Oct. 94 Myers..is a drop-back 'pocket' passer. **1968** *Globe & Mail* (Toronto) 10 July 27/5 He is an accurate passer, either from the pocket or on the roll-out.

12. = *air-pocket* s.v. AIR *sb.*[1] B. III. 1.

1911 G. C. LOENING *Monoplanes & Biplanes* ii. 18 Everywhere in the atmosphere, and especially on windy days, there exist 'pockets' of high density and of low density. **1917** *Boy's Own Paper* Mar. 273/2 Evidently he had dropped into one of those air eddies which were so dangerous to flying men in the early days of aviation. They, in conjunction with 'pockets', accounted for the death of not a few pioneers in flight. **1919** C. P. THOMPSON *Cocktails* 46 The suddenly uncontrolled Hun staggered and whirled in a treacherous 'pocket'. **1978** H. KAPLAN *Damascus Cover* vii. 60 The plane rolled in a pocket of turbulent air.

13. a. *Mil.* An area held by troops who are surrounded by opposing forces; an isolated concentration *of* resistance; also, the men themselves; esp. in phr. ***pocket of resistance*** (also *transf.*).

1918 *Observer* 29 Sept. 7/6 The Anglo-Belgian attack in the north..has reduced the enemy to the necessity of defending..a pocket such as those which brought him to disaster on the Marne and on the Avre. **1927** J. M. KEYNES *Ess. in Biogr.* (1933) I. vi. 62 The strategic surrender, the deliberate withdrawal, the attempt to lure the enemy into a pocket where he could be taken in flank. **1941** *Manch. Guardian Weekly* 10 Jan. 20/2 The Australians engaged strong enemy defence pockets to the south-east of this line. **1943** *Times* (Weekly ed.) 24 Apr. 6 Here the Germans had a small pocket, based on the bridge which carried the highway to Gomel over the Dnieper. **1945** *Daily Express* 12 Apr. 4/8 Full aid to liberated Europe..must wait not only until the German army is beaten, but until pockets of resistance have been wiped out. **1959** *Listener* 12 Feb. 287/1 Except for provincial pockets of resistance it is now as successful as any architecture is ever likely to be. *Ibid.* 29 Oct. 740/2 An enemy 'pocket of resistance' was still occupying a wood about half-a-mile away. **1965** C. D. EBY *Siege of Alcázar* (1966) xi. 230 There was..a large pocket of militia barricaded in the seminary. **1966** T. PYNCHON *Crying of Lot 49* iii. 61 A..battle of attrition in a minor pocket developed during the advance on Rome. **1975** G. ST. GEORGE *Proteus Pact* (1976) i. 5 Kleist sat on top of an armored personnel carrier and watched the systematic elimination of pockets of resistance.

b. A small area contrasted with or differing from its surroundings in some respect; a local concentration *of* something. Cf. senses 7 a, b above.

1926 *Scribner's Mag.* Aug. 163/1 The car swerved into the campus, that green, summer-deserted pocket of peace in the little, dusty, traffic-riddled village. **1932** *Times Educ. Suppl.* 2 Jan. p. iv/4 They walked into a pocket of gas and were asphyxiated. **1935** HUXLEY & HADDON *We Europeans* ii. 53 They do not form definite groups, but occur rather in local pockets where individuals still exhibit characters reminiscent of those remote times. **1937** *Brit. Jrnl. Psychol.* XXVII. 358 We may regard the adjusted group, if it has proceeded to the stage of new, reified institutions, as a small culture pocket or subculture within the larger culture. **1939** *British Birds* XXXIII. 102 The Black-tailed Godwit is increasingly occurring in the British Isles... The increase is greatest on the south coast of England with pockets elsewhere. **1945** *Daily Express* 22 May 2/4 What is to happen when, in the change from war to peace, there occur the inevitable pockets of unemployment? **1959** *Times* 4 Sept. 4/3 We must conclude that the existence of pockets of heat under the lunar surface is probable. **1976** W. H. CANAWAY *Willow-Pattern War* xi. 111 There were edelweiss in soil pockets on the rock outcrops. **1978** J. BLACKBURN *Dead Man's Handle* iii. 36 A pocket of upper-crust suburbia: detached, Regency-style residences with two-car garages.

14. *attrib.* and *Comb.* (passing into adj.).

a. Adapted or intended to be carried in the pocket.

1612 in *Crt. & Times Jas. I* (1849) I. 156 Here is a proclamation coming out this day against pocket-dags. *a* **1625** FLETCHER & MASS. *Cust. Country* II. iii, Out with your bodkin, Your pocket-dagger, your stiletto. **1640** BROME *Antipodes* IV. ix, The multiplicity of pocket-watches. **1640** E. VERNEY *Let.* in F. P. Verney *Mem.* (1892) I. vii. 174, I pray be pleased to send mee a pocket prayer-book. **1688** BOYLE *Final Causes Nat. Things* iv. 153 A pocket-dyal with a magnet needle. **1697** DAMPIER *Voy. round World* (1699) 11 Directing our course by our Pocket Compasses. **1708** *Lond. Gaz.* No. 4422/8 Lost.., a large blue Turkey-Leather Pocket-Case. **1715** *Ibid.* No. 5336/3 A neat Pocket Edition of the Odes..of Horace. **1726** SWIFT *Gulliver* II. III. i. 7, I discovered by my pocket-glass several islands to the south-east. **1740** J. WILLIAMSON (*title*) The British Angler, or a Pocket-Companion for Gentlemen-Fishers. **1793** BEDDOES *Math. Evid.* 138 It is not very easy to believe, that words have the property of shutting up all at once, like pocket telescopes. **1800** M. EDGEWORTH *Parent's Assistant* (ed. 3) IV. 145 Lady Augusta had just shown her a French pocket fan. **1827** J. F. COOPER *Prairie* I. vi. 179 *Quadruped*; seen.. by the aid of a pocket-lamp, in the prairies. **1828** M. WILMOT *Let.* 23 Apr. (1935) 316 They all expect to be your pocket dictionarys and lionizers and walking sticks. **1832** *Chambers's Edin. Jrnl.* 14 Apr. 86/2, I scarcely recollect a single traveller without his pocket-comb. **1837** W. IRVING *Capt. Bonneville* III. xi. 174 The captain now drew forth that grand lure in the eyes of the savage, a pocket mirror. **1848** in H. Howe *Hist. Coll. Ohio* 493 These little pocket editions of humanity are well cared for by kind dames. **1860** TYNDALL *Glac.* I. xxvii. 205, I..looked at the film of liquid through a pocket-lens. **1864** G. MEREDITH *Emilia* xxxiv, I would buy a pocket-dictionary at one of the ports. **1866** 'MARK TWAIN' *Lett. from Hawaii* (1967) 45 We..ran by a pocket compass in the hands of Captain Fish. **1874** *Eng. Mech.* 1 May 165/2 (*title*) How to make a pocket camera. **1885** *Sam Scaramouch* 12 Dec. 247/2 If you must have a drink, gentlemen, carry your pocket flasks. **1903** C. E. WOLFF *Mod. Locomotive Practice* p. ii (Advt.), The 'Mechanical Engineer' Pocket Calculator. **1906** M. CORELLI *Treasure of Heaven* 43 Mrs. Sorrel..drew out a black pocket-fan and fanned herself vigorously. **1913** *Punch* 17 Sept. 252 Portrait of gentleman using pocket-clipper to trim beard at back of neck. **1916** *Daily Colonist* (Victoria, B.C.) 9 July 7/1 (Advt.), Hudson's Bay Company Fine Old Irish Whisky Per Pocket Flasks..50¢. **1917** G. B. MCCUTCHEON *Green Fancy* 56 Barnes found his electric pocket torch and dressed hurriedly. **1921** *Daily Colonist* (Victoria, B.C.) 25 Oct. 8/1 (Advt.), We are now showing an open face pocket watch, in strong nickel case. **1923** CONRAD *Rover* iv. 61 The lieutenant,..with a pocket glass glued to his eye, growled angrily: 'You can see her now, can't you?' **1926** *Daily Colonist* (Victoria B.C.) 16 July 10/7 (Advt.), Matches are dangerous. When you are camping in or around the forests, use a pocket lighter. **1927** S. ERTZ *Now East, now West* xi. 173 Again that keen glance, over her pocket mirror. **1933** M. ARLEN *Man's Mortality* 21 Taking out his pocket-transmitter, he held it near the light. **1939** T. S. ELIOT *Family Reunion* I. i. 21 Reflecting a pocket-torch of observation Upon each other's opacity. **1955** C. SMITH *Speaking Eye* iii. 33 He took out a pocket comb and ran it through his dark wavy hair. **1957** *Practical Wireless* XXXIII. 534/2 Messrs. Cossar announce a neat printed circuit transistor pocket radio. **1972** *Gloss. Electrotechnical, Power Terms* (B.S.I.) IV. iii. 21 *Pocket lamp*, portable luminaire embodying a miniature lamp fed by a dry battery or accumulator. **1972** D. BLOODWORTH *Any Number can Play* xi. 92 Ivansong..kept the pocket radio close to his ear. **1977** *Jrnl. R. Soc. Arts* CXXV. 71/1 Aldus used it [*sc.* italic type] for the pocket editions of classical authors which he printed in Venice around the year 1500. **1977** J. HEDGECOE *Photographer's Handbk.* 20 Most pocket cameras use a fixed lens with a focal length of about 25 mm. **1978** *Daily Tel.* 19 Sept. 8/6 Semiconductors..are an essential part of micro-processor technology and are used in pocket calculators, electronic watches, mini-computers, and many other modern devices.

b. Small enough to be carried in the pocket, or figured as being so; tiny, diminutive.

1621 BP. MOUNTAGU *Diatribæ* 508 Two poore Breuiarists, with our small pocket-learning. **1820** M. EDGEWORTH *Let.* 14 May (1979) 128 My dear little pocket Prince de Beauvoau for me!—worth all the Russian bears and giants put together. **1856** EMERSON *Eng. Traits, Land* Wks. (Bohn) II. 18 A pocket Switzerland, in which the lakes and mountains are on a sufficient scale to fill the eye and touch the imagination. **1860** READE *Cloister & H.* iv, Now this pocket-athlete [a dwarf] was insanely fond of griping the dinner-table with both hands and so swinging. **1936** *Sun* (Baltimore) 18 May 8/3 No decisive victory in the Austrian pocket dictators' duel is possible without profound repercussions. **1951** N. M. GUNN *Well at World's End* xxi. 174 The garden of a gentleman farmer, a pocket laird. **1972** *Listener* 28 Dec. 898/1 The producer is not altogether the little pocket-dictator... He is assisted by a colleague, usually an expert on the topic to be discussed. **1977** *Time* 8 Aug. 30/1 Charles [Prince, of Luxembourg] was long active in promoting business and industry in his pocket principality.

c. (from 2.) Having reference to money; arising from pecuniary considerations.

1705 in W. S. Perry *Hist. Coll. Amer. Col. Ch.* I. 156 The personal interest and pocket gain of one Single person. **1855** J. R. LEIFCHILD *Cornwall Mines* 160 All persons are most open to pocket arguments, and here came one.

d. Private, secret.

1818 CRUISE *Digest* (ed. 2) IV. 543 Being by a secret or pocket deed to be defeated of the incumbrance he has advanced his money for.

e. Of warships: armoured and equipped like a ship of the class named, but smaller.

1930 *Economist* 1 Feb. 227/1 The technical progress represented by Germany's 'pocket battleship' of identical tonnage but heavier armament. **1932** *Sun* (Baltimore) 17 Sept. 1/1 (*heading*) New pocket cruiser to be started October 1. **1941** *Hutchinson's Pictorial Hist. War* 14 May–8 July 89 Some of the latest and fastest motor launches..are known as 'pocket destroyers'. **1942** H. RICHMOND *War at Sea Today* 27 The 'pocket battleships' are protected by armour against which 6-in.-gun fire could not be expected to be fully effective at long ranges. **1951** *Chambers's Jrnl.* Oct. 632/1 Aided by George (now Sir George) Binney, three 'pocket freighters' were rapidly built in British shipyards. **1974** G. JENKINS *Bridge of Magpies* ii. 40 We heard the sound of heavy guns: a raider or a pocket battleship, we thought.

15. Special Comb.: †**pocket allowance** = POCKET-MONEY; **pocket beach** *Physical Geogr.*, a small, narrow beach between two headlands or in a similar sheltered position; **pocket billiards,** (*a*) a North American type of pool (POOL *sb.*[3] 3); (*b*) *slang* (orig. *Schoolboys'*), manipulation of the male genitals (cf. BALL *sb.*[1] 15 b) by the pocketed hands; also phr. ***to play pocket billiards***; **pocket-borough**, a borough of which the parliamentary representation was under the control of one person or family; **pocket-burner** (*humorous*), a coin in the pocket (in allusion to the saying used of one who cannot keep money, that the coin burns a hole in the pocket); †**pocket-cloth**, a pocket-handkerchief; **pocket-cutter**, a thief who cuts pockets; **pocket-expenses**, small personal outlays; **pocket-filled** *a.*, having the pockets full, rich; **pocket-fish** = ANGLER[1] 2; **pocket-flap, pocket-lid**, a lappet covering a pocket; **pocket-gopher** = GOPHER *sb.*[1] 1; †**pocket-hay, pocket-net**: see quot.; †**pocket-hoop**, a hoop consisting of two parts, one worn on each hip, and serving as a pocket; **pocket-hunter** (see quot. 1906); **pocket-judgement**: see quots.; **pocket-like** *a.*, resembling a pocket; **pocket-miner** *U.S.* = *pocket-hunter*; so **pocket-mining** *vbl. sb.*; **pocket-mouse**, a rodent of the family *Saccomyidæ*, a pouched mouse; **pocket pager** = PAGER *sb.*[3]; so **pocket-paging** *vbl. sb.*; **pocket passer** *Amer.* and *Canad. Football*, one who passes from the pocket (POCKET *sb.* 11 b); **pocket-pedlar** *U.S.* (see quot.); **pocket-plum** = *bladder-plum* (BLADDER *sb.* 10): see quots.; **pocket-rat** = GOPHER *sb.*[1] 1; **pocket rot**, a fungus infection causing localized decay in the trunks or roots of trees; also with prefixed defining word (e.g. ***brown pocket rot***); **pocket-sheriff**: see quots.; **pocket-size** *a.*, of a size suitable for carrying in the pocket; hence *fig.*, petty, small-scale; also ***pocket-sized*** adj.; **pocket stay** (see quot.); †**pocket-tortoise**, a pocket tortoise-shell comb; **pocket valley** *Physical Geogr.*, a steep-sided, usu. flat-floored valley at the head of which a stream emerges at the base of a steep slope; **pocket Venus**, a small and beautiful woman; also *transf.*; **pocket veto**: see quot. See also POCKET-BOOK, -HANDKERCHIEF, etc.

1813 JANE AUSTEN *Pride & Prejudice* III. viii. 143 Her board and *pocket allowance, and the continual presents in money, which passed to her, through her mother's hands. **1893** N. S. SHALER in *Ann. Rep. U.S. Geol. Survey* XIII. 141 Where..there are islands or shoals lying on either side of considerable reentrant, a curious action arises, which leads to the formation of what we may term '*pocket beaches'. **1932** W. H. EMMONS et al. *Geol.* ix. 254 On rocky coasts beaches of boulders and cobblestones commonly form at the heads of indentations, although occasionally sand may occupy such positions. These pocket beaches.. are found along the coast of California at Carmel, at La Jolla, and at many other places. **1976** A. N. STRAHLER *Princ. Earth Sci.* xvii. 250 Shingle beaches form in the most sheltered locations—in bays between rocky promontories—and are called pocket beaches... They are typically crescent-shaped and are concave toward the sea. **1913** J. T. STODDARD *Science of Billiards* vii. 152 *Pocket Billiards. The more common pool games are played on tables with pockets, and with balls $2\frac{1}{4}$ inches in diameter,—slightly smaller than the ball used in billiards. **1917** *Billiards Mag.* Dec. 13/1 Greenleaf..began to play pocket billiards 6 years ago... His ambition is to win the pocket billiard championship. **1940** S. SPENDER *Backward Son* ii. 94 He paused, feeling in his trouser pockets with his hands, with a familiar gesture of the class room which the boys knew as 'pocket billiards'. **1949** F. SARGESON *I saw in my Dream* I. 40, I don't remember nothing about when school was in except him playing pocket billiards. **1963** *Landfall* Mar. 14 A pillar of our.. community,..addicted to long volleys of handball, I mean pocket billiards. **1971** A. BURGESS *MF* ii. 31 Saint Face, as if wishing to play pocket-billiards with my balls, thrust his hands in from the rear. **1856** MISS MULOCK *J. Halifax* xxiv, Satisfied that,..despite the unheard-of absurdity of a contested election, his *pocket-borough was quite secure. **1877** BLACK *Green Past.* iv, There was not half as much mischief done by the old pocket-borough system as there is by this money qualification. **1895** C. R. B. BARRETT *Surrey* iii. 80 Horne Tooke..sat for the pocket borough of Sarum. **1848** KINGSLEY *Saint's Trag.* III. iv, One that..never met you after a hail-storm without lightening himself of a few *pocket-burners. *a* **1704** T. BROWN *Two Oxf. Schol.* Wks. 1730 I. 3 Cannot I wipe mine eyes with the fair *pocket-cloth? **1885** *Milnor* (Dakota) *Teller* 5 June 2/3 Deck hands on the steamer..were being robbed by *pocket-cutters among the roustabouts. **1751** SMOLLETT *Per. Pic.* xxxiii, A purse..to defray her *pocket-expenses in her absence. **1905** G. B. SHAW in *Grand Mag.* Feb. 116 If you keep the pocket expenses down to twelve and six. **1886** W. J. TUCKER *E. Europe* 237 Let the empty titles and empty pockets marry the title-mad and *pocket-filled Jewesses. **1896** *Westm. Gaz.* 21 Feb. 8/1 The angler is known by various names, including *Pocket-fish, Sea-devil, Fishing-frog, Toad-fish, Briarbot, and Wide-gab. **1873** E. EGGLESTON *Myst. Metropolisville* iv. 37 She would..explain how the *pocket-gophers built their mounds. **1932** S. ZUCKERMAN *Social Life Monkeys & Apes* iv. 59 The animals of the first sub-group are those that spend the anœstrus in solitude... Examples are the jaguar of Central America and the pocket gopher of the United States. **1977** R. B. COWLES *Desert Jrnl.* xx. 209 A pocket gopher or..a beaver burrowed through the bank. **1704** *Dict. Rust. et Urb.*, **Pocket-Hayes*,..certain short Nets wherewith to take Pheasants alive... They are about a yard long. **1790** R. TYLER *Contrast* I. i, You really think the *pocket-hoop unbecoming. **1834** PLANCHÉ *Brit. Costume* xxii. (1847) 416 The pocket hoop is ridiculed in 1780 by a print in which a girl so attired is placed beside a donkey laden with a pair of panniers. **1906** *Chambers's Jrnl.* Feb. 159/1 They [*sc.* prospectors] include the '*pocket-hunter' who disdains to search for gold except in the form of pockets. **1947** *Field & Stream* June 30/3 Now and then a 'pocket-hunter'..will find a place in the hills containing perhaps a few hundred dollars in gold. **1736–59** M. BACON *Abridgm. Law of Execution* (1778) II. 331 The addition of the King's Seal, which was never required to any Contract at Common Law, was to authenticate and make the Security of a higher Nature than any other then known..thus it must be presumed from the force of them, which is equal to Judgments of the Superior Courts, they obtained the Name of *Pocket Judgments. **1872** *Wharton's Law Lex.* (ed. 5), *Pocket-judgment*, a statute-merchant which was enforceable at any time after non-payment on the day assigned, without further proceedings. **1890** *Pall Mall G.* 15 May 3/2 There is a new tailor-made jacket called the 'Cavalier'... It falls down to the hips and has heavy *pocket-lids and lappels. **1880** A. WILSON in *Gentl. Mag.* CCXLVI. 48 Nose, eyes, and ears..arise as *pocket-like ingrowths from the epiblast or outer layer of the body. **1884** *Cassell's Nat. Hist.* III. 124 These animals [*Saccomyidæ*]..by American writers..are called '*Pocket Mice'. **1902** J. LONDON *Daughter of Snows* 207 The *pocket-miner's eyes sparkled. **1909** 'MARK TWAIN' *Is Shakes. Dead?* vii. 75, I have been a 'pocket' miner—a sort of gold mining not findable in any but one little spot in the world. **1872** —— *Roughing It* 436 In that one little corner of California is found a species of mining.. called '*pocket-mining'. **1975** *Kingston* (Ontario) *Whig-Standard* 6 Dec. 25/1 Off in a side office, MacLean Hunter manager Jack French talks to a client about ordering '*pocket-pagers'. **1977** Pocket pager [see PAGER *sb.*³]. **1973** *Times* 11 Jan. 15/2 The control room is the centre of a vast and flexible intercom system which complements and extends the telephone network..and the *pocket-paging system. **1963** *Pocket passer [see POCKET *sb.* 11 b]. **1977** *Globe & Mail* (Toronto) 26 Nov. 53/6 If Wade, a pocket passer, is harassed by the Eskimoes' blitzing linebackers, he could throw a number of interceptions. **1892** *Nation* (N.Y.) 28 July 66/1 *Pocket-pedlers..who stand on the street corners with a bottle in one pocket and a glass in the other, and will sell you a drink in a doorway or a horse-shed. **1899** MASSEE *Text-bk. Plant Dis.* 85 '*Pocket-plums', or 'Bladder-plums'... The..disease of plum-trees..caused by a minute parasitic fungus [*Exoascus pruni*]... Instead of developing into a normal plum,..grows..into a deformed, useless structure... The entire structure is dry, and not at all fleshy..[and] also hollow, the 'stone' containing the seed not being developed. **1902** *Encycl. Brit.* XXVIII. 560/2 Many of these Taphrineæ are important parasites—*e.g.* Pocket plums and Witches' Brooms on Birches, &c., are due to their action. **1926** *Jrnl. Agric. Res.* XXXIII. 687 As the brown cubical rot produced [by *Trametes subrosea*]..is more or less restricted to definite pockets in the wood, it has been called brown-*pocket rot. **1938** J. S. BOYCE *Forest Pathol.* xvii. 451 Pocket dry rot..is a brown pocket rot of the heartwood of living incense cedar caused by *Polyporus amarus*. **1956** F. W. JANE *Structure of Wood* ix. 208 In the pocket rots the areas of decay are confined to pockets. **1972** *Mycologia* LXIV. 1258 [*Phellinus torulosus*] occurs..mostly on south-western white pine..in which it causes a white pocket rot of the roots. **1765** BLACKSTONE *Comm.* (1768) I. ix. 342 The practice of occasionally naming what are called *pocket-sheriffs, by the sole authority of the crown. **1809** CHRISTIAN *Blackstone's Comm.* I. ix. 341 *note*, When the king appoints a person sheriff, who is not one of the three nominated in the exchequer, he is called a pocket-sheriff. It is probable, that no compulsory instance of the appointment of a pocket-sheriff ever occurred. **1909** *Daily Chron.* 13 Nov. 3/2 They form a serviceable little group of *pocket-size manuals. **1973** P. EVANS *Bodyguard Man* xxx. 183 You know what you are... Just a latter-day Judas, pocket size. **1907** *Daily Chron.* 14 Aug. 3/2 A new *pocket-sized edition of Mr. Edward Hulme's 'Wild Fruits of the Countryside' is being published. **1954** KOESTLER *Invisible Writing* xxiii. 253 Our Jan..was a pocket-sized Stalin. **1964** *McCall's Sewing* ii. 31/2 **Pocket stay*, a strip of interfacing sewn to the wrong side of a pocket opening for reinforcement. **1687** SEDLEY *Bellam.* Prol., Wks. 1722 II. 87 Nor Perruque comb'd, nor *Pocket-Tortoise stirr'd. **1942** O. D. VON ENGELN *Geomorphol.* xxii. 569 Seepage at the bases of the outer scarps [of uplifted coral reefs] promotes the formation of gullies by headward erosion through solution-sapping. *Pocket valleys, with vertical head and side walls and a nearly flat floor, are..opened up by this process. **1966** J. WYCKOFF *Rock, Time, & Landforms* xii. 281 Whereas the blind valley ends at a blank wall, the so-called pocket valley begins at a blank wall. A pocket valley forms where water emerges near the foot of the slope, dissolving out the rock around and below the point of emergence. **1971** J. N. JENNINGS *Karst* vi. 112 A distinction is sometimes made between steepheads incised to an impervious basement and pocket valleys of the same general nature but within the karst rock outcrop. **1869** S. R. HOLE *Bk. about Roses* viii. 125 The lovely little Banksian Rose..this *pocket, or rather button-hole, Venus. **1921** W. DE LA MARE *Memoirs of Midget* xxxiii. 229 Aunt Alice calls you her 'pocket Venus', and she means it, too, in her own sly way. **1969** H. K. FLEMING *Day they kidnapped Queen Victoria* vi. 106 Four years had gone by, since, as the 'Pocket Venus', she had been the rage and toast of society. **1979** 'P. O'CONNOR' *Into Strong City* II. xxvii. 98 Nancy was dark and petite, perfectly formed—the proverbial pocket venus. **1842** *Ohio Statesman* 19 Dec. 3/1 (*heading*) The *pocket vetoes. **1888** BRYCE *Amer. Commw.* I. 74 *note*, If Congress adjourns within the ten days allowed the President for returning the bill, it is lost. His retaining it under these circumstances at the end of a session is popularly called a 'pocket veto'. **1973** *Time* 25 June 20/3 As presidential counsel, he worked out the legal basis for Nixon's impoundment of funds, broad use of pocket vetoes and Executive privilege.

pocket ('pɒkɪt), *v.* [f. POCKET *sb.*: cf. F. *pocheter* (1610 in Godef.).]

1. *trans.* To put into one's pocket. Also with *up*.

1589 *Pasquill's Counter-C.* 4 The goodly frame of this Common-Weale shall fall, and Banck-rouptes and Atheists pocket uppe the peeces. **1615** DAY *Festivals* xii. (1615) 338 Yet would hee not pocket a Penny of it. **1631** MASSINGER *Emperor East* I. ii, Petitions not sweetened With gold,..if received, are pocketed, not read. **1749** SMOLLETT *Gil Bl.* I. ii. I. 5, I stopt short, and pocketing my ducats in a great hurry, took out some rials. **1861** HUGHES *Tom Brown at Oxf.* xviii, He shut up and pocketed his sermon, and followed his flock. **1899** F. T. BULLEN *Log Sea-waif* 219 Our friendly hoveller pocketed his five pounds and departed.

b. To confine or enclose as in a pocket: in quot. 1681, to imprison. (Chiefly in *passive*.)

1681 DRYDEN *Span. Fryar* IV. ii, With Intent to sell the publick Safety, And pocket up his Prince. **1877** WINCHELL *Reconc. Sci. & Rel.* v. (1881) 100 It has been assumed that energy may be pocketed in portions of matter, to be let loose on certain occasions. **1890** *Cent. Dict.* s.v., A pocketed valve. **1897** *Harper's Mag.* Apr. 753 The petty port of Guaymas, pocketed on the California Gulf.

c. *Racing.* To hem in (a competitor) in front and at the sides, so as to prevent him from winning.

1890 in *Cent. Dict.* **1901** *Scotsman* 16 Sept. 3/5 He tried to squeeze through between Fleur d'Eté and Sidus, and for his indiscretion he was very properly pocketed.

2. To take possession of for one's own, to appropriate: sometimes with implication of dishonesty.

1637 R. HUMPHREY tr. *St. Ambrose* II. 41 Pocketing and pursing up..the fruits of other mens labours. **1769** *Junius Lett.* xxix. (1799) I. 204 *note*, She ordered every gown and trinket to be sold, and pocketed the money. **1786** JEFFERSON *Corr.* (1829) II. 11 They [the English] say, they will pocket our carrying trade as well as their own. **1879** J. C. COX *Ch. of Derbysh.* IV. 77 These sums were pocketed by Edward VI, or rather by his advisers. **1898** *Fortn. Rev.* Jan. 99 The object of Sweden being..to realise her long-cherished hopes by quietly 'pocketing' Norway.

3. *fig.* **a.** To take or accept (an affront, etc.) without showing resentment; to submit to, endure meekly, 'swallow'. †Formerly with *up*.

1589 GREENE *Spanish Masquerado* Wks. (Grosart) V. 273 Thus the great Generall of Spaine was content to pockette vppe this Dishonour to saue his life. **1595** SHAKS. *John* III. i. 200 Well ruffian, I must pocket vp these wrongs. **1622** MABBE tr. *Aleman's Guzman d'Alf.* I. 214 If he..pocket a wrong, and hold his hands, he is a coward. **1737** *Common Sense* I. 139 Some great Men who can pocket up a Kick or a Cuff with as good an Air as they cou'd a Bribe. **1769** *Polit. Register* V. 229 Your grace would have pocketed the affront. **1891** *Leeds Mercury* 2 May 7/1 The United States must pocket the rebuff with a pleasant diplomatic smile.

b. To conceal, give no indication of, suppress (pride, anger, or other feeling); to refrain from publishing (a report, letter, etc.); in U.S. politics (of the President or the Governor of a State): To retain (a bill) unsigned, so as to prevent it from becoming law (cf. *pocket veto*, POCKET *sb.* 15).

1610 SHAKS. *Temp.* II. i. 67, *Ant.* If but one of his pockets could speake, would it not say he lyes? *Seb.* I, or very falsely pocket vp his report. **1750** CHESTERF. *Lett.* 1 Nov., Pocket all your knowledge with your watch, and never pull it out in company unless desired. **1878** BOSW. SMITH *Carthage* 115 The other generals, pocketing their pride,..handed over the undivided responsibility to Xanthippus. **1885** [implied at *pocketing* vbl. sb. below].

4. *Billiards.* To drive (a ball) into one of the pockets. (POCKET *sb.* 5.)

1780 *Char.* in *Ann. Reg.* 16/1 It was absolutely necessary to make it rebound from two different parts of the cushion before it could pocket the other. **1873** BENNETT & 'CAVENDISH' *Billiards* 481 After being pocketed or forced off the table, the red ball must be spotted on the top spot.

5. To hold under private control; *esp.* the representation of a constituency. Cf. *pocket-borough*, POCKET *sb.* 15.

1882 SCHOULER *Hist. U.S.* I. 10 He was fond of his State.., and loyal to some one of the blood families who contended for the honor of pocketing the borough in which he voted.

6. To furnish with pockets. (Chiefly in *passive*.)

1896 *Westm. Gaz.* 22 Jan. 2/1 One block of beautiful wavy white quartz was thickly pocketed..with the yellow metal.

7. *Path.* and *Surg.* To convert or form into a pouch, cavity, or depression.

1885–8 FAGGE & PYE-SMITH *Princ. Med.* (ed. 2) II. 612 The exudation being so effused into the meshes of the papillæ and Malpighian layer that the cavity is 'pocketed' and shows a central depression or umbilicus. **1895** *Syd. Soc. Lex.*, *Pocketing* (*Med.* and *Surg.*), forming a pocket or pouch;..a method of treating the pedicle in ovariotomy.

8. *intr.* To form pockets or bag-like recesses.

b. To pucker or become bagged. *rare. U.S.*

1614 CAMDEN *Rem., Apparell* 234 Of the long pocketting sleeues in the time of King Henry the fourth, Hoccliue..song. **1873** MRS. WHITNEY *Other Girls* xxv, That carpet?..why, it hadn't begun to pocket yet. **1884** *N. & Q.* 29 Mar. 259/1 In describing the pocketing sleeve of the twelfth and thirteenth centuries, to draw attention to the fact that it still exists in the heraldic charge known as the *maunch*.

Hence '**pocketed** *ppl. a.*, '**pocketing** *vbl. sb.*, (*a*) the action of the vb.; (*b*) material for pockets; also '**pocketing** *ppl. a.*

1597 *1st Pt. Return Parnass.* v. i. 1448 A lunaticke bawdie trull, a pocketing queane. **1614**, **1884** Pocketing sleeve [see 8]. **1638** FORD *Fancies* IV. i, The pocketing Of some well-looking ducats. **1879** TROLLOPE *John Caldigate* II. xxi. 288 They who were less privileged had fed themselves with pocketed sandwiches. **1885** L. W. SPRING *Kansas* 260 Legislators who..could not be thwarted by any such trifle as the pocketing of a bill. **1885–8** Pocketed [see 7]. **1933** J. E. LIBERTY *Practical Tailoring* v. 64 The pocketing should be about 15½ in. to 16 in. long. **1934** T. S. ELIOT *Rock* i. 10 With pocketed hands..We stand about in open places. **1960** E. ENNION *House on Shore* ix. 108 They would have the greatest difficulty in taking off again: pocketing in snow or sand might easily prevent it. **1963** J. OSBORNE *Dental Mechanics for Students* (ed. 5) ix. 165 The extent of periodontal pocketing will also be shown. **1968** J. IRONSIDE *Fashion Alphabet* 97 *Pocketing*, strong cotton used for men's pockets. **1974** C. RYAN *Bridge too Far* I. iii. 29 Though pocketed—the sea lay behind them to the north and west, and Canadians and British were pressing in from the south and east—they nevertheless controlled most of the southern bank of the estuary.

pocketability (,pɒkɪtə'bɪlɪtɪ). [f. POCKETABLE *a.*: see -ITY.] The capacity to be put or carried in the pocket.

1970 *Amateur Photographer* 22 Apr. 21/1 No modern range-finder camera with a comparable lens..and a built-in selenium meter has its priceless asset of pocketability. **1977** *New Scientist* 10 Feb. p. ii (Advt.), If real pocketability matters, the Sinclair Cambridge Scientific offers a comparable range of functions in a uniquely compact format.

pocketable ('pɒkɪtəb(ə)l), *a.* [f. POCKET *v.* + -ABLE.] That may be put or carried in the pocket.

a **1700** B. E. *Dict. Cant. Crew, Portable*, Pocketable. **1704** DERHAM in *Phil. Trans.* XXV. 1585 (2) These Instruments are..easily carried about,..the latter especially, which may be made pocketable. **1853** *Tait's Mag.* XX. 632 The volume is small and pocketable. **1890** CLARK RUSSELL *My Shipmate Louise* xv, There is pocketable booty in the mail-room.

Hence '**pocketableness**.

1891 *Sat. Rev.* 22 Aug. 230/2 Pocketableness..is the great point of a guide.

pocketa-pocketa ('pɒkɪtə'pɒkɪtə). Also **pockety**. [Echoic.] An imitation of the regular sound made by a smoothly-running internal combustion engine; also *transf.* Also *attrib.* and *adv.*

1939 J. THURBER in *New Yorker* 18 Mar. 19/1 The pounding of the cylinders increased: ta-pocketa-pocketa-pocketa-*pocketa-pocketa*. **1968** L. DEIGHTON *Only when I Larf* i. 11 A helicopter was warming up... Pockety, pockety, pockety. **1971** *Flying* Apr. 93/1, I brought the power back from the standard 1,700 run-up rpm to a pocketa-pocketa idle. **1977** J. AIKEN *Last Movement* ix. 174, I could hear his heart going pocketa-pocketa.

pocket-book ('pɒkɪtbʊk). Also **pocket book**, **pocketbook**.

1. A small book, adapted to be conveniently carried in the pocket. In recent U.S. use, also a cheap edition, esp. paper-bound. Also *attrib.*

1617 *Janua Ling.* Advt., To render the volume as portable ..and if not as a manuall or pocket-booke, yet a pectorall or bosome-booke, to be carried twixt ierkin and doublet. **1648** A. ROWLEY (*title*) The Scholler's Companion, or a Little Library, containing all the Interpretations of the Hebrew and Greek Bible,..brought into a Pocket Book. **1658** A. FOX tr. *Würtz' Surg.* II. Introd. 45 A small Enchiridium and pocket book, easily to be carried about one. **1678** AUBREY in *Ray's Corr.* (1848) 129 A little pocket-book, which may be of use where the larger tables cannot be had. **1882** SAINTSBURY in *Encycl. Brit.* XIV. 318/2 La Rochefoucauld ranks among the scanty number of pocket-books to be read and re-read with ever new admiration, instruction, and delight. **1953** *Amer. Scholar* XXIII. 10 The *Galaxy* serial 'Gravy Planet' (recently republished in a pocket book as *The Space Merchants*). **1959** N. MAILER *Advts. for Myself* (1961) 280 Anyone looking for a fairly close portrait of that outfit is invited to read *The Day the Century Ended*—in pocket-book called *Between Heaven and Hell*. **1962** A. BUCHWALD *How much is that in Dollars?* 167 Always try to get a large advance on pocket-books. **1979** *Maledicta* III. 15, I was paid $50,000 by New American Library in 1968 for the U.S. pocketbook rights of my last novel, *The Man Who Loved Women*.

2. A book for notes, memoranda, etc., intended to be carried in the pocket; a note-book. Also, a book-like case of leather or the like, having compartments for papers, bank-notes, bills, etc.; a woman's hand-bag or other container for bank-notes or coins. Also *fig.* Now chiefly *U.S.*

1685 *Lond. Gaz.* No. 2001/4 Lost.., a Pocket-Book, having an Old Almanack in it of the Date of the Year 80 or 81. **1722** DE FOE *Col. Jack* (1840) 130 A merchant's pocket-book, or letter-case. **1797** HOLCROFT *Stolberg's Trav.* (ed. 2) II. lvii. 325 A lady..makes a memorandum..in her pocket-book. **1816** *Niles' Reg.* X. 216/1 Two methodist preachers were lately robbed of their pocket-books, containing very considerable sums in bank notes. **1862** O. L. JACKSON in *Colonel's Diary* (1922) v. 67, I..thought it best to take my pocket-book out of my pocket and put it under my head. **1867** TROLLOPE *Chron. Barset* I. i. 4 A cheque..said to have been stolen out of a pocket-book. **1897** *Sears, Roebuck Catal.* 223/1 At 50c. Our price poultice for tired..pocket books. **1907** *St. Nicholas* Sept. 1007/2 In her pretty pocket-book..she had found a crisp one-dollar bill. **1936** C. SANDBURG *People, Yes* 111 So dumb he spent his last dollar buying a pocketbook to put it in. **1960** A. SEXTON *To Bedlam & Part Way Back* 13 You guided past groups of robbers.. clutching your pocketbook. **1976** *National Observer* (U.S.) 13 Mar. 18/4 Why should women whose pocketbooks are flatter have to jeopardize their lives..by patronizing sleazy, unqualified nonprofessionals.

3. *attrib.* and *Comb.*

1819 *P.O. Lond. Direct.* 365 Wells, T., Pocket-book-maker. *a* **1860** *Tricks & Traps N. York* 24 (Bartlett), No man, boy, or greenhorn was ever yet victimized by the Pocket-book Droppers..who didn't have so strong a spice of the scamp in his own composition, as to think he was coming a sure and profitable swindle upon some one. *Ibid.*, Pocket-book Dropping may almost be considered as one of the by-gones. **1894** H. H. FURNESS *Address* 4 Our ideal Provost must know the exact location in every rich man's body of the pocket-book nerve.

†**pocke'teer**. *Obs. rare.* [f. POCKET *sb.* + -EER¹.] A pickpocket.

c **1626** *Dick of Devon.* II. iv. in Bullen *O. Pl.* II. 40, I am no pocketeer, no diver into slopps: yet you may please to empty them your selfe, good Don.

pocketer ('pɒkɪtə(r)). [f. POCKET *v.* + -ER¹.] One who pockets or appropriates.

1825 COBBETT *Hist. Prot. Reform.* vi. §176 The tyrant was ..the great pocketter of this species of plunder. **1830** *Fraser's Mag.* I. 501 Nominal editor of the work, but regular pocketer of the salary.

pocketful ('pɒkɪtfʊl). [f. POCKET *sb.* + -FUL.] As much (of anything) as fills a pocket.

1611 COTGR., *Pochée*, a pocket-full, poke-full, sack-full, of. **1718–19** ARBUTHNOT *Let. Swift* Misc. Wks. 1751 II. 120 Formerly, when you had Wit in Pocket-fulls, and no

Money. **1848** THACKERAY *Van. Fair* xiii, A whole pocketful of money. **1866** LIVINGSTONE *Last Jrnls.* (1873) I. ii. 35 They are sitting eating the pocketfuls of corn maize they have stolen.

pocket-handkerchief (ˌpɒkɪtˈhæŋkətʃɪf). **1.** A handkerchief carried in the pocket.

1645 in *Essex* (Mass.) *Inst. Hist. Coll.* (1914) L. 326, 3 pocket handkerchiefs. **1680** ROCHESTER *Poems* 16 Where Critick-like, he sits and squints, Steals Pocket-Handkerchiefs, and hints. **1760** WASHINGTON *Diary* 15 Feb. (1925) I. 126 Pockethandkerchiefs servd the purposes of Table Cloths and Napkins. **1781** MME. D'ARBLAY *Diary* May, She would wave a white pocket-handkerchief out of the coach window. **1825** T. H. LISTER *Granby* x, I am sorry for the poor Duke; he loses his pocket handkerchief at Bath. **1861** MRS. CARLYLE *Lett.* III. 90 Mr. C. saw fit to spread his pocket-handkerchief on the grass..and sit down on it.

2. *transf.* and *fig.* **a.** A very small area (*of* land, etc.).

1866 [see sense 3 below]. **1891** 'GANCONAGH' *John Sherman & Dhoya* 70 This pocket-handkerchief of a garden. **1949** T. RATTIGAN *Browning Version* 27 It's only a pocket handkerchief, I'm afraid, but it's very useful to Andrew. He often works out there. **1961** L. MUMFORD *City in History* xv. 465 The more respectable quarters..with a soiled pocket-handkerchief of grass before their houses. **1973** *Daily Tel.* 8 Dec. 12/3 There is a pocket handkerchief of a dance floor.

b. A light sail.

1936 B. ADAMS *Ships & Women* xi. 239 Martin told me to 'Go get the pocket handkerchiefs off her'. So I called out the watch and hauled down the jib topsail. **1941** *Penguin New Writing* II. 17, I could ride out bad weather with two of the smallest pocket-handkerchiefs.

3. *attrib.* and *Comb.*

1866 GEO. ELIOT *Felix Holt* II. xx. 87 A mere pocket-handkerchief..Pod's End. **1935** N. L. MCCLUNG *Clearing in West* iv. 32 This kind of pocket handkerchief-farming makes people mean. **1953** WODEHOUSE *Performing Flea* 53 Bungalows..each with a little lawn in front and a pocket-handkerchief garden at the back. **1961** *Daily Tel.* 21 Oct. 6/2 The knowledge..helped the Russians to turn the screw..on economic and technical aid to this pocket-handkerchief State [*sc.* Albania]. **1973** N. GRAHAM *Murder in Dark Room* v. 33 A row of little old-fashioned houses with pocket handkerchief lawns.

pocket-hole (ˈpɒkɪthəʊl). The opening in a garment through which the hand is put into the pocket.

a **1658** CLEVELAND *Pet. Poem* 20 The Women call'd me Woman, till the Fools Spy'd their Mistake thorough my Pocket Holes. **1758** JOHNSON *Idler* No. 15 ¶2 She walks.. with her arms through her pocket-holes. **1801** JANE AUSTEN *Lett.* (1884) I. 283 The jacket is all in one with the body, and comes as far as the pocket-holes. **1900** CROCKETT *Fitting of Peats* v. Love Idylls (1901) 35 Take that hand out of your pocket-hole.

pocket-knife (ˈpɒkɪtˌnaɪf). A knife with one or more blades which fold into the handle, for carrying in the pocket.

1727 *Philip Quarll* (1816) 42 Having nothing but a pocket-knife to cut it with. **1875** EMERSON *Lett. & Soc. Aims* i. 16 When a boy finds that his pocket-knife will attract steel filings and take up a needle.

attrib. **1896** *Daily News* 21 Dec. 9/5 One of the largest houses..has nearly 100 pocket knife cutlers and grinders idle.

pocketless (ˈpɒkɪtlɪs), *a.* [f. POCKET *sb.* + -LESS.] Without a pocket; having no pocket.

1889 *Chicago Advance* 3 Jan., Ulster pockets are swept out of existence. The women are pocketless again. **1897** J. A. GRAHAM *On Threshold Three Closed Lands* vii. 101 A scantily clothed and pocketless Lepopa crofter. **1903** *Month* Aug. 161 A charming billiard-room with a long pocketless table.

ˈpocket-ˌmoney. Money carried in the pocket for occasional expenses; *esp.* that allowed to those who have no other money under their control, as schoolchildren.

1632 LITHGOW *Trav.* VIII. 345 We were both robbed of our cloaks and pocket-moneys. *a* **1735** ARBUTHNOT *John Bull* III. xx, One Monday-Morning..he came, as usual, to bring John Bull his Weekly Pocket-Money. **1838** LYTTON *Alice* II. ii, He inquired compassionately, whether she was allowed any pocket-money? **1883** TROLLOPE *Autobiog.* (ed. 2) I. i. 13 Every boy had a shilling a week pocket-money, which we called battels, and which was advanced to us out of the pocket of the second master. **1892** A. W. PINERO *Magistrate* III. i. 114 All my pocket money is in my overcoat at the Hôtel des Princes. **1926** T. E. LAWRENCE *Seven Pillars* (1935) xii. 89 They made pocket-money during their service, if they were ingenious. **1973** *Times* 13 Dec. 21/7 Baroness Marie-Anne..bought from her pocket money Van Gogh's 'L'arlésienne'.

attrib. **1838** DICKENS *Nich. Nick.* i, On pocket-money day, that is to say, on Saturday. **1901** *Daily Chron.* 14 June 6/3 His advice to women was, 'Don't take up pocket-money work'. **1979** *Jrnl. R. Soc. Arts* CXXVII. 135/2 We already live in a pocket-money economy where essentials are provided and we work for the extras.

Hence **ˈpocket-ˌmoneyless** *a.*

1925 A. S. M. HUTCHINSON *One Increasing Purpose* I. xv. 90 The kind of children, well-bred, entirely pocket-moneyless, that retired Anglo-Indians often have.

ˈpocket-ˌpicking, *sb.* 'Picking' of pockets: see PICK *v.*[1] 9; stealing from the pockets of others. So **ˈpocket-ˌpicker,** a pickpocket.

1622 ROWLANDS *Good Newes & Bad N.* 42 A Pocket-picker most exceeding braue (For true mens purses did maintaine the knaue). **1662** PETTY *Taxes* x. Tracts (1769) 56 Such as have abused their dextrous use of them [fingers] by pocket-picking, counterfeiting of seals and writings &c. **1759** STERNE *Tr. Shandy* I. xi, More..people were bubbled out of their goods and money by it in one twelvemonth, than by pocket-picking and shop-lifting in seven. **1864** BURTON *Scot. Abr.* I. iv. 199 As naturally..as the disappearance of watches in a London mob is attributed to pocket-picking.

pocket-picking, *ppl. a.* That picks pockets.

1868 GEO. ELIOT in *Blackw. Mag.* Jan. 3/2 A poor pocket-picking scoundrel, who will steal your loose pence while you are listening round the platform.

ˈpocket-piece.

1. A piece of money carried in the pocket as a charm, a 'lucky' coin; often a coin which is for some reason not current, or is damaged or spurious.

1706 *Lond. Gaz.* No. 4209/4 Lost.., a Silver Snuff-box, ..with some other Silver Things, Pocket-Pieces, and Money. **1726** *Adv. Capt. R. Boyle* (1768) 8 He soon knew the Piece to be his Wife's,..being the same he had some time ago given her for a Pocket-piece. **1837** DICKENS *Pickw.* xlv, He got two doubtful shillin's and sixpenn'orth o' pocket-pieces for a good half-crown. **1905** SIR J. EVANS in *Numismatic Chron.* III. 312 The milled sixpences [of Q. Eliz. 1561–75]..were [not improbably] frequently treasured as pocket-pieces.

2. The socket or cavity on each side of a sash-frame in which the weights run: see POCKET *sb.* 9 a.

1901 *J. Black's Illustr. Carp. & Build., Home Handicr.* 48 We now work along the 'pulley-stile' for a transverse cut, which marks the extremity of the 'pocket-piece', or receptacle for the weights.

ˈpocket-ˈpistol. [See POCKET *sb.* 14.]

1. A small pistol to be carried in the pocket.

1612 S. MOUNTAGU in *Buccleuch MSS.* (Hist. MSS. Comm.) I. 240 There are they say pocket pistols of five and six inches. **1711** ADDISON *Spect.* No. 102 ¶6 It shall make a Report like a Pocket-Pistol. **1784–5** *Chron.* in *Ann. Reg.* 323/2 At Dover..the large gun, well known by the name of Queen Anne's pocket pistol. **1850** in McCrie *Mem. Sir A. Agnew* xi. (1852) 277 It [a pamphlet] served him as a pocket-pistol on such occasions.

2. *humorous.* A pocket spirit-flask.

c **1730** BURT *Lett. N. Scotl.* (1818) I. 298, I had always on my journeys a pocket-pistol loaded with brandy mixed with juice of lemon. **1864** BABBAGE *Passages Life Philos.* xvi. 218 A glass bottle enclosed in a leather case, commonly called a pocket-pistol. **1882** MCQUEEN in *Macm. Mag.* XLVI. 162 The rests had been frequent on the road, as had also been the applications to the pocket-pistols.

ˈpocketwards, *adv.* [-WARDS.] In the direction of one's pocket.

1909 H. G. WELLS *Tono-Bungay* III. i. 280 He made a motion pocketwards, that gave us an invincible persuasion that he had a sample upon him.

pockety (ˈpɒkɪtɪ), *a.* Also **pocketty.** [f. POCKET *sb.* + -Y.]

1. Of a mine or mineral deposit: Characterized by pockets; having the ore unevenly distributed. Also *fig.*

1874 RAYMOND *Statist. Mines & Mining* 370 The vein is irregular and pockety. **1877** *Ibid.* 177 Rich but 'pockety' mineral deposits. **1896** *Naturalist* 289 The sandstones..and seams of lignite rapidly alternate one with another, assuming lenticular, pockety and other forms. **1920** GALSWORTHY *In Chancery* II. x. 204 The atmosphere of his house was strange and pocketty when Jolyon came in and told them of the dog Balthasar's death. The news had a unifying effect.

2. Of the nature of a secluded hollow. Also, characterized by secluded hollows.

1893 E. L. WAKEMAN in *Columbus* (Ohio) *Dispatch* 18 May, A tiny, pockety vale whose surface is almost level on either side to the edges of noble wooded bluffs. **1929** J. BUCHAN *Courts of Morning* II. 257 Days with a bobbery pack of hounds in difficult pockety country. **1932** —— *Gap in Curtain* iv. 190 The river valley was pockety and swampy.

ˈpockify, *v.* ? *Obs.* [f. POCKY *a.*[1] + -FY.] *trans.* To make pocky; to infect with pox or syphilis. Hence **ˈpockified** *ppl. a.*

1624 GEE *Foot out of Snare* 49 If the priests lungs bee but a little vlcerated or pockified. **1658** A. FOX *Würtz' Surg.* III. xvi. 265 If Mercury should be used to a wound of a pockyfied party, that morbus would be rowzed. **1689** T. PLUNKET *Char. Gd. Commander* 26 Thou soul-destroying.. vice,..That dost effeminate and pockifie Those Creatures called men. **1706** PHILLIPS, *Pockified* or *Pocky*, that has got the French-Pox.

ˈpockily, *adv.* [f. POCKY *a.*[1] + -LY[2].] In a pocky manner; with pox or syphilis.

1665 NEEDHAM *Med. Medicinæ* 136 A young Girl that was pockily infected by one that gave her only a kiss as she was dancing.

ˈpockiness. [f. as prec. + -NESS.] The condition of being pocky.

1530 PALSGR. 256/1 Pockynesse, *fossetterie*. **1611** COTGR., *Fossetterie*, pockinesse, or the being full of pock-holes. **1727** BAILEY vol. II, *Pockiness*, pocky State or Condition.

†**ˈpockish,** *a. Obs.* [f. POCK *sb.* + -ISH[1].] Infected with pox (in quot., with small-pox).

1567 Q. MARY *Let.* in Robertson *Hist. Scot.* IV. an. 1567. Note *m*, [Darnley is called a] a pockish man.

pockmanteau. *Sc.* Also **poke-, poak-, pack-, -mantie, -manty, -manky.** Corruption of PORTMANTEAU, confused with *pock*, POKE, bag.

1583 *Leg. Bp. St. Androis* 564 How yt his packmantie was maed, I think it best for to declair. **1638** J. ROW *Red-Shankes Serm.* (1828) B iv b, They were posting to Rome with a Poakmantie behind them, and what was in their Poakmantie, (trow ye?) **1723** MESTON *Poet. Wks., Knight* 9 Bearing his luggage and his lumber,..In a pockmanteau or a wallet. **1815** SCOTT *Guy M.* xlv, It's been the gipsies that took yoar pockmanky when they fand the chaise stickin' in the snaw! **1893** CROCKETT *Stickit Minister* 69 A man canna gang aboot six year wi' a pokemantie withoot seein' somethin' o' baith sides o' life.

pock-mark (ˈpɒkmɑːk), *sb.* Also **pock mark, pockmark.** [f. POCK *sb.* + MARK *sb.*[1]] A scar, mark, or 'pit' left by a pustule, esp. of smallpox. Also *fig.*

1673 *Wedderburn's Vocab.* 20 (Jam.) *Foveae variolarum*, pock-marks. **1851** D. JERROLD *St. Giles* ii. 15 His flat broad face was..thinly sprinkled with deep pock-marks. **1952** G. WILSON *Julien Ware* i. 5 In the yard outside the bail a second cow..stumbled uncertainly..over the sun-dried pock-marks and ridges carved by her own hoofs..when the mud of winter lay there. **1954** G. DURRELL *Bafut Beagles* ix. 156 A steady downpour..turned the red earth of the great courtyard into a shimmering sea of blood-red clay freckled with pockmarks of the falling rain. **1966** L. COHEN *Beautiful Losers* I. 23 Can I yearn after pimples and pock marks? **1976** M. GREEN *Children of Sun* iv. 135 Orwell, while..at Eton, had no powerful defences against the stimulus to dandyism, and..a few pock-marks remained all his life in testimony of his inoculation. **1979** R. BLYTHE *View in Winter* 85 The pock-marks of the shots are still to be seen today on the crinkle-crankle wall.

So **ˈpock-mark** *v. trans.*, to mark or disfigure with pock-marks; also *fig.*; **ˈpock-marked** *a.*, scarred or 'pitted' with pock-marks; also *fig.*

1756 *N. Jersey Archives* (1898) XX. 16 Terence Milford, ..has short brown hair, a little pock-marked. **1899** STEAD in *Review of Rev.* May 493/2 The whole area is pock-marked with public houses. **1908** *Flag* (Union Jack Club) 39 The floors lower down were pock-marked with splashes of the liquid. **1928** *Daily Express* 17 Apr. 10/2 Petrol pumps that pockmark the English countryside. **1952** V. CANNING *House of Seven Flies* xi. 155 The oars pock-marking the dark current with white eddies. **1957** L. DURRELL *Justine* I. 68 The silence pock-marked by the sound of our horses' hooves. **1963** V. NABOKOV *Gift* v. 306 A Georgian socialist with a pockmarked face. **1964** A. WYKES *Gambling* i. 10 He risked his own somewhat pockmarked career. **1973** *Country Life* 14 June 1751/1 Hollyhocks can be sprayed..to suppress rust-disease, whose orange pustules otherwise would soon pock-mark the foliage. **1977** H. INNES *Big Footprints* I. i. 9 Walls pock-marked with bullets. **1979** V. CANNING *Satan Sampler* ix. 183 A fierce spring shower was pock-marking the surface of the lake.

pock-pudding, Sc. var. POKE-PUDDING.

†**ˈpockwood.** *Obs.* [f. POCK *sb.* + WOOD *sb.*] The wood of a tree of the genus *Guaiacum*, formerly used for the cure of syphilis; = GUAIACUM 2, LIGNUM VITÆ 2: cf. *pock-tree* in POCK *sb.* 4. **b.** *attrib.* **pockwood-tree**: = GUAIACUM 1, LIGNUM VITÆ 1.

1590 HESTER *French-Pockes* ¶ iij b, *Lignum Guaiacum*, commonly called Pockwood. **1600** J. PORY tr. *Leo's Africa* IX. 357 That wood..is used by the African phisicians for the curing of the French poxe, whereupon it is commonly called by the name of pock-wood. **1678** PHILLIPS (ed. 4), *Pockwood-tree*,..an Indian Tree, the Wood whereof is brought over in great quantities, by reason of its great virtue, and use in Physick. **1718** QUINCY *Compl. Disp.* 103 Holy-wood, or Pock-wood is the Wood of a Tree that grows very tall in the East-Indies. **1764** GRAINGER *Sugar Cane* I. 37 *note*, The *lignum vitæ* or pockwood-tree.

pocky (ˈpəʊkɪ), *sb. Sc. dial.* [f. *pock*, POKE *sb.*[1] + -Y, dim. suffix.] A small 'pock' or bag.

1889 BARRIE *Window in Thrums* xx. 190 There's the pocky ..ye gae me to keep the sewin' things in.

pocky (ˈpɒkɪ), *a.*[1] Now *rare.* [f. POCK *sb.* + -Y.]

1. Full of or marked with pocks or pustules; *spec.* infected with the pox (i.e., usually, syphilis).

c **1350** *Nominale Gall.-Angl.* 198 (E.E.T.S.) *Femme ad face verolee*, Woman hath face pokky [*MS.* polky]. **1483** *Cath. Angl.* 286/1 Pokky, *porriginosus*. **1530** TINDALE *Pract. Prelates* Wks. (Parker Soc.) II. 313 Our fair young daughter was sent to the old pocky king of France, the year before our mortal enemy. *a* **1548** HALL *Chron., Hen. VIII* 47 b, The Dutchmen..spake shamefully of this mariage, that a feble old & pocky man should mary so fayre a lady. **1640** PARKINSON *Theat. Bot.* 450 Under colour of giving physicke to their pockie patients. **1730** SWIFT *Lady's Dressing-room* 134 To him that looks behind the scene, Statira's but some pocky queen. **1822–34** *Good's Study Med.* (ed. 4) II. 601 *note*, A healthy wet nurse, getting a sore nipple, in consequence of suckling a pocky child.

†**b.** As a coarse expression of reprobation or dislike, or merely intensive. In quot. 1601 as *adv.* (Cf. *mangy.*) *Obs.*

1598–9 B. JONSON *Case is Altered* v. ii, Plaguy boy! he sooths his humour; these French villains have pocky wits. **1601** DEACON & WALKER *Answ. Darrel* 79 Were not this pockie good stuffe..to pester your Pulpit withall? *a* **1619** FLETCHER *Bonduca* v. iii, Oh villain, pocky villain! **1663** DRYDEN *Wild Gallant* IV. i, But that's his pocky humour.

2. Pertaining to, or of the nature of, a pock or pustule, or the pox (i.e., usually, syphilis; sometimes, small-pox); syphilitic or variolous.

1555 BRADFORD in Strype *Eccl. Mem.* (1721) III. App. xlv. 135 With theyr pockeye plasteres and sores. **1600** ROWLANDS *Lett. Humours Blood* ix. 15 But neuer in like pockie heate before. **1658** A. FOX *Würtz' Surg.* II. xviii. 129 Mercurial Ointment is good for lameness and pocky biles. **1752** *Phil. Trans.* XLVII. 504 A pledgit dipp'd in the pocky matter was applied to the excoriated part. **1822–34** *Good's Study Med.* (ed. 4) IV. 499 The pocky itch is so denominated from the resemblance of the pustules to minute small-pox. **1843** SIR T. WATSON *Lect. Princ. Physic* lxxxix. II. 781 This has needlessly been made a separate species of itch, *scabies purulenta*, pocky itch.

pocky, *a.*[2] *Sc. local.* [f. *pock*, POKE *sb.*[1] + -Y.] Characterized by having pokes or bags; baggy; popularly applied in Orkney to a form of cloud, called by some *mammato-cumulus*, the lower surface of which consists of an assemblage of rounded forms like small bags.

(Not in Eng. or general Sc. use.)

1862 C. CLOUSTON in A. Mitchell *Pop. Weather Prognostics Scotl.* 15, I first observed this kind of cloud (cumulous-like festoons of drapery) on 5th March 1822... When properly developed, it was always followed by a storm or gale within twenty-four hours. It is called 'Pocky cloud' by our [Orkney] sailors. **1867** —— *Explan. Pop. Weather Progn. Scotl.* Pref. 4 The festooned or pocky cloud. *Ibid.* 14. **1880** C. LEY in *Nature* XXI. 210/2 The clouds which have been in England [i.e. in Orkney] denominated 'pocky clouds'. **1887** ABERCROMBY *Weather* iii. 78 In Orkney, this is known as the 'pocky cloud', and is there usually followed by a severe gale of wind.

‖**poco** ('poko), *adv. Mus.* [It.] A little, rather: used in musical directions.

1724 *Explication of Foreign Words in Musick Bks.* 56 *Poco*, a little less, and is just contrary to the forgoing Word *Piu.* **1760** L. STERNE *Tristram Shandy* II. vi. 48 How does the *Poco piu* and the *Poco meno* of the *Italian* artists;—the insensible, more or less, determine the precise line of beauty. *a* **1817** [see ALLEGRETTO]. **1884** F. NIECKS *Conc. Dict. Mus. Terms* 194 *Poco* (It.), a little—*Poco a poco*, little by little; *poco allegro*, somewhat quick. **1963** *Times* 16 Jan. 11/1 Perhaps his tone in *mezzo* or *poco forte* should have been more incisive. **1969** *Listener* 4 Sept. 320/2 In the melodic lines of the *Poco Adagio*..the pervading interval not only shapes the..themes but provides the movement of the harmonic bass lines.

‖**poco-curante** (,pokoku'rante), *a.* and *sb.* [It., f. *poco* little + *curante*, pr. pple. of *curare* to care:—L. *cūrāre.*] **a.** *adj.* Caring little; careless, indifferent, *nonchalant.* **b.** *sb.* A careless or indifferent person; one who shows little interest or concern.

1762 STERNE *Tr. Shandy* VI. xx, Leave we my mother —(truest of all the *Poco-curante's* of her sex!) careless about it. **1815** MOORE *Mem.* (1853) II. 76 That idlest of all *poco-curante* places, Dublin. **1823** PRAED *Troubadour* I. 74 Poco-curante in all cases Of furious foes, or pretty faces. **1881** *Sat. Rev.* 9 July 32/1 Lord Granville's pleasant faculty of pococurante conversation.

Hence ,**poco-cu'rantish** *a.*, having a *poco-curante* character, somewhat careless; ,**poco-cu'rantism, -teism**, the character, spirit, or style of a *poco-curante*; indifference; indifferentism.

1821 *Examiner* 491/1 Criticism has been a little Poco-curantish of late years. **1824** *Ibid.* 250/1 This poco-curantish disposition. **1831** MOORE *Mem.* (1854) VI. 228 So far did this poco-curantism of theirs extend, that, even in the trifling article of franking, not one of them..ever offered, when in office, to be of any service to me. **1835** ARNOLD in Stanley *Life* (1845) I. vii. 419, I suppose that Poco-curanteism (excuse the word) is much the order of the day amongst young men. **1846** HT. MARTINEAU *Hist. Peace* III. v. ii. 202 His great and fatal fault..his affectation of scepticism and *pococuranteism.* **1882** *Times* 1 Mar., The House of Commons was counted out... This demonstration of pococurantism may be thought somewhat surprising after the heat and storm of the past few days.

pocok, obs. form of PEACOCK.

Pocomania (pəʊkə'meɪnɪə). Also with lower-case initial. [Origin unknown: prob. Hispanicized form of native name, with second element interpreted as MANIA.] A Jamaican religious rite combining revivalism with ancestor-worship and spirit possession; the cult in which this rite is practised. Also *attrib.* Hence **poco'maniac**, an adherent of this cult; **pocoma'niacal** *a.*

[**1929** M. W. BECKWITH *Black Roadways* 176 Revivalist and Obeah Man unite in the particular religious cult known as the Pukkumerian... The Pukkumerians hold their meetings near a grave-yard, and it is to the ghosts of their own membership that they appeal when spirits are summoned to a meeting... 'They jump and dance and sing and talk in a secret language because the spirits do not talk our language.'] **1938** Z. HURSTON *Voodoo Gods* (1939) ii. 10, I went to the various 'tables' set in Pocomania, which boils down to a mixture of African obeah and Christianity enlivened by very beautiful singing. **1957** F. HENRIQUES *Jamaica* x. 184 Of the specifically native cult groups Pocomania is the most powerful and active. *Ibid.* 185 Native churches..incorporated a degree of physical enthusiasm, evinced in dancing, violent singing, and clapping... It is from this type of activity that such cult groups as Pocomania arose. **1957** *Times Lit. Suppl.* 11 Oct. 612/4 The second part of the book is a study of contemporary Jamaican life... He deals with..the significance of cult-groups such as the Pocomaniacs. **1959** A. SALKEY *Quality of Violence* ii. 36 He told them that the Jamaican celebration of Pocomania closely resembled Haitian Voodoo. *Ibid.* iv. 54 There were about twenty-five people gyrating and uttering Pocomaniacal prayers. **1971** J. BRUNNER *Honky in Woodpile* iv. 31 They broke up religious ceremonies, in particular *pocomania*, rites of possession using the *yoma-xi* drug. **1974** L. WATSON *Romeo Error* I. iii. 80 In Zambia, traditional healers cast out evil spirits by holding a patient's head under a blanket and over a smoking brazier, where he is forced to hyperventilate by breathing very rapidly and shallowly... The pocomania ceremonies in Jamaica are built round 'tromping', which is a rhythm of foot-stamping and peculiar breathing sounds. **1976** BOOT & THOMAS *Jamaica* 82/2 When..the Pocomaniacs feel the spirit quickening in them, they jump and shout and testify till they get so drunk with righteous heaven-sent electricity they froth at the mouth.

pocones, -is: see PUCCOON.

‖**pocosin, poquosin** (pə'kəʊsɪn). *Amer.* Also 7 **pocosen, poquosin, -on,** (8 **percoarson, -koson**), 8–9 **poc(c)oson,** 9 **pocasan.** [Algonquin *poquosin.*

According to W. W. Tooker in *Amer. Anthropologist* Jan. 1899 (N.S.) I. 162–170, meaning 'at or near the opening out or widening', f. *poquo* to break, open out, widen + (*e*)*s* dimin. + *-in(g)* locative suffix. 'The application of the term therefore..was to indicate or describe a locality where water 'backed up' in spring freshets, or in rainy seasons, and which by reason of [this] became more or less marshy or boggy.' As the name of a river in Virginia, the word is found as early as 1635.]

In Southern U.S., A tract of low swampy ground, usually wooded; a marsh, a swamp.

1634 in *Amer. Speech* (1940) XV. 296/2 From that runn along the side of the Pocoson or great Otter pond soe called. **1681** *Rec. Court of New Castle on Delaware* (1904) 504, 74 perches to a Corner marked spannish oake standing neare a pocosen. **1709** J. LAWSON *Hist. Carolina* 26 The Swamp I now spoke of, is not a miry Bog,..but you go down to it thro' a steep Bank, at the Foot of which, begins this Valley... The Land in this Percoarson, or Valley, being extraordinary rich, and the Runs of Water well stor'd with Fowl. *Ibid.* 57 We lay in a rich Perkoson, or low Ground, that was hard-by a Creek, and good dry Land. **1711** in *Virginia Mag. Hist. & Biogr.* V. (1897) July 9 The rest carried the horses 3 mile through a terribly myery Pocoson to a verry great marsh to a River side. **1760** WASHINGTON *Writ.* (1889) II. 163 Black mould taken out of the Pocoson on the creek side. **1784** J. F. D. SMYTH *Tour U.S.* I. 106 Rode along upon a wooden causeway, through a marsh, which is here [North Carolina] called a poccoson. **1875** W. C. KERR *Rep. of the Geol. Survey of N. Carolina* I. 15 There is a large aggregate of territory (between 3,000 and 4,000 square miles), mostly in the counties bordering on the seas and the sounds, known as Swamp Lands. They are locally designated as 'dismals' or 'pocosins', of which the great Dismal Swamp on the borders of North Carolina and Virginia is a good type. **1895** *Educat. Rev.* Nov. 358 The various stages of sound, lagoon, salt marsh, and pocoson are too familiar.

pocques, obs. form of *pocks*: see POCK *sb.*

†**poculary**, *a.* (*sb.*) *Obs. rare*[−1]. [ad. mod.L. *pōculāri-us*, f. *pōcul-um* cup: see -ARY[1].] Pertaining to a cup, i.e. to drinking; in quot. absol. as *sb.* A pardon or indulgence for drinking.

Erroneously explained as = 'cup' by Davies, whence in other Dicts.: cf. note s.v. MANUARY on the same passage.

1537 tr. *Latimer's Serm. bef. Convoc.* D j b, Some brought forth canonizations, some expectations, some pluralities and unions, some tot-quots and dispensations, some pardons, and these of wonderful variety, some stationaries, some jubilaries, some pocularies for drinkers, some manuaries for handlers of relicks..some oscularies for kissers.

pocu'lation. *nonce-wd.* [As if f. L. *pōculārī to frequent the cup, f. *pōcul-um* (see prec.): see -ATION.] Drinking (of wine or other intoxicating liquor).

1837 *New Monthly Mag.* XLIX. 580 The art of poculation, if so it may be termed, being of the highest antiquity, and the claims of Bacchus as the inventor of the art being unquestioned.

†'**poculent**, *a. Obs. rare.* [ad. L. *pōculentus* drinkable.] Fit for drinking; furnishing drink.

1626 BACON *Sylva* §630 Some of those Herbs, which are not Esculent, are notwithstanding Poculent; As Hops, Broom.

poculiform ('pɒkjʊlɪfɔːm), *a. Nat. Hist.* [f. L. *pōcul-um* (see POCULARY) + -(I)FORM.] Of the form of a cup or drinking-vessel; cup-shaped.

1832 LINDLEY *Introd. Bot.* IV. 379 *Poculiform*, cup-shaped, with a hemispherical base and an upright limb; nearly the same as campanulate. **1887** W. PHILLIPS *Brit. Discomycetes* 55 Cup poculiform, oblique, substipitate.

poculum ('pɒkjʊləm). *Rom. Antiq.* Pl. **pocula.** [L.] A cup or drinking-vessel.

1863 W. CHAFFERS *Marks & Monograms Pott. & Porc.* 15 Figure 16 is a poculum of the Castor Ware of white paste. **1884** A. RICH *Dict. Rom. & Gr. Antiq.* 514/1 *Poculum*, a general term for any description of vessel employed as a drinking-cup, and thus including all the special ones. **1965** *Amer. N. & Q.* Mar. 106/1 Visitors can admire a series of cases, bright vases..and decorated 'pocula'.

pocyll(e: see POCILL.

pod (pɒd), *sb.*[1] [Origin obscure: it does not seem to be connected with the later word POD *sb.*[2]]

1. The earlier form of PAD *sb.*[3] 8: the socket of a brace in which the end of the bit is inserted.

1573 TUSSER *Husb.* (1878) 36 Strong exeltred cart, that is clouted and shod, Cart ladder and wimble, with percer and pod. **1823** P. NICHOLSON *Pract. Build.* 254 The lower part of the other limb of the stock is of brass, which is fixed by means of a screw passing through two ears of the brass part, and through the solid of the wood. This brass part is called the pod, and is furnished with a mortise, in the form of a square pyramid, for receiving different pieces of steel, which are secured by means of a spring in the pod. *Ibid.*, Bits are those pieces of steel which are inserted in the pod.

b. 'The straight channel or groove in the body of certain forms of augers and boring-bits'.

1890 in *Cent. Dict.*

2. *Comb.* **pod-bit**: see quot.

1875 KNIGHT *Dict. Mech.*, *Pod-bit*, a boring-tool adapted to be used in a brace. It has a semicylindrical form, a hollow barrel, and at its end is a cutting lip which projects in advance of the barrel.

pod (pɒd), *sb.*[2] [A comparatively recent word, first found with its compounds and derivatives late in 17th c. Origin unknown.

Pod and *podder* appear first *c* 1680, the latter being known earlier than the former; PODWARE occurs 1584, but in origin is not certainly a compound of *pod*. The earlier word for *pod* was *cod*, spec. in *pease-cod*; in 1681 *podders* were explained as 'pease-cod gatherers about London'.]

1. a. A seed-vessel of a long form, usually dry and dehiscent; properly of leguminous and cruciferous plants; a legume or siliqua; but often extended to other long fruits.

1688 R. HOLME *Armoury* II. 85/1 The pod, or berry; is the first knitting of fruit, when the Flower is fallen off. **1706** PHILLIPS, *Pod*, the Husk of any Pulse. **1731–3** MILLER *Gard. Dict.* s.v. *Pisum*, Causing their Leaves to flag, and their Blossoms to fall off without producing Pods. **1760** J. LEE *Introd. Bot.* I. vi. (1765) 13 *Siliqua*, a Pod, is a Pericarpium of two Valves. **1764** GRAINGER *Sugar Cane* I. 604 *note*, The pods [of the cacao]..seldom contain less than thirty nuts of the size of a flatted olive. **1785** MARTYN *Rousseau's Bot.* iii. (1794) 38 You will understand this distinction..if you open the pod of a pea and of a stock at the same time. **1807** J. BARLOW *Columb.* II. 501 From opening pods unbinds the fleecy store. **1833** R. WALKER *Flora Oxfordsh.* 210 The singular figure of the pods of the Horse-shoe vetch must strike the most casual observer. **1866** *Treas. Bot.*, *Pod*, the capsule or seed-case of leguminous and cruciferous plants, those of the former being called legumes, and those of the latter siliques, and silicules. **1882** MRS. RIDDELL *Daisies & B.* I. 114 Where the broad-beans are now in pod. **1904** *Speaker* 23 Apr. 90/1 He gained a copper to buy some pods of red pepper to season the coarse bread. **1905** *Ibid.* 30 Dec. 322/1 These poems are as like as peas in a pod.

b. Colloq. phr. *in pod*: pregnant; also *fig.*

1890 BARRÈRE & LELAND *Dict. Slang* II. 141/2 *Pod, in*, in the family way. **1922** JOYCE *Ulysses* 385 Costello..would sing a bawdy catch..about a wench that was put in pod of a jolly swashbuckler. **1935** L. DURRELL *Spirit of Place* (1969) 33, I am in pod again and am pupping a novel. **1958** P. MORTIMER *Daddy's gone a-Hunting* xi. 60, I married you because you were in pod. **1968** M. BRAGG *Without City Wall* xxvii. 245 Your working-class lad is still a bit worried if he gets his girl in pod. **1972** 'R. GORDON' *Doctor on Brain* xxvi. 190 But why didn't Josephine just tell you she suspected she was in pod? **1976** J. MCNEISH *Glass Zoo* II. xvi. 179 It wasn't Leonard who got Marsh's sister in pod.

c. *slang.* Marijuana. Cf. POT *sb.*[5]

1952 [see JIVE *sb.* 4]. **1952** [see JOINT *sb.* 14c]. **1955** *Amer. Speech* XXX. 304, 'I got no eyes for turning on with pod' (I have absolutely no use for smoking marijuana). **1959** W. BURROUGHS *Naked Lunch* 8 A square wants to come on hip. .. Talks about 'pod', and smokes it now and then. **1979** *High Times* Mar. 19/1 Pod. Say it aloud. It's so much better than 'pot'. A marijuana mantra. *Ibid.*, Pod suggests seeds, buds, pollen, odors, all the multi-dimensional sensual life of the fine plant, while pot ought to remain a word for a thing you plant pod in.

2. *transf.* **a.** The cocoon of the silk-worm. **b.** The case or envelope of the eggs of a locust.

1753 HANWAY *Trav.* (1762) I. v. lxiii. 291 The size which we usually most esteem, is wound off sixteen or eighteen pods or cocoons. **1880** *Times* 10 Nov. 4/6 The cases or 'pods' (as they are called from their shape) of locusts' eggs. **1884** J. G. WOOD in *Sunday Mag.* May 307/1 When these [locusts'] eggs are laid, they are enclosed in a horny envelope called a 'pod', each pod containing thirty-five eggs.

3. A large protuberant abdomen. *dial.*

a **1825** FORBY *Voc. E. Anglia*, *Pod*, a fat protuberant belly. **1888** *Berkshire Gloss.*, *Pod*, a large stomach.

4. A purse-net with a narrow neck for catching eels. Also *pod-net.*

1882 *Blackw. Mag.* Jan. 103 The pods are hauled into the boat and detached from the main net and their contents emptied into a tub. **1883** G. C. DAVIES *Norfolk Broads* xxxii. (1884) 246 The eels passing down the river make their way into the long 'pods' through the narrow necks or apertures of the stops, and cannot find their way back. **1892** *Longman's Mag.* Nov. 88 In this long wall of net are three or four openings, to which purse-nets, about eighteen feet long, stretched on hoops..are attached, the far ends being closed. These 'pods' as they are called, are extended down stream and attached to stakes in the river bottom, their positions being marked by floats. **1893** J. WATSON *Conf. Poacher* 99 The method of working the pod-net is the same in principle.

†**5.** The blade of a cricket-bat. *Obs.*

1833 NYREN *Yng. Cricketer's Tutor* 111 When the practice of bowling length balls was introduced..it became absolutely necessary to change the form of the bat... It was therefore made straight in the pod. **1850** 'BAT' *Crick. Man.* 31 Instead..of the curved form of the pod, it was made straight. *c* **1862** *Handbk. Cricket* (Rtldg.) 11 The regulation size of the bat is thirty-eight inches in length, of which twenty-one inches are taken up by the pod, or, according to the more modern term, the blade.

6. *Geol.* A body of ore or rock whose length greatly exceeds its other dimensions.

1942 T. P. THAYER in *Bull. U.S. Geol. Survey* No. 935. 23 Chromite deposits of the sack-form variety are notable for their variation in size and shape... The majority..might be termed lenses or pods, as their length greatly exceeds their width. **1969** BENNISON & WRIGHT *Geol. Hist. Brit. Isles* iii. 42 They occur as isolated pods distributed very widely through the Scourian granulites and their Inverian derivatives. **1977** *Bulletin* (Sydney) 22 Jan. 69/3 The Darling Range deposits grade only between 28 and 36 percent aluminium oxide. Also, they occur in pods, instead of more or less continuous orebodies.

7. An elongated, streamlined compartment attached to an aircraft and containing an engine, fuel tanks, or the like; a detachable compartment in a spacecraft; also, any protruding or detachable casing on or in a craft or vehicle.

1950 J. V. CASAMASSA *Jet Aircraft Power Systems* 318 Jet pods are mounted beneath the wings. **1951** *Engineering* 6 July 8/2 One of the reasons for mounting jet engines on 'pods'..was because it was impossible to bury the engines in thin wings. **1955** POHL & KORNBLUTH *Space Merchants* ii. 23 The cargo pod of the 'copter hit the concrete a yard from where we stood. **1963** *New Scientist* 9 May 320/3 Rides are being 'hitch-hiked' on Atlas rockets for pods of space instruments. **1965** *Guardian* 25 Aug. 9/2 They [*sc.* two astronauts] had ejected the radar evaluation pod, a 76 lb. satellite. **1967** *Jane's Surface Skimmer Systems 1967–68* 91/2 Power is transmitted through a mechanical right-angle drive transmission to a propeller at the aft end of a strut and pod assembly. **1973** *Sci. Amer.* Aug. 13/1 A rotating radome, or radar pod, is mounted on two struts above the rear section of the fuselage. **1976** *Good Motoring* May 21/2 A particularly quiet car, allowing most of the sound from speakers front and rear to be appreciated. Three pairs fitted at the rear offer a choice from large flush, small flush or pods. **1977** W. MARSHALL *Thin Air* xi. 148 The fuel from the main tanks ran out and was replaced a moment later by the Kerosene from the secondary pods.

8. *attrib.* and *Comb.*, as ***pod-flower***, ***-seed***; (sense 1 c) ***pod smoke***, ***-smoker***; ***pod-bearing***, ***-like***, ***-shaped*** adjs.; **pod corn**, a variety of maize, *Zea mays* var. *tunicata*, in which each kernel, as well as the whole ear, is enclosed in a husk; **pod-fern**, a name of *Ceratopteris thalictroides*, a peculiar tropical aquatic fern, the fertile fronds of which are divided into linear and somewhat siliquose segments; **pod-lover**, collector's name of a noctuid moth, *Dianthœcia capsophila*; **pod maize** = *pod corn*; **pod-pepper**, a common name for capsicum; **pod-shell**, an American kind of razor-shell, *Pharus*; **pod-shrimp**, an entomostracan having the carapace hinged lengthwise upon its back, so as to close like a bivalve shell.

1878 J. R. LUMBY in *Queen's Printers' Bible-Aids* Gloss. s.v. *Pulse*, 'Pulse' in 2 Sam. xvii. 28 means *pod-bearing plants, such as beans, pease, or lentils. **1893** *Science* 17 Nov. 268/1 The kernel of the *pod corn does not present structural differences markedly unlike that of the flint corn ..but this type differs from all others in that each kernel has a husk of its own..; hence the name pod corn. **1923** WALLACE & BRESSMANN *Corn & Corn Growing* xxvi. 147 Pod corn—each kernel enclosed by a husk as well as the entire ear. **1957** E. HYAMS *Speaking Garden* viii. 106 There occurs as a kind of aberration among maize a plant called pod-corn. **1976** R. W. JUGENHEIMER *Corn* iii. 41 Podcorn is not being grown commercially. **1776** MICKLE tr. *Camoens' Lusiad* 386 Yellow *pod-flowers every slope adorn. **1697** *Phil. Trans.* XIX. 396 Plants of a strange Nature, bearing *pod-like Fruit. **1776** WITHERING *Brit. Plants* (1796) I. 260 A very long pod-like capsule. **1904** T. F. HUNT *Cereals in Amer.* x. 164 *Pod maize is rarely grown. **1914** J. BURTT-DAVY *Maize* iv. 103 In 'pod maize'..the glumes are large, completely enclosing the ovary and persisting around the ripe grain. **1866** ROGERS *Agric. & Prices* I. iii. 51 The cheapest corn year is the dearest for *pod-seed. **1830** LINDLEY *Nat. Syst. Bot.* 20 Fruit..*pod-shaped and dehiscent. **1877** *Encycl. Brit.* VI. 663/2 *Nebalia*..seems but the puny and degenerate representative of the once giant *pod-shrimps of Silurian times. **1979** *High Times* Mar. 19/1 The culture that made it possible for jazz musicians to turn sweet *pod smoke into sweet soul sounds. *Ibid.*, Early jazz-musician *pod smokers.

† **pod**, *sb.*[3] *Obs.* [Origin obscure. Cf. early mod.Fris. *pudde* 'mustela piscis' (Kilian).] A young jack or pike (fish).

1587 HARRISON *England* III. iii. (1878) II. 18 The pike as he ageth, receiueth diuerse names, as from a frie to a gilthed, from a gilthed to a pod, from a pod to a iacke, from a iacke to a pickerell, from a pickerell to a pike, and last of all to a luce.

pod, *sb.*[4] orig. *U.S.* [Origin unknown.] A small herd or 'school' of seals or whales, or sometimes of other animals; a small flock of birds.

1832 D. WEBSTER *Let. to White* 14 Sept. in *Priv. Corr.* (1857) I. 526 We saw several small pods of coots go by. **1840** F. D. BENNETT *Whaling Voy.* II. 171 The Sperm Whale is gregarious; and usually occurs in parties, which are termed by whalers 'schools' and 'pods'. **1897** *Speaker* 16 Jan. 68/2 The 'bachelors' [seals] are driven into pods. **1898** F. T. BULLEN *Cruise Cachalot* v. 36 Small pod o cows [whales], an one 'r two bulls layin' off to west'ard of 'em.

pod (pɒd), *v.*[1] [f. POD *sb.*[2]]

1. *intr.* To bear or produce pods.

1734 CURTEIS in *Phil. Trans.* XXXVIII. 273, I planted six Beans in a Pot,..they bloom'd as freely as those which are planted in the Ground, but did not pod so well, having not above a pod or two on each Plant. **1762** MILLS *Syst. Pract. Husb.* I. 464 The best way to make peas pod well. **1833** *Ridgemont Farm Rep.* 141 in *Libr. Usef. Knowl., Husb.* III, Beans certainly pod much better when not crowded together. **1893** *Westm. Gaz.* 17 June 6/2 The peas have failed to pod, and are being cut for fodder.

2. *trans.* To gather (peas, etc.) in the pod.

1805 R. W. DICKSON *Pract. Agric.* II. 587 The business of picking or podding the peas is usually performed by the labourers at a fixed price.

3. To hull or empty (peas, etc.) out of the pods.

1902 *Encycl. Brit.* XXVI. 558/1 By the aid of modern machinery..the peas are podded by a 'huller'.

4. *intr.* To swell out like a pod.

1890 *Columbus Dispatch* 9 July, Twelve intelligent eyes podded until one could have snared them with grape vines.

Hence **'podding** *vbl. sb.*, the production or formation of pods.

1766 *Compl. Farmer* s.v. *Pease*, Both these kinds of..peas are particularly apt to degenerate, and become later in their podding. **1893** *Times* 6 July 4/6 Spring sorts [of beans] shed their flowers without podding.

pod, *v.*[2] Now *dial.* [Origin obscure.] *trans.* To prod, to poke.

1530 PALSGR. 661/2, I podde. **1570** LEVINS *Manip.* 155/38 To Podde, or porre, *pungere*. **1878** *Cumbld. Gloss.*, *Pod*,..to poke. **1903** *Eng. Dial. Dict.* s.v., He podded mi i' t'ribs wi' his walkin' stick.

Hence **'podder**, one who prods.

a **1640** JACKSON *Creed* x. xxxix. §19 To use some in our parliaments as their podders, to drive us into it.

pod, *v.*[3] [f. POD *sb.*[4]] *trans.* To drive (seals, etc.) into a 'pod' or bunch for the purpose of clubbing them.

1887 *Fisheries of U.S.* Sect. v. II. 366 *note*, A singular lurid green light suddenly suffuses the eye of the fur-seal at intervals when it is very much excited, as the 'podding' for the clubbers is in progress. **1897** *Speaker* 17 Jan. 68/2 Females [seals] are often podded with the 'bachelors'.

pod: see PAD *sb.*[1], toad, frog; also PODE.

† **'podage.** *Obs. rare*[−1]. [ad. med.L. *podāgium* (1259 in Du Cange), variant of *pedāgium*.] = PEDAGE: see quot. *c* 1425 s.v.

‖ **podagra** ('pɒdəgrə, pəʊ'dægrə). *Med.* [L. *podagra*, a. Gr. ποδάγρα gout in the feet, lit. a trap for the feet, f. πούς, ποδ- foot + ἄγρα a catching.] Gout in the feet; by extension, gout generally.

1398 TREVISA *Barth. De P.R.* VII. lviii. (Bodl. MS.), Podagra is a sore yuel in þe feete and namelich in þe wrestes and in soles. **1460** CAPGRAVE *Chron.* (Rolls) 40 Podegra, and that seknes thei sey cometh of grete plente of mete and mech rest. **1596** DALRYMPLE tr. *Leslie's Hist. Scot.* IV. 259 The Podagra or Gout, quhilk of the Vehemencie of calde he contracted, Vttirlie ouirthrew his preclare Jugementis. **1799** *Med. Jrnl.* I. 149 According to the opinion of the celebrated Prof. Tode,..hypochondriasis is merely an imperfect podagra residing in the stomach and bowels. **1876** tr. *Wagner's Gen. Pathol.* 577 True gout, Podagra, consists, according to some, of the decreased excretion of uric acid by the urinary organs and an accumulation of it within the blood.

podagral ('pɒdəgrəl), *a.* [f. PODAGRA + -AL[1].] Of or pertaining to gout; gouty.

1822–34 *Good's Study Med.* (ed. 4) II. 685 A long train of dyspeptic, hepatic or podagral symptoms. **1831** *Fraser's Mag.* III. 396 Suspected of making his podagral ailments.. cover a multitude of sins. **1872** JEAFFRESON *Brides & Bridals* I. ii. 159 The land of gouty humours and podagral sufferers.

† **po'dagre**, *sb.*[1] *Obs.* Forms: 3 **poudagre**, 4–6 **podagre**, 4–5 **potagre**, 5 **potacre**. [a. OF. *podagre*, ad. L. *podagra*: see PODAGRA. (The popular repr. of *podagra* in OF. was *poacre*, *pouacre*.)] = PODAGRA.

c **1290** *S. Eng. Leg.* I. 424/128 In his fot ane hote goute, þat poudagre icleopeod is. **1340** HAMPOLE *Pr. Consc.* 2993 Som sal haf in alle þair lymmes obout, For sleuthe, als þe potagre and þe gout. **1398** TREVISA *Barth. De P.R.* VII. viii. (Bodl. MS.), Gelded men haue not podagre for þei serueþ nought venus. *c* **1440** *Promp. Parv.* 411/1 Potacre, or podagre, sekenesse, *potagra*. **1486** *Bk. St. Albans* C iij b, When yowre hawkes fete be swollyn she hath the podagre. **1578** LYTE *Dodoens* III. xv. 337 Good for podagres and aches of ioyntes.

† **po'dagre**, *a.* and *sb.*[2] *Obs.* Also 4 **podagere**, 4–5 **potagre**. [a. OF. (F.) *podagre*, a. L. *podager*, *-grum* (Ennius), ad. Gr. ποδαγρός adj., pertaining to gout: see PODAGRA.]

A. *adj.* Of or pertaining to gout; suffering from gout, gouty.

13.. *Cursor M.* 11825 (Fairf.) þe gutte podagre [*C.* þe potagre, *G.* podagere, *Tr.* potagre] es il to bete. *c* **1422** HOCCLEVE *Jereslaus's Wife* 713 Potagre and gowty & halt he was eek. **1433** LYDG. *S. Edmund* III. 649 Oon was podagre in handis, leggis, knees.

B. *sb.* A sufferer from gout.

1836 E. HOWARD *R. Reefer* xxviii, The port-admiral, for such was the ancient podagre.

podagric (pəʊ'dægrɪk), *a.* and *sb.* [ad. L. *podagric-us*, a. Gr. ποδαγρικός of or pertaining to gout, f. ποδάγρα, PODAGRA.]

A. *adj.* Of or pertaining to gout; gouty.

1702 FLOYER *Cold Baths* I. ii. (1709) 44 Both Hot and Cold Water are good..for Podagrick Pains without Ulcers. **1822–34** *Good's Study Med.* (ed. 4) II. 292 The.. constitution of a podagric patient. **1889** GRETTON *Memory's Harkb.* 197 In later life,..somewhat podagric by inheritance.

B. *sb.* A sufferer from gout.

1737 *Gentl. Mag.* VII. 56 We podagricks you know, primiers imitate, For tho' pains gnaw within, yet without we look great. **1806** A. HUNTER *Culina* (ed. 3) 101 Let the Podagric enjoy his savoury dishes, on condition that every fourth day he submits to eat..plain meat.

† **po'dagrical**, *a.* *Obs.* [f. as prec. + -AL[1].] = prec. adj.

1576 FLEMING *Panop. Epist.* 237 If you meane not to beget to your selfe the Podagricall disease for your daughter. **1646** SIR T. BROWNE *Pseud. Ep.* II. iii. 73 That a Loadstone held in the hand of one that is podagricall doth either cure or give great ease in the gout. **1672** *Phil. Trans.* VII. 4028 Some Podagrical people,..happening to be seized by the Plague, lost the Gout, and recover'd of the Plague too.

podagrous ('pɒdəgrəs), *a.* [ad. L. *podagrōsus* gouty, f. *podagra*: see PODAGRA and -OUS. So obs. F. *podagreux* (Godef.).] Gouty.

1851 COCKERELL in Lady Holland *Mem. Syd. Smith* (1855) I. 249 A podagrous disposition of limbs. **1863** SALA in *Temple Bar Mag.* VIII. 73 If it be a crime to be hereditarily podagrous, take me to the Tower.

† **'podagry.** *Obs. rare.* [a. obs. F. *podagrie* gout (16th c. in Godef.), on med.L. type **podagria*, f. Gr. ποδαγρός: see PODAGRE *a.*] = PODAGRA; in quot., dodder, or the condition of a plant infested with it (a sense of OF. *podagre* and med.L. *podagra*).

[**1640** PARKINSON *Theatr. Bot.* 11 Cuscuta..upon Line or Flax, called *Podagra Lini* and *Angina Lini*.] **1657** TOMLINSON *Renou's Disp.* 237 They..mistake, who take the podagry of other plants for true Cuscuta and Epithyme.

podal ('pəʊdəl), *a.* *Zool.* [irreg. f. Gr. πούς, ποδ- foot + -AL[1].] Belonging to feet, or foot-like organs; *spec.* applied to a membrane fringing the outer margin of the neuropodia and notopodia or ventral and dorsal foot-stumps of certain Annelida.

1896 *Cambr. Nat. Hist.* II. 323 The podal membrane reaches to the tip of the gill in the anterior segments.

‖ **podalgia** (pəʊ'dældʒɪə). [mod.L., f. Gr. πούς, ποδ- foot + ἄλγος pain.] Pain in the foot, as from gout, rheumatism, or the like.

1842 in DUNGLISON *Med. Lex.* **1895** *Syd. Soc. Lex.*, *Podalgia*, pain in the foot: almost the same as Podagra.

podalic (pəʊ'dælɪk), *a.* [irreg. f. Gr. πούς, ποδ- foot, after *cephalic*.] Of or pertaining to the feet.

podalic version (*Obstetrics*), the operation of changing the position of the fœtus so as to bring the feet to present in delivery.

1890 in *Cent. Dict.* **1899** *Syd. Soc. Lex.*, *V[ersion]*, *podalic*, [an operation in obstetrics] when one or both feet are brought down. **1900** *Lancet* 30 June 1886/1 Its aim being 'podalic', as it was to bring the lower limb to present.

podar. *dial.* Also poder. [app. a. Cornish *podar* rotten, worthless.] A local name of MUNDIC or copper pyrites.

[**1754** BORLASE *Antiq. Cornw.* Cornish-Eng. Voc. 403/2 *Podar*, rotten: corrupt: id. Mundic: ugly.] **1816** PARIS *Guide Mount's Bay & Land's End* 117 Upon the first discovery of copper ore, the miner, to whom its nature was entirely unknown, gave it the name of *Poder*... About the year 1735, ..Mr. Coster a mineralogist of Bristol observed this Poder among the heaps of rubbish.

podargus (pə'dɑːgəs). *Ornith.* [mod.L. (L. J. P. Vieillot in *Nouveau Dict. Hist. Nat.* (ed. 2, 1818) XXVII. 151), f. Gr. πόδαργος swift-footed.] A nocturnal, greyish-brown bird of the genus so called, belonging to the family Podargidæ and found in Australia, New Guinea, and the Solomon Islands; esp. the Australian tawny frogmouth, *Podargus strigoides*. Cf. FROG-MOUTH, FROG'S MOUTH 2.

1837 *Proc. Zool. Soc.* V. 67 The sclerotic ring of the great *Podargus* does not present the slightest appearance of distinct plates. **1901** A. J. CAMPBELL *Nests & Eggs Austral. Birds* II. 539 Under the heading of the Tawny-shouldered Podargus..is included *P. cuvieri*, *P. gouldi*, and the ever doubtful *P. megacephalus*. **1933** *Bulletin* (Sydney) 19 Apr. 21/4 My choice for the quietest bush bird is the tawny frogmouth, or podargus. **1961** *Coast to Coast 1959–60* 66 'You know the Podargus.' 'It's a bird. The tawny-shouldered frogmouth.'

‖ **podarthritis** (pɒdɑː'θraɪtɪs). *Med.* [f. Gr. ποδ- (see PODO-) + ARTHRITIS.] Inflammation of joints of the foot.

1857 in DUNGLISON *Dict. Med. Sc.*

poddasway, obs. Sc. f. PADUASOY.

podded ('pɒdɪd), *a.* [f. POD *sb.*[2] + -ED[2].]

1. Bearing pods; leguminous; growing (as a seed) in a pod.

1753 CHAMBERS *Cycl. Supp.* s.v. *Lotus*, The yellow, podded, sea lotus, with a thick, fleshy, and smooth leaf. **1762** MILLS *Syst. Pract. Husb.* I. 465 In the culture of this, and indeed of all other podded grains. **1805** R. W. DICKSON *Pract. Agric.* II. 622 For cleaning and earthing up different sorts of podded crops. **1869** RUSKIN *Q. of Air* (1874) 94 Podded seeds that cannot be reaped, or beaten, or shaken down, but must be gathered green.

2. *fig.* (transl. F. *cossu* podded, fig. well-off.) Well-off, comfortable, snugly secure from harm.
1889 *Spectator* 16 Nov., The working city being tainted with the deep envy of superiors, and especially of superiors leading joyous or 'podded' lives—as the French describe the lives of well-to-do citizens. **1895** *Ibid.* 21 Dec. 886/1 They may trade with profit and live on the profit in podded luxury.

3. *Aeronaut.* Mounted in a pod or pods.
1959 *Times* 26 Feb. 10/6 It has not been British practice to build aircraft with podded engines. **1960** *New Scientist* 5 May 1115/3 Unlike the United States, which has remained faithful to podded engines slung beneath the wing, Russia has resorted to both podded and buried engines in placing the power units of the *Bounder*.

podder[1] ('pɒdə(r)). [f. POD *sb.*[2] or *v.*[1] + -ER[1]; orig. a local term.] A person employed in gathering peas in the pod.
1681 BLOUNT *Glossogr.* (ed. 5), *Podders*, Pescod-gatherers about London, so called. **1706** PHILLIPS, *Podders*, poor People employ'd to gather Pease, Pease-cod Gatherers. **1765** GOLDSM. Ess. Misc. Wks. 1837 I. 248 Those who have seen.. the weeders, podders, and hoppers, who swarm in the fields. **1805** R. W. DICKSON *Pract. Agric.* II. 587 The expence of gathering green peas is different, according to the difficulty of procuring podders [etc.]. **1844** *Cheshire Gloss.*, *Podder*,.. one who gathers field peas for market.

podder[2]: see PODWARE.

podder[3]: see under POD *v.*[2]

†'**poddinger.** *Obs.* exc. *dial.* Forms: 5 puddyngare, 6 podenger, -ynger, (*dial.* -9) poddinger, 8 podinger. [An altered form of POTTINGER, perh. associated with *podyng*, PUDDING. (Intermediate between *pottinger* and *porringer*: cf. PODDISH, PODDIDGE.)] = POTTINGER, PORRINGER.
1483 *Cath. Angl.* 293/1 A Puddyngare, *tucetarius, tucetaria.* **1532** in Weaver *Wells Wills* (1890) 1 A broken krock, a plater, a podynger and a sawcer. **1552** *Bury Wills* (Camden) 142, iiij[or] pewter disshes, sixe sawcers, iij poddingers. **1599** *Acc.-Bk. W. Wray* in *Antiquary* XXXII. 243, iij podengers. **1721** in *Girl's Own P.* (1886) VII. 627 Put ye soup into it [a stewpan] by podingers, and lett every podinger full boyle up as you put it in. *c* **1812** T. WILKINSON in Gilpin *Pop. Poetry* (1875) 204 Poddingers on ivery truncher stood.

'**poddish, poddidge.** Now *dial.* Also 6 podech, 6–7 podge, 9 *dial.* podditch. [Altered form of POTAGE, POTTAGE, perh. due to some analogy: cf. PODDINGER.] = POTTAGE, PORRIDGE; now chiefly applied to oatmeal porridge.
1528 TINDALE *Obed. Chr. Man* 130 Yf the podech [*Wks.* 1573 porage] be burned to or the meate over rosted, we saye, the bysshope hath put his fote in the potte [etc.]. *a* **1590** *Marr. Wit & Wisd.* (1846) 50 How saist thou, Hodge, What, art thou hungrie? wilt thou eat my podge? **1611** COTGR., *Brouët*,.. any liquor, podge, or sauce, of the thicknesse, or consistence of that whereof our pruine-tarts are made. *c* **1746** COLLIER (Tim Bobbin) *View Lanc. Dial.* Wks. (1862) 68 Boh it leet weell atth' Podditch wur naw scawding. **1869** 'EAVESDROPPER' *Vill. Life* 4 (E.D.D.), I can git poddige for mysel' and t' barns. **1886** HALL CAINE *Son of Hagar* I. vii, I know the way to my mouth with a spoonful of poddish, and that's all. *Ibid.* II. xv, May they never lick a lean poddish-stick.

poddle, dial. var. PADDLE *v.*[1] 4.

poddock, dial. f. PADDOCK *sb.*[1], frog, toad.

'**poddy**, *a.* and *sb. colloq.* [f. POD *sb.*[2] + -Y.]
A. *adj.* **1.** Corpulent, obese.
1844 E. FITZGERALD *Lett.* (1889) I. 138 It is a grievous thing to grow poddy: the age of Chivalry is gone then.
2. (See sense B. 1 b below.)
B. *sb.* (Austral.) **1. a.** An unbranded calf.
1893 K. MACKAY *Out Back* (ed. 2) I. v. 75, I did occasionally put my brand by mistake on one of Massey's 'poddies'. **1907** G. B. LANCASTER *Tracks we Tread* iii. 52 [The wild cattle] were a mixed haul: two-year-olds, poddies and pikers. **1950** [see *clean-skins* s.v. CLEAN- 2.].
b. In full *poddy calf* (*foal*, etc.). A calf (less commonly a lamb or foal) fed by hand.
1898 *Bulletin* (Sydney) 8 Jan. (Red Page), Prof. Morris [in *Austral English*] defines 'Poddy' as 'a Vic. name for sand-mullet', but leaves out its meaning of motherless calf or foal (common in the bush). A poddy calf or a poddy foal is heard all over Australia. **1901** M. FRANKLIN *My Brilliant Career* v. 24 It was my duty to 'rare the poddies'. **1908** *Bulletin* (Sydney) 30 Jan. 14, I saw a boy.. driving back to pasture his flock of sixty or seventy newly shorn 'poddies', and it reminded me that the ewe is about the most indifferent mother in the bush. **1911** E. M. CLOWES *On Wallaby* iii. 66 He drives off with the separated milk—due from the day before for his poddy-calves. **1927** B. CRONIN *Red Dawson* xliii. 194 His whole outfit was five old cows and a coupler poddies. **1930** H. S. PALMER *Men are Human* xxv. 235 He's tame as a poddy calf. **1963** A. LUBBOCK *Austral. Roundabout* 5 The kitchen range.. had saucepans of milk, and babies' bottles and teats, boiling on the top to feed the 'poddies', as hand-fed calves and lambs are called.
2. *attrib.* and *Comb.*, as *poddy swill*; *poddy-rearing* vbl. sb.; **poddy-dodger**, one who steals unbranded calves; a cattle rustler; also *poddy-dodging* vbl. sb.
1934 *Bulletin* (Sydney) 1 Aug. 46/3 Nine *poddy-dodgers out of ten gets caught the same way. **1953** A. MOOREHEAD *Rum Jungle* ii. 30 The cattle rustlers—known as 'poddy dodgers'—followed close behind. **1970** *Sunday Mail Mag.* (Brisbane) 30 Aug. 3/5 His practice, as a 'poddy-dodger', was to steal branded cows and cleanskin calves from neighbours, then remove the calves from their mothers before they were ready. **1945** T. RONAN *Strangers on Ophir* 9 He'll be a doctor or a lawyer or a banker with no need to go *poddy-dodging for a living like his old jail-bird of a Dad. **1950** 'N. SHUTE' *Town like Alice* ix. 263 They'll come on to your station and round up the poddys and drive them off on to their own land, and then there's nothing to say they're yours. That's poddy-dodging. **1957** R. S. PORTEOUS *Brigalow* 61 Mick did a bit of poddy-dodging when things were slack... He might lift a few head of cleanskins now and then. **1901** M. FRANKLIN *My Brilliant Career* iii. 17 They do all the milkin' and pig-feedin', and *poddy-rarin'. **1941** *Coast to Coast* 108 Tug Treloar carrying buckets of *poddy swill.

poddy ('pɒdɪ), *v. Austral. colloq.* [f. PODDY *sb.*] *trans.* To feed (a young animal) by hand.
1896 H. LAWSON *While Billy Boils* (1897) 61 Then he 'poddies'—hand-feeds—the calves which have been weaned too early. **1901** M. FRANKLIN *My Brilliant Career* iv. 20 He procured fifty milch-cows, the calves of which had to be 'poddied'. **1908** *Bulletin* (Sydney) 30 Jan. 14 The squatter knows that a deserted lamb will die, also he has no time to 'poddy' it. **1931** V. PALMER *Separate Lives* 176 When her [*sc.* the filly's] mother died, that old drover said I could have her... And I did rear her, bought condensed milk to poddy her for months.

†**pode.** *Obs.* Also 6 poade. [Parallel form of PAD *sb.*[1]] A toad: perh. also applied to other creatures reputed to be venomous; also *transf.* to persons.
c **1250** [see PAD *sb.*[1] 1]. *c* **1425** *Cast. Persev.* 810 in *Macro Plays* 98 Tyl Mankynde fallith to podys prys, Coueytyse schal hym grype & grope. **14..** *Stockh. Med. MS.* I. 156 in *Anglia* XVIII. 298 Rancle.. of venym, As of jrannys or podys or vermyn. **1528** ROY & BARLOW *Rede me* (Arb.) 43 Was nott theare one called Coclaye, A littell pratye foolysshe poade?.. Yett men saye he lacketh no gall. More venemous then any toade. **1549** CHALONER *Erasmus on Folly* Qj, Thei good podes are wholy addicted to fooles and trifle-talkers.

pode, obs. form of POOD.

podel, podell(e, obs. forms of PUDDLE.

podeon ('pɒdiːən). *Entom. rare.* [a. Gr. ποδεών a narrow end, f. πούς, ποδ- foot.] A term for the petiole in the petiolate Hymenoptera: see quots.
1841 E. NEWMAN *Introd. Hist. Insects* 144 The sixth segment, *podeon* or *peduncle*, is usually much smaller than either of the preceding. **1844** GOSSE in *Zoologist* II. 587 That segment which Mr. Newman has called the *podeon* is furnished with a curious hooked spur.

poder, variant of PODAR.

‖**podere** (po'dere). Pl. **poderi** (-i). [It.] A farm or estate.
1884 S. & J. HORNER *Walks in Florence & its Environs* II. xxi. 299 Villas and their surrounding vineyards, olive gardens, and farms (*Poderi*) are enclosed within these walls. **1891** L. SCOTT *Vincigliata & Maiano* 13 The Podere of the Torre.. with its courts, trees, house, huts and vine-yards. *Ibid.* 15 Niccolò, as heir to his father, had a larger claim.. on several lots, especially the Castle of Vincigliata and its *poderi.* **1904** H. JAMES *Golden Bowl* I. iii. 57 The dear contadini of the *podere*, the little girls and the other peasants of the next podere. **1926** D. H. LAWRENCE *Sun* v. 18 Yet she missed him when he did not come to work on the podere. **1961** W. VAUGHAN-THOMAS *Anzio* vii. 137 The peasant farmers had remained in the *poderi* of the countryside. **1970** I. ORIGO *Images & Shadows* v. 116 The steep terraces of the *podere*, partly cultivated with plots of wheat.

‖**podestà** (pode'sta). Also 6–8 **podestate**, 7–8 **podestat**. [It. *podestà*:—OIt. *podestate*:—L. *potestātem*, power, authority, hence public officer, magistrate. So F. *podestat* (1762 in *Dict. Acad.*).] **a.** A governor appointed by the Emperor Frederick I (Barbarossa) over one or more cities of Lombardy. **b.** A chief magistrate elected annually in mediæval Italian towns and republics with judicial functions and almost unlimited powers. Also *transf.* **c.** A subordinate judge or magistrate in modern Italian municipalities.
1548 T. HOBY *Trav.* (1902) 10 No man weareth his weapon within the town, but such as are licensed by the Podesta. **1589** PUTTENHAM *Eng. Poesie* III. xxv. (Arb.) 308, I haue sene of the greatest podestates and grauest iudges and Presidentes of Parliament in Fraunce. **1630** *R. Johnson's Kingd. & Commw.* 135 [In London] we have a Podesta, or Maior, that keepeth a Prince-like house. **1696** tr. *Du Mont's Voy. Levant* 341 The Venitians maintain a Podestat in the Island to gather the Tribute. **1768** BOSWELL *Corsica* ii, Every.. village elects by majority of votes a Podesta and other two magistrates. **1820** BYRON *Mar. Fal.* Pref., When podesta and captain at Treviso. **1832** tr. *Sismondi's Ital. Rep.* ii. 39 When the podestà of the Emperor arrived at Milan to take possession of the tribunal, he was sent contemptuously away. **1860** *All Year Round* No. 53. 71 On the following night, the Podestà of the city suddenly died.
So **po'desterate** [f. It. *podesteria* office of a podestà + -ATE[1]], the rule or office of a podestà.
1787 J. ADAMS *Def. Govt. U.S.* (1794) II. 305 In the next year, 1280, in the podesterate of Alberigo Signoregi of Bologna.

‖**podetium** (pəʊ'diːʃɪəm). *Bot.* Pl. **-ia.** [mod.L., arbitrary f. Gr. πούς, ποδ- foot.] In some lichens (as *Cladoma*), a stalk-like or shrubby outgrowth of the thallus, bearing the apothecium or fruit; also, any stalk-like elevation.
1857 BERKELEY *Cryptog. Bot.* §445. 409 In that genus we have the first indication of a stem to the apothecia, or, as it is called, a podetium. **1870** BENTLEY *Man. Bot.* (ed. 2) 375 In the latter case the stalk has received the name of podetium.
Hence **po'detiiform** *a.*, shaped like or resembling a podetium.

‖**podex** ('pəʊdɛks). Now only *Zool.* [L. *pōdex*, *pōdic-em* anus, fundament.] The fundament, the rump; also, the last dorsal segment of the abdomen of insects, the pygidium.
1598 B. JONSON *Ev. Man in his Hum.* v. i, How Saturn, sitting in an ebon cloud, Disrobed his podex. **1706** PHILLIPS, *Podex*,.. the Fundament, or Breech. **1713** DERHAM *Phys.-Theol.* VIII. vi. 415 The Male is less than the Female,.. and its Podex not so sharp as the Females is. **1822–34** *Good's Study Med.* (ed. 4) IV. 4 These substances are contained in the respective sexes in two bags that unite near the podex. **1826** KIRBY & SP. *Entomol.* III. 390 *Podex*, the last dorsal segment of the abdomen.

pod-fern: see POD *sb.*[2]

podge (pɒdʒ), *sb. dial.* or *colloq.* [A parallel form, app. of later origin, of PUDGE *sb.*] Anything podgy; *spec.* a short fat man or woman; a short stout thick-set animal. Freq. a plump child. Also, excess weight, fat. (In quot. 1833 applied to an epaulette.)
1833 MARRYAT *P. Simple* viii, That man with the gold podge on his shoulder [the first lieutenant]. **1876** *Whitby Gloss.*, *Podge*, a dirty, fat person. **1876** *Mid.-Yorks. Gloss.*, *Podge*,.. the term is.. freely bestowed, in a good-natured manner, upon children of a fleshy appearance.. 'Come hither, thou old podge'. **1901** FARMER & HENLEY *Slang Dict.*, Podge (colloquial). **1903** in *Eng. Dial. Dict.* from Aberdeensh. to Cornwall. **1967** M. SUMMERTON *Memory of Darkness* i. 17 She used to be a horrid little podge, always whining. **1967** A. WILSON *No Laughing Matter* I. 16 Don't tease the poor Podge. Time enough when she loses all that puppy fat. **1976** *Leicester Chron.* 26 Nov., The average man is putting on too much weight, and.. needs clothes designed to help him hide the podge.

podge (pɒdʒ), *v.* Now *dial.* Also **pudge**. *intr.* To walk slowly and heavily. Hence '**podging** *ppl. a.*
1638 N. WHITING *Hist. Albino & Bellama* 141 My Dames will say, I am a podging Asse. **1866** GREGOR *Banffsh. Gloss.*, *Podge*, to walk with short heavy steps. **1876** *Mid.-Yorks. Gloss.* s.v., *Podge* is also a *v*[*erb*] *n.* denoting the heavy irregular gait usual to very fat persons. **1904** H. F. DAY *Kin o' Ktaadn* 193 Old Tay..pudges along to the tin box on the mantel. **1932** *Nat. Geogr. Mag.* July 120 Overtaken by darkness on starless nights, the swamp man crawls into a log for safety or sleep. 'We always "pudge" around first to rout out any copperheads.' **1955** E. POUND *Section: Rock-Drill* xci. 75 Farinata pudg'd still there in the cloister.

podge, obs. form of PODDISH, PODDIDGE.

podger[1] ('pɒdʒə(r)). *rare.* ? A stiff blow.
1816 LD. CAMPBELL in *Life* (1881) I. 334 He cannot deal the knock-me-down blows of old Brough, and if you watch your opportunity you may give him a podger.

podger[2] ('pɒdʒə(r)). [f. PODGE *sb.* + -ER[1].] Any of various tools having the form of a short bar (see quots.).
1888 J. G. HORNER *Dict. Terms Mech. Engin.* 377 *Tommy*, a pointed round iron bar or lever used for insertion in the holes drilled in the circular back nuts of lathes and other machines, for the purpose of tightening them up. Also a metal rod kept for insertion in the eyes of the tightening screws of hand-rest sockets, for tightening the T rest. Sometimes called a podger. **1893** —— *Princ. of Fitting* ii. 22 Fig. 18 shows a podger, employed for two purposes. The tapered end A, of round section, is used for pulling drilled or punched holes into line, so that their bolts or rivets can be inserted. The flattened end B is used like the end of a crowbar for lifting up and slipping along a casting or forging into position, or for prising open.. plates that are in close contact. **1894** W. J. LINEHAM *Textbk. Mech. Engin.* vii. 286 Before riveting a seam, the plates, if punched or drilled separately, are brought into alignment by the podger and bolted. **1971** B. SCHARF *Engin. & Language* ix. 66 A special type of single ended spanner is the podger or prong-ended spanner. This has a long, tapering handle which can be used.. to align holes which do not entirely coincide (e.g. rivet holes in plates).

podgy ('pɒdʒɪ), *a.* [f. PODGE *sb.* + -Y: a parallel form, somewhat later in appearance, of PUDGY.] Short, thick, and fat; squat.
1846 THACKERAY *Cornh. to Cairo* iii. 37, I wish I had had a shake of that trembling, podgy hand. **1856** MAYHEW *Rhine* 143 A shaggy, podgy, black pony. **1858** J. R. GREEN *Lett.* (1901) 26 The slow oily stream, beneath whose willows lurked.. podgy perch. **1861–2** *Vac. Tour.* 24 A priest on the podgy side of forty. **1898** *Allbutt's Syst. Med.* V. 832 Massage is very useful in emaciated or podgy people.
Hence '**podgily** *adv.*, in a podgy way or degree.
1893 'J. S. WINTER' *Aunt Johnnie* I. 2 She was not only fat, but she was podgily fat.

podia, plural of PODION, PODIUM.

podial ('pəʊdɪəl), *a.* [f. PODI-UM + -AL[1].] Of or pertaining to a podium.
1890 in *Cent. Dict.*

podiatry (pə'daɪətrɪ). orig. and chiefly *U.S.* [f. Gr. ποδ-, πούς foot + ἰατρεία healing: see -Y[3].]

The diagnosis and treatment of disorders of the foot; chiropody.

1914 F. von Oefele in M. J. Lewi *Text Bk. Chiropody* i. 3 The practice of foot lesions may hereafter be styled 'Helotomy' or, 'Heliatry', or more generally 'Podiatry'. **1947** P. Lewin *Foot & Ankle* (ed. 3) xxxii. 717 Podiatry is the science of treatment of certain disorders of the feet. **1958** *Technology* Feb. 425/4 The National Association of Chiropodists has announced that it has changed its title to The American Podiatry Association and that its members will henceforth be known by the 'more dignified' style of podiatrists. **1968** F. Weinstein *Princ. & Pract. Podiatry* i. 6/1 More and more hospitals [in the U.S.A.] are working toward the establishment of a regular department or division of podiatry. **1979** *Arizona Daily Star* 22 July B1/6 Podiatry problems can trigger one of many vicious circles affecting the health of the elderly.

So **podi'atric** *a.*; **po'diatrist**, one who practises podiatry; a chiropodist.

1914 F. von Oefele in M. J. Lewi *Text Bk. Chiropody* i. 50 We should prevent the possibility of such a ridiculous misunderstanding by substituting the word 'podiatrist' (physician of the foot) for the unscientific term 'chiropodist'. **1922** *Jrnl. Nat. Assoc. Chiropodists* XII. 35 (Advt.), Bachelet podiatric triplex generator. **1929** E. W. Springs *Above Bright Blue Sky* 97 I've got to hobble along and see my podiatrist. **1950** K. Newton *Geriatric Nursing* xv. 287 The aged patient will avoid serious difficulties with corns and calluses by having his feet cared for regularly by a podiatrist. **1968** T. R. Amberry in F. Weinstein *Princ. & Pract. Podiatry* viii. 138 All too often these factors are either ignored or overlooked by some surgeons, both medical and podiatric. **1974** *Telegraph* (Brisbane) 21 Mar. 16/7 The Australian Chiropody Council wants chiropodists to be called podiatrists. **1976** *Jrnl. Amer. Podiatry Assoc.* LXVI. 15 A wide variety of medications may be necessary during the hospitalization of podiatric surgical patients. **1978** *Detroit Free Press* 16 Apr. 1C/5 Podiatrists and athletes debate endlessly about proper footwear.

podical ('pəʊdɪkəl), *a. Zool.* [f. L. podex, *pōdic-* + -al[1].] Pertaining to the podex, anal.

podical plates, two or more small pieces surrounding the podex in some insects.

1877 Huxley *Anat. Inv. Anim.* vii. 406 When the tenth tergum and the podical plates are removed, a very singular apparatus..comes into view. **1888** Rolleston & Jackson *Anim. Life* 142 Common Cockroach... The anus..lies between two triangular podical plates.

'podicate, *v. humorous nonce-wd.* [f. as prec. + -ate[3].] *intr.* To slide or move along on one's posteriors. So **podi'cation** (in quot. = a blow or kick on the posteriors).

1853 Jerdan *Autobiog.* IV. 180 We managed to roll, slide, stagger and podicate to the foot in the dark. **1884** *World* 20 Aug. 9/1 Unless he wishes to risk podication.

podike: see powdike.

‖**podion** ('pɒdɪɒn). *Zool.* Pl. podia. [mod.L., a. Gr. πόδιον: see podium.] One of the tube-feet of an echinoderm.

1900 E. R. Lankester *Treat. Zool.* iii. 291 Water from the reservoir or ampulla is driven into the podion, and the tube-foot is thus rendered tense and rigid.

podism ('pɒdɪz(ə)m). *rare.* [ad. late L. *podismus* (Veg.), a. Gr. ποδισμός a measuring by feet, f. ποδίζειν to measure by feet, also to bind the feet, f. πούς, ποδ- foot.] †**a.** A measuring by feet. *Obs. rare*⁻⁰. †**b.** A footing. *Obs. rare*⁻¹. **c.** *Path.* Spasm or cramp in the foot. *rare*⁻⁰.

1681 Blount *Glossogr.* (ed. 5), *Podism* (*podismus*), a measuring by feet. **1688** R. Holme *Armoury* iii. xvi. (Roxb.) 89/1 Allowing to euery souldier a larg podisme or place to stand in. **1858** Mayne *Expos. Lex.*, *Podismus*, a term for spasm of the foot, or of the toes..: podism.

podite ('pɒdaɪt). *Zool.* [f. Gr. πούς, ποδ- foot + -ite[1].] A leg or ambulatory limb of an arthropod, esp. of a crustacean. Usually in compounds denoting a part or appendage of such a limb: see quot. 1875, and the words themselves.

1875 Huxley & Martin *Elem. Biol.* (1883) 151 The joints have the following names; the proximal, short and thick, *coxopodite*; the next, small and conical, *basipodite*; next, cylindrical and marked by an annular constriction, *ischiopodite*; the next, longer, *meropodite*; then successively, the *carpopodite*, *propodite*, and *dactylopodite*. **1878** H. Woodward in *Encycl. Brit.* VI. 635/2 These podites are usually seven-jointed, and each bears a gill on its basal-joint.

Hence **poditic** (pəʊ'dɪtɪk) *a.*, belonging to a podite.

1890 in *Cent. Dict.* **1895** in *Syd. Soc. Lex.*

podium ('pəʊdɪəm). Pl. **podia, podiums.** [L. *podium* an elevated place, balcony, ad. Gr. πόδιον, dim. of πούς, ποδ- foot.]

1. *Arch.* **a.** A continuous projecting base or pedestal, a stylobate. **b.** A raised platform surrounding the arena in an ancient amphitheatre. **c.** A continuous seat or bench around a room.

[**1611** Coryat *Crudities* 164 (*Venice*) Euery Palace of any principall note hath a prety walke or open gallery betwixt the wall of the house and the brincke of the riuers banke... Suetonius calleth these kinde of open galleries Podia.] **1743** W. Stukeley *Abury* vii. 28 This was as the *podium* of an amphitheater, for the lower tire of spectators. **1789** P. Smyth tr. *Aldrich's Archit.* (1818) 149 The *podium* (the bottom part of the wall) projects at its lower extremity. **1832** Gell *Pompeiana* I. iv. 54 Along the whole runs a sort of *podium* or base. **1842–76** Gwilt *Archit.* §233 The amphitheatre at Nismes... Its exterior wall has three stories of Tuscan pilasters on the face of the wall, the two upper whereof stand on podia. **1848** B. Webb *Cont. Ecclesiol.* 176 Standing figures..are ranged in two rows on podia between the piers. **1850** S. Dobell *Roman* viii, Up from the podium to the beetling height I turn'd one dying look. **1887** *Pall Mall G.* 4 Mar. 4/1 The podium of the Albert Memorial is almost as fresh as the day the structure was uncovered.

d. A raised platform or dais at the front of a hall or stage; *spec.* that occupied by the conductor of an orchestra.

1947 A. Einstein *Music in Romantic Era* xv. 215 The longer Chopin continued in his career, the more he avoided the concert podium and the expectant masses. **1955** R. Crane *Hero's Walk* v. 94 There was no applause when Dr. Werner took his place at the podium. **1972** *N.Y. Times* 3 Nov. 30/2 Mr. Steinberg stands there, all but motionless,.. and manages to get more from an orchestra than a squadron of podium monkeys jumping up and down. **1973** W. H. Hallahan *Ross Forgery* (1977) iv. 65 The auctioneer stepped off the podium. **1977** *Kuwait Times* 23 Nov. 5/3, I address the following appeal from this podium to the people of Israel. **1978** *Gramophone* Oct. 658/3 He has a genre of courage and determination that enabled him to fight back after a particularly bad car accident and reappear on the podium long before the time appointed by his doctor.

e. A projecting lower structure around the base of a tower block.

1962 *Times* 19 Mar. 13/7 The podium-and-tower pattern is not only a product of daylighting codes. **1970** *Daily Tel.* 21 May 7 At the base of the 220 ft-high tower will be a podium of two and three-story buildings.

2. *Anat.* and *Zool.* **a.** The fore or hind foot (*manus* or *pes*) of a mammal or other vertebrate; in birds, the junction of the toes, or the toes collectively. **b.** In compounds denoting parts of the foot of a mollusc: as epipodium, mesopodium, metapodium, propodium.

1858 Mayne *Expos. Lex.*, Podion, *Podium*, applied by Illiger to the junction of the toes at the extremity of the *tarsus*, upon which the leg rests in birds; to the inferior part of the limb, comprehending, before, the *carpus*, *metacarpus*, and toes; behind, the *tarsus*, *metatarsus*, and toes in the *Mammifera*. **1895** in *Syd. Soc. Lex.*

3. *Bot.* A footstalk or other supporting part. (Chiefly in compounds.)

1866 *Treas. Bot.*, *Podium*, *Podus*, a stalk, or receptacle, or torus; used only in Greek compounds.

podler ('pɒdlə(r)). *Sc.* and *north.* Also **poadler, poodler, puddler.** [An altered or differentiated form of next.] A young coal-fish: see quot. 1838.

1835 S. Oliver *Rambles Northumbld.*, etc. 23 By September they increase to about a foot in length, and are then called poodlers. **1838** Johnston in *Proc. Berw. Nat. Club* I. No. 6. 173 When young it is called with us the Podlie; when somewhat larger the Podler; and when full grown the Coal-sey, or Black-coal-sey. **1859** W. White *Northumbld. & Border* xix. 273 Codlings and puddlers. **1875** G. C. Davies *Rambles Sch. Field-Club* xxxv. 262 Occasionally we got a gurnet or a 'poadler'.

podley ('pɒdlɪ). *Sc.* Forms: 6 podlo, 7 pudlo, 7–8 podly, -lay, 8–9 -lie, 9 podle, -ley, poddle, -lie. [In 16th c. *podlo*' for *podlock*, early form of pollack, q.v. (Cf. *banno*', *banna*, *bannie*, from bannock, *haddo*', *haddie*, from haddock, etc.)]

The fry or young of the coal-fish (*Pollachius* or *Merlangus carbonarius*); also, the true pollack (*Pollachius pollachius*). Cf. podler, pollack.

1525 in *Exc. e Libris Dom. Jac. V* (Bann. Cl.) 8 Bukez, solis, podlois. **1684** Sibbald *Scotia Illustr.* ii. iii. 23 *Asellus fuscus*:..a Podly. **1698** M. Martin *Voy. St. Kilda* (1749) 16 There are also..Pudloes, Herring, and many more. **1753** Maitland *Hist. Edin.* ii. 189 Perches, Podlays, Skate. **1792** *Statist. Acc. Scot.* IV. 537 A few small cod, podlies, and flounders. **1806** D. Graham *Writings* (1883) II. 220 Lobsters, partans, podles. **1838** [see prec.]. **1892** Stevenson *Across the Plains* 209 The podley is hardly to be regarded as a dainty for the table. **1896** J. H. Campbell *Wild Life Scot.* 131 Among the poddles, as the young of the saithe and lythe are called.

podo ('pəʊdəʊ). [f. generic name *Podo(carpus* (see podocarp 2).] An evergreen tree belonging to one of several East African species of the genus *Podocarpus*, or the softwood timber obtained from it. Also *attrib.*

1922 W. Schlich *Man. Forestry* (ed. 4) I. 289 Podo, a medium-sized tree, has a wide distribution. **1940** W. H. Eggeling *Indigenous Trees of Uganda Protectorate* 179 Recently the tendency in Uganda has been to regard musizi ..as a better timber than Podo. **1947** *E. African Ann. 1946–7* 41/1 The north-west point of the Game Reserve..is an impressive mountain with cedar, olive and podo on its summit. **1957** *Handbk. of Softwoods* (Forest Prod. Res. Lab.) 48 Podo is widely used for joinery and interior fittings. **1961** *New Scientist* 24 Aug. 451/3 The cedar, olive and podo forest that covers most of the Mau is being systematically destroyed.

podo- (pɒdəʊ), before a vowel **pod-**, a. Gr. ποδο-, combining form of πούς, ποδ- a foot, an element in terms of Natural History, etc.; e.g.

'podobranch (-bræŋk) *Zool.* [Gr. βράγχια gills], a breathing organ of crustaceans attached to the legs; a foot-gill; so **podobranchial** (-'bræŋkɪəl) *a.*, of or pertaining to podobranchs or foot-gills; **podobranchiate** (-'bræŋkɪət) *a.*, having or provided with foot-gills (*Cent. Dict.* 1890); **podo'cephalous** *a.*, *Bot.* [Gr. κεφαλή head], bearing a head of flowers on a long footstalk; ‖**podogynium** (-'dʒɪnɪəm) *Bot.* [mod.L., f. Gr. γυνή female], = basigynium; so **'podogyn, -gyne** [F. *podogyne*], in same sense; **podogynous** (-'pdʒɪnəs) *a.*; **po'dology** [F. *podologie*], the science which treats of the foot; also, a treatise on the foot; so **po'dologist**; **'podomancy** [Gr. μαντεία divination], divination from signs derived from inspection of the feet (*Syd. Soc. Lex.* 1895); **po'dometer** = pedometer 1; †**po'dometry**: see quots.; **'podoscaph** [Gr. σκάφος ship], a canoe-shaped float attached to the foot, or a pair of these, for moving on water; also, a water-velocipede, or boat propelled by treadles like a bicycle; hence **'podoscapher; po'doscopy** = *podomancy*; **podosomatous** (-səʊmətəs) *a.*, *Zool.*, of or pertaining to the *Podosomata* or sea-spiders, an order of *Arthropoda* having long many-jointed legs; syn. with *Pycnogonidæ*; **'podosperm** *Bot.* [Gr. σπέρμα seed], the stalk of a seed; = funiculus 3; **podo'stomatous** *a.*, *Zool.* [Gr. στόμα mouth], belonging to the *Podostomata*, a group of *Arthropoda* characterized by having a foot-like mouth; ‖**podo'theca** *Zool.* [mod.L., f. Gr. θηκή sheath], the scaly leg-covering of a bird or reptile; also, the sheath covering the leg of an insect; hence **podo'thecal** *a.*

1888 Rolleston & Jackson *Anim. Life* 182 The epipodite (so-called) of the first maxilliped represents the base, stem and lamina of a *podobranch. **1858** Mayne *Expos. Lex.*, *Podocephalus*.., applied to plants that have flowers united into heads borne upon long peduncles..; *podocephalous. **1879** Podocephalous in Webster *Suppl.* **1858** Mayne *Expos. Lex.*, **Podogynium*,..a fleshy and solid projection which.. serves to support the ovary..; a *podogyne. **1895** *Syd. Soc. Lex.*, *Podogyn*, shortened form of the word *Podogynium*. **1818** *Art Preserv. Feet* Pref. 7 Diseases of the Nails, Immoderate Perspiration of the Feet, &c...which merit the attention of the *Podologist. *Ibid.* Pref. 6 It might..be ranked under the new title of *Podology, embracing the whole Art of Preserving the Feet. **1727–41** Chambers *Cycl.*, **Podometer*, or *Pedometer*. **1775** in Ash. **1895** Podometer in *Syd. Soc. Lex.* **1656** Blount *Glossogr.*, **Podemetry*, foot measure, or a measuring by the foot. **1658** Phillips, *Podimetry*, (Greek) a measuring by the foot. **1693** Rymer *Short View Tragedy* 119 They must have played bare foot: the spectators would not have been content without seeing their Podometry. **1858** *Chamb. Jrnl.* X. 349/2 Heer Ochsner of Rotterdam..astonished his countrymen by appearing on the Maas, wearing a *podoscaph fifteen feet long on each foot, and holding a pole, flattened at one end as a paddle, in his hand. **1864** in Webster. [**1868** *Lond. Society* Nov. 414 The latest novelty in the velocipede line is the podoscaphe or vélocipède-marin.] **1884** Knight *Dict. Mech.* Suppl., *Podoscaph*, a foot boat; one in which canoe-shaped floats are attached to or support the feet. **1889** *Pall Mall G.* 9 Sept. 6/3 It bears the peculiar name of podoscaph, and is a sort of tiny raft. **1885** *Encycl. Brit.* XIX. 4/2 The treatises also contain occasional digressions on onychomancy,..*podoscopy, spasmatomancy. **1862** Ansted *Channel Isl.* ii. ix. (ed. 2) 235 A species..of the curious group of *podosomatous crustaceans, resembling a transparent spider, without head or body. **1819** Lindley tr. *Richard's Obs. Fruits & Seeds* 22 When a seed bends back suddenly in a direction contrary to its *podosperm..it is *reclined* by its proper direction. **1857** Henfrey *Bot.* §234 A fully developed ovule is usually attached to the placenta by a short stalk, called the funiculus, podosperm, or umbilical cord. **1872** Coues *Key N. Amer. Birds* 46 The naked part of the leg is covered, like the bill, by a hardened, thickened, modified integument, which varies in texture between corneous and leathery. This is called the *podotheca. **1893** Newton *Dict. Birds* 511 The *podotheca* or covering of the tarsus. **1890** *Cent. Dict.*, *Podothecal.

podocarp ('pəʊdəʊkɑːp). *Bot.* [f. podo- + Gr. καρπ-ός fruit.] **1.** A footstalk bearing the fruit of a plant (Webster *Suppl.* 1879).

2. [f. mod.L. *Podocarpus* (C. L. L'Héritier de Brutelle in C. H. Persoon *Synopsis Plantarum* (1807) II. 580).] A coniferous tree or shrub belonging to the genus *Podocarpus* or the family Podocarpaceæ, including several valuable timber trees native to parts of the Southern Hemisphere. So **podocar'paceous, -'carpous** *adjs.*, belonging to the family Podocarpaceæ. Cf. podo.

1858 G. Gordon *Pinetum* 268 (*heading*) *Eupodocarpus*, Endlicher, or the true podocarps. **1882** J. S. Gardner in *Nature* XXV. 229/1 There are fruits from Sheppey which I believe to be podocarpous, one at least seeming identical with *P[odocarpus] elata* of Queensland. **1918** A. D. Webster *Coniferous Trees* i. 158 The Alpine Podocarp... This distinct and very interesting Tasmanian conifer may be seen in excellent condition in several gardens in the neighbourhood of London. **1923** A. Rehder in L. H. Bailey *Cultivated Evergreens* ii. v. 179 (*heading*) Longleaf Podocarp. **1939** M. Hornibrook *Dwarf & Slow-Growing Conifers* (ed. 2) 216 Of the many podocarps which inhabit Australia and South America, not many of them are fully hardy in north European climates. **1959** A. H. McLintock *Descr. Atlas N.Z.* p. xv, The forest is of silver and mountain beech, with traces of red beech and podocarps at low altitude. **1975** *Nature* 27 Nov. 305/2 Among conifers, the mixture of podocarpaceous and araucarian elements is typical of the Southern Hemisphere early Tertiary. **1977** *N.Z. Listener* 15 Jan. 21/2 Cut down the last of those giant podocarps and you cut down about 800 years of growth. **1978** *Sci. Amer.* July 102/3 At the lower elevations and latitudes the forests were a mixture of broadleaf trees and podocarp conifers, a group of trees peculiar to the southwest Pacific and Chile.

Podolian (pə'dəʊlɪən), *a.* [f. *Podolia* (see below) + -AN.] Of or pertaining to Podolia, a region in south-west Ukraine (see quot. 1974).

c **1850** *Bee Keeper* 18 (*heading*) The construction of the Podolian hive. **1881** *Encycl. Brit.* XIII. 451/2 The breed of cattle most widely distributed throughout Italy is that known as the Podolian. **1911** *Ibid.* XXI. 875/1 The Dniester is an important channel for trade, corn, spirits and timber being exported from Podolian river ports. **1920** *Glasgow Herald* 7/2 Another great Bolshevik offensive in the Southern Polish and Podolian sector has failed absolutely. **1936** C. ROTH *Short Hist. Jewish People* xxvi. 332 The revivalist movement in Poland permeated all sections of society, until it touched a simple Podolian lime-digger, Israel ben Eliezer (1700–1760). **1974** *Encycl. Brit. Micropædia* VIII. 60/2 *Podolia*.. was under Polish rule until 1772, when the part west of the Zbruch River became Austrian; the rest became the Podolian *guberniya* (province) in Russia in 1793. After World War I the region continued to be divided at the Zbruch, between Poland and the U.S.S.R.; after World War II, it was entirely incorporated into the U.S.S.R.

podophthalmate (pɒdɒf'θælmət), *a. Zool.* [f. Gr. πούς, ποδ- foot + ὀφθαλμός eye + -ATE².] Having the eye at the end of a movable stalk, stalk-eyed; of or pertaining to the stalk-eyed crustaceans. So †**podoph'thalma, -'thalmia, -thal'mata** [mod.L. pl.], an order of Crustacea, including those with eyes set on movable foot-stalks, as crabs and lobsters; **podoph'thalmian,** *a.*, pertaining to the *Podophthalmia*; *sb.*, a member of the *Podophthalmia*; **podoph'thalmatous, podoph'thalmic,** *adjs.* = *podophthalmate*; **podoph'thalmite,** the distal joint of the eye-stalk in podophthalmate Crustacea; hence **podophthal'mitic** *a.*; **podoph'thalmous** *a.* = *podophthalmate*.

1835–6 *Todd's Cycl. Anat.* I. 762/1 A corresponding structure is observed in certain Podophthalmia. *Ibid.* 756/1 This dorsal shield.. occurs among the whole of the Podophthalmians. **1841–71** T. R. JONES *Anim. Kingd.* (ed. 4) 442 In the two highest orders of Crustacea, hence called Podophthalmia, the eyes are placed at the extremity of moveable pedicles articulated with the first cephalic ring of the external skeleton. **1855** GOSSE *Marine Zool.* I. 116 Among the *Podophthalma*, or Stalk-eyed Crustacea, the Shrimps or Sand-raisers.. burrow in sand, mostly in shallow water. **1858** MAYNE *Expos. Lex.* 990 *Podophthalmous*, applied by Desmarest and Leach to a vast number of the Crustaceae, having the eyes placed at the extremity of a mobile peduncle. **1874** WOOD *Nat. Hist.* 713 The Podophthalmata, or Stalk-eyed Crustaceans. **1877** HUXLEY *Anat. Inv. Anim.* vi. 369 The organisation of the Stomatopoda is more Edriophthalmian.. than Podophthalmian. *Ibid.* 315 The peduncles of the eye.. are composed of two joints, a small proximal basiophthalmite, and a larger terminal podophthalmite. **1878** BELL tr. *Gegenbaur's Comp. Anat.* 265 A point of affinity to the Podophthalmate Malacostraca. **1880** HUXLEY *Crayfish* vi. 341 Podophthalmatous Crustacea.

podophyllous (pɒdəʊ'fɪləs), *a.* [f. Gr. ποδο-, PODO- + φύλλον leaf + -OUS.]

1. *Entom.* Having, as some insects, compressed leaf-like locomotive organs or feet.

1858 in MAINE *Expos. Lex.* **1895** in *Syd. Soc. Lex.*

2. *Zool.* In ***podophyllous tissue***, the layer of tissue composed of leaf-like vascular lamellæ beneath the coronary cushion of a horse's hoof.

1895 in *Syd. Soc. Lex.*

‖**podophyllum** (pɒdəʊ'fɪləm). [mod. Bot. L., f. Gr. ποδο-, PODO- + φύλλον leaf.] **a.** *Bot.* A genus of *Ranunculaceæ* with two known species, *P. peltatum* of eastern N. America, and *P. Emodi* of the Himalayas, having long thick creeping rhizomes, large long-stalked palmately lobed leaves, and a solitary white flower. **b.** *Pharm.* The dried rootstock of *P. peltatum*. Also *attrib.* Hence **podo'phyllic** *a. Chem.*, of or pertaining to podophyllum; esp. in ***podophyllic acid***, a crystalline acid obtained from podophyllin; **podo'phyllin** *Chem.*, a yellow bitter resin having cathartic properties, obtained from the dried rhizome of *P. peltatum*; = ***resin of podophyllum***.

1760 J. LEE *Introd. Bot.* Table I. (1788) 292 *Podophyllum*, Duck's-Foot, or May Apple. **1842** DUNGLISON *Med. Lex.* (1855) s.v., The root or rhizoma, *Podophyllum* (Ph. U.S.), is purgative in the dose of 20 grains. **1863** *N. Syd. Soc. Year-bk. Med.* 457 The action of podophyllin is favourably contrasted with that of calomel. **1866** AITKEN *Pract. Med.* II. 53 Podophyllin. **1874** GARROD & BAXTER *Mat. Med.* (1880) 183 The resin or Podophylline is a pale greenish-brown amorphous powder. **1875** H. C. WOOD *Therap.* (1879) 471 Podophyllum acts as a purgative like jalap, but more slowly and continuously.

‖**podostemon** (pɒdəʊ'sti:mən). *Bot.* [mod.L., f. PODO- + Gr. στήμων, taken as = stamen: from the two stamens with filaments united for about half their length.] The typical genus of the N.O. *Podostemaceæ*, comprising moss-like aquatic herbs with apetalous flowers, natives chiefly of S. America. So **podostemaceous** (-'eɪʃəs) *a.*, belonging to this order; **podo'stemad** [cf. ARAD], a plant of this order.

1846 LINDLEY *Veg. Kingd.* 482 Hypogynous Exogens. *Rutales... Podostemaceæ.*—Podostemads. **1866** LIVINGSTONE *Last Jrnls.* (1873) I. xliii. 71 This stream is rapid,.. with many podostemons at the bottom. **1880** C. R. MARKHAM *Peruv. Bark* 303 The wet stones were covered with Podostemads, herbaceous branched floating plants, with the habit of liverworts.

Podsnap ('pɒdsnæp). The name of a character in Dickens's 'Our Mutual Friend' (1864–5) used allusively for a person embodying insular complacency and self-satisfaction and refusal to face up to unpleasant facts. So **Pod'snappery, Pod'snap(p)ian** *a.*

[**1864** DICKENS *Mut. Fr.* (1865) I. I. xi. 97 Mr. Podsnap.. stood very high in Mr. Podsnap's opinion... Mr. Podsnap settled that whatever he put behind him he put out of existence... Mr. Podsnap's world was not a very large world ..he considered other countries..a mistake... Mr. Podsnap was sensible of its being required of him to take Providence under his protection... What Providence meant was invariably what Mr. Podsnap meant.] *Ibid.* 98 These may be said to have been the articles of a faith and school which the present chapter takes the liberty of calling after its representative man, Podsnappery. [*Ibid.*, A certain institution in Mr. Podsnap's mind which he called 'the young person'.. was an inconvenient and exacting institution... The question about everything was, would it bring a blush into the cheek of the young person.] **1880** *Daily Tel.* 1 Dec. 5/2 It is all very well to sneer at 'Chauvinism' and 'Podsnappery' but the claim of British children to supremacy among their kind must be resolutely upheld. **1901** *Daily News* 16 Feb. 3/3 The Podsnappian findings of a Commission which.. reported.. that a certain hospital had been infested with bugs, but not in such a degree as to incommode the patients. **1902** *Westm. Gaz.* 21 Nov. 9/3 Podsnap General, Podsnap Financier, Podsnap Statesman we know, but it is my joy to have perceived our old friend in his last incarnation... Podsnap then, Podsnap in crimson tie of The Schools, 'The Red Badge of Culture', but Podsnap still, pervades the Press. **1905** G. K. CHESTERTON *Heretics* 29 None.. will accuse the author of the 'Inferno' of.. a Podsnapian optimism. **1929** A. HUXLEY *Do what you Will* 31 Those detestable Puritans to whom we owe.. Grundyism and Podsnappery. **1944** A. THIRKELL *Headmistress* vii. 149 *As You Like It* might be a suitable play ..for the Young Person in a Podsnappian sense. **1960** *Times* 12 July 13/4 There are too many Podsnaps of officialdom who treat atheletes and *aficionados* alike as noisy nuisances. **1972** G. S. FRASER in Cox & Dyson *20th-Cent. Mind* II. xi. 401 The solid Podsnappian complacencies and unbudgingnesses of the male. **1977** P. N. FURBANK *E. M. Forster* viii. 138 They had a jokey and facetious relationship, based on the fiction of Thompson's extreme Podsnappery and Philistinism.

podsol, var. PODZOL.

‖**podu** ('pəʊdu:). [Telugu.] = KUMRI.

[**1855** H. H. WILSON *Gloss. Indian Terms* 420 *Podu*, Tel., land or lands recently cleared from thickets and prepared for cultivation.] **1938** [see KUMRI]. **1954** O. H. K. SPATE *India & Pakistan* viii. 203 Shifting agriculture—the *jhum* of Assam, the *kumri* or *podu* of the Peninsula—conforms to the standard pattern so widespread in tropical regions.

Podunk ('pəʊdʌŋk). [Algonquian place-name.]

1. Also 7 **Potunck.** A small tribe of Indians formerly inhabiting an area around the Podunk river in Hartford County, Connecticut (chiefly *pl.* or *collect.*) Also *attrib.* or as *adj.*

1656 in *Public Records of Colony of Connecticut* (1850) I. 305 The Court wearied wth their speeches pressed the Potunck Indians to deliver up the murtherer. **1761** E. STILES *Extracts from Itineraries* (1916) 136 Podunk Tribe at the dividing Line between Windsor & Hartford East side; between 2 & 300 Men in Philips War; went off & never returned. **1842** W. L. STONE *Uncas & Miantonomoh* 31 The Podunks resided upon the lands now comprised in the town of East Hartford. **1859** *N.Y. Weekly Tribune* 8 Oct. 3/1 The Numkatunks, Quinnipiacs, Podunks, and Quinnebogs, were present from New-Haven and vicinity. **1910** F. W. HODGE et al. *Handbk. Amer. Indians* II. 271/1 Podunk. A band or small tribe on Podunk r., in Hartford co., Conn., closely related to the Poquonnoc. **1935** *Colony of Connecticut* (Connecticut Board of Educ.) (Senate Doc. 53, 74th Congr., 1st Sess.) 1 A few years previously in 1631 the chief of one of the Indian tribes in the Connecticut Valley, the Podunks, had journeyed to the Massachusetts and Plymouth Colonies to invite them to see the fertile Connecticut Valley. **1937** *Bull. Archaeol. Soc. Connecticut* Apr. 2 The Podunk tribe had two permanent villages during early colonial times... The largest Podunk village was located in South Windsor.

2. *U.S. colloq.* Name for a fictive insignificant, out-of-the-way town; a typical small town.

1846 *Daily National Pilot* (Buffalo, N.Y.) 13 Jan. 3a, Messrs. Editors: I hear you ask, 'Where in the world is Podunk?' It is in the world, sir; and more than that, is a little world of itself. It stands 'high up the big Pigeon', a bright and shining light amid the surrounding darkness. I look back, sir, with pride upon the day when I located in the then unincorporated burgh of Podunk. *Ibid.* 20 Jan. 2a, The distinguished festival of Podunk is the *candy bee*. *Ibid.* 6 Mar. 2b, Podunk is a huge town, not distinguished exactly as the geographies have it, for its 'fertile soil, salubrious and healthy climate', but for some of the characters that here do congregate. **1865** O. W. NORTON *Army Lett.* (1903) 277, I presume that just about this time of day you are sitting in one of the slips in that 'Podunk' or 'Chachunk' (what do you call it?) 'meetin' house'. **1901** *Harper's Weekly* 7 Sept. 903/2 He might just as well have been John Smith, of Podunk Centre. **1933** *Review of Reviews* Feb. 33 It [*sc.* the 18th amendment] required one rule for Podunk, Kansas, and one for New York City. **1947** [see MAIN STREETER, MAINSTREETER]. **1960** *Times Lit. Suppl.* 15 Jan. 27/3 A diploma from Harvard is much more marketable than a diploma from Podunk College. **1976** *National Observer* (U.S.) 30 Oct. 15/5 It won't be just the Podunk liberal-arts colleges that have to hustle. Some of the big state schools, and some well-known large universities, will be out there too —to find new publics.

‖**Podura** (pəʊ'd(j)ʊərə). *Entom.* [mod.L. *podūra* (Linn. 1748), f. Gr. πούς, ποδ- foot + οὐρά tail.] A genus of apterous insects, having a terminal forked springing organ; hence known as spring-tails. Hence **po'duran** *a.*, of or pertaining to the genus *Podura*; *sb.*, an insect of this genus or of the family *Poduridæ*; so **po'durid** *a.* and *sb.*; **po'duroid** *a.*, having the form or character of the *Poduridæ*.

1837 GORING & PRITCHARD *Microgr.* 129 Pray look at these scales of the podura in the engiscope. **1848** CARPENTER *Anim. Phys.* xii. (1872) 498 In one curious family, that of the Poduras or Spring-tails, the leap is accomplished by the sudden extension of the tail. **1867** J. HOGG *Microsc.* I. ii. 58 The Podura scale appears to be a compound structure. **1883** LESLIE *Nordenskiöld's Voy. Vega* 60 Arachnids, acarids, and podurids occur most plentifully.

'**podware.** *Obs.* exc. *dial.* Also 7–9 **podder.** [Of uncertain origin: cf. CODWARE, 1398–1699, and PEDWARE, 1577–1706.

The first element suggests POD of pease, beans, etc.; but this is not known till nearly a century later than *podware*, which moreover in quot. 1584 is not applied to pulse or podded plants, and in quot. 1677 has not necessarily such a sense. In quot. 1736 the word is associated with *pod*.]

Field crops; fodder for cattle; in later use app. pulse, or plants having pods (= CODWARE).

1584 R. SCOT *Discov. Witchcr.* XII. vi. (1886) 179 [They] suffocate and spoile.. grasse, greene corne, and ripe corne, and all other podware. **1617** in *Archæol. Cant.* (1902) XXV. 15 Robert Terry [presented] for profaning of the Sabbath Day, by binding barley, and powting [= stacking] of podder, upon the Sabbath. **1677** PLOT *Oxfordsh.* 153 Dill or Lentills, in poor stone-brash land, which are a good podware for cattle. **1736** J. LEWIS *Hist. Thanet* Gloss. s.v. *Libbit*, The hagister.. was in the poddergrotten. *Ibid.*, *Podder*, podware; beans, peas, tares or vetches, or such ware as has pods. **1794** BOYS *Agric. Kent* 31 Some farmers are bound to sow wheat after beans, on land not fit to produce beans; to leave a quantity of podware gratten, for a wheat tilth on farms where some sorts of podware is the worst tilth known to sow wheat upon. [**1887** *Kentish Gloss.*, *Podder*, a name given to beans, peas, tares, vetches, or such vegetables as have pods.]

† '**pody 'cody,** app. a perversion of *body of God*, in a profane oath.

a **1693** *Urquhart's Rabelais* III. xxxvi. 298 By the Pody Cody, I have fished fair.

podzol ('pɒdzɒl). *Soil Sci.* Also **podsol,** and formerly also with capital initial. [a. Russ. *podzól*, f. *pod-* under- + *zolá* ash.] An acidic, generally infertile soil which is characterized by a well-marked white or grey ash-like subsurface layer from which minerals have been leached into a lower dark-coloured layer, and which occurs esp. under coniferous trees or heath vegetation in moist, usu. temperate climates (typically in parts of N. Russia). Orig. applied only to the ash-like layer itself.

[**1906** E. W. HILGARD *Soils* x. 186 Woodlands of northern countries bearing beech and oak are especially apt to be benefited by the action of lime on the 'raw', acid humous soil and underlying hardpan, which is commonly under-laid by a leaden-blue sandy subsoil ('Bleisand' of the Germans, 'Podzol' of the Russians) colored brown by earth humates.] **1908** *Jrnl. Agric. Sci.* III. 83 The most characteristic feature of the Podzol.. is the dissolution and removal of soluble parts of silicates.. and an increase in the percentage of insoluble silica. **1912** H. B. WOODWARD *Geol. Soils & Substrata* vii. 82 Of mixed soils, the *Podzol* of Russia, as described by Professor Glinka, consists of sands, loams, and clays, locally calcareous, but generally poor in mineral plant food. **1927** C. F. MARBUT tr. *Glinka's Great Soil Groups of World* 71 All these profiles of Russian soils belong to the Podsols. This term is used to designate soils which have a pronounced and well developed whitish A_2 horizon. If this horizon is not well developed, and the corresponding horizon contains whitish specks and stringers the soil is said to be Podsolic. **1928** *Ecology* IX. 177 Originally, the term podsol applied more specifically to the gray-colored zone, though now it is commonly used to describe the entire profile. **1934** *Forestry* VIII. 25 Podzol soils owe their name to the presence of an ashy-grey layer which underlies the surface layer of dead vegetation and plant roots. **1936** *Nature* 17 Oct. 692/2 This utilization of the physical character and colour of the soil.. is a novelty to glacialists from the leached podsol areas of the north-west. **1946** F. E. ZEUNER *Dating Past* v. 124 Brownearth and podsol soils are characteristic of the humid-temperate countries. **1972** J. G. CRUICKSHANK *Soil Geogr.* ii. 63 A coarse sandy deposit in Sherwood Forest.. also showed signs of podsol features only 25–30 years after replanting with pine. **1973** *Sci. Amer.* Dec. 64/2 The tropical podzols are useless even for shifting agriculture; the Dayak peoples of Borneo call them *kerangas*: 'land on which one cannot grow rice'.

Hence **pod'zolic** (or **-ds-**) *a.*, of the nature of or resembling a podzol in possessing a layer from which some leaching of bases has occurred.

1927 C. F. MARBUT tr. *Glinka's Great Soil Groups of World* 44 We can see again the change from Tschernosem to gray forest soils and the latter into Podsolic soils in the vicinity of Borshom. **1932** G. W. ROBINSON *Soils* xvi. 315 The soils of Great Britain belong mainly to the podsolic group. **1952** P. W. RICHARDS *Tropical Rain Forest* ix. 209 If the American view is accepted, a lateritic soil can also be podzolic. **1973** P. A. COLINVAUX *Introd. Ecol.* iii. 46 Some heath lands of northern Europe, with acid litter and leached soils, reveal podzolic profiles.

podzolize (ˈpɒdzəlaɪz), *v. Soil Sci.* Also **-sol-**. [f. prec. + -IZE.] *trans.* and *intr.* To render or become podzolic. Chiefly as **ˈpodzolized** *ppl. a.*, **ˈpodzolizing** *vbl. sb.*

1923 *Soil Sci.* XVI. 97 It is the presence of the acid layer in a definite position in the profile and the strongly marked gray or podsolized horizon which chiefly distinguishes the typical northern from the typical southern profile. **1927** C. F. MARBUT tr. *Glinka's Great Soil Groups of World* 100 Traces of the Podsolizing processes are shown in shallow depressions... The Podsolizing and leaching has reached a more advanced stage of the development. **1932** *Technical Communications Imperial Bureau Soil Sci.* No. 24. 11 Under conditions of poor drainage.. resilication may give rise to a kaolinite red earth which.. may be podsolised into a quartzose, bleached surface soil. **1938** *Geogr. Jrnl.* XCI. 163 The soils of the lower Trent Vale are podsolized sands. **1957** *Soil Sci.* LXXXIII. 215 The parent materials of Swartswood sand loam podzolize with comparative ease. **1976** *Sci. Amer.* Apr. 56/3 The dunes are partly podzolized, and they sustain pines, dwarfed redwoods and shrubs. **1976** *Nature* 15 Apr. 602/2 It would seem to result from percolating solutions removing surface coverings of ferric oxides from quartz sand grains and depositing them again within a short distance, that is, in a typical podzolising process.

Hence **ˌpodzoliˈzation**, the leaching of bases out of the upper parts of a soil and their deposition lower down; the formation of a podzolic soil.

1923 *Soil Sci.* XVI. 103 It is evident.. that podsolization may take place in acid or alkaline [s]oils. **1934** *Discovery* July 200/2 The leaching and subsequent deposition of iron (and aluminium) oxides is a characteristic of all podsols, and is.. generally referred to as 'podsolization'. **1952** P. W. RICHARDS *Tropical Rain Forest* ix. 209 The removal of sesquioxides of iron and aluminium with the accumulation of silica is called podzolization. **1970** E. M. BRIDGES *World Soils* iii. 21/1 The process of podzolization is prevalent in the soils of the cool humid parts of the world and produces soils of the podzolic group and the podzols in particular.

poë, variant of POI[1], Hawaiian food.

poë-bird (ˈpəʊiːbɜːd). Also 8 **poy-**, **pue-bird**. [See quot. 1865.] The name (given by Capt. Cook, and retained in some English ornithological works) for a New Zealand bird, *Prosthemadera novæzelandiæ*, subsequently called by the English settlers PARSON-BIRD (q.v.) and by the Maoris *tui*.

1777 COOK *Voy.* I. 97 Amongst the small birds I must not omit to particularise the wattle-bird, poy-bird. [In the illustration spelt *poe-bird*, and in the list of plates, *poi.*] *Ibid.* 98 The poy-bird is less than the wattle-bird. The feathers of a fine mazarine blue. *a* **1802** BOWLES *Poems* (1855) I. 120 The poe-bird flits,.. With silver neck and blue enamelled wing. **1865** HOWITT *Discov. Austr.* I. vi. 111 This bird they called the Wattle-bird, and also the Poy-bird, from its having little tufts of curled hair under its throat, which they called poies, from the Otaheitan word for ear-rings. **1868** WOOD *Homes without H.* xxv. 470 The splendidly decorated Poe Birds. **1896** *List Anim. Zool. Soc.* (ed. 9) 237 Poë Honey-eater.

‖**Pœcile** (ˈpiːsɪliː). [a. Gr. (ἡ) ποικίλη (στοά) the many-coloured or painted porch.] Name of a famous portico in the market-place of ancient Athens, adorned with a variety of paintings.

1819 in *Pantologia*. **1838** *Encycl. Brit.* (ed. 7) XVIII. 139/1 The only reward Miltiades obtained after the battle of Marathon, was to have his picture drawn.. and to have it hung up in the Pœcile. **1846** ELLIS *Elgin Marb.* I. 32 The Pœcile, or painted piazzas.

†**pœcilite** (ˈpiːsɪlaɪt). *Geol. Obs.* [f. Gr. ποικίλος variegated + -ITE[1]; after F. *terrain pœcilien* (Brongniart 1829).] A name proposed for the Upper New Red Sandstone (cf. Ger. *bunter sandstein*). Hence †**pœcilitic** (piːsɪˈlɪtɪk) *a.*, (*a*) of or pertaining to the Upper New Red Sandstone formation; = POIKILITIC *a.* 1; (*b*) (*Petrogr.*) = POIKILITIC *a.* 2 (*obs.*).

1832 W. D. CONYBEARE in *Rep. Brit. Assoc.* 379 The next geological group.. beneath the lias and oolites, is that.. characterized by the new red or variegated sandstone... I will venture therefore to propose the term Pœcilite.. and hence denominate the group, pœcilitic. Brongniart has already adopted the Gallicised form *Pœcilien*. **1887** G. H. WILLIAMS in *Amer. Jrnl. Sci.* CXXXIII. 139 Here.. we have another example of the structure which the writer has distinguished as pœcilitic* in describing the hornblende of the Cortlandt peridotites. [*Note*] *The word is here changed to the accepted form. **1909** F. P. MENNELL *Introd. Petrol.* xii. 87 (*caption*) Poecilitic structure, in picrite, Belingwe, Rhodesia. (Olivine enclosed in enstatite).

pœcilo- (ˈpiːsɪləʊ), before a vowel **pœcil-**, from Gr. ποικίλο-ς many-coloured, variegated, various, a formative element in scientific terms (in some of which the form POIKILO- is preferred).

ˈpœciloblast, **ˈpœcilocyte**: see POIKILO-; **ˈpœcilomere** [Gr. μέρος part], a part of the body of an animal in which variations of colouring tend to appear first; **ˈpœcilonym** [Gr. ὄνομα, ὄνυμα name], one of various names for the same thing; a synonym (*Cent. Dict.* cites Wilder); hence **pœciloˈnymic** *a.*, having a variety of names; **pœciˈlonymy**; **ˈpœcilopod** [Gr. πούς, ποδ- foot] *Zool.*, a member of the *Pœcilopoda*, in Latreille's classification (now abandoned), a division of *Crustacea* distinguished by limbs of varied form and functions, e.g. prehensory, ambulatory, branchial, and natatory; hence **pœciˈlopodous** *a.*; **pœciloˈthermal**, **pœciloˈthermic**: see POIKILO-.

1905 *Athenæum* 18 Mar. 342/1 That colour-variations tended to appear first of all on certain definite parts of the body, and that these parts, to which the name '*pœcilomeres' had been given, were common to mammals and birds alike. **1889** *Buck's Handbk. Med. Sc.* VIII. 528/2 An unusually complete combination of *pœcilonymic ambiguities. *Ibid.* 517/1 Terminological variety, such as occurs in the passages quoted, may be expressed by the single word, *pœcilonymy. **1835** KIRBY *Hab. & Inst. Anim.* II. xiv. 22 The *Pœcilopods differ [from the Branchiopods] by the different structure and uses of their legs, which are not branching. **1852** DANA *Crust.* II. 1308 Characteristic species of Pœcilopods.

poed, obs. form of POOD.

poee-poee, var. POIPOI.

Poeesque (pəʊˈɛsk), *a.* Also **Poesque**, **Poe-esque**. [f. the name of Edgar Allan *Poe* (1809–49), American author, + -ESQUE.] Of, pertaining to, or resembling E. A. Poe or his work. Also as quasi-*sb.*

1919 *Times Lit. Suppl.* 19 June 335/1 Mr. Harvey's 'The Beast with Five Fingers' is tinged with the Poesque. **1934** R. CAMPBELL *Broken Record* 38 To a stranger they [*sc.* crows] give the English countryside a terrible and sinister, Poeesque atmosphere. **1959** R. FULLER *Ruined Boys* II. xi. 154 He was at a loss to imagine precisely what would indicate any impending disaster, short of some obvious and Poesque symptom like a great fissure in the school walls. **1977** *Times Lit. Suppl.* 20 May 611/3 [Edmund] Wilson's future biographers may want to make something of the Poe-esque inclination.

Similarly **Poeana** (pəʊˈɑːnə), objects associated with E. A. Poe; publications by or about Poe; **ˈPoeish** *a.*; **ˈPoeishly** *adv.*; **ˈPoeist**, a student or devotee of Poe's works; **ˈPoe-like** *a.*

1908 *Westm. Gaz.* 12 Feb. 4/2 There appeared in Paris, in 1836, Gautier's Poe-like story 'La Morte Amoureuse'. **1925** H. ACTON in *Oxf. Poetry* 7 And oh, the Poe-like harmonies of bells! **1929** WYNDHAM LEWIS *Let.* 20 Feb. (1963) 187 My reply to this Poeist.. is that Poe would not have found my writing 'difficult'. **1955** *N. & Q.* May 223/1 All Poeana has been enthusiastically collected for seventy years. **1976** *National Observer* (U.S.) 9 Oct. 24/3, I like the plantation owner brooding Poeishly over the corpse of his too-well-beloved sister. **1977** *Amer. N. & Q.* XV. 70/1 While several contemporary reviewers saw 'Poeish' similarities in Melville's writings, modern critics.. have found little reason to suspect that Melville was influenced by Poe.

poeir, obs. form of POWER.

poele, obs. var. of POLE *sb.*

‖**poêlée** (pwale). Also *erron.* **poêle**. [Fr., a panful; cf. *poêler* to cook in a pan.] A broth or stock (see quots.).

1830 R. DOLBY *Cook's Dict.* 414 *Poelee.* Take two pounds of veal, two pounds of bacon, two large carrots and three onions; cut all these into dice and put them into a stewpan with a pound of butter, the juice of three or four lemons, four cloves, two bay-leaves, bruised, a little thyme, salt, and pepper. **1845** E. ACTON *Mod. Cookery* vii. 185 *Poêlée.* Cut into large dice.. lean veal.. fat bacon.. carrots.. onions;.. add.. butter..; pour.. boiling broth..; strain the *poêlée* through a fine sieve... Use instead of water for boiling. **1861** MRS. BEETON *Bk. Househ. Managem.* 46 *Poêlée*, stock used instead of water for boiling turkeys, sweetbreads, fowls, and vegetables, to render them less insipid. **1877** E. S. DALLAS *Kettner's Bk. of Table* 182 The following receipt is nearly identical with what the French cooks call Poêle... Take two carrots.. onions, two cloves.. sweet-herbs; mince all finely with half a pound of beef fat, and melt it. **1889** J. WHITEHEAD *Steward's Handbk.* IV. 405/1 Poêle is white or colorless broth of bacon and ham with vegetables used to boil chickens, sweetbreads, etc., in instead of water.

poem (ˈpəʊɪm). Also 6–7 **poeme**. [a. F. *poème* (in Oresme 14th c.), ad. L. *poēma* (in Plautus), a. Gr. πόημα (4th c. B.C.), early variant of ποίημα, thing made or created, work, fiction, poetical work, f. ποιεῖν (early variant ποεῖν) to make. (If ποίημα had been the form introduced, the L. would have been *pœēma*.)

The word *poem* was app. not in use till about the middle of the 16th c.; the sense was previously, from 14th c., expressed by POESY, sense 2.]

1. a. 'The work of a poet, a metrical composition' (Johnson); 'a work in verse' (Littré); a composition of words expressing facts, thoughts, or feelings in poetical form; a piece of poetry.

In addition to the metrical or verse form, critics have generally held that in order to deserve the name of 'poem', the theme and its treatment must possess qualities which raise it above the level of ordinary prose. Cf. quots. 1575, 1689, 1841, and see POETRY.

1548 ELYOT *Dict.*, *Poema*.. a poetes inuencion, a poeme [*ed.* 1538 *Poema*.. a poetes warke]. **1568** T. HOWELL (*title*) The Arbor of Amitie; wherin is comprised pleasant Poems and pretie Poesies. **1575** GASCOIGNE *Notes Eng. Verse* §1 in *Steele Glas*, etc. (Arb.) 31 The first and most necessarie poynt.. meete to be considered in making of a delectable poeme is this, to ground it upon some fine inuention. **1581** SIDNEY *Apol. Poetrie* (Arb.) 23 And may not I.. say that the holy Dauids Psalmes are a diuine Poem? **1636** B. JONSON *Discov.* Wks. 1641 II. 126 Even one alone verse sometimes makes a perfect Poeme. *Ibid.*, These three voices differ, as the thing done, the doing, and the doer; the thing fain'd, the faining and the fainer; so the *Poeme*, the *Poesy*, and the *Poet*. **1689–90** TEMPLE *Ess. Poetry* Wks. 1731 I. 236 The Frame and Fabrick of a true Poem, must have something both sublime and just, amazing and agreeable. —— *Ess. Learning* Ibid. I. 298 The Language is but the Colouring; 'tis the Conception, the Invention, the Judgment, that give the Life and Spirit, as well as Beauty and Force, to a Poem. **1706** PHILLIPS, *Poem*, a Piece of Poetry, a Composition in Verse, a Copy of Verses. **1736** SHERIDAN in *Swift's Lett.* (1768) IV. 181, I have written a little pretty birth-day poem against St. Andrew's day, which.. I intend for Faulkner to publish. **1828** WHATELY in *Encycl. Metrop.* I. 290/1 Any composition in verse, (and none that is not,) is always called, whether good or bad, a Poem, by all who have no favourite hypothesis to maintain. **1841–4** EMERSON *Ess.*, *Poet* Wks. (Bohn) I. 157 It is not metres, but a metre-making argument, that makes a poem. **1871** B. TAYLOR *Faust* (1875) I. Notes 319 Everything in this poem is perfect, thought and expression, Rhythm; but one thing it lacks: 'tis not a poem at all.

b. *transf.* (or in more general sense): Applied to a composition which, without the form, has some quality or qualities in common with poetry.

1581 SIDNEY *Apol. Poetrie* (Arb.) 28 Xenophon, who did imitate so excellently.. the portraiture of a iust Empire vnder the name of Cyrus, (as Cicero sayth of him) made therein an absolute heroicall Poem. **1873** RUSKIN *Fors Clav.* III. xxxiv. 6 Do you know what a play is? or what a poem is? or what a novel is?.. You had better first, for clearness' sake, call all the three 'poems', for all the three are so, when they are good, whether written in verse or prose.

2. *fig.* Something (other than a composition of words) of a nature or quality akin or likened to that of poetry (with various implications, as artistic or orderly structure, noble expression, ideal beauty or gracefulness, etc.).

1642 MILTON *Apol. Smect.* Wks. 1851 III. 270 He who would not be frustrate of his hope to write well hereafter in laudable things, ought him selfe to be a true Poem, that is a composition and patterne of the best and honourablest things. **1678** CUDWORTH *Intell. Syst.* I. iv. 421 There being as much continued and coherent Sence.. in this Real Poem of the World, as there is in any Phantastick Poem made by men. **1843** KINGSLEY *Lett.* (1878) I. 108 We shall have no need to write poetry—our life will be a real poem. **1856** EMERSON *Eng. Traits*, *Race* Wks. (Bohn) II. 24 The Celts.. gave to the seas and mountains names which are poems, and imitate the pure voices of nature. **1899** W. R. INGE *Chr. Mysticism* 47 The world is the poem of the Word to the glory of the Father.

3. *attrib.* and *Comb.*, as ***poem-book***, ***-maker***, ***-play***.

1806 R. CUMBERLAND *Mem.* (1807) II. 268 The public did not concern itself about the poem, or the poem-maker. *c* **1843** CARLYLE *Hist. Sk. Jas. I & Chas. I* (1898) 138 A small brown Poem-Book, not without merit. **1878** BROWNING *Poets Croisic* xlvii, 'The Royal Poet' straightway put in type His poem-prophecy. **1887** W. B. YEATS *Let.* 25 June in *Lett. to K. Tynan* (1953) 31 Sparling knows and much admires your 'Flight of the Wild Geese', from which I conclude it will figure in his poem-book. **1949** E. E. CUMMINGS *Let.* 23 Aug. (1969) 193 Poems are nonsellable enough.. without calling the poembook by some foreign word.

Hence (*nonce-wds.*) **ˈpoemet**, **ˈpoemlet** [see -ET[1], -LET], a small or short poem; **ˈpoeming**, composing or reciting of poems.

1799 W. TAYLOR *Let. to Southey* 4 Jan. in Robberds *Mem.* I. 244 A regular receptacle for those *poemets.. which aspire only to a summer's existence. **1871** H. B. FORMAN *Living Poets* 210 We have a great number of these 'poemets', bearing no traces whatever of the triviality of occasional verses. **1708** *Brit. Apollo* No. 84. 2/2 Loud Tawkings and *Poemings. **1887–9** T. A. TROLLOPE *What I remember* II. 369 Many of her verses she set to music, especially one little *poemlet, which I remember to this day.

poeˈmatic, *a. nonce-wd.* [ad. Gr. ποιηματικ-ός (Plut.) poetical.] Of the nature of a poem.

c **1819** COLERIDGE in *Rem.* (1836) II. 321 Conscious of the inferiority, the too poematic *minus*-dramatic nature of his versification.

poemell, obs. form of POMMEL.

poemscape (ˈpəʊɪmskeɪp). [f. POEM + SCAPE *sb.*[3]] The imaginary world envisaged in a poem.

1958 K. PATCHEN (*title*) Poemscapes. **1960** H. KENNER *Invisible Poet* v. 225 The trotting field-mouse is a figure in a poemscape, not like the rat in *The Hollow Men* the synecdoche of some omnipresent world.

‖**pœna** (ˈpiːnə). Also **pena**. In phrases freq. in L. inflected forms. [a. L. *pœna* penalty.]

a. Chiefly *Law* and *Theology*. A punishment.

1632 in *Decisions Court of Session* (1805) XXIV. 10036 They.. were content to pay the L. 100 *loco penae*. **1678** G. MACKENZIE *Laws & Customs Scotl.* II. xxx. 560 Skeen.. observes, that *pœna extraordinaria*, may be sometimes extended to death. **1757** in *Decisions Court of Session* (1805) XXIV. 10049 Expenses of plea.. are in no case due or exigible, unless the Court finds that a party has been litigious, and specially subjects him to the costs of his opponent, *in pœnam* of his offence. **1859** T. C. SANDARS *Inst. Justinian* (ed. 2) 492 *Pœna* is a punishment imposed by some general law, affecting possibly the *caput* and *existimatio* of the person punished. **1863** *Scottish Jurist* XXXV. 588/2 It is plain that here *pœna*—penalty—is used to mean a sum stipulated to be paid in the event of breach of contract. **1916** JOYCE *Portrait of Artist* (1969) 128 This is the greatest torment which the created soul is capable of bearing, *pœna damni*, the pain of loss. **1953** F. DE ZULUETA *Inst. Gaius* II. III. 207 In these cases of negative interest there is no question of dividing the action or the *poena* recovered. **1959**

JOWITT *Dict. Eng. Law* II. 1357/1 *Pœna*, a penalty, the punishment of an offence; generally inflicted for delicts.

b. *School slang.* = IMPOSITION 5 c.

1842 *Eton Bureau* 251 Then the luxury, when told to write out and translate my lesson, to know that beneath the ill-formed letters that disfigured my 'pœna', might safely lurk an intimation to posterity that the reader—charitably supposed to be the inflictor of the punishment—'was a fool'. **1865** *Etoniana* xiv. 201 To such a boy, of course, the usual '*pœna*' of lines from a Greek or Latin poet to learn by heart could be no kind of punishment at all. **1870** 'ETONIAN' *Recoll. Eton* I. viii. 87 He got a pœna for coming in late for morning school one day. **1877** G. N. BANKES *Day of My Life* xiii. 136 It's wretched bad practice for handwriting, this *pœna* writing. **1911** R. NEVILL *Floreat Etona* x. 301 Their usual practice being either to set some tremendous 'poena', which they afterwards revoked, or settle upon the wrong boy. **1941** L. A. G. STRONG *Bay* 70 If you were in disgrace he.. helped you with your poena and shooed you out of the empty classroom.

pœnal(l, obs. form of PENAL.

pœne, obs. var. PAIN, after L. *pœna* (B. Jonson).

poephagous (pəʊ'ɛfəgəs), *a. Zool. rare.* [f. mod.L. *Poēphaga*, neut. pl. (ad. Gr. ποηφάγος (Arist.) eating grass or herbs, f. πόα grass + -φάγος eating) + -OUS.] Eating grass or herbs, herbivorous; *spec.* belonging to the division *Poephaga* of marsupials.

1866 OWEN *Vertebr. Anim.* III. 294 Some palæontologists ..have been led astray in..referring it to the 'Poephagous Potoroos and Kangaroos'.

poer, obs. form of POOR, POWER.

‖**po'esis.** *Obs.* The Greek and Latin word for POESY, formerly sometimes used by English writers.

1567 DRANT *Horace* To Rdr., We write Poesis apace, and of all handes, sum wyth more, and sum with lesse learnynge. **1613** W. SHIPTON *Elegy on Sir T. Overbury* O.'s Wks. (1856) 11 This cynosure in neat poesis.

poeste, var. of POUSTIE *Obs.*, power.

poesy ('pəʊɪsɪ), *sb. arch.* Forms: α. 4 poysi, 4–5 poisie, 4–6 poysee, -ie, -ye, 5 poise, -ei, poyse, poyesye, 6 poisee, poysy. β. 5–7 poesie, -ye, 6 poesi, poezi, 5– poesy. See also POSY. [a. OF. *poesie* (*c* 1335 in Godef. *Compl.*) = Pr., Sp., Pg., It. *poesia*, Common Romanic formation for L. *poēsis* poetry, a poem, a. Gr. πόησις, early variant of ποίησις a making, creation, poetry, a poem. *Poesy* and *poet* occur earlier than *poetry* and *poem.*]

1. = POETRY. **a.** Poetical work or composition; poems collectively or generally; poetry in the concrete, or as a form of literature. (In early use sometimes including composition in prose, esp. works of imagination or fiction: cf. POEM 1 b, POET 1 b, c, POETRY 2.) Now an archaic or poetical synonym of *poetry*.

13.. *Min. Poems fr. Vern. MS.* lv. vii. 73 Salamon seide in his poysi, He holdeþ wel betere wiþ an hounde þat is lykyng and Ioly,..þen be a Leon,..Cold and ded. **1377** LANGL. *P. Pl.* B. XVIII. 406 Thanne piped pees of poysye a note. **1390** GOWER *Conf.* II. 148 Ovide..tolde a tale in Poesie, Which toucheth unto Jelousie. *c* **1400** *Destr. Troy* 418 As put is in poise and prikkit be Ouyd. **1560** WHITEHORNE *Arte Warre* 108 b, The perfeccion that poesie, paintyng, and writing, is now brought vnto. **1581** SIDNEY *Apol. Poetrie* (Arb.) 49 It is not ryming and versing, that maketh Poesie. One may bee a Poet without versing, and a versifier without Poetry. **1605** BACON *Adv. Learn.* II. iv. §1. **1636** DENHAM *Destr. Troy* Pref. (1656) A iij, Poesy is of so subtle a spirit, that in pouring out of one Language into another, it will all evaporate. *a* **1704** T. BROWN *Sat. Antients* Wks. 1730 I. 14 The Satirical poesy of the Greeks. **1841** D'ISRAELI *Amen. Lit.* (1867) 405 Among the arts of English poesie, the most ample and most curious is an anonymous work. **1883** *Congregationalist* Mar. 265 The Book of Psalms ..is the Paradise of Devotion, the Holy Land of poesy.

b. Poetry in the abstract, or as an art. **c.** Faculty or skill of poetical composition.

1579 SPENSER *Sheph. Cal.* Oct. 79 O pierlesse Poesye, where is then the place? **1589** PUTTENHAM *Eng. Poesie* II. i. (Arb.) 79 Poesie is a skill to speake & write harmonically. **1636** B. JONSON *Discov.* Wks. 1641 II. 125 A Poeme..is the worke of the Poet..Poesy is his skill, or Crafte of making. **1686** DRYDEN *Ode Anne Killigrew* 57 O gracious God! how far have we Profaned thy heavenly gift of Poesy! **1807** OPIE in *Lect. Paint.* ii. (1848) 273 Painting..has been called mute poesy. **1879** M. PATTISON *Milton* ii. 29 In *Lycidas* (1637) we have reached the high-water mark of English Poesy and of Milton's own production.

2. (with *a* and *pl.*) †**a.** A poetical composition; a poem. (In early use often in more general sense: An inventive or imaginative composition.)

c **1380** WYCLIF *Wks.* (1880) 124 þei prechen cronyclis & poisies & newe fyndynges of hem self. **1387** TREVISA *Higden* (Rolls) VI. 143 He made wonder poysies as it were of alle þe stories of holy writte. **1412–20** LYDG. *Chron. Troy* II. xii. (MS. Digby 230) lf. 67 b/2 He rehersed many poysies. *c* **1440** *Promp. Parv.* 407/1 Poyse, *poema*. **1552** HULOET s.v., He that maketh such poesies or Balades. **1575** LANEHAM *Let.* (1871) 5 [She] pronounced a proper poezi in English rime and meeter. **1605** BACON *Adv. Learn.* I. iv. §9 Holding them but as diuine poesies. *a* **1727** NEWTON *Chronol. Amended* I. (1728) 194 Thymætes..wrote a poesy called Phrygia. **1843** LYTTON *Last Bar.* II. iii, George of Clarence hath some pretty taste in the arts and poesies.

†**b.** *pl.* Poetical expressions or ideas. *Obs. rare.*

1387–8 T. USK *Test. Love* III. vii. (Skeat) l. 57 Thy wordes may nat be queynt, ne of subtel maner understandinge. Freel-witted people supposen in suche poesies to be begyled.

†**3.** A motto or short inscription (often metrical, and usually in patterned or formal language): = POSY 1, q.v. *Obs.*

c **1430** LYDG. *Min. Poems* (Percy Soc.) 65 And for youre poyesye these lettres v. ye take, Of this name Maria, only for hir sake. *a* **1548** HALL *Chron., Hen. V* 65 b, The tente was replenished and decked with this poysie [**1568** GRAFTON poesie], 'After busie laboure commeth victorious reste'. **1548** UDALL *Erasm. Par. Luke* xxiii. 172 b, There was also a superscripcion or poisee written on the toppe of the crosse, derectely ouer his head, in Greke, in Latin, and Hebrue letters. **1570–6** LAMBARDE *Peramb. Kent* (1826) 450 Out of the very same old word..is framed his Poesie, or woorde upon his armes (Ic Dien) I serve. **1596** SHAKS. *Merch. V.* v. i. 148, 151. **1602** —— *Ham.* III. ii. 162 Is this a Prologue, or the Poesie of a Ring? **1675** *Lond. Gaz.* No. 975/4 A Wedding Ring with this Poesie ('In thee my Choice, I do rejoyce').

†**4.** A bunch of flowers, a nosegay: = POSY 2.

1572 GASCOIGNE (*title*) A Hundreth sundrie Flowres bounde up in one small Poesie. **1629** R. HILL *Pathw. Piety* (ed. Pickering) I. 146 They do offer a poesy of flowers. **1688** R. HOLME *Armoury* II. 64/1 Sweet William is (as it were) many Pinks growing together like a Poesy.

5. *attrib.*

1387–8 T. USK *Test. Love* Prol. 25 There ben some that speken their poysye mater in Frenche, of whiche speche the Frenche men have as good a fantasye as we have in hering of Frenche mennes English. **1861** *Our Eng. Home* 151 The banqueting stuff..spread out on painted trenchers and 'poesie roundels'.

Hence **'poesy** *v. intr.* (*rare*), to compose or recite poetry; to speak or write poetically.

1819 KEATS *Isabella* ix, So said, his erewhile timid lips grew bold, And poesied with hers in dewy rhyme.

poet ('pəʊɪt). Forms: 4–5 poyete, 4–6 poete, 5 poiet, poyte, 5–6 poite, poiett, poyet, 4– poet. [ME. *poete, poyete*, a. OF. *poete* (12th c. in Hatz.-Darm.), mod.F. *poète*, ad. L. *poēta* (Plaut.), ad. Gr. ποητής, early variant of ποιητής maker, author, poet (cf. MAKER 5), f. ποεῖν, ποιεῖν to make, create, produce. (An early Gr. word in L.; if introduced at a later period, the form would have been *pœēta*.)]

1. a. One who composes poetry; a writer of poems; an author who writes in verse. (The ordinary current use; but now usually implying more or less of the sense of c.)

a **1300** *Cursor M.* 8531 (Cott.) Homer þe poet [*v.r.* poete], þat was sa rijf, Liued in þis king dauid lijf. **1388** WYCLIF *Acts* xvii. 28 As also summe of ȝoure poetis seiden, And we ben also the kynde of hym. **14..** *Nom.* in Wr.-Wülcker 680/23 *Hic poeta*, a poyte. *c* **1460** *Towneley Myst.* xvi. 204 Sekys poece [= poets'] tayllys. **1526** TINDALE *Tit.* i. 12 Won.. which was a poyet of their owne. **1567** *Satir. Poems Reform.* viii. 2 Skorner of poitis and sklanderus knaif! **1600** J. PORY tr. *Leo's Africa* III. 146 In Fez there are diuers most excellent poets, which make verses in their owne mother toong. **1604** R. CAWDREY *Table Alph.*, *Poet*, a verse maker. **1623** COCKERAM, *Poet*, one that writeth well in verse. **1665** DRYDEN *Ess. Dram. Poesy* (1889) 67 Shakespeare..was the man who of all modern, and perhaps ancient poets, had the largest and most comprehensive soul. **1755** JOHNSON, *Poet* ..a writer of poems, one who writes in measure. **1765** GRAY *Shaks.* 6 Fumbling baronets and poets small. **1844** BECK & FELTON tr. *Munk's Metres* 30 The poets have not all avoided the hiatus with equal care. **1876** STEDMAN *Victorian Poets* 281 She [Miss Rossetti] is a poet of a profound and serious cast.

†**b.** Formerly (after Gr. and L. use), in more general sense: One who makes or composes works of literature; an author, writer. *Obs.*

1362 LANGL. *P. Pl.* A. XI. 129 Plato þe Poyete I [Studie] put him furste to Boke. **1377** *Ibid.* B. XII. 260 þus þe poete [Aristotle] preues þat þe pecok for his fetheres is reuerenced. *c* **1400** *Destr. Troy* 306 All þat poites haue pricket of his prise dedis, I haue no tome for to telle. *Ibid.* 9075 Ne noght put in our proses by poiettes of old. **1611** CORYAT *Crudities* 319 Cornelius Nepos an eloquent Poet in the time of Cicero. **1678** CUDWORTH *Intell. Syst.* I. iii. 163 The soul,..in sleep or dreams,..seems to be surprized with unexpected answers and reparties, though it self were all the while the poet and inventor of the whole fable. **1755** JOHNSON, *Poet*, an inventor, an author of fiction; [etc.].

c. In select or emphatic sense: A writer in verse (or sometimes, in extended use, in elevated prose) distinguished by special imaginative or creative power, insight, sensibility, and faculty of expression. (Cf. POETRY 3 c.) ***poet's poet***, a poet whose poetry is generally considered to appeal chiefly to other poets.

1530 PALSGR. 256/1 Poet, a connyng man, *poete*. **1531** ELYOT *Gov.* I. xiii, Semblably they that make verses, expressynge therby none other lernynge but the crafte of versifyeng, be nat of auncient writers named poetes, but onely called versifyers. **1581** SIDNEY *Apol. Poetrie* (Arb.) 25 Onely the Poet..lifted vp with the vigor of his owne inuention, dooth growe in effect, another nature, in making things either better then Nature bringeth forth, or quite a newe formes such as neuer were in Nature. *Ibid.* 29 That fayning notable images of vertues, vices, or what els, with that delightfull teaching which must be the right describing note to know a Poet by. **1590** SHAKS. *Mids. N.* v. i. 12 The Poets eye in a fine frenzy rolling, Doth glance from heauen to earth, from earth to heauen. **1609** B. JONSON *Sil. Wom.* II. iii, Euery man, that writes in verse is not a Poet. **1636** —— *Discov.* Wks. 1641 II. 125 Hence he is call'd a Poet, not hee which writeth in measure only, but that fayneth and formeth a fable, and writes things like the Truth. **1806** WORDSW. *Personal Talk* iv, The Poets, who on earth have made us heirs Of truth and pure delight by heavenly lays! **1840** MILL *Diss. & Disc.* (1859) I. 80 Whom, then, shall we call poets? Those who are so constituted, that emotions are the links of association by which their ideas, both sensuous and spiritual, are connected together. **1844** LONGF. *Rain in Summer* 61 These, and far more than these, The Poet sees! .. He can behold Things manifold That have not yet been wholly told. **1844** L. HUNT *Imagination & Fancy* 75 Spenser..has always been felt by his countrymen to be what Charles Lamb called him, the 'Poet's Poet'. He has had more idolatry and imitation from his brethren than all the rest put together. *Ibid.* 107 Spenser emulated the Raphaels and Titians in a profusion of pictures... They give the Poet's Poet a claim to a new title,—that of Poet of the Painters. **1856** RUSKIN *Mod. Paint.* III. IV. i. §14 The power of assembling, by the help of the imagination, such images as will excite these feelings [of 'noble emotion'], is the power of the poet or literally of the 'Maker'. **1867** O. W. HOLMES *Guardian Angel* I. xviii. 280 Master Gridley lifted his eyebrows very slightly, remembering that some had called Spenser the poet's poet. **1873** SYMONDS *Grk. Poets* viii. 249 Aristophanes is essentially a poet—a poet in what we are apt to call the modern sense of the word—a poet, that is to say, endowed with original intuitions into nature, and with the faculty of presenting to our minds the most varied thoughts and feelings in language uniformly beautiful, as the creatures of an exuberant and self-swayed fancy. **1930** *Times Lit. Suppl.* 27 Feb. 149/2 Assuredly, in Lamb's day Spenser was the poet's poet. **1932** J. BUCHAN *Sir W. Scott* iv. 79 Dryden was not a poet's poet, any more than his editor. **1958** *Reporter* 10 July 38/2 (*heading*) A poet's poet looks at his art.

d. Hence occas., by further extension, applied rhetorically in a similar sense to one who practises any of the fine arts.

1839 tr. *Lamartine's Trav. East* 27/1 The poet,..—and by poet I mean whoever creates ideas in bronze, in stone, in prose, in words, or in rhymes—the poet stirs up only what is imperishable in nature and in the human heart. **1874** F. CROWEST (*title*) The Great Tone-Poets, being short memoirs of the greater Musical Composers.

e. ***poet-in-ordinary***, a poet ordinarily employed (after *physician-in-ordinary*, etc., ORDINARY *sb.* 18 b). ***poet-in-residence***, a poet working in or associated with a university or college or a community (see RESIDENCE *sb.*[1] 2 b). ***poet-laureate***: see LAUREATE *a.* 2 b.

c **1386–1843** [see LAUREATE *a.* 2 b]. **1865** KINGSLEY *Herew.* i, Godson of the great earl, and poet-in-ordinary to the band. **1894** A. BIRRELL *Ess.* xiv. 159 Spenser is sometimes [erroneously] reckoned amongst the Poets Laureate. **1972** *Guardian* 8 Feb. 24/5 W. H. Auden..returns to Christ Church, Oxford... Mr Auden..will be what the Americans like to call 'poet in residence'. **1973** *Black World* Jan. 28/2 Buford..is now poet-in-residence at Cleveland State University. **1977** *Canad. N. & Q.* Dec. 15/1 In January 1921 Robert Frost..was invited to visit Queen's and become the first poet-in-residence to occupy such an office in any Canadian University.

Hence **poet-laureateship** = LAUREATESHIP a.

c **1836** in *Byron's Wks.* (1846) 523/2 Pye, the predecessor of Mr. Southey in the poet-laureateship, died in 1813. **1874** C. GIBBON *Casquet of Lit.* V. 358/2 Thomas Warton.. obtained the poet-laureateship in 1785.

f. *fig.* Applied to a singing bird.

a **1748** THOMSON *Ode*, O nightingale! best poet of the grove. **1892** TENNYSON *Throstle* i, Summer is coming, summer is coming, I know it, I know it, I know it... Yes, my wild little Poet.

g. A scholar in the poetry class: see POETRY 6.

1679 *Trials of White & Other Jesuits* 47, Parry. I was a Student there, a Poet.

2. *attrib.* and *Comb.* **a.** appositive (= 'that is a poet'), as ***poet-actor, -artist, -bird, -bishop,*** †***-bounce*** (BOUNCE *sb.*[1] 4 b), ***-boy, -composer, -critic, -dramatist, -historian, -humorist, -king, -musician, -novelist, -painter, -pilgrim, -ploughman, -preacher, -priest, -princess, -prophet, -saint, -satirist, -seer, -singer,*** †***sucker*** (= 'sucking' poet), ***-thinker, -warrior, -woman***, etc. **b.** Of or pertaining to a poet, as ***poet-craft, -heart, -nectar, -song, -soul***, etc.; so ***poet-wise*** adv. **c.** objective, etc., as †***poet-ape*** (one who apes a poet), ***-hater, -whipper, -worship***. **d.** instrumental, etc., as ***poet-haunted, -hymned*** adjs.; ***poet-like*** adj. and adv.

1867 *Cornh. Mag.* XV. 666 The stage whereon the *poet-actor was enacting the counterfeit presentment of a king. **1581** SIDNEY *Apol. Poetrie* (Arb.) 71 The cause why it [Poesie] is not esteemed in Englande, is the fault of *Poet-apes, not Poets. **1817–18** SHELLEY *Rosalind & Helen* 1119 The nightingale..the *poet-bird. **1909** *Westm. Gaz.* 2 June 5/1 The oldest existing wine club, the 'Phœnix', of which the *poet-bishop, Heber, was once a luminary. **1632** BROME *Novella* Prol., Those *Poet-Bownces that write English Greeke. **1838** LYTTON *Alice* VIII. iii, A dream that had hovered over the *poet-boy. **1947** A. EINSTEIN *Music in Romantic Era* xvi. 256 Lortzing..in more modest proportions was comparable to Wagner as a *poet-composer. **1968** *Jrnl. Mus. Acad. Madras* XXXIX. 102 The Tirupati poet-composer. **1977** *Early Music* Oct. 469/2 Machaut..maintained a dual role: one of..poet-composer, detached from the story. **1863** *Edin. Rev.* Apr. 354 A controversy..lost in the mysteries of *poetcraft. **1956** *Essays in Criticism* VI. 212 *Poet-critics as dissimilar as Arthur Symons and Mr. Eliot. **1964** *English Studies* XLV. 290 Of course a poet-critic may be allowed to speak in images. **1581** SIDNEY *Apol. Poetrie* (Arb.) 48 Not onely in these *Mysomousoi*, *Poet-haters, but in all that kinde of people, who seek a prayse by dispraysing others. **1895** MARIE CORELLI *Sorrows of Satan* xxxiii, The beautiful autumnal woods of *poethaunted Warwickshire. **1844** MRS. BROWNING *Lady Geraldine's Courtship* Concl. viii, Is no woman far above me Found more worthy of thy *poet-heart than such a one as I? **1897** *Q. Rev.* Oct. 331 The poet-satirist succeeds the *poet-humorist. **1859** W. Bagehot *Coll. Works* (1965) II. 114 The *poet-king of Israel.. David. **1571** Golding *Calvin on Ps.* vi. 7 Yet dooth not David enlarge his sorowe *Poetlike. **1842** Tennyson *Edwin Morris* 27 Poet-like he spoke. **1903** A. W. Patterson *Schumann* 140 May not the shadow of the gloom that already brooded over him.. already have been overclouding the mental vision of the *poet-musician? **1947** A. Einstein *Music in Romantic Era* iii. 28 Wagner, all his life, thought of himself not merely as a poet-musician. **1957** N. Frye *Sound & Poetry* I. 5 The poet-musician of the Renaissance disappeared, and with few exceptions the major poets of the period gave little thought to the possibilities of musical setting. **1839** Clough *Early Poems* ii. 19 A fount Of the true *poet-nectar whence to fill The golden urns of verse. **1931** R. L. Mégroz *Joseph Conrad's Mind & Method* 154 Three modern *poet-novelists.. might perhaps be bracketed with Wells among the competitors. **1948** F. R. Leavis *Great Tradition* iii. 128 It was the profundity of the pondering that I had in mind when I referred to him [*sc.* Henry James] as a 'poet-novelist'. **1881** O. Wilde *Grave of Keats* in *Poems* 145 O *poet-painter of our English Land! **1943** F. Thompson *Candleford Green* v. 75 Dante Gabriel Rossetti.. that poet-painter. **1892** Zangwill *Childr. Ghetto* I. 164, I sing.. the restoration of our land, and become the *poet-patriot of my people. **1844** Mrs. Browning *Vis. Poets* Concl. ii, That same green forest where had gone The *poet-pilgrim. **1886** Blackie in *19th Cent.* Apr. 534 The great *poet-ploughman of Scotland. **1821** Byron *Elegy on Keats* ii, The *poet-priest Milman (So ready to kill man). **1847** Tennyson *Princ.* III. 256 If that strange *Poet-princess with her grand Imaginations might at all be won. **1963** M. H. Abrams in N. Frye *Romanticism Reconsidered* 41 This voice is that of the *poet-prophets of the Old and New Testaments, now descending on Blake from.. John Milton. **1645** R. Stable *Elegy on Quarles, Sol. Recant.* 64 A *Poet-saint he was. **1842** S. Lover *Handy Andy* xxi, All were silent, for the *poet-singer was a favourite. **1903** L. F. Anderson *Anglo-Saxon Scop* 27 To have seen many lands, to have had a wide and varied experience was considered a qualification for the poet-singer's calling. **1828** Carlyle *Misc., Burns* (1857) I. 200 A true *Poet-soul, for it needs but to be struck, and the sound it yields will be music. **1614** B. Jonson *Bart. Fair* I. i, Gi' mee the man, can.. giue the law to all the Poets, and *Poet-suckers i' Towne, because they are the Players Gossips. **1934** *Publ. Mod. Lang. Assoc.* XLIX. 365 A *poet-warrior sings, adding the name of Grendel's conqueror to the role of Germanic heroes. **1581** Sidney *Apol. Poetrie* (Arb.) 47, I imagine, it falleth out with these *Poet-whyppers, as with some good women, who often are sicke, but in fayth they cannot tel where. **1844** Mrs. Browning *Vis. Poets* cvii, And Sappho.. O *poet-woman! **1856** —— *Aur. Leigh* v. 545 They sound strange As.. lovely *poet-words grown obsolete. **1839** Bailey *Festus* xx. (1852) 370 There is a *poet-worship, one of other Which is idolatry, and not the true Love-service of the soul to God.

e. Combinations with *poets'* or *poet's*: **poets' cassia**, the fragrant shrub anciently called *cassia*, supposed to be *Osyris alba* (see CASSIA[1] 3); **Poets' Corner**, (*a*) name for a part of the south transept of Westminster Abbey, which contains the graves and monuments of several distinguished poets (called, in the *Spectator* 1711, 'the poetical Quarter': see POETICAL *a.* 1); (*b*) applied humorously to a part of a newspaper or other periodical containing short poetical contributions; **poet's daffodil** = *poets' narcissus*; **poets'** (or **poet's**) **narcissus**, the common white narcissus, *N. poeticus*; also = PHEASANT'S EYE 2; **poets' rosemary** = *poets' cassia*.

1760 J. Lee *Introd. Bot.* App. 323 *Poet's Cassia, *Osyris.* **1765** Falconer *Demag.* 235 While his demure Welch goat, with lifted hoof, In *Poet's corner hangs each flimsy woof. **1766** Entick *London* IV. 417 An iron gate opens into the south cross isle; which from the number of monuments erected therein to celebrated English poets, has obtained the name of *The Poets Corner.* **1781** W. Cowper *Let.* 27 Feb. (1908) 60 If you please you may send it [*sc.* a poem] to the Poet's Corner. **1785** Crabbe *Newspaper* ad fin., The Poet's Corner is the place they choose, A fatal nursery for an infant Muse; Unlike that Corner where true Poets lie. **1881** *Antiquary* Oct. 137 Westminster Abbey: a Study on Poets' Corner. [**1772** R. Weston *Universal Botanist* III. 504 Poetic or Common pale Daffodil, or Narcissus.] **1870** W. Robinson *Wild Garden* II. 112 *Poet's Daffodil. *Narcissus poeticus.* Southern Europe. **1841** *Poet's narcissus [see HOOP-PETTICOAT 2]. **1883** W. Robinson *Eng. Flower Garden* 192/2 The finer types of the Poet's Narcissus should be grown for cutting. **1936** L. B. Wilder *Adventures with Hardy Bulbs* 19 The Poets Narcissus is perfect for dampish locations. **1965** H. Ramsbotham tr. *Schauenberg's Bulb Bk.* III. 229 This is the Poet's narcissus, one of the most widely distributed European species. **1977** R. Genders *Scented Flora of World* 322/2 (*heading*) The Poet's Narcissus and Hybrids. **1597** Gerarde *Herbal* III. vi. 1110 The *Poets Rosemarie or Gardrobe, Casia Poetica L'Obelij. **1760** J. Lee *Introd. Bot.* App. 323 Poet's Rosemary, *Osyris.*

poetast ('pəʊɪtæst). Also **poetaste**. [Shortened form of POETASTER.] = POETASTER. Also as *v. trans.* and *intr.*, to write in the manner of a poetaster; hence '**poetasting** *ppl. a.*

1892 Beerbohm *Let.* June (1964) 22 She [*sc.* Mrs Grundy] demands that 'they bring unto her by and by the head of Oscar the Poëtast on a charger'. **1908** *Daily Chron.* 10 Apr. 3/2 In the spring the poetaster poetastes as sure as fate. **1909** G. B. Shaw *Admirable Bashville* Pref. 290, I poetasted The Admirable Bashville in the rigmarole style. **1969** *Daily Tel.* (Colour Suppl.) 14 Nov. 36/1 George Herbert is not there, although.. Herbert's poetasting brother, Lord Herbert of Cherbury, is.

poetaster (pəʊɪ'tæstə(r)). [a. med. or mod.L. *poētaster* (Erasmus *Let.* 25 Mar. 1521), in It. and Sp. *poetastro*, obs. F. *poetastre* (1554 in Sainte-Palaye): see POET and -ASTER.] A petty or paltry poet; a writer of poor or trashy verse; a rimester.

1599 B. Jonson *Cynthia's Rev.* II. i, Madam Moria.. is like one of your ignorant poetasters of the time. **1601** —— (*title*) The Poetaster; or, His Arraignment. **1603** Florio *Montaigne* II. xvii. (1632) 359, I know a Poetaster, gainst whom both weake and strong,.. affirme and say, he hath no skil or judgement in Poesie. **1664** Butler *Hud.* II. iii. 358 Besides all this, He serv'd his Master In quality of Poetaster: And Rhimes appropriate could make, To ev'ry month in th' Almanack. **1762–71** Walpole *Vertue's Anecd. Paint.* (1786) III. 15 One Robert Whitehall, a poetaster of that age, wrote a poem called Urania, or a description of the painting at the top of the Theatre at Oxford. **1849** Macaulay *Hist. Eng.* iii. I. 369 An envious poetaster demonstrated that Venice Preserved ought to have been hooted from the stage. **1883** J. Hawthorne *Dust* I. 201 There are always poetasters enough; but of great poets.. there are never so many as not to leave room for one or two more.

Hence (*nonce-wds.*) **poe'tastering** *sb.* and *a.*, acting the poetaster, composing poor or feeble verse; **poe'tasterism**, **poe'tastery**, **-try**, the work of a poetaster, feeble verse or versification; **poe'tastress**, a female poetaster; **poe'tastric, -ical** (also, erroneously, **poetastic, -tical**) *adjs.*, of, pertaining to, or of the nature of, a poetaster.

1695 Cotton tr. *Martial* II. lxxxvi. (1860) 127 Make not the echo in my verses play, After the Grecian poetastering way! **1823** *Blackw. Mag.* XIII. 645 Examples.. drawn from Italianized poetasterisms. **1830** Mackintosh *Rev. of 1688*, Wks. 1846 II. 223 Mrs. Behn, a loose and paltry poetastress of that age. **1833** *Fraser's Mag.* VIII. 38 Fitzgerald is insulted as much for his politics as his poetastery. **1845** Thackeray *Crit. Rev.* Wks. 1886 XXIII. 83 Away with all poetastering at dinner-parties. **1858** *N.Y. Tribune* 13 Feb. 4/4 May some good genius save them from such poetastical platitudes! **1864** Webster, *Poetastry.* **1867** W. C. Hazlitt *Offspring Th. in Solit.* (1884) 232 The foregoing proverbial poemet or poetastrical proverb. **1893** *Temple Bar Mag.* XCIX. 295 His father thought his poetastic mother a fool. **1894** *Blackw. Mag.* Aug. 205 No more poetry or even poetastery for me.

poetaz ('pəʊɪtæz). [f. *poet*(*icus* + *taz*(*etta*, the specific epithets of two species of *Narcissus*.] In full, ***poetaz daffodil*** or ***narcissus***. A narcissus (*Narcissus* × *medioluteus*) belonging to a group of hybrids produced by crossing *Narcissus poeticus* and *N. tazetta*, bearing fragrant white or yellow flowers in clusters. Also *attrib.*

1906 *Gardeners' Chron.* 17 Mar. 169/3 Narcissus 'Poetaz'.—This name applies to a race derived by crossing *N. poeticus* and *N. Tazetta.* **1910** *Ibid.* 3 Dec. 406/1 Tazetta and Tazetta Hybrids. To include N. Tridymus, Poetaz varieties, [etc.]. **1913** *Daffodil Year-bk.* 51 These Poetaz Daffodils are now well to the front, and are really good decorative plants. **1934** E. A. Bowles *Handbk. Narcissus* xvi. 176 The present-day race classed as Poetaz varieties owes its origin to the Dutch firm of Messrs. R. Van der Schoot. In 1885 large stocks of Tazetta varieties were growing in their Nursery alongside beds of N. poeticus ornatus, and the experiment of crossing them was decided upon. **1959** S. Gibbons *Pink Front Door* xx. 234 The little sitting-room.. smelt of Poetaz narcissus. **1971** *Daffodil & Tulip Year Bk.* XXXVI. 44 There are.. not more than a couple of dozen poetaz in commerce today. **1977** R. Genders *Scented Flora of World* 322/2 Geranium. A poetaz hybrid.. unsurpassed amongst all flowers for its perfume.

'**poetdom.** *rare.* [f. POET + -DOM.] The condition or status of a poet; poetship.

1899 *Westm. Gaz.* 22 Nov. 2/2 Giving him no claim even to the honour of minor poetdom.

‖**poète maudit** (pɔɛt modi). [Fr., = cursed poet.] A poet who is insufficiently appreciated by his contemporaries. Also *transf.*

[**1884** P. Verlaine (*title*) Les poètes maudits.] **1930** L. P. Shanks *Baudelaire* p. vii, Certainly Baudelaire was a *poète maudit*, pursued by the disaster which pursued his fellow-poet Edgar Poe. **1949** M. Turnell tr. *J.-P. Sartre's Baudelaire* 155 The proud free criminal, the Don Juan of hell, the rebel was also at the same time the *poète maudit*, the Devil's marionette. **1958** *Listener* 17 July 98/2 A *poète maudit* is doubly accursed when he exhibits himself and his world with the dry precision of classical prosody. **1963** *Times* 8 Feb. 14/1 It is a loosely assembled collection of episodes,.. following the self-destructive career of a late romantic hero—drunkard, sexual athlete and *poète maudit*. **1977** *Time* 26 Dec. 52/1 Once the ignored art, photography now stands robed in puffery, and armored with analysis; like painting, it has acquired its cast of heroes and *poètes maudits*.

poetese (pəʊɪ'tiːz). [f. POET + -ESE.] The mannered style of language supposed to be characteristic of poets.

1948 I. Brown *No Idle Words* 53 Has Empery, 'the power, status, or dominion of an Emperor', become entirely 'poetese'? In a leading article it would look a trifle odd. **1958** *Listener* 18 Dec. 1049/1 Mr. Bridson, choosing rhymed verse, never let it aspire to the high-poetic style or fall to 'poetese'.

poe'tesque, *a. rare.* [f. POET + -ESQUE.] Suitable for a poem.

a **1849** H. Coleridge *Ess.* (1851) II. 225 Happiness is not very picturesque, or poetesque either, far less dramatic, for it is serious without being tragic.

poetess ('pəʊɪtɪs). [f. POET + -ESS. So It. *poetessa* (Florio 1598), F. *poétesse* (1642 in Hatz.-Darm.), Sp. *poetisa*, etc.] A female poet; a woman who composes poetry.

1530 Tindale *Answ. More* xvi. (Parker Soc.) 92 Our lady hath.. emptied her of much high learning, which, as a goodly poetess, she uttered in rhymes. **1593** G. Harvey *Pierce's Super.* 186 The heauenly deuises of the delitious Poetesse Sappho. **1748** Lady Luxborough *Let. to Shenstone* 28 Apr., I am no Poetess; which reproachful name I would avoid, even if I were capable of acquiring it. **1830** Wordsw. in Chr. Wordsw. *Mem.* (1851) II. 226 British poetesses make but a poor figure in the 'Poems by Eminent Ladies'. **1873** Symonds *Grk. Poets* v. 129 Among the ancients Sappho enjoyed a unique renown. She was called 'the poetess', as Homer was called 'the poet'.

poetette (pəʊɪ'tɛt). *rare.* [f. POET + -ETTE.] A young or minor poetess.

1913 E. Pound *Let.* Nov. (1971) 26, I seem to spend most of my time attending to other peoples' affairs, weaning young poetettes from obscurity into the glowing pages of divers rotten publications, etc.

poethood ('pəʊɪthʊd). [f. POET + -HOOD.] The position or status of poet; the domain or fraternity of poets.

1849 *Fraser's Mag.* XXXIX. 25 Give me.. the healthy, wholesome loveliness, that shines on the face of the poet-hood of Britain. **1888** *Sat. Rev.* 704/2 His flourishing time of poethood and peerhood when Louis Philippe was king.

poetic (pəʊ'ɛtɪk), *a.* and *sb.* Also 6–7 **poetique**, 7 **-icke**, 7–8 **-ick**. [a. F. *poétique* (*a* 1400 in Godef. *Compl.*), ad. L. *poētic-us*, a. Gr. ποητικός, ποιητικός, f. πο(ι)ητής POET: see -IC. So It., Sp. *poético*.]

A. *adj.* **1.** Belonging or proper to poets or poetry. In quot. 1610, Fictitious, fabulous. ***poetic diction***, diction used in or considered to be proper to poetry (see DICTION 4).

poetic JUSTICE, LICENCE: see the sbs.

1530 Palsgr. 321/1 Poeticke in maners, *poetique.* **1585** James I *Ess. Poesie* (Arb.) 13 This onely thing I earnestly requyre, That thou my veine Poetique so inspyre. **1610** Healey *St. Aug. City of God* XVIII. viii. (1620) 626 Her [Minerva's] originall was vnknowne, for that of Ioues braine is absolutely poetique. *a* **1687** Waller *To Ld. Admiral* Wks. (1729) 47 With courage guard, and beauty warm, our age; And lovers fill with like poetic rage. **1693** Congreve in *Dryden's Wks.* (1701) III. Introd. 4 The God of Musick and Poetique Fires. **1728** Pope *Dunc.* I. 52 Poetic Justice, with her lifted scale. **1786** Burns *Brigs of Ayr* 38 What warm, poetic heart, but inly bleeds, And execrates man's savage, ruthless deeds! **1790** Burke *Fr. Rev.* Wks. V. 127 An unjustifiable poetick licence. **1800** Wordsworth *Lyrical Ballads* (ed. 2) I. Pref. p. xxi, There will.. be found in these volumes little of what is usually called poetic diction. *Ibid.* p. xxvii, The distinction of rhyme and metre is regular and uniform, and not, like that which is produced by what is usually called poetic diction, arbitrary and subject to infinite caprices. **1815** G. F. Nott *Works of Henry Howard & Sir T. Wyatt* I. p. clxxxviii, Chaucer did much towards refining our poetic diction, but he left it.. open to subsequent innovation and experiment. **1837** Dickens *Pickw.* ii, 'My friend Mr. Snodgrass has a strong poetic turn', said Mr. Pickwick. **1881** Froude *Short Stud.* (1883) IV. II. ii. 185 The poetic faculty.. secures to those who have it the admiration of every person. **1886** *Encycl. Brit.* XX. 859/2 As a mere question of methods, a reaction against the poetic diction of Pope and his followers was inevitable. **1928** O. Barfield *Poetic Diction: Study in Meaning* 177 The stale Miltonics, which lay at the bottom of so much eighteenth-century 'poetic diction'. **1938** A. Campbell *Battle of Brunanburh* 41 Despite the wealth of poetic diction at his command, he can be, at times, astonishingly simple and direct. **1951** C. Day Lewis *Poet's Task* 5, I hope to devote a number of.. lectures to what is called, somewhat uninvitingly, 'poetic diction'. **1970** M. Swanton *Dream of Rood* 59 The highly formalised nature of Old English poetic diction.

2. a. That is a poet.

a **1640** Day *Peregr. Schol.* (1881) 37 What Perseus.. spoke of the Crowe-poets.. may trewlie be said.. of vs poeticke-pies in this adge. **1841** D'Israeli *Amen. Lit.* (1867) 303 The great reformer of our poetry.. was the poetic Earl of Surrey.

b. Of a poet or poets.

1712–14 Pope *Rape Lock* v. 124 Markt by none but quick, poetic eyes. **1780** Cowper *Table Talk* 768 'Twould thin the ranks of the poetic tribe. **1791** —— *Retired Cat* 89 A long and melancholy mew, Saluting his poetic ears. **1880** L. Stephen *Pope* iii. 71 Chapman was a poet worthy of our great poetic period.

3. a. Of the nature of poetry; consisting of or written in verse; = POETICAL 3.

1656 Sir J. M[ennis] & J. S[mith] (*title*) Musarum Delicæ: or the Muses Recreation. Conteining severall Pieces of Poetique Wit. **1749** *Power Pros. Numbers* 38 When Prosaic Numbers are too much bound, the Stile is Poetic Prose; when Poetic Numbers are too free, it is Prosaic Poetry. **1844** Lingard *Anglo-Sax. Ch.* (1858) I. 377 A poetic paraphrase of certain portions of the service.

b. Having the style or character proper to poetry as a fine art; poetically beautiful or elevated.

1854 Milman *Lat. Chr.* III. vi. (1864) II. 78 Producing a vast mass of what was truly poetic. **1877** Shairp *Poetic Interpr. Nat.* viii. 110 In our own day such poetic descriptions of Nature have burst the bonds of metre altogether, and filled many a splendid page of poetic or imaginative prose.

4. Relating to or dealing with poetry. (= POETICAL 4.) Also, fond of poetry, able to appreciate poetry.

a **1704** T. Brown *Prol. 1st Sat. Persius* Wks. 1730 I. 51 My verse has never yet stood trial Of Poetick Smiths. **1817** Jane Austen *Sanditon* (1925) 91, I have read several of Burn's Poems with great delight.. but I am not poetic enough to separate a Man's poetry entirely from his Character. **1867** Carlyle *Remin.* (1881) II. 332 Wordsworth.. talked a great deal; about 'poetic' correspondents of his own (i.e. correspondents for the sake of his poetry; especially one such who had sent him, from Canton, an excellent chest of tea).

5. Celebrated in poetry; affording a subject for poetry. (Cf. HISTORIC *a.* 2.)

1742 POPE *Dunc.* IV. 489 While thro' Poetic scenes the Genius roves. 1883 WARNER *Roundabout Journ.* xi. 94 When you are on the east coast of Sicily you are in the most poetic locality of the classic world.

6. In etymological sense of Gr. ποιητικός: Making, creative; relating to artistic creation. *rare.*

1872 MORRIS tr. *Ueberweg's Hist. Philos.* I. (Cent.), Poetic philosophy is a form of knowledge having reference to the shaping of material, or to the technically correct and artistic creation of works of art. 1885 J. MARTINEAU *Types Eth. Th.* I. 57 [God] becomes a true Creator, with poetic function (ποιητής) as disposer of the ideas.

B. *sb.* †1. A writer of poetry, a poet. *Obs.*

*c*1650 J. PARRY *To Cleveland* C.'s Wks. (1687) 286 Where all Poeticks else may truckle under. 16.. —— *Elegy on Cleveland* 40 ibid. 285 'Tis your Crime T'upbraid the State-Poeticks of this time.

2. *sing.* and *pl.* That part of literary criticism which treats of poetry; also, a treatise on poetry: applied esp. to that of Aristotle. Also in extended senses.

1727-41 CHAMBERS *Cycl.* s.v., Aristotle's *poetics* is a work infinitely valued... Horace, Vieta, Vossus, and Scaliger, have likewise published *poetics* in Latin. 1776 BURNEY *Hist. Mus.* I. Pref. 8 It is imagined that Plutarch took it either from his [Aristotle's] Treatise on Music, or the second book of his Poetics. 1834 *Penny Cycl.* II. 335/2 Aristotle's genuine extant works may be divided into three classes: 1. Those relating to the philosophy of the mind... To this head may be referred..his Rhetoric and Poetic: the last of which works is imperfect. 1879 M. PATTISON *Milton* xiii. 200 The principle of the Aristotelean Poetic. 1917 T. S. ELIOT *Prufrock & Other Observations* 38 With your air indifferent and imperious At a stroke our mad poetics to confute. 1973 *Word 1970* XXVI. 66 Jakobson avoids the term *stylistics*, preferring instead *poetics*. 1976 *Times Lit. Suppl.* 2 Jan. 11/2 To subscribe to this poetic was to doubt the validity of art and the veracity of dreams. 1976 *Daily Tel.* 5 July 10/3 So autonomous are the poetics of Krzysztof Penderecki's compositional techniques, I found it hardly possible to reconcile words and music in his 'Canticum Canticorum Salomonis'. 1976 *Times Lit. Suppl.* 12 Nov. 1411/2 It is developed theoretically into an alternative poetic, for literature that classical and Coleridgean poetics are unable to treat with justice: a poetic of architectural as against organic form. 1977 A. SHERIDAN tr. *J. Lacan's Écrits* iii. 102 This notion must be approached through its resonances in what I shall call the poetics of the Freudian corpus.

3. *pl.* Poetic composition; the writing of poems.

1851 CARLYLE *Sterling* III. iii. (1872) 194 Our valiant friend..was not to be repulsed from his Poetics either by the world's coldness or by mine.

poetical (pəʊ'ɛtɪkəl), *a.* [f. L. *poēticus* (see prec.) + -AL¹: see -ICAL.]

1. Of, belonging to, or proper to poets or poetry. (= POETIC *a.* 1.)

poetical JUSTICE, LICENCE: see the sbs.

*c*1384 CHAUCER *H. Fame* III. 5 Here art poetical be shewed. 1530 PALSGR. 44 Whiche auctors do rather by a lycence poetycall. 1654 TRAPP *Comm. Job* xxxviii. 19 These are Poetical terms likewise. 1711 ADDISON *Spect.* No. 26 ¶4 In the poetical Quarter [of Westminster Abbey], I found there were Poets who had no Monuments, and Monuments which had no Poets. 1779-81 JOHNSON *L.P., Pope* Wks. IV. 135 Poetical expression includes sound as well as meaning. 1881 FROUDE *Short Stud.* (1883) IV. II. ii. 185 Keble.. possessed..the gift of expressing himself in the musical form which is called poetical.

†b. Such as is found only in poetry or imaginative writing; fictitious, feigned, imaginary, ideal. *Obs.* or merged in prec. sense.

1555 *Lydgate's Chron. Troy* To Rdr., Breakynge out.. into theyr poetycall fictions. 1569 J. SANFORD tr. *Agrippa's Van. Artes* 168b, It is manifest that it is altogether poeticall and fabulous. 1628 F. GREVIL *Sidney* v. (1652) 54 He found many reasons to make question whether it would prove Poetical, or reall on their part. *a*1680 BUTLER *Rem.* (1759) II. 126 Plato, who first banished Poets his Republic, forgot that that very Commonwealth was poetical.

†c. *poetical rising* and *setting* of a star: see quots., and ACRONYCHAL, COSMICAL, HELIACAL.

1594 BLUNDEVIL *Exerc.* III. I. xxxv. (1636) 348 The Poeticall rising is the appearing of some starre above the Horizon, determined by the Sunne. *Ibid.*, The Poeticall setting, is either the going downe of some starre under the Horizon, or else the hiding thereof under the beames of the Sunne. 1704 J. HARRIS *Lex. Techn.* I. s.v., The Ancient Poetical Writers..refer the Rising and Setting of the Stars, always to that of the Sun; and accordingly make three sorts of Poetical Rising and Setting. *Cosmical, Acronycal*, (or as some write it, *Acronychal*) and Heliacal.

2. Characteristic of a poet or poets.

1585 T. WASHINGTON tr. *Nicholay's Voy.* II. viii. 42 This Poet being full of poeticall spyte and indignation. 1876 L. STEPHEN *Eng. Th. 18th Cent.* II. 350 Pope had at least two great poetical qualities. He was among the most keenly sensitive of men, and he had an almost unique felicity of expression.

b. Having the character of a poet; possessing the imaginative power, insight, sensibility, or skill in verse-writing, of a poet.

1581 SIDNEY *Apol. Poetrie* (Arb.) 36 The Historian, bound to tell things as things were, cannot be liberall (without hee will bee poeticall) of a perfect patterne. 1600 SHAKS. *A.Y.L.* III. iii. 16 Truly, I would the Gods hadde made thee poeticall. 1620 T. GRANGER *Div. Logike* 129 Ouid is more Poeticall then Virgil. 1847 L. HUNT *Men, Women, & B.* I. i. 2 And this is most remarkable in proportion as he is a poetical poet—a high lover of fiction.

†c. That is a poet; composing in verse. *Obs.*

1662 STILLINGFL. *Orig. Sacr.* I. iv. §1 That their first writers were Poetical, and apparently fabulous. 1720 SWIFT *Fates Clergymen* Wks. 1755 II. II. 29 He was a thousand times recommended by his poetical friends to great persons.

3. Composed in poetry; written in verse.

1549 *Compl. Scotl.* x. 82 Quhou beit that the said poietical beuk be dytit oratourly. 1601 SHAKS. *Twel. N.* I. v. 207 Alas, I tooke great paines to studie it, and 'tis Poeticall. 1605 CAMDEN *Rem.* 8 Some Poeticall descriptions of our ancient Poets. 1710 SWIFT *Lett.* (1767) III. 21, I am now writing my poetical *Description of a Shower in London*, and will send it to the *Tatler*. 1855 BRIMLEY *Ess., Tennyson* 97 A poetical monument to a personal friend.

b. Of the style or character proper to poetry as a fine art; having the qualities of good poetry.

1447 BOKENHAM *Seyntys* Introd. (Roxb.) 3 The forme of procedyng artificyal Is in no wyse ner poetycal. 1717 POPE in *Lady M. W. Montagu's Lett.* Oct., The poetical manner in which you paint some of the scenes about you. 1868 *Morn. Star* 25 Feb., She combines the real with the poetical in that degree which assuredly marks the true artist.

4. Relating to or dealing with poetry; occupied with or fond of poetry.

1779-81 JOHNSON *L.P., Pope* Wks. IV. 5 Dryden's Fables ..were much in the hands of poetical readers. 1851 BRIMLEY *Ess., Wordsw.* 122 A new poetical philosophy. *Ibid.* 133 His poetical creed.

5. Worthy to be celebrated in poetry: = POETIC *a.* 5. *rare*⁻¹.

1878 SEELEY *Stein* II. 364 A man may also be poetical in the sense of being a good subject for poetry... In this sense, Stein was eminently a poetical person.

†6. In etymological sense of Gr. ποιητικός: Creative, formative; relating to artistic creation or composition. *Obs. rare.* (= POETIC *a.* 6.)

1597 MORLEY *Introd. Mus.* Annot., The second may be called Syntactical, Poetical, or effectiue.

Hence **poeti'cality** = POETICALNESS (in quot. 1575, a poetical expression).

1575 LANEHAM *Let.* (1871) 47 To cum oout of oour poeticalitéez, & too talk no more serioous tearms. 1607 HEYWOOD *Fayre Mayde* Wks. 1874 II. 48 Requires much poeticality in the subscription. 1923 J. M. MURRY *Pencillings* 200 The novel with which he was so enchanted was full of vague poeticalities. 1950 *Scrutiny* XVII. 188 He avoids the opposite danger of bolstering the commonplace by an extraneous poeticality. 1976 *Observer* 17 Oct. 32/2 What he was in fact up to a good deal of the time was spouting frigid poeticalities.

poetically (pəʊ'ɛtɪkəlɪ), *adv.* [f. prec. + -LY².] In a poetical manner, style, or form; in poetry or verse; in a way suitable to poetry or a poet.

1552 HULOET, Poeticallye, *poetice*. 1571 GOLDING *Calvin on Ps.* xviii. 5 To be enlarged poetically, and with glisteringe ornaments of words. 1646 SIR T. BROWNE *Pseud. Ep.* 132 Some have written Poetically as Ovid. 1753 HOGARTH *Anal. Beauty* xi. 90 How poetically doth the action..carry on the allusion to speed. 1847 TENNYSON *Princ.* Concl. 6 What, if you drest it [the story] up poetically!

b. In relation to poetry; as respects poetry.

1697 DRYDEN *Eneid* Ded. a ij b, It is not necessary the Manners of the Heroe should be virtuous. They are Poetically good if they are of a Piece. 1845 MISS MITFORD in L'Estrange *Life* III. xi. 197 Books typographically worth about eightpence—poetically good for nothing.

po'eticalness. [f. as prec. + -NESS.] Poetical quality or style.

1835 *New Monthly Mag.* XLIV. 314 Job stood..brooding in speechless poeticalness on his own thoughts. *a*1881 S. LANIER in *Century Mag.* (1883) May 135 A single fact in proof of this exceeding poeticalness will suffice.

poetician (pəʊɪ'tɪʃən). [f. POETIC + -IAN; cf. *rhetorician, mathematician*, etc.] A student in the poetry class: = POET 2 g: cf. POETRY 6.

1895 J. GILLOW *Bibl. Dict. Eng. Cath.* IV. 34 Guliel. Killick and Jacobus Gooden, poeticians at St. Omers College.

poeticism (pəʊ'ɛtɪsɪz(ə)m). [f. POETIC + -ISM.]

1. The practice of poetry; a being poetic.

1847 *Fraser's Mag.* XXXVI. 15 The sacred flowers and other minor embodiments of a religious poeticism. 1905 *Daily Chron.* 29 May 3/3 As long as the author..is content to confine the expression of his poetry to poeticism, the answer will not matter to him in the least. 1972 *Daily Tel.* 22 June 7/1 The book harks back to the luminous poeticism of much German romantic writing.

2. A poetical expression; an example of poetic diction.

1926 FOWLER *Mod. Eng. Usage* 442/1 *Poeticisms.* Simple reference of words to this article warns the reader that to use them in ordinary prose contexts is dangerous. 1956 *Essays in Criticism* VI. 156 His language avoids conventional poeticisms.

po'eticize (-saɪz), *v.* [f. as prec. + -IZE.]

1. *trans.* To make poetic; to treat poetically; to put into poetry, write poetry about. Hence **po'eticized** *ppl. a.*; **po'eticizing** *vbl. sb.* Also **po'eticizable** *a.*; **poetici'zation, po'eticizer.**

1804 ANNA SEWARD *Lett.* (1811) VI. 141, I think its author has poeticized, if I may be allowed the word, the new and fortunate subject. 1833 S. AUSTIN *Charac. Goethe* I. 315 *note*, Wilhelm Meister's Apprenticeship..is a poeticized, civic and domestic story. 1874 *Contemp. Rev.* XXIV. 870 The working class was..idealized and poeticized by wayward genius. 1923 J. M. MURRY *Pencillings* 189 What he is really lamenting is the absence of poeticisation, of what is called 'imaginative writing'. 1926 FOWLER *Mod. Eng. Usage* 442/2 *Poeticize* makes *-zable*. 1961 *Encounter* XVII. 68 Rossetti appears to me a poeticiser. 1965 *New Statesman* 22 Oct. 617/3 In the studio, he [*sc.* Corot] dropped into tame poeticising, due no doubt to what Mr. Gould calles his 'vein of emotional immaturity'. 1973 *Human World* Feb. 7 The anxiety Mr Maddox senses in the environmentalists comes to no more than a yearning for a universal poeticized prosperity. 1975 *Listener* 11 Sept. 348/1 Francis Ponge..is obsessed with the external world as a series of poetic or poeticisable objects. *Ibid.* 4 Dec. 772/2, I found the sub-Dylan Thomas-ish poeticising here off-putting.

2. *intr.* To write or speak as a poet.

1850 MAZZINI *Royalty & Repub.* 169 It pleases you to poeticize over the ruins of an institution, which was sublime.

po'eticness. *rare.* [f. POETIC + -NESS.] The quality of being poetic.

*a*1631 DONNE *Litany* viii, Pray for mee, That I by them excuse not my excesse In seeking secrets, or poetiquenesse.

poetico- (pəʊ'ɛtɪkəʊ), used as combining form of L. *poēticus* POETIC, with other adjs., to denote a combination of the poetic with some other quality, as ***poetico-antiquarian, -architectural, -commercial, -grotesque, -metaphysical, -philosophic.***

1818 BENTHAM *Ch. Eng.* 109 Ministers of the Established Church are, according to the system of poetico-architectural divinity, 'the pillars of divine truth'. 1827 CARLYLE *Misc., Goethe* (1869) 183 Götz became the parent of an innumerable progeny of poetico-antiquarian performances. 1837 J. S. MILL in *Westm. Rev.* XXVII. 50 Much genuine philosophy, disguised though it often be in a poetico-metaphysical vesture of a most questionable kind. 1878 GROSART in *H. More's Poems* Mem. Introd. 31/1 The peculiarity of More is in that poetico-philosophic mist, which..hangs in light and beautiful festoons over his thoughts. 1930 BLUNDEN *Leigh Hunt* viii. 99 It [sc. *Rimini*] almost became fashionable..but..by no means challenged the poetico-commercial achievements of Rogers.

poeticule (pəʊ'ɛtɪkjuːl). [f. L. *poēta* POET + -CULE.] A petty or insignificant poet.

1872 SWINBURNE *Under Microscope* 68 A poor young poeticule of the same breed as his panegyrist. 1880 —— *Stud. Shaks.* 240 The obtuseness of a full-grown poeticule or poetaster. 1882 *Fraser's Mag.* XXVI. 53 All the poeticules and prelatry of the court of Louis X.

poetism ('pəʊɪtɪz(ə)m). [f. POET + -ISM.] a. = POETICISM 1. b. = POETICISM 2.

1848 A. H. CLOUGH *Let.* 16 July in T. Arnold *N.Z. Lett.* (1966) 111 Matt[hew Arnold]..has become sadly cynical again of late. However I think the poetism goes on favourably. 1867 G. MEREDITH *Vittoria* I. xii. 202 Agostino smiles and chuckles, and talks his poetisms. 1977 P. B. & J. S. MEDAWAR *Life Sci.* ii. 23 The myth that geese might be born of such organisms as the attractive barnacle-like crustacean the goose barnacle, *Lepas anatifera*. Such notions belong to 'poetism'.

‖**poe'tito.** *rare.* [It. deriv. of L. *poeta* poet.] A paltry poet, a poetaster.

1632 B. JONSON *Magn. Lady* Induct., We haue diuers, that driue that trade, now; Poets, Poet'accios, Poetasters, Poetitos. 1689 SHADWELL *Bury Fair* Prol., Those wretched poetitos who got praise For writing most confounded loyal plays.

poetize ('pəʊɪtaɪz), *v.* [ad. F. *poétiser* (14th c. in Hatz.-Darm.); see POET and -IZE.]

1. a. *intr.* To play the poet; to compose poetry; to write or speak in verse, or in poetical style.

1581 SIDNEY *Apol. Poetrie* (Arb.) 60 Not onely to read others Poesies, but to poetise for others reading. 1596 FITZ-GEFFRAY *Sir F. Drake* (1881) 23 Free Poesie is made a marchandize, Onlie to flatter is to Poetize. 1630 DRAYTON *Muses Elizium* (1892) 11 They very curiously could Paint, And neatly Poetize. 1731 *Hist. Litteraria* II. 165 It is but a bold and vain Attempt to poetize in any Language learnt only by Grammar. 1826 *Blackw. Mag.* XIX. 355 Go over all the poets who have poetized about the sea. 1895 *Wales* May 240/2 A shoemaker from Llandwrog was with me..the person who poetized to Mr. Williams in the Bangor paper. 1917 J. B. CABELL *Cream of Jest* I. ii. 13 So Horvendile descended, still poetizing: '*Pus ab mi dons no m pot valer.*' 1939 L. M. MONTGOMERY *Anne of Ingleside* xxii. 147 He doesn't look clever but he can poetize.

†b. To deal in poetical fiction; to feign; to 'romance'. *Obs.*

1595 DANIEL *Civ. Wars* I. vi, I versifie the troth, not poetize. 1639 N. N. tr. *Du Bosq's Compl. Woman* II. 58 It seems they no whit Poetize, who say that Arithmetick cannot multiply so farre.

†2. *trans.* (with *simple obj.* or *obj. cl.*) To record or tell in poetry. *Obs.*

1609 HEYWOOD *Brit. Troy* XIV. *Schol.* 383 It is poetised of him that in the Elisian field after his death he espoused Medea. 1614 T. ADAMS *Fatal Banquet* iii, Wks. 1861 I. 212 What Ovid did but poetize, experience doth moralise, our manners actually perform.

3. *trans.* a. To make poetical; to turn into poetry; to imbue with the spirit or style of poetry.

1762 GOLDSM. *Ess.* xv. *Poetry disting.*, Virgil has.. poetized (if we may be allowed the expression) a whole sentence by means of the same word, which is *pendere*. 1847 *Blackw. Mag.* LXII. 473 He had poetised..the commonest objects of external nature. 1878 DOWDEN *Stud. Lit.* 32 Shelley poetizes the doctrine when Leon bids the tyrant Othman go free.

b. To celebrate in poetry; to compose poetry upon; to write or speak poetically about.

1837 EMERSON *Address, Amer. Schol.* Wks. (Bohn) II. 187 Instead of the sublime and beautiful, the near, the low, the common, was explored and poetized. 1884 J. PARKER *Larger*

Ministry 11 It is irrational.. to poetise the moon, and ignore the sun which she modestly reflects.

Hence **'poetized** *ppl. a.*, **'poetizing** *vbl. sb.*; also **,poeti'zation**, the action of poetizing, a turning into poetry; also quasi-*concr.* a poetical version *of* something; **'poetizer**, one who poetizes.

1875 *N. Amer. Rev.* CXX. 191 Would find a *poetization of that enterprise a rather tough morsel to swallow. **1889** CHURCH *Let.* 9 Nov., Life (1894) 341 A most melancholy, but in parts beautiful book, Edwin Arnold's poetisation of Buddhism. **1829** CARLYLE *Misc.* (1857) II. 78 Only *poetised philosophical speeches. **1877** MORLEY *Crit. Misc.* Ser. II. 298 The Religion of Duty lacks a vital mark of religion, and cannot be regarded as more than a highly poetized morality. **1599** T. M[OUFET] *Silkwormes* 20 These be the tales that *Poetisers sing. **1830** *Fraser's Mag.* I. 342 The Eastern poet is superior to the duller poetisers of more western countries. **1651** STANLEY *Cupid* Poems 69, I first admir'd, then transferr'd my excesse of Admiration to the folly of *poetizing. **1888** F. H. WILLIAMS *Atman* (1891) 243 He is probably bilious, but that is no excuse for his threadbare poetizings. **1894** *Athenæum* 2 June 702/3 A poet like Keats.. has no need to subject his lines to the poetizing process of Wordsworth. **1936** F. CLUNE *Roaming round Darling* viii. 74 A freezing night in August and eating cold corned beef! That's what poetizing does to a man. **1948** F. R. LEAVIS *Great Tradition* iii. 129 *The Waves* and *The Years*—works that offer something like the equivalent of Georgian poetizing. **1961** *PMLA* LXXVI. I. 309/1 None of these glimpses of poetizing without writing is intended to incorporate a signature into the epic matter.

'poetless, *a.* [See -LESS.] Destitute of poets.

1875 S. MANNING *Land of Pharaohs* 113 Poetless as they were, they had a national genius.

'poetling. [See -LING.] A young or budding poet; also, a petty or inferior poet, a poetaster.

1772 NUGENT tr. *Hist. Fr. Gerund* II. 117 One of those poetlings in bud which never ripen. **1830** LYTTON in *Select. Corr. M. Napier* (1879) 86 What is the meaning of this Bible mania among the poetlings? **1886** SYMONDS *Renaiss. It., Cath. React.* (1898) VII. xiv. 240 All classes, from popes and princes down to poetlings and pedants.

'poetly, *a. rare.* [See -LY[1].] Befitting a poet, poetical.

1423 JAS. I *Kingis Q.* iv, He, in his poetly report, In philosophy can him to confort.

poetolatry (pəʊɪ'tɒlətrɪ). [f. POET + -OLATRY.] The worship of poets; immoderate veneration for poets. So **poe'tolater**, one who practises poetolatry.

1936 C. S. LEWIS in *Essays & Studies* XXI. 165 There is yet another way in which Personal Heresy offends against personality;.. I am referring to the growth of what may be called Poetolatry. *Ibid.* 167 Most poetolaters hold that a dead man has no consciousness. **1939** LEWIS & TILLYARD *Personal Heresy* v. 104 Naturalism.. wants poets to be a separate race of great souls or *mahatmas.* Poetolatry is the natural result, for if there were such a race.. those who know no higher deity would do well to worship them.

‖**poetomachia** (pəʊ,iːtəʊ'meɪkɪə). [In form L., f. Gr. ποιητ-ής poet + μαχία fighting: see -MACHY.] A quarrel or contest of poets.

1602 DEKKER *Satiromastix* To World, That terrible Poetomachia, lately commenced betweene Horace the second, and a band of leane-witted Poetasters. **1898** *Athenæum* 30 Apr. 562 Never has a clearer picture been drawn of the poetomachia or theatre war, and of the other discordant elements that made up Shakespeare's every-day environment.

†**'poetress.** *Obs.* Also -is, -esse. [a. obs. F. *poetresse, poetrice*, f. L. *poētria* or *poētris* poetess, with suffix conformed to the fem. endings *-esse, -ice*, -ESS.] = POETESS.

1560 ROLLAND *Crt. Venus* III. 24 The Poetris and Maistres eik Sappho. **1591** SPENSER *Tears Muses* 576 [She] is her selfe a peereles Poetresse. **1622** PEACHAM *Compl. Gent.* iv. (1634) 36 Those foure sisters, the learned daughters of Sir Anthony Cooke, and rare Poetresses. *a* **1640** EARL STIRLING *Poems* 285 (Jod.) The poetress's hasty resolution. **1694** MOTTEUX *Rabelais* IV. lvii, Making Poets of Ravens.. and Poetresses of Magpies. **1756** J. KENNEDY *Curiosities of Wilton House* (1786) 47 The Busts of Sulpitia, the Poetress.

†**'poetrize,** *v. Obs. rare*[−1]. [f. POETRY + -IZE.] *intr.* To compose poetry (= POETIZE 1); to write in verse.

1602 CAREW *Cornwall* 78 b, Henry the third, honoured therewith his brother Richard King of the Romanes, a Prince no lesse plentifully flowing in wealth, than his brother was often driuen to extreme shifts through needinesse, which made that barbarous age to poetrize: Nummus ait, pro me nubit Cornubia Romæ.

poetry ('pəʊɪtrɪ). Forms: 4–7 poetrie, 5 -trye, -terye, 6 *Sc.* poyetrie, 5- poetry. [ME. = OF. *poetrie, poeterie* (13–14th c.), old It. *poetria* (Florio); ad. late and med.L. *poetria*, f. *poēta* poet.

Poetria occurs in a scholium on Horace *Epist.* II. i. 103, written (according to O. Keller, *Pseudacro*) *c* 650, perh. in North Italy, and preserved in MSS. of 10th c.; also in 9th or 10th c. MSS. of Martianus Capella. It is used as the title of treatises on the art of poetry, esp. the *Nova Poetria* of Gaufrei de Vinsauf (Galfridus de Vino Salvo, also called Galfridus Anglicus) about or soon after 1200; and in various works of the 13th c., as the *Græcismus* of Eberhardus Bethuniensis *c* 1212 ('Arte poetria fungor dum fingo poema'), the translation of Averroes' paraphrase of Aristotle's Poetics by Hermannus Alemannus *c* 1260, and the *Catholicon* of Joannes de Janua, 1286 ('a *poeta, poeticus*, et hæc *poetria* ars poetica'). (I. Bywater.) The relation of the word to L. *poētria*, Gr. ποιήτρια, poetess, is not clear; but, from its antiquity, its formative suffix cannot be identified with F. *-erie*, Eng. *-ery, -ry*, in such words as *chirurgery, drollery, bigotry, mimicry.* Our earliest English examples are from Chaucer, to whom the *Nova Poetria* of Galfridus was well known, as he makes the Nun's Priest refer to it in his Tale (l. 527) and apostrophize the author as 'O Gaufred deere Maister soueraym'.]

I. In obsolete senses.

†**1.** A rendering of med.L. *poetria* in sense of an *ars poetica* or treatise on the art of poetry. *Obs.*

1447 BOKENHAM *Seyntys* Introd. (Roxb.) 3 Galfridus Anglicus in hys newe poetrye.

†**2.** Applied to imaginative or creative literature in general; fable, fiction: cf. POET *sb.* 1 b. *Obs.*

c **1384** CHAUCER *H. Fame* II. 493 When thou redest poetrie How goddes gonne stellifye Briddes fisshe best. **1387** TREVISA *Higden* (Rolls) II. 279 Of þe bryngynge forþ of mawmetrie com wel nyh al þe feyninge of poetrie [L. *De ortu idolatriæ omnia pene figmenta manarunt*; 1432–50 Alle figmentes toke begynnenge allemoste of ydolatry]. **1484** CAXTON *Fables of Æsop* II. Proem, Fable is as moche to seye in poeterye as wordes in theologye. **1530** TINDALE *Pract. Prelates* Wks. (Parker Soc.) II. 268 They.. feigned Miracles, and gaue themselues only unto poetry, and shut up the scripture. **1601** HOLLAND *Pliny* II. 607 Their profession of Poëtry, that is to say, of faining and deuising fables, may in some sort excuse them.

II. In existing use.

3. The art or work of the poet **a.** With special reference to its form: Composition in verse or metrical language, or in some equivalent patterned arrangement of language; usually also with choice of elevated words and figurative uses, and option of a syntactical order, differing more or less from those of ordinary speech or prose writing.

In this sense, poetry in its simplest or lowest form has been identified with versification or verse: cf. quots. 1658, 1755.

1386 CHAUCER *Clerk's Prol.* 33 Fraunceys Petrak.. whos Rethorik sweete Enlumyned al Ytaille of poetrie, As Lynyan dide of Philosophie. **1412–20** LYDG. *Chron. Troy* III. xxv. (MS. Digby 230), Til þat he [Chaucer] came and with his poetrye Gan our tunge first to magnifye. *c* **1440** *Promp. Parv.* 406/2 Poetrye, *poetria.* **1509** HAWES *Past. Pleas.* (Percy Soc.) 2 Nothinge I am experte in poetry, As the monke of Bury, floure of eloquence. **1567** *Satir. Poems Reform.* vi. 9 Thair plesand flowre of Poyetrie. **1586** W. WEBBE *Eng. Poetrie* (Arb.) 21 Poetrie.. may properly be defined, the arte of making: which word as it hath alwaies beene especially vsed of the best of our English Poets, to expresse ye very faculty of speaking or wryting Poetically. **1658** PHILLIPS, *Poesie*, or *Poetry*, the art of making a Poem, *i.* any kind of subject consisting of Rythm or Verses. **1727–41** CHAMBERS *Cycl.* s.v., The rules of poetry and versifying are taught by art, and acquired by study... Its *matter*, long and short syllables, and feet composed hereof, with words furnished by grammar; and its *form*, the arrangement of all these things in just and agreeable verse, expressing the thoughts and sentiments of the author. **1755** JOHNSON, *Poetry*, metrical composition; the art or practice of writing poems. **1838** THIRLWALL *Greece* II. xii. 116 The first period of Greek poetry.. is entirely filled by the names of Homer and Hesiod. **1906** J. W. MACKAIL (*Communicated*), In general, the essence of poetry as an art is not so much that it is rhythmical (which all elevated language is), or that it is metrical (which not all poetry is, except by a considerable extension of the meaning of the word), as that it is *patterned* language. This is its specific quality as a 'fine art'. The essence of 'pattern' (in its technical use, as applied to the arts) as distinct from 'composition' generally, is that it is composition which has what is technically called a 'repeat'; and it is the 'repeat' which technically differentiates poetry from non-poetry, both being (as arts) 'composition'. The 'repeat' may be obvious, as in the case of rhymed lines of equal length, or it may be more implicit, to any degree of subtlety; but if it does not exist, there is technically no poetry. The artistic power of the pattern-designer is shown in the way he deals with the problem of 'repeat'; and this is true of poetry likewise, and is probably the key (so far as one exists) to any technical definition or discussion of the art.

b. The product of this art as a form of literature; the writings of a poet or poets; poems collectively or generally; metrical work or composition; verse. (Opp. to *prose.*)

1586 WEBBE *Eng. Poetrie* 28 The first wryters of Poetry among the Latines, shoulde seeme to be those, which excelled in the framing of Commedies. **1588** SHAKS. *Tit. A.* IV. i. 14 Cornelia neuer with more care Read to her sonnes, then she hath read to thee, Sweet Poetry, and Tullies Oratour. **1749** *Numbers in Poet. Comp.* 75 Speak here.. of the several Sorts of English Poetry, as divided into Heroic, Pastoral, Elegy, Satire, Comedy, Tragedy, Epigram and Lyric. **1763** J. BROWN *Poetry & Mus.* xiii. 223 If the Poet select and adapt proper Music to his Poem; or the Musician select and adapt proper Poetry to his Music. **1798** WORDSW. *Lyr. Ballads* (ed. 2) Pref. *note*, I here use the word 'Poetry' (though against my own judgment) as opposed to the word Prose, and synonymous with metrical composition. But.. the only strict antithesis to Prose is Metre; nor is this, in truth, a strict antithesis. **1807** *Edin. Rev.* XI. 216 The end of poetry.. is to please—and the name, we think, is strictly applicable to every metrical composition from which we receive pleasure, without any laborious exercise of the understanding. **1828** WHATELY *Rhet.* in *Encycl. Metrop.* I. 290/1 Good Poetry might be defined, 'Elegant and decorated language in metre, expressing such and such thoughts'. **1846** WRIGHT *Ess. Mid. Ages* II. 39 Poetry was the only form of literary composition found in the primeval age.

c. With special reference to its function: The expression or embodiment of beautiful or elevated thought, imagination, or feeling, in language adapted to stir the imagination and emotions, both immediately and also through the harmonic suggestions latent in or implied by the words and connexions of words actually used, such language containing a rhythmical element and having usually a metrical form (as in sense 3 a); though the term is sometimes extended to include expression in non-metrical language having similar harmonic and emotional qualities (*prose-poetry*).

1581 SIDNEY *Apol. Poetrie* (Arb.) 28 Verse being but an ornament and no cause to Poetry: sith there haue beene many most excellent Poets, that neuer versified. **1588** SHAKS. *L.L.L.* IV. ii. 165, I will proue those Verses to be very vnlearned, neither sauouring of Poetrie, Wit, nor Inuention. **1689–90** TEMPLE *Ess. Poetry* Wks. 1731 I. 235 Nor is it any great Wonder that such Force should be found in Poetry, since in it are assembled all the Powers of Eloquence, of Musick, and of Picture, which are all allowed to make so strong Impressions upon humane Minds. **1779–81** JOHNSON *L.P., Waller* Wks. II. 267 The essence of poetry is invention; such invention as, by producing something unexpected, surprises and delights... Poetry pleases by exhibiting an idea more grateful to the mind than things themselves afford. **1798** WORDSW. *Lyr. Ballads* (ed. 2) Pref., Poetry is the breath and finer spirit of all knowledge; it is the impassioned expression which is in the countenance of all Science. **1853** ROBERTSON *Serm.* Ser. II. xx, All Christ's teaching is a Divine Poetry, luxuriant in metaphor, overflowing with truth too large for accurate sentences, truth which only a heart alive can appreciate. *a* **1854** H. REED *Lect. Brit. Poets* vi. (1857) 220 A strain of prose which is poetry in all but poetry's metrical music. **1885** WATTS-DUNTON in *Encycl. Brit.* XIX. 257/2 Absolute poetry is the concrete and artistic expression of the human mind in emotional and rhythmical language. **1906** W. B. YEATS *Poems* Pref., Poetry.. is in the last analysis an endeavour to condense as out of the flying vapours of the world an image of human perfection, and for its own and not for the art's sake.

d. Extended (with reference to the etymology) to creative or imaginative art in general. *rare.*

[**1815** D. STEWART in *Encycl. Brit., Suppl.* I. 5 *note*, The latitude given by D'Alembert to the meaning of the word *Poetry* is a real and very important improvement on Bacon, who restricts it to fictitious History or Fables... D'Alembert, on the other hand, employs it in its natural signification, as synonymous with *invention* or *creation.*] **1856** RUSKIN *Mod. Paint.* III. IV. i. §15 Painting is properly to be opposed to speaking or writing, but not to poetry. Both painting and speaking are methods of expression. Poetry is the employment of either for the noblest purposes.

4. *pl.* Pieces of poetry; poems collectively. *rare.*

c **1384** CHAUCER *H. Fame* III. 388 Oon seyde Omere was [*v.r.* made] lyes Feynynge in hys Poetries. **1587** GOLDING *De Mornay* xxiv. (1592) 372 What shall we say then to the Poetries [of our Scriptures], specially of Dauid, considering that he was afore all the Poetries of the Heathen? **1656** EARL MONM. tr. *Boccalini's Advts. fr. Parnass.* 284 Desired that she might see both their Poetries; which after she had perused several times, and duly considered them, she.. chose Mauro's *Fava.* **1818** SCOTT *Rob Roy* xxiii, And this young birkie here,.. will his stage plays and his poetries help him here, d'ye think..?—Will *Tityre tu patulæ*, as they ca' it, tell him where Rashleigh Osbaldistone is? **1886** M. F. TUPPER *My Life as Author* 222 If some few have appeared among other poetries in print, they shall not be repeated here.

5. *fig.* Something resembling or compared to poetry; poetical quality, spirit, or feeling. Phr. ***poetry of the foot*** or ***of motion***: dancing.

1664 DRYDEN *Rival Ladies* III. 32 The Poetry of the foot takes most of late. **1813** LADY MORGAN *Wild Irish Girl* (ed. 5) II. xix. 156, 'I seldom dance,' said I—'Ill health has for some time coincided with my inclination, which seldom led me to try my skill at the *Poetry of Motion.*' **1816** KEATS *Sonn. Grasshopper & Cricket*, The poetry of earth is never dead:.. a voice will run.. about the new-mown mead; That is the Grasshopper's. **1817** COLERIDGE *Biog. Lit.* II. xiv. 1 The sudden charm, which accidents of light and shade, which moon-light or sun-set diffused over a known and familiar landscape.. these are the poetry of nature. **1818** BYRON *Childe Harold* IV. lviii. 32 That music in itself, whose sounds are song, The poetry of speech. **1846** MACKAY *Poems, Railways* 1 'No poetry in railways!' foolish thought Of a dull brain, to no fine music wrought. *c* **1863** T. TAYLOR *Ticket-of-leave Man* in M. R. Booth *Eng. Plays of 19th Cent.* (1969) II. 101 Come along, Emily, if you're at liberty to give your Montague a lesson in the poetry of motion. **1874** BLACKIE *Self-Cult.* 70 To live poetry, indeed, is always better than to write it. **1874** HARDY *Far from Madding Crowd* I. ii. 13 The poetry of motion is a phrase much in use. **1946** D. C. PEATTIE *Road of Naturalist* iv. 42 There is left only the poetry of speed and wind. **1959** E. H. CLEMENTS *High Tension* i. 10 He had never been back there. He had not.. seen poetry in the small exploit. **1975** *Times* 6 Mar. 13/5 There is a moment of poetry in a sequence where the dancers simply walk about carrying umbrellas. **1975** *Listener* 4 Dec. 747/2 Raffles.. compares the poetry of cricket with the poetry of burglary. **1977** *Zigzag* Apr. 30/3 This song captures what Television are all about: a kind of poetry in motion with a scorching musical backdrop.

6. (With capital initial.) The name given to the sixth, or (reckoning the *Preparatory* as one, the seventh) class from the bottom or third from the top, in English Roman Catholic schools, seminaries, or colleges, on the continent, and subsequently in England. The class so called comes between *Syntax* and *Rhetoric.*

1629 [see GRAMMAR *sb.* 5 c]. **1679** *Trials of White & other Jesuits* 56 *Fall.* I saw him when I was in my Syntax, and now I am in Poetry. **1773** [see GRAMMAR *sb.* 5 c]. **1838** C. WATERTON *Essays on Nat. Hist.* p. xxiv, One day, when I was in the class of poetry..about two years before I left the college.., he called me up to his room. **1887** *Stonyhurst Mag.* Nov. 34/1 Poetry..were granted a most unexpected but none the less welcome holiday on Thursday October 20th. **1906** ['Still in use at Stonyhurst, etc.; also at St. Edmund's or Douay College, now located at Woolhampton in Berks.' (Rev. Sir D. O. Hunter Blair, O.S.B.)] **1946** D. GWYNN *Bishop Challoner* iii. 39 By the summer of 1708 he had passed through the two higher classes of Poetry and Rhetoric.

7. *attrib.* and *Comb.*, as ***poetry professorship, reader, school, work-shop***; ***poetry-loving*** adj.; **poetry-book**, a book containing a collection of poems, esp. one used in schools; **poetry reading**, the reading of poetry, esp. to an audience; a poetry recital; **poetry recital**, a public performance of poetry; **poetry-voice**, a pompous or mannered style of writing poetry or reading it aloud.

1847 THACKERAY *Van. Fair* (1848) xii. 103 She wrote whole pages out of *poetry-books without the least pity. **1877** A. B. EDWARDS (*title*) A poetry-book of elder poets. **1881** R. L. STEVENSON *Virginibus Puerisque* 176 Whether we regard life as a lane leading to a dead wall..or pule in little atheistic poetry-books about its vanity and brevity [etc.]. **1903** 'A. MCNEILL' *Egregious English* 102 The demand for poetry-books by new writers has practically ceased to exist. **1935** E. FARJEON *Nursery in Nineties* v. 271 The poem was 'good enough' for the Poetry-Book. **1980** G. NELSON *Charity's Child* vi. 86 The poetry book, sir. **1798** WOLCOTT (P. Pindar) *Tales of Hoy* Wks. 1812 IV. 410 He scrawls the chairs and tables over, and walls whenever the *poetry-fit is upon him. **1885** *Illustr. Lond. News* 7 Nov. 468/3 The book is one on which every *poetry lover should form his own opinion. **1941** BLUNDEN *T. Hardy* ii. 34 The change was natural to the period and the *poetry-loving author. **1979** E. KOCH *Good Night Little Spy* iv. 24 A poetry-loving, moon faced charmer. **1887** DOWDEN *Transcripts* (1896) 516 The ignominious years of dreaming, *poetry-making, and the receiving of wretched praise. **1793** W. B. STEVENS *Jrnl.* 11 Mar. (1965) I. 72 Received a College letter, requesting me to support the pretensions of Mr. Hurdies to the *Poetry Professorship which will be vacant in Michaelmas Term next. **1940** R. S. LAMBERT *Ariel & all his Quality* v. 127 Few *poetry-readers win its [*sc.* the audience's] general approbation. **1975** 'G. BLACK' *Big Wind for Summer* ii. 32 The voice of the British Broadcasting Corporation's top poetry reader. **1917** A. HUXLEY *Let.* 11 Dec. (1969) 140 After that to Eliot, whom I found as haggard..as usual; we held a council of war about a *poetry reading, in which both of us are supposed to be performing. **1945** 'G. ORWELL' in *New Saxon Pamphlets* III. 35 That grisly thing, a 'poetry reading'. **1975** O. SELA *Bengali Inheritance* xvi. 139 She..organised poetry readings and prescribed reading books. **1966** J. BETJEMAN *High & Low* 73 A *poetry recital we are giving to the troops. **1978** J. SYMONS *Blackheath Poisonings* I. 34 The Rink Hall in the village, where the poetry recital was to take place. **1976** *Poetry school [see *poetry workshop* below]. **1846** THACKERAY *L. Blanchard* Wks. 1900 XIII. 477 The young fellow..*poetry-stricken, writing dramatic sketches. **1971** *Guardian* 28 Dec. 13/5, I hate the *poetry-voice; the poetry should speak for itself. **1972** *Country Life* 1 June 1418/3 Stevie Smith..was not one for the Poetry Voice. She mixes nonsense and its opposite. **1976** *Times* 1 Mar. 3/1 Mr Lovibond and his supporters..operate a *poetry school and workshop. **1977** *Time Out* 28 Jan.–3 Feb. 40/5 Audio-visual poetry workshop last Fri of month.

Hence '**poetryless** *a.*, devoid of poetry.

1854 H. STRICKLAND *Trav. Th.* 28 A soulless, poetryless, utilitarian, money-making Englishman is bad enough.

poetship ('pəʊɪt-ʃɪp). [f. POET + -SHIP.] The position or function of a poet; also with *poss. adj.* as a mock title for a poet.

1781 COWPER *Let. to J. Newton* 25 Aug., Johnson uses the discretion my poetship has allowed him, with much discernment. **1834** SIR J. STEPHEN in *Sir H. Taylor's Corr.* (1888) 59 Do not let your poetship snort and grow saucy. **1878** BROWNING *Poets Croisic* l, Fury of favour, Royal Poetship, Prophetship.

poeuere, poeure, obs. forms of POOR.

po-faced ('pəʊfeɪst), *a.* [Perh. f. POH *int.* or f. PO *sb.*³ + FACED *ppl. a.*², infl. by *poker-faced* adj.] Having or assuming an expressionless or impassive face, poker-faced; priggish, narrow-minded, or smug. So '**po-face**.

1934 C. LAMBERT *Music Ho!* III. 191, I do not wish, when faced with exoticism, to adopt an attitude which can best be described by the admirable expression 'po-faced'. We cannot live perpetually in the rarefied atmosphere of the austerer classics. **1937** T. RATTIGAN *French without Tears* I. 11 What's he like, though, really? Po-faced, I suppose? **1951** N. BALCHIN *Way through Wood* xvii. 239 You sounded po-faced on the telephone. **1958** *Economist* 11 Oct. 133/3 That 'middle class' which Low used to symbolise by a po-faced woman in a big fur coat. **1965** [see GALUMPH *v.*]. **1967** *Listener* 24 Aug. 232/2, I glimpsed [him]..being lightly grilled by a deliciously po-faced Joan Bakewell. **1973** K. GILES *File on Death* iii. 75 Her po face. **1973** *Times* 11 Dec. 5/3 We do not want to appear po-faced or ministry Scrooges, but on the other hand we should not like to see the country flooded with blazes of extravagant light. **1975** *Globe & Mail* (Toronto) 1 Sept. 7/1 Ted Stuebing..had one of his minions come on the tube all po-faced Saturday night to say that CFTO couldn't let the press in because it would have cluttered up the production studio.

poff, obs. form of PUFF.

‖**poffertje** ('pɒfərtjə). Also (*S. Afr.*) **poffartje, poffertjie** (-cə). [a. Du. *poffertje*, Afrikaans *poffertjie*, f. Fr. *pouffer* to blow up.] A small light doughnut or fritter dusted with sugar. Also *attrib.*

1872 *Cape Monthly Mag.* V. 230 Shall we take offence if an English host..set before our craving appetite..the dainty though untranslatable pumpkin 'poffartjes'? **1890** *Cent. Mag.* Nov. 49 Beside her..sat Jan Wisenkerke watching a buxom darky in a scarlet turban frying poffertjes. *Ibid.*, The kitchen walls were covered with..waffle-irons, poffertje pans. **1905** *Speaker* 11 Mar. 563/1 Poffertjes..are little round pancaky blobs, twisted and covered with butter and sugar. **1942** H. W. VAN LOON *Van Loon's Lives* 850 There is no use trying to describe them to outsiders, for *poffertjes* are the one dish that waxes only in the Low Countries. They are a cross between a very small kind of pancake and a fritter and are the main delicacy of..village fairs. **1949** [see MELKTERT]. **1974** D. WINSOR *Death Convention* viii. 68, I took a poffertje. It was a rather basic lump of dough fried in butter and dusted in icing sugar.

poffle ('pɒf(ə)l). *Sc.* Also **paffle**. [Deriv. obscure: cf. PIGHTLE and the phonetic variations under HICKWALL.] A small parcel of land: cf. PENDICLE 2 b.

(*Max poffil*, the poffle of Maccus, now Maxpoffle in Roxburghshire, is mentioned in 1317.)

1797 *Statist. Acc. Scot.* XIX. 328 Some places are parcelled out into small poffles or farms, few of which are above 30 acres each. **1818** SCOTT *Hrt. Midl.* Ded., Disclaiming all intention of purchasing that pendicle or poffle of land called the Carlinescroft. **1901** A. LANG in *Longm. Mag.* Feb. 380 In Spot itself he purchased a poffle or pendicle of land.

†**poge.** *Obs. rare*⁻¹. [app. repr. It. *appoggio* leaning place, stay, help: cf. *poggio* mounting block:—L. *podium*; see PEW.] Stay, support.

c **1525** BP. CLERKE *Let. to Wolsey* in Ellis *Orig. Lett.* Ser. II. I. 308 His Holynes being excluded frome the help and poge of other Princes.

poge, var. POGUE.

pogey ('pəʊgɪ). *N. Amer. slang* (now chiefly *Hist.*). Also **pogie, pogy**. [Origin unknown.]

a. A hostel for the needy or disabled; a poorhouse; a local relief centre or welfare office.

1891 *Contemporary Rev.* Aug. ii. 255 Begging is called 'battering for chewing'; railway brakemen, 'brakies'; poorhouses, 'pogies'. **1927** *Amer. Speech* June 387/2 A *pogey* is a poorhouse. Government homes for disabled veterans are also known as pogies. **1936** K. MACKENZIE *Living Rough* 269, I was in the Pogey a couple of nights. It stinks. **1953** D. M. LEBOURDAIS *Nation of North* 211 Thousands of self-respecting workmen..sat at home while their wives made the dreary pilgrimage to the 'pogie'. **1959** *Maclean's Mag.* (Toronto) 15 Aug. 21/1 Lean and hungry alley-cat men swung down from the freights and headed for a fifteen-cent mission meal or the innumerable pogies and scratch houses for a ten-cent cot. **1974** P. GZOWSKI *Bk. about This Country* 18 We had lived in teacherages, pogies and scratch houses and boarding houses. **1976** *Whig-Standard* (Kingston, Ont.) 9 Jan. 1/1 Unemployment insurance has indeed come a long way since the days of the pogey houses of turn-of-the-century England—dank, gloomy places where the indigent could do menial tasks in exchange for food and lodging.

b. Relief given to the needy from national or local funds; unemployment benefit.

1960 *Maclean's Mag.* (Toronto) 2 Apr. 54/2 Today unemployment-insurance payments are often referred to as pogey. But pogey in the depths of the thirties meant something as different from present-day unemployment insurance as panhandling is from drawing money from your bank account. **1961** *Time* 31 Mar. 9/2 Said a jobless Hamilton steelworker, father of six children: 'Why should I sweat for $40 a week? I'm getting more than that from the pogey, the welfare and the baby bonus.' **1964** H. T. BARKER *Ice Road* 49 During the winter we lived on turnips, potatoes, canned clams and the pogy, and Mother and I would hook rugs for the tourist trade. **1976** *Whig-Standard* (Kingston, Ont.) 6 Jan. 1/6 The Kingston area's fourth largest and fastest growing industry is unemployment insurance—pogey or, if you wish, the dole.

pogey bait ('pəʊgɪ beɪt). *U.S. slang.* Also **poggy, pogie, poguey bait.** [perh. f. POGY + BAIT *sb.*¹] Candy, sweets. (See also quot. 1970.)

1918 L. E. RUGGLES *Navy Explained* 88 While going through the war zone, the pockets are used for ciggies and poggy bait. **1929** *Papers Mich. Acad. Sci., Arts & Lett.* X. 315 *Poggy bait*, the sailor's designation for sweets. **1935** A. J. POLLOCK *Underworld Speaks* 90/1 *Pogey bait*, candy. **1953** M. DIBNER *Deep Six* xv. 154 A candy bar's called poguey-bait. **1970** *Esquire* Nov. 116 Pogie bait is any snack that is not prepared..in a government mess-hall.

pogge (pɒg). [Origin unascertained.] A name given to certain fishes. **a.** The armed bull-head, *Cottus cataphractus*, having a large broad flat head and sharply tapering body, armed with spines and bony plates. **b.** *Aspidophorus*, an acanthopterygian genus, armed with shield-like scales.

a **1672** WILLUGHBY *Ichthyogr.* (1686) Tab. N. 6, 2 Cataphractus supinus Schonfeldij. 3 idem. a Pogge. **1740** R. BROOKES *Art of Angling* II. xxix. 137 The Pogge..is about two Hands breadth in Length. **1753** CHAMBERS *Cycl. Supp.*, *Pogge*, or *Cataphractus.* **1769** PENNANT *Zool.* III. 178 The pogge is very common on most of the British coasts. **1823** CRABB *Technol. Dict.*, *Pogge*,..a sort of Bull-Head, the *Cottus cataphractus* of Linnæus, a fish having the head larger than the body. **1856** GOSSE *Marine Zool.* II. 200 *Aspidophorus* (Cuv.). Pogge. Body eight-angled, enclosed in plates; recurved spines on the snout; teeth only on the jaws; lower jaw fringed.

Poggendorff ('pɒgəndɔːf). [Name of J. C. *Poggendorff* (1796–1877), German physicist and chemist, who pointed out the illusion (see *Ann. der Physik und Chem.* (1860) CX. 502).] ***Poggendorff illusion***: an optical illusion in which the two ends of a straight line whose central portion is obscured by a rectangular strip crossing at an angle seem not to be in line.

1898 *Psychol. Rev.* V. 540 The Poggendorff illusion... This illusion is due to the fact that the two ends of the transversal, sundered by the vertical strip, are made to belong to two different systems, each suggesting its own perspective interpretation and being under no necessity..of appearing as parts of a continuous line. **1976** *Nature* 1 Apr. 397/2 (*caption*) The Poggendorff illusion in geological contexts; the illusory perceptual data are more likely to mislead when they favour an investigator's geological hypothesis than when they do not.

poggle ('pɒg(ə)l), *sb.* and *a. slang* (orig. Anglo-Ind. *colloq.*). Also **puggle, puggly, pugley.** [ad. Hind. *pāgal, paglā* (fem. *paglī*) madman, idiot.]

A. *sb.* A crazy or foolish person, an idiot. ? *Obs.*

1829 J. SHIPP *Memoirs* II. viii. 233 It's true, the people call me, I know not why, the 'pugley'. **1863** 'N. BROUGHTON' *Dawk Bungalow* II. 37, I was foolish enough to pay these hurrumzarders beforehand, and they have thrown me over. I must have been a poggle to do it! **1886** YULE & BURNELL *Hobson-Jobson* 542 *Poggle, puggly*, etc... Properly Hind. *pāgal*; a madman, an idiot; often used colloquially by Anglo-Indians.

B. *adj.* Mentally unbalanced, crazy; also, drunk, mad-drunk.

1925 FRASER & GIBBONS *Soldier & Sailor Words* 225 *Poggle* (also *puggle*), mad. An idiot. An old Army term. **1936** H. GRAHAM *Private Life of Gregory Gorm* 229, I can't quite make up my mind whether he is a genius, as some people seem to think, or only slightly poggle. **1971** B. W. ALDISS *Soldier Erect* 80 A woman in this bloody dump? You're going *puggle*, Page, that's your trouble! Too much tropical sun.

poggled ('pɒg(ə)ld), *a. Army slang* and *Sc.* Also **puggled**, *Sc.* **pagard, pagart.** [f. prec. + -ED².] = POGGLE *a.*

1923 G. WATSON *Roxburghshire Word-bk.* 227 *Pagart, a.* Also *pagard*... Breathless: 'A was fair pagard; A couldna rin another fitlenth.' **1925** FRASER & GIBBONS *Soldier & Sailor Words* 231 *Puggled*.., Insane. Mad-drunk. **1933** PARTRIDGE *Words, Words, Words!* III. 202 *Poggle(d), puggled*, 'rattled' as well as eccentric and mad-drunk, is a pre-war Regular-Army word. **1968** *Sc. Nat. Dict.* VII. 274/2 *Puggled, -t*, at a standstill from exhaustion or frustration, done for, at the end of one's resources. **1973** 'J. PATRICK' *Glasgow Gang Observed* xii. 112 One guest in particular..was 'stoatin' aw ower the place—pure puggled she wis'.

poggy ('pɒgɪ). Also **poggie.** [Origin unknown.] A small arctic whale; supposed to be the young of the common whale, *Balæna mysticetus.*

1874 SCAMMON *Marine Mamm.* I. v. 60 The whales of this sea [Sea of Okhotsk]..are the same species as those of the Arctic; although in the bays is found, in addition, a very small whale called the 'Poggy', which yields but little oil.

poggy, var. POGY.

poggy bait, var. POGEY BAIT.

pogh(e: see POH *int.*, POUGH *sb. Obs.*

poghaden, the menhaden: see PAUHAUGEN.

pogie, var. POGEY.

pogo ('pəʊgəʊ). Also **Pogo.** [Orig. unknown.]

1. A stilt-like pole (also called a *pogo stick*) on which one jumps about (see quot. 1921²); the pastime of jumping on or as on such a pole.

Formerly registered in the U.S. as a proprietary term.

1921 *Glasgow Herald* 30 Aug. 7 What is a Pogo? It is a four-foot pole, hollowed at the foot for the insertion of a strong spring, with a rubber cushion at the end of it. About half a foot above the spring are two steps. To Pogo you place one foot on each step, clutch the top of the pole firmly in both hands, and hop. **1921** *Punch* 21 Sept. 225/1 Charlie Chaplin intends to give a 'Pogo' to each of the children who are now attending his old schools. **1942** *Official Gaz.* (U.S. Patent Office) 1 Sept. 14/2 Philip de Journo, Forest Hills, Long Island, N.Y. *Pogo* for jumping sticks. Claims use since Feb. 28, 1941.

b. = *pogo-dance.*

1978 *New Society* 19 Jan. 115/2 The wildly exuberant punk dance—the pogo—..derives from the celebratory 'knees-up' of the football terraces. Basically, the participants leap up and down, two-footed, some of them alone, more in two or threes, with their arms linked... It's hot work, pogoing.

2. *attrib.* and *Comb.* **a.** Simple *attrib.* (sense 1 a), as ***pogo carnival, club, -player, stick*** (also *transf.*: see sense 2 b).

1921 *Glasgow Herald* 30 Aug. 7 On the Continent there are Pogo clubs, which conduct Pogo carnivals where the principal items are the high and the long jumps, and there are halls where you Pogo under much the same conditions as obtained on the roller skating rinks. **1921** *Oxford Times* 11 Nov. 16/4 On Thursday afternoon two undergraduates were seen racing along Cornmarket Street on Pogo sticks. **1924** *Punch* 24 Sept. 338 A dozen well-mounted pogo-players. **1958** *Daily Mail* 8 July 6/4 On stilts and pogo sticks (their latest craze). **1973** *Nature* 30 Nov. 313/1 The hopping of kangaroos is reminiscent of a bouncing ball or the action of a pogo stick.

b. With reference to low-frequency longitudinal oscillations of a space rocket.

1968 *New Scientist* 19 Dec. 653/2 The first stage of the three-stage rocket went into 'pogo-stick' oscillations. **1971** *Nature* 10 Dec. 316/2 The Diamant B [booster rocket] has been used successfully on three previous occasions, but a strong vibrational 'pogo effect' was noticed. **1976** SUTTON & ROSS *Rocket Propulsion Elements* (ed. 4) viii. 259 Techniques for damping Pogo instability tendency include..properly designed engine, interstage, and payload support structures.

c. Applied to dancing (esp. to punk-rock music) with movements suggestive of jumping on a pogo stick, as ***pogo dance, -dancing***.

1977 *Zigzag* Mar. 8/1 I've never subscribed to the theory that up to the age of thirty it was all pogo dancing down the Roxy. **1977** *Chicago Tribune* 2 Oct. VI. 14/4 The..punks' hopping 'pogo' dance.

Hence **'pogo** *v.*, (*a*) *trans.* to traverse on a pogo stick; (*b*) *intr.* to jump on or as on a pogo; to perform a pogo dance; also **'pogoer**; **'pogoing** *vbl. sb.* and *ppl. a.*

1921 Pogo *v.* [see sense 1 a of the sb.]. **1921** *Punch* 21 Sept. 225/1 Three men..expressed their intention of 'Pogoing' the Channel. *Ibid.*, A small girl has 'pogo-ed' five hundred miles. **1977** *Zigzag* June 6/4 'I want him thrown out,' he snapped to a roadie, pointing to the pogoing culprit. **1977** *Oxford Times* (City ed.) 30 Sept. 16 The dancers at the front jumping up and down on one leg (they call it pogoing, m'dear). *Ibid.*, Despite the vigorous pogoers, many members of the audience stood on the sidelines. **1977** *New Wave Mag.* No. 7. 3 They just arrived and pogoed through the front door. **1978** Pogoing *vbl. sb.* [see sense 1 b of the sb.]

‖**pogoniasis** (pəʊgəʊ'naɪəsɪs). *Phys.* [mod.L., f. Gr. πωγώνι-ον, dim. of πώγων beard + -ASIS.] Excessive growth of beard; also, growth of beard in a woman.

1842 DUNGLISON *Med. Lex.*, *Pogoniasis*, a female beard. Also, great strength or quantity of beard. **1895** *Syd. Soc. L.*

po'goniate, *a.* [Cf. Gr. πωγωνιάτης bearded man.] **a.** *Zool.* Bearded. **b.** *Ornith.* Webbed, as a feather.

[**1786** *Pogonologia* 19 The emperor Constantine is distinguished by the epithet of Pogonate, which signifies the Bearded.] **1890** in *Cent. Dict.* **1895** in *Syd. Soc. Lex.*

pogonic (pəʊ'gɒnɪk), *a.* [f. Gr. πώγων beard + -IC.] Of or pertaining to a beard.

1858 MAYNE *Expos. Lex.*, *Pogonicus*, of or belonging to the beard: pogonic.

So **pogo'nologist**, a writer on beards; **pogo'nology**, a treatise on beards; **pogo'notomy** [Gr. τομή cutting], the cutting of the beard; shaving; **pogo'notrophy** [Gr. τροφή nourishment], cultivation of the beard, beard-growing.

[**1786** (*title*) Pogonologia, or a Philosophical Essay on Beards, translated from the French.] **1788** V. KNOX *Winter Even.* I. ii. 24 It would not be surprising to see a barber style himself..Pogonologist. **1801** W. TAYLOR in *Monthly Mag.* XII. 422 Some years ago we had to read the Pogonology. **1861** *Temple Bar Mag.* III. 261 Ten years' experience may have made ourselves a little enthusiastic in favour of pogonotrophy. **1883** ROLLESTON in *Archæologia* XLVII. 455 There appears to be some necessary correlation between Hippophagy, Pogonotrophy, and perhaps Paganism. **1897** *Columbus* (Ohio) *Dispatch* Jan., Pogonotomy is what the Greeks used to call the gentle art of self-shaving. **1942** BERREY & VAN DEN BARK *Amer. Thes. Slang* §125/3 *Pogonotomy*, shaving. **1960** *Times* 28 Sept. (Advertising Suppl.) p. iii/2 This is the age, in fact, of pogonotomy. **1966** J. S. COX *Dict. Hairdressing & Wigmaking* 119/1 *Pogonotomy*, beard-cutting or shaving. **1966** *Daily Mail* 29 Oct. 1/1 This week's picture of Beatle George Harrison wearing a moustache—and a particularly sad, droopy looking one at that—caught students of pogonotrophy the world over in two minds.

pogonion (pə'gəʊnɪən). *Anat.* [f. Gr. πώγων beard + -ION².] The foremost point on the midline of the chin.

1897 in *Lippincott's Med. Dict.* **1920** H. H. WILDER *Lab. Man. Anthropometry* I. i. 47 *Pogonion* (pg), the most projecting median point of the chin, on the anterior surface (mental process). **1977** *Proc. R. Soc. Med.* LXX. 433/2 Mandibular length is of particular interest following mandibular osteotomy and it was measured from articulare to pogonion on cephalometric radiographs, using calipers.

pogonophore (pə'gəʊnəʊfɔː(r)). [a. mod.L. *Pogonophora* (K. E. Johannson 1937, in *Zool. Bidrag från Uppsala* XVIII. 253), f. Gk. πώγων beard + -φόρος bearing: see -PHORE.] A worm-like marine invertebrate belonging to the phylum Pogonophora. So **pogo'nophoran**, **pogo'nophorous** *adjs.*, of or pertaining to an animal of this kind or the phylum as a whole.

1955 *Systematic Zool.* III. 184/1 The large size of pogonophorous animals is interesting. **1958** *New Scientist* 20 Nov. 1303/2 All pogonophores look like bits of string or trawl twine. **1959** L. H. HYMAN *Invertebrates* V. xviii. 210 Pogonophores are exclusively marine and are mostly limited to abyssal depths. **1964** *New Scientist* 24 Dec. 842/3 Pogonophores are to be found in all seas, even in those places where the marine fauna had been previously studied with care. **1973** *Nature* 21 Dec. 452/1 Pogonophoran Phylogeny. .. The first international symposium on Pogonophora.. took place in the University of Copenhagen on November 1–3. *Ibid.* 452/3 Gupta finally expressed a doubt that pogonophores are coelomate animals at all. **1976** *Ibid.* 18 Mar. 218/2 The author devotes most space to the few species of animals, such as the ostracod *Gigantocypris* and the pogonophoran worm *Siboglinum*, that have been used by physiologists.

pogrom (pə'grɒm, 'pɒgrɒm), *sb.* [Russian *pogrom*, devastation, destruction.] **a.** An organized massacre in Russia for the destruction or annihilation of any body or class: orig. and esp. applied to those directed against the Jews.

[**1882** *Times* 17 Mar. 3/6 That the 'Pogromen' (riots against the Jews) must be stopped.] **1905** *Daily News* 12 June 5 The only means of combating the 'pogroms' is armed resistance. **1906** *Westm. Gaz.* 21 June 12/1 The Russian word 'pogrom' (pronounced with stress on the final syllable) is generally translated 'desolation, devastation'. The word is related to the Russian words *grom*, thunder, the thunder-clash, and to *gromit*, to thunder, to batter down as with a thunderbolt, to destroy without pity. **1919** N. SOKOLOW *Hist. Zionism* II. p. li, Not even the dark ages extracted so heavy a toll of Jewish blood: something like 1400 pogroms took place all over the Ghetto. **1968** *New Left Rev.* Jan.–Feb. 65 Then came the years of galloping inflation, of the pogroms, of acute social, political and intellectual ferment. **1979** O. SELA *Petrograd Consignment* 142 Wasn't he eager to go back to Russia..to read the Protocols of the Elders of Zion again; wasn't another pogrom all he lived for.

b. In general use: an organized, officially tolerated, attack on any community or group. Also *fig.*

1906 *Tribune* 16 June 7/2 This was the immediate signal for a *pogrom*, or organized riot. **1920** H. J. C. GRIERSON in *Proc. Brit. Acad.* 1919–1920 433 Only Henley refused to take part in the 'pogrom'; and he alas! died before completing his work as champion, critic, and editor of Byron. **1928** 'S. S. VAN DINE' *Greene Murder Case* i. 13, I note that our upliftin' Press bedecked its front pages this morning with headlines about a pogrom at the old Greene mansion last night. **1936** H. A. L. FISHER *Hist. Europe* I. xviii. 232 The Greek Empire..had disgraced itself by a *pogrom* against the French and Italian colony in Constantinople. **1964** *New Statesman* 13 Mar. 405/1 On 20 March 1914 58 British cavalry officers, stationed in Ireland, announced that they would not obey the orders of their lawful superiors... The cry of 'mutiny' was answered by the charge that there had been a plot—a 'pogrom' in the contemporary phrase—to crush Ulster's resistance to Home Rule by force of arms. **1967** T. GUNN *Touch* 27 Am I Your mother or The nearest human being to Hold on to in a Dreamed pogrom. **1971** *Sunday Times* 13 June 12/4 The army units, after clearing out the rebels, pursued the pogrom in the towns and villages. **1975** R. BROWNING *Emperor Julian* iii. 51 Hannibalianus had been killed in 337 in the pogrom of his relations engineered by Constantius.

c. *attrib.* and *Comb.*

1931 *Times Lit. Suppl.* 5 Nov. 855/2 Refugees to England from pogrom-haunted Russia. **1941** KOESTLER *Scum of Earth* 85 The French Government discovered a welcome diversion from the general discontent by exploiting the people's natural hostility to foreigners, and appealing to their pogrom instincts. **1949** —— *Promise & Fulfilment* I. vii. 69 Many of these young men had been members of the Jewish self-defence organizations in the pogrom-threatened small towns of Russia. **1978** D. MURPHY *Place Apart* viii. 167 Few of us would wish to see our army crossing the [Irish] border to fight Loyalist paramilitaries... If another 'pogrom' situation did arise..it would make more sense to welcome..refugees into the Republic.

Hence **po'gromist** (also stressed **'*pogromist***), an organizer of or participant in a pogrom.

1907 *Athenæum* 26 Jan. 99 Small wonder that the 'pogromists' laugh at Europe, and now pursue their work without intermission or disguise. **1960** S. BECKER tr. *A. Schwarz-Bart's Last of Just* (1961) II. 87 The pogromists were White Guards. **1962** *Guardian* 13 Oct. 6/3 Hate-mongers and pogromists. **1963** *Times* 24 Jan. 8/7 However, he criticized the 'complete lack of publicity in the Soviet press' and said that neither the pogromists nor the local police and prosecutors who abetted them had been punished or reprimanded. **1978** I. B. SINGER *Shosha* xiv. 254 People sacrificed themselves for Stalin, for Petlura, for Machno, for every pogromist.

pogrom (pəʊ'grɒm, 'pɒgrɒm), *v.* [f. the sb.] *trans.* To massacre (persons) in a pogrom; to destroy (a place) in a pogrom. Hence **pogromed**, **pogrommed** *ppl. a.*, that has experienced a pogrom.

1915 *Boston Jrnl.* 2 Feb. 3/2 [The Jews in Galicia] are being..pogromed. **1918** G. FRANKAU *One of Them* II. xv. 107 Its East End drab bits..Where toiled..The pogromed horde, and multiplied like rabbits. **1919** *Daily Chron.* 10 Oct. 1/1 The total number of places pogrommed was 353, and the Jews killed 20,500. **1946** KOESTLER *Thieves in Night* 217 They [*sc.* the Jews] are the most admirable salesmen in the world, regardless of whether they sell carpets, Marxism, ..or their own pogromed infants. **1979** *Country Life* 8 Nov. 1688 Such a gathering is, to Mr Pirates, vile enough to justify his decision to pogrom the lot.

pogue (pəʊg). *slang.* Also **poge**. [Perh. related to POUGH *sb.*] A bag, purse, wallet or container. Also by metonymy, money, takings. Also *attrib.*, as **pogue-hunter**, a thief who steals purses, a pickpocket.

1812 J. H. VAUX *Vocab. Flash Lang.* in *Mem.* (1964) 259 *Pogue*, a bag, (probably a corruption of poke.) **1879** J. W. HORSLEY in *Macm. Mag.* XL. 504/2, I went out the next day to Maidenhead, and touched for some wedge and a poge (purse), with over five quid in it. **1896** A. MORRISON *Child of Jago* xxiii. 229 The pogue-hunter, emptying the pogues in his pocket by sense of touch. **1906** E. PUGH *Spoilers* vi. 66 When the tiggies made a raid for a 'ot poge-hunter or snidesman. **1942** BERREY & VAN DEN BARK *Amer. Thes. Slang* §88/15 Purse, dummy, hide,..poge, poke. **1975** M. CRICHTON *Great Train Robbery* v. 29 What's your pogue up there, anyway? *Ibid.* vii. 39 It was the stickman's job to take the pogue once Teddy had snaffled it, thus leaving Teddy clean, should..a constable stop him.

poguey bait, var. POGEY BAIT.

pogy ('pəʊgɪ). *local U.S.* Also **poggy**, **pogie**. [Contr. from *pauhaugen*.] Local name of the menhaden: see PAUHAUGEN. Also *attrib.* and *Comb.*, as ***pogy-fisherman***, ***steamer***; **pogy-catcher**, a vessel employed in the menhaden fishery; **pogy chum** (see quot. 1858); **pogy-gull**, a sea-gull found near Cape Cod, Massachusetts; **pogy-press**, a press for extracting oil from fish; **pogy-seiner**, a boat used in seining for pogy (see SEINE *v.*).

1858, **1859** [see CHUM *sb.*²]. **1864** *Rep. Maine Board Agric.* 42 Rock weed, muscle bed and pogy chum will make grass grow. **1880** *Harper's Mag.* Aug. 341/1 A cast-off 'pogy'-press..had been piled upon an old wharf. *Ibid.* 347/1 The 'pogy' business was the catching of porgies and menhaden for their oil. **1888** GOODE *Amer. Fish* 385 North of Cape Cod the name Pogy is almost universally in use, while in southern New England the fish is known only as the menhaden. **1913** *Oysterman & Fisherman* 10 July 31/1 The new pogy steamer E. B. Thomas the largest ever built for the menhaden fishing industry made her official trip off Portland Monday. **1949** *Sun* (Baltimore) 29 July 2/1 Owners of the Virginia Pogy-Seiner Pluck today planned to advertise for a crew of licensed Maine fishermen. *Ibid.*, Newspaper ads would be tried tomorrow to see whether enough trained pogy-fishermen are available in this area. *Ibid.*, Pogies, or menhaden, are good only for their oil and fish-meal content.

pogy, var. POGEY.

poh (pəʊ), *int.* Also 7–8 **pough**, 8 **pogh**, 9 **po**. An ejaculation of contemptuous rejection. (Cf. POOH.)

1679 PRANCE *Narr. Pop. Plot* 13 Pough, Pough, said Sr. Edmundbury, refusing at first to trouble himself. **1708** MRS. CENTLIVRE *Busie Body* II i, *Sir Fran.* For what? *Marpl.* Po'gh, for a hundred Things. *c* **1738** SWIFT *Lit. Ho. at Castleknock* Wks. 1755 IV. I. 306 Poh! fellow, keep not such a pother. **1787** *Minor* 174 Pogh; thought I, why should I fear a man. **1820** COBBETT *Gram. Eng. Lang.* §210 Poh! Never think a man either learned or good merely on account of his being called a Doctor. **1824** GALT *Rothelan* I. vii, Po! yours are as the pebble stones on the seashore to the jewels that may be bought in Ghent.

pohutukawa (pɔˌhuːtuˈkawa). [Maori.] A New Zealand evergreen tree, *Metrosideros excelsus*, belonging to the family Myrtaceæ and bearing clusters of red flowers with projecting stamens; also called the Christmas tree, as it flowers in December and January. Also *attrib.*

1832 G. BENNETT in *London Med. Gaz.* 7 Jan. 508/1 There is an unpublished species of Metrosideros..named Pohutakawa by the natives of New Zealand. **1851** V. LUSH *Jrnl.* 1 Sept. (1971) 84 Passing now at the foot of lofty perpendicular cliffs, in the crevices and the tops of which were the beautiful Pohutukawa trees. **1867** [see CHRISTMAS-TREE b]. **1886** J. A. FROUDE *Oceana* xviii. 308 Low down on the shores the graceful native Pohutukawa was left undisturbed. **1935** J. GUTHRIE *Little Country* xxi. 316 Along the edge of the coast road are the pohutukawa trees, flowering like bonfires. **1944** [see CHRISTMAS-TREE b]. **1959** M. SHADBOLT *New Zealanders* 22 We..picnicked in the shade of a crimson-blooming pohutukawa grove. **1965** F. SARGESON *Memoirs of Peon* iv. 62 A travelling Frenchman.. had not long since visited the Auckland beaches and painted the pohutukawas in flower. **1977** *N.Z. Herald* 5 Jan. 1-6/10 The cliffs rise behind, dotted with tiny pohutukawas, some little bigger than their first blooms.

‖**poi**¹ (pɔɪ). Also **poe**. [Hawaiian name.] A dish made in Hawaii from the root of the taro or kalo plant, by grinding, mixing, and allowing it to ferment; also, a dish made from the banana and pandanus fruit. Also *attrib.*

1823 C. S. STEWART *Jrnl.* 18 May (1828) vi. 133 This immense bulk of person is supposed to arise..from the abundance and nutritious quality of their food, especially that of poe, a kind of paste made from the taro, an esculent root, a principal article of diet. **1826** W. ELLIS *Tour through Hawaii* xi. 293 The house..was soon furnished. A sleeping mat spread on the ground,..a few calabashes for water and poë. **1829** [see POIPOI]. **1833** A. SMITH in M. D. Frear *Lowell & Abigail* (1934) 72 Their [*sc.* the Hawaiians'] 'staff of life' is poi, which is made by baking taro in the ground and pounding to the consistency of thin flour paste. **1840** F. D. BENNETT *Whaling Voy.* I. 213 They eat it in the form of a paste, or poë. **1862** M. HOPKINS *Hawaii* iii. 34 This succulent root [*sc.* taro] was sometimes cooked, but was more generally pounded into a semi-fluid mess, and allowed partially to ferment, when it was called *poi*. **1877** LADY BRASSEY *Voy. Sunbeam* (1878) 289 Poi is generally eaten from a bowl placed between two people, by dipping three fingers into it, giving them a twirl round, and then sucking them. **1894** *Outing* (U.S.) XXIII 392/1 The poi-pudding tasted like fig-pudding and was extremely palatable. **1905** [see LUAU]. **1924** J. M. BROWN *Riddle of Pacific* xvii. 182 The low coralline islands had not breadfruit, and yet made the fermented paste called sometimes *poi* and sometimes *mai*; and even volcanic islands like the Marquesas, which had breadfruit, preferred to make their *poi* of *taro*. **1951** *Amer. Speech* XXVI. 23 *Poi* dog (a nondescript cur; formerly the native breed of dog was fattened on 'poi' and served at feasts). **1954** [see LAULAU]. **1964** *Asia Mag.* 16 Aug. 20/1 *Poi*. .. Made from starchy taro roots, it is a pinkish-gray goo of one, two, or three-finger thickness depending upon the consistency of the paste. **1968** O. WYNDETTE *Islands of Destiny* II. 85 All five of his wives were enjoying with him a typical Hawaiian meal: baked pork, poi, and sweet potatoes.

poi² (pɔɪ). *N.Z.* [Maori.] A ball made of leaves and fibre attached to a string; a dance to the accompaniment of traditional songs, performed by Maori women and girls using such a ball. Also *attrib.*

1843 E. DIEFFENBACH *Travels in N.Z.* II. iv. 57 Another game is with one ball (poi) suspended from a string. **1859** A.

S. Thomson *Story of N.Z.* I. I. x. 196 Poi is a game played with variegated balls, about the size of large oranges, to which strings are attached. The string is held in one hand and the ball is struck with the other. **1905** W. BAUCKE *Where White Man Treads* 87 When the feasting and gaiety had subsided..we all lazily awaited the lining up of the poi maidens. **1935** J. GUTHRIE *Little Country* vii. 147 The tiny pois danced against arms and shoulders and breasts. **1938** [see HAKA]. **1943** N. MARSH *Colour Scheme* ii. 36 He's going round your younger lot talking about teams of *poi* girls. **1945** R. PARK in *Coast to Coast 1944* 42 There'll be girls dancing the poi. **1949** P. BUCK *Coming of Maori* (1950) II. ix. 243 The women's *poi* dance..used an accessory in the form of the *poi* ball... The *poi* balls in common use in modern times are made of dry bullrush leaves (*raupo*), about the size of an orange but slightly elongated, and with a short string... The movements with the long *poi* were slower than with the modern short *poi*. The string of the *poi* was held in the right hand and the ball was twirled and beaten back with the left hand while various movements were made over the shoulder, to the sides, the thighs, the knees, the head, the *poi* balls being kept twirling in perfect time to the songs sung by the leaders. **1950** *N.Z. Jrnl. Agric.* Jan. 89/1 One of the pois ..is interwoven with raw doghide, a custom which, because it pertained only to very early times, makes this poi a rarity. **1958** S. ASHTON-WARNER *Spinster* 47 The Maori love-songs ..and the poi tunes and the melodies they use in canoes. **1977** *N.Z. Woman's Weekly* 10 Jan. 35/2 A calendar which features Maori poi dancing at Rotorua.

poi, var. PWE.

†**poid**, *a.* (*sb.*) *Sc. Obs.* Also **poyd**. [perh. a. OF. *puit, puet, put*, etc., good for nothing, dirty, evil.] Vicious, evil, vile; as *sb.* a vile person.

1501 DOUGLAS *Pal. Hon.* I. 641 And all the court in haist thair horsis renȝeit, Proclamand loude, quhair is ȝone poid that plenȝeit, Quhilk deith deseruis committand sic dispite. **1513** —— *Æneis* IV. Prol. 190 Sic poyd makrellis for Lucifer bene leche.

poiesis (pɔɪˈiːsɪs). [f. Gr. ποίησις a making, creation; cf. POESIS, POESY *sb.*] Creative production, esp. of a work of art.

1934 in WEBSTER. **1962** *Listener* 24 May 901/2 The tutelary figure of all that belongs to poiesis. **1971** G. STEINER *In Bluebeard's Castle* III. 72 The equivocations between *poiesis*—the artist's, the thinker's creation—and death. **1973** MATIAS & WILLEMEN tr. Cegarra & Metz in *Screen* Spring/Summer 152 Metz uses the term realism to characterise both types [of filmic modernity]: in the case of Godard, 'a copiously disorganised *realism*, a brilliant and euphoric avatar of poiesis'.

-poiesis (pɔɪˈiːsɪs), comb. form of Gr. ποίησις (see prec.), used to form terms in *Med.*, as *hæmopoiesis* s.v. HÆMO-, HEMO-, *lymphopoiesis* s.v. LYMPHO-.

poiet, obs. form of POET.

poietic (pɔɪˈɛtɪk), *a. rare.* [ad. Gr. ποιητικ-ός active, effective, f. ποιεῖν to do, make. (So spelt and pronounced to differentiate the sense from *poetic*, of identical origin.)] Creative, formative, productive, active.

1905 *Athenæum* 29 Apr. 519/3 There are four classes in the State: the Poietic, the Kinetic, the Dull, and the Base. **1905** *Edin. Rev.* July 73 As its organisation becomes settled and efficient the State loses its poietic activity.

poietic, -al, obs. Sc. ff. POETIC, -AL.

poignado, poinado (pɔɪnˈɑːdəʊ). *Obs.* or *arch.* Also 6 **poineado, poinardo,** 6–7 **poynado,** (7 **poinadoe, -adow, poynedo**). [An alteration of PONIARD, app. through *poniardo*: see -ADO.] A small dagger; a poniard.

1567 J. SANFORD *Epictetus* To Rdr. A iv, A short dagger; which is vsed in the warres, or a Poineado. **1581** PETTIE *Guazzo's Civ. Conv.* III. (1586) 168 Perchance they perswade themselues that their seruaunts can not helpe themselues with their Poignadoes. **1587** *Mirr. Mag., Q. Cordila* xxxviii, Poynadoes all bedyde With bloud. **1593** G. HARVEY *Pierce's Super.* Wks. (Grosart) II. 226 What will he do..with the tempestuous Engins of his owne wit, that keepeth such a horrible coile with his Schoole-fellowes poinardo? **1611** CORYAT *Crudities* 408 Duke John his nephew drew his poinado out of his sheath. **1654** R. CODRINGTON tr. *Iustine* XXIV. 341 Brennus..did end his life with his Poynedo. **1658** PHILLIPS, *Poinard*, or *Poinado*. **1694** MOTTEUX *Rabelais* v. ix. (1737) 34 Poinadoes, Skenes, Penknives. **1821** SCOTT *Kenilw.* xxix, A melancholy gallant; who..has his hand on his poignado, and swears death and fury!

poignance (ˈpɔɪnəns, ˈpɔɪnjəns). *rare.* [f. POIGNANT: see -ANCE.] = next.

1769 O. RUFFHEAD *Life A. Pope* 114 The solemn air.. greatly heightens the poignance of the ridicule. *Ibid.* 119 The poet's closing the climax with the highest disaster of all, gives additional poignance to the ridicule. **1782** ELPHINSTON tr. *Martial* III. ii. 132 To lend the pepper poignance. **1812** E. WYNNE *Let.* 6 Apr. in *Wynne Diaries* (1952) xxx. 514 All the poignance of his sufferings. **1893** A. L. HADDON *What ails the House?* I. 129 Everything that surrounded me..lent poignance to my uneasiness.

poignancy (ˈpɔɪnənsɪ, ˈpɔɪnjənsɪ). [f. POIGNANT: see -ANCY.] The quality or fact of being poignant.

1. Pungency of taste or smell. Also *fig.*

1730 SWIFT *Let. to Gay* 19 Nov., I..sat down quietly at my morsel, adding only..a principle of hatred to all succeeding measures..by way of sauce..; and..one point of conduct in my lady duchess's life has added much poignancy to it. **1786** tr. *Beckford's Vathek* (1868) 50 Aromatic herbs of the most acrid poignancy. **1814** SCOTT *Chivalry* (1874) 11 Sated with indulgencies which soon lose their poignancy.

2. Keenness or sharpness of pain, distress, or grief; also, of pleasure (cf. next, 3 b).

17.. J. RYLAND in Spurgeon *Treas. Dav.* Ps. lxxvii. 6 Sometimes this reflection..adds a poignancy to our distress. **1787** J. BARLOW *Oration 4th July* 15 The tidings [were] received with a peculiar poignancy of grief. **1885** *Manch. Exam.* 15 June 5/4 The remembrance..gives our regrets a poignancy due to something like personal gratitude.

3. Piercing quality of words, expressions, looks, etc.; sharpness, keenness; piquancy.

a **1688** VILLIERS (Dk. Buckhm.) *Militant Couple* Wks. (1775) 125 Those words..have lost all the poignancy of their signification. **1719** J. WELWOOD in *Rowe's Lucan* Pref. 36 The first [Virgil] surpasses all in solid strength; the latter [Lucan] excells in vigour and poynancy. **1838** THIRLWALL *Greece* III. xviii. 83 Feelings..deeply stung by the poignancy of their wit. **1934** M. BODKIN *Archetypal Patterns in Poetry* 310 In each poem the lovely image gains poignancy from its imagined background of frustration and pain.

poignant (ˈpɔɪnənt, ˈpɔɪnjənt), *a.* Forms: 4–6 **poynaunt,** 4–8 **-ant,** 7–8 **poinant,** 7– **poignant,** (5 **pugnaunt, ponȝeand, -yaunt, -yawnt, poygnaunt, poyngnant**). [ME. a. OF. *puignant* (12th c. in Godef.), *poignant* (13th c.), pr. pple. of *poindre*:—L. *pungĕre* to prick, pierce.]

†**1. a.** Of weapons, or other pointed material objects: Sharp-pointed, piercing. *Obs.*

c **1400** *Rom. Rose* 1879 The God of Love an arowe took; Ful sharp it was and ful pugnaunt. *c* **1470** HENRY *Wallace* III. 141 The Scottis..With ponȝeand speris throuch platis prest of steylle. **1567** TURBERV. *Ovid's Epist.* 69 b, Poynant hornes of fell and yrefull bulles. **1624** GEE *Hold Fast* 51 This weapon, being made so poinant and deadly, that it would pearce..reasonable good armour. **1695** J. EDWARDS *Perfect. Script.* 339 They were dispatch'd themselves by a more poinant stroke.

b. *fig.* Of the eye or look: Piercing, keen.

1787 'G. GAMBADO' *Acad. Horsemen* (1809) 15 Jeffery was not so slim, or was his eye so poignant. **1820** MISS MITFORD in L'Estrange *Life* II. v. 120 Jeffrey has a singular expression—poignant, bitter, piercing—as if his countenance never lit up but at the perception of some weakness in human nature.

2. Sharp, pungent, piquant to the taste or smell.

c **1386** CHAUCER *Nun's Pr. T.* 14 Of poynaunt sauce hir neded neuer a deel. *c* **1450** LYDG. & BURGH *Secrees* 1949 Wyn..Ponyaunt, delectable, sharp in savour. *c* **1450** *Douce MS.* 55 (Bodl.) iii, Sesyn hit..so that hit be poynant. **1610** B. JONSON *Alch.* II. ii, Drest with an exquisite, and poynant sauce. **1728** YOUNG *Love Fame* VI. 44 Those charms are greatest which decline the sight, That makes the banquet poignant and polite. **1864** HAWTHORNE *Dolliver Rom.* (1879) 61 The rich, poignant perfume spread itself through the air. **1883** STEVENSON *Silverado Sq.* 237 A laboratory of poignant scents.

3. a. Painfully sharp to the physical or mental feelings, as hunger, thirst, a pang, an affront; also said of a state of feeling, as grief, regret, despair.

c **1386** CHAUCER *Pars. T.* ¶ 56 And this sorwe..shal been heuy and greuous and ful sharpe and poynant in herte. **1651** N. BACON *Disc. Govt. Eng.* II. I. (1739) 3 The last affront was from France, and that..more poinant. **1728** ELIZA HEYWOOD *Mme. de Gomez's Belle A.* (1732) II. 10 This final Answer threw the King of Portugal into the most poinant Despair. **1809–10** COLERIDGE *Friend* (1818) III. 233 Those rare excellencies which make one grief poignant. *a* **1881** ROSSETTI *Ho. Life* ii, Creature of poignant thirst And exquisite hunger. **1887** LOWELL *Democr.*, etc. 48 This pang is made more poignant by exile.

b. Stimulating to the mind, feelings, or passions; pleasantly or delightfully piquant.

1649 G. DANIEL *Trinarch., Hen. V*, ccclxvi, Better rellish, [which] in this poynant State Might give an Edge to Witt, at less expence. **1668** H. MORE *Div. Dial.* II. viii. (1713) 113 That Delights thereby may become more poinant and triumphant. **1772** GOUV. MORRIS in Sparks *Life & Writ.* (1832) I. 17 Those poignant joys, which are the lot of the affluent. **1860** HAWTHORNE *Marb. Faun* xliii, Sensible of a more poignant felicity than he had yet experienced.

4. Of words or expressions: Sharp, stinging; severe; also, pleasantly keen or pointed, piquant.

1542 UDALL *Erasm. Apoph.* 270 b, With these sharpe & poynaunte woordes he clene putte awaye yᵉ fearefull trembleyng of all the legions. **1668** DRYDEN *Dram. Poesy* Ess. (Ker) I. 103 Quick and poynant brevity. **1678** WYCHERLEY *Pl. Dealer* III. i, Poinant and sower Invectives. **1706** *Reflex. upon Ridicule* 208 Witticisms which you think so delicate and poignant. **1773** MRS. CHAPONE *Improv. Mind* (1774) I. v. 157 A witty repartee or a stroke of poignant raillery. **1821** LAMB *Elia* Ser. I. *Mrs. Battle's Opinions on Whist*, Her illustrations were apposite and poignant. **1844** DISRAELI *Coningsby* III. i, Poignant sarcasm.

poignantly (ˈpɔɪnəntlɪ), *adv.* [f. prec. + -LY².] In a poignant manner; piercingly, pungently, acutely, keenly.

1794 G. ADAMS *Nat. & Exp. Philos.* II. xvii. 250 How poignantly this loss [of sight] was felt by our great poet is painfully evident from his own words. **1818** MRS. SHELLEY *Frankenst.* xii. (1865) 147 They often..suffered the pangs of hunger very poignantly. **1837–9** HALLAM *Hist. Lit.* II. II. v. §16. 192 Burlesque poetry, sometimes poignantly satirical. **1871** RUSKIN *Fors Clav.* I. iv. 8, I have a piece of red oxide of copper..which grieves me poignantly by losing its colour.

poignard, variant of PONIARD.

†**poigne** (pɔɪn). *Obs. rare.* [a. OF. *poigne*, fem. form parallel to *poing*:—L. *pugn-um* fist.] The closed hand or fist: in phr. ***kept in poigne*** (fig.).

a **1734** NORTH *Exam.* I. ii. §139 (1740) 107 The Witnesses, which the Faction kept in Poigne (like false Dice, high and low Fullhams) to be played forth upon Plots, and to make Discoveries as there was Occasion. *Ibid.* II. v. §126. 393 The Engineers..determined what was to be communicated,.. and what to be kept in Poigne, secret from them.

†**poignet**, *sb. Obs.* Forms: 5 **ponyet, poinett, punȝet,** 5–6 **poynett,** 6 **poygniet,** 9 **poignet**. [a. F. *poignet* wrist, in 14th c. *poingnet*, OF. *pugnet* (13th c.), deriv. of *poing* fist.]

1. An ornament for the wrist or hand; a wristlet or bracelet.

1402 *Will of Matilda Sweeton* (Fairholt), I par de ponyets de scarlet. **1416** *Maldon, Essex, Court Rolls* (Bundle 10 No. 3), Poynetts, iid. *c* **1440** *Promp. Parv.* 408/2 Ponyet, of a sleue,..*premanica, mantus*. **1483** CAXTON *Gold. Leg.* 44/1 Whan he had seen the ryngis in his susters eeris & her poynettis or armyllis on her hondes. **1530** PALSGR. 256/1 Poygniet for ones sleves, *poignet*. *c* **1540** J. HEYWOOD *Four P.P.* B j b, Theyr bonettes and theyr poynettes. **1575** LANEHAM *Let.* (1871) 38 Hiz doobled sleeuez of blak woorsted, vpon them a payr of poynets of towny Chamblet laced a long the wreast wyth blu threeden points.

¶**2.** *erron.* The handle or hilt of a dagger. (For F. *poignée*.) *rare*⁻¹.

1820 SCOTT *Monast.* xvi, The *poignet* being of silver exquisitely hatched.

Hence †ˈ**poignet** *v. Obs. trans.*, to put cuffs on (a garment); whence †ˈ**poigneting** *vbl. sb.*

1555 T. MARSHE *Instit. Gentleman* I vj b, A certayne kyng of Inglande caused his doublet to bee half stocked with foresleues of veluet, called in those dayes, poignetting of a doublet.

poigniard, poik: see PONIARD, POKE *sb.*¹

poikilitic (pɔɪkɪˈlɪtɪk), *a.* Also **poic-**. [var. of PŒCILITIC.] †**1.** *Geol.* (Usu. with capital initial.) A term formerly applied to the Triassic and Permian systems, as being mainly composed of variegated rocks. *Obs.*

1836 BUCKLAND *Geol. & Min.* II. 38 The word *Pœcilitic* is in sound so like to *Pisolite*, that it may be better to adhere more literally to the Greek root ποικίλος, and apply the common name of *Poikilitic* group to the strata in question. **1846** DE LA BECHE in *Mem. Geol. Surv. Gt. Brit.* I. 239 Poicilitic or New Red Sandstone Series. **1861** *Eng. Wom. Dom. Mag.* III. 59 The reconstruction of the cretaceous, poikilitic, oolitic, or silurian landscape, peopled with revivified Batrachians. **1885** GEIKIE *Text-Bk. Geol.* (ed. 2) 748 The term 'Poikilitic' was formerly proposed for them, on account of their characteristic mottled appearance.

2. *Petrogr.* Applied to the structure or texture of a rock (now only an igneous rock), or to the rock itself, in which small crystals of one mineral are enclosed within crystals of another. Cf. PŒCILITIC *a.* 2.

1886 G. H. WILLIAMS in *Amer. Jrnl. Sci.* CXXXI. 30 This structure is so common in many massive rocks, especially in the more basic kinds, that I would venture to suggest the use of the term '*poicilitic*' (derived from the Greek ποικίλος, mottled) for it. **1893** —— in *Jrnl. Geol.* I. 176 (*heading*) On the use of the terms poikilitic and micro-poikilitic in petrography. *Ibid.* 177 This term was at first incorrectly spelled *poicilitic* and subsequently corrected by Prof. Dana to its Latin form, *poecilitic*... Its preferable orthography is, however, that given above [*sc. poikilitic*]. At the time it was proposed the writer was not familiar..with the designations ..*poecilitic* and *poikilitic*, given successively..to the 'New Red' sandstone. **1920** [see *poikiloblastic* adj. s.v. POIKILO-]. **1923** *Jrnl. Geol.* XXXI. 177 The feldspar grains of the arkose are set, in a sort of poikilitic fashion, in a matrix of much more coarsely crystalline quartz. **1954** H. WILLIAMS et al. *Petrography* ii. 19 (*caption*) Poikilitic texture in hornblende peridotite, Odenwald, Germany. **1970** *Nature* 25 July 366/1 The poikilitic chromitite harzburgite..could well be formed from dunite by permeation by silica-bearing solutions.

Hence **poiˈlitically** *adv.*

1912 *Meddelelser om Grønland* XXXVIII. 150 Each anhedron encloses a large number of sodalite-crystals poikilitically. **1932** F. F. GROUT *Petrogr. & Petrol.* vi. 371 Less commonly some rounded granules in a hornfels may be enclosed in a coarser mineral developed poikilitically. **1963** W. A. DEER et al. *Rock-Forming Min.* IV. 263 Kalsilite.. occurs as an interstitial mineral poikilitically enclosing the ferromagnesian constituents.

ˈ**poikilo-**, a formative element from Gr. ποικίλος variegated, various, used in modern scientific terms (in some of which the Latinized form PŒCILO- is preferred):

ˈ**poikiloˌblast**, (*a*) = *poikilocyte* (*Syd. Soc. Lex.*); (*b*) (also **pœcilo-**) *Petrol.*, each of the inclusions in a poikiloblastic rock; ˌ**poikiloˈblastic** *a.* (also **pœcilo-**) *Petrol.* [ad. G. *poikiloblastisch* (F. Becke 1903, in *Compt. Rend. IX Sess. Congr. Géol. Internat.* (1904) II. 570): see -BLAST], applied to the structure or texture of a metamorphic rock, or to the rock itself, in which small crystals of an original mineral occur within crystals of its metamorphic product (cf. POIKILITIC *a.* 2); ˈ**poikiloˌcyte**, a name for red blood-corpuscles of irregular shape, elongated, pyriform, etc. (*Syd. Soc. Lex.*); so

ˌ**poikilocyˈtosis**, the condition of the blood when it contains poikilocytes.

1944 *Trans. R. Soc. Edin.* LXI. 225 Accessories are apatite and sphene,.. the latter in rounded red-brown pleochroic *poeciloblasts in the same minerals. **1969** A. Spry *Metamorphic Textures 169 (heading)* Poikiloblasts. **1920** A. Holmes *Nomencl. Petrol.* 187 **Poikiloblastic*, a metamorphic texture due to the development, during recrystallisation, of a new mineral around numerous relics of the original minerals, thus simulating the poikilitic texture of igneous rocks. **1932** A. Harker *Metamorphism* xiii. 191 *(caption)* A large porphyroblast of green horn-blende showing typical pœciloblastic or sieve-structure. **1954** H. Williams et al. *Petrography* ix. 168 *(caption)* Poikiloblastic (sieve) texture in skarn, Doubtful Sound, New Zealand. **1969** A. Spry *Metamorphic Textures* vi. 170 Inclusions increase the total free energy and thus a poikiloblastic crystal is not in its most-stable.. condition. **1897** *Allbutt's Syst. Med.* IV. 578 Irregular forms of red corpuscles which are generally included under the name of *poikilocytes. **1899** Cagney tr. *Jaksch's Clin. Diagn.* i. (ed. 4) 42 Gräber believes that the poikilocytes do not exist in the circulating blood. **1880** A. Flint *Princ. Med.* 62 The name *poikilocytosis has been proposed to designate the condition of blood in which the corpuscles present manifold variations in shape.

poikiloderma (ˌpɔɪkɪləˈdɜːmə). *Path.* [mod.L., ad. G. *poikilodermia* (E. Jacobi 1907, in *Verhandl. der deutsch. dermatol. Gesellschaft: IX. Kongr. 1906* 322), f. Gr. ποικίλο-ς variegated + δέρμα skin.] An atrophic condition of the skin characterized by reticular pigmentation and associated with telangiectasia. Hence ˌ**poikiloˈdermatous** *a.*

1907 *Index Medicus* 173/2 (Index), Poikiloderma. **1936** *Arch. Dermatol. & Syphilol.* XXXIII. 289 The word poikiloderma.. is used indiscriminately, to indicate variegated lesions, instead of being limited to eruptions presenting a definite picture of poikiloderma atrophicans vasculare. *Ibid.* 290 Poikilodermatous changes may be part of the picture of many chronic inflammatory dermatoses. **1967** H. Montgomery *Dermatopath.* xi. 246/2 Various types of poikiloderma, including poikiloderma of Civatte, do not reveal the typical changes in the blood vessels or in the collagenous fibers although telangiectasia is present clinically and histologically. **1968** A. Rook in A. Rook et al. *Textbk. Dermatol.* II. xlii. 1271/2 Some inflammatory dermatoses, such as lichen planus may also give rise to poikilodermatous changes.

poikilosmotic (ˌpɔɪkɪlɒzˈmɒtɪk), *a. Physiol.* Also **poikilo-osmotic** (ˌpɔɪkɪləʊɒzˈmɒtɪk). [ad. G. *poikilosmotisch* (R. Höber *Physikal. Chem. der Zelle und der Gewebe* (1902) ii. 26): see POIKILO- and OSMOTIC *a.*] Of an animal: that allows the concentration of solute in its body fluids to vary with fluctuations in that in the surrounding medium. Opp. *homœo-osmotic* s.v. HOMŒO-.

1905 *Biol. Bull.* VIII. 262 All of the marine invertebrates which we have worked with are truly 'poikilosmotic'. Two factors may be at work in producing the variations in the osmotic pressure, viz., the interchange of water, and of salts. **1931** *Biol. Rev.* VI. 473 Characteristically marine forms such as *Hyas, Cancer* and the polychaete *Nereis cultrifera* only respond to lowered external salinity by passive swelling till their blood is isotonic with the medium. Such 'poikilosmotic' organisms show no change in oxygen consumption during this process. **1953** E. Palmer tr. *Ekman's Zoogeogr. Sea* vi. 118 The marine invertebrates were until recently considered to be poikilo-osmotic. **1971** *Biol. Abstr.* LII. 5434/1 Poikilosmotic animals are actually slightly hyperosmotic as against their external medium in the normal circumstances of the animal's existence.

Hence ˌ**poikilosˈmosis**, ˌ**poikilosmoˈticity**, the state or property of being poikilosmotic.

1935 *Proc. Linnean Soc. N.S.W.* LX. 244 A 'law of poikilosmoticity' is by no means applicable to all marine invertebrates when the surrounding water is of lower salinity than ordinary sea-water. **1939** A. Krogh *Osmotic Regulation in Aquatic Animals* 242 (Index), Poikilosmosis. **1955** Elkinton & Danowski *Body Fluids* ii. 50 In many invertebrates the poikilosmoticity is only relative and.. steady states are maintained with respect to both total osmolarity and individual ionic levels. **1971** *Biol. Abstr.* LII. 5434/1 *(heading)* On poikilosmosis and iso-osmosis.

poikilothermia (ˌpɔɪkɪləʊˈθɜːmɪə). *Physiol.* Also anglicized as ˈ**poikilothermy**. [f. as next: see -IA[1], -Y[3].] The state or property of being poikilothermic. Also ˌ**poikiloˈthermism** (*rare*).

1903 *Jrnl. Physiol.* XXIX. 369 *(heading)* Poikilothermism in rabies. **1921** *Physiol. Rev.* I. 304 Increased surface blood flow promotes poikilothermia because it facilitates the conduction of heat either to or from the body. **1939** *Nature* 22 Apr. 684/1 Torpidity [in humming-birds] appears to be a temporary poikilothermy, rather similar to that already described for bats. **1968** D. W. Wood *Princ. Animal Physiol.* viii. 122 Social methods of overcoming the disadvantages of poikilothermy are also found. Larvae of the butterfly *Vanessa* cluster together in the cold. **1974** *Nature* 22 Feb. 568/1 In most newborn animals there is a physiological hypothermia and poikilothermia.

poikilothermic (ˌpɔɪkɪləʊˈθɜːmɪk), *a. Physiol.* [ad. G. *pökilotherm* (now *poik-*) (C. Bergmann 1847, in *Göttinger Studien* I. 613): see POIKILO- and THERMIC *a.*] Characterized by a body temperature that varies with the temperature of the environment; cold-blooded. Also ˌ**poikiloˈthermal**, **-ˈthermous** *adjs.*, in the same sense. Opp. HOMŒOTHERMIC *a.*

1884 tr. *Claus' Zoöl.* I. 74 Most of the lower animals are poikilothermic, or, as they have less appropriately been called, cold-blooded. **1885** W. Stirling tr. *Landois's Text-bk. Human Physiol.* I. vi. 426 The so-called cold-blooded animals are called poikilothermal. **1928** Pearse & Hall *Homoiothermism* i. 2 The change from the poikilothermic to the homoiothermic condition. *Ibid.* iv. 27 The extreme minimum temperature which poikilothermal animals can tolerate. **1933** R. H. Wolcott *Animal Biol.* lxiv. 456 Animals which can maintain a constant temperature are termed homoiothermous..; animals unable to do so are termed poikilothermous, or cold-blooded. **1956** *Sci. News* XL. 71 Under ordinary circumstances most poikilothermous animals have body temperatures that fall when the environment becomes cooler, and rises when it becomes warmer. **1963** *Lancet* 5 Jan. 29/1 Newborn infants are poikilothermic, and their temperatures may be rapidly reduced. **1973** *Marine Biol.* XXI. 262/2 Lower poikilothermal animals (protozoans, sponges, some coelenterates). **1973** P. A. Colinvaux *Introd. Ecol.* xx. 288 Poikilothermous lizards are not excluded from the Arctic because they are poikilothermous, but because, on the average, they cannot balance their heat budgets if the ambient temperature is low.

Hence ˈ**poikilotherm**, a poikilothermic animal.

1934 in Webster. **1950** C. L. Prosser in C. L. Prosser et al. *Compar. Animal Physiol.* x. 349 Aquatic poikilotherms follow changes in environmental temperature rapidly and precisely. **1965** B. E. Freeman tr. *Vandel's Biospeleol.* xix. 326 Resistance to starvation is a general property of poikilotherms. **1968** [see HOMŒOTHERM].

‖**poil.** *Obs. rare.* [F. *poile, poêle* a stove, OF. *poisle, peisle*:—L. *pēsile, pensile* adj. neut. hung, suspended, f. *pendĕre* to hang.] A furnace, a stove.

1756 in Ellis *Orig. Lett.* Ser. II. IV. 374 (from Berlin) He would find the ashes in the poil or furnace where they were burnt. *Ibid.* 377 They immediately put them into the poil or furnace, and set fire to them.

poil, poill, obs. Sc. ff. POLE, POLL.

poile. Also poil. [a. F. *poil*:—L. *pil-um* hair.] †**a.** Down, fine hair. *Obs. rare.*

1746 *Phil. Trans.* XLIV. 180 (transl. fr. French) Its Substance was crumbling.. like the Membrane of the Bladder, having a fungous Poile on it. **1806** M. Lewis *Jrnl.* 15 May in *Orig. Jrnls. Lewis & Clark Expedition* (1905) V. xxviii. 38 The poil of these [grizzly] bear were infinitely longer finer and thicker than the black bear.

b. poil(e) de chèvre (see quot. 1960).

1873 F. B. Palliser *Descr. Catal. Lace S. Kensington Mus.* (ed. 2) 9 Lace is made of gold, silver, silk, cotton, and flax, to which may be added poil-de-chèvre. **1927** E. Sitwell *Rustic Elegies* 86 And splashed the red and white striped poil de chèvre short gown. **1960** C. W. Cunnington et al. *Dict. Eng. Costume* 269/2 *Poile de Chèvre*,.. a textile of goat's hair (weft) and silk (warp) in plain weave; having a shiny satin-like lace.

Poilite (ˈpɔɪlaɪt). Also **poilite**. A proprietary name for a building material made of asbestos and cement, used in the form of tiles, sheets, etc.

1903 *Trade Marks Jrnl.* 11 Feb. 154 Poilite... A fire-resisting lining and roofing material.., manufactured of a mixture of asbestos, lime, and Portland cement, for use in building. Bell's Asbestos Company, Limited,.. London. **1922** *Daily Mail* 7 Nov. 3 The amalgamation of the company's poilite (asbestos-cement) section with the British Everite and Asbestilite Works. **1925** E. G. Blake *Roof Coverings* vii. 157 The cost of Poilite slates at the present time is about twenty per cent. less than that of the ordinary Welsh slates. **1936** *Discovery* Apr. 117/1 Wainscotings, skirtings, panelling, poilite sheets, etc., are loosened to allow entry of the gas. **1968** *Laxton's Building Price Bk.* (ed. 141) 726/1 'Poilite' Asbestos-Cement Flat Sheets &c., Turners Asbestos-Cement Co. Ltd.

poilu (pwaly). *colloq.* [Fr., hairy, virile.] A soldier in the French army, *esp.* one who fought in the war of 1914–18. Also *attrib.* and *Comb.*

1914 in *Further Lett. from Man of No Importance* (1932) 15, I hear dear old Madame Waddington is busy as a bee with comforts for *poilus*. **1915** G. Adam *Behind Scenes at Front* 183 France has every reason to be proud of her infantry, the 'poilus' as they have been called in this war. **1916** 'Taffrail' *Pincher Martin* xvi. 303 *Poilus* in their slate-blue uniforms. **1918** E. M. Roberts *Flying Fighter* 54 We were away north of the French lines, but that made no difference to the poilus, who also were to attend the ceremony. **1923** *Daily Mail* 28 Feb. 1 (Advt.), In shades of Coral,.. Poilu-Blue, Lemon, Brique, Mole. **1926** *Glasgow Herald* 30 Nov. 8 He depicts.. the adventures of two poilus who miss the train that should have brought them back to barracks in time for roll-call. **1930** Kipling *Limits & Renewals* (1932) 324 He pointed downward to the little cast-iron *poilu*, which seemed to be standard pattern for War memorials in that region. **1940** 'Gun Buster' *Return via Dunkirk* I. x. 79 The room was packed with poilus, singing songs. **1946** G. Millar *Horned Pigeon* xvii. 263 There were fierce yellowish photographs of men posed in *poilu* uniform all round the walls of her room. **1966** J. Dos Passos *Best Times* (1968) ii. 43 The Boche.. scattered a few salvoes of artillery.. just to keep the poilus on their toes. **1975** P. Fussell *Gt. War & Mod. Memory* (1977) vii. 240 During the 1917 mutinies in the French army, the *poilus* being marched up to the line frequently made loud *baa*-ing noises.

poimenic (pɔɪˈmɛnɪk), *a.* and *sb.* [ad. Gr. ποιμενικ-ός relating to a shepherd (ποιμήν): see -IC.]

A. *adj.* Of or pertaining to pastoral care.

1902 in Webster *Suppl.*

B. *sb.* (Chiefly pl. *poimenics.*) Pastoral theology, or the study of it.

1883 W. G. Blaikie *Ministry of Word* 296 Ample treatises on Homiletics, Liturgics, Catechetics and Poimenics. **1892** Schaff *Theol. Propædeut.* Pref. 3 (Funk), I beg the indulgence of the English reader for introducing a uniform terminology in the singular form for the several departments, as Isagogic,.. Poimenic, Evangelistic.

†**poin**, *v. Obs.* Also **poyn.** [f. stem *poign-* of OF. *poindre* to pierce, prick:—L. *pungĕre*: cf. *join* from *joindre*.]

1. *trans.* To prick; to harass, annoy.

c **1330** R. Brunne *Chron. Wace* (Rolls) 16218 The power of Cadwalyn was mikel, Penda poyned hym [Oswy] als a prykel.

2. To stitch or sew through and through, to quilt (cf. BROCHE *v.*); to ornament with stitching.

13.. *E.E. Allit. P.* A. 217 Pyȝt watz poyned & vche [*ed. Gollancz* pyght and poyned wacz uche] a hemme. **1395** *E.E. Wills* (1882) 6 A keuerlit of selk ypoynet. ?*a* **1400** *Morte Arth.* 2623, I poyne alle his pavelyouns þat to hym-selfe pendes, Dyghttes his dowblettez for dukes and erles. *a* **1440** *Sir Degrev.* 1491 Quyltus poyned of that ylk.

3. To thrust (a spear).

c **1400** *Laud Troy Bk.* 14263 Eyther on other her speres poygned, Wel hard to-geder tho thei Ioyned.

Hence †ˈ**poining** *vbl. sb.*, piercing, stitching.

c **1430** *Pilgr. Lyf Manhode* I. cxi. (1869) 59 Riht as the doublet is maad with poynynges.

poinado, -ardo: see POIGNADO.

poinard, variant of PONIARD.

poinciana (pɔɪnsɪˈɑːnə). [mod.L. (J. P. de Tournefort *Institutiones Rei Herbariæ* (1700) I. 619), f. the name of M. de *Poinci*, a 17th-century governor of the Antilles + *-ana*.] An evergreen tree or a deciduous prickly shrub of the genus formerly so called, now divided between *Delonix* and *Cæsalpinia*, belonging to the family Leguminosæ, native to the West Indies, Madagascar, or northern Africa, and bearing racemes of scarlet or yellow flowers.

1731 P. Miller *Gardeners Dict.* s.v. Poinciana; Barbadoes Flower-Fence, or Spanish Carnations. **1807** *Curtis's Bot. Mag.* XXV. 995 The name of Poinciana was given to this splendid shrub by Tournefort. **1824** H. E. Lloyd tr. *Spix & Martius's Travels in Brazil* I. II. i. 174 The beautiful bushes of the poinciana are planted. **1859** J. Froebel *Seven Years' Travel in Central Amer.* iii. 34 The way down from the city passes through thickets of shrubbery covered with the most splendid flowers, amongst which the Poinciana, with scarlet panicles, is most prominent. **1908** *Daily Chron.* 11 Sept. 7/2 The Royal Poinciana crowns itself with cardinal magnificence. **1927** *Transition* Apr. 101 Under the poinciana, of a noon or afternoon Let fiery blossoms clot the light. **1954** *Coast to Coast 1953–54* 86 The house was.. enclosed by gardens and shaded by tamarind- and poinciana-trees. **1969** T. H. Everett *Living Trees of World* 196/2 A native of Madagascar, but freely planted as an ornamental in most warm climates, the royal poinciana is one of the showiest of flowering trees. **1978** 'A. York' *Tallant for Disaster* xi. 167 A larger than average wave.. smashing at the base of the poinciana trees.

poind (see next), *sb. Sc.* [f. POIND *v.*] **a.** An act of poinding, a distraint. **b.** A beast or other chattel poinded. ***dead poind***, a poinded article of goods as opposed to live cattle.

1563–4 *Reg. Privy Council Scot.* I. 259 The poindis takin thairfoir to be restorit to the said George. **1609** Skene *Reg. Maj.* I. 71 Gif ane takes ane poynde for debt, within ane other mans land, without licence of him, or of his Baillie. *Ibid.* [see POINDER]. **1676** Ld. Fountainhall in M. P. Brown *Suppl. Dict. Decis.* (1826) III. 61 Poinded goods,.. if they be a dead poind, that puts the creditor poinder to no .. expence in keeping it. **1813** N. Carlisle *Topogr. Dict. Scot.* II. s.v. *Priestwick*, Sometimes Poinds are driven, and executed at the Cross of Priestwick. **1868** J. Salmon *Gowodean* 63 (E.D.D.) Glad to catch him with your poind and horn.

poind (pynd, pɪnd), *v. Sc.* Forms: α. 5–7 **pund**, 6 **puind, pwynd**. β. 5–8 **poynd**, 6– **poind.** [Sc. repr. of OE. *pyndan* to enclose, shut in, impound, = Eng. PIND. The *u, ui, wy*, symbolized the vowel (y), representing, as in BUILD (*Sc.* byld), an OE. *y*. Of this, *oi* is a 16th c. spelling, retained in the law-courts. The Sc. pronunciation is (pynd) or (pɪnd: cf. *mither, brither*); (pɔɪnd), given in dictionaries, is merely founded on the spelling.]

1. *trans.* To distrain upon (a person or his goods); to seize and sell under warrant (the goods of a debtor): = PIND *v.* 2.

α. *a* **1400** *Burgh Laws* iii. (*Sc. Stat.* I), Of punding of uplandis men in burgh. **1500** *Exch. Rolls Scotl.* XI. 393 To pund Thomas Fresale for viijli. vijs. vjd. **1531** *Acc. Ld. High Treas. Scotl.* VI. 54 To pas to pwynd the Shereff off Renfrew and utheris for restis of the chakkar. **1604** *Urie Crt.-bk.* (1892) 4 The transgressouris thairof to be punddit preceislie as is aboun wryttin.

β. **1516** *Acc. Ld. High Treas. Scotl.* V. 85 To Dauid Lowry .. to poynd xxxiij lordis and lardis absent fra the assis. **1564–5** *Reg. Privy Council Scot.* I. 317 Lettres to be direct to poind.. the said complenaris and thair gudis for the soum of thre hundreth pund stirling. **1698** *Min. Baron Crt. of Stitchell* (1905) 132 He was poynding the defender at the instance of James Hoggart. **1786** Burns *Twa Dogs* 98 He'll apprehend them, poind their gear. *a* **1803** *Lament Border-Widow* iii. in Child *Ballads* IV. (1886) 429/2 He slew my knight, and poind his gear. **1886** *Act 49 Vict.* c. 23 §3 (2), The right to poind the ground hereinafter provided.

b. *absol.* To distrain.

a. **1500** *Exch. Rolls Scotl.* XI. 457 Falyeing of the said preif the said schiref sal pund for the said thre termez. **1532** *Aberdeen Regr.* (1844) I. 146 Tha ordanit Henry Irvein, bailȝe,.. gif neid beis, to cause puind for the same.

β. **1545** *Reg. Privy Council Scot.* I. 21 Quhair his officiaris ar deforcit in poynding for the said taxt. **1641** *Ferguson's Sc. Prov.* (1785) §936 Ye may poind for debt but not for unkindness.

2. To impound (stray cattle, contraband goods, etc.): = PIND 1 b.

[*c* **1450**: see POINDER.] **1536** BELLENDEN *Cron. Scot.* x. xii. (1541) 144/1 All othir beistis that eittis mennis corne or gres salbe poyndit quhil the awnar thairof redres the skaithis. **1637–50** Row *Hist. Kirk* (Wodrow Soc.) 9 What shall poore sillie sheep doe that are poyndit in a fold where there is no meat? **1678** SIR G. MACKENZIE *Crim. Laws Scot.* I. xxvi. §ii. 259 The Customers Officers were about to poynd some unfree goods. **1815** SCOTT *Guy M.* vii, Their asses were poinded by the ground-officer when left in the plantation.

†**3.** *intr.* To plunder. *Obs. rare.*

c **1425** WYNTOUN *Cron.* VIII. xliv. 6960 The qwhethir offt ryot wald thai ma To pryk, and poynd, bathe to and fra.

Hence **'poinded** *ppl. a.*, **'poinding** *vbl. sb.* and *ppl. a.*: see also MULTIPLE-*poinding*.

1401 *Aberdeen Regr.* (1844) I. 380 Sa that hym nedit nocht in tyme to cum til mak sic pundyng and namly in our toon. **1540** *Records of Elgin* (New Spald. Cl.) I. 50 The vrangus punding of Robert Dauidsone. **1585** *Reg. Privy Council Scot.* IV. 10 Ane actioun and caus of double-poinding. **1676** Poinded [see POIND *sb.*]. **1678** SIR G. MACKENZIE *Crim. Laws Scot.* I. xxvi. §iii. (1699) 131 Poyndings..cannot be execute after the Sun is set, because a Poynding is a sentence. **1746–7** *Act 20 Geo. II*, c. 43 §28 It shall..be lawful for the officer executing such poyndings, to carry the goods poynded..to the market cross. **1899** *Scotsman* 6 July, Notes of expenses of carrying through sales under sequestration or poindings, and also..of carrying back poinded or sequestrated effects.

'poindable, *a. Sc.* [f. POIND *v.* + -ABLE.] Liable to be, or capable of being, poinded.

15.. *Aberdeen Regr.* XXV. (Jam.), To seiss geir poindabill quhaireuir he may apprehend the same. **1566** *Reg. Privy Council Scot.* I. 457 Substantious inlandit men, poindabill. **1772** *Weekly Mag.* 25 June 398/1 He has poindable goods.

'poinder. *Sc.* Also 5 pundar, 9 -er. [f. POIND *v.* + -ER[1].] A person, esp. an official, who poinds or distrains goods; also, **b.** 'A person who has the charge of hedges, woods, etc., and who pounds cattle that trespass' (Jam.).

c **1450** HOLLAND *Howlat* 783 The Corn Crake, the pundar at hand, Had pyndit all his pryss horss in a pundfald. **1609** SKENE *Reg. Maj.* II. 12 The poynds..salbe reteined..in sic ane place pertaining to the poynder..quhere sic poynds or distresse may remaine and be keeped. **1676** [see POIND *sb.*]. **1805** A. SCOTT *Poems* (1808) 146 The punder's axe, with ruthless rap, Fell'd down their favourite tree. *Ibid.* 147 For sure this tree's enormous trunk Defies the punder's axe. **1816** SCOTT *Antiq.* xxiv, I'll..get my bit supper frae Ringan the poinder up by. **1886** *Act 49 Vict.* c. 23 §3 (1) Any arrester or poinder..who shall be thus deprived of the benefit of his diligence.

†**poindfald, poyndfauld,** obs. Sc. ff. PINFOLD.

1494 *Acta Audit.* (1839) 185/1 Anent..doune castin of xii Rudis of dik of þe said Samellis landis, and doune castin of the poyndfalt of Akinbar. **1650** in *Spottiswood Misc.* (1844) I. 211 Ther were neuer such a company of bedlames driuin wnto ane poyndfauld as wee.

†**poindlar, pundler.** *Sc. Obs.* Also 7 poundler, 8 punler. [A parallel form of POINDER, with changed suffix. Cf. PANTLER.] = POINDER.

1533 *Aberdeen Regr.* (1844) I. 149 The prouest, bailȝeis, and counsaill,..ordanit Georg. Annan pvndler of thar kirk yard, and ordanit the pundlene of euery best to be four d. **1583** *Reg. Privy Council Scot.* III. 603 To poind thame, letting thame out for reasonable poindlaris fee, unhoundit, slayne, or hocht. **1673** *Min. Baron Court of Stitchell* (1905) 64 For scandallizing Andro Burn poundler. **1715** PENNECUIK *Poems* 52 The trusty Punler of the Newland pease. **1808** JAMIESON s.v. *Pundler*, Even of late, a person employed to watch the fields, in order to prevent the grain from being stolen or injured, was called a pundler. *Angus.*

poineado, poinred: see POIGNADO, PONIARD.

poiner, dial. var. of PINER[1], labourer.

‖**poinsettia** (pɔɪn'sɛtɪə). [mod.L. (R. Graham 1836, in *Edinb. New Philos. Jrnl.* XX. 412), f. the name of J. R. *Poinsett* (1779–1851), American minister to Mexico + -IA[1].] A Mexican species of Euphorbia, *E.* (*Poinsettia*) *pulcherrima*, formerly made the type of a genus, having large scarlet floral leaves surrounding small greenish-yellow flowers; much cultivated in conservatories as Mexican Flame-leaf and Lobster-flower, called in America Easter-flower or Christmas-flower. Also *attrib.*

1836 *Curtis's Bot. Mag.* LXIII. 3493 (*heading*) Showy Poinsettia. **1871** KINGSLEY *At Last* iv, What is this that hangs over into the road, some fifteen feet in height..? What but the Poinsettia, paltry scions of which..adorn our hothouses and dinner-tables. **1872** DARWIN in *Life & Lett.* (1887) III. 170, I have been more than once assured that butterflies like bright colours—for instance, in India the scarlet leaves of Poinsettia. **1883** V. STUART *Egypt* 3 Over the rubbish..still waved magnificent poinsettias and oleander trees. **1906** P. PENNINGTON *Jrnl.* 9 Mar. in *Woman Rice Planter* (1913) ix. 302 Mr. Poinsett..brought many rare plants from Mexico, among others the Flor de la Noche Buena, which has borne in this country the name Poinsettia in his honor. **1947** K. TENNANT *Lost Haven* vii. 99 The town on the slope was aflame with red poinsettias. **1964** 'R. MACDONALD' in H. Waugh *Merchants of Menace* (1969) 78 Plaster painted adobe color, poinsettia-red curtains. **1968** J. C. HOLMES *Nothing More to Declare* 43 A few luxuriant poinsettias bloomed among the crumbling buildings and the blistered streets. **1977** WARD & WELLSTED *Indoor Plants* 25 (*caption*) These [developments] culminated in the dwarf poinsettias now so common in florists' displays. **1978** *Detroit Free Press* 16 Apr. 1D/2 It is an eclectic and nurturing environment where poinsettias thrive long after Christmas.

point (pɔɪnt), *sb.*[1] Forms: 3- point; also 3–6 **pointe, poynte,** 4–8 **poynt,** (4 *pl.* **poyns**), 5 **pointt(e, puynt, pynt, pyntte,** 6 **poinct, -e, poynct, -e,** *Sc.* **pwint.** *β.* 4–5 **pont, -e,** 5–6 **pounte,** 6 **pownt,** 6–9 *Sc.* **pount.** Also **punt**: see PUNCT. [In origin, two, or perh. three, words. In A., a. F. *point* = Pr. *punt*, Sp., It. *punto*, Pg. *ponto*:—L. *punct-um* that which is pricked, a prick, a minute mark like a prick, a dot, a point in writing, a point in space, a point of time, a small measure, a particular of a discourse, etc.; subst. use of pa. pple. neuter of L. *pungĕre, punct-*, F. *poindre*, *point* to prick, pierce. In B., a. F. *pointe* = Pr., Sp., It. *punta*, Pg. *ponta*:—Com. Romanic (and med.L.) *puncta* the action of piercing, the piercing part of anything, a sharp or pointed extremity (in med.L. the point of a knife, shoe, foot, promontory, etc.); ppl. sb. fem. from *pungĕre* (parallel to those in *-āta, -ada, -ée*). In C., in some senses, app. an independent derivative, as a noun of action, from F. *poindre*, or *pointer*, or from Eng. POINT *v.*[1] In ME., through the loss or non significance of final *-e*, *point* and *pointe* ran together, combining under the same form two senses which in all other langs. are kept apart (e.g. Ger. *punkt, spitze*). Transferred and fig. senses subsequently arose related to both primary notions, so that in senses where there is no corresponding F. *point* or *pointe*, the development is often very difficult to determine. The occasional spellings *pynt*, *pyntte* prob. indicate a pronunciation formerly prevalent and still dialectal of *oi* as (iː), *point* being pronounced like *pint*. The *β*-forms in *pont, pount, pownt*, are difficult to place; perh. they ought to be equated with *punt*, and so rather to be included under the by-form PUNCT.]

A. = F. *point.*

I. A prick, a dot.

†**1.** A minute hole or impression made by pricking; a prick, a puncture. *Obs. rare.*

c **1400** *Lanfranc's Cirurg.* 142 Make a poynt bi þe space of a litil fyngre from þe oon eende of þe wounde, & anoþer poynt at þe oþere eende of þe wounde. *c* **1440** *Promp. Parv.* 406/2 Poynte, *punctus* vel *punctum*. [**1826** KIRBY & SP. *Entomol.* IV. 270 *A Point* (*Punctum*), a minute impression upon the surface, but not perforating it.]

2. A minute mark on a surface, of the size or appearance of a fine puncture; a dot, a minute spot or speck; also, anything excessively small or appearing like a speck.

1390 GOWER *Conf.* III. 65 Which [Astrolabe] was of fin gold precious With pointz and cercles merveilous. **1600** E. BLOUNT tr. *Conestaggio* 202 Now he only subscribed *Rey* :: pointed with fiue points, called by the Portugals the fiue wounds. **1655** MRQ. WORCESTER *Cent. Inv.* §4 This invention..so abbreviated that a point onely sheweth distinctly and significantly any of the 24. Letters. **1732** LAW *Serious C.* xiii. (ed. 2) 228 As the fix'd Stars..appear but as so many points. **1822–34** *Good's Study Med.* (ed. 4) III. 468 The pupil, instead of being dilated, is contracted to a point. **1828** STARK *Elem. Nat. Hist.* I. 468 Body dotted with numerous red points. **1899** *Allbutt's Syst. Med.* VIII. 550 The lesions begin as minute scaly points in the epidermis.

3. A dot or other small mark used in writing or printing.

a. A punctuation-mark; *esp.* the ***full point*** or full stop; also extended to the marks of exclamation (!) and interrogation (?); and sometimes to reference-marks, as the asterisk, obelisk, etc.

c **1386** CHAUCER *Can. Yeom. Prol. & T.* 927 And þer a poynt, for ended is my tale; God send euery trewe man boote of his bale. **1530** PALSGR. 15 b, A poynt, whether it be suche as the Latins call *punctum planum* thus made . ,..or with suche as the Latins cal *comma* thus made : , or *uirgula* thus made /. **1587** F. CLEMENT *Petie Schole* 25 The perfect pause, or full point is set down in the line immediatly after the last word. **1589** NASHE *Anat. Absurd.* 40 In ye pause of a ful point. **1623** LISLE *Ælfric on O. & N. Test.* ad init., The Saxon vseth our note of Full-point commonly for all other distinctions. **1735** POPE *Prol. Sat.* 161 Commas and points they set exactly right. **1771** LUCKOMBE *Hist. Print.* 258, ¶ The Paragraph. † The Obelisk. ‡ The Double Dagger. ‖ The Parallel. § The Section. * The Asterism. These are the Names and Figures of what Founders reckon among Points, and Printers call References. *Ibid.* 262 He assigned the former Points their proper places..and added the Semicolon..to come in between the Comma and the Colon. **1824** L. MURRAY *Eng. Gram.* (ed. 5) I. 406 The point of Interrogation, ? The point of Exclamation, !. **1891** *N. & Q.* 7th Ser. XII. 99/2 All abbreviations being uniformly denoted by the full-point.

b. In Semitic alphabets, Any one of the dots, minute strokes, or groups of these, which are placed over, under, or within the letters or consonants, in order to indicate the vowels; in Hebrew also to indicate variation or doubling of the consonant, stress accent, punctuation, etc.; in Arabic and Persian to distinguish consonants otherwise identical in form, as ﻧ *n*, ﺗ *t*, ﺛ *þ*, ﺑ *b*, ﻳ *i*, ﭘ *p*, etc., called ***diacritical points***.

1614 SELDEN *Titles Hon.* 102 The three words haue ouer the Aliphs their point Vashlu. **1620** T. GRANGER *Div. Logike* 167 They added the points (which wee call vowels). **1668** WILKINS *Real Char.* 365 That Argument..against the Antiquity of the Hebrew Points, or Vowels. **1748** HARTLEY *Observ. on Man* I. iii. 312 The Manner of writing Hebrew without Points. **1776** J. RICHARDSON *Arab. Gram.* iii. 11 When final..it [ه] has often two points above. *Ibid.*, Like ا and و..it [ي] is considerably influenced by the vowel points. **1834** *Penny Cycl.* II. 219/1 In it [the Cufic character] the Koran was written, originally without diacritical points and vowels. **1837** G. PHILLIPS *Syriac Gram.* 3 The points of the vowel Zekofo may coalesce with the point of the letter. **1891** A. F. KIRKPATRICK *Bk. Psalms* I. Introd. vii. 51 The present elaborate system of vowel marks or 'points', commonly called the 'Massoretic punctuation' or 'vocalisation'.

c. A dot used in writing numbers. (*a*) In decimals, separating the integral from the fractional part; also, placed over a repeating decimal, or over the first and last figures of the period in a circulating decimal. (*b*) A dot or stroke used to separate a line of figures into groups.

1704 [see DECIMAL *a.* 1 b]. **1797** *Encycl. Brit.* (ed. 3) II. 312/2 Decimals are distinguished by a point, which separates them from integers, if any be prefixed. **1900** *Daily News* 9 June 5/3 Two 'four-point-sevens',..two naval twelve-pounders.., and two five-inch guns. *Mod.* We read 4·6 as 'four point repeating six'.

4. A dot or mark used in mediæval musical notation (med.L. *punctus* or *punctum*).

a. A mark indicating a tone or sound; corresponding to the modern 'notes'. (Cf. COUNTERPOINT *sb.*[1])

1674 PLAYFORD *Skill Mus.* III. 1 Counterpoint..was the old manner of Composing Parts together, by setting Points or Pricks one against another. **1782** BURNEY *Hist. Mus.* II. i. 39 Points were first used simple, afterwards with tails.

b. = DOT *sb.*[1] 5 d.

point of alteration or ***duplication***, a dot placed before two short notes in 'perfect' or triple rhythm, to indicate that the second of them is to be reckoned as of twice its ordinary length. ***point of augmentation***, a dot placed after a note in 'imperfect' or duple rhythm, to lengthen it by one half (as in modern music). ***point of division*** or ***imperfection***, a dot placed between two short notes in 'perfect' rhythm, of which the first is preceded and the second followed by a long note; indicating a division of the rhythm (like the bar in modern music), and rendering the two long notes 'imperfect'. ***point of perfection***, a dot placed in 'perfect' rhythm after a long note which would otherwise be 'imperfect' by position, to indicate that it is to be 'perfect'.

1597 MORLEY *Introd. Mus.* 12, I pray you say what Prickes or poynts..signifie in singing.

II. 5. a. A separate or single article, item, or clause in an extended whole (usually an abstract whole, as a course of action, a subject of thought, a discourse, etc.); an individual part, element, or matter, a detail, a particular; sometimes, a detail of nature or character, a particular quality or respect; †an instance (of some quality, etc.). Also used with preceding numeral to form an *attrib. phr.* designating a statement or document that has the number of items specified by the numeral.

a **1225** *Ancr. R.* 178 Ȝif eni ancre is þet ne veleð none uondunges, swuð drede hire iðet point. *c* **1290** *S. Eng. Leg.* I. 27/30 Fondede in eche pointe to answerien heom wel quoynteliche. *a* **1300** *Cursor M.* 23261 (Cott.) Bot a point es þar þam pines mare, þan elles al þair oþer fare. *Ibid.* 26092 þe toþer pont es scrift o muth. **1340** *Ayenb.* 33 And yet eft þer byeþ zix poyns kueade, huerby sleuþe brengeþ man to his ende. **1389** in *Eng. Gilds* (1870) 6 These ben þe poyntz & þe articles ordeyned of the bretheren of seint Katerine. *c* **1394** *P. Pl. Crede* 6 In my pater-noster iche poynt after oþer. *c* **1400** *Rule St. Benet* 657 Ther er the pontes of perfite lifyng That nedful er to old and ȝing. *c* **1400** *Brut* (E.E.T.S.) 157 He sent worde..þat þai shulde done out and put awey þat o pynt of restitucion. **1500–20** DUNBAR *Poems* xlv. 17 It is ane pount of ignorance To lufe in sic distemperance. **1526** TINDALE *Jas.* ii. 10 Whosoeuer shall kepe the whole lawe, and yet fayle in one poynt, he is gyltie in all. **1533** GAU *Richt Vay* 55 The ix artikil. I trou that thair is ane halie chrissine kirk and ane communione of sanctis. Thir ii pwintis ar baith bot ane thing. **1541** *Test. Ebor.* VI. 135 That..this my last will and testament be fulfillid in every poynte. **1641** J. JACKSON *True Evang. T.* I. 7, I have prefaced and scholied sufficiently unto the Text, I come now to seek out first the parts, and then the points of it. **1663** GERBIER *Counsel* 49 The censure of the Surveyor, on the point of all the materialls which are brought in. **1701** NORRIS *Ideal World* I. ii. 74 This is the point upon which the whole reasoning turns. **1784** J. POTTER *Virtuous Villagers* II. 23 We shall never agree on these points, so we'll drop them. **1833** HT. MARTINEAU *Manch. Strike* v. 55 If they had known what point was in dispute. **1866** G. MACDONALD *Ann. Q. Neighb.* v, Is it a point of conscience with you? **1897** J. T. TOMLINSON *Prayer Bk., Articles & Hom.* VII. 211 We shall find..that..he [Cosin] never adopted any one of the 'six points' of modern Ritualism. **1945** *Richmond* (Va.) *Times-Dispatch* 26 Oct. 5/1 He proposed, in its stead, a six-point program as a foundation for world peace. **1961** *Chicago Daily Tribune* 25 Oct. I. 16/3 If the parties failed to sign an eight point program agreeing on Gen. Gursel as president. **1975** *New Yorker* 21 Apr. 134/2 The basic policy of the Communists, set forth in a ten-point statement.., is constantly rebroadcast. **1977** *Time* 10 Jan. 20/2 The CPI supported Mrs. Gandhi's 20-point program for social reform, but pointedly witheld support from Sanjay's five-point youth program.

†**b.** *to stand (up)on (one's) points*, to insist upon details of conduct or manners which one has espoused; to be punctilious or scrupulous. *Obs.*

c **1590** GREENE *Fr. Bacon* i. 122 Our country Margret is so coy, And stands so much vpon her honest points, That marriage or no market with the mayd. **1590** SHAKS. *Mids. N.* v. i. 118. **1601** B. JONSON *Ev. Man in Hum.* (Qo.) I. ii. 32 He stood vpon poynts with me too. **1685** BUNYAN *Pharisee & Publican* Wks. 1861 II. 237 For a man here to stand thus upon his points, it is death.

c. *to* STRAIN or STRETCH *a point*: see the verbs.

III. A minute part or particle of anything; the smallest unit of measurement.

†**6. a.** The very least or a very small part *of* something; a jot, whit, particle. *Obs.*

a **1300** *Body & Soul* in *Map's Poems* (Camden) 338 O poynt of ore pine to bate in the world ne is no leche. *c* **1450** LOVELICH *Grail* lv. 182 Neuere Man On hym Cowde Aspye that Evere he hadde poynt of Meselrye. *c* **1450** *Mirour Saluacioun* 368 Nor neuer hafe felt a poynt of vnhelth, nor sekenesse. **1477** NORTON *Ord. Alch.* vii. in Ashm. *Theat. Chem. Brit.* (1652) 104 By one point of excesse all your Warke is shent.

†**b.** *no point* (cf. F. *ne point*): not a bit, not at all, not in the least. *Obs.*

1542 UDALL *Erasm. Apoph.* 137 Diogenes esteemed the fruite to bee no poyncte the more polluted. **1588** SHAKS. *L.L.L.* II. i. 190 *Boy.* Will you prick't with your eye? *La. Ro.* No poynt, with my knife. **1610** *Histrio-m.* III. 266 The Players now are growne so proud, Ten pound a play, or no point Comedy.

†**7.** The smallest or a very small portion of time; a moment, instant. *Obs.*

1382 WYCLIF *Isa.* liv. 7 At a poynt in a litil I forsoc thee. **1434** MISYN *Mending Life* 106 In a poynt we lyfe, ȝa les þen a poynt, for [if] all our lyfe to lyfe euerlastynge we wald likkyn, noȝt it is. *a* **1533** LD. BERNERS *Gold. Bk. M. Aurel.* (1546) Kkj b, Theyr felicitie hath been but a shorte poynt.

†**8.** *sensible point*: the least discernible portion of matter or space. *Obs. rare.*

1690 LOCKE *Hum. Und.* II. xv. §9 A sensible Point, meaning thereby the least Particle of Matter or Space we can discern, which is ordinarily about a Minute, and to the sharpest Eyes seldom less than thirty Seconds of a Circle, where the Eye is the Center. **1704** in J. HARRIS *Lex. Techn.* I.

9. *Mus.* **a.** A short strain or snatch of melody; esp. in phr. *point of war*, etc., a short phrase sounded on an instrument as a signal. *arch.*

13.. *E.E. Allit. P.* A. 890 Of þat songe myȝt synge a poynt. **1578** GOSSON in T. N. tr. *Conq. W. India* ad fin., When.. threatnying trumpet sounde the poyntes of warre. **1597** SHAKS. *2 Hen. IV*, IV. i. 52. **1602** MARSTON *Ant. & Mel.* IV. Wks. 1856 I. 48 Make me a straine;.. Breath me a point that may inforce me weepe. **1814** SCOTT *Wav.* xlvi, To perform the beautiful and wild point of war. **1867** MORRIS *Jason* I. 127 His guardian drew The horn from off his neck, and thereon blew A point of hunting known to two or three. **1871** RUSKIN *Fors Clav.* viii. (1896) I. 152 Bid him put ghostly trump to lip and breathe a point of war.

b. An important phrase or subject, usually in a contrapuntal composition, esp. in relation to its entry in a particular part; the entry of such a phrase or subject.

1597 MORLEY *Introd. Mus.* 76 There can bee no point or Fuge taken without a rest. *a* **1646** J. GREGORY *Posthuma* (1649) 48 The Contrapunctum figuratum, consisting of Feuges, or maintaining of Points. **1881** in Grove *Dict. Mus.* III. 7 *Points*, a term applied.. to the opening notes of the Subject of a Fugue, or other important Motivo, to which it is necessary that the attention of the Performer should be particularly directed.

†**10.** In mediæval measurement of time: The fourth (or according to some, the fifth) part of an hour. (See ATOM *sb.* 7.) *Obs.*

1495 *Trevisa's Barth. De P.R.* IX. ix. (W. de W.) 354 An houre conteynyth foure poyntes [*Bodl. MS.* punctes] and a poynt ten momentes. [*Ibid.* xxi. 359 A puncte is the fourth partye of an houre.] **1844** LINGARD *Anglo-Sax. Ch.* (1858) II. xi. 158 Twenty-four hours, each of which admits of four different subdivisions, into four points [etc.].

†**11.** The twelfth part of the side or radius of a quadrant, etc.: *spec.* in *Astron.* One of the 24 (or, according to some, 12) equal divisions of the diameter of the sun or moon, by which the degree of obscuration in an eclipse was measured.

c **1391** CHAUCER *Astrol.* I. §12 The skale.. that seruith by hise 12 poyntes.. of ful many a subtil conclusioun. *c* **1400** in Halliwell *Rara Mathem.* (1841) 59 Þe 12 departynges of aiþer of þo sides are called poyntes, þan es a poynte þe twelft parte of any thyng, namely of ouþer side of þe quadrat in þe quadrant. **1550** W. LYNNE *Carion's Cron.* 252 b, The third Eclipse was of the Moone.. the Moone was darkened .xvii. pointes and .xxv. minutes. **1594** BLUNDEVIL *Exerc.* III. I. xv. (1636) 309 The Astronomers do divide the Diameter as well of the Sunne, as of the Moone into 12, and some into 24 parts, which they call points.

12. *nine* or *eleven points*, usually in the saying 'Possession is nine (*formerly* eleven) points of the law', i.e. is = nine or eleven out of a supposed ten or twelve points (= a vast majority of the points) that may be raised in a legal action. So by hyperbole, *ninety-nine points* (out of a hundred).

1697–8 WATTS *Reliq. Juv.* (1789) 149 Prejudice and education had eleven points of the law, and it was impossible for arguments to dispossess them. **1809** MALKIN *Gil Blas* X. x. ⁋20 She had possession, and that is nine points of the law. **1863** READE *Very Hard Cash* xliii, Possession is ninety-nine points of Lunacy law.

13. a. A unit of count in the score of a game.

1746 HOYLE *Whist* (ed. 6) 69 *Points.* Ten of them make a Game. **1816** SINGER *Hist. Cards* 261 *note*, The five is called Towser. The six, Tumbler, which reckon in hand for their respective number of points. **1856** LT. COL. B. *Whist-player* (1858) 21 The party revoking forfeit three points. **1873** BENNETT & 'CAVENDISH' *Billiards* 14 The game (1200 up) was won by Cook by 117 points. **1895** *Westm. Gaz.* 3 Dec. 7/1 Cumberland scored 14 points [at Football].

b. Hence, *to give points to* [F. *donner, rendre des points*], to allow (a rival) to count so many points at starting, to give odds to; *colloq.* to have the advantage of; so *to gain a point, to get points*, to gain an advantage.

1871 FREEMAN *Hist. Ess.* Ser. I. xii. 400 The English Minister can often gain a point by dexterous dealing in Parliament. **1881** *Confess. Frivolous Girl* 106, I got more [bouquets] than she did; thereby (to use a bit of slang) getting points on her for the time being. **1883** *American* VI. 333 Any average Eton boy could give points to His Holiness in the matter of Latin verses. **1895** F. E. TROLLOPE *F. Trollope* II. i. 16 She could give points to many younger women and beat them.

c. *spec.* in *Piquet*: The number of cards of the most numerous suit in one's hand after discarding; the number scored by the player who holds the highest number of one suit. See PIQUET[1].

1719 R. SEYMOUR *Court Gamester* 75 He who reckons most in this Manner [either by greater number of cards, or, in case of equality, of Pips, Ace = 11, Court cards 10 each] is said to win the Point. **1727–41** CHAMBERS *Cycl.* s.v. *Piquet*, The carte blance [sic] is the first thing that reckons; then the point. **1809** MALKIN *Gil Blas* I. xvii. ⁋3 Point, quint, and quatorze. **1824** SCOTT *St. Ronan's* xviii, By an infraction of the laws of the game [piquet],.. Lord Etherington called a point without showing it.

d. *pl.* Name of a particular game at bowls.

1902 J. A. MANSON in *Encycl. Brit.* XXVI. 329/1 (*Bowls*) On Scottish greens the game of Points is occasionally played... Three points are scored if the bowl come to rest within one foot of the jack... It is obvious that the Points game demands an ideally perfect green.

e. *on points* (Boxing): according to or as a result of the points scored in a number of rounds, esp. in phr. *to beat* (or *defeat*) *on points*: to beat (an opponent) in a contest by winning more points and not by achieving a knockout. Also *to lose* (or *win*) *on points*, etc. Also *fig.*

1904 *C. B. Fry's Mag.* June 301/1 Aeneas called 'time', and gave a decision.. 'on points'. **1929** *Daily Express* 7 Nov. 13/5 Young Stribling, the American boxer, defeated Maurice Griselle, France, on points in a ten-round.. contest. **1929** *Evening News* 18 Nov. 16/4 Rolland.. beat Wilhelm Bech on points. **1930** *Cambridge Daily News* 25 Sept. 7/4 Campolo.. will probably retire for good.. if Sharkey gives him the full count, or if he loses on points. **1948** J. B. PRIESTLEY *Linden Tree* I. 38 'Daddy had a blazing row with the man at the bookshop. Didn't you, Daddy?'.. 'Yes, but I thought he won on points.' **1955** *Times* 12 May 4/3 He landed a fair number of swings and a few straight lefts... It was not enough and Eddington won on points. **1957** E. GOWERS *H. W. Fowler* 11 The draftsman was attacked for using this construction... If I had been the referee in that contest I should have awarded Jespersen a win on points. **1968** *Listener* 18 July 90/3 Mrs Vlachou was as icily contemptuous of the colonels' intentions as she used once to be of British intentions at the time of the Cyprus troubles; Mr Sparrow was eloquent in their defence. On points I should give the victory to Mrs Vlachou. **1975** *Oxf. Compan. Sports & Games* 116/1 This championship, for which Clay and Frazier, the winner on points over 15 rounds, each received $2,500,000, must have grossed more than $20 million.

14. a. A unit in appraising the qualities of a competitor, or of an exhibit in a competitive show. Also *fig.*

1777 SHERIDAN *Sch. Scand.* IV. iii, Charles's imprudence and bad character are great points in my favour. **1867** TROLLOPE *Chron. Barset* I. xxi. 179, I cannot accept it as a point in a clergyman's favour, that he should be opposed to his bishop. **1886** STEVENSON *Dr. Jekyll* ii, All these were points against him.

b. A unit of credit towards an award or benefit, *spec.* (*a*) an academic qualification (*U.S.*); (*b*) allocation of local authority housing; (*c*) discharge from the armed forces or return from overseas service.

1903 *N.Y. Times* 29 Aug. 3/4 For university credit, each 30 hours' course counts one point, and laboratory work, at the rate of 60 hours, to one point. **1950** B. WOOTTON *Testament for Social Science* ii. 41 The local authority's decision to give x points for size of family, y points for service in the armed forces, plus z points for being bombed out may be regarded as entirely subjective value-judgments. **1953** *Manch. Guardian Weekly* 5 Feb. 7 Into San Francisco come the wounded, come the soldiers who have accumulated enough rotation 'points' to be sent home. **1959** N. MAILER *Advts. for Myself* (1961) 120 The regiment was disbanded, and those men who did not have enough points to go home were sent to other outfits. **1963** [see CREDIT *sb.* 13 b]. **1974** M. BIRMINGHAM *You can help Me* i. 10 The Bengalis.. have not enough points yet to live in tower blocks so they pay exorbitant rents to private landlords. **1974** *Times* 14 Nov. 17/7 Housing lists are so long.. I think.. they [*sc.* agricultural workers] should be given points for the number of years they have lived in a tied house. **1977** E. AMBLER *Send no more Roses* v. 89 It's to be first in, first out, with a points bonus for every month of overseas service. **1977** *Jrnl. R. Soc. Arts* CXXV. 550/2 Usually points were allocated according to the inadequacy of the existing accommodation, the degree of overcrowding, the health of the occupier, the length of time that these conditions had prevailed, and the extent to which the dwelling was unsuited to the needs of the occupier. When a household had acquired enough points to reach the top of the housing list, then their own preference as to location and dwelling type would be taken into account.

c. *Bridge.* A unit by which a hand is evaluated.

1959 *Listener* 5 Mar. 434/2 A balanced hand with less than 25 points is considered insufficient to make a mandatory force to game. *Ibid.* 434/3 A ten-point hand. **1964** *Official Encycl. Bridge* 431/1 This [*sc.* the high-card valuation] gives a total of 40 points in the pack, and makes an average hand worth ten points. **1977** *Times* 10 Dec. 13/4 The text-books advise you to pass, because you have four points only and six points are needed for a positive response.

15. a. A recognized unit in quoting variations in price of stocks, shares, and various commodities, differing in value according to the commodity in question; also used in quoting variations in interest rates (one point representing one per cent) and exchange rates (one point being one-hundredth of the smallest monetary unit). In *Betting*, a unit in stating fluctuations of the odds.

1814 *Sporting Mag.* XLIII. 54 Betting reduced two points. **1890** *Daily News* 13 Nov. 2/4 Cotton.—Liverpool... 'Futures' advanced 2 points, but the improvement has not been maintained, and prices are now one point below yesterday's closing rates. **1901** *Westm. Gaz.* 4 Oct. 9/3 An important advance in American cotton has set in in Liverpool, the rise at noon to-day being nine points, or one-eighth per pound. **1901** MARY E. WILKINS *Portion Labor* 159 The mining stock dropped fast—a point or more a day. **1902** *Westm. Gaz.* 20 Jan. 11/1 The Brighton dividend is 3½ per cent. on ordinary, preferred, and A stock alike. The price has fallen 3 points. **1906** L. C. CORNFORD *Defenceless Islands* 98 Prices have dropped six points. A point is the hundredth part of a penny. **1930** M. CLARK *Home Trade* 163 Prices in the case of spot transactions are not stated in terms of pence per lb., but as so many 'points on' or 'points off' the price of cotton.., a 'point' being one hundredth of a penny. **1971** *Daily Tel.* 5 Apr. 7/2 Bank Rate is now 2½ points higher than at the beginning of 1956, and mortgage rates are also 2½ points higher over the same period. *Ibid.*, This would save the building societies about ½ of a point of interest. **1974** *Ibid.* 23 Feb. 19/4 Metal Box at 206p managed an 11-point rise while Pilkington jumped 13 to 302p. **1980** *Times* 12 Feb. 19/3 Sterling.. continued to maintain a firm position closing 60 points ahead at 2·3045.

b. A unit of value and exchange in rationing; *on points*, (rationed) on the basis of such units.

1940 *Economist* 31 Aug. 280/2 Textiles are sharply rationed [in Holland]... On August 12th, the German system of a clothing card of 100 points was introduced. **1942** *Business Week* 9 May 15/1 The rationing method—according to current OPA thinking—will be to establish a secondary currency of points alongside the dollar currency. Essential articles.. will be listed and given a price in points. Then every person in the country will be given a book of stamps representing a certain number of points. **1944** M. LASKI *Love on Supertax* i. 13 You always seem to forget that breakfast cereals cost points. **1944** *Times* 23 Feb. 2/3 From April 2 imported tinned marmalade will be available on points, and will not be, as hitherto, part of the preserve ration. **1947** *Ann. Reg. 1946* 55 Surplus [Bread] Units would be exchangeable for Points entitling to other foodstuffs. **1948** J. BELL *Wonderful Mrs Marriott* ii. 36 Mrs Dale's worries with points and coupons. **1950** 'P. WOODRUFF' *Island of Chamba* vii. 109 The Sultana sounds like something you get from the grocer if you have enough points. **1965** N. FREELING *Criminal Conversation* II. xv. 169 England during the reign of Sir Stafford Cripps.. with points and coupons and austerity. **1975** S. BRIGGS *Keep Smiling Through* (1976) 155 People could distribute their 16 monthly points as they liked, sometimes spending the lot on a delicious tin of salmon, sometimes cautiously stocking up on sensible spam and pilchards.

†**16. a.** A measure of length, the twelfth part of a French line: cf. LINE *sb.*[2] 16. *Obs.*

1815 J. SMITH *Panorama Sc. & Art* I. 472 The smallest no more than one-half of a Paris point, or the 144th part of an inch in diameter.. is said to magnify the diameter of an object 2560 times.

b. *Printing.* A unit of measurement for type bodies: in the French or Didot system the seventy-second part of a French inch (i.e. twice the amount of prec.); in the U.S. system slightly smaller (in the proportion of about twelve to thirteen), i.e. ·0138 of an inch.

1890 *Cent. Dict.* s.v., The American point was adopted by the United States Type-Founders' Association in 1883. **1900** H. HART *Century of Oxford Typog.* 154 The typographical unit is the point. *Ibid.*, Oxford Press Type-bodies.. Nonpareil, 5·68 Didot Points.. Brevier, 7·35 Didot Points. **1901** *Westm. Gaz.* 6 Feb. 4/3 The type.. must be at least 'eight point', and the lines must be separated by at least two points.

17. In Australian use: A unit in measuring rainfall, the hundredth part (·01) of an inch.

1889 *Australasian* 20 Apr., The following reports have been received:—Brewarrina, 40 points; Bourke, 47 points;.. Ivanhoe, 100 points; Mossagiel, 188 points;.. Hillston, 288 points. **1893** *Westm. Gaz.* 17 May 2/1 In the district of the Thompson River there had only been nine points of rain in 15 months. **1895** *Queenslander* 7 Dec. 1061 Rain set in early this morning, ninety-eight points having fallen up to 2.30 p.m.

18. A measure of weight used for diamonds and other precious stones, equal to one hundredth of a carat.

1931 KRAUS & HOLDEN *Gems* (ed. 2) vii. 99 The weight of a diamond is often expressed in points. Thus, a stone weighing 65 points actually weighs 0·65 carats. **1974** *Encycl. Brit. Micropædia* II. 546/3 The metric carat, equal to 0·200 grams, and the point, equal to 0·01 carat, was adopted by the U.S. in 1913 and, subsequently, by most other countries.

1979 *Guardian* 3 Nov. 17/7 (Advt.), A dazzling 1½ point diamond, handset in a brilliant star-burst of gold 'vermeil'.

IV. Something having definite position, without extension; a position in space, time, succession, degree, order, etc.

19. a. *Geom.* That which is conceived as having position, but not magnitude (as the extremity of a line, or the intersection of two lines).

c **1391** CHAUCER *Astrol.* I. §18 This forseide cenyth is ymagened to ben the verrey point ouer the crowne of thyn heued. **1551** RECORDE *Pathw. Knowl.* I. Defin., A Poynt or a Prycke, is named of Geometricians that small and vnsensible shape, whiche hath in it no partes, that is to say: nother length, breadth, nor depth. **1570** DEE *Math. Pref.* *j, A Point is a thing Mathematicall, indiuisible, which may haue a certayne determined situation. **1660** BARROW *Euclid* I. Defin., i. A Point is that which has no part... iii. The ends, or limits, of a line are Points. **1704** J. HARRIS *Lex. Techn.* I. s.v., If a Point be supposed to be moved any way, it will by its Motion describe a Line. **1828** J. H. MOORE *Pract. Navig.* (ed. 20) 11 To draw a Circle through any Three given Points not situated in a right Line. **1866** BRANDE & COX *Dict. Sc.*, etc. II. 946/1 It is sometimes convenient to consider a point as an evanescent circle or sphere.

b. In various phrases with *of* (in *Geom.*, *Optics*, and *Perspective*), as *point of contrary flexure*, *p. of convergence*, *p. of dispersion*, *p. of distance*, *p. of divergence*, *p. of incidence*, *p. of inflexion*, *p. of osculation*, *p. of reflection*, *p. of refraction*, *p. of sight*, *p. of vision*, etc.: see these words. See also VANISHING *point*.

c. *Astron.*, etc. Applied with qualifying adjs. to special points of the celestial sphere, etc.: see CARDINAL, EQUINOCTIAL, SOLSTITIAL, VERTICAL.

cardinal points = Fr. *points cardinaux*; but *the 32 points of the compass* (sense B. 9) = Fr. *pointes de la boussole, ou du compas*.

†**d.** Middle or central point, centre. *Obs. rare.*

1481 CAXTON *Myrr.* I. xx. 59 No more than hath the poynt or pricke in the myddle of the most grete compaas that may be. **1614** W. B. *Philosopher's Banquet* (ed. 2) 227 Our Ecclesiasticall writers haue thought Iudea to be the middle of the Earth, and Ierusalem the very poynt.

20. a. A place having definite spatial position but no extent, or of which the position alone is considered; a spot.

13.. *E.E. Allit. P.* C. 68 In þat Cete my saȝes soghe alle aboute, þat, in þat place at þe poynt, I put in þi hert. *c* **1400** *Destr. Troy* 564 The perlouse pointtes þat passe you behoues. **1568** GRAFTON *Chron.* II. 698 King Edward.. was not a little troubled.. and driuen to seeke the furthest poynt of his witte. **1669** STURMY *Mariner's Mag.* IV. xi. 178 If you keep a true Account of the Ship's way.., you may at any time have the true Point where the Ship is. **1710** J. CLARKE *Rohault's Nat. Phil.* (1729) I. 263 All the Rays which come from any Point of the Object, and fall upon the whole Superficies of the Glass do.. enter into the Pupil. **1837** LADY W. DE ERESBY in *C. K. Sharpe's Corr.* (1888) II. 498 The nearest way from point to point. **1864** PUSEY *Lect. Daniel* (1876) 411 Susa was a good point, whence to invade Babylon.

b. *spec.* The spot at which a policeman is stationed. (Cf. POINT-DUTY.) Also, a rallying point or rendezvous for police, military personnel, etc.

1888 *Pall Mall G.* 11 Oct. 2/1, I came.. in search of a constable: the one on 'point' at Holborn Town Hall could not come. **1898** J. D. BRAYSHAW *Slum Silhouettes* 201 'Here, John,' he shouts to the potman, 'fetch the man from the point.'.. In a few minutes up comes the potman with a sergeant an' p'liceman. **1963** N. MARSH *Dead Water* (1964) vii. 191 Shall I return to my point, sir? **1967** 'S. WOODS' *And shame Devil* ii. 36, I made my point with t'sergeant... Corner of Badger's Way, that was. **1968** P. N. WALKER *Carnaby & Gaol-breakers* viii. 80 P. C. Williams... His last point was in Romanby village. **1972** J. ROSSITER *Rope for General Dietz* ix. 128 They're waiting until half-past ten. That's when the *Guardia* make their point near the *Bar El Toro Blanco* and wait for thirty minutes.

c. *Hunting. colloq.* A spot to which a straight run is made; hence a straight run from point to point, a cross-country run. *to make his point* (of a fox, etc.), to run straight to a spot aimed at. Cf. D. 11.

1875 WHYTE-MELVILLE *Riding Recoll.* (1879) xi. 185 In Leicestershire especially, foxes.. will make their point with a stiff breeze blowing in their teeth. *Ibid.* xii. 211 A sportsman must.. admit that 'ten mile points' over grass with one of the handsomest packs of [stag-]hounds in the world, are most enjoyable. **1883** R. E. EGERTON-WARBURTON *Hunting Songs* (ed. 7) Introd. 36 The increase of.. dwellings prevents a fox, headed at every corner, from making straight to his point. **1896** *Westm. Gaz.* 25 Nov. 9/1 The Belvoir hounds made an eight mile point in a little over 45 minutes. **1920** *Blackw. Mag.* Jan. 108/1 These marshy channels.. are the invariable point of any hunted boar. **1939** *Country Life* 11 Feb. p. xxxii/1 After running in all for an hour and forty minutes and making a six and a half miles point. **1977** *Field* 13 Jan. 52/1 Our fox crossed the valley and made his point to Moorhill.

d. *pl.* Localities or places considered in some special connection, esp. as being in a particular direction from a specified place. (Influenced by sense B. 9.)

1885 U. S. GRANT *Personal Mem.* I. xxx. 422 From there [*sc.* Vicksburg] a railroad runs east, connecting with other roads leading to all points of the Southern States. **1895** *Montgomery Ward Catal.* Spring & Summer 589/1 Freight paid by us to all points east of the west line of Dakota, Kansas, Nebraska and Louisiana. To points farther west we apply $1 00 on the payment of freight. **1903** *N. Y. Even. Post* 19 Aug. 7/6 The number here is now estimated at 21,000 persons from Eastern points, with fully 35,000 persons in addition from California. **1926** *Publishers' Weekly* 22 May 1684/2 Some of us here get supplies from other points that they know nothing about. *Ibid.* 18 Dec. 2256 The business must be going to distant points—New York, Chicago, etc. **1933** *Fortune* Aug. 94 Loring F. ('Red') Nichols, of Cleveland and points Mid-West, is a crack director and trumpeter. **1969** R. TASHKENT *Ambiguous Man* i. 14 She and a friend had started off for Athens and points East. **1969** D. BARRON *Man who was There* i. 11 I've been in Pakistan and points East for six weeks. **1973** A. ROSS *Dunfermline Affair* 38 We.. took the road through Kilmany and Auchtermuchty and all points south west. **1978** *Jrnl. R. Soc. Arts* CXXVI. 712/1, I will be testing that later this month in Washington and other points West.

e. (See quot. 1926); *spec.* a socket fixed in a wall or the like which is connected to an electricity supply and designed to receive the plug of an electrical appliance; = OUTLET *sb.* 1 e. Cf. also *power point* s.v. POWER *sb.*[1] 18 f.

1904 H. WALTER *Electric Lighting for Inexperienced* viii. 82 The cost per point depends.. on the materials used for protecting the wires, and whether the wires are run on or under the surface of walls. **1913** D. S. MUNRO *Practice of Electr. Wiring* xiv. 126 The stamped boxes are not so useful for variety of outlet point. **1921** J. H. HAVELOCK *Electr. Installation Work* xiii. 155 The lamps may be varied at one of the switch points. **1925** J. C. CONNAN *Electr. Estimating* ix. 167 If the area in square feet to be illuminated is divided by the total number of points (including ceiling roses, wall brackets, and wall plugs), the average area illuminated per point is obtained. **1926** *Gloss. Terms Electr. Engin.* (Brit. Engin. Stand. Assoc.) 111 *Point*, in wiring. The termination of the wiring intended for attachment to a fitting for one or more lamps or other consuming devices. **1940** G. D. H. & M. COLE *Murder at Munition Works* 138 Presumably there was a lead to that reading lamp point over there. **1967** *Listener* 21 Dec. 831/2 There is no electric point in her room, so she uses the ceiling light festooned with wires to plug in her iron. **1972** M. BABSON *Murder on Show* ix. 107 Helena Keswick plugged an electric kettle into a point underneath the table. **1976** *Cumberland & Westmorland Herald* 4 Dec. 16/6 (Advt.), Kitchen/breakfast room,.., floor units and matching wall cupboards and electric cooker point.

21. a. *Her.* One of nine particular spots or places upon a shield, which serve to determine accurately the position a charge is to occupy. **b.** *Her.* The middle part of the chief or base, as distinguished from the dexter or sinister divisions. **c.** *Her.* One of a number of horizontal stripes of different tinctures into which a shield may be divided. (See also B. 3 c, D. 4 c.)

c **1394** *P. Pl. Crede* 562 þe penounes & þe pomels & poyntes of scheldes Wiþ-drawen his deuocion. **1508** KENNEDIE *Flyting w. Dunbar* 414 A stark gallowis, ane wedy, and a pyn, The hede poynt of thyne elderis armes ar. **1658** PHILLIPS, *Points*, in Heraldry are certain places in an Escutcheon diversly named according to their several positions. **1725** COATS *Dict. Her.* s.v., There are nine principal Points in any Escutcheon... A... the Dexter Chief. B. the.. Middle Chief. C. the Sinister Chief. D. the Honour Point. E. the Fesse Point, call'd also the Center. F. the Nombril Point, that is, the Navel Point. G. the Dexter Base. H. the Sinister Base. I. the precise Middle Base. **1865** *Chambers' Encycl.* VII. 626 In order to facilitate the description of a coat-of-arms, it is the practice to suppose the shield to be divided into nine points.

d. *Sculpture.* Any one of a series of holes drilled in a piece of stone or marble or on the model to be copied to the depth to which the material has to be cut away. Also, the position of such a hole.

1841 *Penny Cycl.* XXI. 142/1 This process is repeated till the numerous points at fixed depths, corresponding throughout with the surface of the model, are attained, and a rough copy of the sculptor's original work is thus mechanically made. **1911** A. TOFT *Modelling & Sculpture* 254 A good pointer will keep all his 'points' a little 'full', by never allowing the needle to go quite home. **1947** J. C. RICH *Materials & Methods of Sculpture* ix. 261 The indirect method of stone carving involves the use of previously prepared three-dimensional models, built up in most cases of plastic clay and then cast in a more durable substance, such as plaster of Paris. The casts are then utilized as master models from which to take points or otherwise copy. **1970** *Oxf. Compan. Art* 884/2 Sometimes hundreds and even thousands of points will be taken to ensure a meticulously exact copy. **1974** *Encycl. Brit. Micropædia* VIII. 68/1 The final points on the stone are usually left about $\frac{1}{16}$ inch (about one millimetre) higher than those on the model to enable the sculptor to put the finishing touches on the stone.

†**22.** One of the squares of a chessboard. *the four points*, the four centre squares. *Obs.*

c **1407** LYDG. *Reson & Sens.* 6044 The vnkouth craft of the tabler And the poyntes of the chekker. *c* **1440** *Gesta Rom.* xxi. 71 (Harl.) The chekir or þe chesse hath viij. poyntes in eche partie. **1474** CAXTON *Chesse* 135 The bordeure about is hygher than the squarenes of the poyntes. *a* **1500** *MS. Ashmole* 344 (Bodl.) 10 This is a fair Jupertie to mate a man in on of the iiij poyntes for it cumyth offt in play.

23. a. A definite position in a scale of any kind; a position reached in a course (e.g. DEAD POINT); a step, stage, or degree in progress or development, or in increase or decrease; an exact degree of some measurable quality or condition, as temperature (e.g. *boiling-point*, *dew-point*, *freezing-point*, *melting-point*).

a **1425** *Chaucer's Pars. T.* ¶847 (Harl. MS.) Whan naturel lawe was in his first [6-*text* right] poynt in paradis. **1526** *Pilgr. Perf.* (W. de W. 1531) 5 b, [This] declareth some poynt of our iourney. **1568** GRAFTON *Chron.* II. 678 The extreme poynt of decay of his house and estate. **1639** S. DU VERGER tr. *Camus' Admir. Events* 206 Her beauty and comely grace.. amounted unto a high point. **1747** Freezing Point [FREEZING *vbl. sb.* 2]. **1773** Boiling point [BOILING *vbl. sb.* 5]. **1792** WASHINGTON *Lett.* Writ. 1891 XII. 177 Differences in political opinions are as unavoidable, as, to a certain point, they may perhaps be necessary. **1871** B. STEWART *Heat* §89 The melting points of various substances. **1886** RUSKIN *Præterita* I. 324, I was brought to the point of trying to learn to sing. **1891** *Law Times* XCII. 93/2 The shares reached their highest point on the 13th June 1890, when they might have been sold for £600.

b. A critical position in the course of affairs; a decisive state of circumstances, a juncture; the precise moment for action, an opportunity. Now only in phrases ***when it comes (came) to the point***, and ***at, on, upon the point of*** (see D. 1 c, 5).

1375 BARBOUR *Bruce* VII. 500 In all that tyme schir Amery, .. In carleill lay, his poynt to se. **1489** CAXTON *Faytes of A.* II. xiii. 114 Atte laste he sawe hys poynte whan that his enemyes were wery. *a* **1533** LD. BERNERS *Huon* liii. 178 When it cometh to the poynt ther as strokes shold be gyuen. **1612** BP. HALL *Contempl.*, *O.T.* IV. iii, But now, when it comes to the point, 'Who am I?' **1796** JANE AUSTEN *Pride & Prej.* xxvii, Her father.. who, when it came to the point, so little liked her going, that he told her to write to him.

c. Phr. ***up to a (certain) point***: to a certain extent, but by no means absolutely.

1823 BYRON *Don Juan* XIII. lxxxi. 95 For good society Is no less famed for tolerance than piety: That is, up to a certain point; which point Forms the most difficult in punctuation. **1916** G. B. SHAW *Androcles & Lion* p. xv, As they [*sc.* Savonarolas and Knipperdollings] know, very sensibly, that a little religion is good for children and serves morality, keeping the poor in good-humor or in awe by promising rewards in heaven or threatening torments in hell, they encourage the religious people up to a certain point. **1936** —— *Simpleton* II. 53 Well, it has worked, up to a point. **1951** E. PAUL *Springtime in Paris* xvi. 296 He had been an understanding husband up to a certain point. **1961** *Chicago Daily Tribune* 10 Feb. III. 9/7 But he had in Walter Hendl a willing conductor able only up to a point. **1978** P. MCCUTCHAN *Blackmail North* vi. 69 'There's been a threat, Shard!' 'Being taken seriously?' 'Up to a point.'

24. a. In time, that which has 'position' but not duration (as the beginning or end of a space of time); the precise time at which anything happens; an instant, moment, as the moment of noon, the moment of death.

a **1400** *R. Brunne's Chron. Wace* (Rolls) 8080 Drecchynge by tymes haue [*Petyt MS.* poyntes haf] þey wrought. *c* **1400** *Apol. Loll.* 28 To ani man in þe poynt of deþ. **1413** *Pilgr. Sowle* (Caxton) II. xlii. (1859) 47 In this poynt I herde.. a lusty melodye of wonder swete songe. **1653** HOLCROFT *Procopius* IV. 151 The point of opportunity being past, the greatest endeavours afterward faile. **1737** WHISTON *Josephus, Hist.* I. iii. §5 Four hours.. are over already, which point of time renders the prediction impossible. **1833–6** J. H. NEWMAN *Hist. Sk.* (1873) II. IV. ii. 380 There is.. no assignable point at which the belief was introduced. **1844** MRS. BROWNING *Drama of Exile* Poems 1850 I. 30 Though at the last point of a million years.

b. ***at*** or ***on the point of***: see D. 1 c, 5.

†**25.** A (specified) degree of condition; condition, plight, state, case (good, evil, better, etc.). (Cf. F. *en bon point.*) *Obs.*

1297 R. GLOUC. (Rolls) 8868 Engelond & normandie in god point he broȝte. **1340–70** *Alex. & Dind.* 315 To godus pay is our peple in bettur point founde. *c* **1386** CHAUCER *Prol.* 200 A lord ful fat and in good poynt. **1481** CAXTON *Godeffroy* cxv. 173 The barons toke counseyl.. how they myght conteyne them in this greuous poynt in whiche they were. *a* **1533** LD. BERNERS *Huon* xcv. 307 She demaundyd of hym yf he were hole and in good poynt. **1563** *Reg. Privy Council Scot.* I. 246 The said kirk is at sik ane point that throw decaying thairof, .. the wallis in sindrie partis ar revin. **1685** EVELYN *Mrs. Godolphin* 176 Daniell and his companions.. looked fairer and in better point than all the rest. **1732** POPE *Ess. Man* I. 283 Know thy own point.. this due degree Of blindness, weakness, Heav'n bestows on thee.

V. Figurative and transferred senses.

†**26.** The highest part or degree; the height, summit, zenith, acme. *Obs.*

13.. *E.E. Allit. P.* B. 1502 In þe poynt of her play he poruayes a mynde. **1576** FLEMING *Panopl. Epist.* 17 *margin*, It is the point of folly to shew a will to hurte him, whom thou canst not.. by any meanes annoy. **1640** QUARLES *Enchirid.* (1641) Ded., Your Highnesse is the Expectation of the present Age, and the Poynt of future Hopes. **1728** RAMSAY *Bonny Chirsty* v, This point of a' his wishes, He wadna with set speeches bauk.

27. a. A distinguishing mark or quality; a distinctive trait or feature; a characteristic.

c **1470** HENRYSON *Mor. Fab.* v. (*Parl. Beasts*) xxiv, This suddane semblie.. Haifand the pointis of ane parliament. *c* **1530** H. RHODES *Bk. Nurture* 438 in *Babees Bk.* 94 To forbeare in anger is the poynt of a friendly leeche. **1581** J. BELL *Haddon's Answ. Osor.* 449 b, A shyft of subtle sophisters, and not a poynt of sober Divynes. **1604** JAMES I *Counterbl.* (Arb.) 111 It is become.. a point of good fellow-ship.. to take a pipe of Tobacco. **1694** ATTERBURY *Serm.*, *On Prov.* xiv. 6 (1726) I. 184 To be cautious, and upon our Guard, in receiving Doctrines.. is a Point of great Prudence. **1889** T. A. GUTHRIE *Pariah* I. ix, Description was not Lettice's strong point.

b. *spec.* A physical feature in an animal; *esp.* one by which excellence or purity of breed is judged. (Cf. 14.) *pl.* Of persons and things: good features, advantages; usu. in phr. ***to have one's*** (or ***its***) ***points***.

1546 J. HEYWOOD *Prov.* (1867) 52 She hath one poynt of a good hauke, she is hardie. **1841** BORROW *Zincali* II. ii. 56 Much better versed in the points of a horse than in points of theology. **1859** G. MEREDITH *R. Feverel* xxxvii, She seemed to scan his points approvingly. **1894** G. ARMATAGE *Horse* ii. 14 They [American and Canadian horses] are not remarkable for beauty, though not showing any peculiarly unsightly points. *Ibid.* 20 That the race horse should have all his various points in true relative development. *Ibid.* iv. 47 The points essential to a hunter are a lean head and neck [etc.]. **1897** A. BEARDSLEY *Let.* 16 Sept. (1970) 369 It was a sad moment when I tore myself from Dieppe... Paris however has points and I am forgetting my sorrow. **1931** *Times Lit. Suppl.* 26 Feb. 157/1 A simple story, but it has its points. **1934** E. O'NEILL *Days without End* I. 24 What the devil's got into Walter lately, anyway? Getting drunk as a pastime may have its points, but as an exclusive occupation —. **1946** —— *Iceman Cometh* I. 24 *Parritt.* (*With a disparaging glance around*) Must be hard up for a place to hang out. *Larry.* It has its points for him. He never runs into anyone he knows in his business here. **1953** B. GORDON-CUMMING *Gentle Rain* 38 She had her points, certainly... In her occasional dreamy moods she was lovely. **1961** F. & R. LOCKRIDGE (*title*) Murder has its points.

c. An area of contrasting colour in the fur of certain cats, usually on the face, paws, and tail. Cf. also SEAL POINT.

1903 F. SIMPSON *Bk. of Cat* xxiii. 259/2 The [Siamese] kittens are born absolutely white.. and gradually all the points come. **1935** E. B. SIMMONS *Cats* xxix. 149 Blue points are rare, a sort of 'sport'. **1955** R. TENENT *Pedigree Cats* vi. 53 The points—marking the mask, ears, legs, feet, and tail—are all a dense and clearly defined seal-brown. **1972** ING & POND *Champion Cats of World* II. 87/2 The colouring and points [of Birmans] are as for the Siamese.

28. a. ***the point***: the precise matter in discussion or to be discussed; the essential or important thing. Often in phr. ***to come to the point, to keep to the point***, etc.: see also ***in point, to the point*** (D. 4 d, 6 c).

c **1381** CHAUCER *Parl. Foules* 372 But to the poynt, nature held on hire hond A formele egle of shap the gentilleste That euere she a-mong hire werkis fond. *c* **1386** —— *Prol.* 790 This is the poynt, to speken short and pleyn. *a* **1533** LD. BERNERS *Huon* lxix. 236 Come to yᵉ poynt, and vse no more such langage nor suche serymonyes. **1602** *2nd Pt. Return fr. Parnass.* v. iii. (Arb.) 68 But the point is, I know not how to better my selfe. **1693** CREECH in *Dryden's Juvenal* xiii. Argt. (1697) 319 Then coming closer to his Point, he tells him,.. The Wicked are severely punish'd by their own Consciences. **1738** tr. *Guazzo's Art Conversation* 12 Let us now come to the Point in Hand. **1791** MRS. RADCLIFFE *Rom. Forest* ii, 'Is it impossible for you to speak to the point?' said La Motte. **1868** HELPS *Realmah* (1876) 256 Do keep to the point, my excursive friends. **1875** JOWETT *Plato* (ed. 2) I. 18 The point is not who said the words, but whether they are true or not.

b. ***to make a point of*** (= F. *faire un point de*): to treat or regard (something) as essential or indispensable; to make (it) a special object. Usually with vbl. sb. or gerund: formerly also ***to make a point to do*** something.

a **1778** GOLDSMITH in Boswell *Johnson* 9 Apr., Whenever I write any thing, the publick make a point to know nothing about it. *a* **1806** FOX *Hist. Jas. II* (1808) 12 The King made no point of adhering to his concessions. **1823** W. TENNANT *Cdl. Beaton* IV. iii. 121, I mak a pount to be an e'e-witness o' ilka business o' that sort. **1833** HT. MARTINEAU *Brooke Farm* vii. 88 Her husband made such a point of his tea that she had little hope of persuading him to give it up. **1868** FREEMAN *Norm. Conq.* II. App. 581 A former colleague of mine in the Oxford Schools always made a point of describing him as 'William the Purchaser'.

29. a. That at which one aims, or for which one strives or contends; aim, object, end. Also, (the expression of) an important fact or truth; a noteworthy comment. Phrases ***to carry one's point***: see CARRY *v.* 17 b; ***to have a point***: to have made a convincing or significant remark; to be correct (in a particular matter).

13.. *De Sancta Anastasia* 86 in Horstmann *Altengl. Leg.* (1881) 26 Þe prynce.. Opon a day his poynt wold proue. **1580** SIDNEY *Ps.* xxxi. vii, They their counsells led All to this point, how my poore life to take. **1607** SHAKS. *Cor.* II. ii. 43 It remaines, As the maine Point of this our after-meeting. **1689** POPPLE tr. *Locke's Toleration* L.'s Wks. 1727 II. 250 The Magistrate.. will have his Will, and carry his Point. **1700** PEPYS *Diary*, etc. (1879) VI. 217 The old East India Company have.. obtained their great point against the new, by having got their Bill passed. **1776** SIR J. REYNOLDS *Disc.* vii. (1876) 408 If they make it the point of their ambition. **1857** W. COLLINS *Dead Secret* III. ii, She ended.. by carrying her own point, and having her own way. *c* **1939** A. D. LINDSAY *Let.* in D. Scott *A. D. Lindsay* (1971) xv. 258, I have now read the article with interest and appreciation but it doesn't meet my point at all. **1962** *Listener* 22 Feb. 342/2 Is it possible that the Doctor had a point? **1963** *Ibid.* 21 Feb. 350/2 What most convinced me they had a point was the line taken by the interviewer. **1978** L. THOMAS *Ormerod's Landing* ii. 20 'Right,' he agreed sportingly. 'You've got a point, Ormerod.'

b. ***to make a point***: to establish a proposition, to prove a contention; also *gen.* to attain something that one is aiming at.

1809 J. MARSHALL *Const. Opin.* v. (1839) 112 Two points have been made in this cause. **1865** M. ARNOLD *Ess. Crit.* ii. (1875) 87 All it exists for is to get its ends, to make its points. **1886** *Manch. Exam.* 3 Nov. 3/1 His evident desire to make every point that can possibly be made against the Clark lecturer.

c. ***to take*** (***someone's***) ***point*** (and variants): to understand the import or significance of what is being said; to concede the truth or value of a particular contention.

1898 G. B. SHAW *You never can Tell* II. 254 Do I take your point rightly, Mr McComas? **1901** —— *Capt. Brassbound's Conversion* III. 276 *Rankin* (cannily). I take your point, Leddy Ceecily. It alters the case. **1916** JOYCE *Portrait of Artist* (1969) v. 187, I see. I quite see your point. *Ibid.* 188 Yes, yes: I see, said the dean quickly, I quite catch the point. **1943** N. MARSH *Colour Scheme* x. 187 'The point is quite well taken,' he said at last. **1961** C. WILLOCK *Death in Covert* viii. 168 'You have absolutely nothing to go on except your sixth sense.' 'Point taken.' **1964** R. BRADDON *Year Angry Rabbit* xii. 104 'But this is dusk,' Fitzgerald objected. 'Yes, dear,' Karen got the point quickly, 'which for nocturnals is what dawn is to us.' **1966** *Listener* 3 Nov. 658/2, I take his point about Laszlo Rajk. **1969** V. GIELGUD *Necessary End* xxiii. 205 'A First Officer who doesn't play along to an extent with female passengers would probably be considered to be neglecting his job.' 'Point taken.' **1974** E. LEMARCHAND *Buried in Past* x. 168 'The affair'll have to be shelved.' 'I take your point, sir,' Pollard replied. **1976** J. WAINWRIGHT *Bastard* ii. 35 He nods and says, 'Okay. Point taken.'

d. Sense, purpose, or advantage (*in* or *of* a course of action, state of affairs, etc.). Chiefly in negative contexts, esp. in phr. ***there is no point in***, it has no purpose, it is pointless.

In some cases there are connotations of sense B. 10.

1903 G. B. SHAW *Man & Superman* II. 60 Look here, Ann: if theres no harm in it theres no point in doing it. **1923** W. S. MAUGHAM *Our Betters* II. 85 Thornton has plenty of money. Do you think there is any point in his spending his life making more? **1934** J. B. PRIESTLEY *Eden End* I. 6 What's the point of reading if it makes you feel uncomfortable? **1947** —— *Inspector Calls* II. 49 *Inspector.* And if her story is true—that he was stealing money—. *Mrs. Birling.*.. There's no point in assuming that. **1953** K. AMIS *Lucky Jim* xix. 208 'Give me your address, Christine.' She looked at him scornfully... 'That'll do no good at all. What on earth would be the point?' **1957** J. OSBORNE *Look Back in Anger* III. ii. 90 *Helena.* There doesn't seem much point in trying to explain everything, does there? **1966** M. FRAYN *Russian Interpreter* xxxvii. 207 Was there any possible point for Manning in trying to deny all knowledge of those activities? **1968** C. CHURCHILL in *New Eng. Dramatists* XII. 96 *Tim.* Was it nice in the aeroplane? *Grandfather.* I didn't really notice. *Tim.* What's the point of being in it then? **1971** P. MORTIMER *Home* viii. 80 'Will you.. get married?'.. 'There doesn't seem any point.' **1973** G. GREENE *Hon. Consul* v. ii. 262 Tell Pablo to come in. If they have spotted us, there is no point in leaving him outside to be picked off alone. **1977** *Times* 1 June 17/5 If.. it were true that many Anglican or Roman Catholic Christians could not accept this fundamental affirmation.. we should have to ask whether there is any point in continuing to search for unity.

e. ***debating point***: see DEBATING *vbl. sb.* b.

30. A conclusion, completion, culmination, end, 'period'. Also ***full point***. ? *Obs.*

c **1325** *Spec. Gy Warw.* 278 Habent mortem sine morte et finem mortis sine fine. Hij sholen haue deþ wid-oute deiing And point of deþ wid-outen ending. *c* **1386** CHAUCER *Knt's T.* 2107 But shortly to the point thanne wol I wende, And maken of my longe tale an ende. *c* **1540** HEYWOOD *Four P.P.* in Hazl. *Dodsley* I. 352 Ye shall never have them at a full point. **1555** W. WATREMAN *Fardle Facions* Ded. 3 To bring that to some good pointe, that earst I had begonne. **1590** SHAKS. *Mids. N.* I. ii. 10 First,.. say what the play treats on: then read the names of the Actors: and so grow on to a point. **1633** DURIE in *Presbyt. Rev.* (1887) 307 Thought it necessarie to put the matter to some poynt at that diet. **1686** BURNET *Trav.* v. (1750) 245, I thought I had made so full a Point at the Conclusion of my last Letter, that I should not have given you the Trouble of reading any more Letters. **1833** HT. MARTINEAU *Tale Tyne* i. 7 He is bringing his invention to a point.

†**31.** Determination, decision, resolution. *Obs.*

1477 [see *at a point*, D. 1 d]. **1481** CAXTON *Godeffroy* xxxii. 68 At thende the kyng cam so to poynt that they were appeased goodly. **1530** CRANMER in Strype *Life* (1694) App. 5 After all this he commeth to the poynte to save the Kyngs honour. **1578** T. WILCOCKS *Serm. Pawles Cr.* 22 A great sorte are at a playne poynt, they are carelesse of their soules, so their bodye maye bee free. **1678** BUNYAN *Pilgr.* I. 6, I begin to come to a point; I intend to go along with this good man. **1738** [see *at a point*, D. 1 d].

VI. From 16th c. F. *point* = 15–16th c. It. *punto*; derived from the sense *prick*, through that of *stitch, work done with stitches* with the needle.

As English used the native word *stitch* (OE. *stice*, from OTeut. **stikan* to prick, stab, etc.) for the prick of the needle in sewing, the corresponding Fr. use of *point* was not adopted, and the development of this sense was entirely in Italian and French. The It. name *punto in aria* occurs at Venice in 1476.

32. a. Thread lace made wholly with the needle (also called more fully ***point lace, needle-point lace, needle-point***); also improperly applied to pillow lace imitating that done with the needle, and sometimes to lace generally: often named from the place of manufacture, as ***Alençon point, Venetian point, point of Genoa, Spain***, etc.: cf. POINT *sb.*³ b.

1662 EVELYN *Chalcogr.* 56 Isabella, who was his wife, publish'd a book of all the sorts of Points, Laces, and Embroderies. **1673** RAY *Trav.* 156 Venice is noted.. for Needle-work Laces called Points. *a* **1680** BUTLER *Rem.* (1759) I. 148 To know the Age and Pedigrees Of Poynts of Flandres or Venise. **1686** *Lond. Gaz.* No. 2150/4 Lost.., Two Pieces of Old Point of Spain Three Yards long; and a Quarter of a Yard broad, some of it sowed upon a Parchment, and new Purled. **1745** WESLEY *Wks.* (1872) VIII. 186 Another would not for the world wear lace; but she will wear point, and sees no harm in it at all. **1864** MRS. PALLISER *Hist. Lace* xiii. (1902) 198 A costly work of Alençon point appeared in the Exhibition of 1855. **1882** A. S. COLE in *Encycl. Brit.* XIV. 186/1 The different sorts of early Venetian point laces are called 'flat Venetian point', 'rose (raised) point', 'caterpillar point', 'bone point', &c. **1900** *Westm. Gaz.* 24 May 3/1 The Irish crochet point is.. the best-known of all Irish laces. **1906** *Ibid.* 28 Feb. 12/1 Bucks lace, or 'Bucks pillow point', as the fine work is usually called, dates back.. as far as the sixteenth century.

attrib. **1672** DRYDEN *Marr. à la Mode* III. i, My new point gorget shall be yours upon't. *c* **1710** CELIA FIENNES *Diary* (1888) 252 Fine point or Lace sleeves and Ruffles.

b. A piece of lace used as a kerchief or the like.

1663 PEPYS *Diary* 18 Oct., My wife in her best gowne and new poynt that I bought her the other day, to church with me. **1687** SEDLEY *Bellam.* I. Wks. 1722 II. 90 She.. had but one poor Point of her own making. **1756** MRS. CALDERWOOD *Jrnl.* (1884) 308 Her hair curled and powdered, with a little cap, or perhaps but a point, and nothing more on their heads.

33. A marking on a Hudson's Bay or Mackinaw blanket indicating weight.

1780 in *Beaver* (1935) June 47 [They] had misunderstood him about the price of the pointed plankets as the points were known to every Indian to be the price to be paid for each as 2½ points, 2½ beaver, 3 points, 3 beaver, etc. **1818** T. L. MCKENNEY *Mem.* (1846) I. 309 Northwest Company blankets—so called—three points, to measure six feet six inches long. **1921** *Outing* Nov. 82/1 Hudson Bay blankets run as follows: Three point, 60 × 72 inches, double, weight, 8½ lbs.; 3½ point, 63 × 81 inches, double, weight, 10 lbs.; 4 point, 72 × 90 inches, double, weight, 12 lbs. 'Points' refer to the markings on the blankets and indicate their size. **1935** *Beaver* June 47 The 'point' on the blanket in its present standardized form is comparatively modern, being introduced in 1850. Prior to that date blankets of the Hudson's Bay Company were made with the bar only by individuals in their own homes, each maker putting a distinctive mark, a 'point' on his product to show the size and weight. These 'points' were usually in coloured wools and usually about one inch long. **1954** E. E. RICH *Moose Fort Jrnl., 1783–85* 371 Originally the points and staves of the blankets were blue, but the colour was changed to red in 1786.

B. = F. *pointe*. (L. *cuspis, mucro*, Ger. *spitze*.)

I. 1. a. A sharp end to which anything tapers, used for pricking, piercing, scratching, pointing out, etc.: as of a weapon, tool, pin, pen, pencil, pointer.

a **1330** *Syr Degarre* 1059 Thi swerd.. The point is in min aumenere. He tok the point, and set ther to. *c* **1385** CHAUCER *L.G.W.* 1791 *Lucrece*, This swerd thour out thyn herte shal I ryue.. And sette the poynt [*v.r.* swerd] al sharp vp-on hire herte. *c* **1391** —— *Astrol.* II. §40, I tok a subtil compas, & cleped þat on poynt of my compas A, & þat oþer poynt F. Than tok I the point of A, & set it in [the] Ecliptik line euene in my zodiak. *c* **1400** MAUNDEV. (Roxb.) vii. 27 Take also a litill bawme on þe poynt of þi knyffe. *a* **1425** *Cursor M.* 10626 (Trin.) May no mon write wiþ penne point. *c* **1440** *Promp. Parv.* 406/2 Poynte, of a scharpe toole,.. *cuspis, mucro, pennum.* **1483** *Wardr. Acc. 1 Rich. III*, iij swerdes whereof oon with a flat poynt, called curtana. *c* **1500** *Lancelot* 798 It lyith one your speris poynt. **1526** *Pilgr. Perf.* (W. de W. 1531) 7 It is not so moche as a pynnes poynt, compared to yᵉ hole erth. **1611** BIBLE *Jer.* xvii. 1 The sinne of Iudah is written with a pen of yron, and the point of a diamond. **1722** QUINCY *Lex. Physico-Med.* (ed. 2) 5 Particles that affect the Taste with Points sharp and piercing. **1808** SCOTT *Marm.* VI. xxv, Scarce could they hear, or see their foes, Until at weapon-point they close. **1826** M. R. MITFORD *Our Village* II. 248 A pencil without a point. **1834** MᶜMURTRIE *Cuvier's Anim. Kingd.* 316 Scorpions have.. an arcuated and excessively acute point or sting. **1840** LARDNER *Geom.* i. 6 The point of the finest needle. **1886** C. F. WOOLSON *East Angels* vii. 129 He sharpened all the pencils industriously, taking pains to give each one a very fine point. **1897** MERRIMAN *In Kedar's Tents* xxvii, It is a pretty spot for the knife—nothing to turn a point. **1963** C. FREMLIN *Trouble Makers* xviii. 140 Hundreds of coloured pencils without points went back into their dozens of boxes without lids. **1979** 'J. LE CARRÉ' *Smiley's People* (1980) xvi. 189 Herr Kretzschmer owned a fine gold pencil... He popped out the point and.. drew a pure circle.

†**b.** Rendering L. *acies* ('front of an army').

1382 WYCLIF *Deut.* xx. 2 The preest shal stoond bifore the poynt [Vulg. *aciem*], and thus he shal spek to the puple.

c. Short for ***point of the sword*** (or other weapon). ***to come to points***: to begin fighting (with swords).

1596 SHAKS. *1 Hen. IV*, v. iv. 21, I saw him hold Lord Percy at the point. **1652** TATHAM *Scotch Figgaries* IV. i, But mayn't I Bar points, being the Challenged? **1762** SMOLLETT *Sir L. Greaves* iii. (1793) I. 70 They would have come to points immediately, had not the gentlemen interposed. **1887** SIR F. POLLOCK in *Encycl. Brit.* XXII. 801/2 The effective use of the point is a mark of advanced skill. *Ibid.*, St. Louis anticipated Napoleon in calling on his men to use the point.

d. *fig. phr.* ***to put too fine a point upon***: to express with unnecessary delicacy; not to state bluntly or in plain terms.

1852 DICKENS *Bleak Ho.* xi, He was—not to put too fine a point upon it—.. hard up! **1911** H. S. HARRISON *Queed* iv. 45 The *Post*, not to put too fine a point upon it, had for a time run fast to seed. **1926** F. W. CROFTS *Inspector French & Cheyne Mystery* iii. 40 Not to put too fine a point on it the situation is this: You are there, and you can't get out, and you can't attract attention to your predicament. **1935** C. ISHERWOOD *Mr. Norris changes Trains* x. 155 He seems to have suggested, not to put too fine a point upon it, that you were an accomplice in my nefarious crimes. **1952** A. J. CRONIN *Adventures in Two Worlds* I. vi. 52 This outbreak of scarlet fever... It's spreading, you know, and I find that in all my cases.., well, not to put too fine a point on it—the milk has come from Shawhead. **1971** 'E. CANDY' *Words for Murder Perhaps* iv. 44 One of the doctor's most cherished personal finds, now happily in the City Museum, was not to put too fine a point on it, a fake. **1977** *It* May 10/3 Not to put too fine a point on it, one could say that the real picture consists of nothing but exceptions to the rule.

e. Phr. ***to a*** (***fine***) ***point***: to a precise form; completely.

1888 in Farmer & Henley *Slang* (1902) V. 241/2 Boiled down to a fine point bondsmen are in demand. **1902** G. H. LORIMER *Lett. Self-Made Merchant* xvii. 253 When she was through I knew that I'd been licked—polished right off to a point.

2. a. The (or a) salient or projecting part of anything, of a more or less tapering form, or ending in an acute angle; a tip, apex; a sharp prominence.

c **1391** CHAUCER *Astrol.* II. §7 At the poynt of thy label in the bordure set a prikke..at the point of thi label set a-nother prikke. *c* **1400** MAUNDEV. (Roxb.) xvii. 80 Stanes, þe whilk er noȝt so hard as dyamaundes, and comounly þaire poyntes er broken off. **1483** *Cath. Angl.* 285/2 A Poynte of a nese, *pirula*. **1596** SHAKS. *1 Hen. IV*, II. i. 7, I prethee Tom, beate Cuts Saddle, put a few Flockes in the point: the poore lade is wrung in the withers. **1644** BULWER *Chirol.* 69 Hold up the Hand hollow above the Shoulder points. **1687** A. LOVELL tr. *Thevenot's Trav.* II. 154 The Stern is very low, but the Head is as high again, and draws into a sharp point as the Gondolos of Venice. **1748** *Anson's Voy.* II. xiii. 276 By spreading their sails horizontally, and by putting bullets in the centers of them to draw them to a point, they caught as much [rain] water, as filled all their cask. **1834** McMURTRIE *Cuvier's Anim. Kingd.* 441 The chrysalides are always rounded, or without angular elevations or points. **1841** JAMES *Brigand* iii, Let them get round yon point of the rock. **1881** C. GIBBON *Heart's Problem* iii, Mr. Calthorpe tapped the points of the fingers of each hand together.

fig. **1625** B. JONSON *Staple of N.* II. v, He is my Nephew, and my Chiefe, the Point, Tip, Top, and Tuft of all our family!

b. *spec.* The tapering extremity of any promontory or piece of land running into the sea; a tapering promontory, a cape: often in geographical names, as Start Point, Point of Ardnamurchan. Also *transf.* (chiefly *U.S.*), such a feature on a river; the tapering extremity of any woodland reaching down into a prairie or other treeless area; any tapering extremity *of* land, or *of* rocks, woods, etc., constituting a special feature of this. Also, A peak of a mountain or hill.

1553 EDEN *Treat. Newe Ind.* (Arb.) 32 He discouered a corner or poynt of the sayd mayne land. **1585** T. WASHINGTON tr. *Nicholay's Voy.* II. xviii, The point of the Sarail, whereupon the sea beateth. **1603** OWEN *Pembrokeshire* i. (1892) 4 From Kemes head called Pen Kemes pointe North, to St. Gouens pointe in the Southe. **1604** E. G[RIMSTONE] *D' Acosta's Hist. Indies* III. xxvii. 201 The land..casting his capes, points and tongues farre into the sea. **1637** in *Amer. Speech* (1940) XV. 297/2 Easterly butting out with a point of wood. **1660** *Early Rec. Warwick, Rhode Island* (1926) 256 His point of Meddowe on the south side of Occupessuatuxet Cove. **1662** J. DAVIES tr. *Olearius' Voy. Ambass.* 260 The Mountain of Elwend, which is discover'd..by the whitenesse of its sand and by the extraordinary height of its points. **1682** *Early Rec. Providence, Rhode Island* (1899) XIV. 101 A black Oake tree standing upon a point of Rocks. **1704** J. HARRIS *Lex. Techn.* I. s.v., The Seamen also call the Extremity of any Promontary (which is a Piece of Land running out into the Sea) a Point; which is of much the same Sense with them as the Word Cape. **1772** D. TAITT in N. D. Mereness *Trav. Amer. Col.* (1916) 501, I..viewed this Town which Stands upon a point of Land on the North west side of the River. **1826** T. FLINT *Recollections* 15 You hear of..sawyers, and points, and bends, and shoots. *Ibid.* 258 The entire uniformity of the meanders of the rivers [in Arkansas] called, in the phrase of the country, 'points and bends'. **1836** W. IRVING *Astoria* I. 144 The party landed, and encamped at the bottom of a small bay within point George. **1837** —— *Capt. Bonneville* II. vii. 108 The whole band soon disappeared behind a point of woods. **1857** P. CARTWRIGHT *Autobiogr.* xxi. 328 We rode two miles, and the point of timber was plain in view. **1859** 'MARK TWAIN' in *New Orleans Daily Crescent* 17 May, The point at Cairo, which has not even been moistened by the river since 1813, is now entirely under water. **1883** —— *Life on Miss.* iii. 61 The big raft was away out of sight around the point. **1964** W. C. PUTNAM *Geol.* xi. 275/2 The common name for a broadly curving part of a river is a bend. The convex bank in such a curve is a point.

†**c.** The wing of a fleet or army. *Obs.*

1550 T. NYCOLLS *Thucidides* 222 b, The Peloponesians auaunced..to the ende to haue enclosed with their left poyncte, the ryght poynct of the Athenians. **1614** RALEIGH *Hist. World* v. v. §8. 698 The Latines, as vsually, were in the points; the Romans, in the maine battell.

d. *Mil.* The small leading party of an advanced guard (consisting usually of an experienced non-commissioned officer and four men).

1589 *Discourse Voy. Spain & Port.* 30 Sir Henrie Norris (whose Regiment had the poynt of the Vangard). **1903** LD. WOLSELEY *Story of a Soldier's Life* I. ii. 62 What is now commonly called 'the point of the advanced guard' consisted of four privates and myself.

e. *pl.* The extremities of a horse.

1855 SMEDLEY *H. Coverdale* xliii, A particularly fast mare ..bay, with black points. **1872** R. F. BURTON *Zanzibar* I. ix. 347 The favourite charger of the late Sayyid is a little bay with black points. **1883** W. H. BISHOP in *Harper's Mag.* Oct. 720/2 He is sixteen hands high, dark bay, and has black points.

f. *the Point*: the United States Military Academy at West Point, N.Y. *U.S. colloq.*

1828 J. F. COOPER *Notions of Americans* I. 274 To these relics of a former age, must be added the actual and flourishing establishment at the 'Point', which comprises a village of academic buildings, barracks, and other adjuncts. **1922** *Frontier* (Missoula, Montana) Nov. 14 Ada's father had been C.O. when we were in the Point, and nearly every member of the class had been at one time or another in love with her. **1968** *Michelin: New York City* 139 West Point... Among the war heroes who graduated from the Point are Generals MacArthur (1903), Patton (1909) and Eisenhower (1915). **1971** C. FICK *Danziger Transcript* (1973) 167 Sam had worked his way into Dartmouth..and then transferred to the Point. **1973** E. PACE *Any War* (1974) III. 239 'I've been learning karate... We had the fundamentals at the Point.' 'You went to West Point?'

g. The tip of the lower jaw; the spot on which a knock-out blow is dealt.

1898 [see OUT *adv.* 19 e]. **1901** R. FITZSIMMONS *Phys. Cult. & Self-Defense* 159, I saw Fitzsimmons' right hand reach the point of Corbett's jaw. **1915** E. CORRI *30 Yrs. Boxing Referee* 229 There is no sleeping-draught like a punch on the point. **1923** *Daily Mail* 16 Feb. 8 He once caught Lewis with a hard right near the point. **1924** *Truth* (Sydney) 27 Apr. 6 *Point*, sensitive portion of the jaw. **1942** BERREY & VAN DEN BARK *Amer. Thes. Slang* §121/18 Point,..the vulnerable point of the chin.

h. Either of the extensions at the front end of a saddle-tree.

1908 *Animal Managem.* 166 The front arch extends below the side bars; the extension is known as the 'points', and these are intended to help the girths and prevent the saddle from heeling over.

i. *Ballet.* The tips of the toes. Usu. with *on* and *pl.* = POINTE.

1912 *Dancing Times* Aug. 449/2 *Points.*—Exposition of Principles. **1928** A. L. HASKELL *Some Studies in Ballet* 153 A solo on the points. **1936** L. SOKOLOVA in 'C. Brahms' *Footnotes to Ballet* v. 227, I held myself poised on my points, before literally collapsing exhausted in the middle of the stage. **1936** N. STREATFEILD *Ballet Shoes* iv. 52 The children were most impressed by the way the children in the photographs stood on their points. **1949** A. CHRISTIE *Crooked House* x. 71 'He stopped me learning to be a ballet dancer.'.. She..kicked off her shoes and endeavoured to get on to what are called technically..her points. **1967** 'LA MERI' *Spanish Dancing* (ed. 2) vii. 89 Very rarely it [*sc.* the Bolero] is danced on point. **1975** *New Yorker* 26 May 31/1 Mr. Griforovich, who was watching a tiny blond ballerina rise on point with the single-minded intensity of an adult star, put a hand across his face to conceal a smile. **1977** *Time* 24 Jan. 36/3 In a pas de deux with Ted Kivitt, she stepped majestically on point..as if there were magnets concealed in her toe shoes.

j. *U.S.* The position at the front of a herd of cattle, etc.; the position at the head of a column or wedge of troops (cf. sense B. 2 d); also quasi-*adv.* in phrases ***to ride*** or ***walk point***. Also *fig.*

1916 'B. M. BOWER' *Phantom Herd* xiv. 245 You see a herd drifting before a storm maybe—a blizzard like yesterday, with your pal riding point. **1927** *Scribner's Mag.* Feb. 178/1 Consider the passing herd, anyone of the many that went up the Long Trail. At the 'point' ride two men, at the 'drag' two more, while other horsemen loiter on either flank. **1959** C. OGBURN *Marauders* (1960) ii. 64 Major Osborne looked around and his eye alighted on me. 'You take the point,' said he... He thought the way to use a communications officer was to have him lead the battalion column into action. **1962** J. ONSLOW *Bowler-Hatted Cowboy* xxi. 205, I was riding 'point', not as a leader to the cattle, but to warn oncoming traffic of the herd. **1964** F. O'ROURKE *Mule for Marquesa* 118 Fardan trotted past the mules and took the point. **1969** I. KEMP *Brit. G.I. in Vietnam* v. 102 Goad walked point and I..took the tail, with the rest of squad well spaced out between us. **1970** *Times* 9 May 8/8 Daniel Lepointe, aged 21, a sergeant..was walking point—the front position of his platoon—when..a helicopter observer told him about two huts. **1975** W. SAFIRE *Before Fall* I. iv. 45 He said no: 'Let Romney take the point.' (In military tactics, the soldier 'on the point' of a wedge is the most likely to be shot.) **1977** 'J. LE CARRÉ' *Hon. Schoolboy* iv. 100 Let me send you an advocate. Somebody who can ride point for you, draft your submission, carry it to the barricades.

k. *N.Z.* The hocks of a sheep; the wool that grows on them.

1922 W. PERRY *Sheepfarming in N.Z.* iv. 44 The wool should be..well spread on the back, belly, and points. *a* **1948** L. G. D. ACLAND *Early Canterbury Runs* (1951) 379 *Fribby*,..the yolky locks round the points taken off by the roller from a decently skirted fleece. **1956** G. BOWEN *Wool Away!* (ed. 2) xii. 132 The Corriedale..grows more wool than hair on the hocks, thereby making it imperative that they be shorn trimmed to the feet. These points or socks do not have a tendency to lift or rise off the skin.

3. An object or instrument consisting of or characterized by a point (in sense 1), or which pricks or pierces. **a.** A pointed weapon or instrument for stabbing or piercing; a dagger, pointed sword, or the like; also, a bodkin.

1488 *Inv. R. Wardr.* (1815) 5 Item,..within the said box a point maid of perle contenand xxv perle with hornis of gold. *c* **1520** *Treat. Galaunt* 134 in Hazl. *E.P.P.* III. 157 Howe many poyntes were they nowe a dayes And yet a good poynte amonge them were to fynde Daggers of vengeaunce, redy to make frayes. **1598** B. JONSON *Ev. Man in Hum.* I. iv, I will learne you..to controll any enemies point i' the world. **1627** *Lisander & Cal.* III. 54 Lidian, who entring with a point upon his enemy,..run him cleane thorow. **1719** YOUNG *Busiris* III. i, Let each man bear A steady point, well levell'd at his heart.

b. 'An iron or steel instrument used with some variety in several arts' (Chambers *Cycl.*); e.g. a pin-pointed tool used by etchers and engravers, an etching-needle: cf. *dry-point* (DRY *a.* C. 3); a small punch or chisel used by stone-workers, etc.

1727-41 CHAMBERS *Cycl.* s.v., Engravers, etchers, wooden-cutters, stone-cutters, etc. use points to trace their designs on the copper, wood, stone, etc... Statuaries..have likewise points in manner of little chissels, used in first forming or sketching out their work... Lapidaries have iron points, to the ends whereof are fastened pieces of diamonds, serving to pierce the precious stones withal. *c* **1790** IMISON *Sch. Art* II. 40 If the lines are too small, pass over them again with a short but round point. **1823** P. NICHOLSON *Pract. Build.* 341 The Point is the smallest kind of chisel used by masons. **1860** RUSKIN *Mod. Paint.* V. VII. ii. §6. 115 *note*, No cloud can be drawn with the point: nothing but the most delicate management of the brush. **1880** *Print. Trades Jrnl.* XXXI. 9 The Royal sketches evince a true feeling for art, and much ability with the etching point.

c. *Her.* A bearing resembling a pile, usually occupying the base of the shield; reckoned a 'diminution' or mark of dishonour.

1562 LEIGH *Armorie* 124 He beareth a poynte playne, Geules, in a fielde, Or. This is for hym yt telleth lyes, to hys soueraigne. **1830** ROBSON *Hist. Her.* Gloss., *Point*, according to Edmondson, (meaning the point pointed), is an ordinary somewhat resembling the Pile, issuing from the Base.

d. A tine of a deer's horn.

1863 KINGSLEY *Water-Bab.* ii. (1874) 69 You may know some day..what his rights mean, if he has them, brow, bay, tray, and points. **1884** JEFFERIES *Red Deer* iv. 68 An antler is judged by the number of points or tines which spring from the beam. The beam is the main stem, and the points are the branches. **1885** ROOSEVELT *Hunting Trips* iv. 107 He was a fine buck of eight points.

e. *Electr.* A metallic point at which electricity is discharged or collected; *spec.* (*a*) the tapering extremity of a lightning conductor; (*b*) in an internal-combustion engine, either of the metal pieces on a sparking plug between which the spark jumps, or either of the metal surfaces of a contact-breaker which touch to complete the circuit; usu. *pl.*; also, each of the carbon points or pencils in an electric light (see CARBON *sb.* 2).

1766 in *Essex Inst. Hist. Coll.* (1916) LII. 275 A new Meeting-House building..was struck with Lightning; it had Points and a Conductor as far as the Bellfree. **1775** in *Ibid.* (1877) XIII. 208 They have a handsome clock, points to the house, a fine walk on the top, [etc.]. **1836-41** BRANDE *Chem.* (ed. 5) 261 The influence of points in receiving and carrying off electricity has already been adverted to. **1849** CRAIG, *Point*,..in Electricity, the acute termination of a body which facilitates the passage of the fluid to or from the body. *c* **1865** LETHEBY in *Circ. Sc.* I. 136/2 As the points burn away, the springs keep up a fresh supply. **1870** 'MARK TWAIN' in *Galaxy* Sept. 424/1 He said it would be necessary to know exactly how many 'points' I wanted put up, what parts of the house I wanted them on, and what quality of rod I preferred. **1902** *Westm. Gaz.* 7 Apr. 10/1 At the rate of a foot in five minutes the carbon point wrought its way, and in a short time the enormous mass of steel had been reduced to fragments that could be easily handled. **1902** J. E. HUTTON in A. C. Harmsworth *Motors & Motor-Driving* viii. 150 The points may be sooty and require cleaning. **1927** R. T. NICHOLSON *Austin Seven Bk.* xiii. 116 The rapid separation of the points of the contact-breaker. **1961** J. MILLS *Car Repair & Maintenance* iv. 41 If this happened, there would not be a suitably fat spark at the plug points and the contact breaker points would become burned. **1968** K. WEATHERLY *Roo Shooter* 111, I must have dried the flamin' plugs and points twenty times.

f. On a railway: A tapering movable rail by which vehicles are directed from one line of rails to another. Usually in *pl.*

1838 SIMMS *Public Wks. Gt. Brit.* 27 Moveable points or sliding rails, and the requisite machinery for moving them. **1885** *Scotsman* 11 June, A south bound goods train..ran into the safety points, crashing against the buffer end with great violence. **1889** G. FINDLAY *Eng. Railway* 53 It is impossible for the signalman to lower the signals..until the 'points' or 'switches' have been placed in their proper position.

g. One of the twelve tapered divisions on each 'table' of a backgammon board.

1588 GREENE *Pandosto* (1843) 9 That his friend Egistus had entered a wrong pointe in his tables. **1595** SOUTHWELL *Tri. Death* (1596) 22 God casteth the dice, and giueth vs our chaunce; the most we can doe, is, to take the poynt that the cast will affoord vs. **1680** COTTON *Gamester* xxv. 109 Of Irish... The men which are thirty in number are equally divided between you and your Adversary, and are thus placed, two on the Ace point, and five on the sice of your left hand Table. *Ibid.* xxvii. 114 (*Tick-tack*) Boveries is when you have a man in the eleventh point of your own Tables, and another in the same point of your Adversaries directly answering. **1870** HARDY & WARE *Mod. Hoyle, Backgammon* 142 The next best point..is to make your bar-point. **1905** FISKE *Chess in Iceland* 279 Some confusion is caused by the fact that we English use *point* both for the 'dots' on the dice and the twenty-four *points* (Fr. 'flèches') on the board.

In other applications.

h. †A kind of nail or spike (*obs.*); a glazier's sprig (*Cent. Dict.*). †**i.** An agnail or hangnail; = AGNAIL 3 *Obs.* †**j.** A small piece of heavy wood pieced into the butt of an arrow to counterbalance the head. *Obs.* **k.** †A rough diamond of a certain shape (*obs.*); also, an angular fragment of diamond adapted for glass-cutting (Knight *Dict. Mech.* 1875). **l.** A thorn. **m.** One of the interchangeable pointed legs of a pair of compasses. **n.** A name of certain surgical instruments.

h. 1590 *Acc. Bk. W. Wray* in *Antiquary* XXXII. 374 A gr[oss] doble hard poyntes, iis. iiid.

i. 1653 R. SANDERS *Physiogn.* 73 If about these nails be an excoriation of the flesh, which is commonly called 'points'.

j. 1545 ASCHAM *Toxoph.* (Arb.) 127 Two poyntes in peecing be ynough, lest the moystnes of the earthe enter to moche into the peecinge, and so leuse the glue. Therefore many poyntes be more pleasaunt to the eye, than profitable for the vse.

k. 1698 FRYER *Acc. E. India & P.* 213 The Names of Rough Stones [diamonds], according to their Forms and Substance... A Point... An ½ Point [etc.].

l. 1604 E. G[RIMSTONE] *D' Acosta's Hist. Indies* v. xvii. 373 Every one tooke a poynt of Manguay, which is like vnto an awle or sharpe bodkin, with the which..they pierced the calfes of their legges neare to the bone, drawing foorth much blood. **1893** P. H. EMERSON *On Eng. Lagoons* xxxix. 231 That's good for drawing points..out of your hand.

m. 1669 STURMY *Mariner's Mag.* II. ii. 53 A Brass pair of Compasses to go with an Arch and Screws..and four Steel Points to take in and out.

n. 1890 A. WHITELEGGE *Hygiene & Public Health* xii. 263 The lymph may be sealed in capillary tubes or dried upon ivory points. *Ibid.* 264 If stored calf-lymph is used, two large 'points' are needed for each child. **1897** *Allbutt's Syst. Med.*

IV. 776 Our practice is confined to two methods, namely tonsillotomy and the galvano-caustic point.

o. *Archæol.* (See quot. 1959.)

1912 *Archaeologia* LXIII. 129 (*caption*) A symmetrical 'point' of laurel-leaf form.., but the surface flaking only partial. **1932** *Antiquity* VI. 190 The true Mousterian industries are characterized by flake-tools such as side-scrapers, points and Levallois flakes. **1943** J. & C. HAWKES *Prehist. Britain* i. 19 The Levalloisian, an outstanding culture during the last interglacial, when it was responsible for beautifully finished points and scrapers which..were partially trimmed before the flake was struck from the parent core. **1949** W. F. ALBRIGHT *Archaeol. Palestine* iii. 59 The Natufian was a thorough-going microlithic culture, consisting largely of blades and points. **1959** J. D. CLARK *Prehist. S. Africa* ii. 42 *Point*, a pointed flake or blade, often with careful secondary retouch, or a pointed tool of bone. Believed to have sometimes formed the heads of spears and arrows. **1963** J. HAWKES in Hawkes & Woolley *Prehist. & Beginnings of Civilization* I. iii. 71 Implements found..in the Solo valley..include..points and picks made from bone and antler. **1971** J. BORDAZ *Tools of Old & New Stone Age* iv. 31 In regions where good stone is comparatively abundant,..it is not unusual to find Levallois points up to six inches long.

4. a. *Printing.* One of the short sharp pins fixed on the tympan of a press so as to perforate the sheet and serve to make register.

1683 MOXON *Mech. Exerc., Printing* xi. ¶ 19 This Point is made of a piece of small Wyer about a quarter and half quarter of an Inch high. *Ibid.* xxiv. ¶ 7 To large Paper he chuses Short Shanked Points, and to small Paper Long Shanked Points. **1727–41** CHAMBERS *Cycl.* s.v. *Printing*, To regulate the margins, and make the lines and pages answer each other when printed on the other side; in the middle of the wood, in the sides of this tympan, are two iron points, which make two holes in the sheet. **1825–88** [see *paste-point*, PASTE *sb.* 8].

b. Short for *point-plate* (see D. 19).

1683 MOXON *Mech. Exerc., Printing* xi. ¶ 19 The Points are made of Iron Plates about the thickness of a Queen Elizabeth Shilling:..at the end of this Plate..stands upright the Point. **1824** J. JOHNSON *Typogr.* II. 514 Points are made of sheet iron, of different lengths, about the sixteenth part of an inch thick... The spur of the point is rivetted at the small end, and projects about three eighths of an inch.

II. 5. A tagged lace or cord, of twisted yarn, silk, or leather, for attaching the hose to the doublet, lacing a bodice, and fastening various parts where buttons are now used; often used as a type of something of small value (esp. *blue point*). Now *arch.* or *Hist.*

[In this sense *point* renders F. *aiguillette*, orig. an aglet or metal point of a lace or cord, thence a lace with an aglet. English (on the whole) retained *aglet* for the metal point or tag, and translated it by *point* for the cord.]

1390 *Earl Derby's Exp.* (Camden) 35 Johanni Dounton pro j gros poyntes, iij s. *a* **1450** *Knt. de la Tour* (1868) 33 Y might, and y satte lowe, breke sum of my pointes. *c* **1450** *Cov. Myst.* (Shaks. Soc.) 241 Two doseyn poyntys of cheverelle, the aglottes of sylver feyn. **1530** PALSGR. 256/1 Poynt for ones hose, *esguillette*. **1532** MORE *Confut. Tindale* Wks. 675/2 It is not al worth an aglet of a good blewe poynte. **1549** LATIMER *4th Serm. bef. Edw. VI* (Arb.) 117 He made hys pen of the aglet of a poynte that he plucked from hys hose. ? *a* **1550** *Debate Somer & Wynter* 132 in Hazl. *E.P.P.* III. 41 All is not worthe a poynte of lether. **1603** KNOLLES *Hist. Turks* (1621) 1094 [They] made thongs and points of the skins of men and women, whom they had flaine quick. **1615** SIR E. HOBY *Curry-combe* vi. 265 He hath hardly earned a blew point for his daies worke. **1647** PEACHAM *Worth of Penny* 17 So naturally sparing, that if a point from his hose had broken, he would have tied the same upon a knot, and made it to serve againe. **1739** 'R. BULL' tr. *Dedekindus' Grobianus* 260 A chilling Fear surprizes all his Joints, And makes him ready to untruss his Points. **1819** SCOTT *Ivanhoe* xx, Assistance in tying the endless number of points, as the laces which attached the hose to the doublet were then termed. [See also AGLET *sb.* 1.]

†**6.** A plait of hair; a pigtail. *Obs.*

1603 B. JONSON *Entertainm. Coronat. K. Jas.* Wks. (1616) 844 Her hayre bound into foure seuerall points.

7. *Naut.* One of the short pieces of flat braided cord attached near the lower edge of a sail for tying up a reef; a reef-point: see REEF *sb.*[1] 3.

1769 FALCONER *Dict. Marine* (1789) H h iv, The courses of large ships are either reefed with points or..reef-lines. **1801** *Chron.* in *Ann. Reg.* 44 [He] called to the boatswain to bring a point (a rope doubled with knots at the end), and give the plaintiff a 'starting'. **1859** *All Year Round* No. 17. 399 Midshipmen into the tops to see the points tied!

8. A short buckling strap.

1875 KNIGHT *Dict. Mech., Point*..17. (*Harness.*) A short strap stitched to a wide one for the purpose of attaching the latter to another strap by a buckle. The end of any strap that is provided with holes for the buckle-tongue.

III. 9. Each of the equidistant points on the circumference of the mariner's compass, indicated by one of the thirty-two rays drawn from the centre, which serve to particularize the part of the horizon whence the wind is blowing or in the direction of which an object lies; also *transf.* the angular interval between two successive points (one-eighth of a right angle, or 11° 15′). Hence, any of the corresponding points, or in general any point, of the horizon; thus often nearly = Direction. (In ordinary use, usually ***point of the compass***; in absol. use chiefly *Naut.*)

a **1500** in Arnolde *Chron.* (1811) 86 When the wynde is in any poynte of the northe all the fowle stynke is blowen ouer the citee [London]. **1527** R. THORNE in Hakluyt *Voy.* (1589) 257 The roses of the windes or pointes of the compasse. **1556** BURROUGH *ibid.* (1886) III. 117 The land lyeth North and halfe a point Westerly. **1592** LYLY *Gallathea* I. iv. 33 The two and thirty poynts for the winde. **1634** SIR T. HERBERT *Trav.* 206 To this day they [Chinese] haue but eight points vnto their Compasse. **1720** DE FOE *Capt. Singleton* vi. (1840) 103 They bent their course one point of the compass..to the southward of the east. **1798** MILLAR in Nicolas *Disp. Nelson* (1846) VII. p. cliv, The leading Ship to steer one point more to starboard. **1856** STANLEY *Sinai & Pal.* xiv. (1858) 463 The Latin Church..regardless of all points of the compass, has adopted for its Altar the Holy Tomb itself. **1885** *Law Times Rep.* LIII. 54/1 Lights..were seen from four to five points on the port bow of the *J. M. Stevens*.

IV. 10. a. The salient feature of a story, discourse, epigram, joke, etc.; that which gives it application; effective or telling part. Also, A witty or ingenious turn of thought.

1694 J. SAVAGE tr. C. de St. Evremont in T. Brown *Misc. Ess. M. de St. Evremont* II. II. 96 Points, Antithesis's and Paradoxes. **1728** POPE *Dunc.* I. 254 All arm'd with points, antitheses and puns. **1844** DICKENS *Mart. Chuz.* xi, The young ladies might have rather missed the point and cream of the jest. **1861** M. PATTISON *Ess.* (1889) I. 45 An inscription..in which the moral was better than the point. **1871** BLACKIE *Four Phases* I. 29 So as to be able to turn the point of an argument. **1876** *World* V. No. 106. 3 Full of capital points, blunted in delivery. **1891** LD. COLERIDGE in *Law Times Rep.* LXV. 581/1 He has somewhat misapprehended the point of those observations. *Mod.* He did not see the point of the joke.

b. That quality in speech or writing which arrests attention; appealing, convincing, or penetrating quality; pungency, effect, value.

a **1643** W. CARTWRIGHT *On Fletcher* Comedies, etc. (1651) 8 All point! all edge! all sharpness! **1675** VILLIERS (Dk. Buckhm.) *Ess. Poetry* 114 'Tis epigram, 'tis point, 'tis what you will, But not an elegy. **1791** BOSWELL *Johnson* (1816) I. Introd. 10 Anything..which my illustrious friend thought it worth his while to express, with any degree of point. **1847** L. HUNT *Men, Women, & B.* II. viii. 135 A stanza, which has the point of an epigram with all the softness of a gentle truth. **1901** H. JAMES *Sacred Fount* 17 Having a reputation for 'point' to keep up, she was always under arms.

c. *Theatr.* A gesture, vocal inflection, or some other piece of theatrical technique used to underline a climactic moment in a speech, rôle, or situation; a moment so underlined. Usu. used with the implication that the integrity of the performance as a whole is being subordinated to the desire for immediate applause. Also *fig.*

1822 C. MATHEWS *Let.* 4 Oct. in A. Mathews *Mem. Charles Mathews* (1839) III. 314, I don't know an instance of a point failing which I considered to be really good myself. **1864** [see GRAVY 2c]. **1870** O. LOGAN *Before Footlights & Behind Scenes* 135, I began to practice the effects, the stage walks, the managing of the voice, the general bearing of the person, the making of 'points', the attaining of 'climax'. **1897** G. B. SHAW *Our Theatres in Nineties* (1932) III. 124 It lends itself to people talking at each other rhetorically from opposite sides of the stage, taking long sweeping walks up to their 'points'. *Ibid.* 132 He succumbed to the temptation to utter the two or three most fatuously conceited of Helmer's utterances as 'points'. **1900** T. E. PEMBERTON *Kendals* ix. 259 So natural is she at all times that she never seems to be 'making points' after the crude fashion of inferior actresses. **1916** J. R. TOWSE *Sixty Years of Theater* 29 Woe to the unfortunate actor who was not on his appointed spot and instant in his speech when he was a factor in one of Macready's laboriously calculated 'points'. **1952** GRANVILLE *Dict. Theatrical Terms* 139 A player who is not capable of 'making his *points*' (i.e. stressing his lines at the right time) will never get over.

V. 11. a. *Cricket.* The position of the fieldsman who is stationed more or less in a line with the popping-crease, a short distance on the off-side of the batsman (orig. close to the point of the bat); also *transf.* the fieldsman himself.

1816 W. LAMBERT *Cricketer's Guide* (ed. 6) 41 The Fieldsmen... The Point. The person who stands at the Point should place himself in a line with the popping crease, about seven yards from the striker. **1833** NYREN *Yng. Cricketer's Tutor* 41 The point of the bat... The young fieldsman who is appointed to this situation, should possess a quick eye... For the position of body in the point, I can do no better than refer him to instructions..given to the wicket-keeper. *Ibid.* 42 The point all the while must keep his face towards the batter, and his arms and hands in their proper position. **1849** *Laws of Cricket* in 'Bat' *Crick. Man.* (1850) 57 No substitute..shall be allowed to..stand at the point, cover the point, or stop behind. **1850** *Ibid.* 43 The Point requires a fieldsman with a very quick eye... The distance at which he stands from the point of the bat, varies from five to seven yards. **1851** LILLYWHITE *Guide Cricketers* 68 Templar..has succeeded to his [brother's] place as point. **1870** SEELEY *Lect. & Ess.* 165 What can be more serious than a game of Cricket?.. Point does not chat with cover-point. **1904**, etc. [see BACKWARD *a.* 1]. **1916** *Anzac Book* 128 Was it a boundary hit or a catch at point? **1951** *People* 3 June 8/7 When he was out—to a brilliant catch by Ken Graveney at point—the bowling had been tamed.

b. In *Lacrosse*, The position of the player who stands a short distance in front of the goal-keeper, or the player himself. **c.** In *Baseball*, The positions occupied by the pitcher and catcher.

1868 *Chambers's Encycl.* X. 597/1 In the arrangement of the men on each side, the *goal-keeper* defends the goal; *point* is the first man out from the goal; *cover-point* is a little in advance of point. **1872** *Boy's own Bk., La Crosse*, There is a goal-keeper; a point, placed twenty yards a-head of the goal-keeper; and a coverpoint. **1935** *Encycl. Sports* 379/1 'Point' takes his position immediately in front of goal. **1967** *Globe & Mail* (Toronto) 16 May 39/9 Actually, the goaltender led a charmed life. Most of the danger was involved with the fellow who played between point and cover-point. **1975** *Oxf. Compan. Sports & Games* 588/2 The ten-a-side team consists of a goalkeeper, three defences (known historically as point, cover point, and third man), a left wing defence, [etc.].

C. Noun of action of French or English origin (including some senses of doubtful origination).

†**1.** A feat; *esp.* a feat of arms, a deed of valour, an exploit; also, an encounter, skirmish. [OF. *pointe.*] ***points of war***: warlike exercises. *Obs.*

1375 BARBOUR *Bruce* IX. 631 This wes a richt fair poynt, perfay! *c* **1400** *Destr. Troy* 540 And puttes you to perell in pointis of armes. *c* **1450** *Merlin* 345 For that the kynge hadde slain oon of his nevewes at a poynt, that hadde be by-fore the town. **1513** DOUGLAS *Æneis* III. iv. 138 With oile anoynt, Nakit worsling and strougling at nyse poynt. **1580** SIDNEY *Ps.* XVIII. ix, He me warr points did show, Strengthning mine arms, that I could break an iron bow. **1591** SPENSER *M. Hubberd* 696 Besides he could doo manie other poynts, The which in Court him served to good stead. **1602** *2nd Pt. Return fr. Parnass.* II. vi. 945 Seeing him practise his lofty pointes, as his crospoynt and his backcaper.

†**2.** A hostile charge or accusation. *Obs.*

c **1400** *Destr. Troy* 7900 The triet men of Troy traitur hym cald, And mony pointtes on hym put for his pure shame. *Ibid.* 11751 Er any troiens with truthe might telle suche a fawte, Or soche a point on me put in perlament her aftur. **1480** CAXTON *Chron. Eng.* ccxlii. (1482) 277 To ansuere to all maner poyntes that the kyng and his counceyll wold put vpon hym.

†**3.** Trial, examination: in phr. ***put to point***. *Obs.*

1469 in *Archæologia* XV. 168 That the money..be newe molton and reforged..till it be putte to poynt. **1583** *Reg. Privy Council Scot.* III. 611 To have thair maters callit and put to poynt in ordour. **1584** *Ibid.* 687 Quhill the samin be decydit or utherwise put to point.

4. *Falconry.* Of a hawk: The action of rising vertically in the air; esp. in phr. ***to make*** (***her***) ***point***. [F. *la pointe de l'oiseau.*]

1651 N. BACON *Disc. Govt. Eng.* II. xxvii. (1739) 125 Like the Eagle they make many points before they stoop to their Prey. **1828** SIR J. S. SEBRIGHT *Observ. Hawking* 23 The hawk will make his point—that is, rise perpendicularly in the air over the spot where the bird got into cover. **1852** R. F. BURTON *Falconry in Valley of Indus* iii. 29 The Shikrah ..'makes her point' and takes her stand on some neighbouring tree or eminence. **1883** SALVIN & BRODRICK *Falconry in Brit. Isles* Gloss. 152 *To make its point*, the mode a Hawk has of rising in the air, by which the place is marked where the quarry has 'put in.'

5. A direct forward advance, a charge. [F. *faire pointe* to make a charge.]

1755 J. SHEBBEARE *Lydia* (1769) II. 27 It seems they had all in turn made a dead point at this young earl, though unsuccessfully. **1768** *Woman of Honor* III. 239 Just in my way as I was making my point for Lancashire.

6. Of a pointer or setter: The act of pointing; the rigid attitude assumed on finding game, with the head and gaze directed towards it. Usually in phrases ***to make, come to a point***. Also *fig.*

1771 MACKENZIE *Man Feel.* Introd. 3, My dog had made a point on a piece of lee-ground. **1892** *Field* 7 May 695/1 Raffle made two good points on birds. **1903** *Blackw. Mag.* Oct. 510/2 The method of approaching the point is explained. *Mod.* A dog that comes to a point well.

7. The act of pointing: in the humorous phrase ***bread*** or ***potatoes and point***, the action of merely pointing or looking at the relish, such as cheese, bacon, fish, etc., and making one's meal of bread or potatoes only. (*dial.*)

1831 CARLYLE *Sart. Res.* III. x. (1871) 195 The victual Potatoes-and-Point not appearing, at least not with specific accuracy of description, in any European Cookery-Book whatever. **1897** *Ch. Times* 15 Oct., A poor family, who could not afford to eat meat, and who, we will say, dine on potatoes, would..be commonly said to have for dinner potatoes and point.

8. An indication; a hint, suggestion, direction.

1882 B. HARTE *Flip* iv, One of these officials comes up to this..ranch..to get points about diamond-making. **1886** *Halford's Adviser* 20 Jan., There are friends who honestly and in all good faith give a 'point' as to buying this or that Stock. **1892** *Nation* (N.Y.) 6 Oct. 263/2 A clever young man easily makes the mistake of supposing that he could have given Solomon points about women.

9. *Arch.* Amount or degree of pointedness: in phrase ***of the third*** (or ***fourth***) ***point***, rendering It. *di terzo* (or *quarto*) *acuto*.

1703 T. N. *City & C. Purchaser* 8 Arches of the 3d. and 4th. Point..So our English Authors call 'em, but the Tuscan Authors calls them *di terzo*, and *di quarto acuto*, because they always concur in an acute Angle at the Top. **1842–76** GWILT *Archit.* Gloss., *Tierce point*, the vertex of an equilateral triangle. Arches or vaults of the third point, which are called by the Italians *di terzo acuto*, are such as consist of two arcs of a circle intersecting at the top.

D. Phrases and Combinations (chiefly from A.).

* With prepositions.

1. at point. [= F. *à point.*] †**a.** Aptly, fitly, properly, suitably, conveniently. *Obs.*

1375 BARBOUR *Bruce* III. 702 For wynd at poynt blawand thai had. *Ibid.* VI. 406 He wes arayit at poynt clenly, Outakyn that his hede wes bair. *Ibid.* x. 283 He wes..Curtas at poynt, and debonar And of richt sekir contenyng. **1456** SIR G. HAYE *Law Arms* (S.T.S.) 113 Ane gude knycht..suld sett all his study till arm him at poynt, and hors him. *a* **1547** SURREY *Æneid* II. 25 The fame wherof so wandred it at point [L. *ea fama vagatur*].

†**b.** (Also ***at a point.***) In readiness, prepared.

1605 SHAKS. *Lear* I. iv. 347 Tis politic and safe to let him keep At point a hundred knights. **1611** FLORIO s.v. *Punto*, *Essere in punto*, to be in a readinesse, to be at a point.

c. ***at point to, at the point to*** (with inf.): ready to, on the point of, just about to. Cf. *at the point of* (see f.); *on or upon the point of* (see 5). *arch.*

1526 *Pilgr. Perf.* (W. de W. 1531) 17 Whan they were at the poynt to haue passed ouer the seconde flode called Jordayn. **1564** Haward *Eutropius* II. 15 Pyrrhus was at the poynte to have fled. *a* **1600** Montgomerie *Sonn.* lii. 12 My hairt..At poynt to speid, or quikly to despair. **1605** Shaks. *Lear* III. i. 33 Who already..are at point To show their open banner. **1611** Bible *Gen.* xxv. 32, I am at the point to die. **1621** T. Williamson tr. *Goulart's Wise Vieillard* 195 Being at the poynt to leaue this world. **1870** Morris *Earthly Par.* III. 228 He seemed at point his whole desire to gain.

†**d.** ***at a point***: agreed; settled, decided, determined, resolved. See A. 31. *Obs.*

1477 *Paston Lett.* III. 169 Ye promysyd me, that ye wold never breke the mater to Margrery unto suche tyme as ye and I were at a point. **1513** More *Rich. III* (1883) 60 Yet was [he] at a pointe in his owne mynde, toke she it wel or otherwise. **1555** in Foxe *A. & M.* (1583) 1562/1, I..was at poynt with my selfe, that I woulde not flye. **1562** J. Heywood *Prov. & Epigr.* (1867) 189 Is he at a poynte with his creditors? **1660** Bunyan in *Life* (1870) 97 When they saw that I was at a point, and would not be moved nor persuaded. **1738** Neal *Hist. Purit.* IV. 85 His Highness [Cromwell] was at a point, and obliged them to deliver up the island of Polerone in the East Indies.

e. ***at all points***: in every part, in every particular or respect. (Usually with *armed.*) (Cf. a.)

c **1350** *Will. Palerne* 3332 Wel armed ȝe arn at alle maner poyntes. *c* **1420** Lydg. *Assembly of Gods* 607 Armyd at all poyntes, for a day ys sette. **1470–85** Malory *Arthur* IV. viii. 129 A good knyght that was redy to doo bataill at all poyntes. **1602** Shaks. *Ham.* I. ii. 200 Arm'd at all points exactly, *Cap a Pe.* **1734** tr. *Rollin's Anc. Hist.* (1827) I. Pref. 39 They were armed at all points. **1894** G. Armatage *Horse* ii. 13 Easily beaten at all points by an English horse of second-rate powers.

f. ***at the point of***, on the very verge of, just about to do something. † ***at the point of day*** [F. *au point de jour*], at daybreak (*obs.*). (See also c.)

c **1450** *Merlin* 585 Be redy at the poynte of day for to ride. **1484** Caxton *Fables of Poge* vi, Whanne he was atte thartycle and at the poynt of dethe he wold make his testament. **1604** E. G[rimstone] *D' Acosta's Hist. Indies* v. xxiv. 396 This should be eaten at the point of day. **1696** Luttrell *Brief Rel.* (1857) IV. 74 The lord Berkley was at the point of sayling. **1875** Jowett *Plato* (ed. 2) III. 285 A rich man who was at the point of death. **1897** Hall Caine *Christian* III. ix, I..told him they were at the point of going.

g. ***at this*** (or ***that***) ***point in time***: at this (or that) particular moment (cf. moment *sb.* 1 c).

1974 R. B. Parker *Godwulf Manuscript* viii. 68 You don't understand the situation..at this point in time. **1975** *Atlantic Monthly* Jan. 32/2 The phrase 'at that point in time'..quickly became an early trademark of the whole Watergate affair. **1975** G. V. Higgins *City on Hill* iii. 89 'At that point in time I came away with the impression' that she was the best thing in the world. **1977** *Irish Times* 8 June 12/2 At this point in time the private rented sector of the housing market was shrinking.

†**2. by point of.** By virtue or force of. *rare*$^{-1}$.

1472–3 *Rolls of Parlt.* VI. 156/2 Governours afore rehersed, or other entitled by poynt of Chartour.

3. from point to point. From one point or detail to another, in every particular, in detail. *Obs.* or *arch.* [OF. *de point en point.*]

1390 Gower *Conf.* III. 333 Fro point to point al sche him tolde, That sche hath longe in herte holde. *a* **1450** *Knt. de la Tour* (1868) 43 And than thei..tolde it hym from point to point. **1581** Pettie *Guazzo's Civ. Conv.* I. (1586) 8 It standeth me upon to answere from point to point, to the reasons which you have brought. **1653** H. Cogan tr. *Pinto's Trav.* x. 31 Then I recounted to him from point to point how I was cast away. **1813** Scott *Rokeby* I. xv, From point to point I frankly tell The deed of death as it befell.

4. in point [OF. *en point*]. †**a.** In proper condition, in order. *Obs.*

1481 Caxton *Godeffroy* cxxxi. 145 They toke counseyl..and made theyr shippes to be in poynt and redy. **1490** —— *Eneydos* vii. 30 They dyd doo repayre theyr nauyre, & sette it..alle in poynte, wyth alle thynges to theym necessarye.

†**b.** At once, on the instant. *Obs. rare*$^{-1}$.

1699 R. L'Estrange *Erasm. Colloq.* (1725) 247 To cut off his Head if he had not done it in point.

c. *Her.* (*a*) Said of two piles borne in a shield so as to meet at their points. (*b*) ***point in point***: a bearing (sense B. 3 c) issuing from the base, resembling a pile reversed, but with concavely curved sides; reckoned a mark of dishonour.

1562 Leigh *Armorie* 124 He beareth a pointe in pointe, Or, in a fielde Sable. This is for them yᵗ are slowthfull in warres. **1704** J. Harris *Lex. Techn.* I. s.v., He beareth two Piles in Point.

d. *predicatively.* (Cf. F. *à point = à propos.*) Apposite; appropriate.

1658–9 *Burton's Diary* (1828) IV. 254 Some play or other is in point. **1748** Richardson *Clarissa* (1811) VIII. 274 They are in point to the present subject. **1796** Mrs. J. West *Gossip's Story* I. 198 Not recollecting any similitude in point. **1885** Sir N. Lindley in *Law Rep.* 30 Ch. Div. 14 The case of *Stokes* v. *Trumper* is not really in point. **1888** Burgon *Lives 12 Gd. Men* I. iii. 340, I recall another humble incident somewhat in point.

e. ***in point of***: in the matter of; with reference or respect to; as regards. ***in point of fact***: see also fact *sb.* 6 b. (From A. 5.)

1605 Bacon *Adv. Learn.* I. iii. §3 States were too busy with their laws and too negligent in point of education. **1656** Earl Monm. tr. *Boccalini's Advts. fr. Parnass.* I. iii. (1674) 4 France may vie and weigh even with Greece it self, in point of Learning. **1656** H. Phillips *Purch. Patt.* (1676) 2 Much might be said to this in point of law. **1777** A. Hamilton *Wks.* (1886) VII. 515 He agrees with me in point of the enemy's numbers. **1812** *View State Parties in U.S.* (ed. 2) 32 In point of date, the two events correspond with a singular exactness. **1887** Sir E. Fry in *Law Times Rep.* LVIII. 163/2 The evidence..amply justifies the verdict and judgment in point of fact, if they can be justified in point of law.

†**f.** ***in point to*** (***of***): in a position ready to, on the point of; in immediate peril or danger of. Cf. *at the point* (1 c, f), *on the point* (5). *Obs.*

c **1325** *Poem Times Edw. II.* 432 in *Pol. Songs* (Camden) 343 That al Engelond i-wis was in point to spille. *a* **1350** *Cursor M.* 4760 (Gött.) Iacob and his sonis ware wid hunger in point to for-fare. *c* **1400** Maundev. (Roxb.) xiii. 57 He..was in poynt to drowne, and Criste tuke him by þe hand. **1456** Sir G. Haye *Law Arms* (S.T.S.) 87 [He] put all the lave in poynt of perdicioun. **1479** *Presentm. Juries* in *Surtees Misc.* (1888) 28 The crosse in the merkythe place, that it is in pounte to fall. **1513** Douglas *Æneis* IV. xi. 55 Dido standis redy to cum in point to de. **1572–3** *Reg. Privy Council Scot.* II. 189 Quhairof he hes lyne continewalie bedfast sensyne, and in poynt and dangeare of his lyff. **1641** W. Hakewill *Libertie of Subject* 90 The people were in point to rebell had not the king stayed the proceedings.

5. on or **upon the point of** (†**to**). [F. *sur le point de.*] On the very verge of; usually in reference to action, Just about to, just going to do something (now with vbl. sb. or n. of action, formerly also with inf.). Formerly also in reference to a specified time or a number: Very near, close upon.

c **1290** *S. Eng. Leg.* I. 55/52 A churche..þat ope þe poynte was to falle a-doun. **1297** R. Glouc. (Rolls) 1457 þe brutons were vpe þe pointe to fle. **1525** *St. Papers Hen. VIII*, IV. 320 The gales [= galleys]..ar not yet departed, but upon the pointe of departing; tarying for wynde and weder. *a* **1548** Hall *Chron., Hen. VIII*, 32 b, He had askryed a number of horsemen..vppon the poynct of syx thowsand. **1607** Middleton *Your Five Gallants* II. iii. 247 *Tai.* What's a' clock?..*Gol*...'Tis upon the point of three. **1638** Baker tr. *Balzac's Lett.* II. 10, I was upon the point of sending my footman to you. **1670** Cotton *Espernon* I. II. 100 When he was upon the point to fall upon the City, and Castle of Clisson. **1712** Budgell *Spect.* No. 307 ¶12 He..was upon the Point of being dismissed. **1771** T. Hull *Sir W. Harrington* (1797) I. 75 Such a father!..upon the point to die! **1867** H. Macmillan *Bible Teach.* ii. 31 Everything seemed on the point of moving.

6. to point. †**a.** Into proper condition; to rights. [F. *à point.*] *Obs.*

1481 Caxton *Myrr.* I. xii. 37 So in lyke wyse trauaylleth Phisyque to brynge Nature to poynt, that disnatureth in mannes body whan ony maladye or sekenes encombreth hit.

b. To the smallest detail; exactly, completely. *arch.* (Cf. *at point, at all points*, 1 a, e.)

1590 Spenser *F.Q.* I. i. 16 Seeing one in mayle, Armed to point. **1610** Shaks. *Temp.* I. ii. 194 Hast thou, Spirit, Performd to point, the Tempest that I bad thee? *a* **1625** Fletcher *Chances* I. iv, *Duke.* Are ye all fit? *1 Gent.* To point, sir. **1873** Browning *Red Cott. Nt.-cap* III. 282 All things thus happily performed to point.

c. ***to the point*** (of speech or writing, or *transf.* of the speaker or writer): Apposite, apt, pertinent. (Cf. A. 28.)

1817 Jas. Mill *Brit. India* III. i. 34 Show, that..the evidence which you call for is evidence to the point. **1875** Jowett *Plato* (ed. 2) I. 111 He makes a long speech not much to the point. **1892** *Law Times* XCII. 146/2 The notes are short and to the point.

7. upon point. †**a.** On peril, on penalty. *Obs.*

1642 W. Bird *Mag. Honor* 40 The Clerks of the Chancery..shall not leave out or make omission of the said Additions..upon point to be punished.

†**b.** As a matter of fact, in reality. *Obs.*

1642 Rogers *Naaman* To Rdr. §2 In this sense it is (upon point) no other then the old Adam. **1677** W. Hubbard *Narrative* (1865) II. 15 Diligence..and Faithfulness..is all that is upon point required of him.

c. ***upon the point of***: see 5.

** With other sbs.

†**8. point and blank** (***points and blank***): = point-blank. *Obs. rare.*

1590 Sir J. Smyth *Disc. Weapons* 14 b, The Mosquet ranforced and well charged with good powder, would carrie a full bullet poynt and blancke 24 or 30 scores. *Ibid.* 28 The arrowes doo not onelie wound, and sometimes kill in their points and blank, but also in their discents and fall.

9. point of honour [F. *point d'honneur*]. A matter regarded as vitally affecting one's honour. Hence, the obligation to demand satisfaction (esp. by a duel) for a wrong or an insult.

1612 E. Grimstone tr. *Turquet's Gen. Hist. Spain* XXVII. 971 *margin*, Moderne combats and the Maximes of the point of honour at this day. **1659** B. Harris *Parival's Iron Age* 52 Points of honour make them run into the Field..in such sort, as that the greatest part of the Nobility unhappily falls in Duels. **1703** *Rules of Civility* 233 When we say a Point of Honour, we mean a Rule, a Law, and a Maxim of Honour. **1711** Addison *Spect.* No. 99 ¶2 The great Point of Honour in Men is Courage, and in Women Chastity. **1782** Cowper *Conversation* 163 The Point of Honour has been deemed of use, To teach good manners, and to curb abuse. **1850** Merivale *Rom. Emp.* (1865) II. xiii. 91 To obey the call of the commonwealth was the point of honour with the Roman statesman.

10. point of horse (*Mining*): see horse *sb.* 11.

1882 Ogilvie (Annandale), *Point of horse*,..the spot where a vein, as of ore, is divided by a mass of rock into one or more branches.

11. point-to-point, *a.* **a.** (Made, reckoned, etc.) from one point or place to another in a direct line: chiefly of a cross-country race; hence *ellipt.* as *sb.* a cross-country race, a steeplechase. See A. 20 c. Also, from one point to another in turn (not necessarily in a direct line). Hence **point-to-pointer, point-to-pointing.**

1883 C. Pennell-Elmhirst *Cream Leicestersh.* 236 The winner of the Quenby point-to-point chase. **1895** *Baily's Mag.* May 333/1 The so-called 'point-to-point' steeplechase—i.e., the original form of the sport. **1900** *Pall Mall G.* 18 Apr. 3 Major—conducted the point to point meetings. **1920** *Isis* 10 Mar. 2/2 No one..would go to a Point-to-point without a hat. **1930** *Telegr. & Teleph. Jrnl.* XVI. 110/2 The State wireless services only undertake 'Ship-to-shore'..and 'Point-to-point' internal traffic. **1934** *Sun* (Baltimore) 30 Mar. 3/2 The running of the Maryland Hunt Cup Point-to-Point. **1945** *Salt* 10 Sept. 10 The point-to-point voyages of air transport. **1952** F. A. Brown *Sport from Within* v. 163 Why not do the job properly and buy a racehorse instead of a point-to-pointer? *Ibid.* 177 It might be as well to confine hunters to Point-to-Pointing for the future, instead of encouraging race-horses to masquerade as hunters at race meetings. **1957** *Practical Wireless* XXXIII. 520/1 The arrangement and layout of main components is illustrated in Figs. 2 and 3, which also show partial point-to-point wiring. **1960** *Times* 12 Mar. 9/7 One of the great criticisms of point-to-pointing is the 'readying' of some of the horses. **1962** *Listener* 12 July 62/3 This instrument [*sc.* the electron microprobe] can provide information about the composition of, say, a copper-zinc alloy by point-to-point exploration of tiny areas one-thousandth of a millimetre square. **1964** A. Wykes *Gambling* viii. 187 Hunting's most direct descendant is a form of horse racing called 'point-to-point'. **1967** M. Chandler *Ceramics in Mod. World* iv. 117 These pores..make it possible for charged ions to carry a current over a comparatively easy point-to-point route through it [*sc.* the insulator]. **1970** M. Williams *Continuing Story of Point-to-Point Racing* xxiii. 146 The champion point-to-pointer of the 1964 season was Mr. W. J. A. Shepherd's Straight Lady. **1975** *Oxf. Compan. Sports & Games* 496/2 The major event of the point-to-point season is the Player's Gold Leaf Championship. **1976** *Horse & Hound* 3 Dec. 55/2 She got much pleasure and fun out of owning some useful point-to-pointers, in particular her good horse Brough. **1979** *Guardian* 31 Aug. 10/1 BMW..decided to sponsor point-to-points. *Ibid.*, The point-to-pointer interviewed thought it all very subtle.

b. Direct, straight, categorical.

1905 *Daily Chron.* 15 July 4/3 Random assertions are at once challenged and point-to-point question and answer are sometimes insisted upon.

c. In every particular or respect.

1934 C. Lambert *Music Ho!* v. 326 A book that..has purposely avoided a point-to-point analysis of individual works. **1949** R. K. Merton *Social Theory & Social Structure* xiv. 330 Discussions of the why and wherefore of science bore a point-to-point correlation with the Puritan teachings. **1958** *Listener* 27 Nov. 885/3 Changes of shape in the retinal image will necessarily be reproduced in the occipital lobe of the brain since there is a point-to-point correspondence between them.

12. point of view [F. *point de vue*]: the position from which anything is viewed or seen, or from which a picture is taken; also, the position or aspect in which anything is seen or regarded. *lit.* and *fig.* Also *attrib.*

1727–41 Chambers *Cycl.*, *Point of view*, with regard to building, painting, etc., is a point at a certain distance from a building, or other object, wherein the eye has the most advantageous view or prospect of the same. **1760** Sterne *Sermons* II. xi. 112 Look at a man in one light..behold him in another point of view. **1793** Burke *Remarks on Policy of Allies* in *Three Memorials on French Affairs* (1797) 193 It is not the point of view in which we are in the habit of viewing guilt. **1809–10** Coleridge *Friend* (1865) 143 That he has seen the disputed subject in the same point of view. **1844** Macaulay *Misc. Writ.* (1860) II. 114 In a literary point of view, they are beneath criticism. **1845** M. Pattison *Ess.* (1889) I. 2 Every generation..demands that the history of its forefathers be rewritten from its own point of view. **1860** Tyndall *Glac.* II. xxvi. 367 From no single point of view..can all the Dirt-Bands of the Mer de Glace be seen at once. **1893** *Bookman* June 85/1 From the world's point of view his unpopularity was richly deserved. **1905** S. L. Whitcomb *Study of a Novel* iii. 66 The narrator takes some general point of view for the entire action, and specific points of view for every part of it, in reference to time, place,..etc. The unity of a passage or a plot depends largely on the clearness and stability of this position. **1909** H. James *Wings of Dove* I. p. xvi, There is no economy of treatment without an adopted, a related point of view, and though I understand, under certain degrees of pressure, a represented community of vision between several parties to the action when it makes for concentration, I understand no breaking-up of the register, no sacrifice of the recording consistency, that doesn't rather scatter and weaken. **1921** P. Lubbock *Craft of Fiction* xvii. 251 The whole intricate question of method, in the craft of fiction, I take to be governed by the question of the point of view—the question of the relation in which the narrator stands to the story. **1927** E. M. Forster *Aspects of Novel* iv. 109 The problem of a point of view..is peculiar to the novel. **1948** M. Schorer in *Hudson Review* I. 69 Let it [*sc.* technique in fiction] be thought of in two respects particularly: the uses to which language, as language, is put to express the quality of the experience in question; and the uses of point of view not only as a mode of dramatic delimitation, but more particularly, of thematic definition. **1958** *N. & Q.* CCIII. 85/2 The experimentation with dramatic forms in *The Blithedale Romance* is clearly a prefiguration of the point-of-view technique. Eschewing the novelist's omniscience, Hawthorne had his narrator cloud in vague terms the nature of Moodie's early crime. **1961** W. J. Harvey *Art of George Eliot* i. 14 His [*sc.* Henry James's] insistence on dramatic representation, point of view, elimination of the author..has undergone a subtle critical change into something like dogma. **1973** R. Fowler *Dict. Mod. Critical Terms* 149 Some contemporary experimental novelists..transcend the issue altogether by abrupt and unsignposted shifts from one point of view to another. **1976** *Amer. Speech 1974* XLIX. 232 *Stephen Hero* is written from a heavily omniscient point of view.

13. point of order. In a debate, meeting, etc., an objection or query respecting procedure.

a **1751**, **1781** [see ORDER *sb.* 18]. **1885** *Encycl. Brit.* XVIII. 312/1 A member may speak once only to any question, except to explain, or upon a point of order, [etc.]. **1903** G. B. SHAW *Man & Superman* III. 75 The anarchist (*rising*) A point of order, Mendoza—. Mendoza (*forcibly*) No, by thunder: your last point of order took half an hour. **1952** *Oxf. Jun. Encycl.* X. 194/1 If a member wishes to raise a 'point of order', that is, to suggest that a rule of debate is being broken, he must remain seated and put on a hat to call the attention of the Speaker. **1974** *Encycl. Brit. Micropædia* VIII. 68/1 If the point of order is overruled by the presiding officer, the speaker resumes the floor.

14. point of departure. *fig.* The starting point of a thought or action; the initial assumption, procedure, etc., which is developed. Also (with hyphens) *attrib.*

1857 DICKENS *Dorrit* II. xiii. 438 In the relief of having this companion, and of feeling that he could trust him, he passed on to both [subjects], and both brought him round again.. to his point of departure. **1876** [see DEPARTURE 5]. **1927** R. H. WILENSKI *Mod. Movement in Art* 31 The French romantics of the early nineteenth century made the romantic elements in his art their point of departure. **1959** J. KIRKUP tr. *S. de Beauvoir's Memoirs of Dutiful Daughter* (1963) III. 218 He looked upon marriage as a solution and not as a point of departure. **1961** *Listener* 17 Aug. 257/1 Schönberg began as an heir to Wagner. His point of departure was the intense chromaticism of *Tristan* and *Parsifal*. **1962** *Amer. Speech* XXXVII. 216 Every grammarian analyzes, using his own language as a point of departure. **1965** *Language* XLI. 189 The original point-of-departure vocabulary. **1976** *Early Music* Oct. 469/1 Seebass's point of departure is the tonary contained in the manuscript Paris, Bibliothèque nationale, fonds lat. 1118 from the mid-11th century.

15. point of no return. (See quot. 1941.) Freq. *transf.* and *fig.*

1941 *Jrnl. R. Aeronaut. Soc.* XLV. 306 This three-engined operation data is used to determine our so-called 'Point of No Return'. Laymen are inevitably intrigued by this fatalistic expression. As a matter of fact it is merely a designation of that limit-point, before which any engine failure requires an immediate turn around and return to the point of departure, and beyond which such return is no longer practical. **1946** E. HODGINS *Mr Blandings* x. 141 It would be delightful.. to.. die of old age in a rented apartment... But.. he had reached and passed the crucial mark known, in the poetic language of the air navigator, as the Point of No Return. **1948** 'N. SHUTE' *No Highway* iv. 98 They passed the point of no return, and as a routine matter the navigator reported to him. **1953** R. LEHMANN *Echoing Grove* 281 You were admitting to one another, weren't you, your secret knowledge that you—hadn't reached, together, the—the point of no return? **1956** *Jrnl. Educ.* July 312 But now he stopped [stealing] long enough to write a book (this is usually the point of no return) about his approved school, Borstal and prison experiences. **1958** *Times* 9 Jan. 10/3 When we were on the way to the Pole we received a request from Dr. Fuchs to establish a further depôt, but we were 240 miles from the Pole, and beyond the point of no return. **1960** J. LEHMANN *I am my Brother* vii. 314, I finally decided that Leonard and I had reached a point of no return: if our partnership remained the same.. not only would the Hogarth Press come to a standstill, but my own career would finally be frustrated. **1966** D. VARADAY *Gara-Yaka's Domain* ix. 105 To my consternation I realised that I had let the matter run to the 'point of no return'. For me to refuse to go on now would.. hurt his feelings. **1970** *Times* 7 May 12/7 Forbes.. says all the A.B.P. films have a financial 'point of no return'. **1977** *Oxford Diocesan Mag.* Oct. 20/3 Scholars may well 'have passed the point of no return' in this matter.

16. point-of-lay, *a.* The stage of a hen's life-cycle at which it is able to begin laying eggs. Chiefly *attrib.*

1950 *Starting Poultry Keeping* (Poultry World) (ed. 8) 108 (Advt.), One of the largest suppliers of laying and point-of-lay pullets.. in England. **1953** L. ROBINSON *Mod. Poultry Husbandry* (ed. 3) xxi. 612 During both the autumn and spring the early hatches produced birds of heavier weights at point of lay. **1960** *Farmer & Stockbreeder* 16 Feb. 147/3 Losses to point-of-lay have averaged only 2½ per cent. *Ibid.*, This system of rearing.. enables him to offer a point-of-lay pullet at a really economical price. **1964** J. PORTSMOUTH *Practical Poultry Keeping* (ed. 6) iii. 44 As a pullet approaches the point of lay stage its body undergoes great changes. **1975** A. C. STEWART *Dark Dove* vi. 41 Rhode Island Red pullets, six, point-of-lay—thirty-five shillings. **1977** D. KAY *Poultry Keeping for Beginners* v. 70 At the age of 20 weeks.. the pullet becomes a point of lay bird.

17. point-of-sale. The place at which retail transactions are made. Chiefly *attrib.*

1953 D. RIESMAN *Individualism Reconsidered* (1955) 222 Using the retail store as the point-of-sale as in the Supermarket. **1959** *Design* Sept. 49/1 The coin operated food vending machine is required to carry its own point-of-sale appeal. **1960** *Times* 28 Sept. (Advt. Suppl.) p. ii/5 Posters and point-of-sale displays. **1962** H. E. BEECHENO *Introd. Bus. Stud.* x. 88 Point-of-sale advertising consists of using special display material in shop windows. **1974** *Encycl. Brit. Micropædia* VIII. 68/1 Early point-of-sale displays consisted of stock designs (that is, the brand name of the product or a picture of the product or the factory) on strawboard placed in shop windows and on stands and counters. **1978** *Bookseller* 17 June 3197/3 The time when point-of-sale data was run against a local stock-control system.

*** Attributive uses and Combinations.

18. General Combinations, as ***point-aglet***, ***-cleaner***, ***-current***, ***-end***, ***-holder***, ***-hole*** (Printing), ***-law*** (LAW *sb.*[3]), ***-making***, ***-mark***, ***-pair***, ***-pinner***, ***-rod***, ***-shape***, ***-side***, ***-size***, ***-strap***, ***-system***, ***-triplet***; ***points system***; ***point-eared***, ***-free***, ***-leafed***, ***-tipped*** adjs. In Phonetics, used to describe a consonant articulated with the point of the tongue, as *t*, *d*; also in Comb. as ***point-element***, ***-lingual*** adj., ***-open*** adj. (sb.), ***-side*** (as *l*) adj., ***-stop***, ***-teeth*** (as *þ*) adj., ***-trill***.

1634 SIR T. HERBERT *Trav.* 151 Larrees [Persian coins] fashioned like *point-aglets, and are worth ten pence. **1867** *Point consonant [see BACK *a.* 1 c]. **1888** SWEET *Hist. Eng. Sounds* §11 Point consonants admit of inversion.. and protrusion. **1902** Point consonant [see *fan consonant* s.v. FAN sb.[1] 11]. **1857** DICKENS *Perils Eng. Prisoners* iii, in *Househ. Words* Extra Christmas No., 7 Dec. 30/2 The off-settings and *point-currents of the stream. **1894** GLADSTONE *Odes of Horace* III. xix. 4 Goat-footed, *point-eared Satyrs too. **1933** O. JESPERSEN *Essentials Eng. Gram.* iv. 39 Sometimes the *point-element [of *r*] remains though without any trill. **1771** LUCKOMBE *Hist. Print.* 335 [He] presses a little gently upon the Tympan just over the *Point-ends of each Point. **1897** MARY KINGSLEY *W. Africa* 330 A shallow half-moon cut out of the back [of a bowie-knife] at the point end. **1947** *People* 22 June 1/3 Small quantities of biscuits originally intended for the Services are *point-free—if you can get them. **1897** *Daily News* 17 Sept. 7/3 *Point holder, employed by the Midland Railway Company. **1770** P. LUCKOMBE *Conc. Hist. Printing* 500 **Point-holes*, holes made by the Points in a worked off sheet of paper. **1940** *Chambers's Techn. Dict.* 658/1 *Point holes* (*Print.*), punctures made in the printed sheet by the spurs of the register points. **1602** *Aberdeen Regr.* (1848) II. 229 The said schip sall ly on the *poyntlaw within the herbrie. **1932** R. LEHMANN *Invitation to Waltz* I. 5 And there growing up the side of the house.. is that kind of thick, bristling, woody, *point-leafed shrub. **1931** G. O. RUSSELL *Speech & Voice* xiv. 133 *Point-lingual fricative consonants. **1889** G. B. SHAW *London Music in 1888–89* (1937) 129 Signor Novara, who played the part with unexpected success.. acting without any senseless posturing and *point-making. **1900** *Daily Chron.* 4 Dec. 3/3 The book depends for effect rather upon its natural, facile 'talkativeness' than upon any sort of conscious pointmaking. **1902** *Ibid.* 23 May 6/5 Dialogue sure to evoke laughter when delivered by such experts in point-making. **1975** *New Yorker* 28 Apr. 124/2 The cut between the two scenes is not a piece of easy point-making. **1897** *Archæologia* Ser. II. V. 402 A complete circle, with the *point-mark of the compass in the middle. **1877** H. SWEET *Handbk. Phonetics* II. 37, *rh*, *r* (*point-open). **1927** J. J. HOGAN *Eng. Lang. in Ireland* 29 Point-open and stops: *thedynge* 'tiding,' *onther* 'under,' *tanked* 'thanked'. **1934** —— *Outl. Eng. Philol.* I. i. 8 English has two Point-Opens, þ as in *think*, ð as in *then*. **1858** CAYLEY *Coll. Math. Papers* II. 563 [The] equation.. represents.. a system of *m* points, or point-system of the order *m*... When *m* = 1 we have of course a single point, when *m* = 2 we have a quadric or *point-pair, when *m* = 3 a cubic or point-triplet, and so on. **1877** —— in *Encycl. Brit.* VI. 727/1, 2 μ – ν point-pairs (that is, conics, each of them a pair of points). **1808** E. SLEATH *Bristol Heiress* II. 34 She is as vain of the.. breadth and texture of her *point-pinners as of her coronet. **1889** G. FINDLAY *Eng. Railway* 75 '*Point-rod Compensator', which automatically compensates for the expansion or contraction from heat or cold of the rods which actuate the points. **1684** *Lond. Gaz.* No. 1911/4 Mantua's, Petticoats, *Point shapes, etc. **1884** W. S. B. MCLAREN *Spinning* (ed. 2) 199 There is in every card what is called the *point side and the smooth side, the former being the side towards which the wires point. **1901** *N.E. Dict.* s.v. L, The 'point-side' consonant admits of considerable diversity in mode of articulation and consequently in acoustic quality. **1931** A. ESDAILE *Student's Man. Bibliogr.* 143 Easily available to English printers,.. are the following types, which can, of course, be had in different normal *point-sizes and with their own italic. **1973** S. JENNETT *Making of Books* (ed. 5) ii. 41 These two lines appear to be set in two quite different sizes of type, yet they are both in the same point size and a dozen lines of either would occupy exactly the same depth of space. **1899** W. RIPPMANN tr. *Viëtor's Elements of Phonetics* 142/1 *Point stops, etc. = dental stops, etc. **1934** J. J. HOGAN *Outl. Eng. Philol.* I. i. 6 The English Point Stops, *t*, *d*, *n*. **1963** E. H. EDWARDS *Saddlery* xv. 111 An additional girth known as a '*point strap' and fixed under the point itself, which allows the girth to be fastened to this strap and.. will place the girth much farther forward and help to keep it and the saddle in place. **1888** *Point system [see POINTSMAN 2]. **1931** A. ESDAILE *Student's Man. Bibliogr.* iv. 131 Simon Pierre Fournier,.. best known by.. being the first author of the Continental point-system of measuring types. **1941** *New Statesman* 26 Apr. 430/1 The 'point system' is based on the allocation of so many points per head and if you squander them on caviare instead of on corned beef, it is just too bad for you. **1944** *Ann. Reg. 1943* 40 The *points system was securing an equitable distribution of non-perishable foodstuffs. **1953** R. J. C. ATKINSON *Field Archaeol.* ii. 50 *The point system*, a fairly close grid of pegs is laid out to divide the site into squares. On one side of each peg a small pit is dug. **1959** *Chambers's Encycl.* XI. 533/1 Under the point system [of rationing], there is obviously greater freedom of choice than under specific rationing. **1964** *Listener* 1 Oct. 505/2 The 'points system'.. determines the amount of money which can be spent for special allowances for teaching staff and other purposes. **1974** *Guardian* 23 Jan. 9/3 Council houses are allocated on a points system. **1888** H. SWEET *Hist. Eng. Sounds* (rev. ed.) 5 þ (as in *thin*) [is] a *point-teeth consonant. **1906** H. C. WYLD *Hist. Study Mother Tongue* ii. 32 *th* (þ) in 'think', made between the *Point* of the tongue and the *Teeth* (Point-Teeth-Open). **1952** C. L. B. HUBBARD *Pembrokeshire Corgi Handbk.* 2 Erect and *point-tipped ears. **1877** H. SWEET *Handbk. Phonetics* II. 49, *rhr* (*point-trill). **1927** J. J. HOGAN *Eng. Lang. in Ireland* 75, *r*. This consonant is everywhere retained [in Irish] as in M.E... A strong point-trill is heard in the South. **1933** O. JESPERSEN *Essentials Eng. Gram.* iv. 39 Originally *r* was a full point-trill everywhere.

19. Special Combs.: **point-action** *Gram.*, applied to an aspect which is not durative; **point bar**, (*a*) in the Jacquard apparatus, one of the needles governing the warp-threads, by the motion of which the pattern is produced; (*b*) *Physical Geogr.*, an alluvial deposit that forms by accretion inside the loop of a river as the loop expands outwards, usu. consisting of low, curved, parallel ridges; **point blanket**, a Hudson's Bay or Mackinaw blanket with points (sense A. 33) to indicate weight; **point block**, a high building with flats, offices, etc., built around a central lift or staircase; **point-brass** (see quot.); **point break** *Surfing*, a type of wave characteristic of a coast with a headland; **point charge** *Electr.*, a charge regarded as concentrated in a mathematical point, without spatial extent; **point-circle**, a point considered as an infinitely small or evanescent circle; **point-constable**, a constable on point-duty; **point contact**, the state of touching at a point only; *spec.* in *Electronics*, the contact of a metal point with the surface of a semiconductor so as to form a rectifying junction; freq. *attrib.*; **point-count** *Bridge*, the value of a hand in points; also, any system of allocating points to a hand; hence ***point-counting*** vbl. sb.; **point-counter** *Physics*, an early version of the Geiger counter in which discharges occur between positively-charged chamber walls and a central, earthed, metal point; **point defect** *Cryst.*, any defect in a crystal structure which involves only one lattice site; **point discharge**, an electrical discharge in which current flows between an earthed pointed object and the surrounding gas; also *attrib.*; so **point discharger**, such an object; **point-draughtsman**, one who draws with the point, an engraver; **point-event**, something conceived of as having a definite position in space and time but no extent or duration; **point-finder**, an instrument for determining the vanishing point in making projections (Knight *Dict. Mech.* Suppl. 1884); **point focus** *Physics*, a focus (of a beam of light or particles, etc.) which is small enough to be considered as a point; **Point Four** (or **IV**, **4**) *U.S. Pol.*, the fourth point of President Harry S. Truman's Fair Deal programme (FAIR DEAL) which made provision for technical aid to underdeveloped countries; freq. *attrib.*; **point ground**, in lace-making, a type of *réseau* ground; also *attrib.*; **point-handle**, the lever by which a point or railway switch is moved; **point-head**, a head-dress of point-lace (see HEAD *sb.*[1] 5); **point-instant**, the minimal unit of space-time; a mere position in space-time; **point-iron** (cf. *point-brass*); **point-lever** = *point-handle*; **point load** *Engin.*, a load that acts at a single point; **point mass** *Physics*, a mass regarded as concentrated in a mathematical point, without spatial extent; also *attrib.*; **point mutation** *Genetics*, a mutation not distinguishable by recombinational analysis from a point change within a gene; **point net**, simple point-lace; **point number**, in a musical, a song which is integral to the action; **point paper**, pricked paper for making, copying, or transferring designs (Knight *Dict. Mech.* 1875); **point-plate** (*Printing*), the adjustable plate carrying the points (B. 4); **point-policeman** = *point-constable*; **point rationing**, a system of rationing whereby goods are priced in terms of points (sense A. 15 b) and a certain number of points are assigned to each consumer; so ***point-rationed*** adj.; **point resistance** *Engin.*, the upward force exerted by soil on the base of a pile; **point-screw** (*Printing*), the screw by which the point-plate is fastened down; **points food**, rationed food available on points only; **point shoes**, shoes with pointed toes, *spec.* of a type used by ballet dancers; **point-shooting**, shooting game from a fixed point; **point-shot**, point-blank distance (see POINT-BLANK); **point source**, a source (as of light or sound) of negligible dimensions; **point-sphere**, a point regarded as an infinitesimal sphere; **points rationing** = *point rationing*; **points value** = *point value*; **points victory**, a victory won on points; **points win** = *points victory*; †**point-tag**, the aglet of a lace; †**point-tagger**, a maker of point-tags; **point-tool** (*Turning*), a flat tool having the end ground to a point; **point-trusser**, a valet or page who trussed or tied his master's points; **point value**, value in terms of rationing points; **point-work** *Ballet*, dancing on the points. Also POINT-DUTY, POINT GROUP, POINT-LACE, etc.

1925 G. O. CURME *College English Gram.* II. 56 The *point-action aspect calls attention, not to an act as a whole, but to only one point, either the beginning or the final point. **1932** *Jrnl. Eng. & Gmc. Philol.* XXXI. 251 Most scholars recognize in English a durative aspect and a point-action aspect. **1970** *Language* XLVI. 300 It is particularly noteworthy in the latter case that the headline to this news item read 'Man may not have smelt killer gas', the *-t* form co-occurring with an effective or 'point-action' aspect. **1977** *Ibid.* LIII. 437 The ungrammaticality of 3d would be acounted for by the fact that *arrive*, like all (non-iterable) point-action predicates, does not co-occur with duration adverbials like *until*. **1836** URE *Cotton Manuf.* II. 350 Projects of bobbins, pushers, lockers, *point-bars, and needles. **1945** H. N. FISK in *Geol. Investigation Alluvial Valley of Lower Mississippi River* (U.S. Mississippi River Commission) 20 The point bar, the composite accretion within a bend, consists of an alternation of sand bar ridges, capped with thin top-stratum, and swales underlain by clay plugs. **1963** D. W. & E. E. HUMPHRIES tr. *Termier's Erosion & Sedimentation* v. 110 Alluvial plains appear to be composed chiefly (80–90%) of 'point bars'. **1974** C. H. CRICKMAY *Work of River* ii. 25 The land round which a meander winds is termed the tongue, and the tip of the tongue is the point, whence the term point bar. **1976** K. W. BUTZER *Geomorphol. from Earth* viii. 157 Point bars, developed as a series of low levees on the inside meander bends, form arcuate or parallel ridges and swales. **1783** in E. E. Rich *Moose Fort Jrnl.* (1954) 152, I have enclosed instructions for your Guidance and the Standard of the *point Blankets I now send you. **1797** in *Georgia Hist. Soc. Collections* (1916) IX. 347, 2 2½ point blankets. **1855** J. H. CHAMBERS in *Contrib. Montana Hist. Soc.* (1940) X. 116 We have..30 prs. 3 pt. blkts 20 Pr W 20 1 Blkt 10 blue blkt 18 Scan & 25 Hudson Bay blkts. **1926** *Beaver* Dec. 22 The earliest reference found in a search of the minutes of the.. Hudson's Bay [Co.] to Hudson's Bay 'Point' Blankets is one dated 22nd December 1779, where a notation is made of an order for one hundred pairs of each of five sorts of pointed blankets. **1962** W. STEGNER *Wolf Willow* II. v. 67 The somewhat obscure source of the red point blankets that I slept under. **1954** *Ann Reg. 1953* 371 The London County Council's large sites..were of special interest on account of their carefully landscaped mixture of terrace houses, maisonettes, and 11-storey '*point-blocks'. **1958** *Listener* 6 Nov. 727/1 Eight-storey point-blocks are contrasted with low, gable-ended, four-storey blocks. **1970** *New Scientist* 5 Mar. 460/1 A series of disasters, or near disasters,.. involving a wide range of modern structures from cooling-tower shells to point blocks of flats. **1975** *Times Lit. Suppl.* 5 Sept. 988/4 The London skyline today, peppered with point blocks, tower-blocks, and slabs. *c* **1850** *Rudim. Navig.* (Weale) 138 *Point-iron* or **brass*, a larger sort of plumb, formed conically and terminating in a point, for the more nicely adjusting anything perpendicularly to a given line. **1966** *Surfabout* III. vi. 8/1 The original concept was to have three separate events. A *point break, reef break, and a beach break contest. **1968** W. WARWICK *Surfriding in N.Z.* 21/1 There are four main types of breaks in New Zealand. They are the beach break, the reef break, point break and the river bar break. *Ibid.* 21/2 The point break wave..is formed when swells move almost at right angles along a peninsula or headland. **1970** *Studies in English* (Univ. of Cape Town) I. 26 A headland, point or pier, bends the wave into a *point break*, which gives a consistent ride in one direction, often in a perfect tubing shape, so that the surfer slides along the face of the wave with a tube of water continually breaking behind him. **1903** S. J. BARRETT *Electro-Magn. Theory* 66 The law of inverse squares..is due to the continuity of the electric displacement.., the flux from a *point-charge being distributed equally in all directions. **1975** D. G. FINK *Electronics Engineers' Handbk.* I. 11 A combination of two point charges of equal magnitude and opposite polarity separated by a distance small compared to that at which the field of the dipole is to be determined is called an electric dipole. **1866** BRANDE & COX *Dict. Sc.* II. 946 A **point-circle* has the equation $x^2 + y^2 = 0$, and a *point-sphere* the equation $x^2 + y^2 + z^2 = 0$. **1905** *Westm. Gaz.* 19 Aug. 8/2 A *point constable is on duty twenty yards away. **1914** *Proc. Physical Soc.* XXVII. 70 The present paper relates..to the conductivity of '*point contacts' when a steady, or slowly varying, E.M.F. is applied. *Ibid.*, The behaviour of a typical point contact (zincite and tellurium). **1945** R. K. ALLAN *Rolling Bearings* vi. 143 In roller bearings..we..have 'line contact' as distinct from the 'point contact' of ball bearings. **1947** C. F. EDWARDS in *Proc. IRE* XXXV. 1181/2 In view of the fact that the crystalline state of the silicon is more nearly like that of iron and copper, which are not ordinarily regarded as crystals,..it seems desirable to eliminate the terms 'crystal' and 'crystal detector' and designate these devices by the term 'point-contact rectifier'. **1948** *Physical Rev.* LXXIV. 230/2 When the two point contacts are placed close together on the surface and d.c. bias potentials are applied, there is a mutual influence which makes it possible to use the device to amplify a.c. signals. **1959** [see *junction transistor* s.v. JUNCTION *sb.* 4]. **1962** SIMPSON & RICHARDS *Physical Princ. Junction Transistors* i. 1 The event that opened this era of 'solid-state electronics' was the invention of the point-contact transistor by Bardeen and Brattain in 1948. **1970** H. J. WATSON *Mod. Gear Production* ii. 24 Crossed helical gears theoretically make point contact only which, under load sufficient to cause deflection of the contacting surfaces, becomes a line. **1975** D. G. FINK *Electronic Engineers' Handbk.* IX. 61 The point contact is fabricated by a metal whisker forming a rectifying junction in contact with the semiconductor. **1959** T. REESE *Bridge Player's Dict.* 149 The Milton Work *point-count remains the most popular..because of its simplicity and convenience. **1963** *Times* 9 Jan. 12/7 The Souths who were influenced more by their point-count than their distribution. **1979** *Guardian* 5 Sept. 2/6 The Bridge Challenger..run by two micro-processors..bids the point-count system. **1925** *Proc. Cambr. Philos. Soc.* XXII. 676 The *point counter has also been studied as a unit of an electrical circuit containing capacity and resistance, and an analogy established between its discharges, and the 'flashing' of a neon lamp. **1938** R. W. LAWSON tr. *Hevesy & Paneth's Man. Radioactivity* (ed. 2) i. 18 When we are concerned with the measurement of a very small flux of radiation,..the sensitivity of the point-counter is often inadequate. **1964** J. B. BIRKS *Theory & Practice Scintillation Counting* x. 394 The observation of the time relationship between two or more ionizing events, as represented by pulses from radiation detectors, forms the basis of the coincidence method... It was originally introduced..for use with point-counters and Geiger counters. **1963** *Times* 6 Mar. 13/1 The conventional openings, combined with *point-counting, brought greater refinements into bidding. **1973** *Times* 6 Jan. 9/3, I have written on many occasions that no expert relies upon point-counting alone to value his hand. **1960** H. G. VAN BEUREN *Imperfections in Crystals* ii. 41 *Point defects can be introduced in large numbers into solids by plastic deformation. **1974** D. M. ADAMS *Inorg. Solids* ix. 292 For many years it seemed that non-stoichiometric systems of wide compositional range could be understood in terms of a parent lattice with a high concentration of randomly distributed point defects. **1886** R. WORMELL *Electricity in Service of Man* 49 (*heading*) *Point discharge. **1927** *Proc. R. Soc.* A. CXV. 443 The important part played by the point-discharge currents in the total exchange of electricity between the earth and the atmosphere. **1938** R. W. LAWSON tr. *Hevesy & Paneth's Man. Radioactivity* (ed. 2) i. 17 Each time an ionizing particle..passes the neighbourhood of the point [of the needle], a point discharge takes place by virtue of ionization by collision. **1973** R. H. GOLDE *Lightning Protection* ii. 8 Point-discharge currents and the resulting space charges play an important part in the development of the lighting discharge and in the action of a lightning conductor. **1928** *Proc. R. Soc.* A. CXVIII. 255 Wormell..used a single *point-discharger at a height of 8 metres, which is stated to be likely to produce similar effects to those from a small tree. **1965** S. C. CORONITI *Problems of Atmospheric & Space Electricity* iii. 174 (*heading*) The behavior of trees as point dischargers. **1872** RUSKIN *Eagle's Nest* Pref. 7 The four greatest *point-draughtsmen hitherto known, Mantegna, Sandro Botticelli, Dürer, and Holbein. **1920** A. S. EDDINGTON *Space, Time & Gravit.* xii. 186 In the relativity theory of nature, the most elementary concept is the **point-event*. In ordinary language a point-event is an instant of time at a point in space. *Ibid.*, The aggregate of all the point-events is called the *world*. **1928** C. E. M. JOAD *Future of Life* 36 Faced with a universe consisting of ephemeral point-events, the mind selects from it certain characteristics which have a particular interest for it. **1948** *Mind* LVII. 298 The idea of a mile or a day is an everyday idea. So are those of above and below, east and west, or before and after. Those of a point, an instant, and still more of a point-event, are relatively sophisticated, and much less used. **1965** P. CAWS *Philos. of Sci.* xli. 316 This calls for a solution of the problem of rendering point events (particles interacting and so on) in terms of experiences. **1908** L. LAURANCE *Gen. & Pract. Optics* xii. 329 Thus, rays in the pencil do not have a *point focus, since there are two focal lines. **1923** GLAZEBROOK *Dict. Appl. Physics* IV. 213/1 Whilst the geometrical theory claims a perfect point-focus, the undulatory theory merely demonstrates that there is a maximum of intensity at that point. **1966** D. G. BRANDON *Mod. Techniques Metallogr.* 135 The incident intensity can be increased by using a point-focus X-ray source with the sample close to the source. **1949** *Manch. Guardian Weekly* 27 Oct. 15 The much admired '*point four' also fell by the wayside. **1953** A. HUXLEY *Let.* 21 June (1969) 675 It [*sc.* an M.A. in Public Health] would surely be helpful in all manner of fields—e.g. the UN if you wanted to enter it later, or any other of the international agencies, or Point Four. **1955** *Bull. Atomic Sci.* Mar. 98/2 The Point IV program of technical assistance stirred the imagination throughout the undeveloped areas of the world. **1961** L. D. STAMP *Gloss. Geogr. Terms* 466/1 An official definition used to determine countries qualifying for American Point IV aid was national income per capita. **1965** H. S. TRUMAN *Memoirs* II. xvi. 269 The Point Four program was a practical expression of our attitude toward the countries threatened by Communist domination. **1972** *Times* 27 Dec. 5/1 The Point 4 programme inaugurated technical aid to underdeveloped countries. **1832** J. R. MCCULLOCH *Dict. Commerce* 697 About 1777, or 1778, quite a *new* ground was attempted by the inhabitants of Buckingham and its neighbourhood, which quickly superseded all the others; this was the '*point ground*, which had (as is supposed) been imported from the Netherlands. **1865** F. B. PALLISER *Hist. Lace* xxx. 361 In 1778, according to M'Culloch, was introduced the 'point' ground, as it is locally termed, from which period dates the staple pillow lace trade of these counties. **1968** J. ARNOLD *Shell Book of Country Crafts* 305 'Buckingham Point' or 'Point-ground' lace was that lace containing Lille or Mechlin elements. **1969** E. H. PINTO *Treen* 311 *A* is a 'Trolly'..used for the gimp thread—the thick, soft thread which outlines the design in point ground lace. **1899** *Daily News* 1 July 4/5 The *point handles always stop half-way while being moved over. **1702** FARQUHAR *Twin Rivals* II. iii, 'Tis conscience I warrant that buys her the *point-heads and diamond necklace! **1718** LADY M. W. MONTAGU *Let. to Abbé Conti* 31 Oct., She had bought a fine point head. **1920** S. ALEXANDER *Space, Time, & Deity* I. 58 It is assumed that at each *point-instant (the name is due to Mr. Lorentz, *Ortzeit*) there exists some perceptible 'substance'. **1959** *Listener* 8 Jan. 57/2 The suggestions he [*sc.* Samuel Alexander] made about these 'pervasive features'—for instance, that everything in the world is ultimately composed of complexes of 'space-time point-instants'—are certainly not such as could be either reached or confirmed by any kind of direct observation. **1899** *Westm. Gaz.* 7 Oct. 8/1 In Edinburgh Station the lines are worked from 565 signal and *point levers. **1941** *Jrnl. Inst. Civil Engin.* XVI. 524 A single load was connected with a much higher ultimate moment, owing to a better stress-distribution and a rapid decrease of the moment, than was obtained with two *point-loads. **1976** ATTEWELL & FARMER *Princ. Engin. Geol.* iv. 193 It is possible to relate the point load strength index to the uniaxial compressive strength. **1955** W. HEISENBERG in W. Pauli et al. *Niels Bohr* 17 For Bohm, the particles are 'objectively real' structures, like the *point masses of classical mechanics. **1968** M. S. LIVINGSTON *Particle Physics* iii. 47 This hypothesis had a built-in 'irrationality'..in attempting to correlate the divergent concepts of point-mass particles and of wave motion. **1968** R. A. LYTTLETON *Myst. Solar Syst.* i. 20 The action of the stars once the collision is over can safely be regarded as pure attraction by point-masses. **1925** *Genetics* X. 117 If one thinks of mutations as being simply inherited changes, it becomes necessary to distinguish changes that involve whole chromosomes.., changes that involve several adjacent genes.., and what have been called '*point-mutations' or 'gene-mutations'. **1928** *Jrnl. Genetics* XIX. 223 If such parallel forms were due simply to the special action of a single factor, 'point-mutation' might afford a reasonable basis of explanation. **1974** GOODENOUGH & LEVINE *Genetics* v. 195 A mutation that affects only one or a few nucleotides in a chromosome is known as a point mutation. **1977** *Sci. Amer.* Dec. 94/3 Such mutants of influenza virus are considered to be 'point mutations' that might affect only one of the nucleotide building blocks of the RNA. **1829** *Glover's Hist. Derby* I. 243 The *point-net machine. **1865** F. B. PALLISER *Hist. Lace* xxxvi. 418 In 1777, Else and Harvey introduced at Nottingham the 'pin' or point net machine, so named because made on sharp pins or points. **1953** M. POWYS *Lace & Lace-Making* xi. 196 In working *point net ground* the pin is not enclosed, but after it is placed, two extra twists are given to the pairs which have formed the half stitch. **1937** N. COWARD *Present Indicative* III. 105 There was a sentimental ballad..and a bright '*Point' number. **1958** B. NICHOLS *Sweet & Twenties* 16, I heard a cabaret artist use the word Hiroshima as a comic gag in a point number. **1960** A. KIMMINS *Lugs O'Leary* iii. 35 It was a 'point' number, and she was singing it like a 'pop'. **1960** *News Chron.* 31 Mar. 4/5 'Point numbers'..arise directly out of the play's action—often carrying the plot..forward while they are being sung. **1967** *Stage* 2 Mar. 6/2 (Advt.), Glam. Singer: Pop, Ballad, Point Nos. **1899** J. W. MACKAIL *Life W. Morris* II. xiii. 44 '*Point-paper'—paper, that is, divided into minute spaces, each representing a single knot of the carpet. **1940** *Chambers's Techn. Dict.* 658/1 *Point paper*,..ruled paper upon which the interlacing of the threads in a fabric is shown. **1683** MOXON *Mech. Exerc., Printing* xi. ¶ 19 A round Pin filed with a Male-Screw upon it, to..hold the *Point-Plate fast in its Place. **1771** LUCKOMBE *Hist. Print.* 321. **1895** *Westm. Gaz.* 2 Dec. 7/1 One o'clock in the morning, at which hour the '*point' policeman outside the house goes off duty. **1928** *Evening News* 18 Aug. 6/3 The point policemen at spacious centres like the Marble Arch and Hyde Park Corner seem to be waving the wide world around and the exhilaration of moderate speed can be enjoyed. **1939** H. HODGE *Cab, Sir?* 236 People don't realise how dangerous it is for a point-policeman. **1944** *Times* 15 Feb. 2/2 The increase has been due to higher expenditure on unrationed or '*point' rationed foods. **1944** A. M. TAYLOR *Lang. World War II* 56 **Point Rationing*, a rationing method announced by the Office of Price Administration (OPA), establishing a secondary currency of points alongside the dollar currency. **1959** *Chambers's Encycl.* XI. 533/1 Under point rationing, the group may be extended to cover a combination of several different kinds of article. **1943** K. TERZAGHI *Theoret. Soil Mech.* viii. 136 One part Q_f of the total load on the pile is carried by the skin friction. The balance Q_p is transferred onto the soil through the base or the point of the pile and is called the *point resistance. **1972** L. ZEEVAERT *Foundation Engin. for Difficult Subsoil Conditions* v. 278 The lower part of the piles will work under ultimate point resistance and positive friction. **1683** MOXON *Mech. Exerc., Printing* x. ¶ 10 In the middle of each long Rail of the Tympan, is..an Hole..for the square Shanks of the *Point Screws to fit into. **1941** *New Statesman* 6 Dec. 475 When the retailer sells '*points' food, he can replenish his supplies only by handing over the 'points' that he has collected. **1948** *Hansard Commons* 8 Mar. 795 [He] has been given a licence to sell points foods. **1957** G. B. L. WILSON *Dict. Ballet* 218 **Point shoes*, the silk or satin shoes, tying up the ankle with ribbon, used by dancers when dancing sur les pointes. *Ibid.*, Point shoes cost about 17s a pair. **1970** R. LOWELL *Notebook* 150 My coat limp chestnut-colored suede Cut to match my point shoes that hurt my toes. **1977** *Times* 20 Jan. 8/6 American mothers just want to see their children in point shoes as early as possible. **1874** J. W. LONG *Wild-Fowl Shooting* 71 For *point-shooting, shooting from a blind on shore, or in the edge of the willows from a boat, a few hints may be welcome. **1876** *Fur, Fin & Feather* Sept. 90 We prepared to move out into the clear water onto a log, and there get some point shooting. **1747** *Gentl. Mag.* 521/1 She engaged within *point musket shot, every ship of the enemy from rear to van. **1903** *Nature* 1 Jan. 202/2 for a *point source of strength Q, the V it produces is [etc.]. **1949** [see ANGULAR *a.* 2 c]. **1971** I. G. GASS et al. *Understanding Earth* xiii. 178 Contrast this with a deep ocean floor, lacking in relief, and far from any strong point-sources of debris. **1866** *Point-sphere [see *point-circle*]. **1941** *New Statesman* 6 Dec. 475 '*Points' rationing of canned meat, canned fish etc., from December 1st onwards makes disposal of these goods to 'black market' merchants singularly unattractive. **1950** *Times* 20 May 4/1 The ending..of the points rationing system, which has been in operation for more than eight years, was announced by the Minister of Food yesterday. **1947** *People* 22 June 1/3 More 'ups' and 'downs' in the *points values of food come into force today. **1929** *Daily Express* 7 Nov. 13/2 Jackson's *points victory was about the most easily gained of the night. **1976** *New Musical Express* 12 Feb. 30/3 Theoretically this bout should have provided at least a *points-win decision in favour of Harold Melvin's The Blue Notes. **1976** *Rhyl Jrnl. & Advertiser* 9 Dec. 31/1 One of Rhyl Star Boys Club's most promising boxers, Philip Siddall, gained a classy points win over Peter Williams, of Llay ABC, at Llay last week. **1649** DAVENANT *Love & Honour* II. i, Her Fingers I think they are smaller than thy *point tags. *a* **1652** BROME *New Acad.* II. i. Wks. 1873 II. 23 Thought'st ha' me like the hair brain'd *Point-tagger. **1594** NASHE *Unfort. Trav.* Induct. Wks. (Grosart) V. 10 This fore-mentioned catalogue of the *point trussers. **1602** *2nd Pt. Return fr. Parnass.* III. iii, Let me be a point-trusser while I liue if he vnderstands any tongue but English. **1946** *Mod. Lang. Notes* LXI. 443 Prestige value, cash value, *point value. **1959** *Chambers's Encycl.* XI. 533/1 In the case of foodstuffs, the point value may be related to calorie value. **1936** S. J. SIMON tr. A. Benois in 'C. Brahms' *Footnotes to Ballet* iv. 206 The 'classical ballet' in the steel support does endow *point-work with a special brilliance. **1957** G. B. L. WILSON *Dict. Ballet* 217 Dancing on the point or 'point work' is said to have been practised by the cossacks since time immemorial. *Ibid.* 218 A danced stage performance need not necessarily include 'point work' to be termed ballet. **1975** *New Yorker* 26 May 89/2 Its a question whether 'The Sleeping Beauty' can be danced within the limitations of Bolshoi technique, which stresses big jumps at the expense of brilliance in turns and pointwork.

†**point**, *sb.*[2] *Obs. rare*$^{-1}$. [f. POINT *v.*[2]] An appointment, a preferment.

c **1380** WYCLIF *Wks.* (1880) 250 ȝif thei [poor priests] schullen haue ony heiȝe sacramentis or poyntis of þe heiȝe prelatis, comynly þei schulle bie hem wiþ pore mennus goodis wiþ hook or wiþ crok.

‖**point** (pwæ̃), *sb.*[3] The French for POINT *sb.*[1] A., in various senses; occurring in several phrases used in English, as ***point d'appui***, point of support, fulcrum; also *fig.*, esp. *Mil.*, a strategic point; ***point d'arrêt***, ***point saillant*** (Geom.); ***point d'attache***, point of connection;

point de départ = *point of departure* s.v. POINT *sb.*[1] D. 14; *point de repère*: see quots.; *point d'orgue* (see quots. 1876 and 1883).

1819 LADY MORGAN *Fl. Macarthy* I. iv. 241 (Stanf.) The boatman, with his spoon-shaped paddle fixed against a jutting rock, for a *point d'appui. **1823** BYRON *Don Juan* XIV. lxxxiv. 7 This I could prove beyond a single doubt, Were there a jot of sense among mankind; But till that point d'appui is found, alas! Like Archimedes, I leave earth as 'twas. **1833** *Edin. Rev.* LVI. 383 She [*sc.* the Bank of England] is then, as it were, the *point d'appui* of the whole moneyed and commercial interests. **1836** H. GREVILLE *Diary* 20 Feb. (1883) I. 88 England being now in the hands of *Democrats*, she is no longer useful as a *point d'appui* to France. **1876** C. M. YONGE *Three Brides* II. ii. 35 Raymond used to arm himself with the newspapers as the safest *point d'appui*. **1895** E. MALET *Dispatch* 7 Sept. in *F.O. 64/1351* No. 201 (Public Record Office), The acquisition of a 'point d'appui' in East Asia. **1915** 'I. HAY' *First Hundred Thousand* II. xviii. 264 The wood itself is a *point d'appui*, or fortified post. **1920** S. ALEXANDER *Space, Time, & Deity* II. 136 Some *point d'appui* is needed for our thinking. **1934** C. LAMBERT *Music Ho!* II. 127 His [*sc.* Satie's] progressions have.. no trace of the *point d'appui* that we usually associate with the word progression. **1945** R. HARGREAVES *Enemy at Gate* 103 Gibraltar.. furnished a perfect example of the value of sea power, combined with that ability to retain physical possession of a *point d'appui*. **1967** G. F. FIENNES *I tried to run Railway* vii. 87 The point d'appui was the results in general. **1973** D. AARON *Unwritten War* VII. xix. 294 This defense of the past was.. a *point d'appui* for the Southern traditionalist. **1871** TODHUNTER *Diff. Calculus* (ed. 5) xxii. §304 A *point d'arrêt is a point at which a single branch of a curve suddenly stops. **1939** A. TOYNBEE *Study of Hist.* V. 624 For this linguistic legacy of the Napoleonic Empire—a legacy which is the *point d'attache of the present Annex to the main thread of this Study of History—see V. C.. above. **1923** G. ARTHUR *Further Lett. from Man of No Importance* (1932) 146 King Edward was, however, equally determined that his *point de départ for the Vatican should be the British Embassy and not the English College which Cardinal Rampollá (I think) urged. **1933** *Psychoanalytic Q.* II. 156 However this may be, Freud's formulation serves as the *point de départ* for the author's subsequent discussion of the subject. **1956** *N. & Q.* CCI. 254/2 The Restoration of King Charles II.. provided an invaluable *point de départ* for all those who had economic schemes to present to government and people. **1977** *N.Y. Rev. Bks.* 13 Oct. 27/3 History, in this instance, will largely be the reflection of the historian's *point de départ*. **1886** GURNEY, etc. *Phantasms of Living* I. 468 Some point of external space at or near the seat of the imagined object plays a real part in the phenomenon. To this M. Binet gives the name of *point de repère; and he regards it as producing a nucleus of sensation to which the hallucination accretes itself. **1903** MYERS *Hum. Personality* I. Gloss., *Point de repère*, guiding mark. Used of some (generally inconspicuous) real object which a hallucinated subject sometimes sees along with his hallucination, and whose behaviour under magnification, &c., suggests to him similar changes in the hallucinatory figure. **1904** H. JAMES *Golden Bowl* I. xvi. 288 You give me a *point de repère* outside myself—which is where I like it. Now I can work round you. **1933** *Times Lit. Suppl.* 3 Aug. 527/1 It is this very uncertainty that causes him to regret at the outset the absence of *points de repère* in modern literature, which would enable him to fit his authors into schools and categories. **1937** *Burlington Mag.* Apr. 192/2 This picture.. will now take its place as the *point de repère* for the identification of this painter's individual style. **1958** *Listener* 20 Nov. 846/1 There are, of course, a few *points de repère*, significant works that represent a moment of apocalyptic vision. **1967** V. NABOKOV *Speak, Memory* (rev. ed.) iv. 85 Where a crack or a shadow afforded a *point de repère* for the eye. **1876** STAINER & BARRETT *Dict. Mus. Terms* 363/2 *Point d'orgue,.. a pedal-point. **1883** GROVE *Dict. Mus.* III. 6/2 *Point d'orgue*, organ point, appears.. to be used (1) for an organ point or pedal, that is, a succession of harmonies carried over a holding note ..; and (2),.. for the cadenza in a concerto. **1893** G. B. SHAW *Music in London 1890–94* (1932) III. 12 It gives him [*sc.* Brahms] no trouble to pile up *points d'orgue*, as in the Requiem. **1902** —— *Perfect Wagnerite* (ed. 2) 61 A specifically contrapuntal theme, *points d'orgue*, and a high C for the soprano. **1977** *Listener* 15 Dec. 797/3 Fluctuations of pitch.. must either be confined to a single line of melody, or the accompaniment must simply be a drone—as is recognised in our classical system with the pedal-point or *point d'orgue*. **1871** TODHUNTER *Diff. Calculus* (ed. 5) xxii. §305 A *point saillant is a point at which two branches of a curve meet and stop without having a common tangent.

b. *esp.* In names of various kinds of lace (POINT *sb.*[1] A. 32), as (from the real or supposed place of manufacture) ***point d'Alençon, point d'Argentan, point d'Espagne, point de France, point de Paris, point de Venise***, etc.; also ***point d'Angleterre***: see quot. 1865[3]; ***point d'esprit***, applied to small square or oblong figures used to diversify the net ground of some kinds of lace; also in names of various stitches in lace and embroidery, as ***point coupé***, cut work, ***point à l'aiguille, point de minute, point de neige, de reprise, point russe, de Sorrento***, etc.

1645 EVELYN *Diary* June, Broad but flat tossells of curious Point de Venize. **1676** ETHEREDGE *Man of Mode* III. ii, *Sir Fop.* I never saw anything prettier than this high work on your *point d'Espagne*. *Emil.* 'Tis not so rich as *point de Venise*. **1688** SHADWELL *Sq. Alsatia* II. i. (1699) 18 *Termagant.* Devil! I'll spoil your Point de Venice for you! (*Flies at him.*) **1824** SCOTT *Redgauntlet* ch. xi. His hat laced with *point d'Espagne*. **1842** Point d'Argentan [see BERTHA, BERTHE]. **1850** *Harper's Mag.* I. 431 A Pelerine.. made of embroidered net trimmed with three rows of *point d'Alençon*. **1865** Point coupé [see LACIS]. **1865** F. B. PALLISER *Hist. Lace* iii. 28 Point also means a particular kind of stitch, as point de Paris, point de neige, [etc.]. *Ibid.* vii. 102 They [*sc.* English lace merchants] bought up the choicest laces of the Brussels market, and then smuggling them over to England, sold them under the name of Point d'Angleterre, or 'English Point'. *Ibid.* 106 There are two kinds of flowers: those made with the needle are called 'point à l'aiguille'. *Ibid.* ix. 143 The point de France supplanted that of Venice; but its price confined its use to the rich. *Ibid.* xvii. 216 Point de Paris, mignonette, bisette, and other narrow cheap laces were made. *Ibid.* xxxvi. 424 This was followed by the 'spot', or 'point d'esprit', and various other fancy nets. **1872** *Young Englishwoman* Oct. 555/1 Stars worked in point russe. *Ibid.* Nov. 611/2 Fill up the grey rows ..with scarlet wool in point de reprise. **1879** *Sylvia's Embroidery Bk.* 242 The chain stitch and point russe embroidery is worked with red silk. **1881** C. C. HARRISON *Woman's Handiwork* I. 43 *Point russe* is best known by small block patterns worked in fine back stitch. *Ibid.* 59 Surplices of fine lace resembling point d'esprit. *Ibid.* 89 Modern point coupé.. is made on a shut linen foundation, of which some of the threads are cut away and the remainder worked over with buttonhole stitch, making regular square spaces. **1882** *Encycl. Brit.* XIV. 186/2 'Point d'Argentan' has been thought to be especially distinguished on account of its ground of hexagonally arranged *brides*. **1882** A. S. COLE in *Ibid.* XIV. 188/1 In the 17th century pillow lace in imitation of the scroll patterns of point lace.. produced chiefly in Flanders, went under the name of 'point d'Angleterre'. **1882** Point de reprise [see *darning-stitch* (*b*) s.v. DARNING *vbl. sb.* 3]. **1883** *Truth* 31 May 769/2 A skirt of lilac satin covered with a *point d'Alençon* tunic. *c* **1890** *Weldon's Pract. Needlework* VIII. No. 90. 6/2 A network of button-hole stitches worked in pairs—the same stitch which by lace workers is technically termed 'Point de Sorrento'. *Ibid.* 7/2 Point de reprise is familiar to workers of point lace, and is also used in drawn thread embroidery. *Ibid.* IX. No. 100. 13/2 Worm stitch, also known as 'twisted stitch', 'bullion', 'roll picot', or 'point de minute'. **1895** *Montgomery Ward Catal.* Spring & Summer 78/1 Point de Paris Ivory Lace. **1898** *Daily News* 3 Dec. 6/4 Spotted net, or point d'esprit, ..has come into fashion again for evening dresses for girls. **1902** *Mrs. Palliser's Hist. Lace* vii. 123 *Brussels point à l'aiguille, point de gaze*, is the most filmy and delicate of all point lace. *Ibid.* xvi. 229 Embroidered tulle or point d'esprit was made in Brittany.. Denmark, and around Genoa. **1919** Point d'esprit [see LEADWORK]. **1953** M. POWYS *Lace & Lace-Making* iv. 14 *Point d'Argentan...* This lace is generally known from the Point d'Alençon by the ground, the Brides Bouclées, a hexagonal ground with buttonhole stitches on each of the six sides. *Ibid.* vi. 47 Point de France was used by distinguished prelates in the 18th century. **1958** *Times* 18 Nov. 12/3 All wore Empire dresses of white *point d'esprit* net over pale blue trimmed with blue satin ribbons. **1959** *Chambers's Encycl.* VIII. 293/2 *Point de neige*—a variety of *rosalino*. **1960** H. HAYWARD *Antique Coll.* 223/1 *Point d'Angleterre lace*: this is not an English lace but is a pillow lace made in Brussels. **1971** *Country Life* 4 Nov. 1197/3 At first the same as the Venetian product, this lace had its own evolution into distinctive *Point de France*. **1974** *Encycl. Brit. Micropædia* VIII. 66/3 In modern usage, *point de Paris* has come to mean any bobbin-made lace.. with a six-pointed star mesh that is twisted, as opposed to that of Chantilly which is plaited. **1975** *Oxf. Compan. Decorative Arts* 522/1 It was not until Colbert under Louis XIV set up his state factory at Lonray near Alençon and Argentan that French Needlepoint lace under the general name of *point de France* established its reputation.

point (pɔɪnt), *v.*[1] Also (4 pownt), 4–6 poynte. [orig. ME. a. OF. *point-er*, in its twofold capacity, 'to prick, to mark with pricks or dots', deriv. of F. *point*, and 'to furnish with a point', deriv. of *pointe*: parallel to It. *puntare*, Sp. *puntar*, from *punto*, *punta*, and med.L. *punctāre* from *punctum*, *puncta*. But some of the senses app. arose immediately from the Eng. POINT *sb.*[1], from which indeed, if no such verb had existed in French, the Eng. vb. might have arisen independently.]

I. †**1.** *trans.* To prick with something sharp; to pierce, puncture. *Obs.*

? *a* **1366** CHAUCER *Rom. Rose* 1058 But aftirward they prile [? prike] and poynten, The folk right to the bare boon. **1413** *Pilgr. Sowle* (Caxton 1483) III. viii. 55 It is hye tyme that they brenne, and poynte [other folk] no more. *c* **1420** *Pallad. on Husb.* XII. 46 So goodly by & by hit is to poynt. *c* **1490** *Promp. Parv.* 407/1 (MS. K) Poyntyn, *puncto*. **1570** LEVINS *Manip.* 215/37 To Poynt, *pungere*.

†**2.** To mark with, or indicate by, pricks or dots; to jot down, note, write, describe. *Obs.*

13.. *Gaw. & Gr. Knt.* 1009 To poynte hit ȝet I pyned me parauenture. *a* **1375** *Lay Folks Mass Bk.* App. iv. 105 Eueri fote þat þou gas, þyn Angel poyntep hit vch a pas. **1565–73** COOPER *Thesaurus* s.v. *Diductus*, *Diuisio in digitos diducta*, a deuision poynted or noted vpon the fingers. **1669** STURMY *Mariner's Mag.* IV. xvii. 205, I draw or point out an occult Parallel, and reckon 52 deg. 35 min. from.. Lundy towards the West.

3. a. To insert the proper points or stops in (writing); to make the proper stops or pauses in (something read or spoken); to indicate the grammatical divisions, or the pauses, by points or stops; to punctuate. Also *absol.* Now *rare*.

c **1400** *Rom. Rose* 2161 A reder that poyntith ille, A good sentence may ofte spille. *c* **1440** *Promp. Parv.* 407/1 Poynton, or pawson, yn redynge, *pauso*. **1450–1530** *Myrr. our Ladye* 67 They also that rede in the Couente ought.. to ouerse theyr lesson before.. that they may poynte yt as it oughte to be poynted. **1551** T. WILSON *Logike* (1580) 70 When sentences be euill pointed, and the sence thereby depraued. **1602** MARSTON *Ant. & Mel.* IV. Wks. 1856 I. 51 Weele point our speech With amorous kissing, kissing commaes. **1699** BENTLEY *Phal.* 265 Neither written nor pointed right. **1760** LLOYD *Actor* (1790) 15 Some.. Point ev'ry stop, mark ev'ry pause so strong. **1886** W. D. MACRAY in *Pilgr. Parnass.* Pref. 11, I have supplied the punctuation, the MS. itself being but scantily pointed.

b. To mark (the Psalms, etc.) for chanting, by means of points.

1604 (*title*) The Psalmes of David after the Translation of the Great Bible, pointed. **1636** (*title*) The Booke of Common Prayer, and administration of the Sacraments, etc. of the Church of England; with the Psalter pointed. **1887** *Cong. Ch. Hymnal* II. Editorial Note, Selections from the Book of Psalms, and from other parts of Holy Scripture, pointed and arranged for chanting.

c. To insert the vowel (and other) points in the writing of Hebrew and other Semitic languages; also, in shorthand.

1631 GOUGE *God's Arrows* III. §71. 315 Where they found *Iehovah* expressed, they read *Adonai*, which is pointed with the same pricks. **1681** H. MORE *Exp. Dan.* Pref. 7 They did not know how to point them or vowel them. **1847** J. KIRK *Cloud Dispelled* x. 152 The men who pointed the prophet's language.

d. To separate or mark *off* (figures) into groups by dots or points; *esp.* to mark *off* the decimal fraction from the integral part.

1706 W. JONES *Syn. Palmar. Matheseos* 28 Having placed the Numbers, and pointed them as the Rule Directs. **1827** HUTTON *Course Math.* I. 130 Also, to divide by 100, is done by only pointing off two figures for decimals. *c* **1850** *Rudim. Navig.* (Weale) 37 Point off as many decimals.

II. 4. a. To furnish with a point or points; to work or fashion to a point, to sharpen. Also *fig.*

c **1330** R. BRUNNE *Chron. Wace* (Rolls) 5831 A pale wel y-poynt. **1480** *Wardr. Acc. Edw. IV* (1830) 120 John Poyntmaker for poynting of xl dosen points of silk pointed with ageletts of laton. **1570** LEVINS *Manip.* 215/38 To Poynt a knife, *acuere*. **1611** SHAKS. *Cymb.* I. iii. 19 Till the diminution Of space, had pointed him sharpe as my Needle. **1776** G. SEMPLE *Building in Water* 35 Point them or burn the Points of them in a Fire to harden them. *Mod.* An instrument for pointing pencils.

b. ***to point a cable*** or ***rope***: see quots.

1625–44 MANWAYRING *Sea-mans Dict.* 76 They use also to undoe the Strond at the end of a Cabell (some 2 foot long) and so make Synnet of the Roape-Yarne, and lay them one over another againe, making it lesse towards the end, and so at the end, make them all fast with a peece of Marling, or the like. This is called pointing the Cabell. The use whereof is to keepe the Cabell from farssing, but chiefly to see that none of the end be stolne off, and cut away. **1688** R. HOLME *Armoury* III. xv. (Roxb.) 50/1. **1704** J. HARRIS *Lex. Techn.* I, *Pointing the Cable.* **1706** in PHILLIPS. *c* **1860** H. STUART *Seaman's Catech.* 31 How do you point and graft a rope? If it is a small rope measure five inches from the end you intend to point, then put on a good whipping, unlay the rope and strands to the whipping, take all the outside yarns, and bring them back on the rope, and stop them there, then take all the inside yarns, scrape and taper them down, until the end will be half the size of the rope, marl it down taut with twine, split the outside yarns, and lay them up each into two (two-yarn nettles); when they are all laid up, see that there is an even number, then take every alternate nettle and lay along the pointing, pass the filling, and work down once and a-half the round of the rope, and then finish off.

5. *fig.* †**a.** To make (food) pungent or piquant.

c **1430** *Two Cookery-bks.* 29 Do þer-to hwyte Hony or Sugre, poynte it with Venegre.

b. To give point to (words, actions, etc.); to give force, piquancy, or sting to; to lend prominence, distinction, or poignancy to.

a **1704** T. BROWN *Eng. Sat.* Wks. 1730 I. 25 That Poet.. pointed his verses with revenge and wit. **1726** POPE *Odyss.* XVIII. 396 And now the Martial Maid, by deeper wrongs To rouze Ulysses, points the Suitors tongues. **1727** GAY *Fables* I. xxxix. 38 Beauty with early bloom supplies His daughter's cheeks, and points her eyes. **1748** JOHNSON *Van. Hum. Wishes* 222 To point a moral, or adorn a tale. **1781** COWPER *Conversat.* 29 Who vote for hire, or point it with lampoon. **1839** DE QUINCEY *Recoll. Lakes* Wks. 1862 II. 29 The circumstances.. which pointed and sharpened the public feelings on that occasion. **1885** *Manch. Exam.* 7 Jan. 4/7 Pointing his remarks by reference to art matters in this city.

c. ***to point up***: to emphasize, draw attention to. orig. *U.S.*

1934 in WEBSTER. **1940** *Sun* (Baltimore) 3 Feb. 8/1 The warnings which Finnish spokesmen have recently given to the world that this resistance cannot continue indefinitely have been sharply pointed up by the renewal of very heavy Russian assaults along all sections of the front. **1941** L. TRILLING in D. Lodge *20th Cent. Lit. Crit.* (1972) 286 An analysis of this sort is not momentous and not exclusive of other meanings; perhaps it does no more than point up and formulate what we all have already seen. **1951** *Jrnl. Aeronaut. Sci.* XVIII. 622/1 The introduction of the automatic control system, particularly in pilotless aircraft, points up another basic change in our philosophy of aircraft control. **1958** *Listener* 20 Nov. 814/2 The Federal Government.. should point up the dangers of prolonging the *status quo*. **1967** *Ibid.* 22 June 826/3 Another instance of this is the imagery at the beginning of *Pincher Martin*, which the authors ingeniously point up by comparison with a passage from *Robinson Crusoe*. **1969** A. COCKBURN in Cockburn & Blackburn *Student Power* 20 In a key concluding section he points up the lessons to be drawn from this record. **1972** *Daily Tel.* 17 Nov. 19/7 The [census] returns point up the discrepancies which occur in unemployment figures. **1978** *Verbatim* May 5/2 He points up the ambiguity in the application of the epithet *unabridged*.

†**6.** To fasten or lace with tagged points or laces; to adorn with such points. *Obs.*

1470–85 MALORY *Arthur* V. x. 177 To poynte his paltockes. **1473** *Acc. Ld. High Treas. Scot.* I. 55, j½ elne of vellus to be Bell a pair of sleifis with cuffis, and to poynt his jaket. **1563** *Homilies* II. *Place & Time of Prayer* I. (1640) 126 Poynting and painting themselves to be gorgeous and gay. **1597–8** BP. HALL *Sat.* IV. iv. 44 Poynted on the shoulders for the nonce.

III. 7. a. To work or deepen with a point or graving-tool. ? *Obs.*

1662 EVELYN *Chalcogr.* 75 Which he engrav'd after a new way, of Etching it first, and then pointing it (as it were) with the Burine afterwards.

b. *Sculpture.* To mark at a series of points on (a block of stone or marble) the depth to which the initial working or roughing-out is to be done.

1841 *Penny Cycl.* XXI. 142/1 The statue being rudely blocked out or pointed, the marble is in this state put into the hands of a superior workman called a carver. **1877** A. B. Edwards *Thousand Miles up Nile* 423 A recent writer..is of opinion that the Egyptian sculptors did not even 'point' their work beforehand. **1911** A. Toft *Modelling & Sculpture* 254 The appearance of a work when pointed is not pleasing, covered all over with innumerable holes, and little mounds of marble projecting between these holes. **1947** J. C. Rich *Materials & Methods of Sculpture* ix. 261 Occasionally an indirect sculptor may personally point a work, or have his studio assistants or students do this for him.

8. a. *Building.* To fill in the lines of the joints of (brickwork) with mortar or cement, smoothed with the point of the trowel: cf. POINTING *vbl. sb.*^{1} 5.

1375 in Willis & Clark *Cambridge* (1886) I. 9 [The roll of 1374–5 contains an account..for] powntyng [the chambers]. [**1391** *Mem. Ripon* (Surtees) III. 167 In salar. Willelmi Sklater punctantis super dictam domum per iiij dies, 20d.] *a* **1400–50** *Alexander* 5546 In at a wicket he went. ..Princes pointid it with pik. **1488** *Acc. Ld. High Treas. Scot.* I. 89 Item, to a sclatar for the poyntin of al the place off Stirling. **1572** *Ludlow Churchw. Acc.* (Camden) 151 Paid for ijth horse loode of lyme to point the wales. **1694** Addison *Virgil* Misc. Wks. 1726 I. 16 Point all their chinky lodgings round with mud. **1793** Smeaton *Edystone L.* §239 The joints having been carefully pointed up to the upper surface. **1881** Young *Ev. Man his own Mechanic* §1061 To repair and 'point' a piece of garden wall.

b. *Gardening.* To prick *in* (manure, etc.) to a slight depth with the point of the spade; also, to turn *over* (the surface of the soil) in this way; to prick *over*.

1828 Steuart *Planter's G.* 496 Let it be pointed with the spade, to the depth of two inches only, into the original soil. **1881** Eleanor A. Ormerod *Man. Injur. Insects* 44 Gas-lime, sown broadcast and then pointed in. **1897** *Garden* 16 Jan. 42/1, I do not dig the borders at all, and the surface is merely lightly pointed over.

c. *Naut.* To insert the point of (a mast or spar) through an eye or ring which secures its foot; to thread.

1882 Nares *Seamanship* (ed. 6) 116 How is a topmast pointed?

IV. 9. a. *intr.* To indicate position or direction by or as by extending the finger; to direct attention *to* or *at* something in this way. (With *indirect passive*.)

c **1470** Henry *Wallace* viii. 291 Til him thai ȝeid..; On athir sid fast poyntand at his ger. **1553** T. Wilson *Rhet.* (1580) 148 He shewed hym, pointyng with his finger, a man with a bottle Nose. **1560** Daus tr. *Sleidane's Comm.* 343 They them selues [were] poynted at with fingers. **1613** Purchas *Pilgrimage* (1614) 877 There (wold the father point to the child) goes a Viracochi. **1709** Steele *Tatler* No. 44 ⁋1, I turned to the Object he pointed at. **1715** De Foe *Fam. Instruct.* (1841) I. Introd. 5 Pointing this way and that way. **1726** Shelvocke *Voy. round World* 416, I shall therefore, as I go along, point at the rocks on which we split. **1898** Rider Haggard *Doctor Therne* i. 14 She pointed through the window of the coach.

b. *fig.* To direct the mind or thought in a certain direction: with *at* or *to*; to indicate, suggest, hint *at*, allude *to*.

1393 Langl. *P. Pl.* C. ix. 298 By seynt paul,..thou poyntest neih þe treuthe. **1598** R. Haydocke tr. *Lomazzo* ii. 10 They do..point to the rootes whence they spring, and discover the causes. **1637** Heylin *Antid. Lincoln.* ii. 109, I rather shold conceive, that the word..points not to a table. **1663** Gerbier *Counsel* g ij, This little Manuall doth..point at the Choise of Surveyors. **1885** Sir N. Lindley in *Law Times Rep.* LII. 319/2 Criminal informations are within the mischief pointed at by sect. 2. **1886** *Manch. Exam.* 2 Jan. 5/3 Everything pointed to the probability of a French protectorate being proclaimed over Burmah.

c. *trans.* To indicate or state.

1928 *Publishers' Weekly* 12 May 1957 The effect on books by established authors like Galsworthy's 'Silver Spoon' and Ferber's 'Show Boat' could not be as clearly pointed. **1975** *Language for Life* (Dept. Educ. & Sci.) xxi. 303 There should be an appraisal of the kind of support schools can be given, and this points the need for close consultation between the education authority's advisers, the schools themselves, and the library staff.

10. *trans.* To indicate the place or direction of (something) with the finger or otherwise; to indicate, direct attention to, show. Now almost always *point out*. Also with obj. clause.

c **1489** Caxton *Sonnes of Aymon* ix. 239 Men shall poynte me wyth the fynger, and shall say. **1526** Skelton *Magnyf.* 727 My purpose is to spy and to poynte euery man. **1530** Palsgr. 661/2, I poynte or shewe a thyng with my fyngar. **1579** Lodge *Def. Poetry* C iij b, Then should the wicked bee poynted out from the good. **1695** Woodward *Nat. Hist. Earth* i. (1723) 43 To detect the erroneous Ways, and to point forth the true. **1726** Pope *Odyss.* xxiv. 106 All..May point Achilles' tomb, and hail the mighty ghost. **1777** S. Martin in *Sc. Paraphr.* xii. i, She has no guide to point her way. **1801** *Med. Jrnl.* V. 166 He has pointed out a method of cure. **1885** *Athenæum* 18 July 76/1 He has always pointed out the necessity of rigorous observance of ascertained phonetic law. *Mod.* He pointed out that there were certain formalities to be observed.

11. Of a hound: To indicate the presence and position of (game) by standing rigidly looking towards it. See POINT *sb.*^{1} C. 6. **a.** *intr.*

[**1717**: implied in POINTER 4.] **1742** Somerville *Field-Sports* 257 My setter ranges in the new-shorn fields,..there he stops..And points with his instructive nose upon The trembling prey. **1837–9** Hallam *Hist. Lit.* IV. iv. ii. §21. 13 This wise and faithful animal..had acquired..the habit of standing still, and as it were *pointing*, when he came near an antiquity. **1840** *Penny Cycl.* XVIII. 306/2 Trained to stop and point where the game lies.

b. *trans.*

1821 Clare *Vill. Minstr.* I. 94 The lurking spaniel points the prize. **1850** Keightley *Fairy Mythol.* 310 He knew an old man whose dog had *pointed* a troop of fairies. **1879** Jefferies *Wild Life in S. Co.* 328 Young pointers will point birds' nests in hedges or trees. **1892** *Field* 7 May 695/1 In the next field Satin pointed a leveret.

12. a. To direct (the finger, a weapon, etc.) *at*, to level or aim (a gun) *at*; to direct (a person, his attention, or his course) *to*; to turn (the eyes or mind) *to* or *upon*.

1547 Boorde *Introd. Knowl.* xxxii. (1870) 205, I..poynted them to my hostage [landlord]. **1604** Shaks. *Oth.* iv. ii. 55 To make me The fixed Figure for the time of Scorne To point his slow, and mouing finger at. **1611** —— *Wint. T.* iv. iv. 539 On mine honor, Ile point you where you shall haue such receiuing As shall become your Highnesse. *a* **1704** T. Brown *Sat. agst. Woman* Wks. 1730 I. 57 They point fools swords against each other's breasts. **1706** Phillips, To *Point a Cannon*, to level it against a Place. **1797** Mrs. Radcliffe *Italian* xii, Whenever she ventured to look round, the eyes of the abbess seemed pointed upon her. **1842** Tennyson *Love & Duty* in *Poems* II. 87 Should it [*sc.* my shadow] cross thy dreams, So might it..point thee forward to a distant light. **1850** E. B. Browning *Prometheus Bound* in *Poems* I. 175 Point me not to a good, To leave me straight bereaved. **1855** Bain *Senses & Int.* ii. i. §6 (1864) 83 These influences..seem merely to direct or point the course of the current. *a* **1862** Buckle *Civiliz.* (1869) III. ii. 113 It was they who pointed the finger of scorn at kings and nobles. **1922** Joyce *Ulysses* 399 Yes, Pious had told him of that land and Chaste had pointed him to the way. **1972** J. Philips *Vanishing Senator* (1973) i. ii. 16 They're simply using Lloyd to point us in the wrong direction. **1976** S. George *Fatal Shadows* 106 Someone..had pointed me in her direction, had wanted me to see what she was doing.

b. Fig. phr. ***to point the finger*** (*of scorn*) (*at* a person).

1829 P. Egan *Boxiana* 2nd Ser. II. 499 It was a shame..that pure and honourable men should be suspected of such doings..for even at him the finger of scorn had been pointed. *a* **1862** [see sense 12 a]. **1939** G. B. Shaw *Geneva* iii. 81 You can point the finger of the whole world at the slayer of my husband and say 'You are guilty of murder.' *a* **1966** 'M. na Gopaleen' *Best of Myles* (1968) 93 The finger of scorn is pointed at you. **1978** 'J. Horbury' *Diplomatic Affair* x. 126 We [*sc.* the British] naturally hesitate to point the finger..but the fact is that all these..leaks have been date-lined Washington.

c. *Anthrop.* Esp. in phr. ***to point the bone***. Amongst Australian Aborigines, to will or to bring about the death of a person by a ritual involving special bones or sticks and incantations. Also *transf.* and *fig.* Cf. *pointing-bone* s.v. POINTING *vbl. sb.*^{1} 12.

1897 W. E. Roth *Ethnol. Stud. N.-W.-Central Queensland Aborigines* xi. 156 It is most important to remember that in all cases while the death bone is being 'pointed', the blood of the victim passes invisibly across the intervening space to the 'pointer', and so along the connecting string, into the receptacle..: at the same time one of the doctor's gew-gaws, or..bone, pebble, &c., passes invisibly from the 'pointer' to be inserted in the body of the victim. **1904** Spencer & Gillen *Northern Tribes of Central Australia* xiv. 458 If it were known that any one had 'pointed the bone', that man would at once be killed. **1913** J. G. Frazer *Golden Bough: Balder the Beautiful* (ed. 3) I. 14 The magical bone, which the native sorcerer points at his victim as a means of killing him, is never by any chance allowed to touch the earth. *Ibid.*, The custom of killing a man by pointing a bone or stick at him, while the sorcerer utters appropriate curses. **1934** [see BONE *sb.* 1 e]. **1939** Joyce *Finnegans Wake* i. 193 He points the deathbone and the quick are still. **1953** A. Upfield *Murder must Wait* xvii. 148 Buttons and ends came from me, are a part of me, are necessary objects required for the practice of pointing the bone. **1967** B. Jefferis *One Black Summer* x. 184 You're asking me to point the bone at someone on no real evidence at all. **1974** J. Cleary *Peter's Pence* vii. 197 He was..convinced that the bloody God-botherers had pointed the bone at him just like the blacks did back home in Aussie.

13. a. *intr.* Of a line or a material object: To lie or be situated with its point or length directed *to* or *towards* something; to have a specified direction; also, of a house, etc., to look or face.

1678 Moxon *Mech. Exerc.* v. 95 The Teeth are filed to an angle, pointing towards the end of the Saw. **1788** Charlotte Smith *Emmeline* (1816) III. 205 A boat..was pointing to land just where she had been sitting. **1859** Jephson *Brittany* vi. 71 The churches of Europe were ordinarily built pointing to the east. **1896** *Allbutt's Syst. Med.* I. 102 Such loops..'point' as it were at right angles to the denuded surface. **1901** *J. Black's Illustr. Carp. & Build., Home Handicr.* 37 This may be noticed in any house which points on to a busy thoroughfare.

b. *intr.* To aim *at*, have a motion or tendency *towards* to *to* (also with *inf.*).

1771 Wesley *Wks.* (1872) V. 498 Dost thou point at him [Jesus] in whatsoever thou doest? **1795** Nelson in Nicolas *Disp.* (1845) II. 12 Our Ships endeavouring to form a junction, the Enemy pointing to separate us, but under a very easy Sail. **1864** Bryce *Holy Rom. Emp.* v. (1875) 58 It was the goal towards which the policy of the Frankish kings had for many years pointed.

c. *U.S.* In sport, to make special preparations *for* a particular oppponent or game.

1933 *Sun* (Baltimore) 15 Nov. 12/7, I suppose there is a good deal of hooey in the talk of Army and Navy 'pointing' for each other: they do not like to be licked at any time. **1937** *Ibid.* 1 Sept. 18/2 We are not pointing for any team in particular, but are trying to develop for our major games without being knocked off. **1944** *Ibid.* 19 Oct. 21/2 The Jackets also are pointing for another bowl bid and defeats are anathema to gridsters with January 1 on their minds.

†**14.** *intr.* To project or stick *out* in a point. *Obs.*

1612 Drayton *Poly-olb.* ii. 24 Which running on, the Isle of Portland pointeth out. **1615** G. Sandys *Trav.* 233 The market place..out of which the streets do point on the Round. **1670** Narborough *Jrnl.* in *Acc. Sev. Late Voy.* i. (1694) 76 It shews like a great building of a Castle; for it points off with a Race from the other Mountains. **1703** T. N. *City & C. Purchaser* 271 They..are each about 4 Inches broad, and 8 Inches long, pointing out short at the narrow end, about 2 Inches.

15. *intr.* Of an abscess: To form a point or head; to come to a head.

1876 *Trans. Clinical Soc.* IX. 177 The skin is inflamed, and shows a tendency to point. **1879** *St. George's Hosp. Rep.* IX. 176 The abscess..pointed and became red. **1885–8** Fagge & Pye-Smith *Princ. Med.* (ed. 2) II. 56 The thinning of the roof of an abscess which is about to point.

16. *trans.* To place (a man) in Backgammon, etc., on a point. *rare*.

1680 Cotton *Gamester* xxvi. 112 (*Backgammon*) The advantage of this Game is to be forward if possible upon safe terms, and to point his men at that rate that it should not be possible for you to pass.

†**17.** *intr. Cricket.* To field at point. *Obs.*

1862 *Baily's Mag.* Aug. 85 The Surrey people..selecting ..a Lyttelton to bowl; a John Walker to keep; an F. Burbidge to point. **1863** *Ibid.* Sept. 44 The bowling of Tarrant and Grundy, the wicket-keeping of Lockyer, the pointing of Carpenter,..was all cricket in perfection.

18. *Naut.* Of a sailing vessel: to lay a course close to the wind. Freq. with *up* or in phr. ***to point high***.

1899 in *Cent. Dict.* **1941** H. I. Chapelle *Boatbuilding* i. 37 The sailing qualities of the V-bottom hull are somewhat like those of the flat-bottom types, but with improved windward qualities if well designed. They will rarely point as high as a well-designed round-bottom boat. **1947** A. Ransome *Great Northern?* xiii. 162 'The Gael's castle is behind the ridge beyond it,' said Dorothea. 'She won't point up for our inlet,' said John. **1950** E. C. Hiscock *Cruising under Sail* i. iv. 73 It [*sc.* the ketch] cannot point so high as a sloop, cutter, or yawl. **1954** G. Bradford *Gloss. Sea Terms* 146/2 A vessel *points well* if she sails close to the wind.

19. *trans. U.S.* To turn, guide, or deflect (cattle) in a particular direction.

1903 A. Adams *Log of Cowboy* iv. 42 Priest sent Officer to the left and myself to the right to point in the leaders. **1916** 'B. M. Bower' *Phantom Herd* xiv. 244 You're trying to point the herd then. **1947** C. Price *Trials I Rode* 184 One time we were pointing a herd, Bill on one side and I on the other.

20. To insert white hairs (into a self-coloured fur). Usu. as pa. pple.

1911 in Webster. **1913** [see POINTED *ppl. a.*^{1} 5 c]. **1916** *Fur Trade Directory* (N.Y.) 95 We point either skins or made-up goods. **1922** W. E. Austin *Princ. & Pract. Fur Dressing* i. 10 They are dyed black in imitation of the black fox, or these when pointed with badger or other white hair to imitate the silver fox. **1936** F. Grover *Practical Fur Cutting & Furriery* xv. 22 A black fox is often pointed with silver badger hairs. **1957** M. B. Picken *Fashion Dict.* 260/1 Fox fur pointed to imitate silver fox.

†**point**, *v.*^{2} *Obs.* [Aphetic form of APPOINT *v.*]

1. *intr.* To agree, settle *upon*: = APPOINT *v.* 1.

1560 Daus tr. *Sleidane's Comm.* 107 b, The counsell, so often tymes promysed and poynted vpon.

2. *trans.* To fix, determine (a time or place); to prescribe, ordain, decree; to nominate (a person) *to* an office: = APPOINT *v.* 7, 8, 11, 12.

c **1440** *Alphab. Tales* 275 So þai poyntid a day of disputacion. *c* **1449** Pecock *Repr.* ii. viii. 184 If God..pointe and chese the placis. **1485** in Drake *Eboracum* i. iv. (1736) 120 There to poynt such Personnes as shuld take Wages. **1533** J. Heywood *Play of Wether* (1903) 1045 Poynt us a day to pay hym agayne. **1598** Bp. Hall *Sat.* iv. i. 124 Go bid the banes, and poynt the bridall-day. **1625** Bacon *Ess., Building* (Arb.) 550 If you doe not point any of the lower Roomes for a Dining Place of Seruants. **1711** Steele *Spect.* No. 114 ⁋7 If..every Man would point to himself what Sum he would resolve not to exceed.

3. To equip, furnish, fit up: = APPOINT *v.* 14, 15.

1449 J. Metham *Amor. & Cleopes* 303 Qwat yt myght be, that poyntyd was with so merwulus werkys. *c* **1489** Caxton *Blanchardyn* xiv. 47 The prouostis men, whiche was all prest and redy poyntted to the Iouste. **1514** Barclay *Cyt. & Uplondyshm.* (Percy Soc.) p. liv, Yet shall they..poynt the place nothing after thy intent, Eyther nere a privy, a stable or a sinke.

Hence †**pointing** *vbl. sb.*

c **1449** Pecock *Repressor* ii. viii. 184 Eny such pointing, chesing, or assignyng.

†**point**, *a. Obs. rare.* [Erroneously deduced from *point-device*.] Complete; ready.

1633 B. Jonson *Tale Tub* iii. iv, And if the dapper priest Be but as cunning..point in his device, As I was in my lie.

†**point**, *adv. Obs. rare.* [Short for POINT-BLANK.] Directly.

1754 Richardson *Grandison* (1811) II. iv. 64 All the Christian doctrines..are point against it [*sc.* duelling].

ˈ**pointable**, *a. rare*$^{-1}$. [f. POINT *v.*^{1} + -ABLE.] Capable of being pointed out; visible, apparent.

a **1555** Bradford *Wks.* (Parker Soc.) I. 552 In Elias' time, both in Israel and elsewhere, God's church was not pointable; and therefore cried he out that he was left alone.

pointage ('pɔɪntɪdʒ). [f. POINT *sb.*[1] + -AGE.] Points collectively, *spec.* the number of ration points needed to make a particular purchase.

1934 in WEBSTER. **1944** *Times* 23 Feb. 2/3 From April 2 imported tinned marmalade will be available on points... The pointage will be announced later. **1946** *Evening News* 15 Aug. 1/7 Mr. Strachey said..that he had not contemplated increasing pointage to compensate for the estimated demand for points.

pointal, variant of POINTEL.

'point angle. [f. POINT *sb.*[1] + ANGLE *sb.*[2]] The angle at a vertex of a solid body; *spec.* (*a*) the angle between two diametrically opposite edges or surfaces at the tip of a tool; (*b*) the re-entrant solid angle at a vertex of an artificial cavity in a tooth.

1869 BOUTELL *Arms & Arm.* iv. (1874) 67 The blade [of the Roman sword] was straight..and cut at an obtuse angle to form the point. In process of time this point-angle becomes more and more acute. **1908** G. V. BLACK *Operative Dentistry* II. 9 All point angles are formed by the junction of three walls at a point, and are named by joining the names of the walls forming the angle. They are, therefore, named in three terms. *Ibid.*, The point angles are formed where the line angles of one set meet the other set at the angle of the cavity. **1919** G. W. BURLEY *Machine & Fitting Shop Practice* II. v. 142 The standard point-angle of lathe centres is 60° for small and medium-sized work-pieces. **1950** P. GATES in A. W. Judge *Machine Tools & Operations* I. iv. 149 When drilling soft or ductile materials, drills ground with a smaller point angle tend to throw up considerable burrs on the back of the work. **1973** W. W. HOWARD *Rev. Operative Dentistry* i. 9 Point angles are named for the line angles that form them.

point-blank ('pɔɪnt 'blæŋk), *a.*, *sb.*, and *adv.* Also 8–9 -blanc. [app. f. POINT *v.*[1] + BLANK, the white spot in the centre of a target, = F. *blanc*, Sp. *blanco* (in Eng. also called 'the WHITE').

It has been conjectured that *point-blank* represents a F. **point blanc* meaning the *white point* or white spot on the target, but no such use is found in Fr., or in any Romanic lang. The phrase appears exclusively of English origin and use; and there is no evidence that in Eng. the 'blank' or 'white' was ever called the *point blank*. The probability therefore is that *blank* is here the sb. (BLANK *sb.* 2), and *point* the vb. (POINT *v.*[1] 12 a), referring to the pointing of the arrow or gun at the 'blank' or 'white'; *point-blank* being a combination of the same class as *break-neck*, *cut-throat*, *save-all*, *stop-gap*, etc. It may have started as an adj., in *point-blank shot*, *distance*, *reach*, or *range*, i.e. that in which one *points* or aims at the *blank* or white spot.]

A. *adj.*

1. That points or aims straight at the mark, esp. in shooting horizontally; hence, aimed or fired horizontally; level, direct, straight; as in ***point-blank shot, fire, firing, trajectory***. ***point-blank distance, range, reach***: the distance within which a gun may be fired horizontally at a mark; the distance the shot is carried before it drops appreciably below the horizontal plane of the bore.

(As to the inexactness of the notion that the course of the projectile is level within this distance, see quot. 1804.)

1591 DIGGES *Pantom.* 179 The first parte of the violent course of Gunners, commonly termed the peeces pointe blanke reache. **1627** *Taking of St. Esprit* in *Harl. Misc.* (Malh.) III. 551 Some ships of our fleet..have bestowed divers shot on the French, though without point-blank distance. **1748** J. LIND *Lett. Navy* ii. (1757) 89 They were.. within point blank shot of the enemy. **1769** FALCONER *Dict. Marine* (1789) G g iv, The *point-blank* range of the piece.. may be defined the extent of the apparent right line, described by a ball discharged from a cannon. **1804** *Europ. Mag.* XLV. 327/2 It is generally thought that the ball goes out of the piece in a straight line to a certain distance, which they call the point-blank shot. This is a mistake; for the ball immediately falls from the axis of the gun, the tangent of the curve described, though but insensibly for a short time; but the line in which gunners take sight is usually contrived to make a small angle with the axis, so that..the ball will rise above the line of sights, and then, by the force of gravity, be made to fall again into it, at the place called the point-blank shot. **1818** HAZLITT *Eng. Poets* iv. (1870) 106 The battery is not so point-blank. **1838** *Penny Cycl.* X. 375/2 Large muskets, whose point-blanc range is estimated at about 300 yards. **1864** TREVELYAN *Compet. Wallah* (1866) 89 Then they..endeavoured to crush our line with a heavy point-blank musketry fire. **1888** BURGON *Lives 12 Gd. Men* II. xii. 361 At archery..his arrows had a more point-blank trajectory than those of his competitors.

2. Straightforward, direct, plain, 'flat', blunt.

1656 EARL MONM. tr. *Boccalini's Advts. fr. Parnass.* II. liv. (1674) 204 [They] hoped to hear..excellent discourse in that point-blank argumentation. **1770** FOOTE *Lame Lover* I. Wks. 1799 II. 56 This is point blank treason against my sovereign authority. **1779** MME. D'ARBLAY *Diary* Jan., What a point-blank question! who but Sir Joshua would have ventured it! **1817** *Edin. Rev.* XXVIII. 513 The dialogues in *Othello* and *Lear* furnish the most striking instances of plain, point-blank speaking. **1830** GEN. P. THOMPSON *Exerc.* (1842) I. 294 The English people give this a point-blank denial. **1901** *Scotsman* 6 Mar. 9/3 A point-blank refusal to go into the division lobbies.

B. *sb.*

1. a. = *point-blank range* or *distance*: see A. 1.

1571 DIGGES *Pantom.* I. xxx. I iv, Hauing a table of Randons made, mounting your peeces accordingly, no vessel can passe by your platfourme (though it be without poynte blancke) but you may with your ordinaunce at the first bouge hir and neuer bestow vayne shotte. **1587** HARRISON *England* II. xvi. (1877) I. 281 How manie scores it [the shot] doth flee at point blanke. **1671** S. PARTRIDGE *Double Scale Proportion* 85 If the best Randon and point blank of the one Piece be given. **1708** *Lond. Gaz.* No. 4422/7 We receiv'd not one Shot from them, though within point blank, six of them at once bore down upon us. **1846** GREENER *Sc. Gunnery* 381 As many opinions exist as to the exact distance for what is termed *point blank*..it may be expedient to come to some determination.

†**b.** *fig.* Range, reach (of jurisdiction, etc.). *Obs.*

1593 SHAKS. *2 Hen. VI*, IV. vii. 28 Now art thou within point-blanke of our Iurisdiction Regall. **1652** *Persuasive to Compliance* 16 The King professeth His Person..out of the point-blank of Law.

†**2.** A point-blank shooting or shot. *Obs.*

1614 RALEIGH *Hist. World* III. (1634) 100 Training..his Archers to shoot compasse, who had bin accustomed to the point blanke. *a* **1657** R. LOVEDAY *Lett.* (1663) 169 He should not receive them thus by a glance, but by a level point-blank from my pen. **1669** PEPYS *Diary* 20 Apr., She carried the same bullet as strong to the mark, and nearer and above the mark at a point blank than their's. **1781** M. MADAN *Thelyphthora* III. 275 No necessity of circumstances..can turn the point-blank of this dreadful canon from the unhappy objects of its vengeance.

¶**3.** 'The second point at which the line of sight intersects the trajectory of a projectile' (*Cent. D.*).

18.. *U.S. Army Tactics*, When the natural line of sight is horizontal, the point where the projectile first strikes the horizontal plane on which the gun stands is the point-blank, and the distance to the point-blank is the point-blank range.

¶This is a faulty use, arising from misinterpretation of *point* in 'point-blank.'

C. *adv.*

1. With a direct aim; esp. in a horizontal line. Of a missile: Without dropping below the horizontal plane in which the barrel lies. Of a gun: With the axis of the bore horizontal.

1594 PLAT *Jewell-ho.* III. 23 How to make a Pistol whose barrell is two foote in length to deliver a bullet point blank at eight skore. **1598** SHAKS. *Merry W.* III. ii. 34 This boy will carrie a letter twentie mile as easie as a Canon will shoot point-blanke twelue score. **1611** FLORIO, *Tiráre la giòia*, to shoote by the vpper superficies of the cornish of the mouth of the piece, which the Italians call point blanke. **1667** SIR R. MORAY in *Phil. Trans.* II. 473 To know how Far a Gun Shoots Point-blank (as they call it) that is, so near the Level of the Cylinder of the Peece, that the difference is either not discernable, or not considerable. **1669** STURMY *Mariner's Mag.* v. xi. 46 If the Piece lie point blank. **1868** *Rep. to Govt. U.S. Munitions War* 70, Fig. 1 shows the movable stock and sights arranged for firing point-blank. **1885** *New Bk. Sports* 20 Any man..can fire point-blank into a hustling mob of animals.

2. a. In a direct line, directly, straight (in space).

1607 *Lingua* IV. i, This done, he sets me a boy sixty paces off, just point blank over-against the mouth of the piece. **1641** HOBBES *Lett.* Wks. 1845 VII. 459 The motion of the water, when a stone falls into it, is point blanke contrary to the motion of the stone. **1664** BUTLER *Hud.* II. iii. 437 Unless it be that Cannon-Ball, That, shot i' th' air point-blank upright Was borne to that prodigious height. **1675** TEONGE *Diary* (1825) 51 Wee..doe steare our course poynt-blanke for Trypoly. **1800** WEEMS *Washington* ii. (1877) 17 Led him point blank to the bed. **1876** F. E. TROLLOPE *Charming Fellow* II. ix. 137 [He] stood for a second, staring point-blank at her.

b. *fig.* Directly, exactly (in purport or effect). Now *rare* or *Obs.*

1621 BURTON *Anat. Mel., Democr. to Rdr.* (1676) 6/1 If it be not point-blank to his humour, his method, his conceit. **1704** NORRIS *Ideal World* II. ii. 77 So point-blank against the common sentiment and appearance. **1756** J. WARTON *Ess. Pope* (1782) II. x. 134 If you calmly read every particular of that description you'll find almost all of 'em point-blank the reverse of that persons villa.

3. *fig.* Of a statement, declaration, question, etc.: **a.** Without qualification or circumlocution; directly, flatly. **b.** Without deliberation or consideration; straight away, offhand.

a. 1598 J. FLORIO *Worlde of Wordes* 104/2 *A dirittura*, foorthright, point blanke. **1627** E. F. *Hist. Edw. II* (1680) 61 Spencer is point-blanck charg'd with Insolency. **1663** BUTLER *Hud.* I. i. 528 Thus Ralph..Spoke Truth point blank, tho' unaware. **1672** CAVE *Prim. Chr.* I. iii. (1673) 47 Origen point blanck denies the charge. **1722** DE FOE *Relig. Courtsh.* I. i. (1840) 16, I would ask him point blank what religion he was of. **1851** MRS. CARLYLE *Lett.* I. 146 She.. had offers every week; refused them point-blank. *a* **1914** JOYCE *Stephen Hero* (1944) 45 McCann always represented a member of the Opposition and he spoke point-blank. Then a member would protest. **1938** E. WAUGH *Scoop* II. v. 233, I read the newspapers with lively interest. It is seldom that they are absolutely, point blank wrong. **1968** *Punch* 6 Nov. 658/2 However, I took the oranges home just the same, with marmalade in mind, but my wife refused pointblank.

b. 1679 *Trials of Wakeman*, etc. 24, I cannot point blank tell the time. **1887** LOWELL *Democr.* 4 Called upon to deliver his judgement point-blank and at the word of command.

point-blanker. [f. POINT-BLANK *a.* + -ER[1].] A point-blank shot.

1830 J. F. COOPER *Water Witch* II. vii. 202 'Run in the quoin, and..give her a point-blanker!' said the gruff old seaman... 'None of your geometry calculations for me!'

point-de'vice, *phrase*, *a.*, *adv.* Forms: see POINT *sb.*[1]; 4–5 **devys**, 4–6 **devyse**, 5 **devis**, 5–7 **deu-**, **devise**, 6 **devyce**, 5– **device**. [Orig. in ME. phrase *at point devis*, *at poynt devys*, app. representing an OF. or AF. phrase **à point devis*, not actually cited in Old French, which had however both the advb. phrase *à point* 'to point, to the point aimed at, to the proper or utmost point or degree, to the point of perfection', and the word *devis*, as ppl. adj. 'devised, arranged', and as sb. 'a device, arrangement, will, wish, desire'. The construction in *à point devis* requires the adj. sense, so that the phrase may be construed either 'to (the) point arranged', or, as *devis à point*, 'arranged to a proper point or degree, arranged properly or to perfection'. The latter appears to M. Paul Meyer the better construction of the words.

OF. had also the phrase *à devis, tout à devis*.]

A. *phrase.* **a.** †***at point device***, at or to the point of perfection, perfectly; precisely; with extreme nicety or correctness. *Obs.*

? *a* **1366** CHAUCER *Rom. Rose* 830 So faire, so joly, so fetys, With lymes wrought at poynt devys. *Ibid.* 1215 Hir nose was wrought at poynt devys. *c* **1380** WYCLIF *Serm.* Sel. Wks. I. 122 Jesus, siþ he was boþe God and man, dide alle his dedis at point devys. *c* **1384** CHAUCER *H. Fame* II. 409 That saw in dreme, at poynt devys, Helle and erthe and paradys. *c* **1386** —— *Sqr.'s T.* 552 So peynted he and kembde at point deuys As wel hise wordes as his contenance. *c* **1440** *Generydes* 5995 Armyd thei be eche on atte poynte device. [**1609** SIR E. HOBY *Let. to Mr. T. H.* 75 You think to blow him vp with a Syllogisme: Now then haue at your Point-deuice.]

†**b.** So ***to the point device, by point device***.

1542 UDALL *Erasm. Apoph.* 204 He sawe..all other thynges after a woondreful gorgeous sorte furnished euen to yͤ pointe deuise. **1575** CHURCHYARD *Chippes* (1817) 104 And seld they past the boundes of reasons lore; By poynte deuise they skirmished at will.

B. *adj.* **point-device** (**-yse**, etc.). Perfectly correct, perfect, at the point of perfection; neat or nice to the extreme; extremely precise or scrupulous.

1526 SKELTON *Magnyf.* 852 Properly drest, All poynte deuyse. **1593** PEELE *Chron. Edw. I*, Wks. (Rtldg.) 379/2, I pray thee, then, defer it till the spring, That we may have our garments point-device. **1600** SHAKS. *A.Y.L.* III. ii. 401 You are rather point deuice in your accoustrements. **1639** J. SALTMARSH *Policy* 261 Thomas his faith was the worse for being so point-device. **1872** LONGF. *Wayside Inn* III. *Emma & Eginhard* 35 Thus he grew up, in Logic point-device, Perfect in Grammar, and in Rhetoric nice;..A Minnesinger. **1885** R. L. STEVENSON *Prince Otto* II. i. 64 Otto looked so gay, and walked so airily, he was so well dressed and brushed and frizzled, so point-de-vice, and of such a sovereign elegance. **1900** C. M. YONGE *Modern Broods* xvii. 161 He is a little too point device, too obviously got up for the occasion! **1928** D. L. SAYERS *Ld. Peter views Body* xii. 283 His double-breasted suit of navy-blue and his socks, tie, and handkerchief, all scrupulously matched, were a trifle more point-device than the best taste approves. **1958** *Observer* 28 Dec. 7/7 Odd how neat and point-device and sane they all looked.

C. *adv.* Completely, perfectly, to perfection; in every point; = *at point device* in A. *arch.*

c **1500** MEDWALL *Nature* (Brandl) 591, I know dyuers persones..That can you serue alway poynt deuyce. **1530** PALSGR. 436 This shyppe is armed or decked poynte devyse, *ceste nauire est betreschée en tous poynts.* **1533** J. HEYWOOD *Play of Love* C ij, But thus was I deckt at all poyntes poynt deuyce. **1601** SHAKS. *Twel. N.* II. v. 176. **1627** W. SCLATER *Exp. 2 Thess.* (1629) 290 When..point deuice a man must iumpe in Iudgment and practise with vs. **1632** HOLLAND *Cyrupædia* 212 To set every thing about the body, point device by art and number. **1887** *Daily Tel.* 13 Apr. 5/2 These latter..attired point-device in the garb of ancient Athens.

'point-duty. The duty of a police constable stationed at a particular point in a thoroughfare, to regulate the traffic, etc. Also *attrib.*

1888 *Pall Mall G.* 11 Oct. 3/2 A policeman was standing on point duty at the corner of the street, within twenty yards, without..perceiving him. **1894** *Times* 16 Apr. 6/5 No one happened to be near except a constable on point duty. **1901** *Daily Tel.* 14 Nov. 4/3 The policeman on point duty had signalled to the traffic going west to stop. **1908** *Daily Chron.* 30 June 1/3 A point-duty constable..was knocked down..by a taxi-cab. **1967** N. LUCAS *C.I.D.* vi. 72 Ignoring a point-duty policeman's signal to stop. **1974** *Drive* Autumn 62/2 These days, alas, only small boys want to be point-duty policemen!

‖**pointe** (pwɛ̃t). *Dancing.* [Fr.] The tip of the toes. Also, a dance-movement executed on the tip of the toes. Also *attrib.*

1830 R. BARTON tr. *Blasis's Code of Terpsichore* VI. 505 To waltz properly, all the beats, or *tems*, should be clearly marked, being attentive not to turn upon *les pointes*, or toes, in the same beats. **1846** *Musical World* 21 Nov. 587/2 The *pirouette* and the *pointe*, which she achieves with great facility. **1912** J. C. FLITCH *Mod. Dancing & Dancers* iv. 58 The *pointes*..came to be regarded as the highest form of accomplishment. **1912** *Dancing Times* Aug. 449/2 Various Pointe Steps and..Enchaînements of Steps on the Pointes. **1920** *Ibid.* Feb. 413/1 Second and fourth couples run on the pointe under arch round first and third couples. *Ibid.* Dec. 182/2 The damage that can be done by too early pointe work is incalculable. **1949** *Ballet Ann.* III. 93 The advent of the Italian ballerina and her steel-like *pointes* and brilliant *fouettés*. **1959** T. MARA *On your Toes!* (1961) 18/1 In standing correctly on the pointes the dancer stands on the pads of the toes. **1961** S. LESTER in *Ballet here & Now* i. 29 The swift exploitation of the use of the *pointe* for the female dancer. **1974** P. L. MOLDON *Your Bk. of Ballet* ii. 27 Dancing on the tips of the toes (on *pointe*)..enhanced the ballerina's lightness.

pointed ('pɔɪntɪd), *ppl. a.*[1] [f. POINT *v.*[1] and *sb.*[1] + -ED.]

1. a. Having a point or points; tapering to or ending in a point. ***pointed box***: see quot. 1881.

1297 R. GLOUC. (Rolls) 6342 Smot him.. Wiþ a long ipointed [*v.r.* pointed] knif iegged in eiþer side. *c* **1400** MAUNDEVILLE (1839) xiv. 158 Thei [diamonds] ben square and poynted of here owne kynde. **1552** HULOET, Poynted, or hauynge a poynte, *cuspidatus, mucronatus.* **1575** LANEHAM *Let.* (1871) 51 Beautifyed with great Diamons, Emerauds, Rubyes, and Saphyres: poynted, tabld, rok, and roound. **1725** COATS *Dict. Her.*, *Pointed*, a *Cross pointed*, is that which has the Extremities turn'd off into Points by strait Lines. **1747** FRANKLIN *Lett.* Wks. 1887 II. 67 The wonderful effect of pointed bodies, both in drawing off and throwing off the electrical fire. **1860** TYNDALL *Glac.* I. xxii. 158, I saw a row of pointed rocks at some distance below me. **1881** RAYMOND *Mining Gloss.*, *Pointed boxes*, boxes in the form of inverted pyramids or wedges in which ores, after crushing and sizing, are separated in a current of water.

b. *Arch.* In ***pointed arch***, an arch with a pointed crown; hence applied to the style of architecture characterized by this feature: cf. GOTHIC 3 b.

1750 S. WREN in *Parentalia* 273 They had not yet fallen into the Gothick pointed-arch. **1812** RICKMAN *Archit.* (1817) 41 Pointed arches are either equilateral..or drop arches..or lancet arches. **1823** P. NICHOLSON *Pract. Build.* Gloss., *Pointed architecture*, that style vulgarly called Gothic, more properly English. **1848** B. WEBB *Cont. Ecclesiol.* 47 The apse-windows are late Pointed, of two lights trefoiled. **1874** PARKER *Goth. Archit.* I. ii. 21 The First Pointed style in England is..the style of the twelfth century. *a* **1878** SIR G. G. SCOTT *Lect. Archit.* (1879) I. 18 The round-arch variety [was perfected] in the twelfth, and the pointed-arch in the two succeeding centuries.

2. *fig.* Having the quality of penetrating or piercing the sensations, feelings, or mind; piercing, cutting, stinging, pungent, 'sharp'; having point.

1665 DRYDEN *Ind. Emperor* I. ii, Turn hence those pointed Glories of your Eyes. **1701** DE FOE *True-born Eng.* 3 'Tis pointed Truth must manage this Dispute. *a* **1704** T. BROWN *Sat. on Quack* Wks. 1730 I. 62 Th' impartial muse, in pointed stabbing verse, Shall all thy several villanies rehearse. **1769** SIR W. JONES *Pal. Fortune* Poems (1777) 25 A weak defence from hunger's pointed sting. *a* **1839** PRAED *Poems* (1864) II. 92 Some put their trust in answer smart or pointed repartee. **1882** STEVENSON *New Arab. Nts.* (1884) 245 The air was raw and pointed. **1897** *Westm. Gaz.* 10 May 2/3 The most pointed thing to say about a person is that he 'means well'. **1904** E. RICKERT *Reaper* 261 A wee thing with pointed black eyes.

3. Fitted or furnished with tagged points or laces; wearing points; laced. *Obs.* exc. *Hist.*

1508 *Acc. Ld. High Treas. Scotl.* IV. 21 For xj elne satin to be ane pointit cote to the King. **1552** HULOET, Poynted, or tyed wyth poyntes, *ligulatus.* **1904** M. HEWLETT *Queen's Quair* I. vi, Young men, trunked, puffed, pointed, trussed and doubleted.

4. a. Directed, aimed; *fig.* particularly directed or aimed; marked, emphasized, clearly defined, made evident.

1578 WHETSTONE *2nd Pt. Promos & Cass.* I. i. G iij, So ofte as men, with poynted fingers tell Their friendes, my faultes. **1778** MISS BURNEY *Evelina* (1791) II. xxvii. 167 His attention..is so pointed, that it always confuses me. **1798** JANE AUSTEN *Northang. Abb.* xxix, Only ten days ago had he elated her by his pointed regard. **1870** FREEMAN *Norm. Conq.* I. App. 646 The pointed marking out of Thored as 'Eorl'..is an unusual piece of accuracy.

b. Exact to a point; precise.

1727 P. WALKER *Life Peden* (1827) 85, I doubt nothing of the Truth of them in my own Mind, tho' I be not pointed in Time and Place. **1860** GEN. P. THOMPSON *Audi Alt.* III. cxv. 48 The identical member..who was most pointed in showing up the dishonesty of the act inculpated. **1878** GLADSTONE *Prim. Homer* vi. 63 Its harbour is described with pointed correctness. **1893** MRS. OLIPHANT *Lady William* I. viii. 130 How often must I tell you not to be so pointed with your half-hours?

5. a. In various other senses of the verb: see quots.

c **1440** *Promp. Parv.* 406/2 Poyntyd, or prykkyd, *punctatus.* **1659** LEAK *Waterwks.* 29 Another marked with pointed lines. **1874** KNIGHT *Dict. Mech.* I. 168/2 *Pointed Ashlar*, the face-marking done by a pointed tool or one very narrow. *a* **1907** *Mod.* Such is the reading of the pointed Hebrew text. **1934** PRIEBSCH & COLLINSON *German Lang.* 357 In German documents it [*sc.* Anglo-Saxon type] occurs usually in the *pointed* (Lowe: *miniscule*) form. **1947** *Hansard Commons* 15 Dec. 1451 Mr. Lipson asked..if smaller tins of pointed foodstuffs can be provided. **1957** *Encycl. Brit.* XIX. 664/2 The pointed runes were generally known and used in the whole of the Scandinavian North throughout the Middle Ages as the writing of cultured laymen.

b. ***pointed blanket*** = *point blanket.*

1779 in *Beaver* (1935) June 47 Sends samples of five different sorts of Pointed blankets with their respective prices per pair. **1780** in E. E. Rich *Moose Fort Jrnl., 1783–85* 356 We now send..pointed Blankets of different sizes..to be delivered to him. **1926** [see *point blanket* s.v. POINT *sb.*[1] D. 19]. **1956** *Beaver* Summer 50 It can be no coincidence that while Maugenest was in London enquiries were put in hand for *Pointed* blankets.

c. ***pointed fox***: (see quots.). Cf. POINT *v.*[1] 20.

1911 *Directory Fur Trade* (N.Y.) 11 Fine Kamchatka and American Foxes in Sitka, Pointed, Black and Baumarten. **1913** J. W. JONES *Fur-Farming in Canada* iv. 100 Latterly, the Germans have developed a large trade in 'pointed fox', which is an ordinary cheap fox dyed black, and afterwards 'pointed' by sewing in white hairs. **1939** M. BYERS *Designing Women* III. xix. 250 Pointed Fox is red fox dyed black with white hairs stuck into it artificially. **1952** LAPICK & GELLE *Scientific Fur Servicing* 7 In pointed fox the inserted hairs are generally all white. **1969** R. T. WILCOX *Dict. Costume* (1970) 142/1 *Fox, pointed*, the common red fox dyed black and pointed with silvery badger hairs to simulate silver fox.

6. *Comb.*, as ***pointed-arched, -butted, -toed*** adjs., ***-wise*** adv.

1611 FLORIO, *A spicchio*, made pointed-wise, like the streakes of the Sunne. **1891** 'L. MALET' *Wages of Sin* III. v. vi. 33 Presenting his cousin with a fine view of a pointed-toed shoe sole. **1900** in *Archæol. Jrnl.* Mar. 66 The wide pointed-arched window in the west wall. **1928** PEAKE & FLEURE *Steppe & Sown* iii. 46 Pointed-butted axes of jadeite and other hard stone came into use as well as flint. **1962** *Times* 30 Jan. 12/5 Pointed-toed backless shoes.

† '**pointed**, *ppl. a.*[2] *Obs.* [f. POINT *v.*[2] + -ED[1].] = APPOINTED.

1523 SKELTON *Garl. Laurel* 420 Before the quenes grace, In whose court poynted is your place. **1580** SIDNEY *Ps.* XXI. xii, Thou shalt a-row Set them in pointed places. **1596** SHAKS. *Tam. Shr.* III. i. 19 Ile not be tied to howres, nor pointed times. **1697** DRYDEN *Virg. Georg.* IV. 152 At pointed Seasons. **1709** PRIOR *Ode to Col. Villiers* 17 Poems (1711) 136 Pow'r, To hasten or protract the pointed Hour.

pointedly ('pɔɪntɪdlɪ), *adv.* [f. POINTED *ppl. a.*[1] + -LY[2].] In a pointed manner. **a.** With point or piquancy; wittily. **b.** With directness; explicitly; markedly. **c.** With precision or exactitude; exactly, definitely, punctually.

1680 DRYDEN *Pref. Ovid's Ep.* Ess. (Ker) I. 234 He often writ too pointedly for his subject. **1775** in Sparks *Corr. Amer. Rev.* (1853) I. 7 At this post I have pointedly recommended vigilance and care. **1786** WASHINGTON *Writ.* (1891) XI. 18 Whatever agreement is previously made shall be pointedly fulfilled on my part. **1792** MARY WOLLSTONECR. *Rights Wom.* v. 229 The contempt and obloquy that men..have pointedly levelled at the female mind. **1828** *Life Planter Jamaica* 63 The negroes turned out pointedly to the hour. **1870** E. PEACOCK *Ralf Skirl.* I. 168 Pointedly refusing the offered hand. **1895** H. A. KENNEDY in *19th Cent.* Aug. 324 He..has more to say and says it more pointedly.

pointedness ('pɔɪntɪdnɪs). [f. as prec. + -NESS.] The quality of being pointed; chiefly in reference to the expression of thought.

1636 B. JONSON *Discov.* Wks. (Rtldg.) 759/1 The vicious language is vast, and gaping, swelling and irregular: when it contends to be high, full of rock, mountain, and pointedness. **1693** DRYDEN *Disc. Orig. & Progr. Sat.* Ess. (Ker) II. 19 You add that pointedness of thought, which is visibly wanting in our great Roman. **1801** *Hist. Eur.* in *Ann. Reg.* 124 The eulogium..united pointedness and energy with the simplicity of truth. **1843** *P. Parley's Ann.* IV. 113 This pointedness of wing constitutes the great advantage of the falcons as sporting birds. **1882** C. E. TURNER in *Macm. Mag.* XLV. 480 The contrast is brought out with a force that is almost stern in its pointedness.

pointel ('pɔɪntəl). Now *rare.* Forms: 3– **pointel**; also 3 **pontel**, 4 **poyntele, -til**, 4–6 **-tell, -e**, 4–7 **-tel**, 6 **-tyl(l**, *Sc.* **poyntal**, 6–7 **pointell**, 7–8 **-til**, 7–9 **pointal**. [a. OF. *pointel* (mod. *pointeau*) point of a spear, etc. = It. *puntello, pontello* a bodkin, a prick (Florio), dim. of *punto* point; cf. late L. *punctillum* little point, dot, dim. of *punctum.*]

†**1.** A small pointed instrument. **a.** A writing or graving instrument; a stylus, a pencil. (Also erron. written *pointrell, poitrel(l.)* *Obs.* exc. *Hist.*

a **1300** *Cursor M.* 11087 (Gött.) Þan asked þaim sir Zachari, Tablis and a pointel [*Cott.* pontel] tite, And he bigan þe name to write. *c* **1374** CHAUCER *Boeth.* I. pr. i. 2 While þat I... markede my weply compleynte with office of poyntel. **1432–50** tr. *Higden* (Rolls) VI. 331 Iohn Scotte.. was sleyne with poyntells of childer whom he tauȝhte at Malmesbury. **1561** T. NORTON *Calvin's Inst.* III. iv. (1634) 312 The Lord doth..grave them with an yron pointell in an adamant stone. [**1659** HOOLE *Comenius' Vis. World* xci. (1672) 186 The Ancients writ in Tables done over with wax with a brasan poitrel [*stilo*]. **1678** PHILLIPS (ed. 4), *Poitrel*, a Brasen or Iron Instrument, with the sharp end whereof Letters are ingraven, and rubbed out with the broad end.] **1853** ROCK *Ch. of Fathers* III. II. 129 The stilus, or graphium, was called a pointel.

†**b.** (In form *pointal.*) A stiletto or dagger. †**c.** A plectrum. *Obs.*

1513 DOUGLAS *Æneis* VI. x. 46 Now with gymp fingeris doing stringis smyte, And now with.. poyntalis lyte. *Ibid.* VII. xii. 59 Wyth round rok stok suerdis faucht thai in melle, Wyth poyntalis.

2. The pistil or style of a flower; formerly also applied to a stamen. Now *rare* or *Obs.*

1597 GERARDE *Herbal* II. li. 267 Small white flowers with yellow pointels in the middle. **1657** W. COLES *Adam in Eden* ciii, In the middle part of them [lily flowers] do grow small tender Poyntels, tipped with a dusty yellow colour. **1712** tr. *Pomet's Hist. Drugs* I. 166 With a Pointal or Rudiment of a Seed in the Cavity of the Flower. **1770–4** A. HUNTER *Georg. Ess.* (1803) I. 487 The pointal, or female part of the flower. **1785** MARTYN *Rousseau's Bot.* i. (1794) 23 This, taken in its whole, is called the pistil or pointal. **1831** HOWITT *Seasons* (1837) 263 Saffron,..consisting of the pointals of the crocus.

†**3.** A slender style-like organ on the body of an animal, as the 'horn' of a snail, the *halteres* or poisers of a dipterous insect. *Obs.*

1613 PURCHAS *Pilgrimage* (1614) 560 (Creatures in Africa), The Basiliske..is not halfe a foot long, and hath three pointels (Galen saith) on the head. **1689** J. BANISTER in *Phil. Trans.* XVII. 670 These..have growing out of their Body, under each Wing, a small flexible..Pointel, with which they poise their Body. **1713** DERHAM *Phys.-Theol.* VIII. iv. (1727) 366 Such as have but two [wings, have] Pointels, and Poises placed under the Wings, on each Side of the Body.

†**4.** *Glass-blowing.* = PONTIL, PUNTY. *Obs.*

[**1788** REES *Chambers' Cycl.* s.v. *Glass*, They dip an iron rod, or ponteglo, in the melting-pots.] **1865** *Chambers' Encycl.* IV. 779 A little boy now comes forward with an iron rod, the pointel, upon the end of which has been gathered a small lump of metal.

¶An alleged sense 'a floor set into squares, or lozenge forms', in Parker *Gloss. Arch.*, ed. 3, 1840, s.v. *Poyntell* or *Poyntill* (copied in Gwilt 1842–76, Halliwell 1847–78 (*Pointel*), Webster, Knight, Ogilvie, Cassell, *Century Dict.*, Funk's *Standard Dict.*) following Warton *Hist. Eng. Poetry* ix, is an attempt to explain *poynttyl*, an erroneous reading, in the 1553 print of *Piers Plowman's Crede*, of the two words *peynt tyl*, i.e. painted tile.

pointer ('pɔɪntə(r)). [f. POINT[1] + -ER[1].]

†**1.** A maker of points or laces for fastening clothes. *Obs.*

1500 *Nottingham Rec.* III. 72 Ricardi Byrch, poynter. **1520** WHITINTON *Vulg.* (1527) 16 b, In the townes ende be pynners, poynters,..dyers, tanners. **1609** in *Digby Myst.* (1882) p. xxii, Hatters, Poynters, Girdlers.

2. One who points anything, who puts on or sharpens to a point, as a pointer of pins, pencils, etc.

1839 URE *Dict. Arts* 956 The intermediate portions are handed over to the pointer.

3. One who or that which points out. **a.** A person who points or indicates with his finger or otherwise. *rare.* **b.** A rod used by a teacher or lecturer to point to what is delineated or written on a map, diagram, blackboard, or the like.

The meaning in quot. 1621 is doubtful.

1621 FLETCHER *Pilgrim* III. iii, Do'st thou hear boy, thou pointer? **1658** J. SPENCER in Spurgeon *Treas. Dav.* Ps. cxix. 71 God's rod is as the schoolmaster's pointer to the child, pointing out the letter. **1887** *Overland Monthly* (Farmer *Amer.*), On the march the mighty herd sometimes strings out miles in length, and then it has pointers, who ride abreast at the head of the column. **1897** *Daily News* 28 Sept. 6/5 He has died from the results of a blow from either a ruler or pointer. *Mod.* No pointer had been supplied to the lecturer.

c. The index-hand or indicator of a clock, balance, or other instrument.

1667 HOOKE in *Phil. Trans.* II. 544 The distance of the Object-glass from the Pointers. **1672** *Vestry Bks.* (Surtees) 338 For putting on the pointer of the clocke, 6*d.* **1774** M. MACKENZIE *Maritime Surv.* 37 The Pointer of the Vernier. **1834** J. TODD *Lect. Childr.* i. 3 You hear it tick and see the pointers move. **1879** THOMSON & TAIT *Nat. Phil.* I. I. §424 The divisions being read off by a pointer or vernier attached to the frame of the instrument. **1894** BOTTONE *Electr. Instr. Making* (ed. 6) 119 A small pointer..is to be lightly glued to the top of the pivot at right angles to the needle below.

d. An indicator used in whale-fishery to point out to the boats the place of the whale: see quots.

1877 W. H. MACY *There she blows!* 143 The extended 'pointer' (a light pole with a black ball on the end of it, to be used at the masthead, when the boats are down) told us that the whale was off the ship's lee bow. **1887** *Fisheries U.S.* Sect. v. II. 258 *note*, In right whaling, a pointer..is often used. The pointer is a large basket or frame of wood covered with canvas and painted black, placed at the end of a 12 foot pole, used at mast-head and pointed in the direction of the whale.

e. Short for STATION-POINTER.

1875 in KNIGHT *Dict. Mech.*

f. *colloq.* (orig. *U.S.*). A hint, a point; a piece of information; a suggestion.

1884 *Lisbon* (Dakota) *Star* 10 Oct. 5/2 There's a pointer for you! **1887** BULLOCH *Pynours* v. 41 In this fact there seems to be another pointer to the fishing population. **1891** *Anthony's Photogr. Bull.* IV. 247 Let me give any equestrian photographer a pointer. Don't tie your instrument to yourself, tie it to your horse. **1957** V. BRITTAIN *Testament of Experience* I. iii. 104, I liked the sound of the Bill not better than she; it was another 'pointer' towards the impending shadow of war and its threat to human liberty. **1961** *Lancet* 29 July 245/1 Experimental evidence provides some pointers. **1977** J. F. FIXX *Compl. Bk. Running* vii. 82 An experienced runner may occasionally offer some pointers to a friend, but most of the time we coach ourselves. **1977** *Oxford Diocesan Mag.* Nov. 8/3 Other significant pointers to the future.

g. (See quot. 1872.)

1866 in *Nebraska Hist. Mag.* (1932) XIII. 149 After awhile I get my last pointer yoked, drive the whole team around and hitch it on the wagon tongue. **1872** C. H. EDEN *My Wife & I in Queensland* 36 Twelve bullocks is the usual number in a team, the two polers and the leaders being steady old stagers; the pair next to the pole are called the 'pointers'. **1941** BAKER *Dict. Austral. Slang* 55 *Pointers*, two of the bullocks in a team, placed next to the 'polers'.

4. A dog of a breed nearly allied to the true hounds, used by sportsmen to point at or indicate the presence of game, especially birds; on scenting which the dog stands rigidly, with muzzle stretched toward the game, and usually one foot raised. (In quot. 1717, the proper name of a dog.) Also *attrib.*

1717 PRIOR *Alma* I. 319 The sport and race no more he minds; Neglected Tray and Pointer lie: And covies unmolested fly. **1768** PENNANT *Zool.* I. 54 The Pointer, which is a dog of foreign extraction, was unknown to our ancestors. **1784** COWPER *Task* II. 753 Booted sportsmen, oftener seen With belted waist and pointers at their heels. **1797** J. WOODFORDE *Diary* 15 Jan. (1931) V. 5 One of his Pointer Dogs..was gone mad. **1811** JANE AUSTEN *Sense & S.* III. viii. 181 He reminded me of an old promise about a pointer puppy. **1822** J. WOODS *Two Years' Residence Eng. Prairie* 287, I lately saw a young pointer-dog,..that had three days before been bitten by a rattle-snake. **1837** T. BELL *Hist. Brit. Quadrupeds* 217 The Spanish Pointer was formerly well known as a stanch, strong, and useful, but heavy and lazy dog. The English breed, however, is now very much preferred. **1849** J. W. AUDUBON *Western Jrnl.* (1906) 46 Some of the men had stolen a valuable pointer dog. **1859** DARWIN *Orig. Spec.* i. (1873) 25 The English pointer has been greatly changed within the last century. **1979** *Times* 24 Nov. 26/6 (Advt.), *For sale*: Pointer puppies.

5. *pl.* The two stars α and γ in the Great Bear, a straight line through which points nearly to the pole-star. Sometimes also applied to the two stars α and γ in the Southern Cross, which are nearly in a line with the South Pole of the heavens.

1574 BOURNE *Regiment for Sea* vi. (1577) 28 b, If the two Starres of Charles wayne, called the poynters, be due East from the north Starre. **1669** STURMY *Mariner's Mag.* II. x. 76 The lower of the Pointers. The White or North Pointer. **1879** NEWCOMB & HOLDEN *Astron.* 4 The two stars which form the pointers in the constellation *Ursa Major.* **1892** E. REEVES *Homeward Bound* 34 High overhead..the noble Southern Cross and its pointers gleam like a piece of jewelry in a deep blue setting.

†**6.** *pl.* The antennæ of an insect or crustacean.

1664 H. POWER *Exp. Philos.* I. 2 The Flea..hath..two pointers before which grow out of the forehead, by which he tryes and feels all objects. *Ibid.* 11 A Wood-Louse..hath two pointers..like a pair of pincers.

7. *Printing.* A layer-on who secures the register in printing the reverse side by 'threading' the sheet through the point-holes made in printing the first side.

1882 SOUTHWARD *Pract. Printing* II. xxiii. 543 The word 'pointer' has lately come into use to describe a man who can do work requiring exact register, with points. **1888** in JACOBI *Printer's Voc.* 102.

8. *Naut.* (*pl.*) Timbers sometimes fixed diagonally across the hold, to support the beams.

1769 FALCONER *Dict. Marine* (1789) H iij b, The pointers, if any, are..fixed across the hole diagonally to support the beams. **1820** SCORESBY *Arctic Regions* II. 191–3. **1830** *Encycl. Brit.* (ed. 7) XIX. 219/2 In the plates of a Dutch work of the date of 1697, there are diagonal pointers in an athwartship direction. **1867** SMYTH *Sailor's Word-bk.* s.v., All braces placed diagonally across the hold of any vessel, to support the bilge and prevent loose-working, are called pointers.

9. In various technical applications:

a. A name of particular pointed tools used in various trades, for boring, cutting, graving, etc., e.g. a pointed chisel used by stonemasons, a silversmith's pointer. **b.** A bricklayer's tool for clearing out the old mortar between the courses of bricks in a wall which is being pointed. **c.** In U.S., the lever by which a railway switch is moved, a point-lever.

1875 in KNIGHT *Dict. Mech.*

d. A person who does the ornamental work on the backs of gloves.

1903 *Sci. Amer.* Suppl. 24 Jan. 22629/3 Some make the gloves,..others, called 'pointers', work the ornamental lines on the back. **1921** *Dict. Occup. Terms* (1927) §411.

e. The person who lays or points a gun. *U.S.*

1904 *Sci. Amer.* 18 June 475 The turrets are trained by one man, the trainer; and each gun is pointed by another man, the pointer, who fires the gun.

f. The person who 'points' a block of marble, etc.

1911 [see POINT *sb.*[1] A. 21 d].

g. A person who points furs.

1929 *Fur Trade Directory* (N.Y.) 73 James Feuerlicht, Inc. 'The Old Reliable Fur Pointer'. **1930** M. BACHRACH *Fur* xxiii. 431 The other use of the Badger is by a separate branch of the Industry known as the Pointers. These people furnish new hairs for a peltry by a method known as pointing. **1936** F. GROVER *Practical Fur Cutting & Furriery* xv. 23 Badger hairs are also used for pointing of other furs; the pointer taking the skins for pointing ascertains the sort of pointing necessary. **1953** *Fur Trade Directory* (N.Y.) 66 Artistic Fur Pointers. Lydia Silver Fox Pointing Co.

10. [f. POINT *sb.*[1]] With a prefixed numeral: A stag having horns bearing so many points, e.g. ***ten-pointer, fourteen-pointer***, etc.

1893 *Westm. Gaz.* 18 Sept. 6/3 The magnificent 20-pointer shot..in Glenquoich is said to be the only stag of the kind ever killed in a Scottish forest. **1899** H. MAXWELL in *Pall Mall G.* 3 Oct. 3/2, I stood beside a ten-pointer.

11. *U.S.* A herdsman riding at the head of a herd of cattle on the march to keep it going in the desired direction.

1869 *Overland Monthly* III. 126 On the march the mighty herd sometimes strings out miles in length, and then it has 'pointers', who ride abreast of the head of the column, and 'siders', who keep the stragglers out of the chaparral. **1908** *Pacific Monthly* Mar. 324/2 The pointer is the herdsman who rides at the head of a straggling herd of cattle on the march, a sort of Cowboy John the Baptist. **1943** L. V. HAMNER *Short Grass* 50 Two men, his best, were put near the front of the line... These were the pointers.

12. Either of two sharks belonging to the family Isuridæ, the ***blue pointer***, *Isurus glaucus*, or the ***white pointer***, *Carcharodon carcharias*.

1882 J. E. TENISON-WOODS *Fishes & Fisheries N.S.W.* iv. 95 On the appearance of a 'blue pointer' among boats fishing for schnapper..the general cry is raised. **1896** F. G. AFLALO *Sketches Nat. Hist. Austral.* III. 222 The Blue-Pointer..is the favourite shark of that particular form of fiction which passes for popular natural history. *Ibid.* 223 Such are the chief sharks, the others being the huge White-Pointer [etc.]. **1963** H. W. MCCORMICK et al. *Shadows in Sea* iv. 101 The Mako shark of the western Atlantic is a very close relative of the Blue Pointer (*Isurus glaucus*) of the Indian and Pacific Oceans. *Ibid.*, The Blue Pointer, in turn, is a name given by some South African Fishermen to the shark elsewhere known as the Great White, called in Australia the White Death or White Pointer. **1973** *Parade* (Melbourne) Sept. 63/1 The shark was a white pointer, of the maneater variety. **1975** *Daily Colonist* (Victoria, B.C.) 20 Dec. 7/6 Terry Page also offered odds in favour of Australian diver Wally Gibbons killing the white pointer shark before it kills him.

13. *Canad.* A rowing boat, pointed at both ends and having a shallow draught, used by loggers.

1901 'R. CONNOR' *Man from Glengarry* 13 Swiftly the pointer shot down the current, the swaying bodies and swinging oars in perfect rhythm with the song that rose and fell with melancholy but musical cadence. **1947** J. J. ROWLANDS *Cache Lake Country* 96 And all the while men in pointers..big boats with high pointed ends, move about picking up drivers, working logs off rocks. **1950** J. HAMBLETON *Abitibi Adventure* 140 They would use 'pointers', twenty-foot heavily built craft with steeply sloping sides, which seemed very tippy but actually were the most practical craft ever devised for Canadian logging. **1961** PRICE & KENNEDY *Notes on Hist. Renfrew County* 156 At the suggestion of J. R. Booth, who wanted a useful river craft, John Cockburn in 1883 designed the 'pointer', a sharp-pointed boat that is still widely used in the lumbering business. **1964** *Canad. Geogr. Jrnl.* Feb. 67/3 If you ask Emmett Chartrand about the driving boat or 'pointer' he has a faraway look when he answers, '—— used them, wore them out, broke them.' **1970** *Canad. Geogr. Mag.* Feb. 51/1 But now that Mr. John A. Cockburn has retired and his family's boatbuilding workshop has been demolished, the red Pointer will slowly disappear from the Canadian scene.

14. *Comb.* **pointer reading**, the reading of an instrument as shown by a pointer; also *fig.*

1933 *Mind* XLII. 108 The reduction of the objects of physics to pointer-readings is not for him..a mark of the finality of physics. **1961** *Listener* 17 Aug. 245/2 There are no public pointer-readings in religion. **1967** *Philos.* XLII. 285 The doctrine that science is all about pointer-readings.

pointful ('pɔɪntfʊl), *a.* [f. POINT *sb.*[1] + -FUL.] Full of point; apposite, pertinent. So **'pointfulness**.

1897 *Daily Tel.* 4 Jan. 5/4 Similarly, and with greater pointfulness, it was remarked that the Select Committee..never consulted any person who was not in full work. **1931** *Cath. Gaz.* Feb. 71/2 The story—old, even apocryphal, it may be, but certainly typical and pointful—of Queen Victoria. **1960** *Guardian* 15 July 6/5 The guileless burbling is often very entertaining, and sometimes even pointful. **1970** *Daily Tel.* 27 June 7 Boulez will agree that for such randomness to be pointful the difference between one realisation and another needs to be rendered perceptible. **1976** P. DONOVAN *Relig. Lang.* vii. 81 A surrounding describable in words sets the act in the appropriate light, making it profound and religiously pointful. **1977** *Gramophone* Dec. 1164/1 Another pointful contrast came when we compared this latest RCA version of *La forza del destino* with that company's 1965 version also recorded with Leontyne Price. **1978** *Hi-fi News* Dec. 159/3 The finale is particularly fine, imbued with an urgency and pointfulness that has rarely been equalled.

'point group. *Math.* and *Cryst.* [f. POINT *sb.*[1] + GROUP *sb.*] †**a.** [tr. G. *punktgruppe* (Brill & Noether 1873, in *Nachrichten von der K. Ges. der Wiss. zu Göttingen* 117).] A set of points. *Obs.*

1895 *Proc. London Math. Soc.* XXVI. 495 The following paper deals with the properties of point-groups in relation to algebraic curves drawn through them. **1900** *Rep. Brit. Assoc. Adv. Sci. 1900* 121 (*heading*) Report on the present state of the theory of point-groups. **1900** K. FINK *Hist. Math.* 240 This theorem..introduced point groups, or systems of points of intersection of two curves, into geometry.

b. Any subgroup of the symmetry group of a sphere; *esp.* any of the thiry-two sets of symmetry operations which are used to classify crystal types.

[**1896** *Amer. Jrnl. Math.* XVIII. 172 We mark on the faces of the regular bodies a general point group.] **1903** H. HILTON *Math. Crystallogr.* iv. 48 Finite groups whose operations all leave one point unmoved are called point-groups. **1924** R. W. G. WYCKOFF *Structure of Crystals* i. 21 The point groups, or classes of crystal symmetry, thus formed may be uniquely defined either by stating their symmetry properties or, more analytically, by giving the coördinates of the equivalent points which arise from any arbitrarily chosen point by the operation of each of their elements of symmetry. **1950** W. J. MOORE *Physical Chem.* xiii. 364 The possible combinations of these symmetry elements that can occur in crystals have been shown to number exactly 32. These define the 32 crystallographic point groups, which determine the 32 crystal classes. **1973** T. JANSSEN *Crystallographic Groups* iii. 72 Each subgroup of *O*(3) is called a point group, because it leaves the origin invariant. Point groups occur as symmetry groups of molecules and of atoms in a crystal.

-pointic, *a.* *Math.* [arbitrarily f. POINT *sb.*[1] + -IC.] An element of adjectives, as ***two-pointic, three-pointic, n-pointic***, = having, pertaining to, or passing through two, three, or *n* points.

1879 SALMON *Higher Plane Curves* vi. 214 An ordinary (two-pointic) contact of two branches of the curve.

‖**pointillage** (pwɛ̃tijaʒ). [F., f. *pointiller* to dot: see -AGE.] 'Dotting; in Therapeutics, term for massage with the finger-tips' (*Syd. Soc. Lex.*).

1888 D. MAGUIRE *Art of Massage* iii. (ed. 4) 48 Pointillage vibrations, or pointed vibrations..by striking with the points of the fingers formed into a small or a large circle.

‖**poin'tille.** *Obs. rare.* [F. *pointille* (pwɛ̃tij), ad. It. *puntiglio*, dim. of *punto* point; L. type **puncticulum*, dim. of *punctum* point.] A small point, a trifle, a fine distinction; = PUNCTILIO.

1626 C. POTTER *Hist. Quarrels* 427 The Cardinall..omitting pointilles and subtilties, did not say at Venice all that which the Court of Rome had wished.

‖**pointillé** (pwɛ̃tije), *a.* (*sb.*) [F., pa. pple. of *pointiller* to mark with small points or dots, f. *pointille* (see prec.), L. type **puncticulāre*.] Ornamented with designs engraved or drawn with a sharp-pointed tool or style. Also *fig.* and as *sb.*

1903 *Tregaski's Catal.* Jan. 10/1 Old French Locket Case, ..red morocco faded, gold tooled with small pointille scrolls and border of similar style. **1931** A. ESDAILE *Student's Man. Bibliogr.* vi. 207 The sprays are lighter, not only in themselves but because impressed by pointillé tools, i.e. tools with a dotted surface. **1933** T. E. LAWRENCE *Let.* 1 Aug. (1938) 773 His style disintegrates and not integrates, this time. Too pointillé. **1940** *Proc. Prehistoric Soc.* VI. 173 Sherds ornamented with three bands decorated in pointillé. **1964** H. HODGES *Artifacts* iv. 78 Strictly speaking, a surface that has been backgrounded by stabbing all over with a small pointed punch is referred to as *pointillé*, although some archaeologists are in the habit of using the term to describe any surface with a fine dot pattern, be the dots bosses or pits. **1974** *Times Lit. Suppl.* 23 Aug. 910/2 The English binders showed a liveliness and originality... The new designs included..the all-over pattern, introduced in the 1670s and generally composed of *pointillé* flowers and drawer-handle tools.

pointillism ('pwɛ̃tɪlɪz(ə)m, 'pwæn-). Also ‖-isme. [ad. F. *pointillisme*, f. *pointiller*: see prec. and -ISM.] **1.** A method, invented by French impressionist painters, of producing luminous effects by crowding a surface with small spots of various colours, which are blended by the eye.

1901 *Daily Chron.* 22 Oct. 3/2 Segantini..has broken the *banalité* of Alpine lines by the shimmering of his *pointillisme*. **1901** [see NEO-IMPRESSIONISM]. **1902** *Nation* (N.Y.) 2 Jan. 16/3 He [Segantini] painted without any adherence to systematic process, but used pointillisme as it served his purpose. **1904** *Athenæum* 2 Apr. 441/1 Modern Dutch artists..seem to be taking pointillism with a stolid seriousness which its inventors never can have intended. **1947** BERGSTRÖM & TAYLOR tr. *Bergström's Dutch Still-Life Painting 17th Cent.* vi. 232 His broad and free handling is set off by a spirited *pointillisme* in some passages. **1976** *New Yorker* 15 Mar. 28/2 The murals are a triumph of Japanese pointillism.

2. *transf.* spec. *Mus.*, the breaking up of the musical texture into thematic, rhythmic, and tonal fragments.

1934 C. LAMBERT *Music Ho!* I. 32 In the pointillism of its scoring, *La Mer* represents the apex of Debussy's impressionist manner. **1959** *Times* 4 Apr. 10/2 Hamilton's music has been moving towards serialism for some time, and in this sonata he finds himself up to the elbows in neo-Webernist *pointillisme*. **1972** S. HYNES *Edwardian Occasions* 166 Mrs [Beatrice] Webb..created another character..by a large number of small strokes—a kind of literary pointillism. **1973** *Daily Tel.* 19 Mar. 14/2 A happy synthesis of recent techniques and time-hallowed devices, of chords and clusters, speech-slides and sung intervals, pointillism and canon. **1976** *Visible Language* X. 59 A piece of the once-voguish art of typewriter pointillisme.

pointillist ('pwɛ̃tɪlɪst, 'pwæn-), *sb.* (*a.*). Also ‖-iste [ad. F. *pointilliste*: see prec.] **A.** *sb.* An artist who follows the style of pointillism.

1891 *Academy* 6 June 544/3 'Impressionists', 'tâchistes', 'plein airistes', and 'pointillistes', to use the jargon of the day. **1892** *Mag. of Art* p. xxxv/1 Among the painters who devote themselves to the application of colour in minute subdivision—called *pointillistes*, which may be freely rendered stipplers—the most conspicuous were M. Signac and M. Van Rysselberghe. **1893** *Westm. Gaz.* 18 Mar. 3/3 Mad imaginings of the various modern schools of impressionists, pointillistes, and so on. **1899** *Daily News* 30 May 9/3 Of the Seasons by the pointillist Pissarro, 'L'Automne' is the most realistic and spacious. **1916** A. BENNETT *Lion's Share* xii. 93 Also she was acquainted with the names and styles of all known modern painters from pointillistes to cubistes. **1929** E. LINKLATER *Poet's Pub* ii. 34 We ought to learn from the pointillistes. Put your colour on pure, in spots, and you get a luminous spectrum in verse as well as in painting. **1954** W. LEWIS *Demon of Progress in Arts* I. v. 23 The theory was that the colours would mix in the eye of the spectator—they must never be allowed to mix anywhere else... The Pointillistes adhered most rigidly to this rule. **1961** *Encycl. World Art* V. 184 By employing the color theories of Michel Chevreul..and refining the principle of optical mixture from brush strokes to tiny dots, the pointillists arrived at..'the logical consequence of impressionism'. **1963** F. GETTINGS *Golden Pleasure Book of Art* 59 Because of the way Seurat and his friends used small points of colour, they were called *Pointillistes*.

B. *attrib.* passing into *adj.*

1902 *Encycl. Brit.* XXIX. 414/1 There are several fallacies however, theoretical and practical, in this 'spectral palette' and pointillist method. **1905** *Sat. Rev.* 11 Feb. 174 The 'Neo-Impressionist' or Pointillist painting. **1934** C. LAMBERT *Music Ho!* I. 25 The methods of the pointillist painters have something in common with the use of the orchestra as displayed in Debussy's works. **1940** O. SITWELL *Left Hand, Right Hand!* II. 132 Those figures, full of latent movement, seen in a pointillist picture. **1971** [see DIVISIONISM]. **1975** D. THOMAS *Impressionists* 87 He [*sc.* Van Gogh] met Pissaro, who was then moving towards the pointillist technique of Seurat.

b. *transf.*

1921 E. SAPIR *Language* 243 We cannot assimilate the luxurious periods of Latin nor the pointilliste style of the Chinese classics. **1934** C. LAMBERT *Music Ho!* I. 46 This pointillist orchestration gives to many of Schönberg's works an impressionist effect in performance that an inspection of the score with the eye alone would hardly lead one to expect. **1958** *Observer* 27 Apr. 16/4 Thackeray's..effective 'pointillist' method. **1959** *Ibid.* 14 June 24/3 Although its style was largely *pointilliste*, the music did not strike me as derivative. **1970** *Daily Tel.* 30 Apr. 16/5 A certain lack of eloquence became most clearly discernible during a few melodious lines given to the oboe in this largely pointillist piece. **1976** *Times Lit. Suppl.* 1 Oct. 1229/4 Neither the satire nor the pointillist plotting adds up to much that is coherent and compelling.

Hence **pointi'llistic** *a.*

1922 H. Crane *Let.* 19 Apr. (1965) 84 All this talk of Matty's is..metallic and pointillistic. **1954** *Grove's Dict. Mus.* (ed. 5) IX. 226/1 His [*sc.* Webern's] next compositions ..are still more highly concentrated, still more transparent and pointillistic in texture. **1972** *Village Voice* (N.Y.) 1 June 44/3 Philip Corner adds sporadic pointillistic piano gestures. **1977** *Times* 22 Oct. 10/6 A new and exclusive pointillistic dyeing method... You can shade your carpet from dark to pale.

pointing ('pɔɪntɪŋ), *vbl. sb.*[1] [f. POINT *v.*[1] + -ING[1].] The action of POINT *v.*[1], or its result.

1. †**a.** Pricking or marking with a pointed instrument. *Obs. rare.*

c **1440** *Promp. Parv.* 407/1 Poyntynge, or prykkynge, *punctacio.*

†**b.** *Hunting.* (*concr.*) The foot-print or track left by a beast. *Obs.*

c **1410** *Master of Game* (MS. Digby 182) xxxiv, þat somme man mete þer with and bloweth þe reghtes and halowes, or elles þat he fynde her poyntynge, or pryckynge.

c. The preparation of slates for roofing. ? *Obs.*

1703 T. N. *City & C. Purchaser* 244 The Pointing of Slates..is hewing them, and making them fit for the Work.

d. *Printing.* Placing the sheets on the points of the press. See POINT *sb.*[1] B. 4.

1880 *Printing Times* 15 Feb. 31/1 The pointing and taking-off at the machines are done by intelligent-looking boys or young men.

e. *Sculpture.* (See quot.) Also **pointing-up**.

1845 *Encycl. Metrop.* V. 465/2 The construction of these instruments for pointing is not always the same, but the principle on which they act is exactly similar. **1883** *Mag. of Art* Oct. 514/1 Here is done the pointing, as it is called; the marking out with mathematical accuracy upon the marble the points that shall guide the workman whose labour it is to block out from the rough..the potentiality of a statue, its rude semblance. **1947** J. C. Rich *Materials & Methods of Sculpture* ix. 272 The process of pointing consists of marking with pencil all projections and recessions or 'points' on the model, which is generally a plaster cast, and making position measurements with the adjustable rods of the pointing machine, which are capable of measuring at intervals a fraction of an inch apart. **1969** L. R. Rogers *Sculpture* vi. 199 The pointing-up in marble of clay models in a mechanical fashion by craftsmen assistants. **1974** *Encycl. Brit. Micropædia* VIII. 68/1 Although pointing has limitations as a technique of creative sculpture, it has been used widely, especially in the 19th century.

2. a. The insertion of stops; punctuation; the marks made, or the method of punctuating.

c **1440** *Promp. Parv.* 407/1 Poyntynge, or pawsynge in redynge, *punctuacio.* **1579** Fulke *Heskins's Parl.* 456, I passe ouer howe M. Heskins hath corrupted Tertullian by false pointing. **1706** A. Bedford *Temple Mus.* viii. 162 The Sence ..may seem to require another Pointing. **1896** T. L. De Vinne *Moxon's Mech. Exerc., Printing* 420 The compositor should amend bad spelling and pointing. **1896** J. Hunter *Hymns Faith & Life* (new ed.) Pref., Mr. B. Sykes..has revised the pointing of the Psalms and Canticles.

b. In Semitic languages: The insertion of the vowel (and other) points; the system of doing this.

1659 J. Owen *Integr. & Purity Hebr. & Grk. Text* Wks. 1853 XVI. 376 What is the state and condition of the present Hebrew pointing. **1847** J. Kirk *Cloud Dispelled* x. 153 In the Hebrew the sense is obscured by false pointing.

3. a. Furnishing with a point; sharpening.

1875 Knight *Dict. Mech.* 1705 A finer file-wheel by which the process of pointing is finished.

b. *Naut.* (See quot. 1867.) Also *concr.* The tapered end of a rope.

1840 R. H. Dana *Bef. Mast* xxxv. 134 The neat work upon the rigging,—the knots, Flemish eyes, splices, seizings, coverings, pointings, and graffings. *c* **1860** H. Stuart *Seaman's Catech.* 31 Take every alternate nettle and lay along the pointing. **1867** Smyth *Sailor's Word-bk.*, *Pointing*, the unlaying and tapering the end of a rope, and weaving some of its yarns about the diminished part.

4. The removing of points.

1879 Webster Suppl. (citing Horsford). **1884** Knight *Dict. Mech.* Suppl., *Pointing*, a preliminary in the preparation of grain for the mill in the modern process; it consists in rubbing off the points of the grain, clipping the brush, and removing the germ end.

5. The filling up with special strong mortar of the exterior face of the joints in brickwork; *concr.* the protecting facing thus given to the joints. (In the earlier quots. applied to a similar operation in reference to the tiles or slates of a roof.)

flat pointing: that in which the mortar is left even with the wall. ***tuck pointing***: that in which the mortar slightly projects from the joints, and the lines of mortar have parallel edges contrasting in colour with the central part.

1483–5 *Rec. St. Mary at Hill* 120 Payde to a tyler for iiij dayes & di. in poyntyng of dyuers houses. **1502–3** *Durham Acc. Rolls* (Surtees) 102 Pro le puyntyng super le caponhous. **1609** *Vestry Bks.* (Surtees) 61 Item payed to Nichollas Yonger for laying the lead and for pointing of the slates, xviij d. **1793** Smeaton *Edystone L.* §228 The swell had washed some of the pointing out of the exterior joints. *Ibid.* §233 We took this..opportunity of carefully making good all our pointings and groutings. **1825** J. Nicholson *Operat. Mechanic* 354 Pointing..consists in raking out some of the mortar from the joints, and filling them again with blue mortar. **1881** Young *Ev. Man his own Mechanic* §1201 In building there are two kinds of pointing, distinguished as flat pointing and tuck pointing, the latter being more ornamental than the former.

6. a. The action of indicating or directing; the indication of place or direction, as with the finger or the point of anything; expression by sign or gesture, dumb show; also *fig.* a prompting, impulse; a hint in words.

1553 *Short Catech.* in *Lit. & Doc. Edw. VI* (1844) 495 That by certain questions, as it were by pointing, the ignorant might be instructed. **1553** Eden *Treat. Newe Ind.* (Arb.) 34 With sygnes and poyntinges (as the dumme are wont to speake with the dumme). **1648** Boyle *Seraph. Love* xiii. (1700) 76 The Needle's pointing at the Poles. **1726** Swift *Gulliver* III. i. 181, I found by their pointing towards me..that they plainly discovered me. **1742** Richardson *Pamela* IV. 318 One of those natural Pointings, as I may call it, that is implanted in every Creature, teaching it to chuse its Good, and to avoid its Evil. **1873** M. Arnold *Lit. & Dogma* (1876) 98 The Old Testament abounds..in pointings and approximations to it.

b. Of a yacht, etc.: The action of sailing with the prow close to the wind.

1899 *Daily News* 17 Oct. 6/6 The Shamrock footed the faster, but the Columbia counteracted this by her superior pointing. **1901** *Daily Chron.* 28 Aug. 6/1 The spin showed that she is not only very fast in a breeze that puts her rail awash, but that she is a wonder at pointing.

c. Of a pointer or other dog: see POINT *v.*[1] 11.

1877 J. Gibson in *Encycl. Brit.* VII. 328/2 This habit [of crouching], like that of pointing, is probably..'merely the exaggerated pause of an animal about to spring on its prey'. *Ibid.* 330/1 The strength of this pointing propensity.

7. The coming of an abscess to a point or head; *concr.* the conical head thus formed.

1858 Mayne *Expos. Lex.*, *Pointing*, term for the conical softish projection, of a light yellow colour, observable in an abscess when nearly ripe. **1884** M. Mackenzie *Dis. Throat & Nose* II. 451 Tumours..which after 'pointing' opened spontaneously.

8. a. The disposition of the points (POINT *sb.*[1] B. 3 f) on a railway.

1902 *Westm. Gaz.* 29 Sept. 6/2 The cause of the accident was undoubtedly an error in the pointing.

b. The disposition and colouring of the points in a cat's fur. Cf. POINT *sb.*[1] A. 27 c.

1978 R. Hill *Pinch of Snuff* v. 50 The room was filled with cats..of various ages and pointings.

9. *Needlework.* A kind of ornamental stitch.

1888 *Catholic Househ.* 1 Sept. 14/1 The fine needlework on muslin which includes 'veining', 'stroking', 'pointing' and 'lace stitching'.

†**10.** *Fishing.* (?) The action of using the point of the rod as a means of hooking a fish: a practice followed by poachers. *Sc. Obs.*

1860 *Act 23 & 24 Vict.* c. 45 §1 That it shall not be lawful ..to fish for trout or other fresh water fish.. with any net, ..or by striking the fish with any instrument, or by pointing. **1902** *Act 2 Edw. VII.* c. 29 §2 Fishing for trout..by what is known as double rod fishing, or cross line fishing, or set lines,..or by striking the fish..or by pointing.

11. *Furs.* The insertion of hairs into a pelt, usu. to repair damage or to simulate another fur. Cf. POINT *v.*[1] 20.

1900 *Fur Trade Rev.* 1 May 213/2 Pointing will be one of the popular methods of enhancing the attractiveness of some of the most desirable furs. **1910** *Encycl. Brit.* XI. 354/1 The process of inserting white hairs is called in the trade 'pointing', and is either done by stitching them in with a needle or by adhesive caoutchouc. **1922** W. E. Austin *Princ. & Pract. Fur Dressing* i. 7 Badger hair is very extensively used for 'pointing'. **1930** M. Bachrach *Fur* xix. 275 Rubbed spots on the rumps are judged according to the damaged area, which, in the Silver Fox, can be somewhat restored to its original appearance by the process of pointing. **1936** F. Grover *Practical Fur Cutting & Furriery* xv. 22 Pointing of furs is often resorted to, to make an imitation of another fur. **1950** *N.Z. Jrnl. Agric.* June 597/1 Pointing refers to the practice of glueing in white hairs to improve inferior silver fox furs. **1952** Lapick & Gelle *Scientific Fur Servicing* 4 Pointing may be detected by the fact that the badger hairs used are glued in groups of two or three to the natural fox hairs and the leather.

12. *attrib.* and *Comb.* in names of things used for pointing (see quots. and various senses of POINT *v.*[1]), as ***pointing-breed***, ***-dog***, ***-forge***, ***-trowel***, ***-wire***; **pointing-bone** *Anthrop.*, a bone, or apparatus consisting of bones, and usually a string made of woven hair, used by Australian Aborigines in a secret ritual to bring about the death or illness of the person at whom it is pointed; also *attrib.*; **pointing-machine**, (*a*) (see quot. 1875); (*b*) an apparatus used in sculpture for taking points; †**pointing-mark** = *pointing-stock*; †**pointing-ribbon**, a ribbon used as a lace or point (POINT *sb.*[1] B. 5); so **pointing-silk**; **pointing-rods**, rods used in the exercise of guns and mortars; **pointing-stick** *Anthrop.*, a stick used for the same purpose as a pointing-bone; †**pointing-stock**, a person pointed at; an object of scorn, derision, or ridicule.

1839 Ure *Dict. Arts* 956 A carrier, which takes the pin to the *pointing apparatus. **1904** Spencer & Gillen *Northern Tribes of Central Austral.* xiv. 459 The pointing apparatus.. consists of a long strand of human hair-string, to one end of which five small *pointing-bones are affixed. **1959** S. H. Courtier *Death in Dream Time* v. 50 He..saw a piece of bone, sharp at one end, blunt at the other, and bound round the middle with strands of black fur or hair..a native pointing bone or death bone. **1965** *Austral. Encycl.* I. 67/1 The 'pointing bone' sorcery (widely distributed throughout southern and central northern Australia). **1754–6** *Connoisseur* No. 64 (1767) II. 224 [Dogs] of the *Pointing-breed. **1752** Fielding *Amelia* v. iv, A great *Pointing-dog bit him through the Leg. **1900** H. Lawson *On Track* 139 We would stand by his *pointing forge when he'd be sharpening picks in the early morning. **1875** Knight *Dict. Mech.*, **Pointing-machine*, one for pointing rails, pickets, matches, etc. **1886** *Encycl. Brit.* XXI. 571/2 Partly by eye and partly with the constant help of the pointing machine, which is used to give any required measurements, the workman almost completes the marble statue, leaving only the finishing touches to be done by the sculptor. **1947** J. C. Rich *Materials & Methods of Sculpture* ix. 271 There is evidence that during the Late Hellenistic period the Romans used a primitive version of the pointing machine, and this mechanical device may partly account for the large number of Roman copies of Greek sculpture. **1959** P. & L. Murray *Dict. Art & Artists* 249 A pointing machine measures the depth from a given vertical, of, for example, the receding planes of the nose of a plaster cast and transfers the measurement to a hole drilled in the marble block. **1592** Kyd *Murther I. Brewen* Wks. (1901) 292 Suffer mee not to be a *poynting marke for others, and a shame among my neighbours. **1572** in Cunningham *Revels at Court* (Shaks. Soc.) 19 *Poynting Ribbon of golde sylv[r] and sylke 102 yardes at viij[d] the yarde. **1591** Percivall *Sp. Dict.*, *Trena o trença*, a lace, a pointing ribbon, *taenia, offendix.* **1859** F. A. Griffiths *Artil. Man.* (1862) 121 The mortar is..laid, not directly on the object, but upon two pickets, called **pointing rods.* **1571** *Inventory* in Beck *Draper's Dict.* 190, ij peces and ix yeardes of *pointinge silk, 6*s.* 8*d.* **1904** Spencer & Gillen *Northern Tribes of Central Austral.* xiii. 433 A Thakomara man of the Karinji totem..had special *pointing sticks. **1959** *Chambers's Encycl.* XIV. 629/2 He [*sc.* the person who has caused illness or death] can be put out of the way by means of the 'pointing stick' or 'pointing bone' made efficacious by the spells of witch or sorcerer (usually a man). **1593** Shaks. *2 Hen. VI*, II. iv. 46, I, his forlorne Duchesse, Was made a wonder, and a *pointing stock. **1606** G. W[oodcocke] *Hist. Ivstine* xix. 75 Not to liue pleasantly, but to be a pointing stock for the multitude, and a remembrancer of calamities. **1703** Moxon *Mech. Exerc.* 249 A small *Pointing Trowel, to go into sharp Angles. **1875** Knight *Dict. Mech.*, **Pointing-wire*, an iron wire with a loop at one end, used for sighting mortars by, when the proper line of fire has once been found.

pointing, *vbl. sb.*[2]: see POINT *v.*[2]

pointing ('pɔɪntɪŋ), *ppl. a.* [f. POINT *v.*[1] + -ING[2].] That points, in various senses of the vb.

1630 Milton *Epit. Shaks.* 4 Or that his hallow'd reliques should be hid Under a Star-ypointing Pyramid. **1667** —— *P.L.* I. 223 The flames Drivn backward slope their pointing spires. **1693** Dryden *Persius* i. (1697) 408 To see The Crowd, with pointing Fingers, cry, That's he. **1880** Barwell *Aneurism* 61 The tumor..became conical like a pointing abscess.

b. ***pointing doors*** (in a canal, etc.), two doors of a sluice closing against each other in a point or mitre, or at an angle, so as to resist the pressure of the water; ***pointing sills***, also called ***pointings***, the sills of such doors.

1795 J. Phillips *Hist. Inland Navig.* Add. 178 A new sea sluice, with pointing doors to sea and land. *Ibid.*, The new cut..is to be not less than four feet below the pointings of the present sluice. [A depth of '4 feet below the pointings' means 4 feet below the upper surface of the sills of the lock or sluice, called pointing sills or pointings. (H. Congreve, M. Inst. C.E., Manchester.)]

'pointingly, *adv. rare.* [f. POINTING *ppl. a.* + -LY[2].] In a way that points out; pointedly.

1607 B. Jonson *Volpone* Ded., Where haue I bin particular? Where personall, except to..creatures (for their insolencies) worthy to be tax'd? or to which of these so pointingly, as he might not, either ingeniously haue confest, or wisely dissembled his disease?

'point 'lace. [f. POINT *sb.*[1] A. 32 + LACE *sb.* 6.] Lace made with the needle on a parchment pattern, as distinguished from that made with bones or bobbins on a pillow. Also *attrib.*

1672 *Lond. Gaz.* No. 736/4 A Lawn Pocket handkerchief, ..laced round with a fine Point lace about 4 fingers broad. **1714** *Fr. Bk. of Rates* 41 Furniture for Beds of raised Point-Lace, &c. 6 per Cent. *ad valorem.* **1775** Mrs. Harris in *Priv. Lett. Ld. Malmesbury* (1870) I. 311 Mrs. Howard had a point-lace trimming that cost 500 l. **1881** A. Lang *Library* 65 The..pattern of the gilding resembles the Venetian point-lace. **1882** A. S. Cole in *Encycl. Brit.* XIV. 184/1 Drawn and cut works were ancient forms of embroidery which directly developed into point lace.

Hence **point-laced** *a.*, adorned with point lace.

1665 *Intelligencer* 5 June II. 402 Six Handkerchers,..one point-laced set on Tiffany.

pointless ('pɔɪntlɪs), *a.* [f. POINT *sb.*[1] B. + -LESS.]

1. Without a point; having a rounded or blunt end; blunt.

a **1330** *Syr Degarre* 1047 The Fader amerueiled wes Whi his sword was point les. *a* **1548** Hall *Chron., Rich. III* 25 b, After the procession folowed therle of Northumberlande with a poincteless sword naked. **1687** Dryden *Hind & P.* II. 420 You lay that pointless clergy-weapon by, And to the laws, your sword of justice, fly. **1791** Cowper *Iliad* xx. 539 For I wield also not a pointless beam. **1848** Dickens *Dombey* xxvii, 'My pencils are all pointless', she said.

2. Without point or force (POINT *sb.*[1] B. 10); ineffective, meaningless. Also (in the sense of POINT *sb.*[1] A. 29d), without purpose or advantage; having no good effect.

1726 POPE *Odyss.* xx. 448 The suitors..aim to wound the Prince with pointless wit. **1760** WESLEY *Jrnl.* 7 Aug. (1827) III. 13 Why should a little pointless raillery make us ashamed? **1844** DISRAELI *Coningsby* III. iv, He said something rather pointless about admiring everything that is beautiful. **1884** *Manch. Exam.* 1 Dec. 3/1 This is a pointless little story. **1934** E. WAUGH *Handful of Dust* ii. 33 It sometimes seems to me rather pointless keeping up a house this size if we don't now and then ask some other people to stay in it. **1954** I. MURDOCH *Under Net* xiii. 179 It seems pointless to conceal our identity. Sammy would guess it anyway as soon as we announced our terms. **1966** H. ROSEVEARE *Give me this Mountain* i. 18 Without Him, it was a weary, stupid, empty, pointless, useless life. **1970** G. F. NEWMAN *Sir, You Bastard* v. 147 Flowers didn't occur to Sneed until he had arrived at the hospital, and there the gesture was pointless. **1978** M. BIRMINGHAM *Sleep in Ditch* 193 'He died..soon after six.'.. 'S-so all last night's h-horror was quite pointless.'

3. Of a competitor or side: Not having scored a point. Of a game or contest: In which no point is scored.

1882 *Daily News* 17 Feb. 3/5 Ben-y-Lair..was beaten almost pointless. **1891** *Ibid.* 6 Nov. 2/6 The latter did not long remain pointless, and after a long run by Hubbard, Fegan registered a try. **1892** *Standard* 3 Oct. 7/6 A pointless draw was the result of the meeting.

4. Having no characteristic or distinctive marks.

1879 STEVENSON *Trav. Cevennes* 26 It was the most pointless labyrinth.

Hence '**pointlessly** *adv.*; '**pointlessness**.

1885 *Sat. Rev.* 7 Nov. 599 The greatest charm of Lord Iddesleigh's performance was, to speak paradoxically, its pointlessness. **1894** H. DRUMMOND *Ascent Man* 436 It is not the monotony of life which destroys men, but its pointlessness. **1895** *Funk's Stand. Dict.*, Pointlessly.

pointlet ('pɔɪntlɪt). [f. as prec. + -LET.] A small point. Hence '**pointleted** *a. Bot.*, terminating in a minute point; apiculate.

1847 W. E. STEELE *Field Bot.* 80 *Dianthus cæsius*... Bracts adpressed, ovate, obtuse, pointleted. **1866** *Treas. Bot.*, *Pointletted*, the same as Apiculate. **1866** BLACKMORE *Cradock Nowell* xii, Below were tassels, tufts, and pointlets.

'**pointling**, *sb. nonce-wd.* [? f. POINT *v.*[1] + -LING[1] 2.] A little index-finger.

1840 *Blackw. Mag.* XLVII. 608 There was not a syllable said either of thumbkin, or pointling, or gold-finger.

† '**pointling, -lings**, *adv. Obs.* [f. POINT *sb.*[1] B. + -LING[2], -LINGS.] Point foremost.

1470-85 MALORY *Arthur* XI. iv. 578 He myght wel see a spere grete & longe that streyghte vpon hym poyntelynge. **1596** DALRYMPLE tr. *Leslie's Hist. Scot.* II. 135 Gret kairnis of stanes,..scharpe abone, ryseng vpe poyntlings lyke a steiple.

† '**point-maker**. *Obs.* A maker of points or laces (for fastening apparel): see POINT *sb.*[1] B. 5.

1436 *Libel Eng. Policy* in *Pol. Poems* (Rolls) II. 160 Iren, wolle, wadmole, gotefel, kydefel also, For poynt-makers fulle nedefulle be the ij. **1530** PALSGR. 256/1 Poynt maker, *esguilletier*. *a* **1548** HALL *Chron., Hen. VIII* 234 He was a citezen and poynt-maker of London. **1591** PERCIVALL *Sp. Dict.*, *Agujetero*, a point maker.

pointman. [f. POINT *sb.*[1] or *v.*[1] + MAN *sb.*[1]]

1. = POINTER 11.

1903 A. ADAMS *Log of Cowboy* iii. 28 Two riders, known as point men rode out and well back from the lead cattle. **1942** BERREY & VAN DEN BARK *Amer. Thes. Slang* §913/10 Point men or riders, cowboys riding near the head of a herd of cattle. **1977** M. HERR *Dispatches* iii. 35 Classic essential American types; point men, *isolatos* and outriders.

2. = POINTSMAN 2.

1927 *Observer* 20 Nov. 11/3 It..bore a number of legends; on the footboard, 'Step on the gas'; on the bonnet, 'Don't look inside', and 'Pointman, let us pass'.

3. (Usu. as two words.) The soldier who walks at the head of a patrol. Also *transf.*

1944 *Yank* 4 Feb. 9/1 The Jap point man was on the scene before any camouflaging could be done. **1969** I. KEMP *Brit. G.I. in Vietnam* v. 96 Next to the commander..the point man was the most important member of the squad on jungle patrols. It was his duty to walk at the head of the formation ..and to act as scout for the rest. **1970** *Time* 5 Jan. 14 Cisneros survived 42 patrols in Viet Nam, mostly as the exposed point man, and saw his unit chewed up behind him several times. **1977** *Time* 21 Mar. 56/1 In Young's view, his role is to be a kind of 'point man' for the Administration in foreign policy, charged with getting out in front with new ideas and possibilities. **1978** *Guardian Weekly* 25 June 18/2 Although Carter started his term as no friend of Kennedy.. Kennedy has, ironically, become Carter's point man in the senate.

4. = POINTSMAN 1.

1945 G. MILLAR *Maquis* ix. 180 This pointman would not presumably be antagonistic to us, since he would be an ordinary 'cheminot'.

'**pointment**. *Obs.* exc. *dial.* [Aphetic form of APPOINTMENT: cf. POINT *sb.*[2], *v.*[2] (Cf. OF. *poyntement* (1418 in Godef.).)] = APPOINTMENT 2, 3, 6.

c **1400** *Song Roland* 145 The sairsins be set the poyntment to hold. *a* **1440**, *c* **1440**, **1521** [see APPOINTMENT 2, 3, 6]. **1466** *Cal. Anct. Recds, Dublin* (1889) I. 326 The..poyntment of their wages. **1519** *Interl. Four Elem.* in Hazl. *Dodsley* I. 33 Did ye not erewhile Make pointment openly, To come again all to supper? **1581** RICH *Farewell* (Shaks. Soc.) 149 Accordyng to poinctmente comes Maister Doctour, disguised like a right porter. **1885** *Rep. Provinc.* (E.D.D.), I have made a pointment with Mr. —— to-morrow.

Pointolite ('pɔɪntəlaɪt). Also **pointolite**. A proprietary name for a type of lamp containing a small but bright source of light, produced by the incandescence of a small knob of tungsten heated by an arc struck between it and a cathode.

1916 *Illuminating Engineer* IX. 32/1 A very interesting new form of lamp for projection purposes..has just been brought out by the Edison and Swan United Electric Light Co., Ltd. The 'Pointolite' lamp is in reality an arc within a sealed bulb. **1923** *Trade Marks Jrnl.* 25 July 1558 Pointolite... Electric lamps... The Edison Swan Electric Company, Limited,..London..; manufacturers. **1926** W. E. WOODWARD *Metallogr. Steel & Cast Iron* i. 42 For taking photomicrographs a 500 c.p. 'pointolite' gives excellent results. **1949** A. PEREIRA *Man. Sub-Standard Cinematogr.* vi. 234 A form of arc light which has found wide application for comparatively low power projection is the enclosed tungsten arc known as Pointolite. **1964** M. HYNES *Med. Bacteriol.* (ed. 8) v. 57 A good illumination of sufficient intensity is essential. This is given by an arc-light or a 'pointolite' lamp.

pointrel ('pɔɪntrəl). *rare.* [dim. of POINT *sb.*[1] B.: cf. *cockerel*.] **a.** = POINTEL 1. **b.** The pointed extremity of the lobe of a leaf.

1688 R. HOLME *Armoury* III. xv. (Roxb.) 19/2 The Poitrell or Pointrell is a brasse Instrument formerly used to write withall on tables. **1875** KNIGHT *Dict. Mech.*, *Pointrel*, a graving-tool. **1881** BLACKMORE *Christowell* i, Broad leaves spreading into pointrels, waved and cut with crisp indenture.

pointsman ('pɔɪntsmən). [f. POINT *sb.*[1] + MAN *sb.*[1]]

1. A man who has charge of the points on a railway: see POINT *sb.*[1] B. 3 f.

1849 SIR F. B. HEAD *Stokers & Pokers* viii. (1851) 79 To increase precaution, the pointsman has always the signal of danger on. **1878** F. S. WILLIAMS *Midl. Railw.* 624 Pointsmen have very responsible duties.

2. A police constable stationed on point-duty.

1883 *Globe* 5 Apr. 5/1 Supplemental police 'pointsmen' have been placed at several of the public buildings. **1888** *Pall Mall G.* 12 Oct., If the 'point' system is retained, a pointsman ought to be kept on duty throughout the night.

So '**pointswoman** (cf. sense 1).

1865 A. MUNBY *Diary* 17 Mar. in M. Hiley *Victorian Working Women* (1979) II. i. 86/2 In the cutting I found a girl ..the pointswoman, whose duty it is to mind the rails whenever a train of coalwaggons goes by. **1871** MISS MULOCK *Fair France* ii. 66 Much it amazed us to see continually on French railways these female officials, down to signalwomen and pointswomen.

† '**pointure**. *Obs.* Also 5 -yr. [a. F. *pointure* = Pr. *pointura*:—L. *punctūra* PUNCTURE.] Pricking.

1390 GOWER *Conf.* III. 119 The lusti Maii, Whanne every brid upon his lay Among the griene leves singeth And love of his pointure stingeth.. The youthe of every creature. **1461** *Liber Pluscardensis* XI. viii, The pointyr of a preyn.

† **point-vice**, *a.* and *adv. Obs.* [var. of POINT-DEVICE.] Perfect; perfectly, exactly.

a **1607** BRIGHTMAN *Revelation* (1615) 48 Men..who thinke all that to be point-vice, which they read to haue been in vse in these tymes. *a* **1663** SANDERSON *Serm.* (1681) II. 127 Clamour against the Times, because everything is not point-vise just as we would have it.

'**pointways**, *adv.* [f. as next + *ways*, genitive of WAY *sb.*] = next; with projecting points.

1892 J. T. BENT *Ruined Cities Mashonaland* iv. 107 A pretty little bit of wall with the stones placed pointways for about a yard..formed a sort of dentelle pattern.

'**pointwise**, *adv.* [f. POINT *sb.*[1] B. + -WISE.]

1. In the manner or way of a point.

1545 ELYOT, *Cuspidatim*, poyntyng, or poyntwyse. **1611** FLORIO, *Stipula*, the spindling vp point-wise of any thing namely of corne. **1616** J. LANE *Cont. Sqr.'s T.* IX. 197 Gnartolite..whome Akafir, well eienge, point wise smote. **1904** *Westm. Gaz.* 25 Feb. 4/1 The bodice..enriched with further appliqués of guipure to extend the fronts pointwise.

2. *Math.* With regard to individual points; esp. in ***pointwise convergent***, that converges for each individual point in a space, but not necessarily for the space as a whole (so ***pointwise convergence***).

1932 *Colloquium Publ. Amer. Math. Soc.* XV. i. 26 The term 'convergence in the mean' was introduced to distinguish convergence in the space $\mathfrak{L}_2$..from ordinary point-wise convergence. **1955** HALL & SPENCER *Elem. Topology* iv. 133 This sequence is said to converge pointwise to a mapping $f:S \to T$, if and only if, for each point x of S, the sequence $\{f_n(x)\}$ of points of T converges to the point $f(x)$ of T. **1966** A. FEINSTEIN tr. *G. Choquet's Topology* i. 92 Every sequence (f_n) which converges uniformly to f converges pointwise to f, but it is important to note that the converse is incorrect. **1970** *Manifold* VI. 17 A student produced three new specimens... They came from adding the blackboard examples point-wise. **1971** POWELL & HIGMAN *Finite Simple Groups* iii. 138 And r leaves a hyperplane pointwise fixed. **1974** G. J. O. JAMESON *Topology & Normed Spaces* ix. 90 A decreasing sequence of continuous functions on a compact space can certainly be pointwise convergent to a discontinuous function.

pointy ('pɔɪntɪ), *a.* [f. POINT *sb.*[1] B. + -Y.]

1. Characteristically or notably pointed. Also *fig.*

1644 DIGBY *Nat. Bodies* XV. § 1. 130, I haue seen some very high, and pointy spire steeples do the like. **1906** *Daily Chron.* 2 Oct. 3/4 Puck of the pointy-ears. **1927** J. MASEFIELD *Midnight Folk* 113 She has..pointy, black shiny shoes. **1953** A. MILLER *Crucible* I. 20 Let either of you breathe a word,..and I will bring a pointy reckoning that will shudder you. **1969** M. PUZO *Godfather* IV. xix. 263 Conny stood with hands on hips, her face pointy and white with rage. **1975** J. MCCLURE *Snake* ix. 116 Her nails..were long and pointy. **1977** *Rolling Stone* 19 May 69/3 Zbigniew Brzezinski, the president's national security adviser and a man whose every feature is pointy, enters the office.

2. Of a fleece: Having many points; bearing wool of uneven length.

1844 H. STEPHENS *Bk. Farm* III. 891 A good fleece should have the points of all its staples of equal length, otherwise it will be a pointy one.

3. Full of point; pithy, terse. *slang.*

4. a. Special collocations, as **pointy-head** *U.S. colloq.*, a supposed expert or intellectual (used derogatorily); also *attrib.*; hence ***pointy-headed*** adj.

1972 *Guardian* 21 Feb. 2/4 George Wallace..attacked Muskie, Humphrey, and his other 'pointy-head' opponents. **1972** *Times* 5 May 6/3 Mr Wallace..dismissed it quickly at the end of his address as 'the most callous, asinine, stupid thing that was ever conceived by some pointy-head in Washington DC'. **1972** *National Observer* (N.Y.) 27 May 12/1, I am not ashamed of being a 'pointy headed intellectual snob' who notices the correlation between our 'leadership' and the many distressing phenomena 'coinciding' with those sages' descriptions. **1973** J. DI MONA *Last Man at Arlington* (1974) 178 Idiots... Pointy heads that didn't know how to operate. **1975** *N.Y. Times* 12 Nov. 42/2 Let the dust gather on the pointy-headed bureaucrats and all the other props from yesteryear.

b. *Comb.*, as ***pointy-eared***, ***-toed*** adjs.: see also *pointy-headed* adj. above.

1906 KIPLING *Puck of Pook's Hill* 7 They saw a small, brown, broad-shouldered, pointy-eared person with a snub nose. **1968** A. YOUNG in A. Chapman *New Black Voices* (1972) 147 Sport shirt, creased pants, shiny black pointy-toed stetsons [*sc.* shoes]. **1971** E. BULLINS in W. King *Black Short Story Anthol.* (1972) 61 His snake-skinned, pointy-toed shoes. **1978** *N.Y. Times* 18 Jan. 1/3 A scene normally dominated by men with Western twangs in ten-gallon hats and pointy-toed boots.

poinyard, obs. form of PONIARD.

poiology (pɔɪ'ɒlədʒɪ). [f. Gr. ποῖο-ς of what kind or nature (= L. *quālis*) + -LOGY.] Bentham's proposed term for the doctrine of quality, as opposed to *posology* the doctrine of quantity. Hence **poio'logical** *a.*

1816 BENTHAM *Chrestomathia* Wks. 1843 VIII. 119 Exhibiting Posology and Poiology together, in the character of two branches comprehending between them the whole contents of Somatology. *Ibid.* 86 Poiological Somatology.

‖ **poipoi** ('pɔɪpɔɪ). Also **poee-poee, poi-poi, popoi.** [Polynesian word.] A Polynesian dish, usu. made from fermented bread-fruit (see quot. 1829). Also *attrib.* Cf. POI[1].

1829 W. ELLIS *Polynesian Researches* I. xiii. 377 The most general dish in the Southern Islands is what they call *popoi*, nearly resembling the *poe* of the Sandwich Islands. It is made with the ripe mountain plantain, either raw or baked, beaten up into a paste or jelly, and diluted with cocoa-nut milk. Another kind of *popoi* is made with bread-fruit, or *opio*, beaten up and diluted with cocoa-nut or plain water. **1846** H. MELVILLE *Narr. Residence Marquesas Islands* xv. 128 The great staple articles of food into which the breadfruit is converted by these natives are known respectively by the names of Amar and Poee-Poee. **1888** M. I. STEVENSON *Let.* 25 Aug. in M. C. Balfour *From Saranac to Marquesas* (1903) 121 Madame Stanislas gave Fanny a very finely carved *poi-poi* bowl of *mio* wood. **1910** F. W. CHRISTIAN *Eastern Pacific Lands* xii. 160 To a European palate *Popoi* tastes like an acid custard. **1919** *Century Mag.* Aug. 450/1 The players halted briefly to eat a bowl of *poipoi*. **1970** I. GOLDMAN *Ancient Polynesian Society* vii. 125 The fermented breadfruit mash (*poipoi*) stored well in leaf-lined pits. **1974** T. HEYERDAHL *Fatu-Hiva* iii. 122 *Poipoi*, the staple diet in most of Polynesia. Nowhere else was *poipoi* made as strong as in the Marquesas group.

poire (pwɑː(r)). [abbrev. of Canad. Fr. *poire sauvage*, lit. 'wild pear'.] A name formerly used in Canada for a tree or shrub of the genus *Amelanchier*, belonging to the family Rosaceæ, or its fruit, a blue-black berry; = SASKATOON, *shad-bush* s.v. SHAD *sb.* 4 b.

1789 A. MACKENZIE *Jrnl.* 14 Aug. in *Voyages from Montreal* (1801) vii. 107 There were plenty of berries, which my people called *poires*; they are of a purple hue, somewhat bigger than a pea, and of a luscious taste. **1807** G. KEITH *Let.* 7 Jan. in L. F. R. Masson *Les Bourgeois de la Compagnie du Nord-Ouest* (1890) II. 66 There are *poire*, gooseberry and raspberry bushes. **1837** *Trans. Lit. & Hist. Soc. Quebec* III. 126 In the country parts this small fruit is dignified with the name of poire, more from its fine flavor, it is presumed, than from any resemblance to pears. **1865** MILTON & CHEADLE *N.W. Passage by Land* xiv. 266 The Indians brought in a plentiful supply of the poire, wild pear, or service berry. **1951** W. O'MEARA *Grand Portage* xviii. 102 He found..a large purple berry called the poire that was the most delicious of all.

pois, obs. form of POSE *Sc.*, treasure, etc.

†'**poisable**, *a. Obs. rare.* [a. late AF. *poisable*, f. *poiser* to POISE + -ABLE.] That may be weighed.
[**1429-30** *Act 8 Hen. VI* c. 5 Toutz manners des choses poisablez.] **1502** ARNOLDE *Chron.* 82 The ferme of the grete beame shall bye nor selle any wares or marchaundises peysed or poysable at y^e grete beame.

†'**poisage**. *Obs. rare.* [a. obs. F. *poisage*, = PEISAGE.] Weighing, expense of weighing.
1611 COTGR., *Droict de poisage*, poisage; or, a fee due in some places, vnto the king, for the weighing of wares in the Market-hall, or Towne-house.

†'**poisant**, *a. Obs.* In 4-5 **poysaunt**, 6 **-sent**. [a. OF. *poisant*, variant of *pesant*, *peisant*: see PEISANT, and POISE *v.*] Weighing; heavy, weighty (in various senses): = PEISANT.
1389 in *Eng. Gilds* (1870) 26 Two candels poysaunt viij. pounde. *c* **1477** CAXTON *Jason* 17 Gyuyng to hys enemye many strokes terryble and poysaunt. **1489** —— *Faytes of A.* I. ix. 24 More poysaunt and namely bygger armures. **1592** WYRLEY *Armorie* 111 Right poysent bloe he stroke.

DOMI MINA
NVS TIO
ILLV MEA